The Complete Directory to Prime Time Network and Cable TV Shows

1946–Present

The Complete Directory to Prime Time Network and Cable TV Shows

1946–Present

The Complete Directory to Prime Time Network and Cable TV Shows

1946–Present

(Eighth Edition)

Tim Brooks and Earle Marsh

Ballantine Books • New York

A Ballantine Book
Published by The Random House Publishing Group

www.ballantinebooks.com

Library of Congress Control Number: 2003105447

ISBN: 0-345-45542-8

Cover design by Derek Walls

Front cover photos: *Sex and the City* (THE KOBAL COLLECTION / DARREN STAR PRODUCTIONS / ROY, NORMAN JEAN); *The Andy Giffith Show* (THE KOBAL COLLECTION / CBS-TV); *The Jeffersons* (THE KOBAL COLLECTION / CBS-TV); *MASH* (THE KOBAL COLLECTION / 20TH CENTURY FOX); *The Simpsons* (FOX); *The X-Files* (THE KOBAL COLLECTION / 20TH CENTURY FOX TELEVISION); *Charlie's Angles* (THE KOBAL COLLECTION / SPELLING-GOLDBERG)

Spine photos: *Bewitched* (THE KOBAL COLLECTION / COLUMBIA); *The Sopranos* (HBO)

Manufactured in the United States of America

First Edition: May 1979
Second (Revised) Edition: November 1981
Third (Revised) Edition: May 1985
Fourth (Revised) Edition: October 1988
Fifth (Revised) Edition: May 1992
Sixth (Revised) Edition: October 1995
Seventh (Revised) Edition: December 1999
Eighth (Revised) Edition: October 2003
10 9 8 7 6 5 4 3 2

CONTENTS

PREFACE TO THE EIGHTH EDITION

What a different world it was 24 years ago, when the first edition of this book was published. Three networks, a nice orderly prime time schedule, and all decisions about what we saw made (as the saying went) "by three middle-aged white guys in New York." For most people television was still relatively new, something that had begun during their lifetime, and we were just beginning to see inklings that it had a history. The first major TV retrospectives appeared in the late 1970s, starting with NBC's fiftieth anniversary special in 1976. Not everyone believed there was value in TV's past. Twenty publishers turned this book down, telling us that no one would be interested in a book about old TV shows. What did *they* know?

Ballantine Books said yes and now, half a million copies later, we bring you the eighth edition of this chronicle of American prime time TV. If we had known back then what TV would look like 24 years later—more than 100 networks (including cable), hundreds of new series every year, Ozzy Osbourne as a sitcom dad—we might never have begun. We are sincerely grateful to our readers for the support that has made it possible to continually update and refine this volume. Popular television may still not get the respect accorded films or the theater—you will never see this book reviewed in *The New York Times*—but we the viewers don't care, do we?

We are also grateful for your feedback and suggestions. This book is not a "factory" production but handcrafted, by the two of us, and it is quite a challenge to keep up. As Earle mentioned over lunch the other day, the real miracle is not that the book has grown so much, but that we are still talking to each other, and still friends.

We've tried to give you the most complete, accurate and interesting book possible on prime time TV. As always, your comments and suggestions are welcome, in care of the publisher.

—T.B. and E.M.

ACKNOWLEDGMENTS

Many people both inside and outside of the television industry have helped by providing information used in this edition, and we offer our sincere thanks to them here. We are grateful to our friends at the broadcast and cable networks, many of whom use this book. On the broadcast side they include Brent Petersen at ABC; John Behrens and Nancy Delaney at CBS; Niki Ostin at Fox; Sari DeCesare, Curt King, Claudine Ricanor and Brian Robinette at NBC; and Jay Potashnick and Cathy Schaper at the WB. At the cable networks there were Jennifer Marburg at Animal Planet; Roy Giacopelli at Comedy Central; Matt Katzive at Discovery Channel; Patricia Kollappallil and Gary Morgenstein at Lifetime; Betsy Frank at MTV Networks; Thomas Vitale at the Sci-Fi Channel; and Kat Stein at USA Network.

Others who contributed to the eighth edition included Marc Berman, editor of the industry newsletter *The Programming Insider* from *Mediaweek* (mberman@mediaweek.com), who provided "The Ph.D. Trivia Quiz," Ron Simon, curator of The Museum of Television and Radio in New York; and actress Nancy McKeon.

Our readers, who obviously love television as much as we do, continue to write in with (usually) good-natured comments and suggestions. We appreciate your input. All suggestions for additions and corrections are checked and included in future editions if we can confirm them (but note, please be sure of your facts, providing sources if possible; memories, no matter how certain, can be mistaken!). We regret that we cannot personally answer every letter, but we do read them and want to thank the following whose contributions will be found in this edition: Barbara Arnstein, Aaron Barnhart, Robert E. Blank, James Clink, Phyllis Cohen, Emily V. Dais, Charleen Dale, Brandon Haleamau, Nelson T. Hall, David P. Jackino, Jeff Jourdan, Katalin Korossy, Joy Lewis, Barrie Pick, Edward J. Powers, Rick Rofman and Stephen Tuttle.

Finally, our thanks to our understanding and helpful editors at Ballantine Books for this edition, Patricia Peters and Mark Tavani.

Comments are welcome c/o Ballantine Books, 1745 Broadway, New York, NY 10019.

INTRODUCTION

Wait no more, here it is—nearly 60 years of television at your fingertips. From *I Love Lucy* to *Everybody Loves Raymond*, *Milton Berle* to *Malcolm in the Middle*, *Toast of the Town* to *Touched by an Angel*—detailed information on all the shows you loved, whatever their era. Television shows never really die, you know, they just keep being rerun, on and on. So if you stumble into the middle of *The X-Files* or *Buffy the Vampire Slayer*, we'll help you untangle the plot. If you're a romantic, you can relive the love affairs on *Moonlighting* and *Mad about You*. For the historians we've exhumed information on the first network news programs, on *Amos 'n' Andy*, and on the first major TV production, the now-forgotten *Hour Glass* (1946). And there are thousands of others, flickering through the years—*The Lone Ranger*, *Arthur Godfrey's Talent Scouts* (who says *American Idol* is a new idea?), *Gunsmoke*, *The Beverly Hillbillies*, *Gomer Pyle*, *Rowan & Martin's Laugh-In*, *All in the Family*, *Happy Days*, *Hill Street Blues*, *Dallas* (about which we get lots of letters), *Dynasty* (not so many), *The Cosby Show*, *ER*, *South Park*, *The Real World*, *The West Wing*, *Rugrats*, *Lizzie McGuire*, *Survivor*, *The Bachelor*, and many more.

We both work, or have worked, in the TV industry, care about its history, and have done everything possible to get the facts correct. That doesn't mean there are no mistakes—we will surely hear about them!—but we hope not many. If you have an earlier edition of this book, there are thousands of additions and improvements, appearing on almost every page. The book has been carefully researched for the scholar, but it is also, like television itself, for your enjoyment (as well as for trivia quizzes, bet settling, and spouse pacifying on a birthday or holiday). Guard your copy, though. People get so interested in what's in here that the book might "walk away." You can still watch many of these shows, on broadcast stations, cable networks, tape or DVD. We hope this book will help you enjoy them even more.

What Is in This Book

This encyclopedia lists regular series carried on the commercial broadcast and cable networks between 6:00 P.M. and roughly 3:00 A.M. eastern time—in other words, "prime time" plus early evening and late-night programs. In addition, we have included all the top syndicated programs that have aired primarily in the evening hours. We cover the entire history of TV networking in the United States, from its inception on a regular basis in 1944 through April 15, 2003. Our definition of a "series" is a program that ran for at least four consecutive weeks in the same time slot—or was intended to!

A few generic program types are found under general headings. Newscasts are summarized under *News*; sports events such as football, boxing, wrestling, etc., under the name of the sport; and feature film series under *Movies*. All other series are arranged by title in alphabetical order. There is a full index in the back to every cast member, plus appendixes listing the highest rated programs each season, network schedules for each season at a glance, major TV awards, and other information.

Network series are those that are fed out by broadcast or cable networks and seen simultaneously across most of the country. The following broadcast networks are covered, beginning with the year shown. Although individual program clearance information for the earliest years is anything but clear, we'll also indicate our best guess as to each network's first regular prime-time series.

NBC—1944, *Voice of Firestone Televues*
DuMont—1946, *Serving Through Science*
CBS—1948, *Tonight on Broadway*
ABC—1948, *Hollywood Screen Test**
Fox—1986, *The Late Show* (Joan Rivers)
WB—1995, *The Wayans Brothers*
UPN—1995, *Star Trek: Voyager*

*on an ad hoc network

Original cable series are listed in two different ways. Major programs seen on the largest networks (those reaching at least 50% of U.S.

homes) are listed alphabetically and in detail; other cable series, including those appearing on less widely circulated networks or on networks without regular series-oriented schedules (such as CNN, the Weather Channel and movie and documentary channels), may be listed under the network's name. Programming on more than 100 national cable networks from ABC Family Channel to the Weather Channel, is described here. We believe this is the most extensive description of original cable programming ever undertaken. Look for a cable series first under its own name, and if you don't find it there, under the name of the cable network.

Syndicated series are sold by their producers to individual stations, and are therefore seen at different times in different cities, and not at all in some areas. Thousands of syndicated programs have been produced over the years, many with very limited distribution. Only the principal ones are included here. As with cable series, and with some exceptions, the general rule is that they must have been available to at least half of all U.S. television homes. Other programs that may have been seen in your city after 6:00 P.M.—but are not included here—are local programs and syndicated series which did not achieve widespread distribution.

This is the first book to trace programming back to the very founding of the networks, and, consequently, it includes some very early network series that were seen in only two or three cities on the East Coast. The networks spread quickly, however, first by sending out kinescopes (films) of their shows to nonconnected stations, and soon after with live connections to stations in the Midwest (in 1949) and on the West Coast (in 1951).

Under each series' main heading you will find the following:

First/Last Telecast: The dates on which the series was first and last seen on a network. This includes repeats on a network during its original run, but not later reruns on local stations, which will be at a different time in each city, and may go on long after the program has ceased production. Generally the first and last telecast dates indicate the original production run of a network series.

Broadcast History: The days, times, and networks on which the series was carried (eastern time). Special episodes which ran for only one or two weeks in other than the normal time slot are not reflected. DUM indicates the DuMont TV network, and (OS) indicates that the program was off during the summer months. For syndicated and cable series, we have indicated the years the program was in production, and when it was first telecast.

Cast: Regular cast members, those who were seen on a recurring basis, are listed along with the years in which they were seen during the original run. We have gone to considerable effort to separate regulars from guests making occasional appearances, as the latter were not part of the continuing casts. Notable guests may be listed in the series description, however.

Principal sources of scheduling information were the files of the networks, cross-checked against detailed logs maintained over the years by NBC and ratings reports from Nielsen Media Research. For the very earliest programs, listings in *TV Guide* and various newspapers were consulted; however, readers should be aware that pretelecast publicity does not always reflect what actually aired. Nielsen rating reports are useful as they indicate, after the fact, what was actually telecast. Cast and content data were drawn from a multitude of sources including network and syndicator files, press releases, listings in *TV Guide*, reviews in *Variety*, *Billboard*, and *Television* magazines, Internet Web sites, and, of course, our viewing of the shows. Yes, we watch almost everything.

—T.B. and E.M.

A Short History of Network Television

by Tim Brooks

Television goes back a good deal further than most people realize. There was no single inventor of television, although Dr. Vladimir Zworykin's invention of the iconoscope in 1923 provided a basic element, the "eye" of the TV camera. Demonstrations of various kinds of experimental TV were made in the late 1920s, including even primitive color television in 1929. General Electric began semiregular telecasts from its laboratories in Schenectady in May 1928, mostly for the benefit of a few nearby engineers who had receiving sets. NBC opened experimental TV station W2XBS in New York in 1930, followed by a similar CBS station in 1931. But for the next several years TV seemed to go nowhere. Pictures were fuzzy, screens tiny, and costs astronomical. In addition, there were several incompatible types of transmission, and engineers spent much time arguing over a single set of technical standards—something we take for granted today.

For the public at large the 1930s was the decade of radio, when virtually every home had a set, and superstars and hit shows became a familiar phenomenon. Comedies, dramas, quiz shows, and variety hours were all developed for a mass market, establishing formats that would later be transferred virtually intact to television. While radio and TV are only vaguely related technically, there is no doubt that the great radio networks of the 1930s were the direct entertainment predecessors of today's TV.

By the end of the 1930s interest in TV was picking up. In 1938 NBC transmitted several notable telecasts from its New York station, including scenes from the Broadway play *Susan and God* starring Gertrude Lawrence and Paul McGrath from the original cast. Also in that year the NBC station carried the first live, unscheduled coverage of a news event in progress. An NBC mobile unit happened to be working in a park in Queens, New York, when a fire broke out on Ward's Island, across the river. The TV crew swung their cameras around and telecast live pictures of the raging fire to surprised viewers.

Looking for a memorable event with which to inaugurate regular TV service, NBC decided upon the official opening of the World's Fair in New York on April 30, 1939. President Franklin D. Roosevelt was seen arriving and delivering the opening address, thus becoming the first incumbent president to appear on television. NBC announcer Bill Farren described the proceedings and also conducted interviews at the fairground. Thereafter, from 1939–1941, both NBC and CBS presented a surprisingly extensive schedule of programs over their New York stations for the several thousand sets then in use. There were few regular "series," however—every night was an event. If you had a set, you simply turned it on at night (there was seldom anything telecast during the day) and saw what was being sent out from the studios that night. Anything that moved was worth watching.

A sample night's entertainment, shortly after the World's Fair inaugural, was called simply *The Wednesday Night Program* and ran from 8:00–9:07 P.M. It opened with a fashion show described by commentators Renee Macredy and Nancy Turner, followed by songs by The Three Smoothies, a sketch called "The Smart Thing" (cast included Martha Sleeper, Ned Wever, and Burford Hampden), dancer Hal Sherman from the show *Hellzapoppin'*, and finally a magic act by Robert Reinhart, who also served as emcee of the program. If you've never heard of most of these names, neither had most viewers in 1939. Appearances by stars, especially the big names of radio, were few and far between, and television had to rely primarily on cabaret talent and young, lesser-known Broadway actors and actresses for many years to come.

Viewers didn't mind. There was a common bond of pioneering between viewers and broadcasters in those days, and in fact a good deal of communication both ways. NBC kept a card file listing every known set owner and sent out postcards each week listing the programs to be telecast, asking the viewer's opinion of each one. These were the first TV "ratings."

Most television programs were seen in New York only, which was, throughout the 1940s, America's TV "capital." It was the first city with more than one station operating, and it had by far the largest number of sets in people's homes. However, the possibility of networking, along the lines of the great radio chains, was pursued from the very beginning. As early as 1940 NBC began to relay some telecasts to the General Electric station in Schenectady, thus forming history's first network of sorts. (The feasibility of transmitting pictures between two widely separated cities had been demonstrated in 1927, when Secretary of Commerce Herbert Hoover, speaking in Washington, D.C., was seen in a New York laboratory, by special hookup.) The New York–Schenectady link was accomplished by the simple method of having General Electric pick up the signal off the air from New York, 130 miles away, and rebroadcast it. The picture quality thus obtained was not very good. In 1941 some NBC New York telecasts began to be fed to the Philco station in Philadelphia as well, giving NBC a three-station "network." But all of this was intermittent, and there were still no regular series as we know them today.

Commercial television first saw the light of day in 1941, when both NBC and CBS were granted commercial licenses for their New York stations, both on July 1st (so neither could claim a "first"). NBC's call letters became WNBT on channel one (now WNBC-TV on channel four), and CBS got WCBW on channel two (now WCBS-TV).

Just as commercial television was beginning to take root, World War II put a stop to everything. Little was telecast during the war years, except for some training programs. The DuMont Laboratories, which had been experimenting with TV for years, received a commercial license in 1944 for WABD, New York (now WNYW-TV on channel five), serving as the cornerstone of that company's ill-fated network venture.

With the war over, work started anew. The year 1946 marked the true beginnings of regular network series. NBC's WNBT began feeding its programs on a more or less regular basis to Philadelphia and Schenectady, forming NBC's "East Coast Network." DuMont opened a second station, WTTG, in Washington, D.C., to which it fed programs—even though there were in mid-1946 only a bare dozen sets in the nation's capital. Network television's first major series effort, and the program which set many precedents for programs to come, was a regular Thursday night big-budget variety hour called *Hour Glass*, which ran for ten months beginning in May 1946. It was a pioneer in many ways and helped spread the word that television could provide not only a novelty gadget for the gadget-minded, but regular high-quality family entertainment as well.

Several other network series began in 1946, including the long-running *You Are an Artist*, Mrs. Carveth Wells's *Geographically Speaking*, *Television Screen Magazine* (an early version of *60 Minutes*), *Play the Game* (charades), *Cash and Carry* (quiz), *Face to Face* (drawings), *I Love to Eat* (cooking), and *Faraway Hill* (the first network soap opera). All of these programs can be found under their individual headings in this book.

Most early programming was quite experimental, just to see what would work in the new medium. Costs were kept to a minimum, and advertising agencies were given free time by the stations, to get them into the studio to try out TV. (Programs were often produced by the advertisers themselves.) Such visual formats as charades, cartooning, and fashion shows were favorites, along with sports events and adaptations of radio shows, telecast on a one-time tryout basis.

A landmark was the premiere of *Kraft Television Theatre* in May 1947. This was not only the first regularly scheduled drama series to go out over a network, but was also blessed with sufficient money from a sponsor to insure uniformly high-quality productions.

Gradually stations were added to NBC's and DuMont's chains, two more stations in Washington, D.C., additional facilities in Philadelphia, then Baltimore, then Boston. Stations not connected with the East Coast opened in the Midwest and Far West, often receiving network programs on kinescope.

But where were CBS and ABC?

Both were fully committed to the idea of networking, but each hung back for a different reason. ABC did not yet have a New York flagship station on the air from which to originate programming. ABC had in fact been buying time on other stations and producing programs on their schedules just to give its own technicians experience in studio production techniques, against the day when ABC would have its own station. An early example was *Play the Game* (1946), which was produced by ABC using DuMont's facilities. In early 1948 ABC lined up a network of four stations, a curious amalgam of DuMont and independent stations, for a series called *On the Corner* with radio star Henry Morgan—which it now considers its first "network" program (although *Play the Game* was also seen over a network). Finally, in August 1948 ABC got its own New York station and production center on the air and began network service on a regular basis.

CBS delayed its entry into network television for quite a different reason. It had had an active New York station for years. But CBS was committed to the idea of color TV, and tried hard to get its own color system accepted by the Federal Communications Commission as the industry standard. This would have meant color TV from the start for everyone, and would also have made obsolete all of the equipment in use by CBS' rivals because the different systems were incompatible. The choice had to be color or black and white, but not both. Unfortunately, the CBS system was clumsy and unreliable compared with the fairly well-developed black-and-white TV of the day, and its adoption would probably have set TV back several years. (Eventually the CBS electromechanical system, with its spinning disc within every set, was discarded altogether. It is RCA's all-electronic, black-and-white compatible color system that we use today.) While the verdict was out, CBS delayed investment in a network.

Two events changed CBS' mind. First, a critical government decision went against the CBS color system. Then the NBC network's coverage of the 1947 World Series—the first World Series on TV—suddenly made it very apparent that an explosion in TV set ownership was about to take place. CBS, if it did not move quickly, was in danger of being left at the starting gate. A crash program of series development was instituted, and early in 1948 CBS began feeding programs out over its own small network.

The 1947 World Series brought in television's first mass audience. It was carried in New York, Philadelphia, Schenectady, and Washington, D.C., and was seen by an estimated 3.9 million people—3.5 million of them in bars! The TV set over the corner bar was a first introduction to the new medium for many people, and it helped sell thousands of sets for the home. After that, TV ownership was contagious. The first set on the block always brought in dozens of curious neighbors, who eventually went out and bought sets of their own.

By 1948 television networking was on its way. Several of the longest running programs included in this book premiered in that year, including Ted Mack's *Original Amateur Hour* in January, Milton Berle's *Texaco Star Theater* in June, Ed Sullivan's *Toast of the Town* in June, and *Arthur Godfrey's Talent Scouts* in December. NBC opened its midwestern network of stations in September 1948, and in a special ceremonial telecast on January 11, 1949, East and Midwest were linked. For a time Chicago was an important production center for network programs, but without the talent pool available in New York it could not compete for long. *Kukla, Fran & Ollie* and *Garroway at Large* were probably the most important series to come out of Chicago in its TV heyday.

In September 1951 the link was completed to the West Coast, and America at last had nationwide television. Los Angeles was not to become the principal network production center until Hollywood-produced filmed dramatic shows became the TV norm during the second half of the 1950s, however.

In the early years of network operation NBC had the largest audiences, with *Milton Berle, Kraft Television Theatre, Your Show of Shows, Dragnet*, and other top hits. But by the mid-1950s, through a combination of astute program development *(I Love Lucy, Ed Sullivan)* and carryovers from its top radio shows *(Arthur Godfrey, Jack Benny)*, CBS took the lead, which it proudly retained for two decades thereafter. Nevertheless, NBC and CBS, the two giants of TV, were never far apart. ABC and DuMont were far behind, fighting for survival—for it was rapidly becoming apparent that there was room for only one other network in the U.S. There were several reasons for this. For one thing the talent pool available for successful TV shows was severely limited and very high priced. NBC and CBS had so many of the trump cards that there just wasn't very much left over for another network, much less for two others. Whenever a new talent emerged on DuMont or ABC, such as Ted Mack *(Original Amateur Hour)* or Jackie Gleason, he would soon be stolen away by the "majors" with the promise of much more money.

Even more important, there were a limited number of stations to go around. Outside of New York and a few other large cities, very few places in the U.S. were serviced by more than two, or perhaps three, stations (some areas still aren't). NBC and CBS always got the best stations in each city, leaving ABC and DuMont to fight for the scraps, or perhaps be seen only part-time on a "shared" station.

In many ways DuMont seemed to be in a good position to become America's third network. The company was led by a brilliant and progressive engineer, Dr. Allen B. DuMont, who seemed to have made all the right decisions at the right times. He was involved in experimental television broadcasting from his laboratory in New Jersey in the early 1930s, long before ABC was even founded (in 1943, as a spin-off from NBC). DuMont had a base in manufacturing, and in fact marketed the first large screen (14-inch) home TV set in 1938. Knowing that large amounts of capital would be needed for television development, he obtained financing from giant Paramount Pictures in 1938 and began active TV programming in the early 1940s. DuMont was close on the heels of NBC in setting up a network in 1946–1947, and its production facilities were the most elaborate in the industry. What went wrong?

One important factor working against DuMont was the fact that the company did not operate a radio network, as did NBC, CBS, and ABC. An established radio network not only provided its competitors with a ready talent pool to draw on, but also gave them a foot in the door in signing up choice affiliates (which were usually associated with network radio stations) in many cities. Another devastating blow was a ruling by the government that DuMont, unlike the other three networks, could not own the legal maximum of five television stations.

Most of the affiliates over which the TV networks send their programs are locally owned. Each network could by law own outright only five VHF stations. These five were critically important because they provided the base of revenues to support the network (for years the networks themselves all lost money). They also guaranteed that all of the network's programs would be seen in at least those five markets. NBC, CBS, and ABC each obtained their quota of five stations early in the game. But because of a series of complicated legal rulings involving its relationship with Paramount Pictures (which also owned stations), DuMont could not, and thus was denied both the revenues and guaranteed program clearances that a full roster of five big-market stations could provide. In addition, Paramount refused to give DuMont any further financial support after 1939.

ABC had financial problems too, but in 1953 it got the boost it needed by merging with United Paramount Theaters. With a heavy infusion of capital provided by the merger, ABC began developing programs in earnest, including the landmark deal in 1954 that brought *Walt Disney* to television and in 1955 the arrangement with Warner Brothers that produced many hit series (see under *Warner Brothers Presents*). With the ABC–Paramount Theaters merger, DuMont's fate was sealed, and the latter network finally went out of business in 1956.

Structurally, little changed in TV networking for the next thirty years. In the mid-1950s, compatible color TV was introduced, pushed hard by NBC (whose parent company, RCA, manufactured the sets). Video tape effected a behind-the-scenes revolution in the 1960s by freeing producers from the cumbersome aspects of film and the hectic uncertainty of live production. There was periodic talk of a fourth national network, such as the ill-fated Overmyer Network ("ON") in the 1960s, but nothing came of it until 20th Century–Fox launched its Fox Network in 1986 (with the ill-fated *Late Show Starring Joan Rivers*). Even network ownership remained unchanged until the 1980s. The giant conglomerate ITT and later billionaire Howard Hughes each tried to buy ABC, but no one succeeded until a cash-rich station owner, Capital Cities Broadcasting, swallowed the network in January 1986. Five months later the giant General Electric Co. gobbled up RCA, and with it NBC. CBS was taken over by investor Laurence Tisch three months after that.

It took ABC nearly thirty years to reach parity with CBS and NBC in audience size. It did not have a number-one rated series until *Marcus Welby, M.D.*, in the 1970s, and it did not rank number one as a network for a full season until 1976–1977, when long-time leader CBS was finally deposed. In the 1980s CBS recaptured first place, then yielded to NBC. But the race among them became increasingly irrelevant compared to the decline in viewership of all three as viewers flocked to cable TV, which offered both convenient reruns of classic network fare and original programming of its own. The "big three" still command the largest audiences, but with more than 80 percent of American homes receiving alternative programming via cable or satellite, that is changing. TV itself is flourishing. It once seemed that people might finally be getting tired of it; today they're watching more than ever, from a greater and greater variety of sources.

Trends in Programming: The Eight Eras of Prime Time

Television programming has changed a great deal over the years, both in style and content. Each decade has had its program trends, reflecting not only the evolving tastes of the American public, but also important behind-the-scenes changes in the business that determine what we see. We have come a long way from the silly slapstick of Milton Berle to today's raunchy relevance.

Prime time program history can be divided into eight principal eras.

The First Era: "Vaudeo" (1948–1957)

In the beginning there was Milton Berle. His time at the top was actually rather short—his series ranked number one for three seasons (1948–1951), in a period when relatively few people even had a TV set. Later major hits such as *I Love Lucy*, *Gunsmoke*, and *All in the Family* were number one for a longer time and were seen by far more people. But Uncle Miltie's influence was enormous. Not only was he TV's first superstar, but the excitement he created for the new medium helped television ownership spread like wildfire, from less than 2 percent of U.S. homes when he premiered in 1948 to over 70 percent by the time he left the air in 1956.

Berle's Tuesday night *Texaco Star Theater* was typical of the first wave of television programming—frantic, corny, but always highly visual. If ordinary people were going to spend $400 for a small-screen "radio with pictures," they wanted to see movement and action, and lots of it. Berle gave them fall-down slapstick with crazy costumes and sight gags galore. Ed Sullivan offered a three-ring circus of comedians, acrobats, opera singers, scenes from plays, and dancing bears. *The Ed Wynn Show*, *The All Star Revue* with Jimmy Durante, *Your Show of Shows* with Sid Caesar, *Fireball Fun-For-All* with Olsen and Johnson, and *The Colgate Comedy Hour* with practically everybody (Eddie Cantor, Martin and Lewis, Abbott and Costello, Bob Hope) all did the same. Such broadly played slapstick and variety looked so old fashioned that some called it "vaudeo"—a wedding of vaudeville and the new video medium.

Other types of series exploited the new medium's visual possibilities even further. *I'd Like to See* and *You Asked for It* brought viewers their own visual requests. *Photographic Horizons* showed models posing so that home viewers could take pictures of them right off the screen. Pantomime shows like Mike Stokey's *Pantomime Quiz* were popular.

Variety programs, however, drew the largest audiences. Talent shows proliferated, led by *Arthur Godfrey's Talent Scouts* (for up-and-coming professionals) and *The Original Amateur Hour* (for your local tap dancers and kazoo players). Future stars like Jack Klugman, Pernell Roberts, and Martin Balsam could be seen trying out on *Hollywood Screen Test*, but Godfrey's audition staff flunked a greasy-haired young singer named Elvis Presley before he could even get on the air!

Early situation comedies frequently used broadly played physical comedy. The number one hit in the mid-1950s was *I Love Lucy*, with the inspired mugging of Lucy and the continual exasperation of her bandleader husband, Desi. There were many others, including *The Life of Riley*, *The Stu Erwin Show*, Jackie Gleason's *Honeymooners*, and *Red Skelton*. Of the major stars of the day, only Jack Benny and Groucho Marx seemed to rely primarily on verbal humor. Another popular genre was the family comedy, full of warm, homey values and typified by *The Adventures of Ozzie & Harriet*, *The Danny Thomas Show (Make Room for Daddy)*, *Father Knows Best*, and *Mama*. Such family shows have been among TV's longest running series.

Although vaudeville dominated early TV, some series tried a more intimate approach. Much of Arthur Godfrey's appeal was due to his folksy, down-to-earth humor, and his weekly variety show, *Arthur Godfrey & His Friends*, had an easygoing pace. Godfrey did not showcase stars; instead, his regular "family" of performers including Tony Marvin, the Chordettes, Julius LaRosa, and Frank Parker and Marion Marlowe were seen every week. Dave Garroway was also known for his wry, low-key style, while singer/host Perry Como was so relaxed that he became the butt of jokes: "Wake up, Perry!"

"Serious" television was represented mainly by dramatic anthology series, which offered a different play with a new cast each week. Some of these series had a unifying theme, like the newsworthiness of *Armstrong Circle Theatre* and *The Big Story*, but most simply presented good drama drawn from a variety of sources (original scripts, short stories, adaptations of the classics). Among the more popular of these stage-type series were *Kraft Television Theatre*, *General Electric Theater*, *Philco/Goodyear TV Playhouse*, *Ford Theatre*, *Fireside Theatre*, *Robert Montgomery Presents*, and *Studio One*. The last of these great series, *Playhouse 90*, left the air in 1961. Another kind of innovation was represented by the daring, though never highly popular, series of Ernie Kovacs, who experimented with the visual comedy effects possible in the new medium.

There were relatively few action or adventure shows in the early days, largely because of the studio-bound technical requirements of TV. *Dragnet* was the most popular police show, and one of the few series filmed in Hollywood—most of the big variety, comedy, and playhouse series originated live from New York. But that was to change.

The "Adult Westerns" Era (1957–early 1960s)

Saturday, September 10, 1955, was an important night in television history. If you were watching CBS at 10 P.M. that evening you saw big John Wayne, standing by a corral, introducing a new series that he had been asked to star in. He couldn't take the role, but he had recommended a lanky young actor to take his place. It proved to be a lucky break for Jim Arness, who would star for the next 20 years in *Gunsmoke*. The series started off slowly in the ratings, but quickly gained momentum and was followed by a veritable stampede of others: *Cheyenne*; *Have Gun, Will Travel*; *Tales of Wells Fargo*; *Wagon Train*; *Rawhide*; *Wanted: Dead or Alive*; *The Virginian*. There were variations on the theme, including true-history Westerns *(Life & Legend of Wyatt Earp)*, anthology Westerns *(Zane Grey Theater)*, "family" Westerns *(The Rifleman)*, and even a Western that satirized the other Westerns *(Maverick)*. By 1958–1959, seven out of the top ten series were Westerns—a dominance seldom achieved by any program type.

What set these series apart from earlier kids' Westerns like *The Lone Ranger* and *Hopalong Cassidy* was that they were written for adults, in the style of such recent movie hits as *High Noon* and *Shane*. They often tackled adult subjects and relationships: Just what *was* the relationship between Matt Dillon and Miss Kitty, anyway? Kids could still enjoy the action, while adults got something more than a Saturday-matinee plot and a moral.

TV violence took its first major upswing during the era of the adult Western, to the dismay of critics. The range of weapons used by TV's horseback crusaders was truly remarkable.

The adult Westerns signaled a major change in the source of prime-time TV programming. All of them were on film, and most of them were produced by the major Hollywood movie studios, which had previously avoided involvement with television as if it were the

Series	Weapon
Wanted: Dead or Alive	Steve McQueen's sawed-off carbine
The Rifleman	Chuck Connors's fast-cocking Winchester with a large ring that supposedly allowed him to fire off the first round in three tenths of a second
Wyatt Earp	Hugh O'Brian's oversized Buntline pistol
Shotgun Slade	Scott Brady's unique two-in-one shotgun
Adventures of Jim Bowie	Scott Forbes's Bowie knife
Cisco Kid	Pancho's bullwhip
Hotel de Paree	The shiny little discs in Earl Holliman's Stetson, with which he could blind adversaries

plague. From this time on most TV series would be products of Hollywood's dream factories rather than the live, theater-influenced New York stage. Like a product's switch from wood to plastic, this change made an important difference in the texture and "feel" of all future entertainment programs.

The last hurrah for live, Eastern-originated programming was the big-money quiz show fad which began in the summer of 1955 with the fabulous success of *The $64,000 Question*. The quiz shows were marvelous theater; a contestant agonized in an isolation booth while the host ticked off a complicated, multipart question which could be worth a fabulous amount of money. There was usually just one climactic question per week, for ever greater amounts of money. The suspense from week to week was palpable, and contestant-heroes like Charles Van Doren on *Twenty-One* became national celebrities as they slowly climbed from obscurity to wealth before America's eyes—on live TV. Unfortunately some of the shows turned out to have been fixed (contestants were given the answers beforehand, and coached on how to triumph or fail on cue). They were all swept off the air in 1958–1959 in one of television's most embarrassing scandals.

While the adult Westerns were at their zenith another type of filmed program took root, a type that proved to be one of the most durable formats of all. The "swinging detectives" were sexy, as fast with a wisecrack as with a gun, and usually operated in an exotic locale. They began with *77 Sunset Strip* in 1958, which combined a couple of hip private eyes, some beautiful women, a colorful sidekick (Kookie), and the glamorous backdrop of L.A.'s Sunset Strip. In the wake of its success came *Hawaiian Eye*, *Peter Gunn*, *Checkmate*, *Burke's Law*, and many others right up to *Magnum, P.I.* and *Remington Steele* in the 1980s.

By the early 1960s the flood of adult Westerns was beginning to abate. There were simply too many of them on the air—as many as 31 in a single season—and new entries found it hard to attract attention. Does anyone today remember 1960–1961's *Gunslinger* (Tony Young), *Stagecoach West* (Wayne Rogers), or *The Westerner* (Brian Keith with a mongrel dog)?

Number of Westerns In Prime Time, By Season

Season	Number
1955–1956:	9
1956–1957:	11
1957–1958:	20
1958–1959:	31
1959–1960:	30
1960–1961:	26
1961–1962:	16
1962–1963:	13
1963–1964:	8
1964–1965:	7

A second factor in the demise of the Westerns was concern over TV violence, which had centered on crime shows such as *The Untouchables* and *Bus Stop*, but which spilled over into Westerns as well. By 1961 Congress was holding hearings on the subject, and network executives were under heavy pressure to tone things down.

Even more important forces were at work behind the scenes—forces which would ultimately change all TV programming. The research companies that measured TV audiences were beginning to report those audiences in increasing detail—not only how many homes were tuned in, but detailed ages and incomes of the people who watched each show. It turned out that the adult Westerns were attracting older people, while young adults and kids were tuning to situation comedies. Since advertisers wanted to reach high-consuming young families, sitcoms were in.

The "Idiot Sitcom" Era (early to late 1960s)

The 1960s was the youth decade, and many of the comedies that poured onto the screen seemed to be aimed at the young. Most of them had a gimmick to attract attention. *Beverly Hillbillies,* the number-one program from 1962–1964, put hayseeds in high society, while *Gomer Pyle* had its bumpkin turning the Marine Corps upside down. In *Green Acres* the premise was reversed, with city folks out on the farm. *My Favorite Martian* offered reporter Bill Bixby the biggest story of his career, except that "Uncle Martin" wouldn't reveal his powers to anyone else; meanwhile pretty Samantha on *Bewitched* used her witchly powers more than husband Darrin would have liked. TV's sexiest genie, Barbara Eden, frustrated her "master" (Larry Hagman) and delighted viewers on *I Dream of Jeannie*. Bizarre, comical characters turned up on *The Addams Family*, *The Munsters*, *The Flying Nun*, and *Batman*, and slapstick silliness was alive and well on *Gilligan's Island*, *Mr. Ed*, *McHale's Navy*, *F Troop*, *Hogan's Heroes*, and many other shows.

Kids themselves were the stars of some of the comedies as in *Dennis the Menace*, *Leave It to Beaver*, *The Donna Reed Show*, and *The Many Loves of Dobie Gillis*. Kids like cartoons, so we had *The Flintstones* and *The Jetsons* in prime time; animals turned up on *Flipper* and *Daktari*; rock music on *Shindig* and *Hullabaloo*; science fiction on *Lost in Space* and *Star Trek*.

Of the many fads that swept America in the 1960s, probably the biggest was the James Bond–super agent vogue, which started with the Bond movies in 1963–64. The trend was soon reflected on the TV screen in such hits as *The Man From U.N.C.L.E.*, *I Spy*, *Secret Agent*, and *Mission: Impossible*. One of the funniest comedies of the 1960s, *Get Smart*, satirized the whole genre.

A few Westerns lingered on, notably *Bonanza* (the number-one series from 1964–1967) and *Gunsmoke*, which enjoyed a revival as a 7:30 P.M. kid's show. Drs. Kildare and Ben Casey kept women enthralled, as did the continuing anguish on prime time's first hit soap opera, *Peyton Place*. Men could find excitement on a wave of war shows, among them *Combat!*, *Twelve O'Clock High*, and *Garrison's Gorillas*.

Was there anything serious on TV in the early 1960s? The answer is "not much"; even the network newscasts were only 15 minutes long until 1963. *The Dick Van Dyke Show* did offer comedy written on an adult level, and *The Defenders* sometimes presented serious, relevant drama. More typical was the fate of George C. Scott's first network TV series, *East Side/West Side,* a gritty 1963 drama about an inner-city social worker; it lasted a single season opposite *Sing Along with Mitch*. The following year, *That Was the Week That Was ("TW3")*, a pioneering attempt at social satire, was driven off the air by *Petticoat Junction*.

The Relevance Era (late 1960s–1975)

East Side/West Side and *TW3* were shows ahead of their time. America was changing, and the gap between TV's land of make-believe and the real world was becoming a gulf. While Jed Clampett and Pvt. Gomer Pyle cavorted on our television screens, Kennedy and Khrushchev had brought the world to the brink of nuclear war over Cuba, and black Americans were burning and looting the slums of Los Angeles. Television, like many of society's other institutions, had to change.

The first major series of the period to acknowledge that there was a world beyond *Gilligan's Island* was *I Spy* in 1965, the series that reintroduced blacks to prime-time starring roles. Blacks had scarcely been seen on television since the early 1950s, and never in respectable, nondemeaning leading roles. *I Spy*, *Julia*, *Room 222*, and *The Mod Squad* changed all that, and dozens of black or minority series followed in the 1970s. The portrayal of women began to change as well, from the dependent housewives of *I Love Lucy* and *Donna Reed* to the liberated singles of *That Girl* and *Mary Tyler Moore*.

Direct political commentary within an entertainment format was a little longer in coming, but when it did it produced some enormous hits. *The Smothers Brothers Comedy Hour* premiered in February 1967 as a lightweight, youth-oriented variety show, but quickly swung toward biting political satire which caused the CBS censors to have fits. On NBC, *Rowan & Martin's Laugh-In* premiered in 1968 with a similarly topical approach, and shot straight to the top of the ratings; it was the number-one program on television from 1968–1970.

Ratings for the fall 1970 schedule seemed to suggest that "relevant TV" might have passed its peak. A slew of highly contemporary, youth-oriented shows were introduced that fall, among them *The Storefront Lawyers*, *The Young Lawyers*, *The Senator*, and *The Young Rebels* (the 1960s youth movement transplanted to the Revolutionary War). All of them failed. But a midseason replacement, scheduled with great trepidation by CBS, gave relevance new life. *All in the Family*, about a blue-collar bigot and the folly of his ways, ranked number one among all series for five years, the longest time on top for any series in television history. In its wake came spin-offs *(Maude, The Jeffersons)* and a new wave of shows dealing with issues TV had scarcely ever touched before: interfaith marriage *(Bridget Loves Bernie)*, anti-war sentiments *(M*A*S*H)*, life at the bottom of the economic ladder *(Good Times, Chico & The Man)*. Maude had an abortion, and Edith Bunker was attacked by a rapist—comedy had never been like this before!

Some shows stayed away from serious issues. Action-adventure was represented by the descendants of *77 Sunset Strip*, including *Mannix*, *Hawaii Five-O*, *Kojak*, *Columbo*, and *The Rockford Files*. *The Waltons* and *Little House on the Prairie* were gentle reminders of a simpler time, carrying a message about the value of love and the nuclear family.

A situation comedy that premiered on ABC in 1974 seemed to be even more of a throwback—but *Happy Days* would prove to be a harbinger of the next era of prime-time TV programming. Major changes were about to take place, in part due to government complaints about TV violence and the increasing frankness of the relevance shows, especially in time periods when children were watching. In 1975 the networks were forced to "sanitize" their early evening lineups with a curiously cynical concept called the 8:00–9:00 P.M. Family Viewing Time (cynical because children hardly view only between 8:00–9:00 P.M.). Henceforth, programs in that time slot would have to be suitable for "family viewing." No rapes and no abortions.

The ABC "Fantasy" Era (1975–1980)

As prime-time programming had swung like a pendulum from the escapism of the early 1960s to the relevance of the early 1970s, it now swung back again—at least partway. *Happy Days*, the perfect inoffensive 8:00 P.M. show, grew steadily in popularity, paralleling the vogue for one of its secondary characters, the Fonz. By 1976 it was the number-one program on television. At that time ABC's fortunes were in the hands of Fred Silverman, a master programmer who knew how to milk a rising series for all it was worth. Using *Happy Days* as his launching pad, he built a whole evening of similarly lightweight programs on Tuesdays with *Laverne & Shirley* at 8:30 followed by the progressively sexier *Three's Company*, *Soap*, and *Family*. The same thing worked on Wednesday, where *Eight Is Enough* captured the kids at 8 o'clock and *Charlie's Angels* gave adults something to leer at at nine.

Other hits were carefully nurtured in strategic places throughout the week, almost all of them thoroughly escapist comedy/action (for the kids) or sexually titillating. Thursday had *Welcome Back, Kotter* and *Barney Miller*; Friday, *Donny and Marie*; Saturday; *The Love Boat* and *Fantasy Island*; and Sunday, *The Six Million Dollar Man*. *Mork and Mindy* was spun off from *Happy Days*, and *The Bionic Woman* from *The Six Million Dollar Man*. ABC, long the number-three network, vaulted to number one in the ratings for the first time in its history.

As ABC's fantasy and sex filled the air, the other two networks struggled to compete. They managed a few imitations of the ABC style (CBS' *Dukes of Hazzard*, NBC's *CHiPs*), but CBS survived mostly on carryovers from its glory days of the early 1970s (it had been in the vanguard of the relevance movement), while NBC floundered with an uneven hodgepodge typified by *The Big Event*. Few new "relevant" series were able to get a foothold; among them were *Lou Grant* and *Quincy, M.E.* "Serious" TV was relegated mostly to mini-series, such as the spectacularly successful *Roots*. In addition, *60 Minutes*, an obscure CBS public affairs series that had been bumping around the schedule since 1968, enjoyed a remarkable surge in popularity, aided by fortuitous scheduling Sunday night at 7 P.M. It happened that a peculiarity in government regulations prevented the networks from competing with entertainment series in that time slot; only "public service" was allowed. Given this protection from normal competition, *60 Minutes* caught on in a big way, eventually becoming the number-one program on television—the only news series ever to do so.

Soap Operas and the "Real People" Era (1980s)

By 1980 ABC's escapist hits were in decline, their novelty worn thin. Fred Silverman had defected to NBC, and new hits were hard to come by. In addition the competitive environment was changing radically. Cable TV networks were spreading across the country, and commercial broadcasters found an increasing portion of their audience siphoned off to watch commercial-free movies and specialty channels (all news, sports, rock music, etc.). With so many viewing alternatives, the commercial network schedules looked increasingly stale and derivative.

Gradually two new trends emerged. The soap opera, that serialized format so popular in daytime, became a hit in prime time as well, introducing a continuing-story element missing from most prime-time series. *Dallas* was the first major hit, followed by *Dynasty*, *Falcon Crest*, and *Knots Landing*. Other series also began to work in continuing stories, such as the rocky romances on *Hill Street Blues* and *Cheers*.

The other trend was sparked by the much talked-about *Real People* in 1979 and was, in a sense, a swing back to reality. These programs set out to reflect the real world, especially its lighter, more entertaining aspects, without necessarily trying to change it (as the relevance shows had tended to do). *That's Incredible* and *Ripley's Believe It or Not* followed closely in the spirit of *Real People*. *20/20* was a cross between *60 Minutes* and a celebrity magazine, while *TV's Bloopers and Practical Jokes* was a close relation to that old snoop, *Candid Camera*. The number-one hit, *The Cosby Show*, presented a realistic view of child rearing; *Hill Street Blues* and *St. Elsewhere* brought reality to police and doctor shows. Numerous syndicated programs picked up on the reality trend, among them *PM Magazine*, *Entertainment Tonight*, and *The People's Court*.

There were still escapist fantasies like *The A-Team*, *Knight Rider*, *The Fall Guy*, and *Magnum, P.I.*, some of them so slapstick they bordered on comedy. Wildly careening automobiles, a favorite since the days of *Starsky & Hutch* and *The Dukes of Hazzard*, were a favorite device. In *Knight Rider*, the vehicle (a talking Pontiac Trans-Am named KITT) could actually fly through the air. Landings were often hard, but no one ever got hurt.

The Era of Choice (1990s)

When I first wrote about the (then) "Six Eras of Prime Time" in 1984, it looked as if future updates would be easy. One network would sooner or later stumble upon the next trend, the other two would immediately copy it, and the viewing public would be inundated with clones—the next programming "era." But it hasn't worked out that way. Instead, the once tightly controlled world of national television has exploded into hundreds of channels, all with their own independent voices. No longer can three powerful networks dictate what you will see, and no longer does programming move in lockstep. For the first time viewers have a real choice, all the time, and they are using it.

The principal engine of change was cable, a minor force until the early 1980s when changes in government regulations (which had previously favored broadcasters) ignited rapid growth. By 1987 cable had wired 50 percent of U.S. TV homes, and today it is in about 70 percent, with an additional close-to-20 percent receiving "cable" networks via satellite—a real force in the marketplace. At first the cable networks, lacking the vast financial resources of the entrenched broadcasters, could afford only old movies and reruns of old network shows. But necessity led to ingenuity, resulting in viewing alternatives that the older networks would never provide. There was continuous news (CNN), music (MTV, VH1), documentaries (Discovery), instruction (The Learning Channel, Mind Extension University), cultural programs (A&E, Bravo), and services (The Weather Channel, QVC). Movie channels offered films that were new (HBO), old (AMC), and in between (TNT, TBS, USA). Nickelodeon offered a safe yet exciting environment for kids, while The Family Channel and TNN were built around traditional family values (something the broadcast networks seemed to care little about). Other entertainment channels were thematic, such as The Sci-Fi Channel and Comedy Central. Rather than copycat programming, cable networks tended to provide something different. When the broadcast networks all flocked to make torn-from-the-headlines "reality" movies, USA Network produced a steady stream of original romantic thrillers, TNT filmed sweeping historical epics such as *Gettysburg* and *Geronimo*, and HBO offered Hollywood-style "events" *(Barbarians at the Gate, Stalin)*.

As the 1990s dawned, the cable networks expanded into original series in a big way. CNN's *Larry King Live* was a major force in the 1992 Presidential elections; Nick's *Double Dare*, *Clarissa Explains It All*, and *Ren and Stimpy* were hits with kids; USA's *Swamp Thing* and *Ray Bradbury Theater* enthralled sci-fi fans; and MTV mirrored its own restless "MTV generation" with innovative series such as *Liquid TV* and *The Real World*. Later, *Biography*, *Rugrats*, *South Park*, *The Statler Brothers Show*, and *WWF Wrestling* drew big audiences.

Cable was not the only source for new viewing alternatives in the 1990s. Original syndicated series, which bypassed the networks and were sold directly to stations, were booming. There had always been some successful shows of this type, such as *Lawrence Welk* and *Hee Haw*, but a new era began with the fabulously successful *Star Trek: The Next Generation* (1987)—a franchise which NBC had refused to give a second chance after its original *Star Trek* series in the 1960s. The same network shot itself in the foot again in 1990 when it discarded a lightweight hour called *Baywatch*, only to see it continue in production for syndication and become, reportedly, the most popular TV series in the world. By the 1990s scores of original non-network series filled the early evening, weekend, and (on independent stations) prime-time hours, among them *American Gladiators, Arsenio Hall, A Current Affair, Entertainment Tonight, Hercules, Highlander, Renegade, Rush Limbaugh, Star Trek: Deep Space Nine*, and *Xena: Warrior Princess*.

The reaction of the three old-line networks to all this new competition was largely business as usual. As the prime-time soap operas faded in the late 1980s, all three turned to reality, in forms as diverse as *America's Funniest Home Videos, Unsolved Mysteries*, and *Rescue 911*. *Roseanne* and *Grace Under Fire* were funny looks at the real-life problems of lower middle-class parents during hard times; *Murphy Brown* welcomed a parade of real-life newscasters to her fictional newsroom (and took on the real-life Vice President of the United States, Dan Quayle, in a debate about the morality of choosing to raise a child alone); *Major Dad* worried about his base being closed due to Pentagon cutbacks. Quirkiness was in *(Northern Exposure, Picket Fences)*, as were shows about spoiled young singles bonding *(Seinfeld, Friends, Ellen)*. Two of the three major networks were now run by bottom-line oriented investors who treated them as mere factories, not show business, leading to a proliferation of low-cost and sometimes sleazy prime-time "newsmagazines" which often screamed as loudly as the supermarket tabloids *(Dateline NBC, Day One, Turning Point, 48 Hours, Primetime Live, Street Stories, Eye to Eye with Connie Chung*, et al.). Every mass murderer and sexual deviant in America seemed to have his fifteen minutes of fame on these "informational" shows.

Because the older networks steadfastly refused to differentiate themselves, competition even sprang up from new broadcast networks. The first was the hip, racy Fox Network in 1987, which scored hits with several shows the older networks had turned down as too "different" *(Cops, Married with Children)*. Later, Warner Bros.' WB Network and Paramount's UPN launched a mix of prime-time comedy and action serving youth and ethnic minorities.

The "Real" Reality Era (early 2000s)

As the chaotic '90s, with its mixture of spoiled-singles sitcoms and gritty reality-drama *(ER, N.Y.P.D. Blue, Law & Order)* wound to an end, network television stumbled on to the "next big thing" in *real* reality shows. Imagine, putting real people on the screen and watching them worry, scheme and sweat! The vanguard of this new wave was the quiz show *Who Wants to Be a Millionaire* in the late summer of 1999, which reminded networks of the value of audience participation (anyone could get on the show by calling in and taking some tests) and of showing us ourselves on the screen. *Survivor* in 2000 clinched it, with its soap opera backbiting and theatricality as one contestant after another was "voted off the island." MTV had been doing this sort of thing for youth since *The Real World* premiered in 1992, but now adults discovered it, and a flood of imitators followed, including *Big Brother, Temptation Island, Making the Band, Fear Factor, Chains of Love, The Amazing Race, The Mole, The Bachelor/Bachelorette, Joe Millionaire* and *American Idol*. Cable had its own strange variations in shows like *Jackass, The Osbournes* and *The Anna Nicole Show*. There were also some pretty brutal game shows, including *The Weakest Link* and torture-quizzes *The Chamber* and *The Chair*; for the most bizarre variation, however, one had to turn to the Game Show Network, which had a show called *Russian Roulette* in which losing contestants literally dropped out of sight through a suddenly sprung trapdoor!

For a time cable seemed to be the refuge of scripted drama, with hits like *La Femme Nikita, Any Day Now, Strong Medicine, The Shield, Monk, Dead Zone* and *The Sopranos*. But a new wave of reality-based drama spread on the broadcast networks as well, including *CSI, The West Wing, Third Watch* and *Boston Public*, while fantasy escapism, in shows like *Alias* and *Thieves*, struggled. Women became more empowered (*Judging Amy, Crossing Jordan, Charmed*, anything on Lifetime). In sitcoms there was a subtrend toward challenged (or slobbish) guys with smart, sexy wives, as in *The King of Queens, According to Jim, Yes Dear* and *Everybody Loves Raymond*. Youth was served more than ever before, with teen angst on *Dawson's Creek* and *7th Heaven* (and, humorously, on *Buffy the Vampire Slayer*), as well as with whole networks like MTV and the Cartoon Network. Kids were in heaven with cable hits like *The Powerpuff Girls, SpongeBob Square-Pants, Lizzie McGuire* and *Yu-Gi-Oh!*

All this choice has not deterred viewers from their time-honored tradition of complaining about TV. However, Bruce Springsteen's 1992 song "57 Channels (And Nothin' On)" seems supremely ironic, given the diversity mentioned above; the problem may well be a generation unwilling to give anything more than five seconds of its attention, rather than a lack of quality alternatives. As the authors are acutely aware, as we try to keep up with it all on your behalf, this is television's Golden Age of Choice.

Over the years America's love affair with television has matured from initial infatuation to an accepted, and pervasive, part of everyday life. It happened very fast. The percentage of U.S. homes with one or more TV sets leaped from 1 percent to 50 percent in five short years (1948–1953), and passed 90 percent in the early 1960s. Today 98 percent of U.S. homes have TV—it is everywhere. And the average home has its set on seven hours a day, every day, watching and taping. The explosion in cable channels has only added to the enormous variety of programs available.

As for the programs we've watched, they're all in these pages. Leaf through the book, guided perhaps by the year-by-year network schedules and top program rankings in the back. A panorama of the series and the stars who captivated America for fifty-plus years is on display.

A&E (Network), see *Arts & Entertainment Network*

ABC ALBUM, see *Plymouth Playhouse*

ABC BARN DANCE (*Music*)
FIRST TELECAST: *February 21, 1949*
LAST TELECAST: *November 14, 1949*
BROADCAST HISTORY:
Feb 1949–Jun 1949, ABC Mon 8:30–9:00
Jul 1949–Oct 1949, ABC Mon 9:00–9:30
Oct 1949–Nov 1949, ABC Mon 9:30–10:00
EMCEE:
Hal O'Halloran
Jack Stillwell

The *National Barn Dance*, begun in 1924 on radio station WLS, Chicago, and long a radio favorite, was carried on ABC television in 1949 as the *ABC Barn Dance*. Among the *Barn Dance* favorites appearing on this half-hour Monday night version were the Sage Riders instrumental quartet, Lulu Belle and Scotty, Cousin Tifford, the De Zurick Sisters (a yodeling duet), caller John Dolce, and comic Holly Swanson. The series was telecast from Chicago.

ABC COMEDY HOUR (*Comedy/Variety*)
FIRST TELECAST: *January 12, 1972*
LAST TELECAST: *August 9, 1972*
BROADCAST HISTORY:
Jan 1972–Apr 1972, ABC Wed 8:30–9:30
Jun 1972–Aug 1972, ABC Wed 9:30–10:30
REGULARS:
Rich Little
Frank Gorshin
George Kirby
Marilyn Michaels
Charlie Callas
Joe Baker
Fred Travalena

Most of the telecasts that were aired under the title *ABC Comedy Hour* featured a guest host plus a regular repertory company of impressionists called The Kopycats, listed above. (Fred Travalena replaced Charlie Callas in the company in mid-series.) The series also included a number of other comedy specials, among them two Friars' Roasts, an Alan King special, and an updated version of *Hellzapoppin'*. Reruns of the Kopycats episodes were aired during the summer of 1972 under the title *ABC Comedy Hour Presents the Kopycats*.

ABC COMEDY SPECIAL (*Comedy Anthology*)
FIRST TELECAST: *June 6, 1986*
LAST TELECAST: *August 8, 1986*
BROADCAST HISTORY:
Jun 1986–Jul 1986, ABC Fri 9:30–10:00
Aug 1986, ABC Fri 9:00–10:00

A collection of pilots for comedies that did not make ABC's Fall 1986 schedule. Among those starring in this particular crop of "busted pilots" were Caroline McWilliams, Annie Potts, Blair Brown, Ted Bessell, Robert Klein, Madeline Kahn, and Pat Harrington.

ABC DRAMATIC SHORTS—1952–1953 (*Dramatic Films*)

ABC had problems in the early 1950s. It had fewer stations than NBC or CBS, few advertisers, and therefore little revenue with which to pay for new programming. In order just to stay on the air, the "other network" was forced to schedule dozens of low-budget quiz shows, interview programs, and documentary films (most obtained free from government and industry). Needless to say, this did not attract much of an audience to the network. In 1952 ABC tried an experiment. It assembled a package of several dozen low-budget 30-minute dramatic films, most of them made by MCA Films in Hollywood. Many of them had been seen on TV before, on ABC (*Gruen Guild Theater*), DuMont (*Gruen Playhouse*), and some even on NBC (*Campbell Soundstage*). These shopworn films were sprinkled liberally throughout the ABC schedule during the 1952–1953 season, on multiple "theater" series. Each film ran up to half a dozen times on different nights and on different series. Not every film would turn up on every series, but if you watched ABC long enough you would frequently get the impression that you had "seen that film before."

Most of the films were grade "B" productions, starring some Hollywood old-timers as well as lesser-known young actors and actresses (some of whom were to gain fame in later years). Among them were Buddy Ebsen, Raymond Burr, Cesar Romero, Ann Rutherford, Helen Parrish, Vincent Price, Anita Louise, Hans Conried, Cliff Arquette, Onslow Stevens, and many others. The scripts included mysteries (such as "The Cavorting Statue" with Cesar Romero), romantic tales ("A Little Pig Cried" with Frances Rafferty), and comedies.

Following is a list of the theater series among which the films rotated, mostly during 1952–1953. It is not guaranteed to be complete!

APPOINTMENT WITH LOVE
Dec 1952–Sep 1953, ABC Fri 9:00–9:30
CARNIVAL
Feb 1953–Sep 1953, ABC Thu 8:00–8:30
DARK ADVENTURE
Jan 1953–Jul 1953, ABC Mon 8:30–9:00
DOUBLE EXPOSURE
Jan 1953–Sep 1953, ABC Wed 9:00–9:30
FABLE FOR A SUMMER NIGHT
Jul 1953–Oct 1953, ABC Thu 10:30–11:00
FEAR AND FANCY
May 1953–Aug 1953, ABC Wed 8:00–8:30
FILM FESTIVAL
Jul 1953–Sep 1953, ABC Sun 6:30–7:00
GRUEN GUILD THEATER
Sep 1951–Dec 1951, ABC Thu 9:30–10:00
HALF HOUR THEATRE
Jun 1953–Sep 1953, ABC Fri 9:30–10:00
HOUR GLASS
Jan 1953–Sep 1953, ABC Wed 8:30–9:00
LITTLE THEATRE
Dec 1952–Jan 1953, ABC Wed 7:30–8:00
Aug 1953–Sep 1953, ABC Tue 9:00–10:30 (3 films)
PLAYHOUSE NUMBER 7
Oct 1952–Nov 1952, ABC Sun 9:00–9:30
Nov 1952–Jan 1953, ABC Wed/Sun 9:00–9:30
Jan 1953–Mar 1953, ABC Sun 7:30–8:00
RETURN ENGAGEMENT
Jul 1953–Sep 1953, ABC Mon 9:30–10:00

STRAW HAT THEATER
Jul 1953–Sep 1953, ABC Sun 7:30–8:00
SUMMER FAIR
Jun 1953–Sep 1953, ABC Thu 9:30–10:00
TURNING POINT, THE
Jan 1953–Mar 1953, ABC Thu 9:00–9:30
May 1953–Jan 1953, ABC Sat 7:30–8:00
TWENTIETH CENTURY TALES
Jan 1953–Jul 1953, ABC Wed 8:00–8:30
Jul 1953–Sep 1953, ABC Mon 8:30–9:00
WHITE CAMELLIA, THE
Jan 1953–Mar 1953, ABC Tue 8:30–9:30 (2 films)

ABC FAMILY CHANNEL, THE (Network) (*General Entertainment Cable Network*)

LAUNCHED:
April 1977
SUBSCRIBERS (MAY 2003):
84.7 million (79% U.S.)

This cable network has gone through some major changes during its long history. It was launched in 1977 as CBN, the Christian Broadcasting Network, and originally featured a heavy dose of religious programming. A vestige of that era remains on its schedule today in *The 700 Club* (q.v.), a Christian news and features magazine hosted by network founder Pat Robertson. Among CBN's drama series during the 1980s were *Another Life* (1981–1984), a Christian soap opera; and *The Campbells* (1986–1989), about a Scottish family in the Canadian wilderness in the 1830s. CBN's big production center in Virginia Beach, Virginia, said to be the largest facility in the world for the production of Christian TV programming, was dubbed the "Video Vatican."

The network gradually broadened its focus, acquiring a wide range of broadcast reruns, especially westerns but also including cartoons, game shows, and dramas (*The Waltons, Rescue 911*). In 1989, CBN was renamed the Family Channel. Although it promoted itself as the home of "positive-value, upbeat programming the whole family can enjoy," its schedule was hardly without violence, particularly in rerun westerns such as *Gunsmoke, Bonanza,* and *The Young Riders.* However, it generally avoided the contemporary sex and violence that is so widespread on broadcast channels. Family also became one of the more prolific producers of original series programming on cable, most of it light action/adventure emphasizing relationships and individual courage. There were also some sitcoms. Among its earlier series were *Bordertown, Rin Tin Tin K-9 Cop,* and *Zorro*; later entries included *Big Brother Jake, Maniac Mansion, Snowy River: The MacGregor Saga, Madeline,* and *That's My Dog.*

In 1998, Pat Robertson sold the network to Rupert Murdoch's News Corporation, which operates the Fox Network and is known for precisely the kind of edgy (often sexy and violent) programming the Family Channel traditionally abhorred. Effective August 15, 1998, the name was changed to the Fox Family Channel, and there were major on-air changes—though not, initially at least, toward the kind of raunchy programming critics feared. Daytime was given over to cartoons and other kids' programming, while in the evening there were lightweight family shows including *I Can't Believe You Said That* (quiz), *Show Me the Funny* (videos), *Life, Camera, Action!* (more videos), *Ohhh, Noooo! Mr. Bill Presents* (English comedy sketches), and *The New Addams Family* (sitcom). There were also nightly movies, including some produced by the channel.

Later entries included *Higher Ground, The Fearing Mind* and the critically acclaimed *State of Grace.* None of these was terribly successful, and after only three years Fox sold the network to Disney/ABC, which in November 2001 renamed it the ABC Family Channel. It then began to air reruns of current ABC series such as *Whose Line Is It Anyway?, Alias, According to Jim, Life with Bonnie, Less Than Perfect, Celebrity Mole* and *The Bachelor.* It also produced some reality programs of its own, including *The Last Resort* (specials, 2002) and *My Life Is a Sitcom* (series, 2003).

The network first reached more than half of all U.S. television homes in June 1989, and its principal original evening series after that date (including those mentioned above) can be found in this book under their individual titles.

ABC FEATURE FILM, see *Movies—Prior to 1961*

ABC IN CONCERT (*Music*)

FIRST TELECAST: *June 7, 1991*
LAST TELECAST: *September 11, 1998*
BROADCAST HISTORY:
Jun 1991–Dec 1992, ABC Fri 12:00 midnight–1:00 A.M.
Jan 1993–Jan 1997, ABC Fri 12:05–12:35 A.M.
Jan 1997–Sep 1998, ABC Fri 12:35–1:05 A.M.
HOST:
Madison Michele (1996–1998)

From 1973 to 1975, as part of its *Wide World of Entertainment,* ABC aired a series of late-night rock concerts called *In Concert* on Fridays (see under *ABC Late Night*). In 1991 the network revived the tradition as a stand-alone series. The performances were taped in stadiums all over the world and featured a mix of newer acts (Poison, George Michael, Sinéad O'Connor, INXS, L.L. Cool J) and longer-established performers (Cher, the Grateful Dead, Judas Priest, the Scorpions, Phil Collins). Concert staging had grown a lot more elaborate since the 1970s. Poison leader Brett Michaels said at the premiere, "It's about time live rock & roll is returning to the airwaves, and this show will give fans the chance to see bands with all their sound and lights." There was no regular host until 1996, although *General Hospital*'s Vanessa Marcil frequently handled the honors beginning in 1994.

The concerts were simulcast in stereo on the ABC radio networks. Originally titled *ABC's In Concert,* the series was renamed *ABC In Concert* in January, 1992.

ABC IN CONCERT COUNTRY (*Music*)

FIRST TELECAST: *June 4, 1994*
LAST TELECAST: *August 10, 1994*
BROADCAST HISTORY:
Jun 1994–Aug 1994, ABC Sat 11:30 P.M.–12:30 A.M.
HOST:
Billy Dean

A companion program to Friday night's *ABC In Concert* rock series, featuring contemporary country artists such as Trisha Yearwood, Billy Ray Cyrus, Sawyer Brown, and Travis Tritt.

ABC LATE NIGHT (*Various*)
FIRST TELECAST: *January 1, 1973*
LAST TELECAST: *October 21, 1982*
BROADCAST HISTORY:

Jan 1973–Nov 1979, ABC Mon–Fri 11:30–Conclusion
Nov 1979–Mar 1980, ABC Mon–Fri 11:50–Conclusion
Mar 1980–Jan 1981, ABC Mon–Thu 11:50–Conclusion + Fri 11:30–Conclusion
Jan 1981–Mar 1981, ABC Mon–Thu 12:00–Conclusion + Fri 11:30–Conclusion
Mar 1981–Oct 1982, ABC Mon–Fri 12:00–Conclusion

With the failure of Les Crane, Joey Bishop, or Dick Cavett to attract a substantial following for ABC in the late-night area, the network decided in 1973 to try a new tack. Johnny Carson could have the talk-show audience; ABC countered with a diversified potpourri that, it was hoped, would offer something of interest to everyone. ABC officially premiered *Wide World of Entertainment* on January 1, 1973, following a tryout run from November 21–December 8, 1972. There were nights, in fact whole weeks, with Cavett or Jack Paar hosting talk shows, but there were also comedy specials, mysteries, documentaries, rock-music shows, and just about anything else that could be done on a small budget. The first telecast was in two parts: "Let's Celebrate," a comedy-variety show starring Tony Roberts, followed by a short "Bedtime Story" in which a young married couple talked about their day as they prepared for bed. Other specials included "In Concert" (rock music), "Comedy News," Truman Capote interviewing convicts, and "The Roger Miller Show."

It soon became apparent that the improvisational comedy and offbeat specials were not attracting weary viewers, but the occasional mystery thrillers and TV-movie repeats were. Eventually these became the bulk of the presentations, followed in the later 1970s by reruns of prime-time series. With the change in program content, the umbrella title for this series was changed from *ABC Wide World of Entertainment* to *ABC Late Night* on January 12, 1976. During the fall, when ABC carried *Monday Night Football*, there was no *ABC Late Night* programming on that night.

Summarized below is a night-by-night history of *ABC Late Night*. In cases where there was a double feature on a given night, a semicolon is used to separate the first and second features. If more than one series alternated in the same time slot on different weeks, they are separated by a slash.

CHRONOLOGY OF ABC LATE NIGHT BY NIGHT OF THE WEEK

Monday
Jan 1973–Sep 1973, Movie/*Jack Paar Tonight*/Movie/*Dick Cavett Show*
Jan 1974–Aug 1974, ABC Late Night Special
Jan 1975–Sep 1975, Wide World Mystery (Movie)
Jan 1976–Sep 1976, ABC Monday Night Special
Jan 1977–Apr 1977, The Streets of San Francisco; Dan August
Apr 1977–Sep 1977, The Streets of San Francisco; Toma
Jan 1978–May 1978, Police Story
Jun 1978–Aug 1978, Soap; Police Story
Dec 1978–Aug 1979, Police Story
Jan 1980–Mar 1980, Barney Miller; Police Story
Apr 1980–Jul 1980, Barney Miller; Police Woman
Jul 1980–Aug 1980, Barney Miller
Jan 1981–Aug 1981, Fantasy Island
Jan 1982–Aug 1982, Movie

Tuesday
Jan 1973–Oct 1973, ABC Late Night Special/Jack Paar Tonight/Movie/*Dick Cavett Show*
Nov 1973–Dec 1973, Movie/*Dick Cavett Show*
Dec 1973–Jan 1976, Wide World Mystery (Movie)
Jan 1976–May 1978, Tuesday Movie of the Week
Jun 1978–Aug 1978, Soap; Tuesday Movie of the Week
Aug 1978–Sep 1979, Tuesday Movie of the Week
Sep 1979–Dec 1979, Barney Miller; Tuesday Movie of the Week
Jan 1980–Apr 1980, Tuesday Movie of the Week
Apr 1980–Aug 1980, Soap; Tuesday Movie of the Week
Aug 1980–Sep 1981, Tuesday Movie of the Week
Sep 1981–Oct 1982, Fantasy Island

Wednesday
Jan 1973–Oct 1973, ABC Late Night Special/Jack Paar Tonight/ABC Late Night Special/Dick Cavett Show
Nov 1973–Dec 1973, ABC Late Night Special/Dick Cavett Show
Dec 1973–Sep 1975, Wide World Special
Sep 1975–Sep 1976, Wednesday Movie of the Week
Sep 1976–Aug 1977, The Rookies; Mystery of the Week (Movie)
Sep 1977–Dec 1977, Starsky and Hutch; Mystery of the Week (Movie)
Jan 1978–Aug 1978, Police Story; Mystery of the Week (Movie)
Sep 1978–Jan 1979, Police Woman; S.W.A.T.
Jan 1979–Jul 1979, Police Woman; Mannix
Jul 1979–Sep 1979, Police Woman; Baretta
Sep 1979–Sep 1980, Love Boat; Baretta
Sep 1980–Feb 1981, Love Boat; Police Woman
Mar 1981–Apr 1981, Love Boat; Joe Forrester
Apr 1981–Oct 1982, Love Boat

Thursday
Jan 1973–Nov 1973, ABC Late Night Special/Jack Paar Tonight/Movie/*Dick Cavett Show*
Nov 1973–May 1974, ABC Late Night Special/Dick Cavett Show
Jun 1974–Sep 1974, Good Night America/Dick Cavett Show
Sep 1974–Dec 1974, Wide World Special/Dick Cavett Show
Jan 1975–Sep 1975, Wide World Special
Oct 1975–Mar 1976, Mannix; Longstreet
Mar 1976–Sep 1976, Mannix; The Magician
Sep 1976–Dec 1976, The Streets of San Francisco; Dan August
Jan 1977–Jun 1977, ABC Thursday Night Special
June 1977–Sep 1977, S.W.A.T.; ABC Thursday Night Special
Sep 1977–Dec 1977, Police Story; ABC Thursday Night Special
Jan 1978–Aug 1978, Starsky and Hutch; Toma
Sep 1978–Jan 1979, Starsky and Hutch; S.W.A.T.
Jan 1979–Jul 1979, Starsky and Hutch; Mannix
Jul 1979–Sep 1979, Starsky and Hutch; Baretta

Sep 1979–Apr 1980, Police Woman; Baretta
Apr 1980–Sep 1980, Charlie's Angels; Baretta
Sep 1980–Jan 1981, Charlie's Angels; Police Woman
Jan 1981–Sep 1981, Charlie's Angels
Oct 1981–Oct 1982, Vega$

Friday
Jan 1973–Nov 1973, In Concert/Jack Paar Tonight/In Concert/ Dick Cavett Show
*Dec 1973–May 1975, In Concert/*Movie
*May 1975–Jan 1976, Wide World Special/*Movie
Jan 1976–Sep 1976, The Rookies
Sep 1976–Apr 1977, S.W.A.T.
Apr 1977–Mar 1979, Baretta
Apr 1979–Jul 1979, Soap; Baretta
Jul 1979–Aug 1979, Soap
Sep 1979–Apr 1980, Charlie's Angels
Apr 1980–Oct 1982, Fridays

ABC MONDAY MYSTERY MOVIE, THE, see *ABC Mystery Movie, The*

ABC MONDAY NIGHT COMEDY SPECIAL, THE (*Various*)
FIRST TELECAST: *May 16, 1977*
LAST TELECAST: *September 5, 1977*
BROADCAST HISTORY:
May 1977–Sep 1977, ABC Mon 8:00–8:30

This was an umbrella title, covering an assortment of films for proposed series that did not make the schedule and leftovers from series that had been canceled. Included was a John Byner situation comedy, an unusual rock music show (30 minutes of music—no dialogue), and leftover episodes from the canceled *Blansky's Beauties, Nancy Walker Show,* and *Holmes and Yoyo.*

ABC MYSTERY MOVIE, THE (*Police/Detective Drama*)
FIRST TELECAST: *February 6, 1989*
LAST TELECAST: *August 4, 1990*
BROADCAST HISTORY:
Feb 1989–May 1989, ABC Mon 9:00–11:00
Aug 1989–Aug 1990, ABC Sat 9:00–11:00

Seeking to recapture the success—and programming flexibility—of the *NBC Mystery Movie* of the 1970s, which had spawned *Columbo, McMillan and Wife,* and other hits, ABC launched this version in early 1989. Originally there were three elements; *Columbo* was back, alternating with *B.L. Stryker* and *Gideon Oliver.* When the series moved to Saturday nights in the fall, *Gideon Oliver* was dropped and two new series were added, *Christine Cromwell* and a revival of *Kojak.* Details on each of these will be found under their separate title headings.

During the Monday run the formal title was the *ABC Monday Mystery Movie*; on Saturday it was the *ABC Saturday Mystery Movie.*

ABC NEWS REPORTS (*Documentary/Public Affairs*)
FIRST TELECAST: *July 7, 1963*
LAST TELECAST: *August 13, 1964*
BROADCAST HISTORY:
Jul 1963–Dec 1963, ABC Sun 10:30–11:00
Jan 1964–Aug 1964, ABC Thu 10:30–11:00
ANCHORMAN:
Bob Young (1963)

Some of the documentaries in this ABC News series were newly produced; others had been aired previously under the title *ABC Closeup.* A major production during August and September 1963 was a five-part series of special reports entitled "Crucial Summer: The 1963 Civil Rights Crisis," produced by Bill Kobin and anchored by newsman Ron Cochran. From September through December 1963, correspondent Bob Young, who was reportedly being groomed as a major on-camera news "personality" by ABC, served as the regular host. Later the anchor responsibilities rotated among various ABC correspondents.

ABC PENTHOUSE PLAYERS, see *ABC Television Players*

ABC PRESENTS (*Documentary*)
FIRST TELECAST: *July 22, 1957*
LAST TELECAST: *October 3, 1957*
BROADCAST HISTORY:
Jul 1957–Sep 1957, ABC Mon 9:00–9:30
Sep 1957–Oct 1957, ABC Thu 8:00–8:30

A documentary film series seen during the summer of 1957. This program was also known as *Quest for Adventure.*

ABC ROCKS (*Music Videos*)
FIRST TELECAST: *June 22, 1984*
LAST TELECAST: *August 2, 1985*
BROADCAST HISTORY:
Jun 1984–Aug 1985, ABC Fri 12:00 midnight–12:30 A.M.

One year after the premiere of NBC's *Friday Night Videos,* network television's first attempt to respond to the popularity of cable television's MTV (Music Television), ABC entered the fray with this half hour of music videos. Each weekly show consisted of a number of currently popular rock music videos, by such artists as Prince, The Cars, Cyndi Lauper, Bonnie Tyler, Eurythmics, Billy Idol, David Bowie, Huey Lewis and the News, and A Flock of Seagulls.

ABC SATURDAY COMEDY SPECIAL, THE (*Comedy Anthology*)
FIRST TELECAST: *June 24, 1978*
LAST TELECAST: *August 5, 1978*
BROADCAST HISTORY:
Jun 1978–Jul 1978, ABC Sat 8:30–9:00
Jul 1978–Aug 1978, ABC Sat 8:00–9:00

This was a collection of pilots for shows which did not make ABC's Fall 1978 schedule, along with miscellaneous reruns. Included were three Harvey Korman comedy episodes and a comedy-variety hour featuring characters from the Archie comic strip, with Dennis Bowen as Archie, Mark Winkworth as Reggie, and Hilary Thompson as Veronica.

ABC SATURDAY MYSTERY MOVIE, THE, see *ABC Mystery Movie, The*

ABC SCOPE (*Documentary/Public Affairs*)
FIRST TELECAST: *November 11, 1964*
LAST TELECAST: *March 2, 1968*
BROADCAST HISTORY:
Nov 1964–Sep 1965, ABC Wed 10:30–11:00
Sep 1965–Mar 1968, ABC Sat 10:30–11:00

Filmed reports, interviews, and roundtable discussions of current issues were all part of the format of this weekly public affairs series. ABC has also run many one-time documentary specials under this umbrella title over the years.

ABC SHOWCASE (*Drama/Variety*)
FIRST TELECAST: *June 22, 1950*
LAST TELECAST: *July 26, 1950*
BROADCAST HISTORY:
Jun 1950–Jul 1950, ABC Thu 9:00–9:30
Jul 1950, ABC Wed 9:00–9:30

This was a blanket title for a series of dramatic and variety specials run during the summer of 1950 and starring, among others, Betty Furness, Peter Donald, and George O'Hanlon.

ABC STAGE 67 (*Various*)
FIRST TELECAST: *September 14, 1966*
LAST TELECAST: *May 11, 1967*
BROADCAST HISTORY:
Sep 1966–Jan 1967, ABC Wed 10:00–11:00
Jan 1967–May 1967, ABC Thu 10:00–11:00

This was an umbrella title for a potpourri of assorted specials. Among them were serious dramas with distinguished international casts, variety shows, an occasional documentary, and such unique formats as Jack Paar with examples of the Kennedy wit and David Frost on a tour of London with Peter Sellers, Albert Finney, and Laurence Olivier. The program had no regular host.

ABC TELEVISION PLAYERS (*Dramatic Anthology*)
FIRST TELECAST: *January 16, 1949*
LAST TELECAST: *October 30, 1949*
BROADCAST HISTORY:
Jan 1949–Mar 1949, ABC Sun 9:00–9:30
Mar 1949–Oct 1949, ABC Sun 7:30–8:00
NARRATOR:
Don Gallagher

This was a series of low-budget live dramatic presentations from Chicago, fed to the East Coast network in the months immediately following the opening of the East-Midwest coaxial cable. Little-known Midwestern actors and actresses were used.

In April the title of the series was changed to *ABC Tele-Players,* and in August to *ABC Penthouse Players.*

ABC WIDE WORLD OF ENTERTAINMENT, see *ABC Late Night*

ABC'S NIGHTLIFE (*Talk*)
FIRST TELECAST: *November 9, 1964*
LAST TELECAST: *November 12, 1965*
BROADCAST HISTORY:
Nov 1964–Nov 1965, ABC Mon–Fri 11:15–1:00
REGULARS:
Les Crane (Nov 1964–Feb 1965, Jun–Nov 1965)
William B. Williams (1965)
Nipsey Russell (1965)
Jimmy Cannon (1965)
ORCHESTRA:
Cy Coleman (1965)
Donn Trenner (Mar–Jun 1965)
Elliot Lawrence (Jun–Nov 1965)

ABC's Nightlife was an early and abortive attempt by that network to compete in the late-night area long dominated by NBC's *Tonight Show.* The star was Les Crane, a handsome, young talk-show host from San Francisco who had attracted considerable attention there. Les's style was informal, highly spontaneous, and often controversial. The setting was a sort of studio-in-the-round, with the audience seated in circular tiers surrounding the stage, arena-style. Les, perched on his stool, often conversed with audience members by using a long-nosed "shotgun microphone," which he could focus on someone a long distance off. He strove for diversity and intelligence in his guests; the first show featured conservative commentator William F. Buckley and liberal Representative John V. Lindsay, actress Betsy Palmer, columnist Max Lerner, and comedian Groucho Marx, who acted as "instant critic" of the show.

Other critics were not very friendly, and Les left the show after only four months, to be replaced by a succession of guest hosts, including Shelley Berman, Dave Garroway, and Pat Boone, among others. Radio personality William B. Williams acted as aide-de-camp for all of them. At the end of June, however, Les was back, with Nipsey Russell as his sidekick. Soon after, the program moved from New York to Hollywood, but that couldn't save it. It ended its run just a year and three days after its premiere. Johnny Carson remained king of late-night television.

During its first four months the program was known as *The Les Crane Show.*

ACTS (Network), see *Faith & Values Channel*

A.E.S. HUDSON STREET (*Situation Comedy*)
FIRST TELECAST: *March 23, 1978*
LAST TELECAST: *April 20, 1978*
BROADCAST HISTORY:
Mar 1978–Apr 1978, ABC Thu 9:30–10:00
CAST:
Dr. Antonio "Tony" Menzies .... Gregory Sierra
Nurse Rosa Santiago .... Rosana DeSoto
J. Powell Karbo .... Stefan Gierasch
Ambulance Driver Foshko .... Susan Peretz
Ambulance Aide Stanke .... Ralph Manza
Nurse Newton .... Ray Stewart
Dr. Mackler .... Bill Cort
Dr. Glick .... Allan Miller

This medical comedy starred Gregory Sierra as Dr. Menzies, the harried chief resident of an inner city emergency ward; "A.E.S." stood for Adult Emergency Services. The location was Hudson Street, New York City, an area as run down as the hospital itself. Perpetually short of funds and surrounded by a staff of lunatics, Dr. Menzies nevertheless dealt with the various accident victims coming through the door as best he could, with good humor and only an occasional yearning to be somewhere else in the medical profession—anywhere else. Dr. Glick was the resident psychiatrist and J. Powell Karbo the bureaucratic hospital administrator.

AFP: AMERICAN FIGHTER PILOT (*Military Documentary*)
FIRST TELECAST: *March 29, 2002*
LAST TELECAST: *April 5, 2002*
BROADCAST HISTORY:
Mar 2002–Apr 2002, CBS Fri 8:00–9:00
REGULARS:
Lt. Todd Giggy

Lt. Marcus Gregory
Lt. Mike Love
Lt. Col. David Freaney ("Beans")
Maj. Robert Garland ("Shark")
Lt. Col. Monty Cooper ("Stump")
Maj. David Nahoum ("Abu")
Capt. Kevin Nicholson ("Divot")
Maj. Dennis Scarborough ("Cons")

This patriotic quasi-documentary series followed three young men as they went through the air force's rigorous F-15 fighter pilot training program at Tyndall Air Force Base near Panama City, Florida. The three aspiring pilots were Giggy, an enthusiastic newlywed whose father had been a fighter pilot; Gregory, a serious and religious young man about to become a first-time father; and Love, the most experienced of the three, father of two sons, with previous experience as a bomber pilot. The training staff included Freaney, the operations officer who oversaw the training program; Garland, the weapons instructor; Cooper, the classroom instructor; and the flight instructors assigned to each of the trainees—Nahoum (for Gregory), Nicholson (for Gibby) and Scarborough (for Love).

There was footage of the pilots training in their F-15s at more than 1,100 miles per hour along with coverage of their ground training and off-duty lives, all done in a disjointed cinema verité style that made everything seem dramatic and important. Apparently neither the subject matter nor the technique appealed to viewers. After two episodes failed to attract much of an audience, CBS abruptly grounded *AFP*.

AJ AFTER HOURS (*Talk/Variety*)

BROADCAST HISTORY:
E! Entertainment
30 minutes
Original episodes: *2001*
Premiered: *May 31, 2001*

HOST:
A. J. Benza

Leather-jacketed columnist and all-around cool dude A. J. Benza hosted this late-night variety show, which was set in a funky New York City club. Equally cool guests such as singer Luther Vandross, model Frederique, disk jockey Grand Master Flash and comic Vanessa Hollingshead appeared as A. J. fawned, hiply. He also did interviews in such places as a New York City rooftop or fire escape at night.

A. J., by the way, stood for Alfred Joseph, but probably only his mother called him that.

A.K.A. PABLO (*Situation Comedy*)

FIRST TELECAST: *March 6, 1984*
LAST TELECAST: *April 17, 1984*
BROADCAST HISTORY:
Mar 1984–Apr 1984, ABC Tue 8:30–9:00

CAST:
Paul (Pablo) Rivera .... Paul Rodriguez
Domingo Rivera .... Joe Santos
Rosa Maria Rivera.................... Katy Jurado
Sylvia Rivera .... Alma Cuervo
Lucia Rivera Del Gato .... Martha Velez
Hector Del Gato .... Arnaldo Santana
Manuel Rivera....................... Bert Rosario
Carmen Rivera................... Maria Richwine
José Sanchez/Shapiro .... Hector Elizondo
Linda Rivera .... Edie Marie Rubio
Nicholas Rivera....................... Antonio Torres
Anna Maria Del Gato .... Claudia Gonzales
Susana Del Gato .... Martha Gonzales
Tomas Del Gato .... Mario Lopez
Mario Del Gato....................... Beto Lovato
Elena Del Gato.................... Michelle Smith

EXECUTIVE PRODUCER:
Norman Lear

Short-lived comedy about a struggling young Hispanic comedian and his large, noisy family, who rooted for his success while wanting him to treat his Mexican-American heritage with almost solemn dignity. Paul Rivera—still called Pablo by his family—used a lot of ethnic jokes in his act, which sometimes offended his traditionalist parents, Domingo and Rosa Maria. But every Mexican joke he used seemed to spring from his home situation, whether it was about sister Lucia and her swaggering husband Hector, stuffy brother Manuel and his coquettish wife Carmen, or unmarried (but anxious) sister Sylvia. José was Paul's fast-talking but inexperienced agent, while the rest of the regulars consisted of the Rivera/Del Gato children.

A-TEAM, THE (*Adventure*)

FIRST TELECAST: *January 23, 1983*
LAST TELECAST: *June 14, 1987*
BROADCAST HISTORY:
Jan 1983, NBC Sun 10:00–11:00
Feb 1983–Aug 1986, NBC Tue 8:00–9:00
Aug 1986–Dec 1986, NBC Fri 8:00–9:00
Dec 1986, NBC Tue 8:00–9:00
May 1987–Jun 1987, NBC Sun 7:00–8:00

CAST:
Col. John "Hannibal" Smith .... George Peppard
Sgt. Bosco "B.A." Baracus .... Mr. T
Lt. Templeton Peck ("Faceman") (pilot only)
.... Tim Dunigan
Lt. Templeton Peck ("Faceman") ..... Dirk Benedict
Capt. H.M. "Howling Mad" Murdock
.... Dwight Schultz
Amy Allen (1983).................. Melinda Culea
Col. Lynch (1983–1984) .... William Lucking
Col. Roderick Decker (1983–1986)... Lance LeGault
Tawnia Baker (1984)............... Marla Heasley
Gen. Hunt Stockwell (1986–1987) .. Robert Vaughn
"Dishpan" Frankie Sanchez (1986–1987)
.... Eddie Velez
Carla (1986) .... Judy Ledford

MUSIC:
Mike Post and Pete Carpenter

It opened with machine-gun-like music, followed by the title stamped across the screen in stenciled, military-style letters, which were then punctured by bullet holes containing pictures of the stars. From opening title to closing credits, *The A-Team* was a veritable weekly demolition derby—and it was a smash hit.

The premise, like the plots, was standard-issue TV. A crack team of soldiers in Vietnam was caught while on a super-secret mission behind enemy lines. Seems that four days after the war had ended, they had knocked over the Bank of Hanoi for one hundred million yen, but could not prove who had given them their orders, and so were imprisoned by their own government. They had escaped, but now were outcasts, pursued as criminals by a relentless Col. Lynch (and later by Col. Decker), who was determined to put them behind bars again. They not only managed to evade the colonel's clutches, however, but became freelance soldiers of fortune, righting wrongs across the country and in exotic foreign locales.

It was a colorful team. Col. Hannibal Smith, the cigar-chomping, remarkably fit leader, was a master of disguises. B.A. (officially "Bad Attitude," but you can use your imagination) was big, black, and menacing—and also an expert mechanic. Howling Mad Murdock was their pilot, whose sanity was seriously in question (they had to spring him from a mental hospital for their missions), but who could apparently fly anything from a crop duster to a 747. Faceman was the pretty boy, a smooth talker who could hustle practically anything they needed for their missions. Joining them in the first episode was Amy Allen, a pretty reporter who was understandably taken with this odd bunch and their far-flung adventures.

The destruction they wrought may have seemed appalling to some, but it was carried off with such panache, such a twinkle in the eye, that viewers knew it was not for real. Despite jeeps spinning through the air and buildings leveled in fiery explosions, hardly anyone—even the bad guys—ever got hurt. One furious chase scene ended with the pursuing villains' car in a spectacular high-speed crash. The camera lingered for a moment on the overturned wreck; one voice from inside grunted, "You okay, Al?" and another answered, "Yeah, I'm all right."

Nor were the team members ever at a loss for firepower, even when separated from their innocuous-looking but well-armed van. B.A. could build machine guns out of old washing machines, rocket launchers out of used water heaters, and an armored tank out of a broken-down school bus. Mr. T (as B.A.) was the cult hero of the show, with his macho chains (35 lbs. of gold) draped around his neck and his favorite scowling line, "You better watch out, sucker!" For all his threatening appearance, however, he did have one abiding fear—flying in a plane piloted by Howling Mad. So the team regularly drugged, hypnotized, or tricked him to get him to the scene of the action.

In the fall of 1986 the team's status changed dramatically. Tricked into capture by the mysterious Gen. Stockwell, they were tried and sentenced to die—but Stockwell arranged for them to "pay their debt" by becoming undercover government agents instead, under his heavy-handed control. Joining the team was a sneaky little special-effects expert known as "Dishpan" Frankie.

A.U.S.A. (*Situation Comedy*)
FIRST TELECAST: *February 4, 2003*
LAST TELECAST: *April 1, 2003*
BROADCAST HISTORY:
Feb 2003–Apr 2003, NBC Tue 9:30–10:00
CAST:
Adam Sullivan .... Scott Foley
Susan Rakoff .... Amanda Detmer
Geoffrey Laurence .... Peter Jacobson
Wally Berman .... John Ross Bowie
Ana Rivera .... Ana Ortiz
Owen Harper .... Eddie McClintock
Courtroom comedy centering on handsome young New York Assistant U.S. Attorney Adam, who bumbled his way through his first days on the job even while showing some surprising backbone when cases got serious. His chief foil was pretty public defender Susan, who felt that all A.U.S.A.'s were enemies of the people and who regularly put him down. Of course that made him lust for her all the more. Geoffrey was Adam's mousy supervisor, Wally his grinning, goofball paralegal (obsessed with stapling everything), and Ana a street-smart fellow A.U.S.A., who came to the rescue when gullible Adam was about to let his naïveté get the best of him. Owen was his shaggy, party-guy roommate, who hung around the office looking for chicks.

AAAHH!!! REAL MONSTERS (*Cartoon*)
BROADCAST HISTORY:
Nickelodeon
30 minutes
Produced: *1994–1997* (52 episodes)
Premiered: *October 29, 1994*
VOICES:
Ickis .... Charlie Adler
Oblina .... Christine Cavanaugh
Krumm .... David Eccles
The Gromble .... Gregg Berger
One of the gross-you-out cartoons so popular with kids in the nineties, this series centered on the comic adventures of three "real monsters." Ickis was an insecure little creature with big teeth and rabbit ears, Oblina a bad-tempered stick figure, and Krumm a lazy, smelly blob who carried his eyes in his hands. Ugly, disgusting, and smelly, they all attended a monster school located under a huge garbage dump run by imperious headmaster, the Gromble. Despite their inadequacies the three practiced hard at scaring the wits out of people by popping out of unlikely places (a favorite was toilet bowls).

AARON'S WAY (*Drama*)
FIRST TELECAST: *March 9, 1988*
LAST TELECAST: *May 25, 1988*
BROADCAST HISTORY:
Mar 1988–May 1988, NBC Wed 8:00–9:00
CAST:
Aaron Miller .... Merlin Olsen
Sarah Miller .... Belinda Montgomery
Roseanne Miller (age 15) .... Samantha Mathis
Martha Miller (12) .... Erin Chase
Frank Miller (11) .... Scott Curtis
Susannah Lo Verde .... Kathleen York
Connie Lo Verde .... Jessica Walter
Mickey Lo Verde (16) .... Christopher Gartin
Mr. Benvenuto .... Pierrino Mascarino
Merlin Olsen, best known for his roles in such "warm and wonderful" dramas as *Little House on the Prairie* and *Father Murphy*, starred in another one in 1988. Aaron Miller was a strict, bearded Amish patriarch who uprooted his tight-knit family from their cloistered environment in Pennsylvania and moved to California when his eldest son died there. Noah Miller had forsaken Amish ways, and when he perished in a surfing accident he left behind a pregnant girlfriend (Susannah) with a vineyard she couldn't maintain alone. So, unbidden, the Millers moved in to help.

Stories revolved around the Millers' culture shock as they adjusted to modern California ways, while trying to retain their deep-rooted moral values and peculiar style of dress; and conservative Aaron's clashes with free-spirited Susannah and her tart-tongued mother, Connie, who ran the local beauty salon. Underneath, of course, there was a lot of love. Susannah's teenaged brother Mickey had his own plan for bridging the culture gap, with eyes for Miller's daughter, Roseanne.

ABBOTT AND COSTELLO SHOW, THE (*Situation Comedy*)

BROADCAST HISTORY:

Syndicated and network daytime
30 minutes
Produced: *1951–1953* (52 episodes)
Released: *Fall 1952*

CAST:

Bud Abbott .... Himself
Lou Costello .... Himself
Hillary Brooke .... Herself
Sid Fields .... Himself
Mike the Cop .... Gordon Jones
Mr. Bacciagalupe .... Joe Kirk
Stinky .... Joe Besser

VARIOUS SUPPORTING ROLES:

Joan Shawlee
Bobby Barber
Milt Bronson

PRODUCER:

Alex Gottlieb
Pat Costello

DIRECTOR:

Jean Yarborough

Critics hated this show. Audiences found it screamingly funny, so much so that it became one of the most successful and most repeated syndicated programs in television history.

It certainly was low-brow slapstick in its purest form, full of terrible puns, improbable situations, and lots of knockabout, physical comedy. There was a story line of sorts, which had Bud (the tall, debonair one) and Lou (the short, silly one) as unemployed actors sharing an apartment in a rooming house run by Mr. Fields, who was always hounding them for back rent. Lou's girlfriend, Hillary, lived across the hall. Also living in the boardinghouse was Stinky, a malevolent brat who'd grab Lou's arm and threaten, "I'll harm you!" (Though a grown man, Stinky was always dressed in a Little Lord Fauntleroy outfit.) Other more or less regular characters were Mike the Cop and Mr. Bacciagalupe, who had different occupations depending on the episode. Appearing frequently in different roles were Joan Shawlee, Bobby Barber (the short, bald one), and Milt Bronson.

Each program began with a premise, often some scheme of Lou's to make money or avoid paying bills, but soon disintegrated into a succession of unrelated skits and gags. Essentially, the series was a showcase for all the old material Bud and Lou had been using on stage and in films since the 1930s. They might be at a charity bazaar (where they could work in the "Lemon Bit"), or stranded in a haunted house (good excuse for the "Moving Candle" routine), or in an old folks' home full of loonies who were having a baseball game with an imaginary ball (up popped their classic "Who's on First?" routine). Some episodes were complete steals from old silent comedies, including a virtual reenactment of Buster Keaton's 1920 short *One Week*, in which a jealous suitor sabotages the house Lou has built for his fiancée.

Lou Costello was the spark plug of all this frenzy. He was a natural comic, full of gags and practical jokes on screen and off. During filming, even when the action shifted elsewhere, the director kept one camera on Costello so as not to miss any impromptu bits of business. Lou owned the show, and after the first half-dozen episodes installed his brother, Pat Costello, as producer.

After the first 26 episodes were filmed, changes were made. Brooke, Kirk, Besser, and Shawlee departed (as did the boys' pet, Bingo the Chimp, who had made the mistake of biting Costello). Director Jean Yarborough tried to get things more organized, with more consistent story lines and a new gag writer, Clyde Bruckman, for Abbott and Costello were running out of their old material. In all, only 52 episodes of the program were filmed, but these were highly popular—critics notwithstanding—and were rerun endlessly over the next decades (starting with six months on CBS' Saturday morning lineup from September 1954 to February 1955). One New York station is said to have aired each one of the 52 more than 200 times. It was one of the last great successes for the top comedy team of the 1940s, whose films, radio show, and *Colgate Comedy Hour* appearances entertained millions. The pair finally broke up in 1957. Costello, the human dynamo, was worn out by the time he reached his fifties; he died in 1959, at the age of 52. Abbott passed away in 1974.

A cartoon version of *The Abbott and Costello Show* was syndicated in 1966, with Abbott providing his own voice.

A detailed and appreciative account of Abbott and Costello's career, including full details on the TV series, can be found in *The Abbott and Costello Book* by Jim Mulholland, published in 1975.

ABBY (*Situation Comedy*)

FIRST TELECAST: *January 6, 2003*
LAST TELECAST: *March 4, 2003*

BROADCAST HISTORY:

Jan 2003, UPN Mon 9:30–10:00
Jan 2003, UPN Tue 9:30–10:00
Jan 2003–Mar 2003, UPN Tue 9:00–9:30

CAST:

Abby Walker .... Sydney Tamiia Poitier
Joanne "Jo" Walker .... Tangie Ambrose
Will Jeffries .... Kadeem Hardison
Roger Tomkins .... Sean O'Bryan
Max Ellis .... Randy J. Goodwin

This comedy centered on the personal and professional life of Abby Walker, who had recently been promoted to producer of the *West Coast Sports Report* on WCSR-TV in San Francisco. Pretty Abby had just broken up with Will, her self-absorbed, professional photographer boyfriend, but was attempting to maintain a platonic live-in relationship with him so that they could keep their rent-controlled apartment. Will still had the hots for Abby and spent considerable time trying to rekindle their romance. Roger, Abby's chauvinistic boss and Will's buddy, wanted to get them back together, while her outspoken sister, Jo, thought it was time for Abby to move on. Max, the handsome anchor of the *West Coast Sports Report*, was Abby's uncomfortable confidant—he had a crush on Abby that was obvious to everyone but her.

ABE BURROWS' ALMANAC (*Comedy/Variety*)
FIRST TELECAST: *January 4, 1950*
LAST TELECAST: *March 29, 1950*
BROADCAST HISTORY:
Jan 1950–Mar 1950, CBS Wed 9:00–9:30
REGULARS:
Abe Burrows
Milton Delugg and his Orchestra

This live variety series starred comedian Abe Burrows, "the bald-headed baritone from Brooklyn," who chatted with orchestra leader Milton Delugg and welcomed different guest stars each week. Burrows had hosted two short-lived radio series in the late 1940s, but his greatest fame came as a writer-director for radio *(Duffy's Tavern)*, Broadway *(Guys and Dolls, How to Succeed in Business Without Really Trying)*, and Hollywood *(The Solid Gold Cadillac)*.

ACADEMY THEATRE (*Dramatic Anthology*)
FIRST TELECAST: *July 25, 1949*
LAST TELECAST: *September 12, 1949*
BROADCAST HISTORY:
Jul 1949–Sep 1949, NBC Mon 8:00–8:30

This series of eight live half-hour dramas replaced *Chevrolet on Broadway* for the summer of 1949. It had a different cast each week, consisting of lesser-known actors and actresses in playlets by such authors as Thornton Wilder, Edna St. Vincent Millay, and Robert Finch. *Academy Theatre* was produced by Curtis Canfield, Professor of Dramatics at Amherst College.

ACAPULCO (*Adventure*)
FIRST TELECAST: *February 27, 1961*
LAST TELECAST: *April 24, 1961*
BROADCAST HISTORY:
Feb 1961–Apr 1961, NBC Mon 9:00–9:30
CAST:
Patrick Malone .... Ralph Taeger
Gregg Miles .... James Coburn
Mr. Carver .... Telly Savalas
Chloe .... Allison Hayes
Bobby .... Bobby Troup
Max .... Jason Robards, Sr.

Ralph Taeger and James Coburn starred as two Korean War buddies turned action-prone "beachcombers" in sunny Acapulco. Mr. Carver, a retired criminal lawyer, had supplied them with a beach cottage adjoining his sumptuous estate in return for their help in protecting him from enemies made during his career as a gangbusting lawyer. The two ex-GIs were constantly forced to give up their girl-chasing to protect Mr. Carver, but they still managed to spend much time at a small club run by musician Bobby Troup and at a more opulent club run by Chloe, a beautiful woman who knew everything about everybody in Acapulco.

ACAPULCO H.E.A.T. (*Adventure/Foreign Intrigue*)
BROADCAST HISTORY:
Syndicated only
60 minutes
Produced: *1993–1994, 1996* (48 episodes)
Released: *September 1993*
CAST:
Ashley Hunter-Coddington (1993–1994)
.... Catherine Oxenberg
Mike Savage (1993–1994) .... Brendan Kelly
Cat (Catherine Avery Pascal) .... Alison Armitage
Brett (1993–1994) .... Spencer Rochfort
Krissie Valentine (1993–1994) .... Holly Floria
Tommy Chase .... Michael Worth
Marcos (1993–1994) .... Randy Vasquez
Arthur Small (1993–1994) .... Graham Heywood
Claudio (1993–1994) .... Fabio
Mr. Smith (1993–1994) .... John Vernon
Nicole Bernard (1996–1997) .... Lydie Denier
Joanna Barnes (1996–1997) .... Christa Sauls
THEME:
"I Feel the Heat," composed by Michael Lloyd, Tommy Oliver, and Jim Ervin; performed by Pepper Mashay

This updated high-tech variation on *Mission: Impossible* focused on the activities of the Hemisphere Emergency Action Team (H.E.A.T.), a top-secret unit that fought international crime and terrorism from their base in a hotel in glamorous Acapulco. The leaders of the team were Ashley, an aristocratic onetime British agent, and Mike, a cool former operative of the CIA. The other members of the team were Cat, a sexy ex–cat burglar; Brett, an attractive guy who often worked undercover; Krissie, the pretty computer expert who provided the rest of the team with useful data; Tommy, a martial arts expert; Marcos, a former Mexican cabdriver who was romantically involved with Krissie; and Arthur, the uptight guy who worked out logistics for most of their missions. Claudio was the hunky owner of the hotel where their headquarters was located and Mr. Smith, seen only via video link, the government official who gave them their assignments.

The team's cover was fashion photography, with Ashley and Mike as photographers and Cat and Krissie as two of their models. (The same plot device had been used by CBS a decade earlier in *Cover Up*.) There was plenty of action and lots of beaches and bikinis—the opening credits lingered lovingly on scantily clad cast members and others on the beach. Fabio, the self-promoting romance novel model, was in those credits but was seldom seen. His acting was wooden, and he had been completely dropped from the show by early 1994.

When the series returned for its second season, only Cat and Tommy were still around. New to the cast were Joanna, their computer expert, and Nicole, a sexy former spy who had reconstituted the team to help her track down a stolen necklace. The people they worked for on the initial case provided the money to keep the H.E.A.T. team (no longer funded by the government) operational, including all the high-tech resources they used to aid in solving cases. They were now based in Puerto Vallarta and their new cover was running Acapulco Beach Fashions, a clothing store on the beach, and selling a line of beachwear called—surprise!—"Acapulco Heat."

The second season of *Acapulco H.E.A.T.* was produced in 1996 for European distribution but was not aired by any stations in the U.S. It surfaced in the States for the 1998–1999 season. Both seasons' episodes were filmed on location in Puerto Vallarta, Mexico.

ACCENT ON AN AMERICAN SUMMER (*Travelogue*)
FIRST TELECAST: *June 7, 1962*
LAST TELECAST: *September 6, 1962*

BROADCAST HISTORY:

Jun 1962–Sep 1962, CBS Thu 7:30–8:00

HOST:

John Ciardi

Accent on an American Summer was a summer series that took viewers on tours of various places of historic or general interest. Hosted by John Ciardi, the series went to Monticello, Thomas Jefferson's home; the American Shakespeare Festival, to see excerpts from two plays; the wilds of Yellowstone National Park; the gambling environment of Reno, Nevada; and other varied locales.

ACCESS HOLLYWOOD (*Magazine*)

BROADCAST HISTORY:

Syndicated only
30 minutes
Produced: *1996–*
Released: *September 9, 1996*

ANCHORS:

Weekday: Larry Mendte (1996–1997)
Giselle Fernandez (1996–1998)
Pat O'Brien (1997–)
Nancy O'Dell (1998–)
Weekend: Larry Mendte (1996–1997)
Nancy O'Dell (1996–1999)
Giselle Fernandez (1997–1998)
Pat O'Brien (1998–1999)
Shaun Robinson (1999–)
Tony Potts (1999–)

This series was launched in the fall of 1996 to provide the NBC-owned television stations, and other stations, a glitzy show business news and feature-laden alternative to the long-running *Entertainment Tonight.* Fawning, Hollywood-centric, and celebrity-chasing like its role model, it was taped daily at NBC's Burbank studios. After a year, original co-host Larry Mendte was replaced by Pat O'Brien. Late in 1998 Giselle Fernandez was replaced by Nancy O'Dell, who had been co-hosting the weekend edition.

ACCIDENTAL FAMILY (*Situation Comedy*)

FIRST TELECAST: *September 15, 1967*
LAST TELECAST: *January 5, 1968*
BROADCAST HISTORY:

Sep 1967–Jan 1968, NBC Fri 9:30–10:00

CAST:

Jerry Webster........................ Jerry Van Dyke
Sue Kramer........................ Lois Nettleton
Sandy Webster........................ Teddy Quinn
Tracy Kramer........................ Susan Benjamin
Ben McGrath........................ Ben Blue
Marty Warren........................ Larry D. Mann

Jerry Van Dyke played nightclub comedian Jerry Webster, one of TV's many widowers, confronted with the problems of raising a young son, Sandy, played by Teddy Quinn. In this series Father decided literally to "farm out" his son by purchasing a farm in California's San Fernando Valley as a full-time home for the boy and part-time home for himself, between performing commitments. Farm manager Sue Kramer, a pretty divorcée whose daughter, Tracy, just happened to be Sandy's age, served as de facto governess for the boy and foil for Jerry. Ben McGrath, the farm handyman, and Marty Warren, Jerry's friend and lawyer, rounded out the cast of regulars.

ACCORDING TO JIM (*Situation Comedy*)

FIRST TELECAST: *October 3, 2001*
LAST TELECAST:
BROADCAST HISTORY:

Oct 2001–Jul 2002, ABC Wed 8:30–9:00
Jul 2002–Sep 2002, ABC Tue 8:00–9:00
Sep 2002–Mar 2003, ABC Tue 8:30–9:00
Apr 2003–May 2003, ABC Tue 8:30–9:30
May 2003– , ABC Tue 9:00–9:30

CAST:

Jim........................ Jim Belushi
Cheryl........................ Courtney Thorne-Smith
Ruby (age 6)........................ Taylor Atelian
Gracie........................ Billi Bruno
Andy........................ Larry Joe Campbell
Dana........................ Kimberly Williams

This was another one of those sunny family sitcoms in which a lovable lug was married to a beautiful and much smarter wife. Jim was a contractor who worked with his brother-in-law in a small design firm. He liked to posture and act macho, and always thought first of himself, but underneath he was a big pussycat who adored his wife and kids. Putting up with him was Cheryl, who was as smart and sophisticated as Jim was crude; but he made her laugh, and they were truly in love. The kids were adorable little Ruby and Gracie, and baby Kyle. Often visiting in Jim's suburban kitchen were Cheryl's chubby, cheerful architect brother Andy, who worked with Jim and played with him in his garage blues band; and Cheryl's neurotic sister Dana, a vice president in an ad agency, who verbally sparred with Jim. Dana was desperately trying to find a man. Unfortunately, due to her insecurities she had many first dates but few second ones.

ACCUSED (*Courtroom Drama*)

FIRST TELECAST: *December 10, 1958*
LAST TELECAST: *September 30, 1959*
BROADCAST HISTORY:

Dec 1958–Sep 1959, ABC Wed 9:30–10:00

CAST:

Presiding Judge........................ Edgar Allan Jones, Jr.
**Presiding Judge*........................ William Gwinn
Bailiff........................ Tim Farrell
Clerk........................ Jim Hodson
Reporter........................ Violet Gilmore

*Occasional

Accused was a prime-time spin-off from *Day in Court,* a popular ABC daytime program that presented filmed reenactments of actual cases. Realism was the keynote of the series; the judge for most of the trials was Edgar Allan Jones, Jr., a UCLA law professor, and the prosecution and defense attorneys were also real-life lawyers. Only the defendants and witnesses were actors, usually obscure ones but occasionally such well-known performers as Pamela Mason and Robert Culp (who appeared with his wife, actress Nancy Ash). The cases were almost invariably criminal proceedings.

Accused was produced by Selig J. Seligman, a former State Department attorney and ABC-TV Vice President, who kept a whole staff of lawyers and law students busy digging through court records and law books to provide authenticity for the show.

During its first few weeks on the air the nighttime series was known as *Day in Court.* The daytime version continued under that name from 1958 until 1965.

ACE CRAWFORD, PRIVATE EYE (*Situation Comedy*)
FIRST TELECAST: *March 15, 1983*
LAST TELECAST: *April 12, 1983*
BROADCAST HISTORY:
Mar 1983–Apr 1983, CBS Tue 8:00–8:30
CAST:
Ace Crawford .... Tim Conway
Toomey .... Joe Regalbuto
Inch .... Billy Barty
Luana .... Shera Danese
Mello .... Bill Henderson
Lt. Fanning .... Dick Christie

Imagine Bogie's Sam Spade played for laughs, and you've got *Ace Crawford.* A hard-nosed private detective, attired in the requisite trench coat, Ace was all business. But blind luck and fortuitous accidents were more responsible for his solving cases than his sleuthing skill. His incredible run of luck had given him an undeserved reputation and brought him a continuous stream of clients. It also made Ace irresistible to the ladies, although he was usually too busy fumbling through cases to pay any attention to them. Ace's bumbling part-time assistant Toomey, a full-time CPA, idolized Ace and hung out with his "boss" at the Shanty, a sleazy club located on the wharf. Inch (played by midget Billy Barty) was the owner and bartender at the Shanty, where Ace's not-quite-girlfriend Luana was the featured singer. Mello, Luana's blind accompanist, was played by jazz great Bill Henderson. Also featured was an incredulous Lt. Fanning, who couldn't understand how Ace seemed to solve difficult cases without any effort.

ACT IT OUT, see *Say It with Acting*

ACTION (*Situation Comedy*)
FIRST TELECAST: *September 16, 1999*
LAST TELECAST: *December 2, 1999*
BROADCAST HISTORY:
Sep 1999–Oct 1999, FOX Thu 9:00–9:30
Dec 1999, FOX Thu 9:00–10:00
CAST:
Peter Dragon .... Jay Mohr
Wendy Ward .... Illeana Douglas
Lonnie Valiant .... Buddy Hackett
Adam Rafkin .... Jarrad Paul
Stuart Glazer .... Jack Plotnick
Bobby Gianopolis .... Lee Arenberg
Jane Gianopolis .... Cindy Ambuehl

One of television's periodic attempts to build a comedy around a thoroughly despicable leading character, *Action* delighted critics but turned off audiences during its short run in 1999. Peter, the head of DragonFire Films, was an obnoxious, morally corrupt Hollywood producer. Suave and self-assured, he insulted everyone and laced his language with obscenities—the more vulgar ones were bleeped out, while the mild ones were left in. Sex and backstabbing were everywhere. Not surprisingly, each episode opened with the disclaimer, "Portions of *Action* may be inappropriate for younger viewers. . . ."

Peter's arrogance seldom got him what he wanted. As the series opened, his latest release, *Slow Torture,* was proving to be a $150 million bomb. Wendy was a former TV child star who was now a high-class hooker, and who so impressed Peter with her honesty and film instincts that he gave her a development job with the studio. Also seen regularly were Stuart, Peter's well-meaning but incompetent head of production; Uncle Lonnie, his cheerful limo driver; Adam, the nerdy former TV writer whose script was going to be made into DragonFire's big summer movie, *Beverly Hills Gun Club;* and Bobby, the billionaire studio owner, who had married Peter's former wife, Jane. The gay and well-endowed Bobby often called meetings when he was naked so that he could cow his underlings with "the majesty of his organ."

Among the real stars appearing as themselves on this wild parody of Hollywood were Keanu Reeves, Salma Hayek, Sandra Bullock (who beat Peter up after she discovered he was selling nude videos of her), David Hasselhoff (taking bids on himself at a charity auction), and Scott Wolf (who was told he was too short for the movie role he was pitching).

Action was pulled from the Fox schedule with five episodes still unaired; these appeared the following summer on the FX cable network. During the course of these episodes, Peter had a heart attack and was pronounced dead, but miraculously recovered and returned to his ruthless ways.

ACTION AUTOGRAPHS (*Documentary*)
FIRST TELECAST: *April 24, 1949*
LAST TELECAST: *January 8, 1950*
BROADCAST HISTORY:
Apr 1949–Jun 1949, ABC Sun 10:00–10:15
Sep 1949–Jan 1950, ABC Sun 6:30–6:45
HOST:
Jack Brand *(Apr–Jun)*
Ed Prentiss *(Sep–Jan)*

This short filmed program was sponsored by Bell & Howell Cameras, evidently to show how the medium of film could allow viewers to drop in on many interesting people and watch their activities. Interviews, demonstrations, and performances were included. Among the subjects were the national barbershop quartet champions, a water show, singer Burl Ives, and Dr. Beryl Orris psychoanalyzing the thoughts and actions of a character played by actor Richard Basehart in a scene from the play *She Walks at Night.*

ACTION TONIGHT (*Dramatic Anthology*)
FIRST TELECAST: *July 15, 1957*
LAST TELECAST: *September 2, 1957*
BROADCAST HISTORY:
Jul 1957–Sep 1957, NBC Mon 8:30–9:00

This series presented filmed reruns of dramas originally seen on *Schlitz Playhouse* and *Pepsi-Cola Playhouse.*

ACTORS STUDIO (*Dramatic Anthology*)
FIRST TELECAST: *September 26, 1948*
LAST TELECAST: *June 23, 1950*
BROADCAST HISTORY:
Sep 1948–Mar 1949, ABC Sun 8:30–9:00
Mar 1949–Apr 1949, ABC Thu 8:30–9:00
May 1949, ABC Thu 9:30–10:00
Sep 1949–Oct 1949, ABC Wed 8:00–8:30
Nov 1949–Jan 1950, CBS Tue 9:00–9:30
Feb 1950–Jun 1950, CBS Fri 9:00–10:00
HOST:
Marc Connelly

PRODUCER:

Donald Davis

This was one of the first "prestige" dramatic showcases on the fledgling ABC network. It was produced live each week by the Actors Studio, Inc., a nonprofit organization for professional actors and actresses. Most productions were serious dramas, encompassing both adaptations of classic stories and occasional original scripts. Among the authors represented were William Saroyan, James Thurber, Ring Lardner, Edgar Allan Poe, Irwin Shaw, and Budd Schulberg. Performers included such first-rate talent as Julie Harris, Cloris Leachman, Martin Balsam, and Kim Hunter. The first telecast was "Portrait of a Madonna" and starred Jessica Tandy. Young Marlon Brando made his first television appearance here in January 1949.

Actors Studio made a strong impression during its first months on the air, and received a Peabody Award for its "uninhibited and brilliant pioneering in the field of televised drama" during the year of 1948.

During its final four months the program expanded to a full hour and was seen every other week, alternating with *Ford Theatre*. The series name was changed to *The Play's the Thing* in March 1950.

ACTUALITY SPECIALS (*Documentary*)

FIRST TELECAST: *July 16, 1962*

LAST TELECAST: *September 13, 1968*

BROADCAST HISTORY:

Jul 1962–Sep 1962, NBC Mon 10:00–11:00
Oct 1965–Jun 1967, NBC Sun 6:30–7:30 (OS)
Sep 1967–Sep 1968, NBC Fri 10:00–11:00

Actuality Specials was a collection of NBC News documentary specials. Some were reruns of programs shown earlier; others were new programs made specifically for this series. Narrators were usually NBC newsmen such as Robert MacNeil, Edwin Newman, Frank McGee, and Chet Huntley; however, celebrities such as Lorne Greene or Raymond Burr sometimes provided narration. *Actuality Specials* frequently alternated with other documentary series such as *NBC White Paper*, *NBC News Special*, *Campaign and the Candidates*, and *American Profile*.

AD LIBBERS (*Improvisation*)

FIRST TELECAST: *August 3, 1951*

LAST TELECAST: *August 31, 1951*

BROADCAST HISTORY:

Aug 1951, CBS Fri 8:00–8:30

HOST:

Peter Donald

REGULARS:

Charles Mendick
Patricia Hosley
Joe Silver
Jack Lemmon
Cynthia Stone
Earl Hammond

This live series of improvisations was the 1951 summer replacement for *Mama*. Peter Donald, the host, would read a brief outline of a situation to the performers, who would then ad-lib dialogue to fit the situation. There were three or four sketches performed during each episode of this five-week show.

ADAM 12 (*Police Drama*)

FIRST TELECAST: *September 21, 1968*

LAST TELECAST: *August 26, 1975*

BROADCAST HISTORY:

Sep 1968–Sep 1969, NBC Sat 7:30–8:00
Sep 1969–Jan 1971, NBC Sat 8:30–9:00
Jan 1971–Sep 1971, NBC Thu 9:30–10:00
Sep 1971–Jan 1974, NBC Wed 8:00–8:30
Jan 1974–Aug 1975, NBC Tue 8:00–8:30

CAST:

Officer Pete Malloy .... Martin Milner
Officer Jim Reed .... Kent McCord
Sgt. MacDonald .... William Boyett
Officer Ed Wells .... Gary Crosby
Dispatcher's voice .... Shaaron Claridge
Officer Jerry Walters (1968–1969) . William Stevens
Sgt. Jerry Miller (1969) .... Jack Hogan
Jean Reed (1969) .... Mikki Jamison
Officer Norm Green (1970–1971) .. Claude Johnson
Officer Grant (1974–1975) .... William Elliott
Officer Woods (1974–1975) .... Fred Stromsoe

Produced by Jack Webb, whose realistic portrayal of police work had scored a major hit in *Dragnet*, *Adam 12* dealt with the day-to-day working world of two uniformed policemen assigned to patrol-car duty. Officer Pete Malloy was a senior officer who at the start of the series was teamed with a probationary rookie cop, Jim Reed. As members of the Los Angeles Police Department, they encountered a wide range of cases in each episode, some serious, some trivial, some amusing, and some tragic. Running as it did for seven seasons, *Adam 12* saw changes in the status of the officers as the years passed. During the 1970–1971 season Jim Reed was promoted from rookie to officer, and in the following year Officer Malloy was upped to Policeman 3, one notch below the rank of sergeant.

ADAM 12 (*Police Drama*)

BROADCAST HISTORY:

Syndicated only
30 minutes
Produced: *1989–1990* (52 episodes)
Released: *September 1989*

CAST:

Officer Gus Grant .... Peter Parros
Officer Matt Doyle .... Ethan Wayne
Sgt. Harry Santos .... Miguel Fernandes

A very routine remake of the famous series; nothing much had changed except for the faces and the police cars (which were newer). Gus and Matt were the uniformed L.A.P.D. cops on patrol this time, in a squad car code-named "Adam 12"—hence the title of the series. As before, episodes contained a mixture of serious crimes and trivial or amusing incidents on the streets of L.A., augmented by running byplay between married Gus and single Matt about their off-duty lives. Sgt. Santos was the watch commander.

Produced during 1989–1990, this series aired only in New York and Los Angeles at that time, going into national syndication the following season.

ADAM'S RIB (*Situation Comedy*)

FIRST TELECAST: *September 14, 1973*

LAST TELECAST: *December 28, 1973*

BROADCAST HISTORY:

Sep 1973–Dec 1973, ABC Fri 9:30–10:00

CAST:

Adam Bonner .... Ken Howard

Amanda Bonner.................. Blythe Danner
Gracie............................ Dena Dietrich
Asst. D.A. Roy Mendelsohn............ Ron Rifkin
Kip Kipple........................ Edward Winter
District Attorney Donahue........ Norman Bartold

CREATOR/PRODUCER/DIRECTOR:

Peter H. Hunt

THEME:

"Two People," by Perry Botkin, Jr., and Gil Garfield

This romantic comedy was based on the Spencer Tracy–Katharine Hepburn movie classic of the same title. The show concerned a young Assistant D.A. and his wife, a junior partner in a law firm, whose jobs often put them on opposite sides in the courtroom as well as at home. *Adam's Rib* made overtures to the Women's Lib movement by building many stories around Amanda's crusades for women's rights (50 percent of the show's writers were women), but the program never found an audience.

Dena Dietrich ("Mother Nature" of commercials fame) played Amanda's secretary, and Edward Winter her law partner, while Norman Bartold and Ron Rifkin were on Adam's side.

ADDAMS FAMILY, THE (*Situation Comedy*)

FIRST TELECAST: *September 18, 1964*
LAST TELECAST: *September 2, 1966*
BROADCAST HISTORY:

Sep 1964–Sep 1966, ABC Fri 8:30–9:00

CAST:

Morticia Frump Addams........... Carolyn Jones
Gomez Addams.......................... John Astin
Uncle Fester Frump................ Jackie Coogan
Lurch................................ Ted Cassidy
Grandmama Addams............... Blossom Rock
Pugsley Addams................ Ken Weatherwax
Wednesday Friday Addams............ Lisa Loring
Cousin Itt............................ Felix Silla
Thing.............................. Ted Cassidy

The strange, macabre, but somehow amusing cartoon characters created by Charles Addams for *The New Yorker* magazine made their live-action debut in the fall of 1964, one of two almost identical "ghoul comedies" to premiere that year (see also CBS' *Munsters*). Morticia was the beautiful but somber lady of the house. Her husband Gomez had strange eyes and rather destructive instincts, as did Uncle Fester. Lurch, the butler, was a seven-foot-tall warmed-over Frankenstein monster whose dialogue usually consisted solely of the two words, "You rang?" The children also had a rather ghoulish quality about them. Grandmama, although a witch, was the most normal-looking one of the bunch. They all lived in a musty, castle-like home full of strange objects—such as a disembodied hand, called "Thing," which kept popping out of a black box—and they scared almost everyone—except viewers—half to death.

An animated version of *The Addams Family* aired Saturday mornings on NBC from September 1973 to August 1975, with Jackie Coogan and Ted Cassidy providing the voices of their animated characters. A second animated *Addams Family* ran on Saturday mornings on ABC from September 1992 to January 1995, with John Astin returning to provide the voice of Gomez.

Astin was back again in a recurring role in *The New Addams Family*, which premiered on the Fox Family Channel in 1998 (see separate entry).

ADDERLY (*Comedy Drama*)

FIRST TELECAST: *September 24, 1986*
LAST TELECAST: *September 13, 1989*
BROADCAST HISTORY:

Sep 1986–Jul 1987, CBS Wed 11:30–12:40 A.M.
Aug 1987–Sep 1987, CBS Fri 10:00–11:00
Sep 1987–Jul 1988, CBS Wed 11:30–12:40 A.M.
Jun 1989–Sep 1989, CBS Mon/Wed 1:00–2:00 A.M.

CAST:

V.H. Adderly...................... Winston Rekert
Melville Greenspan.............. Jonathan Welsh
Mona Ellerby.......................... Dixie Seatle
Major Jonathan B. Clack................ Ken Pogue

Adderly had been a top operative of the department of International Security and Intelligence (I.S.I.) until he lost the use of his left hand while being tortured by enemy agents. His superior, Major Clack, in order to keep him on the payroll, assigned him to work for the department of "Miscellaneous Affairs," which usually got involved with minor and harmless diplomatic assignments. V.H.'s new boss was a petty bureaucrat named Greenspan who had no desire to rock the boat and was exasperated by Adderly's predilection for making real cases out of seemingly mundane—and often nonsensical—assignments. Greenspan's secretary, Mona, who had a bit of a crush on Adderly, was more than willing to bypass normal channels and procedures to help V.H., despite the complaints from her boss.

Produced in Toronto.

ADMIRAL BROADWAY REVUE (*Variety*)

FIRST TELECAST: *January 28, 1949*
LAST TELECAST: *June 3, 1949*
BROADCAST HISTORY:

Jan 1949–Jun 1949, NBC & DUM Fri 8:00–9:00

REGULARS:

Sid Caesar
Imogene Coca
Mary McCarty
Marge and Gower Champion
Tom Avera
Ronnie Cunningham
Judson Laire
Estelle Loring
Loren Welch

Sid Caesar won his first regular starring role in this program, which united him in a comedy team with Imogene Coca for the first time. Neither of them was new to television in 1949, Caesar having guest-starred on Milton Berle's show during the previous fall and Coca having appeared on television as early as 1939.

Though short lived, *Admiral Broadway Revue* was one of early television's most spectacular productions, completely dominating Friday night viewing the way that Milton Berle dominated Tuesday and Ed Sullivan, Sunday. The series was produced and directed by Max Liebman and was built along the lines of a Broadway music and comedy revue, with top-name guest stars and big production numbers. For example, the opening program included half a dozen comedy skits and closed with an elaborate burlesque on opera in the style of Billy Rose, called "No No Rigoletto." The program was telecast live from the newly completed International Theatre in New York and was one of the few major programs ever to be carried on two networks simultaneously (NBC and DuMont). It was seen in every city in the United States that had television facilities, either live from the networks or on kinescope in markets not yet having network connections.

Judson Laire, who was the featured baritone singer on *Admiral Broadway Revue*, turned up one month after this series left the air in a straight dramatic role on CBS' series *Mama*. He played Lars Hansen, the father figure in the show, for the next eight years.

ADMIRAL PRESENTS THE FIVE STAR REVUE—WELCOME ABOARD, see *Welcome Aboard*

ADMISSION FREE, see *Movies—Prior to 1961*

ADORN PLAYHOUSE (*Dramatic Anthology*)
FIRST TELECAST: *May 13, 1958*
LAST TELECAST: *July 1, 1958*
BROADCAST HISTORY:
May 1958–Jul 1958, CBS Tue 8:30–9:00
This 1958 summer series consisted of reruns of episodes from other CBS anthologies, primarily *Schlitz Playhouse.*

ADVENTURE (*Wildlife/Adventure*)
FIRST TELECAST: *June 28, 1953*
LAST TELECAST: *September 27, 1953*
BROADCAST HISTORY:
Jun 1953–Sep 1953, CBS Sun 6:00–7:00
NARRATOR:
Charles Collingwood
Produced in cooperation with the American Museum of Natural History, *Adventure* was composed of interviews with naturalists, anthropologists, and other authorities, coupled with filmed reports of expeditions to remote areas and primitive peoples. Charles Collingwood was the host of the series, which actually had its premiere as a late-Sunday-afternoon program on May 10, 1953. Following its run as an evening program, it returned to Sunday afternoons where it remained on the air until July 1956.

ADVENTURE INC. (*Adventure*)
BROADCAST HISTORY:
Syndicated only
60 minutes
Produced: *2002–*
Released: *October 2002*
CAST:
Judson Cross .... Michael Biehn
Mackenzie Previn .... Karen Cliche
Gabriel Patterson .... Jesse Nilsson
The jungles were full of ruthless thugs, blazing machine guns and beautiful women in this comic-book-style adventure series, a kind of low-rent *Indiana Jones.* Judson Cross was a famous archeologist (he had specials on the Discovery Channel!) who was in the business of finding things, but, as he put it, "Adventure really is our business." Judson's crew at Adventure Inc.—tough sexy Mac, who was totally fearless, and young hunk Gabe, who had left college to travel the world—lived on his salvage boat, the *Vast Explorer.* Among the artifacts they sought were a Romanoff icon with mystical properties that turned out to be a transceiver used by a group of Russians with ESP, a magical scepter in a quicksand tunnel in the desert, a Mayan jade altar and the remains of a helicopter downed in Cambodia during the Vietnam War.

There was lots of action and fighting, and many of the episodes had supernatural overtones, not surprising since the producers' previous project, *Relic Hunter,* had many of the same qualities. The series was supposedly inspired by the adventures of real-life explorer Barry Clifford.

ADVENTURE PLAYHOUSE, see *Movies—Prior to 1961*

ADVENTURE SHOWCASE (*Adventure Anthology*)
FIRST TELECAST: *August 11, 1959*
LAST TELECAST: *September 1, 1959*
BROADCAST HISTORY:
Aug 1959–Sep 1959, CBS Tue 9:00–9:30
This four-week summer series consisted of unsold pilots for proposed adventure series.

ADVENTURE THEATER (*Adventure Anthology*)
FIRST TELECAST: *June 16, 1956*
LAST TELECAST: *August 31, 1957*
BROADCAST HISTORY:
Jun 1956–Sep 1956, NBC Sat 10:30–11:00
Jun 1957–Aug 1957, NBC Sat 10:30–11:00
HOST:
Paul Douglas
Aired as a summer replacement for *Your Hit Parade,* this program presented filmed, two-act plays that were produced in England. Host Paul Douglas introduced the plays, appearing as a storyteller who had been to England and returned with various objects such as a fur coat or a scarf, each of which led into the story with which it was associated. The 1957 series consisted of repeats of the 1956 episodes.

ADVENTURE THEATER (*Dramatic Anthology*)
FIRST TELECAST: *August 4, 1960*
LAST TELECAST: *September 22, 1961*
BROADCAST HISTORY:
Aug 1960–Sep 1960, CBS Thu 10:00–10:30
Jul 1961–Sep 1961, CBS Fri 9:30–10:00
The dramas seen in this summer series were all reruns of episodes originally telecast on *Schlitz Playhouse.* There was no host.

ADVENTURES AT SCOTT ISLAND, see *Harbourmaster*

ADVENTURES IN JAZZ (*Music*)
FIRST TELECAST: *January 28, 1949*
LAST TELECAST: *June 24, 1949*
BROADCAST HISTORY:
Jan 1949–Jun 1949, CBS Fri 8:00–8:30
HOST:
Fred Robbins
Bill Williams
Disc jockey Fred Robbins—noted for his unique chatter, concocted vocabulary, and floppy bow tie—was host of this live show, which brought jazz musicians and singers to television. After appearing on the show's premiere telecast, Robbins departed for other commitments and did not return to the series until May. Bill Williams hosted in Robbins's absence.

ADVENTURES IN PARADISE (*Adventure*)
FIRST TELECAST: *October 5, 1959*
LAST TELECAST: *April 1, 1962*
BROADCAST HISTORY:

Oct 1959–Sep 1961, ABC Mon 9:30–10:30
Oct 1961–Apr 1962, ABC Sun 10:00–11:00

CAST:

Capt. Adam Troy .... Gardner McKay
Oliver Lee (1959–1961) .... Weaver Levy
Renee (1960–1961) .... Linda Lawson
Bulldog Lovey (1960–1961) .... Henry Slate
Clay Baker (1960–1962) .... James Holden
Trader Penrose (1960–1961) .... George Tobias
Sondi (1960–1961) .... Sondi Sodsai
Kelly (1960–1962) .... Lani Kai
Chris Parker (1961–1962) .... Guy Stockwell
Inspector Bouchard (1961–1962) ... Marcel Hillaire

This series featured handsome Gardner McKay as Adam Troy, the captain of a freelance schooner plying the South Pacific in search of passengers, cargo, and adventure. Troy was a Korean War veteran who had found the Pacific to his liking. His schooner, the *Tiki*, ranged across the area from Hong Kong to Pitcairn Island with all sorts of adventurers, schemers, and island beauties aboard. Troy's original partner was a Chinese-American named Oliver Lee. In 1960 he hired a first mate named Clay Baker. The following season Baker went ashore to become manager of the Bali Miki hotel (replacing Trader Penrose), and Troy took on Chris Parker as his first mate. The females in the cast were young Tahitians and other lovely young women who seemed to abound in this series.

James A. Michener created *Adventures in Paradise* and sold the original idea to television, but then he apparently dropped out of the project. Critics complained that the series contained none of the scripting one would expect from such an eminent author. Even the sets looked like the 20th Century–Fox back lot—which it was—though after a couple of years, some location filming was actually done in the South Pacific.

ADVENTURES IN SHERWOOD FOREST,
syndicated title for *Adventures of Robin Hood, The*

ADVENTURES OF BRISCO COUNTY, JR., THE (*Western*)
FIRST TELECAST: *August 27, 1993*
LAST TELECAST: *August 28, 1994*
BROADCAST HISTORY:

Aug 1993–Jul 1994, FOX Fri 8:00–9:00
Jul 1994–Aug 1994, FOX Sun 7:00–8:00

CAST:

Brisco County, Jr. .... Bruce Campbell
John Bly .... Billy Drago
Lord Bowler (James Lonefeather) ...... Julius Carry
Socrates Poole .... Christian Clemenson
Prof. Albert Wickwire .... John Astin
Cartwright .... James Greene
Peter Hutter .... John Pyper-Ferguson
Dixie Cousins .... Kelly Rutherford
Whip Morgan (1994) .... Jeff Phillips

This whimsical western fantasy, set in 1893, chronicled the adventures of jut-jawed hero Brisco County, Jr., a Harvard-educated attorney who had become a bounty hunter because he didn't like practicing law. For much of the season Brisco hunted a creepy, ruthless criminal named John Bly, who had murdered Brisco's father, a U.S. Marshal, during a train robbery. Working with Brisco, often against his better judgment, was a black bounty hunter with expensive tastes named Lord Bowler. Socrates Poole, who gave Brisco most of his assignments, was an attorney for the San Francisco–based Westerfield Club, which had hired Brisco to work for its interests in the West. Comet was Brisco's incredibly intelligent and resourceful horse. Seen on a recurring basis were Professor Wickwire, an eccentric inventor; Cartwright, one of the senior members of the Westerfield Club; Pete Hutter, a dumb thief who sometimes worked with Bly; Whip Morgan, a likable con artist; and Dixie, the sexy adventuress who was Brisco's on-again off-again love interest.

There was a tongue-in-cheek quality to *Brisco*, with each episode divided into "chapters" that usually ended in cliff-hangers. A running theme related to a mystical golden orb that had strange powers to bring people back to life and heal people who would otherwise be dead—and everyone wanted it for their own. In a January 1994 episode it was revealed that Bly was a time traveler from 2506 who had come back to the 1890s to get the orb and take it to his time to use its power to rule his future world. In February, Brisco, with the help of Carina, a woman from the year 5502 whose people had placed the orbs in the past to help mankind develop, destroyed Bly, thus preventing him from returning to his time and initiating a 2,000-year-long reign of terror. At the end of that episode Brisco and Bowler agreed to become special agents working on cases for President Cleveland when he needed them.

ADVENTURES OF CHAMPION, THE (*Adventure*)
FIRST TELECAST: *September 30, 1955*
LAST TELECAST: *February 3, 1956*
BROADCAST HISTORY:

Sep 1955–Feb 1956, CBS Fri 7:30–8:00

CAST:

Ricky North .... Barry Curtis
Sandy North .... Jim Bannon
Will Calhoun .... Francis McDonald
Sheriff Powers .... Ewing Mitchell

This series was produced by Gene Autry and starred Champion the Wonder Horse, his mount. In *The Adventures of Champion*, the talented horse was owned by 12-year-old Ricky North, the only person Champion would allow to ride him. Ricky also owned a German Shepherd named Rebel, and both the horse and the dog were his constant companions. Ricky, who lived on a ranch owned by his Uncle Sandy, had a penchant for getting involved in dangerous situations. But whether he was faced with natural disasters or with evil men who would steal, murder, or in some other way cause trouble, Champion and Rebel would come to his rescue by performing some feat not normally associated with horses or dogs.

ADVENTURES OF ELLERY QUEEN, THE (*Detective Drama*)
FIRST TELECAST: *October 14, 1950*
LAST TELECAST: *September 5, 1976*
BROADCAST HISTORY:

Oct 1950–Dec 1951, DUM Thu 9:00–9:30 (OS)

Dec 1951–Mar 1952, ABC Sun 7:30–8:00
Apr 1952–Dec 1952, ABC Wed 9:00–9:30
Sep 1958–Aug 1959, NBC Fri 8:00–9:00
Sep 1975–Dec 1975, NBC Thu 9:00–10:00
Jan 1976–Sep 1976, NBC Sun 8:00–9:00

CAST:
Ellery Queen (1950–1951) .... Richard Hart
Ellery Queen (1951–1952) .... Lee Bowman
Inspector Richard Queen (1950–1952) .... Florenz Ames
Ellery Queen (1958–1959) .... George Nader
Inspector Richard Queen (1958–1959) .... Les Tremayne
Ellery Queen (1959) .... Lee Philips
Ellery Queen (1975–1976) .... Jim Hutton
Inspector Richard Queen (1975–1976) .... David Wayne
Sgt. Velie (1975–1976) .... Tom Reese
Simon Brimmer (1975–1976)....... John Hillerman
Frank Flannigan (1975–1976) ...... Ken Swofford

Fictional mystery writer–supersleuth Ellery Queen had been the main character in a number of popular mystery novels, written by Frederic Dannay and Manfred Bennington Lee, before he became a regular feature on the CBS Radio Network in 1939. A decade later he made the first of four appearances on television. Ellery was a slightly absentminded mystery writer who would sort through a mass of evidence and a large collection of suspects to determine the guilty party in a crime, usually murder. His aid was regularly sought by his father, an inspector with the New York Police Department. Inspector Queen never ceased to marvel at the way his son could reach the proper conclusion by unearthing the most obscure clues—often left by the dying victim—and piecing them together.

Richard Hart was television's first Ellery Queen, portraying the role in *The Adventures of Ellery Queen,* a live series that premiered on DuMont in the fall of 1950. The following January, Hart died of a sudden and unexpected heart attack—he was in his 30s—and was replaced by Lee Bowman. Bowman stayed with the series when it moved to ABC in December of 1951 and played Ellery until its cancellation in December 1952. In 1954 a syndicated film version appeared, also titled *The Adventures of Ellery Queen,* and starring Hugh Marlowe, one of four actors who had played the role on radio. Florenz Ames continued as Inspector Queen in these films. The title of the syndicated version was changed in 1956 to *Mystery Is My Business.*

Ellery returned to live network television on NBC in the fall of 1958 with George Nader in the title role. To distinguish it from its predecessors, this edition was titled *The Further Adventures of Ellery Queen* but, effective with the October 24, 1958, telecast, the title was shortened to *Ellery Queen.* When production of this edition shifted from Hollywood to New York, and went from live to videotape, both of the principal actors—George Nader and Les Tremayne—left the series. The role of Ellery was assumed by Lee Philips and that of Inspector Queen was dropped.

After a gap of 16 years, NBC once more brought the series back to television, with Jim Hutton in the title role. This version, also titled *Ellery Queen,* was done as a period piece set in New York City in the late 1940s. Sergeant Velie, the plainclothes assistant to Inspector Queen, was now a regular in the cast; he had appeared in the novels and the radio series, but had not been seen regularly in any of the previous TV versions. Also added to this latest TV cast were Simon Brimmer, a radio detective who vied with Ellery in trying to solve the murders, and newspaper columnist Frank Flannigan. At the climax of each episode, just before resolving the case, Ellery would turn to the television audience and ask, "Have you figured it out? Do you know who the murderer is?"

ADVENTURES OF FU MANCHU, THE (*Crime Drama*)

BROADCAST HISTORY:
Syndicated only
30 minutes
Produced: *1955–1956* (39 episodes)
Released: *Early 1956*

CAST:
Dr. Fu Manchu........................ Glen Gordon
Sir Dennis Nayland-Smith .... Lester Matthews
Dr. John Petrie .... Clark Howat
Betty Leonard .... Carla Balenda
Karamanch .... Laurette Luez
Kolb .... John George

The *Fu Manchu* series must be unique in that it starred the villain. An extraordinary villain he was, a brilliant and powerful scientist operating out of Macao and other points in the Orient, with one goal: the destruction, or at least discomfiture, of the Western democracies, to avenge old wrongs. Each week Dr. Fu sent his agents on missions of subversion, such as extorting secret information from a U.S. diplomat, waging germ warfare, undermining the U.S. currency, or subverting a peace conference. On the side, he engaged in smuggling and other criminal activities. Fu had apparently unlimited resources, including diabolical scientific devices of his own invention. Battling the evil genius was Sir Dennis Nayland-Smith of Scotland Yard, his sworn enemy for generations, who succeeded in foiling each scheme but never got Fu himself.

Fu Manchu has had a long and varied media history beginning with his invention in the stories and novels of Sax Rohmer around 1910. At that time he was the embodiment of the "Yellow Peril," threatening Western civilization, but the racial elements were later downplayed. He appeared in numerous silent movies and in sound films in the 1930s and 1940s, and was on radio from 1929 on. A pilot film for a TV series was made in 1952, starring Sir Cedric Hardwicke, but this did not make it to the screen. Finally in 1955 Sax Rohmer, then 72, sold the rights to his famous creation to Republic Pictures for $4 million, and another TV pilot was made. This one resulted in the syndicated series shown above. However, the series was not very successful, and only 39 episodes were made.

More recent appearances of Fu Manchu include a number of English movies made in the 1960s, starring Christopher Lee, and a 1980 feature starring Peter Sellers in his final appearance.

ADVENTURES OF HIRAM HOLIDAY, THE (*Situation Comedy*)

FIRST TELECAST: *October 3, 1956*

LAST TELECAST: *February 27, 1957*
BROADCAST HISTORY:
Oct 1956–Feb 1957, NBC Wed 8:00–8:30
CAST:
Hiram Holiday .... Wally Cox
Joel Smith .... Ainslie Pryor

Hiram was a meek, mild-mannered proofreader for a New York newspaper who was discovered to possess physical and technical skills in a remarkable assortment of activities, such as fencing, scuba diving, airplane piloting, and art forgery. This so impressed his publisher that the newspaper sent him on a trip around the world, along with reporter Joel Smith as companion and recorder of his adventures.

ADVENTURES OF JIM BOWIE, THE (*Western*)
FIRST TELECAST: *September 7, 1956*
LAST TELECAST: *August 29, 1958*
BROADCAST HISTORY:
Sep 1956–Aug 1958, ABC Fri 8:00–8:30
CAST:
Jim Bowie .... Scott Forbes
John James Audubon .... Robert Cornthwaite
Rezin Bowie .... Peter Hanson

This Western was unusual in at least two respects: it was based—somewhat loosely, to be sure—on a real historical character, and its hero wielded a knife instead of a gun. According to the scriptwriters, Jim Bowie invented his famous knife after an encounter with a grizzly bear in which his standard blade broke at a critical moment. His new Bowie knife became his favorite weapon, although ABC, sensitive to parental reaction, played down its explicit use as a weapon in this series.

The Adventures of Jim Bowie was set in the Louisiana Territory of the 1830s, which provided backdrops of French-American New Orleans, and backwoods settings. Bowie was a wealthy young planter and adventurer, and his path crossed those of many interesting people, including his good friend John James Audubon (the naturalist painter), pirate Jean Lafitte, Sam Houston, Andrew Jackson, and even Johnny Appleseed. In one episode Jim ran for Congress against Davy Crockett. A young Michael Landon appeared in a 1956 episode.

The show was adapted from the book, *Tempered Blade,* by Monte Barrett.

ADVENTURES OF JIMMY NEUTRON: BOY GENIUS, THE (*Cartoon*)
BROADCAST HISTORY:
Nickelodeon
30 minutes
Original episodes: *2002–*
Premiered: *September 6, 2002*
VOICES:
James Isaac "Jimmy" Neutron ..... Debi Derryberry
Goddard .... Frank Welker
Carl Wheezer .... Rob Paulsen
Sheen .... Jeffrey Garcia
Cindy Vortex .... Carolyn Lawrence
Libby .... Crystal Scales
Hugh Beaumont Neutron .... Mark DeCarlo
Judy Neutron .... Megan Cavanagh
Nick Dean .... Candi Milo
Ms. Winifred Fowl .... Andrea Martin

Jimmy Neutron, a little imp with a big hairdo, was the smartest kid in Retroville. He spent his time dreaming up silly inventions to make his life more fun—pants folders, lightning-fast running shoes for a school race, a NanoBot to protect him from bullies, youth tonic for his granny—but most of the time they went awry. The pants took on a life of their own, the shoes made him disappear, the NanoBot terrorized his friends, Granny turned into a baby, and so on. Goddard was his pet mechanical dog; Carl, his loyal but scared, chubby friend (allergic to almost everything); and Sheen, his geeky friend obsessed with the Ultra-Lord action figure. Jimmy's chief rival was bossy Cindy, who was almost as smart as he was, and who was always putting him and his inventions down. Libby was Cindy's boy-crazy best friend, Hugh and Judy were Jimmy's indulgent parents, and Ms. Fowl was a teacher who looked and sounded like a chicken.

The Adventures of Jimmy Neutron was first seen in two special telecasts, on July 20 and August 5, 2002, in conjunction with the theatrical film of the same name.

ADVENTURES OF KIT CARSON, THE (*Western*)
BROADCAST HISTORY:
Syndicated only
30 minutes
Produced: *1951–1955* (104 episodes)
Released: *Fall 1951*
CAST:
Kit Carson .... Bill Williams
El Toro .... Don Diamond

One of the popular early kids' Westerns, with the famous frontier scout played by Hollywood leading man Bill Williams. His Mexican sidekick, El Toro, was played by Brooklyn-born Don Diamond. Kit and El Toro roamed the Old West, righting wrongs and eating dust from Wyoming to the Texas Panhandle, for 104 episodes. A couple of years later, when Williams was beginning work on a distinctly less rugged series, *Date with the Angels,* he remarked, "I never want to see or hear of Kit Carson again."

Hank Peterson played the occasional role of Sierra Jack.

ADVENTURES OF MARK AND BRIAN, THE (*Comedy*)
FIRST TELECAST: *September 9, 1991*
LAST TELECAST: *May 31, 1992*
BROADCAST HISTORY:
Sep 1991, NBC Mon 8:30–9:00
Sep 1991, NBC Thu 8:30–9:00
Sep 1991–Nov 1991, NBC Sun 7:00–7:30
May 1992, NBC Sun 7:00–7:30
REGULARS:
Brian Phelps
Mark Thompson

In the early days of television there were many successful adaptations of radio shows, including dramas, comedies, quiz shows, and public affairs series (see appendix). Since radio became a rock 'n' roll jukebox, however, there have been none—and that includes this loose adaptation of the radio routines of Los Angeles disc jockeys Mark and Brian. On their morning radio show, which began on KLOS-FM in 1987, the boys staged numerous stunts that must have been hilarious when heard but not seen. Imagine Robert

Goulet serenading Los Angeles on Valentine's Day from a helicopter with a giant loudspeaker, or a giant 8-by-16-foot head of Elvis Presley being towed across the country to Graceland in Memphis, in homage to the King. The premise of the TV series was that each week Mark and Brian would think up a new fantasy they wanted to fulfill. For the remainder of the half hour a film crew followed them around as they prepared and then did it. Among their "adventures": floating weightless above the earth during real astronaut training, performing on stage with the Temptations during an actual concert, and going underwater sharkdiving (with advice from *Sea Hunt*'s Lloyd Bridges).

Perhaps it sounded better than it looked. *The Adventures of Mark and Brian* was one of the lowest-rated new shows of the 1991–1992 season.

ADVENTURES of MCGRAW, THE, see *Meet McGraw*

ADVENTURES OF OKY DOKY (*Children's*)

FIRST TELECAST: *November 4, 1948*
LAST TELECAST: *May 26, 1949*
BROADCAST HISTORY:

Nov 1948–Mar 1949, DUM Thu 7:00–7:30
Mar 1949–May 1949, DUM Tue/Thu 6:45–7:00

HOST/HOSTESS:

Wendy Barrie
Burt Hilber

REGULARS:

Pat Barnard
Mellodaires

VOICE OF OKY DOKY:

Dayton Allen

Oky Doky was a large (30-inch) mustachioed puppet created by Raye Copeland, which was first seen on a local New York kids' fashion show called *Tots, Tweens and Teens.* He later got his own show on the DuMont network, called first *Adventures of Oky Doky* and later *Oky Doky Ranch.* The setting was a dude ranch to which the kids flocked, to watch Oky's latest Western adventure and to take part in games and junior talent performances. There was a certain amount of roughhouse in Oky's sketches, with knockdown drag-out fights with the bad guys and lots of smashed furniture, but Oky triumphed in the end, thanks to his magic strength pills (they contained good wholesome MILK, kids!).

ADVENTURES OF OZZIE & HARRIET, THE (*Situation Comedy*)

FIRST TELECAST: *October 3, 1952*
LAST TELECAST: *September 3, 1966*
BROADCAST HISTORY:

Oct 1952–June 1956, ABC Fri 8:00–8:30 (OS)
Oct 1956–Sep 1958, ABC Wed 9:00–9:30
Sep 1958–Sep 1961, ABC Wed 8:30–9:00
Sep 1961–Sep 1963, ABC Thu 7:30–8:00
Sep 1963–Jan 1966, ABC Wed 7:30–8:00
Jan 1966–Sep 1966, ABC Sat 7:30–8:00

CAST:

Ozzie Nelson .... Himself
Harriet Nelson .... Herself
David Nelson .... Himself
Eric "Ricky" Nelson .... Himself
"Thorny" Thornberry (1952–1958) .... Don DeFore
Darby (1955–1961) .... Parley Baer
Joe Randolph (1956–1966) .... Lyle Talbot
Clara Randolph (1956–1966) ...... Mary Jane Croft
Doc Williams (1954–1965) .... Frank Cady
Wally (1957–1966) .... Skip Young
Butch Barton (1958–1960) .... Gordon Jones
June (Mrs. David Nelson) (1961–1966) ... June Blair
Kris (Mrs. Rick Nelson) (1964–1966) .... Kristin Harmon
Fred (1958–1964) .... James Stacy
Mr. Kelley (1960–1962) .... Joe Flynn
Connie Edwards (1960–1966) ... Constance Harper
Jack (1961–1966) .... Jack Wagner*
Ginger (1962–1965) .... Charlene Salerno
Dean Hopkins (1964–1966) .... Ivan Bonar
Greg (1965–1966) .... Greg Dawson
Sean (1965–1966) .... Sean Morgan

*Played numerous other roles in late 1950s.

PRODUCER/DIRECTOR/HEAD WRITER:

Ozzie Nelson

One of TV's longest-running family comedies, this program was as much a picture of reality in its own way as the "relevance" comedies of the 1970s. *The Adventures of Ozzie & Harriet* was the real-life Nelson family on the air, with all the little adventures that an active and interesting middle-class American family might have, and two young boys growing up before their parents'—and the television audience's—eyes. Even the house they lived in was modeled on the Nelsons' real-life home in Hollywood. About the only liberties taken with reality, for dramatic purposes, was in Ozzie's role. On TV he had no defined source of income, and always seemed to be hanging around the house. (However, on at least one episode, "Ricky the Drummer," Ozzie referred to his former life as an orchestra leader, with Harriet as his vocalist.) In real life Ozzie Nelson was a hard worker indeed, having been the nation's youngest Eagle Scout at age 13, an honor student and star quarterback at Rutgers, and a nationally known bandleader in the 1930s. His wife, Harriet, had once been his band's vocalist.

Their two sons were the real stars of the program. When *The Adventures of Ozzie & Harriet* began on radio in 1944, the boys' roles were played by professional actors, but in 1949 Ozzie finally allowed his actual offspring to go on the air. From then until the TV version ended, America watched the two boys grow up. From 1952 to 1966 Ricky went from a crew-cut 11-year-old, to a real-life teenage singing idol, to a 25-year-old husband.

In the early episodes the stories revolved mostly around the four Nelsons, with only a few friends and neighbors featured—notably Thorny Thornberry, a holdover from radio days, who regularly offered Ozzie bits of ill-timed advice. Later, as the boys began to date, a succession of girlfriends and school buddies began to appear. In 1956 David went off to college, followed four years later by Ricky. In the meantime Ricky had begun a show business career of his own, which gave *The Adventures of Ozzie & Harriet* quite a boost among younger viewers. A fall 1956 episode had him organizing a rock 'n' roll band in high school. Then in an April 1957 telecast he was drafted to perform with a local band and sang a currently popular Fats Domino hit, "I'm Walkin' "—which, backed with "A Teenager's Romance," promptly became a real-life million-selling record for him. It was no flash-in-the-pan. Ricky went on to become one of the biggest stars of the rock era, and all of his songs were featured in *Ozzie & Harriet* episodes, or in an unconnected short segment tacked on to the end of the show.

In time both David and Ricky were married, and both real-life wives (June and Kris) appeared on the show. David emerged from "college" as a lawyer, and joined a law office, in which Ricky later worked as a part-time clerk. Their boss during most of this period was Mr. Kelley, and their secretary, Miss Edwards. Toward the end *The Adventures of Ozzie & Harriet* became almost a living exercise in nostalgia, with a number of episodes from the early 1950s being rerun during the last two seasons. The final original telecast in 1966 was wistful; it had Ozzie deciding to buy a pool table and convert David and Ricky's now-vacant bedroom into a game room—until he met with stiff opposition from Harriet.

For a short time in 1960 the series ran under the title *The Adventures of the Nelson Family*.

In 1973, the senior Nelsons returned with a syndicated series called *Ozzie's Girls*. With their two sons married and away, Ozzie and Harriet took in two college-coed boarders—Susie Hamilton (played by Susan Sennett) and Brenda MacKenzie (Brenda Sykes). In the first few episodes Brenda's first name was Jennifer. Stories revolved around the problems of the parents of two sons adjusting to the presence of two "daughters."

ADVENTURES OF PETE & PETE, THE (*Situation Comedy*)

BROADCAST HISTORY:

Nickelodeon
30 minutes
Produced: *1993–1996* (39 episodes)
Premiered: *December 5, 1993*

CAST:

Big Pete Wrigley .... Michael Maronna
Little Pete Wrigley .... Danny Tamberelli
Don Wrigley .... Hardy Rawls
Joyce Wrigley .... Judy Grafe
Ellen Hickle .... Alison Fanelli
Artie .... Toby Huss
Nona Mecklenberg .... Michelle Trachtenberg
Mr. Mecklenberg .... Iggy Pop

THEME:

performed by the rock group Polaris (on the Wrigleys' lawn)

Surreal comedy, reminiscent of NBC's *Eerie, Indiana*, in which a peaceful suburban neighborhood was a strange and skewed world as seen through the eyes of a preteen—in this case hyperactive "Little Pete" Wrigley. Strangeness abounded in the quiet town of Wellsville. For one thing Pete's teenage brother was also named Pete, for no particular reason. Don, his dad, was a balding goofball obsessed by his lawn, and Joyce, his mom, had a plate in her head on which she could pick up police radio and other odd signals. Artie, the truly nutty neighbor, was a rubber-faced inventor who dressed in red tights and maybe really was a comic-book superhero. Certainly he was Little Pete's hero. Ellen was Big Pete's friend and Nona the oddly perceptive little girl next door; only Big Pete, who narrated, was half normal. Nimbus was the family dog, and Petunia was Little Pete's bizarre tattoo. Parents, teachers, neighbors, school crossing guards, and others all acted illogically (as adults often do from a kid's point of view), but Little Pete's adventures usually worked out in the end.

The Adventures of Pete & Pete originated as a series of one-minute vignettes in 1990, was expanded into a series of five specials, and then became a regular series in late 1993. Filmed in Leonia, New Jersey.

ADVENTURES OF RIN TIN TIN, THE (*Western*)

FIRST TELECAST: *October 15, 1954*
LAST TELECAST: *August 28, 1959*
BROADCAST HISTORY:

Oct 1954–Aug 1959, ABC Fri 7:30–8:00

CAST:

Rusty .... Lee Aaker
Lt. Rip Masters .... James Brown
Sgt. Biff O'Hara .... Joe Sawyer
Cpl. Boone .... Rand Brooks

TRAINER:

Lee Duncan

The Adventurers of Rin Tin Tin was TV's "other" dog show. Despite some similarities to *Lassie*—it featured a heroic dog, with a small boy as his companion—there were considerable differences between the two shows. *Rin Tin Tin* was set in the Old West and was full of violent action, including gunfights, rampaging Indians, and the like. The boy, Rusty, had in fact been orphaned in an Indian raid, after which he and his dog Rin Tin Tin ("Yo ho, Rinty!") were adopted by the cavalry soldiers at Fort Apache, Arizona. The two were made honorary troopers and for the next five seasons proceeded to help the cavalry and the townspeople of nearby Mesa Grande establish law and order on the frontier.

Rin Tin Tin was a movie favorite of long standing, the first *Rin Tin Tin* feature having been made in 1922. Three different German Shepherds filled the role in the TV series, two of them descendants of the original Rinty (who died in 1932) and the other the offspring of another movie canine, Flame, Jr.

Reruns of *The Adventures of Rin Tin Tin* aired on ABC late afternoons from September 1959 to September 1961 and on CBS' Saturday morning lineup from September 1962 to September 1964.

When the old episodes of *Rin Tin Tin* were revived for a new life in reruns in 1976, former star James Brown came out of retirement to film new introductions for them. Remarkably, he looked only slightly older than he had two decades earlier when the series had been in production. Although the episodes were in black-and-white, the 1976 reruns had been tinted a light brown.

Rinty's saga continued on *Rin Tin Tin K-9 Cop*, which premiered on the Family Channel in 1988 (see separate entry).

ADVENTURES OF ROBIN HOOD, THE (*Adventure*)

FIRST TELECAST: *September 26, 1955*
LAST TELECAST: *September 22, 1958*
BROADCAST HISTORY:

Sep 1955–Sep 1958, CBS Mon 7:30–8:00

CAST:

Robin Hood .... Richard Greene
Maid Marian (1955–1957) .... Bernadette O'Farrell
Maid Marian (1957–1958) .... Patricia Driscoll

Sir Richard .... Ian Hunter
Friar Tuck...................... Alexander Gauge
Little John (1955, 1956–1958)....... Archie Duncan
Little John (1955–1956) .... Rufus Cruikshank
Sheriff of Nottingham .... Alan Wheatley
Prince John .... Donald Pleasence

Filmed completely on location in England, *The Adventures of Robin Hood* brought the famous swashbuckler to American television. Robin and his Merry Men made their home in Sherwood Forest. Their efforts to rob from the rich to give to the poor were frowned upon by Prince John and the Sheriff of Nottingham. Robin's true love, Maid Marian, was a member of Prince John's court who provided Robin with useful information, which helped him frustrate the efforts of the sheriff to capture him.

CBS aired reruns of this series on Saturday mornings from October 1958 to September 1959. See also *The New Adventures of Robin Hood*.

ADVENTURES OF SINBAD, THE (*Fantasy Adventure*)

BROADCAST HISTORY:

Syndicated only
60 minutes
Produced: *1996–1998* (42 episodes)
Released: *September 1996*

CAST:

Sinbad .... Zen Gesner
Doubar .... George Buza
Maeve (1996–1997) .... Jacqueline Collen
Firouz .... Tim Progosh
Rongar .... Oris Erhuero
Bryn (1997–1998)................ Mariah Shirley

In this over-the-top fantasy loosely based on the *Arabian Nights*, Sinbad was an attractive youth who set out from Baghdad on sailing adventures throughout the known world. Sinbad's crew included Doubar, his beefy much older brother, and Maeve, the sexy apprentice to Master Din Din, a magician friend of Sinbad's. Dermott, Maeve's trained falcon, served them as an advance scout. Also sailing with them in search of adventure were the well-meaning but nerdy Firouz and Rongar, a silent Nubian. They traveled the seas on their ship, the *Nomad*. Along with lots of magic, monsters, sorcerers, and witchcraft—all produced with cheap special effects—there was some truly mythical dialogue (sneering villain to damsel in distress: "Come, my pretty"; Sinbad, battling sea monster: "If we miss, we're seafood!"; Sinbad, about to be beheaded, to cohort: "I'll think of something").

At the beginning of the second season's premiere episode, Maeve was washed overboard during a fierce storm and died. Replacing her was Bryn, another sexy young sorceress, who rescued Sinbad on the beach where he washed up after his failed attempt to save Maeve. At the end of the episode the crew found out that Maeve was being protected from a powerful wizard and Bryn was to take her place with them. The tone of the show became more serious, and Sinbad, who had looked incredibly boyish during the first season, began sporting a stubbly beard.

ADVENTURES OF SIR FRANCIS DRAKE, THE (*Adventure*)

FIRST TELECAST: *June 24, 1962*
LAST TELECAST: *September 9, 1962*
BROADCAST HISTORY:

Jun 1962–Sep 1962, NBC Sun 8:30–9:00

CAST:

Sir Francis Drake .... Terence Morgan
Queen Elizabeth I .... Jean Kent
Richard Trevelyan .... Patrick McLoughlin
Walsingham .... Richard Warner
Morton, Earl of Lenox .... Ewan Roberts
Mendoza, the Spanish Ambassador .... Roger Delgado
John Drake .... Michael Crawford
Diego.............................. Milton Reid
Grenville .... Howard Lang
Bosun .... Peter Diamond

Filmed in England, and used as a summer replacement for *Car 54, Where Are You?*, this series consisted of fictional stories about Sir Francis Drake, the 16th-century adventurer. His varied skills as a seaman, soldier, pirate, explorer, and spy made him an invaluable asset to the court of Queen Elizabeth I. Included in his exploits were the rescue of Sir Walter Raleigh's lost colony in Virginia; an attack on the Spanish fort at St. Augustine in what is now Florida; and the release of a captive Seminole Indian princess. The producers made every effort to replicate exactly Drake's ship, *The Golden Hind*, and emphasis was placed on accuracy in historical detail.

ADVENTURES OF SIR LANCELOT, THE (*Adventure*)

FIRST TELECAST: *September 24, 1956*
LAST TELECAST: *June 24, 1957*
BROADCAST HISTORY:

Sep 1956–Jun 1957, NBC Mon 8:00–8:30

CAST:

Sir Lancelot .... William Russell
Queen Guinevere .... Jane Hylton
King Arthur .... Ronald Leigh-Hunt
Merlin .... Cyril Smith
Leonides .... Peter Bennett
Brian......................... Bobby Scroggins

This series, consisting of stories of the most famous knight of the Round Table, was filmed in England after extensive research had been done by Oxford University to guarantee the authenticity of the sixth- and seventh-century settings. Themes for the episodes came from assorted legends surrounding the chivalrous acts of Sir Lancelot and the other members of King Arthur's court.

ABC aired reruns of *The Adventures of Sir Lancelot* on Tuesday afternoons from October 1957 to September 1958.

ADVENTURES OF SUPERBOY, see *Superboy*

ADVENTURES OF SUPERMAN, THE (*Adventure*)

BROADCAST HISTORY:

Syndicated and network daytime
30 minutes
Produced: *July 1951–Nov 1957* (104 episodes)
Released: *Fall 1952*

CAST:

Superman/Clark Kent .... George Reeves
Lois Lane (1951) .... Phyllis Coates
Lois Lane (1953–1957) .... Noel Neill
Jimmy Olson .... Jack Larson
Perry White .... John Hamilton

Inspector William Henderson .... Robert Shayne

"Faster than a speeding bullet!" exclaimed the announcer. "More powerful than a locomotive! Able to leap tall buildings at a single bound.... Superman... strange visitor from another planet who came to Earth with powers and abilities far beyond those of mortal men! Superman, who can change the course of mighty rivers, bend steel in his bare hands, and who, disguised as Clark Kent, mild-mannered reporter for a great metropolitan newspaper, fights a never-ending battle for truth, justice, and the American way!"

Superman was one of the most fabulously successful media creations of modern times—and, if you think about it, an interesting reflection on what we would like to be. Following a highly successful career in comic books, radio, and movies in the 1940s, he came to television in a syndicated (not network) version that was a major hit of the 1950s.

His now-familiar genealogy was spelled out in the first episode. Kal-El was born on the faraway planet Krypton, the son of scientist Jor-El and his wife Lara (played by Robert Rockwell and Aline Towne in "Superman on Earth," the establishing TV episode). When destruction of their planet became imminent, the parents of Kal-El sent the infant to Earth in a miniature rocket. The rocket landed in Smallville, U.S.A., where the infant was discovered and raised by a childless couple named Eben and Sarah Kent. They named him Clark. As he grew older, Clark began to discover that he was different from other children, endowed with superhuman powers. The Kents told him about his origin and Clark began to consider how he might use these powers for the good of mankind.

At age 25, after Eben Kent's death, Clark moved to Metropolis and landed a job as a reporter for *The Daily Planet*, a crusading newspaper. When danger loomed he quickly changed from mild-mannered Clark Kent to Superman, leapt out a convenient window, and flew to the rescue! His familiar red-and-blue costume had been given him by Mrs. Kent, who had made it from the blankets that had swaddled him in the rocket as an infant (with no explanation how she cut and sewed it, since the completed costume was bulletproof, tearproof, and virtually as indestructible as Superman himself).

Clark's boss at the newspaper was blustery editor Perry White, whose most common expletive was "Great Caesar's ghost!" Jimmy Olson was the ambitious, but timid, young cub reporter, and Lois Lane was the top reporter on the paper. She was chief competitor to Clark, and chief female admirer of Superman, but she never connected the two men. Lois was in fact rather hard-nosed and aggressive as portrayed by Phyllis Coates, but became more sensitive and vulnerable in the later characterization of Noel Neill. Inspector Henderson of the Metropolis Police Department was hard-working, but somehow never managed to solve a case without the help of Superman, the *Planet* staff, or both. Jimmy and Lois also seemed to depend on Superman's help—he was constantly called upon to rescue them from criminals—but no one suspected his true identity.

Superman did have an incredible collection of powers—super-strength, super-hearing, X-ray vision, telescopic and microscopic vision, super-breath—and the abilities to split himself into two functioning entities, to will himself through solid matter, to levitate people, and, most important, to fly. The only thing to which he was vulnerable was Kryptonite, fragments of green rock that were the remnants of his exploded home planet. The bad guys on *Superman*, including semiregulars Ben Welden, Herb Vigran, Tris Coffin, and Billy Nelson (they turned up in different roles on different episodes), used everything they could get their hands on, including Kryptonite, to defeat and destroy Superman, but good always triumphed.

Although the first batch of 26 *Superman* films were made in 1951, the series did not reach local TV stations until late 1952. From 1953 to 1957 additional groups of films were made. Production, as with most non-network series, was low budget, and the actors wore virtually the same outfits all the time so that footage from different episodes could be shot at the same time without having to worry about matching costumes. The special effects were limited to having Superman crash through walls, lots of explosions, and scenes of Superman flying around—the latter accomplished by suspending him from invisible wires. The same flying sequences were used over and over, sometimes running as long as 30 or 40 seconds, to fill time. In one episode Superman changed direction while flying, which was accomplished by simply turning the film around—making the "S" on his uniform backward! There was a good deal of action and violence on *Superman* initially, but over the years it began to take itself less seriously and, by the last season, many of the episodes were played more for laughs than for action.

The media history of Superman is certainly varied. He was created by two teenagers, writer Jerry Siegel and artist Joe Shuster in the 1930s, and was initially rejected by all the major newspaper syndicates. He finally appeared in a comic book in 1938, and became an instantaneous hit. This led to a regular newspaper strip that ran 28 years (1939–1967); a radio series from 1940 to 1951, with Bud Collyer initially providing the voice of Superman; 17 animated Paramount cartoons from 1941 to 1943; theatrical serials in 1948 and 1950; and a feature-length movie, *Superman and the Mole Men*, in 1951 (later re-edited and shown as a two-part episode of the TV series).

George Reeves, who had made his movie debut in *Gone with the Wind*, became so typecast by his TV Superman role that he could not get other work. Although there were conflicting stories surrounding his death on June 16, 1959—including one that the series was about to return to production—the coroner's verdict was that he had committed suicide by shooting himself in the head. Nothing, however, could end the fictional Superman's life. ABC reran the syndicated films from October 1957–September 1958 on Wednesday afternoons, and CBS revived the Man of Steel in animated form on its Saturday morning lineup in 1966 (with Bud Collyer again doing the voice). The CBS cartoons, under the titles *Superman*, or *The New Adventures of Superman*, or as part of *The Superman-Aquaman Hour* and *The Batman-Superman Hour*, ran until September 1970. Superman then moved to ABC on Saturday mornings where he was an integral part of the animated *Superfriends* from 1973 to 1985. CBS brought the Man of Steel back to its animated Saturday morning lineup for the 1988–1989 season, and the WB network aired *The New Batman/Superman Adventures* on both Saturday mornings and weekday afternoons from September 1997 until the fall of 2000. In 1978 Superman got his first big-budget production, *Superman—The Movie*, starring Christopher Reeve, Margot Kidder, and Marlon Brando (with Noel Neill in an unbilled cameo role). It was a huge hit at the box office and precipitated a series of films about the superhero. There have also been a Superman play on Broadway, a novel, a Superman museum in Illinois, and endless nostalgia books about the Man of Steel. He will no doubt be seen on videodisks and on holographic TV in years to come. A thorough and comprehensive history of the Superman character can be found in *Superman—Serial to Cereal* by Gary Grossman, published by Popular Library in 1977.

ADVENTURES OF THE BLACK STALLION, THE
(*Adventure*)

BROADCAST HISTORY:
The Family Channel
30 minutes
Produced: *1990–1993* (78 episodes)
Premiered: *September 15, 1990*

CAST:
Henry Dailey .... Mickey Rooney
Alec Ramsey .... Richard Ian Cox
Belle Ramsey (1990–1992) .... Michele Goodger
Pierre Chastel (1990–1992) .... Jean-Paul Solal
Catherine Varnier (1990–1992) .. Virginie Demians
Nicole Berthier (1992–1993) .... Marianne Filali
Nathaniel MacKay (1992–1993) ...... David Taylor

A boy and his horse were at the center of this serialized adventure, adapted from the classic children's novel by Walter Farley. Alec was the teenage jockey determined to ride "the Black" to fame and glory with the aid of his grumpy trainer, Henry Dailey. Unfortunately a steady stream of rival trainers, bounders, cads, and crooks got in their way, often leading to tense showdowns and even gunplay.

During the first two seasons Henry and Alec operated out of a stable run by Pierre; Alec's mother, Belle, helped out (his father was deceased). During the second season the action moved for a time to France, where Alec and Henry toured the racing circuits with the Black and met young Nicole, a feisty teenager with a crush on Alec. Nathaniel was Henry's young nephew, an orphan.

The story had previously been told in two movies, *The Black Stallion* (1979), also starring Mickey Rooney, and *The Black Stallion Returns* (1983). Kelly Reno played the boy in both films.

ADVENTURES OF THE NELSON FAMILY, THE,
see *Adventures of Ozzie & Harriet, The*

ADVENTURES OF TUGBOAT ANNIE, THE
(*Comedy Adventure*)

BROADCAST HISTORY:
Syndicated only
30 minutes
Produced: *1956* (39 episodes)
Released: *March 1958*

CAST:
Tugboat Annie .... Minerva Urecal
Capt. Horatio Bullwinkle .... Walter Sande

Salt spray, insults, and action marked this expensively produced comedy, which had a short but well-publicized run in syndication in the late 1950s. Rival tugboat captains in the Pacific Northwest, Annie, a widow, and Bullwinkle were both built like oxes. The two of them were constantly trading jibes, stealing jobs from one another, and sharing adventure. Pinto was the weakling cook on Annie's tug, the *Narcissus*.

The character of Tugboat Annie had been created many years earlier by Norman Reilly Raine in a long series of stories for *The Saturday Evening Post*. These were made into a famous movie in 1933, in which Marie Dressler traded salty insults with a drunken Wallace Beery. A Hollywood production company obtained TV rights to the stories in 1954, but had great trouble both in casting the leads and in the actual filming, on location in San Pedro Harbor and on the Pacific. The pilot episode was said by *Variety* in 1956 to have been the most expensive ever made, costing upward of $130,000. It took two more years to get the series on the air, and then it only lasted for 39 episodes.

ADVENTURES OF WILD BILL HICKOK, THE
(*Western*)

BROADCAST HISTORY:
Syndicated and network daytime
30 minutes
Produced: *1951–1958* (113 episodes)
Released: *April 1951*

CAST:
Marshal James Butler Hickok .... Guy Madison
Jingles .... Andy Devine

"James Butler Hickok, mister," the hero announced. Whereupon his fat sidekick, Jingles, would pipe up in his shrill, raspy voice, "That's *Wild Bill Hickok*, mister! The bravest, strongest, fightingest U.S. Marshal in the whole West!" It was just as well that Jingles kept filling people in, because Guy Madison, the star of this early oater, was so handsome he might otherwise have been mistaken for a Hollywood matinee idol (which, in fact, he was). Good looks aside, Wild Bill could beat up on the baddies with the best of them, while his 300-pound companion added comic relief and not a little serious help at times. Despite his girth and blundering manner, Jingles was good at disguises. Buckshot was Wild Bill's horse, while Jingles' suffering steed was named Joker.

There was a real Wild Bill Hickok in the 1800s, who was variously a Pony Express rider, Union scout during the Civil War, scout for Colonel Custer, and Marshal of Abilene, Kansas. He did *not* look like a matinee idol.

Begun as a syndicated program for local broadcast, *Wild Bill Hickok* was also seen on CBS from 1955–1958 and on ABC from 1957–1958, in the daytime or late afternoon. There was a concurrent radio version on Mutual from 1951–1956, also starring Madison and Devine.

AEON FLUX (*Cartoon*)

BROADCAST HISTORY:
MTV
30 minutes
Produced: *1995–1996*
Premiered: *August 8, 1995*

VOICES:
Aeon Flux .... Denise Poirier
Trevor Goodchild .... John Lee

She was gorgeous, seductive, and deadly. She fought powerful and mystical foes, but whose side she was on was never entirely clear. Animator Peter Chung's strikingly sexy secret agent Aeon Flux possessed extraordinary powers, but she existed in a dark, futuristic netherworld where the lines between good and evil, hope and despair, were blurred. Trevor Goodchild was both her chief nemesis and her soul mate. *Aeon Flux* was first seen in 1991 as a short subject on MTV's *Liquid Television*, then expanded to a full half hour in 1995.

AFRICAN SKIES (*Adventure*)

BROADCAST HISTORY:

The Family Channel
30 minutes
Produced: *1992–1994* (52 episodes)
Premiered: *October 11, 1992*

CAST:

Margo Dutton .... Catherine Bach
Rory Dutton .... Simon James
Sam Dutton .... Robert Mitchum
Jam Mathiba .... Rouxnet Brown
Nyasa Mathiba..................... Nakedi Ribane
Raimund .... Raimund Harmstorf

Two South African teenagers, one white and one black, were best friends in this light adventure series. Rory was the son of Margo Dutton, who lived at Freedom Ranch, a modern spread located in the bush country. His dad had been killed some years earlier, but his grandfather Sam (Margo's father-in-law), a wealthy industrialist who ran the huge Acanco Corporation, looked after them from afar. (Sam was usually seen phoning from his office; actor Mitchum literally "phoned in" his role.) Jam was Rory's intelligent, soft-spoken African buddy. His seldom-seen father, a doctor, ran a clinic in the mountains; Nyasa was his mother. Rounding out the regular cast was Raimund, Margo's rugged companion, who helped her run the ranch and added comic relief with his heavy German accent.

Most of the stories revolved around Rory and Jam's adventures, which often forced them to use their wits and ingenuity to get out of scrapes. There were plenty of family values and little lessons about helping each other. Rhythmic African music punctuated the sound track.

AFTER HOURS (*Magazine*)

BROADCAST HISTORY:

Syndicated only
30 minutes
Produced: *1989–1990*
Released: *September 1989*

HOSTS:

Heidi Bohay
John Majhor

This entertainment magazine series aired on weekday evenings, with an offbeat assortment of short features ranging from interviews with rock music stars to coverage of celebrity baseball games, to a report on a car wash with topless and/or nude attendants. The pacing was extremely fast, originating in a large control room from which viewers could watch the director move from one story to the next. The producers categorized this as "zapless TV"—with so many stories in each half hour that viewers would feel like the channel was being changed automatically.

AFTERMASH (*Situation Comedy*)

FIRST TELECAST: *September 26, 1983*
LAST TELECAST: *December 18, 1984*
BROADCAST HISTORY:

Sep 1983–Mar 1984, CBS Mon 9:00–9:30
Apr 1984–Jun 1984, CBS Sun 8:00–8:30
Jul 1984–Oct 1984, CBS Tue 8:00–8:30
Dec 1984, CBS Tue 8:30–9:00

CAST:

Dr. Sherman Potter .... Harry Morgan
Max Klinger .... Jamie Farr
Father Francis Mulcahy ...... William Christopher
Mildred Potter .... Barbara Townsend
Mildred Potter (1984) .... Ann Pitoniak
Soon-Lee Klinger.................. Rosalind Chao
Mike D'Angelo...................... John Chappell
Wally Wainwright (1984) ...... Peter Michael Goetz
Dr. Gene Pfeiffer.................... Jay O. Sanders
Alma Cox .... Brandis Kemp
Nurse Coleman......................... Lois Foraker
Bonnie Hornbeck.................. Wendy Schaal
Bob Scannell........................ Pat Cranshaw
Nurse Crown.......................... Shirley Lang
Dr. Boyer (1984).................. David Ackroyd
Sarah (1984) .... Carolsue Walker
Nurse Weber (1984)...................... Susan Luck
Nurse Parker (1984) .... Joan Sweeny
Sunshine (1984)................. Sunshine Parker
Lenore Dudziek (1984) .... Wendy Girard

The Korean War was over and the men of the 4077th M.A.S.H. unit had returned to civilian life. Most of them scattered to the four corners of the States but three—Sherman Potter, Max Klinger, and Father Mulcahy—were reunited on the staff of the General Pershing Veterans Administration Hospital in River Bend, Missouri. Potter was chief of staff at the hospital, and it was through his recruiting efforts that Klinger joined the staff as his administrative assistant, and Mulcahy as the hospital chaplain. Others on staff included bureaucratic, ineffectual hospital administrator Mike D'Angelo; his pushy secretary Alma; another secretary, Bonnie; and a somewhat ingenuous young surgical resident named Gene. Most notable among the patients was absentminded old-timer Bob Scannell. Stories alternated between light comedy and serious depictions of the human wreckage created by war.

There was also a home scene. Klinger's Korean war bride, Soon-Lee, had come with him to America, and Potter's unassuming wife, Mildred, who was often talked about but never seen on *M*A*S*H* (except in a picture on Potter's desk), was on hand as well. By the spring of 1984 another cast member was on the way: Soon-Lee was about to give birth to her first child, a boy. The baby was born on the first episode of the show's second season but the series, despite a number of cast changes, including the arrival of a more serious administrator in the person of Wally Wainwright, died before the end of the year.

AGAINST ALL ODDS (*Documentary*)

FIRST TELECAST: *April 19, 1992*
LAST TELECAST: *July 19, 1992*
BROADCAST HISTORY:

Apr 1992–May 1992, NBC Sun 7:30–8:00
May 1992, NBC Sun 8:00–8:30
Jul 1992, NBC Sun 7:30–8:00

HOSTS:

Lindsay Wagner
Everett McGill

A pilot clings to life from the open door of his plane! A heroic rottweiler saves the life of an epileptic child during the 1989 San Francisco earthquake! A man heroically stops a runaway train transporting deadly gas! Everyday heroes were the subject of this half-hour reality show that used both re-creations and actual videotape shot at the scene by amateurs and others.

AGAINST THE GRAIN (*Adventure*)
FIRST TELECAST: *October 1, 1993*
LAST TELECAST: *July 22, 1994*
BROADCAST HISTORY:

Oct 1993–Dec 1993, NBC Fri 8:00–9:00
Jul 1994, NBC Fri 8:00–9:00

CAST:

Ed Clemons .... John Terry
Maggie Clemons .... Donna Bullock
Jill Clemons .... Robyn Lively
Joe Willie Clemons (age 16) .... Ben Affleck
Jenny Clemons (11) .... Vanessa Lee Evigan
Niles Hardeman .... Stephen Tobolowsky
Bobby Taylor .... Rick Peters
Abel .... Derek McGrath

A small-town insurance salesman and former high school football star found a new lease on life coaching his old team in this warm, down-home drama. Sumpter, Texas, was football-obsessed, but its team, the Sumpter Mustangs, was in a prolonged slump. Ed Clemons was given exactly one year to turn things around. He knew it was a big challenge, but it was also a lot more fun than insurance, so he turned the business over to his eager-to-prove-herself wife, Maggie, and tackled his new job with awesome, sometimes blinding, self-confidence. Trouble arose immediately when he replaced insolent quarterback Bobby with his own son, Joe Willie, who just happened to be a star in the making. Pushing Ed hard from the sidelines was loud auto salesman Niles ("Niles Autorama"), president of the team booster club, and just about everyone else in town.

Jill was Ed's oldest daughter, who visited sometimes from college, and Jenny his youngest. Abel was his assistant coach. GO MUSTANGS!

AGAINST THE LAW (*Legal Comedy/Drama*)
FIRST TELECAST: *September 23, 1990*
LAST TELECAST: *April 12, 1991*
BROADCAST HISTORY:

Sep 1990–Nov. 1990, FOX Sun 10:00–11:00
Nov 1990–Apr 1991, FOX Fri 9:00–10:00

CAST:

Simon MacHeath .... Michael O'Keefe
Yvette Carruthers .... Suzzanne Douglas
Elizabeth Verhagen .... Elizabeth Ruscio
J. T. Meigs (Miggsy) .... M. C. Gainey

Simon MacHeath had left a lucrative position with a prestigious Boston law firm (whose senior partner was the father of his former wife) to establish his own practice. A short-tempered maverick with strong principles, MacHeath was renowned for his unconventional legal techniques, courtroom histrionics, and confrontations with judges. But he was a good attorney. Although he did have some clients with money, many of them were the downtrodden and disadvantaged. Typical of the latter were a victim of hospital negligence, a woman who had been date-raped, a comedian arrested for using obscene language, and an illiterate college basketball star who was about to lose his scholarship because of a knee injury. Yvette was MacHeath's young black researcher/assistant, Elizabeth, his secretary, and Miggsy, his scruffy legman.

AGENCY, THE (*Foreign Intrigue*)
FIRST TELECAST: *September 27, 2001*
LAST TELECAST: *July 5, 2003*
BROADCAST HISTORY:

Sep 2001–Aug 2002, CBS Thu 10:00–11:00
Mar 2002, CBS Sat 9:00–10:00
Jul 2002–Jul 2003, CBS Sat 10:00–11:00

CAST:

Dir. Alex Pierce III (2001) .... Ronny Cox
Matt Callan (2001–2002) .... Gil Bellows
Carl Reese .... Rocky Carroll
Lisa Fabrizzi (2001–2002) .... Gloria Reuben
Terri Lowell .... Paige Turco
Joshua Nankin .... David Clennon
Jackson Haisley .... Will Patton
Robert Quinn .... Daniel Benzali
Lex .... Richard Speight, Jr.
Dir. Tom Gage (2002–) .... Beau Bridges
A. B. Stiles (2002–) .... Jason O'Mara

The covert activities of America's Central Intelligence Agency (CIA) served as the central focus of this sneaky series. Alex Pierce, the agency's white-haired director, was a career intelligence officer who had weathered everything from the Cold War to the fight against terrorism. He had seen the business of espionage evolve from a primary reliance on fieldwork to an emphasis on technology, including sophisticated monitoring equipment and an ever-growing dependence on computers. Carl, his sardonic deputy, served as both mediator and hatchet man. Matt was one of the CIA's top undercover operatives who, when *The Agency* premiered, was recovering from the mysterious death of his brother. Lisa, in charge of the counterterrorism team, had been engaged to Matt's brother. Terri, who had recently been hired, used sophisticated computer graphic design capabilites and other aids to forge documents and create counterfeit items needed by agents in the field. Occasionally she was sent out with other agents on undercover assignments. Others seen regularly included Lex, a young computer wizard who worked with her; their boss Joshua, head of the Office of Technical Services; and Jackson, the brilliant and introspective intelligence officer who spent most of his time in the office and often agonized about the moral implications of the Agency's activities.

Late in the year Pierce was fired, ostensibly for lying to a government committee about a mission involving spy planes in Peru—but in reality because someone had to take the fall for a number of recent intelligence failures. Quinn, a former CIA director, was brought in as his temporary replacement. In February, when Sen. Tom Gage was appointed new director of the CIA, Quinn became CIA liaison to the Office of Homeland Security but continued to maneuver to get his old job back. At the end of the first season Lisa, who had brooded over the intelligence failures that had enabled the September 11 terrorist attacks in New York and Washington, resigned from the Agency for psychological reasons. Matt was killed while on assignment in the season finale, and that fall Stiles was added to the team as his replacement. While working together on an assignment in Afghanistan, Terri and Stiles began an on-again, off-again affair.

In the season finale it was revealed that Joshua, whom the North Koreans thought had been a mole for them for the last 12 years, had actually been working for Quinn. In the cliffhanger ending Stiles was trying to remove an explosive-laden necklace from a captured Terri but the North Koreans, who had Joshua with them, set it off. No renewal, no resolution.

AIR AMERICA (*Adventure/Foreign Intrigue*)

BROADCAST HISTORY:

Syndicated only
60 minutes
Produced: *1998–1999* (23 episodes)
Released: *September 1998*

CAST:

Rio Arnett .... Lorenzo Lamas
Wiley Farrell .... Scott Plank
Alison Stratton .... Diana Barton
Edward Furman .... Gary Wood
Will Jenner .... Arthur Roberts
Dominique .... Shauna Sand
Pablo .... Gilbert Montoya

Rio was a hunky undercover agent for the O.S.I. (Office of Strategic Implementation) whose cover, and code name, was Air America, an air transport service based in exotic Costa Perdida in Latin America. He worked with his buddy, Wiley, the deputy base chief of the Costa Perdida airfield. Furman was the local State Department official who gave the guys most of their assignments, and white-haired Jenner was their State Department contact in Washington. Furman was a problem because he was looking to line his pockets and occasionally ran deals of his own that got Rio in trouble. They performed rescues, provided witness protection, conducted covert intelligence activities, and, thanks to the hot climate, got to take off their shirts a lot. Alison, who had romantic designs on Rio, ran the Hotel Parador, while Dominique (played by series star and producer Lamas's real-life wife) was a cocktail waitress at the hotel and Pablo was a young man who helped out at the airfield.

AIR POWER (*Documentary*)

FIRST TELECAST: *November 11, 1956*
LAST TELECAST: *October 19, 1958*
BROADCAST HISTORY:

Nov 1956–May 1957, CBS Sun 6:30–7:00
May 1958–Oct 1958, CBS Sun 6:30–7:00

NARRATOR:

Walter Cronkite

Air Power was a documentary series produced with the cooperation of the U.S. Air Force. Using filmed footage from all over the world, it traced the history of the airplane and gave an appraisal of its impact on the history and lifestyles of the 20th century. From its infancy at the turn of the century to the jet planes that were flying when the series was produced in the 1950s, the airplane was portrayed as both a weapon and a servant. The 1958 summer series consisted of reruns of the 1956–57 films.

AIR TIME '57 (*Musical Variety*)

FIRST TELECAST: *December 27, 1956*
LAST TELECAST: *April 4, 1957*
BROADCAST HISTORY:

Dec 1956–Apr 1957, ABC Thu 10:00–10:30

REGULARS:

Vaughn Monroe
Bobby Hackett
Elliot Lawrence Orchestra

Singer Vaughn Monroe was the host and star of this live musical variety series, jazz trumpet player Bobby Hackett and his group were featured regulars, and there was one or more guest stars each week.

AIRWOLF (*Adventure/Foreign Intrigue*)

FIRST TELECAST: *January 22, 1984*
LAST TELECAST: *July 23, 1986*
BROADCAST HISTORY:

Jan 1984, CBS Sun 9:30–11:30
Jan 1984–Apr 1984, CBS Sat 9:00–10:00
Aug 1984–Jan 1985, CBS Sat 8:00–9:00
Jan 1985–Jul 1985, CBS Sat 9:00–10:00
Jul 1985–Mar 1986, CBS Sat 8:00–9:00
May 1986–Jun 1986, CBS Sat 9:00–10:00
Jun 1986–Jul 1986, CBS Wed 9:00–10:00
(First run on USA Cable Network in 1987)

CAST:

Stringfellow Hawke (1984–1986)
.... Jan-Michael Vincent
Dominic Santini (1984–1986) ..... Ernest Borgnine
Michael Archangel (1984–1986) .... Alex Cord
Marella (1984–1985) .... Deborah Pratt
Caitlin O'Shannessy (1984–1986)
.... Jean Bruce Scott
St. John Hawke (1987) .... Barry Van Dyke
Jason Lock (1987) .... Anthony Sherwood
Jo Santini (1987) .... Michele Scarabelli
Maj. Mike Rivers (1987) .... Geraint Wyn Davies

Nineteen eighty-four was the year of the helicopter. The success of the theatrical film *Blue Thunder* in the summer of 1983 resulted, the following spring, in series on all three networks featuring copters—CBS' *Airwolf*, ABC's *Blue Thunder*, and NBC's less serious *Riptide*.

Most advanced of all the aircraft was Airwolf, a high-tech attack helicopter of the future. It could outrace conventional jets, travel halfway around the world, and blast away with enormous firepower. When its creator stole it and attempted to sell it to Libya, a supersecret U.S. Government agency known only as "The Firm" recruited reclusive pilot Stringfellow Hawke to get it back. He did, but then refused to turn it over until the government tracked down his brother, who was missing in action in Vietnam.

While the government was obligingly hunting up his brother, Hawke agreed to use Airwolf—which he had hidden in the Southwestern desert—on dangerous missions for The Firm. Hawke was not easy to deal with, however. A sullen and uncommunicative type, he could usually be found holed up in his mountain cabin, surrounded by his collection of impressionistic paintings, playing his cello. Women found this handsome loner fascinating, but he disdained them. His contact at The Firm was the suave, mysterious Archangel—identifiable by his white suit, eye patch, and cane. Helping Hawke on missions was his sensible, middle-aged war buddy, Dominic, and sometimes one of The Firm's agents, the beautiful Marella. Added to the cast at the start of the show's second season was spunky Caitlin O'Shannessy, a lady helicopter pilot who became part of the team.

When new episodes of *Airwolf* premiered on the USA Cable network in January of 1987, the cast was completely changed. In the story line Dominic was killed and Stringfellow badly injured when one of their regular helicopters, sabotaged by foreign agents, exploded. Dom's niece, Jo; Archangel's replacement, Jason Locke; and a talented but hard-to-control young agent, Mike Rivers, took Airwolf on a mission to rescue Stringfellow's brother, St. John Hawke. After getting back to the states, St. John took over for his injured brother as head of the Airwolf team. They still hid the super copter from "The Company" (it used to be "The Firm"), but were willing to use it on assignments they felt were worthwhile.

In order to keep the budget down on the cable version of *Airwolf*, production was moved from Hollywood to various locations in Canada.

AL MORGAN (*Music*)

FIRST TELECAST: *September 5, 1949*
LAST TELECAST: *August 30, 1951*
BROADCAST HISTORY:
Sep 1949–Feb 1951, DUM Mon 8:30–9:00
May 1951–Aug 1951, DUM Thu 8:00–8:30
HOST:
Al Morgan

This musical variety program from Chicago featured popular singer-pianist Al Morgan (whose big hit, in 1949, was a song called "Jealous Heart"). Most of the program consisted of Al's own easygoing playing and singing, although guests also appeared.

ALAN BURKE SHOW, THE (*Talk*)

BROADCAST HISTORY:
Syndicated only
2 hours *(1966–1969)*, 1 hour *(1969–1970)*
Produced: *1966–1970*
Released: *Spring 1966*
HOST:
Alan Burke

Alan Burke, former news editor, ad man, and real estate broker, was the caustic host of this New York–based discussion program. It was representative of the "crackpot" school of talk shows, generally eschewing celebrity or serious political guests for more bizarre or sensational subjects—witchcraft, UFOs, censorship, political extremists, belly dancers, and the like. Originally two hours in length, it was later cut to an hour without noticeable improvement. Seen mostly in large cities.

ALAN DALE SHOW, THE (*Music*)

FIRST TELECAST: *August 10, 1948*
LAST TELECAST: *January 16, 1951*
BROADCAST HISTORY:
Aug 1948–Sep 1948, DUM Tue 7:00–7:15
Jun 1950–Nov 1950, CBS Fri 11:00–11:30
Dec 1950–Jan 1951, CBS Mon/Wed/Fri 6:30–6:45 and Tue/Thu 6:30–7:00
HOST:
Alan Dale
REGULARS:
Janie Ford (1948)
Milt Green Trio (1950–1951)

Young Alan Dale (whose real name was Aldo Sigismundi) was considered one of the more promising crooners of the late 1940s and early 1950s. He was only 21 when he began his first local television show over DuMont's New York station in May 1948. The setting was a record shop supposedly run by Alan and his singing partner Janie Ford, which gave him plenty of opportunities to demonstrate his smooth baritone (actually he lip-synched to his own recordings). This series, which continued until March 1949, was fed out over the DuMont network for a time during the fall of 1948. Later Alan Dale was seen on CBS, in late-night and early-evening shows. Guest singers and comedians also appeared on his shows.

ALAN YOUNG SHOW, THE (*Comedy/Variety*)

FIRST TELECAST: *April 6, 1950*
LAST TELECAST: *June 21, 1953*
BROADCAST HISTORY:
Apr 1950–Mar 1952, CBS Thu 9:00–9:30 (OS)
Feb 1953–Jun 1953, CBS Sun 9:30–10:00
REGULARS:
Alan Young................................Himself
Kay Prindall (1953).................Dawn Addams
WRITERS:
Leo Solomon, David R. Schwartz, Alan Young

Young Canadian comedian Alan Young seemed to have a very bright future when he first moved to the new medium of television in 1950 (he had previously been on radio for a number of years). Critics applauded his gentle, intelligent humor, his versatility, and the excellent writing for his shows. "The Charlie Chaplin of television," *TV Guide* called him. "Without benefit of purloined gags, squirting seltzer, bad grammar, insults, references to his family, wornout guest stars, or women's hats, [he has] quietly become the rave of a growing legion of loving fans."

Young generally played a well-meaning young man who constantly wound up in a predicament. His half-hour shows consisted of a brief monologue, a song or two by a vocalist, and two complete skits—ranging from the first-time airline passenger who turns a peaceful flight into chaos, to a small boy in a world of very large furniture.

Despite his talents, Young's shows never really caught on. After two and a half seasons of the skits format, he returned in the spring of 1953 in a situation comedy, cast as a bank teller, with a girlfriend played by Dawn Addams. This version of the *Alan Young Show* was aired on alternate weeks with the *Ken Murray Show* under the umbrella title, *Time to Smile*. After two unsuccessful months Young returned to his familiar two-skit format, but this failed to save the series from final cancellation in June 1953.

ALASKANS, THE (*Adventure*)

FIRST TELECAST: *October 4, 1959*
LAST TELECAST: *September 25, 1960*

BROADCAST HISTORY:

Oct 1959–Sep 1960, ABC Sun 9:30–10:30

CAST:

Silky Harris .... Roger Moore
Reno McKee .... Jeff York
Nifty Cronin .... Ray Danton
Rocky Shaw .... Dorothy Provine

The Alaskan gold rush of the 1890s brought adventurers Silky Harris and Reno McKee to less-than-beautiful Skagway, Alaska, in search of their fortunes. With them went a singer friend, Rocky Shaw. Hunting for gold did not really appeal to the trio—it was too much like work—so they cast about for other means of obtaining money. Rocky went to work for saloon owner Nifty Cronin, who was only slightly more devious than Rocky's two friends but noticeably less honest. Silky and Reno would fleece their victims gently and rarely did anything completely harmful. Nifty would resort to robbery, murder, and any other means to attain his ends.

ALCOA HOUR, THE (*Dramatic Anthology*)

FIRST TELECAST: *October 16, 1955*
LAST TELECAST: *September 22, 1957*
BROADCAST HISTORY:

Oct 1955–Sep 1957, NBC Sun 9:00–10:00

One of the major drama series of TV's "Golden Age," *The Alcoa Hour* was telecast live from New York on alternate Sundays. The premiere presented Ann Todd in her American TV debut in "The Black Wings," co-starring Wendell Corey. Among the others who performed on *Alcoa* during its two-year run were Laurence Harvey (in his United States TV debut), Martin Balsam, Walter Matthau, Joanne Woodward, Sal Mineo, Helen Hayes, Eddie Albert, and Maureen Stapleton.

Although the majority of plays presented on *Alcoa Hour* were dramas, there were some musicals as well. These included "Amahl and the Night Visitors"; an adaptation of Dickens's *Christmas Carol* entitled "The Stingiest Man in Town," starring Vic Damone, Johnny Desmond, and Basil Rathbone (singing!); and an original TV musical entitled "He's for Me," with Roddy McDowall, Jane Kean, and Larry Blyden.

ALCOA PREMIERE (*Dramatic Anthology*)

FIRST TELECAST: *October 10, 1961*
LAST TELECAST: *September 12, 1963*
BROADCAST HISTORY:

Oct 1961–Sep 1962, ABC Tue 10:00–11:00
Oct 1962–Sep 1963, ABC Thu 10:00–11:00

HOST:

Fred Astaire

This filmed dramatic series featured Fred Astaire as host and occasional star. The premiere telecast was "People Need People," a powerful drama about the rehabilitation of psychologically disturbed war veterans, starring Lee Marvin and Arthur Kennedy and directed by Alex Segal. Subsequent telecasts maintained this high standard, with appearances by Charlton Heston, Brian Keith, Shelley Winters, Cliff Robertson, Janis Paige, Telly Savalas, and many others. Among the notable productions were "End of a World," a big-budget documentary drama about the assassination of Archduke Ferdinand, the event that triggered World War I; "Hornblower," based on the C. S. Forester books and pilot for a series that never materialized; "The Jail," by science-fiction writer Ray Bradbury; and "Flashing Spikes," a baseball drama starring James Stewart and real-life pitcher Don Drysdale, directed by movie giant John Ford.

Astaire generally appeared in dramatic roles too, but perhaps his most notable performance was in a comedy called "Mr. Lucifer," co-starring Elizabeth Montgomery—in which he played the Devil, in six different disguises.

ALCOA PRESENTS (*Occult Anthology*)

FIRST TELECAST: *January 20, 1959*
LAST TELECAST: *October 3, 1961*
BROADCAST HISTORY:

Jan 1959–Oct 1961, ABC Tue 10:00–10:30

HOST:

John Newland

Actual case histories of supernatural phenomena and the occult were dramatized for this filmed series. Confrontations with ghosts and various forms of ESP were frequent themes, and the stories were always told with a suitably eerie and mysterious air. The subtitle of the show (later used as the title when the series went into syndication) was more descriptive of its contents: *One Step Beyond*.

Almost two decades later a much grayer John Newland turned up as the host of a new syndicated series of tales of the occult and supernatural, *The Next Step Beyond*. Unlike the original series, which was in black-and-white, the syndicated version was shot in color. This may have actually hurt its chances, because it lacked the moody texture of the original. At any rate, it was in production only during 1978 and never attracted much of an audience.

ALCOA THEATRE (*Dramatic Anthology*)

FIRST TELECAST: *October 7, 1957*
LAST TELECAST: *September 19, 1960*
BROADCAST HISTORY:

Oct 1957–Sep 1960, NBC Mon 9:30–10:00

ROTATING STARS:

David Niven (1957–1958)
Robert Ryan (1957–1958)
Jane Powell (1957–1958)
Jack Lemmon (1957–1958)
Charles Boyer (1957–1958)

When Alcoa transferred its dramatic efforts from Sunday (see *Alcoa Hour*) to Monday nights in 1957, several major changes were made. A rotating company of five stars was introduced, and the format was reduced from a full hour live to half an hour on film. Though the quality remained high, the program had a less spectacular air. Many of the presentations were dramas, with titles such as "On Edge," "Circumstantial," "In the Dark," and "Ten Miles to Doomsday." However, there were occasional light comedies as well.

In 1958 the rotating stars were dropped and the program became a true anthology once again, featuring such varied talents as Cornel Wilde, Janet Blair, John Cassavetes, Jack Carson, Cliff Robertson, Agnes Moorehead, Walter Slezak, and Gary Merrill, among others. Throughout its run *Alcoa Theatre* was seen on alternate weeks. During its first four months it alternated with *Goodyear Theatre* under the umbrella title *A Turn of Fate*.

ALDRICH FAMILY, THE (*Situation Comedy*)
FIRST TELECAST: *October 2, 1949*
LAST TELECAST: *May 29, 1953*
BROADCAST HISTORY:
Oct 1949–Jun 1951, NBC Sun 7:30–8:00
Sep 1951–May 1953, NBC Fri 9:30–10:00
CAST:
Henry Aldrich (1949–1950) .... Robert Casey
Henry Aldrich (1950–1951) .... Richard Tyler
Henry Aldrich (1951–1952) .... Henry Girard
Henry Aldrich (1952) .... Kenneth Nelson
Henry Aldrich (1952–1953) .... Bobby Ellis
Mr. Sam Aldrich .... House Jameson*
Mrs. Alice Aldrich (1949–1950) .... Lois Wilson
Mrs. Alice Aldrich (1950–1951) ...... Nancy Carroll
Mrs. Alice Aldrich (1951) .... Lois Wilson
Mrs. Alice Aldrich (1951–1953) ... Barbara Robbins
Mary Aldrich (1949–1950) .... Charita Bauer
Mary Aldrich (1950–1952) .... Mary Malone
Mary Aldrich (1952–1953) .... June Dayton
Homer Brown (1949–1951) .... Jackie Kelk*
Homer Brown (1951–1952) .... Robert Barry
Homer Brown (1952–1953) .... Jackie Grimes
Mrs. Brown .... Leona Powers*
Mr. Brown .... Howard Smith
Kathleen .... Marcia Henderson
Aunt Harriet .... Ethel Wilson
Anna Mitchell .... Ann Sorg
George Bigelow .... Lionel Wilson
Mr. Bradley (1949) .... Richard Midgley
Mr. Bradley (1950–1953) .... Joseph Foley
Eleanor (1952–1953) .... Loretta Leversee
*Same role in radio series.

This television version of the long-running radio situation comedy concerned the adventures of teenager Henry Aldrich, his "typical American family," his high school buddies (including best friend Homer Brown), and his puppy loves. The locale was the Aldrich household on Elm Street, Centerville. There was considerable turnover in casting of the principal roles, with only House Jameson remaining throughout the television run as Henry's long-suffering father. Viewers must have wondered at Mr. Aldrich's marital life, what with five different sons, three daughters, and three wives all within the space of four years!

Still another actress was supposed to play the role of Henry's mother, but was dropped at the last minute in one of the television industry's most celebrated cases of political blacklisting. Jean Muir, a movie and radio actress for nearly 20 years, was hired during the summer of 1950 to portray Mrs. Aldrich in the coming season. Immediately, protests began to come in from right-wing groups, accusing Miss Muir of left-wing sympathies—it seems her name was listed in *Red Channels*, a vicious pamphlet that cited the alleged left-wing activities of dozens of performers. The sponsor, General Foods, and its advertising agency, Young and Rubicam, canceled the opening episode of the season as a result, and Miss Muir was summarily fired—with no opportunity to defend herself. Later, before a Congressional committee, she stated that she was not and had never been a Communist. But the truth didn't really matter. As in the cases of Philip Loeb of *The Goldbergs* and Ireene Wicker, *The Singing Lady*, the accusations alone had been enough virtually to destroy her career.

The Aldrich Family was created by Clifford Goldsmith, based on his play *What a Life*. The opening lines each week became something of a national catch phrase, with Mrs. Aldrich's call, "Henry! Henry Aldrich!," and Henry's pained reply, "Coming, Mother!"

ALF (*Situation Comedy*)
FIRST TELECAST: *September 22, 1986*
LAST TELECAST: *June 18, 1990*
BROADCAST HISTORY:
Sep 1986–Feb 1990, NBC Mon 8:00–8:30
Mar 1990, NBC Sat 8:00–8:30
Apr 1990–May 1990, NBC Sun 8:00–8:30
May 1990–Jun 1990, NBC Mon 8:00–8:30
CAST:
ALF (Gordon Shumway) (voice only) .... Paul Fusco
Willie Tanner .... Max Wright
Kate Tanner .... Anne Schedeen
Lynn Tanner .... Andrea Elson
Brian Tanner .... Benji Gregory
Dorothy Halligan (1987) .... Anne Meara
Raquel Ochmonek .... Liz Sheridan
Trevor Ochmonek .... John LaMotta
Jake Ochmonek (age 15) (1988–1989) .... Josh Blake
**Neal Tanner (1989–1990)* .... JM J. Bullock
*Occasional

Well, what would *you* do if an alien's spaceship crashed into your garage? Call the police? If you lived in a TV sitcom, you would probably do just what the Tanners did—hide him in the kitchen and enjoy years of laughs. Actually, there was little more to the plot of *ALF* than that. The furry little creature, nicknamed ALF (for "Alien Life Form"), landed on the Tanners' garage when his spacecraft went out of control. Unfortunately the ship couldn't be fixed, and anyway, his home planet of Melmac had just blown up, so ALF took up residence in the pleasant suburban Tanner home, disrupting their formerly boring life and commenting sarcastically (in a gravelly voice provided by the show's co-creator Paul Fusco) on the foibles of earthlings. The dense neighbors, the Ochmoneks, like all sitcom neighbors, never figured out what was going on.

A baby named Eric was born to the Tanner household in 1989, giving ALF new human customs to wisecrack about, and Willie's eager-to-please younger brother Neal showed up a few times in the last season to add variety. In a final episode cliffhanger in March 1990, ALF was contacted by Melmacians Skip and Rhonda, who invited him to leave with them and colonize a new planet—just as the U.S. government's Alien Task Force closed in to capture the furry little wiseacre.

ALF was a novelty hit in the 1986–87 season, leading to ALF dolls and other kids' paraphernalia. NBC even issued an official biography of its Monday night star. He was said to be 229 years old ("I've got dandruff older than your country") and had attended Melmac high school for 122 years, where he majored in software and was co-captain of the Bouillabaisseball team. Adult occupations included Assistant Boxleitner, part-time male model, and operator of his own phlegm dealership. Hobbies included gerrymandering and snacking on cats, a Melmackian delicacy (the Tanners' cat, Lucky, was often seen scurrying from the room). Height: "Fluctuates with weight." Weight: "Till the Sun Shines Nellie."

The creators of this fanciful comedy were Fusco

and actor/producer Tom Patchett; a frequent director was TV comic Peter Bonerz. A three-foot-tall midget by the name of Michu Meszaros was inside the ALF costume (when scenes called for it to walk around) during the first season.

An animated version of *Alf*, recounting Gordon Shumway's exploits on the planet Melmac, ran on NBC's Saturday morning lineup from September 1987 to August 1990.

ALFRED HITCHCOCK PRESENTS (*Suspense Anthology*)

FIRST TELECAST: *October 2, 1955*
LAST TELECAST: *July 20, 1986*
BROADCAST HISTORY:

Oct 1955–Sep 1960, CBS Sun 9:30–10:00
Sep 1960–Sep 1962, NBC Tue 8:30–9:00
Sep 1962–Dec 1962, CBS Thu 10:00–11:00
Jan 1963–Sep 1963, CBS Fri 9:30–10:30
Sep 1963–Sep 1964, CBS Fri 10:00–11:00
Oct 1964–Sep 1965, NBC Mon 10:00–11:00
Sep 1985–Jul 1986, NBC Sun 8:30–9:00
(First run on USA Cable Network in 1987–1988)

HOST:

Alfred Hitchcock

MUSICAL THEME:

Based on Gounod's "Funeral March of a Marionette"

The benign countenance of pudgy film director Alfred Hitchcock welcomed viewers to stories of terror, horror, suspense, and twisted endings for an entire decade. His clipped British accent and catlike theme music became television standbys as the series appeared on two different networks and was later seen for years in syndication. The stories would often appear to end with evil triumphant, in strict violation of the television code of ethics. This situation was always resolved following the last commercial, when Hitchcock would return to explain, in his deadpan sardonic way, what silly mistake or chance occurrence had finally done the villain in. When the show was expanded to an hour in the fall of 1962, the title was changed to *The Alfred Hitchcock Hour*.

Twenty years after the original series left the air, and five years after Hitchcock's death, the famous director achieved a unique distinction: he became the first person in history to return from the dead to host a new series. Films of his original black-and-white introductions were computer processed into color and used to introduce new episodes. Some of the color films made for the 1985 revival series were new stories, while others were remakes of original scripts. Hitchcock's black humor took on an eerie quality coming, as it were, from the grave. It was the sort of macabre touch the master would have enjoyed.

Following a one-year network run, additional episodes were filmed for the USA Cable Network beginning in 1987. The last of the additional episodes had its cable premiere early in 1988.

ALIAS (*Espionage*)

FIRST TELECAST: *September 30, 2001*
LAST TELECAST:
BROADCAST HISTORY:

Sep 2001– , ABC Sun 9:00–10:00

CAST:

Sydney Bristow.................... Jennifer Garner
Jack Bristow......................... Victor Garber
Arvin Sloane.......................... Ron Rifkin
Marcus Dixon......................... Carl Lumbly
Marshall Flinkman............... Kevin Weisman
Michael Vaughn.................. Michael Vartan
Will Tippin......................... Bradley Cooper
Francie Calfo (2001–2003)......... Merrin Dungey
Irina Derevko/Laura Bristow (2002–).. Lena Olin
Mr. Sark (2002–)................. David Anders

A beautiful young woman found herself drawn into a dangerous world of spies and counterspies in this action-packed, complicated and somewhat cartoonish thriller. Sydney had been approached by SD-6, a top secret division of the CIA, during her freshman year in college. Now she was a graduate student, and her hair-raising secret assignments took her all over the world, chasing down bad guys and blowing up their lairs (in between school assignments, apparently) in true James Bond fashion. Then she discovered that SD-6 was not a branch of the CIA at all but a rogue organization involved in espionage, extortion and weapons sales and an enemy of the United States. Her fiancé was killed and her life was placed in mortal danger. Sydney turned to the real CIA and became a double agent, determined to bring down SD-6—if it did not terminate her first.

Dixon was her partner at SD-6, a calm, cool married man who apparently did not know the organization's evil purpose; Marshall, the brilliant young tech guy, who provided its weapons, and Sloane, the grizzled, intense and totally ruthless chief who had mysterious connections and goals. Even more startling was Sydney's discovery that Jack, a trusted senior agent, was her long-absent father, and also a double agent for the CIA. Michael was her CIA handler, with whom she furtively met. Others in her life were Will, a hunky reporter friend who grew increasingly suspicious about her activities, and Francie, her clueless roommate, a party planner.

Much of the first season was spent chasing around the world in search of clues to a mysterious, mystical and potentially all-powerful weapon designed in the fifteenth century by a seer named Milo Rambaldi. SD-6's initial adversary in this pursuit was the Russian K-Directorate, but by the end of the season another evil network was revealed involving the devious Mr. Sark and run by none other than Sydney's supposedly dead mother, Laura Bristow, aka Irina Derevko. Will was drawn into one of Sydney's missions and learned the secret of what was going on.

In season two Irina surrendered to the CIA, but Sydney and her father could not decide whether to trust her or kill her. Sloane was revealed to be working independently not only of SD-6 but also of its governing body, the evil Alliance of Twelve, and in a complicated scheme in early 2003 he brought down the entire criminal enterprise so that he could pursue world domination on his own! With limitless resources and ruthless cunning, all he needed was the infernal Rambaldi device. As the season ended Francie was killed, the CIA, Sloane and Irina (who had escaped) jockeyed for the scattered pieces of the Rambaldi device, and Sydney disappeared for two years, waking up in Hong Kong unaware that her entire world had changed again.

ALIAS SMITH AND JONES (*Western*)

FIRST TELECAST: *January 21, 1971*
LAST TELECAST: *January 13, 1973*

BROADCAST HISTORY:

Jan 1971–Sep 1971, ABC Thu 7:30–8:30
Sep 1971–Aug 1972, ABC Thu 8:00–9:00
Sep 1972–Jan 1973, ABC Sat 8:00–9:00

CAST:

Hannibal Heyes (Joshua Smith) (1971–1972) .... Peter Deuel
Hannibal Heyes (Joshua Smith) (1972–1973) .... Roger Davis
Jed "Kid" Curry (Thaddeus Jones) ..... Ben Murphy
Clementine Hale .... Sally Field

NARRATOR:

Roger Davis (1971–1972)
Ralph Story (1972–1973)

CREATOR/PRODUCER:

Glen A. Larson

The main characters in this Western adventure were two gallant and amiable ex-outlaws trying to go straight. The governor had promised them a pardon for their past crimes if they could stay out of trouble for one year, but what with a price still on their heads, a lot of grudges against them, and a bit of larceny still in their hearts, that was no easy proposition. Chased across two TV seasons by posses, bounty hunters, and old outlaw friends who wanted them to join in on some escapade, they never did get their pardon. The occasional role of Clementine Hale, another lovable rogue, was added in October 1971 to give the program some continuing female interest.

On December 31, 1971, star Peter Deuel, age 31, was found shot to death in his Hollywood Hills apartment, an apparent suicide. With only a few episodes already in the can, the role of Joshua Smith quickly had to be recast. Roger Davis, who had been doing the program's opening and closing narrations, was chosen, and a partially completed episode was finished with Davis redoing scenes already filmed by Deuel.

ALICE (*Situation Comedy*)

FIRST TELECAST: *August 31, 1976*
LAST TELECAST: *July 2, 1985*

BROADCAST HISTORY:

Aug 1976, CBS Mon 9:30–10:00
Sep 1976–Oct 1976, CBS Wed 9:30–10:00
Nov 1976–Sep 1977, CBS Sat 9:30–10:00
Oct 1977–Oct 1978, CBS Sun 9:30–10:00
Oct 1978–Feb 1979, CBS Sun 8:30–9:00
Mar 1979–Sep 1982, CBS Sun 9:00–9:30
Oct 1982–Nov 1982, CBS Wed 9:00–9:30
Mar 1983–Apr 1983, CBS Mon 9:00–9:30
Apr 1983–May 1983, CBS Sun 9:30–10:00
Jun 1983–Jan 1984, CBS Sun 8:00–8:30
Jan 1984–Dec 1984, CBS Sun 9:30–10:00
Jan 1985–Mar 1985, CBS Tue 8:30–9:00
Jun 1985–Jul 1985, CBS Tue 8:30–9:00

CAST:

Alice Hyatt .... Linda Lavin
Tommy Hyatt .... Philip McKeon
Mel Sharples .... Vic Tayback
Florence Jean Castleberry ("Flo") (1976–1980) .... Polly Holliday
Vera Louise Gorman .... Beth Howland
Belle Dupree (1980–1981) .... Diane Ladd
Jolene Hunnicutt (1981–1985) .... Celia Weston
Carrie Sharples (1982–1984) .... Martha Raye
Eliot Novak (1983–1985) .... Charles Levin
Nicholas Stone (1984–1985) .... Michael Durrell
Henry (1977–1985) .... Marvin Kaplan
Andy (1976–1978) .... Pat Cranshaw
Jason (1978–1979) .... Patrick J. Cronin
Cecil (1978–1979) .... Bob McClurg
Earl Hicks (1978–1985) .... Dave Madden
Chuck (1978–1985) .... Duane R. Campbell
Marie (1978–1980) .... Victoria Carroll
Mike (1979–1980) .... Michael Ballard
Brian (1979–1980) .... Alan Haufrect
Charlie (1979–1981) .... Ted Gehring
Ralph (1979–1981) .... Michael Alldredge
Raleigh (1979–1981) .... Raleigh Bond
Mitch Aames (1981–1982) .... Phillip R. Allen
Jerry (1982–1982) .... Jerry Potter
Artie (1982–1985) .... Tony Longo
Danny (1984–1985) .... Jonathan Prince
Doug (1984–1985) .... Doug Robinson

THEME:

"There's a New Girl in Town," by Alan and Marilyn Bergman and David Shire, sung over the opening credits by Linda Lavin

When this comedy premiered in 1976, it was the story of a recently widowed aspiring singer with a very precocious 12-year-old son. Alice Hyatt had moved from her home in New Jersey to look for work in Phoenix. While attempting to find a singing job, she kept her household together by working as a waitress at Mel's Diner. The two other waitresses at Mel's provided quite a contrast. Flo, the old hand, was lusty, outspoken, and crude (her favorite expression was "Kiss my grits"), but had difficulty hiding a soft heart. Vera, on the other hand, was young, impressionable, and rather quiet. Mel Sharples, the owner of the diner, was also its cook and the creator of Mel's Famous Chili, which was so popular in the area that it (along with fun-loving Flo) attracted a loyal and regular clientele. In fact, all of the listed cast members from Henry on down (with the exception of Mel's sometime girlfriend Marie) were regulars at the diner.

The series was based on the movie *Alice Doesn't Live Here Anymore*, the title role of which was played by Ellen Burstyn, who received an Academy Award for her performance. The only member of the movie cast to make the transition to the TV series in 1976 was Vic Tayback, re-creating his role as the crusty owner of Mel's Diner. He was joined in the spring of 1980 by Diane Ladd, who had played Flo in the movie but turned up as Belle in the TV series. Belle was hired by Mel as a waitress when Flo moved to Houston to run her own restaurant (see the spin-off series *Flo*). She was from Mississippi, wrote country-and-western songs, and lived in the Phoenix Palms Apartments, where Alice and Tommy also resided. Belle admirably filled the void left by Flo—the accent may have been different, but her earthy outlook on life and aggressive personality endeared her to Mel's regulars. She left after one year and was replaced by Jolene. Carrie, Mel's pushy, loudmouthed mother, moved to Phoenix after her divorce, took up residence with her son, and practically took over the diner. Next to her, Mel was a real softie. In the fall of 1983, after a whirlwind courtship, shy Vera married policeman Elliot Novak and the following fall found Alice with a new boyfriend, Nicholas Stone.

In the last original episode of the series (March 19, 1985) Mel sold the diner and, despite his reputation for cheapness over the years, gave each of his waitresses a $5,000 farewell bonus. All worked out for the best, however, since Jolene was planning to quit to open a beauty shop, Vera had become pregnant and was looking forward to becoming a full-time mother, and Alice, after all the years at the diner, was moving to Nashville as lead singer with a band.

CBS aired reruns of *Alice* on weekday mornings from June 1980 to September 1982.

ALICE PEARCE (*Musical Variety*)

FIRST TELECAST: *January 28, 1949*
LAST TELECAST: *March 4, 1949*
BROADCAST HISTORY:
Jan 1949–Mar 1949, ABC Fri 9:45–10:00
REGULARS:
Alice Pearce
Mark Lawrence, piano

This short—and short-lived—program presented fifteen minutes of music and comedy, hosted by comedienne Alice Pearce.

ALIEN NATION (*Science Fiction*)

FIRST TELECAST: *September 18, 1989*
LAST TELECAST: *July 26, 1991*
BROADCAST HISTORY:
Sep 1989–Sep 1990, FOX Mon 9:00–10:00
Jun 1991–Jul 1991, FOX Fri 9:00–10:00
CAST:
Det. Matthew Sikes .... Gary Graham
Det. George Francisco .... Eric Pierpoint
Susan Francisco .... Michele Scarabelli
Buck Francisco (age 17) .... Sean Six
Emily Francisco (9) .... Lauren Woodland
Cathy Frankel .... Terri Treas
Albert Einstein .... Jeff Marcus
Burns (1989) .... Jeff Doucette
Sgt. Dobbs .... Lawrence-Hilton Jacobs
Capt. Brian Grazer .... Ron Fassler
Jill (1989) .... Molly Morgan

Set in Los Angeles in 1995, *Alien Nation* was both a futuristic cop show and a thinly veiled commentary on racial intolerance. Matt and George were partners on the L.A.P.D., whose backgrounds were, literally, worlds apart. Matt was a divorced, streetwise, hardened cop, just trying to survive. George was a Newcomer, one of the hundreds of thousands of "people" from the planet Tencton whose spaceship—a slave transport in transit to another planet—had crashed in the Mojave Desert a few years earlier. The Newcomers, who were derisively referred to by the prejudiced as Slags, had taken on Earth names and tried to assimilate into the population of Los Angeles. Although generally humanoid in appearance, they had enlarged craniums (they were smarter than humans), mottled skin pigmentation instead of hair, and vestigial ears. Newcomers learned faster than humans, aged much more slowly, and were physically much stronger—all traits that did nothing to endear them to the Purists who wanted them out of Los Angeles and off the planet.

George was the first Newcomer to rise to the rank of detective on the L.A.P.D. He was generally gentle, quiet, and introspective. His analytical approach to crime fighting was often at odds with Matt's impulsive tendency to violent action. George's wife, Susan, worked at an advertising agency, and their two children, teenage Buck and preteen Emily, were both in school. It was through the eyes of the Francisco family that viewers saw the problems of cultural prejudice. Other Newcomers in the cast were Cathy Frankel, a biochemist who lived in Matt's building (to whom Matt was attracted, despite his confusion over what to do about it), and Albert Einstein, a maintenance man at the police station where Matt and George worked.

One of the most unusual story lines dealt with the pregnancy of the Franciscos. Susan only carried the fetus for the first part of the pregnancy, with George carrying it to term and actually giving birth to little Vesna late in the season.

Fox aired reruns of *Alien Nation* during the summer of 1991. Adapted from the 1988 movie of the same name starring James Caan and Mandy Patinkin.

ALIENS IN THE FAMILY (*Situation Comedy*)

FIRST TELECAST: *March 15, 1996*
LAST TELECAST: *March 22, 1996*
BROADCAST HISTORY:
Mar 1996, ABC Fri 9:00–9:30
CAST:
Doug Brody .... John Bedford Lloyd
Cookie Brody .... Margaret Trigg
Heather Brody (age 14) .... Paige Tiffany
Adam Brody (9) .... Chris Marquette
Spit (14)(voice) ... Joey Mazzarino & Michelan Sisti
Snizzy (10)(voice)
.... Alice Dinnead & Michael Gilden
Bobut (baby)(voice)
.... David Rudman & John Kennedy
Sally Hagen .... Julie Dretzin
THEME:
by Todd Rundgren

Can an alien abduction lead to romance? Perhaps, but not for long, judging by this sitcom that lasted just two weeks on ABC's prime-time lineup. Doug was an easygoing office worker and single dad who was abducted by alien scientist Cookie; they fell in love and married, combining his earthly and her otherworldly families. Doug's kids were self-absorbed Heather and cute Adam. Hers were supercool teen son Spit, rambunctious daughter Snizzy, and sarcastic baby Bobut, who acted as if he was the Emperor of the Universe—because he was. Sally was the harried Nanny.

The aliens were portrayed by life-sized muppets designed in the Jim Henson studios. Leftover episodes of the failed series aired in ABC's Saturday morning kids' lineup—where they perhaps belonged in the first place—from July 27 through August 31, 1996.

ALKALI IKE (*Comedy*)

FIRST TELECAST: *April 17, 1950*
LAST TELECAST: *May 11, 1950*
BROADCAST HISTORY:
Apr 1950–May 1950, CBS Mon/Thu/Fri 7:45–8:00
REGULARS:
Al Robinson
Beverly Fite
The Slim Jackson Quartet

Ventriloquist Al Robinson was a discovery of Arthur Godfrey's. For a short time in the spring of 1950 he had his own live show featuring his Western dummy, Alkali Ike. Ike was trying to learn to live a varied and interesting life with the help of Al and an attractive female tutor. The action took place at Ike's ranch "somewhere in the West" and included vocal numbers by Beverly Fite and The Slim Jackson Quartet.

ALL-AMERICAN GIRL (*Situation Comedy*)
FIRST TELECAST: *September 14, 1994*
LAST TELECAST: *August 23, 1995*
BROADCAST HISTORY:
Sep 1994, ABC Wed 9:30–10:00
Sep 1994–Mar 1995, ABC Wed 8:30–9:00
Aug 1995, ABC Wed 9:30–10:00
CAST:
Margaret Kim .... Margaret Cho
Katherine Kim .... Jodi Long
Benny Kim .... Clyde Kusatsu
Stuart Kim .... B. D. Wong
Eric Kim (age 12) .... J. B. Quon
Grandma .... Amy Hill
Ruthie .... Maddie Corman
Gloria .... Judy Gold
Casey Emerson (1994) .... Eric and Ashley Johnson

Culture-clash comedy about a hip, thoroughly assimilated Korean-American girl and her very traditional mother. Twenty-one-year-old Margaret and her mother, Katherine, fought constantly, mostly over dates; Mom wanted her to become the deferential wife of some nice Korean boy, while Margaret favored Caucasians in leather biker garb. Stuart was Margaret's Goody Two-shoes older brother, engaged and studying to become a cardiologist while deferentially spending most of his time at his parents' home. Eric, the younger brother, looked up to his sister, much to Mom's chagrin. Dad (Benny) just ducked for cover as the women lobbed one-liners at each other.

The scene alternated between the Kims' nice white town house, their family business ("Kim's Books"), and the department store where Margaret worked at a cosmetics counter, all presumably in San Francisco. Ruthie and Gloria were coworkers who egged Margaret on. Another unexpected ally was Grandma, a stereotype-buster in her younger days, who was now either senile or very wise.

ALL AMERICAN GIRL (*Talent*)
FIRST TELECAST: *March 12, 2003*
LAST TELECAST: *April 24, 2003*
BROADCAST HISTORY:
Mar 2003, ABC Wed 9:00–10:00
Mar 2003–Apr 2003, ABC Wed 10:00–11:00
Apr 2003, ABC Thu 8:00–9:00
(Additional episodes on ABC Family on May 8 and 24, 2003)
HOST:
Mitch Mullany
JUDGES:
Geri Halliwell
John Salley
Suzanne de Passe

Young women vied for $100,000, a management contract and the title of "All American Girl" in this straightforward talent competition. The process began with open auditions in four cities, which led to a field of 45 finalists who were flown to a Disney theme park in California to face three celebrity judges: former Spice Girl Geri Halliwell, NBA star John Salley, and entertainment executive Suzanne de Passe. The contestants could perform in any manner, and there were singers, dancers, comediennes, gymnasts, a poetry reader, a Michael Jackson imitator (de Passe, who knew Jackson, trashed that one) and even a young pianist performing Beethoven's "Für Elise." There were also intelligence quizzes, and tests of personality and athletic ability. The judges whittled the group down to 24, and then the fun began. Each judge had to pick five girls for his or her "team," and the judges squabbled and plotted against each other to snare the most talented. If a contestant was picked by more than one judge, she got to choose which judge she wanted to go with.

Once the teams were formed the show moved to the training camps, where the judges, with the help of professional coaches, put the girls through a rigorous training program. During the process one to two girls were cut from each team, resulting in a final field of ten. The final ten then strutted their stuff for the TV audience, and viewers at home voted who would be crowned the "All American Girl." Due to low ratings ABC aired the last two episodes on the co-owned ABC Family Channel cable network in May 2003. The winner was 22-year-old Jessica Felice.

ALL AROUND THE TOWN (*Interview*)
FIRST TELECAST: *November 10, 1951*
LAST TELECAST: *June 7, 1952*
BROADCAST HISTORY:
Nov 1951–Jan 1952, CBS Sat 6:00–6:45
May 1952–Jun 1952, CBS Sat 9:00–9:30
REGULARS:
Mike Wallace
Buff Cobb

Mike Wallace and his wife Buff Cobb hosted this live interview show on CBS during the 1951–1952 season. They traveled around New York City to places such as Coney Island, the New York City Ballet, and numerous restaurants from which they telecast their informal interviews with patrons and promoters.

The series began as a thrice-weekly late-afternoon entry in June 1951, then moved into the evening hours in November.

ALL IN ONE (*Comedy Variety*)
FIRST TELECAST: *December 27, 1952*
LAST TELECAST: *April 2, 1953*
BROADCAST HISTORY:
Dec 1952–Jan 1953, CBS Sat 9:00–9:30
Apr 1953, CBS Thu 8:00–8:30
HOST:
George de Witt

In addition to functioning as host, George de Witt participated in sketches with the guest comics who were the stars of this short-lived variety show. Everything was done on a bare stage, and the audience was required to use its imagination to visualize sets and props. *All in One* had a four-week run and then returned in April for a single encore. It originated live from New York.

ALL IN THE FAMILY (*Situation Comedy*)
FIRST TELECAST: *January 12, 1971*
LAST TELECAST: *September 21, 1983*
BROADCAST HISTORY:
Jan 1971–Jul 1971, CBS Tue 9:30–10:00
Sep 1971–Sep 1975, CBS Sat 8:00–8:30
Sep 1975–Sep 1976, CBS Mon 9:00–9:30
Sep 1976–Oct 1976, CBS Wed 9:00–9:30
Nov 1976–Sep 1977, CBS Sat 9:00–9:30

Oct 1977–Oct 1978, CBS Sun 9:00–9:30
Oct 1978–Mar 1983, CBS Sun 8:00–8:30
Mar 1983–May 1983, CBS Mon 8:00–8:30
May 1983, CBS Sun 8:00–8:30
Jun 1983, CBS Mon 9:30–10:00
Jun 1983–Sep 1983, CBS Wed 8:00–8:30

CAST:

Archie Bunker .... Carroll O'Connor
Edith Bunker (Dingbat) (1971–1980) .... Jean Stapleton
Gloria Bunker Stivic (1971–1978) .... Sally Struthers
Mike Stivic (Meathead) (1971–1978) .... Rob Reiner
Lionel Jefferson (1971–1975)........... Mike Evans
Louise Jefferson (1971–1975)........ Isabel Sanford
Henry Jefferson (1971–1973) .... Mel Stewart
George Jefferson (1973–1975) .... Sherman Hemsley
Irene Lorenzo (1973–1975) .... Betty Garrett
Frank Lorenzo (1973–1974) ...... Vincent Gardenia
Bert Munson (1972–1977).............. Billy Halop
Tommy Kelsey (1972–1973)........ Brendon Dillon
Tommy Kelsey (1973–1977) .... Bob Hastings
Justin Quigley (1973–1976)............ Burt Mustin
Barney Hefner (1973–1983) .... Allan Melvin
Jo Nelson (1973–1975).............. Ruth McDevitt
Stretch Cunningham (1974)....... James Cromwell
Teresa Betancourt (1976–1977).......... Liz Torres
Stephanie Mills (1978–1983) .... Danielle Brisebois
Harry Snowden (1977–1983) ...... Jason Wingreen
Hank Pivnik (1977–1981) .... Danny Dayton
Murray Klein (1979–1981) .... Martin Balsam
Mr. Van Ranseleer (1978–1983) .... Bill Quinn
Veronica Rooney (1979–1982) .... Anne Meara
Jose (1979–1983) .... Abraham Alvarez
Linda (1980–1981) .... Heidi Hagman
Raoul (1980–1983) .... Joe Rosario
Ellen Canby (1980–1982)........... Barbara Meek
Polly Swanson (1980–1981 ...... Janet MacLachlan
Ed Swanson (1980–1981) .... Mel Bryant
Billie Bunker (1981–1983)............ Denise Miller
Gary Rabinowitz (1981–1983) .... Barry Gordon
Bruce (1982–1983) .... Bob Okazaki
Marsha (1982–1983)................ Jessica Nelson

THEME:

"Those Were the Days," by Strouse and Adams, sung at the opening of each show by Archie and Edith until 1979, replaced by an instrumental version after that.

PRODUCER:

Norman Lear

All in the Family changed the course of television comedy. It brought a sense of harsh reality to a TV world which previously had been populated largely by homogenized, inoffensive characters and stories that seemed to have been laundered before they ever got on the air. Its chief character, Archie Bunker, was anything but bland. A typical working-class Joe, he was uneducated, prejudiced, and blatantly outspoken. He was constantly lambasting virtually every minority group in existence. His views on blacks (or, as he often called them, "jungle bunnies" or "spades"), Puerto Ricans ("spics"), Chinese ("chinks"), and any other racial or religious group not his own, were clear and consistent. Archie believed in every negative racial and ethnic stereotype he had ever heard.

Unfortunately, he could never get away from the people he despised. Archie was a dock foreman for the Prendergast Tool and Die Company, and he had to work with a racially mixed group of people. Next door to his small house at 704 Houser Street, in the Corona section of Queens, New York, lived a black family, the Jeffersons. His daughter Gloria had married a Pole. On top of it all, Archie, the bigoted arch-conservative, even had to share his house with his egghead liberal son-in-law, Mike Stivic. (Mike was studying for his degree in sociology, and so was unemployed.) Completing the Bunker household was Archie's slow-witted but honest and unprejudiced wife, Edith.

The Jefferson family next door consisted of Louise, one of Edith's closest friends, her husband George, who ran a small dry-cleaning store, and their son Lionel, a close friend of Mike's. Lionel loved to come to the Bunker house to tease Archie about his prejudices, while George Jefferson's brother Henry, who was as opinionated from the black point of view as Archie was from the white, also provided conflict.

Over the years changes took place. Edith's cousin Maude Findlay, played by Bea Arthur, appeared in several episodes, provoking Archie with her loud, liberal opinions. She got her own show, *Maude*, in 1972. The Jeffersons moved away to Manhattan and into their own show, *The Jeffersons*, early in 1975, whereupon Mike, who had finally graduated from college, moved into their old house. This allowed Mike to continue to torment Archie, but as a next-door neighbor. Then Gloria became pregnant; the baby, Joey, was born in December 1975. The Lorenzos, an Italian couple, moved in as neighbors for a while. Frank Lorenzo loved to clean and cook (woman's work, according to Archie) while his wife Irene was an accomplished fixer of anything mechanical. Irene also possessed a sarcastic wit, with which she put down Archie regularly. When Archie was temporarily laid off from his job in October 1976, the Bunkers were forced to take in a Puerto Rican boarder, Teresa Betancourt, which provided still another source of irritation.

The 1977–1978 season brought a major change to *All in the Family*. In the opening three-part story, Archie gave up his job to pursue the American dream of owning his own business. Along with Harry the bartender, he purchased Kelsey's Bar from an ailing Tommy Kelsey, and reopened it as Archie's Place. This season included episodes with some very adult themes, including one in which an intruder attempted to rape Edith. Then at the end of the season Rob Reiner and Sally Struthers announced that they were leaving *All in the Family* for ventures of their own. The final episode of the season saw Mike, Gloria, and little Joey (played by twins Jason and Justin Draeger) moving to California, where Mike was to take a teaching position. The episode was a tearful and sentimental farewell, leaving Archie and Edith with an "empty nest." Temporarily, as it turned out, for in the fall of 1978, Archie and Edith were joined by little Stephanie Mills, a niece who had been abandoned by her father.

During the 1979–1980 season the program grew even further away from its original format, as the action shifted to Archie's bar. Edith was seen only infrequently—Jean Stapleton, feeling that she had exhausted the potential of her character, wished to be phased out of the series. New regulars were introduced at the bar, as Archie expanded it to include a short-order restaurant and took on a Jewish partner named Murray Klein. Murray's liberal intellectual background was in sharp contrast to, and sometimes in sharp conflict with, Archie's views. The ethnic mix at Archie's Place included Veronica, the sardonic Irish cook, Jose, the Puerto Rican busboy, and a wide variety of customers. Coincident with these changes, in the fall of 1979, the name of the series was changed to *Archie Bunker's Place*.

Then came a development which in the early days of the series would have seemed unthinkable. Edith died suddenly, of a stroke. This was not treated directly; rather, in the premiere episode of the 1980–1981 season Archie and Stephanie—whom the Bunkers had adopted—were seen grieving over Edith's unexpected death. Life did go on, however, and Archie hired a black housekeeper, Ellen Canby, to help look after his niece. Mrs. Canby was the sister-in-law of one of his neighbors, Polly Swanson. With Edith gone, Archie gingerly moved into the dating scene, for the first time in more than 25 years.

In the spring of 1981, Archie took over sole operation of the bar when partner Murray moved to San Francisco with his new wife (Martin Balsam had tired of his limited role in the series and wanted to bow out). That fall, without the business expertise of his now-absentee partner, Archie got needed financial help from young lawyer/business manager Gary Rabinowitz. Gary's involvement was more than strictly business, however, since he was dating Archie's 18-year-old niece, Billie. She had arrived at the start of the season on a visit, only to become a permanent member of the Bunker household and a waitress at Archie's Place.

Throughout all of these changes *All in the Family* remained one of the top hits on television. It did not begin that way, however. It took 1971 audiences several months to adjust to the blunt, outrageous humor of the show. There was considerable publicity about Archie's railings against "spics and spades," and it seemed possible that the show might be canceled. But by the summer of 1971 *All in the Family* had become a controversial hit, and the number-one program on television—a position it retained for five years. Part of its appeal was based on the fact that it could be interpreted in several different ways. Liberals and intellectuals could cite it as an example of the absurdity of prejudice, while another large segment of the viewing audience could agree with Archie's attitudes and enjoy him as their kind of guy. Like *The Honeymooners'* Ralph Kramden in the 1950s, the loudmouthed yet vulnerable Archie Bunker was a man for all audiences.

All in the Family was based on the British series, *Till Death Us Do Part*.

CBS telecast reruns of *All in the Family* weekdays from December 1975 to September 1979 and in prime time during the summer of 1991, in the latter instance paired with Norman Lear's new (and decidedly less successful) series *Sunday Dinner*. Selected reruns also surfaced in prime time in January 1992.

ALL IS FORGIVEN (*Situation Comedy*)

FIRST TELECAST: *March 20, 1986*
LAST TELECAST: *June 12, 1986*
BROADCAST HISTORY:

Mar 1986, NBC Thu 9:30–10:00
Mar 1986–Apr 1986, NBC Sat 9:30–10:00
May 1986–Jun 1986, NBC Thu 9:30–10:00

CAST:

Paula Russell .... Bess Armstrong
Matt Russell.......................... Terence Knox
Nicolette Bingham .... Carol Kane
Sonia Russell .... Shawnee Smith
Lorraine Elder .... Valerie Landsburg
Cecile Porter-Lindsey .... Judith-Marie Bergan
Oliver Royce .... David Alan Grier
Wendell Branch........................ Bill Wiley
Sherry Levy .... Debi Richter

"She has a love nest at home and a cuckoo's nest at work," read the ad for this short-lived comedy. Paula Russell went through two of life's great traumas on the same day, March 29th—getting married and starting a new job. The new hubby was Matt, a young donut executive who came complete with a loud and somewhat jealous teenage daughter named Sonia. The job was that of producer of the soap opera *All Is Forgiven* (yes, the same title as this series), providing a crew of loony co-workers. Nicolette, a spaced-out, syrupy transplanted Southern belle, was the head writer; Wendell, the insecure director; Cecile, the pushy star who did everything possible to make sure that no one usurped her status; Oliver, the talented but unsure new member of the writing staff; Sherry, one of the production assistants; and Lorraine, the receptionist/secretary who seemed to be eternally preoccupied with her social life.

For some reason NBC repeated the premiere episode of this forgettable series as a "special presentation" on August 23, 1986, two months after the regular run had ended.

ALL SOULS (*Supernatural Medical Drama*)

FIRST TELECAST: *April 17, 2001*
LAST TELECAST: *September 7, 2001*
BROADCAST HISTORY:

Apr 2001–May 2001, UPN Tue 9:00–10:00
Aug 2001–Sep 2001, UPN Fri 9:00–10:00

CAST:

Dr. Mitchell Grace .... Grayson McCouch
Dr. Nicole de Brae .... Serena Scott Thomas
Dr. Philomena Cullen............ Reiko Aylesworth
Glory St. Clair, R.N...................... Irma P. Hall
Patrick Fortado .... Adam Rodriguez
Dr. Bradley Sterling............... Daniel Cosgrove
Joey the Orderly .... Christian Tessier
Dr. Dante Ambrosious .... Jean Leclerc

In this spooky drama Dr. Mitchell Grace had just graduated from medical school and taken a position as a resident at Boston's huge, old All Souls Hospital, where his father, a janitor, had died mysteriously when Mitchell was still a child. There were all sorts of strange things going on at All Souls, which appeared to be haunted with spirits dating back to the Civil War. Nobody was allowed in the old hospital tower—formerly an insane asylum—where some people believed the souls of former patients were still resident. An assortment of weird people were seen in the hospital's halls, including a ghostly woman in black pushing an antique baby carriage. The mysterious Dr. Ambrosious, the hospital's chairman of the board, seemed to be in league with evil spirits, or demons, or something. Others on the hospital staff were Dr. de Brae, the nononsense chief of staff; Dr. Cullen, the staff psychiatrist; and Dr. Sterling, a fellow first-year resident whose privileged background was a far cry from Grace's working-class roots. Nurse St. Clair, a veteran at All Souls who had been on staff when Mitchell's father died, had psychic visions and served as Mitchell's spiritual guide through the haunted maze around the hospital. Wheelchair-bound computer expert Patrick, whose parents had taken Mitchell in after his father's death, was Mitchell's best friend.

ALL STAR REVUE (*Comedy Variety*)
FIRST TELECAST: *October 4, 1950*
LAST TELECAST: *April 18, 1953*
BROADCAST HISTORY:
Oct 1950–Jul 1951, NBC Wed 8:00–9:00
Sep 1951–Apr 1953, NBC Sat 8:00–9:00
STARS:
Ed Wynn (1950–1952)
Danny Thomas (1950–1952)
Jack Carson (1950–1952)
Jimmy Durante (1950–1953)
Martha Raye (1951–1953)
George Jessell (1952–1953)
Tallulah Bankhead (1952–1953)

This variety series originally featured a rotating roster of four famous comedians—Ed Wynn, Danny Thomas, Jack Carson, and Jimmy Durante—who alternated as hosts. First known as *Four Star Revue,* the series was retitled *All Star Revue* in the fall of 1951 when a number of additional entertainers began to headline episodes. Among them were Martha Raye (who starred in four episodes), Olsen & Johnson, Spike Jones, Victor Borge, Bob Hope, the Ritz Brothers, and Paul Winchell.

During the summer of 1952 there was no regular star and the program adopted a vaudeville flavor, with both new and established performers appearing. This summer version was titled *All Star Summer Revue.* When the fall season began there was a new lineup of regular hosts, with only Jimmy Durante remaining from prior seasons. The other performers starring in single episodes of the series in 1952–1953 were Dennis Day, the Ritz Brothers, Walter O'Keefe, Perry Como, Sonja Henie, and Ben Blue.

ALL THAT (*Comedy/Variety*)
BROADCAST HISTORY:
Nickelodeon
30 minutes
Produced: *1994–*
Premiered: *January 21, 1995*
REGULARS:
Anglique Bates (1995–1996)
Lori Beth Denberg (1995–1998)
Katrina Johnson (1995–1997)
Kel Mitchell (1995–1999)
Alisa Reyes (1995–1997)
Josh Server (1995–2001)
Kenan Thompson (1995–2000)
Amanda Bynes (1997–2000)
Tricia Dickson (1997)
Danny Tamberelli (1998–2001)
Christy Knowings (1998–2001)
Leon Frierson (1998–2001)
Zachary McLemore (1998–1999)
Nick Cannon (1999–2001)
Mark Saul (1999–2001)
Gabriel Iglesias (2000–2001)
Louisette Geiss (2002)
Jamie Lynn Spears (2002)
Chelsea Brummett (2002–)
Jack De Sena (2002–)
Lisa Renee Foiles (2002–)
Bryan Hearne (2002–)
Shane Lyons (2002–)
Giovonnie Samuels (2002–)
Kyle Sullivan (2002–)

Sketch-comedy show with a cast of youngsters. Recurring characters included Walter the "Ear-boy," a high school teen cursed with enormous ears; "Super Dude," a superhero who could only be stopped with dairy products; "Baggin' Saggin' Barry," a kid who pulled unlikely objects out of his baggy pants; and a pair of cooking-show chefs who insisted on mixing massive amounts of chocolate into every possible food. Two of the most popular cast members were Kenan Thompson and Kel Mitchell, whose routine built around the "Good Burger" fast food joint led to a series of their own (*Kenan & Kel*) and the 1997 feature film *Good Burger.* Rock and R&B musical acts were also featured.

All That was created by former *Head of the Class* stars Brian Robbins and Dan Schneider.

ALL'S FAIR (*Situation Comedy*)
FIRST TELECAST: *September 20, 1976*
LAST TELECAST: *August 15, 1977*
BROADCAST HISTORY:
Sep 1976–Aug 1977, CBS Mon 9:30–10:00
CAST:
Richard C. Barrington .... Richard Crenna
Charlotte (Charley) Drake .... Bernadette Peters
Lucy Daniels .... Lee Chamberlain
Allen Brooks .... J. A. Preston
Ginger Livingston .... Judy Kahan
Sen. Wayne Joplin .... Jack Dodson
Lanny Wolf (1977) .... Michael Keaton

As if the difference in their ages wasn't enough of a problem, 49-year-old political columnist Richard Barrington and his vivacious 23-year-old girlfriend Charley, a freelance photographer, were also at the opposite ends of the political spectrum: he was an arch-conservative and she was a "liberated" liberal. Love somehow managed to keep them together, despite the stormy outbursts that occurred when the subject of government and governmental policies happened to come up, which was quite often, since this series was set in Washington, D.C. Al Brooks was Richard's black assistant; his girlfriend Lucy was a reporter for CBS News in Washington. Charley's roommate Ginger was involved with a married Congressman; Wayne Joplin was a liberal senator and a friend of Richard's who usually sided with Charley in any disagreement between the couple. When Richard became a special assistant to President Carter, Ginger became his secretary and "superhip" Carter aide Lanny Wolf became a permanent member of the cast.

ALLY McBEAL (*Legal Comedy/Drama*)
FIRST TELECAST: *September 8, 1997*
LAST TELECAST: *July 8, 2002*
BROADCAST HISTORY:
Sep 1997–Jul 2002, FOX Mon 9:00–10:00
CAST:
Ally McBeal .... Calista Flockhart
Georgia Thomas (1997–2000)
.... Courtney Thorne-Smith

Richard Fish .... Greg Germann
Renee Raddick (1997–2001) .... Lisa Nicole Carson
Elaine Bassell .... Jane Krakowski
Billy Alan Thomas (1997–2000) .... Gil Bellows
Vonda Shepard .... Herself
John Cage .... Peter MacNicol
**Jennifer "Whipper" Cone (1997–2000)*
.... Dyan Cannon
Jennifer Higgin (1997) .... Brooke Burns
The Dancing Twins (1997–1999)
.... Eric and Steven Cohen
Dr. Greg Butters (1998–1999) .... Jesse L. Martin
Nell Porter (1998–2002) .... Portia de Rossi
Ling Woo (1998–2002) .... Lucy Liu
**Dr. Tracy Clark (1998–2000)* .... Tracey Ullman
Judge Seymore Walsh (1998–2002) ..... Albert Hall
Sandy Hingle (1999–2000) .... Gina Philips
Mark Albert (2000–2001) .... James LeGros
Brian (2000) .... Tim Dutton
Larry Paul (2000–2001) .... Robert Downey, Jr.
Cindy McCauliff (2000–2001) .... Lisa Edelstein
Jackson Duper (2001) .... Taye Diggs
Coretta Lipp (2001–2002) .... Regina Hall
Jenny Shaw (2001–2002) .... Julianne Nicholson
Glenn Foy (2001–2002) .... James Marsden
Raymond Millbury (2001–2002) ...... Josh Hopkins
**Steven Milter (2001–2002)* ... John Michael Higgins
Melanie West (2001) .... Anne Heche
Claire Otoms (2001–2002) ..... Dame Edna Everage
Victor Morrison (2002) .... Jon Bon Jovi
Maddie Harrington (2002) ...... Hayden Panettiere
Liza "Lolita" Bump (2002) .... Christina Ricci
Wilson Jade (2002) .... Bobby Cannavale

*Occasional

THEME:

"Searching My Soul" sung by Vonda Shepard

In this quirky comedy/drama Ally was a Boston trial attorney who, despite her confidence in the courtroom, was incredibly neurotic about her personal life, especially her failure to sustain a romantic relationship. The slender, almost anorexic-looking Ally struck a chord with many young working women who could relate to the emotional and professional struggles of the impulsive young lawyer. She was smart and successful but had her flaws—a short temper, a tendency to make mistakes, and sometimes an incredible naiveté. It had all started with her childhood friend Billy, who became her lover but broke it off when he transferred from Harvard to Michigan Law School and she stayed in Boston. Now Ally found herself working for Cage/Fish & Associates, where Billy was the star litigator. A novel aspect of the show was the humorous fantasy sequences, with voice-over commentary by Ally, illustrating her personal turmoil: seeing a bully's head grow, herself making love in a coffee cup, and a dancing baby that only she could see.

Other regulars were Elaine, Ally's brassy, busybody assistant, who knew where all the firm's skeletons were buried; Georgia, the beautiful attorney Billy had married while at Michigan Law School (Ally wanted to hate her but became her friend instead); Ally's sensible roommate Renee, a deputy District Attorney who gave her advice on how to deal with men; former classmate Richard, the money-hungry shark who had hired Ally; and John ("The Biscuit") Cage, the weird but brilliant senior partner famous for his courtroom histrionics. John often sat in at meetings saying nothing and even referred to himself as an enigma. The firm had one large unisex bathroom where gossip and embarrassing encounters were common occurrences.

Like *L.A. Law* before it, *Ally McBeal* mixed so many romantic liaisons in with its legal cases that at times it resembled a soap opera—with a comic twist. During the first season, Richard was dating older lady judge Whipper Cone, but she broke off the relationship early in 1998 because he somehow became obsessed with other women's wattles—the loose skin under the chin. During the second season, he moved on to Ling Woo, an aggressive businesswoman/attorney whom he eventually hired as an associate in the firm. Ally dated Greg, an African-American physician, then almost got back together with Billy until she learned during a session with her shrink, Dr. Clark, that he didn't really respect her. Even eccentric John, who was shy and painfully insecure with women, was lured into a relationship with a sexy new member of the firm, Nell.

In the fall of 1999 Whipper resigned her post as a judge and went into private practice with Renee; they were soon joined by Georgia, who divorced Billy when she found him in his office kissing a client (Farrah Fawcett). Billy went off the deep end, hiring a succession of sultry women to accompany him around and then dating his sexy 25-year-old assistant, Sandy. In March 2000 he discovered he had a brain tumor, and the following week he suffered a cerebral hemorrhage while in court and died—but his ghost showed up occasionally to give his old flame Ally advice. Ling broke up with Richard and Nell left John and the firm to start her own practice, attempting to steal Elaine in the process. Nell's new venture foundered when her underhanded methods were discovered, and Elaine testified against her in a hearing about her violation of legal ethics. Nell was soon back at Cage/Fish.

In the 2000–2001 season Ally found new love with handsome attorney Larry Paul (played by film star Robert Downey, Jr.), while loyal Elaine dated Mark and John got involved with Melanie, a client suffering from Tourette's syndrome. None of these affairs ended well. Mark was gone by the end of the season, and John and Melanie broke up after she turned down his marriage proposal. Ally's rocky relationship with Larry ended when he moved to Detroit to help raise his son from a former marriage (actor Downey was fired after being arrested twice during the season for drug possession). A new hunk on the scene was black attorney Jackson Duper, who ricocheted between Ling and Renee.

The final season saw several new attorneys join the firm, including Jenny (who brought with her a class-action lawsuit involving 72,000 plaintiffs), Jenny's exboyfriend Glenn, Glenn's friend Raymond, and Larry's former partner, Coretta. Ally engineered a reconciliation between Jenny and Glenn, but her own love life remained empty until she fell for Victor, the contractor sent to fix an electrical problem in her new brownstone. *Anyone* wandering into this series could become the subject of a romantic story line! Then, in the spring, 10-year-old Maddie arrived. She was the product of an egg donation Ally had made to an infertility program when she was in college. After initial shock and misgivings, Ally decided to take temporary custody of her orphaned "daughter." The following week Richard told the firm that John was cutting back his workload and would no longer be a name partner. He made Ally a name partner, and the firm became Cage & McBeal. Meanwhile, Ling left the firm when she received a judicial appointment and then an offer to star in a syndicated TV show.

As the series came to a close, Richard and Nell were struggling with a tough case in which the opposing counsel, Liza, was a sexy 21-year-old with a Lolita-like personality. Richard begged John, who was playing in a mariachi band at a Mexican restaurant, to take the case. John won the case, hired Liza as a new associate and gave her his office. On her first day she informed the firm that she had hired Wilson Jade, an effective but totally unprincipled litigator, as an associate. Ally broke up with Victor the electrician, while Richard fell in love with Liza. In the final episode Richard and Liza were married and Ally resigned from the firm to move to New York with emotionally troubled Maddie. At the postwedding party Ally bid tearful farewells to her coworkers and friends—including Billy's spirit.

In the fall of 1999 Fox premiered *Ally*, a half-hour version of *Ally McBeal*, on Tuesday nights. *Ally* was an edited-down version of the regular hour, omitting the courtroom sequences and adding some new footage. A novel attempt to get double usage out of a popular series, it was gone in three months.

Vonda Shepard, who sang the songs used to punctuate the show's story lines, was the featured entertainer at the bar where the gang went to unwind. The Dancing Twins, regulars at the bar, often danced with Ally and Renee if they were there without dates.

ALMOST ANYTHING GOES (*Competition*)
FIRST TELECAST: *July 31, 1975*
LAST TELECAST: *April 10, 1976*
BROADCAST HISTORY:
July 1975–Aug 1975, ABC Thu 8:00–9:00
Jan 1976–Apr 1976, ABC Sat 8:00–9:00
PLAY BY PLAY:
Charlie Jones
COLOR COMMENTATOR:
Lynn Shackleford
FIELD INTERVIEWER:
Dick Whittington (1975)
Regis Philbin (1976)

Originally conceived as a one-month summer fill-in show, this uninhibited free-for-all was sufficiently popular to win a regular season tryout in early 1976 and also give birth to a Saturday morning kids' edition (called *Junior Almost Anything Goes*). The format was an expansion of the old *Beat the Clock*, pitting teams from different towns and states against each other in all sorts of bizarre stunts. The setting was outdoors and the coverage was handled as in a sports event, complete with play-by-play, color, and field interviews. Winning teams got to participate in regional championships.

The first telecast, for example, had contestants carry a loaf of bread while sliding across a greased pole suspended over a pool; balance an egg on the head while riding down an obstacle course in a golf cart; and dive into a pool and climb onto a raft to dress up in formal garb. Greased runways, swimming pools filled with peanuts, and chocolate pies in the face were also stock-in-trade for this series.

ALMOST GROWN (*Drama*)
FIRST TELECAST: *November 27, 1988*
LAST TELECAST: *February 27, 1989*
BROADCAST HISTORY:
Nov 1988, CBS Sun 9:00–11:00
Nov 1988–Feb 1989, CBS Mon 10:00–11:00
CAST:
Norman Foley .... Timothy Daly
Suzie Long Foley .... Eve Gordon
Joan Foley .... Rita Taggart
Frank Foley .... Michael Alldredge
Vi Long .... Anita Gillette
Dick Long .... Richard Schaal
Joey Long .... Albert Macklin
Anya Foley .... Ocean Hellman
Jackson Foley (first 2 episodes)... Nathaniel Moreau
Jackson Foley .... Raffi Diblasio

Norman and Suzie had been part of each other's lives for almost 25 years, and viewers saw every bit of it in this flashback-laden series. They had dated through high school and college, been married for 14 years, and, now divorced, were sharing responsibility for raising their two children, Anya (age 16) and Jackson (age 10). Despite the divorce they still loved each other—they just couldn't live together without fighting. Originally from New Jersey, they were now living in Los Angeles where Suzie was a filmmaker and Norman the program director for a rock radio station. It was music that gave this series a unique feel. In every episode there was at least one point when either Norman or Suzie, upon hearing a fondly remembered oldie, would be transported back through time (via flashback) to some significant event in their relationship that had occurred when the oldie had been popular.

Other regulars in the cast included Norman's best friend Joey (who was also Suzie's brother) and both of their parents.

ALMOST HOME, see *The Torkelsons*

ALMOST PERFECT (*Situation Comedy*)
FIRST TELECAST: *September 17, 1995*
LAST TELECAST: *October 30, 1996*
BROADCAST HISTORY:
Sep 1995–Mar 1996, CBS Sun 8:30–9:00
Mar 1996–Apr 1996, CBS Mon 8:30–9:00
Jul 1996–Sep 1996, CBS Mon 8:30–9:00
Oct 1996, CBS Wed 8:30–9:00
Oct 1996, CBS Wed 9:00–9:30
CAST:
Kim Cooper .... Nancy Travis
Mike Ryan .... Kevin Kilner
Neal Luder .... David Clennon
Rob Paley .... Matthew Letscher
Gary Karp .... Chip Zien
Patty Shapiro Karp .... Lisa Edelstein

The travails of two young, ambitious professionals in Los Angeles trying to develop a relationship while coping with the demands of their jobs was the focus of this romantic comedy. Kim, the only woman on the writing staff of the hit TV cop series *Blue Justice*, had just been promoted to executive producer when she met "Mr. Right," handsome district attorney Mike Ryan. The chemistry between them was strong, and romance blossomed—but they had their problems. Hers were the nutty writers on *Blue Justice*, as well as the insecure and/or overbearing actors on the show. The writers were Neal, a burned-out hack with a penchant for one-liners; Rob, the young innocent from the Midwest who desperately wanted to become a "cool" Angelino; and Gary, a world-class neurotic who wanted her job. Gary's personal problems included his obnoxious wife, Patty, from whom he separated in November. Mike's schedule with the D.A.'s office kept him busy, and his friendship with the writers working for Kim tended to get in the way of the relationship. Both were very competitive, and each of them needed to be in control of their relationship, but their love seemed to be strong enough to overcome the difficulties; by the end of the season they were living together.

When *Almost Perfect* returned in the fall, Kim and Mike were breaking up and she was adjusting to life without a serious romantic relationship. The change in the series' focus didn't have much time to evolve; it was canceled after the fourth episode of the 1996–1997 season.

ALOHA PARADISE (*Situation Comedy*)
FIRST TELECAST: *February 25, 1981*
LAST TELECAST: *April 29, 1981*
BROADCAST HISTORY:
Feb 1981–Apr 1981, ABC Wed 9:00–10:00
CAST:
Sydney Chase .... Debbie Reynolds
Curtis Shea .... Bill Daily
Fran Linhart .... Pat Klous
Evelyn Pahinui .... Mokihana
Richard Bean .... Stephen Shortridge

Aloha Paradise was a rather obvious clone of *The Love Boat*, and was produced by the same people. The captain in this case was Sydney Chase, the female manager of the glamorous Paradise Village resort in sun-drenched Hawaii. As on *The Love Boat*, there was a perky social director (Fran) and an understanding bartender (Evelyn), who dispensed tropical drinks and wise counsel. Also on board—or on hand—were Curtis, the somewhat uncertain assistant manager and Richard, the handsome lifeguard.

The plot also bore more than a passing resemblance to *Love Boat*'s: three or four different stories were told within each episode, each about people in love, out of love, or looking for love, and finding that their dreams could come true—at any age—in a romantic vacation setting. The guest stars who appeared in these little stories were mostly retreads from other TV series, also a *Love Boat* practice. Even the lush theme song sounded like *Love Boat*'s.

One almost expected *Aloha Paradise* to toot its whistle and set sail.

ALRIGHT ALREADY (*Situation Comedy*)
FIRST TELECAST: *September 7, 1997*
LAST TELECAST: *July 5, 1998*
BROADCAST HISTORY:
Sep 1997–Apr 1998, WB Sun 9:30–10:00
Apr 1998, WB Mon 9:30–10:00
May 1998–Jul 1998, WB Sun 9:30–10:00
CAST:
Carol Lerner .... Carol Leifer
Renee .... Amy Yasbeck
Alvin Lerner .... Jerry Adler
Miriam Lerner .... Mitzi McCall
Jessica Lerner .... Stacy Galina
Vaughn Lerner .... Maury Sterling

Carol was a man-hungry, thirtysomething optometrist in Miami coping with an iffy social life and a dysfunctional family. Alvin and Miriam were her retired, overbearing, perpetually squabbling parents. Jessica, her spaced-out younger sister, and Vaughn, her lazy unemployed brother, were living with her folks in a senior citizens complex while she had her own apartment. Renee, her partner in Collins Avenue Optical, was Carol's best friend and confidante—the two of them did the singles bar scene together. Carol was so serious about guys she never seemed to find one, while Renee, a free spirit, had an active social life.

ALVIN SHOW, THE (*Cartoon*)
FIRST TELECAST: *October 4, 1961*
LAST TELECAST: *September 5, 1962*
BROADCAST HISTORY:
Oct 1961–Sep 1962, CBS Wed 7:30–8:00
VOICES:
Ross Bagdasarian
Shepard Menken

Ross Bagdasarian, whose professional name was David Seville, had a huge success with a novelty record "The Chipmunk Song." In the seven weeks following its original release in 1958, it sold over four million copies. Subsequent success with Chipmunk albums and singles eventually resulted in this animated series. Bagdasarian was the voice of three chipmunks; Alvin, an aggressive, ambitious, impulsive, and often foolish little fellow and his more conservative brothers Simon and Theodore. Bagdasarian was also the voice of the animated David Seville, in whose home Alvin and his brothers lived. In addition to stories about their relationship and one or two musical numbers, each episode included an adventure of Clyde Crashcup, a nutty inventor who took credit for inventing anything and everything. His voice was done by Shepard Menken.

Reruns of *The Alvin Show* aired on Saturday mornings on CBS from June 1962 to September 1965 and were revived on NBC's Saturday morning lineup from March to November 1979.

An all-new animated series, *Alvin & the Chipmunks* premiered on NBC's Saturday morning lineup in September of 1983, with Ross Bagdasarian, Jr. filling the role his late father had filled in the original series. The new version, which was later retitled *The Chipmunks* and *The Chipmunks Go to the Movies*, left the air in September 1991. Reruns of this newer version of *Alvin & the Chipmunks* aired on the Fox weekday morning lineup throughout the 1992–1993 season.

AMANDA SHOW, THE (*Comedy/Variety*)
BROADCAST HISTORY:
Nickelodeon
30 minutes
Original episodes: *1999–2002* (38 episodes)
Premiered: *October 16, 1999*
REGULARS:
Amanda Bynes
Drake Bell
Raquel Lee (1999–2000)
Josh Peck (2000–2002)
Nancy Sullivan

John Kassir (1999–2000)
Amy Elizabeth
Reagan Gomez-Preston
Lance Kinsey
Tracy Swain

Frenetic sketch-comedy show starring winsome tween star Amanda Bynes from Nickelodeon's *All That.* Skits depicted the efforts of Amanda's overly enthusiastic "number one fan," Penelope Taynt (also played by Bynes), to meet her idol; the Klutz family, who fell over everything; the courtroom of Judge Trudy, where kids always won; a pretty girl who turned unexpectedly gross; a woman with an extremely large derriere; and recurring appearances by the dancing lobsters. The show was created by one-time kid star Dan Schneider.

AMANDA'S (*Situation Comedy*)
FIRST TELECAST: *February 10, 1983*
LAST TELECAST: *May 26, 1983*
BROADCAST HISTORY:
Feb 1983–Mar 1983, ABC Thu 8:30–9:00
May 1983, ABC Thu 9:30–10:00
CAST:
Amanda Cartwright .... Beatrice Arthur
Marty Cartwright .... Fred McCarren
Arlene Cartwright................. Simone Griffeth
Earl Nash .... Rick Hurst
Aldo .... Tony Rosato
Clifford Mundy......................... Keene Curtis
Zack Cartwright .... Kevin McCarthy

Bea Arthur returned briefly to series television in this obvious (though unacknowledged) copy of the popular British series *Fawlty Towers.* Amanda was the formidable owner of "Amanda's By The Sea," a homey little hotel overlooking the Pacific. Her fractious staff included Marty, her hotel-management-graduate son; Arlene, his spoiled and citified wife; Earl, the excitable chef; and Aldo, the confused bellhop of indeterminate foreign extraction. Stories concerned burnt steaks, fussy guests, travel-guide writers who had to be impressed, and the threatening banker, Mr. Mundy, who was always about to foreclose. In the last few episodes brother-in-law Zack showed up to meddle and to woo Amanda.

AMATEUR HOUR, THE, see *Original Amateur Hour, The*

AMAZING DUNNINGER, THE (*Mind Reading/Audience Participation*)
FIRST TELECAST: *June 25, 1955*
LAST TELECAST: *October 10, 1956*
BROADCAST HISTORY:
Jun 1955–Sep 1955, NBC Sat 8:30–9:00
May 1956–Oct 1956, ABC Wed 8:30–9:00
REGULAR:
Joseph Dunninger

Titled *The Dunninger Show* on NBC and *The Amazing Dunninger* on ABC, this summer series featured the unique skills of the famed mentalist. His ability to read minds was tested each week by celebrity guests and by members of the studio audience.

AMAZING GRACE (*Drama*)
FIRST TELECAST: *April 1, 1995*
LAST TELECAST: *April 22, 1995*
BROADCAST HISTORY:
Apr 1995, NBC Sat 8:00–9:00
CAST:
Hannah Miller .... Patty Duke
Jenny Miller (age 16) .... Marguerite Moreau
Brian Miller.......................... Justin Garms
Harry Kramer......................... Dan Lauria
Det. Dominick Corso .... Joe Spano
Link (19) .... Gavin Harrison
Yvonne Price.................. Lorraine Toussaint
Arthur Sutherland .... Robin Gammell
THEME:
"Amazing Grace," by Reverend John Newton (hymn, written in 1779)

In this earnest drama, Hannah Miller was a small-town nurse whose difficult life and failed marriage had caused her to become addicted to pills and almost kill herself. A near-death experience changed her life, and she became a minister. Now at her first parish, she struggled to rebuild her life and help others in need. Young son Brian was cheerful and helpful, but self-absorbed teenage daughter Jenny was not (she called herself agnostic, complained about their new life, and took up with Link, a scruffy 19-year-old musician/drifter she found in the park). Others in Hannah's "family" were Harry, a blustery attorney and former boyfriend who still cared for her and who was a father figure to her kids; Dominick, a tough local cop who could, however, be faced down; Yvonne, an understanding former colleague from the emergency room where Hannah had worked; and Arthur Sutherland, a stiff-necked deacon at her church who opposed her appointment and was suspicious of her abilities.

AMAZING MR. MALONE, THE (*Crime Drama*)
FIRST TELECAST: *September 24, 1951*
LAST TELECAST: *March 10, 1952*
BROADCAST HISTORY:
Sep 1951–Mar 1952, ABC Mon 8:00–8:30
CAST:
John J. Malone........................... Lee Tracy

Lee Tracy, who perhaps was better known as *Martin Kane—Private Eye,* enacted the role of the "brilliant criminal lawyer" John J. Malone in this live mystery series. Malone, who had been a cynical, humorless character on radio, became a lighthearted sleuth with a ready quip and an affinity for pretty girls in this TV version.

It was based on the Malone novels by Craig Rice, and on the radio series which began in 1947; the TV version alternated with *Mr. District Attorney.*

AMAZING POLGAR, THE (*Hypnosis*)
FIRST TELECAST: *September 16, 1949*
LAST TELECAST: *October 21, 1949*
BROADCAST HISTORY:
Sep 1949–Oct 1949, CBS Fri 7:45–7:55
STAR:
Dr. Franz Polgar

This extremely short, live series—it was only ten minutes long and was on the air for five weeks—examined the effects of hypnosis, the power of suggestion, the immunity to pain, the ability to recall incidents that the conscious mind does not remember, and other mental feats. It starred professional hypnotist Dr. Franz Polgar, who possessed doctorates in psychology and economics.

AMAZING RACE, THE (*Reality/Adventure*)
FIRST TELECAST: *September 5, 2001*
LAST TELECAST:
BROADCAST HISTORY:
Sep 2001–Dec 2001, CBS Wed 9:00–10:00
Mar 2002–May 2002, CBS Wed 9:00–10:00
Mar 2002, UPN Fri 9:00–10:00
Oct 2002–Dec 2002, CBS Wed 9:00–10:00
May 2003– , CBS Thu 8:00–9:00
HOST:
Phil Keoghan

The Amazing Race was, in many respects, a big-money scavenger hunt, produced with glitzy, movie-style techniques by big-screen producer Jerry Bruckheimer. Eleven teams of two people who had some type of relationship—best friends, lovers, husband and wife, father and son, mother and daughter, fraternity brothers, etc.—competed in an around-the-world race to win $1 million. The participants were given a limited amount of money and had to overcome mental and physical challenges to best their competition without exhausting their finances. Although some air travel was permitted, much of their time was spent on buses, trains, taxis, bicycles and animals. Because they had to conserve their money, they were sometimes forced to camp out and sleep in bus stations or on park benches.

The first *Amazing Race* started and ended in New York City. As the race progressed the contestants looked for "Route Markers," yellow-and-white flags at the sites of their next instructions. In many cases the instructions gave them two options to complete a task or get to their next destination, but they had to be careful—what appeared to be the easier option might include something unexpected that made it more difficult than the other choice. The final destination for each segment of the race was the "Pit Stop," where they clocked in and, in most cases, the last team to get there was eliminated from the race. Each leg of the race included one "Fast Forward." The first team to complete the task to win the Fast Forward could use it to go directly to the next Pit Stop without having to perform any tasks, but they had to be judicious—they could use only one Fast Forward during the entire race.

The first leg of *The Amazing Race* sent the teams from New York to South Africa. From there the clues took them to France, Tunisia, the Sahara Desert, Italy, England, India, Thailand, mainland China and Alaska. As the race wore on, some of the teams got closer while others bickered with each other and saw their relationships deteriorate. When the final leg from Alaska back to New York began, there were three teams left. The winners, the first to arrive at the final Pit Stop in Flushing Meadows Park, were Rob Frisbee and Brennan Swain, two attorneys from Los Angeles who were best friends.

Amazing Race 2 started in the Nevada desert. The quest took the teams to Brazil, South Africa, Namibia, Thailand, Hong Kong, Australia, New Zealand, Hawaii, Alaska and California. The final Pit Stop was at Fort Baker in the Golden Gate National Recreation Area near San Francisco. The first to arrive were Chris Luca and Alex Boylan, lifelong friends from Jacksonville, Florida. UPN aired reruns of *Amazing Race 2*, but they were dropped after three weeks because of minuscule ratings.

Amazing Race 3, which started with 12 teams instead of the 11 that began the previous editions of the series, originated in the Florida Everglades. The teams' travels took them from there to Mexico, Scotland, Portugal, Spain, Morocco, Germany, Switzerland, Malaysia, Singapore, Vietnam, Hawaii and Seattle. The winners, at Lincoln Park in Seattle, were Flo Pesenti and Zach Behr, friends from New York City.

AMAZING SPIDER-MAN, THE (*Adventure*)
FIRST TELECAST: *April 5, 1978*
LAST TELECAST: *May 3, 1978*
BROADCAST HISTORY:
Apr 1978–May 1978, CBS Wed 8:00–9:00
CAST:
Peter Parker/Spider-Man ..... Nicholas Hammond
Capt. Barbera .... Michael Pataki
J. Jonah Jameson .... Robert F. Simon
Rita Conway .... Chip Fields

Spider-Man, the Marvel comics creation of Stan Lee, was brought to life for this limited run CBS series. Peter Parker was a young college science major and a part-time news photographer for the *Daily Bugle*. When he was accidentally bitten by a radioactive spider, he suddenly found himself endowed with superhuman abilities. He could sense the presence of danger and possessed strength far superior to that of ordinary men; he could scale sheer walls without ropes and had a magic web concealed in a wrist band that helped him to "fly" and to subdue attackers. But the transformation to Spider-Man was a mixed blessing for young Peter. He was, by nature, a rather simple, nonviolent man who found himself forced to lead a double life, possessing powers he didn't quite understand and didn't really want. Peter's boss at the *Daily Bugle* was publisher J. Jonah Jameson. Jameson's secretary, Rita, was Peter's good friend and protector.

Spider-Man returned to the air in the fall of 1978, but as a number of specials rather than as a regular series. For these seven new episodes, the last of which aired on July 6, 1979, Ellen Bry was added to the cast as freelance photographer Julie Mason.

An animated *Spider-Man* series ran on ABC's Saturday morning lineup from September 1967 to August 1969, and on its Sunday morning lineup from March to September 1970. Spider-Man then resurfaced in animation as part of NBC's Saturday morning lineup for five seasons beginning in September 1981. Another new animated version of *Spider-Man* premiered on Fox's Saturday morning lineup in February 1995 and on Fox's weekday afternoon lineup in November 1996. The weekday telecasts ran until September 1999 and the Saturday morning telecasts until August 2001.

AMAZING STORIES (*Fantasy Anthology*)
FIRST TELECAST: *September 29, 1985*
LAST TELECAST: *May 15, 1987*
BROADCAST HISTORY:
Sep 1985–Jun 1986, NBC Sun 8:00–8:30
Jun 1986–Feb 1987, NBC Mon 8:30–9:00
Mar 1987–May 1987, NBC Fri 8:30–9:00
EXECUTIVE PRODUCER:
Steven Spielberg

As a child, Steven Spielberg was a fan of such TV anthology series as *The Outer Limits*, *One Step Beyond*, and *The Twilight Zone*. He began his career at age 21

(1969) as a director of the pilot for Rod Serling's *Night Gallery*, and first gained attention for his unusual TV movie *Duel* (between a man and a mysterious truck), in 1971. Then he moved on to the big screen to create such monster hits as *Jaws*, *Close Encounters of the Third Kind*, *Raiders of the Lost Ark*, and *E.T.*

In 1985 NBC lured him back to produce a series that was supposed to mark the revival of the kind of short story TV anthologies he had loved as a child. It didn't, but during its two-year run *Amazing Stories* did provide innovative, sometimes scary, sometimes whimsical "little films" from some of Hollywood's leading talents—people who otherwise had little to do with television. Episode directors included Spielberg himself ("Ghost Train," "The Mission"), Martin Scorsese, Clint Eastwood, Paul Bartel, and Burt Reynolds. Among the guest stars were Drew Barrymore, Kevin Costner, Sid Caesar, Mark Hamill, Sam Waterston, Milton Berle, David Carradine, Stan Freberg, and Charlie Sheen.

AMAZING WORLD OF KRESKIN, THE (*Mind Reading/Audience Participation*)

BROADCAST HISTORY:

Syndicated only
30 minutes
Produced: *1971–1975* (90 episodes)
Released: *1971*

STAR:

Kreskin

HOST:

Bill Luxton

This was one of those sideshows that TV sometimes puts forth. Like Dunninger and Kuda Bux in the 1950s, Kreskin specialized in mind reading and ESP—he knew where you had been that morning, what was in the sealed envelope, where the lady in the third row went for her vacation. Celebrity guests ranging from William Shatner to Meadowlark Lemon dropped in. *Kreskin* was taped in Canada, for broadcast on the CTV network, and was syndicated in the U.S. A later batch of episodes, made in 1975, were called *The New Kreskin Show*.

AMAZON, see *Peter Benchley's Amazon*

AMEN (*Situation Comedy*)

FIRST TELECAST: *September 27, 1986*
LAST TELECAST: *July 27, 1991*
BROADCAST HISTORY:

Sep 1986–Apr 1987, NBC Sat 9:30–10:00
Jun 1987–Sep 1988, NBC Sat 9:30–10:00
Oct 1988–Jul 1989, NBC Sat 8:30–9:00
Aug 1989, NBC Sat 8:00–8:30
Sep 1989–July 1990, NBC Sat 8:30–9:00
Aug 1990, NBC Sat 8:00–8:30
Dec 1990–Jul 1991, NBC Sat 8:00–8:30

CAST:

Deacon Ernest Frye .... Sherman Hemsley
Rev. Reuben Gregory .... Clifton Davis
Thelma Frye .... Anna Maria Horsford
Casietta Hetebrink (1986–1990)
 .... Barbara Montgomery
Amelia Hetebrink .... Roz Ryan
Rolly Forbes .... Jester Hairston
**Lorenzo Hollingsworth (1986–1987)*
 .... Franklyn Seales
**Leola Forbes (1987–1989)* .... Rosetta LeNoire
Inga (1988–1990) .... Elsa Raven
Chris (1988–1990) .... Tony T. Johnson
Clarence (1990–1991) .... Bumper Robinson

*Occasional

Amen was a breakthrough of sorts—the first hit comedy in TV history to be based on religion. Sherman Hemsley, who played pushy, egotistical George Jefferson on *The Jeffersons* for ten years, played a similar character here as an insufferable deacon (and lawyer) whose father had founded the First Community Church of Philadelphia, and who intended to keep it under his thumb. Unfortunately the new minister, Rev. Gregory, had other ideas and every week he quietly deflated the strutting deacon. Both, of course, really had the church's best interests at heart. Thelma was the deacon's 30-year-old, unmarried, romantically frustrated daughter, who eventually began dating the handsome new pastor; Casietta and Amelia, chattering sisters who were members of the Church board; and Rolly, the board's wise old voice of reason.

Developments in later seasons included the marriage of Rolly to Thelma's great aunt Leola in November 1987; Deacon Frye's "fantasy wedding" to colorful guest star Jackee later that season; and the long-awaited moment when Thelma finally tied the knot with the man of her dreams, Rev. Gregory, in February 1990. In the final season Deacon Frye was appointed a judge, so he could wreak havoc in the courts, too.

Younger faces on the show included a charismatic 12-year-old preacher, Rev. Johnny Tolbert (played in several 1987 guest appearances by real-life child minister Rev. William Hudson III); six-year-old parishioner Chris, who was not shy about his opinions; and in the last season, a hip street kid and aspiring rapper named Clarence, who was taken in by the Deacon and who looked up to him admiringly. The final original episode was memorable. Deacon Frye staged a telethon to raise money to save the church, culminating in his wild imitation of James Brown—which was topped when Brown himself walked on and launched into his patented "I Feel Good!" His screams were echoed by screams offstage as an overdue Thelma went into labor and gave birth to the Deacon's first grandchild.

Actor Clifton Davis, best known as the star of the 1974 series *That's My Mama*, was also a real-life minister. While appearing in the top-rated *Amen* he served as assistant pastor at the Loma Linda, Calif., Seventh-Day Adventist Church.

AMERICA (*Documentary*)

FIRST TELECAST: *November 14, 1972*
LAST TELECAST: *April 10, 1973*
BROADCAST HISTORY:

Nov 1972–Apr 1973, NBC Tue 10:00–11:00

HOST:

Alistair Cooke

Through pictures and the commentary of Englishman Alistair Cooke, these documentaries traced the history of the United States from the last of the Mohicans to the hippies of the 1970s; they were filmed on location over a period of two years. Cooke, who had spent the last 35 years living in the United States as a foreign correspondent and reporter, narrated the series, which he regarded as a "personal history of America."

America was one of the few series ever to be shown first on commercial television and later rerun on public television (the Public Broadcasting Service network).

AMERICA IN VIEW (*Travelogue*)
FIRST TELECAST: *May 31, 1951*
LAST TELECAST: *October 28, 1953*
BROADCAST HISTORY:
May 1951–Jul 1951, ABC Thu 10:30–11:00
Aug 1951–Oct 1951, ABC Fri 10:30–11:00
Jan 1952–Mar 1952, ABC Sat 10:45–11:00
Jun 1952–Jun 1953, ABC Sun 9:00–9:30 (most weeks)
Oct 1953, ABC Wed 8:00–8:30
Film travelogues of the United States.

AMERICA SONG (*Music*)
FIRST TELECAST: *April 21, 1948*
LAST TELECAST: *April 25, 1949*
BROADCAST HISTORY:
Apr 1948–Jul 1948, NBC Wed 8:00–8:15
Jul 1948–Sep 1948, NBC Tue 7:30–7:50
Oct 1948–Feb 1949, NBC Mon 7:30–7:50
Mar 1949–Apr 1949, NBC various 15-minute spots
REGULARS:
Paul Arnold
Nellie Fisher, dancer
Ray Harrison, dancer
A program of traditional American folk songs and dances, hosted by singer-guitarist Paul Arnold. A number of singers and dancers rotated in and out of the cast during the program's run, including 12-year-old Jimsey Somers and 8-year-old Dickie Orlan in early 1949. The program was renamed *American Songs* during its last four months.

AMERICA SPEAKS (*Opinion Poll*)
FIRST TELECAST: *September 5, 1948*
LAST TELECAST: *October 31, 1948*
BROADCAST HISTORY:
Sep 1948–Oct 1948, CBS Sun 10:00–10:15
HOST:
Dr. George Gallup
George Gallup was probably the most famous poll taker in America. In the fall of 1948, a presidential election year, he was the star of a nine-week live series in which he presented the results of a series of public opinion polls he had taken to the television audience. In addition to displaying the results, the series showed reenactments of the actual polling techniques.

AMERICA 2-NIGHT, see *Fernwood 2-Night*

AMERICA TONIGHT (*News*)
FIRST TELECAST: *October 1, 1990*
LAST TELECAST: *March 29, 1991*
BROADCAST HISTORY:
Oct 1990–Mar 1991, CBS Mon–Fri 11:30–12:00 midnight
ANCHORS:
Charles Kuralt
Lesley Stahl
Robert Krulwich
Edie Magnus
This nightly summary of the important news of the day included interviews, features, and editorial analysis. On Monday through Thursday Charles Kuralt anchored from New York, and Lesley Stahl, from Washington, while on Friday Robert Krulwich and Edie Magnus co-anchored from New York.

AMERICA TONIGHT (*Newsmagazine*)
FIRST TELECAST: *June 1, 1994*
LAST TELECAST: *August 10, 1994*
BROADCAST HISTORY:
Jun 1994–Aug 1994, CBS Wed 9:00–10:00
ANCHORWOMEN:
Dana King
Deborah Norville
CORRESPONDENTS:
Bob McKeown
Peter Van Sant
Bill Geist
A fairly standard newsmagazine offering a mix of informative and/or amusing investigative reports and features. Starting in mid-June, a weekly segment on the developing O. J. Simpson murder case was added. The show's one distinguishing feature was a segment in which a guest commentator "sounded off" on an issue of current interest followed by a live segment in which home viewers could phone in their reactions to the commentary. Although originally planned for each episode, in actuality these "sound-off" segments only aired occasionally. Former Vice President Dan Quayle commented on the public's reaction to his "Murphy Brown" speech about single-mother households and welfare, author Ishmael Reed talked about the positive and negative exposure blacks get in broadcast media, and Susan Estrich bemoaned high-profile murder cases that made the defendants seem like the victims.

AMERICAN BANDSTAND (*Music*)
FIRST TELECAST: *October 7, 1957*
LAST TELECAST: *December 30, 1957*
BROADCAST HISTORY:
Oct 1957–Dec 1957, ABC Mon 7:30–8:00
HOST:
Dick Clark
Dick Clark's *American Bandstand* is best known as the networks' longest-running (30 years) afternoon show for teens, but it did have a short run in prime time as well, as indicated above. The show had begun as a local dance program in Philadelphia in 1952, moving to the full ABC network as a Monday–Friday late afternoon entry in August 1957. Its immediate success prompted ABC to give it a brief run on Monday nights that fall.

The nighttime version was identical to its daytime counterpart. Clark hosted one or two guest performers whose records were currently on the pop charts. They lip-synched their hits, chatted about their careers, and signed autographs. Most of these young singers and groups were at the beginnings of their careers, and Clark wisely kept the tapes of their appearances and got full permission to use them in the future. These clips are often seen in rock music retrospectives today, and in some cases are the only film available of some rock legends (and "one-shot" wonders) early in their careers.

During the remainder of the show Clark played current hits, while the studio audience danced to the music. There was also the infamous "rate-a-record" feature ("Umm, it's got a good beat . . . I'll give it a 95").

The daytime network version of *American Band-*

stand continued on ABC's weekday lineup until August 1963, and then became a once-a-week Saturday afternoon show from 1963–1987. In the fall of 1987 it was finally canceled by ABC, but Clark continued production of original episodes for syndication, which were seen on many stations in the same time period—Saturday afternoons—for another year. In the spring of 1989 *Bandstand* surfaced again, this time on the USA cable network, airing from noon to 1:00 P.M. on Saturday afternoons. Clark still produced the series but the host was now 26-year-old David Hirsch. The USA Network version of *American Bandstand* lasted less than a year, leaving the air in late 1989. In the 1950s and early '60s the show (both daytime and nighttime versions) originated live from Philadelphia; production moved to Hollywood in February 1964. For a loving, illustrated history of the program see *The History of American Bandstand* by Michael Shore with Dick Clark (Ballantine, 1985).

Dick Clark also produced and hosted a number of other prime-time rock music shows, including the Saturday night *Dick Clark Show* (q.v.), which ran from 1958 until 1960.

AMERICAN CHRONICLES (*Documentary*)
FIRST TELECAST: *September 8, 1990*
LAST TELECAST: *December 15, 1990*
BROADCAST HISTORY:
Sep 1990–Dec 1990, FOX Sat 9:30–10:00
NARRATOR:
Richard Dreyfuss

Produced by David Lynch, the man responsible for ABC's quirky *Twin Peaks,* this series was a collection of decidedly eccentric documentaries bearing his stamp. Odd camera angles, slow eerie music, and a focus on the violent, sexual, and bizarre aspects of life—all Lynch trademarks—predominated. Subjects included "Farewell to the Flesh" (the New Orleans Mardi Gras), "Semper Fi" (Marine boot camp), "Eye of the Beholder" (the Miss Texas beauty pageant), and short features on circus life, Beverly Hills, and the comeback of heavyweight boxer George Foreman, all arguably bizarre threads of the American social fabric.

AMERICAN DETECTIVE (*Documentary*)
FIRST TELECAST: *May 2, 1991*
LAST TELECAST: *June 26, 1993*
BROADCAST HISTORY:
May 1991, ABC Thu 9:00–10:00
May 1991, ABC Wed 10:00–11:00
Aug 1991–Sep 1991, ABC Thu 9:00–11:00
Sep 1991–Dec 1991, ABC Thu 9:30–10:00
Jan 1992–Jul 1992, ABC Mon 8:30–9:00
Nov 1992–May 1993, ABC Mon 8:30–9:00
Jun 1993, ABC Sat 9:30–10:00
HOST:
Lt. John Bunnell (1992–1993)
THEME:
performed by Southside Johnny

A documentary series that followed big-city detectives at work on major cases, usually violent crimes or drug investigations. The program also offered glimpses of their personal lives, as in the case of one real-life detective who was faced with a tough choice: nail down his first Federal drug case, or be with his wife in the delivery room.

In January 1992, Lt. John Bunnell of the Multnomah County (Portland, Oregon) Sheriff's Department, who had been frequently featured during 1991, was officially named the show's host. Other cities visited included Las Vegas, Sacramento, Naples, Florida, and New York City. In February 1993, Lt. Bunnell took viewers to Russia for a view of law enforcement there.

AMERICAN DREAM (*Drama*)
FIRST TELECAST: *April 26, 1981*
LAST TELECAST: *June 10, 1981*
BROADCAST HISTORY:
Apr 1981, ABC Sun 9:30–11:00
Apr 1981, ABC Mon 9:00–10:00
May 1981–Jun 1981, ABC Wed 9:00–10:00
CAST:
Danny Novak .... Stephen Macht
Donna Novak .... Karen Carlson
Casey Novak .... Tim Waldrip
Todd Novak .... Michael Hershewe
Jennifer Novak .... Andrea Smith
Abe Berlowitz .... Hans Conried
Sam Whittier .... John McIntire

Family drama about the Novaks, who made the unusual decision to move from the sunny suburbs back into the grimy inner city, partly of necessity, partly to put a little "reality" into their lives. Danny Novak's decision came about when he began looking for a new house—to accommodate an expected baby, and Donna's aging father Sam—and found that the only place the family could afford was a creaky old structure in downtown Chicago. It was a far cry from the neat lawns of Park Ridge, and most of the family was apprehensive, particularly 17-year-old Casey, a pasty-faced youth who seemed to have a great deal of trouble adjusting. Todd, the 12-year-old, was a natural-born "operator" and could adjust anywhere. Jennifer, the 5-year-old, thought it was all great fun. Abe Berlowitz was the neighborhood old-timer who had sold them the house, and who became their new best friend.

Filmed on location in Chicago and Park Ridge, Illinois.

AMERICAN DREAMER (*Situation Comedy*)
FIRST TELECAST: *September 13, 1990*
LAST TELECAST: *June 22, 1991*
BROADCAST HISTORY:
Sep 1990, NBC Thu 9:30–10:00
Sep 1990–Dec 1990, NBC Sat 10:30–11:00
May 1991–Jun 1991, NBC Sat 8:30–9:00
CAST:
Tom Nash .... Robert Urich
Rachel Nash (age 14) .... Chay Lentin
Danny Nash (12) .... Johnny Galecki
Joe Baines .... Jeffrey Tambor
Lillian Abernathy .... Carol Kane
Holly Baker .... Margaret Walsh

An amiable, low-key comedy about a high-powered, globe-trotting network reporter who, following the death of his wife, decided to chuck the job, pack up the kids, and pursue his own version of the "American Dream." He moved to a small town in Wisconsin where he could write a philosophical column about "real people" for a Chicago newspaper. Tom found plenty of subjects for his musings. Joe Baines, his dour editor, drove into the boonies (which he detested) every week to try to persuade Tom to come back to the rat race and chase "real" news. Replied Tom, "Why do you torture yourself by coming up here once a week? You know the fresh air and the general decency of the people upset you." Tom's winsome kids were Rachel and Danny, who wouldn't have minded a return trip. Lillian was his dippy-but-not-so-dumb secretary, and Holly, the earthy waitress at his favorite roadside diner.

A certain reflectiveness permeated this series, with Tom sometimes addressing the viewer directly, or seen in free-form daydream sequences that illustrated his thoughts and fears.

AMERICAN DREAMS (*Comedy/Drama*)
FIRST TELECAST: *September 29, 2002*
LAST TELECAST:
BROADCAST HISTORY:
Sep 2002– , NBC Sun 8:00–9:00
CAST:
Jack Pryor .... Tom Verica
Helen Pryor .... Gail O'Grady
JJ Pryor .... Will Estes
Meg Pryor (age 15) .... Brittany Snow
Will Pryor .... Ethan Dampf
Patty Pryor .... Sarah Ramos
Roxanne Bojarski .... Vanessa Lengies
Henry Walker .... Jonathan Adams
Sam Walker .... Arlen Escarpeta
Rebecca Sandstrom .... Virginia Madsen
Michael Brooks .... Joey Lawrence
Beth Mason .... Rachel Boston

The '60s were back with a vengeance in his nostalgia-fest, which juxtaposed family drama against the popular culture, and especially the music, of that era. The setting was Philadelphia in 1963 and the family was the Irish Catholic Pryors—Jack, the rigid, football-obsessed father, who ran an appliance store that sold both black-and-white and the new *color* TVs; his stressed-out wife, Helen, who tried to calm down his rants; his eldest son, JJ, a handsome jock who chafed under his father's iron hand; bubbly Meg, starry-eyed and radiant; bratty Patty, and sweet youngest son Will, who was physically disabled and wore a leg brace. Others in their circle included Meg's brassy friend Roxanne, Helen's progressive friend Rebecca, Jack's black employee Henry and Henry's shy teenage son Sam.

Much of the action revolved around Dick Clark's teen dance show *American Bandstand*, which originated from the studios of WFIL-TV in Philadelphia. Pushy Roxanne got Meg on the show, with the help of young associate producer Michael, and they both became featured regulars on the nationally televised dance floor. Stories involved the family's reactions to the events of the day, such as the assassination of President Kennedy, Jack's determination for JJ to play football at Notre Dame, and the brewing civil rights struggle as seen through the eyes of Henry and Sam, who were treated as second-class citizens. All of this was heavily overlaid with the music of the era, lots of it and loud, from songs like "Stay" and "Let's Dance"—which punctuated scenes—to the girls singing along with "Will You Still Love Me Tomorrow." Scenes on the *American Bandstand* set cleverly intercut films of '60s pop artists performing their hits (seen on studio monitors in original black-and-white films from the real *American Bandstand*) with modern imitators doing the same songs. Among the modern performers who appeared as '60s icons were Backstreet Boy Nick Carter as Jay Black (of Jay and the Americans), Usher as Marvin Gaye, Ashanti as Dionne Warwick, Keb' Mo' as Sunnyland Slim and Wayne Brady as Jackie Wilson.

AMERICAN EMBASSY, THE (*Political Drama*)
FIRST TELECAST: *March 11, 2002*
LAST TELECAST: *April 1, 2002*
BROADCAST HISTORY:
Mar 2002–Apr 2002, FOX Mon 9:00–10:00
CAST:
Emma Brody .... Arija Bareikis
Doug Roach .... David Cubitt
Jack Wellington .... Jonathan Cake
Consul General Elque Polk .... Jonathan Adams
Vice Consul Carmen Jones .... Davenia McFadden
Dep. Chief Janet Westerman .... Helen Carey
Vice Consul Liz Shoop .... Reiko Aylesworth
Gary Forbush .... Michael Cerveris
James Wellington .... Nicholas Irons
Rob Goodwin .... Eric Dane
Drew Barkley .... Lee Willliams

Twenty-eight-year-old Emma Brody left her native Toledo, Ohio, to start a new job as a vice consul for the American embassy in London in this light drama. Cosmopolitan London and embassy politics provided serious culture shock for the wide-eyed young woman from the American heartland. Doug, an American C.I.A. agent working out of the embassy whom she had met on her flight to London, seemed romantically attracted to her, as did Jack, a young English lord with a huge castle. Members of the embassy staff included Elque, Emma's imposing and demanding boss; Carmen, who was both cynical and supportive; Janet, the embassy's organized administrator; and Liz, Emma's new flatmate, who was a veteran diplomat and former lover of Elque. Gary, the sociable cross-dressing lead singer of an underground band, was one of their neighbors.

Emma's assignments were both light and serious, ranging from helping a dog breeder get her champion Afghan out of quarantine, to tracking down an American father who had taken his 12-year-old daughter to London after losing a custody battle. At the end of the first episode the embassy was damaged by a car bomb. Emma provided narration in letters she was writing to her brother, Jules.

AMERICAN FORUM OF THE AIR (*Discussion*)
FIRST TELECAST: *February 4, 1950*
LAST TELECAST: *September 21, 1952*
BROADCAST HISTORY:
Feb 1950–Sep 1950, NBC Sat 7:00–7:30
Sep 1950–Oct 1950, NBC Sat 6:00–6:30
Jul 1951–Sep 1951, NBC Sun 10:00–10:30
May 1952–Sep 1952, NBC Sun 10:30–11:00
MODERATOR:
Theodore Granik

This long-running discussion program was founded and moderated by Theodore Granik. It originated in Washington, D.C., usually before a live audience, with Granik interviewing two distinguished guests, one on each side of a major national or international issue. *Forum* began on radio in 1928 and appeared on television from 1949 to 1957, generally on Sunday afternoons. However, during the periods indicated above it was a prime-time series. Granik, who was also founder and moderator of *Youth Wants to Know*, relinquished the role of moderator in 1953 due to ill health, but continued to produce the program with newsman Stephen McCormick as moderator.

AMERICAN GIRLS, THE (*Adventure/Drama*)

FIRST TELECAST: *September 23, 1978*
LAST TELECAST: *November 10, 1978*
BROADCAST HISTORY:
Sep 1978–Nov 1978, CBS Sat 9:00–10:00
CAST:
Rebecca Tomkins .... Priscilla Barnes
Amy Waddell .... Debra Clinger
Francis X. Casey .... David Spielberg
Jason Cook .... William Prince

Rebecca and Amy were two very attractive young reporters working for *The American Report*, a fictitious TV newsmagazine similar to the real-life *60 Minutes*. Rebecca was the older and more experienced of the two, a witty and sophisticated big-city girl. Amy was fresh out of college, a small-town girl who was eager to succeed. The two of them traveled around the country on assignments in an elaborately equipped van that provided them with a remote production studio to work on their stories. Casey was the show's producer in New York, who gave the girls their assignments and helped them out of dangerous or embarrassing situations. The on-air personality who anchored *The American Report* was Jason Cook.

AMERICAN GLADIATORS (*Sports/Audience Participation*)

BROADCAST HISTORY:
Syndicated only
60 minutes
Produced: *1989–1997* (208 episodes)
Released: *September 1989*
HOSTS:
Mike Adamle
Joe Theismann (1989)
Todd Christensen (1989–1990)
Larry Czonka (1990–1993)
Lisa Malosky (1993–1995)
Dan Clark (1995–1997)
REFEREE:
Larry Thompson
GLADIATORS:
Male—Michael Horton—"Gemini" (1989–1992)
Dan Clark—"Nitro" (1989–1992, 1994–1995)
Darren McBee—"Malibu" (1989)
Jim Starr—"Laser"
David Nelson—"Titan" (1989–1990)
Billy Smith—"Thunder" (1990–1992)
Galen Tomlinson—"Turbo" (1990–1997)
Steve Henneberry—"Tower" (1991–1994)
Chuck Berlinger—"Viper" (1992–1993)
Lynn "Red" Williams—"Sabre" (1992–1997)
Lee Reherman—"Hawk" (1993–1997)
Female—Sha-ri Pendleton—"Blaze" (1989–1992)
Marisa Paré—"Lace" (1989–1992)
Cheryl Barldinger—"Sunny" (1989)
Tonya Knight—"Gold" (1989–1992)
Ray Hollitt—"Zap" (1989–1990, 1991–1995)
Lori Fetrick—"Ice" (1990–1992, 1993–1997)
Erika Andersch—"Diamond" (1990–1993)
Debbie Clark—"Storm" (1991–1993)
Shirley Eson—"Sky" (1992–1997)
Salina Bartunek—"Elektra" (1992–1993)
Shelley Beattie—"Siren" (1992–1997)
Victoria Gay—"Jazz" (1993–1997)

In this highly stylized physical competition contestants were pitted not against each other but against muscular, highly trained professional "gladiators." Four contenders began each week, each in a separate contest, two men facing male gladiators and two women battling female foes. Contenders found their strength, agility, endurance, and strategy tested as the gladiators attempted to defeat them at every step. The ever-changing games were bruising, tough, and unusual. Among them were The Joust, Powerball, Assault, Breakthrough and Conquer, Human Cannonball, Atlasphere, Hang Tough, The Wall, Swingshot, and The Maze. The final event was The Eliminator, a taxing obstacle course during which gladiators attacked the contestants with mock weapons (everyone was well padded), or blocked their way, trying to slow them down. Contenders earned points according to how well they fought their way through all this, and high scorers advanced to an elimination tournament. The male and female grand champions at season's end each won $35,000—and viewers knew that they had earned it.

Mike Adamle and Joe Theismann co-hosted the show, with Todd Christensen replacing Theismann midway through the first season. Larry Czonka took over as co-host in the fall of 1990, replaced by Lisa Malosky three years later. Tryouts, which attracted thousands of hopeful contenders, were conducted in various cities around the country. Staying in shape was important to the gladiators. Zap, who left the series after the first season to have a baby, returned a year later looking fitter than ever. Although the names of the gladiators were not generally revealed, Marisa Paré (Lace) revealed a lot more than just her name when she was featured in the October 1990 issue of *Playboy*.

At the start of the 1995–1996 season gladiator Dan Clark traded in his costume for a microphone—taking over as Mike Adamle's co-host.

AMERICAN GOTHIC (*Horror*)

FIRST TELECAST: *September 22, 1995*
LAST TELECAST: *July 11, 1996*
BROADCAST HISTORY:
Sep 1995–Nov 1995, CBS Fri 10:00–11:00
Jan 1996, CBS Wed 10:00–11:00
Jul 1996, CBS Wed 8:00–10:00
Jul 1996, CBS Wed 9:00–10:00
CAST:
Sheriff Lucas Buck .... Gary Cole
Dr. Matt Crower .... Jake Weber
Caleb Temple .... Lucas Black
Gail Emory .... Paige Turco
Selena Coombs .... Brenda Baake
Merlyn Temple .... Sarah Paulson
Deputy Ben Healy .... Nick Searcy
Boone MacKenzie .... Christopher Fennell

Dr. Billy Peele (1996) .... John Mese
Rita Barber (1996) .... Lynda Clark

Rural Trinity, South Carolina, seemed tranquil and non-threatening: beautiful old homes, manicured lawns, and a quaint central shopping district. But something was not quite right. That something was Sheriff Lucas Buck. He seemed like an affable law officer but in reality was a demonic presence with an insatiable need to control everything and everyone in town. If anyone got in his way, he either killed them himself, used his supernatural powers to force other people to kill them, or caused them to have fatal "accidents." Lucas's deputy, Ben, was aware of what his boss was doing, but perhaps out of fear, perhaps because he was indebted to the sheriff for his job, he never intervened. This was true of many people in town. Lucas did favors for people—but there were always strings attached.

The sheriff's one weak spot was Caleb, the young boy who didn't know Lucas had raped his mother and was, in fact, his father. To gain custody of the boy, Lucas set out to destroy his family. In the series premiere, on Caleb's tenth birthday, Lucas broke the neck of Caleb's older sister Merlyn, arrested Caleb's father for the murder, and then induced the tortured man to commit suicide in his jail cell. Lucas was thwarted by newly arrived doctor Matt Crower, who, along with Caleb's recently returned cousin Gail, kept the boy from the sheriff's clutches. Caleb moved in with Matt at the local boardinghouse, and Gail, a newspaper reporter, proceeded to search for incriminating evidence against Lucas for all the strange murders and disappearances that had occurred in Trinity over the years. Other regulars were Merlyn's ghost, who appeared in visions to protect and advise her brother; Selena, Caleb's sexy teacher, who was having an affair with Lucas and did favors for him; and Boone, Caleb's classmate and friend.

When *American Gothic* returned to the air in January, the previously passive ghost of Merlyn had become a powerful and active threat to Lucas's control. New to the cast was Dr. Peele, who originally arrived to fight an epidemic and stayed to have an affair with Selena. Merlyn and Buck had several confrontations, including one in which she almost broke his neck in the same way that he had killed her. By July, Caleb was spending time with the sheriff and learning some of his evil skills, despite Merlyn's admonitions. As the series wound to a close, Lucas was stabbed and almost died. When he recovered, Merlyn pleaded with him to release Caleb, who was turning into a sick, power-hungry little monster. Lucas told her the only solution was to kill the boy, but when he attempted to do so, Merlyn gave up her ethereal existence to save her brother after he was thrown from the top of a staircase by the sheriff. When young Caleb woke up, apparently back to normal, Lucas told him that he would probably never see Merlyn again.

Former teen heartthrob Shaun Cassidy was the creator and supervising producer of this creepy series.

AMERICAN HIGH (*Documentary*)

FIRST TELECAST: *August 2, 2000*
LAST TELECAST: *August 9, 2000*
BROADCAST HISTORY:
Aug 2000, FOX Wed 9:00–10:00

This documentary series provided an unusually realistic look at the lives of 14 students at Illinois' Highland Park High School during the 1999–2000 school year, with an emphasis on their emotional angst as they approached adulthood. Everything was covered—classrooms, sports, detention halls, social activities, and home life with demanding parents and squabbling siblings. The producers also provided the students with cameras with which they could record their own personal video diaries, documenting their hopes, fears, dreams, insecurities and relationships. Featured students included Morgan, determined not to let homework get in the way of his partying; Anna, a bright and pretty girl looking forward to college; Robby and Sarah, who had been a couple for "ages"; Kiwi, the field goal kicker whose family had moved back and forth to New Zealand several times since he was an infant; and Brad, who was openly gay.

Critics loved *American High* but, despite heavy promotion, few viewers watched it. The 14 half-hour episodes were scheduled to run in seven hourly installments, but Fox pulled it after the second week. It was picked up by PBS, which aired the entire series beginning the following April and won an Emmy Award for Outstanding Nonfiction Program (Reality).

AMERICAN IDOL: THE SEARCH FOR A SUPERSTAR (*Talent*)

FIRST TELECAST: *June 11, 2002*
LAST TELECAST:
BROADCAST HISTORY:
Jun 2002–Sep 2002, FOX Tue 9:00–10:00
Jun 2002–Sep 2002, FOX Wed 9:30–10:00
Jan 2003– , FOX Tue 8:00–9:00
Jan 2003– , FOX Wed 8:30–9:00

HOSTS:
Brian Dunkleman (2002)
Ryan Seacrest

JUDGES:
Simon Cowell
Paula Abdul
Randy Jackson

SPECIAL CORRESPONDENT:
Kristin Holt (2003–)

Modeled on the popular British talent show *Pop Idol*, *American Idol* was a smash hit with American viewers. It was basically a simple talent contest for aspiring young singers, age 16 to 24 (older need not apply), with the grand prize being a recording contract. There are evidently a lot of starry-eyed young people out there, as more than 10,000 auditioned—some good, some mediocre, and some truly awful. The first episode hilariously recapped the auditions held in various cities, as the field was narrowed by the judges to 100, and then to 30.

What set *American Idol* apart were its three judges. Paula Abdul was an authentic '80s diva who had many hits of her own, but who had entered, for most people, the "whatever happened to . . . ?" category. She was kind and encouraging to the young performers. Music producer Randy Jackson was a true pro who sat at the judges' table chewing on ice from his Coke, and occasionally chewing on the performers as well. Then there was BMG Records A&R executive Simon Cowell. With those he felt had real talent Simon could be quite supportive, but to the rest he was brutal. When he had served as a judge on *Pop Idol* in Britain, the tabloids gave him the nickname "Mr.

Nasty." Among his observations were such gems as, "I think you just killed my favorite song of all time," "That's probably the worst audition I've ever heard. Honestly, it was appalling," "You're too fat. You really need to lose 20 pounds," "Really dreadful. And I'm saying that to be kind, because you will never, ever, ever, ever have a career in singing" and this exchange with a young hopeful:

Simon: "Do you have a singing instructor?"

Hopeful: "Yes."

Simon: "Do you have a lawyer?"

Hopeful: "No."

Simon: "Then I suggest you get a lawyer and sue your instructor."

American audiences ate it up and Simon became the star of the show. Not only did he belittle the contestants, but he also constantly made fun of Brian and Ryan, *Idol*'s cheerful young hosts, and occasionally even squabbled with his fellow judges ("Judge fight!" onlookers would exclaim).

After the judges had whittled the number of hopefuls to 30, viewers got their chance. For each of the next three weeks ten semifinalists performed on Tuesday, after which viewers cast their votes via toll-free phone numbers. The live Wednesday telecast, which included chats with the contestants and highlights from Tuesday, revealed which three would move on to the next round. On the first July telecast Delano, one of the ten scheduled to sing, was disqualified for lying about his age (he had told the producers he was 23 but was actually 29) and replaced by an alternate. The following week the judges added a "wildcard" contestant, from among the 21 not voted in by viewers, to bring the number to ten.

Starting the following Tuesday the songs on *Idol* were tied into specific themes, with the lowest vote-getter eliminated on Wednesday. Themes included Motown, '60s week, '70s week, big-band songs, Burt Bacharach love songs and songs from the '80s and '90s. The final telecast included three songs each by the last two finalists—Justin Guarini and Kelly Clarkson. Kelly won.

When *American Idol* returned for its second season, there were a few changes. Ryan was the sole host and Kristin Holt, a former Dallas Cowboys cheerleader and contestant from the first season of *Idol*, was added to provide behind-the-scenes features on the participants. According to the producers, the number of preliminary auditions (held in New York, Miami, Los Angeles, Detroit, Atlanta, Nashville and Austin, Texas) had exploded to almost 50,000. When the number had been reduced to 32, viewers again got their chance to vote. For each of the next four weeks, eight contestants sang on Tuesday and the two with the most votes, who went on to the finals, were announced on Wednesday. There was also a "best of the worst" episode that featured terrible performances and some of Simon's more caustic critiques.

This time around the wildcard round provided a little surprise. Each of the judges picked one hopeful and viewers phoned in their votes for a fourth, increasing the number of finalists from eight to 12. Each week a single contestant was eliminated, and on most weeks there was a guest celebrity judge, among them Lamont Dozier, Gladys Knight, Olivia Newton-John, Lionel Ritchie, Smokey Robinson and Neil Sedaka. In the first week of April contestant Corey Clark was booted off the show after he had been arrested for assaulting his sister. When it finally got down to the two finalists, Ruben Studdard, the humble gentle giant with the velvet voice, and Clay Aiken, who may have had a better voice but certainly didn't have the personality, the vote was incredibly close. In an overlong two-hour finale that included everything from an appearance by former winner Kelly Clarkson, to shameless plugs for the upcoming *American Idol* tour, to a presidential-election-style rundown of which finalist had received the most votes in each state, Ruben was declared the winner—by a margin of 130,000 votes out of the 24 million cast.

AMERICAN INVENTORY (*Documentary/Drama*)

FIRST TELECAST: *July 1, 1951*

LAST TELECAST: *August 23, 1952*

BROADCAST HISTORY:

Jul 1951–Aug 1951, NBC Sun 8:00–8:30

Jun 1952–Aug 1952, NBC Sat 7:30–8:00

HOST:

Ray Morgan (1951)

Produced by NBC in cooperation with the Alfred P. Sloan Foundation, *American Inventory* was an experimental series that tried out new techniques in adult education. Episodes included panel discussions on various issues, documentary films, ballet, drama, and other features to make it, according to its producers, "the living newspaper." It premiered as a Sunday evening show in July of 1951 and moved to an earlier time period on Sunday afternoons in September. The host of the original series was Ray Morgan, who left in May 1952 when the program ended. When returned to nighttime television on June 28, 1952, it was as a series of documentary-style dramatizations under the broad subtitle "American Gallery." The dramatizations dealt with the people who contributed, in their modest ways, to the betterment of American society—doctors, lawyers, teachers, and so on. In September 1952 it again moved into an earlier time slot on Sunday afternoons, where it remained on the air until December 1955.

AMERICAN JOURNAL (*Magazine*)

BROADCAST HISTORY:

Syndicated only

30 minutes

Produced: *1993–1998*

Released: *September 1993*

HOSTESS:

Nancy Glass (1993–1997)

Michele Dabney-Perez (1997–1998)

Charles Perez (1997–1998)

This was Nancy Glass's second opportunity to front a tabloid magazine series. In 1989 she had hosted *This Evening*, a similar show that had limited distribution and lasted little more than a year, the last several months on the Lifetime cable network. After *This Evening* folded Ms. Glass moved to *Inside Edition*, where she was a senior correspondent for the next three years. In 1993 the producers of *Inside Edition* decided it was time for her to helm her own show again, and *American Journal* was launched that fall.

When Glass departed in the fall of 1997, she was replaced by the brother and sister team of Michele Dabney-Perez and Charles Perez, and the series was retitled *American Journal—Coast to Coast*.

AMERICAN MINSTRELS OF 1949 (*Variety*)
FIRST TELECAST: *January 13, 1949*
LAST TELECAST: *March 17, 1949*
BROADCAST HISTORY:
Jan 1949–Mar 1949, ABC Thu 8:00–9:00
EMCEE:
Jack Carter
REGULARS:
Pick and Pat (Pick Malone and Pat Padgett)
Mary Small
Jimmy Burrell
Estelle Sloane

This was more vaudeville than a true minstrel show, but it featured some real old-time acts, such as Smith and Dale in their "Doctor Kronkheit" routine. Regulars included blackface comics Pick and Pat, singers Mary Small and Jimmy Burrell, and dancer Estelle Sloane. Also seen were such big-time TV acts as Nelson's Cats.

AMERICAN MOVIE CLASSICS (Network) (*Cable Movie Network*)
LAUNCHED:
October 1, 1984
SUBSCRIBERS (MAY 2003):
83.8 million (79% U.S.)

AMC was originally the home of Turhan Bey, Randolph Scott, Piper Laurie, and all those other stars of Hollywood past whose films were not quite big enough to be featured on the broadcast (or bigger cable) networks. Most of AMC's schedule consisted of movies and short subjects from the 1930s through the 1970s, shown without commercial interruption. In addition there were occasional interviews, quiz and panel shows, and original documentaries about the movie world. Comics called AMC the "Ancient Movie Channel," but viewers made it one of the more popular on cable.

Although there were occasional celebrity hosts, the principal hosts for AMC's movie presentations were former actors Bob Dorian and Nick Clooney.

In 1996 AMC launched its first original dramatic series, *Remember WENN*, followed in 1999 by *The Lot*. In the early 2000s AMC began to switch its emphasis to somewhat more recent films (1970s–1990s), leaving lovers of older classics to Turner Classic Movies.

AMERICAN MUSIC SHOP (*Music*)
BROADCAST HISTORY:
The Nashville Network
60 minutes
Produced: *1990–1993*
Premiered: *March 31, 1990*
HOST:
David Holt

A Saturday-night concert series featuring assorted country artists performing together in improvisational jam sessions. Earl Scruggs, Marty Stuart, and Vince Gill were among the early guests. David Holt hosted along with a guest co-host each week. After 1993 the program continued to appear on TNN as a series of specials.

AMERICAN ODYSSEY (*Documentary*)
FIRST TELECAST: *March 24, 1958*
LAST TELECAST: *June 9, 1958*
BROADCAST HISTORY:
Mar 1958–Jun 1958, ABC Mon 7:30–8:00

American Odyssey focused on the various roles played by American institutions and individuals and presented a half-hour filmed documentary on a given topic each week. Subjects ranged from the grueling experiences of a plebe at West Point to dramatized cases from the files of the American Medical Association to a tour of the famous sights in Washington, D.C.

AMERICAN PARADE, THE (*Magazine*)
FIRST TELECAST: *March 27, 1984*
LAST TELECAST: *September 5, 1984*
BROADCAST HISTORY:
Mar 1984–May 1984, CBS Tue 8:00–9:00
Jun 1984–Sep 1984, CBS Wed 8:00–9:00
ANCHORMEN/HOSTS:
Charles Kuralt
Bill Moyers
CORRESPONDENTS:
Morton Dean
Andrew Lack
Bill Kurtis
Diane Sawyer
Maria Shriver
Art Buchwald

This unabashedly patriotic magazine series featured stories about the triumphs and tragedies of individuals both well known and obscure. It was dedicated to an exploration of the "vitality of the American spirit." Most weeks the show was a potpourri of pieces ranging from the likes of Muhammad Ali or ex-president Richard Nixon to a report on a Vietnamese refugee's accomplishments as a female cadet at West Point. Humorist Art Buchwald was also seen with his irreverent, satirical views of the American scene, and host Kuralt did whimsical features on the quirky and eccentric folks he had encountered over the years doing his "on the road" featurettes for CBS News. After dismal early ratings Bill Moyers was added as co-host, covering more serious subjects. The show was retitled *Crossroads* and moved to Wednesdays in June, but none of this seemed to help and the revamped show ground to a halt by the end of the summer.

AMERICAN PROFILE (*Documentary*)
FIRST TELECAST: *September 29, 1967*
LAST TELECAST: *July 5, 1968*
BROADCAST HISTORY:
Sep 1967–Jul 1968, NBC Fri 10:00–11:00

Various aspects of American life and the natural beauty of the country were covered in this series of seven documentaries, which were aired on a rotating basis with *The Bell Telephone Hour, Actuality Specials*, and *NBC News Reports*. The subjects included an examination of endangered species of American wildlife, discussions of politics, and a tour through the National Gallery of Art in Washington, D.C. NBC newsmen narrated most of the telecasts; however, Eddy Arnold was host for "Music from the Land" and Robert Culp led the tour through the National Gallery of Art.

AMERICAN SCENE, THE (*Documentary*)
FIRST TELECAST: *July 6, 1952*
LAST TELECAST: *September 28, 1952*

BROADCAST HISTORY:

Jul 1952–Sep 1952, ABC Sun 6:30–7:00

American Scene presented documentary films on assorted subjects. The title was also used by ABC for various one-time telecasts of films in 1952–1953.

AMERICAN WEEK, THE (*News/Commentary*)

FIRST TELECAST: *April 4, 1954*

LAST TELECAST: *October 10, 1954*

BROADCAST HISTORY:

Apr 1954–Oct 1954, CBS Sun 6:00–6:30

CORRESPONDENT:

Eric Sevareid

A summary of the major happenings in the world during the previous week was presented each Sunday evening by CBS News' chief Washington correspondent, Eric Sevareid. In addition to summarizing the news, Mr. Sevareid included observations and analysis of his own. The show featured original filmed interviews with people prominent in the week's news. Although it left the nighttime slot in the middle of October 1954, this series remained on the air in an earlier time period on Sunday afternoons until the following June.

AMERICAN YOUTH FORUM, see *Youth Wants to Know*

AMERICANA (*Quiz*)

FIRST TELECAST: *December 8, 1947*

LAST TELECAST: *July 4, 1949*

BROADCAST HISTORY:

Dec 1947, NBC Mon 8:10–8:40
Jan 1948–Apr 1948, NBC Wed 8:00–8:30
Apr 1948–Nov 1948, NBC Mon 8:30–9:00
Dec 1948–Jul 1949, NBC Mon 9:30–10:00

MODERATOR:

John Mason Brown (Dec 1947–Jan 1948)
Ben Grauer (1948–1949)

This quiz program dealt with American history and folklore, using questions submitted by viewers. The person submitting "the most interesting question of the week" received a set of the *Encyclopedia Americana*. At first the questions were put to a panel of adult experts, but in February 1948 this was changed to teams of high school students.

AMERICANS, THE (*Civil War Drama*)

FIRST TELECAST: *January 23, 1961*

LAST TELECAST: *September 11, 1961*

BROADCAST HISTORY:

Jan 1961–Sep 1961, NBC Mon 7:30–8:30

CAST:

Ben Canfield .... Darryl Hickman
Jeff Canfield .... Dick Davalos

Two young brothers who grew up in Harpers Ferry, then in the state of Virginia, were faced with a major decision when Virginia seceded from the Union in 1861. Jeff, the younger brother, somewhat impetuous and rebellious, decided to fight for the Confederacy. Ben, the elder brother, was torn between loyalty to his home state and loyalty to the Union. After their father died in a fire during the first episode, Ben swam across the river to Maryland and enlisted in the Union Army. During the remainder of the series each brother was showcased on alternate weeks, Ben fighting for the Union and Jeff with the Confederates in the Virginia Militia.

AMERICA'S DUMBEST CRIMINALS (*Comedy/Police*)

BROADCAST HISTORY:

Syndicated only
30 minutes
Produced: *1996–2000* (96 episodes)
Released: *September 1996*

HOSTS:

Daniel Butler
Debbie Alan (1998–2000)

This series showed reenactments and documentary footage of incompetent criminals screwing up their attempted crimes. The show was a celebration of the dumb, brainless, dopey, and dull—the elite of the criminally inept. Real police officers related experiences, and then viewers saw either surveillance footage or a reenactment of the bungled crime. Host Daniel Butler was also the producer of this reassuring series. Debbie Alan was added as co-host in the fall of 1998.

AMERICA'S FUNNIEST HOME VIDEOS (*Comedy*)

FIRST TELECAST: *January 14, 1990*

LAST TELECAST:

BROADCAST HISTORY:

Jan 1990–Feb 1993, ABC Sun 8:00–8:30
Mar 1993–May 1993, ABC Sun 7:00–7:30
May 1993–Sep 1993, ABC Sun 8:00–8:30
Sep 1993–Dec 1994, ABC Sun 7:00–7:30
Jan 1995–Jun 1996, ABC Sun 7:00–8:00
Jun 1996–Jul 1996, ABC Sun 7:30–8:00
Jul 1996–Dec 1996, ABC Sun 7:00–8:00
Jan 1997, ABC Sun 8:00–9:00
Feb 1997, ABC Sun 7:00–8:00
Mar 1997, ABC Sun 8:00–9:00
Apr 1997–May 1997, ABC Sun 7:00–8:00
May 1997–Sep 1997, ABC Sun 8:00–9:00
Jan 1998–Aug 1998, ABC Mon 8:00–9:00
Jul 1998–Dec 1998, ABC Sat 8:00–9:00
Mar 1999–Apr 1999, ABC Thu 8:00–9:00
May 1999–Aug 1999, ABC Sat 8:00–8:30
Jul 2001–Aug 2001, ABC Fri 8:00–9:00
Nov 2001–, ABC Fri 8:00–9:00
Mar 2002–Apr 2002, ABC Mon 8:00–9:00
Sep 2002–Oct 2002, ABC Fri 9:00–10:00
Jan 2003–Jun 2003, ABC Fri 9:00–10:00

HOST:

Bob Saget (1990–1997)
Daisy Fuentes (1998–1999)
John Fugelsang (1998–1999)
Tom Bergeron (2001–)

A dog joins a conga line. Kamikaze fish take revenge on fishermen. Tots wear their food. A horse collapses under the weight of a portly woman. Hilarious pictures from real life, captured on tape by America's growing army of camcorder owners, were the subject of this first surprise hit of the 1990s. The premise was extremely simple. Viewers were invited to send in their tapes, from which the funniest short segments were shown. The studio audience voted for the best in each show: first prize took away $10,000, second prize $3,000, third prize $2,000. Several times each season a grand prize of $100,000 was offered, and viewers at home could vote by a special 900 number (more than 250,000 called in the first competition).

Comedian Bob Saget hosted the fast-paced proceedings with inane jokes, but the videos were the stars. Most were unintended slapstick, such as people falling down or getting hit with objects (Saget had to constantly assure viewers that "no one was hurt"—even that poor horse). There was certainly no lack of material. A groom gallantly picked up his bride and both fell over. A man stepped into a portable toilet which was promptly blown away by a gust of wind. And perhaps best—a crocodile unmistakably expressed his dislike of camcorders.

First seen as a special telecast in November 1989.

AMERICA'S FUNNIEST PEOPLE (*Comedy*)
FIRST TELECAST: *September 8, 1990*
LAST TELECAST: *August 28, 1994*
BROADCAST HISTORY:
Sep 1990, ABC Sat 8:30–9:00
Sep 1990–Feb 1993, ABC Sun 8:30–9:00
Mar 1993, ABC Sun 7:30–8:00
May 1993–Aug 1993, ABC Sun 8:30–9:00
Sep 1993–Aug 1994, ABC Sun 7:30–8:00
HOSTS:
David Coulier
Arleen Sorkin (1990–1992)
Tawny Kitaen (1992–1994)

TV is famous for immediately cloning its hits, and this cheerful low-budget series did just that for ABC's surprise sensation *America's Funniest Home Videos.* It followed the earlier show on the schedule, serving as the second half of an ABC "videos" hour on Sunday night. There were some differences between the two shows. On *Videos,* the clips were shot by amateurs, and in most cases supposedly not staged. On *People,* sequences were deliberately staged, as ordinary people performed gags and stunts for the camera. Some of the clips were shot by amateurs, and others by the show's own crews. The same prize structure as on *Videos* was used, $10,000 for first prize each week, $3,000 for second, and $2,000 for third.

The gags were certainly high class. Four businessmen painted their bellies with eyes and mouths, placed big hats over the top half of their bodies, and "whistled" with their belly buttons; a man used a vacuum cleaner to form bizarre shapes with his mouth; and kids blurted out variations on jokes far older than they were ("Why did the chicken cross the playground? To get to the other slide!"). Critics groaned, but they were drowned out by the audience laughter.

In the fall of 1993 the program was renamed *The New America's Funniest People* and a guest co-host from a different ABC show joined David and Tawny each week, all to no particular effect.

AMERICA'S GREATEST BANDS (*Music*)
FIRST TELECAST: *June 25, 1955*
LAST TELECAST: *September 24, 1955*
BROADCAST HISTORY:
Jun 1955–Sep 1955, CBS Sat 8:00–9:00
HOST:
Paul Whiteman

Serving as the 1955 summer replacement for *The Jackie Gleason Show, America's Greatest Bands* presented four different big-name bands each week. Appearing on a giant rotating stage, each of the bands took turns performing. The permanent host of the series was bandleader Paul Whiteman, whose own band was featured on the first telecast. Among the other bands that appeared were those of Duke Ellington, Sammy Kaye, Xavier Cugat, Perez Prado, Bob Crosby, Les Brown, and Count Basie.

AMERICA'S GREATEST PETS (*Animals*)
FIRST TELECAST: *October 28, 1998*
LAST TELECAST: *July 2, 1999*
BROADCAST HISTORY:
Oct 1998–Nov 1998, UPN Tue 9:00–9:30
Dec 1998–Jan 1999, UPN Tue 9:00–10:00
Mar 1999–Jul 1999, UPN Fri 8:00–9:00
HOSTS:
Ali Landry
Jules Sylvester

This cross between *Those Amazing Animals* and *America's Funniest Home Videos* was hosted by actress and "pet lover extraordinaire" Ali Landry and Jules Sylvester, an animal expert and owner of Reptile Rentals, a firm that provided animals for movies and TV. There were segments on a surfboarding, scuba-diving dog, turtle racing, a hotel that provided guests with pet cats for the duration of their stay, a visit to a 32-year-old hippo at the Sacramento Zoo, a plumber who used his pet pig to sniff out broken sewer lines, a dog trainer with her pet-trained ferret, and a veterinarian who had rigged a cart to provide mobility for a partially paralyzed cat.

Each episode provided a number of animal-related questions (and answers) to the home audience—the record for kittens born to a single cat (420), how pigs are like people (they can get sunburned), who has the most bones, humans, cats, or dogs (dogs, with almost 300). Viewers were asked to send in tapes or write to the show about their own special pets.

The rather wooden Sylvester was phased out in the spring, with Landry becoming the sole host.

AMERICA'S HEALTH (*Documentary*)
FIRST TELECAST: *August 20, 1951*
LAST TELECAST: *March 6, 1952*
BROADCAST HISTORY:
Aug 1951–Sep 1951, ABC Mon 10:00–10:30
Sep 1951–Oct 1951, ABC Sat 9:30–10:00
Feb 1952–Mar 1952, ABC Thu 10:00–10:15

This series consisted of documentary films on health subjects, provided by such organizations as the Veterans Administration and the American Cancer Society. A sample title was "Doctor Speaks His Mind."

AMERICA'S MOST TALENTED KID (*Talent*)
FIRST TELECAST: *March 28, 2003*
LAST TELECAST: *May 2, 2003*
BROADCAST HISTORY:
Mar 2003–May 2003, NBC Fri 8:00–9:00
HOST:
Mario Lopez
REGULAR JUDGE:
Lance Bass

The antidote for the cutthroat vote-'em-off-the-island reality shows and brutal talent shows so popular in the early 2000s was this sweet show, in which fresh-faced, talented youngsters age three to 15 strutted their stuff before an adoring audience. The kids were divided into three age categories, three to seven, eight to 12, and 13 to 15, with three contestants in each category competing each week. They could do anything—sing, dance, rap, play an instrument—while parents lovingly watched and boyish host Mario Lopez and the audience clapped, laughed and offered encouragement. At the end of the performances in each category the judges punched in their scores for talent and showmanship, and the contestant with the highest average score advanced to the next round. There were no cutting remarks or evaluations, although at the end of each round the judges offered a few comments on how great the kids were. Lance Bass (of 'NSYNC) was the sole permanent judge, joined each week by two guest judges such as Sisqo, Maureen McCormick, Jermaine Jackson or Daisy Fuentes.

Almost every kid here was rated nine or better on a ten-point scale, and they were quite talented, a parade of pint-sized rappers and tiny tykes with booming voices. Occasionally one was a bit bizarre, such as the spike-haired white teenager who gave an impassioned delivery of "We Shall Overcome" while black rapper Sisqo looked on in disbelief.

The first winner was 12-year-old guitarist/songwriter Cheyenne Kimball, who took home a grand prize of $50,000.

AMERICA'S MOST WANTED (*Public Service*)

FIRST TELECAST: *April 10, 1988*

LAST TELECAST:

BROADCAST HISTORY:

Apr 1988–Aug 1990, FOX Sun 8:00–8:30

Sep 1990–Jul 1993, FOX Fri 8:00–9:00

Jul 1993–Jan 1994, FOX Tue 9:00–10:00

Jan 1994– , FOX Sat 9:00–10:00

HOST:

John Walsh

This series billed itself as a "weekly nationwide criminal manhunt." In cooperation with law enforcement agencies ranging from the F.B.I. to local municipalities, *America's Most Wanted* provided the general public with detailed information about violent criminals on the loose. Each week two or three cases were covered with re-creations of the crimes, interviews with victims and law officers, and, if available, pictures of the actual criminals themselves. Viewers were given a toll-free number to call (1-800-CRIME-88) if they had information that might help in apprehending the criminals.

The show certainly got off to a good start. Four days after the first episode aired (in February 1988 on the Fox-owned stations), calls from viewers led to the capture of one of the criminals depicted—David James Roberts, a murderer and rapist on the F.B.I.'s ten most wanted list. Over the next few months several other criminals wanted by the F.B.I. were captured with the help of viewers. In early April, *America's Most Wanted* became a prime-time series on the Fox network.

In the fall of 1990 *America's Most Wanted* moved to Friday nights and expanded from thirty minutes to a full hour. Added to the profiles of wanted criminals were features on such things as legal organizations and victims' rights groups, tips on how to protect life and property from criminals, and interviews with law enforcement officers from around the country. Each year the last two digits of the 800 number were changed to reflect the calendar year until 1994, when the number was permanently changed to 1-800-CRIME-TV. In May 1992 the total number of profiled criminals apprehended passed 200, and it reached 430 at the time of the show's cancellation in September 1996. Two months later, prompted by weak ratings for the two sitcoms that had replaced it, Fox brought the show back with the modified title *America's Most Wanted: America Fights Back*. By February of 1999 the total captured had passed 550, and four years later it passed 750.

Host John Walsh had more than a professional interest in this program. His six-year-old son Adam had been kidnapped and murdered in the 1970s and he and his wife had lobbied Congress to pass the Missing Children's Bill that gave parents access to F.B.I. records that might help them find their lost kids. His story was dramatized in the 1983 Emmy-winning TV movie *Adam*, in which he was played by Daniel J. Travanti.

AMERICA'S TALKING (Network) (*All-Talk Cable Network*)

LAUNCHED:

July 4, 1994

CEASED OPERATION:

July 1996

SUBSCRIBERS (JUL. 1996):

20 million (21% U.S.)

An all-talk cable channel launched by NBC to fill the extra channels it was given on cable systems as a result of the 1992 cable reregulation act. The initial schedule consisted of one- and two-hour call-in talk fests hosted by lesser-known personalities in the field, including E. Jean Carroll, Mike Jerrick, Brian O'Connor, Brian Tracey, and the network's own president, Roger Ailes. The format did not attract sufficient viewers to satisfy NBC, so in July 1996 the format was changed and the channel renamed MSNBC (q.v.).

AMERICA'S TOWN MEETING (*Debate*)

FIRST TELECAST: *October 5, 1948*

LAST TELECAST: *July 6, 1952*

BROADCAST HISTORY:

Oct 1948–Jun 1949, ABC Tue 8:30–9:30

Jan 1952–Jul 1952, ABC Sun 6:30–7:00

MODERATOR:

George V. Denny, Jr. (1948–1952)

John Daly (Apr–Jul 1952)

This venerable radio series, which began in 1935 and ran for 21 years thereafter, had two runs on network television, in 1948–1949 and in 1952. The format was the same as that of the radio show, consisting of debates by politicians, writers, and other prominent persons on such topics as "Are We Too Hysterical About Communism?", "Has the Korean War Been a Failure?", and "Should We Have Uniform Federal Divorce Laws?" The program originated from New York's Town Hall Auditorium before a vociferous and involved audience. George V. Denny, Jr., who created the series, served as moderator for all telecasts except for a brief period in 1952 when ABC newsman John Daly took over.

AMOS BURKE—SECRET AGENT, see *Burke's Law*

AMOS 'N' ANDY (*Situation Comedy*)
FIRST TELECAST: *June 28, 1951*
LAST TELECAST: *June 11, 1953*
BROADCAST HISTORY:
Jun 1951–Jun 1953, CBS Thu 8:30–9:00
CAST:
Amos Jones .... Alvin Childress
Andrew Hogg Brown ("Andy") .... Spencer Williams, Jr.
George "The Kingfish" Stevens .... Tim Moore
Lawyer Algonquin J. Calhoun .... Johnny Lee
Sapphire Stevens .... Ernestine Wade
Lightnin' .... Horace Stewart (a.k.a. Nick O'Demus)
Sapphire's Mama (Ramona Smith) .... Amanda Randolph
Madame Queen................. Lillian Randolph
THEME:
"Angel's Serenade," by Gaetano Braga

Amos 'n' Andy, one of the most popular and long-running radio programs of all time, was brought to television in the summer of 1951. The series was produced by Freeman Gosden and Charles Correll, the two actors who had created and starred in the radio version. Since they were white, and the entire cast of the show on television had to be black, a much ballyhooed search was held, over a period of four years, to find the right actors to play the parts. Only Ernestine Wade and Amanda Randolph were brought over from the radio cast.

Set in Harlem, *Amos 'n' Andy* centered around the activities of George Stevens, a conniving character who was always looking for a way to make a fast buck. As head of the Mystic Knights of the Sea Lodge, where he held the position of "Kingfish," he got most of the lodge brothers involved in his schemes. That put him at odds not only with them, but with his wife, Sapphire, and her mother. Mama, in particular, didn't trust him at all. Andy Brown was the most gullible of the lodge members, a husky, well-meaning, but rather simple soul. The Kingfish was constantly trying to swindle him in one way or another, but the "big dummy" (as Kingfish called him) kept coming back for more. More often than not, Kingfish would get them both into trouble, but win Andy's cooperation with an appeal to fraternal spirit—"Holy mackerel, Andy! We's all got to stick together in dis heah thing . . . remember, we is brothers in that great fraternity, the Mystic Knights of the Sea."

Amos was actually a rather minor character, the philosophical cabdriver who narrated most of the episodes. Madame Queen was Andy's girlfriend and Lightnin' was the slow-moving janitor at the lodge.

Civil rights groups such as the NAACP had long protested the series as fostering racial stereotypes, to little avail. *Amos 'n' Andy* drew sizable audiences during its two-year CBS run, and was widely rerun on local stations for the next decade. The turning point came in 1963 when CBS Films, which was still calling *Amos 'n' Andy* one of its most widely circulated shows, announced that the program had been sold to two African countries, Kenya and Western Nigeria. Soon afterward, an official of the Kenya government announced that the program would be banned in his country. This focused attention anew on the old controversy and in the summer of 1964, when a Chicago station announced that it was resuming reruns, there were widespread and bitter protests. CBS found its market for the films suddenly disappearing, and in 1966 the program was withdrawn from sale, as quietly as possible.

As to whether the program was in fact racist, there was no agreement on that. The creators certainly didn't think so, and actor Alvin Childress (Amos) was quoted as saying, "I didn't feel it harmed the Negro at all. . . . Actually the series had many episodes that showed the Negro with professions and businesses like attorneys, store owners, and so on, which they never had in TV or movies before. . . ." Others pointed out that the situations were no different than those found in many comedy programs with white characters. Nevertheless the humor certainly derived from the fact that these were shiftless, conniving, not-too-bright *blacks.* The very stereotypes that had so long been unfairly applied to an entire race were used throughout. As a result, it is unlikely that *Amos 'n' Andy* will ever be seen again on television.

For an interesting, but disguised, sequel by Correll and Gosden, see *Calvin and the Colonel.*

AMY PRENTISS (*Police Drama*)
FIRST TELECAST: *December 1, 1974*
LAST TELECAST: *July 6, 1975*
BROADCAST HISTORY:
Dec 1974–Jul 1975, NBC Sun 8:30–10:30
CAST:
Amy Prentiss .... Jessica Walter
Det. Tony Russell .... Steve Sandor
Det. Rod Pena.................... Arthur Metrano
Det. Contreras .... Johnny Seven
Jill Prentiss.......................... Helen Hunt
Joan Carter .... Gwenn Mitchell

When the chief of detectives of the San Francisco Police Department died unexpectedly, the person at the top of the service list was Amy Prentiss, an attractive 35-year-old widow with a young daughter. There had never been a woman chief of detectives before, and many of the male officers who suddenly found themselves reporting to Amy resented it. A measure of grudging respect gradually emerged, however, when her skill as an investigator became apparent in a series of cases that otherwise constituted standard crime-show fare. Unfortunately, viewers took less readily to the idea of woman as boss, and the program was canceled after a short run.

Amy Prentiss was one of the four rotating elements that made up the 1974–1975 edition of *NBC Sunday Mystery Movie.* The others were *Columbo, McCloud,* and *McMillan and Wife.*

AND EVERYTHING NICE (*Fashions*)
FIRST TELECAST: *March 15, 1949*
LAST TELECAST: *January 2, 1950*
BROADCAST HISTORY:
Mar 1949–June 1949, DUM Tue 7:00–7:30
Jul 1949–Aug 1949, DUM Mon 8:30–9:00
Sep 1949–Jan 1950, DUM Mon 9:00–9:30
HOSTESS:
Maxine Barrat

This was an early program that presented fashions, style tips, and guests.

AND HERE'S THE SHOW (*Comedy Variety*)
FIRST TELECAST: *July 9, 1955*
LAST TELECAST: *September 24, 1955*
BROADCAST HISTORY:
Jul 1955–Sep 1955, NBC Sat 10:00–10:30
REGULARS:
Ransom Sherman
Jonathan Winters
The Double Daters
John Scott Trotter, musical director
Bob LeMond, announcer

This live variety program served as a summer replacement for the *George Gobel Show.* Ransom Sherman and Jonathan Winters were the co-stars, with Sherman also acting as host. Both of the stars functioned as monologists and appeared together in skits. The Double Daters introduced the guest stars and the comedy skits and performed a featured musical number each week. The program's title was derived from one of George Gobel's familiar lines.

ANDROS TARGETS, THE (*Newspaper Drama*)
FIRST TELECAST: *January 31, 1977*
LAST TELECAST: *July 9, 1977*
BROADCAST HISTORY:
Jan 1977–May 1977, CBS Mon 10:00–11:00
Jul 1977, CBS Sat 10:00–11:00
CAST:
Mike Andros....................... James Sutorius
Sandi Farrell......................... Pamela Reed
Chet Reynolds .... Roy Poole
Norman Kale.......................... Alan Mixon
Wayne Hillman....................... Ted Beniades
Ted Bergman...................... Jordan Charney

Mike Andros was an investigative reporter for *The New York Forum.* Much in the style of the real-life reporters who had become celebrities in the aftermath of the Watergate scandal, Andros focused his efforts on corruption in the biggest city in the nation. Unethical use of amphetamines by doctors, underworld activities in areas of pornography, prostitution, and narcotics, and unusual criminal cases that had been hushed up by the police all came under his scrutiny. Sandi Farrell was Mike's young assistant and Chet and Norman were the managing and city editors, respectively, of *The New York Forum.* Wayne Hillman was a fellow reporter and friend, and Ted Bergman was the paper's metropolitan editor.

ANDY AND DELLA RUSSELL (*Music*)
FIRST TELECAST: *December 18, 1950*
LAST TELECAST: *June 15, 1951*
BROADCAST HISTORY:
Dec 1950–Jun 1951, ABC Mon–Fri 7:00–7:05
REGULARS:
Andy Russell
Della Russell
Mort Lippman, piano

Andy Russell, a radio and recording star of the 1940s, and his wife Della hosted this brief but pleasant musical interlude, which originated live from New York every weeknight. A month after its premiere the series' name was changed to *Cook's Champagne Party,* in honor of the sponsor.

ANDY DICK SHOW, THE (*Comedy*)
BROADCAST HISTORY:
MTV
30 minutes
Original episodes: *2001–2002* (21 episodes)
Premiered: *February 27, 2001*
REGULARS:
Andy Dick

Comedian Andy Dick turned up the raunch meter on this MTV sketch series that featured bleeps and digitally obscured body parts. Skits, many of them filmed on location, ranged from a coach making his team play football in the nude (ouch!), to a butt puppet interviewing Ben Stiller, to Andy teaching a prison guard how to intimidate prisoners, to Andy's personal assistant changing his diapers and prechewing his food, to a mock *E! True Hollywood Story* about the star ("Fresh from Chicago, Dick penetrated Hollywood with ease"). There was much mockery of MTV, including Andy's recurring character of a pop diva called Daphne Aguilera.

ANDY GRIFFITH SHOW, THE (*Situation Comedy*)
FIRST TELECAST: *October 3, 1960*
LAST TELECAST: *September 16, 1968*
BROADCAST HISTORY:
Oct 1960–Jul 1963, CBS Mon 9:30–10:00 (OS)
Sep 1963–Sep 1964, CBS Mon 9:30–10:00
Sep 1964–June 1965, CBS Mon 8:30–9:00
Sep 1965–Sep 1968, CBS Mon 9:00–9:30
CAST:
Andy Taylor......................... Andy Griffith
Opie Taylor .... Ronny Howard
Barney Fife (1960–1965) .... Don Knotts
Ellie Walker (1960–1961) .... Elinor Donahue
Aunt Bee Taylor................... Frances Bavier
Clara Edwards .... Hope Summers
Gomer Pyle (1963–1964) .... Jim Nabors
Helen Crump (1964–1968) .... Aneta Corsaut
Goober Pyle (1965–1968) .... George Lindsey
Floyd Lawson .... Howard McNear
Otis Campbell (1960–1967) .... Hal Smith
Howard Sprague (1966–1968) .... Jack Dodson
Emmett Clark (1967–1968) .... Paul Hartman
Thelma Lou (1960–1965).............. Betty Lynn
Warren Ferguson (1965–1966) .... Jack Burns
Mayor Stoner (1962–1963) .... Parley Baer
Jud Crowley (1961–1966).............. Burt Mustin
Sam Jones (1968) .... Ken Berry

The small town of Mayberry, North Carolina, was the setting of this highly successful homespun situation comedy. Sheriff Andy Taylor was a widower with a young son, Opie. They lived with Andy's Aunt Bee, a combination housekeeper and foster mother for Opie. Andy's deputy was his cousin Barney Fife, the most inept, hypertense deputy sheriff ever seen on television. The tone of the show was very gentle, giving Andy the opportunity to state and practice his understanding, philosophical outlook on life. Since there was practically no crime in Mayberry, the stories revolved mostly around the personal relationships of its citizens.

Two of the show's regulars graduated to series of their own. The first was Jim Nabors. He had become a member of the cast in the spring of 1963 in the role of

Gomer Pyle, the naive, lovable gas station attendant at Wally's filling station. After a year and a half he left to join the marines and become *Gomer Pyle, U.S.M.C.* Co-star Don Knotts left the show in 1965 for his own variety series, *The Don Knotts Show*. Among the other regulars, Andy's original girlfriend, druggist Ellie Walker, was seen only during the first season, and for the following three years Andy had no regular romantic interest. Schoolteacher Helen Crump filled the void in 1964, and, when Andy Griffith decided to quit the show in 1968, she also provided his means of escape. On the first episode of *Mayberry R.F.D.*, the successor to *The Andy Griffith Show*, Andy and Helen married and moved away, leaving the supporting cast to carry on with a new star, Ken Berry, in the role of Sam Jones—another widower with a young son.

Daytime reruns of this series, as well as some syndicated versions, were titled *Andy of Mayberry*. CBS aired weekday daytime reruns from October 1964 to September 1970, with the title reverting to *The Andy Griffith Show* when the prime-time version left the air. A nostalgic reunion of the series' original cast—the made-for-TV film "Return to Mayberry"—aired in April 1986 and was the highest-rated movie of the entire 1985–1986 season.

ANDY OF MAYBERRY, see *Andy Griffith Show, The*

ANDY RICHTER CONTROLS THE UNIVERSE
(*Situation Comedy*)

FIRST TELECAST: *March 19, 2002*
LAST TELECAST: *January 12, 2003*
BROADCAST HISTORY:
Mar 2002–Apr 2002, FOX Tue 8:30–9:00
Apr 2002, FOX Thu 9:30–10:00
May 2002–Jun 2002, FOX Tue 8:30–9:00
Dec 2002–Jan 2003, FOX Sun 9:30–10:00
Dec 2002, FOX Tue 8:30–9:00

CAST:
Andy Richter .... Andy Richter
Jessica Green .... Paget Brewster
Byron Togler .... Jonathan Slavin
Wendy McKay .... Irene Molloy
Keith Richards .... James Patrick Stuart
Mr. Pickering .... John Bliss

Andy was an aspiring short-story writer with a vivid imagination who was reduced to writing technical manuals for Chicago-based Pickering Industries, the "fifth largest company in America," in this surrealistic comedy. As he narrated what was going on in his life Andy fantasized about the way things might have been—but weren't. Most of the action took place at work, where the much put-upon Andy did his best to cope with various indignities. Coworkers included Jessica, the insensitive supervisor he had known for years; Byron, the creepy neurotic illustrator with whom Andy was forced to share a tiny office; Keith, the good-looking ladies' man who never seemed to have any problems; and Wendy, the pretty young receptionist. Andy was infatuated with her but, unfortunately for him, she was dating Keith. One of Andy's fantasy people, who gave him constant grief, was nasty old Mr. Pickering, the long-dead founder of the company.

ANDY WILLIAMS AND JUNE VALLI SHOW, THE
(*Music*)

FIRST TELECAST: *July 2, 1957*
LAST TELECAST: *September 5, 1957*
BROADCAST HISTORY:
Jul 1957–Sep 1957, NBC Tue/Thu 7:30–7:45

REGULARS:
Andy Williams
June Valli
Alvy West, orchestra conductor

THEME:
"On a Summer Evening"

On this live summer series, Andy Williams and June Valli sang both individually and together.

ANDY WILLIAMS PRESENTS RAY STEVENS
(*Comedy Variety*)

FIRST TELECAST: *June 20, 1970*
LAST TELECAST: *August 8, 1970*
BROADCAST HISTORY:
Jun 1970–Aug 1970, NBC Sat 7:30–8:30

REGULARS:
Ray Stevens
Lulu
Dick Curtis
Steve Martin
Carol Robinson
Solari and Carr
Billy Van
"Mama" Cass Elliot

Singer-composer-comedian-impressionist Ray Stevens starred in this summer replacement for *The Andy Williams Show*. Ray, who was a frequent guest on Andy's show, was featured in production numbers and comedy skits in the summer program, which was taped in Toronto. The skits tended to be very broad and often verged on the physical violence associated with Mack Sennett slapstick.

ANDY WILLIAMS SHOW, THE (*Musical Variety*)

FIRST TELECAST: *July 3, 1958*
LAST TELECAST: *July 17, 1971*
BROADCAST HISTORY:
Jul 1958–Sep 1958, ABC Thu 9:00–9:30
Jul 1959–Sep 1959, CBS Tue 10:00–11:00
Sep 1962–Jun 1963, NBC Thu 10:00–11:00
Sep 1963–May 1964, NBC Tue 10:00–11:00
Oct 1964–May 1966, NBC Mon 9:00–10:00
Sep 1966–May 1967, NBC Sun 10:00–11:00
Sep 1969–Jul 1971, NBC Sat 7:30–8:30 (OS)

REGULARS:
Andy Williams
Dick Van Dyke (1958)
The Bob Hamilton Trio (1958)
The Mort Lindsey Orchestra (1958)
The Dick Williams Singers (1959)
The Peter Gennaro Dancers (1959)
The Jack Kane Orchestra (1959)
Randy Sparks and the New Christy Minstrels (1962–1963)
Jimmy Gaines (1962–1963)
Marian Mercer (1962–1963)
R. G. Brown (1962–1963)
The Osmond Brothers (1962–1971)
The Colin Romoff Orchestra (1962–1963)
The Dave Grusin Orchestra (1963–1966)
The Allyn Ferguson Orchestra (1966–1967)

The Mike Post Orchestra (1969–1971)
The Good Time Singers (1963–1966)
Jonathan Winters (1965–1967, 1970–1971)
Irwin Corey (1969–1970)
Janos Prohaska (1969–1971)
Ray Stevens (1969–1971)
The Lennon Sisters (1970–1971)
Charlie Callas (1970–1971)
The Nick Castle Dancers (1963–1966)
The James Starbuck Dancers (1966–1967)
The Jaime Roger Dancers (1969–1970)
The Andre Tayri Dancers (1970–1971)

THEME (AFTER 1962):
"Moon River," by Henry Mancini and Johnny Mercer

Smooth-voiced popular singer Andy Williams starred in a number of variety shows in the late 1950s and 1960s. The first two were summer shows, in 1958 and 1959, followed by his own regular season series on NBC beginning in 1962. Big-name guest stars appeared, usually of the adult variety (rarely a rock act), and a large number of regulars were seen. Originally the New Christy Minstrels were the chief backup act, but they were soon superseded by the quartet of talented youngsters discovered by Williams performing at Disneyland (they had also appeared once on a *Disneyland* TV special). The Osmond Brothers, billed as "youthful barbershop harmony group from Ogden, Utah," were first seen on December 20, 1962, singing "I'm a Ding Dong Daddy from Dumas" and "Side by Side." They stayed with Williams for the rest of his run. The original four were periodically augmented by brothers and sisters, with six-year-old Donny Osmond making his debut on December 10, 1963.

In 1967 Andy cut back to a schedule of only three specials per year, but in 1969 he returned with a regular weekly series once again. This time the look was decidedly contemporary, including rock acts, psychedelic lighting, and a futuristic set that had the audience seated on movable platforms which followed Andy around through the show. Among the regular features were "The Informal Spot" and "The Williams Weirdos"—Little General, Walking Suitcase, Big Bird, and The Bear. Williams's 1958 summer show, which had filled in for vacationing Pat Boone, was titled *The Chevy Showroom Starring Andy Williams.* All of his subsequent series were simply titled *The Andy Williams Show*, including a syndicated half-hour musical variety series he hosted during the 1976–1977 season. The only featured regular on the syndicated show was comic/ventriloquist Wayland Flowers.

ANDY'S GANG, see *Smilin' Ed McConnell and His Buster Brown Gang*

ANGEL (*Situation Comedy*)
FIRST TELECAST: *October 6, 1960*
LAST TELECAST: *September 20, 1961*
BROADCAST HISTORY:
Oct 1960–Dec 1960, CBS Thu 9:00–9:30
Dec 1960–Apr 1961, CBS Thu 8:00–8:30
April 1961–Sep 1961, CBS Wed 9:00–9:30
CAST:
Angel .... Annie Farge
John Smith .... Marshall Thompson
Susie .... Doris Singleton
George .... Don Keefer

Angel was a petite French girl who had just moved to America and become the bride of a young architect, John Smith. Her efforts to adjust to the American way of life provided the humor in this series. Her problems with English, misunderstanding of situations, and attempts to be a responsible housewife all contributed to the amusement of her husband and their next-door neighbors, Susie and George, who were also their closest friends.

ANGEL (*Supernatural Drama*)
FIRST TELECAST: *October 5, 1999*
LAST TELECAST:
BROADCAST HISTORY:
Oct 1999–May 2001, WB Tue 9:00–10:00
Jun 2001–Jun 2002, WB Mon 9:00–10:00
Jan 2002, WB Thu 8:00–9:00
Jun 2002–Dec 2002, WB Sun 9:00–10:00
Jan 2003–May 2003, WB Wed 9:00–10:00
CAST:
Angel .... David Boreanaz
Doyle (Francis) (1999) .... Colin Quinn
Cordelia Chase .... Charisma Carpenter
Wesley Wyndham Price .... Alexis Denisof
**Det. Kate Lochley (1999–2001)* ..... Elisabeth Rohm
Charles Gunn (2000–) .... J. August Richards
Lindsey McDonald (1999–2001) .... Christian Kane
Lilah Morgan (2000–2003) .... Stephanie Romanov
**Holland Manners (2000–2001)* ..... Sam Anderson
Darla (2000–2001) .... Julie Benz
Lorne, The Host (2000–) .... Andy Hallett
Winifred "Fred" Burkle (2001–) ...... Amy Acker
Daniel Holtz (2001–2002) .... Keith Szarabajka
**Gavin Park (2001–2003)* .... Daniel Dae Kim
**Sahijhan (2001–2002)* .... Jack Conley
**Linwood Murrow (2001–2002)* .... John Rubinstein
Justine (2001–2002) .... Laurel Holloman
Groosalugg (2001–2002) .... Mark Lutz
Connor (2002–) .... Vincent Kartheiser
The Beast (2002–2003) .... Vladimir Kuzich

*Occasional

This spin-off from *Buffy the Vampire Slayer*, featured Angel, Buffy's vampire lover, who moved to Los Angeles in search of redemption for his sins. As part of his penance he vowed to protect humans in L.A. from other predatory vampires and demons. Doyle, his guide, was a half-demon Irishman sent to Angel by "The Powers That Be" to guide him to those in need of help. Doyle had visions—in splitting migraine headaches—about the people who needed Angel's assistance. *Buffy*'s Cordelia, a struggling unemployed actress, worked as the office manager for Angel Investigations. Their nemesis was the powerful law firm of Wolfram & Hart, which worked with vampires, demons and other assorted bad guys and didn't appreciate Angel's interference.

In November Doyle sacrificed himself to save Cordelia and Angel, but a kiss he gave Cordelia just before his death saddled her with the visions—and the accompanying headaches—that gave Angel his new link to The Powers That Be. In the same episode Wesley showed up as a rogue demon hunter, and later went to work with Angel and Cordelia. In January, while trying to help Det. Lochley solve a series of murders committed by a vampire he had known 200 years earlier, Angel told her that he was a vampire. While researching the case she uncovered Angel's brutal past and had problems dealing with him. Lindsey, one of the attorneys at Wolfram & Hart, had evidenced a good side, but still took a promotion to run the firm's L.A. office.

That fall Gunn, a disgruntled black former gang member who wanted to do good, joined Angel. Darla, the vampire who had originally made Angel a vampire, was prepared by the folks at Wolfram & Hart to do battle with him. She had become human and set Angel up for the murder of a guy posing as her husband. Angel kidnapped Darla and she tried to return him to his dark ways—unsuccessfully—and then, after she realized she had a soul, Darla sought his help. Meanwhile, Lochley had to reconsider her belief in Angel's evil when he saved her from a monster. In late November Holland (the head of Wolfram & Hart) told Darla she was dying from syphilis—she had contracted it before becoming a vampire and, now that she was human again, it was killing her. Lindsey showed up with Drusilla, who drank Darla's blood and remade her as a vampire, after which the two of them went on a rampage, killing Holland and other members of the Wolfram & Hart staff who were at a party at his home. Lindsey and Lilah were the only survivors, and the senior partners made them co-executive vice presidents of special projects.

Angel, obsessed with Darla, fired his entire staff and went after her and Drusilla. The rest of the staff decided to keep the agency open and, after a shaky start, seemed to be doing okay. The powers at Wolfram & Hart wanted Angel alive because there were prophecies that he would be a major player in the coming apocalypse and they wanted him on their side. Angel worked with Lorne, a psychic karaoke demon, to help him with his search. Lochley, whose superiors were upset with her preoccupation with macabre cases that were mostly Angel-related, was fired from the LAPD. Angel destroyed Wolfram & Hart's demon "senior partner" when it arrived from Hell and, when he attempted to go to Hell himself to wreak havoc, found that evil was an integral part of all people. Depressed, he returned home and had a night of meaningless sex with Darla—which, miraculously, caused him to regain his conscience and sense of purpose. He then revived Lochley, who had attempted suicide and saved the rest of his team from a group of demons determined to destroy them. Afterward he went to work for the people he had previously fired—he just wanted to help people. At season's end Cordelia was swept into an alternate universe, to Pylea, Lorne's home world. He joined the gang trying to get her back and was beheaded by his people—but got his body back and was okay.

At the start of the 2001–2002 season neurotic Fred, who had helped the gang get back from Pylea, and had returned with them, was in love with Angel. Darla was very pregnant with Angel's child and in November, when she showed up at his office, he did everything he could to protect her and their unborn child from both Wolfram & Hart and a vampire cult that believed the baby was The Miracle Child. At the same time a demon brought Holtz, a man whose family had been destroyed by Angel 250 years earlier, to the present to exact vengeance on Angel and Darla. Angel and his gang sought sanctuary in Caritas, Lorne's club, and Darla destroyed herself to allow the baby, Connor, to be born. Holtz let them leave with the baby but vowed not to show Angel any mercy. Still trying to figure out how to be a good father, Angel saw his problems get worse as Holtz and several other groups tried to kidnap Connor and kill him.

In January Cordelia, in order to survive her visions, was made into a partial demon by a guide from The Powers That Be. Fred and Gunn were attracted to each other, upsetting Wesley (who was also interested in her), and Angel began to acknowledge a growing feeling for Cordelia. He was a bit jealous when Groosalugg, who had been in love with Cordelia in Pylea, turned up in Los Angeles and romanced her. Sahijhan, the demon who had brought Holtz to the present to destroy Angel, was upset with his progress and sought Lilah's help. In March Wesley kidnapped Connor to protect him from a suddenly violent and bloodthirsty Angel. His plan fell apart when Justine, who worked for Holtz, stole Connor and took him to Holtz. They wanted to take him to live with them in Utah but Sahijhan, who wanted the baby dead, opened a portal to a Hell dimension through which Holtz ran with Connor in his arms. Angel wanted revenge on Wesley for letting Holtz get his son, and Wesley found himself ostracized from the people with whom he had previously worked. In the spring Connor returned from the Hell dimension as a teenage warrior determined to destroy Angel because Holtz had told him about his bloody past. Meanwhile, Lilah had an affair with Wesley as part of her effort to recruit him to work for Wolfram & Hart. At the end of the season Angel and Connor were starting to bond when Holtz, who had made peace with things and wanted to die, convinced Justine to kill him. Justine then made it look like Angel was responsible for Holtz's death and, with Connor's help, sealed Angel in a coffinlike box, which they dumped into the ocean. At the same time The Powers That Be told Cordelia it was time for her to move on to another dimension, and she had to leave before she could tell Angel she loved him.

That fall, with Angel and Cordelia both missing and Lorne having moved to Las Vegas, Fred and Gunn were the only ones left at Angel Investigations. Wesley pressured Justine into telling him what they had done to Angel, rescued him and told Fred and Gunn about Connor's betrayal. Despite everything, Angel tried to convince Connor he loved him, but the boy was having none of it. Meanwhile, Lilah beheaded Linwood, one of the senior people at Wolfram & Hart, and took over his office. After Angel and the gang brought Lorne back from Las Vegas, Cordelia showed up suffering from amnesia. Connor rescued her from a demon and became her protector, but when her memory returned she remembered that she loved Angel and her apocalyptic nightmares came true.

That frightening reality was The Beast from the center of the Earth, a superdemon who caused earthquakes, created firestorms and, in January, blotted out the sunlight in Los Angeles. Angel eventually defeated The Beast and the sunlight returned, but he found out that it had been controlled by Cordelia who, in turn, had been under the control of a higher being. That being had orchestrated everything from Connor's birth to Cordelia's ascension to the higher plane to Angel turning into his soulless self (Angelus) to Cordelia's pregnancy (Connor was the "father"). All this to give birth to something even more powerful—Jasmine (Gina Torres)—born as a sexy adult in April, with the hypnotic power to compel everyone to love her. She appeared benign but was, in reality, the incarnation of pure evil. Fred was the first to realize the truth, and she helped the rest of the gang—except for Connor—break free from Jasmine's spell.

As the season ended Connor was battling the gang on behalf of Jasmine, but Angel returned from an alternative dimension with a way to destroy her as she was broadcasting to a worldwide TV hook-up, breaking her hypnotic spell over the populace. Connor, realizing what she was, then killed her. Wolfram & Hart turned over control of its L.A. office to Angel, and placed teenage Connor with a suburban family whose memories were altered to make them believe he was their son. Everyone else's memory of Connor was erased—except that of Angel, the only one who now knew who he was.

ANGEL FALLS (*Drama*)

FIRST TELECAST: *August 26, 1993*

LAST TELECAST: *September 30, 1993*

BROADCAST HISTORY:

Aug 1993–Sep 1993, CBS Thu 10:00–11:00

CAST:

Eli Harrison .... Brian Kerwin
Genna Harrison .... Kim Cattrall
Rae Dawn Snow .... Chelsea Field
Sonny Snow .... Jeremy London
Luke Larson .... James Brolin
Hadley Larson .... Peggy Lipton
Toby Riopelle .... Robert Rusler
Irene Larson .... Jean Simmons
Molly Harrison .... Cassidy Rae
Sophie Harrison .... Ashlee Lauren
Brandi Dare .... Marlee Shelton
Rowena Dare .... Shannon Wilcox
Edie Wren Cox .... Shirley Knight
Sheriff Bailey .... William Frankfather
Robbie Larson .... Jimmy Baker

Set in rural Angel Falls, Montana, this drama focused on the intertwined relationships of three families—the Snows, the Harrisons, and the Larsons. Rae Dawn Snow, whose father had recently passed away, had moved back to town to run the family business, the Red Eye Pool Hall. It took very little time for her to get involved with rancher Eli Harrison, her high school sweetheart who was now married with two teenaged daughters. Her own 16-year-old, Sonny, was having problems adjusting to his new home and the rumors about his mother's promiscuous youth in Angel Falls. He found comfort in the arms of Molly Harrison, Eli's older daughter. Eli's former beauty queen wife, Genna, had been unhappy with their marriage for some time and was having an affair with young ranch hand Toby Riopelle. High school basketball coach Luke Larson and his wife, Hadley, were trying to cope with the loss of their infant son.

CBS premiered *Angel Falls* before the start of the 1993–1994 season to help it find an audience, to no avail.

ANGEL STREET (*Police Drama*)

FIRST TELECAST: *September 15, 1992*

LAST TELECAST: *October 3, 1992*

BROADCAST HISTORY:

Sep 1992, CBS Tue 9:00–11:00
Sep 1992–Oct 1992, CBS Sat 10:00–11:00

CAST:

Det. Anita King .... Robin Givens
Det. Dorothy Paretsky .... Pamela Gidley
Det. Kenny Branigan .... Ron Dean
Sgt. Ciamacco .... Joe Guzaldo
Det. Kanaskie .... Rick Snyder
Det. Llewellyn .... Luray Cooper
Det. Delaney .... Danny Goldring

Anita King and Dorothy Paretsky made an unlikely team. As the only female homicide detectives working out of a precinct in a rundown section of Chicago, they could hardly have been more different. Anita was a sophisticated, college-educated black woman with ambitions of making captain in a hurry, while Dorothy was a street-smart, working-class, Polish-American single parent. The series spent almost as much time dealing with their uneasy relationship with each other and with the good ol' boys at the station house (who considered them "Affirmative Action Babies"), as with the murders they were trying to solve.

The off-screen hostility between the two stars, coupled with very low ratings, made *Angel Street* the first casualty of the 1992–1993 season. It was dropped after only three episodes.

ANGIE (*Situation Comedy*)

FIRST TELECAST: *February 8, 1979*

LAST TELECAST: *October 2, 1980*

BROADCAST HISTORY:

Feb 1979–Aug 1979, ABC Thu 8:30–9:00
Sep 1979–Jan 1980, ABC Tue 8:30–9:00
Jan 1980–Feb 1980, ABC Mon 8:30–9:00
Apr 1980, ABC Sat 8:00–8:30
Jul 1980–Oct 1980, ABC Thu 8:30–9:00

CAST:

Angie Falco Benson .... Donna Pescow
Brad Benson .... Robert Hays
Theresa Falco .... Doris Roberts
Marie Falco .... Debralee Scott
Joyce Benson .... Sharon Spelman
Randall Benson .... John Randolph
Diedre "DiDi" Malloy .... Diane Robin
Hillary (1979) .... Tammy Lauren
Phipps .... Emory Bass
Mary Mary .... Valri Bromfield
Mary Grace .... Susan Duvall
Mary Katherine .... Nancy Lane
Gianni .... Tim Thomerson

THEME:

"Different Worlds," by Gimbel and Fox, sung by Maureen McGovern

Cinderella-story comedy about a pert young waitress who finds her handsome—and rich—young prince. When Brad Benson first walked into the Liberty Coffee Shop, Angie thought he was poor and began slipping him pastries. It turned out he was not only a pediatrician from the medical building across the street, but scion of one of Philadelphia's richest families. They fell in love and were married, much to the dismay of Brad's overbearing big sister, Joyce, and stuffy father, Randall, and to the bemusement of Angie's down-to-earth mama, Theresa. Mr. Falco had walked out 19 years earlier—"He went to get the paper"—but Theresa still kept a place at the table for him. She had raised Angie and younger sister Marie by running a newsstand. The Bensons had a different set of problems. Snobbish Joyce was three times divorced and undergoing therapy with a psychiatrist who hated her. DiDi was Angie's big-hearted, big-mouthed best friend at the coffee shop, and Phipps was the butler.

The newlyweds moved into Brad's mansion, but the palatial surroundings were too much so they later bought a smaller house, where Brad set up his practice on the first floor. At first Angie bought the coffee shop, to keep herself busy, but later she traded it for a beauty parlor, where Gianni was the pleasure-seeking hairstylist.

ABC aired reruns of *Angie* on weekday mornings from June–September 1985.

ANGRY BEAVERS (*Cartoon*)

BROADCAST HISTORY:

Nickelodeon
30 minutes
Produced: *1997–2001* (63 episodes)
Premiered: *April 19, 1997*

VOICES:

Norbert .... Nick Bakay
Daggett.............................. Richard Horvitz
Treeflower.............................. Cynthia Mann
Bing .... Victor Wilson
Big Rabbit .... Scott Weil
Barry the Bear .... John Garry
Truckee .... Mark Klastorin

After being kicked out of their parents' lodge, a couple of adolescent beavers with attitude built a bachelor pad dam of their own, and proceeded to cause chaos across the land, in this frantic Nichelodeon cartoon. Norbert was the bossy, hip, lazy one, and Daggett his dumb brother, who was constantly getting flattened. Why were they angry? Producer Matt Schauer explained, "cartoons are typically soft, everything's happy. I just went in the opposite direction."

ANIMAL CRACK-UPS (*Wildlife/Nature*)

FIRST TELECAST: *August 8, 1987*
LAST TELECAST: *September 12, 1987*
BROADCAST HISTORY:

Aug 1987–Sep 1987, ABC Sat 8:00–8:30

HOST:

Alan Thicke

What does an orangutan eat for lunch? Why do giraffes neck? Does an elephant have eyelashes? For those who have always wanted to know the answers to such questions, ABC presented this nature documentary cum quiz show about comical oddities of the animal world. A panel of guest celebrities made educated guesses, then viewers saw the answers in film clips supplied by the Tokyo Broadcasting System. The series moved to a more appropriate time slot (for kids) on Saturday morning effective September 12, 1987. The Saturday morning version ran for three seasons, leaving the air in September 1990.

ANIMAL KINGDOM, see *Animal World*

ANIMAL PLANET (Network) (*Documentary Cable Network*)

LAUNCHED:

June 1, 1996

SUBSCRIBERS (MAY 2003):

81.6 million (76% U.S.)

This specialty channel billed itself as "all animals, all the time," with programs such as *Amazing Tails; Petsburgh, U.S.A.; Crocodile Hunter; Pick of the Litter;* and *Breed: All About It.* The network's programming crown jewel during the late '90s was *Judge Wapner's Animal Court,* in which the famed judge sorted out disputes between pet owners. Most programs were documentary or instructional in nature, although reruns of a few entertainment series such as *Lassie* and *Gentle Ben* were also seen. Perhaps its most successful early program was the death-defying *Crocodile Hunter* with Australians Steve and Terri Irwin, first seen on Discovery in 1996 and a regular feature on Animal Planet beginning in early 1997. The show the network would rather forget was a scripted sitcom called *Beware of Dog,* which premiered in 2002 but was canceled after one telecast!

Animal Planet was launched in 1996 as a spin-off from the Discovery Channel, and because of its family-friendly content, was quickly picked up by a majority of cable systems across the country.

ANIMAL RESCUE WITH ALEX PAEN (*Documentary*)

BROADCAST HISTORY:

Syndicated only
60 minutes
Produced: *1997–*
Released: *September 1997*

HOST:

Alex Paen

This was the animal version of *Emergency Call,* another rescue series produced by host Alex Paen. Each episode followed the activities of rescue workers—firemen, veterinarians, police officers, and ordinary people—saving stranded, trapped, and endangered animals all over the world. In addition to actual rescue coverage, there were interviews with the lifesavers talking about their jobs, their love of animals, and the special problems involved in non-human rescues.

ANIMAL SECRETS (*Wildlife Documentary*)

FIRST TELECAST: *July 2, 1967*
LAST TELECAST: *August 27, 1967*
BROADCAST HISTORY:

Jul 1967–Aug 1967, NBC Sun 7:00–7:30

HOST:

Dr. Loren Eiseley

The mysteries of animal behavior were explored in this nature series hosted by Dr. Loren Eiseley, Professor of Anthropology at the University of Pennsylvania. Each episode dealt with a specific mystery—why do birds migrate, what makes bees buzz, how do fish talk. NBC got a lot of mileage out of this pleasant little series. It first ran on Saturday afternoons from October 1966 to April 1967, was rerun Sunday at 7 P.M. during the summer of 1967, then was rerun again on Sunday afternoons from January until May 1968.

ANIMAL WORLD (*Wildlife Documentary*)

FIRST TELECAST: *June 16, 1968*
LAST TELECAST: *September 12, 1971*
BROADCAST HISTORY:

Jun 1968–Sep 1968, NBC Sun 6:30–7:00
May 1969–Sep 1969, CBS Thu 7:30–8:00
Apr 1970–Sep 1970, ABC Thu 7:30–8:00
Jul 1971–Sep 1971, CBS Sun 7:30–8:00

HOST:

Bill Burrud

Bill Burrud, who had previously made several true-life adventure films for theatrical release, produced and hosted this nature series, which showed wild animals in their natural habitats from locations all over the world. The title of the series was originally *Animal Kingdom,* but was changed to *Animal World* with the telecast that was aired on August 11, 1968. After a season on NBC, it moved to CBS as a late Sunday afternoon series in the fall of 1968. It returned to prime time on three occasions: on CBS in the summers of 1969 and 1971, and on ABC in the summer of 1970, followed by a final network run on Sunday afternoons on NBC from January to September of 1972. *Animal World* then went into syndication, with a mixture of reruns and new episodes. The last of the new episodes were produced in 1976.

ANIMALS ARE PEOPLE, TOO (*Animal Reality*)

FIRST TELECAST: *April 17, 1999*

LAST TELECAST: *August 21, 1999*

BROADCAST HISTORY:

Apr 1999–May 1999, PAX Sat 8:00–9:00

Jul 1999–Aug 1999, PAX Sat 8:00–9:00

HOST:

Alan Thicke

At the start of the first episode of this gentle series host Alan Thicke came out with his dog, Max, and told viewers that "Animals see each day as a chance to have a good time with their human friends." He then proceeded to prove it with funny and heartwarming stories and vignettes about a dancing border collie, a polar bear that played in a pool with its human friend, a brown Labrador that served as caretaker and helper for its injured young owner, a cat "super-model," a veterinarian in Thailand who only treated elephants, a "wedding" of two dogs, an orphaned beluga whale adopted by a small village in Nova Scotia and a cat therapist in New York. Between segments Thicke made silly jokes about the stories.

ANIMORPHS (*Science Fiction*)

BROADCAST HISTORY:

Nickelodeon

30 minutes

Produced: *1998–1999* (26 episodes)

Premiered: *September 4, 1998*

CAST:

Jake Berenson .... Shawn Ashmore

Rachel Berenson .... Brooke Nevin

Marco .... Boris Cabrera

Cassie .... Nadia Nascimento

Tobias .... Christopher Ralph

Aximili-Esgarrouth-Isthill .... Paulo Costanzo

Five teenagers were the world's only defense against a race of invading aliens in this adaptation of K. A. Applegate's rather derivative science fiction books. It seems that the evil Yeerks planned to conquer Earth by implanting slugs into the ears of unsuspecting humans, who thereupon became their slaves, called "controllers." Anyone might be a controller—the traffic cop, that obnoxious teacher, maybe your own brother. (Is the plot beginning to sound familiar?) In the premiere, Jake and his friends were warned of this nefarious scheme by a dying Andalite "good alien," who also gave them a special power: the ability to morph into any animal they touched, for two hours. (Evidently it was easier to fight the Yeerks as a dog or pussycat than as a human!)

Jake, the leader, had a special grudge to settle, as his brother Tom had been turned into a controller. The rest of the team consisted of Jake's mall rat cousin Rachel; his buddy Marco; sensitive Cassie, whose parents were veterinarians; and a quiet new kid in town named Tobias. None would reveal their last names or where they lived, because "the Yeerks are after us." Homer was Jake's dog.

ANN JILLIAN (*Situation Comedy*)

FIRST TELECAST: *November 30, 1989*

LAST TELECAST: *August 19, 1990*

BROADCAST HISTORY:

Nov 1989, NBC Thu 8:30–9:00

Dec 1989–Jan 1990, NBC Sun 8:00–8:30

Aug 1990, NBC Sun 7:00–7:30

CAST:

Ann McNeil .... Ann Jillian

Lucy McNeil .... Lisa Rieffel

Robin Winkle .... Amy Lynne

Kaz Sumner .... Zachary Rosencrantz

Duke Howard .... Noble Willingham

Melissa Santos .... Chantel Rivera-Batisse

Sheila Hufnagel .... Cynthia Harris

A single-mom sitcom starring Ann Jillian as a widow who, after the death of her fireman husband, decided to move from New York to the northern California village of Marvel—the town where she and her late husband had honeymooned. Teenage daughter Lucy was mortified at the thought of going to California ("They're all gonna be tan and blond and say things like 'bitchin' and 'shoot the crawl' . . . we're gonna lose our New York edge!"), but mom was determined to start a new life. Start she did, with a job at a gift shop run by a sarcastic Easterner named Mrs. Hufnagel. Local teens included overhormoned Kaz, stuck-up Melissa, and insecure Robin. Kaz's easygoing grandfather Duke dropped in from time to time to try to help Ann and Lucy adjust, before their early departure to sitcom heaven.

ANN SOTHERN SHOW, THE (*Situation Comedy*)

FIRST TELECAST: *October 6, 1958*

LAST TELECAST: *September 25, 1961*

BROADCAST HISTORY:

Oct 1958–Jul 1960, CBS Mon 9:30–10:00 (OS)

Oct 1960–Dec 1960, CBS Thu 9:30–10:00

Dec 1960–Mar 1961, CBS Thu 7:30–8:00

Jul 1961–Sep 1961, CBS Mon 9:30–10:00

CAST:

Katy O'Connor .... Ann Sothern

Jason Macauley (1958–1959) .... Ernest Truex

Olive Smith .... Ann Tyrrell

Johnny Wallace (1958–1960) .... Jack Mullaney

Paul Martine (1958–1959) .... Jacques Scott

Flora Macauley (1958–1959) .... Reta Shaw

James Devery (1959–1961) .... Don Porter

Dr. Delbert Gray (1960–1961) .... Louis Nye

Woody (1960–1961) .... Ken Berry

Oscar Pudney (1960–1961) .... Jesse White

Katy O'Connor was the assistant manager of the plush Bartley House Hotel in New York. Her first boss, Jason Macauley, was transferred to Calcutta in the March 9, 1959, episode, but Katy's hopes of succeeding him as manager were torpedoed when James Devery arrived to fill the job. Katy's secretary, roommate, and best friend was Olive Smith, who developed a romantic interest during the 1960–1961 season in the person of dentist Delbert Gray. Don Porter and Ann Tyrrell had been Ann Sothern's co-stars in her previous series, *Private Secretary*, and they joined her here in amusing tales of the problems encountered in running a big-city hotel.

ANNA AND THE KING (*Situation Comedy*)
FIRST TELECAST: *September 17, 1972*
LAST TELECAST: *December 31, 1972*
BROADCAST HISTORY
Sep 1972–Dec 1972, CBS Sun 7:30–8:00
CAST:
King of Siam........................ Yul Brynner
Anna Owens..................... Samantha Eggar
Kralahome.......................... Keye Luke
Louis Owens........................ Eric Shea
Crown Prince Chulalongkorn.......... Brian Tochi
Lady Thiang.......................... Lisa Lu

It was in 1951, while preparing for his starring role in Rodgers and Hammerstein's new musical *The King and I*, that Yul Brynner first shaved his head, to add realism to his portrayal. The role and the bald pate both became Brynner trademarks; he brought them to the film version of the musical in 1956 and to this short-lived television comedy version in 1972. Based on Margaret Landon's novel *Anna and the King of Siam*, the story was set in the 1860s and involved a young schoolteacher, a widow with a 12-year-old son, who had been hired by the King of Siam to educate his royal offspring. (The king's many wives, of whom Lady Thiang was most important, had borne him a whole schoolful of children.) There was much conflict between the autocratic king and the stubborn, strong-willed teacher, but there was also a developing respect and affection.

ANNA NICOLE SHOW, THE (*Documentary*)
BROADCAST HISTORY:
E! Entertainment
30 minutes
Original episodes: *2002–*
Premiered: *August 4, 2002*
REGULARS:
Anna Nicole Smith
Howard K. Stern
Kim Walther
Daniel Smith

One of Hollywood's more colorful denizens, Anna Nicole Smith, a large blonde with huge breasts and a bizarre life, was the subject of this humorous documentary series. The cartoon opening mocked her story—from waitress in a Texas diner, to topless dancer, to *Playboy* Playmate (1993), to Guess? jeans model, to her marriage (in 1994) to 89-year-old oil billionaire J. Howard Marshall II, who died shortly thereafter. Her squeaky voice, impulsive behavior and little-girl innocence led some to call her "a human train wreck," but viewers made *The Anna Nicole Show* one of the top cable hits of the summer of 2002. In her entourage were devoted friend and lawyer Howard K. Stern (no relation to the radio personality); tattooed, purple-haired young assistant Kim; shy, 16-year-old son Daniel, and pampered black toy poodle Sugar Pie. Episodes dealt with Anna's search for a house, attempts to furnish it (including a long-running battle between Stern and decorator Bobby Trendy), an impromptu trip to Las Vegas for lap dancing and revelry, and appearances at celebrity events as well as *The Tonight Show* and *Larry King Live*. "Ah love mah paparazzi," she drawled.

Anna had previously been the subject of one of the top-rated episodes of *E! True Hollywood Stories*, which gave the network the idea for this show.

ANNIE MCGUIRE (*Situation Comedy*)
FIRST TELECAST: *October 26, 1988*
LAST TELECAST: *December 28, 1988*
BROADCAST HISTORY:
Oct 1988–Dec 1988, CBS Wed 8:30–9:00
CAST:
Annie McGuire................. Mary Tyler Moore
Nick McGuire......................... Denis Arndt
Emma Block...................... Eileen Heckart
Red McGuire...................... John Randolph
Lenny McGuire (age 14)............. Adrien Brody
Debbie McGuire (9)........... Cynthia Marie King
Lewis Block (12)................ Bradley Warden

Mary Tyler Moore had been one of CBS' biggest stars in the 1960s *(The Dick Van Dyke Show)* and the 1970s *(The Mary Tyler Moore Show)*. Although she had considerable later success in both films and on Broadway, she seemed unable to repeat her earlier triumphs on the small screen. *Annie McGuire* was her fourth consecutive TV failure (see her two *Mary* series and *The Mary Tyler Moore Hour*).

Annie and Nick were newlyweds, each with children from their first marriages. She was a divorcee working as Deputy Coordinator of Human Relations for the Manhattan borough president's office, and he was a recently widowed structural engineer. She had a son named Lewis and he had two children, Lenny and Debbie. Stories revolved around the adjustments made by both the adults and children in this merged household as well as the additional conflicts caused by Annie's flaming liberal mother Emma and Nick's ultra-conservative father Red.

ANNIE OAKLEY (*Western*)
BROADCAST HISTORY:
Syndicated and network daytime
30 minutes
Produced: *Apr 1953–Dec 1956* (81 episodes)
Released: *January 1954*
CAST:
Annie Oakley.......................... Gail Davis
Deputy Sheriff Lofty Craig........... Brad Johnson
Tagg Oakley...................... Jimmy Hawkins

Pigtails and pistols were the formula in one of the 1950s' more unusual Westerns. Five-foot-two, 95 pounds, and cute as a button, Annie was also a crack shot and the scourge of badmen around her hometown of Diablo, where she lived with her kid brother, Tagg (the rest of the immediate family was unaccounted for). Towering Deputy Lofty Craig was her friend and silent suitor, and Annie's uncle, Luke MacTavish, was the seldom-seen town sheriff. Co-starring were the horses—Annie's Target, Lofty's Forest, and Tagg's Pixie.

Gail Davis was discovered by Gene Autry, who featured her in nearly 20 of his movies, 30 of his own program's episodes, and then spun her off into this series of her own, which was produced by his company. She really was a good rider and trick shot, performing in Autry's traveling rodeo as well. She once said, "So far as I'm concerned, I'm going to be Annie Oakley for the rest of my born days," and apparently she was right. She later managed other celebrities.

The real Annie Oakley lived from 1859 to 1926, and was an exhibition sharpshooter for Buffalo Bill and other traveling shows. She traveled around the world, and once shot a cigarette from the mouth of Kaiser Wilhelm II.

Annie Oakley reruns were seen on ABC on Saturday and Sunday daytime from 1959 to 1960, and 1964 to 1965.

ANOTHER DAY (*Situation Comedy*)

FIRST TELECAST: *April 8, 1978*
LAST TELECAST: *April 29, 1978*
BROADCAST HISTORY:
Apr 1978, CBS Sat 9:00–9:30
CAST:
Don Gardner .... David Groh
Ginny Gardner .... Joan Hackett
Olive Gardner .... Hope Summers
Kelly Gardner .... Lisa Lindgren
Mark Gardner .... Al Eisenmann

Don Gardner was a somewhat old-fashioned young businessman trying to live up to his expectations of the American dream despite limited finances. Even with the extra income provided by his wife Ginny, who had recently returned to work, there never seemed to be enough money. With an inhibited 12-year-old son, Mark, and a totally uninhibited teenage daughter, Kelly, things were never normal in the Gardner family. Adding to the confusion was Don's complaining mother, Olive, who completed the household.

ANSWER YES OR NO (*Quiz*)

FIRST TELECAST: *April 30, 1950*
LAST TELECAST: *July 23, 1950*
BROADCAST HISTORY:
Apr 1950–Jul 1950, NBC Sun 10:30–11:00
EMCEE:
Moss Hart

This quiz show featured a celebrity panel. Arlene Francis was the only panelist to remain for the entire three-month run of the program. The typical question asked of the panel was "What would you do in this situation?", to which they responded with comic answers.

ANSWERS FOR AMERICANS (*Discussion*)

FIRST TELECAST: *November 11, 1953*
LAST TELECAST: *February 24, 1954*
BROADCAST HISTORY:
Nov 1953–Feb 1954, ABC Wed 8:30–9:00
MODERATOR:
Hardy Burt
PERMANENT PANEL:
Brig. General Frank Howley, Vice Chancellor, New York University
Devin Garrity, publisher
John K. Norton, Columbia University
Dr. Charles Hodges, New York University

This public affairs program was presented in cooperation with *Facts Forum*. The prestigious panel discussed with equally prestigious guests such lofty issues as "Where Does the Eisenhower Administration Stand Today?", "Should Red China Be Admitted to the UN?", and "What Can Be Done About Korea?" After a brief prime-time run the program continued on Sunday afternoon until June 1954.

ANTAGONISTS, THE (*Legal Drama*)

FIRST TELECAST: *March 26, 1991*
LAST TELECAST: *May 30, 1991*
BROADCAST HISTORY:
Mar 1991, CBS Tue 9:30–11:00
Mar 1991–May 1991, CBS Thu 9:00–10:00
CAST:
Jack Scarlett .... David Andrews
Kate Ward .... Lauren Holly
Joanie Rutledge .... Lisa Jane Persky
Asst. D.A. Marvin Thompson .... Brent Jennings
Clark Munsinger .... Matt Roth

Set in Los Angeles, *The Antagonists* was the story of Jack Scarlett, an ambitious defense attorney noted for his unpredictable and unconventional style, and Kate Ward, a bright, young, by-the-book prosecutor for the District Attorney's office. Away from the courtroom they were friends with a developing relationship, but their confrontations in court, particularly when Jack's approach and point of view were at odds with Kate's, kept getting in the way. Other regulars were Joanie, Kate's good friend and fellow prosecutor; Marvin, their politically ambitious boss; and Clark, a bookish law student who worked as a clerk at Jack's law firm.

ANY DAY NOW (*Drama*)

BROADCAST HISTORY:
Lifetime
60 minutes
Produced: *1998–2002* (88 episodes)
Premiered: *August 18, 1998*
CAST:
Mary Elizabeth (M.E.) O'Brien Sims .... Annie Potts
Mary Elizabeth (as child) (1998–2001)
.... Mae Middleton
Mary Elizabeth (as child) (2001–2002)
.... Olivia Hack
Rene Jackson .... Lorraine Toussaint
Rene (as child) (1998–2001) ...... Shari Dyon Perry
Rene (as child) (2001–2002) .. Maya Elise Goodwin
Sara Jackson .... Donzaleigh Abernathy
Colliar Sims .... Chris Mulkey
Colliar (as child) .... Dan Byrd
Kelly Sims Williams .... Olivia Friedman
**Davis Sims (age 12)* .... Calvin Devault
**Catherine O'Brien* .... Nancy McLoughlin
**Bill Moody (1999–2000)* .... Richard Biggs
Joe Lozano (1999–2002) .... Bronson Picket
Lakeisha Reynolds (1999–2002) ... Taneka Johnson
Ajoni Williams (1999–2002) .... Derrex Brady
**Teresa O'Brien* .... Elise Shirley
**James Jackson* .... John Lafayette
**Clyde "Turk" Terhune (2001–2002)*
.... William Allen Young

*Occasional

THEME:
"Any Day Now," by Bob Hilliard and Burt Bacharach

A renewed friendship between two very different women was the theme of this sensitive drama on cable's Lifetime network. White tomboy Mary Elizabeth and shy black girl Rene had been best friends when they were growing up in 1960s Birmingham, Alabama. That friendship had ended abruptly when M.E. became pregnant by ne'er-do-well local boy Colliar Sims, and Rene had refused to be supportive.

M.E. went on to become a mother of three by the good-hearted but none-too-successful Colliar, a laborer, and their life together had brought many disappointments. Their firstborn, Bobby, drowned at age five; teenage Kelly was a constant challenge, as rebellious as M.E. had been in her youth; Davis was their 12-year-old. The family eked out a living, as M.E. dreamed of becoming a writer. Meanwhile Rene, the daughter of a successful and progressive civil rights lawyer, had left Birmingham and become an attorney herself, rising to join the power elite in Washington, D.C. Her dream of raising a family had been put on hold as she pursued her career.

It was the death of Rene's father, James, that brought Rene and M.E. back together in 1998, thirty years after they had parted. To the disgust of her self-absorbed boyfriend Garret, Rene moved back to Alabama to take up her father's work and renew her friendship with her feisty white friend from "the other side of the tracks." Scenes alternated between their exploits as children (shown in sepia tones) and as adults.

During the course of the series' run Rene dated first Bill and then Turk, to whom she ultimately proposed (the women were in charge here!). M.E. got her book *Port Dixie* published and began writing articles. The biggest change in the Sims household, however, came when Kelly brought home a black boyfriend, Ajoni, by whom she became pregnant, married, and had a baby (Emmett), in that order. In the final episode M.E. was offered a teaching position at a local college, and Rene finally wed her Turk.

ANYBODY CAN PLAY (*Quiz*)

FIRST TELECAST: *July 6, 1958*
LAST TELECAST: *December 8, 1958*
BROADCAST HISTORY:
Jul 1958–Sep 1958, ABC Sun 8:30–9:00
Oct 1958–Dec 1958, ABC Mon 9:30–10:00
EMCEE:
George Fenneman
ASSISTANT:
Judy Bamber (Nov–Dec)

In this quiz show, four studio contestants competed for cash and prizes by answering questions on a point system. The questions ranged over many subjects; for instance, contestants were asked to name a celebrity, identify a song or movie from short clips, or identify an object solely by touch. Contestants remained on the show for four weeks (later reduced to two), and viewers at home had the opportunity to participate in a $10,000 jackpot competition by sending in estimates of the contestants' age, weight, ability, and related data. Judy Bamber joined George Fenneman as cohost during the program's final month.

ANYONE CAN WIN (*Quiz*)

FIRST TELECAST: *July 14, 1953*
LAST TELECAST: *September 1, 1953*
BROADCAST HISTORY;
Jul 1953–Sep 1953, CBS Tue 9:00–9:30
MODERATOR:
Al Capp

Each week a different panel of four celebrities competed in a general quiz, with cartoonist Al Capp serving as moderator. Before the show started, all members of the studio audience were asked to pick which celebrity they thought would answer the most questions correctly. At the end of each show, those who had correctly guessed the winner shared $2,000 in cash.

ANYTHING BUT LOVE (*Situation Comedy*)

FIRST TELECAST: *March 7, 1989*
LAST TELECAST: *June 10, 1992*
BROADCAST HISTORY:
Mar 1989–Apr 1989, ABC Tue 9:30–10:00
Aug 1989, ABC Tue 9:30–10:00
Oct 1989–Mar 1990, ABC Wed 9:30–10:00
Jul 1990–Sep 1990, ABC Wed 9:30–10:00
Feb 1991–Jun 1991, ABC Wed 9:30–10:00
Aug 1991–Oct 1991, ABC Wed 10:00–10:30
Nov 1991–Feb 1992, ABC Wed 9:30–10:00
May 1992–Jun 1992, ABC Wed 9:30–10:00
CAST:
Hannah Miller .... Jamie Lee Curtis
Marty Gold .... Richard Lewis
Norman Keil (1989) .... Louis Giambalvo
Catherine Hughes .... Ann Magnuson
*Jules "Julie" Kramer/Bennett** .... Richard Frank
Robin "Mrs. Schmenkman" Dulitski... Holly Fulger
Leo Miller (1989) .... Bruce Kirby
Pamela Peyton-Finch (1989) .... Sandy Faison
Brian Allquist (1989–1990) .... Joseph Maher
Harold (1989–1990) .... Billy Van Zandt
Kelly (1989–1990) .... Kate McNeil
Mike Urbanek (1991–1992)............ Bruce Weitz
*Name changed in 1989.

When cheerful, aspiring writer Hannah met neurotic investigative reporter Marty on a plane and calmed his frazzled nerves, she did not imagine it would lead to a new career, much less to romance. Marty got her an interview at *Chicago Weekly* magazine, where she landed a job as a researcher sitting right across from his desk. It wasn't love at first (or even fiftieth) sight for these two opposites, but their mutual attraction grew until they were indeed in love by the second season.

Looking on and kibitzing as the budding romance developed were an assortment of eccentric friends and co-workers. Norman was the blustery editor, replaced in the fall of 1989 by hard driving, super chic Catherine (who promoted Hannah to writer); Julie was the editor's fawning assistant; Pamela, a catty writer; and Leo, Hannah's outdoorsman dad. Brian arrived in the fall of 1989 as a very British TV critic; he lasted only one season before going berserk in Marshall Field's department store and smashing all the TV sets on display. Hannah got encouragement from landlady and best friend Robin, but none from no-nonsense columnist Mike, who joined the staff in 1991.

ANYWHERE, U.S.A. (*Documentary Drama*)

FIRST TELECAST: *November 9, 1952*
LAST TELECAST: *December 14, 1952*
BROADCAST HISTORY:
Nov 1952–Dec 1952, ABC Sun 10:30–11:00

CAST:

Doctor .... Eddie Dowling

Dramatized documentary films on health subjects, produced by the Health Information Foundation, covered such topics as physical therapy, the need for checkups, and new drugs. Robert Preston also appeared as a doctor on some telecasts of this series.

APT. 2-F (*Situation Comedy*)

BROADCAST HISTORY:

MTV
30 minutes
Produced: *1997* (13 episodes)
Premiered: *July 13, 1997*

CAST:

Randy .... Randy Sklar
Jason .... Jason Sklar
Zach .... Zach Galifianakis
Danny .... Matt Price

Also:

Florence Clutch
Emmy Laybourne
Leila Sbitiani

Randy and Jason Sklar were twin brothers from St. Louis who moved to Manhattan in search of a life, finding nutty friends and unexpected situations in this rather traditional sitcom. Earnest brother Randy was a New York University film student who worked at a video store called The Village Vidiot. His goofy sibling Jason worked for a large corporation called Products Inc. Their little adventures together were periodically interrupted by short, strange films they had made, such as *The Bleeding Fist of Liberty*. Zach was a funny friend, Danny a jumpy teen, and Stacy, Randy's sensible girlfriend.

APOLLO COMEDY HOUR, THE (*Comedy Variety*)

BROADCAST HISTORY:

Syndicated only
60 minutes
Produced: *1992–1995* (78 episodes)
Released: *October 1992*

REGULARS:

Derrick Fox
Kent Jackman
Paula Jai Parker (1992–1993)
Yusuf Lamont
Randl Ask (1992–1994)
Lisa Carson (1992–1993)
Kool Bubba Ice
Deborah Magdalena (1993–1994)
Grace Garland (1993–1995)
Michael Maburn (1993–1995)
Ronda Fowler (1994–1995)
Karen June Sanchez (1994–1995)
Ilan Kwittken (1994–1995)

This sketch-comedy series was produced by the same people who produced *It's Showtime at the Apollo*. There was a regular troupe of young, primarily black and Hispanic performers (Randl Ask and later Ilan Kwittken were the only whites), along with guest performers, standup comedians, and musical acts.

APPLE PIE (*Situation Comedy*)

FIRST TELECAST: *September 23, 1978*
LAST TELECAST: *September 30, 1978*
BROADCAST HISTORY:

Sep 1978, ABC Sat 8:30–9:00

CAST:

Ginger-Nell Hollyhock .... Rue McClanahan
"Fast Eddie" Murtaugh .... Dabney Coleman
Grandpa Hollyhock .... Jack Gilford
Anna Marie Hollyhock .... Caitlin O'Heaney
Junior Hollyhock .... Derrel Maury

"You can't pick your own relatives" goes the old saying, but that's exactly what a lonely hairdresser named Ginger-Nell Hollyhock did in this 1978 comedy. Placing classified ads in the local papers, she recruited a con man husband ("Fast Eddie"), a tap-dancing daughter (Anna Marie), a son who wanted to fly like a bird (Junior), and a tottering old grandfather (Grandpa), all of whom came to live together—for the laughs. The setting was Kansas City, Missouri, in 1933, which added period color.

The program was based on the play *Nourish the Beast*, by Steve Tesich.

APPLE'S WAY (*General Drama*)

FIRST TELECAST: *February 10, 1974*
LAST TELECAST: *January 12, 1975*
BROADCAST HISTORY:

Feb 1974–Jan 1975, CBS Sun 7:30–8:30

CAST:

George Apple .... Ronny Cox
Barbara Apple .... Lee McCain
Paul Apple .... Vincent Van Patten
Cathy Apple .... Patti Cohoon
Patricia Apple (1974) .... Franny Michel
Patricia Apple (1974–1975) .... Kristy McNichol
Steven Apple .... Eric Olson
Grandfather Aldon .... Malcolm Atterbury

This drama concerned the successful architect George Apple, who decided to leave the rat race of big-city life and return with his wife Barbara and their four children to his home town of Appleton, Iowa. This small rural community, which had been founded by George's ancestors, was a far cry from Los Angeles. It provided even more adjustment problems for George's city-bred children than for his wife and himself, but in time the entire family came to appreciate their new surroundings. George was an idealist, with compassion for his fellow man and strong religious convictions, and he found himself getting involved in numerous causes, sometimes being looked upon by the townspeople as a bit of a kook.

APPOINTMENT WITH ADVENTURE (*Dramatic Anthology*)

FIRST TELECAST: *April 3, 1955*
LAST TELECAST: *April 1, 1956*
BROADCAST HISTORY:

Apr 1955–Apr 1956, CBS Sun 10:00–10:30

This live half-hour series, using studio sets, took viewers to various parts of the world, as well as different locations in the United States. Its contemporary and period stories were set in such locales as World War II Europe and Civil War America. Among the better-known performers who appeared in these plays were Polly Bergen, Betsy Palmer, Gena Rowlands, Phyllis Kirk, Dane Clark, Tony Randall, Gene Barry, and Paul Newman.

APPOINTMENT WITH LOVE, see *ABC Dramatic Shorts—1952–1953*

AQUANAUTS, THE (*Adventure*)
FIRST TELECAST: *September 14, 1960*
LAST TELECAST: *September 27, 1961*
BROADCAST HISTORY:
Sep 1960–Sep 1961, CBS Wed 7:30–8:30
CAST:
Drake Andrews .... Keith Larsen
Larry Lahr .... Jeremy Slate
Mike Madison .... Ron Ely
The Captain (1961) .... Charles Thompson

Taking the same format as the highly successful syndicated series *Sea Hunt, The Aquanauts* told stories of the adventures of two professional salvage divers based in Southern California. The human and marine perils they faced on assignments created the suspense and action. Drake Andrews and Larry Lahr were the two young divers at the start of the season. Andrews was last seen in the episode that was aired on January 18. The following week Larry Lahr recruited Mike Madison as a replacement. On February 15, the title of the series was changed to *Malibu Run.* Although the principals still participated in salvage operations, they had moved into the Malibu Beach area and set up an aquatic sports shop. A new member of the cast was the Captain, an old salt who lived nearby and who became their good friend.

ARCHER (*Detective Drama*)
FIRST TELECAST: *January 30, 1975*
LAST TELECAST: *March 13, 1975*
BROADCAST HISTORY:
Jan 1975–Mar 1975, NBC Thu 9:00–10:00
CAST:
Lew Archer .... Brian Keith
Lt. Barney Brighton .... John P. Ryan

Lew Archer was the antithesis of the slick, sexy, superefficient detective so often seen on television. He was a real person, a man of simple tastes, who used his analytic ability rather than brute strength or gimmicks to solve crimes. Although he was a former cop, and generally worked with the police, Archer was not above bending the law if it would help him nail the culprit. Perhaps the lack of gimmicks is why the program failed to catch on.

The series was based on the central character in Ross Macdonald's highly successful mystery novels.

ARCHIE BUNKER'S PLACE, see *All in the Family*

ARE YOU AFRAID OF THE DARK? (*Supernatural Anthology*)
BROADCAST HISTORY:
Nickelodeon
30 minutes
Produced: *1992–1996, 1999–2000* (91 episodes)
Premiered: *August 15, 1992*
CAST ("THE MIDNIGHT SOCIETY"):
Frank (1992–1996) .... Jason Alisharan
Gary (1992–1996) .... Ross Hull
Betty Ann (1992–1996) .... Raine Pare-Coull
Kiki (1992–1996) .... Jodie Resther
Kristen (1992–1993) .... Rachel Blanchard
David (1992–1993) .... Nathaniel Moreau
Eric (1992–1993) .... Jacob Tierney
Tucker (1994–2000) .... Daniel De Santo
Sam (1994–1996) .... Joanna Garcia
Stig (1995–1996) .... Codie Wilbee
Quinn (1999–2000) .... Kareem Blackwell
Meghan (1999–2000) .... Elisha Cuthbert
Andy (1999–2000) .... David Deveau
Vange (1999–2000) .... Vanessa Lengies

A scary, but never gory, anthology of ghost stories featuring kids of various ages. Each episode began with a group of kids called "The Midnight Society" seated around a flickering campfire. As one of them began a yarn the scene shifted and the story, usually involving haunted houses, phantom cars, mysterious neighbors, or the like, unfolded. The series went out of production in 1996, but returned in 1999 with a new "Midnight Society" to host the creepy tales. The leader and only holdover was Tucker, brother of original Midnighter, Gary.

ARE YOU HOT? THE SEARCH FOR AMERICA'S SEXIEST PEOPLE (*Reality*)
FIRST TELECAST: *February 13, 2003*
LAST TELECAST: *April 5, 2003*
BROADCAST HISTORY:
Feb 2003–Mar 2003, ABC Thu 9:00–10:00
Apr 2003, ABC Sat 9:00–11:00
HOST:
J. D. Roberto
JUDGES:
Randolph Duke
Rachel Hunter
Lorenzo Lamas

In case the title didn't adequately describe this skin parade, host J. D. Roberto made it clear at the start: "We are the show that thinks talent is completely overrated." What followed was a parade of young hunks and hunkettes baring as much skin as legally permissible on network television, while a rowdy audience cheered and three judges offered blunt assessments, rating each contestant on face, body and sex appeal ("Too big a jaw, thin lips, I give you a five"). The judges were fashion designer Randolph Duke, who could be rather cutting; heartthrob actor Lorenzo Lamas, the hip one ("Hey, man"), and supermodel Rachel Hunter. Hunter seemed a bit embarrassed by the proceedings, but Lamas went with the flow, at one point even using a laser pointer to highlight a woman's crotch and slightly saggy rear end. There were plenty of close-ups of breasts and buns, and a bright sign flashed HOT or NOT while flames danced on a screen behind the contestants.

The first four episodes each featured 32 "hotties" (16 men, 16 women) from a different Hot Zone—the Northeast, Southeast, Northwest and Southwest. The four men and four women in each Hot Zone with the highest scores went on to the finals. The winner for each sex was then chosen via voting by viewers at home. Everybody on this show looked pretty buff, but taking home the grand prizes were Chantille Boudousque from New Orleans and David Maxwell from San Diego, who each got $50,000 and a vacation in Tahiti.

ARE YOU POSITIVE (*Sports Quiz/Panel*)
FIRST TELECAST: *July 6, 1952*
LAST TELECAST: *August 24, 1952*

BROADCAST HISTORY:

Jul 1952–Aug 1952, NBC Sun 6:00–6:30

EMCEE:

Bill Stern (Jul 6–20)

Frank Coniff (Jul 27–Aug 24)

REGULAR PANELISTS:

Jimmy Cannon (*New York Post* columnist)

Frank Fisch (radio and TV sports commentator)

This weekly live sports quiz program, which premiered as *Bill Stern's Sports Quiz,* featured Stern and a panel of three people familiar with all aspects of sports. The panelists were asked to identify a sports personality from photographs taken when he/she was a child, or occasionally from a negative of a photograph. Suggestions for personalities to be used were sent in by the viewing audience. Frank Coniff replaced Bill Stern as emcee on July 27.

ARMCHAIR DETECTIVE (*Detective Drama*)

FIRST TELECAST: *Jul 6, 1949*

LAST TELECAST: *September 28, 1949*

BROADCAST HISTORY:

Jul 1949–Sep 1949, CBS Wed 9:00–9:30

CAST:

Mr. Crime Interrogator .... John Milton Kennedy

Mr. Crime Authority .... H. Allen Smith

Each week two one-act whodunit plays were presented in this series of films. The plays contained clues that pointed to the solution, which was explained in detail at the end of each story by H. Allen Smith, a member of the California State Legislature.

ARMED FORCES HOUR, THE (*Musical Variety*)

FIRST TELECAST: *February 4, 1951*

LAST TELECAST: *May 6, 1951*

BROADCAST HISTORY:

Feb 1951–May 1951, DUM Sun 8:00–9:00

This was a frankly promotional half hour for the U.S. Armed Forces, produced by the Department of Defense and using a musical variety format to lure viewers to watch short films about the services. Entertainment was by servicemen-performers such as The Singing Sergeants and the U.S. Navy Dance Band appearing on a USO Club set, joined by professional entertainers such as Frances Langford and Marion Morgan. Acts were interspersed with films about the army, the navy, and the air force.

ARMSTRONG BY REQUEST (*Dramatic Anthology*)

FIRST TELECAST: *July 8, 1959*

LAST TELECAST: *September 16, 1959*

BROADCAST HISTORY:

Jul 1959–Sep 1959, CBS Wed 10:00–11:00

The summer 1959 replacement for *Armstrong Circle Theatre* was a series of repeats of six documentary dramas that had been presented on that program during the 1958–1959 season. The program alternated with *The U.S. Steel Hour.*

ARMSTRONG CIRCLE THEATRE (*Dramatic Anthology*)

FIRST TELECAST: *June 6, 1950*

LAST TELECAST: *August 28, 1963*

BROADCAST HISTORY:

Jun 1950–Jun 1955, NBC Tue 9:30–10:00

Sep 1955–Jun 1957, NBC Tue 9:30–10:30

Oct 1957–Aug 1963, CBS Wed 10:00–11:00 (OS)

HOST/NARRATOR:

Nelson Case (1950–1951)

Joe Ripley (1952–1953)

Bob Sherry (1953–1954)

Sandy Becker (1954–1955)

John Cameron Swayze (1955–1957)

Douglas Edwards (1957–1961)

Ron Cochran (1961–1962)

Henry Hamilton (1962–1963)

Armstrong Circle Theatre was one of the major dramatic anthology series of television's "Golden Age." At the outset it featured original dramas set in the contemporary world, many by noted writers. Serious treatments of such sensitive subjects as mental illness and racial intolerance alternated with occasional spoofs and comedies. Violence and morbidity were specifically avoided as Armstrong intended its program to be suitable for family viewing. Among the early telecasts was "The Parrot" (March 24, 1953), the first operetta commissioned for commercial television.

In 1955, when *Armstrong Circle Theatre* expanded to an hour, the format was changed to emphasize dramas based on real-life events, both headline-making ("S.O.S. from the *Andrea Doria*") and personal ("I Was Accused," the story of an immigrant threatened with deportation). One of the most notable telecasts of this period was "Nightmare in Red," a documentary on the history of Communism in Russia (December 27, 1955).

When it moved to CBS in 1957, as the program alternating with *The U.S. Steel Hour, Armstrong Circle Theatre* retained the documentary-drama format. The most popular topics during this period were related to the cold war. "The Vanished," about an Iron Curtain victim; "Thunder Over Berlin"; "Security Risk," about army counterintelligence; "The Spy Next Door"; "Crime Without a Country," about Interpol; "Window on the West," about Radio Free Europe; "Tunnel to Freedom," about refugees escaping to West Berlin; and "The Assassin," about a Soviet espionage agent. The other most prevalent format was the exposé: "The Meanest Crime in the World," about fraudulent medical practices; "Sound of Violence: The Juke Box Rackets"; "Full Disclosure," about security swindles; "The Antique Swindle"; "Smash-Up," about auto insurance company fraud; and "The Thief of Charity," among others.

ARMY SHOW, THE (*Situation Comedy*)

FIRST TELECAST: *September 13, 1998*

LAST TELECAST: *December 20, 1998*

BROADCAST HISTORY:

Sep 1998–Dec 1998, WB Sun 9:30–10:00

CAST:

Master Sgt. Dave Hopkins ... David Anthony Higgins

Pvt. Johnny Caesar .... John Sencio

Cpl. Rusty Link .... Toby Huss

Lt. Branford R. Handy .... Craig Anton

Col. John Henchy .... Harold Sylvester

Pvt. Eddie Mitterand .... Brian Posehn

Pvt. Ozzie .... Victor Togunde

Pvt. Lana Povic .... Ivana Milicevic

Sgt. Madeleine Tipton .... Mary Lynn Rajskub

This military comedy was set at mythical Fort Bendix, Florida, where Sgt. Dave was a fat, scheming con man running the mail depot on the base. Sarge was in charge of a group of misfits who did his bidding while he maneuvered around uptight Lt. Handy and newly arrived Col. Henchy. Hopkins's charges included Johnny, a long-haired party animal serving in the military instead of jail for his computer hacking activities; Eddie, a brilliant but incredibly neurotic nerd; Ozzie, a well-meaning man content to follow orders and not rock the boat; Lana, a tough, sexy young woman who didn't take any crap from the guys; and Rusty, a mechanic with delusions of Rambo and the hots for Lana. Sgt. Tipton was Col. Henchy's marginally competent, and totally insecure, administrative assistant.

Any resemblance between this series and the classic 1950s military comedy *The Phil Silvers Show* was purely intentional.

ARNIE (*Situation Comedy*)
FIRST TELECAST: *September 19, 1970*
LAST TELECAST: *September 9, 1972*
BROADCAST HISTORY:
Sep 1970–Sep 1971, CBS Sat 9:00–9:30
Sep 1971–Dec 1971, CBS Mon 10:30–11:00
Dec 1971–Sep 1972, CBS Sat 9:30–10:00
CAST:
Arnie Nuvo .... Herschel Bernardi
Lillian Nuvo .... Sue Ane Langdon
Hamilton Majors, Jr. .... Roger Bowen
Felicia Farfiss .... Elaine Shore
Neil Ogilvie .... Herb Voland
Richard Nuvo .... Del Russel
Andrea Nuvo .... Stephanie Steele
Julius .... Tom Pedi
Fred Springer .... Olan Soule
Randy Robinson (1971–1972)
.... Charles Nelson Reilly

Arnie Nuvo, a perfectly content loading dock foreman for the Continental Flange Company, unexpectedly found himself promoted to head of the Product Improvement Division. The sudden shift from blue-collar worker to white-collar executive made many drastic changes in Arnie's life. Suddenly he had all sorts of new challenges, new responsibilities, new sources of aggravation, and a substantial increase in pay. His social status was changed, and, with the exception of his good friend Julius, he was removed from the contact with his former co-workers. The adjustments he and his wife Lillian had to make, and the problems they had making them, provided the material for the comedy in this series.

AROUND THE TOWN, see *Girl about Town* for 1949 program by this name

AROUND THE TOWN (*Documentary*)
FIRST TELECAST: *January 7, 1950*
LAST TELECAST: *February 18, 1950*
BROADCAST HISTORY:
Jan 1950–Feb 1950, NBC Sat 9:30–10:00
HOST:
Bob Stanton

In this program, a mobile unit visited interesting places around New York City.

ARREST & TRIAL (*Police Documentary*)
BROADCAST HISTORY:
Syndicated only
30 minutes
Produced: *2000–2001*
Released: *September 2000*
HOST:
Brian Dennehy

Dramatized reenactments, interviews, and actual news footage of brutal crimes were interwoven with an explanation of the procedures the police used to solve them in this documentary series. Each segment started with the initial investigation of the crime and followed through to the trial verdict, accompanied by somewhat sensationalized narration ("The crime threatened to tear a small town apart!"). Produced by Dick Wolf, creator of the long-running NBC hit series *Law & Order*.

ARREST AND TRIAL (*Crime Drama*)
FIRST TELECAST: *September 15, 1963*
LAST TELECAST: *September 6, 1964*
BROADCAST HISTORY:
Sep 1963–Sep 1964, ABC Sun 8:30–10:00
CAST:
Det. Sgt. Nick Anderson .... Ben Gazzara
Attorney John Egan .... Chuck Connors
Deputy D.A. Jerry Miller .... John Larch
Assistant Deputy D.A. Barry Pine .... John Kerr
Det. Sgt. Dan Kirby .... Roger Perry
Det. Lt. Bone .... Noah Keen
Mitchell Harris .... Don Galloway
Jake Shakespeare .... Joe Higgins
Janet Okada .... Jo Anne Miya

Arrest and Trial was actually two separate but interwoven 45-minute programs, the first showing the commission of a crime, the police investigation, and the arrest; and the second depicting the trial. Ben Gazzara starred as Los Angeles police detective Nick Anderson in the first part, while Chuck Connors portrayed defense attorney John Egan (who tried to get Anderson's arrestees off the hook) in the second.

ARRESTING BEHAVIOR (*Situation Comedy*)
FIRST TELECAST: *August 18, 1992*
LAST TELECAST: *September 9, 1992*
BROADCAST HISTORY:
Aug 1992, ABC Tue 9:30–10:00
Aug 1992–Sep 1992, ABC Wed 9:30–10:00
CAST:
Officer Bill Ruskin .... Leo Burmester
Officer Donny Walsh .... Ron Eldard
Officer Pete Walsh .... Chris Mulkey
Connie Ruskin .... Lee Garlington
Rhonda Ruskin .... Amy Hathaway
Bill Ruskin, Jr. .... Eric Balfour
Seth Ruskin .... Joey Simmrin

This odd little comedy cop show was a takeoff on the numerous police "reality" series on television in the 1990s, such as *Cops* and *Real Stories of the Highway Patrol*. Middle-aged Bill and young, enthusiastic Donny were squad-car partners who were followed by hand-held cameras as they freed babies from locked cars, investigated unlikely cases of abuse, and arrested their neighbors in the peaceful town of Vista Valley, California. Meanwhile they never seemed to notice the real crimes taking place around them. There were running gags about their family lives as well, Bill getting into trouble with wife, Connie (a dog groomer), and his three kids, while Donny's ex and kids hoped he wouldn't show up. Pete was Donny's helpful brother.

ARROW SHOW, THE (*Comedy/Variety*)
FIRST TELECAST: *November 24, 1948*
LAST TELECAST: *May 19, 1949*
BROADCAST HISTORY:
Nov 1948–Dec 1948, NBC Wed 8:30–9:00
Dec 1948, NBC Wed 7:30–7:55
Nov 1948–May 1949, NBC Thu 8:00–8:30
HOST:
Phil Silvers (Nov 1948–Mar 1949)
Hank Ladd (Apr–May 1949)
REGULAR:
Jack Gilford
This was a comedy/variety show with guest stars and a rotating stable of "regulars," of whom only Jack Gilford remained for the full season. Also known as *The Phil Silvers Arrow Show* and *Arrow Comedy Theatre.*

ARSENIO (*Situation Comedy*)
FIRST TELECAST: *March 5, 1997*
LAST TELECAST: *April 9, 1997*
BROADCAST HISTORY:
Mar 1997–Apr 1997, ABC Wed 9:30–10:00
CAST:
Michael Atwood .... Arsenio Hall
Vivian Atwood .... Vivica A. Fox
Matthew Deveaux .... Alimi Ballard
Al O'Brien .... Kevin Dunn
Laura Lauman .... Shawnee Smith
Onetime late-night sensation Arsenio Hall took a stab at sitcom stardom in this surprisingly pedestrian series. Michael Atwood was an announcer for ASTV, an all-sports cable network in Atlanta. After 37 years of "confirmed bachelorhood," he had just married a sharp, good-looking attorney named Vivian. But women remained the greatest of mysteries to our cool dude, especially overachievers like his new bride, who hogged the bed and lived for her next promotion. Michael commiserated with his best friend Al, the big, somewhat dense six o'clock anchorman, while Vivian turned to her sarcastic, bleached-blond, punk friend Laura. Matthew was Vivian's lazy, Harvard-educated brother, who mooched off them.

The Cosby Show, it wasn't.

ARSENIO HALL SHOW, THE (*Talk*)
BROADCAST HISTORY:
Syndicated only
60 minutes
Produced: *1989–1994* (1,248 episodes)
Released: *January 3, 1989*
HOST:
Arsenio Hall
BAND:
Michael Wolff
ANNOUNCER:
Burton Richardson
Arsenio Hall had been the interim host on Fox's *The Late Show* during the summer of 1987 following Joan Rivers's departure. Although he had started to build an audience, his 13-week contract was not renewed and he moved on to act in the theatrical film *Coming to America* with his buddy Eddie Murphy. By the time Fox decided they wanted him back, Arsenio had been signed by Paramount to host his own syndicated late-night talk show.

When *The Arsenio Hall Show* premiered early in 1989, one week before CBS' competing *The Pat Sajak Show,* there was much speculation about whether either show could dent the ratings of Johnny Carson's *Tonight Show.* Arsenio, whose core audience of urban blacks broadened considerably with this series, prospered, while Pat Sajak floundered for fifteen months and went off the air.

Although the basic format was standard talk show—opening monologue, chat with celebrity guests, musical or comedy act performances—*The Arsenio Hall Show* quickly set itself apart from the competition. Mr. Hall's hip monologues, contemporary attitudes, choice of musical guests, and generally party-like atmosphere drew a sizable and loyal audience of younger viewers. Unlike his competition, he showcased black celebrity guests and rock, soul, and rap musicians. Even the house band (which Arsenio referred to as his "posse"), led by Michael Wolff, had a distinctly upbeat rock 'n' roll look and sound.

By the time Jay Leno replaced the retiring Johnny Carson on *The Tonight Show* the ratings for Arsenio Hall were already starting to slide. Arsenio's well-publicized feud with Leno over celebrity bookings and his threat to "kick Jay's ass" in the ratings provided more bad publicity than good. When David Letterman's new show on CBS started off by consistently winning the ratings war, many CBS affiliates that had previously been carrying Arsenio's show either canceled it or moved it to the wee small hours of the morning. In the spring of 1994 Arsenio announced that his show would air its last original episode in May. Among his guests during his last months were controversial black figures including Spike Lee, and Nation of Islam leader Louis Farrakhan. Reruns of *The Arsenio Hall Show* continued to air until September.

ART BAKER SHOW, THE, see *You Asked For It*

ART FORD ON BROADWAY (*Interview*)
FIRST TELECAST: *April 5, 1950*
LAST TELECAST: *June 30, 1950*
BROADCAST HISTORY:
Apr 1950–Jun 1950, ABC Wed/Thu/Fri 7:15–7:30
HOST:
Art Ford
On this short-lived Broadway chatter program, host Art Ford interviewed such guests as the manager of the Astor Hotel, a Broadway detective, and the author of a new book. During its final month on the air the program's title was altered to *Art Ford on the Broadways of the World.*

ART FORD SHOW, THE (*Quiz/Audience Participation*)
FIRST TELECAST: *July 28, 1951*
LAST TELECAST: *September 15, 1951*
BROADCAST HISTORY:
Jul 1951–Sep 1951, NBC Sat 7:30–8:00
EMCEE:
Art Ford
Each week three disc jockeys from stations around the country served as panelists trying to guess composers, vocalists, and orchestras of various records

played on the air. The disc jockey with the most correct answers at the end of the program received a special "Disc Jockey Oscar." Mr. Ford, himself a disc jockey on radio station WNEW in New York, also introduced each week a recording artist with a "million seller" who performed on the show.

An unusual feature of this program was that it also sought to publicize the good works done by many disc jockeys, such as their support of charities and their involvement in other public service activities.

ART LINKLETTER SHOW,THE (*Quiz/Audience Participation*)

FIRST TELECAST: *February 18, 1963*
LAST TELECAST: *September 16, 1963*
BROADCAST HISTORY:
Feb 1963–Sep 1963, NBC Mon 9:30–10:00
HOST:
Art Linkletter
REGULARS:
Carl Reiner (Apr–Sep)
Jayne Meadows (Apr–Sep)

This short-lived variation on *Candid Camera* presented amusing incidents in everyday life, some filmed with a hidden camera and some acted out by a group of players. Celebrity guests and the studio audience then tried to guess the outcome; by April the guessing was being done by a celebrity panel alone. In a typical episode, the panel had to guess whether a woman would buy an atrocious hat, if told it was by a famous French designer; whether a man with both his arms in slings could persuade a stranger to feed him ice cream; and if a customer in a pet shop would be willing to conduct his business with a chimpanzee, in the absence of the proprietor.

ART LINKLETTER'S HOLLYWOOD TALENT SCOUTS, see *Hollywood Talent Scouts*

ARTHUR GODFREY AND HIS FRIENDS (*Musical Variety*)

FIRST TELECAST: *January 12, 1949*
LAST TELECAST: *April 28, 1959*
BROADCAST HISTORY:
Jan 1949–Jun 1957, CBS Wed 8:00–9:00 (OS)
Sep 1958–Apr 1959, CBS Tue 9:00–9:30
HOST:
Arthur Godfrey
REGULARS:
Tony Marvin
The Chordettes (Virginia Osborn, Dorothy Schwartz, Carol Hagedorn, Janet Ertel) (1949–1953)
Janette Davis (1949–1957)
Bill Lawrence (1949–1950)
The Mariners (Jim Lewis, Tom Lockard, Nat Dickerson, Martin Karl) (1949–1955)
Haleloke (1950–1955)
Frank Parker (1950–1956)
Marion Marlowe (1950–1955)
Julius LaRosa (1952–1953)
Lu Ann Simms (1952–1955)
The McGuire Sisters (Christine, Dorothy, Phyllis) (1952–1957)
Carmel Quinn (1954–1957)
Pat Boone (1955–1957)
The Toppers (1955–1957)
Miyoshi Umeki (1955)
Frank Westbrook Dancers (1958–1959)
ORCHESTRA:
Archie Bleyer (1949–1954)
Jerry Bresler (1954–1955)
Will Roland and Bert Farber (1955–1957)
Bernie Green (1958–1959)

The arrival of Arthur Godfrey on television was the most widely publicized event of the 1948–1949 season. Godfrey had been one of the biggest stars on radio in the late 1940s, and his folksy, person-to-person style looked like a natural for TV. It was.

Both *Arthur Godfrey and His Friends* and its companion show, *Arthur Godfrey's Talent Scouts,* shot to the top of the TV ratings and stayed there for several years. Part of the appeal was in Godfrey's repertory company of singers, all of them good clean kids who had been lifted out of obscurity by Godfrey (he never hired an established performer as a regular). But mostly it was "the old redhead" himself that the viewers adored. Ben Gross of the New York *Daily News* summed up his appeal: "It is his friendliness, his good cheer, his small-boy mischievousness and his kindly philosophy . . . or maybe it's his magnetism, his personal attractiveness." As on radio, Godfrey frequently kidded his sponsors and refused to advertise any product for which he could not personally vouch. Frequently he would throw away the script and improvise his way through a testimonial. When Godfrey talked about how much he liked that cup of Lipton Tea, he sounded like he meant it.

The show itself was a variety hour built around Godfrey and his "friends." Frank Parker and Marion Marlowe were the mature, romantic duet, Julius LaRosa was the bright young boy singer, Haleloke the shy, exotic Hawaiian, and the Chordettes the well-scrubbed young barbershop harmonizers from Sheboygan, Wisconsin. Tony Marvin was the deep-voiced announcer who added a certain urbanity to the show. In and out of the proceedings flitted Godfrey, sometimes plunking his ukulele, sometimes singing (the term is used generously), sometimes just adding encouragement or folksy chatter.

For several years there seemed to be no stopping him. Arthur Godfrey was practically deified by the press. When he underwent surgery in May 1953 for an old hip injury (the painful result of an auto smashup 20 years before), the whole country, it seemed, sent get-well cards.

Then, in one of the most dramatic turnarounds in any star's history, Godfrey became the subject of tremendous controversy, vilified by the same columnists who had heaped praise on him only a few years before. Probably no personality got more press coverage in the mid-1950s, often with sensational headlines. Godfrey brought it on himself. Most publicized was his firing of the "little Godfreys," one by one, for what often seemed petty reasons. By far the most dramatic incident was the on-the-air dismissal in October 1953 of Julius LaRosa, who, Godfrey said, had gotten to be too big a star. His remark to the press that LaRosa had lost his "humility" was to haunt Godfrey for the rest of his days. (LaRosa, who had only humble praise for his former boss, immediately went on to some well-publicized appearances on the *Ed Sullivan Show*, several hit records, and a series of his own, but his career faded after a few years.) Others who got the ax included orchestra leader Archie Bleyer, who was running a record company on the side and who made the mistake of recording Godfrey's archrival, Don McNeill (Bleyer's dating of Chordette Janet Ertel, whom he later married, was also given as a reason); producer Larry Puck (who was dating Marion Marlowe); and the Chordettes (they never could figure out why). Then, in April 1955, in one fell swoop he fired Marion Marlowe, Haleloke, and the Mariners, plus three writers.

All this might not have been so bad if Godfrey had not been so thin-skinned about press criticism. A regular feud erupted, with the vituperous star variously labeling his detractors as "Dope!" (Ed Sullivan), "Liar!" (or words to that effect, for Dorothy Kilgallen), "Fatuous ass!" (John Crosby), "These jerk newspapermen!" and "Muckrakers!" for all and sundry. When his private pilot's license was suspended because he allegedly buzzed an airport tower in his private DC-3, the papers had a field day with that, too.

Godfrey's bad press adversely affected his goodwill, and his ratings began to drop. The fired "friends" were all replaced, almost on a one-for-one basis. Pretty Marion Marlowe with her long, flowing black hair was replaced by pretty Carmel Quinn with long, flowing red hair; earnest young Julius LaRosa by earnest young Pat Boone; the harmonizing Chordettes by the harmonizing McGuire Sisters. Godfrey even signed up a Japanese girl, Miyoshi Umeki, to take the place of the Hawaiian Haleloke. It was not quite the same, though, and while Godfrey kept both his shows until he voluntarily decided to give them up, their popularity in the later days never matched that of the spectacular early 1950s.

After a final season in a half-hour format in 1958–1959, with only Tony Marvin as a regular, Godfrey left nighttime TV. He turned up briefly on *Candid Camera* in 1960–1961, then continued on radio for many years, until a tearful farewell broadcast on CBS in 1972. Having survived a bout with cancer, he devoted himself to conservationist causes until his death in 1983.

ARTHUR GODFREY AND HIS UKULELE (*Instruction*)

FIRST TELECAST: *April 4, 1950*
LAST TELECAST: *June 30, 1950*
BROADCAST HISTORY:

Apr 1950, CBS Tue/Thu 7:45–8:00
Apr 1950–Jun 1950, CBS Tue/Fri 7:45–8:00

STAR:

Arthur Godfrey

For a three-month period in 1950, in addition to his other CBS radio and television programs, Arthur Godfrey appeared twice a week to give lessons on how to play the ukulele to his television audience. For the first three weeks these live lessons ran on Tuesday and Thursday nights at 7:45, after which the Thursday lesson moved to Friday.

ARTHUR GODFREY SHOW, THE, see *Arthur Godfrey and His Friends*

ARTHUR GODFREY'S TALENT SCOUTS (*Talent*)

FIRST TELECAST: *December 6, 1948*
LAST TELECAST: *July 21, 1958*
BROADCAST HISTORY:

Dec 1948–Jul 1958, CBS Mon 8:30–9:00 (OS)

HOST:

Arthur Godfrey

ANNOUNCER:

Tony Marvin

ORCHESTRA:

Archie Bleyer (1948–1954)
Jerry Bresler (1954–1955)
Will Roland and Bert Farber (1955–1958)

Arthur Godfrey was the only personality in TV history to have two top-rated programs running simultaneously in prime time for an extended period (eight and a half seasons). On Mondays viewers could see him on the *Talent Scouts,* on Wednesdays on *Arthur Godfrey and His Friends. Talent Scouts* was slightly higher-rated, reaching No. 1 for the 1951–1952 season. But it was hard to tell the two programs apart. In 1952–1953 *Talent Scouts* and *Friends* ranked No. 2 and 3 among all programs on TV, just behind *I Love Lucy.*

Talent Scouts had "scouts" bring on their discoveries to perform before a live national audience. Most of these "discoveries" were aspiring professionals with some prior experience, and the quality of the acts was therefore quite high. Godfrey's folksy banter and interviews added the icing to the cake. Winners for each show were chosen by an audience applause meter. Several of the winners were invited to join Godfrey as regulars on his other show, and of these some went on to become major stars in their own right. Among the Godfrey regulars who were discovered on *Talent Scouts* were the Chordettes, Carmel Quinn, Pat Boone, and the McGuire Sisters.

Others who appeared here before they became famous included Rosemary Clooney, Tony Bennett, and 13-year-old Connie Francis (playing her accordion), all in 1950; Steve Lawrence and Al Martino in 1951; Marian McPartland and Leslie Uggams in 1952; the Diamonds and Roy Clark in 1956; and Johnny Nash and Patsy Cline in 1957. The Godfrey screening staff missed a few big ones, though. Elvis Presley (in early 1955) and Buddy Holly (in 1956) both flunked auditions for the show.

ARTHUR MURRAY PARTY, THE (*Musical Variety*)

FIRST TELECAST: *July 20, 1950*
LAST TELECAST: *September 6, 1960*
BROADCAST HISTORY:

Jul 1950–Sep 1950, ABC Thu 9:00–9:30
Oct 1950–Jan 1951, DUM Sun 9:00–10:00
Jan 1951–Mar 1951, DUM Sun 9:00–9:30
Apr 1951–Jun 1951, ABC Mon 9:00–9:30
Sep 1951–Dec 1951, ABC Wed 9:00–9:30
Jan 1952–May 1952, ABC Sun 9:00–9:30
Jul 1952–Aug 1952, CBS Fri 8:00–8:30
Oct 1952–Apr 1953, DUM Sun 10:00–10:30
Jun 1953–Oct 1953, CBS Sun 9:30–10:00
Oct 1953–Apr 1954, NBC Mon 7:30–7:45
Jun 1954–Sep 1954, NBC Tue 8:30–9:00
Jun 1955–Sep 1955, NBC Tue 8:30–9:00
Apr 1956–Sep 1956, CBS Thu 10:00–10:30
Apr 1957–Jun 1957, NBC Tue 8:00–8:30
Jul 1957–Sep 1957, NBC Mon 9:30–10:00
Sep 1958–Sep 1959, NBC Mon 10:00–10:30
Sep 1959–Jan 1960, NBC Tue 9:00–9:30
Jan 1960–Sep 1960, NBC Tue 9:30–10:00

REGULARS:

Kathryn Murray
Arthur Murray

The Arthur Murray Dancers
The Stanley Melba Orchestra (1950)
The Emil Coleman Orchestra (1951–1952)
The Ray Carter Orchestra (1953–1960)

This was, without a doubt, the longest-running commercial in the history of television. For a full decade, Arthur and Kathryn Murray built an entire program around dancing as an incentive for viewers to take courses with the Arthur Murray Dance Studio. In the early years, through spring of 1953, the show was actually sponsored by the dance studios. A regular feature was a mystery dance segment, in which viewers could win two free lessons at their nearest Arthur Murray Studio by mailing in a postcard correctly identifying the week's mystery dance.

Throughout its long run, the format of *The Arthur Murray Party* remained virtually unchanged. The setting was a large party at which Kathryn was the cheerful, vivacious hostess. There were always one or two guest stars on hand, from the world of show business or sports, and a substantial group of Arthur Murray dance instructors from the various studios in the New York area. Kathryn chatted with the guests; they in turn sang, danced, and occasionally participated in comedy sketches. Arthur acted as the instructor who taught the home audience, and often the guest stars as well, a particular dance step. The instructors who appeared in the party group would often be singled out to demonstrate their proficiency at unusual or complex dances. As the show drew to a close, Arthur and Kathryn would glide majestically into a Strauss waltz with the rest of the party group joining in. There were subtle additions and subtractions to the format over the years but the basic structure remained intact. Kathryn's closing line each week was, "Till then, to put a little fun in your life, try dancing."

The Arthur Murray Party was the perennial summer replacement series. It was easy to produce and always attracted a respectable audience. It was one of only four series to appear, at one time or another, on four broadcast television networks. For its premiere on ABC in 1950 it was called *Arthur Murray Party Time*. That fall, the first DuMont version was titled *The Arthur Murray Show*, but by the autumn of 1951 it had become *The Arthur Murray Party*, the name it retained throughout the rest of its ten years on the air.

ARTS & ENTERTAINMENT NETWORK (Network)

(*General Entertainment Cable Network*)

LAUNCHED:

February 1, 1984

SUBSCRIBERS (MAY 2003):

85.8 million (80% U.S.)

Often compared to PBS, A&E's schedule consists largely of cultural programs, dramas, and documentaries. In the 1980s *TV Guide* referred to it as "a kind of BBC-West" due to its heavy reliance on reruns from the BBC (more than two thirds of its schedule at the time). In later years, however, it broadened its sources. Some series were still acquired from England, including *The Sherlock Holmes Mysteries* and *Lovejoy*, but its top-rated series in later years was that hoary old standby *Biography*, updated with pop-culture profiles of Great Americans such as Madonna and Howard Cosell. The show was also the basis of a second channel launched in 1998 called the Biography Channel.

Following is a sample of A&E's first-run (in the U.S.) series programming.

American Justice (documentary about twentieth-century crimes, hosted by Bill Kurtis), 1993–
America's Castles (great homes), 1996–
Ancient Mysteries (documentary on unexplained historical mysteries), 1993–2000
Arts & Entertainment Review (arts magazine), 1990–1992
*Behind Closed Doors with Joan Lunden** (newsmagazine), 2000–
*Biography** (documentary), 1987–
*Caroline's Comedy Hour** (standup comedy), 1990–1995
Challenge of the Seas (documentary), c. 1991
Civil War Journal (documentary, hosted by Danny Glover), 1993–1995 (later seen on History Channel)
Cold Case Files (crime documentary), 2002–
Dogs (documentary), 1993
Dream Chasers (aka *Ultimate Reality*) (documentary), 2001–2002
Eagle and the Bear (documentary)
*Evening at the Improv, An** (standup comedy), 1985–1995
Heroes (documentary), c. 1990
Investigative Reports (news documentary on a current issue, hosted by Bill Kurtis), 1991–
L.A. Detectives (documentary about cops, hosted by Bill Kurtis), 1998–1999
Living Dangerously (documentary), c. 1988
Lovejoy (comedy-thriller produced by the BBC, starring Ian McShane as the art dealer/sleuth), 1991–1994
*Nero Wolfe** (drama), 2001–2002
*100 Centre Street** (drama), 2001–2002
Pole to Pole (travelogue hosted by Michael Palin), 1993
Rave (entertainment magazine), 1992
Real West, The (documentary hosted by Kenny Rogers), 1992
Sherlock Holmes Mysteries (mystery starring Jeremy Brett as Holmes and David Burke as Watson), 1991–1998
Spies (documentary), 1992
Travelquest (travelogue hosted by Alan Thicke), 1992
The Unexplained (paranormal, aliens, etc.), 1997–2001

*See separate alphabetical entry.

The rest of the A&E schedule was composed of movies and network reruns such as *Lou Grant*, *Columbo*, *The Rockford Files*, *In Search of . . .* , and *Law & Order*.

A&E was created in 1984 by the merger of two failed cable channels, ARTS (launched 1981) and The Entertainment Channel (1982). It first reached more than half of all U.S. television homes in May 1990.

AS IF (*Drama*)

FIRST TELECAST: *March 5, 2002*
LAST TELECAST: *March 12, 2002*
BROADCAST HISTORY:

Mar 2002, UPN Tue 9:00–9:30

CAST:

Alex Stanton .... Robin Dunne
Nicki.......................... Adrienne Wilkinson
Sooz .... Emily Corrie

Jamie Collier........................Derek Hughes
Rob..................................Chris Engen
Sasha...............................Tracie Thoms

Life was a party set to pulsing, contemporary music in this odd little series about six urban teenagers in New York City. Shot in cinema verité style at an extremely fast pace (most scenes seemed to last no more than 20 seconds), each episode was shown from the perspective of one of the six—making each the star of an episode. Sexy Nicki, the tease, loved to turn on guys but was smarter than she acted, while Sooz, a counterculture creative type, used a sharp wit, wildly colored hair and body piercings to mask her insecurities. Sasha, an ambitious, aggressive college freshman, was working on a plan to be a successful career woman. As for the guys, Alex was the bright one who was much better at giving advice to others than to himself, while Jamie was a girl chaser who was honest to a fault. Nineteen-year-old Rob was a shaggy-haired hunk who was having difficulty dealing with the responsibilities of becoming an adult.

The first episode was shot from Jamie's perspective and the second from Sooz's, but the others never got their chance—UPN pulled the plug with five episodes unaired. Adapted from the popular British series of the same name (set in London), with Emily Corrie reprising her role as the colorful Sooz.

AS TOLD BY GINGER (*Cartoon*)

BROADCAST HISTORY:

Nickelodeon
30 minutes
Original episodes: *2000–*
Premiered: *October 25, 2000*

VOICES:

Ginger Foutley (age 12) (2000–2002)
...................................Melissa Disney
Ginger Foutley (2003–).............Shayna Fox
Carl Foutley........................Jeannie Elias
Lois Foutley.....................Laraine Newman
Deidre Hortense "Dodie" Bishop......Aspen Miller
Macie Lightfoot.....................Jackie Harris
Darren Patterson....................Kenny Blank
Robert Joseph "Hoodsie" Bishop... Tress MacNeille
Courtney Gripling....................Liz Georges
Miranda Killgallen.................Cree Summer
Blake Gripling (7)....................Kath Soucie
Brandon Higsby.....................Grey DeLisle
Winston..............................John Kassir
Chet Zipper...........................Hope Levy
Mrs. Gordon....................Kathleen Freeman
Ms. Zorski.....................Elizabeth Halpern

The trials of middle school from a girl's point of view was the theme of this Nick cartoon, whose exaggerated characters all seemed to have small bodies and large heads. Ginger was a nervous but nice seventh-grader who lived in the town of Sheltered Shrubs with her grungy little brother Carl (who liked anything that was dirty) and mom Lois, a nurse. Her best friends at Lucky Jr. High School were gossipy Dodie, geeky Macie and Darren, whose entire head was in a head brace. Her chief nemesis was rich, snobbish Courtney, who was frequently egged on by friend and snob-wannabe Miranda. Troublemaker Carl hung out with Dodie's brother Hoodsie, a little runt who habitually wore a purple hood, and fended off the schemes of Courtney's preppy brother Blake, who employed a variety of high-tech toys to torment them. Winston was Blake's chauffeur, who often wound up rescuing him.

In later episodes Courtney began to warm up to Ginger, treating her as a "popularity experiment"; the gang began high school; and Ginger and Carl's absent dad Jonah (Tom Virtue), who had apparently abandoned the family, occasionally showed up to make amends.

ASIA PERSPECTIVE (*Documentary/Public Affairs*)

FIRST TELECAST: *September 4, 1966*
LAST TELECAST: *September 25, 1966*
BROADCAST HISTORY:

Sep 1966, CBS Sun 6:00–6:30

The four documentaries that were shown under the collective title *Asia Perspective* covered the then-current ideological purges in Communist China, the elections taking place in South Vietnam, and a two-party history of the political, economic, and social changes that had taken place on the Chinese mainland since the fall of Manchuria in 1931. Various CBS correspondents contributed to the reports

ASK DR. RUTH, see *Dr. Ruth*

ASK HARRIET (*Situation Comedy*)

FIRST TELECAST: *January 4, 1998*
LAST TELECAST: *January 29, 1998*
BROADCAST HISTORY:

Jan 1998, FOX Sun 8:30–9:00
Jan 1998, FOX Thu 8:30–9:00

CAST:

Jack Cody/Sylvia Coco.......Anthony Tyler Quinn
Ron Rendall........................Willie Garson
Trey Anderson.................Patrick Y. Malone
Melissa Peters.........................Lisa Waltz
Joplin Russell.........................Julie Benz
Marshall "Old Man" Russell.........Edward Asner
Blair Cody....................Jamie Renee Smith
Marty............................Damien Leake

Jack was a divorced, womanizing sports reporter who had written the column "A Man's World" for the *New York Dispatch* until he was fired by Melissa, his editor and vengeful former girlfriend. Somehow he got a new job writing the paper's advice-to-the-lovelorn column, "Ask Harriet," by dressing in drag and submitting material under the name Sylvia Coco. Others on the staff were Trey, the young former assistant who took over Jack's column, and Ron, Jack's mousy friend and the paper's restaurant critic. Ron was the only one who knew that Jack and Sylvia were the same person—everyone else was too dense, or too busy staring at Sylvia's exaggerated bosom. Joplin was the sexy young granddaughter of Old Man Russell, who owned the paper and had the hots for Sylvia. Although Joplin had been home-schooled and had no college education, Russell told Melissa to groom her to take over her job as managing editor. Blair was Jack's young daughter, who showed up frequently at his apartment, and Marty was the vagrant who solicited in front of the building housing the *Dispatch*'s offices.

ASK ME ANOTHER (*Quiz/Panel*)

FIRST TELECAST: *July 3, 1952*
LAST TELECAST: *September 25, 1952*

BROADCAST HISTORY:

Jul 1952–Sep 1952, NBC Thu 10:30–11:00

EMCEE:

Joe Boland

REGULAR PANELISTS:

Johnny Lujack (football player)
Warren Brown (sports editor, *Chicago Tribune*)
Kay Westfall (TV actress)
Tom Duggan (sports commentator)

The four panelists on this quiz show tried to guess the identities of famous sports personalities, who appeared as guests. Each guest would stand behind a shadow curtain while the panelists asked questions to try to figure out his or her identity. A special feature of the show was the appearance of one "performing guest" each week, who would perform his or her specialty behind the shadow curtain while the panelists tried to guess who it was.

ASPEN, see *Innocent and the Damned, The*

ASPHALT JUNGLE, THE (*Police Drama*)

FIRST TELECAST: *April 2, 1961*
LAST TELECAST: *September 24, 1961*
BROADCAST HISTORY:

Apr 1961–Sep 1961, ABC Sun 9:30–10:30

CAST:

Matthew Gower .... Jack Warden
Capt. Gus Honochek .... Arch Johnson
Sgt. Danny Keller .... Bill Smith

Fighting crime in a big city is often a job that requires specialists. Deputy Police Commissioner Matthew Gower was one of them. Helping him break up the large organized crime rings that infiltrated his town was a special squad of select men headed by Gus Honochek and Danny Keller. Often they had undercover assignments, and Commissioner Gower, not one to leave the dirty work to his men, would pitch in and go undercover with them. The most memorable aspect of this police series was the background music, composed by the great jazz musician Duke Ellington.

ASSIGNMENT DANGER, see *Martin Kane, Private Eye*

ASSIGNMENT FOREIGN LEGION (*Adventure Anthology*)

FIRST TELECAST: *October 1, 1957*
LAST TELECAST: *December 24, 1957*
BROADCAST HISTORY:

Oct 1957–Dec 1957, CBS Tue 10:30–11:00

HOSTESS:

Merle Oberon

Actress Merle Oberon was the narrator of and occasional performer in this British dramatic series about the French Foreign Legion. Each episode opened with Miss Oberon, as a foreign correspondent stationed in North Africa, introducing a story about the officers and men of the Legion. Occasionally, as the foreign correspondent, she appeared in the story as well. The series was filmed on location in Morocco, Algiers, and Spain and was first seen on British television.

ASSIGNMENT MANHUNT, see *Manhunt*

ASSIGNMENT VIENNA (*Spy Drama*)

FIRST TELECAST: *September 28, 1972*
LAST TELECAST: *June 9, 1973*
BROADCAST HISTORY:

Sep 1972–Dec 1972, ABC Thu 9:00–10:00
Jan 1973–Jun 1973, ABC Sat 10:00–11:00

CAST:

Jake Webster .... Robert Conrad
Maj. Caldwell .... Charles Cioffi
Inspector Hoffman .... Anton Diffring

This international spy drama was one of three rotating elements of the series *The Men.* It starred Robert Conrad as Jake Webster, a rugged, independent American expatriate with a shady past who operated Jake's Bar & Grill in Vienna. Jake's bistro was only a cover for his undercover work for the United States government, however, as he tracked down assorted spies and international criminals in convoluted plots. He maintained an uneasy liaison with Major Caldwell of U.S. Intelligence who, in return for Jake's services, kept the American out of jail. The series was filmed on location in Vienna.

ASSOCIATES, THE (*Situation Comedy*)

FIRST TELECAST: *September 23, 1979*
LAST TELECAST: *April 17, 1980*
BROADCAST HISTORY:

Sep 1979–Oct 1979, ABC Sun 8:30–9:00
Mar 1980–Apr 1980, ABC Thu 9:30–10:00

CAST:

Emerson Marshall .... Wilfrid Hyde-White
Eliot Streeter .... Joe Regalbuto
Leslie Dunn .... Alley Mills
Tucker Kerwin .... Martin Short
Sara James .... Shelley Smith
Johnny Danko .... Tim Thomerson

THEME:

"Wall Street Blues," by Albert Brooks, sung by B. B. King.

ABC had high hopes for this lawyer-comedy show, which, though well received by critics, never attracted a large audience. It revolved around three young law school graduates who had just joined the prestigious Wall Street firm of Bass and Marshall as associates, beginning their five- to seven-year trial period. Daughter of a poor New York family, Leslie was recently graduated from Columbia, and felt for the oppressed. Bass and Marshall did not usually represent the oppressed. Tucker, Leslie's beau, was a Midwesterner slightly out of step with his Ivy League colleagues, a little naive but very charming. Sara was a Boston blueblood, bright as well as sexy. They were all at the mercy of a hierarchy including such oddballs as formidable but slightly dotty Senior Partner Emerson Marshall, 81 (played to perfection by British character actor Wilfrid Hyde-White), and dedicated Junior Partner Eliot Streeter, who had only one goal—to take over the firm. Waving his hand he exclaimed, in the first episode, "I love this firm. . . . I never told it so, but it *knows.*"

Counterpointing all this class was Johnny Danko, the 21-year-old mailboy, whose one goal was to make time with beautiful chicks.

AT EASE (*Situation Comedy*)

FIRST TELECAST: *March 4, 1983*
LAST TELECAST: *July 15, 1983*
BROADCAST HISTORY:

Mar 1983–Jul 1983, ABC Fri 8:30–9:00

CAST:

Sgt. Val Valentine .... Jimmie Walker
PFC Tony Baker .... David Naughton
Col. Clapp .... Roger Bowen
Maj. Hawkins .... Richard Jaeckel
Cpl. Lola Grey .... Jourdan Fremin
Cpt. Wessel .... George Wyner
Maxwell .... Joshua Mostel
Cardinel .... John Vargas
Maurice .... Jeff Bannister

This short-lived military comedy was billed as the 1980s version of the classic Sgt. Bilko series *(The Phil Silvers Show)*. Without a strong lead to match Phil Silvers, it attracted few viewers. As in the original, the setting was a sleepy peacetime army post in the heartland—this time a computer base called Camp Tar Creek, in Texas. The scheming Sgt. Bilko was replaced by scheming Sgt. Valentine and his buddy PFC Baker, and the dense Col. Hall by the equally credulous Col. Clapp. The greatest threat to Val and his pals in Company J was the Colonel's by-the-book security chief, Maj. Hawkins, whose informant was the weasely Cpl. Wessel. Hawkins was always trying to close down Val's scams and shape things up, but to no avail. A little sex appeal was added by Baker's luscious girlfriend Lola, and a contemporary slant by the computers from Apple Computer Co. But some things never change: the platoon also had a klutzy, always-hungry private named Maxwell (remember Doberman?).

AT HOME SHOW, see *Earl Wrightson Show*

AT ISSUE (*Interview*)

FIRST TELECAST: *July 12, 1953*
LAST TELECAST: *February 24, 1954*
BROADCAST HISTORY:

Jul 1953–Aug 1953, ABC Sun 9:00–9:15
Oct 1953–Feb 1954, ABC Wed 8:00–8:15

HOST:

Martin Agronsky

News commentator Agronsky interviewed public figures on important issues of the day in this 15-minute public-affairs program. After its prime-time run the program continued on Sunday afternoons until June 1954.

AT LIBERTY CLUB (*Music*)

FIRST TELECAST: *June 25, 1948*
LAST TELECAST: *September 16, 1948*
BROADCAST HISTORY:

Jun 1948–Jul 1948, NBC Fri 8:00–8:30
Jul 1948–Sep 1948, NBC Thu 8:00–8:15

HOSTESS:

Jacqueline (Turner)

This short musical interlude was set in a mythical nightclub for "at liberty" youngsters, presided over by Parisian singer Jacqueline, with guests. The program was formerly local on WPTZ, Philadelphia.

AT THE MOVIES (*Commentary*)

BROADCAST HISTORY:

Syndicated only
30 minutes
Produced: *1982–1990*
Released: *September 1982*

HOSTS:

Roger Ebert (1982–1986)
Gene Siskel (1982–1986)
Rex Reed (1986–1990)
Bill Harris (1986–1988)
Dixie Whatley (1988–1990)

Film critics Roger Ebert of the *Chicago Sun-Times* and Gene Siskel of the *Chicago Tribune* first gained national notoriety in 1977 as the contentious hosts of the popular PBS series *Sneak Previews.* In 1982 they left public television to launch this syndicated program for commercial stations, using virtually the same format and theater setting. Each week, from "the balcony," they watched clips from several new movies, argued about them, and then individually gave a "thumbs up/thumbs down" evaluation of each one.

When Ebert and Siskel ran into contractual difficulties with Tribune Entertainment, the producer of the show, in the fall of 1986, they departed for a new movie review series, *Siskel & Ebert & the Movies. At the Movies* acquired two new hosts, movie critic Rex Reed and critic/gossip columnist Bill Harris. Added to the format, in addition to the movie reviews, were show business news and short pieces on movie production. Dixie Whatley, who had been seen regularly on *Entertainment Tonight*, took over as Rex Reed's cohost in 1988.

AUCTION-AIRE (*Auction*)

FIRST TELECAST: *September 30, 1949*
LAST TELECAST: *June 23, 1950*
BROADCAST HISTORY:

Sep 1949–Jun 1950, ABC Fri 9:00–9:30

EMCEE:

Jack Gregson

REGULAR:

"Rebel" (Charlotte) Randall

COMMERCIAL ANNOUNCER:

Durward Kirby

In this fast-paced auction program from Chicago, the audience had a chance to bid on valuable merchandise—using, instead of cash, the labels from products of The Libby Company, the program's sponsor. Among the bargains were a $250 home freezer that went for 88 labels, a $355 refrigerator for 225 labels, and a $450 sterling silver set for 225 labels. Out-of-town viewers could call their bids in to their local station, which relayed them to the stage of the Ritz Theater in New York, where the program originated live. There was also a "Mystery Chant," in which contestants who could identify the total of the numbers rattled off in an auctioneer's chant won an automobile. Auction-Aire Gregson's assistant, buxom model "Rebel" Randall, was mainly decorative.

AUSTIN STORIES (*Situation Comedy*)

BROADCAST HISTORY:

MTV
30 minutes
Produced: *1997* (12 episodes)
Premiered: *September 10, 1997*

CAST:

Howard .... Howard Kremer
Laura .... Laura House
Chip .... Brad "Chip" Pope

MTV's "slacker-com" about three twentysomething friends goofing off, and getting by (more or less), in easygoing Austin, Texas. Laura was the relatively responsible one, with a real job at an alternative newspaper, *The Austin Weekly.* Howard was her goofy, and goofy-looking, friend, who lived out of his car (when he had one) and spent his days doing little scams like stuffing his pockets with free maps at the local tourist office, then selling them on the steps of the Capitol, or trying to slip into a theater for free. He always got caught, of course, but he was so amiable that no one could really get mad at him. Chip was the somewhat dense hanger-on, who kept getting fired from menial jobs, and whose ill-conceived schemes blew up even faster than Howard's.

AUTHOR MEETS THE CRITICS (*Book Discussion*)

FIRST TELECAST: *April 4, 1948*
LAST TELECAST: *October 10, 1954*
BROADCAST HISTORY:

Apr 1948–Mar 1949, NBC Sun 8:00–8:30
Mar 1949–Jul 1949, NBC Sun 8:30–9:00
Oct 1949–Nov 1949, ABC Mon 7:30–8:00
Nov 1949–Dec 1949, ABC Wed 9:00–9:30
Dec 1949–Mar 1950, ABC Thu 9:30–10:00
Mar 1950–Sep 1950, ABC Wed 8:30–9:00
Sep 1951–Dec 1951, NBC Mon 10:00–10:30
Mar 1952–Oct 1952, DUM Thu 10:30–11:00
Oct 1952–May 1953, DUM Thu 10:00–10:30
May 1953–Oct 1953, DUM Wed 9:30–10:00
Mar 1954–Jul 1954, DUM Sun 7:00–7:30
Jul 1954–Oct 1954, DUM Sun 10:00–10:30

MODERATOR:

John K. M. McCaffery (1948–1951)
Faye Emerson (1952)
Virgilia Peterson (1952–1954)

An author defending his current work against a panel of critics was the premise of this durable program, which began on local television in New York on July 10, 1947, and later saw service on an assortment of nights and networks. The critics, one pro and one con each week, were generally literary figures, although some were TV celebrities as well, such as Bennett Cerf and Dr. Mason Gross. Authors ranged from Ezra Stone and Cornelia Otis Skinner to Henry Morgan (whose latest movie was dissected) and cartoonist Al Capp. Their debates sometimes generated real verbal fireworks.

In addition to current books, such as *U.S.A. Confidential* and *The Execution of Private Slovik,* occasional movies and magazine articles were considered. John K. M. McCaffery, who had been one of the hosts of *Author Meets the Critics* on radio, where it originated in 1946, was the first host of the TV series; he was later succeeded by actress Faye Emerson and then by Virgilia Peterson.

AUTOMAN (*Police/Science Fiction*)

FIRST TELECAST: *December 15, 1983*
LAST TELECAST: *April 2, 1984*
BROADCAST HISTORY:

Dec 1983–Jan 1984, ABC Thu 8:00–9:00
Mar 1984–Apr 1984, ABC Mon 8:00–9:00

CAST:

Walter Nebicher .... Desi Arnaz, Jr.
Automan .... Chuck Wagner
Lt. Jack Curtis .... Robert Lansing
Capt. Boyd .... Gerald S. O'Loughlin
Roxanne .... Heather McNair

Computers were becoming part of everyday life, from the checkout counter and the automatic bank teller to home-video games, and *Automan* tried to make them part of television fantasy as well. Walter Nebbish—er, Nebicher—was a mousy police computer expert who liked to develop computer games in his spare time. One day he really blew his circuits: a computer creation called "Automan" jumped right off the screen and started Walter on a career as an international crime fighter. Since Walter had programmed in everything that Automan knew, this handsome superhero in his sparkling uniform was really Walter's alter ego, but able to do all the things that Walter couldn't. He could walk through walls, make objects appear and disappear, and make beautiful women swoon (Automan's broad smile showed more teeth than an Osmond brother). Automan also had lots of friends; practically any computer he ran into would help him out, which was handy for commandeering elevators and causing security systems to keep their bells quiet. If Walter and his creation got into serious trouble while on a case, Walter could even merge into Automan for a time and evade flying bullets!

As if Automan were not enough, there was also Cursor—the little glowing dot that normally moves around a computer screen to show you where you are. This Cursor followed Automan and Walter, and on their command would outline a superfast getaway car or even a tank (which would then materialize, ready for use).

There were, of course, problems. Automan used so much energy that lights tended to dim around him. He faded away entirely at daybreak, when the city's electrical consumption began to rise, often leaving Walter in some dangerous predicament. Then there was Walter's grumpy, old-fashioned boss, Capt. Boyd, who thought that all computers were worthless, to say nothing of the people who ran them. Neither he nor Walter's protector on the force, Lt. Curtis, knew about Automan, but Curtis knew that somehow Walter was able to crack cases and he shamelessly used Walter's leads to further his own career.

AVENGERS, THE (*Spy Drama*)

FIRST TELECAST: *March 28, 1966*
LAST TELECAST: *September 15, 1969*
BROADCAST HISTORY:

Mar 1966–July 1966, ABC Mon 10:00–11:00
Jul 1966–Sep 1966, ABC Thu 10:00–11:00
Jan 1967–Sep 1967, ABC Fri 10:00–11:00
Jan 1968–Sep 1968, ABC Wed 7:30–8:30
Sep 1968–Sep 1969, ABC Mon 7:30–8:30

CAST:

John Steed .... Patrick Macnee
Emma Peel (1966–1968)................ Diana Rigg
Tara King (1968–1969) .... Linda Thorson
"Mother" (1968–1969)............. Patrick Newell
Purdey (1976)...................... Joanna Lumley
Mike Gambit (1976)................... Gareth Hunt

The Avengers first appeared on British television more than five years before it was imported to the United States in 1966. Pure escapist entertainment, it centered on John Steed, a suave, imperturbable, and very proper British secret agent, who was joined after a few episodes by a female partner. Their missions, whether planned or accidental, involved all sorts of diabolical geniuses who planned to take over the world through various fantastic schemes. Improbable technical devices, wittily absurd villains, and the clever and efficient Steed combined to make this fantasized espionage series unique. Like the American-made *Man From U.N.C.L.E.*, it attempted to out-James-Bond James Bond.

Macnee's original female partner in the British version of the series was Honor Blackman, who played Pussy Galore in the James Bond film *Goldfinger*. By the time *The Avengers* reached American audiences she had been replaced by the lithe, jumpsuited Diana Rigg. Steed and Mrs. Peel were separated in the March 20, 1968 episode, when the lady agent was reunited with her long-lost husband. Linda Thorson, a younger and more voluptuous woman, then became the female partner.

The series was resurrected in Britain in 1976 with a new title, *The New Avengers*, and a new supporting cast for Mr. Steed—young agents Purdey and Gambit. It was this version that joined the CBS late-night lineup in the fall of 1978, the only original programming (at least to American audiences) amid CBS' late-night movie reruns and episodes of former prime-time network series.

The popularity of this late-night *Avengers* prompted CBS to subsequently rerun both it and the earlier version that aired on ABC in the 1960s. The end date above refers to the original ABC prime-time run of *The Avengers*. For information on the later reruns see *The CBS Late Movie*.

AWARD THEATER, syndicated title for *Alcoa Theatre* and *Goodyear Theater*

AWAY WE GO (*Musical Variety*)

FIRST TELECAST: *June 3, 1967*
LAST TELECAST: *September 2, 1967*
BROADCAST HISTORY:
Jun 1967–Sep 1967, CBS Sat 7:30–8:30
REGULARS:
George Carlin
Buddy Greco
Buddy Rich
The Miriam Nelson Dancers
The Allyn Ferguson Orchestra

Comedian George Carlin, singer Buddy Greco, and drummer Buddy Rich and his orchestra were the stars of this variety show, which was the 1967 summer replacement for *The Jackie Gleason Show*. The series title was based on one of Gleason's pet expressions, "And away we go!"

B

B.A.D. CATS (*Police Drama*)
FIRST TELECAST: *January 4, 1980*
LAST TELECAST: *February 8, 1980*
BROADCAST HISTORY:
Jan 1980–Feb 1980, ABC Fri 8:00–9:00
CAST:
Officer Nick Donovan .... Asher Brauner
Officer Ocee James .... Steve Hanks
Officer Samantha Jensen .... Michelle Pfeiffer
Capt. Eugene Nathan .... Vic Morrow
Rodney Washington............... Jimmie Walker
Ma................................ LaWanda Page

Another of TV's hot-rod cops series. Nick and Ocee were ex–racing drivers who had been recruited by the Los Angeles Police Department for its B.A.D. C.A.T. squad (Burglary Auto Detail, Commercial Auto Thefts)—apparently on the theory that if you can't catch the crooks peaceably, run 'em down in the streets. Bystanders dove for cover as Nick and Ocee went chasing miscreants down the streets of L.A. in their souped-up Nova, tires squealing. Like all good TV cops, they were willing to "bend the rules" (which they hardly knew anyway) to get their prey. Helping were shapely lady cop Samantha, crusty Captain Nathan, restaurant owner Ma, and gangling Rodney, a comic car-thief-turned-auto-repossessor.

The series was canceled after only five telecasts, leading producer Everett Chambers to admit ruefully, "It was an ill-conceived and ineptly executed series. The network is responsible for some of it and I'm responsible for some of it. We bought $40,000 worth of cars to smash up, and we never got a chance to smash them up. I think that's kind of immoral, $40,000 worth of cars to smash up when people are starving in India." He concluded, "I'm not putting this on my credits."

BBC AMERICA (Network) (*General Entertainment Cable Network*)
LAUNCHED:
March 1998
SUBSCRIBERS (MAY 2003):
35.2 million (33% U.S.)

Britain's BBC, which had long leased its shows and formats to American networks, created its own U.S. beachhead with this cable network, whose slogan was "Completely British, Completely Different." Programming included contemporary BBC fare such as the *BBC World News, Changing Rooms* (the inspiration for TLC's *Trading Spaces*), *What Not to Wear* and *So Graham Norton*, as well as classics including *Cracker, Inspector Morse, Monty Python's Flying Circus, Fawlty Towers* and *Blackadder*. It was an Anglophile's delight.

BET (Network), see *Black Entertainment Television*

B.J. AND THE BEAR (*Comedy/Adventure*)
FIRST TELECAST: *February 10, 1979*
LAST TELECAST: *August 1, 1981*
BROADCAST HISTORY:
Feb 1979–Mar 1980, NBC Sat 9:00–10:00 (OS)
Mar 1980–Aug 1980, NBC Sat 8:00–9:00
Jan 1981–Apr 1981, NBC Tue 9:00–10:00
Apr 1981–Aug 1981, NBC Sat 9:00–10:00
CAST:
B.J. (Billie Joe) McCay .... Greg Evigan
Sheriff Elroy P. Lobo (1979)........... Claude Akins
Deputy Perkins (1979)................ Mills Watson
Sheriff Masters (1979)............. Richard Deacon
Sheriff Cain (1979–1980) .... Ed Lauter
Sgt. Beauregard Wiley (1979) .... Slim Pickens
Wilhelmina "The Fox" Johnson (1979–1980)
.... Conchata Ferrell
Deputy Higgins (1979–1980)............. Otto Felix
Tommy (1979–1980) .... Janet Louise Johnson
Bullets (1979–1980) .... Joshua Shelley
Rutherford T. Grant (1981)....... Murray Hamilton
Lt. Jim Steiger (1981) .... Eric Server
Stacks (1981) .... Judy Landers
Callie (1981) .... Linda McCullough
Samantha (1981).................. Barbra Horan
Teri Garrison (1981)................ Candi Brough
Geri Garrison (1981)................ Randi Brough
Cindy Grant (1981)................ Sherilyn Wolter
Angie Cartwright (1981) .... Sheila DeWindt
THEME:
"B.J. and the Bear," written by Glen A. Larson and sung by Greg Evigan

In the mid-1970s NBC had aired an adventure series about two truckers traveling around the country, titled *Movin' On*. A few years later, and about the same time CBS premiered its hit "good ole boy" rural adventure series *The Dukes of Hazzard*, this countrified version of *Movin' On* turned up on NBC. *B.J. and the Bear* was played more for laughs than adventure, and did seem to put stronger emphasis on pretty girls and wild car and truck chases, but it had a distinct family resemblance to its predecessor on NBC.

B.J. McCay was a good-looking young trucker who traveled around the country in his big red-and-white rig, with a single companion, his pet chimp Bear. Although he logged a lot of miles, B.J. was based in rural Georgia, where he was confronted by a succession of corrupt local sheriffs—Elroy P. Lobo (who was later given his own series, *Lobo*), followed in the fall of 1979 by Sgt. Wiley of Winslow County and his two fellow lawmen, Sheriffs Cain and Masters. The only honest cop B.J. seemed to encounter was the Fox, who spent much of her time trying to trap the crooked local cops. Tommy was a lady trucker friend of B.J.'s and Bullets ran the local hangout, the Country Comfort Truck Stop.

When *B.J. and the Bear* returned for its second season in January 1981 (delayed several months by an actors' strike), B.J. had settled down to run a trucking business in Los Angeles called Bear Enterprises. For B.J., however, corruption seemed to follow wherever he went. His new adversary was Rutherford T. Grant, a corrupt politician who headed the state Special Crimes Action Team. Grant was a silent partner in TransCal, the largest trucking firm in the state, and stopped at nothing to stamp out potential competition. Because of Grant's intervention, B.J. found it impossible to get regular male truck drivers to work for him and had to settle for a crew of seven young, beautiful lady truckers (in the cast credits from Stacks to Angie), including a pair of identical twins, and Grant's daughter, Cindy.

B. L. STRYKER (*Detective*)
FIRST TELECAST: *February 13, 1989*
LAST TELECAST: *August 4, 1990*
BROADCAST HISTORY:
Feb 1989–May 1989, ABC Mon 9:00–11:00
Aug 1989–Aug 1990, ABC Sat 9:00–11:00
CAST:
B. L. Stryker .... Burt Reynolds
Oz Jackson .... Ossie Davis
Lyynda Lennox .... Dana Kaminski
Chief McGee .... Michael O. Smith
Oliver .... Alfie Wise
Kimberly Baskin .... Rita Moreno
EXECUTIVE PRODUCER:
Tom Selleck

Burt Reynolds, who had begun his career on TV (he was a regular on four different series between 1959 and 1970—see index), returned many years and more than a few bad movies later to do this rather routine private eye series. Stryker was a Vietnam war hero and burned-out New Orleans police detective who moved to Palm Beach, Florida, to bum around and work occasionally as a low-rent p.i. Living on a houseboat and tooling around in a beat-up old Caddy, he solved murders mostly among the rich and famous of that golden resort. Oz was his pal and enforcer, a former boxer; Lyynda, his free-spirited secretary; Oliver, his wealthy but trouble-prone landlord; and Kimberly, his oft-married ex-wife.

B. L. Stryker was one of the rotating elements of the *ABC Mystery Movie* and was seen every three weeks or so.

BAA BAA BLACK SHEEP (*War Drama*)
FIRST TELECAST: *September 21, 1976*
LAST TELECAST: *September 1, 1978*
BROADCAST HISTORY:
Sep 1976–Aug 1977, NBC Tue 8:00–9:00
Dec 1977–Mar 1978, NBC Wed 9:00–10:00
Mar 1978–Apr 1978, NBC Thu 9:00–10:00
Jul 1978, NBC Wed 9:00–10:00
Aug 1978–Sep 1978, NBC Fri 8:00–9:00
CAST:
Maj. Gregory "Pappy" Boyington .... Robert Conrad
Col. Lard, USMC .... Dana Elcar
Capt. James W. Gutterman (1976–1977)
.... James Whitmore, Jr.
Lt. Jerry Bragg .... Dirk Blocker
Lt. T. J. Wiley .... Robert Ginty
Lt. Bob Anderson .... John Larroquette
Lt. Lawrence Casey .... W. K. Stratton
Gen. Moore .... Simon Oakland
Hutch (1976–1977) .... Joey Aresco
Lt. Don French .... Jeff MacKay
Lt. Bob Boyle .... Larry Manetti
Sgt. Andy Micklin (1977–1978) .... Red West
Cpl. Stan Richards (1977–1978) ... Steve Richmond
Capt. Tommy Harachi (1977–1978) ... Byron Chung
Capt. Dottie Dixon (1977–1978) .. Katherine Cannon
Lt. Jeb Pruitt (1978) .... Jeb Adams
Nurse Samantha Green (1978) ..... Denise DuBarry
Nurse Ellie (1977–1978) .... Kathy McCullen
Nurse Susan (1977–1978) .... Brianne Leary
Nurse Nancy Gilmore (1977–1978) ... Nancy Conrad
TECHNICAL ADVISOR:
Gregory Boyington

Based loosely on the book *Baa Baa Black Sheep*, by the World War II Marine Corps flying ace Gregory Boyington, this series was the story of a squadron of misfit fliers in the South Pacific. Squadron 214 was composed of men who had been on the verge of court-martial before Boyington provided them with reprieves. They had been charged with everything from fighting with officers, to stealing booze, to being general nuisances and nonconformists. Pappy (he was so named because at age 35 "he was an old man" by the standards of his men) maintained almost no discipline, ignored military regulations, and did not care what his men did when they weren't on missions. As long as they could fly and do the job when necessary, nothing else mattered. Given this personal code, Pappy was completely at home with his men, whether they were chasing women, getting into brawls, conning the military hierarchy or civilian populations, or—in a more serious vein—intercepting the Japanese.

Baa Baa Black Sheep was dropped from the NBC lineup at the end of the 1976–1977 season, only to be revived in December 1977 when most of the new 1977–1978 series failed and the network ran short of programming. It was retitled *Black Sheep Squadron*, and Capt. Dottie Dixon was added to the cast. She was in charge of the nursing force on Vella La Cava, the island where Pappy and his men were based, and her young charges were seemingly always available for fun and games with the men of the 214th Squadron. Four of the girls became regular cast members in early 1978. They were christened "Pappy's Lambs," perhaps as a parody of ABC's popular *Charlie's Angels*, who were scheduled opposite *Black Sheep Squadron*. One of the lambs, Nurse Nancy, was played by the daughter of Robert Conrad.

BABES (*Situation Comedy*)
FIRST TELECAST: *September 13, 1990*
LAST TELECAST: *August 10, 1991*
BROADCAST HISTORY:
Sep 1990–Jun 1991, FOX Thu 8:30–9:00
Jul 1991–Aug 1991, FOX Sat 9:30–10:00
CAST:
Charlene Gilbert .... Wendie Jo Sperber
Darlene Gilbert .... Susan Peretz
Marlene Gilbert .... Lesley Boone
**Ronnie Underwood (1990)* .... Rick Overton
**Mrs. Florence Newman (1991)* .... Nedra Volz
*Occasional

Charlene, Darlene, and Marlene were sisters living together in a studio apartment in Manhattan. Charlene, the outgoing and vivacious middle sister, made her living as a makeup artist for a commercial photographer; Darlene, the cynical, divorced eldest sister, worked as a dog groomer; and Marlene, the trusting, naive youngest sister, was unsure of what she wanted to do. Episodes dealt with their social lives (Ronnie was Charlene's boyfriend early on), the problems they had sharing a small apartment, and their working lives. In the spring of 1991 Darlene went to work at a day-care center. Mrs. Newman lived in their building.

What set this show apart from other comedies was the size of its stars. All three actresses were considerably overweight, in stark contrast to the svelte women usually seen on television. Early in its run *Babes* made liberal use of fat jokes and situations that focused on girth. As time went on, however, this aspect of the show was de-emphasized and their size became incidental to the stories.

BABY BLUES (*Cartoon*)
FIRST TELECAST: *July 28, 2000*
LAST TELECAST: *September 15, 2000*
BROADCAST HISTORY:
Jul 2000–Sep 2000, WB Fri 8:00–9:00
Sep 2000, WB Fri 8:00–8:30
VOICES:
Darryl MacPherson .... Mike O'Malley
Wanda MacPherson .... Julia Sweeney
Zoe MacPherson.............. Elizabeth E. G. Daily
Carl Bitterman .... Joel Murray
Melinda Bitterman.................. Arabella Field
Kenny............................ Diedrich Bader
Bizzy the Baby-Sitter .... Nicole Sullivan
Rodney Bitterman (age 8) .... Kath Soucie
Megan Bitterman (5) .... Kath Soucie

The tribulations of a young married couple were the center of this rather bland animated comedy. Darryl was a wimpy, red-haired office worker who had ironic fantasies, and Wanda his sensible wife. Zoe was their cute baby daughter who constantly presented them with parenting challenges, from nursing to napping. Adding a bit of color were their white-trash next-door neighbors, Carl, a loud, chunky slob who installed sprinkler systems, and his chain-smoking wife, Melinda. Their three kids, who paid no attention to Carl's rants, were hell-raiser Rodney, giggling Megan and 4-year-old Shelby, who never spoke. Wanda and Melinda were good friends, but Darryl couldn't stand the pushy Carl. Kenny was Darryl's best friend at work, constantly belittling his buddy's efforts to work things out at home, despite the fact that his own family life was no bargain. Bizzy was the MacPherson's baby-sitter, a boy-crazy teenager with horrible taste in men.

Eight episodes aired on the WB, with five more premiering on the Cartoon Network beginning in January 2002. Based on the comic strip "Baby Blues" by Rick Kirkman and Jerry Scott.

BABY BOB (*Situation Comedy*)
FIRST TELECAST: *March 18, 2002*
LAST TELECAST:
BROADCAST HISTORY:
Mar 2002–Apr 2002, CBS Mon 8:30–9:00
Jun 2003, CBS Fri 8:00–8:30
CAST:
Walter Spencer .... Adam Arkin
Lizzy Spencer......................... Joely Fisher
Sam Spencer......................... Elliott Gould
Madeline .... Holland Taylor
Teala .... Marissa Tait
Baby Bob (voice) .... Ken Campbell

Walter, a Santa Monica public relations executive, and his fussy wife, Lizzy, were first-time parents who in the premiere of *Baby Bob* made a startling discovery—their six-month-old son could talk. Not just baby talk, but talk like a full-grown adult—although a lot of things about the adult world mystified him. Lizzy wanted to tell the world but Walter, fearing that their son would be treated like a freak, swore both her and Bob to secrecy. Unfortunately Bob sometimes spoke when others could hear him, making it difficult to keep the secret. Walter's cantankerous widowed father, Sam, was a doting grandparent, while Lizzy's divorced mother, Madeline, was forever bragging about her other grandchildren. In the fourth episode, after Bob slipped and talked in front of both of them, it was hard for Walter to convince them to keep the secret. Although none of the adults knew it, Bob had been chatting for some time with his baby-sitter, Teala.

BABY BOOM (*Situation Comedy*)
FIRST TELECAST: *September 10, 1988*
LAST TELECAST: *January 4, 1989*
BROADCAST HISTORY:
Sep 1988, NBC Sat 9:30–10:00
Nov 1988–Jan 1989, NBC Wed 9:30–10:00
CAST:
J. C. Wiatt .... Kate Jackson
Elizabeth (age 2)
.... Michelle & Kristina Kennedy (alternating)
Fritz Curtis .... Sam Wanamaker
Charlotte .... Susie Essman
Arlene Mandell .... Robyn Peterson
Ken Arrenberg .... Daniel Bardol
Helga Von Haupt....................... Joy Behar

Yet another movie-turned-TV series that flopped was this comedy based on the 1987 Diane Keaton film of the same name. J. C. was the picture of Yuppiedom, a stylish, single, Harvard-educated lawyer aggressively pushing her way up the executive ladder at a large corporation. Dates called her "The Tiger Lady." Then on her doorstep appeared baby Elizabeth, left to her by a recently deceased English relative. J. C.'s high-powered career was thrown into turmoil. She tried hard to juggle the demands of instant motherhood and career, but never could seem to decide which life she wanted. Seemingly oblivious to her plight were Mr. Curtis, her demanding boss (played by Sam Wanamaker, who also appeared in the movie); secretary Charlotte; fellow lawyer Arlene; and officious young assistant Ken, who was constantly angling for her job. Helga was the fearsome nanny who took care of Elizabeth while J. C. played office politics.

Seen occasionally in flashbacks were J. C. as a career-obsessed child (played by Nikki Feemster) and as a teen (played by Jill Whitlow).

Viewers were apparently unamused by the idea of baby-as-career-obstacle, and the series was soon canceled. Two leftover episodes aired on August 14 and September 10, 1989.

BABY, I'M BACK (*Situation Comedy*)
FIRST TELECAST: *January 30, 1978*
LAST TELECAST: *August 12, 1978*
BROADCAST HISTORY:
Jan 1978–Aug 1978, CBS Mon 8:30–9:00
CAST:
Raymond Ellis.................... Demond Wilson
Olivia Ellis....................... Denise Nicholas
Luzelle Carter .... Helen Martin
Angie Ellis .... Kim Fields
Jordan Ellis......................... Tony Holmes
Col. Wallace Dickey........................ Ed Hall

Seven years after he had deserted his wife because he couldn't take the pressures of being married, Raymond Ellis discovered that she had just had him declared legally dead. His interest in reconciliation suddenly revived, Raymond moved into the apartment building where his ex-wife, Olivia, lived with their two young children, Angie and Jordan, and her mother Luzelle. Not only did Ray try to rekindle a romance with his estranged wife, but he also had to contend with a mother-in-law who had never thought very much of him in the first place, and with Olivia's fiancé, Col. Dickey. Col. Dickey was a Pentagon official for whom Olivia worked and to whom she was planning to get married—until Ray showed up. A backdrop to this romantic conflict was Ray's attempts to have himself legally declared alive.

BABY MAKES FIVE (*Situation Comedy*)
FIRST TELECAST: *April 1, 1983*
LAST TELECAST: *April 29, 1983*
BROADCAST HISTORY:
Apr 1983, ABC Fri 8:00–8:30
CAST:
Eddie Riddle .... Peter Scolari
Jennie Riddle .... Louise Williams
Blanche Riddle .... Janis Paige
Edna Kearney .... Priscilla Morrill
Michael Riddle .... André Gower
Laura Riddle .... Emily Moultrie
Annie Riddle .... Brandy Gold

Babies and other small children were the focus of this super-cute family comedy. Accountant Eddie Riddle was the young husband who found his family growing faster than expected; his wife Jennie was about to give birth to twins to add to the three small children already creating havoc in their household. Eddie's madcap mother Blanche and Jennie's stodgy, old-fashioned mom Edna were also on hand.

BABY RACES (*Game*)
BROADCAST HISTORY:
Family Channel
30 minutes
Produced: *1993–1994* (26 episodes)
Premiered: *September 12, 1993*
HOST:
Fred Travalena

A game show in which tots and their families competed in a variety of events. The prizes were toys.

BABY TALK (*Situation Comedy*)
FIRST TELECAST: *March 8, 1991*
LAST TELECAST: *July 3, 1992*
BROADCAST HISTORY:
Mar 1991, ABC Fri 8:30–9:00
Mar 1991–Apr 1991, ABC Fri 9:30–10:00
Apr 1991–May 1991, ABC Tue 8:30–9:00
Sep 1991–Dec 1991, ABC Fri 9:30–10:00
Jan 1992–Mar 1992, ABC Fri 9:00–9:30
Mar 1992–Jun 1992, ABC Fri 9:30–10:00
Jul 1992, ABC Fri 8:30–9:00
CAST:
Maggie Campbell (1991) .... Julia Duffy
Maggie Campbell .... Mary Page Keller
Mickey Campbell .... Paul & Ryan Jessup
Mickey Campbell (voice) .... Tony Danza
Joe (1991) .... George Clooney
Fogarty (1991) .... William Hickey
Howard (1991) .... Lenny Wolpe
Dr. Elliot Fleisher (1991) .... Tom Alan Robbins
Nurse Andrea (1991) .... Michelle Ashlee
James Halbrook .... Scott Baio
Doris Campbell .... Polly Bergen
Anita Craig .... Francesca P. Roberts
Danielle Craig .... Alicia & Celicia Johnson
Danielle Craig (voice) ..... Vernee Watson-Johnson
Susan Davis .... Jessica Lundy
Tony Craig .... Wayne Collins
THEME:
"Bread and Butter" (1964 pop song)

The idea of a TV baby whose thoughts could be heard was at least as old as the 1960 series *Happy*. Television had made progress in thirty years, however, as this time *all* the babies could be heard making unspoken wisecracks. In the Spring 1991 version, harried young single mom Maggie and infant Mickey lived in a Manhattan loft that was still under construction. Joe, Fogarty, and Howard were the incompetent construction workers who were always underfoot. By the fall, Maggie (now played by Mary Page Keller) had moved to an apartment in nearby, trendy Brooklyn Heights, where fun-loving young superintendent James, an aspiring songwriter, became her special friend. Also joining the cast in the fall were Doris, her meddling mom; Susan, a friend and co-worker at the accounting office where she worked; and Anita, a neighbor with a talkative infant of her own.

Nothing seemed to deter ABC from trying to make this inane sitcom a success. Not the fact that two leading ladies quit in the first six months (Connie Sellecca before it even premiered, and Julia Duffy at the end of the Spring 1991 run). Not the fact that gimmicky movies (in this case 1989's *Look Who's Talking*) hardly ever become successful TV series. And certainly not the fact that *Baby Talk* was voted the dubious honor of "Worst Series on Television" in the 1991 *Electronic Media* critics' poll.

BABYLON 5 (*Science Fiction*)
BROADCAST HISTORY:
Syndicated only (1992–1997)
TNT Network (1998)
60 minutes
Produced: *1992–1998* (110 episodes)
Released: *January 1994*
CAST:
Commander Jeffrey Sinclair (1994)
.... Michael O'Hare
Commander John Sheridan (1994–1998)
.... Bruce Boxleitner
Lt. Cmdr. Susan Ivanova (1994–1997)
.... Claudia Christian
Security Chief Michael Garibaldi .... Jerry Doyle
Dr. Stephen Franklin .... Richard Biggs
Talia Winters (1994–1995) ...... Andrea Thompson
Londo Mollari .... Peter Jurasik
Vir Cotto .... Stephen Furst
Delenn .... Mira Furlan
Lennier .... Bill Mumy
Ambassador G'Kar .... Andreas Katsulas
Na'Toth (1994) .... Julie Caitlin Brown
Na'Toth (1994–1995) .... Mary Kay Adams
**Kosh (1994–1996)* .... Ardwight Chamberlain
Lt. Warren Keffer (1994–1995) .... Robert Rusler
Sgt. Zack Allan (1995–1998) .... Jeff Conaway
Marcus Cole (1995–1997) .... Jason Carter
Lyta Alexander (1996–1998) ...... Patricia Tallman
**Alfred Bester (1994–1998)* .... Walter Koenig
Emperor Cartagia (1996–1997) . Wortham Krimmer
Lorien (1996–1997) .... Wayne Alexander

Capt. Elizabeth Lochley (1998) ..... Tracy Scoggins
**Morden (1996–1998)*..................... Ed Wasser
**Number One (1997–1998)*..... Marjorie Monaghan
**Lise Hampton-Edgars (1997–1998)*.. Denise Gentile
Lt. David Corwin (1998) .... Joshua Cox
Byron (1998) .... Robin Atkin Downes
Drazi Ambassador (1998) .... Kim Strauss
Centauri Defense Minister (1998)
.... Thomas MacGreevy

*Occasional

This space opera was set in the year 2258 aboard Babylon 5, a space station where 250,000 beings from different worlds could work and play together. It was big enough to include seamy slums as well as areas housing aliens whose environmental needs were decidedly nonhuman. It was also neutral turf, a place to keep the peace, its regularly scheduled council meetings with government representatives from many worlds serving as an interplanetary UN trying to resolve disputes among the League of Non-aligned Worlds. Visitors to Babylon 5 included diplomats, hustlers, entrepreneurs, and wanderers. The series opened ten years after the end of the Earth-Minbari war, at a time when the Centauri and the Narn, longtime enemies whose ambassadors barely tolerated each other, were on the verge of starting a war of their own.

Jeffrey Sinclair was the senior military officer on Babylon 5, charged with keeping the peace among often hostile entities. On his staff were Ivanova, a dedicated officer with very little sense of humor; Garibaldi, the grizzled security chief with a checkered past; Dr. Franklin, the compassionate head physician; and Winters, the telepath who verified sincerity of individuals during negotiations. Among the diplomats on Babylon 5 were Mollari, the ebullient Centauri ambassador, and his aide, Vir; Delenn, the Minbari ambassador, and her aide, Lennier; G'Kar, the often hostile Narn ambassador, and his aide, Na'Toth; and Kosh, the mysterious, clairvoyant nonhumanoid Vorlon ambassador.

At the start of the 1994–1995 season things started to heat up on Babylon 5. Sinclair had been reassigned to the Minbari home world and was replaced by Sheridan, a decorated officer. Early on he promoted Ivanova to Commander and gave Garibaldi, unsure of his position with the new commanding officer, a vote of confidence. Delenn, who had been hibernating, came out of a cocoon looking more like an Earth woman than a Minbari as she metamorphosed into a hybrid entity. That February the Centauri attacked a Narn base and, despite having ambassadors on Babylon 5, the Narn declared war on the Centauri. The station struggled to remain neutral territory.

The Narn were defeated by the Centauri in the fall of 1995. In November the station was caught up in the year of the Shadow War (2260) with mysterious aliens. Meanwhile, Earth's corrupt President Clark was embroiled in a dispute with the Mars colony, which escalated into a violent war when he attempted to put it under martial law. When Babylon 5 gave refuge to Martian colonists, it precipitated a dispute with Earth, and Sheridan seceded from the Earth alliance to join with the Martians and other rebellious colonies. Babylon 5's staff found out from arrogant, telepathic Psy-corp officer Bester that the "Shadow" people had worked with the Centauri to defeat the Narn and were allied with President Clark. When Sheridan got Kosh's Vorlons to engage the Shadow ships to prove to the unaligned worlds that they were not invincible, the Shadows' human liaison on Babylon 5 provided them access to Kosh's quarters, where they killed him.

That fall Delenn took over as head of the station's Rangers fighting against the Shadows. As they prepared to battle the Shadows, with the help of a strike force built by the Minbari, Sheridan and Delenn fell in love. He went on a secret mission to the Shadow home world and set off a nuclear device that destroyed much of their capital city and "killed" him. Sheridan was reanimated by Lorien (the last of an ancient race of near-immortals), but the process would only give him twenty more years of life. Londo returned to Centauri Prime to take a state position, and after realizing that his emperor, who had been working with the Shadows, was crazy, plotted to assassinate him (Vir actually did it, with a drug that stopped his heart). After the assassination Londo was appointed Prime Minister of Centauri Prime and, as he had promised, gave Narn its freedom in return for the help G'Kar had provided during his coup. In the final Shadow War confrontation the Vorlons and the Shadows, along with Lorien, who had been around since the beginning of time, went beyond the rim to follow the other ancient races and leave the galaxy to humans and other younger races.

After the end of the Shadow War, President Clark set about to undermine Sheridan and shut down Babylon 5, using Bester and Psy-corp as his minions. Londo and Vir returned to Babylon 5, and Garibaldi, who had been emotionally readjusted as a pawn of Psy-corp, resigned his post, with Zack being promoted to head of security. Franklin and scout Cole went to Mars to rally the resistance forces and gain support for Babylon 5's fight with President Clark, and Sheridan declared war on the Earth forces to force the evil Clark out of power. Garibaldi worked with Martian business interests to capture Sheridan and stop the rebellion so that they could do business with President Clark and the Psy-corp, but Garibaldi's conditioned mind alerted Bester, who foiled their plan and freed Garibaldi's mind. Garibaldi told the Mars leadership and his former crew mates what had been done to him and led a group that freed Sheridan. The Council of Non-aligned Worlds voted to help Sheridan fight Earth, resulting in President Clark's suicide. He almost took Earth with him, but Sheridan's forces destroyed the booby-trapped defense grid around the planet. Ivanova, badly hurt in a confrontation during the war with Earth, was saved when Cole used an alien healing machine to transfer his life energy to save her—and perished.

When new *Babylon 5* episodes surfaced on TNT, Sheridan, now married to Delenn, was elected first president of the Interstellar Alliance. Garibaldi was made head of security for the Alliance, and new to the cast was Elizabeth Lochley, replacing Sheridan as Captain of Babylon 5. Ivanova had left. Londo was in transition—he was the Centauri Emperor-to-be—and he told Vir that when he became emperor, Vir would be appointed ambassador to Babylon 5. After Lennier went on a Ranger mission that proved the Centauri were responsible for attacks plaguing Alliance shipping, a surprised Londo was informed that the Centauri were being tossed out of the Alliance and a blockade placed around Centauri Prime. He returned to his home world with G'Kar as his bodyguard, and the two of them were thrown into jail by the conspirators responsible for the attacks. A war ensued, Centauri Prime fell, and G'Kar became a hero to his people. G'Kar, who didn't want to return home to be idolized, departed on a trip across the universe with Lyta, the telepath who had replaced Winters two years earlier. Garibaldi married Lise and took over control of Edgars Industries on Mars, while Sheridan and Delenn, who was carrying his child, moved to Minbari.

Babylon 5's last original episode served as an epitaph for the series. It took place in 2281, twenty years after Sheridan's reanimation on the Shadow home world. Sheridan, knowing he was dying, got his old Babylon 5 gang back together for a final dinner and reminiscences at his home on Minbari, where the Alliance's headquarters had been for almost two decades. In 2279, Sheridan had refused to continue as President and Delenn was elected to replace him. They all came—Vir, now Emperor of the Centauri; Garibaldi, still living on Mars with Lise and their young daughter; Ivanova, a General with a desk job on Earth; and Franklin, doing medical research on Earth. The next morning Sheridan took a one-man scout ship to Babylon 5 for a last farewell, and on to the star system where they had won the Shadow War. He was met by Lorien, who materialized inside Sheridan's ship and took him beyond the rim. Zack, who had returned to Babylon 5 in its waning days, was there for its decommissioning, he was joined by Delenn, Garibaldi, Franklin, Vir, and Ivanova. After the ceremony Zack went to work for Vir on Centauri Prime and Delenn appointed Ivanova head of the Rangers.

The two-hour pilot episode for *Babylon 5* was produced in 1992 and aired early in 1993, but the series did not premiere until a year later.

BACHELOR, THE (*Romance/Reality*)
FIRST TELECAST: *March 25, 2002*
LAST TELECAST:
BROADCAST HISTORY:

Mar 2002–Apr 2002, ABC Mon 9:00–10:00
Sep 2002–Nov 2002, ABC Wed 9:00–10:00
Jan 2003–Feb 2003, ABC Wed 9:00–10:00
Mar 2003–May 2003, ABC Wed 9:00–10:00

HOST:

Chris Harrison

The premise of *The Bachelor* was simple and compelling. Twenty-five women were driven by limousine to a luxurious Malibu estate to meet one eligible bachelor. Over the next six weeks they partied, dated, went on glamorous excursions and talked, while cameras watched. One by one the women were eliminated until at the end the bachelor picked just one to be his possible future bride.

The first bachelor was darkly handsome Alex Michel, a 31-year-old Harvard-educated management consultant from Virginia who bore more than a passing resemblance to John F. Kennedy, Jr. The bachelorettes ranged in age from 22 to 31 and were attractive, accomplished (and white); they included doctors, attorneys, an actress and a photographer. They all met at a big, formal party, at the end of which Alex had to go alone into the "deliberation room" and decide which 15 would get long-stemmed roses, meaning they could come back the following week. In week two cameras followed three dates with five women each, in Las Vegas, Palm Springs and Santa Barbara, after which eight got roses and seven more candidates were cut. (At any point a candidate could decline the rose and leave, but none did.) In week three two of Alex's friends arrived to give the eight remaining candidates a "compatibility test," after which three got private dates and then four more were eliminated. During the following weeks he met the families of the four remaining candidates, had "dream dates" in New York, Lake Tahoe and Hawaii, and eventually eliminated two more. Then, following a special "the women tell all" episode, Alex took the last two—Trista Rehn and Amanda Marsh—home to meet his folks. He then made his final choice, 23-year-old event planner Amanda. However, to the great dismay of the producers, he didn't propose, but said he'd hold on to the ring until they got to know each other better. (They later broke up.)

It was glossy, catty, opulent and romantic all at once. A male reviewer in *Variety* grumped that the show was "insulting to women . . . as if the network bankrolled a brothel and positioned cameras to catch the action." But female viewers loved it, and made it one of the biggest ratings hits of 2002, guaranteeing a second edition in the fall. In that one the bachelor was hunky young Aaron Buerge, a budding restaurateur, banker (in his family's bank) and classical pianist all rolled into one. Seeking to deflect criticism that the first bachelor had been a little too slick and devious, this one, from Missouri, looked as all-American as you can get. After seven weeks of glamorous dates and meeting the folks he proposed to his final choice, New Jersey psychologist Helene Eksterowicz, and she accepted. (It didn't last.)

The next edition, in early 2003, was called *The Bachelorette*, and it turned the tables by having the rejected Trista from the first *Bachelor* date 25 eligible men. A sexy, vivacious dancer for the Miami Heat, and a physical therapist, she had the time of her life doing to two dozen guys (age 24 to 42) what Alex had done to her. The guys were clearly a little more uncomfortable in this situation (host Chris kept asking, "How's it feel?"), but they went along. In the end she chose shaggy-haired Ryan Sutter, who had read her a poem he wrote called "Something About Her."

The next edition added a new twist with the bachelor being Andrew Firestone, the great-grandson of tire entrepreneur Harvey Firestone, a very rich bachelor indeed. After weeks of lavish parties, romantic dates and tours of his family's vineyards, he proposed to 26-year-old Chicago account executive Jennifer Schefft, and she accepted.

BACHELOR FATHER (*Situation Comedy*)
FIRST TELECAST: *September 15, 1957*
LAST TELECAST: *September 25, 1962*
BROADCAST HISTORY:

Sep 1957–Jun 1959, CBS Sun 7:30–8:00 (OS)
Jun 1959–Sep 1961, NBC Thu 9:00–9:30
Oct 1961–Sep 1962, ABC Tue 8:00–8:30

CAST:

Bentley Gregg .... John Forsythe
Kelly Gregg .... Noreen Corcoran
Peter Tong .... Sammee Tong
Ginger Farrell/Loomis/Mitchell
.... Bernadette Withers

Howard Meechim (1958–1961) .... Jimmy Boyd
Elaine Meechim (1959) .... Joan Vohs
Cal Mitchell (1960–1962) .... Del Moore
Adelaide Mitchell (1960–1962) .... Evelyn Scott
Cousin Charlie Fong (1961–1962)
.... Victor Sen Yung
Warren Dawson (1962)............... Aron Kincaid
Vickie (1957–1958) .... Alice Backus
Kitty Deveraux (1958–1959)....... Shirley Mitchell
Kitty Marsh (1959–1961)......... Sue Ane Langdon
Suzanne Collins (1961) .... Jeanne Bal
Connie (1961–1962)............... Sally Mansfield

Bentley Gregg was a wealthy, successful Hollywood attorney, whose clients included many glamorous and available women. He lived with his niece Kelly, his houseboy Peter, and a large shaggy dog named Jasper in posh Beverly Hills. Uncle Bentley had become Kelly's legal guardian after her parents had been killed in an automobile accident when she was 13 years old. Between his large and active law practice, his social life with beautiful women, and the responsibilities of raising a teenage girl, Bentley's time was more than adequately filled. Peter, the helpful but often inscrutable Oriental houseboy, was a jack-of-all-trades who ran the Gregg home and was indispensable to his boss.

Kelly was a typical teenager—exuberant and enthusiastic—who at times tried to find a wife for her uncle. During her high school years she had a regular boyfriend, lanky Howard Meechim. Her best friend was Ginger, whose parents and last name were changed twice during the five-year run of the show; only the last set of parents, Cal and Adelaide Mitchell, appeared often enough to be listed as regulars. At the end of the 1960–1961 season, in the last episode aired on NBC, Kelly graduated from high school. Two weeks later, when new episodes began on ABC, she had started college. The following spring brought her true love, in the person of Warren Dawson, a young lawyer who became Bentley's junior partner and Kelly's fiancé. *Bachelor Father* concluded its network run at the end of that season, however, so that Kelly and Warren never did get married.

As for Bentley, he may have been an irresistible ladies' man, but he certainly had trouble holding on to a secretary. Five different actresses filled that role in succession: Alice Backus, Shirley Mitchell, Sue Ane Langdon, Jeanne Bal, and Sally Mansfield.

In what would later become a bit of irony, actress Linda Evans appeared in one episode of *Bachelor Father* as a girlfriend of Bentley's niece Kelly. Two decades later, on the series *Dynasty*, she and John Forsythe, who had played Bentley, were man and wife.

BACHELORETTE, THE, see *The Bachelor*

BACK THAT FACT (*Audience Participation*)
FIRST TELECAST: *October 22, 1953*
LAST TELECAST: *November 26, 1953*
BROADCAST HISTORY:
Oct 1953–Nov 1953, ABC Thu 9:00–9:30
EMCEE:
Joey Adams
ASSISTANTS:
Al Kelly
Hope Lange
Carl Caruso

As host of this short-lived audience-participation show, Joey Adams interviewed members of the studio audience about such matters as their backgrounds, hobbies, and accomplishments. From time to time an offstage voice (Carl Caruso) would challenge a statement they made, calling on them to "back that fact." If they could (in the estimation of a panel chosen from the audience), they won a prize. The program was presented live from New York.

BACKGROUND (*News/Documentary*)
FIRST TELECAST: *August 16, 1954*
LAST TELECAST: *September 6, 1954*
BROADCAST HISTORY:
Aug 1954–Sep 1954, NBC Mon 8:30–9:00
COMMENTATOR:
Joseph C. Harsch

On this program, Joseph C. Harsch each week presented an analysis of a different issue of current world importance. Special film reports produced by NBC News were used; the thrust of the program was to take the audience beyond the headlines to the people who were actually living the news. After a brief run in prime time the series moved to Sunday afternoons, where it continued until June 1955.

BACKSTAGE WITH BARRY WOOD (*Variety*)
FIRST TELECAST: *March 1, 1949*
LAST TELECAST: *May 24, 1949*
BROADCAST HISTORY:
Mar 1949–May 1949, CBS Tue 10:00–10:15
HOST:
Barry Wood

Singer Barry Wood was the producer and host of this series, which gave young entertainers an opportunity to perform on live television to a full network audience. The slogan of the show was that it "featured tomorrow's stars today."

BACKSTAIRS AT THE WHITE HOUSE
(*Documentary/Drama*)
FIRST TELECAST: *January 29, 1979*
LAST TELECAST: *February 19, 1979*
BROADCAST HISTORY:
Jan 1979–Feb 1979, NBC Mon 9:00–11:00
CAST:
Maggie Rogers .... Olivia Cole
Lillian Rogers (as a child) .... Tania Johnson
Lillian Rogers Parks (as an adult).... Leslie Uggams
Levi Mercer .... Louis Gossett, Jr.
Ike Hoover......................... Leslie Nielsen
Mrs. Jaffray .... Cloris Leachman
Mays .... Robert Hooks
Coates .... Hari Rhodes
Dixon.......................... David Downing
Jackson .... Bill Overton
Annie............................ Helena Carroll
Pres. William Howard Taft .... Victor Buono
Helen "Nellie" Taft..................... Julie Harris
Pres. Woodrow Wilson .... Robert Vaughn
Ellen Wilson .... Kim Hunter
Edith Galt Wilson .... Claire Bloom
Pres. Warren Harding .... George Kennedy
Florence Harding.................. Celeste Holm
Pres. Calvin Coolidge.............. Ed Flanders
Grace Coolidge........................ Lee Grant
Pres. Herbert Hoover .... Larry Gates

Lou Hoover .... Jan Sterling
Pres. Franklin D. Roosevelt .... John Anderson
Eleanor Roosevelt .... Eileen Heckart
Pres. Harry S Truman .... Harry Morgan
Bess Truman .... Estelle Parsons
Pres. Dwight D. Eisenhower .... Andrew Duggan
Mamie Eisenhower .... Barbara Barrie

This mini-series presented an unusual glimpse into the private lives of eight American Presidents—from Taft to Eisenhower—as seen through the eyes of the permanent White House staff. The central characters were Chief Maid Maggie Rogers and her daughter, Lillian, who succeeded her. A continuing subplot concerned Maggie's efforts to hold her own little family together, despite many problems: a missing husband, survival on the edge of poverty (White House servants, though they worked amid the trappings of wealth and power, were paid very little), a son permanently scarred by wartime service, and daughter Lillian's affliction with polio. Lillian, though occasionally hotheaded, overcame her affliction and went on to a long and successful career serving the Presidents and their sometimes more demanding wives.

Others on the White House staff included Mrs. Jaffray, the head housekeeper; Ike Hoover, the chief usher; and Levi Mercer, the serving man. Coates and Dixon were butlers, Mays and Jackson, doormen, and Annie, another maid.

Based on *My Thirty Years Backstairs at the White House*, by Lillian Rogers Parks with Frances Spatz Leighton, a book which created a furor when first released because of its frank and intimate portrayal of presidential families. At the beginning of each episode of the mini-series it was announced that in some instances real names and settings had been changed to advance the story.

BAD NEWS BEARS, THE (*Situation Comedy*)

FIRST TELECAST: *March 24, 1979*

LAST TELECAST: *July 26, 1980*

BROADCAST HISTORY:

Mar 1979–Sep 1979, CBS Sat 8:00–8:30
Sep 1979–Oct 1979, CBS Sat 8:30–9:00
Jun 1980, CBS Sat 8:00–8:30
Jul 1980, CBS Sat 8:30–9:00

CAST:

Morris Buttermaker .... Jack Warden
Dr. Emily Rappant .... Catherine Hicks
Roy Turner .... Phillip R. Allen
Leslie Ogilvie .... Sparky Marcus
Tanner Boyle .... Meeno Peluce
Rudi Stein .... Billy Jacoby
Regi Tower .... Corey Feldman
Timmy Lupus .... Shane Butterworth
Ahmad Abdul Rahim .... Christoff St. John
Mike Engelberg .... J. Brennan Smith
Miguel Agilar .... Charles Nunez
Jose Agilar .... Danny Nunez
Amanda Whirlitzer .... Tricia Cast
Frosty .... Bill Lazarus
Kelly Leek .... Gregg Forrest
Josh Matthews .... Rad Daly

Former minor-league baseball player Morris Buttermaker was trying to make a living as a swimming-pool cleaner, but his temper got him another, part-time job. When one of his clients refused to pay him, Morris drove the client's car into the pool. Dragged into court, he was given the alternative of "volunteering" to coach the baseball team at Hoover Junior High or going to jail. He chose baseball, but soon found that jail might have been more rewarding—the Hoover Bears were as sorry a pack of youthful misfits and bumblers as could be found anywhere. It was a miracle that he managed to get them to accomplish anything. Dr. Emily Rappant was Hoover's principal, Roy Turner, the coach of the hated rival Lions, and Amanda Whirlitzer, the Bears' star pitcher. Morris had dated Amanda's mother at one time, and Amanda was always looking for ways to get them back together. The only member of the Bears who was not on the team when the series premiered was Josh Matthews, who transferred to Hoover in the fall of 1979.

Based on the 1976 motion picture, *The Bad News Bears*, starring Walter Matthau and Tatum O'Neal. Two sequels to the theatrical movie, *The Bad News Bears in Breaking Training* and *The Bad News Bears Go to Japan*, were released prior to the start of the television series.

BADGE 714, syndicated title for *Dragnet* (before 1967)

BAGDAD CAFE (*Situation Comedy*)

FIRST TELECAST: *March 30, 1990*

LAST TELECAST: *November 23, 1990*

BROADCAST HISTORY:

Mar 1990–May 1990, CBS Fri 9:00–9:30
Sep 1990–Nov 1990, CBS Fri 8:30–9:00

CAST:

Brenda .... Whoopi Goldberg
Jasmine Zweibel .... Jean Stapleton
Juney (age 22) .... Scott Lawrence
Debbie (16) .... Monica Calhoun
Rudy .... James Gammon
**Sal* .... Cleavon Little
Dewey Kunkle .... Sam Whipple

*Occasional

THEME:

"Calling You," written by Bob Telson and sung by Jevetta Steele

Brenda and Jasmine were, in their way, a female "Odd Couple"—two women with seemingly incompatible personalities who became fast friends. Brenda was the owner and operator of the Bagdad Cafe diner and motel, an isolated, fleabitten rest stop in the middle of the Mojave Desert between Los Angeles and Las Vegas. Jasmine had been traveling through the desert with her husband when their car broke down. The argument that followed was, for her, the last straw. She abandoned him and dragged her luggage through the desert until she staggered into the Bagdad Cafe. With limited funds and no desire to return to her former life, Jasmine went to work for Brenda and took up residence in one of the rooms at the motel.

Jasmine was a perfect complement to Brenda. She was very neat, structured, and organized while Brenda was a disorganized slob. She was philosophical and optimistic while Brenda was a crude, loudmouthed cynic. The one thing they had in common was being separated from their husbands—Brenda having thrown out her philandering Sal when she caught him in bed with a guest at the motel. Other regulars were Juney, Brenda's talented piano-playing son who served as the diner's cook and was raising his infant daughter, Amarah; Debbie, Brenda's daughter who was much more interested in boys than in her schoolwork; and Rudy, a regular at the diner who took an immediate fancy to Jasmine. When *Bagdad Cafe* returned in the fall, Rudy's nervous nephew Dewey, unable to cope with a high-stress job in the space industry, arrived and took over as the diner's cook. Juney had departed to seek his fortune, leaving Brenda with the additional burden of raising her granddaughter.

Adapted from the 1988 theatrical film of the same name, with Monica Calhoun reprising her role as Debbie.

BAILEYS OF BALBOA, THE (*Situation Comedy*)
FIRST TELECAST: *September 24, 1964*
LAST TELECAST: *April 1, 1965*
BROADCAST HISTORY:
Sep 1964–Apr 1965, CBS Thu 9:30–10:00
CAST:
Sam Bailey .... Paul Ford
Buck Singleton .... Sterling Holloway
Jim Bailey .... Les Brown, Jr.
Stanley .... Clint Howard
Commodore Cecil Wyntoon .... John Dehner
Barbara Wyntoon .... Judy Carne

Paul Ford portrayed crusty old Sam Bailey, a widower who ran a small charter fishing boat called *The Island Princess.* The boat was based on a little island Sam owned in the middle of Balboa, California, an exclusive yachting community. Sam's unpretentious nature and dislike for fancy society trappings antagonized the surrounding community, particularly the aristocratic Commodore Wyntoon. Sam's son Jim was infatuated with the commodore's daughter Barbara, however, and their romance forced a degree of civility on the two fathers. Buck was the forgetful first mate and entire crew of *The Island Princess*, and Stanley was an obnoxious little boy who was one of Sam's neighbors.

BAKER'S DOZEN (*Situation Comedy*)
FIRST TELECAST: *March 17, 1982*
LAST TELECAST: *April 21, 1982*
BROADCAST HISTORY:
Mar 1982–Apr 1982, CBS Wed 9:30–10:00
CAST:
Mike Locasale .... Ron Silver
Terry Munson .... Cindy Weintraub
O.K. Otis Kelly .... Alan Weeks
Harve Schoendorf .... Sam McMurray
Desk Sgt. Martin .... Thomas Quinn
Jeff Diggins .... John Del Regno
Capt. Florence Baker .... Doris Belack

Much in the style of *Barney Miller, Baker's Dozen* sought to show the human and often funny side of police work. It followed the offbeat activities of an undercover anti-crime unit of the N.Y.P.D. under the direction of no-nonsense Capt. Florence Baker. Mike and Terry, two of the undercover cops, struggled to maintain their rather rocky romantic relationship, though their assignments often got in the way. Kelly and Harve were also members of Baker's team and Jeff Diggins, one of the many street people they dealt with, was a neighborhood con man who sometimes helped them out with information. Sgt. Martin, the precinct philosopher, was forever spouting homilies and making long-winded observations about life to anyone who would sit still and listen.

The program was filmed on location in New York City.

BAKERSFIELD P.D. (*Situation Comedy*)
FIRST TELECAST: *September 14, 1993*
LAST TELECAST: *August 25, 1994*
BROADCAST HISTORY:
Sep 1993–Jan 1994, FOX Tue 8:30–9:00
Jul 1994–Aug 1994, FOX Thu 9:30–10:00
CAST:
Det. Wade Preston .... Ron Eldard
Det. Paul Gigante .... Giancarlo Esposito
Off. Denny Boyer .... Chris Mulkey
Off. Luke Ramirez .... Tony Plana
Capt. Aldo Stiles .... Jack Hallett
Sgt. Phil Hampton .... Brian Doyle-Murray

Most episodes of this quirky police comedy opened with morning roll call, as had the critically acclaimed *Hill Street Blues*, but this loony series more closely resembled *Police Squad*. The central character was Detective Paul Gigante, a reserved officer who relocated from Washington, D.C., following a separation from his wife, to start a new life on the police force of Bakersfield, California. Half black and half Italian, Paul was the only black on the force and was often mistaken for a criminal simply because of his race. Wade, his partner, was a well-meaning redneck and a trivia freak. Sgt. Hampton, a 22-year veteran of the force, was the long-suffering aide to inept, indecisive Capt. Stiles. Hampton spent much of his time covering for Stiles's mistakes and making decisions for him. Also seen were Officer Boyer, a hunky but incredibly dumb officer and his partner, Ramirez, who was highly emotional and sensitive.

BALANCE YOUR BUDGET (*Quiz/Audience Participation*)
FIRST TELECAST: *October 18, 1952*
LAST TELECAST: *May 2, 1953*
BROADCAST HISTORY:
Oct 1952–May 1953, CBS Sat 10:00–10:30
EMCEE:
Bert Parks

Contestants on *Balance Your Budget* were asked to describe what had caused "their personal or family budgets to slip into the red"; they were then given an opportunity to win some money by answering a series of questions asked by emcee Bert Parks. Winners were also given the opportunity to pick from among a large number of keys, one of which would open the show's "Treasure Chest," containing an additional jackpot of $1,500 or more. Because the contestants had the chance to explain why they needed the money, CBS billed this as a "human interest" quiz show.

BALL FOUR (*Situation Comedy*)
FIRST TELECAST: *September 22, 1976*
LAST TELECAST: *October 27, 1976*
BROADCAST HISTORY:
Sep 1976–Oct 1976, CBS Wed 8:30–9:00
CAST:
Jim Barton .... Jim Bouton
"Cap" Capogrosso .... Jack Somack

Bill Westlake.................. David-James Carroll
"Rhino" Rhinelander................ Ben Davidson
Coach Pinky Pinkney............. Bill McCutcheon
Lenny "Birdman" Siegel .... Lenny Schultz
Rayford Plunkett.................... Marco St. John
Orlando Lopez .... Jaime Tirelli
C. B. Travis .... Sam Wright

Ball Four was truly "locker-room" comedy, since most of its action took place in the locker room of a major league baseball team, the Washington Americans. In the first episode pitcher Jim Barton informed his teammates and coaches that he was going to write a series of articles on baseball life "off the field." Manager Capogrosso and most of the others were not very keen on the idea, and neither was the viewing audience. The show folded after less than two months on the air. *Ball Four* was based on a book of the same title by former major league pitcher Jim Bouton. Not only did he star in a semi-autobiographical role in the series, he was also one of the writers.

BANACEK (*Detective Drama*)
FIRST TELECAST: *September 13, 1972*
LAST TELECAST: *September 3, 1974*
BROADCAST HISTORY:
Sep 1972–Dec 1973, NBC Wed 8:30–10:00
Jan 1974–Sep 1974, NBC Tue 8:30–10:00
CAST:
Thomas Banacek .... George Peppard
Jay Drury............................ Ralph Manza
Felix Mulholland................ Murray Matheson
Carlie Kirkland (1973–1974)...... Christine Belford

The gimmick in this private-eye series was ethnic: Banacek was a cool, smooth, shrewd Polish-American. His game was collecting rewards from insurance companies by solving crimes involving stolen property, and he was successful enough to live in the exclusive Beacon Hill section of Boston. Banacek's buddies were his chauffeur Jay and his good friend Felix, who ran a bookstore. During the show's second season Carlie, an insurance agent, was added for romantic interest. Polish proverbs were liberally sprinkled throughout the series, and the positive image of its hero made the show very popular with such groups as the Polish-American Congress, which gave the program an award for portraying Polish-Americans in a positive manner. *Banacek* originally aired as one of the rotating segments of NBC's *Wednesday Mystery Movie*.

BAND OF AMERICA, see *Cities Service*

BAND OF THE WEEK, see *Music at the Meadowbrook*

BANDS ON THE RUN (*Competition*)
BROADCAST HISTORY:
VH1
60 minutes
Original episodes: *2001* (16 episodes)
Premiered: *April 1, 2001*
HOSTS ("TOUR MANAGERS"):
Brendon Carter
Katina Turner

A kind of *Survivor* for rock-band wannabes, this intriguing series followed four unknown bands (four to five members each) as they traveled across the country competing for a shot at stardom. The "tour" started in San Francisco, where each band was given a van, phone cards, and $20 a day allowance. After that they moved from city to city playing separate small-time gigs, scaring up their own publicity via posters and radio interviews, schmoozing fans and meeting challenges posed by the producers. Viewers voted on-line for the best band in each challenge, which included the band with the coolest outfits, best original songs, best self-designed album art, coolest answering-machine message, wildest road story, craziest publicity stunt, and finally "the band that rocks hardest on stage." The bands also had to hustle to sell CDs, T-shirts, and other souvenirs to raise cash, and were graded on how much money they brought in. There were plenty of squabbling and partying, highs and lows (as when one band played to an empty club), making this like a noisy version of MTV's *Road Rules*.

The four bands were hard-rocking Flickerstick, pop-rock SoulCracker, exotic girl group Harlow, and the art-rock Josh Dodes Band. Flickerstick won in a landslide, getting the $25,000 grand prize and a contract with Epic Records; ranking a distant last was the arty Josh Dodes Band.

BANK ON THE STARS (*Quiz/Audience Participation*)
FIRST TELECAST: *June 20, 1953*
LAST TELECAST: *August 21, 1954*
BROADCAST HISTORY:
Jun 1953, CBS Sat 9:00–9:30
Jun 1953–Aug 1953, CBS Sat 9:30–10:00
May 1954–Aug 1954, NBC Sat 8:00–8:30
EMCEE:
Jack Paar (1953)
Bill Cullen (May–Jul 1954)
Jimmy Nelson (Jul–Aug 1954)

Contestants on this game show were drawn from the studio audience and divided into teams. Each two-person team would be shown a film clip from a famous motion picture and asked questions about the scene, for cash prizes. A bonus round involved answering more difficult questions about a different movie scene, which the contestants could only hear and not see.

BANYON (*Detective Drama*)
FIRST TELECAST: *September 15, 1972*
LAST TELECAST: *January 12, 1973*
BROADCAST HISTORY:
Sep 1972–Jan 1973, NBC Fri 10:00–11:00
CAST:
Miles C. Banyon .... Robert Forster
Peggy Revere .... Joan Blondell
Lt. Pete McNeil .... Richard Jaeckel
Abby Graham .... Julie Gregg

This period private-eye series was set in Los Angeles during the late 1930s. Banyon, a tough but honest detective, would take on any case, from murder to missing persons, for $20 a day. Peggy Revere, whose secretarial school was located in the same building as Banyon's office, provided him each week with a new free secretary, ranging from sexpot to country farm girl. Banyon's eyes were fixed on his girlfriend Abby Graham, a nightclub singer—though he successfully evaded her constant efforts to get him to marry and settle down.

BARBARA MCNAIR SHOW, THE (*Musical Variety*)

BROADCAST HISTORY:

Syndicated only
60 minutes
Produced: *1969–1971* (52 episodes)
Released: *Fall 1969*

HOSTESS:

Barbara McNair

This was one of those pleasant musical variety shows that made the rounds in the late 1960s and early 1970s. Barbara McNair, a good-looking black songstress, hosted such diverse musical guests as John Gary and the Turtles, along with such comics as Bob Hope, Soupy Sales, and Rich Little.

BARBARA MANDRELL & THE MANDRELL SISTERS (*Musical Variety*)

FIRST TELECAST: *November 18, 1980*
LAST TELECAST: *June 26, 1982*
BROADCAST HISTORY:

Nov 1980, NBC Tue 10:00–11:00
Nov 1980–Jan 1982, NBC Sat 8:00–9:00
Jan 1982–Feb 1982, NBC Sat 9:00–10:00
Mar 1982, NBC Tue 10:00–11:00
Apr 1982–Jun 1982, NBC Sat 9:00–10:00

REGULARS:

Barbara Mandrell
Louise Mandrell
Irlene Mandrell
The Krofft Puppets

Country-and-western music star Barbara Mandrell hosted this variety series with the help of her talented younger sisters, Louise and Irlene. All three sang and played musical instruments: Barbara the banjo, steel guitar, piano, and saxophone; Louise, the banjo and fiddle; and Irlene, the drums. They engaged in a certain amount of tongue-in-cheek sibling rivalry, and throughout each telecast there was byplay among the sisters, including comedy sketches describing their relationship over the years. Barbara was usually portrayed as the serious, pushy sister, and Irlene the sexy, vain one.

The main emphasis of the show was on music, however, with such well-known country stars as Dolly Parton, Marty Robbins, Tennessee Ernie Ford, Kenny Rogers, and Charley Pride making appearances. A group of life-size Krofft puppets called Truck Shackley & the Texas Critters—five musicians and a dog—served as the resident band. The series was produced by Sid and Marty Krofft.

Midway through the second season, series star Barbara Mandrell announced that the show would cease production in early 1982. The weekly grind was more work than she had anticipated and, in conjunction with her busy concert schedule, left her on the verge of exhaustion. Health problems, not ratings problems, canceled this series.

BARBARA STANWYCK SHOW, THE (*Dramatic Anthology*)

FIRST TELECAST: *September 19, 1960*
LAST TELECAST: *September 11, 1961*
BROADCAST HISTORY:

Sep 1960–Sep 1961, NBC Mon 10:00–10:30

HOSTESS/STAR:

Barbara Stanwyck

Hollywood leading lady Barbara Stanwyck hosted this anthology of original 30-minute filmed teleplays and starred in all but four of them. The four were pilots for possible series and starred Lloyd Nolan ("The Seventh Miracle"), Milton Berle ("Dear Charlie"), Peggy Cass ("Call Me Annie"), and Andy Devine ("Big Jake"). None of them made it on to the next fall's schedule.

The dramas in which Miss Stanwyck appeared tended to be on the serious side. Three of them were pilots for a proposed new series of her own, in which she would star as an American adventuress running an import-export business in exotic Hong Kong. The original pilot was aired on November 14, 1960, as "The Miraculous Journey of 'Tadpole Chan' " and established the character of Josephine Little. Viewers were requested to write to the network if they liked the idea, and the response was strong enough to result in two other episodes, in January and March. However, the Josephine Little series never went into full production.

BARBARY COAST, THE (*Western*)

FIRST TELECAST: *September 8, 1975*
LAST TELECAST: *January 9, 1976*
BROADCAST HISTORY:

Sep 1975–Oct 1975, ABC Mon 8:00–9:00
Oct 1975–Jan 1976, ABC Fri 8:00–9:00

CAST:

Cash Conover .... Doug McClure
Jeff Cable .... William Shatner
Moose Moran .... Richard Kiel
Thumbs, the piano player .... Dave Turner

This Western was set in the 1870s in a square-mile section of San Francisco called the Barbary Coast, a wide-open, rip-roaring district whose inhabitants ranged from flashy ladies to sourdoughs. Cable was a special agent working for the Governor of California, gathering information on criminals in the district. He traveled incognito and was a master of disguise. Conover was the flamboyant owner of the Golden Gate Casino (which he had won in a poker game) and was Cable's unlikely ally.

BARE ESSENCE (*Drama*)

FIRST TELECAST: *February 15, 1983*
LAST TELECAST: *April 29, 1983*
BROADCAST HISTORY:

Feb 1983–Mar 1983, NBC Tue 9:00–10:00
Mar 1983–Apr 1983, NBC Fri 10:00–11:00

CAST:

Tyger Hayes .... Genie Francis
Lady Bobbi Rowan .... Jennifer O'Neill
Ava Marshall .... Jessica Walter
Hadden Marshall .... John Dehner
Niko Theophilus .... Ian McShane
Sean Benedict .... Michael Woods
Marcus Marshall .... Jonathan Frakes
Muffin Marshall .... Wendy Fulton
Laura Parker .... Penny Fuller
Margaret Marshall .... Susan French
Barbara Fisher .... Jaime Lyn Bauer
Cathy .... Laura Bruneau
Natasha .... Anulka Dziubinska
Larry DeVito .... Morgan Stevens

The perfume business was the setting for this tale of corruption, sex, and power. Tyger Hayes—young and beautiful, ambitious and energetic—was entering the business world after the death of her wealthy playboy husband, Chase Marshall. Chase's father, Hadden, was the patriarch of the Marshall family and the head of Kellico, the family's privately held conglomerate. With the help of her staunchest supporter, Hadden's sister Margaret, Tyger attempted to make a name for herself developing "Ma Femme" perfume. But she soon found herself in conflict with her conniving in-laws. Ava, the widow of Hadden's other son, Hugh, was determined to see her ineffectual son Marcus take over Kellico. Marcus's wife Muffin agreed. Ava's efforts to secure the Marshall empire for her son led her to woo and eventually marry Hadden himself (her father-in-law). Meanwhile Tyger's mother, international beauty Lady Bobbi, was having an affair with Niko Theophilus, a Greek millionaire with a long-standing vendetta against the Marshalls. He hoped to use this liaison as a means of destroying them.

This series was the continuation of a highly popular TV movie of the same name seen on CBS in October 1982. It was based on a popular novel, and starred one of the hottest young stars of the daytime soap-opera world, *General Hospital*'s Genie Francis. Despite a heavy infusion of jet-set glamour (settings included Manhattan, the Marshalls' country estate, Niko's yacht, and locations in Paris and along the Mediterranean), the audience for this weekly series was small, and *Bare Essence* soon left the air.

BAREFOOT IN THE PARK (*Situation Comedy*)
FIRST TELECAST: *September 24, 1970*
LAST TELECAST: *January 14, 1971*
BROADCAST HISTORY:
Sep 1970–Jan 1971, ABC Thu 9:00–9:30
CAST:
Paul Bratter .... Scoey Mitchlll
Corie Bratter .... Tracy Reed
Mabel Bates .... Thelma Carpenter
Honey Robinson .... Nipsey Russell
Mr. Kendricks .... Harry Holcombe
Mr. Velasquez .... Vito Scotti

This black version of Neil Simon's hit play and movie concerned two young newlyweds trying to establish their life on a shoestring budget in New York. Their home was a one-room walk-up apartment on the top floor of an old brownstone. At least they had each other—plus Corie's busybody mother Mabel, Mabel's persistent suitor Honey, Paul's boss Mr. Kendricks, and the bumbling building superintendent Mr. Velasquez.

BARETTA (*Police Drama*)
FIRST TELECAST: *January 17, 1975*
LAST TELECAST: *June 1, 1978*
BROADCAST HISTORY:
Jan 1975–Mar 1975, ABC Fri 10:00–11:00
Apr 1975–Jul 1975, ABC Wed 10:00–11:00
Sep 1975–Aug 1977, ABC Wed 9:00–10:00
Aug 1977–Jan 1978, ABC Wed 10:00–11:00
Feb 1978–Jun 1978, ABC Thu 10:00–11:00
CAST:
Det. Tony Baretta .... Robert Blake
Inspector Shiller (1975) .... Dana Elcar
Lt. Hal Brubaker .... Edward Grover
Billy Truman .... Tom Ewell
Rooster .... Michael D. Roberts
Fats .... Chino Williams
THEME:
"Keep Your Eye on the Sparrow," sung by Sammy Davis, Jr.

Baretta was half a spin-off from another detective show. Robert Blake had originally been scheduled to take over the lead role in *Toma* after Tony Musante left that series. But *Toma* had not been a big hit, and rather than risk being tied to an unsuccessful series the title was changed and alterations were made in the locale and other details. In essence, *Toma* became *Baretta*, moved to California.

Tony Baretta was, like Toma, an unconventional cop. He was streetwise, single, with a decidedly funky lifestyle: he holed up in a run-down old hotel when he wasn't on the job, which was seldom. He was usually seen in T-shirt and jeans, with his trademark cap pulled down over his forehead. The orphaned son of poor Italian immigrants, Tony knew the city inside out. He was a master of disguise, and because of his rough appearance was able to infiltrate such groups as motorcycle gangs and even "the Mob." Needless to say, he refused to have a partner and always worked alone. Inspector Shiller was his original boss, later succeeded by Lt. Brubaker. Billy Truman was a retired cop who was a combined manager and house detective at the hotel where Baretta lived.

There was plenty of hard action in this series, despite Blake's public protestations that he opposed wanton violence on TV. The show had a "with-it" light sense of humor; comic relief was provided by Tony's fancy-dude informant-friend Rooster and by Fred, Tony's pet cockatoo. Blake's real-life wife Sondra Blake was an occasional guest star.

BARNABY JONES (*Detective Drama*)
FIRST TELECAST: *January 28, 1973*
LAST TELECAST: *September 4, 1980*
BROADCAST HISTORY:
Jan 1973–Jun 1974, CBS Sun 9:30–10:30
Jul 1974–Sep 1974, CBS Sat 10:00–11:00
Sep 1974–Aug 1975, CBS Tue 10:00–11:00
Sep 1975–Nov 1975, CBS Fri 10:00–11:00
Dec 1975–Nov 1979, CBS Thu 10:00–11:00
Dec 1979–Sep 1980, CBS Thu 9:00–10:00
CAST:
Barnaby Jones .... Buddy Ebsen
Betty Jones .... Lee Meriwether
Jedediah Romano (J.R.) Jones (1976–1980)
.... Mark Shera
Lt. Joe Taylor (1973) .... Vince Howard
Lt. John Biddle (1974–1980) .... John Carter
EXECUTIVE PRODUCER:
Quinn Martin

After a long and successful career as a private investigator, Barnaby Jones had retired, leaving the business to his son Hal. When Hal was murdered while on a case, Barnaby came out of retirement to help track down his son's killer. Hal's widow, Betty, worked with her father-in-law to solve the case and remained with him, as his assistant, when he decided to keep his Los Angeles–based firm in operation. His keen analytic skills were often masked by a homespun exterior, drawing guilty parties into a false sense of security that led to their downfall. Until *Cannon*—another Los Angeles detective series—went off the air in the fall of 1975, there was occasional interplay between it and *Barnaby Jones*.

In the fall of 1976 Barnaby's young cousin J.R. joined the firm, initially to track down the murderer of *his* father, but eventually as a permanent partner. One of the things that most fascinated him was Barnaby's home crime laboratory, something rarely seen in other detective series. It was in the lab that various clues were analyzed and possible bits of evidence evaluated. J.R., in addition to his work with Barnaby, was also studying to pass the bar exam and become a lawyer.

BARNEY BLAKE, POLICE REPORTER (*Crime Drama*)

FIRST TELECAST: *April 22, 1948*
LAST TELECAST: *July 8, 1948*
BROADCAST HISTORY:
Apr 1948–Jul 1948, NBC Thu 9:30–10:00
CAST:
Barney Blake .... Gene O'Donnell
Jennifer Allen .... Judy Parrish

Reporter Barney Blake, assisted by his secretary Jennifer, solved assorted homicides in this live series, which NBC claims was television's first regularly scheduled mystery series. It set at least one precedent when it was canceled by the sponsor, American Tobacco Company, after only thirteen weeks.

BARNEY MILLER (*Situation Comedy*)

FIRST TELECAST: *January 23, 1975*
LAST TELECAST: *September 9, 1982*
BROADCAST HISTORY:
Jan 1975–Jan 1976, ABC Thu 8:00–8:30 (OS)
Jan 1976–Dec 1976, ABC Thu 8:30–9:00 (OS)
Dec 1976–Mar 1982, ABC Thu 9:00–9:30
Mar 1982–Apr 1982, ABC Fri 8:30–9:00
Apr 1982–Sep 1982, ABC Thu 9:00–9:30
CAST:
Capt. Barney Miller .... Hal Linden
Det. Phil Fish (1975–1977) .... Abe Vigoda
Det. Sgt. Chano Amenguale (1975–1976) .... Gregory Sierra
Det. Stanley Wojohowicz ("Wojo") .... Maxwell Gail
Det. Nick Yemana (1975–1978) .... Jack Soo
Det. Ron Harris .... Ron Glass
Elizabeth Miller (pilot only) .... Abby Dalton
Elizabeth Miller (1975–1976) .... Barbara Barrie
Rachael Miller (1975) .... Anne Wyndham
David Miller (1975) .... Michael Tessier
Bernice Fish (1975–1977) .... Florence Stanley
Det. Janice Wentworth (1975–1976) .... Linda Lavin
Inspector Frank Luger .... James Gregory
Officer Carl Levitt (1976–1982) .... Ron Carey
Det. Baptista (1976–1977) .... June Gable
Det. Arthur Dietrich (1976–1982) .... Steve Landesberg
Lt. Scanlon (1978–1982) .... George Murdock

Barney Miller grew out of a rejected comedy pilot called "The Life and Times of Captain Barney Miller," which aired as part of an ABC summer anthology called *Just for Laughs* in 1974. In that pilot the action revolved equally around Barney's problems at the police precinct house and his home life, with his wife Elizabeth and kids prominently featured. But when *Barney Miller* made it to the regular ABC schedule the following January, the family played a much smaller role (eventually they were written out) and the locale became the Greenwich Village station house where Barney and his motley crew spent their day.

Three actors besides Hal Linden came over from the pilot to the series: Barney's two kids, David and Rachael, who soon disappeared, and a broken-down old cop named Fish. Fish was the hit of the show. Not only did he look incredible, he sounded and acted like every breath might be his last. Fish was always on the verge of retirement, and his worst day was when the station house toilet broke down. He was constantly complaining about everything, especially his seldom-seen wife Bernice.

There were ironies in Abe Vigoda's portrayal of Fish. Vigoda, 54, was in real life an active athlete (he jogged and played handball), and the role for which he was previously best known was quite different indeed—that of the ruthless Mafia leader Tessio, in *The Godfather*. Vigoda became so popular that he eventually got his own series, *Fish*, though he also continued on *Barney Miller* for a time. He left the series ("retiring" from the police force) in September 1977.

Others around the 12th Precinct station house were Det. Amenguale, the Puerto Rican; Wojo, the naive, trusting one; Yemana, the philosophical one who made coffee for them all; Dietrich, the know-it-all; and Harris, the wisecracking, ambitious black. Seen occasionally were Inspector Luger, the sometimes incoherent superior; Levitt, the 5'3" uniformed officer who wanted to be a detective, but was "too short"; Lt. Scanlon of Internal Affairs; and female officers Wentworth and Baptista. A continuous parade of crazies, crooks, con men, hookers, juvenile muggers, and other street denizens passed through.

Among the notable events of later seasons were Harris's emergence as a published author, with a lurid novel about police work called *Blood on the Badge*; and, in January 1979, the death of actor Jack Soo. Soo was last seen as Yemana in October 1978, but was so loved that a special episode was devoted to him the following May, with clips from past shows and reminiscences by the cast. At the end they all raised their coffee cups in a poignant farewell toast.

As the series declined in audience share during 1981–1982, the producers decided to end its run with an ironic twist. The discovery of an antique gun in the precinct house revealed that the building had been the headquarters of Teddy Roosevelt when he was president of the New York Police Board in the 1890s. In fact, Barney's office may have been President Roosevelt's office. As a result, the building was declared a historic landmark and the precinct forced to vacate. In the last episode, Barney received the long-awaited phone call from headquarters. The news was bittersweet: Barney was promoted to deputy inspector and Levitt had finally made sergeant; but the men of the precinct would be scattered to different locations throughout the city. The 12th was no more.

BARON, THE (*Spy Drama*)

FIRST TELECAST: *January 20, 1966*
LAST TELECAST: *July 14, 1966*
BROADCAST HISTORY:
Jan 1966–Jul 1966, ABC Thu 10:00–11:00
CAST:
John Mannering, "The Baron" .... Steve Forrest
Cordelia Winfield .... Sue Lloyd

John Alexander Templeton-Green ... Colin Gordon
David Marlowe .... Paul Ferris

John Mannering, otherwise known as "The Baron," was the handsome, cultured, American-born owner of fine antique shops in London, Paris, and Washington, D.C. When not appraising expensive objets d'art for his exclusive clientele, he was pursuing dangerous missions around the world on behalf of British Intelligence. He was called in whenever priceless art objects were involved, as often seemed to happen in cases of espionage, blackmail, and murder. His contact at British Intelligence was John Templeton-Green, to whom the beautiful secret agent Cordelia Winfield also reported. David Marlowe served occasionally as Mannering's assistant. The name "The Baron" derived from the Mannering family's sprawling ranch in Texas, where John grew up.

The series was filmed in England and was based on the novels of John Creasey.

BASEBALL (*Sports*)

FIRST TELECAST: *May 26, 1951*
LAST TELECAST: *September 29, 1995*
BROADCAST HISTORY:

May 1951–Sep 1951, ABC Sat 9:00–11:00
May 1952–Jun 1952, ABC Sat 8:30–10:30
Jun 1972–Sep 1975, NBC Mon 8:15–Conclusion (summers only)
Apr 1976–Aug 1982, ABC Mon 8:30–Conclusion (summers only)
Jun 1983–Aug 1988, ABC Mon 8:00–Conclusion (summers only)
Jun 1989–Jul 1989, ABC Thu 8:00–Conclusion
Jul 1994–Aug 1994, ABC Mon 8:00–Conclusion
Jul 1995–Aug 1995, ABC Sat 8:00–Conclusion
Aug 1995–Sep 1995, NBC Fri 8:00–Conclusion

SPORTSCASTERS:

Pat Flanagan (1951)
Don Dunphy (1952)
Bob Finnegan (1952)
Curt Gowdy (1972–1975)
Tony Kubek (1972–1975)
Jim Simpson (1972–1975)
Sandy Koufax (1972)
Maury Wills (1973–1975)
Joe Garagiola (1975)
Bob Prince (1976)
Warner Wolf (1976–1977)
Bob Uecker (1976–1982)
Al Michaels (1976–1989)
Norm Cash (1976)
Bob Gibson (1976–1977)
Bill White (1977–1979)
Howard Cosell (1977–1985)
Keith Jackson (1978–1982, 1986)
Don Drysdale (1978–1985)
Jim Lampley (1978–1979)
Lou Brock (1980)
Earl Weaver (1983–1984)
Steve Stone (1983)
Jim Palmer (1984–1989)
Tim McCarver (1984–1989)
Gary Bender (1987–1988)
Joe Morgan (1988–1989)
Gary Thorne (1989)

Baseball has always had a home on television, at both the local and the network level. The first baseball game ever telecast was a college, rather than a professional game. On May 17, 1939, NBC telecast a game between Princeton and Columbia to the few sets in operation in the New York City area. In 1947 the World Series had its first network telecast, over a four-station NBC network; it has been a popular fall attraction ever since. Although locally originated baseball networks were set up in the late 1940s and early 1950s, they were primarily weekend afternoon games and were beamed to the limited area in which the originating team had most of its fans. Later, on both local stations and networks, Saturday and Sunday afternoons were reserved for "the national pastime."

The first nighttime network baseball series, aired on ABC in 1951 and 1952, featured women rather than men. There was a women's professional league at that time, and the ABC series, known popularly as *Girls' Baseball*, was officially titled *National Women's Professional Baseball League Games*. In 1951 it was telecast from Chicago and followed the home games of the Queens of America. The following year it originated from New York, with Don Dunphy doing the play-by-play and Bob Finnegan providing color commentary on the home games of the Arthur Murray Girls.

It was not until two decades later that NBC decided to bring men's major-league baseball to prime-time television as the regular summer replacement for *NBC Monday Night at the Movies*. Curt Gowdy and Tony Kubek provided coverage of the major game telecast each week, with other sportscasters covering secondary games. After four years on NBC, *Monday Night Baseball* moved to ABC in the spring of 1976. ABC expanded the number of people in the broadcast booth from two to three, as they had done with *Monday Night Football*, and during the summer of 1976 the primary game team was composed of Bob Prince, Warner Wolf, and Bob Uecker. Others seen frequently on the "first team" in subsequent years included Al Michaels, Howard Cosell, Keith Jackson, Don Drysdale, and former Baltimore Orioles manager Earl Weaver.

CBS paid a reported one billion dollars for the exclusive network rights to all major-league baseball for four years beginning in 1990—including the All-Star Game, the League Championships, and the World Series. Curiously enough, the network decided not to schedule prime-time games on a regular basis, so for the first time in eighteen years viewers were without nighttime coverage except on local stations and the ESPN cable network.

Fans eagerly anticipated the return of nighttime games when ABC won coverage rights back from CBS, beginning in 1994. For the first time there would not be a single national game but instead as many as 14 regional games carried in different parts of the country, each with its own announcing team. (The major East/West Coast game was announced by Michaels, McCarver, and Palmer.) But after only four weeks of this coverage the unthinkable happened; the players went on strike and the entire remainder of the season, including the World Series, was canceled. After one additional season, regular season baseball was once again gone from the prime-time broadcast schedule, although games continued on weekends and on cable.

BASEBALL CORNER (*Sports Discussion*)
FIRST TELECAST: *June 1, 1958*
LAST TELECAST: *August 27, 1958*
BROADCAST HISTORY:
Jun 1958–Jul 1958, ABC Sun 9:00–9:30
Jul 1958–Aug 1958, ABC Wed 9:30–10:00
HOST:
Buddy Blattner
Buddy Blattner broadcast sports news, narrated films, and conducted interviews with a panel of four guests. The program emanated from Chicago.

BASEBALL WORLD OF JOE GARAGIOLA, THE (*Sports Commentary*)
FIRST TELECAST: *June 12, 1972*
LAST TELECAST: *September 1, 1975*
BROADCAST HISTORY:
Jun 1972–Sep 1975, NBC Mon 8:00–8:15 (summers only)
HOST:
Joe Garagiola
Former major league baseball player Joe Garagiola was the host of this show that preceded the Monday night *NBC Major League Baseball* game. The show featured interviews with players and the humorous anecdotes and observations of Mr. Garagiola.

BASKETBALL (*Sports*)
FIRST TELECAST: *November 13, 1948*
LAST TELECAST: *March 15, 1952*
BROADCAST HISTORY:
Nov 1948–Mar 1949, NBC Sat 9:00–Conclusion
Feb 1949–Mar 1949, CBS Thu 9:00–Conclusion
Dec 1951–Mar 1952, ABC Sat 9:00–Conclusion
Basketball has rarely been seen on a regular basis on nighttime broadcast network television. Back in the early days of network television it was tried by three different networks, all four networks if its frequent appearance on DuMont's *Saturday Night at the Garden* is considered.

The earliest appearance of network basketball was on NBC during the 1948–1949 season, with Bob Stanton announcing the games of the semipro New York Gothams. That same spring CBS gave Mel Allen the mike to cover various college games during the college tournament season. College games did somewhat better than the semipros in terms of audience appeal, and ABC gave them another try during the 1951–1952 college season, with Curt Gowdy and Vince Garrity doing the play-by-play.

Cable changed the picture dramatically, as it did with many other types of programming long denied prime-time broadcast carriage. Since the 1970s nighttime college basketball has been regularly featured on ESPN, USA, WTBS, and regional networks. NBA professional basketball was carried on USA from the 1980–1981 season through the 1983–1984 season, and ESPN provided additional coverage during the last two. WTBS, which had always carried Atlanta Hawks games since Ted Turner owned both the station and the team, took over full nighttime NBA coverage from the 1984–1985 season through the 1988–1989 season. The following fall, TNT, also owned by Turner, became the NBA's cable network, as it still is today. During the first TNT season WTBS did not carry any pro basketball, but since the fall of 1989 it has been airing Hawks games in addition to the broader NBA coverage offered by its sister network.

BASSMASTERS, THE (*Instruction*)
BROADCAST HISTORY:
The Nashville Network/ESPN2
30 minutes
Produced: *1985–*
Premiered: *August 11, 1985* (TNN); *2001* (ESPN2)
HOST:
Ray Scott (earlier)
Bob Cobb (later)
A Sunday-night program about sport fishing, with coverage of competitions and tips for the novice.

BAT MASTERSON (*Western*)
FIRST TELECAST: *October 8, 1958*
LAST TELECAST: *September 21, 1961*
BROADCAST HISTORY:
Oct 1958–Sep 1959, NBC Wed 9:30–10:00
Oct 1959–Sep 1960, NBC Thu 8:00–8:30
Sep 1960–Sep 1961, NBC Thu 8:30–9:00
CAST:
Bat Masterson .... Gene Barry
Bat Masterson was a lawman, Indian fighter, scout, and professional gambler. He was also, by Western standards, quite a dandy. With a derby hat, a gold-topped cane, and clothes that were more at home in New York than in Tombstone, Arizona, he did not look like he belonged in the Old West. Preferring to use his wits and his cane to disarm opponents, rather than his gun, Masterson provided quite a contrast to the general run of violent Western heroes. He was a debonair charmer of women and roamed the Southwest romancing the ladies and helping to protect the innocent, especially in situations where they had been wrongly accused of crimes. The real William Bartley "Bat" Masterson may not have been quite as glamorous a personality as Gene Barry's portrayal indicated, but he was quite a character in his own right. The derby, cane, and a specially designed gun were presented to him by the grateful citizens of Dodge City during his tenure as sheriff; he was a close friend of Wyatt Earp, another legendary Western hero; and his exploits created the legend upon which this series was based.

BATMAN (*Fantasy Adventure*)
FIRST TELECAST: *January 12, 1966*
LAST TELECAST: *March 14, 1968*
BROADCAST HISTORY:
Jan 1966–Aug 1967, ABC Wed/Thu 7:30–8:00
Sep 1967–Mar 1968, ABC Thu 7:30–8:00
CAST:
Bruce Wayne (Batman) .... Adam West
Dick Grayson (Robin) .... Burt Ward
Alfred Pennyworth .... Alan Napier
Aunt Harriet Cooper .... Madge Blake
Police Commissioner Gordon .... Neil Hamilton
Chief O'Hara .... Stafford Repp
Barbara Gordon (Batgirl) (1967–1968)
.... Yvonne Craig
MUSICAL THEME:
"Batman," by Neal Hefti
Cartoonist Bob Kane's *Batman* first appeared in comic-book form in *Detective Comics* in 1939 and was featured on radio's *Superman* series and in two movie

serials in the 1940s. In January of 1966 it took television by storm. But in slightly over two years it blew itself out. *Batman* was the ultimate "camp" show of the 1960s and was definitely not to be taken seriously, even by those who acted in it. The fight scenes were punctuated by animated "Pows," "Bops," "Bangs," and "Thuds" that flashed on the screen when a blow was struck, obliterating the actors. The situations were incredibly contrived and the acting was intentionally overdone by everyone except Adam West, who was so wooden that he was hilarious.

The general structure of the series was true to Bob Kane's original comics. Bruce Wayne had been orphaned in his teens when his parents were killed by a criminal. Inheriting their fortune, Bruce built a complex crime lab under the Wayne mansion and, as the mysterious Batman, waged war on the evildoers who plagued Gotham City. His young ward, the orphaned Dick Grayson, joined him; they were known individually as the Caped Crusader and The Boy Wonder, and together as The Dynamic Duo. The only person who knew their real identity was the Wayne family butler, Alfred, who had raised Bruce after his parents' murder. In addition to the underground Batlab (where every device was carefully labeled with its function), they used a marvelously equipped car, the Batmobile, to chase and apprehend criminals. Whenever their services were needed, Police Commissioner Gordon could summon them with the searchlight-like Batsignal or call them on the special Batphone.

Batman was an overnight sensation when it premiered in 1966, airing two-part stories that ran on Wednesday and Thursday. The climax of the first part always left the pair in a dire predicament from which they managed to extricate themselves on the following night. The public's fancy was caught by the silliness, the absurdity, and Robin's horrible puns (attempting to scale a building with Batman in the first episode, he was heard to say, "Holy fire escape, Batman!"). Both the Wednesday and Thursday episodes ranked among the ten most popular programs of the 1965–1966 season. Appearing as a guest villain on the show became something of a status symbol. Among the more celebrated foes were The Penguin (Burgess Meredith), The Joker (Cesar Romero), The Riddler (Frank Gorshin and, later, John Astin), Egghead (Vincent Price), King Tut (Victor Buono), and the Catwoman (played variously by Julie Newmar, Lee Ann Meriwether, and Eartha Kitt).

By the fall of 1967, however, the novelty had passed and the ratings began to fall. A new role was added, the part of Commissioner Gordon's daughter Barbara, a young librarian who fought crime on her own as Batgirl and who regularly teamed up with Batman and Robin (she had also been in Kane's comics). But it didn't help. Cut back to once a week in the fall of 1967, the surprise hit of 1966 was gone by the following spring.

The Dynamic Duo didn't completely disappear from network television, however. Six months after the ABC prime-time series faded from the air, the animated *Batman-Superman Hour* premiered on CBS' Saturday morning schedule. This first animated version lasted two seasons. Batman and Robin surfaced again on ABC's *Super Friends* in the fall of 1973. From February 1977 to September 1978 CBS aired *The New Adventures of Batman* with Adam West and Burt Ward providing the voices, and *Super Friends* on ABC, despite numerous title changes, remained on the air until 1985.

They resurfaced as part of *The New Batman/Superman Adventures* on the WB network in September 1997, where they aired on Saturday mornings and weekday afternoons until the fall of 2000.

BATMAN—THE ANIMATED SERIES (*Cartoon*)
FIRST TELECAST: *December 13, 1992*
LAST TELECAST: *March 14, 1993*
BROADCAST HISTORY:
Dec 1992–Mar 1993, FOX Sun 7:00–7:30
VOICES:
Bruce Wayne/Batman .... Kevin Conroy
Commissioner James Gordon .... Bob Hastings
Det. Bullock .... Robert Costanzo
Alfred .... Efrem Zimbalist, Jr.
Dick Grayson/Robin .... Loren Lester
Barbara Gordon/Batgirl .... Melissa Gilbert
Leslie Thompkins .... Diana Muldaur
Summer Gleeson .... Mari Devon
The Joker .... Mark Hamill
The Riddler .... John Glover
The Penguin .... Paul Williams

Gotham City's Caped Crusader returned to prime-time television in this animated series that was much more somber in tone than either the 1960s live-action *Batman* or the animated versions that had run in the 1970s and 1980s. Featured were an uncharacteristically moody Bruce Wayne plus Robin, Alfred the butler, Commissioner Gordon, and Gordon's daughter Barbara. New to this version were Det. Bullock; Leslie Thompkins, Bruce Wayne's love interest; and TV reporter Summer Gleeson. All of the traditional villains, including the major ones listed in the cast credits above, were back as well.

This animated series was produced by Tim Burton, whose live-action theatrical *Batman* films in the late 1980s and 1990s were equally dark in mood and had a similar Art Deco look. *Batman: The Animated Series* had premiered in September of 1992 and was a fixture on the Fox weekday afternoon lineup for the next two years, including the four months when it was running on Sunday nights as well. When it moved to Saturday mornings in September 1994 the title was changed to *The Adventures of Batman and Robin.* It kept that title when it moved back to the Fox weekday lineup a year later, and remained there until the fall of 1997, when it moved to the WB network as part of *The New Batman/Superman Adventures.* The WB aired episodes on both Saturday mornings and weekday afternoons through the summer of 2000.

In the most unusual variation on the Batman franchise, the WB premiered an animated series titled *Batman Beyond* in January 1999. In this version an aged Bruce Wayne gave his Batman outfit to teenager Terry McGinnis. McGinnis, who had tracked down the location of the Batcave, took over as the Caped Crusader. *Batman Beyond* aired on the WB on Saturday mornings from January 1999 to April 2001 and on weekdays from November 1999 to September 2001.

BATTERY PARK (*Situation Comedy*)
FIRST TELECAST: *March 23, 2000*
LAST TELECAST: *April 13, 2000*
BROADCAST HISTORY:
Mar 2000–Apr 2000, NBC Thu 9:30–10:00

CAST:

Capt. Madeleine Dunleavy .... Elizabeth Perkins
Lieut. Ben Hardin .... Justin Louis
Det. Elena Vera .... Jacqueline Obradors
Det. Kevin Strain .... Robert Mailhouse
Det. Carl Zernial .... Jay Paulson
Det. Antony (Stig) Stigliano .... Frank Grillo
Det. Derek Finley .... Bokeem Woodbine
Ray Giddeon .... Sam Lloyd
Maria Di Cenzo .... Wendy Moniz

One-liners abounded in this silly cop comedy, set in New York City's Battery Park district. Capt. Dunleavy was the tough, sarcastic boss who was mostly interested in advancing her political career, and Ben, the level-headed chief detective with an annoyingly impeccable record. Others at the station house included smart, flirty Elena, self-absorbed publicity hound Kevin (often seen reading *Variety*), slightly dense Carl, and the overeager team of Stig and Derek, who had to be reined in before they blew away every perp. Ray was the precinct's sad sack perpetual victim, and Maria a mob boss' cute daughter whom Ben, unwisely, was dating.

BATTLE DOME (*Sports Competition*)

BROADCAST HISTORY:

Syndicated only
60 minutes
Produced: *1999–2001*
Released: *September 1999*

HOST:

Steve Albert, Announcer

COLOR ANALYSTS:

Scott Ferrall (1999–2000)
Ed Lover (2000–2001)

SIDELINE INTERVIEWERS:

Kathleen McClellan (1999–2000)
Brien Blakely (2000–2001)

REFEREE:

Seth Stockton

CAST:

Michael O'Dell .... Mike O'Hearn
T-Money .... Terry Crews
The Commander .... Christian Boeving
Cuda .... Randolph Jones
Jake Fury .... Gary Kasper
Bubba King .... Tim Elwell
Payne (1999–2000) .... John Sperandeo
Sleepwalker (1999–2000) .... Woon Park
Bobbie Haven (1999–2000) .... Bobbie Brown
Angel (1999–2000) .... Karen Taucher
Karen Ko (1999–2000) .... Karen Kim
D.O.A. .... Chad Bannon
The Dahm Triplets (1999–2000)
.... Erica, Jaclyn, & Nicole Dahm
Mad Dog Steele (2000–2001) .... Stefan Gamlin
Suzy Wood (2000–2001) .... Tiffany Richardson
Moose (2000–2001) .... Scott Milne
Snake (2000–2001) .... Justice Smith
The Prince (2000–2001) .... Maximilien Atoki
Crystal Sunset (2000–2001) .... Teresa Politi
Nikkie Hart (2000–2001) .... Enya Flack
Monica Fox (2000–2001) .... Monica Hansen
Sindy Ko (2000–2001) .... Mara Clinch
Stacy & Jessica (2000–2001)
.... Stacy Fuson & Jessica Asher
The Perfect 10 Dome Girls (2000–2001)
Jennifer Leone, Carla Alapont, & Ashley Degenford

In this cross between *American Gladiators* and professional wrestling, the warriors were challenged each week by three contestants. The events—all of which had the potential to seriously injure the combatants—included Aerial Kickboxing, Take Down, Rollercage of Fire, Anti-Gravity, and Battle Wheel. The regular warriors were much like professional wrestlers. They had managers, scantily clad assistants and hangers-on. They fought with each other, disrupted the contests, and bragged to the audience.

After preliminary rounds, the top two contestants wrestled each other on a platform with the winner the one who knocked the other off the platform. The week's champion won $1,000 and title of Battle Dome Champion—with a chance to advance to the ultimate finals, where he or she could win $100,000. In case of a draw the one with the most points going in was declared the winner.

Taped at the Los Angeles Sports Arena.

BATTLE OF THE AGES (*Talent*)

FIRST TELECAST: *January 1, 1952*
LAST TELECAST: *November 29, 1952*
BROADCAST HISTORY:

Jan 1952–Jun 1952, DUM Tue 9:00–9:30
Sep 1952–Nov 1952, CBS Sat 10:30–11:00

EMCEE:

John Reed King (Jan–Jun)
Morey Amsterdam (Sep–Nov)

Each week *Battle of the Ages* presented two teams of professional performers competing for audience applause. The teams' distinguishing characteristic was the age of the participants. All members of one team had to be over 35 (veterans), and all members of the other team under 35 (youngsters). When the older team won the sponsor made a donation to the Actors Fund of America, and when the younger team won a similar donation was made to the Scholarship Fund of the Professional Children's School.

BATTLE REPORT (*Documentary/Public Affairs*)

FIRST TELECAST: *August 13, 1950*
LAST TELECAST: *August 31, 1951*
BROADCAST HISTORY:

Aug 1950–Sep 1950, NBC Sun 8:00–8:30
Jun 1951–Aug 1951, NBC Fri 9:30–10:00

HOST:

Robert McCormick

This weekly documentary program on the United States' involvement in the Korean War used filmed interviews and reports from both the home front and battlefront. Although produced by NBC News, it was virtually an official government presentation, with regular weekly commentary by Dr. John Steelman, assistant to President Truman, and reports from many high-ranking officials. The series was telecast on Sunday afternoon during most of its 1950–1952 run, but moved to prime time during the periods shown above.

BATTLEBOTS (*Sports/Audience Participation*)

BROADCAST HISTORY:

Comedy Central
30/60 minutes
Original episodes: *2000–*
Premiered: *August 23, 2000*

ANNOUNCERS:
Bil Dwyer
Sean Salisbury (2000–2001)
Tim Green (2001–2002)
Bill Nye, technical expert
Mark Beiro, announcer

FEATURE REPORTERS:
Donna D'Errico (2000)
Jason Sklar (2000–2001)
Randy Sklar (2000–2001)
Heidi Mark (2000–2001)
Traci Bingham (2001)
Carmen Electra (2002)
Arj Barker (2002)
Brad Wollack (2002)
Tony Rock (2002)

This high-tech demolition derby had small radio-controlled robots bashing each other into submission in a large metal cage dubbed the "Battle Box." The robots, mostly squat, armor-plated machines mounted on wheels and equipped with rams, hammers and saws, were built and operated by amateurs who were interviewed and shown in their shops prior to the competition. Each match lasted three to five minutes, and was enlivened by buzz saws that would spring out of the floor and a sledgehammer that might suddenly slam down on a robot. It was a riotous smash-fest, complete with screaming audience, flashing strobe lights and thundering music, and covered like a regular sporting event. Judges awarded points based on aggression, damage inflicted and hits, and the teams with the most points (or a knockout) won $5,000 and a giant gold nut.

BATTLESTAR GALACTICA (*Science Fiction*)

FIRST TELECAST: *September 17, 1978*
LAST TELECAST: *August 17, 1980*
BROADCAST HISTORY:
Sep 1978–Apr 1979, ABC Sun 8:00–9:00
Jun 1979–Aug 1979, ABC Sat 8:00–9:00
Jan 1980–Aug 1980, ABC Sun 7:00–8:00

CAST:
Commander Adama................Lorne Greene
Capt. Apollo (1978–1979)...........Richard Hatch
Lt. Starbuck (1978–1979)...........Dirk Benedict
Lt. Boomer (1978–1979).........Herb Jefferson, Jr.
Athena (1978–1979).................Maren Jensen
Flight Sgt. Jolly (1978–1979).........Tony Swartz
Boxey (1978–1979)...............Noah Hathaway
Col. Tigh (1978–1979)................Terry Carter
Cassiopea (1978–1979)............Laurette Spang
Count Baltar (1978–1979)............John Colicos
Sheba (1979).......................Anne Lockhart
Capt. Troy (1980)...................Kent McCord
Lt. Dillon (1980)..................Barry Van Dyke
Jamie Hamilton (1980)............Robyn Douglass
Dr. Zee (1980).........................Robbie Risk
Dr. Zee (1980)......................Patrick Stuart
Col. Sydell (1980)....................Allan Miller
Xavier (1980)......................Richard Lynch

SPECIAL EFFECTS:
John Dykstra

MUSIC:
The Los Angeles Philharmonic Orchestra

Battlestar Galactica was the most highly publicized new series of the fall 1978 schedule. Reported to have cost one million dollars per hour to produce—the highest budget ever for a regular series—it used spectacular special effects to depict a mighty life and death struggle between the forces of good and evil in outer space, thousands of years in the future. Lasers flashed, majestic spaceships lumbered through deep space, and dashing, caped heroes fought half-human, half-robot villains for no less than the survival of mankind.

If this sounds like a copy of the movie *Star Wars*, it was. *Battlestar Galactica* was such a literal imitation of *Star Wars* that the producers of the movie sued ABC for "stealing" their film. Part of the similarity lay in the special effects, such as laser battles and closeups of the spacecraft, which were created by John Dykstra, the same man who worked on *Star Wars*.

The setting was the seventh millennium, A.D. Galactica was the only surviving battlestar after a surprise attack by the evil Cylons, aided by the treacherous Count Baltar, had shattered the interplanetary peace and wiped out most of humankind. Now the Cylons were pursuing Galactica and her attendant fleet of 220 smaller spacecraft as they sped through space toward a last refuge, a distant, unknown planet called Earth.

Commanding the mile-wide Galactica was the stoic, silver-haired Adama. His son Apollo led Galactica's fighter squadron (another son was killed off by the Cylons in the premiere). Starbuck was his ace pilot, as well as a smooth-talking con artist and ladies' man. Muffit was the mechanical canine daggit. Many other characters came and went from the large cast, including the singing Android Sisters, who entertained with two sets of mouths apiece, in a surrealistic outer-space bar peopled by oddly shaped creatures from other civilizations (remember *that* scene in *Star Wars*?).

Despite the hype, the audience for *Galactica* declined sharply, until eventually only the kids were left watching. It left the air after a single season, then returned in early 1980 retitled *Galactica 1980*.

This new series of films was set 30 years later, and only Lorne Greene remained from the original regular cast. Galactica had finally reached Earth, only to find that the Cylons were planning to destroy that, too. Capt. Troy (Boxey as an adult) and Lt. Dillon were sent to the planet's surface, incognito, to enlist the aid of California's high-powered Pacific Institute of Technology in preparing Earth for the forthcoming battle. Novice TV newswoman Jamie Hamilton of United Broadcasting latched on to them, and, sensing a big story, insisted that she accompany them when they were called back to the mother ship. Also in the revamped cast were Dr. Zee, a 14-year-old boy genius, and Xavier, a renegade member of Galactica's 12-man ruling council.

BAXTERS, THE (*Situation Comedy/Audience Participation*)

BROADCAST HISTORY:
Syndicated only
30 minutes
Produced: *1979–1981* (25 episodes)
Released: *September 1979*

CAST (1979–1980):
Fred Baxter............................Larry Keith
Nancy Baxter........................Anita Gillette
Naomi Baxter (age 19)................Derin Altay

Jonah Baxter (14) .... Chris Petersen
Rachael Baxter (10) .... Terri Lynn Wood

CAST (1980–1981):

Jim Baxter .... Sean McCann
Susan Baxter......................... Terry Tweed
Allison Baxter (age 19)......... Marianne McIsaac
Gregg Baxter (14) .... Sammy Snyders
Lucy Baxter (10) .... Megan Follows

Surely one of the most unusual programs telecast nationally in the U.S., this comedy gave viewers the chance to do "instant analysis" of a program they'd just seen, and to do it on the air. The format consisted of an 11-minute vignette about the Baxters, a middle-class family living in a suburb of St. Louis, as they faced a controversial issue. In one episode they had to decide whether to commit Mother Baxter to a nursing home; in another, whether the fact that Jonah's teacher was a homosexual would harm their son; in another, Fred faced a dilemma over whether to turn a small, money-losing apartment house he owned into condominiums, thus forcing out some of the tenants.

This short episode was played as a situation comedy, but it always ended with several options open. A studio audience assembled at the local station where the program was being carried, then discussed what *they* thought should be done. In some cities, viewers could call in and voice their reactions.

In the vignettes, Fred Baxter was an insurance salesman and Mary a housewife. Naomi (adopted) was their college-aged daughter, and Jonah and Rachael the youngsters. The discussion moderator in the second segment was, of course, different in each city.

Despite its good intentions, *The Baxters* came across as rather heavy-handed, and never reached a very large audience. The program had begun as a local production at WCVB-TV, Boston, in early 1977, where it had been created by an ex–divinity student named Hubert Jessup as part of his Sunday morning public-affairs show. Jessup persuaded station management to try it in the early evening, and to everyone's surprise it attracted a loyal, if not large, cult following. Producer Norman Lear happened to find out about it, offered to produce the program in Hollywood, and put it into nationwide syndication for the 1979–1980 season—a move that, because of Lear's many past hits, attracted wide attention. High costs and a generally disappointing reception caused Lear to withdraw after a year, and for the 1980–1981 season the program reverted to its Boston originators, who syndicated it themselves. The 1980–1981 episodes were produced in Toronto with an all-new cast, and even new first names for the Baxters. Mr. Baxter became a schoolteacher and Mrs. Baxter returned to work, but otherwise the format was essentially the same.

BAY CITY BLUES, THE (*Drama*)

FIRST TELECAST: *October 25, 1983*
LAST TELECAST: *November 15, 1983*
BROADCAST HISTORY:

Oct 1983–Nov 1983 NBC Tue 10:00–11:00

CAST:

Joe Rohner .... Michael Nouri
Sunny Hayward .... Kelly Harmon
Ray Holtz................................ Pat Corley
Ozzie Peoples........................ Bernie Casey
Frenchy Nuckles....................... Perry Lang
Terry St. Marie .... Patrick Cassidy
Angelo Carbone .... Dennis Franz
Lynwood Scott .... Larry Flash Jenkins
Judy Nuckles....................... Michele Greene
Rocky Padillo .... Ken Olin
Lee Jacoby .... Tony Spiridakis
Deejay Cunningham .... Mykel T. Williamson
Vic Kresky.......................... Jeff McCracken
Mitch Klein .... Peter Jurasik
Cathy St. Marie...................... Sharon Stone
Lynn Holtz .... Sheree North
Bird................................ Marco Rodriguez
Mickey Wagner........................ Barry Tubb

The private and public lives of the members of a minor-league baseball team provided the focus for this highly touted but short-lived series. The working-class town of Bay City, California, was the setting, and the Bluebirds were the local pro baseball team. Practically everyone on the team wanted to get out of Bay City and into the majors, including manager Joe Rohner, who meanwhile did his best to nurture the promising young players and deal with the frustrations of the older has-beens and never-weres who were also on the team. Ray Holtz was the Bluebirds' slippery owner, who also ran a local used-car lot; Ozzie Peoples and Angelo Carbone were two coaches; Mitch Klein was the team's motormouth announcer; and Bird, the colorful mascot, who paraded around the stands decked out as "The Bluebird of Happiness."

There was a lot of sex in this series, including Joe's clandestine affair with Sunny, the wife of a local banker. There were personal problems galore, among them the hotshot young pitcher's secret agony—he regularly wet his bed. *Bay City Blues* was produced by the people responsible for *Hill Street Blues*, and attempted the same gritty realism, but succeeded mostly in being depressing and so had a short run.

BAYWATCH (*Adventure*)

FIRST TELECAST: *September 22, 1989*
LAST TELECAST: *August 28, 1990*
BROADCAST HISTORY:

Sep 1989–Aug 1990, NBC Fri 8:00–9:00
(In first-run syndication September 1991–September 2001)

CAST:

Lt. Mitch Bucannon (1989–2000). David Hasselhoff
Jill Riley (1989–1990)........... Shawn Weatherly
Craig Pomeroy (1989–1990, 1997–1999)
.... Parker Stevenson
Eddie Kramer (1989–1992) .... Billy Warlock
Shauni McLain (1989–1992) .... Erika Eleniak
Trevor Cole (1989–1990) .... Peter Phelps
Gina Pomeroy (1989–1990).......... Holly Gagnier
Hobie Bucannon (1989–1990)........ Brandon Call
Hobie Bucannon (1991–1999)...... Jeremy Jackson
J. D. Cort (1989–1990) .... John Allen Nelson
Garner Ellerbee (1989–1995)
.... Gregory Alan-Williams
Capt. Don Thorpe (1989–1992) ... Monte Markham
**Sid Wilson (1989–1990)* .... Michael McManus
Harvey Miller (1991–1992) .... Tom McTigue
Lt. Ben Edwards (1991–1992)...... Richard Jaeckel
**Kay Morgan (1991–1992)* .... Pamela Bach
**Megan (1991–1992)*.................. Vanessa Angel

Michael "Newmie" Newman (1989–1999)
.... Michael Newman
**Barnett (1989–1996)* .... Gregory Barnett
**Jackie Quinn (1992–1994)* .... Susan Anton
Roberta "Summer" Quinn (1992–1994)
.... Nicole Eggert
Casey Jean (C.J.) Parker (1992–1997)
.... Pamela Anderson Lee
Matt Brodie (1992–1995) .... David Charvet
Jimmy Slade (1992–1993) .... Kelly Slater
Lt. Stephanie Holden (1992–1997) . Alexandra Paul
**Guido Torzini (1992–1993)* .... Buzz Belmondo
Logan Fowler (1994–1996) .... Jaason Simmons
Caroline Holden (1994–1997) ...... Yasmine Bleeth
Cody Madison (1995–1999) .... David Chokachi
Neely Kapshaw (1995–1998) .... Gena Lee Nolin
**Joey Weaver (1995)* .... Ashley Gorrell
Donna Marco (1996–1998) .... Donna D'Errico
Manny Gutierrez (1996–1999) .... Jose Solano
Jordan Tate (1996–1998) .... Traci Bingham
Samantha "Sam" Thomas (1996–1997)
.... Nancy Valen
Lani McKenzie (1997–1998) .... Carmen Electra
April Giminski (1997–1999) .... Kelly Packard
Jack "J. D." Darius (1997–2001) ..... Michael Bergin
Lt. Taylor Walsh (1997–1998) ..... Angelica Bridges
Skylar Bergman (1997–1998) .... Marliece Andrada
Alex Ryker (1998–1999) .... Mitzi Kapture
Jessie Owens (1998–2000) .... Brooke Burns
Dawn Masterton (1999–2000) ..... Brandy Ledford
Allie Reese (1999–2000) ..... Simmone MacKinnon
Jason Ioane (1999–2001) .... Jason Momoa
Kekoa Tanaka (1999–2001) .... Stacy Kamano
Sean Monroe (1999–2001) .... Jason Brooks
**Kai (1999–2000)* .... Kala'i Miller
Brian Kealulana (1999–2001) .... Himself
Jenna Avid (2000–2001) .... Krista Allen
Leigh Dyer (2000–2001) .... Brande Roderick
Zach McEwan (2000–2001) .... Charlie Brumbly
Carrie Sharpe (2000–2001) .... Alicia Rickter
**Hidecki Tanaka (2000–2001)* .... Pat Morita

*Occasional

THEME:

"Save Me," by Peter Cetera (1989–1990); later "I'm Always Here," performed by Jim Jamison and "Current of Love," sung by David Hasselhoff; changed for fall 2000 to "Let Me Be the One" written by Glenn Medeiros, Carlos Villalobos and Fiji, performed by Fiji and Glenn Medeiros.

"Bodywatch" is what critics dubbed this hour of bare-chested hunks and scantily clad women in the sun and surf of Southern California. Mitch was the earnest and able new lieutenant in charge of Los Angeles county lifeguards at Malibu Beach; Thorpe, his rather officious captain; Jill and Craig (a married lawyer who preferred life on the beach), his most experienced pros; Eddie and Shauni, the eager young rookies; Garner, the beach patrol officer from the L.A.P.D.; and J. D., the manager of Sam's Surf & Dive, which rented surfboards and scuba equipment. Eddie and Shauni, the street kid from Philadelphia and the rich girl from Beverly Hills, were the station house sweethearts.

Although there was the predictable buddy-banter, daring rescues, and puppy loves on and off the beach—and, of course, lots of skin—*Baywatch* was not all lightweight fun-in-the-sun. Mitch was locked in an ugly custody battle with his ex-wife Gayle (Wendie Malick) over his son Hobie (he won); unwanted "friends" from Eddie's troubled past reappeared; Trevor, the arrogant but incompetent lifeguard from the private beach next door, caused problems; and murderers, robbers, and rapists seemed to stalk the beach with uncommon frequency. In March 1990 Jill died from an embolism she suffered while recovering from a shark attack.

The soap opera elements gave the characters surprising dimension and drew a loyal enough following to convince star Hasselhoff to invest his own money in reviving the series for the first-run syndication market. When the new episodes premiered in the fall of 1991 there were two new lifeguards—Ben, a grizzled but good-natured veteran who manned the radio and coordinated rescue activities, and Harvey, a young prankster who was constantly on the lookout for ways to make extra money. And Mitch, who had not dated much at all since his divorce, was starting to take interest in Kay Morgan (played by the real-life Mrs. Hasselhoff), a pretty former reporter who had just started up a neighborhood newspaper, the *Venice Voice*.

The 1992–1993 season brought major changes. In the season premiere Shauni and Eddie got married and moved to Australia. New to the cast were rookie lifeguard Summer, who had just moved to California with her mother, Jackie, a would-be lounge singer working as a singing cocktail waitress. They lived in the house trailer in which they had made the move from Pittsburgh. Other new lifeguards were Mitch's onetime lover Stephanie, who had been reassigned and was his new boss; his friend C.J., an incredibly sexy woman who moved back from Northern California to rejoin the Baywatch team; and Matt, who vied with surfer Jimmy Slade for Summer's affections.

In the fall of 1993 Summer's mother rented the restaurant at the beach and renamed it "Jackie's Summer Place." Slade was away surfing professionally, and Matt, who had moved in with Stephanie and C.J. when his parents left town, got more serious with Summer. Their romance didn't last because at the start of the 1994–1995 season, Summer went off to college at Penn State and Jackie, after losing her house trailer in an earthquake, moved back to Pittsburgh.

Logan, a brash new lifeguard from Australia, joined the Baywatch team that fall, as did Stephanie's younger sister, Caroline. She had just separated from her husband and, when she successfully retested as a lifeguard, moved in with C.J. and her sister. Later that year Matt and C.J. started to date and Logan got involved with Caroline.

Two new lifeguards were added to the regular cast in the fall of 1995: Cody, an aspiring Olympic swimmer who was being trained by Stephanie and Neely, whose phony sexual harassment suit had precipitated Matt's resignation earlier that year. In the spring Cody found out he had an irregular heartbeat, making it impossible for him to train for the Olympic trials, and Stephanie had successful surgery to remove a malignant melanoma from one of her legs. The 1996–1997 season started with three new lifeguards (Donna, Manny, and Jordan), and Michael Newman, the real lifeguard who had served as technical consultant and acted as one of the on-camera lifeguards since *Baywatch*'s NBC days, finally showed up in the opening credits. Logan resigned to direct movies, Cody and

C.J. were dating, and Mitch got a new boss, Samantha. In a February episode Stephanie got married, but the following week she died from injuries suffered when she was hit by the mast of a sailboat that fell on her during a storm. Later that spring Mitch started dating Samantha, but she was gone at the end of the season, and that fall he was promoted into her job.

When the 1997–1998 season started, C.J. was gone, having left Baywatch after marrying a rock star she had met in Mexico, and Cody was infatuated with Lani, a new lifeguard who also wanted to be a professional dancer. Caroline, who returned from a New York audition in early November, went back East when she got a job on a soap opera. Later that month Neely, addicted to painkillers she was taking for a slipped disk, quit Baywatch to take a lifeguard position with a local beach club. In the same episode Craig, Mitch's buddy from the first season, returned. A Washington lawyer newly separated from his wife, he chucked it all to become a lifeguard again (he only appeared occasionally). That spring Neely, after giving birth to a little girl, Ashley, moved in (platonically) with Mitch. In the season finale, while on a cruise in Alaska, she found out that Ashley's father was married, realized she was in love with Mitch (who subsequently proposed to her), and got married by the ship's captain before the cruise ended.

That fall Mitch's marriage to Neely (played briefly by Jennifer Campbell because Ms. Nolin had quit the show) fell apart and she and Mitch separated. She turned up again in the spring trying to get Mitch in trouble with false charges of harassment but, when her lies were exposed, Neely was forced to quit Baywatch. Alex, who had been running a competing lifeguard service, joined Baywatch in an administrative capacity—initially bumping heads with Mitch—and Jessie, originally hired to do maintenance, was promoted to rookie lifeguard. Cody, in college, was living with J.D. and no longer seen regularly.

At the start of the 1999–2000 season the series was retitled *Baywatch: Hawaii*. Mitch (who only showed up on about half the episodes) was on a solitary quest to find himself in Hawaii. His dad had died, his mom was suffering from Alzheimer's disease, and Hobie was in college. Mitch decided to set up a lifeguard training center on the north shore of Oahu, at which lifeguards from all over the world could come to learn new skills. He recruited J. D. and Jessie, who were dating, from Baywatch. He also hired Allie, an Australian helicopter pilot who was skilled in surf rescues, and Sean, a Californian working in Hawaii, to run the training center. Others were Kekoa, a Hawaiian lifeguard; Jason, an arrogant guy from Galveston, Texas; and Dawn, a human body training specialist from the University of Florida and an old flame of J. D.'s. They wore yellow swimsuits instead of the traditional California red ones. Newmie, who had brought the scarab rescue boat with him from L.A., was still in the credits but appeared only occasionally. In November they moved into their new headquarters and were ready to tackle all sorts of rescues. In February Jenna, head of the North Shore Lifeguards, tried to absorb Sean's rescue team into her group—a plan he resisted. In the season finale Mitch was killed while trying to prevent ecoterrorists from blowing up a coral reef—while setting the charges, they made a mistake, and the explosion killed them all.

Baywatch's final season began with Jenna, whose affair with Sean had petered out, trying to shut down the training center. Working with Sean was Leigh, a lifeguard he had recruited who was good with the business side of the operation. He also had a bunch of lifeguard trainees including Zach, a former Chicago lifeguard who was full of himself. J. D. had problems dealing with his breakup with Jessie, who had moved back to the mainland. Jenna tried to make up with a disinterested Sean, then turned vindictive and tried to make his life miserable. In December Zach, whose attitude and impulsiveness had created problems, was not promoted to trainer. He was so determined to succeed that he cashed in his return flight ticket and took the training course again. In February J. D., who was dating Kekoa, made friends with her dad after saving him from drowning, but the old man was still unwilling to accept him as a potential son-in-law because his earning prospects were limited. Zach, after graduation, was assigned to work with a junior lifeguard program that Sean had just instituted. When Kekoa got into a fight with her father over her plans to marry J. D., the old man suffered a stroke. In the series finale J. D. and Kekoa tried to make peace with her ailing father but it didn't work, and Sean never managed to tell Leigh—who had just gotten engaged—how much he cared about her.

Baywatch was first seen as a made-for-TV movie on April 23, 1989.

BAYWATCH NIGHTS (*Detective Drama*)

BROADCAST HISTORY:

Syndicated only
60 minutes
Produced: *1995–1997* (44 episodes)
Released: *September 1995*

CAST:

Mitch Bucannon .... David Hasselhoff
Garner Ellerbee (1995–1996) .... Gregory Alan-Williams
Ryan McBride .... Angie Harmon
Destiny Desimone (1995) .... Lisa Stahl
Lou Raymond (1995–1996) .... Lou Rawls
Griff Walker (1996–1997) .... Eddie Cibrian
Donna Marco (1996–1997) .... Donna D'Errico
Diamont Teague (1996–1997) ..... Dorian Gregory

*Occasional

THEMES:

Opening—"After the Sun Goes Down," sung by David Hasselhoff and Lou Rawls (1995–1996 season)

Closing—"Into the Night," sung by David Hasselhoff (1995–1996 season)

David Hasselhoff moonlighted as a private detective in this series that was spun off from *Baywatch*, in which he still starred. He and his buddy Garner, who had resigned from the police force, were partnered with pretty young P.I. Ryan in a struggling detective agency with offices near the beach. Also seen were Destiny, a cute tarot card reader at the beach who really believed she could see the future, and Lou, the owner and featured singer at Nights, the club housing Mitch's office and where they hung out in their spare time. In February 1996 sexy Donna Marco bought Nights and became their new landlord. Also added to the cast was Griff, a young photographer who did some of their legwork.

When *Baywatch Nights* returned for its second season, it had been completely retooled. The vocal opening and closing themes had been dropped, Garner was gone, Mitch and Ryan were working mostly alone, and the tone of the show—lighthearted the first year—had suddenly become somber and spooky. New regular Teague was an agent for a secret organization, and Mitch and Ryan worked with him when he asked for their help—in cases almost always involving the bizarre and the supernatural. They fought cannibal demons, lady vampires, a genetically mutated female fugitive, a sea creature that resembled the blob, witches, demons, and other supernatural villains. Griff and Donna (who was now doing double duty as a lifeguard on *Baywatch*) were still in the opening credits, but only appeared occasionally.

BE OUR GUEST (*Musical Variety*)
FIRST TELECAST: *January 27, 1960*
LAST TELECAST: *June 1, 1960*
BROADCAST HISTORY:
Jan 1960–Jun 1960, CBS Wed 7:30–8:30
REGULARS:
George De Witt (Jan–Mar)
Keefe Brasselle (Mar–Jun)
Mary Ann Mobley
Ray McKinley and the Glenn Miller Orchestra

A number of performers, some well known and some not, some professional and some amateur, some very young and others very old, were invited each week to *Be Our Guest* and participate in this informal musical variety program. George De Witt was the original host, replaced by Keefe Brasselle on March 16; Mary Ann Mobley (a former Miss America) was the featured singer.

BEACH PATROL (*Documentary*)
BROADCAST HISTORY:
Syndicated only
60 minutes
Produced: *1996* (26 episodes)
Released: *September 1996*
HOST:
Ian Ziering

A diversified series covering the activities of law enforcement and rescue agencies that served and protected the nation's waterways. Some of the stories used actual documentary film; others used re-creations. Among the organizations whose operations were profiled were the Coast Guard; Department of Alcohol, Tobacco, and Firearms; D.E.A.; U.S. Marshals; the F.B.I.; lifeguards; and local police and sheriff's departments. An episode might cover such topics as a parasailing accident on Lake Tahoe, a multi-agency task force busting drug smugglers, a party that got out of control on Lake Havasu, Arizona, fighting a fire caused by the collision of two ships in Tampa Bay, and host Ian Ziering flying with the Blue Angels at the Florida Air & Water Show.

BEACON HILL (*Drama*)
FIRST TELECAST: *August 25, 1975*
LAST TELECAST: *November 4, 1975*
BROADCAST HISTORY:
Aug 1975, CBS Mon 9:00–11:00
Sep 1975–Nov 1975, CBS Tue 10:00–11:00
CAST:
Trevor Bullock .... Roy Cooper
Robert Lassiter .... David Dukes
Benjamin Lassiter .... Stephen Elliott
Richard Palmer .... Edward Herrmann
Mary Lassiter .... Nancy Marchand
Maude Palmer .... Maeve McGuire
Emily Bullock .... Deann Mears
Giorgio Bellonci .... Michael Nouri
Betsy Bullock .... Linda Purl
Mr. Hacker .... George Rose
Terence O'Hara .... David Rounds
Brian Mallory .... Paul Rudd
Harry Emmet .... Barry Snider
Mrs. Hacker .... Beatrice Straight
Eleanor .... Sydney Swire
Marilyn Gardiner .... Holland Taylor
Fawn Lassiter .... Kathryn Walker
William Piper .... Richard Ward
Rosamond Lassiter .... Kitty Winn

Hoping to capitalize on the success that public television had had with the British import *Upstairs, Downstairs,* CBS launched this lavish, period soap opera in prime time in the fall of 1975. *Beacon Hill* was set in Boston in the early 1920s. The various continuing story lines revolved around the lives of the wealthy Lassiter family and the members of their household staff, led by Mr. Hacker, the Lassiters' head butler. The cast was huge, the sets and production values the best, and a special two-hour advance premiere on August 2 received top ratings. But after that the audience shrank steadily with each succeeding episode. CBS, which had hoped to parlay a successful British program into a new trend in American television (as it had done with *All in the Family*), was forced to cancel the program after only 13 episodes.

BEANY & CECIL, see *Matty's Funday Funnies*

BEARCATS (*Adventure*)
FIRST TELECAST: *September 16, 1971*
LAST TELECAST: *December 30, 1971*
BROADCAST HISTORY:
Sep 1971–Dec 1971, CBS Thu 8:00–9:00
CAST:
Hank Brackett .... Rod Taylor
Johnny Reach .... Dennis Cole

Set in the American Southwest around 1914, *Bearcats* was the story of two adventurers who traveled around looking for lucrative, difficult, and dangerous assignments. Their mode of transportation was a fancy Stutz Bearcat. Rather than charge a fee for taking on an assignment, they requested a blank check from each of their clients. After completing the job they filled in the amount according to what they felt their services were worth. In one episode they were hired to find out who was setting fire to oil wells in a small border town; in another, their task was to stop mercenaries from sabotaging medical supplies that were being shipped overseas to the Allies during World War I.

BEAST, THE (*Drama*)
FIRST TELECAST: *June 13, 2001*
LAST TELECAST: *July 18, 2001*
BROADCAST HISTORY:
Jun 2001–Jul 2001, ABC Wed 10:00–11:00

CAST:

Jackson Burns .... Frank Langella
Reese McFadden.................... Jason Gedrick
Ted Fisher .... Peter Riegert
Tamir Naipaul.................. Naveen Andrews
Mrs. Sweeny.............. Harriet Sansom Harris
Sonya Topple .... April Grace
Maggie Steech.................... Wendy Crewson
Alice Allenby.................. Elizabeth Mitchell
Harry. .... Gary Werntz

The "beast" of this series was a 24-hour cable TV news service with a unique twist. All of the behind-the-scenes activities of its staff—in the halls, in the conference rooms, in its vehicles, everywhere—were monitored by cameras and fed live over the Internet. The idea was to keep news gathering and reporting completely honest, by letting viewers watch its inner workings. Jackson Burns was the owner of WNS (World News Service), a powerful mogul who had made his millions from violent video games and now wanted to do something worthwhile. His driven staff included cocky young anchor Reese (who was fond of leather jackets), anger-prone newsman Ted, personable cameraman Tamir, blunt secretary Mrs. Sweeny and idealistic reporter Alice. They all agonized mightily over issues such as the death penalty and the rights of people in the news, while Burns paced back and forth on his catwalk high above the newsroom floor. Harry was the director in the "feed box," seen only in the shadows, who controlled the cameras that allowed those watching on the Internet to follow their every move. Why was this 24-hour news station called "the beast"? As newcomer Alice was told in the premiere episode, "Because it's always hungry."

BEASTMASTER (*Adventure*)

BROADCAST HISTORY:

Syndicated only
60 minutes
Produced: *1999–2002* (66 episodes)
Released: *October 1999*

CAST:

Dar.............................. Daniel Goddard
Tao................................ Jackson Raine
The Sorceress (1999–2000, 2001–2002)
.... Monika Schnarre
The Sorceress (2000–2001)........... Dylan Bierk
Kyra (1999) .... Natalie Mendoza
The Ancient One (1999–2001)...... Grahame Bond
King Zad............................ Steven Grives
Demon Curupira (1999–2000) ..... Emilie de Ravin
Demon Iara (2000–2001) .... Sam Healy
Arina (2000–2002) .... Marjean Holden
King Voden (2000–2001) .... David Patterson
Dartanus (2001–2002) .... Marc Singer

Dar was the last surviving male member of the Sula tribe in this cross between *Tarzan* and a sorcery series. After his tribe had been massacred by the Terrons led by evil King Zad, Dar had been given sacred powers by Curupira, the demon guardian of the animals, and charged with protecting all the creatures of the forests. A noble warrior who could now communicate with the animals, Dar traveled with Ruh, a tiger, and Kodo and Podo, two impish ferrets. He could also see through the eyes of Sharak, a flying black eagle. Dar's loyal human companion, Tao, was a young man from a tribe of intellectuals whose mission was to educate those with whom he came in contact. They had met when Dar rescued Tao from a Terron prison camp while searching for Kyra, the woman he had planned to marry. She had been enslaved by the Terrons and forced to join King Zad's harem. Midway through the first season Kyra died saving Dar's life, by blocking a hatchet thrown at him and taking it herself. Also seen were The Ancient One, the enigmatic, all-powerful sorcerer who had existed before animals or people had evolved on the Earth; and The Sorceress, a beautiful but amoral temptress who had been learning from The Ancient One for ages. When it suited her purposes she provided assistance to Zad, but she had a soft spot in her heart for Dar. Long ago she and Sharak, then a sorcerer himself, had been lovers, but when The Ancient One found out, he turned Sharak into an eagle to keep them apart.

Early in the 2000–2001 season The Ancient One, upset at the insolence of his pupil, encased her in an amber prison and started working with a new student of his magical arts. Also called The Sorceress, she was eager to learn about the world into which he had brought her to life. A lover of the animals of the forest, she befriended Dar—but still followed the teachings of The Ancient One. New to the cast was young Voden, the evil Nord king who had shown up after his homeland had been destroyed by glacial movement and fought with Zad to take over his land. Arina, who worked for Voden, was a treacherous warrior whose only real loyalty was to herself. She and Dar fought the obvious chemistry between them and eventually became friends. Dar also had several confrontations with the evil serpent demon Iara, who was infatuated with him and had conspired with the original Sorceress to trap Curupira in an underwater prison. In the season finale Zad defeated Voden, who survived the assault on his capital city and fled.

That fall, guided by his spirit warrior, Dartanus, Dar began a quest to discover his true destiny, enduring a number of trials in the process that tested his resolve. Early in 2001 the original Sorceress, who was back, made a deal with the devil to have Sharak, her one-time lover whom The Ancient One had turned into an eagle ages ago, returned to human form. Their time together was brief, however, since at episode's end Sharak gave up his human form to help Dar continue his quest. As the series drew to a close Zad, working with Balcifer, the Lord of Darkness, attempted to stop Dar from completing the quest to find his family. They had been turned into animals to protect them, and Dar collected them in a crystal ark for safety. In the series-ending two-parter Dar confronted Balcifer, who wanted him to abandon his quest to save Tao and Arina. Instead Dar defeated Balcifer, who subsequently used King Zad to get the key to the ark. Balcifer took the key and killed Zad, but Dar defeated him again and restored his family to life. He joined them to rule in a golden land but had to leave his friends Tao and Arina behind.

Beastmaster was adapted from a novel by Andre Norton. It was produced as a theatrical film in 1982 with Marc Singer as Dar. He also starred in two sequels, *Beastmaster 2: Through the Portal of Time* (1991) and the TV movie *Beastmaster III: The Eye of Braxus* (1996).

BEAT, THE (*Police Drama*)
FIRST TELECAST: *March 21, 2000*
LAST TELECAST: *April 25, 2000*
BROADCAST HISTORY:
Mar 2000–Apr 2000, UPN Tue 9:00–10:00
CAST:
Officer Mike Dorigan .... Derek Cecil
Officer Zane Marinelli .... Mark Ruffalo
Elizabeth Waclawek .... Poppy Montgomery
Beatrice Felsen .... Heather Burns
Capt. Howard Schmidt .... Tom Noonan
Sgt. Jack Nicorella .... Vincent Guastaferro
Officer Ray .... David Zayas
Officer Joey Kilmer .... Domenick Lombardozzi
Steve Dorigan .... Lee Tergesen
Officer Craig Newell .... David Eigenberg
Officer Brad Ulrich .... Jeffrey Donovan

Mike and Zane were two young New York Police Department beat cops assigned to the 12th precinct on the Lower East Side of Manhattan. Mike, the more sensible one—although he did have a drinking problem—had just gotten engaged to Elizabeth, a medical student. Wild, impetuous Zane was dating Beatrice, a psycho nymphomaniac who, in the series premiere, torched his apartment not long after she had moved in with him. She split, and when he found her, instead of arresting her he had sex with her. Mike's brother Steve was a fire inspector investigating the torching of Zane's apartment. Zane was trying to prove that his father, in prison, was not guilty of the 1976 murder of his mother. He was also in trouble with Internal Affairs for slugging Beatrice's obnoxious new boyfriend. She got the new guy to drop charges and told Zane that she had decided to go to school to become a funeral director.

This gritty series was from the producers of *Homicide: Life on the Street.* It used handheld cameras, extreme close-ups, unusual camera angles and *Cops*-style cinema verité video cutting to add to the tension.

BEAT THE CLOCK (*Quiz/Audience Participation*)
FIRST TELECAST: *March 23, 1950*
LAST TELECAST:
BROADCAST HISTORY:
Mar 1950, CBS Thu 9:45–10:30
Apr 1950–Sep 1950, CBS Sat 8:00–9:00
Sep 1950–Mar 1951, CBS Fri 10:30–11:00
Mar 1951–Sep 1956, CBS Sat 7:30–8:00
Sep 1956–Feb 1957, CBS Sat 7:00–7:30
Feb 1957–Sep 1957, CBS Fri 7:30–8:00
Oct 1957–Feb 1958, CBS Sun 6:00–6:30
Sep 2002, PAX Mon–Thu 11:00–11:30
Sep 2002–Jul 2003, PAX Mon–Fri 6:30–7:00
Mar 2002– , PAX Mon–Thu 11:00–11:30
EMCEE:
Bud Collyer (1950–1958)
Gary Kroeger (2002–)
ASSISTANT:
Roxanne (1950–1955)
Beverly Bentley (1955–1956)
Joanne Jorden (1956–1957)
Bern Bennett (1957–1958)
PRODUCERS:
Mark Goodson and Bill Todman

This durable game show started on CBS radio in 1949 with Bud Collyer as emcee and moved to television in March 1950. The format was certainly simple. Contestants were chosen from the studio audience and attempted to perform various stunts within a given time limit (in most cases 60 seconds or less), depending on the difficulty of the stunt. Prizes were awarded for succeeding within the time limit, and occasionally there was a bonus if the contestant completed it faster than that. A large clock ticked off the seconds so that the audience and contestants could see how much time was left.

What made *Beat the Clock* a hit were the stunts themselves, which were full of whipped cream, custard pies, and exploding balloons, always frantic yet always ingenious. Most of them were dreamed up by production staffers Frank Wayne and Bob Howard, who maintained "a stunt factory" where each feat was tried out before the show to make sure that it wasn't either too hard or too easy. Unemployed actors were used for the testing (including a young unknown named James Dean, who was described as so well-coordinated he could do *anything* the producers dreamed up). The stunts were so popular that the sponsor even issued a book of them.

A typical stunt had a contestant put on an oversize set of long underwear, then try to stuff 12 inflated balloons into it without breaking any, all in 45 seconds. Another presented the contestant with a fishing pole and line, with a frankfurter tied at the end. He would then have to lower the frankfurter onto a series of mousetraps and try to spring a total of six of them in 40 seconds. His teammate would release the frankfurter from each trap after it sprang. Yet a third stunt, one that was pretty messy, involved three marshmallows and a bowl of Jell-O. The marshmallows were buried deep in the bowl and the contestant had to dig out two of them with a spoon held in his mouth, and deposit them carefully on the table next to the bowl. If a marshmallow fell off the spoon it was reburied in the gelatin (time limit: 35 seconds). Some stunts were even messier. One interesting statistic quoted in 1955 was that, up to that point, approximately 1,100 gallons of whipped cream had been squirted into the faces of hapless contestants on the program, an average of three and a half gallons per week.

Before the advent of the big-money quiz shows in 1955, the prizes on *Beat the Clock* had always been secondary to the game. Even the "bonus stunt," which was harder than most, had rarely been worth more than $100. By 1956, however, with competition from NBC's *The Big Surprise,* the ante for successfully completing the "bonus stunt" had gone up considerably, starting at $5,000 and rising by $1,000 for every attempt until somebody finally managed to complete it successfully. In September 1956 one winning couple took home $64,000, by far the biggest prize ever given on the show.

Bud Collyer's original assistant and the show's official photographer, who snapped photos of contestants amid the debris after their stunts, was a shapely blonde named Roxanne (real name: Dolores Rosedale). She became a celebrity in her own right, often appearing in magazine articles about beauty or fashion and making personal appearance tours with her boss. At one time there were rumors that her celebrity status did not endear her to Collyer, who was, after all, supposed to be the star of the show. In August 1955 she left the show on maternity leave and was replaced by Beverly Bentley.

Bud Collyer also hosted the network daytime version of *Beat the Clock*, which ran on CBS from September 1957 to September 1958 and on ABC from October 1958 to January 1961. A syndicated version was in production from 1969 to 1975, with Jack Narz emceeing for the first three years and Gene Wood, who had been the announcer for Narz, taking over as emcee for the last three. *Beat the Clock* returned briefly to CBS' weekday daytime lineup in the fall of 1979. Monty Hall hosted this last version, which ran from September to February.

Two decades after its last telecast on CBS, *Beat the Clock* returned to network TV on Pax. On this new version three couples competed answering questions and completing stunts; the winning couple entered the swirling "Whirlwind of Money," where they grabbed as much cash as they could, with potential winnings of $50,000 in cash and prizes.

BEAT THE GEEKS (*Quiz*)

BROADCAST HISTORY:

Comedy Central
30 minutes
Original episodes: *2001–2002* (130 episodes)
Premiered: *November 7, 2001*

REGULARS:

J. Keith van Straaten, host (2001–2002)
Blaine Capatch, host (2002)
Tiffany Bolton, cohost
Paul Goebel, TV geek
Marc Edward Heuck, movie geek
Michael Jolly, music geek (2001–2002)
Michael Farmer, music geek (2002)
Andy Zax, music geek (2002)

Contestants on the pop trivia quiz *Beat the Geeks* would have been well advised to study this book from cover to cover—and a lot more. The show opened with three contestants facing four geeks, each an expert in his or her field. The geeks wore robes and medallions, sat on a raised platform and projected a certain air of superiority, like judges in some Supreme Court of Trivia. In round one the contestants were given a series of fast questions, with the geeks commenting. In rounds two and three the two surviving contestants each went one-on-one with a geek of their choice, for the geek's medal (worth points). In the final round the last surviving contestant faced off against a geek in a showdown round; whoever got to seven points first, won. (Later the rules were modified to allow contestants to compete directly with the geeks in all rounds.) Prizes were worth up to $5,000.

The rather hip original host, J. Keith van Straaten, was replaced in season two by the geekier Blaine Capatch. There were three "permanent" geeks for the general areas of TV, movies and music; joining them each week was a guest geek who specialized in a more specific area, such as The Beatles, *Star Wars*, or "Nudity in Movies" (that geek called himself simply "Mr. Skin"). Appearing occasionally were guest stars who were themselves the subject of trivia, such as Jimmie Walker, Hugh Hefner, Coolio and Jerry Springer.

BEAUTIFUL PHYLLIS DILLER SHOW, THE (*Comedy/Variety*)

FIRST TELECAST: *September 15, 1968*
LAST TELECAST: *December 22, 1968*
BROADCAST HISTORY:

Sep 1968–Dec 1968, NBC Sun 10:00–11:00

REGULARS:

Phyllis Diller
Norm Crosby
Rip Taylor
Dave Willock
Bob Jellison
Merryl Joy
The Curtain Calls
The Jack Regas Dancers
The Jack Elliott Orchestra

This comedy-variety hour had as its star the comedienne Phyllis Diller, known for her fright-wig hair and rasping cackle; the supporting performers were comics Norm Crosby and Rip Taylor, guest stars, and the Curtain Calls, a song-and-dance group. Each week's show featured a big production-number "salute" to a famous person, ranging from Ponce de León to Luther Burbank to P. T. Barnum—all classified, at least as far as Phyllis was concerned, as forgotten Americans.

BEAUTY AND THE BEAST (*Fantasy/Drama*)

FIRST TELECAST: *September 25, 1987*
LAST TELECAST: *August 4, 1990*
BROADCAST HISTORY:

Sep 1987, CBS Fri 10:00–11:00
Oct 1987–Sep 1988, CBS Fri 8:00–9:00
Nov 1988–Aug 1989, CBS Fri 8:00–9:00
Dec 1989–Jan 1990, CBS Wed 8:00–9:00
Jun 1990–Aug 1990, CBS Sat 9:00–10:00

CAST:

Asst. D.A. Catherine Chandler (1987–1989) .... Linda Hamilton
Vincent .... Ron Perlman
Father (Jacob Wells) .... Roy Dotrice
Deputy D.A. Joe Maxwell .... Jay Acavone
Edie (1987–1988) .... Ren Woods
Kipper (pilot only) .... Jason Allen
Kipper (1987–1988) .... Cory Danziger
Mouse (1988–1990) .... David Greenlee
Mary (1988–1990) .... Ellen Geer
Zach (1988–1989) .... Zachary Rosencrantz
William (1988–1990) .... Ritch Brinkley
Diana Bennett (1989–1990) .... Jo Anderson
Gabriel (1989–1990) .... Stephen McHattie
Elliot Burch (1989–1990) .... Edward Albert
Mark (1989–1990) .... Lewis Smith

New York City was the setting for this unusual romantic fantasy. Catherine was a young attorney who had been attacked by criminals and left to die in Central Park. It was there that she was found by Vincent, a powerful but sensitive man-beast with the facial features of a lion, who lived in a strange, serene world of caverns and tunnels deep beneath Manhattan Island. He took her to this underground tunnel world to nurse her back to health. Although she returned to the surface world after her recovery, Catherine and Vincent had fallen in love—despite his beastly appearance, the vast differences in their worlds, and their lack of physical contact—and they developed a strong psychic bond. He could sense when she was in danger and always reached her before she could be hurt, sometimes riding on the tops of subway cars (so he wouldn't be seen in public). Her new job, working in the D.A.'s office under Joe Maxwell, seemed to put her in jeopardy regularly.

Edie was Catherine's researcher, Father the brilliant recluse who had raised Vincent from infancy and was the nominal leader of the "Tunnel World" people, and Kipper and Mouse two of its other residents who often ran errands for Father.

During its second season *Beauty and the Beast* spent considerable time with the inhabitants of the Tunnel World, where Catherine had been accepted as a protector and friend. More people from the outside world turned up for emotional support and healing in the Tunnel World's secure womb. There were assorted threats to its secrecy. Mourning her father's death, Catherine decided to abandon the upper world and move full-time to the Tunnel World but eventually returned to the surface. The season-ending three-parter ended with an emotionally distraught Vincent fleeing into the depths with Catherine following.

When *Beauty and the Beast* returned for its abbreviated third season late in 1989, Catherine rescued Vincent from his inner demons but was kidnapped by Gabriel, the head of a vast criminal empire she had been investigating, which was trying to corrupt the D.A.'s office itself. She was killed, but not before giving birth to Vincent's son, who was held hostage by the evil Gabriel. Catherine's boss Joe hired Diana Bennett, a top investigator, to find her killer, and Diana's investigation led to the shadowy Vincent. She became his new ally and protector. With the help of Elliot Burch, a businessman who was being ruined by Gabriel, they eventually tracked down the ruthless Gabriel in his secret headquarters. In the final episode, Vincent, who had been captured by Gabriel, broke free and rescued his son; a force organized by Diana, Joe, and Father cornered Gabriel, who was shot by Diana with Catherine's gun; and Vincent returned with his son to the peace and tranquillity of the Tunnel World.

BEAVIS & BUTT-HEAD SHOW, THE (*Cartoon*)

BROADCAST HISTORY:

MTV
30 minutes
Produced: *1993–1997* (196 episodes)
Premiered: *March 8, 1993*

VOICES:

Beavis, Butt-head .... Mike Judge

"Beavis and Butt-head are not real," read a disclaimer at the beginning of this notorious cartoon. "They are stupid cartoon people made up by this Texas guy who we hardly even know. Beavis and Butt-head are dumb, crude, thoughtless, ugly, sexist, self-destructive fools. But for some reason, the little wiener-heads make us laugh."

They were all that, and cult favorites too, and they excited just the sort of controversy that in-your-face MTV viewers like. Blond, toothy Beavis and brownhaired Butt-head were two moronic teens who sat around all day watching videos (their highest compliment: "It sucks"), abusing animals, sniffing glue, making bad jokes about bodily functions, and generally getting into trouble wherever they could. All of this was interspersed with their trademark grating laugh ("heh, heh, heh"). Sometimes they went over the line, as in the fall of 1993 when they made fun of starting fires. One five-year-old viewer imitated them, burning down his home; his little sister died in the blaze. MTV said it wasn't its fault but moved the program to a later time period.

Mike Judge, who voiced both characters (heh, heh, heh), created them on an amateur animating kit he bought for $200. He stoutly defended them against critics who maintained they were terrible role models for kids and downright dangerous to those who might imitate their all-too-imitable destructiveness. "These characters are like guys I knew in junior high," he said. "Vulgar schoolyard humor is just the way they are." As for the critics, he said, "I think they really need to lighten up."

The antisocial duo starred in their own feature film, *Beavis and Butt-head Do America*, in late 1996.

BECKER (*Situation Comedy*)

FIRST TELECAST: *November 2, 1998*
LAST TELECAST:
BROADCAST HISTORY:

Nov 1998–Sep 2002, CBS Mon 9:30–10:00
Aug 2000, CBS Wed 8:30–9:00
Sep 2002–Feb 2003, CBS Sun 8:00–8:30
Mar 2003–Apr 2003, CBS Sun 8:30–9:00
May 2003– , CBS Sun 8:00–8:30

CAST:

Dr. John Becker .... Ted Danson
Regina "Reggie" Kostas (1998–2002)... Terry Farrell
Nurse Margaret Wyborn............ Hattie Winston
Nurses' Aide Linda............... Shawnee Smith
Jake Malinak .... Alex Desert
Bob .... Saverio Guerra
Chris Connor (2002–)............. Nancy Travis

John Becker may have been a good doctor but he had no bedside manner. Sarcastic, opinionated, and cranky, with a short fuse that only made things worse, he could drive anyone up a wall. His attitude was a source of irritation to Reggie, the attractive woman who had recently taken over the diner where he stopped for breakfast every morning on the way to his office. Becker had been practicing in the Bronx for years, and most of the people in the neighborhood, including Jake, the blind newsstand operator, were used to his tirades. Margaret, Becker's longtime nurse, kept things under control at his busy office and calmed him down when he got upset about something in the news or when he alienated one of his patients. New to the office was Linda, a young nurses' aide who was part flower child and part airhead. Bob, an obnoxious, sleazy guy who had gone to high school with Reggie and still had the hots for her (despite being married) also frequented the diner.

Becker's bluster often masked a tender heart. In the premiere he used the money he had planned to spend on a new car to pay for special treatments for a 7-year-old patient whose mother couldn't afford them. He made sure that nobody knew it was his money.

In November 1999 Becker was accidentally shot in the shoulder trying to break up a fight. He and Elizabeth (Frances Fisher), the doctor who treated him, had an affair, but both were afraid of commitment and eventually broke up. The following February Linda took pity on Bob, who was in the throes of a divorce and had no place else to live, and let him move into her fancy Manhattan apartment (it was owned by her parents). That fall Bob was hired as the super of Becker's building and spent most of his time complaining about the work—which he rarely did, anyway.

In the spring 2002 season finale Becker found himself attracted to his perky new neighbor Chris, who kissed him passionately in his apartment. In the last scene Reggie planted one on him at her restaurant, and he looked very confused. That fall it was revealed that Becker had spent the night with Reggie, but decided he was really interested in Chris. Reggie, however, had realized how desperate she must have been to sleep with him and had left town to sort out her life. When Becker tried to clear things up with Chris he made a fool of himself and she stalked out, refusing to date him—but they continued to spar verbally, particularly after she took over the diner.

BECOMING (*Documentary*)

BROADCAST HISTORY:

MTV
30 minutes
Original episodes: *2001–*
Premiered: *June 11, 2001*

Fans got to "become" their favorite musical stars in this fantasy series. With the help of family and friends, one or more fans were surprised, whisked away in an MTV limo, then made over by experts to look and perform like their idols—from hair and makeup to wardrobe and choreography. The show culminated with the filming of a video in the style of their idol, who was usually a current pop fave such as Britney Spears, Destiny's Child or the Backstreet Boys.

BEFORE THEY WERE STARS (*Documentary*)

FIRST TELECAST: *February 1, 1996*
LAST TELECAST: *June 20, 1996*
BROADCAST HISTORY:

Feb 1996–Jun 1996, ABC Thu 8:30–9:00

HOST:

Scott Baio

Tony Danza was an executive producer of this clip-show which spotlighted appearances by celebrities before they were well known. The first installment featured young comics David Letterman, Michael Keaton, and Jerry Seinfeld doing standup, Kathy Bates playing a convict on *All My Children,* early movie work by Sean Connery and Whoopi Goldberg, and home movies of Andre Agassi. *Before They Were Stars* was first seen as a series of specials, beginning on May 15, 1994.

BEHIND CLOSED DOORS (*Spy Drama*)

FIRST TELECAST: *October 2, 1958*
LAST TELECAST: *April 9, 1959*
BROADCAST HISTORY:

Oct 1958–Apr 1959, NBC Thu 9:00–9:30

CAST:

Commander Matson .... Bruce Gordon

Incidents of American counterespionage were dramatized in this series based on the files of Rear Admiral Ellis M. Zacharias, USN (Ret.), who had spent 25 years in naval intelligence. The stories were connected with the cold war, which required updating and relocating the real-life incidents supplied by Adm. Zacharias, who served as technical consultant for the series. Commander Matson was the program host and was occasionally featured in the stories themselves.

BEHIND CLOSED DOORS WITH JOAN LUNDEN
(*News Magazine*)

BROADCAST HISTORY:

Arts & Entertainment Network
60 minutes
Original episodes: *2000–*
Premiered: *October 4, 2000*

HOST:

Joan Lunden

News magazine in which ABC reporter Lunden took her cameras behind the not-so-closed doors of government agencies such as the Secret Service and the Coast Guard, as well as backstage with showgirls in Las Vegas. She also took a look at how to spend $1 million in New York City in 24 hours.

BEHIND THE MUSIC (*Documentary*)

BROADCAST HISTORY:

VH1
60 minutes
Original episodes: *1997–*
Premiered: *August 24, 1997*

NARRATOR:

Jim Forbes

Behind the Music started out as VH1's "other" biography series, meant to cover those artists whose careers didn't qualify them for *Legends*, but it quickly became the more popular of the two because of its tabloid focus on one-hit wonders, drug excesses, sensational rises and dramatic falls from fame and other musical flame-outs. The first artist profiled was Milli Vanilli—certainly an act whose career collapsed spectacularly (after they won a Grammy it was discovered that they didn't even sing on their own records)—but it soon expanded to cover the likes of Jefferson Starship, Metallica, Gloria Estefan and others who could hardly be called one-hit wonders. A running theme was the perils of rock stardom, and sometimes the series seemed to be a morality play saying, "Don't take crack like Mötley Crüe," or "Don't get your arm chopped off like the drummer in Def Leppard." One fan called the series "a historic dent in the history of rock and roll."

BEHIND THE NEWS WITH HOWARD K. SMITH
(*News Analysis*)

FIRST TELECAST: *April 12, 1959*
LAST TELECAST: *September 20, 1959*
BROADCAST HISTORY:

Apr 1959–Jun 1959, CBS Sun 6:00–6:30
Sep 1959, CBS Sun 6:00–6:30

HOST:

Howard K. Smith

The purpose of this series was to take the most significant news story of the previous week and do an in-depth analysis of its background, significance, and consequences. CBS News Washington correspondence Howard K. Smith served as analyst, host, moderator, or discussion leader, depending on the way in which the story was presented. Film coverage, interviews, and round-table discussions were all used at one time or another. The program was originally seen on Sunday afternoons, beginning in January 1959.

BEHIND THE SCREEN (*Drama*)
FIRST TELECAST: *October 9, 1981*
LAST TELECAST: *January 8, 1982*
BROADCAST HISTORY:
Oct 1981–Jan 1982, CBS Fri 11:30–12:05 A.M.
CAST:
Evan Hammer .... Mel Ferrer
Zina Willow .... Joanne Linville
Gerry Holmby .... Joshua Bryant
Dory Ranfield Holmby.............. Loyita Chapel
Bobby Danzig .... Bruce Fairbairn
Lynette Porter .... Debbi Morgan
Sally Dundee..................... Catherine Parks
Brian Holmby .... Michael Sabatino
Janie-Claire Willow................. Janine Turner
Jeanne .... Momo Yashima
Karl Madison .... Mark Pinter
Tony, the Director .... Terry Alexander
Joyce .... Erica Yohn
Jordan Willow .... Scott Mulhern
Merritt Madison................. Warren Stevens
Angela Aries.................... Claudette Nevins

The behind-the-scenes activities and manipulations of people involved with a successful daytime soap opera provided the focus of this short-lived late-night soap opera. Gerry Holmby was the creator/producer of the daytime drama *Generations.* His wife Dory was a screenwriter, and Brian, his son by a former wife, was one of *Generations*' actors. Brian's girlfriend, on and off the soap opera, was Janie-Claire Willow. Writer Jordan Willow was Janie-Claire's brother, and Zina their invalid mother. Brian's former girlfriend Sally Dundee was an actress sharing an apartment with another young actress, Lynette Porter. Unscrupulous Evan Hammer served as personal manager to both Janie-Claire and Lynette. Evil Merritt Madison was the overbearing head of a major movie studio and the father of Dory's former lover, Karl. And on, and on, and on . . .

BEING (*Documentary*)
BROADCAST HISTORY:
VH1
30 minutes
Original episodes: *2002*
Premiered: *March 4, 2002*

Another of VH1's many rock-documentary shows, this one was a fly-on-the-wall view of stars' worlds from their own point of view using hidden cameras—"who they rub elbows with, who they hang out with, who commands their respect and who kisses their ass" (as VH1 delicately put it). Among the subjects were Brandy, Jewel, Nelly Furtado, Rob Zombie and Shakira.

BELIEVE IT OR NOT, see *Ripley's Believe It or Not*

BELL AND HOWELL CLOSEUP (*Documentary*)
FIRST TELECAST: *November 14, 1961*
LAST TELECAST: *June 4, 1963*
BROADCAST HISTORY:
Nov 1961–Dec 1961, ABC Tue 10:30–11:00
Oct 1962–Dec 1962, ABC Tue 10:30–11:00
Apr 1963–Jun 1963, ABC Tue 10:30–11:00

This series of documentaries, produced by ABC News, covered subjects ranging from international politics to a day in the life of a concert pianist. It began on an occasional basis in September 1960 and was seen in sporadic regular runs from 1961–1963.

BELL SUMMER THEATRE, see *Bell Telephone Hour, The*

BELL TELEPHONE HOUR, THE (*Music*)
FIRST TELECAST: *October 9, 1959*
LAST TELECAST: *April 26, 1968*
BROADCAST HISTORY:
Oct 1959–Apr 1960, NBC Fri 8:30–9:30
Sep 1960–Apr 1961, NBC Fri 9:00–10:00
Sep 1961–Apr 1962, NBC Fri 9:30–10:30
Oct 1963–May 1965, NBC Tue 10:00–11:00
Sep 1965–Apr 1967, NBC Sun 6:30–7:30 (OS)
Sep 1967–Apr 1968, NBC Fri 10:00–11:00
FEATURING:
The Bell Telephone Orchestra conducted by Donald Voorhees
EXECUTIVE PRODUCER:
Barry Wood (1959–1967)
Henry Jaffe (1967–1968)
THEME:
"The Bell Waltz," by Donald Voorhees

For nearly a decade *The Bell Telephone Hour* provided a prestigious television showcase for fine music, always presented with elegance and style. The music ranged across the spectrum from popular to jazz to classical, performed by the top names among established Broadway, Hollywood, and recording stars (no rock 'n' roll here). A different host presided over each telecast. The featured performers appearing over the years included Benny Goodman, Mahalia Jackson, Carol Lawrence, Paul Whiteman (conducting "Rhapsody in Blue"), Marge and Gower Champion, the Kingston Trio, Ray Bolger, Richard Tucker, and Bing Crosby.

Among the classical highlights were the American TV debuts of ballet dancer Rudolf Nureyev in January 1961 (he was a last-minute substitute for the injured Erik Bruhn), Joan Sutherland in March 1961, and pianists Albert Casadesus in February 1964 and Clifford Curzon in April 1965.

Just as the performers tended to be standard adult favorites, so did the music. *The Bell Telephone Hour,* though certainly classy, was not overly adventuresome. During the first few seasons, popular and show music predominated, though there was usually a classical spot in each telecast. Programs were built around tributes to popular composers such as Gershwin, Berlin, and Porter, or around holiday themes or topics such as small-town shindigs. In 1966 a new format was introduced—that of filmed musical documentaries, generally of great performers—and the emphasis was shifted to more classical music. Among the subjects were Van Cliburn, Pablo Casals, Zubin Mehta, Arturo Toscanini, Duke Ellington, and even George Plimpton (in his brief career as a percussionist with the New York Symphony Orchestra).

The Bell Telephone Hour had been a radio standby for 19 years when it moved to television in 1959, first as a series of specials in the spring and then as a regular alternate weekly series in the fall. Bell had previously sponsored a series of science specials and for a time these alternated with the music hour. Later, news and other programs ran on the alternate weeks; *Bell* continued as a biweekly or monthly series throughout its television history. During the summer of 1964 the program featured some newer talent and was subtitled *The Bell Summer Theatre*.

Conductor Donald Voorhees, who was associated with the program throughout its radio and TV history, was also the composer of its lilting theme, "The Bell Waltz."

BEN CASEY (*Medical Drama*)
FIRST TELECAST: *October 2, 1961*
LAST TELECAST: *March 21, 1966*
BROADCAST HISTORY:
Oct 1961–Sep 1963, ABC Mon 10:00–11:00
Sep 1963–Sep 1964, ABC Wed 9:00–10:00
Sep 1964–Mar 1966, ABC Mon 10:00–11:00
CAST:
Dr. Ben Casey .... Vince Edwards
Dr. David Zorba (1961–1965) .... Sam Jaffe
Dr. Maggie Graham .... Bettye Ackerman
Dr. Ted Hoffman .... Harry Landers
Nick Kanavaras .... Nick Dennis
Nurse Wills .... Jeanne Bates
Jane Hancock (1965) .... Stella Stevens
Dr. Mike Rogers (1965) .... Ben Piazza
Dr. Daniel Niles Freeland (1965–1966)
.... Franchot Tone
Dr. Terry McDaniel (1965–1966) .... Jim McMullan
Sally Welden (1965–1966) .... Marlyn Mason

"Man, woman, birth, death, infinity," intoned the opening narration of *Ben Casey*, one of the great medical dramas in television history. It premiered in October 1961 and quickly became the most popular program on the ABC network. Much of its success was due to its lead, the handsome, virile Vince Edwards, who was discovered by Bing Crosby (the show was produced by Crosby's production company). Casey's original mentor, in the Kildare-Gillespie tradition, was Dr. David Zorba, who guided the gifted young resident surgeon in his battles with disease and the medical establishment. *Ben Casey* frequently tackled controversial subjects and exuded a feeling of realism and tension, which was emphasized by extreme closeup shots in moments of crisis. A *Time* review noted that it "accurately captures the feeling of sleepless intensity in a metropolitan hospital."

Some important changes took place at County General Hospital at the beginning of the 1965–1966 season. Dr. Zorba departed and was replaced as Chief of Surgery by Dr. Daniel Freeland. A greater thread of continuity from week to week was introduced, including some "cliff-hangers," and Casey was even allowed a brief love affair with Jane Hancock, a beautiful young woman who had just awakened from a 13-year coma. This was established in a five-part story early in the season, which involved a romantic triangle between Casey, Hancock, and the young intern Mike Rogers. (There had always been a hint of love between Casey and Dr. Maggie Graham, but it was not openly stated.) There was also a stormy romance between the new doctor Terry McDaniel and a disturbed patient, Sally Welden. The role of the orderly Nick Kanavaras was downplayed, although quiet, likable Dr. Ted Hoffman and Nurse Wills remained.

Ben Casey was produced by James Moser, who also created *Medic*. Reruns were aired on ABC's weekday daytime lineup from September 1965 to March 1967.

BEN GRAUER SHOW, THE (*Talk*)
FIRST TELECAST: *January 3, 1950*
LAST TELECAST: *June 27, 1950*
BROADCAST HISTORY:
Jan 1950–Jun 1950, NBC Tue 11:00–11:15
HOST:
Jon Gnagy (Jan)
Warren Hull (Jan–Feb)
Ben Grauer (Feb–Jun)

This show was nothing more than an extended commercial for its sponsor, the book publishers Doubleday and Company. It started as a local program in New York, with Jon Gnagy as the host and the title *You Are an Artist*, the same title as Gnagy's previous art-instruction program on NBC. In this case, since Doubleday had published Gnagy's new book, the emphasis was on convincing the viewing audience to run out and buy it to help them learn to draw. The show started in October of 1949 and went network at the start of the new year.

At the end of January, Warren Hull took over, with the title changed to *The Warren Hull Show*. Hull had no book to plug but, instead, chatted each week about a new book (offered by Doubleday) and then interviewed the author. Hull left the show after a month and was replaced by Ben Grauer. Again the title was changed, to identify the host, but the format remained the same. Grauer would interview authors about their new books, and there were plugs for both the books themselves and the various Doubleday book clubs—such as the Doubleday Dollar Book Club and the Mystery Guild—through which they could be obtained at discount.

BEN STILLER SHOW, THE (*Comedy*)
BROADCAST HISTORY:
MTV
30 minutes
Produced: *1990*
Premiered: *January 2, 1990*
REGULARS:
Ben Stiller
Jeff Kahn

A weekly behind-the-scenes look at the world of TV comedy in which host Stiller was constantly getting grief from co-writer and sidekick Kahn and other cast members.

BEN STILLER SHOW, THE (*Comedy*)
FIRST TELECAST: *September 27, 1992*
LAST TELECAST: *January 31, 1993*
BROADCAST HISTORY:
Sep 1992–Dec 1992, FOX Sun 7:30–8:00
Dec 1992–Jan 1993, FOX Sun 10:30–11:00
REGULARS:
Ben Stiller
Andy Dick
Janeane Garofalo
Bob Odenkirk
John F. O'Donohue

Talented young Ben Stiller, son of well-known comedians Jerry Stiller and Anne Meara, was the host, producer, director, and one of the writers of this inventive sketch-comedy series that may have been a little too offbeat to attract a large audience.

The focus of each episode was a collection of short comedic films. TV series parodies were prime fodder for the show—Melrose Heights 902102402 (*Beverly Hills 90210* and *Melrose Place*); *COPS* in Salem, Massachusetts (witch hunters), and in ancient Egypt; *Studs* (with shy, conservative Amish participants); Information 411 (*Rescue 911*), Low Budget Tales of Clichéd Horror; and *Tonight Show* replacement host auditions. Other recurring features were spoofs of commercials and rock groups, Ben's Video Diary chronicling "major" events in his life, and John O'Donohue's Cop Stories.

Guest stars included Roseanne and Tom Arnold, Garry Shandling, Bobcat Goldthwait, James Doohan, Run DMC, Todd Bridges, Susan Anton, Danny Bonaduce, and Rip Taylor.

The series was produced by cable television giant HBO.

BEN VEREEN . . . COMIN' AT YA (*Musical Variety*)

FIRST TELECAST: *August 7, 1975*
LAST TELECAST: *August 28, 1975*
BROADCAST HISTORY:
Aug 1975, NBC Thu 8:00–9:00
REGULARS:
Ben Vereen
Lola Falana
Liz Torres
Avery Schreiber
Arte Johnson
Lee Lund
The Jack Elliott and Allyn Ferguson Orchestra

This was a summer musical variety hour hosted by the versatile black actor/singer Ben Vereen.

BENNY HILL SHOW, THE (*Comedy*)

BROADCAST HISTORY:
Syndicated only
30 minutes
Produced (U.K.): *1969–1989* (111 episodes)
Released (U.S.): *January 1979*
REGULARS:
Benny Hill
Henry McGee
Bob Todd
Jackie Wright
Nicholas Parsons

A pudgy comedian named Benny Hill, who had been convulsing British TV audiences for a decade, suddenly became a cult hit on American screens in 1979. The shows were all edited versions of his British programs, but the humor was universal. Sly, lecherous, and good at slapstick, knockabout comedy, Benny appeared in several skits per show, in roles ranging from a passenger on a Cunard liner in the 1930s to an astronaut about to blast off with a bevy of beautiful "helpers." In fact, leggy girls in skimpy outfits abounded in the sketches, as in Benny as a shepherd with three naughty shepherdesses, or Benny as a nervous bridegroom. Stock characters included Capt. Fred Scuttle, Prof. Marvel, and the Firemen's Choir. In the supporting cast, along with the girls, were Jackie Wright (the little bald guy) and Henry McGee (the straight man/announcer).

With all the mugging and sight gags, Benny, at times, resembled a slightly blue version of Red Skelton, on occasion even using Skelton's sincere closing, "Good night, God bless."

One of the oddities of this series was that, because the episodes were actually compiled sketches from his British programs, without regard to when the individual sketches had originally aired, Benny's age could vary as much as fifteen years from sketch to sketch within a single episode.

BENNY RUBIN SHOW, THE (*Comedy/Variety*)

FIRST TELECAST: *April 29, 1949*
LAST TELECAST: *June 24, 1949*
BROADCAST HISTORY:
Apr 1949–Jun 1949, NBC Fri 9:00–9:30
REGULARS:
Benny Rubin
Vinnie Monte
Mady Sullivan
Charlie Ford, the organist
The Creators
The Rex Maupin Orchestra

In this comedy-variety program, a succession of singers, dancers, and comedians visited Benny Rubin's Theatrical Agency to show him their latest routines. Vinnie Monte played the young office boy at the agency and Mady Sullivan served as Benny's secretary.

BENSON (*Situation Comedy*)

FIRST TELECAST: *September 13, 1979*
LAST TELECAST: *August 30, 1986*
BROADCAST HISTORY:
Sep 1979–Jul 1980, ABC Thu 8:30–9:00
Aug 1980–Mar 1983, ABC Fri 8:00–8:30
Mar 1983–Apr 1983, ABC Thu 8:00–8:30
May 1983–Mar 1985, ABC Fri 8:00–8:30
Mar 1985–Sep 1985, ABC Fri 9:00–9:30
Oct 1985–Jan 1986, ABC Fri 9:30–10:00
Jan 1986–Aug 1986, ABC Sat 8:30–9:00
CAST:
Benson DuBois .... Robert Guillaume
Governor James Gatling .... James Noble
Katie Gatling .... Missy Gold
Gretchen Kraus .... Inga Swenson
Marcy Hill (1979–1981) ...... Caroline McWilliams
John Taylor (1979–1980) .... Lewis J. Stadlen
Clayton Endicott III (1980–1986)
.... René Auberjonois
Pete Downey (1980–1985) .... Ethan Phillips
Frankie (1980–1981) .... Jerry Seinfeld
Denise Stevens Downey (1981–1985) .... Didi Conn
Mrs. Cassidy (1984–1986) .... Billie Bird
Sen. Diane Hartford (1985–1986) .... Donna LaBrie

In this spin-off from *Soap*, Benson the black butler—the only sane member of the Tate household—was sent by Jessica Tate to help her widowed cousin, Gov. James Gatling. Benson found himself moved from one loony bin to another.

Gov. Gatling was a sweet, well-meaning man, but terribly naive; Katie, his precocious daughter; Gretchen, the formidable German housekeeper; and Marcy, his secretary (married in a February 1981 episode). Benson, though theoretically only in charge of the governor's household, kept order around the executive mansion, did constant battle with Gretchen, helped raise little Katie, and generally assisted the meek governor in deciding what to do, both politically and personally. Of less help to the chief executive were his political aide Taylor (replaced by Clayton), bumbling press assistant Pete, and messenger boy Frankie.

In 1981 Benson was appointed state budget director, giving him added responsibilities as well as his own secretary, Denise (who later married Pete). The promotion came just in time for Benson to help the governor in his campaign for a second term, which fortunately for the series he won, as an Independent—after his party dumped him. Benson's former employer, Jessica Tate, showed up in ghostly form in 1983 to remind him how far he had progressed. Benson's remarkable rise continued. In 1984 he was elected Lieutenant Governor, and in 1986—in the series' final original episodes—he ran against his mentor Gov. Gatling for the governorship itself, with his new fiancée Diane serving as his campaign manager. The bitter campaign strained the two men's friendship, but in the end they reconciled, reminisced, and settled in to watch the election results together. In true TV cliff-hanger tradition, the outcome was not revealed, so viewers never did find out who won. However one thing was clear—Benson the insolent butler had come a long way.

ABC aired reruns of *Benson* on weekday mornings from September 1983–June 1984.

BERNIE MAC SHOW, THE (*Situation Comedy*)

FIRST TELECAST: *November 14, 2001*
LAST TELECAST:
BROADCAST HISTORY:

Nov 2001–Aug 2002, FOX Wed 9:00–9:30
Sep 2002–Jan 2003, FOX Wed 8:00–8:30
Feb 2003–   , FOX Wed 9:00–9:30

CAST:

Bernie Mac .... Bernie Mac
Wanda Mac .... Kellita Smith
Vanessa "Nessa" Tompkins (age 13) .... Camille Winbush
Jordan Tompkins (8) .... Jeremy Suarez
Bryanna "baby girl" Tompkins (5) ... Dee Dee Davis
W. B .... Reginald Ballard
Chuy (2002–   ) .... Lombardo Boyer
Kelly .... Michael Ralph

Bernie Mac was a successful black stand-up comedian in Los Angeles living in a comfortable home with his wife, Wanda, a busy vice president with AT&T. They had not planned to raise kids, but when Bernie's sister was sent to jail her three kids moved in with them. Vanessa, the oldest, was going through puberty and the most likely to chafe at authority; intellectual, bespectacled Jordan was certainly not what macho Bernie would have chosen for his own son; and cute little Bryanna could get away with almost anything. Bernie tried to lay down the law and maintain his idea of order but, despite all the bluster when he reprimanded the kids, he really did care about them. He claimed he believed in tough love but rarely implemented it, usually because his old-fashioned concepts of child rearing were no longer politically correct.

Bernie's experiences with the kids, both good and bad, were chronicled on a weekly basis. He would sit in his easy chair and address the viewing audience directly ("Listen here, America"), explaining the latest problem and how he planned to resolve it—even though his plans frequently went awry. Being a "stay at home" dad was not easy but, as time passed, Bernie and the kids adjusted to each other and things did get better—for the most part. When there were disagreements Wanda often sided with the kids, which irritated Bernie—and sometimes even his poker-playing buddies, W. B., Chuy and Kelly, seemed unsympathetic to his plight.

BERRENGER'S (*Drama*)

FIRST TELECAST: *January 5, 1985*
LAST TELECAST: *March 9, 1985*
BROADCAST HISTORY:

Jan 1985–Mar 1985, NBC Sat 10:00–11:00

CAST:

Billy Berrenger .... Robin Strand
Paul Berrenger .... Ben Murphy
Simon Berrenger .... Sam Wanamaker
Shane Bradley .... Yvette Mimieux
Babs Berrenger .... Anita Morris
Stacey Russell .... Jonelle Allen
Laurel Hayes .... Laura Ashton
Melody Hughes .... Claudia Christian
John Higgins .... Jeff Conaway
Todd Hughes .... Art Hindle
Cammie Springer .... Leslie Hope
Nick Morrison .... Steve Kahan
Gloria Berrenger .... Andrea Marcovicci
Danny Krucek .... Jack Scalia
Julio Morales .... Eddie Velez
Connie Morales .... Connie Ramirez
Mami Morales .... Alma Beltran
Ana Morales .... Jeannie Linero
Max Kaufman .... Alan Feinstein
Mr. Allen .... Michael David Lally
Frank Chapman .... Richard Sanders
Allison Harris .... Donna Dixon

This short-lived nighttime soap opera attempted to find sex and scandal at a fancy New York department store, but instead went out of business in two months. Sam Wanamaker portrayed ruthless Simon Berrenger, the head of the high-class store that bore his name (why didn't they call it Wanamaker's?). His two sons were both working in the business—Paul, the president of Berrenger's, who was trapped in a loveless marriage to his wife Gloria and was carrying on an affair with Shane Bradley, the chain's merchandise v.p.; and Billy, in charge of P.R., who was fighting a losing battle with booze and gambling. Simon's daughter, Babs, was a divorcée who had spent her entire life trying to win her father's love and respect. Babs's daughter, Melody, was married to ambitious Todd Hughes, who ran Berrenger's only branch store. They, and the others on the payroll of Berrenger's, were all involved in the licit and illicit affairs, power struggles, and assorted other intrigues that were the staple of all serial dramas. Telecast so briefly, however, *Berrenger's* never had the opportunity to become as convoluted as its more successful brethren.

BERT D'ANGELO/SUPERSTAR (*Police Drama*)

FIRST TELECAST: *February 21, 1976*
LAST TELECAST: *July 10, 1976*
BROADCAST HISTORY:

Feb 1976–Jul 1976, ABC Sat 10:00–11:00

CAST:

Sgt. Bert D'Angelo .... Paul Sorvino
Inspector Larry Johnson .... Robert Pine
Capt. Jack Breen..................... Dennis Patrick

EXECUTIVE PRODUCER:

Quinn Martin

The superstar in this case was a TV cop, this one a 10-year veteran of the New York City force who had transferred to new turf—San Francisco. Tough, direct, and often in trouble with his superiors, D'Angelo handled cases that cut across departmental lines, including homicides, narcotics, and robberies. He found lots of action but not much audience, and was canceled after half a season.

BEST COMMERCIALS YOU'VE NEVER SEEN, THE (AND SOME YOU HAVE) (*Informational*)

FIRST TELECAST: *June 30, 2001*
LAST TELECAST: *July 28, 2001*
BROADCAST HISTORY:

Jun 2001–Jul 2001, ABC Sat 8:00–9:00

Repeats of previously aired specials featuring funny commercials. A number of different hosts were seen, including Art Landry, Kenny Mayne and John Henson.

BEST IN MYSTERY, THE (*Dramatic Anthology*)

FIRST TELECAST: *July 16, 1954*
LAST TELECAST: *August 31, 1956*
BROADCAST HISTORY:

Jul 1954–Sep 1954, NBC Fri 9:00–9:30
Jul 1955–Sep 1955, NBC Fri 9:00–9:30
Jul 1956–Aug 1956, NBC Fri 9:00–9:30

This program was aired for three years as a summer replacement for *The Big Story.* During 1954 and 1955 it was a true anthology composed of reruns from other dramatic series. The suspense dramas during this period included "Lullaby," starring Agnes Moorehead and Tom Drake; "Death Makes a Pass," starring Jay Novello and Lloyd Corrigan; "Accounts Closed," starring George Nader and Carolyn Jones; and "Passage Home," starring John Doucette, James McCallion, and Brian Keith. The 1956 version, however, consisted solely of episodes of *Four Star Playhouse*, seen previously on CBS, starring Dick Powell as the gambling-house owner Willie Dante. See also under series: *Dante.*

BEST OF BROADWAY, THE (*Anthology*)

FIRST TELECAST: *September 15, 1954*
LAST TELECAST: *May 4, 1955*
BROADCAST HISTORY:

Sep 1954–May 1955, CBS Wed 10:00–11:00

Hard as it may be to believe, this series of classic Broadway plays and musical comedies shared its time period with one of the more popular boxing shows on network television. Every fourth Wednesday, for the entire 1954–1955 season, *Pabst Blue Ribbon Bouts* were preempted by *The Best of Broadway*—one of the more unlikely marriages in television history. Produced live in New York, the plays included *The Royal Family* with Helen Hayes, Fredric March, Claudette Colbert, and Charles Coburn; *The Man Who Came to Dinner* with Monty Woolley, Merle Oberon, Joan Bennett, and Bert Lahr; *The Philadelphia Story* with Dorothy McGuire, John Payne, Richard Carlson, and Mary Astor; and *Arsenic and Old Lace* with Helen Hayes, Boris Karloff, Peter Lorre, Billie Burke, Orson Bean, and Edward Everett Horton.

CBS was very proud of its ability to present these plays in color, utilizing a giant new color studio recently completed in New York. They even ballyhooed the fact that "for the first time the Westinghouse product demonstrations will be done in color by Betty Furness."

BEST OF GROUCHO, THE, see *You Bet Your Life*

BEST OF THE WEST (*Situation Comedy*)

FIRST TELECAST: *September 10, 1981*
LAST TELECAST: *August 23, 1982*
BROADCAST HISTORY:

Sep 1981, ABC Thu 8:00–8:30
Sep 1981–Jan 1982, ABC Thu 8:30–9:00
Feb 1982, ABC Fri 9:00–9:30
Jun 1982–Aug 1982, ABC Mon 8:00–8:30

CAST:

Marshal Sam Best..................... Joel Higgins
Elvira Best........................ Carlene Watkins
Daniel Best .... Meeno Peluce
Parker Tillman .... Leonard Frey
Doc Jerome Kullens..................... Tom Ewell
Laney Gibbs .... Valri Bromfield
Frog .... Tracey Walter
Mayor Fletcher .... Macon McCalman

The brave marshal, the evil saloonkeeper who "owns" the town, the drunken old sawbones—*Best of the West* was a rollicking spoof of the clichés of TV Westerns. "Best" was Sam Best, a Civil War veteran from Philadelphia who journeyed west in 1865. With him were his ten-year-old son Daniel and his new wife Elvira, a Southern belle whom he had met while burning her father's plantation to the ground. Fluttery Elvira and smart-mouthed Daniel were not exactly at home on the rough-and-tumble frontier. Elvira did her best to tidy up their new cabin, though. Dabbing daintily at the floor with a broom, she sighed, "I just can't seem to get the dirt off this floor"—to which Sam deadpanned, "It's a dirt floor." And from city kid Daniel came: "I want you to understand, Dad, I'm never going outside."

But Sam's problems weren't confined to home. First there was the Calico Kid, an incompetent gunfighter who terrorized the town until Sam accidentally drove him off, thereby earning himself the job of town marshal. A more continuing source of aggravation was Parker Tillman, the villainous proprietor of the Square Deal Saloon (and of most of the rest of Copper Creek). Though his fastidious, prissy demeanor seemed totally out of place in the West, Tillman had his manicured fingers in every racket imaginable. When his construction company put up the new jail, the building promptly collapsed; when the townspeople had to fight a flood, he rented them shovels.

Also in the cast was Tillman's dim-witted henchman Frog, bawdy mountain woman Laney Gibbs, and—of course—drunk old Doc Kullens.

BEST OF THE WORST (*Comedy*)

FIRST TELECAST: *August 17, 1991*
LAST TELECAST: *January 24, 1992*
BROADCAST HISTORY:

Aug 1991–Nov 1991, FOX Sat 9:30–10:00
Nov 1991, FOX Fri 9:00–9:30
Dec 1991–Jan 1992, FOX Fri 9:30–10:00

HOST:

Greg Kinnear

This series was a weekly, lighthearted celebration of the dumb, stupid, and non-functional things in life. Each week brought a collection of features that might include the worst stores, competitions, human interest news items, places to get married, movies, Elvis impersonators, airline food, world records (a spoof of Guinness), celebrity souvenirs, museums, or practical jokes. Although most of the "worst" things that were aired were American, *The Best of the Worst* did employ the services of a Japanese correspondent, David Spector, who proved that Americans had no monopoly on the ridiculous.

BEST TIMES, THE (*Drama*)

FIRST TELECAST: *April 19, 1985*
LAST TELECAST: *June 7, 1985*
BROADCAST HISTORY:
Apr 1985–Jun 1985, NBC Fri 8:00–9:00
CAST:
Joanne Braithwaite .... Janet Eilber
Mia Braithwaite .... Beth Ehlers
Dan Bragen .... Jim Metzler
Tony Younger .... Jay Baker
Annette Dimetriano .... Liane Curtis
Chris Henson .... Darren Dalton
Dionne MacAllister .... LaSaundra Hall
Giselle Kraft .... Tammy Lauren
Neil "Trout" Troutman .... David Packer
Dale Troutman .... K.C. Martel
Joy Villafranco .... Melora Hardin

Southern California's John F. Kennedy High School was the setting for this drama about teachers, students, and the trials of growing up. Divorcée Joanne Braithwaite and her daughter Mia had both just entered the school—Joanne as a nervous new English teacher, and Mia as a student trying hard to fit in. Joanne, at least, found support and a fledgling love interest in science teacher Dan Bragen. Among the students who were seen regularly were Tony, a fast-talking jock who was not very interested in classwork; Annette, Mia's tough-talking friend who didn't want to be in school at all; Chris, a former dropout who had returned to complete his education; Dionne and Giselle (Mia's best friend), both of whom worked part-time at the Potato Palace fast food restaurant; "Trout," the ambitious young night manager at the Potato Palace who was going steady with Joy; and Trout's trouble-prone younger brother, Dale.

BETTE (*Situation Comedy*)

FIRST TELECAST: *October 10, 2000*
LAST TELECAST: *March 7, 2001*
BROADCAST HISTORY:
Oct 2000–Feb 2001, CBS Wed 8:00–8:30
Feb 2001–Mar 2001, CBS Wed 8:30–9:00
CAST:
Bette .... Bette Midler
Roy .... Kevin Dunn
Roy (2001) .... Robert Hays
Rose (pilot only) .... Lindsay Lohan
Rose (age 12) .... Marina Malota
Connie Randolph .... Joanna Gleason
Oscar .... James Dreyfus

This ill-fated knockabout comedy starred Bette Midler playing a caricature of her real-life self. Bette was a successful and high-energy entertainer trying, with limited success, to also be a loving wife and mother—but her hectic schedule and big ego kept getting in the way. Roy was her understanding husband and Rose, her active daughter. Rounding out the cast were Connie, her cynical, overworked, and underappreciated business manager, and Oscar, her sarcastic, long-suffering accompanist. Episodes dealt with such topics as the Golden Globe Awards (she won), appearances on talk shows, a recording session, faking a nervous breakdown to rejuvenate her sagging career and volunteering at Rose's school.

A number of celebrities—Danny DeVito, George Segal, Dolly Parton, Oprah Winfrey, Tony Danza, and Olivia Newton-John among them—appeared as themselves on *Bette* but, despite their presence and the preseason hype, the series was unable to attract much of an audience. Kevin Dunn, upset with the limited role he had on the show, departed, and Robert Hays took over the role—but not for long. His first episode, in which Bette made a none-too-subtle reference to her "new" Roy, was the last one aired.

BETTER DAYS (*Situation Comedy*)

FIRST TELECAST: *October 1, 1986*
LAST TELECAST: *October 29, 1986*
BROADCAST HISTORY:
Oct 1986, CBS Wed 8:30–9:00
Oct 1986, CBS Wed 8:00–8:30
CAST:
Brian McGuire .... Raphael Sbarge
Harry Clooney .... Dick O'Neill
Luther Cain .... Chip McAllister
Anthony "The Snake" Johnson .... Guy Killum
Harriet Winners .... Randee Heller
Terence Dean .... Randall Batinkoff
Beat-Box .... Richard McGregor

Brian was a blond California teenager whose world was turned upside down when his parents suffered severe financial reversals. To help ease the burden, he moved in with his grandfather, Harry, and tried to adjust to life in Brooklyn, New York—a far cry from the sunny surfer's life he had led in Beverly Hills. Helping him to adjust, although they never completely accepted him, were Luther and the Snake, two of his street-smart teammates on the Braxton High School basketball team. Miss Winners was their cynical, nononsense English teacher.

The first casualty of the 1986–1987 season, this culture-shock comedy lasted only five weeks.

BETTER HOME SHOW, THE (*Instruction*)

FIRST TELECAST: *May 5, 1951*
LAST TELECAST: *April 26, 1952*
BROADCAST HISTORY:
May 1951–Apr 1952, ABC Sat 6:30–7:00
REGULARS:
Norman Brokenshire
Dick Wilson
Doreen Wilson

An interesting "how-to" program with kindly old radio announcer Norman Brokenshire, assisted by his neighbors the Wilsons, who often dropped in. "Broke's" topics ranged from how to build cabinets out of orange crates to how to use luminous paint on garden tools and how to get bats out of your belfry. The program was previously aired locally.

BETTER LIVING TV THEATRE (*Documentary/Discussion*)
FIRST TELECAST: *April 21, 1954*
LAST TELECAST: *August 29, 1954*
BROADCAST HISTORY:
Apr 1954–Jun 1954, DUM Wed 10:30–11:00
Jun 1954–Aug 1954, DUM Sun 10:30–11:00
HOST:
Fischer Black

This program promoted private industry through interviews, discussions, and film clips illustrating the contribution made by industry toward better living in the United States. Fischer Black, editor of *Electrical World,* served as moderator. The show had originally aired Sundays at noon on ABC for two months in the summer of 1953, and then turned up almost a year later in prime time on DuMont.

BETTY HUTTON SHOW, THE (*Situation Comedy*)
FIRST TELECAST: *October 1, 1959*
LAST TELECAST: *June 30, 1960*
BROADCAST HISTORY:
Oct 1959–Jun 1960, CBS Thu 8:00–8:30
CAST:
Goldie Appleby .... Betty Hutton
Pat Strickland .... Gigi Perreau
Nicky Strickland .... Richard Miles
Roy Strickland .... Dennis Joel
Lorna .... Joan Shawlee
Rosemary .... Jean Carson
Howard Seaton .... Tom Conway
Hollister .... Gavin Muir

The leading character in this comedy was Goldie, an outspoken showgirl turned manicurist. When Mr. Strickland, one of her regular customers, died suddenly, Goldie found herself the inheritor of his considerable estate, as well as legal guardian of his three teenage children. The adjustments made by all concerned—Goldie to the luxury and social status of her new wealth, the children to their unsophisticated and unconventional guardian, and family lawyer Howard Seaton to his new employer—created many comic story situations. Goldie's ex-roommates, Lorna and Rosemary, also spent time at the Strickland mansion and remained her closest friends.

BETTY WHITE SHOW, THE (*Comedy/Variety*)
FIRST TELECAST: *February 5, 1958*
LAST TELECAST: *April 30, 1958*
BROADCAST HISTORY:
Feb 1958–Apr 1958, ABC Wed 9:30–10:00
REGULARS:
Betty White
Johnny Jacobs
Del Moore
Reta Shaw
Frank Nelson
Frank DeVol Orchestra

After the cancellation of her situation comedy *Date with the Angels,* comedienne Betty White filled the same time slot by starring for a few months in this comedy-variety show. Each show generally consisted of three skits, in which Miss White portrayed a variety of roles, assisted by her regulars and guest stars, such as Charles Coburn and Billy De Wolfe. Jimmy Boyd, who had played the role of Wheeler in *Angels,* was a regular guest, and orchestra leader Frank DeVol also took part in the skits.

BETTY WHITE SHOW, THE (*Situation Comedy*)
FIRST TELECAST: *September 12, 1977*
LAST TELECAST: *January 9, 1978*
BROADCAST HISTORY:
Sep 1977–Nov 1977, CBS Mon 9:00–9:30
Dec 1977–Jan 1978, CBS Mon 9:30–10:00
CAST:
Joyce Whitman .... Betty White
John Elliot .... John Hillerman
Mitzi Maloney .... Georgia Engel
Tracy Garrett .... Caren Kaye
Doug Porterfield .... Alex Henteloff
Fletcher Huff .... Barney Phillips
Hugo Muncy .... Charles Cyphers

Betty White and Georgia Engel, two alumnae from *The Mary Tyler Moore Show,* starred in this comedy spoof of television and the people who work in it. Joyce Whitman was a fortyish movie actress whose career had been on the decline until she was offered the starring role in a new television series *Undercover Woman* (a loose parody on the real TV series, *Police Woman*). Joyce jumped at the chance, only to discover that the director was her suave, sarcastic ex-husband, John Elliot. None of the mutual antagonism that had ended their marriage had ebbed, and the two of them spent much of their time on the set putting each other down. Others working on *Undercover Woman* were Joyce's TV "partner," Tracy Garrett, a sexy young actress who was mindlessly clawing her way to the top, using anybody and anything to get there; Fletcher Huff, a fidgety actor who played the police chief for whom Undercover Woman worked; and Hugo Muncy, her stuntman double. Also wandering around the set was Doug Porterfield, the network liaison man assigned to the series by CBS (yes, they did refer to the network producing the mythical series as CBS). Doug was forever trying to assert himself as a network "executive," but his weak, bumbling personality kept getting in his way, making it difficult for anyone to take him seriously.

Away from the studio, Joyce's best friend was flaky Mitzi Maloney, a lovable dumb blonde (virtually the same role Georgia Engel had played on *The Mary Tyler Moore Show*). Mitzi had worked at the unemployment office when Joyce was collecting unemployment checks, prior to getting the part in *Undercover Woman,* and she subsequently became Joyce's roommate.

BETWEEN BROTHERS (*Situation Comedy*)
FIRST TELECAST: *September 11, 1997*
LAST TELECAST: *August 24, 1999*
BROADCAST HISTORY:
Sep 1997–Jan 1998, FOX Thu 8:30–9:00
Jan 1999–Aug 1999, UPN Tue 9:30–10:00
CAST:
James Winston .... Dondre T. Whitfield
Charles Winston .... Kadeem Hardison
Dusty Canyon .... Kelly Perine
Mitchell Ford .... Tommy Davidson
Terri (1997) .... Rachael Crawford
Stuart Franklin .... Brian Doyle-Murray
May Ford (1999) .... Sandy Brown

Buddy comedy about four black men sharing an apartment in Chicago. Charles and James were brothers. Charles, the responsible older one, was a sports writer for *The Chicago Examiner*, while irresponsible James sold real estate. Mitchell-the-mooch, a junior high school history teacher, had just returned to the apartment after his second wife, Audrey, had thrown him out. Dusty, the short fellow with the loud clothes, had moved up from Indiana to take a job as a weekend TV weatherman on WEQT-TV, Channel 64. Terri (dropped from the cast in November) was a friend who worked at their hangout, The Corner Pub, and Stuart was Charles's boss at the paper. Most of the episodes focused on their job and dating problems and the not-always-helpful advice they gave to each other.

When the series was picked up by UPN, the new episodes included Mitchell's dippy sister May, who moved to Chicago and got a job working as a waitress at The Corner Pub. Cynical Stuart, who had been a minor character in the Fox episodes, was more prominently featured on UPN.

BEULAH (*Situation Comedy*)

FIRST TELECAST: *October 3, 1950*
LAST TELECAST: *September 22, 1953*
BROADCAST HISTORY:

Oct 1950–Sep 1953, ABC Tue 7:30–8:00

CAST:

Beulah (1950–1952) .... Ethel Waters
Beulah (1952–1953) .... Louise Beavers
Harry Henderson (1950–1952) .... William Post, Jr.
Harry Henderson (1952–1953) .... David Bruce
Alice Henderson (1950–1952) .... Ginger Jones
Alice Henderson (1952–1953) .... Jane Frazee
Donnie Henderson (1950–1952) ..... Clifford Sales
Donnie Henderson (1952–1953) ...... Stuffy Singer
Oriole (1950–1952) .... Butterfly McQueen
Oriole (1952–1953) .... Ruby Dandridge
Bill Jackson (1950–1951) .... Percy (Bud) Harris
Bill Jackson (1951–1952) .... Dooley Wilson
Bill Jackson (1952–1953) .... Ernest Whitman

"Somebody bawl fo' Beulah?" she exclaimed, as TV's favorite black maid came once again to the rescue of her ever-bumbling employers. *Beulah*, one of the most popular comedy characters of the 1940s and 1950s, originated as a supporting role on radio's *Fibber McGee and Molly* program in 1944. Its creator was a white male actor, Marlin Hurt, who eventually began a separate *Beulah* series on radio. When ABC brought the popular show to television in 1950 the role was filled by veteran singer-actress Ethel Waters, with Percy Harris as her shiftless boyfriend Bill and Butterfly McQueen as her girlfriend Oriole. Her employers, the Hendersons, were a virtual caricature of a white middle-class family, giving Beulah plenty to do as one crisis after another overtook the household (such as Mr. Henderson's burning the steaks at a picnic, falling into the water while fishing, or trying to stop his young son Donnie from running away from home).

In April 1952, there was a major cast change. Hattie McDaniel, another Hollywood veteran (*Gone With the Wind*), was hired to take over the role of Beulah, but she suddenly became ill and the part went to Louise Beavers, who had a long list of movie credits of her own. (McDaniel played the role in only a few episodes.) At the same time the entire Henderson family changed faces. *Beulah* was still receiving high ratings in September 1953 when it went off the air because Miss Beavers decided to leave the role.

BEVERLY HILLBILLIES, THE (*Situation Comedy*)

FIRST TELECAST: *September 26, 1962*
LAST TELECAST: *September 7, 1971*
BROADCAST HISTORY:

Sep 1962–Sep 1964, CBS Wed 9:00–9:30
Sep 1964–Sep 1968, CBS Wed 8:30–9:00
Sep 1968–Sep 1969, CBS Wed 9:00–9:30
Sep 1969–Sep 1970, CBS Wed 8:30–9:00
Sep 1970–Sep 1971, CBS Tue 7:30–8:00

CAST:

Jed Clampett .... Buddy Ebsen
Daisy Moses (Granny) .... Irene Ryan
Elly May Clampett .... Donna Douglas
Jethro Bodine .... Max Baer, Jr.
Milburn Drysdale .... Raymond Bailey
Jane Hathaway .... Nancy Kulp
Cousin Pearl Bodine (1962–1963) ... Bea Benaderet
Mrs. Margaret Drysdale (1962–1969)
.... Harriet MacGibbon
Jethrene Bodine (1962–1963) .... Max Baer, Jr.
John Brewster (1962–1966) .... Frank Wilcox
Edythe Brewster (1965–1966) .... Lisa Seagram
Jasper DePew (1962–1963) .... Phil Gordon
Ravenswood, the butler (1962–1965)
.... Arthur Gould Porter
Marie, the maid (1962–1963) .... Sirry Steffen
Sonny Drysdale (1962) .... Louis Nye
Janet Trego (1963–1965) .... Sharon Tate
Lawrence Chapman (1964–1967) .... Milton Frome
Studio Guard (1964–1966) .... Ray Kellogg
John Cushing (1964–1967) .... Roy Roberts
Dash Riprock (nee Homer Noodleman)
(1965–1969) .... Larry Pennell
Homer Cratchit (1968–1971) .... Percy Helton
Elverna Bradshaw (1969–1971) .... Elvia Allman
Shorty Kellems (1969–1971)
.... George "Shug" Fisher
Miss Switzer (1969–1970) .... Judy Jordan
Helen Thompson (1969–1971) ...... Danielle Mardi
Miss Leeds (1969) .... Judy McConnell
Susan Graham (1969–1971) .... Mady Maguire
Gloria Buckles (1969–1971) .... Bettina Brenna
Shifty Shafer (1969–1971) .... Phil Silvers
Flo Shafer (1969–1971) .... Kathleen Freeman
Joy Devine (1970–1971) .... Diana Bartlett
Mark Templeton (1970–1971) .... Roger Torrey

One of CBS' longest-running situation comedies, this was the slapstick treatment of the Clampetts, an Ozark hillbilly family who struck it rich (an oil well sprouted in their front yard) and moved to a Beverly Hills mansion. They deposited the $25 million given them by John Brewster, of the OK Oil Company, for drilling rights to their land, in Milburn Drysdale's Commerce Bank. As Drysdale's biggest depositors, they received special treatment. The banker, concerned about their naiveté and ignorance of "big city ways," moved them into the mansion next door to his own home, in hopes of keeping an eye on them and helping them become more civilized.

The Clampetts were quite a group. Jed was the patriarch of the clan, a widower with much more common sense than anyone else in his slightly scatterbrained family. Jed's mother-in-law, Granny, spent most of her time concocting potions and trying to find a husband for Elly May. Elly May was a gorgeous young thing who loved "critters" (from cats and dogs to skunks and goats) and was incredibly naive. Many viewers put up with the inane stories just to see her in a pair of jeans that looked like they were painted on. Cousin Jethro Bodine was a hulking giant of a man, as stupid as he was strong, always chasing any attractive lady he saw. The Clampetts' encounters with corrupt politics, unfamiliar fashions, indoor plumbing, and the other trappings of modern life provided grist for years of comedy.

Mrs. Drysdale, the banker's wife, could not stand living next door to the Clampetts. A socially prominent, status-conscious lady, she could never civilize them and, at one point, suffered the indignity of having her prize poodle Claude bear a litter fathered by Jed's lazy bloodhound, Duke. Despite her constant efforts, she could never get the Clampetts to move away. That her husband fawned over them, and indulged them as his best customers, only made matters worse. To help him with the monumental task of dealing with the Clampetts, Mr. Drysdale had the able help of his highly efficient assistant, Jane Hathaway.

In its first season, *The Beverly Hillbillies* spent much time in the hill country, as well as in Los Angeles. Jethro's mother, Cousin Pearl Bodine, was a prominent member of the cast, and there was a running story line covering the romance of Jethro's sister, Jethrine, with Jasper DePew. In later years, when *Petticoat Junction* was on the air, the Clampetts would travel to Hooterville around Christmastime to spend the holidays with their friends "back home." They were even there in the fall of 1970, after *Petticoat Junction* had been canceled as a regular series.

In June of 1966 Jethro finally got his grade-school diploma and began a succession of schemes to become successful in business and, more important, as a playboy. None of his schemes worked but, since the oil kept flowing (by the last season the Clampett fortune had swelled to $95,000,000), it really didn't matter. In the fall of 1964 Mr. Drysdale purchased controlling interest in Mammoth Studios for the Clampetts, who spent the next several seasons giving studio boss Lawrence Chapman fits. Elly May even found a long-term, but unsuccessful, suitor in movie star Dash Riprock, who tried to help Jethro in his quest to become a playboy. There was also an extended running battle between Mr. Drysdale and John Cushing, who ran the Merchant's Bank in Beverly Hills, since the latter was always trying to get the Clampetts to move their funds to his bank. In the last season *The Beverly Hillbillies* was in production Elly May had a serious beau in Mark Templeton, a navy frogman, something Granny never quite understood. Interestingly, during the previous season, the same actor had played a backwoods hillbilly named Matthew Templeton during a story line in which Granny returned home to Bug Tussle with Elly May to find her a husband.

The Beverly Hillbillies was an instantaneous hit, and during its first two seasons ranked as the number-one program on television, attracting as many as 60 million viewers per week. It entertained audiences for nine years in prime time but was finally canceled because its ratings declined gradually and its audience was too heavily concentrated in rural areas to suit Madison Avenue advertisers.

The theme song "The Ballad of Jed Clampett," was specially composed for the program by blue-grass musicians Lester Flatt and Earl Scruggs, and was on the national hit parade in early 1963. Not only did they sing the theme song, but Flatt and Scruggs made annual appearances on the show, playing themselves as friends of the Clampetts. These annual appearances, which ran until 1968, included actress Joi Lansing in the role of Gladys Flatt, Lester's wife, an ambitious but untalented singer and actress.

CBS aired reruns of *The Beverly Hillbillies* weekday mornings from September 1966 to September 1972.

BEVERLY HILLS BUNTZ (*Situation Comedy*)
FIRST TELECAST: *November 5, 1987*
LAST TELECAST: *April 22, 1988*
BROADCAST HISTORY:

Nov 1987–Jan 1988, NBC various previews
Mar 1988–Apr 1988, NBC Fri 9:30–10:00

CAST:

Norman Buntz .... Dennis Franz
Sidney Thurston .... Peter Jurasik
Rebecca Giswold .... Dana Wheeler-Nicholson
Lt. James Pugh .... Guy Boyd

Television lost its most beloved police series but gained two seedy private eyes in this spin-off from the much honored *Hill Street Blues.* In the final *Hill Street* episode Buntz punched out pompous Chief Daniels and resigned. He then moved with his friend Sid "the Snitch" to sunnier climes, opening his own low-rent private detective business in Los Angeles. Fish out of water in trendy L.A. ("Knights in shining polyester," the ads called them), the two shifty sleazeballs took on the dregs of detective work, but somehow managed to get things done when higher priced talent could not. Sid, true to his code, cooked up a succession of scams to augment their meager income.

Neither drama nor outright comedy, *Beverly Hills Buntz* confused critics and viewers alike. NBC was so uncertain of its chances that it ran four "try out" episodes in various time periods from November to January, before beginning a regular run in March.

BEVERLY HILLS 90210 (*Drama*)
FIRST TELECAST: *October 4, 1990*
LAST TELECAST: *May 17, 2000*
BROADCAST HISTORY:

Oct 1990–Aug 1992, FOX Thu 9:00–10:00
Jul 1992–May 1997, FOX Wed 8:00–9:00
Jun 1993–Aug 1993, FOX Tue 8:00–9:00
Sep 1997–May 2000, FOX Wed 8:00–9:00 (OS)

CAST:

Brenda Walsh (1990–1994) ...... Shannen Doherty
Brandon Walsh (1990–1998) .... Jason Priestley
Jim Walsh (1990–1995) .... James Eckhouse
Cindy Walsh (1990–1995) .... Carol Potter
Kelly Taylor .... Jennie Garth
**Jackie Taylor Silver* .... Ann Gillespie
Steve Sanders .... Ian Ziering
Dylan McKay (1990–1995, 1998–2000) .. Luke Perry
Andrea Zuckerman-Vasquez (1990–1995)
.... Gabrielle Carteris
David Silver .... Brian Austin Green
**Mel Silver (1991–2000)* .... Matthew Laurance
Donna Martin .... Tori Spelling

Scott Scanlon (1990–1991) ...... Douglas Emerson
Nat Bussichio .... Joe E. Tata
Chris Suiter (1991) .... Michael St. Gerard
Henry Thomas (1991)............ James Pickens, Jr.
Emily Valentine (1991–1992)........ Christine Elise
**Felice Martin (1991–2000)* ...... Katherine Cannon
**Dr. John Martin (1991–1999)*........ Michael Durrell
Nikki Witt (1992) .... Dana Barron
Gil Meyers (1992–1993) .... Mark Kiely
Sue Scanlon (1992).................. Nicholle Tom
Herbert (1992).......................... Cory Tyler
Mrs. Yvonne Teasley (1992–1993)
.... Denise Y. Dowse
**Jordan Bonner (1992–1993)*
.... Michael Anthony Rawlins
**Jack McKay (1991–1993, 2000)* .... Josh Taylor
**Tony Miller (1992–1993)* .... Michael Cudlitz
Celeste Lundy (1993–1994).......... Jennifer Grant
Dan Rubin (1993–1994).......... Matthew Porretta
Josh Richland (1993–1994) .... Joshua Beckett
Howard Rubin (1993–1994) .... Zachary Throne
Leslie Sumner (1993)................ Brooke Theiss
John Sears (1993–1994)............ Paul Johansson
Stuart Carson (1993–1994) .... David Gail
D'Shawn Hardell (1993–1994)...... Cress Williams
Professor Corey Randall (1993–1994) ... Scott Paulin
Lucinda Nicholson Randall (1993–1994)
.... Dina Meyer
Laura Kingman (1993–1994) .... Tracy Middendorf
Jesse Vasquez (1993–1995) . Mark Damon Espinoza
**Erin Silver (1993–1994)*
.... April and Arielle Peterson
**Erin Silver (1994–1995)* ... Paige and Ryanne Kettner
**Erin Silver (1995–1996)*.......... Megan Lee Braley
**Erin Silver (1997)* .... Mercedes Villamil
**Erin Silver (1998–2000)* .... Mercedes Kastner
Erica Steele (1993–1994) .... Noley Thornton
Suzanne Steele (1993–1994).......... Kerrie Keane
**Chancellor Milton Arnold (1993–1997)*
.... Nicholas Pryor
Clare Arnold (1994–1997) ..... Kathleen Robertson
Kevin Weaver (1994)............... David Hayward
Valerie Malone (1994–1998)
.... Tiffani-Amber Thiessen
**Rush Sanders (1994–1998)*.............. Jed Allan
Ray Pruit (1994–1995).............. Jamie Walters
Griffin Stone (1994)............... Casper Van Dien
**Arnold Muntz (1994–1998, 2000)*
.... Ryan Thomas Brown
**Janice Williams (1994–1995)*....... Natalie Belcon
**LuAnn Pruitt (1994–1995)* ... Caroline McWilliams
Dr. Peter Tucker (1995) .... James C. Victor
Charlie Rollins (1995) .... Jeffrey King
Colin Robins (1995–1996) .... Jason Wiles
Tony Marchette (1995)............. Stanley Kamel
Susan Keats (1995–1996) .... Emma Caulfield
Antonia Marchette (1995) .... Rebecca Gayheart
**Sheila Silver (1995–1996)* .... Caroline Lagerfelt
Bruno (1995)...................... Cliff Weissman
Joe Bradley (1995–1996) .... Cameron Bancroft
Jonathan Casten (1996)............... Carl T. Evans
**Joan Diamond Bussichio (1996)* .... Julie Parrish
Tara (1996) .... Paige Moss
Prince Carl (1996).................. Nick Kiriazis
Kenny Bannerman (1996)................ Joey Gian
Mark Reese (1995–1997) .... Dalton James
Tracy Gaylian (1996–1997) ... Jill Elizabeth Novick
**Bill Taylor (1996–1998)* .... John Reilly
Cliff Yeager (1996–1997)........... Greg Vaughan
Dick Harrison (1996–1997) .... Dan Gauthier
Tom Miller (1997)...................... Kane Picoy
**Abby Malone (1997–1998)*........ Michelle Phillips
Carly Reynolds (1997–1998) .... Hilary Swank
Noah Hunter (1997–2000) .... Vincent Young
Zach Malloy (1997–1998) .... Myles Jeffrey
Terri Spar (1997)...................... Fatima Lowe
Dr. Monahan (1997–1998)........ George Del Hoyo
Emma Bennett (1997–1998) .... Angel Boris
Janet Sosna (1998–2000) .... Lindsay Price
Jasper (1998)...................... Paul Popowich
Sophie Burns (1998) .... Laura Leighton
Matt Durning (1998–2000)........ Daniel Cosgrove
Gina Kincaid (1998–1999) .... Vanessa Marcil
Lauren Durning (1999)................ Cari Shayne
Wayne Moses (1999).............. Shawn Christian
Camille Desmond (2000) .... Josie Davis
Ellen (2000)................. Heidi Noelle Lenhart

*Occasional

Premiering in a season loaded with new series about high school life, several of which were more heavily promoted (*Ferris Bueller*, *Hull High*, *Parker Lewis Can't Lose*, *Fresh Prince of Bel Air*), *Beverly Hills 90210* emerged as the most popular among young people. One thing that distinguished it from the others was its realistic portrayal of issues that concerned teens—grades, peer group acceptance, money, drugs, sex, parents, and just fitting in. There were episodes that dealt with safe sex, alcoholism (both teen and adult), date rape, and suicide. Although most episodes were self-contained, the series did, on occasion, have the look of a serial drama.

The central focus of *Beverly Hills 90210* was the Walsh family, recently moved to opulent, expensive, status-conscious Beverly Hills from Minneapolis. In an environment where almost every child was living with a single parent, the Walshes were an anachronism. Jim, an executive with an accounting firm, and his homemaker wife, Cindy, were supportive and obviously still in love with each other, and their fraternal 16-year-old twins, Brandon and Brenda, were relatively normal and free of neuroses. Nor were the Walshes as concerned with the trappings of success—the size of their house, the make of their car, designer clothes—as were their new neighbors.

When the series premiered, Brandon and Brenda were starting their sophomore year at West Beverly Hills High. The fellow students with whom they became involved were Kelly, Brenda's snobbish, beautiful best friend, whose mother was an alcoholic; Steve, Kelly's jaded, arrogant former boyfriend, whose mother, TV actress Samantha Sanders, was the star of *Hartley House*; Dylan, Brandon's best friend and Brenda's boyfriend, the hunky surfer who lived alone in a fancy hotel suite until his father was indicted for corporate financial fraud; Andrea, the bright editor of the school newspaper where Brandon worked, who actually lived in the San Fernando Valley but used her grandmother's Beverly Hills address so she could go to a better school; Donna, Brenda and Kelly's insecure friend; David Silver, the freshman who tried too hard to be liked by upperclassmen; and Scott, David's buddy, who died tragically in a gun accident on his birthday. Nat was the owner of The Peach Pit, the restaurant where Brandon worked part time to make extra spending money.

In a rather unusual move, Fox aired new episodes of *Beverly Hills 90210* during the summer of 1991 and, appropriately, they dealt with what the kids did during summer vacation. Brandon worked for Henry Thomas, as a cabana boy at The Beverly Hills Beach Club, while Brenda, Kelly, Donna, and David took an acting class in summer school, with Chris Suiter as their teacher. The summer episodes helped the show build a large and devoted audience of young viewers and made stars Jason Priestley and Luke Perry teen heartthrobs.

Subsequent seasons consisted of a seemingly endless parade of romances. During 1991–1992 Kelly's mother, Jackie, became pregnant by David's father, Mel; they then married and had a baby, Erin. During the summer of 1992 Donna and Brenda joined a "study" program in Paris. Big mistake—back home Brenda's boyfriend, Dylan, took up with Kelly (Brenda wouldn't speak to her for months).

The 1992–1993 season was the senior year for all the regulars, including David, who had skipped a grade. His father almost immediately started cheating on his new wife, Jackie, so she threw him out of the house and filed for divorce. Dylan inherited $10 million after his father, who was out of prison working undercover for the government, was killed by a car bomb. He took Kelly to Europe for the summer, but by the time they returned they too had broken up.

The fall of 1993 saw most of the regulars beginning their freshman year at California University (Brenda enrolled at the University of Minnesota, but finding it somewhat less romantic than Southern California, she soon returned). Kelly, Donna, and David shared an apartment at the beach in Santa Monica (convenient since David and Donna were dating), and he developed a drug problem. Kelly and Dylan got back together, then split up again (she for Brandon, he for Brenda). Andrea had affairs with graduate assistant Dan Rubin and Hispanic law student Jesse. She got pregnant by Jesse, married him, and at season's end gave birth prematurely to a daughter, Hannah. Newly minted millionaire Dylan bought half interest in the Peach Pit, where he got his late father's old girlfriend Suzanne a job as a waitress. Suzanne married Kevin, and together they scammed Dylan out of his inheritance and left the country, taking her daughter, Erica, with them.

The fall of 1994 marked the departure of Brenda, ostensibly to study acting at the Royal Academy in London (actress Shannen Doherty had been getting bad publicity for years for her attitude and extracurricular activities and was fired by the producers). Brandon and Kelly had gotten serious, and Donna had dumped David, who had cheated on her (partially because she didn't believe in premarital sex). Moving into Brenda's old room was manipulative Valerie, a friend of the Walshes from Buffalo who moved to L.A. following her father's suicide and had an affair with Dylan, who was now broke (though nobody knew it). He had a recurrence of his drinking problem but eventually went to Mexico and, with Valerie's help, got his money back from Kevin and Suzanne. Clare, who had chased Brandon the previous spring, was Kelly and Donna's new roommate. She got involved with David, while Brandon became student body president and Steve promoted the nightclub After Dark, which was in the same building as the Peach Pit. Donna started dating Ray, a carpenter and musician whom her parents felt was beneath her, and Kelly was badly burned in a fire caused by Steve's sleazy fraternity brother Griffin. Valerie used some of her take from helping Dylan to buy Peach Pit After Dark and put pressure on Ray, lead singer of its house band, to have an affair. Andrea had an affair with Peter, and it almost broke up her marriage to Jesse. As the 1994–1995 season ended, Andrea and Jesse moved east (he for a teaching assistant position at Yale and she into its pre-med program), while Jim and Cindy Walsh moved to Hong Kong after he got a big promotion.

In the fall Dylan fell in love with Antonia, the daughter of the gangster who had his father killed. They got married in November, but after her father's hit man killed her by mistake (he was supposed to get Dylan), a despondent Dylan left town to sort things out. Other romances included Steve with Clare, David with Val and with Donna, Colin with Val and with Kelly, and Brandon with Susan, the editor of the school paper. Kelly made the worst choice with artist Colin, who had a cocaine problem. She started to use the drug and ended up in rehab. In the season finale Steve and Brandon cornered Colin near the harbor, where he was trying to skip the country on a tramp steamer, and the cops arrested him. Nat's girlfriend Joan found out she was pregnant and they decided to get married, while Brandon and Kelly talked about rekindling their romance and found out that Dylan and Brenda were living together in London.

In the fall of 1996, Kenny, a married guy who worked for Jim Walsh's firm, helped Val with After Dark's financial problems and they had an affair. Joan went into labor at her wedding and gave birth to a son, Frankie. David received $250,000 from his grandfather's estate and went on a spending spree, including buying half interest in After Dark from Val, who promptly got scammed out of her windfall by a crooked financial manager. Donna was stalked by a psycho student during the winter, and in March her dad suffered a stroke. After a fling with Tracy, Brandon got back together with Kelly, and she moved into the Walsh house. In May the gang graduated from C.U. and Brandon won the award as the school's outstanding senior.

At the start of the 1997–1998 season Kelly was shot in the stomach by drive-by car thieves, and when she recovered, she had partial amnesia—and didn't remember Brandon. It was several months before she got all her memories back. Noah, whom the gang had met during a vacation in Hawaii, moved to L.A. and got a job at After Dark through Val, with whom, naturally, he ended up in the sack. Steve was at loose ends after an affair with single mom Carly, so to give him something to do, his father, Rush, bought him a defunct weekly, *The Beverly Hills Shopper,* and told him to turn it into a viable paper. Steve talked Brandon into becoming the paper's editor and they renamed it *The Beverly Beat*. Noah, who turned out to be the heir to a corporate fortune, was dating Donna, and Val convinced David to pretend they were having an affair to make their former lovers jealous. David sold After Dark to Noah to get out of debt, and Noah took Val in as his business partner. The season finale was to be Brandon and Kelly's wedding, but as the ceremony was starting, they called it off.

That fall, as Kelly and Brandon tried to resolve their relationship, Sophie, a sexy young con artist who knew Val, turned up and started moving in on David, who was working as a disc jockey on radio station KBIB (his show aired live from After Dark). Steve had the hots for Sophie and got her a job as a "columnist" at *The Beverly Beat.* Noah found out that he and his family were broke after the IRS had fined his father for questionable business dealings. After his disgraced father committed suicide, Noah developed a serious drinking problem. Brandon and Kelly's long relationship was apparently over. She opened a dress store with Donna, and began a relationship with Matt, the handsome lawyer with offices in the same building. In November, Brandon got a job with the *New York Chronicle* and left town. With Brandon gone, Steve decided to turn *The Beverly Beat* into a tabloid, since he didn't have to do any real research and could make up the articles.

At Thanksgiving 1998, Val moved back home to Buffalo to be with her mother, Donna's scheming cousin Gina arrived and moved into the beach house with Donna and Kelly, and Dylan returned after a three-year absence. After failing to get together with Kelly, he started dating Gina. Matt, whose law practice was struggling, traded legal services for Steve's rag for a room at the Walsh house, and Steve found out his mother was gay. In the spring, Matt's girlfriend Kelly was raped by a small-time crook he was defending; she later shot and killed the crook when he attacked her a second time. Meanwhile, Dylan bought the building that housed the Peach Pit and After Dark to keep a financially strapped Noah from evicting Nat for a more lucrative tenant.

At the start of the 1999–2000 season Noah dumped Donna for cheating on him. They patched things up and moved in together, but in the spring they broke up. Gina moved in with Dylan, who had moved into the Beverly Royale Hotel. Janet was four months pregnant with Steve's baby and, after initial misgivings, he proposed. In November they got married in an informal ceremony with just their friends; on their honeymoon Janet went into early labor and gave birth to a girl, Madeline. Donna discovered that her father had had an affair with her aunt and that Gina was actually her sister. In December she told Gina, who didn't take it well. Dr. Martin and Gina finally made up, but at the end of the episode he died from a stroke. At Christmas Matt proposed to Kelly, who accepted and quit her job at Donna's dress shop. Donna took in Camille, who was getting serious with David, as a small-percentage partner. Dylan found out that his father had faked his death in the explosion seven years earlier and had spent the last seven years in the witness protection program and had difficulty reconciling with him. David got a job with a radio station in New York, had misgivings about leaving his friends and realized he still loved Donna. He turned down the job and broke up with Camille. Matt's brother, who worked in New York, was killed in a car accident; after he returned from the funeral, Matt decided to move to New York and be father to his late brother's unborn child. David proposed to Donna and, in the series finale, they got married, Kelly and Dylan acknowledged that they had a bond that time and circumstance had been unable to break, and Noah was about to commit to Ellen, the woman he had fallen in love with after breaking up with Donna.

BEWARE OF DOG (*Situation Comedy*)

BROADCAST HISTORY:

Animal Planet
30 minutes
Original episodes: *2002*
Premiered: *August 13, 2002*

CAST:

Jack the Dog (voice).................... Park Bench
Bill Poole.......................... Richard Waugh
Mary Poole .... Carolyn Dunn
Jessica Poole (age 16).................. Alex Appel
Matt Poole (12)......................... Gage Knox

This rather clichéd sitcom was the first such series on Animal Planet, but it got a quick yank of the collar. Jack, an adorable shaggy bearded collie, didn't think much of human owners and said so in his sarcastic voice-over comments (leashes were "postdomestication tools of oppression"). But he needed to eat, so he insinuated himself into the sunny suburban home of the Pooles, a family consisting of one goofy dad, Bill, a Civil War buff; Bill's smarter wife, Mary; one slightly snotty teen, Jessica; and a cheerful younger son, Matt. Jack saved the day more than once—for example, phoning in an order for flowers when Bill forgot Mary's birthday—but he couldn't save this show. Two "preview" episodes aired in August 2002, with a regular run planned for 2003, but it was never seen again. Jack was played by a pooch named Chip. And, yes, the actor who gave him voice was named "Park Bench."

BEWITCHED (*Situation Comedy*)

FIRST TELECAST: *September 17, 1964*
LAST TELECAST: *July 1, 1972*
BROADCAST HISTORY:

Sep 1964–Jan 1967, ABC Thu 9:00–9:30
Jan 1967–Sep 1971, ABC Thu 8:30–9:00
Sep 1971–Jan 1972, ABC Wed 8:00–8:30
Jan 1972–Jul 1972, ABC Sat 8:00–8:30

CAST:

Samantha Stephens/Serena
.... Elizabeth Montgomery
Darrin Stephens (1964–1969)............ Dick York
Darrin Stephens (1969–1972)......... Dick Sargent
Endora......................... Agnes Moorehead
**Maurice* .... Maurice Evans
Larry Tate........................... David White
Louise Tate (1964–1966) .... Irene Vernon
Louise Tate (1966–1972)............. Kasey Rogers
Tabitha Stephens (1966–1972)
.... Erin and Diane Murphy
Adam Stephens (1971–1972)
.... David and Greg Lawrence
Abner Kravitz .... George Tobias
Gladys Kravitz (1964–1966) . . Alice Pearce (d. 3/66)
Gladys Kravitz (1966–1972) .... Sandra Gould
Aunt Clara (1964–1968)............ Marion Lorne
**Uncle Arthur (1965–1972)* .... Paul Lynde
**Esmerelda (1969–1972)* .... Alice Ghostley
Dr. Bombay (1967–1972).............. Bernard Fox

*Occasional

PRODUCER/DIRECTOR:

William Asher

Bewitched was a comedy about an exceptionally

pretty young witch named Samantha and her earnest attempts to abandon her witchcraft to please her mortal husband, Darrin. The couple was married on the first telecast, but that was the last "normal" event in their union. Samantha was continually tempted to use her witchly powers, invoked by a twitch of her nose, to get her way around the house. There was also a bevy of her relatives, none of whom wanted her to go straight: her mother Endora, her father Maurice, practical-joking Uncle Arthur, and forgetful Aunt Clara, witches and warlocks all. Esmerelda the housekeeper, who came along in 1969, was also a witch, but her powers were declining; a timid soul, she would fade away when spoken to harshly. Samantha's mischievous look-alike cousin Serena, was also played by Miss Montgomery.

Also in the cast were Larry Tate, Darrin's long-suffering boss at the New York advertising agency of McMann and Tate, Larry's wife Louise, and the Stephens's easygoing but somewhat nosy neighbors, the Kravitzes.

Samantha's first child, Tabitha, was "born" on the telecast of January 13, 1966. The newborn infant was played briefly by identical twins Heidi and Laura Gentry and then by Tamar and Julie Young; beginning in the fall of 1966, two-year-old Erin and Diane Murphy assumed the role (later it was played by Erin alone). A son, Adam, came along on the night of October 16, 1969, although he was not seen regularly until the 1971–1972 season.

Visitors to the Stephens household included Julius Caesar (summoned up by mistake when Samantha asked Esmerelda to make a Caesar salad), George Washington, and Henry VIII.

Bewitched was an imaginative and well-written show that earned several Emmys. Extremely popular, it was in fact the biggest hit series produced by the ABC network up to that time (it ranked number two among all programs on the air during its first season). Reruns have entertained viewers for many years, on the ABC weekday schedule from January 1968 to July 1973, on ABC's Saturday morning lineup from September 1971 to September 1973, and on local stations.

Elizabeth Montgomery, the star of the series, was in real life married to its producer/director, William Asher.

BEYOND BELIEF: FACT OR FICTION (*Supernatural Anthology*)

FIRST TELECAST: *May 25, 1997*
LAST TELECAST: *September 5, 2002*
BROADCAST HISTORY:

May 1997–Jun 1997, FOX Sun 7:00–8:00
Aug 1997–Sep 1997, FOX Sun 7:00–8:00
Jan 1998–Jul 1998, FOX Fri 8:00–9:00
Jun 2000–Aug 2000, FOX Fri 8:00–9:00
Jun 2002–Sep 2002, FOX Thu 8:00–9:00

HOSTS:

James Brolin (1997)
Jonathan Frakes (1998–2002)

Each episode of this summer series included three to five stories depicting "normal" people confronted with unexplainable incidents. At the opening, the host challenged viewers to figure out which were based on real events and which were pure fabrications by the series' writers. At the end of each episode he revealed which were real and which were faked. For example: e-mail from a dead man stops a crime (true); three frightened girls driving in the rain narrowly escape disaster (true); dead relatives in a family tomb fight with each other (true); a boy's psychic dog is run over, but comes back from the dead (fiction); a false obituary leads to a man who later died (true). The series returned with new episodes during the summers of 2000 and 2002.

BEYOND CHANCE (*Documentary*)

BROADCAST HISTORY:

Lifetime
60 minutes
Original episodes: *1999–2002* (66 episodes)
Premiered: *August 16, 1999*

HOST:

Melissa Etheridge

A somewhat mystical series featuring gentle, life-affirming stories about ordinary people who encountered unusual situations that seem "beyond chance." There were several stories per episode—for example, a woman in Pennsylvania goes on the Internet and meets a man in England, who winds up saving her life via a kidney transplant; a birth mother and her long-lost daughter are reunited after they place ads seeking each other in the same newspaper on the same day; a beautiful woman in a coma nevertheless manages to establish communication with her therapist, write poetry and ultimately author a book; and a man is struck by lightning *twice* while trying to get his pregnant wife to a hospital on a stormy night. The series was hosted by soft-spoken rock star Melissa Etheridge, usually seen in eerie surroundings with lots of candles.

BEYOND REALITY (*Science Fiction*)

BROADCAST HISTORY:

USA Network
30 minutes
Produced: *1991–1993* (44 episodes)
Premiered: *October 4, 1991*

CAST:

Laura Wingate .... Shari Belafonte
J.J. Stillman .... Carl Marotte
Celia .... Nicole deBoer

Two university parapsychologists investigated reports of ghosts, out-of-body experiences, telekinesis, and other unexplained phenomena that had occurred in ordinary people's lives in this series, which was more thoughtful than scary. Laura tended to be the believer, and by the end of each episode she had usually convinced her skeptical young co-worker J.J. that maybe . . . just maybe . . .

Celia was a graduate assistant who sometimes helped. The series was set in an unnamed city that looked remarkably like Toronto, where it was in fact filmed. Stories were loosely based on actual reports of unexplained phenomena.

BEYOND TOMORROW (*Informational*)

FIRST TELECAST: *September 10, 1988*
LAST TELECAST: *December 16, 1989*
BROADCAST HISTORY:

Sep 1988–Mar 1989, FOX Sat 9:00–10:00
Mar 1989–Dec 1989, FOX Sat 9:30–10:00

CORRESPONDENTS:

Randy Meier
Gary Cubberley
Susan Hunt
Richard Wiese
Renee Chenault (1989)
Barry Nolan (1989)
Dave Marash (1989)

Beyond Tomorrow gave viewers an opportunity to see how their lives might be vastly changed in the coming decades. Each week its correspondents roamed the world in search of new products that might eventually impact the lives of everyone. Among them were a sonic clothes washer that worked without detergent, a house run completely by computer, a laser device for performing facial cosmetic surgery, office bomb shelters, hydrogen-powered cars, and new prosthetic devices for young amputees. In addition to covering technological and scientific advances, the series also featured stories on environmental issues—acid rain, depletion of the ozone layer, cryogenics, protection of endangered species, and other efforts to save the environment. Only Randy Meier stayed with *Beyond Tomorrow* throughout its run. The other three original correspondents were all replaced in the fall of 1989.

Beyond Tomorrow was an American adaptation of the Australian series *Beyond 2000.*

BEYOND WESTWORLD (*Science Fiction*)

FIRST TELECAST: *March 5, 1980*
LAST TELECAST: *March 19, 1980*
BROADCAST HISTORY:
Mar 1980, CBS Wed 8:00–9:00

CAST:

John Moore.......................... Jim McMullan
Simon Quaid.................. James Wainwright
Joseph Oppenheimer .... William Jordan
Pamela Williams .... Connie Sellecca
Foley .... Severn Darden
Roberta............................ Ann McCurry

The Delos Corporation was the world's largest and most powerful multinational company. Among its many enterprises was the futuristic amusement park, Westworld, where visitors were waited on by sophisticated robots that looked and acted exactly like real people. With their help, Westworld's visitors could live out their wildest fantasies.

Enter the mad scientist, Simon Quaid, who with Joseph Oppenheimer had invented these lifelike robots for Delos. Quaid, an unstable genius, decided to reprogram his children "to take over the world (what else!) and turn it into a utopian" society under his guidance. Charged with foiling this fiendish plot were John Moore, head of Delos Security, and his lovely assistant, Pamela Williams. Actually, Quaid's efforts were thwarted more by this series' viewers than by anything else. There were so few of them that it was canceled after only three episodes.

Beyond Westworld was an offshoot of the 1973 movie *Westworld*, in which the robots ran amok (with no explanation why) and destroyed the amusement park, killing many of the guests in the process. Yul Brynner, as one of the robots, was the star of the movie *Westworld* and was its only cast member to appear in its sequel, *Futureworld.*

BID 'N' BUY (*Quiz/Audience Participation*)

FIRST TELECAST: *July 1, 1958*
LAST TELECAST: *September 23, 1958*
BROADCAST HISTORY:
Jul 1958–Sep 1958, CBS Tue 10:00–10:30

EMCEE:

Bert Parks

At the start of each telecast of this auction game show, each of four contestants was given $10,000 in real money, which they then used to bid for clues that would help them identify a silhouette of some common object. The winner received an expensive prize, such as a sports car, a fancy wardrobe, or a cabin cruiser, plus the right to return the following week.

BIFF BAKER U.S.A. (*Adventure*)

FIRST TELECAST: *November 13, 1952*
LAST TELECAST: *March 26, 1953*
BROADCAST HISTORY:
Nov 1952–Mar 1953, CBS Thu 9:00–9:30

CAST:

Biff Baker........................... Alan Hale, Jr.
Louise Baker......................... Randy Stuart

Traveling all over the world in search of goods for his profitable importing business, Biff Baker often found himself involved in some form of international intrigue. Never looking for trouble, he nevertheless encountered it with remarkable frequency, and was always ready to deal with it. Biff and his wife Louise, with whom he traveled, most often found themselves caught up in some form of espionage, which was bad for the importing business but good for the plot.

BIG APPLE (*Police Drama*)

FIRST TELECAST: *March 1, 2001*
LAST TELECAST: *April 5, 2001*
BROADCAST HISTORY:
Mar 2001–Apr 2001, CBS Thu 10:00–11:00

CAST:

Det. Mike Mooney .... Ed O'Neill
Det. Vincent Trout.................. Jeffrey Pierce
Agent Will Preecher .... David Strathairn
Agent Jimmy Flynn .... Titus Welliver
Agent Teddy Olsen................ Glynn Turman
Agent Sarah Day.................... Kim Dickens
Terry Maddock.................. Michael Madsen
Chris Scott .... Donnie Wahlberg
Vlad .... Sebastian Roche
Mitya .... Pasha Lynchnikoff
Lt. Swenson...................... Michael Rispoli
Sandra Reynolds .... Elizabeth Regen
Howard Klein .... Frank Pellegrino
Brigid McNamara .... Samantha Buck
John Corelli .... Peter Appel
Bobby Rizutto .... Anthony Alessandro
Officer Cruz .... Yul Vazquez
Lois Mooney .... Brooke Smith
Rosemary........................... Maria Thayer

This dark, moody police drama starred sitcom veteran Ed O'Neill (*Married . . . with Children*) as Mike Mooney, a brooding, cynical detective on the N.Y.P.D. Mooney and his ambitious young partner, Trout, were investigating the murder of a stripper in a fancy Park Avenue penthouse, which got them involved in an undercover F.B.I. operation at a strip club controlled by the Russian mob. Preecher and Flynn, the senior F.B.I. agents overseeing the operation, "deputized" Mooney and Trout so they could keep things under their control and keep the N.Y.P.D. out. Day was a recently arrived F.B.I. agent who was tentatively scheduled to replace Olsen, a veteran unhappy with the methods being used by the younger agents. Also featured were Flynn's friend Maddock, an informant whose Hell's Kitchen bar was wired for surveillance purposes by the F.B.I.; Scott, a young neighborhood tough whom Maddock was trying to reform; and Vlad and Mitya, two Russian mobsters. As if things weren't depressing enough, Mooney had to cope with the suffering of his terminally ill sister, Lois, who died in the last episode aired, and Flynn had a confrontation with Maddock, who had taken the law into his own hands and may have been responsible for some local murders.

Despite airing directly after CBS' megahit series *Survivor*, *Big Apple* attracted a minuscule audience and was canceled after six episodes.

BIG BEAT, THE (*Music*)
FIRST TELECAST: *July 12, 1957*
LAST TELECAST: *August 2, 1957*
BROADCAST HISTORY:
Jul 1957–Aug 1957, ABC Fri 10:00–10:30
HOST:
Alan Freed

Alan Freed was the New York City disc jockey who is credited with coining the term "rock 'n' roll" and who did much to popularize "the big beat" in the mid-1950s. A flamboyant showman and promoter, Freed packaged this series of four rock spectaculars for ABC in the summer of 1957. The list of guests reads like a Who's Who of rock in the 1950s; the first show alone starred Connie Francis, The Everly Brothers ("Bye Bye Love"), Ferlin Husky ("Gone"), Don Rondo ("White Silver Sands"), the Billy Williams Quartet ("I'm Gonna Sit Right Down and Write Myself a Letter"), Nancy Wiskey ("Freight Train"), and Johnny and Joe ("Over the Mountain"). Later guests included Andy Williams, Chuck Berry, Frankie Lymon and the Teenagers, Bobby Darin, the Fontane Sisters, Fats Domino, Clyde McPhatter, Dale Hawkins, Gogi Grant, Mickey and Sylvia, Jerry Lee Lewis, and more—all in four half-hour telecasts! The Big Beat was probably a better representation of the current hit parade, all with original artists doing their own hits, than was ever heard on *Your Hit Parade*. In addition to serving as host, Freed led his own orchestra on the show, which included star saxophonists "Big Al" Sears and Sam "the Man" Taylor.

BIG BREAK (*Talent Contest*)
BROADCAST HISTORY:
Syndicated only
60 minutes
Produced: *1990* (26 episodes)
Released: *September 1990*
HOST:
Natalie Cole

Singer Natalie Cole hosted this weekly talent contest in which musical performers competed in three categories—solo vocalist, group performance, and young performance. Despite the multiple categories, each week's panel of celebrity judges determined a single winner. *Big Break* offered a grand prize of $100,000.

BIG BROTHER (*Reality/Competition*)
FIRST TELECAST: *July 5, 2000*
LAST TELECAST:
BROADCAST HISTORY:
Jul 2000–Aug 2000, CBS Wed 9:00–10:00
Jul 2000, CBS Thu 8:00–9:00
Jul 2000–Sep 2000, CBS Fri 8:00–8:30
Jul 2000–Sep 2000, CBS Sat 8:00–9:00
Jul 2000–Sep 2000, CBS Mon/Tue 8:00–8:30
Aug 2000–Sep 2000, CBS Wed 8:00–9:00
Aug 2000–Sep 2000, CBS Thu 8:00–8:30
Jul 2001–Aug 2001, CBS Thu/Sat/Tue 8:00–9:00
Aug 2001–Sep 2001, CBS Thu/Sat/Tue 9:00–10:00
Sep 2001, CBS Thu 10:00–11:00
Jul 2002–Sep 2002, CBS Wed 9:00–10:00
Jul 2002–Sep 2002, CBS Thu/Sat 8:00–9:00
Jul 2003– , CBS Tue/Fri 8:00–9:00
Jul 2003– , CBS Wed 9:00–10:00
HOST:
Julie Chen

Big Brother provided audiences with the ultimate in voyeurism. Not only could viewers watch five nights a week on TV, but computer users could access streaming video coverage 24 hours a day, seven days a week. The show placed ten strangers together in a specially designed "house" built at CBS facilities in Studio City, California, with 28 cameras and 60 microphones to spy on everything that happened. The housemates had no contact with the outside world—no telephones, newspapers, radio or TV—and all of their activities, interactions and confrontations were monitored. Periodically each of the housemates went to the confession room, where they vented their feelings and plans to outwit the others to the viewing audience. There were few amenities in the house, and they had to grow some of their own food in the garden. They were provided with a limited household allowance for food and supplies, which could be supplemented if they successfully completed challenges—the first two being to decipher a cryptographic message and to make a working clock using two potatoes as the battery.

The first *Big Brother* ran for 87 days, with the original contestants being beauty queen Jamie, pudgy dad George, hunky Eddie, happy college guy Josh, thirty-ish Cassandra, exotic dancer Jordan, Asian Curtis, unhappy suburban mom Karen (who appeared to be headed for a divorce), party animal Brittany and ladies' man William. Once every two weeks the housemates nominated two of their fellow participants for elimination and viewers voted by telephone to determine who was ousted. After leaving the house banished contestants were reunited with their families and interviewed by host Chen. At the end of the three months, when the number of survivors was down to three, a final telephone vote determined their winnings—$500,000 to the winner, $100,000 for second place and $50,000 for third. Participants could leave the house at any time (nobody did) but, if they left, they couldn't go back in and lost their shot at the prize money. If anyone had left, they would have been replaced by an alternate.

Big Brother was produced by a Dutch company, Endemol Entertainment, and had been a big hit in the Netherlands, where it had premiered in 1999, as well as in Germany and Spain. American viewers were less enthralled than their European counterparts and found the show incredibly boring. Home viewers kept voting out the most interesting and controversial housemates (first to go was African American William, who turned out to be a supporter of the Black Panthers), and the surviving group became progressively more bland and uninteresting. The winner, Eddie McGee, was an affable 21-year-old college student from Arlington, Texas, who had lost a leg to bone cancer as a child.

When *Big Brother 2* premiered in the summer of 2001, there were a number of changes designed to spice up the show. It was broadcast three nights a week instead of five, the initial number of housemates was increased to 12 from ten, housemates were evicted by each other, rather than by the viewing audience, evictions occurred every week and males and females shared bedrooms (night cams watched the action there). There was also the introduction of the Head of Household (HOH), determined by a weekly competition. The winner of the HOH competition spent the week in a private bedroom complete with maid service and a well-stocked refrigerator but was responsible for nominating the two housemates to be voted on for eviction. In addition to the Food Competitions, which sometimes pitted housemates against each other, there were Luxury Competitions with winnings ranging from getting access to the hot tub to spending one night out in the real world. Some of the competitions included cash incentives for the winners. Although 24-hour-a-day viewing via the Internet was still available, CBS began charging computer users for access, which generated a considerable amount of negative response.

One week after *Big Brother 2* premiered Justin Sebik, a bartender from Bayonne, New Jersey, was expelled from the house for intimidating other housemates and threatening them with physical violence—including holding a kitchen knife to the throat of one of the women while he was kissing her. Among the other housemates were hunks Will and Hardy, who always seemed to have their shirts off, amazingly hairy Bunky, whom viewers hoped would keep his shirt *on*, and conservative family man Kent, who surprisingly bonded with gay Bunky. The revised format resulted in more alliances, double-crossing and sexual activity than in the first season, but it was still a marginal ratings success. In order to maintain a sense of viewer participation there were periodic America's Choice votes on such things as allowing one housemate a short phone call from home or choosing what kind of clothes they could buy on a short shopping spree. When the number of survivors was down to three Nicole, the winner of the final HOH competition, picked which of the two others to evict and thereby chose whom she would vie with for the $500,000 grand prize, with the winner determined by a vote of the seven previous evictees. Each of the evictees asked the finalists questions to help them make their decisions, after which the finalists made their final pleas to the group. The winner was Will Kirby, a 28-year-old physician from Miami, Florida.

The major change for *Big Brother 3* was the addition of a weekly competition for the "power of veto." The person who won the competition could force the HOH to replace one of the two people he or she had nominated for eviction—except that the HOH couldn't replace the nominee with the veto winner, and a veto winner couldn't veto his or her own nomination. After four people had been evicted the producers added a new twist, allowing one of them to negotiate back into the house. Host Chen asked each of them how much of the $500,000 first prize they would be willing to give up for a chance to get back into the game. Three of the four were willing to give up half and two of them, when asked, said they'd be willing to subsist on only peanut butter and jelly for the remaining 42 days of the competition. Chen then told the two finalists that if they won they could keep the money and they wouldn't have to live on peanut butter and jelly. The seven housemates still in the game voted to bring Amy back—but she was evicted again five weeks later. The winner of *Big Brother 3* was Lisa Donahue, a 26-year-old bartender from Los Angeles.

BIG BROTHER JAKE (*Situation Comedy*)

BROADCAST HISTORY:

The Family Channel
30 minutes
Produced: *1990–1994* (100 episodes)
Premiered: *September 2, 1990*

CAST:

Jake Rozzner .... Jake Steinfeld
Connie Duncan ("Ma") .... Barbara Meek
Gary MacLamore .... Ben Siegler
Loomis "Lou" Washington .... Josiah Trager
Kateri Monroe .... Gabrielle Carmouche
Andy King .... Jeremy Wieand
Dave King .... Daniel Hilfer
Jill Kenyon (1990–1992) .... Elizabeth Narvaez
Jane O'Hara (1991–1993) .... Melody Combs
Caroline (1992–1994) .... Rachelle Guzy
**Miss Meg Morgan (1990–1991)* ...... Denise Devin
**Miss Roberta Domedian (1991–1994)*
.... Jane Connell

*Occasional

Love was all around in this sunny sitcom set in a bustling interracial foster home in Brooklyn. At the center of things was Jake, a beefy former Hollywood stuntman who had returned to the home in which he was raised to help his foster "mom," a sweet black woman named Connie, raise her next generation of foster kids. She certainly needed the help. Her husband, Isaac, had passed away, and there were kid problems everywhere. Her charges were Lou, a chubby teenager; Kateri, a bright, studious young black girl; Jill, an older, boy-obsessed teen; and Andy and Dave, preteen terrors who looked like twins but were not in fact related. After two seasons grownup Jill left and was replaced by Caroline, a little abandoned Oriental girl.

Gary was Jake's amiable pal from high school, now a Manhattan lawyer, and Jane was Jake's former high school girlfriend. Miss Morgan was the original social worker, replaced in year two by the dreaded and cranky Miss Domedian. The older kids attended Frederick Douglass High School. Jake narrated.

BIG DEAL (*Game/Audience Participation*)

FIRST TELECAST: *September 1, 1996*
LAST TELECAST: *September 29, 1996*
BROADCAST HISTORY:

Sep 1996, FOX Sun 7:00–8:00

HOST:

Mark DeCarlo

BAND:

Big Bad VooDoo Daddy

In this variation on *Let's Make a Deal*, host DeCarlo picked members of the studio audience to compete in stunts and games. The winners could either keep the prizes or trade them for things behind curtains and screens. Many of the stunts were designed to make the contestants look foolish and/or mess them up, like the stunts from *Family Double Dare*. The first episode included inept people attempting to milk cows to provide milk for a kitten, with the winner trading the kitten to win what was behind a curtain: a sailboat. The person who kept the kitten got a diamond tennis bracelet masked as its collar. A family, filmed on location, won a big prize for breaking every window in the front of their house in 60 seconds by hitting them with baseballs. At the end of each episode the two big winners could trade everything they had won for the "Big Deal" of the week.

BIG EASY, THE (*Police Drama*)

BROADCAST HISTORY:

USA Network
60 minutes
Produced: *1996–1997* (35 episodes)
Premiered: *August 11, 1996*

CAST:

Det. Remy McSwain .... Tony Crane
Anne Osborne .... Susan Walters
Sheriff C. D. LeBlanc .... Barry Corbin
Det. Darlene Broussard .... Karla Tamburrelli
Smiley Dupree .... Eric George
Asst. D.A. Lightnin' Hawkins .... Troy Bryant
Janine Rebbenack .... Leslie Bibb

In this atmospheric cop show with a drawl, Det. Remy McSwain, a smooth-talking ladies' man, tracked down criminals in the colorful alleyways of New Orleans. Always ready to bend the law to get things done—as was everyone else in the Crescent City, apparently—Remy met his match in uptight federal attorney Anne Osborne, who came to town to investigate a crime and decided to stay. Civil War buff C.D. was both Remy's uncle and his boss on the police force, Darlene his man-hungry co-worker, Smiley his jazzman friend and street informant, and Lightnin' the scheming Assistant D.A. Actress Walters left the series after about two-thirds of its run. Based on the 1987 movie starring Dennis Quaid and Ellen Barkin.

BIG EDDIE (*Situation Comedy*)

FIRST TELECAST: *August 23, 1975*
LAST TELECAST: *November 7, 1975*
BROADCAST HISTORY:

Aug 1975–Sep 1975, CBS Sat 8:30–9:00
Sep 1975–Nov 1975, CBS Fri 8:00–8:30

CAST:

Eddie Smith .... Sheldon Leonard
Honey Smith .... Sheree North
Ginger Smith .... Quinn Cummings
Monte "Bang Bang" Valentine .... Billy Sands
Jessie Smith .... Alan Oppenheimer
Raymond McKay .... Ralph Wilcox

Eddie Smith was a reformed gambler who was trying to make it as the owner-promoter of New York's Big E Sports Arena. Despite the gruff exterior, accentuated by the thickest New York accent ever heard on television, Eddie was a softie at heart and really wanted to broaden his intellectual horizons and improve his manners. His family consisted of his wife Honey, an ex-stripper; his granddaughter Ginger; and his brother Jessie, the accountant for Eddie's business. Bang Bang was Eddie's cook, and Raymond a stereotyped, jive-talking young black man working for Eddie. *Big Eddie* was given a preseason preview run on Saturday nights before moving into a Friday time period, but it faded quickly when pitted against *Sanford and Son*, its regular competition, in September.

BIG EVENT, THE (*Various*)

FIRST TELECAST: *September 26, 1976*
LAST TELECAST: *September 27, 1981*
BROADCAST HISTORY:

Sep 1976–Sep 1981, NBC Sun Various times
Jan 1978–Sep 1979, NBC Tue Various times

The Big Event was NBC's regular weekly showcase for special programming. Many of the specials lumped under this generic title were two hours in length, and some were even longer. "The First Fifty Years," a retrospective of NBC's half-century in broadcasting, occupied the entire evening of November 21, 1976, from 7:00 to 11:30 P.M. Major theatrical motion pictures were aired as Big Events; *Earthquake, 2001: A Space Odyssey,* and *Gone With the Wind* made their network television debuts here. In addition several major original television films were produced for the show (*Sybil, The Moneychangers, Holocaust,* and *Jesus of Nazareth*—the latter having previously aired in Europe) as well as more standard specials ("An Evening with Diana Ross," "The Father Knows Best Reunion," "The Story of Princess Grace").

The *Big Event* concept soon spread to other nights of the week as NBC, which was suffering from a shortage of hit series at the time, sought to boost its ratings with short-run but spectacular programming. A number of two- and three-part series such as "Harvest Home" and "The Godfather Saga" (an amalgam of the two *Godfather* theatrical films plus unused footage left over from the making of the films), ran partly or entirely under the *Big Event* title, usually extending from Saturday through Monday or Tuesday nights. A second regular *Big Event* night was added on Tuesday from 1978 to 1979.

BIG GAME, THE (*Quiz/Audience Participation*)

FIRST TELECAST: *June 13, 1958*
LAST TELECAST: *September 12, 1958*
BROADCAST HISTORY:

Jun 1958–Sep 1958, NBC Fri 7:30–8:00

EMCEE:

Tom Kennedy

An unusual variation on quiz shows, this program tried to create the atmosphere of a big-game hunt. Each contestant was first given three plastic animals to place wherever he chose in his "jungle" (game board). He then answered multi-part questions, giving him opportunities to "shoot" at his opponent's animals. Although unable to see his opponent's board, a contestant could "shoot" at specific locations on the board (marked by a grid), hoping that the animals had been placed there. The first hunter to bag all of his opponent's animals won $2,000 and the right to face a new challenger.

BIG HAWAII (*Adventure*)
FIRST TELECAST: *September 21, 1977*
LAST TELECAST: *November 16, 1977*
BROADCAST HISTORY:
Sep 1977–Nov 1977, NBC Wed 10:00–11:00
CAST:
Mitch Fears .... Cliff Potts
Barrett Fears .... John Dehner
Karen "Keke" Fears .... Lucia Stralser
Oscar Kalahani .... Bill Lucking
Lulu Kalahani .... Elizabeth Smith
Garfield Kalahani .... Moe Keale
Kimo Kalahani .... Remi Abellira

The sprawling Paradise Ranch on the island of Hawaii was the private domain of autocratic Barrett Fears. He had built it into an empire that had made him one of the richest and most powerful men in all the Hawaiian islands. Recently returned to help him run the ranch was his only son, 29-year-old Mitch, a free spirit whose anti-establishment, radical attitudes were a source of constant conflict with his traditional father. Mitch's best friend, and the mediator between the two strong-willed Fears men, was Oscar Kalahani, the foreman of Paradise Ranch. Keke was Mitch's spoiled, tomboyish 18-year-old cousin who also lived on the ranch; Big Lulu, Oscar's mother and the family housekeeper, whose son Garfield did odd jobs around the ranch; and Kimo, Lulu's son and a good friend of Keke. Stories revolved around the problems of running the ranch, the conflicts between its owners, and the adjustments forced on the traditional Hawaiian lifestyle by the inroads of change.

BIG IDEA, THE (*Inventions*)
FIRST TELECAST: *December 15, 1952*
LAST TELECAST: *October 15, 1953*
BROADCAST HISTORY:
Dec 1952–May 1953, DUM Mon 9:00–9:30
May 1953–Oct 1953, DUM Thu 10:00–10:30
HOST:
Donn Bennett
REGULAR PANELIST:
Ray Wood

This unusual program displayed new inventions, with commentary by a panel and interviews with guest inventors. The presentations were entirely straight, and most of the inventions shown were useful, if prosaic, aids to everyday life, though there were some screwball exceptions. A sample of what the viewer might see on *The Big Idea*: a woman's inflatable bathing suit, an inflatable coat hanger, a dartboard that lit up, a golf bag that stood up by itself, a complete miniature orchestra, a lunch box with self-contained hot plate, a refrigerated lunch box, a self-snuffing ashtray, a collapsible smoking pipe, spring-loaded shoe heels, rotating shoe heels, a clothesline with permanently attached clothespins, a device for preventing storm windows from falling off, a device to allow cars to park sideways, the "Dickey-Dout" (a device to hold blouses and shirts in place), and individual plastic nose filters for allergy sufferers.

The Big Idea was first scheduled against CBS' *I Love Lucy,* where it was probably seen by nobody except friends and families of the inventors. It later moved to Thursday night but expired after a year's run.

BIG ISSUE, THE (*Public Affairs*)
FIRST TELECAST: *April 7, 1953*
LAST TELECAST: *January 18, 1954*
BROADCAST HISTORY:
Apr 1953–Jun 1953, DUM Tue 8:30–9:00
Sep 1953–Jan 1954, DUM Mon 8:30–9:00
MODERATOR:
Martha Rountree
REGULAR PANELIST:
Lawrence E. Spivak

This discussion program covered important issues of the day and was moderated for most of its run by Martha Rountree, who is better known for her *Meet the Press.* Two guests, on opposing sides of the "big issue," appeared on each telecast. DuMont considered this to be "throwaway" programming, scheduling it first against *Milton Berle* on Tuesday and then opposite *Arthur Godfrey's Talent Scouts* on Monday.

BIG MOMENT, THE (*Sports Drama*)
FIRST TELECAST: *July 5, 1957*
LAST TELECAST: *September 13, 1957*
BROADCAST HISTORY:
Jul 1957–Sep 1957, NBC Fri 9:30–10:00
HOST:
Bud Palmer

Films of sports highlights from the early 1920s to the present were featured on this summer replacement for *The Big Story.* Among the stories covered were famous finishes, arguments and riots, upsets, comebacks, sports characters, and women athletes.

BIG MOMENT, THE (*Audience Participation*)
FIRST TELECAST: *April 3, 1999*
LAST TELECAST: *June 26, 1999*
BROADCAST HISTORY:
Apr 1999, ABC Sat 8:00–9:00
Apr 1999, ABC Sat 8:30–9:00
Jun 1999, ABC Sat 8:30–9:00
HOST:
Brad Sherwood

In this show happy, middle-class Americans, most of them with adorable, squealing kids, were given the chance to win $25,000 in prizes if they could perform a specified stunt while their family cheered them on. Ironically, most contestants were lawyers or nurses or other professionals who didn't look like they really needed the money—one man said he wanted to buy a ball machine to improve his tennis game! The stunts, however, were neither silly (usually) nor easy, for example memorizing pi to the 100th decimal point, learning to pull a tablecloth out from under a fully set dinner table, teaching a puppy five new tricks, or properly identifying thirty different flavors of ice cream. The contestants were given seven days to practice mastering their challenge at home, and a video camera to record their efforts. Then, in the studio, came the "big moment" when they would have to prove they could do it, resulting in triumph—or humiliation—in front of a national audience.

Ratings for *The Big Moment* were so low that in its third week ABC abruptly cut the show to half an hour—making it, in effect, "Half a Big Moment." Based on *The Happy Family Plan Show,* which was popular in Japan, where viewers seem to like public humiliation of this kind.

BIG PARTY, THE (*Variety*)
FIRST TELECAST: *October 8, 1959*
LAST TELECAST: *December 31, 1959*

BROADCAST HISTORY:

Oct 1959–Dec 1959, CBS Thu 9:30–11:00

The full title of this biweekly series was *The Big Party by Revlon,* paying homage to its sponsor. Each telecast presented a different host or hostess and a large roster of guest stars in a lavish 90-minute variety show. The program filling the alternate weeks was the prestigious *Playhouse 90.* Originally there were to have been a total of 20 of these live variety shows, but the series was canceled with the New Year's Eve telecast. Despite the appearance of such well-known performers as Rock Hudson, Tallulah Bankhead, Sammy Davis, Jr., Mort Sahl, and Esther Williams, all of whom were on the first telecast, *The Big Party* never found a big audience.

BIG PAYOFF, THE (*Quiz/Audience Participation*)

FIRST TELECAST: *June 29, 1952*
LAST TELECAST: *September 27, 1953*
BROADCAST HISTORY:

Jun 1952–Sep 1952, NBC Sun 8:00–9:00
Jun 1953–Sep 1953, NBC Sun 8:00–9:00

EMCEE:

Randy Merriman

HOSTESS:

Bess Myerson

Contestants for this summer series were selected from letters in which men told why the women in their lives deserved the wonderful prizes offered by the program. The Big Payoff itself included jewelry, clothes, a mink coat for the woman, a new car for the man, and a trip to anywhere in the world via Pan American World Airways. To win, the man had to answer a series of progressively more difficult questions. Added features were the Big Little Payoff for children and the Turn About Payoff, in which women had a chance to win prizes for their men. Randy Merriman was also the emcee of the daytime version of this show, which premiered December 31, 1951. Bess Myerson appeared on both the daytime and the nighttime versions, chatting with contestants and displaying prizes.

The daytime version ran on NBC until March 1953 and was then carried by CBS until it went off the air in October 1959. Hosts who succeeded Mr. Merriman on the daytime version were Bert Parks, Mort Lawrence, and Robert Paige. When Miss Myerson left the daytime version of *The Big Payoff* her role as assistant/model was taken by Betty Ann Grove and later by Denise Lor.

BIG PICTURE, THE (*Documentary*)

FIRST TELECAST: *October 5, 1953*
LAST TELECAST: *September 30, 1959*
BROADCAST HISTORY:

Oct 1953–Dec 1954, ABC Mon 9:30–10:00
Jan 1954–Aug 1954, ABC Wed 9:00–9:30
Aug 1954–Feb 1955, ABC Sun 8:30–9:00
Mar 1955–Jun 1955, ABC Sat 7:30–8:00
Aug 1955, ABC Tue 8:30–9:00
Sep 1955–Jan 1956, ABC Mon 10:00–10:30
Mar 1956–Apr 1956, ABC Sun 10:00–10:30
Jun 1956–Oct 1956, ABC Tue 10:00–10:30
Jul 1957, ABC Thu 8:00–8:30
Aug 1957–Oct 1957, ABC Fri 10:00–10:30
Sep 1958–Oct 1958, ABC Fri 9:00–9:30
Jun 1959–Aug 1959, ABC Sat 10:00–10:30
Aug 1959–Sep 1959, ABC Wed 7:30–8:00

NARRATOR:

Capt. Carl Zimmerman

Many films produced by government and industry to promote their own interests were shown on television during the 1950s, especially by the impoverished ABC and DuMont networks. Probably no such series had as long a run or was as well received by viewers as the U.S. Army's *Big Picture.* This program aired straight documentary films produced by the Army Pictorial Center and depicted various facets of the U.S. Army in action, including great battles, biographies of generals, new weaponry, and the roles played by various divisions and branches. Professional actors were rarely used; instead most of the footage came from the army's own vast historical and training film libraries.

The Big Picture was the brainchild of Lt. Carl Bruton, a commercial broadcaster called to active duty at the Pentagon during the Korean War. Seeing the vast amount of film available, and realizing the impact made by such privately made documentaries as *Crusade in Europe,* he sensed an excellent public relations opportunity for the army. (The films were also used for training purposes and were shown to foreign audiences.) The series began on WTOP in Washington, D.C., in 1951 and was soon being offered free to stations all over the country, to be shown in any manner they pleased. ABC picked it up in 1953 and ran it off and on for six years, seemingly whenever there was a hole to plug in the network schedule.

BIG PICTURE, THE (*Movie News*)

BROADCAST HISTORY:

MTV
30 minutes
Produced: *1988–1993*
Premiered: *June 9, 1988*

REGULARS:

Chris Connelly

A magazine show about movies with interviews and clips from the latest flicks. Host Chris Connelly was senior editor of *Premiere* magazine.

BIG QUESTION, THE (*News/Discussion*)

FIRST TELECAST: *September 9, 1951*
LAST TELECAST: *October 21, 1951*
BROADCAST HISTORY:

Sep 1951–Oct 1951, CBS Sun 6:00–6:30

MODERATOR:

Charles Collingwood

This live discussion program, which originated from Washington, D.C., attempted to cover a major issue of domestic or world importance each week. CBS White House correspondent Charles Collingwood served as moderator. When the subject warranted, the program might be filmed in advance on location, as in the case of a discussion with the delegates to the San Francisco conference on the Japanese Peace Treaty. At the end of October 1951 the program moved to an afternoon time slot, where it remained until early 1952.

BIG RECORD, THE (*Music*)

FIRST TELECAST: *September 18, 1957*
LAST TELECAST: *June 11, 1958*
BROADCAST HISTORY:

Sep 1957–Mar 1958, CBS Wed 8:00–8:30
Mar 1958–Jun 1958, CBS Wed 8:30–9:00

HOSTESS:

Patti Page

Singer Patti Page, who had sold millions of her own records, was the hostess of this live musical showcase. The program's guest stars were well-established recording artists singing their biggest-selling or trademark songs; those currently on the popular record charts; and up-and-coming young singers who were, in the words of the producers, "due to hit the jukebox jackpot within the near future." The range of selections included show music and standards in addition to rock 'n' roll, then a fairly new trend in music. Emphasis was placed on standards, however, to attract a wider audience than the teenage-oriented top-40 songs.

BIG SHAMUS, LITTLE SHAMUS (*Detective Drama*)

FIRST TELECAST: *September 29, 1979*
LAST TELECAST: *October 6, 1979*
BROADCAST HISTORY:

Sep 1979–Oct 1979, CBS Sat 9:00–10:00

CAST:

Arnie Sutter .... Brian Dennehy
Max Sutter .... Doug McKeon
George Korman .... George Wyner
Stephanie Marsh .... Kathryn Leigh Scott
Jerry Wilson .... Ty Henderson
Jingles Lodestar .... Cynthia Sikes

Atlantic City's Ansonia Hotel would have gone bankrupt were it not for the legalization of gambling in that seaside resort community. With new management and a brand-new casino to help bring in money, the Ansonia had a new lease on life. One of the survivors from the Ansonia's past was its veteran house detective, Arnie Sutter. With his 13-year-old son, Max, he attempted to cope with the tremendous increase in crime accompanying the legalization of gambling. Along with the bettors came an influx of prostitutes, thieves, and con men, all trying to "hit it big" in their own way. George Korman was Arnie's boss, the security chief at the Ansonia; Stephanie Marsh was the new assistant manager; Jerry Wilson was the desk clerk; and Jingles Lodestar was an undercover security agent posing as a cocktail waitress. *Big Shamus, Little Shamus* was so poorly done, and so poorly received, that it was canceled after only two episodes had aired.

BIG SHOW, THE (*Variety*)

FIRST TELECAST: *March 4, 1980*
LAST TELECAST: *June 3, 1980*
BROADCAST HISTORY:

Mar 1980–Jun 1980, NBC Tue 9:00–10:30

REGULARS:

Joe Baker
Graham Chapman
Paul Grimm
Charlie Hill
Mimi Kennedy
Edie McClurg
Pamela Myers
Owen Sullivan
Adolfo Quinones and his dance group, Shabba-Doo
The Big Show Water Ballet
The Big Show Ice Skaters
The Tony Charmoli Dancers
The Nick Perito Orchestra

NBC tried gamely to bring back the big, splashy variety show with this 1980 series. It offered lavish sets, big budgets, major stars, and a full 90 minutes (sometimes two hours) of entertainment every week. There was a regular company of resident comedians for sketches, a huge pool for water ballets, a giant rink for ice-skating numbers, and a pair of big-name cohosts each week. Steve Allen hosted on three occasions, and other hosts included Dean Martin, Tony Randall, Victor Borge, Gene Kelly, Flip Wilson, and Don Rickles. Singers Mel Tillis and Debby Boone made multiple guest appearances, as did comics Sid Caesar and Gallagher, and ice skaters Peggy Fleming and Dorothy Hamill. The reviewers thought it was wonderful, but the viewing audience stayed with ABC's Tuesday night comedies, leading to *The Big Show*'s early demise.

BIG STORY, THE (*Dramatic Anthology*)

FIRST TELECAST: *September 16, 1949*
LAST TELECAST: *June 28, 1957*
BROADCAST HISTORY:

Sep 1949–Mar 1951, NBC Fri 9:30–10:00
Mar 1951–Jul 1956, NBC 9:00–9:30 (OS)
Sep 1956–Jun 1957, NBC Fri 9:30–10:00

NARRATOR:

Bob Sloane (1949–1954)
Norman Rose (1954–1955)
Ben Grauer (1955–1957)

This long-running documentary-drama series was based on the actual case histories of reporters who solved crimes, uncovered corruption, or otherwise performed significant public service through their diligent reporting. Some episodes were local human-interest stories, and some were national scandals, such as the story of labor columnist Victor Riesel, who was blinded by racketeers for his exposé. Each week, the sponsor, American Tobacco Company, gave a $500 cash award (initially called the Pall Mall Award) to the reporter whose story was used. Starting in 1955 Ben Grauer appeared in a newsroom at the beginning and end of each episode, in the role of the program's editor. He introduced the evening's "big story," and then, after the drama, would present the real-life reporter with his "Big Story Award." The series was presented on alternate weeks during part of its run.

Following its cancellation by NBC in 1957, *The Big Story* continued in production for another season as a syndicated series. Burgess Meredith narrated the syndicated version.

BIG SURPRISE, THE (*Quiz*)

FIRST TELECAST: *October 8, 1955*
LAST TELECAST: *April 2, 1957*
BROADCAST HISTORY:

Oct 1955–Jun 1956, NBC Sat 7:30–8:00
Sep 1956–Apr 1957, NBC Tue 8:00–8:30

EMCEE:

Jack Barry (1955–1956)
Mike Wallace (1956–1957)

In the wake of the sudden and dramatic success of CBS' *The $64,000 Question*, which had premiered during the summer of 1955, NBC brought out its own big-money quiz show that fall. During its first six months on the air *The Big Surprise* underwent numerous modifications in format. There was a period during which the contestant could be "rescued" if he or she missed a question, by having someone else correctly answer a substitute question; the "rescuer" then got 10 percent of the regular contestant's total winnings. There was a period when the contestant could be asked easy or hard questions. Missing an easy question cost the contestant all his or her winnings, while missing a hard one cost only half the winnings. There were other variations as well. In April 1956 the program finally settled down with a less complicated format. The subject area was chosen by the contestant. There were ten questions ranging in value from $100 to $100,000, and the contestant could also answer two insurance questions. Correct answers to the insurance questions guaranteed the contestants all the money they had won up to that point, regardless of future misses.

Unlike *The $64,000 Question*, there was no isolation booth on *The Big Surprise*. Contestants stood on a pedestal while pondering the answers to questions. Jack Barry left the show on March 3, 1956, and was replaced the following week by Mike Wallace.

BIG TOP (*Circus*)
FIRST TELECAST: *July 1, 1950*
LAST TELECAST: *January 6, 1951*
BROADCAST HISTORY:
Jul 1950–Sep 1950, CBS Sat 7:00–8:00
Sep 1950–Jan 1951, CBS Sat 6:30–7:30
REGULARS:
Jack Sterling
Dan Lurie
Ed McMahon
Chris Keegan

Each week a full hour of live circus acts was presented on this series, which originated from the Camden, New Jersey, Convention Hall. Jack Sterling was the ringmaster, Ed McMahon (later of *The Tonight Show*) and Chris Keegan were the resident clowns, and Dan Lurie was the strongman. In addition to the regulars, at least six different acts, ranging from trapeze to trained animals, were presented on each show. After its six-month run at night, *Big Top* moved to Saturday afternoons (noon–1:00 P.M.), where it remained a fixture on the CBS lineup for the next seven years.

BIG TOWN (*Newspaper Drama*)
FIRST TELECAST: *October 5, 1950*
LAST TELECAST: *October 2, 1956*
BROADCAST HISTORY:
Oct 1950–Sep 1954, CBS Thu 9:30–10:00
Feb 1953–Jul 1953, DUM Fri 8:00–8:30
Oct 1954–Sep 1955, NBC Wed 10:30–11:00
Sep 1955–Oct 1956, NBC Tue 10:30–11:00
CAST:
Steve Wilson (1950–1954) .... Patrick McVey
Steve Wilson (1954–1956) .... Mark Stevens
Lorelei Kilbourne (1950–1951)....... Mary K. Wells
Lorelei Kilbourne (1951–1952)........ Julie Stevens
Lorelei Kilbourne (1952–1953)........... Jane Nigh
Lorelei Kilbourne (1953–1954) .... Beverly Tyler
Lorelei Kilbourne (1954–1955)......... Trudy Wroe
Charlie Anderson (1954–1956)........ Barry Kelley
Lt. Tom Greggory (1954–1955)....... John Doucette
"Rush" (1954–1955)................. Lyn Stalmaster
Diane Walker (1955–1956) .... Doe Avedon

This long-running melodrama centered on *The Illustrated Press*, the largest and most influential newspaper in Big Town, whose driving force was crusading editor Steve Wilson. Steve's concerns were thwarting the spread of organized crime, exposing political corruption, establishing various types of reforms, and any other cause that seemed worthy. His star reporter was Lorelei Kilbourne, who had a certain romantic interest in her boss. *Big Town* had run from 1937 to 1948 on radio (where Steve Wilson had once been played by Edward G. Robinson), and when it moved to television as a live weekly series in 1950 it was an immediate hit. In April 1952 series production moved from New York to Hollywood, and *Big Town* was thereafter a filmed rather than live show. Patrick McVey portrayed editor Wilson throughout the CBS run, but Lorelei Kilbourne's face kept changing. After the end of its first season on NBC, her part was dropped completely from the show and Steve's love interest became Diane Walker, a commercial artist. City editor Charlie Anderson was also added as a regular cast member by NBC, as was ambitious young cub reporter "Rush."

Repeats of *Big Town* were seen on DuMont under the title *City Assignment* while the program was still running on CBS. The DuMont episodes starred Patrick McVey, as did other episodes later syndicated under the title *Heart of the City*. The episodes in which Mark Stevens had starred were later syndicated as *Headline* (1954–1955 episodes) and *Byline Steve Wilson* (1955–1956 episodes).

BIG URBAN MYTH (*Information*)
BROADCAST HISTORY:
MTV
30 minutes
Original episodes: *2003*
Premiered: *February 18, 2003*

A helpful-hints show, as only MTV would do it. Each episode covered half a dozen "myths" relevant to teenagers, illustrated with interviews, demonstrations and fast and funny videos. Some of the subjects were reasonably serious—for example, "Can carrying a backpack hurt your back?"; "Does wearing briefs really lower your sperm rate?"; and "Can your parents send you to a mental hospital against your will?" Others were goofs, like "Is there a hole to hell?" (various weirdos were interviewed); "Did Courtney Love's dog choke to death trying to ingest one of her breast implants?"; and "Did Justin Timberlake and Britney Spears have toilet seats with pictures of each other on them made?"

BIG VALLEY, THE (*Western*)
FIRST TELECAST: *September 15, 1965*
LAST TELECAST: *May 19, 1969*
BROADCAST HISTORY:
Sep 1965–Jul 1966, ABC Wed 9:00–10:00
Jul 1966–May 1969, ABC Mon 10:00–11:00
CAST:
Victoria Barkley................ Barbara Stanwyck
Jarrod Barkley....................... Richard Long
Nick Barkley .... Peter Breck
Heath Barkley .... Lee Majors
Audra Barkley......................... Linda Evans
Silas .... Napoleon Whiting

This action-filled Western adventure was set on the sprawling Barkley ranch in California's San Joaquin Valley in the 1870s. The matriarch of the clan was Victoria Barkley, who ran the family empire with a strong hand and the help of her four adult offspring: lawyer Jarrod, bold, brawling young Nick, ruggedly handsome Heath, and beautiful daughter Audra. (Another son, 19-year-old Eugene, played by Charles Briles, was seen occasionally in early episodes.) Like other settlers, the Barkleys were continually fighting the lawless elements of the Old West, and *Big Valley* stories were peopled with schemers, murderers, bank robbers, Mexican revolutionaries, and con men; one of the latter was delightfully portrayed by Milton Berle, in a guest appearance.

The Big Valley was Lee Majors's first TV series, and was in fact the first acting role he read for after completing a mere six months of drama instruction. He played the illegitimate son of Victoria's late husband, Tom.

BIG WAVE DAVE'S (*Situation Comedy*)
FIRST TELECAST: *August 9, 1993*
LAST TELECAST: *September 13, 1993*
BROADCAST HISTORY:
Aug 1993–Sep 1993, CBS Mon 9:30–10:00
CAST:
Dave Bell .... David Morse
Marshall Fisher .... Adam Arkin
Karen Fisher .... Jane Kaczmarek
Richie Lamonica .... Patrick Breen
Jack Lord .... Kurtwood Smith
Danny Kinimaka .... Ray Bumatai

Dave, Marshall, and Richie were three buddies who decided to give up their traditional lifestyles in Chicago (and the frigid winter weather) and move to the north shore of sunny Oahu to run a Hawaiian surf shop. Dave, the free spirit after whom the shop "Big Wave Dave's" was named, was a stockbroker whose wife had just left him; Marshall was a neurotic attorney who had just been squeezed out of the law firm his father had founded; and Richie was an insecure high school typing teacher desperately in search of a more positive self-image. Marshall's wife, Karen, who had more common sense than the three of them combined, agreed to do most of the administrative and creative work to keep the fledgling business afloat. Also seen were an eccentric, freeloading local resident who claimed his name was Jack Lord (of *Hawaii Five-O* fame) and Danny, the owner of the rival surf shop, who had seen many mainlanders try, unsuccessfully, to compete with him.

BIGELOW SHOW, THE (*Variety*)
FIRST TELECAST: *October 14, 1948*
LAST TELECAST: *December 28, 1949*
BROADCAST HISTORY:
Oct 1948–Jul 1949, NBC Thu 9:30–10:00
Oct 1949–Dec 1949, CBS Wed 9:00–9:30
REGULARS:
Paul Winchell and Jerry Mahoney
Dunninger

This two-part program featured the ventriloquist Paul Winchell and his dummy Jerry Mahoney in one segment, and mental telepathist Dunninger in another. Winchell and Mahoney did a regular weekly comedy routine, sometimes with the aid of a guest star. Dunninger's act consisted of reading the minds of members of the studio audience or special guests, and sometimes other tricks, always with a noted personality present to judge the honesty of the performance; he had a standing offer of $10,000 to anyone who could prove that he used an accomplice. In one telecast a United States Congressman was shown on the steps of the Capitol in Washington, while from New York Dunninger read his mind—via split screen.

BIGELOW THEATRE, THE (*Dramatic Anthology*)
FIRST TELECAST: *December 10, 1950*
LAST TELECAST: *December 27, 1951*
BROADCAST HISTORY:
Dec 1950–Jun 1951, CBS Sun 6:00–6:30
Sep 1951–Dec 1951, DUM Thu 10:00–10:30

This series of filmed dramas appeared first on CBS before moving to DuMont. Some of the telecasts in the DuMont run had originally been seen on CBS—among them, "The Big Hello" with Cesar Romero, "Charming Billy" with Spring Byington, and "A Man's First Debt" with Lloyd Bridges; others were originals appearing for the first time. Ward Bond, Gig Young, Lynn Bari, Chico Marx, and Gale Storm appeared in episodes.

BILL & TED'S EXCELLENT ADVENTURES (*Situation Comedy*)
FIRST TELECAST: *June 28, 1992*
LAST TELECAST: *September 20, 1992*
BROADCAST HISTORY:
Jun 1992–Sep 1992, FOX Sun 7:00–7:30
CAST:
Bill Preston, Esq. .... Evan Richards
Ted Logan .... Christopher Kennedy
Mr. Keilson .... Danny Breen
Mr. Preston .... Don Lake
Missy Preston .... Lisa Wilcox
Rufus .... Rick Overton

San Dimas, California, in the suburban sprawl of Los Angeles, was the setting for this youth-oriented comedy/adventure series. Bill and Ted were best buddies who had formed a two-man band, the Wyld Stallyns. They longed to be rock and roll superstars but, for now, were still in school and working part-time at Mr. Keilson's hardware store at Mall World. The boys had a language all their own—they were "righteous dudes," and most things in their world were "awesome," "totally awesome," "bogus," or "heinous." When things weren't going well they were "totally bummed." Their adventures took them to the past and the future with the help of Rufus, their spaced-out guide from the future, and the "Circuits of Time" phone booth from the twenty-seventh century, which provided transportation. Missy was Bill's incredibly sexy young stepmother.

Adapted from the 1989 theatrical film *Bill & Ted's Excellent Adventure* starring Alex Winter, Keanu Reeves, and George Carlin. All three principals from the film provided the voices for an animated *Bill & Ted's Excellent Adventures* series that ran Saturday mornings on CBS during the 1990–1991 season and was rerun on Fox the following season.

BILL COSBY SHOW, THE (*Situation Comedy*)
FIRST TELECAST: *September 14, 1969*
LAST TELECAST: *August 31, 1971*
BROADCAST HISTORY:
Sep 1969–May 1971, NBC Sun 8:30–9:00
Jun 1971–Aug 1971, NBC Tue 7:30–8:00

CAST:

Chet Kincaid .... Bill Cosby
Rose Kincaid (1969–1970)........ Lillian Randolph
Rose Kincaid (1970–1971) .... Beah Richards
Brian Kincaid .... Lee Weaver
Verna Kincaid......................... Olga James
Mr. Langford.......................... Sid McCoy
Mrs. Marsha Peterson .... Joyce Bulifant
Max Waltz .... Joseph Perry

Comic Bill Cosby, who scored his first TV success in the adventure series *I Spy*, played a high school physical education teacher and coach, Chet Kincaid, in this warmhearted comedy. The setting was a school in a lower-middle-class neighborhood of Los Angeles. Chet's relationships with family, students, and fellow teachers were emphasized, giving free rein to Cosby's gentle sense of humor and philosophy. His family life with his mother, Rose, his brother, Brian, and his sister-in-law, Verna, were as much a part of the program as his professional life with the principal, Mr. Langford; the guidance counselor, Mrs. Peterson; and lots of kids.

BILL DANA SHOW, THE (*Situation Comedy*)

FIRST TELECAST: *September 22, 1963*
LAST TELECAST: *January 17, 1965*
BROADCAST HISTORY:

Sep 1963–Sep 1964, NBC Sun 7:00–7:30
Sep 1964–Jan 1965, NBC Sun 8:30–9:00

CAST:

Jose Jimenez............................ Bill Dana
Mr. Phillips .... Jonathan Harris
Eddie (1963–1964) .... Gary Crosby
Byron Glick .... Don Adams
Susie .... Maggie Peterson

Writer-comedian Bill Dana, whose character Jose Jimenez had a very successful career on records and in nightclubs following its creation on *The Steve Allen Show*, brought him to life for this series. Jose was a Mexican immigrant who worked as a bellhop at the Park Central Hotel. Not only did he work there, it was practically his entire world: he lived in special bachelor quarters provided for hotel employees, ate in the hotel kitchen, and had social contact only with employees and guests of the hotel. In his goodhearted naiveté he saw only the good in the people around him. His biggest problems were his fellow bellhop Eddie, who was constantly trying to get him to wise up; the less-than-understanding hotel manager Mr. Phillips; and the not-too-brilliant hotel detective Byron Glick. Walter Mitty–like dream sequences were occasionally used to extricate Jose from the hotel environment.

BILL DANCE OUTDOORS (*Outdoors*)

BROADCAST HISTORY:

The Nashville Network
30 minutes
Produced: *1995–*
Premiered: *January 7, 1996*

HOST:

Bill Dance

THEME:

"I've Gone Fishing Today"

Good ol' boy outdoorsman Bill Dance hosted this fishing show with a sense of humor, occasionally falling down as he tried to load his truck, or jumping out of his rowboat to avoid a swarm of bees. Between the lame comic bits were instructional segments and talk about fishing—mostly out on the water—and a lot of product endorsements. Dance had been seen in first-run syndication since the 1970s.

BILL GWINN SHOW, THE (*Audience Participation*)

FIRST TELECAST: *February 5, 1951*
LAST TELECAST: *April 21, 1952*
BROADCAST HISTORY:

Feb. 1951–Mar 1951, ABC Mon 10:30–11:00
Mar 1951–Jun 1951, ABC Mon 8:30–9:30
Jun 1951–Sep 1951, ABC Wed 9:00–9:30
Oct 1951–Mar 1952, ABC Mon 10:00–10:30
Mar 1952–Apr 1952, ABC Mon 9:30–10:00

EMCEE:

Bill Gwinn

In this audience-participation show, three couples competed for prizes by enacting scenes showing how favorite songs had influenced their lives. The program underwent several title changes, beginning as *It Could Be You*, changing to *This Could Be You* two weeks later, *The Bill Gwinn Show* in April 1951, and *This Is My Song* shortly before its demise in April 1952.

BILL STERN'S SPORTS QUIZ, see *Are You Positive?*

BILLY (*Situation Comedy*)

FIRST TELECAST: *February 26, 1979*
LAST TELECAST: *April 28, 1979*
BROADCAST HISTORY:

Feb 1979–Mar 1979, CBS Mon 8:00–8:30
Mar 1979–Apr 1979, CBS Sat 8:30–9:00

CAST:

Billy Fisher .... Steve Guttenberg
George Fisher....................... James Gallery
Alice Fisher .... Peggy Pope
Gran .... Paula Trueman
Norval Shadrack................. Michael Alaimo
Arthur Milliken................. Bruce Talkington

There were many ways of looking at 19-year-old Billy Fisher. His mother, Alice, thought he had a vivid imagination; his father, George, was sure he was a compulsive liar; and his grandmother put it more succinctly than either of his parents—as far as she was concerned, Billy was just "nuts." Billy's real world revolved around his menial job as an assistant mortician's clerk at the funeral home of Shadrack and Shadrack. In his fantasy life, however, he was everything from a famous surgeon, to a rock-music superstar appearing on *The Merv Griffin Show*, to the world's most irresistible bachelor. In Billy's daydreams, at least two of which were shown in each episode of this short-lived series, appeared such personalities as Don Adams, Suzanne Somers, and football star Larry Czonka—all playing themselves.

BILLY (*Situation Comedy*)

FIRST TELECAST: *January 31, 1992*
LAST TELECAST: *July 4, 1992*
BROADCAST HISTORY:

Jan 1992–Mar 1992, ABC Fri 9:30–10:00
Mar 1992–Apr 1992, ABC Sat 8:30–9:00
May 1992–Jun 1992, ABC Sat 9:00–9:30
Jun 1992–Jul 1992, ABC Sat 8:00–8:30

CAST:

Billy MacGregor .... Billy Connolly
Mary Springer MacGregor .... Marie Marshall
David (age 14) .... Johnny Galecki
Laura (10) .... Natanya Ross
Annie (5) .... Clara Bryant
Phoebe .... Mary Gross
Shana .... Maureen Mueller
Giselle .... Kathy Wagner
Norman .... Peter Vogt

THEME:

"I've Told Every Little Star" (1932 pop song)

Another of TV's periodic attempts to find comedy in breaking those silly immigration laws (for another, see *I Married Dora*). Billy was a college instructor from Scotland who "forgot to renew his visa" and was about to be deported when Mary, one of his students, mentioned that she desperately needed a boarder for her basement apartment in order to make ends meet. So Billy married Mary, got his green card, and she got her boarder. Her rules: He stayed in the basement, and there would be no drinking, smoking, pets, or sex. Marriage was just a formality.

Marrying an alien for the purpose of avoiding deportation may be illegal, but divorcée Mary's three kids (girl-chasing David and musically inclined Laura and Annie) thought the ebullient Billy was pretty neat, even as he provided a much-needed father figure and taught them little lessons in life.

BILLY BOONE AND COUSIN KIB (*Children's*)

FIRST TELECAST: *July 9, 1950*
LAST TELECAST: *August 27, 1950*
BROADCAST HISTORY:

Jul 1950–Aug 1950, CBS Sun 6:30–7:00

REGULARS:

Carroll "Kib" Colby
Patti Milligan

As the 1950 summer replacement for *Mr. I Magination*, another children's show, this series featured cartoonist "Kib" Colby and Patti Milligan as Suzy, his ten-year-old helper and friend. Each episode consisted of Billy Boone comic strips sketched by Mr. Colby, drawing games with members of the studio audience, and children's folk songs sung by the audience.

BILLY CRYSTAL COMEDY HOUR, THE (*Comedy Variety*)

FIRST TELECAST: *January 30, 1982*
LAST TELECAST: *February 27, 1982*
BROADCAST HISTORY:

Jan 1982–Feb 1982, NBC Sat 10:00–11:00

REGULARS:

Billy Crystal
Phyllis Katz
Monica Ganas
Tino Insana
Jane Anderson
Brother Theodore Gottlieb
The Dee Dee Wood Dancers
The Van Dyke Parks Orchestra

Veteran nightclub comic (and former star of *Soap*) Billy Crystal starred in this short-lived variety hour. Each episode included comedy monologues, celebrity impersonations, and comedy skits, as well as an occasional musical number. In addition to the resident comedians, Billy played host to a wide range of guest performers—actors Robert Urich and Morgan Fairchild, funny men Rob Reiner and Gallagher, and musical performers Smokey Robinson and the Manhattan Transfer.

BILLY DANIELS SHOW, THE (*Music*)

FIRST TELECAST: *October 5, 1952*
LAST TELECAST: *December 28, 1952*
BROADCAST HISTORY:

Oct 1952–Dec 1952, ABC Sun 6:30–6:45

FEATURING:

Billy Daniels
Benny Payne Trio

HOST:

Jimmy Blaine

This brief program consisted of songs performed by "That Old Black Magic" singer, Billy Daniels, with rhythm accompaniment.

BILLY GRAHAM CRUSADE, THE (*Religion*)

FIRST TELECAST: *June 1, 1957*
LAST TELECAST: *April 11, 1959*
BROADCAST HISTORY:

Jun 1957–Aug 1957, ABC Sat 8:00–9:00
May 1958–Jun 1958, ABC Sat 10:00–11:00
Sep 1958–Oct 1958, ABC Sat 8:00–9:00
Feb 1959–Apr 1959, ABC Sat 10:00–11:00

HOST:

Rev. Billy Graham

On four occasions in the late 1950s, the world-famous evangelist Dr. Billy Graham had a regular series of televised religious services from his various crusades.

BILLY ROSE SHOW, THE (*Dramatic Anthology*)

FIRST TELECAST: *October 3, 1950*
LAST TELECAST: *March 27, 1951*
BROADCAST HISTORY:

Oct 1950–Mar 1951, ABC Tue 9:00–9:30

DIRECTOR:

Jed Harris

Billy Rose, the legendary Broadway producer and songwriter, had a brief fling with television in this early dramatic series, most of whose stories were adaptations from his syndicated newspaper column, "Pitching Horseshoes." Sample titles were "The Night They Made a Bum out of Helen Hayes" and "The Night Billy Rose Shoulda Stood in Bed." Billy had a reputation for doing things in a big way. The talent he used here was respectable—Burgess Meredith, Alfred Drake, Leo G. Carroll—but the project never quite measured up to the Rose reputation. What did Billy, the producer of so many theatrical spectaculars, finally think of the new medium? "It shapes up like a shortcut to an ulcer," he told *TV Guide*, ". . . but a darn interesting one."

BILLY WALKER'S COUNTRY CARNIVAL, see *Grand Ole Opry*

BING CROSBY SHOW, THE (*Situation Comedy*)

FIRST TELECAST: *September 14, 1964*
LAST TELECAST: *June 14, 1965*
BROADCAST HISTORY:

Sep 1964–Jun 1965, ABC Mon 9:30–10:00

CAST:

Bing Collins .... Bing Crosby
Ellie Collins .... Beverly Garland
Janice Collins .... Carol Faylen

Joyce Collins........................Diane Sherry
Willie Walters........................Frank McHugh

Bing Collins was a former singer who had left the hectic world of show business to settle down with his family and work as an electrical engineer. But life around the Collins household was hardly peaceful. Bing's wife Ellie had visions of making it in show business herself. Their two daughters provided quite a contrast: Janice was a normal, boy-crazy 15-year-old, but 10-year-old Joyce was so intellectual she seemed to belong in college. Willie Walters was the family's live-in handyman. Bing managed to sneak a song into almost every episode of this series, in between mediating disputes and dispensing sage advice to all.

BING! THE SOUND OF SOMETHING NEW (*Kids' Magazine*)

BROADCAST HISTORY:

Nickelodeon
30 minutes
Produced: *1994–1995* (10 episodes)
Premiered: *January 13, 1995*

HOST:

David Sidoni

Kids' lifestyle magazine with segments on music, fashion, video games, and movies. A "Top Things Bing" list ranked what was hot with kids each week.

BIOGRAPHY (*Documentary*)

SYNDICATION HISTORY:

Syndicated only
30 minutes
Produced: *1961–1964, 1979* (91 episodes)
Released: *February 1962*

CABLE HISTORY:

Arts & Entertainment Network
60 minutes
Produced: *1987–*
Premiered: *April 6, 1987*

NARRATOR/HOST:

Mike Wallace (1961–1964)
David Janssen (1979)
Peter Graves (1987–1999)
Jack Perkins (1994–1999)
Harry Smith (1999–)

PRODUCERS (1960s):

David Wolper
Jack Haley, Jr.

Biography was pretty much what the title implied, filmed biographies of great men and women of the twentieth century, assembled from film clips, still photos, and recordings. It covered politicians such as Fiorello La Guardia, Huey Long, Sen. Joseph McCarthy, and all the modern presidents; world leaders (Churchill, Hitler, etc.); sports figures (Babe Ruth, Knute Rockne); as well as generals, explorers, authors, scientists, actors, and humanitarians. A modest and rather obvious project, it nevertheless became a very popular syndicated feature in the 1960s, and many of its episodes are still used as the "standard" filmed biographies of the subjects involved.

Narrator and script consultant in the original series was Mike Wallace, who was then at a low point in his career. Originally an actor and game-show host, Wallace had made his name in news as a fire-breathing interviewer in the late 1950s, but was made to tone down his approach by nervous network executives, and eventually forced out of network news work altogether. The considerable success of *Biography* helped reestablish his name. Soon he landed a position with CBS News, and a few years later he emerged once again as a biting, relentless inquisitor on CBS' *60 Minutes*.

A 1979 revival of *Biography*, covering a new set of celebrities ranging from Idi Amin to Walt Disney, was narrated by David Janssen. Yet another revival of *Biography*, narrated by Peter Graves, began airing on the Arts & Entertainment cable network in April 1987. In the 1990s this new series began to focus increasingly on pop culture icons such as James Dean, O. J. Simpson, Elizabeth Taylor, and Princess Diana, making it one of the most popular series on cable TV, and leading to many imitators on other networks. In May 1994 it expanded from Tuesday nights at 8:00 P.M. to five nights a week.

BIONIC WOMAN, THE (*Adventure*)

FIRST TELECAST: *January 14, 1976*
LAST TELECAST: *September 2, 1978*

BROADCAST HISTORY:

Jan 1976–May 1977, ABC Wed 8:00–9:00
Sep 1977–Mar 1978, NBC Sat 8:00–9:00
May 1978–Sep 1978, NBC Sat 8:00–9:00

CAST:

Jaime Sommers, the Bionic Woman
................................Lindsay Wagner
Oscar Goldman................Richard Anderson
Dr. Rudy Wells..................Martin E. Brooks
Jim Elgin (1976)........................Ford Rainey
Helen Elgin (1976)..................Martha Scott

The Bionic Woman was one of a wave of comic-book-style superheroes brought to TV in the wake of the enormous success of *The Six Million Dollar Man*. *The Bionic Woman* was in fact a spin-off from, and closely linked to, that program. Jaime Sommers was originally introduced on *The Six Million Dollar Man* as Steve Austin's one-time fiancée. The couple had drifted apart when Steve became an astronaut, while Jaime went to college and then became a successful tennis pro. Then Jaime was nearly killed in a skydiving accident, and the doctors who had reconstructed Steve bionically after his accident decided to try again with Jaime. Steve and Jaime renewed their romance, but too late it seemed, for when the four-part story ended in early 1975 Jaime was in a coma and apparently near death.

Unbeknownst to Steve, Jaime recovered and began a new life as a schoolteacher on an army base near her home town of Ojai, California. Her bionic operation had given her superhuman abilities—two legs for great speed, a right arm of great strength, and an ear for acute, long-distance hearing. Grateful for having been saved, she, like Steve, undertook dangerous underground missions for the government's Office of Scientific Information (OSI), fighting international spies, smugglers, kidnappers, and an occasional extraterrestrial being. Among her disguises were those of a nun, a roller-derby queen, and a lady wrestler.

When Steve Austin learned of all this he rushed to her, but Jaime's problems had left her with a partial memory loss, and she had forgotten her love for Steve. So for the time being there was no bionic marriage. They sometimes were seen jointly on missions, however, and Jaime for a time lived in an apartment over the coach house at the farm of Steve's mother and stepfather, the Elgins, in Ojai.

Other regulars in the cast were Oscar Goldman, Jaime's supervisor at OSI, and Dr. Rudy Wells, who had devised the bionic operations, both of whom also appeared on *The Six Million Dollar Man*. Peggy Callahan (played by Jennifer Darling) was seen occasionally as Oscar's secretary on both series.

When *The Bionic Woman* moved to NBC another regular character was added to the cast in the person of Max, the bionic dog, a German Shepherd that became Jaime's loyal pet. Toward the end of that NBC season, with the popularity of science fiction movies on theater screens, more and more episodes of *The Bionic Woman* found Jaime encountering visitors from other planets.

The series was based on the novel *Cyborg*, by Martin Caidin.

BIORHYTHM (*Documentary*)

BROADCAST HISTORY:

MTV
30 minutes
Produced: *1998–1999*
Premiered: *June 23, 1998*

MTV's answer to *Biography*, featuring profiles of rock musicians and others of interest to the network's young viewers, set to music. Among the subjects were Tupac Shakur, Aerosmith's Steven Tyler, rapper Queen Latifah, and Britain's Princess Diana.

BIRDLAND (*Medical Drama*)

FIRST TELECAST: *January 5, 1994*
LAST TELECAST: *February 9, 1994*
BROADCAST HISTORY:

Jan 1994–Feb 1994, ABC Wed 10:00–11:00

CAST:

Dr. Brian McKenzie .... Brian Dennehy
Dr. Lewis Niles .... Jeff Williams
Dr. Alan Bergman .... John Rothman
Dr. Jessie Lane....................... Lindsay Frost
Nurse Lucy.......................... C.C.H. Pounder
Nurse Mary............................ Leslie Mann
Mr. Horner...................... Kevin J. O'Connor
Hector .... Julio Oscar Mechoso
Dr. Gil Zuchetti .... David Packer

Big, burly Brian Dennehy portrayed a compassionate chief of psychiatry at a big-city hospital in this interestingly textured but short-lived drama. While McKenzie's imposing stature certainly lent him authority, he had reason to be sensitive to the problems of others. His own troubled life included compulsive gambling, an ex-wife who hated him, estranged children, and a secret affair with independent Dr. Jessie. He cared deeply for his patients at Riverside Hospital and constantly bent the rules to help them. Bergman was the officious administrator and chief rule-enforcer, Niles the without-a-clue young resident, and Lucy the nononsense head nurse. Mr. Horner was the nervous inmate who "ran" the ward while sending psychic signals to Kathie Lee Gifford on the TV screen.

BIRDS OF PREY (*Science Fiction*)

FIRST TELECAST: *October 9, 2002*
LAST TELECAST: *January 8, 2003*
BROADCAST HISTORY:

Oct 2002–Jan 2003, WB Wed 9:00–10:00

CAST:

Barbara Gordon (Oracle) .... Dina Meyer
Helena Kyle (Huntress) .... Ashley Scott
Dinah Lance/Redmond .... Rachel Skarsten
Det. Jesse Reese .... Shemar Moore
Alfred Pennyworth............... Ian Abercrombie
Dr. Harleen Quinzel (Harley Quinn)
.... Mia Sara
Wade Brixton .... Shawn Christian

Seven years earlier Batman had mysteriously disappeared from the dark and crime-ridden city of New Gotham after The Joker had attacked the two women most dear to him—Catwoman, his lover, and Barbara Gordon, who had fought beside him as Batgirl. The attack resulted in Catwoman's death and left Barbara confined to a wheelchair. Despite her handicap, Barbara was still leading a double life, by day a computer science teacher at New Gotham High, by night as Oracle, monitoring the activities of the local criminals from her hidden high-tech base in the city's Clocktower. Barbara had raised Helena, the secret daughter of Catwoman and Batman who, with her mother's meta-human abilities and her father's sense of justice, had grown into Huntress, and who now worked with Oracle as a black-leather-clad crime fighter in New Gotham. Joining them was Dinah, a girlish 17-year-old who showed up with her own budding meta-human abilities, including the ability to see into the future. Together the three women were the "Birds of Prey." Others seen regularly were Jesse, an honest cop whose father was a ruthless crime lord; Alfred, Batman's loyal butler who now worked for Barbara; Harley, The Joker's former lover whose goal was to build her own criminal empire; and Wade, a fellow teacher who was romantically interested in Barbara.

Helena was the central focus of the series. Beside actively fighting crime, she helped Jesse solve cases and gave him a signal ring with which he could call her in an emergency. She shared her personal demons with her therapist, Dr. Quinzel, unaware of Quinzel's evil alter ego, Harley. In the series finale Alfred brought Wade, whose relationship with Barbara had gotten pretty serious, to the Clocktower, where he discovered her secret life. After Helena told her "therapist" she was Huntress, the evil madwoman used a meta-human power she had acquired to hypnotize Helena into helping her gain control of The Clocktower. Harley killed Wade and sent a hypnotic signal to all the TVs in New Gotham in order to take over the city. Barbara managed to break Helena out of her hypnotic trance and the two of them, with the help of Alfred, Dinah and Jesse, defeated Harley and her cohorts. In the final scene Alfred was on the phone with Batman telling him what had happened.

The last original episode aired on February 19, 2003, after the series had ended its regular run.

BIRTHDAY PARTY (*Children's*)

FIRST TELECAST: *May 15, 1947*
LAST TELECAST: *June 23, 1949*
BROADCAST HISTORY:

May 1947–Jan 1948, DUM Thu 7:30–8:00
Jan 1948–Aug 1948, DUM Thu 7:00–7:30
Sep 1948–Mar 1949, DUM Wed 7:00–7:30

Mar 1949–May 1949, DUM Sun 6:00–6:30
May 1949–Jun 1949, DUM Thu 7:00–7:30

HOST:

Bill Slater (1947)
Aunt Grace (1948)
Ted Brown as "King Cole" (1949)

This early children's show was built around a birthday party for a visiting child, complete with ice cream and cake, with performances by talented youngsters. Although it began on DuMont's New York station in May 1947, the exact date when it was first fed over the network is not known; it was a network entry by early in 1948. It was also known as *King Cole's Birthday Party.*

BISHOP SHEEN PROGRAM, THE, syndicated title for *Life Is Worth Living*

BLACK BOOKS (*Situation Comedy*)

BROADCAST HISTORY:

Comedy Central
30 minutes
Original episodes: *2001–*
Premiered: *December 9, 2001*

CAST:

Bernard Black .... Dylan Moran
Manny Bianco .... Bill Bailey
Fran Katzenjammer .... Tamsin Greig

British comedy about the disheveled, neurotic young owner of a small bookshop called Black Books, who, unfortunately for a shopkeeper, disliked people. Manny was his balding accountant, of questionable sanity, and Fran the sardonic owner of the Nifty Gifty gift shop next door.

BLACK ENTERTAINMENT TELEVISION (BET) (Network) (*General Entertainment Cable Network*)

LAUNCHED:

January 25, 1980

SUBSCRIBERS (MAY 2003):

74.5 million (70% U.S.)

BET presents programming reflecting African-American popular culture. Due to financial constraints there have been few high-profile original programs on the network; instead, it has become the rerun home of black-themed series from the broadcast networks, such as *Sanford and Son, What's Happening!!,* and *Frank's Place.* A large portion of the schedule is given over to music videos featuring black artists, making BET in part the African-American counterpart to MTV (which in the 1980s was accused of underrepresenting black artists). At one time there was a heavy dose of movies, including black films of the 1930s and 1940s that were rarely seen elsewhere, but these have largely been phased out.

Original series have included *BET Uptown Comedy Club, BET on Jazz* (Ramsey Lewis, host), *NBA Off the Court* (Ahmad Rashad, host), *Bobby Jones Gospel, Our Voices* (issue-oriented talk show), *Triple Threat* (quiz show hosted by Spencer Christian), and newscasts. One of its longer-running shows was a showcase for stand-up comics called *BET's ComicView* (1992–), whose hosts included D. L. Hughley (1992), Cedric The Entertainer (1993), Sommore (1994), Don "D. C." Curry (1995), Montana Taylor (1997), Rickey Smiley (2000), Bruce Bruce (2001), Arnez J (2002) and Reynaldo Rey. In March 2003 BET launched its first animated series, *Hey Monie!,* about the exploits of a vivacious young black woman named Simone (aka Monie, voiced by Angela Shelton) and her best friend Yvette (Frances Collier).

BET was started on a shoestring by black entrepreneur Robert L. Johnson in 1980 and at first provided only two hours of programming per day. It expanded to 24 hours per day in 1984. In 2000 BET was sold to Viacom, which operates CBS, UPN and the MTV networks.

A companion jazz channel, BET Jazz: The Jazz Channel, was launched in January 1996, but to date has achieved limited distribution.

BLACK JACK SAVAGE, see *Disney Presents the 100 Lives of Black Jack Savage*

BLACK ROBE, THE (*Courtroom Reenactments*)

FIRST TELECAST: *May 18, 1949*
LAST TELECAST: *March 30, 1950*

BROADCAST HISTORY:

May 1949–Aug 1949, NBC Wed 8:30–9:00
Aug 1949–Oct 1949, NBC Mon Various times
Nov 1949–Dec 1949, NBC Sat 10:00–10:30
Jan 1950–Mar 1950, NBC Thu 8:00–8:30

REGULARS:

Judge .... Frank Thomas
Police Officer .... John Green

Dramatic reenactments of cases tried in New York City's Police Night Court. Although the judge and court officers were portrayed by actors, the persons appearing in court were often actual defendants and witnesses re-creating their own cases; their names and appearance were "altered for reasons in the public interest." Various public figures appeared as guests of the court, and on at least one occasion a remorseful criminal was induced to surrender to authorities as the result of an appeal made on the show. The appearance of three orphans on another telecast drew 500 offers of adoption in the New York City area. *The Black Robe* received a number of commendations for its public service and humanitarian work, but could not find a sponsor and so was canceled after ten months on the air.

BLACK SADDLE (*Western*)

FIRST TELECAST: *January 10, 1959*
LAST TELECAST: *September 30, 1960*

BROADCAST HISTORY:

Jan 1959–Sep 1959, NBC Sat 9:00–9:30
Oct 1959–Sep 1960, ABC Fri 10:30–11:00

CAST:

Clay Culhane .... Peter Breck
Marshal Gib Scott .... Russell Johnson
Nora Travers .... Anna Lisa

Clay Culhane came from a family of gunfighters, but after losing his brothers in a shootout he decided that the practice of law might be a less violent way to settle personal disputes. Carrying his law books in his saddle bags, he traveled throughout the New Mexico Territory during the post–Civil War years, helping those in need of legal assistance. U.S. Marshal Gib Scott, who could not quite believe that Clay had really given up the gun for good, was never far behind.

BLACK SASH (*Adventure*)

FIRST TELECAST: *March 30, 2003*
LAST TELECAST: *June 1, 2003*

BROADCAST HISTORY:

Mar 2003–Jun 2003, WB Sun 9:00–10:00

CAST:

Tom Chang .... Russell Wong
Allie Bennett .... Sarah Carter
Bryan Lanier .... Ray J. Norwood
Tory Stratton .... Missy Peregrym
Trip Brady .... Corey Sevier
Nick Reed .... Drew Fuller
Master Li .... Mako
Beth Rodgers .... Ona Grauer
Claire Rodgers .... Valerie Tian

While working as an undercover narcotics cop, Tom Chang had been framed and convicted of smuggling heroin and spent five years in a Hong Kong prison. After his release he returned home to San Francisco to rebuild his life. Unfortunately, while he was in prison his wife, Beth, had divorced him and remarried. He was determined to regain Beth's respect and to establish a relationship with their preteen daughter, Claire. Unable to resume his former career, Tom, a martial-arts master, turned to his former teacher and mentor, Master Li. The elderly Master Li, who continued to provide Tom sage counsel, let him run his martial-arts school and live in the building. Tom's youthful students became his new family. They included sexy Tory, a 17-year-old trying to channel the rage she still felt over the death of her policeman father; sensitive Trip, who had suffered at the hands of an abusive father; street-smart Bryan, whose bravado masked how much he cared about Tom and his fellow students; gentle Allie, who wanted to become more assertive and make new friends, and Nick, a rebel desperately in need of learning to control his hostility. Tom not only taught them the physical aspects of the martial arts but also provided them with discipline and spiritual guidance as they dealt with their troubled lives.

BLACK SCORPION (*Adventure*)

BROADCAST HISTORY:

Sci-Fi Channel
60 minutes
Original episodes: *2001* (22 episodes)
Premiered: *January 5, 2001*

CAST:

Det. Darcy Walker (Black Scorpion)
.... Michelle Lintel
Det. Steve Rafferty .... Scott Valentine
Argyle .... B. T. (aka Brandon Terrill)
Tender Lovin' (Veronica) .... Enya Flack
Slugger .... Steven Kravitz
Specs .... Shane Powers
Capt. Strickland .... Guy Boyd
Don MacDonald .... Ben McCain
Mayor Arthur Worth .... Robert Pine
Babette (Agnes) .... Shae Marks

The ads read, "23 lightning bolts, 18 shots fired, 8 chick slaps, 6 car crashes, 4 deadly kisses, 3 action figures, it all adds up to one hour of ass-kicking vigilante justice!" There certainly was a lot of comic-book action in this *Batman* imitation, with the roles reversed—Our Hero was a sexy woman in black leather, her partner a clueless young guy. Darcy was an Angel City cop by day who became the masked crime fighter Black Scorpion by night, originally to avenge the death of her policeman father at the hands of super-villain The Breathtaker. Her partner, Steve, didn't know about her nightlife. Helping her were cool black dude Argyle, a brilliant scientist who "reorganized the atoms" in her white Corvette so that it could morph into the Scorpionmobile, a supercharged weapons platform in which she chased down bad guys. Tender Lovin' was Argyle's bossy girlfriend, and Slugger and Specs, two nerdy cops. Worth was the worthless, corrupt mayor, who spent most of his time chasing his scantily clad secretary Babette.

There were lots of martial-arts kicks and cartwheels, and an impressive array of over-the-top villains played by such guest stars as Adam West (The Breathtaker), Lou Ferrigno (Slave Master), Frank Gorshin (Clockwise), Soupy Sales (Professor Prophet), Stoney Jackson (Gangster Prankster) and *Playboy* playmate Victoria Silvestedt (Hour Glass). One of the producers of this series was B-film legend Roger Corman.

BLACK SHEEP SQUADRON, see *Baa Baa Black Sheep*

BLACK TIE AFFAIR (*Situation Comedy*)

FIRST TELECAST: *May 29, 1993*
LAST TELECAST: *June 19, 1993*
BROADCAST HISTORY:

May 1993–Jun 1993, NBC Sat 10:00–10:30

CAST:

Dave Brodsky .... Bradley Whitford
Margo Cody .... Kate Capshaw
Christopher Cody .... John Calvin
Eve Saskatchewan .... Alison Elliott
Philip Wingate .... Patrick Bristow
Cookie .... Maggie Han

Jay Tarses produced this offbeat comedy satirizing 1940s detective movies that aired briefly in the summer of 1993. Brodsky was a world-weary San Francisco private eye who ran a used record store on the side. His latest caper was tailing philandering clothing-catalog tycoon Christopher Cody on behalf of his suspicious socialite wife, Margo. No sooner did Brodsky uncover Cody's love item, voluptuous model Eve, than he found himself entangled in a murder case and in romantic liaisons with both Margo and Eve. The serialized story followed the case through nonsensical twists and turns for four weeks before NBC abruptly pulled the plug, leaving the Cody caper to *Unsolved Mysteries*.

BLACKE'S MAGIC (*Detective Drama*)

FIRST TELECAST: *January 5, 1986*
LAST TELECAST: *September 9, 1988*
BROADCAST HISTORY:

Jan 1986, NBC Sun 9:00–11:00
Jan 1986–Jun 1986, NBC Wed 9:00–10:00
Jul 1988–Sep 1988, NBC Fri 9:00–10:00

CAST:

Alexander Blacke .... Hal Linden
Leonard Blacke .... Harry Morgan

Old pros Hal Linden and Harry Morgan were teamed in this rather thin series about a magician-detective and his dad. Alexander Blacke was the debonair detective, who had recently retired as a society magician (after he almost killed himself in a particularly difficult stunt) and who now used his bag of tricks to nab murderers and other scoundrels. His understanding of illusion and deception often proved useful in figuring out how seemingly impossible crimes had been committed. Assisting Alexander was his father Leonard, a not quite reformed flim-flam man and master of disguise, whose skills came in handy in setting up ways to expose the bad guys. Unfortunately Dad still found it difficult to stay on the right side of the law, requiring his son to periodically bail him out.

Most of the magic tricks performed on this series were real, performed by star Hal Linden, who had no previous experience as an illusionist.

NBC aired reruns of *Blacke's Magic* during the summer of 1988.

BLAME GAME, THE (*Quiz/Audience Participation*)

BROADCAST HISTORY:

MTV
30 minutes
Produced: *1999–2000*
Premiered: *February 8, 1999*

CAST:

Judge Chris Reed
Kara McNamara
Jason Winer

A sort of halfway house between *The Dating Game* and *Divorce Court*, MTV's raucous *The Blame Game* pitted couples against each other in a mock trial intended to assign blame for the breakup of their relationship. As mad-hatter Judge Reed presided, gal and guy each took their turns on the stand, aided by their "counselors" (Kara for the gal, Jason for the guy). Witnesses testified, evidence was introduced (e.g., sexy nightclothes, discarded love letters, sweaty socks). The rowdy audience voted twice on who they thought caused the breakup: on first sight (based on looks alone), and then after the trial (based on the evidence). The winner (i.e., the one not at fault) got prizes including a romantic getaway—presumably with someone else—while the loser got his or her picture published like a mug shot in a national magazine. The couple was also given one last chance to make up, which they seldom did.

Created by Dr. Stuart Atkins.

BLANSKY'S BEAUTIES (*Situation Comedy*)

FIRST TELECAST: *February 12, 1977*
LAST TELECAST: *May 21, 1977*
BROADCAST HISTORY:

Feb 1977–May 1977, ABC Sat 8:00–8:30

CAST:

Nancy Blansky .... Nancy Walker
Bambi Benton .... Caren Kaye
Ethel "Sunshine" Akalino .... Lynda Goodfriend
Emilio .... Johnny Desmond
Joey DeLuca .... Eddie Mekka
Anthony DeLuca .... Scott Baio
Horace "Stubbs" Wilmington ..... George Pentecost
Hillary S. Prentiss .... Taaffe O'Connell
Arkansas .... Rhonda Bates
Lovely Carson .... Bond Gideon
Jackie Outlaw .... Gerri Reddick
Gladys "Cochise" Littlefeather .... Shirley Kirkes
Sylvia Silver .... Antoinette Yuskis
Misty Karamazov .... Jill Owens
Bridget Muldoon .... Elaine Bolton
Arnold .... Pat Morita

Nancy Blansky was den mother to a bevy of beautiful Las Vegas showgirls in this short-lived comedy. In addition to keeping order in the chaotic apartment complex where they all lived, Nancy staged the girls' big numbers at the Oasis Hotel, where her boss—the second-in-command at the hotel—was Horace Wilmington. Emilio, the maître d', was Nancy's boyfriend. To help Nancy defray the costs of her apartment, Sunshine and Bambi shared it with her, along with her nephews Joey DeLuca (a choreographer) and leering, 12-year-old ("going on 28") Anthony. Anthony was forever trying to make time with Bambi, who much to his chagrin treated him like a kid brother, as did almost all of Nancy's girls. Also sharing Nancy's apartment was a huge Great Dane named Black Jack.

Pat Morita, after the failure of his series *Mr. T. and Tina*, was added to the cast as Arnold, the same name (and virtually the same character) he had had in a similar supporting role on *Happy Days*. There he had run a drive-in restaurant, while here he ran the coffee shop at the Oasis. (Nancy, in turn, was supposed to be the cousin of *Happy Days* dad Howard Cunningham.) Morita's presence on *Blansky's Beauties* gave both him and star Nancy Walker the dubious distinction of being in two program failures in the same season; she had starred in *The Nancy Walker Show* five months before the premiere of *Blansky's Beauties*.

BLESS THIS HOUSE (*Situation Comedy*)

FIRST TELECAST: *September 11, 1995*
LAST TELECAST: *January 17, 1996*
BROADCAST HISTORY:

Sep 1995, CBS Mon 8:30–9:00
Sep 1995–Nov 1995, CBS Wed 8:00–8:30
Nov 1995–Jan 1996, CBS Wed 8:30–9:00

CAST:

Burt Clayton .... Andrew Clay
Alice Clayton .... Cathy Moriarty
Danny Clayton (age 12) .... Raegan Kotz
Sean Clayton .... Sam Gifaldi
Phyllis .... Molly Price
Lenny .... Don Stark
Cuba .... Wren T. Brown
Vicki Shetski .... Patricia Healy
Jane .... Kimberly Cullum

Foul-mouthed standup comic Andrew Dice Clay shortened his name and attempted to change his image in this short-lived sitcom that could be described as *The Honeymooners* with kids. Burt and Alice were a working-class couple living in an aging apartment complex in Trenton, New Jersey, with their 12-year-old daughter, Danny, and young son Sean. Blustery Burt was a post office supervisor, and sharp-tongued Alice worked in the parts department of a local car dealership. Sure they fought—often—but they loved each other and their kids. Living on the floor below were new parents Phyllis, Alice's best friend, and klutzy, well-meaning Lenny, who worked with Burt at the post office. Others seen regularly were Cuba, another postal worker, Vicki, the sexy divorced mother on the make who lived in their building, and Jane, Danny's best friend. Throughout much of the series' short run the Claytons were trying to buy a house and move out of their apartment, but when they finally succeeded, the costs were such that they had to rent the house to one of Burt's coworkers (who moved in with 22 of his relatives) and ended up back in the apartment.

BLIND DATE (*Audience Participation*)

FIRST TELECAST: *May 5, 1949*
LAST TELECAST: *September 15, 1953*

BROADCAST HISTORY:

May 1949–Jul 1949, ABC Thu 7:30–8:00
Jul 1949–Sep 1949, ABC Thu 9:30–10:00
Sep 1949–Feb 1950, ABC Fri 8:30–9:00
Mar 1950–Jun 1950, ABC Thu 9:00–9:30
Aug 1950–Sep 1951, ABC Thu 9:30–10:00
Jun 1952–Jul 1952, NBC Sat 9:00–9:30
May 1953–Sep 1953, DUM Tue 8:00–8:30

EMCEE:

Arlene Francis (1949–1952)
Melvyn Douglas (May–Jun 1953)
Jan Murray (Jun–Sep 1953)

REGULAR:

Ray Bloch Orchestra (1953)

College boys attempted to win a date with an unseen—but beautiful—model in this audience-participation program, which was adapted from the radio series of the same name. The boys and their quarry were separated by a wall, but they could talk to each other via a special telephone hookup. The boys with the best "line" won the date and a night on the town. During the Korean War the program did its patriotic bit by substituting eager young servicemen for the college crowd, as its radio predecessor had done during World War II.

After a two-year run on ABC, *Blind Date* returned in 1952 as an NBC summer replacement and in 1953 as a DuMont summer show. The DuMont version began under the title *Your Big Moment*, with a slightly different format; the host helped arrange blind dates for people writing in requesting a certain type of individual—a sort of TV dating service. After a few weeks the title was changed back to *Blind Date* and the duties of host passed from Melvyn Douglas to Jan Murray.

BLIND DATE (*Dating*)

BROADCAST HISTORY:

Syndicated only
30 minutes
Produced: *1999–*
Released: *September 1999*

HOST:

Roger Lodge

In this variation on *Love Connection*, the producers arranged blind dates for couples who didn't know each other and sent a camera crew to follow them on the date. The host opened the show by referring to the proceedings as "a lighthearted look at that romantic crapshoot known as the setup." There was some background material on the participants, including what they were looking for in a date; then viewers were shown the film of the date—with humorous animated on-screen commentary on the progress of their relationship. After the date the producers filmed the observations of each of the participants—first impressions, how they felt the date went, and whether or not they thought there was any future in the relationship.

BLONDIE (*Situation Comedy*)

FIRST TELECAST: *January 4, 1957*
LAST TELECAST: *January 9, 1969*

BROADCAST HISTORY:

Jan 1957–Sep 1957, NBC Fri 8:00–8:30
Sep 1968–Jan 1969, CBS Thu 7:30–8:00

CAST (1957):

Dagwood Bumstead.................. Arthur Lake
Blondie.......................... Pamela Britton
J. C. Dithers........................ Florenz Ames
Alexander.......................... Stuffy Singer
Cookie............................. Ann Barnes
Cora Dithers........................ Elvia Allman
Herb Woodley........................ Hal Peary
Mr. Beasley..................... Lucien Littlefield

CAST (1968):

Dagwood Bumstead................ Will Hutchins
Blondie.......................... Patricia Harty
J. C. Dithers........................ Jim Backus
Alexander......................... Peter Robbins
Cookie.......................... Pamelyn Ferdin
Cora Dithers...................... Henny Backus
Tootsie Woodley.................... Bobbi Jordan
Mr. Beasley...................... Bryan O'Bourne

There were two attempts to bring to television the adventures of the Bumstead household, long a favorite of comic-strip readers and movie fans. In 1957 NBC brought Dagwood, Blondie, their children Alexander and Cookie, and Daisy and the other dogs to TV. Arthur Lake, the Dagwood of this version, had played the role in the movie series of the 1940s. The stories were all familiar to regular readers of the strip, with Dagwood getting into misunderstandings both at home and at work with Mr. Dithers, his boss. CBS gave *Blondie* a second chance a decade later, with a completely different cast, but that version also failed to catch on.

BLOOMBERG TELEVISION (Network) (*Business News Cable Network*)

LAUNCHED:

January 1995

SUBSCRIBERS (JAN 2003):

26.0 million (24% U.S.)

A no-frills 24-hour news and business channel known for its multilayered screen containing numerous bands of constantly changing stock market data, news crawls and inserts, with the announcer relegated to a small box in the corner. The network was founded by and named after entrepreneur Michael Bloomberg, a former Wall Street executive who founded his financial services company in 1981, opened a business news wire service in 1990 and expanded into television in 1995. In 2001 he was elected mayor of New York City.

BLOSSOM (*Situation Comedy*)

FIRST TELECAST: *January 3, 1991*
LAST TELECAST: *June 5, 1995*

BROADCAST HISTORY:

Jan 1991, NBC Thu 8:30–9:00
Jan 1991–Jun 1991, NBC Mon 8:30–9:00
Aug 1991–Mar 1995, NBC Mon 8:30–9:00
May 1995–Jun 1995, NBC Mon 8:30–9:00

CAST:

Blossom Russo...................... Mayim Bialik
Anthony Russo.................. Michael Stoyanov
Joey Russo........................ Joey Lawrence
Nick Russo............................ Ted Wass
Six LeMuere........................ Jenna Von Oy
Buzz Richman.................... Barnard Hughes
Vinnie Bonitardi (1992–1994)....... David Lascher
Rhonda Jo Applegate (1992–1993)... Portia Dawson
Shelly Russo (1993–1995)........ Samaria Graham
Carol (1994–1995)................. Finola Hughes
Kennedy (age 6) (1994–1995)...... Courtney Chase
Frank (1994–1995)............ Kevin James Woods

THEME:

"My Opinionation," by Mike Post, performed by Dr. John

Life as seen through the eyes of a sassy and adventuresome 13-year-old, '90s style. Though the youngest of the three Russo children, Blossom was mature beyond her years. Her family was distressingly modern: dad was divorced, eldest brother Anthony, a recovering substance abuser, and Joey, a teenage Lothario. In an early episode Nick, her studio musician dad, was served with final divorce papers which the kids tried to keep from him—hardly the sort of comic situation viewers would have seen in the 1960s! Joining the family in the fall of 1991 was Grandpa Buzz, a freewheeling oldster undergoing a delayed midlife crisis.

Blossom herself was not the prettiest girl on the block. She dealt with life and the fracturing of her family partly through spunk, and partly through fantasies in which she got hilarious advice from celebrities including Phil Donahue, Little Richard, Sonny Bono, and ALF. Her thoughts were related each day to her "video diary." Six was her teenage best friend (so-named because she was the sixth child in her family) and Vinnie her hip, streetwise boyfriend. Rhonda was Anthony's girlfriend for a season.

During the 1993–1994 season Anthony, who worked as a paramedic, began dating a black girl named Shelly. They were eventually married and had a baby, Nash, during the November 1994 ratings period (of course!). For a time they lived in a garage apartment, but in March 1995 they moved back east. Close on the heels of the marriage of his oldest son, Nick began seeing a worldly British woman named Carol. They were married in the fall of 1994, whereupon the household gained a new youngster in Carol's six-year-old daughter, Kennedy. Joey, whose cheerfulness was exceeded by his incredible denseness, somehow graduated from high school and went on the road with a minor-league baseball team, while becoming engaged to girlfriend Melanie.

In the May 1995 series finale, dumb Joey abruptly proposed to Melanie, who said yes. Carol announced that she was pregnant, and Nick arranged to sell the house so that he and Carol could move into a place of their own. Blossom, seeing the family as she knew it coming to an end, at first tried to sabotage the deal, but finally realized that it was all about "moving on."

Blossom was first seen in a single pilot telecast on July 5, 1990.

BLUE ANGEL, THE (*Variety*)

FIRST TELECAST: *July 6, 1954*
LAST TELECAST: *October 12, 1954*
BROADCAST HISTORY:

Jul 1954–Aug 1954, CBS Tue 10:30–11:00
Sep 1954–Oct 1954, CBS Tue 8:30–9:00

HOST:

Orson Bean
Norman Paris Trio

This variety series was the 1954 summer replacement for *See It Now*. In a nightclub setting patterned after the famous Blue Angel in the 1930 movie of the same title, host Orson Bean introduced and chatted with the various guest stars and occasionally added his own humor to the show. After *See It Now* returned to the air, *The Blue Angel* was given another four-week run at an earlier time.

BLUE ANGELS, THE (*Adventure*)

BROADCAST HISTORY:

Syndicated only
30 minutes
Produced: *1960* (39 episodes)
Released: *Fall 1960*

CAST:

Cdr. Arthur Richards .... Dennis Cross
Cdr. Donovan .... Morgan Jones
Capt. Wilbur Scott .... Warner Jones
Lt. Russ MacDonald .... Michael Galloway
Lt. Hank Bertelli .... Don Gordon

This was an adventure series tracing the "exploits" of the U.S. Navy's four-man precision flying team, the Blue Angels. Cdr. Richards was the original skipper (replaced after the first 12 episodes by Cdr. Donovan), and Scott, MacDonald, and Bertelli his fellow pilots. There were no other continuing characters, but one of the more frequent supporting actors, appearing in various roles, was Burt Reynolds (in three episodes). For the precision flying scenes, films were used of the real Blue Angels tooling around in their Grumman F11Fs.

Since the real Blue Angels spent most of their time simply flying, at one air show after another, considerable ingenuity was needed to lend this series variety. The producers managed to concoct all sorts of unlikely plots, such as having the pilots, on the spur of the moment, chase smugglers, romance pretty bystanders, fly life-saving supplies to a dying woman, scare a juvenile delinquent into going straight by giving him a wild airplane ride, and even stop a holdup—much of this off duty. The U.S. Navy, which cooperated in the production of the series, protested some of this, but producer Sam Gallu barked back, "How the hell does the Pentagon know what happens to a Blue when he's off duty?"

BLUE KNIGHT, THE (*Police Drama*)

FIRST TELECAST: *December 17, 1975*
LAST TELECAST: *October 27, 1976*
BROADCAST HISTORY:

Dec 1975–Oct 1976, CBS Wed 10:00–11:00

CAST:

Bumper Morgan .... George Kennedy
Sgt. Newman .... Phillip Pine
Sgt. Cabe (1976) .... Charles Siebert
Lt. Hauser (1976) .... Lin McCarthy

Joseph Wambaugh, the author of the novel *The Blue Knight*, had once been a member of the Los Angeles Police Department, and his portrayal of police officers at work bore a note of strong realism missing from many TV police series. Wambaugh's first brush with TV was as consultant for NBC's police anthology *Police Story*, where he continued to write about the day-to-day world of big-city cops. Bumper Morgan, *The Blue Knight*'s leading character, first came to television in an NBC mini-series of the same name in the spring of 1973, with William Holden in the lead role. In both the mini-series and the series itself, Bumper Morgan was a cop who walked his beat, had no squad car for transportation, and knew virtually everyone in his territory. He was not beyond overlooking the existence of "good" prostitutes and other harmless types living on the fringes of the law, for his main concern was maintaining order in his inner-city neighborhood. He was stubborn, loyal, and determined, often resorting to physical force when it served his needs. An old-fashioned cop, he had a certain amount of trouble adjusting to the red tape and concern for suspects' rights that had grown up over the years.

BLUE LIGHT (*Spy Drama*)
FIRST TELECAST: *January 12, 1966*
LAST TELECAST: *August 31, 1966*
BROADCAST HISTORY:
Jan 1966–Aug 1966, ABC Wed 8:30–9:00
CAST:
David March .... Robert Goulet
Suzanne Duchard .... Christine Carere

Filmed in Germany and set in Europe during World War II, *Blue Light* was the story of American espionage agent David March. March posed as a foreign correspondent who had officially renounced his American citizenship, but he actually belonged to a highly secret organization called "Code: Blue Light," whose purpose was to infiltrate the German high command and pass information on to the Allies. In addition to eluding German counterintelligence, who managed to uncover and execute 17 members of the Blue Light unit, March also had to watch out for Allied intelligence agencies, who never seemed to realize that he was on their side. Suzanne Duchard was his girl Friday.

BLUE MEN, THE, see *Brenner*

BLUE RIBBON BOUTS, see *Boxing*

BLUE SKIES (*Drama*)
FIRST TELECAST: *June 13, 1988*
LAST TELECAST: *August 1, 1988*
BROADCAST HISTORY:
Jun 1988–Aug 1988, CBS Mon 8:00–9:00
CAST:
Frank Cobb .... Tom Wopat
Annie Pfeiffer Cobb .... Season Hubley
Henry Cobb .... Pat Hingle
Zoe Pfeiffer (age 12) .... Kim Hauser
Sarah Cobb (12) .... Alyson Croft
Charley Cobb (10) .... Danny Gerard
Claire Ordway .... Lois Foraker

Frank Cobb was starting a new life in almost every way—new family, new home, and new job. A widower with two young children, Sarah and Charley, he had just married Annie Pfeiffer, a sophisticated New York divorcée with a daughter of her own (Zoe). Wanting to begin his new life at a less hurried pace, Frank gave up his successful advertising career in San Francisco to return to his native Eagle Falls, Oregon, and run the old sawmill founded by his father, Henry. There were all sorts of problems to overcome—convincing Annie she would be happy living in a small town, dealing with the sibling rivalry between Zoe and Sarah, getting all of the children to adjust to the slower pace of rural America, and coping with the resentment his father harbored over Frank's abandonment of a promising career to do manual labor. But Frank did work hard at making a go of it, even convincing his dad, who was himself engaged to be married to Claire Ordway, to come out of retirement and help him run the mill.

BLUE SKIES (*Situation Comedy*)
FIRST TELECAST: *September 12, 1994*
LAST TELECAST: *October 24, 1994*
BROADCAST HISTORY:
Sep 1994–Oct 1994, ABC Mon 8:30–9:00
CAST:
Russell Evans .... Matt Roth
Joel Goodman .... Corey Parker
Ellie Baskin .... Julia Campbell
Oak .... Stephen Tobolowsky
Kenny .... Richard Kind
Eve Munroe .... Adilah Barnes
THEME:
"Blue Skies," by Irving Berlin (1927)

Lightweight sitcom about two young buddies, suave, charming Russell and creative, excitable Joel, who formed an outdoor-goods catalog business in a Boston loft. The Blue Skies Trading Company (a frank rip-off of L.L. Bean) scored big sales but no profits until the boys discovered that Joel's cousin Kenny, the firm's loud, sleazy accountant, was ripping them off, so in came smart, savvy, nineties woman Ellie with her Harvard M.B.A. and big plans to straighten things out.

Ellie tried to keep her two new partners, who acted like big kids, thinking of business while fending off the continuing schemes of bumbling Kenny (who looked and acted a lot like the late Paul Lynde). Oak was the nutty product tester, who stood in ice water all weekend to try out wading boots, and Eve the sarcastic but remarkably resourceful black secretary.

BLUE THUNDER (*Police Drama*)
FIRST TELECAST: *January 6, 1984*
LAST TELECAST: *September 7, 1984*
BROADCAST HISTORY:
Jan 1984–Mar 1984, ABC Fri 9:00–10:00
Apr 1984, ABC Mon 8:00–9:00
May 1984–Jun 1984, ABC Fri 9:00–10:00
Aug 1984–Sep 1984, ABC Fri 9:00–10:00
CAST:
Frank Chaney .... James Farentino
Clinton Wonderlove ("Jafo") .... Dana Carvey
Lyman "Bubba" Kelsey .... Bubba Smith
Richard "Ski" Butowski .... Dick Butkus
Capt. Braddock .... Sandy McPeak
J. J. Douglas .... Ann Cooper

One of the hit movies of the summer of 1983 was *Blue Thunder*, an action-adventure "starring" a seemingly impregnable police helicopter. Perfect for television, someone said, so six months later ABC and CBS both produced television copies, the CBS version called *Airwolf* and this one direct from the movie. Honcho of the Blue Thunder team was Frank Chaney, an argumentative, determined pilot who was constantly in trouble with his boss, Capt. Braddock. Flying with him in the high-tech chopper was a youthful electronics whiz named Clinton, who was simultaneously awed and frustrated by do-it-my-way Chaney ("Please stop calling me Jafo!" "Sorry, Jafo."). Two other members of the team drove a truck—for some reason this super-helicopter had to be followed around on the ground by a mobile support vehicle. The two, Bubba and Ski, both ex-football players and built like mountains, helped out in the pinches and added comic relief during the dull spots.

The real star of the show, as of the movie, was the ominous black chopper. It could eavesdrop at 10,000 feet, "map" the interior of other aircraft, switch to a "whisper mode" and tiptoe through the sky undetected, deflect machine-gun fire, or blaze away with its own awesome firepower. It could not, however, outrace conventional jet aircraft—as Airwolf could.

BLUES BY BARGY (*Music*)
FIRST TELECAST: *April 23, 1949*
LAST TELECAST: *April 22, 1950*
BROADCAST HISTORY:
Apr 1949–Aug 1949, CBS Sat 7:45–8:00
Aug 1949–Feb 1950, CBS Sat 7:45–7:55
Mar 1950–Apr 1950, CBS Sat 7:15–7:30
HOSTESS:
Jean Bargy

Jean Bargy, daughter of veteran pianist-conductor Roy Bargy, sang ballads and played the piano in this short musical interlude that ran for a full year on CBS. She was also seen locally in New York on other nights of the week in an end-of-the-evening "filler" program on WCBS-TV.

BOB (*Situation Comedy*)
FIRST TELECAST: *September 13, 1992*
LAST TELECAST: *December 17, 1993*
BROADCAST HISTORY:
Sep 1992, CBS Fri 8:30–9:00
Sep 1992–Mar 1993, CBS Fri 9:30–10:00
Apr 1993–May 1993, CBS Mon 8:30–9:00
Oct 1993–Nov 1993, CBS Fri 9:00–9:30
Dec 1993, CBS Mon 9:30–10:00
CAST:
Bob McKay .... Bob Newhart
Kaye McKay .... Carlene Watkins
Trisha McKay .... Cynthia Stevenson
Harlan Stone .... John Cygan
Albie Lutz .... Andrew Bilgore
Chad Pfefferle .... Timothy Fall
Iris Frankel .... Ruth Kobart
Mr. Terhorst (voice only) .... Michael Cumpsty
Shayla .... Christine Dunford
**Jerry Fleisher* .... Tom Poston
**Patty Fleisher* .... Dorothy Lyman
**Kathy Fleisher* .... Lisa Kudrow
**Buzz Loudermilk* .... Dick Martin
Sylvia Schmitt (1993) .... Betty White
Pete Schmitt (1993) .... Jere Burns
Whitey van de Bunt (1993) .... Eric Allan Kramer
Chris Szelinski (1993) .... Megan Cavanagh
*Occasional

Comedian Bob Newhart had starred in two highly successful ensemble comedy series for CBS, *The Bob Newhart Show* (1972–1978) and *Newhart* (1982–1990)—then came *Bob*. With his track record most TV critics thought he was destined for another long run, but viewers never warmed up to this show as they had to his earlier series. Part of the problem may have been the changed nature of his character. In previous incarnations Bob's character had always been lovable and understanding of the foibles of others. In *Bob* he had a temper, railed about the shortcomings and faults of his co-workers and friends, and even threatened to microwave Otto, the family cat. This was not the same "Mr. Nice Guy" that viewers had loved for more than twenty years.

Bob McKay had been working as an artist for the Chicago-based Schmitt Greeting Card Company for 20 years when he thought his dream had come true. In his younger days he had created a canine comic-book character called "Mad-Dog" that had lasted for only 12 issues, and now ACE Comics wanted to revive the character. What Bob didn't realize was that Harlan, the obnoxious, manipulative senior story editor at ACE, had taken Bob's decent superhero and turned Mad-Dog into a bloodthirsty vigilante. The president of ACE, Mr. Terhorst, who only communicated by phone, decided that if the two worked together they could create a truly great comic-book hero. Theirs was an uneasy alliance, with constant bickering about the way Mad-Dog stories should go. Other eccentrics at ACE were Trisha, Bob's flaky daughter, who colored the comic frames; Albie, the klutzy gofer with a crush on Trisha; Chad, the spaced-out cartoon inker; and Iris, the crotchety old-timer who had seen it all. Kaye was Bob's sensible wife of 25 years and Shayla was Harlan's pushy bimbo girlfriend.

In the last episode of the 1992–1993 season the conglomerate that owned ACE Comics sold out to a millionaire who hated comic books and the entire Mad-Dog staff, including Bob, was fired. When the series returned that fall Sylvia Schmitt, the wife of his former boss, offered Bob the presidency of Schmitt Greetings to replace her husband, who had run off with his dental hygienist. Sylvia's obnoxious son, Pete, the sales VP who had expected to take over the company and now had to work for Bob, was irate. Others at Schmitt were Chris, the sarcastic bookkeeper, and Whitey, a huge dumb guy from the production area who adored Bob. The changes in the cast and a softening of Bob Newhart's character didn't help. Only five episodes of the "new" *Bob* aired before it was canceled.

BOB & CAROL & TED & ALICE (*Situation Comedy*)
FIRST TELECAST: *September 26, 1973*
LAST TELECAST: *November 7, 1973*
BROADCAST HISTORY:
Sep 1973–Nov 1973, ABC Wed 8:00–8:30
CAST:
Bob Sanders .... Robert Urich
Carol Sanders .... Anne Archer
Ted Henderson .... David Spielberg
Alice Henderson .... Anita Gillette
Sean Sanders, son .... Brad Savage
Elizabeth Henderson, daughter .... Jodie Foster

This comedy concerned two Los Angeles couples who were close friends, but rather distant in values and attitudes. Filmmaker Bob Sanders and his wife Carol were in their twenties, "young, aware, and with-it." Lawyer Ted Henderson and his wife Alice, in their thirties, were much more conventional. Overly cute stories about nude swimming, premarital sex, and unmarried friends living together helped hasten this generation-gap comedy to an early end. The program was based on the movie of the same name.

BOB AND MARGARET (*Cartoon*)
BROADCAST HISTORY:
Comedy Central
30 minutes
Produced: *1998* (13 episodes)
Premiered: *June 22, 1998*
VOICES:
Dr. Bob Fish .... Andy Hamilton
Margaret Fish .... Alison Snowden

Penny .... Sarah Hadland
Beany .... Steve Brody
Boney .... Trevor Cooper

Based on the 1995 Academy Award–winning short subject, "Bob's Birthday," this adult 'toon traced the rather pedestrian lives of a childless, middle-aged professional couple in London, England. Dr. Bob Fish was a neurotic dentist, who jabbered while his patients gurgled; his dumpy wife Margaret was a podiatrist who offered him little solace. At home they were beset by their two fat, yapping dogs, William and Elizabeth, while work was a world of self-absorbed patients, ruthless competitors, and Bob's marginally helpful receptionist, Dorothy. Created by husband-and-wife filmmakers Alison Snowden (who also did voice work) and David Fine.

BOB AND RAY (*Comedy Variety*)
FIRST TELECAST: *November 26, 1951*
LAST TELECAST: *September 28, 1953*
BROADCAST HISTORY:
Nov 1951–Feb 1952, NBC Mon–Fri 7:15–7:30
Feb 1952–May 1952, NBC Tue/Thu 7:15–7:30
Jul 1952–Aug 1952, NBC Sat 7:30–8:00
Apr 1953–Sep 1953, NBC Mon 7:30–7:45
REGULARS:
Bob Elliott
Ray Goulding
Audrey Meadows
Cloris Leachman (1952)

Satirists Bob Elliott and Ray Goulding were already well known to radio audiences when they first appeared on television in the early 1950s. Although their gentle, intelligent humor had always relied more on puns and vocal delivery than on sight gags, they nevertheless adapted well enough to the new medium to survive nearly two years on NBC, first on a Monday-through-Friday show, then on Tuesdays and Thursdays, and later once a week. Among their stock characters were Mary Margaret McGoon, cooking "expert," commentator, and all-purpose giver of advice; Tex, the drawling cowboy; and an assortment of travesties on current radio and TV personalities. Singer and actress Audrey Meadows played the part of Linda Lovely in Bob and Ray's continuing satire of soap operas. During the summer of 1952, when the show served as summer replacement for the soap opera *One Man's Family* (their version was *One Feller's Family*), Miss Meadows's place was taken by Cloris Leachman. Her primary role was in their spoof *Mary Backstage, Noble Wife* (a takeoff on the indomitable heroine of the radio serial *Mary Noble, Backstage Wife*). Audrey Meadows returned to the cast in the spring of 1953.

BOB CRANE SHOW, THE (*Situation Comedy*)
FIRST TELECAST: *March 6, 1975*
LAST TELECAST: *June 19, 1975*
BROADCAST HISTORY:
Mar 1975–Jun 1975, NBC Thu 8:30–9:00
CAST:
Bob Wilcox .... Bob Crane
Ellie Wilcox .... Trisha Hart
Marvin Susman .... Todd Susman
Dean Lyle Ingersoll .... Jack Fletcher
Mr. Ernest Busso .... Ronny Graham
Pam Wilcox .... Erica Petal
Jerry Mallory .... James Sutorius

In this short-lived series, Bob Crane played a fortyish insurance executive who abruptly decided to quit his job and enter medical school. The family pitched in, but the problems inherent in being twice the age of the other students and dependent on his working wife Ellie created constant comic situations, as did such resident characters as the overzealous Dean Ingersoll and nutty landlord Mr. Busso.

BOB CROSBY SHOW, THE (*Musical Variety*)
FIRST TELECAST: *June 14, 1958*
LAST TELECAST: *September 6, 1958*
BROADCAST HISTORY:
Jun 1958–Sep 1958, NBC Sat 8:00–9:00
REGULARS:
Bob Crosby
The Bobcats
Gretchen Wyler
The Peter Gennaro Dancers
The Clay Warnick Singers
The Carl Hoff Orchestra

Singer-bandleader Bob Crosby hosted and starred in this 1958 summer replacement for *The Perry Como Show*. With Bob were his band, The Bobcats, and musical-comedy star Gretchen Wyler.

BOB CUMMINGS SHOW, THE (*Situation Comedy*)
FIRST TELECAST: *January 2, 1955*
LAST TELECAST: *September 15, 1959*
BROADCAST HISTORY:
Jan 1955–Sep 1955, NBC Sun 10:30–11:00
Jul 1955–Sep 1957, CBS Thu 8:00–8:30
Sep 1957–Sep 1959, NBC Tue 9:30–10:00
CAST:
Bob Collins .... Bob Cummings
Margaret MacDonald .... Rosemary DeCamp
Charmaine "Shultzy" Schultz .... Ann B. Davis
Chuck MacDonald .... Dwayne Hickman
Pamela Livingston .... Nancy Kulp
Paul Fonda .... Lyle Talbot
Collette DuBois .... Lisa Gaye
Francine Williams (1955–1956) ...... Diane Jergens
Harvey Helm (1955–1958) .... King Donovan
Ruth Helm (1956–1958) .... Mary Lawrence
Mary Beth Hall (1956–1957) .... Gloria Marshall
Shirley Swanson (1956–1959) .... Joi Lansing
Olive Sturgess (1956–1957) .... Carol Henning
Ingrid Goude, Miss Sweden 1956 (1957–1958) .... Herself
Tammy Johnson (1959) ..... Tammy Lea Marihugh

Clean-cut Bob Cummings played swinging bachelor Bob Collins in this comedy about a professional photographer who spent all his working time with beautiful models. In his spare time Bob squired the lovely ladies around town, but he never seemed able to settle on any one woman, causing endless problems at home and "in the harem." Bob lived with his widowed sister Margaret and her son Chuck; Margaret never quite understood her brother's social life, and Chuck was always trying to get in on Uncle Bob's action, despite the fact that he had attractive, wholesome girlfriends of his own (Francine and later Olive). Bob's devoted assistant was Shultzy, who had a crush on her boss but couldn't compete with glamorous models like Collette, Mary Beth, Shirley, and Ingrid.

Bob had his own private plane and occasionally

flew to his home town of Joplin, Missouri, to visit his grandfather, Josh Collins (also played by Bob Cummings). Despite his age, the elder Collins had not lost his eye for the ladies, which he proved when it was his turn to visit his grandson—and all the sexy young models at the photography studio. When this series moved to daytime after concluding its evening run, the title was changed to *Love That Bob*, the same title later used in syndication. The network daytime run was on ABC from October 1959 to December 1961.

BOB CUMMINGS SHOW, THE (*Comedy/Adventure*)
FIRST TELECAST: *October 5, 1961*
LAST TELECAST: *March 1, 1962*
BROADCAST HISTORY:
Oct 1961–Jan 1962, CBS Thu 8:30–9:00
Feb 1962–Mar 1962, CBS Thu 7:30–8:00
CAST:
Bob Carson........................ Bob Cummings
Lionel................................ Murvyn Vye
Hank Gogerty....................... Roberta Shore

Bob Cummings, long an airplane enthusiast, managed to mix his avocation with his vocation in this adventure series. Bob Carson was a suave, high-living adventurer who made his living as a combination charter pilot and amateur detective. His assignments, both with and without passengers, took him all over the world. When his travels were short domestic hops close to his California base, Bob flew an aerocar, an unusual vehicle that could be used as an automobile or, when its removable wing was attached, converted into a small single-engine aircraft. When carrying passengers or traveling longer distances, Bob used a more luxurious twin-engine plane. His operating motto was that he would do anything that wasn't "illegal, immoral, or underpaid" and, with his expensive lifestyle, keeping in the black financially demanded regular employment. Lionel was his bodyguard/assistant and Hank the teenage daughter of the owner of the airstrip where Bob kept his planes. A tomboy, who rode a motor scooter to the airstrip every day, she spent much of her time flirting with Bob and trying to get him to take her on assignments. Effective with the episode that aired on December 28, 1961, the title of this series was changed to *The New Bob Cummings Show*.

BOB HOPE PRESENTS THE CHRYSLER THEATRE (*Dramatic Anthology*)
FIRST TELECAST: *September 27, 1963*
LAST TELECAST: *September 6, 1967*
BROADCAST HISTORY:
Sep 1963–Sep 1965, NBC Fri 8:30–9:30
Sep 1965–Sep 1967, NBC Wed 9:00–10:00
HOST:
Bob Hope

A mixed bag of drama, variety, and "event" specials, all involving Bob Hope in one role or another. In addition to serving as host on the dramatic telecasts, he starred in several of them. Among the more memorable telecasts of the series were "One Day in the Life of Ivan Denisovich," starring Jason Robards, Jr., Albert Paulsen, and Harold J. Stone (from the novel by Alexander Solzhenitsyn, later made into a movie); "The Seven Little Foys," with Mickey Rooney, Eddie Foy, Jr., and the Osmond Brothers; and "Think Pretty," a musical with Fred Astaire and Barrie Chase. Performers who starred in at least two of the episodes in this series were Peter Falk, Hugh O'Brian, Shelley Winters, Cliff Robertson, John Cassavetes, Jack Lord, William Shatner, Angie Dickinson, Suzanne Pleshette, Robert Stack, Dina Merrill, Darren McGavin, Broderick Crawford, and Stuart Whitman.

The variety shows were pure Hope, full of his topical one-liners, beautiful girls, sports heroes, and elaborate skits. The title of the variety hours was altered slightly to *Chrysler Presents a Bob Hope Special*. The highlight of the year, however, must be classed as one of TV's annual "events." This was the Bob Hope Christmas Show, filmed before an audience of G.I.s in Vietnam and carried as a 90-minute special telecast in January.

BOB NEWHART SHOW, THE (*Comedy/Variety*)
FIRST TELECAST: *October 10, 1961*
LAST TELECAST: *June 13, 1962*
BROADCAST HISTORY:
Oct 1961–Jun 1962, NBC Wed 10:00–10:30
REGULARS:
Bob Newhart
Mickey Manners (1961)
Joe Flynn
Jackie Joseph
Andy Albin
Dan Sorkin
Kay Westfall (1961)
Jack Grinnage (1961)
Ken Berry (1962)
Paul Weston and His Orchestra

On the heels of the success of his "Button Down Mind" comedy albums, the young comic Bob Newhart was given this variety hour in the fall of 1961. Borrowing the format of his nightclub and album routines, each telecast opened with a monologue in which Newhart talked on the telephone with an unseen, and unheard, adversary. The conversation usually concluded with Newhart's regular tag line, "Same to you, fella." The show featured great musical talent and a large group of comic actors and actresses who appeared in various sketches about contemporary life. None of them were truly regulars appearing on each telecast, but those listed above showed up at least half a dozen times during the season.

BOB NEWHART SHOW, THE (*Situation Comedy*)
FIRST TELECAST: *September 16, 1972*
LAST TELECAST: *August 26, 1978*
BROADCAST HISTORY:
Sep 1972–Oct 1976, CBS Sat 9:30–10:00
Nov 1976–Sep 1977, CBS Sat 8:30–9:00
Sep 1977–Apr 1978, CBS Sat 8:00–8:30
Jun 1978–Aug 1978, CBS Sat 8:00–8:30
CAST:
Robert (Bob) Hartley................ Bob Newhart
Emily Hartley.................. Suzanne Pleshette
Howard Borden........................ Bill Daily
Jerry Robinson...................... Peter Bonerz
Carol Kester Bondurant............ Marcia Wallace
Margaret Hoover (1972–1973)....... Patricia Smith
Dr. Bernie Tupperman (1972–1976)
.... Larry Gelman
Ellen Hartley (1974–1976).............. Pat Finley
Larry Bondurant (1975–1977)..... Will Mackenzie
Elliot Carlin............................ Jack Riley

Mrs. Bakerman .... Florida Friebus
Miss Larson (1972–1973) .... Penny Marshall
Michelle Nardo (1973–1976) .... Renee Lippin
Mr. Peterson (1973–1978) .... John Fiedler
Mr. Gianelli (1972–1973) .... Noam Pitlik
Mr Vickers (1974–1975)............... Lucien Scott
Mr. Herd (1976–1977)................ Oliver Clark

Bob Hartley was a successful Chicago psychologist who lived in a high-rise apartment with his wife Emily, an elementary school teacher. Bob shared the services of his receptionist Carol with a bachelor dentist, Jerry Robinson. Carol was a brash, nutty individual who could dish it out pretty well to both her bosses. In the fall of 1975, she married Larry Bondurant, a travel agent, after a whirlwind courtship. Originally two of the Hartleys' neighbors were seen on a regular basis: Howard Borden, a divorced commercial airline pilot who had an annoying habit of barging into their apartment without knocking; and Margaret Hoover, a friend of Emily's. For a period Bob's sister Ellen lived with him and Emily, and at one point almost married Howard, but that passed.

Bob was a very low-key fellow, which was handy at the office but did not always prove effective in dealings with his wife and friends. He had a number of regular patients, including all of the above cast of characters from Elliot Carlin to the bottom of the list. Bob's patients had problems ranging from ordinary, everyday neuroses to homosexuality to extreme paranoia. They were all trying to find themselves. The character who appeared most regularly—and the one with the biggest problems—was Elliot, without doubt one of the most neurotic individuals ever seen on television. He was completely lacking in self-confidence, had a persecution complex, and was forever putting himself down.

In addition to treating his patients individually, Bob was a firm believer in group therapy, and his patients interacted in various groups in hilarious fashion.

BOB PATTERSON (*Situation Comedy*)
FIRST TELECAST: *October 2, 2001*
LAST TELECAST: *October 31, 2001*
BROADCAST HISTORY:
Oct 2001, ABC Tue 9:00–9:30
Oct 2001, ABC Wed 9:30–10:00
CAST:
Bob Patterson .... Jason Alexander
Janet............................. Jennifer Aspen
Landau .... Robert Klein
Claudia .... Chandra Wilson
Vic................................. Phil Buckman
Jeffrey............................ James Guidice

Bob Patterson was America's self-proclaimed "number three motivational speaker," the author of the best-selling *I Know More Than You* (and its sequel, *I Still Know More Than You*). Despite his success, and his swank home in the Hollywood Hills, his own life was a mess. A voluble, insecure little runt, he mugged, gave exaggerated reactions and strutted around, but usually botched everything he touched. Janet was his goofy ex-wife, a New Age type; Jeffrey, his chubby, smart-mouthed son (by another wife); Landau, his loud, sycophantic assistant; Claudia, his clumsy, wheelchair-bound secretary, who kept running into things; and Vic, his incompetent intern. The jokes were stale or offensive—or both. Endless negative comparisons with Jason Alexander's previous series, the infinitely better-written *Seinfeld*, brought a quick demise for this pedestrian effort.

BOBBIE GENTRY SHOW, THE (*Musical Variety*)
FIRST TELECAST: *June 5, 1974*
LAST TELECAST: *June 26, 1974*
BROADCAST HISTORY:
Jun 1974, CBS Wed 8:00–9:00
REGULARS:
Bobbie Gentry
Michael Greer
Earl Pomerantz
Valri Bromfield

The star and host of this short summer variety series was country and western singer Bobbie Gentry, whose biggest hit was "Ode to Billy Joe," a ballad she had written herself.

The series was also known as *Bobbie Gentry's Happiness.*

BOBBY DARIN AMUSEMENT COMPANY, THE, see *Dean Martin Presents The Bobby Darin Amusement Company*

BOBBY DARIN SHOW, THE (*Musical Variety*)
FIRST TELECAST: *January 19, 1973*
LAST TELECAST: *April 27, 1973*
BROADCAST HISTORY:
Jan 1973–Apr 1973, NBC Fri 10:00–11:00
REGULARS:
Bobby Darin
Dick Bakalyan
Geoff Edwards
Tommy Amato
THEME:
"Mack the Knife"

Pop singer Bobby Darin appeared as both a singer and a sketch comedian in this short-lived series. In the sketches he became Groucho, Dusty John the hippie poet, Angie the tenement dweller, or the Godmother. He also performed several musical numbers each week, backed by a full orchestra. A consistent theme of the show was a salute to a different city each week, in song and in blackout comedy sketches.

BOBBY GOLDSBORO SHOW, THE (*Music*)
BROADCAST HISTORY:
Syndicated only
30 minutes
Produced: *1972–1975* (78 episodes)
Released: *Early 1973*
HOST:
Bobby Goldsboro

Mop-topped young singer Bobby Goldsboro, who looked like a rock 'n' roller but did strictly middle-of-the-road material, hosted this pleasant little half hour of songs. His guests were generally non-rock artists such as Johnny Mathis, Bobby Vinton, the Lennon Sisters, and B. J. Thomas. He also had a hand puppet named Jonathan Rebel to contribute to the patter.

BOBBY SHERMAN SHOW, THE, see *Getting Together*

BOBBY VINTON SHOW, THE (*Musical Variety*)
BROADCAST HISTORY:
Syndicated only

30 minutes
Produced: *1975–1978* (52 episodes)
Released: *Fall 1975*

REGULARS:

Bobby Vinton
Freeman King (1975–1976)
Jack Duffy (1975–1976)
Billy Van (1975–1976)
Jimmy Dale Orchestra
The Peaches (1976–1978)

Popular singer Bobby Vinton who had a long string of ballad hits in the 1960s ("Roses Are Red, My Dear," "Blue on Blue," "Mr. Lonely"), was host of this slick musical-comedy series produced in Toronto. He described his style as "sentimental and sincere," and so was most of the music presented here. There were also sketches, comedy blackouts, and short animated sequences, and most of the guests were comedians—Arte Johnson, Foster Brooks, John Byner, and Henny Youngman making multiple appearances.

During the first season there was a cast of regulars, and a lot of "Polish Power" jokes (Bobby was of Polish extraction). Both these elements were dropped in the second season, to give the boyish star broader appeal. A shapely backup group called the Peaches was also added.

BODIES OF EVIDENCE (*Police Drama*)

FIRST TELECAST: *June 18, 1992*
LAST TELECAST: *May 28, 1993*
BROADCAST HISTORY:

Jun 1992–Aug 1992, CBS Thu 10:00–11:00
Apr 1993–May 1993, CBS Fri 10:00–11:00

CAST:

Lt. Ben Carroll .... Lee Horsley
Det. Ryan Walker .... George Clooney
Det. Nora Houghton .... Kate McNeil
Det. Walt Stratton .... Al Fann
Sgt. Jimmy Houghton .... Francis X. McCarthy
Lemar Samuels .... Leslie Jordan
Dr. Mary Rocket (1992) .... Lorraine Toussaint
Bonnie Carroll .... Jennifer Hetrick
Chief Frank Leland .... Alan Fudge
Maggie Holland (1993) .... Kimberly Scott

Lt. Ben Carroll was the veteran head of the homicide department of an unnamed big-city police department in this gritty series that attempted to show how the stress of police work affected the personal lives of officers. Working with Ben were Ryan Walker, an able cop who tended to get too emotionally involved in his cases; Nora Houghton, a young officer who sometimes questioned her own competence and dedication; and Nora's partner, Walt Stratton, a grizzled veteran who had seen it all and was close to retirement. Lemar was the department's forensic specialist, Mary a psychiatrist who worked with them, and Maggie a psychic who started dating Ben after helping him solve a case. Ben's ex-wife, Bonnie, who had divorced him because of the stress of being a "police wife," remarried in 1993 and moved to another city with their son.

BODY & SOUL (*Medical Drama*)

FIRST TELECAST: *September 16, 2002*
LAST TELECAST: *December 29, 2002*
BROADCAST HISTORY:

Sep 2002–Oct 2002, PAX Mon 9:00–10:00
Sep 2002–Oct 2002, PAX Sun 10:00–11:00
Oct 2002–Nov 2002, PAX Tue 9:00–10:00
Nov 2002–Dec 2002, PAX Sun 11:00–12:00

CAST:

Dr. Isaac Braun .... Peter Strauss
Dr. Rachel Griffen .... Larissa Laskin
Dr. Marshall Banks .... Conrad Coates
Dr. Quinton Bremmer .... Currie Graham
Dr. Phillip Grenier .... Duncan Regehr
Oz, the orderly .... Gil Birmingham
Nurse Yolanda Rosales .... Idalis DeLeon
Dr. Jerry Donovan .... Brian McNamara
Dr. Edward A. Esseff .... William B. Davis

Columbus, Ohio's, Century Hospital was the setting for this medical drama that mixed conventional with alternative medicine. Dr. Rachel Griffen, recently back from a two-year fellowship in the Far East, had become a convert to the benefits of alternative therapies and treatments—healing the mind and spirit as well as the body. There was strong opposition to her plans for an alternative center at the hospital, primarily from traditionalist Dr. Braun, the chief of surgery and Griffen's former mentor, and Dr. Grenier, Century's profit-hungry administrator. The alternative center became a reality after Griffen saved the life of Wallace Beaton (James Callahan), the hospital's wealthy benefactor, who demanded that Grenier fund the project. Others on the staff included gay Dr. Bremmer, who was enthusiastic about the center; Dr. Banks, a young black intern unsure about the direction his medical career should take; philosophical Dr. Esseff, who performed autopsies; and Dr. Donovan, Griffen's ex-husband, who was still romantically interested in her. In a bizarre accident, a patient attempting suicide jumped out of his window and landed on Dr. Braun, almost killing him. Braun had a near-death experience and, after his recovery, discovered that he had the ability to see into the bodies of patients and sense their internal medical problems.

BOING BOING SHOW, THE (*Cartoon*)

FIRST TELECAST: *May 30, 1958*
LAST TELECAST: *October 3, 1958*
BROADCAST HISTORY:

May 1958–Oct 1958, CBS Fri 7:30–8:00

NARRATOR:

Bill Goodwin

The Gerald McBoing-Boing cartoon series—a combination of animation and live action—made its debut on CBS in December of 1956, on Sunday afternoons. Unable to talk, little Gerald would make himself understood by using pantomime and various noises rather than speech. When this didn't work, actor-announcer Bill Goodwin was always on hand to serve as a live interpreter. The series was aired in prime time during the summer of 1958.

BOLD JOURNEY (*Travel Documentary*)

FIRST TELECAST: *July 16, 1956*
LAST TELECAST: *August 31, 1959*
BROADCAST HISTORY:

Jul 1956–Feb 1957, ABC Mon 7:30–8:00
Feb 1957–Jun 1957, ABC Thu 9:30–10:00
Jun 1957–Aug 1959, ABC Mon 8:30–9:00

HOST:

John Stephenson (1955–1957)
Jack Douglas (1957–1959)

Home movies were shown on this series, but not normal everyday home movies. These films were taken by explorers and adventurers on trips to remote or highly unusual places around the world. The host of the show would introduce each week's guest, interview him about his experiences during the expedition, and then help narrate the film that had been taken during the trip. Los Angeles personality, Jack Douglas, took over as host on October 28, 1957.

BOLD ONES, THE (*Drama*)
FIRST TELECAST: *September 14, 1969*
LAST TELECAST: *June 22, 1973*
BROADCAST HISTORY:
Sep 1969–Sep 1972, NBC Sun 10:00–11:00
Sep 1972–Jan 1973, NBC Tue 9:00–10:00
May 1973–Jun 1973, NBC Fri 10:00–11:00

The Bold Ones was the umbrella title for a number of rotating series that were aired within the same time slot. During the 1969–1970 season there were three elements in the program: *The New Doctors*, *The Lawyers*, and *The Protectors*. In its second season, *The Senator* replaced *The Protectors*. For 1971–1972 only two elements were aired—*The New Doctors* and *The Lawyers*—and in its last season the program was composed solely of new episodes of *The New Doctors*. For information on specific elements in this series, see their respective titles.

BOLD VENTURE (*Adventure*)
BROADCAST HISTORY:
Syndicated only
30 minutes
Produced: *1958–1959* (39 episodes)
Released: *January 1959*
CAST:
Slate Shannon .... Dane Clark
Sailor Duval .... Joan Marshall
King Moses .... Bernie Gozier

Swaying palms, beautiful women, and high adventure filled this action series set in the Caribbean. Slate Shannon was an expatriate American, owner of a hotel called Shannon's Place and a 60-foot sloop named *The Bold Venture*. His constant companion was Sailor Duval, a good-looking young woman who had been left as his ward by her deceased father, Slate's best friend (although why, in her 20s, she needed to be anybody's ward was never explained). From their base in Trinidad, Slate and his charge stumbled into one adventure after another, involving smugglers, killers, and the other shady characters who populate series such as this.

An unusual feature of the series was its calypso music, which not only served as background but sometimes tied the story together through bits of narrative by calypso singer King Moses.

Bold Venture originated as a syndicated radio series in 1951–1952, in which Humphrey Bogart and Lauren Bacall wisecracked their way around the West Indies. They were a hard act to follow, and only 39 episodes of this television sequel were filmed.

BON VOYAGE, see *Treasure Quest*

BONANZA (*Western*)
FIRST TELECAST: *September 12, 1959*
LAST TELECAST: *January 16, 1973*
BROADCAST HISTORY:
Sep 1959–Sep 1961, NBC Sat 7:30–8:30
Sep 1961–Sep 1972, NBC Sun 9:00–10:00
May 1972–Aug 1972, NBC Tue 7:30–8:30
Sep 1972–Jan 1973, NBC Tue 8:00–9:00
CAST:
Ben Cartwright .... Lorne Greene
Little Joe Cartwright .... Michael Landon
Eric "Hoss" Cartwright (1959–1972) ... Dan Blocker
Adam Cartwright (1959–1965) ..... Pernell Roberts
Hop Sing .... Victor Sen Yung
Sheriff Roy Coffee (1960–1972) .... Ray Teal
Candy (1967–1970, 1972–1973)...... David Canary
Dusty Rhoades (1970–1972) .... Lou Frizzel
Jamie Hunter (1970–1973) .... Mitch Vogel
Griff King (1972–1973).............. Tim Matheson
**Deputy Clem Foster (1961–1973)*...... Bing Russell
*Occasional
THEME:
"Bonanza," by Jay Livingston and Ray Evans

Set in the vicinity of Virginia City, Nevada, during and after the Civil War, soon after the discovery of the fabulous Comstock Silver Lode, *Bonanza* was the story of a prosperous family of ranchers. Widower Ben Cartwright was the patriarch of the all-male clan and owner of the thousand-square-mile Ponderosa Ranch. Each of his three sons had been borne by a different wife, none of whom was still alive. Adam, the oldest of the half brothers, was the most serious and introspective, the likely successor to his father as the controlling force behind the sprawling Cartwright holdings. Hoss, the middle son, was a mountain of a man who was as gentle as he was huge, at times naive, and not particularly bright. Little Joe was the youngest, most impulsive, and most romantic of the Cartwright offspring. The adventures of these men, individually and collectively, their dealings with the mining interests and the ranching interests, and the people whose paths crossed theirs made up the stories on *Bonanza*.

The program was not a traditional shoot-'em-up Western; it relied more on the relationships among the principals and the stories of the characters played by weekly guest stars than it did on violence. Many of the episodes explored serious dramatic themes.

Bonanza premiered on Saturday night in the fall of 1959, and was the first Western to be televised in color. It was at first only moderately successful, but two years later, when it moved to Sunday night as the replacement for *The Dinah Shore Chevy Show*, it soared in popularity. For most of the 1960s *Bonanza* ranked as one of the highest-rated programs on television, placing number-one for three seasons between 1964–1967. Its driving theme song, written by two Hollywood songsmiths who had written many top movie hits of the 1940s and 1950s, was on the hit parade. *Bonanza* finished second only to *Gunsmoke* as the longest-running, most successful Western in the history of television.

There were cast changes over the years. Pernell Roberts left the series at the end of the 1964–1965 season and his role was written out of the show. At the start of the 1967–1968 season a wanderer named Candy was hired as a ranch hand for the Cartwrights and practically became one of the family. Three years later, when Candy left the series (he later returned), two other new cast members arrived to join the

Ponderosa household. Dusty Rhoades was a friend of Ben's, and Jamie Hunter, his charge, was an orphaned teenaged son of a rainmaker who had been killed. Prior to the start of production for the 1972–1973 season Dan Blocker died unexpectedly. His loss, coupled with a move to a new day and time, after 11 years on Sunday night, may have contributed to the poor rating performance that resulted in *Bonanza*'s cancellation in the middle of its 14th season.

During the summer of 1972, while *Bonanza* was still being aired on Sundays, reruns from the 1967–1970 period were shown on Tuesdays at 7:30 P.M. under the title *Ponderosa. Bonanza* itself moved to Tuesdays that September.

Pax aired a prequel, *The Ponderosa,* during the 2001–2002 season.

BONINO (*Situation Comedy*)

FIRST TELECAST: *September 12, 1953*
LAST TELECAST: *December 26, 1953*
BROADCAST HISTORY:
Sep 1953–Dec 1953, NBC Sat 8:00–8:30

CAST:
Bonino .... Ezio Pinza
Edward .... Conrad Janis
Doris .... Lenka Peterson
Jerry .... Chet Allen
Jerry (beg. 11/18, 1953) .... Donald Harris
Carlo .... Oliver Andes
Francesco .... Gaye Huston
Andrew .... Van Dyke Parks
Martha, the maid .... Mary Wickes
Rusty, the former valet .... Mike Kellin
Walter Rogers .... David Opatoshu
John Clinton .... Fred (Anthony) Eisley

This live situation comedy starred the operatic basso Ezio Pinza as Bonino, a world-famous concert singer. Bonino's wife had died, leaving him with eight children to support. He abandoned his professional touring—much to the chagrin of his concert manager, Walter Rogers, and his valet—but found that his children had grown very independent during his absence. Mr. Pinza sang once during each episode.

BONKERS (*Comedy*)

BROADCAST HISTORY:
Syndicated only
30 minutes
Produced: *1978–1979* (24 episodes)
Released: *September 1978*

CAST:
The Hudson Brothers (Bill, Brett, Mark)
Bob Monkhouse
The Bonkettes

"But *who* are the Hudson Brothers?" asked the *TV Guide* reporter, echoing a question that bedeviled this talented comedy trio throughout their career. Despite a network summer series in 1974, the Saturday morning *Hudson Brothers Razzle Dazzle Show* in 1974–1975, this syndicated entry in 1978, a number of moderately popular records, and innumerable guest spots, they still were not—well, household names.

On *Bonkers* they did their usual thing, which was frantic, knockabout comedy somewhat reminiscent of the Marx Brothers, combined with contemporary music, real and parodied. Guest stars, a dazzling chorus line called the Bonkettes, and production by the company responsible for *The Muppets* didn't help.

BONNIE HUNT SHOW, THE (*Situation Comedy*)

FIRST TELECAST: *September 22, 1995*
LAST TELECAST: *April 7, 1996*
BROADCAST HISTORY:
Sep 1995–Oct 1995, CBS Fri 8:30–9:00
Mar 1996–Apr 1996, CBS Sun 8:30–9:00

CAST:
Bonnie Kelly .... Bonnie Hunt
Holly Jankofsky .... Holly Wortell
Bill Kirkland .... Mark Derwin
Diane Fulton .... Janet Carroll
Joe Briggs .... Richard Gant
Andrew Wiggins .... Eamonn Roche
Tom Vandoozer .... Tom Virtue
Sammy Sinatra .... Brian Howe
Keith Jetzek .... Don Lake

EXECUTIVE PRODUCERS:
Rob Burnett
Bonnie Hunt
David Letterman

Terminally nice, relentlessly naive Bonnie Kelly had recently moved to Chicago from her native Wisconsin to take her "dream job" as a human interest reporter for WBDR-TV. The fast pace and competitive pressure at the Chicago station took some getting used to. Her best friend from high school, chatterbox Holly, lived in Bonnie's apartment building and worked as a makeup artist and hairstylist at WBDR. Among Bonnie's other co-workers were Bill, the always-in-a-rush news director; Diane, Bill's bossy, deceitful assistant who had it in for Bonnie; Joe, the news department's tough assignment editor; Andrew, the spaced-out videotape editor; Tom, the cameraman, who usually teamed with her; Sammy, the coffee guy; and Keith, a limo driver who also lived in her apartment building. Each episode included a charming segment in which Bonnie and Tom went on location and interviewed real people on the streets of Chicago in unscripted encounters.

This was the second failed star vehicle for Ms. Hunt and her fellow Second City alumni Wortell, Virtue, and Lake. As with the first, 1993's *The Building,* Ms. Hunt was one of the show's creators, writers, and, along with her good friend David Letterman, executive producers. Pulled from the fall schedule after five episodes had aired, the series returned the following March with its title shortened to *Bonnie*; after five more weeks, it was gone for good.

BONNY MAID VERSATILE VARIETIES, see *Versatile Varieties*

BOOK OF LISTS, THE (*Variety*)

FIRST TELECAST: *May 4, 1982*
LAST TELECAST: *May 25, 1982*
BROADCAST HISTORY:
May 1982, CBS Tue 8:00–9:00

HOST:
Bill Bixby

Each week host Bill Bixby, along with a co-host and a couple of other assistants, brought to life some of the odd, unusual, and intriguing facts gleaned from *The Book of Lists* and *The Book of Lists II,* two best-sellers compiled by David Wallechinsky, Irving Wallace, and

Amy Wallace. Other items were tailored to the guest personalities who appeared on the show. Guest helper Ruth Buzzi described the "Ten Physical Attributes Women Most Admire in Men," Shecky Greene told "His Five Favorite Stories," Foster Brooks explained his "Favorite Hangover Cures," co-host Lorna Patterson sang a medley of "Songs Made Famous by Blondes," and co-host Steve Allen discussed the "Seven Things Married Couples Fight About Most."

This summer series lasted four weeks and may well turn up itself someday on a list of "Ten Most Obscure TV Series."

BOOKER (*Detective Drama*)

FIRST TELECAST: *September 24, 1989*
LAST TELECAST: *August 26, 1990*
BROADCAST HISTORY:

Sep 1989–Mar 1990, FOX Sun 7:00–8:00
Apr 1990–Aug 1990, FOX Sun 10:00–11:00

CAST:

Dennis Booker.................... Richard Grieco
Elaine Grazzo .... Katie Rich
Charles "Chick" Sterling ...... Carmen Argenziano
Alicia Rudd..................... Marcia Strassman
Suzanne Dunne (1990) .... Lori Petty

THEME:

"Hot in the City," performed by Billy Idol

On *21 Jump Street*, Dennis Booker had been an outspoken rebel, constantly fighting the system. No longer a cop, he was now working as the in-house investigation department for the huge multinational, Japanese-owned Teshima Corporation. Not that he had given in to societal pressures. Dennis was still the rebel, wearing jeans, T-shirt, and leather jacket to work, going unshaved, tooling around on his motorcycle (although he had also acquired an old Firebird convertible), and still fighting for his personal independence with his boss, Alicia Rudd, and her boss, Chick Sterling, head of Teshima's American operations. Alicia was aghast at his flaunting of corporate conformity, but he was a first-rate investigator. One of his secrets was his network of "friends in low places." Every female clerk and computer operator swooned when he came around, and got him whatever inside information he needed.

Booker worked on the cases Teshima gave him and managed to get the corporation to do the right thing for the little guy, even when it didn't intend to. He also had time to work on outside cases as a private investigator. His original and enthusiastic young assistant and secretary was Elaine; when she left to get married he hired Suzanne, a former bail-jumping con woman.

Filmed in Vancouver.

BOOMTOWN (*Drama*)

FIRST TELECAST: *September 29, 2002*
LAST TELECAST:
BROADCAST HISTORY:

Sep 2002–Apr 2003, NBC Sun 10:00–11:00

CAST:

Det. Joel Stevens................. Donnie Wahlberg
Det. "Fearless" Bobby Smith ... Mykelti Williamson
Dep. D.A. David McNorris .... Neal McDonough
Off. Tom Turcotte.................. Jason Gedrick
Off. Ray Hechler................... Gary Basaraba
Teresa Ortiz......................... Lana Parrilla
Andrea Little .... Nina Garbiras

Crime in Los Angeles was seen from a variety of viewpoints in this unusually formatted drama. First on the scene were usually the street cops, hunky Tom and chunky wiseguy Ray, along with compassionate paramedic Teresa. Then came the detectives, moody Joel and his partner "Fearless" Bobby Smith. They didn't call Bobby fearless for nothing. This black dude had almost been killed while in the army in the Gulf War, and had decided to start living for today. He was the kind who would walk up to a distraught murderer and simply jive him out of his gun while the perp was trying to figure him out. Close behind the detectives was Deputy D.A. David, a slick, buttoned-down media manipulator who, though dedicated, frequently played to the cameras. Andrea was an aggressive reporter for the *Tribune* who was having an affair with David, even though she was suspicious of him. They all converged on the scene of the homicide, and the events that occurred were often replayed two or three times, depicting what each of them saw. The story might also jump around in time—for example, showing a young shooter in a flashback as a once happy, innocent kid. There was plenty of hard-boiled sarcasm, some sex and infuriating encounters with arrogant L.A. "power broker" types, flanked by their lawyers, who wouldn't even let the detectives past the front gates of their mansions. Nevertheless, in the end the cops usually got their man.

BOONE (*Drama*)

FIRST TELECAST: *September 26, 1983*
LAST TELECAST: *August 11, 1984*
BROADCAST HISTORY:

Sep 1983–Dec 1983, NBC Mon 8:00–9:00
Jul 1984–Aug 1984, NBC Sat 10:00–11:00

CAST:

Boone Sawyer.......................... Tom Byrd
Rome Hawley.......................... Greg Webb
Merit Sawyer .... Barry Corbin
Faye Sawyer..................... Elizabeth Huddle
Susannah Sawyer.................... Kitty Moffat
Squirt Sawyer.................. Amanda Peterson
Uncle Link............... William Edward Phipps
Aunt Dolly................. Ronnie Claire Edwards
Mr. Johnson......................... Davis Roberts
Banjo........................ Julie Anne Haddock
Norman .... Chris Hebert
Amanda .... Robyn Lively

Boone Sawyer was a young man with a guitar and a dream. It was 1953, in rural Trinity, Tennessee, not far from Nashville, and Boone was about to graduate from high school. He was an earnest and decent young man, and his family had down-to-earth plans for him. But Boone had other ideas. Upbeat country music, the kind that would soon evolve into rockabilly, was his first love, and he hoped it would be his ticket to stardom. Unfortunately the management of the Grand Ole Opry thought otherwise—they threw him out on his ear. Boone's father, Merit, who ran a local garage, and his loving mother, Faye, were not very supportive either, preferring that Boone stay close to home and either take over Dad's gas station or become a minister—the career intended for his older brother Dwight, who had been killed in World War II. Parents never understand.

Boone found encouragement elsewhere, however, especially from his best buddy, leather-jacketed, motorcycle-riding Rome Hawley, who backed him on stage and shared wild times with him. Older sister Susannah and younger sister Squirt were sympathetic to his ambitions, too, as were Aunt Dolly and Uncle Link, who ran Link's Lounge, a local saloon where Boone and Rome hung out and sometimes performed. Mr. Johnson was an old, blind black man, a former blues guitarist who gave Boone helpful advice. Follow your dream, he said, so Boone kept a-pickin' and a-grinnin'—right up to the time this *Waltons*-esque series bit the dust after only three and a half months.

BOOT CAMP (*Reality/Adventure*)
FIRST TELECAST: *March 28, 2001*
LAST TELECAST: *May 23, 2001*
BROADCAST HISTORY:
Mar 2001–May 2001, FOX Wed 9:00–10:00
DRILL INSTRUCTORS:
Dave Francisco
Leo McSweeney
Tony Rosenbum
Annette Taylor

This variation on the megahit *Survivor* began with 16 civilian "recruits" who were subjected to grueling physical challenges and mental discipline in a military setting. For 30 days they were pushed, prodded and screamed at by four real marine drill instructors, enduring sleep deprivation, push-ups, three-mile runs, rock climbing, and mess-hall food. Each week the troop selected a squad leader who helped the instructors train the recruits for a "combat mission" such as Demolition, Reconnaissance, or Hostage Rescue. If the mission was successful, the squad leader won amnesty and could not be eliminated in that episode. Each episode ended with a ceremony at "Dismissal Hill," in which two recruits were eliminated—one by a vote of the contestants and, in an opportunity for revenge, another picked by the person who had just been voted out.

At the conclusion of the series the last two survivors, Ryan Wolf and Jennifer Whitlow, competed in The Gauntlet, an exceptionally brutal 48 hours of physical and mental challenges including 5 hours standing at attention with a full pack, a two-mile obstacle course, a 1.5-mile run, rappels, a slide recognition memory test, a 10-mile march with a heavy pack, and holding a pair of dogtags over a tank of blood without dropping them. The winner (who got $500,000) was to be determined by a combination of points from the competition and a vote by previously dismissed constants. In an ironic ending that must have disgusted real marines, tough, arrogant Ryan won almost all the physical challenges but Jennifer got the money based on the vote because the other contestants thought she was "nicer" and "tried hard."

The true stars of *Boot Camp*, however, were the real-life marine drill instructors who screamed at, harassed and, occasionally, cajoled the recruits. Dave, the imposing head instructor, had joined the show because he wanted to show the world "how to do it right." Leo, who had served in Japan, Africa, Australia and the Persian Gulf, said "being a drill instructor was the last challenge in the Marine Corps," and Tony said it gave him "the greatest impact and influence over a group of people in a short amount of time."

BORDEN SHOW, THE (*Various*)
FIRST TELECAST: *July 6, 1947*
LAST TELECAST: *September 28, 1947*
BROADCAST HISTORY:
July 1947–Sep 1947, NBC Sun 9:00–9:30
DIRECTOR:
Fred Coe

The Borden Show was the overall title for a 1947 series, sponsored by Borden, that presented a different format each week. Such "sampler" programs were typical in the early days of TV broadcasting when networks and sponsors alike were experimenting with the new medium. Among the formats tried out on *The Borden Show* were variety shows, dramas, films, and marionette shows. The first telecast, subtitled "Borden Club," is illustrative. Set in an intimate supper club, it opened outside the club with a shot of a group of autograph-seekers besieging an unseen celebrity—who turned out to be Elsie the Borden Cow, in marionette form. The camera then moved inside where emcee Wally Boag entertained with his rubber balloons, followed by singer Lisa Kirk, impressionist Patricia Bright, and the Dominicans dance team.

The Elsie marionette also appeared on other *Borden Show* telecasts, providing a thread of continuity for the series.

BORDERTOWN (*Adventure*)
BROADCAST HISTORY:
The Family Channel
30 minutes
Produced: *1988–1991* (78 episodes)
Premiered: *January 7, 1989*
CAST:
Marshal Jack Craddock .... Richard Comar
Corporal Clive Bennett .... John H. Brennan
Marie Dumont .... Sophie Barjac
**Otto Danzinger* .... Fritz Bergold
**Bruno Danzinger* .... Wyatt Orr
**Sally Duffield* .... Beverly Elliott
**Zachary Denny* .... Duncan Fraser
**Diane Denny* .... Freda Perry
**Willie Haddon* .... Gregory Togal
**Clara* .... Kimberly Sheppard
**Jake Epple* .... Bill Pepperall
**Liam Gleeson* .... Hagan Beggs
**Dominic* .... Dom Fiore
**Wendell MacWherter* .... Paul Batten
*Occasional

Cable's Family Channel, last resting place of many of the great westerns of the 1950s and '60s such as *Wagon Train*, *Gunsmoke*, and *Bonanza*, added its own with this low-budget series set in the Canadian Northwest. The setting was an 1880s town that straddled the U.S.–Canadian border, necessitating cooperation between lawmen from the two countries. They were Marshal Jack Craddock, a rough-hewn gunfighter rooted in the rough-and-ready law-keeping ways of Dodge City, and Corporal Clive Bennett, a young, earnest Mountie who seemed to prefer twentieth-century procedure ("Do we have a warrant?"). Their chief clash, however, was over the affections of the town's doctor and storekeeper, pretty Marie Dumont, who, diplomatically, did not favor either. Gunfights abounded in *Bordertown*, but this being the Family Channel there was very little sex.

Historical figures such as Teddy Roosevelt and Bat

Masterson passed through, and a large number of townspeople were seen on an occasional basis. Filmed in Maple Ridge and Pitt Meadows, British Columbia, as a coproduction with Canadian TV.

BORN FREE (*Adventure*)

FIRST TELECAST: *September 9, 1974*

LAST TELECAST: *December 12, 1974*

BROADCAST HISTORY:

Sep 1974–Dec 1974, NBC Mon 8:00–9:00

CAST:

George Adamson .... Gary Collins
Joy Adamson .... Diana Muldaur
Makedde .... Hal Frederick
Nuru .... Peter Lukoye
Awaru .... Nelson Kajuna
Joe Kanini .... Joseph De Craft

Filmed entirely on location in East Africa, where the action took place, *Born Free* chronicled the adventures of George and Joy Adamson with the lioness Elsa. The Adamsons were game wardens whose job was to watch over the wildlife in the area and protect the animals from poachers and natural disasters. The show was based on the popular book and movie of the same name.

BORN TO THE WIND (*Adventure*)

FIRST TELECAST: *August 19, 1982*

LAST TELECAST: *September 5, 1982*

BROADCAST HISTORY:

Aug 1982, NBC Thu 8:00–9:00
Aug 1982, NBC Sat 8:00–9:00
Aug 1982–Sep 1982, NBC Sun 7:00–8:00

CAST:

Painted Bear .... Will Sampson
Low Wolf .... A Martinez
One Feather .... Dehl Berti
Star Fire .... Rose Portillo
Prairie Woman .... Linda Redfearn
White Bull .... Emilio Delgado
Two Hawks .... Guillermo San Juan

This summer series had an unusual setting: a small Indian tribe somewhere in North America, around 1800, prior to the arrival of white settlers. The Indians' attempts to cope with an often hostile environment, relationships with each other, and the strong moral and ethical code by which they lived were all explored. Painted Bear was the leader (but not designated chief) of the group, and made most of the major decisions. Prairie Woman was his squaw, Star Fire his daughter, and Two Hawks his teenage son. One Feather was the village medicine man, and Low Wolf and White Bull were two other prominently featured braves.

BOSOM BUDDIES (*Situation Comedy*)

FIRST TELECAST: *November 27, 1980*

LAST TELECAST: *September 15, 1984*

BROADCAST HISTORY:

Nov 1980–Sep 1981, ABC Thu 8:30–9:00
Oct 1981, ABC Thu 9:00–9:30
Nov 1981–Jan 1982, ABC Fri 8:30–9:00
Feb 1982–Mar 1982, ABC Thu 8:30–9:00
May 1982–Jun 1982, ABC Thu 8:30–9:00
Jul 1984–Sep 1984, NBC Sat 9:00–9:30

CAST:

Henry Desmond/Hildegarde .... Peter Scolari
Kip Wilson/Buffy .... Tom Hanks
Amy Cassidy .... Wendie Jo Sperber
Sonny Lumet .... Donna Dixon
Isabelle .... Telma Hopkins
Lilly Sinclair (1980–1981) .... Lucille Benson
Ruth Dunbar .... Holland Taylor

THEME:

"My Life," written by Billy Joel

The old guys-in-drag gag was revived in this 1980 sex farce. Henry and Kip were two young studs working at a New York City advertising agency, Henry as a junior copywriter (and aspiring novelist) and Kip as a junior illustrator (and aspiring painter). They were also roommates, but one day they found a wrecking ball in the bedroom—seems the building was being demolished. Office receptionist Amy, who was smitten with Henry, came up with the bright idea that they move into her building, which just happened to be an all-girl residence—the Susan B. Anthony Hotel. Henry and Kip liked the low rent and the idea of being surrounded by beautiful women in various stages of undress, so in they went, gussied up as Hildegarde and Buffy. Amy was the only one who knew their true identities, even though Henry and Kip kept showing up at the hotel as themselves (passed off as Hildegarde's and Buffy's brothers). Sonny and Isabelle were two sexpots at the hotel, and Lilly Sinclair its fearsome manager. Ruth Dunbar was the idea-appropriating boss at the office.

Eventually the boys revealed their ruse to the girls at the hotel, but nobody else seemed to catch on. They also went into the commercial production business with Amy, taking over the failing firm owned by Henry's Uncle Mort. Sonny pursued her career as a nurse, while being pursued by Kip, and Isabelle took over as manager of the hotel, while waiting for her big break as an actress.

NBC aired reruns of *Bosom Buddies* during the summer of 1984.

BOSS LADY (*Situation Comedy*)

FIRST TELECAST: *July 1, 1952*

LAST TELECAST: *September 23, 1952*

BROADCAST HISTORY:

Jul 1952–Sep 1952, NBC Tue 9:00–9:30

CAST:

Gwen F. Allen .... Lynn Bari
Gwen's Father .... Nicholas Joy
Jeff Standish .... Glenn Langan
Chester Allen .... Charlie Smith
Aggie .... Lee Patrick
Roger .... Richard Gainer

In this summer replacement of *Fireside Theatre*, Lynn Bari played Gwen F. Allen, the beautiful chief executive of a highly successful construction firm, Hillandale Homes. Her two major problems, around which most of the stories were based, were finding a general manager who would not fall in love with her and maintaining her well-intentioned but inept father in his position as chairman of the board.

BOSTON BLACKIE (*Detective Drama*)

BROADCAST HISTORY:

Syndicated only
30 minutes
Produced: *1951–1953* (58 episodes)
Released: *September 1951*

CAST:

Boston Blackie .... Kent Taylor

Mary Wesley .... Lois Collier
Inspector Faraday .... Frank Orth

Boston Blackie, hero of more than a dozen 1940s B movies, a B radio series, and B-grade magazine stories dating back decades, appeared in a memorable B-grade television series in the early 1950s. The term "B" is used in all the best senses: a certain vitality and sense of humor substituted more than adequately for the normal criteria of expensive production and famous stars.

Blackie, "enemy of those who make him an enemy, friend of those who have no friend," was a dapper reformed crook living in Los Angeles. Aided by his helper and girlfriend Mary, he regularly solved crimes several steps ahead of the local police, who were represented by the somewhat dimwitted Inspector Faraday. There were a lot of wisecracks and light asides along with the murders, and the whole series looked a little like a stock-company version of *Mr. and Mrs. North*, or Nick and Nora Charles in *The Thin Man* (Blackie and Mary had a dog too, named Whitey). Some episodes, in fact, were played more for comedy than crime.

The original Boston Blackie was a rather disreputable character, created by Jack Boyle in the pages of *Cosmopolitan* and *Redbook* magazines in the early 1900s (though the character was possibly inspired by black-eyed Blackie Daw, an elegant con man who was a major character in the "Get-Rich-Quick Wallingford" stories of George Randolph Chester, beginning in 1908). Boyle's Blackie was a burglar and bank robber by trade, and though well educated and extremely clever, he spent a lot of time in prison while Mary patiently waited. After one particularly brutal incarceration, he decided to go straight and started solving crimes instead of committing them. He was a popular character, appearing in several silent movies of the 1910s and 1920s, and in the feature-film series of the 1940s starring Chester Morris. There was also a 1940s radio series with Morris and, later, Richard Kollmar.

BOSTON COMMON (*Situation Comedy*)

FIRST TELECAST: *March 21, 1996*
LAST TELECAST: *April 28, 1997*
BROADCAST HISTORY:

Mar 1996–Apr 1996, NBC Thu 8:30–9:00
Aug 1996–Apr 1997, NBC Sun 8:30–9:00
Apr 1997, NBC Mon 8:30–9:00

CAST:

Boyd "Bo" Pritchett .... Anthony Clark
Wyleen Pritchett .... Hedy Burress
Joy Byrnes .... Traylor Howard
Leonard Prince .... Steve Paymer
Tasha King .... Tasha Smith
Prof. Jack Reed .... Vincent Ventresca

Wyleen was an enthusiastic 18-year-old from a small town in Virginia, eager to start a new life as a freshman at Randolph Harrington College in Boston. Unfortunately, her old life wasn't entirely left behind. Her doting older brother Bo had the car, so he drove her to Boston—then took a job in the student union and moved into her small apartment, just to make sure his little sis was "all right." The backwoods handyman surprised everyone with his cleverness and charm, and indeed seemed smarter than most of the oddballs who populated Harrington. Joy was a ditzy grad student studying southern culture for whom Bo had eyes; she, however, was taken with young Professor Jack, who in turn was in love mostly with himself. Leonard was the dour college archivist who hung out at their apartment, and Tasha the surly administrative assistant. Other students and faculty members stumbled, fumbled, and leered their way through various episodes during the series' one-year run.

BOSTON PUBLIC (*School Drama*)

FIRST TELECAST: *October 23, 2000*
LAST TELECAST:
BROADCAST HISTORY:

Oct 2000–Aug 2002, FOX Mon 8:00–9:00
Oct 2002–May 2003, FOX Mon 8:00–9:00
Jul 2003– , FOX Fri 9:00–10:00

CAST:

Principal Steven Harper .... Chi McBride
Lauren Davis (2000–2002) .... Jessalyn Gilsig
Milton Buttle (2000–2001) .... Joey Slotnick
Harry Senate (2000–2002) .... Nicky Katt
Harvey Lipshultz .... Fyvush Finkel
Vice Principal Scott Guber .... Anthony Heald
Kevin Riley (2000–2001) .... Thomas McCarthy
Marylin Sudor .... Sharon Leal
Louisa Fenn (2000–2002) .... Rashida Jones
Marla Hendricks .... Loretta Devine
**Dana Poole (2000–2002)* .... Sarah Thompson
**Sheryl Holt (2000–2001)* .... Lamya Jezek
**Anthony Ward (2000–2001)* .... John Francis Daley
Lisa Greer (2000–2001) .... Bianca Kajlich
**Kevin Jackson (2000–2001)* .... Antwon Tanner
**Superintendant Marsha Shinn (2000–2001)*
.... Debbi Morgan
**Bob Lick* .... Dwight "Heavy D" Myers
**Jamaal Crenshaw (2000–2002)* ...... Edwin Hodge
Ronnie Cooke (2001–) .... Jeri Ryan
Danny Hanson (2001–) .... Michael Rapaport
Meredith Peters (2001–2002) .... Kathy Baker
Jeremy Peters (2001–2002) .... Kaj-Erik Eriksen
Brooke Harper (2001–) ... China Jesusita Shavers
Tina Knowels (2001) .... Alexondra Lee
Jenna Miller (2001) .... Gina Philips
**Mrs. Parks (2001–2002)* .... Cleo King
**Dr. Benjamin Harris (2001–2002)* ..... Leslie Jordan
Debbie Nixon (2001–2002) .... Tamara Bass
Zach Fischer (2002–) .... Jon Abrahams
Colin Flynn (2002–) .... Joey McIntyre
Marcie Kendall (2002–) .... Cara DeLizia
Kimberly Woods (2002–2003) . Michelle Monaghan
**Cheyenne (2002–2003)* .... Indigo
Claire Ellison (2003–) .... Missy Yager
Aisha Clemens (2003–) .... Tamyra Gray
Dave Fields (2003–) .... David Conrad
**Becky Emerson (2003–)* .... Courtney Peldon
Allison (2003–) .... Lyrica Woodruff
**Joannie Hanson (2003–)* .... Kate Norby

*Occasional

Steven Harper was the dedicated principal of Winslow High School in an inner-city section of Boston in this school-drama-*cum*-soap-opera. A big, physically imposing man, Steven tried to do what was best for the students and faculty at Winslow and, although he usually kept it under control, his temper did, on occasion, get the better of him. It was Steven's calming influence that kept vice principal Scott, a stern disciplinarian despised by most of the students, from turning Winslow into a detention center. Others on the faculty were Lauren, the attractive head of the social studies department; Milton, the nerdy English teacher who was frequently the butt of student jokes; Harry, an eccentric geology teacher stuck in "the dungeon" with the most disruptive kids at Winslow (he sometimes packed a gun to class); well-meaning Harvey, the elderly American history teacher whose racist attitudes kept slipping out; hefty Marla, the emotionally fragile special education teacher who was recovering from a partial nervous breakdown; Marylin, the beautiful music teacher; Louisa, Steven's secretary, and Kevin, the intense young football coach. Seen occasionally was Bob, the guidance counselor.

In November Milton fell madly in love with Lisa, a senior he thought was a sophomore at Harvard. After he found out she was a student at Winslow, they continued to have sex at his apartment despite warnings from his friend Kevin to break it off. In February Lisa's father caught her and Milton in the act and told Steven and Scott, who asked Milton to resign. When Kevin told Scott he had been trying to get Milton to break off the affair, Scott fired him for not notifying him. Steven subsequently found out that Lisa had been teaching her English class for months (the teacher had decided she knew more about Shakespeare than he did and stopped showing up). In May Lauren had a torrid affair with a young man who had been her student four years earlier, but quit when she realized he was obsessed with her; after he stalked her, she threatened him with a gun. When Steven found out, he suspended her for two months. At the end of the season it was revealed that bright Jeremy Peters, after suffering emotional abuse at the hands of his mother, Meredith, had handcuffed her in the basement of their house.

That fall two new English teachers joined the Winslow faculty—Harry's friend Ronnie, a corporate lawyer who gave up a lucrative practice to become a teacher, and opinionated Danny, who immediately started to have problems with Marla. Meredith, who had accidentally cut one of her hands off with a chain saw trying to get out of the handcuffs in her basement, surfaced as a teacher's assistant, and Steven's headstrong daughter, Brooke, enrolled at Winslow after she was kicked out of the private school she had been attending. As the holidays approached, Steven and his ex-wife, Luanna (Lynn Whitfield), considered getting back together, but didn't, while Scott was trying to come to terms with his developing relationship with Meredith, made more complicated when he realized her son, Jeremy, was gay. Things fell apart when Scott didn't believe her denial that she had struck a student and fired her—she left her prosthetic arm with him and stalked out in a huff.

One of the great ironies occurred in April when Harvey was visited by Aaron Lipshultz (Troy Winbush), a 58-year-old black man who turned out to be his son. Harvey had had a one-night stand with Aaron's mother the night before he went off to war. At the end of the month Ronnie told Harry she cared about him but that he was afraid of letting anyone get too close to him. As the prom approached, a very nervous Scott asked Lauren to go with him but he was so anxiety-ridden that, when she accepted, he fainted. Despite his embarrassment, they went together and had a great time. Harry was stabbed by the older brother of one of his students after failing to convince him to turn himself in for killing a store clerk during a robbery; while he was recovering, Ronnie told him she loved him.

Three new teachers joined the Winslow staff in the fall of 2002—Colin, a popular English literature teacher who identified with his students; Zach, a science teacher who had graduated from Winslow a few years earlier; and Kimberly, an idealistic social studies teacher hired to replace Lauren, whose departure was not explained. Louisa was also gone, and Marcie took over part of her job as Steven's student aide. Kimberly's tenure was short—after the first of the year Steven had her transferred to a school out of state to protect her from a psychotic student stalker. The relationship between Danny and Marla, who had never gotten along, got worse after he filed a grievance with the union accusing her of being a racist (she was black). Although Harry recovered from his stab wounds, he was constantly depressed, and after Ronnie broke up with him, he had a nervous breakdown and went to Florida on an unapproved medical leave. Steven convinced Ronnie, who was dating much younger Zach, to take over Harry's misfit class in the dungeon.

After the first of the year Marcie admitted she was two months' pregnant and Scott, surprisingly, fought to keep her in school. Danny started dating Claire, an investment banker friend of Ronnie's, despite believing she was "out of his league," while Colin had an ill-fated affair with the mother of one of his students. Dave Fields, an investigator for the mayor's office, showed up in the spring. He convinced Steven to promote Ronnie, to whom he was attracted, to assistant principal and have her develop a program to improve Winslow's dismal performance on citywide standardized tests—which would help with funding for the school. Her success and the subsequent publicity did not sit well with Scott, who believed she was out to get him, or with Zach, who was jealous of Dave. Despite Dave's promises, the city's financial crisis threatened Winslow with draconian budget cuts, and Scott's radical solution—supported by Steven—was to drop all athletic programs (unless the city or the parents of the affected students were willing to fund them) and save academic programs and teachers' jobs. Danny, who had grown attached to his niece Allison, living with him because her mother was a drug addict, wanted to adopt the little girl. At the end of the season finale he and Claire, who both loved her, entered a judge's chambers to be married.

BOTH SIDES (*Debate*)

FIRST TELECAST: *March 15, 1953*
LAST TELECAST: *June 21, 1953*
BROADCAST HISTORY:

Mar 1953–Jun 1953, ABC Sun 10:30–11:00

MODERATOR:

Quincy Howe

This public-affairs debate was sponsored by the American Federation of Labor. Prominent politicians, organized into opposing teams of two members each (the debater and his "counsel"), engaged in lively verbal jousting on a major issue of the day. On the first telecast Sen. Hubert Humphrey (D—Minn.) and Sen. Homer Ferguson (R—Mich.) practically tore each other apart.

BOTH SIDES WITH JESSE JACKSON (*Discussion*)

BROADCAST HISTORY:
CNN
30 minutes
Produced: *1992–2001*
Premiered: *January 4, 1992*

HOST:
Reverend Jesse Jackson

A weekly discussion program addressing current social and political issues, hosted by onetime presidential candidate Jesse Jackson. Originally seen on Saturday nights, it later moved to weekend afternoons and lasted until Jackson became mired in a paternity scandal in 2001.

BOUNTY HUNTERS (*Reality*)

BROADCAST HISTORY:
Syndicated only
60 minutes
Produced: *1996–1998* (50 episodes)
Released: *September 1996*

THEME:
"You Can Run But You Can't Hide," written by Wayne Hubbard and Nick Richards, performed by Boys Don't Cry

They looked like bikers, with their beefy physiques, black T-shirts, and ponytails, and they weren't cops, but they could break down doors—legally. Similar in style to *Cops*, *Bounty Hunters* used a cinema verité style and on-location coverage of real bounty hunters in search of their prey. An 1873 federal law gave them the power to enter residences and cross state lines in search of bail jumpers. The bounty hunters' motto was "You can run but you can't hide." The show followed bounty hunters who talked to the camera crew about the fugitives they were after and the techniques they used to capture them. They were shown working with local cops on stakeouts, and breaking into places where the people they were after were hiding. One of the featured bounty hunters—beefy, bearded Dan Cueller—served as technical advisor for the series.

BOURBON STREET BEAT (*Detective Drama*)

FIRST TELECAST: *October 5, 1959*
LAST TELECAST: *September 26, 1960*

BROADCAST HISTORY:
Oct 1959–Sep 1960, ABC Mon 8:30–9:30

CAST:
Cal Calhoun .... Andrew Duggan
Rex Randolph .... Richard Long
Melody Lee Mercer .... Arlene Howell
Kenny Madison .... Van Williams

Bourbon Street Beat was the least successful of the imitation *77 Sunset Strip* detective shows churned out by Warner Bros. for ABC in the late 1950s and early 1960s. It had the requisite team of detectives (Cal and Rex), the aspiring young junior-grade detective (Kenny), the attractive female (Melody), and was set in an interesting locale (New Orleans), but somehow it just never caught on. The only casualty from its passing, however, was senior partner Cal Calhoun. Rex Randolph moved to Los Angeles and joined the detectives at *77 Sunset Strip* and Kenny Madison moved to Miami Beach to set up his own agency. He remained in the same time slot in the fall of 1960 as one of the stars of *Surfside Six*.

BOWLING HEADLINERS (*Sports*)

FIRST TELECAST: *January 2, 1949*
LAST TELECAST: *October 30, 1949*

BROADCAST HISTORY:
Jan 1949–Apr 1949, ABC Sun 10:00–10:30
May 1949–Jun 1949, ABC Sun 10:15–11:00
Jul 1949–Oct 1949, ABC Sun 10:30–11:00 (OS)
Oct 1949, ABC Sun 11:00–12:00

ANNOUNCERS:
Al Cirillo
Jimmy Powers
Joe Hasel

This show, broadcast live from the Rego Park Lanes in Queens, New York, has the distinction of being television's first regularly scheduled bowling show. Each week two nationally known professional bowlers competed in matches of a round-robin elimination tournament. There was prize money, but it was minimal by today's standards, since bowling in the late 1940s was still a sport with limited appeal that was trying to change its lower-middle-class image. It was during this period, as a matter of fact, that the first major effort to change bowling terminology was launched to give it universal appeal; "lanes" was substituted for "alleys," "channel ball" for "gutter ball," and so on.

Al Cirillo, who produced the show, was the announcer throughout its run, assisted by sportswriter Jimmy Powers until the middle of March, and by Joe Hasel thereafter. For a two-month period, from mid-July until mid-September, when the heat in an un-air-conditioned bowling establishment became unbearable, the show took a summer break.

BOWLING STARS, see *National Bowling Champions*

BOXING (*Sports*)

FIRST TELECAST: *November 8, 1946*
LAST TELECAST: *September 11, 1964*

BROADCAST HISTORY:
Monday—
Nov 1946–May 1949, NBC 9:00–Conclusion
Mar 1949–May 1949, DUM 10:00–Conclusion
May 1952–Aug 1956, DUM 9:00–Conclusion
May 1954–May 1955, ABC 9:30–11:00
Tuesday—
July 1948–Jan 1949, DUM 9:00–11:00
Jan 1949–Sep 1950, ABC 10:00–Conclusion
Apr 1949–May 1949, DUM 9:30–Conclusion
Feb 1953–Aug 1953, ABC 9:00–10:00
Wednesday—
Jul 1948–Jan 1949, DUM 9:00–11:00
Jun 1949–Aug 1949, DUM 9:30–Conclusion
Oct 1948–May 1949, CBS 9:00–Conclusion
Oct 1949–May 1950, CBS 9:30–Conclusion
Sep 1950–May 1955, CBS 10:00–Conclusion
Jun 1955–Sep 1960, ABC 10:00–Conclusion
Thursday—
Aug 1949–Sep 1950, DUM 9:30–Conclusion
Jan 1952–Jun 1952, ABC 9:30–10:00
Mar 1953–Jun 1953, ABC 9:00–10:00
Friday—
Nov 1946–Jan 1949, NBC 9:30–Conclusion

Jan 1949–May 1949, NBC 10:00–Conclusion
Sep 1949–Jun 1960, NBC 10:00–Conclusion (OS)
Sep 1949–Jul 1950, DUM 10:00–Conclusion
Oct 1963–Sep 1964, ABC 10:00–Conclusion
Saturday—
Jan 1953–Jan 1955, ABC 9:00–Conclusion
Oct 1960–Sep 1963, ABC 10:00–Conclusion

Boxing was an institution in early television for several reasons. It was easy to produce, the camera-coverage area was limited to the relatively small space occupied by the ring, and it had tremendous appeal to the first purchasers of television sets in the late 1940s—bars. Even a TV with a ten-inch screen could become a magnet to sports-minded drinkers. All the great names of the era—Sugar Ray Robinson, Rocky Marciano, Willie Pep, Rocky Graziano, and Archie Moore—appeared on the screen, as well as multitudes of lesser-known boxers who would probably not have had careers if it were not for the voracious appetite of television. Unlike today, when the main interest is in the heavyweight class, boxers in all weight divisions had strong fan appeal when television was new.

There were periods in the late 1940s and early 1950s when it was common to have as many as five or six network boxing shows on during the same week, not to mention the local shows that were also available. Those who complain about the saturation of football on television today need only look at the boxing picture in the early 1950s to see what *real* saturation was. A summary of the boxing shows carried by each network follows.

NBC was the first network to carry televised boxing. *Cavalcade of Sports* began on local TV in the mid-1940s and added network coverage in 1946, with Bob Stanton at the TV mike from St. Nicholas Arena in Manhattan on Mondays and from Madison Square Garden on Fridays. The Friday telecasts, which became the *Gillette Cavalcade of Sports* in 1948, ran for 14 years, by far the longest continuous run of any televised boxing show. When Stanton, who worked with Ray Forrest for part of the 1948–1949 season, left the series in 1949, he was replaced by Jimmy Powers. Powers remained the principal NBC announcer until the show went off the air in 1960. In its later years, the *Gillette Cavalcade of Sports* traveled all over the country to cover top bouts, and other announcers occasionally substituted for Powers.

CBS' boxing coverage was aired exclusively on Wednesday nights. Russ Hodges was the first CBS announcer for bouts originating from White Plains, New York, and St. Nicholas Arena. The series was given the title *International Boxing Club Bouts* in the fall of 1949, not long before Hodges left to be replaced by Ted Husing in March of 1950. Husing remained for roughly 16 months; Hodges returned in the summer of 1951, when the title was changed to *Blue Ribbon Bouts*; and Jack Drees arrived in 1954. Drees and Hodges shared announcing duties during that last CBS year and both stayed with the show when ABC took it over in June of 1955. As was true on NBC, coverage was extended beyond the New York area in the early 1950s, to locations where the most promotable fights were being staged.

DuMont's programming was heavy with both boxing and wrestling in the late 1940s and early 1950s. With its limited finances, inexpensive programming that had a ready audience was something that DuMont could not resist. Dennis James was DuMont's sports announcer for boxing and wrestling. The DuMont boxing shows, however, could not afford traveling to locations where there were no DuMont stations, so most of them originated from the New York area. Dennis James covered bouts from Jamaica Arena, Queens, on Mondays, from Park Arena on Tuesdays, from White Plains, New York, on Wednesdays, and from Sunnyside Gardens and Dexter Arena on Thursdays. The longest-running DuMont boxing show, however, did not have James at the helm. Ted Husing was the announcer when *Boxing from Eastern Parkway* (Brooklyn) went on the air in May of 1952. He left in March of 1953 and was replaced by young Chris Schenkel. When ABC picked up the show in May of 1954, DuMont and Schenkel moved shop to St. Nicholas Arena where they stayed until DuMont went out of the network business in 1956. *Boxing from St. Nicholas Arena* was the last DuMont network series, its last network telecast coming on August 6, 1956, though it remained on as a local program in New York for another two months.

ABC's first major entry into the boxing wars came with *Tomorrow's Boxing Champions*, a show featuring young, unranked boxers that was aired on Tuesday nights in 1949. It originated from Chicago, with Bob Elson at the mike. January of 1952 brought *Meet the Champ*, a collection of bouts involving members of the armed forces, on Thursday nights, with Wally Butterfield announcing. In 1953 ABC's boxing coverage really expanded. In January *The Saturday Night Fights* premiered with Bill Stern doing the blow-by-blow; Jack Gregson took over from Stern in the fall. In February a series of *Boxing from Ridgewood Grove* bouts began on Tuesdays, with Jason Owen as the announcer in the first month and Bob Finnegan taking over until its cancellation in August. March brought *Motor City Boxing* from Detroit for three months of Thursdays, with Don Wattrick at the mike. In 1954 *Boxing from Eastern Parkway* moved to ABC from DuMont, with the announcing chores taken over by Tommy Logran, occasionally helped by Bob Finnegan and Fred Sayles. ABC also picked up the CBS *Blue Ribbon Bouts* when it was canceled and renamed it *The Wednesday Night Fights*. Russ Hodges and Jack Drees both stayed with the show, but Hodges left in October and Drees was the only regular announcer for the five years it stayed on ABC. When it moved to Saturday, and eventually Friday, the title was again changed, this time to *The Fight of the Week*. Don Dunphy, released from NBC radio with the cancellation of the *Cavalcade of Sports* show on Fridays, took over the television commentary in the fall of 1960 and remained with it until it faded in September of 1964, the last regular nighttime network boxing series on a broadcast network. In later years boxing found a home on cable, with numerous pay-per-view fights, irregularly scheduled bouts on HBO and other premium channels, and the long-running series *Tuesday Night Fights* on USA Network, which aired from 1981 to 1998. *Toughman Boxing,* on which out-of-shape guys who looked like they were more at home in bars than in the ring, premiered on FX in July 1999 and ran for three years.

BOY MEETS WORLD (*Situation Comedy*)
FIRST TELECAST: *September 24, 1993*
LAST TELECAST: *September 8, 2000*

BROADCAST HISTORY:

Sep 1993–Mar 1995, ABC Fri 8:30–9:00
May 1995–Sep 1996, ABC Fri 8:30–9:00
Sep 1996–Oct 1996, ABC Fri 9:30–10:00
Oct 1996–May 1998, ABC Fri 8:30–9:00
Sep 1997, ABC Fri 9:30–10:00
Apr 1998–May 1998, ABC Fri 9:30–10:00
May 1998–Sep 1998, ABC Fri 9:00–9:30
Sep 1998–Jul 1999, ABC Fri 8:30–9:00
Jul 1999–Sep 1999, ABC Fri 9:30–10:00
Sep 1999–Oct 1999, ABC Fri 8:30–9:00
Oct 1999–May 2000, ABC Fri 8:00–8:30
Jun 2000–Sep 2000, ABC Fri 8:30–9:00

CAST:

Cory Matthews (age 11) .... Ben Savage
Alan Matthews .... William "Rusty" Russ
Amy Matthews....................... Betsy Randle
Eric Matthews .... Will Friedle
Morgan Matthews (1993–1995) .... Lily Nicksay
Morgan Matthews (1995–2000) . Lindsay Ridgeway
Shawn Hunter .... Rider Strong
George Feeny.................... William Daniels
Stuart Lempke/Minkus (1993–1994) .... Lee Norris
Topanga Lawrence................ Danielle Fishel
Jonathan Turner (1994–1997) Anthony Tyler Quinn
**Harley Kiner (1994–1998)* .... Danny McNulty
**Joey (1994–1998)* .... Blake Soper
**Frankie (1994–1998)*................ Ethan Suplee
Eli Williams (1996).................... Alex Désert
**Chet Hunter (1996–1999)* .... Blake Clark
Jack Newman (1997–2000)..... Matthew Lawrence
Angela (1997–2000) .... Trina McGee-Davis
Rachel McGuire (1998–2000)....... Maitland Ward

*Occasional

Life through the eyes of an 11-year-old starring Ben Savage, younger brother of Fred Savage of *The Wonder Years,* and loosely modeled on that hit series. Cory was an inquisitive, brash junior high student beset with the problems of the tween years. Where to turn for advice? His mom (Amy) and blue-collar dad (Alan) were solicitous, but they were grown-ups. Supercool older brother Eric ignored him. Cute little sis Morgan had plenty of opinions but was too young to know anything. So Cory and his best pal, Shawn, explored life's mysteries on their own. The number-one mystery was demanding, acerbic teacher Mr. Feeny, who either hated Cory or liked him—it was hard to tell. Feeny lived next door to the Matthews, so Cory got to see a lot of him. Topanga was the girl of Cory's dreams and Stuart a bookish friend.

In 1994 Cory and Shawn entered John Adams High School, and there to greet them was Mr. Feeny, the new acting principal! Their new homeroom/English teacher was cool Mr. Turner, who read poetry in class but wore a leather jacket and rode a motorcycle outside. Harley (Cory's new nemesis), Joey, and Frankie were schoolmates, along with a host of others who were occasionally seen in the school corridors and hanging out at Chubbie's Malt Shoppe.

The relationship between Cory and Topanga grew over time, from puppy love to hesitant dating, breakups, and reconciliations. Finally, on their graduation day in 1998, Topanga proposed! Cory wavered, but by the fall they had become engaged. Meanwhile, Cory's best buddy Shawn, the product of a failed marriage, faced some pretty heavy concerns of his own. For a time he lived with Mr. Turner, who was appointed his legal guardian. Then his irresponsible, truck-driver father Chet showed up, and Shawn lived with him for a season.

In the fall of 1998, Cory and Topanga enrolled in Pennbrook College, the same college that Cory's older brother Eric had entered (with great difficulty) the preceding year. For Topanga it was a choice of the heart; she turned down Yale in order to be with Cory. Party-guy Eric was rooming with a studious young man named Jack, who turned out to be Shawn's long-lost half brother. Chet had left town again, so Shawn had moved in with them for a while, sampling college life even though he wasn't officially enrolled. He then moved into a dormitory with his pal Cory. Topanga, meanwhile, roomed with Shawn's new girlfriend, an African-American girl named Angela. The series was widely complimented for never mentioning the interracial aspect of Shawn and Angela's relationship.

The 1998–1999 season brought other changes. With Shawn gone, Eric and Jack needed a new roommate: enter Rachel, a red-haired beauty who kept them both in their places. Feeny retired and moved to Wyoming, but not for long. Returning, he met a pretty dean named Bolander (played by William Daniels's real-life wife, Bonnie Bartlett) and began a relationship of his own. Back at the nearly empty Matthewses' nest, Cory's mom Amy was pregnant with her fourth child.

During the last season Amy gave birth to a boy, Joshua, and Cory and Topanga were married. In the finale the newlyweds moved to New York where Topanga had been offered an internship, while Shawn and Jack joined the Peace Corps. Before they all left, however, Mr. Feeny had once last piece of advice: "Believe in yourselves. Dream. Try. Do good. I love you all. Class dismissed."

BOYS, THE (*Situation Comedy*)

FIRST TELECAST: *August 20, 1993*
LAST TELECAST: *September 17, 1993*
BROADCAST HISTORY:

Aug 1993, CBS Fri 9:00–9:30
Sep 1993, CBS Fri 9:30–10:00

CAST:

Herbert Francis (Bert) Greenblatt .... Ned Beatty
Doug Kirkfield .... Chris Meloni
Molly Rich .... Isabella Hofmann
Doris Greenblatt...................... Doris Roberts
Harlan Cooper........................ John Harkins
Al Kozarian .... Richard Venture

THEME:

"Bethena: A Concert Waltz," by Scott Joplin (1905)

Relationship comedy about a hip young writer who is inexplicably drawn to three grumpy old men and their weekly card game next door. Writer Doug Kirkfield and his girlfriend, Molly, moved from New York to a small town outside of Seattle, Washington, so he could work on his second novel away from the pressures of the big city. Still suffering from writer's block, he was befriended by three eccentric older neighbors who convinced him to join their "boys" club and participate in their weekly gatherings to replace a fourth man who had died. The three were Bert, a loud, antagonistic retired fireman; Harlan, the unmarried owner of a local antique store; and Al, a widower who had worked his entire career at a tar factory and was euphoric when talking about tar. Bert's knowing wife, Doris, who was much friendlier than he was, helped smooth the waters when necessary.

BOYS ARE BACK, THE (*Situation Comedy*)
FIRST TELECAST: *September 11, 1994*
LAST TELECAST: *January 28, 1995*
BROADCAST HISTORY:
Sep 1994, CBS Sun 8:00–8:30
Sep 1994–Nov 1994, CBS Wed 8:00–8:30
Nov 1994–Dec 1994, CBS Wed 8:30–9:00
Jan 1995, CBS Sat 9:00–9:30
CAST:
Fred Hansen.......................... Hal Linden
Jackie Hansen .... Suzanne Pleshette
Rick Hansen .... Kevin Crowley
Mike Hansen .... George Newbern
Judy Hansen .... Bess Meyer
Peter Hansen (age 10) .... Ryan O'Donohue
Sarah Hansen (6) .... Kelsey Mulrooney
Nicky Hansen (5) .... Justin Cooper

Fred and Jackie Hansen had just packed the youngest of their three sons off to college, leaving Fred delighted at the prospect of finally enjoying his recent retirement, while Jackie suffered a little empty-nest syndrome. Their solitude was short-lived. Son Mike, who had just lost his job, moved back home with his wife, Judy, and their three rambunctious kids. Then Rick, a Portland, Oregon, cop, arrived after his wife threw him out of their house. There was a predictable uproar as these three generations tried to live together. Fred, who spent more time at home than any of the other adults in the family, groused about the loss of his peace and quiet; Jackie, who worked as a real estate agent, skirmished with her daughter-in-law; Mike, who was very neurotic, felt pressured to find a job and get his family out of his parents' house; and Rick agonized over the failure of his marriage.

BOYS OF TWILIGHT, THE (*Western*)
FIRST TELECAST: *February 29, 1992*
LAST TELECAST: *March 21, 1992*
BROADCAST HISTORY:
Feb 1992–Mar 1992, CBS Sat 10:00–11:00
CAST:
Sheriff Cody McPherson ...... Richard Farnsworth
Deputy Bill Huntoon............. Wilford Brimley
Deputy Tyler Clare .... Ben Browder
Genelva McPherson .... Louise Fletcher
Mayor Suzanne Troxell .... Amanda McBroom

Cody McPherson and Bill Huntoon had been the peace officers in the scenic, sleepy little mountain town of Twilight, Utah, for generations. Now they were having to adjust to the explosive growth caused by the arrival of jet-setters wanting to make Twilight the latest playground of the rich and famous. Cody was the easygoing, methodical, dignified sheriff and Bill his blustery, impetuous best friend and chief deputy. Newly added to the force was "city-slicker" Tyler Clare, whose efforts to modernize law enforcement in Twilight grated on both of the old-timers. They had to tread lightly, however, since Tyler was the nephew of the town's mayor, Suzanne Troxell. Cody's wife, Genelva, did her best to keep peace among the men, but it was not an easy task.

BOYS WILL BE BOYS, see *Second Chance*

BRACKEN'S WORLD (*Drama*)
FIRST TELECAST: *September 19, 1969*
LAST TELECAST: *December 25, 1970*
BROADCAST HISTORY:
Sep 1969–Dec 1970, NBC Fri 10:00–11:00
CAST:
Sylvia Caldwell (1969–1970)........ Eleanor Parker
Kevin Grant.......................... Peter Haskell
Davey Evans (1969–1970) .... Dennis Cole
Laura Deane...................... Elizabeth Allen
John Bracken (voice only; 1969–1970)
.... Warren Stevens
John Bracken (1970)................ Leslie Nielsen
Diane Waring.................... Laraine Stephens
Rachel Holt.......................... Karen Jensen
Paulette Douglas.................. Linda Harrison
Marjorie Grant (1969–1970) .... Madlyn Rhue
Tom Hudson (1970)................ Stephen Oliver
Grace Douglas (1970)............... Jeanne Cooper
Mark Grant (1970).................... Gary Dubin

The personal and professional lives of fictitious people in the movie business were the focus of this melodrama. Filmed at 20th Century–Fox, and featuring many real-life movie stars in cameo roles, *Bracken's World* was set at fictional Century Studios. Studio head John Bracken, though never seen, dominated the lives of the principals in the series through his executive secretary, Sylvia Caldwell. Among his many scheming underlings were writer-producer Kevin Grant; Laura Deane, who ran the studio's new-talent school; stuntman Davey Evans; and a number of aspiring young actors and starlets.

Bracken's World was only moderately successful during its first season, and so major surgery was performed at the start of the second. Bracken, now played by Leslie Nielsen, became visible as he struggled to guide the studio through troubled economic times. Gone were his executive secretary, stuntman Evans, and Kevin Grant's alcoholic wife Marjorie—who was killed off in the season's premiere episode. The series itself outlived her by only three months.

BRADY BRIDES, THE (*Situation Comedy*)
FIRST TELECAST: *February 6, 1981*
LAST TELECAST: *April 17, 1981*
BROADCAST HISTORY:
Feb 1981–Apr 1981, NBC Fri 8:30–9:00
CAST:
Marcia Brady Logan .... Maureen McCormick
Jan Brady Covington .... Eve Plumb
Wally Logan.......................... Jerry Houser
Philip Covington III .... Ron Kuhlman
Alice Nelson .... Ann B. Davis
Harry .... Keland Love
Carol Brady .... Florence Henderson

In this spin-off from the successful ABC comedy of the early 1970s, *The Brady Bunch,* the two older Brady girls, Marcia and Jan, got married. They then began house-hunting with the help of their mother, Carol, who became a real estate agent after the kids had grown up. But Los Angeles was an expensive place to live, and the only solution seemed to be to set up housekeeping together in a big old house that they had all fallen in love with. This created some problems, as their lifestyles were rather different—Marcia and her toy-salesman husband Wally were much less traditional than Jan and her college-instructor husband Philip. There were also the little strains of new marriage. Helping work things out, as in the old days, was Alice, their former housekeeper, who lived nearby. Harry was a kid from the slums who had been befriended by Wally.

BRADY BUNCH, THE (*Situation Comedy*)
FIRST TELECAST: *September 26, 1969*
LAST TELECAST: *August 30, 1974*
BROADCAST HISTORY:
Sep 1969–Sep 1970, ABC Fri 8:00–8:30
Sep 1970–Sep 1971, ABC Fri 7:30–8:00
Sep 1971–Aug 1974, ABC Fri 8:00–8:30
CAST:
Mike Brady .... Robert Reed
Carol Brady .... Florence Henderson
Alice Nelson .... Ann B. Davis
Marcia Brady .... Maureen McCormick
Jan Brady .... Eve Plumb
Cindy Brady .... Susan Olsen
Greg Brady .... Barry Williams
Peter Brady .... Christopher Knight
Bobby Brady .... Mike Lookinland

The Brady Bunch was one of the last of the old-style fun-around-the-house situation comedies, full of well-scrubbed children, trivial adventures, and relentlessly middle-class parents. The premise here was a kind of conglomerate family, formed by a widow with three daughters who married a widower with three sons; a nutty housekeeper, Alice, thrown in to act as referee; plus, of course, a shaggy dog, Tiger.

All of these smiling faces lived in a four-bedroom, two-bathroom house in the Los Angeles suburbs, from which Dad pursued his nice, clean profession as a designer and architect. Typical stories revolved around the children going steady, family camping trips, competition for the family telephone (at one point Dad installed a pay phone), and of course war in the bathroom.

The children ranged in age from 7 to 14 at the series' start, and the oldest son, Greg, played by Barry Williams, soon became something of a teenage idol; he was receiving 6,500 fan letters per week during 1971. Barry and several of the others tried to parlay their TV success into recording careers in the early 1970s, but without notable success.

Reruns of *The Brady Bunch* were aired as part of ABC's weekday daytime lineup from July 1973 to August 1975, and an animated spin-off titled *The Brady Kids* ran Saturday mornings on ABC from September 1972 to August 1974.

BRADY BUNCH HOUR, THE (*Comedy/Variety*)
FIRST TELECAST: *January 23, 1977*
LAST TELECAST: *May 25, 1977*
BROADCAST HISTORY:
Jan 1977–Feb 1977, ABC Sun 7:00–8:00
Mar 1977–Apr 1977, ABC Mon 8:00–9:00
May 1977, ABC Wed 8:00–9:00
CAST:
Carol Brady .... Florence Henderson
Mike Brady .... Robert Reed
Alice .... Ann B. Davis
Marcia Brady .... Maureen McCormick
Jan Brady .... Geri Reischl
Cindy Brady .... Susan Olsen
Greg Brady .... Barry Williams
Peter Brady .... Christopher Knight
Bobby Brady .... Mike Lookinland

This was an attempt to revive the *Brady Bunch* comedy of the early 1970s, in an hour-long format. The original cast returned intact except for Eve Plumb, who was replaced by Geri Reischl as Jan. The format now contained more variety than situation comedy, as father Mike had given up his career as an architect so that the family could star in their own TV variety show. The setting also changed, to a new beachfront home in California, and a group called the Water Follies Swimmers made regular appearances.

Originally scheduled to be seen only every fifth week in the *Nancy Drew/Hardy Boys Mysteries* time slot on Sunday, *The Brady Bunch Hour* later turned up in various ABC time periods on different nights.

BRADYS, THE (*Drama*)
FIRST TELECAST: *February 9, 1990*
LAST TELECAST: *March 9, 1990*
BROADCAST HISTORY:
Feb 1990–Mar 1990, CBS Fri 8:00–9:00
CAST:
Carol Brady .... Florence Henderson
Mike Brady .... Robert Reed
Marcia Brady Logan .... Leah Ayres
Jan Brady Covington .... Eve Plumb
Cindy Brady .... Susan Olsen
Greg Brady .... Barry Williams
Peter Brady .... Christopher Knight
Bobby Brady .... Michael Lookinland
Alice Nelson .... Ann B. Davis
Wally Logan .... Jerry Houser
Phillip Covington III .... Ron Kuhlman
Jessica Logan .... Jaclyn Bernstein
Mickey Logan .... Michael Melby
Nora Brady .... Caryn Richman
Tracy Brady .... Martha Quinn
Gary Greenberg .... Ken Michelman
Kevin Brady .... Jonathan Weiss
Patty Covington .... Valerie Ick

The Bradys were back again, but this time in a rather bizarre drama laden with the worries of the '90s. Mike had opened his own architectural firm, Carol was now selling real estate, and four of the six kids were married. Jan and her college professor husband Phillip, unable to conceive, had just adopted a young Korean girl (Patty); obstetrician Greg and his wife Nora had one son (Kevin); Marcia and her salesman husband Wally had two children (Jessica and Mickey); disc jockey Cindy had just gotten serious with her older widowed boss, Gary; and businessman Peter was a worried playboy in the age of AIDS. The first crisis the family had to face involved Bobby, a race car driver and newly married to Tracy, who had just been paralyzed from the waist down as the result of an accident. Was this the prototypical happy TV family of the 1970s?

The Bradys was launched in the wake of the success of the 1988 TV movie *A Very Brady Christmas* and was the fourth series starring the "family that won't go away." Despite the presence of almost the entire original cast (Maureen McCormick was the only one missing), the downbeat themes doomed this incarnation to the quickest cancellation yet.

BRAINS & BRAWN (*Quiz/Audience Participation*)
FIRST TELECAST: *September 13, 1958*
LAST TELECAST: *December 27, 1958*

BROADCAST HISTORY:

Sep 1958–Dec 1958, NBC Sat 10:30–11:00

EMCEE:

Jack Lescoulie ("brawn")
Fred Davis ("brains")

Each team on this unusual show consisted of an athlete (the "brawn") and someone with high intellectual skills (the "brains"). The teams were determined by lot before the show went on the air. Two such teams were then pitted against each other, the "brawn" competing in athletic events and the "brains" answering questions. Two emcees handled the two parts of the competition.

BRAK SHOW, THE (*Cartoon*)

BROADCAST HISTORY:

Cartoon Network
30 minutes
Original episodes: *2001–*
Premiered: *September 2, 2001*

VOICES:

Brak .... Andy Merrill
Zorak .... C. Martin Croker
Mom (2001–2002) .... Marsha Crenshaw
Mom (2002–) .... Joanna Daniel
Dad .... George Lowe
Thundercleese .... Carey Means

Brak was a diminutive and rather vicious-looking space monster with narrow eyes and sharp teeth who was Space Ghost's studio sidekick on the mock talk show *Space Ghost: Coast to Coast*. This cartoon looked back at Brak's idyllic youth, growing up with his human mom and dad in a nice suburban house somewhere in space. Brak was as dumb and whiny as ever, while Mom was a pleasant homemaker and Dad a suave Latin with slick hair and a mustache. Causing trouble were best friend Zorak, a foulmouthed destructive mantis, and neighbor Thundercleese, a giant armed robot usually seen tending his lawn. The stories were typical little-kid adventures at home and school, in sharp contrast with the frightening appearance of most of the principals.

BRAM AND ALICE (*Situation Comedy*)

FIRST TELECAST: *October 6, 2002*
LAST TELECAST: *October 27, 2002*
BROADCAST HISTORY:

Oct 2002, CBS Sun 8:30–9:00

CAST:

Bram Shepherd .... Alfred Molina
Alice O'Connor .... Traylor Howard
Paul Newman .... Roger Bart
Katie Hoover .... Katie Finneran
Michael .... Michael Rispoli

Bram was a blustery, conniving author whose only successful novel, the Pulitzer Prize–winning *Matthew Kent*, had been published more than twenty years earlier. Despite his subsequent lack of productivity, Bram lived off his reputation and the continuing sales of *Kent*, which was still required reading at many colleges, and milked his publisher for money to live in a huge, book-filled Dickensian apartment in Manhattan. Then one day a perky aspiring writer named Alice showed up at his door and informed him that she was his daughter. Her mother had had a one-night stand with Bram when he was a guest lecturer at Vassar. Despite their mutual wariness—he was concerned that she would cramp his style, and she detested his drinking and womanizing—Alice moved into the apartment and they attempted to establish a functional father-daughter relationship. Paul was the earnest young assistant who tried to organize Bram's life and keep him from getting into too much trouble. Also seen were obnoxious Katie, one of Bram's neighbors, and Michael, a former priest who was the bartender in the lounge on the ground floor of Bram's apartment building.

The critics hated *Bram and Alice* and, apparently, so did the television audience. After four low-rated telecasts CBS pulled the plug.

BRAND NEW LIFE, A, see *Walt Disney*

BRANDED (*Western*)

FIRST TELECAST: *January 24, 1965*
LAST TELECAST: *September 4, 1966*
BROADCAST HISTORY:

Jan 1965–Sep 1966, NBC Sun 8:30–9:00 (OS)

CAST:

Jason McCord .... Chuck Connors

Set in America in the 1880s, this series told the story of Jason McCord, who had had a successful military career following his graduation from West Point. He had risen to the rank of captain before he was dismissed from the service after being unjustly accused of cowardice. McCord traveled around the country in his attempt to gain proof that he was not a coward. In his travels he encountered people who believed in him and others who accepted his cowardice as fact. His previous experience as an engineer and mapmaker also led him into assorted adventures.

BRAVE EAGLE (*Western*)

FIRST TELECAST: *September 28, 1955*
LAST TELECAST: *June 6, 1956*
BROADCAST HISTORY:

Sep 1955–Jun 1956, CBS Wed 7:30–8:00

CAST:

Brave Eagle .... Keith Larsen
Keena .... Keena Nomkeena
Morning Star .... Kim Winona
Smokey Joe .... Bert Wheeler

In a turnabout from the normal pattern of TV Westerns, *Brave Eagle* presented the white man's expansion into the American Southwest during the middle of the 19th century from the Indian point of view. Brave Eagle was the young chief of a peaceful tribe of Cheyenne, Keena was his foster son, Morning Star was the attractive young Indian girl in whom he showed some romantic interest, and Smokey Joe was an old half-breed who was the tribal sage. Stories told in the series detailed their struggles with nature, other Indian tribes, and the ever-encroaching white man.

BRAVEST, THE (*Documentary*)

BROADCAST HISTORY:

Syndicated only
60 minutes
Produced: *2001–2002* (22 episodes)
Released: *September 2001*

Filmed in the same cinema verité style as *Cops*, this series chronicled the working lives of firefighters around the country. Not only did it cover fires, rescues and other emergencies, but it also showed what life was like in firehouses during the rest of the working day—eating, sleeping, training, and killing time. The film crews spent long days with the firemen; when they were on a call, the pace was often frenetic. In promotional ads for *The Bravest* the producers said, "You'll feel the heat of the action and the bond between firefighters that stems from sharing moments of fear, life and death . . . as these heroes risk their own lives to save the lives of strangers."

In the first episode a New York brownstone went up in flames; a 600-pound man trapped in his house had a heart attack; firefighters put out a blaze that jeopardized a block of connecting homes; firefighters thought they had put out a house fire only to find that it was still active in the walls; a fire department was called to check out potentially hazardous material; and the fire department rescued a fugitive stuck on a roof.

The Bravest premiered less than two weeks after more then 300 firefighters lost their lives in the aftermath of the terrorist attack that destroyed New York's World Trade Center.

BRAVO (Network) (*Cultural Cable Network*)

LAUNCHED:

December 7, 1980

SUBSCRIBERS (MAY 2003):

70.9 million (66% U.S.)

Bravo was for years a small, struggling cultural channel that survived several industry shakeouts and gained a foothold in the cable world. Unlike A&E, which wooed a wider audience with reruns of such popular fare as *Columbo* and *The Rockford Files*, Bravo stuck to fairly narrow interest programming. Tony foreign and domestic movies made up much of the schedule (e.g., *The Great Gatsby, Monsieur Hire*), along with reruns of prestigious mini-series (*Brideshead Revisited; I, Claudius*), network series (*Brooklyn Bridge*), and occasional concerts. Among its signature series have been *The Lenny Henry Show* and *The South Bank Show*, both produced by British television. Original series have included *Inside the Actor's Studio* (1995), hosted by James Lipton, *Bravo Profiles* (performer biographies, 1997), *The Awful Truth* (1999) with muckraking filmmaker Michael Moore, *Louis Theroux's Weird Weekends* (1999) and *Breaking News* (2002), a drama made for TNT but aired on Bravo instead.

BREAK THE BANK (*Quiz*)

FIRST TELECAST: *October 22, 1948*

LAST TELECAST: *January 15, 1957*

BROADCAST HISTORY:

Oct 1948–Sep 1949, ABC Fri 9:00–9:30
Oct 1949–Jan 1952, NBC Wed 10:00–10:30
Jan 1952–Feb 1953, CBS Sun 9:30–10:00
Jun 1953–Sep 1953, NBC Tue 8:30–9:00
Jan 1954–Oct 1955, ABC Sun 10:00–10:30
Oct 1955–Jun 1956, ABC Wed 9:30–10:00
Oct 1956–Jan 1957, NBC Tue 10:30–11:00

HOST:

Bert Parks

CO-HOST:

Bud Collyer (1948–1953)

PAYING TELLER:

Janice Gilbert

MUSIC:

Peter Van Steeden Orchestra
The Song Spinners

This popular quiz show began on radio in 1945 and started television simulcasts in 1948. Bert Parks, who had begun as one of *Break the Bank*'s several radio hosts in 1945, when he was fresh out of the army, was closely associated with the program throughout its television run.

Break the Bank was always considered a big-money show, with cash prizes sometimes running over $10,000 even in the early days. The questions were tough, too. Contestants, who were drawn from the studio audience, chose a category and were asked a series of questions in that category for increasing amounts of money. If successful, they eventually had a chance to "break the bank," which was usually worth thousands of dollars (depending on how long it was since it had last been "broken").

A number of gimmicks were added to the show from time to time, including guest celebrities during the early years, and a "Wish Bowl Couple." These were viewers chosen by postcard drawing who won an expense-paid trip to New York to compete on the show.

In October 1956 *Break the Bank* jumped on the super-money bandwagon and was renamed *Break the $250,000 Bank*. Instead of studio contestants, "experts" were brought in to answer complex questions worth thousands of dollars. They did this while standing in a specially designed "Hall of Knowledge" and could sometimes be assisted by members of their families seated to the side of the stage. Among the unusual contestants during this period were two Hungarian refugees just arrived in the United States (their category was "Fight for Freedom") and the veteran actress-singer Ethel Waters, who said she needed the money to pay off back taxes (she won $10,000). No one ever reached $250,000 during the program's brief run.

Efforts to launch other versions of this old warhorse have been notably unsuccessful. Bud Collyer hosted an NBC daytime version that ran from March to September 1953, while Tom Kennedy gamely tried a revival on ABC from April to July 1976. There was also a syndicated version hosted by Jack Barry in 1976 and another hosted by Gene Rayburn for the 1985–1986 season.

BREAKING AWAY (*Situation Comedy*)

FIRST TELECAST: *November 29, 1980*

LAST TELECAST: *July 6, 1981*

BROADCAST HISTORY:

Nov 1980–Jan 1981, ABC Sat 8:00–9:00
Jun 1981–Jul 1981, ABC Mon 8:00–9:00

CAST:

Dave Stohler . . . . Shaun Cassidy
Ray Stohler . . . . Vincent Gardenia
Evelyn Stohler . . . . Barbara Barrie
Moocher . . . . Jackie Earle Haley
Cyril . . . . Thom Bray
Mike . . . . Tom Wiggin
Roy . . . . John Ashton

Breaking Away was another example of the fact that hit movies do not necessarily make hit TV series. The setting was the college town of Bloomington, Indiana, where four high school buddies spent their time playing pranks on the lordly University of Indiana fraternity men (who disdainfully called them "cutters," after the town's blue-collar stone cutters), dealing with their parents, and just growing up. Dave was the central character, an intelligent, dreamy boy whose great passion was bicycle racing, and whose prized possession was a $1,200 La Strada bike he'd won. His buddies were easygoing Moocher, sardonic Cyril, and aggressive football star Mike. Dave's father was Ray, a stone-cutter-turned-used-car-salesman who wished Dave would settle down to a meat-and-potatoes existence like his own. Evelyn was the mediating mother, and Roy was buddy Mike's brother, a campus cop.

Re-creating their roles from the film *Breaking Away* were Barrie (who had been nominated for an Academy Award), Haley, and Ashton.

BREAKING NEWS (*Newsroom Drama*)

BROADCAST HISTORY:

Bravo
60 minutes
Original episodes: *2002* (13 episodes)
Premiered: *July 17, 2002*

CAST:

Peter Kozyck .... Clancy Brown
Rachel Glass .... Lisa Ann Walter
Bill Dunne .... Tim Matheson
Janet LeClaire .... Myndy Crist
Mel Thomas .... Jeffrey D. Sams
Jamie Templeton .... Rowena King
Ethan Barnes .... Scott Bairstow
Quentin Druzinski .... Vincent Gale
Julian Kerbis .... Paul Adelstein
Jacqui Savard .... Gabrielle Miller

The intensity of modern news gathering was captured in this straightforward drama set at I-24, a 24-hour cable news channel with the motto "Around the Clock, Around the World." Peter was the newly appointed president of the news division, struggling to boost the ratings while maintaining his journalistic integrity (everyone here worried about integrity). Rachel was his savvy, bustling executive producer. Among the on-air talent were loud, idealistic anchorman Bill ("Murrow said . . ."); his insecure, young coanchor Janet, brought in to satisfy the younger viewing demographic and trying hard to prove herself; stylish black reporter Jamie and her white field producer Julian, who were romantically involved; and star reporter Mel, who was having marital troubles. Behind the cameras were young producer Ethan, who happened to be the son of the network president, and eager beaver Quentin. Plane crashes, maniacal hostage takers, sleazy politicians, and overreaching judges (who wanted that tape!) filled their days.

The behind-the-scenes story of *Breaking News* was more interesting than what was on the screen. Modeled on CNN, the show was originally produced for sister network TNT, which got cold feet and canceled it before it even aired—even though 13 expensive episodes had been produced. A year later it was finally picked up by Bravo (which presumably got it cheap), but failed to attract an audience and was not renewed.

BREAKING POINT (*Medical Drama*)

FIRST TELECAST: *September 16, 1963*
LAST TELECAST: *September 7, 1964*
BROADCAST HISTORY:

Sep 1963–Sep 1964, ABC Mon 10:00–11:00

CAST:

Dr. McKinley Thompson .... Paul Richards
Dr. Edward Raymer .... Eduard Franz

McKinley Thompson, called Dr. Mac by almost everyone on the staff, was the chief resident psychiatrist at fictitious York Hospital in Los Angeles. His superior, the director of the hospital's psychiatric clinic, was Dr. Edward Raymer. Running what amounted to an outpatient service for the emotionally distraught, they tried to help the various people who came to the clinic. Their roles in the series were rather peripheral, as the action dealt more with the situations that had caused people to seek their help than with life at the hospital.

BRENNER (*Police Drama*)

FIRST TELECAST: *June 6, 1959*
LAST TELECAST: *September 13, 1964*
BROADCAST HISTORY:

Jun 1959–Oct 1959, CBS Sat 9:00–9:30
Jun 1961–Sep 1961, CBS Mon 10:30–11:00
Jun 1962–Sep 1962, CBS Thu 9:00–9:30
May 1964–Sep 1964, CBS Sun 9:30–10:00

CAST:

Det. Lt. Roy Brenner .... Edward Binns
Officer Ernie Brenner .... James Broderick

Filmed entirely on location in New York, *Brenner* was the story of two generations of police officers learning from each other. Roy Brenner was a career cop who had risen to the rank of detective lieutenant. His son Ernie was a rookie patrolman. The approach of the veteran father, who had been hardened by the experiences of more than 20 years on the force, was often radically different from that of the young, inexperienced, and idealistic son. Nevertheless, their love and respect for each other enabled both of them to grow as individuals and learn from each other. The series was produced in 1959 and selected reruns were aired by CBS in the summers of 1961, 1962, and 1964. In order to freshen the series during its 1964 run, ten new episodes were produced and aired in addition to the original 1959 shows.

BRET MAVERICK (*Western*)

FIRST TELECAST: *December 1, 1981*
LAST TELECAST: *August 3, 1990*
BROADCAST HISTORY:

Dec 1981–Mar 1982, NBC Tue 9:00–10:00
Mar 1982–Jul 1982, NBC Tue 8:00–9:00
Jul 1982–Aug 1982, NBC Tue 9:00–10:00
Jul 1990–Aug 1990, NBC Fri 8:00–9:00

CAST:

Bret Maverick .... James Garner
Tom Guthrie .... Ed Bruce
Philo Sandine .... Stuart Margolin
Mary Lou Springer .... Darleen Carr
Cy Whittaker .... Richard Hamilton
Rodney Catlow .... David Knell
Sheriff Mitchell Dowd .... John Shearin
Elijah Crow .... Ramon Bieri
Jack, the bartender .... Jack Garner
Shifty Delgrado .... Luis Delgado
Deputy Sturgess .... Tommy Bush
Mrs. Springer .... Priscilla Morrill
Kate Hanrahan .... Marj Dusay
Jasmine DuBois (1982) .... Simone Griffeth

More than 20 years after leaving *Maverick*, the TV series that had made him a star, James Garner returned to the role that had launched his career. Set in the town of Sweetwater, in the Arizona Territory, during the late 1880s, this series provided a more mature, less adventuresome Bret Maverick than the one who had wandered from town to town in search of poker games and excitement. The sense of humor and friendliness were still there, but Bret had become a solid citizen and full-time resident of a community trying to shed its untamed rural Western image. He owned a ranch outside Sweetwater and was part owner of the Red Ox Saloon in town. Cranky, irritable Cy Whittaker was the caretaker at the Lazy Ace, Bret's ranch, and former sheriff Tom Guthrie was his partner in the saloon. Guthrie, an old-fashioned lawman, had recently lost the sheriff's election to young, ambitious Mitchell Dowd, who struggled to bring "civilization" to Sweetwater with the marginal help of his stupid deputy, Sturgess. Feisty Mary Lou Springer ran the local newspaper, the *Territorian*, with the help of her mother and young printer's apprentice, Rodney Catlow. Also seen regularly were the local banker, Elijah Crow, who was not above stretching the law to his advantage; Shifty Delgrado, the house dealer at the Red Ox who cheated at cards whenever he thought he could get away with it; and Philo Sandine, a self-styled Indian scout who was more small-time con man than anything else (a role similar to the one Stuart Margolin had played on Garner's previous series, *The Rockford Files*). The actor playing the bartender at the Red Ox was James Garner's brother, Jack.

NBC aired reruns of *Bret Maverick* during the summer of 1990.

BREWSTER PLACE (*Drama*)

FIRST TELECAST: *May 1, 1990*
LAST TELECAST: *July 11, 1990*
BROADCAST HISTORY:
May 1990, ABC Tue 9:30–10:00
May 1990–Jul 1990, ABC Wed 9:30–10:00
CAST:
Mattie Michael .... Oprah Winfrey
Etta Mae Johnson .... Brenda Pressley
Miss Sophie .... Olivia Cole
Jessie.............................. Oscar Brown, Jr.
Kiswana Browne................. Rachael Crawford
Abshu Kamau .... Kelly Neal
Ralph Thomas .... John Cothran, Jr.
Margaret Thomas................ DeLeon Richards
Matthew Thomas.................... Jason Weaver
Miles Thomas .... Steven Crump
Mickey Adriano................. John Speredakos
Mr. Willie .... John Beasley

The heartwarming side of life in a black inner-city tenement in 1967 was portrayed in this "warmedy" starring daytime talk show host Oprah Winfrey. Mattie, a strong-willed, caring woman who had suffered many trials in her life, was the center of activity at Brewster Place. With her best friend Etta Mae, she ran a small neighborhood restaurant called LaScala, where neighbors could partake of both her food and her sensible advice. Miss Sophie was the resident gossip and troublemaker, Jessie was Sophie's husband, and Kiswana and Abshu, a young couple that were dating (more advice!). Ralph was Mattie's widowed cousin, with three children (still more advice!). Mickey was the cook at the restaurant, and Willie the mailman.

Based on the hit 1989 TV movie *The Women of Brewster Place*, which was in turn based on a novel of the same name by Gloria Naylor. Filmed on location in Chicago. Oprah continued to host her hit daytime talkfest during the brief run of this series.

BRIAN BENBEN SHOW, THE (*Situation Comedy*)

FIRST TELECAST: *September 21, 1998*
LAST TELECAST: *October 12, 1998*
BROADCAST HISTORY:
Sep 1998–Oct 1998, CBS Mon 9:30–10:00
CAST:
Brian Benben .... Brian Benben
Beverly Shippel................. Susan Blommaert
Chad Rockwell .... Charles Esten
Kevin La Rue....................... Wendell Pierce
Billy Hernandez .... Luis Antonio Ramos
Tabitha Berkeley .... Lisa Thornhill
Julie Martin............................. Lisa Vidal

A sad-sack newsman was demoted and divorced, but wore a silly grin through it all, in this slapstick sitcom. Brian was co-anchor on the KYLA-TV news in Los Angeles who had been replaced, along with his co-anchor, in favor of two incompetent but attractive young news personalities: Chad (most recently, a VJ on cable's VH1) and Tabitha (who had scored highly in audience testing when males were asked, "Who would you most like to screw?"). Despite having been dumped, Brian returned to the station as the emergency replacement for the human interest reporter who had been mauled and killed covering an ape exhibit at the zoo. He did have his allies at KYLA—Kevin, the sports anchor, and Billy, the weatherman. Beverly, the station manager who had dumped him, was a constant thorn in his side. His friend Julie provided a sympathetic ear and good advice.

BRIAN KEITH SHOW, THE (*Situation Comedy*)

FIRST TELECAST: *September 15, 1972*
LAST TELECAST: *August 30, 1974*
BROADCAST HISTORY:
Sep 1972–Aug 1973, NBC Fri 8:30–9:00
Sep 1973–May 1974, NBC Fri 9:30–10:00
May 1974–Aug 1974, NBC Fri 8:30–9:00
CAST:
Dr. Sean Jamison .... Brian Keith
Dr. Anne Jamison .... Shelley Fabares
Nurse Puni.......................... Victoria Young
Ronnie (1972–1973)................. Michael Gray
Alfred Landis (1972–1973) .... Steven Hague
Stewart............................ Sean Tyler Hall
Dr. Austin Chaffee (1973–1974) ...... Roger Bowen
Mrs. Gruber (1973–1974) .... Nancy Kulp

Titled *The Little People* during its first season, this was a "heartwarming" comedy about two pediatricians, a father and a daughter, who ran a free clinic as well as private practices on the Hawaiian island of Oahu. The concern that the Jamisons had for their "little people" formed the crux of most of the stories. The type of humor was similar to that on *Family Affair*, Mr. Keith's previous hit series. In its second season the situation changed somewhat, as did the title, which became *The Brian Keith Show*. The very proper Dr. Chaffee now shared office space with Sean and found that adjusting to Sean's informality could be rather difficult. Wealthy widow Mrs. Gruber, owner of the free clinic, as well as of much of Hawaii, was added to the cast to help provide problem situations for the easygoing doctor and his attractive and equally competent daughter.

BRIDGES TO CROSS (*Drama*)

FIRST TELECAST: *April 24, 1986*
LAST TELECAST: *June 12, 1986*

BROADCAST HISTORY:

Apr 1986–Jun 1986, CBS Thu 9:00–10:00

CAST:

Tracy Bridges.................. Suzanne Pleshette
Peter Cross....................... Nicolas Surovy
Morris Kane.......................... Jose Ferrer
Maria Talbot.......................... Eva Gabor
Norman Parks................. Roddy McDowall

Fictional *World/Week* magazine, a major news weekly headquartered in Washington, D.C., was the focal point of this romantic drama. Veteran reporter Tracy Bridges's accumulated contacts gave her entree to the movers and shakers in the capital's political and economic circles. One of Tracy's fellow reporters was her former husband, Peter Cross, with whom she continually sparred, romantically and professionally. Keeping *World/Week* on schedule was hard-nosed editor Morris Kane; keeping Tracy on schedule was her efficient male executive secretary, Norman. One of Tracy's closest friends, and an invaluable contact, was Washington socialite Maria Talbot.

This was CBS' second attempt to place Miss Pleshette in a series as a reporter, after they had failed with the comedic approach of *Suzanne Pleshette Is Maggie Briggs* in the spring of 1984.

BRIDGET LOVES BERNIE (*Situation Comedy*)

FIRST TELECAST: *September 16, 1972*
LAST TELECAST: *September 8, 1973*
BROADCAST HISTORY:

Sept 1972–Sep 1973, CBS Sat 8:30–9:00

CAST:

Bernie Steinberg..................... David Birney
Bridget Fitzgerald Steinberg....... Meredith Baxter
Sam Steinberg..................... Harold J. Stone
Sophie Steinberg................. Bibi Osterwald
Amy Fitzgerald.................... Audra Lindley
Walt Fitzgerald...................... David Doyle
Uncle Moe Plotnick.................... Ned Glass
Father Mike Fitzgerald........... Robert Sampson
Otis Foster........................ William Elliott
Charles, the butler...................... Ivor Barry

This show was part of a wave of ethnic comedies in the early 1970s that followed on the success of *All in the Family* and *Sanford and Son*. Bernie was Jewish, a struggling young writer who supplemented his income by driving a cab. Bridget, his young bride, was an elementary school teacher whose parents were wealthy Irish Catholics. The couple shared a small apartment above a New York City delicatessen owned by Bernie's parents. The widely divergent ethnic, cultural, and social backgrounds of the Steinberg and Fitzgerald families, and their attempts to reconcile for the sake of the young couple, provided most of the plot situations. Any resemblance to the vintage Broadway play *Abie's Irish Rose* was hardly coincidental.

Despite reasonably good ratings, *Bridget Loves Bernie* was canceled at the end of its first season. One contributing factor may have been the furor created by the unhappiness of religious groups, primarily Jewish, over the show's condoning and publicizing mixed marriages. An interesting sidelight is that the two stars of the series, David Birney and Meredith Baxter, married each other in real life the year after this series left the air (they were divorced in 1989).

BRIMSTONE (*Supernatural Drama*)

FIRST TELECAST: *October 23, 1998*
LAST TELECAST: *March 12, 1999*
BROADCAST HISTORY:

Oct 1998–Mar 1999, FOX Fri 8:00–9:00

CAST:

Ezekiel Stone........................ Peter Horton
The Devil............................. John Glover
Maxine................................. Lori Petty

A strange, dark drama about the afterlife of a New York City cop. Detective Stone was a highly decorated hero whose wife had been raped; when the rapist beat the rap, he tracked the slimeball down and killed him. Two months later Stone himself was killed in a hail of bullets from a petty thief he had cornered, and, because he had killed a man in cold blood, he went straight to Hell.

Damnation is supposed to be forever, but fifteen years later Stone received an unusual reprieve. One hundred thirteen of the vilest creatures in Hell had escaped to Earth, and the Devil offered Stone a deal if he would track them down and bring them back. If Stone succeeded, he would be transferred into Heaven. When cornered, the escapees fought fiercely, often with fearsome powers; the way he sent them back was to shoot them in their eyes—the windows into their souls. Stone himself could be shot without being killed, and could leap off buildings without injury. He had a tattoo on his body for each quarry, and every time he sent one back, that tattoo disappeared. Periodically the Devil himself would show up, in various guises, to mock Stone and egg him on.

Stone, a creepy, shuffling sort, spent most of his time in Los Angeles, where evil apparently likes to congregate. He became romantically involved with Detective Ash (Teri Polo) of the L.A.P.D. She turned out to be Ashara Badaktu, a 4,000-year-old demon who had masterminded the escape from Hell and who was number-one on the Devil's list to get back. Stone almost dispatched her in December, but she escaped. She surfaced again in February, apparently still infatuated with Stone, and almost killed his wife, Rosalyn (Stacy Haiduk). Maxine, a strange aspiring writer and fortune-teller, worked at the desk of a rundown L.A. hotel where Stone was staying.

BRING 'EM BACK ALIVE (*Adventure*)

FIRST TELECAST: *September 24, 1982*
LAST TELECAST: *June 21, 1983*
BROADCAST HISTORY:

Sep 1982, CBS Fri 9:00–10:00
Sep 1982–Dec 1982, CBS Tue 8:00–9:00
Jan 1983–Feb 1983, CBS Sat 8:00–9:00
May 1983–Jun 1983, CBS Tue 8:00–9:00

CAST:

Frank Buck..................... Bruce Boxleitner
Gloria Marlowe.................... Cindy Morgan
H.H., the Sultan of Johore............. Ron O'Neal
Myles Delany...................... Sean McClory
G. B. VonTurgo......................... John Zee
Ali................................ Clyde Kusatsu
Bhundi............................ Harvey Jason
Chaing, the bartender.......... George Lee Cheong

Inspired by the box-office success of the film *Raiders of the Lost Ark*, CBS brought this period adventure series to TV viewers the following year. Frank Buck was a legendary guide and Great White Hunter, living in Malaya during the years just prior to World War II. Operating out of the Raffles Hotel bar in Singapore, an establishment run by his good friend Myles Delaney, Frank donned pith helmet and ventured forth every week to deal with the baddies of Southeast Asia. His foes ran the gamut from smugglers, warlords, and bounty hunters to spies, strutting Nazis, and menacing Japs. Lantern-jawed Frank dispatched them all with élan, although G. B. VonTurgo, top man in the Singapore underworld, did manage to create recurring problems for Frank and his friends. On the side of the good guys were Gloria Marlowe, the pretty new American vice consul in Singapore; the regal Sultan of Johore; and Frank's loyal assistant, Ali. Bhundi was an associate of VonTurgo who, though essentially a criminal, would switch sides if he thought it would benefit him.

There was a real Frank Buck, a famous animal trapper in the 1940s, and the book which provided the title for this series was about his exploits. Any resemblance, however, between the real Buck and the character portrayed in this series, was purely coincidental.

BRINGING UP BUDDY (*Situation Comedy*)

FIRST TELECAST: *October 10, 1960*
LAST TELECAST: *September 25, 1961*
BROADCAST HISTORY:
Oct 1960–Sep 1961, CBS Mon 8:30–9:00
CAST:
Aunt Violet Flower .... Enid Markey
Aunt Iris Flower .... Doro Merande
Buddy Flower .... Frank Aletter

Making his home with two lovable but wacky maiden aunts kept investment counselor Buddy Flower pretty busy. As if he didn't have enough to cope with at the office, when he came home he was likely to discover that they had found the perfect girl for him to marry, had made some other major decision about the way he was to live, or had gotten themselves into some kind of trouble from which he would have to extricate them.

BRINGING UP JACK (*Situation Comedy*)

FIRST TELECAST: *May 27, 1995*
LAST TELECAST: *June 24, 1995*
BROADCAST HISTORY:
May 1995–Jun 1995, ABC Sat 8:30–9:00
CAST:
Jack McMahon .... Jack Gallagher
Ellen McMahon .... Harley Jane Kozak
Ryan (age 15) .... Matthew Lawrence
Molly (10) .... Kathryn Zaremba
Artie .... Jeff Garlin

Standup comic Jack Gallagher starred in this short-lived family sitcom about a Philadelphia sports talk show host and his new family. Jack McMahon had recently married Ellen, who was pregnant with their first child, and who also brought along two kids by a previous marriage—long-haired Ryan, and cute little Molly. Goofy Jack tried to bond with his new stepkids, while sensible Ellen dealt with the one "in the oven." Down at station WST ("AM 1040"), Jack confided in his fat co-host and best friend Artie, who, frankly, was more interested in that plate of doughnuts over there.

BRISTOL-MYERS TELE-VARIETIES (*Various*)

FIRST TELECAST: *January 5, 1947*
LAST TELECAST: *April 13, 1947*
BROADCAST HISTORY:
Jan 1947–Mar 1947, NBC Sun 8:15–8:30
Mar 1947–Apr 1947, NBC Sun 8:00–8:15

This was a series of short program tryouts by sponsor Bristol-Myers in the new medium of television. The variety show was the most common format, using an assortment of little-known talent, but perhaps the most successful experiment was a TV adaptation in March of Tex and Jinx McCrary's radio talk show, *Hi Jinx.* The McCrarys were naturals for TV, and with their combination of friendly chatter, interviews, and features, they later became two of the leading personalities in the new medium.

Tele-Varieties was first seen as a local show in New York in December 1946.

BROADSIDE (*Situation Comedy*)

FIRST TELECAST: *September 20, 1964*
LAST TELECAST: *September 5, 1965*
BROADCAST HISTORY:
Sep 1964–Sep 1965, ABC Sun 8:30–9:00
CAST:
Lt. (j.g.) Anne Morgan .... Kathy Nolan
Cdr. Rogers Adrian .... Edward Andrews
Lt. Maxwell Trotter .... Dick Sargent
Machinist's Mate Molly McGuire ...... Lois Roberts
Machinist's Mate Selma Kowalski .... Sheila James
Machinist's Mate Roberta Love .... Joan Staley
Machinist's Mate Marion Botnik ...... Jimmy Boyd
Ship's Cook 1st Class Stanley Stubbs (1965)
.... Arnold Stang
Ensign Beasley .... George Furth
Nicky D'Angelo (1964) .... Don Edmonds

This military comedy featured a group of U.S. Navy WAVES who were assigned to a South Pacific island during World War II and found themselves surrounded by thousands of sailors and an unappreciative CO. As an experiment, Lt. Morgan and her girls had been sent to Ranakai Island as replacements for male motor pool personnel, but Cdr. Adrian, the base CO, did not appreciate the resulting disruption. Ranakai was one of the quietest posts in the Pacific, and until they arrived Adrian had had a soft tour, complete with a Persian rug in his office, Rolls-Royce staff car, and gourmet meals (prepared by his eccentric but world-famous chef, Stanley Stubbs).

Most episodes consisted of Adrian's attempts to get the WAVES to transfer Stateside, by such clever ploys as cutting off their lipstick supply. Some concerned the "plight" of M/M Marion Botnik, who had been assigned to the WAVES by mistake when a personnel clerk mistook his name for that of a female.

Broadside was produced by the creator of *McHale's Navy,* Edward J. Montagne.

BROADWAY JAMBOREE (*Musical Variety*)

FIRST TELECAST: *May 10, 1948*
LAST TELECAST: *June 28, 1948*
BROADCAST HISTORY:
May 1948–Jun 1948, NBC Mon 8:00–8:30

This early live variety show was originally conceived as network television's first all-black series. The first telecast was described by NBC as an "all colored revue . . . featuring the Deep River Boys, colored quartet dressed in regular business suits and singing the songs popular with a minstrel show, and Derby Wilson, colored tap rhythm dancer." The second week offered the Deep River Boys, Maxine Sullivan, Tom Fletcher, Theodore Hines, and the dance team of Carl & Haryette. Thereafter the format suffered some turmoil, and featured both black and white performers. The third telecast was a straight variety show, and the next two starred Jack Albertson as a Broadway columnist trying to fend off his job-hunting girlfriend while talking about various acts (who then performed). The final week tied together the acts by leafing through the pages of *Variety*, then cutting to performers who were named in ads or stories. Among those appearing during the later telecasts were comedian Gus Van, dancers Ellsworth and Fairchild, the Melodeers (a black quintet), and a square-dance team from New Rochelle.

The series was originally called *Broadway Minstrels* (for the first two, all-black episodes), and thereafter *Broadway Jamboree*.

BROADWAY MINSTRELS, see *Broadway Jamboree*

BROADWAY OPEN HOUSE (*Talk/Variety*)

FIRST TELECAST: *May 29, 1950*
LAST TELECAST: *August 24, 1951*
BROADCAST HISTORY:
May 1950–May 1951, NBC Mon–Fri 11:00–12:00
May 1951–Aug 1951, NBC Tue/Thu/Fri 11:00–12:00
REGULARS:
Jerry Lester
Morey Amsterdam (1950)
Dave Street
Jane Harvey (1950)
Andy Roberts
The Mellolarks
Bob Warren (1951)
Richard Hayes (1951)
Helen Wood (1951)
Elaine Dunn (1951)
Jack Leonard (1951)
Eileen Barton (1951)
Buddy Greco (1951)
The Milton Delugg Quartet
Dagmar
Ray Malone
Wayne Howell
The Honeydreamers
Dell and Abbott (1951)
Estelle Sloane (1951)
Earl Barton (1951)
The Kirby Stone Quintet (1951)
Maureen Cannon (1951)
Marion Colby (1951)
Frank Gallop (1951)
Barbara Nichols (1951)

Broadway Open House was the granddaddy of all of television's informal talk shows, and preceded *The Tonight Show* as NBC's post-11 P.M. nightly attraction. Actually, however, it was two shows in one. Jerry Lester was on three days a week (Tuesday, Thursday, and Friday), while Morey Amsterdam was the initial emcee on Mondays and Wednesdays. They each had their own group of regulars, the most famous being the statuesque "dumb" blonde Dagmar, on Lester's nights. Stars were invited to drop in and chat, or perform if they felt like it, and the regulars performed in comedy skits, songs, and dances. There was also byplay with orchestra leader/accordionist Milton Delugg. Delugg was a songwriter as well and at least one of his numbers, "Orange Colored Sky," was plugged so much on this show that it became a major record hit—probably the first song ever to become a hit through television exposure.

Morey Amsterdam left in November of 1950, and the cast on his two nights underwent a number of changes. Finally, in May 1951, Jerry Lester also left the show; he was replaced by Jack Leonard as star, and the entire show was cut back to three nights a week. Original cast member Dagmar was retained, new singers, dancers, and musicians were added, and the Kirby Stone Quintet moved over from the canceled Monday and Wednesday show.

The circumstances surrounding Jerry Lester's departure from *Broadway Open House* involved an ongoing feud with Dagmar, the show's biggest star next to Jerry. A young actress named Jennie Lewis (although her real name was Virginia Ruth Egnor), Dagmar had been signed by Jerry to do a walk-on early in the run of the show, reading inane poetry with a deadpan delivery. It was for that part that Jerry renamed her Dagmar. She was an instant hit and became a regular feature, her salary rising quickly to the point where only Jerry made more. A veteran performer, Jerry resented the publicity and popularity of what he felt was his "creation" and tried to minimize her role. In the spring of 1951, to divert attention from Dagmar, he even added another statuesque blonde to the cast, Barbara Nichols (whom he renamed Agathon). The friction became intolerable, for Dagmar had become Jerry's Frankenstein monster, too popular for him to deal with, and Jerry abandoned the series to pursue other interests. Neither the show nor Dagmar's newfound career survived without him.

BROADWAY SPOTLIGHT (*Variety*)

FIRST TELECAST: *March 10, 1949*
LAST TELECAST: *September 4, 1949*
BROADCAST HISTORY:
Mar 1949–Apr 1949, NBC Wed 8:00–8:30
May 1949–Jul 1949, NBC Sun 7:00–7:30
Jul 1949–Sep 1949, NBC Sun 7:30–8:00
REGULARS:
Danton Walker (Mar–Jun)
Richard Kollmar (Jun–Sep)
Ving Merlin Orchestra
Joey Faye, comedian (Jun–Sep)
June Taylor Dancers (Jul–Sep)

This live variety program was originally hosted by Broadway columnist Danton Walker, later by radio personality Richard Kollmar. Singers, comedians, and stage actors and actresses appeared as guests, with the emphasis on past and present stars of the Broadway stage. One early feature involved a major star performing one of his or her great successes of the past, together with a newcomer whom that star had discovered. The title of the series varied from *Show Business, Inc.* (March–April) to *Danton Walker's Broadway Scrapbook* (April–June) to *Broadway Spotlight* (June–September).

BROADWAY TO HOLLYWOOD—HEADLINE CLUES (*News/Interview/Quiz*)
FIRST TELECAST: *July 20, 1949*
LAST TELECAST: *July 15, 1954*
BROADCAST HISTORY:
Jul 1949–Sep 1949, DUM Wed 8:30–9:00
Oct 1949–May 1950, DUM Fri 8:30–9:00
May 1950–Jan 1951, DUM Wed 10:00–10:30
Jan 1951–Jul 1954, DUM Thu 8:30–9:00
HOST:
George F. Putnam (1949–1951)
Bill Slater (1951–1953)
Conrad Nagel (1953–1954)

This magazine show featuring news, gossip, and quiz elements ran for five years on the DuMont TV network. Early in the program's history the quiz element was stressed; host-commentator George Putnam would call viewers at home and offer prizes for the correct answers to news-related questions or identification of photos shown on the air. There were also guest celebrities and new talent discoveries; Eddie Fisher is said to have made his first TV appearance on this show.

By the time Bill Slater took over as host in March 1951, the quiz segment had been dropped, and emphasis was placed on late-breaking news stories and timely features on world and national issues and show business. The day assassins attempted to kill President Truman, for instance, *Headline Clues* flew an eyewitness to its New York studios to give a first-hand account of the incident. Human-interest stories were also featured, as in the meeting—on the show—of two doctors who had developed the wonder drug cortisone and a little girl who had been cured of a crippling infirmity by their discovery. New movies and nightclub acts were reviewed, and guest celebrities performed.

First known simply as *Headline Clues*, the program changed its name to *Broadway to Hollywood—Headline Clues* in October 1949.

BROKEN ARROW (*Western*)
FIRST TELECAST: *September 25, 1956*
LAST TELECAST: *September 18, 1960*
BROADCAST HISTORY:
Sep 1956–Sep 1958, ABC Tue 9:00–9:30
Apr 1960–Sep 1960, ABC Sun 7:00–7:30
CAST:
Tom Jeffords .... John Lupton
Cochise .... Michael Ansara
Duffield .... Tom Fadden
Nukaya .... Steven Ritch

The cowboys and Indians got together to battle injustice in this Western, which starred John Lupton as Indian agent Tom Jeffords and Michael Ansara as Apache Chief Cochise. Jeffords was originally an army officer given the assignment of getting the U.S. Mail safely through Apache territory in Arizona. Adopting the novel approach of making friends with the Indians instead of shooting at them, Jeffords soon became blood brother to Cochise. Together they fought both renegades from the Chiricahua Reservation and dishonest "white eyes" who preyed upon the Indians. The show was based on the novel *Blood Brother*, by Elliott Arnold, which had been made into a movie in 1950.

Repeats of *Broken Arrow* were seen on the network on Sunday afternoons in 1959–1960 and in an early-evening time slot during the summer of 1960.

BROKEN BADGES (*Police Drama*)
FIRST TELECAST: *November 24, 1990*
LAST TELECAST: *June 20, 1991*
BROADCAST HISTORY:
Nov 1990–Dec 1990, CBS Sat 9:00–10:00
Jun 1991, CBS Thu 9:00–10:00
CAST:
Beau Jack Bowman .... Miguel Ferrer
J.J. "Bullet" Tingreedes .... Eileen Davidson
Stanley "Whipusall" Jones .... Jay Johnson
Toby Baker .... Ernie Hudson
Priscilla Mather .... Charlotte Lewis

These were not your run-of-the-mill cops. J.J. was addicted to the thrill of dangerous situations, Stanley was a mild-mannered, pint-sized ventriloquist who exploded whenever anyone made derogatory comments about his size, and Toby was a depressed, accident-prone kleptomaniac. All three of them were on psychiatric leave from the Bay City, California, Police Department. With former New Orleans Cajun cop Beau Jack Bowman as their leader, and the support of police psychiatrist Priscilla Mather, they formed an unlikely crime-fighting team. Viewers apparently found them too unlikely a team, with low ratings resulting in the series' cancellation barely a month after its premiere. The following June CBS aired three episodes not broadcast during the series' initial run.

BRONCO (*Western*)
FIRST TELECAST: *September 23, 1958*
LAST TELECAST: *August 20, 1962*
BROADCAST HISTORY:
Sep 1958–Sep 1960, ABC Tue 7:30–8:30
Oct 1960–Aug 1962, ABC Mon 7:30–8:30
CAST:
Bronco Layne .... Ty Hardin

Bronco, as portrayed by newcomer Ty Hardin, was born of the fight between Clint Walker and Warner Bros. Studios over the series *Cheyenne* (see *Cheyenne* for details). When Walker quit his successful series in 1958, Hardin was brought in to replace him. Although the series continued under the title *Cheyenne*, Hardin starred in it as Bronco Layne, an ex-Confederate Army captain who had wandered west after the war in search of adventure. There were no other regulars, but the handsome young Bronco did encounter plenty of interesting characters in his exploits, including Billy the Kid, Jesse James (played by James Coburn), Cole Younger, Belle Starr, and Wild Bill Hickok.

In 1959 Clint Walker returned to *Cheyenne*, and *Bronco* became a separate series. In both the 1958–1959 and 1959–1960 seasons Hardin's series alternated with another Western, *Sugarfoot*. Then in 1960 *Bronco* was brought back under the *Cheyenne* umbrella title, as part of a rotating anthology consisting of Walker's *Cheyenne*, Will Hutchins's *Sugarfoot*, and Hardin's *Bronco*; the three stars were seen separately, in different episodes. *Sugarfoot* was dropped from the rotation in 1961, leaving only *Bronco* and *Cheyenne* to alternate in 1961–1962.

BRONK (*Detective Drama*)
FIRST TELECAST: *September 21, 1975*
LAST TELECAST: *July 18, 1976*

BROADCAST HISTORY:

Sep 1975–Jul 1976, CBS Sun 10:00–11:00

CAST:

Lt. Alex Bronkov .... Jack Palance
Mayor Pete Santori .... Joseph Mascolo
Harry Mark .... Henry Beckman
Sgt. John Webber .... Tony King
Ellen Bronkov .... Dina Ousley

Tough guy Jack Palance, who frequently played heavies in movies, turned contemplative cop for this single-season series. Pipe-smoking Lt. Alex Bronkov had been enlisted by his old friend Pete Santori, mayor of Ocean City, in Southern California, to help clean up that corruption-ridden town. Bronk worked on special assignments from the mayor, with the assistance of fellow officer Sgt. John Webber. Also featured in the cast were retired policeman Harry Mark, a close friend of Bronk's who was now in the auto-junkyard business, and Bronk's daughter Ellen, who had been confined to a wheelchair by an accident that had crippled her and killed Bronk's wife.

BRONX ZOO, THE (*Drama*)

FIRST TELECAST: *March 19, 1987*
LAST TELECAST: *June 29, 1988*
BROADCAST HISTORY:

Mar 1987, NBC Thu 10:10–11:10
Mar 1987–May 1987, NBC Wed 10:00–11:00
Aug 1987–Sep 1987, NBC Wed 9:00–10:00
Dec 1987–Jan 1988, NBC Wed 10:00–11:00
Mar 1988–Apr 1988, NBC Wed 10:00–11:00
Jun 1988, NBC Wed 10:00–11:00

CAST:

Principal Joe Danzig .... Edward Asner
Jack Felspar .... Nicholas Pryor
Sara Newhouse .... Kathryn Harrold
Harry Barnes .... David Wilson
Mary Caitlin Callahan .... Kathleen Beller
Matthew Littman .... Jerry Levine
Gus Butterfield .... Mykel T. Williamson
Carol Danzig .... Janet Carroll
Roz .... Gail Boggs
Roberta .... Tyra Ferrell
Virginia Biederman .... Betty Karlen
Snyder .... Adam Carl
Chris Barnes (1988) .... Chelsea Field

"Are you *bad*?" sneered the smart-mouthed black girl to the new principal. "Can be," he shot back, smiling. Ed Asner, stung by the quick cancellation of his lightweight 1985 sitcom *Off the Rack,* essayed a meatier role in this tough-as-nails drama. It was set in an inner-city high school whose violent atmosphere made viewers wince. The producer called it "a show of small victories," and that's the most viewers got amid the muggings, vandalism, and worse (Asner's character was even shot in one episode). Despite the problems, Principal Joe Danzig was determined to keep order and perhaps impart a little hope to the mostly poor and underprivileged students who (sometimes) attended Benjamin Harrison High. Jack was the often insufferable but basically decent Vice Principal, who had wanted Danzig's job; Sara the beautiful, upper-class English teacher, dubious about her assignment to such a hellhole; Harry the streetwise history teacher who helped, and romanced, her; Callahan the free-spirited art and drama teacher; Littman, a drop-out lawyer and neophyte math teacher; and Gus the black basketball coach and science teacher. Carol was Joe's wife of 29 years, who wished he would get out of such a dangerous assignment, but understood his idealism. She passed away shortly after giving birth to a late-in-life baby, leaving him with an additional burden.

BROOKLYN BRIDGE (*Comedy/Drama*)

FIRST TELECAST: *September 20, 1991*
LAST TELECAST: *August 6, 1993*
BROADCAST HISTORY:

Sep 1991–Oct 1991, CBS Fri 8:30–9:00
Oct 1991, CBS Fri 8:00–8:30
Nov 1991–Dec 1991, CBS Wed 8:00–8:30
Dec 1991–Jun 1992, CBS Wed 8:30–9:00
Sep 1992–Oct 1992, CBS Sat 8:30–9:00
Oct 1992–Nov 1992, CBS Sat 8:00–8:30
Apr 1993, CBS Sat 9:30–10:00
Jul 1993–Aug 1993, CBS Fri 8:30–9:00

CAST:

Alan Silver (age 14) .... Danny Gerard
Sophie Berger .... Marion Ross
Jules Berger .... Louis Zorich
Phyllis Berger Silver .... Amy Aquino
George Silver .... Peter Friedman
Nathaniel Silver (9) .... Matthew Louis Siegel
Nicholas Scamperelli .... Adam LaVorgna
Katie Monahan .... Jenny Lewis
Benny Belinksy .... Jake Jundef
Warren Butcher .... Aeryk Egan
Sid Elgart .... David Wohl
**Uncle Willie* .... Alan Blumenfeld
**Aunt Miriam (1991–1992)* .... Natalia Nogulich
**Aunt Sylvia (1991–1992)* .... Carol Kane
**Uncle Buddy (1991–1992)* .... Murray Rubin
**Cousin Bernie (1991–1992)* ..... Armin Shimerman

*Occasional

THEME:

"Just Over the Brooklyn Bridge," written by Marvin Hamlisch and Alan & Marilyn Bergman, performed by Art Garfunkel

Brooklyn, New York, in 1956 was the setting for this nostalgic series. The focus of the show was 14-year-old Alan Silver, a middle-class Jewish youngster growing up in a time when the beloved Dodgers were still in Brooklyn, candy was a penny at Sid Elgart's neighborhood candy store, doctors made house calls, and street crime was virtually nonexistent. Alan lived in an apartment house with his parents, postal worker George and working mom Phyllis, and his kid brother, Nathaniel. Living in the same building were Alan's maternal grandparents, Jules and Sophie Berger. Sophie, the unquestioned matriarch of the family, was a loving but strong-willed woman whose word was almost always law to her family. Although she was perfectly at home with her grandson's multi-ethnic friends—Nicholas, Benny, and Warren—Sophie found it difficult to accept Katie Monahan, the Catholic girl he was dating.

For creator/producer Gary David Goldberg, who had also created the long-running *Family Ties,* this series was a semi-autobiographical labor of love. He had grown up in Brooklyn in the 1950s, and his fond remembrances of those years provided the framework on which *Brooklyn Bridge* was built—everything from the radio coverage of Dodger baseball games (voiced by longtime Los Angeles Dodger announcer Vin Scully) to the vintage rock 'n' roll songs used in the background to set the mood.

BROOKLYN SOUTH (*Police Drama*)
FIRST TELECAST: *September 22, 1997*
LAST TELECAST: *April 27, 1998*
BROADCAST HISTORY:
Sep 1997–Apr 1998, CBS Mon 10:00–11:00
CAST:
Patrol Sgt. Francis X. Donovan .... Jon Tenney
Off. Phil Roussakoff .... Michael DeLuise
Off. Jimmy Doyle .... Dylan Walsh
Capt. Stan Jonas .... James B. Sikking
Off. Anne-Marie Kersey .... Yancy Butler
Sgt. Richard Santoro .... Gary Basaraba
Off. Jake Lowery .... Titus Welliver
Off. Nona Valentine .... Klea Scott
Off. Clement Johnson .... Richard T. Jones
Off. Hector Villaneuva .... Adam Rodriguez
Terry Doyle .... Patrick McGaw
Kathleen Doyle .... A. J. Langer
Off. Kevin Patrick .... Mark Kiely
Noreen Patrick .... Star Jasper
Emmeline Flannagan .... Brigid Brannagh
Capt. Lou Zerola (1997) .... Bradford English
Off. Ray MacElwaine (1998) .... John Finn

Another gritty cop show from producer Steven Bochco, whose previous credits included *Hill Street Blues* and *N.Y.P.D. Blue*. The nominal focus of the show was Sgt. Francis Donovan, who presided over the morning shift assignments given to the officers of the 74th Precinct in Brooklyn, New York. He reported to Captain Jonas, who early in the season made the uneasy transition from being a hated Internal Affairs Bureau lieutenant to precinct commander. Their relationship was complicated by the fact that Donovan had been recruited as an undercover informant for I.A.B. when he first graduated from the police academy (to protect his retired cop father from indictment for corruption).

Each of the many officers had his own story. In the series premiere Anne-Marie's policeman boyfriend was killed in a shootout, and the wounded madman responsible died from internal injuries in the station house after she kicked him in the stomach while growling, "Die, you scumbag." This precipitated an I.A.B. investigation that eventually exonerated everyone. Later in the season she and Donovan had an affair and she was promoted to Detective.

Jimmy Doyle was a well-liked street cop whose younger brother, Terry, left the police academy "in disgrace" in order to take an undercover assignment to infiltrate a local Irish gang. Jimmy's beefy partner, Phil, was a recent transfer who was a little too quick to use his fists or open his big mouth—usually regretting his actions later. He was attracted to Jimmy's sister, Kathleen, but was awkward and uncomfortable when it came to dating. Jack, whose wife had left him early in the season, was a tough cop coping with personal demons. He had a developing romance with his partner, Nona, which did not sit well with Clement, her former lover. Desk sergeant Richard Santoro, a veteran who had seen it all, was the voice of reason in the station house, keeping things calm and supporting Donovan when the latter admitted his I.A.B. activities to his fellow officers. Donovan had fessed up in order to keep a crooked I.A.B. lieutenant from ruining Santoro's reputation with trumped-up charges of extortion. In the series finale Santoro was promoted to Lieutenant.

BROTHERLY LOVE (*Situation Comedy*)
FIRST TELECAST: *September 17, 1995*
LAST TELECAST: *June 1, 1997*
BROADCAST HISTORY:
Sep 1995–Nov 1995, NBC Sun 7:00–7:30
Mar 1996–Apr 1996, NBC Mon 8:30–9:00
Aug 1996–Nov 1996, WB Sun 7:30–8:00
Nov 1996–Jan 1997, WB Sun 7:00–8:00
Jan 1997–Jun 1997, WB Sun 7:00–7:30
CAST:
Joe Roman .... Joey Lawrence
Matt Roman .... Matthew Lawrence
Andy Roman (age 7) .... Andrew Lawrence
Claire Roman .... Melinda Culea
Louise David (Lou) .... Liz Vassey
Lloyd Burwell .... Michael McShane
Kristen .... Rebecca Herbst
THEME:
performed by Joey Lawrence

The three shaggy-haired Lawrence brothers costarred in this energetic sitcom about three brothers and their widowed mom. Joe was a free spirit who returned to Philadelphia to collect his inheritance when he learned that his late dad had left him one-quarter of the family business, Roman Customizing. But after meeting his two half brothers who needed a father figure, and a stepmom, Claire, who needed help keeping the auto shop afloat (although she wouldn't admit it), Joe reluctantly decided to stay. In-charge Claire and easygoing Joe had their tiffs, but they basically liked each other. Dumb, insecure teenager Matt could use a guiding hand, and hyper little Andy was delighted to have a new brother to play with. Dim-witted Lloyd was a portly mechanic, and Lou a talented female mechanic.

After the series moved to the WB, Joe and Lou realized they were attracted to each other, but didn't want to date, fearing it would ruin their friendship. In May 1997, Lloyd married his girlfriend Sheila (Suzanne Kent) in a spur-of-the-moment ceremony at the end of the formal remarriage of Joe's hippie mom Amber (Jane Fleiss) to the "aura" photographer she had met at a seminar.

BROTHERS, THE (*Situation Comedy*)
FIRST TELECAST: *October 2, 1956*
LAST TELECAST: *September 7, 1958*
BROADCAST HISTORY:
Oct 1956–Mar 1957, CBS Tue 8:30–9:00
Jun 1958–Sep 1958, CBS Sun 7:30–8:00
CAST:
Harvey Box .... Gale Gordon
Gilmore Box .... Bob Sweeney
Dr. Margaret Kleeb .... Ann Morriss
Capt. Sam Box (1956) .... Frank Orth
Capt. Sam Box (1956–1957) ...... Howard McNear
Marilee Dorf .... Nancy Hadley
Carl Dorf .... Oliver Blake
Barrington Steel .... Robin Hughes

Harvey and Gilly Box were two brothers who owned a photography studio in San Francisco. Harvey, the older brother, was somewhat blustery and overbearing, but at heart was a good man whose bark was worse than his bite. Gilly was a shy, naive, and inoffensive soul who seemed happy to let his older brother run things. Both of them had girlfriends whose personalities seemed well matched to those of their men, Harvey's the strong-willed Dr. Margaret Kleeb, and Gilly's the quiet Marilee Dorf. Most of the episodes of *The Brothers* revolved around their social and personal lives, their friends, and family. During the summer of 1958, reruns of this series alternated with *Bachelor Father.*

BROTHERS AND SISTERS (*Situation Comedy*)
FIRST TELECAST: *January 21, 1979*
LAST TELECAST: *April 6, 1979*
BROADCAST HISTORY:

Jan 1979, NBC Sun 8:10–8:40
Jan 1979–Feb 1979, NBC Fri 8:30–9:00
Feb 1979–Apr 1979, NBC Fri 9:00–9:30

CAST:

Milos "Checko" Sabolcik .... Chris Lemmon
Ronald Holmes III .... Randy Brooks
Stanley Zipper .... Jon Cutler
Harlan Ramsey .... Larry Anderson
Mary Lee .... Amy Johnston
Suzi Cooper .... Mary Crosby
Seymour .... Roy Teicher
Larry Krandall .... William Windom
Isabel St. Anthony .... Susan Cotten

Following the success of the movie *Animal House* in 1978, all three networks came up with their televersions of college life. ABC had *Delta House,* CBS had *Co-Ed Fever,* and NBC had *Brothers and Sisters.* None of them succeeded.

The setting for this comedy was the campus of Larry Krandall College, run by its founder and namesake. Living at Pi Nu Fraternity were three buddies, Checko, Ronald, and Zipper. They inhabited the frat house's boiler room, nicknamed "Le Dump," and made quite a group. Checko was sincere and dedicated to getting an education, Ron was the fraternity's token black, and Zipper its resident slob. The Pi Nu president, Harlan Ramsey, was as obnoxious and overbearing as he was rich. Harlan's girlfriend, the social-climbing and equally obnoxious Mary Lee, was a member of Gamma Iota sorority, as was Zipper's dream girl, Suzi Cooper. Stories centered around activities at the two houses, with emphasis on pranks and social activities.

BROTHERS GARCIA, THE (*Situation Comedy*)
BROADCAST HISTORY:

Nickelodeon
30 minutes
Original episodes: *2000–*
Premiered: *July 23, 2000*

CAST:

Ray Garcia .... Carlos Lacamara
Sonia Garcia .... Ada Maris
Carlos Garcia (age 13) .... Jeffrey Licon
George Garcia (12) .... Bobby Gonzalez
Larry Garcia (11) .... Alvin Alvarez
Larry (as adult; voice only) .... John Leguizamo
Lorena Garcia .... Vaneza Leza Pitynski

Billed as the first English-language sitcom with an all-Latino cast and creative team, *The Brothers Garcia* was an affectionate look at a middle-class Mexican American family living in San Antonio, Texas. In fact it was so relentlessly middle class that it could have been called *Leave It to Beaver Español.* Ray, the dad, was a history professor, while his wife, Sonia, ran a hair salon. Their rambunctious kids were cool Carlos the operator ("don't worry, I have a plan"), chubby George, an Internet freak, and put-upon Larry, who wanted to be an astronaut, and who sometimes lapsed into black-and-white fantasy sequences. Lorena was Larry's melodramatic twin sister, who was obsessed with Mexican soap operas. Stories revolved around little misunderstandings, puppy loves and family excursions. Larry narrated the stories as an adult, making this perhaps more like a Latino *Wonder Years.*

BROTHERS GRUNT, THE (*Cartoon*)
BROADCAST HISTORY:

MTV
30 minutes
Produced: *1994* (30 episodes)
Premiered: *August 15, 1994*

This gross-you-out cartoon was MTV's attempt to top its own *Beavis & Butt-head.* It certainly was gross. The leading characters did not speak, only grunt, and they looked as disgusting as imagination could make them—flabby, belching, oozing, pale-white half-humans with bulging veins and bloodshot eyes, clad only in polka-dot boxer shorts. The six grotesque siblings had been raised in a secluded monastery and were content there until Brother Perry was anointed "The Chosen One" and ran off into the real world. The other five (Frank, Tony, Bing, Dean, and Sammy—sort of a rat pack?) chased after him.

The cartoon world into which they escaped didn't seem to mind them much, but their toilet humor, beer-guzzling, nipple-twisting, and other gross habits did annoy some adults. Which was presumably the intent. Executive producer Abby Terkuhle commented, "Creatively, we've never judged things according to what parents or critics think." Fart.

BROTHER'S KEEPER (*Situation Comedy*)
FIRST TELECAST: *September 25, 1998*
LAST TELECAST: *July 16, 1999*
BROADCAST HISTORY:

Sep 1998–Jul 1999, ABC Fri 9:30–10:00

CAST:

Porter Waide .... William Ragsdale
Bobby Waide .... Sean O'Bryan
Oscar Waide (age 8) .... Justin Cooper
Dena Draeger .... Bess Meyer

Imagine *The Odd Couple* plus a kid, and you pretty much have the premise of this lightweight sitcom. Widower Porter Waide was an uptight young San Francisco history professor, oh-so-carefully raising his young son Oscar to be as quiet and logical as himself. Who should arrive on his doorstep, ready to move in and disrupt his orderly world, than his free-wheeling brother Bobby? Bobby, it seems, was an NFL star kicker who'd just been traded to the hometown team. There was just one catch to his new multi-million-dollar contract: trouble-prone Bobby was required to find a "responsible adult" to live with. And the most responsible adult he knew was brother Porter.

Little Oscar hit it off immediately with his fun-loving uncle, while Porter fussed and stewed and tried to keep everyone down to earth. Dena was the team's sports agent who had been given the unenviable task of keeping Bobby out of trouble.

BRUTALLY NORMAL (*Situation Comedy*)
FIRST TELECAST: *January 24, 2000*
LAST TELECAST: *February 14, 2000*
BROADCAST HISTORY:
Jan 2000–Feb 2000, WB Mon 9:00–9:30
CAST:
Russell Wise (age 16) .... Eddie Kaye Thomas
Robert "Pooh" Cutler .... Mike Damus
Anna Pricova .... Lea Moreno
Dru .... Tangie Ambrose
Gogi Pricova .... Joanna Pacula
Shaheem .... Antwon Tanner

This short-lived comedy focused on the day-to-day lives of a group of sophomores at Wacker H. Normall High School. Russell, the hunky, aggressive one, was much more concerned with being a celebrity among his peers than with his grades. Pooh, Russell's neurotic best friend and gofer, was obsessed with the potential disaster that loomed in any situation. Anna, their studious Russian friend and confidante, was a first-generation American whose divorced mother, Gogi, dated a succession of overly amorous suitors. When Anna needed advice, she sought it from her friend Dru, a bright, cynical, self-sufficient young woman who didn't take crap from anyone—including Russell.

BUCCANEERS, THE (*Adventure*)
FIRST TELECAST: *September 22, 1956*
LAST TELECAST: *September 14, 1957*
BROADCAST HISTORY:
Sep 1956–Sep 1957, CBS Sat 7:30–8:00
CAST:
Captain Dan Tempest .... Robert Shaw
Lt. Beamish .... Peter Hammond
Crewman Armando .... Edwin Richfield
Crewman Gaff .... Brian Rawlinson
Crewman Taffy .... Paul Hansard
Crewman Van Bruch .... Alex Mango
Crewman Dickon .... Wilfrid Downing

Set in the West Indies during the early 1700s, *The Buccaneers* featured adventure on the high seas as well as swashbuckling on land. After clearing the island of New Providence (Nassau) of pirates, the original governor was sent back to England by the Admiralty and replaced by young Lt. Beamish. Fresh out of the Royal Navy's Midshipman's School, the inexperienced Beamish found that, with Blackbeard threatening to take over the island, the situation there was more than he could handle. To cope with it, he made an ally of Dan Tempest, a reformed pirate who had been pardoned by the previous governor. Tempest helped rout the pirates and enjoyed himself so much in the process that he decided to return permanently to the sea on his ship *The Sultana.* His travels to places as far away as New York, and battles with pirates and Spaniards, provided the central plots of episodes of this series. *The Buccaneers* was filmed entirely in England.

ABC aired reruns on Monday afternoons from September 1957 to September 1958.

BUCK JAMES (*Medical Drama*)
FIRST TELECAST: *September 27, 1987*
LAST TELECAST: *May 5, 1988*
BROADCAST HISTORY:
Sep 1987–Jan 1988, ABC Sun 10:00–11:00
Mar 1988–May 1988, ABC Thu 10:00–11:00
CAST:
Dr. Buck James .... Dennis Weaver
Clint James .... Jon Maynard Pennell
Dinah James .... Elena Stiteler
Jenny James .... Shannon Wilcox
Vittorio .... Dehl Berti
Dr. Rebecca Meyer .... Alberta Watson
Henry Carliner .... John Cullum

Dennis Weaver starred in this routine medical drama, which resembled *McCloud* in a surgical gown. Buck James was a dedicated trauma surgeon at Holloman University Hospital in Texas. His laconic, down home manner and common-sense approach to the constant crises in the emergency room made him an excellent doctor—despite a certain amount of verbal sparring with newcomer Rebecca (who was female, East-Coast, and Jewish) and hospital administrator Henry, a well-meaning bureaucrat. When Buck put on his stetson and drove home to the ranch things did not go smoothly, however. His ex-wife Jenny still loved him, but their marriage had ended in divorce due to his total dedication to his work. Daughter Dinah, 22, had come home unmarried and pregnant; son Clint, 19, worked at the ranch and felt alienated from his busy father. Vittorio was the ranch foreman, who dispensed sage advice and had become a kind of second father to Clint. "It's not that I like my job more than my family," opined Buck. "I'm just better at my job."

BUCK ROGERS (*Science Fiction*)
FIRST TELECAST: *April 15, 1950*
LAST TELECAST: *January 30, 1951*
BROADCAST HISTORY:
Apr 1950–Sep 1950, ABC Sat 7:00–7:30
Sep 1950–Jan 1951, ABC Tue 8:30–9:00
CAST:
Buck Rogers (1950) .... Kem Dibbs
Buck Rogers (1950–1951) .... Robert Pastene
Wilma Deering .... Lou Prentis
Dr. Huer .... Harry Sothern
Black Barney .... Harry Kingston

This was the first TV version of the famous hero of comic books, radio, and movie serials, also known as *Buck Rogers in the 25th Century.* As in the other versions Buck alone was responsible for the safety of the universe; aided by various pseudo-scientific gadgets, he always managed to outwit such interstellar villains as Killer Kane. Lou Prentis played Buck's beautiful companion Wilma; Harry Sothern his ally, the brilliant Dr. Huer; and Harry Kingston his Martian crony, Barney. His home base was Niagara, capital of the world. Handsome Ken Dibbs first played the role of Buck on television with suitable derring-do, but was nevertheless replaced after a few months by Robert Pastene.

Production was on the cheap side, though perhaps not as cheap as for DuMont's long-running hit *Captain Video,* which *Buck Rogers* preceded on Saturdays for a time. *Buck Rogers* was also seen in later years as a local series, consisting of edited versions of the movie serials starring Buster Crabbe in the title role.

BUCK ROGERS IN THE 25TH CENTURY (*Science Fiction*)
FIRST TELECAST: *September 20, 1979*
LAST TELECAST: *April 16, 1981*

BROADCAST HISTORY:

Sep 1979–Jul 1980, NBC Thu 8:00–9:00
Aug 1980–Sep 1980, NBC Sat 8:00–9:00
Jan 1981–Apr 1981, NBC Thu 8:00–9:00

CAST:

Capt. William "Buck" Rogers .... Gil Gerard
Col. Wilma Deering .... Erin Gray
Dr. Huer (1979–1980) .... Tim O'Connor
Twiki .... Felix Silla
Twiki's voice .... Mel Blanc
Twiki's voice (1981 temporary replacement)
.... Bob Elyea
Dr. Theopolis (voice only) (1979–1980) ....
.... Eric Server
Princess Ardala (1979–1980) ...... Pamela Hensley
Kane (1979) .... Henry Silva
Kane (1979–1980) .... Michael Ansara
Hawk (1981) .... Thom Christopher
Dr. Goodfellow (1981) .... Wilfred Hyde-White
Admiral Asimov (1981) .... Jay Garner
Crichton (voice only) (1981) .... Jeff David
Lt. Devlin (1981) .... Paul Carr

This updated *Buck Rogers* was far more elaborate than the version aired on ABC almost 30 years earlier. It benefited from much-improved technology, the interest generated by theatrical films like *Star Wars* and *Close Encounters of the Third Kind*, and a budget that enabled the utilization of fancy special effects. Also, unlike earlier versions of *Buck*, in the comics and on film, radio, and television, this series didn't take itself seriously. It was good escapist entertainment with a tongue-in-cheek quality that prevented it from getting pretentious.

Capt. Buck Rogers was an astronaut whose deep-space probe, launched in 1987, was lost for 500 years. Fortunately for Buck, he was frozen in suspended animation, awakening when his craft was discovered by Draconians in the year 2491. The Draconians, led by beautiful but evil Princess Ardala and her henchman, Kane, hoped to take over Earth and thought that Buck was a spy. So, too, did the Earth Defense Directorate, based in the city of New Chicago. Buck, using a combination of wit, charm, brains, and brute strength, eventually prevented the Draconians from achieving their ends (though they did keep reappearing with new plans to defeat Earth) and became a valued ally in defending Earth. He became a good friend of Dr. Huer, the most renowned scientist on Earth, and of Wilma Deering, the beautiful commander in charge of Earth's defenses. Dr. Huer provided Buck with a small robot aide, Twiki, and the services of a talking computer, Dr. Theopolis (usually seen in the form of a large disk around Twiki's neck). Together, they fought the Draconians and others who threatened peace and security. Buck's acclimation to the world of the 25th century was not always easy and his use of 20th-century slang tended to rub off on both Twiki and his human associates.

When *Buck Rogers in the 25th Century* returned for its second season in 1981 (delayed several months by an actors' strike), it had been completely overhauled. No longer based on Earth, Buck and Wilma were now crew members aboard the *Searcher*, an interstellar spaceship seeking survivors of the "great holocaust" that had sent many Earthmen into space not long after Buck's original probe had been lost. In many respects this new format had elements of both *Star Trek* and *Battlestar Galactica*. Other members of the *Searcher*'s crew included its commander, Admiral Asimov (descended from science-fiction writer Isaac Asimov); Lt. Devlin, Asimov's assistant; Dr. Goodfellow, an elderly, eccentric scientist with an insatiable curiosity; and Hawk, part man and part bird, searching for other members of his race. In addition to Twiki, the *Searcher* carried Crichton, a highly intelligent but very obnoxious robot that could not believe it had been built by humans, and especially by its creator, Dr. Goodfellow. Missing from the second season, in addition to the departed cast members, was the narration provided by William Conrad during *Buck Rogers'* initial year.

The pilot for this series, titled *Buck Rogers in the 25th Century*, was released theatrically in March 1979, six months before the series premiered on NBC.

BUCKSKIN (*Western*)

FIRST TELECAST: *July 3, 1958*
LAST TELECAST: *August 29, 1965*
BROADCAST HISTORY:

Jul 1958–Sep 1958, NBC Thu 9:30–10:00
Oct 1958–Jan 1959, NBC Fri 7:30–8:00
Jan 1959–Sep 1959, NBC Mon 7:30–8:00
Jul 1965–Aug 1965, NBC Sun 8:30–9:00

CAST:

Jody O'Connell .... Tommy Nolan
Mrs. Annie O'Connell .... Sallie Brophy
Marshal Tom Sellers .... Michael Road
Ben Newcomb (1959) .... Michael Lipton

Jody O'Connell was a ten-year-old boy living in his mother's boardinghouse in the frontier town of Buckskin, Montana, in 1880. Annie's boardinghouse was the center of social and business activity for the area, and the series showed life through the eyes of young Jody as he became involved both with guests passing through town and with residents of Buckskin. The series ran for about a year in 1958–1959 and was rerun during the summer of 1965.

BUDDIES (*Situation Comedy*)

FIRST TELECAST: *March 5, 1996*
LAST TELECAST: *March 27, 1996*
BROADCAST HISTORY:

Mar 1996, ABC Tue 9:30–10:00
Mar 1996, ABC Wed 9:30–10:00

CAST:

Dave Carlisle .... Dave Chappelle
John Butler .... Christopher Gartin
Lorraine Butler .... Paula Cale
Phyllis .... Tanya Wright
Maureen (Mo) DeMoss .... Judith Ivey
Henry Carlisle .... Richard Roundtree

Two Chicago buddies, one black and one white, went into business together despite the objections of their racially challenged elders in this short-lived sitcom. Dave (black) and John (white) had been friends since childhood, and joked about everything, including their racial differences. Their business, "Hi-Intensity," was a small film and videotaping company which they hoped would lead to Hollywood, but for now they settled for taping bar mitzvahs and weddings. Supporting them were John's nutty new bride, Lorraine, and Dave's spunky girlfriend and wannabe bride, Phyllis. Lobbing sarcastic comments into the mix were Lorraine's drawling, bigoted mom, Mo ("the white-trash queen"), and Dave's rigid father Henry, their landlord, whose motto was "black-owned, black-operated."

Buddies was a spin-off from *Home Improvement*, with the characters first being seen on the March 14, 1995, episode of the latter series (with Jim Breuer as John).

BUDDY FARO (*Detective*)

FIRST TELECAST: *September 25, 1998*
LAST TELECAST: *December 4, 1998*
BROADCAST HISTORY:
Sep 1998–Dec 1998, CBS Fri 9:00–10:00
CAST:
Buddy Faro .... Dennis Farina
Bob Jones .... Frank Whaley
Julie Barber .... Allison Smith
El Jefe .... Charlie Robinson

Stylish, offbeat detective show about a legendary private eye who surfaced unchanged after two decades in obscurity, just as the '60s were once again becoming cool. Talk about timing! Bob Jones, a competent but incredibly dull private investigator, had been hired by Julie to find the colorful but long-missing Buddy Faro—one of Bob's childhood heroes—so she could pass along an inheritance. Buddy had disappeared on September 9, 1978, just as his star was beginning to fade. Tracking Buddy down in a small town in Mexico, Jones dragged him back to L.A., cleaned him up, and watched him resume his lifestyle as if it were still the '60s. Suave and debonair, he looked like a member of the Rat Pack, was politically incorrect, and alternately charmed women and treated them like the male chauvinist pig he was. He was also very good at solving crimes. Bob and Julie, his new partners, vainly tried to update him on the radically changed times and keep him out of trouble.

El Jefe was Buddy's compadre from the Mexican slums ("You owe me money!"), who followed him to L.A. and ended up becoming part of the team. There was plenty of violence, mixed liberally with off-the-wall comedy, as the '60s collided with the '90s in present-day L.A. Some episodes featured real retro-celebrities appearing as themselves, including singer Jack Jones, actor George Hamilton (who had supposedly played Faro in a '70s TV detective series), and *Playboy*'s Hugh Hefner.

BUDWEISER SUMMER THEATRE, see *Movies—Prior to 1961*

BUFFALO BILL (*Situation Comedy*)

FIRST TELECAST: *May 31, 1983*
LAST TELECAST: *April 5, 1984*
BROADCAST HISTORY:
May 1983—Aug 1983, NBC Wed 9:30–10:00
Dec 1983–Apr 1984, NBC Thu 9:30–10:00
CAST:
Bill Bittinger .... Dabney Coleman
Jo Jo White .... Joanna Cassidy
Woody .... John Fiedler
Karl Shub .... Max Wright
Wendy Killian .... Geena Davis
Newdell .... Charles Robinson
Tony .... Meshach Taylor
Stan Fluger .... Claude Earl Jones

Surely one of the most unusual comedies of the 1980s, *Buffalo Bill* flouted a basic rule of series TV—that the leading character must, if nothing else, be likable. Bill Bittinger was arrogant, insensitive, and a thorough cad. As the garrulous host of an inexplicably popular local TV talk show in Buffalo, New York, he regularly played the role of "star," shamelessly used everyone around him, and blamed others for anything that went wrong. He did all this, it must be said, with style; Bill, as played by the talented Dabney Coleman, was a fascinating character, even if he did make you squirm at times. And—honoring one of TV's other basic rules, that good *must* win out in the end—he usually failed to get his way. Practically everybody was on to him, and Bill spent many a lonely night after his latest scheme or attempted amorous conquest had fallen through.

Among the people Bill worked with at WBFL-TV was Jo Jo, the beautiful director of his show, with whom he had an on-again, off-again romantic involvement. She harbored no illusions about his nature, however. Once he had proposed to her, with the gallant comment, "You're better than 90 percent of the bimbos out there." Woody was his mousy stage manager, who seemed incredibly naive (he worshiped Bill) but underneath it all, understood. Just to rub it in, the little guy happened to be extremely successful on the side, owning an auto dealership and Bill's apartment building. Karl was the nervous station manager at Channel 12, constantly beset by lawsuits brought on by Bill's outrageous on-air comments; Wendy, the ingenuous research assistant; and Newdell, the black makeup man, who took no grief from anyone, Bill included. Seen occasionally was Bill's daughter Melanie, portrayed by Pippa Peartree. Some rather sensitive subjects were dealt with in this comedy setting, including Jo Jo's abortion (after Bill had pompously decided for her that she should have the child), and Bill's racist dream, after he had had a run-in with Newdell. The dream was filled with Zulu warriors, pushy black hookers, and other outrageous stereotypes, all in pursuit of Bill, accompanied by the music of Ray Charles's "Hit the Road, Jack."

BUFFY THE VAMPIRE SLAYER (*Supernatural*)

FIRST TELECAST: *March 10, 1997*
LAST TELECAST:
BROADCAST HISTORY:
Mar 1997–Jan 1998, WB Mon 9:00–10:00
Jul 1997–Aug 1997, WB Sun 8:00–9:00
Jan 1998–May 2001, WB Tue 8:00–9:00
Jun 1998–Sep 1998, WB Mon 9:00–10:00
May 1999–Jun 1999, WB Mon 9:00–10:00
Jun 2001–Jul 2001, WB Wed 9:00–10:00
Jun 2001–Aug 2001, WB Sun 7:00–8:00
Oct 2001– , UPN Tue 8:00–9:00
Jul 2002, UPN Wed 9:00–10:00
CAST:
Buffy Summers .... Sarah Michelle Gellar
Alexander "Xander" Harris ..... Nicholas Brendon
Willow Rosenberg .... Alyson Hannigan
Cordelia Chase (1997–1999)... Charisma Carpenter
Rupert Giles (1997–2001, 2002–2003)
.... Anthony Stewart Head
The Master (1997) .... Mark Metcalf
Angel (1997–1999) .... David Boreanaz
Joyce Summers (1997–2002)... Kristine Sutherland
Colin, The Anointed (1997) ... Andrew J. Ferchland
Jenny Kalender (1997–1998)........ Robia LaMorte

Principal Snyder (1997–1999) ... Armin Shimerman
Spike (1997–1998, 1999–2003)..... James Marsters
Drusilla (1997–1998) .... Juliet Landau
Oz (1997–2000)........................ Seth Green
Mr. Trick (1998–1999)............ K. Todd Freeman
Faith (1998–1999, 2003) .... Eliza Dushku
Mayor Richard Wilkens III (1998–1999)
.... Harry Groener
Wesley Wyndham Price (1999) ...... Alexis Denisof
Anya Emerson (1998–2003)....... Emma Caulfield
Riley Finn (1999–2000) .... Marc Blucas
Maggie Walsh (1999–2000) .... Lindsay Crouse
Forrest (1999–2000).............. Leonard Roberts
Graham Miller (1999–2000) .... Bailey Chase
Tara Maclay (2000–2002) .... Amber Benson
Adam (2000)..................... George Hertzberg
Dawn Summers (2000–2003)
.... Michelle Trachtenberg
**Harmony Kendall (1999–2001)* .. Mercedes McNab
Ben (2000–2001) .... Charlie Weber
**Jonathan (2000–2003)* .... Danny Strong
Glory (2000–2001)................... Clare Kramer
Jinx (2001)....................... Troy T. Blendell
**Warren Meers (2001–2003)*........... Adam Busch
Andrew (2001–2003)................... Tom Lenk
Halfrek (2002) .... Kali Rocha
Principal Robin Wood (2002–2003)
.... D. B. Woodside
Amanda (2002–2003)................ Sarah Hagan
Kennedy (2002–2003)................. Iyari Limon
Molly (2002–2003) .... Clara Bryant
Rona (2003).................................. Indigo
Caleb (2003)......................... Nathan Fillion

*Occasional

This campy horror drama was set in Sunnydale, California. Bright, perky Buffy had just moved to town with her divorced mother Joyce, having been thrown out of her Los Angeles high school for burning down the school gym. (She did so to destroy a nest of vampires, but who knew?) Buffy was about to start her sophomore year at Sunnydale High, but unfortunately, her new hometown sat over the very mouth of Hell, and was about to be invaded by a horde of bloodsucking vampires. She was the vampire slayer charged with protecting the populace. Giles, the eccentric new librarian, was the "watcher" assigned to prepare her to fight the demonic creatures. Helping them were fellow students Willow, a brilliant but shy girl who was Buffy's best friend; Xander, a gawky, good-natured guy who was infatuated with Buffy; and Cordelia, the popular sexy girl whose contributions were more accidental than intentional. The local teen hangout was a club called The Bronze, where the youthful vampires looked like normal people until they morphed into their scaly demonic selves. In addition to vampires, Buffy fought witches, a giant praying mantis that took the form of a teacher at school, students possessed by demonic hyenas who ate the original principal, and a girl who was such a nonentity at school she had become invisible—all the better to get revenge on those who had ignored her. Angel, the mysterious hunk who gave Buffy advice, turned out to be a good vampire who had once been under the control of The Master, a powerful evil vampire Buffy killed in the first season.

During 1997–1998 the main threat was a sadistic, recently arrived vampire named Spike who, it turned out, had been sired by Angel. By the end of the year Xander and Cordelia, who didn't like each other very much, were struggling with a strong sexual attraction, and Buffy's relationship with Angel was changing—they slept together in January but the true happiness he had found when they made love activated a Gypsy curse and caused him to revert back to his evil vampire self. Oz, a computer nerd friend, started dating Willow and found out he was a werewolf (which was okay as long as he locked himself up during the full moon). In February, Jenny, the teacher Giles loved, told Giles she loved him, but Angel then broke her neck to keep her from working out a way to restore Angel's soul. In addition Spike lost his beloved Drusilla to Angel, who was working with Drusilla and a demon to send the entire town of Sunnydale to Hell. Spike teamed with a reluctant Buffy to foil their plan; in the final confrontation, he skipped town with Drusilla, and Buffy stabbed Angel, forcing him into the demon's vortex. At episode's end a depressed Buffy left town to work things out.

That fall Buffy returned to Sunnydale after several months of soul searching and started her senior year—after convincing nasty Principal Snyder to let her back into school. Angel returned from the demon dimension as an animalistic creature but slowly got back to "normal," and Mayor Wilkens, himself a demon, was plotting to gain for himself unlimited power. In January, Giles proved to be too emotionally involved with Buffy's welfare to suit his superiors, and Price was sent to take over responsibilities as her watcher. Meanwhile Faith, another slayer who had seen her watcher killed by an ancient vampire, showed up in Sunnydale and joined the team. She accidentally killed an assistant mayor and subsequently changed sides, becoming the mayor's evil aide. He set her up in a fancy apartment and she helped him get the Books of Ascension, which would enable him to gain power. Angel told Buffy he was leaving Sunnydale, for her sake, before this happened, but then Faith shot him with a poisoned arrow. Since the only thing that could save him was the blood of a slayer, Buffy confronted Faith and stabbed her to death.

Amidst the turmoil Buffy and Willow were both accepted to the University of California at Sunnydale, and at the senior prom Buffy was given an award as "class protector" for, at one time or another, saving the lives of most of her classmates.

The 1998–1999 season finale was delayed until July due to controversy over its depiction of school violence. In it, Mayor Wilkens morphed into a towering serpent while addressing the graduating class, and Buffy and her classmates battled him and his undead minions with medieval weapons and flamethrowers they had hidden under their gowns. He was destroyed, and after the battle Angel slipped away to begin a new life in Los Angeles.

That fall Buffy, Willow and Oz were starting college at UC Sunnydale and Xander, though not in college, was still around to help, as was Giles, who was no longer the librarian at Sunnydale High. Anya, an ex-demon from the gang's high school days, returned and began an affair with Xander. In November Oz, after almost killing Willow during one of his werewolf phases, left town. It was revealed that Ben, one of Buffy's fellow students, was a secret agent for The Initiative, a group of scientific demon hunters, under the leadership of Prof. Maggie Walsh. Spike, who was back, escaped from their laboratory with a chip implanted in his body that kept him from feeding on the blood of humans. He was forced to align himself with the gang, though he was not always honest with them. Just before Christmas Buffy and Riley (an agent for The Initiative) were developing a relationship when they discovered they were both hunting demons and vampires. When Riley found out that Prof. Walsh wanted to eliminate Buffy, whom she considered a rival, he joined Buffy's group. Walsh's creation Adam (a sort of Frankenstein monster—part human, part demon, part machine) killed Walsh, took control of the vampire/demon community and began a reign of terror. In May Oz returned, supposedly cured of his werewolf curse by Tibetan monks. Unfortunately, when he found out that Willow was involved with Tara, an apprentice witch she had befriended, he reverted and was caught by The Initiative. Riley got him out but he left town for good. With the help of a spell cast by Willow, Buffy and Riley were able to destroy Adam, who was in the process of creating a race of superhuman hybrids.

At the start of the 2000–2001 season Buffy convinced Giles to be her watcher again and he opened a magic shop, The Magic Box. At the end of the episode Buffy discovered Dawn, who appeared to be her kid sister (but wasn't). Spike was determined to rid himself of the chip that prevented his returning to his vampire ways and to get revenge on Buffy but, after failing, realized he was in love with her (in the spring Dawn found out and told Buffy). Buffy's relationship with Riley deteriorated, and he left town. In January Giles' superiors showed up in Sunnydale seeking Buffy's help dealing with Glory, who had been causing trouble since the fall. They told her Glory was a god and, if she activated the "key," the barriers between dimensions would be breached and the universe thrown into chaos. Monks had sent the key to Buffy for protection, in human form—Dawn. It was revealed that Ben, a shy intern at the hospital, was sharing his body with Glory, and he periodically morphed into her. At the end of February Buffy's mom died from a brain aneurysm and the whole gang was depressed. Buffy dropped out of college to help Dawn, who had been skipping school, and Willow and Amber broke up. Glory thought Amber was the key and damaged her mind before she found out it was Dawn she was after. In the season finale Xander proposed to Anya, Willow got Amber's mind back and the gang fought it out with Glory—Buffy defeated her, with Giles killing the body after it had morphed back into Ben. At the end, in order to save both Dawn and the world from the interdimensional breach, Buffy sacrificed her own life. The last scene was a shot of her tombstone in the Sunnydale cemetery.

With Buffy gone the gang was having difficulty finishing off vampires despite Willow coordinating and the "help" of a robot Buffy. Giles returned to England, leaving Anya to run The Magic Box. Willow cast a spell at Buffy's grave site that brought the slayer back to life, but the resurrected Buffy was somewhat disoriented and not particularly happy. Warren, who had created the Buffy robot, and his two friends Jonathan and Andrew were the Troika, troublemakers who wanted to make the real Buffy their love slave. Willow's compulsion to use magic to solve problems—not always with the results she expected—created problems and alienated Tara, who left. Spike and Buffy had a confrontation that turned them both on and they had sex— she forbade him from letting anyone know, but they continued to have an affair. In the spring Xander and Anya were supposed to get married, but at the last moment he got cold feet and bailed out, leaving her devastated. In late April she let her demon friend, Halfrek, convince her to go back to being a vengeance demon and she tried to get even with Xander for the pain he had caused her, but eventually her conscience got the best of her and she was made human again. Willow and Tara were patching up things when a crazed Warren, during a fight with Buffy, accidentally shot and killed Tara. Willow went nuts, killing Warren and hunting down Jonathan and Andrew, who had fled to Mexico, but the gang managed to calm her down before she harmed them. Meanwhile Spike, who had left town in an ugly mood, passed a test and was given a soul by an African demon.

Buffy's final season began with Dawn starting her first day at the newly restored Sunnydale High; Spike living in the school's basement and adapting to his new soul, and Willow temporarily in England with Giles, working on her redemption. Principal Wood gave Buffy a job as guidance counselor because she seemed so in tune with the students. Dawn was the first of the gang to encounter their ultimate threat, The First Evil, a shapeshifting demon. Meanwhile, after they returned from Mexico, Andrew killed Jonathan while Spike, under temporary control of The First, went on a murder spree but eventually got his senses back. Giles was back in town, along with three potential slayers, with word that The First was killing potential slayers to rid the world of good and leave the Hellmouth under Sunnydale High free to open. Buffy got Spike to help her train the potential slayers and, when she realized that the chip in his body was malfunctioning, managed to get it removed. She subsequently found out that Principal Wood's mother had been a slayer and that Spike was responsible for her death.

Faith returned to Sunnydale to help and made peace with Buffy. The new menace was Caleb, who was living at a nearby vineyard with his "bringers" and had a mysterious something that belonged to Buffy. When the gang confronted him Caleb broke Rona's arm, killed Molly and a few of the apprentice slayers and blinded Xander in one eye. Buffy had her next encounter with Caleb at the high school, where he knocked her out. After an argument the potential slayers decided they wanted to report to Faith, not Buffy, and tossed Buffy out of her own home.

Buffy found a trapdoor that led to a scythe lodged in a rock. The scythe, which she removed, would turn out to be a potent weapon. At a tomb she met an old woman who told her the scythe was created to destroy the last pure demon. Caleb arrived, killed the old woman and almost got Buffy, but she was saved when long-departed Angel showed up. Buffy thought she had killed Caleb and gave Angel a passionate kiss. Their reunion was interrupted by Caleb, who had somehow survied, and this time she finished the job. Angel, who could smell Spike's scent on her, was jealous and after an argument she told him to leave.

To defeat The First, Buffy had Willow invoke a spell that took the power from Buffy and the scythe and gave it to every potential slayer in the world, making everyone a slayer. With the help of the new slayers the gang fought a climactic battle in which many died, including Anya. Most of Sunnydale was swallowed into the Hellmouth and Spike, whose fate was to return to Hell, told Buffy to leave with her friends and have a normal life. She departed, secure in the knowledge that there were now millions of girls who could fight the eternal evil.

Adapted from the 1992 movie starring Kristy Swanson, Donald Sutherland, and Luke Perry.

BUG JUICE (*Documentary*)

BROADCAST HISTORY:

Disney Channel
30 minutes
Original episodes: *1999–2002*
Premiered: *March 1998*

A kids' version of MTV's *The Real World* that followed a group of teens and tweens at summer camp. The locations featured were Camp Waziyatah in Maine (1998), Camp Highlander in North Carolina (1999) and Brush Ranch Camp in New Mexico (2001). Approximately 10 campers were highlighted in each series, participating in competitions and other camp activities, and talking to the camera about their reactions and feelings toward each other, both good and bad. A notorious moment among fans was when Eve and Jen were expelled from Brush Ranch for bringing "inappropriate materials."

For those who have never experienced summer camp, "bug juice" is the flavored drink of uncertain origin commonly fed to campers. Kids have many theories about it, as in the old scout song (to the tune of "On Top of Old Smoky"): "At the camp with the Boy Scouts / they gave us a drink / we thought it was Kool-Aid / because it was pink. But the thing that they told us / would've grossed out a moose / for that great-tasting pink drink / was really bug juice."

BUGS BUNNY/ROADRUNNER SHOW, THE (*Cartoon*)

FIRST TELECAST: *April 27, 1976*
LAST TELECAST: *June 1, 1976*
BROADCAST HISTORY:

Apr 1976–Jun 1976, CBS Tue 8:00–8:30

For a five-week period in the spring of 1976, CBS aired a collection of cartoon shorts from the Warner Bros. cartoon library as a prime-time series. Although titled *The Bugs Bunny/Roadrunner Show*, the series included appearances by such famous cartoon characters as Elmer Fudd, Sylvester and Tweety, Yosemite Sam, Daffy Duck, and Pepe le Pew. Voice characterizations were done by veteran Mel Blanc. This series ran concurrently with other Warner Bros. cartoons that were aired on Saturday mornings by CBS under the same title.

BUGS BUNNY SHOW, THE (*Cartoon*)

FIRST TELECAST: *October 11, 1960*
LAST TELECAST: *September 25, 1962*
BROADCAST HISTORY:

Oct 1960–Sep 1962, ABC Tue 7:30–8:00

HOST:

Dick Coughlan

VOICES:

Mel Blanc

Bugs Bunny and the entire Warner Bros. inventory of theatrical cartoon characters first appeared on network television in this prime-time series, which premiered in the fall of 1960, the same season that saw the premiere of ABC's most successful venture in prime-time animation, *The Flintstones.* Along with Bugs were Porky Pig, Tweety and Sylvester, Yosemite Sam, the Roadrunner, Henry Hawk, Hippity Hopper, Daffy Duck, and others. All voices were done by veteran Mel Blanc. By the time this series departed from prime time in September 1962 a Saturday morning version had already started (in April 1962). That Saturday morning version became the longest continuously running Saturday morning children's program in the history of network television.

Under an assortment of titles—*The Bugs Bunny Show, The Bugs Bunny–Road Runner Show, The Bugs Bunny/Looney Tunes Comedy Hour,* and *The Bugs Bunny & Tweety Show*—it ran on ABC (1962–1968, the final season on Sunday morning), CBS (1968–1973), ABC again (1973–1975), CBS (1975–1985), and ABC (1985–2000). In addition, the WB aired *Bugs 'n' Daffy* on weekday afternoons from 1996 to 1998.

BUICK ACTION THEATER (*Dramatic Anthology*)

FIRST TELECAST: *August 22, 1958*
LAST TELECAST: *October 3, 1958*
BROADCAST HISTORY:

Aug 1958–Oct 1958, ABC Fri 9:30–10:00

The plays telecast in this short summer series consisted of filmed reruns of episodes from other anthology series.

BUICK BERLE SHOW, THE, see *Milton Berle Show, The*

BUICK CIRCUS HOUR, THE (*Musical Drama*)

FIRST TELECAST: *October 7, 1952*
LAST TELECAST: *June 16, 1953*
BROADCAST HISTORY:

Oct 1952–Jun 1953, NBC Tue 8:00–9:00

CAST:

The Clown .... Joe E. Brown
Bill Sothern .... John Raitt
Kim O'Neill .... Dolores Gray
The Ringmaster .... Frank Gallop

Set within the framework of a circus, this was the story of an aging clown who tries to help a young singer, Kim O'Neill, who has just joined the troupe. Kim had joined the circus to be near its owner, Bill Sothern, a boisterous, fun-loving giant of a man with whom she had fallen in love. Musical production numbers as well as real circus acts were featured in this series, all interwoven with the stories of the personal and professional conflicts of circus life. Originating live from New York, the series was aired every fourth week in the time slot normally occupied by Milton Berle's *Texaco Star Theatre.*

BUILDING, THE (*Situation Comedy*)

FIRST TELECAST: *August 20, 1993*
LAST TELECAST: *September 17, 1993*
BROADCAST HISTORY:

Aug 1993, CBS Fri 9:30–10:00
Sep 1993, CBS Fri 9:00–9:30

CAST:

Bonnie Kennedy .... Bonnie Hunt
Finley .... Michael G. Hagerty
Big Tony .... Richard Kuhlman
Brad .... Don Lake
Stan .... Tom Virtue
Holly .... Holly Wortell

EXECUTIVE PRODUCERS:

Bonnie Hunt
David Letterman

Rapid-fire comedy centering on Bonnie, a timid, conservative, struggling actress who had moved back to Chicago and into her old apartment across from Wrigley Field after her fiancé had dumped her. Her fellow tenants provided a dubious support group—Holly, her loud, Jewish best friend; Finley, a fireman and a part-time bartender at the local hangout; Big Tony, a boisterous man with the vocabulary of a stevedore; Brad, an unemployed journalist who always showed up in time to get a free meal from Bonnie; and Stan, Brad's roommate and a fellow actor. Bonnie's main gig at the moment was as a TV model—"The Randolph Carpet Girl."

All of the regulars in this series were friends and alumni of Chicago's Second City improvisational comedy theater, where they had worked together. Miss Hunt was the series' creator, wrote all of the scripts, and was co-executive producer with her good friend David Letterman.

BUILT TO LAST (*Situation Comedy*)

FIRST TELECAST: *September 24, 1997*
LAST TELECAST: *October 15, 1997*
BROADCAST HISTORY:

Sep 1997–Oct 1997, NBC Wed 8:30–9:00

CAST:

Royale Watkins .... Royale Watkins
Robert Watkins .... Geoffrey Owens
Randal Watkins .... J. Lamont Pope
Tammy Watkins .... Natalie Desselle
Ryce Watkins (age 9) .... Jeremy Suarez
Russel Watkins .... Paul Winfield
Sylvia Watkins .... Denise Dowse
Stanley Taylor .... Richard Speight, Jr.

This ironically named sitcom, which aired just three times on NBC's fall schedule, was based on the real-life family of black comedian Royale Watkins. In the series, Royale was a young computer whiz who put his career on hold in order to help run the family's small construction business in Washington, D.C., after his proud father Russel suffered a mild heart attack. Crusty, cranky Russel could do little but complain loudly as Royale dueled with bossy eldest son Robert, an architect, teenage Randal, and loud, chubby Tammy. Sylvia was the bossy mom, and Stanley the sycophantic young white assistant. There was a lot of yelling at Watkins Construction.

Actor Royale's real-life father ran a real Watkins Construction in Washington, which was far more successful than this series.

BULL (*Drama*)

BROADCAST HISTORY:

TNT
60 minutes
Original episodes: *2000* (22 episodes)
Premiered: *August 15, 2000*

CAST:

Robert "the Kaiser" Roberts .... Donald Moffat
Robert "Ditto" Roberts III .... George Newbern
Corey Granville .... Malik Yoba
Alison Jeffers .... Elisabeth Rohm
Marty Decker .... Ian Kahn
Marissa Rufo .... Alicia Coppola
Carson Boyd .... Christopher Wiehl
Hunter Lasky .... Stanley Tucci
Pam Boyd .... Elizabeth Anne Allen

TNT was a little late in dramatizing the stock market boom days of the late 1990s in this overheated Wall Street drama. Robert "Ditto" Roberts III was the grandson of the ruthless head of the prestigious firm of Meriwether & Mark. Rebelling at his grandfather's autocratic ways (so autocratic he was known on the trading floor as "the Kaiser"), Ditto rallied five of his colleagues to quit and start their own firm, HSD Capital. Joining him to "make some green, people" were Corey, the brilliant black trader who chafed at the Kaiser's prejudice; ice queen Alison; new kid Marty; no-nonsense Marissa, who was set up by the Kaiser to take the fall for an illegal trade; and eager, idealistic trainee Carson. The Kaiser immediately tried to crush them through lawsuits and scaring off clients, and his seeming henchman, weasily Hunter Lasky, did the same. But Hunter, a hard-hitting negotiations shark, ultimately joined the rebels.

Everybody plotted and schemed, slept around, and talked of making a killing from arbitrage and IPOs, but with the real-life market crumbling, disillusioned viewers fled; *Bull* was canceled after 11 episodes. Eleven additional episodes were filmed but not seen during the original run. Several new characters were introduced in these unaired episodes (which may turn up somewhere), including Stubby Frye (Dave Ruby), Nora (Heather Dawn) and Walt Wesley (Rick Peters).

BULLWINKLE SHOW, THE (*Cartoon*)

FIRST TELECAST: *September 24, 1961*
LAST TELECAST: *September 16, 1962*
BROADCAST HISTORY:

Sep 1961–Sep 1962, NBC Sun 7:00–7:30

VOICES:

Bullwinkle Moose, Dudley Doright, Mr. Peabody
.... Bill Scott
Rocky J. Squirrel, Natasha Fatale .... June Foray
Boris Badenov .... Paul Frees
Aesop .... Charles Ruggles
Snidley Whiplash .... Hans Conried
Sherman .... Walter Tetley
Narrator of "Fractured Fairy Tales"
.... Edward Everett Horton
Narrator of "Bullwinkle" segments
.... William Conrad

This cartoon show included clever satire designed to appeal to adults as well as children. The principal characters in the series were Bullwinkle and his friend Rocket J. (Rocky) Squirrel. Boris and Natasha were the cynical but rather ineffectual spies with whom they were were most often involved. Other featured segments, not seen in every episode, included "Fractured Fairy Tales"; "Peabody's Improbable History," in which a wealthy dog, Mr. Peabody, traveled back through time with his adopted boy, Sherman; "Adventures of Dudley Doright," a noble mountie confronted with the evil Snidley Whiplash; and "Aesop and Son," in which fables were recounted in unusual ways.

The characters of Rocky and Bullwinkle had originally appeared in a series called *Rocky and His Friends*, in ABC's weekday afternoon lineup during the 1959–1960 season. That series, which had different supporting segments than *The Bullwinkle Show*, ran on ABC until September 1961. *The Bullwinkle Show* then appeared on NBC, Sunday at 7 P.M. from 1961–1962 (above); moved to NBC's Sunday afternoon and then Saturday morning schedule in 1962–1964; and finally went back to ABC, where it remained on Sunday mornings until September 1973. *The Bullwinkle Show* returned home to NBC's Saturday morning lineup almost a decade later, for the 1981–1982 season.

BURKE'S LAW (*Police/Detective Drama*)

FIRST TELECAST: *September 20, 1963*

LAST TELECAST: *August 3, 1995*

BROADCAST HISTORY:

Sep 1963–Sep 1964, ABC Fri 8:30–9:30
Sep 1964–Sep 1965, ABC Wed 9:30–10:30
Sep 1965–Jan 1966, ABC Wed 10:00–11:00
Jan 1994–Sep 1994, CBS Fri 9:00–10:00
May 1995–Aug 1995, CBS Wed 8:00–9:00

CAST:

Capt. Amos Burke .... Gene Barry
Det. Tim Tilson (1963–1965) .... Gary Conway
Det. Sgt. Les Hart (1963–1965) .... Regis Toomey
Henry (1963–1965) .... Leon Lontoc
Sgt. Ames (1964–1965) .... Eileen O'Neill
"The Man" (1965–1966) .... Carl Benton Reid
Peter Burke (1994–1995) .... Peter Barton
Henry (1994–1995) .... Danny Kamekona
Lily Morgan (1994–1995) ..... Bever-Leigh Banfield
Vinnie Piatte (1994–1995) .... Dom DeLuise

Gene Barry played a Los Angeles chief of detectives who also was a millionaire, a role not unlike his cowboy-dandy in the earlier *Bat Masterson* series. The character of Amos Burke was first seen two seasons earlier in a *Dick Powell Theatre* presentation ("Who Killed Julia Greer?"), where it was played by Dick Powell. As portrayed by Barry, Amos Burke was high-living, elegant, and witty, yet cagey and tough when required. He lived in a palatial mansion and habitually arrived at the scene of a crime in a Rolls-Royce driven by his chauffeur, Henry. Burke also had a magnetic attraction for beautiful women, and interrupted his romances only for interesting homicide cases, usually involving the elite.

His sidekicks were Det. Tim Tilson, a smart, young college type; Det. Les Hart, a seasoned veteran of the force; and in 1964–1965 a pretty policewoman, Sgt. Ames. *Amos Burke* was highly promoted during its first season and featured dozens of Hollywood stars as guests, ranging from Annette Funicello to Sir Cedric Hardwicke; 63 stars appeared in the first eight episodes, according to one press release.

An important change in format and title was made in September 1965. Glamour and sophistication remained the series' trademarks, but Amos Burke severed his connection with the police and became a debonair, globe-trotting secret agent for a United States intelligence agency. His only contact at the agency, and the only other regular during the last season, was known simply as "The Man." The title of the series was simultaneously changed to *Amos Burke—Secret Agent*.

Almost three decades after the original series had left the air, *Burke's Law* returned to television. Gene Barry was back as the remarkably well-preserved and still debonair cop, now chief of homicide for the L.A.P.D. During the intervening years the womanizing Burke had been married and fathered a son, Peter. Peter had inherited his father's good looks, charm, wit, and love of the law. He was now a homicide detective solving murder cases with his dad. Despite differences in both style and attitude—Peter was more impulsive and less patient than Amos—together they made an effective team. Other regulars were Amos's loyal manservant, Henry, who chauffeured him around in his Rolls-Royce; Lily, the forensics expert; and Amos's friend Vinnie, a gourmet chef who popped up in almost every episode.

The *Burke's Law* revival looked a bit like a land-locked *Love Boat*. The dialogue was incredibly corny, and every episode was populated with stars long past their prime. Among them were George Segal, Polly Bergen, Carol Channing, Connie Stevens, Buddy Ebsen, Anne Francis, Tanya Roberts, Edd Byrnes, Milton Berle, Jack Carter, Eva Gabor, Ed McMahon, John Astin, Audrey Meadows, Roddy McDowall, Bonnie Franklin, Florence Henderson, Efrem Zimbalist, Jr., and Don Knotts.

BURNING ZONE, THE (*Drama*)

FIRST TELECAST: *September 3, 1996*

LAST TELECAST: *June 24, 1997*

BROADCAST HISTORY:

Sep 1996–Jun 1997, UPN Tue 9:00–10:00

CAST:

Dr. Edward Marcase .... Jeffrey Dean Morgan
Dr. Kimberly Shiroma .... Tamlyn Tomita
Michael Hailey .... James Black
Dr. Daniel Cassian .... Michael Harris
Dr. Brian Taft (1997) .... Bradford Tatum
Henry Newland (1997) .... Todd Susman

Marcase was a brilliant young virologist who headed a highly trained bio-crisis team that fought biologically spread plagues and catastrophes *Mission Impossible*–style. Working with him were Shiroma, a molecular geneticist whose fiancé had lost his life to ebola while working with Marcase, and Hailey, a security specialist who had previously worked with the CIA. Dr. Cassian was the mysterious, politically connected physician who had assembled the team and gave them their assignments. In the first episode, in which the team was formed, they found a way to destroy an intelligent virus, recently resurrected in the jungles of Costa Rica, that used human bodies as its hosts. Later they fought viruses and other contagions—both natural and man-made—all over the world.

In January the team was reconstituted after Marcase and Shiroma were caught up in a political firestorm after some research in Zimbabwe. Added to the team was Dr. Taft, a Los Angeles–based expert in neuropathology with a big ego. Later Cassian got a new boss, Henry Newland, director of the Institute of Public Health, a humorless former N.S.A. executive who tried to do everything by the book.

BURNS AND ALLEN SHOW, THE, see *George Burns and Gracie Allen Show, The*

BURNS AND SCHREIBER COMEDY HOUR, THE (*Comedy/Variety*)

FIRST TELECAST: *June 30, 1973*
LAST TELECAST: *September 1, 1973*
BROADCAST HISTORY:
Jun 1973–Sep 1973, ABC Sat 9:00–10:00
REGULARS:
Jack Burns
Avery Schreiber
Teri Garr
Frank Welker
Fred Willard
Frank Link
Lisa Todd
Jack Elliott and Allyn Ferguson Orchestra
Tony Mordente Dancers

Comedians Jack Burns (the thin one) and Avery Schreiber (the rotund, mustachioed one) starred in this summer series, which featured their own brand of offbeat humor in sketches and blackouts. Various guest stars, including many popular singers, also appeared.

BUS STOP (*Drama*)

FIRST TELECAST: *October 1, 1961*
LAST TELECAST: *March 25, 1962*
BROADCAST HISTORY:
Oct 1961–Mar 1962, ABC Sun 9:00–10:00
CAST:
Grace Sherwood................Marilyn Maxwell
Will Mayberry....................Rhodes Reason
Elma Gahringer.....................Joan Freeman
Glenn Wagner.................Richard Anderson

The bus stop of this series was a diner in Sunrise, Colorado, a small town in Rocky Mountain country. The continuing characters included Grace Sherwood, the working owner of the diner; Elma Gahringer, its only waitress; Sheriff Will Mayberry; and District Attorney Glenn Wagner. The stories revolved around the people passing through Sunrise, and many an unusual character stepped off that interstate bus. The program earned national notoriety—and probably an early cancellation—due to an episode titled "A Lion Walks Among Us," which was based on a Tom Wicker novel and starred rock singer Fabian Forte as a youthful psychopath bent on murder and mayhem. This segment was widely denounced for its explicit violence and sadism and was cited in Congressional hearings on violence in television. The president of ABC-TV, when challenged by an angry senator as to whether he allowed his own children to watch such a series, stammered and admitted no—he did not.

Bus Stop was based on the successful play of the same name and had the original playwright, William Inge, as a script consultant.

BUSTIN' LOOSE (*Situation Comedy*)

BROADCAST HISTORY:
Syndicated only
30 minutes
Produced: *1987–1988* (26 episodes)
Released: *September 1987*
CAST:
Sonny Barnes......................Jimmie Walker
Mimi Shaw..........................Vonetta McGee
Rudey Butler.......................Larry Williams
Trish Reagan..........................Tyren Perry
Nikky Robison.........................Aaron Lohr
Sue Anne Tyler................Marie Lynn Wise

Sonny Barnes was a small-time con man in Philadelphia with a penchant for telling tall tales about his nonexistent exploits and relationships with famous people. When one of his scams landed him in court, the judge sentenced him to five years' community service—helping social worker Mimi Shaw take care of the four orphans who lived with her. Sonny moved into the basement of her home and took over, however reluctantly, most of the work around the house. He also endeared himself to the orphans, who were fascinated by his bragging. Rudey, the oldest, was a well-meaning klutz who was blind without his glasses; Trish was a popular teen who was the most "adult" of the group; Nikky was street-smart and had the potential to become a junior-grade Sonny; and little Sue Anne was just too cuddly and adorable for words.

Based loosely on the 1981 movie of the same name starring Richard Pryor.

BUSTING LOOSE (*Situation Comedy*)

FIRST TELECAST: *January 17, 1977*
LAST TELECAST: *November 16, 1977*
BROADCAST HISTORY:
Jan 1977–May 1977, CBS Mon 8:30–9:00
Jul 1977–Nov 1977, CBS Wed 8:30–9:00
CAST:
Lenny Markowitz...................Adam Arkin
Melody Feebeck...............Barbara Rhoades
Sam Markowitz.....................Jack Kruschen
Pearl Markowitz.......................Pat Carroll
Lester Bellman....................Danny Goldman
Allan Simmonds....................Steve Nathan
Vinnie Mordabito................Greg Antonacci
Woody Warshaw......................Paul Sylvan
Ralph Cabell..........................Paul B. Price
Raymond St. Williams..............Ralph Wilcox
Jackie Gleason...................Louise Williams

After graduating from engineering school, young Lenny Markowitz decided it was time to find his own place, away from his overprotective parents Sam and Pearl. He secretly moved into a run-down apartment building and set up housekeeping. Since he could not even afford to cover up the ducks on the wallpaper left by the previous tenant, it was not exactly a swinger's pad. It did have compensations, however, most notably his next-door neighbor Melody, a beautiful young woman who worked for an escort service. To make money on a temporary basis, until he could find more suitable employment, Lenny went to work as a salesman at Mr. Cabell's shoe store, where he worked with a "hip" black named Raymond. Lenny's buddies, Lester, Allan, Vinnie and Woody, were frequent visitors to his place and partners in mischief, as when they left the New York setting of the series to hunt girls at a fashionable Catskills resort. In the fall of 1977, Lenny found a regular girlfriend in a curvaceous young beauty named "Jackie Gleason" (no relation, or resemblance, to the famous TV comedian).

BUTT UGLY MARTIANS (*Cartoon*)

BROADCAST HISTORY:

Nickelodeon
30 minutes
Original episodes: *2001–2002* (26 episodes)
Premiered: *November 9, 2001*

VOICES:

Cmdr. B-bop-A-Luna .... Charlie Schlatter
Do Wah-Diddy .... Jess Harnell
2-T Fru-T, Mike, Ronald .... Rob Paulsen
Angela .... Kath Soucie
Cedric .... Ogie Banks
Emperor Bog, Dr. Damage .... S. Scott Bullock
Stoat Muldoon .... Robert Stack

Three aliens—yes, they were pretty ugly—landed on earth in the year 2053 in this nonsensical sci-fi parody. Discovering video games, burgers and hover boards, they decided they'd rather hang with some teenagers than conquer the place. B-bop-A-Luna was the fun-loving leader; Do Wah-Diddy, the slightly dense alien who was, however, a great mimic; and 2-T Fru-T, the all-around handyman. "Dog" was their versatile, robotic pet canine. Their new teen friends were hunky Mike, the kids' somewhat reluctant leader ("My parents will kill me!"); smart, independent Angela; and technical whiz Cedric. The only problem with the arrangement was the aliens' evil boss, a raving lunatic named Bog, who was circling Earth in a spaceship with his scientist henchman Dr. Damage ("dah-mahge") waiting for the planet to be subdued. So each week the aliens sent back phony reports making it look like they were doing just that. Meanwhile they had to fend off attacks from other aliens by chanting "B-K-M" (butt-kicking-mode) and morphing into fearsome, armored fighters. Observing all this were humorless Stoat Muldoon, host of the cable TV show *Stoat Muldoon: Alien Hunter,* and his geeky assistant, Ronald. Muldoon tried constantly to expose or capture the little guys, unaware that they were actually protecting Earth, but he never succeeded.

BUZZKILL (*Comedy*)

BROADCAST HISTORY:

MTV
30 minutes
Produced: *1996–1997*
Premiered: *June 18, 1996*

REGULARS:

Dave Sheridan
Travis Draft
Frank Hudetz

Three young guys drove around various cities in a beat-up van playing pranks in this MTV variation on *Candid Camera.* In one segment they intercepted nubile young sunbathers while posing as the "Miami Beach Safety Patrol"; in another they became fake paparazzi, always shooting the wrong people; and in another, they conned people into posing as models for ridiculous clothes. The series was created by comic Dave Sheridan.

BUZZY WUZZY (*Comedy/Variety*)

FIRST TELECAST: *November 17, 1948*
LAST TELECAST: *December 8, 1948*
BROADCAST HISTORY:

Nov 1948–Dec 1948, ABC Wed 7:30–7:45

HOST:

Jerry Bergen
Imogene Coca

Hollywood comedian Jerry Bergen had just finished work on *The Pirate,* a Judy Garland film, when he was recruited to try television in this short comedy-variety show. It lasted only four weeks. Imogene Coca was seen with him.

BY POPULAR DEMAND (*Variety*)

FIRST TELECAST: *July 2, 1950*
LAST TELECAST: *September 22, 1950*
BROADCAST HISTORY:

Jul 1950–Aug 1950, CBS Sun 7:30–8:00
Aug 1950–Sep 1950, CBS Fri 10:00–10:30
Sep 1950, CBS Fri 10:30–11:00

REGULARS:

Robert Alda
Arlene Francis (Sep)
The Harry Sosnik Orchestra

Robert Alda was the master of ceremonies for this series, which featured four professional entertainment acts competing with each other in an elimination competition to determine which act would return the following week. Winners were determined by the applause-meter vote of the studio audience. Robert Alda left the show at the beginning of September and was replaced by Arlene Francis for the last three telecasts.

BYLINE (*Drama*)

FIRST TELECAST: *November 4, 1951*
LAST TELECAST: *December 9, 1951*
BROADCAST HISTORY:

Nov 1951–Dec 1951, ABC Sun 7:30–8:00

CAST:

Betty Furness

Betty Furness starred in this brief series of live mysteries, which filled in ABC's Sunday 7:30 P.M. time slot until *Ellery Queen* moved over from DuMont in December 1951. Miss Furness was introduced in the first episode as a reporter on the trail of international criminals.

The official title of the program must surely be one of the longest in TV history: *Your Kaiser Dealer Presents Kaiser-Frazer "Adventures in Mystery" Starring Betty Furness in "Byline."*

For two weeks prior to its evening run, the program had run Saturday at noon under the rather simpler title *News Gal.*

BYLINE—STEVE WILSON, syndicated title for *Big Town*

BYRDS OF PARADISE (*Family Drama*)

FIRST TELECAST: *March 3, 1994*
LAST TELECAST: *June 23, 1994*
BROADCAST HISTORY:

Mar 1994–Jun 1994, ABC Thu 8:00–9:00

CAST:

Prof. Sam Byrd .... Timothy Busfield
Harry Byrd (age 16) .... Seth Green
Franny Byrd (15) .... Jennifer Love Hewitt
Zeke Byrd (11) .... Ryan O'Donohue
Healani Douglas .... Elizabeth Lindsey
Valentina Aguilar .... Betty Carvalho
Sonny Kaulukukui .... Robert Kekaula
Manu Kaulukukui .... Lani Opunui-Ancheta
Alan Moon .... Arlo Guthrie
Dr. Murray Rubenstein .... Bruce Weitz
Mo Pa .... Matthew Stephen Liu
Crystal Sapolu .... Elsa Awaya

Todd Matsuoka .... Todd Yamashita
Rex Palmer .... Warren Frost

Sun, surf, and anguish marked this family drama about a Yale professor whose wife had been killed at a cash machine in New Haven and who then moved his family to Hawaii to "get away from the memories." No sooner was Sam installed as the new headmaster of Palmer School than conflicts with the locals (to whom all newcomers were "haoles") and with his own kids darkened the azure sky.

Harry was hip, quick-witted, and smart but troubled by what had happened; rebellious, self-centered Franny was even worse off. Zeke, the scrappy eleven-year-old, seemed to be bearing up best. On campus Sam dealt with Healani, the feisty (and attractive) dean of students, while being counseled in island ways by Val, his motherly secretary. Sonny and Manu, the hefty handyman and housekeeper for the Byrds, also provided entree into island culture. Also seen were Alan Moon, a warmed-over hippie and 45-year-old high school student, and Dr. Rubenstein, a psychiatrist who gave the family much-needed counseling. Heidi was the family's Labrador retriever.

Filmed on Oahu in the Hawaiian Islands.

BYRON ALLEN SHOW, THE (*Talk*)

BROADCAST HISTORY:

Syndicated only
60 minutes
Produced: *1989–1992* (131 episodes)
Released: *September 1989*

REGULARS:

Byron Allen
Terry Wollman
John Cramer

Byron Allen, former co-host of *Real People* in the early 1980s, resurfaced five years later with this weekly late-night talk show that aired in most markets on Saturday night after the local news. Terry Wollman directed the studio orchestra and John Cramer was the off-camera announcer.

In the fall of 1992 Allen's show was cut to half an hour in length and reworked as a comedy/talk show in which he did a lot of out-of-studio comic bits. There was almost no talk, only comedy sketches and performances by guest comics. By the end of the year the reworked *Byron Allen Show*, which aired Monday through Friday in a limited number of markets, had faded from the air.

C

CBN (Christian Broadcasting Network) (Network), see ABC Family Channel

CBS CARTOON THEATRE (*Cartoons*)
FIRST TELECAST: *June 13, 1956*
LAST TELECAST: *September 5, 1956*
BROADCAST HISTORY:
Jun 1956–Sep 1956, CBS Wed 7:30–8:00
HOST:
Dick Van Dyke

This summer cartoon series featured the characters from Hollywood's "Terrytoons," Heckle and Jeckle, Gandy Goose, Sour Puss, Dinky Duck, and Little Roquefort. Through the use of special film techniques, host Dick Van Dyke was seen chatting with the animated characters between cartoons.

CBS LATE MOVIE, THE (*Various*)
FIRST TELECAST: *February 14, 1972*
LAST TELECAST: *January 6, 1989*
BROADCAST HISTORY:
Feb 1972–Jan 1989, CBS Mon–Fri 11:30–Conclusion

In the early 1970s CBS had attempted to compete in the late-night audience sweepstakes with *The Merv Griffin Show.* When *Griffin* failed to make a significant dent in the ratings of NBC's highly successful *Tonight Show,* CBS decided to take a different approach to late-night programming, airing the same thing local stations had been showing for years—movies. *The CBS Late Movie* at first consisted of theatrical and made-for-television films, mostly reruns of material that had previously been seen in prime time. In the fall of 1976 reruns of *Kojak* started airing two nights a week and by the end of the 1970s, despite the umbrella title *The CBS Late Movie,* the bulk of CBS' late-night lineup actually consisted of reruns of former prime-time series (*Kojak, Hawaii Five-O, Barnaby Jones, The Jeffersons,* etc.). There were also first American runs of such British series as *The New Avengers* and *Return of the Saint,* and limited runs of original programming (*NBA Basketball Playoffs* and *No Holds Barred*). In the fall of 1985, finally acknowledging the obvious, the series' title was changed to *CBS Late Night.*

Summarized below is a night-by-night history of *The CBS Late Movie.* In cases where there was a double feature on a given night, a semicolon is used to separate the first and second features. If more than one series alternated in the same time slot on different weeks they are separated by a slash.

CHRONOLOGY OF CBS LATE MOVIE BY NIGHT OF THE WEEK

Monday
Feb 1972–Jan 1977, Movie
Jan 1977–Sep 1977, Kojak; Movie
Sep 1977–Sep 1978, Movie
Sep 1978–Sep 1979, The Rockford Files; Movie
Sep 1979–Dec 1979, Harry-O; McMillan & Wife
Jan 1980–Sep 1980, Harry-O; Movie
Sept 1980–Oct 1980, Quincy, M.E.; The Saint
Oct 1980–Mar 1981, Quincy, M.E.; The New Avengers
Mar 1981–Nov 1981, Quincy, M.E.; Harry-O
Dec 1981–Feb 1982, Quincy, M.E.; Banacek
Feb 1982–Sep 1982, Quincy, M.E.; Columbo
Sep 1982–Jun 1983, Trapper John, M.D.; Columbo
Jun 1983–Jul 1983, Hart to Hart; Columbo
Jul 1983–Sep 1983, Hart to Hart; Movie
Sep 1983–Jun 1984, Hart to Hart; Columbo
Jul 1984–Aug 1984, Magnum, P.I.; Movie
Sep 1984–May 1985, Simon & Simon; McMillan & Wife
May 1985–Aug 1985, Simon & Simon; Columbo
Aug 1985–Sep 1985, Simon & Simon; Movie
Sep 1985–May 1986, Remington Steele; Movie
Jun 1986–Sep 1986, Magnum, P.I.; Movie
Sep 1986–Aug 1987, Simon & Simon; Movie
Sep 1987–Jan 1989, Hunter; Movie

Tuesday
Feb 1972–Sep 1976, Movie
Sep 1976–Jan 1977, Kojak; Movie
Jan 1977–Sep 1977, Movie
Sep 1977–Nov 1977, Kojak; Movie
Nov 1977–Aug 1978, Movie; *Kojak*
Aug 1978–Sep 1978, Movie
Sep 1978–May 1980, Barnaby Jones; Movie
May 1980–Jun 1980, Barnaby Jones; Mary Hartman, Mary Hartman
Jul 1980–Sep 1980, Cannon; Barnaby Jones
Sep 1980–Mar 1981, Lou Grant; Movie
Mar 1981–May 1981, Columbo; NBA Basketball Playoffs
May 1981–Jul 1981, Columbo
Jul 1981–Sep 1981, Cannon; The Saint
Sep 1981–Jan 1982, Alice; McCloud
Jan 1982–Jul 1982, Alice; WKRP In Cincinnati; McCloud
Aug 1982–Sep 1982, Alice; McCloud
Sep 1982–Aug 1983, Quincy, M.E.; McMillan & Wife
Aug 1983–Sep 1983, Movie
Sep 1983–Jun 1984, Magnum, P.I.; McCloud
Jul 1984–Aug 1984, McGarrett; Columbo
Sep 1984, Campaign '84; McGarrett; Columbo
Oct 1984, Campaign '84; The Fall Guy; Columbo
Nov 1984–May 1985, The Fall Guy; Columbo
May 1985, The Fall Guy; McCloud
Jun 1985–Sep 1985, Magnum, P.I.; McCloud
Sep 1985–Oct 1985, Simon & Simon; Movie
Oct 1985–Nov 1985, Simon & Simon; Cool Million
Nov 1985–Dec 1985, Simon & Simon; McCoy
Jan 1986, Simon & Simon; Madigan
Feb 1986–Sep 1986, Simon & Simon; Movie
Sep 1986–Dec 1986, Hot Shots; Movie
Dec 1986–Sep 1987, T.J. Hooker; Movie
Sep 1987–Sep 1988, Diamonds; Movie
Sep 1988–Jan 1989, Night Heat; Movie

Wednesday
Feb 1972–Sep 1977, Movie
Sep 1977–Nov 1977, Hawaii Five-O; Movie
Dec 1977–Aug 1978, Hawaii Five-O; Kojak
Aug 1978–Sep 1978, Hawaii Five-O; Movie
Sep 1978–Nov 1978, Hawaii Five-O; Kojak
Nov 1978–Dec 1978, Movie; *Kojak*
Jan 1979–Apr 1979, The Rockford Files; Kojak
May 1979, The Rockford Files; Hawaii Five-O
Jun 1979–Sep 1979, Switch; Kojak
Sep 1979–Oct 1979, Switch; Hawaii Five-O
Oct 1979–Dec 1979, Black Sheep Squadron; Hawaii Five-O

Dec 1979–Jan 1980, Black Sheep Squadron; Movie
Jan 1980–Mar 1980, Mary Hartman, Mary Hartman; Movie
Mar 1980–Jun 1980, Black Sheep Squadron; Movie
Jul 1980, The Saint; Black Sheep Squadron
Jul 1980–Sep 1980, The Saint; Movie
Sep 1980–Nov 1980, Campaign Countdown; Movie
Nov 1980–Mar 1981, Movie
Apr 1981, NBA Basketball Playoffs
May 1981–Sep 1981, Movie
Sep 1981–Jan 1982, WKRP in Cincinnati; Movie
Jan 1982–Sep 1982, Movie
Sep 1982–Dec 1982, Archie Bunker's Place; Movie
Dec 1982–Jun 1983, Hart to Hart; Movie
Jun 1983–Sep 1983, Police Story
Sep 1983–Jun 1984, Police Story; Movie
Jun 1984–Aug 1984, The New Avengers; McCloud
Sep 1984–May 1985, Magnum, P.I.; Movie
Jun 1985–Jul 1985, Night Heat; Movie
Jul 1985–Sep 1985, Movie; *The New Avengers*
Sep 1985–Sep 1986, T.J. Hooker; Movie
Sep 1986–Jul 1987, Adderly; Movie
Jul 1987–Sep 1987, Hot Shots; Movie
Sep 1987–Jul 1988, Adderly; Movie
Aug 1988, Diamonds; Movie
Aug 1988–Sep 1988, Movie
Sep 1988–Jan 1989, Night Heat; Movie

Thursday
Feb 1972–Sep 1976, Movie
Sep 1976–Sep 1977, Kojak; Movie
Sep 1977–Mar 1978, Movie
*Mar 1978–Sep 1979, M*A*S*H;* Movie
Sep 1979–Jan 1980, Columbo; McCloud/Banacek/Madigan
Jan 1980–Mar 1980, Columbo; Black Sheep Squadron
Mar 1980–Apr 1980, Columbo; Mary Hartman, Mary Hartman
May 1980–Sep 1980, The Jeffersons; Movie
Sep 1980–May 1981, The Jeffersons; McMillan & Wife
Jun 1981–Aug 1981, The Jeffersons; Hec Ramsey
Aug 1981–Sep 1981, The Jeffersons; Madigan
Sep 1981–Feb 1982, Quincy, M.E.; The Saint
Feb 1982–Sep 1982, Quincy, M.E.; McMillan & Wife
Sep 1982–Jul 1983, Quincy, M.E.; McCloud
Jul 1983–Sep 1983, Movie
Sep 1983–Jun 1984, Trapper John, M.D.; Movie
Jul 1984–Aug 1984, Hart to Hart; Movie
Sep 1984–Jan 1985, Newhart; Movie
Jan 1985–Mar 1985, Night Heat; Movie
Mar 1985–Apr 1985, Newhart; Movie
May 1985, Night Heat; Movie
Jun 1985–Jul 1985, The Fall Guy; Movie
Jul 1985–Aug 1985, The New Avengers; Movie
Aug 1985–Sep 1985, Columbo; The New Avengers
Sep 1985–Jul 1987, Night Heat; Movie
Aug 1987–Sep 1987, Movie
Sep 1987–Jan 1989, Night Heat; Movie

Friday
Feb 1972–Sep 1977, Movie
*Sep 1977–Dec 1977, M*A*S*H; Kojak*
*Dec 1977–Mar 1978, M*A*S*H;* Movie
Mar 1978–May 1978, NBA Basketball Playoffs
May 1978–Sep 1978, Movie
Sep 1978–Mar 1979, The New Avengers; Movie
Mar 1979–May 1979, NBA Basketball Playoffs
May 1979–Jul 1979, Kolchak: The Night Stalker; Movie
July 1979–Aug 1979, Hawaii Five-O; Movie
Sep 1979–Dec 1979, Kolchak: The Night Stalker; Movie
Dec 1979–Mar 1980, The Avengers; Return of the Saint
Mar 1980–Apr 1980, NBA Basketball Playoffs
May 1980–Aug 1980, The Avengers; Return of the Saint
Aug 1980–Sep 1980, The Avengers; Movie
Sep 1980–Oct 1980, No Holds Barred; The New Avengers
Oct 1980–Mar 1981, Movie
Mar 1981–May 1981, NBA Basketball Playoffs
June 1981–Sep 1981, Kolchak: The Night Stalker; Movie
Sep 1981–Oct 1981, Movie
Oct 1981–Jan 1982, Behind the Screen; Movie
Jan 1982–Mar 1982, Movie
Mar 1982–May 1982, NCAA/NBA Basketball Playoffs
May 1982–Apr 1983, Movie
Apr 1983–May 1983, NBA Basketball Playoffs
May 1983–Jan 1986, Movie
Feb 1986, Magnum, P.I
Feb 1986–Mar 1986, Magnum, P.I.; Movie
Mar 1986–May 1986, Magnum, P.I.; McGarrett
Jun 1986–Sep 1986, Movie
Sep 1986–Dec 1986, T.J. Hooker; Movie
Jan 1987–Jun 1987, Keep On Cruisin'; McGarrett
Jun 1987–Aug 1987, In Person from the Palace; Movie
Aug 1987–Sep 1987, Movie
Sep 1987–Mar 1988, Top of the Pops; Kolchak: The Night Stalker
Apr 1988–Jan 1989, Movie

CBS LATE NIGHT (*Various*)
FIRST TELECAST: *February 5, 1990*
LAST TELECAST: *March 28, 1991*
BROADCAST HISTORY:
Feb 1990–Apr 1990, CBS Mon–Fri 12:30–Conclusion
Apr 1990–Sep 1990, CBS Mon–Fri 11:30–Conclusion
Oct 1990–Mar 1991, CBS Mon–Fri 12:00 midnight–Conclusion

For almost seventeen years, ending in early 1989, CBS had aired a potpourri of late-night programming under the umbrella title *The CBS Late Movie* (changed to *CBS Late Night* in 1985). When *The Pat Sajak Show* premiered in 1989, the umbrella title was dropped. Thirteen months later, *Sajak* was cut back from ninety to sixty minutes, and the *CBS Late Night* umbrella title was revived to describe the programming following it. When *Sajak* went off the air in April, the umbrella was expanded to cover all CBS' post–11:30 P.M. weeknight action programming. As can be seen from the details below, there was little stability during the fourteen months *CBS Late Night* remained on the air. Things finally settled down when a collection of entirely first-run series, under the new umbrella title *CrimeTime After Primetime,* replaced *CBS Late Night* in April of 1991. In cases where there was a double feature on a given night, a semicolon is used to separate them.

CHRONOLOGY OF CBS LATE NIGHT
BY NIGHT OF THE WEEK

Monday
Feb 1990–Apr 1990, Stingray
Apr 1990–Jun 1990, Wiseguy; Stingray
Jul 1990, Stingray; Night Heat
Jul 1990, Stingray; The Midnight Hour
Aug 1990, 21 Jump Street; The Midnight Hour
Aug 1990, Stingray; The Midnight Hour
Sep 1990, Night Heat; The Midnight Hour
Sep 1990–Nov 1990, Wiseguy; Stingray
Nov 1990–Dec 1990, Mission: Impossible; Stingray
Jan 1991, Mission: Impossible; Night Heat
Jan 1991, Wolf; Night Heat
Feb 1991, Stingray; Night Heat
Mar 1991, Wiseguy; Night Heat

Tuesday
Feb 1990–Apr 1990, Stingray
Apr 1990–Jun 1990, Wiseguy; Stingray
Jul 1990, Stingray; Night Heat
Jul 1990–Sep 1990, Stingray; The Midnight Hour
Sep 1990–Nov 1990, Wiseguy; Wolf
Nov 1990–Jan 1991, Mission: Impossible; Wolf
Jan 1991, Mission: Impossible; Night Heat
Jan 1991, Wolf; Night Heat
Jan 1991–Mar 1991, Stingray; Night Heat
Mar 1991, Wiseguy; Night Heat

Wednesday
Feb 1990–Apr 1990, Night Heat
Apr 1990–Jun 1990, Wiseguy; Night Heat
Jul 1990, Stingray; Night Heat
Jul 1990, Wolf; Night Heat
Jul 1990–Sep 1990, Wolf; The Midnight Hour
Sep 1990–Nov 1990, Wiseguy; Night Heat
Nov 1990, Mission: Impossible; Night Heat
Dec 1990, Mission: Impossible; Stingray
Jan 1991, Mission: Impossible; Wolf
Jan 1991, Mission: Impossible; Night Heat
Jan 1991, Wolf; Night Heat
Jan 1991–Mar 1991, Stingray; Night Heat
Mar 1991, Wiseguy; Night Heat

Thursday
Feb 1990–Apr 1990, The Prisoner
Apr 1990–Jun 1990, Wiseguy; The Prisoner
Jul 1990, Stingray; The Prisoner
Jul 1990, Night Heat; The Prisoner
Jul 1990–Aug 1990, Night Heat; The Midnight Hour
Aug 1990, 21 Jump Street; The Midnight Hour
Sep 1990, Stingray; The Midnight Hour
Sep 1990–Nov 1990, Wiseguy; The Prisoner
Nov 1990–Dec 1990, Mission: Impossible; The Prisoner
Jan 1991, Mission: Impossible; Wolf
Jan 1991, Mission: Impossible; Night Heat
Jan 1991, Wolf; Night Heat
Jan 1991–Mar 1991, Stingray; Night Heat
Mar 1991, Wiseguy; Night Heat

Friday
Feb 1990–Apr 1990, Movie
Apr 1990–Jun 1990, Wiseguy; Movie
Jun 1990–Jul 1990, 21 Jump Street; Movie
Jul 1990–Aug 1990, 21 Jump Street; The Midnight Hour
Aug 1990, Overtime . . . With Pat O'Brien; The Midnight Hour
Aug 1990, 21 Jump Street; The Midnight Hour
Sep 1990, Stingray; The Midnight Hour
Sep 1990–Nov 1990, Wiseguy; Movie
Nov 1990, Mission: Impossible; Movie
Dec 1990, Mission: Impossible; Stingray
Jan 1991, Mission: Impossible; Wolf
Jan 1991, Mission: Impossible; Night Heat
Jan 1991, Wolf; Night Heat
Feb 1991, Stingray; Night Heat
Mar 1991, UnSUB; Night Heat
Mar 1991, Wiseguy; Night Heat

CBS NEWCOMERS (*Variety*)

FIRST TELECAST: *July 12, 1971*
LAST TELECAST: *September 6, 1971*
BROADCAST HISTORY:
Jul 1971–Sep 1971, CBS Mon 10:00–11:00
REGULARS:
Dave Garroway
David Arlen
Cynthia Clawson
Raul Perez
Rex Allen, Jr.
Gay Perkins
Peggy Sears
The Californians
Joey Garza
Rodney Winfield
The Good Humor Company
Nelson Riddle and His Orchestra

This summer variety show marked the return to a regular network series of Dave Garroway after a nine-year absence. He introduced performances by a wide range of young entertainers, all new to network television, who had been discovered in nightclubs and theaters during the previous year. None of them, alas, went on to become a major star.

CBS NEWS ADVENTURE (*Documentary*)

FIRST TELECAST: *March 20, 1970*
LAST TELECAST: *April 17, 1970*
BROADCAST HISTORY:
Mar 1970–Apr 1970, CBS Fri 7:30–8:30
NARRATOR:
Charles Kuralt

This adventure documentary series examined in depth one or two subjects each week. Among the topics were an auto race from London, England, to Sydney, Australia; people who dive to remarkable depths without diving equipment; and a round-the-world sailing trip by five men and a woman, using a 47-foot boat.

CBS NEWS RETROSPECTIVE (*Documentary/Public Affairs*)

FIRST TELECAST: *July 8, 1973*
LAST TELECAST: *September 1, 1974*
BROADCAST HISTORY:
Jul 1973–Sep 1973, CBS Sun 6:00–7:00
Jul 1974–Sep 1974, CBS Sun 6:00–7:00
HOST:
John Hart

The documentaries that were aired in this summer series had originally been telecast during the 1950s and 1960s and were considered classics of TV journalism. Many of them came from Edward R. Murrow's *See It Now*; others were from the *CBS News Reports* and *CBS News Special* series that succeeded it. John Hart was the host, setting the background for the period in which the specials had originally been aired and putting them in historical perspective.

CBS REPORTS/NEWS HOUR/NEWS SPECIAL (*Documentary*)

FIRST TELECAST: *January 5, 1961*
LAST TELECAST: *September 7, 1971*
BROADCAST HISTORY:
Jan 1961–Sep 1962, CBS Thu 10:00–11:00
Sep 1962–Dec 1964, CBS Wed 7:30–8:30
Dec 1964–Aug 1965, CBS Mon 10:00–11:00
Sep 1965–Jun 1970, CBS Tue 10:00–11:00
Apr 1966–May 1966, CBS Fri 10:00–11:00
Sep 1970–Sep 1971, CBS Tue 10:00–11:00

On October 27, 1959, fifteen months after the demise of Edward R. Murrow's *See It Now*, the CBS News Department premiered a new, incisive, in-depth documentary program entitled *CBS Reports*. It was patterned after Murrow's precedent-setting program and employed many of the same production staff, including Murrow's former partner Fred Friendly. It was aired during 1959–60 on an irregular basis as a series of specials. Murrow himself appeared on the first telecast, "Biography of a Missile," though he was later only an infrequent participant in the new series.

In January of 1961 CBS began airing *CBS Reports* as a regular alternate-week series on Thursday nights, opposite ABC's enormously successful *The Untouchables*. The rationale seemed to be that since CBS could not compete for the escapist-entertainment audience, it would at least telecast something worthwhile opposite the violence on ABC. For almost a full decade *CBS Reports* remained a regular series on various nights, at times alternating with *CBS News Hour*, *CBS News Special*, and other shows and at times as a weekly series. It remained CBS' most prestigious news analysis program and generally ran for a full hour, while the other CBS news programs varied between 30 and 60 minutes depending on subject. *CBS Reports* has continued to appear since 1971 on an irregular basis, in the form of specials.

During its ten-year run as a regular series, a number of the documentaries aired on *CBS Reports* won Emmy awards. Among them were "KKK—The Invisible Empire" (1966), "Eric Hoffer, the Passionate State of Mind" (1968), "CBS Reports: What About Ronald Reagan" (1968), "Gauguin in Tahiti: The Search for Paradise" (1968), "CBS Reports: Hunger in America" (1969), "Justice Black and the Bill of Rights" (1969), "The Great American Novel" (1969), "The Japanese" (1970), and "The Selling of the Pentagon" (1971).

CBS SUMMER PLAYHOUSE (*Dramatic Anthology*)

FIRST TELECAST: *June 12, 1987*
LAST TELECAST: *August 22, 1989*
BROADCAST HISTORY:
Jun 1987–Sep 1987, CBS Fri 8:00–9:00
Jun 1988–Sep 1988, CBS Tue 8:00–9:00
Jun 1989–Aug 1989, CBS Tue 8:00–9:00
HOSTS:
Tim Reid (1987)
Daphne Maxwell Reid (1987)

This summer anthology series was comprised entirely of pilot episodes for series—both comedy and drama—that CBS had not picked for its fall lineup. In an unusual twist, viewers were given the opportunity to say whether or not they liked each of the pilots by voting via special "900" phone numbers after each evening's pilot (or pilots) had aired.

The series' hosts, married couple Tim and Daphne Maxwell Reid, took advantage of their role here to promote *Frank's Place*, the CBS series in which they would co-star in September. Among the more familiar faces featured in the pilots (none of which were "saved" by viewer call-ins) were Kevin Tighe, Valerie Perrine, Brenda Vaccaro, Barbara Bain, Buddy Ebsen, Linda Purl, and Darren McGavin.

When *CBS Summer Playhouse* returned in 1988 it was without hosts or viewer voting.

C. EVERETT KOOP, M.D. (*Educational*)

FIRST TELECAST: *June 4, 1991*
LAST TELECAST: *July 7, 1991*
BROADCAST HISTORY:
Jun 1991, NBC Tue 10:00–11:00
Jun 1991–Jul 1991, NBC Sun 7:00–8:00
HOST:
Dr. C. Everett Koop

NBC got an "A" for effort but few viewers for this series of specials hosted by the controversial former U.S. Surgeon General. Koop, a pediatric surgeon known for both his strong opinions and his distinctive full beard, remarked "I'm not trying to be an unbiased commentator," and he wasn't. Subjects included teenage sexuality (in which teens shared their views with the 74-year-old Koop), the doctor-patient relationship, and problems with the entire U.S. health care system.

CMT: COUNTRY MUSIC TELEVISION (Network) (*Music Cable Network*)

LAUNCHED:
March 6, 1983
SUBSCRIBERS (MAY 2003):
67.8 million (64% U.S.)

The country equivalent of MTV and VH-1, playing contemporary country music videos, interviews, and occasional specials 24 hours a day. When sister network TNN abandoned country music in 2001 it also became the TV home of Saturday night's *Grand Ole Opry*. However, new owner Viacom Inc. gradually began to decrease its emphasis on music in favor of "lifestyle" programs, like those of MTV, to woo Madison Avenue advertising agencies who neither like nor understand country music. As a New York agency executive put it, "It's had an unbelievable makeover from what it was . . . I don't know if they're going to alienate the hayseeds."

CNBC (Network) (*News and Talk Cable Network*)

LAUNCHED:
April 17, 1989
SUBSCRIBERS (MAY 2003):
84.2 million (79% U.S.)

A cable channel run by NBC, featuring business news in the daytime and talk shows at night. The initials originally stood for "Consumer News and Business Channel."

CNBC first reached 50 percent of all U.S. television homes in March 1992. Following are its principal original evening series since that date. Hosts' names are given in parentheses when they are not part of a show's title.

Al Roker (talk), 1994–1996
Business Insiders (talk, Neil Cavuto), 1992–1997
Business Tonight (news, Sue Herara), 1992–1997
Business Weekly/Weekly Business, 1993–1994
Cal Thomas (talk), 1994–1996
*Charles Grodin** (talk), 1995–1998
CNBC Talks (repeats of other talk shows, Al Roker), 1994–1996
Daisy Fuentes (youth talk), 1994–1995
The Dick Cavett Show (talk), 1989–1996
Edge, The (investor news), 1997–2002
*Equal Time** (talk), 1993–1998
Fortune Week, 1993–1994
*Hardball with Chris Matthews** (talk), 1996–2002
How to Succeed in Business, 1993–1998
Kudlow & Cramer (discussion, Larry Kudlow, Jim Cramer), 2002–
Louis Rukeyser's Wall Street (discussion), 2002–
McLaughlin (talk, John McLaughlin), 1989–1994
Money Talk (advice, Sue Herera), 1992–1994
Money Tonight (advice, Sue Herera, Janice Lieberman), 1994–1995
Mutual Fund Investor (advice, Bill Griffeth), 1994–1995
*National Geographic Explorer** (documentary), 1999–2001
Pozner/Donahue (talk, Vladimir Pozner, Phil Donahue), 1992–1995
Real Life (lifestyle magazine, Cassandra Clayton, Boyd Matson), 1992
Real Personal (advice, Bob Berkowitz), 1992–1996
The Real Story (investigative reports, Cassandra Clayton, Boyd Matson), 1992–1993
*Rivera Live** (talk, Geraldo Rivera), 1994–2001
Smart Money (advice, Ken and Daria Dolan), 1990–1993
Steals and Deals (consumer information, Janice Lieberman), 1989–1997
Strictly Business (roundtable discussion), 1993–1994
Talk Live (talk, various), 1992–1996
Tim Russert (talk), 1994–
Tom Snyder (talk), 1993–1995
Upfront Tonight (talk, Geraldo Rivera), 1998–2000
Ushuaia (adventure/travelogue with French adventurer Nicolas Hulot; originally produced for syndication in 1996), 1998–2002
Your Portfolio (discussion, Bill Griffeth), 1992–1994

*See separate alphabetical entry.

CNBC was founded in 1989 as a business news channel in competition with FNN. Experiencing difficulty in obtaining distribution, it became the first major network literally to buy its way on to cable systems across the country, first by paying systems for carriage and in 1991 by buying its competitor, shutting it down, and taking over its channels.

CNN (CABLE NEWS NETWORK) (Network) (*All-News Cable Network*)

LAUNCHED:
June 1, 1980

SUBSCRIBERS (MAY 2003):
86.3 million (81% U.S.)

A cornerstone of the cable revolution, CNN broadcasts live news coverage, features, and analysis 24 hours a day. It is one of the great success stories of modern television.

Founded by Atlanta TV station owner R. E. "Ted" Turner in 1980, it was widely dismissed at first as puny competition to the mighty news operations of ABC, CBS, and NBC (legend has it that it was once dubbed the "Chicken Noodle Network"). CBS and Post-Newsweek had considered starting a cable news network a year or so earlier but had concluded that there would not be a sufficient audience. CNN got no respect in its early days and in fact had to sue to obtain access to White House press conferences.

No one is laughing anymore. While CNN's normal viewership is lower than that of entertainment networks such as USA and TBS, during crises it has often become the "network of record" with continuous, live coverage of unfolding events. Perhaps its finest hour to date was during the January 1991 Gulf War, when correspondents Bernard Shaw, Peter Arnett, and John Holliman telecast live from behind enemy lines in Baghdad as the city underwent a nighttime attack by allied planes. Broadcast stations and even, reluctantly, the major networks switched to its dramatic coverage.

It was not only Americans who were watching. CNN is carried in more than 90 countries around the world, through a special international feed, and has enormous influence as a primary news source for world leaders. It spun off a second U.S. channel in January 1982, originally known as CNN-2, to fend off competitive services being planned by ABC and Group W. This second channel, now known as CNN Headline News, has fewer features and concentrates on short, frequently repeated updates of current headlines. It is seen in more than 80 million homes, only slightly fewer than CNN itself.

Principal reporters on CNN over the years, besides those mentioned above, have included Daniel Schorr, Bill Zimmerman, Catherine Crier, Mary Alice Williams, Susan Rook, Frank Sesno, Wolf Blitzer, and Judy Woodruff. Perhaps its best-known prime-time series has been *Larry King Live* (1985–), a weeknight interview show that made headlines during 1992 with multiple appearances by the presidential candidates. Others include *The Capital Gang*, *Crossfire*, *Evans & Novak*, *Moneyline*, and *Showbiz Today*.

CNN first reached more than half of all U.S. television homes in December 1987, and its principal regular series after that date (other than news coverage) are listed in this book under their individual titles.

CNN launched several subsidiary networks in addition to Headline News, including CNN/FN (financial news, 1995), CNNI (international news, 1985, U.S. launch 1995), CNN/SI (sports news, 1996) and CNN en Español (1997). CNN/SI shut down in 2002.

CNN NEWSSTAND (*Newsmagazine*)

BROADCAST HISTORY:
CNN
60 minutes
Produced: *1998–2001*
Premiered: *June 7, 1998*

REGULARS:
Jeff Greenfield
Bernard Shaw
Judd Rose
Willow Bay

Stephen Frazier
Perri Peltz

In a veritable fit of corporate "synergy" Time-Warner Communications, which owned both CNN and a vast publishing empire, introduced this multi-part series built around three of its leading newsmagazines. Originally airing four nights a week, installments were introduced from trendy, high-tech newsstands in various cities. *CNN Newsstand: Time* focused on hard news stories similar to those featured in *Time*; *CNN Newsstand: Entertainment Weekly* covered the hype-filled world of entertainment; and *CNN Newsstand: Fortune* dealt with the world of business and finance. All of them adopted the tabloid tone so popular on TV newsmagazines in the '90s ("Millionaire NBA Deadbeat DADS!" "Spin Doctors at Work!" "Luxury CEO Jets!"). The tendency toward sensationalism got the series into trouble during its first week, as *CNN Newsstand: Time* aired a story (also published in *Time*) alleging that the U.S. military had used nerve gas on its own troops behind enemy lines in Vietnam in "Operation Tailwind." When serious doubt was cast on the story, three producers resigned or were fired, correspondent Peter Arnett was suspended (and eventually left the network), and mighty Time-Warner apologized to all concerned.

Interspersed with the regular *Newsstand* telecasts were *People* magazine celebrity biographies, called *People Profiles* and billed as "a special presentation of *CNN Newsstand*."

C.P.O. SHARKEY (*Situation Comedy*)

FIRST TELECAST: *December 1, 1976*
LAST TELECAST: *July 28, 1978*
BROADCAST HISTORY:

Dec 1976–Jan 1977, NBC Wed 8:00–8:30
Feb 1977–Apr 1977, NBC Wed 9:00–9:30
Jul 1977–Aug 1977, NBC Wed 9:00–9:30
Oct 1977–Jan 1978, NBC Fri 8:30–9:00
Feb 1978–Apr 1978, NBC Fri 8:30–9:00
Jun 1978–Jul 1978, NBC Fri 8:00–8:30

CAST:

C.P.O. Otto Sharkey .... Don Rickles
Seaman Pruitt .... Peter Isacksen
Daniels .... Jeff Hollis
Kowalski .... Tom Ruben
Skolnick .... David Landsberg
Capt. Quinlan (1976–1977) .... Elizabeth Allen
Chief Robinson .... Harrison Page
Mignone (1976–1977) .... Barry Pearl
Apodaca (1977–1978) .... Philip Simms
Rodriguez .... Richard Beauchamp
Lt. Whipple .... Jonathan Daly
Chief Gypsy Koch .... Beverly Sanders
Capt. "Buck" Buckner (1977–1978)
.... Richard X. Slattery

Insult comic Don Rickles found the perfect vehicle for his humor in this situation comedy, in which he was cast as Chief Petty Officer Sharkey of the U.S. Navy. Sharkey, a 24-year veteran of navy service, was stationed at the Navy Training Center in San Diego, California. He was in charge of a company of new recruits, and it was his job to make sailors out of a collection of diverse ethnic types, most of whom had never been away from home before. The various ethnic backgrounds and stereotypes were all targets of Sharkey's verbal barbs, but beneath that harsh, nasty exterior beat the heart of an old softie, especially when he sensed the suffering of a recruit who either could not take his bluster or was suffering the problems of adjusting to life away from home. Sharkey's immediate superior was the long-winded and overbearing Lt. Whipple; the base commander was Capt. Quinlan, who was, of all things, an attractive woman.

When *C.P.O. Sharkey* returned in October 1977, to replace the short-lived *The Sanford Arms*, Sharkey had a new, and male, commanding officer in Capt. "Buck" Buckner.

C.P.W., see *Central Park West*

CSI: CRIME SCENE INVESTIGATION (*Police Drama*)

FIRST TELECAST: *October 6, 2000*
LAST TELECAST:
BROADCAST HISTORY:

Oct 2000–Jan 2001, CBS Fri 9:00–10:00
Feb 2001–Aug 2001, CBS Thu 9:00–10:00
Aug 2001–Sep 2001, CBS Thu 10:00–11:00
Sep 2001– , CBS Thu 9:00–10:00
Apr 2002–May 2002, CBS Fri 8:00–9:00
Aug 2002–Sep 2002, CBS Mon 10:00–11:00
Sep 2002, CBS Thu 10:00–11:00

CAST:

Gil Grissom .... William Petersen
Catherine Willows .... Marg Helgenberger
Warrick Brown .... Gary Dourdan
Nick Stokes .... George Eads
Sara Sidel .... Jorja Fox
Capt. Jim Brass .... Paul Guilfoyle
Dr. Al Robbins .... Robert David Hall
David Phillips .... David Berman
Greg Sanders .... Eric Szmanda
Sgt./Det. O'Riley (2000–2002) .... Skip O'Brien

Gil Grissom was a senior forensics officer working in the Criminalistics Bureau of the Las Vegas Police Department. A calm and relentless investigator, Grissom and his team used all of the advanced techniques available to analyze evidence found at crime scenes and determine how the crimes, mostly gruesome murders, had been committed. Grissom's primary assistant was Catherine, a veteran investigator who had worked her way through college as a stripper. She was divorced and raising a young daughter. Others on the team were Warrick, whose analytical skills were complemented by his extensive knowledge of the gambling world of Las Vegas; Nick, the hunky guy who was very competitive with Warrick; and Sara, the rookie, who buried herself in work because she had problems with social relationships. Others seen regularly were Brass, their surly former boss who had been reassigned to homicide; Dr. Robbins, the chief medical examiner; Phillips, Dr. Robbins' assistant, and Greg, an eccentric, but very bright, lab technician.

Most episodes of *CSI* covered two separate and unrelated cases, with the members of the team working diligently to piece together the evidence that would help the police solve the crimes. There were graphic close-ups of the individual bits of evidence and the crimes (for example, the camera zooming up a nostril), along with constantly altered reconstructions of the events as the investigators pondered the various ways the crime might have been committed.

In the spring of 2002 Grissom was diagnosed with a degenerative hearing disorder, and during the 2002–2003 season there were several occasions on which he suffered temporary hearing loss. In February 2003 Catherine's ex-husband died from a gunshot wound.

CSI: MIAMI (*Police Drama*)
FIRST TELECAST: *September 23, 2002*
LAST TELECAST:
BROADCAST HISTORY:
Sep 2002– , CBS Mon 10:00–11:00
CAST:
Horatio Caine .... David Caruso
Megan Donner (2002) .... Kim Delaney
Calleigh Duquesne .... Emily Procter
Tim Speedle .... Rory Cochrane
Eric Delko .... Adam Rodriguez
Alexx Woods .... Khandi Alexander
Det. Adell Sevilla .... Wanda de Jesus
Det. Yelina Salas (2003–) .... Sofia Milos

Set in steamy South Florida, *CSI: Miami* was a virtual clone of *CSI: Crime Scene Investigation*. As with its predecessor, episodes followed the criminologists as they collected and analyzed the evidence found at crime scenes to determine how the crimes, mostly murders, had been committed. Horatio Caine, a moody former homicide detective, was the leader of the unit. Horatio had his problems with Megan, a DNA specialist and former head of the unit, who had returned to work and took issue with his tendency to rely on hunches as well as the scientific evidence. Others on the team included sexy Calleigh, whose specialty was ballistics; street-smart Tim, a former jock who could charm almost anyone; easygoing Eric, who did most of the underwater recovery, and Alexx, the brilliant young coroner whose sometimes condescending attitude could be irritating.

Many episodes covered two separate and unrelated cases, with the members of the team working to assemble the evidence and solve the crimes. There were graphic close-ups of the individual bits of evidence and the crimes, along with constantly altered reconstructions of the events as the investigators built their cases. In December Megan resigned because the work was a constant reminder of her husband's death. The pilot for *CSI: Miami* aired as a special episode of *CSI: Crime Scene Investigation* in May 2002.

C-16 (*Police Drama*)
FIRST TELECAST: *September 27, 1997*
LAST TELECAST: *July 2, 1998*
BROADCAST HISTORY:
Sep 1997–Nov 1997, ABC Sat 8:00–9:00
May 1998–Jul 1998, ABC Thu 8:00–9:00
CAST:
John Olansky .... Eric Roberts
Scott Stoddard .... D.B. Sweeney
Annie Rooney .... Christine Tucci
Jack DiRado .... Zach Grenier
Mal Robinson .... Morris Chestnut
Amanda Reardon .... Angie Harmon
Dennis Grassi .... Michael Cavanaugh
Andrew Pritchett .... Glenn Morshower

A by-the-book action series about the 16th Squad, Criminal Division, of the F.B.I.'s Los Angeles field office. Bearded, intense John Olansky headed the elite squad, which took on only the toughest cases of kidnapping, drug smuggling, terrorism, and hostage taking (what did you expect them to do, rescue kitties from trees?). His experienced team included womanizer Scott, loose cannon Jack, worried single mom Annie, and rookies Mal and Amanda. Dennis was the head of the L.A. office, with whom John frequently fought since his team had a tendency to "bend the rules." The team was tight and highly professional, employing all the high-tech tools the agency could provide, although most cases seemed to end with gunfights and explosions.

Viewers who survived all those clichés noticed at least one innovation in this series: the first several episodes were telecast in letterbox, like a major, widescreen theatrical film.

C-SPAN (Network) (*Public Affairs Cable Network*)
LAUNCHED:
March 19, 1979
SUBSCRIBERS (FEB 2003):
86.6 million (81% U.S.)

A noncommercial public affairs network, funded by the cable industry, which carries live, gavel-to-gavel coverage of the U.S. House of Representatives. When the house is out of session it covers various Washington speeches and forums and carries discussion programs (some of which take viewer calls). A series called *Booknotes* (1989) presents interviews with authors. A second channel, C-SPAN 2, was launched in June 1986 to provide coverage of the U.S. Senate and is currently available in more than 70 million homes. Another spin-off, C-SPAN 3, carrying a variety of public affairs programming, launched in September 1997.

In case you were wondering, the acronym stands for "Cable-Satellite Public Affairs Network."

CACTUS JIM (*Children's*)
FIRST TELECAST: *October 31, 1949*
LAST TELECAST: *October 26, 1951*
BROADCAST HISTORY:
Oct 1949–Oct 1951, NBC Mon–Fri 6:00–6:30
HOST:
Cactus Jim (1949–1951) .... Clarence Hartzell
Cactus Jim (1951) .... Bill Bailey

This children's program was built around Western feature movies, which were shown in segments on succeeding days. Cactus Jim, a "range-riding oldtimer," introduced each episode and spun a few yarns. The program emanated from WNBQ, Chicago. It later turned up on NBC's Saturday morning lineup for a brief run from January to March 1952.

CADE'S COUNTY (*Police Drama*)
FIRST TELECAST: *September 19, 1971*
LAST TELECAST: *September 4, 1972*
BROADCAST HISTORY:
Sep 1971–Aug 1972, CBS Sun 9:30–10:30
Aug 1972–Sep 1972, CBS Mon 10:00–11:00
CAST:
Sam Cade .... Glenn Ford
J. J. Jackson .... Edgar Buchanan
Arlo Pritchard .... Taylor Lacher
Rudy Davillo .... Victor Campos
Pete .... Peter Ford
Joannie Little Bird (1971) .... Sandra Ego
Betty Ann Sundown .... Betty Ann Carr

Sprawling Madrid County, California, was the setting for this contemporary Western/police drama. Sheriff Sam Cade, based in the town of Madrid, was responsible for law enforcement throughout the county. He was assisted by veteran deputy J. J. Jackson and three younger deputies, Arlo, Rudy, and Pete. Sandra Ego initially had the role of police dispatcher but was replaced early on by Betty Ann Carr. Both of them were American Indians. The role of Pete, one of Cade's young deputies, was played by the son of Glenn Ford, the show's star.

CAESAR PRESENTS (*Comedy/Variety*)

FIRST TELECAST: *July 4, 1955*
LAST TELECAST: *September 12, 1955*
BROADCAST HISTORY:
Jul 1955–Sep 1955, NBC Mon 8:00–9:00
HOST:
Bobby Sherwood
CAST:
Charles Williams .... Phil Foster
Barbara Williams .... Barbara Nichols
Sandy Williams .... Sandra Deel
Vocalist .... Bill Hayes
Various Parts .... Sid Gould
Various Parts .... Cliff Norton
Various Parts .... Judy Tyler

This combination variety and situation-comedy show was a summer replacement for Caesar's Hour. In addition to production numbers and comedy skits, a weekly feature of the program was the situation-comedy sketch "The Pharmacist," starring Phil Foster as an overworked and underpaid pharmacist with problems at home and at work. Sid Caesar, who produced this show, appeared live to introduce each episode.

CAESAR'S HOUR (*Comedy/Variety*)

FIRST TELECAST: *September 27, 1954*
LAST TELECAST: *May 25, 1957*
BROADCAST HISTORY:
Sep 1954–Jun 1956, NBC Mon 8:00–9:00
Sep 1956–May 1957, NBC Sat 9:00–10:00
CAST:
Bob Victor .... Sid Caesar
George Hansen .... Carl Reiner
Fred Brewster .... Howard Morris
Ann Victor (1954–1956) .... Nanette Fabray
Betty Hansen (1954–1955) .... Virginia Curtis
Betty Hansen (1955–1956) .... Sandra Deel
Betty Hansen (1956–1957) .... Shirl Conway
Alice Brewster (1954–1956) .... Ellen Parker
Alice Brewster (1956–1957) .... Pat Carroll
Jane Victor (1956–1957) .... Janet Blair
REGULARS:
William Lewis (1955–1957)
Earl Wild (1955–1957)
Dave Caesar (1955–1957)
Paul Reed (1955–1957)
Milt Kamen (1956–1957)
Bea Arthur (1956–1957)
Hugh Downs (1956–1957), announcer

The highly imaginative and creative comedy of Sid Caesar was the moving force in this successor to his famous *Your Show of Shows,* With him in this venture, also from *Your Show of Shows,* were comedians Carl Reiner and Howard Morris. The format of the series varied from a full hour of situation comedy, to musical revues, to a variety show or any combination of the three. Although the three male leads remained the same throughout the duration of the series, there was considerable turnover among the women.

The most successful sketch used in the series was "The Commuters," in which Caesar, Reiner, and Morris typified the suburbanite who takes the same train to work in the big city every morning and the same train home every evening. The lives of these people became to *Caesar's Hour* what "The Honeymooners" was to *The Jackie Gleason Show.* A featured part of the program, on occasion this sketch was expanded to fill the entire hour. The cast credits above are for the parts played by the participants in this sketch. Other featured comedy skits were "The Three Haircuts," in which Caesar, Reiner, and Morris satirized rock 'n' roll musicians, and Caesar's characterization of "The Professor."

CAFÉ AMERICAIN (*Situation Comedy*)

FIRST TELECAST: *September 18, 1993*
LAST TELECAST: *February 8, 1994*
BROADCAST HISTORY:
Sep 1993, NBC Sat 9:30–10:00
Sep 1993–Dec 1993, NBC Sat 8:30–9:00
Jan 1994–Feb 1994, NBC Tue 9:30–10:00
CAST:
Holly Aldridge .... Valerie Bertinelli
Margaret Hunt .... Lila Kaye
Fabiana Borelli .... Sofia Milos
Marcel .... Maurice Godin
Madame Ybarra .... Jodi Long
Steve Sullivan .... Graham Beckel

Holly Aldridge was a flighty young divorcée from Minneapolis seeking adventure in glamorous Paris in this quaint, rather old-fashioned comedy. It was all rather like a 1950s MGM musical without the music—naive American damsel faces mixups and struggles with the language, cranky French landladies, and suave roués who had only romance on their minds. Holly ostensibly came to take a job translating English to English [*sic*] for a French firm, but when that fell through she stumbled into the Café Americain, a fabled hangout for oddballs and expatriates. Among the habitués were Margaret, the worldly, no-nonsense owner, who gave her a job; Fabiana, an egocentric supermodel; Marcel, a suave Frenchman (and mineral water salesman) with eyes for Holly; Madame Ybarra, regal former first lady of an unspecified Asian country, whose husband had been deposed; and Steve, a grumpy American businessman.

Holly lived in a tiny apartment that was once Balzac's closet. In one concession to the 1990s, she videotaped letters home to her sister. Two leftover episodes of this series were aired on May 28, 1994. Then we bid adieu to Holly.

CAGNEY & LACEY (*Police Drama*)

FIRST TELECAST: *March 25, 1982*
LAST TELECAST: *August 25, 1988*
BROADCAST HISTORY:
Mar 1982–Apr 1982, CBS Thu 9:00–10:00
Oct 1982–Sep 1983, CBS Mon 10:00–11:00
Mar 1984–Dec 1987, CBS Mon 10:00–11:00
Jan 1988–Apr 1988, CBS Tue 10:00–11:00
Apr 1988–Jun 1988, CBS Mon 10:00–11:00
Jun 1988–Aug 1988, CBS Thu 10:00–11:00

CAST:

Det. Mary Beth Lacey .... Tyne Daly
Det. Chris Cagney (1982) .... Meg Foster
Det. Chris Cagney (1982–1988) .... Sharon Gless
Lt. Bert Samuels .... Al Waxman
Det. Mark Petrie .... Carl Lumbly
Det. Victor Isbecki .... Martin Kove
Det. Paul La Guardia (1982–1985) ..... Sidney Clute
Deputy Inspector Marquette (1982–1983)
.... Jason Bernard
Desk Sergeant Ronald Coleman ...... Harvey Atkin
Harvey Lacey .... John Karlen
Harvey Lacey, Jr. .... Tony La Torre
Michael Lacey .... Troy Slaten
Sgt. Dory McKenna (1984–1985) ..... Barry Primus
Insp. Knelman (1984–1988) ...... Michael Fairman
Det. Jonah Newman (1985–1986) .... Dan Shor
David Keeler (1985–1988) .... Stephen Macht
Alice Lacey (1985–1987) ... Dana & Paige Bardolph
Alice Lacey (1987–1988) .... Michelle Sepe
Det. Manny Esposito (1986–1988) ... Robert Hegyes
Det. Al Corassa (1986–1988) .... Paul Mantee
Josie (1986–1988) .... Jo Corday
Kazak (1986–1987) .... Stewart Coss
Beverley Faverty (1986–1987) .... Beverley Faverty
Tom Basil (1986–1988) .... Barry Laws
Verna Dee Jordan (1987–1988) ...... Merry Clayton

"We had a shot," said producer Barney Rosenzweig, "at television history." *Cagney & Lacey* was certainly unusual for commercial TV, asserting that two women could be best buddies in the Starsky-and-Hutch, Paul Newman–Robert Redford tradition and do a "man's job" just as well as any man could. With male leads it would have been a rather ordinary TV police series. Mary Beth Lacey was the married one, trying to be a wife and mother, as well as a New York City police officer. Chris Cagney was single, ambitious, and full of the joys of living. Though beautiful, she was often disappointed in love. Despite their different lifestyles, Mary Beth and Chris were partners and fast friends, determined to break the stereotypes often ascribed to women in jobs not traditionally associated with them. They fought criminals, the chauvinism of their male fellow officers, the ignorance of their friends regarding their unusual careers, and sometimes each other—with shouting sessions in the ladies' room. Working primarily as undercover cops, they infiltrated criminal organizations and sometimes served as decoys to capture street criminals.

Not all of the cases worked out, either. Like *Hill Street Blues* and other "reality" shows, *Cagney & Lacey* reflected the real world of the big-city cop.

The offscreen troubles of this series were almost as dramatic as the onscreen problems of its stars. Conceived by Rosenzweig with the help of feminists Barbara Corday and Barbara Avedon in 1974, it was turned down as a series by all three networks, finally airing as a made-for-TV movie on CBS in October 1981 with Loretta Swit as Cagney. The movie drew a tremendous audience, and a limited-run series was commissioned for the following spring. Loretta Swit was unavailable, so Meg Foster was cast as Cagney. This time the ratings were poor, and CBS thought it knew why. "They were too harshly women's lib," said an unnamed CBS executive in *TV Guide*, "too tough, too hard, and not feminine." "The American public doesn't respond to the bra burners, the fighters, the women who insist on calling manhole covers peoplehole covers," he continued. "We perceived them as dykes."

That last remark set off a storm of protest, but the role of Cagney was once again recast, this time with beautiful Sharon Gless, who was to provide a softer, more feminine counterpart for Lacey. Gay groups protested *that* ("She's from the Copacabana school of acting," complained the Gay Media Task Force, "very kittenish and feminine . . ."), but the decision stuck.

Despite the changes, audiences were disappointingly small in 1982–1983, and the series was canceled at the end of the season amid a flurry of publicity about the cop show that had tried to be "different." Loyal viewers thereupon inundated CBS with letters, and summer reruns began to pick up new viewers who were curious about the fuss. In September the show won an Emmy. Much to everyone's surprise, CBS relented and the series surfaced once again in the spring of 1984—accompanied by the *TV Guide* headline "Welcome Back, *Cagney & Lacey*," and advertising that proclaimed "You Want Them! You've Got Them!"

The series flourished after being brought back and the personal lives of Cagney and Lacey became more prominent in the story lines. Mary Beth had another child, a daughter named Alice. Chris's social life, first her relationship with drug-addicted fellow cop Dory McKenna and later with attorney David Keeler, was featured. At one point she was even the victim of date rape. Her personal problems, including the fear of never marrying and having a family and a bout with alcoholism, were also depicted. Chris's father, Charlie (Dick O'Neill), also turned up from time to time, until he passed away in the spring of 1987. That year she was promoted to sergeant.

CAIN'S HUNDRED (*Police Drama*)

FIRST TELECAST: *September 19, 1961*
LAST TELECAST: *September 11, 1962*
BROADCAST HISTORY:

Sep 1961–Sep 1962, NBC Tue 10:00–11:00

CAST:

Nicholas "Nick" Cain .... (Peter) Mark Richman

Nick Cain had spent years as a gangland lawyer. He knew who the important people in organized crime were; and now that he had become an agent of the federal government, he was determined to ferret out and bring to prosecution the 100 men controlling the many-tentacled monster of organized crime in America. Roving about the country with a special squad of assistants, Nick Cain assembled the necessary evidence to help the government bring big-time gangsters to justice. Based on actual case histories, *Cain's Hundred* dramatized, often in quasi-documentary fashion, the personalities, lives, and methods of the members of the underworld fraternity in the United States.

CAITLIN'S WAY (*Drama*)

BROADCAST HISTORY:

Nickelodeon
30 minutes
Original episodes: *2000–2002* (47 episodes)
Premiered: *March 11, 2000*

CAST:

Caitlin Seeger (age 14) .... Lindsay Felton
Dr. Dori Lowe .... Cynthia Belliveau

Sheriff Jim Lowe .... Ken Tremblett
Griffen Lowe (14)..................... Jeremy Foley
Brett Stevens .... Stephen Warner
Eric .... Brendan Fletcher
Nikki (2001–2002)................. Alana Husband
Mr. Watson.......................... Philip Akin
Taylor Langford .... Tania Saulnier

A rebellious, troubled kid from inner-city Philadelphia was sent to live with a family in rural Montana in this fish-out-of-water drama. Caitlin had had a tough life since her mother died of an aneurysm, shuffling from one foster home to another while getting into trouble on the streets. Finally a judge told her she could either go live with her closest relatives, the Lowes, in High River, Montana, or spend the rest of her youth in juvenile hall. Cousin Dori, a veterinarian, and Jim, the local sheriff, were decent and kind people, but it took a lot of patience to get through to wild Caitlin. Their son Griffen, who was trying very hard to be cool in school, had an even harder time dealing with the upheaval in his life ("It figures—where there's trouble there's Caitlin"), but he did try, and eventually they started to bond. His pals Brett and Eric were sometimes not so kind. Caitlin began to express herself through photography, and she made a friend at school in Taylor. However, her closest companion was probably Bandit, a wild buckskin stallion, whom she befriended after he saved her from a rabid wolf.

CALIFORNIA FEVER (*Adventure*)
FIRST TELECAST: *September 25, 1979*
LAST TELECAST: *December 11, 1979*
BROADCAST HISTORY:
Sep 1979–Dec 1979, CBS Tue 8:00–9:00
CAST:
Vince Butler.................... Jimmy McNichol
Ross Whitman....................... Marc McClure
Laurie Newman .... Michele Tobin
Rick............................ Lorenzo Lamas
Bobby.............................. Cosie Costa
Sue.................................. Lisa Cori

This is what middle-aged network executives think is meant by the term "youth appeal." Vince, Ross, and Laurie were three high school students living the carefree life in suburban Los Angeles. With a background of disco music, surfing, souped-up cars, and the Sunset Strip, this series followed the adventures of Vince and Ross. Vince was into music, and ran an underground radio station from the back room of Rick's, the local hangout that served snacks and rented roller skates. Ross was the mechanic supreme, and drove a personally customized monstrosity that he had named "The Grossmobile." Together they sought fun and excitement in the sun-drenched, fad-oriented environment of Southern California. Like the fads, however, *California Fever* didn't have much staying power.

CALIFORNIANS, THE (*Western*)
FIRST TELECAST: *September 24, 1957*
LAST TELECAST: *August 27, 1959*
BROADCAST HISTORY:
Sep 1957–Mar 1959, NBC Tue 10:00–10:30
Apr 1959–Jun 1959, NBC Tue 9:00–9:30
Jul 1959–Aug 1959, NBC Thu 7:30–8:00
CAST:
Dion Patrick (1957–1958).......... Adam Kennedy
Jack McGivern (1957–1958) .... Sean McClory
Martha McGivern (1957–1958).......... Nan Leslie
Sam Brennan (1957–1958)......... Herbert Rudley
Matthew Wayne .... Richard Coogan
Schaab (1957–1958)................ Howard Caine
Wilma Fansler (1958–1959) ...... Carole Matthews
Jeremy Pitt (1958–1959) .... Arthur Fleming

Set in San Francisco during the 1850s, at the height of the Gold Rush, *The Californians* was the story of the honest men trying to clean up a wild city overrun by criminals and con men. Dion Patrick had been drawn to San Francisco by the prospect of Gold Rush riches, but went to work instead as a crusading reporter for newspaperman Sam Brennan—and also joined storekeeper Jack McGivern's vigilantes, the only functioning law-enforcement organization in town. In the middle of the first season Matthew Wayne arrived and was elected sheriff of San Francisco; he became the leading character as vigilantes Patrick and McGivern were eased out of the show. In the second season Wayne, by then city marshal, continued his fight against crime with a newly reorganized 50-man police force. He remained the focal point with the addition of love interest Wilma Fansler, a young widow who ran a gambling house, and attorney Jeremy Pitt, friend and foil to the marshal.

CALL MR. D, syndicated title for *Richard Diamond, Private Detective*

CALL OF THE WEST, see *Death Valley Days*

CALL TO GLORY (*Drama*)
FIRST TELECAST: *August 13, 1984*
LAST TELECAST: *February 12, 1985*
BROADCAST HISTORY:
Aug 1984–Dec 1984, ABC Mon 8:00–9:00
Jan 1985–Feb 1985, ABC Tue 10:00–11:00
CAST:
Col. Raynor Sarnac .... Craig T. Nelson
Vanessa Sarnac .... Cindy Pickett
RH Sarnac .... Gabriel Damon
Jackie Sarnac..................... Elisabeth Shue
Wesley Sarnac .... David Hollander
Carl Sarnac........................ Keenan Wynn
Patrick Thomas .... Thomas O'Brien
Airman Tom Bonelli .... David Lain Baker
General Hampton.................... J.D. Cannon
Lillie............................ Priscilla Pointer

The Cold War of the early 1960s provided the backdrop for this drama about a military family headed by patriotic Air Force Colonel Raynor Sarnac. Sarnac commanded a group of jet pilots, and he seemed to become involved in many of the earthshaking events of the time, from the Cuban Missile Crisis to the incipient U.S. involvement in Vietnam. He also faced turmoil at home, from his worried wife, Vanessa, and his three growing children: Jackie, 15, who was dating a somewhat confused young man named Patrick; Wesley, the fun-loving 14-year-old; and RH, the 8-year-old. They all felt the pressures of military life, with its danger and constant relocation. Carl was the colonel's walrus-mustached dad, who offered sage advice about duty to family and country.

Bits of 1960s songs, vintage news film, and references to such issues of the day as air raid drills and the Civil Rights movement helped give the series a period flavor.

CALUCCI'S DEPARTMENT (*Situation Comedy*)
FIRST TELECAST: *September 14, 1973*
LAST TELECAST: *December 28, 1973*
BROADCAST HISTORY:
Sep 1973–Dec 1973, CBS Fri 8:00–8:30
CAST:
Joe Calucci .... James Coco
Shirley Balukis .... Candy Azzara
Ramon Gonzales .... Jose Perez
Cosgrove .... Jack Fletcher
Elaine Fusco .... Peggy Pope
Woods .... Bill Lazarus
Frohler .... Bernard Wexler
Mitzi Gordon .... Rosetta LeNoire

Roly-poly comic James Coco portrayed the supervisor of a branch of the New York State Unemployment Office in this ethnic sitcom. Calucci had to cope with the problems of unemployed claimants, the frictions among various members of his staff (who were carefully picked to represent every race, religion, and creed imaginable), and the frustrations of governmental red tape. As if that wasn't enough, he was in love with his secretary, Shirley—or at least infatuated with her—but the series was canceled before their relationship really developed. Apparently most Americans did not find an unemployment office very amusing.

CALVIN AND THE COLONEL (*Cartoon*)
FIRST TELECAST: *October 3, 1961*
LAST TELECAST: *September 22, 1962*
BROADCAST HISTORY:
Oct 1961–Nov 1961, ABC Tue 8:30–9:00
Jan 1962–Sep 1962, ABC Sat 7:30–8:00
VOICES:
The Colonel .... Freeman Gosden
Calvin .... Charles Correll
Maggie Belle .... Virginia Gregg
Sister Sue .... Beatrice Kay
Oliver Wendell Clutch .... Paul Frees

This animated series concerned the exploits of a bunch of animals from the Deep South who had taken up residence in a large Northern city. The Colonel was a very foxy fox, and Calvin was his best friend, a lovable but not particularly bright bear. Other regulars on the series were the Colonel's wife Maggie Belle, her sister Sue, and Oliver Wendell Clutch, a lawyer who was a weasel. If the plot line sounds vaguely like that of *Amos 'n' Andy*, don't be surprised. Gosden and Correll, the creators and principal voices of this series, played *Amos 'n' Andy* on radio for years. The use of animals here avoided creating what could have been a touchy racial situation in the early 1960s.

CAMEL CARAVAN, see *Vaughn Monroe Show, The*

CAMEO THEATRE (*Dramatic Anthology*)
FIRST TELECAST: *May 16, 1950*
LAST TELECAST: *August 21, 1955*
BROADCAST HISTORY:
May 1950–Sep 1950, NBC Wed 8:30–9:00
Jun 1951–Aug 1951, NBC Mon 8:00–8:30
Jan 1952–Apr 1952, NBC Sun 10:00–10:30
Jul 1955–Aug 1955, NBC Sun 10:00–10:30
CREATOR AND PRODUCER:
Albert McCleery

An interesting early experiment in the unique dramatic possibilities of television, this occasional series of live plays was produced in the round, using a minimum of props. It made considerable use of close-ups and other camera techniques to focus attention on the characterizations of individual actors. High-quality scripts were used, both originals and adaptations for television. The first telecast was "It Takes a Thief," by Arthur Miller; later presentations included a three-part adaptation of Ibsen's *Peer Gynt* and a version of the Broadway musical *Dark of the Moon*.

After an absence of three years the series returned for a final run during the summer of 1955, as a replacement for *The Loretta Young Show*.

CAMP RUNAMUCK (*Situation Comedy*)
FIRST TELECAST: *September 17, 1965*
LAST TELECAST: *September 2, 1966*
BROADCAST HISTORY:
Sep 1965–Sep 1966, NBC Fri 7:30–8:00
CAST:
Senior Counselor Spiffy .... Dave Ketchum
Commander Wivenhoe .... Arch Johnson
Mahala May Gruenecker .... Alice Nunn
Pruett .... David Madden
Doc Joslyn .... Leonard Stone
Caprice Yeudleman .... Nina Wayne
Eulalia Divine .... Hermione Baddeley
Malden .... Mike Wagner
The Sheriff .... George Dunn

Nuttiness abounded in this comedy of two summer camps for children, Camp Runamuck for boys and, on the other side of the lake bordering it, Camp Divine for girls. The four characters in charge of the boys' camp, Spiffy, Wivenhoe, Pruett, and Doc Joslyn, created constant chaos in their own camp and maintained a strong, and often hilarious, rivalry with the counselors of Camp Divine.

Bandleader Frank DeVol was originally scheduled to play Doc, and did so in the first episode, but health problems forced him to quit the series. Leonard Stone replaced him.

CAMP WILDER (*Situation Comedy*)
FIRST TELECAST: *September 18, 1992*
LAST TELECAST: *February 26, 1993*
BROADCAST HISTORY:
Sep 1992–Feb 1993, ABC Fri 9:30–10:00
CAST:
Ricky Wilder .... Mary Page Keller
Brody Wilder (age 16) .... Jerry O'Connell
Melissa Wilder (13) .... Meghann Haldeman
Sophie Wilder (6) .... Tina Majorino
Dorfman .... Jay Mohr
Danielle .... Hilary Swank
Beth .... Margaret Langrick

Ricky Wilder was a 28-year-old divorced nurse with an unusual brood. Returning to her family home upon the sudden death of her parents, she became "mom" not only to her own six-year-old, Sophie, but to her teenaged brother Brody and sister Melissa. In addition, Ricky's lively, laissez-faire household made the Wilder kitchen a favored hangout for neighborhood teens, who preferred it to their own stricter homes.

Among the hangers-out were Brody's dim-witted buddy Dorfman and Beth and Danielle. Though their parents did not always approve of Ricky's methods, everyone learned sitcom lessons in life around "Camp Wilder's" kitchen table.

CAMPAIGN AND THE CANDIDATES, THE (*News*)
FIRST TELECAST: *September 17, 1960*
LAST TELECAST: *November 5, 1960*
BROADCAST HISTORY:
Sep 1960–Nov 1960, NBC Sat 9:30–10:30
ANCHORMAN:
Frank McGee

This series of weekly summaries followed the campaigns of presidential candidates John F. Kennedy and Richard M. Nixon as they stated their cases to the American public in the fall of 1960. Coverage was narrated by numerous NBC reporters assigned to the campaigns, with Frank McGee acting as host and coordinator.

CAMPAIGN COUNTDOWN (*News*)
FIRST TELECAST: *September 10, 1980*
LAST TELECAST: *November 5, 1980*
BROADCAST HISTORY:
Sep 1980–Nov 1980, CBS Wed 11:30–12:00
ANCHORMAN:
Walter Cronkite

As the 1980 Presidential campaign reached its final stages, CBS aired this weekly wrap-up of political news. Four regular features were: summaries of the campaign activities of the candidates; "Inside Politics," dealing with the impact of finances, media consultants, and polls; latest results of the CBS News —*New York Times* poll; and interviews conducted by George Crile, discussing the major issues. Various CBS news correspondents contributed reports.

CAMPAIGN ROUNDUP (*News Analysis*)
FIRST TELECAST: *May 12, 1958*
LAST TELECAST: *June 9, 1958*
BROADCAST HISTORY:
May 1958–Jun 1958, ABC Mon 8:00–8:30
MODERATOR:
Quincy Howe

Continuing analysis of the various congressional and gubernatorial campaigns taking place throughout the country was provided by the ABC news staff during the 1958 primary season. Different correspondents contributed information regarding the races in different parts of the country.

CAMPAIGN '72 (*News*)
FIRST TELECAST: *June 25, 1972*
LAST TELECAST: *September 17, 1972*
BROADCAST HISTORY:
Jun 1972–Sep 1972, CBS Sun 6:00–7:00

During the summer of 1972, a presidential election year, CBS aired a regular series of reports on the activities of both parties as they prepared for their conventions, planned their campaign strategies, and sought to determine the way in which their respective nominees would handle themselves in the post-convention campaign.

CAMPAIGN '76 (*News*)
FIRST TELECAST: *September 3, 1976*
LAST TELECAST: *October 31, 1976*
BROADCAST HISTORY:
Sep 1976–Oct 1976, CBS Fri 7:30–8:00

As the 1976 presidential campaign drew to a close, CBS News provided a weekly report on the activities of Gerald Ford and Jimmy Carter in their "race for the White House." In addition to the latest poll results, CBS correspondents were shown on location with the candidates and in various parts of the country discussing issues with citizens and evaluating how regional climate of opinion was affected by the rhetoric. Various CBS News correspondents served as anchormen on individual telecasts.

CAMPAIGN '84 (*News*)
FIRST TELECAST: *September 11, 1984*
LAST TELECAST: *October 30, 1984*
BROADCAST HISTORY:
Sep 1984–Oct 1984, CBS Tue 11:30–12:00
ANCHORMAN:
Dan Rather

This weekly program updated viewers on the presidential campaigns of Republican President Ronald Reagan and Democratic challenger Walter Mondale. Dan Rather coordinated the proceedings, which included coverage of the preceding week's major political stories and features on various aspects of the campaigns—economic, ideological, social, and political.

CAMPBELL PLAYHOUSE, see *Campbell Soundstage*

CAMPBELL SOUNDSTAGE (*Dramatic Anthology*)
FIRST TELECAST: *June 6, 1952*
LAST TELECAST: *September 3, 1954*
BROADCAST HISTORY:
Jun 1952–Aug 1952, NBC Fri 9:30–10:00
Jul 1953–Sep 1954, NBC Fri 9:30–10:00

This dramatic series premiered in 1952 as the summer replacement for the vacationing *Aldrich Family*. Initially it was a collection of filmed dramas under the title *Campbell Playhouse*. Among the dramas were "The Cavorting Statue," starring Cesar Romero and Ann Rutherford, "Return to Vienna," with Ruth Warrick and Cameron Mitchell, and "This Little Pig Cried," with Frances Rafferty and Robert Rockwell.

The show returned in 1953 under the title *Campbell Soundstage*, this time as the permanent replacement for the canceled *Aldrich Family*. With the new name came a change in format. The plays were produced live in New York, starred big-name talent, and all had surprise endings reminiscent of O. Henry's short stories. Among the performers who starred in these live plays were Jack Lemmon, Walter Matthau, James Dean, E. G. Marshall, Betsy Palmer, Roddy McDowall, Brian Keith, and Lillian Gish.

On June 4, 1954, the title became *Campbell Summer Soundstage* and the presentations reverted to film. Many of these were reruns of episodes previously aired on *Ford Theatre*.

CAMPUS COPS (*Situation Comedy*)
BROADCAST HISTORY:
USA Network
30 minutes
Produced: *1995–1996* (13 episodes)
Premiered: *January 6, 1996*
CAST:
Wayne Simko.......................... Ryan Hurst
Andy MacCormack..................... Ben Bode

Capt. Mack Hingle .... David Sage
Roy Raskin .... J. D. Cullum
Meg DuVry .... LaRita Shelby
Elliot Royce .... Jerry Kernion
Dean Walter Pilkington.......... Monte Markham

Slapstick sitcom about two bumbling young campus policemen, Wayne and Andy, who spent more time chasing coeds than protecting them at Canfield University, located at Schlicter Falls. Capt. Hingle was their exasperated boss, and Pilkington the clueless dean, while Raskin, DuVry, and Royce were members of the squad.

CAMPUS CORNER (*Music*)
FIRST TELECAST: *March 18, 1949*
LAST TELECAST: *April 11, 1949*
BROADCAST HISTORY:
Mar 1949–Apr 1949, CBS Mon/Fri 7:45–8:00
REGULAR SINGERS:
Beverly Fite
Frank Stevens
Buzz Davis
Dean Campbell
Bob Burkhardt

Singer Beverly Fite was the hostess and star of this short-lived musical series, which was aired twice a week in the spring of 1949. She sang, with a quartet as backup, and chatted with a guest or two. The series was also called *The Quadrangle.*

CAMPUS HOOPLA (*Sports/Variety*)
FIRST TELECAST: *December 27, 1946*
LAST TELECAST: *December 19, 1947*
BROADCAST HISTORY:
Dec 1946–Dec 1947, NBC Fri 8:00–8:30 (OS)
HOST:
Bob Stanton
COMMERCIALS:
Eva Marie Saint

Campus Hoopla was a combination sports and variety show aimed at teenage viewers. The setting was a campus soda shop, complete with "cheerleaders" and "students" who talked about sports, participated in quiz segments, and sang and danced to the music of a jukebox. The latest sports scores were given by NBC sportscaster Bob Stanton, who also narrated films of recent games.

CAN DO (*Quiz/Audience Participation*)
FIRST TELECAST: *November 26, 1956*
LAST TELECAST: *December 31, 1956*
BROADCAST HISTORY:
Nov 1956–Dec 1956, NBC Mon 9:00–9:30
EMCEE:
Robert Alda

This short-lived game show offered contestants the opportunity to win up to $50,000 for correctly guessing whether famous show-business personalities could successfully perform certain stunts. The first round was worth $1,500, with the price doubling on each successive round. A contestant could quit at any time, with the threat of losing most of his winnings to be weighed against doubling his money. An incorrect guess meant that the contestant only took home 10 percent of the amount he was trying for, or roughly 20 percent of what he had already won. Among the celebrities featured were Sal Mineo operating a construction crane and Rory Calhoun performing an archery feat.

CAN YOU TOP THIS? (*Comedy*)
FIRST TELECAST: *October 3, 1950*
LAST TELECAST: *March 26, 1951*
BROADCAST HISTORY:
Oct 1950–Dec 1950, ABC Tue 9:30–10:00
Dec 1950–Mar 1951, ABC Mon 8:00–8:30
EMCEE:
Ward Wilson
PANEL:
Joe Laurie, Jr.
Harry Hershfield
Peter Donald
"Senator" Ed Ford

In the simple format of this show, four old-time gagsters sat around a table and told funny stories, including some sent in by viewers. A laugh meter measured the audience reaction to each and determined the winner of each round. The program was based on the radio show of the same name.

Here's a typical story: A very fussy school inspector arrived to inspect a little country schoolhouse. Hearing a commotion in one of the classrooms, he walked in and found the boys and girls raising a ruckus. One of them, a little taller than the rest, was making most of the noise. So the inspector promptly took this lad into another room, bent him over his knee, and spanked him. "Now, you stand in that corner and behave yourself or else I'll spank you again," the inspector warned sternly. So the fellow stood in the corner. A while later, there was a timid knock on the door. A little girl stuck her head in and said, "Please, sir, can we have our teacher back now?"

During the 1969–1970 season, almost two decades after the network version left the air, *Can You Top This?* returned in a syndicated version. Wink Martindale (replaced during the season by Dennis James) was the emcee, Richard Dawson assisted, and Morey Amsterdam was the only permanent panelist.

CANDID CAMERA (*Humor*)
FIRST TELECAST: *August 10, 1948*
LAST TELECAST:
BROADCAST HISTORY:
Aug 1948–Sep 1948, ABC Sun 8:00–8:30
Oct 1948, ABC Wed 8:30–8:45
Nov 1948–Dec 1948, ABC Fri 8:00–8:30
May 1949–Jul 1949, NBC Sun 7:30–8:00
Jul 1949–Aug 1949, NBC Thu 9:00–9:30
Sep 1949–Sep 1950, CBS Mon 9:00–9:30
Jun 1953, NBC Tue 9:30–10:00
Jul 1953, NBC Wed 10:00–10:30
Oct 1960–Sep 1967, CBS Sun 10:00–10:30
Jul 1990–Aug 1990, CBS Fri 8:30–9:00
Feb 1998–Jan 2000, CBS Fri 8:30–9:00
Jan 2000–Feb 2000, CBS Sat 8:30–9:00
Jun 2000–Sep 2000, CBS Fri 8:30–9:00
Jan 2001– , PAX Sun 7:00–8:00
Jun 2001– , PAX Wed 8:00–9:00
Jan 2003– , PAX Sat 8:00–9:00
HOST:
Allen Funt (1948–1990)
Dom DeLuise (1991–1992)
Peter Funt (1998–)

CO-HOST:

Arthur Godfrey (1960–1961)
Durward Kirby (1961–1966)
Bess Myerson (1966–1967)
Phyllis George (1974–1976)
Jo Ann Pflug (1976–1977)
John Bartholomew Tucker (1977–1978)
Peter Funt (1990)
Suzanne Somers (1998–2000)
Dina Eastwood (2001–)

A patron at a bowling alley would roll a ball, and back down the chute it would come—minus finger holes. *Candid Camera* viewers watched as the poor fellow tried to figure out *what the*—!

A tiny foreign car would pull into a service station and the driver would casually ask for a "fill up." The hidden camera focused on the attendant's growing astonishment as the midget auto practically drained the station dry. (There was a tank concealed in the trunk.)

"Smile, you're on *Candid Camera*!"

The premise of Allen Funt's long-running *Candid Camera* was simply to snoop on unsuspecting citizens with hidden cameras and see how they would react to bizarre situations. Cars were a favorite device. In one sequence, innocent-looking Dorothy Collins (frequently seen on the show during the 1960s) would come driving down a hill and pull up in front of a passerby, asking for help—the car "won't seem to start." Up went the hood to reveal . . . no engine. Other ploys included vending machines that talked back, actors who got into unbelievable predicaments and then asked passersby for help, diners served impossibly small portions, and so on—*ad infinitum*. The reactions of the surprised victims were often hilarious.

Allen Funt, who appeared in many of the gags, may have been one of the nerviest actors in TV history. Yet he got few rejections, even fewer punches in the nose, for his presumptions upon innocent citizens. His greatest coup was a special filmed in Moscow—without the permission, or even knowledge, of the Russian authorities. Funt managed to smuggle himself, cameramen, hidden cameras, and 90,000 feet of film into and out of the Soviet Union undetected (the border guards, taking him for a tourist, never opened his bags). On the streets of the Russian capital he staged many of his favorite stunts, including the newspaper routine (start reading someone's paper over their shoulder, gradually get your hands on it to position it better, and then work it away from them entirely) and the two-suitcase caper. (A pretty girl with two suitcases asks a passing male to help her carry one; hers is empty, his is filled with 200 pounds of concrete. To Funt's astonishment, a burly Russian blithely picked up the trick suitcase and trotted off with it, never blinking an eye.)

Some of the best sequences were not setups, but simply cameos from life; for instance, the husky traffic cop at a busy intersection who seemed to perform a classical ballet as he motioned cars hither and yon.

Allen Funt first brought his established *Candid Microphone* radio program to television in 1948, and it continued off and on for 30 years thereafter. The first TV version was in fact called *Candid Microphone*, but the title was changed to *Candid Camera* when it moved to NBC in 1949. In addition to its prime-time runs, listed above, *Candid Camera* was aired as a local program in New York in the mid-1950s; as part of the commercials within *Pontiac Presents Playwrights '56* in 1955–1956; as a segment within the *Garry Moore Show* in 1959–1960; and in reruns on CBS daytime TV, from September 1966 to September 1968.

Six years later, Allen Funt brought *Candid Camera* back in a syndicated version that included both new and old material. The syndicated version, which ran from 1974 to 1978, utilized the services of Phyllis George, Jo Ann Pflug, and John Bartholomew Tucker as co-hosts with Funt, and comedienne Fannie Flagg as a semi-regular participant in the setups.

CBS had aired a number of *Candid Camera* specials during the 1989–1990 season, with Funt's son Peter joining his dad as co-host. At the end of the summer, they were rerun as part of CBS' regular weekly schedule. The success of the specials prompted Funt to produce a new *Candid Camera* for first-run syndication. It premiered in the fall of 1991, with Dom DeLuise serving as host and Eva LaRue as his announcer/assistant. Failing to attract much of an audience, it was canceled after a single season.

The venerable series was revived again in 1998 after four new *Candid Camera* specials had garnered strong ratings on CBS during the previous year. Peter Funt was back, with actress Suzanne Somers serving as his co-host. In addition to segments produced for the new version, there were "Then and Now" segments featuring clips from the series' earlier incarnations followed by updated versions of the same stunts. At the end of each episode viewers were shown an address to which they could mail in their own suggestions for future stunts. On the episode that aired on September 24, 1999, host Peter Funt introduced a video tribute to his father, Allen, the creator of *Candid Camera*, who had died earlier that month, and in December the series aired a special one-hour episode featuring the senior Funt. The first November episode saw the debut of a new rock 'n' roll version of the series theme song performed by legendary rocker Little Richard.

When CBS canceled the show it moved to Pax, at first airing reruns of the CBS episodes, and later new episodes with Dina Eastwood replacing Somers as co-host.

CANNON (*Detective Drama*)

FIRST TELECAST: *September 14, 1971*
LAST TELECAST: *September 19, 1976*
BROADCAST HISTORY:

Sep 1971–Sep 1972, CBS Tue 9:30–10:30
Sep 1972–Sep 1973, CBS Wed 10:00–11:00
Sep 1973–Jul 1976, CBS Wed 9:00–10:00
Jul 1976–Sep 1976, CBS Sun 10:00–11:00

CAST:

Frank Cannon .... William Conrad

Balding, middle-aged, and portly, detective Frank Cannon represented quite a change from the traditional suave, handsome private detectives TV had brought to its viewers. He occasionally let his conscience dictate his choice of cases, but more often his wallet took precedence. To most clients he charged a high fee, in order to provide himself with the money to indulge in personal luxuries such as an expensive convertible and fine cuisine. Cannon rarely fired a shot, was in no condition to beat up his adversaries, and was generally seen driving around Los Angeles in his big, shiny Continental. The car took more physical abuse than Cannon did, often getting dented, scraped, and mangled during chase sequences.

William Conrad, the only regular in the series, had previously been more familiar to the ears than to the eyes of Americans. During the 1950s he had been the voice of Matt Dillon in the radio version of *Gunsmoke*, but was manifestly unsuited to portray the tough Western marshal when the series moved to television—so young James Arness got the role, in what became the longest-running dramatic series in TV history.

CAN'T HURRY LOVE (*Situation Comedy*)
FIRST TELECAST: *September 18, 1995*
LAST TELECAST: *July 31, 1996*
BROADCAST HISTORY:
Sep 1995–Feb 1996, CBS Mon 8:30–9:00
Jul 1996, CBS Wed 8:30–9:00
CAST:
Annie O'Donnell .... Nancy McKeon
Didi Edelstein .... Mariska Hargitay
Roger Carlucci .... Louis Mandylor
Elliot Tenney (pilot only) .... David Pressman
Elliot Tenney .... Kevin Crowley

This was not a copy of *Friends*, claimed the producers and stars of this series which focused on the social and working lives of four attractive friends in their late 20s in New York. Three of them worked together at a Manhattan personnel agency—Annie, who over the years had "kissed too many frogs looking for a prince"; lovable, womanizing Roger, whose rough edges made finding a classy lady rather difficult; and Elliot, the married confidant who found all the dos and don'ts of dating in the '90s hard to keep track of. Annie's neighbor, sexy divorced Didi, was always giving her advice, often unsolicited, on everything from what to buy to how far to go on the first date. The four of them regularly provided emotional support and helpful advice—not always good advice—to each other. By December, Elliot's marriage was in trouble; in January he moved in with Roger, and after his wife served him with divorce papers in February, it looked like he would be back in the dating game along with the others.

CAPE, THE (*Adventure*)
BROADCAST HISTORY:
Syndicated only
60 minutes
Produced: *1996–1997* (22 episodes)
Released: *September 1996*
CAST:
Col Henry J. "Bull" Eckert .... Corbin Bernsen
Lt. Col. Jack Riles .... Adam Baldwin
Mission Specialist Tamara St. James ... Tyra Ferrell
Maj. Reggie Warren .... Bobby Hosea
Capt. Zeke Beaumont .... Cameron Bancroft
Lt. Cmdr. Barbara DiSantis .... Bobbie Phillips
Lt. Cmdr. D. B. Woods .... David Kelsey
Peter Engel .... Chad Willett
Andrea Wyler .... Katie Mitchell
Harry Krause .... Larry Black
**Sweets McCain* .... Whitman Mayo
*Occasional
TECHNICAL CONSULTANT:
Buzz Aldrin

"Bull" Eckert, a veteran of three shuttle missions, was the stern director of astronaut training at Florida's Kennedy Space Center in this hard-edged action series that featured intense, buzz-cut space jockeys, personal jealousies, and constant crises in outer space. Other veterans in the program were Jack, the aggressive Air Force officer who had piloted a number of shuttle missions; Reggie, a Marine who terrorized the trainees and nurtured major resentments until he got his own first space assignment after six years at the Cape; and Tamara, the mission specialist. Among the newer trainees (known as AsCans) were Zeke, an Air Force veteran of the Gulf War; Barbara, a Navy pilot who had had an affair with Reggie and was incapacitated for a time after a motorcycle accident; D.B., a Ph.D. in astrophysics and aeronautical engineering whose father, now a senator, had himself been an astronaut; and Peter, an elementary school teacher who felt insecure about his lack of military training. Harry was Bull's boss, and Andrea the astronaut program's worried public affairs director (all those crises!). A personal friend of newly separated Bull, she started dating him in the spring of 1997. Episodes dealt with their training, personal lives, and the politics surrounding the space program. Sweets ran the Moonshot Bar & Grill, where the astronauts and trainees hung out in their spare time. In February, due to budget cuts, trainee Zeke Beaumont, who was about to graduate, was dropped from the astronaut program, and in May 1997 he decided to resign from the Air Force—but was recalled to help run a rescue mission to repair a shuttle with damaged heat tiles.

The series was filmed on location at the Kennedy Space Center and the Cape Canaveral air station in Florida. Former astronaut Buzz Aldrin served as the technical consultant.

CAPITAL GANG, THE (*Discussion*)
BROADCAST HISTORY:
CNN
30 minutes
Produced: *1988–*
Premiered: *October 15, 1988*
REGULARS:
Pat Buchanan (1988–1991)
Mark Shields
Robert Novak
Al Hunt
Margaret Warner (1991–1993)
Mona Charen (1991–1997)
Margaret Carlson (1993–)
Kate O'Beirne (1995–)

A lively weekend discussion program focusing on the week's political events. The moderators have been Pat Buchanan (1988–1991), Al Hunt (1991–1993), and Mark Shields (1993–).

CAPITAL NEWS (*Newspaper Drama*)
FIRST TELECAST: *April 9, 1990*
LAST TELECAST: *April 30, 1990*
BROADCAST HISTORY:
Apr 1990, ABC Mon 10:00–11:00
CAST:
Jonathan "Jo Jo" Turner .... Lloyd Bridges
Clay Gibson .... Michael Woods
Edison King .... Mark Blum

Redmond Dunne .... William Russ
Anne McKenna .... Helen Slater
Haskell Epstein .... Daniel Roebuck
Doreen Duncan...................... Jenny Wright
Todd Lunden .... Christian Clemenson
Miles Plato.......................... Kurt Fuller
Conrad White.................... Wendell Pierce
Cassy Swann .... Chelsea Field
Vinnie DeSalvo .... Charles Levin
Richie Fineberg .... Richard Murphy

ABC yelled "stop the presses!" after only four episodes of this noble newspaper drama set in Washington, D.C. Heroic Editor-in-Chief "Jo Jo" Turner ran *The Washington Capital* with a firm hand, alternately encouraging and admonishing his dedicated, hard-working reporters. The newsroom was divided into two very different worlds. Metro, headed by Clay Gibson, explored the seamy underside of Washington, America's "murder and drug capital." National, led by Edison King, stalked the corridors of governmental power, uncovering scandal and abuse. Undistracted by all this nobility, iconoclastic, seasoned reporter Dunne was having an affair with newcomer McKenna. Plato was a worried columnist, and most of the rest of the regular cast (above) were reporters chasing hot scoops while anguishing about current journalistic issues such as checkbook journalism and reporter objectivity.

Although producer David Milch said "I'll go to my grave denying that the series is based on *The Washington Post*," it obviously was. Bridges looked and acted like the *Post*'s legendary editor Ben Bradlee, the giant newsroom looked like that of the *Post*, co-creator Christian Williams worked there for 13 years, *Post* staffers were interviewed and their work habits studied in developing the series, and several of them actually worked behind the scenes on the show.

CAPITOL CAPERS (*Music*)

FIRST TELECAST: *August 1, 1949*
LAST TELECAST: *September 7, 1949*
BROADCAST HISTORY:
Aug 1949–Sep 1949, NBC Mon/Wed 7:30–7:45
REGULARS:
Cliff Quartet, instrumental
Gene Archer, baritone

This live musical program emanated from NBC's Washington, D.C., studios.

CAPITOL CLOAK ROOM (*Public Affairs/Discussion*)

FIRST TELECAST: *October 14, 1949*
LAST TELECAST: *September 8, 1950*
BROADCAST HISTORY:
Oct 1949–Sep 1950, CBS Fri 10:30–11:00
PANELISTS:
Griffing Bancroft
Eric Sevareid
Bill Shadel

CBS simulcast this live political discussion program from Washington, D.C., on both its television and radio networks. Each week a key political figure was interviewed by a panel of three CBS correspondents. The panel was chaired by Griffing Bancroft. Following its prime-time run, *Capitol Cloak Room* moved to Sunday afternoons, where it remained until the following January.

CAPITOL CRITTERS (*Cartoon*)

FIRST TELECAST: *January 28, 1992*
LAST TELECAST: *March 14, 1992*
BROADCAST HISTORY:
Jan 1992, ABC Tue 8:30–9:00
Jan 1992, ABC Fri 8:30–9:00
Feb 1992–Mar 1992, ABC Sat 8:00–8:30
VOICES:
Max.......................... Neil Patrick Harris
Muggle .... Bobcat Goldthwait
Moze .... Dorian Harewood
Jammet .... Charlie Adler
Berkeley....................... Jennifer Darling
Trixie .... Pattie Deutsch
Presidential felines.................. Frank Welker

Steven Bochco, a producer known for some of television's bolder experiments *(Hill Street Blues, Cop Rock)*, was responsible for this satiric cartoon about mice, rats, and roaches living under the White House. The central character was Max, a friendly Nebraska field mouse whose family had been wiped out by exterminators and who then came to Washington to live with his cousin Berkeley. Besides Berkeley, an unrepentant sixties radical, his new world included Muggle, a lab rat prone to spontaneous combustion and other unexpected reactions due to the tests done on him; Moze, a streetwise roach who befriended him; Jammet, a headstrong teenage pack rat; and Trixie, Jammet's world-weary mother.

Stories were a mix of social commentary on such issues as gun control, interracial violence, and political corruption, and Tom & Jerry chases as the critters dodged exterminators and the ever-present, but fortunately fat and incompetent, Presidential cats.

CAPTAIN AND TENNILLE, THE (*Musical Variety*)

FIRST TELECAST: *September 20, 1976*
LAST TELECAST: *March 14, 1977*
BROADCAST HISTORY:
Sep 1976–Mar 1977, ABC Mon 8:00–9:00
REGULARS:
Daryl Dragon
Toni Tennille
THEME:
"Love Will Keep Us Together"

This youth-oriented variety hour was built around the "soft rock" husband-and-wife team of Daryl Dragon and Toni Tennille, who had several big record hits in 1975–1976 and who, ABC hoped, might become another Sonny and Cher on TV. They didn't.

Toni was a pretty but somewhat antiseptic version of Cher, while Daryl ("The Captain," after his ever-present captain's hat) was decidedly quieter than Sonny. In fact, he scarcely said a word, and much of the comedy was built around his extremely taciturn nature. He also had a chance to show off his musical wizardry—he was a master of all sorts of keyboard instruments. Daryl came from a background of music, if not comedy, being the son of the well-known concert conductor Carmen Dragon.

Among the featured segments on the show were "The Charcoal House," with Daryl and Toni as two struggling young performers, and "Master-joke Theater." The only other regulars on the show were the Dragons' two English bulldogs, Elizabeth and Broderick.

CAPTAIN BILLY'S MISSISSIPPI MUSIC HALL (*Variety*)
FIRST TELECAST: *October 1, 1948*
LAST TELECAST: *November 26, 1948*
BROADCAST HISTORY:
Oct 1948–Nov 1948, CBS Fri 8:30–9:00
REGULARS:
Ralph Dumke
Betty Brewer
Johnny Downs
Juanita Hall
George Jason
Bibi Osterwald
The Vic Smalley Orchestra

Loosely based on incidents related in the book *Old Man River and His Chillun*, written by Captain Billy Bryant, this live variety series was set on a Mississippi paddle-wheel showboat. It was hosted by Ralph Dumke, in the role of Captain Billy, and included musical numbers, comedy, and dramatic interludes performed by guest stars. The series had premiered on August 16 as a local show under the title *Captain Billy's Showboat*, changed its name on September 17, and two weeks later became a network program.

CAPTAIN NICE (*Situation Comedy*)
FIRST TELECAST: *January 9, 1967*
LAST TELECAST: *August 28, 1967*
BROADCAST HISTORY:
Jan 1967–Aug 1967, NBC Mon 8:30–9:00
CAST:
Carter Nash (Captain Nice)........ William Daniels
Mrs. Nash.......................... Alice Ghostley
Sgt. Candy Kane..................... Ann Prentiss
Mayor Finney........................ Liam Dunn
Chief Segal...................... William Zuckert
Mr. Nash.......................... Byron Foulger

Captain Nice was created and written by Buck Henry, co-creator of *Get Smart*, and it was to superheroes what *Get Smart* was to secret agents—a parody. Carter Nash was a police department chemist who had accidentally discovered a liquid that, when drunk, would transform him into Captain Nice. Unfortunately Captain Nice was no stronger a personality than Carter was normally—shy, quiet, unassuming, and mother-dominated. In fact if it had not been for his mother, who demanded that her son wage war on the evil forces that constantly threatened society, he would not have gotten actively involved in fighting crime at all. The sight of Captain Nice trying to maintain his composure while flying over Bigtown (he had an acute fear of heights) in his baggy, moth-eaten, red-white-and-blue leotards (made for him by his mother) did not exactly terrify evildoers.

CAPTAIN VIDEO AND HIS VIDEO RANGERS (*Children's*)
FIRST TELECAST: *June 27, 1949*
LAST TELECAST: *April 1, 1955*
BROADCAST HISTORY:
Jun 1949–Aug 1949, DUM Mon/Tue/Thu/Fri 7:00–7:30
Aug 1949–Sep 1953, DUM Mon–Fri 7:00–7:30
Sep 1953–Apr 1955, DUM Mon–Fri 7:00–7:15
also
Feb 1950–Sep 1950, DUM Sat 7:30–8:00
Sep 1950–Nov 1950, DUM Sat 7:00–7:30
CAST:
Captain Video (1949–1950)....... Richard Coogan
Captain Video (1951–1955)............. Al Hodge
The Ranger........................ Don Hastings
Dr. Pauli (1949)................... Bran Mossen
Dr. Pauli (later).................... Hal Conklin
CREATOR/PRODUCER:
James Caddigan
WRITER:
Maurice C. Brock
THEME:
Overture to *The Flying Dutchman*, by Richard Wagner

"Guardian of the Safety of the World"—on a prop budget of $25 per week! *Captain Video* was one of the low-budget wonders of television history, and one of the most popular children's programs of the early 1950s. It was the first of a trio of "space operas" popular at the time—*Space Patrol* and *Tom Corbett—Space Cadet* were mere imitations—and the one most frequently seen (Monday–Friday during most of its run).

Captain Video, as played by handsome, jut-jawed Richard Coogan, and later by handsome, jut-jawed Al Hodge (formerly the voice of radio's *Green Hornet*), was a scientific genius who took it upon himself, as a private citizen, to insure the safety of the universe. Operating from his secret, mountaintop headquarters, sometime in the 21st or 22nd century, he controlled a vast network of "Video Rangers" as well as an impressive arsenal of futuristic weaponry of his own invention. His sidekick The Ranger—idol of half the kids in America—was played by young Don Hastings, who was 15 when the series began.

Captain Video's adversaries were legion, among them Nargola, Mook the Moon Man, Kul of Eos, Heng Foo Seeng, Dr. Clysmok, and Dahoumie. But the most persistent was Dr. Pauli, head of the Astroidal Society and an evil genius whose scientific weaponry was almost equal to Video's own.

Captain Video and The Ranger were constantly coming up with new devices with which to fight off these assorted villains. The Opticon Scillometer (which looked suspiciously like a length of pipe with some spare parts bolted on) allowed one to see through things; the Atomic Rifle could blow up almost anything; the Discatron was a sort of portable TV set; the Radio Scillograph was a long-range two-way radio that fit in the palm of the hand; and the Cosmic Ray Vibrator a handy device that literally shook adversaries into submission—seldom was anyone killed outright on *Captain Video*. Not to be outdone, Dr. Pauli countered with his Trisonic Compensator, which could curve bullets around a house; his Barrier of Silence, so he couldn't be heard; and the Cloak of Invisibility—how many kids would have liked to get their hands on *that*!

Perhaps the most terrifying piece of machinery seen on *Captain Video*, however, was Tobor ("robot" spelled backward). Designed as the ultimate, unstoppable, indestructible robot to work for the good of mankind, he had been appropriated by a beautiful villainess named Atar. She programmed him, naturally, to "get Captain Video." But the captain also managed to get on Tobor's secret frequency and in a magnified climactic scene, the hulking brute was reduced to a pile of scrap metal by conflicting orders from Atar and Video.

Since DuMont was perpetually impoverished, the

sets and props on *Captain Video* were constructed on the smallest possible budget. Most of the controls in the captain's spaceship, the *Galaxy*, were painted on, and one suspected that a single swift kick at his master control board would destroy the entire headquarters. The unkindest limitations were on the network of Video Rangers, whom the captain would look in on, using his Remote Carrier Beam, once during each telecast. Most of them looked exactly like cowboys in the Old West—DuMont was running pieces of ancient Westerns to pad out the half hour! (This practice ceased after a time.)

There was tremendous viewer interest in *Captain Video*, heightened by offers of premiums such as plastic replicas of the captain's weapons, his decoder ring, and his space helmet. A theatrical serial was made based on his exploits. The program won several awards from impressed adults, too, for the captain's regular short talks to "Rangers at home" on the value of tolerance, fair play, and personal integrity.

Captain Video was, in all, a splendid example of innovative programming that was perfect for the TV medium. Had DuMont been able to devise more such breakthroughs, the network might have survived longer than it did. As it was, *Captain Video and His Video Rangers* lasted until the network itself crumbled away, in 1955. During the last stages of its run it was also known as *The Secret Files of Captain Video*.

The reader interested in a detailed, and loving, description of *Captain Video* and other "space operas" is referred to *The Great Television Heroes*, by Donald F. Glut and Jim Harmon.

CAPTAINS AND THE KINGS (*Drama*)

FIRST TELECAST: *September 30, 1976*

LAST TELECAST: *April 25, 1977*

BROADCAST HISTORY:

Sep 1976–Nov 1976, NBC Thu 9:00–10:00
Mar 1977–Apr 1977, NBC Thu 9:00–11:00
Apr 1977, NBC Mon 9:00–11:00

CAST:

Joseph Armagh .... Richard Jordan
Katherine Hennessey .... Joanna Pettet
Big Ed Healey .... Charles Durning
Martinique .... Barbara Parkins
Tom Hennessey .... Vic Morrow
Harry Zieff .... Harvey Jason
Miss Emmy .... Beverly D'Angelo
Charles Desmond .... Robert Vaughn
Elizabeth Healey Hennessey .... Blair Brown
Bernadette Hennessey Armagh ... Patty Duke Astin
Moira/Mary Armagh .... Katherine Crawford
Marjorie Chisholm Armagh .... Jane Seymour
Rory Armagh .... Perry King
Claudia Desmond .... Cynthia Sikes
Kevin Armagh .... Douglas Heyes, Jr.

Adapted from Taylor Caldwell's novel, *Captains and the Kings* was the saga of Joseph Armagh, a poor Irish immigrant who rose to great prominence in America in the latter part of the nineteenth century. Episodes chronicled the period from his arrival in New York as a young man in 1857 till the death of his last son around 1912. His rise to wealth and power through investments in the oil industry, his affairs both public and private, and his consuming desire to have one of his sons become the first Irish Catholic president of the United States were all woven into the story. The latter plan, on the verge of success, was abruptly destroyed when Rory was assassinated during the campaign.

Captains and the Kings was one of the four novels dramatized under the collective title *NBC's Best Sellers*. Although most of the chapters ran only one hour, as indicated in the broadcast history above, the first and last chapters ran from 9–11 P.M. It was also the only one of the four novels to be rerun, in the spring of 1977, with all rerun installments running two hours in length. The concluding chapter of the *Captains and the Kings* reruns aired on Monday night, April 25, 1977.

CAPTURED, syndicated title for *Gangbusters*

CAR 54, WHERE ARE YOU? (*Situation Comedy*)

FIRST TELECAST: *September 17, 1961*

LAST TELECAST: *September 8, 1963*

BROADCAST HISTORY:

Sep 1961–Sep 1963, NBC Sun 8:30–9:00

CAST:

Officer Gunther Toody .... Joe E. Ross
Officer Francis Muldoon .... Fred Gwynne
Lucille Toody .... Bea Pons
Captain Martin Block .... Paul Reed
Officer O'Hara .... Albert Henderson
Officer Anderson (1961–1962) ...... Nipsey Russell
Officer Antonnucci (1961–1962) ....
.... Jerome Guardino
Officer Riley (1961–1962) .... Duke Farley
Officer Murdock (1961–1962) ...... Shelley Burton
Officer Steinmetz .... Joe Warren
Officer Leo Schnauser .... Al Lewis
Officer Kissel .... Bruce Kirby
Officer Ed Nicholson .... Hank Garrett
Officer Nelson .... Jim Gormley
Sylvia Schnauser .... Charlotte Rae
Officer Wallace (1962–1963) ..... Frederick O'Neal

CREATOR AND PRODUCER:

Nat Hiken

Officers Toody and Muldoon were among the most unlikely patrol-car partners ever seen on a police force. Toody was short, stocky, friendly, and just a bit nosy, a marked contrast to the tall, quiet Muldoon. Although they were assigned to New York's 53rd precinct—a run-down area in the Bronx not generally considered a hotbed of hilarity—they always seemed to encounter more comedy than crime. Much of the action took place in the precinct house itself, particularly in the locker room as the officers got into uniform, and the comedy was invariably of the broad slapstick variety reminiscent of Mack Sennett.

One unusual aspect of this series was the partners' patrol car, which looked identical to those used by real-life New York City police—but only because the show was filmed in black and white. The car was actually painted red and white to distinguish it from real police cars during the shooting (all of which was done on location). On the home screen the red and white car looked identical to the dark green and white of genuine New York City police cars.

Nat Hiken of the *Phil Silvers Show* was the creator, producer, and one of the writers of *Car 54, Where Are You?*

CARA WILLIAMS SHOW, THE (*Situation Comedy*)

FIRST TELECAST: *September 23, 1964*

LAST TELECAST: *September 10, 1965*
BROADCAST HISTORY:
Sep 1964–Apr 1965, CBS Wed 9:30–10:00
May 1965–Sep 1965, CBS Fri 8:30–9:00
CAST:
Cara Bridges/Wilton .... Cara Williams
Frank Bridges .... Frank Aletter
Damon Burkhardt .... Paul Reed
Mrs. Burkhardt......................... Reta Shaw
Fletcher Kincaid .... Jack Sheldon
Mary Hammilmeyer .... Jeanne Arnold
Agnes .... Audrey Christie

A secret marriage in the face of a company rule against employing married couples provided the basis for much of the comedy in this series. Cara and Frank Bridges, the secret spouses, had to pretend to be singles as they went to work each day at Fenwick Diversified Industries. Frank was the company efficiency expert, and Cara, who used her maiden name of Wilton in the office, was a secretary with an incredibly complex filing system. She was indispensable to her boss, Mr. Burkhardt, because she was the only one who could find anything in her files. The Bridges' problems at home and at work, as they tried to protect their secret, made for amusing and complicated situations.

CARIBE (*Police Drama*)

FIRST TELECAST: *February 17, 1975*
LAST TELECAST: *August 11, 1975*
BROADCAST HISTORY:
Feb 1975–Aug 1975, ABC Mon 10:00–11:00
CAST:
Lt. Ben Logan .... Stacy Keach
Sgt. Mark Walters .... Carl Franklin
Deputy Commissioner Ed Rawlings, Miami P.D.
.... Robert Mandan

This action-adventure was set in Miami and throughout the Caribbean. Ben Logan and his black partner, Sgt. Mark Walters, constituted a two-man law-enforcement unit working for Caribbean Force, an international agency fighting crime wherever Americans were involved.

CARMEL MYERS SHOW, THE (*Interviews*)

FIRST TELECAST: *June 26, 1951*
LAST TELECAST: *February 21, 1952*
BROADCAST HISTORY:
Jun 1951–Oct 1951, ABC Tue 7:15–7:30
Oct 1951–Feb 1952, ABC Thu 10:45–11:00
HOSTESS:
Carmel Myers

Carmel Myers, formerly a queen of the silent movies, hosted this weekly 15-minute program of interviews, chats, and reminiscences on ABC in 1951–1952. Among her guests were Abe Burrows, Jule Styne, and Richard Rodgers.

CARNIVAL, see *ABC Dramatic Shorts—1952–1953*

CAROL & COMPANY (*Comedy Anthology*)

FIRST TELECAST: *March 31, 1990*
LAST TELECAST: *July 20, 1991*
BROADCAST HISTORY:
Mar 1990–Apr 1990, NBC Sat 9:30–10:00
Apr 1990–Jun 1990, NBC Sat 10:00–10:30
Aug 1990–Mar 1991, NBC Sat 10:00–10:30
Mar 1991–May 1991, NBC Sat 10:00–11:00
Jul 1991, NBC Sat 10:30–11:00
REPERTORY GROUP:
Carol Burnett
Terry Kiser
Meagan Fay
Richard Kind
Anita Barone
Jeremy Piven
Peter Krause

Rubber-faced comedienne Carol Burnett hosted and starred in this weekly comedy anthology. Each week there was a single half-hour "playlet" about someone in an unusual situation. Among the subjects: a temperamental soap opera star, a sex-starved 82-year-old in a rest home, a Pollyanna-ish housewife having a nightmare day, a woman applying for a bank loan while her son robs the bank, a Las Vegas preacher who makes the mistake of advertising that she'll "marry anyone," and a recently released asylum inmate struggling to maintain her sanity while applying for a license at the Motor Vehicle Department.

Supporting players included a repertory troupe of actors (above), and occasional guest stars including Hal Linden, Christopher Reeve, Nell Carter, and Burnett's daughter Carrie Hamilton.

CAROL BURNETT SHOW, THE (*Comedy/Variety*)

FIRST TELECAST: *September 11, 1967*
LAST TELECAST: *September 8, 1979*
BROADCAST HISTORY:
Sep 1967–May 1971, CBS Mon 10:00–11:00 (OS)
Sep 1971–Nov 1972, CBS Wed 8:00–9:00 (OS)
Dec 1972–Dec 1977, CBS Sat 10:00–11:00 (OS)
Dec 1977–Mar 1978, CBS Sun 10:00–11:00
Jun 1978–Aug 1978, CBS Wed 8:00–9:00
Aug 1979–Sep 1979, ABC Sat 8:00–9:00
REGULARS:
Carol Burnett
Harvey Korman (1967–1977)
Lyle Waggoner (1967–1974)
Vicki Lawrence
Tim Conway (1975–1979)
The Ernest Flatt Dancers
The Harry Zimmerman Orchestra (1967–1971)
The Peter Matz Orchestra (1971–1978)
Dick Van Dyke (1977)
Kenneth Mars (1979)
Craig Richard Nelson (1979)
THEME:
"It's Time to Say Goodbye"

In an era in which variety shows were rapidly disappearing from television, *The Carol Burnett Show* survived for more than a decade. The life span for other variety series in the 1970s rarely exceeded two seasons, and their total number had dwindled substantially from the heyday of variety shows in the 1950s. Only Carol managed to remain popular and successful. The small nucleus of her regular cast remained constant for several years, with none of her original supporting troupes leaving until 1974. Their chemistry helped hold the show together. The binding force, however, was Carol, one of television's most versatile variety performers, who could sing, dance, act, clown, and mime with equal facility.

Over the years certain basic aspects of the show remained the same. There was one point in each telecast, usually at the beginning, when Carol and the evening's guest star would answer questions from the studio audience. There were comedy sketches that spoofed TV series, popular movies, or other forms of mass entertainment. Among Carol's extensive repertoire of comic characterizations were a few recurring sketches that persisted for years. In "Mr. Tudball and Mrs. Wiggins" she played an inept, blonde office worker with a frustrated, ever-suffering boss played by Tim Conway. In "Ed & Eunice" (which several years later ran as a series titled *Mama's Family* on NBC) she and Harvey Korman were an uptight married couple constantly at odds with Eunice's mother, played by Vicki Lawrence. In "Old Folks at Home" Carol and Roger, played by Miss Burnett and Harvey Korman, were an unhappily married couple who fought almost all the time and had problems with Carol's kid sister Chrissy, played by Vicki Lawrence (who, disconcertingly, looked enough like Carol to really have been her sister). "As the Stomach Turns" was a continuing soap-opera satire.

Jim Nabors, one of Carol's close friends, was her good-luck charm and always appeared as the guest star on the opening telecast of each season. Tim Conway, who had been a frequent guest in *The Carol Burnett Show*'s early years, joined the regular cast in the fall of 1975. Harvey Korman decided to leave the series in the spring of 1977, a loss that was felt deeply by Carol, who had worked so well with him for so long. The resulting need for a strong lead actor-comic was met by Dick Van Dyke, who was assigned to be Carol's co-star that fall.

The chemistry that had existed between Carol and Harvey Korman was not present with her new co-star and Dick Van Dyke left the show only three months after he had arrived. For the first time in years, Carol's ratings faltered, forcing the move to Sunday nights in December of 1977. Semi-regular guest stars Ken Berry and Steve Lawrence tried to help fill the void caused by the lack of a strong male lead, but by the following spring, after eleven years on the air, Carol decided to give up the weekly grind. In a special two-hour finale, on March 29, 1978, highlights from past shows were intermixed with new material.

This was not quite the end, however. Reruns were aired during the summer of 1978, and during the summer of 1979 four new episodes were produced for ABC featuring two new regulars, and aired under the title *Carol Burnett & Company*. Also in 1979, the comedy sketches (only) from the original CBS programs were edited into a series of half-hour shows and syndicated to local stations to be rerun under the title *Carol Burnett and Friends*.

CAROL BURNETT SHOW, THE (*Comedy/Variety*)
FIRST TELECAST: *November 1, 1991*
LAST TELECAST: *December 27, 1991*
BROADCAST HISTORY:

Nov 1991–Dec 1991, CBS Fri 9:00–10:00

REGULARS:

Carol Burnett
Chris Barnes
Meagan Fay
Roger Kabler
Richard Kind
Jessica Lundy
The Tom Scott Orchestra

Carol Burnett returned to the format, the style of sketches, and even the title that had made her a star in the 1960s with this familiar-looking, short-lived comedy variety series. It was déjà vu all over again: just as before, she opened by taking questions from the audience, then welcomed a guest star, then performed in a number of unrelated sketches with her guest and a repertory company of regulars. Jim Nabors was even on hand on the premiere to wish her luck, as he had been at the beginning of every season in the old days. Carol adopted many faces in the short sketches, which were much like those she had been doing for years—and seemingly a little conservative for the let-it-all-hang-out 1990s. Her repertory players were mostly young faces, including Meagan Fay and Richard Kind (the heavyset guy) who had been with her on her NBC anthology, *Carol & Company*, during the previous season.

CAROLINE IN THE CITY (*Situation Comedy*)
FIRST TELECAST: *September 21, 1995*
LAST TELECAST: *April 26, 1999*
BROADCAST HISTORY:

Sep 1995–Jul 1996, NBC Thu 9:30–10:00
Aug 1996–Jul 1997, NBC Tue 9:30–10:00
Jun 1997–Jun 1998, NBC Mon 9:00–9:30
Jun 1998–Jul 1998, NBC Mon 8:30–9:00
Sep 1998–Nov 1998, NBC Mon 9:00–9:30
Dec 1998–Jan 1999, NBC Mon 8:30–9:00
Mar 1999–Apr 1999, NBC Mon 8:30–9:00

CAST:

Caroline Duffy .... Lea Thompson
Richard Karinsky .... Malcolm Gets
Del Cassidy .... Eric Lutes
Charlie .... Andy Lauer
Annie Spadaro .... Amy Pietz
Julia Mazzone (1997–1998) .... Sofia Milos
Remo (1997–1998) .... Tom La Grua

A romantic comedy set in Manhattan. Perky Caroline had found success with her autobiographical comic strip, "Caroline in the City," about the experiences of a young single woman in the big city, which had expanded into greeting cards, books, and calendars. Working out of her Tribeca apartment, she hired stiff, eccentric Richard, a frustrated painter, to work with her as her colorist. Romantic sparks quickly began to fly, but both denied it. Instead, Caroline became engaged to ex-boyfriend Del, the president of Eagle Greeting Cards, which published her work. Annie, a sometimes employed dancer who was Caroline's best friend, helped the affair along, neither of them realizing that it was quiet Richard who was Caroline's true love.

After Caroline called off her impending marriage to Del in early 1997, she and Richard still denied their mutual attraction and dated others. During the following season, Caroline dated Trevor (Richard Gant), while Richard met, and eventually married, bartender Julia. But Richard's marriage blew up, and by 1998 Caroline and Richard had finally accepted the obvious and begun dating. In the same year, Del's company merged with a large corporation, and Caroline began working at its offices, changing the setting for the show. Charlie was the energetic gofer for the card company, and Remo ran the Italian restaurant where the gang hung out. Salty was Caroline's cat (referred to by Richard as "beast").

The series was illustrated with the cartoons of Bonnie Timmons.

CAROLINE'S COMEDY HOUR (*Comedy*)
BROADCAST HISTORY:
Arts & Entertainment Network
60 minutes
Produced: *1989–1995*
Premiered: *January 7, 1990*

Standup comedy and sketches taped at the New York club, generally aired by A&E Sunday nights at 11:00 P.M. The debut featured Carol Leifer as host, with Richard Belzer, Bobby Collins, and Ron Darian performing. Later, Richard Jeni was a regular host.

CAROLYN GILBERT SHOW, THE (*Music*)
FIRST TELECAST: *January 15, 1950*
LAST TELECAST: *July 30, 1950*
BROADCAST HISTORY:
Jan 1950–Jul 1950, ABC Sun 7:30–7:45
REGULARS:
Carolyn Gilbert
Don Tennant

This musical variety program was hosted by singer-pianist Carolyn Gilbert. The young puppeteer and vocalist Don Tennant provided skits to introduce Miss Gilbert's numbers.

CARTER COUNTRY (*Situation Comedy*)
FIRST TELECAST: *September 15, 1977*
LAST TELECAST: *August 23, 1979*
BROADCAST HISTORY:
Sep 1977–Mar 1978, ABC Thu 9:30–10:00
May 1978–Aug 1978, ABC Tue 9:30–10:00
Sep 1978, ABC Sat 8:00–8:30
Oct 1978–Jan 1979, ABC Sat 8:30–9:00
Mar 1979–Aug 1979, ABC Thu 9:30–10:00
CAST:
Chief Roy Mobey .... Victor French
Sgt. Curtis Baker.................... Kene Holliday
Mayor Teddy Burnside .... Richard Paul
Deputy Jasper DeWitt, Jr. .... Harvey Vernon
Deputy Harley Puckett .... Guich Koock
Cloris Phebus .... Barbara Cason
Lucille Banks .... Vernee Watson
Tracy Quinn (1978–1979) .... Melanie Griffith
Julia Mobey (1978–1979)......... Amzie Strickland

This racial comedy was set in the small Georgia town of Clinton Corners, "just down the road from Plains" (home of President Jimmy Carter). Chief Roy Mobey was the lovable redneck police chief and Sgt. Curtis Baker his ultra-sharp black deputy, who had been trained in big-city police methods in New York. Despite the obvious points of conflict—black *vs.* white, big city *vs.* backwoods—the two had a basic respect for each other. Also on the force was Cloris Phebus, a man-hungry policewoman; young Harley; and "good old boy" Jasper. Teddy Burnside was the chubby, weak-willed mayor, a mama's boy who was elected because nobody else wanted the job. He also ran the local bank, Burnside Savings & Loan, though he usually preferred to pass the buck; his favorite departing words were: "Handle it!" Curtis was always trying to make time with the mayor's secretary, Lucille, and finally, in May 1979, they were married.

Added to the cast in the second season were Tracy Quinn, a cub reporter, and Roy's mother, Julia Mobey.

CARTOON NETWORK, THE (Network) (*All-Cartoon Cable Network*)
LAUNCHED:
October 1, 1992
SUBSCRIBERS (MAY 2003):
82.7 million (77% U.S.)

This network began with a wide range of mostly older classic cartoons, including *The Flintstones, The Jetsons, Yogi Bear, Jonny Quest, The Bugs Bunny Show,* and *The Daffy Duck Show.* Initially it offered little that was original, notably the cartoon/talk show *Space Ghost: Coast to Coast* (1994) and *The Moxy Pirate Show* (1994). However, by 1996 it had begun to debut new 'toons of its own, such as *Dexter's Laboratory, Big Bag, Cow and Chicken, Johnny Bravo, Ed, Edd and Eddy,* and *Powerpuff Girls.* Beginning in 2000 it introduced quite a few action cartoons drawn in the stark, angular Japanese anime style, including *Tenchi Muyo, Samurai Jack, Transformers Armada, He-Man Masters of the Universe* and *Yu-Gi-Oh!*

Cartoon Network first reached more than half of all U.S. television homes in March 1998, and its principal original nighttime series after that date are listed in this book under their individual titles.

CARTOON SUSHI (*Cartoons*)
BROADCAST HISTORY:
MTV
30 minutes
Produced: *1997–1998*
Premiered: *July 17, 1997*

A collection of short, mostly sick and sadistic cartoons airing in the late evening on MTV.

CARTOON TELETALES (*Children's*)
FIRST TELECAST: *November 14, 1948*
LAST TELECAST: *September 24, 1950*
BROADCAST HISTORY:
Nov 1948–Sep 1949, ABC Sun 6:00–6:30
May 1950–Aug 1950, ABC Sun 6:30–7:00
Aug 1950–Sep 1950, ABC Sun 6:00–6:30
HOSTS:
Chuck Luchsinger
Jack Luchsinger

This children's program was hosted by cartoonist Chuck Luchsinger and his brother Jack. Jack, a professional actor, narrated stories from the big *Cartoon TeleTales* storybook while his brother drew amusing illustrations to match. For a time the program was highly popular with both children and their parents, and a continuing art contest drew as many as 5,600 entries a month during 1949. Among the characters introduced were Usta the Rooster, Bumsniff the Bloodhound, Madcap the Mountain Goat, and Mimi the Mole. *Cartoon TeleTales* began in Philadelphia in May 1948, moved to New York as a late-afternoon entry in June, and became a 6:00 P.M. network entry in November.

CASABLANCA (*International Intrigue*)
FIRST TELECAST: *September 27, 1955*
LAST TELECAST: *September 3, 1983*
BROADCAST HISTORY:
Sep 1955–Apr 1956, ABC Tue 7:30–8:30
Apr 1983, NBC Sun 10:00–11:00
Aug 1983–Sep 1983, NBC Sat 10:00–11:00

CAST (1955–1956):

Rick Jason .... Charles McGraw
Capt. Renaud .... Marcel Dalio
Ferrari .... Dan Seymour
Sasha .... Michael Fox
Sam .... Clarence Muse
Ludwig .... Ludwig Stossel

CAST (1983):

Rick Blaine .... David Soul
Capt. Louis Renault .... Hector Elizondo
Ferrari .... Reuven Bar-Yotam
Sacha .... Ray Liotta
Sam .... Scatman Crothers
Carl .... Arthur Malet
Major Heinrik Strasser .... Patrick Horgan
Lt. Heinz .... Kai Wulff

Casablanca, based on the classic 1942 film of the same name, presented stories of romance and adventure in a North African setting. Rick was an American expatriate and owner of the Club Americain in Casablanca, a bistro that attracted both intrigue and beautiful women. Despite his gruff and indifferent exterior, Rick had a penchant for getting involved in other people's problems. He also worked, quietly, to undermine the activities of the Nazis who were occupying Casablanca during World War II. Capt. Renaud/Renault was the unsympathetic police captain, Ferrari a black marketeer, Sasha/Sacha the bartender at Rick's place, and Sam the inimitable piano player.

Casablanca first surfaced as a series in 1955 as one of three rotating elements airing under the umbrella title *Warner Bros. Presents.* In this version Rick's last name was Jason; when NBC revived the program as a weekly series in 1983, the name had changed to Blaine, the one used by Humphrey Bogart in the film. The names of some of the other regulars were also spelled differently in the two series. Seen regularly in the 1983 version were Nazi commander Strasser and his aide, Heinz.

CASE CLOSED (*Information*)

BROADCAST HISTORY:

USA Network
60 minutes
Produced: *1993–1994* (22 episodes)
Premiered: *September 17, 1993*

HOST:

Stacy Keach

This short-lived reality series offered to send private investigators to help those who had not been able to solve their legitimate grievances by other means. Camera crews snooped as the investigators set up hidden cameras and caught a woman's stalker; reunited a boy, who was about to undergo a serious operation, with his long-lost father; exposed a child-support dodger; and vindicated an innocent man who had been accused of murder. Reenactments were intermixed with actual footage of the case being solved. Crime tips were offered to help viewers help themselves in this dangerous world.

CASE HISTORIES OF SCOTLAND YARD,

syndicated title for *Scotland Yard*

CASH AND CARRY (*Quiz/Audience Participation*)

FIRST TELECAST: *June 20, 1946*
LAST TELECAST: *July 1, 1947*
BROADCAST HISTORY:

Jun 1946–Jan 1947, DUM Thu 9:00–9:30
Apr 1947–Jul 1947, DUM Tue 7:30–8:00

EMCEE:

Dennis James

Sponsored by Libby's, this early quiz show was set in a grocery store, its shelves lined with cans of the sponsor's products to which were attached questions worth $5, $10, or $15. There were also studio stunts, such as a man assigned to pantomime a woman taking off her clothes for a bath, or a blindfolded wife trying to feed her husband ice cream. At home viewers could also participate, via phone, in a segment that involved guessing what was under a large barrel.

As with some other early programs, it is not known whether this was fed over a network from the start, though it was being networked by early 1947 at the latest.

CASSIE & COMPANY (*Detective Drama*)

FIRST TELECAST: *January 29, 1982*
LAST TELECAST: *August 20, 1982*
BROADCAST HISTORY:

Jan 1982–Feb 1982, NBC Fri 10:00–11:00
Jun 1982–Jul 1982, NBC Tue 10:00–11:00
Jul 1982–Aug 1982, NBC Fri 10:00–11:00

CAST:

Cassie Holland .... Angie Dickinson
Lyman "Shack" Shackelford .... John Ireland
Meryl Foxx .... Dori Brenner
Benny Silva .... A Martinez
Mike Holland .... Alex Cord

This series could have been subtitled "*Police Woman* Goes Private," since the role played by star Angie Dickinson was essentially the Pepper Anderson character she had played in the earlier series. Though no youngster, former police officer Cassie Holland was a private detective who took advantage of her looks and sex appeal as well as her analytical skills to solve cases. She had taken over the business of retired private eye Shack Shackelford, and often sought his help with tough cases. Young ex-con Meryl worked as Cassie's secretary, and part-time gym manager Benny was her legman, doing most of the physical work. Cassie's friendship with her ex-husband, City District Attorney Mike Holland, came in handy when she needed to get her hands on inside information.

CATDOG (*Cartoon*)

BROADCAST HISTORY:

Nickelodeon
30 minutes
Produced: *1998–2000* (66 episodes)
Premiered: *April 4, 1998*

VOICES:

Cat, T. Rex .... Jim Cummings
Dog, Cliff .... Tom Kenny
Winslow Oddfellow, Lube .... Carlos Alazraqui
Mr. Sunshine, Rancid Rabbit .... Billy West
Shriek, Tallulah, Fredo .... Maria Bamford

The gag in this cartoon was purely visual: CatDog was a two-headed lead character that looked like a dachshund, but with a dog at one end and a cat at the other. Fussy feline and slobbering canine coexisted as best they could, but cats and dogs being what they are, there was a lot of running and chasing, smashing and crashing. They (it?) lived in a weird house on a high cliff with Winslow, a big blue mouse. Cliff, Lube, and Shriek were three dumb "greaser dogs," while Rancid Rabbit was a nitpicking teacher and Mr. Sunshine a cranky, glum individual.

CATWALK (*Drama*)

BROADCAST HISTORY:

Syndicated and MTV
60 minutes
Produced: *1992–1994*
Released: *October 1992*

CAST:

Johnnie Camden (1992–1993) .... Keram Malicki-Sanchez
Daisy McKenzie (1992–1993) .... Neve Campbell
Mary Owens .... Kelli Taylor
Jesse (Andrew Joseph) Carlson ..... Paul Popowich
Sierra Williams .... Lisa Butler
Addie ("Atlas") Robinson (1992–1993) .... Christopher Lee Clements
Billy-K (William Kramer) .... Joel Wyner
**Joe Owens (1992–1993)* .... Johnie Chase
**Julia Owens (1992–1993)* .... Brenda Bazinet
**Aunt Ellen (1992–1993)* .... Jackie Richardson
**Eddie Camden (1992–1993)* .... Victor Ertmanis
Frank Calfa (1994) .... David Lee Russek
Benny Doulon (1994) .... Rob Sefaniuk
Gus Danzig (1994) .... Ron Lea
Maggi Holden (1994) .... Nicole deBoer
Wendy (1994) .... Chandra West
Pamela (1994) .... Tracey Cook

*Occasional

Premiering the same fall as Fox's *The Heights*, *Catwalk* had a similar premise, a group of people in their early twenties forming a band and trying to succeed in the pop music business. Johnnie, the lead guitarist and driving force behind the band, had formed Catwalk after getting fed up performing with a dull group. He wanted to play R&B, funk, and jazz. Others in the group were Daisy (keyboard), who taught dancing to make a living; Mary (bass guitar), an auto mechanic with a black father and white mother who had played with Johnnie in the other band; Jesse, the son of a wealthy family who had the hots for Mary and learned to play drums so he could get into the band; Sierra (steamy vocals), an assistant at a recording studio; and Atlas, the band's muscular, energetic rapper/hip-hop dancer who made a living as an enforcer for loan shark/club owner Billy-K in Toronto, where *Catwalk* was set.

During the season Jesse and Mary, who had been a virgin, became lovers, but later their romance cooled; Billy-K eventually became a good guy, giving up his underworld activities and managing Catwalk while trying to get them a record deal; Jesse moved in with Johnnie; and Daisy, who knew accounting, became Billy-K's bookkeeper and, later, lover. In the last episode of the season Billy-K started his own record label to release Catwalk's album. The head of a major label heard the CD, liked it, and made a distribution deal with him. Catwalk became a major hit on CD and went on tour.

In March of 1994 *Catwalk* surfaced on MTV with new episodes and a number of cast changes. Atlas had left to join another group and Johnnie and Daisy had gone together to L.A. to seek their fortune. Sierra was now playing keyboard, and new to the group were young Benny (lead guitar) and Frank, a great singer with a drinking problem. Unfortunately, their record deal fell through when the executive who had signed them lost his job. Mary, now writing most of Catwalk's songs, moved in with Jesse on a platonic basis. She got involved with Frank, who sponged off them and often crashed at their apartment. Jesse, meanwhile, had an affair with Wendy, his boss at the construction job he worked days. They eventually got engaged after she got pregnant. Gus owned Phoebe's, the club where the band performed regularly, and Maggi was one of his waitresses. She had an on-again, off-again affair with Billy-K, who was still trying to get Catwalk a record deal. Their relationship soured after he slept with Pamela, a former classmate of hers who now worked for a big record company that was interested in Catwalk. In June Billy-K's record deal with Pamela fell through, but she wanted to use Frank as a single. He quit the band at the same time Maggi's wealthy mother bought Phoebe's from Gus and made her manager.

CAVALCADE OF AMERICA (*Dramatic Anthology*)

FIRST TELECAST: *October 1, 1952*
LAST TELECAST: *June 4, 1957*
BROADCAST HISTORY:

Oct 1952–Jun 1953, NBC Wed 8:30–9:00
Sep 1953–Jun 1955, ABC Tue 7:30–8:00 (OS)
Sep 1955–Jun 1957, ABC Tue 9:30–10:00 (OS)

Cavalcade of America was one of the most prestigious dramatic shows of network radio, sponsored for 18 years (1935–1953) by DuPont as a means of enhancing the company's image and bringing great events in American history to an audience of millions. In 1952 DuPont brought the *Cavalcade* to TV, and viewers were treated to the same meticulously accurate stories of American heroes both famous and obscure, in historical periods ranging from colonial days to the Revolution to the early 1900s. The first telecast was a humorous piece about Benjamin Franklin's lighter side.

In 1955 the format was modified to include contemporary stories, such as a biography of Dr. Ralphe Bunche and an account of a 1948 Olympic swimming star's battle with polio. In this season and the one following, an increasing number of episodes dealt with ordinary people unconnected with great events, but triumphing over some adversity or showing some act of courage.

Actors and actresses appearing on *Cavalcade* were generally lesser-known talent, as the focus was always on the story.

For the first season the program was seen every two weeks, alternating with *Scott Music Hall*. In 1955 it changed its name to *DuPont Cavalcade Theater* and in 1956 to *DuPont Theater*.

CAVALCADE OF BANDS (*Musical Variety*)

FIRST TELECAST: *January 17, 1950*
LAST TELECAST: *September 25, 1951*
BROADCAST HISTORY:

Jan 1950–Sep 1951, DUM Tue 9:00–10:00

EMCEE:

Fred Robbins (Jan 1950)
Warren Hull (Jan–Apr 1950)
Ted Steele (May 1950–Feb 1951)
Buddy Rogers (Feb–Sep 1951)

This was one of the DuMont network's major efforts in the musical variety field, and was designed to lure some of the NBC audience away following the top-rated Milton Berle hour (which ran Tuesday 8–9 P.M.). The "star" of this series was a different big-name band each week, ranging from the "sweet" music of Guy Lombardo and Lawrence Welk to the big-band swing of Lionel Hampton and Duke Ellington. Virtually every major dance band in the country appeared on this program at one time or another.

In addition to the "Band of the Week," top-line singers and comedians filled out the bill, including such names as Jackie Gleason, Kitty Kallen, and Peggy Lee, as well as a number of lesser lights. Four different hosts presided over the *Cavalcade of Bands* during its year-and-a-half run: New York disc jockey Fred Robbins at the beginning, replaced almost immediately by Warren Hull, who was followed by Ted Steele and finally by former matinee idol Buddy Rogers.

CAVALCADE OF SPORTS, see *Boxing* and *Gillette Summer Sports Reel*

CAVALCADE OF STARS (*Comedy/Variety*)

FIRST TELECAST: *June 4, 1949*
LAST TELECAST: *September 26, 1952*
BROADCAST HISTORY:

Jun 1949–Sep 1950, DUM Sat 9:00–10:00
Sep 1950–Sep 1952, DUM Fri 10:00–11:00

EMCEE:

Jack Carter (1949–1950)
Jerry Lester (1950)
Jackie Gleason (1950–1952)
Larry Storch (summer 1951, 1952)

REGULARS:

Art Carney (1950–1952)
Pert Kelton (1950–1952)
June Taylor Dancers (1950–1952)
Sammy Spear/Charlie Spear Orchestra

Big-budget variety shows seemed to be taking over television in 1949. DuMont's answer to such hits as NBC's *Texaco Star Theatre* and CBS' *Ed Sullivan Show* was the *Cavalcade of Stars*, which gave early exposure to a number of talented performers who later became major TV celebrities.

The first host was Jack Carter, who maintained a lightning pace throughout the 60 minutes, mugging, tossing off gags, and working with the guests in skits. Just as he began to build a following, NBC stole him away in February 1950, to front the first hour of its *Saturday Night Revue*, on the same night as *Cavalcade*. His replacement was round-faced comic Jerry Lester, who was no less manic but who remained on the show for only four months, until July 1950. (He later became TV's first late-night star, on NBC's original *Broadway Open House*.) Lester's replacement, and one of the major talents on DuMont during the next two years, was Jackie Gleason.

Gleason, who had starred in the first, unsuccessful version of *The Life of Riley* in 1949–1950, immediately began to build a large and loyal following, a process that was helped when *Cavalcade* moved to a more propitious time period on Friday night, away from the competition of Saturday's Sid Caesar–Imogene Coca hour. One of the chief delights of *Cavalcade* was the variety of comic characterizations Gleason introduced on the show, many of which he was to continue throughout his TV career. The first to become enormously popular, in 1950, was "The Bachelor," in which he portrayed a helpless, spouseless male bedeviled by the necessities of housekeeping for one. Typical routines, all in pantomime, were "The Bachelor Gets His Own Breakfast," "Doing the Laundry," and "Dressing for a Date," all to the soft music of "Somebody Loves Me."

Later additions included the dissolute, top-hatted playboy Reggie Van Gleason III; The Poor Soul; the garrulous Joe the Bartender, talking about his patrons Crazy Guggenheim, Moriarty the undertaker, Duddy Duddleston, and Bookshelf Robinson; the continually oppressed Fenwick Babbitt; and Charlie Bratten, "The Loudmouth." The best, however, was probably "The Honeymooners," introduced in the fall of 1951. Bus driver Ralph Kramden was the perfect incarnation of the always boastful, always scheming, always thwarted "poor slob" who would never get away from his dingy apartment and nagging wife.

Part of Gleason's success lay with his excellent supporting cast—which included Pert Kelton as the original Alice Kramden and Art Carney as his foil in many of the sketches—and his stable of top-notch writers (Joe Bigelow and Harry Crane helped him develop "The Honeymooners"). But most of the appeal lay with Gleason himself, and when CBS lured him away in 1952—with a reported offer of $8,000 per week instead of the $1,600 he was getting from DuMont—there was nowhere for *Cavalcade* to go but down. After lingering through the summer with comedian Larry Storch as host, it ended in September 1952.

CAVALIER THEATRE (*Dramatic Anthology*)

FIRST TELECAST: *December 5, 1951*
LAST TELECAST: *December 26, 1951*
BROADCAST HISTORY:

Dec 1951, NBC Wed 10:30–11:00

A short-lived anthology series that filled NBC's Wednesday 10:30 P.M. time slot between the last telecast of *The Freddy Martin Show* and the premiere of *Pantomime Quiz* on January 2, 1952.

CAVANAUGHS, THE (*Situation Comedy*)

FIRST TELECAST: *December 1, 1986*
LAST TELECAST: *July 27, 1989*
BROADCAST HISTORY:

Dec 1986–Mar 1987, CBS Mon 9:30–10:00
Aug 1988–Oct 1988, CBS Mon 8:30–9:00
Jun 1989–Jul 1989, CBS Thu 9:00–9:30

CAST:

Francis "Pop" Cavanaugh .... Barnard Hughes
Kit Cavanaugh .... Christine Ebersole
Chuck Cavanaugh .... Peter Michael Goetz
Mary Margaret Cavanaugh .... Mary Tanner
Father Chuck Cavanaugh, Jr. .... John Short
Kevin Cavanaugh .... Danny Cooksey
John Cavanaugh .... Parker Jacobs

Crochety old Barnard Hughes played crochety old "Pop" Cavanaugh—as Irish as a shillelagh, and about as blunt—in this ethnic family comedy. His daughter Kit had left Boston 20 years earlier in search of fame, but now she was back, an aging and much-divorced showgirl, to help raise her widowed brother Chuck's family. Sparks flew between strong-willed Pop and his wayward daughter, but underneath there was a lot of love. Often caught in the comic crossfire were Chuck, a busy executive with the family-run Cavanaugh Construction Company, and his four kids: Chuck, Jr., a young priest with the demeanor of a talk show host; Mary Margaret, a shy teenager who idolized the freewheeling Kit; and the obnoxious young twins, Kevin and John. A frequent guest star was Art Carney as Pop's brother James "the weasel" Cavanaugh, the owner of Cavanaugh Construction and Chuck's boss.

CEDRIC THE ENTERTAINER PRESENTS (*Comedy Variety*)

FIRST TELECAST: *September 18, 2002*
LAST TELECAST:
BROADCAST HISTORY:

Sep 2002–Jan 2003, FOX Wed 8:30–9:00
Feb 2003–Mar 2003, FOX Wed 9:30–10:00
May 2003–, FOX Wed 9:30–10:00

REGULARS:

Cedric The Entertainer
Amy Brassette
Shaun Majumder
Wendy Raquel Robinson
JB Smoove
The Ced-sation Dancers

Cedric The Entertainer opened each episode of this variety series with a small-scale production number featuring the Ced-sation dancers and a short chat with his studio audience. The remainder of the half hour was filled with comedy sketches satirizing everything from movies to TV shows to social mores. Among Cedric's recurring characters were Mrs. Cafeteria Lady, a bossy, fat lunchroom worker who knew all the school gossip and could dish it out much better than she could take it; the satin-robed Love Doctor, a marriage therapist who was totally infatuated with himself, and Li'l Holla, a street hustler who talked in rap-style rhymes and riddles.

CELANESE THEATRE (*Dramatic Anthology*)

FIRST TELECAST: *October 3, 1951*
LAST TELECAST: *June 25, 1952*
BROADCAST HISTORY:

Oct 1951–Dec 1951, ABC Wed 10:00–11:00
Dec 1951–Jun 1952, ABC Wed 10:00–10:30

A live dramatic series telecast from New York, *Celanese Theatre* presented high-quality plays by leading playwrights. The first *Celanese* telecast was Eugene O'Neill's *Ah, Wilderness!*, followed by such classics as O'Neill's *Anna Christie*, Maxwell Anderson's *Winterset*, and Elmer Rice's *Street Scene*. Stars appearing included Alfred Drake, David Niven, Mickey Rooney, and Lillian Gish. *Celanese Theatre* appeared on alternate weeks throughout its run.

CELEBRITY CHALLENGE OF THE SEXES (*Sports*)

FIRST TELECAST: *January 31, 1978*
LAST TELECAST: *February 28, 1978*
BROADCAST HISTORY:

Jan 1978–Feb 1978, CBS Tue 8:00–8:30

HOST:

Tom Brookshier

COACHES:

McLean Stevenson (men)
Barbara Rhoades (women)

This series was an offshoot of the CBS Sunday afternoon sports series *Challenge of the Sexes*. As the title implies, *Celebrity Challenge of the Sexes* pitted show business personalities against each other in various sporting events. To make the contests more competitive, the men were given handicaps to compensate for their superior size or strength. Sports announcer Tom Brookshier acted as host and commentator, while McLean Stevenson and Barbara Rhoades coached the competitors, although the "coaches" played their roles primarily for laughs. Among the stars participating were Karen Black and Don Adams in Ping-Pong, Barbi Benton and baseball star Reggie Jackson in a bicycle race, and Elke Sommer and Pat Harrington on an obstacle course.

CELEBRITY DEATH MATCH (*Puppets*)

CABLE HISTORY:

MTV
30 minutes
Produced: *1998–2002* (76 episodes)
Premiered: *May 14, 1998*

NETWORK HISTORY:
FIRST TELECAST: *January 12, 2001*
LAST TELECAST: *March 23, 2001*

Jan 2001–Mar 2001, UPN Fri 8:30–9:00
Mar 2001, UPN Fri 9:30–10:00

VOICES:

Johnny Gomez .... Maurice Schlafer
Nick Diamond .... Len Maxwell
Referee Mills Lane .... Himself

A bizarre, violent puppet show in which clay figures representing real life celebrities battled each other to the death in wild wrestling bouts. Sometimes skewered, sometimes flattened (literally), sometimes dismembered, they could always stick themselves back together and fight on. Among the matches were Oprah vs. Rosie O'Donnell, Jerry Seinfeld vs. Tim Allen, Monica Lewinsky vs. Hillary Clinton, and Jim Carrey vs. Mariah Carey. Johnny Gomez and Nick Diamond were the tuxedo-clad ringside announcers, and bald, snarling Mills Lane the referee. Sexy reporter Stacy Cornbred sometimes appeared as a supporting character. A special preview aired during the 1998 Super Bowl.

For two months in 2001 UPN aired repeats of episodes that had previously aired on MTV.

CELEBRITY GAME, THE (*Quiz/Panel*)

FIRST TELECAST: *April 5, 1964*
LAST TELECAST: *September 9, 1965*
BROADCAST HISTORY:

Apr 1964–Sep 1964, CBS Sun 9:00–9:30
Apr 1965–Sep 1965, CBS Thu 9:30–10:00

EMCEE:

Carl Reiner

At times this series seemed more like a comedy-variety program than a quiz show. There were three contestants each week and a rotating panel of nine celebrities. Reiner would pose a question such as "Can a man love two women at the same time?," "Should nude scenes be banned from Hollywood movies?," or "Can most women keep a secret?" The individual panelists decided yes or no, and each contestant tried to guess which way a given panelist had voted, and why. The "why" gave the panelists the opportunity to make funny responses. Contestants won money for correct guessing but the money was incidental to the humor.

Reruns were aired by CBS on Sunday afternoons from October 1967 to June 1968.

CELEBRITY HOMES AND HIDEAWAYS (*Magazine*)

BROADCAST HISTORY:
The Nashville Network
60 minutes
Produced: *1998*
Premiered: *August 19, 1998*

HOST:
Martina McBride

THEME:
"This Ole House"

Lifestyles of the Rich and Famous, with a twang. In the premiere, perky host McBride took viewers into the 27,000-square-foot "log cabin" estate of Barbara Mandrell, the swank bachelor pad of towheaded young country star Bryan White, and Wynonna's homey digs, while gushing compliments and posing viewers' questions.

CELEBRITY JUSTICE (*Legal*)

BROADCAST HISTORY:
Syndicated only
30 minutes
Produced: *2002–*
Released: *September 2002*

HOST:
Holly Herbert

This daily newsmagazine focused exclusively on legal issues involving celebrities, including criminal trials and civil disputes. The series' producers maintained that the show gave balanced reports of both sides of each story as it examined the rights of the rich and famous as they dealt with the legal system.

There were numerous recurring segments on *Celebrity Justice.* "You Be the Judge" was a mock trial of a real case with viewers voting on-line to decide the outcome; "C.J. Spin" examined the behind-the-scenes strategies used by attorneys in celebrity cases; "Equal Justice" looked at whether the treatment celebrities received was better or worse than ordinary citizens got in similar situations; "Real Estate Wars" covered celebrity property disputes; "Family Matters" tracked divorces; "Art of the Deal" covered negotiations between stars and studios, including the money paid and the incredible perks demanded; "Celebrity Wills" chronicled the battles over estates, and "Court Appearance" critiqued the courtroom wardrobe choices of the rich and famous. Finally, "Power Players" provided profiles of the high-priced law firms and attorneys who made a great deal of money off the foregoing shenanigans.

CELEBRITY MOLE, see *Mole, The*

CELEBRITY OUTDOORS (*Travel*)

BROADCAST HISTORY:
The Nashville Network
30 minutes
Produced: *1987–1996*
Premiered: *July 5, 1987*

HOST:
Bobby Lord (1987–1989)

Sunday-night travelogue in which celebrities explored various outdoor sports and exotic locales around the world. It succeeded a program called *Country Sportsman* (1983–1986), which Lord also hosted.

CELEBRITY TALENT SCOUTS (*Variety*)

FIRST TELECAST: *August 1, 1960*
LAST TELECAST: *September 26, 1960*

BROADCAST HISTORY:
Aug 1960–Sep 1960, CBS Mon 9:00–9:30

HOST:
Sam Levenson

This series was the 1960 summer replacement for *The Danny Thomas Show.* Each week Sam Levenson introduced three or four celebrities who had new young "discoveries" they felt deserved national television exposure. The "discoveries" then performed their specialties, generally comedy, singing, or dancing.

CELEBRITY TIME (*Quiz/Audience Participation*)

FIRST TELECAST: *January 23, 1949*
LAST TELECAST: *September 21, 1952*

BROADCAST HISTORY:
Jan 1949–Mar 1949, CBS Sun 8:30–9:00
Mar 1949–Jun 1949, ABC Sun 8:30–9:00
Jul 1949–Mar 1950, ABC Sun 10:00–10:30
Apr 1950–Jun 1950, CBS Sun 10:00–10:30
Oct 1950–Sep 1952, CBS Sun 10:00–10:30

EMCEE:
Conrad Nagel

PANELISTS:
John Daly (1948–1950)
Ilka Chase (1948–1950)
Kyle MacDonnell (1950–1951)
Herman Hickman (1950–1952)
Martha Wright (1950–1951)
Mary McCarty (1951–1952)
Jane Wilson (1951–1952)

This program began as a combination guessing game and battle of the sexes, teaming regular panelists with guest celebrities of their own sex to compete against a similar team of the opposite sex. Guests ranged from Sir Thomas Beecham to Slapsie Maxie Rosenbloom. At first the questions were reasonably intelligent, involving, for example, guessing names in the news, identifying famous places from film clips, or providing information about live demonstrations or skits performed on the show. Later, skits and performances by the guests began to predominate until the proceedings resembled a variety show more than a quiz. Finally, in June 1952, the panel was dropped altogether; during its final months *Celebrity Time* became a straight musical variety program, with Conrad Nagel as host.

The series underwent quite a few title changes during its career, beginning in November 1948 as a local New York program called *The Eyes Have It* (Douglas Edwards, host), quickly changing to *Stop, Look and Listen* (Paul Gallico, host), then *Riddle Me This* in December 1948 (with Nagel), *Goodrich Celebrity Time* in March 1949, and finally *Celebrity Time* in April 1950.

CENTENNIAL (*Historical Drama*)

FIRST TELECAST: *October 1, 1978*
LAST TELECAST: *October 25, 1980*

BROADCAST HISTORY:
Oct 1978–Feb 1979, NBC Sun (or Sat) Various times
Sep 1980–Oct 1980, NBC Sat (& other days) Various times

CAST:

Pasquinel .... Robert Conrad
Alexander McKeag .... Richard Chamberlain
Bockweiss .... Raymond Burr
Lisa Bockweiss .... Sally Kellerman
Clay Basket .... Barbara Carrera
Lame Beaver .... Michael Ansara
Levi Zandt .... Gregory Harrison
Elly Zahm .... Stephanie Zimbalist
Lucinda .... Cristina Raines
Jake Pasquinel .... Stephen McHattie
Mike Pasquinel .... Kario Salem
Maxwell Mercy .... Chad Everett
Hans Brumbaugh .... Alex Karras
John McIntosh .... Mark Harmon
R. J. Poteet .... Dennis Weaver
Oliver Seccombe .... Timothy Dalton
Col. Frank Skimmerhorn .... Richard Crenna
John Skimmerhorn .... Cliff DeYoung
Nate Person .... Glynn Turman
Bufe Coker .... Les Lannom
Axel Dumire .... Brian Keith
Clemma .... Adrienne LaRussa
Nacho .... Rafael Campos
Mervin Wendell .... Anthony Zerbe
Philip Wendell .... Doug McKeon
Charlotte Buckland Seccombe Lloyd
.... Lynn Redgrave
Jim Lloyd .... William Atherton
Maude Wendell .... Lois Nettleton
Tranquilino .... A Martinez
Paul Garrett .... David Janssen
Morgan Wendell .... Robert Vaughn
Lew Vernor .... Andy Griffith
Sidney Enderman .... Sharon Gless

This epic television series (twenty-four hours in all), which reportedly cost more than $20,000,000 to produce, faithfully transferred James A. Michener's massive novel *Centennial* to the screen. Michener himself appeared at the beginning of the first episode to ask the viewing audience if it was aware of the way in which the land on which man depends was being used and exploited. Citing the historical events described in *Centennial*, Michener reminded viewers that their actions (and inactions) have an impact on the quality of life for future generations.

Centennial chronicled the settlement and development of and the controversies surrounding a piece of land in the Rocky Mountain area, from 1795 to the present day. It began with the arrival of the first white men to stake claims on the land, French trapper Pasquinel and Scottish trader Alexander McKeag. Over the years the area, which would eventually become the town of Centennial, Colorado, attracted all types of men. Some were settlers who cared for the land and tried to co-exist with the original Pawnee and Cheyenne Indian inhabitants. Among these were Mennonite Levi Zandt, founder of the town, German immigrant Hans Brumbaugh, the first to raise crops in the area, and Englishman Oliver Seccombe, who saw the potential of the land as a grazing area for vast herds of cattle. As more people arrived, the land began to lose its unspoiled natural beauty. Many later arrivals wanted to manipulate events for their own ends, some out of greed and others out of a mistaken sense of righteousness. The unscrupulous Wendell family was willing to do anything to gain the power and wealth offered by Centennial, while the misguided Col. Frank Skimmerhorn was convinced that only white men belonged, and that the remaining Indians must be driven off or killed. Many of these basic struggles continued for generations and some were still apparent in the Colorado of today, where rancher Paul Garrett, whose family line could be traced all the way back to Pasquinel, fought to prevent the senseless exploitation of the land by wealthy businessman Morgan Wendell.

Originally aired during the 1978–1979 season, *Centennial* was repeated in the fall of 1980, when an actors' strike delayed the availability of new programs.

CENTER STAGE (*Dramatic Anthology*)

FIRST TELECAST: *June 1, 1954*
LAST TELECAST: *September 21, 1954*
BROADCAST HISTORY:

Jun 1954–Sep 1954, ABC Tue 9:30–10:30

Center Stage consisted of filmed dramas presented on alternate weeks during the summer of 1954, as a replacement for *Motorola TV Theatre*. An assortment of notable actors and actresses was seen, including Walter Matthau, Lee Marvin, Vivian Blaine, and Charles Coburn.

CENTRAL PARK WEST (*Serial Drama*)

FIRST TELECAST: *September 13, 1995*
LAST TELECAST: *June 28, 1996*
BROADCAST HISTORY:

Sep 1995–Nov 1995, CBS Wed 9:00–10:00
Jun 1996, CBS Wed/Fri 10:00–11:00

CAST:

Stephanie Wells (1995) .... Mariel Hemingway
Mark Merrill .... Tom Verica
Carrie Fairchild .... Madchen Amick
Peter Fairchild .... John Barrowman
Allen Rush .... Ron Leibman
Linda Fairchild Rush .... Lauren Hutton
Nikki Sheridan .... Michael Michele
Gil Chase .... Justin Lazard
Alex Bartoli .... Melissa Errico
Rachael Dennis .... Kylie Travis
Jordan Tate (1996) .... Noelle Beck
Adam Brock (1996) .... Gerald McRaney
Dianna Brock (1996) .... Raquel Welch

A glitzy prime-time soap opera that focused on behind-the-scenes backstabbing at *Communiqué*, a slick, struggling, New York magazine. Earnest Stephanie had just moved from Seattle to take the editorial reins of the magazine, which was owned by Allen Rush, the notorious "Darth Vader of Publishing." A wealthy businessman whose wife, Linda, had come from one of the city's most socially prominent families, Allen hoped that Stephanie would be able to both breathe new life into the magazine and fire his spoiled, lazy stepdaughter Carrie, who made $200,000 a year as *Communiqué* society columnist. Carrie, an amoral manipulative bitch who lived for Manhattan's night life and rarely showed up at work before noon, responded by gaining the confidence of Stephanie's insecure husband Mark, a novelist/teacher/playwright, and eventually dragged him into an affair.

Others seen regularly were Peter, Carrie's hunky, well-intentioned brother, an assistant D.A. trying to live down his playboy image and keep his name out of the tabloids; Peter's best friend Gil, an unscrupulous stockbroker; Carrie's friend Nikki, the owner of a SoHo art gallery, who was having an affair with Allen; Alex, a tabloid reporter with whom Peter had fallen in love; and Rachel, whom Stephanie hired as the new fashion editor. Rachel almost immediately went after Stephanie's job, doing everything in her power to undermine her boss. She was also obsessed with Peter and tried vainly to break up his relationship with Alex, settling for an affair with Gil. In the last fall episode Mark's affair with Carrie was rekindled when she became the editor of his first article for *Communiqué*.

Low ratings prompted CBS to pull struggling *Central Park West* from its schedule in November for extensive retooling and a relaunch in the spring. When the new episodes finally surfaced in June, the series had been retitled *CPW*. *Communiqué* was taken over by Allen's hated rival, Adam Brock, and Rachel was promoted to editor-in-chief as a favor to Gil, Adam's broker. Allen brought Adam's ex-wife, Dianna, to New York in a plot to regain control of the company, but Dianna reached a compromise with Adam and got a place on his Board of Directors. Mark split with Stephanie and began pitching his latest novel.

Alex, who had been sweet and sincere in the fall, had become totally psychotic. She faked a pregnancy to get Peter to marry her, and then faked a miscarriage by blackmailing her doctor. When Peter found out, Alex tried to kill him with a knife, and in the ensuing struggle, stabbed herself fatally. The cops thought it was a murder, and Peter was the prime suspect. Allen helped him skip the country after Adam gave Linda $2 million for his bail. In the last episode, Allen attempted a hostile takeover of Brock Global Communications, which failed when Adam's duplicitous son, Tyler (Michael Reilly Burke), found out he wasn't going to have a major job with the company after Allen took control. Mark, who had been terrorizing Carrie, accidentally killed himself with his own gun. Dianna married Allen for purely mercenary reasons, and on the night after their marriage—the same day his hostile takeover failed—he died from a heart attack.

CHAINS OF LOVE (*Romance/Reality*)
FIRST TELECAST: *April 17, 2001*
LAST TELECAST: *May 22, 2001*
BROADCAST HISTORY:

Apr 2001–May 2001, UPN Tue 8:00–9:00
May 2001, UPN Tue 9:00–10:00

HOST:

Madison Michele

This bizarre series, which the producers classified as a relationship game show, followed the activities of a contestant, referred to as the "picker," and four members of the opposite sex to whom he or she was chained—literally. In each episode viewers were "treated" to taped highlights of four days during which the chained-together group lived in a luxurious mansion overlooking the Pacific Ocean. The picker's job was to evaluate each of his or her companions for their potential in a long-term relationship.

At unspecified times the show's beefy, brooding chauffeur, known as "The Locksmith," would show up with a cash box, and the picker would have to set one of his or her companions free. It was at this time that monetary considerations were involved. The producers provided the picker with $10,000. Whenever companions were released, the picker could give them whatever portion of the $10,000 he or she thought they were worth (usually a few hundred dollars). At the end of the episode, the picker had to decide whether he or she had made a "love connection" with the last chainee. If so, the two split whatever was left of the $10,000; if not, the picker gave the survivor whatever he or she wished and kept the rest.

Chains of Love originated in the Netherlands, and was produced by the same people responsible for *Big Brother* and *Blind Date*. It was full of skin, backbiting and sexual innuendo, and critics crucified it as tacky, awkward and embarrassing. Anemic viewing levels led to cancellation after six episodes had aired.

CHAIR, THE (*Quiz/Audience Participation*)
FIRST TELECAST: *January 15, 2002*
LAST TELECAST: *March 4, 2002*
BROADCAST HISTORY:

Jan 2002–Feb 2002, ABC Tue 8:00–9:00
Mar 2002, ABC Mon 9:00–10:00

EMCEE:

John McEnroe

The Chair was one of two nearly identical "torture" quiz shows that premiered in January 2002 (the other: Fox's *The Chamber*). Tennis star John McEnroe, a man who was said to be "used to pressure," introduced contestants to a large chair that looked something like a dentist's chair. One player at a time was seated, wired to a heart monitor, and challenged to bring his or her heart rate down to a certain range before giving the answer. For the first question the rate had to be no more than 60 percent above contestants' previously determined resting heart rate, but as the questions became increasingly difficult the bar dropped to 55 percent, then 50, and so on. Music thundered and surprises popped up (like an alligator dangling above the chair, or flames shooting up around it) to further unnerve them. The grand prize was $250,000, but for each second contestants had to wait to bring down their heart rate money melted away, in some cases leaving them with nothing at all at the end. Questions were generally of the pop-culture variety, such as, "Name three movies for which Tom Hanks was nominated for an Academy Award," or "What is the name of Oprah Winfrey's production company?"

CHALKZONE (*Cartoon*)
BROADCAST HISTORY:

Nickelodeon
30 minutes
Original episodes: *2002–*
Premiered: *March 22, 2002*

VOICES:

Rudy Tabootie .... Elizabeth (E. G.) Daily
Penny Sanchez .... Hynden Walch
Snap, Reggie Bullnerd, Bullynerd .... Candi Milo
Mr. Wilter .... Robert Cait

Rudy was a dreamy elementary schoolkid in the town of Plainsville who loved to draw. One day in detention he picked up a magic piece of chalk that allowed him to enter Chalkzone, that magical place behind the chalkboard where drawings come to life. Soon he was having adventures in strange lands, where villains would chase him and he would draw birds to pick him up and fly him away, or bridges over which to escape. Penny was a smart classmate who liked Rudy's imaginative drawings, but wanted him to use a little science in his tales. Reggie was the school bully whose big, dumb alter ego Bullynerd roamed Chalkzone terrorizing Rudy. Fortunately Rudy had his own fearless blue superhero, Snap, whom he could call up at the last minute to protect him. Mr. Wilter was Rudy's incredibly boring teacher, who thought all this was nonsense, and that Rudy should stop drawing and pay attention like the other kids.

CHALLENGERS, THE (*Quiz/Audience Participation*)

BROADCAST HISTORY:

Syndicated only
30 minutes
Produced: *1990–1991* (260 episodes)
Released: *September 1990*

EMCEE:

Dick Clark

TV veteran Dick Clark was the emcee and producer of this nightly game show that emphasized contestants' knowledge of current events. The game started with a 60-second "sprint" round, in which contestants, who started with a $200 bankroll, won $100 for each correct answer (or lost $100 for each wrong answer) about subjects in the news. The leader after the sprint round could choose, from among six choices, the next question category. Each category had three questions of increasing difficulty, with dollar values of $150, $200, and $250. Contestants could choose which question to answer, and if all three chose the same category, the dollar value was doubled. After four rounds, and a commercial break, six new categories were displayed with the dollar values doubled and five more rounds were played. The winner was determined by the "Final Challenge," in which contestants could wager any portion of their accumulated winnings on one of three questions from a new category with the options of doubling, tripling, or quadrupling the wagered amount. If more than one contestant opted for the same question, only the one with the largest wager played. Unlike most game shows, all contestants kept the money they had won, regardless of whether they won or lost. The winner, however, returned to compete the following day, with a large bonus if he/she could win for three consecutive days.

CHAMBER, THE (*Quiz/Game*)

FIRST TELECAST: *January 13, 2002*
LAST TELECAST: *January 25, 2002*

BROADCAST HISTORY:

Jan 2002, FOX Sun 8:00–9:00
Jan 2002, FOX Sun 9:00–10:00
Jan 2002, FOX Fri 8:00–9:00

EMCEE:

Rick Swartz

Contestants on this sadistic game show competed to enter "The Chamber," where they tried to answer questions while being subjected to physical and psychological pressures. As the time spent in The Chamber increased, the value of correct answers grew, but so did the physical suffering of the contestants. Among the ordeals were being turned upside down while subjected to vibrations registering up to 9.0 on the Richter scale, hit with up to 100-mile-per-hour winds, poked in the back, and subjected to temperature extremes ranging from 150 degrees above zero to 10 degrees below. Contestants responded with such colorful exclamations as "ow!" "son of a bitch!" and "oh, crap!"

In the preliminary round two contestants were asked trivia questions, with the winner given the choice of going into The Chamber or taking a $500 "bailout" fee. If they chose The Chamber they were stripped to their shorts, were wired with health-monitoring equipment and took their chances. Once in The Chamber they were asked $1,000 questions as their environment got progressively more hostile. Two misses in a row and they were out, along with half of their accumulated winnings. Twenty-five correct answers and the prize money was tripled, with a potential total of more than $100,000.

All contestants were required to take preshow physicals to establish their individual "Stress Quotients" based on blood pressure and pulse rate. Anyone whose Quotient rose above the level the series' doctors deemed dangerous, for more than 20 seconds, was terminated from the game. Contestants could also quit by yelling "Stop The Chamber!"

Fox premiered *The Chamber* earlier than originally planned to get a head start on ABC's similar torture quiz, *The Chair.* Two special preview telecasts aired on Sundays, and the format and rules were tinkered with prior to the first telecast in its regular Friday time slot. It then lasted only two weeks before viewers screamed "Stop The Chamber!"

CHAMBER MUSIC HOUR, see *Chicago Symphony Chamber Orchestra*

CHAMPAGNE AND ORCHIDS (*Music*)

FIRST TELECAST: *September 6, 1948*
LAST TELECAST: *January 10, 1949*

BROADCAST HISTORY:

Sep 1948–Nov 1948, DUM Mon 8:00–8:15
Nov 1948–Jan 1949, DUM Mon 7:45–8:00

HOSTESS:

Adrienne (Meyerberg)

ANNOUNCER:

Robert Turner

ALSO:

David Lippman at the theremin

This musical interlude featured Adrienne, a svelte brunette who sang sultry torch songs in French, Spanish, and English. The setting was a fancy nightclub, and the atmosphere of elegance was enhanced by Adrienne's glamorous gowns, lent by some of New York's leading stores. Even the announcer, with whom she sometimes danced, wore a tux.

Seen originally as a local New York show beginning in December 1947, *Champagne and Orchids* was sent out over the DuMont network beginning in September 1948.

CHAMPIONS, THE (*Adventure*)

FIRST TELECAST: *June 10, 1968*
LAST TELECAST: *September 9, 1968*

BROADCAST HISTORY:

Jun 1968–Sep 1968, NBC Mon 8:00–9:00

CAST:

Craig Stirling .... Stuart Damon
Sharon Macready .... Alexandra Bastedo
Richard Barrett .... William Gaunt
Tremayne .... Anthony Nicholls

Craig, Sharon, and Richard were three international crime fighters with special "powers," which had been given to them by members of an unknown race from a lost civilization deep in the wastelands of Tibet. The powers included extraordinary mental abilities, the ability to see in the dark, superhuman strength, and assorted other physical talents. All these special skills were put to good use by the trio in their missions for Nemesis, a Geneva-based international agency similar to Interpol. Tremayne, head of Nemesis, was their boss and principal contact.

CHAMPS (*Situation Comedy*)
FIRST TELECAST: *January 9, 1996*
LAST TELECAST: *August 7, 1996*
BROADCAST HISTORY:
Jan 1996–Feb 1996, ABC Tue 9:30–10:00
Jul 1996–Aug 1996, ABC Wed 9:30–10:00
CAST:
Tom McManus .... Timothy Busfield
Linda McManus .... Ashley Crow
Phoebe McManus (age 12) .... Libby Winters
Jesse McManus .... Danny Pritchett
Marty Heslov .... Kevin Nealon
Doris Heslov .... Julia Campbell
Vince Massilli .... Ed Marinaro
Dr. Herb Barton .... Paul McCrane
Coach Harris .... Ron McLarty

Arrested-development men and the smart women who tolerate them seemed to be the theme of this sitcom. The five fortyish guys were all former members of a championship school basketball team, 20 years before, and they seemed to live to reminisce about their glory days on the court. Male chauvinist Tom was now a loving dad to supersmart Phoebe and underachieving young son Jesse; Marty was tall and taciturn, and breaking up with his wife Doris; Vince, still horny after all these years, was in law school; Dr. Herb was the balding M.D.; and Coach Harris was old and a little spaced out.

The guys shot hoops in the backyard, punched each other in the shoulder, and made gross jokes, while savvy law student Linda and the other women made fun of their male piggery.

CHANCE OF A LIFETIME (*Quiz*)
FIRST TELECAST: *September 6, 1950*
LAST TELECAST: *November 28, 1951*
BROADCAST HISTORY:
Sep 1950–Nov 1951, ABC Wed 7:30–8:00
EMCEE:
John Reed King
REGULARS:
Dick Collier
Russell Arms
Liza Palmer
Joseph Biviano Orchestra

This quiz show, which was also heard on radio, used singers and comedians to provide clues for contestants. A female contestant might be placed in a mock-Egyptian setting and wooed by rotund comic Dick Collier, to hint that the correct answer was "Cleopatra." Or, a couple of professional wrestlers might come on stage and the contestant would be asked to name the holds they were using. Singers Russell Arms and Liza Palmer gave musical clues.

Thirty-five years after this series went off the air another quiz show using essentially the same title, *The $1,000,000 Chance of a Lifetime*, turned up in the first-run syndication market, emceed by Jim Lange. The syndicated revival ran from early 1986 through the summer of 1987.

CHANCE OF A LIFETIME (*Talent*)
FIRST TELECAST: *May 8, 1952*
LAST TELECAST: *June 23, 1956*
BROADCAST HISTORY:
May 1952–Aug 1953, ABC Thu 8:30–9:00
Sep 1953–Jun 1955, DUM Fri 10:00–10:30
Jul 1955–Feb 1956, ABC Sun 9:00–9:30
Mar 1956–Jun 1956, ABC Sat 10:00–10:30
EMCEE:
Dennis James
REGULAR:
Bernie Leighton Orchestra

This talent show gave network exposure to aspiring young performers who had some prior professional experience. Winners, chosen by the studio audience, got $1,000 and a week's engagement at New York's Latin Quarter, while runners-up often landed bookings at lesser night spots. Those competing ranged from banjo players to opera singers, but surprisingly, despite their professional orientation, few seem to have gone on to become big names in show business. According to a review of the show after its first year, the top "find" up to that time was a comedienne named Helen Halpin, who subsequently had a minor career on Broadway and TV. A more notable later find was teenage singer Diahann Carroll, who won three weeks in a row.

CHANGE OF HEART (*Audience Participation*)
BROADCAST HISTORY:
Syndicated only
30 minutes
Produced: *1998–*
Released: *September 1998*
HOSTS:
Chris Jagger
Lynne Koplitz (2001–2002)

On each weeknight episode of this variation on *The Dating Game*, couples who had reached crossroads in their relationships voluntarily went on blind dates with new people picked to match requirements that they had specified. First the couples talked with the host about the good and bad aspects of their relationships, and then, after a commercial break, they were joined by their blind dates and discussed how the dates had gone. At the end of the episode they decided whether they wanted to stay in their original relationship or start dating others.

When production moved from Los Angeles to New York for the 2001–2002 season, Lynne Koplitz took over as host and a couple of changes were made. Added were follow-up interviews with the couples after they had left the show and "rate-a-date" testimonials from parents, siblings and close friends. The following fall Chris Jagger returned as host.

CHANNING (*Drama*)
FIRST TELECAST: *September 18, 1963*
LAST TELECAST: *April 8, 1964*
BROADCAST HISTORY:
Sep 1963–Apr 1964, ABC Wed 10:00–11:00

CAST:

Dean Fred Baker....................... Henry Jones
Prof. Joseph Howe..................... Jason Evers

Mythical Channing University was the setting for this series of dramas revolving around life on a college campus. Fred Baker was the school's dean, and Joseph Howe was a professor of English. Their personal and professional lives provided the basis for many stories, as they related to students, faculty, and the nonacademic world. At times the action focused more strongly on the students or other faculty members.

CHAPPELLE'S SHOW (*Comedy*)

BROADCAST HISTORY:

Comedy Central
30 minutes
Original episodes: *2003–*
Premiered: *January 22, 2003*

REGULARS:

Dave Chappelle

Sketch-comedy show featuring lanky black comic Dave Chappelle. Typical skits included a video training employees how to be rude to customers, an ad pitching home stenographers (to capture your every thought), a crack addict giving an antidrug speech to an elementary school class, and a blind Ku Klux Klan leader who didn't know he was black.

CHARADE QUIZ (*Charades*)

FIRST TELECAST: *December 4, 1947*
LAST TELECAST: *June 23, 1949*
BROADCAST HISTORY:

Dec 1947–May 1948, DUM Thu 8:30–9:00
May 1948–Jul 1948, DUM Thu 8:00–8:30
Aug 1948–Jan 1949, DUM Thu 8:30–9:00
Jan 1949–Apr 1949, DUM Wed 8:00–8:30
May 1949–Jun 1949, DUM Thu 8:30–9:00

EMCEE:

Bill Slater

PANEL:

Minnabess Lewis
Herb Polesie
Bob Shepard
Jackson Beck

REPERTORY COMPANY:

Allan Frank
Richard Seff
Ellen Fenwick

Charades were a favorite type of program on early television, since they were so obviously visual. This show used subjects suggested by viewers and acted out by a varying repertory company of young actors (those remaining on the show for several months are listed above). If the actors stumped the panel, the viewer who sent in the suggestion got $15.

CHARLES GRODIN (*Talk*)

BROADCAST HISTORY:

CNBC
60 minutes
Produced: *1995–1996*
Premiered: *January 9, 1995*

HOST:

Charles Grodin

Actor-writer-comedian Charles Grodin showed an unexpected gift of gab in this nightly talk show, which included a viewer call-in segment. The first week's guests ranged from actors Martin Short and Marlo Thomas to New York governor Mario Cuomo.

CHARLES IN CHARGE (*Situation Comedy*)

FIRST TELECAST: *October 3, 1984*
LAST TELECAST: *July 24, 1985*
BROADCAST HISTORY:

Oct 1984–Apr 1985, CBS Wed 8:00–8:30
Apr 1985, CBS Sat 8:00–8:30
Jun 1985–Jul 1985, CBS Wed 8:00–8:30
(In first-run syndication from January 1987 to December 1990)

CAST:

Charles.................................. Scott Baio
Jill Pembroke (1984–1985).............. Julie Cobb
Stan Pembroke (1984–1985)....... James Widdoes
Lila Pembroke (1984–1985).......... April Lerman
Douglas Pembroke (1984–1985).... Jonathan Ward
Jason Pembroke (1984–1985)... Michael Pearlman
Buddy Lembeck..................... Willie Aames
Gwendolyn Pierce (1984–1985)... Jennifer Runyon
Walter Powell (1987–1990)........ James Callahan
Ellen Powell (1987–1990)........... Sandra Kerns
Jamie Powell (1987–1990)........... Nicole Eggert
Sarah Powell (1987–1990).............. Josie Davis
Adam Powell (1987–1990)..... Alexander Polinsky
Lillian (1987–1990)................. Ellen Travolta
Anthony (1988)...................... Justin Whalin
Stephanie Curtis (1988–1989)........ Erika Eleniak

One of two 1984 series featuring hunky guys working as domestics (the other was ABC's *Who's the Boss*), *Charles in Charge* was the saga of a 19-year-old college student who went to work as a male governess for a busy working couple. In exchange for room, board, and a little spending money, Charles tried valiantly to keep a rein on Stan and Jill's three rambunctious children; cute, boy-crazy Lila (14); sarcastic Douglas (12); and happy-go-lucky Jason (10). Charles worked hard at the job and at his studies, but still managed to find time to hang out with his best friend Buddy and to pursue the girl of his dreams, beautiful sexy coed Gwendolyn Pierce.

When *Charles in Charge* returned to the air as a first-run syndicated series in early 1987, only Charles and Buddy were left from the original cast. The Pembrokes had moved to Seattle and sold their house to the Powells, who became Charles's new employers. The man of the house was not Mr. Powell, a Navy commander stationed in the South Seas, but his cranky father Walter, himself a retired career Navy man. Also in the house were Walter's daughter-in-law Ellen, and his three grandchildren, Jamie (14), Sarah (13), and Adam (12). Jamie was much more outgoing, worldly, and boy-crazy than her younger sister and seemed to be forever preoccupied with getting Sarah out of her shell, while Sarah was moving at a much slower, but for her more comfortable, pace. Rambunctious Adam could have been a clone of Jason Pembroke.

That fall Charles's loving mother, Lillian, came from Scranton for a short visit. She bought his favorite hangout, Sid's Pizza Parlor, and took up permanent residence in New Brunswick. Not only did he have to deal with her good-natured meddling, but picking up girls at Sid's, when she was there, was not what it used to be.

During the 1988–1989 season, Lillian converted the

pizza parlor to a nostalgic diner named The Yesterday Cafe, her hip young nephew, Anthony, came to live with her for awhile, and Charles was involved with sexy Stephanie—his most serious romance since Gwendolyn. In the last original episode, which aired in December 1990, Charles was accepted to graduate school at Princeton.

CHARLEY WEAVER SHOW, THE, see *Hobby Lobby*

CHARLIE & CO. (*Situation Comedy*)
FIRST TELECAST: *September 18, 1985*
LAST TELECAST: *July 23, 1986*
BROADCAST HISTORY:
Sep 1985–Dec 1985, CBS Wed 9:00–9:30
Jan 1986, CBS Tue 8:30–9:00
Apr 1986–Jun 1986, CBS Fri 8:00–8:30
Jun 1986–Jul 1986, CBS Wed 8:30–9:00
CAST:
Charlie Richmond .... Flip Wilson
Diana Richmond .... Gladys Knight
Lauren Richmond (15) .... Fran Robinson
Charlie Richmond, Jr. (16) .... Kristoff St. John
Robert Richmond (9) .... Jaleel White
Walter Simpson .... Ray Girardin
Milton Bieberman .... Richard Karron
Ronald Sandler .... Kip King
Jim Coyle .... Terry McGovern
Miguel Santana .... Eddie Velez
Aunt Rachel (1986) .... Della Reese

Chicago's south side was the setting for this domestic comedy which many critics accused of being a poor-man's version of NBC's highly successful *The Cosby Show.* Charlie Richmond was an administrative assistant with the Chicago Department of Highways. He and his wife Diana, an elementary school teacher, had three outspoken children—Junior, Lauren, and Robert. Since none of them were afflicted with shyness, life at home, particularly at meals, tended to resemble a verbal free-for-all. Walter Simpson was Charlie's boss, and Bieberman, Sandler, Coyle, and Miguel were his co-workers. Early in 1986 Diana's sarcastic Aunt Rachel, not one of Charlie's favorite people, turned up, adding to the already contentious atmosphere in Charlie's home.

CHARLIE CHAN, see *New Adventures of Charlie Chan, The*

CHARLIE DANIELS' TALENT ROUND UP (*Talent*)
BROADCAST HISTORY:
The Nashville Network
60 minutes
Produced: *1994–1996*
Premiered: *October 1, 1994*
HOST:
Charlie Daniels
Williams and Ree

Talent competition hosted by the country star, with contestants competing for cash prizes in three categories: male, female and group.

CHARLIE FARRELL SHOW, THE (*Situation Comedy*)
FIRST TELECAST: *July 2, 1956*
LAST TELECAST: *September 19, 1960*
BROADCAST HISTORY:
Jul 1956–Sep 1956, CBS Mon 9:00–9:30
Jul 1957–Sep 1957, NBC Mon 8:00–8:30
Aug 1960–Sep 1960, CBS Mon 7:30–8:00
CAST:
Charlie Farrell .... Himself
Dad Farrell .... Charles Winninger
Sherman Hull .... Richard Deacon
Mrs. Papernow .... Kathryn Card
Pierre .... Leon Askin
Rodney .... Jeff Silver
Doris Mayfield .... Noreen Nash

The Charlie Farrell Show was originally telecast as the 1956 summer replacement for *I Love Lucy.* It was the semi-autobiographical story of its star, as the stories were all based on actual incidents that had occurred at the Racquet Club, the exclusive Palm Springs, California, resort owned and managed by Mr. Farrell. Charlie had problems with everybody—the resort's manager, Sherman Hull; the chef, Pierre; his nephew, Rodney; his housekeeper, Mrs. Papernow; and even his lovable father. Reruns of the series were aired by NBC in 1957 and by CBS in 1960.

CHARLIE GRACE (*Detective Drama*)
FIRST TELECAST: *September 14, 1995*
LAST TELECAST: *October 19, 1995*
BROADCAST HISTORY:
Sep 1995–Oct 1995, ABC Thu 8:00–9:00
CAST:
Charlie Grace .... Mark Harmon
Jenny Grace (age 12) .... Leelee Sobieski
Leslie Loeb .... Cindy Katz
Artie Crawford .... Robert Costanzo

Private eyes don't come any handsomer than Mark Harmon, but that did little for this pedestrian series about the private and professional life of small-time L.A. investigator Charlie Grace. Charlie was a former cop who had been run off the force after exposing crooked fellow cops. Now he was a P.I., operating out of a pool parlor and going about his cases (which usually escalated into murder and mayhem) with a whimsical smirk. Leslie was his ex-girlfriend, a criminal attorney who used him on her cases, and Artie a pudgy former cop and fellow P.I. whose street connections often proved useful.

Just to prove he was a sensitive guy, the producers also gave Charlie a cute daughter named Jenny, who was the love of his life, and made one of his cases getting his ex-wife Holly (played by Harley Jane Kozak) off the rap for murdering her rich second husband.

CHARLIE HOOVER (*Situation Comedy*)
FIRST TELECAST: *November 9, 1991*
LAST TELECAST: *February 2, 1992*
BROADCAST HISTORY:
Nov 1991–Dec 1991, FOX Sat 9:00–9:30
Dec 1991–Feb 1992, FOX Sun 10:30–11:00
CAST:
Charlie Hoover .... Tim Matheson
Hugh .... Sam Kinison
Helen Hoover .... Lucy Webb
Doris .... Julie Hayden
Paul Hoover .... Michael Manasseri
Emily Hoover .... Leslie Engel
Mr. Culbertson .... Kevin McCarthy
Elliott Weedle .... Bill Maher

Charlie was a 40-year-old accountant suffering a midlife crisis when his alter ego, outspoken, hedonistic Hugh materialized to offer him advice on how to spice up his dull life. Hugh was twelve inches tall and visible only to Charlie, but his advice was certainly welcome. Charlie's boss, Mr. Culbertson, ignored him; his wife, Helen, and his two teenaged kids only cared about the money he provided; and Warren, the family bulldog, regularly urinated on his shoes. Only his secretary, Doris, had any sympathy for him, and she had her own problems. Hugh wanted Charlie to be assertive, spontaneous, and adventuresome, but it wasn't easy for him to change.

Comic Sam Kinison's outrageous videos and appearances on *Saturday Night Live* and *HBO*, as well as his struggles with drugs and alcohol, had given him a wild-man image that was toned down so much for this series that, comparatively, he was almost as dull as Charlie. Only six original episodes of *Charlie Hoover* were produced before Fox pulled the plug. A few months after the series left the air, Kinison was killed in an automobile crash.

CHARLIE WILD, PRIVATE DETECTIVE (*Detective Drama*)

FIRST TELECAST: *December 22, 1950*
LAST TELECAST: *June 19, 1952*
BROADCAST HISTORY:

Dec 1950–Mar 1951, CBS Fri 9:00–9:30
Apr 1951–Jun 1951, CBS Wed 9:00–9:30
Sep 1951–Mar 1952, ABC Tue 8:00–8:30
Mar 1952–Jun 1952, DUM Thu 10:00–10:30

CAST:

Charlie Wild (1950–1951) .... Kevin O'Morrison
Charlie Wild (1951–1952) .... John McQuade
Effie Perrine .... Cloris Leachman

Charlie Wild was a tough New York City private eye who got into a fight in almost every episode of this live detective series, one of many on the air in the late 1940s and early 1950s. The series had started on CBS radio in the late 1940s, and was brought to television with Kevin O'Morrison in the lead. He was replaced in May 1951 by John McQuade, who remained in the part through the show's rapid movement from CBS to ABC to DuMont. The show's only other regular cast member was Charlie's secretary, Effie Perrine.

CHARLIE'S ANGELS (*Detective Drama*)

FIRST TELECAST: *September 22, 1976*
LAST TELECAST: *August 19, 1981*
BROADCAST HISTORY:

Sep 1976–Aug 1977, ABC Wed 10:00–11:00
Aug 1977–Oct 1980, ABC Wed 9:00–10:00
Nov 1980–Jan 1981, ABC Sun 8:00–9:00
Jan 1981–Feb 1981, ABC Sat 8:00–9:00
Jun 1981–Aug 1981, ABC Wed 8:00–9:00

CAST:

Sabrina Duncan (1976–1979)......... Kate Jackson
Jill Munroe (1976–1977) .... Farrah Fawcett-Majors
Kelly Garrett .... Jaclyn Smith
Kris Munroe (1977–1981) .... Cheryl Ladd
Tiffany Welles (1979–1980) .... Shelley Hack
Julie Rogers (1980–1981)............ Tanya Roberts
John Bosley.......................... David Doyle
Charlie Townsend (voice only)....... John Forsythe

Sex, pure and simple, seemed to be the principal ingredient in the considerable success of this detective show. Denunciations of "massage parlor television" and "voyeurism" only brought more viewers to the screen, to see what the controversy was about. Often they were rather disappointed, as a lot more seemed to be promised than delivered, but *Charlie's Angels* nevertheless ended its first season as one of the top hits on television.

The plot involved three sexy police-trained detectives working for an unseen boss named Charlie, who relayed assignments by telephone. Charlie's assistant, Bosley, was on hand to help the girls and fret about costs, but he hardly seemed likely to make a pass at any of them. Most of the cases involved health spas, Las Vegas night spots, or other places where the girls could appear in bikinis or other scanty attire.

Sabrina was the cool, multilingual leader, Jill the athletic type, and Kelly the former showgirl who had "been around." Usually they worked as an undercover team. When they investigated a killing in the army, Jill and Kelly became recruits and Sabrina a base nurse; when it was the death of a roller-derby queen, Sabrina posed as an insurance investigator, Kelly as a magazine writer, and Jill as a derby competitor.

Farrah Fawcett-Majors was the last of the Angels to be cast (the show needed a blonde) and was little known compared to the lead, Kate Jackson, when the series began. Farrah quickly became the object of a tremendous fad, based partially on her gorgeous, flowing blond hair, and partially on some cheesecake publicity photos, including one now-famous swimsuit pose which showed the fine points of her anatomy in marvelous detail. Farrah Fawcett-Majors dolls were marketed, as were T-shirts with her picture and dozens of other gimmicks. Heady with all the sudden adulation, she walked out on the series, with the intention of launching a career in feature films. This started a series of lawsuits, which ended when she finally agreed to make a limited number of guest appearances on the show during the next three seasons. Thereafter, the introduction of a new "Angel" became an almost annual occurrence. First, Jill was replaced by her spunky younger sister, Kris (1977); two years later, Sabrina left and was replaced by Tiffany Welles, daughter of a Connecticut police chief (1979); a year after that, Tiffany was out, replaced by street-smart Julie Rogers (1980).

CHARMED (*Fantasy*)

FIRST TELECAST: *October 7, 1998*
LAST TELECAST:
BROADCAST HISTORY:

Oct 1998–Sep 1999, WB Wed 9:00–10:00
Sep 1999–Jun 2002, WB Thu 9:00–10:00
Apr 2000–May 2000, WB Sun 8:00–9:00
Aug 2000–Sep 2000, WB Thu 8:00–9:00
Jul 2001–Aug 2001, WB Fri 9:00–10:00
Feb 2002–Mar 2002, WB Thu 8:00–9:00
May 2002, WB Thu 8:00–9:00
Jun 2002–Aug 2002, WB Sun 8:00–9:00
Aug 2002–Sep 2002, WB Sun 7:00–9:00
Sep 2002– , WB Sun 8:00–9:00

CAST:

Prudence "Pru" Halliwell (1998–2001)
.... Shannen Doherty
Piper Halliwell .... Holly Marie Combs
Phoebe Halliwell.................... Alyssa Milano

Inspector Andrew Trudeau (1998–1999) . . . T.W. King
Inspector Daryl Morris . . . . Dorian Gregory
Rex Buckland (1998–1999) . . . . Neil Roberts
Leo Wyatt (1999–) . . . . Brian Krause
Dan Gordon (1999–2000) . . . . Greg Vaughan
Jack Sheridan (1999–2000) . . . . Lochlyn Munro
Asst. D.A. Cole Turner (2000–2003)
. . . . Julian McMahon
Paige Matthews (2001–) . . . . Rose McGowan
The Seer (2002–2003) . . . . Debbi Morgan

In this offbeat fantasy/horror series, three sisters were reunited in the big old Victorian family home in San Francisco, only to discover something their mother had never told them: they were all witches, each with unique powers. Because they hadn't known about the powers, they had been protected from evil, but now that they knew about and could use their powers, they were targets. Each week they fought the good fight against evil. It all started when Phoebe invoked an incantation that activated their powers. She could see into the future, Pru could move objects at will (telekinesis), and Piper could stop time. As protectors of the innocent, they were known as the charmed ones. Collectively they used incantations from *The Book of Shadows*, a book of witchcraft, to cast spells. Holding hands and chanting, "The Power of Three Will Set Us Free," they destroyed an evil warlock in the premiere. They could use incantations to fight demons, warlocks, and other spirits, but had to be together chanting as a team for the incantations to work. Pru worked for the Buckland Auction House, Piper was a student chef at The Quake restaurant and catered on the side, and Phoebe bounced from job to job. Andy, Pru's former boyfriend, was a cop. In the Thanksgiving episode she told him she was a witch and, not surprisingly, he had problems dealing with it.

In January they were threatened by Pru's boss Rex, a warlock who was after their powers. They were saved by Leo the hunky handyman who had had a brief affair with Piper. He turned out to be a white lighter, a guardian angel for good witches. Claire, a tough businesswoman, took over management of the auction house. In May Andy was suspended during an Internal Affairs investigation of his unsolved cases—all of which related to the activities of the three witches. In the season finale he was killed trying to save them from a demon, the I.A. investigator responsible for his suspension.

That fall Piper opened a club, P3 (for Piper, Prudence and Phoebe), and hired Dan, a contractor who was their new neighbor, to do the renovations. Phoebe was still unemployed. Despite finding out, in an episode in which the three sisters went into the future, that she and Leo eventually would get married and have a daughter, Piper started to date Dan. Leo had told her to date Dan because there was no future in relationships between witches and white lighters. Jack, a rival at acquiring antiques and other artifacts, got a job working at Buckland's and tried to kindle romantic sparks with Pru, but she resigned from Buckland's because she felt the new ownership was engaging in unethical practices. In January the Halliwells told Daryl they were witches and Pru acquired a new power, astral projection. At the end of the month Leo used his powers to save Piper's life—she had contracted a rare fatal disease—and was put on temporary suspension, making him mortal. Piper gave Leo a job as a bartender at P3 and in late February admitted to him that he was her true love. In April Pru got a job as a photographer for *415 Magazine*, and at the end of the season, with the help of a genie (French Stewart), Piper's wish that Dan could move on with his life and forget her was granted. He got a new job out of town.

In October Phoebe, still unemployed, started dating Cole, a prosecutor who seemed normal but was actually Belthazor, a demon determined to destroy the charmed ones. Leo proposed to Piper and she accepted. In November the witches were made aware that Belthazor posed a threat but had no idea that he was Cole. Cole really loved Phoebe but The Triad, to whom Belthazor reported, did not appreciate his involvement with her, since they wanted him to kill the three Halliwell witches. Before they could destroy him he managed to destroy them, along with a demon bounty hunter. He declared that he was no longer evil and sought Phoebe's love, but she told him he had to stay out of her life. In February Piper and Leo got married and in May Cole, manipulated by demons he had previously been associated with, reverted—with regrets—to his evil ways. Meanwhile, a TV news crew caught the witches in action vanquishing a demon, they were hounded by publicity seekers and a crazed would-be witch mortally wounded Piper. Phoebe, who had gone to the netherworld to bring Cole back, made a deal to stay in the netherworld if a powerful demon would reset time and make everything okay. It did but, at episode's end, the demon that had started the trouble appeared to have killed a doctor, Pru and Piper.

That fall Piper had survived but everyone was preparing for Pru's funeral. Mother Patty (Finola Hughes) showed up and told the surviving sisters that, after her divorce from their father, she and her white lighter lover had had a daughter, Paige. Since Paige was their half sister she could fill in for Pru and enable them to reconstitute the "Power of Three." The evil demon responsible for Pru's death tried to tempt Paige to become an evil witch, but in the end she joined her half sisters and moved into the Halliwell house. Like Pru, she had could cause objects to move. In November a stripping potion destroyed Belthazor but left Cole's human self intact. Unsure of what he should do with his life—he had been a demon for more than 100 years—he left town to find himself. He was back in February to save the witches from The Source, a powerful demon who took first Piper's, and then Paige's, powers. It worked, but Cole suffered a residual problem—The Source took over his body.

The Seer, a manipulative demon, helped Cole maneuver Phoebe into marrying him, ensuring that their future son would be an all-powerful demon. Cole got a fancy high-paying job as an attorney and plotted to impregnate Phoebe with his evil. Meanwhile, Phoebe started writing an advice column for a local paper, the *Bay Mirror*, where Elise (Rebecca Balding) was her demanding boss. In April Phoebe found out she was pregnant. Phoebe and Paige teamed up with a wizard to stop the coronation of the new Source, not realizing it was Cole, and Phoebe was soon to be his queen of the Underworld. Phoebe tried to accept her new role in Cole's life but, despite her love for him, ultimately helped her sisters to vanquish him. The Seer stole Phoebe's unborn baby, transferring it to her own body, but when the sisters vanquished her, she took the baby and many other demons with her. As the season ended Cole was trapped in another realm, holding on to his love for Phoebe, and Piper found out she was pregnant.

By the start of the 2002–2003 season Phoebe had become the star advice columnist for the *Bay Mirror* and had started divorce proceedings when Cole showed up. He claimed he was good but still had demonic powers. A demon told him he was still destined to become the new Source, and Cole tried to get the charmed ones to vanquish him to avoid returning to the Underworld—in January he finally succeeded. Paige gave up her job as a social worker to spend full time helping the innocent, while Piper and Leo were having problems adjusting to Piper's pregnancy. In February she gave birth to Wyatt Matthew Halliwell (after Leo's last name, Paige's last name and Piper's last name). Wyatt could generate force fields to protect himself from demons, which explained why Piper had been virtually invincible during her pregnancy.

CHARMINGS, THE (*Situation Comedy*)

FIRST TELECAST: *March 20, 1987*
LAST TELECAST: *February 11, 1988*
BROADCAST HISTORY:
Mar 1987–Apr 1987, ABC Fri 8:00–8:30
Aug 1987–Jan 1988, ABC Thu 8:30–9:00
Jan 1988–Feb 1988, ABC Thu 8:00–8:30
CAST:
Snow White Charming (Spring 1987) .... Caitlin O'Heaney
Snow White Charming .... Carol Huston
Prince Eric Charming .... Christopher Rich
Queen Lillian White .... Judy Parfitt
Thomas Charming .... Brandon Call
Cory Charming .... Garette Ratliffe
Luther .... Cork Hubbert
The Mirror .... Paul Winfield
Sally Miller .... Dori Brenner
Don Miller .... Paul Eiding

Snow White and Prince Charming fell asleep in the Enchanted Forest and woke up in 20th-century California in this slightly off-center continuation of the Brothers Grimm fairy tale. According to the legend, the beautiful couple threw Snow's wicked stepmother, Queen Lillian, into a bottomless pit and lived happily ever after. Unfortunately the pit was not really bottomless, just very, very deep, and when the furious Queen managed to climb out she cast a spell so powerful that even she couldn't control it. Everybody—Snow White, the Prince, their two young sons, the dwarf, the Magic Mirror, and even the Queen herself—fell asleep for centuries.

They all woke up in 1987 in Van Oaks, California, and found themselves coping with the modern, not-so-quaint world of American suburbia. The handsome Prince, still in his tights and referring to his "castle" (a suburban home), became a writer of children's stories; Snow, a dress designer; and their young sons Thomas and Cory, schoolchildren. The dwarf Luther helped around the house. Spoiling the fun was Queen Lillian, a vain, vengeful, and still powerful in-law who lived upstairs. Jealous of the happy lovebirds, she would periodically cast spells to disrupt their plans and alarm the neighbors, who didn't understand the new couple on the block at all. A botched attempt to send everyone back to the Forest just brought Cinderella into the 20th century, to flirt with Eric; a few magic beans carelessly thrown out her window produced Jack and the Beanstalk in their yard. Even Lillian's sole companion, the Magic Mirror (which had a sarcastic personality of its own), failed to calm her down.

Sally and Don were the befuddled neighbors who, in true sitcom fashion, never caught on.

CHASE (*Police Drama*)

FIRST TELECAST: *September 11, 1973*
LAST TELECAST: *August 28, 1974*
BROADCAST HISTORY:
Sep 1973–Jan 1974, NBC Tue 8:00–9:00
Jan 1974–Aug 1974, NBC Wed 8:00–9:00
CAST:
Capt. Chase Reddick .... Mitchell Ryan
Officer Norm Hamilton .... Reid Smith
Officer Steve Baker .... Michael Richardson
Officer Fred Sing .... Brian Fong
Sgt. Sam MacCray .... Wayne Maunder
Inspector Frank Dawson .... Albert Reed
Officer Ed Rice .... Gary Crosby
Officer Tom Wilson .... Craig Gardner

One of the variations on the police-show format so popular in the early 1970s was the "special cop," the policeman or unit with special skills solving otherwise unsolvable crimes with unconventional means. Cpt. Chase Reddick's plainclothes unit, though nominally part of the Los Angeles Police Department, was accountable only to the Chief of Detectives and had a virtual free hand in solving cases none of the other police divisions could crack. Reddick had only four men, each with a useful skill: Sam MacCray, a specialist in the training and handling of police dogs; Norm Hamilton, a former Vietnam War helicopter pilot; Steve Baker, a hot-rod car driver; and Fred Sing, an expert motorcycle rider. Occasional "straight" cops also appeared in the series, including officer Ed Rice, played by Gary Crosby—who on other duty tours turned up in Jack Webb's *Adam 12,* the model of the "straight cop" genre.

CHECK IT OUT (*Situation Comedy*)

BROADCAST HISTORY:
USA Cable Network and Syndicated
30 minutes
Produced: *1985–1988* (66 episodes)
Released: *Spring 1986*
CAST:
Howard Bannister .... Don Adams
Edna Moseley .... Dinah Christie
Jack Christian .... Jeff Pustil
Marlene Weimaraner .... Kathleen Laskey
Jennifer Woods (1985–1986) .... Tonya Williams
Leslie Rappaport .... Aaron Schwartz
Marvin (1985) .... Jason Warren
Murray Amherst (1985–1987) ..... Simon Reynolds
Alf Scully (1985–1986) .... Henry Beckman
Mrs. Alfreda Cobb (1985–1986) .. Barbara Hamilton
Viker (1986–1988) .... Gordon Clapp
T. C. Collingwood (1987) .... Elizabeth Hanna

*Occasional

Don Adams returned to series television as a bumbling supermarket manager in this low-budget sitcom. The setting was Cobb's, part of a chain of stores in the town of Brampton. Jack was the ambitious, obnoxious young assistant manager; Marlene, Jennifer, and overtly homosexual Leslie worked the checkout registers; Marvin, and later Murray, were both bagboys and stock clerks; Alf was the ancient security guard who had been working in the same store for more than 40 years; and Edna was Howard's secretary. They had been having an affair, which the entire town knew about, for more than six years. Although she would have loved to become Mrs. Bannister, Edna was resigned to tolerating Howard's inability to make a binding commitment. Mrs. Cobb, the overbearing owner of the small grocery chain, turned up periodically to disrupt the already less-than-efficient operation of the store.

Viker was added to the cast in the second season as Cobb's inept handyman and T. C. Collingwood arrived in the fall of 1987 as the ambitious young v.p. of corporate development for Cendrax Corporation, the conglomerate to which Mrs. Cobb had sold the chain. T. C. was all business, and determined to make her name by turning around the slipshod operation. Fat chance.

Check It Out was based on the British series *Tripper's Day*. It had originally been produced in Toronto as a joint venture of the CTV Television Network in Canada and the USA Cable Network in the United States. It aired first-run on both, with the reruns sold into syndication in the United States.

CHECKING IN (*Situation Comedy*)
FIRST TELECAST: *April 9, 1981*
LAST TELECAST: *April 30, 1981*
BROADCAST HISTORY:
Apr 1981, CBS Thu 8:00–8:30
CAST:
Florence Johnston .... Marla Gibbs
Lyle Block.......................... Larry Linville
Elena Beltran .... Liz Torres
Earl Bellamy .... Patrick Collins
Hank Sabatino .... Robert Costanzo
Betty .... Ruth Brown
Dennis, the bellboy.................. Jordan Gibbs

In this comedy spin-off from *The Jeffersons*, Florence, the Jeffersons' outspoken maid, left domestic work to become executive housekeeper at the St. Frederick, one of Manhattan's better hotels. Her new responsibilities included managing most of the hotel's staff. Elena was her efficient assistant; Earl, the barely competent house detective; Hank, the beefy chief engineer in charge of heat, air conditioning, and plumbing; and Betty, one of the floor supervisors. Florence's biggest problem, however, and the target of the most of her jibes, was her stuffy boss, hotel manager Lyle Block. Block was in fact reminiscent of another character played by actor Larry Linville in the series *M*A*S*H*, the insufferable Major Frank Burns.

CHECKMATE (*Detective Drama*)
FIRST TELECAST: *September 17, 1960*
LAST TELECAST: *September 19, 1962*
BROADCAST HISTORY:
Sep 1960–Sep 1961, CBS Sat 8:30–9:30
Oct 1961–Sep 1962, CBS Wed 8:30–9:30
CAST:
Don Corey.......................... Anthony George
Jed Sills .... Doug McClure
Carl Hyatt .... Sebastian Cabot
Chris Devlin (1962) .... Jack Betts

Checkmate, Inc., was the name of a very fancy, very expensive investigative agency operated in San Francisco by Don Corey and Jed Sills. The goal of the company was to prevent crimes and to forestall death. In most of their cases, Don and Jed tried to protect the lives of people who had been threatened or who suspected they were possible targets of criminals. Helping them with the analytical side of the operation was Carl Hyatt, a bearded and very British former Oxford professor of criminology, who acted as special consultant to the firm. Added to the firm in 1962, on an irregular basis, was investigator Chris Devlin.

CHEER TELEVISION THEATRE (*Dramatic Anthology*)
FIRST TELECAST: *May 30, 1954*
LAST TELECAST: *June 27, 1954*
BROADCAST HISTORY:
May 1954–Jun 1954, NBC Sun 7:00–7:30

This five-week series of filmed dramas filled the period between the cancellation of *The Paul Winchell Show* and the start of *Kollege of Musical Knowledge*.

CHEERS (*Situation Comedy*)
FIRST TELECAST: *September 30, 1982*
LAST TELECAST: *August 19, 1993*
BROADCAST HISTORY:
Sep 1982–Dec 1982, NBC Thu 9:00–9:30
Jan 1983–Dec 1983, NBC Thu 9:30–10:00
Dec 1983–Aug 1993, NBC Thu 9:00–9:30
Feb 1993–May 1993, NBC Thu 8:00–8:30
CAST:
Sam Malone .... Ted Danson
Diane Chambers (1982–1987) .... Shelley Long
Carla Tortelli LeBec .... Rhea Perlman
Ernie "Coach" Pantusso (1982–1985)
.... Nicholas Colasanto
Norm Peterson .... George Wendt
Cliff Clavin..................... John Ratzenberger
Dr. Frasier Crane (1984–1993) .... Kelsey Grammer
Woody Boyd (1985–1993)........ Woody Harrelson
Rebecca Howe (1987–1993)........... Kirstie Alley
Dr. Lilith Sternin (1986–1993) ...... Bebe Neuwirth
**Evan Drake (1987–1988)*.............. Tom Skerritt
**Eddie LeBec (1987–1989)*.............. Jay Thomas
Robin Colcord (1989–1991)............ Roger Rees
**Kelly Gaines (1989–1993)*.......... Jackie Swanson
Paul (1991–1993)...................... Paul Willson
Phil (1991–1993)................... Philip Perlman
*Occasional
THEME:
"Where Everybody Knows Your Name," by Judy Hart Angelo and Gary Portnoy, sung by Gary Portnoy

The witty gang at a Boston bar called Cheers provided the focus of this comedy. Sam was the owner and bartender, a tall, rugged, and rather self-assured man with a knack for good conversation, an eye for the ladies, and an interesting past. Once a pitcher for the Boston Red Sox, he'd had a bout with alcoholism but was now sworn off the stuff for good. Helping him out behind the great oak bar was "Coach," a kindly, absentminded gent who had been in pro ball as a coach and manager, and who regaled the customers with his experiences. Carla was a wisecracking waitress, while Norm (an accountant) and Cliff (the mailman) were regular patrons.

Into this bastion of locker-room chatter came Diane, a bright, attractive graduate student whose interests leaned toward the arts. Stopping by one snowy evening with her fiancé, literature professor Sumner Sloan, on their way to the Caribbean to be married, Diane expected never to see the place again. But her fiancé jilted her, and Diane found herself in need of immediate employment. Sam hired her for the only job she was qualified to do, that of waitress. She despised him at first, and the barbs flew thick and fast, but in time a romantic attraction grew. By the beginning of the second season Sam and Diane—despite their sarcastic jibes—were the latest "item" at Cheers.

Their off-again, on-again romance lasted only about a year until, in the fall of 1984, Diane found a new boyfriend in obnoxious, insecure psychologist Frasier Crane. They went to Europe to get married but, unable to get Sam out of her mind, Diane jilted Frasier and eventually returned to working at Cheers. Meanwhile in early 1985 "Coach" passed away (actor Nicholas Colasanto had died), and a new bartender joined the ensemble. Young Woody, a naive farmboy from Indiana, had been taking a mail-order course in bartending from Coach and had come to Cheers to meet him. The dejected Frasier also joined the gang.

The 1985–1986 season ended with a cliff-hanger worthy of a prime-time soap opera. Sam's whirlwind romance with attractive city councilwoman Janet Eldridge (Kate Mulgrew) was coming to a head and Sam was ready to propose—but to whom? In the last scene of the season he was on the phone asking someone to marry him. It turned out to be Diane, but she said no and the two returned to another season of sparring, ending when Diane announced in 1987 she was leaving for "just six months" to write her long-awaited novel. As she walked out the door—and out of his life—a knowing Sam whispered after her, "have a good life."

Sam then sold the bar and embarked on an around-the-world trip in a sailboat, but the boat sank and he was soon back looking for a job at the establishment he once ran. The new manager was Rebecca, a buxom, determined lady who took him in, but only on *her* terms. Her main interest in life seemed to be to score points with her boss Evan, in order to advance in the corporation that now owned the bar. When that didn't work out, she turned her attention to Robin, a sleazy corporate raider who promised riches but wound up in jail. She eventually dumped him at the altar, all the time fighting her attraction to Sam. But it was a rocky relationship. The boss-employee tables were turned when Sam regained control of the bar and demoted the haughty Rebecca to barmaid.

Meanwhile, sarcastic Carla married Eddie LeBec in the 1987–1988 season, and had twins named Elvis and Jesse—making her the mother of eight. No-good Eddie was then run over by a Zamboni skating-rink machine, leaving her once again a single mother. Frasier recovered from his rejection by Diane and married acerbic fellow psychiatrist Lilith, in early 1988, and they had a son named Frederick. Woody dated and eventually married girlfriend Kelly. Other friends and relatives of the regulars showed up from time to time, perhaps the most talked about among fans being Vera, the wife of the now-unemployed Norm. Only her feet were shown—except once when viewers did see her face, but covered with pie! The actress undergoing these indignities was George Wendt's real-life wife, Bernadette Birkett.

Cheers became something of an institution during its long run and was the number-one series on television during its final season. The final episode was one of the top-rated TV events of all time. In it, not-so-naive Woody was elected to the City Council; Rebecca abruptly married plumber Dan; and Diane, now a successful TV writer, returned for a visit. Sam and Diane ran off to get married but at the last minute called it off, leaving the gang to sit around the soon-to-be-closed bar and muse on the meaning of life (Cliff said it was "shoes"). They then turned out the lights and went home.

CHER (*Musical Variety*)
FIRST TELECAST: *February 16, 1975*
LAST TELECAST: *January 4, 1976*
BROADCAST HISTORY:
Feb 1975–Jun 1975, CBS Sun 7:30–8:30
Sep 1975–Jan 1976, CBS Sun 8:00–9:00
REGULARS:
Cher Bono
Gailard Sartain
The Tony Charmoli Dancers (1975)
The Anita Mann Dancers (1975–1976)
The Jimmy Dale Orchestra (1975)
The Jack Eskew Orchestra (1975–1976)

Following their divorce in 1974, pop singers Sonny and Cher Bono, who had formerly starred together on *The Sonny and Cher Comedy Hour*, each hosted a series of their own. His was a short-lived variety series on ABC in the fall of 1974 (see *The Sonny Comedy Revue*), and hers was *Cher*, a musical variety hour with guest stars that premiered the following February. Steve Martin, Teri Garr, and Sonny and Cher's daughter Chastity were frequent guest stars during Cher's solo period.

The magic Sonny and Cher had had together did not survive the transition to singles. Cher's solo venture limped along on CBS for almost a year, with a new dance group and orchestra in the fall of 1975, by which time she and Sonny decided to try it again as a team, at least professionally. One month after *Cher* left the air, *The Sonny and Cher Show* reappeared in the time period that had been vacated.

CHESTERFIELD PRESENTS (*Dramatic Anthology*)
FIRST TELECAST: *January 10, 1952*
LAST TELECAST: *March 6, 1952*
BROADCAST HISTORY:
Jan 1952–Mar 1952, NBC Thu 9:00–9:30

This dramatic anthology series, also known as *Dramatic Mystery*, alternated with *Dragnet* on Thursday nights during the latter's first two months on network television.

CHESTERFIELD SOUND OFF TIME (*Comedy/Variety*)
FIRST TELECAST: *October 14, 1951*
LAST TELECAST: *January 6, 1952*
BROADCAST HISTORY:
Oct 1951–Jan 1952, NBC Sun 7:00–7:30
STARS:
Bob Hope
Jerry Lester
Fred Allen

This half-hour comedy variety series was emceed on a rotating basis by three major stars. The programs involved skits, monologues, and production numbers keyed to each star's brand of comedy. The original version of *Dragnet* was previewed as a special edition of *Chesterfield Sound Off Time* on December 16, 1951. Jack Webb starred in the preview, while his superior was played by Raymond Burr, later of *Perry Mason* and *Ironside*.

CHESTERFIELD SUPPER CLUB, see *Perry Como*

CHET HUNTLEY REPORTING
(*News/Documentary*)
FIRST TELECAST: *December 22, 1957*
LAST TELECAST: *June 18, 1963*
BROADCAST HISTORY:
Dec 1957–Sep 1959, NBC Sun 6:30–7:00
Jan 1962–Sep 1962, NBC Fri 10:30–11:00
Oct 1962–Jun 1963, NBC Tue 10:30–11:00
HOST/REPORTER:
Chet Huntley

This documentary series premiered on Sunday afternoons in April 1956 under the title *Outlook*. It began as a weekend news program that included news headlines and covered four or five stories at greater length, with filmed reports. Narration and commentary was by Huntley. When the program moved to Sunday evenings in December 1957, the format was changed to provide in-depth exploration of a single subject. From 1959 to 1961 the program was aired on Sunday afternoons at 5:30 P.M. On January 12, 1962, it moved to Friday nights and continued in the evening hours for another year and a half, retaining the same news-documentary format with Huntley interviewing news personalities and exploring topical issues in depth.

The program title changed several times during its seven-year run. Originally *Outlook*, it later became *Chet Huntley . . . Reporting* (November 1958) and *Time: Present . . . Chet Huntley Reporting* (October 1959) before going back to *Chet Huntley Reporting* (September 1960).

CHEVROLET ON BROADWAY (*Musical Variety*)
FIRST TELECAST: *July 17, 1956*
LAST TELECAST: *September 13, 1956*
BROADCAST HISTORY:
Jul 1956, NBC Tue/Thu 7:30–7:45
Aug 1956–Sep 1956, NBC Thu 7:30–7:45
REGULARS:
Snooky Lanson
Mellolarks, vocal quartet
The Hal Hastings Orchestra

This summer replacement for *The Dinah Shore Show* featured Snooky Lanson, star of the popular *Your Hit Parade*. For its first three weeks it ran as a twice-weekly series on Tuesdays and Thursdays, then switched to once a week for the duration of the summer.

CHEVROLET SHOWROOM, see *Your Chevrolet Showroom*

CHEVROLET TELE-THEATRE (*Dramatic Anthology*)
FIRST TELECAST: *September 27, 1948*
LAST TELECAST: *June 26, 1950*
BROADCAST HISTORY:
Sep 1948–Jan 1949, NBC Mon 8:00–8:30
Feb 1949–Apr 1949, NBC Mon 8:30–9:00
May 1949–Jun 1950, NBC Mon 8:00–8:30

Chevrolet Tele-Theatre was a big-budget, live dramatic series that presented an original play or adaptation each week during the 1948–1949 and 1949–1950 seasons. Top-flight writers and actors were used, the latter including such names as Paul Muni, Eddie Albert, Nanette Fabray, Basil Rathbone, Mercedes McCambridge, Rex Harrison, and E. G. Marshall. Gertrude Berg made her TV debut on the October 18, 1948, telecast in the comedy "Whistle, Daughter, Whistle." This was based on her highly popular radio series *The Goldbergs* and became the prototype for the TV series of the same name which premiered a few months later. *Chevrolet Tele-Theatre* was known as *Chevrolet on Broadway* during parts of the 1948–1949 season.

CHEVY CHASE SHOW, THE (*Talk*)
FIRST TELECAST: *September 7, 1993*
LAST TELECAST: *October 15, 1993*
BROADCAST HISTORY:
Sep 1993–Oct 1993, FOX Mon–Fri 11:00–12:00 A.M.
HOST:
Chevy Chase
ORCHESTRA:
Tom Scott and the Hollywood Express
ANNOUNCER:
Ron Russ

Fox hoped to end its string of late-night talk-show failures with this much-ballyhooed entry, but what it got was one of the worst TV debacles of the early 1990s. The idea was to use movie star Chevy Chase, who had not done regular TV since the glory days of *Saturday Night Live* two decades earlier, to inject some irreverence into the relatively staid late-night talk-show format. The publicity buildup was huge, and Fox even went so far as to rename the building from which it aired The Chevy Chase Theatre. Then came opening night.

Few who saw it will forget it. Chevy's opening monologue fell flat, and he seemed painfully uncomfortable throughout the entire hour. Opening guest Goldie Hawn tried desperately to salvage the show, but by the end of the hour it was apparent that Fox had grievously miscalculated. Viewers had left in droves, and the reviews the following morning were devastating—critics called it the worst hour on TV. About the only bright spot was the "News Update" at the midpoint of the show, obviously lifted from the "Weekend Update" segment of *SNL*. Other segments included comedy bits done in and around the theater, "Ask Dr. Chase" (bad medical advice), taped mime pieces with multiple disembodied Chevy Chase heads, and silly out-of-studio show openings. Eccentric sound effects man Archie Hahn was a sometime sidekick.

The show changed writers and producers and sought advice from a media consultant, but to no avail. Six weeks after its premiere *The Chevy Chase Show* bit the dust. Fox presumably ate the $3 million guarantee to Chase and quickly renamed the theater. As for Chevy, he showed great humor about the whole thing, even doing product commercials later on that spoofed his disaster-prone image.

CHEVY MYSTERY SHOW, THE (*Dramatic Anthology*)

FIRST TELECAST: *May 29, 1960*

LAST TELECAST: *September 17, 1961*

BROADCAST HISTORY:

May 1960–Sep 1960, NBC Sun 9:00–10:00
Jul 1961–Sep 1961, NBC Sun 9:00–10:00

HOSTS:

Walter Slezak
Vincent Price (1960)

Aired as a summer replacement for *The Dinah Shore Chevy Show,* these dramas were hosted by Walter Slezak through September 4, 1960, and by Vincent Price for the last three telecasts that year. The host introduced the program, introduced each act, and then closed the program. Reruns of the plays hosted by Walter Slezak were aired the following summer under the title *Sunday Mystery Hour.* Among the plays, which emphasized suspense and mystery without resorting to violence, were: "The Summer Hero," written by Charlotte Armstrong and starring Zachary Scott and Patty McCormack; "Dead Man's Walk," starring Robert Culp and Abby Dalton; "Trial by Fury," starring Agnes Moorehead and Warren Stevens; and an adaptation of the A. A. Milne story "The Perfect Alibi," starring Janet Blair.

CHEVY SHOW, THE (*Variety*)

FIRST TELECAST: *October 4, 1955*

LAST TELECAST: *September 4, 1956*

BROADCAST HISTORY:

Oct 1955–Sep 1956, NBC Tue 8:00–9:00

There was no regular star on this variety series, which aired every third Tuesday during the 1955–1956 season on a rotating basis with *The Milton Berle Show* and *The Martha Raye Show.* Bob Hope and Dinah Shore—who later had her own *Chevy Show* series—appeared frequently during the winter season, and Betty Hutton and Ethel Merman each starred in one show apiece. During the summer of 1956 *The Chevy Show* continued to appear every third week, alternating with assorted specials. Gisele Mackenzie, Fred Waring, and Janet Blair appeared as hosts for the summer edition.

CHEVY SHOW, THE (*Musical Variety*)

FIRST TELECAST: *June 22, 1958*

LAST TELECAST: *September 27, 1959*

BROADCAST HISTORY:

Jun 1958–Sep 1958, NBC Sun 9:00–10:00
Jun 1959–Sep 1959, NBC Sun 9:00–10:00

REGULARS:

Janet Blair
John Raitt
Edie Adams (1958)
Dorothy Kirsten
Stan Freberg (1958)
Rowan and Martin (1958)
The Harry Zimmerman Orchestra

This *Chevy Show* was the summer replacement for *The Dinah Shore Chevy Show* in 1958 and 1959. The format was a mixed bag of popular and classical music, skits, and monologues. During the summer of 1958 the show had three musical-comedy stars—Janet Blair, John Raitt, and Edie Adams—who appeared each week and took turns as host. The opera singer Dorothy Kirsten was a featured regular; Stan Freberg and Rowan and Martin provided humor. During the summer of 1959 Blair and Raitt returned as co-hosts, with Miss Kirsten the only other returning regular.

CHEVY SHOWROOM STARRING ANDY WILLIAMS, THE, see *Andy Williams Show, The*

CHEYENNE (*Western*)

FIRST TELECAST: *September 20, 1955*

LAST TELECAST: *September 13, 1963*

BROADCAST HISTORY:

Sep 1955–Sep 1959, ABC Tue 7:30–8:30
Sep 1959–Dec 1962, ABC Mon 7:30–8:30
Apr 1963–Sep 1963, ABC Fri 7:30–8:30

CAST:

Cheyenne Bodie....................... Clint Walker
Smitty (1955–1956)..................... L. Q. Jones

The behind-the-scenes story of this series was fully as interesting as what appeared on the screen. Probably no series in TV history has undergone so much production turmoil and absorbed and spun off as many other series as did *Cheyenne.*

The on-screen story was simple enough. Cheyenne Bodie was a tall, strapping Western adventurer in the days following the Civil War—he was 6'7", or 6'5", or 6'8", depending on the press release—and a mean hombre. He drifted from job to job, encountering plenty of villains, beautiful girls, and gunfights. In one episode he could be seen as the foreman on a ranch, in another as trail scout for a wagon train, in another as a recently deputized lawman. The show was lavishly produced, movie-style, by Warner Bros., but the attraction was obviously Clint Walker himself. He had a sidekick, Smitty, for the first season, but after that he worked alone.

Cheyenne was first seen as one of three rotating elements of *Warner Bros. Presents,* the studio's first venture into TV, and quickly emerged as the most popular of the three. Hour-long Westerns were difficult to produce on a once-a-week basis, however, so the program continued to alternate with other series, first *Conflict* (1956–1957) and then *Sugarfoot* (1957–1959). In fact, Clint Walker's *Cheyenne* was seldom seen on an every-week basis at any time during its original run.

In 1958 the brooding fighter of the screen walked out on Warner Bros., after they refused to release him from some of the more stringent requirements of his contract, which had been signed before *Cheyenne* became a hit. Among other things Walker did not want to have to kick back 50 percent of all personal-appearance fees to the studio, wanted higher payment for reruns, and wanted permission to make records for labels other than Warner's own. Stripped of its star, the studio nevertheless refused to give an inch and continued the series under the name *Cheyenne,* with an unknown actor named Ty Hardin in the leading role, which was now that of Bronco Layne. Walker, meanwhile, was legally prevented from working anywhere.

In early 1959 Walker and the studio finally came to terms, and Walker returned to the series. Ty Hardin continued in a series of his own called *Bronco.* Clint Walker was obviously not happy with the settlement, for although the pot had been sweetened somewhat he felt he had simply worn out the Cheyenne character and was becoming typecast. But the program was in the top 20, and Warner Bros. was not about to let him go. "I am like a caged animal," he complained to reporters.

For part of the 1959–1960 season *Cheyenne* alternated with *Shirley Temple's Storybook*. Then for 1960–1961 *Cheyenne* became *The Cheyenne Show*, a rotating anthology in which Walker was seen on a majority of weeks, interspersed with episodes of Ty Hardin as *Bronco* and Will Hutchins as *Sugarfoot*. In 1961–1962 *Sugarfoot* was dropped and only *Cheyenne* and *Bronco* were seen. Finally, in the fall of 1962, for the last three months, the series consisted of episodes of Walker's *Cheyenne* alone. Reruns of *Cheyenne* episodes were also seen during the summer of 1963.

Cheyenne was based, rather loosely, on a 1947 movie of the same name that starred Dennis Morgan.

See *Bronco* and *Sugarfoot* for details of those series, including the period when they ran under the *Cheyenne* title.

CHICAGO HOPE (*Medical Drama*)

FIRST TELECAST: *September 18, 1994*
LAST TELECAST: *May 4, 2000*
BROADCAST HISTORY:

Sep 1994, CBS Sun 8:00–9:00
Sep 1994, CBS Thu 10:00–11:00
Oct 1994–Dec 1994, CBS Thu 9:00–10:00
Dec 1994–Sep 1997, CBS Mon 10:00–11:00
Oct 1997–Jun 1999, CBS Wed 10:00–11:00
Sep 1999–May 2000, CBS Thu 9:00–10:00

CAST:

Dr. Jeffrey Geiger (1994–1995, 1999–2000) .... Mandy Patinkin
Dr. Aaron Shutt .... Adam Arkin
Dr. Arthur Thurmond (1994–1995) .. E. G. Marshall
Dr. Phillip Watters .... Hector Elizondo
Nurse Camille Shutt (1994–1996) .... Roxanne Hart
Alan Birch (1994–1995) .... Peter MacNicol
Dr. Daniel Nyland (1994–1997) .... Thomas Gibson
**Angela Giandamenico (1994–1995)* .. Roma Maffia
Dr. Karen Antonovich (1994) .... Margaret Colin
Dr. Billy Kronk (1995–1999) .... Peter Berg
**Laurie Geiger (1994–1995)* .... Kim Griest
Nurse Maggie Atkisson (1994–1995) .. Robyn Lively
Dr. Geri Infante (1994–1995) .... Diane Venora
Dr. Dennis Hancock (1995–1999) .... Vondie Curtis-Hall
Dr. Diane Grad (1995–1999) .... Jayne Brook
**Judge Harold Aldrich (1994–1996)* .... Stephen Elliott
Dr. Kathryn Austin (1995–1999) .... Christine Lahti
**Maggie Murphy (1996–1997)* ...... Maggie Murphy
Dr. John Sutton (1995–1996) .... Jamey Sheridan
Tommy Wilmette (1996–1997) .... Ron Silver
**Sara Wilmette (1996–1999)* .... Mae Whitman
Dr. Jack McNeil (1996–2000) .... Mark Harmon
Dr. Keith Wilkes (1996–2000) .... Rocky Carroll
Dr. Grace Carr (1996) .... Vanessa L. Williams
Dr. Sean Underhill (1996) .... John DiMaggio
Dr. Caroline Eggert (1996) .... Sam Jenkins
**Dr. Lloyd Chernow (1996–1998)* .... Stu Charno
**Karen Wilder (1996–1998)* .... Kathryn Harrold
Tracey Doyle, R.N. (1997–1998) .... Vanessia Valentino
Dr. Joseph Cacaci (1997–1999) .... Bob Bancroft
Dr. Lisa Catera (1997–1999) .... Stacy Edwards
Danny Blaines (1997–1998) .... Jason Beghe
Dr. Scott Frank (1997–1998) ...... George Newbern
Dr. Robert Yeats (1998–1999) .... Eric Stolz
Dr. Jeremy Hanlon (1999–2000) ...... Lauren Holly
Dr. Gina Simon (1999–2000) .... Carla Gugino
Dr. Francesca Alberghetti (1999–2000) .... Barbara Hershey
Stuart Brickman (1999–2000) ..... Alan Rosenberg
Hugh Miller (2000) .... James Garner

*Occasional

Chicago Hope Hospital, a high-tech medical facility in America's second city, was the setting for this drama about the professional and personal lives of its talented staff. Dr. Geiger was a brilliant, but difficult, surgeon. His proclivity for trying experimental, and often unauthorized, procedures, insensitive bedside manner, and hair-trigger temper did not endear him to his fellow doctors. His best friend, neurosurgeon Aaron Shutt, was as compassionate as Geiger was brusque; he had been served with divorce papers by his wife, Camille, the chief surgical operating nurse, but at midseason they were working at saving their marriage. Other featured members of Chicago Hope's staff were Dr. Watters, the overburdened chief of staff who tried to balance his and his fellow surgeons' wants with the economic realities of modern medical care; Dr. Thurmond, the renowned but aging former star of the surgical staff who had trouble accepting his increasingly secondary role; and Alan Birch, the hospital's legal counsel, who spent most of his time trying to keep the doctors, usually Geiger, and Chicago Hope itself, out of major lawsuits.

When it premiered in 1994, directly opposite NBC's more successful medical drama *ER*, *Chicago Hope* struggled to find an audience. Part of the problem may have been its tone, which was deadly serious. By the end of the year the episodes began to include lighter elements, a number of younger staff members were introduced—Dr. Kronk, Dr. Grad, and Nurse Atkisson—and even Geiger started to soften up. His wife, Laurie, who had been institutionalized after murdering their young son, was seeking a divorce, and he had begun a relationship with Dr. Infante, the best reconstructive (cosmetic) surgeon on Chicago Hope's staff.

In Fall 1995 outspoken, contentious Kate Austin joined the staff as a new cardiothoracic surgeon, and soon alienated Geiger by suggesting ways Chicago Hope could cut costs. In November, Birch was shot seven times by an agitated street gang member, and just when everyone thought he was recovering, had a relapse and died. Geiger took a leave of absence to care for Birch's adopted baby daughter, Alicia, leaving Austin as the hospital's star surgeon—she applied for the position of Chief of Surgery in February. Kronk and Nyland founded an unlicensed clinic for the poor, and Nyland decided to keep it running to serve the community. He got some help and supplies from Hancock, who eventually took over the reins. In the spring Diane and Billy began dating. They went to Africa to do research, and after they both got back, their relationship became serious. Camille, who had divorced Aaron earlier in the season, quit Chicago Hope because of a dispute over the lack of support E.R. nurses received from the staff. The season ended with the hospital on the verge of being sold to a group headed by Austin's vindictive ex-husband, Tommy Wilmette, to whom she had lost custody of their daughter, Sara.

There were two major staff additions in 1996: Keith Wilkes, who replaced Nyland as head of the trauma unit when the latter was suspended for an indiscretion with a patient's wife; and Jack McNeil, a gifted orthopedic surgeon with a gambling problem. McNeil had an on-again, off-again relationship with Karen Wilder, a classmate who had quit medical school before graduating. Austin was also on suspension for leaving Chicago with Sara in violation of her visitation agreement. When the suspensions were reviewed, Nyland was forced to work under Wilkes—they were constantly at odds—and left the hospital at the end of the season. Austin was also reinstated, but with her salary reduced and stripped of the Chief of Surgery title. In the spring Tommy gave custody of Sara back to Austin when he moved to Washington, D.C.

The 1997–1998 season brought a number of changes. Many of the doctors had invested in what was now the restructured Hope HealthCare consortium, in which the absent Dr. Geiger (who showed up once or twice a season as a guest star, after his departure) had purchased controlling interest. A new regular was annoying Dr. Cacaci, a pompous ass with no bedside manner who alienated anyone—staff or patient—with whom he came in contact. Billy and Diane were engaged, and because of cutbacks in her research funding, she was working in the E.R. Diane found out she was pregnant just before Billy left for a four-month medical sabbatical in South America, and they got married at the airport just before his departure. In October, McNeil joined Gamblers Anonymous, Hancock revealed he was gay, and Shutt suffered a brain aneurysm that left his ability to perform delicate surgery in doubt. Lisa Catera was hired to assist him, and eventually took over most of the work while he began a psychiatric residency. In April, Diane gave birth to a daughter, Emily, and the following week Dr. Watters's son committed suicide.

In the fall of 1998, Austin was accepted into NASA's "Doctors in Space" program, and Shutt, who had recently regained his ability to operate, was torn between neurosurgery and psychiatry. New to the staff was Robert Yeats, a brilliant but eccentric young diagnostician—a Buddhist, and proponent of yoga and Eastern medicine. In the spring Kate suffered internal injuries in a car accident that forced her out of the space program, Watters successfully fought an attempt by nasty Cacaci to have him removed for a romantic encounter he had had with a former patient and, in the season finale, Geiger returned as chairman of the hospital board of directors and summarily fired Austin, Hancock, Catera, Yeats, and Kronk (Grad also left to be with her husband), because, as he said—"This reflects a new direction in hospital policy. We'd like to see more of our patients discharged . . . alive."

New to the cast that fall were Dr. Simon, a neurosurgeon specializing in pediatrics; Dr. Hanlon, a plastic surgeon who used money from her lucrative cosmetic surgery to fund her experimental work in reconstructive surgery; Dr. Alberghetti, a dedicated thoracic surgeon; and Stuart Brickman, Chicago Hope's new legal counsel. In October obnoxious Cacaci, who had been seeing a psychiatrist for a long time, committed suicide by jumping off the sixth-floor roof of the hospital. In April Hugh Miller, a smooth-talking medical care manipulator from Stanwood Consolidated Enterprises, arrived and told the staff that he had purchased Chicago Hope and was turning it into a for-profit HMO. The following week he fired McNeil for performing an unauthorized hip replacement. In the series finale, with Chicago Hope still losing money, Stanwood decided to sell off the equipment and fire the doctors. Miller, however, gambled on the stock of a company owned by a paralyzed genius with the idea for a microchip that would give mobility back to the paralyzed. McNeil performed the surgery on him, the stock took off, and Miller sold at a big enough profit to bail out the hospital. Unfortunately, while they were celebrating, the genius went into cardiac arrest and, in the last scene, had gone flatline.

CHICAGO JAZZ (*Music*)
FIRST TELECAST: *November 26, 1949*
LAST TELECAST: *December 31, 1949*
BROADCAST HISTORY:
Nov 1949–Dec 1949, NBC Sat 8:30–8:45
REGULARS:
Art Van Damme Quintette
The Tailgate Seven

A live musical interlude from Chicago, this short-lived program was also known as *Sessions*. The Art Van Damme Quintette was featured on the first telecast, and The Tailgate Seven on the rest.

CHICAGO SONS (*Situation Comedy*)
FIRST TELECAST: *January 8, 1997*
LAST TELECAST: *July 2, 1997*
BROADCAST HISTORY:
Jan 1997–Mar 1997, NBC Wed 8:30–9:00
Jun 1997–Jul 1997, NBC Wed 9:30–10:00
CAST:
Harry Kulchak .... Jason Bateman
Mike Kulchak .... D.W. Moffett
Billy Kulchak .... David Krumholtz
Lindsay Sutton .... Paula Marshall

The testosterone flowed freely in this lightweight sitcom about three skirt-chasing brothers living in a bachelor dream pad overlooking Chicago's Wrigley Field. Harry, the most responsible (relatively speaking), worked as a junior architect and had the hots for co-worker Lindsay. She, unfortunately, already had a boyfriend of five years. In the spare bedroom was Harry's dumb, insensitive older brother Mike, who had been kicked out of his house by his fed-up wife, but nevertheless had babes hanging on him. On the couch was college dropout Billy, the wisecracking, boyish-looking youngest of the clan. They all hung out at Murphy's Bar, when not drinking milk right out of the carton or watching a Cubs game from the roof.

CHICAGO STORY (*Drama*)
FIRST TELECAST: *March 6, 1982*
LAST TELECAST: *August 27, 1982*
BROADCAST HISTORY:
Mar 1982–Apr 1982, NBC Sat 8:30–10:00
Apr 1982–Aug 1982, NBC Fri 8:30–10:00
CAST:
Dr. Judith Bergstrom .... Maud Adams
Lou Pellegrino .... Vincent Baggetta
Megan Powers .... Molly Cheek
Officer Joe Gilland .... Dennis Franz
Annie Gilland .... Connie Foster
Det. Frank Wajorski .... Daniel Hugh-Kelly

Det. O. Z. Tate .... Richard Lawson
Kenneth A. Dutton .... Craig T. Nelson
Dr. Max Carson .... Kristoffer Tabori
Lt. Roselli .... John Mahoney
Carol .... Jill Shellabarger

Set in Chicago, this series followed the professional and personal lives of three groups of people—doctors, lawyers, and police officers—whose paths often crossed. Judith Bergstrom and Max Carson were surgeons in the trauma unit at Cook County Hospital. Lou Pellegrino was a stubborn public defender whose penniless clients were often prosecuted by young assistant D.A. Kenneth Dutton. Outside the courtroom Lou and Ken were good friends, but in it they were sworn enemies, a situation that tended to make things uncomfortable for their mutual friend and fellow attorney, Megan Powers. The Chicago police included hardworking, married beat cop Joe Gilland and two plainclothes detectives, old pro O. Z. Tate and young partner Frank Wajorski. When the people being pursued by the police got hurt they often ended up in the Cook County Hospital trauma unit and, when they got out of the hospital, they went to trial. Because of the 90-minute format of the show, each of the principals in *Chicago Story* was regularly featured, along with plenty of Chicago scenery.

CHICAGO SYMPHONY (*Music*)

FIRST TELECAST: *January 6, 1954*
LAST TELECAST: *April 6, 1955*
BROADCAST HISTORY:
Jan 1954–Mar 1954, DUM Wed 8:30–9:00
Sep 1954–Apr 1955, DUM Wed 9:00–10:00
CONDUCTORS:
Fritz Reiner
George Schick
COMMENTATOR:
George Kuyper

George Kuyper, orchestra manager of the Chicago Symphony, introduced the various pieces performed in this weekly classical-music series. During the intermissions, he also provided commentary and information about the composers and their works from "The Music Room." The principal conductor of the Chicago Symphony at this time was Fritz Reiner, who for most of this series shared the podium with associate conductor George Schick. During the first four weeks of the 1954–1955 season, before the start of the Chicago Symphony season, this time period was occupied by *Concert Tonight,* performances by the New York Concert Choir and Orchestra under the baton of Margaret Hillis.

CHICAGO SYMPHONY CHAMBER ORCHESTRA (*Music*)

FIRST TELECAST: *September 25, 1951*
LAST TELECAST: *March 18, 1952*
BROADCAST HISTORY:
Sep 1951–Mar 1952, ABC Tue 10:30–11:00
ANNOUNCER:
Ken Nordine

With 25 to 30 members of the Chicago Symphony under the baton of Rafael Kubelik, this program featured soloists from the orchestra and guest vocalists. Some of the presentations were not carried over the full ABC network. ABC also carried occasional telecasts of the Chicago Symphony during the fall of 1948 under the titles *Chamber Music Hour* and *Chamber Music.* The 1951–1952 series was also known simply as *The Symphony.*

CHICAGO TEDDY BEARS, THE (*Situation Comedy*)

FIRST TELECAST: *September 17, 1971*
LAST TELECAST: *December 17, 1971*
BROADCAST HISTORY:
Sep 1971–Dec 1971, CBS Fri 8:00–8:30
CAST:
Linc McCray .... Dean Jones
Nick Marr .... Art Metrano
Marvin .... Marvin Kaplan
Duke .... Mickey Shaughnessy
Lefty .... Jamie Farr
Julius .... Mike Mazurki
Dutch .... Huntz Hall
Uncle Latzi .... John Banner

Linc McCray and his Uncle Latzi were partners in a Chicago speakeasy during the late 1920s in this period comedy. The speakeasy did good business and was coveted by a small-time gangster, Big Nick Marr, whose efforts to muscle in on the operation provided much of the action. It was all a family affair, since Linc and Nick were cousins and both were nephews of Uncle Latzi, who couldn't believe that his nephew Nicholas could be anything but a nice young man. Everyone else was terrified of Big Nick, however, including Marvin, Linc's bookkeeper, and the club's four inept bodyguards, Duke, Lefty, Julius, and Dutch.

CHICAGOLAND MYSTERY PLAYERS (*Police Drama*)

FIRST TELECAST: *September 18, 1949*
LAST TELECAST: *July 30, 1950*
BROADCAST HISTORY:
Sep 1949–Jul 1950, DUM Sun 8:00–8:30
CAST:
Jeffrey Hall .... Gordon Urquhart
Sgt. Holland .... Bob Smith

Chicagoland Mystery Players was a good example of Chicago-based dramatic programming in the early days of television. The format was that of a straight crime drama, with criminologist Jeffrey Hall and his partner, Sgt. Holland, tracking down criminals in stories such as "The Fangs of Death," "Tryst with a Dummy," and "Kiss of Death." The program had been seen locally on Chicago television for two years before its network run. During its local days viewers were not shown the solution of the night's crime, but were told to pick up a copy of the next day's *Chicago Tribune* for the outcome—a nice commercial tie-in.

CHICKEN SOUP (*Situation Comedy*)

FIRST TELECAST: *September 12, 1989*
LAST TELECAST: *November 7, 1989*
BROADCAST HISTORY:
Sep 1989–Nov 1989, ABC Tue 9:30–10:00
CAST:
Jackie Fisher .... Jackie Mason
Maddie Peerce .... Lynn Redgrave
Bea Fisher .... Rita Karin
Patricia Peerce (age 17) .... Kathryn Erbe
Donnie Peerce (11) .... Johnny Pinto

Molly Peerce (8) .... Alisan Porter
Mike Donovan .... Brandon Maggart
Barbara Donovan .... Cathy Lind Hayes

One of the more celebrated flops of the 1989–1990 season was this comedy of mixed religions. The premise was the same as in *Bridget Loves Bernie* seventeen years earlier: a New York Jewish man falls in love with an Irish Catholic woman, to the intense disapproval of their families. Jackie was a short, 52-year-old former pajama salesman who had given up his job to do volunteer work at an inner-city community center. His neighbor and co-worker Maddie was a tall, somewhat younger widow with three kids. Jackie's stereotypical nagging Jewish mother Bea disliked the relationship, as did Maddie's bigoted brother Mike. Unfortunately, wisecracking comic Jackie Mason did not seem to generate much electricity onscreen with English actress Lynn Redgrave. Probably the best part of each show was when Jackie went up to his rooftop alone to *kvetch* about life—essentially his standup comedy routine.

There were predictable complaints from protest groups about the series (the Jewish Defense League wanted an all-Jewish cast, or for Maddie to convert), but they scarcely had time to get out their placards before *Chicken Soup* was canceled a few weeks into the season.

CHICKEN SOUP FOR THE SOUL (*Dramatic Anthology*)

FIRST TELECAST: *August 24, 1999*
LAST TELECAST: *July 23, 2000*
BROADCAST HISTORY:

Aug 1999–Jul 2000, PAX Tue 8:00–9:00
Aug 1999–Oct 1999, PAX Sun 7:00–8:00
Oct 1999, PAX Fri 11:00–midnight
Nov 1999–Jul 2000, PAX Sun 11:00–midnight

HOST:

Michael Tucker

This anthology series provided viewers with heart-warming, uplifting stories about the human condition and the ways in which individuals obtained emotional nourishment from others in their times of need. Each episode contained several separate vignettes, varying in length, but all with positive messages. Among those appearing were Shirley Knight, Teri Garr, Ray Walston, Harold Gould, Shelley Long, William Windom, Joe Piscopo, Stephanie Zimbalist, Tracey Gold, Marion Ross, and Jill Eikenberry (in a segment with her husband, series host Michael Tucker).

Adapted from the *Chicken Soup for the Soul* books written by Jack Canfield and Mark Victor Hansen.

CHICO AND THE MAN (*Situation Comedy*)

FIRST TELECAST: *September 13, 1974*
LAST TELECAST: *July 21, 1978*
BROADCAST HISTORY:

Sep 1974–Jan 1976, NBC Fri 8:30–9:00
Jan 1976–Mar 1976, NBC Wed 9:00–9:30
Apr 1976–Aug 1976, NBC Wed 9:30–10:00
Aug 1976–Feb 1978, NBC Fri 8:30–9:00
Jun 1978–Jul 1978, NBC Fri 8:30–9:00

CAST:

Ed Brown (The Man)................ Jack Albertson
Chico Rodriguez (1974–1977)....... Freddie Prinze
Louie .... Scatman Crothers
Mabel (1974–1975)................ Bonnie Boland
Mando (1974–1977).................... Isaac Ruiz
Rev. Bemis (1975–1976)............ Ronny Graham
Della Rogers (1976–1978).............. Della Reese
Raul Garcia (1977–1978)........... Gabriel Melgar
Aunt Charo (1977–1978)..................... Charo

THEME:

"Chico and the Man," written and performed by Jose Feliciano

Set in the barrio of East Los Angeles, *Chico and the Man* was the story of two men from radically different cultural backgrounds who grew to respect each other. Chico, the enterprising young Chicano, was determined to go into partnership with cranky, sarcastic, cynical Ed Brown. Ed operated a small, run-down garage and spent most of his time complaining and alienating people. A lonely widower, he at first fought Chico's determined efforts to help him make the business work, but underneath it all he was both flattered and touched to have someone show genuine interest in him. Chico cleaned the place up, moved into a beat-up old truck in the garage, and brought in business. As often as Ed complained about Chico, and as often as he made token efforts to get rid of him, he felt an attachment that he would never publicly admit.

Regularly seen were Louie the garbageman, Mabel the mailwoman, and Chico's friend Mando. Della Rogers was added to the cast in the fall of 1976 as the civic-minded owner of the diner across the street from Ed's Garage, who also happened to be the new owner of the property on which the garage was located. She was more than capable of dishing out as much as she took from Ed.

When Freddy Prinze took his own life early in 1977, prior to the completion of the season's episodes, there was serious consideration given to the cancellation of the series. That was not done, however, as a new "Chico" was added to the cast for the following fall.

He was not an adult, though, or even someone whose name was really Chico. In the opening episode of the 1977–1978 season it was established that Chico had left Ed's garage to go into business with his successful father, a character introduced the previous year and played by Cesar Romero. Later, Ed and Louie returned from a fishing trip to Tijuana to discover a 12-year-old stowaway in their car trunk. The boy, Raul, ingratiated himself with Ed and became his personal resident alien. At the end of that first episode, when the two of them were preparing to go to bed, Ed inadvertently said "Good night, Chico" to his new friend and, when corrected, simply said, "You're all Chicos to me." Thus a new "Chico" for "The Man." Ed eventually adopted Raul and found himself contending with Raul's protective, and very sexy, Aunt Charo, an entertainer who had recently arrived from Spain to work in Los Angeles. She spent so much time at Ed's garage with her nephew that she, too, became part of the family.

NBC aired reruns of *Chico and the Man* from May to December 1977 in its weekday daytime lineup.

CHILDREN'S SKETCH BOOK (*Children's*)

FIRST TELECAST: *January 7, 1950*
LAST TELECAST: *February 4, 1950*
BROADCAST HISTORY:

Jan 1950–Feb 1950, NBC Sat 7:00–7:30

STORYTELLER:

Edith Skinner

ILLUSTRATOR:

Lisl Weil

In this live children's program, Edith Skinner told stories in rhyme, accompanied by songs and drawings made by Lisl Weil. The show had formerly been on the network during the afternoon.

CHILD'S WORLD (*Children's Discussion*)
FIRST TELECAST: *November 1, 1948*
LAST TELECAST: *April 27, 1949*
BROADCAST HISTORY:
Nov 1948–Jan 1949, ABC Tue 7:30–7:45
Jan 1949–Apr 1949, ABC Wed 7:15–7:30
HOSTESS:
Helen Parkhurst

Child's World was an experiment in drawing out children's real feelings through spontaneous discussions. Youngsters ranging in age from 8 to 13 met in Miss Parkhurst's apartment and discussed such topics as jealousy, God, prejudice, and school.

CHIMP CHANNEL, THE (*Situation Comedy*)
BROADCAST HISTORY:
TBS
30 minutes
Original episodes: *1999* (13 episodes)
Premiered: *June 10, 1999*
VOICES:
Ford Carter, George W. Heinlein ..... Richard Doyle
Harry Waller, Bernard the Sarcastic Cockatoo ..... Maurice LaMarche
Brock Hammond, Announcer .... Daran Norris
Murray Price .... Eugene Roche
Marina .... Jennifer Hale
Candy Yuponce .... Mindy Cohn
Bif .... Michael Donovan
Stan .... Dwight Schultz
Timmy Briar .... Richard Steven Horvitz
Joel .... Dan Redican
Old Rose .... Deborah Theaker

The Chimp Channel resembled *Saturday Night Live* played by chimps. It was set at a cable network called TCC (The Chimp Channel), where everyone from the executives behind the scenes to the stars were costumed, chattering chimps. Ford Carter was the tycoon owner, Harry his cultured network president (complete with a British accent) and Timmy an intern. In front of the cameras were studly superstar Brock, talk-show host Murray, stately anchorman George, and screaming diva Marina, among others. Their shows, depicted in skits, included such favorites as *NYPD Zoo, Touched by an Anvil, Treewatch, Ally McSqueal, Buffy* (she killed everyone) and *America's Most Uncomfortable Videos.*

This mercifully short-lived sitcom was spun off from the short "Monkey-ed Movies" parodies previously seen within and between regular TBS films.

CHINA BEACH (*War Drama*)
FIRST TELECAST: *April 26, 1988*
LAST TELECAST: *July 22, 1991*
BROADCAST HISTORY:
Apr 1988, ABC Tue 9:00–11:00
Apr 1988–Jun 1988, ABC Wed 10:00–11:00
Aug 1988–Sep 1988, ABC Wed 10:00–11:00
Nov 1988–Mar 1990, ABC Wed 10:00–11:00
Apr 1990, ABC Mon 9:00–10:00
Jul 1990–Aug 1990, ABC Wed 10:00–11:00
Aug 1990–Dec 1990, ABC Sat 9:00–10:00
Jun 1991–Jul 1991, ABC Tue 10:00–11:00
Jul 1991, ABC Mon 9:00–11:00
CAST:
Nurse Colleen McMurphy .... Dana Delany
Cherry White (1988–1989) .... Nan Woods
Laurette Barber (1988) .... Chloe Webb
Karen Charlene (K. C.) Koloski . Marg Helgenberger
Pvt. Sam Beckett .... Michael Boatman
Dr. Dick Richard .... Robert Picardo
Natch Austen (1988–1989) .... Tim Ryan
Maj. Lila Garreau .... Concetta Tomei
Boonie Lanier .... Brian Wimmer
Wayloo Marie Holmes (1988–1989) ..... Megan Gallagher
Pvt. Frankie Bunsen .... Nancy Giles
Dodger .... Jeff Kober
Jeff Hyers (1989) .... Ned Vaughn
Sgt. Pepper (1989–1991) .... Troy Evans
Holly the Donut Dolly (1989–1990) ...... Ricki Lake
THEME:
"Reflections," sung by Diana Ross and the Supremes

Television has had a difficult time adapting the Vietnam war to the small screen. How do you get women (the audience advertisers want to reach) to watch a mostly male war, especially one that was considered rather unheroic? CBS tried and failed with the gritty *Tour of Duty*, but ABC had better luck by treating the conflict as soap opera, set on a beach and with plenty of women. Like *M*A*S*H,* this version also had a strong anti-war point of view.

The premise was plausible, even if it did not look like the Vietnam most veterans probably remember. China Beach was a combination evacuation hospital and USO entertainment center near the big U.S. base at Da Nang, on the South China Sea. Most of the stories revolved around McMurphy, a conscientious nurse who had affairs with pilot Natch and several others who passed through the base. Her true love was Dr. Dick, but he was married; although his marriage was troubled, their love was never to be. Early episodes also featured Laurette, a professional singer with plans for the big time; Wayloo Marie, an ambitious on-air personality; and Cherry, a Red Cross worker who was killed in the 1968 Tet Offensive. Others whose lives and loves unfolded over the years included officious Major Lila (who eventually married Sgt. Pepper from the motor pool!); her assistant, ambitious K. C. (a hooker and heroin addict); and Dodger, who fathered an Amerasian child. Adding some black humor were sarcastic Beckett, who ran the morgue, and portly Holly, the Donut Dolly, from the Red Cross.

The series did not flinch from a graphic portrayal of the horror and stress of war, and there was much period flavor, including incessant 1960s rock 'n' roll songs and references to contemporary turmoil in the United States. By the final season episodes were alternating between Vietnam and the States, with "flash-forwards" to the 1980s as the principals looked back on their wartime experiences.

CHINA SMITH (*Adventure*)
BROADCAST HISTORY:
Syndicated only
30 minutes
Produced *Jun 1952–1955* (52 episodes)
Released: *Fall 1952*

CAST:

China Smith .... Dan Duryea
Inspector Hobson .... Douglas Dumbrille
Shira ("Empress") .... Myrna Dell

Tough-guy movie actor Dan Duryea, who made a name for himself slugging Joan Bennett in *The Woman in the Window* (1944), carried on in two-fisted style in this 1950s syndicated adventure. China Smith was an opportunistic con artist and sometimes private eye, operating out of a bar in Singapore, who roamed the Orient in search of adventure and a fast buck. He had an eye for beautiful women, and they all seemed to fall for his wisecracks and Irish brogue, despite—or perhaps because of—his tendency to play rough. Douglas Dumbrille was the very British police inspector, and Myrna Dell the scheming and powerful "Empress."

Two groups of *China Smith* films were made, the first 26 in 1952 (shot in Mexico), and the second 26 in 1954–1955, the latter being syndicated as *The New Adventures of China Smith.* Also known as *The Affairs of China Smith.*

CHiPS (*Police Drama*)

FIRST TELECAST: *September 15, 1977*
LAST TELECAST: *July 17, 1983*
BROADCAST HISTORY:

Sep 1977–Mar 1978, NBC Thu 8:00–9:00
Apr 1978, NBC Sat 8:00–9:00
May 1978–Aug 1978, NBC Thu 8:00–9:00
Sep 1978–Mar 1980, NBC Sat 8:00–9:00
Mar 1980–Mar 1983, NBC Sun 8:00–9:00
Apr 1983–May 1983, NBC Sun 7:00–8:00
May 1983–Jul 1983, NBC Sun 8:00–9:00

CAST:

Officer Jon Baker (1977–1982) .... Larry Wilcox
Officer Frank "Ponch" Poncherello .... Erik Estrada
Sgt. Joe Getraer .... Robert Pine
Officer Gene Fritz (1977–1981) ...... Lew Saunders
Officer Baricza (1977–1982) .... Brodie Greer
Officer Sindy Cahill (1978–1979) .... Brianne Leary
Harlan (1978–1983) .... Lou Wagner
Officer Grossman .... Paul Linke
Officer Bonnie Clark (1979–1982) ..... Randi Oakes
Officer Turner (1980–1982) .... Michael Dorn
Officer Bobby Nelson (1982–1983) ...... Tom Reilly
Officer Kathy Linahan (1982–1983) ..... Tina Gayle
Cadet Bruce Nelson (1982–1983) .... Bruce Penhall
Officer Webster (1982–1983) ... Clarence Gilyard, Jr.

CHiPs, an acronym for California Highway Patrol, was the motorcycle equivalent to a previous episodic police series, *Adam 12.* Jon Baker and "Ponch" Poncherello were two state motorcycle patrolmen, both young bachelors, whose adventures helping citizens, fighting crime, and leading active social lives were all woven into the series. The two men worked as a team, and spent most of their working time around the vast Los Angeles freeway system. Each episode was a composite of four or five separate incidents, both on the job and off, with violence downplayed in favor of human interest and the humorous elements of their work. Jon was rather straight and serious, while "Ponch" was the romantic free spirit, whose happy-go-lucky attitude did not always sit well with their superior, Sgt. Getraer. Added in 1978 were Harlan, a police mechanic who worked on their "choppers," and Sindy, a female "Chippie" who worked out of a patrol car. She was replaced, the following fall, by another female "Chippie," Bonnie Clark.

Former Olympic decathlon champion Bruce Jenner appeared as Officer Steve McLeish in several episodes in the fall of 1981 as a temporary replacement for Erik Estrada, who was embroiled in a salary dispute with *CHiPs'* producers. When Estrada returned, Jenner left the show. The fall of 1982 brought a number of cast changes. Larry Wilcox, who had had a stormy relationship with Estrada for several years, quit the series. Ponch got a new partner, Bobby Nelson, and Nelson's kid brother Bruce (played by professional motorcycle racer Bruce Penhall) joined the force as a trainee. The new resident "Chippie" was Kathy Linahan.

NBC aired reruns of *CHiPs* on weekday afternoons from April 1980–September 1980.

CHISHOLMS, THE (*Western*)

FIRST TELECAST: *March 29, 1979*
LAST TELECAST: *March 15, 1980*
BROADCAST HISTORY:

Mar 1979–Apr 1979, CBS Thu 8:00–9:00
Jan 1980–Mar 1980, CBS Sat 8:00–9:00

CAST:

Hadley Chisholm .... Robert Preston
Minerva Chisholm .... Rosemary Harris
Will Chisholm .... Ben Murphy
Gideon Chisholm (1979) .... Brian Kerwin
Gideon Chisholm (1980) .... Brett Cullen
Bo Chisholm .... James Van Patten
Bonnie Sue Chisholm (1979) .... Stacey Nelkin
Bonnie Sue Chisholm (1980) .... Delta Burke
Annabel Chisholm (1979) .... Susan Swift
Mercy Hopwell (1980) .... Susan Swift
Cooper Hawkins (1980) .... Mitchell Ryan
Kewedinok .... Victoria Racimo
Lester Hackett (1979) .... Charles Frank
Lester Hackett (1980) .... Reid Smith
Betsy O'Neal (1980) .... Devon Ericson
Frank O'Neal (1980) .... Guich Koock
Jeremy O'Neal (1980) .... Les Lannom
McVeety (1980) .... Frank Noel
Tehohane (1980) .... Nick Ramus

Originally aired as a four-part mini-series in the spring of 1979, *The Chisholms* attracted a sufficiently large audience to encourage CBS to bring it back the following January. It was soap-opera-cum-Western. The Chisholm clan, led by patriarch Hadley and his wife Minerva, were a poor but industrious Virginia family of the 1840s who lost their land in a legal dispute. With little money but a lot of gumption they began a journey to California, in search of a new life. The original mini-series chronicled the arduous trip from Virginia to Fort Laramie, Wyoming, in the course of which the youngest daughter Annabel died during an Indian attack; son Will married an Indian woman, Kewedinok; and daughter Bonnie Sue had an illegitimate child by con man and gambler Lester Hackett, who had joined them in Louisville. When *The Chisholms* returned in 1980, the family was part of a wagon train, led by Cooper Hawkins, traveling from Fort Laramie to California. En route Hadley, having fallen ill, passed away. Not long thereafter, so did the entire series.

CHOPPER ONE (*Police Drama*)

FIRST TELECAST: *January 17, 1974*

LAST TELECAST: *July 11, 1974*

BROADCAST HISTORY:

Jan 1974–Jul 1974, ABC Thu 8:00–8:30

CAST:

Officer Don Burdick .... Jim McMullan
Officer Gil Foley .... Dirk Benedict
Capt. McKeegan .... Ted Hartley
Mitch .... Lou Frizzel

In this action drama, two young "chopper cops" were assigned to police helicopter duty in a large California city. Among their adversaries were rooftop snipers, muggers in the parks, and other desperados foolish enough to work in the open—including one sniper whose goal in life was to shoot down police helicopters. Lou Frizzel played Mitch, the copter mechanic.

CHRIS WYLDE SHOW, THE (*Talk/Comedy*)

BROADCAST HISTORY:

Comedy Central
30 minutes
Original episodes: *2001* (3 episodes?)
Premiered: *August 5, 2001*

CAST:

Chris Wylde .... Himself
Forty .... Brian Walsh
Corey Feldman .... Himself

A short-lived late-night talk/sketch-comedy show hosted by Wylde, a young guy with wild hair, a hip "baggy" look, and gross-out humor that Comedy Central executives obviously thought would appeal to the younger generation. It didn't. "Forty" was his slacker sidekick, and Cousin Michael (Michael Ghegan) and the All Stars his funky band.

CHRISTINE CROMWELL (*Crime Drama*)

FIRST TELECAST: *November 11, 1989*

LAST TELECAST: *March 24, 1990*

BROADCAST HISTORY:

Nov 1989–Mar 1990, ABC Sat 9:00–11:00

CAST:

Christine Cromwell .... Jaclyn Smith
Samantha Cromwell .... Celeste Holm
Cyrus Blain .... Ralph Bellamy
Sarah .... Rebecca Cross

Murder mysteries among the super-rich. Elegant Christine Cromwell was born to wealth and privilege, but she was nevertheless a self-made woman. After earning degrees in business and law, she had worked as a public defender and then accepted a position with one of San Francisco's most prestigious investment management firms. As a financial advisor to the rich, she was drawn into their affairs, which usually led her to dastardly crimes, including murder. Samantha was Christine's oft-married mother; Cyrus, the avuncular head of her investment firm; and Sarah, her well-meaning but naive secretary.

Christine Cromwell was one of the rotating elements of the *ABC Mystery Movie* and was seen every month or so.

CHRISTY (*Drama*)

FIRST TELECAST: *April 3, 1994*

LAST TELECAST: *August 2, 1995*

BROADCAST HISTORY:

Apr 1994, CBS Sun 8:00–10:00
Apr 1994–May 1994, CBS Thu 8:00–9:00
Aug 1994–Sep 1994, CBS Wed 9:00–10:00
Jun 1995–Aug 1995, CBS Wed 8:00–9:00

CAST:

Christy Huddleston .... Kellie Martin
Alice Henderson .... Tyne Daly
Rev. David Grantland .... Randall Batinkoff
Fairlight Spencer .... Tess Harper
Miss Ida Grantland .... Annabella Price
Dr. Neil MacNeill .... Stewart Finlay-McLennan
Ruby Mae Morrison .... Emily Schulman
Little Burl Allen .... Andy Nichols
Uncle Bogg .... Frank Hoyt Taylor
Creed Allen .... Clay Jeter
Jeb Spencer .... Bruce McKinnon
Zady Spencer .... Jenny Krochmal
Mountie O'Teale .... Alyssa Hmielewski
Sam Houston Holcombe .... Kyle Hudgens
Ben Pentland .... Chelcie Ross
Rob Allen .... Jack Landry
Bob Allen .... Jeffrey Ford
Mary Allen .... Bonita Allen
John Spencer .... Sam Tyler-Wayman
Opal McHone .... Dale Dickey
Daniel Scott (1995) .... LeVar Burton

Adapted from the novel by Catherine Marshall, *Christy* was the heartwarming story of a spunky young woman who, in 1912 at the age of nineteen, left a comfortable life in Asheville, Tennessee, to teach at a missionary school in the remote Appalachian community of Cutter Gap. Christy's inspiration had come from a speech made at her church by Alice Henderson, the imposing, strong-willed Quaker who ran the mission school with her towering son-in-law, the Reverend David Grantland, who had built it. It was Miss Alice's support and counsel that kept Christy in Cutter Gap when she had misgivings about being there, and it was her newfound friendship with Fairlight, a local mountain woman, that gave her insights into the customs and lifestyles of the residents of the impoverished, almost illiterate community. Christy persevered, despite the harsh living conditions, the blood feuds among local families, and the hostility of many of the natives threatened by the educated, more civilized lifestyle she represented. Christy also had her problems with Miss Ida, David's older sister, the mission's housekeeper and cook, who feared he and Christy would become romantically involved.

In the summer of 1995, Cutter Gap got its first black resident, Daniel Scott, who moved to Cutter Gap to study medicine as an apprentice to Dr. MacNeill.

CHRONICLE (*Documentary*)

FIRST TELECAST: *October 2, 1963*

LAST TELECAST: *April 22, 1964*

BROADCAST HISTORY:

Oct 1963–Apr 1964, CBS Wed 7:30–8:30

HOST:

Charles Collingwood

Chronicle was aired during the 1963–1964 season on an alternating basis with *CBS Reports.* Whereas *CBS Reports* was known for its hard-news documentaries, *Chronicle* sought to look at the cultural side of contemporary society and the roots from which that culture developed. Episodes in the series covered such diverse subjects as the British music hall, the writings of Edgar Allan Poe, political and social revolution in the 20th century, and the Constitution of the United States.

CHRONICLE, THE (*Science Fiction*)

BROADCAST HISTORY:

Sci-Fi Channel
60 minutes
Original episodes: *2001–2002* (22 episodes)
Premiered: *July 14, 2001*

CAST:

Tucker Burns .... Chad Willett
Grace Hall .... Rena Sofer
Wes Freewald .... Reno Wilson
Donald Stern .... Jon Polito
Sal the Pig-Boy .... Curtis Armstrong
Kristen Martin .... Elaine Hendrix
Vera .... Sharon Sachs
Ruby .... Octavia L. Spencer

Disgraced journalist Tucker Burns, whose career had been ruined when he was "tricked" into writing a false exposé for the *New York Times*, thought he had hit rock bottom when he wound up working for the disreputable *World Chronicle*, a sensationalizing tabloid that reported on ghosts, mermaids, alien abductions and dragons in the sewers. To his surprise he found that most of its bizarre stories were true, even if they were not always what they seemed (the dragon in the sewer, for example, turned out to be man-made). Helping the altruistic Tucker were saucy reporter Grace, herself an alien abductee, and foxy black dude Wes, their photographer. Stern was the grumpy, bald boss ("Good job, kid"); Sal, the mutant researcher with a pig's nose; and Kristen, Tucker's girlfriend. In the final episode the police, who were investigating Stern, shut down the *Chronicle* and put everyone under arrest. "To Not Be Continued."

Based on the *News from the Edge* series of books by Mark Sumner.

CHRONOLOG, see *First Tuesday*

CHRONOSCOPE (*Discussion*)

FIRST TELECAST: *June 11, 1951*
LAST TELECAST: *April 29, 1955*
BROADCAST HISTORY:

Jun 1951–Sep 1951, CBS Mon 11:00–11:15
Sep 1951–Jun 1953, CBS Mon/Wed/Fri 11:00–11:15
Aug 1953–Apr 1955, CBS Mon/Wed/Fri 11:00–11:15

MODERATOR:

Frank Knight (1951)
William Bradford Huie (1951–1953)
Edward P. Morgan (1953)
Larry Le Sueur (1953–1955)

Current issues in world affairs were discussed on this late evening series. Each telecast featured a guest who was either personally involved in, or an expert on, a situation of major significance on the world scene—politics, finance, natural disasters, or the Korean War, for example. Two other panelists from a rotating group of journalists chatted with the guest panelist about the implications of the event or trend under discussion.

CHRYSLER THEATRE, see *Bob Hope Presents The Chrysler Theatre*

CHUCK BARRIS RAH RAH SHOW, THE (*Comedy Variety*)

FIRST TELECAST: *February 28, 1978*
LAST TELECAST: *April 11, 1978*
BROADCAST HISTORY:

Feb 1978–Apr 1978, NBC Tue 8:00–9:00

REGULARS:

Chuck Barris
Jaye P. Morgan
Milton Delugg Orchestra

The Chuck Barris Rah Rah Show was one of the less conventional variety shows of the 1970s, as well as one of the shortest-lived. Barris was a longtime producer of game shows who had first been seen on camera on *The Gong Show*, a parody on talent shows which was seen on the NBC daytime lineup. He was supposed to be simply the program's producer, but had taken over as host at the last minute before the premiere, when the original host proved unsuitable. He was perfect in the role.

The *Gong Show* idea—a succession of no-talent amateurs doing dreadful acts (and often getting "gonged" off the stage)—caught on, and soon produced both a syndicated version and this nighttime adaptation. Unlike *Gong* the *Rah Rah Show* included professional acts, doing their bits in quick succession on a simple stage. Barris's choice of guests was a bit odd, combining old-timers such as Slim Gaillard ("Flat Foot Floogie") and Cab Calloway with 1950s rock artists such as The Coasters and Chuck Berry, along with contemporary talent such as Jose Feliciano and Anson Williams. Comics Fred Travelena and Henny Youngman made repeat appearances, and singer Jaye P. Morgan was a regular. In addition there were always several amateurs displaying their questionable talents, such as the lady who chirped and barked while singing "The Sound of Music" and Dr. Flame-O, who played "Smoke Gets in Your Eyes" on a row of burning candles.

CHURCH STREET STATION (*Music*)

BROADCAST HISTORY:

The Nashville Network
30 minutes
Produced: *1984–1987, 1989–1992*
Premiered: *March 10, 1984*

One of TNN's earliest and longest-running concert series, *Church Street Station* featured country artists performing at the Cheyenne Saloon and Opera House in Orlando, Florida. Many classic acts appeared (Rex Allen, Sr., Hank Thompson, Asleep at the Wheel), although there were also more recent artists such as Mary Chapin Carpenter and Garth Brooks.

CIMARRON CITY (*Western*)

FIRST TELECAST: *October 11, 1958*
LAST TELECAST: *September 16, 1960*
BROADCAST HISTORY:

Oct 1958–Sep 1959, NBC Sat 9:30–10:30
Jun 1960–Sep 1960, NBC Fri 7:30–8:30

CAST:

Matthew Rockford .... George Montgomery
Beth Purcell .... Audrey Totter

Lane Temple .... John Smith
Art Sampson .... Stuart Randall
Martin Kingsley .... Addison Richards
Burt Purdy .... Fred Sherman
Alice Purdy .... Claire Carleton
Tiny Budinger .... Dan Blocker
Jesse Williams .... George Dunn
Dody Hamer .... Pete Dunn
Silas Perry .... Tom Fadden
Jed Fame .... Wally Brown

George Montgomery was both star and narrator of this saga of a boomtown on the western frontier during the 1890s. Oil and gold had created a booming economy in the Oklahoma Territory, and Cimarron City had mushroomed into a sprawling, rough-hewn metropolis, with hopes of becoming the capital of the future state of Oklahoma. Matthew Rockford, son of the town's founder, was mayor and a leading cattle rancher; Beth Purcell, the owner of a boardinghouse; and Lane Temple, the town sheriff. These three, singly or together, were the focus of most episodes. Dan Blocker, who later starred as Hoss on *Bonanza*, was featured as a local citizen who often helped the sheriff in the cause of law and order. Montgomery narrated the episodes from the perspective of an older man recalling the adventures and happenings of his younger days. Those that were telecast during the summer of 1960 were reruns of earlier shows.

CIMARRON STRIP (*Western*)
FIRST TELECAST: *September 7, 1967*
LAST TELECAST: *September 7, 1971*
BROADCAST HISTORY:
Sep 1967–Sep 1968, CBS Thu 7:30–9:00
Jul 1971–Sep 1971, CBS Tue 8:30–10:00
CAST:
U.S. Marshal Jim Crown .... Stuart Whitman
Mac Gregor .... Percy Herbert
Francis Wilde .... Randy Boone
Dulcey Coopersmith .... Jill Townsend

The Cimarron Strip was the border region between the Kansas Territory and Indian territory during the late 19th century. Patrolling this vast area was the job of U.S. Marshal Jim Crown, who was based in Cimarron City. Marshal Crown had no full-time deputies but he often availed himself of the assistance of Mac Gregor, an itinerant Scot, and Francis Wilde, a young photographer. Also seen as a regular in this series was Dulcey, a young woman from the East who had moved to the frontier to take over an inn that had been run by her late father. *Cimarron Strip* was an attempt by CBS to copy the success of NBC's *The Virginian* (the first 90-minute Western series), and like *The Virginian* it centered largely on characters acted by guest stars. Reruns of the original series aired during the summer of 1971.

CINDY MARGOLIS SHOW, THE (*Variety*)
BROADCAST HISTORY:
Syndicated only
60 minutes
Produced: *2000* (13 episodes)
Released: *August 2000*
REGULARS:
Cindy Margolis
D. J. Skribble
Lance Krall

Internet pinup Cindy Margolis hosted this short-lived variety show. Taped in Miami Beach's trendy South Beach in a club setting, it featured dance music, hip-hop, and guests. The scantily clad Ms. Margolis was assisted by disk jockey D. J. Skribble and announcer Lance Krall. This frenetic series' audience appeared to be almost all under 25, and sexy talk was a staple of the show. Cindy would have her guests—usually playmates like Devin Devasquez—join her on a big waterbed to answer questions from her horny audience. Regular features included videos covering the South Beach social scene, a webkini contest in which local girls paraded around in skimpy swimsuits with the drooling guys cheering for their favorites and the voting done at Cindy's Internet Web site, and a dance contest in which three couples competed simultaneously with the winner determined by audience applause.

CINEMA VARIETIES, see *Movies—Prior to 1961*

CINEMA-SCOPE, see *Movies—Prior to 1961*

CIRCLE OF FEAR, see *Ghost Story*

CIRCLE THEATER, see *Armstrong Circle Theater*

CIRCUIT RIDER (*Religion*)
FIRST TELECAST: *March 5, 1951*
LAST TELECAST: *May 7, 1951*
BROADCAST HISTORY:
Mar 1951–May 1951, ABC Mon 11:00–11:30
NARRATOR:
Rex Marshall
MODERATOR:
Rev. George Pigueron

This series began with dramatizations of the efforts of clergymen to bring religion to the early American frontier, and later broadened to dramatizations emphasizing the significance of Christianity in everyday life. There was also a weekly guest who discussed current religious problems and activities. Sponsored by America for Christ, Inc.

CIRCUS (*Variety*)
BROADCAST HISTORY:
Syndicated only
30 minutes
Produced: *1971–1973* (52 episodes)
Released: *Fall 1971*
HOST:
Bert Parks

Leading European circus acts were taped on location for this series, which was much in the style of the earlier *International Showtime* (by the same producers).

CIRCUS BOY (*Adventure*)
FIRST TELECAST: *September 23, 1956*
LAST TELECAST: *September 11, 1958*
BROADCAST HISTORY:
Sep 1956–Sep 1957, NBC Sun 7:30–8:00
Sep 1957–Sep 1958, ABC Thu 7:30–8:00
CAST:
Corky .... Mickey Braddock
Joey, the Clown .... Noah Beery, Jr.
Big Tim Champion .... Robert Lowery
Hank Miller .... Leo Gordon

Little Tom, the Midget .... Billy Barty
Swifty.................................. Olin Howlin
Barker .... Eddie Marr
Big Boy .... Guinn Williams

Circus life at the turn of the century as seen through the eyes of a young boy. Corky, a 12-year-old orphan, had been adopted by the members of a traveling circus owned by Big Tim Champion. His life with the colorful performers and behind-the-scenes workers, as the circus traveled from town to town, formed the basis for the series. Corky's personal pet was Bimbo, a baby elephant, for whom he was water boy.

Although the series left prime time after two seasons on two networks, reruns continued on Saturday mornings until September 1960.

Nearly a decade after *Circus Boy* left the air, its star, Mickey Braddock, surfaced again on another series. Now an adult, and using his real last name, Dolenz, he was one of the four stars of *The Monkees*.

CIRCUS TIME (*Variety*)
FIRST TELECAST: *October 4, 1956*
LAST TELECAST: *June 27, 1957*
BROADCAST HISTORY:
Oct 1956–Jun 1957, ABC Thu 8:00–9:00
REGULARS:
Paul Winchell
Betty Ann Grove (1957)
Ralph Herman Orchestra

This variety show with the flavor of a traditional circus presented both circus performers and traditional entertainment acts. Paul Winchell was the "ringmaster-host," assisted by his dummies Jerry Mahoney and Knucklehead Smith. Guests included popular music acts such as Mickey and Sylvia and the Dell Vikings.

CISCO KID, THE (*Western*)
BROADCAST HISTORY:
Syndicated only
30 minutes
Produced: *1950–1956* (156 episodes)
Released: *Late 1950*
CAST:
The Cisco Kid .... Duncan Renaldo
Pancho .... Leo Carrillo

One of the most popular kids' Westerns of early television never ran on a network. Sold individually to local stations, *The Cisco Kid* was not only the first big syndicated film hit, but was in fact one of the first popular filmed programs on TV (most shows at that time were done live). Eventually 156 half-hour episodes were made by Ziv Television, surprisingly all of them in color, although most stations showed them in black-and-white during the 1950s.

The Cisco Kid was a Mexican adventurer who ranged the old Southwest with his trusty sidekick, Pancho. Dressed immaculately in a highly embroidered black outfit, and endowed with an excess of Latin charm, he usually swept some señorita off her feet after running the criminals to earth. All she got was a kiss and a dashing sweep of the sombrero, however, before the two knights on horseback rode off with a laugh. Cisco's horse was Diablo, and Pancho's was Loco.

Fat old Pancho was always ready with a crack and some fractured English that kids loved to imitate ("Ceesco? Let's went! The shereef, he ees getting closer!"). But he was brave in a fight, and an expert with the bullwhip. They saw a lot of action together, but relatively little gunplay. Usually Cisco's fast draw was to shoot the gun out of the bad guy's hand. The ready, fun-loving camaraderie between Cisco and Pancho was what made the series work.

The Cisco Kid had a long and glorious history before coming to TV. Invented by O. Henry in the short story "The Caballero's Way," he was originally a scruffy bandito who victimized the rich and helped the poor. He turned up in early silent movies, and then in many sound features beginning with *In Old Arizona* in 1929 (for which Warner Baxter, as Cisco, won one of the first Academy Awards). Dozens of films followed with Cesar Romero, Gilbert Roland, and Duncan Renaldo in the lead role, and there was a popular radio series off and on during the 1940s. Beginning simultaneously with the TV series, there was also a comic strip, which lasted until 1968.

Renaldo was in his 50s and Leo Carrillo in his 70s when the TV films were made, but they nevertheless did much (though not all) of the hard riding and stunts themselves. They were both excellent horsemen. Years after production finally ended, Renaldo continued to tour with aging Diablo, and he will always be, in his own and the public's eye, the Cisco Kid. Carrillo died in 1961 at the age of 81.

CITIES SERVICE BAND OF AMERICA (*Music*)
FIRST TELECAST: *October 17, 1949*
LAST TELECAST: *January 9, 1950*
BROADCAST HISTORY:
Oct 1949–Jan 1950, NBC Mon 9:30–10:00
CONDUCTOR:
Paul Lavalle
ANNOUNCER:
Ford Bond

This simulcast of the popular NBC radio program featured Paul Lavalle and the 48-piece Band of America. Various soloists from the band were spotlighted, as well as the Green and White Vocal Quartette and a 12-voice glee club. Baton-twirling majorettes and an occasional film clip were added as a concession to television, but the program faced withering competition from *The Goldbergs*, running opposite it on CBS, and was soon canceled.

CITIZEN BAINES (*Drama*)
FIRST TELECAST: *September 29, 2001*
LAST TELECAST: *November 3, 2001*
BROADCAST HISTORY:
Sep 2001–Nov 2001, CBS Sat 9:00–10:00
CAST:
Elliott Baines .... James Cromwell
Ellen Baines Croland .... Embeth Davidtz
Reeva Baines Eidenberg .... Jane Adams
Dori Baines .... Jacinda Barrett
Shel Eidenberg .... Arye Gross
Arthur Croland .... Matt McCoy
Claude Waverly .... McCaleb Burnett
Otis Croland .... Emmett Shoemaker
Sam Eidenberg .... Easton Gage
Ruthie Eidenberg .... Bryn Lauren Lemon
David Goldman .... David Kriegel
Dr. Judith Lin .... Rosalind Chao

Grant Tanaka .... Clyde Kusatsu
Randy .... Dave Engfer
Tony Keaton .... Vyto Ruginis
Maxine .... Stacey Silverman
Andy Carlson .... Tom Verica

Elliott Baines was at a major turning point in his life. In the series premiere the tall, rather cold three-term senator from the state of Washington lost his reelection bid and had to return home to Seattle to figure out what to do with the rest of his life. His first challenge was dealing with his fractious family. Divorced Elliott had three daughters: Ellen, the eldest, was a high-powered attorney planning to run for Congress, but unsure of herself; Reeva, the insecure middle daughter, was the frazzled mother of two young children whose college professor husband, Shel, was having an affair; and free-spirited Dori, the youngest, was the wild child, just out of school and working as a photographer for a local newspaper. Claude, a musician, was Dori's sometime boyfriend. Reeva, in the early stages of pregnancy, separated from Shel and, with her two kids, Sam and Ruthie, moved into the family home with Elliott and Dori.

CBS abruptly canceled *Citizen Baines* after only six episodes had aired. In what would have been the next episode, Ellen's husband, Arthur, suffered a heart attack while jogging.

CITY (*Situation Comedy*)
FIRST TELECAST: *January 29, 1990*
LAST TELECAST: *June 8, 1990*
BROADCAST HISTORY:
Jan 1990–Apr 1990, CBS Mon 8:30–9:00
Jun 1990, CBS Fri 8:30–9:00
CAST:
Liz Gianni .... Valerie Harper
Roger Barnett .... Todd Susman
Wanda Jenkins .... Tyra Ferrell
Ken Resnick .... Stephen Lee
Lance Armstrong .... Sam Lloyd
Anna-Maria Batista .... Liz Torres
Gloria Elgis .... Mary Jo Keenen
Victor Sloboda .... James Lorinz
Penny Gianni .... LuAnne Ponce
Sean .... Shay Duffin

The Department of City Services for a moderately large, unnamed American city (even the seal shown in the opening credits only referred to it as "city") was the setting for this comedy. Liz Gianni was the harried city manager, trying to get as much as possible out of her limited budget and off-the-wall staff. Assistant City Manager Roger Barnett was her right-hand man, an unflappable career civil servant who had seen it all. Others were Wanda, Liz's secretary; Lance, the obsessive and obnoxious head of the records department; Anna-Maria, the outspoken, Cuban-born, purchasing agent whose revolutionary husband was incarcerated in her homeland; Gloria, the flighty social services coordinator; and Victor, the overly enthusiastic acting chief of security. Liz's nemesis was Deputy Mayor Ken Resnick, a pompous, manipulative, petty bureaucrat who was not above using his position to try to line his pockets with "gifts" from favored contractors. A widow, Liz also had to deal with Penny, her 19-year-old daughter, who had dropped out of college and returned home. Penny wanted to be treated as a "friend," not as a daughter, something Liz found difficult to accept, particularly when it came to Penny's offbeat social relationships.

CITY ASSIGNMENT, see *Big Town*

CITY DETECTIVE (*Police Drama*)
BROADCAST HISTORY:
Syndicated only
30 minutes
Produced: *1953–1955* (65 episodes)
Released: *Fall 1953*
CAST:
Det. Lt. Bart Grant .... Rod Cameron

This bare-knuckles detective show was one of several such vehicles for lanky Rod Cameron *(State Trooper, Coronado 9)*, of whom *TV Guide* once remarked, "Most of his acting ability is in his fists." Despite the "city" in the title, Lt. Grant ranged far and wide fighting crime, from Mexico to the Mojave Desert to New York City. Most episodes involved murder, extortion, or similar crimes.

CITY HOSPITAL (*Medical Drama*)
FIRST TELECAST: *March 25, 1952*
LAST TELECAST: *October 1, 1953*
BROADCAST HISTORY:
Mar 1952–Jun 1953, CBS Tue 9:00–9:30
Jun 1953–Oct 1953, CBS Thu 10:30–11:00
CAST:
Dr. Barton Crane .... Melville Ruick
Dr. Kate Morrow .... Ann Burr

The daily crises of a large metropolitan hospital, and the personal and professional lives of its staff members, were dramatized in this live series. Dr. Barton Crane was the medical director of City Hospital, and it was from his position, either as an active participant or advisor to those involved, that the stories were developed. The presence of a female doctor, Kate Morrow, was rather uncommon for medical shows of this period.

City Hospital was aired on a biweekly basis throughout its run, alternating with *Crime Syndicated* on Tuesdays and with *Place the Face* on Thursdays. It had originally been seen as a Saturday afternoon series on ABC, where it ran from November 1951 to April 1952, barely overlapping the start of its prime-time run on CBS.

CITY OF ANGELS (*Detective Drama*)
FIRST TELECAST: *February 3, 1976*
LAST TELECAST: *August 10, 1976*
BROADCAST HISTORY:
Feb 1976–Aug 1976, NBC Tue 10:00–11:00
CAST:
Jake Axminster .... Wayne Rogers
Marsha .... Elaine Joyce
Lt. Murray Quint .... Clifton James
Michael Brimm .... Philip Sterling

Set in Los Angeles (the "City of Angels") in the 1930s, this period detective series was patterned after the hit motion picture *Chinatown.* It concerned the exploits of Jake Axminster, an often broke but always freewheeling private investigator who was not above stretching the law and his ethics to get the information he wanted. Possibly as a reflection of his own standards, Jake trusted nobody completely, not even his attorney, Michael Brimm. Jake's office was run by a beautiful but daffy secretary, Marsha, who also ran a switchboard that took messages for call girls. A midseason replacement, *City of Angels* was notable more for its vintage automobiles and period fashions than for dramatic involvement, and it was soon canceled.

CITY OF ANGELS (*Medical Drama*)
FIRST TELECAST: *January 16, 2000*
LAST TELECAST: *December 21, 2000*
BROADCAST HISTORY:
Jan 2000, CBS Sun 8:30–9:30
Jan 2000–Apr 2000, CBS Wed 8:00–9:00
Jul 2000–Dec 2000, CBS Thu 9:00–10:00
CAST:
Dr. Ben Turner .... Blair Underwood
Dr. Lillian Price .... Vivica A. Fox
Ron Harris.................. Michael Warren
Edwin O'Malley .... Robert Morse
Dr. Wesley Williams.................. Hill Harper
Dr. Arthur Jackson .... T. E. Russell
Dr. Geoffrey Weiss .... Phil Buckman
Nurse Grace Patterson .... Maya Rudolph
Nurse Lynette Peeler.................. Viola Davis
Barney Fisk.................. Mike Scriba
E.R. Nurse Bernice Cottrel ...... Octavia L. Spencer
Dr. Ana Syphax .... Tamara Taylor
Dr. Ted Gill .... Gregg Daniel
Dr. Ethan Carter .... Ron Canada
Wendell Loman .... Harold Sylvester
Paramedic Carla.................. Mari Weiss
Paramedic Rafi.................. Lawrence LeJohn
Dr. Courtney Ellis .... Gabrielle Union
Dr. Raleigh Stewart.................. Kyle Secor
Nurse Mandy Harmon .... Arminae Azarian
Dr. Ambrose.................. GregalanWilliams

Angels of Mercy was a struggling hospital in the inner city of Los Angeles with a primarily minority staff. Dr. Turner, the acting chief of surgery, was a dedicated surgeon who was deeply concerned with the needs of the community. He reported to Price, a former lover, the recently hired medical director charged with improving staff morale. Harris, the hospital's chief executive officer, wasn't convinced she was the right person for the job, and O'Malley, the politically powerful chairman of the board of supervisors, attempted to manipulate people and situations to serve his own purposes. Others on the hospital's staff included Williams, a young black resident trying to overcome his personal prejudices; Weiss, an inexperienced but enthusiastic resident; Jackson, the five-year resident who had seen it all; Peeler, a veteran surgical nurse; and attractive Nurse Patterson, who was dating Dr. Weiss, one of the few white doctors at Angels of Mercy.

When *City of Angels* started its second season in the fall of 2000 there were a number of changes. Gone were the dark, moody lighting and background gospel music that had helped set the brooding tone for the series. Dr. Price had left for another job; Dr. Ambrose was the new medical director, a by-the-book bean counter who alienated most of the staff. Despite her feelings for Dr. Weiss, Nurse Patterson also left for a job in another city. New to the staff were Dr. Stewart, a talented young plastic surgeon, and Dr. Ellis, a new resident whose father was a famous surgeon. For several weeks the hospital's female staff was terrorized by a serial rapist who turned out to be Dr. Damon Sullivan (Bokeem Woodbine), one of its medical residents.

CIVIL WARS (*Legal Drama*)
FIRST TELECAST: *November 20, 1991*
LAST TELECAST: *March 2, 1993*
BROADCAST HISTORY:
Nov 1991–Feb 1992, ABC Wed 10:00–11:00
Mar 1992–Apr 1992, ABC Tue 10:00–11:00
May 1992–Jan 1993, ABC Wed 10:00–11:00
Jan 1993–Mar 1993, ABC Tue 10:00–11:00
CAST:
Sydney Guilford.................. Mariel Hemingway
Charlie Howell.................. Peter Onorati
Denise Iannello.................. Debi Mazar
Jeffrey Lassick .... David Marciano
Eli Levinson .... Alan Rosenberg

The emotional warfare of divorce was the subject of this drama, in which almost everyone's problems were settled with a lawsuit. Sydney and Eli were successful Manhattan divorce lawyers who added Charlie to their firm after Eli suffered a nervous breakdown and decided to work on "less stressful," nondivorce cases. Workaholic divorcée Sydney and earthy, impulsive Charlie immediately hit it off and over time began to develop a romantic attraction for one another. Meanwhile Denise, their efficient legal secretary, was wooed by likable messenger boy Jeffrey, whom she eventually married. He turned out to be a wealthy young eccentric, and their marriage, too, was threatened with divorce.

Bitter, vengeful divorces and custody spats alternated with lighter cases (e.g., the woman who wanted to divorce her hubby because he thought he was Elvis), but the overall tone of the series was rather depressing. As if that weren't enough, a running story in the second season was Charlie's father's battle with prostate cancer. The series attempted to attract attention with a September 1992 episode in which Sydney posed nude for a famous photographer (viewers didn't see much), but by the following spring Judge A. C. Nielsen had ruled—"Canceled!"

CLAPPROOD LIVE (*Talk*)
BROADCAST HISTORY:
Lifetime Network
30 minutes
Produced: *1994* (37 episodes)
Premiere: *January 2, 1994*
HOST:
Marjorie Clapprood

A weekly Sunday-night talk show oriented toward current affairs and women's issues. Host Marjorie Clapprood was a former three-term Massachusetts state legislator, Boston radio talk-show host (on WRKO), and part-time standup comic who kept things interesting without getting too ponderous. She examined one topic per show, usually with a well-known guest, and took viewer calls. The series originated from WCVB-TV in Boston.

CLARISSA EXPLAINS IT ALL (*Situation Comedy*)
BROADCAST HISTORY:
Nickelodeon
30 minutes
Produced: *1991–1994* (65 episodes)
Premiered: *March 23, 1991*

CAST:

Clarissa Darling (age 14) .... Melissa Joan Hart
Ferguson W. Darling (12) .... Jason Zimbler
Janet Darling .... Elizabeth Hess
Marshall Darling .... Joe O'Connor
Sam Anders .... Sean O'Neal

Sunny sitcom centering around Clarissa Darling, an uncommonly glib, energetic high school student. Each episode opened with Clarissa in her bright suburban bedroom talking to the camera about one of life's little mysteries—friends, love, boys, parents, and so on. Then a story along those lines would unfold. Ferguson was her scheming dweeb of a younger brother, Janet her understanding mom, and Marshall her somewhat goofy dad, an architect. Sam was her oldest friend and confidant, who routinely arrived by climbing up a ladder and through her bedroom window unannounced. Lots of friends passed through (Clarissa was a popular girl), each helping illustrate another story about growing up.

In the final episode Clarissa, looking very mature, graduated from high school and accepted an offer to become a cub reporter/intern for the *New York Daily Post* before going to college. Sam, after being rejected by almost every institution of higher education in the U.S., was accepted as the first male student at all-girl Bibbington College in Maine. Heaven!

CLASS OF '96 (*Drama*)

FIRST TELECAST: *January 19, 1993*
LAST TELECAST: *May 25, 1993*
BROADCAST HISTORY:

Jan 1993–May 1993, FOX Tue 8:00–9:00

CAST:

David Morrissey .... Jason Gedrick
Whitney Reed .... Brandon Douglas
Samuel (Stroke) Dexter .... Gale Hansen
Antonio Hopkins .... Perry Moore
Jessica Cohen .... Lisa Dean Ryan
Robin Farr .... Kari Wuhrer
Patty Horvath .... Megan Ward
Janet Keeler .... Bridgid Coulter

Havenhurst College, a fictional Ivy League school in the Northeast, was the setting for this ensemble drama about a group of college freshmen. David, who served as the show's narrator through the letters he wrote regularly to his Uncle Joe back home in New Jersey, was the first of his family ever to go to college. He had an on-again, off-again romance/friendship with Jessica, an English major from a wealthy family. David's roommate, Stroke, was an avaricious computer genius constantly coming up with schemes to make easy money. Jessica's roommates were Patty and Robin. Patty, the daughter of a prominent actress who wanted to follow in her mother's footsteps, befriended Stroke (who would have preferred more than just friendship) and got romantically involved with Whitney. Robin, a sexually active free spirit who lost her security when money problems caused her parents to ask her to transfer to a state school, was determined to stay at expensive Havenhurst. She sought both financial aid and a job to pay her college bills and started an affair with English literature professor Jameson Howe (David Beecroft). The other featured roommates were Whitney and Antonio. Whitney, the insecure son of an autocratic Havenhurst alumnus, had a drinking problem that he eventually got under control, while Antonio, a serious and bright black student on an academic scholarship, clashed with the father of his girlfriend, Janet, a wealthy and successful black who found it difficult to accept his daughter dating a guy from the ghetto.

Filmed in Toronto with the University of Toronto used for exteriors.

CLAUDE'S CRIB (*Situation Comedy*)

BROADCAST HISTORY:

USA Network
30 minutes
Produced: *1996–1997* (13 episodes)
Premiered: *January 5, 1997*

CAST:

Claude .... Claude Brooks
Kaylene .... Tembi Locke
Julie .... Jennifer Aspen
Bailey .... Matt Champagne
Des .... James Wong
Shorty .... Anthony C. Hall
Al .... Larry Hankin

Black comic Claude Brooks created this homey little sitcom which aired briefly on Sunday nights. Claude was a twenty-something guy who had a lot going on in his life, what with college studies, a part-time job as a DJ at a local club, and being landlord to the diverse group of young tenants who lived in the house he had inherited from his grandmother. Most of the action took place in the house (his "crib"), where the multi-racial boarders were bossy black aerobics instructor Kaylene, naive midwesterner Julie, bumbling geek Bailey, and Asian-American slacker Des. Shorty was Claude's six-foot-three-inch pal, and Al the irritable next-door neighbor who had a fetish for statues of toads.

CLAUDIA, THE STORY OF A MARRIAGE (*Drama*)

FIRST TELECAST: *January 6, 1952*
LAST TELECAST: *June 30, 1952*
BROADCAST HISTORY:

Jan 1952–Mar 1952, NBC Sun 6:30–7:30
Mar 1952–Jun 1952, CBS Mon 9:30–10:00

CAST:

Claudia Naughton .... Joan McCracken
David Naughton .... Hugh Reilly
Mrs. Brown .... Margaret Wycherly
Bertha .... Lilia Skala
Julia Naughton .... Faith Brook
Harley Naughton .... Alex Clark
Fritz .... Paul Andor
Roger .... Mercer McCloud

Claudia was a study in contrasts, at once both very childish and remarkably mature for her age. She married aspiring architect David Naughton at the age of 18, and the problems and joys of their young marriage were explored realistically in this series. Claudia's dealings with her new family, including David's sister Julia and brother Harley, and her attempts to break away from her possessive mother, Mrs. Brown, all served as subject matter. The series was broadcast live from New York.

Claudia had had a highly successful career before coming to TV, having been the heroine in three novels by Rose Franken (published between 1939–1941), a Broadway play, a radio series, and two movies starring Dorothy McGuire and Robert Young. On television, however, her story was brief.

CLEGHORNE! (*Situation Comedy*)
FIRST TELECAST: *September 10, 1995*
LAST TELECAST: *January 28, 1996*
BROADCAST HISTORY:
Sep 1995–Oct 1995, WB Sun 9:00–9:30
Oct 1995–Dec 1995, WB Sun 8:30–9:00
Dec 1995, WB Sun 9:00–9:30
Jan 1996, WB Sun 9:30–10:00
CAST:
Ellen Carlson .... Ellen Cleghorne
Akeyla Carlson (age 9) ... Cerita Monet Bickelmann
Lena Carlson .... Alaina Reed Hall
Sidney Carlson .... Garrett Morris
Victoria Carlson .... Sherri Shepherd
Brad .... Steve Bean
Tyrell Livingston .... Michael Ralph
Coral .... Cathy Silvers

Ellen was a stylish, black, single parent living on Manhattan's Upper West Side with her smart-mouth daughter Akeyla. With her partner, Brad (who was in the opening credits for the show but rarely seen on camera), she ran a small TV commercial production company in the SoHo section of lower Manhattan. Life got complicated when her overbearing parents and lazy, unemployed, 25-year-old sister, Victoria, moved into the apartment next door. Tyrell, Akeyla's father, whom Ellen had never married, was a Jamaican-born cabdriver trying to avoid deportation, who harbored delusions of racial persecution. In her free time Ellen hung out at Piccolo's, a local restaurant where Coral was the sarcastic bartender.

CLEOPATRA 2525 (*Science Fiction*)
BROADCAST HISTORY:
Syndicated only
30 minutes (60 minutes effective February 2001)
Produced: *1999–2001* (28 episodes)
Released: *January 2000*
CAST:
Cleopatra .... Jennifer Sky
Hel .... Gina Torres
Sarge (née Rose) .... Victoria Pratt
Edward Mauser .... Patrick Kake
Voice .... Elizabeth Hawthorne
Creegan .... Joel Tobeck
THEME:
"In the Year 2525"

Cleopatra 2525 was a campy action series that used much of the same tongue-in-cheek humor as *Hercules: The Legendary Journeys,* created by the same production team. Cleopatra was a spaced-out stripper whose 2001 breast implant operation had gone wrong. She went into a coma and was cryogenically frozen, only to be revived 500 years later into an Earth in which the human population had been driven underground by robotic machines called Baileys and other mechanical devices. She joined with two female warriors, Hel and Sarge, to help humankind regain control of the planet from the robots. Cleo often used dated expressions—"No pain, no gain," "Make my day," "All for one and one for all," "Live long and prosper," "May the Force be with you." Mauser was a good robot who helped them, and Voice was the unseen woman who gave them their orders. Seen regularly were Betrayers, evil robots that looked human and shot death rays from their eyes.

Creegan, a recurring villain, was a crazed joker-like character who had once been a scientist working with Hel's father, whom he killed in the hour-long episode that launched the series. The following week the imprisoned Creegan was sentenced to death, but when the gang paid him a last visit, he kissed Hel and swapped bodies with her in order to escape. Hel finally managed to switch back, but unfortunately by then Creegan was on the loose. In the last original episode he was caught and revealed that he, like Cleo, was a 500-year-old "thaw." He had been in control of the Baileys (in fact, his real name was George Bailey), which he had created as environmental control units to clean up the mess of nuclear war, but eventually they had developed wills of their own and decided to clean humanity off the planet. As the episode ended there was a climactic, but unresolved, battle between the Baileys and Voice's forces.

Packaged with *Jack of All Trades* in a syndicated hour titled "Back 2 Back Action."

CLERKS (*Cartoon*)
FIRST TELECAST: *May 31, 2000*
LAST TELECAST: *June 7, 2000*
BROADCAST HISTORY:
May 2000–Jun 2000, ABC Wed 9:30–10:00
VOICES:
Dante Hicks .... Brian O'Halloran
Randal Graves .... Jeff Anderson
Jay .... Jason Mewes
Silent Bob Plutarski .... Kevin Smith

Nothing made much sense in this offbeat cartoon about four young slackers in Leonardo, New Jersey. Bearded Dante manned the cash register at the Quick Stop convenience store while his buddy, tall, shaggy Randal (the one with the backward baseball cap), was the unmotivated clerk at RST Video next door. Dim-witted Jay and hefty biker Silent Bob hung out with them. Stories started out with a little incident, then evolved into fantasy sequences or parodies of pop culture—for example Jay slipped on the floor and sued the store for $10 million, leading to an elaborate trial in which Judge Reinhold presided and George Lucas, Steven Spielberg and Spike Lee appeared on the stand defending their movies.

Clerks originated in 1994 as a low-budget independent black-and-white film by Smith that won a Sundance Film Festival award and two prizes at Cannes. It came to TV in 2000, but was canceled after two episodes. As Randal would say, "Yeah, whatever."

CLIENT, THE, see *John Grisham's The Client*

CLIFF EDWARDS SHOW, THE (*Music*)
FIRST TELECAST: *May 23, 1949*
LAST TELECAST: *September 19, 1949*
BROADCAST HISTORY:
May 1949–Sep 1949, CBS Mon/Wed/Fri 7:45–8:00
Sep 1949, CBS Mon 7:45–8:00
REGULARS:
Cliff Edwards
The Tony Mottola Trio

Show-business veteran Cliff "Ukulele Ike" Edwards was the host of this informal live musical series, which filled out the remainder of the half-hour in which CBS aired its nightly network news program. Cliff would recount homespun stories, play his ukulele, and model some of his huge collection of unusual hats. He also sang songs and occasionally chatted with a guest. Some of the songs were no doubt taken from Cliff's long career on records, radio, and in movies, during which he had introduced such hits as "Fascinating Rhythm" (in a 1924 Broadway show), "Singin' in the Rain" (in a 1929 movie musical), and "When You Wish Upon A Star" (in the 1939 Disney feature *Pinocchio*, for which Edwards provided the voice of Jiminy Cricket).

CLIFF HANGERS (*Serials*)

FIRST TELECAST: *February 27, 1979*
LAST TELECAST: *May 1, 1979*
BROADCAST HISTORY:
Feb 1979–May 1979, NBC Tue 8:00–9:00

From the 1910s to the 1950s, cliff-hangers were a staple form of movie entertainment for America's young. Saturday afternoons meant a trip to the neighborhood theater where the latest chapter of the current *Zorro*, *Superman*, or *Commando Cody* serial was on display. All of the movie serials—whether Westerns, melodramas, science fiction, or gothic horror stories—had one element in common. At the end of each episode (full series ran 10 to 15 episodes) the hero or heroine was left in a perilous, potentially fatal situation. Miraculously, however, the first minutes of the succeeding episode would show how he or she had escaped. The kids at the Saturday matinees knew their heroes would survive, the only question was how. Not knowing gave them something to talk about all week until they faithfully returned to the movie house the following week to find out.

More than two decades after the last movie serial was produced, NBC tried the format on television. *Cliff Hangers* was the umbrella title for three separate serials all sharing the same hour on Tuesday nights. Each week viewers saw the latest 20-minute chapter of *Stop Susan Williams*, *The Secret Empire*, and *The Curse of Dracula*. To add to the "in progress" feeling, each of the three was picked up at a different stage on February 27, 1979: *Stop Susan Williams* at Chapter II, *The Secret Empire* at Chapter III, and *The Curse of Dracula* at Chapter VI. The idea was to begin new serials while others were still in progress, but only *The Curse of Dracula* managed to reach its conclusion in the brief time *Cliff Hangers* was on the air. For more detail, see the individual serial titles.

CLIMAX! (*Dramatic Anthology*)

FIRST TELECAST: *October 7, 1954*
LAST TELECAST: *June 26, 1958*
BROADCAST HISTORY:
Oct 1954–Jun 1958, CBS Thu 8:30–9:30
HOSTS:
William Lundigan
Mary Costa (1956–1958)

Climax! was one of the longer-running dramatic series aired on network television during the 1950s. Hosted by William Lundigan, who was joined by permanent co-host Mary Costa in the summer of 1956, each week it presented a one-hour drama originating from CBS' facilities in Hollywood. When it first went on the air, *Climax!* was done live every week, but as time wore on, filmed (and later taped) productions were added to the mix. Even in its last season, however, there were several live programs presented. Among the plays aired were adaptations of *Casino Royale*, with Barry Nelson playing an American James Bond; *A Farewell to Arms*, with Guy Madison and Diana Lynn; and *Dr. Jekyll and Mr. Hyde*, with Michael Rennie playing the dual role.

CLOAK OF MYSTERY (*Dramatic Anthology*)

FIRST TELECAST: *May 11, 1965*
LAST TELECAST: *August 8, 1965*
BROADCAST HISTORY:
May 1965, NBC Tue 9:30–10:00
May 1965–Aug 1965, NBC Tue 9:00–10:00

This summer anthology series consisted of reruns of episodes of *Alcoa Premiere*, *Alfred Hitchcock Presents*, *Pepsi-Cola Playhouse*, and *G. E. Theatre*. In addition, two episodes were pilots for series that never made it to the schedule.

CLOCK, THE (*Suspense Anthology*)

FIRST TELECAST: *May 16, 1949*
LAST TELECAST: *January 9, 1952*
BROADCAST HISTORY:
May 1949–Aug 1949, NBC Mon 8:30–9:00
Aug 1949–Mar 1950, NBC Wed 8:30–9:00
Apr 1950–Feb 1951, NBC Fri 9:30–10:00
Jul 1951–Aug 1951, NBC Fri 8:30–9:00
Oct 1951–Jan 1952, ABC Wed 9:30–10:00
NARRATOR:
Larry Semon
THEME:
"Sands of Time"

"Sunrise and sunset, promise and fulfillment, birth and death—the whole drama of life is written in the Sands of Time." So began this mystery-suspense series, composed for the most part of live original dramas written for TV and starring a wide range of guest actors and actresses. A clock was prominently featured, and time played a vital role in each story. Typically, murder or insanity was the theme. The program was based on a preceding ABC radio series (1946–1948).

CLONE HIGH, USA (*Cartoon*)

BROADCAST HISTORY:
MTV
30 minutes
Original episodes: *2003* (13 episodes)
Premiered: *January 20, 2003*
VOICES:
Abe Lincoln, narrator .... Will Forte
Gandhi .... Michael McDonald
Joan of Arc .... Nicole Sullivan
Cleopatra .... Christa Miller Lawrence
JFK, Mr. B (Butlerton) .... Christopher R. Miller
George Washington Carver, Toots, Wally .... Donald Adeosun Faison
Caesar, Gandhi's dad .... Neil Flynn
Principal Cinnamon J. Scudworth .... Phil Lord

All of the students in Clone High were clones of famous historical figures, but they acted like and were faced with the trials of ordinary present-day teenagers. Most frequently seen were tall, gangly Abe Lincoln, with his historically accurate goatee and the hots for sexy Cleopatra, who looked very ancient Egyptian; Gandhi, a little brown party animal with an affinity for dangly earrings, rap music and junk food; and Joan of Arc, a smart do-gooder who was into community service but had an odd aversion to fire. Abe's chief nemesis was preppy jock JFK, a big, buff guy with an outrageous Massachusetts accent who was always getting laid. Running the school was mad scientist Principal Scudworth, who reported to "shadowy figures," and his squat, foulmouthed robot Mr. B. Numerous other familiar faces passed through the halls, including Eleanor Roosevelt (a macho gym teacher), Moses (who looked a lot like Charlton Heston) and Genghis Khan (a big dumb bully with a T-shirt reading SCREW TIBET).

Clone High was produced in Canada but it got MTV into a lot of trouble when activists in India staged a fast to protest the "disrespectful" depiction of Mahatma Gandhi, a revered figure in that country. MTV backpedaled quickly, saying it meant no offense and that "various cultures may view this programming differently" (!). The show was pulled before all 13 episodes were aired.

CLORETS SUMMER THEATRE (*Dramatic Anthology*)

FIRST TELECAST: *July 12, 1955*
LAST TELECAST: *August 23, 1955*
BROADCAST HISTORY:
Jul 1955–Aug 1955, NBC Tue 9:00–9:30

Clorets Summer Theatre alternated with *Kleenex Summer Theatre* as a replacement series for *Fireside Theatre*. The dramas shown were all filmed reruns of episodes from *Four Star Playhouse*.

CLOSER, THE (*Situation Comedy*)

FIRST TELECAST: *February 23, 1998*
LAST TELECAST: *May 4, 1998*
BROADCAST HISTORY:
Feb 1998–May 1998, CBS Mon 9:00–9:30
CAST:
Jack McLaren .... Tom Selleck
Carl "Dobbs" Dobson .... Edward Asner
Erica Hewitt .... Penelope Ann Miller
Bruno Verma .... David Krumholtz
Alex McLaren .... Hedy Burress
Suzy Nakamura .... Beverly Andolini

Jack was a slick, self-centered Denver advertising executive who had been fired from his previous job after beating the President at golf and losing the agency's biggest client, the U.S. Army. Instead of taking a job at another agency, Jack started his own, in a run-down factory building, so he could provide work for the support team that had been let go with him. They were Carl, the crusty sarcastic creative director; Bruno, a boyish young copywriter with few strong convictions about anything; Suzy, Jack's sexy and efficient secretary; and Erica, an easily flustered Ivy League accountant who wanted to do something more exciting than spreadsheets. Also seen regularly was Jack's daughter, Alex, an independent young woman immune to any of his slick lines. Jack and her mother, Claire (Joanna Kerns), were in the final stages of an almost amicable divorce. The series title referred to Jack's legendary reputation for always being able to close a deal.

There had been press rumors of creative problems with *The Closer* even before it got on the air, and things apparently didn't improve. Co-star Miller, unhappy with the development of her role, jumped ship after taping only four episodes, and five episodes later the show had its last airing.

CLUB DANCE (*Dance*)

BROADCAST HISTORY:
The Nashville Network
60 minutes
Produced: *1991–1999* (1,848 episodes)
Premiered: *April 1, 1991*
HOST:
Shelley Mangrum
Phil Campbell (1993–1999)

Club Dance was country music's version of *American Bandstand*, a real, down-home dance party with jeans, fringed skirts, and cowboy boots. Unlike the usual TV dance show, however, this one was truly multigenerational: dancers spanned the gamut from teens to senior citizens (more than a few potbellies bounced here) and from the talented to the strictly amateur. Some came simply to sit on the sidelines and watch. Viewers came to know the regulars, including Gayle and Mike, Debbie and Johnny, Georgia and Jerry, and Joyce and James, as they high-stepped through such popular dances as the Tush Push and the Achy Breaky.

Shelley Mangrum was the friendly host, wandering the floor chatting with guests, and was joined in 1993 by fatherly Phil Campbell, the soda-pop bartender. *Club Dance* was first telecast in the afternoon on TNN but later moved into the early evening. The show originated from Knoxville, Tennessee.

CLUB EMBASSY (*Variety*)

FIRST TELECAST: *October 7, 1952*
LAST TELECAST: *June 23, 1953*
BROADCAST HISTORY:
Oct 1952–Jun 1953, NBC Tue 10:30–10:45
REGULARS:
Bob Elliott (Oct–Dec)
Ray Goulding (Oct–Dec)
Audrey Meadows (Oct–Dec)
Florian Zabach
Julia Meade (Oct–Dec)
Mindy Carson (Dec–May)
The Embassy Quartet (Dec–Jun)
Danny Hoctor (Dec–Jun)
Connie Russell (May–Jun)

This comedy-variety show originally starred Bob and Ray doing their own brand of offbeat, satirical humor, in the setting of a nightclub (the first telecast was under the title *Embassy Club*). Audrey Meadows sang and acted in various skits, violinist Florian Zabach (famous for his showpiece number "The Hot Canary") was the featured instrumental soloist, and Julia Meade was the emcee and cigarette girl. On December 30, 1952, the cast and format underwent major changes. Bob and Ray, Audrey Meadows, and Julia Meade were replaced by singer Mindy Carson, and the emphasis was shifted from comedy to music. Backing up Miss Carson were the Embassy Quartet and dancer Danny Hoctor. On May 19, 1953, Miss Carson was in turn replaced by singer Connie Russell, but the "club" closed down a month later.

CLUB MTV (*Music*)

BROADCAST HISTORY:
MTV
30/60 minutes
Produced: *1987–1992*
Premiered: *August 31, 1987*

HOSTESS:

Downtown Julie Brown

A daily dance show, originally from the Palladium in New York City and hosted by popular MTV veejay Downtown Julie Brown. The show was generally seen in the afternoon, although there were also various early- and late-evening telecasts.

CLUB OASIS (*Variety*)

FIRST TELECAST: *September 28, 1957*

LAST TELECAST: *September 6, 1958*

BROADCAST HISTORY:

Sep 1957–Aug 1958, NBC Sat 9:00–9:30
Sep 1958, NBC Sat 10:30–11:00

REGULARS:

Spike Jones and His City Slickers (1958)
Helen Grayco (1958)
Joyce Jameson (1958)
Billy Barty (1958)

Club Oasis was a simulated nightclub that headlined a different popular entertainer each week. Depending on the performer, the material might be comedy or singing or full-scale production numbers. Among those featured were Jimmy Durante, Martha Raye, Eddie Fisher, Jo Stafford, Dean Martin, Kay Starr, and Frank Sinatra, along with supporting acts each week to fill out the bill. During the summer of 1958 Spike Jones became the permanent star of the show and the title was changed to *Club Oasis Starring Spike Jones.* Featured along with Spike's lunatic band were his wife, singer Helen Grayco; comedienne Joyce Jameson; and midget comic Billy Barty. *Club Oasis* was a biweekly series throughout its run, first alternating with *The Polly Bergen Show* and during the summer of 1958 with *Opening Night.*

CLUB SEVEN (*Musical Variety*)

FIRST TELECAST: *August 12, 1948*

LAST TELECAST: *August 24, 1951*

BROADCAST HISTORY:

Aug 1948–Sep 1948, ABC Thu 8:00–8:30
Oct 1948, ABC Thu 8:30–9:00
Nov 1948–Jan 1949, ABC Wed 8:00–8:30
Jan 1949–Mar 1949, ABC Thu 10:30–11:00
Sep 1950–Aug 1951, ABC Mon–Fri 7:00–7:30

REGULARS:

Johnny Thompson (1948–1949)
Bobby Byrne Orchestra (1948–1949)
Tony Bavaar (1950–1951)
Eadie and Rack, piano team (1950–1951)

This informal, low-budget musical variety program in the early days of the ABC network featured new talent, ranging from singers and dancers to acrobats and "Hank the Mule." After a hiatus in 1949–1950 the program returned as a nightly feature, hosted by vocalist Tony Bavaar. This later version varied in length from 10 to 30 minutes, since it was often truncated by five- or ten-minute newscasts or other series on either end.

CLUELESS (*Situation Comedy*)

FIRST TELECAST: *September 20, 1996*

LAST TELECAST: *August 24, 1999*

BROADCAST HISTORY:

Sep 1996–Oct 1996, ABC Fri 9:00–9:30
Oct 1996–Feb 1997, ABC Fri 9:30–10:00
Jun 1997–Aug 1997, ABC Fri 9:30–10:00
Sep 1997–Oct 1997, UPN Tue 8:00–8:30
Nov 1997–May 1998, UPN Tue 8:30–9:00
May 1998–Jul 1998, UPN Mon 9:00–10:00
Jul 1998–Aug 1999, UPN Tue 8:30–9:00
Jul 1998–Sep 1998, UPN Tue 9:30–10:00

CAST:

Cher Horowitz .... Rachel Blanchard
Dionne (Dee) Davenport .... Stacey Dash
Murray Lawrence Duvall .. Donald Adeosun Faison
Amber Princess Mariens .... Elisa Donovan
Sean Holliday .... Sean Holland
Mel Horowitz (1996–1997) .... Michael Lerner
Mel Horowitz (1997–1999) .... Doug Sheehan
Josh (age 19) (1996–1997) .... David Lascher
Miss Geist (1996–1997).............. Twink Caplan
Mr. Hall (1996–1997) .... Wallace Shawn
Tai (1996–1997).................. Heather Gottlieb
**Coach Millie Diemer* .... Julie Brown

*Occasional

THEME:

"Ordinary Girl" written by Charlotte Caffey and Anna Waronker, performed by China Forbes

This fluffy teen sitcom, painted in a riot of bright colors and easy gags, was based on the equally fluffy hit 1995 movie of the same name starring Alicia Silverstone. It was set in Beverly Hills, where the teens cruise swank Rodeo Drive, compete for fashion plate of the day, and call each other across the classroom on their cell phones instead of passing notes. At the center of the action was Cher, the perky, way-cool daughter of rich, widowed lawyer Mel. Dee was her stylish, African-American best friend, and Amber her obnoxious fashion rival at Bronson Alcott High. Murray was Dee's hip boyfriend, and Sean his none-too-bright buddy. Watching the kids have a groovy time was Miss Geist, the disheveled guidance counselor, whom Cher, in an effort to head off more homework, had fixed up with nerdy debate coach Mr. Hall. Josh was Cher's handsome, idealistic "non-stepbrother," Mel's stepson from another marriage. In the Spring 1998 season finale Mel broke the news that his business manager had skipped town with all their money, and he was going to have to sell the mansion and take a job in blue-collar Bakersfield. What a bummer! Resourceful Cher wound up working as a waitress in Bakersfield, briefly, until Mel got rich again (funny how that happens) and they moved back to Beverly Hills. In April 1999 Cher and Dee, who was their class valedictorian, were accepted to Stanhope College. As graduation approached it was revealed that Sean had gotten into Bronson Alcott because Cher's dad was friendly with his mother and had faked his address—he actually lived in East Los Angeles. After graduation Murray and Dee got back together.

Five members of the initial cast—Dash, Faison, Donovan, Caplan, and Shawn—reprised their roles from the 1995 film, which was produced by the same producer, Amy Heckerling. In fact, Ms. Heckerling claimed that the story was originally conceived as a TV series, and was loosely based on the Jane Austen novel *Emma.*

COACH (*Situation Comedy*)

FIRST TELECAST: *February 28, 1989*

LAST TELECAST: *August 6, 1997*

BROADCAST HISTORY:

Feb 1989, ABC Tue 9:30–10:00

Mar 1989–Jun 1989, ABC Wed 9:00–9:30
Jun 1989–Aug 1989, ABC Tue 9:30–10:00
Aug 1989–Sep 1989, ABC Wed 9:30–10:00
Nov 1989–Nov 1992, ABC Tue 9:30–10:00
Nov 1992–Jul 1993, ABC Wed 9:30–10:00
Jul 1993–Jul 1994, ABC Tue 9:30–10:00
Aug 1994–Oct 1994, ABC Mon 8:00–8:30
Oct 1994–Dec 1994, ABC Mon 8:00–9:00
Jan 1995–Mar 1995, ABC Mon 8:00–8:30
Mar 1995–May 1995, ABC Wed 9:30–10:00
Jun 1995–Jan 1996, ABC Tue 9:30–10:00
Feb 1996–May 1996, ABC Tue 8:30–9:00
May 1996–Sep 1996, ABC Tue 9:30–10:00
Sep 1996–Oct 1996, ABC Sat 9:00–9:30
Dec 1996–Aug 1997, ABC Wed 8:30–9:00

CAST:
Coach Hayden Fox................ Craig T. Nelson
Assistant Coach Luther Van Dam... Jerry Van Dyke
Christine Armstrong Fox.......... Shelley Fabares
Dauber Dybinski.................. Bill Fagerbakke
Kelly Fox (1989–1993)................ Clare Carey
Stuart Rosebrock (1989–1991)......... Kris Kamm
**Coach Judy Watkins (1989–1995)*....... Pam Stone
Howard Burleigh.................... Ken Kimmins
**Fred Webb (1989–1990)*.......... Travis McKenna
**Shirley Burleigh (1991–1997)*........ Georgia Engel
Doris Sherman (1995–1997)... Katherine Helmond
**Ruthanne (1994–1995)*............... Rita Taggart
**Rosemary (1995–1997)*............... Vicki Juditz
**Eddie (1995–1996)*............. Shashawnee Hall
**John (1995–1997)*................. John Valdetero
**Martin (1995–1996)*.......... Julio Oscar Mechoso
**Timothy David (T.D.) Fox (1996–1997)*
.... Brennan and Brian Felker

*Occasional

Hayden Fox had both football and women on his mind in this broad comedy. As head coach of Minnesota State University's Screaming Eagles, he had to build up his bumbling team with dubious assistance from cheerful, but vacuous, Luther and perennial student Dauber, a big, dumb hulk of a player. The women in his life were considerably smarter: Christine was Hayden's steady girlfriend, a TV newswoman who wanted a little more attention; and Kelly was "daddy's little girl," his 18-year-old daughter by a previous marriage, who now attended Minnesota State. Everyone's love life went through comic twists and turns. To her doting dad's dismay, Kelly dated and eventually wed theater mime Stuart, but they then broke up. Hayden and Christine broke up, and then became engaged. Dumb Dauber fell for Hayden's college rival, girls' basketball coach Judy.

By 1990 the Screaming Eagles were on a winning streak, and eventually they bumbled their way to the Pioneer Bowl. Christine also flirted with the big time, as she was offered network anchor jobs, and her impending departure finally moved Hayden to propose on the air in the fall of 1992. Three times during the 1992–1993 season they tried to get married (once during each TV ratings period!)—first in her home state of Kentucky, then in Las Vegas, and finally in a peaceful setting in the woods. The first two were comic disasters, but the third was the lucky charm.

Kelly left for an ad agency job in New York in 1993 but returned to visit from time to time. Luther played the field with a succession of unlikely love interests (rich Mrs. Rizzendough, Lorraine, raucous Ruthanne), while Dauber's long-running relationship with Coach Judy continued. Howard was the tall, bald college administrator with authority over Hayden's budget, and Shirley was his nutty wife.

The 1995 season brought major changes when Hayden got his big break, leaving Minnesota to coach a Pro expansion team, the Orlando Breakers. The Breakers were owned by eccentric millionairess Doris Sherman, whose ideas for promotion and publicity sometimes collided with Hayden's love of the game. Most of the old gang moved to Florida with him, and new faces were seen representing the Breakers coaching staff. Dauber did leave Coach Judy behind, and dated the field, including a girl who played Snow White at the local GrimmWorld theme park. The Breakers got off to a slow start, and Hayden was thrown into a funk when he was asked to write a book called *Learning to Live with Losing*. Instead, Luther picked up the idea, wrote something called *Just Short of the Goal*, and scored a major success.

In 1996, having exhausted every natural and scientific means of conceiving a child, Hayden and Christine adopted an adorable baby named Timothy. The final original episode, in May 1997, brought closure and a look into the future for the principal characters. Hayden was offered contracts by several Pro teams, including $17 million to stay with the Breakers for ten more years. After much agonizing, he turned them all down and returned to Minnesota in order to help Christine build her career. Luther quit and opened his own version of Graceland; Howard was fired, and with Shirley, opened a dinner theater in Florida; and Dauber stayed with the Breakers, winning two Super Bowls and eventually becoming a star commentator. And baby Timothy? He, we were told, grew up to be just like Hayden.

COAST GUARD (*Documentary*)

BROADCAST HISTORY:
Syndicated only
30 minutes
Produced: *1995–1997* (68 episodes)
Released: *September 1995*

HOST:
Scott Morris

The work of the U.S. Coast Guard was chronicled in this reality series. Episodes featured rescues and crime prevention and apprehension. In addition to filmed footage of Coast Guard personnel in action, there were re-creations of events and interviews with participants. A representative episode included a helicopter crew rescuing three people trapped on the side of a cliff, Coast Guard boats keeping the Great Lakes shipping lanes clear of ice during the winter, medevacking a man with a head injury to a hospital, and a Coast Guard cutter patrolling the waterways of Southern California.

COAST TO COAST (*Newsmagazine*)

FIRST TELECAST: *January 15, 1997*
LAST TELECAST: *September 3, 1997*
BROADCAST HISTORY:
Jan 1997, CBS Wed 9:00–10:00
Jul 1997–Sep 1997, CBS Wed 9:00–10:00

CORRESPONDENTS:
Bernard Goldberg
Cynthia Bowers

Vicki Mabrey
Peter Van Sant
Derek McGinty
Alison Stewart
Jennifer Laird
David Turecamo
Steve Hartman

Unlike most TV newsmagazines, *Coast to Coast* originated not in a studio, but in different towns and cities across America where its human-interest stories took place. In the grand tradition of the late Charles Kuralt's "On the Road" segments for *The CBS Evening News*, its correspondents took viewers on trips to the backwaters of America to cover offbeat, real-life stories about people, places, and policies that they felt were making life in America better. Segments included an Idaho farmer who trained newborn sandhill cranes to follow his ultralight airplane in an effort to teach the endangered species how to migrate, a St. Louis doctor helping schizophrenics battle their illness, a feature to determine whether or not a man with no money could travel across the state of Iowa in a week relying exclusively on the generosity and help of strangers, a woman trying to save the last herd of wild horses on the Outer Banks of North Carolina, a prison in Columbus, Ohio, where the inmates trained seeing-eye dogs, and the first female boxer to win a fight at New York's Madison Square Garden.

Coast to Coast was pulled from the CBS schedule after only three episodes had aired. It returned that summer with five more episodes.

COBRA (*Adventure*)

BROADCAST HISTORY:

Syndicated only
60 minutes
Produced: *1993–1994* (22 episodes)
Released: *September 1993*

CAST:

Robert "Scandal" Jackson .... Michael Dudikoff
Danielle LaPointe .... Allison J. Hossack
Dallas Cassel .... James Tolkan

Supercool former Navy SEAL Scandal Jackson had a lot to be thankful for. Shot in the face and left for dead, he had been given a complete facial reconstruction and a new identity by Cobra, a secret foundation funded by billionaire Quentin Avery to help victims of crime who had not received justice. Cobra even faked his death so he could function as its crime fighter with nobody looking for him. Danielle, Avery's savvy, beautiful daughter, became his partner, and Dallas, who often ended up out in the field with them, was their supercompetent boss. Scandal drove a vintage A.C. Cobra sports convertible (coincidence?) that he and his dad had restored. Although the team's offices were in Bay City, California, they traveled all over the country, often using high technology and military tactics and lingo ("Bogey moving toward you . . . watch out!") to nail the bad guys.

CODE NAME: FOXFIRE (*Foreign Intrigue/Secret Agent*)

FIRST TELECAST: *January 27, 1985*
LAST TELECAST: *March 22, 1985*
BROADCAST HISTORY:

Jan 1985, NBC Sun 8:00–10:00
Feb 1985–Mar 1985, NBC Fri 8:00–9:00

CAST:

Elizabeth "Foxfire" Towne .... Joanna Cassidy
Larry Hutchins .... John McCook
Maggie Bryan .... Sheryl Lee Ralph
Danny O'Toole .... Robin Johnson
Phillips .... Henry Jones

The fate of the nation (or at least of NBC's Friday night schedule) rested in the hands of three sexy government agents in this hard-action cross between the James Bond movies and *Charlie's Angels*. The leader was former CIA operative Liz "Foxfire" Towne, who had just served four years in prison for a crime she hadn't committed. She had been sprung by Larry Hutchins, the brother of the President, to organize a special counterespionage team reporting directly to him. Liz's partners were Maggie "the cat," a reformed thief from Detroit and Danny "the driver," a resourceful, streetwise, former hansom cabdriver from New York. They were hard-nosed and tough, or elegant and sophisticated, as the assignment demanded. Also on Liz's mind, understandably, was tracking down the former lover who had abandoned her in Bogotá and thereby been responsible for her imprisonment. Phillips was Hutchins's stuffy valet who helped out at unexpected times.

CODE R (*Adventure*)

FIRST TELECAST: *January 21, 1977*
LAST TELECAST: *June 10, 1977*
BROADCAST HISTORY:

Jan 1977–Jun 1977, CBS Fri 8:00–9:00

CAST:

Rick Wilson .... James Houghton
George Baker .... Martin Kove
Walt Robinson .... Tom Simcox
Suzy .... Susanne Reed
Ted Milbank .... Ben Davidson
Bobby Robinson .... Robbie Rundle
Harry .... W. T. Zacha

Scenic Channel Island, off the southern California coast, was the setting for this adventure series, which resembled NBC's *Emergency* but was laid in a self-contained locale. Rick Wilson was the fire chief, George Baker the chief of beaches, and Walt Robinson the police chief on Channel Island. They all managed to get involved in at least one of the several stories that unfolded in any given episode. Suzy was the dispatcher for the Island's Emergency Services Department and doubled as secretary to all three men, since their offices were in the same building. Ted was a deputy of police, Bobby was Walt's ten-year-old son, and Harry was the owner and bartender at the Lighthouse Bar, a favorite off-duty hangout of the three chiefs. Typical situations included rescuing two young boys floating out to sea on a homemade raft, tracking down a bootleg whiskey operation, coping with an arsonist, and helping a man trapped in the water in his dune buggy.

CODE RED (*Adventure*)

FIRST TELECAST: *September 20, 1981*
LAST TELECAST: *September 12, 1982*
BROADCAST HISTORY:

Sep 1981, ABC Sun 8:00–9:30
Nov 1981–Mar 1982, ABC Sun 7:00–8:00
Jul 1982–Sep 1982, ABC Sun 7:00–8:00

CAST:

Battalion Chief Joe Rorchek .... Lorne Greene
Ann Rorchek .... Julie Adams
Ted Rorchek .... Andrew Stevens
Chris Rorchek .... Sam J. Jones
Haley Green .... Martina Deignan
Danny Blake .... Adam Rich
Capt. Mike Benton .... Joe Maross
Rags Harris .... James Crittenden
"Stuff" Wade .... Dennis Haysbert
Al Martelli .... Jack Lindine

PRODUCER:

Irwin Allen

Lorne Greene headed a family of firefighters in this instructional series. Joe Rorchek was a 30-year veteran of the Los Angeles City Fire Department who specialized in arson investigations. His sons were also firemen—Ted on the ground and Chris from the air, as a helicopter pilot. Haley was a young woman trying to prove herself as the city's first female "smoke eater," and Danny was a homeless 13-year-old adopted by the Rorcheks. Naturally he joined the fire department's Explorer Program so he could learn all about firefighting, too.

Along with lessons in fire safety, viewers saw examples of the work of paramedics, rescue operations, and even "scuba diving for underwater fire prevention"—a danger most people would find unlikely!

CODE 3 (*Documentary*)

FIRST TELECAST: *April 11, 1992*
LAST TELECAST: *June 12, 1994*
BROADCAST HISTORY:

Apr 1992–Jan 1993, FOX Sat 9:00–9:30
Feb 1993–Jun 1993, FOX Sat 9:00–10:00
Jun 1993–Jul 1993, FOX Fri 9:30–10:00
Nov 1993–Jan 1994, FOX Mon–Fri 11:00–11:30
Jan 1994–Jun 1994, FOX Sun 7:00–8:00

HOST:

Gil Gerard

Actor Gil Gerard hosted this documentary series that focused on the activities of paramedics, airlift rescue teams, fire department rescue units, police, and ordinary citizens. Each episode featured several segments showing the diverse ways in which these people worked to help others in dangerous, often life-threatening situations. There were no re-creations on *Code 3*; everything shown was real-life footage.

Code 3 was canceled at the end of the 1992–1993 season, but returned in reruns as a weekday late-night show for a couple of months that November, and with a mix of new and repeat episodes on Sunday evenings during the first half of 1993.

CODENAME: KIDS NEXT DOOR (*Cartoon*)

BROADCAST HISTORY:

Cartoon Network
30 minutes
Original episodes: *2002–*
Premiered: *December 6, 2002*

VOICES:

Numbah 1 (Nigel Uno), Numbah 2 (Hoagie P. Gilligan, Jr.) .... Ben Diskin
Numbah 3 (Kuki Sanban) .... Lauren Tom
Numbah 4 (Wallabee Beetles) ... Dee Bradley Baker
Numbah 5 (Abigail "Abby" Lincoln) .. Cree Summer

Five ten-year-olds, known by their numbers, banded together to battle the domination of the world by adults in this fantasy series. Numbah 1 was the British-accented leader, resourceful and cool in his ever-present sunglasses; Numbah 2, the mechanical genius and pilot; Numbah 3, the little charmer, in charge of diversionary tactics; Numbah 4, the enforcer, skilled in hand-to-hand combat, and Numbah 5, the quiet, stealthy one and team spy. From their tree-house headquarters they launched missions on behalf of children everywhere, "liberating" an ice cream factory, taking back "adult swim time" at the local pool and defeating homework. They used fantastic technology, including flying machines, catapults and an improvised cannon. Their chief adversaries were not the adults of town but the scary Delightful Children from Down the Lane, five immaculately groomed kids who stood together, spoke in unison and fought the very idea of childhood. The KND slogan: "Either you're in or you're old."

CO-ED FEVER (*Situation Comedy*)

FIRST TELECAST: *February 4, 1979*
LAST TELECAST: *February 4, 1979*
BROADCAST HISTORY:

Feb 1979, CBS Sun 10:30–11:00

CAST:

Tuck .... David Keith
Mousie .... Alexa Kenin
Doug .... Christopher S. Nelson
Elizabeth .... Cathryn O'Neil
Gobo .... Michael Pasternak
Hope .... Tacey Phillips
Mrs. Selby .... Jane Rose
Sandi .... Heather Thomas
Mr. Peabody .... Hamilton Camp
Melba .... Jillian Kesner

One of the biggest theatrical movie hits of 1978 was a slapstick look at college life titled *Animal House*. Whether by pure coincidence or not, each of the three networks rushed to television early in 1979 a comedy series that centered around college hijinks. ABC had *Delta House* and NBC, *Brothers and Sisters*, but to CBS went the distinction of a series so dreadful that it never even made it to its regular time slot (on Monday). *Co-Ed Fever* was seen just once, as a "special preview" on Sunday, February 4, 1979.

The setting for *Co-Ed Fever* was a co-educational dormitory at rustic Baxter College. The dormitory, Brewster House, was peopled by a wide assortment of kooky college students, one ultra-sexy blonde named Sandi, and a spaced-out housemother, Mrs. Selby.

COKE TIME WITH EDDIE FISHER (*Music*)

FIRST TELECAST: *April 29, 1953*
LAST TELECAST: *February 22, 1957*
BROADCAST HISTORY:

Apr 1953–Feb 1957, NBC Wed/Fri 7:30–7:45 (OS)

REGULARS:

Eddie Fisher
Don Ameche (1953)
Freddy Robbins
Axel Stordahl and His Orchestra
The Echoes (1956–1957)

Handsome young Eddie Fisher was fresh out of the army and at the height of his career when this popular 15-minute show began in 1953. The idol of bobbysoxers all over the country, he sang many of his million-selling recordings here, including "I'm Walking Behind You" (which reached number-one on the hit parade shortly after the series began), "Oh! My Papa," and "Anytime." Each live telecast—occasionally the show was filmed in advance or on location—opened with Eddie singing his theme song, "May I Sing to You." Guest stars appeared frequently and a permanent backup group, the Echoes, was added in the fall of 1956. Actor Don Ameche was the original host of the show, through October 23, 1953. Freddy Robbins, who had been announcing the commercials, subsequently took on the added duty of host.

COLBYS, THE (*Drama*)

FIRST TELECAST: *November 20, 1985*
LAST TELECAST: *March 26, 1987*
BROADCAST HISTORY:

Nov 1985, ABC Wed 10:00–11:00
Nov 1985–Mar 1987, ABC Thu 9:00–10:00

CAST:

Jason Colby .... Charlton Heston
Sable Scott Colby............. Stephanie Beacham
Francesca Scott Colby Hamilton Langdon
.... Katherine Ross
Jeff Colby .... John James
Fallon Carrington Colby............. Emma Samms
Monica Colby...................... Tracy Scoggins
Miles Colby.................... Maxwell Caulfield
Bliss Colby......................... Claire Yarlett
Zachary Powers .... Ricardo Montalban
Constance Colby (1985–1986)... Barbara Stanwyck
Lord Roger Langdon............... David Hedison
Garrett Boydston (1985–1986) .... Ken Howard
Hutch Corrigan (1985–1986) ... Joseph Campanella
Sean McAllister (1985–1986).... Charles Van Eman
Neil Kittredge (1985–1986)........... Philip Brown
Henderson Palmer (1985–1986) .... Ivan Bonar
Arthur Cates (1985–1986) .... Peter White
Wayne Masterson (1986) .... Gary Morris
L.B. ("Little Blake") Colby (1986)
.... Ashley Mutrux; also Brandon Bluhm
Spiros Koralis (1986).................... Ray Wise
Asst. D.A. John Moretti (1986) ...... Vince Baggetta
Channing Carter Colby (1986–1987)
.... Kim Morgan Greene
Sen. Cash Cassidy (1986–1987)... James Houghton
Adrienne Cassidy (1986–1987)....... Shanna Reed
Kolya (Nikolai) Rostov (1986–1987).... Adrian Paul
Anna Rostov (1986–1987) .... Anna Levine
Sacha Malenkov (1986).............. Judson Scott
Lucas Carter (1986–1987)......... Kevin McCarthy
Dr. Waverly (1986–1987) .... Georgann Johnson
Phillip Colby (a.k.a. Hoyt Parker) (1987)
.... Michael Parks

A strong emphasis on glamour and the trappings of the super-rich marked this close copy of (and spin-off from) ABC's hit soap opera *Dynasty*. Perhaps it was too close a copy; *The Colbys* never caught on as its parent program had, and was canceled after only two seasons.

At the center of the turmoil was Jason Colby, head of giant Colby Enterprises, a multinational conglomerate with interests in oil, shipping, real estate, and the aerospace industry. The family's opulent estate Belvedere, overlooking Los Angeles, was a veritable hotbed of intrigue, much of it between Jason's glamorous, scheming wife Sable and her much-married sister Francesca ("Frankie"), her rival for Jason's affections. Maintaining a degree of civility between the squabbling sisters was Jason's sensible older sister Constance, who owned half of Colby Enterprises.

Stories during the first season included the arrival (from *Dynasty*) of Jason's nephew Jeff, to take his place in the family empire and to search for his missing bride Fallon, who had developed amnesia; Sable's scheme to have Constance declared incompetent so she couldn't leave her half of the family fortune to Jeff; Connie's relationship with rancher Hutch and Francesca's short marriage to British diplomat Roger Langdon; Zach Powers's incessant plotting against the Colbys; and the revelation that Jeff was in fact Jason's son, the product of a tryst with Francesca many years before. Along the way each of Jason and Sable's three children had their own entanglements: lawyer Monica with blind country singer Wayne and married man Neil (with whom she worked at Titania Records); playboy Miles with Fallon, whom he maneuvered into marriage; and sexy young Bliss with Clean Earth activist Sean. As the season ended, Jason and Sable were embroiled in a messy divorce proceeding, sons Miles and Jeff were accused of murdering minor characters, and Jason was in jail for wife-beating and attempted murder.

During the second season Sable plotted to hold on to Jason, but was ultimately unsuccessful as he prepared to marry Francesca. At the last minute Frankie's long-lost husband (and Jason's brother) Phillip showed up, however, spoiling that idea. Monica had an affair with Senator Cash Cassidy, whose wife Adrienne and young son Scott were not pleased; Miles bedded and then married a magazine reporter named Channing, who found that before she could get the lurid story of the Colbys into print she had become part of it; and Bliss fell in love with a Russian ballet dancer named Kolya, who cheerfully defected on her behalf. There was death and birth: word of Constance Colby's death in Nepal was received, while Fallon gave birth to a baby girl prematurely after a fall, as current husband Jeff and her ex, Miles, wondered which of them was the father. As if that was not enough, poor Fallon soon after found herself in one of the most bizarre end-of-season cliff-hangers ever devised for a prime-time soap: driving down a remote country road, she was abducted and carried away in an alien spaceship! (In retrospect, that was probably not a bad thing; the aliens transported her back to *Dynasty* the following season, while most of the other characters in *The Colbys* disappeared as the show was canceled.)

So that viewers would have no doubt about its origins, the series was officially called *Dynasty II—The Colbys* during its first two months.

COLD FEET (*Comedy/Drama*)

FIRST TELECAST: *September 24, 1999*
LAST TELECAST: *October 29, 1999*
BROADCAST HISTORY:

Sep 1999–Oct 1999, NBC Fri 10:00–11:00

CAST:

Adam Williams .... David Sutcliffe
Shelley Sullivan .... Jean Louisa Kelly
Pete Lombardi .... William Keane
Jenny Lombardi....................... Dina Spybey
David Chandler .... Anthony Starke
Karen Chandler.................... Alicia Coppola

Three relationships, marriage, parenthood, and the

"cold feet" of dating were explored in this short-lived series about six self-absorbed yuppies living in Seattle. The newlyweds were harried Pete and his pregnant wife, Jenny, whose sex drive seemed to have spun out of control since she became pregnant—she wanted it all the time, exhausting him. David and Karen already had their baby, little Joshua, but David wanted Karen to stay home and nurture while she wanted to get a nanny and have a little freedom. Representing the dating scene was Pete's shaggy-haired work pal Adam, a romantic goofball who did nutty things like standing outside the window of his desired stark naked, singing, with a rose up his butt. Shelley was the object of this disconcerting affection, and since she had just been dumped by her last no-good boyfriend, well, maybe there was a chance.

Based on the 1997 British series of the same name.

COLGATE COMEDY HOUR, THE (*Variety*)
FIRST TELECAST: *September 10, 1950*
LAST TELECAST: *December 25, 1955*
BROADCAST HISTORY:
Sep 1950–Dec 1955, NBC Sun 8:00–9:00
PRINCIPAL HOSTS:
Eddie Cantor (1950–1954)
Dean Martin and Jerry Lewis (1950–1955)
Fred Allen (1950)
Donald O'Connor (1951–1954)
Abbott and Costello (1951–1954)
Bob Hope (1952–1953)
Jimmy Durante (1953–1954)
Gordon MacRae (1954–1955)
Robert Paige (1955)

This big-budget series of comedy spectaculars, featuring most of the top names in show business, was NBC's first successful counterprogramming against *The Ed Sullivan Show*, which ran opposite it on Sunday nights. It boasted numerous television firsts, and was the first starring vehicle for such names as Eddie Cantor, Fred Allen, Abbott and Costello, Spike Jones, Tony Martin, and Ray Bolger. It was also the first commercial series to originate in Hollywood (September 30, 1951), and it included the first network color telecast, on November 22, 1953 (as an experimental test of RCA's new compatible color system, under special permission from the FCC).

When *The Colgate Comedy Hour* began in the fall of 1950 the intention was to have three rotating elements, each a complete series of its own, starring Eddie Cantor, Martin and Lewis, and Fred Allen, respectively. Allen was dropped in December 1950, and the series thereafter began to include other big-name hosts on an occasional basis, in addition to the principals, who appeared approximately once a month. Among those hosting one or two shows during 1950–1951, for example, were Abbott and Costello, Jerry Lester, Spike Jones, Tony Martin, and Phil Silvers. In September 1951 the program began telecasts from the El Capitan Theatre in Hollywood, though there continued to be occasional telecasts from the International Theatre in New York.

In September 1952 Eddie Cantor suffered a heart attack immediately following one of his telecasts and was off the air for several months. He returned in January 1953 and completed one more season with the show. Beginning with the 1952–1953 season Colgate also began to vary the revue format, with occasional "book" musicals, such as *Anything Goes*, starring Ethel Merman and Frank Sinatra (February 28, 1954); *Revenge With Music*, with Anna Maria Alberghetti (October 24, 1954); and *Roberta*, with Gordon MacRae (April 10, 1955). In early 1954 the program began to "hit the road," with special broadcasts from all over the United States, including Pebble Beach, California; the Coconut Grove and Hollywood Bowl in Hollywood; Miami; Las Vegas; Jones Beach, New York; and the liner *S.S. United States* docked at a pier in New York. Some shows featured special events, such as the Ice Capades or various awards presentations and salutes. Always the emphasis was on big names and "event" television.

In the summer of 1955 Colgate began a tie-in with Paramount Pictures, in which scenes from a new film were shown, and stars from the movie appeared. Charlton Heston even hosted several telecasts. The name of the series was changed at this time to *Colgate Variety Hour*. However, a superbudget series such as this proved harder and harder to sustain, and in December 1955 one of TV's most notable early comedy variety programs finally reached the end of its run—with a December 25th hour devoted to Christmas music by Fred Waring and his Pennsylvanians, from Hollywood.

COLGATE THEATRE (*Dramatic Anthology*)
FIRST TELECAST: *January 3, 1949*
LAST TELECAST: *October 7, 1958*
BROADCAST HISTORY:
Jan 1949–Oct 1949, NBC Mon 9:00–9:30
Oct 1949–Jun 1950, NBC Sun 8:30–9:00
Aug 1958–Oct 1958, NBC Tue 9:00–9:30

The first program to use this name was a live dramatic series presenting adaptations of short stories and plays, as well as scripts especially written for television. Comedies, dramas, and mysteries alternated, and a wide variety of talent appeared (usually not top names, however). A "Broadway Theater" theme opened the show, with the camera following theatergoers into their seats, scanning the program for the title of the night's production, and then focusing on the stage as the curtain began to rise. Among the first season's productions were the first TV adaptations of two popular radio series, *Mr. and Mrs. North* (July 4, 1949) and *Vic and Sade* (July 11–July 25, 1949).

The second *Colgate Theatre* was a summer film series in 1958, consisting primarily of pilots for projected series that did not make it to the network's fall schedule. However, one episode, "Fountain of Youth," written, directed, and narrated by Orson Welles, won a Peabody Award.

COLGATE VARIETY HOUR, THE, see *Colgate Comedy Hour, The*

COLGATE WESTERN THEATRE (*Western Anthology*)
FIRST TELECAST: *July 3, 1959*
LAST TELECAST: *September 4, 1959*
BROADCAST HISTORY:
Jul 1959–Sep 1959, NBC Fri 9:30–10:00

This summer series consisted of reruns of films of Western dramas originally seen, for the most part, on *G.E. Theatre* and *Schlitz Playhouse*.

COLIN QUINN'S MANLY WORLD (*Comedy*)
BROADCAST HISTORY:
MTV
30 minutes
Produced: *1990*
Premiered: *January 22, 1990*
REGULAR:
Colin Quinn
Comedy by MTV veejay Colin Quinn and various professional sports figures, intercut with music videos.

COLISEUM (*Variety*)
FIRST TELECAST: *January 26, 1967*
LAST TELECAST: *June 1, 1967*
BROADCAST HISTORY:
Jan 1967–Jun 1967, CBS Thu 7:30–8:30
Each week a different star hosted this variety series, which traveled around the world to film such spectacles as the New Vienna Ice Extravaganza and the Moscow State Circus. In addition there were many New York–based programs featuring popular entertainers in a straight variety format.

COLLEGE BOWL, THE (*Musical Comedy*)
FIRST TELECAST: *October 2, 1950*
LAST TELECAST: *March 26, 1951*
BROADCAST HISTORY:
Oct 1950–Mar 1951, ABC Mon 9:00–9:30
REGULARS:
Chico Marx
Jimmy Brock
Stanley Prager
Barbara Ruick
Kenny Buffert
Evelyn Ward
Andy Williams
Paula Huston
Tommy Morton
Joan Holloway
Lee Lindsey
PRODUCER:
Martin Gosch
A weekly miniature musical comedy featuring Chico Marx, of the Marx Brothers, as the proprietor of a campus soda fountain. The supporting cast was a lively group of young actors and actresses from Broadway shows and nightclubs, most notably 18-year-old Andy Williams. The show was telecast live from New York.

COLLEGE OF MUSICAL KNOWLEDGE, THE, see *Kay Kyser's Kollege of Musical Knowledge*

COLLEGE PRESS CONFERENCE, see *Junior Press Conference*

COLONEL HUMPHREY FLACK (*Situation Comedy*)
FIRST TELECAST: *October 7, 1953*
LAST TELECAST: *July 2, 1954*
BROADCAST HISTORY:
Oct 1953–Dec 1953, DUM Wed 9:00–9:30
Jan 1954–May 1954, DUM Sat 10:00–10:30
May 1954–Jul 1954, DUM Fri 10:30–11:00
(In first-run syndication during the 1958–1959 season)
CAST:
Col. Humphrey Flack............... Alan Mowbray
Uthas P. Garvey........................ Frank Jenks
By 1953, Britisher Alan Mowbray was one of Hollywood's most experienced character actors, having appeared in nearly 300 B films since 1923. (Contrary to popular belief, in only five of them did he play the butler.) DuMont could not have picked a more suitable performer to play Col. Humphrey Flack, a dapper, witty, somewhat paunchy modern-day Robin Hood. Flack was a con man's con man, outswindling assorted swindlers in order to aid the poor—and retaining a percentage for himself, of course, to "cover expenses." His sidekick was Uthas P. (for Patsy) Garvey, who was no slouch himself, but not up to the colonel's suave standards.

The program was based on a series of *Saturday Evening Post* stories by Everett Rhodes Castle and was telecast live. In 1958 a film syndicated version, simply titled *Colonel Flack*, starring Mowbray and Jenks, was released. This series was also known as *The Fabulous Fraud.*

COLT .45 (*Western*)
FIRST TELECAST: *October 18, 1957*
LAST TELECAST: *September 27, 1960*
BROADCAST HISTORY:
Oct 1957–Dec 1957, ABC Fri 10:00–10:30
Jan 1958–Apr 1958, ABC Fri 8:30–9:00
Oct 1958–Sep 1959, ABC Sun 9:00–9:30
Oct 1959–Mar 1960, ABC Sun 7:00–7:30
Apr 1960–Sep 1960, ABC Tue 9:30–10:00
CAST:
Christopher Colt.................. Wayde Preston
Sam Colt, Jr. (1959–1960) .... Donald May
Christopher Colt was a handsome young government undercover agent posing as a gun salesman in this Western adventure. Most of his missions involved tracking down notorious outlaws, and in the process he had plenty of opportunities to use his famous Colt .45 pistol.

Not long after the series began, Warner Bros. Studios began to have trouble with its star. Eventually Wayde Preston joined the growing list of "Warner Bros. walkouts" (for some others see *Cheyenne, Maverick,* and *77 Sunset Strip*), and a considerable number of repeats had to be interspersed with original episodes to keep the series on the air through the 1958–1959 season. In 1959 Christopher Colt was gradually replaced as the leading character by his cousin Sam Colt, Jr. Also a government agent, Sam was the focal point of some episodes and appeared jointly with Christopher Colt at least once. Although actor Preston did rejoin the fold, Donald May eventually took over as the lead full-time.

COLUMBIA UNIVERSITY SEMINAR (*Instruction*)
FIRST TELECAST: *October 4, 1952*
LAST TELECAST: *January 3, 1953*
BROADCAST HISTORY:
Oct 1952–Jan 1953, ABC Sat 6:30–7:00
INSTRUCTOR:
Donald N. Bigelow
This was a course on American Civilization, presided over by Donald N. Bigelow, Assistant Professor of History at Columbia University. Prof. Bigelow

and his eleven students were seen seated at a round table. Academic credit was also given to viewers actively participating in the course. After its prime-time run the series continued on Sunday afternoons until May 1953.

COLUMBO (*Police Drama*)

FIRST TELECAST: *September 15, 1971*
LAST TELECAST: *February 20, 1993*
BROADCAST HISTORY:

Sep 1971–Sep 1972, NBC Wed 8:30–10:00
Sep 1972–Jul 1974, NBC Sun 8:30–10:00
Aug 1974–Aug 1975, NBC Sun 8:30–10:30
Sep 1975–Sep 1976, NBC Sun 9:00–11:00
Oct 1976–Sep 1977, NBC Sun 8:00–9:30
Feb 1989–May 1989, ABC Mon 9:00–11:00
Aug 1989–Jul 1990, ABC Sat 9:00–11:00
Aug 1990, ABC Sun 9:00–11:00
Jan 1992–May 1992, ABC Thu 8:00–10:00
Nov 1992–Feb 1993, ABC Sat 8:00–10:00

CAST:

Lt. Columbo............................Peter Falk

At the beginning of each *Columbo* episode the audience witnessed a clever murder and saw the ingenious measures the murderer took to prevent detection by the police. Then into the case came Lt. Columbo (he never did have a first name). He drove a beat-up old car, wore a dirty, rumpled trench coat that looked at least ten years old, and acted for all the world like an incompetent bumbler. He was excessively polite to everyone, went out of his way not to offend any of the suspects, and seemed like a hopeless choice to solve any crime, especially a well-conceived murder. But all that was superficial, designed to lull the murderer into a false sense of security. Despite his appearance, Columbo was one of the shrewdest, most resourceful detectives on the Los Angeles police force. Slowly and methodically he pieced together the most minute clues leading to the identity of the killer, who, when his guilt was revealed, was always incredulous that such an unlikely cop had managed to find him out.

Columbo was one of the three original rotating elements of the *NBC Sunday Mystery Movie*, the other two being *McMillan and Wife* and *McCloud*. It was by far the most popular of the elements and would have become a separate series in its own right if actor Peter Falk had permitted it to. But a 60- or 90-minute movie every week was too much for one actor to carry, not to mention the dangers of being typecast in such a distinctive role. Toward the end of the program's original run Falk was said to be making more than a quarter of a million dollars per episode, but even at that refused to do more than a few per year. He continued to film an occasional new episode after 1977.

In 1989, more than a decade after the original series ended, Falk returned with some new *Columbo* films for the *ABC Mystery Movie*. Nothing had changed, and in fact the writers had begun to tease viewers about the series' little gimmicks. In an episode in which Mrs. Columbo's murder was faked, the missus was never actually seen in person, only referred to. She was never seen in the original series either, even though there was a spin-off series called *Mrs. Columbo*. ABC used the new films made in 1989–1990 to plug various holes in its schedule during the early 1990s.

An interesting sidelight is that Peter Falk was the producers' second choice to portray Columbo. The first actor approached for the role was Bing Crosby. Crosby, 67 years old and a millionaire many times over, declined, reportedly because it would interfere with his golf game. And so Falk got the part, and stardom.

COMBAT! (*War Drama*)

FIRST TELECAST: *October 2, 1962*
LAST TELECAST: *August 29, 1967*
BROADCAST HISTORY:

Oct 1962–Aug 1967, ABC Tue 7:30–8:30

CAST:

Lt. Gil Hanley..........................Rick Jason
Sgt. Chip Saunders....................Vic Morrow
*PFC Paul "Caje" Lemay**..............Pierre Jalbert
Pvt. William G. Kirby (1963–1967)......Jack Hogan
PFC Littlejohn (1963–1967)...........Dick Peabody
Doc Walton (1962–1963).............Steven Rogers
Doc (1963–1967).....................Conlan Carter
Pvt. Braddock (1962–1963).........Shecky Greene
Pvt. Billy Nelson (1963–1964)..........Tom Lowell

*Character originally named Caddy Cadron in pilot.

Combat depicted the exploits of a U.S. Army platoon fighting its way across Europe during World War II, following D-Day. Realism was the keynote of this mud-splattered series, whose cast was sent to army camp for a week of actual "boot camp" training before production began. Original World War II battle footage was included in some episodes. The stories ranged from straight combat adventure to human interest and sometimes humorous themes. Among the regulars were Pvt. Braddock, the platoon comic and resident hustler, played by nightclub comedian Shecky Greene; Caje, the sly, dark-haired Cajun; and Doc Walton, the young, sensitive medical aidman. Out in front were the tough, hard-boiled leaders, Lt. Gil Hanley and Sgt. Chip Saunders.

COMBAT MISSIONS (*Competition*)

BROADCAST HISTORY:

USA Network
60 minutes
Original episodes: *2002*
Premiered: *January 16, 2002*

REGULARS:

Rudy Boesch, Base Commander
James D. Dever, Sergeant Major
T. J. Myers, Executive Officer
Leigh Koechner, Bartender
Katie Morgan, Bartender

Possibly the most macho entry in the reality-show wave of the early 2000s was this gung-ho competition between real soldiers and law enforcement agents in California's hot, dusty Mojave Desert. The setting was fictional Camp Windstorm, commanded by "Colonel" Rudy Boesch of *Survivor* fame. (In reality Boesch was a retired navy chief petty officer.) Twenty-four veterans of such organizations as the Navy SEALS, Green Berets, Army Rangers, C.I.A. and police S.W.A.T. teams, ranging in age from their 20s to their 50s, were organized into four teams of six each. Two teams competed each week in mock military operations such as Tank Take-Out, Fuel Dump Demolition, Urban Assault and Hostage Rescue, triggering explosions and firing infrared lasers from authentic weapons and vehicles. They also fought a "Shadow Squad" of specially trained opponents. Each week the losing team had to vote out one member in a discharge ceremony and replace him with a new member from a pool. The series culminated with the winning team taking home a $150,000 team prize, and a *mano a mano* showdown for the best single soldier, who won $250,000.

It was all extremely strenuous and realistic, down to the almost total absence of women (except for a couple of female bartenders in the Snake Pit clubhouse). *Combat Missions* was produced by *Survivor* creator Mark Burnett.

COMBAT SERGEANT (*War Drama*)
FIRST TELECAST: *June 29, 1956*
LAST TELECAST: *September 27, 1956*
BROADCAST HISTORY:
Jun 1956–Aug 1956, ABC Fri 8:00–8:30
Sep 1956, ABC Thu 9:00–9:30
CAST:
Sgt. Nelson .... Michael Thomas
Gen. Harrison .... Cliff Clark
Abdulla .... Dominick Delgarde

This wartime adventure was set in North Africa during World War II. Sgt. Nelson, receiving his orders direct from Gen. Harrison, found himself involved in various dangerous assignments, including coordination between the Allied forces, espionage against the Germans, and sometimes even romance. Actual World War II film footage was used in this series.

COME CLOSER (*Quiz/Audience Participation*)
FIRST TELECAST: *September 20, 1954*
LAST TELECAST: *December 13, 1954*
BROADCAST HISTORY:
Sep 1954–Dec 1954, ABC Mon 8:00–8:30
EMCEE:
Jimmy Nelson
DUMMIES:
Danny O'Day
Humphrey Higby
Farfel the Dog

This audience-participation show starred the ventriloquist Jimmy Nelson and his dummies, with questions calling for comic answers by studio contestants. The contestant "coming closest" to the correct answer won cash and prizes. A jackpot prize, based on a clue given in song by "Danny O'Day," was also featured.

COMEBACK STORY, THE (*Drama/Interview*)
FIRST TELECAST: *October 2, 1953*
LAST TELECAST: *February 5, 1954*
BROADCAST HISTORY:
Oct 1953–Feb 1954, ABC Fri 9:30–10:00
EMCEE:
George Jessel (Oct 1953–Jan 1954)
Arlene Francis (Jan–Feb 1954)

This heartwarming series presented, through interviews and dramatizations, the stories of persons stricken with physical disabilities or bad fortune who had fought to rebuild their lives. Some of the guests were ordinary people, but most were notable personalities such as Norman Brokenshire, the pioneer radio announcer who won his battle with alcoholism; athlete Mildred "Babe" Didrikson Zaharias; and blind jazz pianist George Shearing. The program was telecast live from New York.

COMEDY BREAK (*Comedy/Variety*)
BROADCAST HISTORY:
Syndicated only
30 minutes
Produced: *1985–1986* (125 episodes)
Released: *Fall 1985*
HOSTS:
Mack Dryden
Jamie Alcroft

Comedians Dryden and Alcroft hosted this collection of comedy skits, standup routines, and funny clips from old TV shows. Their guests were primarily veteran comics like Morey Amsterdam, Rose Marie, Ruth Buzzi, Bill Dana, and Arte Johnson, along with current TV series regulars like John Larroquette, Tim Reid, John Hillerman, Christopher Hewett, Markie Post, Katherine Helmond, and Marla Gibbs.

COMEDY CENTRAL (Network) (*General Entertainment Cable Network*)
LAUNCHED:
April 1, 1991
SUBSCRIBERS (MAY 2003):
82.1 million (77% U.S.)

This cable channel specializes in comedy programming with a distinctly contemporary attitude. Its first well-known original series was *Mystery Science Theater 3000*, a daily movie (usually old and awful) "hosted" by a human and two robots. Another series that attracted attention was *Politically Incorrect*, a mock political talk show. In addition the channel carried standup comedy and live comic "coverage" of major events such as the President's State of the Union address to Congress *(State of the Union UnDressed)*.

The remainder of the schedule consists of reruns of such series as *Saturday Night Live*, *Soap*, and *The Kids in the Hall*, with an occasional old classic *(The Abbott and Costello Show, The Ernie Kovacs Show)* mixed in. In 1994 the network made news by running the racy British sitcom *Absolutely Fabulous* after it had been turned down by other U.S. broadcasters.

Comedy Central was created in 1991 by the merger of two struggling limited-distribution comedy networks, The Comedy Channel (launched in November 1989) and Ha! (launched in April 1990). Following are some of its early original series. Hosts or stars are in parentheses.

A-List, The (standup comedy, Richard Lewis, Sandra Bernhard), 1992–1994
Absolutely Fabulous (British sitcom, Jennifer Saunders, Joanna Lumley), 1994–1999
Comic Justice (urban standup, A. J. Jamal), 1993–1996
Comics Only (comedy talk, Paul Provenza), 1991–1995
Exit 57 (sketch comedy, with repertory troupe), 1995
French and Saunders (British variety, Dawn French, Jennifer Saunders), 1994–1995
London Underground (British standup, Arthur Smith, Dennis Leary, Kevin Meaney), 1990–1996
**Mystery Science Theater 3000*, 1989–1996
**Politically Incorrect with Bill Maher* (comedy talk, Bill Maher), 1993–1996
StandUp, StandUp (standup, Walli Collins, Kristen Wilson, Laura Kightlinger), 1990–1995
Vacant Lot, The (sketch comedy, with repertory company), 1994–1995

Whose Line Is It Anyway? (ad-lib sketch comedy, with repertory company), 1990–1998

*See separate alphabetical entry.

The network increased its original production in the mid-'90s, attracting attention with such offbeat series as *Dr. Katz: Professional Therapist* (1995), *The Daily Show* (1996), and *Win Ben Stein's Money* (1997). It hit the jackpot with an irreverent cartoon about four foul-mouthed third-graders, called *South Park* (1997), a smash hit. Comedy Central first reached more than half of all U.S. television homes in April 1998, and its principal regular series after that date (as well as those just mentioned) are listed in this book under their individual titles.

COMEDY CIRCUS (*Films*)

FIRST TELECAST: *July 13, 1951*
LAST TELECAST: *September 28, 1951*
BROADCAST HISTORY:

July 1951, ABC 7:30–8:00
Aug 1951–Sep 1951, ABC Fri 8:00–8:30

Comedy Circus consisted of vintage comedy films starring such actors as Buster Keaton and Harry Langdon.

COMEDY FACTORY, THE (*Comedy Anthology*)

FIRST TELECAST: *June 21, 1985*
LAST TELECAST: *August 9, 1985*
BROADCAST HISTORY:

Jun 1985–Aug 1985, ABC Fri 8:30–9:00

REGULARS:

Mary Ann McDonald
Geoffrey Bowes
Derek McGrath
Mary Long

This unusual summer series featured a repertory company of players, plus a guest star, in a different half-hour situation comedy sketch each week. The guest stars included Bill Daily, Avery Schreiber, Judy Landers, Pat Harrington, and Richard Kline.

COMEDY HOUR SPECIAL (*Comedy/Variety*)

FIRST TELECAST: *July 29, 1963*
LAST TELECAST: *September 16, 1963*
BROADCAST HISTORY:

Jul 1963–Sep 1963, CBS Mon 9:00–10:00

Reruns of eight specials formed the contents of this summer series. Originally aired during the 1959–1960 season, they starred Jack Benny and Phil Silvers, appearing both separately and together.

COMEDY PARADE, see *Movies—Prior to 1961*

COMEDY PLAYHOUSE (*Comedy Anthology*)

FIRST TELECAST: *August 1, 1971*
LAST TELECAST: *September 5, 1971*
BROADCAST HISTORY:

Aug 1971–Sep 1971, CBS Sun 8:00–8:30

The situation comedies that made up this 1971 summer anthology were all pilots for proposed series that had not made it to the fall schedule. Around the networks this kind of summer runoff of busted pilots—which every network has in quantity—is irreverently known as "garbage can theater."

COMEDY SHOP, THE (*Comedy*)

BROADCAST HISTORY:

Syndicated only
30 minutes
Produced: *1978* (25 episodes)
Released: *Fall 1978*

HOST:

Norm Crosby

Standup comics, most of them little known, had a chance to do their stuff before a studio audience in this 1978 series. Some established comedians also appeared, among them Larry Storch, Shirley Hemphill, Ted Knight, and Red Buttons. The format called for a three-minute monologue from each performer.

COMEDY SPOT, THE (*Comedy Anthology*)

FIRST TELECAST: *June 28, 1960*
LAST TELECAST: *September 18, 1962*
BROADCAST HISTORY:

Jun 1960–Sep 1960, CBS Tue 9:30–10:00
Jul 1961–Sep 1961, CBS Tue 9:00–9:30
Jul 1962–Sep 1962, CBS Tue 9:00–9:30

HOST:

Art Gilmore (1960)

This series filled in for *The Red Skelton Show* for three consecutive summers. The 1960 and 1962 versions were called *The Comedy Spot*, while the 1961 edition was titled *Comedy Spotlight*. Although some of the episodes were reruns of previously aired episodes from other anthologies, most were pilots for proposed comedy series that had not made it to the fall schedule. There was one notable exception: the July 19, 1960, comedy titled "Head of the Family," starring Carl Reiner as a television comedy writer, Robert Petrie. This was the pilot for what would become, the following season, *The Dick Van Dyke Show*. Reiner, the creator of the show, was the only member of the pilot's cast to have a role in *The Dick Van Dyke Show* when it went on the air, though it was not the role he had had in the pilot. Instead of the series' star, he played Rob's tyrannical boss, Alan Brady (Alan Sturdy in the pilot), star of the variety show for which Rob was head writer.

COMEDY THEATER (*Comedy Anthology*)

FIRST TELECAST: *July 17, 1981*
LAST TELECAST: *August 28, 1981*
BROADCAST HISTORY:

Jul 1981–Aug 1981, NBC Fri 8:30–9:00

Each episode of this summer series was a pilot for a series that NBC had decided not to carry on its regular fall lineup. Among the series pilots shown were "Pals" starring Tony Lo Bianco and Jeffrey Tambor, "The Grady Nutt Show" starring Rev. Grady Nutt and Elinor Donahue, and "Dear Teacher" starring Melinda Culea, Rebecca York, and Ted Danson.

COMEDY THEATRE (*Comedy Anthology*)

FIRST TELECAST: *July 26, 1976*
LAST TELECAST: *June 28, 1979*
BROADCAST HISTORY:

Jul 1976–Sep 1976, NBC Mon 8:00–9:00
May 1979–Jun 1979, NBC Thu 8:30–9:00

This was a collection of pilot episodes from series that were not purchased for regular weekly presentation. Among the more recognizable names who appeared in these proposed shows were Don Knotts and Peter Isacksen in "Piper's Pets," Cleavon Little and Adam Wade in "Uptown Saturday Night," and Carol Wayne and William Daniels in "Heaven on Earth."

COMEDY TIME (*Comedy Anthology*)
FIRST TELECAST: *July 6, 1977*
LAST TELECAST: *September 1, 1977*
BROADCAST HISTORY:
Jul 1977, NBC Wed 9:30–10:00
Jul 1977–Sep 1977, NBC Thu 8:00–9:00

NBC used this blanket title for a collection of situation-comedy pilots that were aired during the summer of 1977 on two different nights. All of them were half-hour shows, with two different pilots running back-to-back on Thursdays. None of them made the fall schedule as regular series.

COMEDY TONIGHT (*Comedy/Variety*)
FIRST TELECAST: *July 5, 1970*
LAST TELECAST: *August 23, 1970*
BROADCAST HISTORY:
Jul 1970–Aug 1970, CBS Sun 9:00–10:00
REGULARS:
Robert Klein
Peter Boyle
Macintyre Dixon
Judy Graubart
Madeline Kahn
Lynn Lipton
Marty Barris
Barbara Cason
Boni Enten
Laura Greene

Comedian Robert Klein was the host and star of this summer comedy series that spoofed such things as soap operas, politics, and almost anything else that its cast felt topical and worth satirizing. The tone was highly improvisational. Two members of the cast, Peter Boyle and Madeline Kahn, went on to successful careers in motion pictures.

COMEDY TONIGHT (*Comedy/Variety*)
BROADCAST HISTORY:
Syndicated only
30 minutes
Produced: *1985–1986* (65 episodes)
Released: *Fall 1985*
HOST:
Bill Boggs

New York talk-show personality Bill Boggs hosted this series, which featured standup comedians doing their routines. Although some veteran comedians (Rich Little, Henny Youngman, and George Burns among them) appeared, most of the performers were relatively new faces, like Pudgy, Rita Rudner, Marsha Warfield, Dennis Wolfberg, Harvey Fierstein, Yakov Smirnoff, Paul Provenza, Danitra Vance, Eric Bogosian, Bob Saget, John Mulrooney, Sinbad, and Bob Duback.

COMEDY ZONE (*Comedy*)
FIRST TELECAST: *August 17, 1984*
LAST TELECAST: *September 7, 1984*
BROADCAST HISTORY:
Aug 1984–Sep 1984, CBS Fri 8:00–9:00
REGULARS:
Bob Gunton
Ann Lange
Mark Linn-Baker
Joe Mantegna
Audrie J. Neenan
Bill Randolph

Comedy Zone was a collection of short sketches, ranging in length from two to twelve minutes apiece, performed by a repertory company of comic actors and guest stars. There was no host. The show tried to achieve a fresh look by originating from New York and featuring the work of Broadway and Off-Broadway comedy writers rather than using the Hollywood-based writers employed by most TV series. Some of their ideas were certainly unusual: a musical production number, "They've Got No Cocaine In Cancun," performed by a full mariachi band and dancers; "The Blind Dating Game"; and a musical takeoff on the Heimlich maneuver. In between the skits there were short blackouts; often two stick figures on a road sign (representing pedestrians) who came to life and did strange things to each other. Apparently the audience didn't notice much difference between this and traditional TV comedy, and the show soon disappeared.

COMIC STRIP: LIVE (*Comedy*)
FIRST TELECAST: *August 12, 1989*
LAST TELECAST: *January 15, 1994*
BROADCAST HISTORY:
Aug 1989–Jan 1994, FOX Sat 11:00–12:00 midnight
Nov 1990–Apr 1991, FOX Sun 10:00–11:00
HOST:
John Mulrooney (1989–1990)
Gary Kroeger (1990–1991)
Wayne Cotter (1991–1994)

Comic Strip: Live was a weekly hour of standup comedy, originating from The Laugh Factory on the Sunset Strip in Hollywood. Both established comedians and newcomers (mostly young) were featured, among them The Amazing Jonathan, Jack Gallagher, Richard Belzer, Jeff Joseph, Judy Tenuta, Dennis Wolfberg, Rich Hall, Rick Overton, Shirley Hemphill, Will Shriner, Carol Suskind, and Wayne Cotter.

The series began as a local show on KTTV-TV, Los Angeles, in the summer of 1988, with John Mulrooney as host. Mulrooney remained with the show when it expanded to the Fox-owned stations that October and to the full Fox Network in August 1989. Later hosts were Gary Kroeger (January 1990) and Wayne Cotter (January 1991). The title of the show varied somewhat. The Saturday edition, originally *Comic Strip: Live,* became *Comic Strip: Late Night* when a prime-time version premiered on Sunday in November 1990; when the Sunday hour ended its run in 1991, the Saturday version reverted to its original title. The Sunday hour at first used the *Comic Strip: Live* name, switching to *Comic Strip: Prime Time* in February 1991.

The Sunday show was taped at various locations around the country and featured guest hosts, including Dave Thomas from Key West, Sinbad from the New Orleans Mardi Gras, Paul Rodriguez from a cruise ship, Martin Mull from Aspen, Colorado, and Bob Uecker from spring training in Arizona.

COMIKAZE (*Comedy*)
BROADCAST HISTORY:
MTV
30 minutes
Produced: *1993*
Premiered: *March 22, 1993*

HOST:

Jon Bauman

Daily standup comedy series featuring many of the hot young comedians who had previously appeared on MTV's *Half Hour Comedy Hour.*

COMING OF AGE (*Situation Comedy*)

FIRST TELECAST: *March 15, 1988*
LAST TELECAST: *July 27, 1989*
BROADCAST HISTORY:

Mar 1988, CBS Tue 9:00–9:30
Oct 1988–Nov 1988, CBS Mon 8:30–9:00
Jun 1989–Jul 1989, CBS Thu 9:30–10:00

CAST:

Dick Hale .... Paul Dooley
Ginny Hale .... Phyllis Newman
Ed Pepper .... Alan Young
Trudie Pepper .... Glynis Johns
Brian Binker .... Kevin Pollak
Pauline Spencer .... Ruta Lee
Wilma Salzgaber .... Lenore Woodward

"Old age is the most unexpected of all things that happen to a man," mused this sitcom, borrowing a quote from Leon Trotsky. Dick Hale was an airline pilot forced into an unwanted retirement at age 60 by company policy. He and his wife Ginny moved to The Dunes, an Arizona retirement community, to begin a new life. She had a positive outlook but Dick, whose grumpy personality did not help, found it difficult to make the adjustment. He didn't like retirement, he didn't like the climate, he didn't like condescending young Brian Binker, who managed The Dunes, and he wasn't particularly fond of many of his fellow residents. Their next-door neighbors—and the walls between the apartments were so thin you could hear right through them—were perpetually perky Ed and Trudie Pepper. Among the other residents were Wilma, who worked in the management office, and Pauline, The Dunes' resident sexpot.

An unmitigated disaster—it was pulled from the CBS schedule after only three weeks—*Coming of Age* was given two more chances and failed to last more than a month in each outing.

COMMAND POST (*Instruction*)

FIRST TELECAST: *February 14, 1950*
LAST TELECAST: *April 4, 1950*
BROADCAST HISTORY:

Feb 1950–Apr 1950, CBS Tue 8:00–9:00

Produced by and for the U.S. Army, this series was designed as an eight-week course to train the army reserves via television. Subjects covered in the series included planning attacks, self-defense, and combat theory and technique.

COMMENT (*Public Affairs*)

FIRST TELECAST: *June 17, 1954*
LAST TELECAST: *September 10, 1972*
BROADCAST HISTORY:

Jun 1954–Aug 1954, NBC Mon 8:30–9:00
Jan 1958–Aug 1958, NBC Fri 10:45–11:00
Jan 1971–Sep 1971, NBC Sun 6:00–6:30
Jan 1972–Sep 1972, NBC Sun 6:00–6:30

HOST:

Edwin Newman (1971–1972)

In the first two series aired by NBC under the title *Comment,* NBC News correspondents made personal observations about current news issues. That was in 1954 and 1958. More than a decade later, when *Comment* returned to the NBC lineup, the personal opinions voiced were those of spokesmen for various causes or noted public figures discussing significant issues. NBC newsman Edwin Newman was the host for the 1970s version of *Comment* but rarely voiced any opinions of his own on the series.

COMMISH, THE (*Police Drama*)

FIRST TELECAST: *September 28, 1991*
LAST TELECAST: *September 7, 1995*
BROADCAST HISTORY:

Sep 1991–Jan 1995, ABC Sat 10:00–11:00
Aug 1994, ABC Thu 9:00–10:00
Feb 1995–Apr 1995, ABC Thu 9:00–10:00
May 1995, ABC Sat 10:00–11:00
Aug 1995–Sep 1995, ABC Thu 9:00–10:00

CAST:

Commissioner Tony Scali .... Michael Chiklis
Rachel Scali .... Theresa Saldana
David Scali .... Kaj-Erik Eriksen
Sarah Scali (1992–1994)
.... Dayna and Justine Cornborough
Arnie Metzger (1991–1992) .... David Paymer
Det. Irv Wallerstein (1991) .... Alex Bruhanski
Off. Enrico "Ricky" Caruso (1991–1994)
.... Nicholas Lea
Off. Carmela Pagan (1991–1993) .... Gina Belafonte
Off. Stan Kelly (1991–1994) .... Geoffrey Nauffts
Det. Cyd Madison (1992–1994) ... Melinda McGraw
Det. Paulie Pentangeli (1991–1992, 1994–1995)
.... John Cygan
**Lucille Carter* .... Kimberly Scott
Officer Mike Rose (1991–1994) .... Pat Bermel
Officer Ronnie Lopez .... Jason Scott Schombing
Officer Gordy Tuefel (1991–1993) ... Michael Patten
**Freddie* .... David "Squatch" Ward
Officer Jonathan Papdakis (1992–1994)
.... Ray Scrivano
**Mayor Louise Hinton* .... Linda Darlow

*Occasional

A rather easygoing series about the paunchy, balding top cop in suburban Eastbridge, just north of New York City. Brooklyn-born Tony, the "commish" to his officers, was tough on criminals but ebullient around others, and had a sense of fun that belied his serious title. His approach to police work was entirely practical—he'd rather eat lunch than chase a criminal down an alley. "Chases usually lead to friggin' injuries," he observed, "but no one ever got hurt by a bowl of linguini." In addition to busting "perps" (sometimes personally), Tony dealt with a bustling home life including supportive wife Rachel, impressionable young son David, and freeloading brother-in-law Arnie. Irv was his longtime friend and second-in-command at the p.d., and Ricky and Carmela, two squabbling young patrol car officers. Freddie was the dense maintenance man.

Quite a few officers were seen over the years. Irv was succeeded almost immediately as Chief of Detectives by Paulie, who gave way to Cyd Madison in 1992. When she left for a better position in 1994 Paulie returned. Other continuing stories included the birth of daughter Sarah to the Scalis in 1992 and the assassination attempt on Tony in 1994, which left him paralyzed and in rehab for a time.

Based on a real-life police commissioner, Tony Schembri of Rye, New York, who had previously been an advisor to producer Stephen J. Cannell on other cop shows.

Two *Commish* movies aired in late November and early December 1995, after the series had ended.

COMMON LAW (*Situation Comedy*)

FIRST TELECAST: *September 28, 1996*

LAST TELECAST: *October 19, 1996*

BROADCAST HISTORY:

Sep 1996–Oct 1996, ABC Sat 9:30–10:00

CAST:

John Alvarez .... Greg Giraldo
Nancy Slaton .... Megyn Price
Luis Alvarez .... Gregory Sierra
Henry Beckett .... David Pasquesi
Peter Gutenhimmel .... Carlos Jacott
Maria Marquez .... Diana-Maria Riva

THEME:

performed by Los Lobos

Attorney John Alvarez was considered a bit out of place at the conservative, upscale Manhattan law firm where he worked. Although he had a Harvard law degree, he was a Hispanic raised in blue-collar Queens, wore his hair long, strummed a guitar, and liked to look out for the "the little guy." The firm was more interested in looking out for the Big Guys. John's unconventional attitude was just what attracted WASPy associate Nancy, so they moved in together, which had to be kept secret since the firm frowned on interoffice romances. Henry was a stuffy, ambitious associate, Peter the insecure yuppie son of one of the firm's partners, and Maria the chattering office manager. Back in the 'hood John kept in touch with his old-fashioned dad Luis, a barber, who disapproved of his son's "hippie" ways.

COMPASS (*Travelogue*)

FIRST TELECAST: *October 23, 1954*

LAST TELECAST: *October 6, 1957*

BROADCAST HISTORY:

Oct 1954–Feb 1955, ABC Sat 7:30–8:00
Mar 1955–Sep 1955, ABC Sat 10:00–10:30
Jul 1956–Sep 1956, ABC Thu 10:00–10:30
Jun 1957–Jul 1957, ABC Thu 9:30–10:00
Jul 1957–Oct 1957, ABC Sun 9:00–9:30

These documentary travel films were fed out over the ABC network for the benefit of stations that did not wish to schedule local series in these time periods. *Compass* was never carried on ABC's flagship station in New York.

CONAN: THE TELEVISION SERIES (*Adventure*)

BROADCAST HISTORY:

Syndicated only
60 minutes
Produced: *1997–1998* (22 episodes)
Released: *September 1997*

CAST:

Conan .... Ralf Moeller
Otli .... Danny Woodburn
Zzeben .... Robert McRay
Vulkar (1997) .... Andrew Craig
Hissah Zul .... Jeremy Kemp
Bayu .... T. J. Storm
Talking Skull .... A. C. Qart-Hadosht
Karella .... Aly Dunne

A sword-and-sorcery epic set in the Hyborian Age. Conan, a muscular Sumerian warrior descended from the people of the fabled Atlantis, was destined to become king through battle. Helping him in his quest were a disparate group of companions. Otli was a minion of the evil wizard Yara, who had escaped from him to seek freedom helping Conan. Vulkar, the beefy bald fighter (who left the series after a few weeks), joined Conan when they had escaped together from the gladiator arena, along with mute but muscular Zzeben. Vulkar was replaced by the short-tempered Bayu. Karella, a sexy amoral bandit queen with the hots for Conan, showed up periodically—sometimes to help and sometimes to cause trouble. Their mutual enemy was the evil sorcerer Hissah Zul, a ruler determined to kill Conan before Conan could kill him. Zul got advice from his oracle, a talking skull in a vat that apprised him of what was happening away from his castle. *Conan* featured lots of fighting and bloody swordplay. In May, with the help of three treacherous, duplicitous wizards, Conan and his men were able to storm Hissah Zul's castle and Conan beheaded him with his sword. He was in line to become the new king, while each of the wizards tried, unsuccessfully, to get the ear of one of Conan's men in their efforts to betray each other and gain power.

Based on the Conan character created by Robert E. Howard. There were 60 Conan novels, comic books, and three feature films with Arnold Schwarzenegger in the title role. Filmed in Puerto Vallarta, Mexico.

CONCENTRATION (*Quiz/Audience Participation*)

FIRST TELECAST: *October 30, 1958*

LAST TELECAST: *September 11, 1961*

BROADCAST HISTORY:

Oct 1958–Nov 1958, NBC Thu 8:30–9:00
Apr 1961–Sep 1961, NBC Mon 9:30–10:00

EMCEE:

Jack Barry (1958)
Hugh Downs (1961)

Concentration, a fixture on the NBC daytime lineup from August 1958 until March 1973, had two runs as a nighttime network series. It first appeared in the fall of 1958 as a temporary replacement for *Twenty-One,* after the latter was suddenly pulled off the air because of the quiz-show scandals that were developing at the time. The host of this version of *Concentration,* which ran for only four weeks, was Jack Barry, who had been host of the suspended *Twenty-One. Concentration* made its second appearance on the nighttime schedule as a summer show in 1961, with Hugh Downs, who had hosted the daytime version since its inception.

The format of the show was based on an old children's game of the same name. Two contestants were faced with a game board containing 30 squares. Behind each square was a prize. There were two squares on the board for each prize, and to win the prize the contestant had to match the two correct squares. In order to keep the prizes, however, the contestant also had to be first to guess a rebus, which was gradually revealed as the chosen squares were rotated.

After Hugh Downs left the daytime edition of *Concentration* early in 1969, he was replaced by Bob Clayton, who had been the announcer and substitute host on the show for more than five years. Clayton emceed *Concentration* for the remainder of its network run (except for six months in 1969 when Ed McMahon held the reins). Others who filled in as substitute emcees over the years were Art James, Jim Lucas, and Bill Mazur. James and Lucas were *Concentration* announcers when the regular emcee was around.

The series returned to NBC's weekday daytime lineup under the title *Classic Concentration* in May of 1987, with Alex Trebek as emcee. He remained with the revival throughout its NBC run, which ended in December 1993.

CONCERT TONIGHT, see *Chicago Symphony*

CONCRETE COWBOYS (*Adventure*)
FIRST TELECAST: *February 7, 1981*
LAST TELECAST: *March 21, 1981*
BROADCAST HISTORY:
Feb 1981, CBS 10:00–11:00
Feb 1981–Mar 1981, CBS Sat 9:00–10:00
CAST:
Jimmy Lee (J.D.) Reed .... Jerry Reed
Will Ewbanks .... Geoffrey Scott
THEME:
"Breakin' Loose," written and performed by Jerry Reed

This was a countrified version of the early 1960s hit *Route 66*. J.D. and Will were two carefree cowpokes traveling around the country in search of adventure. J.D. was the fast-talking instigator, who usually made the decisions, while Will was his sidekick, more inhibited and more romantic than his buddy. They were slick operators in a card game, but when their gambling luck failed them they could still pick up a few bucks by taking on various odd jobs. Never staying long in one place, they roamed the concrete trails of modern-day America, sometimes finding trouble, always looking for adventure. Their home on wheels was a beat-up old camper.

Country music star Jerry Reed starred in the series and also served as its narrator. There was usually at least one opportunity in each episode for him to grab his guitar and do a little pickin'.

CONDO (*Situation Comedy*)
FIRST TELECAST: *February 10, 1983*
LAST TELECAST: *June 16, 1983*
BROADCAST HISTORY:
Feb 1983–Mar 1983, ABC Thu 8:00–8:30
Mar 1983–Apr 1983, ABC Thu 8:30–9:00
May 1983–Jun 1983, ABC Thu 8:00–8:30
CAST:
James Kirkridge .... McLean Stevenson
Kiki Kirkridge .... Brooke Alderson
Scott Kirkridge .... Mark Schubb
Billy Kirkridge .... Marc Price
Jesse Rodriguez .... Luis Avalos
Maria Rodriguez .... Yvonne Wilder
Linda Rodriguez .... Julie Carmen
Jose Montoya .... James Victor

The declining fortunes of an opinionated WASP brought him next door to an upwardly mobile Latino family in this 1983 comedy. Insurance salesman James Kirkridge found it necessary to move his All-American family from their rambling house to a smaller condominium, where his next-door neighbor turned out to be Jesse Rodriguez, whose success in the landscaping business had recently allowed him to move up from the barrio. As if the clash of cultures wasn't enough for traditionalist Kirkridge, his son Scott and Jesse's daughter Linda soon announced that they were getting married and expecting a baby. Race and religion jokes flew thick and fast between James and Jesse, but not fast enough to save this series.

CONFESSION (*Interview/Discussion*)
FIRST TELECAST: *June 19, 1958*
LAST TELECAST: *January 13, 1959*
BROADCAST HISTORY:
Jun 1958–Sep 1958, ABC Thu 10:00–10:30
Sep 1958–Jan 1959, ABC Tue 10:00–10:30
HOST:
Jack Wyatt

This series sought to probe the underlying causes of criminal acts. Filmed in Dallas, Texas, and moderated by Jack Wyatt, each show opened with an interview between Mr. Wyatt and a convicted criminal. Following the interview, Mr. Wyatt led a discussion group that attempted to analyze the reasons for the crime. The discussion group consisted of a lawyer, a clergyman, a penologist or sociologist, and a psychiatrist or psychologist.

CONFESSIONS OF CRIME (*Information*)
BROADCAST HISTORY:
Lifetime Network
30 minutes
Produced: *1991* (13 episodes)
Premiered: *July 23, 1991*
HOSTESS:
Theresa Saldana

Reality series that used police interrogation tapes and reenactments to reconstruct a different violent crime each week and explore the reasons behind it. The emphasis was on attacks on everyday people, especially women, such as a wife held hostage by her husband, parents who were murdered by their son, or the actions of a violent cult. The host was petite and somewhat frightened looking movie actress Theresa Saldana, who had herself been attacked by a deranged fan and subsequently founded the advocacy group Victims for Victims.

CONFIDENTIAL REPORT, syndicated title for *Dragnet*

CONFLICT (*Dramatic Anthology*)
FIRST TELECAST: *September 18, 1956*
LAST TELECAST: *September 3, 1957*
BROADCAST HISTORY:
Sep 1956–Sep 1957, ABC Tue 7:30–8:30

These hour-long dramas, produced in Hollywood by Warner Bros., featured varying casts and were seen on alternate weeks with *Cheyenne*. The general theme was people in conflict, in settings ranging across time from Elizabethan England to the present. One of the better productions was "The Magic Brew," starring Jim Backus as a medicine-show pitchman attempting to peddle his wares in a small town. At least two episodes served as prototypes for future series; in one, Will Hutchins appeared as an inept cowboy (his role a year later in *Sugarfoot*), and in the other Efrem Zimbalist, Jr., portrayed private detective Stuart Bailey (as he did in 1958's *77 Sunset Strip*). Among the others seen on *Conflict* were Tab Hunter, Virginia Mayo, and Jack Lord.

CONGRESSIONAL REPORT (*Discussion*)
FIRST TELECAST: *June 15, 1969*
LAST TELECAST: *August 31, 1969*
BROADCAST HISTORY:
Jun 1969–Aug 1969, NBC Sun 6:00–6:30
MODERATOR:
Bill Monroe

Each week four members of Congress participated in a round-table discussion of an issue of current interest to the congressmen and their constituencies. Two members of the panel supported the issue and the other two opposed it. NBC newsman Bill Monroe was the moderator of this series, which had premiered as a Sunday afternoon show on April 13, 1969.

CONRAD BLOOM (*Situation Comedy*)
FIRST TELECAST: *September 21, 1998*
LAST TELECAST: *December 28, 1998*
BROADCAST HISTORY:
Sep 1998–Nov 1998, NBC Mon 8:30–9:00
Dec 1998, NBC Mon 9:30–10:00
CAST:
Conrad Bloom .... Mark Feuerstein
Molly Davenport .... Lauren Graham
Nina Bloom .... Ever Carradine
Florie Bloom .... Linda Lavin
Faye Reynolds .... Paula Newsome
Shelley Rudetsky .... Jessica Stone
George Dorsey .... Steve Landesberg

An amiable copywriter at a New York advertising agency was dominated by women in this rather bland workplace comedy. Conrad dated a lot, but never seemed to get very far, perhaps because he let every woman in sight tell him what to do. There was wholesome ex-girlfriend Molly; dippy, cause-obsessed sister Nina; guilt-inducing mom Florie ("Don't change your plans just for *me*"); domineering boss Faye (she stood with her hands on her hips a lot), and new coworker Shelley. They all wanted him to take care of their problems, and he willingly obliged. George was the burned-out adman still living in the '70s, whom Conrad for some reason admired.

CONSPIRACY ZONE, THE (*Discussion*)
BROADCAST HISTORY:
TNN
30 minutes
Original episodes: *2002–*
Premiered: *January 6, 2002*
HOST:
Kevin Nealon

"If we've made just one person a little paranoid, we've done our job" was the tagline for this mock talk show. Comic Kevin Nealon appeared with three or four guest "experts" on a bare stage discussing such subjects as "Do psychics have paranormal powers?" "Did aliens land in Roswell?" "Was Marilyn Monroe murdered by the Kennedys?" "Was Sirhan Sirhan a mind-controlled CIA assassin?" and "Are we all unwitting puppets in Satan's master plan to corrupt the world?" Guests included conspiracy specialists, authors (Harlan Ellison), intellectuals and a variety of celebrities (Coolio, Eric Idle, Lisa Ann Walter, Jimmy Kimmel).

CONTENDER, THE (*Drama*)
FIRST TELECAST: *April 3, 1980*
LAST TELECAST: *May 1, 1980*
BROADCAST HISTORY:
Apr 1980–May 1980, CBS Thu 10:00–11:00
CAST:
Johnny Captor .... Marc Singer
Jill Sindon .... Katherine Cannon
George Beifus .... Moses Gunn
Brian Captor .... Alan Stock
Alma Captor .... Louise Latham
Missy Dinwittie .... Tina Andrews
Harry .... Don Gordon
Andy .... William Watson
Lucinda (Lou) Waverly .... Susan Walden

Johnny Captor was from a middle-class Oregon family. While he was in college, his father, a lumberjack, was paralyzed in a freak mill accident and committed suicide rather than face a life of total dependency on others. Johnny, trying to decide what to do with his life, and with the added burden of supporting his mother and his kid brother, Brian, decided to leave college and concentrate on a boxing career. This did not sit well with his girlfriend, Jill Sindon, a teacher at the college, who failed to understand why an intelligent person would want to earn a living in such a dangerous way. Former fighter George Beifus was Johnny's trainer and manager and Missy Dinwittie, the teenage sister of "Killer" Dinwittie, another fighter. Missy seemed more interested in Johnny's career than in her brother's. Lou Waverly was a sportswriter working on an article about Johnny.

CONTINENTAL, THE (*Romantic Monologue*)
FIRST TELECAST: *January 22, 1952*
LAST TELECAST: *January 6, 1953*
BROADCAST HISTORY:
Jan 1952–Apr 1952, CBS Tue/Thu 11:15–11:30
Oct 1952–Jan 1953, ABC Tue/Fri 11:00–11:15
HOST:
Renzo Cesana

For bored housewives looking to add a little excitement to their lives, CBS offered this live program, which followed the 11:00 P.M. local news twice a week. Suave, debonair, sultry-voiced Renzo Cesana, Italian by birth but American by choice, was the only performer. Each night, in a glamorous setting, he would provide a romantic monologue directed to the women in the audience. He was promoted as an Italian count and member of one of the leading families of Rome, and had been doing a similar program on a local station in Los Angeles for several months before CBS brought him to New York to perform on the network.

After a short tenure on that network he showed up on ABC in the fall for another brief run, this time meeting with couples out on their first date.

CONTINENTAL SHOWCASE (*Variety*)
FIRST TELECAST: *June 11, 1966*
LAST TELECAST: *September 10, 1966*
BROADCAST HISTORY:
Jun 1966–Sep 1966, CBS Sat 7:30–8:30
REGULARS:
Jim Backus
The Kessler Twins
Heidi Bruhl

Bibi Johns
Esther & Abi Ofarim
The Peanuts
The Continental Showcase Dancers
The Hazy Osterwald Sextet
The Harry Segers Orchestra

Continental Showcase was the 1966 summer replacement for *The Jackie Gleason Show.* Host Jim Backus traveled throughout Europe with the production company filming many popular local acts, including singers, dancers, acrobats, and other European (and occasionally Oriental) performers. Although they were not officially regulars, the artists shown above appeared on more than half of the shows.

CONVERSATION WITH DINAH, A (*Talk*)
BROADCAST HISTORY:
The Nashville Network
30 minutes
Produced: *1989–1991* (30 episodes)
Premiered: *August 28, 1989*
HOST:
Dinah Shore

Dinah Shore talked with celebrities from the worlds of entertainment, politics, and sports in this intimate interview series, her last.

CONVERSATIONS WITH ERIC SEVAREID (*Discussion*)
FIRST TELECAST: *July 13, 1975*
LAST TELECAST: *August 31, 1975*
BROADCAST HISTORY:
Jul 1975–Aug 1975, CBS Sun 6:00–7:00
HOST:
Eric Sevareid

CBS News correspondent Eric Sevareid had an informal chat each Sunday with a person who had a background in, and understanding of, world affairs. Their talks usually dealt with developing economic and political situations. Among the guests were former West German President Willy Brandt and novelist Leo Rosten.

CONVOY (*War Drama*)
FIRST TELECAST: *September 17, 1965*
LAST TELECAST: *December 10, 1965*
BROADCAST HISTORY:
Sep 1965–Dec 1965, NBC Fri 8:30–9:00
CAST:
Comdr. Dan Talbot .... John Gavin
Merchant Capt. Ben Foster .... John Larch
Chief Officer Steve Kirkland .... Linden Chiles
Lt. Dick O'Connell .... James Callahan

The problems of transporting troops and supplies across the high seas during World War II provided the thrust for this series. Commander Dan Talbot of the U.S. Navy Destroyer Escort *DD 181* was responsible for insuring the safety of a convoy of merchant ships, while civilian Captain Ben Foster ran the merchant freighter *Flagship,* the nerve center for the entire convoy. These two men, one military and one civilian, contended with the problems caused by war—air and U-boat attacks—as well as fogs, high seas, and other perils of the ocean. Foster's chief aide was Chief Officer Steve Kirkland; his counterpart on the destroyer escort was Lt. Dick O'Connell.

COOK'S CHAMPAGNE PARTY, see *Andy and Della Russell*

COOL MILLION (*Detective Drama*)
FIRST TELECAST: *October 25, 1972*
LAST TELECAST: *July 11, 1973*
BROADCAST HISTORY:
Oct 1972–Jul 1973, NBC Wed 8:30–10:00
CAST:
Jefferson Keyes .... James Farentino
Elena .... Adele Mara
Tony Baylor .... Ed Bernard

Jefferson Keyes was a former CIA agent who had become an extremely successful private investigator. He was so successful, in fact, that he demanded a $1 million fee for his services. With that kind of money he could afford to have his own executive jet, which he piloted himself to whatever destination, business or pleasure, he had in mind. His popularity as a raconteur as well as a sleuth created strong demands on his time whenever he was not occupied professionally. *Cool Million* was one of the three elements in the 1972–1973 version of *NBC Wednesday Mystery Movie* along with *Banacek* and *Madigan.*

COP AND THE KID, THE (*Situation Comedy*)
FIRST TELECAST: *December 4, 1975*
LAST TELECAST: *March 4, 1976*
BROADCAST HISTORY:
Dec 1975, NBC Thu 8:30–9:00
Jan 1976–Mar 1976, NBC Thu 8:00–8:30
CAST:
Officer Frank Murphy .... Charles Durning
Lucas Adams .... Tierre Turner
Mrs. Brigid Murphy .... Patsy Kelly
Mary Goodhew .... Sharon Spelman
Shortstuff .... Curtiz Willis
Mouse .... Eric Laneuville
Sgt. Zimmerman .... William Pierson

This was another of the ethnic comedies so popular in the 1970s. Through a strange circumstance, portly, middle-aged Irish cop Frank Murphy found himself assigned custody of Lucas, a young, black, streetwise orphan. Murphy had suffered an asthma attack while chasing Lucas, following a shoplifting incident. Knowing that the asthma could be cause for Murphy's dismissal from the force, Lucas blackmailed Murphy into asking for leniency for him at his trial. Murphy did this so well that the court made him Lucas's guardian. The efforts of Murphy and his mother to reform young Lucas provided the comedy.

COP ROCK (*Police Musical/Drama*)
FIRST TELECAST: *September 26, 1990*
LAST TELECAST: *December 25, 1990*
BROADCAST HISTORY:
Sep 1990–Dec 1990, ABC Wed 10:00–11:00
CAST:
Mayor Louise Plank .... Barbara Bosson
Chief Roger Kendrick .... Ronny Cox
Capt. John Hollander .... Larry Joshua
Det. Vincent LaRusso .... Peter Onorati
Off. Andy Campo .... David Gianopoulos
Off. Vicki Quinn .... Anne Bobby

Det. Ralph Ruskin .... Ron McLarty
Off. Franklin Rose .... James McDaniel
Det. Joseph Gaines .... Mick Murray
Det. Bob McIntire .... Paul McCrane
Cdr. Warren Osborne .... Vondie Curtis-Hall
Det. William Donald Potts ..... William Thomas, Jr.
Trish Vaughn .... Teri Austin
Sidney Weitz .... Dennis Lipscomb
Ray Rodbart .... Jeffrey Allan Chandler

THEME:

"Under the Gun," written and performed by Randy Newman

Critics who complain that TV never tries anything really different must have missed this bizarre series from otherwise sane producer Steven Bochco (*Hill Street Blues, L.A. Law*). The premise was not just singing cops, as in the BBC's absurdist farce *The Singing Detective*. This was a tough, brutal crime show with singing murderers, singing crack house denizens, singing corrupt politicians, and singing juries—just before they hanged someone.

The stories were similar to those on *Hill Street Blues*, set in the seediest parts of Los Angeles, where cops fought an often losing war against drugs, racism, and murder. Capt. Hollander was the no-nonsense, honest commander reporting to Chief Kendrick, an old-timer with a cowboy fixation and a developing affair with ambitious and corrupt Mayor Plank ("the Iron Lady"). Campo and Quinn were young patrol-car partners who were romantically attracted to each other, causing problems because Quinn was married to the much older Ruskin, a portly, balding forensics expert. Tough guy LaRusso caused the most problems, killing a murder suspect in cold blood in the opening episode; his subsequent trial, replete with cover-ups and sex with his cold-blooded defense attorney Trish, tore apart department loyalties. They all sang about their problems.

Unfortunately, it was less engrossing than disconcerting when an angry crowd of blacks taunted white cops making a ghetto bust by going into a rap song, "In these streets, *we* got the power." Or when an agitated yuppie, watching his BMW being impounded after he was arrested for buying cocaine in a seedy parking lot, wailed the soulful lyrics "I want my Beemer back!" Critics and viewers applauded the effort, but reluctantly concluded that the "shotgun marriage of musical fantasy and inner-city mayhem" (as one writer put it) just didn't work.

COP TALK: BEHIND THE SHIELD

(*Interview/Discussion*)

BROADCAST HISTORY:

Syndicated only
60 minutes
Produced: *1989* (26 episodes)
Released: *January 1989*

MODERATOR:

Sonny Grosso

Former policeman and current TV producer Sonny Grosso hosted this weekly series in which he talked with law enforcement officers from around the country about the real nature of their work, their actual experience and problems, and how police work affected their personal lives.

COPS (*Police Documentary*)

FIRST TELECAST: *March 11, 1989*
LAST TELECAST:
BROADCAST HISTORY:

Mar 1989–Jun 1989, FOX Sat 9:00–9:30
Jun 1989–Jul 1990, FOX Sat 8:00–8:30
Aug 1990–Dec 1990, FOX Sat 9:00–9:30
Dec 1990–Jul 1991, FOX Sat 9:00–10:00
Jul 1991– , FOX Sat 8:00–9:00

THEME:

"Bad Boys," by Ian Lewis, performed by Inner Circle

"Bad boys, bad boys . . . *whatcha gonna do when they come for you?*" chanted the hypnotic theme song of this unusual and gripping cinéma vérité series about patrol cops and the dark underside of America. *Newsweek* called it "unlike anything in prime time," and *USA Today* added that this was "real cops chasing real criminals down really mean streets." It certainly was real. Production crews accompanied actual cops on their rounds, often at night, typically shooting one hundred 20-minute videotapes to get 22 minutes of broadcast material. Nothing was spared: dead bodies being pulled out of the water, drug dealers being slammed against the hood of a patrol car, scantily clad hookers being busted on their rounds, violence of all kinds. Adding to the realism, there was no narrator; the voices were those of the cops themselves on the scene.

The initial episodes of *Cops* were shot in 1988 in Broward County, Florida (Ft. Lauderdale), and aired on the Fox-owned television stations in early 1989. In March 1989 the series went on the full Fox network, and subsequent episodes were shot in many other locations including Portland, Oregon, and San Diego in 1989, Los Angeles, Minneapolis, Anchorage, and Jersey City in 1990, and Tucson, Houston, and Kansas City in 1991. By the start of the 1998–1999 season *Cops* had chronicled the activities of police officers in more than 100 U.S. cities. There were also episodes following street cops in London, Hong Kong, Central and South America, Moscow, and Leningrad, where things weren't much prettier than in the United States. The chief criticism of *Cops* in fact, was that it was exploitative and intensely voyeuristic. Indeed, the camera often lingered on the sleaziest aspects of a scene (at least one suspect mooned the camera) or on intense emotional trauma. Who could forget the close-up of a small boy screaming in terror as cops broke down the door and dragged off his drug-dealing father? On the other hand, *Cops* made it vividly clear that there was nothing glamorous about the pain and suffering brought on by crime.

The concept for *Cops* was originally proposed to and rejected by the major networks. Executive Producer John Langley later commented, "They had no faith in our concept and told us it was a legal nightmare." But Fox took a chance and scored a notable success. Probably the most frequently asked question about the show was why the suspects allowed themselves to be put on TV in such an unflattering light. "It perplexes me," said Langley. "Maybe it's fame or immortality, or to have a videotape to claim innocence, but most people want to be on." (About 50 percent signed the required release; others who were shown appeared with their faces electronically obscured.)

When *Cops* expanded to an hour in December 1990, each show consisted of two half-hour episodes from different cities, usually an original episode followed by a rerun.

CORLISS ARCHER, see *Meet Corliss Archer*

CORNER BAR, THE (*Situation Comedy*)
FIRST TELECAST: *June 21, 1972*
LAST TELECAST: *September 7, 1973*
BROADCAST HISTORY:
Jun 1972–Aug 1972, ABC Wed 8:30–9:00
Aug 1973–Sep 1973, ABC Fri 9:30–10:00
CAST:
Harry Grant (1972).................... Gabriel Dell
Fred Costello .... J. J. Barry
Phil Bracken................................ Bill Fiore
Joe (1972) .... Joe Keyes
Peter Panama (1972)............ Vincent Schiavelli
Meyer Shapiro .... Shimen Ruskin
Mary Ann (1972) .... Langhorn Scruggs
Mae (1973) .... Anne Meara
Frank Flynn (1973)................. Eugene Roche
Donald Hooten (1973) .... Ron Carey
EXECUTIVE PRODUCER:
Alan King
PRODUCER:
Howard Morris
This comedy about contemporary life focused on the patrons who frequented Grant's Toomb, a neighborhood tavern in New York City. During the summer of 1972 Gabriel Dell (one of the original Bowery Boys) portrayed bartender-owner Harry Grant, but in 1973 the place was taken over by Mae and Frank (Anne Meara and Eugene Roche). The regular patrons in one or both seasons were Fred, a griping, hard-hat cab-driver; Phil, a scheming Wall Street lawyer; Peter Panama, a gay set designer; and Donald, a flamboyant actor. The hired help included Joe, the "liberated" black cook; Meyer, the long-suffering waiter; and Mary Ann, the sexy and slightly daft waitress.

CORONET BLUE (*Mystery*)
FIRST TELECAST: *May 29, 1967*
LAST TELECAST: *September 4, 1967*
BROADCAST HISTORY:
May 1967–Sep 1967, CBS Mon 10:00–11:00
CAST:
Michael Alden .... Frank Converse
Anthony............................ Brian Bedford
Max Spier................................ Joe Silver
Michael Alden was not his real name. It was the name he used because he had suffered almost total amnesia after having been dumped off a freighter in New York harbor by someone trying to kill him. The only clue he could remember was that he had been mumbling the words "Coronet Blue" when the police fished him out of the water. In his attempt to ascertain his identity, Alden was befriended by a monk named Anthony and a coffee-shop owner named Max Spier. Danger and intrigue were the keynotes of this summer series as the unknown villains who had dumped Alden into the river pursued him to finish the job. *Coronet Blue* never made it to a full season's run and no conclusion was ever filmed, so Alden—and the viewers—never did find out the meaning of those mysterious words.

CORRUPTORS, THE, see *Target! The Corruptors*

COS (*Comedy/Variety*)
FIRST TELECAST: *September 19, 1976*
LAST TELECAST: *November 7, 1976*
BROADCAST HISTORY:
Sep 1976–Nov 1976, ABC Sun 7:00–8:00
REGULARS:
Bill Cosby
Jeffrey Altman
Tim Thomerson
Marion Ramsey
Buzzy Linhart
Willie Bobo
Mauricio Jarrin
Cos was one of the few attempts to design a prime-time television series specifically for two- to twelve-year-olds. It was essentially a variety program, with guest celebrities, sports stars, puppets, and comedy and music that would appeal to the younger set. Bill Cosby opened each show with a monologue, which he never got to finish, because he was invariably interrupted in some fashion. Then he went through a "magic door" to various adventures. A "Cos" Repertory Company of youngsters was on hand to assist in the skits.

COSBY (*Situation Comedy*)
FIRST TELECAST: *September 16, 1996*
LAST TELECAST: *April 28, 2000*
BROADCAST HISTORY:
Sep 1996–Aug 1998, CBS Mon 8:00–8:30
Aug 1998–Sep 1998, CBS Mon 8:00–9:00
Sep 1998–Jul 1999, CBS Mon 8:00–8:30
Jul 1999–Dec 1999, CBS Wed 8:00–8:30
Jan 2000–Apr 2000, CBS Fri 8:30–9:00
CAST:
Hilton Lucas............................ Bill Cosby
Ruth Lucas .... Phylicia Rashad
Pauline Fox .... Madeline Kahn
Erica Lucas............. T' Keyah Crystal Keymah
Griffin Vesey......................... Doug E. Doug
Angelo (1997–1998) .... Angelo Massagli
Jurnee (age 11) (1998–1999)........ Jurnee Smollett
Darien Hall (1998–2000)........ Darien Sills-Evans
Four years after the long-running *Cosby Show* left the air, Bill Cosby returned to sitcom TV (with Phylicia Rashad again playing his wife) as a considerably less affluent New Yorker. Hilton Lucas was a cranky but lovable curmudgeon who, at age 60, was adjusting to a major life change: being unemployed. After thirty years of working for an airline, he had just been pink-slipped as part of a corporate downsizing. In addition to the frustrations attendant with having too much free time, Hilton was put out by all the little things he found wrong with the world—everything from misleading advertising, to having to take a number and stand in line at his doctor's office, to the way people parked in front of his home. Ruthie, his loving wife, worked part-time with her eccentric best friend, Pauline, at a flower shop in their Queens, New York, neighborhood. Hilton's daughter, Erica, a young attorney with a Manhattan law firm, was unsure about her career, which annoyed him no end. Griffin, Erica's jittery high school classmate and current platonic roommate, was intent on wooing her, but she wasn't interested.

At the start of *Cosby*'s second season, the living arrangements at the Lucas household got considerably more crowded. Erica left the law firm to become a chef. She moved back into her old room, and Griffin, licking his wounds after a failed business deal, moved into their attic. That way he could rent the house next door to Hilton's, which he had just purchased, to a preschool. Angelo was one of the children at the preschool. The struggling flower shop started serving Erica's cookies and coffee and and became so popular it was converted into a coffee shop and rechristened The Flower Café.

In the fall of 1998, Hilton took on the responsibility of watching young Jurnee after school until her dad, Del (Sinbad), got home from work. Griffin and Erica were about to move into his house when it burned to the ground, leaving the living arrangements as they had been for the previous year. Griffin, still trying to find himself, decided he wanted to become a teacher. He took courses so he could get a teaching license and did a little substitute teaching. In the spring of 1999 Erica and her new boyfriend, Darien, an airline flight attendant, got engaged. Their marriage took place in the second episode of the 1999–2000 season; Erica was working as a substitute teacher, which eventually led to a full-time position. In October Ruth took over the neighborhood bookstore and annexed it to The Flower Café. The last episode aired in 1999 was a special tribute to Madeline Kahn, who had passed away early in December.

Based on the British series *One Foot in the Grave.*

COSBY MYSTERIES, THE (*Detective Drama*)

FIRST TELECAST: *September 21, 1994*
LAST TELECAST: *April 12, 1995*
BROADCAST HISTORY:

Sep 1994–Apr 1995, NBC Wed 8:00–9:00

CAST:

Guy Hanks .... Bill Cosby
Det. Adam Sully .... James Naughton
Barbara Lorenz (1994) .... Lynn Whitfield
Dante (1994) .... Dante Beze
Angie Corea .... Rita Moreno
Robert Chapman .... Robert Stanton

Guy Hanks was a criminologist and forensics expert for the New York City Police Department who had struck it rich by winning the state lottery. Although he had taken early retirement and no longer needed to work, he missed the challenges and continued to consult on difficult cases, which, of course, he alone was able to solve with his shambling, *Columbo*-esque approach. Others populating this rather routine detective show included Detective Sully, his longtime colleague; Barbara, his good friend and widow of his former partner; Dante, an eager young street kid who was his unofficial assistant; and Angie, his fussy housekeeper.

COSBY SHOW, THE (*Situation Comedy*)

FIRST TELECAST: *September 20, 1984*
LAST TELECAST: *September 17, 1992*
BROADCAST HISTORY:

Sep 1984–Jun 1992, NBC Thu 8:00–8:30
Jul 1992–Sep 1992, NBC Thu 8:30–9:00

CAST:

Dr. Heathcliff (Cliff) Huxtable .... Bill Cosby
Clair Huxtable .... Phylicia Rashad
Sondra Huxtable Tibideaux (age 20) .... Sabrina Le Beauf
Denise Huxtable Kendall (16) (1984–1991) .... Lisa Bonet
Theodore Huxtable (14) .... Malcolm-Jamal Warner
Vanessa Huxtable (8) .... Tempestt Bledsoe
Rudy Huxtable (5) .... Keshia Knight Pulliam
**Anna Huxtable* .... Clarice Taylor
**Russell Huxtable* .... Earle Hyman
**Peter Chiara (1985–1989)* .... Peter Costa
Elvin Tibideaux (1986–1992) ...... Geoffrey Owens
**Kenny ("Bud") (1986–1992)* .... Deon Richmond
**Cockroach (1986–1987)* ..... Carl Anthony Payne II
**Denny (1987–1991)* .... Troy Winbush
Lt. Martin Kendall (1989–1992) .. Joseph C. Phillips
Olivia Kendall (1989–1992) .... Raven-Symone
Pam Tucker (17) (1990–1992) ..... Erika Alexander
**Dabnis Brickey (1991–1992)* ... William Thomas, Jr.

*Occasional

This gentle yet hip family comedy was the number-one program on television during the mid 1980s, and a striking reminder that TV series don't have to be built on gimmicks to succeed. Most of the action took place at the Huxtable residence, a New York City brownstone where Cliff (an obstetrician) also maintained his office. He and his wife Clair (a legal aid attorney) tried to bring up the kids with a combination of love and parental firmness, while leading their own active professional lives. Sondra, the oldest daughter, was a senior at Princeton University during the first season, graduating early in the second; Denise and Theo ("No problem!") were the know-it-all teenagers; Vanessa the rambunctious 8-year-old; and Rudy the adorable, if mischievous, little girl. "I just hope they get out of the house before we die," murmured an exhausted Cliff as he sank into bed at the end of the premiere episode.

He would not be so lucky. As seasons went by and the children grew up, they brought home friends, then surprise spouses, and eventually babies. The first to wed was Sondra, who met Elvin at Princeton. They married during the 1986–1987 season and had twins, Winnie and Nelson, in November 1988. She was calm during the delivery, but Elvin almost passed out; he then decided to enroll in medical school. Independent-minded Denise was next, departing for Hillman College (and her own series, *A Different World*) in 1987, dropping out a year later and going to Africa to work as a photographer's assistant. She returned home unexpectedly in 1989 complete with a husband, Navy Lieutenant Martin, and his four-year-old daughter, Olivia. The tyke won everybody's heart, especially Cliff's, as he now had a new cute child in the house to mug with.

Theo, the underachiever, enrolled at nearby New York University during the fifth season, while Vanessa later chose Lincoln University. She shocked everyone at the start of the eighth season by announcing that she had been engaged for the past six months to a maintenance man at her college, Dabnis, who was twelve years older than she was!

Although the main focus was on the immediate family, a number of other characters were seen occasionally. Cliff's parents Anna and Russell and Clair's folks Carrie and Al Hanks turned up once in a while, as did Rudy's little friends Peter (one of the few whites in the cast) and Bud, and Theo's buddies Cockroach and Denny. Clair's cousin Pam, an underprivileged youth from the Bedford-Stuyvesant slums, came to live with the family in 1990, giving them all a taste of the "other half."

About the only celebrities to appear on the show were some very famous musicians who reflected Cosby's wide-ranging tastes in black music. Among them were Sammy Davis, Jr., Stevie Wonder, B. B. King, Nancy Wilson, Joe Williams (who played the occasional role of Clair's dad, Al), and the entire Count Basie Band.

The Cosby Show had an interesting history. Originally proposed as a comedy about a blue-collar worker, it was turned down by ABC and NBC. Bill Cosby's wife reportedly urged the comedian to change the lead characters to upscale professionals, whereupon the show was again rejected by ABC but was picked up by NBC, which agreed to Cosby's condition that, unlike most network series, it would be taped in New York (he disliked working in Hollywood). Cosby also insisted on total creative control, which he used to shape the series into a showcase for the educational and child-rearing theories he had developed while pursuing his doctorate in education in the 1970s (the actor proudly included the redundant line "Dr. William H. Cosby, Jr., Ed.D." in the credits for early episodes). Not everyone agreed with his approach: *The Cosby Show* was criticized for its unrealistic portrayal of blacks as wealthy, well-educated professionals, and for its lack of attention to black-white relations. Others defended it as providing role models for what blacks could achieve, and lessons for all races in how to raise a family in a calm and loving manner.

COSMOPOLITAN THEATRE (*Dramatic Anthology*)

FIRST TELECAST: *October 2, 1951*
LAST TELECAST: *December 25, 1951*
BROADCAST HISTORY:
Oct 1951–Dec 1951, DUM Tue 9:00–10:00

This major dramatic effort by DuMont presented live TV adaptations of stories from the pages of *Cosmopolitan* magazine, many of them mysteries or romantic dramas. Among the stars that appeared were Lee Tracy, Marsha Hunt, and Lon Chaney, Jr.

COSTELLO (*Situation Comedy*)

FIRST TELECAST: *September 15, 1998*
LAST TELECAST: *October 13, 1998*
BROADCAST HISTORY:
Sep 1998–Oct 1998, FOX Tue 8:30–9:00
CAST:
Sue Murphy .... Sue Costello
James "Spud" Murphy .... Dan Lauria
Lottie Murphy .... Jenny O'Hara
Trish .... Kerry O'Malley
Jimmy Murphy .... Chuck Walczak
Mary McDonough .... Josie DiVencenzo

Sue was a spunky, outspoken, 27-year-old barmaid at The Bull and Dog Bar, in a working-class neighborhood of South Boston. She was trying to better herself and took a lot of abuse about it from her family and the beer-guzzling customers at the bar. Spud, her father, was a carpenter who frowned on her intellectual ambitions; Lottie, her mother, was a waitress at The Bull and Dog; and Jimmy, her dim-witted, pretty-boy kid brother, made a career out of not having a real job. Trish, Sue's best friend, was a fellow barmaid/bartender at the bar where Mary, her slutty nemesis who worked at the Department of Motor Vehicles, was a regular.

Although all the yelling and punching each other around was in good humor, *Costello* was lambasted by critics for being crude and offensive. (Jimmy, looking at a University of Massachusetts catalog: "These bitches need to get laid!") The language was pretty salty by the standards of prime-time television, but the real problems with the show were its one-dimensional stereotyping of Boston's working-class Irish, and its inability to find an audience. After a month on the air it became one of the first casualties of the season.

COULD IT BE A MIRACLE? (*Religious/Paranormal*)

BROADCAST HISTORY:
Syndicated only
60 minutes
Produced: *1996–1997* (24 episodes)
Released: *September 1996*
HOST:
Robert Culp
MIRACLE RESEARCH TEAM:
Sayer (1996) .... Nicholas de Wolff
Lucia (1996) .... Carla Jo Bailey
Michele (1996) .... Michelle O'Bryant
Rob (1996) .... Christopher Davis
Andee (1996) .... Dawn Gray
Jim (1996) .... P.J. Lambert
MIRACLE RESEARCH CENTER HOSTS:
Michele Wolford
Bob B. Evans

A look at paranormal phenomena with a religious focus. Episodes featured interviews with actual participants and re-creations of unexplained events. Each episode opened with the "Miracle Research Team" discussing cases they had been investigating individually, and as they went into the details, the re-creations would start. After the recreations the "team" discussed the implications and whether or not the incident was, in fact, a miracle. Regularly featured were Brad Steiger and Sherry Hanson Steiger, Karen Goldman, and Joan Wester Anderson, all of whom had written books on miracles, along with guest authors who related miraculous events to home viewers. These included incidents involving visions, mysterious dreams, ghosts and other apparitions. The unifying factor was that all of those who were touched by "miraculous" experiences had faith in miracles: the "team" considered this the most vital tool in investigating cases.

After a month the "team," along with their discussion and evaluation segments, was dropped, and two of the show's producers—Michele Wolford and Bob Evans—introduced the interview and re-creation segments.

COUNTERATTACK: CRIME IN AMERICA (*Information/Public Affairs*)

FIRST TELECAST: *May 2, 1982*
LAST TELECAST: *May 23, 1982*
BROADCAST HISTORY:
May 1982, ABC Sun 7:00–8:00
HOST:
George Kennedy

This unusual program featured a national telephone hot line intended to help solve real-life crimes. It was produced in cooperation with WeTip, a California organization that had been operating a similar statewide hot line for ten years. Operators were seen standing by as host George Kennedy described recent crimes around the country that had baffled police, among them the "Catch Me Killer" in St. Paul, Minnesota, and the "Rotten Tooth .45-caliber Thief" in Nassau County, New York. Reenactments were also shown, and tips given on how to prevent crime.

COUNTERSTRIKE (*Foreign Intrigue*)

BROADCAST HISTORY:

USA Network
60 minutes
Produced: *1990–1993* (66 episodes)
Premiered: *July 1, 1990*

CAST:

Alexander Addington .... Christopher Plummer
Peter Sinclair .... Simon MacCorkindale
Nikki Beaumont (1990–1991) .... Cyrielle Claire
Luke Brenner (1990–1991) .... Stephen Shellen
Suzanne Addington (1990–1991)
.... Laurence Ashley-Taboulet
Gabrielle Germont (1991–1993) ... Sophie Michaud
Hector Stone (1991–1993) .... James Purcell
Helene Previn (1991–1993) .... Patricia Cartier
J.J. .... Andre Mayers
Bennett .... Tom Kneebone

Toronto billionaire Alexander Addington had reason to be angry. Terrorists had kidnapped and killed his beloved wife, but instead of blowing someone up he decided to use his considerable resources to form a crack international crime-fighting team, one that would take on similar cases that the authorities could not—or would not—tackle. Suave Peter, an ex–Scotland Yard operative, was the team's leader, assisted in the first season by beautiful Nikki and strong-man Luke. At the beginning of year two Nikki got married and Luke was killed on a mission; they were replaced by Gabrielle, a nosy magazine writer, and Stone, an ex-Marine and Navy SEAL.

They all jetted about in Addington's high-tech command plane, linked to the world and to his Paris headquarters by picture phones and other state-of-the-art communications devices. J.J. was the pilot, Bennett the butler, Helene was Addington's efficient secretary, and Suzanne his beloved daughter.

COUNTRY CARNIVAL/COUNTRY MUSIC CARAVAN/COUNTRY MUSIC MEMORIES/COUNTRY SHOW, THE, see *Grand Ole Opry*

COUNTRY MUSIC JUBILEE, see *Ozark Jubilee*

COUNTRY MUSIC SPOTLIGHT (*Music*)

BROADCAST HISTORY:

The Family Channel
60 minutes
Produced: *1993–1994* (13 episodes)
Premiered: *January 8, 1994*

Country music concert series spotlighting such stars as Johnny Cash, Tammy Wynette, and the Gatlins along with up-and-comers including John Michael Montgomery and Tracy Lawrence. Taped at various locations including Branson, Missouri, and Myrtle Beach, South Carolina.

COUNTRY STYLE (*Musical Variety*)

FIRST TELECAST: *July 29, 1950*
LAST TELECAST: *November 25, 1950*
BROADCAST HISTORY:

Jul 1950–Nov 1950, DUM Sat 8:00–9:00

REGULARS:

Peggy Ann Ellis
Gordon Dilworth
Pat Adair
Emily Barnes
Bob Austin
The Folk Dancers
Alvy West and the Volunteer Firemen, band

This rustic musical variety hour was designed to simulate a Saturday night's entertainment in a small town. The town bandstand, manned by the Volunteer Firemen's band, was the setting around which musical numbers, square dancing, and comedy vignettes took place.

COUPLE OF JOES, A (*Variety*)

FIRST TELECAST: *October 27, 1949*
LAST TELECAST: *July 12, 1950*
BROADCAST HISTORY:

Oct 1949–Dec 1949, ABC Thu 11:15–12 Mid
Dec 1949–Feb 1950, ABC Wed 8:00–9:00
Mar 1950–Jul 1950, ABC Wed 9:00–9:30

REGULARS:

"Big" Joe Rosenfield
Joe Bushkin
Joan Barton (Sep–Feb)
Warren Hull (Dec–Mar)
Beryl Richards (Mar–Jul)
Pat Harrington (Mar–May)
Allyn Edwards (Mar–Jul)
Morgan the Dog
Mike Reilly Orchestra
Bobby Sherwood Orchestra (1950)

This combination music, variety, and giveaway program starred "Big" Joe Rosenfield and jazz pianist Joe Bushkin, with an assortment of regulars that included singer Joan Barton and, later, comic Pat Harrington. One of the biggest stars of the show seemed to be Morgan the Dog, who attracted much publicity and survived numerous cast changes. *A Couple of Joes* premiered as a local New York show in August 1949, moved to the network in a late-night time slot in October, and in December became a prime-time entry.

COURAGE (*Documentary*)

BROADCAST HISTORY:

Fox Family Channel
60 minutes
Original episodes: *2000* (13 episodes)
Premiered: *August 7, 2000*

HOST:

Danny Glover

True-life stories of courage, heroism, and triumph narrated by a reverent Danny Glover. One episode profiled little Rudy, who ran, biked, and swam with artificial steel legs; an army medic recognized after many years for his incredible bravery during the war; a family in a plane crash saved by their brave teenage son; and a 66-year-old crossing guard who dived in front of a truck to save some children (with close-ups of the adorable kids).

COURAGE THE COWARDLY DOG (*Cartoon*)

BROADCAST HISTORY:

Cartoon Network
30 minutes
Original episodes: *1999–*
Premiered: *November 12, 1999*

VOICES:

Courage.......................... Marty Grabstein
Muriel Bagge......................... Thea White
Eustace Bagge (1999–2002)......... Lionel Wilson
Eustace Bagge (2002–)......... Arthur Anderson
The Computer..................... Simon Prebble
**Katz*.............................. Paul Schoeffler
**Di Lung*................................ Tim Chi Ly
**Ma Bagge*.......................... Billie Lou Watt
**Shirley the Medium*................... Mary Testa

*Occasional

This rather surrealistic cartoon centered on Courage, a plump pink dog who was afraid of almost everything. Abandoned as a pup, he now lived in a big ramshackle house in the middle of "Nowhere, Kansas" (portrayed as a vast empty plain), with his elderly owners, kindly, white-haired Muriel and her cranky husband, Eustace. The place was regularly invaded by aliens and monsters bent on demolishing it and its inhabitants, and it was up to Courage, with chattering teeth and frightened look, to outwit them. He got some help from his talking Computer, but none from self-centered Eustace, who could only mutter, "Stupid dog!" Katz was an evil red cat who walked on his hind legs and caused much trouble; Di Lung, a punk kid with a scientific bent; and Ma, Eustace's irritable mother.

COURT, THE (*Legal Drama*)

FIRST TELECAST: *March 26, 2002*
LAST TELECAST: *April 9, 2002*
BROADCAST HISTORY:

Mar 2002–Apr 2002, ABC Tue 10:00–11:00

CAST:

Justice Kate Nolan...................... Sally Field
Chief Justice Amos Townsend........... Pat Hingle
Justice Roberto Martinez......... Miguel Sandoval
Justice Lucas Voorhees............ Chris Sarandon
Justice Angela DeSett............. Diahann Carroll
Harlan Brandt......................... Craig Bierko
Betsy Tyler................... Christina Hendricks
Alexis Cameron.................... Nicole DeHuff
Christopher Bell....................... Hill Harper
Dylan Hirsch.......................... Josh Radnor

Feisty, pixie-ish Sally Field was cast in the unlikely role of a Supreme Court justice in this short-lived drama. Kate Nolan was the governor of an unnamed midwestern state when she was appointed to the Court to replace a popular justice who had died unexpectedly in an auto accident. A wide-eyed idealist, she found a panel full of good ol' boys and schemers, split evenly between liberals and conservatives, who treated her like the green new kid. Of course being the swing vote she promptly stirred up the pot and showed *them* a thing or two! Jowly Townsend was the chief justice, and Voorhees, an abrupt, domineering colleague. Alexis, Christopher and Dylan were eager clerks. Bedeviling Kate outside the marble halls were Harlan, an aggressive reporter trying to dig up dirt on her past, and his young production assistant Betsy. This was one of two Supreme Court dramas premiering in early 2002, the other being CBS' *First Monday*.

COURT-MARTIAL (*Drama*)

FIRST TELECAST: *April 8, 1966*
LAST TELECAST: *September 2, 1966*
BROADCAST HISTORY:

Apr 1966–Sep 1966, ABC Fri 10:00–11:00

CAST:

Capt. David Young.............. Bradford Dillman
Maj. Frank Whittaker................. Peter Graves
M/Sgt. John MacCaskey......... Kenneth J. Warren
Sgt. Wendy............................ Diane Clare

At the center of this World War II drama were the officer-lawyers of the U.S. Army Judge Advocate General's Office, headquartered in England, who investigated and prosecuted crimes committed during wartime. The court-martial itself, the climactic part of each show, was preceded by lengthy investigations ranging across war-torn Europe. The series was filmed in England.

COURT OF CURRENT ISSUES (*Debate*)

FIRST TELECAST: *February 9, 1948*
LAST TELECAST: *June 26, 1951*
BROADCAST HISTORY:

Feb 1948–Jul 1948, DUM Tue 8:00–8:30
Jul 1948–Nov 1948, DUM Mon 9:30–10:00
Nov 1948–Jan 1949, DUM Mon 8:00–9:00
Jan 1949–Feb 1949, DUM Mon 10:00–11:00
Mar 1949–Apr 1949, DUM Mon 9:00–10:00
May 1949–Jun 1949, DUM Wed 9:00–10:00
Jun 1949–Jun 1951, DUM Tue 8:00–9:00

CREATOR/PRODUCER:

Irvin Paul Sulds

Court of Current Issues was one of a number of early programs that presented debates on public affairs, this one within the framework of a courtroom trial. A real judge or attorney sat on the bench, prominent persons on each side of the issue represented opposing counsel and witnesses, and a jury of 12 drawn from the audience handed down a verdict. During its last two years *Court* was scheduled on Tuesday night, opposite NBC's Milton Berle, and a reviewer complained that a fine public-affairs show was being wasted—not a single person called in an audience survey was watching it.

The program was known during its early months as *Court of Public Opinion*.

COURT OF LAST RESORT, THE (*Crime Drama*)

FIRST TELECAST: *October 4, 1957*
LAST TELECAST: *February 17, 1960*
BROADCAST HISTORY:

Oct 1957–Apr 1958, NBC Fri 8:00–8:30
Aug 1959–Sep 1959, ABC Wed 8:00–8:30
Oct 1959–Feb 1960, ABC Wed 7:30–8:00

CAST:

Sam Larsen............................ Lyle Bettger
Erle Stanley Gardner.................... Paul Birch
Dr. LeMoyne Snyder........... Charles Meredith
Raymond Schindler............... Robert H. Harris
Harry Steeger.................... Carleton Young
Marshall Houts........................ John Launer

Alex Gregory........................John Maxwell
Park Street, Jr...................Robert Anderson

The Court of Last Resort, in real life, was a committee of crime experts who investigated cases in which there was a possibility that the convicted prisoner was innocent. This series dramatized some of the actual cases taken on by this renowned group, founded in the early 1950s by the famous mystery writer Erle Stanley Gardner. Each episode depicted the crime for which a given person was imprisoned, and then followed the efforts of the members of the Court of Last Resort to verify his guilt or find evidence of his innocence. The names of the people involved were changed, since the cases were all based on real situations.

In the series Sam Larsen was a special investigator working with the seven members of the Court in their search for truth. At the close of each story, the actual seven-member board was seen briefly and one of them would discuss a specific point of law that was crucial in the drama just finished. On occasion this function was taken over by judges, law-enforcement officers, or district attorneys.

The ABC telecasts consisted of reruns from the original NBC series.

COURT OF PUBLIC OPINION, see *Court of Current Issues*

COURT TV (Network) (*Cable Network*)

LAUNCHED:
July 1, 1991
SUBSCRIBERS (MAY 2003):
75.3 million (71% U.S.)

Another of the "niche," or specialty, networks founded in the 1990s. Court TV (whose formal name is Courtroom Television Network) carried live coverage of trials during the day, via in-court cameras, and summaries and analysis at night. The network claimed to cover over 125 trials per year in more than 75 municipalities. For obvious reasons the focus was often on high-profile or celebrity cases. In its first months it highlighted the trial of the Los Angeles policemen accused of beating Rodney King, the rape trial of William Kennedy Smith, and a case in which American Nazis defended their right to burn crosses. In early 1995 the network attracted much attention with its live, continuous coverage of the O. J. Simpson double-murder trial in Los Angeles.

Among the network's early prime-time series were *Prime Time Justice* (a summary of the day's legal events), *Lock & Key* (parole and death penalty hearings), *In Context* (analysis by Harvard law professor Arthur Miller), *Trial Story* (high-profile cases, summarized in an hour), *Washington Watch* (legal news from the capital), and various series hosted by famed attorney Johnnie Cochran. Court TV's original chief anchor was former CBS law correspondent Fred Graham.

Beginning around 2000 the network started to shift its prime-time lineup away from trial-related subjects (trials continued during daytime) and toward the broader subject of crime and punishment. Among the documentary series introduced were *Mugshots*, *Hollywood & Crime*, *Forensic Files*, *The System*, and *I, Detective*. Off-network reruns included *Cops*, *Homicide: Life on the Street*, *Wiseguy*, *Profiler*, and *N.Y.P.D. Blue*. One documentary series that caused a storm of protest was *Confessions* (September 2000), in which real murderers and rapists described their horrific crimes. It was quickly pulled from the schedule.

COURT TV—INSIDE AMERICA'S COURTS
(*Legal/Information*)

BROADCAST HISTORY:
Syndicated only
30 minutes
Produced: *1993–1997*
Released: *October 1993*
HOST:
Gregg Jarrett
Jami Floyd (1996–1997)
Chris Gordon (1996–1997)
REPORTER:
Cynthia McFadden (1993–1994)
June Grasso (1994–1995)
Kristin Jeannette-Meyers (1995–1997)

This weekly series summarized activities in cases from cable's Court TV (The Courtroom Television Network). In addition to highlights from current and past cases, viewers were shown parole hearings and provided with information on the legal process and other related issues. Host Gregg Jarrett provided background material and Cynthia McFadden, later replaced by June Grasso and Kristin Jeannette-Meyers, updated currently active court cases.

When the series expanded to a weekday half hour in the fall of 1995, a weekend wrap-up edition, *Court TV: Justice this Week*, was added. The following fall Chris Gordon relieved Jarrett as host of the weekend show, and two months later Jami Floyd joined Jarrett as co-host of the weekday version. The following February the syndicated series ended its run, with all of its staff returning to full-time duty for its source, cable's *Court TV*.

COURTHOUSE (*Legal Drama*)

FIRST TELECAST: *September 13, 1995*
LAST TELECAST: *November 15, 1995*
BROADCAST HISTORY:
Sep 1995–Nov 1995, CBS Wed 10:00–11:00
CAST:
Judge Justine Parkes...............Patricia Wettig
Lenore Laderman.................Annabeth Gish
Suzanne Graham...................Robin Givens
Judge Homer Conklin................Bob Gunton
Judge Wyatt E. Jackson.............Brad Johnson
Judge Myron Winkelman..........Michael Lerner
Judge Rosetta Reide.................Jenifer Lewis
Edison Moore.....................Jeffrey D. Sams
Veronica Gilbert.......................Nia Peeples
Jonathan Mitchell..................Dan Gauthier
Amy Chen........................Jacqueline Kim
Nell..........................Shelley Morrison
Andrew Rawson.....................Cotter Smith
Sean..........................George Newbern
Gabe...............................John Mese

Violent, sex-laden serial drama about the judges, lawyers, and staff working in an unnamed big-city courthouse in mythical Clark County. In the eye of the judicial hurricane, in a rotting building with limited budgetary resources and an overcrowded case load, was no-nonsense presiding judge Justine Parkes. The two Criminal Court judges on her staff were polar opposites—Conklin, the autocratic, by-the-book traditionalist; and Wyatt Earp Jackson, the hunky, recently arrived non-conformist from Montana. The other judges on the staff were Winkelman, the neurotic who presided over Family Court; and Reide, a struggling, gay single mother responsible for Juvenile Court. Among the others working in and around the courthouse were conceited prosecutor Mitchell, who was dating public defender Gilbert; ambitious young prosecutor Moore, who was carrying on a torrid secret affair with Graham, an investigator for the D.A.'s office; and young prosecutor Laderman, who was adjusting to reassignment to the sex crimes unit.

Series star Patricia Wettig, dissatisfied with the direction of her character, had announced her intention to leave *Courthouse*, but the show was canceled before her character was written out.

COURTSHIP OF EDDIE'S FATHER, THE (*Situation Comedy*)

FIRST TELECAST: *September 17, 1969*
LAST TELECAST: *June 14, 1972*
BROADCAST HISTORY:
Sep 1969–Sep 1970, ABC Wed 8:00–8:30
Sep 1970–Sep 1971, ABC Wed 7:30–8:00
Sep 1971–Jan 1972, ABC Wed 8:30–9:00
Jan 1972–Jun 1972, ABC Wed 8:00–8:30
CAST:
Tom Corbett .... Bill Bixby
Eddie Corbett .... Brandon Cruz
Mrs. Livingston .... Miyoshi Umeki
Norman Tinker .... James Komack
Tina Rickles .... Kristina Holland
THEME:
"Best Friend" by Harry Nilsson

Magazine publisher Tom Corbett was one of television's many widowers saddled with the responsibility of running a motherless household. In this case his son, freckle-faced young Eddie (played by Brandon Cruz, who was seven years old when the series began), did most of the plotting. Eddie had a special penchant for getting his father romantically involved with prospective brides, which led to many warm and comic moments. Mrs. Livingston was Tom's dependable, philosophical, but sometimes confused housekeeper; Tina his secretary; and Norman Tinker a mod photographer at the magazine. Although not a regular on the show, young Jodie Foster appeared from time to time as Eddie's friend, Joey Kelly. The series was based on a novel by Mark Toby, also made into a 1963 movie starring Glenn Ford and Ronny Howard, and had a theme song ("Best Friend") written by pop singer Harry Nilsson.

COUSIN SKEETER (*Situation Comedy*)

BROADCAST HISTORY:
Nickelodeon
30 minutes
Produced: *1998–2000* (52 episodes)
Premiered: *September 1, 1998*
CAST:
Skeeter (voice) .... Bill Bellamy
Bobby Walker .... Robert Ri'chard
Andre Walker .... Rondell Sheridan
Vanessa Walker .... Angela Means
Nina .... Meagan Good
Nicole .... Tisha Campbell
Sweetie .... Christine Flores

Cousin Skeeter, a sort of updated version of *Alf*, was a live-action sitcom about a shy 13-year-old black kid whose family moved from Los Angeles to New York City and promptly took in a cousin from Atlanta who became his new best friend. Bobby was your typical insecure teen, but there was nothing typical about Skeeter—he was a loud, wisecracking, trouble-causing, girl-chasing, cool dude, who also happened to be a puppet (though nobody seemed to notice). Skeeter dragged cautious Bobby into all sorts of exploits, which in the end, we were told, helped the lad open up and "bring some fun into his life." Andre and Vanessa were Bobby's easygoing parents, and Nina was the chatterbox neighbor girl, on whom Bobby had a crush.

COVER ME (*Crime Drama*)

BROADCAST HISTORY:
USA Network
60 minutes
Original episodes: *2000–2001* (25 episodes)
Premiered: *March 5, 2000*
CAST:
Danny Arno .... Peter Dobson
Barbara Arno .... Melora Hardin
Celeste Arno (age 16) .... Cameron Richardson
Ruby Arno (14) .... Antoinette Picatto
Chance Arno (11) .... Michael Angarano
Chance (older, voice only) .... David Faustino

Danny Arno was an excitable undercover agent who moonlighted for the F.B.I., D.E.A., Department of Justice, Interpol and other law enforcement agencies. He came with an unusual extra: his family. Rather than shield his wife and kids from his dangerous work, he brought them in on the gig. Barbara was his supportive wife who tried to provide a "normal" home life for the children when she wasn't playing a floozy on some undercover assignment; Celeste was the eldest teen, who could flirt with a criminal's son to gain information; Ruby, the brainy 14-year-old, who combined baby-sitting and surveillance; and Chance, the eager youngest, who adored his dad and filled in on such roles as bagman and lookout. (Who would suspect a *kid*?) Despite the risks they took—there were explosions and shoot-outs galore—the family seemed relatively bulletproof, although parents at home might have been a little uncomfortable seeing wacko Danny hand five-year-old Chance a loaded gun (in a flashback) and telling him, "Shoot it!" The show was narrated by Chance as an adult.

Believe it or not, the series was supposedly based on the true story of the Brown family, Carolyn Brown Brannon, Laura Brown, and Cory Patrick Brown. Its full title was *Cover Me: Based on the True Life of an FBI Family*.

COVER STORY (*Interview*)

BROADCAST HISTORY:
USA Network
30 minutes
Produced: *1984–1989* (106 episodes)
Premiered: *March 2, 1984*

An inexpensive series of celebrity profiles utilizing film clips and interviews. The first subject was Carl Reiner; others included Stephanie Mills, Dennis Weaver, and Anthony Quinn.

COVER UP (*Detective/Foreign Intrigue*)
FIRST TELECAST: *September 22, 1984*
LAST TELECAST: *July 6, 1985*
BROADCAST HISTORY:
Sep 1984–Apr 1985, CBS Sat 10:00–11:00
May 1985–Jul 1985, CBS Sat 8:00–9:00
CAST:
Mac Harper (1984) .... Jon-Erik Hexum
Danielle Reynolds .... Jennifer O'Neill
Henry Towler .... Richard Anderson
Jack Striker .... Antony Hamilton
Rick .... Mykel T. Williamson
Gretchen .... Ingrid Anderson
Billie .... Irena Ferris
Ashley .... Dana Sparks
Cindy (1984) .... Heather McNair

They traveled around the world on fashion assignments—Dani, the gorgeous professional photographer, and Mac, her handsome male model. At least that was their public job; actually they were secret agents working on a freelance basis for a mysterious U.S. government agency. They were well-suited to their clandestine roles—Mac was a former Green Beret who had served in Vietnam and was a specialist in karate, chemical interrogation, and foreign languages. Dani was no novice either, having been married to an agent whose death she and Mac avenged in the series' premiere episode. Under the loose supervision of Towler they traveled from country to country, staging fashion shows and photo sessions with their scantily clad models, while rescuing Americans from dangerous situations. Rick was Dani's photographic assistant and helped both her and Mac on espionage assignments, while Gretchen, Billie, Ashley, and Linda were her most frequently used models.

Antony Hamilton replaced Jon-Erik Hexum as Dani's partner after Hexum's tragic death following an accident in which he had shot himself in the head on the set of *Cover Up*.

COVER WARS (*Talent*)
BROADCAST HISTORY:
VH1
60 minutes
Original episodes: *2001*
Premiered: *June 23, 2001*
REGULARS:
Paul Shaffer, Host
Sky Nellor, Assistant/Disk Jockey

Three cover bands competed on adjacent stages in front of a panel of three celebrity judges to win exposure and a van full of music gear in this fast-paced show. First came the Human Juke Box round in which each band had to play a song picked by one of the judges to test their repertoire; in the Style Jam round, they played a single song in different styles to test their versatility. One band was then eliminated, and the two remaining advanced to the Chops competition, where one band started and the other had to pick up the song without missing a beat or screwing up the lyrics. Judges were mostly music industry insiders such as Sebastian Bach, Duncan Sheik and Spacehog singer Royston Langston. Super-cool Paul Shaffer (all in black) hosted, and sidekick Sky boogied in her hot pants as the audience screamed.

COVINGTON CROSS (*Adventure*)
FIRST TELECAST: *August 25, 1992*
LAST TELECAST: *October 31, 1992*
BROADCAST HISTORY:
Aug 1992, ABC Tue 10:00–11:00
Sep 1992, ABC Fri 9:00–10:00
Sep 1992–October 1992, ABC Sat 8:00–9:00
CAST:
Sir Thomas Gray .... Nigel Terry
Richard Gray .... Jonathan Firth
Cedric Gray .... Glenn Quinn
Armus Gray .... Tim Killick
Eleanor Gray .... Ione Skye
Lady Elizabeth .... Cherie Lunghi
Sir John Mullens .... James Faulkner
Friar .... Paul Brooke

Political correctness, women's liberation, and other wonders of the late twentieth century were transported to medieval England, much to the surprise of the villagers, in this rather silly swashbuckler filmed in the English countryside. Sir Thomas was an imposing but sensitive lord who shared his castle with four active offspring, manly Knights Richard and Armus, young Knight-wannabe Cedric (who was desperately trying to avoid the fate his late mother wished on him, to go into a monastery), and spunky, independent young daughter Eleanor. Sir Thomas's main squeeze was fiercely independent Lady Elizabeth, who lived in her own castle down the road. The principal villain of the piece was evil-hearted Sir John, who plotted constantly to destroy the Grays and steal their land.

Another son, William, left for the Crusades in the first episode, apparently unaware that they had ended more than one hundred years earlier (historical accuracy was never the series' strong point!). The villages were sparkling clean, and everyone looked ruddy and healthy, also unlikely for the period. At least the locale was authentic. *Covington Cross* was filmed on location at Allington Castle, Kent, and Penshurst Place, Kent, in England.

COW AND CHICKEN (*Cartoon*)
BROADCAST HISTORY:
Cartoon Network
30 minutes
Produced: *1997–1999* (52 episodes)
Premiered: *c. July 1, 1997*
VOICES:
Cow, Chicken, The Red Guy .... Charlie Adler
Mom .... Candi Milo
Dad .... Dee Bradley Baker
Flem .... Dan Castellaneta
Earl .... Howard Morris

"Mama had a chicken, Mama had a cow, Dad was proud, he didn't care how," went the jazzy theme of this frantic, *Ren and Stimpy*–style cartoon. Cow was the big, dumb sister, complete with a bulging udder, while her brother Chicken was a scrawny schemer. Their fast-paced adventures around the neighborhood often involved a big red bully who looked like a cross between a pig and the devil, called The Red Guy. Flem and Earl were Chicken's school friends. Squabbling Mom and Dad were seen only from the knees down.

Originally seen on Cartoon Network's *World Premiere Toons*.

COWBOY IN AFRICA (*Adventure*)
FIRST TELECAST: *September 11, 1967*
LAST TELECAST: *September 16, 1968*
BROADCAST HISTORY:
Sep 1967–Sep 1968, ABC Mon 7:30–8:30
CAST:
Jim Sinclair .... Chuck Connors
John Henry .... Tom Nardini
Wing Comdr. Howard Hayes....... Ronald Howard
Samson .... Gerald Edwards

After TV had run through adult Westerns, dude Westerns, "empire" Westerns, contemporary Westerns, and comedy Westerns, ABC decided to try an African Western. *Cowboy in Africa* starred Chuck Connors as the world champion rodeo cowboy Jim Sinclair, who had been hired by an English landowner, Commander Hayes, to bring modern ranching methods to his game ranch in Kenya. Sinclair was assisted by his Navajo blood brother John Henry and was "adopted" by an orphaned, ten-year-old Kikuyu native boy named Samson.

The series was based on Ivan Tors's theatrical film *Africa—Texas Style* and was shot in Africa (for the backgrounds) and the Africa, U.S.A., park in southern California.

COWBOY THEATRE (*Western Anthology*)
FIRST TELECAST: *June 9, 1957*
LAST TELECAST: *September 15, 1957*
BROADCAST HISTORY:
Jun 1957, NBC Sun 6:30–7:00
Jun 1957–Sep 1957, NBC Sun 6:30–7:30
HOST:
Monty Hall

Re-edited Western feature films produced by Columbia Pictures in the 1930s and 1940s provided the material for this anthology, which was hosted and narrated by Monty Hall. The series began on Saturday afternoons in September 1956.

COWBOYS, THE (*Western*)
FIRST TELECAST: *February 6, 1974*
LAST TELECAST: *August 14, 1974*
BROADCAST HISTORY:
Feb 1974–Aug 1974, ABC Wed 8:00–8:30
CAST:
Jebediah Nightlinger .... Moses Gunn
Mrs. Annie Andersen............... Diana Douglas
U.S. Marshal Bill Winter .... Jim Davis
Cimarron.............................. A Martinez
Slim........................... Robert Carradine
Jimmy .... Sean Kelly
Homer .... Kerry MacLane
Steve............................... Clint Howard
Hardy .... Mitch Brown
Weedy .... Clay O'Brien

The Cowboys was a kind of teenage Western in which seven young boys, aged 9 to 17 years, faced the trials of growing into manhood while helping a widow run a ranch in the New Mexico Territory of the 1870s. The ranch foreman, Jebediah Nightlinger, and the widow, Mrs. Andersen, were around for adult supervision as the boys fought off teenage Comanches and adult rustlers. The series was based on the novel by William Dale Jennings and the movie starring John Wayne. Four of the boys in the series—Martinez, Carradine, Kelly, and O'Brien—also appeared in the film.

COWBOYS & INJUNS (*Children's*)
FIRST TELECAST: *October 15, 1950*
LAST TELECAST: *December 31, 1950*
BROADCAST HISTORY:
Oct 1950–Dec 1950, ABC Sun 6:00–6:30
HOST:
Rex Bell

This was an unusually informative children's show, consisting of demonstrations of real cowboy and Indian folklore. It was filmed in an outdoor corral and an Indian village as well as in indoor settings. Originally it was a local program in Los Angeles.

COWTOWN RODEO (*Rodeo*)
FIRST TELECAST: *August 1, 1957*
LAST TELECAST: *September 8, 1958*
BROADCAST HISTORY:
Aug 1957–Sep 1957, ABC Thu 8:00–9:00
Jun 1958–Sep 1958, ABC Mon 7:30–8:30
COMMENTATORS:
Marty Glickman
Howard "Stony" Harris

Top rodeo performers competed for cash prizes on this summertime show. Bronco busting, saddle and bareback riding, and calf roping were among the featured events. The program was produced at Cowtown Ranch in New Jersey, whose owner, Stony Harris, was one of the commentators.

CRACKER (*Detective Drama*)
FIRST TELECAST: *September 18, 1997*
LAST TELECAST: *January 24, 1998*
BROADCAST HISTORY:
Sep 1997–Dec 1997, ABC Thu 9:00–10:00
Jan 1998, ABC Sat 9:00–10:00
CAST:
Gerry "Fitz" Fitzgerald............ Robert Pastorelli
Judith Fitzgerald .... Carolyn McCormick
Michael Fitzgerald (age 17)............ Josh Harnett
Det. Hannah Tyler............ Angela Featherstone
Det. Danny Watlington .... Robert Wisdom
Lt. Fry .... R. Lee Ermey

Fitz was an eccentric psychologist who drank too much, gambled too much, fought too much, and seemed to have a direct connection to the dark side of the human soul. Oddly enough, it was those very traits that made him valuable as a consultant to the Los Angeles Police Department homicide squad. Lt. Fry was his grouchy boss, who grudgingly put up with Fitz's antics because he was so effective in cracking the most gruesome, difficult cases. In fact, Fitz could look into the criminal mind. Hannah was the intense detective who both charmed and annoyed Fitz, and Danny the resident skeptic ("What do we need him for?").

Fitz's personal life was no less tortured. His wife Judith, a feminist lecturer, agonized about their rocky relationship, but stuck with him for the sake of their baby daughter. Insecure teenage son Michael had a hard time relating to his unreachable father. Fitz also lectured at the County University of Los Angeles, and hosted a radio show on station KZAB.

Based on the successful British series of the same

name, starring Robbie Coltrane, which was seen in the U.S. on the A&E cable network.

CRAM (*Quiz*)
BROADCAST HISTORY:
Game Show Network
30 minutes
Original episodes: *2003–*
Premiered: *January 6, 2003*
REGULARS:
Graham Elwood, emcee
Andrea Hutchman (as Miss Pickwick)
Cram was billed as "the only game show that gives you the answers," the hitch being that it provided far more answers than questions and wore you out in the process. Before each show was taped, two teams of two contestants each were sequestered for 24 hours and given a mountain of reference materials to study, including magazines, books of riddles, instruction manuals and trivia lists. Then, with no opportunity for sleep, the teams were given a series of quizzes based on those materials while simultaneously engaged in physical stunts designed to drain their energy. In round one the teams were put in two huge hamster wheels and told to talk on a subject continuously while running, weaving in a list of key words; every time they said "um" or went off topic they were buzzed. In round two the teams did physical matchups—for example, matching spiders with their scientific names or placing weather symbols on a map—while simultaneously answering unrelated questions. In round three one member of each team pedaled furiously on a stationary bicycle while the other answered questions. In round four the contestants were tucked into nice comfy beds and read a droning series of facts by Miss Pickwick, while trying to stay awake; they then had to jump out of the beds and punch in answers using those facts, in a speed round.

The team with the highest score won a grand prize of as much as $10,000, and then got a good night's sleep.

CRANK YANKERS (*Situation Comedy*)
BROADCAST HISTORY:
Comedy Central
30 minutes
Original episodes: *2002–*
Premiered: *June 2, 2002*
VOICES:
Dick Birchum .... Adam Carolla
Elmer Higgins, The Nudge, Terrence, Karl Malone .... Jimmy Kimmel
Special Ed, Bobby Fletcher .... Jim Florentine
Spoonie Luv .... Tracy Morgan
Hadassah Guberman .... Sarah Silverman
Tony DeLoge, Bob Carlman .... Bob Einstein (as Super Dave Osborne)
Most people consider crank phone calls an annoyance, but on this series they were the joke. A wide range of comedians made crank calls to unsuspecting ordinary people, and the results were then used on the show, with the callers (and victims) portrayed by foam puppets living in the strange town of Yankerville. Among its inhabitants were gross disc jockey The Nudge, who called a 7-Eleven employee and convinced him to scream, "I peed in the slurpee machine!"; Birchum, an angry war veteran looking for a job; Elmer, an old coot who called for a hearing aid but couldn't hear the salesperson; Bobby, who called about a job but kept belching throughout the conversation; Tony, a candidate for district selectman who offended everyone, and Spoonie Luv, a cool black dude who called a very proper flower shop to dictate an obscene greeting card to his ex. Among the guest stars making calls were Jack Black, David Alan Grier and Kevin Nealon.

Interspersed with the calls were short visual jokes, such as a Chinaman with a large gong announcing, "Confucius say: girl who sit on judge's lap get honorable discharge." Gong!

Crank Yankers was created by those princes of puerile humor, Adam Carolla and Jimmy Kimmel, who were also responsible for *The Man Show*. Reportedly, all calls used were made in Nevada and New York, the only two states where harassment prosecution is not possible.

CRASH CORRIGAN'S RANCH (*Children's*)
FIRST TELECAST: *July 15, 1950*
LAST TELECAST: *September 29, 1950*
BROADCAST HISTORY:
Jul 1950–Aug 1950, ABC Sat 7:00–7:30
Aug 1950–Sep 1950, ABC Sun 6:30–7:00
Sep 1950, ABC Fri 7:30–8:00
HOST:
Ray (Crash) Corrigan
This variety show for children, starring Ray (Crash) Corrigan, featured musical and other acts in a Western setting.

CRAWFORD MYSTERY THEATRE (*Drama/Quiz*)
FIRST TELECAST: *September 6, 1951*
LAST TELECAST: *September 27, 1951*
BROADCAST HISTORY:
Sep 1951, DUM Thu 9:30–10:00
HOST/MODERATOR:
John Howard
Warren Hull
Detective-fiction writers and other guests guessed solutions to filmed mysteries in this early series, which was sponsored by Crawford Clothes. John Howard was host for the first two telecasts, after which he was replaced by Warren Hull (Howard later appeared as an actor in some of the dramas). The program was also known as *Public Prosecutor*. It was under the latter title that it remained on the air locally in New York until the end of February 1952.

CRAZY LIKE A FOX (*Detective*)
FIRST TELECAST: *December 30, 1984*
LAST TELECAST: *September 4, 1986*
BROADCAST HISTORY:
Dec 1984–Jan 1986, CBS Sun 9:00–10:00
Jan 1986–Mar 1986, CBS Wed 9:00–10:00
Apr 1986–Jun 1986, CBS Sat 8:00–9:00
Jun 1986–Jul 1986, CBS Thu 8:00–9:00
Aug 1986–Sep 1986, CBS Thu 9:00–10:00
CAST:
Harry Fox .... Jack Warden
Harrison K. Fox .... John Rubinstein
Cindy Fox .... Penny Peyser

Josh Fox .... Robby Kiger
Allison Ling (1984–1985) .... Lydia Lei
Allison Ling (1985–1986)
.... Patricia Ayame Thomson
Lt. Walker (1985–1986) .... Robert Hanley
Ernie (1985–1986) .... Theodore Wilson

Harrison K. Fox was a conservative young attorney trying to develop a successful law practice in San Francisco to support his wife, Cindy, and his young son, Josh. Unfortunately his life was endlessly complicated by his unconventional father Harry, a lovable con artist and private eye who was constantly getting involved in murder cases. Harry was a real character. When he got involved in a dicey case, he would inevitably drag Harrison in with him—sometimes to get free legal advice (he had, after all, paid for Harrison's education), sometimes to get Harrison to take on one of his trouble-prone friends as a client, most often to help with the legwork. That usually meant chasing people, breaking into offices, and getting shot at—just the sort of diversion a conservative attorney enjoys! Harrison's secretary Allison grew used to seeing Harry barge into the office, interrupting important meetings.

Despite all this, and regardless of his better judgment, Harrison could never turn Harry down. He was, after all, a lovable old coot.

CREW, THE (*Situation Comedy*)
FIRST TELECAST: *August 31, 1995*
LAST TELECAST: *June 30, 1996*
BROADCAST HISTORY:
Aug 1995–Jan 1996, FOX Thu 8:30–9:00
May 1996–Jun 1996, FOX Sun 9:30–10:00
CAST:
Jess Jameson .... Rose Jackson
Maggie Reynolds .... Kristin Bauer
Paul Steadman .... David Burke
Randy Anderson .... Charles Esten
MacArthur Edwards .... Dondre T. Whitfield
Lenora Zwick .... Christine Estabrook
Capt. Rex Parker .... Lane Davies

A group of young people working for a small airline were at the center of this wacky sitcom, a sort of "*Friends* takes *Wings*." Jess and Maggie were flight attendants for Miami-based Regency Airlines and lived in the trendy South Beach section of Miami Beach. Jess was a sexy woman whose temper sometimes got the best of her, even when she was on the job, and Maggie was her sensible roommate. Gay Paul and good-ole-boy Randy were fellow flight attendants, and mature Lenora, who made cracks about Paul's gayness, was their obnoxious supervisor. Mac, the bartender at Mambo Mambo, the restaurant where the gang hung out, was in love with Jess, while Lenora had the hots for stately, clueless Regency pilot, Rex Parker. Spats was Jess's never seen but overly possessive cat.

When the show returned in May, after a hiatus, Mac convinced Jess to move in with him. In June, Rex proposed to Lenora and she accepted. In the last episode—in the aftermath of a hurricane—Maggie and womanizing Randy ended up in bed, while Mac left Jess because he thought she couldn't commit.

CRIME & PUNISHMENT (*Police Drama*)
FIRST TELECAST: *March 3, 1993*
LAST TELECAST: *April 7, 1993*
BROADCAST HISTORY:
Mar 1993, NBC Wed 10:00–11:00
Mar 1993, NBC Thu 10:00–11:00
Apr 1993, NBC Wed 9:00–10:00
CAST:
Det. Ken O'Donnell .... Jon Tenney
Det. Annette Rey .... Rachel Ticotin
Lt. Anthony Bartoli .... Carmen Argenziano
Jan Sorenson .... Lisa Darr
Tanya .... Maris Celedonio
"Interrogator" .... James Sloyan

Detectives O'Donnell and Rey were partners in the L.A.P.D. in this cop-show-with-a-gimmick. In addition to their police work, much time was spent on their personal lives—Ken's relationship with his longtime girlfriend, Jan, a medical intern, and Rey's troubled home life with her once-estranged 17-year-old daughter, Tanya. Lt. Bartoli was their understanding boss.

The gimmick? Each crime was followed from the point of view of the criminal, the victim, and the police, with an unseen "Interrogator" questioning characters in midaction. *Variety* called that "pretentious and interruptive," but it made little difference as the series lasted for only six episodes.

CRIME & PUNISHMENT (*Legal Documentary*)
FIRST TELECAST: *June 16, 2002*
LAST TELECAST:
BROADCAST HISTORY:
Jun 2002–Sep 2002, NBC Sun 10:00–11:00
Jun 2003– , NBC Sun 10:00–11:00

This documentary series looked at real-life criminal cases handled by the prosecutors in the San Diego District Attorney's office. Though not quite as "behind the scenes" as ABC's similar *State v.*, which aired at the same time (and which even had access to jury deliberations), *Crime & Punishment* did show prosecutors conferring, talking to witnesses, building their case, and then appearing in the courtroom. Most of the crimes were violent, including murders, rapes and child molestation. Since the point of view was that of the prosecutors, the accused were almost always portrayed from the start as scumbags who were guilty as charged.

One case per episode was profiled, involving attorneys from the family protection unit, gang unit, high-tech crimes division and superior court division. They included supervisor Eugenia Eyherabide and deputies Dan Goldstein, Jill DiCarlo, Chris Lindberg, Garry Haehnle, Lisa Weinreb, Mark Amador, Michael Runyon, Michael Groch and Blaine Bowman.

CRIME PHOTOGRAPHER (*Newspaper Drama*)
FIRST TELECAST: *April 19, 1951*
LAST TELECAST: *June 5, 1952*
BROADCAST HISTORY:
Apr 1951–Jun 1952, CBS Thu 10:30–11:00
CAST:
Casey (Apr–Jun 1951) .... Richard Carlyle
Casey (Jun 1951–1952) .... Darren McGavin
Ethelbert (Apr–Jun 1951) .... John Gibson
Ethelbert (Jun 1951–1952) .... Cliff Hall
Ann Williams .... Jan Miner
Captain Logan .... Donald McClelland
Jack Lipman .... Archie Smith

The adventures of Casey, crack photographer for *The Morning Express*, were told in this series, which moved to television after a highly successful run on radio in the 1940s. Casey hung out at the Blue Note Cafe, where the music was provided by the Tony Mottola Trio, and was friendly with Ethelbert the bartender, to whom he recounted his various exploits. Richard Carlyle and John Gibson portrayed the roles when the series premiered in April 1951, but by June they were replaced by Darren McGavin and Cliff Hall. Ann Williams, a reporter on *The Morning Express*, was Casey's girlfriend. During the summer of 1951, he acquired a partner in cub reporter Jack Lipman, who wrote copy to go with Casey's pictures. This live series was set in, and broadcast from, New York City. It was based on the *Casey* novels by George Harmon Coxe.

CRIME STOPPERS 800 (*Public Service*)

BROADCAST HISTORY:

Syndicated only
30 minutes
Produced: *1989–1991* (104 episodes)
Released: *October 1989*

HOSTS:

Edwin Hart
Det. Larry Gross (1989–1990)
Officer Marete Edillo (1990–1991)

In this variation of Fox's successful *America's Most Wanted*, three to five cases involving wanted criminals were dramatized each week. Viewers were given a telephone-800 number to call, but unlike the Fox show, *Crime Stoppers 800* offered possible rewards for information leading to the capture and conviction of the criminals profiled. Edwin Hart shared the hosting duties with real police officers.

CRIME STORY (*Serial Drama*)

FIRST TELECAST: *September 18, 1986*
LAST TELECAST: *May 10, 1988*
BROADCAST HISTORY:

Sep 1986, NBC Thu 9:00–11:00
Sep 1986, NBC Fri 10:00–11:00
Sep 1986–Nov 1986, NBC Tue 9:00–10:00
Dec 1986–Mar 1987, NBC Fri 10:00–11:00
Jun 1987–Sep 1987, NBC Fri 10:00–11:00
Sep 1987–May 1988, NBC Tue 10:00–11:00

CAST:

Lt. Mike Torello .... Dennis Farina
Ray Luca .... Anthony Denison
Pauli Taglia .... John Santucci
Atty. David Abrams .... Stephen Lang
Det. Danny Krychek .... Bill Smitrovich
Det. Joey Indelli .... William Campbell
Det. Walter Clemmons .... Paul Butler
Det. Nate Grossman .... Steve Ryan
Frank Holman .... Ted Levine
Manny Weisbord .... Joseph Wiseman
Cori Luca .... Johann Carlo
Max Goldman .... Andrew Clay
Julie Torello (1986–1987) .... Darlanne Fluegel
Inga Thorson (1986–1987) ... Patricia Charbonneau
Ted Kehoe (1986–1987) .... Mark Hutter
Chief Kramer (1986–1987) .... Ron Dean
Phil Bartoli (1986–1987) .... Jon Polito
Steven Kordo (1987–1988) .... Jay O. Sanders

THEME:

"Runaway," sung by Del Shannon

Crime Story was an unusual serialized police drama. It began in Chicago in the early 1960s, where Lt. Mike Torello was head of the city's MCU (Major Crime Unit), and rising young gangster Ray Luca his chief target. Liberal prosecutor David Abrams, the son of a mobster himself, had forsaken the underworld and joined Torello in pursuing Luca. Julie was Torello's estranged wife (they were divorced after a few episodes, whereupon Torello had an affair with Inga); Danny, Joey, Walter, and Nate were his team of hard-bitten detectives. Despite their efforts—and his own blundering sidekick Pauli—Luca prospered, building a violent criminal empire with nationwide tentacles. Old-line crime lords Manny Weisbord and Phil Bartoli provided support. When Luca moved his base of operations to Las Vegas, Torello followed, as part of a federal task force headed by Abrams. Although Torello dogged Luca's every step, he never could shut him down completely; the resilient gangster even survived an A-bomb blast at the end of the first season when he fled across Yucca Flats in the middle of a test.

Period flavor was a major component of this series, as was authenticity. Star Dennis Farina had been a real-life cop in Chicago for 18 years before shifting his beat to TV.

CRIME SYNDICATED (*Police Anthology*)

FIRST TELECAST: *September 18, 1951*
LAST TELECAST: *June 23, 1953*
BROADCAST HISTORY:

Sep 1951–Jun 1953, CBS Tue 9:00–9:30

NARRATOR:

Rudolph Halley
Herbert R. O'Conor

Dramatizations of actual cases from the files of the Senate Crime Investigating Committee, the F.B.I., and local law-enforcement agencies were presented each week on this live series. Rudolph Halley, former chief counsel for the Senate Crime Investigating Committee, was the original host. When he became president of the New York City Council in late 1951 he decided to alternate narrator responsibilities with Sen. Herbert R. O'Conor of Maryland, former chairman of the Senate Crime Investigating Committee. In March 1952 *Crime Syndicated* was cut back from a weekly series to a biweekly series, alternating with *City Hospital*.

CRIME WITH FATHER (*Police Drama*)

FIRST TELECAST: *August 31, 1951*
LAST TELECAST: *January 18, 1952*
BROADCAST HISTORY:

Aug 1951–Jan 1952, ABC Fri 9:00–9:30

CAST:

Capt. Jim Riland .... Rusty Lane
Chris Riland .... Peggy Lobbin

This father-and-daughter detective show revolved around the cases of Capt. Jim Riland of the homicide squad. Jim's daughter Chris was of greater help in solving cases than any of his plainclothesmen.

CRIMES OF THE CENTURY (*Documentary*)

BROADCAST HISTORY:

Syndicated only
30 minutes
Produced: *1988* (28 episodes)
Released: *January 1989*

HOST:

Mike Connors

Hosted by former TV detective Mike Connors (*Mannix*), this weekly series focused on bizarre, strange, or violent crimes that had happened all over the country. Each episode included dramatizations of the actual cases and interviews with some of the real people involved in them.

CRIMETIME AFTER PRIMETIME (*Various*)
FIRST TELECAST: *April 1, 1991*
LAST TELECAST: *January 4, 1995*
BROADCAST HISTORY:
Apr 1991–Dec 1992, CBS Mon–Fri 11:30–12:30 A.M.
Jan 1993–Aug 1993, CBS Mon–Thu 11:30–1:30 A.M.
Jan 1993–Aug 1993, CBS Fri 11:30–12:30 A.M.
Sep 1993–Dec 1993, CBS Mon–Thu 12:35–1:35 A.M.
Dec 1993–Feb 1994, CBS Mon–Wed 12:35–1:35 A.M.
Mar 1994–Dec 1994, CBS Mon–Thu 12:35–1:35 A.M.
Dec 1994–Jan 1995, CBS Mon–Wed 1:05–2:05 A.M.

After almost two decades of airing a mix of original programs and reruns of former prime-time series under the titles *The CBS Late Night Movie* and *CBS Late Night* (see those entries for details), CBS put together a completely first-run late-night schedule under the umbrella title *CrimeTime After Primetime*. Listed below are the series that comprised *CrimeTime After Primetime*. Details on each can be found under their separate title headings.

Monday
Apr 1991–Dec 1992, Sweating Bullets
Jan 1993–Aug 1993, Sweating Bullets; Scene of the Crime
Sep 1993–Jan 1995, Sweating Bullets

Tuesday
Apr 1991–Oct 1991, The Exile
Oct 1991–Feb 1992, Urban Angel
Mar 1992–Apr 1992, Scene of the Crime
Apr 1992–Dec 1992, Forever Knight
Jan 1993–Mar 1993, Forever Knight; Urban Angel
Apr 1993–Aug 1993, Forever Knight; The Exile
Sep 1993–Nov 1993, Dark Justice
Nov 1993–Aug 1994, Forever Knight
Aug 1994–Jan 1995, Fly By Night

Wednesday
Apr 1991–Mar 1992, Scene of the Crime
Mar 1992–Dec 1992, Dangerous Curves
Jan 1993–Jun 1993, Dangerous Curves; Fly By Night
Jun 1993–Aug 1993, Johnny Bago; Fly By Night
Sep 1993–Dec 1993, Dangerous Curves
Dec 1993–Feb 1994, Dark Justice
Mar 1994–Aug 1994, Scene of the Crime
Aug 1994–Jan 1995, The Exile

Thursday
Apr 1991–Oct 1991, Fly By Night
Nov 1991–Dec 1992, Silk Stalkings
Jan 1993–Aug 1993, Silk Stalkings; Scene of the Crime
Sep 1993–Nov 1993, Silk Stalkings
Nov 1993–Dec 1993, Dark Justice
Mar 1994–Apr 1994, Dark Justice
Apr 1994–Dec 1994, Sweating Bullets

Friday
Apr 1991–Aug 1993, Dark Justice

CRIMEWATCH TONIGHT (*Public Service*)
BROADCAST HISTORY:
Syndicated only
30 minutes
Produced: *1989–1990*
Released: *September 1989*
HOST:
Ike Pappas
REPORTERS:
Jose Grinan
Jim Hill
Elizabeth Robinson

This Monday–Friday evening series was a potpourri of news on currently active criminal cases, stories on the activities of criminal justice agencies in various communities, and assorted anti-crime tips. Among the regular features were information on fugitives from justice, crime quizzes to test viewers' knowledge of the law and the ways in which criminals operate, crime tips to help viewers reduce their chances of being victimized, and acknowledgment of the outstanding achievements of individual law enforcement professionals.

CRISIS, syndicated title for *Kraft Mystery Theater*

CRISIS, THE (*Drama*)
FIRST TELECAST: *October 5, 1949*
LAST TELECAST: *December 28, 1949*
BROADCAST HISTORY:
Oct 1949–Dec 1949, NBC Wed 8:00–8:30
INTERVIEWER:
Adrian Spies
"DIRECTOR":
Arthur Peterson (Oct)
Bob Cunningham (Nov–Dec)

This unusual series used a real-life crisis as the subject of a studio dramatization. First a guest would describe for interviewer Spies the events leading up to a critical moment in his or her life. At the major turning point in the story the guest's narrative was stopped, and professional actors—who were unaware of what actually happened next—would carry on, playing the scene as they imagined it might have been resolved. The actors worked unrehearsed and without scripts, improvising dialogue. An on-camera "director" provided some instructions and called for props. After each scene was played, the guest would return to explain what had actually happened. The show was produced live in Chicago and was directed by Norman Felton.

CRISIS CENTER (*Medical Drama*)
FIRST TELECAST: *February 28, 1997*
LAST TELECAST: *April 4, 1997*
BROADCAST HISTORY:
Feb 1997–Apr 1997, NBC Fri 10:00–11:00
CAST:
Kathy Goodman .... Kellie Martin
Dr. Rick Buckley .... Matt Roth
Lily Gannon.......................... Nia Peeples
Tess Robinson .... Tina Lifford
Nando Taylor.......... Clifton Gonzales Gonzales
Off. Gary McDermott .... Dana Ashbrook

A suicide, a hostage situation, and a mother giving birth on a desk were all in a day's work in this aptly named series, set in the hectic, bustling world of the San Francisco Assistance Center. Kathy was the innocent young intern, traumatized because the guy she was counseling on the telephone blew his brains out. Trying to give her a little support was the center's earnest founder and co-director, Dr. Rick, a psychiatrist, and his businesslike co-director, Lily, who was trying to keep the place afloat. Tess was the center's attorney (they needed one after that phone incident), and Nando the streetwise youth counselor. Gary was a young officer on the local beat who had eyes for Kathy. They were all terribly committed and frantically busy, giving this short-lived series an intensity that was apparently too much for viewers to take. It closed its doors after just six episodes.

CRITIC, THE (*Cartoon*)
FIRST TELECAST: *January 26, 1994*
LAST TELECAST: *July 30, 1995*
BROADCAST HISTORY:
Jan 1994–Mar 1994, ABC Wed 8:30–9:00
Jun 1994–Jul 1994, ABC Wed 8:30–9:00
Mar 1995–Jul 1995, FOX Sun 8:30–9:00
VOICES:
Jay Sherman .... Jon Lovitz
Marty Sherman (age 11) ...... Christine Cavanaugh
Franklin .... Gerrit Graham
Eleanor .... Judith Ivey
Margo (16) .... Nancy Cartwright, others
Duke Phillips .... Charles Napier
Doris .... Doris Grau
Jeremy Hawke .... Maurice LaMarche
Vlada .... Nick Jameson
Alice Tompkins (1995) .... Park Overall
Penny Tompkins (4)(1995) .... Russi Taylor
Various voices .... Kath Soucie

Pudgy, balding, sweater-clad movie critic Jay Sherman skewered movies and celebrities in this lampoon of popular culture. His own life was a bit of a mess. He was divorced and had no social life and no self-esteem. His wealthy adoptive parents, Franklin and Eleanor, paid little attention to him, and his chubby son, Marty, liked his ex-wife's new boyfriend. At New York's Channel 67, where Jay hosted *Coming Attractions*, he was constantly being put down by megalomaniacal owner Duke Phillips and makeup lady Doris. Only his pal Jeremy, an Australian actor (and the spitting image of Paul Hogan), offered some understanding. Despite all these slings and arrows, Jay never lost his wit when reviewing the latest ridiculous films, such as *Home Alone 8, Rabbi P.I.* (with Arnold Schwarzenegger), *The Red Ballooon Part II—Revenge of the Balloon, Honey, I Ate the Kids,* and *Crocodile Gandhi.* His usual review: "It stinks."

The Critic had a short run on ABC, then returned the following year on Fox. Added to the cast was Southern divorcée Alice, who finally brought a little love interest into Jay's life. Penny was Alice's four-year-old daughter.

Among the show's closing credits was this arch statement: "All impersonations were parodical . . . No celebrities were harmed in the filming of this episode."

CRITIC AT LARGE (*Discussion*)
FIRST TELECAST: *August 18, 1948*
LAST TELECAST: *April 20, 1949*
BROADCAST HISTORY:
Aug 1948–Nov 1948, ABC Wed 7:30–8:00
Nov 1948–Jan 1949, ABC Thu 8:30–9:00
Jan 1949–Apr 1949, ABC Wed 8:30–9:00
MODERATOR:
John Mason Brown

Author and critic John Mason Brown, who once commented that "some television programs are so much chewing gum for the eyes," offered this intellectual alternative in 1948–1949. It consisted of an informal living-room discussion on the arts with two or three guests, of the caliber of author James Michener, producer Billy Rose, publisher Bennett Cerf, and critic Bosley Crowther. The subjects ranged from modern art to new novels, films, the theater, and fashions.

CROCODILE HUNTER, THE (*Documentary*)
BROADCAST HISTORY:
Animal Planet
60 minutes
Original episodes: *1997–*
Premiered: *January 1997*
REGULARS:
Steve Irwin
Terri Irwin

The show that arguably put Animal Planet on the TV map was this over-the-top documentary series by Australian herpetologist Steve Irwin, a true wild man when it came to wrangling crocodiles. Irwin, who seemed to be completely fearless around the big beasts, took viewers into the Australia Outback, where he relocated rogue crocs using muscle, ropes and clever stratagems while doing as little harm to them (and himself) as possible in the process. All of this was accompanied by a big smile, enthusiastic narration ("Holy smokes that was close!"; "She's a little ripper"; "Beaut bonza mate!") and assistance from his sensible wife, Terri.

The first *Crocodile Hunter* documentary was filmed at Irwin's Australia Zoo, in Queensland, in 1992. *Crocodile Hunter* premiered in the U.S. on the Discovery Channel in October 1996, and moved to sister Channel Animal Planet in January 1997 where it became that network's flagship series. It was so popular that it spawned spin-off series *Croc Files* (1999), following Steve's life in and around the zoo and featuring Steve, Terri, infant daughter Bindi Sue, best mate Wes Mannion and family dog Sui; and *The Crocodile Hunter Diaries* (2001).

CROOK AND CHASE (*Magazine*)
BROADCAST HISTORY:
The Nashville Network
30/60 minutes
Produced: *1986–1993*
Premiered: *April 28, 1986*
REGULARS:
Lorianne Crook
Charlie Chase

Their sunny dispositions and playful banter led some to call them the Regis and Kathie Lee of country music (to which they responded, "Our next goal is to be the Beavis and Butt-head of country"). Crook and Chase began their live, nightly, Nashville-based show in 1986, quickly becoming a staple of the TNN schedule. Virtually every major star and up-and-comer in the field stopped by at one time or another. Originally half an hour in length, the series expanded to an hour in March 1991. In 1993 Crook and Chase moved to a 90-minute nightly variety format under the title *Music City Tonight* (q.v.).

CROOK AND CHASE TONIGHT (*Magazine*)
BROADCAST HISTORY:
The Nashville Network
60 minutes
Produced: *1999*
Premiered: *January 6, 1999*
HOSTS:
Lorianne Crook
Charlie Chase
TNN favorites Crook and Chase hosted this homey prime-time hour consisting of entertainment news, on-location interviews, and comedy bits.

CROSS CURRENT, see *Foreign Intrigue*

CROSS QUESTION, see *They Stand Accused*

CROSSFIRE (*Discussion*)
BROADCAST HISTORY:
CNN
30 minutes
Produced: *1982–*
Premiered: *June 1982*
REGULARS:
Pat Buchanan (1982–1999)
Tom Braden (1982–1989)
Michael Kinsley (1989–1995)
John Sununu (1992–1998)
Bill Press (1996–2002)
Robert Novak (1985–)
Mary Matalin (1999–2001)
James Carville (2002–)
Paul Begala (2002–)
Tucker Carlson (2002–)
A long and noisy political discussion that raged Monday through Friday nights at 7:30 P.M. for most of its history. The principal combatants have included conservative Pat Buchanan and liberal Tom Braden, although Buchanan periodically left the show to make his quixotic runs for the presidency.

CROSSING JORDAN (*Police Drama*)
FIRST TELECAST: *September 24, 2001*
LAST TELECAST:
BROADCAST HISTORY:
Sep 2001–May 2003, NBC Mon 10:00–11:00
Jun 2003– , NBC Fri 8:00–9:00
CAST:
Dr. Jordan Cavanaugh .... Jill Hennessy
Dr. Garret Macy .... Miguel Ferrer
Dr. Trey Sanders (2000–2001)
.... Mahershalalhashbaz Ali
Dr. Mahesh "Bug" Vijayaraghavensatyanaryanamurthy .... Ravi Kapoor
Max Cavanaugh..................... Ken Howard
Lily Lebowski...................... Kathryn Hahn
Dr. Nigel Townsend............... Steve Valentine
Elaine Duchamps (2002–2003) . Lorraine Toussaint
Det. Woody Hoyt (2002–) .... Jerry O'Connell
**Abby Macy* .... Alex McKenna
Dr. Peter Winslow (2002–) .... Ivan Sergei
*Occasional

Jordan was a crusading medical examiner whose single-mindedness got her into trouble. Having screwed up her career in Los Angeles, she had come back to her hometown of Boston to plead with Dr. Macy, the man who had given her her start, for her old job back. She got it, but continued to skate on the edge of "acceptable behavior," badgering witnesses, pilfering evidence and sometimes flouting laws in her quest to track down the guilty in the murders she was assigned (and sometimes in cases she was not assigned). Macy was her stressed-out boss, a man with many demons of his own, including his troubles with his drug-prone daughter Abby. Trey was a trainee who helped Jordan while angling for a date; Bug, the eccentric medical examiner who chased butterflies; Lily, the slightly strange office coordinator/grief counselor, and Nigel, the tall British criminalist. Also helping Jordan crack cases was her dad, a retired cop with a Down East accent (he called her "Jerden"), whose personal demon was the unsolved murder of his wife, Jordan's mother, which haunted him as it did Jordan. He helped by role playing the events of a crime with Jordan. Joining in the second season were Woody, a boyish detective who reluctantly tagged along on Jordan's investigations, and Elaine, an aggressive medical examiner assigned to Macy's department against his will by the DA's office.

In the 2002–2003 season finale Jordan and Woody edged closer to unraveling the mystery of her mother's 1979 murder, which appeared to be connected to a police coverup of crooked cops involving both her father and her long-missing half-brother, James Horton (Michael T. Weiss).

CROSSING OVER WITH JOHN EDWARD (*Psychic*)
BROADCAST HISTORY:
Sci-Fi Channel and syndicated
30 minutes
Original episodes: *2000–*
Premiered: *July 10, 2000* (Sci-Fi Channel); *September 2001* (syndication)
HOST:
John Edward
Dapper, casually dressed John Edward was a medium who fascinated audiences with his apparent ability to contact the deceased in this fast-moving talk show. John claimed that he couldn't control who "came through" when he was channeling the spirits of the dead. As his Web site stated, "John has read the cameraman, soundman, and someone in the next room during rehearsals. If you feel you'll be too embarrassed, too frazzled, or just not interested, we ask that you give up your seat to someone who's anxious for a reading." In addition to reading random people from the audience, there were also one-on-one segments with celebrities, such as Linda Dano from a soap opera named, appropriately enough, *Another World*. Many of the readings were teary attempts to put the subjects in touch with deceased loved ones, but some were amusing (Edward: "Is there a new animal in your family?" Subject: "My boyfriend?" Edward: "Not unless he crawls").

Although skeptics claimed they could explain everything he did, and disclaimers were prominently displayed at the end of each episode, *Crossing Over* was an immediate hit as a late-night entry on the Sci-Fi Channel. In 2001 it went into daily syndication.

CROSSROADS (*Dramatic Anthology*)
FIRST TELECAST: *October 7, 1955*
LAST TELECAST: *September 27, 1957*
BROADCAST HISTORY:
Oct 1955–Sep 1957, ABC Fri 8:30–9:00

Crossroads would have been indistinguishable from many other competently done dramatic anthologies of the early and mid-1950s were it not for its unusual subject matter. The series dealt exclusively with dramatizations of the experiences of clergymen. The problems they faced in both their personal and professional lives were depicted by many fine actors, Vincent Price and Luther Adler among them. Clergymen of all faiths were treated at one time or another, and the dramas successfully made the point that these were real people, as well as representatives of their respective faiths.

CROSSROADS, see *American Parade, The*

CROSSROADS (*Adventure*)
FIRST TELECAST: *September 14, 1992*
LAST TELECAST: *July 15, 1993*
BROADCAST HISTORY:
Sep 1992, ABC Mon 8:00–9:00
Sep 1992, ABC Wed 10:00–11:00
Sep 1992–Oct 1992, ABC Sat 9:00–10:00
Jun 1993–Jul 1993, ABC Thu 9:00–10:00
Jul 1993, ABC Thu 8:00–9:00
CAST:
Johnny Hawkins .... Robert Urich
Dylan Hawkins .... Dalton James

Father-son bonding series in which Johnny Hawkins, a star New York City prosecutor in line for D.A., put his career on hold in order to rescue his rebellious 16-year-old son from a life of crime. Johnny had only himself to blame, since ten years earlier when his wife died he had left Dylan with his grandparents in Atlanta. Now the kid was getting into increasingly serious trouble. Making up for lost time, Johnny got them both leather jackets, set Dylan on the back of his vintage motorcycle, and embarked on a tour of America. Along the way they encountered and helped an assortment of people in the best *Fugitive* tradition.

CROSS-WITS, THE (*Quiz/Audience Participation*)
BROADCAST HISTORY:
Syndicated only
30 minutes
Produced: *1975–1980, 1986–1987*
Released: *Fall 1975*
HOST:
Jack Clark (1975–1980)
David Sparks (1986–1987)
EXECUTIVE PRODUCER:
Ralph Edwards

This popular syndicated quiz show was a word game, based on a crossword puzzle. Two teams, each composed of two celebrities and one civilian, competed to fill in words in a crossword puzzle, from clues provided by the host. Points were awarded, and the winner advanced to the "Crossfire" finale, where he or she was assisted by a celebrity of his choice. The object here was to fill in 10 words in 60 seconds. The grand prize on the premiere was a trip to Paris.

Among the celebrities making frequent appearances were Alice Ghostley, Jo Anne Worley, Jamie Farr, Stu Gilliam, and Vicki Lawrence.

Six years after the original series had left the air, *The New Cross-Wits* surfaced, with David Sparks replacing the original host, Jack Clark.

CROW: STAIRWAY TO HEAVEN, THE (*Adventure*)
BROADCAST HISTORY:
Syndicated only
60 minutes
Produced: *1998–1999* (22 episodes)
Released: *September 1998*
CAST:
Eric Draven .... Mark Dacascos
Det. Daryl Albrecht .... Marc Gomes
Shelly Webster .... Sabine Karsenti
Sarah Mohr .... Katie Stuart
Darla Mohr .... Lynda Boyd
Lt. David Vicennes .... Jon Cuthbert
Det. Jessica Capshaw .... Christina Cox

The tone of this brooding series was set in the opening narration by the lead character: "People once believed that when someone dies the crow carries their soul to the land of the dead—but sometimes something so bad happens that a terrible sadness is carried with it and the soul can't rest. And sometimes, just sometimes, the crow can bring the soul back to put things right. . . ."

Eric was one who had come back, a musician who returned from the dead to seek vengeance on the inner-city thugs who had killed him and his fiancée, Shelly, a year earlier. The crow had brought Eric back to Port Columbia, and served as his earthly spirit guide as he attempted to right the wrongs that had befallen them. Most of the time he looked normal, if a bit creepy, but in crises his pallor turned ghostly, his face had bizarre eye makeup, and his strength became superhuman. Eric could not be killed since he was actually in a sort of limbo between astral planes, his cuts healed almost immediately and bullet holes sealed themselves. There were flashbacks to happier times with his beloved Shelly, with whom he longed to be reunited.

Eric moved back into the seedy apartment building where he had been murdered, where he met Sarah, an intelligent child who befriended him and helped him deal with his demons. Darla, Sarah's mother, was a former drug addict who worked at the local police precinct. Detective Albrecht was a local cop who was understandably skeptical of Eric's incredible story. Already *dead*? They later worked out a deal in which Eric helped him on some of his cases and he cut the young man some slack. However, in February, Eric was put on trial and convicted of conspiracy to commit Shelly's murder. Seeing him "alive," the jury believed he had faked his death and was responsible for the crime, but the judge set him free on a technicality. Because of his association with Eric, Albrecht was demoted to beat cop (eventually he was reinstated) and his new partner, Capshaw, took over his case load.

Based on the comic book series by James O'Barr and the 1994 theatrical film *The Crow*, starring Brandon Lee as Eric and Ernie Hudson as Albrecht. Filmed in Vancouver, British Columbia.

CRUSADE (*Science Fiction*)

BROADCAST HISTORY:

TNT Network
60 minutes
Original episodes: *1999* (13 episodes)
Premiered: *June 9, 1999*

CAST:

Capt. Matthew Gideon .... Gary Cole
Lt. John Matheson .... Daniel Dae Kim
Max Eilerson .... David Allen Brooks
Galen .... Peter Woodward
Dr. Sarah Chambers .... Marjean Holden
Dureena Nafeel .... Carrie Dobro
Capt. Elizabeth Lochley .... Tracy Scoggins

This sequel to *Babylon 5* took place a few years after the end of the Great War with the Shadows. In the series premiere Earth was quarantined after the insect-like Drakh, who had been allied with the Shadows, spread a biogenetic plague into the atmosphere. The plague would take five years to adapt itself to humanity and then would kill everyone on the planet. Since there was not enough time to develop a cure on Earth, the only hope was to search through the ruins of alien civilizations on other planets looking for a medical technology that could cure the disease. The vessel entrusted with this vital mission was the *Excalibur,* an advanced prototype starship whose no-nonsense captain, Matthew Gideon, had been chosen because of his extensive experience dealing with alien races. Among his crew members were First Officer Matheson, a telepath who had worked with Gideon before and was very familiar with the commander's way of doing things; Galen, a hooded technomage who, nine years ago, had used his almost magical skills to save Gideon's life after his ship had been destroyed; Eilerson, an arrogant archeologist and linguist whose ability to translate alien languages was invaluable; Nafeel, a member of the Thieves Guild who could break into otherwise impenetrable places; and Dr. Chambers, the ship's chief medical officer. Elizabeth Lochley, commander of the Babylon 5 space station, was Gideon's longtime friend and sometimes lover. Some episodes focused on their explorations and contacts with alien races and civilizations, while others dealt with other assignments and political issues.

Crusade was originally intended to run for five seasons, as had *Babylon 5,* but disagreements between its producers and TNT resulted in its premature cancelation. They never did find the cure.

CRUSADE IN EUROPE (*Documentary*)

FIRST TELECAST: *May 5, 1949*
LAST TELECAST: *October 27, 1949*

BROADCAST HISTORY:

May 1949–Oct 1949, ABC Thu 9:00–9:30

NARRATOR:

Westbrook Van Voorhis
Maurice Joyce

PRODUCER:

Richard de Rochemont

ADAPTED BY:

Fred Feldkamp

This film documentary series on the European theater of action during World War II was assembled from combat footage shot during the war. *Crusade in Europe* was one of the first major documentary series produced especially for television (by the March of Time film unit), and was based on General Dwight D. Eisenhower's best-selling book of the same name. Its success led to a syndicated sequel titled *Crusade in the Pacific.* Westbrook Van Voorhis provided narration, while Maurice Joyce read quotes from Eisenhower's book.

CRUSADER (*International Intrigue*)

FIRST TELECAST: *October 7, 1955*
LAST TELECAST: *December 28, 1956*

BROADCAST HISTORY:

Oct 1955–Dec 1956, CBS Fri 9:00–9:30

CAST:

Matt Anders........................... Brian Keith

Freelance writer Matt Anders devoted much of his time to one cause: helping the oppressed peoples living under dictatorial or Communist regimes escape to free countries. The reason for his devotion to this cause was simple. After overthrowing the Polish government, the Communists had kept his mother in Poland and sent her to a concentration camp, where she died. Holding the Communists responsible for her death, Matt used every means at his disposal to help save others from her fate.

CRUSADERS, THE (*Newsmagazine*)

BROADCAST HISTORY:

Syndicated only
60 minutes
Produced: *1993–1995*
Released: *September 1993*

SENIOR REPORTERS/HOSTS:

Mark Hyman (1993)
William LaJeunesse (1993)
Howard Thompson
Carla Wohl

When this investigative series premiered in 1993 its producer told the viewing audience that *The Crusaders* would provide a new brand of TV journalism, that there was someone on their side and that the stories it covered would make a difference, right wrongs, give help, and open doors that would lead to improvements in the legal and social systems around the country. There were features on blind cords that strangled children, an inner-city gang member who wanted to straighten out his life, a cop who almost lost his job after arresting a drunken driver city councilman, death benefits for a firefighter dying of cancer, cemetery fraud, and help for Midwest flood victims.

When the series premiered, the four senior reporters chatted with field reporters at the end of most stories and were occasionally out in the field themselves. By the end of the year two of them, Mark Hyman and William LaJeunesse, were gone, although Hyman stayed with the show as a field reporter. The producers provided a phone number, toll-free during the show's first season, for people involved in their own crusades who needed assistance or who knew of other "crusaders" who needed help.

CRUSH (*Audience Participation*)

BROADCAST HISTORY:

USA Network
30 minutes
Original episodes: *2000*
Premiered: *March 27, 2000*

HOST:
Andrew Krasny

Three contestants claimed they had a crush on the same person—and tried to prove it—on this rather awkward early-evening show. Three girls talked about the same guy, and the guy then asked them questions designed to find out who really had a crush on him. At the end he picked the one he thought was his admirer, and they got a romantic vacation (if he picked wrong, the real admirer was "crushed"). When three guys confronted a girl, the talk generally got raunchier ("her butt's tight and round—the best"), but the game was the same. The girls bounced around in short skirts and tight blouses while the audience shrieked.

CRYSTAL ROOM (*Variety*)
FIRST TELECAST: *August 15, 1948*
LAST TELECAST: *September 12, 1948*
BROADCAST HISTORY:
Aug 1948–Sep 1948, ABC Sun 8:30–9:00
HOSTESS:
Maggi McNellis

This short-lived variety program was set in an imaginary nightclub and featured Maggi McNellis, one of early TV's ubiquitous personalities, and guests.

CUPID (*Fantasy*)
FIRST TELECAST: *September 26, 1998*
LAST TELECAST: *February 11, 1999*
BROADCAST HISTORY:
Sep 1998–Dec 1998, ABC Sat 10:00–11:00
Jan 1999–Feb 1999, ABC Thu 9:00–10:00
CAST:
Trevor Hale (Cupid).................Jeremy Piven
Dr. Claire Allen ....Paula Marshall
Champ Terrace.....................Jeffrey D. Sams
THEME:
"Human," performed by the Pretenders

Trevor was a glib, sarcastic young man, just released from a Chicago mental hospital, who claimed he was Cupid. Yeah, sure. He had no special powers ("they took away my bow and arrow"), although he did have a rather intimate knowledge of the denizens of Mount Olympus. He also seemed to have a knack, in his own pushy way, for helping couples discover, or rediscover, romance. He was on Earth, he claimed, as punishment for his sloppy work in the '60s and '70s (too many divorces); in order to be allowed back on Olympus, he would have to reunite a hundred couples, without the use of magic.

All this attracted uptight psychologist Claire, who didn't believe the Cupid bit for a moment, but thought the delusional young man might be an interesting subject for her next book. Assigned by the mental health board to "monitor his progress," she did begin to wonder. Champ, Trevor's roommate, was a frustrated actor who groused a lot but usually helped him out when needed.

CURRENT AFFAIR, A (*Newsmagazine*)
BROADCAST HISTORY:
Syndicated only
30 minutes
Produced: *1986–1996*
Released: *July 28, 1986*
HOST: (Mon–Fri)
Maury Povich (1986–1990)
Maureen O'Boyle (1990–1994)
Jim Ryan (1994)
Penny Daniels (1994–1995)
John Scott (1995–1996)
HOST: (weekend)
Maureen O'Boyle (1990–1991, 1993)
Bill McGowan (1991–1992)
Alexander Johnson (1993)
Terry Willesee (1993–1995)
Penny Daniels (1995)
Mary Garofalo (1995–1996)

The first, and arguably the most successful, of what became known as the "Tabloid News" series in the late 1980s was *A Current Affair.* Hosted by former Washington TV anchorman Maury Povich, this nightly magazine series was bizarre, exploitive, and unabashedly sexy.

It was produced by Fox television, which was owned by Australian publisher Rupert Murdoch, whose newspapers around the world were themselves prime examples of the "tabloid" style. *A Current Affair* often resembled a TV version of Murdoch's weekly *Star* magazine. Each episode contained two to four stories, favoring messy divorce and palimony cases, religious cults, gruesome murders, the troubles of the rich and famous, assorted show business gossip (often reported by gossip columnist Cindy Adams), and anything involving sexy women in bikinis or lingerie.

Occasionally, while looking for the dirt, the "investigative reporters" of *A Current Affair* ran across stories that actually made news. Two of the most notable involved videotapes they managed to acquire. The first was recorded at a 1988 party and showed Robert Chambers, who had strangled young Jennifer Levin in New York's Central Park during what he claimed was rough sex, making a macabre joke of the murder only days before asking for leniency in a courtroom plea bargain. The second, which surfaced in the summer of 1989, was a tape made by actor Rob Lowe during the 1988 Democratic Convention in Atlanta. It showed a 16-year-old girl having sex with both another woman and with Lowe himself.

Although Povich was the only on-camera regular, *A Current Affair* utilized the services of a whole host of Fox reporters including Rafael Abramovitz, Steve Dunleavy, Gordon Elliott, Bob Martin, Bill McGowan, Steve McPartlin, Maureen O'Boyle, and Krista Bradford. When Maury was on vacation or assignment, Maureen and Krista were the most frequent substitute hosts, and Maureen took over full-time in the fall of 1990 when Maury left to host his own daytime talk show.

It was also that fall that an hour-long weekend version, *Current Affair Extra,* premiered. Aussie Terry Willesee had been the original host of the Australian *A Current Affair* and was the only person to host the show in both countries.

CURSE OF DRACULA, THE (*Serial*)
FIRST TELECAST: *February 27, 1979*
LAST TELECAST: *May 1, 1979*
BROADCAST HISTORY:
Feb 1979–Mar 1979, NBC Tue 8:40–9:00
Mar 1979–May 1979, NBC Tue 8:00–8:20
CAST:
Count Dracula ....Michael Nouri
Kurt von Helsing................Stephen Johnson

Mary Gibbons .... Carol Baxter
Antoinette .... Antoinette Stella
Darryl .... Mark Montgomery
Christine .... Bever-Leigh Banfield
Amanda Gibbons .... Louise Sorel

In this contemporary serial, Count Dracula was "undead and well, and living in California." The 500-year-old vampire was located in San Francisco and teaching a course in European history at South Bay College (Evening Division). One of the principal advantages of his teaching post was that it brought him in contact with attractive young students—Antoinette, Christine, and Darryl—who could be turned into vampires and join the legions of the undead. Seeking to destroy Dracula was Kurt von Helsing, grandson of Prof. von Helsing, a former nemesis of the count. Helping Kurt was Mary Gibbons, whose mother had been turned into a vampire by Dracula years before. Mary herself almost fell victim to the fatal charm of the count, but was saved by the intervention of her vampire mother, Amanda. In the climactic chapter, Mary drove a wooden stake through the heart of her mother, freeing her from the curse of the undead, and Kurt shot Dracula with a wooden arrow from a crossbow, destroying him . . . or so it seemed. After the others had escaped the burning wax museum where the confrontation had taken place, Dracula was seen regaining consciousness, pulling the stake from his chest and fleeing the building. Would he be back?

The Curse of Dracula was one of three serials aired under the umbrella title *Cliff Hangers*, and was the only one to reach its conclusion by the time the series was canceled.

CURSED (*Situation Comedy*)
FIRST TELECAST: *October 26, 2000*
LAST TELECAST: *April 26, 2001*
BROADCAST HISTORY:
Oct 2000–Jan 2001, NBC Thu 8:30–9:00
Mar 2001–Apr 2001, NBC Thu 8:30–9:00
CAST:
Jack Nagle .... Steven Weber
Melissa Taylor .... Amy Pietz
Dr. Larry Heckman .... Chris Elliott
Wendell Simms .... Wendell Pierce
Katie .... Paula Marshall

Everything was going wrong for ladies' man Jack, and for good reason—he was "cursed." Literally. It seems that he had gone on a blind date with a woman who had put a hex on him. From that point forward his life was full of misunderstandings, little annoyances and irate dates. Melissa was his perky ex-girlfriend, an avant-garde artist, with whom he kept breaking up all over again; Larry, his gross, freeloading roommate, who happened to be a doctor; and Wendell, his wide-eyed, insecure boss in the marketing department at Flashware, an interactive software company. Katie was a gorgeous friend who was a lesbian. Drat! The setting was Chicago.

This series itself seemed to be cursed, judging by its behind-the-scenes history. Almost as soon as it went on the air NBC executives decided the premise was a mistake, so they fired the producers and ordered up scripts in which the "curse" was no longer mentioned. In December they changed the title to *The Weber Show*. Then, after numerous preemptions, they canceled it. Cursed, indeed.

CURTAIN CALL, syndicated title for *Lux Video Theater*

CURTAIN CALL (*Dramatic Anthology*)
FIRST TELECAST: *June 20, 1952*
LAST TELECAST: *September 26, 1952*
BROADCAST HISTORY:
Jun 1952–Sep 1952, NBC Fri 8:00–8:30

Curtain Call, the 1952 summer replacement for *The RCA Victor Show,* was composed of live plays telecast from Hollywood.

CURTAIN TIME, syndicated title for *Telephone Time*

CURTAIN UP, see *Movies—Prior to 1961*

CUSTER (*Western*)
FIRST TELECAST: *September 6, 1967*
LAST TELECAST: *December 27, 1967*
BROADCAST HISTORY:
Sep 1967–Dec 1967, ABC Wed 7:30–8:30
CAST:
Lt. Col. George A. Custer .... Wayne Maunder
California Joe Milner .... Slim Pickens
Sgt. James Bustard .... Peter Palmer
Crazy Horse .... Michael Dante
Brig. Gen. Alfred Terry .... Robert F. Simon
Capt. Miles Keogh .... Grant Woods

This action Western was based on the career of George A. Custer between 1868 and 1875, the year before his death in the Battle of the Little Big Horn. In 1868, after losing his Civil War rank of brevet major general, Custer was posted to Fort Hays, Kansas, to take command of the 7th Cavalry Regiment. The 7th was a ragtag outfit of low reputation, made up of ex-Confederates, thieves, and renegades. With the help of California Joe Milner, a leathery old army scout and friend; Capt. Keogh, a shrewd and witty Irishman; and towering Sgt. Bustard, Custer managed to whip this sorry regiment into an effective force capable of protecting the settlers on the surrounding plains. Gen. Terry, commanding officer of Fort Hays, disliked Custer's unconventional methods and appearance (including his shoulder-length blond hair), but supported him in his battles with Crazy Horse's Sioux.

CUT, THE (*Talent*)
BROADCAST HISTORY:
MTV
30 minutes
Produced: *1998–1999*
Premiered: *September 28, 1998*
HOST:
Lisa Lopes

A fairly straightforward talent competition, in which three music business professionals (including artists and executives) judged aspiring young musicians on a scale of one to ten, with the winner getting to appear in his or her own music video. The host was a saucy sexpot in a halter, who boogied to the acts and urged the audience to "Give it up!" for the contestants.

CUTTER TO HOUSTON (*Medical Drama*)
FIRST TELECAST: *October 1, 1983*
LAST TELECAST: *December 31, 1983*
BROADCAST HISTORY:
Oct 1983, CBS Sat 8:00–9:00
Dec 1983, CBS Sat 8:00–9:00
CAST:
Dr. Andy Fenton .... Jim Metzler
Dr. Beth Gilbert .... Shelley Hack
Dr. Hal Wexler .... Alec Baldwin
Nurse Connie Buford .... K Callan
Mayor Warren Jarvis .... Noble Willingham
Nurse Patty Alvarez .... Susan Styles

TV's hotshot young doctors usually work their miracles in sprawling urban medical centers, but in this series three of them were dumped in the boondocks—with varying reactions. Rural Cutter, Texas, pop. 5231, was only 60 miles from Houston, but it seemed like a million miles to ambitious young surgeon Beth Gilbert, who had to serve her apprenticeship in the town's newly opened clinic before returning to the prestigious Texas Medical Center. Andy Fenton didn't mind it, though; he was a local boy and was eager to repay the townsfolk who had encouraged his career. Internist Hal Wexler hadn't made up his mind about Cutter. Since he had been convicted of writing illegal prescriptions and was serving his probation in Cutter, he was glad to be working at all.

Though the town was small it was mighty proud of its new facility, and provided plenty of business, including victims of bar brawls, oil-well explosions, and crimes, as well as normal cases of pregnancy and disease. Whenever things got worse than could be handled with Cutter's limited equipment, Houston's Texas Medical Center could be reached by helicopter, radio, or computer linkup (hence the call, "Cutter to Houston . . .").

CUTTERS (*Situation Comedy*)
FIRST TELECAST: *June 11, 1993*
LAST TELECAST: *July 9, 1993*
BROADCAST HISTORY:
Jun 1993–Jul 1993, CBS Fri 8:30–9:00
CAST:
Joe Polachek .... Robert Hays
Harry Polachek .... Dakin Matthews
Adrienne St. John .... Margaret Whitton
Lynn Fletcher .... Julia Campbell
Deborah Hart .... Robin Tunney
Troy King .... Julius Carry
Chad Connors .... Ray Buktenica

Joe Polachek had returned home to Buffalo, New York, to work with his grumpy widowed father, Harry, in the family barbershop after an unsuccessful career as a professional golfer. Despite Harry's misgivings, Joe convinced the old man to tear down the wall between the failing barbershop and "Adrienne of Buffalo," the very successful and trendy beauty salon next door. Harry had never been happy about renting the space to Adrienne, but now he had to share space with her expanding business to keep his from going under. Harry and his old-line customers, including Chad, felt particularly uncomfortable in the frilly pink world of Adrienne's. Working for Adrienne were Lynn, a beautician infatuated with Joe; Deborah, the manicurist; and—much to Harry's chagrin—Troy, an openly gay black stylist who was once an Olympic track star.

CYBILL (*Situation Comedy*)
FIRST TELECAST: *January 2, 1995*
LAST TELECAST: *July 13, 1998*
BROADCAST HISTORY:
Jan 1995–Sep 1995, CBS Mon 9:30–10:00
Sep 1995–Apr 1996, CBS Sun 8:00–8:30
Apr 1996–Feb 1997, CBS Mon 9:30–10:00
Mar 1997–Dec 1997, CBS Mon 9:00–9:30
Mar 1998–Apr 1998, CBS Wed 8:30–9:00
May 1998–Jun 1998, CBS Mon 9:00–9:30
Jun 1998–Jul 1998, CBS Mon 9:30–10:00
CAST:
Cybill Sheridan .... Cybill Shepherd
Maryann Thorpe .... Christine Baranski
Jeff Robbins (1995–1996) .... Tom Wopat
Rachel Blanders (1995–1997) .... Dedee Pfeiffer
Zoey Woodbine .... Alicia Witt
Ira Woodbine .... Alan Rosenberg
Waiter .... Tim Macaulan
Kevin Blanders (1995–1997) .... Peter Krause
Sean (1995–1996) .... Jay Paulson
Justin Thorpe (1997–1998) .... Danny Masterson
Dr. Richard Thorpe (1997–1998) .... Ray Baker

Cybill was a wisecracking actress in Los Angeles whose professional and personal life was in constant turmoil. At fortysomething, the roles she was offered were mostly small parts for older women—each episode opened with her filming a scene from a movie or TV show in which she had a small part—not the glamorous roles she had been offered when she was a young beauty. She wasn't unattractive, she was just starting to show her age. Then there were the leftovers from her two failed marriages. Her first hubby was Jeff, a handsome stuntman currently living on the couch in Cybill's living room. Their married daughter Rachel had recently announced that Mom was going to be a grandmother. Zoey, the moody 16-year-old from her second marriage, was also living with her. Zoey's father, Ira, a successful but incredibly neurotic novelist, still had strong feelings for Cybill and was hoping to rekindle their romance. Fat chance. Cybill's best friend was Maryann, a cynical divorcée whose ex-husband had left her quite well off. Maryann had been to the Betty Ford Clinic to cure her drinking problem but desperately needed a booster shot. The two of them dished the dirt, which included their respective dating problems, at the trendy restaurant where they lunched in almost every episode.

Maryann's obsession with making life miserable for her ex, the notorious Dr. Dick, continued to get her and Cybill into precarious situations in slapstick adventures reminiscent of *I Love Lucy*. In the fall of 1995 Rachel gave birth to a son, and two years later, to a daughter. Jeff moved out of Cybill's home in late 1995 and was seen only occasionally from 1996 on. In the spring of 1996, Ira and Maryann started dating (it didn't last) and Zoey broke up with Sean, the busboy.

That fall Rachel and her family moved in with Cybill, while Kevin looked for a new job, and Zoey got her own apartment. Cybill starred for a time in a new science fiction series, and when Jeff's career got hot, he gave Rachel and Kevin money for a down payment on a new home. Early in 1997, Maryann started dating a nice veterinarian who—ugh!—was another Dr. Dick.

In the spring of 1998, Maryann's son, Justin, who had been friendly with Zoey, moved to San Francisco for a new job. In the series finale Maryann was left broke after Dr. Dick bribed her business manager into having her sign a form giving him power of attorney. He cleaned her out and, at the episode's end, she and Cybill were arrested for murdering Dr. Dick. He had apparently been in the Chris-Craft boat that, among other things, they had gleefully blown up on his property. As they were led off, "To be continued" flashed on the screen, but since *Cybill* had been canceled, there was no resolution.

D

D.A., THE (*Courtroom Drama*)

FIRST TELECAST: *September 17, 1971*
LAST TELECAST: *January 7, 1972*
BROADCAST HISTORY:
Sep 1971–Jan 1972, NBC Fri 8:00–8:30
CAST:
Deputy D.A. Paul Ryan .... Robert Conrad
Chief Deputy D.A. "Staff" Stafford .. Harry Morgan
D.A. Investigator Bob Ramirez .... Ned Romero
Public Defender Katherine Benson ...... Julie Cobb

Collecting the evidence necessary to bring criminals to trial and following the course of the trial provided the thrust for this short-lived series. The program had two segments: first Deputy D.A. Ryan and his team would investigate the crime, then Ryan would function as prosecuting attorney. His courtroom adversary in most cases was Public Defender Katherine Benson, representing the accused. The courtroom portion of the series was done in quasi-documentary style with Ryan doing voice-over narration to explain legal terminology and procedures to the audience. The series was replaced after a few months by the highly successful *Sanford and Son.*

D.A.'S MAN, THE (*Police Drama*)

FIRST TELECAST: *January 3, 1959*
LAST TELECAST: *August 29, 1959*
BROADCAST HISTORY:
Jan 1959–Aug 1959, NBC Sat 10:30–11:00
CAST:
Shannon .... John Compton
Al Bonacorsi .... Ralph Manza
Frank LaValle .... Herb Ellis

Working as an undercover investigator for the New York City District Attorney's Office, ex-private eye Shannon spent most of his time infiltrating the New York underworld. Hijacking rings, prostitution, narcotics, and any other source of "mob" income were appropriate targets for his sleuthing. Shannon's contact at the D.A.'s office was First Assistant D.A. Al Bonacorsi.

D.C. (*Political Drama*)

FIRST TELECAST: *April 1, 2000*
LAST TELECAST: *April 23, 2000*
BROADCAST HISTORY:
Apr 2000, WB Sun 8:00–9:00
CAST:
Pete Komisky .... Mark-Paul Gosselaar
Mason Scott .... Gabriel Olds
Sarah Logan .... Kristanna Loken
Lewis Freeman .... Daniel Sunjata
Finley Scott .... Jacinda Barrett
THEME:
performed by Angry Salad

Short-lived drama about five earnest 20-somethings trying to make it in the cutthroat world of Washington, D.C. Pete was an animal rights lobbyist; Mason, an idealistic correspondent (gofer) for the senior senator from Virginia, who lost his job in the series premiere; Sarah, a hard-driving associate field producer for CNL (Cable NewsLink), a local cable news station; Lewis, a Supreme Court law clerk; and Finley, Mason's flaky twin sister who had just dropped out of grad school and was trying to find herself. In the premiere Finley hustled a job house-sitting a large brownstone in Georgetown, into which all five of them moved. Sarah shared a room with Lewis, whom she had been dating since they were undergrads at Yale.

In subsequent episodes Mason got a job working for Representative Owens of Michigan, Pete went to work for a lobbying group specializing in guns, and Finley was hired as a guide at a museum. And then, after only four weeks on the air, *D.C.* was abruptly canceled.

D.C. FOLLIES (*Situation Comedy*)

BROADCAST HISTORY:
Syndicated only
30 minutes
Produced: *1987–1989* (72 episodes)
Released: *September 1987*
REGULARS:
Fred Willard
The Krofft Puppets
VOICES:
Louise DuArt
John Roarke
Maurice LaMarche
Joe Alaskey (1987–1988)

D.C. Follies was a bar located in Washington not far from the White House. Its owner and bartender was Fred Willard, who was, in fact, the only live regular on this series—the patrons were virtually all puppets designed by Sid and Marty Krofft. They included dummies (no pun intended) of President and Mrs. Reagan; former presidents Carter, Ford, and Nixon; other political personalities; assorted news types like Andy Rooney, Dan Rather, and Ted Koppel; and celebrities such as Woody Allen, Jack Nicholson, and Oprah Winfrey. The humor tended to be on the satirical side, often taking potshots at politicians and the political process. In addition to the puppets, each episode brought a celebrity guest into the bar, with Martin Mull, Robin Leach, Bob Uecker, and Betty White appearing early on.

DEA (*Police Drama*)

FIRST TELECAST: *September 7, 1990*
LAST TELECAST: *June 7, 1991*
BROADCAST HISTORY:
Sep 1990–Nov 1990, FOX Fri 9:00–10:00
Apr 1991–Jun 1991, FOX Fri 9:00–10:00
CAST:
Nick Biaggi .... Chris Stanley
Bill Stadler .... Tom Mason
Teresa Robles .... Jenny Gago
Phil Jacobs .... David Wohl
Jimmy Sanders .... Byron Keith Minns
Ricky Prado (1990) .... John Vargas
Rafael Cordera (1990) .... Miguel Sandoval
Carl Schleimann (1990) .... Alan Scarfe
Isabella Solana .... Roya Megnot
Severo De Lasera (1991) .... Joseph Gian
Ellen Brunner (1991) .... Terri Treas

D.E.A. was a highly unusual, though ultimately unsuccessful, attempt to integrate the popular cinéma vérité style of the 1990s into the framework of a traditional police drama with a continuing cast. While actors were used and most scenes were staged, the cases were real and actual surveillance and news footage was incorporated to lend authenticity.

The series followed the tense and often violent work of a small group of Drug Enforcement Agency field agents as they fought the influx of illegal narcotics to the United States. Nick, Teresa, and Jimmy were the younger members of the team, Bill Stadler was their veteran leader, and Phil Jacobs was the group 9 supervisor to whom they all reported. When *DEA* premiered, the group's target was an Ecuador-based crime family smuggling cocaine into New York. Rafael Cordera was the head of the crime family; Ricky Prado, a Cordera lieutenant who, in the series' first episode, killed a DEA agent and was eventually killed himself in a sting operation; Carl Schleimann, Cordera's trusted German-born aide; and Isabella Solana, the sexy, cold-blooded daughter of another crime family leader who had her father killed so she could take over the business. In the spring she, too, was killed by another mobster.

The series was taken off in the fall because of low ratings, but returned in April with its title changed to *DEA—Special Task Force*. More emphasis was put on the agents' personal lives and the violence was toned down a bit, but it still attracted few viewers.

DADDIO (*Situation Comedy*)
FIRST TELECAST: *March 23, 2000*
LAST TELECAST: *October 23, 2000*
BROADCAST HISTORY:
Mar 2000–Apr 2000, NBC Thu 8:30–9:00
Jul 2000–Aug 2000, NBC Thu 8:30–9:00
Oct 2000, NBC Mon 8:00–8:30
CAST:
Chris Woods .... Michael Chiklis
Linda Woods .... Anita Barone
Shannon Woods (age 13) .... Cristina Kernan
Max Woods (12) .... Martin Spanjers
Jake Woods (5) .... Mitch Holleman
Emily Woods (infant) ... Ashlen and Whitney Steidl
Emily Woods .... Cassidy and Savannah Clark
Rod Krolak .... Kevin Crowley
Barb Krolak .... Amy Wilson
Holly Martin .... Suzy Nakamura
Bobick .... Steve Ryan

In between two famous stints as a cop, one of them light (*The Commish,* 1991) and the other brutal (*The Shield,* 2002), pudgy Michael Chiklis played a cheerful stay-at-home dad in this little-known comedy. Chris was a gruff-but-lovable unemployed restaurant supply salesman who was now "mommy" to his four kids, since his high-powered attorney wife, Linda, had taken a new job. The kids, uncertain Shannon, little operator Max, cute Jake and baby Emily, were a handful. Chris' days were filled with diapers, dirty laundry and getting Jake to stop wearing a tiara. Even more frustrating were the adults he now interacted with in the local mommies group, including the annoyingly upbeat Barb (Linda's best friend) and pregnant, sarcastic Holly. While they chattered and breast-fed, he looked embarrassed. Among the neighborhood men were Barb's slightly dense husband, Rod, and next-door neighbor Bobick, an insensitive ex-marine who thought Chris was a wimp and never missed an opportunity to tell him so.

DADDY DEAREST (*Situation Comedy*)
FIRST TELECAST: *September 5, 1993*
LAST TELECAST: *November 7, 1993*
BROADCAST HISTORY:
Sep 1993–Nov 1993, FOX Sun 9:30–10:00
CAST:
Dr. Steven Mitchell .... Richard Lewis
Al Mitchell .... Don Rickles
Helen Mitchell .... Renée Taylor
Christine Winters, Ph.D. .... Sydney Walsh
Lisa .... Alice Carter
Larry Mitchell .... Carey Eidel
Danny Mitchell (pilot only) .... Jonathan Gibby
Danny Mitchell (age 11) .... Jeffrey Bomberger
Pete Peters .... Barney Martin

Set in New York, this loud sitcom was the story of Dr. Steven Mitchell, a neurotic, divorced psychologist living in Manhattan with his wimpy young son, Danny, and his obnoxious father, Al. A used-car salesman, Al had recently separated from his wife, Helen, and Steven was trying to get them back together so that he could reduce the rather considerable amount of hostility at home. Despite their underlying love for each other, whenever Steven and Al were together the insults and put-downs flew fast and furious. Also seen were Christine, the attractive psychologist with whom Steven had a joint practice; Lisa, their sexy but somewhat eccentric secretary/receptionist; Larry, his married brother, who was more than happy to have their overpowering father living with Steven; and Pete, Al's buddy, who seemed to spend more time at Steven's home than at his own. Each episode ended with flubbed moments from takes of scenes aired behind the closing credits.

DADDY'S GIRL (*Situation Comedy*)
FIRST TELECAST: *September 21, 1994*
LAST TELECAST: *October 12, 1994*
BROADCAST HISTORY:
Sep 1994–Oct 1994, CBS Wed 8:30–9:00
CAST:
Dudley Walker .... Dudley Moore
Samantha Walker .... Meredith Scott Lynn
Amy Walker .... Stacy Galina
Phoebe Walker (age 16) .... Keri Russell
Dennis Dumont .... Harvey Fierstein
Lenny .... Alan Ruck
Scar .... Phil Buckman

Dudley Walker's world was full of aggravation in this single-parent sitcom. Dudley's ex-wife, Annette, had run off with his partner, leaving him to run their struggling Los Angeles–based women's clothing business by himself. Dudley's three daughters contributed to his angst. Amy, the eldest, had married Lenny, the world's most boring opthalmologist; Samantha, the ambitious middle daughter, had taken on much of the responsibility of his ex-partner and wanted to be a partner herself; and Phoebe, the teenager, was a free spirit with a very dumb, long-haired boyfriend named Scar. Dennis Dumont, the firm's fussy designer, who had an incredibly gravelly voice, despite his bizarre behavior, was a sort of father figure who dispensed generally sound advice.

DADS (*Situation Comedy*)
FIRST TELECAST: *December 5, 1986*
LAST TELECAST: *June 27, 1987*

BROADCAST HISTORY:

Dec 1986–Jan 1987, ABC Fri 9:00–9:30
Jan 1987–Feb 1987, ABC Fri 9:30–10:00
Jun 1987, ABC Sat 9:30–10:00

CAST:

Rick Armstrong .... Barry Bostwick
Louie Mangiotti.................... Carl Weintraub
Kelly Armstrong (age 13) .... Skye Bassett
Allan Mangiotti (16) .... Eddie Castrodad
Kenny Mangiotti (12) .... Jason Naylor

Two single fathers shared a house in Philadelphia, and the joys of child rearing, in this short-lived comedy. Yuppie Rick, a reporter, worried a lot about his teenage daughter Kelly, while his blue-collar pal Louie, a stonemason, just played it loose with his young sons Kenny and Allan.

DAG (*Situation Comedy*)

FIRST TELECAST: *November 14, 2000*
LAST TELECAST: *April 10, 2001*
BROADCAST HISTORY:

Nov 2000–Apr 2001, NBC Tue 9:30–10:00

CAST:

Agent Jerome Daggett .... David Alan Grier
First Lady Judith Whitman .... Delta Burke
**President Whitman* .... David Rasche
Camilla Whitman .... Lea Moreno Young
Agent Morton......................... Mel Jackson
Agent Edward Pillows .... Stephen Dunham
Agent Susan Cole .... Emmy Laybourne
Ginger Chin .... Lauren Tom
Sullivan Pope .... Paul F. Thompkins

*Occasional

Jerome Daggett was a Secret Service agent whose career had taken a giant leap in the wrong direction. Assigned to protect the president, he had inadvertently leapt *away* from the chief executive during a failed assassination attempt, and his blunder had been plastered all over the evening news, making him the object of ridicule. Instead of firing him, however, the president demoted him to head of the White House B-team, assigned to protect his bothersome wife, Judith. Daggett, stuffy and all business, found himself little more than an errand boy for the bossy, frustrated first lady, who resented the fact that she had worked so hard on behalf of her husband's career and now he ignored her. Besides taking care of her fluffy dog, "Betsy Ross," and baby-sitting her sassy teenage daughter, Camilla, Dag now had to deal with Judith's rude secretary Ginger, a former grifter, and her power-hungry chief of staff, Sullivan. His motley security team included Pillows, a tall, handsome but dumb guy who used to head the team but kept forgetting his gun, and Cole, a sexy, tough, incredibly obsessive agent who slept three hours a night and pumped iron the rest of the time. Morton, the new head of the president's A-team, ragged Dag endlessly. The occasionally seen president was portrayed as a clueless doofus.

Despite their differences, Dag and the first lady hit it off in a odd sort of way, and amid the banter and nonsensical assignments there was a kind of camaraderie between these two "people left behind." In the series finale Dag was promoted back to the A-team and Pillows got the B-team again; Ginger and Sullivan fell in love, and Cole was sent to Harvard with Camilla, who had enrolled there. Although the series ended its regular run in April, one leftover episode aired on May 29, 2001.

DAGMAR'S CANTEEN (*Variety*)

FIRST TELECAST: *March 22, 1952*
LAST TELECAST: *June 14, 1952*
BROADCAST HISTORY:

Mar 1952–Jun 1952, NBC Sat 12:15–12:45 A.M.

REGULARS:

Dagmar (Jennie Lewis)
Ray Malone
Tim Herbert
Jeanne Lewis
Milton Delugg and His Orchestra

Dagmar, the statuesque, well-endowed blonde made famous on Jerry Lester's *Broadway Open House*, starred in this late-night live variety show as the hostess of a real canteen for servicemen. She interviewed, sang songs, and danced, but the most amusing part of the show was her weekly reading of one of her original plays (similar to her hilarious "poetry readings" on *Broadway Open House*). Roles in the plays were also read by servicemen chosen from the audience, as well as by the other cast members. One of the regulars was Dagmar's sister Jeanne, who was the assistant hostess.

DAILY SHOW, THE (*Comedy*)

BROADCAST HISTORY:

Comedy Central
30 minutes
Produced: *1996–*
Premiered: *July 22, 1996*

HOST:

Craig Kilborn (1996–1998)
Jon Stewart (1999–)

This comedy newscast, seen nightly at 11:00 P.M., was one of the more popular features on the saucy Comedy Central cable network. Stories large and small were reported with deadpan seriousness: an actor cat dies in Florida; a clueless reporter covers the Olympics, mocking the foreign athletes in the process. Among the "correspondents" were A. Whitney Brown, Beth Littleford, Brian Unger, and Lizz Winstead.

DAKOTAS, THE (*Western*)

FIRST TELECAST: *January 7, 1963*
LAST TELECAST: *September 9, 1963*
BROADCAST HISTORY:

Jan 1963–Sep 1963, ABC Mon 7:30–8:30

CAST:

Marshal Frank Ragan.................. Larry Ward
Deputy J. D. Smith....................... Jack Elam
Deputy Del Stark .... Chad Everett
Deputy Vance Porter .... Mike Greene

This Western adventure depicted the efforts of a U.S. marshal and his three deputies to maintain law and order across the Black Hills and Badlands of the Dakota Territory. The deputies were a study in contrasts: young, volatile Del Stark; big, gruff Vance Porter; and J. D. Smith, an ex-gunfighter.

DAKTARI (*Adventure*)

FIRST TELECAST: *January 11, 1966*
LAST TELECAST: *January 15, 1969*
BROADCAST HISTORY:

Jan 1966–Sep 1968, CBS Tue 7:30–8:30
Sep 1968–Jan 1969, CBS Wed 7:30–8:30

CAST:

Dr. Marsh Tracy .... Marshall Thompson
Paula Tracy .... Cheryl Miller
Jack Dane (1966–1968) .... Yale Summers
Hedley .... Hedley Mattingly
Mike .... Hari Rhodes
Bart Jason (1968–1969) .... Ross Hagen
Jenny Jones (1968–1969) .... Erin Moran

Filmed at Africa, U.S.A., a wild-animal park near Los Angeles, *Daktari* told the story of an American doctor and his daughter living in Africa. "Daktari" is a native word for doctor. Marsh Tracy was a veterinarian who ran an animal study center with the assistance of his daughter Paula, an American named Jack Dane, and a native named Mike. The Tracys had two distinctive pets, a lion named Clarence and a chimpanzee named Judy. (Clarence had previously starred in an Ivan Tors movie called *Clarence the Crosseyed Lion.*) Also featured was Hedley, the British game warden, who often called on Marsh for help in dealing with animals, natives, and poachers. Added to the cast in 1968 were Bart Jason, a former ranger and hunter who had become a guide for camera safaris, and Jenny Jones, a seven-year-old orphan who became part of the Tracy household.

DALLAS (*Drama*)

FIRST TELECAST: *April 2, 1978*
LAST TELECAST: *May 3, 1991*
BROADCAST HISTORY:

Apr 1978, CBS Sun 10:00–11:00
Sep 1978–Oct 1978, CBS Sat 10:00–11:00
Oct 1978–Jan 1979, CBS Sun 10:00–11:00
Jan 1979–Nov 1981, CBS Fri 10:00–11:00
Dec 1981–May 1985, CBS Fri 9:00–10:00
Sep 1985–May 1986, CBS Fri 9:00–10:00 (OS)
Sep 1986–May 1988, CBS Fri 9:00–10:00
Oct 1988–Mar 1990, CBS Fri 9:00–10:00 (OS)
Mar 1990–May 1990, CBS Fri 10:00–11:00
Nov 1990–Dec 1990, CBS Fri 10:00–11:00
Jan 1991–May 1991, CBS Fri 9:00–10:00

CAST:

John Ross (J.R.) Ewing, Jr. .... Larry Hagman
Eleanor Southworth (Miss Ellie) Ewing (1978–1984, 1985–1990) .... Barbara Bel Geddes
Eleanor Southworth (Miss Ellie) Ewing (1984–1985) .... Donna Reed
John Ross (Jock) Ewing (1978–1981) ...... Jim Davis
Bobby Ewing (1978–1985, 1986–1991) .... Patrick Duffy
Pamela Barnes Ewing (1978–1987) .... Victoria Principal
Lucy Ewing Cooper (1978–1985, 1988–1990) .... Charlene Tilton
Sue Ellen Ewing (1978–1989) .... Linda Gray
Ray Krebbs (1978–1989) .... Steve Kanaly
Cliff Barnes .... Ken Kercheval
Julie Grey (April 1978, 1979) .... Tina Louise
Willard "Digger" Barnes (1978) .... David Wayne
Willard "Digger" Barnes (1979–1980) .... Keenan Wynn
Gary Ewing (1978) .... David Ackroyd
Gary Ewing (1979–1981) .... Ted Shackelford
Valene Ewing (1978–1981) .... Joan Van Ark
Liz Craig (1978–1982) .... Barbara Babcock
Willie Joe Garr (1978–1979) .... John Ashton
Jeb Ames (1978–1979) .... Sandy Ward
Marilee Stone (1979–1987, 1989) ... Fern Fitzgerald
Jackie Dugan .... Sherril Lynn Rettino
Kristin Shepard (1979–1981) .... Mary Crosby
Mrs. Patricia Shepard (1979, 1985) .... Martha Scott
Dusty Farlow (1979–1982, 1985) ...... Jared Martin
Alan Beam (1979–1980) .... Randolph Powell
Dr. Elby (1979–1981) .... Jeff Cooper
Teresa (1982–1991) .... Roseanna Christiansen
Donna Culver Krebbs (1979–1987) .... Susan Howard
Dave Culver (1979–1983, 1986–1988) .... Tom Fuccello
Harve Smithfield (1979–1991) ..... George O. Petrie
Vaughn Leland (1979–1981, 1984) .. Dennis Patrick
Connie (1979–1981) .... Jeanna Michaels
Louella (1978–1981) .... Megan Gallagher
Jordan Lee (1979–1990) .... Don Starr
Mitch Cooper (1980–1982) .... Leigh McCloskey
John Ross Ewing III (1980–1983) .... Tyler Banks
John Ross Ewing III (1983–1991) .... Omri Katz
Punk Anderson (1980–1987) .... Morgan Woodward
Mavis Anderson (1982–1988) .... Alice Hirson
Brady York (1980–1981) .... Ted Gehring
Alex Ward (1980–1981) .... Joel Fabiani
Les Crowley (1980–1981) .... Michael Bell
Afton Cooper (1981–1984, 1989) ... Audrey Landers
Arliss Cooper (1981) .... Anne Francis
Clint Ogden (1981) .... Monte Markham
Leslie Stewart (1981) .... Susan Flannery
Rebecca Wentworth (1981–1983) .. Priscilla Pointer
Craig Stewart (1981) .... Craig Stevens
Jeremy Wendell (1981, 1984–1989) .... William Smithers
Clayton Farlow (1981–1991) .... Howard Keel
Jeff Farraday (1981–1982) .... Art Hindle
Sly Lovegren (1981–1991) .... Deborah Rennard
Phyllis (1981–1991) .... Deborah Tranelli
Katherine Wentworth (1981–1984) .... Morgan Brittany
Charles Eccles (1982) .... Ron Tomme
Bonnie Robertson (1982) .... Lindsay Bloom
Blair Sullivan (1982) .... Ray Wise
Holly Harwood (1982–1983) .... Lois Chiles
Mickey Trotter (1982–1983) .... Timothy Patrick Murphy
Walt Driscoll (1982–1983) .... Ben Piazza
Jarrett McLeish (1982–1983) ... J. Patrick McNamara
Thornton McLeish (1982–1983) .... Kenneth Kimmins
Dora Mae (1983–1991) .... Pat Colbert
Eugene Bullock (1982–1983) .... E. J. Andre
Mark Graison (1983–1984, 1985–1986) ... John Beck
Aunt Lil Trotter (1982–1983) .... Kate Reid
Roy Ralston (1983) .... John Reilly
Serena Wald (1983–1985, 1990) .... Stephanie Blackmore
Peter Richards (1983–1984) .... Christopher Atkins
Paul Morgan (1983–1984, 1986–1988) .... Glenn Corbett
Kendall Chapman (1982–1991) ... Danone Simpson
Jenna Wade (1983–1988) .... Priscilla Presley
Charlie Wade (1983–1988) .... Shalane McCall
Edgar Randolph (1983–1984) ..... Martin E. Brooks
Armando Sidoni (1983–1984) ...... Alberto Morin
Betty (1984–1985) .... Kathleen York
Eddie Cronin (1984–1985) .... Fredric Lehne
Pete Adams (1984–1985) .... Burke Byrnes
Dave Stratton (1984) .... Christopher Stone

Jessica Montfort (1984, 1990) ....Alexis Smith
Mandy Winger (1984–1987) ......Deborah Shelton
Jamie Ewing Barnes (1984–1986) ...Jenilee Harrison
Christopher Ewing (1985–1991)......Joshua Harris
Scotty Demarest (1985).............Stephen Elliott
Jack Ewing (1985–1987) ....Dack Rambo
Angelica Nero (1985–1986)........Barbara Carrera
Dr. Jerry Kenderson (1984–1986)......Barry Jenner
Nicholas (1985–1986)..............George Chakiris
Grace (1985–1986) ....Merete Van Kamp
Matt Cantrell (1986)..................Marc Singer
Luis Rueda (1986) ....Alejandro Rey
Tony (1986)..................Solomon Smaniotto
April Stevens (1986–1991) ....Sheree J. Wilson
Ben Stivers/Wes Parmalee (1986) .....Steve Forrest
B. D. Calhoun (1986–1987)........Hunter von Leer
Ozwald Valentine (1986–1988) ....Derek McGrath
Bruce Harvey (1986–1987, 1989)
..........................Jonathan Goldsmith
Senator Dowling (1986–1987).......Jim McMullan
Nancy Scottfield (1986–1987).......Karen Carlson
Nicholas Pearce (1987–1988)...........Jack Scalia
Casey Denault (1987–1989) ....Andrew Stevens
"Dandy" Dandridge (1987)............Bert Remsen
Kimberly Cryder (1987–1989)..Leigh Taylor-Young
Lisa Alden (1987–1988) ....Amy Stock
Laurel Ellis (1988) ....Annabel Schofield
Sen. Henry Harrison O'Dell (1988)....Howard Duff
Brett Lomax (1988)........Mark Lindsay Chapman
Kay Lloyd (1988–1989) ....Karen Kopins
Carter McKay (1988–1991)........George Kennedy
Tracy Lawton (1988–1989) ....Beth Toussaint
Cally Harper Ewing (1988–1991)...Cathy Podewell
Tommy McKay (1989) ....J. Eddie Peck
Rose McKay (1988–1991).................Jeri Gaile
Don Lockwood (1989)................Ian McShane
James Richard Beaumont (1989–1991)
..............................Sasha Mitchell
Michelle Stevens (1989–1991).....Kimberly Foster
Debbie (1988–1990).........Deborah Marie Taylor
Vanessa Beaumont (1989–1991)...Gayle Hunnicut
Alex Barton (1989) ....Michael Wilding
Ratagan (1989–1991)..................John Hogue
Nancy (1989–1990)...............Evelyn Guerrero
Billy Joe Bates (1989–1990)...........Bill McIntyre
Stephanie Rogers (1990) ....Lesley-Anne Down
Arlen Ward (1990) ....John Larch
Eugene Inagaki (1990)..............Richard Narita
Liz Adams (1990–1991) ....Barbara Stock
Det. Marshall (1990) ....Daryl Roach
Anita (1990) ....Shannon Wilcox
Keller (1990)....................Michael P. Keenan
Donia (1990) ....Zane Lasky
Goldman (1990)...................Hugh Maguire
Ryan (1990).........................Arthur Malet
Del Greco (1990)......................Marty Schiff
Sheila Foley (Hillary Taylor) (1990–1991)
.................................Susan Lucci
Breslin (1990–1991) ....Peter White
LeeAnn De La Vega (1990–1991) .....Barbara Eden
Jory (1991)......................Deirdre Imershein
Debra Lynn (1991) ....Deborah Tucker

Soap operas have always been a staple of daytime television, but ABC's mid-1960s *Peyton Place* was the last prime-time soap opera to be a major viewer attraction—until *Dallas*. It was not a big hit when it premiered in 1978, but *Dallas*'s audience continued to build and, by the 1980–1981 season, it was the runaway most popular series on network television, having spawned one spin-off (*Knots Landing*) and a host of imitators, including *Dynasty*, *Flamingo Road*, and *Secrets of Midland Heights*.

Dallas had all of the elements that make for a successful soap opera—characters that were larger than life, conflicts based on the struggle for money and power, and lots and lots of sex. It was appropriate that the series was set in Texas, with its reputation for the excesses of the wealthy. Patriarch of the Ewing clan was Jock Ewing, who 40 years before had struck it rich as an oil wildcatter and then maneuvered his partner Digger Barnes out of both his share of their company and his true love, Eleanor Southworth. Jock and Miss Ellie had three sons, J.R., Bobby, and Gary. J.R., the eldest, was the man viewers loved to hate. He was power-hungry, unscrupulous, and conniving in his business dealings, and continually unfaithful to his wife, Sue Ellen—even after she bore him a son, J.R. Ewing III, in 1979. When J.R. wanted something or someone, he stopped at nothing to attain his goal. Bobby, the youngest brother, had the morals and integrity his older brother lacked, and was a constant thorn in J.R.'s side. Bobby was married to Digger Barnes's sexy young daughter Pamela, and seemed to J.R. to represent a continual threat to his control of Ewing Oil. Jock, J.R., Bobby, and their families all lived under one roof, a sprawling ranch owned by the Ewings called Southfork, which was located outside the city in rural Braddock, Texas.

The middle Ewing brother, Gary, was rarely seen on *Dallas*. Unable to compete with his strong-willed brothers, and suffering from emotional instability, Gary only appeared occasionally to see his daughter Lucy (he eventually got his own series, *Knots Landing*). Lucy also lived at Southfork and spent most of her time seducing every man in sight, a not too difficult task in light of her blond sexiness. Management of the Southfork ranch fell to Ray Krebbs, one of Lucy's first conquests. Cliff Barnes, the son of Jock's ex-partner Digger Barnes, had become a Ewing in-law when his sister Pam married Bobby. But Cliff was an assistant district attorney and was determined to avenge his father's ruination by the Ewings, so he spent most of his time working with the government attempting to expose the family's corruption of public officials and other illegal business practices.

Most of the major conflicts on *Dallas* centered around J.R., aptly described in *Time* magazine as "that human oil slick." He had, among other things, sold worthless Asian oil leases to the family banker Vaughn Leland and a number of other investors, mortgaged Southfork without telling his parents, attempted to get Sue Ellen institutionalized for alcoholism, thwarted the efforts of unscrupulous Alan Beam to marry Lucy and get his hands on part of the Ewing fortune, and left a trail of disillusioned mistresses whom he had discarded like so much garbage. It was one of these mistresses, his wife's sister Kristin (played briefly in early 1979 by Colleen Camp), who became the focal point of the major TV story of 1980. In the last original episode of the 1979–1980 season, J.R. was shot by an unknown assailant and rushed to the hospital in critical condition. All summer the question raged—"Who shot J.R.?" *Dallas* was by this time a huge international hit, and all over the world viewers were trying to figure out which of the 15 or so characters who had just cause had actually pulled the trigger. Betting parlors took in millions of dollars in wagers. Security was extraordinarily tight at the studio where *Dallas* was filmed, and even the actors themselves did not know for sure (several alternative endings had been filmed). Finally, on November 21, 1980, the world found out: Kristin had pulled the trigger. Pregnant with J.R.'s child, and about to be framed by him for prostitution because she refused his order to get out of Dallas, she shot him for revenge. The episode in which her guilt was revealed was seen by more people than any program in the history of television up to that time. Nearly 80 percent of all viewers watching television that night were tuned to *Dallas*.

In true *Dallas* style, however, J.R. lived and Kristin was never prosecuted, although she did finally leave town. J.R. recovered and waged a new war to unseat his brother Bobby, who had taken over Ewing Oil during his convalescence. There were also two Ewing marriages that season. Lucy married young pre-med student Mitch Cooper, and Ray Krebbs (who was revealed to be Jock's illegitimate son, and therefore a Ewing) married attractive, politically powerful widow Donna Culver. J.R. was as malevolent as ever, engineering a foreign coup to regain some of his holdings as well as hiring a sexy (of course) public-relations woman to promote a new image for himself as an "All-American Businessman." If she could pull that off, she would deserve an Academy Award!

As time passed, marriages alternated with divorces. J.R. and Sue Ellen divorced and later remarried, although neither remained faithful to the other. Lucy and Mitch also divorced, and she subsequently had an ill-fated romance with Mickey Trotter. Mickey was grievously injured in a car accident caused by a drunken Sue Ellen; while he was lying brain-dead at the hospital, Ray Krebbs pulled the plug on his life-support system. The jury called it manslaughter. Meanwhile, Pam had an emotional breakdown, separated from, and eventually divorced Bobby (while retaining custody of their adopted son Christopher, Kristin and Jeff Farrady's child).

Pam's brother Cliff proved to be just as greedy as everyone else—if somewhat less talented at it—when he went to work for his mother. His manipulations became more complicated as the stakes got higher and, when he became president of Barnes/Wentworth Oil, he even had hopes of besting J.R. in the world of dirty deals. His conniving and beautiful half sister Katherine Wentworth first tried to ally herself with J.R. to break Cliff, and then fell in love with Bobby—who by that time was back together with an old girlfriend, Jenna Wade (played once in 1978 by Morgan Fairchild and a few times in early 1980 by Francine Tacker).

Even Miss Ellie found a new romance, after Jock passed away in 1982 (actor Jim Davis had died), marrying the wealthy Clayton Farlow. Through it all her sons J.R. and Bobby fought over control of Ewing Oil. Eventually, to neither's satisfaction, they ended up running the family business together, constantly trying to outmaneuver each other to gain total control.

The year 1984 saw the arrival of still another troublemaker, cousin Jamie, who teamed with Cliff Barnes to fight J.R. for a piece of Ewing Oil; eventually she and Cliff were married. Donna struck oil in an independent venture, introducing strains in her marriage to Ray; and J.R., in between battles with everyone, found time to pursue hard-to-get Mandy Winger. Brother Bobby had a bad year all around. First he was shot by an assassin, then he broke up with Jenna (who married and then was convicted of murdering Marchetta), and finally he was "killed" in a hit-and-run accident.

Bobby's demise left a major hole in *Dallas*. During 1985–1986 his two loves tried to find happiness in new relationships, Pam with the long-missing Mark Graison and Jenna with Jamie's brother Jack Ewing. The season's major new manipulator was Marinos Shipping executive Angelica, who allied with Cliff while flirting with Jack. J.R.'s boozy wife Sue Ellen was committed to a sanitarium (her mother Patricia bailed her out), had a fling with Dusty, and wound up in a nasty custody fight with J.R. over little John Ross. But still the memory of Bobby lingered. It was renewed when a childhood friend named Matt turned up looking for an extension of the financing Bobby had given him for an emerald mine in South America. Pam obliged and a series of adventures in the jungle ensued.

What Pam—and viewers—longed for, of course, was not ghosts from Bobby's past but Bobby himself. With ratings sagging, star Larry Hagman made a personal appeal to Patrick Duffy to rejoin the cast. No matter that his character had been killed and buried in an elaborate funeral. In one of the most celebrated cop-outs in soap opera history the 1986–1987 season opened with a very live Bobby lathering up in Pam's shower. How did he get there? It seems she had *dreamt* the entire 1985–1986 season, and Bobby had not died at all! With that minor detail out of the way it was back to normal, and he remarried Pam. Pam, however, was grievously injured in a fiery auto accident and then disappeared, while Jenna was preoccupied with her trouble-prone teenaged daughter Charlie. Over in J.R.'s story, a bitter Sue Ellen found a new way to embarrass him by manufacturing a line of "Valentine's Girl" erotic lingerie—which became an instant hit with Mandy as the model. Inspired, perhaps, by Bobby's miraculous resurrection, a ranch hand named Parmalee surfaced, claiming to be the long-dead Jock Ewing, causing great distress in the family. The Krebbs's marriage disintegrated further when Donna went to Washington as a lobbyist, and fell in love with Senator Dowling. Back home Jack's ex-wife April was the latest newcomer scheming to snag a piece of Ewing Oil.

The Ewings suffered a major setback in 1987 when proof of J.R.'s illegal dealings finally caused him to lose control of Ewing Oil. Ever resourceful but on the defensive, wily J.R. worked with Casey Denault to regain some of his lost power. He also tried his celebrated bedroom ploy with Kimberly Cryder, the beautiful wife of his new nemesis Winston Cryder. Jenna and Ray were married; Bobby was pursued by Lisa (who sought custody of his son, Christopher) and by April; and Miss Ellie threw Clayton out of the house. Sue Ellen had the right product for them all—she pursued the lingerie business with intimate help from banker Nicholas Pearce.

Three major stories dominated the 1988–1989 season. J.R., on a hunting trip to Arkansas, seduced a rural lass named Cally and was promptly imprisoned on a work farm by her vengeful brothers and their friend, the local judge. He escaped only after agreeing to marry her, then spent the next two seasons trying to get rid of her, while his hayseed bride insinuated herself into his affairs and even bore him a child. J.R.'s previous wife, Sue Ellen, bought a movie studio in order to make (with screenwriter Don Lockwood) a filmed exposé about J.R. that would surely "destroy him." On the business front, Colorado rancher Carter McKay teamed with Weststar Oil chairman Jeremy Wendell to mount a full-scale range war against the Ewings (complete with fatigue-clad mercenaries), as well as to take over Ewing Oil, which was now controlled by Bobby. McKay had his own family problems with wife Rose, drug-addicted son Tommy, and daughter Tracy, but Weststar (which he eventually took over) and Ewing Oil battled it out in Dallas, Washington, D.C., and even Austria and Russia (where episodes were filmed on location).

At the start of the 1989–1990 season, a Weststar and a Ewing tanker collided, resulting in a huge oil spill. A government investigation ensued, chaired by none other than Cliff Barnes, who had launched a political career as a new way to get back at J.R. Assisted by public relations expert Stephanie, he eventually won (and then lost) the position of national energy czar. Bobby, despondent over the death of his beloved Pam, became obsessed with Pam-look-alike Jeanne, but eventually married April. J.R. learned that he had a second son by former flame Vanessa. The now 20-year-old James proved to be a "junior J.R.," wheeling and dealing, bedding many women, and eventually ganging up with the disillusioned Cally against his dad. By the end of the season they actually had J.R. confined to a mental institution (part of a convoluted plot in which J.R. had entered the facility to try to wheedle Weststar stock out of Clayton's crazy sister Jessica, who had earlier tried to kill half the population of Dallas). J.R. in a straitjacket seemed a perfect reward!

J.R. managed to escape the following season (1990–1991), but what little control he still had over Ewing Oil slipped further from his grasp. Bobby, weary of the battle and grieving over the sudden death of his new bride April (she had been kidnapped by Hillary during their Paris honeymoon), sold his controlling interest to manipulative newcomer LeeAnn, whom J.R. had jilted in college. LeeAnn in turn sold to Michelle (married to J.R.'s plotting son James), who after murdering her sister April's killer (Hillary) turned half interest over to J.R.'s old rival, boozy Cliff. Cliff soon snared the other half as well. McKay had left town so J.R. made a play for Weststar, but when that failed he was locked out of the oil business altogether.

In the series' final episode, J.R.'s entire world seemed to have crashed down around him. His business was gone: Ewing Oil now belonged to Cliff. His family was dispersed: Ellie and Clayton were traveling in Europe, beloved son John Ross left him to live with Sue Ellen in London, not-so-beloved son James and his bride Debra Lynn departed with grandson Jimmy, and ex-wife Cally now lived happily in Palm Beach with his other child. Even Southfork had been turned over to Bobby by Miss Ellie. J.R. was left with a bank account and the promise of his ever-forgiving brother that he could stay in the big, now-empty house as long as he wished.

As J.R. drank and contemplated suicide, an apparition named Adam (Joel Grey) appeared to show him what life would have been like if he had never been born. It was *It's a Wonderful Life* turned upside down—some *Dallas* characters were seen with better lives, others with even worse ones. Finally the "angel" Adam's eyes flashed red (was he the devil?), J.R. raised the pistol, and a shot rang out. Bobby burst into the room. Only he, not the viewer, saw what had happened.

DALTON'S CODE OF VENGEANCE (*Adventure*)
FIRST TELECAST: *July 27, 1986*
LAST TELECAST: *August 24, 1986*
BROADCAST HISTORY:
Jul 1986–Aug 1986, NBC Sun 8:00–9:00
CAST:
David Dalton .... Charles Taylor

A short-run series about a rootless young Vietnam veteran who prowled around the country stumbling upon wrongs to right. The character was originally seen in two TV movies, telecast in June 1985 and May 1986; the first of these was chopped in two and rerun as two episodes of the series' four-episode run in the summer of 1986, which was the last network viewers saw of Dalton.

DAMON (*Situation Comedy*)
FIRST TELECAST: *March 22, 1998*
LAST TELECAST: *July 20, 1998*
BROADCAST HISTORY:
Mar 1998–Apr 1998, FOX Sun 8:30–9:00
Apr 1998–Jul 1998, FOX Mon 8:00–8:30
Jul 1998, FOX Mon 8:00–9:00
CAST:
Det. Damon Thomas .... Damon Wayans
Bernard Thomas .... David Alan Grier
Captain Carol Czynencko .... Andrea Martin
Det. Carrol Fontain .... Dom Irrera
Det. Stacy Phillips .... Melissa De Sousa
Det. Jimmy Tortone .... Julio Oscar Mechoso
Off. Billy Cavanaugh .... Greg Pitts
Tracy Ward .... Veronica Webb

In this farcial series, Damon Wayans played an undercover cop in the Chicago Police Department who relished the opportunity to disguise himself as everything from a flashy pimp, in order to break up an escort service, to a warehouse worker, to catch a cocaine smuggler. His inept older brother, Bernard, worked as a security guard but wanted desperately to be a real cop. He had just separated from his wife and moved in with Damon. Tough cookie Stacy was Damon's sometimes partner; Billy the ignorant new recruit; and Fontain an officer who hated to do the paperwork to close his cases. Captain Czynencko, their pint-sized female boss, was pretty abrasive despite trying to find ways to "relate" to her less-than-receptive squad. Tracy was the sexy, divorced reporter for the *Chicago Times* with whom Damon was in love. For a time she lived into the apartment across the hall along with Bernard, who'd had a falling out with his brother, but after three weeks she took a Peace Corps assignment and Bernard moved back in with Damon.

DAMON RUNYON THEATRE (*Dramatic Anthology*)
FIRST TELECAST: *April 16, 1955*
LAST TELECAST: *June 30, 1956*

BROADCAST HISTORY:

Apr 1955–Jun 1956, CBS Sat 10:30–11:00

HOST:

Donald Woods

Most of the episodes in this filmed anthology were based on the short stories of Damon Runyon. Best known through the musical *Guys and Dolls,* which was adapted from his writings, Runyon was unique in his use of hip New York language and characters. Vivian Blaine, who created the role of Adelaide in *Guys and Dolls,* appeared in a variation on that role in the premiere episode of the program.

DAN AUGUST (*Police Drama*)

FIRST TELECAST: *September 23, 1970*

LAST TELECAST: *June 25, 1975*

BROADCAST HISTORY:

Sep 1970–Jan 1971, ABC Wed 10:00–11:00
Jan 1971–Aug 1971, ABC Thu 9:30–10:30
May 1973–Oct 1973, CBS Wed 9:00–10:00
Apr 1975–Jun 1975, CBS Wed 10:00–11:00

CAST:

Det. Lt. Dan August .... Burt Reynolds
Sgt. Charles Wilentz .... Norman Fell
Sgt. Joe Rivera .... Ned Romero
Chief George Untermeyer .... Richard Anderson
Katy Grant .... Ena Hartmann

Burt Reynolds portrayed Dan August, a police detective, in this straight police-action show. Since August had grown up with many of the people he had to deal with officially in Santa Luisa, California, he became more personally involved in his cases than would most big-city detectives. Despite—or perhaps because of—this, he always got his man, in true TV-detective fashion.

Dan August was aired on ABC during the 1970–1971 season to mediocre ratings and was not renewed. However, shortly thereafter Reynolds became a major celebrity through feature-film and other exposure, and CBS telecast reruns during two subsequent summers to larger audiences than had seen the original series.

DAN RAVEN (*Police Drama*)

FIRST TELECAST: *September 23, 1960*

LAST TELECAST: *January 6, 1961*

BROADCAST HISTORY:

Sep 1960–Jan 1961, NBC Fri 7:30–8:30

CAST:

Lt. Dan Raven .... Skip Homeier
Det. Sgt. Burke .... Dan Barton
Perry Levitt .... Quinn Redeker

The Sunset Strip in Hollywood provided the setting for this police-action series. Lt. Dan Raven and his partner Sgt. Burke were assigned by the Los Angeles sheriff's office (West Hollywood Division) to the maze of jazz spots, nightclubs, coffeehouses, and other entertainment emporiums that lined the famous Strip. While covering his beat, Raven often became involved with show business personalities—such as Bobby Darin, Paul Anka, Buddy Hackett, and Gogi Grant—who worked on the Strip. The plots often revolved around these guest stars, some of whom played themselves and some of whom portrayed fictional characters. Magazine photographer Perry Levitt, who also had the Hollywood beat, was often seen where the action was.

DAN TEMPEST, see *Buccaneers, The*

DANA CARVEY SHOW, THE (*Comedy/Variety*)

FIRST TELECAST: *March 12, 1996*

LAST TELECAST: *May 7, 1996*

BROADCAST HISTORY:

Mar 1996–May 1996, ABC Tue 9:30–10:00

REGULARS:

Dana Carvey
Steve Carell
Bill Chott
Stephen Colbert
Heather Morgan
Robert Smigel

Boyish comedian Dana Carvey stirred up a hornet's nest of controversy with this over-the-top sketch comedy series, which showed how far "edgy" sponsors were willing—or not willing—to go on American broadcast television. The idea was for each week's sponsor to get title billing—the first episode was called *The Taco Bell Dana Carvey Show*—and then demonstrate its sense of humor by allowing its product to be gently spoofed in the sketches that followed. But when Taco Bell saw what it got, it canceled all future advertising, as did several other sponsors. What caused the ruckus? The premiere opened with a chorus of dancing Taco Bell clerks introducing Carvey by singing, "We paid him a fortune to use our name, 'cause he's a shameless whore . . ." This segued into *Saturday Night Live*-style political sketches, including President Bill Clinton ripping off his shirt to reveal a chest full of nipples, with which he suckled babies and small animals (to show how nurturing he was), and First Lady Hillary Clinton locked in a White House room, under "house arrest," screaming like a banshee demanding to be let out. (Note to readers in future centuries: at this time the assertive First Lady was considered an embarrassment to the President; later, *he* would become an embarrassment to *her*.)

Pizza Hut, explaining its pull-out, said its audience was "family and children . . . we only align with projects that meet the family brand." The sponsor's name was omitted from the title in later episodes, but Carvey, to his credit, did not let up; later sketches included a scatological takeoff on *The Wizard of Oz* and first ladies as dogs, with Jackie Kennedy barking and eating dog biscuits. With sponsors heading for the door, and only moderately large audiences, the series was canceled after two months.

DANCE FEVER (*Dance*)

BROADCAST HISTORY:

Syndicated only
30 minutes
Produced: *1978–1987* (234 episodes)
Released: *January 1979*

HOST:

Deney Terrio (1979–1985)
Adrian Zmed (1985–1987)

REGULARS:

Freeman King (1979–1980)
Motion—Dianne Day (1979–1980, 1981–1985)
Flo Solder (1980–1981)
Toni Yuskis (1979–1980)
Janet Marie Jones (1980–1985)

Debra Johnson (1985–1987)
Jeanie Thompson (1985–1987)
Debby Harris (1985–1987)
Cindy Millican (1985–1987)

This pulsating series offered the best amateur disco dancers from around the country a chance for national exposure. Each week four couples competed and were rated by a guest panel of show-business celebrities. The top-rated team could go on to win as much as $50,000 if they made it to the annual Grand Prix finals. The music was hot and continuous, with flashing lights and spectacular routines straight out of *Saturday Night Fever*. A rock music act and the show's own dancers (Terrio and two women called "Motion") also performed each week. Freeman King was the show's "video disc jockey" during the first two seasons. When Terrio left *Dance Fever* in 1985 he was replaced by actor Adrian Zmed, who had previously been a celebrity panelist on the show.

DANCIN' AT THE HOT SPOTS (*Dance*)

BROADCAST HISTORY:
The Nashville Network
60 minutes
Produced: *1993–1994*
Premiered: *May 1, 1993*

REGULARS:
Rebecca Holden
James Hill

This Saturday-night country music program was taped in dance clubs across the country.

DANCIN' TO THE HITS (*Music*)

BROADCAST HISTORY:
Syndicated only
30 minutes
Produced: *1986* (30 episodes)
Released: *September 1986*

HOST:
Lorenzo Lamas

DANCERS:
Sweet Dreams
(Jeff, Cheryl, Eartha, Aurorah, Priscilla, Barry, Andrea, Bill)

Music series which emphasized the athletic and erotic dancing of its regular troupe of young, attractive dancers. Hosted by sexy Lorenzo Lamas, star of CBS' *Falcon Crest, Dancin' to the Hits* looked like *American Bandstand* with professional dancers and choreography. In addition to dancing to current top-40 recordings, each episode included a live song by such new performers as the S.O.S. band, the Stabilizers, Melissa Morgan, the Rainmakers, Dramarama, Jean Carn, and Howard Hewitt.

DANCING ON AIR (*Instruction*)

FIRST TELECAST: *February 2, 1947*
LAST TELECAST: *March 2, 1947*
BROADCAST HISTORY:
Feb 1947–Mar 1947, NBC Sun 8:00–8:15

EMCEE:
Ed Sims

Dancing on Air was a five-week dance-instruction program, with instructors from the Fred Astaire Studios.

DANGER (*Dramatic Anthology*)

FIRST TELECAST: *September 19, 1950*
LAST TELECAST: *May 31, 1955*
BROADCAST HISTORY:
Sep 1950–Aug 1954, CBS Tue 10:00–10:30
Aug 1954–Dec 1954, CBS Tue 9:30–10:00
Jan 1955–May 1955, CBS Tue 10:00–10:30

HOST/NARRATOR:
Richard Stark

The title of this series was fully descriptive of its content. Psychological dramas and various types of murder mysteries were the weekly fare in these live plays telecast from New York. "Death and Murder," in fact, might have been an even more appropriate title, since those words kept popping up in titles of individual episodes. There were "Murder Takes the 'A' Train," "Operation Murder," "Murder's Face," "Motive for Murder," and "Inherit Murder" on the one hand, and "Death Gamble," "Death Among the Relics," "Death Beat," "Prelude to Death," "Death for the Lonely," "Flowers of Death," and "Death Signs an Autograph" on the other. The players were not particularly well known and, at the time, neither were the directors. Three of the directors subsequently did become highly successful. Yul Brynner, who worked frequently as a director in the early days of television, was the director of *Danger* when it went on the air in the fall of 1950. He was replaced early on by Sidney Lumet, who later gave way to John Frankenheimer.

Among the young performers featured on *Danger* were several who would go on to successful careers in the movies. They included John Cassavetes, James Dean, Charlton Heston, Paul Newman, Walter Matthau, Jack Lemmon, Rod Steiger, and Anthony Quinn. On the distaff side, Grace Kelly, Lee Grant, Carroll Baker, Nina Foch, Kim Stanley, and Cloris Leachman appeared.

DANGER MAN (*International Intrigue*)

FIRST TELECAST: *April 5, 1961*
LAST TELECAST: *September 13, 1961*
BROADCAST HISTORY:
Apr 1961–Sep 1961, CBS Wed 8:30–9:00

CAST:
John Drake.................... Patrick McGoohan

Filmed on diverse locations around the world, ranging from major European capitals to remote African jungles, *Danger Man* told of the exploits of John Drake, an internationally famous security investigator whose services were available only to governments or highly placed government officials. Working in affiliation with NATO, the suave, calculating, and highly efficient Mr. Drake was equally at home in the best restaurants or eating raw meat with a native tribe in some remote outpost as he pursued his quarry to the four corners of the earth. This British-produced series was the first of three similar series starring Patrick McGoohan to reach American audiences in the 1960s. The other two were *Secret Agent* and *The Prisoner*.

DANGER THEATRE (*Comedy/Adventure*)

FIRST TELECAST: *July 11, 1993*
LAST TELECAST: *August 22, 1993*
BROADCAST HISTORY:
Jul 1993–Aug 1993, FOX Sun 7:30–8:00

HOST:

Robert Vaughn

Robert Vaughn hosted *Danger Theatre*, "the show that dares to take a bite out of the butt of crime," with his tongue so far in his cheek it was amazing he could still talk. He tried to sound serious, but looked and acted embarrassed, distracted, and clumsy as he provided introductions and previews of upcoming episodes. Most weeks consisted of 15-minute segments of *The Searcher*, a parody of *Knight Rider*, followed by similarly short segments of *Tropical Punch*, a send-up of *Hawaii Five-O*. The last segment of *Tropical Punch* aired on August 15, and on *Danger Theatre*'s last telecast it was replaced by a single episode of *357 Marina del Rey*, a private-eye spoof in the *77 Sunset Strip* mold starring Todd Field and Ricky Harris. For detailed information on *The Searcher* and *Tropical Punch* see the listings under those titles.

DANGEROUS ASSIGNMENT (*Foreign Intrigue*)

BROADCAST HISTORY:

Syndicated only
30 minutes
Produced: *1951–1952* (39 episodes)
Released: *Early 1952*

CAST:

Steve Mitchell .... Brian Donlevy

Action and intrigue in exotic places marked the exploits of Steve Mitchell, undercover agent for the U.S. government. In each episode he was dispatched by "The Commissioner" to a place like Mexico City, Casablanca, or Burma, or behind the Iron Curtain, to tidy up some international problem. The scenery was nice, but only a backdrop for violence. In the first episode, for example, he was sent to pick up a turncoat's son in Stockholm. He got slugged with an automatic, leapt from a speeding car just before it hurtled over a cliff and burst into flames, and finally zapped the villain with the bare wires of a light fixture. Nice trip.

Donlevy also starred in an NBC radio version of *Dangerous Assignment* from 1949 to 1953.

DANGEROUS CURVES (*Detective Drama*)

FIRST TELECAST: *February 26, 1992*
LAST TELECAST: *December 15, 1993*
BROADCAST HISTORY:

Feb 1992–Jun 1993, CBS Wed 11:30–12:30 A.M.
Sep 1993–Dec 1993, CBS Wed 12:35 A.M.–1:35 A.M.

CAST:

Gina McKay .... Lise Cutter
Holly Williams .... Michael Michele
Lt. Ozzie Bird .... Gregory McKinney
Marina Bonnelle (1992) .... Diane Bellego
Alexandre Dorleac .... Francois-Eric Gendron

Gina and Holly were two former policewomen working as operatives for the Personal Touch security service in Dallas. Their assignments included protecting people and property from thieves and assassins. When the series premiered their boss was Marina Bonnelle, but she was transferred a couple of months later. Her replacement, Alexandre Dorleac, was actually an agent for an Interpol-like agency that dealt with international criminals and terrorists around the world. He used Personal Touch as a cover for his international activities, and under him Gina and Holly's work expanded to include assignments for this agency in addition to their local security work. Ozzie, Gina's lover, was a Dallas cop who provided them with information and sometimes got personally involved in their cases.

DANGEROUS MINDS (*Drama*)

FIRST TELECAST: *September 30, 1996*
LAST TELECAST: *July 12, 1997*
BROADCAST HISTORY:

Sep 1996–Feb 1997, ABC Mon 8:00–9:00
Mar 1997, ABC Sat 8:00–9:00
Jun 1997–Jul 1997, ABC Sat 9:00–10:00

CAST:

Louanne Johnson .... Annie Potts
Callie Timmons .... Tamala Jones
James Revill .... Cedrick Terrell
Amanda Bardales .... Jenny Gago
Gusmaro Lopez .... Greg Serano
Blanca Guerrero .... Maria Costa
Alvina Edwards .... LaToya Howlett
Cornelius Hawkins .... Vicellous Reon Shannon
Jerome Griffin .... Michael Jace
Bud Bartkus .... Stanley Anderson
Hal Gray .... William Converse-Roberts
Jean Warner .... Jenny O'Hara

THEME:

by Coolio

The students at inner-city Parkmont Sr. High School, in East Palo Alto, California, were surly, intimidating street kids. They had run three English teachers out of school since the beginning of the year. Then in strode drawling Louanne Johnson, a petite but tough former Marine, the latest in a long and honorable line of TV teachers who "really cared." She could spit back at them, but she also used humor, clever gimmicks, and real caring to win them over. She went to their homes, took in their babies, and covered for them on their jobs so they could study. Their bad-ass friends tried to pull them back to the mean streets, but when violence loomed, others would come to her aid. The streets were no match for Louanne.

Among the kids, Callie was a young single mom, Gusmaro a tough gang member, and Cornelius a big brooding kid who expressed himself through graffiti. Jerome was the gang services counselor, Hal the history teacher, and Bud the disillusioned computer teacher who was particularly hard on Louanne. To him, her kids were all thugs. "If I can save just one . . ." she snapped back. The ghost of *The White Shadow* surely walked these halls. Mickey's Tavern was the faculty hangout.

Based on the memoirs of the real Louanne Johnson *(My Posse Don't Do Homework)*, and the subsequent 1995 film starring Michelle Pfeiffer.

DANIEL BOONE (*Western*)

FIRST TELECAST: *September 24, 1964*
LAST TELECAST: *August 27, 1970*
BROADCAST HISTORY:

Sep 1964–Aug 1970, NBC Thu 7:30–8:30

CAST:

Daniel Boone .... Fess Parker
Yadkin (1964–1965) .... Albert Salmi
Mingo (1964–1968) .... Ed Ames
Rebecca Boone .... Patricia Blair
Jemima Boone (1964–1966) ... Veronica Cartwright
Israel Boone .... Darby Hinton
Cincinnatus .... Dal McKennon

Jericho Jones (1965–1966) .... Robert Logan
Gideon (1968–1969) .... Don Pedro Colley
Gabe Cooper (1969–1970) .... Roosevelt Grier
Josh Clements (1968–1970) .... Jimmy Dean

Fess Parker, who gained fame portraying Davy Crockett for Walt Disney in the mid-1950s, became even more successful as another frontiersman, Daniel Boone, in the 1960s. Like Crockett, Daniel Boone was one of America's great folk heroes. He lived in the North Carolina–Tennessee–Kentucky area just before and during the Revolutionary War, and his exploits were legendary. The stories in this series revolved around Boone's encounters with Indians, both friendly and hostile, his survey work and pioneering expeditions, and his relationships with family and friends.

The family included his wife Rebecca, his daughter Jemima, and his son Israel. The friends were originally his traveling companion Yadkin, his Indian friend Mingo, and Cincinnatus, tavern-keeper of Boonesborough, Daniel's home base. Only Cincinnatus remained through the entire six-year run of the show. Later added to the cast were young pioneer Jericho Jones; Gideon, a black Indian; Josh Clements, a fur trapper; and Gabe Cooper, a runaway slave living with the Indians.

DANNY (*Situation Comedy*)
FIRST TELECAST: *September 28, 2001*
LAST TELECAST: *October 5, 2001*
BROADCAST HISTORY:
Sep 2001–Oct 2001, CBS Fri 8:30–9:00
CAST:
Danny G .... Daniel Stern
Lenny .... Robert Prosky
Chickie .... Roz Ryan
Sally (age 14) .... Julia McIlvaine
Henry (13) .... Jon Foster
Molly .... Joely Fisher
Rachel .... Mia Korf

Danny was a 40-year-old idealistic dreamer who was still adjusting to his recent divorce. He and his friendly ex-wife, Molly, had two teenage children, Sally and Henry, who were living with Danny, as was his grumpy father, Lenny. Danny, who was a big kid himself, was the director of "The Wreck Center," the local community center, where he worked with Chickie, whose tough-talking exterior masked a kind heart. Rachel, the bubbly young ballet teacher at the center, liked him, but Danny was too shy to ask her out.

The first casualty of the 2001–2002 season, *Danny* was canceled after only two telecasts.

DANNY KAYE SHOW, THE (*Musical Variety*)
FIRST TELECAST: *September 25, 1963*
LAST TELECAST: *June 7, 1967*
BROADCAST HISTORY:
Sep 1963–Jun 1967, CBS Wed 10:00–11:00 (OS)
REGULARS:
Danny Kaye
Harvey Korman (1964–1967)
Joyce Van Patten (1964–1967)
Laurie Ichino (1964–1965)
Victoria Meyerink (1964–1967)
The Johnny Mann Singers (1963–1964)
The Earl Brown Singers (1964–1967)
The Tony Charmoli Dancers
Paul Weston and His Orchestra

The multitalented Danny Kaye starred for four seasons in his own musical comedy–variety series on CBS. He did monologues, pantomime, and comedy sketches; he sang, danced, and even played an instrument or two. The most remarkable aspect of the series was its use of inventive comedy sketches with Danny's guest stars. Although neither Harvey Korman nor Joyce Van Patten appeared on every episode during the three years in which they frequented the series, they were given featured-performer status by CBS in all press releases about the show, as were child performers Laurie Ichino and Victoria Meyerink.

DANNY THOMAS HOUR, THE (*Various*)
FIRST TELECAST: *September 11, 1967*
LAST TELECAST: *June 10, 1968*
BROADCAST HISTORY:
Sep 1967–Jun 1968, NBC Mon 9:00–10:00
HOST/STAR:
Danny Thomas

This weekly series was a potpourri of different entertainment forms. Included were musical-variety specials, dramatic plays, and light comedies. Danny Thomas starred in all the musical-variety episodes and comedies and was host of the serious dramas. A number of comedies were long versions of his own previous hit series, *Make Room for Daddy (The Danny Thomas Show).*

DANNY THOMAS SHOW, THE (*Situation Comedy*)
FIRST TELECAST: *September 29, 1953*
LAST TELECAST: *September 2, 1971*
BROADCAST HISTORY:
Sep 1953–Jun 1956, ABC Tue 9:00–9:30
Oct 1956–Feb 1957, ABC Mon 8:00–8:30
Feb 1957–Jul 1957, ABC Thu 9:00–9:30
Oct 1957–Sep 1964, CBS Mon 9:00–9:30 (OS)
Apr 1965–Sep 1965, CBS Mon 9:30–10:00
Sep 1970–Jan 1971, ABC Wed 8:00–8:30
Jan 1971–Sep 1971, ABC Thu 9:00–9:30
CAST:
Danny Williams .... Danny Thomas
Mrs. Margaret Williams (1953–1956) ... Jean Hagen
Mrs. Kathy Williams ("Clancey") (1957–1971) .... Marjorie Lord
Rusty Williams........................ Rusty Hamer
Terry Williams (1953–1958) .... Sherry Jackson
Terry Williams (1959–1960)......... Penney Parker
Linda Williams (1957–1971) .... Angela Cartwright
Louise (1953–1954) .... Louise Beavers
Louise (1955–1964) .... Amanda Randolph
Horace (1953–1954) .... Horace McMahon
Benny (1953–1959) .... Ben Lessy
Jesse Leeds (1953–1957) .... Jesse White
Uncle Tonoose (1956–1971) .... Hans Conried
Liz (1956–1957) .... Mary Wickes
Phil Brokaw (1957–1961) .... Sheldon Leonard
Pat Hannigan (1959–1960) ...... Pat Harrington, Jr.
Gina (1959) .... Annette Funicello
"Uncle Charley" Halper (1959–1971).... Sid Melton
Bunny Halper (1961–1964) .... Pat Carroll
Rosey Robbins (1970–1971)........ Roosevelt Grier
Michael (1970–1971) .... Michael Hughes
Henry (1970–1971) .... Stanley Myron Handleman
THEME:
"Danny Boy" ("Londonderry Air")

Danny Thomas's first major exposure on television had been as one of the hosts of NBC's *All Star Revue*. His nightclub routine was a flop on TV, as a result of which he blasted the new medium as being suitable "only for idiots" and vowed never to return. But return he did, in 1953, with one of the longest-running family comedies of the 1950s and 1960s. *Make Room for Daddy*, as it was called for its first three seasons, was a reflection of Danny's own life as an entertainer and the problems created by his frequent absences from his children. The title came from a phrase used in the real-life Thomas household: whenever Danny returned home from a tour, his children had to shift bedrooms, to "make room for Daddy." In the series, Danny played nightclub entertainer Danny Williams, a sometimes loud but ultimately soft-hearted lord of the household, who was constantly being upstaged by his bratty but lovable kids. The kids were, at the outset, 6-year-old Rusty and 11-year-old Terry. Jean Hagen played Danny's loving wife, Margaret.

A number of major changes took place as the show matured. In 1956 Jean Hagen quit. Instead of replacing her, Danny had her written out of the show as having died, which led to a season (1956–1957) of his courting eligible women—with frequent assistance from the kids. He eventually proposed to an Irish lass, Kathy O'Hara. The wedding did not take place on the show, but when the program returned in the fall of 1957 Danny and Kathy were just returning from their honeymoon, and little Linda, Kathy's daughter by a previous marriage, had also joined the Williams household.

Sherry Jackson left the cast in 1958. At first the character she played, Terry, was supposed to be away at school, but in 1959 a new actress assumed the role. Terry then had a season-long courtship with a young nightclub performer named Pat Hannigan, whom she eventually married. Terry then left the household for good.

A number of other youngsters also passed through the series, including Gina, a foreign exchange student living in the Williams home. Picola Pupa, a young Italian singer discovered by Danny, was also seen in a few episodes. Other regulars included a succession of Danny's agents, the first played by Horace McMahon, later ones by Jesse White—who simultaneously was appearing as the agent on *Private Secretary*—and Sheldon Leonard. (Leonard was the real-life producer of *The Danny Thomas Show* and had appeared in 1953 episodes as Danny's masseur.) Benny was Danny's original accompanist, Louise the family housekeeper, and Charley Halper the owner of the Copa Club, where Danny Williams frequently performed.

No doubt the most memorable regular was Hans Conried in the role of Uncle Tonoose, eccentric patriarch of the Williams family. Conried was seen in several guest roles on the show, including those of ne'er-do-well Cousin Carl, Uncle Oscar, and visiting Derik Campbell, and he turned up as Tonoose as early as 1956. The role was perfect, and he continued to appear in it, periodically, for the rest of the series' run. Others who made guest appearances were songwriter Harry Ruby as himself, Bill Dana as José Jiminez, the elevator operator, and many top names from the entertainment world, playing themselves.

The Danny Thomas Show ended its original run in 1964, although repeat telecasts were seen on CBS during 1965. Then in 1970 Danny Williams returned in a new series called *Danny Thomas in Make Room for Granddaddy*, complete with Kathy, Rusty (now 23 and married), and Linda (now 17) from the original cast. A newcomer was a roguishly cute little terror named Michael, age 6. Michael made Danny the "Granddaddy," since he was cast as Terry's son, left with the Williamses while Terry and her soldier husband were abroad. Charley Halper and Uncle Tonoose were back, joined by a new accompanist (played by ex–football star Roosevelt Grier) and Henry, the neurotic elevator operator in Danny's apartment building. Despite guest appearances by such stars as Bob Hope, Frank Sinatra, Milton Berle, and Lucille Ball, the format was rather old-hat for the 1970s, and *Make Room for Granddaddy* expired after a single season.

NBC aired reruns of *The Danny Thomas Show*, under the title *Make Room for Daddy*, as part of its weekday daytime lineup from October 1960–March 1965 and as part of its Saturday morning lineup for various periods between September 1961 and October 1964.

DANTE (*Mystery Adventure*)
FIRST TELECAST: *October 3, 1960*
LAST TELECAST: *April 10, 1961*
BROADCAST HISTORY:
Oct 1960–Apr 1961, NBC Mon 9:30–10:00
CAST:
Willie Dante .... Howard Duff
Stewart Styles...................... Alan Mowbray
Biff .... Tom D'Andrea
Inspector Loper .... James Nolan

Adventurer Willie Dante had a history of running clip joints and gambling casinos around the country, a reputation he planned to change when he opened his own legitimate nightclub in San Francisco. With him were his two sidekicks from the gambling days, Biff the bartender and Stewart the maître d'. Unfortunately, neither the police nor the underworld believed that Dante had really gone straight, and his confrontations with both provided much of the action of the show. Played in a tongue-in-cheek manner, *Dante* had more humor than violence. The contrast among the three leads—suave, urbane, ladies' man Willie Dante; Biff, who kept bringing up incidents from their sordid past; and Stewart, whose proper British image did not fit with his encyclopedic knowledge of underworld characters and activities—was the source of much of the humor.

The role of Willie Dante had been played by Dick Powell in a number of episodes of *Four Star Playhouse* during the 1950s.

DARIA (*Cartoon*)
BROADCAST HISTORY:
MTV
30 minutes
Produced: *1997–2002* (69 episodes)
Premiered: *March 3, 1997*
VOICES:
Daria Morgendorffer .... Tracy Grandstaff
Quinn Morgendorffer, Helen Morgendorffer,
Jayne Lane .... Wendy Hoopes
Jake Morgendorffer.............. Julian Rebolledo

Trent Lane .... Alvaro J. Gonzalez
Brittany Taylor .... Janie Mertz
Kevin Thompson, Mr. DeMartino, Mr. O'Neill
.... Marc Thompson

In this spin-off from *Beavis and Butt-head*, the boys' sardonic friend Daria—the brainy girl with the big glasses and the permanent smirk—got a life of her own, at Lawndale High School. But what a life. Her successful parents, Jake and Helen, couldn't figure her out. Her self-esteem teacher couldn't remember her name. And her fellow students, well, they were dummies anyway. What made it all bearable was that Daria viewed such nonsense with wry bemusement. When her parents worried that she had low self-esteem, she merely replied, "I have low esteem for everyone else." Quinn was her dumb, sexy sister, and Jayne Lane her sarcastic friend.

In the series finale (a TV movie called *Is It College Yet?*), Daria failed to get into fancy Ivy League college Bromwell, but was accepted at Raft College; Jayne, after some agonizing, went to Boston Fine Arts College; and Brittany (and the other cheerleaders) wound up at Great Prairie State University.

DARK ADVENTURE, see *ABC Dramatic Shorts—1952–1953*

DARK ANGEL (*Science Fiction*)
FIRST TELECAST: *October 3, 2000*
LAST TELECAST: *June 28, 2002*
BROADCAST HISTORY:
Oct 2000–Jul 2001, FOX Tue 9:00–10:00
Jul 2001–Sep 2001, FOX Fri 9:00–10:00
Sep 2001–Jan 2002, FOX Fri 8:00–9:00
Jan 2002–May 2002, FOX Fri 9:00–10:00
May 2002–Jun 2002, FOX Fri 8:00–9:00
CAST:
Max Guevara (X-452) .... Jessica Alba
Logan Cale (Eyes Only) .... Michael Weatherly
Herbal Thought (2000–2001) .... Alimi Ballard
Kendra Maibaum (2000–2001) ...... Jennifer Blanc
Calvin Simon Theodore "Sketchy" .. Richard Gunn
Normal (Reagan Ronald)........... J. C. Mackenzie
Original Cindy .... Valarie Rae Miller
Donald Michael Lydecker (2000–2001) John Savage
Bling (2000–2001) .... Peter Bryant
Dan Vogelsang (2000)................ Stephen Lee
**Young Max (2000–2001)* .... Geneva Locke
**Det. Matt Sung* .... Byron Mann
**Zack (2000–2001)*............ William Gregory Lee
Director Renfro "Madame X" (2001) ... Nana Visitor
Asha Barlow (2001–2002)............. Ashley Scott
Alec (2001–2002) .... Jensen Ackles
Ames White (2001–2002) .... Martin Cummins
Joshua (2001–2002)................ Kevin Durand
Otto (2001–2002).................... Craig Veroni
Operative (2002) .... Mark Lukyn
*Occasional

Max was a genetically enhanced woman working as a bicycle messenger for Jam Pony X-Press in postapocalyptic Seattle in 2019. Normal was the uptight dispatcher, while others working there were Original Cindy, her best friend; Herbal, the fastest rider at Jam Pony; and Sketchy, who was always looking for get-rich-quick schemes. Ten years earlier Max, along with a number of her genetically enhanced "siblings" (they were classified as X-5s), had escaped from Project Manticore, the government research project that had created them. Logan was a wheelchair-bound underground cyberjournalist and crusader who ran Streaming Freedom Video, an alert service that overrode local TV to inform citizens about corruption and other things the authorities didn't want them to know. When on the air he was "Eyes Only." He befriended Max and helped her find other X-5s like herself. Also seen regularly were Kendra, Max's roommate; Bling, Logan's physical therapist; Dan, the detective Max had hired to help find her siblings; and Lydecker, the evil government agent determined to recapture Max and the other escapees.

In February Logan realized that a transfusion of Max's unique blood was regenerating nerve cells and helping him regain the use of his legs. Soon he was back on his feet, although as his immune system fought the transfusion he lost some of his newfound mobility. Original Cindy got a job telemarketing insurance and quit the messenger service but was kidnapped by people hunting Max. After rescuing her, Max told Cindy what she really was. The following week Cindy moved in with Max, since Kendra was spending most of her time at her boyfriend's place. In May Max's sister gave herself up to save her daughter and Manticore put her in a stasis tank. Max found the lab and broke the tank in which her sister was stored, killing her. Max was captured by Lydecker, but he was being pursued by the even more evil Madame X so he sided with Max and her friends to help them bring down Manticore. They blew up the genetics lab, but Max was shot and almost died. When Zack, a fellow X-5, found her, she appeared to die in his arms before she could tell him she loved him. He was also shot and caught, and the two of them were taken to a Manticore hospital ward where he committed suicide to provide her with a new heart and a chance at new life.

At the start of the 2001–2002 season Max was being trained by Manticore and Madame X was trying hard to break her spirit. Max dug her way out of her cell and into Manticore's basement, where she befriended a transhuman named Joshua, who had traits of both a dog and a human. There were many like him being kept underground. Joshua and Alec, another X-5, helped Max escape, but when she went to Logan's apartment she found out, after kissing him, that Alec had injected her with a genetically targeted virus that would prove fatal to Logan if they had physical contact. Max returned to Manticore, which was on fire, and freed all the X-series and transhumans. Then she got the antidote from Madame X, who died taking a bullet meant for her. Although the antidote cured Logan, the fact that subsequent contact would cause a relapse strained his relationship with Max

Max went back to work for Jam Pony. A new team of agents trying to kill off the X-5s, led by Ames White, captured Max (they were aware that her DNA made her very special), but she was rescued by Alec and four of the other X-5s. Asha, a member of a resistance group, had come to Seattle and was working as Logan's assistant. Although she became attracted to him, she realized he was only interested in Max. Late in the year it became apparent that White was more than just a government agent, and had his own agenda. He had certain powers and was part of a secret group that had been around for centuries. In the spring Joshua's friendship with a blind woman led to his becoming the target of a transgenic manhunt in the city's sewer system. White planted leaks in the media about the human-looking X-5s, resulting in widespread attacks on the "freaks." Joshua sought safety in the shambles of bombed-out Terminal City, where most of the other mutant transgenics were living.

In the series finale there was a hostage situation in which Max, Logan and a number of transgenics were barricaded in the Jam Pony office while White, who had precipitated most of the trouble, was outside with cops and soldiers hoping to kill all the transgenics. After the governor put White in charge of the operation, he and his men stormed the building. The transgenics won the battle and, wearing the soldiers' uniforms, Logan, Alec and others "arrested" Max and a number of other transgenics and took them in a truck to Terminal City. When the police went after them, the transgenics made a stand and the police called a truce. In the last scene, with Terminal City still under siege by the police, Max, who had become the de facto leader of the transgenics, was on a rooftop holding gloved hands with Logan.

DARK JUSTICE (*Legal/Detective Drama*)

FIRST TELECAST: *April 5, 1991*
LAST TELECAST: *April 14, 1994*
BROADCAST HISTORY:

Apr 1991–Aug 1993, CBS Fri 11:30–12:30 A.M.
Aug 1993, CBS Tue 11:30–12:30 A.M.
Sep 1993–Nov 1993, CBS Tue 12:35–1:35 A.M.
Nov 1993–Dec 1993, CBS Thu 12:35–1:35 A.M.
Dec 1993–Feb 1994, CBS Wed 12:35–1:35 A.M.
Mar 1994–Apr 1994, CBS Thu 12:35–1:35 A.M.

CAST:

Judge Nicholas Marshall (1991) .... Ramy Zada
Judge Nicholas Marshall (1992–1993) .... Bruce Abbott
Arnold "Moon" Willis .... Dick O'Neill
Jericho "Gibs" Gibson .... Clayton Prince
Catalana "Cat" Duran (1991) .... Begona Plaza
Maria Marti (1991) .... Viviane Vives
Tara McDonald (1991–1993) .... Carrie-Anne Moss
D.A. Ken Horton .... Kit Kincannon
Kelly Cochran (1992–1993) .... Janet Gunn
Kari-Lynn (1992–1993) .... Joanne Haas
Samantha "Sam" Collins (1993) .... Elisa Heinsohn

Shades of *Hardcastle & McCormick*! Judge Nicholas Marshall was a respected, if rather young, criminal court jurist who had worked his way up from policeman. He had formerly been a D.A. His faith in the system was shaken, however, when his wife and daughter were killed by a car bomb meant for him, and the criminals got off scot-free. Determined to bring them to justice, and to do the same for other criminals, he was forced to release on "legal technicalities," Marshall began living a double life. When he let someone go whom he *knew* to be guilty, he would tell them from the bench that "Justice may be blind but it can see in the dark."

Usually, in their arrogance at beating the rap, they didn't hear. But that night Marshall would take off his glasses, shake loose his pulled-back black hair, don a leather jacket, and roar off on his motorcycle to get the ones who got away. Like Judge Hardcastle he needed help in setting up his stings (in which the guilty would incriminate themselves), so working with him were Moon, a former forger and counterfeiter, Gibs, a special-effects expert, and beautiful Cat. After Cat was killed in a gunfight, Maria, a former Interpol agent, joined the team. Collectively, they were The Night Watchmen. Tara was Judge Marshall's secretary/researcher and Ken Horton, the beleaguered prosecutor whose cases always seemed to collapse due to those pesky legal technicalities.

Although the series was supposed to be set in an unnamed American city, it was actually filmed on location in Barcelona, Spain. When production moved from Spain to L.A. in 1992 Bruce Abbott took over the role of Judge Marshall. Also new to the cast was Kelly Cochran, a private detective who had discovered Nick's dual identity and joined his team. That summer Moon sold his gym and bought a bar where everyone hung out. Kari-Lynn was a waitress working for Moon, and Sam the sexy woman who replaced Tara, who had moved to Boston early in 1993. Sam, who was very attracted to Nick, eventually found out about the Night Watchmen and became an occasional member of the team.

All of the episodes airing during the 1993–1994 season were reruns.

DARK OF NIGHT (*Dramatic Anthology*)

FIRST TELECAST: *October 10, 1952*
LAST TELECAST: *May 1, 1953*
BROADCAST HISTORY:

Oct 1952–May 1953, DUM Fri 8:30–9:00

The stars of this unusual drama series were its locations. *Dark of Night* was telecast live each week from locations all over the New York City area, such as stores, factories, railroad yards, docks, and hospitals. Apparently most of the budget was used in getting the cameras and crew to the locations, since the performers and writers were for the most part unknown. Among the starring locations were Brentano's Book Store on Fifth Avenue, a hangar at Idlewild (now Kennedy) Airport, an old English-style castle in Paterson, New Jersey, the Parke-Bernet art galleries in Manhattan, a Coca-Cola bottling plant, a coffee company (for a comedy about the trials of a coffee taster), the F. & M. Shaeffer Brewing Company, and the American Red Cross Blood Bank. Appropriately, the final telecast was from the DuMont television set factory in East Paterson, New Jersey.

During a two-month period, from mid-November 1952 to mid-January 1953, *Dark of Night* was seen on alternate weeks.

DARK SHADOWS (*Supernatural*)

FIRST TELECAST: *January 13, 1991*
LAST TELECAST: *March 22, 1991*
BROADCAST HISTORY:

Jan 1991, NBC Sun 9:00–11:00
Jan 1991, NBC Mon 9:00–11:00
Jan 1991, NBC Fri 10:00–11:00
Jan 1991–Mar 1991, NBC Fri 9:00–10:00
Mar 1991, NBC Fri 10:00–11:00

CAST:

Barnabas Collins .... Ben Cross
Victoria Winters/Josette .... Joanna Going
Elizabeth Collins Stoddard/Naomi .... Jean Simmons
Roger Collins/Rev. Trask .... Roy Thinnes
David Collins/Daniel (age 8) ... Joseph Gordon-Levitt
Dr. Julia Hoffman/Natalie .... Barbara Steele

Prof. Woodard/Joshua	Stefan Gierasch
Angelique	Lysette Anthony
Willie Loomis/Ben	Jim Fyfe
Mrs. Johnson/Abigail	Julianna McCarthy
Sheriff Patterson	Michael Cavanaugh
Joe Haskell/Peter	Michael T. Weiss
Maggie Evans	Ely Pouget
Sarah Collins	Veronica Lauren
Carolyn Stoddard	Barbara Blackburn

Television's most famous vampire stalked the screen once again, briefly, in this prime-time revival of the daytime serial that ran on ABC from 1966 to 1971. The trouble began when Willie, the lurching, dim-witted groundskeeper at the musty Collins estate in seaside Collinsport, Maine, opened the family crypt during a treasure hunt. Big mistake, Willie. Out crawled Barnabas, the family's 200-year-old vampire, who dusted himself off and began feeding on the local townspeople—particularly the beautiful women—by night. By day he passed himself off as a long-lost relative recently arrived from England.

Barnabas was an unhappy vampire, however, who longed to be rid of his "curse." Dr. Julia, discovering his secret, resolved to help him, producing a serum that reduced his blood lust—a little—and even let him walk in the sunlight and show a reflection in a mirror. Of course she loved him, but a triangle developed because his heart belonged to young family governess Victoria, a dead ringer (get it?) for his beloved Josette, whom he had loved and lost two centuries before.

Elizabeth was the aristocratic matriarch of Collinwood, Roger, her brooding brother, and David was Roger's incorrigible son. After a few episodes, the action began to alternate between Collinsport in the present day and in 1790, when most of the principal cast members seemed to have alter egos (second cast names above). Angelique was the eighteenth-century witch who lusted after Barnabas and caused a great deal of trouble, while Barnabas's modern-day nemesis, Professor Woodard, turned out to be his father two centuries earlier.

The 1991 version of *Dark Shadows* focused almost exclusively on the character of Barnabas (who had not even appeared in the original serial until its second year), with spectacular and scary special effects that had been notably absent from the low-budget original. Perhaps the emphasis on horrific effects rather than on character limited its appeal; perhaps a fad belongs to its own day. Whatever the reason, the revival did not catch on and Barnabas returned to his crypt. He may rise again in another twenty years.

DARK SKIES (*Science Fiction*)

FIRST TELECAST: *September 21, 1996*

LAST TELECAST: *May 31, 1997*

BROADCAST HISTORY:

Sep 1996–Mar 1997, NBC Sat 8:00–9:00
May 1997, NBC Sat 8:00–9:00

CAST:

John Loengard	Eric Close
Kimberly Sayers	Megan Ward
Capt. Frank Bach	J.T. Walsh
Phil Albano	Conor O'Farrell
Dr. Charlie Halligan	Charley Lang
Jim Steele	Tim Kelleher
Juliet (1997)	Jeri Lynn Ryan

How's this for paranoia: according to this series, most of American history for the last fifty years was a gigantic fraud, a cover-up for government efforts to thwart an alien invasion. Eisenhower, Kennedy, Francis Gary Powers, Howard Hughes, and Dr. Timothy Leary were all involved, in one way or another—only Ronald Reagan (as Governor of California) was too clueless to realize what was going on! The series began in 1961, as two idealistic college graduates arrived in Washington to become part of John F. Kennedy's New Frontier. Kim got a job in Jackie Kennedy's office, and John became an aide to a congressman, who assigned him to a cost-cutting investigation that led to the discovery of a super-secret government agency called Majestic-12, run by ruthless Navy Capt. Frank Bach. Its incredible mission: to battle the infiltration of Earth by the alien Hive, while keeping the terrible threat a secret from the American public. The war had begun in Roswell, New Mexico, in 1947. President Truman had met with the aliens to try to arrange a truce (film existed!), but they demanded total surrender, and began taking over human bodies. Anyone could be an alien slave—they had infected people in all walks of life and all levels of government (including the congressman for whom John worked). Soon, John and Kim were on the run, chased by Bach's men to prevent them from squealing, and by the Hive because they knew too much. Albano was Majestic's security chief, and Steele a Hive spy within the project.

John and Kim criss-crossed the country, investigating strange happenings (all based on real events of the '60s), alternately fighting and working with Bach. Kim was infected with the Hive ganglion, eventually having a baby and turning to the alien side. John then partnered with Juliet, a Soviet counter-alien specialist he met in Vietnam (the Vietnam War had been started by Majestic, to increase its funding). Another alien race, the Gray, surfaced to help, before they too were taken over by the powerful Hive.

In the dramatic conclusion John and Juliet infiltrated the Hive mother ship, and rescued his young son from the aliens' clutches. Back on Earth the governing board of Majestic was manipulated to vote on whether to remove Bach. The eleven-member board was split: Hubert Humphrey, Dr. Edward Teller, Dr. Rozinsky, Governor Rockefeller, and Prof. Kissinger voted yes, while William Paley, General Twining, George Bush, Admiral Poindexter, and Allen Dulles voted no. Bobby Kennedy, whose brother had allegedly been killed by Majestic as part of a cover-up, waffled, then cast the deciding vote—yes. Bach was taken away and shot to death by Albano, who was in fact a Hive agent ("We will take over"). Learning that America's last defense against the invading Hive had been neutralized, John nevertheless vowed that the fight would go on.

DARKROOM (*Occult Anthology*)

FIRST TELECAST: *November 27, 1981*

LAST TELECAST: *July 8, 1982*

BROADCAST HISTORY:

Nov 1981–Jan 1982, ABC Fri 9:00–10:00
Jul 1982, ABC Thu 8:00–9:00

HOST:

James Coburn

An imaginative teenager suspects that her sister's handsome boyfriend is a vampire; a Vietnam veteran gives his son an army of toy soldiers, only to have them come to life and attack him; a ruthless young hoodlum finds himself stalked by an eerie black cat; a French rogue tries to escape the guillotine by an ingenious plot to execute the executioner. Stories of suspense and terror characterized this short-run anthology series, which featured different guest stars each week. Among those appearing were Steve Allen, Esther Rolle, Lawrence-Hilton Jacobs, David Carradine, and June Lockhart.

DATE WITH JUDY, A (*Situation Comedy*)

FIRST TELECAST: *July 10, 1952*
LAST TELECAST: *September 30, 1953*
BROADCAST HISTORY:

Jul 1952–Oct 1952, ABC Thu 8:00–8:30
Jan 1953–Sep 1953, ABC Wed 7:30–8:00

CAST:

Judy Foster .... Mary Linn Beller
Melvyn Foster .... John Gibson
Dora Foster .... Flora Campbell
Randolph Foster .... Peter Avramo
Oogie Pringle .... Jimmy Sommers

WRITER:

Aleen Leslie

The trials of a hyperactive bobby-soxer and her harassed parents were the subject of this live situation comedy, which was the TV version of a popular radio series begun in 1941. In addition to Judy and her sedate, middle-class parents, the characters included her pesky younger brother Randolph and her boyfriend Oogie. First seen as a Saturday daytime series on June 2, 1951 (with Pat Crowley as Judy), *A Date with Judy* changed casts and moved to prime time in July 1952.

DATE WITH THE ANGELS (*Situation Comedy*)

FIRST TELECAST: *May 10, 1957*
LAST TELECAST: *January 29, 1958*
BROADCAST HISTORY:

May 1957–Jun 1957, ABC Fri 10:00–10:30
Jul 1957–Dec 1957, ABC Fri 9:30–10:00
Jan 1958, ABC Wed 9:30–10:00

CAST:

Vicki Angel .... Betty White
Gus Angel .... Bill Williams
Wilma Clemson .... Natalie Masters
George Clemson .... Roy Engle
Mrs. Cassie Murphy .... Maudie Prickett
Mr. Murphy (Murph) .... Richard Reeves
Mrs. Drake .... Lillian Bronson
Dr. Gordon .... Gage Clark
Mr. Finley .... Burt Mustin
Roger Finley .... Richard Deacon
Wheeler .... Jimmy Boyd

Betty White starred in this domestic comedy about a new bride and her husband, an insurance salesman. An unusually wide assortment of neighbors and friends passed through the series, usually serving as foils for one of Vicki's or Gus's schemes. Most frequently seen were their friend Murph, the Clemsons, and an erratic neighbor, Mr. Finley. Jimmy Boyd appeared periodically as their teenage nephew Wheeler.

DATELINE EUROPE, see *Foreign Intrigue*

DATELINE NBC (*Newsmagazine*)

FIRST TELECAST: *March 31, 1992*
LAST TELECAST:
BROADCAST HISTORY:

Mar 1992– , NBC Tue 10:00–11:00
Jun 1994–Sep 1994, NBC Thu 10:00–11:00
Sep 1994–Sep 1996, NBC Wed 9:00–10:00
Oct 1994–May 1996, NBC Fri 9:00–10:00
Mar 1996–Apr 1996, NBC Sun 7:00–8:00
May 1996–Jun 1996, NBC Fri 8:00–9:00
Jun 1996–Apr 1998, NBC Sun 7:00–8:00
Jun 1996–Jan 1998, NBC Fri 9:00–10:00
Jun 1997–May 1999, NBC Mon 10:00–11:00
Jan 1998–Feb 1998, NBC Fri 8:00–9:00
Mar 1998–May 1998, NBC Fri 9:00–10:00
Mar 1998–Sep 1998, NBC Sun 8:00–9:00
Apr 1998–Jul 1998, NBC Fri 8:00–9:00
Jul 1998–Aug 1998, NBC Fri 10:00–11:00
Aug 1998–Sep 2000, NBC Wed 8:00–9:00
Sep 1998–Jan 1999, NBC Fri 8:00–9:00
Sep 1998–Oct 1998, NBC Sun 7:00–8:00
Oct 1998–Nov 1998, NBC Sun 8:00–9:00
Nov 1998–Dec 1998, NBC Sun 7:00–8:30
Dec 1998–Jan 1999, NBC Sun 7:00–8:00
Jan 1999–Jun 2002, NBC Fri 9:00–10:00
Apr 1999–Jul 1999, NBC Sun 8:00–9:00
May 1999–Jun 1999, NBC Mon 8:00–9:00
Jun 1999–Dec 1999, NBC Mon 10:00–11:00
Jul 1999–Jan 2000, NBC Sun 7:00–8:00
Jan 2000–Feb 2000, NBC Mon 9:00–10:00
Feb 2000–Jun 2000, NBC Sun 8:00–9:00
Apr 2000–Jul 2000, NBC Mon 8:00–9:00
Jul 2000–Nov 2000, NBC Sun 7:00–8:00
Oct 2000–Nov 2000, NBC Mon 8:00–9:00
Dec 2000–May 2001, NBC Sun 8:00–9:00
Dec 2000–May 2001, NBC Mon 9:00–10:00
Jun 2001–Nov 2001, NBC Sun 7:00–8:00
Jul 2001– , NBC Mon 10:00–11:00
Jan 2002–Feb 2002, NBC Sun 8:00–9:00
Jun 2002–Jul 2002, NBC Sun 7:00–8:00
Jun 2002–Aug 2002, NBC Fri 8:00–10:00
Jul 2002–Aug 2002, NBC Sun 7:00–9:00
Aug 2002– , NBC Sun 7:00–8:00
Aug 2002–Sep 2002, NBC Fri 8:00–9:00
Sep 2002– , NBC Fri 9:00–10:00
Mar 2003–May 2003, NBC Wed 8:00–9:00
May 2003–Jun 2003, NBC Fri 8:00–9:00

ANCHORS:

Jane Pauley (1992–2003)
Stone Phillips

"CONTRIBUTING ANCHORS"

Tom Brokaw (1994–)
Katie Couric (1994–)
Bryant Gumbel (1994–1997)
Maria Shriver (1994–)

REGULAR CORRESPONDENTS:

Dr. Bob Arnot (1998–)
Robert Bazelle (2002–)
Mike Boettcher (1995–1996)
Les Cannon (1995–)
Victoria Corderi (1995–)
Bob Costas (1997–2000)
Ann Curry (1996–2000, 2002–)
Faith Daniels (1993–1995)
Steve Daniels (1998–1999)
Dawn Fratangelo (1996–)
Ed Gordon (1996–2000)
Michele Gillen (1992–1993)
David Gregory (1999–)
Chris Hansen (1995–)

John Hockenberry (1996–)
Sarah James (1996–)
Arthur Kent (1992)
Hoda Kotbe (1998–)
John Larson (1994–)
Margaret Larson (1998–)
Edie Magnus (1999–)
Josh Mankiewicz (1996–)
Bob McKeown (1995–)
Keith Morrison (1995–)
Dennis Murphy (1994–)
Deborah Roberts (1992–1995)
Brian Ross (1992–1994)
Lisa Rudolph (1994–)
Jon Scott (1995–1996)
Rob Stafford (1997–)
Mike Taibbi (1997–)
Lea Thompson (1995–)
Elizabeth Vargas (1995–1996)

After years of futile attempts to compete with the top-rated newsmagazines on CBS and ABC by trying something different, NBC finally succeeded with this carbon copy of its competitors' shows. Stories included the usual range of government and business exposés, with an unusually high quotient of tabloid sensationalism: a piece on selling machine tools to Iraq was intercut with shots of grieving parents of dead U.S. soldiers, one on the Weather Service dwelled on a woman whose husband had been killed by a freak storm, and one on prescription mixups seemed preoccupied with exploiting the grief of parents of dead children. Jailhouse interviews with the likes of Mike Tyson, Amy Fisher, and Jeffrey Dahmer tended to overshadow more substantive reports, such as an exposé of deceptive practices by the Wal-Mart chain, which won several awards.

Dateline created its own scandal with a phony exposé of the crashworthiness of certain types of General Motors trucks in November 1992. It turned out that the producers had rigged a crash to show a dramatic explosion. General Motors threatened to sue, and in the aftermath the president of NBC News resigned.

Once *Dateline* became successful in its original Tuesday night time slot, NBC began scheduling additional hours on other nights, until it was airing on as many as five nights per week. This led to a considerable increase in the number of correspondents, as indicated above.

DATING GAME, THE (*Audience Participation*)
FIRST TELECAST: *October 6, 1966*
LAST TELECAST: *January 17, 1970*
BROADCAST HISTORY:
Oct 1966–Jan 1967, ABC Thu 8:30–9:00
Jan 1967–Jan 1970, ABC Sat 7:30–8:00
HOST:
Jim Lange
PRODUCER:
Chuck Barris

The premise of *The Dating Game* was to take one young person plus three "candidates" of the opposite sex and arrange a date. There were two rounds in each show, one in which a girl asked questions of three guys, and one in which a guy asked questions of three girls. The questioner could not see the three candidates, which eliminated appearance as a consideration. At the end of each round the questioner picked the date he or she thought would be most interesting, and the newly matched pair were then sent off on a night on the town or an expense-paid trip to some exotic fun spot. (Follow-up reports in later months told how many of these first dates blossomed into romance and marriage.) The questions, which were prepared by the show's staff, were generally of the titillating variety.

Originally a daytime program on ABC, *The Dating Game* came to prime time as a stop-gap replacement for *The Tammy Grimes Show*, the first casualty of the 1966–1967 season. It was popular enough to remain in the nighttime lineup for more than three years, after which it continued in daytime only. The daytime edition of *The Dating Game* ran on ABC from December 1965 to July 1973. It then turned up in a number of syndicated versions. Jim Lange hosted the first two, during the 1973–1974 season and from 1977–1980. In the fall of 1986 Elaine Joyce served as hostess of *The New Dating Game*. A year later it had a new name, *The All New Dating Game*; a new host, Jeff MacGregor; and a modified format. In addition to the quiz segments, some of the daters returned together to tell all about their date, in a manner similar to the highly successful syndicated daytime series *Love Connection*. The modified format didn't help, however, and the series faded from view at the end of the 1988–1989 season.

In the fall of 1996 another syndicated version of *The Dating Game* surfaced, this time hosted by Brad Sherwood. The format had been changed somewhat—potential dates were scored on looks and personality, with the final choice based on how important each of these factors was to the chooser. Sherwood was replaced by Chuck Woolery in the fall of 1997. Woolery remained with the show until it was canceled in 2000.

For the companion program by the same producers, which ran in the adjacent time slot on Saturday night, see *The Newlywed Game*.

DAVE GARROWAY SHOW, THE, see *Garroway at Large*

DAVE KING SHOW, THE, see *Kraft Music Hall Presents the Dave King Show*

DAVE THOMAS COMEDY SHOW, THE (*Comedy Variety*)
FIRST TELECAST: *May 28, 1990*
LAST TELECAST: *June 25, 1990*
BROADCAST HISTORY:
May 1990–Jun 1990, CBS Mon 10:30–11:00
HOST:
Dave Thomas
REGULARS:
Anson Downes
Julie Fulton
Teresa Ganzel
Don Lake
Fran Ryan
David Wiley

Summer variety series starring former *SCTV* writer and performer Dave Thomas. Each episode consisted of a number of short comedy sketches featuring Mr. Thomas, his comedy troupe, and weekly guest stars. The guest stars were mostly comedians with previous experience on *SCTV* and *Saturday Night Live*—John Candy, Dan Aykroyd, Chevy Chase, Martin Short, and Catherine O'Hara.

DAVE'S WORLD (*Situation Comedy*)
FIRST TELECAST: *September 20, 1993*
LAST TELECAST: *July 18, 1997*
BROADCAST HISTORY:
Sep 1993–Apr 1994, CBS Mon 8:30–9:00
Apr 1994–Jun 1994, CBS Mon 8:00–8:30
Jul 1994–Sep 1995, CBS Mon 8:30–9:00
Aug 1995–Nov 1995, CBS Wed 8:30–9:00
Nov 1995–Apr 1996, CBS Wed 8:00–8:30
Apr 1996–Jun 1996, CBS Mon 8:30–9:00
Jul 1996, CBS Wed 8:00–8:30
Aug 1996, CBS Wed 8:30–9:00
Sep 1996–Mar 1997, CBS Fri 8:00–8:30
Apr 1997–May 1997, CBS Wed 8:30–9:00
Jun 1997–Jul 1997, CBS Fri 8:00–8:30
Jul 1997, CBS Fri 8:00–9:00
CAST:
Dave Barry .... Harry Anderson
Beth Barry .... DeLane Matthews
Sheldon Baylor .... Meshach Taylor
Kenny Beckett .... Shadoe Stevens
Mia .... J. C. Wendel
Tommy Barry (age 8) .... Zane Carney
Willie Barry (5) .... Andrew Ducote
Eric (1994–1997) .... Patrick Warburton
Carly Baylor (1993) .... Shannon Sharp
Carly Baylor (1994–1995) .... Angell Conwell
Julie (1994–1995) .... Tammy Lauren
THEME:
"You May Be Right," by Billy Joel, performed by Southside Johnny

Dave Barry was a syndicated newspaper columnist living in Miami with his perky, supportive wife, Beth, and their two young sons, Tommy and Willie. Dave was a kind of whimsical, overgrown kid who didn't quite understand how to deal with children, technology, changing social values, or the world of the nineties. His off-center reactions to things and observations about the absurdities of life were all grist for his column in the Miami *Record-Dispatch*, called "Barry's World." Since Dave worked at home, Beth's decision to go back to teaching should not have created problems, but like everything else in Dave's world, the adjustment did not go smoothly. Dave had two close friends, his self-centered womanizing editor, Kenny, who was incapable of sustaining a meaningful relationship, and his college buddy and neighbor Shel, a recently divorced plastic surgeon with a cute young daughter, Carly. Others seen were Kenny's secretary, Mia, with more ambition than talent; Mia's boyfriend, Eric, a handyman with limited skills; and Beth's sister, Julie, a recent divorcée. Earnest, a bloodhound, was the Barry family dog.

In the fall of 1995, Julie threw herself at Eric, and when Mia saw them together, she dumped him. In the spring, with Julie having departed, Mia and Eric reconciled and he proposed to her. She moved in with him and they almost got married, but in December they broke up again. Kenny was fired when it was discovered he'd had an affair with the publisher's wife, and after a difficult job search, he found one recording books-on-tape. In the spring of 1997, Shel discovered that his accountant had skipped the country with all his money. He had a tough time adjusting to a more spartan lifestyle.

Adapted from the Pulitzer Prize–winning columns of the real Dave Barry.

DAVID BRINKLEY'S JOURNAL (*Documentary*)
FIRST TELECAST: *October 11, 1961*
LAST TELECAST: *August 26, 1963*
BROADCAST HISTORY:
Oct 1961–Sep 1962, NBC Wed 10:30–11:00
Oct 1962–Aug 1963, NBC Mon 10:00–10:30
COMMENTATOR:
David Brinkley

David Brinkley, who had been the co-anchor of NBC's nightly *Huntley-Brinkley Report* since 1956, hosted his own prime-time documentary series in the early 1960s. From one to three stories were examined each week, each of them treated from Brinkley's own unique perspective. His caustic wit and incisive observations gave the program a very personal flavor, quite different from the run of TV documentaries. The subject matter ranged from light pieces on professional wrestler Antonino Rocca, the birth of a Broadway musical, and after-dinner speeches by political figures, to probing evaluations of domestic and foreign political issues.

The critical response to *David Brinkley's Journal* was positive, and the program won Emmy Awards in both 1962 and 1963 as the best public-affairs series on television. However, viewership was low and the series survived as a weekly entry for only two seasons. It was later seen on an occasional basis, until 1965.

DAVID CASSIDY—MAN UNDERCOVER (*Police Drama*)
FIRST TELECAST: *November 2, 1978*
LAST TELECAST: *August 2, 1979*
BROADCAST HISTORY:
Nov 1978–Jan 1979, NBC Thu 10:00–11:00
Jul 1979–Aug 1979, NBC Thu 10:00–11:00
CAST:
Officer Dan Shay .... David Cassidy
Joanne Shay .... Wendy Rastatter
Cindy Shay .... Elizabeth Reddin
Sgt. Walt Abrams .... Simon Oakland
Officer T. J. Epps .... Ray Vitte
Officer Paul Sanchez .... Michael A. Salcido

Dan Shay was a policeman in his late 20s working as part of an undercover team headed by Sgt. Abrams. As an undercover cop, Dan generally played the youth angle, infiltrating a gang of young bank robbers, posing as a college student to crack an illegal adoption racket, pretending to be a drug addict to nail a doctor selling narcotics prescriptions. Dan's wife Joanne worried constantly, but kept a stiff upper lip for the sake of their little girl, Cindy. The setting for this series, as with most televised police shows over the years, was Los Angeles.

DAVID FROST REVUE, THE (*Comedy*)
BROADCAST HISTORY:
Syndicated only
30 minutes
Produced: *1971–1973* (52 episodes)
Released: *Fall 1971*
REGULARS:
David Frost
Marcia Rodd
Jack Gilford
Jim Catusi
George S. Irving
Lynn Lipton

Cleavon Little
Whitney Blake

In this program of satire, David Frost returned to the format that had made him famous. Each week's skits concentrated on a different subject, such as sports, medicine, women's lib, the telephone company, or TV talk shows. There were barbs and blackouts, but little of the topical bite with which Frost had made his name. Celebrity guests included Alan Alda, Lucille Ball, Jack Klugman, and Arte Johnson.

DAVID FROST SHOW, THE (*Talk*)

BROADCAST HISTORY:
Syndicated only
90 minutes
Produced: *1969–1972*
Released: *Summer 1969*

REGULARS:
David Frost
Billy Taylor Orchestra

David Frost, the *enfant terrible* of British and American political satire in the 1960s (see *That Was The Week That Was*), here tried to become a celebrity talk-show host in the Merv Griffin–Johnny Carson mold. The program originated in New York and ran 60 to 90 minutes, depending on the local station. Guests ranged across the map, and included the likes of Paul Newman, Gore Vidal, Billy Graham, Averill Harriman, and Dr. Timothy Leary, musicians Pete Seeger, James Brown, Tex Ritter, and the Rolling Stones, actors Burt Reynolds, Shirley MacLaine, and Elizabeth Taylor, comics Rich Little and Henny Youngman, *et al.* A minor tempest raged among critics as to whether Frost had "sold out," but all remarked on his singular interviewing style: hunched forward, staring at the guest with rapt attention, like a "bemused and slightly undernourished bird of prey transfixed by a being it finds too fascinating to attack" (in the words of Peter Heller). He seemed constantly enthralled by everyone, regularly exclaiming, "Marvelous! Smashing! Terrific! It's been a *joy* having you here!"

The program ran for three years, while Frost jetted back and forth across the Atlantic (he was simultaneously hosting a weekly variety show in England). Produced by the Westinghouse station group, *The David Frost Show* got its start when Merv Griffin left afternoon and evening syndication for a late-night network run on CBS; Frost filled the gap on many stations. When Griffin returned to local syndication in 1972, Frost folded.

DAVID NIVEN SHOW, THE (*Dramatic Anthology*)

FIRST TELECAST: *April 7, 1959*
LAST TELECAST: *September 15, 1959*
BROADCAST HISTORY:
Apr 1959–Sep 1959, NBC Tue 10:00–10:30

HOST:
David Niven

David Niven appeared before each episode of this summer anthology series to introduce the drama being presented, and personally starred in one of the episodes.

DAVID STEINBERG SHOW, THE (*Comedy/Variety*)

FIRST TELECAST: *July 19, 1972*
LAST TELECAST: *August 16, 1972*
BROADCAST HISTORY:
Jul 1972–Aug 1972, CBS Wed 8:00–9:00

REGULAR:
David Steinberg

Controversial comedian David Steinberg was referred to in *TV Guide* as "offbeat, racy, outrageous and establishment-baiting—all of which makes him a particular favorite of the young and disenchanted." In 1972 he starred in his own summer comedy series, introducing two or three guest stars each week and performing with them.

DAVID SUSSKIND SHOW, THE (*Talk*)

BROADCAST HISTORY:
Syndicated only
2 hours
Produced: *1958–1987*
Released: *1961*

HOST:
David Susskind

David Susskind talked on television for a very long time. An aggressive former talent agent and Broadway and TV producer (responsible for many of the top TV plays of the 1950s), he began the chatter in October 1958 with a local show in New York. It was called *Open End*, because it started at 11 P.M. and ran until the subject—or participants—were exhausted (which led unkind critics to dub it "Open Mouth"). The guests were literate, provocative, and often controversial. In perhaps his most celebrated confrontation, Susskind took on Nikita Khrushchev during the latter's visit to the U.S. in 1960; the leader of the Communist world made mincemeat of him.

Over the years, topics ranged across all sorts of social problems (race relations, the draft, organized crime, etc.) as well as less weighty subjects such as clairvoyants, sex-change operations, and testing your I.Q. In the early 1960s the program was mercifully cut to two hours (though the name remained *Open End* for several years more), and went into national syndication. In later years it was seen largely on PBS stations, although it was on commercial channels in some cities.

Mr. Susskind passed away in 1987.

DAVIS RULES (*Situation Comedy*)

FIRST TELECAST: *January 27, 1991*
LAST TELECAST: *July 15, 1992*
BROADCAST HISTORY:
Jan 1991, ABC Sun 10:15–10:45
Jan 1991–Apr 1991, ABC Tue 8:30–9:00
Jul 1991, ABC Tue 8:30–9:00
Aug 1991–Sep 1991, ABC Wed 9:30–10:00
Jan 1992–Apr 1992, CBS Wed 8:00–8:30
Apr 1992–May 1992, CBS Wed 8:30–9:00
May 1992–Jun 1992, CBS Wed 8:00–8:30
Jul 1992, CBS Wed 8:30–9:00

CAST:
Dwight Davis .... Randy Quaid
Gunny Davis .... Jonathan Winters
Robbie Davis (1991) .... Trevor Bullock
Charlie Davis .... Luke Edwards
Ben Davis .... Nathan Watt
Cosmo Yeargin (1991) .... Patti Clarkson
Rigo Cordona (1991) .... Rigoberto Jiminez
Mrs. Elaine Yamagami .... Tamayo Otsuki

Mrs. Rush .... Debra Mooney
Ms. Higgins (1991) .... Debra Jo Rush
Skinner Buckley (1992) .... Vonni Ribisi
Gwen Davis (1992) .... Bonnie Hunt

Newly appointed grammar school principal Dwight Davis had disciplinary problems around the clock in this light comedy—at school with the kids, and at home as a single dad with three rambunctious boys, Robbie (the oldest), Charlie, and Ben (the youngest). The biggest kid of all, however, was Dwight's eccentric father Gunny, who lived with them and regularly dispensed outlandish advice. They all cheered Dwight on in his developing relationship with Cosmo, an intelligent, offbeat new teacher at his school. Rigo was Robbie's teenage pal.

When *Davis Rules* moved to CBS in 1992 there were a number of changes in the cast. Robbie was away at college, Cosmo had left Seattle to become a nun, and Dwight's sister Gwen had moved in to help raise the family. Also living with the Davises was Skinner Buckley, the 15-year-old son of two of Dwight's college friends who were away doing research in South America.

DAWSON'S CREEK (*Drama*)

FIRST TELECAST: *January 20, 1998*
LAST TELECAST: *May 28, 2003*
BROADCAST HISTORY:

Jan 1998–May 1998, WB Tue 9:00–10:00
Jul 1998–Sep 1998, WB Tue 9:00–10:00
Sep 1998–Jul 2001, WB Wed 8:00–9:00
Sep 2001–Jun 2002, WB Wed 8:00–9:00
May 2002–Jun 2002, WB Wed 9:00–10:00
Oct 2002–May 2003, WB Wed 8:00–9:00

CAST:

Dawson Leery .... James Van Der Beek
Josephine "Joey" Potter .... Katie Holmes
Pacey Witter .... Joshua Jackson
Jennifer "Jen" Lindley .... Michelle Williams
Gayle Leery (1998–2002) ... Mary-Margaret Humes
Mitch Leery (1998–2001) .... John Wesley Shipp
Evelyn "Grams" Ryan .... Mary Beth Peil
**Bessie Potter (1998–2002)* .... Nina Repeta
Miss Tamara Jacobs (1998) .... Leann Hunley
Cliff Elliott (1998) .... Scott Foley
Andie McPhee (1998–2001) ..... Meredith Monroe
Jack McPhee .... Kerr Smith
Abby Morgan (1998–1999) .... Monica Keena
Chris Wolfe (1998–1999) .... Jason Behr
**Bodie Wells (1998, 2000–2002)* .... Obi Ndefo
**Doug Witter* .... Dylan Neal
**Mike Potter (1998–1999)* .... Gareth Williams
**Mr. McPhee (1999–2000)* .... David Dukes
**Principal Green (1999–2000)* ..... Obba Babatunde
Henry Parker (1999–2000) .... Michael Pitt
Gretchen Witter (2000–2001) ..... Sasha Alexander
Drew Valentine (2000–2001) ...... Mark Matkevich
Mrs. Valentine (2000–2001) ...... Carolyn Hennesy
Arthur Brooks (2000–2001) .... Harve Presnell
**Toby (2000–2001)* .... David Monahan
Prof. David Wilder (2001–2002) .... Ken Marino
Audrey Liddell (2001–2003) .... Busy Philipps
Charlie Todd (2001–2002) ... Chad Michael Murray
Todd Carr (2001–2003) .... Hal Ozsan
Karen Torres (2001) .... Lourdes Benedicto
Danny Brecher (2001–2002) .... Ian Kahn
Oliver Chirkchick (2001–2002) ..... Jordan Bridges
Eric (2001–2002) .... Ryan Bittle
Eddie Dooling (2002–2003) .... Oliver Hudson
CJ (2002–2003) .... Jensen Ackles
Emma Jones (2002–2003) .... Megan Gray
Rich Rinaldi (2002–2003) .... Dana Ashbrook
Prof. Greg Hetson (2002–2003) ..... Roger Howarth
Prof. Mark Freeman (2002) ...... Sebastian Spence
Natasha Kelly (2002–2003) .... Bianca Kajlich
**Harley Hetson (2002–2003)* .... Mika Boorem
**David (2002–2003)* .... Greg Rikaart

*Occasional

THEME:

Written and performed by Paula Cole

Dawson, Joey, Pacey, and Jen were four 15-year-old friends in their sophomore year at Capeside High School in coastal Massachusetts in this overheated teen soap opera. Dawson, the show's intense, brooding heartthrob, loved movies and was determined to become a filmmaker (he worshiped Steven Spielberg). His best buddy since childhood was Joey, a tomboy who was emerging into womanhood, and who was beginning to view their weekly sleepovers in a whole new light. Joey lived with her sister, Bessie, because her dad was in jail for selling marijuana and her mother had died from cancer. Jen, the sexy blonde with the promiscuous past, had just moved from New York to help her grandmother, Evelyn, nurse her ailing grandfather (who died in September), and began dating Dawson. Early on, Pacey, a mediocre student with an active libido, had an affair with his sexy English teacher, Miss Jacobs, who left town to avoid a scandal.

In fact, sex was on pretty much everyone's mind. This was the kind of series where teens would show their anguish with lines like, "Repressing our desire can only make it more powerful!" (Typical teen to teacher dialogue: "You blew it, lady, 'cause I'm the best sex you'll never have".)

When Dawson's mother Gayle, a local TV news anchor, told her husband Mitch that she had had an affair, their "perfect" marriage began to fracture. Later they would file for divorce, which Dawson didn't handle well at all. Meanwhile, unmarried Bessie gave birth to a boy, Alex, in the Leery living room. Dawson and Jen broke up, and by the end of the first season Dawson's feelings toward Joey had become more than platonic. In the season finale they shared their first passionate kiss, and that fall started to date. They later broke up because Joey had problems dealing with Dawson's unwavering conviction that they were destined to be together. He saw everything in black-and-white, while her world was filled with shades of gray.

New at school in Fall 1998 were Abby, a manipulative bitch who tried to befriend Jen, and Andie and her brother Jack, who had recently arrived from Rhode Island. None of the three newcomers fared very well. While Abby and Jen were out drinking, Abby fell off a bridge and drowned. Pacey dated Andie and they got pretty serious, while Jack, her brother, who dated Joey for a time, realized he was gay. His admission was a source of great embarrassment. Andie later suffered a breakdown, and returned to Providence with her dad, leaving Jack alone. Dawson, mooning over Joey, made a film about his relationship with her. In February, Mitch lost the restaurant he had been running, and a month later took a job as an English teacher at Capeside High—with Dawson in one of his classes.

Dawson's mom, Gayle, got a job offer from a TV station in Philadelphia, allowing Mitch to move back into the house with Dawson.

At the start of the 1999–2000 season Andie, recovered from her illness, returned, but Jack continued to live with Jen and her grandmother. Mitch, now the football coach, convinced Jack to play for the team—he was a talented pass receiver. Dawson's mother returned from Philadelphia after she lost the anchor job and opened a restaurant, Leary's Fresh Fish, hiring Mitch as general manager and Jen as the hostess. In January Joey and Bessie reopened their restaurant as the Potter Bed and Breakfast and Jack moved back home with Andie and their dad. Jen began dating Henry, a freshman who was in love with her, and later Pacey started dating Joey. This created a rift between him and a jealous Dawson. They fought over her, much to her consternation, but Dawson eventually told her to go to Pacey. Meanwhile, Mitch and Gayle got back together but Jen and Henry, after a falling-out at the junior prom, broke up. In the season finale Mitch and Gayle were remarried, Jen made up with Henry, who was on his way to football camp, and Joey decided to spend the summer sailing with Pacey.

They returned that fall to start their senior year at Capeside High. Pacey's older sister Gretchen, who had decided to take time off from college, moved in with their brother, Doug, and took a job as a waitress at Gayle's restaurant. Dawson and Jen had dated over the summer, and Henry had transferred to a new school. Pacey, whose academic problems threatened his graduating with their class, asked Joey to help him get through the year. Meanwhile, after Dawson had saved Pacey and Jen from a storm that destroyed Pacey's boat, they started to rebuild their friendship. Early in November Gayle found out she was pregnant (in the spring she had a daughter, Lily) and Andie was accepted to Harvard. She left to spend the rest of the school year with an aunt in Italy because she already had enough credits to graduate on time. Dawson made a documentary film about the life of Arthur Brooks, a cranky retired filmmaker for whom he had done odd jobs, and, after the old man succumbed to cancer in February, was surprised by a bequest Brooks had made to him. Joey was accepted to Worthington College and Dawson, to U.S.C. film school. After the prom Pacey, feeling inadequate, broke up with Joey—but they remained friends—and Gretchen, who had been dating Dawson, went back to school. Grams sold her home to pay for Jen's tuition, and Jen convinced her to move to Boston to be close to her. Pacey took a summer job as a boat hand on a yacht, and Dawson was off to a L.A. for a summer film program at U.S.C.

In the fall of 2001 Joey was struggling with a writing class taught by Prof. Wilder and adjusting to life with Audrey, her uninhibited new roommate from Beverly Hills. Dawson was in L.A. where his film internship turned into a disaster when Todd, the egotistical director, fired him. Jen and Jack were attending Boston Bay College while Pacey, who was living on his boat, got a job at Civilization, a trendy Boston restaurant where he befriended Karen, a waitress who was having an affair with Danny, Civilization's married chef. Jen was dating Charlie, a moody bass player, and hosting a talk show on the college radio station. Dawson returned to Capeside to tell his folks he was dropping out of U.S.C. and suffered severe depression when Mitch was killed in a car accident. He stayed in Boston because he was seeing a psychiatrist, began an affair with Jen and later enrolled in a local film school. In January Pacey was promoted to assistant chef at Civilization and Audrey took a job as a waitress there. Jack moved into his fraternity house but has problems because some of the brothers were uncomfortable living with someone who was gay. Pacey and Audrey got involved, as did Joey and Prof. Wilder. In April Joey went out with Charlie, despite his tendency to act like a sexual slimeball, but they broke up when his band went on tour and he dropped out of school. Jack, struggling to keep from flunking out, got help from Eric, a former frat brother who had concluded that he, too, was gay. As the school year drew to a close Pacey and Audrey drove cross-country to her home in L.A., and Joey and Dawson both admitted they still loved each other.

The last season began with Dawson returning to Boston after spending the summer as an assistant film director in L.A. He was working on Todd's horror film, *Wicked Dead*, which was doing location shooting in Boston, and having an affair with its star, Natasha. Audrey and Pacey were also back. He got a sales job with a brokerage firm working for wheeler-dealer Rich and, with Jack, convinced Emma, who ran a local bar, to take them in as her new roommates. Jen was attracted to CJ, a peer counselor at school, and Joey began a relationship with Eddie, a bartender at the restaurant where she worked. Audrey became the lead singer in Emma's punk band "Hell's Bells." At Halloween Audrey broke up with Pacey because he was more involved with his job than with her, and she developed a drinking problem.

In January Dawson was back in L.A., directing reshoots of *Wicked Dead* after Todd refused to do it, to salvage the film for the production company. Despite the financial rewards, Pacey was having misgivings about the way he was making a living, while Audrey's drinking got worse. Eddie drove to L.A. to join a writers' workshop and took Joey and Audrey, who was going into alcohol rehab, with him. In April Pacey and Joey almost rekindled their romance but Eddie returned from L.A. and she realized she really loved him—for now. With Grams' prodding Jen finally went out with CJ but, just as things started to blossom, Jen was devastated when her grandmother told her she had breast cancer. Despite his misgivings, Pacey agreed to invest Dawson's life savings to refinance his semiautobiographical film project, but the investment went bad. Sober Audrey returned from L.A., Eddie broke up with Joey and Jen and Jack moved to New York with Grams. Back in Capeside Joey got the gang to help Dawson start production on his film, serving as both actors and crew. She also worked on rebuilding his relationship with Pacey, who helped out by raising money for the film from local merchants.

The *Dawson's Creek* series finale took place five years later as everyone returned to Capeside for Gayle's wedding. Jack was teaching English at Capeside High and in love with Pacey's brother, Doug, the chief of police, who was afraid to come out of the closet, and Pacey, who had also moved back home, ran the new Ice House restaurant. Dawson was living in L.A. where he was producing an autobiographical

TV series, *The Creek,* while Joey was a book editor in New York and Jen was a single mother living with Grams and managing a Soho art gallery. While visiting Capeside Jen died from a congenital heart problem, but not before arranging for Jack to adopt her infant daughter, Amy. In the end the friendship/romantic triangle that had provided the centerpiece of the series—Dawson, Pacey and Joey—survived. She was in love with both Dawson, who would always be her soulmate, and Pacey, who moved to New York to be with her.

DAY BY DAY (*Situation Comedy*)
FIRST TELECAST: *February 29, 1988*
LAST TELECAST: *June 25, 1989*
BROADCAST HISTORY:
Feb 1988, NBC Mon 8:30–9:00
Mar 1988, NBC Thu 8:30–9:00
Mar 1988–Jun 1989, NBC Sun 8:30–9:00 (OS)
CAST:
Brian Harper .... Douglas Sheehan
Kate Harper.......................... Linda Kelsey
Ross Harper .... Christopher Daniel ("C.B.") Barnes
Eileen Swift .... Julia Louis-Dreyfus
Kristin Carlson........... Courtney Thorne-Smith
Molly.. Thora
Blake............................... Garrett Taylor
Justin O'Donnell .... Chris Finefrock
Sammy Schrom .... Robert Chavez
Buddy Schrom (1988) .... Mark Gordon
Stiv Miltman....................... Gino de Mauro
Emily Harper .... Catherine & Mary Donahue
THEME:
"Day By Day," by Sammy Cahn, Axel Stordahl, and Paul Weston (1945 popular song), sung by Clydine Jackson

One of the wave of "yuppie comedies" that swept TV in the late '80s, *Day By Day* was about a couple of suburban overachievers who dropped out and opened a day-care center in their home. Why? Well, with the arrival of their second child, stockbroker Brian and his wife Kate, a lawyer, decided that they were missing their children's best years and wanted to be at home. Gangly teenager Ross, who enjoyed his independence and girl chasing, was not sure that was such a good idea—especially the "quality time" his underfoot dad now wanted to spend with him. But there were compensations, notably the sexy 19-year-old assistant Kristin whom his parents had hired to help run the center.

Eileen, Brian's single and sarcastic former business associate, could not understand the Harpers' decision at all (observing the children in organized activities: "Oh, you've got them to march around in a circle. Are you going to enter them in a show?"). Numerous cute kids were seen, including super-smart little Molly, who the Harpers hoped would not turn out as they almost had.

DAY DREAMING WITH LARAINE DAY
(*Interviews/Variety*)
FIRST TELECAST: *May 17, 1951*
LAST TELECAST: *July 19, 1951*
BROADCAST HISTORY:
May 1951–Jul 1951, ABC Thu 7:15–7:30
HOSTESS:
Laraine Day

Celebrity interviews, songs, and Broadway and Hollywood gossip with actress Laraine Day were the features of this program. Among other things, Miss Day asked her guests to describe alternative careers they might prefer to have chosen. A similar series with Miss Day ran concurrently on Saturday afternoons.

DAY IN COURT, see *Accused*

DAY ONE (*Newsmagazine*)
FIRST TELECAST: *March 7, 1993*
LAST TELECAST: *September 21, 1995*
BROADCAST HISTORY:
Mar 1993–May 1993, ABC Sun 8:00–9:00
Jun 1993–Jul 1994, ABC Mon 8:00–9:00
Jan 1995–Sep 1995, ABC Thu 10:00–11:00
ANCHOR:
Forrest Sawyer
REGULAR CORRESPONDENTS:
John Hockenberry
Michel McQueen
John McKenzie
Sheila MacVicar (1993–1994)
Jay Schadler (1993–1994)
Lloyd Kramer (1993–1994)
Robert Krulwich (1994–1995)
Brian Ross (1994–1995)

A tabloid newsmagazine full of screaming headlines and sensational exposés. Among them: a man deliberately infects his girlfriends with AIDS! Voodoo still being practiced in Haiti! Sexual abuse in a Georgia women's prison! Black-market babies! Most of the stories were told in stark black-and-white tones, but at least the show had the sense of humor to include in its first telecast a Jeff Greenfield piece on "TV's Greatest Flops"—on the assumption, presumably, that this would not be one of them.

DAYS AND NIGHTS OF MOLLY DODD, THE
(*Comedy/Drama*)
FIRST TELECAST: *May 21, 1987*
LAST TELECAST: *June 29, 1988*
BROADCAST HISTORY:
May 1987–Aug 1987, NBC Thu 9:30–10:00
Mar 1988–Apr 1988, NBC Thu 9:30–10:00
May 1988–Jun 1988, NBC Wed 9:00–9:30
Jun 1988, NBC Wed 9:30–10:00
(New episodes on Lifetime cable network from 1989–1991)
CAST:
Molly Dodd .... Blair Brown
Florence Bickford............. Allyn Ann McLerie
Fred Dodd............... William Converse-Roberts
Mamie Grolnick (1987–1988) .... Sandy Faison
Davey McQuinn...................... James Greene
**Nina Shapiro*.................. Maureen Anderman
Dennis Widmer (1987–1988)......... Victor Garber
**Moss Goodman (1988–1990)* ..... David Strathairn
**Nick Donatello*............................ Jay Tarses
Det. Nathaniel Hawthorne (1989–1991)
.... Richard Lawson
Arthur Feldman (1989–1991)....... George Gaynes
Sara Reddick (1989–1990) ...... Jennifer Van Dyck
Brice (1989–1991) .... Drew McVety
Ron Luchesse (1990–1991)........... John Pankow
Ramona Luchesse (1990–1991).. J. Smith-Cameron
Jimmy McQuinn (1990–1991)....... James Gleason

Dr. Kim Rosenthal (1990) .... Mia Korf
* Occasional

Critics loved this mellow, reality-based "dramedy" (combination drama and comedy) about the life and times of an attractive divorced woman in her mid-30s, living in New York City. Molly spent a good deal of time musing about herself—her love life, her goals, her ever-changing career, her apartment, her . . . you get the idea. Molly changed jobs rather often. First she was a singer with Fred Dodd's band, then she sold real estate (Dennis was her boss), and then worked at a Greenwich Village bookstore (where Moss was the boss). All of her bosses were also sometime love interests. Fred was her irresponsible ex-husband, a jazz saxophone player, who kept hanging around; Florence her worrywart mother; Mamie her unhappily married sister; Davey the philosophical elevator operator; and Nina her best friend.

When NBC canceled *The Days and Nights of Molly Dodd*, the Lifetime cable network telecast reruns and, the following year, began airing newly produced episodes. In 1989 Molly found a job as an editor at a small publishing house and began dating black policeman Nathaniel Hawthorne. Her widowed mother, Florence, was also dating someone new, wealthy theatrical producer Arthur Feldman. The following year saw Molly dealing with two major crises—trying to find the money for a down payment on her apartment, which was converting from a rental to a co-op, and dealing with an unplanned pregnancy. Arthur eventually helped with the money but the pregnancy was more complicated, primarily because she wasn't sure whether the father was Nat or Moss Goodman, a writer with whom she had had a brief fling. That year also saw the arrival of quirky new neighbors, Ron and Ramona, who had purchased the apartment next to her; and Davey's son, Jimmy, a would-be actor working part-time for his dad as an apprentice doorman.

In 1991 there were many changes and resolutions. Molly's boss at the publishing house, Sara Reddick, was fired and, much to her amazement, Molly was promoted into her job. She found out that Nat was the father of her unborn child but, after they had gotten engaged, he died in a freak allergic reaction to MSG in the food at a restaurant where he was having lunch with his partner. Following the birth of her daughter, Emily, Molly got much closer to her ex, but before anything could develop Fred moved to Los Angeles to write the music for a movie.

Series producer Jay Tarses appeared occasionally as Nick Donatello who, in keeping with the quirky nature of this series, started as her garbageman, during the 1990 season had become a chauffeur-driven mayoral aide and, by the end of 1991, had gone back to being a garbageman.

DEAD AT 21 (*Science Fiction*)

BROADCAST HISTORY:

MTV
30 minutes
Produced: *1994* (13 episodes)
Premiered: *June 9, 1994*

CAST:

Ed Bellamy .... Jack Noseworthy
Maria Cavalos .... Lisa Dean Ryan
Agent Winston .... Whip Hubley

Teen paranoia and distrust of the adult world were the themes of this odd series about two 20-year-olds on the run. Ed, a quiet, Harley-riding hunk, learned on his twentieth birthday that he had been the victim of an infernal government experiment to implant neurochips in the brains of babies in order to increase their intelligence. Unfortunately, all that smartness caused sensory overload. When, and if, he reached 21 his brain would literally explode. Now he understood why he was having those vivid and terrifying dreams.

Ed got his warning via a posthumous videotape left by an unfortunate pal named Dan who had also been a "neurocybernaut." After seeing it he promptly took off on his cycle to try to track down the one man who might save him, Dr. Victor Heisenberg, the chip's elusive inventor. At his side was Maria, a sexy companion his own age, who was as smart as he was and just wanted to help. On *their* trail was ruthless government agent Winston, with orders to kill anyone who knew about the experiments. He had framed them on a murder rap as a cover, so there was no authority they could turn to. Only the beat of the hard-rock sound track, and hope, drove them on.

DEAD LAST (*Supernatural Comedy/Drama*)

FIRST TELECAST: *August 14, 2001*
LAST TELECAST: *September 25, 2001*
BROADCAST HISTORY:

Aug 2001–Sep 2001, WB Tue 9:00–10:00

CAST:

Vaughn Parrish .... Kett Turton
Scotty Sailback .... Tyler Labine
Jane Cahill .... Sara Downing
Dennis Budny .... Wayne Pere

Vaughn, Scotty and Jane were the members of a struggling rock band appropriately named The Problem—not because of their music but due to the strange occurrence that changed their lives. Vaughn was the egocentric lead singer and guitar player; Scotty, the easygoing beefy drummer; and Jane, the sexy bass player and songwriter with an ability to keep the peace when the guys started yelling at each other (which was often). While conducting a sound check in a 400-year-old building, Scotty stumbled across the amulet of Soren, an artifact that enabled the three musicians to see ghosts walking among the living because their earthly work was unfinished and, until things were resolved, they couldn't move on. Some of the ghosts were hundreds of years old, while others were contemporaries, but they all had one thing in common—they needed help.

No matter where they went—their uptight manager, Dennis, kept them on the road while trying to get them a record deal—the members of The Problem were besieged by an endless stream of spirits seeking the assistance that would free them to depart for the next world. Not only was this unsought companionship a nuisance, but it could also be dangerous—assisting the apparitions sometimes put their own lives in jeopardy. In New York, where the ghost density was higher than anyplace else they had been, they even attempted to conduct group counseling sessions for the ghosts.

Thirteen episodes of *Dead Last* were produced and aired on YTV in Canada. Only the first six aired on the WB in the U.S.

DEAD ZONE, THE (*Drama*)

BROADCAST HISTORY:

USA Network
60 minutes
Original episodes: *2002–*
Premiered: *June 16, 2002*

CAST:

Johnny Smith .... Anthony Michael Hall
Sarah Bracknell Bannerman .... Nicole deBoer
Sheriff Walt Bannerman .... Chris Bruno
Bruce Lewis .... John L. Adams
Rev. Gene Purdy .... David Ogden Stiers
Dana Bright .... Kristen Dalton

Johnny Smith was a respected science teacher with a lovely fiancée, Sarah, until a terrible car accident left him in a coma for six years. When he awoke he found he had strange new powers, which allowed him to see into the lives of anyone he touched. Touching his Vietnamese doctor he saw that the doctor's mother, thought killed many years earlier, was still alive; touching a nurse led to the discovery that her house was on fire; simply shaking hands with a politician brought vivid pictures of the evil the man would one day do. He was, it was said, tapping into his brain's "dead zone." Johnny's life had changed in other ways as well. Despairing of his recovery, Sarah had married amiable friend Walt, now the sheriff in their little town of Cleaves Mills, Maine, and had a son named Johnny ("J. J."). His mother had died and left his inheritance in the care of slippery Rev. Purdy, head of the ultraconservative Faith Heritage Alliance. Bruce was Johnny's levelheaded therapist and friend, and Dana a reporter interested in his case.

Johnny, a quiet, moody sort, was uncomfortable with his new abilities and what they foretold, and tended to push people away. He didn't smile much. But as his psychic abilities became widely known, he was called on to help in many difficult situations. He also wanted to reestablish some sort of relationship with Sarah and her son J. J., who was in fact his son.

Based on the Stephen King novel of the same name, which was made into a 1983 film starring Christopher Walken.

DEADLINE (*Newspaper Drama*)

FIRST TELECAST: *October 2, 2000*
LAST TELECAST: *October 30, 2000*
BROADCAST HISTORY:

Oct 2000, NBC Mon 9:00–10:00

CAST:

Wallace Benton .... Oliver Platt
Brooke Benton .... Hope Davis
Beth Khambu .... Christina Chang
Charles Foster .... Damon Gupton
Nikki Masucci .... Bebe Neuwirth
Hildy Baker .... Lili Taylor
Si Beekman .... Tom Conti

Wallace Benton was a larger-than-life crusading journalist in this earnest newspaper drama. He had won a Pulitzer Prize for his work, and made headlines of his own with his rabble-rousing column "Nothing But the Truth" in the *New York Ledger.* A chubby, bossy guy with dapper clothes and an imperious manner, he clashed regularly with his colleagues, including sharp-witted managing editor Nikki, vitriolic gossip columnist Hildy, and hard-driving feature writer Brooke, his estranged wife. Si was the overbearing owner of the *Ledger.* Stoking his ego was a group of graduate students from his seminar on investigative journalism, notably eager Beth and racially uptight black student Charles. He used them to do his legwork, drive him around, and as a sounding board, but they clearly held him in awe (student to Wallace, after watching him smooth-talk a source: "You lie with such incredible ease"). So did the cops, who seemed to let him barge in on any crime scene.

Audiences were less impressed, and NBC pulled *Deadline* after only five episodes. Eight additional episodes aired on Bravo in the fall of 2002.

DEADLINE FOR ACTION, see *Wire Service*

DEADLY GAMES (*Science Fiction*)

FIRST TELECAST: *September 5, 1995*
LAST TELECAST: *January 9, 1996*
BROADCAST HISTORY:

Sep 1995–Jan 1996, UPN Tue 8:00–9:00

CAST:

Sebastian Jackal .... Christopher Lloyd
Gus Lloyd .... James Calvert
Lauren Ashborne .... Cynthia Gibb
Peter Rucker .... Stephen T. Kay

Scientist Gus Lloyd designed video games as a hobby, modeling the bad guys on real people who bothered him in this wild comedy-adventure. In a freak accident, the evil supervillain Jackal and all of the other game characters (programmed to destroy anything and anyone who got in their way) were unleashed on an unsuspecting Los Angeles. Their goals, in classic video-game fashion, included removing all happiness from Earth and most of the good people from the planet. Gus, the model for the computer hero, the "Cold Steel Kid," was forced to play each level of the game for real—coping with the villains' strengths but also knowing their programmed weaknesses—while he and his assistant Peter tried to find a way to force the characters back into the computer. Gus's ex-wife, Lauren, was reluctantly sucked into this mess since he had made her the heroine of the game and a primary target of the evil characters. She tolerated him and was a remarkably good sport about helping out, but he hoped they could get back together since he still loved her. Each episode featured guest stars, often playing both the evil villains and the real people in Lloyd's life on whom they were based. Jackal was modeled after Gus's dad, with whom he'd had an unsettled relationship as a child. At one point Gus and Lauren were even sucked into his computer when an attempt to delete Jackal's file went awry. Among the guest villains was Shirley Jones as Gus's ex-mother-in-law.

DEALER'S CHOICE (*Quiz*)

BROADCAST HISTORY:

Syndicated only
30 minutes
Produced: *1973–1975* (210 episodes)
Released: *Early 1974*

HOST:

Bob Hastings
Jack Clark

Syndicated game show taped at the Tropicana Hotel in Las Vegas, and built around various gambling-casino games—blackjack, roulette, slot machines, etc.

Garish surroundings and the betting fever prevalent in Las Vegas helped add excitement. The original host, Bob Hastings, was later replaced by Jack Clark.

DEAN MARTIN COMEDY WORLD, THE (*Comedy Variety*)

FIRST TELECAST: *June 6, 1974*
LAST TELECAST: *August 15, 1974*
BROADCAST HISTORY:
Jun 1974–Aug 1974, NBC Thu 10:00–11:00
HOSTS:
Jackie Cooper
Nipsey Russell
Barbara Feldon

Jackie Cooper served as "anchorman in the control room from the center of the comedy world," coordinating and introducing many of the comedy acts that appeared on this summer replacement for *The Dean Martin Comedy Hour*. The show included taped performances by new comedy talent from all over the world, excerpts from both old and new comedy films, and performances by well-established comedy stars. Nipsey Russell and Barbara Feldon were on location to do introductions from such diverse spots as London, Hollywood, and San Francisco.

DEAN MARTIN PRESENTS (*Musical Variety*)

FIRST TELECAST: *June 20, 1968*
LAST TELECAST: *September 6, 1973*
BROADCAST HISTORY:
Jun 1968–Sep 1968, NBC Thu 10:00–11:00
Jul 1969–Sep 1969, NBC Thu 10:00–11:00
Jul 1970–Sep 1970, NBC Thu 10:00–11:00
Jul 1972–Sep 1972, NBC Thu 10:00–11:00
Jul 1973–Sep 1973, NBC Thu 10:00–11:00
REGULARS:
Joey Heatherton (1968)
Frank Sinatra, Jr. (1968)
Paul Lynde (1968–1969)
The Golddiggers (1968–1970)
Barbara Heller (1968)
Stu Gilliam (1968)
Stanley Myron Handleman (1968, 1969)
Skiles and Henderson (1968)
Times Square Two (1968)
Gail Martin (1969)
Allison McKay (1969)
Darleen Carr (1969)
Fiore and Eldridge (1969)
Lou Rawls (1969)
Tommy Tune (1969–1970)
Albert Brooks (1969)
Danny Lockin (1969)
Joyce Ames (1969)
Charles Nelson Reilly (1970)
Marty Feldman (1970)
Julian Chagrin (1970)
Bobby Darin (1972)
Rip Taylor (1972)
Steve Landesberg (1972)
Sara Hankboner (1972)
Cathy Cahill (1972)
Dick Bakalyan (1972)
Schnecklegruber (1972)
Loretta Lynn (1973)
Lynn Anderson (1973)
Jerry Reed (1973)
Ray Stevens (1973)
Les Brown and His Band (1968–1969)
The Jack Parnell Orchestra (1970)
The Eddie Karam Orchestra (1972)

Dean Martin Presents . . . was the umbrella title for a series of summer replacements for *The Dean Martin Show*. They were all musical variety shows featuring mostly young talent; their actual titles were as follows:

1968—*Dean Martin Presents the Golddiggers*
1969—*Dean Martin Presents the Golddiggers*
1970—*Dean Martin Presents the Golddiggers in London*
1972—*Dean Martin Presents the Bobby Darin Amusement Co.*
1973—*Dean Martin Presents Music Country*

The regular casts of these summer shows remained relatively stable through 1972. The country and western version aired during the summer of 1973 had, in addition to the four regulars who appeared in almost every episode, a large number of country music performers who appeared irregularly. The Golddiggers also had a syndicated variety show in 1971.

DEAN MARTIN SHOW, THE (*Comedy/Variety*)

FIRST TELECAST: *September 16, 1965*
LAST TELECAST: *May 24, 1974*
BROADCAST HISTORY:
Sep 1965–Jul 1973, NBC Thu 10:00–11:00 (OS)
Sep 1973–May 1974, NBC Fri 10:00–11:00
REGULARS:
Dean Martin
The Golddiggers (1967–1971)
The Ding-a-Ling Sisters (1970–1973)
Kay Medford (1970–1973)
Lou Jacobi (1971–1973)
Marian Mercer (1971–1972)
Tom Bosley (1971–1972)
Dom DeLuise (1972–1973)
Nipsey Russell (1972–1973)
Rodney Dangerfield (1972–1973)
Ken Lane
Les Brown and His Band
THEME:
"Everybody Loves Somebody"

Singer-comedian Dean Martin was host and star of this long-lived variety hour, which was for most of its run a fixture on the NBC Thursday night lineup. At first Dean had no regular supporting cast other than his accompanist, pianist Ken Lane. Guest stars were featured each week in comedy skits and songs, both alone and with Dean. Some of the young talent appearing during the regular season also starred in Dean's summer replacement series, *The Dean Martin Summer Show* and later *Dean Martin Presents*. A bevy of pretty young dancers called the Golddiggers were added as regulars in 1967, and four of these later became the Ding-a-Ling Sisters (1970–1973).

Beginning in 1970 a supporting case of comics and singers was gradually assembled around Dean, some of whom appeared regularly (see credits) and others occasionally, such as Foster Brooks with his "drunk" routine. The hallmark of the show remained Dean's own easy informality, as he welcomed guests into his cozy living room through the ever-present door, or sang or clowned beside (or on, or under) Ken Lane's grand piano. In fact, a stipulation in Dean's contract helped foster this air of informality by allowing Dean not to show up until the day of the taping each week, when the show would be done with only minimal rehearsal.

In 1973 the title and format were changed, as well as the time slot. The new title was *The Dean Martin Comedy Hour*, and Dean and Ken Lane were once again the only regulars. Two new features were added. The first was a country music spot, with top-name country performers, to hold some of the audience that had been attracted to Dean's summer replacement in 1973, *Dean Martin Presents Music Country*. The second was the "Man of the Week Celebrity Roast," in which several celebrities seated at a banquet dais tossed comic insults at the guest of honor. This feature proved so popular that after Dean's regular series ended in 1974, the "roasts" continued on NBC as a series of occasional specials.

DEAN MARTIN SUMMER SHOW, THE (*Variety*)
FIRST TELECAST: *June 16, 1966*
LAST BROADCAST: *August 19, 1971*
BROADCAST HISTORY:
Jun 1966–Sep 1966, NBC Thu 10:00–11:00
Jun 1967–Sep 1967, NBC Thu 10:00–11:00
Jul 1971–Aug 1971, NBC Thu 10:00–11:00
REGULARS:
Dan Rowan (1966)
Dick Martin (1966)
Dom DeLuise (1966)
Lainie Kazan (1966)
Frankie Randall (1966)
Judi Rolin (1966)
Wisa D'Orso (1966)
Vic Damone (1967)
Carol Lawrence (1967)
Gail Martin (1967)
Don Cherry (1967)
Les Brown and His Band

Nearly two years before their hit *Laugh-In*, comedians Dan Rowan and Dick Martin starred as the 1966 summer replacements for Dean Martin. Because of the stars, the emphasis was more on comedy than on music. The 1967 replacement, however, which was aired under the title *The Dean Martin Summer Show Starring Your Host Vic Damone*, relied more on music. Selected episodes of the Vic Damone series were rerun as Dean's summer replacement during the summer of 1971.

DEAR DETECTIVE (*Police Drama*)
FIRST TELECAST: *March 28, 1979*
LAST TELECAST: *April 18, 1979*
BROADCAST HISTORY:
Mar 1979–Apr 1979, CBS Wed 9:00–10:00
CAST:
Det. Sgt. Kate Hudson .... Brenda Vaccaro
Prof. Richard Weyland .... Arlen Dean Snyder
Det. Brock......................... Michael McRae
Det. Clay.................... John Dennis Johnston
Det. Chuck Morris....................... Jack Ging
Det. Schwartz .... Ron Silver
Mrs. Hudson....................... Lesley Woods
Lisa .... Jet Yardum
Capt. Gorcey..................... M. Emmet Walsh

Kate Hudson juggled three roles—policewoman, lover, and mother—in this short-lived series. Det. Sgt. Hudson was a dedicated professional, who also happened to be in love with Prof. Richard Weyland, a teacher of English literature at U.C.L.A. The fact that she was always "on call" complicated their relationship, as did his distinct lack of enthusiasm for the police and their methods. Kate was also saddled with the responsibility of raising young Lisa, her daughter from a dissolved marriage.

DEAR JOHN (*Situation Comedy*)
FIRST TELECAST: *October 6, 1988*
LAST TELECAST: *July 22, 1992*
BROADCAST HISTORY:
Oct 1988, NBC Thu 9:00–9:30
Oct 1988–Jan 1990, NBC Thu 9:30–10:00
Jan 1990–Mar 1990, NBC Wed 9:30–10:00
May 1990–Oct 1990, NBC Wed 9:30–10:00
Oct 1990–Dec 1990, NBC Wed 9:00–9:30
Dec 1990–Mar 1991, NBC Sat 10:30–11:00
Mar 1991–Jun 1991, NBC Wed 9:30–10:00
Jul 1991, NBC Sat 10:00–10:30
Aug 1991–Sep 1991, NBC Sat 9:30–10:00
Sep 1991–Oct 1991, NBC Fri 9:00–9:30
Oct 1991–Jan 1992, NBC Fri 9:30–10:00
Apr 1992, NBC Wed 9:30–10:00
Jul 1992, NBC Wed 9:30–10:00
CAST:
John Lacey............................ Judd Hirsch
Louise Mercer .... Jane Carr
Kirk Morris .... Jere Burns
Ralph Drang (1988–1991).......... Harry Groener
Kate McCarron................. Isabella Hofmann
Mrs. Margie Philbert .... Billie Bird
Mary Beth Sutton (1990–1992) ...... Susan Walters
Tom .... Tom Willett
Denise (1990–1991) .... Olivia Brown
**Matthew Lacey (1988–1990)* .... Ben Savage
**Matthew Lacey (1990)* .... Billy Cohen
**Wendy Lacey (1988–1989)* .... Carlene Watkins
**Wendy Lacey (1990–1991)* .... Deborah Harmon
Ben (1991–1992) .... William O'Leary
Annie Marino (1991–1992) ...... Marietta DePrima
* Occasional
THEME:
"Dear John," by John Sullivan, sung by Wendy Talbot

Character comedy can work in almost any setting, as evidenced by the success of this popular series based on the unfunny subject of divorce. John Lacey was an easygoing high school English teacher from New Rochelle, New York, who came home one day to discover that his wife had dumped him for his best friend. Her note began, "Dear John . . ."

Wendy got the house, their son Matthew, and everything else that mattered, so John moved into an apartment in Queens and joined the "One-Two-One Club," a singles support group at the Rego Park Community Center, whose offbeat members seemed guaranteed to cheer anybody up. Kirk was the swaggering ladies' man who was oblivious to his own boorishness; Ralph, the shy, owlish toll collector; Kate, the compassionate but somewhat out-of-touch beauty; Mrs. Philbert, the daft, chattering retiree; and Tom (her boyfriend), the older man who hardly ever said anything. Mary Beth, a sexy but naive Southerner, and Denise, who was in the weight control group across the hall, surfaced later, as did maintenance man Ben. The group leader was

Louise, a bubbly, sex-obsessed Englishwoman. Most of them had lost spouses in one hilarious manner or another, and they helped each other fumble through the endless trials of readjustment.

A surprising development in the third season occurred when Wendy decided to have another child by unwilling John. First she tried to withdraw his deposit at a sperm bank, then she handcuffed him to a bed and made love!

Based on the English television series of the same name.

DEAR PHOEBE (*Situation Comedy*)
FIRST TELECAST: *September 10, 1954*
LAST TELECAST: *September 11, 1956*
BROADCAST HISTORY:
Sep 1954–Sep 1955, NBC Fri 9:30–10:00
Jun 1956–Sep 1956, NBC Tue 8:00–8:30
CAST:
Bill Hastings .... Peter Lawford
Mickey Riley .... Marcia Henderson
Mr. Fosdick .... Charles Lane
Humphrey Humpsteader .... Joe Corey

In this comedy, a college instructor gave up teaching to become the writer of the advice-to-the-lovelorn column in the *Los Angeles Daily Blade.* Bill Hastings, who wrote under the name Phoebe Goodheart, had a lovelorn admirer of his own in the person of the paper's female sportswriter, Mickey Riley. Mickey tried to hide her affection by being extremely competitive with Bill for choice assignments from Mr. Fosdick, the flinty old managing editor. Bill made no secret of his love for Mickey, however, and many of the episodes developed around their rocky romance. Humphrey Humpsteader was the typical copyboy trying to make it in the newspaper game. The 1956 edition of *Dear Phoebe* was composed entirely of reruns.

DEATH VALLEY DAYS (*Western Anthology*)
BROADCAST HISTORY:
Syndicated only
30 minutes
Produced: *1952–1975* (558 episodes)
Released: *Fall 1952*
HOST:
Stanley Andrews ("The Old Ranger") (1952–1965)
Ronald Reagan (1965–1966)
Robert Taylor (1966–1968)
Dale Robertson (1968–1972)
Merle Haggard (1975)

This modestly produced but very popular anthology was one of the longest-running series in the history of television—and of radio. It began on radio in 1930, as a means of promoting the products of sponsor 20 Mule Team Borax. The stories were all based in fact, and revolved around the legends and lore of Death Valley, California, where borax was mined. Mostly they tended to be human-interest stories, sometimes little more than vignettes, from the days when miners and homesteaders first fanned across the western United States in search of a better life. There were both gentle comedy and drama, for example the story of the Bennett-Arcane party trapped in the sweltering, arid valley in 1849; that of a prospector who bought a white hearse believing that it was a pleasure vehicle; and that of Tiger Lil, the queen of Virginia City in gold-rush days. Hundreds of actors appeared in the series, most of them not big names; the emphasis was clearly on the story.

The only regular, in fact, was the host and narrator, originally Stanley Andrews as "The Old Ranger." When Andrews left the series in the mid-1960s he was succeeded by a number of hosts, including Ronald Reagan, who dropped out after he was elected governor of California in 1966. Other familiar aspects of the show were the opening bugle call, the scenes of the 20-mule team hauling the borax wagons out of the desert, and Rosemary DeCamp doing the homey commercials for the product. Nearly 600 episodes were filmed, most of them on location in Death Valley.

Death Valley Days was created in 1930 by Ruth Woodman, a New York advertising-agency scriptwriter who had never seen the place. After the series went on the air she became fascinated with the area, and made many trips there to gather lore and ideas for stories. She even found a real "old ranger," a grizzled old desert rat named Wash Cahill, who seemed to know everybody and everything in the valley, and who served as her guide on many of the trips. For Mrs. Woodman, *Death Valley Days* became a career, and she wrote scripts throughout its long radio run (1930–1945) and when it began on TV as well. In 1960 she claimed that there had never been a script without a solid basis in fact. When asked about the show's extraordinary durability, she remarked, "Sometimes it seems it will go on forever."

Death Valley Days has been seen in reruns under a variety of titles and with various hosts, including *Call of the West* (John Payne), *Frontier Adventure* (Dale Robertson), *The Pioneers* (Will Rogers, Jr.), *Trails West* (Ray Milland), and *Western Star Theatre* (Rory Calhoun).

DEBBIE REYNOLDS SHOW, THE (*Situation Comedy*)
FIRST TELECAST: *September 16, 1969*
LAST TELECAST: *September 1, 1970*
BROADCAST HISTORY:
Sep 1969–Sep 1970, NBC Tue 8:00–8:30
CAST:
Debbie Thompson .... Debbie Reynolds
Jim Thompson .... Don Chastain
Charlotte Landers .... Patricia Smith
Bob Landers .... Tom Bosley
Bruce Landers .... Bobby Riha

Debbie Reynolds made her series television debut in this comedy about the unpredictable wife of a successful sports columnist for the *Los Angeles Sun.* Debbie's efforts to create more excitement for herself than her life in the suburbs offered got her into all sorts of strange situations, much to the consternation of her husband Jim. Debbie's schemes, which were in some ways reminiscent of Lucille Ball's screwball exploits in the old *I Love Lucy* series, were often helped along by her sister Charlotte. The long-suffering members of Charlotte's family were her husband Bob and their son Bruce.

DEBT (*Quiz*)
BROADCAST HISTORY:
Lifetime
30 minutes
Produced: *1996–1998*
Premiered: *June 3, 1996*

HOST:

Wink Martindale

An early evening game show, with an unusual twist. Contestants began with a negative total reflecting their real-life debt (up to $10,000), and then competed to reduce their totals by answering pop culture questions. A bonus round at the end allowed a contestant to have all his debt paid off, and even go home with money in the pocket—or lose it all and be right back in the hole.

DECEMBER BRIDE (*Situation Comedy*)

FIRST TELECAST: *October 4, 1954*
LAST TELECAST: *April 20, 1961*
BROADCAST HISTORY:

Oct 1954–Jun 1958, CBS Mon 9:30–10:00 (OS)
Oct 1958–Sep 1959, CBS Thu 8:00–8:30
Jul 1960–Sep 1960, CBS Fri 9:30–10:00
Apr 1961, CBS Thu 7:30–8:00

CAST:

Lily Ruskin .... Spring Byington
Ruth Henshaw .... Frances Rafferty
Matt Henshaw .... Dean Miller
Hilda Crocker .... Verna Felton
Pete Porter .... Harry Morgan

Lily Ruskin was that truly rare individual, a mother-in-law who could live with and be loved by her son-in-law. An attractive widow who was very popular with the older set—hence her potential as a "December bride"—Lily's social life revolved around her family as well. Her daughter Ruth and son-in-law Matt were always looking for suitable marriage prospects for Lily, as was her friend and peer, Hilda Crocker. Pete Porter, the next-door neighbor who couldn't stand *his* mother-in-law, was often seen around the Henshaw household, and he became so popular that he eventually got his own series, *Pete and Gladys*, after *December Bride* went off the air. Pete complained constantly about his wife, Gladys, but she was never seen on *December Bride*—only heard. Reruns of this series were aired in prime time during 1960 and 1961 and had been part of the CBS weekday morning lineup from October 1959 to March 1961.

DECISION (*Dramatic Anthology*)

FIRST TELECAST: *July 6, 1958*
LAST TELECAST: *September 28, 1958*
BROADCAST HISTORY:

Jul 1958–Sep 1958, NBC Sun 10:00–10:30

This series of filmed dramas was the 1958 summer replacement for *The Loretta Young Show*. Half the shows were reruns of episodes from other dramatic-anthology series; the remainder were pilots for proposed series. One of the latter was a short version of *The Virginian* starring James Drury, who played the same role when the show became a series in the fall of 1962.

DECISION '80 (*News*)

FIRST TELECAST: *September 14, 1980*
LAST TELECAST: *November 2, 1980*
BROADCAST HISTORY:

Sep 1980–Nov 1980, NBC Sun 11:30–12:00

ANCHORMAN:

Robert Abernethy

NBC News presented this series of campaign reports leading up to the 1980 Presidential election. There were also discussions of other important races, and each week a special report centered on voter attitudes in a different key state.

DEFENDERS, THE (*Courtroom Drama*)

FIRST TELECAST: *September 16, 1961*
LAST TELECAST: *September 9, 1965*
BROADCAST HISTORY:

Sep 1961–Sep 1963, CBS Sat 8:30–9:30
Sep 1963–Nov 1963, CBS Sat 9:00–10:00
Nov 1963–Sep 1964, CBS Sat 8:30–9:30
Sep 1964–Sep 1965, CBS Thu 10:00–11:00

CAST:

Lawrence Preston .... E. G. Marshall
Kenneth Preston .... Robert Reed
Helen Donaldson (1961–1962) .... Polly Rowles
Joan Miller (1961–1962) .... Joan Hackett

The law firm of Preston & Preston was composed of a father and son, two lawyers involved in a weekly courtroom drama. Lawrence, the father, was a knowledgeable, seasoned attorney with more than 20 years of experience at the bar. Kenneth, the son, was a recent law school graduate. The learning process he went through as his father's partner was an integral part of this series. During the first season the firm's secretary, Helen Donaldson, and Kenneth's girlfriend, Joan Miller, had regular featured roles.

At a time when most TV entertainment series avoided any hint of controversy or topicality, *The Defenders* occasionally addressed such real-life issues as abortion, mercy killing, and the U.S. government's restriction of its citizens' right to travel to unfriendly countries. A January 1964 episode entitled "Blacklist" was TV's first hard look at its own practice of political blacklisting, and won actor Jack Klugman and writer Ernest Kinoy Emmy awards.

The Defenders was based on an original story by Reginald Rose, which was first telecast as a two-part episode of *Studio One* in February–March, 1957. That presentation was titled "The Defender," and starred Ralph Bellamy and William Shatner as the father and son attorneys, with Steve McQueen as a young defendant accused of murder.

DELL O'DELL SHOW (*Variety*)

FIRST TELECAST: *September 14, 1951*
LAST TELECAST: *December 14, 1951*
BROADCAST HISTORY:

Sep 1951–Dec 1951, ABC Fri 10:00–10:30

EMCEE:

Dell O'Dell

Lady magician Dell O'Dell performed on this short-lived variety program, which included audience participation in the stunts as well as special guests. Wonder if she sawed any men in half?

DELLAVENTURA (*Detective Drama*)

FIRST TELECAST: *September 23, 1997*
LAST TELECAST: *January 13, 1998*
BROADCAST HISTORY:

Sep 1997–Jan 1998, CBS Tue 10:00–11:00

CAST:

Anthony Dellaventura .... Danny Aiello
Teddy Naples .... Ricky Aiello
Jonas Deeds .... Byron Keith Minns
Geri Zarias .... Anne Ramsay
Frankie Bongiorno .... Himself

Anthony Dellaventura was a tough guy with style and swagger. A former N.Y.P.D. detective who had become a highly successful private detective, he and his staff took on cases that the police couldn't or wouldn't handle. Many of his clients came to him because the legal system had either failed them or didn't seem interested in their problems. Dellaventura didn't come cheap; for customers who could afford it, his rate was $100 per hour per associate. He may have come across as arrogant, but he did have a heart. Most episodes included subplots in which he helped out people, sometimes without charge—working with a landlord to get drug dealers out of his building, finding out the identity of an apparently homeless man, exposing an auto mechanic who made expensive unneeded repairs, and aiding an accountant trying to track down the mystery woman of his dreams. Dellaventura's associates were Teddy (played by the series star's son), a smart ex-cop who wasn't above using a little muscle; Jonas, skilled in electronics surveillance; and Geri, a tough recent arrival in New York who used her beauty and sex appeal to her advantage, particularly on undercover assignments. When they needed to unwind, they hung out at Dellaventura's favorite restaurant, Trattoria Spaghetto, owned by his good friend, Frankie.

Filmed on location in New York.

DELORA BUENO (*Music*)
FIRST TELECAST: *March 10, 1949*
LAST TELECAST: *May 5, 1949*
BROADCAST HISTORY:
Mar 1949–May 1949, DUM Thu 7:00–7:15
HOSTESS:
Delora Bueno

Songs and piano stylings were performed by Delora Bueno, a Latin beauty born in Dubuque, Iowa. (She was raised, however, in Brazil.)

DELPHI BUREAU, THE (*Spy Drama*)
FIRST TELECAST: *October 5, 1972*
LAST TELECAST: *September 1, 1973*
BROADCAST HISTORY:
Oct 1972–Jan 1973, ABC Thu 9:00–10:00
Mar 1973–Sep 1973, ABC Sat 10:00–11:00
CAST:
Glenn Garth Gregory .... Laurence Luckinbill
Sybil Van Loween .... Anne Jeffreys

The Delphi Bureau was an obscure government agency ostensibly intended to do research for the President of the United States; in fact it carried out super-secret missions to protect and defend the security of the nation against various foes. Its office was a moving limousine, and its chief operative, Glenn Gregory, a most reluctant hero. Gregory's only contact at the Delphi Bureau was Sybil Van Loween, a delightful but slightly mysterious Washington hostess. Secret ciphers, hidden islands, and bizarre international operators showed up regularly in the plots.

Celeste Holm was originally announced to play the role of Sybil, but she never appeared in the series, being replaced by Anne Jeffreys. *The Delphi Bureau* was one of three rotating elements of *The Men.*

DELTA (*Situation Comedy*)
FIRST TELECAST: *September 15, 1992*
LAST TELECAST: *August 25, 1993*
BROADCAST HISTORY:
Sep 1992, ABC Tue 9:30–10:00
Sep 1992–Dec 1992, ABC Thu 8:00–8:30
Apr 1993, ABC Tue 9:30–10:00
Jul 1993–Aug 1993, ABC Wed 9:30–10:00
CAST:
Delta Bishop .... Delta Burke
Lavonne Overton .... Gigi Rice
Buck Overton .... Bill Engvall
Darden Towe .... Earl Holliman
Thelma Wainwright .... Beth Grant
Connie Morris .... Nancy Giles

Delta Bishop was a hefty woman with a hefty dream—to make it in the glittering world of country music like her idol, the late Patsy Cline. When her no-good husband, Charlie, proved no help she dumped him, quit her job at Mona's House of Hair, and set out on her own. While working for her big break she waited tables in a Nashville bar run by understanding Darden and stayed with her cousin and biggest fan, Lavonne. Friends and co-workers Thelma and Connie offered encouragement, but Lavonne's husband, Buck, who spent most of his time eating Cocoa Puffs, had little use for her dreams. Men!

DELTA HOUSE (*Situation Comedy*)
FIRST TELECAST: *January 18, 1979*
LAST TELECAST: *April 28, 1979*
BROADCAST HISTORY:
Jan 1979, ABC Thu 8:30–9:00
Jan 1979–Mar 1979, ABC Sat 8:00–8:30
Mar 1979–Apr 1979, ABC Sat 8:30–9:00
CAST:
Dean Vernon Wormer .... John Vernon*
Kent "Flounder" Dorfman .... Stephen Furst*
Daniel Simpson Day ("D-Day") ...... Bruce McGill*
Robert Hoover .... James Widdoes*
Jim "Blotto" Blutarsky .... Josh Mostel
Eric Stratton ("Otter") .... Peter Fox
Doug Neidermayer .... Gary Cookson
Larry Kroger ("Pinto") .... Richard Seer
Mandy Pepperidge .... Susanna Dalton
Muffy .... Wendy Goldman
Greg Marmalard .... Brian Patrick Clarke
Einswine .... Lee Wilkof
Prof. Dave Jennings .... Peter Kastner
The Bombshell .... Michelle Pfeiffer

* Played same role in the movie

Following the enormous success of the movie *Animal House,* all three networks rushed imitations onto the small screen. ABC had a leg up on the competition, however, as it had acquired the production team responsible for the movie as well as rights to the story—everything except the title itself. So *Delta House* was *Animal House* brought to TV.

The setting was the same, Faber College in the early 1960s, where the riotous members of Delta House fraternity pulled pranks on Dean Wormer (who was constantly trying to get them kicked off campus) and his allies, the stuffy, rich brothers of Omega House. The series opened with the arrival of Blotto, younger brother of the legendary Bluto Blutarsky (John Belushi's unforgettable character in the film). Belushi wasn't available for the TV series, so the role was played by Josh Mostel, Zero Mostel's son. The other Deltas included portly Flounder, greasy, mustachioed D-Day, and Hoover. Doug Neidermayer and Greg

Marmalard represented Omega House, and there were assorted girlfriends and faculty (although nobody studied much).

It all was a pretty pale imitation without Belushi, and it lasted only about three months. That was longer than NBC's *Brothers and Sisters* (two and a half months) or CBS' *Co-Ed Fever* (one telecast)!

DELVECCHIO (*Police Drama*)

FIRST TELECAST: *September 9, 1976*

LAST TELECAST: *July 17, 1977*

BROADCAST HISTORY:

Sep 1976, CBS Thu 9:00–10:00
Sep 1976–Jul 1977, CBS Sun 10:00–11:00

CAST:

Sgt. Dominick Delvecchio .... Judd Hirsch
Sgt. Paul Shonski .... Charles Haid
Lt. Macavan .... Michael Conrad
Tomaso Delvecchio .... Mario Gallo
Sgt. Rivera .... Jay Varela
Asst. D.A. Dorfman .... George Wyner

Delvecchio was the story of a tough, independent big-city police detective fighting crime in Los Angeles. Delvecchio and his partner Shonski were assigned cases that ranged from narcotics investigations to murders to auto thefts. His boss, and the man who assigned most of his cases, was Lt. Macavan. Also seen regularly was Delvecchio's father, Tomaso, an Old World type who ran a small barbershop and was constantly perplexed about why his stubborn, determined son had become a cop. The series was shot on location in Los Angeles.

DEMPSEY & MAKEPEACE (*Police Drama*)

BROADCAST HISTORY:

Syndicated only
60 minutes
Produced: *1985* (19 episodes)
Released: *September 1985*

CAST:

Lt. James Dempsey .... Michael Brandon
Det. Sgt. Harriet Makepeace (Harry) ... Glynis Barber
Chief Superintendent Gordon Spikings ... Ray Smith
Det. Sgt. Charles Jarvis (Chas) .... Tony Osoba

Produced in England, *Dempsey & Makepeace* chronicled the exploits of two members of SI-10, a special undercover group working out of London's Scotland Yard. Jim Dempsey was a New York City cop who had discovered corruption in the New York City police force and had been sent to England for his own protection. He was brash, impetuous, occasionally obnoxious, and much quicker to use his gun than the British. His reluctant partner was Lady Harriet Makepeace, a member of the nobility who, for reasons never clearly explained on the show, had decided to make a career out of police work. Her connections with those in high places often proved handy when they were looking for information or assistance on various cases. Although a grudging mutual respect developed between them, and there was a certain sexual tension, a social relationship never materialized. Spikings was the blustery head of SI-10 and Chas was one of the other members of the team.

DENNIS DAY SHOW, THE, see *RCA Victor Show, The*

DENNIS MILLER SHOW, THE (*Talk*)

BROADCAST HISTORY:

Syndicated only
60 minutes
Produced: *1992*
Released: *January 1992*

REGULARS:

Dennis Miller
Nick Bakay
Andy Summers
David Goldblatt

Cynical comedian and *Saturday Night Live* alumnus Dennis Miller hosted his own relatively short-lived talk show in 1992. Unlike most of his competitors, Miller rarely opened the show with the traditional opening monologue. Instead he would do a variation of *Saturday Night Live*'s "Weekend Update"—which he had done when he was a regular on that show—making comments about stories and personalities in the news. The rest of the show was the usual mix of celebrity (usually second-tier) interviews and performances by young comics and music groups. Miller was popular with young people, who liked his hip, smart-alecky style, but he was unable to attract viewers from *The Arsenio Hall Show*, his principal competition. Six months after its premiere Miller's show went out of production, with reruns airing until September. Nick Bakay was the show's occasionally seen announcer and Andy Summers, former guitarist with The Police, led the house band. Barely a month after the show's premiere, Summers left and was replaced by keyboardist David Goldblatt.

DENNIS O'KEEFE SHOW, THE (*Situation Comedy*)

FIRST TELECAST: *September 22, 1959*

LAST TELECAST: *June 7, 1960*

BROADCAST HISTORY:

Sep 1959–Jun 1960, CBS Tue 8:00–8:30

CAST:

Hal Towne .... Dennis O'Keefe
Sarge .... Hope Emerson
Randy Towne .... Rickey Kelman
Karen Hadley .... Eloise Hardt
Eliot .... Eddie Ryder

This comedy starred Dennis O'Keefe as the syndicated columnist Hal Towne, one of TV's many widowers, with a precocious, friendly ten-year-old son named Randy. Helping Hal keep his home together while he was out getting material for his column was a housekeeper aptly named Sarge. Karen Hadley, an aggressive, career-oriented publicity agent, was Hal's regular girlfriend, but his work on his column, called "All Around Towne," was constantly introducing Hal to some very attractive competition. The story was set in Los Angeles.

DENNIS PRAGER SHOW, THE (*Discussion*)

BROADCAST HISTORY:

Syndicated only
30 minutes
Produced: *1994–1995* (195 episodes)
Released: *September 1994*

HOST:

Dennis Prager

Conservative Los Angeles radio talk-show host Dennis Prager, who had a religiously oriented commonsense approach to issues of personal or public concern, followed Rush Limbaugh into the TV wars in 1994. Each night he opened the show with a monologue reacting to topical stories in the news and then talked with people involved in the news or advocating a point of view on a specific issue. The show was taped in front of a small studio audience that asked questions after the initial discussion. Among his early guests were actor Gregory Alan-Williams, who had tried to help people being assaulted in Los Angeles during the riots following the Rodney King verdict, flight attendants talking about dealing with passengers, an animal rights advocate decrying the killing of animals for medical research, a group of prostitutes, and a panel on both sides of the welfare issue.

DENNIS THE MENACE (*Situation Comedy*)

FIRST TELECAST: *October 4, 1959*
LAST TELECAST: *September 22, 1963*
BROADCAST HISTORY:
Oct 1959–Sep 1963, CBS Sun 7:30–8:00

CAST:
Dennis Mitchell .... Jay North
Henry Mitchell.......... Herbert Anderson
Alice Mitchell.......... Gloria Henry
George Wilson (1959–1962) .... Joseph Kearns
Martha Wilson (1959–1962) .... Sylvia Field
Joey McDonald (1959–1960) .... Gil Smith
Mrs. Lucy Elkins.......... Irene Tedrow
Tommy Anderson .... Billy Booth
Margaret Wade .... Jeannie Russell
Mr. Quigley .... Willard Waterman
Miss Esther Cathcart (1959–1961) .... Mary Wickes
Grandma Mitchell (1961) ...... Kathleen Mulqueen
Sgt. Theodore Mooney (1961–1963).... George Cisar
Seymour (1962–1963)......... Robert John Pittman
John Wilson (1962–1963) .... Gale Gordon
Eloise Wilson (1962–1963).......... Sara Seeger

Cartoonist Hank Ketcham's mischievous imp was brought to television in 1959 in the person of Jay North. *Dennis the Menace* had been a comic-strip fixture for years, with its little boy who was always trying to help out but who usually managed to make everything worse. Dennis's long-suffering parents put up with him as best they could, which was more than could be said for Mr. Wilson, their next-door neighbor in suburban Hillsdale. If Mr. Wilson planted some fancy tulips, Dennis was sure to uproot them and plant some "prettier" potatoes in their place. If Dennis happened upon some of Mr. Wilson's rare coins, he was sure to donate them to the March of Dimes. Adding to the general confusion was Mr. Wilson's dog, Fremont.

Joseph Kearns, the first Mr. Wilson, died before filming was completed for the 1961–1962 season. He was replaced in May 1962 by Gale Gordon, who was initially introduced as Mr. Wilson's brother John, a houseguest of Mrs. Wilson. The next fall, John returned complete with a wife of his own, Eloise, as if he had always been the sole Mr. Wilson.

Reruns of *Dennis the Menace* aired Saturday mornings on NBC from October 1963 to September 1965. A quarter-century after the live-action *Dennis the Menace* left the air, CBS brought an animated version to its Saturday morning lineup in January 1988. The animated *Dennis* only lasted for nine months. A second animated series, *The New Dennis the Menace*, aired Saturday mornings on CBS during the 1993–1994 season.

DEPUTY, THE (*Western*)

FIRST TELECAST: *September 12, 1959*
LAST TELECAST: *September 16, 1961*
BROADCAST HISTORY:
Sep 1959–Sep 1961, NBC Sat 9:00–9:30

CAST:
Marshal Simon Fry .... Henry Fonda
Clay McCord .... Allen Case
Marshal Herk Lamson (1959–1960)... Wallace Ford
Fran McCord (1959–1960) .... Betty Lou Keim
Sgt. Hapgood Tasker (1960–1961).... Read Morgan

Set in the Arizona Territory in the early 1880s, *The Deputy* was built around the conflict in ideals between Chief Marshal Simon Fry, a dedicated lawman, and young storekeeper Clay McCord. Although an expert shot, Clay was opposed to the use of weapons because they contributed to the high level of violence on the frontier. Despite his pacifist feelings, however, Clay was frequently persuaded to serve as "the deputy" in Silver City to help the aging town marshal, Herk Lamson, defend the local populace when Marshal Fry was out of town. The basis for many of the stories was the ongoing conflict between the oldtimers in Silver City and the younger townspeople, who wanted to see it settle down, grow, and prosper. Added to the cast at the start of the second season was "Sarge" Tasker, an army sergeant assigned to set up a supply office in Silver City. At the same time, Herk Lamson and Clay's younger sister Fran were dropped from the cast. Henry Fonda appeared as narrator in all episodes but was featured in the cast only when Marshal Fry was in town.

DES O'CONNOR SHOW, THE, see *Kraft Music Hall Presents The Des O'Connor Show*

DESIGNING WOMEN (*Situation Comedy*)

FIRST TELECAST: *September 29, 1986*
LAST TELECAST: *May 24, 1993*
BROADCAST HISTORY:
Sep 1986–Nov 1986, CBS Mon 9:30–10:00
Dec 1986–Jan 1987, CBS Thu 9:30–10:00
Feb 1987, CBS Sun 9:00–9:30
Mar 1987–Feb 1988, CBS Mon 9:30–10:00
Feb 1988–Jun 1988, CBS Mon 8:30–9:00
Jun 1988–Sep 1989, CBS Mon 9:30–10:00
Sep 1989–Oct 1989, CBS Mon 10:00–10:30
Nov 1989–Jun 1992, CBS Mon 9:30–10:00
Aug 1992–Sep 1992, CBS Mon 9:30–10:00
Sep 1992–May 1993, CBS Fri 9:00–9:30
May 1993, CBS Mon 9:00–10:00

CAST:
Suzanne Sugarbaker (1986–1991) ..... Delta Burke
Julia Sugarbaker.......... Dixie Carter
Charlene Frazier Stillfield (1986–1991)
.... Jean Smart
Mary Jo Shively.......... Annie Potts
Anthony Bouvier .... Meshach Taylor
**Claudia Shively (1986–1990)*...... Priscilla Weems
**Quinton Shively (1986–1991)* .... Brian Lando
**Reese Watson (1986–1989)* .... Hal Holbrook
**J. D. Shackleford (1986–1991)*.... Richard Gilliland
Bernice Clifton (1987–1993) .... Alice Ghostley

**Bill Stillfield (1988–1991)* .... Doug Barr
**Rusty (1991)*.................. Michael Goldfinger
Allison Sugarbaker (1991–1992) .... Julia Duffy
Carlene Frazier Dobber (1991–1993)..... Jan Hooks
B. J. Poteet (1992–1993) .... Judith Ivey
Etienne Toussant Bouvier (1992–1993)
.... Sheryl Lee Ralph

* Occasional

THEME:

"Georgia on My Mind," performed by Doc Severinsen (Ray Charles performed a vocal version during the 1991–1992 season)

Designing Women was the story of the four outspoken women who ran Sugarbakers, a recently opened interior decorating business in Atlanta, which they operated out of an attractive suburban home that served as both office and showplace for their work. The founder, guiding force, and most sharp-tongued of the four was widowed Julia Sugarbaker. She was bright, classy, and had great taste and good connections. Her younger sister Suzanne was sexy, flashy, and prone to use her physical charms to mask a limited knowledge of decorating. A former beauty contest winner, she flirted with any and all attractive, successful, and/or wealthy men—and was collecting alimony from three ex-husbands. Their two partners were Mary Jo, a recent divorcée with a teenaged daughter, Claudia, and a young son, Quinton; and Charlene, the firm's business manager who had never been married but was not averse to the prospect if the right man came along. There was plenty of good-natured bitchiness and, by the standards of network TV, a lot of sexual innuendo. Helping them with the heavy work was their deliveryman-handyman, Anthony, a cheerful, black ex-con. Reese (played by Ms. Carter's real-life husband, Hal Holbrook) was Julia's boyfriend and J.D. (played by Ms. Smart's husband Richard Gilliland—they had met on the *Designing Women* set) was dating Mary Jo.

The critics loved *Designing Women*, and so did its loyal audience. They howled when CBS moved the show all over the schedule following initial ratings success on Monday nights, and then canceled it in the spring of 1987. Viewer protests (encouraged by the network's own publicity) prompted the programmers to reconsider, and *Designing Women* was saved from the Nielsen axe.

Once it became firmly entrenched on Monday evenings that fall, *Designing Women* flourished as part of a strong CBS Monday comedy lineup. Additions to the cast were Bernice Clifton, a lovably eccentric older woman who became friendly with all the partners at Sugarbakers, and Air Force Captain Bill Stillfield, Charlene's new boyfriend. In April 1989 Charlene and Bill were married and, the following January, they had a baby girl, Olivia (Ms. Smart had a baby in real life). Suzanne's biggest crisis occurred when her pet pig, Noel, ran away in the fall of 1989. In the last original episode of the 1989–1990 season, Anthony, who had been going to night school, graduated from college and the following season he became a partner in Sugarbakers. In March of 1991 Julia suffered a major emotional trauma when her longtime boyfriend, Reese, died suddenly from a heart attack.

Although the ratings were fine, a behind-the-scenes situation created problems on the set of *Designing Women*. Star Delta Burke had, over the years, put on considerable weight, which the producers felt made it difficult for her to maintain her sexy on-screen image. They wanted her to lose weight and, when she didn't, an acrimonious feud developed, which was grist for the supermarket and TV tabloids. There were numerous attempts to patch things up but none succeeded, and she was dropped from the show at the end of the 1990–1991 season. In the story line, Suzanne moved to Japan and sold her share of the business to her cousin Allison, an obnoxious, pushy young woman who had failed to find success in New York and had returned to Atlanta. Also added to the cast was Charlene's naive, newly divorced kid sister, Carlene, who arrived to help care for Olivia and who stayed in Atlanta when Charlene moved to England where her husband was stationed.

When Allison pulled out her money to buy a Victoria's Secret franchise at the start of the 1992–1993 season, the financially strapped firm took in a new partner, eccentric wealthy widow B.J. Poteet. It was B.J.'s infusion of cash that kept Sugarbakers from going bankrupt. Later that fall Anthony, while on a trip to Las Vegas to forget his broken engagement, woke up in his hotel room to find out he had married beautiful Folies-Bergère showgirl Etienne Toussant.

CBS aired reruns of *Designing Women* on weekday mornings from May 1991–June 1992.

DESILU PLAYHOUSE, see *Westinghouse Desilu Playhouse*

DESTINATION STARDOM (*Talent*)

FIRST TELECAST: *August 23, 1999*
LAST TELECAST: *July 23, 2000*
BROADCAST HISTORY:

Aug 1999–Oct 1999, PAX Mon 8:00–9:00
Aug 1999–Sep 1999, PAX Sat 7:00–8:00
Sep 1999–Feb 2000, PAX Sat 8:00–9:00
Oct 1999, PAX Thu 11:00–midnight
Nov 1999–Jul 2000, PAX Sun 6:00–7:00
Dec 1999–Jan 2000, PAX Tue 11:00–midnight

HOST:

Lisa Canning

ISLAND HOST:

Kalai Miller

Produced by the people responsible for the long-runnng syndicated talent show *Star Search, Destination Stardom* included both variety and talent elements and was taped in Hawaii. There were six performance categories on *Destination Stardom*—singers age 16-plus, singers age 5–15, comedians, family acts, runway models, and variety acts. It offered more cash prizes than its predecessor, and 100 members of the evening's studio audience served as judges. Winners in each category won $2,000 and the opportunity to return the following week to defend their championship. Home viewers could also vote for their favorite Performance of the Week on the Internet; the Internet-winning act won an additional $1,000.

DESTINY (*Dramatic Anthology*)

FIRST TELECAST: *July 5, 1957*
LAST TELECAST: *September 26, 1958*
BROADCAST HISTORY:

Jul 1957–Sep 1957, CBS Fri 8:30–9:00
Jul 1958–Sep 1958, CBS Fri 8:30–9:00

HOST:

Francis L. Sullivan

Reruns of episodes from other anthologies were aired by CBS in this time slot for two summers, as replacement for *Dick Powell's Zane Grey Theater.*

DESTRY (*Western*)

FIRST TELECAST: *February 14, 1964*
LAST TELECAST: *September 11, 1964*
BROADCAST HISTORY:

Feb 1964–Sep 1964, ABC Fri 7:30–8:30

CAST:

Harrison Destry .... John Gavin

At the center of this comedy-Western was Harrison Destry, a tall, easygoing chap who wasn't exactly a coward—just a mite careful. He'd just as soon dive under the table as shoot it out. Young Destry, the son of famed lawman Tom Destry, had once been a sheriff, until he was packed off to prison on a trumped-up embezzlement charge. In this series he wandered about the West trying to stay out of further trouble as he looked for the scalawags who had framed him.

The Destry character has had a lengthy career; he was portrayed in films by Tom Mix, James Stewart (in a 1939 movie classic co-starring Marlene Dietrich), and Audie Murphy, and later in a hit Broadway musical starring Andy Griffith. The character was originally based on the Max Brand novel *Destry Rides Again.*

DETECTIVE IN THE HOUSE (*Detective*)

FIRST TELECAST: *March 15, 1985*
LAST TELECAST: *April 19, 1985*
BROADCAST HISTORY:

Mar 1985–Apr 1985, CBS Fri 8:00–9:00

CAST:

Press Wyman .... Judd Hirsch
Diane Wyman .... Cassie Yates
Todd Wyman .... Meeno Peluce
Deborah Wyman .... Mandy Ingber
Dunc Wyman .... R. J. Williams
Nick Turner .... Jack Elam

This was not your everyday mid-life crisis. Press Wyman was a successful engineer who wanted to be a private detective. Since he knew very little about sleuthing, Press sought the assistance of retired private eye Nick Turner. In his time, Nick had been a legend—in retirement he was a bit loony, living on his unkempt estate furnished completely with lawn furniture. While Press bumbled his way through cases and did most of the household chores when he wasn't busy, his loving wife Diane went back to work to provide them with a regular income. Todd, Deborah, and Dunc were their three children, who didn't really understand why their father was doing this.

DETECTIVE SCHOOL (*Situation Comedy*)

FIRST TELECAST: *July 31, 1979*
LAST TELECAST: *November 24, 1979*
BROADCAST HISTORY:

Jul 1979–Aug 1979, ABC Tue 8:30–9:00
Sep 1979–Nov 1979, ABC Sat 8:30–9:00

CAST:

Nick Hannigan .... James Gregory
Eddie Dawkins .... Randolph Mantooth
Charlene Jenkins .... LaWanda Page
Teresa Cleary (Jul–Aug) .... Jo Ann Harris
Maggie Ferguson (Sep–Nov) .... Melinda Naud
Leo Frick .... Pat Proft
Robert Redford .... Douglas V. Fowley
Silvio Galindez .... Taylor Negron

James Gregory (Inspector Luger of *Barney Miller*) headed the cast in this short-lived comedy. Nick Hannigan's flea-bitten detective school and agency was supposed to be a night school for sleuths, nothing more. Unfortunately his motley collection of students was constantly getting involved in real cases, to comic effect, and Nick more than once had to bail them out. Sometimes they had to bail *him* out. Dawkins was an enthusiastic young man who worked in a shoe store; Jenkins, a black housewife with a smart mouth, often aimed at aging fellow student Robert Redford (who was obviously no kin to the movie star!). Frick sold vacuum cleaners door-to-door; Galindez was an oily Argentinian hooked on the disco scene. Petite Teresa Cleary, the sixth student, was replaced by gorgeous Maggie Ferguson in September.

The show did well in the summer, against soft competition, but died when it was added to the regular schedule in the fall.

DETECTIVE'S DIARY, see *Mark Saber*

DETECTIVES, STARRING ROBERT TAYLOR, THE (*Police Drama*)

FIRST TELECAST: *October 16, 1959*
LAST TELECAST: *September 21, 1962*
BROADCAST HISTORY:

Oct 1959–Sep 1961, ABC Fri 10:00–10:30
Sep 1961–Sep 1962, NBC Fri 8:30–9:30

CAST:

Capt. Matt Holbrook .... Robert Taylor
Lt. John Russo .... Tige Andrews
Lt. James Conway (1959–1960) .... Lee Farr
Lt. Otto Lindstrom (1959–1961) ... Russell Thorson
Sgt. Chris Ballard (1960–1962) ...... Mark Goddard
Lisa Bonay (1960–1961) .... Ursula Thiess
Sgt. Steve Nelson (1961–1962) .... Adam West

Screen star Robert Taylor played a humorless, hard-nosed, doggedly effective captain on a big-city police force in this unassuming series. He led a team of three plainclothes detectives, which allowed individual episodes of the program to vary the lead (seldom were all four men assigned to the same case). The original trio consisted of Lt. Jim Conway of Homicide, a young ladies' man; Lt. Johnny Russo of Burglary, cigar-smoking and tough-talking; and Lt. Otto Lindstrom of the Bunco squad, an old-timer. Each week one or more of them would tackle a murder, con game, drug operation, or other crime.

Capt. Holbrook was a widower with little time for anything but his job. His only romantic involvement during the three-year run of the series was a brief, antiseptic affair with a police reporter named Lisa Bonay—played by Taylor's real-life wife, German actress Ursula Thiess.

During its season on NBC the program was retitled *Robert Taylor's Detectives.*

DETECTIVE'S WIFE (*Detective Comedy*)

FIRST TELECAST: *July 7, 1950*
LAST TELECAST: *September 29, 1950*
BROADCAST HISTORY:

Jul 1950–Sep 1950, CBS Fri 8:30–9:00

CAST:

Connie Conway .... Lynn Bari
Adam Conway .... Donald Curtis

Detective's Wife was the live summer replacement in 1950 for the popular detective series *Man Against Crime*. Adam Conway was a private detective who wanted to run a peaceful little agency but had received so much publicity after solving a murder that homicides were the only kind of cases he could get. The emphasis in this series was mostly on Adam's wife Connie, who got more involved in his cases than either of them would have preferred.

DEVLIN CONNECTION, THE (*Detective Drama*)

FIRST TELECAST: *October 2, 1982*
LAST TELECAST: *December 25, 1982*
BROADCAST HISTORY:

Oct 1982–Dec 1982, NBC Sat 10:00–11:00

CAST:

Brian Devlin .... Rock Hudson
Nick Corsello .... Jack Scalia
Lauren Dane .... Leigh Taylor-Young
Lt. Earl Borden .... Louis Giambalvo
Mrs. Watanabe .... Takayo
Otis Barnes .... Herb Jefferson, Jr.

The contrast was striking. Brian Devlin was suave, debonair, and independently wealthy, leading a life of quiet elegance. After retiring from a most successful career as a private investigator, he had taken on the distinctly civilized position of Director of the Los Angeles Cultural Arts Center. Into this classy world burst coarse and impetuous Nick Corsello, 28, an aspiring private eye of the "tough" school—and Brian's long-lost son! Nick had been raised in New York by his mother, and now wanted to make it on his own as a gumshoe—though he still worked part-time as a racquetball pro at a health club.

Understandably taken aback, Dad still wanted to get to know this rough gem of a son a little better. Keeping an eye on Nick's cases, he helped out wherever possible, preferably without Nick's knowledge or damage to the Mercedes. Usually they wound up solving the cases together, each using his own special skills.

Lauren was Brian's beautiful assistant at the arts center, and Mrs. Watanabe his efficient housekeeper and cook. Lt. Borden was the friendly, if less than competent, contact on the L.A.P.D. and Otis was Nick's nightclub owner friend.

The series was originally scheduled to premiere in 1981, but was delayed when Rock Hudson underwent open-heart surgery.

DEXTER'S LABORATORY (*Cartoon*)

BROADCAST HISTORY:

Cartoon Network and syndicated
30 minutes
Original episodes: *1996–1998, 2001–* (187 episodes)
Premiered: *April 27, 1996*

VOICES:

Dexter (age 7) (1996–1998, 2001)
.... Christine Cavanaugh
Dexter (2001–) .... Candi Milo
Dee Dee (rotating, 1996–1997, 2001–)
.... Allison Moore
Dee Dee (rotating, 1997–)...... Kathryn Cressida
Mom .... Kath Soucie
Dad .... Jeff Bennett
Mandark (Astro Nomenoff) .... Eddie Deezen
Major Glory .... Rob Paulsen
ValHallen .... Tom Kenny
Krunk, monkey .... Frank Welker

Dexter was an inquisitive seven year-old with horn-rimmed glasses who routinely saved the world with amazing inventions from his secret—but remarkably well-equipped—bedroom laboratory. In addition to robots, monsters, alien fighters, and secret spells, he came up with tricks to improve his own geeky life, such as turning himself (and others) into odd things, or laminating himself so that he wouldn't have to take baths. He also tried to invent a magnetic field to keep his annoying sister Dee Dee out of the lab, but that was hopeless; she regularly wreaked havoc with his experiments. Mom and Dad were their pleasant, clueless parents, and Mandark his archrival at Huber Elementary School, a brainy kid who had his own laboratory and was even smarter than Dexter. Mandark had a crush on Dee Dee, but she was more interested in ballet and candy.

Among the more frequently seen supporting characters were action hero Major Glory, guitar-strumming ValHallen ("the Viking God of Rock"), and Krunk, the "infragable one." Stories were filled with puns, like "Jurassic Pooch" and "Dead Mc Mann and the Publisher's Sweeping House." *Dexter* was first seen on Cartoon Network's "World Premiere Toons" in 1995, becoming a regular series the following year.

DHARMA & GREG (*Situation Comedy*)

FIRST TELECAST: *September 24, 1997*
LAST TELECAST: *April 30, 2002*
BROADCAST HISTORY:

Sep 1997–Jul 1998, ABC Wed 8:30–9:00
Jul 1998–Jul 1999, ABC Wed 8:00–8:30
Jul 1998–Sep 1998, ABC Tue 9:30–10:00
Jul 1999–Sep 2001, ABC Tue 9:00–9:30
Sep 2001–Jan 2002, ABC Tue 8:00–8:30
Mar 2002–Apr 2002, ABC Tue 8:00–8:30

CAST:

Dharma Finkelstein .... Jenna Elfman
Greg Montgomery .... Thomas Gibson
Larry Finkelstein .... Alan Rachins
Abby O'Neill .... Mimi Kennedy
Edward Montgomery .... Mitchell Ryan
Kitty Montgomery .... Susan Sullivan
Pete Cavanaugh .... Joel Murray
Jane (1997–2001) .... Shae D'lyn

Opposites attracted quickly indeed in this romantic comedy, a hit of the 1997 fall season. Dharma was a free-spirited San Francisco yoga instructor and dog trainer, living life on impulse. When she spotted ruggedly handsome attorney Greg on a subway platform, she knew at once he was her spiritual mate. Greg was as stiff and conservative as Dharma was wild and impetuous, but somehow he knew, too, and they were married on their first date. The news did not sit well with either set of parents, for different reasons. Dharma's bohemian mom Abby liked to paint in the nude, while her father Larry was a bumbling anti-war radical from the '60s who acted as if he was still hiding from the authorities (although nobody seemed to care). To them, Dharma had married into the hated establishment (Greg was an Assistant U.S. Attorney). Greg's rich parents, Edward and Kitty, were blue bloods from the country-club crowd, to whom Dharma was utterly incomprehensible. Pete was Greg's gross co-worker, and Jane was Dharma's flaky friend.

During later seasons Greg left the U.S. Attorney's office, went on a "voyage of self-discovery," and eventually set up a private practice with his friend Pete; Abby had a baby; and Dharma and Greg were both injured in a car accident, which led them to be even more appreciative of their lives with each other.

DIAGNOSIS MURDER (*Detective Drama*)
FIRST TELECAST: *October 29, 1993*
LAST TELECAST: *September 7, 2001*
BROADCAST HISTORY:
Oct 1993–Sep 1995, CBS Fri 8:00–9:00
Dec 1995–Aug 1996, CBS Fri 9:00–10:00
Sep 1996–Jul 1997, CBS Thu 8:00–9:00
Jul 1997–Jan 1999, CBS Thu 9:00–10:00
Jan 1999–Mar 1999, CBS Thu 8:00–9:00
Apr 1999–Sep 1999, CBS Thu 9:00–10:00
Jul 1999–May 2000, CBS Thu 8:00–9:00
May 2000–Jun 2000, CBS Thu 8:00–10:00
Oct 2000–Dec 2000, CBS Thu 10:00–11:00
Dec 2000–Jan 2001, CBS Thu 8:00–9:00
Jan 2001, CBS Thu 9:00–10:00
Feb 2001–Sep 2001, CBS Fri 8:00–9:00
Jun 2001, CBS Thu 9:00–10:00
CAST:
Dr. Mark Sloan .... Dick Van Dyke
Dr. Jack Stewart (1993–1995) .... Scott Baio
Amanda Bentley Livingston .... Victoria Rowell
Det. Steve Sloan .... Barry Van Dyke
Norman Briggs (1993–1997)......... Michael Tucci
Nurse Delores Mitchell (1993–1995) ... Delores Hall
Dr. Jesse Travis (1995–2000) ...... Charlie Schlatter
Nurse Susan Hilliard (1998–1999) .... Kim Little
Dr. Madison Wesley (1999–2000) ... Joanna Cassidy
Alex Smith (1999–2001) .... Shane Van Dyke
Det. Cheryl Banks (1999–2001) .... Charmin Lee

Dr. Mark Sloan was the chief of internal medicine at fictional Community General Hospital in Los Angeles in this lighthearted whodunit. Dr. Sloan was a busy guy. Not only did he treat patients and teach young doctors at Community General, but he also maintained a private practice and served as a special consultant to the L.A.P.D. It was consulting to the police that gave Dr. Sloan the most pleasure. An amateur detective, in many ways similar to Jessica Fletcher of *Murder, She Wrote*, the good doctor combined his medical knowledge with keen analytical skills to solve murders that had confounded the police. Working with him were Jack, a handsome young resident at the hospital who did double duty as Mark's legman; Amanda, another resident at Community General, who specialized in pathology; and his son, Steve, a detective on the L.A.P.D. Also seen regularly were Norman, the penny-pinching fussbudget hospital administrator, and Delores, a longtime friend of Mark's and a nurse at the hospital.

When *Diagnosis Murder* returned in December 1995, Jack was gone. He had finished his residency and set up a private practice in Vail, Colorado. New to the cast was Jesse, an enthusiastic young intern who was friendly with Dr. Sloan. Dr. Sloan himself was no longer head of internal medicine but serving as a teaching physician at the hospital and working out of his beach house. In the fall of 1996, Amanda got married and took her spouse's surname—Livingston. The following fall she had become a medical examiner for the L.A.P.D. Norman, who had been injured in the 1996–1997 season finale, went off to recuperate and never showed up again.

In 1998 Amanda got divorced and went back to her maiden name; the following year Steve got a new partner, Cheryl. At the start of the 1999–2000 season Dr. Wesley was the new dean of Community General's medical school. She and Mark had a mutual attraction, but it was offset by their divergent views regarding medical school policy issues. Alex, played by Barry Van Dyke's son Shane, showed up occasionally as a medical student at Community General.

The character of Dr. Mark Sloan had been introduced in an episode of *Jake and the Fatman* and appeared in three made-for-TV movies on CBS before this series premiered.

DIAGNOSIS: UNKNOWN (*Detective Drama*)
FIRST TELECAST: *July 5, 1960*
LAST TELECAST: *September 20, 1960*
BROADCAST HISTORY:
Jul 1960–Sep 1960, CBS Tue 10:00–11:00
CAST:
Dr. Daniel Coffee .... Patrick O'Neal
Doris Hudson .... Phyllis Newman
Dr. Motilal Mookerji .... Cal Bellini
Link .... Martin Huston
Det. Capt. Max Ritter .... Chester Morris

Daniel Coffee, the head pathologist at a large metropolitan hospital, worked closely with the police department to solve bizarre murders. Working with him were his two close friends and assistants, Motilal Mookerji and Doris Hudson. Also seen regularly was Link, the young boy who cleaned up the lab and worked as a handyman for Dr. Coffee. Dr. Coffee's contact on the New York City police department was Captain Ritter.

DIAHANN CARROLL SHOW, THE (*Musical Variety*)
FIRST TELECAST: *August 14, 1976*
LAST TELECAST: *September 3, 1976*
BROADCAST HISTORY:
Aug 1976–Sep 1976, CBS Sat 10:00–11:00
REGULARS:
Diahann Carroll
The Carl Jablonski Dancers
The Earl Brown Orchestra

Singer Diahann Carroll was the star of this four-week mini-series, which included comedy and repartee with guest performers as well as musical numbers.

DIAMONDS (*Detective*)
FIRST TELECAST: *September 22, 1987*
LAST TELECAST: *September 13, 1988*
BROADCAST HISTORY:
Sep 1987–Sep 1988, CBS Tue 11:30–12:40 A.M.
Aug 1988, CBS Wed 11:30–12:40 A.M.
CAST:
Mike Devitt .... Nicholas Campbell
Christina Towne .... Peggy Smithhart
Lt. Lou Gianetti .... Tony Rosato
Darryl .... Alan Feiman

A TV series about TV private eyes who decided to tackle the real thing. Mike and Christina had been married and played married private detectives on their once-popular TV detective series *Diamonds*. Now that they were divorced and their series had been canceled, they decided to try and make a go of it as real-life detectives, opening an agency appropriately called "Two of Diamonds." Helping them was Darryl, the special-effects expert from their former studio, whose plans and tricks got them into and out of numerous tight situations. Also providing assistance was Mike's cousin, police Lt. Gianetti.

When *Diamonds* turned up on the USA cable network after its cancellation by CBS, it included a number of episodes that had not run on American broadcast network television.

Produced in Toronto.

DIANA (*Situation Comedy*)
FIRST TELECAST: *September 10, 1973*
LAST TELECAST: *January 7, 1974*
BROADCAST HISTORY:
Sep 1973–Jan 1974, NBC Mon 8:30–9:00
CAST:
Diana Smythe .... Diana Rigg
Norman Brodnik .... David Sheiner
Howard Tolbrook .... Richard B. Shull
Norma Brodnik .... Barbara Barrie
Marshall Tyler .... Robert Moore
Holly Green .... Carol Androsky
Jeff Harmon .... Richard Mulligan
Smitty, the bellboy .... Liam Dunn

Diana Rigg had been introduced to American audiences as Emma Peel in the British spy-adventure series *The Avengers*. In *Diana* she played an English divorcée in her mid-30s who had moved to New York to begin a new life and a new career. Soon after taking over her absent brother's Manhattan apartment, however, Diana discovered that a number of his men friends had duplicate keys to the place, a situation that resulted in both embarrassing and comic confrontations. Commercial model Holly Green was Diana's friendly neighbor, helping her cope with the unexpected visitors. Diana's co-workers at Butley's Department Store on Fifth Avenue, where she was employed as a fashion coordinator, included Norman Brodnik, the president of the store; Norma, his wife; Howard Tolbrook, a cantankerous copywriter who shared an office with Diana; and Marshall Tyler, a window dresser. Jeff Harmon was a mystery-writer friend of hers.

DIANE DOXEE SHOW, THE (*Music*)
FIRST TELECAST: *August 6, 1950*
LAST TELECAST: *September 24, 1950*
BROADCAST HISTORY:
Aug 1950–Sep 1950, ABC Sun 7:30–8:00
REGULARS:
Diane Doxee
Jimmy Blade

This program featured songs by Miss Doxee, accompanied by Jimmy Blade on piano.

DIARY (*Documentary*)
BROADCAST HISTORY:
MTV
30 minutes
Original episodes: *2000–*
Premiered: *February 16, 2000*

MTV's candid look inside the life of pop idols, from their own point of view. Cameras followed as the celebrity narrated his or her activities, whether recording, staging a concert, hanging with their homies, or talking to the camera (rapper DMZ: "I hate being in the studio!"). Those profiled were favorites of the MTV generation, such as Christina Aguilera, Blink-182, Jackie Chan, Sean "P. Diddy" Combs, Snoop Dogg, Jennifer Lopez, Adam Sandler, and Chris Tucker.

DICK AND THE DUCHESS (*Comedy/Adventure*)
FIRST TELECAST: *September 28, 1957*
LAST TELECAST: *May 16, 1958*
BROADCAST HISTORY:
Sep 1957–Mar 1958, CBS Sat 8:30–9:00
Mar 1958–May 1958, CBS Fri 7:30–8:00
CAST:
Dick Starrett .... Patrick O'Neal
Jane Starrett .... Hazel Court
Peter Jamison .... Richard Wattis
Inspector Stark .... Michael Shepley
Mathilda .... Beatrice Varley
Rodney .... Ronnie Stevens

Dick Starrett was an American living in London and married to Jane, his "duchess." He often found himself in perplexing situations with members of Jane's upper-crust English family, who were less than enchanted with her marriage to a commoner—and an American at that. Dick was employed as an insurance investigator/adjuster by a large multinational company, and to complicate matters, Jane frequently managed to get herself involved in his claims investigations, trying to help but only causing problems. Peter Jamison was Dick's friend and associate at the office, and Inspector Stark was a Scotland Yard investigator with whom he often worked.

DICK CAVETT SHOW, THE (*Talk/Variety*)
FIRST TELECAST: *May 26, 1969*
LAST TELECAST: *December 29, 1972*
BROADCAST HISTORY:
May 1969–Sep 1969, ABC Mon/Tue/Fri 10:00–11:00
Dec 1969–Dec 1972, ABC Mon–Fri 11:30 P.M.–1:00 A.M.
REGULARS:
Dick Cavett
Bobby Rosengarden
Fred Foy

Dick Cavett was one of the few TV personalities ever to star in major programs in daytime, prime time, and late nighttime, all in quick succession, and to fail to attract a large audience with any of them. His shows were well received by the critics and were generally acknowledged to be witty, intelligent, and interesting compared to what was scheduled around them. Perhaps it was his intelligence that did Cavett in, for he never hesitated to bring in thought-provoking people as well as show-biz types as guests. Viewers, evidently, didn't much care to have their thoughts provoked.

All three of Cavett's ABC shows were essentially talk programs with some singing or performing guests. The daytime version was a 90-minute affair, five days a week, and lasted from March 1968 until January 1969. The prime-time summer show was on three nights a week from May until September 1969, and the late-night edition (11:30 P.M.-1:00 A.M.) lasted from December 1969 until December 1972. Guests in prime time included the usual run of movie and sports stars (including a full hour with Groucho Marx) mixed in with such heady fare as political pundit I. F. Stone, maverick Federal Communications Commission member Nicholas Johnson, and Cavett's own former philosophy professor, Paul Weiss.

In December 1969 Cavett moved to late-night television, with Bobby Rosengarden as orchestra leader and Fred Foy as announcer. The guests continued to be diverse. At one point Cavett presented a series of one-guest shows with Anthony Quinn, Fred Astaire, Charlton Heston, Jack Lemmon, and Woody Allen, followed by a program on which a group of children gave their views of contemporary life. On another famous occasion, in December 1971, former Governor Lester Maddox of Georgia walked off the show when challenged on his segregationist views.

While the show continued to receive excellent reviews, ABC continued to run a poor third behind NBC and CBS in late-night viewership. Finally in April 1972 the network announced that unless audience levels improved by July 28, the program would be canceled. This set off a controversy almost unparalleled in TV history. ABC was deluged with more than 15,000 letters in a few weeks, running nine to one in favor of Cavett. Several ABC affiliates ran "Save the Dick Cavett Show" advertisements, and notable public figures urged that the series be continued. Columnists around the country had a field day, castigating ABC and the Nielsen audience measurement system, and lauding Cavett as—in the words of one—"infinitely more valuable than another old movie." Perhaps Cavett could not attract as many viewers as Johnny Carson, editorialized *Time* magazine, but "should the more than 3,200,000 viewers who want his brand of intelligent alternative programming be summarily disenfranchised?"

Viewership did not increase significantly and, after a temporary reprieve, *The Dick Cavett Show* was cut back to occasional status in January 1973, when it became part of the new *ABC Wide World of Entertainment*. It left ABC entirely in 1975.

DICK CAVETT SHOW, THE (*Variety*)

FIRST TELECAST: *August 16, 1975*
LAST TELECAST: *September 6, 1975*
BROADCAST HISTORY:
Aug 1975–Sep 1975, CBS Sat 10:00–11:00
REGULARS:
Dick Cavett
Leigh French
Marshall Efron

Host Dick Cavett did a little bit of everything in this four-week summer series. He interviewed guest stars, sang a little, and acted in comedy sketches with comedienne Leigh French and comedian Marshall Efron. Mr. Efron, in addition to performing, was one of the writers of the show.

DICK CAVETT SHOW, THE (*Talk/Discussion*)

FIRST TELECAST: *September 23, 1986*
LAST TELECAST: *December 30, 1986*
BROADCAST HISTORY:
Sep 1986–Dec 1986, ABC Tue/Wed 12:00 midnight-1:00 A.M.
HOST:
Dick Cavett

Dick Cavett returned to network TV in 1986, briefly, with another of his wide-ranging, thought-provoking, and little-viewed discussion shows. Part of an ABC plan to provide meatier fare for late-night viewers (*Nightline* at 11:30 P.M., followed by Cavett on Tuesday and Wednesday, and Jimmy Breslin on Thursday and Friday). *The Dick Cavett Show* featured authors, screenwriters, politicians, and thinkers along with some interesting actors (Lily Tomlin, Carol Burnett, Veronica Hamel). The last telecast consisted of a group of children explaining their views on a number of issues.

DICK CLARK PRESENTS THE ROCK AND ROLL YEARS (*Music*)

FIRST TELECAST: *November 28, 1973*
LAST TELECAST: *January 9, 1974*
BROADCAST HISTORY:
Nov 1973–Jan 1974, ABC Wed 8:00–8:30
HOST/EXECUTIVE PRODUCER:
Dick Clark
REGULARS:
Jeff Kutash Dancers

This series presented a nostalgic portrait of the rock 'n' roll era through performances by its top artists, laced with chatter about the styles, dances, and news events of the period. Each program consisted of three acts taped before a live audience at Santa Monica Civic Auditorium in California, five acts from the past shown in film clips, and one spot titled "The Immortal," in which a superstar of the past performed. Many of the top recording stars of the 1950s and 1960s appeared, such as Chuck Berry, Pat Boone, Danny and the Juniors, the Shirelles, Duane Eddy, and Little Richard; there were also some more recent acts, such as Chicago and Three Dog Night. The "Immortals" (most of them deceased) included Jimi Hendrix, James Dean, Clyde McPhatter, and Jim Croce. Unfortunately, Clark never managed to sign Elvis.

DICK CLARK SHOW, THE (*Music*)

FIRST TELECAST: *February 16, 1958*
LAST TELECAST: *September 10, 1960*
BROADCAST HISTORY:
Feb 1958–Sep 1960, ABC Sat 7:30–8:00
HOST:
Dick Clark

Dick Clark, host of the highly successful afternoon series *American Bandstand*, was featured in this nighttime derivative of his daytime show. Each week a number of recording artists, whose records were currently on the "Top 40" charts, performed their hits on *The Dick Clark Show*. Although some of them actually sang on the show, most of them lip-synched to their own recordings. Some of the numbers were performed simply; others were done as production numbers. The highlight of the show was the unveiling of the "American Bandstand Top Ten" records for the following week at the conclusion of the program. The series was also known as *The Dick Clark Saturday Night Beechnut Show*.

DICK CLARK'S GOLDEN GREATS (*Music*)

BROADCAST HISTORY:
Syndicated only

30 minutes
Produced: *1988–1989* (26 episodes)
Released: *October 1988*

HOST:
Dick Clark

He was no longer hosting *American Bandstand*, but Dick Clark was still finding ways to mine the vaults. Taking his cue from the popularity of current and vintage music videos, Clark put together this show which featured taped and filmed performances by rock performers over the decades. Many of the videos were excerpted from *Bandstand* and other Clark properties, along with others that he licensed for the show. Among those appearing were the Beach Boys, Linda Ronstadt, Lionel Ritchie, Roy Orbison, The Supremes, Michael Jackson, Gladys Knight and the Pips, Bill Haley and the Comets, James Brown, The Beastie Boys, Jerry Lee Lewis, Kiss, and The Four Tops.

DICK CLARK'S LIVE WEDNESDAY (*Variety*)

FIRST TELECAST: *September 20, 1978*
LAST TELECAST: *December 27, 1978*
BROADCAST HISTORY:
Sep 1978–Dec 1978, NBC Wed 8:00–9:00

HOST/PRODUCER:
Dick Clark

Dick Clark, who was a major force in bringing rock 'n' roll to TV in the 1950s, became the chief exponent of nostalgia for the music of that decade, 20 years later. Looking just as young as he had on *American Bandstand* in 1957, Clark hosted a series of highly popular specials which led to his own live prime-time musical variety series in 1978. The program featured a mix of current popular music and that of the 1950s and 1960s, performed by the original artists. Sometimes singers would be introduced with clips of themselves performing years before, as when Ricky Nelson was seen as a child on *The Adventures of Ozzie & Harriet*, before he came on to perform. There was chatter about the fads of the past, and a feature called "Where Are They Now?", but all was not nostalgia. Current stars performed as well. Dozens of famous faces flashed across the screen each week, many in cameo appearances, ranging from such current teenage favorites as Jimmy and Kristy McNichol to old pros like Bob Hope and Danny Kaye, and old rock 'n' rollers like Chuck Berry and Bo Diddley. To emphasize the show's live origination (from Hollywood), a death-defying stunt was performed on each telecast by a professional stuntman.

Six months after it left the air, *Dick Clark's Live Wednesday* returned for a single telecast on July 11, 1979.

DICK CLARK'S NIGHTTIME (*Musical Variety*)

BROADCAST HISTORY:
Syndicated only
60 minutes
Produced: *1985–1986* (26 episodes)
Released: *September 1985*

HOST:
Dick Clark

Dick Clark, host of ABC's long-running *American Bandstand*, produced and hosted this late-night syndicated music series. The format was a mix of performances and interviews with rock artists, videos, and *Bandstand*-style in-studio dancing to recorded music. Most of the stations carrying the show aired it on Saturday nights after their late-evening local news.

DICK CLARK'S WORLD OF TALENT (*Variety*)

FIRST TELECAST: *September 27, 1959*
LAST TELECAST: *December 20, 1959*
BROADCAST HISTORY:
Sep 1959–Dec 1959, ABC Sun 10:30–11:00

REGULARS:
Dick Clark
Jack E. Leonard

Each week Dick Clark was the host to three young performers who presented their acts to the viewing audience and a panel composed of Jack E. Leonard and two celebrity guests. The panel would then comment on the performances and offer suggestions to the entertainers. Most of the performers had already begun their professional careers; they ranged from 15-year-old concert pianist Lorin Hollander to folksingers Bud and Travis. Comedians, dancers, and soloists were also seen (despite Clark's identification with the current hit parade, there were few rock acts). Some of the performers had been in show business quite a while, in fact, stretching the "young artist" theme a bit; among these were singers Don Cornell, Della Reese, Alan Dale, and The Four Aces.

DICK POWELL SHOW, THE (*Dramatic Anthology*)

FIRST TELECAST: *September 26, 1961*
LAST TELECAST: *September 17, 1963*
BROADCAST HISTORY:
Sep 1961–Sep 1962, NBC Tue 9:00–10:00
Sep 1962–Sep 1963, NBC Tue 9:30–10:30

HOST/STAR:
Dick Powell

Dick Powell, the boyish star of some of the 1930s' most glittering movie musicals, was a seasoned veteran when he appeared in this, his last TV series. Many of the episodes aired were pilots, and two of them actually became regular series in their own right. Powell himself starred in the first telecast, "Who Killed Julie Greer," playing the role of wealthy policeman Amos Burke; the following fall Gene Barry took on the same role in the series *Burke's Law*. "Savage Sunday" starred Nick Adams as a crusading New York newspaper reporter, a role he kept when *Saints and Sinners* premiered the next fall. Among the pilots that didn't succeed was "Safari," based on the movie *The African Queen* and starring Glynis Johns and James Coburn. A noteworthy episode was "The Price of Tomatoes," for which a young Peter Falk won an Emmy.

In addition to serving as host, Powell periodically appeared in individual episodes. During the first season he co-starred with his wife June Allyson in a play called "A Time to Die." It is not known whether Powell knew at the time that he had cancer, but by the beginning of the second season he was in declining health. His last acting role was in "The Court-Martial of Captain Wycliff," which was aired on December 12, 1962, and his last appearance as host (on film) was on New Year's Day 1963. He died the following day. In deference to his family the filmed introductions that he had already prepared for future telecasts were deleted, and a succession of guest stars appeared as hosts for the remainder of the season. The title of the program was also changed to *The Dick Powell Theatre.*

DICK POWELL'S ZANE GREY THEATER (*Western Anthology*)

FIRST TELECAST: *October 5, 1956*
LAST TELECAST: *September 20, 1962*
BROADCAST HISTORY:

Oct 1956–Jul 1958, CBS Fri 8:30–9:00 (OS)
Oct 1958–Sep 1960, CBS Thu 9:00–9:30
Oct 1960–Jul 1961, CBS Thu 8:30–9:00
Apr 1962–Sep 1962, CBS Thu 9:30–10:00

HOST/STAR:

Dick Powell

During its early seasons, *Dick Powell's Zane Grey Theater* was comprised completely of adaptations of the short stories and novels of famous Western author Zane Grey. Eventually, when the Grey material began to run out, Western stories from other authors were included. Host Dick Powell was frequently the star of individual episodes, more often in the early years than later in its run. The episodes telecast in the summer of 1962 were all reruns.

DICK TRACY (*Police Drama*)

FIRST TELECAST: *September 11, 1950*
LAST TELECAST: *February 12, 1951*
BROADCAST HISTORY:

Sep 1950–Oct 1950, ABC Wed 8:30–9:00
Oct 1950–Dec 1950, ABC Mon 8:30–9:00
Jan 1951–Feb 1951, ABC Tue 8:00–8:30

CAST:

Dick Tracy .... Ralph Byrd
Sam Catchem .... Joe Devlin

Chester Gould's famous comic-strip hero appeared briefly on network television in 1950–1951 in this very violent series. With him were the famous supporting characters, including his sidekick Sam Catchem, Chief Murphy, and an array of incredible villains ranging from The Mole (a counterfeiter who tunneled underground) to the laughing Joker. Ralph Byrd, who had been slugging it out in Dick Tracy theatrical movies and serials since the 1930s, also appeared in this TV version.

Byrd continued to make new *Tracy* films for TV syndication after the series left the network, until his death in 1952. Joe Devlin co-starred. *Dick Tracy* had also been heard on radio from 1935–1948, the latter part of its run on ABC. Edited versions of theatrical movies, as well as a cartoon version, were seen on TV in later years.

DICK VAN DYKE SHOW, THE (*Situation Comedy*)

FIRST TELECAST: *October 3, 1961*
LAST TELECAST: *September 7, 1966*
BROADCAST HISTORY:

Oct 1961–Dec 1961, CBS Tue 8:00–8:30
Jan 1962–Sep 1964, CBS Wed 9:30–10:00
Sep 1964–Sep 1965, CBS Wed 9:00–9:30
Sep 1965–Sep 1966, CBS Wed 9:30–10:00

CAST:

Rob Petrie .... Dick Van Dyke
Laura Petrie .... Mary Tyler Moore
Sally Rogers .... Rose Marie
Maurice "Buddy" Sorrell .... Morey Amsterdam
Ritchie Petrie .... Larry Mathews
Melvin Cooley .... Richard Deacon
Jerry Helper .... Jerry Paris
Millie Helper .... Ann Morgan Guilbert
Alan Brady .... Carl Reiner

CREATOR

Carl Reiner

PRODUCER/DIRECTOR/WRITER (VARIOUS EPISODES):

Carl Reiner
Sheldon Leonard
Jerry Paris

This highly successful series is often considered one of television's classic comedies, primarily because of its first-class scripting and excellent casting. Most of the principals were show-business veterans and several went on to star in series of their own. The setting, appropriately enough, was behind the scenes on a mythical TV comedy show. Rob Petrie was the head comedy writer for *The Alan Brady Show*, a popular New York-based comedy-variety series whose neurotic star was seldom seen here. Working with Rob were two other writers, Sally and Buddy, both of whom were close friends of Rob and his wife Laura. Their nemesis at the office, and the butt of much humor, was balding Melvin Cooley, the pompous producer of *The Alan Brady Show* and the brother-in-law of its star. Episodes generally revolved around the problems of the writers and the home life of the Petries in New Rochelle. Early episodes often included flashbacks to Rob and Laura's courtship, while Rob was still in the army, the early days of their marriage, and the development of Rob's career. Frequently seen were their next-door neighbors, Jerry and Millie Helper. Writer-director Carl Reiner played the occasional role of Alan Brady, who was heard but never seen until the show had been on for several seasons.

The Dick Van Dyke Show took several seasons to develop into a major hit and was still very popular in 1966, when it finally left the air because Van Dyke and other cast members wanted to try new material. Van Dyke was never able to repeat the spectacular success of this series, but his co-star Mary Tyler Moore went on to greater fame on her own *Mary Tyler Moore Show* in the 1970s. See the index for other series starring Morey Amsterdam and Sheldon Leonard.

Reruns of *The Dick Van Dyke Show* were a staple on the CBS weekday daytime lineup from August 1965 to September 1969.

DIFF'RENT STROKES (*Situation Comedy*)

FIRST TELECAST: *November 3, 1978*
LAST TELECAST: *August 30, 1986*
BROADCAST HISTORY:

Nov 1978–Oct 1979, NBC Fri 8:00–8:30
Oct 1979–Oct 1981, NBC Wed 9:00–9:30
Oct 1981–Aug 1982, NBC Thu 9:00–9:30
Aug 1982–Aug 1985, NBC Sat 8:00–8:30
Sep 1985–Mar 1986, ABC Fri 9:00–9:30
Jun 1986–Aug 1986, ABC Sat 8:00–8:30

CAST:

Philip Drummond .... Conrad Bain
Arnold Jackson .... Gary Coleman
Willis Jackson .... Todd Bridges
Kimberly Drummond (1978–1984) ...... Dana Plato
Mrs. Edna Garrett (1978–1979) .... Charlotte Rae
Adelaide Brubaker (1980–1982) .... Nedra Volz
Pearl Gallagher (1982–1986) .... Mary Jo Catlett

Aunt Sophia (1981–1982) .... Dody Goodman
Dudley Ramsey (1981–1986) .... Shavar Ross
Mr. Ted Ramsey (1981–1985) .... Le Tari
Miss Chung (1982–1983) .... Rosalind Chao
Charlene DuPrey (1981–1982)........ Janet Jackson
Robbie Jason (1982–1983)............ Steven Mond
Lisa Hayes (1982–1986) .... Nikki Swasey
Sam McKinney (1984–1986)....... Danny Cooksey
Maggie McKinney (1984–1985)........ Dixie Carter
Maggie McKinney (1985–1986) ... Mary Ann Mobley
Charlie (1985–1986) .... Jason Hervey

Pint-sized Gary Coleman was one of the comedy discoveries of the late 1970s. Pudgy cheeks, twinkling eyes, and flawless timing made him seem like an old pro packed into the body of a small child—and he helped turn this improbable comedy into one of the hits of the 1978–1979 season.

Eight-year-old Arnold and his 12-year-old brother Willis were two black kids from Harlem who found themselves quite suddenly in the lap of luxury. Their dying mother, a housekeeper for wealthy Philip Drummond, had extracted from her employer the promise that he would look after her boys. Unlike some of TV's other accidental parents (see, for example, *Family Affair*), Drummond didn't mind at all, and welcomed the two into his Park Avenue apartment as his own. No matter that there were endless double takes when the rich, white Drummond, president of the huge conglomerate Trans Allied, Inc. (though he never seemed to work much), introduced the two spunky black kids as his "sons." They didn't care. There was always plenty of love around—though Willis seemed a bit reserved—and everybody learned little lessons in Living Right in each episode. There were also episodes on such serious subjects as child abuse and the dangers of hitchhiking. First Lady Nancy Reagan appeared in a 1983 episode dealing with drug abuse. Rounding out the household was widower Drummond's 13-year-old daughter, Kimberly, and the new housekeeper, the scatterbrained Mrs. Garrett.

As years passed, new characters were introduced. Mrs. Garrett left to become a housemother at the prestigious Eastland School for Girls, which Kimberly was attending, in a spin-off series called *The Facts of Life*. She was replaced as housekeeper first by the somewhat grumpy Adelaide, and then by cheerful Pearl. Dudley arrived on the scene in 1981 as Arnold's best buddy, while Charlene was Willis's girlfriend for a time. Perhaps the most notable addition to all their lives came in 1984. After years of fruitless matchmaking by his sister Sophia and by the kids, Drummond finally fell in love—with a feisty TV-exercise-show hostess named Maggie. They were married in February 1984, adding her young son Sam to the Drummond household. In the fall of 1984 Kimberly graduated from high school and went away to study in Paris.

When *Diff'rent Strokes* premiered NBC had few comedies on its schedule, and it used its new hit to help out some of the others. First *Facts of Life* began with a crossover episode. Then Drummond just happened to buy the Portland, Oregon, radio station where Larry Adler (principal character on *Hello, Larry*) was a talk-show host, leading to some visits there; Larry and Philip, it seemed, were old army buddies.

Coleman was 10 when this series began. He was born with a congenital kidney problem and received a kidney transplant at the age of five, which resulted in his being smaller than normal for his age (a condition that would continue throughout his life). An uncommonly bright and articulate youngster, he seemed quite happy to be alive, and became a frequent and popular guest on talk shows and other series.

NBC aired reruns of *Diff'rent Strokes* on weekdays from April 1982 to December 1983 and from July to September 1984.

DIFFERENT WORLD, A (*Situation Comedy*)

FIRST TELECAST: *September 24, 1987*
LAST TELECAST: *July 9, 1993*
BROADCAST HISTORY:
Sep 1987–Jun 1992, NBC Thu 8:30–9:00
Jul 1991–Aug 1991, NBC Mon 8:30–9:00
Jul 1992–Nov 1992, NBC Thu 8:00–8:30
Nov 1992–Jan 1993, NBC Thu 8:30–9:00
May 1993–Jun 1993, NBC Thu 8:00–8:30
Jul 1993, NBC Fri 8:00–8:30

CAST:
Denise Huxtable (1987–1988) .... Lisa Bonet
Whitley Gilbert .... Jasmine Guy
Jaleesa Vinson (1987–1992) .... Dawnn Lewis
Dwayne Wayne .... Kadeem Hardison
Ron Johnson.......................... Darryl Bell
Maggie Lauten (1987–1988) .... Marisa Tomei
Millie (1987–1988)........... Marie-Alise Recasner
Stevie Rallen (1987–1988) .... Loretta Devine
J. T. Rallen (1987–1988)............ Amir Williams
Gloria (1987–1988) .... Bee-be Smith
Allison (1987–1988) .... Kim Wayans
Walter Oakes (1987–1991) .... Sinbad
Lettie Bostic (1988–1989).............. Mary Alice
Col. Clayton Taylor (1988–1993) .... Glynn Turman
**Terrence Johann Taylor (1990–1992)*.... Cory Tyler
Winifred "Freddie" Brooks (1988–1993)
.... Cree Summer
Kim Reese (1988–1993) .... Charnele Brown
Vernon Gaines (1988–1993) .... Lou Myers
Ernest (1989–1990) .... Reuben Grundy
**Julian (1990–1991)* .... Dominic Hoffman
Lena James (1991–1993)............... Jada Pinkett
Charmaine Brown (1992–1993)
.... Karen Malina White
Gina Devereaux (1991–1992) .... Ajai Sanders
Byron Douglas III (1991)............... Joe Morton
Shazza Zulu (1992) .... Gary Dourdan
Clint (1992–1992) .... Michael Ralph

* Occasional

THEME:
"A Different World," by Stu Gardner, Bill Cosby, and Dawnn Lewis, sung by Phoebe Snow during the first season and Aretha Franklin thereafter

Fresh from her movie debut in the controversial film *Angel Heart*, 19-year-old Lisa Bonet starred in this spin-off from the top-rated *Cosby Show*. The "different world" for Denise Huxtable was college, where for the first time in her life she was out from under the protective wing of her family and trying to make it on her own. As the series began she was a sophomore at Hillman College, a mostly black institution which both her father and grandfather had attended. Dad (Bill Cosby) and the family were only a phone call away, but Denise was determined to show that she was "all grown up" and wasn't going to come running home for money and support at every crisis. That wasn't easy, since the crises came every week, sitcom-style. Denise's roommates were Jaleesa, a 26-year-old freshman who had already been married and divorced, and who had a no-nonsense attitude toward life; and Maggie, a flighty, naive, eternally optimistic chatterbox (and one of the few whites at Hillman).

There were numerous cast changes as the series, which began as a rather pale offshoot of *The Cosby Show*, began to find a character of its own. The ostensible star, Lisa Bonet, was eased out after the first season. Various professors came and went, and dorm director Stevie was replaced by Lettie—a colorful woman who had left Hillman to "walk on the wild side," then returned to finish her education—and eventually by Walter, who also ran a local community center. Also prominently featured were uppity Southern belle Whitley, super-cool math major Dwayne and his best friend Ron, as well as Col. Taylor ("Dr. War"), free-spirit Freddie, strong-willed Kim, streetwise Lena, chatty Charmaine, and sassy Gina in later seasons. Gaines ran the campus eatery and hangout, The Pit.

Hillman proved such a rewarding place that several of the principals stayed around even after graduation. Jaleesa became a marketing executive, opened her own temporary employment agency, and married Col. Taylor; Dwayne continued as a graduate student; and Whitley (whom Dwayne eventually married) was for a time dorm director of Gilbert Hall.

DILBERT (*Cartoon Situation Comedy*)
FIRST TELECAST: *January 25, 1999*
LAST TELECAST: *August 15, 2000*
BROADCAST HISTORY:
Jan 1999–Jul 1999, UPN Mon 8:00–8:30
Sep 1999–Oct 1999, UPN Tue 8:00–8:30
Oct 1999–Jan 2000, UPN Tue 8:30–9:00
Jan 2000–Feb 2000, UPN Tue 9:30–10:00
May 2000–Aug 2000, UPN Tue 8:30–9:00
VOICES:
Dilbert .... Daniel Stern
Dogbert .... Chris Elliott
Wally .... Gordon Hunt
Alice .... Cathy Griffin
The Boss .... Larry Miller
Dilmom .... Jackie Hoffman

While Fred Savage, the innocent Kevin of *The Wonder Years*, went on to star in one wild parody of corporate America in the '90s (*Working*), his alter ego (Daniel Stern) provided the lead voice on another. Dilbert was an everyman for modern office workers, coping with the absurdities and frustrations of a bureaucracy gone mad. The Company, for which he worked as a lowly, cubicle-bound engineer, was gigantic and totally dysfunctional. At one point it marketed a throat lozenge laced with anthrax spores, and when that failed, planned another product called "Salmonella." When layoffs took place, there was actual rioting in the offices. Lazy Wally and hyperactive, aggressive Alice were fellow engineers. They all worked for the Boss, a pointy-haired incompetent who took credit for the work of others and was totally insensitive to the needs of his people. Since The Company only cared about profits, Dilbert's work was closely scrutinized by the dreaded marketing department, and he was constantly under pressure to come up with new products and ideas. The ultimate threat, should he fail to produce, was a transfer to Albany, the Siberia of The Company. Dilbert's most beloved invention was the Gruntmaster 6000, whose purpose was never explained—although his superiors had great hopes for its success. Dogbert was Dilbert's sarcastic canine roommate, an opportunist and master manipulator who turned every situation into a profitable business opportunity for himself. In one episode he even orchestrated a takeover of The Company and installed himself as CEO. Dilmom, Dilbert's condescending mother, came to visit occasionally, invariably beating him at Scrabble.

In the series-ending two parter, Dilbert sent a small rocket probe to find samples of life and return to him. It accumulated DNA from aliens, a hillbilly, a cow, an engineer and a robot. When it returned, it struck Dilbert in the buttocks and impregnated him. Because The Company had cut back on his health insurance and wouldn't cover his pregnancy, he went to a literary agent, who manipulated the media into a frenzy. At the televised custody hearing for his unborn "baby," presided over by Judge "Stone Cold" Steve Austin, Dilbert lost custody, attempted suicide by jumping out the courtroom window, and was saved by Dogbert. After Dilbert gave birth to a hybrid baby, Dogbert kept it out of the hands of the people by sending it to Jor-El and Lara on the planet Krypton—which apparently had not been destroyed after they had sent *their* infant son to Earth decades earlier.

Based on the highly successful syndicated comic strip by Scott Adams, who also created the TV series.

DINAH AND HER NEW BEST FRIENDS (*Musical Variety*)
FIRST TELECAST: *June 5, 1976*
LAST TELECAST: *July 31, 1976*
BROADCAST HISTORY:
Jun 1976–Jul 1976, CBS Sat 10:00–11:00
REGULARS:
Dinah Shore
Diana Canova
Bruce Kimmel
Gary Mule Deer
Mike Neun
Leland Palmer
Michael Preminger
Avelio Falana
Dee Dee Rescher

This 1976 summer variety series, a replacement for the vacationing Carol Burnett, starred the most successful female variety series performer of the 1950s and 1960s, the versatile Dinah Shore. Working with Miss Shore was a company of regular players who had had little, if any, previous television exposure. They participated in comedy sketches, did their own solos, and blended their talents with those of the guest stars for the week.

DINAH SHORE CHEVY SHOW, THE (*Musical Variety*)
FIRST TELECAST: *October 5, 1956*
LAST TELECAST: *May 12, 1963*
BROADCAST HISTORY:
Oct 1956–Jun 1957, NBC Fri 10:00–11:00
Oct 1957–Jun 1961, NBC Sun 9:00–10:00 (OS)

Oct 1961–Jun 1962, NBC Fri 9:30–10:30
Dec 1962–May 1963, NBC Sun 10:00–11:00

REGULARS:

Dinah Shore
The Skylarks (1956–1957)
The Even Dozen (1961–1962)
The Tony Charmoli Dancers (1957–1962)
The Nick Castle Dancers (1962–1963)
The Harry Zimmerman Orchestra (1957–1961, 1962–1963)
Frank DeVol and His Orchestra (1961–1962)

Dinah Shore, one of the few women to achieve major success as a variety-series host on TV, starred in her own full-hour musical variety show on NBC for seven seasons, following a successful run with the much simpler and shorter *Dinah Shore Show,* which was only 15 minutes long. A full hour enabled Dinah to play host to top-name guest stars, include skits and large production numbers, and expand on her own varied talents. Besides her warm and friendly style, her trademarks on this series were the theme song "See the U.S.A. in your Chevrolet" and the resounding kiss she gave the audience at the end of each show.

When *The Dinah Shore Chevy Show* premiered in 1956 it was as a series of monthly specials. The following fall it moved to Sunday night and became a weekly series. It vacated the Sunday time slot to *Bonanza* in 1961, moved to Friday with the new title *The Dinah Shore Show,* and continued on a rotating basis with assorted specials for two more seasons.

DINAH SHORE SHOW, THE (*Music*)

FIRST TELECAST: *November 27, 1951*
LAST TELECAST: *July 18, 1957*
BROADCAST HISTORY:

Nov 1951–Jul 1957, NBC Tue/Thu 7:30–7:45 (OS)

REGULARS:

Dinah Shore
The Notables, vocal quintet (1951–1955)
The Skylarks, vocal quintet (1955–1957)
Ticker Freeman, pianist
The Vic Shoen Orchestra (1951–1954)
The Harry Zimmerman Orchestra (1954–1957)

Twice weekly for six years, Dinah Shore starred in this live 15-minute musical show that occupied the remainder of the half hour that included the NBC network news. Dinah sang, often gave her accompanist Ticker Freeman a chance to do featured solos, and occasionally had guest stars with whom she chatted and performed.

DINNER DATE WITH VINCENT LOPEZ, see *Vincent Lopez*

DINOSAURS (*Situation Comedy*)

FIRST TELECAST: *April 26, 1991*
LAST TELECAST: *July 20, 1994*
BROADCAST HISTORY:

Apr 1991–May 1991, ABC Fri 8:30–9:00
Aug 1991–Feb 1992, ABC Wed 8:00–8:30
Mar 1992–Feb 1993, ABC Fri 9:00–9:30
Apr 1993–May 1993, ABC Sun 7:30–8:00
Jun 1993–Sep 1993, ABC Fri 9:00–9:30
Jun 1994–Jul 1994, ABC Wed 8:00–8:30

VOICES:

Earl Sinclair.......................... Stuart Pankin
Fran Sinclair.......................... Jessica Walter
Robbie Sinclair (age 14)............ Jason Willinger
Charlene Sinclair (12).............. Sally Struthers
Baby Sinclair......................... Kevin Clash
Grandma Ethyl....................... Florence Stanley
Roy Hess.............................. Sam McMurray
B. P. Richfield...................... Sherman Hemsley

Modern-day life and its foibles were seen through the eyes of a domesticated family of dinosaurs in this unusual comedy, conceived by muppet creator Jim Henson before his death. The puppet-like figures were brought to life by a complex process called "audio-animatronics" at Henson Productions' Creature Shop in London by his son, Brian Henson, and the same craftsmen who created the Muppets and the Teenage Mutant Ninja Turtles.

The puppets were funny and strikingly realistic, but the plot was Stone Age sitcom, derived from *The Honeymooners* by way of *The Flintstones.* The year was 60,000,003 B.C. on the Super-continent of Pangaea. Earl Sinclair was a henpecked, blustery, cigar-smoking megalosaurus who worked as a tree-pusher for the Wesayso Development Corporation, which leveled forests to make way for suburban tract homes like his own. His sensible wife Fran, a ten-ton allosaurus, ran both the household and Earl's life. Teenage son Robbie was in his rebellious phase, but also the most enlightened member of the family, questioning all the foolish dinosaur customs; Charlene was his shop-till-you-drop sister; and Baby, the most recently hatched member of the family, a smart-mouthed brat who got on Earl's nerves. Everyone, in fact, got on Earl's nerves, especially his nagging mother-in-law Ethyl, who despised him, and his tyrannical boss B. P. Richfield, a triceratops with fearsome teeth. Earl's best friend, a confirmed bachelor tyrannosaurus who lived in a condo at the marina, was Roy Hess. (Notice how everyone here seems to have a name derived from an oil company? There were many levels of parody in *Dinosaurs.*) Occasionally, for comic relief, a few caveman humans were seen scampering around like wild animals trying to invent the wheel.

Although the series ended its regular run at the end of the 1992–1993 season, a few additional original episodes were aired during the summer of 1994.

DINOTOPIA (*Fantasy/Adventure*)

FIRST TELECAST: *November 28, 2002*
LAST TELECAST: *December 26, 2002*
BROADCAST HISTORY:

Nov 2002–Dec 2002, ABC Thu 8:00–9:00

CAST:

Karl Scott........................ Erik von Detten
David Scott....................... Shiloh Strong
Frank Scott...................... Michael Brandon
Princess Marion............... Georgina Rylance
Mayor Waldo.................... Jonathan Hyde
Rosemary......................... Sophie Ward
Le Sage........................... Lisa Zane
Zippo (voice).................... Omid Djalili

MUSIC:

performed by the London Symphony Orchestra, conducted by Geoffrey Alexander

This fantasy-adventure, modeled after the *Jurassic Park* movies, was a festival of special effects. Bull-headed Frank Scott and his handsome, squabbling teenage sons Karl and David had crashed their private plane in the Caribbean and washed up on a "lost" tropical island. There they found others who had been similarly stranded, some descended from castaways from as much as 400 years earlier—and, most incredibly, friendly dinosaurs. The inhabitants had built a spectacular, medieval-style city called Waterfall City where kindly Mayor Waldo welcomed the Scotts as the latest "Off Worlders" and enrolled them in the capital's academy so they could learn to become Dinotopians. The strangest thing to which the newcomers had to adjust was the sight of dinosaurs both large and small, some of whom could speak, and most of whom were quite domesticated. The Scotts even got their own erudite stenonychosaurus, Zippo, who helped them around the house. Frank and the boys wanted to return to modern civilization, and even tried to do so, but found that the island was surrounded by "razor reefs" that prevented escape.

Karl, the younger son, went to work at a Saurian "hatchery" where he was assigned to oversee the birth of an infant chemosaurus, while curly-haired David became a Skybax "pilot" in the Dinotopian Air Force, which meant clinging to the back of a large-winged terrasaur and guiding it through the air. Marion was the mayor's winsome daughter, and Rosemary, his supportive wife. Le Sage was the warrior leader of a renegade group known as the Outsiders who mainly seemed to be interested in killing the wildlife and plundering the peaceful Dinotopians.

Worse than the Outsiders were the wild tyrannosaurus rexes who roamed the countryside gobbling up villagers (no blood was ever seen) and periodically threatening Waterfall City itself. Why the inhabitants insisted on "living peacefully" with these huge beasts who kept trying to kill them was another of Dinotopia's mysteries.

Dinotopia was based on the books by James Gurney, and was first seen as a miniseries in May 2002.

DIONE LUCAS SHOW, THE, see *To the Queen's Taste*

DIONNE AND FRIENDS (*Music*)

BROADCAST HISTORY:

Syndicated only
30 minutes
Produced: *1990* (13 episodes)
Released: *January 1990*

HOSTESS:

Dionne Warwick

MUSICAL DIRECTOR:

Rocky Davis

Short-lived musical series in which Miss Warwick and her weekly guest stars performed and chatted. Among those appearing were veteran performers Freddie Jackson, Peter Allen, Stevie Wonder, Johnny Mathis, Gladys Knight, Deniece Williams, Olivia Newton-John, and Stephanie Mills. At the end of each show, Miss Warwick added a new member to her personal "Walk of Fame." Most of her choices were black singers with long and distinguished careers—Sammy Davis, Jr., Sarah Vaughan, and Ella Fitzgerald, etc.—but also included was Martin Luther King, Jr.

DIRESTA (*Situation Comedy*)

FIRST TELECAST: *October 5, 1998*
LAST TELECAST: *March 1, 1999*

BROADCAST HISTORY:

Oct 1998, UPN Mon 8:30–9:00
Nov 1998–Jan 1999, UPN Mon 9:30–10:00
Jan 1999–Mar 1999, UPN Mon 8:30–9:00

CAST:

Off. John DiResta.................... John DiResta
Kate DiResta .... Leila Kenzle
Sgt. Kazmerek .... Joe Guzaldo
Off. Liz Labella.................. Sandra Purpuro
Cal .... David Batiste
Tully .... Erik Palladino
Anna DiResta (age 5) .... Karle Warren
Dakota DiResta (2)........... Ruairi & Sean Kenna
Vic DiResta (1999) .... Robert Costanzo

John was a pudgy New York City transit policeman living with his family on Long Island in this blue-collar comedy. Also in the bustling DiResta household were his wife, Kate, his two young kids, Anna and Dakota, and Tully, his unemployed cousin, who slept in the basement and sometimes babysat for them. John's fellow officers included Liz, Kate's outspoken single sister, and Sgt. Kazmerek, their obnoxious boss. Cal worked at Yankee Frank's, a diner in the Bronx where the transit cops hung out. Stories dealt with both the work and home life of the well-meaning but somewhat blustery DiResta, who looked like and seemed to be patterned after *The Honeymooners'* Ralph Kramden. In February, Tully married a woman he'd been dating for less than two months, and John was thrilled to be getting rid of his freeloading cousin. His dad, a retired fireman, who took over the subway newsstand on John's beat, became a regular about this time.

Comedian John DiResta didn't go far from home with this series, having himself been a New York City transit cop before turning to comedy for a living.

DIRTY DANCING (*Comedy/Drama*)

FIRST TELECAST: *October 29, 1988*
LAST TELECAST: *January 14, 1989*

BROADCAST HISTORY:

Oct 1988–Dec 1988, CBS Sat 8:00–8:30
Jan 1989, CBS 9:30–10:00

CAST:

Johnny Castle .... Patrick Cassidy
Frances "Baby" Kellerman.......... Melora Hardin
Norman Bryant............................ Paul Feig
Penny Rivera..................... Constance Marie
Sweets Walker........................ John Wesley
Robin Kellerman.................... Mandy Ingber
Neil Mumford .... Charles Stratton
Max Kellerman .... McLean Stevenson

Set in the 1960s, *Dirty Dancing* was the musical story of two young people falling in love while working at Kellerman's, a summer resort in the Catskills. The young lovers were 17-year-old Baby, daughter of resort owner Max, and Johnny, the resort's sexy dance instructor. Baby had come to Kellerman's to spend the summer between high school and college with her dad, after living with her mom since her parents' divorce. It was a summer to be remembered. Dad made her talent coordinator, which irked Johnny, who had been doubling in that capacity. But when Johnny began to teach her "dirty dancing" the relationship between upscale Baby and working-class Johnny blossomed into romance—much to her doting father's disgust. Complicating matters was Penny, Johnny's fiery Latin dance partner, who did not appreciate the boss's daughter butting in. Also seen were Norman, an obnoxious pre-med student working as a waiter; Sweets, the resort's talented jazz pianist; Norman, the young comic and bellhop; and Robin, Baby's spoiled, boy-crazy cousin and confidante.

Loosely adapted from the 1987 movie of the same name, which starred Jennifer Grey and Patrick Swayze. As with the movie, sensual dancing, albeit somewhat sanitized for TV, was an integral part of each episode.

DIRTY DOZEN, THE (*War Drama*)

FIRST TELECAST: *April 30, 1988*

LAST TELECAST: *July 30, 1988*

BROADCAST HISTORY:

Apr 1988–Jul 1988, FOX Sat 9:00–10:00

CAST:

Lt. Danko .... Ben Murphy
Johnny Farrell .... John Bradley
Jean Lebec .... John DiAquino
Vern Beauboff .... Mike Jolly
Roy Beauboff .... Glenn Withrow
Janosz Feke .... Jon Tenney
Pvt. Dylan Leeds .... John Slattery
Master Sgt. Cutter .... Barry Cullison
Maj. Gen. Worth .... Frank Marth

This short-lived series took a group of prisoners from Marston Military Prison and followed their exploits on secret missions for the Allied command in Europe during World War II. The group's leader, and the only non-prisoner among them, was no-nonsense, Lt. Danko. A dedicated, independent, authority-hating rebel himself, he had previously been busted from major to private but his superiors needed someone the prisoners would respect. Danko had arranged the release of this collection of hardened criminals because each of them had specific useful skills. Among them were Farrell, a former actor; Lebec, a demolitions expert; Feke, a brilliant strategist; Leeds, a forger; and the muscular but crazed Beauboff brothers. Sgt. Cutter coordinated their activities, and General Worth was Danko's commanding officer.

Filmed on the cheap in Yugoslavia, this series caused a publicized rift between Fox and its production company, MGM/UA. Although thirteen episodes were filmed, poor initial ratings, not helped by being scheduled opposite CBS' Vietnam War series *Tour of Duty*, resulted in Fox's decision to air—and pay for—only seven episodes. The production company wanted to be paid for all thirteen.

Adapted from the 1967 movie of the same name starring Lee Marvin.

DIRTY ROTTEN CHEATER (*Quiz*)

FIRST TELECAST: *January 6, 2003*

LAST TELECAST: *April 14, 2003*

BROADCAST HISTORY:

Jan 2003–Apr 2003, PAX Mon 8:00–9:00

EMCEE:

Bil Dwyer

Six contestants competed in each telecast of this comedy/quiz show. The questions were all survey questions, and the contestants won money by coming up with one of the ten most popular answers. Unlike *Family Feud*, which used similar surveys for its questions, the least popular answer was worth the most money ($2,500) and the most popular worth the least ($250). At the end of each round there were bonuses of $10,000 for highest-value answer, $7,500 for second highest and $5,000 for third highest. Among the survey questions were, "What body part would you be willing to sell for $1 million?"; "Name something little boys hate to do," and "What is a reason to take your clothes off?"

There was an unusual twist on *Dirty Rotten Cheater*—one of the contestants, The Cheater, was secretly given the answers. Since this player knew the answers, he or she could build up the cash balance, but had to be careful to avoid detection. After every round the contestants declared whom they thought The Cheater was, followed by a vote to eject. If nobody received the minimum number of votes necessary to eject, everybody lost half their money and The Cheater could eject one of them. If The Cheater was ejected, another contestant was made the new secret Cheater. The fourth round consisted of three questions with no bonus money, and the audience voted on who The Cheater was. If less than half the audience correctly identified The Cheater then The Cheater got to eliminate one of the two honest players.

In the Final Showdown there were two questions, and each of the two surviving contestants could give three answers for each question. The audience again tried to identify The Cheater. The first three eliminated players indicated to the audience whom they thought was cheating and won money if they were right. If The Cheater fooled the audience, he or she won; otherwise the honest player took home the winnings.

DIRTY SALLY (*Western*)

FIRST TELECAST: *January 11, 1974*

LAST TELECAST: *July 19, 1974*

BROADCAST HISTORY:

Jan 1974–Jul 1974, CBS Fri 8:00–8:30

CAST:

Sally Fergus .... Jeanette Nolan
Cyrus Pike .... Dack Rambo

Dirty Sally was a far cry from the traditional violent Western. Sally Fergus was a hard-drinking, crusty old lady who was traveling west to the California gold fields in a wagon pulled by her faithful mule, Worthless. Her traveling companion was Cyrus Pike, a young ex-gunfighter. His desire to reach their destination met with constant frustration from Sally, who got herself involved in the lives of almost everyone they met along the way.

DISC MAGIC, see *Musical Merry-Go-Round*

DISCOVERY CHANNEL, THE (Network)

(*Documentary/Instruction Cable Network*)

LAUNCHED:

June 17, 1985

SUBSCRIBERS (MAY 2003):

86.4 million (81% U.S.)

Cable's home for documentaries on Tasmanian divers, 2,000-year-old pottery, the Buddhist legend of Shambhala, Jim Henson's puppet magic, Caribbean shipwrecks, pirates, wars, natural disasters, and just about every other subject in the areas of science, nature, history, and real-life adventure. Although the subjects were often engrossing, the delivery could be ponderous (in *Wings*, about the history of aviation, every warplane seemed to be "the plane that won the war!"). One of the network's most popular features was its annual "Shark Week" (1988) consisting of specials on that subject. Another early event was its presentation of 60 hours of Soviet television programming in 1987.

Discovery is not the most heavily viewed cable network, but it is one of the best loved by subscribers, and so it is carried on almost every system in America. It first reached more than half of all U.S. television homes in October 1989, and its principal original prime-time series telecast after that date are listed below. All are documentaries, unless otherwise noted. Also shown are host or narrator (if not included in the title), years, and number of episodes made.

Adventures (Doug McConnell), 1991–1994 (39 eps.)
Adventures in Diving, 1990–1993 (13 eps.)
Amazing America (human interest, Kevin Nealon), 1994–1995 (13 eps.)
America Coast to Coast (travelogue, Susan Hunt), 1991–1995 (18 eps.)
American Album, An, c. 1989–1990
American Chopper (aviation), 2003– (13 eps.)
American Diary, The (E. G. Marshall), 1987–1990 (6 eps.)
Animal World Down Under (Australian wildlife), 1986–1993 (13 eps.)
Arctic, The (E. G. Marshall), 1992–1994 (13 eps.)
Arthur C. Clarke's Mysterious Universe (phenomena), 1994–1996 (26 eps.)
Arthur C. Clarke's Mysterious World (supernatural), 1992–1997 (13 eps.)
Arthur C. Clarke's World of Strange Powers (paranormal), 1989–1996 (26 eps.)
Bear Hunter, The, 1990–1991 (6 eps.)
Beyond 2000 (science magazine, Henry Tenenbaum), 1988–1994 (174 eps.)
Buckman Treatment, The, 1987–1990 (12 eps.)
Carriers, 1990–1993 (13 eps.)
Casino Diaries, 2001 (13 eps.)
Centenary of the Motorcar, 1989–1991 (13 eps.)
Choppers (helicopters), 1991–1993 (13 eps.)
Deadline: Discovery (news), 2001–2002 (41 eps.)
Deaf Mosaic (documentary on deafness, Gil Eastman, Mary Lou Novitsky), 1987–1995 (101 eps.)
Disappearing World (Portrait of a People) (ancient cultures), 1985–1995 (43 eps.)
Discover Magazine (science & technology, Jim Lovell), 1996–2000 (112 eps.)
Discovery News (science & technology, Steve Aveson), 1997–2001 (163 eps.)
Discovery Sport (unusual sports), 1990–1993 (13 eps.)
Discovery Sunday, 1996– (160 eps.)
Dive to Adventure (underwater), 1988–1992 (13 eps.)
Earth Guide (environmental magazine, Wade Davis), 1991–1992 (13 eps.)
Extreme Engineering (science and technology), 2003– (10 eps.)
Fangs (wildlife), 1995–1998 (13 eps.)
FBI Files, The (James Kallstrom), 1998– (85 eps.)
Fields of Armor (tanks), 1993–1995 (12 eps.)
Firepower (military), 1990–1994 (45 eps.)
Frank Capra's The War Years, 1990–1992 (8 eps.)
From Monkeys to Apes (apes), 1990–1993 (12 eps.)
Frontiers of Flight (aviation), 1992–1994 (13 eps.)
GI Diary (history), c. 1991–1992 (25 eps.)
Global Family (wildlife), 1992–1993 (19 eps.)
Great Days of the Century (history), 1991–1992 (13 eps.)
Heart of Courage (everyday heroes, Alex Trebek), 1992–1993 (22 eps.)
Himalayas, 1994–1995 (13 eps.)
Hollywood Chronicles, 1989–1991 (26 eps.)
Hollywood Stuntmakers (James Coburn), 1991–1993 (13 eps.)
How the West Was Lost (history), 1993–1995 (13 eps.)
Hunters (wildlife), 1994–1995 (10 eps.)
Hunters in the Sky (WWII pilots), 1991–1993 (13 eps.)
In Care of Nature (wildlife conservation), 1994–1995 (26 eps.)
In the Wild with Harry Butler (nature, Harry Butler), 1985–1990 (26 eps.)
Incredibly Strange Film Show, The (low-budget filmmakers, Jonathan Ross), 1991–1993 (15 eps.)
Into the Unknown (science), 1997–1999 (10 eps.)
Invention (inventions, Lucky Severson), 1990–1997 (60 eps.)
Just for the Record, 1989–1990 (50 eps.)
Justice Files (true crime stories, Forrest Sawyer, Jay Schadler, John Quinones), 1992–2002 (125 eps.)
Know Zone (scientific breakthroughs, Don Bleu, Soledad O'Brien, Craig Miller), 1994–1996 (18 eps.)
Looking East (Asia documentary, Yue-Sai Kan), 1989–1992 (52 eps.)
Magical Worlds (anthropology), 1993–1995 (14 eps.)
Moments of Courage (adventure, Tom Jarriel), c. 1991–1993 (13 eps.)
**Monster Garage* (cars, Jesse James), 2002– (26 eps.)
Mother Nature (children's nature documentary), 1992–1994 (12 eps.)
Movie Magic (movies), 1993–1998 (44 eps.)
Natural World (nature), 1989–1990 (8 eps.)
Nature, 1990 (21 eps.)
Nature Connection (children's nature documentary, Dr. David Suzuki), 1993–1994 (13 eps.)
Nature of Things (science, Dr. David Suzuki), 1985–1996 (166 eps.)
Nature Watch (environmental), 1992–1993 (35 eps.)
New Detectives (forensic science), 1996– (103 eps.)
Next Step (scientific breakthroughs, Richard Hart), 1992–1997 (52 eps.)
On the Inside (people), 1998– (63 eps.)
Orphans of the Wild, 1987–1991 (13 eps.)
Pacifica: Tales from the South Seas, 1993–1994 (13 eps.)
Pet Connection (pets, Dr. Berney Pukay), 1993–1995 (65 eps.)
Pirates (historical), 1994–1995 (13 eps.)
Predators and Prey (Charles Adler), 1989–1992 (8 eps.)
Profiles of Nature (Canadian nature), 1992–1993 (39 eps.)

Prosecutors, The (legal), 2000–2002 (31 eps.)
Rendezvous, c. 1989–1991
Safari (wildlife), c. 1989–1996 (26 eps.)
Sci-Trek (science), 1995– (169 eps.)
Science Mysteries (science), 1999– (13 eps.)
Search for Adventure (travelogue), 1988–1993 (34 eps.)
Search for the World's Most Secret Animals (wildlife), 1994 (12 eps.)
Secret Life of Machines (science, Tim Hunkin), 1990–1994 (18 eps.)
Secret Weapons (military, John Palmer), 1992–1995 (13 eps.)
Secrets of the Deep (ocean documentary), 1992–1997 (16 eps.)
Skybound (aviation), 1992–1994 (13 eps.)
Smithsonian Treasures (David McCullough), 1990–1992 (25 eps.)
Spirit of Survival (disasters) 1994–1996 (38 eps.)
Sporting Life, c. 1989–1990 (7 eps.)
Survival (disasters), c. 1989–1993 (20 eps.)
Terra X (historical documentary), 1989–1997 (67 eps.)
Those Incredible Animals (wildlife, Loretta Swit), 1992–1994 (26 eps.)
Those Who Dare (adventure), 1993–1994 (13 eps.)
Timewatch (historical events), 1991–1992 (18 eps.)
Treasure Hunters (treasure hunting), 1992–1996 (24 eps.)
Unsolved History (history, Daniel Martinez), 2002– (22 eps.)
Walk on the Wild Side (nature, Simon King), 1993–1995 (6 eps.)
War Stories, c. 1989–1990 (13 eps.)
Wheels in Sport, 1990–1991 (13 eps.)
Wild About Wheels (autos), 1990–1993 (39 eps.)
Wild Discovery (nature), 1995–2003 (451 eps.)
Wild Sanctuaries (nature), 1993–1995 (13 eps.)
Wild Side (wildlife), 1989–1991 (48 eps.)
Wild Things, c. 1991 (36 eps.)
Wild West (history, Jack Lemmon), 1994–1995 (13 eps.)
Wildlife Chronicles (nature), 1987–1995 (125 eps.)
Wildlife International (Fred Keating), 1991–1993 (13 eps.)
Wildlife Journeys (wildlife), 1992–1994 (13 eps.)
Wildlife Tales (wildlife), 1991–1993 (26 eps.)
Wings: Great Planes (aviation), 1988–1989 (46 eps.)
Wings of the Luftwaffe (German aviation), 1992–1995 (13 eps.)
Wings of the Red Star (Soviet aviation), 1993–1994 (13 eps.)
Wonder of Our World (travelogue, Guy Baskin), 1993 (8 eps.)
World Alive (wildlife), 1987–1993 (18 eps.)
World Away, A (travelogue, Nancy Glass), 1990–1992 (52 eps.)
World of Discovery (people & places), 1994–1995 (27 eps.)
World of Valor (military), 1992–1994 (26 eps.)
World of Wonder (science, Dr. Mae Jemison), 1994–1998 (26 eps.)
X-Planes (experimental planes), 1993–1995 (13 eps.)

*See separate alphabetical entry

Discovery operates a large number of subsidiary networks, running the same (or similar) informational programming. Among them are Animal Planet (animals, 1996), Discovery Civilization (history, 1996), Discovery Home & Leisure (homemaking, 1996), Discovery Kids Channel (1996), The Science Channel (1996), Discovery Wings Channel (aviation, 1998), Discovery en Español (1998) and Discovery Health Channel (1998). Another short-lived venture, Discovery People, operated 1997–2000.

DISH, THE (*Magazine*)

BROADCAST HISTORY:
Lifetime
30 minutes
Produced: *1997*
Premiered: *January 24, 1997*

HOST:
Tracee Ross

A Friday night guide to the coming week in television, movies, music, and other aspects of popular culture, from a woman's point of view. Included were mini-features such as "Guerrilla Girls" stalking celebrities.

DISMISSED (*Documentary*)

BROADCAST HISTORY:
MTV
30 minutes
Original episodes: *2001–*
Premiered: *October 8, 2001*

A dating show in which a young guy or gal was sent on a date with two members of the opposite sex. After a certain amount of flirting, partying, and sexual banter ("She gave him a 'checkup from the neck up,' " said one catty female of her competitor), and challenges for the two suitors (off with the shirts, guys, who's got the best pecs?), the show ended at "dismissal," when the guy or gal chose one of the two dates and dismissed the other.

DISNEY CHANNEL, THE (Network) (*General Entertainment Cable Network*)

LAUNCHED:
April 18, 1983

SUBSCRIBERS (MAY 2003):
81.4 million (76% U.S.)

The Disney Channel was for many years offered as a noncommercial premium channel on most cable systems and thus had more limited distribution than other "family"-oriented networks such as The Family Channel and Nickelodeon. It began as a children's service, featuring cartoons, documentaries, and kid-flicks from the vast Disney library (and other sources). In the late 1990s its programming expanded to include family fare in the early evening and "adult" (but never offensive) programs after 9 P.M. These consisted mostly of specials, concerts (e.g., Billy Joel, Roger Daltrey), and movies such as *Topaz* and *Guess Who's Coming to Dinner?* At the same time, cable systems began to make Disney part of their basic service, expanding its coverage considerably.

Early original series on Disney included revivals of *Leave It to Beaver* in 1985 (see *The New Leave It to Beaver*), *The Mickey Mouse Club* in 1989 and the following notable evening series:

Danger Bay (1985), a kids' adventure about a biologist and his teenage children, set in the modern Canadian Northwest. Donnelly Rhodes starred as biologist Grant "Doc" Roberts, with Christopher Crabb and Ocean Hellman as his kids, Jonah and Nicole, and

Deborah Wakeman as bush pilot Joyce Carter, who airlifted them into and out of trouble.

Avonlea (1990), a serialized drama about the residents of a small town on picturesque Prince Edward Island, centering on young Sara Stanley (Sarah Polley) and her relatives, the King family. Recurring roles were played by such noted actors as Michael York, Colleen Dewhurst, Peter Coyote, and Madeline Kahn. Based on the turn-of-the-century stories of Lucy Maud Montgomery, previously filmed as *Anne of Green Gables* (1934, 1985) and *Anne of Avonlea* (1987).

Ocean Girl (1994), adventure about a mysterious aquatic girl with amazing powers named Neri (Marzena Godecki) who lived in the tropical waters of Australia's Great Barrier Reef. There she was discovered and befriended by Jason and Brett (David Hoflin, Jeffrey Walker), teenage sons of marine biologist Dr. Dianne Bates (Kerry Armstrong). At first, neither Mom nor her scientist-partner Winston Seth (Alex Pinder) were in on the boys' secret.

Disney first reached more than half of all U.S. television homes in August 1999, and its principal original series after that date are listed in this book under their individual titles. Among them are *The Famous Jett Jackson, So Weird, Even Stevens, Lizzie McGuire, The Proud Family, Kim Possible* and *That's So Raven.*

DISNEY PRESENTS THE 100 LIVES OF BLACK JACK SAVAGE (*Adventure*)

FIRST TELECAST: *March 31, 1991*
LAST TELECAST: *May 26, 1991*
BROADCAST HISTORY:

Mar 1991, NBC Sun 9:00–11:00
Apr 1991, NBC Fri 8:00–9:00
May 1991, NBC Sun 7:00–8:00

CAST:

Barry Tarberry .... Daniel Hugh-Kelly
Black Jack Savage (pilot only) ...... Stoney Jackson
Black Jack Savage .... Steven Williams
Logan "F. X." Murphy................ Steve Hytner
Governor General Abel Vasquez....... Bert Rosario
Danielle St. Clair .... Roma Downey

This action hour was reminiscent of the high-spirited, swashbuckling adventure series of the 1950s (*Robin Hood*, et al.), complete with a sly sense of humor. Barry Tarberry was a high-profile Wall Street wheeler-dealer who, indicted for securities violations, had fled to the small Caribbean island of San Pietro to escape prosecution. There he sublet an old castle, only to find it haunted by another fugitive—Black Jack Savage, a colorful (and rather young) 17th-century pirate, who had been hiding there for the last 300 years to avoid *his* fate (hellfire) for the hundred lives he took during his days on the bounding main.

It seems as long as Black Jack stayed in the castle he was safe; the moment he ventured out he was subject to pursuit by the "Snarks," screeching, otherworldly bounty hunters from hell, who would drag him to his fiery fate. He had to get out, though, to save the one hundred lives that would compensate for those he had taken, and commute his sentence. Tarberry realized that he had the same problem. Unless he teamed up with Black Jack, he would one day face the same fate for his many misdeeds.

So the two of them struck a thief's bargain, venturing out each week to save a few lives and reduce their mutual outstanding balance of misdeeds. Barry conned nerdy inventor F. X. Murphy into letting them use his high-tech super-speedboat to zip around the beautiful blue waters chasing bad guys; F. X. also provided them with a "snark buster" (which looked a lot like an old vacuum cleaner) to ward off those pesky bats from hell.

Vasquez was the corrupt petty dictator who ran the island (with whom Tarberry struck another thief's deal), and Danielle, the beautiful, socially conscious activist who defended the villagers against the governor's injustices. Naturally she enlisted the reluctant Barry in more than one crusade.

A running gag was the handsome Tarberry's unwanted celebrity status. While a stateside billionaire he had regularly appeared on quiz shows and magazine covers, and now practically everybody he ran into did a second take and exclaimed "didn't I see you on *Hollywood Squares*?"

Filmed in Dade County, Florida.

DISNEY SUNDAY MOVIE, THE, see *Walt Disney*

DISNEYLAND, see *Walt Disney*

DISNEY'S HONEY, I SHRUNK THE KIDS (*Comedy/Science Fiction*)

BROADCAST HISTORY:

Syndicated only
60 minutes
Produced: *1997–2000* (66 episodes)
Released: *September 1997*

CAST:

Wayne Szalinski .... Peter Scolari
Diane Szalinski .... Barbara Alyn Woods
Amy Szalinski......................... Hillary Tuck
Nicholas Szalinski .... Thomas Dekker
**Mr. Jennings* .... Bruce Jarchow
**Ms. Elders*...................... Hilary Alexander
Jake McKenna (1998–2000).......... George Buza
Joel McKenna (1998–2000)........ Andrew T. Grant

*Occasional

This fanciful series might better have been called "Dad's Gadgets." Wayne was an eccentric inventor in Matheson, Colorado, who created things like a shrink ray, a spaceship, the robotic-armed Szalinski Breakfast Buddy, the retinal rotator (allowing one to see ghosts), and the Szalinski Time Hopper (a time machine). Unfortunately, his devices often went awry, getting various family members into bizarre predicaments—as when Wayne inadvertently shrunk the family van with most of the family in it, and it was promptly swallowed by Grandpa. Diane was Wayne's long-suffering wife, a new attorney; Amy, their nearly normal teenage daughter; and Nicholas a younger version of nutty Dad. Quark was the family dog, which at the beginning of the second season changed breeds, morphing from a border collie to a border terrier. (No one was safe around the Szalinski household.)

When Wayne wasn't creating an uproar at home, he worked for Jentech, a high-tech development firm, where Mr. Jennings was his oblivious boss and Ms. Elders, the boss's secretary. Joining the cast in the second season was Nicholas's friend Joel and Joel's gruff father, Jake, a cop. In May 1999 Mr. Jennings was "shipped off to the laughing academy" and his twin brother,

William, took over the company, but in October Jennings had been released and was back in charge.

Based on the 1989 theatrical film starring Rick Moranis, although most of the stories in the series had nothing to do with "shrinking the kids."

DISTRICT, THE (*Police Drama*)

FIRST TELECAST: *October 7, 2000*

LAST TELECAST:

BROADCAST HISTORY:

Oct 2000–Jun 2002, CBS Sat 10:00–11:00
Jun 2002–Jul 2003, CBS Sat 9:00–10:00
Jul 2003– , CBS Sat 10:00–11:00

CAST:

Chief Jack Mannion .... Craig T. Nelson
Ella Farmer (2000–2003) .... Lynne Thigpen
Mary Ann Mitchell (2000) .... Jayne Brook
Deputy Chief Joe Noland ...... Roger Aaron Brown
Det. Temple Page .... Sean Patrick Thomas
Nick Pierce (2000–2001) .... Justin Theroux
Det. Danny "Mac" McGregor (2000–2001) .... David O'Hara
Off. Nancy Parras .... Elizabeth Marvel
Mayor Ethan Baker (2000–2001) .... John Amos
Sgt. Phil Brander .... Wayne Duvall
Helen York (2000) .... Michelle Forbes
**U.S. Attorney Bruce Logan* .... Richard Fancy
**Ricky Alvarez (2000–2001)* .... Segun Ajaga
**Ricky Alvarez (2001–2003)* .... William Turner
Det. Kevin Debreno (2001–) ... Jonathan LaPaglia
Sgt. Ray Cutter (2001–) ... Christopher B. Duncan
**Clive Rodgers (2001–2003)* ..... Gregalan Williams
**Attorney General Troy Hatcher (2002–)* .... Ving Rhames
**Vanessa Cavanaugh (2002–)* .... Jaclyn Smith
**Melinda Lockhart (2002–)* ..... Kelly Rutherford
**Carol Bodine (2002–)* .... Helen Cates
**Mayor Morgan Douglas (2002–)* .... Joseph C. Phillips
Kendall Truman (2002–) .... Kristen Wilson
Ferris Gluck (2002–) .... Rita S. Jett

*Occasional

Jack Mannion was the newly appointed chief of police in Washington, D.C., a dapper dresser with a wry sense of humor, tremendous compassion and an indomitable drive to fight crime. Mannion's prior successes in Boston and Newark, New Jersey, had attracted the attention of ambitious Deputy Mayor Mitchell and led her to convince Mayor Baker to hire him. His arrival was met with less than unbridled enthusiasm by the Metro Police Department (MPD) brass, particularly Deputy Chief Noland, who had expected to get the job and who for a time tried to undermine him. With the help of Nick, his brilliant young PR aide, Mannion set out to build a more effective department that could reduce the obscenely high crime rate in the nation's capital. Possibly the single most important member of his inner circle was Ella, a statistics clerk for whom he obtained a high-tech computer system to analyze crime patterns and help senior officers make the most effective deployment of their men. Featured officers included ex-marine Temple, a street-smart young cop; Temple's partner Mac, formerly a Royal Ulster Constabulary cop from Belfast; and Nancy, the bright officer assigned as Mannion's administrative assistant. It took a while, but eventually most of the senior officers, including Noland, came to respect and admire Mannion.

Ella was caring for her nephew, Ricky, whose mother had been murdered by his father, and eventually got custody. Early on Helen York, the muckraking chief of staff for Sen. Reese, initiated hearings on the mayor's activities, but was unable to prove anything. Nancy and Mac began an affair, which Mannion found out about in March. In the season finale Giselle (Daphnee Duplaix), the nurse who was Temple's fiancée, was killed by a random shot from a crazed guy in the hospital, and Ella found out that the breast cancer she'd had five years ago had returned. At the end of the episode Mac was killed by a car bomb planted by the Russian mob and intended for Chief Mannion.

That fall Temple, mourning his double loss, got a new partner, Debreno, a cynical officer with whom he constantly disagreed. Nancy went back on patrol and was frequently partnered with Brander, who was very fond of her. In October Ella started to date Clive, a lobbyist she had met on a bus, and their relationship, tentative at first, blossomed. In the spring Temple, working undercover on a drug case, was forced to take crack to prove he wasn't a cop, and having previously had a drug problem, it took him a while to quit. Clive asked Ella to move to Seattle with him but, when she refused, decided to stay in Washington and marry her.

In the third season Kendall was Mannion's new press secretary and Ferris was his new administrative assistant. He had ongoing problems with Attorney General Hatcher and later with newly elected Mayor Douglas, who resented his popularity and independence and wanted to get rid of him (Mannion himself had been urged several times to run for mayor). After a contentious beginning, Mannion became friendly with Vanessa, a beautiful and well-connected civil rights attorney, and there were hints of a possible romance. In November Nancy was hurt chasing a purse snatcher and, while in the hospital, found out she was in the early stages of Huntington's disease. Later that month Noland's wife gave birth to a baby girl, Ashley. In the spring the mayor's efforts to oust Mannion intensified and, after riots broke out following the death of a PCP addict in Brander's police car, he fired Mannion in May, with Noland taking over as acting chief of police. At the end of the episode Clive called Mannion to tell him that Ella had died from a stroke (actress Lynne Thigpen had died from a heart attack in March). After Ella's funeral Vanessa was working on ways to get Mannion reinstated—she discovered that the only hard evidence the mayor had was from an illegal wiretap on Mannion's cell phone—while Nancy proved that Brander, who had been fired, was not responsible for the PCP addict's death.

Based on the experiences of New York City Deputy Police Commissioner Jack Maple.

DIVISION, THE (*Police Drama*)

BROADCAST HISTORY:

Lifetime
60 minutes
Original episodes: *2001–*
Premiered: *January 7, 2001*

CAST:

Capt. Kaitlyn "Kate" McCafferty .... Bonnie Bedelia
Inspector Jinny Exstead .... Nancy McKeon
Inspector Magdalena Ramirez .... Lisa Vidal
Inspector Peter Torriano (2001) David Gianopoulos
Inspector Candace "C. D." DeLorenzo .... Tracey Needham

Inspector Angela Reide (2001)
.... Lela Rochon Fuqua
Inspector Nathan "Nate" Russo (2002–)
.... Jon Hamm
Inspector Raina Washington (2002–)
.... Taraji Henson
**Benjamin Herrara (age 7)* .... Jacob Urrutia
**Gabriel Herrara* .... Jose Yenque
**Dep. Chief Charles Haysbert (2002–)*
.... James Avery

*Occasional

San Francisco's Central Station was a precinct house with a difference—the captain and most of the inspectors were women. As the perps quickly found out, however, they were just as tough as their male counterparts—they had to be, given their personal lives. Kate was the seasoned boss, in her forties, hardened by having to fight her way up through the male-dominated ranks; Jinny, the maverick with a drinking problem, who came from a dysfunctional family of cops; Magda the stretched-thin Puerto Rican single mom; Peter, Magda's original partner; C. D., the cynical overachiever dedicated to her job and saddled with a cheating husband, and Angela, C. D.'s idealistic but inexperienced black partner.

Early stories dealt with Jinny's sexual promiscuity and alcoholism (which almost got her thrown off the force); Kate's angry, defiant daughter Amanda, and the death of Kate's mother. Magda was beset with almost constant travail, having to deal with her irresponsible ex (Gabriel, whom she called a "magician"—he had disappeared when she told him she was pregnant), her son Ben's leukemia, her married partner Peter's attraction to her, her troubled sister Lily and then her remarriage. Joining the squad in the second season were Nate, a handsome, unflappable former vice cop, and Raina, a young former Olympic hopeful who had decided to try a new career. In January 2003, Jinny impulsively married Insp. Jack Ellis (Dean Cain), but the marriage was troubled from the start due to her drinking and drug problems.

DO IT YOURSELF (*Comedy/Information*)

FIRST TELECAST: *June 26, 1955*

LAST TELECAST: *September 18, 1955*

BROADCAST HISTORY:

Jun 1955–Sep 1955, NBC Sun 7:30–8:00

REGULARS:

Dave Willock
Cliff Arquette (as Charley Weaver)

Do It Yourself was a short-lived attempt to mix situation comedy with useful household information. Hobbyist-builder Dave Willock was seen each week in his workshop with two or three projects on his schedule, ranging from the repair of broken appliances to building various objects from scratch. He was "helped" by his friend Charley Weaver, who spent most of the time clowning around, and by other friends who happened to drop by. Despite the horseplay, Willock managed to convey all the information needed to build or repair the projects at hand.

DO OVER (*Situation Comedy*)

FIRST TELECAST: *September 19, 2002*

LAST TELECAST: *December 26, 2002*

BROADCAST HISTORY:

Sep 2002–Dec 2002, WB Thu 8:30–9:00

CAST:

Joel Larsen (age 14) .... Penn Badgley
Cheryl Larsen (16) .... Angela Goethals
Isabelle Meyers .... Natasha Melnick
Bill Larsen .... Michael Milhoan
Karen Larsen .... Gigi Rice
Pat Brody .... Josh Wise
Joel Larsen (adult, voice only) .... Tom Everett Scott
Holly Kent .... Melinda Sward

Newton, Massachusetts, outside Boston, was the setting for this fantasy comedy, one of two "back to the future" failures that premiered in the fall of 2002 (the other: ABC's *That Was Then*). Joel was an unhappy, unmarried 34-year-old salesman whose life changed completely when his sister, Cheryl, accidentally used the defibrillation panels from an EMS van on his head. When Joel woke up, it was 1981 and he was a 14-year-old who knew what would happen over the next 20 years. He was all too aware of the problems that would beset his family. Cheryl was a rebellious teen whose future drug abuse would mess up her life, and his parents were on the road to divorce. Bill, his dad, was an unromantic chauvinist pig who didn't want anything to change, while Karen, his mom, was enthusiastic and creative and stifled by her husband's lack of interest in her ideas. Joel had two close friends at school—Isabelle, the intellectual, and Pat, to whom he had confided his secret (Pat called him "future guy"). Holly was the sexy girl he was too shy to ask out. Pat wanted Joel to take advantage of his knowledge of the future but Joel just wanted to change things for the better. He won a class election that he had originally lost, prevented the teacher who broke up his parents' marriage from hitting on his mom, tried to save Cheryl from a succession of bad relationships and encouraged his mom when she wanted to start her own business. Much of his time was spent trying to keep his parents' marriage together by getting Bill to show more interest in Karen. *Do Over* was narrated by the adult Joel.

DO YOU TRUST YOUR WIFE? (*Quiz*)

FIRST TELECAST: *January 3, 1956*

LAST TELECAST: *March 26, 1957*

BROADCAST HISTORY:

Jan 1956–Mar 1957, CBS Tue 10:30–11:00

EMCEE:

Edgar Bergen

ANNOUNCER:

Ed Reimers
Bob LeMond (1956–1957)

Ventriloquist Edgar Bergen was the host of this comedy quiz show, which derived its title from the fact that when Mr. Bergen asked each married team of contestants to answer questions on a given topic, the husband had to decide whether he—or his wife—would try to answer. The jackpot available at the end of each telecast was $100 per week for a full year. Featured on the series along with Mr. Bergen were his assorted dummies: Charlie McCarthy, Mortimer Snerd, and Effie Klinker. The program later moved to daytime where it was seen under the title *Who Do You Trust?* During most of its run as a daytime show, Johnny Carson was the emcee and Ed McMahon the onstage announcer. The daytime version ran from September 1957 to December 1963. When Carson left it to take over *The Tonight Show* in the fall of 1962, he was replaced by Woody Woodbury.

DOBIE GILLIS, syndicated title for *Many Loves of Dobie Gillis, The*

DOC (*Situation Comedy*)
FIRST TELECAST: *August 16, 1975*
LAST TELECAST: *October 30, 1976*
BROADCAST HISTORY:
Aug 1975–Oct 1976, CBS Sat 8:30–9:00
CAST:
"Doc" Joe Bogert .... Barnard Hughes
Annie Bogert .... Elizabeth Wilson
Miss Tully .... Mary Wickes
"Happy" Miller .... Irwin Corey
Laurie Bogert Fenner .... Judy Kahan
Fred Fenner .... John Harkins
Ben Goldman .... Herbie Faye
Janet Scott (1976) .... Audra Lindley
Stanley Moss (1976) .... David Ogden Stiers
Woody Henderson (1976) .... Ray Vitte
Teresa Ortega (1976) .... Lisa Mordente

During its first season, *Doc* was the story of an old-fashioned doctor practicing medicine in New York City. Joe Bogert was a kindly, soft-spoken doctor who was more concerned with his patients' health than with his fees (similar to *The Practice*, which premiered the following January). He was happily married to a woman who was much tougher with his patients than he was; his daughter and son-in-law (a fellow he disliked intensely) rented the apartment above his. Doc often sought refuge in the company of his friends Ben and Happy.

Marginal ratings during the first season prompted a major overhaul in the fall of 1976. Doc now worked at the Westside Clinic, run by Stanley Moss, and had a new nurse in Janet Scott. Gone were his wife and family and friends from the previous season. The new characters in the series consisted of the people who worked at the clinic with him, including Woody and Teresa. The change didn't help the show, which lasted only two months in the new format before being canceled.

DOC (*Medical Drama*)
FIRST TELECAST: *March 11, 2001*
LAST TELECAST:
BROADCAST HISTORY:
Mar 2001– , PAX Sun 8:00–9:00
Mar 2001–Jul 2001, PAX Tue 9:00–10:00
Aug 2001–Dec 2001, PAX Tue 8:00–9:00
Dec 2001–Sep 2002, PAX Tue 9:00–10:00
Jul 2002–Sep 2002, PAX Sun 9:00–10:00
Sep 2002– , PAX Wed 9:00–10:00
CAST:
Dr. Clint Cassidy .... Billy Ray Cyrus
Dr. Derek Hebert .... Derek McGrath
Off. Nate Jackson .... Richard Leacock
Nurse Nancy Nichol .... Andrea Robinson
Dr. Phillip Crane .... Ron Lea
Raul Garcia (age 8) .... Tyler Garcia Posey
Donna DeWitt .... Ruth Marshall
Beverly Jackson .... Tracy Shreve
Dr. Harley "Doc" Johanson .... Neil Dainard
Tippy Williams .... Paula Boudreau
Justin (8) .... Demetrius Joyette
**Junior* .... Billy Otis
**Jelly Bean* .... Kenny Robinson
Dr. Kate Westin (2001–2002) ...... Nancy Sakovich
**Nellie Hebert (2002–)* .... Linda Kash
**Capt. Steven Doss* .... Kevin Jubinville
*Occasional

THEME:
"Stand Still," performed by Billy Ray Cyrus

Clint was a hunky, long-haired country doctor from Montana who moved to New York to be with a woman he loved and, when she dumped him, decided to stay. Taking a job with the Westbury Clinic, a Manhattan HMO, he quickly became the clinic's dreamboat doctor (female patient: "*That's* my doctor?"). His polite, honest country ways brought a breath of fresh air to the big bad city. The staff at Westbury included kindly Dr. Hebert, stuffy Dr. Crane, pretty Nurse Nichol, who was attracted to Clint (as was almost every other woman), and Ms. DeWitt, the bossy administrative director. Nate was a friendly black police officer who befriended Clint and found him an apartment in his building, and Beverly was Nate's wife. In the premiere Nate and Beverly adopted young Raul, after Clint promised the boy's dying mother he would take care of him. Others in the cast included Tippy, the clinic's flighty new receptionist; Justin, Raul's classmate and best friend, and Junior and Jelly Bean, eccentric friends of Clint's.

Dr. Hebert liked Clint but Dr. Crane, who was interested only in the bottom line, could barely tolerate his folksy ways and willingness to do anything for his patients. On Christmas Eve Dr. Hebert's wife, Nellie, went into premature labor and gave birth to a girl, Grace. In the spring of 2001 Clint started dating Kate, although it was apparent that Nancy was also interested in him. A serious injury to her former fiancé motivated Kate to rethink her relationship. By that time Nancy had started to date a guy Tippy had found for her.

That fall Beverly found out she was pregnant and Kate, whom Clint hadn't seen in months, was suffering from Hodgkin's disease. Tippy was dating uptight Capt. Doss. In February Clint's mentor Doc came to New York for a conference and suffered a heart attack. He received a valve replacement and returned to Montana. Each episode ended with Clint corresponding, via e-mail, with Doc, who was still practicing in Montana.

DOC CORKLE (*Situation Comedy*)
FIRST TELECAST: *October 5, 1952*
LAST TELECAST: *October 19, 1952*
BROADCAST HISTORY:
Oct 1952, NBC Sun 7:30–8:00
CAST:
Doc Corkle .... Eddie Mayehoff
Melinda .... Billie Burke
Winfield Dill .... Arnold Stang
Nellie Corkle .... Hope Emerson
Laurie Corkle .... Connie Marshall

Doc Corkle was a neighborhood dentist who was continually beset with money problems and a collection of nutty relatives. The wackiest was his stepsister Melinda, whose well-meaning blunders got Doc and his sister Nellie in all sorts of trouble. His teenage daughter Laurie was engaged to marry Winfield Dill, a youthful millionaire who had inherited six businesses.

This filmed series ran only three weeks. The sponsor, Reynolds Metals, was so disappointed with it that it was quickly canceled and replaced with *Mr. Peepers*.

The part of Melinda was played by the famous and, by this time, aging film and theater star, Billie Burke.

DOC ELLIOT (*Medical Drama*)
FIRST TELECAST: *January 23, 1974*
LAST TELECAST: *August 14, 1974*
BROADCAST HISTORY:
Jan 1974–Aug 1974, ABC Wed 10:00–11:00
CAST:
Dr. Benjamin Elliot .... James Franciscus
Mags Brimble .... Neva Patterson
Barney Weeks .... Noah Beery
Eldred McCoy .... Bo Hopkins
PRODUCER:
Sandor Stern, M.D.
MAIN THEME:
by Marvin Hamlisch

This contemporary drama concerned a drop-out doctor who gave up his career in New York City to become a blue-jeaned G.P. in Gideon, Colorado. Doc's new patients, most of them as independent as he, were spread over a 600-square-mile area of rugged terrain, and his house calls (better named cabin calls) were made by plane or in a four-wheel-drive camper outfitted with medical equipment. Mags Brimble was the widow of the area's former G.P. and Doc's helper and confidante; Barney Weeks the owner of the general store; and Eldred McCoy a bush pilot. There was a lot of attractive mountain scenery in this series.

DOCTOR, THE (*Medical Anthology*)
FIRST TELECAST: *August 24, 1952*
LAST TELECAST: *June 28, 1953*
BROADCAST HISTORY:
Aug 1952–Jun 1953, NBC Sun 10:00–10:30
CAST:
The Doctor .... Warner Anderson

The Doctor was a series of dramas centering more on situations of high emotional stress than on physical ailments. An assortment of actors and actresses appeared, among them Jay Jostyn, Anne Jackson, Ernest Truex, Mildred Natwick, and Lee Marvin. Except for the infrequent occasions on which he also starred in the story, Warner Anderson appeared only at the beginning and end of each episode, to set the scene and discuss the outcome.

DOCTOR, DOCTOR (*Situation Comedy*)
FIRST TELECAST: *June 12, 1989*
LAST TELECAST: *July 6, 1991*
BROADCAST HISTORY:
Jun 1989–Jul 1989, CBS Mon 10:30–11:00
Nov 1989–Feb 1990, CBS Mon 10:30–11:00
Aug 1990–Sep 1990, CBS Mon 8:30–9:00
Sep 1990–Oct 1990, CBS Wed 8:30–9:00
Oct 1990–Jan 1991, CBS Thu 9:30–10:00
Jun 1991–Jul 1991, CBS Sat 10:00–10:30
CAST:
Dr. Mike Stratford .... Matt Frewer
Dr. Abraham Butterfield .... Julius Carry
Dr. Grant Linowitz .... Beau Gravitte
Dr. Dierdre Bennett .... Maureen Mueller
Nurse Faye Baryiski .... Audrie J. Neenan
Pia Bismark .... Sarah Abrell
Richard Stratford .... Tony Carreiro
Elizabeth McQueen (1989) .... Jane Brucker
Dr. Harold Stratford (1989) .... Dakin Matthews
Hugh Persons (1989–1990) .... Brian George
Connie Stratford (1989) .... Inga Swenson
Dr. Leona Linowitz (1990–1991)
.... Anne Elizabeth Ramsay
Emily (1990) .... Anna Slotky
THEME:
"Good Lovin' "

Mike Stratford was an idealistic, eccentric physician working in a group medical practice in Providence, Rhode Island. A general practitioner whose principal motivation was caring for the sick rather than getting rich, Mike was often at odds with his more cash-flow conscious partners—Abe, his best friend and the group's mediator; Grant, a talented but avaricious cardiologist; and Dierdre, Mike's sarcastic former girlfriend whose medical practice was much more successful than her social life. Faye was their know-it-all nurse/receptionist and Richard was Mike's gay brother, a college English professor. Mike was also co-host, with Pia Bismark, of "Wake Up, Providence," a local morning TV show on which he provided off-beat (but sound) medical information. A renaissance man, he had also written an unsuccessful novel, *Panacea.*

In the fall of 1990 Grant's neurotic, recently divorced younger sister, Leona, moved to Providence with her 8-year-old daughter, Emily. A psychiatrist, she set up her office in the same building in which her brother's group practice was located. She had a brief fling with Mike. The following spring Abe separated from his wife of almost twenty years and made his first tentative steps back into the dating world.

DR. FIX-UM (*Information*)
FIRST TELECAST: *May 3, 1949*
LAST TELECAST: *August 6, 1950*
BROADCAST HISTORY:
May 1949–Jun 1949, ABC Tue 9:30–10:00
Nov 1949–Jan 1950, ABC Sun 6:45–7:00
Jan 1950–Aug 1950, ABC Sun 7:45–8:00
HOST:
Arthur Youngquist
Ed Prentiss

Dr. Fix-Um was a program of helpful household hints in which Arthur Youngquist showed how to repair broken gadgets and gave solutions to various other household problems. The program was telecast from Chicago, where it continued to be seen as a local program after the network run.

DR. HUDSON'S SECRET JOURNAL (*Medical Drama*)
BROADCAST HISTORY:
Syndicated only
30 minutes
Produced: *1955–1957* (78 episodes)
Released: *Fall 1955*
CAST:
Dr. Wayne Hudson .... John Howard
Kathy Hudson .... Cheryl Callaway
Mrs. Grady .... Olive Blakeney
Nurse Ann Talbot .... Frances Mercer
Dr. Bennett .... Jack Kelly

This syndicated medical series was based on a character in one of the best-selling novels of the 20th century. Dr. Wayne Hudson was killed off at the start of Lloyd C. Douglas's *Magnificent Obsession* (1929), but his private journal, written in a secret code, helped guide young Bobby Merrick spiritually and professionally as he struggled to become a doctor and save the eyesight of Hudson's widow. A subsequent book by Douglas, *Dr. Hudson's Secret Journal* (1939), reprinted the journal in full, and served as the basis for this program.

The TV series largely dispensed with the religious overtones of Douglas's books (as had the two weepy movie versions of *Magnificent Obsession*, made in 1935 and 1954). Nevertheless it was clear that Hudson, a noted neurosurgeon at Center Hospital, had a strange and rather mysterious gift in his ability to help others psychologically as well as physically. He needed such talents, as he encountered a succession of shattered lives as well as shattered bodies in his weekly rounds. A widower, he lived with his young daughter, Kathy, and their housekeeper, Mrs. Grady.

An unusual aspect of the series was the nationwide competition held in the pages of *TV Guide* in 1955 to find a young actor to play the role of Hudson's protégé, Tim Watson, in several episodes. Those entering had to submit a photograph and a recording ("professional or amusement-park type") in which they read some emotional dialogue. The winner, one Joe Walker, does not appear to have found fame in show business, however.

DOCTOR I.Q. (*Quiz*)

FIRST TELECAST: *November 4, 1953*
LAST TELECAST: *March 23, 1959*
BROADCAST HISTORY:

Nov 1953, ABC Wed 9:30–10:00
Dec 1953–Jan 1954, ABC Thu 9:00–9:30
Jan 1954–Mar 1954, ABC Mon 8:30–9:00
Apr 1954–Oct 1954, ABC Sun 9:30–10:00
Dec 1958–Mar 1959, ABC Sun 9:30–10:00

EMCEE:

Jay Owen (1953–1954)
James McClain (1954)
Tom Kennedy (1958–1959)

Doctor I.Q., one of radio's more popular quiz shows, came to television for two brief runs in the 1950s. "The Doctor" stood behind a podium on the stage and fired questions at people seated in the studio audience. Roving assistants with hand microphones located the contestants and shot back to the Doctor such familiar phrases as "I have a lady in the balcony, Doctor." The questions were reasonably intelligent, and winners were always paid off in silver dollars ("Give that lady ten silver dollars!").

DOCTOR IN THE HOUSE (*Situation Comedy*)

BROADCAST HISTORY:

Syndicated only
30 minutes
Produced: *1970–1973* (78 episodes)
Released (U.S.): *Fall 1971*

CAST:

Dr. Michael Upton (1970–1972) .... Barry Evans
Dr. Duncan Waring .... Robin Nedwell
Dr. Dick Stuart-Clark .... Geoffrey Davies
Prof. Geoffrey Loftus .... Ernest Clark
The Dean .... Ralph Michael
Paul Collier .... George Layton
Huw Evans .... Martin Shaw
Dave Briddock .... Simon Cuff
Danny Hooley .... Jonathan Lynn
Dr. Bingham .... Richard O'Sullivan
Nurses:
Donna Reading, Sammie Winmill, Siobhan Quinlan, Madeline Smith, others

This English comedy about a group of madcap medical students was set at crumbling St. Swithin's Teaching Hospital in London—which, as the Dean informed us in the opening episode, "is not one of the oldest but was founded in 1560, after a severe outbreak of venereal disease that followed closely on the discovery of America."

The three principals were newly arrived and youthful Dr. Michael Upton, his newfound friend Duncan Waring, and perpetual malingerer Dick Stuart-Clark. Their nemesis was the crotchety and ever put-upon Prof. Loftus. The boys were constantly in trouble, whether hatching schemes or pranks, throwing up in anatomy class, or chasing the shapely nurses who populated St. Swithin's. A large cast of semi-regulars also appeared.

Doctor in the House was originally a series of books popular in England in the early 1950s. The author, a newly graduated and bored Dr. Richard Gordon, wrote the first while he was a ship's doctor on a cargo vessel en route to Australia. The books led to a hugely successful (in England) series of movies starring Dirk Bogarde, and, around 1970, to a London Weekend Television network series which became a national craze. The TV scripts were supervised by Dr. Gordon himself, and the show was taped before a live audience. Although it was quickly exported to, and popular in, many other countries, cracking the U.S. market was difficult. American station managers resisted (1) anything English and (2) anything making fun of doctors. It finally made it to the U.S. and became a popular program here for several seasons.

DR. KATZ: PROFESSIONAL THERAPIST (*Cartoon*)

BROADCAST HISTORY:

Comedy Central
30 minutes
Produced: *1995–1999* (78 episodes)
Premiered: *May 28, 1995*

VOICES:

Dr. Katz .... Jonathan Katz
Benjamin Katz .... H. Jon Benjamin
Laura Sweeney .... Laura Silverman
Stanley .... Will Lebow
Julie, the bartender .... Julianne Shapiro

Comedian Jonathan Katz co-created this witty comedy about a deadpan big-city psychologist and his wry conversations with his off-the-wall patients. The patients were usually voiced by real-life fellow comedians, who recorded improvised dialogue which was then fitted to their animated likenesses. For example, Katz with comic Bill Braudis: "Do you remember the first time you had sex?" "Yes, because I kept the receipt." Or with Dom Irrera: "Did you have a problem with bed-wetting as a child?" "No, not as a child."

The divorced doctor also had to deal with his lazy 23-year-old son, Ben, who lived with him and whose chief goal in life seemed to be the permanent avoidance of work. Laura was his insolent receptionist. An unusual feature of the show was its jumpy style of animation, known as "squigglevision." Although it was billed as an innovation, its purpose was much more prosaic: it allowed *Dr. Katz* to be made at far less cost than traditional animation.

DR. KILDARE (*Medical Drama*)
FIRST TELECAST: *September 28, 1961*
LAST TELECAST: *August 30, 1966*
BROADCAST HISTORY:
Sep 1961–Sep 1965, NBC Thu 8:30–9:30
Sep 1965–Aug 1966, NBC Mon/Tue 8:30–9:00
CAST:
Dr. James Kildare .... Richard Chamberlain
Dr. Leonard Gillespie .... Raymond Massey
Dr. Simon Agurski (1961–1962) .... Eddie Ryder
Dr. Thomas Gerson (1961–1962) .... Jud Taylor
Receptionist Susan Deigh (1961–1962) .... Joan Patrick
Nurse Zoe Lawton (1965–1966) .... Lee Kurty
PRODUCER:
Norman Felton
THEME:
"Three Stars Will Shine Tonight"

Dr. Kildare came to television after having been an extremely successful series of movies in the 1940s. There was something immensely appealing about the story of a young intern in a large metropolitan hospital trying to learn his profession, deal with the problems of the patients, and win the respect of the senior doctor in his specialty, internal medicine. Kildare was the young intern, Dr. Gillespie the father figure, and Blair General the hospital in which they practiced medicine. The series did not flinch from realistic portrayals of hospital life and the life-and-death aspect of the work. Interestingly, both *Dr. Kildare* and *Ben Casey*, the two most successful medical shows of the 1960s, arrived in the same season.

During the course of its run, *Dr. Kildare* went through an evolutionary process. By the third season Kildare was promoted to resident. His intern buddies from the first season, Drs. Agurski and Gerson, were not seen in subsequent seasons as the program came to center more closely on the patients and their families. In the 1965–1966 season the show was aired twice a week as a half-hour program rather than once a week for an hour, as previously. Although each episode was self-contained, the series began to take on more of a serial nature, with consecutive episodes developing an overall story. Some of these extended stories ran for only two episodes, others for as many as six.

The Kildare stories were also seen in a 1972 syndicated series called *Young Dr. Kildare*, starring Mark Jenkins as Kildare and Gary Merrill as Gillespie.

DR. QUINN, MEDICINE WOMAN (*Western Drama*)
FIRST TELECAST: *January 1, 1993*
LAST TELECAST: *June 27, 1998*
BROADCAST HISTORY:
Jan 1993, CBS Fri 8:00–10:00
Jan 1993–Dec 1997, CBS Sat 8:00–9:00
Feb 1998–Jun1998, CBS Sat 8:00–9:00
CAST:
Dr. Michaela "Mike" Quinn .... Jane Seymour
Byron Sully .... Joe Lando
Loren Bray (pilot only) .... Guy Boyd
Loren Bray .... Orson Bean
Matthew Cooper (age 17) .... Chad Allen
Colleen Cooper (12) (1993–1995) ...... Erika Flores
Colleen Cooper (1995–1998) ...... Jessica Bowman
Brian Cooper (10) .... Shawn Toovey
Jake Slicker .... Jim Knobeloch
Rev. Timothy Johnson .... Geoffrey Lower
Horace Bing .... Frank Collison
Robert E. .... Henry G. Sanders
Grace .... Jonelle Allen
Emily (1993) .... Heidi Kozak
Cloud Dancing .... Larry Sellers
Hank Claggerty .... William Shockley
Myra Bing (1993–1997) .... Helene Udy
Ingrid (1993) .... Ashley Jones
Ingrid (1993–1995) .... Jennifer Youngs
Dorothy Jennings .... Barbara Babcock
Olive Davis (1993) .... Gail Strickland
**Alice (1993–1996)* .... Andrea Bakkum
Becky (1993–1997) .... Haylie Johnson
**Chief Black Kettle (1993–1995)* .... Nick Ramus
Missy (1993–1994) .... Melissa Flores
Preston A. Lodge III (1995–1998) .... Jason Leland Adams
**Emma (1996)* .... Charlotte Chatton
Dr. Andrew Cook (1995–1998) ... Brandon Douglas
**Anthony (1996–1997)* .... Brandon Hammond
Katie Sully (1996–1998) ...... Megan, Alexandria & McKenzie Calabrese
Teresa Morales (1996–1997) ...... Michelle Bonilla
Teresa Morales (1997–1998) .... Alex Meneses
Sgt. McKay (1997) .... David Beecroft
Daniel Simon (1997–1998) .... John Schneider
*Occasional

Feminism on the frontier was the theme of this drama about an independent young woman doctor making a life for herself in the Old West. Michaela Quinn ("Dr. Mike") had moved from Boston to Colorado Springs, Colorado, in the 1860s following the death of her father and medical partner. The rough-and-ready townspeople, who expected a man when they had advertised for a town physician, greeted Dr. Mike with a mixture of hostility and skepticism. The one person who immediately befriended her was Charlotte Cooper (Diane Ladd), who owned the local boardinghouse. On her deathbed from a snakebite, Charlotte asked Dr. Mike to adopt her three children, Matthew, Colleen, and Brian. Dr. Mike moved them into a homestead owned by Sully, a mysterious mountain man more at home with the Cheyenne Indians and his wolf companion than with the citizens of Colorado Springs. Gradually she gained the grudging respect of the community, since she was virtually always right. Among the featured townspeople were crotchety Loren Bray, owner of the general store; Bray's conniving buddy Jake, the town barber who was elected mayor; Dorothy, Loren's sister-in-law, who worked for him at the store and ran the town newspaper; Hank, who ran the town's saloon/brothel; Myra, one of Hank's barmaids, who eventually quit the business to marry Horace, the telegraph operator; Robert E., the town's black blacksmith, and his wife, Grace, who ran Grace's café; Cloud Dancing, the Cheyenne medicine man; and Ingrid, Matthew's girlfriend.

Dr. Mike was truly a woman ahead of her time. Aside from having chosen a "male" profession, she was an outspoken liberal and avid supporter of all sorts of humanitarian causes. She respected the Indians, sought equality for the blacks in Colorado Springs, and was sympathetic to the barmaids/prostitutes who worked in Hank's saloon. Over time she not only gained the respect of the community but found love with the ruggedly handsome Sully. They got engaged in 1994, and he started building the home they would move into after their marriage. The end of the 1994–1995 season brought three major events—the cavalry massacred the Cheyenne villagers (but Cloud Dancing, who was not there at the time, survived), the railroad link to Colorado Springs was completed, and Sully and Dr. Mike got married.

That fall, Dr. Mike and Sully returned from their honeymoon and it took a while for her foster children to adjust, since she spent more time on her relationship with her new husband than on them. Cloud Dancing was forced onto a government-run reservation. New to the cast was Preston, a Bostonian who arrived to establish the first bank in Colorado Springs and planned to build a big hotel and casino. Tragedy occurred when Matthew's fiancée, Ingrid, was bitten by a rabid dog and died. Dorothy wrote a best-seller about her experiences in Colorado Springs, which irritated the townsfolk because of its revelations, and in January, Dr. Mike became the first woman accepted into the A.M.A. Matthew, still grieving over Ingrid's death, was elected sheriff of Colorado Springs and started dating Emma, who worked in the town bordello. It didn't work out. Sully, who had become the government's Indian agent, had problems with the various tribes. In the season finale, Dr. Mike gave birth to a baby girl, Katie.

When Dr. Mike returned to her practice, the townspeople had problems adjusting because they had gotten used to Andrew Cook, the young doctor who covered for her while she was on maternity leave. Colleen started college and eventually started to date Andrew. In October, Teresa, a Latin American widowed after her husband was mauled by a mountain lion, replaced Rev. Johnson as the schoolteacher, which did not sit well with some of the more prejudiced townspeople. Sully lost his job as Indian agent and was banned from the reservation because of his relationship with Cloud Dancing and the Cheyenne. In February, Sully's old friend Daniel, wealthy from a recent gold strike, showed up for a visit and paid off the entire loan on their homestead. At season's end Sully was on the run, having organized an escape for Cloud Dancing and the Cheyenne from the reservation that resulted in a massacre.

At the start of *Dr. Quinn*'s final season, Daniel, who had stayed in Colorado Springs and replaced Matthew as sheriff, went with Dr. Mike in search of her fugitive husband. Wounded, Sully was in hiding after having killed a soldier in self-defense. He was also pursued by a relentless Sgt. McKay, who blamed Sully for the Indian massacre. After he regained his health, Sully, still in hiding, worked to convince the renegade Indians to go back to the reservation—they finally did, at year's end, signing a treaty that allowed Sully, too, to return home. Dorothy had fallen in love with Cloud Dancing, and Matthew was studying law. In the series finale Colleen graduated from Colorado Seminary College, and was accepted to medical school at the Women's Medical College of Pennsylvania, Dr. Mike's alma mater. Preston, the banker, had serious financial problems when the stock market, in which he had invested his depositors' money, crashed, resulting in a run on the bank. The episode ended at the outdoor wedding reception for Colleen and Andrew, at which Grace told Robert E. she was pregnant, and Loren told Dorothy he had taken out a mortgage on his store to pay off her loan to Preston for the *Colorado Springs Gazette*.

DR. RUTH (*Discussion/Advice*)

CABLE HISTORY:

Lifetime Network
30/60 minutes
Produced: *1984–1991*
Premiered: *August 27, 1984*

SYNDICATION HISTORY:

Syndicated
30 minutes
Produced: *1987*
Released: *January 1987*

HOST:

Dr. Ruth Westheimer

Diminutive psychologist Dr. Ruth Westheimer's subject was sex—"good sex"—and coming from this sweet, grandmotherly lady with a thick German accent, the sometimes graphic discussions of physical and emotional performance problems, techniques, and other ways to make your sex life enjoyable caused quite a sensation. Starting with a late-night local radio show in New York in the early 1980s, she had, by the middle of the decade, become a national phenomenon, with cable and syndicated series, a best-selling book, and scores of personal appearances. The kindest compliment was being lampooned by dozens of comics, notably Johnny Carson on *The Tonight Show*.

Over the years Dr. Ruth hosted at least five different series on Lifetime and one in syndication (she also made pilots for the broadcast networks, for example, *Dr. Ruth's House* for ABC in 1990, but they were too chicken to pick them up!). Her first TV series was *Good Sex! With Dr. Ruth Westheimer*, a half-hour 10 P.M. weeknight show on Lifetime in 1984 that included reenactments. The first telecast dealt with premature ejaculation. In 1985 the show was expanded to an hour nightly and the name changed to *The Dr. Ruth Show*. Dr. Ruth became such a sensation on Lifetime that in 1987 she launched a separate half-hour syndicated series, *Ask Dr. Ruth*, with co-host Larry Angelo, which ran on many broadcast stations in the wee hours.

The irrepressible doctor returned to Lifetime in 1988 with *The All New Dr. Ruth Show*, followed by *What's Up, Dr. Ruth?* (advice for teens, 1989) and *You're on the Air with Dr. Ruth* (call-in, 1990). These were half-hour series seen primarily on weekends; the last one left the air in June 1991. Most of Dr. Ruth's series featured guests and sometimes a studio audience. Naturally, due to the explicit subject matter, nearly all of them aired late at night.

DR. SEUSS, See *Wubbulous World of Dr. Seuss, The*

DR. SIMON LOCKE (*Medical Drama*)

BROADCAST HISTORY:

Syndicated only
30 minutes
Produced: *1971–1974* (78 episodes)
Released: *Fall 1971*

CAST:

Dr. Simon Locke .... Sam Groom
Dr. Sellers (1971–1972) .... Jack Albertson

Nurse Wynn (1971–1972) .... Nuala Fitzgerald
Chief/Det. Lt. Dan Palmer (1971–1973). Len Birman
Lt. Jack Gordon (1973–1974) .... Larry D. Mann

This Canadian-produced medical drama was very cheaply made, and critics found it awful, but nevertheless it survived for three seasons in syndication in the U.S. In the first season Dr. Simon Locke was an earnest young physician newly arrived in the small town of Dixon Mills, where his mentor was the crusty Dr. Sellers. Despite the rural locale, Locke encountered all sorts of excitement, such as murders, battered children, and a typhoid epidemic. In its second season the show moved to the city, where Locke was assigned to the police emergency unit, finding even more crime-oriented (though generally nonviolent) stories. Chief Palmer of Dixon Mills came along as his tough-talking police boss. ("Remember," he growled at Locke, "you're only second line. Don't become a hero.") The title was changed to *Police Surgeon*. In the final season, Lt. Gordon became Locke's police superior. A guest-star policy was also instituted in the second and third seasons, with such well-known actors as William Shatner, Leslie Nielsen, Keenan Wynn, and Susan Strasberg appearing.

The behind-the-scenes story of *Dr. Simon Locke* is an interesting, if extreme, case study in how syndicated programs get on the air. It isn't simply a matter of a producer having a bright idea, followed by the audience voting yea or nay. This one began when the Federal Communications Commission announced that starting in the fall of 1971, the networks had to cut back their evening programming, and local stations would have to fill the vacated time—generally 7:30–8:00 P.M.—with original shows (not reruns). The idea was to encourage localized programming, but that didn't happen. Syndicators, who sell their programs station to station, rushed out all sorts of first-run candidates. The problem was that they had to be very cheap, because without network financing and guaranteed exposure, the risk capital simply wasn't available for big-budget production. As a result, what the public got was mostly inexpensive game shows and nature documentaries. However, the Colgate-Palmolive Co., sponsor of *Dr. Kildare* and the daytime serial *The Doctors*, was persuaded by its advertising agency to finance a dramatic show about a young doctor who moves to a rural town.

The first necessity was to get production out of Hollywood, where expenses were astronomical. The second was to find a way to sell the program to other countries, to help defray costs. Unfortunately many countries had recently instituted severe quotas on the amount of programming that could be imported from the U.S. So production was moved to Toronto, thus qualifying the series as "Canadian"—okay for Canada and the British Empire—and cheap enough for the U.S. Little-known Sam Groom, a refugee from *Another World*, provided an inexpensive lead. Jack Albertson was lured away from Hollywood as the only "name" in the cast.

Still, budgets were so skinflinty that when Albertson arrived to do location filming he found he literally had to change his pants in the bushes. The director refused to screen the results of each day's filming for him (again, to save money), and he never saw a show until the first three were edited and complete. When he did, he was furious at the mess—incredibly sloppy production, microphones in camera range, bad lighting, choppy editing, dreadful scripts. He promptly quit to save his reputation. "You have a contract," insisted the producer. "After what I just saw," exploded Albertson, "there's not a jury in the world that would convict me!"

Albertson was mollified, at least temporarily, but when critics saw the results on the air they were even madder. "Sub-sub par . . . unbelievable . . . It is literally impossible to assume that any viewer would return for a second look. . . . No way, no way!" cried *Variety*. "A syndie quickie," groaned *TV Guide*. "The only way [the producers] could break even with this show would be if they gave something away with it."

So how did it survive? Economics. It was not only cheap, the producers actually *gave* it to stations—with the understanding that two of the commercials in each episode remain with them (called "barter" in the trade). These went to Colgate, who had put up the cash. Although audiences weren't sizable, they did contain a fair number of young women (Colgate's clientele), and the sponsor liked Sam Groom and thought perhaps the show could be juiced up with the move to the city. Things limped along this way until 1974, when Colgate finally found better things to do with its money, and Dr. Locke closed up shop. Without the benefit of the legislative and economic accident that put it on the air, *Dr. Simon Locke* was scarcely seen at all in reruns.

DOCTORS AND THE NURSES, THE, see *Nurses, The*

DOCTORS' HOSPITAL (*Medical Drama*)
FIRST TELECAST: *September 10, 1975*
LAST TELECAST: *January 14, 1976*
BROADCAST HISTORY:
Sep 1975–Jan 1976, NBC Wed 9:00–10:00
CAST:
Dr. Jake Goodwin .... George Peppard
Dr. Norah Purcell .... Zohra Lampert
Dr. Felipe Ortega .... Victor Campos
Janos Varga .... Albert Paulsen
Dr. Chaffey .... Russ Martin
Dr. Paul Herman .... John Larroquette
Dr. Danvers........................ John Pleshette
Dr. Anson Brooks .... James Almanzar
Nurse Connie Kimbrough .... Elizabeth Brooks
Nurse Hester Stanton .... Adrian Ricard
Nurse Forester.................... Barbara Darrow
Nurse Wilson .... Elaine Church
Nurse Franklin .... Susan Franklin
Barney............................... Larry Watson
Scotty .... Maxine Stuart

Set at fictitious Lowell Memorial Hospital in Los Angeles, this medical series sought a unique approach to hospital life: it examined all aspects of that life—the good and the bad—through the eyes of the doctors rather than those of the patients. Dr. Jake Goodwin was the chief of neurosurgical services at the hospital, and Norah Purcell was a second-year resident and his most gifted student. Dr. Ortega was the chief resident at Lowell Memorial and Janos Varga its director. To minimize the roles of the patients, a large number of them were treated in each episode, thereby shifting the emphasis to the work and personalities of the doctors and the other members of the hospital staff.

DOCTORS' PRIVATE LIVES (*Medical Drama*)
FIRST TELECAST: *April 5, 1979*
LAST TELECAST: *April 26, 1979*
BROADCAST HISTORY:
Apr 1979, ABC Thu 10:00–11:00
CAST:
Dr. Michael Wise .... Ed Nelson
Dr. Jeffrey Latimer .... John Gavin
Dr. Rick Calder .... Randolph Powell
Kenny Wise .... Phil Levien
Sheila Castle .... Gwen Humble
Nurse Diane Cooper .... Eddie Benton

This series focused on the personal and professional crises of two famous heart surgeons, Chief Surgeon Dr. Michael Wise and cardiovascular unit chief Dr. Jeffrey Latimer. Worrying along with them were young Dr. Rick Calder, medical students Kenny Wise and Sheila Castle, and Nurse Cooper.

DOG AND CAT (*Police Drama*)
FIRST TELECAST: *March 5, 1977*
LAST TELECAST: *May 14, 1977*
BROADCAST HISTORY:
Mar 1977–May 1977, ABC Sat 10:00–11:00
CAST:
Det. Sgt. Jack Ramsey .... Lou Antonio
Officer J. Z. Kane .... Kim Basinger
Lt. Arthur Kipling .... Matt Clark

This was a police show with a light sense of humor. It had to be, to team an experienced veteran plainclothes cop (Ramsey) with a bright, sexy, and, of course, competent female rookie (Kane) and expect nothing but police work to occur. Lt. Kipling was the boss. The program was filmed in Southern California.

DOG EAT DOG (*Quiz*)
FIRST TELECAST: *June 17, 2002*
LAST TELECAST:
BROADCAST HISTORY:
Jun 2002–Aug 2002, NBC Mon 9:00–10:00
Aug 2002–Sep 2002, NBC Sat 9:00–10:00
May 2003– , NBC Tue 8:00–9:00
EMCEE:
Brooke Burns

One of the many bizarre shows that came and went during the prime time game-show craze of the early 2000's, *Dog Eat Dog* brought six fit, young contestants together for a series of physical and mental challenges. First they spent a day together facing various challenges so they could judge each other's strengths and weaknesses. Then they came together on a huge stage that looked a lot like a cave (complete with steam coming out of the walls), with a 30-foot-tall tower and a 300,000-gallon swimming tank. Tall, sexy host Brooke Burns presented them with more challenges, and for each the group voted who would be the most likely to fail. The chosen contestant then had to take the challenge; a loser went to the "dog pound" (a bench on the side), but if the contestant succeeded, he or she got to send one of the other players there. The last contestant left standing was dubbed "Top Dog" but faced one last challenge, competing in a trivia round against the eliminated players for a grand prize of $25,000. If he or she lost, the money was split among the other five.

Challenges included diving into the pool after various objects, climbing a swinging pole to retrieve flags and answering trivia questions while running on a treadmill that was suspended high above the water, and which picked up speed with each wrong answer. There was a good deal of skin, especially in the water (girls in bikinis, guys in trunks), and an annoying amount of advertising integrated into the show (the NetZero Countdown Clock, the Circuit City Video Screen, etc.).

DOLLAR A SECOND (*Quiz/Audience Participation*)
FIRST TELECAST: *September 20, 1953*
LAST TELECAST: *September 28, 1957*
BROADCAST HISTORY:
Sep 1953–Apr 1954, DUM Sun 10:00–10:30
Apr 1954–Jun 1954, DUM Mon 8:00–8:30
Jul 1954–Aug 1954, NBC Sun 10:00–10:30
Oct 1954–Jun 1955, ABC Fri 9:00–9:30
Jul 1955–Aug 1955, NBC Tue 9:30–10:00
Sep 1955–Sep 1956, ABC Fri 9:00–9:30
Jun 1957–Sep 1957, NBC Sat 9:30–10:00
Sep 1957, NBC Sat 10:00–10:30
EMCEE:
Jan Murray

In this comedy quiz show the contestant could win money in two ways: he or she won a dollar for every correct answer and another dollar for every second he stayed on the show. There was a catch, however, and that was called "the outside event." While the contestant was answering questions, and paying funny but embarrassing penalties for wrong answers (as in *Truth or Consequences*), something was going on outside the studio that might cause him or her to forfeit all winnings. The contestant could choose to quit at any time and keep all winnings up to that point, or continue in the hope that the outside event would not take place until after the show was over. The contestant did not know the nature of the outside event, but viewers did. It might be the arrival of a train at a specified point, or the landing of a given plane at LaGuardia Airport, or the birth of a baby at a designated hospital. A remote camera looked in periodically on the event about to take place, to heighten the suspense for the viewing audience.

$1.98 BEAUTY SHOW, THE (*Comedy*)
BROADCAST HISTORY:
Syndicated only
30 minutes
Produced: *1978–1980* (54 episodes)
Released: *September 1978*
HOST:
Rip Taylor
EXECUTIVE PRODUCER:
Chuck Barris

Critics howled with disgust, but audiences seemed to enjoy this intentionally tacky travesty on the traditional American beauty pageant. "Chuck Barris [the producer] seems determined to become the leading purveyor of bad taste on the tube," groaned *Variety*. The format called for six contestants, some sexy, some gross, to vie for a crown. First they were introduced, to good-natured ribbing by chubby, mustachioed host Rip Taylor and the rambunctious panel;

then came the "talent" competition, in which 200-pound lady plumbers did the "Dance of the Sugar Plum Fairies," and off-key singers bellowed their way through hapless ballads (shades of *The Gong Show*!); and finally there was the swimsuit competition, in which the girls purred, nervously tiptoed, or defiantly waddled through their paces "deprived of all their worldly goods." Hoots and cheers from the audience! Some of the contestants were pretty sexy, but the fat ladies always seemed to do best in this last segment.

The winner got $1.98 plunked into her hand, and a tacky crown. In his gaudy vest, host Taylor presided over the tumult with unctuous charm. Frequently celebrity panelists included Jaye P. Morgan, Jamie Farr, Louis Nye, Marty Allen, and the Unknown Comic (Murray Langston).

DOLLY (*Music*)

BROADCAST HISTORY:

Syndicated only
30 minutes
Produced: *1976* (52 episodes)
Released: *February 1976*

HOSTESS:

Dolly Parton

Country superstar Dolly Parton, with her generous bust, mountainous wig, and sequined pseudo-cowgirl outfit, hosted this half hour of music taped in Nashville. Guests included country-pop talent such as Tennessee Ernie Ford, Bobby Goldsboro, Lynn Anderson, Rod McKuen, and even Captain Kangaroo. Though Miss Parton was a major star in the country field, she had not yet emerged into the popular mainstream at this time; as her fame spread over the next few years, the program was widely repeated.

DOLLY (*Musical Variety*)

FIRST TELECAST: *September 27, 1987*
LAST TELECAST: *May 7, 1988*
BROADCAST HISTORY:

Sep 1987–Jan 1988, ABC Sun 9:00–10:00
Jan 1988–May 1988, ABC Sat 8:00–9:00

REGULARS:

Dolly Parton
A Cappella (singing group)

ABC made a valiant attempt to revive the concept of a big, splashy prime-time variety show in this 1987 series headlined by country superstar Dolly Parton. The petite (5'2") Miss Parton, in her towering blonde wigs and skintight fashions, never looked better ("It takes a lot money to make me look this cheap," she cracked). The accent was on music "with a lot of heart," mostly of the country or country-pop variety, often in cozy settings such as Dolly's rustic living room with its roaring fireplace, rather than on a stage. There were also comedy sketches in recurring settings, including Dixie's Place Cafe (with Dolly as a waitress), the Vanity Fair Beauty Salon, "D.P.'s" country music club, or on "Dolly's Date."

Guests included Burt Reynolds, country groups Alabama and The Oak Ridge Boys, Whoopi Goldberg, Willie Nelson, the Smothers Brothers, and Kermit the Frog. A Cappella was Dolly's backup group, consisting of Richard Dennison, Gene Miller, Dave Rowland, and Howard Smith.

DOLPHIN COVE (*Adventure*)

FIRST TELECAST: *January 21, 1989*
LAST TELECAST: *March 11, 1989*
BROADCAST HISTORY:

Jan 1989–Mar 1989, CBS Sat 8:00–9:00

CAST:

Michael Larson .... Frank Converse
David Larson .... Trey Ames
Katie Larson .... Karron Graves
Didge .... Ernie Dingo
Baron Trent .... Nick Tate
Alison Mitchell .... Virginia Hey
Kevin Mitchell .... Antony Richards

Several months after the death of his wife in a tragic automobile accident, dolphin researcher Michael Larson and his two children moved to Australia to start a new life. Michael had been hired by a wealthy Australian industrialist, Baron Trent, to perfect man-to-dolphin communications. Living at Trent's estate on the Australian coast, Michael worked full-time with the two resident dolphins, Slim and Delbert. But life for these Yanks in Australia was not without its problems. David, the teenage son, felt like an outsider at school and found it hard to adjust to the regimented discipline of the Australian school system. Katie, his younger sister, had yet to regain her speech—lost from the shock of being in the car with her mother during the accident—and was slow to accept her new therapist, Alison Mitchell. Although she was uncomfortable with people, Katie was completely at home with the dolphins, with whom she developed an almost telepathic communication. Alison's son Kevin was David's one close friend at school, and Didge was the Aborigine who ran the estate for Baron Trent and helped Michael with his research.

Filmed entirely on location in Australia and co-created by Peter Benchley, the author of *Jaws*.

DOM DELUISE SHOW, THE (*Comedy/Variety*)

FIRST TELECAST: *May 1, 1968*
LAST TELECAST: *September 18, 1968*
BROADCAST HISTORY:

May 1968–Sep 1968, CBS Wed 10:00–11:00

REGULARS:

Dom DeLuise
Marian Mercer
Bill McCutcheon
Carol Arthur
Paul Dooley
Mike and Joe Gentry
Dick Lynn
The June Taylor Dancers
Sammy Spear and His Orchestra

Pudgy comedian Dom DeLuise hosted and starred in this summer variety series. The emphasis was on comedy, with DeLuise's pantomime routines frequently featured. Guest stars appeared on each telecast, along with a cast of regulars. One of the regulars, Carol Arthur, was Dom's wife.

DOM DELUISE SHOW, THE (*Situation Comedy*)

BROADCAST HISTORY:

Syndicated only
30 minutes
Produced: *1987–1988* (24 episodes)
Released: *September 1987*

CAST:

Dom .... Dom DeLuise
George Henry Wallace .... George Wallace
Maureen .... Maureen Murphy
Penny .... Angela Aames
Michael Chambers .... Michael Chambers
Blanche Maxwell .... Lois Foraker
Rosa .... Lauren Woodland
Charlie .... Charlie Callas
Billy (1987) .... Billy Scudder

This series described itself as "almost, but not quite, a situation comedy" and did so with good reason. Although the regulars, most of whom had considerable experience as standup comics, all stayed in character, individual scenes frequently tended to look like variety-show comedy sketches or comedy monologues. On top of everything else, star Dom DeLuise (and on occasion others in the cast) sometimes talked directly to the viewing audience, much as George Burns had done three decades earlier on *The George Burns and Gracie Allen Show*.

Most of the action took place in Dom's Barber Shop, where Dom and his black partner George held court for their customers and friends. Among them were Maureen, their spaced-out manicurist; Penny, the sexy young aerobics instructor who worked nearby; Michael, the loose-limbed pizza delivery boy who could dance up a storm; Charlie, the paranoid, trench-coated private detective; and Billy, the Chaplinesque (including tramp costume and walk) little man who advertised Dom's Barber Shop with a small sign on his back. Dom, a widower who took pride in being a gourmet cook, lived behind the barbershop with his cute 10-year-old daughter Rosa. His girlfriend Blanche owned a neighborhood pet shop and had given him Max, his pet chimpanzee, as a Christmas present. Located near the big movie studios in Hollywood, the barbershop was visited by celebrities like Burt Reynolds, Sherman Hemsley, Zsa Zsa Gabor, Dean Martin, and Tom Jones.

DOMESTIC LIFE (*Situation Comedy*)

FIRST TELECAST: *January 4, 1984*
LAST TELECAST: *September 11, 1984*
BROADCAST HISTORY:

Jan 1984–Feb 1984, CBS Wed 8:00–8:30
Mar 1984–Apr 1984, CBS Sun 8:00–8:30
Jul 1984–Sep 1984, CBS Tue 8:30–9:00

CAST:

Martin Crane .... Martin Mull
Harold Crane .... Christian Brackett-Zika
Didi Crane .... Megan Follows
Cliff Hamilton .... Robert Ridgely
Candy Crane .... Judith-Marie Bergan
Jane Funakubo .... Mie Hunt
Rip Steele .... Hoyt Axton
Jeff, the floor manager .... J. Alan Thomas

EXECUTIVE PRODUCER:

Steve Martin

Comedian Steve Martin produced this comedy about a slightly offbeat family, which was turned down by one network (NBC) and then had a short and unsuccessful run on another (CBS). Martin Crane had just arrived in Seattle to take a job as a commentator for station KMRT-TV. His regular spot on the station's evening news was called "Domestic Life," and dealt with the humorous side of home and family life. He certainly had a lot to talk about! His wife Candy was a sucker for other people's problems, and vaguely dissatisfied with their own limited finances. Daughter Didi was a typical, semi-controllable 15-year-old. Harold, their chubby ten-year-old son, talked like a businessman, had an office in his room, and had already netted thousands from wise investments. In some ways he was more mature than his parents, though he still wanted a hug and a kiss when he gave them a loan.

Martin's life was usually in an uproar both at home and at the station, where Cliff and Jane were fellow reporters and Rip Steele—an ex–cowboy star of "B" movies—was the colorful, guitar-strumming station owner.

DON ADAMS' SCREEN TEST (*Comedy/Audience Participation*)

BROADCAST HISTORY:

Syndicated only
30 minutes
Produced: *1974–1975* (26 episodes)
Released: *Fall 1975*

HOST/"DIRECTOR":

Don Adams

Comedian Don Adams hosted this original but high-decibel audience-participation show, in which preselected studio contestants were paired with guest stars to reenact famous movie scenes. First the original scene was shown, via a film clip. Then the contestant and celebrity did it, usually for laughs (in the beach scene from *From Here to Eternity*, for example, everybody got drenched with buckets of water). Don Adams served as "director" and sometimes participant in the scenes. A professional TV or movie director picked the winner, who got a bit part in an upcoming real production—although that part was incidental to the laughs. Among the stars appearing were Milton Berle, Mel Brooks, Bob Newhart, and Greg Morris; the movies parodied included *On the Waterfront*, *Pillow Talk*, *Bride of Frankenstein*, and *The African Queen*.

DON AMECHE'S MUSICAL PLAYHOUSE, see *Holiday Hotel*

DON KIRSHNER'S ROCK CONCERT (*Music*)

BROADCAST HISTORY:

Syndicated only
90 minutes
Produced: *1973–1981*
Released: *September 1973*

HOST:

Don Kirshner

This was one of the two principal showcases for rock music in the mid- and late 1970s. Although it was syndicated for local airing anywhere on a station's schedule, it usually ran late at night, like NBC's *Midnight Special*. The emphasis was on progressive rock bands, such as the Allman Brothers, Fleetwood Mac, Black Sabbath, Led Zeppelin, and the Ramones, but a wide variety of contemporary talent appeared—Paul McCartney and Wings, Dr. Hook, Blondie, Chuck Berry, etc. Mick Jagger and the Rolling Stones headlined the much-heralded premiere in 1973. In the later 1970s soft-pop acts started to creep in (Captain and Tennille, Johnny Nash, Shaun Cassidy, even Debby Boone), but the program never abandoned the non-top-40 side of rock. Some hip comics also were seen, among them Martin Mull, the Village Idiots, and Natural Gas.

Don Kirshner had begun his career with Bobby Darin in the 1950s, and was a major figure in the music business by this time (he was responsible for the Monkees, among others). ABC hired him in late 1972 as impresario for its short-lived *In Concert*, but he left to start his own show a few months later. Some of the executives at ABC, he remarked, didn't seem to know the difference between the Allman Brothers and the Osmond Brothers.

There was no regular host at first. Beginning with the second season, Kirshner himself began to do brief introductions (on camera but offstage).

DON KNOTTS SHOW, THE (*Comedy/Variety*)

FIRST TELECAST: *September 15, 1970*
LAST TELECAST: *July 6, 1971*
BROADCAST HISTORY:

Sep 1970–Jan 1971, NBC Tue 7:30–8:30
Jan 1971–Jul 1971, NBC Tue 8:00–9:00

REGULARS:

Don Knotts
Elaine Joyce
Bob Williams and his dog Louie
Frank Welker
Ken Mars
Mickey Deems
John Dehner
Eddie Carroll
Gary Burghoff
The Nick Perito Orchestra

Don Knotts hosted and starred in this comedy-variety show. There were two regular features each week: Don and his guest stars in skits about his frustrations caused by the grind of doing a weekly TV show, and "The Front Porch," in which Don and his guest star would sit in rocking chairs and exchange "philosophies."

DON McNEILL TV CLUB (*Variety*)

FIRST TELECAST: *September 13, 1950*
LAST TELECAST: *December 19, 1951*
BROADCAST HISTORY:

Sep 1950–Jun 1951, ABC Wed 9:00–10:00
Sep 1951–Dec 1951, ABC Wed 9:00–9:30 (alternate weeks)

REGULARS:

Don McNeill
Johnny Desmond
Fran Allison
Sam Cowling
Patsy Lee
Eddie Ballantine Orchestra

Don McNeill seemed like a natural for TV. His easy-going, homey style was much like that of Arthur Godfrey, who in 1950 was scoring an enormous hit with his *Arthur Godfrey and His Friends* and *Talent Scouts* programs. McNeill, like Godfrey, had been a radio fixture for years; his *Breakfast Club,* which began in 1933, had almost singlehandedly turned early-morning network radio into a profitable medium. Thus, in the fall of 1950 ABC brought McNeill and his *Breakfast Club* gang to nighttime network television, live from his hometown of Chicago.

Music and variety acts were featured, all delivered with the down-home charm and sincerity that had endeared McNeill to millions of radio fans. Among the regulars were Fran Allison doing her rural Aunt Fanny characterization, singer Johnny Desmond, portly comic Sam Cowling, and singer-comedienne Patsy Lee, plus show-business guests. The guests never overshadowed the regular cast. Perhaps that was part of the problem; perhaps there was only room for one Godfrey. In any event, McNeill never caught on in television, and after a season and a half in prime time and an attempt at a daytime version of the *Breakfast Club* in 1954, he abandoned the medium to concentrate solely on his radio show (which had continued in the meantime). He continued with it until 1968, a run of over 34 years. His signature was the same on radio and television: "Be good to yourself."

DON RICKLES SHOW, THE (*Comedy/Variety*)

FIRST TELECAST: *September 27, 1968*
LAST TELECAST: *January 31, 1969*
BROADCAST HISTORY:

Sep 1968–Jan 1969, ABC Fri 9:00–9:30

REGULARS:

Don Rickles
Pat McCormick
Vic Mizzy Orchestra

This was a kind of one-man roast, in which Don Rickles directed his famous "insult humor" at guests and audience. Everyone was a "dummy" to Don. Pat McCormick was his gargantuan foil-announcer-factotum, as well as one of the writers of the show. Apparently the viewing audience did not take kindly to this kind of assault, and the show was soon canceled. Those involved bore no grudge, however; at the end of the final telecast the writers and the entire crew and staff carried Rickles off the stage on their shoulders. What they did with him afterward was not revealed.

DON RICKLES SHOW, THE (*Situation Comedy*)

FIRST TELECAST: *January 14, 1972*
LAST TELECAST: *May 26, 1972*
BROADCAST HISTORY:

Jan 1972–May 1972, CBS Fri 10:30–11:00

CAST:

Don Robinson .... Don Rickles
Barbara Robinson .... Louise Sorel
Janie Robinson .... Erin Moran
Tyler Benedict .... Robert Hogan
Audrey .... Judy Cassmore
Jean Benedict .... Joyce Van Patten
Conrad Musk .... Barry Gordon

The life and endless problems of a New York advertising-agency executive were the premise for this comedy starring Don Rickles. Don Robinson's loving wife Barbara and his cute young daughter Janie stood by more or less helplessly while Don, the master of insult humor, did constant battle with the frustrations of corporate society. Battlegrounds included his office at Kingston, Cohen and Vanderpool, Inc., and his pleasant Long Island home. Apparently viewers quickly wearied of the fray, as the series was cancelled after only four months.

DONALD O'CONNOR TEXACO SHOW, THE
(*Situation Comedy*)

FIRST TELECAST: *October 9, 1954*
LAST TELECAST: *September 10, 1955*
BROADCAST HISTORY:
Oct 1954–Sep 1955, NBC Sat 9:30–10:00
CAST:
Donald O'Connor .... Himself
Sid Miller .... Himself
Doreen .... Joyce Smight

During the 1954–1955 season the *Texaco Star Theatre* consisted of two alternating series, *The Donald O'Connor Show* and *The Jimmy Durante Show*. O'Connor's half of the venture, which was subtitled "Here Comes Donald," was a loosely structured situation comedy whose primary function was to let Donald perform as a singer and dancer with his songwriting partner Sid Miller. The basic story line presented Donald and Sid as two young songwriters trying to find buyers for their songs and winding up in situations where they had the opportunity to sing, dance, and be comedians. Joyce Smight had the continuing role of their secretary, Doreen.

DONNA REED SHOW, THE (*Situation Comedy*)

FIRST TELECAST: *September 24, 1958*
LAST TELECAST: *September 3, 1966*
BROADCAST HISTORY:
Sep 1958–Sep 1959, ABC Wed 9:00–9:30
Oct 1959–Jan 1966, ABC Thu 8:00–8:30
Jan 1966–Sep 1966, ABC Sat 8:00–8:30
CAST:
Donna Stone .... Donna Reed
Dr. Alex Stone .... Carl Betz
Mary Stone (1958–1963) .... Shelley Fabares
Jeff Stone .... Paul Petersen
Trisha Stone (1963–1966) .... Patty Petersen
Dr. Dave Kelsey (1963–1965) .... Bob Crane
Midge Kelsey (1963–1966) .... Ann McCrea
Karen Holmby (1964–1965) .... Janet Langard
Smitty (1965–1966) .... Darryl Richard
PRODUCER/EXEC. PRODUCER:
Tony Owen
THEME SONG:
"Happy Days," by William Loose and John Seely

At the center of this family comedy were Donna Stone, her husband Alex, a pediatrician, and their rambunctious teenage kids. The adventures of the Stone family were similar to those of other TV families—measles, girlfriends, school problems, little white lies, and so on—compounded by the fact that Dr. Alex was always running off at odd hours to attend to his patients. The show was set in the small town of Hilldale, and it had a wholesome quality that endeared it to audiences. It won many awards from youth, women's, educational, and medical groups; the president of the American Medical Association even appeared in a cameo role in one telecast.

Over the years changes in the series took place. Mary, the older child, went off to college in 1962, followed by Jeff two years later. About the time that Mary left the series for good, in 1963, the character of Trisha, an eight-year-old orphan who "adopted" the Stones, was added. Played by Patty Petersen, Paul's real-life sister, she was first seen in a January 1963 telecast and stayed for the rest of the series. Dave Kelsey was Alex's colleague and the Stones' next-door neighbor, and Midge was Dave's wife. Various friends and romances of Mary and Jeff appeared from time to time, the most regular of whom were Paul's girlfriend Karen and his college buddy Smitty.

Both of Donna Reed's original TV offspring had short but spectacular recording careers in 1962–1963 with songs introduced on the series. On a January 1962 telecast Paul Petersen sang the novelty ditty "She Can't Find Her Keys," as part of a dream sequence in which Jeff dreamed he was a teenage recording star out on a date. His recording of the song became a major hit during early 1962. Later he had several other best-sellers, including the top-ten hit "My Dad," about Dr. Alex. Shelley Fabares did even better with a teenage love song called "Johnny Angel," which went to number-one on the charts in early 1962 and earned her a gold record, denoting sales of more than a million copies.

Reruns of *The Donna Reed Show* were telecast weekdays on ABC from December 1964 to March 1968.

DONNY AND MARIE (*Musical Variety*)

FIRST TELECAST: *January 16, 1976*
LAST TELECAST: *May 6, 1979*
BROADCAST HISTORY:
Jan 1976–May 1977, ABC Fri 8:00–9:00
Jun 1977–Aug 1977, ABC Wed 8:00–9:00
Aug 1977–Jan 1979, ABC Fri 8:00–9:00 (OS)
Jan 1979–Mar 1979, ABC Sun 7:00–8:00
May 1979, ABC Sun 7:00–8:00
REGULARS:
Donny Osmond
Marie Osmond
Alan Osmond
Wayne Osmond
Merrill Osmond
Jay Osmond
Johnny Dark (1978–1979)
Jimmy Osmond
The Ice Vanities (1976–1977)
The Ice Angels (1977–1978)
The Disco Dozen (1978–1979)
Jim Connell
Larry Larsen

Sid and Marty Krofft, of animated cartoon fame, originally produced this teenage variety hour. Eighteen-year-old Donny and his 16-year-old sister Marie were co-hosts of the show, which also featured other members of the popular musical family, ranging in age from Jimmy (12) to Alan (26). Despite his youth, Donny was a show-business veteran by the time the program premiered, having made his TV debut at the age of four singing "You Are My Sunshine" on *The Andy Williams Show*. In order to keep up the clan's youthful appearance, Merrill introduced another Osmond—his six-month-old son Travis—to the cast on an early telecast.

The format was the usual mixture of comedy and songs, with a liberal sprinkling of the Osmonds' teenybopper hits. The comedy often made fun of Donny's toothy, super-wholesome appearance, as when his brothers ganged up and dumped him into a gigantic nine-foot whipped cream pie in one 1976 broadcast. "I think I finally made a big splash on television," Donny said. Although not credited as a regular, Paul Lynde appeared as a guest star on many of the *Donny and Marie* episodes.

The second season brought changes, as a new production team took over in an attempt to give the show a more "adult" look. Much was made of Marie's stunning new wardrobe, designed by Bob Mackie (Cher's former designer), and her eighteenth birthday party was telecast in October. However, *Donny and Marie* remained, at heart, a homey affair. Tired of the tinsel and glitter of Hollywood, the entire Osmond clan packed up and moved back to their hometown of Orem, Utah, in late 1977; all subsequent telecasts originated from the elaborate studio facility built there by the Osmonds at a cost of $2.5 million, to house their various TV and film activities. The first episode taped in Orem was the 1977 Christmas show, which starred Paul Lynde, the Mormon Tabernacle Choir, and 28 members of the Osmond family.

Midway through the final season, Donny turned 21 (and to prove it had his wife Debbie on the show!). In January 1979 the series moved to Sunday night and was retitled *The Osmond Family Show*.

DON'T CALL ME CHARLIE (*Situation Comedy*)

FIRST TELECAST: *September 21, 1962*

LAST TELECAST: *January 25, 1963*

BROADCAST HISTORY:

Sep 1962–Jan 1963, NBC Fri 9:30–10:00

CAST:

Judson McKay .... Josh Peine
Pat Perry .... Linda Lawson
Col. U. Charles Barker.............. John Hubbard
First Sgt. Wozniak................. Cully Richards
Gen. Steele .... Alan Napier
Cpl. Lefkowitz .... Arte Johnson
Selma Yossarian..................... Louise Glenn
Madame Fatima .... Penny Santon

This "military' comedy centered on Judson McKay, a young veterinarian from Iowa, who was drafted by mistake and assigned to a U.S. Army veterinary station in Paris. The principal conflict was between good-natured country boy McKay and his pompous commander, Col. U. Charles Barker, the "Charlie" of the title. Arte Johnson played the supporting role of Cpl. Lefkowitz, Pat Perry was the general's secretary, Selma Yossarian another secretary, and Mme. Fatima the concierge.

DON'T FORGET YOUR TOOTHBRUSH
(*Quiz/Audience Participation*)

BROADCAST HISTORY:

Comedy Central
30 minutes
Original episodes: *2000* (20 episodes)
Premiered: *June 20, 2000*

EMCEE:

Mark Curry

In this high-energy quiz show, emcee Mark Curry called people out of the audience and challenged them to pranks and stunts as well as asking embarrassing questions—for example, "Can you match six of your grade school classmates who are sitting on the stage with their correct names?" The large, rowdy audience hooted and cheered. Audience members were told in advance to bring their luggage with them, because if they won the grand prize they were immediately whisked away on a weeklong vacation to a surprise destination (hence the title).

Based on a popular British show.

DOODLES WEAVER (*Comedy Variety*)

FIRST TELECAST: *June 9, 1951*

LAST TELECAST: *September 1, 1951*

BROADCAST HISTORY:

Jun 1951–Jul 1951, NBC Sat 10:00–10:15
Aug 1951–Sep 1951, NBC Sat 10:00–10:30

REGULARS:

Doodles Weaver
Marion Colby
Milton Delugg and His Orchestra
Red Marshall
Dick Dana
Peanuts Mann

In the premiere telecast, Doodles Weaver was informed that he had to put together a low-budget summer show without sets, scenery, or dancing girls. He was left with an empty television studio and discarded sets and props from other shows. Although this was supposed to be a joke, it set the tone for a rather formless improvisational comedy series. Veteran burlesque comics Marshall, Dana, and Mann contributed laughs and singer Marion Colby provided musical support.

DOOGIE HOWSER, M.D. (*Situation Comedy*)

FIRST TELECAST: *September 19, 1989*

LAST TELECAST: *July 21, 1993*

BROADCAST HISTORY:

Sep 1989, ABC Tue 8:30–9:00
Sep 1989, ABC Wed 9:30–10:00
Oct 1989–Feb 1992, ABC Wed 9:00–9:30
Feb 1992–May 1992, ABC Wed 8:30–9:00
May 1992–Aug 1992, ABC Wed 9:00–9:30
Aug 1992–Mar 1993, ABC Wed 8:30–9:00
Jun 1993–Jul 1993, ABC Wed 8:30–9:00

CAST:

Dr. Douglas "Doogie" Howser.... Neil Patrick Harris
Dr. David Howser .... James B. Sikking
Katherine Howser .... Belinda Montgomery
Vinnie Delpino .... Max Casella
Dr. Benjamin Canfield .... Lawrence Pressman
Dr. Jack McGuire (1989–1991) .. Mitchell Anderson
Nurse Curly Spaulding............. Kathryn Layng
Wanda Plenn (1989–1992)......... Lisa Dean Ryan
Janine Stewart (1989–1992)........... Lucy Boryer
Raymond Alexander (1990–1993)
.... Markus Redmond
**Dr. Ron Welch (1990–1993)* .... Rif Hutton
**Nurse Michele Faber (1991–1993)*.... Robyn Lively

*Occasional

Life can be complicated for a 16-year-old, what with dating, demanding parents, and being a doctor. A doctor? That was what most people said when they met fresh-faced Doogie Howser, a boy genius who had zipped through high school in nine weeks, graduated from Princeton at age ten, and from medical school at 14, and who was now a second-year resident at Eastman Medical Center in Los Angeles. Though he was an accomplished physician, Doogie had a lot to learn in the growing-up department, and learn he did in this gentle if implausible comedy. His father David (also a doctor) and mother Katherine kept him on an even keel, as did his colleagues at the hospital, including Chief of Services Dr. Canfield and fellow resident McGuire. Doogie's not-so-bright buddy, squeaky-voiced Vinnie, kept him in touch with the teen world, climbing in his bedroom window to share the latest news. Later, when

Vinnie miraculously entered college, Doogie and Vinnie shared an "odd couple" apartment. Janine was Vinnie's girlfriend, while Wanda was the object of Doogie's desires—though their relationship sometimes got complicated. Wanda was mortified when she had an appendix attack while on a date, and Doogie had to examine her. ("Did you put your hand on her conundrum?" blurted an envious Vinnie later.) By the last season both Doogie and Vinnie were playing the field, with Doogie particularly attracted to Nurse Faber. Vinnie, meanwhile, began pursuing a career as a filmmaker.

At the end of each episode Doogie entered his experiences in his electronic diary, on his computer.

For the record, there are no 16-year-old doctors in the United States and, according to most medical authorities, probably never will be. On television, however, there's no telling what might come next.

DOOR WITH NO NAME, see *Doorway to Danger*

DOORWAY TO DANGER (*International Intrigue*)

FIRST TELECAST: *July 6, 1951*
LAST TELECAST: *October 1, 1953*
BROADCAST HISTORY:

Jul 1951–Aug 1951, NBC Fri 9:00–9:30
Jul 1952–Aug 1952, NBC Fri 9:00–9:30
Jul 1953–Oct 1953, ABC Thu 8:30–9:00

CAST:

John Randolph (1951).................... Mel Ruick
John Randolph (1952) .... Roland Winters
John Randolph (1953) .... Raymond Bramley
Doug Carter (1951).................. Grant Richards
Doug Carter (1953)..................... Stacy Harris

NARRATOR:

Westbrook Van Voorhis (1951)

Doorway to Danger was a summer replacement series during the early 1950s. It told, in quasi-documentary style, stories of international intrigue involving operatives of federal agencies. The title referred to the door to the office of John Randolph, chief of a top-secret government agency, who supervised the agents assigned to track down enemies of the United States. These enemies might be either domestic criminals or agents of a foreign power; smugglers and spies seemed to be the usual opponents in this series.

Doug Carter was Randolph's number-one agent during the first and third seasons, and episodes followed Carter around the world on his dangerous assignments. During the second season there was no regular agent, and each week Chief Randolph sent a different trench-coated operative scurrying off to defend the nation.

During its first season this series was known as *Door With No Name.*

DOORWAY TO FAME (*Talent*)

FIRST TELECAST: *May 2, 1947*
LAST TELECAST: *July 11, 1949*
BROADCAST HISTORY:

May 1947–Sep 1947, DUM Fri 7:30–8:00
(approximately)
Oct 1947–Mar 1948, DUM Mon 7:00–7:30
Mar 1949–Jul 1949, DUM Mon 8:30–9:00

REGULARS:

Johnny Olsen
Ned Harvey Orchestra

This was one of the many talent shows that populated early television. Through the doorway came all manner of hopefuls, plus one guest star each week who offered words of encouragement. Some 20,000 New York–area residents were said to have auditioned for the show during its first year, but none are known to have gone on to stardom.

DORIS DAY SHOW, THE (*Situation Comedy*)

FIRST TELECAST: *September 24, 1968*
LAST TELECAST: *September 10, 1973*
BROADCAST HISTORY:

Sep 1968–Sep 1969, CBS Tue 9:30–10:00
Sep 1969–Sep 1973, CBS Mon 9:30–10:00

CAST:

Doris Martin............................ Doris Day
Buck Webb (1968–1970)............... Denver Pyle
Aggie Thompson (1968)................. Fran Ryan
Leroy B. Simpson (1968–1969) .... James Hampton
Billy Martin (1968–1971)............. Philip Brown
Toby Martin (1968–1971).............. Todd Starke
Juanita (1968–1969) .... Naomi Stevens
Myrna Gibbons (1969–1971) .... Rose Marie
Michael Nicholson (1969–1971) McLean Stevenson
Ron Harvey (1969–1971) .... Paul Smith
Angie Palucci (1970–1971) .... Kaye Ballard
Louie Palucci (1970–1971)........... Bernie Kopell
Cy Bennett (1971–1973) .... John Dehner
Jackie Parker (1971–1973)............ Jackie Joseph

THEME:

"Whatever Will Be, Will Be (Que Sera Sera)"

When *The Doris Day Show* premiered in the fall of 1968, Miss Day was cast as a widow with two young sons who had decided to move back to the family ranch after spending most of her life in big cities. The adjustments to rural living provided much of the comedy. The ranch was run by her father Buck, their hired hand Leroy, and the housekeeper Aggie (replaced in December by a new housekeeper, Juanita).

At the start of the second season Doris became a commuter. She got a job as a secretary at *Today's World* magazine in San Francisco and commuted daily from the farm. Mr. Nicholson, the editor of the magazine, was her boss, and Myrna Gibbons was a secretary with whom she became friendly. At the start of the third season Doris, her two boys, and their huge dog Lord Nelson left the farm and moved into a San Francisco apartment owned by the Paluccis, who ran an Italian restaurant on the ground floor. Doris's activities expanded from merely being Mr. Nicholson's secretary to include some writing for the magazine, on assignment from the assistant editor, Ron Harvey.

Still another major change was made at the start of the fourth season, in the fall of 1971, as the show edged still closer to the urban-career-girl format popularized by Mary Tyler Moore. Doris continued to work for *Today's World*, but she suddenly became a carefree, single staff writer; the children, the dog, and the entire cast from previous seasons disappeared. Her new boss was editor Cy Bennett, and the only other regular was his secretary Jackie.

At the end of the fifth season the entire show disappeared.

DOROTHY (*Situation Comedy*)

FIRST TELECAST: *August 8, 1979*
LAST TELECAST: *August 29, 1979*

BROADCAST HISTORY:

Aug 1979, CBS Wed 8:00–8:30

CAST:

Dorothy Banks .... Dorothy Loudon
Frankie .... Linda Manz
Meredith .... Susan Brecht
Cissy .... Elissa Leeds
Margo .... Michele Greene
Burton Foley .... Russell Nype
Jack Landis .... Kenneth Gilman
Lorna Cathcart .... Priscilla Morrill

Fresh from winning a Tony Award for her role in the musical *Annie*, Dorothy Loudon turned up on this summer comedy series as a divorced former showgirl who took a position as music and drama teacher at the exclusive Hannah Hunt School for Girls, a rather stuffy Eastern school. Her background and undisciplined approach to teaching were not always appreciated by the administration, especially by headmaster Burton Foley. But the girls were delighted, and Dorothy was tickled by the chance to do some of her routines for such an appreciative (if underage) audience. Jack and Lorna were two other teachers at the school.

DO'S AND DON'TS (*Instruction*)

FIRST TELECAST: *July 3, 1952*
LAST TELECAST: *August 28, 1952*
BROADCAST HISTORY:

Jul 1952–Aug 1952, ABC Thu 9:30–10:00

This was a brief series of films on safety.

DOT COMEDY (*Comedy*)

FIRST TELECAST: *December 8, 2000*
LAST TELECAST: *December 8, 2000*
BROADCAST HISTORY:

Dec 2000, ABC Fri 8:30–9:00

REGULARS:

Jason Sklar
Randy Sklar
Annabelle Gurwitch
Katie Puckrick

This was one of those rare network series that was so bad it was canceled after a single telecast. *Dot Comedy* attempted to cash in on the Internet boom by reviewing Web sites in a supposedly humorous way. Snarky hosts Jason and Randy Sklar made snide comments, while ultracool, leather-clad assistant Annabelle sat off to the side at a computer keyboard, surfing the Web for sites such as howstuffworks.com and globe xplorer.com. Katie contributed taped interviews, for example, with the guy who ran airsicknessbag.com. Viewers were invited to send in their funny mpegs (music files) and jpegs (pictures), but those who did found that by the time their files got to ABC the show had vanished.

Based on a British series of the same name.

DOTTO (*Quiz*)

FIRST TELECAST: *July 1, 1958*
LAST TELECAST: *August 12, 1958*
BROADCAST HISTORY:

Jul 1958–Aug 1958, NBC Tue 9:00–9:30

EMCEE:

Jack Narz

In *Dotto* two contestants competed to guess the identity of a famous personality whose caricature was drawn on a screen by connecting fifty dots on each contestant's "Dotto" board. The contestants answered questions that allowed them progressively to connect the dots, and the first to identify the picture of the person won. There was also a home game in which viewers sent in postcards, hoping to be called on the phone to identify a special dotted caricature shown on the air. *Dotto*'s biggest claim to fame was that a disgruntled former contestant on the daytime version of the show (which had begun earlier and ran concurrently with this nighttime version) started the famous quiz show scandals by publicly declaring that the game was rigged. His name was Edward Hilgemeier, Jr., and, ironically, he had never actually appeared on the show at all. While waiting in the studio for his opportunity to go on as a contestant, he found a notebook belonging to a woman contestant that contained answers to questions she had been asked on the show. He informed the contestant who had been defeated by the woman and both he and the defeated contestant confronted the producers. They were both paid off, but when Mr. Hilgemeier found out the defeated contestant had been given $4000 while he had only been given $1500, he got angry and precipitated the quiz show scandals by protesting to the New York State Attorney General's office.

DOTTY MACK SHOW, THE (*Music*)

FIRST TELECAST: *February 16, 1953*
LAST TELECAST: *September 3, 1956*
BROADCAST HISTORY:

Feb 1953–Jun 1953, DUM Mon 10:45–11:00
Jul 1953–Aug 1953, DUM Tue 9:00–9:30
Aug 1953–Oct 1953, ABC Thu 9:00–9:30
Oct 1953–Mar 1954, ABC Sat 6:30–7:00
Apr 1954–Oct 1954, ABC Sat 7:30–8:00
Oct 1954–Jun 1955, ABC Sat 8:00–9:00
Jun 1955–Sep 1955, ABC Tue 9:30–10:00
Sep 1955–Mar 1956, ABC Mon 9:00–9:30
Apr 1956–Jul 1956, ABC Thu 10:00–10:30
Jul 1956–Sep 1956, ABC Mon 8:00–8:30

REGULARS:

Dotty Mack
Bob Braun
Colin Male

Dotty Mack had one of the simpler acts on early television: she pantomimed to other performers' hit records. She began her miming on *The Paul Dixon Show* out of Cincinnati, then landed a 15-minute spot by herself on DuMont called, appropriately, *Girl Alone*. Four months later, in July 1953, the program was expanded to 30 minutes, two assistants (Bob Braun and Colin Male) were added, and the title was changed to *The Dotty Mack Show*. Shortly thereafter ABC picked it up. At times the program was a full hour in length, although 30 minutes was normal.

Most of the songs pantomimed were currently popular favorites or novelty songs by such stars as Eddie Fisher, Perry Como, or Patti Page; sometimes puppets or other visual aids accompanied the pantomimes. Things began to get complicated when rock 'n' roll started taking over the hit parade in 1955. Although Dotty gamely included such records as "Rock Around the Clock" in her repertoire, the sight of pleasant young people pantomiming to Bill Haley or Elvis Presley records became slightly ludicrous, and the show quietly passed from the scene in 1956.

DOUBLE DARE (*Detective*)

FIRST TELECAST: *April 10, 1985*
LAST TELECAST: *May 22, 1985*
BROADCAST HISTORY:
Apr 1985–May 1985, CBS Wed 8:00–9:00
CAST:
Billy Diamond .... Billy Dee Williams
Ken Sisko .... Ken Wahl
Sylvester .... Joe Maher
Lt. Samantha Warner (pilot only) .. Jennifer Warren
Lt. Samantha Warner .... Janet Carroll

Billy Diamond was the most successful thief in San Francisco. He lived lavishly on the fruits of his illicit activities—until he got caught in the act by Lt. Samantha Warner of the S.F.P.D. To avoid going to jail he agreed to become an undercover operative for the San Francisco police. It was either that or give up his lifestyle for a drab, dirty prison cell. The one concession that he was able to get from Warner was to have his former partner, Ken Sisko, released from San Quentin to work with him again. Sylvester was Billy's butler.

DOUBLE DARE (*Quiz*)

CABLE HISTORY:
Nickelodeon
30 minutes
Produced: *1986–1993* (482 episodes), *2000*
Premiered: *October 6, 1986*
NETWORK HISTORY:
FIRST TELECAST: *April 3, 1988*
LAST TELECAST: *July 23, 1988*
Apr 1988, FOX Sun 8:00–8:30
Apr 1988–Jul 1988, FOX Sat 8:00–8:30
Jul 1988, FOX Sat 8:00–9:00
EMCEE:
Marc Summers (1986–1993)
Jason Harris (2000)

Start with *Family Feud*, pour on a bucket of *Beat the Clock*, and add a gooey topping of *Truth or Consequences* and you have a pretty good idea what Fox's *Family Double Dare* was like—one of the messiest "stunt shows" on television.

The show began as *Double Dare* on the Nickelodeon cable channel on October 6, 1986, with Marc Summers as host. On the cable version all the contestants were children, and the show was a big hit with Nickelodeon's young audience. Early in 1988 a limited number of Fox television stations began airing a new version of *Double Dare* and a couple of months later *Family Double Dare*, including adults, premiered on the Fox network. If there was one thing young viewers liked more than seeing other kids covered with slop, it was seeing parents making a mess of themselves.

Two families (parents and two children) competed. In the opening rounds the families tried to best each other in a stunt, for example, by being the first to fill a cup sitting on one of the parent's heads with seltzer, from six feet away. The winning family won a cash prize and then was asked a question worth a specified amount. They could either answer or dare the other family to do so for twice as much money; the second family could take the challenge or "double dare" the first family to answer (and the amount would double again). An incorrect answer gave the money and first chance on the next question to the other family.

The family "double-dared" had another option, which was frequently taken. Instead of the question they could choose "the physical challenge," another stunt that had to be completed in a limited time. At the end the family winning the most money ran an obstacle course for grand prizes. The object of most of the stunts and challenges seemed to be to make as big a mess as possible, with the various family members wading through water balloons, puddings and syrups, eggs, pies, and green and red slime. It was no accident that the emcee, while attired in a tuxedo, also wore tennis shoes!

Other versions of the show included *Super Sloppy Double Dare* (Nickelodeon, 1987, 1989), *Celebrity Double Dare* (syndicated, 1989) and *Super Special Double Dare* (Nickelodeon, 1992), all with Summers as host, and *Double Dare 2000* (Nickelodeon, 2000) with Jason Harris.

DOUBLE EXPOSURE, see *ABC Dramatic Shorts—1952–1953*

DOUBLE LIFE OF HENRY PHYFE, THE (*Situation Comedy*)

FIRST TELECAST: *January 13, 1966*
LAST TELECAST: *September 1, 1966*
BROADCAST HISTORY:
Jan 1966–Sep 1966, ABC Thu 8:30–9:00
CAST:
Henry Wadsworth Phyfe .... Red Buttons
Gerald B. Hannahan .... Fred Clark
Judy Kimball .... Zeme North
Mrs. Florence Kimball .... Marge Redmond
Mr. Hamble .... Parley Baer

This short-lived comedy focused on the adventures of Henry Phyfe, a mild-mannered accountant who was recruited by the CIS, a United States counterintelligence agency, to impersonate U-31, a recently deceased foreign agent to whom Henry bore a striking resemblance. The trouble was that U-31 in most other respects had been the opposite of Henry: bon vivant, Don Juan, master linguist, and crack shot, Henry's girlfriend Judy, his future mother-in-law Florence, and his boss at the accounting firm had no idea of his double life. Only Gerald B. Hannahan, the balding, bombastic regional director of CIS, linked him with the world of spies and adventure. Judy and her mother were phased out of the series in March.

DOUBLE OR NOTHING (*Quiz/Audience Participation*)

FIRST TELECAST: *June 5, 1953*
LAST TELECAST: *July 3, 1953*
BROADCAST HISTORY:
Jun 1953–Jul 1953, NBC Fri 9:30–10:00
EMCEE:
Bert Parks
Bob Williams (asst.)

The summer of 1953 brought this familiar radio quiz show—and its emcee, Bert Parks—to television for a five-week stay. Each contestant was asked a series of four questions, respectively worth $10, $20, $40, and double or nothing, for a possible total of $140 in the first round. All contestants, whether or not they were successful in the first round, then participated in the "Red and White Sweepstakes" at the end (the colors referred to those on the label of the sponsor's product, Campbell soups). In the sweepstakes, a question was asked and each contestant wrote his or her answer on a card shaped like a horse. The "race" was won by whoever could provide the correct answer first.

The daytime version of *Double or Nothing* had started on CBS in October 1952 and ran until July 1954.

DOUBLE RUSH (*Situation Comedy*)
FIRST TELECAST: *January 4, 1995*
LAST TELECAST: *April 12, 1995*
BROADCAST HISTORY:
Jan 1995–Feb 1995, CBS Wed 9:00–9:30
Mar 1995–Apr 1995, CBS Wed 8:30–9:00
CAST:
Johnny Verona .... Robert Pastorelli
Hunter .... David Arquette
Zoe Fuller .... Corinne Bohrer
Leo .... Adam Goldberg
Marlon .... D. L. Hughley
The Kid .... Phil Leeds
Barkley .... Sam Lloyd

Johnny Verona was an idealistic free spirit and former musician who owned the Double Rush bicycle messenger service in Manhattan. A gruff but fatherly guy who mused about his failure to become a rock star 25 years before, Johnny took a personal interest in the lives of his employees. Working for him were Barkley, the spaced-out dispatcher; Hunter, the young daredevil who gloried in speeding through midtown traffic on his bike; Zoe, a neurotic Harvard Business School graduate who was biding her time until she found her dream job; Leo, a cynical, self-centered young former delinquent; Marlon, a young husband and father with a legendary ability to con people; and The Kid, who at 75 moved painfully slowly; however, after working as a messenger for 58 years he knew every shortcut in the city.

DOUBLE TROUBLE (*Situation Comedy*)
FIRST TELECAST: *April 4, 1984*
LAST TELECAST: *August 21, 1985*
BROADCAST HISTORY:
Apr 1984–May 1984, NBC Wed 9:30–10:00
Jul 1984–Sep 1984, NBC Wed 8:00–8:30
Dec 1984–May 1985, NBC Sat 8:30–9:00
Jun 1985–Aug 1985, NBC Wed 9:30–10:00
CAST:
Kate Foster .... Jean Sagal
Allison Foster .... Liz Sagal
Art Foster (1984) .... Donnelly Rhodes
Beth McConnell (1984) .... Patricia Richardson
Michael Gillette (1984) .... Jon Caliri
Aunt Margo .... Barbara Barrie
Billy Batalato .... Jonathan Schmock
Charles Kincaid .... James Vallely
Mr. Arrechia .... Michael D. Roberts
Aileen Lewis .... Anne-Marie Johnson

The adventures of a pair of teenage twins were explored in this light comedy. Kate and Allison were 16, identical in appearance, but opposites in personality. Allison was the sober, responsible one, and Kate the spunky troublemaker who often got them both into hot water. Pretending to be Allison was one of Kate's favorite ploys. Art was their widower father, who ran a gym and dance studio in their hometown of Des Moines, Iowa, Beth was one of his adult instructors, and Michael was Kate's boyfriend.

When *Double Trouble* returned for a second season, in December 1984, Kate and Allison had moved to New York to pursue separate careers. Kate wanted to become an actress, while her more practical sister was enrolled in the Fashion Institute of Technology studying design. They lived in a spacious town house with their kooky Aunt Margo, a successful writer of children's stories. Also living in the town house were Billy and Charles, two aspiring actors and kindred spirits of Kate's. Mr. Arrechia was an obnoxious, overbearing instructor at the Fashion Institute and Aileen was Allison's fellow student and best friend.

DOUG (*Cartoon*)
BROADCAST HISTORY:
Nickelodeon
30 minutes
Produced: *1991–1993* (52 episodes)
Premiered: *August 11, 1991*
VOICES:
Doug Funnie, Roger Klotz .... Billy West
Judy Funnie, Theda Funnie .... Becca Lish
Phil Funnie, Lamar Bone .... Doug Preis
Skeeter, Bud Dink, Grandma Opal ... Fred Newman
Patti Mayonnaise .... Connie Shulman
Tippi Dink, Mrs. Wingo .... Doris Belack
Beebe .... Alice Playten
Mayor White .... Greg Lee

The fantasy world of 11-year-old Doug Funnie was explored in this whimsical cartoon. Doug, in his geeky wool sweater and short pants, was the ultimate outsider at the Bluffington School, constantly put upon by leather-jacketed bully Roger. Further embarrassment came from the fact that his older sister, Judy, was a Bohemian free spirit who habitually wore dark glasses and a beret and gave unintelligible one-woman shows billed as "performance art."

With best friend Skeeter and loyal family pooch Porkchop, Doug embarked on little adventures designed to salvage his self-respect, or he simply escaped into a fantasy world inhabited by his alter-ego superhero, Quailman. Despite his visions of failure, Doug usually succeeded in the end by simply using his wits. Theda and Phil were his parents, Patti his secret love, Mrs. Wingo the homeroom teacher, and Mr. Bone the nutty, yodeling assistant principal.

Nickelodeon failed to renew *Doug* after 52 episodes had been produced, whereupon Disney picked up the franchise in early 1996, produced new episodes under the title *Disney's Doug,* and saw them become one of the more popular entries on the ABC Saturday morning lineup, where it ran from September 1996 to September 2001. Meanwhile, Nick continued to run the older episodes, to strong ratings. In early 1999 a big screen version, *The First Doug Movie,* opened in theaters.

DOUGLAS FAIRBANKS, JR., PRESENTS (*Anthology*)
BROADCAST HISTORY:
Syndicated only
30 minutes
Produced: *1952–1957* (117 episodes)
Released: *January 1953*
HOST:
Douglas Fairbanks, Jr.

Douglas Fairbanks, Jr., a Hollywood star since the 1920s, hosted one of television's classiest and most successful anthology series during the 1950s. He also served as executive producer and starred in approximately a fourth of the episodes. The scripts were first-rate and unusually wide-ranging, from psychological studies to light farce, with an occasional murder yarn. Actors were generally lesser known. The series was filmed in England, with an eye to authenticity—if they needed a castle, they went out and got one!

DOWN AND OUT IN BEVERLY HILLS (*Situation Comedy*)
FIRST TELECAST: *April 26, 1987*
LAST TELECAST: *September 12, 1987*
BROADCAST HISTORY:
Apr 1987, FOX Sun 9:00–9:30
Jul 1987–Aug 1987, FOX Sat 8:00–8:30
Aug 1987–Sep 1987, FOX Sat 9:00–9:30
CAST:
Dave Whiteman .... Hector Elizondo
Barbara Whiteman .... Anita Morris
Jerry Baskin .... Tim Thomerson
Max Whiteman (age 17) .... Evan Richards
Jenny Whiteman (20) .... Eileen Seeley
Carmen, the maid .... April Ortiz

Dave Whiteman had made his fortune selling clothes hangers and had moved his family into a sumptuous Beverly Hills mansion. Although he still had middle-class roots and understood the value of a dollar, such could not be said for his flighty wife Barbara or his social-climbing daughter Jenny. Max, his son, was not coping well with either his new peer group at Beverly Hills High or his own adolescence. Into this unsettled household came Jerry Baskin, a flower child of the '60s who had become a derelict in the '80s. When his attempt to commit suicide in the Whiteman pool failed—he was pulled out by Dave—Jerry stayed on to live the good life with them and dispense philosophical and sometimes cryptic answers to the unending questions posed by the Whitemans.

Based on the 1985 feature film starring Richard Dreyfuss, Bette Midler, and Nick Nolte, which in turn was based on characters from the play "Boudu Sauvé des Eaux" by Rene Fauchois and the classic French film *Boudu Saved from Drowning* (1932). Reprising his role in the 1985 movie as the nasty pooch Matisse was a black-and-white Scottish Border collie known professionally as Mike the Dog.

DOWN HOME (*Situation Comedy*)
FIRST TELECAST: *April 12, 1990*
LAST TELECAST: *August 10, 1991*
BROADCAST HISTORY:
Apr 1990, NBC Thu 10:30–11:00
Apr 1990–May 1990, NBC Sat 10:30–11:00
Mar 1991–May 1991, NBC Sat 8:30–9:00
Jun 1991–Aug 1991, NBC Sat 8:30–9:00
CAST:
Kate McCrorey .... Judith Ivey
Wade Prescott .... Ray Baker
Drew McCrorey .... Eric Allan Kramer
Walt McCrorey .... Dakin Matthews
Grover .... Timothy Scott
Tran .... Gedde Watanabe

It wasn't exactly *Green Acres,* but city met country once again in this laid-back comedy. Kate was a high-powered New York executive who came home to the sleepy Gulf Coast fishing village of Hadley Cove, Texas, to visit her dad's dockside bait & tackle shop and café—only to discover that it was about to be leveled for a condominium development. This being a sitcom, she, of course, stayed and tried to save the rickety, money-losing place. Behind the condo scheme was Wade, the boyfriend Kate had dumped many years before, but who still had eyes for her. Drew was Kate's big, dumb brother; Walt, her crotchety dad; Grover, a rustic townfolk; and Tran, the Vietnamese cook at the café.

Cheers star Ted Danson was the co-producer of this series, which featured mostly New York stage actors (Ivey was a multiple Tony winner) and had a uniquely—for TV—"stage" look.

DOWN THE SHORE (*Situation Comedy*)
FIRST TELECAST: *June 21, 1992*
LAST TELECAST: *August 5, 1993*
BROADCAST HISTORY:
Jun 1992, FOX Sun 9:30–10:00
Jun 1992–Aug 1992, FOX Sun 10:00–10:30
Aug 1992–Sep 1992, FOX Sun 10:30–11:00
Dec 1992–Aug 1993, FOX Thu 9:30–10:00
CAST:
Arden .... Anna Gunn
Donna Shipko .... Cathryn de Prume
Miranda Halpern (1992) .... Pamela Segall
Eddie Cheever .... Tom McGowan
Aldo Carbone .... Louis Mandylor
Zach Singer .... Lew Schneider
Sammy .... Nancy Sorel

Three twenty-something guys and three young women shared a weekend summer rental house at Belmar Beach on the Jersey shore in this youth-oriented comedy. The guys, who had been friends since childhood, were Eddie, a fat, shy writer of computer software; Aldo, a self-centered womanizer who was a salesman for a clothing manufacturer in Manhattan's garment center; and Zach, a down-to-earth junior high school social studies teacher. The women, who worked together at a Manhattan advertising agency, were Arden, a bitchy, ice-princess account executive; Donna, a naive receptionist; and Miranda, an idealistic graphic artist.

When *Down the Shore* returned in December, after a three-month hiatus, Miranda had given up her share because some of her canvases were in a gallery and she was staying in New York on weekends to paint. She was replaced by Sammy, a sexy childhood friend of Arden's who designed jewelry.

DOWN YOU GO (*Quiz/Panel*)
FIRST TELECAST: *May 30, 1951*
LAST TELECAST: *September 8, 1956*
BROADCAST HISTORY:
May 1951–Jul 1951, DUM Wed 9:00–9:30
Jul 1951–Sep 1951, DUM Thu 9:30–9:30
Sep 1951–Jun 1952, DUM Fri 9:00–9:30
Jul 1952–Sep 1952, DUM Fri 8:00–8:30
Oct 1952–Apr 1954, DUM Fri 10:30–11:00
May 1954–Jun 1954, DUM Wed 9:30–10:00
Sep 1954–Jan 1955, DUM Wed 10:00–10:30
Jan 1955–May 1955, DUM Fri 10:30–11:00
Jun 1955–Sep 1955, CBS Sat 9:30–10:00
Sep 1955–Jun 1956, ABC Thu 9:30–10:00
Jun 1956–Sep 1956, NBC Sat 7:30–8:00

EMCEE:

Dr. Bergen Evans (1951–1956)
Bill Cullen (1956)

REGULAR PANELISTS:

Francis Coughlin
Prof. Robert Breen (1951–1954)
Toni Gilman (1951–1954)
Carmelita Pope (1951–1954)
Fran Allison (1954)
Phil Rizzuto (1954–1955)
Boris Karloff (1954–1955)
Jean Kerr (1955)
Patricia Cutts (1955–1956)
Basil Davenport (1955)
Phyllis Cerf (1955)
Sherl Stern (1955)
John Kieran, Jr. (1955)
Arthur Treacher (1956)
Hildy Parks (1956)
Jimmy Nelson (1956)
Jayne Mansfield (1956)

Widely regarded as one of the wittiest, most intelligent panel shows on television, *Down You Go* was a deceptively simple word game whose charm derived from its participants. The rules were simple: the panel was asked to guess a word or phrase that had been submitted by a viewer. A few cryptic clues were offered, and then the panelists filled in the words, letter by letter, on a "magic board." An incorrect guess by a panelist and "down you go," out of play until the next round. Viewers received $5 for submitting a phrase that was used, and $25 for one that stumped the panel (later these amounts were increased, but money was never the principal appeal of the show).

Dr. Bergen Evans, a witty and charming professor of English at Northwestern University, was the longtime host of *Down You Go*, which at first was telecast from Chicago over the DuMont network. The program became quite popular, and in 1954 a *Down You Go* game was being sold in stores, complete with tiles, board, and clock. In December 1954 the program moved to New York, with only Evans and Francis Coughlin, a Chicago radio editor, remaining from the original cast. During 1955 and 1956 a succession of regular and guest panelists appeared, but none of these later panels seemed to catch the flavor of the original. Nevertheless the program survived the end of the DuMont network, making a grand tour of the networks from CBS to ABC to NBC before it was canceled in September 1956.

The last version of *Down You Go* little resembled the original. Bergen Evans was replaced for the last two months of the show by Bill Cullen, and the panel was filled by such "literati" as Jimmy Nelson and his dummies, and Jayne Mansfield.

DOWNER CHANNEL (*Comedy Variety*)

FIRST TELECAST: *July 24, 2001*
LAST TELECAST: *August 21, 2001*
BROADCAST HISTORY:

Jul 2001–Aug 2001, NBC Tue 8:30–9:00

REGULARS:

Jeff B. Davis
Wanda Sykes
Lance Krall
Mary Lynn Rajskub

Four goofy young comics rode around in an old station wagon perpetrating short comic bits on the street, as well as in the studio, in this fast-paced show. The running theme was life's frustrations, like "cell phone hell," "awful bosses," "relationship roadshow," "breakup lines" and "annoying comment of the week." There was also turtle wrestling (to overwrought WWF-style narration) and the game show "Spot That Carcinogen." The players were foxy Jeff, doofus Lance, tirade-prone Wanda and versatile Mary Lynn. Comedian Steve Martin, one of the eight executive producers, commented, "It's the perfect show to get you out of an 'up' mood."

DOWNTOWN (*Police Drama*)

FIRST TELECAST: *September 27, 1986*
LAST TELECAST: *September 5, 1987*
BROADCAST HISTORY:

Sep 1986–Dec 1986, CBS Sat 8:00–9:00
Aug 1987–Sep 1987, CBS Sat 8:00–9:00

CAST:

Det. John Forney.................... Michael Nouri
Terry Corsaro .... Blair Underwood
Harriet Conover .... Millicent Martin
Jesse Smith...................... Mariska Hargitay
Dennis Shothoffer................ Robert Englund
Delia Bonner .... Virginia Capers
Capt. David Kiner.................. David Paymer

In addition to fighting crime in Los Angeles, police Det. John Forney was saddled with the responsibility of serving as probation officer for four parolees living together in a sort of halfway house as part of an experimental program administered by social worker Delia Bonner. Forney's charges were Terry, a likable young black and former pickpocket; Harriet, a classy older woman whose financial reverses had prompted her to get involved in land fraud; Jesse, a young woman whose tough, street-smart exterior hid a yearning to be accepted; and Dennis, a neurotic with a penchant for impersonating others. Being a part-time probation officer did not appeal to Forney, but he made the best of it, trying to keep the four of them out of trouble and find them jobs. Their repeated attempts to help him solve cases did not make it any easier. Capt. Kiner was Forney's boss.

DOWNTOWN (*Cartoon*)

BROADCAST HISTORY:

MTV
30 minutes
Original episodes: *1999* (13 episodes)
Premiered: *August 3, 1999*

VOICES:

Alex Henson...................... Gregory Gilmore
Chaka Henson................. Leyora Zuberman
Jen .... Tammy Lang
Serena.................... Phoebe Summersquash
Mecca .... Aurora Lucia-Levey
Goat.................................... Scot Rienecker
Fruity .... Marco H. Rodriguez
Matt .... Hector Fontanez

Easygoing cartoon about eight young friends, mostly in their 20s, living in Manhattan's funky East Village neighborhood. Alex was a shy, geeky kid who worked at the Repro Man copy shop, played video games, and fantasized about a more adventurous life; Chaka, his sexy younger sister, an extroverted motormouth; Jen, his tomboyish best friend and confidante; and Serena, the super-hip girl of his dreams, who affected the goth look. Mecca was Chaka's dreamy, naive sidekick; Goat, an amiable but somewhat seedy older (26!) hanger-on; Fruity, a horny high schooler; and Matt, Fruity's laid-back pal, who was smarter than most of the gang but hid it so he would fit in. One of their principal hangouts was the Starbase 12 comics store, where Matt and Serena worked.

DRACULA: THE SERIES (*Horror*)

BROADCAST HISTORY:

Syndicated only
30 minutes
Produced: *1990* (26 episodes)
Released: *September 1990*

CAST:

Alexander Lucard................Geordie Johnson
Max Townsend (age 12).............Jacob Tierney
Chris Townsend (17).................Joe Roncetti
Gustav Helsing...................Bernard Behrens
Sophie Metternich...................Mia Kirshner
Klaus Helsing.................Geraint Wyn Davies
**Eileen Townsend* ....Lynne Cormack

*Occasional

In this contemporary tongue-in-cheek (fang-in-neck?) adaptation of Bram Stoker's classic *Dracula*, the vampire was the head of a globe-spanning conglomerate with interests in banking, real estate, and chemicals. Unlike previous incarnations, Alexander Lucard (try a mirror) did not have to hide from the sun. The only problem he had during daylight hours was that his vampire powers were inactive until the sun went down. His nemesis, kindly old Gustav Helsing, knew all there was to know about fighting vampires and protecting homes and people from them. Unfortunately, Gustav had been unable to prevent his son Klaus from being bitten by Lucard and becoming a vampire himself.

Living with Helsing, and finding vampire hunting fun, were his young American nephews Max and Chris, and sweet Sophie Metternich. Gustav spent most of his time trying to destroy Lucard and, when things went awry, removing the vampire's curse from those who had been bitten. The latter included Sophie and Max and Chris's mother Eileen, a globe-trotting banker from Philadelphia who had tried to structure a financial deal with Lucard Industries before he put the bite on her.

Filmed entirely on location in Luxembourg.

DRAGNET (*Police Drama*)

FIRST TELECAST: *January 3, 1952*
LAST TELECAST: *September 10, 1970*

BROADCAST HISTORY:

Jan 1952–Dec 1955, NBC Thu 9:00–9:30
Jan 1956–Sep 1958, NBC Thu 8:30–9:00
Sep 1958–Jun 1959, NBC Tue 7:30–8:00
Jul 1959–Sep 1959, NBC Sun 8:30–9:00
Jan 1967–Sep 1970, NBC Thu 9:30–10:00

CAST:

Sgt. Joe Friday..........................Jack Webb
Sgt. Ben Romero (1951).........Barton Yarborough
Sgt. Ed Jacobs (1952)...............Barney Phillips
Officer Frank Smith (1952) ....Herb Ellis
Officer Frank Smith (1953–1959) ...Ben Alexander
Officer Bill Gannon (1967–1970) ....Harry Morgan

THEME:

"Dragnet" (also known as "Dragnet March" and "Danger Ahead"), by Walter Schumann

DIRECTOR:

Jack Webb

Dragnet was probably the most successful police series in the history of television. By providing the prototype of the realistic action series, it marked a major turning point for a medium that had, for its first few years, been dominated by comedy and vaudeville. *Dragnet*'s hallmark was its appearance of realism, from the documentary-style narration by Joe Friday, to the cases drawn from the files of a real police department (Los Angeles, which provided the locale), to its careful attention to the details of police work ("It was 3:55. . . . We were working the day watch out of homicide"). Viewers were reminded of the unglamorous dead ends and the constant interruptions of their private lives that plague real policemen, and this made the final shoot-out and capture of the criminal all the more exciting. At the end of each episode, after the criminal was apprehended, an announcer would describe what happened at the subsequent trial and the severity of the sentence.

The concept, as created by laconic actor-director Jack Webb, caught on immediately, perhaps because it stood out so sharply against the police–private eye caricatures then on the air. *Dragnet* became an enormous hit. Its catchphrases and devices became national bywords and were widely satirized. There was Webb's terse "My name's Friday—I'm a cop," and "Just the facts, ma'am"; the jargon—the criminal's "M.O.," "Book him on a 358"—and, of course, that arresting theme music, with possibly the most famous four-note introduction since Beethoven's Fifth Symphony ("Dum-de-dum-dum"). Music was an important part of *Dragnet*'s success, even aside from the theme. It was laced throughout every episode, dark and tension-filled, then erupting in a loud, sudden "stinger" after an especially significant revelation or denouement. In fact, *Dragnet* inspired two hit records in 1953: a recording of the theme music by Ray Anthony and His Orchestra, and the hilarious "St. George and the Dragonet" by Stan Freberg—probably the only parody of a current TV series ever to sell a million copies and reach number-one on the hit parade. (The record's opening intoned, "The legend you are about to hear is true; only the needle should be changed to protect the record . . .")

Dragnet began on radio in 1949 and, after a special TV preview on *Chesterfield Sound Off Time* in December 1951, opened its official TV run on January 3, 1952. Friday's partner in the preview was played by Barton Yarborough, of the radio series. He died suddenly of a heart attack a few days after the telecast, and four actors subsequently portrayed Friday's sidekick: Barney Phillips in the spring of 1952, Herb Ellis in the fall, Ben Alexander for the remainder of the seven-and-a-half-year original run, and Harry Morgan for the revival in 1967–1970.

During most of its first 12 months on the air *Dragnet* ran every other Thursday, alternating with *Gangbusters*, another transplanted radio police show. From January of 1953 until 1959 it was a weekly series. In 1967, after a hiatus of more than seven years, it returned to the air under the slightly modified title *Dragnet '67*, to distinguish it from the reruns of the original series still being played on many stations. (Reruns were also known as *Badge 714*, after Friday's badge number.) Jack Webb returned to the role of Friday but with a new partner, Officer Bill Gannon. The format was essentially the same as the original *Dragnet* but there was somewhat stronger emphasis on the noncrime aspects of police work, such as community involvement and helping individuals in trouble.

DRAGNET (*Police Drama*)
BROADCAST HISTORY:
Syndicated only
30 minutes
Produced: *1989–1990* (52 episodes)
Released: *September 1989*
CAST:
Vic Daniels .... Jeff Osterhage
Carl Molina .... Bernard White
Capt. Boltz.......................... Thalmus Rasulala
Capt. Lussen .... Don Stroud

This syndicated revival of Jack Webb's venerable crime series featured partners Vic Daniels and Carl Molina, plainclothes detectives working for the Los Angeles Police Department. Each episode detailed the laborious process by which police put together clues to solve crimes. Ongoing narration was provided by Det. Daniels in a matter-of-fact style similar to that used by Joe Friday on the original version of the show. Depending on the episode, the commanding officer was either Capt. Boltz or Capt. Lussen.

Originally produced during the 1989–1990 season, *Dragnet* aired that season only in New York and Los Angeles. It went into national syndication the following year but failed to capture the public's imagination in an era when shows like *Cops* and *America's Most Wanted* showed what police work was *really* like.

DRAGNET (*Police Drama*)
FIRST TELECAST: *February 2, 2003*
LAST TELECAST:
BROADCAST HISTORY:
Feb 2003–May 2003, ABC Sun 10:00–11:00
Jun 2003– , ABC Sat 10:00–11:00
CAST:
Det. Joe Friday.......................... Ed O'Neill
Det. Frank Smith .... Ethan Embry
THEME:
"Danger Ahead," by Walter Schumann

The ghost of Jack Webb must have been hovering over this revival of the classic cop show, which stayed rather close to the original. Back was the team of Joe Friday and Frank Smith, the famous theme (in a new arrangement), the trial results in the coda and the matter-of-fact opening setting the scene: "It was Monday. It was overcast in Los Angeles. My partner and I were working the day shift out of Robbery Homicide." Most of all, back was the laconic, by-the-book, no-frills approach to police work. Some things had changed, however. Despite his trench coat and deadpan expression, this Joe Friday was a little gruffer than his famous predecessor, and his partner Det. Smith was a relatively inexperienced newcomer who tagged along behind (unlike Webb's experienced partners), having just been promoted to Robbery Homicide from the Vice Division. Also, the crimes were definitely gorier, often murders involving rape and dismemberment. But the cops' approach was the same, methodically tracking down clues until they closed in on the perp, usually without gunfire.

DRAMA AT EIGHT (*Dramatic Anthology*)
FIRST TELECAST: *July 9, 1953*
LAST TELECAST: *July 30, 1953*
BROADCAST HISTORY:
Jul 1953, DUM Thu 8:00–8:30

This was a series of filmed dramas featuring lesser-known actors and actresses. The July 30 telecast, a comedy entitled "Uncle Charlie," presented an early TV version of Cliff Arquette's Charley Weaver characterization. That was the last network airing of the program, though it continued locally in New York through October 1, 1953.

DRAMATIC MYSTERY, see *Chesterfield Presents*

DRAW ME A LAUGH (*Cartoon Quiz/Panel*)
FIRST TELECAST: *January 15, 1949*
LAST TELECAST: *February 5, 1949*
BROADCAST HISTORY:
Jan 1949–Feb 1949, ABC Sat 8:30–9:00
EMCEE:
Walter Hurley
Patricia Bright
REGULARS:
Mel Casson
Jay Irving
Oscar Brand

The object of this show was for the participants, who were cartoonists, to draw cartoons based on ideas sent in by viewers. The show's regular cartoonist, Mel Casson, was given a description of the cartoon to be drawn but not the caption; simultaneously, the caption but not the description was given to another cartoonist, who made up his own illustration. The two cartoons were then compared and an audience panel voted on which was funnier. Other segments of the show included making cartoons out of scribbles, drawing blind, and "singing captions" by folksinger Oscar Brand.

The program lasted exactly four weeks.

DRAW TO WIN (*Cartoon Quiz/Panel*)
FIRST TELECAST: *April 22, 1952*
LAST TELECAST: *June 10, 1952*
BROADCAST HISTORY:
Apr 1952–Jun 1952, CBS Tue 8:30–9:00
EMCEE:
Henry Morgan
PANELISTS:
Bill Holman
Abner Dean

Home viewers here were asked to send in slogans, names of objects, or anything else that could be described through a series of cartoon clues. The panel, composed of three cartoonists and a celebrity guest, would then try to guess the solution to the cartoon clues. Depending on how long it took them to identify correctly the meaning of the clues, the sender would receive a prize of up to $25.

DREAM GIRL, U.S.A. (*Beauty Contest*)
BROADCAST HISTORY:
30 minutes
Syndicated only

Produced: *1986* (26 episodes)
Released: *Fall 1986*

HOST:
Ken Howard

ANNOUNCER:
Danny Dark

CHOREOGRAPHER:
Kevin Carlisle

DANCERS:
Alexander Cole
Scott Grossman
Michael Thompson
Jerald Vincent

This prerecorded beauty pageant (the entire series was taped during a few weeks in 1986) featured a series of elimination rounds with four participants in each episode competing in swimsuit, evening gown, and other events.

DREAM HOUSE (*Quiz*)

FIRST TELECAST: *March 27, 1968*
LAST TELECAST: *September 19, 1968*
BROADCAST HISTORY:
Mar 1968–Aug 1968, ABC Wed 8:30–9:00
Sep 1968, ABC Thu 9:30–10:00

EMCEE:
Mike Darrow

Young married couples were offered a roomful of furniture for correct answers on this quiz show. Winners of four consecutive rounds (rooms) received a house worth up to $40,000 as well. The "dream house" might take several forms, a traditional house, mobile home, ski lodge, houseboat, or even a private island. *Dream House* was also seen in a daytime edition that premiered a few weeks after the prime-time version and remained on the air until January 1970.

Thirteen years later, in April 1983, a new version of *Dream House* surfaced on NBC's weekday daytime lineup. The revived version, hosted by Bob Eubanks, ran until June 1984. The cost of housing had gone up considerably over the years. The grand prize "dream house" in the new version of the show was worth $100,000.

DREAM ON (*Situation Comedy*)

FIRST TELECAST: *January 8, 1995*
LAST TELECAST: *July 3, 1995*
BROADCAST HISTORY:
Jan 1995–Apr 1995, FOX Sun 9:30–10:00
Jun 1995–Jul 1995, FOX Mon 9:00–10:00
(Also on HBO, 1990–1996)

CAST:
Martin Tupper .... Brian Benben
Jeremy Tupper (age 11) .... Chris Demetral
Toby Pedalbee .... Denny Dillon
Eddie Charles (early episodes) .... Jeff Joseph
Eddie Charles (later episodes) .... Dorien Wilson
Judith Tupper Stone .... Wendie Malick
**Gibby* .... Michael McKean

*Occasional

A middle-aged man's vivid fantasy life was the centerpiece of this racy comedy. Mild-mannered Martin Tupper was a book editor for a Manhattan publisher and recently divorced from psychologist Judith, the one real love of his life. He had to cope with the sexually liberated dating scene of the nineties and with the fact that Judith was now married to the incredibly perfect Dr. Richard Stone. How perfect? Richard was so perfect that he seemed to be receiving a Nobel Prize, or being nominated for sainthood, almost every week.

Martin, on the other hand, was constantly reminded of his shortcomings—by almost everyone. He was a weekend father to his son, Jeremy, who gave him little respect, and got questionable dating advice from his longtime friend Eddie, the womanizing host of a *Geraldo*-style talk show. At the office he was regularly put down by his sarcastic secretary, Toby, and intimidated by his new boss, Gibby, whose taste in literature ran toward the salacious.

Two things distinguished *Dream On* from other TV comedies: its sexual frankness (including, on HBO, frontal female nudity) and its innovative use of old TV and movie clips to illustrate Martin's musings and reactions and to serve as punch lines for jokes. Martin's fantasies were filled with everyone from Ozzie Nelson to Jack Benny, William Bendix, Bette Davis, Charlton Heston, and Joan Crawford, in glorious black and white. Two versions of each episode were filmed, with and without nudity and strong language, and it was the latter that aired on Fox. Sex was still the focus of most episodes, however.

The last original episode premiered on HBO on March 27, 1996. During the intervening period, Judith's second husband, Richard, had suffered kidney failure and was cryogenically frozen. In the finale the following happened: Judith, who had started seeing Martin again, remarried him. At the wedding, pregnant Toby's boyfriend Irwin Bader (Larry Miller) proposed and they got married in the ambulance in which she delivered their baby girl on the way to the hospital. Martin's buddy Eddie, who had himself gotten married five months earlier, found out from his wife Rema (Dawnn Lewis) that he was going to be a father.

DREAM STREET (*Drama*)

FIRST TELECAST: *April 13, 1989*
LAST TELECAST: *June 7, 1989*
BROADCAST HISTORY:
Apr 1989, NBC Thu 9:30–10:00
Apr 1989–May 1989, NBC Fri 10:00–11:00
Jun 1989, NBC Wed 10:00–11:00

CAST:
Denis DeBeau .... Dale Midkiff
Harry DeBeau .... Peter Frechette
Eric DeBeau .... David Barry Gray
Pete DeBeau .... Tom Signorelli
Lillian DeBeau .... Debra Mooney
Joey Coltrera .... Thomas Calabro
Anthony Coltrera .... Victor Argo
Joni Goldstein .... Cecil Hoffmann
Marianne McKinney .... Jo Anderson
Cesar Clemons .... Charles Brown
Ruben Fundora .... Paul Calderon
Kara .... Christine Moore

Dream Street was from the producers of *thirtysomething* and was billed as offering the same kind of realistic stories of intertwined lives and loves, but among the lower middle class. It bore little resemblance to the earlier series about superachieving married couples, however. Far fewer viewers could relate to this gritty series—unless they happened to live in Hoboken and be connected to the Mob.

At the center was the DeBeau family: Harry, the irresponsible eldest son; Denis, the middle son who was more reliable but also something of a dreamer; and wild teenager Eric. When father Pete suffered a stroke, he turned the family's refrigeration business over to Denis, setting up family tensions. Those problems were nothing compared to the worries of Denis's best friend Joey, whose engagement to Joni was vehemently opposed by her parents because Joey's father was a lower-level Mafioso. A nice Jewish girl marrying into the Mob! Joey's friendship with Denis was also a bit strained when he was forced to collect protection money from his friend ("the cost of doing business").

Marianne was Denis's schoolteacher girlfriend.

Dream Street was filmed on location in Hoboken, New Jersey.

DREAM TEAM, THE (*Foreign Intrigue*)

BROADCAST HISTORY:

Syndicated only
60 minutes
Produced: *1999* (8 episodes)
Released: *September 1999*

CAST:

Zach Hamilton .... Jeff Kaake
Victoria Carrera .... Traci Bingham
Kim Taylor .... Angie Everhart
Eva Kirov .... Eva Halina
Desmond Heath .... Roger Moore
J. W. Garrison .... Martin Sheen

The Dangerous Reconnaissance Emergency Action Mission (D.R.E.A.M.) Team was a group of intelligence agents battling drug dealers, terrorists and other international criminals in this fleetingly seen fantasy adventure. Zach, the hunky team leader, was a former C.I.A. operative. The three sexy agents working with him were Kim, a special agent multiforce instructor for the hostage rescue team; Victoria, a renowned guerrilla fighter; and Eva, a covert operations expert and former K.G.B. agent. The team was based in Puerto Rico and worked undercover as "the Dream Team," doing music videos, fashion shoots, and TV commercials. Behind a sliding wall in the mansion in which they lived was the high-tech communications center from which they communicated with their boss, Garrison, who was based in Washington. The team was his brainchild. In the third episode Garrison was promoted, and the team began reporting to the very British and mysterious Desmond Heath.

A special behind-the-scenes episode, hosted by costar Traci Bingham, aired in December and introduced the newest member of the team, model/singer Caprice Bourret. Her character, Dani West, was a friend of Heath's who joined the Dream Team but, since the show abruptly ceased production after eight episodes, she was never seen as a regular.

DREAM TEAM WITH ANNABELLE AND MICHAEL, THE (*Talk*)

BROADCAST HISTORY:

Sci-Fi Channel
30 minutes
Original episodes: *2003* (22 episodes)
Premiered: *January 20, 2003*

REGULARS:

Annabelle Gurwitch
Michael Lennox

Guests on this odd late-night series described their dreams or nightmares and had them interpreted by the show's mousy, bespectacled "Dream Interpreter," Michael. Some of the dreams had to do with sex, or the lack of it (for example, the girl who dreamed her female friend had a penis); then there was the man who dreamed his deceased mother was on the back of his motorcycle, pregnant with him (fear of loss); the guy who dreamed he was standing at the altar with a fat woman (fear of commitment); and the woman who saw people falling from the sky, including John Goodman (fear of giving birth, fear of becoming fat). Most of the guests were young, and many of the dreams were titillating, but Michael answered them all quite seriously, while slightly saucy cohost Annabelle added a little color. There were also short segments analyzing celebrities' dreams and man-on-the-street dreams. Few watched, and after six weeks the show faded away—or, depending on how you look at it, maybe it was just a TV dream.

DREAMS (*Situation Comedy*)

FIRST TELECAST: *October 3, 1984*
LAST TELECAST: *October 31, 1984*
BROADCAST HISTORY:

Oct 1984, CBS Wed 8:30–9:00

CAST:

Gino Minnelli .... John Stamos
Martha Spino .... Jami Gertz
Phil Taylor .... Cain Devore
Morris Weiner .... Albert Macklin
Lisa Copley .... Valerie Stevenson
Louise Franconi .... Sandy Freeman
Frank Franconi .... Ron Karabatsos
Torpedo .... Bill Henderson

Gino Minnelli, 22, was a welder by day and a rock musician by night. He and the other young members of his group "Dreams" hoped that their music would be the ticket out of their blue-collar Philadelphia neighborhood. Gino was lead singer, lead guitarist, and resident ladykiller. Martha sang backup, Phil wrote most of their songs and also played guitar, and Weiner was the flaky keyboard player. The newest member of "Dreams" was Lisa, whose father was a wealthy U.S. senator, and who had been recruited mostly for her money. The pleasant surprise for all was that Lisa could really belt out a song. While they worked for their big break, "Dreams" performed regularly at a small neighborhood club owned by Gino's uncle Frank. Music video segments were incorporated into each episode of *Dreams* in an attempt to merge a traditional situation comedy format with the hot new fad for music videos.

DRESS REHEARSAL (*Various*)

FIRST TELECAST: *March 21, 1948*
LAST TELECAST: *August 31, 1948*
BROADCAST HISTORY:

Mar 1948–Apr 1948, NBC Thu 8:00–8:30
Jul 1948–Aug 1948, NBC Mon 8:00–8:30
Aug 1948, NBC Tue 9:00–9:30

"DIRECTOR" (ON CAMERA):

Richard Goode

This was an umbrella title for a series of one-time and experimental programs that took the form of dress rehearsals. It included musical revues, quiz shows, and an occasional drama. Perhaps the best show was the last, entitled "Swap Night," which featured the first TV appearance of veteran radio commentator Norman Brokenshire, dressed as a rural Yankee trader and presiding over a swap session between cast members and viewers at home.

DREW CAREY SHOW, THE (*Situation Comedy*)

FIRST TELECAST: *September 13, 1995*

LAST TELECAST:

BROADCAST HISTORY:

Sep 1995–Feb 1996, ABC Wed 8:30–9:00
Apr 1996–May 1996, ABC Wed 8:30–9:00
May 1996–Sep 1996, ABC Tue 8:30–9:00
Aug 1996–Nov 1996, ABC Wed 9:30–10:00
Dec 1996–Jun 2002, ABC Wed 9:00–9:30
Aug 1997–Sep 1997, ABC Wed 8:00–8:30
Jan 1998–Feb 1998, ABC Tue 8:00–8:30
Mar 1999– Apr 1999, ABC Thu 9:00–9:30
Jun 2001–Jul 2001, ABC Wed 8:00–8:30
Jun 2002–Sep 2002, ABC Mon 9:00–10:00
Sep 2002–Oct 2002, ABC Mon 8:00–8:30
Nov 2002–Dec 2002, ABC Fri 9:00–9:30
Dec 2002–Jan 2003, ABC Fri 9:30–10:00
Jun 2003– , ABC Fri 9:00–10:00

CAST:

Drew Carey .... Drew Carey
Oswald Harvey .... Diedrich Bader
Lewis Kiniski .... Ryan Stiles
Kate O'Brien (1995–2002) .... Christa Miller
Mimi Bobeck.......................... Kathy Kinney
Lisa (1995–1996)................ Katy Selverstone
Jay Clemens (1995–1996)............. Robert Torti
Mr. Bell (voice) (1995–1996) .... Kevin Pollak
Nigel Wick (1997–2003)........... Craig Ferguson
**Nicki Fifer (1997–1998, 2001–2003)*.... Kate Walsh
Dottie/Fran Louder (1997–1999) .... Nan Martin
Steve Carey (1999–2003) .... John Carroll Lynch
Kellie Newmark (2002–2003) ...... Cynthia Watros

*Occasional

Crew-cut, heavyset comic Drew Carey starred in this inventive sitcom about four single working-class friends in Cleveland, his own real-life hometown. Drew (the character) was the underpaid assistant personnel director at the Winfred-Louder Department Store, but he spent much of his time hanging out in his kitchen, or at the Warsaw Tavern, with his three best friends. They were Oswald, an easygoing package deliveryman and wannabe disc jockey; Lewis, a janitor at the mysterious DrugCo Pharmaceutical Co.; and Kate, an overgrown tomboy looking for love. At work his chief nemesis was Mimi, the secretary from Hell, a living cartoon whose loud clothes and louder makeup would make the Roadrunner scoot. Mr. Bell was the original loud but usually unseen boss, replaced in 1997 by the more visible Nigel Wick. Dottie (later Fran) Louder was the elderly widow of the store founder.

A succession of Drew's girlfriends passed through, including Lisa, Nicki (whom he almost married), sixtyish Celia (played by Shirley Jones), and Tracy. Jay was Kate's boyfriend for a time, before she and Oswald decided to become engaged during the 1997–1998 season. At the last minute they called it off. Besides the gang's dating misadventures, they started their own micro-brewery, Buzz Beer, hosted a backyard bash for much of Cleveland, and took spur-of-the-moment road trips. Among the highlights of the series were the occasional elaborately produced musical fantasies, in which everyone danced and sang, and the parodies on current films such as *The Full Monty*.

Later seasons brought comic twists and turns as the series verged more and more toward the surrealistic (Drew's fantasies while in a coma, multiple marriages, dance numbers, various takeovers of the department store by unlikely people, etc.). Drew's brother Steve came to town and married Mimi, with whom he eventually had a baby, Gus, in 2001. Drew decided that his true soul mate had been Kate all along, so they began dating during the 1999–2000 season, and at various times he was "married" to Kate, Nicki (who came back) and Mr. Wick (who needed to marry a U.S. citizen to stay in the country). In 2002 Kate abruptly left Cleveland and married handsome fighter pilot Kirk (Cameron Mathison), throwing Drew into a profound depression. Nicki, his sometimes homicidal ex-girlfriend, now badly overweight and with low self-esteem, moved into his house, as did pretty newcomer Kellie, a former schoolmate with a crush on Drew. The two women did not get along. Drew decided to search for a wife, a task hindered by the disruption of his career when Winfred-Louder went bankrupt. The store was taken over by two annoying young techno-nerds and turned into an Internet shopping site, neverendingstore.com. They considered Drew "the old guy," but eventually gave him his old job back.

DREW PEARSON (*Commentary*)

FIRST TELECAST: *May 4, 1952*

LAST TELECAST: *March 18, 1953*

BROADCAST HISTORY:

May 1952–Nov 1952, ABC Sun 11:00–11:15
Dec 1952–Mar 1953, DUM Wed 7:30–7:45

COMMENTATOR:

Drew Pearson

The famous columnist Drew Pearson, who covered the 1952 political conventions and the subsequent presidential election for ABC, presented commentary and his "Predictions of Things to Come" in these network telecasts in 1952–1953.

DREXELL'S CLASS (*Situation Comedy*)

FIRST TELECAST: *September 19, 1991*

LAST TELECAST: *July 9, 1992*

BROADCAST HISTORY:

Sep 1991–Jul 1992, FOX Thu 8:30–9:00

CAST:

Otis Drexell...................... Dabney Coleman
Principal Francine E. Itkin (1991)...... Randy Graff
Roscoe Davis .... Dakin Matthews
Willie Trancas (1991) .... Jason Biggs
Nicole Finnigan (1991).............. Heidi Zeigler
Kenny Sanders............... Damian Cagnolatti
Walker (1991)................ Matthew Lawrence
Melissa Drexell (age 15) .... A. J. Langer
Brenda Drexell (14)............. Brittany Murphy
Principal Marilyn Ridge .... Edie McClurg
George Foster .... Cleavant Derricks
Slash.............................. Phil Buckman
Bernadette .... Jacqueline Donnelly
Lionel.......................... Matthew Slowik

Otis Drexell was a fifth-grade teacher at Grantwood Elementary School in Cedar Bluffs, Iowa. Sarcastic, cynical, and manipulative, he seemed to get along much better with the outspoken youngsters in his class than with the school's staff, especially Principal Itkin, who thought he was an incompetent teacher unable to control his class, and Roscoe Davis, the smug, supercilious fellow fifth-grade teacher who relished putting Drexell down and proving his class was better than Drexell's. Willie, Nicole, Kenny, and Walker were students in Drexell's class and Melissa (the sexy one) and Brenda (the little homemaker) were his beloved teenaged daughters.

When Principal Itkin had a nervous breakdown and left the school in November, she was replaced by Principal Ridge. At this point the focus of the series changed from the classroom (a number of the students were dropped from the cast) to Drexell's family life and adventures outside of school.

This was the latest in several attempts to find the right TV vehicle for Dabney Coleman's lovable (?) misanthrope persona, but was not much more successful than *Buffalo Bill* or *Slap Maxwell*. Its spirit was summed up by two of the titles originally proposed for the series: *Oh No, Not Drexell* and *Shut Up, Kids*.

DRIVEN (*Documentary*)

BROADCAST HISTORY:

VH1
60 minutes
Original episodes: *2002–*
Premiered: *January 15, 2002*

Biographies of contemporary music stars, with an emphasis on their formative years, those who influenced them, and why they were driven to succeed. Subjects ranged from Britney Spears and Christina Aguilera to Notorious B.I.G. and Tupac Shakur ("Thug Angel").

DROODLES (*Cartoon Quiz/Audience Participation*)

FIRST TELECAST: *June 21, 1954*
LAST TELECAST: *September 17, 1954*
BROADCAST HISTORY:

Jun 1954–Sep 1954, NBC Mon 8:00–8:30
Sep 1954, NBC Fri 8:00–8:30

EMCEE:

Roger Price

PANELISTS:

Marc Connelly
Carl Reiner
Denise Lor

"Droodles" were simple line drawings that depicted an object or scene, often from a rather strange perspective. Roger Price, who had written a book called *Droodles*, was the emcee. The three regular panelists were joined by a fourth guest panelist, who started the show by drawing his or her own droodle for the other panelists to try to figure out. After this the guest joined the other panelists in guessing what was depicted in selected droodles submitted by home viewers (who won prizes if they stumped the panel) and some drawn by Price. In addition, there was a "Hundred Dollar Droodle" drawn by Price at the end of each show. Viewers were invited to send in postcards with possible titles for it, and the best title won the $100.

DUCK FACTORY, THE (*Situation Comedy*)

FIRST TELECAST: *April 12, 1984*
LAST TELECAST: *July 11, 1984*
BROADCAST HISTORY:

Apr 1984–May 1984, NBC Thu 9:30–10:00
Jun 1984–Jul 1984, NBC Wed 9:30–10:00

CAST:

Skip Tarkenton .... Jim Carrey
Mrs. Sheree Winkler .... Teresa Ganzel
Brooks Carmichael .... Jack Gilford
Aggie Aylesworth .... Julie Payne
Andrea Lewin .... Nancy Lane
Marty Fenneman .... Jay Tarses
Roland Culp .... Clarence Gilyard, Jr.
Wally Wooster .... Don Messick

The Duck Factory was set in a small, run-down Hollywood animation studio peopled by the loony crew who produced a TV cartoon show called *Dippy Duck*. The newest employee was Skip Tarkenton, an eager young cartoonist fresh from the Midwest and bursting with excitement at his first professional job. His wide-eyed innocence contrasted sharply with the cynicism of his co-workers: Brooks, the fatherly artist full of doubts about his own brilliance; Andrea, the sarcastic, man-hungry film editor; Marty, the two-bit gag writer; Roland, the only black storyboard artist in the business; and Wally, the voice-over narrator who had a repertoire of so many cartoon voices that he had long since forgotten his own voice. Buddy Winkler, the tyrannical owner of the studio, had just died and the place was virtually leaderless when Skip arrived, so the whole crew turned to the reluctant newcomer to save *Dippy Duck*—which was constantly on the verge of cancellation by the network. This brought the enmity of Aggie, the pushy, penny-pinching business manager who thought she should be in charge, but also the appreciation of Mrs. Winkler, the sexy young bimbo whom Buddy had met and married only three weeks before his demise—and who was, therefore, now the studio's owner.

DUCKMAN (*Cartoon*)

BROADCAST HISTORY:

USA Network
30 minutes
Produced: *1993–1997* (70 episodes)
Premiered: *March 5, 1994*

VOICES:

Duckman .... Jason Alexander
Aunt Bernice .... Nancy Travis
Ajax (age 16) .... Dweezil Zappa
Charles (10) .... Dana Hill
Mambo (10) .... E. G. Daily
Cornfed .... Gregg Berger
Fluffy, Uranus .... Pat Musick
**King Chicken* .... Tim Curry

*Occasional

MUSIC:

by Frank Zappa (and others)

"What the hell you starin' at?" snarled this dyspeptic duck who was no relation to Donald. The sticklike hero of this offbeat cartoon was a flop at just about everything. He fancied himself a crack private eye (or "private dick" as he preferred it), but nearly all of his cases were solved by his low-key partner, a pig named Cornfed who droned in a Sgt. Friday monotone. Family life wasn't much better. He had either two or three sons, depending on how you counted them: Ajax, the incredibly dumb surfer-dude oldest, and Charles and Mambo, wisecracking twins whose two heads shared a single body. Then there was Bernice, his domineering, aerobics-obsessed sister-in-law, who had inherited both his house and children when his wife, Beatrice, died and barely tolerated him still living there. At least he could vent his angst on Fluffy and Uranus, the two disgustingly cute teddy bears who helped around his office and whom he mashed, drop-kicked, and mangled on a regular basis. They always bounced back smiling. King Chicken was an occasional foe and Gecko was the family dog.

Duckman was a favorite of critics for its iconoclasm, sarcastic comments on modern life, and bits of social satire amid the fast-paced nonsense. Much of the humor was rather gross. For example, Grandmama never spoke, only sat in her chair and flatulated. Music for the series was composed by rock legend Frank Zappa just before he died. No doubt he would have appreciated the series' in-your-face attitude, even if viewers weren't entirely sure what to make of it.

Based on the underground comic strip by Everett Peck.

DUDLEY (*Situation Comedy*)
FIRST TELECAST: *April 16, 1993*
LAST TELECAST: *May 14, 1993*
BROADCAST HISTORY:
Apr 1993–May 1993, CBS Fri 8:30–9:00
May 1993, CBS Fri 8:00–8:30
CAST:
Dudley Bristol .... Dudley Moore
Laraine Bristol .... Joanna Cassidy
Fred Bristol .... Harley Cross
Harold Krowten .... Joel Brooks
Marta .... Lupe Ontiveros
Paul .... Max Wright

Dudley Bristol was a celebrated New York composer and nightclub pianist whose professional life was much more successful than his personal life, for one simple reason—he was incapable of making personal commitments. In this low-key comedy he was faced with trying to raise his trouble-prone, 14-year-old son, Fred, after his ex-wife, Laraine, had given up. Fred, who had an attitude problem and had spent more than his share of time in juvenile court, grudgingly agreed to the arrangement, while Dudley, who didn't have a clue about parenting, tried to establish a viable relationship with the boy. Others seen regularly were Harold, the owner of Liaisons, the supper club at which Dudley performed; Paul, Dudley's business manager and best friend; and Marta, the Hispanic maid who spoke no English but could at least talk to Fred who, for all his other shortcomings, spoke fluent Spanish.

DUE SOUTH (*Police Drama*)
FIRST TELECAST: *September 15, 1994*
LAST TELECAST: *August 16, 1996*
BROADCAST HISTORY:
Sep 1994–Apr 1995, CBS Thu 8:00–9:00
Jun 1995–Jul 1995, CBS Fri 9:00–10:00
Dec 1995–Aug 1996, CBS Fri 8:00–9:00
(In first-run syndication Sep 1997–Sep 1998)
CAST:
Constable Benton Fraser .... Paul Gross
Det. Ray Vecchio (1994–1996) ..... David Marciano
Capt./Lt. Harding Welsh .... Beau Starr
Det. Louis Guardino (1994–1996) ...... Daniel Kash
Det. Jack Huey .... Tony Craig
Elaine Besbriss (1994–1997) ..... Catherine Bruhier
Francesca Vecchio .... Ramona Milano
Robert Fraser .... Gordon Pinsent
Insp. Meg Thatcher (1995–1998) ..... Camilla Scott
Det. Stanley Raymond Kowalski (1997–1998)
.... Callum Keith Rennie
Det. Thomas E. Dewey (1997–1998) ... Tom Melissis
Constable Turnbull (1997–1998) .. Dean McDermott

Not since the 1950s had an American network aired a prime-time series starring a Mountie, and Benton Fraser was much closer in spirit to Dudley Do-Right of cartoon fame than to the grizzled Sgt. Preston of *Sergeant Preston of the Yukon*. Constable Fraser was an unbelievably polite Royal Canadian Mountie assigned to the Canadian Consulate in Chicago. Although he wasn't there in a law-enforcement capacity, he regularly found himself helping his friend, wisecracking street-smart Chicago cop Ray Vecchio, solve cases. They had met when Fraser was in Chicago searching for his father's murderer. Others in Ray's precinct were his boss, Captain Welsh, who couldn't understand how Fraser kept getting involved in police business; fellow detectives Guardino and Huey; and Elaine, the dispatcher/assistant with eyes for the handsome Mountie. Despite outward appearances and his often unorthodox methods (including using the skills of an animal tracker to locate human prey in the big city), Fraser was an excellent detective. Not only that, but his straight-arrow demeanor even softened up some of the harder cases on the mean streets of Chicago, not the least of whom were his neighbors in the run-down building in which he rented an apartment.

There was a tongue-in-cheek quality about *Due South*. The producers made fun of American stereotypes of Canadians and Canadian stereotypes of Americans and managed to weave spoofs of almost every television genre into the stories. Of particular amusement to Canadian viewers (the show was a joint venture of CBS and Canada's CTV Network) was Fraser's deaf, lip-reading pet wolf Diefenbaker, named after a former Canadian prime minister.

Seen occasionally during the CBS run were Ray's feisty younger sister, Francesca, who had the hots for Fraser and always seemed to be in trouble, and the ghost of Fraser's deceased Mountie father, Robert, who showed up to give his son advice. When *Due South*'s second season began, Fraser had a new boss at the consulate, the attractive but stuffy Margaret "Meg" Thatcher. In keeping with protocol, he always addressed her as "sir."

A year after its network run ended, *Due South* returned in syndication, with star Gross now also serving as executive producer. In the syndicated premiere Fraser returned to Chicago from working in Canada and got a new partner, Kowalski, a fast-talking, cynical cop who spent much of his time bending the rules. Ray (seen only in the premiere and last two episodes of the season) had gone deep undercover, and Kowalski was pretending to be him until the case was resolved. Early on, Francesca replaced Elaine, who had become a real cop. Welsh, who had been a captain in the CBS episodes, was now a lieutenant. Fraser's chats with his deceased father became a regular feature, and when Fraser wanted to talk to his father, he would walk into the closet in his office at the consulate and emerge in his dad's log cabin.

In spring of 1998, Kowalski and Fraser stumbled on the real Ray Vecchio and almost blew his cover (he was working for the A.T.F.) but helped him nail Muldoon (guest star Bo Svenson), the illegal arms dealer who long ago had killed Fraser's mother. When Fraser finally captured Muldoon, with his late father's help, the old man faded away, since he had finally closed his last case. In the epilogue at the end of the episode, Fraser let viewers know that Huey and Dewey became a standup comedy team; Turnbull ran for public office but was accidentally run over by his campaign bus; Ray married Stanley's ex-wife Stella (Anne Marie Loder) and moved to Florida, where they opened a bowling alley; Francesca made *Life* magazine with a record six immaculate conceptions; Inspector Thatcher transferred into the Canadian Security Intelligence Service; and Fraser and Stanley went off together on a quest in the Canadian Rockies.

Filmed in Toronto, Canada.

DUET (*Comedy/Drama*)

FIRST TELECAST: *April 19, 1987*

LAST TELECAST: *August 20, 1989*

BROADCAST HISTORY:

Apr 1987–May 1987, FOX Sun 9:30–10:00
May 1987–Sep 1987, FOX Sun 8:30–9:00
Sep 1987–Oct 1987, FOX Sat 9:30–10:00
Oct 1987–Jul 1988, FOX Sun 9:30–10:00
Jul 1988–Jul 1989, FOX Sun 10:00–10:30
Jul 1989–Aug 1989, FOX Sun 10:30–11:00

CAST:

Ben Coleman .... Matthew Laurance
Laura Kelly .... Mary Page Keller
Richard Phillips .... Chris Lemmon
Linda Phillips .... Alison LaPlaca
Jane Kelly .... Jodi Thelen
Geneva .... Arleen Sorkin
Cooper Hayden (1987–1988) ..... Larry Poindexter
Amanda Phillips (1988–1989) .... Ginger Orsi

This episodic comedy revolved around the intertwined romantic lives of two couples. Ben and Laura were establishing a new relationship while Richard and Linda were trying to maintain one. When *Duet* premiered Ben was an unpublished writer of mystery novels (his first published novel, "Death in the Fast Lane," did become a best-seller) and Laura was running a catering business with the "help" of her flighty younger sister Jane. As their relationship evolved from casual dating to serious dating to living together, Ben and Laura went through periods of uncertainty and misgivings—at one point they even stopped dating—but their love kept bringing them back together. Interspersed through the story of their courtship were Ben's daydream sequences, in black and white, in which he imagined himself as one of his own Sam Spade–like detective creations winning his moll.

Ben's best friend Richard and his wife Linda were stereotypical yuppies, preoccupied with financial success and status. Linda was an executive at World Wide Studios, and had a difficult time dealing with Richard's abrupt decision to quit his lucrative job selling patio furniture for his father and become a professional pianist. She was also not nearly as enthusiastic about their impending parenthood as was Richard (in fact, the prospect terrified her), but after their daughter Amanda was born she became a doting mother. Geneva was the Phillipses' sexy, sharp-tongued maid who took great pleasure in putting down her employers, especially Linda; Cooper was Linda's boss at World Wide, who for some reason was infatuated with Jane; and Reuben was Ben's large dog and, prior to the arrival of Laura in his master's life, Ben's closest confidant.

When *Duet* started its 1988–1989 season, a number of changes had occurred. Amanda, who had been born in the last original episode that spring, was now a talking three-year-old, Ben and Laura were now married, and Linda had been fired by World Wide Studios. Stories that season concerned Richard and Linda's parenthood, the difficulties that arose when Linda prevailed upon Laura to take her in as a partner in the catering business, and Ben and Laura's adjustments to married life. As the season progressed, the focus shifted more and more to stories about Linda and, when *Duet* was canceled, she became the star of *Open House*, the spin-off series that replaced it in the Fox lineup.

DUKE, THE (*Situation Comedy*)

FIRST TELECAST: *July 2, 1954*

LAST TELECAST: *September 3, 1954*

BROADCAST HISTORY:

Jul 1954–Sep 1954, NBC Fri 8:00–8:30

CAST:

"The Duke" London .... Paul Gilbert
Johnny .... Allen Jenkins
Rudy Cromwell .... Claude Stroud
Sam Marco .... Sheldon Leonard
Gloria .... Phyllis Coates

The "Duke" in this comedy was a streetwise professional boxer who had, in his spare time, become an accomplished painter. Through that hobby he met Harvard graduate Rudy Cromwell, who offered to help him expand his intellectual and cultural horizons. Rudy was admirably suited to the purpose and enjoyed introducing Duke to "highbrow" forms of entertainment and diversion. The fighting side of the Duke's life kept intruding, however, in the persons of his trainer, Johnny, and fight promoter Sam Marco, both of whom wanted him to give up his pursuit of the finer things in life and return to what he knew best, boxing. Society blonde Gloria, the Duke's girlfriend, also played a prominent part.

DUKE, THE (*Detective Drama*)

FIRST TELECAST: *April 5, 1979*

LAST TELECAST: *May 18, 1979*

BROADCAST HISTORY:

Apr 1979, NBC Thu 9:30–11:30
Apr 1979–May 1979, NBC Fri 10:00–11:00

CAST:

Oscar "Duke" Ramsey .... Robert Conrad
Joe Cadillac .... Larry Manetti
Sgt. Mick O'Brien .... Red West
Dedra Smith .... Patricia Conwell

After losing a bout to a man almost half his age, 38-year-old prizefighter Duke Ramsey decided to give up the ring and spend more time with outside interests, such as running Duke and Benny's Corner, a bar and grill in his native Chicago. Benny Lyle, his manager and friend, was the person who shared billing on the eatery, but by the time it opened he had been murdered. Duke tracked down his killer, and thereby found himself a new calling—private detective. Friends from his fight days, on both sides of the law, gave him access to numerous sources of information. One of these was Joe Cadillac, a flashy young bookie. Dedra was a jet-setting socialite with romantic designs on tough-guy Duke.

DUKES OF HAZZARD, THE (*Comedy/Adventure*)
FIRST TELECAST: *January 26, 1979*
LAST TELECAST: *August 16, 1985*
BROADCAST HISTORY:
Jan 1979–Nov 1981, CBS Fri 9:00–10:00
Dec 1981–Feb 1985, CBS Fri 8:00–9:00
Jun 1985–Aug 1985, CBS Fri 8:00–9:00
CAST:
Luke Duke .... Tom Wopat
Bo Duke .... John Schneider
Daisy Duke .... Catherine Bach
Uncle Jesse Duke .... Denver Pyle
Sheriff Roscoe P. Coltrane .... James Best
Jefferson Davis "Boss" Hogg .... Sorrell Booke
Deputy Enos Strate (1979–1980, 1982–1985) .... Sonny Shroyer
Cooter Davenport .... Ben Jones
Deputy Cletus (1980–1983) .... Rick Hurst
Lulu Hogg .... Peggy Rea
Miz Emma Tisdale (1981–1983) .... Nedra Volz
Sheriff Little (1981–1984) .... Don Pedro Colley
Laverne (1981–1985) .... Lila Kent
Emery Potter (1981–1985) .... Charlie Dell
Coy Duke (1982–1983) .... Byron Cherry
Vance Duke (1982–1983) .... Christopher Mayer
The Balladeer (voice only) .... Waylon Jennings
THEME:
"The Dukes of Hazzard (Good Ol' Boys)," written and sung by Waylon Jennings

Rural comedies such as *The Beverly Hillbillies* had been a staple of the CBS lineup in the 1960s. *The Dukes of Hazzard* signaled a revival of the "good ol' boy" comedy, nearly a decade later. Luke and Bo Duke were cousins and buddies in Hazzard County, located "east of the Mississippi and south of the Ohio" (no mention of the state, but there is a real Hazard, Kentucky—a city, not a county). Their nemesis was Boss Hogg, a fat, blustery, and thoroughly corrupt local politician always seen in a white flannel suit. The Dukes easily managed to avoid capture by dim-witted Sheriff Coltrane, Boss Hogg's brother-in-law, while acting as Robin Hoods of the county. The boys hot-rodded all over Hazzard County in their souped-up Dodge Charger, "General Lee," occasionally pausing for some sage advice from their wise old uncle Jesse. Moonshine, wild car chases and crashes, and lots of scantily clad young women, including the Dukes' gorgeous cousin Daisy, populated the series. Country star Waylon Jennings served as off-screen narrator, to the accompaniment of fast-paced banjo music.

The considerable success of *Dukes* spawned several imitations, including *Lobo*, *Harper Valley P.T.A.*, and a spin-off from *Dukes* itself starring Sheriff Coltrane's grinning deputy Enos (see *Enos*). When Enos departed the series he was replaced by a new deputy, Cletus.

In the spring of 1982, series stars Tom Wopat and John Schneider walked out on *The Dukes of Hazzard* in a contract dispute over their salaries and share of the merchandising rights royalties from *Dukes* toys, games, T-shirts, and other paraphernalia that were selling like hotcakes to children around the country. The production company, Warner Bros., held a nationwide hunt to find two new Dukes to fill their places in the series and, after screening 2,230 applicants, settled on Byron Cherry and Christopher Mayer. In the premiere episode that fall, it was explained that Luke and Bo had left Hazzard to try their luck on the NASCAR racing circuit, and that their cousins Coy and Vance had returned home, after a six-year absence, to help Uncle Jesse run the farm. Deputy Enos Strate was back, but it just wasn't the same. For those who were convinced that the real star of the series was the "General Lee," it must have come as a surprise to learn that the car's drivers made any difference. The program's ratings and Wopat's and Schneider's careers all suffered as a result of the feud, so a settlement was finally reached and Luke and Bo returned to Hazzard County the following February. That fall Coy and Vance were gone.

The series also took its toll in real automobiles, as a result of all those chases and crashes. Although on-screen the General Lee never seemed to have a scratch, almost 300 look-alikes were wrecked during filming. A regular stable of identically painted Dodge Chargers was kept on hand during production of each episode, so as not to hold things up.

The theme song from this series, sung by Waylon Jennings, was on the charts during 1980. An animated version of the show, titled *The Dukes*, aired on CBS' Saturday morning lineup from February to November 1983 with the series' regulars providing the voices.

DUMONT ROYAL THEATER (*Dramatic Anthology*)
FIRST TELECAST: *April 12, 1951*
LAST TELECAST: *June 26, 1952*
BROADCAST HISTORY:
Apr 1951–Jul 1951, DUM Thu 9:30–10:00
Apr 1952–Jun 1952, DUM Thu 9:00–9:30

This was a series of low-budget 30-minute dramatic films featuring an assortment of lesser-known talent, such as Edgar Barrier, Mary Sinclair, and Hugh O'Brian (later of *Wyatt Earp* fame). The 1952 version alternated with *Gruen Playhouse*. The series was also known as *Royal Playhouse*.

DUMPLINGS, THE (*Situation Comedy*)
FIRST TELECAST: *January 28, 1976*
LAST TELECAST: *March 24, 1976*
BROADCAST HISTORY:
Jan 1976–Mar 1976, NBC Wed 9:30–10:00
CAST:
Joe Dumpling .... James Coco
Angela Dumpling .... Geraldine Brooks
Charles Sweetzer .... George S. Irving
Frederic Steele .... George Furth
Stephanie .... Marcia Rodd
Cully .... Mort Marshall
Bridget McKenna .... Jane Connell
The prude .... Wil Albert

There was a message in *The Dumplings*—fat people can be as kind, good, industrious, and lovable as anyone else. Joe and Angela were a chubby married couple running a lunch counter in a large office building in Manhattan. Among their regular customers were a city councilman, Mr. Steele; an executive of a large corporation with offices in the building, Mr. Sweetzer; his secretary, Bridget; and Angela's sister

Stephanie. Joe and Angela were madly in love with life and each other, exuded good cheer and enthusiasm, and never had a bad word for anyone.

DUNDEE AND THE CULHANE (*Western*)
FIRST TELECAST: *September 6, 1967*
LAST TELECAST: *December 13, 1967*
BROADCAST HISTORY:
Sep 1967–Dec 1967, CBS Wed 10:00–11:00
CAST:
Dundee .... John Mills
Culhane .... Sean Garrison

Although their law offices were in Sausalito, across the bay from San Francisco, British attorney Dundee and his apprentice lawyer, Culhane, traveled throughout the West to help their clients. Dealing with the sort of haphazard justice prevalent in much of the West during the latter part of the 19th century proved more of a problem than the actual courtroom defense. Judges were bribed, prisoners broke out of jails, and many citizens took the law into their own hands.

DUNNINGER SHOW, THE, see *Amazing Dunninger, The*

DUPONT CAVALCADE THEATER, see *Cavalcade of America*

DUPONT SHOW OF THE WEEK, THE (*Various*)
FIRST TELECAST: *September 17, 1961*
LAST TELECAST: *September 6, 1964*
BROADCAST HISTORY:
Sep 1961–Sep 1964, NBC Sun 10:00–11:00

The DuPont Show of the Week presented a potpourri of various types of entertainment and informational programs. For three seasons it was NBC's late Sunday evening "class" showcase, with sponsor E. I. DuPont using the best available talent, both in front of and behind the cameras, to present everything from dramatic plays and documentaries to light comedies and musical revues. One of the aims of the series was to show the latitude and potential of the television medium as a means of communication. This format represented a change in the sponsor's philosophy. For the four years before the start of this weekly NBC series, DuPont had sponsored *DuPont Show of the Month*, an irregularly scheduled collection of culturally impressive 90-minute dramas on CBS. During the CBS period, adaptations of such classics as *Don Quixote*, *Hamlet*, *A Tale of Two Cities*, and *The Browning Version* had been aired. At the time, that was CBS' answer to NBC's *Hallmark Hall of Fame*.

The first telecast on NBC was the documentary "Hemingway," narrated by Chet Huntley, with Andrew Duggan providing Ernest Hemingway's voice. Later, retired actor Ken Murray presented his edited home movies of the stars at home in "Hollywood—My Home Town"; clown Emmett Kelly narrated a documentary on the universal appeal of the circus; and Peter Lind Hayes was narrator of a musical special, "Regards to George M. Cohan." Dramatic programs were not omitted; in fact, they became the primary staple of the series during its last two years. Starring were such people as Richard Conte, Claude Rains, Walter Matthau, Zachary Scott, Teresa Wright, Eddie Albert, Martha Scott, Lloyd Nolan, James Daly, Peter Falk, Arthur Kennedy, and Oscar Homolka. Documentaries also continued; one of the most interesting was "Comedian Backstage," a *cinéma-vérité* look at the real life of comedian Shelley Berman.

DUPONT SHOW WITH JUNE ALLYSON, THE (*Dramatic Anthology*)
FIRST TELECAST: *September 21, 1959*
LAST TELECAST: *June 12, 1961*
BROADCAST HISTORY:
Sep 1959–Sep 1960, CBS Mon 10:30–11:00
Sep 1960–Dec 1960, CBS Thu 10:30–11:00
Jan 1961–Jun 1961, CBS Mon 10:30–11:00
HOSTESS/STAR:
June Allyson

Actress June Allyson was the regular hostess and occasional star of this filmed dramatic-anthology series. The plays, which ranged from light comedy to melodrama, told stories of contemporary American life. The budget for this show was lavish, and it attracted many Hollywood stars, including Ginger Rogers, Bette Davis, David Niven, Joseph Cotten, and Jane Powell. Among the telecasts were "A Summer's Ending," in which Miss Allyson and her husband Dick Powell made their first joint television appearance; "Slip of the Tongue," in which Italian actor Rossano Brazzi made his American television debut; and "Silent Panic," with Harpo Marx in a rare dramatic appearance as a deaf-mute.

DUPONT THEATER, see *Cavalcade of America*

DUSTY'S TRAIL (*Situation Comedy*)
BROADCAST HISTORY:
Syndicated only
30 minutes
Produced: *1973* (26 episodes)
Released: *Fall 1973*
CAST:
Dusty .... Bob Denver
Mr. Callahan .... Forrest Tucker
Mr. Brookhaven .... Ivor Francis
Mrs. Brookhaven .... Lynn Wood
Lulu McQueen .... Jeannine Riley
Betsy .... Lori Saunders
Andy .... Bill Cort

Bob Denver starred in this slapstick comedy, which was rather reminiscent of his earlier hit *Gilligan's Island*—only set in the West. In fact it was an almost exact copy, character for character. Bumbling their way across the prairie in a wagon train were Dusty (Gilligan), wagonmaster Callahan (the Skipper), the rich socialites the Brookhavens (the Thurston Howells), two sexy girls, sassy Lulu (Ginger) and sweet young Betsy (Mary Ann), and the nice young man, Andy (the Professor). The simpleminded, knockabout humor was also the same. Despite saturation coverage when it premiered, *Dusty's Trail* was a derivative flop.

DWEEBS (*Situation Comedy*)
FIRST TELECAST: *September 22, 1995*
LAST TELECAST: *October 27, 1995*
BROADCAST HISTORY:
Sep 1995–Oct 1995, CBS Fri 8:00–8:30
CAST:
Warren Mosbey .... Peter Scolari
Carey .... Farrah Forke

Vic .... Corey Feldman
Morley .... David Kaufman
Karl .... Stephen Tobolowsky
Todd .... Adam Biesk

Warren was a young computer software writer whose programs had made him a legend in the industry. Unfortunately, he was painfully shy and socially maladjusted as well as eccentric (to come up with ideas for the next "killer app," he bounced on a trampoline in his office). His Seattle company, Cyberbyte, was staffed with three talented but similarly socially inept programmers. Karl, the oldest, dressed horribly; Vic, who thought his dark glasses made him "cool," was constantly depressed; and Morley, who had been Vic's buddy since high school, was allergic to everything, especially women. Into their dysfunctional world came Carey, the sexy new office manager, who knew absolutely nothing about computers but much about life. She hired Todd as a gofer who, among other things, translated technospeak into English for her, and set out to give them real lives and some style. Despite their eccentricities, they were nice guys—they just needed help dealing with the outside world.

DYNASTY (*Drama*)

FIRST TELECAST: *January 12, 1981*
LAST TELECAST: *May 11, 1989*
BROADCAST HISTORY:

Jan 1981–Apr 1981, ABC Mon 9:00–10:00
Jul 1981–Sep 1983, ABC Wed 10:00–11:00
Sep 1983–May 1984, ABC Wed 9:00–10:00
Aug 1984–May 1986, ABC Wed 9:00–10:00
Sep 1986–May 1987, ABC Wed 9:00–10:00
Sep 1987–Mar 1988, ABC Wed 10:00–11:00
Nov 1988–May 1989, ABC Wed 10:00–11:00

CAST:

Blake Carrington .... John Forsythe
Krystle Jennings Carrington .... Linda Evans
Alexis Carrington Colby .... Joan Collins
Fallon Carrington Colby (1981–1984)
.... Pamela Sue Martin
Fallon Carrington Colby (1985, 1987–1989)
.... Emma Samms
Steven Carrington (1981–1982) .... Al Corley
Steven Carrington (1982–1988) .... Jack Coleman
Adam Carrington/Michael Torrance (1982–1989)
.... Gordon Thomson
Cecil Colby (1981–1982) .... Lloyd Bochner
Jeff Colby (1981–1985, 1987–1989) .... John James
Claudia Blaisdel (1981–1986) .... Pamela Bellwood
Matthew Blaisdel (1981) .... Bo Hopkins
Lindsay Blaisdel (1981) .... Katy Kurtzman
Walter Lankershim (1981) .... Dale Robertson
Jeannette .... Virginia Hawkins
Joseph Anders (1981–1983) .... Lee Bergere
Kirby (1982–1984) .... Kathleen Beller
Andrew Laird (1981–1984) .... Peter Mark Richman
Sammy Jo Dean .... Heather Locklear
Michael Culhane (1981, 1986–1987)
.... Wayne Northrop
Dr. Nick Toscanni (1981–1982) .... James Farentino
Mark Jennings (1982–1984) .... Geoffrey Scott
Cong. Neal McVane (1982–1984, 1987) .... Paul Burke
Chris Deegan (1983) .... Grant Goodeve
Tracy Kendall (1983–1984) .... Deborah Adair
Farnsworth "Dex" Dexter (1983–1989)
.... Michael Nader
Peter de Vilbis (1983–1984) .... Helmut Berger
Amanda Carrington (1984–1986)
.... Catherine Oxenberg
Amanda Carrington (1986–1987) .... Karen Cellini
Dominique Deveraux (1984–1987) .... Diahann Carroll
Gerard (1984–1989) .... William Beckley
Gordon Wales (1984–1988) .... James Sutorius
Luke Fuller (1984–1985) .... William Campbell
Nicole Simpson (1984–1985) .... Susan Scannell
Charles (1984–1985) .... George DiCenzo
Daniel Reece (1984–1985) .... Rock Hudson
Lady Ashley Mitchell (1985) .... Ali MacGraw
Danny Carrington (1985–1988) .... Jameson Sampley
Joel Abrigore (1985–1986) .... George Hamilton
Garrett Boydston (1985–1986) .... Ken Howard
King Galen (1985–1986) .... Joel Fabiani
Prince Michael (1985–1986) .... Michael Praed
Sen. Buck Fallmont (1986–1987) .... Richard Anderson
Emily Fallmont (1986) .... Pat Crowley
Clay Fallmont (1986–1987) .... Ted McGinley
Ben Carrington (1986–1987) .... Christopher Cazenove
Jackie Deveraux (1986–1987) .... Troy Beyer
Caress Morell (1986) .... Kate O'Mara
Dana Waring Carrington (1986–1988)
.... Leann Hunley
Nick Kimball (1986–1987) .... Richard Lawson
Leslie Carrington (1987–1988) .... Terri Garber
Sean Rowan (1987–1988) .... James Healey
Krystina Carrington (1987–1989) .... Jessica Player
Sarah Curtis (1987) .... Cassie Yates
Karen Atkinson (1987–1988) .... Stephanie Dunnam
Sable Colby (1988–1989) .... Stephanie Beacham
Sgt. Johnny Zorelli (1988–1989) .... Ray Abruzzo
Claire Tennyson (1988) .... Stella Hall
Virginia Metheny (1988–1989) .... Liza Morrow
Capt. William Handler (1988–1989) .... John Brandon
Rudy Richards (1988–1989) .... Lou Beatty, Jr.
Joanna Clauss/Sills (1988–1989) .... Kim Terry-Costin
Monica Colby (1989) .... Tracy Scoggins
Father Tanner McBride (1989) .... Kevin Bernhardt

THEME:

by Bill Conti

One of the most successful prime-time soap operas inspired by *Dallas* was this lavish entry. The setting was Denver, but true to the form, practically everyone was either filthy rich and disgusting or not-so-rich and disgusting.

As in *Dallas*, the money flowed from Big Oil (in fact, the series was originally going to be called *Oil*). Blake Carrington ran his vast holdings from an opulent, 48-room mansion. As the story began, however, his empire was tottering on the brink of collapse because Mideast revolutionaries had expropriated his tankers. Blake's unhappy wife was Krystle, a beautiful former secretary he had wooed and won, but whom he now treated like any other possession. Fallon was his spoiled, arrogant daughter and Steven his homosexual son (both by a previous marriage). Matthew Blaisdel, a crack geologist with the Carrington firm, was Krystle's former lover, but now had his hands full with a psychologically disturbed wife (Claudia) and a sexually blossoming daughter (Lindsay).

As the spring 1981 season ended Blake found himself on trial for the murder of Steven's male lover, Ted. Into the courtroom swept an unexpected witness for the prosecution, a mysterious, veiled woman. Not until the fall did viewers learn her identity; it was none other than Blake's former wife, the glamorous and vengeful Alexis. From that time on, much of the action on *Dynasty* centered on the rivalry between Krystle and Alexis, as Alexis schemed to displace the younger woman and secure her place in the Carrington dynasty.

Alexis soon insinuated herself into everyone's affairs. When her efforts failed to win Blake she wed his archrival, oil tycoon Cecil Colby—who promptly died of a heart attack. Then she schemed to destroy Blake professionally as well as personally, through a merger of Denver-Carrington with Colby's Colbyco. Alexis did tempt Blake briefly, but ultimately he realized the strength of his love for Krystle and Alexis was once again foiled. The war between the two beautiful women continued unabated; Alexis causing Krystle to lose her baby. Krystle attacking Alexis in a spectacular fight in a lily pond, the two of them trapped together in a burning cabin and battling it out in the mud.

On the fringes of this battle royal other stories unfolded. There was Steven's somewhat confused love life, from his homosexual affair with Ted to his marriages with Sammy Jo (who bore him a child, Danny) and Claudia. In 1982 he disappeared into exile in Indonesia, where he was injured in an explosion, necessitating "plastic surgery." His new face solved nothing, however. Always the black sheep of the family, on his return Steven found himself fighting Blake, who thought him unfit for the custody of Danny.

Meanwhile, fickle Fallon knew exactly what *she* wanted, bedding down successively with Michael the chauffeur, Nick the doctor, Jeff the junior executive, and Peter the playboy. Jeff, whom she married briefly and bore a child with, L.B. ("Little Blake"), was the one who really loved her. But it seemed that he might have to settle for Kirby (the butler's daughter!) instead.

A third Carrington offspring arrived in October 1982, calling himself Michael Torrance. He turned out to be Adam Carrington, Blake's long-lost son, who had returned to claim his birthright and whatever ladies were available. Others passing through the early stories included blustery wildcatter Walter Lankershim, an old foe of Blake's who arrived at Blake and Krystle's wedding with gun in hand; Joseph, the majordomo (Kirby's father); lawyer Andrew Laird; Krystle's ex, handsome Mark Jennings; and ruthless Congressman Neal McVane.

After a slow start *Dynasty* rose quickly to the top of the ratings, only slightly behind its prototype *Dallas*. What it may have lacked in depth of characterization and story as compared to the older serial, it made up in style and glamour, as exemplified by that gorgeous mansion (actually the Filoli estate, south of San Francisco). And if "class" is measured by the company one keeps, *Dynasty* won hands down. It was probably the first soap opera in history in which an ex-President and Secretary of State of the United States played on-screen roles: former President and Mrs. Gerald Ford and Henry Kissinger all appeared in a December 1983 episode set at Denver's glittering, real-life Carousel Ball.

As *Dynasty* matured, however, its "campy" approach to soap opera began to wear a little thin. The 1984–1985 season saw Blake fighting to regain his empire from Alexis, who had finally ruined him by undermining his South China Sea oil deal; Alexis herself was convicted of murdering Mark (actually Neal McVane did it, in a wig that made him look like Alexis). New on the scene was black singer Dominique, who arrived with her record-mogul husband Brady Lloyd (played by Billy Dee Williams) to reveal, to Blake's discomfort, that she too was a Carrington—his father's illegitimate daughter! Blake's old man Tom Carrington, seen in a riotous deathbed scene, had apparently been a world-class philanderer. Blake and Krystle's marriage had its problems; after giving birth to their first child, Krystina, Krystle dallied with handsome horsebreeder Daniel Reece (played by Rock Hudson in his last role), while Blake was seen with jet-set photographer Lady Ashley. Son Steven, as sexually confused as ever, alternated between wife Claudia and boyfriend Luke, and Jeff spent most of the season searching for true love Fallon, who had disappeared. The climactic event of the season—and for many the most preposterous story yet—involved the arrival of Alexis's lost daughter Amanda, who made a few passes at Alexis's new husband Dex and was then fixed up with Prince Michael of Moldavia. The Carringtons trooped off to the picturesque European principality for a royal wedding, but in the season finale revolutionaries burst into the palace and machine-gunned them all!

After a certain amount of intrigue in the cardboard kingdom, everybody got out and Prince Michael and King Galen became part of the Denver scene. Other major stories of 1985–1986 included a drawn-out scheme by evil producer Joel and greedy Sammy Jo to abduct Krystle and substitute a look-alike actress named Rita inside the Carrington mansion (Blake didn't seem to notice the difference, even in bed); several episodes featuring the cast of the spin-off serial *The Colbys* (q.v.); and the appearance of Blake's estranged younger brother Ben and Alexis's sister Caress. Caress wrote a scandalous book about Alexis called *Sister Dearest*; there was plenty to write about, but Alexis squashed the project by buying the publisher. Also introduced were the Fallmonts, Senator Buck, indiscreet wife Emily, sons Clay (who eventually married Sammy Jo) and Bart (who made a pass at Steven). Alexis once again "destroyed" Blake, this time throwing him "and that blond tramp" (Krystle) out of the mansion entirely. The season ended with a distraught Blake attempting to physically strangle his ex, while across town his resort hotel La Mirage was engulfed in a fire accidentally touched off by Claudia, who perished in the flames.

The following season saw the marriages of Sammy Jo to Clay and Dana to Adam (who turned out not to be Blake's long-lost son, but was adopted by him anyhow); a story in which three-year-old Krystina needed a heart transplant, then was abducted by the donor's mother, Sarah; the return of Ben's sexy daughter Leslie; and a surreal interlude in which Blake, suffering from "soap opera amnesia" after an accident, thought he was married to Alexis. She loved it. The writers apparently suffered amnesia too, bringing back three characters long since disposed of: Michael Culhane, the sleazy chauffeur from the first season, now with $50 million in his pocket; Neal McVane, who was sprung from prison long enough to blackmail Adam over his non-Carrington parentage; and supposedly deceased Matthew Blaisdel, who burst in on the Adam/Dana wedding reception with a gang of tuxedo-clad gunmen determined to carry off Krystle. At least Blake got his company back from Alexis.

Another spectre appeared in the fall of 1987 in the person of Sean, son of the butler Joseph (who had committed suicide) and brother of Kirby (fled to Europe), seeking revenge against Alexis. Fallon and Jeff were back, having escaped the sinking *Colbys* series; Blake ran for governor against Alexis, enduring her mudslinging attacks on him in her paper the *Denver Mirror* (in the end both lost the election to a third candidate); Adam and Dana, unable to conceive, hired Karen to be a surrogate mother and got into a nasty court fight when Karen decided to keep the child; and Alexis and Krystle fell into yet another hair-pulling fight in the mud.

Much of the final season was occupied by an extended murder investigation resulting from the discovery of a mummified body in a lake on the Carrington estate. It turned out to be architect Roger Grimes, one of Alexis's former lovers, shot long ago by her daughter Fallon (then a child) when he attacked her mommy. Fallon had forgotten all of this, of course, but predictably fell into bed with the macho cop investigating the case, Sgt. Zorelli. Alexis tried to frame Blake for the murder but was distracted as vengeful cousin Sable arrived in Denver to try to destroy *her*. Meanwhile Blake's beloved Krystle began having spells of bizarre behavior as the result of a bump on the head, and wound up in a permanent coma in a Swiss hospital (actress Linda Evans had decided to leave the show). In the final episode Fallon and little Krystina were trapped in a collapsing mine shaft with a buried Nazi art collection and a deranged killer; Blake and crooked police Captain Handler (who was trying to blackmail him) shot each other; and an enraged Adam pushed Alexis and Dex from a balcony. Could they bounce back?

In October 1991 ABC aired a movie sequel called *Dynasty: The Reunion* which tied up these loose ends, but created others. Fallon got out of the mine shaft and the art was "given away." The fate of Alexis and Dex was even more remarkable. "She got off pretty easy . . . they say she managed to turn in midair so she could land on top of him," marveled a minor character. "He didn't fare all that well." As for Blake, he was sent to prison for murder, his company was lost to foreign takeover, and his family scattered. The main story of *Dynasty: The Reunion* involved Blake's attempts to prove that his company—and others in the United States—were being gobbled up by a murderous, secret foreign cartel called "The Consortium." Pardoned after three years, Blake and his "sons" (Steven, Adam, and sons-in-law Jeff and Miles Colby) battled the Swiss-based Consortium, which proved to be headed by the Nazi-like Jeremy Van Dorn (Jeroen Krabbé). They eventually won back the family business—though not before Van Dorn and his agents tried to kill both Blake and Alexis (who had allied with Van Dorn). Blake even got his beloved Krystle back, freed from the Swiss sanitarium where the Consortium had tried to "program" her to kill him. Sneering Van Dorn got away, however, so there may be yet another sequel.

DYNASTY II—THE COLBYS, see *The Colbys*

E.A.R.T.H. FORCE (*Adventure*)
FIRST TELECAST: *September 16, 1990*
LAST TELECAST: *September 29, 1990*
BROADCAST HISTORY:
Sep 1990, CBS Sun 9:00–11:00
Sep 1990, CBS Sat 9:00–10:00
CAST;
John Harding, M.D. .... Gil Gerard
Dr. Carl Dana .... Clayton Rohner
Dr. Catherine Romano .... Tiffany Lamb
Diana Randall .... Joanna Pacula
Charles Dillon .... Stewart Finlay-McLennan

This short-lived series, the first casualty of the 1990–1991 season, was sort of an environmental *Mission: Impossible.* The team, organized by a dying billionaire concerned with the ecological balance of the environment, traveled all over the world using guerrilla tactics to prevent ecological catastrophes. In the three episodes that aired they recovered stolen plutonium that was earmarked for nuclear weapons, stopped animal poachers from selling endangered species on the black market, and prevented unscrupulous developers from building housing on a toxic waste site. Their organization—Earth Alert Research Tactical Headquarters (E.A.R.T.H. for short)—was staffed by John, a trauma care expert; Carl, a maverick nuclear physicist who had become an environmental activist; Catherine, a marine biologist and expert on oil spills; Charles, a mercenary who was in it only for the money; and Diana, director of the Earth Alert Foundation that provided their funding.

E.D.J., see *Personalities*

E! ENTERTAINMENT TELEVISION (Network)
(*General Entertainment Cable Network*)
LAUNCHED:
July 31, 1987
SUBSCRIBERS (MAY 2003):
80.6 million (76% U.S.)

For those who cannot get enough celebrity-gazing from *Entertainment Tonight* or *People* magazine, the E! cable network offers 24 hours a day of entertainment news and chatter. Among its early original series were *Talk Soup* (1991–2002), a recap of the day's broadcast talk shows hosted originally by Greg Kinnear and later by John Henson; *Stand Up/Sit Down Comedy* (1992–1994), hosted by Robert Klein; *Q & E!* (1994–1995), celebrity Q&A by Eleanor Mondale; *Howard Stern* (1994–); and *Celebrity Profile* (1997), E!'s version of *Biography.* Later entries included *E! True Hollywood Story, Fashion Emergency, Wild On, Revealed with Jules Asner* and *The Anna Nicole Show.* E! also programs reruns such as *Late Night with David Letterman, Lifestyles of the Rich and Famous, TV's Bloopers & Practical Jokes,* and even occasional dramatic series such as *Hotel* and *Melrose Place.*

E! attracted controversy in 1995 as a result of its decision to carry gavel-to-gavel coverage of the O. J. Simpson double-murder trial in Los Angeles. Some called its coverage "O. J. Lite," but others argued that the trial was celebrity-driven and a circus anyway.

The network began in 1987 as Movietime, a low-budget service that aired promotional clips and interviews about upcoming motion pictures. The name was changed in June 1990 to reflect the channel's widening coverage of all aspects of the entertainment world.

A spin-off network launched in October 1998, called Style, focused on the world of style, fashion and design.

E.N.G. (*Drama*)
BROADCAST HISTORY:
LIfetime Network
60 minutes
Produced: *1989–1990* (44 episodes)
Premiered: *September 1, 1990*
CAST:
Ann Hildebrandt .... Sara Botsford
Jake Antonelli .... Mark Humphrey
Mike Fennell .... Art Hindle
Jane Oliver .... Sherry Miller
Seth Miller .... Jim Millington
Bruce Foreman .... David Cubitt
J. C. Callahan .... Neil Dainard
Dan Watson .... Karl Pruner
Kyle Copeland .... George R. Robertson
Eric MacFarlane .... Jonathan Welsh
Marge Atherton .... Theresa Tova
Terri Morgan .... Cynthia Belliveau

Soap opera set in the television newsroom of Canadian station CTLS, Channel 10. The initials stood for "electronic news gathering," but the focus was not so much on the news as on who was sleeping with whom. Ann was the savvy and assertive executive producer who was having a clandestine affair with Jake, the station's star cameraman. Her world was upset by the arrival of ratings-minded News Director Mike, whose coverage philosophy clashed with hers. Younger Jane and mature Seth (who was sure he was being pushed aside) were the anchors; Bruce a young schemer; J. C. a cranky, older, wheelchair-bound assignment editor; Dan a smarmy reporter who always turned out to be wrong; and Kyle the fatherly, silver-haired station manager. In addition to the bed-hopping, there was much agonizing over journalistic ethics, even as people's lives were destroyed by the station's aggressive pursuit of ratings-grabbing stories.

This Canadian-produced series was aired by Lifetime daily at 7:00 P.M. for only a few months before it was banished into the wee hours—a victim of the ratings Mike dreaded.

E/R (*Situation Comedy*)
FIRST TELECAST: *September 16, 1984*
LAST TELECAST: *July 24, 1985*
BROADCAST HISTORY:
Sep 1984, CBS Sun 8:00–9:00
Sep 1984–Oct 1984, CBS Tue 8:30–9:00
Nov 1984–Apr 1985, CBS Wed 8:30–9:00
Apr 1985, CBS Sat 8:30–9:00
Jun 1985–Jul 1985, CBS Wed 8:30–9:00
CAST:
Dr. Howard Sheinfeld .... Elliott Gould
Dr. Eve Sheridan (pilot only) ..... Marcia Strassman
Dr. Eve Sheridan .... Mary McDonnell
Nurse Joan Thor .... Conchata Ferrell
Nurse Julie Williams .... Lynne Moody

Maria Amardo .... Shuko Akune
Nurse Cory Smith .... Corinne Bohrer
Off. Fred Burdock .... Bruce A. Young
Dr. Thomas Esquivel .... Luis Avalos
Harold Stickley.................... Jason Alexander
Ace................................ George Clooney
Richard, the orderly .... William G. Schilling
Bert, the paramedic .... Jeff Doucette

Chicago's Clark Street Hospital was the setting for this comedy about the staff and patients populating the hospital's emergency room. Howard Sheinfeld was the sarcastic, talkative doctor who oversaw most of the emergency-room treatment. An ear-nose-and-throat specialist, he moonlighted at Clark Street Hospital doing 48-hour shifts to help him keep up with alimony payments to two ex-wives. Eve, his no-nonsense boss at the hospital, wished he would take things a little more seriously and not work such long shifts. Harold Stickley was the hospital administrator and Ace the inexperienced young physician recently assigned to emergency-room duty. Joan Thor was the head nurse, Julie her industrious assistant, and Cory the perpetually confused floater nurse. Maria was the lazy, smart-mouthed receptionist, and Fred was her boyfriend. Into their emergency room came a constant stream of the sick and the injured, some with minor problems and others in critical condition, in this awkward mixture of gag comedy and serious illness.

ER (*Medical Drama*)

FIRST TELECAST: *September 19, 1994*
LAST TELECAST:
BROADCAST HISTORY:

Sep 1994, NBC Mon 9:00–11:00
Sep 1994–Feb 1997, NBC Thu 10:00–11:00
Apr 1997– , NBC Thu 10:00–11:00

CAST:

Dr. Mark Greene (1994–2002) ... Anthony Edwards
Dr. Douglas Ross (1994–1999) ..... George Clooney
Dr. Susan Lewis (1994–1996, 2001–) .... Sherry Stringfield
Dr. Peter Benton (1994–2001).......... Eriq LaSalle
Dr. John Carter........................ Noah Wyle
Dr. David Morgenstern (1994–1998) .... William H. Macy
Head Nurse Carol Hathaway (1994–2000) .... Julianna Margulies
Jerry Markovic (1994–1999, 2002–) .... Abraham Benrubi
**Jennifer Greene/Simon* .... Christine Harnos
Dr. John Taglieri (1994–1995) ...... Rick Rossovich
**Dr. "Div" Cvetic (1994)*................. John Terry
***Nurse Lydia Wright*................ Ellen Crawford
***Nurse Connie Oligario*...... Conni Marie Brazleton
Nurse Haleh Adams .... Yvette Freeman
Nurse Wendy Goldman (1994–1997) .... Vanessa Marquez
Dr. Angela Hicks (1994–1997) .... CCH Pounder
**Mae Benton (1994–1995)* .... Beah Richards
Chloe Lewis (1994–1995)........ Kathleen Wilhoite
Timmy (1994–1995)............... Glenn Plummer
Nurse Malik McGrath .... Deezer D.
Doris Pickman .... Emily Wagner
Nurse Lily Jarvik...................... Lily Mariye
**Rachel Greene (1994–2000)*.......... Yvonne Zima
**Rachel Greene (2001–2002)*........... Hallee Hirsh
Dr. William Swift (1995) .... Michael Ironside
Jeanie Boulet (1995–1999) .... Gloria Reuben
**Al Boulet (1995–1997)*............... Michael Beach
Dr. Kerry Weaver (1995–)............ Laura Innes
Nurse Chuny Marquez (1995–)...... Laura Ceron
**Dr. Carl Vucelich (1995–1996)* .... Ron Rifkin
Harper Tracy (1995–1996) .... Christine Elise
Ray "Shep" Shepard (1995–1996) ...... Ron Eldard
Pamela Olbes, EMS (1995–) .... Lynn Henderson
Dr. Jing-Mei (Deb) Chen (1995, 2000–) .. Ming-Na
***Dwight Zadro, EMS (1995–)* ...... Monte Russell
***Randi (1995–)*.................... Kristin Minter
**Shirley (1995–)*................... Dinah Lenney
Dr. Abby Keaton (1996–1997)....... Glenne Headly
**Dr. Dennis Gant (1996–1997)* .... Omar Epps
**Carla Reese/Simmons (1996–)* .... Lisa Nicole Carson
***Dr. Donald Anspaugh (1996–)*..... John Aylward
Dr. Maggie Doyle (1996–1999) .... Jorja Fox
***Dumar, EMS (1996–)* .... Brian Lester
Cynthia Hooper (1997–1998) .... Mariska Hargitay
Dr. Anna Del Amico (1997–1998) ...... Maria Bello
Dr. Elizabeth Corday (1997–)...... Alex Kingston
Dr. Robert "Rocket" Romano (1997–) .... Paul McCrane
Lars Audia, EMS (1997–1999) .... J. P. Hubbell
***Yosh (1997–)* .... Gedde Watanabe
Lucy Knight (1998–2000)............. Kellie Martin
**Gabe Morales, EMS (1998–)* .. Demetrius Navarro
**Off. Reggie Moore (1998–2000)* ..... Cress Williams
David Greene (1999–2000) .... John Cullum
Dr. Dave Malucci (1999–2001)....... Erik Palladino
Dr. Luka Kovak (1999–)........... Goran Visnjic
**Harms (1999–)*................. Michelle Bonilla
**Reese (1999–2001)* .... Matthew Watkins
Abby Lockhart (2000–)........... Maura Tierney
Frank (2000–)........................ Troy Evans
Dr. Cleo Finch (2000–2001)....... Michael Michele
Dr. Kim Legaspi (2000–2001).... Elizabeth Mitchell
Michael Gallant (2002–) .... Sharif Atkins
Dr. Gregory Pratt (2002–) .... Mekhi Phifer

*Occasional
**Occasional in some seasons.

CREATOR/CO-EXECUTIVE PRODUCER:
Michael Crichton

This intense yet traditional medical series, set in the emergency room of Chicago's County General Hospital, was the surprise hit of the 1994–1995 season. Perhaps it had simply been too long since TV had a good, by-the-book doctor show. Though *ER* broke no new dramatic ground, it oozed adrenaline, projecting the breathless, high-pressure environment in which a group of young doctors struggled to save lives while trying to maintain their own emotional balance. There was a great deal of yelling and running down corridors, as blood spurted and doctors rattled off diagnoses ("Anterior and lateral right lower extremity, femur articulation, patella, tibia, fibula all appear normal!").

Rushing about were Ross, the womanizing, dreamboat pediatrician at the center of much of the action, both in the ER and out; Greene, the earnest chief resident, whose job stress was augmented by that of his home life with his demanding lawyer-wife, Jennifer; Lewis, the straight-arrow resident still looking for Mr. Right; Benton, the brusque, demanding black supersurgeon; Carter, the wide-eyed, sometimes inept (though not when it really counted) first-year resident assigned to Benton; Hathaway, the troubled chief nurse, who nearly OD'd in the first episode; and Morgenstern, the predictably crusty head of the ER (replaced by Swift in the spring of 1995).

Stories mostly revolved around the tangled romantic relationships of the doctors and staff, set against their heroics in the ER. During the first two years Greene's wife left, returned, and eventually left again, for good. Lewis had a fling with manic-depressive Cvetic, then adopted her drug-addicted sister Chloe's abandoned daughter, fighting to keep the child when the "cleaned up" Chole returned with her husband. Hathaway became engaged to Taglieri, but dumped him at the altar, later taking up with playful paramedic Shep. Benton, in between terrorizing interns, had to deal with his deteriorating mother, Mae, hiring physical therapist Boulet to look after her. Ross slept with almost every female in sight, his personal irresponsibility nearly getting him fired on several occasions. His heroism in a pinch always saved the day, however.

During the second season the rapidly maturing Carter became a doctor, and had an affair with intern Tracy. Benton joined eminent Dr. Vucelich in his research work, only to discover the latter was faking test results; turning on him almost cost Benton his job. He sought solace in Boulet's arms, only to learn that she was HIV-positive due to her philandering husband. Fortunately, she had not infected Benton.

In the 1996 season Greene pursued Lewis, who departed for Arizona, leaving him to play the field. At the end of the season he was severely beaten by an unknown assailant, who was apparently angry over the death of a patient in his care. Hard-driving Benton had a tough year. Dismissed from a prestigious team by Keaton, he caused the suicide of a young intern, Gant, then found himself the father of Carla's baby Reese, who was born deaf. Ross's downward spiral continued as a one-night stand died while with him, and he was forced to tell the authorities he didn't even know her name. He attempted to redeem himself by helping a 14-year-old escape prostitution, but botched it. The 1997 season began with a highly publicized live telecast, in which a documentary film crew followed Greene around the ER. Benton cared for his deaf baby, while working for the manipulative Romano and having an interracial affair with English surgeon Corday. Carter had a tempestuous relationship with Del Amico, while Chief Resident Weaver faced a crisis when she was forced by new hospital boss Anspaugh to lay off staff. She started with Boulet, which was a mistake, since the latter claimed discrimination (due to her HIV-positive condition) and forced the hospital to reinstate her. Ross got into his most serious trouble yet when he and Hathaway performed an unauthorized ultrarapid detox of a methodone-addicted infant. Put on probation, he then helped a dying boy end his life, and was threatened with a murder charge. Early in 1999 he left the hospital, hoping that Hathaway would go with him, but she didn't. Also in the 1998–1999 season, Hathaway opened a clinic; Carter found himself supervising a wide-eyed resident (Knight); Corday broke up with Benton and was demoted to intern by the vengeful Romano; and bad-luck Boulet learned she had hepatitis C, as well as being HIV-positive.

During the 1999–2000 season Romano was promoted to chief of staff, wielding his new power with a vengeance. Weaver became chief of the ER, Boulet and Moore were married, Hathaway gave birth to twins, Chen returned (and eventually became chief resident), Greene dealt with his dying father, nutty "Dr. Dave" Malucci caused an uproar, and Knight and Carter were stabbed by a deranged patient. Knight died and Carter took time to recover, struggling with a drug addiction problem brought on by the trauma. The most dramatic development of 2000–2001 was no doubt Greene's discovery that he had a brain tumor; girlfriend Corday stayed by his side through the treatment, and in April they were married. Shortly thereafter she gave birth to baby Ella. Chen had a baby (which she put up for adoption), Weaver announced she was a lesbian and Lewis returned to the ER after a five-year absence.

The 2001–2002 season was pivotal for Benton and Greene, both of whom had been mainstays of *ER* since the beginning. Carla died in an accident and Benton discovered that he was not the biological father of her son Reese after all. He won a nasty custody dispute, but Romano refused to let him work reduced hours while he raised the deaf boy. Forced to choose between his son and the ER, he quit in December and moved with girlfriend Finch to the suburbs. Greene's ending was tragic. After a short period of remission, his brain tumor returned and was diagnosed as inoperable. With only a few months to live, he moved to Hawaii with his estranged 14-year-old daughter Rachel, hoping to spend his last days reconnecting with her and revisiting the scenes of his youth. Corday had left him, but at the end she returned and he died quietly in his sleep.

During 2002–2003 Romano was seriously injured and forced to stop performing surgery, leading to the promotion of Weaver.

Created by best-selling author Michael Crichton (*Jurassic Park, Rising Sun*) and based on his own experiences as a medical student at Massachusetts General Hospital.

E.S.P. (*Audience Participation/Anthology*)
FIRST TELECAST: *July 11, 1958*
LAST TELECAST: *August 22, 1958*
BROADCAST HISTORY:
Jul 1958–Aug 1958, ABC Fri 9:00–9:30
EMCEE/HOST:
Vincent Price

E.S.P. premiered as a contest show to determine the amount of extrasensory perception possessed by contestants, all of whom were first screened by a staff of psychologists. After only three telecasts the quiz format was replaced by dramas entitled *Tales of E.S.P.*, which depicted people with the abilities that the quiz show had been trying to find. Vincent Price was host of both programs.

ESPN (Network) (*Sports Cable Network*)
LAUNCHED:
September 7, 1979
SUBSCRIBERS (MAY 2003):
86.4 million (81% U.S.)

One of the best-known cable networks, ESPN is a 24-hour sports channel available on virtually every cable system in the country. Over the years it has offered increasing numbers of high-profile events that were once exclusive to the broadcast networks. Two landmark acquisitions were NFL Sunday night games in 1987 and an extensive schedule of major-league baseball games in 1990. Among its other highlights are NHL hockey (including the Stanley Cup Playoffs), NCAA basketball, tennis, golf, boxing, and NASCAR auto racing.

ESPN's schedule is dominated by event coverage, leaving little room for "regular series" as defined in this book. Its best-known series is probably its sports newscast, *SportsCenter* (1979). Other series that have been seen occasionally include *Max Out* (videos), *Up Close* (discussion), and *Sports on Tap* (quiz). In 2002 ESPN presented its first original movie, *Season on the Brink,* about controversial Indiana basketball coach Bobby Knight.

In October 1993 ESPN launched a second network, called ESPN2, specializing in "extreme" sports and presented with a youthful attitude. It is currently seen in more than 80 million homes. Other subsidiary networks are ESPN Classic (sporting events of the past, 1995), ESPNews (sports news, 1996), ESPN Now (barker channel, 1999) and ESPN Today (interactive information, 2001). The initials ESPN originally stood for "Entertainment & Sports Programming Network."

E! TRUE HOLLYWOOD STORY (*Documentary*)

BROADCAST HISTORY:

E! Entertainment
60/120 minutes
Original episodes: *1996–*
Premiered: c. *October 25, 1996*

NARRATORS:

Michael Bell
Phil Crowley
Owen Wilson

Tabloid documentary that promised "the inside scoop on Tinseltown's steamiest secrets," and largely delivered, drawing a substantial audience to the young E! cable network. Early episodes set the tone, including bios of Rebecca Schaeffer (died young), Sam Kinison (died young), River Phoenix (died younger), Natalie Wood (died glamorous), Elvis (died rich), and Macaulay Culkin ("A Child's Rise, A Family's Fall"). Later the series began to mix in "show-ographies" of popular TV series, including behind-the-scenes scandals on *The Facts of Life, Growing Pains,* and *Survivor.* Even sunny show-business icons sometimes got the THS treatment ("Doris Day—Anguish, drama, pain and heartbreak!"). The number one THS profile of all time, according to one poll of the series' discerning viewers, was that of Princess Diana (who died young, rich, *and* glamorous).

E! True Hollywood Story began in the fall of 1996 as a monthly special, expanding to weekly telecasts in April 1998 and later to seemingly every night.

EZ STREETS (*Drama*)

FIRST TELECAST: *October 27, 1996*
LAST TELECAST: *April 2, 1997*

BROADCAST HISTORY:

Oct 1996, CBS Sun 9:00–11:00
Oct 1996, CBS Wed 10:00–11:00
Mar 1997–Apr 1997, CBS 10:00–11:00

CAST:

Det. Cameron Quinn .... Ken Olin
Daniel Rooney .... Jason Gedrick
Jimmy Murtha .... Joe Pantoliano
Theresa Conners .... Debrah Farentino
Captain Geary .... John Finn
Det. Frank Collero .... Richard Portnow
Mickey Kinnear .... Mike Starr
Michael "Fivers" Dugan .... R.D. Call
Elli Rooney .... Sarah Trigger
Mayor Christian Davidson (1997) ..... Carl Lumbly
Christina Quinn .... Rosemary Murphy
Sammy Feathers .... Saverio Guerra
Janie .... Courtney Jacquin
Bobby .... Robert Spillane
Shirt .... Andrew Rothenberg
Bo .... John St. Ryan
Councilman Eeling (1997) .... Gregg Henry
Leo (1997) .... Jack McGee
Fat Man (1997) .... Louis Lombardi

This richly textured crime drama focused on the activities of three men—Cameron Quinn, Danny Rooney, and Jimmy Murtha—living in an unnamed, run-down northern city. Quinn was a police detective who had joined the intelligence division to clear his name after being categorized as a "dirty" cop. He worked undercover for Captain Geary, infiltrating the local underworld. Quinn's prime target, and the man he tried to get close to, was Murtha, an extremely vicious young hood whose rise in the ranks of the mob had been helped by his sexy, unscrupulous attorney, Theresa Conners. She was adept at using every legal loophole and ploy to keep him out of jail. Murtha's primary competition, the guy who ran the other mob in town, was Michael Dugan. Rooney had just gotten out of jail after taking the rap for a robbery he hadn't committed, but despite his desire to go straight, was forced to go to work for his childhood friend Murtha to make a living. He hoped the dirty money would help him get back together with his estranged, drug-addicted wife, Elli, and their young daughter, Janie. Even the proud black mayor was under the thumb of the mob. All of the principals on *EZ Streets* were flawed, with both good and bad sides. Even Murtha, who seemed to be evil incarnate, had one positive goal: to save his neighborhood. The relationships were complex but didn't have a lot of time to develop.

Among the series' other memorable features was the barren, hopeless look of the bombed-out inner city (the title referred to the slums between "E" and "Z" streets), and its distinctive music, consisting in part of Celtic folk songs sung by ethereal soprano Loreena McKennitt. To some it was depressing and self-consciously arty, to others, simply "too good for TV." Predictably, critics loved it but viewers shunned it like the plague. It premiered as a two-hour Sunday movie special and aired just once in its regular time slot before being yanked from the CBS schedule. It was relaunched the following spring but again failed to find an audience and was canceled after six more episodes.

EARL WRIGHTSON SHOW, THE (*Music*)

FIRST TELECAST: *November 27, 1948*
LAST TELECAST: *February 21, 1952*

BROADCAST HISTORY:

Nov 1948–Jan 1949, ABC Sat 7:45–8:00
Jan 1949–Apr 1949, ABC Mon 7:15–7:30
Sep 1949–Jun 1950, CBS Wed 7:45–8:00
Sep 1950–Jun 1951, CBS Mon 11:00–11:15
Aug 1951–Feb 1952, ABC Thu 10:30–10:45

REGULARS:

Earl Wrightson

Buddy Weed, piano and trio (1948–1949)

Norman Paris Trio and Orchestra (1949–1951)

Concert baritone Earl Wrightson was a familiar figure in the early days of television, appearing on his own 15-minute program of songs on both ABC and CBS. Wrightson's forte was Broadway show tunes and music from operettas such as *The Student Prince* and *H.M.S. Pinafore*, and he performed these in program segments called "Spotlight on Showtime" and "Masland Showtime." Guest stars were also featured.

The title of this program changed several times, from the original *Earl Wrightson Show* to *Earl Wrightson at Home* (September 1949), *At Home* (October 1949), *At Home Show* (September 1950), and finally, in honor of the sponsor, *Masland at Home Party* (August 1951).

In later years Wrightson made frequent guest appearances on other programs.

EARLY EDITION (*Fantasy/Adventure*)

FIRST TELECAST: *September 28, 1996*
LAST TELECAST: *June 3, 2000*
BROADCAST HISTORY:

Sep 1996–Jan 1998, CBS Sat 9:00–10:00
Apr 1998–Jun 1998, CBS Sat 9:00–10:00
Jul 1998–Jun 2000, CBS Sat 8:00–9:00

CAST:

Gary Hobson .... Kyle Chandler
Marissa Clark .... Shanesia Davis-Williams
Chuck Fishman (1996–1998) .... Fisher Stevens
Pete, the Bartender (1996–1997) .... Mike Houlihan
Det. Marion Crumb (1996–1998) .... Ron Dean
Boswell (1996–1997) .... James Deuter
Erica Paget (1998–1999) .... Kristy Swanson
Henry Paget (1998–1999) .... Myles Jeffrey
Patrick Quinn (1998–1999) .... Billie Worley

Gary was a young Chicago stockbroker whose life was in a shambles. He'd just been fired from a job he hated, his wife had thrown him out, and he was living in a single room in a run-down hotel. Then, one morning, everything changed. He woke up to find a mysterious cat outside his door sitting on a copy of the *Chicago Sun Times*—a paper that contained the next day's news (the cat would continue to do so every day thereafter). Advance knowledge of what was going to happen left Gary with two choices: use his "inside information" to make himself rich, or try to change other people's lives for the better. Despite the urging of his avaricious friend Chuck, Gary took the latter course, trying to help people and prevent disasters from happening. Marissa, a blind former co-worker, served as his moral compass, offering sounder suggestions than Chuck's selfish advice. With their help, Gary set out to prevent the bad news he read in his daily "Early Edition" of the paper from happening. When he changed things, the next edition of the paper would reveal what the result of his actions had been—sometimes necessitating further intervention. Spike was Marissa's guide dog. Gary's hangout was McGinty's, a friendly neighborhood bar.

In the 1997–1998 season premiere the hotel in which Gary had been living burned down and McGinty's was almost sold to a land developer who planned to replace it with a parking lot—but Gary and Chuck took it over instead. In the spring, when police detective Crumb retired, he took a part-time job as bartender at McGinty's. Chuck moved to Hollywood in the summer of 1998 to become a producer so Gary made Marissa his partner and hired Erica, a divorcée with a young son, Henry, to manage the bar. Patrick was the college-student bartender who worked for them. In November a broke Chuck returned, hoping to film Gary saving people and use the footage to sell Hollywood the concept of a guy who got the news a day early. After Gary saved him from a potential accident he went back and sold a series of cheerleader movies to CBS. In the May 1999 season finale Erica, who had been dating Gary, decided that the only way to break things off was to leave Chicago.

That October well-meaning but incompetent Patrick left to become an elementary school teacher in Bend, Oregon. Chuck showed up a couple of times, and former nemesis Marion Crumb, now a private detective, appeared in a few episodes the following spring.

EARN YOUR VACATION (*Quiz/Audience Participation*)

FIRST TELECAST: *May 23, 1954*
LAST TELECAST: *September 5, 1954*
BROADCAST HISTORY:

May 1954–Sep 1954, CBS Sun 7:00–7:30

EMCEE:

Johnny Carson

Young comedian Johnny Carson hosted this summer quiz show, which asked members of the studio audience where they would most like to go on a vacation and why. The people with the most interesting answers won the chance to become contestants and answer a series of four progressively more difficult questions, which could win them their dream vacation.

EARTH: FINAL CONFLICT, see *Gene Roddenberry's Earth: Final Conflict*

EARTH 2 (*Science Fiction*)

FIRST TELECAST: *November 6, 1994*
LAST TELECAST: *May 28, 1995*
BROADCAST HISTORY:

Nov 1994–May 1995, NBC Sun 7:00–8:00

CAST:

Devon Adair .... Debrah Farentino
Ulysses Adair .... Joey Zimmerman
John Danziger .... Clancy Brown
True Brown .... J. Madison Wright
Dr. Julia Heller .... Jessica Steen
Yale .... Sullivan Walker
Alonzo Solace .... Antonio Sabato, Jr.
Morgan Martin .... John Gegenhuber
Bess Martin .... Rebecca Gayheart

Steven Spielberg's Amblin Studios produced this rather slow-moving cross between a soap opera and *Lost in Space*. It was set 200 years in the future, a time when Earth's pollution had forced humans to live in confining space stations and produced a generation of children who were sick from the lack of a normal environment. Hoping to help her young son Ulysses (who already had to wear clumsy life-support apparatus), courageous scientist Devon Adair hijacked a spaceship and with an intrepid group of adventurers set off for an unspoiled, Earth-like planet that promised a new beginning. Devon's little band included John, a high-tech mechanic, and his resourceful preteen daughter, True; Julia, the group's physician, who turned out to be a spy; Yale, a cyborg; Alonzo, a cocky but gifted pilot; Morgan, a conniving, cowardly government agent; and Morgan's young wife, Bess.

Unfortunately they crash-landed on the wrong side of the planet, so the pioneers patched together their remaining equipment and set off in their big red Hummer vehicle on the long journey to their target destination, New Pacifica, where other humans were supposed to be waiting. Along the way they encountered a variety of bizarre life forms, who looked threatening but were not necessarily unfriendly. Among them were the Terrians, corpselike dwellers of the underground who communicated with them through Alonzo's dreams; Grendlers, raggedy, slobbering scavengers; and little Kobas, who were cute but potentially lethal. Most of the stories were moralistic, about caring, trusting, and how Earth 2 and its denizens will be good to us if we can only be good to them.

EAST SIDE/WEST SIDE (*Drama*)
FIRST TELECAST: *September 23, 1963*
LAST TELECAST: *September 14, 1964*
BROADCAST HISTORY:
Sep 1963–Sep 1964, CBS Mon 10:00–11:00
CAST:
Neil Brock .... George C. Scott
Frieda Hechlinger .... Elizabeth Wilson
Jane Foster .... Cicely Tyson

This dramatic series starred George C. Scott as Neil Brock, a young social worker in the New York slums. The stories involved child abuse, the welfare syndrome, problems of aging, drug addiction, and crime, situations all too familiar to Neil Brock in his daily routine. Frieda Hechlinger was the head of the welfare agency branch for which he worked, and Jane Foster was the office secretary. Critics appreciated the gritty realism of this series in the midst of TV's land of make-believe, but its downbeat subjects proved deadly with viewers and it was dropped after a single season.

EASY ACES (*Humor*)
FIRST TELECAST: *December 14, 1949*
LAST TELECAST: *June 14, 1950*
BROADCAST HISTORY:
Dec 1949–Jun 1950, DUM Wed 7:45–8:00
REGULARS:
Goodman Ace
Jane Ace
Betty Garde

This was a video version of the longtime radio favorite, featuring Goodman and Jane Ace in comedy chatter. As on radio, "Ace" was his witty, intelligent self, and his wife, Jane, was a charming bundle of malapropisms. *Easy Aces* went on the DuMont network in December 1949, but lasted for only six months. Goodman Ace went on to make a much greater impression on the new medium as a top comedy writer for such stars as Perry Como.

Easy Aces was filmed, and was syndicated to other local stations even while it was on the DuMont network.

EASY DOES IT . . . STARRING FRANKIE AVALON (*Musical Variety*)
FIRST TELECAST: *August 25, 1976*
LAST TELECAST: *September 15, 1976*
BROADCAST HISTORY:
Aug 1976–Sep 1976, CBS Wed 8:30–9:00
REGULARS:
Frankie Avalon
Annette Funicello
The War Babies (Marsha Meyers, Susan Nesbitt, Tim Reid, Renny Temple)
Vic Glazer

Frankie Avalon, a pop singer and star of numerous "beach-party" movies in the early 1960s, was the star of this four-week mini-series. With him each week was Annette Funicello, his co-star in several of those movies. In addition to the musical numbers, the show featured blackouts and silly comedy sketches with an improvisational group, The War Babies. Also on camera, in many of the sketches, was the show's musical director, Vic Glazer.

EASY STREET (*Situation Comedy*)
FIRST TELECAST: *September 15, 1986*
LAST TELECAST: *May 27, 1987*
BROADCAST HISTORY:
Sep 1986, NBC Sat 9:30–10:00
Sep 1986–Nov 1986, NBC Sun 8:00–8:30
Nov 1986–Mar 1987, NBC Sun 8:30–9:00
Mar 1987–Apr 1987, NBC Tue 9:30–10:00
Apr 1987–May 1987, NBC Wed 9:30–10:00
CAST:
L.K. McGuire .... Loni Anderson
Uncle Alvin "Bully" Stevenson .... Jack Elam
Ricardo Williams .... Lee Weaver
Eleanor Standard .... Dana Ivey
Quentin Standard .... James Cromwell
Bobby, the butler .... Arthur Malet
THEME:
"Easy Street" (1941 popular song)

This routine clash-of-cultures comedy starred Loni Anderson as a former Las Vegas showgirl who had married a rich playboy ("we were really in love"), and promptly inherited half of his Beverly Hills mansion when he unexpectedly died. The other half was owned and occupied by L.K.'s snooty sister-in-law Eleanor and her milquetoast husband, Quentin, who wished L.K. was out of the house—and their lives. Also sharing the manse was L.K.'s only living relative, elderly Uncle Bully, and his pal Ricardo, who had been pried out of their run-down retirement home to come keep her company in the lonely lap of luxury. Bully and Ricardo's earthy ways vs. Eleanor's pretensions formed the basis of most of the comedy.

EBERT & ROEPER AND THE MOVIES, see *Siskel & Ebert*

ED (*Comedy/Drama*)
FIRST TELECAST: *October 8, 2000*
LAST TELECAST:
BROADCAST HISTORY:
Oct 2000–Nov 2000, NBC Sun 8:00–9:00
Dec 2000–Aug 2001, NBC Wed 8:00–9:00
Oct 2001–Mar 2003, NBC Wed 8:00–9:00
Mar 2003–Apr 2003, NBC Fri 9:00–10:00
CAST:
Ed Stevens .... Tom Cavanagh
Carol Vessey .... Julie Bowen
Dr. Mike Burton .... Josh Randall

Nancy Burton .... Jana Marie Hupp
Molly Hudson .... Lesley Boone
Phil Stubbs .... Michael Ian Black
Shirley Pifgo .... Rachel Cronin
Kenny Sandusky (2000–2002) .... Mike Starr
Warren Cheswick .... Justin Long
**Dr. Walter R. Jerome* .... Marvin Chatinover
**Principal Dennis Martino (2001–2002)*
.... John Slattery
Mark Vanacore (2001–) ..... Michael R. Genadry
Diane Snyder (2001–) .... Ginnifer Goodwin
Eli Goggins (2002–) .... Daryl "Chill" Mitchell
Frankie Hector (2003–) .... Sabrina Lloyd

*Occasional

Ed was a tall, goofy New York attorney who, after being fired and finding his wife cheating on him—both on the same day—decided it was time to start over. He moved to his small hometown of Stuckeyville, Ohio, to pursue the pretty girl he had adored in high school, but whom he had always been too shy to ask out. Carol, a teacher and an aspiring writer, was romantically involved with someone else and wasn't interested. But Ed hung around, buying the local bowling alley, the Stuckeyville Bowl, on a whim and setting up his practice there. He reunited with his school chum Mike, now a doctor married to busy Nancy, and met the staff of his new business: ever-scamming manager Phil, slightly dense Shirley, who tended the food-and-beverage counter, and amiable Kenny, the handyman. Molly was Carol's chubby, brassy best friend and fellow teacher, Warren an awkward student who reminded Ed of his own younger self, and Dr. Jerome the bossy older doctor with whom Mike shared his practice (and who, it seemed, was never going to retire). Mark was a chubby student who competed with Warren for the affections of pretty Diane.

Stories involved Ed's offbeat cases, the town's eccentric citizens, life at the Stuckeyville Bowl ("I'm done bowling. Let's redo my will") and Ed's continuing pursuit of Carol. Sometimes they would start to get together, then break up and date others. During 2002 she became engaged to Dennis, the school principal, and in the fall they made it all the way to the altar before the ceremony was canceled. Ed and Carol continued their mating dance, with Ed taking up with young law school grad Frankie, making Carol jealous. Also during the 2002–2003 season, Kenny left Stuckeyville (after bowling a perfect game) and Ed hired a "supervising manager," Eli.

ED, EDD AND EDDY (*Cartoon*)

BROADCAST HISTORY:

Cartoon Network
30 minutes
Produced: *1998–*
Premiered: *November 16, 1998*

VOICES:

Ed .... Matt Hill
Edd ("Double D") .... Samuel Vincent
Eddy .... Tony Sampson

The loud, manic adventures of three teenage boys named "Ed." Ed was the tall, dumb one with spiked hair; Edd the smart, sensible one who usually figured a way out of the scrapes they got into; and Eddy the short, excitable leader who got them into trouble in the first place. Various other kids were seen in their suburban neighborhood.

ED McMAHON'S NEXT BIG STAR (*Talent*)

FIRST TELECAST: *September 9, 2001*
LAST TELECAST: *August 25, 2002*
BROADCAST HISTORY:

Sep 2001–Aug 2002, PAX Sun 6:00–7:00
Sep 2001, PAX Sat 7:00–8:00

HOST:

Ed McMahon

Six years after his long-running *Star Search* left the air, white-haired, avuncular Ed McMahon returned with this big, glossy talent show that originated from the MGM Grand Hotel in Las Vegas. Professionals and semi-pros competed in singing, dancing, comedy and modeling categories. Each contest cycle started with six weeks of preliminary competition, followed by quarter-finals, semi-finals and the finals.

There were open auditions in cities around the country, bus tours looking for young talent, and a Web site, Nextbigstar.com, where hopefuls could register to compete. Visitors to the site could view auditions and vote for their favorite performers.

ED SULLIVAN SHOW, THE (*Variety*)

FIRST TELECAST: *June 20, 1948*
LAST TELECAST: *June 6, 1971*
BROADCAST HISTORY:

Jun 1948, CBS Sun 9:00–10:00
Jul 1948–Aug 1948, CBS Sun 9:30–10:30
Aug 1948–Mar 1949, CBS Sun 9:00–10:00
Mar 1949–Jun 1971, CBS Sun 8:00–9:00

REGULARS:

Ed Sullivan
Ray Bloch and His Orchestra
The June Taylor Dancers

If any program in the history of American television could be called an institution, it would probably be *The Ed Sullivan Show.* Every Sunday night for more than two decades this homely newspaper columnist with peculiar diction and awkward gestures brought an incredible variety of entertainment into American homes. No pandering to the lowest common denominator here—there was grand opera and the latest rock stars, classical ballet and leggy Broadway showgirls, slapstick comedy and recitations from great dramatic writings, often juxtaposed on a single telecast. Viewers loved it.

It began simply enough. Originally titled *Toast of the Town* (it was going to be called *You're the Top,* but that title was dropped before the first telecast), the program was one of many variety shows on early television—most of which had noticeably short lives. The first telecast, in the summer of 1948, was produced on a meager budget of $1,375. Only $375 was allocated for talent, and the two young stars of that show, Dean Martin and Jerry Lewis, split the lion's share of that—$200. But Ed had class. Also on that first telecast was concert pianist Eugene List, Richard Rodgers and Oscar Hammerstein II, and the six original June Taylor Dancers (then called the Toastettes). The critics of the early Sullivan shows were not kind. They complained about his deadpan delivery, his lack of any noticeable talent as a performer, and the strange collections of acts he put together for a single program. That very variety, and a newspaperman's nose for "events," made Sullivan's show a resounding success. The format only seemed to be that of an old-fashioned vaudeville revue (Ed himself stoutly denied that it was "vaudeo"). Where in vaudeville would you have the Bolshoi Ballet one week, scenes from a hit Broadway show with the original cast on another, and dancing bears on a third?

Numerous performers made their American television debuts on the show, including Charles Laughton, Bob Hope, Lena Horne, Martin and Lewis, Dinah Shore, Eddie Fisher, the Beatles, and Walt Disney. Disney's appearance was ironic. He was featured in a full-hour special edition of *Toast of the Town* on February 8, 1953. The following year he began his own show, on ABC, and it was that program that finally surpassed *Ed Sullivan* as the longest-running prime-time network show. It will be noted that Elvis Presley is missing from the above list of firsts. Although he is best remembered for his appearances on *The Ed Sullivan Show* in the fall of 1956, Elvis actually made his TV debut in January 1956, on Tommy and Jimmy Dorsey's *Stage Show*. No matter. To play Sullivan was to make headlines, and Presley's appearance just at the moment he was revolutionizing popular music did just that. So did the Beatles seven years later.

In addition to the firsts, virtually every "name" act in American music, comedy, theater, and film appeared over the years. There were also a few who never did make it out from under Ed's wing: Topo Gigio, the mechanical Italian mouse, and Señor Wences and his talking box ("S-all right?" "S-all right!"). Those celebrities not appearing on the stage were in the audience. To be picked out by Ed from the stage and introduced on nationwide television was a high honor indeed.

Sullivan's mannerisms became legendary, the butt of a thousand comics. He himself participated in a parody record called "It's a Reeally Big SHEW Tonight!" in the mid-1950s, and his program was brilliantly satirized in the Broadway musical *Bye Bye Birdie* in the early 1960s—in which an all-American family reaches spiritual ecstasy when they learn, "We're going to be on . . . Ed Sullivan!"

The show itself changed little over the years, though its scope certainly widened. The title was changed officially to *The Ed Sullivan Show* on September 18, 1955. Some telecasts and segments originated from foreign countries, including Japan, the Soviet Union, Italy, France, England, Spain, Portugal, Ireland, Mexico, Israel, Cuba, and Hong Kong. Some shows were mini-spectaculars, such as the 90-minute tribute to songwriter Irving Berlin, which ended in true Sullivan fashion with a huge American flag in fireworks and the entire cast singing "God Bless America."

Sullivan's run finally ended in 1971, the victim not so much of falling ratings as of a desire by CBS to "modernize" its programming (Ed's appeal had increasingly been to older viewers). There followed some Ed Sullivan specials and a 25th-anniversary special in 1973, but shortly thereafter Sullivan was dead. He will not soon be forgotten.

ED WYNN SHOW, THE (*Comedy/Variety*)

FIRST TELECAST: *October 6, 1949*
LAST TELECAST: *July 4, 1950*
BROADCAST HISTORY:
Oct 1949–Dec 1949, CBS Thu 9:00–9:30
Jan 1950–Mar 1950, CBS Sat 9:00–9:30
Apr 1950–Jul 1950, CBS Tue 9:00–9:30
REGULARS:
Ed Wynn
Lud Gluskin

One year after being named by his fellow comedians as "the greatest visual comedian of our day," and more than 40 years after he began his career in vaudeville, Ed Wynn became a regular television performer with his own variety show. Although the show had guest stars, its main focus was Ed himself, in his giggling "Perfect Fool" characterization and in other roles he had created over the years on stage and radio. Ed's guests included many of the great names in film comedy. Ben Blue, Buster Keaton, Lucille Ball and Desi Arnaz (before *I Love Lucy*), Leon Errol, the Three Stooges (Moe Howard, Shemp Howard, and Larry Fine), Joe E. Brown, Ben Wrigley, and Marie Wilson all made guest appearances on the show.

The Ed Wynn Show was the first regular show to originate from Hollywood, carried live on the West Coast and kinescoped for rebroadcast from New York to the CBS Eastern and Midwest networks. This was the reverse of the normal procedure of that day, in which live shows were aired from New York and had kinescoped repeats fed from Hollywood.

ED WYNN SHOW, THE (*Situation Comedy*)

FIRST TELECAST: *September 25, 1958*
LAST TELECAST: *January 1, 1959*
BROADCAST HISTORY:
Sep 1958–Jan 1959, NBC Thu 8:00–8:30
CAST:
John Beamer . . . . Ed Wynn
Laurie . . . . Jacklyn O'Donnell
Midge . . . . Sherry Alberoni
Ernest Henshaw . . . . Herb Vigran

Ed Wynn came out of semi-retirement to make one final try at a regular series on television, and this short-lived situation comedy was the result. As John Beamer, he was an elderly widower whose children had also died, leaving him with the responsibility of raising his two granddaughters—Laurie, age 18, and Midge, age 9. With unbounded enthusiasm and optimism he helped not only his own family, but his friends, his neighbors, and anyone else he met. At one point he even got himself elected to the city council.

EDDIE CANTOR COMEDY THEATRE (*Comedy/Variety*)

BROADCAST HISTORY:
Syndicated only
30 minutes
Produced: *1954–1955* (38 episodes)
Released: *January 1955*
HOST:
Eddie Cantor

Eddie Cantor's trademark during 50 years in show business was always manic activity—prancing around the stage, waving his hands, rolling his banjo eyes. He was still at it in the early 1950s on *The Colgate Comedy Hour*, but after a heart attack in 1952 he was forced to slow down. This was his last series, a relatively leisurely, filmed half-hour incorporating many of his old routines, but leaving much of the work to numerous guest stars. Many of the episodes consisted of little playlets, with Cantor only hosting. The guest stars were many and varied—Billie Burke, Eddie Fisher, Peter Lorre, Stan Freberg, Helen O'Connell,

Charles Coburn, Buster Keaton, and the Three Stooges among them.

On the variety stanzas viewers got all of Cantor's old chestnuts: "If You Knew Susie," "Ma!," "Mandy" (he never seemed to sing anything written after 1930); Cantor with a chorus line of leggy beauties; Cantor behind the wheel of a cab as Maxie the Taxi. It all seemed pretty old hat, and a little weary. But these syndicated films got tremendous circulation, and a great deal of press coverage. As Steve Allen remarked, "Let no one underestimate the importance of being venerable. . . ."

EDDIE CAPRA MYSTERIES, THE

(*Lawyer/Detective Drama*)

FIRST TELECAST: *September 8, 1978*
LAST TELECAST: *August 30, 1990*
BROADCAST HISTORY:

Sep 1978–Jan 1979, NBC Fri 10:00–11:00
Jun 1979–Sep 1979, NBC Fri 10:00–11:00
Jul 1990–Aug 1990, CBS Thu 9:00–10:00

CAST:

Eddie Capra . . . . Vincent Baggetta
Lacey Brown . . . . Wendy Phillips
J.J. Devlin . . . . Ken Swofford
Harvey Winchell . . . . Michael Horton
Jennie Brown . . . . Seven Ann McDonald

Capra was introduced as a detective show in the "classic style." No fancy frills, just a straightforward homicide at the opening of each show, followed by an hour in which the viewer could watch the young lawyer-sleuth uncover clues one by one. Eddie Capra, the unconventional star, worked for the conventional, and very prestigious, law firm of Devlin, Linkman and O'Brien. Lacey was his secretary, close to her boss both on the job and off; Harvey was his enthusiastic young legman; J.J. Devlin, the irascible senior partner in the firm; and Jennie was Lacey's precocious daughter.

CBS aired reruns of *The Eddie Capra Mysteries* during the summer of 1990.

EDDIE CONDON'S FLOOR SHOW (*Music*)

FIRST TELECAST: *January 1, 1949*
LAST TELECAST: *June 24, 1950*
BROADCAST HISTORY:

Jan 1949–Jul 1949, NBC Sat 8:30–9:00
Jul 1949–Sep 1949, NBC Sat 9:30–10:00
May 1950–Jun 1950, CBS Sat 7:30–8:00

HOST:

Eddie Condon
Carl Reiner (1950)

Guitarist Eddie Condon hosted this informal weekly jam session, one of the first network series devoted to jazz music. It had run previously on WPIX-TV, New York, and before that on WNBT-TV, New York, during the war, making it one of television's oldest features. Guests included many of the top names in jazz, such as Gene Krupa, Woody Herman, Sidney Bechet, Ella Fitzgerald, Louis Armstrong, and dozens of others, as well as such up-and-coming vocalists as Patti Page and Rosemary Clooney. A special feature during the summer of 1949 was a series of programs dramatizing—musically—great moments in jazz history. During the program's brief run on CBS, Condon was joined by Carl Reiner, who chatted with the guests about their careers.

EDDIE DODD (*Legal Drama*)

FIRST TELECAST: *March 12, 1991*
LAST TELECAST: *June 6, 1991*
BROADCAST HISTORY:

Mar 1991–Apr 1991, ABC Tue 10:00–11:00
May 1991–Jun 1991, ABC Wed 10:00–11:00

CAST:

Eddie Dodd . . . . Treat Williams
Roger Baron . . . . Corey Parker
Kitty Greer. . . . . Sydney Walsh
Billie . . . . Annabelle Gurwitch

Attorney Eddie Dodd was earnest, determined, and movie-star handsome. Just about the only thing he couldn't face was his own fortieth birthday, and what it represented. As a young radical lawyer in the '60s, Eddie had been controversial and famous for shaking up the system. But the system had never really changed, and now he was considered by many—perhaps even by himself—to have become a failure, a burned-out relic of another time.

A few people still believed in Eddie, however. Pumped up by his idealistic young assistant, Roger, and by his former girlfriend, Kitty, a private eye, the angst-ridden attorney could still be pushed into taking on "unwinnable" cases, and righting society's wrongs. Billie was the secretary in his small New York City practice.

EDDIE FISHER SHOW, THE (*Musical Variety*)

FIRST TELECAST: *September 24, 1957*
LAST TELECAST: *March 17, 1959*
BROADCAST HISTORY:

Sep 1957–Mar 1959, NBC Tue 8:00–9:00 (OS)

REGULARS:

Eddie Fisher
George Gobel
Buddy Bregman and His Orchestra
The Bill Thompson Singers (1957–1958)
The Johnny Mann Singers (1959)

After toiling in a limited-format 15-minute program for several years (see *Coke Time*), popular singer Eddie Fisher got his own full-hour variety show in the fall of 1957. It lasted for two seasons, alternating on Tuesdays with *The George Gobel Show*. Although there were no regulars on the show other than Fisher, George Gobel participated in comedy skits in most of the telecasts. To reciprocate, Eddie made frequent guest appearances on George's show.

EDDY ARNOLD SHOW, THE (*Musical Variety*)

FIRST TELECAST: *July 14, 1952*
LAST TELECAST: *September 28, 1956*
BROADCAST HISTORY:

Jul 1952–Aug 1952, CBS Mon/Wed/Fri 7:45–8:00
Jul 1953–Oct 1953, NBC Tue/Thu 7:30–7:45
Apr 1956–Jun 1956, ABC Thu 8:00–8:30
Jun 1956–Sep 1956, ABC Wed 9:30–10:00

REGULARS:

Eddy Arnold
The Russ Case Orchestra (1952)
The Dickens Sisters (1953)
Chet Atkins (1956)
The Paul Mitchell Quintet (1956)

Country and western singer Eddy Arnold spent two summers filling in for vacationing singers with regularly scheduled song shows: Perry Como on CBS in 1952 and Dinah Shore on NBC in 1953. In both cases, these 15-minute programs, which filled the remainder of the half hours in which the networks presented their news programs, provided little opportunity for anything but two or three songs. In the spring of 1956, with a full half hour on ABC, Mr. Arnold could talk with special guest stars and do more involved production numbers as well as perform solos. Chet Atkins provided instrumental solos and the Paul Mitchell Quintet instrumental backup for this later series, which featured both popular and classical numbers, as well as the soft ballads for which Arnold was famous.

EDGE, THE (*Comedy*)
FIRST TELECAST: *September 19, 1992*
LAST TELECAST: *July 18, 1993*
BROADCAST HISTORY:
Sep 1992–Jan 1993, FOX Sat 9:30–10:00
Feb 1993–Jul 1993, FOX Sun 10:30–11:00
REGULARS:
Julie Brown
Jennifer Aniston
Tom Kenny
Wayne Knight
Carol Rosenthal
James Stephens III
Jill Talley
Paul Feig (1992)
Rick Overton
Alan Ruck (1992)
VOICE-OVERS:
Edd Hall
ANIMATION:
Bill Plympton

This sketch comedy series made extensive use of animation and computer graphics to give it an unstructured MTV look. There were commercial satires, celebrity satires, and parodies of TV series—*Beverly Hills 90210, Sally Jessy Raphael, Studs* ("Sluts")—and videos. There was a lot of "cartoon" violence in *The Edge.* Most episodes began with the cast assembling onstage and then being decapitated, crushed, blown up, or otherwise destroyed just before the first commercial break. One recurring sketch showed a giant Delta Burke plucking people from houses and eating them. "Armed Family" was about a pleasant middle-class family who continually shot each other, and everyone else, at the least provocation. Another was a bizarre animation of a guy in a suit who reacted to situations, metamorphosed, and then disassembled. Some of the sketches were gross and tasteless, while others were hilariously funny. Julie Brown, one of the featured performers, also wrote and produced some of the sketches.

The series created an uproar when powerful Hollywood producer Aaron Spelling (*Beverly Hills 90210, Melrose Place,* and others) threatened to sue over its wild lampoons of his sex-driven shows. In one *90210* sendup, an actress portraying Tori Spelling (his real-life actress-daughter) hogged scenes and kicked other cast members, screaming "I can do that because it's Daddy's show!" Spelling demanded a public apology, which producer David Mirkin refused to give. Mirkin subsequently left the show, although the production company claimed there was no connection.

EDIE ADAMS SHOW, THE (*Musical Variety*)
FIRST TELECAST: *September 26, 1963*
LAST TELECAST: *March 19, 1964*
BROADCAST HISTORY:
Sep 1963–Mar 1964, ABC Thu 10:00–10:30
REGULARS:
Edie Adams
Don Chastain
Peter Hanley
The Paul Godkin Dancers
The Randy Rayburn Singers
The Peter Matz Orchestra

Singer Edie Adams starred in this half-hour musical variety series that alternated with *The Sid Caesar Show* on Thursday nights during the 1963–1964 season. Edie and her guest stars sang, danced, and did comedy sketches. To start the season both Edie and Sid Caesar appeared together in a full-hour variety special that aired from 10:00–11:00 P.M. on September 19. This show was also known by the title *Here's Edie.*

EDITOR'S CHOICE (*News Analysis*)
FIRST TELECAST: *June 25, 1961*
LAST TELECAST: *September 24, 1961*
BROADCAST HISTORY:
Jun 1961–Sep 1961, ABC Sun 10:30–11:00
HOST:
Fendall Yerxa

Each week, in either a filmed report, a filmed report with interviews, or interviews alone, members of the ABC News staff sought to treat a current news story or issue in greater depth than was possible within the framework of the regular nightly newscast. *Editor's Choice* returned to the air on Sunday afternoons in January 1962, where it remained until February 1963.

EDUCATION OF MAX BICKFORD, THE (*Drama*)
FIRST TELECAST: *September 23, 2001*
LAST TELECAST: *June 2, 2002*
BROADCAST HISTORY:
Sep 2001–Jun 2002, CBS Sun 8:00–9:00
CAST:
Max Bickford .... Richard Dreyfuss
Andrea Haskell .... Marcia Gay Harden
Judith Hackett Bryant .... Regina Taylor
Erica Bettis .... Helen Shaver
Nell Bickford (age 18) .... Katee Sackhoff
Lester Bickford (11) .... Eric Ian Goldberg
Lorraine Tator .... Molly Regan
Josh Howlett .... Patrick Fabian
Brenda Vanderpool .... Meredith Lieber
Rose Quinley .... Natalie Venetia Belcon
Rex Pinsker .... Stephen Spinella
Walter Thornhill .... David McCallum
Lyla Ortiz .... Jayne Atkinson

Testy, opinionated Max was a history professor at Chadwick College, a small, all-women liberal arts school in New Jersey, who started the fall term facing both major changes at work and his own midlife crisis. Andrea, a former student and ex-lover, had been hired as a professor and given a position he had expected for himself. Worse, she had become an expert in popular culture, a field that traditionalist Max despised. His friend Steve, an anthropology professor, had returned after a sabbatical having had a sex-change operation, and was now Erica. Judith, the

Chadwick president, appointed Max chairman of the American studies department, which meant that he was saddled with Lorraine, the department's outspoken administrative assistant.

A reformed alcoholic, Max was a widower with two children—rebellious Nell, a freshman at Chadwick who was more interested in her rock band than in her studies, and Lester, his intellectually curious, adoring young son. Also seen were friend Josh, a fellow history professor; Rose, Walter and Rex, also history professors; Nell's roommate, Brenda; and Lyla, the woman Max had started to date, despite his ongoing attraction to Andrea.

For the first six months of the season it was not explained why Max, when musing about the frustrations in his life, referred to himself in the third person as Schuyler. Then in March, after three years of hard work, he finished a semi-autobiographical novel with a lead character named Schuyler Hatfield, a thinly disguised Max. When the manuscript leaked out, much of the staff thought they saw unflattering versions of themselves, but Max convinced them that he had taken creative license and meant no offense. At the end of the season he was offered a teaching position at Harvard but, after serious consideration, decided to stay at Chadwick.

EDWIN NEWMAN REPORTING (*News/Documentary*)
FIRST TELECAST: *June 5, 1960*
LAST TELECAST: *September 4, 1960*
BROADCAST HISTORY:
Jun 1960–Sep 1960, NBC Sun 6:30–7:00
HOST/REPORTER:
Edwin Newman

This series was the 1960 summer replacement for *Time Present: Chet Huntley Reporting.* Edwin Newman, then chief of the NBC News Paris bureau, filled in for Chet Huntley, focusing each week on one or two issues of current interest.

EERIE, INDIANA (*Supernatural*)
FIRST TELECAST: *September 15, 1991*
LAST TELECAST: *April 12, 1992*
BROADCAST HISTORY:
Sep 1991–Nov 1991, NBC Sun 7:30–8:00
Dec 1991–Feb 1992, NBC Sun 7:00–7:30
Mar 1992, NBC Sun 7:30–8:00
Mar 1992–Apr 1992, NBC Sun 7:00–7:30
CAST:
Marshall Teller (age 13) .... Omri Katz
Simon Holmes (10) .... Justin Shenkarow
Marilyn Teller.............. Mary-Margaret Humes
Edgar Teller .... Francis Guinan
Syndi Teller .... Julie Condra

The producers of NBC's *Unsolved Mysteries* also produced this odd little comedy-drama about an inquisitive 13-year-old who believed that his new home town was an eerie place indeed. How else to explain the mocking raven with a glass eye in its beak, the mailman who packed a pistol, or Elvis Presley coming out of his suburban house in the morning to pick up his paper from the lawn (on Marshall's route)? Marshall, recently transplanted from New Jersey, and his loyal pal Simon got into and out of many scrapes with the town's nutty residents as they tooled around on their bikes. There was the caretaker of the underground Bureau of Lost Items (where all those misplaced single socks go); and the Donna Reed–perfect neighbor who sealed her twins in vacuum-wear every night to keep them forever young. (Guess what happened when Marshall sneaked in and broke the seal?) Even the dogs in the local pound, it seemed, were plotting an uprising that could be overheard only through a school pal's new dental retainers.

Marshall and Simon saved and tagged the "evidence" of this weirdness each week and stashed it in the Tellers' attic, for they were the only ones who saw the strangeness. Marshall's bland family, including dad Edgar (an inventor for "Things, Inc."), bustling mom Marilyn, and self-absorbed older sister Syndi, didn't have a clue.

Reruns of *Eerie, Indiana* aired on FOX's Saturday morning lineup January–September 1997. New episodes with a new cast, under the title *Eerie,Indiana: The Other Dimension*, ran on FOX's Saturday morning lineup February–May 1998. The two youthful leads were Mitchell Taylor (played by Bill Switzer) and Stanley Hope (Daniel Clark). Also in the cast were Mitchell's parents (Bruce Hunter and Deborah Odell) and his sister Carrie (Lindy Booth).

EIGHT IS ENOUGH (*Comedy/Drama*)
FIRST TELECAST: *March 15, 1977*
LAST TELECAST: *August 29, 1981*
BROADCAST HISTORY:
Mar 1977–May 1977, ABC Tue 9:00–10:00
Aug 1977–Mar 1981, ABC Wed 8:00–9:00
Mar 1981–Aug 1981, ABC Sat 8:00–9:00
CAST:
Tom Bradford .... Dick Van Patten
Joan Bradford (1977) .... Diana Hyland
Sandra Sue Abbott ("Abby") Bradford
.... Betty Buckley
Nicholas Bradford (age 8) .... Adam Rich
Tommy Bradford (14) .... Willie Aames
Elizabeth Bradford (15)
.... Connie Needham (Newton)
Nancy Bradford (18).................. Dianne Kay
Susan Bradford Stockwell (19)
.... Susan Richardson
Joannie Bradford (20).............. Laurie Walters
Mary Bradford (21) .... Lani O'Grady
David Bradford (pilot only) .... Mark Hamill
David Bradford (23)............... Grant Goodeve
Dr. Greg Maxwell (1977–1979) ..... Michael Thoma
Daisy Maxwell (1977–1979) .... Virginia Vincent
Donna (1978–1981) .... Jennifer Darling
Merle "The Pearl" Stockwell (1979–1981)
.... Brian Patrick Clarke
Janet Bradford (1979–1981) .... Joan Prather
Ernie Fields (1979–1981) .... Michael Goodrow
Jeremy Andretti (1980–1981)....... Ralph Macchio

This comedy-drama focused on a family with eight very independent children, aged 8 to 23. When the series began, Tom, the father, was a newspaper columnist for the Sacramento, California, *Register*, and Joan was his wife of 25 years. The death of actress Diana Hyland during production of the spring 1977 episodes of *Eight Is Enough* forced major changes, however. Hyland had completed only four shows and was written out of the remainder as being "away." When the series returned with new episodes that fall, Tom Bradford had become a widower, his wife having died, at least in the story line, about "a year ago." With the help of his best friend Doc Maxwell, Tom set about keeping order among his large brood while reentering, in middle age, the singles world. He soon found romance in the person of Abby, a pretty schoolteacher who came to the Bradford home to tutor one of the youngsters. Their romance blossomed, and on a special two-hour telecast on November 9, 1977, Tom and Abby were married.

As the series continued, Abby pursued and got her Ph.D. in education and began counseling work at Memorial High (as well as at home!). The Bradford kids all became involved with various friends and romances as they grew, and in a special episode in September 1979 David and Susan each got married, in a double wedding—David to attorney Janet, and Susan to pro baseball pitcher Merle "The Pearl" Stockwell (who later signed with the New York Mets). David then went to work for a construction firm, while Susan set about producing the first Bradford grandchild—Sandra Sue, born in October 1980. Meanwhile Joannie got a job at a television station, and became engaged to Jeffrey Trout (played by Nicholas Pryor).

The series was based on the book *Eight Is Enough* by Thomas Braden.

8 SIMPLE RULES FOR DATING MY TEENAGE DAUGHTER (*Situation Comedy*)

FIRST TELECAST: *September 17, 2002*
LAST TELECAST:
BROADCAST HISTORY:
Sep 2002– , ABC Tue 8:00–8:30
Mar 2003–Apr 2003, ABC Fri 9:00–9:30
May 2003–Jun 2003, ABC Tue 8:30–9:00

CAST:
Paul Hennessy .... John Ritter
Cate Hennessy .... Katey Sagal
Bridget Hennessy (age 16) .... Kaley Cuoco
Kerry Hennessy (15) .... Amy Davidson
Rory Hennessy (13) .... Martin Spanjers
Tommy .... Larry Miller
Kyle .... Billy Aaron Brown

Paul was a typical harried dad in this sunny family sitcom. A sportswriter, he had missed much of his kids' growing-up years because he was on the road. Now they were in their teens and his sensible wife, Cate, had gone back to work as a nurse, so it was up to Paul to stay home and "take care of the kids." Trouble was, they were no longer the cute little dumplings he remembered. Bridget had matured (if that is the word) into a sexy, thong-wearing, skin-baring teen vamp, who was also a bit of an airhead; Kerry was the smart one but masked her insecurities with sarcasm, and Rory was a little hustler who bonded with Dad because neither of them understood women. Tommy was Paul's coworker, and Kyle his teenage son, who was Bridget's sometime boyfriend.

There were plenty of generation-gap lines (to Dad: "Stop calling me care-bear!"; "What do you know, you're like, a hundred"), lots of misunderstandings and traumas about dates, but also plenty of love. Based on the best-selling book *8 Simple Rules for Dating My Teenage Daughter: and Other Tips from a Beleaguered Father (Not That Any of Them Work)* by W. Bruce Cameron.

18 WHEELS OF JUSTICE (*Adventure*)

BROADCAST HISTORY:
TNN
60 minutes
Original episodes: *2000–2001* (44 episodes)
Premiered: *January 12, 2000*

CAST:
Agent Michael Cates/"Chance Bowman"
.... Lucky Vanous
Agent Celia "Cie" Baxter .... Lisa Thornhill
Burton Hardesty (2000) .... Billy Dee Williams
Jonathan Snow (2001) .... Bobby Hosea
Jacob Calder .... G. Gordon Liddy

A hunky guy and a *really* big truck combined to fight crime in this formulaic adventure. Michael Cates was a Justice Department undercover agent who testified against Jacob Calder, one of the richest, most ruthless crime lords in America—and had his family blown up as a result. To protect Michael from further retribution his boss, Burton Hardesty, offered him a new undercover identity as trucker Chance Bowman, and an 18-wheel, seven-ton Kenworth T-2000 truck in which to "hide in plain sight." The big rig was outfitted with various high-tech gear, including a tracking system that allowed pretty agent Cie Baxter to follow him and give him instructions on a video screen. Although a rebel by nature, and obsessed with bringing down the extremely slippery and powerful Calder, Michael/Chance took the offer and helped people across America while playing a cat-and-mouse game with Calder and his seemingly limitless army of hitmen. In the second season Hardesty was promoted to assistant attorney general, Agent Snow became Chance's boss, and Calder, now in prison, became a surprising ally when Chance learned that it was not him but someone "higher up" who was orchestrating the whole criminal enterprise.

The soundtrack featured country music, and among the guest stars were Billy Ray Cyrus and Waylon Jennings, along with *Survivor* contestant (and real-life truck driver) Susan Hawk.

87TH PRECINCT (*Police Drama*)

FIRST TELECAST: *September 25, 1961*
LAST TELECAST: *September 10, 1962*
BROADCAST HISTORY:
Sep 1961–Sep 1962, NBC Mon 9:00–10:00

CAST:
Det. Steve Carella .... Robert Lansing
Det. Bert Kling .... Ron Harper
Det. Roger Havilland .... Gregory Walcott
Det. Meyer Meyer .... Norman Fell
Teddy Carella .... Gena Rowlands

Manhattan's 87th precinct was the base for the police detectives of this rather grim, violent series that was based on the mystery stories of Ed McBain (pseudonym of Evan Hunter), which were popular in the 1950s and 1960s. In addition to the various aspects of police work normally seen in action series of this type, the personal lives of the officers provided much of the side drama. Detective Steve Carella was married to a beautiful woman who unfortunately was a deaf-mute; Bert Kling was the young detective learning the ropes; Roger Havilland the hardened old pro; and Meyer Meyer the older officer who, having "seen it all," often injected a dry humor into otherwise serious business. Most of the stories started in the precinct office where all of the detectives gathered to write up reports and wait for assignments.

EISCHIED (*Police Drama*)
FIRST TELECAST: *September 21, 1979*
LAST TELECAST: *September 2, 1983*
BROADCAST HISTORY:
Sep 1979–Dec 1979, NBC Fri 10:00–11:00
Dec 1979–Jan 1980, NBC Sun 10:00–11:00
June 1983–Sep 1983, NBC Fri 10:00–11:00
CAST:
Chief Earl Eischied .... Joe Don Baker
Capt. Finnerty .... Alan Oppenheimer
Dep. Commissioner Kimbrough .... Alan Fudge
Chief Inspector Ed Parks .... Eddie Egan
Carol Wright .... Suzanne Lederer
Rick Alessi .... Vincent Bufano
Det. Malfitano .... Joe Cirillo
Working for the New York City Police Department could harden anyone, and nobody was more hardened than Chief of Detectives Earl Eischied, in this violent, gritty series. A tough, dedicated career cop, Eischied (pronounced "Eye-shyed") knew the rule book and how to get around it when necessary to break a case. Eischied's methods worried politically ambitious, "by-the-book" Deputy Commissioner Kimbrough, but fortunately Earl's friend, Chief Inspector Ed Parks, could serve as a buffer between them. Carol Wright and Rick Alessi were two members of the special squad reporting directly to Eischied, as was trusted friend Capt. Finnerty. They were all dedicated to Eischied, though their only reward was an occasional, gruff "You done good," delivered in his inimitable Southern drawl. A bachelor, Eischied's constant companion both at home and at work was his pet cat, P.C.

Three years after the conclusion of its unsuccessful original run, NBC aired reruns of *Eischied* as a summer replacement series in 1983.

EISENHOWER & LUTZ (*Situation Comedy*)
FIRST TELECAST: *March 14, 1988*
LAST TELECAST: *June 20, 1988*
BROADCAST HISTORY:
Mar 1988–Jun 1988, CBS Mon 9:30–10:00
CAST:
Barnett M. "Bud" Lutz, Jr. .... Scott Bakula
Megan O'Malley .... DeLane Matthews
Kay "K.K." Dunne .... Patricia Richardson
Millie Zamora .... Rose Portillo
Dwayne Spitler .... Leo Geter
Barnett M. "Big Bud" Lutz ..... Henderson Forsythe
Bud Lutz had barely made it through law school and, after failing to establish a practice in Las Vegas, had returned home to Palm Springs, California, to open a law office there. The office, located in a former hot-tub showroom (with a leftover sample in his reception area) in a mini-mall on the outskirts of town, did not attract a high-class clientele—mostly whiplash victims and illegal aliens. Bud's girlfriend Megan, who had returned with him from Vegas, was a cocktail waitress at the nearby Kon Tiki Lounge. Her relationship with Bud was threatened by his high school sweetheart Kay, a partner in the high-powered local law firm of Griffin, McKendrick & Dunne, who still had the hots for him. Others in the cast were Millie, the secretary who Bud never seemed to pay; Dwayne, the eager young law student who did odd jobs for free in order to watch a real lawyer at work (some example!!); and Bud's free-spirited father Big Bud, an eccentric sign painter. It was Big Bud's idea to call his son's firm Eisenhower & Lutz because the Eisenhower name was well respected in the desert. Unfortunately, too many prospective clients asked for the nonexistent Mr. Eisenhower and not enough for Mr. Lutz.

ELDER MICHAUX (*Religion*)
FIRST TELECAST: *October 31, 1948*
LAST TELECAST: *January 9, 1949*
BROADCAST HISTORY:
Oct 1948–Jan 1949, DUM Sun 6:00–6:30
PREACHER:
Elder Lightfoot Solomon Michaux
The black preacher Lightfoot Solomon Michaux (pronounced "Me-show") and his foot-stomping, hand-clapping revival meetings had been heard on radio since the very early days of that medium. The broadcasts emanated from his hometown of Washington, D.C., where he was pastor of the Church of God, and featured his Happy-Am-I Choir and an enthusiastic congregation that shouted ecstatic encouragement as the Elder preached. He became a regular feature on local Washington TV soon after the first station opened there, and his broadcasts were periodically fed over the DuMont network beginning in 1947. The network telecasts included a semi-regular run in 1948–1949, as shown above.

ELEVENTH HOUR, THE (*Medical Drama*)
FIRST TELECAST: *October 3, 1962*
LAST TELECAST: *September 9, 1964*
BROADCAST HISTORY:
Oct 1962–Sep 1964, NBC Wed 10:00–11:00
CAST:
Dr. Theodore Bassett (1962–1963) .. Wendell Corey
Dr. Paul Graham .... Jack Ging
Dr. L. Richard Starke (1963–1964) .. Ralph Bellamy
The role of psychiatry in helping people cope with the world, as well as its use in law-enforcement areas, provided the grist for this dramatic series. Drs. Bassett and Graham were two psychiatrists sharing an office, and the patients who came to them "in the eleventh hour"—on the verge of some form of breakdown—provided the stories. Various forms of analysis and psychotherapy were used, and the two doctors often disagreed on the proper course to take with a specific patient. Dr. Bassett was also an advisor to the State Department of Correction and the police department and was often called upon to evaluate the mental competency of accused criminals.

During the first season the majority of stories dealt with Dr. Bassett's criminal cases. When Wendell Corey left the series, Ralph Bellamy took over his responsibilities, as Dr. Starke, and the emphasis was shifted to involve both of the doctors directly in more of the cases.

ELGIN TV HOUR, THE (*Dramatic Anthology*)
FIRST TELECAST: *October 5, 1954*
LAST TELECAST: *June 14, 1955*
BROADCAST HISTORY:
Oct 1954–Jun 1955, ABC Tue 9:30–10:30
This one-hour Tuesday night series of dramatic presentations on ABC replaced the previous season's *Motorola*

TV Theatre. The dramas were telecast live from New York and featured such top actors as Ralph Bellamy, Gertrude Berg, Franchot Tone, Boris Karloff, Polly Bergen, John Cassavetes, and John Forsythe, to name a few. The series alternated with *The U.S. Steel Hour*.

ELIMIDATE DELUXE (*Dating*)
FIRST TELECAST: *October 11, 2001*
LAST TELECAST: *October 25, 2001*
BROADCAST HISTORY:
Oct 2001, WB Thu 8:30–9:00

Each episode of this dating show gave one guy or girl (The Host) the opportunity to go on a group date with four attractive members of the opposite sex and eliminate them one at a time until only one was left. In order to stay in the game each of the prospects worked hard to outflirt and outsmart the others and keep the interest of the host. Home viewers followed the action, listened to the participants trash each other, and guessed which of them would be the final survivor.

Elimidate Deluxe was canceled after two prime time airings on the WB, but the syndicated version, *Elimidate*, which had premiered a few weeks earlier, thrived.

ELLEN (*Situation Comedy*)
FIRST TELECAST: *March 30, 1994*
LAST TELECAST: *July 29, 1998*
BROADCAST HISTORY:
Mar 1994–May 1994, ABC Wed 9:30–10:00
Aug 1994–Sep 1994, ABC Tue 9:30–10:00
Sep 1994–Mar 1995, ABC Wed 9:30–10:00
Mar 1995–Sep 1995, ABC Wed 8:30–9:00
Apr 1995–May 1995, ABC Tue 9:30–10:00
Sep 1995–Nov 1996, ABC Wed 8:00–8:30
Dec 1996–Feb 1997, ABC Wed 9:30–10:00
Mar 1997–Apr 1997, ABC Tue 8:30–9:00
Apr 1997–Mar 1998, ABC Wed 9:30–10:00
May 1998–Jul 1998, ABC Wed 9:30–10:00
CAST:
Ellen Morgan .... Ellen DeGeneres
Holly (1994) .... Holly Fulger
Anita (1994) .... Maggie Wheeler
Adam Greene (1994–1996) .... Arye Gross
Joe Farrell .... David Anthony Higgins
Paige Clark .... Joely Fisher
**Lois Morgan* .... Alice Hirson
**Harold Morgan* .... Steven Gilborn
**Peter* .... Patrick Bristow
Audrey Penney (1995–1998) .... Clea Lewis
Spence Kovak (1995–1998) .... Jeremy Piven
**Barrett (1996–1998)* .... Jack Plotnick
*Occasional

This *Seinfeld*-esque comedy premiered under the title *These Friends of Mine*, which was descriptive of its content. Ellen was a blond, insecure, somewhat hyper thirty-something single who managed a Los Angeles bookstore/coffee shop called Buy the Book. Dates and friends, new and old, wanted and unwanted, pretty much filled her life. Her original circle included Adam, her sloppy, sarcastic roommate, a struggling photographer who was also playing the field (though not with Ellen); longtime friend Holly; and smart-mouthed Anita. They rated each other's dates, talked about their sexual misadventures (casual sex was big here), and how to dump people they didn't like.

When the series returned in the fall Ellen had done some dumping of her own. The title was changed to *Ellen*, and Holly and Anita were history. Joe, a chubby co-worker at the bookstore (which Ellen now owned), was promoted to full-time "friend," and Paige, a rather pushy childhood friend who usually got her way, joined the gang. Joe became the coffee-brewing "java king," while Paige was a movie development executive. Lois and Harold were Ellen's occasionally seen parents.

In the 1995–1996 season Buy the Book was destroyed in an earthquake. After rebuilding, Ellen decided to sell out to a large chain, while continuing to manage it for them. Her new roommate was her cousin Spence, a deposed doctor from New York (he had been fired for punching a patient) who was looking for a new life; and a new friend was naive, giggly Audrey, an annoying vision in pink. On the dating front, Paige and Spence were soon involved in a volatile romance, but the big news was Ellen herself. Stories began hinting that her pursuit of the perfect man might not be her real desire, and the real-life media began a drumbeat of speculation as to whether Ellen might in fact become the first openly gay leading character on broadcast series television. She did, in an April 30, 1997, "coming out" episode in which she overcame years of denial and fell for her boyfriend's producer, Susan (Laura Dern)—who promptly left her. Ellen's friends stuck by her, however, and clueless Audrey even proved a surprisingly knowledgeable guide to the gay scene. Also lending support on this episode was Ellen's therapist, none other than Oprah Winfrey.

The final season saw Ellen leaving her job at Buy the Book to try new occupations and pay the mortgage on her newly acquired dream home. The final episode was a mock history of Ellen's show business career, from vaudeville in the '20s through the birth of television to the present day. Over the credits a chorus sang, "Who's got a lesbian smile? Ellen!"

ELLEN BURSTYN SHOW, THE (*Situation Comedy*)
FIRST TELECAST: *September 20, 1986*
LAST TELECAST: *September 12, 1987*
BROADCAST HISTORY:
Sep 1986–Nov 1986, ABC Sat 8:30–9:00
Aug 1987–Sep 1987, ABC Sat 8:30–9:00
CAST:
Ellen Brewer .... Ellen Burstyn
Sydney Brewer .... Elaine Stritch
Molly Brewer Ross .... Megan Mullally
Nick Ross .... Jesse Tendler
Tom Hines .... Barry Sobel

Ellen Burstyn starred as a best-selling author whose life seemed to consist mostly of one-liners, in this multigenerational comedy. Sharing her Baltimore brownstone were her acerbic mother, Sydney; her divorced, 25-year-old daughter Molly; and her cute 5-year-old grandson Nick. Tom was an impoverished student who was taking the seminar Ellen taught at a nearby college. Quips flew thick and fast around the kitchen table, but not fast enough to save this series.

ELLEN SHOW, THE (*Situation Comedy*)
FIRST TELECAST: *September 24, 2001*
LAST TELECAST: *January 11, 2002*

BROADCAST HISTORY:

Sep 2001, CBS Mon 9:30–10:00
Sep 2001–Oct 2001, CBS Fri 8:00–8:30
Oct 2001–Nov 2001, CBS Fri 8:30–9:00
Dec 2001, CBS Mon 8:30–9:00
Dec 2001–Jan 2002, CBS Fri 8:30–9:00

CAST:

Ellen Richmond .... Ellen DeGeneres
Dot Richmond .... Cloris Leachman
Mr. Munn............................. Martin Mull
Rusty Carnouk .... Jim Gaffigan
Catherine Richmond .... Emily Rutherfurd
Bunny Hopstetter (2001)............ Diane Delano
Pam.................................. Kerri Kenney

Ellen DeGeneres played a fallen star who returned to her small-town roots in this screwball comedy. Ellen Richmond had become a national celebrity through her L.A.-based Internet company, Homelearn.com, but while on a triumphal visit to her hometown of Clark she learned that the company had suddenly gone bankrupt. She decided to stay in Clark and restart her life without the pressures of the big city. She moved in with her fussy mother, Dot, who had kept Ellen's room exactly the way it was the day she had moved to L.A., and her insecure younger sister, Catherine, who was jealous of Dot's closeness to Ellen. Catherine wanted desperately to find a man but had a history of choosing losers for suitors. Mr. Munn, Ellen's former teacher and now the principal of Clark High School, gave her a job as a school guidance counselor. Other teachers at the school were Ellen's onetime prom date Rusty, a gentle soul who wanted to rekindle their romance and didn't notice that she was openly gay; Bunny, the lesbian gym teacher; and Pam, the home economics teacher with whom Ellen barely got along.

ELLERY QUEEN, see *Adventures of Ellery Queen, The*

ELVIS (*Drama*)

FIRST TELECAST: *February 6, 1990*
LAST TELECAST: *May 19, 1990*
BROADCAST HISTORY:

Feb 1990, ABC Tue 9:30–10:00
Feb 1990–Mar 1990, ABC Sun 8:30–9:00
May 1990, ABC Sat 8:00–8:30

CAST:

Elvis Presley .... Michael St. Gerard
Scotty Moore .... Jesse Dabson
Bill Black .... Blake Gibbons
Vernon Presley.................. Billy Green Bush
Gladys Presley .... Millie Perkins
Mattie Walker .... Kelli Williams
Sam Phillips...................... Jordan Williams

THEME:

"All Shook Up," sung by Ronnie McDowell

One of the most ballyhooed series of the 1989–1990 season was this loving re-creation of Elvis Presley's early years. Though not a ratings success, it was a TV first. Never before had the true story of a real-life superstar been dramatized in a weekly series; and never had the birth of rock 'n' roll been treated with such reverence and authenticity. It was as if the innocent, vital young Elvis, almost forgotten in his later years of dissipation and decline, had come back to life.

The series was based on "vignettes" from Presley's life in 1954–1955, just before he became famous, and featured look-alike actors portraying Elvis and the (real) people around him. Scotty and Bill were his pals and fellow musicians (on guitar and bass), with whom he formed his first combo; Vernon and Gladys, his poor-folks mom and dad; and Sam Phillips, the savvy local entrepreneur and owner of tiny Sun Records, who gave him his first break. Stories followed Elvis through amateur performances, his first primitive but electrifying recordings, life on the road as he tasted regional success, and his resulting breakup with his high school sweetheart Mattie. It was all terribly authentic—perhaps *too* authentic—from the period cars, to the Memphis backdrop (where the series was filmed), to the slow, natural pace. Elvis's actual singing voice was sometimes used, although most songs were dubbed by singer Ronnie McDowell. The co-producer of the series was Elvis's widow, Priscilla Presley.

EMERALD POINT N.A.S. (*Military Drama*)

FIRST TELECAST: *September 26, 1983*
LAST TELECAST: *March 12, 1984*
BROADCAST HISTORY:

Sep 1983–Mar 1984, CBS Mon 10:00–11:00

CAST:

Rear Adm. Thomas Mallory .... Dennis Weaver
Maggie Farrell........................ Maud Adams
Deanna Kincaid .... Jill St. John
Lt. Glenn Matthews .... Andrew Stevens
Lt. Cmdr. Jack Warren............... Charles Frank
Lt. Simon Adams .... Richard Dean Anderson
Hilary Adams .... Sela Ward
Ensign Leslie Mallory .... Doran Clark
Kay Mallory Matthews .... Stephanie Dunnam
Celia Mallory Warren .... Susan Dey
Harlan Adams (1983)............... Patrick O'Neal
Harlan Adams (1983–1984) .... Robert Vaughn
Lt. Alexi Gorichenko .... Michael Carven
Adm. Yuri Bukharin .... Robert Loggia
Scott Farrell........................ Darryl Cooksey
David Marquette .... Michael Brandon

The interlocking worlds of the military and big business provided the backdrop for this prime-time soap opera. Commanding officer at the Emerald Point Naval Air Station was Admiral Thomas Mallory, a widowed career military man with three beautiful young daughters—Celia, married to brilliant military lawyer Jack Warren; Kay, who in midseason wed Glenn Matthews, a former pilot who had been discharged from the navy after being convicted of manslaughter; and youngest daughter Leslie, recently graduated from Annapolis. The local business magnate, appropriately unscrupulous, was Harlan Adams, president of Adams Industries. Harlan's son, navy pilot Simon Adams, was as honorable and good as his father and sister Hilary were bad. There was the usual mix of maneuvering for power, sleeping around, and horrible revelations about flawed characters and hidden pasts, along with the intrigue added by the military setting. Admiral Mallory's bitchy but beautiful sister-in-law, Deanna Kincaid, who wanted power and wealth, had her heart set on marrying Harlan. In the meantime she got involved with KGB spy Yuri Bukharin and, when caught by naval intelligence, became a double agent. The love life of Admiral Mallory was shared with Maggie Farrell, the liaison between the town's military affairs council and the naval base. She and Mallory, who were good friends at the start of the season, were about to be married at its end. The wedding never took place, however, since she was kidnapped by a mentally disturbed David Marquette in the cliff-hanger season-ending episode. Since the series was not renewed, viewers never did find out what happened.

EMERGENCY (*Drama*)

FIRST TELECAST: *January 22, 1972*
LAST TELECAST: *September 3, 1977*
BROADCAST HISTORY:
Jan 1972–Jul 1972, NBC Sat 8:00–9:00
Sep 1972–Sep 1977, NBC Sat 8:00–9:00
CAST:
Dr. Kelly Brackett .... Robert Fuller
Nurse Dixie McCall .... Julie London
Dr. Joe Early .... Bobby Troup
Paramedic Roy DeSoto .... Kevin Tighe
Paramedic John Gage .... Randolph Mantooth
Dr. Mike Morton .... Ron Pinkhard
Captain Hammer (1972) .... Dick Hammer
Captain Hank Stanley (1973–1977)
.... Michael Norell
Fireman Chet Kelly .... Tim Donnelly
Fireman Marco Lopez .... Marco Lopez
Fireman Mike Stoker .... Mike Stoker
Dispatcher .... Sam Lanier
Officer Vince .... Vince Howard
EXECUTIVE PRODUCER:
Jack Webb

Done in the semi-documentary style for which Jack Webb had become famous with *Dragnet, Emergency* followed the efforts of Squad 51 of the Los Angeles County Fire Department's Paramedical Rescue Service. Paramedics DeSoto and Gage were usually at the center of the action, while the emergency staff of Rampart Hospital provided backup assistance. Each telecast depicted several interwoven incidents, some humorous, some touching, others tragic. A typical night's work might have the paramedics called on to help an overweight woman who was having trouble breathing because her girdle was too tight, or aiding a maintenance worker who had broken his back in a 100-foot fall from a smokestack he was painting. Another night they might be saving children trapped in an abandoned building when a wrecking crew began demolishing the place, or rescuing a woman parachutist who had gotten caught in a tree. One of the specialties of the paramedics, in fact, seemed to be saving "danglers"—people trapped in precarious positions because of faulty rigging, collapsing scaffolding, or the like.

Former bandleader Bobby Troup, who played neurosurgeon Joe Early, was in real life married to Julie London, who played Rampart's head nurse. (She had previously been married to producer Jack Webb.) Squad 51's mascot was a dog named Boots, succeeded by Henry (named after the squad's captain) in 1976.

Although *Emergency* ended its run as a series in 1977, special two-hour movie versions, newly filmed, were periodically aired during the following season.

An animated Saturday morning spin-off of this series, titled *Emergency + 4*, aired on NBC from September 1973 to September 1976.

EMERGENCY CALL (*Documentary*)

BROADCAST HISTORY:
Syndicated only
30 minutes
Produced: *1991–1998* (141 episodes)
Released: *September 1991*
HOST:
Joseph Campanella (1991–1992)
Ron Allen (1992–1993)
Alex Paen (1994–1998)
NARRATOR:
Ron Allen

Much like *On Scene—Emergency Response*, which had premiered the previous fall, this series showcased the activities of firefighters, police rescue teams, medical rescue workers, and other lifesavers at work and at home, in action and reflecting on their jobs. In the third season there was no on-screen host, only the off-screen announcer narrating the activity. When the 1994–1995 season began, the series producer, Alex Paen, had taken over the on-camera hosting duties. In the fall of 1996 the series was retitled *Emergency with Alex Paen* and the episodes that had originally aired with other hosts were re-edited with Paen as host.

EMERIL (*Situation Comedy*)

FIRST TELECAST: *September 25, 2001*
LAST TELECAST: *December 11, 2001*
BROADCAST HISTORY:
Sep 2001–Dec 2001, NBC Tue 8:00–8:30
CAST:
Emeril Lagasse .... Himself
Cassandra Gilman .... Lisa Ann Walter
Melva LeBlanc .... Sherri Shepherd
B. D. Benson .... Carrie Preston
Jerry McKenney .... Robert Urich
Trish O'Connell .... Tricia O'Kelley
Nora Lagasse .... Mary Page Keller
James Lagasse .... James Lafferty
**Halo Lagasse* .... Alexis Della Ripa
**Charlie Lagasse* .... Joey Roberts Mercado
*Occasional

Real-life superchef Emeril Lagasse, cooking star of the Food Network, made the odd transition to sitcom in this "cooking comedy." The setting was a fictional show on the "Food Channel," which looked a lot like his real show except for the nutty crew. Cassandra was the brassy blond producer, Melva the hefty, wisecracking stage manager, B. D. the flighty assistant chef, Trish the overbearing network executive, and Jerry—the only other man around—his rather dense agent. Less often seen were his neglected wife Nora and their three kids, James (an intern on the show), Halo and Charlie.

Lagasse seemed to shamble through the plots—except for the cooking sequences, where he came alive with his trademark energy ("Kick it up a notch!"; "Bam!"). There was a good deal of physical comedy, including throwing food around, and at the end usually a big, raucous meal.

EMPIRE (*Western*)

FIRST TELECAST: *September 25, 1962*
LAST TELECAST: *September 6, 1964*
BROADCAST HISTORY:
Sep 1962–Sep 1963, NBC Tue 8:30–9:30
Mar 1964–Sep 1964, ABC Sun 7:30–8:30

CAST:

Jim Redigo .... Richard Egan
Constance Garret .... Terry Moore
Lucia Garret .... Anne Seymour
Tal Garret .... Ryan O'Neal
Chuck Davis (1963) .... Warren Vanders
Paul Moreno (1963) .... Charles Bronson

This drama was set on the sprawling Garret ranch in contemporary New Mexico. The ranch was indeed an empire, a multi-million-dollar operation covering half a million acres and including oil, mining, lumber, and crop-raising industries, plus cattle-, sheep-, and horse-breeding. All of these gave Jim Redigo, the foreman, plenty of opportunity for dramatic adventure.

Production of *Empire* ceased at the end of the 1962–1963 season, but ABC aired reruns of the original episodes during mid-1964. The main character, Jim Redigo, was saved by NBC for a shorter version of this series, simply titled *Redigo*, that was aired in the fall of 1963 but lasted only 13 weeks. (See *Redigo* for details.)

EMPIRE (*Situation Comedy*)

FIRST TELECAST: *January 4, 1984*
LAST TELECAST: *February 1, 1984*
BROADCAST HISTORY:

Jan 1984–Feb 1984, CBS Wed 8:30–9:00

CAST:

Ben Christian .... Dennis Dugan
Calvin Cromwell .... Patrick Macnee
Peg .... Maureen Arthur
Jackie Willow .... Christine Belford
Meredith .... Caren Kaye
Jack Willow .... Richard Masur
Edward Roland .... Michael McGuire
Arthur Broderick .... Dick O'Neill
Roger Martinson .... Howard Platt
T. Howard Daniels .... Edward Winter
Renee .... Patricia Elliott
Bill .... Paul Wilson
Amelia Lapidus .... Francine Tacker

Empire was a wild satire on the shenanigans and paranoia of corporate America. Board of directors meetings at giant Empire Industries resembled open house at a lunatic asylum. Calvin Cromwell was the autocratic chairman of the board who delighted in making his underlings squirm; Meredith was the manipulative director of public relations; Jack Willow, the incompetent sales v.p., whose ambitious wife, Jackie, had to give him detailed instructions on what to say at board meetings (which sometimes backfired when an unexpected question was asked). In addition, Arthur Broderick was the over-the-hill head of marketing, who plastered his hair with artificial coloring in a hopeless attempt to look young; Tom Martinson, the thoroughly unprincipled chief counsel; and Howard Daniels, the neurotic security chief who kept an oxygen mask by his side during board meetings. Edward Roland was another board member rather obviously trying to unseat Cromwell and take over the entire business.

Into this nest of bumbling schemers came naive young Ben Christian, whom Cromwell had just appointed to be vice president of research and development. Friendly toward the company's workers, honest, and with the boss's confidence as well, Ben posed a major threat to the others. Played in serial fashion, and strictly for laughs, *Empire* featured back-stabbing, double-dealing, and even an off-handed murder committed by Martinson as board members jockeyed for power.

EMPTY NEST (*Situation Comedy*)

FIRST TELECAST: *October 8, 1988*
LAST TELECAST: *July 8, 1995*
BROADCAST HISTORY:

Oct 1988–Jul 1991, NBC Sat 9:30–10:00
Aug 1991–Jul 1994, NBC Sat 9:00–9:30
Jan 1993, NBC Sat 8:00–8:30
Aug 1994–Oct 1994, NBC Sat 8:30–9:00
Oct 1994–Mar 1995, NBC Sat 8:00–8:30
Jun 1995–Jul 1995, NBC Sat 8:00–9:00

CAST:

Dr. Harry Weston .... Richard Mulligan
Barbara Weston (1988–1993) ..... Kristy McNichol
Carol Weston .... Dinah Manoff
Nurse LaVerne Todd .... Park Overall
Charley Dietz .... David Leisure
Patrick Arcola (1992–1993) .... Paul Provenza
Emily Weston (1993) .... Lisa Rieffel
Dr. Maxine Douglas (1993–1995). . Marsha Warfield
Sophia Petrillo (1993–1995) .... Estelle Getty

NBC capitalized on the success of the *Golden Girls* with another character comedy from the same producers, on the same night, set in the same Miami neighborhood, and also starring well-known TV actors of the 1970s. Richard Mulligan (of *Soap*) played a pediatrician whose wife, Libby, had died a year before the show began, and whose children were grown. But his nest did not stay empty for long. As one of the most eligible bachelors in Miami, he was constantly pursued by mature females, including on occasion the Golden Girls themselves. As for his kids, both eldest daughter Carol, a neurotic divorcée, and middle daughter Barbara, a self-assured undercover cop, came home to live (the youngest, Emily, was away at college; she called but was not seen). LaVerne was the tart-tongued, prescient nurse with a pronounced Arkansas drawl, and Charley, the obnoxious, skirt-chasing neighbor who worked on a cruise ship but never seemed to be away. He dropped in regularly to mooch food from the Weston kitchen and trade jibes with Carol.

Harry fretted and fussed over his daughters' love lives, as well as his own, finding the most sympathetic (if hairy) ear from his enormous dog, Dreyfuss. Other best buddies were the kids with whom he bantered at the office, including little Jeffrey Millstein (played in a recurring role by Edan Gross).

Harry's home life was disrupted further in 1992 when Carol's eccentric boyfriend, Patrick, moved in, converting the Westons' garage into a sculpture studio. He departed at the start of the next season, but not before Carol became pregnant; their child, Scotty, was born in November 1993. Barbara left midway through the 1992–1993 season (due to actress Kristy McNichol's illness), though she sometimes phoned home; ostensibly she was on "undercover assignment." Globe-trotting youngest daughter Emily returned for a while to fill the void but soon was gone again.

In the fall of 1993 Harry and Nurse LaVerne joined hard-driving Maxine Douglas at her inner-city clinic in downtown Miami. They were not allowed to forget their roots, however. Sophia Petrillo, of *The Golden Girls* and *The Golden Palace*, frequently wandered into Harry's living room, as if she were looking for her own former Saturday-night series. With the demise of her earlier series she had moved back to the Shady Pines Retirement Home nearby.

As the series ended in 1995, Carol married boyfriend Kevin (D. David Morin), LaVerne married Matt (Stephen Nichols), and Harry accepted a job offer from Vermont.

ENCORE! ENCORE! (*Situation Comedy*)

FIRST TELECAST: *September 22, 1998*
LAST TELECAST: *February 3, 1999*
BROADCAST HISTORY:

Sep 1998–Nov 1998, NBC Tue 8:30–9:00
Dec 1998–Feb 1999, NBC Wed 9:30–10:00

CAST:

Joseph Pinoni .... Nathan Lane
Marie Pinoni .... Joan Plowright
Francesca Pinoni .... Glenne Headly
Michael Pinoni (age 16) .... Trevor Fehrman
Leo Wodecki .... Ernie Sabella
Claude Bertrand .... James Patrick Stuart

Mama mia! Joseph Pinoni was on top of the world, a world-famous Italian opera star who ate a bad clam and collapsed in the middle of a performance of *Pagliacci,* only to have the doctor who pumped his stomach botch the job and ruin his precious vocal cords. When egotistical, skirt-chasing Joseph realized that his high-flying career was suddenly over, he returned to the family vineyard in Napa, California, to sulk, meddle, and overact for the only audience he had left—his own family. Marie was his unimpressed mom, who let him know he was no star in *her* home; Francesca, his wimpy, divorced sister, resentful of the fame he had gained while she stayed home and helped run the business; and Michael her shy son, who liked the colorful uncle who added a little *brio* to the orderly household. Claude was Joseph's wealthy friend and co-conspirator from the opera world, and Leo the gruff vineyard manager.

The operatic vocals were dubbed by Thomas Harper.

ENCORE PLAYHOUSE, see *Movies—Prior to 1961*

ENCORE THEATRE (*Dramatic Anthology*)

FIRST TELECAST: *July 7, 1956*
LAST TELECAST: *September 14, 1957*
BROADCAST HISTORY:

Jul 1956–Sep 1956, NBC Sat 10:00–10:30
Jul 1957–Sep 1957, NBC Sat 10:00–10:30

Encore Theatre was the 1956 summer replacement for *The George Gobel Show* and ran in the summer of 1957 after Gobel left the Saturday schedule. The 1956 version consisted of reruns of episodes of *Pepsi-Cola Playhouse* and *Studio 57*. The 1957 version was made up of reruns of episodes of *Ford Theatre*.

ENCOUNTER (*Dramatic Anthology*)

FIRST TELECAST: *October 5, 1958*
LAST TELECAST: *November 2, 1958*
BROADCAST HISTORY:

Oct 1958–Nov 1958, ABC Sun 9:30–10:30

Encounter was a live dramatic series, telecast from Toronto and produced by the Canadian Broadcasting Corporation. For a five-week period in the fall of 1958 these dramas were aired simultaneously by the CBC in Canada and by ABC in the United States, one of the few instances of a live "international network" involving the U.S.

The stories varied between romance, mystery, and adventure, but all involved Canadians as characters and featured such Canadian and British actors as Patrick Macnee and Barry Morse.

ENCOUNTERS: THE HIDDEN TRUTH
(*Supernatural Magazine*)

FIRST TELECAST: *June 24, 1994*
LAST TELECAST: *August 21, 1995*
BROADCAST HISTORY:

June 1994–July 1994, FOX Fri 8:00–9:00
Oct 1994, FOX Sun 7:00–8:00
Dec 1994–Jan 1995, FOX Sun 7:00–8:00
Mar 1995, FOX Sun 7:00–8:00
May 1995–Jun 1995, FOX Sun 7:00–8:00
Jul 1995–Aug 1995, FOX Mon 8:00–9:00

HOST:

John Marshall

REPORTERS:

Russell Rhodes
Sandra Pinckney
Sandra Gin
Linda Deleray (1995)
Mark Thompson (1995)

As a summer series this was the perfect companion for the show that followed it on Friday nights, *The X-Files.* Each week three or four stories dealing with exorcisms, reincarnation, UFOs, prophets, psychics, and other supernatural phenomena, including reenactments of the events and the recollections of the actual participants, were covered in serious *20/20* style by *Encounters'* reporters. Following some stories the reporters and the show's somewhat skeptical host, John Marshall, discussed their reactions to what had just been shown.

Fox had problems with the Sunday 7:00 P.M. hour during the 1994–1995 season and kept bringing *Encounters* back to fill in for canceled series—*Fortune Hunter* in the fall and *The Great Defender*, which lasted only one week, in the spring.

Three more special editions of *Encounters* aired during the 1995–1996 season, with Steven Williams replacing Marshall as host. The first two ran on consecutive Saturdays in mid-November, and the last on January 23, 1996.

ENCOUNTERS WITH THE UNEXPLAINED
(*Documentary*)

FIRST TELECAST: *August 24, 2000*
LAST TELECAST:
BROADCAST HISTORY:

Aug 2000–May 2001, PAX Fri 8:00–9:00
Sep 2000–Jan 2001, PAX Sun 7:00–8:00
Jun 2001–Mar 2002, PAX Fri 9:00–10:00
Sep 2001–Oct 2001, PAX Mon 8:00–9:00
Mar 2002–May 2002, PAX Sun 11:00–12:00
May 2002–Jul 2002, PAX Fri 9:00–10:00
Jun 2003– , PAX Thu 9:00–10:00

HOST:

Jerry Orbach

Encounters with the Unexplained was an updated version of the 1970s syndicated series *In Search Of.* Each episode included documentary segments, actual footage of strange happenings, conjecture, differing interpretations, hypotheses and, ostensibly, new evidence that might change general attitudes about what had really happened. The first episode covered the construction and purpose of the Great Pyramid in Egypt, the largest man-made structure on Earth. Subsequent episodes dealt with Noah's Ark, the 1947 Roswell, New Mexico, UFO mystery, the Shroud of Turin, the existence of Jesus, the intelligence of dolphins, time travel and whether or not ancient seers could actually see the future.

When *Encounters* returned for its second season, each episode covered two unrelated mysteries rather than the single topics that had been investigated during the first season.

END OF THE RAINBOW, THE (*Audience Participation*)

FIRST TELECAST: *January 11, 1958*
LAST TELECAST: *February 15, 1958*
BROADCAST HISTORY:
Jan 1958–Feb 1958, NBC Sat 10:00–10:30
EMCEE:
Art Baker (Jan)
Bob Barker (Feb)
PRODUCER:
Ralph Edwards

The End of the Rainbow was a poor man's traveling version of *This Is Your Life* and was produced by the same man, Ralph Edwards. Each week during its brief run, an unsuspecting person or couple would be surprised in their hometown and honored for being good citizens who had made an outstanding contribution to the community. The chosen people were given "The Surprise of Their Lives," a gift, award, or opportunity that they could only have expected to find "at the end of the rainbow." As on *This Is Your Life*, the subjects were surprised by friends and relatives who were invited to participate in telling their story. The original emcee, Art Baker, left the show after three telecasts and was replaced by Bob Barker for the final three.

ENGELBERT HUMPERDINCK SHOW, THE (*Musical Variety*)

FIRST TELECAST: *January 21, 1970*
LAST TELECAST: *September 19, 1970*
BROADCAST HISTORY:
Jan 1970–Jun 1970, ABC Wed 10:00–11:00
Jul 1970–Sep 1970, ABC Sat 9:30–10:30
REGULARS:
Engelbert Humperdinck
Irving Davies Dancers
The Jack Parnell Orchestra

ABC's success with *This Is Tom Jones*, an English musical variety hour, prompted the network to try this London-based revue starring another singer of similar background and musical style, Engelbert Humperdinck. The star (whose real name was Arnold George Dorsey) was a handsome, likable chap popular in both England and the United States. He had done well enough in an ABC special in December 1969, but his regular series failed to make the grade. It ceased production after six months, although reruns were aired on Saturday nights through the summer.

ENOS (*Police Comedy*)

FIRST TELECAST: *November 5, 1980*
LAST TELECAST: *September 19, 1981*
BROADCAST HISTORY:
Nov 1980–May 1981, CBS Wed 8:00–9:00
May 1981–Sep 1981, CBS Sat 8:00–9:00
CAST:
Officer Enos Strate .... Sonny Shroyer
Officer Turk Adams .... Samuel E. Wright
Lt. Jacob Broggi .... John Dehner
Capt. Dempsey .... John Milford
Det. Bigalow (1980) .... C. Peter Munro
Sgt. Theodore Kick .... Leo V. Gordon

Enos Strate was the reincarnation of Gomer Pyle—a gullible, trusting Southerner who had his own hilarious way of coping with urban life. Enos had been a Hazzard County deputy sheriff on CBS' highly successful series, *The Dukes of Hazzard*. When he accidentally captured two most-wanted criminals, the Los Angeles Police Department was so impressed it offered him a job with the newly organized Special Branch of its Metro Squad. Los Angeles was not quite the same after country bumpkin Enos arrived. His street-smart black partner Turk Adams couldn't believe how naive he was, and their superior, Lt. Broggi, had as much trouble with him as the Marines had with Gomer Pyle. Enos always had an ear-to-ear grin on his face, a Southern homily for every situation, and a love for fast cars and wild chases (and crashes). Dumb, maybe, but by the final scene he always seemed to run down the crooks. His friends from Hazzard made occasional visits to L.A. and Enos narrated each episode as he wrote letters to Daisy telling her what was happening in the big city.

ENSIGN O'TOOLE (*Situation Comedy*)

FIRST TELECAST: *September 23, 1962*
LAST TELECAST: *September 10, 1964*
BROADCAST HISTORY:
Sep 1962–Sep 1963, NBC Sun 7:00–7:30
Mar 1964–Sep 1964, ABC Thu 9:00–9:30
CAST:
Ensign O'Toole .... Dean Jones
Chief Petty Officer Homer Nelson .... Jay C. Flippen
Lt. (jg) Rex St. John .... Jack Mullaney
Seaman Gabby Di Julio .... Harvey Lembeck
Lt. Cdr. Virgil Stoner .... Jack Albertson
Seaman Howard Spicer .... Beau Bridges
Seaman Claude White .... Bob Sorrells

This military comedy followed along the same lines as *McHale's Navy* (which also premiered in 1962), but it was set in peacetime. O'Toole was a junior officer aboard the destroyer *Appleby*, clever and an expert on almost everybody's subject, but seldom to be found when there was work to be done. His foils were the usual assortment of lunatic crew members and the overbearing and ambitious supply officer, Lt. Rex St. John. The ship's executive officer was Lt. Cdr. Virgil Stoner. He relayed orders from the captain, who was never seen but only heard, barking orders over the "squawk box."

Based on two books by Bill Lederer, *All the Ships at Sea* and *Ensign O'Toole and Me*. Lederer served as consultant for the series.

The ABC run consisted of reruns of episodes previously aired by NBC.

ENTERPRISE (*Documentary*)

FIRST TELECAST: *October 19, 1952*
LAST TELECAST: *June 8, 1958*

BROADCAST HISTORY:

Oct 1952–Dec 1952, ABC Sun 7:30–8:00
Dec 1952–Mar 1953, ABC Sun 10:30–10:45
Jan 1954–Sep 1954, ABC Sat 8:00–8:30
Oct 1954–Jan 1955, ABC Wed 9:30–10:00
Jul 1957, ABC Thu 8:30–9:00
Aug 1957–Oct 1957, ABC Fri 9:00–9:30
Mar 1958–Apr 1958, ABC Sun 7:00–7:30
Apr 1958–Jun 1958, ABC Sun 9:30–10:00

These documentary films on American industry were run by ABC to fill various holes in the schedule. The original 1952–1953 series was billed in an interesting fashion: "These films, presented in cooperation with such industries as Bethlehem Steel and General Electric, will point out that America is out to prove democracy in industry and to fight communism in industry."

ENTERPRISE (*Science Fiction*)

FIRST TELECAST: *September 26, 2001*
LAST TELECAST:
BROADCAST HISTORY:

Sep 2001– , UPN Wed 8:00–9:00
Feb 2002–Mar 2002, UPN Wed 9:00–10:00
Aug 2002–Sep 2002, UPN Wed 9:00–10:00

CAST:

Capt. Jonathan Archer .... Scott Bakula
Subcommander T'Pol .... Jolene Blalock
Dr. Phlox .... John Billingsley
Lt. Malcolm Reed .... Dominic Keating
Ensign Travis Mayweather
.... Anthony "A. T." Montgomery
Ensign Hoshi Sato .... Linda Park
Cmdr. Charles "Trip" Tucker III ... Connor Trinneer
Admiral Forrest .... Vaughn Armstrong

THEME:

"Faith of the Heart," written by Diane Warren and performed by Russell Watson

This action-packed entry in the *Star Trek* series was set in the early days of Earth's exploration of the universe. The year was 2151 and the Vulcans had reluctantly released star charts to the humans that would enable them to navigate deep space. Captain Archer was the commanding officer of the starship *Enterprise,* a charismatic leader with an insatiable curiosity who inspired tremendous loyalty among his crew. T'Pol, his sexy Vulcan science officer, had been assigned to the *Enterprise* because Soval (Gary Graham) and the rest of the Vulcan High Council didn't really believe humans were ready to explore deep space and wanted someone on the ship as an observer. Initially arrogant and somewhat more emotional than Vulcans were supposed to be, T'Pol came to respect Archer and eventually supported him even when her Vulcan superiors were opposed to his actions.

Others on Archer's staff included his longtime friend Trip, the ship's resourceful chief engineer; Malcolm, the rather proper British-born munitions expert; Travis, the helmsman, who had spent years on interstellar cargo ships and was more comfortable with aliens than most of his fellow crew; intellectual Hoshi, convinced by Archer to leave her teaching career to serve as his communications officer and the ship's translator, and Phlox, a cheerful Denobulan doctor with a vast knowledge of the physiology of lifeforms throughout the galaxies and a particular fascination with humans. Porthos was Archer's pet beagle.

At the time of *Enterprise* technology was not nearly as advanced as in the *Star Trek* series, set farther in the future. Many aspects of space travel were, for the people of Earth, works in progress. Even the transporters were not completely reliable. Archer's ship, the *Enterprise NX-01,* built by his father, was capable of traveling at Warp Five (100 times faster than any other human ship), and carried a crew of about 80. Unlike the other *Trek* series, on *Enterprise* log dates were standard Earth dates, not stardates. The primary villains were the Suliban, a genetically manipulative race that fought with the Klingons, the Vulcans and most of the other races in the universe.

ENTERTAINERS (*Celebrity Talk*)

BROADCAST HISTORY:

Syndicated only
60 minutes
Produced: *1994–*
Released: *Fall 1994*

INTERVIEWER:

Byron Allen

This weekly series showcased celebrities in informal interview situations along with clips from their work. The first episode featured actor Jean Claude van Damme at a restaurant bar, actor/comedian David Alan Grier in a studio full of paintings, actor David Faustino in his living room, comic Paul Rodriguez at a busy traffic intersection at night, model/actress Garcelle Beauvais on the beach, and singers Bebe and Cece Winans at a pool. A later episode featured Peter Falk in his home, Kate Capshaw on the terrace of a hotel, Bruce Boxleitner on the set of *Babylon 5,* Julia Duffy at home, and Daryl "Chill" Mitchell on the set of *The John Larroquette Show.*

In the fall of 1996 the series title was expanded to *Entertainers with Byron Allen.*

ENTERTAINERS, THE (*Variety*)

FIRST TELECAST: *September 25, 1964*
LAST TELECAST: *March 27, 1965*
BROADCAST HISTORY:

Sep 1964–Dec 1964, CBS Fri 8:30–9:30
Jan 1965–Mar 1965, CBS Sat 9:00–10:00

REGULARS:

Carol Burnett
Caterina Valente
Bob Newhart (1964)
Tessie O'Shea (1964)
Art Buchwald (1964)
Don Crichton (1964)
Ruth Buzzi
John Davidson
Dom DeLuise
The Ernie Flatt Dancers (1964)
The Peter Gennaro Dancers (1965)
The Lee Hale Singers
The Harry Zimmerman Orchestra

The format of this variety series was designed to allow each of its three stars—Carol Burnett, Caterina Valente, and Bob Newhart—at least one week off each month. Sometimes all three of them were on a given episode, sometimes only two, and occasionally only one. There was no formal host; instead, each performer introduced the act to follow at the conclusion of his own act. In an effort to simulate a live show, the taping was done on the same evening that the program was actually aired. The regular repertory company of singers, dancers, and comedians was augmented by one or two guest stars each week.

By the end of 1964 one of the three co-stars, Bob Newhart, had left the series, along with several members of its regular cast, and Carol Burnett and Caterina Valente were seen together as co-stars on every episode in 1965. One interesting sidelight is that on November 13, 1964, *The Entertainers* presented a full-hour documentary on the Beatles' 1964 American tour.

ENTERTAINMENT TONIGHT (*News/Gossip*)

BROADCAST HISTORY:

Syndicated only
30 minutes weeknights/60 minutes weekends
Produced: *1981–*
Released: *September 14, 1981*

ANCHORS:

Weekday
Marjorie Wallace (1981)
Tom Hallick (1981)
Ron Hendren (1981–1984)
Dixie Whatley (1981–1982)
Mary Hart (1982–)
Robb Weller (1984–1986)
John Tesh (1986–1996)
Bob Goen (1996–)

Weekend
Marjorie Wallace (1981)
Tom Hallick (1981)
Ron Hendren (1981–1982)
Dixie Whatley (1981–1984)
Steve Edwards (1982–1983)
Alan Arthur (1983–1984)
Robb Weller (1984–1989)
Leeza Gibbons (1984–1995)
John Tesh (1989–1996)
Bob Goen (1993–1999)
Julie Moran (1995–1999)
Jann Carl (1999–)
Mark Steines (1999–)

The latest news items and gossip from the world of show business were presented in straight newscast fashion on *Entertainment Tonight*. To stay up-to-the-minute, *ET* was fed daily by satellite to stations around the country, most of which carried it live. Many of the stories hardly deserved that urgency—who was leaving what series, who was seen going out with whom, hype for the latest movies and shows—but an audience anxious for the latest celebrity scuttlebutt, no matter how trivial, made the program a hit from coast to coast.

There has been considerable turnover in the host assignments on *ET*, as indicated by the listings above. The original team, which appeared on both the weeknight edition and the one hour weekend recap, consisted of actor Tom Hallick, former Miss World Marjorie Wallace, and critic Ron Hendren. Only Hendren survived; Hallick was dropped after a month and Wallace a month after that. Of their many successors, two became cultural icons of a sort, even doing occasional cameos (as themselves) on other shows and in movies: Mary Hart, with her winsome manner and shapely legs; and John Tesh, the tall, handsome co-host whose parallel career in New Age music endeared him to the middle-aged set, but made him the butt of a thousand jokes among the hipper crowd. Married to actress Connie Sellecca, Tesh left the show in May 1996 to pursue a full-time music career as a keyboardist and writer.

Another familiar face, with the show since its debut, was nerdy but authoritative movie critic Leonard Maltin. Others who have passed through include gossip mavens Bill Harris (1984–1985), Rona Barrett (1985–1986), and Jeanne Wolf (1986–1990). The weekend recap, originally called *Entertainment This Week*, reverted to simply *Entertainment Tonight* in 1990.

EQUAL JUSTICE (*Legal Drama*)

FIRST TELECAST: *March 27, 1990*
LAST TELECAST: *July 24, 1991*
BROADCAST HISTORY:

Mar 1990, ABC Tue 9:00–11:00
Mar 1990–Jun 1990, ABC Wed 10:00–11:00
Aug 1990, ABC Wed 10:00–11:00
Jan 1991–Apr 1991, ABC Wed 10:00–11:00
Jun 1991–Jul 1991, ABC Wed 10:00–11:00

CAST:

D.A. Arnold Bach .... George DiCenzo
Dep. D.A. Eugene "Gene" Rogan .... Cotter Smith
Jesse Rogan .... Kathleen Lloyd
Linda Bauer .... Jane Kaczmarek
Michael James .... Joe Morton
Jo Ann Harris .... Sarah Jessica Parker
Pete "Briggs" Brigman .... Barry Miller
Julie Janovich .... Debrah Farentino
Christopher Searls .... James Wilder
Peter Bauer .... Jon Tenney

The lives and loves of a big city D.A.'s staff were explored in this gritty, semi-serialized legal drama, set in Pittsburgh. It was a sort of downscale *L.A. Law*. Bach was the essentially honest but very political elected D.A.; Gene, his charming, ambitious deputy and Chief of the Felony Bureau, who coveted Bach's job and eventually ran against him for it; Jesse was Gene's supportive wife; Linda, the ever-anguished head of the Sex Crimes Unit; Peter, her younger brother, a public defender; Michael, the department's top prosecutor; and Jo Ann, Briggs, Julie, and Christopher, the eager young attorneys pursuing criminals (mostly the slime of the city) while constantly agonizing over their rights. Country girl Jo Ann and smooth operator Briggs had an affair going, as did several other cast members with assorted love interests who passed through.

EQUAL TIME (*Discussion*)

BROADCAST HISTORY:

CNBC, MSNBC
30 minutes
Produced: *1993–2000*
Premiered: *May 1993* (CNBC); *January 2, 1999* (MSNBC)

REGULARS:

Mary Matalin (1993–1998)
Jane Wallace (1993–1994)
DeeDee Myers (1995–1998)
Cynthia Alksne (1999–2000)
Oliver North (1999–2000)

Political discussion show notable for its female co-hosts, liberal-conservative counterpoint, and "insider's view" of Washington. Mary Matalin was a former campaign aide to President Bush, DeeDee Myers the White House Press Secretary in the Clinton Administration, and Oliver North the famous "Iran-Contra" scandal figure. The series aired on CNBC from 1993 to August 1998, and moved to sister network MSNBC in January 1999.

EQUALIZER, THE (*Detective*)
FIRST TELECAST: *September 18, 1985*
LAST TELECAST: *September 7, 1989*
BROADCAST HISTORY:
Sep 1985–Mar 1986, CBS Wed 10:00–11:00
Mar 1986–Aug 1986, CBS Tue 10:00–11:00
Sep 1986–Feb 1987, CBS Wed 10:00–11:00
May 1987–Jun 1988, CBS Wed 10:00–11:00
Jun 1988–Mar 1989, CBS Wed 9:00–10:00
Mar 1989–May 1989, CBS Thu 9:00–10:00
Jun 1989–Jul 1989, CBS Thu 10:00–11:00
Aug 1989–Sep 1989, CBS Thu 9:00–10:00
CAST:
Robert McCall .... Edward Woodward
Control .... Robert Lansing
Lt. Burnett (1985) .... Steven Williams
Lt. Isadore Smalls (1986–1987) .... Ron O'Neal
**Scott McCall (1986–1989)* .... William Zabka
Mickey Kostmayer (1986–1989) .. Keith Szarabajka
Sgt. Alice Shepherd (1987–1989) .... Chad Redding
Pete O'Phelan (1987–1989).... Maureen Anderman
Lt. Brannigan (1989)................... Eddie Jones
*Occasional

He had served as a secret agent for the government, but Robert McCall had grown disillusioned by all the double-dealing that he had seen over the years. Now retired, McCall, who had been known throughout his espionage career as "The Equalizer," attempted to be just that for people who found themselves facing seemingly hopeless situations. Operating his one-man security force from a plush Manhattan apartment, he found his clients through ads he placed in the local newspapers urging people in dire straits to contact The Equalizer. He was both detective and bodyguard, and was only occasionally helped by his former Agency boss, known only as Control. McCall sought to do good on a personal level—as a form of penance for his previous life—often for little or no pay.

Also seen were Mickey, who did much of McCall's legwork; Scott, his impulsive young son; and assorted members of the N.Y.P.D. Turning up late in 1987, as the owner of a little bistro which McCall began to frequent, was a former friend from his Agency days, Pete O'Phelan.

ERN WESTMORE SHOW, THE, see *Hollywood Backstage*

ERNIE IN KOVACSLAND (*Comedy/Variety*)
FIRST TELECAST: *July 2, 1951*
LAST TELECAST: *August 24, 1951*
BROADCAST HISTORY:
Jul 1951–Aug 1951, NBC Mon–Fri 7:00–7:30
REGULARS:
Ernie Kovacs
Tony DeSimone Trio
Edith Adams

Emanating from Philadelphia during the summer of 1951, *Ernie in Kovacsland* was an unstructured live comedy show that highlighted its star's incredible repertoire of nutty characterizations. The humor was slapstick and almost entirely visual, and was a forerunner of the later Kovacs shows. Appearing as vocalist on *Ernie in Kovacsland* was one Edith Adams, who would later marry the star and shorten her first name to Edie.

ERNIE KOVACS SHOW, THE (*Comedy/Variety*)
FIRST TELECAST: *December 30, 1952*
LAST TELECAST: *September 10, 1956*
BROADCAST HISTORY:
Dec 1952–Apr 1953, CBS Tue 8:00–9:00
Jul 1956–Sep 1956, NBC Mon 8:00–9:00
REGULARS:
Ernie Kovacs
Edith Adams
Ernie Hatrak (1952–1953)
Trigger Lund (1952–1953)
Andy McKay (1952–1953)
Bill Wendell (1956)
Peter Hanley (1956)
Henry Lascoe (1956)
Al Kelly (1956)
Barbara Loden (1956)

Ernie Kovacs, one of the most original TV comedians of the 1950s, turned up on the CBS network for a few months in 1952–1953 in this live hour of comedy sketches (at first titled *Kovacs Unlimited*, the same as his local show). With him were many of the regulars from his local show, including singer Edith (not yet Edie) Adams, pianist Ernie Hatrak, and straight men Trigger Lund and Andy McKay. After an absence of three years Ernie returned in 1956, cigar in hand, as the summer replacement for *Caesar's Hour* on NBC. By then he and Edie were married. The supporting cast was different but the humor was the same, largely visual and always offbeat. Among the regular features were *You Asked to See It*, Percy Dovetonsils, the Nairobi Trio, Mr. Question Man, and Clowdy Faire, Your Weather Girl.

ESCAPE (*Dramatic Anthology*)
FIRST TELECAST: *January 5, 1950*
LAST TELECAST: *March 30, 1950*
BROADCAST HISTORY:
Jan 1950–Mar 1950, CBS Thu 9:00–9:30

This live dramatic series was the television counterpart to a successful CBS radio series of the same name. The plays depicted people attempting to deal with danger, the supernatural, or some fantasized situation, allowing the viewer to escape from reality.

ESCAPE (*Adventure Anthology*)
FIRST TELECAST: *February 11, 1973*
LAST TELECAST: *September 9, 1973*
BROADCAST HISTORY:
Feb 1973–Apr 1973, NBC Sun 10:00–10:30
Aug 1973–Sep 1973, NBC Sun 10:00–10:30
NARRATOR:
Jack Webb

Narrow escapes from danger, both natural and manmade, formed the subject matter of this brief semi-documentary adventure series narrated by Jack Webb. Only four original episodes were aired during February–April 1973, dealing with a submarine trapped on the ocean's floor, a demolition expert racing to avert disaster, two children lost in the woods, and an orphan who saves an American official during the Korean war. The four were repeated during the summer of 1973.

ESPIONAGE (*Spy Drama*)
FIRST TELECAST: *October 2, 1963*
LAST TELECAST: *September 2, 1964*
BROADCAST HISTORY:
Oct 1963–Sep 1964, NBC Wed 9:00–10:00

Filmed on location throughout Europe, *Espionage* was an anthology of spy stories, all based on actual case histories. The periods ranged from World War I to the then-current cold war, and covered all forms of international intrigue, civil war, and underground resistance movements. Although most of the performers in these dramas were Europeans unfamiliar to American audiences, some fairly well-known names were also featured, such as Dennis Hopper, Patricia Neal, Arthur Kennedy, Jim Backus, Anthony Quayle, and, in a small supporting role in one episode, author Ian Fleming (of James Bond fame).

ESQUIRE: ABOUT MEN, FOR WOMEN (*Magazine*)
BROADCAST HISTORY:
Lifetime Network
30 minutes
Produced: *1989–1990 (26 episodes)*
Premiered: *May 6, 1989*
REGULARS:
Matt Lauer (1989)
Guy Martin
Ali MacGraw (1989)
Brianne Leary (1990)

Lifetime, the women's network, offered this weekly female fantasy show about the world of men. Each episode focused on one overall topic and included "First Person Commentaries" by opinionated women and men, "Confessions" by men who revealed their "innermost feelings and secrets" one-on-one to the camera, and profiles of male stars ("The Men You Love"). Matt Lauer was succeeded as host in the second season by Guy Martin, an editor of *Esquire* who had previously contributed commentaries. Ali MacGraw and Brianne Leary conducted interviews.

ETHEL AND ALBERT (*Situation Comedy*)
FIRST TELECAST: *April 25, 1953*
LAST TELECAST: *July 6, 1956*
BROADCAST HISTORY:
Apr 1953–Dec 1954, NBC Sat 7:30–8:00 (OS)
Jun 1955–Sep 1955, CBS Mon 9:30–10:00
Oct 1955–Jul 1956, ABC Fri 10:00–10:30
CAST:
Ethel Arbuckle .... Peg Lynch
Albert Arbuckle .... Alan Bunce

Ethel and Albert was one of many popular radio shows of the 1940s that had a second life on television in the 1950s. The format was extremely simple and down-to-earth, following the middle-aged Ethel and Albert Arbuckle through the minor triumphs and crises of everyday life. A gentle realism was the keynote of this series, with blown fuses, burnt-out lightbulbs, and ruined dinners being about the worst things that happened in Sandy Harbor, where the couple lived. On radio the Arbuckles had generally been the only characters heard, but a few friends and neighbors wandered through the TV version from time to time.

Peggy Lynch, who had created the characters *Ethel and Albert* in the 1930s, played the role of Ethel on TV, and Alan Bunce, also a holdover from radio, was Albert. They first appeared on TV as a featured sketch on *The Kate Smith Hour,* before launching their own series.

EVANS & NOVAK (*Discussion*)
BROADCAST HISTORY:
CNN
30 minutes
Produced: *1982–2002*
Premiered: *September 1982*
REGULARS:
Rowland Evans (1982–2001)
Robert Novak
Al Hunt (1998–2002)
Mark Shields (1998–2002)

Political interview/discussion program that aired Saturday nights on CNN beginning in the network's early days. Prior to that, in the late 1970s, Evans and Novak had a similar syndicated program.

In the late '90s Evans and Novak were joined by permanent panelists Al Hunt and Mark Shields, and the show was renamed *Evans, Novak, Hunt and Shields.* When Evans left in 2001, it became *Novak, Hunt and Shields.*

EVE ARDEN SHOW, THE (*Situation Comedy*)
FIRST TELECAST: *September 17, 1957*
LAST TELECAST: *March 25, 1958*
BROADCAST HISTORY:
Sep 1957–Mar 1958, CBS Tue 8:30–9:00
CAST:
Liza Hammond .... Eve Arden
George Howell .... Allyn Joslyn
Nora .... Frances Bavier
Jenny .... Gail Stone
Mary .... Karen Greene

Following Eve Arden's long association with *Our Miss Brooks,* which had ended the previous season, this comedy series cast the actress as novelist Liza Hammond. Liza was a widow who supplemented her writing income by giving lectures, and George Howell was the head of the lecture bureau that booked her tours. While Liza was out lecturing the population, her 12-year-old twin daughters, Jenny and Mary, were at home being looked after by her mother, Nora. The series was based on the autobiography of the writer Emily Kimbrough.

EVEN STEVENS (*Situation Comedy*)
BROADCAST HISTORY:
Disney Channel
30 minutes
Original episodes: *2000–2003* (65 episodes)
Premiered: *June 17, 2000*
CAST:
Louis Anthony Stevens (*age 13*) ...... Shia LaBeouf
Ren Stevens .... Christy Carlson Romano
Donnie Stevens .... Nick Spano
Eileen Stevens .... Donna Pescow
Steve Stevens .... Tom Virtue
Tawny Dean .... Margo Harshman
Alan Twitty .... A. J. Trauth
Thomas Gribalski .... Fred Meyers
**Principal Conrad Wexler* ..... George Anthony Bell
**Ruby Mendel* (*2001–2003*) .... Lauren Frost

**Bernard "Beans" Aranguren (2001–2003)* ....Steven Anthony Lawrence

*Occasional

Louis Stevens was a typical sitcom kid—an angelic seventh-grade schemer whose best-laid plans were often tripped up—in this sunny comedy set in Sacramento, California. Ren was his smarter older sister, one year ahead of him at Lawrence Junior High School but light-years ahead in grades and popularity. Whereas Louis wanted to get by with as little work as possible, Ren couldn't get enough; to her, Louis was a first-class nuisance. Casting another long shadow was older brother Donnie, a self-absorbed jock who was a sports legend at the local high school. Dad and Mom were over-achievers, too, Steve being a successful attorney and Eileen, a state senator. Friends at school included sometime girlfriend Tawny and pal Twitty, an aspiring musician with a band called The Alan Twitty Project. Tom was the school A/V geek who helped Louis with his schemes. Stories involved braces, school rivalries, puppy loves, and how to get out of homework.

In later seasons Ren gained a best friend in gossipy Ruby, while Louis and Twitty picked up an annoying little eight year-old hanger-on named Beans. On the home front Eileen ran for state attorney general and later, at the end of the series' run, for the U.S. Senate. What's a slacker to do in a family like that?

EVENING AT THE IMPROV, AN (*Comedy*)

BROADCAST HISTORY:

Arts & Entertainment Network
60 minutes
Produced: *1985–1995*
Premiered: *October 6, 1985*

Standup comedy from the famous improvisational comedy club in Los Angeles, usually aired at 11:00 on various nights on A&E. At first the guest hosts were showbiz veterans such as Phyllis Diller and Milton Berle, but later the emphasis changed to attract a younger, hipper crowd (e.g., MTV's Martha Quinn). Performers were mostly young talents such as Richard Belzer, Arsenio Hall, Michael Keaton, and Paula Poundstone.

An earlier version of *An Evening at the Improv* was syndicated in 1981–1983, with Budd Friedman as host.

EVENING SHADE (*Situation Comedy*)

FIRST TELECAST: *September 21, 1990*
LAST TELECAST: *May 30, 1994*

BROADCAST HISTORY:

Sep 1990–Nov 1990, CBS Fri 8:00–8:30
Nov 1990–Jun 1991, CBS Mon 8:00–8:30
Jun 1991, CBS Mon 9:30–10:00
Jul 1991–May 1994, CBS Mon 8:00–8:30
Aug 1991–Sep 1991, CBS Fri 8:00–8:30

CAST:

Wood Newton .... Burt Reynolds
Ava Evans Newton .... Marilu Henner
Evan Evans .... Hal Holbrook
Ponder Blue .... Ossie Davis
Dr. Harlan Elldridge .... Charles Durning
Frieda Evans .... Elizabeth Ashley
Herman Stiles .... Michael Jeter
Taylor Newton (age 15) .... Jay R. Ferguson
Molly Newton (9) (1990–1991) ...... Melissa Martin
Molly Newton (1991–1994) .... Candace Hutson
Will Newton (4) .... Jacob Parker
Merleen Elldridge .... Ann Wedgeworth
Fontana Beausoleil .... Linda Gehringer
Virgil .... Burton Gilliam
Nub Oliver .... Charlie Dell
**Margaret Fouch (1990–1993)* .... Ann Hearn
**Luther* .... Brent Briscoe
**Emily Newton (1993–1994)* .... Alexa Vega
**Aimee (1991–1992)* .... Hilary Swank
**Aimee (1992–1993)* .... Ari Meyers
**Dorothy (1991–1994)* .... Jane Abbott
**Philpott (1991–1992)* .... David A.R. White
**Neal Heck ("Thor") (1991–1993)* .. Pepper Sweeney
**Irma Wallingsford (1992–1994)* ..... Alice Ghostley
Wanda (1993–1994) .... Wanda Jones
**Daisy (1993)* .... Leah Remini

*Occasional

Rural Evening Shade, Arkansas, was the setting for this laid-back ensemble comedy. The focus of the series was easygoing Wood Newton, who had, in his youth, been a star running back on the local high school football team before going on to college and pro football. Now he was back home coaching the team, the Evening Shade Mules, which had not won a game in more than two years. Wood's family consisted of Ava, his wife of sixteen years who, during the series' first season, was elected Evening Shade prosecuting attorney while pregnant with their fourth child; Taylor, the careful quarterback on the high school team; and little Molly and Will. Ava's father, Evan, publisher of the local newspaper, *The Evening Shade Argus*, had never forgiven Wood for cradle robbing (Ava married him when she was eighteen and he was thirty), but was himself dating the town's voluptuous but dimwitted stripper, Fontana Beausoleil. Other regulars included Ava's outspoken aunt Frieda; Harlan Elldridge, the town's cranky physician; Merleen Elldridge, Harlan's lusty wife; Herman Stiles, the wimpy math teacher who served as assistant football coach; and Ponder Blue, the philosophical (he also narrated the series) proprietor of Ponder Blue's Barbecue Villa, the restaurant where many of the townspeople hung out. In the last original episode of the 1990–1991 season Ava gave birth to a daughter, Emily.

Over the years a number of significant events took place. Fontana married Evan in March of 1992 and later gave birth to a little girl, Scout. She also found out that Merleen was her mother and that she had been given up for adoption. Herman lost his teaching job at the high school in April of 1992 as part of a budget cutback. He continued as Wood's assistant coach and took on odd jobs to make a living. That December he moved into Frieda's house when his apartment was converted into a condominium. In the fall of 1993 Taylor, who had been going to college locally, moved into his own apartment; the Mules finally won a football game in early October, breaking a 57-game losing streak; and Wood ran for and was elected mayor of Evening Shade. Little Emily, who had rarely been seen since her birth, was now three years old and showed up in several episodes during *Evening Shade*'s final season.

Although the series' run ended in May 1994, a last rerun episode aired in its regular time slot on July 4 of that year.

EVERWOOD (*Drama*)

FIRST TELECAST: *September 16, 2002*
LAST TELECAST:

BROADCAST HISTORY:

Sep 2002– , WB Mon 9:00–10:00

CAST:

Dr. Andrew Brown.................Treat Williams
Ephram Brown (age 15)............Gregory Smith
Delia Brown (9)..................Vivien Cardone
Edna Wallace.....................Debra Mooney
Dr. Harold Abbott................Tom Amandes
Amy Abbott (15)..................Emily VanCamp
Bright Abbott (17)...............Chris Pratt
Irv Wallace......................John Beasley
Nina Feeny.......................Stephanie Niznik
Rose Abbott......................Merrilyn Gann
Sharon Hart......................Nancy Everhard
Colin Hart.......................Mike Erwin
James Hart.......................Michael Flynn
Brenda Baxworth..................Lee Garlington

Andy Brown was a famous neurosurgeon in New York whose world was turned upside down when his wife was killed in an auto accident. With his wife gone he had the responsibility of raising their two children, moody teenager Ephram and perky young Delia, by himself. In an effort to be a better parent—in New York his focus had been entirely on his career—Andy moved the family to the beautiful, rustic community of Everwood, Colorado. Delia adapted quickly but Ephram, deeply hurt by the loss of his mother and bitter over how little time his father had spent with the family over the years, brooded about almost everything. Financially secure and determined to contribute to his new community, Andy opened a free clinic for the townspeople, alienating uptight Harold, the only other doctor in town. His hiring of Harold's eccentric mother, Edna, as his nurse/office manager only added to the tension between the two physicians. Much to Harold's chagrin, his daughter, Amy, befriended Ephram and tried to help him adjust to his new surroundings. Also seen were Edna's second husband, Irv, the black school bus driver who served as the series' narrator, and Andrew's neighbor Nina, who worked at the local diner.

Because Ephram was romantically attracted to Amy, he was reluctant to ask his father if he would consider operating on her boyfriend Colin, who had been in a coma since being injured in an auto accident. Eventually Andy met with Colin's parents and performed the surgery. While Colin was recovering Amy's obnoxious brother, Bright, admitted to his father that he'd been driving the car when the accident occurred. When Colin returned to school he had limited memory of many of his past relationships, including how serious he had been with Amy. Despite his feelings for Amy, Ephram found himself becoming Colin's friend and confidant, as the recovering young man tried to get his old life and memories back. In the spring there were violent outbursts that indicated Colin's recovery was not going well, and in the season finale Andy performed a second delicate brain operation necessary to save Colin's life.

EVERYBODY LOVES RAYMOND (*Situation Comedy*)

FIRST TELECAST: *September 13, 1996*

LAST TELECAST:

BROADCAST HISTORY:

Sep 1996–Feb 1997, CBS Fri 8:30–9:00
Mar 1997–Jun 1998, CBS Mon 8:30–9:00
Jun 1998–Aug 1998, CBS Mon 8:30–9:30
Aug 1998–Sep 1998, CBS Mon 9:00–10:00
Sep 1998– , CBS Mon 9:00–9:30
Apr 1999–May 1999, CBS Wed 8:00–8:30

CAST:

Ray Barone.......................Ray Romano
Debra Barone.....................Patricia Heaton
Robert Barone....................Brad Garrett
Marie Barone.....................Doris Roberts
Frank Barone.....................Peter Boyle
Ally Barone (age 5)..............Madylin Sweeten
Michael & Geoffrey Barone (2)
..........................Sawyer & Sullivan Sweeten
**Andy*............................Andy Kindler
**Kevin (1996–1998)*...............Kevin James
**Amy MacDougall (1997–)*.........Monica Horan
**Gianni (1997–)*.................Joe Manfrellotti

*Occasional

Ray was a good-natured married father of three and a successful sportswriter for *New York Newsday*. His life would have been perfect were it not for one little thing: his bickering parents who lived across the street from Ray's Long Island home. Even that would not have been so hard to take if they were a little less intrusive. Frank, his father, had the code to Ray's answering machine and monitored his calls, while Marie, his mother, stuck her nose into everything their son did. They treated Ray's home like their own—showing up unannounced at all hours. Frank had the strange habit of sniffing the kids' heads because he believed he could "suck the youth out of 'em," and Marie raided their refrigerator. Debra, Ray's wife, tried to like his parents, but wished they had a little more privacy. Despite agreeing with Debra, Ray was unwilling to complain to his parents because he didn't want to upset them. Robert, Ray's hulking, insecure older brother, was a divorced police officer living with Frank and Marie. He was convinced that they liked Ray more than they liked him because, as he was wont to say, "Everybody loves Raymond." Nemo's was a restaurant where Robert hung out. In November 1998, Robert and his girlfriend Amy broke up because he couldn't commit. Andy was an aspiring sportswriter obsessed with statistics who worked at *Newsday* and played basketball with Ray.

Late in 1998 Robert moved out of his folks' home and into his own apartment, but he eventually moved back. The following April Debra decided to go back to work doing PR. In May 1999 Amy came back into Robert's life but he still couldn't commit and they broke up again. In the fall of 2000, while on vacation in Rome, Robert met Stefania (Alex Maneses), the girl of his dreams. She showed up in New York in the spring but he had misgivings about their relationship and things didn't work out. Her strict father and Frank's friend, Marco (David Proval), bought Nemo's. In the winter of 2003 Robert finally got up the nerve to propose to his long-suffering girlfriend, Amy, and she accepted. Then he had to deal with her very conservative, and unenthusiastic, parents, Hank (Fred Willard) and Pat (Georgia Engel), and her eccentric brother Peter (Chris Elliot)—but the wedding plans continued and, in the season finale, they were finally wed.

The series was adapted from star Romano's standup comedy routine about the problems of a father with three young children—this paralleled his real life. Romano's real-life brother was a divorced cop living with his parents, and when the series premiered, the actor's family included a 6-year-old daughter and 3-year-old twin boys. He had even lived across the street from his parents in Queens, New York. Everything on the show was seen through Ray's eyes as he tried to be a good husband, father, son, and brother to the people in his life.

EVERYBODY'S BUSINESS (*Documentary*)
FIRST TELECAST: *July 2, 1951*
LAST TELECAST: *September 28, 1952*
BROADCAST HISTORY:
Jul 1951–Aug 1951, ABC Sun 10:30–11:00
Jul 1952–Sep 1952, ABC Sun 7:30–8:00
HOST:
Oscar Ewing (1951)
This documentary film series on education, health, and social services was presented in cooperation with the Federal Security Agency during the summers of 1951 and 1952. The host was Oscar Ewing, Federal Security Administrator.

EVERYTHING'S RELATIVE (*Situation Comedy*)
FIRST TELECAST: *October 3, 1987*
LAST TELECAST: *November 7, 1987*
BROADCAST HISTORY:
Oct 1987–Nov 1987, CBS Sat 8:30–9:00
CAST:
Julian Beeby..................... Jason Alexander
Scott Beeby.......................... John Bolger
Emily Cabot.......................... Gina Hecht
Mickey Murphy.............. Tony Deacon Nittoli
Rae Matthews...................... Anne Jackson
A short-lived comedy about two brothers sharing a loft apartment in the SoHo section of lower Manhattan. Julian was older and more sensible, a divorced 33-year-old with a small business that tested consumer products for advertising agencies and companies. Scott was a carefree hunk, a 25-year-old construction worker who was irresistible to women. Stories revolved around their divergent values, lifestyles, and social lives. Julian's partner Emily wanted their relationship to be more than just business, and was vocal about letting him know it; Mickey was the young guy who ran errands for both of the brothers and marveled at Scott's womanizing; and Rae was their mother. Stenciled on the door of their loft apartment was the Latin phrase "Tutto E Possibile" (Everything Is Possible).

EVERYTHING'S RELATIVE (*Situation Comedy*)
FIRST TELECAST: *April 6, 1999*
LAST TELECAST: *April 27, 1999*
BROADCAST HISTORY:
Apr 1999, NBC Tue 9:30–10:00
CAST:
Leo Gorelick.......................... Kevin Rahm
Dr. Marty Gorelick.................. Eric Shaeffer
Jake Gorelick...................... Jeffrey Tambor
Mickey Gorelick.................... Jill Clayburgh
Trina.......................... Maureen Cassidy
Everything was "relatives" in this sitcom about a mild-mannered comedy writer beset by his overbearing family. Leo seemed to be the only calm, well-adjusted member of the Gorelick family, which of course meant that the others were forever imposing on him. There was Jake, his tall, bossy dad, who was long divorced from Leo's mother and fancied himself quite a ladies' man (as well as the world's most loving father). Mickey, his mom, was constantly showing up in his kitchen saying "I'm going to go" but never doing so. A clinical therapist who "wrote the book on obsession," she was nevertheless obsessed both with her beloved sons and with showing up Jake. Marty was Leo's excitable, neurotic, self-centered brother, and Trina his bemused writing partner.

EXCITING WORLD OF SPEED AND BEAUTY, THE (*Magazine*)
BROADCAST HISTORY:
The Nashville Network
30 minutes
Produced: *1989–1992* (117 episodes)
Premiered: *September 3, 1989*
HOST:
Dallas Raines
Weekend magazine show for those into power and SPEED, including drag boats, hydroplanes, vintage airplanes, ice sleds, mud buggies, and jet cars. The program was previously seen in syndication, from 1985 through 1988.

EXCLUSIVELY YOURS, see *Igor Cassini Show, The*

EXECUTIVE SUITE (*Drama*)
FIRST TELECAST: *September 20, 1976*
LAST TELECAST: *February 11, 1977*
BROADCAST HISTORY:
Sep 1976–Jan 1977, CBS Mon 10:00–11:00
Jan 1977–Feb 1977, CBS Fri 10:00–11:00
CAST:
Don Walling........................ Mitchell Ryan
Howell Rutledge.................. Stephen Elliott
Helen Walling...................... Sharon Acker
Brian Walling.................. Leigh McCloskey
Mark Desmond...................... Richard Cox
Astrid Rutledge................ Gwyda DonHowe
Tom Dalessio...................... Paul Lambert
Pearce Newberry.................. Byron Morrow
Yvonne Holland.................... Trisha Noble
Stacey Walling.................. Wendy Phillips
Glory Dalessio...................... Joan Prather
Hilary Madison.................... Madlyn Rhue
Malcolm Gibson................ Percy Rodriguez
Anderson Galt................ William Smithers
Marge Newberry.................. Maxine Stuart
Summer Johnson.................. Brenda Sykes
Harry Ragin...................... Carl Weintraub
Corporate intrigue, family problems, and all sorts of emotional involvements were part of the mix in this nighttime soap opera about the lives of people working for, and affected by, the huge Cardway Corporation. Don Walling was the president, Howell Rutledge the vice president and chief rival to Walling, and their families, business associates, and personal entanglements all had their parts in this short-lived series.

EXILE, THE (*Foreign Intrigue*)
FIRST TELECAST: *April 2, 1991*
LAST TELECAST: *January 4, 1995*
BROADCAST HISTORY:
Apr 1991–Oct 1991, CBS Tue 11:30–12:30 A.M.
Apr 1993–Aug 1993, CBS Tue 12:30–1:30 A.M.
Aug 1994–Sep 1994, CBS Wed 1:05–2:05 A.M.

Sep 1994–Dec 1994, CBS Wed 12:35–1:35 A.M.
Dec 1994–Jan 1995, CBS Wed 1:05–2:05 A.M.

CAST:

John Stone/Phillips .... Jeffrey Meek
Charles Cabot .... Christian Burgess
Danny Montreau .... Patrick Floershim
Nadia Fares .... Jacquie Decaux

A *film-noir* spy series, produced in Europe and reminiscent of *Foreign Intrigue* and similar espionage series of the 1950s.

John Stone had been an intelligence agent working under cover for the DCS in Eastern Europe. When the cold war ended, he thought he would return to the States as a hero but, unfortunately, a double agent in DCS framed him for murder and got him branded a traitor. With the help of his friends, Charles Cabot, Cultural Affairs Attaché to the U.S. Embassy in Paris, and Danny Montreau, a colonel in France's Special Action Directorate, John's death was faked so that the DCS would stop looking for him. With a new identity, as John Phillips, he lived in Paris and worked on covert special assignments for Charles and Danny, while trying to find the people who could clear his name. Also seen regularly was John's pretty young landlord, Nadia Fares, an artist who ran a garage specializing in exotic cars on the ground level of the building in which he lived.

In the last original episode it was revealed that Charles Cabot was the DCS double agent and, in a final confrontation, Danny Montreau killed him. As the episode ended, an exonerated John Stone was on his way to the airport to return to the States.

CBS reran episodes of *The Exile* from 1993 to 1995.

EXPEDITION (*Wildlife/Archeology*)

FIRST TELECAST: *September 20, 1960*
LAST TELECAST: *April 23, 1962*
BROADCAST HISTORY:

Sep 1960–Jun 1961, ABC Tue 7:00–7:30
Sep 1961–Apr 1962, ABC Mon 7:00–7:30

HOST:

Col. John D. Craig

Filmed accounts of safaris to Africa, meetings with remote and primitive tribes, archeological expeditions to ruined cities of antiquity, and studies of animals in their natural habitats were all part of this series. Col. Craig was widely seen in later years in a similar, syndicated series called *Of Lands and Seas*.

EXPLORERS, THE (*Documentary*)

BROADCAST HISTORY:

Syndicated only
30 minutes
Produced: *1972–1973* (22 episodes)
Released: *Fall 1972*

HOST:

Leslie Nielsen

True-life adventure films of explorers, scientists, and others in various remote corners of the world.

EXPOSÉ, syndicated title for *Target: The Corruptors*

EXPOSÉ (*News Documentary*)

FIRST TELECAST: *January 6, 1991*
LAST TELECAST: *October 4, 1991*
BROADCAST HISTORY:

Jan 1991–Feb 1991, NBC Sun 8:30–9:00
Mar 1991–Sep 1991, NBC Sun 8:00–8:30
Sep 1991–Oct 1991, NBC Fri 8:30–9:00

REGULARS:

Tom Brokaw
Brian Ross, correspondent
Ira Silverman, field producer
Michele Gillen, correspondent
Noah Nelson, correspondent

After years of demonstrating its inability to mount a successful newsmagazine like CBS' *60 Minutes* and ABC's *20/20*, NBC decided to try a different tack. The aptly named *Exposé* consisted almost entirely of hard-hitting revelations about real and potential scandals, in America and elsewhere. *NBC Nightly News* anchor Tom Brokaw was paired with one of NBC's (and the industry's) most successful investigative teams, Brian Ross and Ira Silverman, to dig up the dirt. Among the stories: Russian mobsters setting up shop in the United States; buying Uzi submachine guns on the streets of Florida; the Mafia muscling in on small-town garbage collection; and death squads sent to kill beggar children who harass tourists on the streets of Brazil.

EXTRA: THE ENTERTAINMENT MAGAZINE

(*News/Gossip*)

BROADCAST HISTORY:

Syndicated only
30 minutes (60 minutes on weekend)
Produced: *1994–*
Released: *September 5, 1994*

HOSTS:

Weekday: Arthel Neville (1994–1996)
Dave Nemeth (1994–1996)
Brad Goode (1996–1997)
Libby Weaver (1996–1997)
Maureen O'Boyle (1997–2000)
Leeza Gibbons (2000–)
Weekend: Arthel Neville (1994)
Dave Nemeth (1994–1995)
Maureen O'Boyle (1994–1995, 1997–2000)
David Rose (1995–1996)
Libby Weaver (1995–1997)
Brad Goode (1996–1997)
Dayna Devon (2000–)
Jon Kelly (2001–)

The long-running success of Paramount's *Entertainment Tonight* eventually prompted another major entertainment company, Time Warner, to produce its own copycat celebrity news and information show. *Extra* was faster-paced than *Entertainment Tonight* and had more stories and a somewhat jumpier video style. It also utilized the resources of *Time*, *People*, and *Entertainment Weekly* magazines to beef up the content of its stories. Unlike *Entertainment Tonight*, *Extra* often had in-studio interviews with celebrities integrated into the "live" portion of the nightly show. Hosts Arthel Neville and Dave Nemeth did both in-studio and on-location taped interviews and, in December of 1994, correspondent Maureen O'Boyle replaced Neville as co-host of the weekend edition.

In the summer of 1996, Brad Goode and Libby Weaver took over weekdays. Diane Dimond moved to *Extra* from *Hard Copy* as a featured reporter and substitute anchor in the fall of 1996. In 1998 the focus of the show was widened to include more non-entertainment news in an effort to differentiate it from *Access Hollywood*, which was aired on many of the same stations. When Maureen O'Boyle left the show in the summer of 2000, substitute anchor Dayna Devon took over the hosting duties until the fall arrival of new full-time anchor Leeza Gibbons.

EXTRAORDINARY, THE (*Supernatural*)

BROADCAST HISTORY:

Syndicated only
60 minutes
Produced: *1994–1996* (52 episodes)
Released: *September 1994*

HOST:

Corbin Bernsen

INVESTIGATORS:

Rafael Abramovitz (1994–1995)
Alison Holloway
Mary Hughes
Warwick Moss (1994–1995)

The Extraordinary offered viewers a weekly collection of investigations of real-life paranormal experiences—witches, exorcisms, spirits, and UFOs. There was a man immune to snake venom, a man who lost his sight and most of his hearing in a car accident and got them back a decade later after he was struck by lightning, a curse that affected people who violated a Hopi Indian burial ground in Arizona, a ghost in a castle in England, a woman who communicated with animals, and a man going through an exorcism. The show used interviews and reenactments to tell its stories when actual footage was not available. It also included celebrities telling of revelations, personal experiences, and encounters with spirits from the other side. Among those with such stories were Jim Belushi, Robert Mitchum, Loni Anderson, Roger Moore, Lou Gossett, Jr., Jacqueline Bisset, John Forsythe, and Robert Stack. Host Corbin Bernsen was seen in a dark, moody setting smoking a big cigar.

EXTREME (*Adventure*)

FIRST TELECAST: *January 29, 1995*
LAST TELECAST: *April 6, 1995*
BROADCAST HISTORY:

Jan 1995, ABC Sun 10:30–11:30
Mar 1995–Apr 1995, ABC Thu 8:00–9:00

CAST:

Reese Wheeler .... James Brolin
Farley Potts .... Tom Wright
Kyle Hansen .... Cameron Bancroft
Lance Monroe .... Justin Lazard
Andie McDermmott .... Julie Bowen
Sarah Bowen .... Brooke Langton
Bones Bowen .... Micah Dyer
Skeeter .... Danny Masterson
Callie Manners .... Elizabeth Gracen
Sheriff Lynn Roberts .... Patricia Charbonneau
Marnie Shepard .... Dey Young

The spectacular mountains around Park City, Utah, served as the backdrop (some might say the star) of this outdoor adventure series. Reese was the fatherly leader of the Steep Mountain Rescue Group, responsible for plucking foolhardy daredevils off the sheer cliffs of the unforgiving peaks. His team consisted of seasoned helicopter pilot and old friend (from 'Nam) Farley; handsome Kyle, who was tormented by the recent death of his fiancée; even more handsome Lance, a suave self-promoter hoping to break into show business; Andie, a lively, ambitious local girl; and Sarah, a runaway heiress looking for adventure. Bones (Sarah's kid brother) and Skeeter were two teenage schemers who provided comic relief, and Callie was a cunning developer determined to ruin the pristine wilderness.

Besides the daring rescues (always just as the rope was about to break), team members agonized about their lives and engaged in quite a bit of romantic interplay.

EX-TREME DATING (*Audience Participation*)

BROADCAST HISTORY:

Syndicated only
30 minutes
Produced: *2002–*
Released: *July 2002*

HOST:

Jillian Barberie

Yet another of the many voyeuristic dating shows that cluttered the TV landscape at the start of the 21st century. Each episode of *Ex-Treme Dating* followed a date between a subject and a member of the opposite sex chosen to match his or her previously determined "dating profile." What the subject didn't know was that two people he or she had previously dated were in the studio watching the proceedings on a TV monitor. They were able to talk to the date via an earpiece—providing background information, advice and, occasionally, warnings about what to expect. This left the subject at a distinct disadvantage and gave sexy host Jillian the opportunity to make cynical comments about the progress of the date.

EXTREMISTS WITH GABRIELLE REECE, THE (*Sports Anthology*)

BROADCAST HISTORY:

Syndicated only
30 minutes
Produced: *1995–1997* (52 episodes)
Released: *September 1995*

HOSTESS:

Gabrielle Reece (1995–1996)

CORRESPONDENT:

Laird Hamilton (1996–1997)

ANNOUNCER:

Jim Ladd

Statuesque (6-foot-3) professional beach volleyball player Gabrielle Reece hosted this series featuring people engaged in "extreme" sports—those with an unusually high level of personal danger to the participants. Among the sports covered were bungee jumping, motorcycle drag racing, downhill mountain biking, barefoot water skiing, hang gliding, and airplane dog fights. Although some were too dangerous to try herself, she did participate in many of the sports.

Reece was gone when the series returned for the 1996–1997 season and the title was shortened to *The Extremists*. The off-screen narrator remained and Laird Hamilton was added as a correspondent on some segments.

EYE ON HOLLYWOOD (*Magazine*)

FIRST TELECAST: *August 4, 1983*
LAST TELECAST: *July 18, 1986*

BROADCAST HISTORY:

Aug 1983–Sep 1983, ABC Thu 8:00–8:30
Feb 1984–Jun 1984, ABC Mon–Fri 12:00–12:30 A.M.
Jun 1984–Aug 1985, ABC Mon–Thu 12:00–12:30 A.M.
Aug 1985–Dec 1985, ABC Tue–Fri 12:00–12:30 A.M.
Jan 1986–Jul 1986, ABC Mon–Fri 12:00–12:30 A.M.

HOST:

Tawny Schneider (1983–1984)
Chuck Henry
Paul Moyer (1984)
Jann Carl (1985–1986)

CORRESPONDENT:

Johnny Mountain

For those who couldn't get enough of showbiz glamour, this fast-paced magazine series brought video reports on such burning questions as what the truly rich in Los Angeles spend their money on (gold-plated handguns and mink bedspreads, it seems) and "California Girls, the Myth and the Reality." One of the regular features was "Pressed for Time," a 60-second montage of clips showing a famous L.A. location like Sunset Boulevard or Disneyland. The series was based on the local Los Angeles television program "Eye on L.A.," seen on KABC-TV.

EYE TO EYE (*Detective*)

FIRST TELECAST: *March 21, 1985*
LAST TELECAST: *May 2, 1985*
BROADCAST HISTORY:

Mar 1985–May 1985, ABC Thu 9:00–10:00

CAST:

Oscar Poole .... Charles Durning
Tracy Doyle .... Stephanie Faracy

Action series about a mismatched pair of private eyes. Oscar was an overweight, over-the-hill L.A. gumshoe who was semiretired until his ex-partner was murdered, and the man's sexy young daughter insisted that Oscar help her solve the case. They then solved several more, with Tracy providing tight dresses and enthusiasm, and Oscar puffing along behind.

EYE TO EYE WITH CONNIE CHUNG (*Newsmagazine*)

FIRST TELECAST: *June 17, 1993*
LAST TELECAST: *August 31, 1995*
BROADCAST HISTORY:

Jun 1993–Apr 1994, CBS Thu 9:00–10:00
May 1994–Jun 1994, CBS Thu 10:00–11:00
June 1994–Sep 1994, CBS Thu 9:00–10:00
Oct 1994–Dec 1994, CBS Thu 10:00–11:00
Jan 1995–Aug 1995, CBS Thu 9:00–10:00

HOST:

Connie Chung

CORRESPONDENTS:

Bernard Goldberg
Edie Magnus
Russ Mitchell
Roberta Baskin
Bill Lagattuta

Two weeks after becoming co-anchor of *The CBS Evening News* with Dan Rather, Connie Chung added this weekly magazine series to her workload. Subjects ranged from the serious to the frivolous, and four or five stories aired in each episode. Chung covered some of the stories and conducted interviews with newsmakers and celebrities. Among the people she interviewed were basketball star Michael Jordan, accused Los Angeles madam Heidi Fleiss, rap singer Ice-T, actor Hugh Grant, computer software magnate Bill Gates, and actress Jodie Foster.

Perhaps the most controversial moment on *Eye to Eye* occurred during the first 1995 telecast. Chung was interviewing Kathleen Gingrich, mother of Speaker of the House Newt Gingrich, and asked her what her son thought about First Lady Hillary Clinton. When Mrs. Gingrich hesitated, Connie leaned close to her and told her if she whispered the answer it would "just be between us." As the technician turned up the volume on Chung's microphone the answer—"He thinks she's a bitch"—could clearly be heard. The attendant publicity, including airing on almost every news program in the country and a complaint from Gingrich that the network had taken advantage of his unsophisticated mother, proved embarrassing to both Chung and CBS. When Ms. Chung was dropped as co-anchor of *The CBS Evening News* that May, resulting in her departure from CBS, the series title was shortened to *Eye to Eye*.

EYE WITNESS (*Documentary*)

FIRST TELECAST: *November 6, 1947*
LAST TELECAST: *April 13, 1948*
BROADCAST HISTORY:

Nov 1947–Dec 1947, NBC Thu various times
Jan 1948–Apr 1948, NBC Thu 8:00–8:30

HOST:

Ben Grauer

One of the earliest regularly scheduled network programs was this behind-the-scenes introduction to the television medium itself. The program was telecast live with film inserts, and frequently went on location. Subjects included how a TV set works, how a TV studio operates, mobile units on location, and the problems of networking. One telecast, in February 1948, traced the history of television from Joseph May's experiments in 1873 to the present day.

EYE WITNESS (*Dramatic Anthology*)

FIRST TELECAST: *March 30, 1953*
LAST TELECAST: *June 29, 1953*
BROADCAST HISTORY:

Mar 1953–Jun 1953, NBC Mon 9:00–9:30

PRODUCER:

Robert Montgomery

A live dramatic-anthology series produced by Robert Montgomery, with emphasis on the supernatural and strange twists of fate. Scripts were both originals written for TV and adaptations of stories. The guest host or hostess for each program, who was introduced at the start of the show by Mr. Montgomery, starred the following week on Montgomery's principal series, *Robert Montgomery Presents* (Monday 9:30–10:30 P.M.).

EYES HAVE IT, THE, see *Celebrity Time*

EYES HAVE IT, THE (*Quiz/Panel*)

FIRST TELECAST: *November 20, 1948*
LAST TELECAST: *January 27, 1949*
BROADCAST HISTORY:

Nov 1948–Jan 1949, NBC Sat 8:00–8:30

MODERATOR:

Ralph McNair

This quiz program required panelists to identify a famous place or face from a portion of a picture—a picture in pieces, an unusual angle shot, extreme close-up, or a close shot of the eyes, gradually widening to reveal other parts of a face. The program emanated from NBC's station in Washington, D.C., where it had begun as a local show in September 1948. After its prime-time run it continued on the network on Sunday afternoons until June 1949.

EYEWITNESS TO HISTORY (*News Analysis*)

FIRST TELECAST: *September 23, 1960*
LAST TELECAST: *August 2, 1963*
BROADCAST HISTORY:

Sep 1960, CBS Fri 9:00–9:30
Sep 1960–Jun 1961, CBS Fri 10:30–11:00
Sep 1961–Aug 1963, CBS Fri 10:30–11:00

ANCHORMAN:

Charles Kuralt (1960–1961)
Walter Cronkite (1961–1962)
Charles Collingwood (1962–1963)

An in-depth analysis of a major current news story was presented each Friday night on *Eyewitness to History.* The program was originally aired as a series of specials beginning in September 1959, then moved into a regular weekly time slot a year later. The title of the series was shortened to *Eyewitness* in September 1961.

F

F.B.I., THE (*Police Drama*)
FIRST TELECAST: *September 19, 1965*
LAST TELECAST: *September 8, 1974*
BROADCAST HISTORY:
Sep 1965–Sep 1973, ABC Sun 8:00–9:00
Sep 1973–Sep 1974, ABC Sun 7:30–8:30
CAST:
Inspector Lewis Erskine........ Efrem Zimbalist, Jr.
Arthur Ward .... Philip Abbott
Barbara Erskine (1965–1966) .... Lynn Loring
Special Agent Jim Rhodes (1965–1967)
.... Stephen Brooks
Special Agent Tom Colby (1967–1973)
.... William Reynolds
Agent Chris Daniels (1973–1974).... Shelly Novack
EXECUTIVE PRODUCER:
Quinn Martin
MUSICAL THEME
"F.B.I. Theme," by Bronislaw Kaper

The Federal Bureau of Investigation has been the subject of several highly popular radio and TV shows (remember *The F.B.I. in Peace and War*?), but none portrayed the cool, professional operation of the agency so thoroughly as this long-running series starring Efrem Zimbalist, Jr., as Inspector Lewis Erskine. Zimbalist personified the calm, business-suited government agent who always tracked his quarry down, scientifically and methodically, and with virtually no emotion whatever.

The cases were supposedly based on real F.B.I. files. They ranged across the United States and involved counterfeiters, extortionists, organized crime, Communist spies, and radical bombings (during the era of Vietnam dissent). Arthur Ward was the assistant to the F.B.I. director and the man to whom Inspector Erskine reported, while several agents served as Erskine's sidekick over the years. Barbara Erskine, his daughter, appeared only during the first season, later being written out apparently because there was no room for anything so fallible as family ties in *The F.B.I.*

The program always portrayed the agency in a favorable light. It won the commendation of real-life F.B.I. Director J. Edgar Hoover, who gave the show full government cooperation and even allowed filming of some background scenes at the F.B.I. headquarters in Washington. Bringing the program even closer to real life, many telecasts closed with a short segment asking the audience for information on the F.B.I.'s most-wanted men (including, in April 1968, the fugitive James Earl Ray).

Associated with the program as sponsor throughout its run was the Ford Motor Company, which accounted for the fact that those agents were always seen driving Ford cars.

F.B.I.: THE UNTOLD STORIES (*Police Anthology*)
FIRST TELECAST: *September 26, 1991*
LAST TELECAST: *June 26, 1993*
BROADCAST HISTORY:
Sep 1991–Dec 1991, ABC Thu 9:00–9:30
Jan 1992–Aug 1992, ABC Mon 8:00–8:30
Nov 1992–May 1993, ABC Mon 8:00–8:30
Jun 1993, ABC Sat 9:00–9:30
HOST:
Pernell Roberts

A documentary-style dramatization of recent cases from the files of the F.B.I., dating from the 1970s to the 1990s. There were no continuing characters, and the roles of key participants in each case were played by different actors each week. Actual newsreel and surveillance films were used to lend authenticity. Cases included that of the extortionist who held Harvey's Casino in Lake Tahoe hostage with a huge bomb (and wound up blowing the place up); the daring infiltration of the Bonanno crime family by an F.B.I. agent; the 1979 assassination of a federal judge; and a 1986 Miami shoot-out that left two agents dead.

F.D.R. (*Documentary*)
FIRST TELECAST: *January 8, 1965*
LAST TELECAST: *September 10, 1965*
BROADCAST HISTORY:
Jan 1965–Jun 1965, ABC Fri 9:30–10:00
Jun 1965–Sep 1965, ABC Fri 8:00–8:30
NARRATORS:
Arthur Kennedy
Charlton Heston
EXECUTIVE PRODUCER:
Robert D. Graff
PRODUCER:
Ben Feiner, Jr.

Created by the same team that had produced the acclaimed *Winston Churchill: The Valiant Years* several years before, *F.D.R.* was a presentation and analysis of the life of Franklin Delano Roosevelt. Eleanor Roosevelt, FDR's widow, acted as consultant during the development of the program and intended to appear on the telecasts, but she died before the series reached the air. Before her death she was filmed relating her reminiscences of FDR's early days, and these sequences were included in some of the early telecasts of the series. Arthur Kennedy narrated, and Charlton Heston read from the late president's writings.

FM (*Situation Comedy*)
FIRST TELECAST: *August 17, 1989*
LAST TELECAST: *June 28, 1990*
BROADCAST HISTORY:
Aug 1989, NBC Thu 9:30–10:00
Aug 1989–Sep 1989, NBC Wed 9:30–10:00
Mar 1990–Apr 1990, NBC Wed 9:30–10:00
May 1990–Jun 1990, NBC Sat 10:30–11:00
Jun 1990, NBC Thu 9:30–10:00
CAST:
Ted Costas .... Robert Hays
Lee-Ann Plunkett .... Patricia Richardson
Gretchen Schreck.............. DeLane Matthews
Jay Edgar.............................. Leo Geter
Naomi Sayers .... Lynne Thigpen
Don Tupsouni......................... John Kassir
Quentin Lamoreaux................. James Avery
Harrison Green.................... Fred Applegate
Maude Costas (age 15).......... Nicole Huntington
Daryl Tarses (1990) .... Rainbow Harvest

Office comedy set at WGEO-FM, a small, listener-supported station in Washington, D.C., where program director Ted Costas had his hands full with conflicts, both personal and professional. The colorful crew included Lee-Ann, Ted's spitfire ex-wife, whom he had recently hired to co-host a talk show; Harrison, Lee-Ann's pompous conservative co-host; Gretchen, the sexy young office assistant whom Lee-Ann saw as a rival for Ted's affections (or at least for his libido); Jay, the eager but bumbling gofer recently promoted to producer, with the hots for Gretchen; Quentin, who doubled as a classical music announcer and "dat wild reggae mon, the mighty Doctor Q!"; Don, the on-air voice man whose mimicry never seemed to stop; and Naomi, the levelheaded station manager. Popping in from time to time were Daryl, an incredibly sexy computer repairperson, and Maude, Ted and Lee-Ann's teenage daughter, who was constantly trying to get them back together.

F TROOP (*Situation Comedy*)
FIRST TELECAST: *September 14, 1965*
LAST TELECAST: *August 31, 1967*
BROADCAST HISTORY:
Sep 1965–Aug 1966, ABC Tue 9:00–9:30
Sep 1966–Aug 1967, ABC Thu 8:00–8:30
CAST:
Capt. Wilton Parmenter .... Ken Berry
Sgt. Morgan O'Rourke .... Forrest Tucker
Cpl. Randolph Agarn .... Larry Storch
Jane Angelica Thrift (Wrangler Jane)
.... Melody Patterson
Chief Wild Eagle .... Frank deKova
Crazy Cat .... Don Diamond
Bugler Hannibal Dobbs .... James Hampton
Trooper Duffy .... Bob Steele
Trooper Vanderbilt .... Joe Brooks

The "stars" of this military farce were the gallant incompetents of F Troop at Fort Courage, somewhere west of the Missouri, in post–Civil War days. The CO was the wide-eyed, bumbling Capt. Parmenter, who had been promoted from private during the closing days of the war when he accidentally led a charge in the wrong direction—toward the enemy. Unbeknownst to the captain, Sgt. O'Rourke had already negotiated a secret—and highly profitable—treaty with the Hekawi Indians, from whom he also had an exclusive franchise to sell their souvenirs to tourists. There was no peace treaty with the Shugs, however, and they sometimes caused trouble. Cpl. Agarn was O'Rourke's chief aide and assistant schemer, and Wrangler Jane the hard-riding, fast-shooting cowgirl who was out to marry Parmenter.

A lot of colorful Indians and others passed through this series in special appearances, including Roaring Chicken (Edward Everett Horton); 147-year-old Flaming Arrow (Phil Harris); Bald Eagle (Don Rickles); Wise Owl (Milton Berle), an Indian detective; Sgt. Ramsden (Paul Lynde), a singing mountie; and Wrongo Starr (Henry Gibson), a jinxed cavalry trooper.

FX (Network) (*General Entertainment Cable Network*)
LAUNCHED:
June 1, 1994
SUBSCRIBERS (MAY 2003):
79.7 million (75% U.S.)

An entertainment network launched by Fox Television to take advantage of the extra channels that many cable systems were forced to give broadcasters as the result of federal legislation in 1992. Much of its initial schedule consisted of reruns of elderly series such as *Batman*, *The Ghost and Mrs. Muir*, *Mission: Impossible*, *Hart to Hart*, and *Dynasty*, but the network also produced several original daytime shows, including a live morning show, *Breakfast Time*, as well as the prime-time news analysis *Under Scrutiny with Jane Wallace*. Also in the evening was the imported Australian family drama, *Home & Away*, a videos show (*Sound FX*, hosted by Karyn Bryant, Orlando Jones, and Matthew Ostrom), and reruns of the recent Fox hit *In Living Color*.

Perhaps the most novel aspect of FX was its hip, irreverent attitude toward everything on its schedule, including self-mocking promotions (even *Dynasty* was presented as a comedy), and youthful "hosts" who popped on the screen from time to time, live from the network's funky apartment-style studio in Manhattan. The five original "channel hosts" were Peter Chaconas, Jane Fergus, Luann Lee, Jeff Probst, and Vernon Shaw.

In the late '90s FX upgraded its programming somewhat. It added major-league baseball, reruns of more recent series such as *The X-Files* and *NYPD Blue*, and even a few original series, including *Bobcat's Big Ass Show* (1998), a bawdy game show with Bobcat Goldthwait; and *Penn & Teller's Sin City Spectacular* (1998), a variety show from Las Vegas starring the magicians.

Later seasons brought more original series, most of which were by TV standards rather sexy and edgy (or offensive, depending on your point of view). These included *The X Show*, *Son of the Beach*, *The Shield* and *Lucky*. FX first reached half of all U.S. television homes in August 2000, and its principal original series aired after that date are listed in this book under their individual titles.

FX: THE SERIES (*Police Drama*)
BROADCAST HISTORY:
Syndicated only
60 minutes
Produced: *1996–1998* (39 episodes)
Released: *September 1996*
CAST:
Rollie Tyler .... Cameron Daddo
Det. Leo McCarthy (1996–1997) ..... Kevin Dobson
Angie Ramirez .... Christina Cox
Lucinda Scott (1996–1997) ...... Carrie-Anne Moss
Colleen O'Malley (1996–1997) .... Sherry Miller
Det. Francis Gatti .... Richard Waugh
Capt. Marvin VanDuren .... Jason Blicker
Det. Mira Sanchez (1997–1998) .. Jacqueline Torres

Australian-born special effects genius Rollie Tyler, who made his living working on films and TV series, moonlighted with the New York City police solving crimes in this series. His specialties were makeup, mechanical gadgets, and visual effects utilizing a van that served as his mobile workshop. His police work was primarily for his buddy, Leo, a detective working out of Manhattan's Midtown South precinct. Also seen were Rollie's assistant Angie, a recent film school graduate who zipped around on skates; Lucinda, an actress who could do dialects and play almost any age; Frank, Leo's young partner; VanDuren, Leo's smarmy boss; and Colleen, who had a desk job at the precinct and was Leo's sometimes love interest. Blue was Rollie's mobile electronic "dog," complete with bark, that was used to help with the stings they ran on criminals.

In the second season premiere, Leo was set up and killed when a warehouse in which he was negotiating with gun runners was blown up. New to the cast was Det. Sanchez from Internal Affairs, who, after investigating Leo's murder, was transferred to Midtown South. She worked with Rollie and the gang.

Adapted from the feature films *F/X* and *F/X2*, which starred Bryan Brown and Brian Dennehy.

F.Y.I. (*Public Affairs*)
FIRST TELECAST: *June 5, 1960*
LAST TELECAST: *September 25, 1960*
BROADCAST HISTORY:
Jun 1960–Sep 1960, CBS Sun 6:00–6:30
HOST:
Douglas Edwards

F.Y.I. (For Your Information) premiered as a Sunday morning informational program on CBS in January 1960. It moved to Sunday evenings for the summer of 1960, providing filmed reports and interviews covering such subjects as the political problems of shifting city populations, the pressures leading to mental breakdowns, and European attitudes toward the American way of electing political leaders.

FABLE FOR A SUMMER NIGHT, see *ABC Dramatic Shorts—1952–1953*

FABULOUS FRAUD, THE, see *Colonel Humphrey Flack*

FACE IS FAMILIAR, THE (*Quiz*)
FIRST TELECAST: *May 7, 1966*
LAST TELECAST: *September 3, 1966*
BROADCAST HISTORY:
May 1966–Sep 1966, CBS Sat 9:30–10:00
EMCEE:
Jack Whitaker

This summer game show featured two teams of contestants, each consisting of a celebrity guest and a non-celebrity contestant. The teams competed to guess the identity of a familiar face from scrambled sections of a photograph of that face. As each team correctly answered questions from the emcee, increasing sections of the face were revealed. The first team to guess the correct identity won $200 and the chance to win an additional $500 by correctly identifying which sets of eyes, noses, and mouths belonged to specific predesignated celebrities.

FACE OF DANGER, THE (*Dramatic Anthology*)
FIRST TELECAST: *April 18, 1959*
LAST TELECAST: *May 30, 1959*
BROADCAST HISTORY:
Apr 1959–May 1959, CBS Sat 9:00–9:30

The filmed dramas telecast in this short-lived series were all reruns of episodes previously aired in the series *Playhouse of Stars.*

FACE THE MUSIC (*Music*)
FIRST TELECAST: *May 3, 1948*
LAST TELECAST: *May 19, 1949*
BROADCAST HISTORY:
May 1948, CBS Mon/Wed 7:15–7:30
May 1948, CBS Mon/Wed/Fri 7:15–7:30
May 1948–Jun 1948, CBS Mon/Wed/Thu/Fri 7:15–7:30
Jun 1948–Aug 1948, CBS Mon–Fri 7:15–7:30
Aug 1948–Feb 1949, CBS Mon–Fri 7:45–8:00
Feb 1949–Mar 1949, CBS Mon/Tue/Thu/Fri 7:45–8:00
Mar 1949–Apr 1949, CBS Tue/Thu 7:45–8:00
Apr 1949–May 1949, CBS Tue/Thu 7:15–7:30
REGULARS:
Johnny Desmond (1948)
Shaye Cogan (1948)
Carole Coleman
Tony Mottola Trio

This live musical show premiered as a twice-a-week feature starring vocalists Johnny Desmond and Shaye Cogan with music by the Tony Mottola Trio. Within six weeks of its premiere it had expanded to a five-day-a-week schedule. On December 13, 1948, the title was changed to *Make Mine Music* and Carole Coleman took over as featured singer.

FACE THE NATION (*Interview*)
FIRST TELECAST: *October 2, 1960*
LAST TELECAST: *April 6, 1961*
BROADCAST HISTORY:
Oct 1960–Nov 1960, CBS Sun 6:00–6:30
Nov 1960–Dec 1960, CBS Mon 10:30–11:00
Jan 1961–Apr 1961, CBS Thu 10:00–10:30
MODERATORS:
Stuart Novins (1960)
Howard K. Smith (1960–1961)

CBS' well-respected public affairs program, in which leading politicians and other public figures were subjected to questioning by a panel of newsmen, premiered on Sunday, November 7, 1954. Though it has spent most of its long career as a Sunday daytime program, it was seen for short periods in the early 1960s as a nighttime show. When *Face the Nation* premiered in late 1954, CBS newsman Ted Koop was the moderator. He was replaced the following August by Stuart Novins, who was still moderating the show when it moved to prime time in 1960. Howard K. Smith took over in November 1960. His successors have been Paul Niven (1963–1965), Martin Agronsky (1965–1969), George Herman (1969–1983), Lesley Stahl (1983–1991), and Bob Schieffer (since 1991).

FACE TO FACE (*Cartoon Quiz*)
FIRST TELECAST: *June 9, 1946*
LAST TELECAST: *January 26, 1947*
BROADCAST HISTORY:
Jun 1946–Jan 1947, NBC Sun 8:00–8:20
REGULARS:
Eddie Dunn
Bill Dunn
"Sugar"

The idea of this early game show was for an artist to draw a picture of an unseen person from verbal clues, then compare the results with the actual person, when he came into the studio. At first the subject was in a separate room, unseen by viewers and heard only over a telephone line; later he sat on the opposite side of a curtain from the artist, and viewers could compare the sketch as it progressed. There was also a quiz element, with prizes for identifying a celebrity from various clues. Bill Dunn did the sketching and Eddie Dunn the interviewing, with a woman named Sugar present on later telecasts as a kind of emcee.

As with some other early programs, it is not known whether this was carried over the NBC network from the start; however, it was a network feature by early November 1946 at the latest.

FACE TO FACE WITH CONNIE CHUNG, see *Saturday Night with Connie Chung*

FACTS OF LIFE, THE (*Situation Comedy*)

FIRST TELECAST: *August 24, 1979*
LAST TELECAST: *September 10, 1988*
BROADCAST HISTORY:

Aug 1979–Sep 1979, NBC Fri 8:30–9:00
Mar 1980–May 1980, NBC Fri 8:30–9:00
Jun 1980–Jul 1980, NBC Wed 9:30–10:00
Aug 1980–Oct 1980, NBC Fri 8:30–9:00
Nov 1980–Oct 1981, NBC Wed 9:30–10:00
Oct 1981–Aug 1985, NBC Wed 9:00–9:30
Sep 1985–Jun 1986, NBC Sat 8:30–9:00
Jun 1986–May 1987, NBC Sat 8:00–8:30
Jun 1987–Jul 1987, NBC Wed 9:00–9:30
Jul 1987–Sep 1988, NBC Sat 8:00–8:30

CAST:

Edna Garrett (1979–1986) .... Charlotte Rae
Blair Warner .... Lisa Whelchel
Dorothy "Tootie" Ramsey .... Kim Fields
Natalie Green .... Mindy Cohn
Jo Polniaczek (1980–1988) .... Nancy McKeon
Steven Bradley (1979–1980) .... John Lawlor
Miss Emily Mahoney (1979) .... Jenny O'Hara
Nancy Olson (1979–1980) .... Felice Schacter
Sue Ann Weaver (1979–1980) .... Julie Piekarski
Cindy Webster (1979–1980) ... Julie Anne Haddock
Molly Parker (1979–1980) .... Molly Ringwald
Howard (1980–1981) .... Hugh Gillin
Mr. Charles Parker (1981–1983) .... Roger Perry
**Geri Warner (1981–1984)* .... Geri Jewell
Kelly Affinado (1983–1984) .... Pamela Segall
Cliff (1983–1984) .... Woody Brown
George Burnett (1985–1986) .... George Clooney
Andy Moffet (1985–1988) .... MacKenzie Astin
Beverly Ann Stickle (1986–1988) . Cloris Leachman
Pippa McKenna (1987–1988) .... Sherrie Krenn
Jeff Williams (1987–1988) .... Todd Hollowell
Snake Robinson (1987–1988) ..... Robert Romanus
Casey Clark (1987–1988) .... Paul Provenza
Rick Bonner (1988) .... Scott Bryce

*Occasional

THEME:

"The Facts of Life," by Alan Thicke, Gloria Loring, and Al Burton, sung by Gloria Loring

This spin-off from the popular NBC comedy *Diff'rent Strokes* originally focused on Mrs. Garrett, who had been the Drummonds' housekeeper prior to taking a job as housemother at the prestigious Eastland school for young women. Mrs. Garrett was kind and understanding, serving as both confidante and surrogate parent to the girls in her charge, who at the start of the series ranged in age from 11 to 15. Blair, 15, was wealthy, attractive, and spoiled; Nancy, 14, was well-rounded; Sue Ann, 14, was cute and boy-crazy; Tootie, 11, was the resident gossip; and Natalie, the other principal student, was plump and impressionable. The headmaster at Eastland was Mr. Bradley, and Miss Mahoney was a teacher seen only during the tryout run of *The Facts of Life* in the summer of 1979.

As the seasons passed, the series evolved. By 1980 Mrs. Garrett had taken on the additional responsibilities of dietician at Eastland, and there were two new cast members: Jo, a 16-year-old street kid from the Bronx who maintained a tough exterior to hide her insecurities; and Howard, the cook at Eastland. Mr. Bradley was succeeded as headmaster by the seldom-seen Mr. Harris (Kenneth Mars), and then by Mr. Parker. It was Parker's callousness toward Mrs. Garrett that led to a major change in 1983. Frustrated at having been underpaid and taken for granted for so long, Edna vented her frustration to her beloved son Raymond, an accountant who stunned her by offering to buy a run-down store in the nearby town of Peekskill, New York, and letting her reopen it as a gourmet food shop. Thus was born Edna's Edibles. Blair and Jo (who were now attending nearby Langley College) and Tootie and Natalie (still at Eastland) moved in, and their good times continued.

In 1985 a fire destroyed the store and Mrs. Garrett and the girls rebuilt it into a completely new business—an updated version of a 1950s malt shop, selling everything from ice cream to records and T-shirts, and called "Over Our Heads." It was the perfect hangout for students at Langley, and the girls were all partners. Young Andy was the errand boy, and George the good-looking young carpenter who helped with the rebuilding. The following year Mrs. Garrett remarried and tearfully moved away; she was replaced by her chatterbox sister, Beverly Ann, who became the new "housemother" and stepmother to Andy.

By 1987–1988 the "girls" had become young women. It was announced that this would be *The Facts of Life*'s last season, and each of the regulars was seen embarking on adult life, each in her own way. Natalie, the aspiring author, got her first taste of a writer's life in New York City, and was also the first to lose her virginity when she spent the night with her boyfriend Snake. Shortly thereafter Jo, who was headed for a business career, was married to free-wheeling musician Rick. Tootie, who was engaged to Jeff, planned to become an actress, and enrolled at the prestigious Royal Academy of Dramatic Arts in London. But the most surprising was wealthy Blair, by now enrolled at Langley Law School. Watching in despair as her alma mater Eastland went steadily downhill, she decided to do something about it. Putting all her assets on the line, she bought the school and assumed the position of headmistress, planning major changes—including a coed student body—to put Eastland back on the map.

The stories on *The Facts of Life* were funny, but also often touching. The girls faced problems with their parents, including lack of communication, divorce, and death; they also experienced growing pains in a realistic way (it seemed as if teenager Tootie's braces would never come off). Blair's 23-year-old cousin Geri, who was determined to become a comedienne despite the handicap of cerebral palsy, was occasionally seen (played by Geri Jewell, a real-life CP victim). Also seen infrequently were Blair's divorced parents, David and Monica Warner (played by Nicolas Coster and Marj Dusay), and Jo's folks Charlie and Rose Polniaczek (Alex Rocco, Claire Malis).

NBC aired reruns of *The Facts of Life* on weekdays from December 1982 until June 1985.

FACTS WE FACE, THE (*Documentary*)
FIRST TELECAST: *August 27, 1950*
LAST TELECAST: *August 19, 1951*
BROADCAST HISTORY:
Aug 1950–Sep 1950, CBS Sun 9:30–10:00
Sep 1950, CBS Sun 10:15–11:00
Jul 1951–Aug 1951, CBS Sun 6:00–6:30
MODERATOR:
Bill Shadel (1950)
Walter Cronkite (1951)

The Facts We Face was originally a five-week series designed to inform the American public of the impact that the then-current Korean War mobilization would have on their lives. Through filmed reports and interviews the program covered the selective service, production and allocation of resources and manpower, rationing, economic prospects, and civil defense. Following its prime-time run the series moved to Sunday afternoons. It returned to nighttime television during the following summer, with Walter Cronkite as moderator and a new title, *Open Hearing.*

FACULTY, THE (*Situation Comedy*)
FIRST TELECAST: *March 13, 1996*
LAST TELECAST: *August 28, 1996*
BROADCAST HISTORY:
Mar 1996–Apr 1996, ABC Wed 8:30–9:00
Apr 1996–Jun 1996, ABC Wed 9:30–10:00
Jun 1996–Aug 1996, ABC Wed 8:30–9:00
CAST:
Flynn Sullivan .... Meredith Baxter
Herb Adams .... Peter Michael Goetz
Shelly Ray .... Constance Shulman
Amanda Duvall .... Jenica Bergere
Clark Edwards .... Peter Mackenzie
Daisy Skelnick .... Nancy Lenehan
Luis Jackson .... Miguel A. Nunez, Jr.

A cheerful, unmemorable sitcom set in the office and faculty lounge of a contemporary junior high school, Hamilton Middle School. Flynn was the earnest, divorced vice principal, bustling about trying to keep things together despite a slightly off-kilter staff. Her absentminded boss, Principal Herb, was distinguished-looking but totally clueless; best friend Shelly was the drawling, acerbic English teacher; Amanda the flighty young math teacher, a '60s type; Clark the milquetoast history teacher; Daisy the snippy secretary; and Luis the young school nurse. The students were dumb and the laugh track loud. Or was it the other way around?

FAIR EXCHANGE (*Situation Comedy*)
FIRST TELECAST: *September 21, 1962*
LAST TELECAST: *September 19, 1963*
BROADCAST HISTORY:
Sep 1962–Dec 1962, CBS Fri 9:30–10:30
Mar 1963–Sep 1963, CBS Thu 7:30–8:00
CAST:
Eddie Walker .... Eddie Foy, Jr.
Dorothy Walker .... Audrey Christie
Patty Walker .... Lynn Loring
Larry Walker .... Flip Mark
Tommy Finch .... Victor Maddern
Sybil Finch .... Diana Chesney
Heather Finch .... Judy Carne
Neville Finch .... Dennis Waterman
Willie Shorthouse .... Maurice Dallimore

This hands-across-the-sea comedy concerned two middle-class families, the Eddie Walkers of New York City, U.S.A., and the Thomas Finches of London, England, who agreed to swap teenage daughters for a year. Eddie and Tommy had been wartime buddies, and now each had a lovely wife (Dorothy and Sybil), a son, and a daughter. The scene alternated between New York and London as the two daughters, Patty and Heather, explored their new friends and surroundings.

Begun as an unusual experiment in full-hour comedy, *Fair Exchange* ran for only three months and was canceled. The unexpected volume of mail from the show's audience prompted CBS to give it another try. It was trimmed to half an hour and, after a three-month hiatus, returned in March 1963. The shorter format didn't work either, and the program left the air for good at the end of the season.

FAIRLY ODDPARENTS, THE (*Cartoon*)
BROADCAST HISTORY:
Nickelodeon
30 minutes
Original episodes: *2001–*
Premiered: *March 30, 2001*
VOICES:
Timmy Turner (age 10) .... Tara Strong
Timmy Turner (some episodes)
.... Mary Kay Bergman
Cosmo, Mr. Turner .... Daran Norris
Wanda, Mrs. Turner .... Susan Blakeslee
Vicky .... Grey Delisle
Chester McBadbat .... Frankie Muniz
A. J. Ibrahim .... Haneef Muhammad
A. J. .... Gary Leroi Gray
Jorgen Von Strangle .... Rodger Bumpass
Trixie Tang .... Dionne Quan
Mr. Crocker .... Carlos Alazraqui

"Timmy is an average kid / that no one understands" began the theme song of this whimsical cartoon set in the town of Dimmsdale. Ten-year-old Timmy himself put it more bluntly: "Being little stinks!" To his rescue came two fairy godparents whom only he could see, Cosmo and Wanda. Unfortunately they were rather inept fairies, which often landed Timmy in trouble with his loving parents, not to mention his not-so-loving baby-sitter, mean Vicky ("twerp!"). Chester and A. J. were Timmy's pals, and Jorgen was Cosmo and Wanda's boss, the toughest fairy in the universe! The Crimson Chin (voice of Jay Leno) was Timmy's favorite superhero. After a certain amount of frenzy, bright colors and running around, Timmy usually learned a little lesson by the end of each episode.

FAITH & VALUES CHANNEL (Network), see Hallmark Channel

FALCON CREST (*Drama*)
FIRST TELECAST: *December 4, 1981*
LAST TELECAST: *May 17, 1990*
BROADCAST HISTORY:
Dec 1981–May 1985, CBS Fri 10:00–11:00
Sep 1985–Mar 1990, CBS Fri 10:00–11:00 (OS)
Apr 1990–May 1990, CBS Thu 9:00–10:00

CAST:

Angela Channing .... Jane Wyman
Chase Gioberti (1981–1987) ...... Robert Foxworth
Maggie Gioberti Channing (1981–1989) .... Susan Sullivan
Lance Cumson .... Lorenzo Lamas
Tony Cumson (1981–1982, 1986–1988). John Saxon
Cole Gioberti (1981–1986) ...... William R. Moses
Victoria Gioberti Hogan (1981–1983) ... Jamie Rose
Victoria Gioberti Hogan Stavros (1986–1988) .... Dana Sparks
Julia Cumson (1981–1986)........... Abby Dalton
Gus Nunouz (1981–1982) .... Nick Ramus
Phillip Erikson (1981–1984)............ Mel Ferrer
Emma Channing (1981–1989) ...... Margaret Ladd
Douglas Channing (1981–1982)..... Stephen Elliott
Sheriff Turk Tobias (1981–1982) .. Robert Sampson
Mario (1981–1982).............. Mario Marcelino
Chau-Li .... Chau-Li Chi
Melissa Agretti Cumson Gioberti (1982–1988) .... Ana Alicia
Richard Channing (1982–1990) .... David Selby
Carlo Agretti (1982) .... Carlos Romero
Diana Hunter (1982–1983)........ Shannon Tweed
John Costello (1982–1985)............ Roger Perry
Nick Hogan (1982–1983) .... Roy Thinnes
Jacqueline Perrault (1982–1983)...... Lana Turner
Darryl Clayton (1982–1983) ..... Bradford Dillman
Lori Stevens (1982–1983) .... Maggie Cooper
Dr. Howell (1982–1983) .... Richard Eastham
Sheriff Robbins (1982–1983) .... Joe Lambie
Linda Caproni (1982–1984).. Mary Kate McGeehan
Vince Caproni (1982–1984) .... Harry Basch
Dr. Michael Ranson (1983–1984) ... Cliff Robertson
Dr. Hooks (1983–1984) .... Raymond St. Jacques
Dr. Lantry (1983–1984)................. Ron Rifkin
Pamela Lynch (1983–1985) .... Sarah Douglas
Terry Hartford Ranson (1983–1986). Laura Johnson
Corene Powers (1983–1984) .... Victoria Racimo
Dr. Foster (1983–1984) .... Thomas Callaway
Valerie (1983–1984)................. Tina Andrews
Joseph Gioberti (1983–1987) .... Jason Goldberg
Norton Crane (1983–1984)......... Jordan Charney
Spheeris (1983–1985) .... Ken Letner
Padgett (1984)...................... Don Matheson
Francesca Gioberti (1984) .... Gina Lollobrigida
Lorraine Prescott (1984–1985) .... Kate Vernon
Greg Reardon (1984–1986) .. Simon MacCorkindale
Joel McCarthy (1984–1985) ...... Parker Stevenson
Gustav Riebmann (1984–1985) .... J. Paul Freeman
Alan Caldwell (1984) .... George McDaniel
Max Hartman (1984–1985) .... John Carter
Father Bob (1985–1990) .... Bob Curtis
Connie Giannini (1985)............... Carla Borelli
Cassandra Wilder (1985) .... Anne Archer
Robin Agretti (1985–1986)........ Barbara Howard
Jordan Roberts (1985–1986) ..... Morgan Fairchild
Father Christopher (1985–1986).......... Ken Olin
Apollonia (1985–1986) .... Patricia "Apollonia" Kotero
Peter Stavros (1985–1987).......... Cesar Romero
Anna Rossini (1985) .... Celeste Holm
Sheriff Gilmore (1985–1986).... John Bennett Perry
Al Hurley (1985).................. Mike Genovese
B. Riley Wicker (1985–1986)........... Henry Jones
Dwayne Cooley (1985–1986) .... Daniel Greene
Julian J. Roberts (1985–1986)....... John McMartin
Sofia Stavros (1986).................. Julie Carmen
Eric Stavros (1986–1988)........... John Callahan
Erin Jones (1986) .... Jill Jacobson
Jeff Wainwright (1986).............. Edward Albert
Kit Marlowe (1986–1987) .... Kim Novak
Dan Fixx (1986–1988)................. Brett Cullen
Meredith Braxton (1986–1987)......... Jane Badler
Vince Karlotti (1986–1987) .... Marjoe Gortner
Guy Stafford (1986–1987).............. Jeff Kober
Dina Wells (1986–1987)............... Robin Greer
Mrs. Whitaker (1986–1987)........ Laurel Schaefer
Sheriff Jack North (1987)............... John Aprea
Garth (1987–1989) .... Carl Heid
Jay Spence (1987–1988) .... John David Carson
Gabrielle Short (1987–1988) .... Cindy Morgan
Kolinski (1987)................... Jonathan Banks
Roland Saunders (1987)............. Robert Stack
Fred Wilkinson (1987) .... Dick O'Neill
Allison (1987–1988) .... Maggie Cooper
Carly Fixx (1988) .... Mariska Hargitay
Rosemont (1988) .... Roscoe Lee Browne
Frank Agretti (1988–1990) .... Rod Taylor
Senator Ryder (1988)................ Charles Frank
Pilar Ortega Cumson (1988–1990) .... Kristian Alfonso
Cesar Ortega (1988–1989).......... Castulo Guerra
Tommy Ortega (1988–1989) .... Dan Ferro
Gabriel Ortega (1988–1989) .... Danny Nucci
Michael Channing (1988–1990).... Robert Gorman
Kevin Channing (1988–1989)...... Brendon Kasper
Kevin Channing (1989–1990).......... Jesse Stock
Nick Agretti (1988–1989).......... David Beecroft
Ben Agretti (1988–1989) .... Brandon Douglas
R. D. Young (1988–1989)............... Allan Royal
Miguel Aviles (1988–1989) .... Jay Varela
Harriet Anderson (1988–1989)...... Angela Paton
Paco (1988–1989) .... Rick Najera
Amos Fedders (1988–1989) .... Michael Fox
Raoul (1988–1989) .... Israel Juarbe
Sheriff Sanchez (1988–1989)..... Ronald G. Joseph
Kelly (1988–1989)................ Amy Michelson
Cookie Nash (1989).................... Janet Julian
Justin Nash (1989).................... Lee Bergere
Anna Cellini (1989)............... Assumpta Serna
Malcolm Sinclair (1989) .... Alan Feinstein
Samantha Ross (1989)................... Ana Alicia
Michael Sharpe (1989–1990) .... Gregory Harrison
Julius Karnow (1989–1990) .... Norman Parker
Ed Meyers (1989–1990) .... Philip Baker Hall
Brian (1989–1990) .... Thom Adcox
Charley St. John (1989).... Mark Lindsay Chapman
Lauren Daniels (1989–1990) .... Wendy Phillips
Walker Daniels (1989–1990) .... Robert Ginty
Jace Sampson (1989–1990) .... Stuart Pankin
Genele Ericson (1989–1990) .... Andrea Thompson
Sydney St. James (1989–1990)....... Carla Gugino
Danny Sharpe (1990)............. David Sheinkopf
Connie Johnson (1990) .... Diane Behrens
Nick Massoud (1990) .... Shahrad Vossoughi
Johnny Sacco (1990).............. James DiStefano

Airing in the time slot following CBS' immensely popular *Dallas*, *Falcon Crest* sought to hold on to the soap-opera addicts with yet another saga of the rich and greedy fighting for power and sex. The setting was the fictitious Tuscany Valley, located in the beautiful Napa Valley region outside San Francisco, and the industry around which the action centered was wine-making. *Falcon Crest* had all the requisite characters: autocratic, evil power broker Angela Channing, industrious good guy Chase Gioberti, lazy young playboy Lance Cumson, and ambitious newspaper owner Richard Channing, among many others.

The matriarch and principal empire-builder on *Falcon Crest* was powerful Angela Channing, played by veteran actress Jane Wyman. Respected and feared by almost everyone whose life she touched, Angela ran the Falcon Crest winery with an iron hand and lived regally in a palatial house near her sprawling vineyards. Angela tried to manipulate everyone to suit her purposes. As the series began, her nephew Chase had just inherited 50 acres of vineyards from his late father, Angela's brother Jason. Angela was convinced the land should be hers, to add to her already vast holdings, but Chase brought his wife Maggie and two children, Cole and Victoria, west from New York to live in the valley and manage his land. Angela and Chase were constantly in conflict. She first tried to ruin Chase by blocking a badly needed bank loan; then she attempted to undermine his relationship with his son, Cole, by implying that Cole might someday inherit all of Falcon Crest. When she couldn't get her hands on Chase's land, she pushed her grandson, Lance Cumson, into marrying Melissa Agretti, to help her consolidate the large Agretti and Falcon Crest wineries under her control. When she eventually lost control of Falcon Crest to Chase, in a complicated legal maneuver, she devoted her life to getting it back.

Compared to Angela, Chase Gioberti was a knight in shining armor. His concerns were with his family and all the people of the valley, and he fought hard to keep the power-hungry from taking over. When he became a county supervisor, Chase did everything in his power to stop Angela from monopolizing the water supply for the entire Tuscany Valley, which could have bankrupted most of the other vintners there. His mother, Jacqueline Perrault, showed up occasionally, to give him advice on how to deal with Angela, and in the cliff-hanger finale of the 1982–1983 season, the two of them ended up getting shot (fatally for Jacqueline) by Angela's mentally disturbed daughter, Julia Cumson (Lance's mother). Julia had earlier killed another figure who was in her mother's way, Melissa Agretti's father Carlo. Chase eventually recovered and Julia went first to prison and later into a mental institution.

Lance Cumson was the archetypal good-looking, ne'er-do-well playboy. He wanted power and money from Falcon Crest, but was too lazy to work for it. Although he chafed at the control Angela had over him, Lance was tied to her. He had married Melissa, who had plenty of ambition and greed in her own right, but he never stopped fooling around with other women. When he found out that Melissa's newborn son, Joseph, had been fathered not by him but by Cole, he disappeared with his old girlfriend, Lori Stevens. Before long a lack of money brought Lance back to his wife and the luxury he craved.

The only character on *Falcon Crest* who approached Angela in nastiness was Richard Channing. He arrived in San Francisco to run the *Globe*, a newspaper which had been owned by his late father, Angela's ex-husband Douglas Channing. Richard inherited 50 percent, while Angela's two daughters, Julia Cumson and Emma Channing, got the other half. Richard was ambitious and unprincipled. Not only did he want all of the paper, but Carlo Agretti's land and Falcon Crest as well. He worked with Jacqueline (whom he subsequently discovered was his mother) to fight Angela, and connived with Julia to get control of Falcon Crest. When all else failed, he fought for, and got, a permit to build a racetrack in the Tuscany Valley that could destroy the area's entire wine industry.

Others with recurring major roles were Angela's lawyer, Phillip Erikson; Chase's wife, Maggie, who worked as a reporter at the San Francisco *Globe*; Jacqueline's nephew, Dr. Michael Ranson, a neurosurgeon who arrived to help Chase recover from his gunshot wound; and Terry Hartford, Maggie's hooker sister who arrived to get in on the action and found it by moving in with Dr. Ranson.

Murders, bombings, and other violent criminal activity became a trademark of *Falcon Crest* in later seasons. A major story in 1984–1985 involved The Cartel, a shadowy international syndicate headed by an exceptionally vicious man named Gustav Riebmann, who was after wartime Nazi booty that had been buried on the Falcon Crest lands. After assorted plane crashes, bombings, buggings and—when that didn't work—seductions, The Cartel (which had been cofounded by Richard's late mother Jacqueline) was finally smashed. Other main stories that season involved Angela's takeover of Richard's newspaper, *The Globe,* with Lance being installed as Editor; Richard's plot to frame Lance for the attempted murder of Angela; Richard's acquisition of a one-third interest in Falcon Crest from Angela's half sister, Francesca; Cole and Melissa's stormy marriage; and Cassandra's vendetta against Angela for past wrongs to her family.

Cassandra was quite successful, leaving both Angela and her partner/enemy Richard in dire financial straits. Angela fought back by calling on an old flame, shipping magnate Peter Stavros, to bail her out. He did—after being abducted by his own daughter Sophia (who wanted the money herself)—and then persuaded Angela to marry him. It was either that, or he would become her landlord! Peter's son Eric later became an important character. Meanwhile Richard managed to claw his way back to solvency by skimming profits from the Tuscany Downs racetrack, until Terry found out and blackmailed him into marriage. Other main stories of 1985–1986 included Richard's schizophrenic lady attorney Jordan, a hooker ("Monica") by night; Maggie's lapse into amnesia, during which she secretly wrote, then forgot she had written, a tell-all novel about the inhabitants of Tuscany Valley; her subsequent pursuit by crazed book publicist Jeff; and Cole and Melissa's plan to hire a surrogate mother, which backfired when the sexy surrogate (Robin) seduced Cole and then kept the baby. Emma's distraction for the season was rough-hewn trucker Dwayne, while Lance's was rock singer Apollonia ("Babylonia" to his disgusted grandmother Angela). The season ended with a major earthquake shaking the valley.

Richard's private investigator Miss Jones was practically a one-person crime wave in 1986–1987, framing her boss for attempted murder, trying to kill Chase, and blowing up Jeff. Richard finally shipped her off to a prison in Borneo, only to have her sister Meredith show up seeking revenge. Melissa, meanwhile, dabbled in a singing career, then made off with Chase and Maggie's newborn baby Kevin (Chase was killed during the rescue at the end of the season). Emma had an even more bizarre year, dallying with a con man/spiritualist named Karlotti. A new arrival was Kit, a mysterious woman of many disguises, at first thought to be Peter's long-lost daughter Skylar. Instead she was on the run from Eastern criminals who arrived in the person of evil billionaire Roland Saunders. He met an untimely end; Kit poisoned his cigar just before Peter bonked him on the head with a heavy wrench. Another newcomer was trucker Dan Fixx, who schemed to displace Lance as Angela's heir apparent. The Richard-Angela infighting continued, but the squabbling wine moguls had more in common than they realized. As Peter departed for Greece (having "amicably" divorced Angela), he revealed that archenemy Richard was actually her son—the one she had been told was stillborn!

Falcon Crest edged even closer to becoming the *Crime Story* of nighttime serials in 1987–1988 as Richard became deeply involved with a murderous underworld group known as "The Thirteen," which was bent on destroying the world's economy. Maggie, his new wife, was increasingly disturbed by his shady connections, not to mention the bombs going off on their estate. Angela, who had a few shady connections of her own, continued to fight Richard for control of the valley, but expended most of her energy luring runaway grandson Lance back into the fold—Dan having defected and allied with Melissa. (In a curious subplot, Angela tried to drive Melissa crazy by having a special-effects expert make Melissa think there were ghosts in her house.) Emma had a fling running a call-girl business, then tried to sell her experience as a movie, while Vickie was dragged off by a Yugoslavian white slavery ring. At the end of the season Richard turned on "The Thirteen" when forced to testify before a Senate committee. Targeted for death, he nobly gave up his life to an assassin (Eric) in return for a promise of safety for Angela and his family. But Melissa trumped Angela, discovering an old deed that proved that Falcon Crest belonged to *her* family. Angela was escorted out of her beloved mansion by U.S. Marshals as Melissa moved in.

The 1988–1989 season began with the revelation that Richard was not dead but in hiding, protected by the feds (who had staged his "death" and an elaborate funeral). "The Thirteen," including kingpin Rosemont, were themselves assassinated by crazed Senator Ryder, who was eventually shot by Maggie when he tried to do in Richard as well. Melissa came to a fiery end, torching the Falcon Crest mansion (and herself) after losing her child and lover. Angela plotted to regain the place, but faced a new foe in Pilar, savvy daughter of the Falcon Crest foreman Cesar, who married Lance and allied with Richard in a scheme to industrialize the valley under the cover of a Hispanic-improvement group called the "consortium." Richard's ingenious ploy of the year was to kidnap Angela (his own mother), delude her with a look-alike of the dead Melissa (Samantha), and when she escaped make it look as if she had imagined the whole thing. He then forced her into a mental competency hearing in which he would be appointed conservator of her affairs! It almost worked, but at the last minute Angela married Frank Agretti, which somehow got her off the hook, and Richard's schemes were exposed, which landed him in prison. Emma's fling of the year was with reclusive writer R. D. Young; the Agrettis agonized over teenage Ben (Nick's son) and his dying mother Anna; and the Ortegas over their teenager Gabriel who was attacked by a gang and almost killed by faulty treatment in the hospital (prejudice against Hispanics?).

The final season was even more violent. Maggie drowned when her diamond ring caught in a drain at the bottom of her swimming pool. Richard got out of prison but faced a new nemesis in murderous financier Michael Sharpe, who stole Richard's sons (Kevin and Michael) and at one point Falcon Crest itself. (Actually, everyone seems to have "seized control" of Falcon Crest at one time or another.) Romantic butterfly Emma married Charley St. James who, with his violent brother Ian, moved into the Falcon Crest mansion, assaulted Angela (who lay in a resulting coma for most of the season), and held a disastrous Bacchus costume party which was invaded by bikers and from which guests went screaming into the night. Charley and Ian eventually decided to kill their bothersome wives (Emma, Sydney), but were instead stabbed and shot themselves. Michael Sharpe and his ally Genele meddled with his sister Lauren's marriage and with his own troubled son Danny (who turned out to be Richard's son instead; the boy contemplated suicide).

Reality, if there had ever been any in *Falcon Crest*, disappeared entirely in the final episodes. Angela awoke from her six-month coma as if she had been taking a nap, and reentered the fray. Ownership of Falcon Crest bounced between Emma, Sharpe, Richard, and the cleaning lady. Finally everyone had a blinding vision of decency and decided to do the right thing. Richard sold Falcon Crest back to its "rightful owner" Angela, with the provision that half would go to his sons upon her death. The other half would go to Lance, 10 percent now and the remainder when Angela died. Indomitable Angela now could run the place for the rest of her days, then it would go to the next generation; she and her son Richard were at peace. Richard and Lauren were happily married, Emma (who had fled) returned to the valley, and mad Julia was safely tucked away in a convent. As Angela's face floated over the vineyards, toasts were raised. "The land endures."

FALCONE (*Police Drama*)
FIRST TELECAST: *June 10, 2000*
LAST TELECAST: *July 8, 2000*
BROADCAST HISTORY:
Jun 2000–Jul 2000, CBS Sat 10:00–11:00
CAST:
Joe Falcone/Pistone .... Jason Gedrick
Santino "Sonny" Napoli .... Titus Welliver
Jules Weller .... Robert John Burke
Maggie Pistone .... Amy Carlson
Jimmy "Suits" Urizzi .... Sonny Marinelli
Alberto "Lucky" Fema .... Lillo Brancato, Jr.

Amanda Pistone .... Delanie Fitzpatrick
Jess Pistone .... Sarah Hyland
Sal "Sally Soaps" Martini .... Allan Steele
Pasche .... P. R. Paul
Vito .... Joe Murphy
Caesar Nicoletti .... Joaquim de Almeida

Joe Pistone was an FBI special agent working undercover inside the New York Mafia for 29 months. When local mob boss Carlo Volonte was murdered, he was caught in the middle of a territorial power struggle. Sonny, his best friend in the mob, was vying to become the new underboss but, after losing out to Caesar, was working on ways to oust his competition. After Caesar forced him to kill his friend Lucky on a mob contract, it only made things worse. Jules, Joe's boss at the FBI, was getting flak from his superiors, who feared that Joe had been undercover so long that his loyalty to the agency was suspect—especially since he had not provided them with enough information to bring cases against any of the principals in the mob.

On the home front Joe's wife, Maggie, couldn't cope with what his job was doing to her and their two daughters, Amanda and Jess, and suggested they separate until the investigation was over and their life could return to normal.

Falcone was based on the book *Donnie Brasco—My Undercover Life in the Mafia,* a true story by FBI agent Joseph D. Pistone with Richard Woodley. CBS originally ran the nine episodes in miniseries format over eight nights in early April. When it was rerun as a weekly series in June it attracted such low ratings that CBS canceled it after only five episodes had aired.

FALL GUY, THE (*Adventure*)

FIRST TELECAST: *November 4, 1981*
LAST TELECAST: *May 2, 1986*
BROADCAST HISTORY:

Nov 1981–Mar 1983, ABC Wed 9:00–10:00
Apr 1983–Jul 1985, ABC Wed 8:00–9:00
Sep 1985–Oct 1985, ABC Thu 8:00–9:00
Nov 1985–Jan 1986, ABC Sat 8:00–9:00
Jan 1986–May 1986, ABC Fri 10:00–11:00

CAST:

Colt Seavers .... Lee Majors
Howie Munson .... Douglas Barr
Jody Banks .... Heather Thomas
Samantha "Big Jack" Jack (1981–1982) Jo Ann Pflug
Terri Shannon/Michaels (1982–1985) .. Markie Post
Pearl Sperling (1985–1986) .... Nedra Volz

THEME:

"The Unknown Stuntman," by David Somerville, Gail Jensen, and Glen Larson, sung by Lee Majors

Spectacular stunt work was the hallmark of this action series, which was rugged Lee Majors's fifth successful prime-time offering. Majors was cast, appropriately enough, as Hollywood stuntman Colt Seavers, who picked up a little extra money by using his special skills to track down and capture bail jumpers. Helping out were Colt's inexperienced but eager younger cousin, Howie, and stunning stuntwoman Jody. They got their assignments from a sexy bail bondswoman named Big Jack, later replaced by Terri Shannon (whose last name was changed to Michaels in 1983) and then by a feisty old lady named Pearl.

Each episode began with one of Colt's daredevil (and usually high-speed) movie stunts, then shifted to his pursuit of the bail jumper—during which Colt often used the same stunts he had used in the movie. None of these assignments turned out to be as simple as Big Jack or Terri claimed they would be, but with so many beautiful women, famous stars, and exotic locales to see along the way, Colt did not complain—much.

FAME (*Drama*)

FIRST TELECAST: *January 7, 1982*
LAST TELECAST: *August 4, 1983*
BROADCAST HISTORY:

Jan 1982–Aug 1983, NBC Thu 8:00–9:00
(In first-run syndication from fall 1983–fall 1987)

CAST:

Lydia Grant .... Debbie Allen
Coco Hernandez (1982–1983) .... Erica Gimpel
Danny Amatullo .... Carlo Imperato
Bruno Martelli (1982–1984) .... Lee Curreri
Doris Schwartz (1982–1985) .... Valerie Landsburg
Leroy Johnson .... Gene Anthony Ray
Montgomery MacNeil (1982) .... P. R. Paul
Elizabeth Sherwood (1982–1986)
.... Carol Mayo Jenkins
Mr. Benjamin Shorofsky .... Albert Hague
Julie Miller (1982–1983) .... Lori Singer
Mr. Crandall (1982) .... Michael Thoma
Mrs. Charlotte Miller (1982–1983) ...... Judy Farrell
Angelo Martelli (1982–1983) .... Carmine Caridi
David Reardon (1982–1983) ...... Morgan Stevens
Dwight (1982–1985) .... David Greenlee
Mrs. Gertrude Berg (Alice Bowman) .... Ann Nelson
Holly Laird (1983–1986) .... Cynthia Gibb
Christopher Donlon (1983–1987) ...... Billy Hufsey
Quentin Morloch (1983–1985) .... Ken Swofford
Cleo Hewitt (1984–1985) .... Janet Jackson
Jesse Valesquez (1984–1987) .... Jesse Borrego
Nicole Chapman (1984–1987) .... Nia Peeples
Mr. Lou Mackie (1985–1987) .... Dick Miller
Laura Mackie (1986–1987) .... Carolyn J. Silas
Dusty Tyler (1985–1987) .... Loretta Chandler
Mr. Bob Dyrenforth (1985–1987) .... Graham Jarvis
Reggie Higgins (1986–1987) .... Carrie Hamilton
Kate Riley (1986) .... Page Hannah
Ian Ware (1986–1987) .... Michael Cerveris
Jillian Beckett (1986–1987) .... Elisa Heinsohn
Mr. Paul Seeger (1986–1987) .... Eric Pierpoint
Maxie (1986–1987) .... Olivia Barash
Miltie Horowitz (1986–1987) ..... Robert Romanus

THEME:

"Fame," written by Michael Gore and Dean Pitchford, sung by Erica Gimpel

New York City's renowned High School for the Performing Arts was the setting for this series about the hopes and aspirations of a group of students planning to become singers, dancers, actors, musicians, and comedians. Geared specifically to provide a curriculum that would prepare its graduates for careers in show business, the School for the Performing Arts attracted a student body with tremendous talent, energy, and ambition. It was there that they learned to deal with competition and rejection, as well as the problems of growing up.

Among the featured students were Bruno, a talented but somewhat arrogant keyboard artist and composer; Coco, a singer-dancer driven to succeed and in a rush to get into the professional world; Danny, a bright comedian who would break into a monologue at the drop of a hat; Doris, an actress-writer-comedienne whose easygoing manner belied an ego as strong and determined as anyone's; Leroy, a talented dancer from the ghettos of New York, who graduated and became an assistant dance instructor at the school himself; Montgomery, trying to follow in the path of his successful actress mother; and Julie, the outsider from Grand Rapids, Michigan, who was an accomplished cellist adjusting both to the school and the high-energy environment of New York.

If anything, the faculty was even more dedicated than the students, with hard-driving, beautiful dance teacher Lydia Grant the most prominent. Other teachers included Mr. Shorofsky, the bearded music teacher; Mr. Crandall, the drama instructor; and English teacher Elizabeth Sherwood.

Fame was an immediate hit with the critics. They lauded its talented cast of young performers, the well-choreographed production numbers, and its realistic portrayal of the problems of growing up in contemporary society. Unfortunately it attracted a small audience, and after a year and a half on NBC it was finally canceled in the spring of 1983. Undaunted, the producers continued production of new episodes and sold them on a syndicated basis to local stations, which generally aired them on Saturday or Sunday in the early evening.

There were changes in the cast. David Reardon replaced Mr. Crandall (Michael Thoma had died) as drama teacher (later replaced by Paul Seeger); Mrs. Berg, the scatterbrained school secretary, became a regular; and Quentin Morloch, an officious principal (later replaced by Bob Dyrenforth) who gradually came to understand that this was not an ordinary high school, was added. New students included Dwight, an awkward, fat tuba player; Holly, a vivacious drama major; Jesse, an Hispanic dancer who became Leroy's protégé; Nicole, a beautiful black singer and dancer who was tragically killed in an auto accident; Christopher, a talented but cocky dancer; and Ian, an English guitarist who loved rock music. In later years Lou's bowling alley/restaurant became a regular hangout for the students.

Fame was based on the movie of the same name, with a number of its cast members—Debbie Allen, Albert Hague, Gene Anthony Ray, and Lee Curreri—reprising their roles in the series.

FAME FOR 15 (*Documentary*)

BROADCAST HISTORY:

TNN
60 minutes
Original episodes: *2001*
Premiered: *October 22, 2001*

Documentary series about those folks who streak across the headlines and disappear. Among the subjects covered (two per hour) were Donato Dalyrmple, air force captain Scott O'Grady, pitcher Jim Morris, Darva Conger, John Wayne Bobbit, vigilante Ellie Nesler, Divine Brown, Olympian Tommie Smith, and George Holliday. How many do you remember? (Hint: Dalyrmple was the fisherman who rescued Elian Gonzalez; Holliday, the man who shot the Rodney King video.)

FAME L.A. (*Drama*)

BROADCAST HISTORY:

Syndicated only
60 minutes
Produced: *1997–1998* (22 episodes)
Released: *September 1997*

CAST:

David Graysmark................ William R. Moses
Suzanne Carson .... Heidi Noelle Lenhart
Lili Arguelo .... Roselyn Sanchez
Ryan "Flyboy" Legget............... Christian Kane
Adam Lewis.......................... Matt Winston
Liz Clark .... Lesli Margherita
Marcus Carilli.......................... Andy Milder
Reese Toussaint .... Stephanie Dicker
T.J. Baron .... T.E. Russell
Robert Hawkins .... Carlton Wilborn
**Brent Legget* .... Brent David Fraser
**Sylvia Williams*.................. Valarie Pettiford

*Occasional

Venice Beach, California, was where most of this class of aspiring young actors, singers, and dancers lived. They studied acting with David, the owner/operator of Who's Who, a small club on the beach in Venice. David had obtained financing from his former lover, Julie (Diane Dilascio), a successful actress, in return for 30 percent ownership of the club. Ryan, just arrived in L.A., was an aspiring actor with a talented but drug-addicted older brother. Among the young hopefuls were the comedy team of Lewis and Clark, lovers living together; Lili, a dancer/actress whose Hispanic family was not happy about her being in show business; Suzanne, an insecure songwriter/singer/guitarist; and Reese, a sexy actress who resented being seen as a "body" rather than a serious actress. In early May, David and Reese got involved in a torrid but unplanned affair, and Lili, after losing a part in a play, almost gave up acting to apply to medical school. Other regulars were Marcus, David's neurotic partner; T.J., Suzanne's friend, who was an engineer at a recording studio; and Robert, a struggling young filmmaker. A new theme song ("You Gotta Want It") was heard at the beginning of each episode, with the famous '80s theme performed by a hip vocal group at the end.

FAMILY (*Drama*)

FIRST TELECAST: *March 9, 1976*
LAST TELECAST: *June 25, 1980*
BROADCAST HISTORY:

Mar 1976–Feb 1978, ABC Tue 10:00–11:00 (OS)
May 1978, ABC Tue 10:00–11:00
Sep 1978–Mar 1979, ABC Thu 10:00–11:00
Mar 1979–Apr 1979, ABC Fri 8:00–9:00
May 1979, ABC Thu 10:00–11:00
Dec 1979–Feb 1980, ABC Mon 10:00–11:00
Mar 1980, ABC Mon 9:00–10:00
Jun 1980, ABC Wed 8:00–9:00

CAST:

Kate Lawrence..................... Sada Thompson
Doug Lawrence.................. James Broderick
Nancy Lawrence Maitland (1976)... Elayne Heilveil
Nancy Lawrence Maitland (1976–1980)
.... Meredith Baxter-Birney
Willie Lawrence .... Gary Frank
Letitia "Buddy" Lawrence......... Kristy McNichol
Jeff Maitland .... John Rubinstein

Mrs. Hanley (1976–1978) ..... Mary Grace Canfield
Salina Magee (1976–1977) .... Season Hubley
Annie Cooper (1978–1980) ...... Quinn Cummings
Timmy Maitland (1978–1980)
.... Michael David Schackelford

Family was a prime-time soap opera that followed the travails of the middle-class Lawrence family in Pasadena, California. Doug was the father, a highly independent lawyer, and Kate his quiet, steadfast wife. The series opened with daughter Nancy discovering that her husband Jeff was untrue (she walked in on him making love to another woman!) and it was all downhill from there. Nancy had a baby (Timmy), divorced Jeff, then began having affairs of her own. Later she went to work for a law firm, which seemed more interested in her body than in her brains. Brother Willie, age 17, vulnerable and idealistic, was confronted with his first love, an unwed mother (Salina), then married a girl with a terminal illness (Lizzy). Little sister Buddy, age 13, feeling unwanted, ran away from home. Before Kate could worry about *that*, she discovered that she had breast cancer, after which Doug was temporarily blinded in an automobile accident. An 11-year-old waif named Annie joined the household, only to reject everyone's affections. Then there was the dying grandmother, Doug's alcoholic sister, and so on, and on, and on . . .

FAMILY, THE (*Reality*)
FIRST TELECAST: *March 4, 2003*
LAST TELECAST: *March 18, 2003*
BROADCAST HISTORY:
Mar 2003, ABC Tue 10:00–11:00
HOST:
George Hamilton

This *Survivor*-style elimination contest was so preposterous it verged on comedy. The premise was to take an uncultured middle-class family, plunk them down in an opulent Palm Beach mansion complete with servants and have them learn high-class manners while competing for a $1 million fortune. Heading the family were bossy Uncle Michael, a 46-year-old sales manager from Manalapan, New Jersey, and his blunt wife, Donna, a school bus driver (who called herself "the bitch of the family"). Their extended family consisted of playboy son Anthony, wiseguy Cousin Ed, gossipy Cousin Jill, obnoxious Cousin Robert, sweet Cousin Melinda, chubby take-no-crap Cousin Dawn Marie, outsider Cousin Maria and shaven-headed, tattooed Cousin Mike, the misunderstood and surprisingly considerate one.

They all competed in silly games such as stealing each other's gifts or a formal auction where the "art" was paintings of one another, and sometimes in such pastimes of the rich as fencing, boating or polo. Each day one of the day's two lowest scorers was eliminated from the competition by vote of a secret Board of Trustees. Unbeknownst to the contestants, the board was made up of the household staff who served them, chief among whom were very proper English butler Andrew Lowrey, snotty social secretary Ringo Allen, manners-obsessed head housekeeper Linda Levis, epicurean chef Franck Porcher, and elegant stylist Jill Swid. In an unusual twist the eliminated family member stayed in the household interacting with those still competing for the prize, and might even be voted back into the competition at the end. The contestant who won the $1 million had the option of keeping it all, or giving a portion of it to other family members. As this book went to print the show had been pulled from the schedule and the winner was unresolved.

FAMILY AFFAIR (*Situation Comedy*)
FIRST TELECAST: *September 12, 1966*
LAST TELECAST: *March 13, 2003*
BROADCAST HISTORY:
Sep 1966–Sep 1969, CBS Mon 9:30–10:00
Sep 1969–Sep 1971, CBS Thu 7:30–8:00
Sep 2002–Dec 2002, WB Thu 8:00–8:30
Feb 2003–Mar 2003, WB Thu 8:30–9:00
CAST: (1966–1971)
Bill Davis .... Brian Keith
Mr. (Giles) French .... Sebastian Cabot
Buffy .... Anissa Jones
Jody .... Johnnie Whitaker
Cissy .... Kathy Garver
Emily Turner (1970–1971) .... Nancy Walker
CAST: (2002–2003)
Bill Davis .... Gary Cole
Giles French .... Tim Curry
Elizabeth "Buffy" Patterson-Davis (age 6)
.... Sacha Pieterse
Jonathan "Jody" Patterson-Davis (pilot only)
.... Luke Benward
Jonathan "Jody" Patterson-Davis
.... Jimmy "Jax" Pinchak
Sigourney "Sissy" Patterson-Davis (14)
.... Caitlin Wachs
**Bert, the doorman* .... Jack McGee
**Chelsea* .... Marina Malota
*Occasional

Bill Davis's carefree existence as a swinging bachelor was just about perfect. A highly paid consulting engineer, he maintained an elegant apartment off Fifth Avenue in Manhattan and had his domestic needs cared for by a very English gentleman's gentleman, Mr. French. Into this life of independence came three young orphans, the 6-year-old twins Buffy and Jody and 15-year-old Cissy. Their parents, Bill's brother and sister-in-law, had died in an accident, and other relatives felt that Bill could best provide for them. Despite initial misgivings, Bill and French became very attached to the children and learned to adjust their lifestyle to make room for the new members of the household. Mr. French, a stickler for neatness and order, had the toughest adjustment to make—he was with the children all the time while Bill was often out of town on assignments—but he and the children managed to compromise and learn to live with each other.

For a period during the show's first season, co-star Sebastian Cabot was taken ill and was replaced in nine episodes by John Williams. In the story line, Giles French was called away to special service of the Queen of England and his brother Nigel arrived at the Davis residence to serve the family during his absence. Although not a full-time member of the cast, Nancy Walker appeared in the continuing role of Mr. Davis's part-time housekeeper, Emily, during the last season.

CBS aired reruns of *Family Affair* on weekdays from September 1970 to January 1973.

When the WB revived *Family Affair* in 2002 nothing much had changed—the show even used the same instrumental theme song, and Buffy was still attached to her beloved doll, Mrs. Beasley. In the new version Bill was a high-powered corporate executive living in a luxurious Manhattan apartment overlooking Central Park, whose sister, Jenny, prevailed upon him to honor his promise to take his late brother's twins after her own kids had grown up. The adorable tykes, brassy Buffy and blunt Jody, arrived from the Midwest, and later the same day their older sister, Sissy, who had been living with Bill's other sister, Lucy, showed up with a backpack and moved in, too. Bill spoiled them all rotten and French adjusted to the their presence—it wasn't always easy—but there was much love amidst the consternation. French enrolled the twins in the Dovetail School, which had been organized by local parents looking for an alternative to the stuffy private schools in the neighborhood, while Sissy attended a performing-arts high school where Chelsea was her best friend.

FAMILY ALBUM (*Situation Comedy*)
FIRST TELECAST: *September 24, 1993*
LAST TELECAST: *November 12, 1993*
BROADCAST HISTORY:
Sep 1993–Oct 1993, CBS Fri 8:30–9:00
Oct 1993–Nov 1993, CBS Fri 9:30–10:00
CAST:
Dr. Jonathan Lerner .... Peter Scolari
Denise Lerner .... Pamela Reed
Nicki Lerner (age 14) .... Ashlee Levitch
Jeffrey Lerner (11) .... Christopher Miranda
Max Lerner (7) .... Phillip Van Dyke
Lillian Lerner .... Doris Belack
Dr. Sid Lerner .... Alan North
Ruby DeMattis .... Rhoda Gemignani
Sheila DeMattis .... Nancy Cassaro
Elvis DeMattis (18) .... Giovanni Ribisi

After several years in California, physician Jonathan Lerner and his architect wife, Denise, decided it would be a good idea to move their family back to Philadelphia to be close to their parents. Wrong. Jonathan's father, Sid, also a physician, was forever telling Jonathan how to practice medicine, and his mother, Lillian, smothered him and the children with affection. Denise's widowed mother, Ruby, a hairdresser, was critical of everything she did, and her sister, Sheila, an unhappy single parent with an idiot son who bordered on being a juvenile delinquent, couldn't understand why anyone would move back to Philadelphia. As for the older children, Jeffrey was only happy when he was glued to the TV, and Nicki was suffering culture shock, convinced that she could never adjust to being uprooted from California. Zingers flew around the dinner table as all these generations tried to get along.

FAMILY CHANNEL, THE (Network), see ABC Family Channel

FAMILY CLASSICS (*Dramatic Anthology*)
FIRST TELECAST: *March 23, 1989*
LAST TELECAST: *June 1, 1989*
BROADCAST HISTORY:
Mar 1989–Apr 1989, ABC Thu 8:00–9:00
May 1989–Jun 1989, ABC Thu 8:00–10:00

During 1989 ABC ran a series of wholesome movies under this umbrella title to fill time against NBC's unbeatable Thursday schedule. The titles ranged from 1959's *The Shaggy Dog* to 1988's *Rock 'n' Roll Mom.*

FAMILY DOG (*Cartoon*)
FIRST TELECAST: *June 23, 1993*
LAST TELECAST: *July 28, 1993*
BROADCAST HISTORY:
Jun 1993–Jul 1993, CBS Wed 8:00–8:30
Jul 1993, CBS Wed 8:00–9:00
VOICES:
Skip Binsford .... Martin Mull
Bev Binsford .... Molly Cheek
Billy Binsford (age 9) .... Zak Huxtable Epstein
Buffy Binsford (3) .... Cassie Cole
Family Dog .... Danny Mann

Known only as Family Dog, the star of this animated comedy was a happy mongrel whose life was filled with the day-to-day concerns of the doggie world—finding good places to nap, burying and digging up bones, finding canine romance, avoiding confrontations with other animals, and coping with the idiosyncrasies of the human family to whom he belonged. The middle-class family consisted of father Skip, mother Bev, and two children—Billy, who was almost as nasty as Bart Simpson, and Buffy, who spent most of her time planted in front of the TV.

Family Dog was an innovative series that CBS had high hopes for when it was originally put into production in 1990. Creators Steven Spielberg and Tim Burton decided that everything on *Family Dog* would be seen from the dog's perspective, not the human family's. There had been production problems, and the network must have had serious concerns about the results, because the finished series sat on the shelf for two years until finally airing in the summer of 1993.

FAMILY DOUBLE DARE, see *Double Dare*

FAMILY FEUD (*Quiz/Audience Participation*)
BROADCAST HISTORY:
Syndicated and network daytime
30 minutes
Produced: *1977–1985; 1988–1995; 1999–*
Released: *Fall 1977; Fall 1988; Fall 1999*
HOST:
Richard Dawson (1977–1985, 1994–1995)
Ray Combs (1988–1994)
Louie Anderson (1999–2002)
Richard Karn (2002–)

Family Feud was one of the most popular game shows to come along in the 1970s. A hit on ABC's daytime lineup from its debut in July 1976, it quickly spun off this syndicated nighttime version a year later.

Two families of five members each (parents, children, cousins, aunts and uncles, etc.) were introduced at the start of each show, seated opposite each other as if posing for family portraits. Host Richard Dawson spent at least the first five minutes of the show talking to them, asking about their backgrounds and interests, and cracking little jokes. Then the game began. The families were presented with a question; for example: "Name a purchase on which most families spend a great deal of money." The object was to guess how most people would have answered, based on a prior survey. Points were awarded according to what percentage of the survey, if any, gave the same answer (for example, if the family said "buying a house" and

60 percent of the survey said the same thing, the family got 60 points). The family with the most points on the initial answer was given the option of trying to guess all the answers the survey had generated, accumulating points until they had either gotten them all, or gotten three wrong answers. In that case, the other team could win the accumulated points by coming up with one of the remaining correct answers. Preliminary rounds were played until one of the families had won at least 300 points. That family played the final round in which, if successful, they walked away with the $10,000 grand prize and $1 for every point accumulated in the preliminary rounds.

The format was identical to that used in daytime, except for the grand prize ($5,000 in the daytime version). The host of both was Richard Dawson, an English comedian who got his start in the U.S. as Newkirk in *Hogan's Heroes*. It was Dawson's glib familiarity and ready wit that helped make *Family Feud* a hit. The ABC network periodically telecast prime-time specials based on the show, with celebrity casts from various series substituting for the families.

The network version left ABC's daytime lineup in June 1985. Three years later CBS revived the daytime version of *Family Feud*, and that fall a new version went into first-run syndication. Both were emceed by Ray Combs. The network version, which was retitled *The Family Feud Challenge* when it expanded to a full hour format in June 1992, left the air in September 1993. A year later the syndicated version, which was still in production, brought back the show's original host, Richard Dawson, to replace Ray Combs. In 1999 *Family Feud* resurfaced in syndication with comic Louie Anderson as host, replaced in the fall of 2002 by Richard Karn. Reruns of the Louie Anderson episodes aired on Pax starting in September 2002.

FAMILY FOR JOE, A (*Situation Comedy*)

FIRST TELECAST: *February 25, 1990*
LAST TELECAST: *August 19, 1990*
BROADCAST HISTORY:
Feb 1990, NBC Sun 8:00–10:00
Mar 1990–May 1990, NBC Sat 8:00–8:30
Jul 1990–Aug 1990, NBC Sun 7:30–8:00

CAST:
Joe Whitaker .... Robert Mitchum
Nick Bankston (age 16) (pilot) .... Chris Furrh
Nick Bankston .... David Lascher
Holly Bankston (15) (pilot) .... Maia Brewton
Holly Bankston .... Juliette Lewis
Chris Bankston (9) (pilot) .... Jarrad Paul
Chris Bankston .... Ben Savage
Mary Bankston (7) .... Jessica Player
Roger Hightower .... Barry Gordon

For those who had forgotten the unsuccessful TV series careers of screen legends James Stewart (*The Jimmy Stewart Show*), Henry Fonda (*The Smith Family*), and George C. Scott (*Mr. President*), 72-year-old Robert Mitchum proved once again that movie stardom does not necessarily translate to the home screen. *A Family for Joe* would certainly have been forgettable without him. The premise was that four cute upper-middle-class kids had been suddenly orphaned. About to be split up and sent to foster homes, they located a cranky old homeless man and offered him food, a home, and a decent lifestyle if he would live in their nice house and pose as their grandfather (this could only happen in a sitcom!). Of course he took his new responsibilities more seriously than they expected, and amid the quips, little lessons in life were learned by all around the sunny kitchen table. Roger was the helpful next-door neighbor, an air traffic controller turned homemaker.

FAMILY GUY (*Cartoon Situation Comedy*)

FIRST TELECAST: *April 6, 1999*
LAST TELECAST: *April 18, 2002*
BROADCAST HISTORY:
Apr 1999, FOX Tue 9:30–11:00
Apr 1999–Jun 1999, FOX Sun 8:30–9:00
Jun 1999–Sep 1999, FOX Thu 9:00–9:30
Mar 2000–Apr 2000, FOX Tue 8:30–9:00
May 2000–Sep 2000, FOX Tue 9:00–9:30
Jul 2000–Sep 2000, FOX Wed 8:30–9:00
Jul 2001–Sep 2001, FOX Wed 9:30–10:00
Nov 2001–Jan 2002, FOX Thu 8:00–8:30
Jan 2002–Mar 2002, FOX Thu 8:00–9:00
Mar 2002–Apr 2002, FOX Thu 8:00–8:30

VOICES:
Peter Griffin .... Seth MacFarlane
Lois Griffin .... Alex Borstein
Meg Griffin (age 16) .... Mila Kunis
Chris Griffin (13) .... Seth Green
Stewie Griffin (1) .... Seth MacFarlane
Brian, the dog .... Seth MacFarlane
Officer Joe Swanson .... Patrick Warburton

This animated sitcom about a dysfunctional New England family living in Quahog, Rhode Island, was created by 25-year-old Seth MacFarlane, who also wrote the stories, drew some of the cartoons, and provided voices for some of the characters. Peter, the heavyweight, fun-loving father, worked as a product safety inspector at the Happy-Go-Lucky Toy Company. He may have been lazy, dense, and insensitive, but he loved his family. He would do anything for them—as long as it didn't interfere with his TV viewing. Lois, his homemaker wife, tried—not always successfully—to maintain some order in their household. The three Griffin children were Meg, an awkward, unpopular teenager desperately searching for peer group acceptance; Chris, a spaced-out, fat underachiever; and Stewie, a homicidal, power-hungry toddler with a clipped British accent. No one seemed to notice Stewie's bizarre schemes to destroy his family—or the world—which almost succeeded, being foiled at the last minute by some accident. The most normal member of the household was Brian, their intellectual talking dog—although he did have a drinking problem. Peter's boss, Mr. Weed, overlooked his marginal performance because, for some unknown reason, he considered him "eye candy" on the assembly line.

Late in 1999 Joe Swanson, a handicapped police officer, became one of the Griffins' new neighbors. In September 2001, while having dinner at Peter's home, Mr. Weed choked to death on a roll; the Happy-Go-Lucky Toy Company went out of business. Jobless Peter tried various means of making a living, including becoming a fisherman, but nothing seemed to work out and the family suffered from money problems throughout the rest of the show's run.

When *Family Guy* premiered, the Fox Network press department said that the actress who provided Meg's voice had a clause in her contract prohibiting the release of her name. It was later revealed that she was Mila Kunis, a regular on *That '70s Show*.

The *Family Guy* pilot aired after the Super Bowl on January 31, 1999.

FAMILY HOLVAK, THE (*General Drama*)

FIRST TELECAST: *September 7, 1975*
LAST TELECAST: *June 28, 1977*
BROADCAST HISTORY:

Sep 1975, NBC Sun 7:30–8:30
Sep 1975–Oct 1975, NBC Sun 8:00–9:00
Oct 1975, NBC Mon 8:00–9:00
Dec 1975, NBC Sun 8:00–9:00
May 1977–Jun 1977, CBS Tue 8:00–9:00

CAST:

Rev. Tom Holvak .... Glenn Ford
Elizabeth Holvak .... Julie Harris
Ramey Holvak .... Lance Kerwin
Julie Mae Holvak .... Elizabeth Cheshire
Chester Purdle .... Ted Gehring
Ida.............................. Cynthia Howard
Deputy Jim Shanks .... William McKinney

Life in the South during the Depression was hard on everyone, and a preacher was no exception. Rev. Tom Holvak was the poverty-stricken clergyman trying to scrape together enough money to support his wife Elizabeth and his two children, 13-year-old Ramey and 8-year-old Julie Mae. To add to his meager income, he sold produce grown on a small plot of land owned by the church. This unsuccessful series was, in many ways, patterned after the highly successful CBS series *The Waltons*, in that it stressed how love and understanding helped a Depression family survive, even though they lacked many of the comforts that most people now take for granted.

Reruns of *the Family Holvak* were aired briefly on CBS during the summer of 1977.

FAMILY LAW (*Legal Drama*)

FIRST TELECAST: *September 20, 1999*
LAST TELECAST: *April 15, 2002*
BROADCAST HISTORY:

Sep 1999–May 2000, CBS Mon 10:00–11:00
Jul 2000–May 2001, CBS Mon 10:00–11:00
Jul 2001–Apr 2002, CBS Mon 10:00–11:00

CAST:

Lynn Holt .... Kathleen Quinlan
Danni Lipton (1999–2001) .... Julie Warner
Rex Weller................ Christopher McDonald
Randi King .... Dixie Carter
Andres Diaz (1999–2001) ..... Cristian de la Fuente
Viveca Foster .... Salli Richardson
Patricia Dumar .... Merrilee McCommas
Cassie Holt (pilot only) .... Rosemarie Martin
Cassie Holt......................... Michelle Horn
Rupert "Rupie" Holt (pilot only)
.... Elliott & Jordan Dolling
Rupert "Rupie" Holt (1999) .... Blake Rossi
Rupert "Rupie" Holt................ David Dorfman
**Michael Holt (1999–2001)* .... Gregg Henry
**Judge Alice Kingston (1999–2001)* ..... Tina Lifford
**Judge Richard Prentiss* .... Michael Rothaar
**Judge Walter Neff (1999–2001)* .... Alberto Isaac
Joe Celano (2000–2002) .... Tony Danza
Naoise O'Neill (2001) .... Orla Brady
Emily Resnick (2001–2002) .... Meredith Eaton

*Occasional

THEME:

"War," performed by Edwin Starr

When her husband and law partner, Michael, left her (he also cleaned out their joint office in Century City), Lynn was forced to rebuild her Los Angeles–based family law practice from scratch. Not only had he dumped her, but he had set up offices in an adjacent building and taken most of the staff and clients with him. Spunky Danni, talented and ambitious, was the only associate attorney who stayed with Lynn, and Patricia was their secretary, Viveca was their paralegal, and young Andres did menial work for the firm. Lynn hired Southern belle Randi, a barracuda of a divorce attorney who had spent time in prison for killing her abusive husband, to build the case against Michael. Because she needed people to help offset the rent on her offices, she brought in Rex, a suave criminal defense attorney who advertised for clients on cable TV. His partners had skipped the country with the retainer moneys from their clients, and he was trying to reestablish himself. At home, Lynn dealt with her two children, 12-year-old Cassie and young Rupie. In January, when Viveca passed the bar exam and quit working for Lynn, Rex hired her as an associate. In the season finale Randi found out that Andres, with whom she was having a hot affair, was on the verge of being deported for marrying an American woman to get a green card. In order to avoid prison, he returned to his native Chile.

In the fall of 2000 Lynn offered a partnership to Joe, a lawyer with a blue-collar background and a reputation as a civil rights attorney helping underdogs fight big business and big government. She hadn't cleared it with Rex and Randi, but despite some friction, they managed to work things out. When Andres returned to the firm from Chile in November Randi found out he had a wife and child back home and she broke up with him. In the spring Danni was trying to adopt Raphael (Billy Campos), a young boy she had defended from his abusive foster father.

At the start of the 2001–2002 season the firm moved from expensive Century City to Venice, near the beach, where they got a deal on space vacated by a dotcom company that had folded. They also added two new associates—Naoise, an ambitious young attorney from Ireland, and Emily, a bright and aggressive dwarf who refused to let her height affect her performance. In the second episode of the season Danni obtained custody of Raphael and left the firm. Randi, who had been given custody of her young granddaughter after the death of her estranged daughter, was a little less caustic than in prior years. Joe, the bleeding-heart liberal whose tactics often got him in trouble with the authorities, wanted to do nothing but pro bono work for the downtrodden, alienating his partners. Viveca, who had been having an affair with Joe since the spring, was working hard to make partner. In November sparks heated up between Lynn and Rex, and they, too, began an affair. Tragedy struck when Naoise, at the home of one of the firm's clients, was shot by gangsters and later died in the hospital. In March Viveca, pregnant with Joe's child, objected so strongly to his representing a teacher contesting the validity of a statewide teachers' proficiency exam that she resigned and argued the case for the opposing side. When Joe objected to bringing Viveca back as a partner, Lynn, Rex, and Randi voted him out of his partnership. He stayed, but on his own terms. In the series' final episode, which aired as a special on May 27, 2002, Lynn and Rex, who had gotten married earlier in the season to make a point in a case they were handling, went to Las Vegas to have their marriage annulled, while Joe, who had expressed misgivings about fatherhood, seemed to be warming to the idea.

FAMILY MAN (*Situation Comedy*)

FIRST TELECAST: *March 18, 1988*

LAST TELECAST: *April 29, 1988*

BROADCAST HISTORY:

Mar 1988–Apr 1988, ABC Fri 9:30–10:00

CAST:

Shelly Tobin .... Richard Libertini
Andrea Tobin .... Mimi Kennedy
Rosie Tobin (age 10) .... Alison Sweeney
Josh Tobin (7) .... Whitby Hertford
Sara Tobin (3) .... Keeley Mari Gallagher

A routine family comedy with lots of close-ups of cute kids. Shelly was a tall, balding TV comedy writer who worked at home, where he was evidently surrounded by comedy one-liners. Wife Andrea provided loyal support, along with two children from her previous marriage (Rosie, Josh) and one of their own (Sara).

FAMILY MAN, THE (*Situation Comedy*)

FIRST TELECAST: *September 11, 1990*

LAST TELECAST: *July 17, 1991*

BROADCAST HISTORY:

Sep 1990, CBS Tue 8:30–9:00
Sep 1990–Dec 1990, CBS Sat 8:00–8:30
Jun 1991–Jul 1991, CBS Mon/Wed 8:30–9:00

CAST:

Jack Taylor .... Gregory Harrison
Jeff Taylor (age 16) .... John Buchanan
Steve Taylor (14) .... Scott Weinger
Brian Taylor (11) .... Matthew Brooks
Allison Taylor (5) .... Ashleigh Blair Sterling
Joe Alberghetti .... Al Molinaro
Patrick Kozak .... Josh Byrne
Hilary Kozak .... Gail Edwards
**Bus Harbrook (1990)* .... Ed Winter
**Eddie Cooper* .... Peter Parros
**Ted Reinhard (1990)* .... Adam Biesk
Jill Nichols (1991) .... Nancy Everhard

*Occasional

The Family Man was another of TV's endless stream of series about single-parent households. Southern California fire captain Jack Taylor had lost his wife in an automobile accident and now had the added responsibilities of being both father and mother to his four children. It was chaos in the kitchen. Jack's handsome children were Jeff, very concerned with his image at school; Steve, still trying to develop a positive self-image; Brian, who was having the hardest time accepting the loss of his mother; and Allison, the stereotypically wise-beyond-her-years little girl. Helping out around the house was Jack's bumbling but good-hearted father-in-law Joe, who gave up his home in New York to move in with them and help raise his grandchildren. Patrick, the little boy living next door with his divorced mother, was Allison's best friend, and Bus, Eddie, and Ted were fellow firefighters with whom Jack played poker every week. Jack's social life did perk up in the summer of 1991 when he started dating pretty TV reporter Jill Nichols.

FAMILY MATTERS (*Situation Comedy*)

FIRST TELECAST: *September 22, 1989*

LAST TELECAST: *July 17, 1998*

BROADCAST HISTORY:

Sep 1989–Apr 1991, ABC Fri 8:30–9:00
Aug 1990–Sep 1990, ABC Tue 8:30–9:00
Apr 1991–May 1991, ABC Fri 9:00–9:30
May 1991–Aug 1991, ABC Fri 8:30–9:00
Aug 1991–May 1997, ABC Fri 8:00–8:30
Jun 1997–Aug 1997, ABC Sat 8:00–8:30
Sep 1997–Oct 1997, CBS Fri 8:00–8:30
Nov 1997–Jan 1998, CBS Fri 9:00–9:30
Jun 1998–Jul 1998, CBS Fri 9:00–10:00

CAST:

Harriette Winslow .... Jo Marie Payton**
Carl Winslow .... Reginald VelJohnson
Eddie Winslow (age 15) .... Darius McCrary
Laura Winslow (13) ...... Kellie Shanygne Williams
Judy Winslow (9) (1989–1993) .... Jaimee Foxworth
Grandma Winslow (1989–1997) ... Rosetta LeNoire
Rachel Crawford (1989–1995) ...... Telma Hopkins
Richie Crawford (1989) ..... Joseph & Julius Wright
Richie Crawford (1990–1997) ..... Bryton McClure
Steve Urkel (1990–1998) .... Jaleel White
**Rodney (1989–1991)* .... Randy Josselyn
Lt. Murtagh (1990–1992) .... Barry Jenner
Waldo Faldo (1991–1996) .... Shawn Harrison
**Maxine Johnson (1992–1998)* ...... Cherie Johnson
**Weasel (1992–1994)* .... Shavar Ross
**Myra Monkhouse (1993–1998)* ... Michelle Thomas
"3J" (8) (1996–1998) .... Orlando Brown
**Commissioner Geiss (1997–1998)* ..... Dick O'Neill
**Greta (1997–1998)* .... Tammy Townsend

*Occasional
**Also Payton-France (earlier) and Payton-Noble (later)

THEME:

"What a Wonderful World," sung by Louis Armstrong (1989); "As Days Go By" thereafter

Standard-issue sitcom about the misadventures of a middle-class black family living in suburban Chicago. Blustery, heavyset Carl was a Chicago cop, Harriette, his sharp-tongued wife, and Eddie, Laura, and Judy, their rambunctious children. Further stoking the laugh meter were Carl's cantankerous mother and Harriette's recently widowed sister Rachel, who moved in with her infant Richie. Something of an entrepreneur, Rachel operated a local lunch counter and teen hangout called "Rachel's Place." The real star of the show emerged halfway through the first season, however. Steve Urkel, the ultimate nerd, was a neighborhood kid with a serious crush on mortified Laura. With his oversized glasses, hiked-up trousers, and high-pitched voice, he was a walking cartoon and an instant sensation.

In later years *Family Matters* began to focus almost exclusively on skinny Urkel and his foil, the ever-frustrated big guy, Carl. Slapstick comedy and Urkel's ever more bizarre inventions made the show a living cartoon. Judy disappeared from the scene without explanation, and Eddie (who was off to college) and Rachel were seldom seen after 1993. Eddie's dim-bulb buddy Waldo and Laura's friend Maxine were seen from time to time, but perhaps the most surprising addition was Myra, a bright, beautiful teenager in pursuit of Urkel, who still had eyes only for disdainful Laura.

Urkel moved in with the Winslows in 1995, when

his parents left the country without him. Yet another kid joined the household the following year, as the Winslows became foster parents to frisky "3J," whom Urkel had met as a Big Brother. By now the older "kids" were growing up, and Urkel, Laura, and Myra joined Eddie as students at a local community college. However, episodes were frequently based on Urkel's fantastic inventions, as when he transported the entire family to Paris on the Urk-Pad, or time-traveled with Carl back to an eighteenth-century pirate ship. He also learned the secret of cloning, and Urkels began to multiply. There was Myrtle Urkel, his outrageous cousin from Biloxi; he also dreamed up the debonair Stefan Urquelle, as a way to get to Laura.

In the last season, on CBS, Urkel helped get Carl promoted to Captain, while Eddie quit college to enter the police academy. Two new characters were Commissioner Geiss and Eddie's new girlfriend, Greta (a rival to Myrtle). In the final episode Urkel and Laura were engaged, when he learned he had won a contest to become the first student astronaut, and blasted off on a shuttle mission that went awry. After a series of disasters (some caused by himself), he did a space walk to remove an errant satellite that had crashed into the hull, and saved the day. He was reunited on Earth with his fiancée Laura, and everybody hugged.

Family Matters was a spin-off from *Perfect Strangers*, on which Harriette appeared as the sarcastic elevator operator.

FAMILY RULES (*Situation Comedy*)

FIRST TELECAST: *March 9, 1999*
LAST TELECAST: *April 13, 1999*
BROADCAST HISTORY:
Mar 1999–Apr 1999, UPN Tue 8:30–9:00

CAST:
Nate Harrison .... Greg Evigan
Hope Harrison (age 16) .... Maggie Lawson
Ann Harrison (15) .... Shawna Waldron
C. J. Harrison (14) .... Andi Eystad
Lucy Harrison (11) .... Brooke Garrett
Phil Bennett .... Markus Redmond

Nate was a widower raising four daughters in suburban Baltimore in this formula sitcom. He was the basketball coach at nearby Morgan College, although virtually all of the activity in this series took place at home with his kids. Hope was the sexy popular blond senior; Ann, the smart responsible one; C.J. the adventurous tomboy sports junkie; and Lucy the impressionable preteen. Phil, Nate's best friend and neighbor, was a freelance magazine writer who worked at home. He was a frequent visitor in the Harrison household, giving generally helpful advice to Nate and his daughters. There was plenty of good-natured sibling rivalry, and Nate worked at being a sensitive, understanding father, but he was a little overwhelmed by the women in his life.

FAMILY TIES (*Situation Comedy*)

FIRST TELECAST: *September 22, 1982*
LAST TELECAST: *September 17, 1989*
BROADCAST HISTORY:
Sep 1982–Mar 1983, NBC Wed 9:30–10:00
Mar 1983–Aug 1983, NBC Mon 8:30–9:00
Aug 1983–Dec 1983, NBC Wed 9:30–10:00
Jan 1984–Aug 1987, NBC Thu 8:30–9:00
Aug 1987–Sep 1987, NBC Sun 8:00–9:00
Sep 1987–Sep 1989, NBC Sun 8:00–8:30

CAST:
Elyse Keaton .... Meredith Baxter-Birney
Steve Keaton .... Michael Gross
Alex P. Keaton .... Michael J. Fox
Mallory Keaton .... Justine Bateman
Jennifer Keaton .... Tina Yothers
Andrew Keaton (1986–1989) .... Brian Bonsall
Irwin "Skippy" Handelman .... Marc Price
Ellen Reed (1985–1986) .... Tracy Pollan
Nick Moore (1985–1989) .... Scott Valentine
Lauren Miller (1987–1989) .... Courteney Cox

THEME:
"Without Us," by Jeff Barry and Tom Scott, sung by Johnny Mathis and Deniece Williams

The mellow 1960s clashed with the conservative 1980s in this generation-gap comedy, which in some ways reflected America's changing values in the Reagan era. President Reagan, in fact, called *Family Ties* his favorite show. It was set in middle America—Columbus, Ohio—where one-time flower children Elyse and Steven Keaton still espoused the liberal values of the idealistic '60s, although they were now parents and professionals (she an architect, he the manager of public TV station WKS-TV). Their children's ideals were something else. Seventeen-year-old Alex was Mr. Conservative, habitually dressed in suit and tie and with a picture of William F. Buckley, Jr., over his bed. Mallory, 15, was into designer jeans, boys, and junk food, while cute little Jennifer, 9, just wanted to be a kid. They were a loving family, though the kids never could understand those Bob Dylan records their parents kept playing.

During the 1984–1985 season Elyse gave birth to baby Andrew, and by the following fall superstudent Alex had entered Leland College, espousing, what else, the virtues of the Reagan administration's supply-side economics. There he became seriously involved with another student, perky Ellen Reed, while back home sister Mallory was dating a poorly educated aspiring sculptor named Nick Moore. Mallory, an academic underachiever, narrowly graduated from high school in 1986, entered Grant Junior College, and set her sights on a career in fashion design, more or less. In 1987 another love interest entered Alex's life in the person of psychology student Lauren Miller. Alex's chief sidekick, though, was little brother Andrew (already four years old!), who idolized him. Every week they watched *Wall Street Week* on TV together. Skippy was Alex's rather dense friend.

Besides its continuing parody of Reagan-era values, *Family Ties* tackled some sensitive subjects in unusual episodes. Perhaps the most famous episode was "A, My Name Is Alex," performed theater-style on a nearly bare stage, in which Alex worked through his grief and disorientation following the sudden death of a young friend in an auto accident. During the 1988–1989 season, the Keatons confronted racism when a black family moved into the neighborhood; and faced their own greatest crisis when Steve suffered a heart attack and had to undergo bypass surgery. In the last original episode, the nuclear family was finally, and inevitably, dissolved as Alex graduated, accepted a plum job with a large Wall Street brokerage firm, and moved away. There would be no *Family Ties* reunions, said creator/producer

Gary David Goldberg. The 1980s and all that it stood for were over.

NBC aired reruns of *Family Ties* on weekday mornings from December 1985 to January 1987.

FAMILY TREE, THE (*Drama*)

FIRST TELECAST: *January 22, 1983*
LAST TELECAST: *August 10, 1983*
BROADCAST HISTORY:
Jan 1983–Feb 1983, NBC Sat 10:00–11:00
Jul 1983–Aug 1983, NBC Wed 10:00–11:00
CAST:
Kevin Nichols .... Frank Converse
Annie Benjamin Nichols .... Anne Archer
Jake Nichols .... James Spader
Toby Benjamin .... Jonathan Hall Kovacs
Tess Benjamin .... Melora Hardin
Sam Benjamin .... Martin Hewitt
Dr. David Benjamin .... Alan Feinstein
Elizabeth Nichols .... Joanna Cassidy
Molly Nichols Tanner .... Ann Dusenberry

Remarriage for divorced people with children takes understanding and patience from all the family members involved. That was the theme of *The Family Tree.* Kevin Nichols, owner of a successful lumber company, and Annie Benjamin, who worked part-time selling real estate, were the couple starting a second life together. Kevin's grown daughter Molly was married, and his teenaged son Jake lived with Kevin's exwife, Elizabeth. Annie's three children were all still part of her household, with Toby, her deaf young son, particularly upset about the divorce from her first husband, David. Annie's children were still very close to their father and had problems adjusting to the arrival of their stepfather. Coping with the altered relationships caused by divorce and remarriage provided the focus for this series.

FAMOUS ADVENTURES OF MR. MAGOO, THE (*Cartoon*)

FIRST TELECAST: *September 19, 1964*
LAST TELECAST: *August 7, 1965*
BROADCAST HISTORY:
Sep 1964–Dec 1964, NBC Sat 8:00–8:30
Jan 1965–Aug 1965, NBC Sat 8:30–9:00
VOICES:
Mr. Quincy Magoo .... Jim Backus
Various .... Marvin Miller, Howard Morris, Paul Frees

Mr. Magoo, that clumsy, crusty, nearsighted old man, had a long history of success in theatrical cartoons and on TV. At Christmastime in 1962 and 1963, NBC aired a feature-length cartoon version of Dickens's *The Christmas Carol,* featuring Mr. Magoo as Ebenezer Scrooge and retitled "Mr. Magoo's Christmas Carol." This prompted the development of a series in which Magoo played assorted characters of historic significance, both fictional and real. Long John Silver, Friar Tuck, William Tell, Dr. Watson (of the Sherlock Holmes stories), and Rip Van Winkle were among the characters played by Magoo in this humorous animated series.

FAMOUS FAMILIES (*Documentary*)

BROADCAST HISTORY:
Fox Family Channel
60 minutes
Original episodes: *1999–2000*
Premiered (series): *September 27, 1999*
HOST:
Mariel Hemingway

Celebrity biographies. *Famous Families* began as a series of occasional specials on October 5, 1998 (with "The Jacksons"), becoming weekly in September 1999. Subjects included the Presleys, the Osmonds, the Ozzie Nelsons, and the Barrymores, along with non-show-business families including the Kennedys and racing legends the Unsers.

FAMOUS FIGHTS (*Sports*)

FIRST TELECAST: *September 15, 1952*
LAST TELECAST: *December 17, 1957*
BROADCAST HISTORY:
Sep 1952–Dec 1952, DUM Mon 9:45–10:00
Jul 1957–Dec 1957, ABC Wed 10:45–11:00
COMMENTATOR:
Jimmy Powers (1952)

Filmed highlights of outstanding boxing matches in the history of Madison Square Garden were shown preceding or following the live fights in 1952 and 1957.

FAMOUS FILM FESTIVAL, see *Movies—Prior to 1961*

FAMOUS JETT JACKSON, THE (*Situation Comedy*)

BROADCAST HISTORY:
Disney Channel
30 minutes
Original episodes: *1998–2001* (64 episodes)
Premiered: *October 25, 1998*
CAST:
Jett Jackson/Silverstone ..... Lee Thompson Young
J. B. Halliburton .... Ryan Sommers Baum
Kayla West .... Kerry Duff
Sheriff Wood Jackson .... Gordon Greene
Miz Coretta .... Montrose Hagins
Jules Jackson .... Melanie Nicholls-King
Marvin "Cubby" Cubolsky .... Jeffrey Douglas
Deputy Booker Murray .... Andrew Tarbet
Riley Grant/Hawk Hawkins (*1999–2001*) .... Lindy Booth
Artemus/Nigel Essex (*1999–2001*) .... Nigel Shawn-Williams

This popular kids' show was about a black teenage celebrity who returned home to Wilsted, North Carolina, to try to live a normal life with his family and friends. Jett Jackson was a happy, handsome kid who starred in the network action series *Silverstone* as a secret agent for M.O.M. (Mission Omega Matrix), an organization out to save the world from villains like Dr. Hypnoto and The Rat. Production of the show followed Jett to his hometown, but during the first season the focus was primarily on his offscreen exploits with his buddies J. B. and Kayla, as he tried to balance fame and being a regular guy. Sheriff Wood was his dad, and Miz Coretta, his wise grandma. Jules, his actress mom who had divorced Wood and continued her career in Los Angeles, sometimes showed up to cause problems. Beginning in the second season, scenes from *Silverstone* alternated with Jett's offscreen life, and his costar "Hawk" and fictional mentor Artemus were frequently seen. The contrast between Jett's on-screen heroics and offscreen screw-ups added to the humor.

Jett's world was thoroughly integrated both off screen and on (J. B. and Hawk were white, Kayla and Artemus, black), and some of the stories were gentle lessons about race relations, while others were simply about growing up.

FAMOUS JURY TRIALS (*Courtroom Drama*)
FIRST TELECAST: *October 12, 1949*
LAST TELECAST: *March 12, 1952*
BROADCAST HISTORY:
Oct 1949–May 1950, DUM Wed 9:30–10:00
May 1950–May 1951, DUM Wed 9:00–9:30
Nov 1951–Mar 1952, DUM Wed 9:00–9:30

This series presented reenactments of real-life criminal trials and the crimes that led to them. Typically the story would open in the courtroom. While opposing witnesses related their versions of the events, the scene would shift to another set and a reenactment of the crime according to each witness's version. At the end the jury was given the case, and the viewer found out what really happened. Staged with little-known actors on a minuscule budget, this DuMont production nevertheless managed to survive off and on for two and a half years.

FAMOUS TEDDY Z, THE (*Situation Comedy*)
FIRST TELECAST: *September 18, 1989*
LAST TELECAST: *May 12, 1990*
BROADCAST HISTORY:
Sep 1989–Oct 1989, CBS Mon 9:30–10:00
Nov 1989–Jan 1990, CBS Mon 8:30–9:00
May 1990, CBS Sat 9:00–9:30
CAST:
Teddy Zakalokis .... Jon Cryer
Abe Werkfinder .... Milton Selzer
Laurie Parr .... Jane Sibbett
Al Floss .... Alex Rocco
Richie Herby.......................... Tom La Grua
Deena Zakalokis .... Erica Yohn
Aristotle Zakalokis .... Josh Blake
**Harland Keyvo* .... Dennis Lipscomb
**Al Floss's secretary* .... Andrew Philpot
*Occasional

Teddy Zakalokis was working for his cousin Richie in the mailroom of the Unlimited Talent Agency when fate changed his life. Teddy had no interest in show business—he had only taken the job to make some money between a stint in the Army and going to work in the family bakery. Everything changed when he was assigned to a limo picking up the agency's biggest client, movie star Harland Keyvo, and Keyvo impetuously decided Teddy should become his new agent. Teddy didn't even know what an agent was, but the prospect of at least $50,000 a year to start and a fancy office at Unlimited's swank Los Angeles headquarters was more than he could resist. Abe Werkfinder, the venerable, fatherly president of the agency, who found it impossible to pronounce his last name, dubbed him "Teddy Z" and the nickname stuck.

Most upset with Teddy's meteoric rise was Al Floss, the fast-talking obnoxious agent who had represented Keyvo until Teddy's arrival. Running Al a close second was Laurie Parr, an ambitious young college graduate who had been working in the mailroom for months, hoping to move up at the agency. She knew almost everything about the business while Teddy knew nothing. Laurie was dumbfounded by his sudden rise and was less than thrilled when, because he was romantically interested in her and thought proximity would help his cause, he had her "promoted" to his secretary. Despite his newfound fortune, Teddy was still living in a middle-class Los Angeles neighborhood with his grandmother Deena, who couldn't understand how he could get paid so much money for doing nothing but making phone calls and going to expensive restaurants; and his kid brother Aristotle, a high school student who thought it was great.

The Famous Teddy Z was inspired by the real-life story of agent Jay Kantor, who was working in the mailroom of talent agency MCA in 1947 when he was sent with a limo driver to pick up Marlon Brando at the Los Angeles airport. Brando took an immediate liking to young Kantor and, on the way to the office, informed him he wanted him to be his agent. Kantor became the boy wonder of the talent agency business and later, a successful producer in partnership with Alan Ladd, Jr.

FANATIC (*Documentary*)
BROADCAST HISTORY:
MTV
30 minutes
Produced: *1998–1999*
Premiered: *July 6, 1998*

One of MTV's innovative reality shows involving its own viewers (for others, see *The Real World, Road Rules, Singled Out,* etc.). In this one, a "major fan" of some celebrity was abruptly plucked out of their everyday life and whisked off to meet their idol. Friends and family usually conspired in the surprise "abduction," which sometimes came at an inopportune moment. In the premiere a geeky young kid was pulled out of the family pool and packed into a limo and then a plane, still dripping wet ("Can I have a towel?"), to travel to meet his idol, Van Halen.

FANELLI BOYS, THE (*Situation Comedy*)
FIRST TELECAST: *September 8, 1990*
LAST TELECAST: *February 16, 1991*
BROADCAST HISTORY:
Sep 1990, NBC Sat 9:30–10:00
Sep 1990–Oct 1990, NBC Wed 9:00–9:30
Oct 1990–Nov 1990, NBC Wed 9:30–10:00
Dec 1990–Feb 1991, NBC Sat 8:30–9:00
CAST:
Theresa Fanelli.............. Ann Morgan Guilbert
Anthony Fanelli.................... Ned Eisenberg
Ronnie Fanelli .... Andy Hirsch
Frankie Fanelli .... Chris Meloni
Dominic Fanelli .... Joe Pantoliano
Father Angelo .... Richard Libertini
Eddie DeTucci .... Nick DeMauro
**Philamena*.......................... Vera Lockwood
*Occasional

Now that her husband had passed away, and the boys were grown and out on their own, mom Fanelli was ready to sell the family home in Brooklyn and move to Florida. But who's that at the door? Ronnie has just dropped out of school; girl-chasing Frankie's engagement is off; Anthony, who took over the family funeral parlor, is $25,000 in debt; and Dom, the hustler, is between scores. They all moved back home so mom could straighten out their lives, once again. Father Angelo was Theresa's tall, balding brother who offered dubious advice, though not so dubious as that of the neighborhood fortune-teller Philamena. Could Philamena have foreseen—cancellation by the time snow flies?

FANFARE (*Dramatic Anthology*)
FIRST TELECAST: *July 7, 1959*
LAST TELECAST: *September 8, 1959*
BROADCAST HISTORY:
Jul 1959–Sep 1959, NBC Tue 9:00–9:30
HOST:
Richard Derr
This summer series consisted of repeats of *Loretta Young Show* plays in which Miss Young had not appeared. Actor Richard Derr was the host, introducing each play and giving a summary of the following week's offering at the conclusion of the telecast.

FANFARE (*Musical Variety*)
FIRST TELECAST: *June 19, 1965*
LAST TELECAST: *September 11, 1965*
BROADCAST HISTORY:
Jun 1965–Sep 1965, CBS Sat 7:30–8:30
REGULARS:
Al Hirt
The Don McKayle Dancers
The Mort Lindsey Orchestra
Al Hirt, the hefty, bearded New Orleans trumpet player, was the host and star of this summer musical variety series. In addition to his own flashy renditions of popular and classical trumpet pieces, Hirt presented various guest stars, all of whom participated in some type of musical number, whether or not they were themselves musicians.

FANTASTIC FACTS (*Informational*)
FIRST TELECAST: *August 9, 1991*
LAST TELECAST: *September 13, 1991*
BROADCAST HISTORY:
Aug 1991–Sep 1991, CBS Fri 8:00–8:30
HOST:
Merlin Olsen
Former professional football player Merlin Olsen hosted this summer show that resembled a contemporary "Ripley's Believe It or Not." Each episode focused on what the producers described as "real facts about real things." Using demonstrations filmed for the series, as well as documentary/news footage, *Fantastic Facts* provided information on such natural phenomena as hurricanes, volcanoes, and sinkholes; the odds of winning at gambling casinos; the secrets behind movie special effects; the discovery/development of inventions; and hidden treasures around the world. In addition there were regular features on unusual people, ranging from a couple married for 82 years, to the workers putting out the oil fires in Gulf War–ravaged Kuwait, to the accomplishments of the Edomites who lived in what is now Jordan, more than 2,000 years ago.

FANTASTIC JOURNEY (*Science Fiction*)
FIRST TELECAST: *February 3, 1977*
LAST TELECAST: *April 13, 1977*
BROADCAST HISTORY:
Feb 1977–Apr 1977, NBC Thu 8:00–9:00
CAST:
Varian .... Jared Martin
Dr. Fred Walters .... Carl Franklin
Scott Jordan .... Ike Eisenmann
Liana .... Katie Saylor
Dr. Jonathan Willoway .... Roddy McDowall
This science-fantasy series began with a group of university scientists exploring the area of the Bermuda Triangle. Their boat ran aground on an uncharted land mass, which turned out to be the source of a strange "time and space warp" in which past, present, and future were all intermingled. One of the scientists, Dr. Fred Walters, was drawn into the warp, along with young Scott, where they met three people from various eras, each of whom was trying to find the way back to his or her own time. They were Varian, a telepathic individual from the 23rd century; Liana, a survivor from the lost continent of Atlantis; and Dr. Jonathan Willoway, a scientist from the 1960s who was living with androids. The adventures of these wanderers in time and space, the bizarre creatures they encountered, and the conflicts between them were all interwoven in the series.

FANTASY ISLAND (*Romantic Drama*)
FIRST TELECAST: *January 28, 1978*
LAST TELECAST: *August 18, 1984*
BROADCAST HISTORY:
Jan 1978–Aug 1979, ABC Sat 10:00–11:00
Aug 1979–Oct 1979, ABC Fri 8:00–9:00
Oct 1979–Aug 1984, ABC Sat 10:00–11:00
CAST:
Mr. Roarke .... Ricardo Montalban
Tattoo (1978–1983).............. Herve Villechaize
Julie (1981–1982) .... Wendy Schaal
Lawrence (1983–1984) .... Christopher Hewett
When ABC realized it had a major hit with *Love Boat*, it immediately began developing a second program using a similar theme. That program was *Fantasy Island*, and, scheduled right after *Love Boat* on Saturday night, it soon became an equally big hit.

Both programs were episodic, consisting of several different stories each week played out against a common background. The backdrop of *Fantasy Island* was romantic indeed: a remote island resort, where each visitor could have one lifelong dream come true. A homely young man wanted to become, during his stay, a sex symbol to beautiful girls (bikini-clad beauties abounded on *Fantasy Island*); a frustrated salesman whose career was going nowhere wanted to score the business coup of his life; a henpecked family man wanted a weekend of respect from his clan. Many of the stories involved glamour and excitement for ordinary people whose lives normally had none, and ABC obviously felt that viewers would relate this to their own lives. There was sometimes an element of danger, or a twist of fate, but everything always worked out for the best.

Overseeing the two or three little dramas each week was the island's owner, the suave and slightly mysterious Mr. Roarke, and his midget helper Tattoo (replaced in 1983 by Lawrence). In later seasons, Roarke became increasingly mysterious, in fact, dispensing magic spells and potions, calling up events from the past and future, and even doing battle with the devil. The plots got ever more fanciful. Visitors on the island were played by a wide range of guest stars, among them Henry Gibson, Georgia Engel, Christopher George, Marcia Strassman, Dennis James, and Roddy McDowall (as Mephistopheles). Mr. Roarke's god-daughter Julie was seen as a regular for a single season.

Fantasy Island was originally filmed at a real tropical paradise, a public park called the Arboretum, 25 miles from Los Angeles.

FANTASY ISLAND (*Romantic Drama*)
FIRST TELECAST: *September 26, 1998*
LAST TELECAST: *January 23, 1999*
BROADCAST HISTORY:
Sep 1998–Dec 1998, ABC Sat 9:00–10:00
Jan 1999, ABC Sat 10:00–11:00
CAST:
Mr. Roarke .... Malcolm McDowell
Cal .... Louis Lombardi
Harry .... Edward Hibbert
Ariel .... Madchen Amick
Fisher .... Fyvush Finkel
Clia .... Sylvia Sidney

Here's one revival that looked very little like the original on which it was based. Unlike the bright and saccharine *Fantasy Island* of the '70s, this version had an air of mystery about it, and a strong sense of the supernatural. The new Mr. Roarke, dressed in a stylish black suit, was by turns charming and slightly sinister. He also had mysterious powers that defied even the forces of nature, as he summoned up roiling clouds and bolts of lightning. Like his predecessor, he presided over a beautiful, remote, usually sun-drenched island where guests could come to realize their fantasies and look into their souls. Meeting the arrivals at the dock with him were Cal, the chubby, dumb bellhop, and Harry, the redheaded concierge. Ariel was his beauteous assistant, a shape-shifter who could morph into whatever guests wished her to be. All three seemed to be working off some karmic debt to Roarke. Fisher and his secretary Clia were the eccentric elderly couple who ran the quaint, out-of-the-way Fantasy Island travel agency back on the mainland, recruiting unsuspecting guests for the island. As in the original, stories involved people confronting their jealousies and obsessions, though here they tended to shift between the real world and the surreal, and between the past, present, and future.

Filmed on location in Hawaii.

FARADAY AND COMPANY (*Detective Drama*)
FIRST TELECAST: *September 26, 1973*
LAST TELECAST: *August 13, 1974*
BROADCAST HISTORY:
Sep 1973–Jan 1974, NBC Wed 8:30–10:00
Apr 1974–Aug 1974, NBC Tue 8:30–10:00
CAST:
Frank Faraday .... Dan Dailey
Steve Faraday .... James Naughton
Holly Barrett .... Sharon Gless
Lou Carson .... Geraldine Brooks

Frank Faraday was a private detective who had served 25 years in a South American jail for a crime that he had not committed. When he was finally released he was forced to adjust to a world very much changed, including a son, Steve, he had never known (born to his secretary, Lou Carson, after his imprisonment). After tracking down and bringing to justice the man who had actually committed the crime for which he had been imprisoned, Frank joined forces with his son—who had himself become a detective—in operating a Los Angeles detective agency that specialized in security investigations. The contrast in styles between the two men created constant tensions and strains in the relationship, for father Frank often resorted to old-style physical force against a new generation of technologically and legally astute criminals. *Faraday and Company* was one of the four rotating elements in the 1973–1974 version of the *NBC Wednesday Mystery Movie.* The others were *Banacek, The Snoop Sisters,* and *Tenafly.*

FARAWAY HILL (*Romantic Drama*)
FIRST TELECAST: *October 2, 1946*
LAST TELECAST: *December 18, 1946*
BROADCAST HISTORY:
Oct 1946–Dec 1946, DUM Wed 9:00–9:30
CAST:
Karen St. John .... Flora Campbell
ALSO:
Mel Brandt
Ann Stell
Lorene Scott
Frederic Meyer
Melville Galliart
Jacqueline Waite
Jack Halloran
Ben Low
Bill Gale
Vivian King
Eve McVeagh
Julie Christy
Hal Studer
Barry Doig
Munroe Gabler
WRITER/DIRECTOR:
David P. Lewis

Faraway Hill was the first example on network television of a durable and tear-stained program type—the soap opera. The network wasn't very big (New York and Washington) and the program didn't last very long (12 weeks), but it had all the elements that today's serial viewers have come to know and love—two women after the same man, family jealousies, incredible complications, and the inevitable "tune in next time" to find out what happened.

Some of the specifics, such as character names, have been lost in the mists of history. The basic plot concerned a wealthy New York woman who, following the death of her husband, traveled to the country to visit relatives and get away from it all. The relatives, who lived on a farm, turned out to be a little more rural than she had expected, which resulted in conflict between her sophistication and their lack of it. Staying with them was an adopted farm boy, with whom the widow soon became romantically involved. Unfortunately, he was already promised to the farmer's daughter, which led to the inevitable romantic triangle. Widow St. John tried all her wiles to win him away, but—well, tune in next week.

Flora Campbell, a Broadway actress with numerous credits, played the leading role of Karen St. John, and Mel Brandt was the object of her affections.

Faraway Hill was an experiment to see how this kind of series would look on TV, and some of the devices used were interesting. On the initial episode the various characters were introduced with their names and relationships shown on the screen, so that viewers could keep everyone straight. Each subsequent episode began with a recap of what had gone before (illustrated by slides from the shows) and a reminder of who was who, narrated in emotional tones by Karen. Within the show an off-screen voice would relate Karen's thoughts, to serve as a bridge between scenes, and occasional film sequences were worked into the otherwise live show to depict such details as passing trains. The whole production was done on an absolutely minimal budget of $300 per week.

Though *Faraway Hill* was the first soap opera to be carried on a network, it was not the first one on television. During the summer of 1946 WRGB, the pioneering General Electric station in Schenectady, aired a 13-part serial called *War Bride*, about a GI returned from the war with a new love, much to the consternation of his mother and his former fiancée. There may have been a few others, also telecast on a local basis. In any event it was not until the networks moved into daytime telecasting in a big way in the 1950s that the TV soap opera really caught on, and the serialized grief has been endless ever since.

FARMER'S DAUGHTER, THE (*Situation Comedy*)

FIRST TELECAST: *September 20, 1963*

LAST TELECAST: *September 2, 1966*

BROADCAST HISTORY:

Sep 1963–Nov 1963, ABC Fri 9:30–10:00
Dec 1963–Sep 1964, ABC Wed 8:30–9:00
Sep 1964–Jun 1965, ABC Fri 8:00–8:30
Jun 1965–Oct 1965, ABC Mon 9:30–10:00
Nov 1965–Sep 1966, ABC Fri 9:30–10:00

CAST:

Katrin "Katy" Holstrum .... Inger Stevens
Congressman Glen Morley .... William Windom
Agatha Morley, Glen's Mother..... Cathleen Nesbitt
Steve Morley...................... Mickey Sholdar
Danny Morley .... Rory O'Brien
Cooper, the butler (1963–1964) .... Philip Coolidge

This comedy concerned Katy, a naive, sexy farm girl of Swedish descent, who came to Washington, D.C., to look for help from her congressman. Instead she wound up working for him, as governess of his two motherless boys, Danny (age 8) and Steve (age 14). Through simple charm and native intelligence Katy managed to loosen up the sometimes stuffy politicians around her and to further Glen's bumbling political career. On the telecast of November 5, 1965, Katy married Glen, but this failed to reverse the declining ratings, and the show concluded its run at the end of that season.

The program was based on the 1947 movie of the same name starring Loretta Young, for which Miss Young won an Oscar.

FARSCAPE (*Science Fiction*)

BROADCAST HISTORY:

Sci-Fi Channel
60 minutes
Original episodes: *1999–2003* (88 episodes)
Premiered: *March 14, 1999*

CAST:

Cdr. John Crichton .... Ben Browder
Officer Aeryn Sun...................... Claudia Black
General Ka D'Argo .... Anthony Simcoe
Pa'u Zotoh Zhaan (1999–2001) .... Virginia Hey
Rygel XVI (voice).................. Jonathan Hardy
Capt. Bialar Crais (1999–2002)/pilot (voice) .... Lani John Tupu
Chiana................................. Gigi Edgley
Stark (2000–2002) .... Paul Goddard
Scorpius/Harvey (2000–2003) ..... Wayne Pygram
**Lt./Capt. Braca (2000–2003)*........ David Frankin
**Noranti (2000–2003)* .... Melissa Jaffer
**Jool (2001–2002)*............... Tammy MacIntosh
**Sikozu (2002–2003)*.................. Raelee Hill

*Occasional

A twentieth-century astronaut was accidentally blasted to the far reaches of space, only to find it populated by a mixture of humanoids, monsters, and muppets in this odd, imaginative action series. John Crichton was test-flying the experimental *Farscape* vehicle near the Earth when he was suddenly swallowed up by a wormhole, which flung him far, far away, into the midst of a pitched battle between the warlike Peacekeepers and a small band of rebels. Seeking refuge, he was taken aboard *Moya*, a huge but nearly empty rebel ship. The few rebels on board were a strange and sometimes fractious bunch: D'Argo, a large, brutish member of the Luxan warrior race; Aeryn, an equally fierce female former Peacekeeper soldier; Zhaan, a serene, thoughtful Delvian priestess, totally blue from head to toe (although 812 years old, she didn't look a day over 30); and Rygel, the disdainful, 26-inch-high Hynerian Emperor, sovereign to more than 600 billion subjects—none of whom, unfortunately, were anywhere nearby. All of them were on the run from the Peacekeepers, whose ruthless Captain Crais was determined to kill them and especially the intruder Crichton, who while blundering through the battle had inadvertently caused the death of Crais's brother, a pilot. The spaceship *Moya* was a living organism (it even gave birth in one episode!), and was operated by Pilot, a sort of living control panel that obediently implemented the shouted orders of D'Argo and Aeryn.

Together this small band battled Peacekeepers and other threatening life-forms, explored strange planets, and squabbled amongst themselves, sometimes humorously. The races they encountered were many and varied, including Draks, Delvians, Acquarians, Charrids, Nebaris, Litigarians (from a world where lawyers comprised 90 percent of the population!) and Zenetans. Major story lines included Crichton's continuing search for the secrets of wormholes, so that he could return to Earth (which he did several times, to little advantage); his realization that knowledge of wormholes had been implanted in his brain by a race called The Ancients; and Moya's pregnancy and delivery of a baby warship, Talyn, which was commandeered by Crais (who defected from the Peacekeepers) and eventually killed. New characters were Chiana, a seductress and scoundrel who joined the crew; Stark, a former slave with healing powers who became an ally; and Scorpius; a corpselike villain who chased Crichton around the universe trying to steal his knowledge of wormholes. ("Harvey" was Scorpius' neuro-clone.) Jool was a feisty, brilliant young woman whom Crichton saved from death during one of his rescue missions, but who blamed him anyway for the death of her two friends. Zhaan died during a battle in 2001 (actress Virginia Hey left the series because the heavy makeup was damaging her health).

In the final episode Crichton made it back to Earth again, landing in the 1980's (before he had left!), and tried to prevent his astronaut-father Jack (Kent McCord) from joining the crew of the ill-fated *Challenger.* John and Aeryn had become romantic, and she revealed she was having his baby; he proposed to her just before an intruding alien blasted them to bits. The episode ended oddly, with a big "To Be Continued." This was reportedly because the Sc-Fi Channel had abruptly canceled the series in the middle of a story line (John and Aeryn were not really dead), and the producers were not able to film a finale.

The novel special effects were created at Jim Henson's Creature Shop. A preview episode of *Farscape* aired on USA Network on March 14, 1999, followed by the series' debut on the Sci-Fi Channel five days later.

FASHION STORY, THE (*Fashion/Comedy*)

FIRST TELECAST: *November 4, 1948*
LAST TELECAST: *March 1, 1949*
BROADCAST HISTORY:
Nov 1948–Jan 1949, ABC Thu 8:00–8:30
Jan 1949–Mar 1949, ABC Tue 7:30–8:00
REGULARS:
Marilyn Day
Carl Reiner
Don Saxon
Pamela O'Neill
Dennis Bohan
Doris Lane
Patsy Davis
Elaine Joyce
Aina Shields
Hayes Gorden
MUSIC
Walter Fleicher Trio
Roger Stearns, piano

This was a fashion show combined with a slight comedy story line to provide continuity. Marilyn Day was seen in the role of Lucky Marshall, a young model who hoped to break into show business as a singer (thus providing an excuse for periodic songs). Her young boss, who was forever causing problems, was played by Dennis Bohan. A bevy of fashion models paraded through each show, providing its main reason for being. Pamela O'Neill was the fashion commentator. Carl Reiner, as a comic photographer, was also a regular, but his talents were largely wasted, causing one reviewer to remark that he and Miss Day deserved "a good spot of their own on a variety show, without the drawback of tying together a fashion show." They both got one, working together two months later on *The Fifty-fourth Street Revue.* For Miss Day that was the end of the network line, but Carl Reiner went on to *Your Show of Shows* and a long succession of writing/performing/producing jobs in television.

FASHIONS ON PARADE (*Fashion/Variety*)

FIRST TELECAST: *August 20, 1948*
LAST TELECAST: *January 7, 1949*
BROADCAST HISTORY:
Aug 1948–Jan 1949, DUM Fri 8:00–8:30
NARRATOR:
Adelaide Hawley

This combination fashion show and musical revue featured guest celebrities and the famous Conover (Modeling Agency) Cover Girls as models. A thin story line each week tied together the performances and the showing of the latest fashions. Among the guests were Vincent Lopez and Jerry Wayne.

The show was also seen locally in New York during various periods in 1948 and 1949.

FAST TIMES (*Situation Comedy*)

FIRST TELECAST: *March 5, 1986*
LAST TELECAST: *April 23, 1986*
BROADCAST HISTORY:
Mar 1986–Apr 1986, CBS Wed 8:00–8:30
CAST:
Jeff Spicoli .... Dean Cameron
Mr. Arnold Hand .... Ray Walston
Mike Damone .... Patrick Dempsey
Mark Ratner .... Wally Ward
Stacey Hamilton .... Courtney Thorne-Smith
Brad Hamilton .... James Nardini
Linda Barrett .... Claudia Wells
Mr. Hector Vargas .... Vincent Schiavelli
Ms. Leslie Melon .... Kit McDonough
Barbara DeVilbiss .... Moon Unit Zappa
Dennis Taylor .... Paul Willson
The Surfer .... Bill Calvert
Curtis Spicoli .... Jason Hervey
THEME:
"Fast Times," written by Danny Elfman and performed by Oingo Boingo

This contemporary high-school comedy was centered around the lives of the students and faculty at Ridgemont High in Los Angeles's San Fernando Valley. The students included spaced-out Spicoli, who would rather go surfing than waste his time in school; Brad Hamilton, a popular guy who worked at the burger stand in the neighborhood shopping mall; Stacey, Brad's cute but somewhat insecure younger sister; Linda Barrett, a beautiful, popular cheerleader and Stacey's best friend; Damone, the school's resident con man and source for anything from a phony ID to tickets for a sold-out rock concert; and Ratner, a shy guy who worked as a ticket taker at the movie theater in the mall. The faculty members showing up regularly were Mr. Hand, a disciplinarian history teacher frustrated by the casual attitude of so many of his students; Mr. Vargas, the eccentric science teacher; and Ms. Melon, the Life Studies teacher with a penchant for getting personally involved in the personal lives of her students.

Based on the theatrical feature *Fast Times at Ridgemont High,* with Ray Walston and Vincent Schiavelli re-creating the roles they played in the film. Cameron Crowe, who had written the article on which a book, and later the film, had been based, served as creative consultant for the series.

FASTLANE (*Police Drama*)

FIRST TELECAST: *September 18, 2002*
LAST TELECAST: *June 20, 2003*
BROADCAST HISTORY:
Sep 2002–Jan 2003, FOX Wed 9:00–10:00
Jan 2003–Apr 2003, FOX Fri 8:00–9:00
Jun 2003– , FOX Fri 8:00–10:00
CAST:
Off. Van Ray .... Peter Facinelli
Off. Deaqon ("Deaq") Hayes .... Bill Bellamy

Lt. Wilhemina "Billie" Chambers . . . Tiffani Thiessen
Aquarius . . . . Big Boy (Kurt Alexander)

THEME:

performed by Snoop Dogg

Fast cars, fast women, over-the-top violence and lots of skin (male and female)—all punctuated by throbbing music and fast editing—were the signature elements of *Fastlane*, the *Miami Vice* wannabe of the new millennium. Van and Deaq were two cops working undercover as wealthy gangsters in the glitzy world of Los Angeles. Van's black partner Andre had been killed by a sniper during a bust gone bad, whereupon Andre's younger brother, Deaq, an NYPD narcotics cop, arrived in town determined to avenge his murder. They were recruited by sexy Billie, who ran a specialized unit within the LAPD and who was looking for a couple of cool cats to work deep undercover to bring down the wealthiest and most powerful of the bad guys. She worked out of the "Candy Store," a downtown warehouse that housed the latest in high-tech monitoring equipment and a huge cache of confiscated goodies—expensive and exotic sports cars, jewelry, clothes, cash, etc.—all of which were at their disposal to help maintain their flashy covers. Deaq's hefty friend Aquarius, a well-connected club owner, was a frequent source of information.

Although the majority of their cases involved drug dealers, the guys brought down everyone from Russian gunrunners to counterfeiters and jewel thieves. They were very effective as a team, but they rarely saw eye to eye and often squabbled like little boys. Billie, who could be as tough as she was beautiful, did her best to keep them under control. Although she usually worked out of the Candy Store, when necessary she was ready to go into the field and blast away with the best of them. (There were a lot of spectacular firefights and explosions in this cartoonish series.) Despite her success, Billie's operation was under the constant scrutiny of the Internal Affairs division of the LAPD, which was concerned about her unorthodox tactics.

FATHER DOWLING MYSTERIES (*Detective*)

FIRST TELECAST: *January 20, 1989*
LAST TELECAST: *September 5, 1991*
BROADCAST HISTORY:

Jan 1989–Mar 1989, NBC Fri 8:00–9:00
Jan 1990–Jul 1991, ABC Thu 8:00–9:00
Aug 1991, ABC Thu 9:00–10:00
Aug 1991–Sep 1991, ABC Thu 8:00–9:00

CAST:

Father Frank Dowling . . . . Tom Bosley
Sister Stephanie ("Sister Steve") . . . . . . Tracy Nelson
Father Prestwick . . . . James Stephens
Marie . . . . Mary Wickes
Sgt. Clancy . . . . Regina Krueger

Frank Dowling was an amiable, unassuming Chicago priest with an inquisitive nature. Each week his curiosity would draw him into a new murder mystery which he would unravel with the help of Sister Steve, an unusually savvy young nun. Steve, who had a rather worldly background, was equally adept at picking a lock, cutting a deck of cards, or picking up information on the streets. The unthreatening appearance of a mild-mannered priest and nun got the pair in many doors, and out of many a scrape, and there was hardly any violence as they tracked down the bad guys in Dowling's beat-up old station wagon. Sharing the St. Michael's rectory were Marie, the busybody housekeeper, and Father Prestwick, a bumbling younger priest who never seemed to understand what was going on.

Based on the *Father Dowling* mystery novels by Ralph McInerny.

FATHER KNOWS BEST (*Situation Comedy*)

FIRST TELECAST: *October 3, 1954*
LAST TELECAST: *April 5, 1963*
BROADCAST HISTORY:

Oct 1954–Mar 1955, CBS Sun 10:00–10:30
Aug 1955–Sep 1958, NBC Wed 8:30–9:00
Sep 1958–Sep 1960, CBS Mon 8:30–9:00
Oct 1960–Sep 1961, CBS Tue 8:00–8:30
Oct 1961–Feb 1962, CBS Wed 8:00–8:30
Feb 1962–Sep 1962, CBS Mon 8:30–9:00
Sep 1962–Dec 1962, ABC Sun 7:00–7:30
Dec 1962–Apr 1963, ABC Fri 8:00–8:30

CAST:

Jim Anderson . . . . Robert Young
Margaret Anderson . . . . Jane Wyatt
Betty Anderson (Princess) . . . . Elinor Donahue
James Anderson, Jr. (Bud) . . . . Billy Gray
Kathy Anderson (Kitten) . . . . Lauren Chapin
Miss Thomas . . . . Sarah Selby
Ed Davis (1955–1959) . . . . Robert Foulk
Myrtle Davis (1955–1959) . . . . Vivi Jannis
Dotty Snow (1954–1957) . . . . Yvonne Lime
Kippy Watkins (1954–1959) . . . . Paul Wallace
Claude Messner (1954–1959) . . . . Jimmy Bates
Doyle Hobbs (1957–1958) . . . . Roger Smith
Ralph Little (1957–1958) . . . . Robert Chapman
April Adams (1957–1958) . . . . Sue George
Joyce Kendall (1958–1959) . Jymme (Roberta) Shore

Father Knows Best was the classic wholesome family situation comedy. It was set in the typical Midwestern community of Springfield, where Jim Anderson was an agent for the General Insurance Company. Every evening he would come home from work, take off his sports jacket, put on his comfortable sweater, and deal with the everyday problems of a growing family. In contrast with most other family comedies of the period, in which one or the other of the parents was a blundering idiot, both Jim and his wife Margaret were portrayed as thoughtful, responsible adults. When a family crisis arose, Jim would calm the waters with a warm smile and some sensible advice.

When *Father Knows Best* went on television in 1954, the three children were aged 17 (Betty), 14 (Bud), and 9 (Kathy). As the seasons passed two of them graduated from high school, first Betty (1956) and then Bud (1959). Neither left home, however, both electing to go to Springfield's own State College.

The Andersons were truly an idealized family, the sort that viewers could relate to and wish to emulate. The children went through the normal problems of growing up, including those concerning school, friends, and members of the opposite sex. They didn't always agree with their parents and occasionally succeeded in asserting their independence (as when Jim and Margaret almost succeeded in pushing Betty into going to their alma mater, until they realized that she had to make her own decisions and let her choose State instead). But the bickering was minimal, and everything seemed to work out by the end of the half-hour.

Father Knows Best began as an NBC radio series in 1949, with Robert Young in the starring role. He was the only member of the radio cast that made the transition to TV in 1954. The TV series was not particularly successful at first, and CBS canceled it in March 1955. A flood of viewer protests, demanding that the program be reinstated and moved to an earlier time slot so that the whole family could watch it, prompted NBC to pick it up for the following season with an 8:30 P.M. starting time. *Father Knows Best* prospered for the next five years.

The series became such a symbol of the "typical" American family that the U.S. Treasury Department commissioned the producers to film a special episode to help promote the 1959 U.S. Savings Bond Drive. The story, "24 Hours in Tyrant Land," told how the Anderson children attempted to live for a day under a make-believe dictatorship. Never aired on television, this special episode was distributed to churches, schools, and civic organizations to show the importance of maintaining a strong American democracy.

During the 1959–1960 season, its last with original episodes, *Father Knows Best* had its most successful year, ranking sixth among all television programs. By the end of that season, however, star Robert Young had tired of the role, which he had been playing for 11 years, and decided it was time to move on to other things. This was one of the rare occasions in the history of television when production on a series ceased when it was at the peak of its popularity. CBS scheduled rerun episodes in prime time for another two years, also a rarity, and ABC reran them for another season after that. From November 1962 until February 1967, reruns were also seen on ABC daytime.

FATHER MURPHY (*Drama*)

FIRST TELECAST: *November 3, 1981*

LAST TELECAST: *June 17, 1984*

BROADCAST HISTORY:

Nov 1981–Mar 1982, NBC Tue 8:00–9:00
Mar 1982–Jul 1982, NBC Sun 7:00–8:00
Jul 1982–Dec 1982, NBC Tue 8:00–9:00
Apr 1984–Jun 1984, NBC Sun 7:00–8:00

CAST:

John Michael Murphy .... Merlin Olsen
Moses Gage .... Moses Gunn
Mae Woodward Murphy .... Katherine Cannon
Will Adams .... Timothy Gibbs
Lizette Winkler .... Lisa Trusel
Ephram Winkler .... Scott Mellini
Eli (1982) .... Chez Lister
Howard Rodman .... Charles Tyner
Miss Tuttle .... Ivy Bethune
Father Joe Parker .... Richard Bergman
Dr. Thompson .... Warren Munson
Sheriff .... Charles Cooper

CREATOR/PRODUCER:

Michael Landon

Michael Landon created and produced this wholesome series about love and caring on the American frontier featuring Merlin Olsen, his beefy co-star from *Little House on the Prairie*. Set in the Dakota Territory town of Jackson during the 1870s, the story began when drifter John Murphy sought to rally the local prospectors against the depredations of the town boss. The boss and his henchmen retaliated by blowing up the miners' camp, thereby creating a new career for Murphy—establishing and running an orphanage for two dozen now-parentless children. To make the orphanage appear legitimate, the bearded frontiersman had to pose as a priest; hence he became "Father" Murphy.

With Murphy at the Gold Hill School were a young teacher named Mae and a friendly dog named Mine. Danger was constantly at their doorstep. While Murphy and Mae attempted to teach and care for the orphans, they were constantly threatened by two pompous and officious representatives of the Dakota Territory Authority, Mr. Rodman and Miss Tuttle, who sought to have the children sent to the territorial workhouse at Claymore. In the spring of 1982, when Murphy's deception was exposed, he and Mae got married, adopted all the orphans, and continued to struggle to hold the "family" together. Black miner Moses Gage was Murphy's good friend, and Will, Lizette, and Ephram were the most prominently seen of the 25 children under Murphy's care. Eli, an orphaned young black boy, became part of the household at the start of *Father Murphy*'s second season. Episodes of *Father Murphy* were rerun in 1984.

FATHER OF THE BRIDE (*Situation Comedy*)

FIRST TELECAST: *September 29, 1961*

LAST TELECAST: *September 14, 1962*

BROADCAST HISTORY:

Sep 1961–Sep 1962, CBS Fri 9:30–10:00

CAST:

Stanley Banks .... Leon Ames
Ellie Banks .... Ruth Warrick
Kay Banks Dunston .... Myrna Fahey
Tommy Banks .... Rickie Sorensen
Buckley Dunston .... Burt Metcalfe
Herbert Dunston .... Ransom Sherman
Doris Dunston .... Lurene Tuttle
Delilah .... Ruby Dandridge

The adjustments parents must make when their children grow up and seek a life of their own were the subject of this comedy. Attorney Stanley Banks was not quite ready to accept his daughter Kay's decision when she announced that she was engaged to Buckley Dunston. Despite the enthusiasm of his wife, Ellie, his son, Tommy, his maid, Delilah, and almost everyone else, Stanley was not happy about it at all. Episodes on the series involved Stanley's tribulations at getting used to his prospective son-in-law and the son-in-law's parents, the planning and carrying out of the wedding, and learning to live without Kay around.

FATHERS AND SONS (*Situation Comedy*)

FIRST TELECAST: *April 6, 1986*

LAST TELECAST: *May 4, 1986*

BROADCAST HISTORY:

Apr 1986–May 1986, NBC Sun 7:30–8:00

CAST:

Buddy Landau .... Merlin Olsen
Lanny Landau .... Jason Late
Ellen Landau .... Kelly Sanders
Sean Flynn .... Andre Gower
Matty Bolen .... Ian Fried
Dr. Richard Bolen .... Nicholas Guest
Brandon Russo .... Hakeem

The focus of this limited-run series was on the relationships of a group of adolescent boys with each other and with Buddy Landau, one of the boys' fathers. Buddy, a former athlete, loved sports and served as the coach of various little league teams. The boys included Buddy's chubby son Lanny, whose involvement in sports seemed to be more a function of his father's enthusiasm than his own; Sean, the budding ladies' man of the group; Matt, the resident intellectual whose father was unable to spend as much time with his son as he would have liked; and Brandon, a diminutive ball of fire who almost made up in energy and determination what he lacked in size.

FAVORITE STORY (*Dramatic Anthology*)

BROADCAST HISTORY:

Syndicated only
30 minutes
Produced: *1952–1954* (78 episodes)
Released: *January 1953*

HOST/OCCASIONAL STAR:

Adolphe Menjou

Debonair Adolphe Menjou hosted and sometimes starred in this popular syndicated anthology series. Stories were adapted from the classics and ranged from farce to tragedy, sometimes treading a delicate line between the two. The scripts and casting were generally first-rate. Raymond Burr played a land-hungry Russian peasant in the first episode, a little morality play adapted from Tolstoy and called "How Much Land Does a Man Need?"

Adapted from the *Favorite Story* radio series of 1946–1949, hosted by Ronald Colman. Menjou presided over another, somewhat different TV anthology series in the late 1950s—see *Target*.

FAY (*Situation Comedy*)

FIRST TELECAST: *September 4, 1975*
LAST TELECAST: *June 2, 1976*
BROADCAST HISTORY:

Sep 1975–Oct 1975, NBC Thu 8:30–9:00
May 1976–Jun 1976, NBC Wed 9:30–10:00

CAST:

Fay Stewart .... Lee Grant
Lillian .... Audra Lindley
Jack Stewart .... Joe Silver
Linda Stewart Baines .... Margaret Willock
Dr. Elliott Baines .... Stewart Moss
Danny Messina .... Bill Gerber
Letty Gilmore .... Lillian Lehman
Al Cassidy .... Norman Alden

The exploits of an attractive, fortyish divorcée who decides to become a swinging single were the subject of this short-lived and somewhat risqué comedy. After divorcing Jack, her philandering husband of 25 years, Fay first got herself a job as secretary to two off-the-wall attorneys, Danny Messina and Al Cassidy. She then moved into an apartment of her own and started dating. Onlookers to Fay's new lifestyle were Jack, who kept trying to get her back again, daughter Linda and son-in-law Elliott, who were appalled, and Fay's unhappily married friend Lillian, who lived vicariously through Fay's affairs.

FAYE EMERSON SHOW, THE (*Interview*)

FIRST TELECAST: *March 13, 1950*
LAST TELECAST: *December 23, 1950*
BROADCAST HISTORY:

Mar 1950–Apr 1950, CBS Mon 11:00–11:15
Apr 1950–May 1950, NBC Sat 10:30–10:45
May 1950–Jul 1950, CBS Sun various 15-minute spots
Jun 1950–Aug 1950, NBC Wed 8:00–8:15
Sep 1950–Dec 1950, CBS Tue/Thu/Sat 7:45–8:00

HOSTESS:

Faye Emerson

Faye Emerson seemed to be everywhere on early television. In addition to numerous guest appearances on fashion, quiz, and dramatic shows, she hosted her own 15-minute "chat" on a variety of nights in 1950, sometimes appearing on two networks simultaneously. The format of *The Faye Emerson Show* was informal and gossipy, with Miss Emerson discussing fashions, the theater, and current celebrities and welcoming a guest from some area of show business. Perhaps her most widely publicized contributions to the new medium, however, were the gowns she wore—her trademark plunging neckline was the subject of considerable controversy during television's formative years.

From June to August 1950 Miss Emerson's NBC series was known as *Fifteen with Faye.* She also hosted several similarly formatted local programs in New York, prior to and following her network run.

FAYE EMERSON'S WONDERFUL TOWN (*Variety*)

FIRST TELECAST: *June 16, 1951*
LAST TELECAST: *April 12, 1952*
BROADCAST HISTORY:

Jun 1951–Apr 1952, CBS Sat 9:00–9:30

HOSTESS:

Faye Emerson

Each week Faye Emerson spotlighted a different city in America, using musical, dramatic, and narrative elements to convey the flavor of the city, both past and present. Guest stars for each telecast either were born in the city or had some strong association with it. In time, the scope of the show expanded to include interesting foreign cities, such as Paris and Mexico City.

FEAR (*Game*)

BROADCAST HISTORY:

MTV
60 minutes
Original episodes: *2001–2002* (17 episodes)
Premiered: *February 18, 2001*

In this spooky twist on the reality-show genre, six young people were taken blindfolded to a frightening location, where they spent two or three nights looking for paranormal activity. If they carried out their assignments without giving in to their fears they could win as much as $5,000 each. In the initial special episode three girls and three guys between the ages of 18 and 24 were led into an abandoned maximum-security prison in West Virginia, where they were left completely alone (there was no film crew; producers watched them via infrared security cameras). Each was given a video camera and a walkie-talkie; one member (the "Navigator") stayed behind in a safe room accessing assignments from a special Web site and directing others in the field, generally in teams of two. Assignments included spending 15 minutes alone in the death chamber (to "determine abnormal activity"), in a dark, deserted underground chamber where inmates had been beaten and killed, and in the deserted infirmary, where other prisoners met mysterious deaths. All of the assignments were at night; by day the contestants stayed in a safe house, where they slept or watched movies such as *The Shining, The Exorcist,* and *Rosemary's Baby*. A contestant could quit at any time, but then forfeited winnings and was sent home; in the first installment one of the girls broke down, babbling "I want to get out of here—*now!*"

Fear was first telecast as two specials, on September 21 and October 27, 2000, followed by the weekly series in 2001.

FEAR AND FANCY, see *ABC Dramatic Shorts—1952–1953*

FEAR FACTOR (*Audience Participation*)

FIRST TELECAST: *June 11, 2001*
LAST TELECAST:
BROADCAST HISTORY:
Jun 2001–Aug 2001, NBC Mon 8:00–9:00
Jan 2002– , NBC Mon 8:00–9:00

HOST:
Joe Rogan

Fear Factor was one of the most popular shows of the reality fad, and at times the grossest. The premise was simple. Six healthy young contestants—three men and three women—faced a series of physical challenges designed to test their greatest fears. Macho host Joe Rogan (often seen in a leather jacket) shouted encouragement as they attempted such stunts as being dragged a fixed distance by galloping horses, stripping to their underwear and being lowered into a pit full of rats, walking across a six-and-one-half-inch-wide beam suspended more than 100 feet in the air, driving a car off a three-story parking structure, and crawling out of a car hanging 150 feet in the air over a river, retrieving a flag, then crawling back in—while being hosed. Many of the stunts involved being covered with rodents or insects, or eating disgusting things (such as bull's testicles or live beetles). There was also plenty of skin, with the gals always good looking and in bikinis. In one segment contestants had to confront their "fear of nudity" by going naked in public.

Contestants who failed a challenge or dropped out because of fear left with nothing, and there was a certain amount of byplay as players tried to "spook" each other before a stunt. The last contestant standing won the grand prize of $50,000. There were also celebrity editions, including one with *Playboy* Playmates. Contestants were always given safety gear, such as goggles, helmets and safety wires for the high-altitude stunts, but the challenges, supervised by professionals, were still dangerous. Said host Rogan, "They should not be attempted by anyone, anywhere, anytime."

Besides its regular run, *Fear Factor* appeared as a special at various times on NBC.

FEARING MIND, THE (*Drama*)

BROADCAST HISTORY:
Fox Family Channel
60 minutes
Original Episodes: *2000* (13 episodes)
Premiered: *October 21, 2000*

CAST:
W. M. "Bill" Fearing .... Harry Van Gorkum
Cynthia Fearing .... Susan Gibney
Lenore Fearing .... Katee Sackhoff
Grandma Lucy Fearing .... Rae Allen
Howard .... John Fleck

The strange, dark imaginings of a writer of mystery/horror stories intersected with his family life in this odd little series. Bill Fearing was a somewhat distracted, put-upon writer living in a small town in Oregon. Cynthia was his resourceful, sharp-tongued wife; Lenore, his self-absorbed teenage daughter; and Lucy, his bossy, live-in mother-in-law. Howard, his fussy friend, ran a nearby bookstore. Little incidents in this traditional world morphed into Bill's imaginary world of horror; for example, an ant that landed on his hand might lead to a story about the skin being torn off a woman, ants devouring a man, and a psycho with army ants living inside him.

To those around him Bill acted a little odd, but none saw what he—or the viewer—saw. Said Lenore, "I love you, Dad, but it must be really strange to be inside your head." Thirteen episodes of *The Fearing Mind* were produced, but only six were telecast in its original run.

FEARLESS FOSDICK (*Children's*)

FIRST TELECAST: *July 13, 1952*
LAST TELECAST: *September 28, 1952*
BROADCAST HISTORY:
Jul 1952–Sep 1952, NBC Sun 6:30–7:00

PUPPETS:
The Mary Chase Marionettes

Straight from Al Capp's comic strip "Li'l Abner" came this filmed summer series using puppets and animation. Fosdick—a parody of Dick Tracy—was Li'l Abner's favorite detective and, according to him, the world's greatest. The lantern-jawed Fosdick was abused by his boss on the police force and made barely enough money to live on, but he valiantly fought on against crime and evil. *Fearless Fosdick* premiered on June 15, 1952, on Sunday afternoon and later moved into an evening slot.

FEATHER AND FATHER GANG, THE (*Crime Drama*)

FIRST TELECAST: *March 7, 1977*
LAST TELECAST: *August 6, 1977*
BROADCAST HISTORY:
Mar 1977–Apr 1977, ABC Mon 10:00–11:00
May 1977–Aug 1977, ABC Sat 10:00–11:00

CAST:
Toni "Feather" Danton .... Stefanie Powers
Harry Danton .... Harold Gould
Enzo .... Frank Delfino
Margo .... Joan Shawlee
Michael .... Monte Landis
Lou .... Lewis Charles

"Feather" was a beautiful young attorney, her father a suave, shrewd ex-con man. Together with their little band of grafters and bunco artists they comprised a crack investigative team, determined to "cheat the cheaters," the swindlers and murderers who were the targets of their investigations. Lots of disguises and elaborate ruses were used.

Harold Gould, the "father" in this show, was a rarity in show business—a Ph.D. and a former full professor of drama at UCLA who decided to practice what he taught.

FEATURE PLAYHOUSE, see *Movies—Prior to 1961*

FEATURE THEATRE, see *Movies—Prior to 1961*

FEDERAL MEN, syndicated title for *Treasury Men in Action*

FEDS (*Legal Drama*)

FIRST TELECAST: *March 5, 1997*
LAST TELECAST: *April 9, 1997*
BROADCAST HISTORY:
Mar 1997–Apr 1997, CBS Wed 9:00–10:00
CAST:
U.S. Atty. Erica Stanton .... Blair Brown
Asst. U.S. Atty. Sandra Broome ...... Regina Taylor
Chief Asst. U.S. Atty. Michael Mancini .... John Slattery
Asst. U.S. Atty. C. Oliver Resor ...... Adrian Pasdar
Asst. U.S. Atty. Jessica Graham ...... Grace Phillips
Special Agent Jack Gaffney .... Dylan Baker
Agent Katz .... John Rothman
Tony Garufi .... George DiCenzo
Charles Resor .... George Martin
Alfonse Bucci .... John Ventimiglia
Tommy Iradesco .... Frank Senger
Rod Nesbitt .... Scott Cohen

The Manhattan Federal Prosecutor's office was the setting for this short-lived crime drama. Running the office was U.S. Attorney Erica Stanton, the second most powerful federal law enforcement officer in the country after Attorney General Janet Reno. Stanton supervised a staff of ambitious hard-driving prosecutors. Mancini, in charge of organized crime and terrorism, was obsessed with bringing down mob boss Tony Garufi, whom he suspected was responsible for gunning down his wife and kids. Broome was in charge of civil rights cases; Resor, whose father wanted him to resign and join his law firm, handled corporate crime; and Graham handled cases ranging from Internet pornography to theft of museum artifacts. Gaffney was head of the investigative unit. They all ran around in their blue jackets emblazoned "FBI," with guns drawn.

In a television first, episodes of *Feds* were aired in letter-box format, giving the series the wide-screen look of a theatrical film (see *C-16* for another series that did this). The novelty didn't attract many viewers, and *Feds* was not renewed after the initial six-episode run.

FELICITY (*Drama*)

FIRST TELECAST: *September 29, 1998*
LAST TELECAST: *May 22, 2002*
BROADCAST HISTORY:
Sep 1998–Sep 1999, WB Tue 9:00–10:00
Sep 1999–Apr 2000, WB Sun 8:00–9:00
Apr 2000–Dec 2000, WB Wed 9:00–10:00 (OS)
Apr 2001–Dec 2001, WB Wed 9:00–10:00 (OS)
Mar 2002–May 2002, WB Wed 9:00–10:00
CAST:
Felicity Porter .... Keri Russell
Ben Covington .... Scott Speedman
Noel Crane .... Scott Foley
Julie Emrick (1998–2000) .... Amy Jo Johnson
Elena Tyler .... Tangi Miller
Meghan Rotundi .... Amanda Foreman
Sean Blumberg .... Greg Grunberg
Javier Frantata .... Ian Gomez
Richard Coad .... Robert Patrick Benedict
**Sally (voice, 1998–2000)* .... Janeane Garofalo
Lynn (1999) .... Dash Mihok
Guy (1998–1999) .... Brian Klugman
Ruby (1999–2000) .... Amy Smart
Maggie Sherwood (1999) .... Teri Polo
**Dr. Toni Pavone (2000–2002)* .... Amy Aquino
Tracy (2000–2001) .... Donald Faison
Greg Stenson (2000) .... Chris William Martin
Molly (2000–2001) .... Sarah-Jane Potts
**Dr. Edward Porter* .... Erich Anderson
Carol Anderson (1999–2000) ...... Jane Kaczmarek
Dr. McGrath (1999) .... Chris Sarandon
Professor Annie Sherman (1999) .... Sally Kirkland
David Sherman (1999) .... Henry Lubatti
**Andrew Covington (2000–2002)* .... John Ritter
**Professor Bill Hodges (2001–2002)* ...... Jim Ortlieb
Trevor O'Donnell (2001–2002) .... Christopher Gorham
**Lauren (2001–2002)* .... Lisa Edelstein
Zoe Webb (2001–2002) .... Sarah Jane Morris

*Occasional

Felicity was a starry-eyed freshman at the University of New York, located in Manhattan's Greenwich Village in this angst-ridden drama. Back home in California she had developed a crush on handsome high school classmate Ben, and on an impulse (and against her parents' wishes) followed him to New York and enrolled in his college—unbeknownst to him—in order to be near him. When she caught up with him she found out that he really wasn't that interested in her—oops! Felicity decided to stay in New York anyway and fell in love with the city. She narrated each episode with pithy and often introspective observations recorded on audiocassette letters to her friend Sally, in Santa Fe, detailing everything that was going on in her life.

Other students included Julie, her new best friend; Meghan, her never-there spooky roommate; Elena, who came from a poor family and got a scholarship to stay in school; Noel, Felicity's dorm advisor, who had a crush on her; Sean, who shared an off-campus apartment with Ben and was forever trying to develop a product that would make him rich; and Richard, the dorm's entrepreneur. Felicity and Noel developed a relationship but had a rocky time, particularly after his old girlfriend, Hanna, moved to New York in March, prompting Felicity to lose her virginity to Eli, an art student who was infatuated with her. Julie, who had been date-raped in the fall, got seriously involved with Ben in the spring and started searching for her birth mother, who had given her up. In February, Javier, Felicity's boss at Dean & DeLuca, the restaurant in which she worked part-time, moved back to Spain with his male lover. As the season, and her freshman year, drew to a close, Felicity and Noel were trying to rebuild their relationship. Things got complicated when Ben, who had broken up with Julie, started to express feelings for Felicity.

Felicity's feelings for both Ben and Noel, and everyone's romantic entanglements, provided the thread that ran through the rest of the series' run. During the summer of 1999 Felicity traveled cross-country with Ben, and as her sophomore year began she had to smooth things over with both Noel and Julie. As part of an attempt to restart her life, Felicity had her trademark long tresses shorn and then changed her major from pre-med to art. Ben had an affair with Maggie, a caterer, but they broke up after he found out she was married. Noel started dating Ruby, a freshman on Felicity's floor, but when he found out she was pregnant with someone else's baby they broke up and she left school. Julie moved in (awkwardly) with Ben and Sean, who was attracted to her but was never able to verbalize his feelings. Ambitious Sean then started a documentary film about Felicity and some of the other students, with Richard as his assistant, and was both intrusive and obnoxious in his filming. Elena dated Tracy but, when he told her he wouldn't have sex until he got married, she thought they might be better off as friends. After dumping Maggie, Ben decided he really was in love with Felicity after all, but she started dating Greg, who ran the health center where she volunteered. Later she went back to Ben, who got a construction job for the summer in Palo Alto. They planned to be together—but Felicity took a summer internship at the Metropolitan Museum of Art with her art history professor. Also during this season Felicity's dad was offered a teaching position in the medical school and took it because he and her mom had decided to separate. Felicity didn't take the impending divorce well and sought help from Dr. Pavone, a school psychologist. Javier got a work visa and was back at the restaurant. In the season finale he married his boyfriend, with Ben as an usher and Felicity as his "best man."

Felicity returned for her junior year and rented a small apartment in Brooklyn with Ben instead of moving into a university apartment. Noel had spent the summer partying with Natalie (Ali Landry), whom he had met at Javier's wedding; by the end of the premiere episode, they had gotten married and he was planning to drop out of school. The gang helped him realize he had made a mistake, and he got an annulment. Julie, needing to find herself, dropped out of school—leaving an explanatory videotape for the gang to watch. Elena cheated on Tracy with Finn, a white guy to whom she was strongly attracted. Tracy found out and had trouble forgiving her, but in December they made up and finally made love—after which he left for an exchange program in Africa. Joining the cast was Molly, an English girl taking her junior year abroad. Also showing up during the fall of 2000 was Ben's recovering alcoholic father, Andrew, who made a pass at Felicity.

In a December cliffhanger finale, Molly's drug-dealing boyfriend appeared at the gang's Christmas party and shot someone. When *Felicity* returned in April, one girl had been seriously injured and Elena had been shot in the shoulder. In the aftermath Molly's boyfriend was apprehended and sent to prison, she went back to England to sort things out (she eventually returned), and Elena became a self-defense fanatic. Noel, who was about to graduate, got a job supervising graphic design for a Web site in Seattle and offered Felicity a job for the summer. In the last episode of the season it became apparent that Noel's love for Felicity had rekindled, causing problems for her and Ben. Ruby came to New York with her baby, Eva, for Noel's graduation. Elena got back together with Tracy, who had returned from Africa, and he proposed. Sean and Meghan, who had been having a hot affair, went to Switzerland for the summer; Ben went to Kansas City for E.M.T. training; and Noel, whose job offer fell through, spent the summer in New York with Felicity.

At the start of the senior year Ben returned from E.M.T. training convinced he wanted to be a doctor and changed his major to pre-med. When Felicity's visiting father accused her of wasting her college years, she decided to pay for her senior year. She then tried to get into the honors program but, failing, had sex with sympathetic Noel instead. Tracy and Elena bailed out on their wedding day because he was convinced she was only getting married out of fear of losing him; he left school to think things out. In a surprise replacement Sean and Meghan got married instead, with the ceremony performed by Felicity, who had been ordained by the Universal Life Church. Elena then started an affair with Trevor, a pre-med student and friend of Ben's. Noel got $50,000 from his ex-wife Natalie's inheritance and used it to bail Sean out of a financial jam. Then, after he fell into a position as a guidance counselor at the university, he got Felicity a teaching assistant position to help her with her school costs. Noel, who had finally decided to get on with his life and not pine over Felicity, started a graphics business with Sean as his outspoken, and sometimes troublesome, partner.

As graduation approached, Felicity resumed sending tapes to Sally. Noel and Sean went to work for Webb Graphics, a company they had beaten out of an account, and Noel started dating Zoe, the boss's daughter. Lauren, a former lover of Ben's father with whom Ben had a brief affair, told him she was pregnant with his child. They decided that she would raise it alone, a decision that shocked Felicity. Ben then decided he wanted to be involved in his child's life and considered transferring to the University of Arizona, near Lauren's family's home. As this was going on, an understandably distracted Felicity couldn't concentrate on a term paper and copied one she found in the library. When the professor submitted it for publication, Felicity had to admit what she had done. The sympathetic professor failed her on the paper but gave her a passing grade in the course so she could graduate. Ben left for Philadelphia to be with Lauren when she gave birth to his son, Andrew, then moved to Arizona.

Six months later and back home in Palo Alto, Felicity sent Ben a letter updating him on their friends. Sean and Noel, who restarted their own design business after being laid off by Mr. Webb, were doing well, and Sean's wife, Meghan, had decided to become a psychiatrist. Felicity was at Stanford taking pre-med courses and was surprised when Ben turned up on campus. He had convinced Lauren to move to California with Andrew so that he could transfer to Stanford and be with Felicity.

After Elena, who had been in medical school, died in an auto accident, Felicity went into a severe depression and distanced herself from Ben, eventually breaking up with him. Then, while in New York for Noel and Zoe's wedding, she told Meghan she would have been better off if she had chosen Noel instead of Ben, leading to the series' last and most bizarre story line. Meghan cast a spell that sent Felicity back in time to the night she had slept with Noel. In this alternate reality Felicity's life was changed as she tried to reshape the past. Ben gave up pre-med after failing a test, Elena and Tracy called off their wedding plans, and, because they never got to the altar, Sean and

Meghan didn't get married. Stuck in her alternate reality, Felicity asked Meghan to undo the spell, but Meghan had no idea what her friend was talking about. Noel was also confused by Felicity's strange behavior and almost broke up with her, but they made up and moved in together. Motivated by Noel's reunion with Felicity, Sean told Meghan he wanted to break up, and gave Julie a call. But Julie ignored him and made a move on Ben. Noel then dumped Felicity because he was sure she couldn't get over Ben, and when she told him she had time-traveled to get him back, he thought she was crazy. (Are you following this?) Later Noel died in a fire—which really upset Felicity, because he was alive before she had gone into the spell. She finally went to the man who had written the book from which Meghan had obtained the time-travel spell, and he conducted a reverse spell.

Felicity woke up on the night before Noel's wedding, surrounded by concerned friends who told her she'd had a high fever and been delirious. Ben asked her to forgive him, and she took him back; Noel married Zoe; and everything was as it had been, except for one thing—Elena was alive and back together with Tracy.

FELONY SQUAD (*Police Drama*)

FIRST TELECAST: *September 12, 1966*
LAST TELECAST: *January 31, 1969*
BROADCAST HISTORY:

Sep 1966–Sep 1968, ABC Mon 9:00–9:30
Sep 1968–Jan 1969, ABC Fri 8:30–9:00

CAST:

Det. Sgt. Sam Stone .... Howard Duff
Det. Jim Briggs .... Dennis Cole
Desk Sgt. Dan Briggs................ Ben Alexander
Capt. Nye.......................... Frank Maxwell
Capt. Franks (1967–1968).......... Barney Phillips
Det. Cliff Sims (1968–1969).......... Robert DoQui

THEME:

"Felony Squad Theme," by Pete Rugolo

This police action drama was set in a large city in the West. The principals were 20-year veteran Sam Stone, his young partner Jim Briggs, and Briggs's father, Desk Sgt. Dan Briggs, a kind of paunchy housemother to the younger cops in the station house. Capt. Nye was their commanding officer during the first and last seasons, temporarily replaced by Capt. Franks in 1967–1968. The series was filmed on location in the Los Angeles area.

FERNWOOD 2-NIGHT (*Satire*)

BROADCAST HISTORY:

Syndicated only
30 minutes
Produced: *1977–1978* (125 episodes)
Released: *July 1977*

CAST:

Barth Gimble .... Martin Mull
Jerry Hubbard........................ Fred Willard
Happy Kyne.......................... Frank DeVol

FREQUENT GUESTS:

Garth Gimble, Sr................ Robert B. Williams
Verne Taylor........................... Verne Rowe
Virgil Sims............................. Jim Varney
Aunt Edity .... Irma Seigel
Linda Barry .... Barrie Youngfellow
Tony Roletti.................... Bill Kirchenbauer

CREATED BY:

Norman Lear

Introduced as the summer replacement for *Mary Hartman, Mary Hartman*, this was one of the most talked-about programs of 1977. In it, denizens of Fernwood, Ohio (Mary's hometown), mounted a talk show on local station WZAZ-TV, Channel 6, down on Acacia Street. It did look like an ordinary talk show, with desk and couch, slick, smiling host and his eager sidekick, and guests like a piano player, an insufferable child dancer, and a couple who had lost their son to a religious cult. But the pianist was rolled out in an iron lung, and proceeded to play a Mozart sonata upside down and backward while the Shirley Temple look-alike tap-danced alongside; the son, whom the parents complained had been programmed to keep "falling on his knees and mumbling in a foreign tongue," and who always dressed in black and kept "leading cockamamie parades down church aisles," turned out to be a Catholic priest.

Fernwood 2-Night was a wild, and some said patently offensive, parody on TV talk shows. The host, Barth Gimble, was natty and egotistical, his sidekick, Jerry Hubbard, a fatuous idiot ("Any comparison to Johnny Carson and Ed McMahon is, of course, purely intentional," smirked *Time* magazine). Martin Mull had previously appeared on *Mary Hartman, Mary Hartman* as Garth Gimble, a wife beater who eventually impaled himself on an aluminum Christmas tree in the closet. Barth was presented here as his twin brother, and there were occasional visits by their father, Garth, Sr. The guests were parodies of every mind-numbing act that ever paraded across the Carson/Douglas/Griffin shows, from Vietnamese refugee Mian Co Tiam, who had written a patriotic book titled *Yankee Doodle Gook*, to a housewife who was campaigning to have her late Aunt Dora made a saint because she made "remarkable raisin bread," to a Jewish man named Morton Rose who had been caught speeding through all-WASP Fernwood. He was brought on because Barth was sure many of the local viewers had never seen "a person of the Jewish persuasion." "What tribe are you from?" asked Hubbard. "I'm originally from Toledo," responded the guest eagerly. Then they opened the phone lines for a "Talk-to-a-Jew" call-in segment, in which one woman wanted to know, "When is Barbra Streisand's next movie coming out?"

The writers spared no one. "We will offend the sensitivities of a number of Americans, for which we apologize out front," admitted producer Alan Thicke. "But we're not being discriminating in our satire," he added cheerfully, "we're offending everybody, regardless of race, creed, color, or income level." A few jokes, though very few, were off-limits. A line about recent suicide Freddie Prinze was deleted; as was a skit about two brothers fighting over whether to pull the plug on their comatose mother. ("Now," interjected Gimble, "is it Mom or the money you want?")

Other guests included Linda Barry, owner of the Fernwood Nudist Colony, mechanic Virgil Sims, Barth's aunt Edity, a couple discussing the La Fromage method of childbirth, the founder of the Church of the Divine Lemonade, and the Salvation Army Singers performing "Da Do Ron Ron." Happy Kyne led the ragged, four-piece studio band, the Mirth Makers, when not touting his franchised dental service.

Although this bizarre program was only marginally successful in its summer 1977 run, Norman Lear brought it back in April 1978 as *America 2-Night*. Barth and Jerry had moved to Alta Coma, California, "the unfinished furniture capital of the world," and hoped to boost the show with appearances by major Hollywood stars. (Many did appear, playing parodies of themselves, including Charlton Heston, Robin Williams, George Gobel, Elke Sommer, and Gary Burghoff.) The new series got off to a grand start with a week-long buildup for "Electrocution Night '78," in which a convict was to be executed on stage while his wife lined up book, movie, and T-shirt deals. Viewers had a chance to participate by entering an "I would like to throw the switch because . . ." contest.

FERRIS BUELLER (*Situation Comedy*)
FIRST TELECAST: *August 23, 1990*
LAST TELECAST: *December 16, 1990*
BROADCAST HISTORY:
Aug 1990, NBC Thu 8:30–9:00
Sep 1990–Dec 1990, NBC Mon 8:30–9:00
Dec 1990, NBC Sun 7:00–7:30
CAST:
Ferris Bueller (age 16) .... Charlie Schlatter
Jeannie Bueller (17) .... Jennifer Aniston
Bill Bueller .... Sam Freed
Barbara Bueller .... Cristine Rose
Cameron Frye .... Brandon Douglas
Principal Ed Rooney .... Richard Riehle
Grace .... Judith Kahan
Sloan Peterson .... Ami Dolenz
Arthur Petrelli .... Jeff Maynard

The fall 1990 schedule brought two conniving teenager series, *Parker Lewis Can't Lose* and this adaptation of the 1986 Matthew Broderick movie that had inspired them both, *Ferris Bueller's Day Off*. Ferris was the more mean-spirited of the two. His colorful scams and flimflams at Ocean Park High School in Santa Monica, California, were mostly self-centered and often seemed designed to humiliate and punish. A lot depended on high-tech gadgetry: his portable computer that could patch into the school system and alter course assignments, his portable phone for impersonating authorities, his remote control for setting off little disasters at school assemblies. No one was his match—not pompous principal Rooney, his assistant Grace, or Ferris's fuming sister Jeannie, who despised how he got away with things. Bill and Barbara were his vacuous parents, who believed whatever he told them, Cameron, his dim-witted best friend, and beautiful Sloan, the object of his affections—and the one person he couldn't bamboozle.

A leftover episode of this failed series aired on August 11, 1991.

FESTIVAL OF STARS (*Dramatic Anthology*)
FIRST TELECAST: *June 30, 1956*
LAST TELECAST: *September 17, 1957*
BROADCAST HISTORY:
Jun 1956–Sep 1956, NBC Sat 9:30–10:00
Jul 1957–Sep 1957, NBC Tue 8:00–8:30
HOST:
Jim Ameche (1957)

The 1956 edition of this summer series of dramas was made up of reruns of episodes of *Ford Theatre*. When it returned the following summer, *Festival of Stars* consisted of reruns of episodes from *The Loretta Young Show* in which Miss Young had not appeared. Jim Ameche served as host of the latter series.

FIBBER MCGEE AND MOLLY (*Situation Comedy*)
FIRST TELECAST: *September 15, 1959*
LAST TELECAST: *January 19, 1960*
BROADCAST HISTORY:
Sep 1959–Jan 1960, NBC Tue 8:30–9:00
CAST:
Fibber McGee .... Bob Sweeney
Molly McGee .... Cathy Lewis
Doc Gamble .... Addison Richards
Mayor La Trivia .... Harold Peary
Teeny .... Barbara Beaird
Hazel Norris .... Elisabeth Fraser
Roy Norris .... Paul Smith
Fred Nitney .... Jack Kirkwood

Fibber McGee and Molly was one of the most popular radio shows of all time, running from 1935 until 1957. In the fall of 1959 it came to television, but with much less success. The McGees were the residents of 79 Wistful Vista and, as on radio, had to cope with friends and neighbors who made life rather hilarious. Fibber's tendency to overstate—some people called it fibbing—constantly got him into trouble. Fortunately, Molly's common sense and talents as a peacemaker prevented most situations from getting out of hand. Symptomatic of the problems involved in bringing *Fibber McGee and Molly* to television was McGee's famous overcrowded hall closet, which always unleashed its contents in a crash whenever it was opened. Somehow this was not as funny seen on television as it had been when only heard on radio.

Most of the actors in the TV version had not been associated with the show on radio, but one did have an interesting connection with the earlier version. Harold Peary had created the role of Throckmorton P. Gildersleeve on *Fibber McGee and Molly* in 1939, later moving it to a series of his own as *The Great Gildersleeve*. When *Fibber McGee* came to TV, he returned as Mayor La Trivia.

FIFTEEN (*Drama*)
BROADCAST HISTORY:
Nickelodeon
30 minutes
Produced: *1991–1993* (65 episodes)
Premiered: *February 2, 1991*
CAST:
Roxanne .... Roxanne Alexander
Jake .... Ken Angel
Chris .... Andrew Baskin
John .... John Boyd
Courtney .... Sarah Douglas
Ashley .... Laura Elizabeth Harris
Erin .... Erin Inglis
Dylan .... Corky Martin
Billy .... Ryan Reynolds
Brooke .... Robyn Ross
Matt .... Todd Talbot
Stacy .... Lisa Warner
David .... David Wight
Arseman .... Arseman Yohannes

An issue-oriented soap opera revolving around the

lives and loves of a group of high school teens. According to Nickelodeon, it was not related to a series of the same name that was briefly syndicated in 1987, even though the name of the high school ("Hillside High") was the same in both shows.

FIFTEEN WITH FAYE, see *Faye Emerson Show, The*

FIFTH CORNER, THE (*Espionage*)
FIRST TELECAST: *April 17, 1992*
LAST TELECAST: *April 24, 1992*
BROADCAST HISTORY:
Apr 1992, NBC Fri 10:00–11:00
CAST:
Richard Braun .... Alex McArthur
Erica Fontaine .... Kim Delaney
Dr. Grandwell .... James Coburn
Boone .... J.E. Freeman
The Hat .... Anthony Valentine

Serialized espionage series about an undercover agent whose past was a mystery even to him. Richard Braun woke up in Mexico next to a dead woman, with no recollection of who he was or why he was there. On the lam, he found clues: multiple passports with his picture but different names, an assortment of murders of which he was accused, a crusading journalist (Erica) on his trail, a scruffy chauffeur (Boone) who materialized with a limo to drive him around, and, behind it all, a ruthless, shadowy billionaire (Grandwell) who was evidently his employer. "The Fifth Corner" was a reference to Braun's ability to find his way out of any situation, even when all four corners were blocked.

Unfortunately neither Braun nor viewers had time to make much sense out of this tangled muddle, as NBC pulled the plug on *The Fifth Corner* after only two weeks.

5TH WHEEL, THE (*Dating*)
BROADCAST HISTORY:
Syndicated only
30 minutes
Produced: *2001–*
Released: *October 2001*
HOST:
Aisha Tyler

Each episode of this show started with two guys and two girls in a fully loaded luxury bus, making small talk and trying to size up the members of the opposite sex as they started out on their group date. Over the course of the evening they tried to impress each other while seeking a romantic connection. Just when things were starting to get interesting another person, "The 5th Wheel," joined and attempted to get one of them to dump whomever they were with, in favor of him or her.

Host Tyler introduced the participants and made comments—sometimes pretty snide—about the activities. There was pop-up on-screen commentary about things that were happening and observations made by the players. At the end of the episode each of the five participants evaluated the members of the opposite sex and picked who they wanted to spend more time with. If there was a match, they "scored."

Produced by the folks responsible for *Blind Date.* Their slogan for *The 5th Wheel* was "Where strangers become friends, friends become lovers and lovers become bitter suicidal exes all on the same show."

FIFTY-FOURTH STREET REVUE, THE (*Variety*)
FIRST TELECAST: *May 5, 1949*
LAST TELECAST: *March 25, 1950*
BROADCAST HISTORY:
May 1949–Sep 1949, CBS Thu 8:00–9:00
Sep 1949–Jan 1950, CBS Fri 9:00–10:00
Jan 1950–Mar 1950, CBS Sat 8:00–9:00
HOST:
Jack Sterling (1949)
Al Bernie (1949)
Billy Vine (1949–1950)
Joey Faye (1950)
REGULARS:
Russell Arms
Marilyn Day
Carl Reiner (1949)
Pat Bright (1949)
Cliff "Ukulele Ike" Edwards (1949)
Wynn Murray (1949)
Mort Marshall
Joe Silver
Joan Diener
Fosse and Niles
Virginia Gorski
Harry Sosnik Orchestra

This live musical and comedy revue derived its name from the street address of the New York studio in which it was produced. Its regular cast changed constantly, depending on what other jobs its members could find that were more substantial than employment in early television. Jack Sterling was the original host, soon replaced by Al Bernie. Bernie lasted until December 1949, to be replaced by Billy Vine, who lasted only two months, and finally by Joey Faye. Carl Reiner, Pat Bright, Cliff Edwards, and Marilyn Day were also early departures, with Miss Day returning for a second stint during Joey Faye's tenure as host.

The male half of the young dance team of Fosse and Niles was Bob Fosse, who would become a very successful choreographer and director of Broadway musicals and films in the 1960s and 1970s.

FIGHT BEAT (*Sports Commentary*)
FIRST TELECAST: *April 4, 1958*
LAST TELECAST: *December 26, 1958*
BROADCAST HISTORY:
Apr 1958–Dec 1958, NBC Fri 10:45–11:00
HOST:
Bud Palmer

Bud Palmer interviewed the winning fighters and other boxing celebrities in this short sports commentary program designed to fill the time remaining between the conclusion of the featured bout on *Cavalcade of Sports* and the 11 o'clock news. The title of the program was originally *Post Fight Beat,* but this was shortened to *Fight Beat* on May 23.

FIGHT OF THE WEEK, THE, see *Boxing*

FIGHT TALK (*Sports Commentary*)
FIRST TELECAST: *January 24, 1953*
LAST TELECAST: *January 15, 1955*
BROADCAST HISTORY:
Jan 1953–Jan 1955, ABC Sat 9:45–10:00
COMMENTATOR:
Don Dunphy
Red Smith (1953–1954)
Bob Cook (1954–1955)

This show followed ABC's *Saturday Night Fights* and provided its two commentators with an opportunity to analyze the bout that had just been seen and make predictions and observations about other major fights that were coming up in the near future. Don Dunphy was with the show throughout its run, while Red Smith left and was replaced by Bob Cook.

FIGHTING FITZGERALDS, THE (*Situation Comedy*)

FIRST TELECAST: *March 6, 2001*
LAST TELECAST: *May 29, 2001*
BROADCAST HISTORY:
Mar 2001, NBC Tue 8:30–9:00
Mar 2001–May 2001, NBC Tue 8:00–8:30
CAST:
Mr. Fitzgerald.......... Brian Dennehy
Jim Fitzgerald.......... Justin Louis
Sophie Fitzgerald.......... Connie Britton
Terry Fitzgerald.......... Christopher Moynihan
Patrick Fitzgerald.......... Jon Patrick Walker
Marie Fitzgerald (age 6) (pilot only)
.... Dakota Fanning
Marie Fitzgerald.......... Abigail Mavity
Beth.......... Constance Zimmer

Blustery, barrel-chested "Fitz" Fitzgerald was a retired fire captain and a widower, but he wasn't enjoying his retirement. The modern world where adult men go to therapy, kids call their teachers by their first names and political correctness reigns was too much for him. So were his three grown sons, who, seemingly, would never leave the house. Jim was the sensible gym teacher, married to tart-tongued Sophie and father to adorable Marie. Terry was a goofy, layabout bartender, who could hardly say a word without getting slapped upside the head by Fitz. Patrick, the youngest, was the biggest disappointment of all, a successful stockbroker who had chucked it all in order to "find himself," while returning home to sleep on the family couch. They squabbled and sparred, sometimes hanging out at Gibson's Tavern, but by the end of each episode Fitz was revealed to be, under that gruff exterior, a sentimental pussycat.

Loosely based on the 1995 film *The Brothers McMullen.*

FIGURE IT OUT (*Quiz/Audience Participation*)

BROADCAST HISTORY:
Nickelodeon
30 minutes
Produced: *1997–1999*
Premiered: *July 7, 1997*
HOST:
Summer Sanders

Imagine debonair '50s panel show host John Daly turned into Olympic swimmer Summer Sanders, and his erudite panel morphed into four young actors cracking jokes; a large vat of gelatinous slime hanging over the panelists' heads, which would drench them whenever they said the secret word; and kids as the contestants—and you have Nickelodeon's '90s version of *What's My Line? Figure It Out* may have been derivative, but its youthful audience was unlikely to ever figure *that* out. The panelists, who had to guess each contestant's special talent via a series of yes or no questions, were mostly drawn from Nickelodeon's own series. Danny Tamberelli from *The Adventures of Pete & Pete* and Lori Beth Denberg from *All That* were frequent guests. Besides the gags and sliming, the series did have one redeeming feature: most of the young contestants had accomplished something notable, in sports, science, or some other field, and their achievements were profiled at the end of the game as an inspiration to other kids.

FILM FAIR, see *Movies—Prior to 1961*

FILM FESTIVAL, see *ABC Dramatic Shorts—1952–1953*

FILM SHORTS, see *Movies—Prior to 1961*

FILM THEATRE OF THE AIR, see *Movies—Prior to 1961*

FILTHY RICH (*Situation Comedy*)

FIRST TELECAST: *August 9, 1982*
LAST TELECAST: *June 15, 1983*
BROADCAST HISTORY:
Aug 1982, CBS Mon 9:30–10:00
Oct 1982–Nov 1982, CBS Wed 9:30–10:00
Jan 1983–Feb 1983, CBS Mon 8:30–9:00
Jun 1983, CBS Wed 8:30–9:00
CAST:
Big Guy Beck (1982).......... Slim Pickens
Big Guy Beck.......... Forrest Tucker
Kathleen Beck.......... Delta Burke
Carlotta Beck.......... Dixie Carter
Stanley Beck.......... Charles Frank
Wild Bill Weschester.......... Jerry Hardin
Marshall Beck.......... Michael Lombard
Bootsie Weschester.......... Ann Wedgeworth
Winona "Mother B" Beck.......... Nedra Volz
George Wilhoit (pilot only).......... David Healy
George Wilhoit.......... Vernon Weddle

Filthy Rich was an unabashed sendup of the *Dallas/Dynasty/Falcon Crest* school of prime-time soap opera about the machinations of the unscrupulous rich. The founder of the family fortune, Tennessee land baron Big Guy Beck, was dead, but he still controlled the lives of his heirs. Before dying, and being cryogenically frozen, he had produced a living will on videotape, and each week another section of it was played for the family. The terms of the will were hardest on socially prominent elder son Marshall and his equally status-conscious wife Carlotta. They were forced to welcome Big Guy's illegitimate son, Wild Bill Weschester, and Bill's flaky wife, Bootsie, into the family mansion, Toad Hall. For the simple Weschesters this was paradise, but for the Becks it was humiliating. Big Guy's greedy, social-climbing, sexy young widow, Kathleen, was looking for a new meal ticket, while his first wife, elderly Mother B, belied her age by repeatedly escaping from the nursing home where she was living. Only Big Guy's younger son, Stanley, who was independently wealthy, seemed to be normal. He was considerate and charming, and spent much of his time foiling the devious plans of Marshall and Carlotta to rid themselves of both the Weschesters and the constraints of the will. George Wilhoit was the attorney who administered Big Guy's taped will.

When this limited-run series returned to the air in

October 1982 Forrest Tucker was seen as Big Guy in the tapes, since actor Slim Pickens had died after the first few episodes had been produced.

FINAL APPEAL: FROM THE FILES OF UNSOLVED MYSTERIES (*Documentary*)
FIRST TELECAST: *September 18, 1992*
LAST TELECAST: *October 16, 1992*
BROADCAST HISTORY:
Sep 1992–Oct 1992, NBC Fri 8:00–8:30
HOST:
Robert Stack

Short-lived spin-off from NBC's *Unsolved Mysteries,* based on a popular segment that reopened criminal cases in which the person convicted may have been innocent. The show looked at each case from the perspective of the prosecution and defense, leaving it up to the viewer to decide whether the criminal deserved a "final appeal." It was not recorded whether anyone profiled during its short run was subsequently exonerated.

FINAL JUSTICE (*Documentary*)
BROADCAST HISTORY:
Lifetime
60 minutes
Original episodes: *2003–*
Premiered: *January 17, 2003*
HOST:
Erin Brockovich
THEME:
Co-written and performed by Wynonna Judd

The real-life woman who was the subject of the hit 2000 Julia Roberts' film *Erin Brockovich* stepped in front of the cameras to host this inspiring series about ordinary people—like herself—who made a difference. Tall, determined-looking Erin narrated as stories unfolded, such as that of the Louisiana woman who was spied on in her own home by an obsessed neighbor, and eventually got a law passed against video voyeurism; the parents who lost their four-year-old son in an auto accident because the seat belts didn't work, and got a law passed fixing that; and the black woman whose husband was killed because of his race and who brought the killer to justice herself after the police had given up on the case. What was Erin's secret? To those fighting injustice in their lives, she said, "If you believe in yourself, you can do anything." One of the victims profiled put it this way—when asked, "How did you get law enforcement professionals to take you seriously?" she replied, "I wouldn't take no for an answer!"

FINANCIAL NEWS NETWORK (Network)
(*Business News Cable Network*)
LAUNCHED:
November 1981
CEASED OPERATION:
June 1991
SUBSCRIBERS (JUN. 1991):
36.3 million

One of the casualties of the cable network wars was FNN, a well-regarded network devoted to business news, stock market reports, and programs about personal money management. Although it never had a large total audience, it was a favorite of business professionals, and it pioneered the idea of a stock ticker at the bottom of the screen, continuously reporting current stock prices. Among its series were *FNN Money Talks* and *The Insiders* with Jack Anderson.

Ironically FNN fell prey to a financial scandal similar to those that rocked Wall Street (its chief subject) in the late 1980s. In the early 1990s allegations were made of financial mismanagement and the network was forced into bankruptcy. A lively bidding war for its assets ensued; some bidders intended to put its affairs in order and continue operation. The bidding, however, was won by its chief competitor, CNBC (owned by General Electric), which was trailing in viewership. The new owner shut down the network, fired its employees, and took over its channel space on cable systems around the country.

FINDER OF LOST LOVES (*Detective Drama*)
FIRST TELECAST: *September 22, 1984*
LAST TELECAST: *August 24, 1985*
BROADCAST HISTORY:
Sep 1984–Aug 1985, ABC Sat 10:00–11:00
CAST:
Cary Maxwell .... Tony Franciosa
Daisy Lloyd .... Deborah Adair
Rita Hargrove .... Anne Jeffreys
Brian Fletcher .... Richard Kantor
Lyman Whittaker (1985) .... Larry Flash Jenkins

Mix a little bit of *Love Boat* with a touch of *Fantasy Island,* wrap the entire package as a detective series, and you have *Finder of Lost Loves.* Cary Maxwell was a wealthy widower who, after the untimely death of his beloved wife Kate, had decided to devote the remainder of his working life reuniting star-crossed lovers and tracking down old flames. With the help of his beautiful assistant, Daisy (Kate's sister), his young trainee, Brian, and his efficient office manager, Rita, Cary sought to bring romance back into the lives of others. In this high-tech contemporary world it was not surprising that his most valued asset was Oscar, the computer he used to tie pieces of information together and locate the missing people his clients sought. Each episode contained two or three separate stories, and most resolved themselves into appropriately satisfying happy endings, the trademark of producer Aaron Spelling, who was also responsible for the aforementioned *Love Boat* and *Fantasy Island.*

FINE ROMANCE, A (*Adventure*)
FIRST TELECAST: *January 18, 1989*
LAST TELECAST: *March 16, 1989*
BROADCAST HISTORY:
Jan 1989, ABC Wed 10:00–11:00
Jan 1989–Mar 1989, ABC Thu 8:00–9:00
CAST:
Louisa Phillips .... Margaret Whitton
Michael Trent .... Christopher Cazenove
George Shipman .... Ernie Sabella
Miles Barrish .... Kevin Moore
Friday .... Dinah Lenney
Francois Boyer .... Xavier Kuentz
Francois Boyer (one episode) ..... Gerard Grobman

A stylish romantic comedy about a feuding couple who, though divorced, couldn't seem to stay away from each other. Louisa and Michael co-hosted a successful TV travel show called *Ticket to Ride,* which kept them chasing around the glamour spots of Europe—Paris, Dublin, Budapest, Malta. Amid the banter and Louisa's pranks on the exasperated Michael, they seemed to stumble into a murder mystery at every turn.

Filmed on location in Europe.

FIREBALL FUN-FOR-ALL (*Comedy/Variety*)
FIRST TELECAST: *June 28, 1949*
LAST TELECAST: *October 27, 1949*
BROADCAST HISTORY:
Jun 1949–Aug 1949, NBC Tue 8:00–9:00
Sep 1949–Oct 1949, NBC Thu 9:00–10:00
REGULARS:
Ole Olsen and Chick Johnson
Bill Hayes
Marty May
June Johnson
J. C. Olsen
The Buick Belles
Al Goodman Orchestra (Jun–Jul)
Charles Sanford Orchestra (Jul–Oct)

This comedy free-for-all, hosted by old-time vaudevillians Olsen and Johnson, was based on their Broadway hit *Hellzapoppin'*. Gimmick props, midgets running frantically across the stage, leggy showgirls, seltzer water, and custard pies were all the stock-in-trade of this noisy and unpredictable revue, which generally resembled organized mayhem. At the beginning many of the gags took place in the studio audience, but when the show returned after a brief summer hiatus the action tended to be more confined to the stage.

The program was directed and staged by Ezra Stone, one of the stars of the *Henry Aldrich* series. June Johnson and J. C. Olsen were the daughter and son, respectively, of the show's hosts.

FIRED UP (*Situation Comedy*)
FIRST TELECAST: *April 10, 1997*
LAST TELECAST: *February 9, 1998*
BROADCAST HISTORY:
Apr 1997–May 1997, NBC Thu 9:30–10:00
Jun 1997–Nov 1997, NBC Mon 8:30–9:00
Dec 1997–Jan 1998, NBC Mon 9:30–10:00
Jan 1998–Feb 1998, NBC Mon 8:30–9:00
CAST:
Gwen Leonard .... Sharon Lawrence
Terry Reynolds .... Leah Remini
Danny Reynolds .... Mark Feuerstein
Guy Mann .... Jonathan Banks
Mrs. Francis .... Francesca P. Roberts
Ashley .... Mark Davis

Gwen was an imperious, high-powered public relations executive, and Terry her long-suffering assistant. They were fired on the same day from a large Manhattan firm in this unusual "change of career" sitcom. Rather than go their separate ways, they decided to combine their talents—Gwen's contacts and Terry's smarts—and start their own small promotions firm, living in and operating out of Terry's SoHo loft. Boss and bossee were now partners, leading to many adjustments, especially for selfish Gwen. Danny was Terry's smart-mouth brother, a struggling writer who lived with them and worked at Guy's bar downstairs. Ashley was Guy's son, a female impersonator, and Mrs. Francis an unemployment office worker.

FIREFLY (*Science Fiction*)
FIRST TELECAST: *September 20, 2002*
LAST TELECAST: *December 20, 2002*
BROADCAST HISTORY:
Sep 2002–Dec 2002, FOX Fri 8:00–9:00
CAST:
Captain Malcolm "Mal" Reynolds ... Nathan Fillion
Inara Serra ("The Ambassador") .. Morena Baccarin
Jayne Cobb ("The Mercenary") ...... Adam Baldwin
Book ("The Shepherd") .... Ron Glass
River Tam ("The Fugitive") .... Summer Glau
Simon Tam .... Sean Maher
Kaylee Frye ("The Mechanic") .... Jewel Staite
Zoe ("The Soldier") .... Gina Torres
Wash ("The Pilot") .... Alan Tudyk

This series took place 400 years in the future and followed the exploits of Mal Reynolds, a renegade who had fought, unsuccessfully, against the unification of planets by The Alliance in a civil war that had ended a few years earlier. As captain of his transport ship, *The Serenity,* Mal traversed the border planets trying to make a living while avoiding confrontations with The Alliance. Some of the jobs he took on were legitimate salvage runs while others were decidedly illegal—he had no qualms about working for crime lords or selling medical supplies his crew had stolen from The Alliance. Mal's crew consisted of Zoe, who had served with Mal during the war and was fiercely loyal to him; Wash, Zoe's soft-spoken husband and *Serenity*'s pilot; Kaylee, the ship's brilliant engineer who was more comfortable with machines than with people; Jayne, Mal's tough, ill-tempered warrior crewman, and Simon, the ship's doctor who often disagreed with Mal's decisions. Also on *The Serenity* were Inara, a high-class courtesan who lived primarily on the ship's shuttlecraft; Book, a wise and thoughtful priest who was uncertain of his place in the universe, and River, Simon's troubled, psychic sister who could read minds. She had fled from The Alliance, which wanted to utilize her talents to serve its own ends.

FIREHOUSE (*Adventure*)
FIRST TELECAST: *January 17, 1974*
LAST TELECAST: *August 1, 1974*
BROADCAST HISTORY:
Jan 1974–Aug 1974, ABC Thu 8:30–9:00
CAST:
Capt. Spike Ryerson .... James Drury
Hank Myers .... Richard Jaeckel
Sonny Caputo .... Michael Delano
Billy Dalzell .... Brad David
Cal Dakin .... Bill Overton
Scotty Smith .... Scott Smith

In 1972 a crudely written but true-to-life book titled *Report from Engine Co. 82*, whose author was a real-life fireman, shot to the top of the best-seller list. About a year and a half later, a crudely produced but hopefully true-to-life television series called *Firehouse* premiered on the ABC network. Was it coincidence? Where do you suppose TV producers find their inspirations?

James Drury portrayed the father figure to the young smoke-eaters of Engine Co. 23 in this action drama. They encountered various disasters and performed various rescues each week; one of the more interesting of these was a man in traction whose house was about to slide off a hill. The firemen couldn't get into his room to maneuver him out without setting off the tilting house. How did they get him out? Sorry, series canceled.

FIRESIDE ARENA THEATRE (*Dramatic Anthology*)

FIRST TELECAST: *July 3, 1951*
LAST TELECAST: *August 21, 1951*
BROADCAST HISTORY:
Jul 1951–Aug 1951, NBC Tue 9:00–9:30
PRODUCER/DIRECTOR:
Albert McCleery

This summer replacement for *Fireside Theatre* was quite a different program, presenting eight weeks of live drama in a theater-in-the-round setting. A minimum of scenery and props was used, as the camera focused closely on the actors and the story.

FIRESIDE THEATRE (*Dramatic Anthology*)

FIRST TELECAST: *April 5, 1949*
LAST TELECAST: *September 8, 1963*
BROADCAST HISTORY:
Apr 1949–Jun 1957, NBC Tue 9:00–9:30 (OS)
Sep 1957–May 1958, NBC Thu 10:30–11:00
Jun 1963–Sep 1963, ABC Sun 8:00–8:30
HOST:
Frank Wisbar (1952–1953)
Gene Raymond (1953–1955)
Jane Wyman (1955–1958)

Fireside Theatre was one of the earliest filmed dramatic shows produced especially for television. However, for its first three months this series was a showcase of new program ideas, some live and some on film, which were being tried out for possible inclusion on the network schedule. These included dramas, comedies, and musical revues. The very first episode was a situation comedy, "Friend of the Family," starring Virginia Gilmore, Yul Brynner, and Peter Barry. One of the musical revues was Leonard Sillman's "New Faces." Win Elliot was the original announcer for the show, but he left after eight telecasts, after which there was no regular announcer or host for the next few years.

In the fall of 1949 *Fireside Theatre* switched to filmed stories, mostly dramas, featuring a wide range of actors and actresses (generally not big names). According to *TV Guide* these were "quickie" films, each one ground out in two or three days at the Hal Roach studios in Hollywood. Most of them were produced by Frank Wisbar. During the 1949–1950 season the majority of these little dramas were 15 minutes long (there were two per week), but beginning in the fall of 1950 and for the rest of the series each telecast was a self-contained 30-minute presentation.

In the fall of 1952 producer Frank Wisbar began appearing at the start of each week's telecast, in an effort to give the series greater continuity. From 1953–1955 actor Gene Raymond was the host, in addition to appearing in many of the dramas. For the 1954–1955 season an effort was also made to develop a regular repertory company of actors and actresses, including William Bendix, George Brent, and Dorothy Malone.

The hostess who is most identified with the show in viewers' minds—Jane Wyman—made her first appearance in 1955. The movie actress also starred in many of the episodes during her association with the show. The program was renamed in her honor (eventually it became simply *The Jane Wyman Show*) and special theme music was written for her. Well-known actors and actresses were engaged for the weeks when Miss Wyman did not star, among them Keenan Wynn, Peter Lawford, Dan Duryea, Ozzie Nelson, John Ireland, Gene Lockhart, Imogene Coca, Gene Barry, Joseph Cotten, and Vincent Price, plus many lesser-known Hollywood standbys. The program continued until the spring of 1958, when it was finally retired—to begin a very long run in syndication.

Reruns were shown on NBC as a summer replacement in 1954 and on the ABC network during the summer of 1963 (as *Jane Wyman Presents*).

Fireside Theatre, with and without Miss Wyman, was one of the most durable dramatic anthologies of the 1950s. Though generally not rising to the star-studded heights of *Studio One* or *Robert Montgomery Presents,* it did produce hundreds of fine dramas and also proved the practicality and value of a filmed series for the TV medium.

FIRST CAMERA, see *Monitor*

FIRST DATE, see *Continental, The*

FIRST IMPRESSIONS (*Situation Comedy*)

FIRST TELECAST: *August 27, 1988*
LAST TELECAST: *October 1, 1988*
BROADCAST HISTORY:
Aug 1988–Oct 1988, CBS Sat 8:00–8:30
CAST:
Frank Dutton .... Brad Garrett
Dave Poole .... Thom Sharp
Lindsay Dutton (age 9) .... Brandy Gold
Donna Patterson .... Sarah Abrell
Raymond Voss .... James Noble
Mrs. Madison .... Ruth Kobart

Set in Omaha, Nebraska, this short-lived summer sitcom chronicled the trials and tribulations of Frank Dutton. Frank, who had been divorced for a year, was raising his daughter Lindsay, gingerly reentering the social scene, and trying to get his business, Media of Omaha, off the ground. A talented impressionist, he put his vocal skills to good use on the commercials produced by his company. Working with him were his best friend and partner Dave, whose delusions of grandeur and neuroses were pretty hard to take; Donna, Media's absurdly naive receptionist; and Raymond, their eccentric audio engineer whose compulsive gambling kept him constantly on the verge of bankruptcy. Mrs. Madison was Frank's widowed next-door neighbor with a penchant for offering unsolicited, and usually unwanted, motherly advice for both Frank and his daughter.

FIRST LOOK (*Magazine*)

BROADCAST HISTORY:
Syndicated only
30 minutes
Produced: *1991–1992* (26 episodes)
Released: *September 1991*
HOSTS:
Chuck Henry
Paula McClure

This series was a spin-off from one of the failures of the previous season, *Preview.* Co-hosted by Chuck

Henry and Paula McClure, both alumni from *Preview*, *First Look* was a weekly look at breakthroughs in medicine, science, and technology that were in development and might reach the general public in the next few years.

FIRST MONDAY (*Legal Drama*)
FIRST TELECAST: *January 15, 2002*
LAST TELECAST: *June 7, 2002*
BROADCAST HISTORY:
Jan 2002, CBS Tue 9:00–10:00
Jan 2002–Jun 2002, CBS Fri 9:00–10:00
CAST:
Justice Joseph Novelli .... Joe Mantegna
Chief Justice Thomas Brankin .... James Garner
Justice Henry Hoskins .... Charles Durning
Justice Esther Weisenberg .... Camille Saviola
Justice Jerome Morris .... James McEachin
Justice Michael Bancroft .... James Karen
Justice Deborah Szwark .... Gail Strickland
Justice Theodore Snow .... Stephen Markle
Justice Brian Chandler .... Lyman Ward
Ellie Pearson .... Hedy Burgess
Miguel Mora .... Randy Vasquez
Jerry Klein .... Christopher Wiehl
Julian Lodge .... Joe Flanigan
Sarah Novelli .... Linda Purl
Andrew Novelli .... Brandon Davies
Beth Novelli .... Rachel Grate
Charles Bierbauer .... Himself
Kayla Turner .... Sandra Prosper
Court Crier .... Mark Costello
Janet Crowley .... Liz Torres
Idealistic attorney Joe Novelli had recently moved to Washington with his wife, Sarah, and their two teenage children, Beth and Andrew, to take a dream job. As the newly appointed associate justice on the U.S. Supreme Court, Joe was often the swing vote on a panel whose other members were evenly divided—four conservatives, led by scheming Chief Justice Brankin and his geriatric, wheelchair-bound friend Justice Hoskins, and four liberals. Joe's enthusiastic young law clerks were spunky liberal Ellie, suave, conservative Miguel and green Jerry. Julian was the snotty, bow-tied chief law clerk who was attracted to Ellie. Each episode centered on one or two cases before the Court, including testimony, evidence provided to the Court, discussions and maneuvering among the justices, and the Court's final determination. Novelli regularly agonized over his vote, but usually seemed to side with the heroic liberals over the well-meaning but clueless conservatives. Several real-life attorneys appeared in small roles as themselves, among them Barry Scheck, Johnnie Cochran, Gerry Spence, Vincent Bugliosi and Marcia Clark.

There was an attempt to get Joe thrown off the bench because his uncle in Chicago had a relationship with a known member of the Mafia, and later Joe's wife Sarah quit her job as a real estate agent to keep others from manipulating Joe through her. In April, while the Court was trying a case on the right to bear arms, it was revealed that a gun he had once owned had been used in a drive-by shooting. The title *First Monday* referred to the Court's annual opening session on the first Monday in October.

FIRST NIGHTER, see *Movies—Prior to 1961*

FIRST PERSON, see *Gulf Playhouse: 1st Person*

FIRST TIME OUT (*Situation Comedy*)
FIRST TELECAST: *September 10, 1995*
LAST TELECAST: *December 17, 1995*
BROADCAST HISTORY:
Sep 1995–Oct 1995, WB Sun 9:30–10:00
Oct 1995–Dec 1995, WB Sun 9:00–9:30
CAST:
Jackie Guerra .... Jackie Guerra
Dominique Costellano .... Leah Remini
Susan Gardner .... Mia Cottet
Nathan Fisk .... Craig Anton
Rosa .... Tracy Vilar
Madeline .... Roxanne Beckford
Freddy Tudor .... Harry Van Gorkum
Jackie was the receptionist at the trendy Tudor Hair Salon in L.A. and shared an apartment with her two friends, Dominique and Susan, in this single-girl comedy. Recently graduated from Yale, she was going to law school at night and longed for the day when she could make a difference in the world—and find a man. Cynical Dominique was a production assistant at Ventura Records; and neurotic, analytical Susan was about to get her license as a psychotherapist. Working with Jackie at the salon were her good friend Rosa, and Freddy, an obnoxious, womanizing English hairstylist. Madeline was the yuppie executive who lived across the hall, and Nathan was Jackie's klutzy, sex-obsessed childhood friend who worked at the *L.A. Review*. He had a million ideas but was incapable of staying focused long enough to finish anything.

Comedienne Guerra, who according to the WB network was "the first Latina to star in her own television series," was quoted in the press complaining about the stereotypical nature of her character, but since *First Time Out* only lasted for 13 episodes, she had little time to do much about it.

FIRST TUESDAY (*Newsmagazine*)
FIRST TELECAST: *January 7, 1969*
LAST TELECAST: *August 8, 1973*
BROADCAST HISTORY:
Jan 1969–Sep 1971, NBC Tue 9:00–11:00
Oct 1971–Jul 1972, NBC Fri 9:00–11:00
Sep 1972–Aug 1973, NBC Tue 10:00–11:00
ANCHORMAN:
Sander Vanocur (1969–1970)
Garrick Utley (1971–1972)
First Tuesday premiered four months after CBS' *60 Minutes*, but its roots went back to the early 1960s when *David Brinkley's Journal* provided viewers with a magazine/documentary format. Unlike all of the other magazine series, *First Tuesday* ran for a full two hours. With that much time to fill, the number of stories covered in each telecast often ran from six to eight. Among the subjects treated in depth were chemical-biological warfare, student revolts, occultism, the rise in beef prices, and the miracle of heart transplants. *First Tuesday* also had its lighter side, covering such topics as baton twirling, bathrooms in America, the romantic mystique surrounding stewardesses, and honeymoon trips to Guam.

Sander Vanocur was the original anchorman/reporter on *First Tuesday*, which, as the title indicates, aired in place of the NBC Tuesday movie once a month. When Vanocur left, he was replaced by Garrick Utley, who stayed with the series when it moved to the fourth Friday of every month and was retitled *Chronolog*. After a season on Fridays, it returned to its original day and title, but was trimmed to an hour in length. For its last season on the air, *First Tuesday* had no regular anchorman, although reporters Tom Pettit and Patrick Trese made frequent appearances. NBC did not give up on the newsmagazine concept, trying in later years with *Weekend*, *Prime Time Sunday*, and, returning to the source, with *NBC Magazine With David Brinkley*.

FIRST WAVE (*Science Fiction*)

BROADCAST HISTORY:

Sci-Fi Channel
60 minutes
Produced: *1999–2001* (66 episodes)
Premiered: *March 14, 1999*

CAST:

Cade Foster .... Sebastian Spence
Eddie Nambulous/Larry Pisinski ...... Rob LaBelle
Joshua/Cain........................ Roger R. Cross
Jordan Radcliffe (2000–2001) .... Traci Lords

This alien-invasion series used an alleged prophecy as its premise, claiming that "in 1564, Nostradamus predicted that the world would be destroyed in three waves of attack: infiltration, invasion from above, and Armageddon. The 'First Wave' is already here." According to the prophet, Earth's only hope to lead a resistance was a mysterious "twice-blessed man," who turned out to be a former thief named Cade Foster. Cade had turned his life around, abandoning his criminal ways, when he stumbled on the vast conspiracy of the alien Gua to enslave the Earth. The Gua destroyed his life, killed his wife, and framed him for the murder, but he slipped through their fingers—and a police dragnet—and set out on a long journey to expose the plot before the terrible Second Wave could begin. His guidebook was a hitherto unknown, secret text of Nostradamus. Gua agents were everywhere, posing as humans and seeking to undermine civilization in various ways. When Cade found one and managed to kill it, it would dissolve into a phosphorescent glow. Most people would not believe him, of course, but Cade did find two unlikely allies. Crazy Eddie was the publisher of a Web site called *The Paranoid Times*, who shared valuable information on strange, possibly alien-instigated happenings around the country. Joshua was a turncoat alien who gave Cade an inside link to the aliens' plans. In the final episode of the first season, the Gua Assembly prepared to vote on whether the "First Wave" infiltration had been successful and when the fiery Second Wave invasion should begin, but Cade and his little band of true believers managed to hold them off. Cade was joined in the third season by beautiful Jordan, who added a female touch to the previously all-male battle.

A preview episode of *First Wave* aired on USA Network on March 14, 1999, followed by the series' debut on the Sci-Fi Channel five days later.

FIRST YEARS (*Legal Drama*)

FIRST TELECAST: *March 19, 2001*
LAST TELECAST: *April 9, 2001*
BROADCAST HISTORY:

Mar 2001–Apr 2001, NBC Mon 9:00–10:00

CAST:

Anna Weller...................... Samantha Mathis
Warren Harrison .... Mackenzie Astin
Riley Kessler .... Sydney Tamiia Poitier
Edgar "Egg" Ross.................... James Roday
Miles Lawton .... Ken Marino
Sam O'Donnell .... Eric Schaeffer
Bruce.............................. Bruce Winant
Joe............................... Kevin Connolly

Five young lawyers struggled to get their careers, and their love lives, off the ground in this San Francisco–based drama. Anna slept around and was beset by moral crises; Warren was the closet gay, who agonized over coming out (especially when a gay rights organization planned to honor him); Riley, the dedicated black female, who acted so refined that a black client thought she had abandoned her heritage; Egg, Riley's shaggy-haired boyfriend, who had disgraced his Peace Corps family by becoming a lawyer, and Miles, the dark, charming smart guy from a rich family. Sam was their rude, authoritative mentor at the law firm of Hoberman, Spain, McPherson, O'Donnell.

The young lawyers lived together in a big old house, like college roommates, and worked in a downtown office tower where they seemed to be given the most obnoxious cases (evicting an old lady, defending a sexual harasser, representing two arrogant teens in a case involving ownership of a Web site). At least there was plenty of sex, inside and outside the office. Based on the 1996 British series *This Life*.

FISH (*Situation Comedy*)

FIRST TELECAST: *February 5, 1977*
LAST TELECAST: *June 8, 1978*
BROADCAST HISTORY:

Feb 1977–May 1977, ABC Sat 8:30–9:00
Jun 1977–Aug 1977, ABC Thu 9:30–10:00
Aug 1977–Nov 1977, ABC Sat 8:00–8:30
Jan 1978–Apr 1978, ABC Thu 8:30–9:00
May 1978–Jun 1978, ABC Thu 9:30–10:00

CAST:

Det. Phil Fish......................... Abe Vigoda
Bernice Fish .... Florence Stanley
Mike................................ Lenny Bari
Loomis.......................... Todd Bridges
Victor Kreutzer .... John Cassisi
Jilly Papalardo .... Denise Miller
Diane Pulaski .... Sarah Natoli
Charlie Harrison.................. Barry Gordon

Detective Fish, the dilapidated cop in the hit series *Barney Miller*, got his own show in 1977. It was unusual in that he not only remained in character, but for several months continued to appear in *Barney Miller* as well. *Fish* simply presented the domestic side of his life.

Fish and his wife Bernice had decided to move out of their New York apartment and into a run-down house, in order to become foster parents to five P.I.N.S.—the social workers' term for "Persons in Need of Supervision." The term was an understatement, for the five racially mixed street kids were constantly causing problems. Loomis was the cut-up of the lot, the preteen hipster who befriended the dead cat in Fish's basement. Mike was the oldest, charming but streetwise. Victor was the blustery tough guy, Jilly the angelic con artist, and Diane the young TV addict. Psychologist Charlie Harrison (played by onetime child star Barry Gordon) tended to be too impractical to help very much, leaving huffing, puffing Fish and chattering Bernice to quell each uproar and reestablish normalcy.

FISH POLICE (*Cartoon*)

FIRST TELECAST: *February 28, 1992*
LAST TELECAST: *March 13, 1992*
BROADCAST HISTORY:
Feb 1992–Mar 1992, CBS Fri 8:30–9:00
VOICES:
Inspector Gil .... John Ritter
Chief Abalone .... Edward Asner
Goldie.......................... Georgia Brown
Sharkster .... Tim Curry
Calamari .... Hector Elizondo
Det. Catfish .... Robert Guillaume
Crabby .... Buddy Hackett
Pearl .... Megan Mullally
Tadpole .... Charlie Schlatter
Mussels Marinara/Doc Croaker ...... Frank Welker
Angel .... JoBeth Williams
Mayor Cod .... Jonathan Winters

Fish Police was a strange animated police series with allusions to the Raymond Chandler film noir detective movies of the 1940s, but set in underwater Fish City. Inspector Gil was a no-nonsense cop trying to rid Fish City of organized crime. Others on the force were Chief Abalone, Det. Catfish, young Tadpole, and Goldie, the secretary. The head of the local underworld was Calamari, owner of the Shell Shack, the sleazy nightclub where sexy Angel was the singer; his tentacles were everywhere. Others on the wrong side of the law were Sharkster, Calamari's crooked attorney, and Mussels Marinara, his bodyguard. There were two females in Gil's life, Angel and innocent Pearl, who ran the local diner.

Fish Police was full of dreadful fish puns (Angel was a "fin-fatale" and a "sole" singer), the choice of which fish would portray what character was stereotypical, and even lines in the press releases were ridiculous ("All the characters are fish—well, some are crustaceans, but why carp?"). The concept may have been funny, but the finished product smelled like, well, dead fish. It lasted three weeks.

FISHIN' WITH ORLANDO WILSON (*Fishing*)

BROADCAST HISTORY
The Nashville Network
30 minutes
Produced: *1992–2000*
Premiered: *January 2, 1993*
HOST:
Orlando Wilson

Only on the Nashville Network would half an hour of prime time be devoted to watching a couple of guys fish. Guest celebrities and fishing experts joined host Orlando Wilson as he toured top fishing spots around the country and provided amiable commentary on the finer points of fishing. The series was previously seen on Saturday afternoons on TBS.

FISHING AND HUNTING CLUB (*Sports*)

FIRST TELECAST: *September 30, 1949*
LAST TELECAST: *March 31, 1950*
BROADCAST HISTORY:
Sep 1949–Mar 1950, DUM Fri 9:00–9:30
HOST:
Bill Slater

This sports interview and demonstration program featured Bill Slater and experts from various fields. The title was changed on January 20, 1950, to *Sports for All.*

FISHING WITH ROLAND MARTIN (*Instruction*)

BROADCAST HISTORY:
The Nashville Network/Outdoor Life Network
30 minutes
Produced: *1992–*
Premiered: *January 2, 1993* (TNN); *January 2002* (OLN)
HOST:
Roland Martin

Champion bass angler Roland Martin shared expert advice and fishing experiences on location across North America on this Sunday-night fishing series, which was more explicitly instructional than the companion program *Fishin' with Orlando Wilson.* Martin's show began in syndication from 1976 to 1985, and was later seen on TBS on Saturday afternoon before moving to TNN in 1993.

FITZ AND BONES (*Comedy/Drama*)

FIRST TELECAST: *October 24, 1981*
LAST TELECAST: *November 14, 1981*
BROADCAST HISTORY:
Oct 1981–Nov 1981, NBC Sat 10:00–11:00
CAST:
Ryan Fitzpatrick .... Dick Smothers
Bones Howard .... Tom Smothers
Terri Seymour..................... Diana Muldaur
Robert Whitmore....................... Mike Kellin
Lt. Rosie Cochran .... Lynette Mettey
Lawrence Brody .... Roger C. Carmel

Ryan Fitzpatrick and Bones Howard were an oddly matched pair. Ryan was an aggressive investigative reporter for Newsline 3, on a San Francisco television station, and Bones was his somewhat inept cameraman. Together they pursued a wide range of leads throughout the city, from human-interest vignettes about little kids to deadly serious stories of terrorism, racism, and crime. Ryan's style was unorthodox and he would stop at nothing to get a scoop on his rival, Lawrence Brody, who worked for a competing station. He also had to contend with his director at the station, Robert Whitmore, and the no-nonsense news editor, Terri, who often thought he was off on another wild-goose chase. One connection that often helped was Fitz's good relationship with his ex-wife, Rosie, whose position on the police force enabled her to feed him leads.

FITZPATRICKS, THE (*Drama*)

FIRST TELECAST: *September 5, 1977*
LAST TELECAST: *January 10, 1978*
BROADCAST HISTORY:
Sep 1977, CBS Mon 9:00–10:00
Sep 1977–Jan 1978, CBS Tue 8:00–9:00
CAST:
Mike Fitzpatrick..................... Bert Kramer
Maggie Fitzpatrick............. Mariclare Costello
Sean Fitzpatrick .... Clark Brandon

Jack Fitzpatrick .... James Vincent McNichol
Maureen (Mo) Fitzpatrick .... Michele Tobin
Max Fitzpatrick .... Sean Marshall
R.J. .... Derek Wells
Kerry Gerardi .... Helen Hunt

Flint, Michigan, was the setting for this warm family drama about a middle-class Catholic family trying to make ends meet. The father, Mike Fitzpatrick, was a steelworker who put in lots of overtime, and mother Maggie worked part-time at a diner to help supplement the family income. The rest of the family consisted of four children—Sean (16), Jack (15), Mo (14), and Max (10)—and a mangy dog named Detroit. Seen regularly were Max's best friend R.J. and Kerry, the cute girl next door whose flirting with both of the older Fitzpatrick boys intensified their sibling rivalry. The stories were often little lessons in morality and growing up, making this series something like a modern-day *Waltons*. Previewed by CBS on a Monday night early in September, *The Fitzpatricks* moved into its regular Tuesday time slot two weeks later.

FIVE FINGERS (*Spy Drama*)

FIRST TELECAST: *October 3, 1959*
LAST TELECAST: *January 9, 1960*
BROADCAST HISTORY:
Oct 1959–Jan 1960, NBC Sat 9:30–10:30
CAST:
Victor Sebastian .... David Hedison
Simone Genet .... Luciana Paluzzi
Robertson .... Paul Burke

Victor Sebastian was an American counterspy posing as a Communist agent in Europe. His code name was "Five Fingers," and his mission, to feed information on Communist activities to the United States government. Sebastian's public cover was that of a theatrical booking agent who placed musical talent in clubs and cafés all over the Continent. In this capacity he traveled with a beautiful young fashion model, Simone Genet, who aspired to become a singer. Romance blossomed between them, which complicated their relationship since she was not aware of his espionage activities. The only person who did know was Robertson, Sebastian's American contact. Victor and Simone's relationship provided both humorous and romantic counterpoint to the main theme of international intrigue.

The series was based, rather loosely, on a successful 1952 film of the same name directed by Joseph L. Mankiewicz and starring James Mason and Danielle Darrieux.

5 MRS. BUCHANANS, THE (*Situation Comedy*)

FIRST TELECAST: *September 24, 1994*
LAST TELECAST: *April 15, 1995*
BROADCAST HISTORY:
Sep 1994–Dec 1994, CBS Sat 9:00–9:30
Jan 1995, CBS Sat 9:30–10:00
Mar 1995–Apr 1995, CBS Sat 9:30–10:00
CAST:
Emma Buchanan .... Eileen Heckart
Alex Buchanan .... Judith Ivey
Delilah Buchanan .... Beth Broderick
Vivian Buchanan .... Harriet Sansom Harris
Bree Buchanan .... Charlotte Ross

This ensemble comedy centered on the conflicts among four women with very little in common except a fearsome mother-in-law. Gravel-voiced Emma "Mother" Buchanan was the matriarch of the Buchanan clan in suburban Mercy, Indiana, outside of Indianapolis. A tough, opinionated widow, she loved her four sons but barely tolerated the women they had married. Alex, married to Roy, was a fast-talking Jewish New Yorker who kept busy running a small thrift store. Delilah, married to Charles, was a sexy, sugary-sweet but somewhat dim-witted Southerner who helped out at the thrift store. Vivian, married to Ed, was an obnoxious, class-conscious Midwesterner, and Bree, who had just married Jesse, was an outgoing, if somewhat naive, Californian whose youthful blond good looks were the envy of her sisters-in-law. What kept the younger women from having serious catfights with each other was their mutual dislike of their mother-in-law. Most of the action took place at the thrift shop, where they compared the cheap engagement rings they had all been given, complained about how Mother Buchanan had spoiled their husbands, and plotted ways to get under her thick skin. The husbands themselves were almost never seen.

FIVE STAR JUBILEE (*Musical Variety*)

FIRST TELECAST: *March 17, 1961*
LAST TELECAST: *September 22, 1961*
BROADCAST HISTORY:
Mar 1961–Apr 1961, NBC Fri 8:00–8:30
May 1961–Sep 1961, NBC Fri 8:30–9:00
STARS:
Snooky Lanson
Tex Ritter
Jimmy Wakely
Carl Smith
Rex Allen
REGULARS:
The Promenaders
The Wagon Wheelers
The Jubilaires
The Tall Timber Trio
Slim Wilson and His Jubilee Band

The five stars of this country music variety show appeared separately, on a rotating basis. The program featured square dancing as well as guest stars and originated from Springfield, Missouri. Although a network offering, *Five Star Jubilee* was never telecast in New York because of its primarily rural appeal.

FLAMINGO ROAD (*Drama*)

FIRST TELECAST: *January 6, 1981*
LAST TELECAST: *July 13, 1982*
BROADCAST HISTORY:
Jan 1981–Mar 1981, NBC Tue 10:00–11:00
Jun 1981–Aug 1981, NBC Mon 9:00–10:00
Nov 1981–Mar 1982, NBC Tue 10:00–11:00
Mar 1982–Jun 1982, NBC Tue 9:00–10:00
Jun 1982–Jul 1982, NBC Tue 10:00–11:00
CAST:
Sheriff Titus Semple .... Howard Duff
Sam Curtis .... John Beck
Claude Weldon .... Kevin McCarthy
Eudora Weldon .... Barbara Rush
Skipper Weldon .... Woody Brown

Constance Weldon Carlyle .... Morgan Fairchild
Fielding Carlyle .... Mark Harmon
Jasper, the butler .... Glenn Robards
Elmo Tyson .... Peter Donat
Lane Ballou .... Cristina Raines
Lute-Mae Sanders .... Stella Stevens
Michael Tyrone .... David Selby
Sande Swanson .... Cynthia Sikes
Julio Sanchez .... Fernando Allende
Alicia Sanchez .... Gina Gallego
Christie Kovacs .... Denise Galik
Alice Kovacs .... Marcia Rodd
Beth MacDonald .... Sandra Kearns
Deputy Tyler .... John Shearin

Produced by the same company responsible for CBS' *Dallas, Flamingo Road* was a similar mix of corruption, sex, financial manipulation, and political jockeying, albeit on a smaller scale. Here the setting was the sleepy town of Truro, Florida. Most of the action involved Sheriff Titus Semple, a crafty power broker who had a vast knowledge of potentially embarrassing or incriminating facts about most of the town's residents. Truro's wealthiest family was the Weldons, residing on exclusive Flamingo Road. Claude Weldon had made his money from the family paper mill, which his son Skipper now ran. Claude's spoiled, adopted daughter Constance was married to Fielding Carlyle, the ambitious protégé of Sheriff Semple, who had orchestrated Fielding's successful campaign for state senator. Semple had insisted that Fielding marry into the influential Weldon family, despite the young man's love for Lane Ballou, a pretty singer at Lute-Mae Sanders' casino-cum-bordello. Lane still harbored romantic feelings for Fielding, though she was also involved with Sam Curtis, a successful construction-company developer. Elmo Tyson was the publisher of the *Clarion*, Truro's newspaper.

The fall of 1981 brought ruthless tycoon Michael Tyrone to Truro, intent on avenging the execution, many years before, of his father for a murder he had not committed. Michael stopped at nothing to achieve his goal. When money, power, and deceit were not enough, he used black magic and murder (including that of his sister, reporter Sande Swanson) to get revenge on the citizens of Truro. Fielding had an affair with Sande, and Michael ended up in bed with both Lute-Mae and Constance (who, it had been revealed, was Lute-Mae's illegitimate daughter). The only healthy relationship was that of Constance's brother, Skipper, and Alicia Sanchez, younger sister of one of Constance's former lovers, Julio. Skipper and Alicia, truly in love, eloped and tried to make a life for themselves despite the turmoil around them.

Flamingo Road was based on the best-selling novel by Robert Wilder and the 1949 movie starring Joan Crawford.

FLASH, THE (*Fantasy/Adventure*)
FIRST TELECAST: *September 20, 1990*
LAST TELECAST: *July 19, 1991*
BROADCAST HISTORY:
Sep 1990–Feb 1991, CBS Thu 8:30–9:30
Feb 1991–Mar 1991, CBS Thu 9:00–10:00
Apr 1991–Jun 1991, CBS Sat 8:00–9:00
Jul 1991, CBS Fri 9:00–10:00

CAST:
Barry Allen/The Flash .... John Wesley Shipp
Tina McGee .... Amanda Pays
Julio Mendez .... Alex Desert
Off. Michael Francis Murphy .... Biff Manard
Off. Bellows .... Vito D'Ambrosio
Lt. Warren Garfield .... Mike Genovese

Barry Allen was a mild-mannered police chemist working in Central City's crime lab when a lightning bolt hit the lab and caused him to be soaked with a mixture of electrically charged chemicals. The chemicals caused a metabolic change in his body that gave him the ability to move with superhuman speed—so fast, in fact, that he was virtually invisible to the naked eye. At first Barry sought to return to normal with the help of Tina McGee, a research scientist working for Star Labs, but eventually he decided to use his super speed to thwart criminals under the guise of The Flash, a masked crimefighter in a fire-engine-red costume. Julio was Barry's lab assistant, who never figured out he was The Flash, and Murphy and Bellows were two comical local cops who turned up frequently at locations where The Flash had been in action. Although they, and most of the general public, appreciated his help, there were many in power, particularly the corrupt, who resented his intrusions.

Adapted from the comic-book hero that had been created more than fifty years earlier by Gardner Fox and Harry Lampert, *The Flash* had an appropriately campy style and comic-book look, along with great special effects—especially the scenes of The Flash running at super speed. Alas, it didn't attract super ratings and was canceled after a single season.

FLASH GORDON (*Science Fiction*)
BROADCAST HISTORY:
Syndicated only
30 minutes
Produced: *1953–1954* (39 episodes)
Released: *Fall 1953*

CAST:
Flash Gordon .... Steve Holland
Dale Arden .... Irene Champlin
Dr. Zharkov .... Joe Nash

Flash Gordon was one of the great comic-book heroes of the 1930s and 1940s, fighting daring intergalactic battles with merciless foes for the safety of mankind. In this syndicated TV version, produced in Germany, he was portrayed by an obscure actor named Steve Holland. His companions, as always, were the lovely Dale and the bearded Dr. Zharkov. Together they battled the androids and death rays of such exotic enemies as the Evil Queen of Cygnil, the archcriminal Bizdar, the Great God Em of Odin, and the Mad Witch of Neptune.

The blond hero was created for a comic strip in 1934 by Alex Raymond. Science-fiction heroes were very popular at the time (*Buck Rogers* had begun five years earlier), and Flash captured the imagination of the nation's youth. He was introduced as a Yale graduate and polo player who set off with Dale and Dr. Zharkov to the planet Mongo, where the fearsome Emperor Ming was plotting to destroy the Earth. In wild and woolly battles they managed to defeat Ming and his legions, then set about dealing with other villains of the galaxy. *Flash Gordon* quickly became a radio serial in 1935 (starring Gale Gordon), and was immortalized in a series of three movie serials starring Buster Crabbe, made between 1936 and 1940. These movies have been widely shown on television since the early 1950s, and are probably more familiar to viewers than the Steve Holland TV films.

In 1979 *Flash Gordon* was seen as a Saturday morning cartoon series on NBC. In 1980 an expensive, frequently witty theatrical film of *Flash Gordon* was released, but it failed to attract a public large enough to make it a financial success.

FLATBUSH (*Situation Comedy*)

FIRST TELECAST: *February 26, 1979*
LAST TELECAST: *March 12, 1979*
BROADCAST HISTORY:
Feb 1979–Mar 1979, CBS Mon 8:30–9:00
CAST:
Presto Prestopopolos .... Joseph Cali
Socks Palermo .... Adrian Zmed
Turtle Romero .... Vincent Bufano
Joey Dee .... Randy Stumpf
Figgy Figueroa .... Sandy Helberg
Esposito .... Antony Ponzini
Mrs. Fortunato .... Helen Verbit
Detective Bosko .... Jack Murdock
Clean Otto .... John Quade

The exploits of five recent high school graduates living in a middle-class Italian neighborhood in the Flatbush district of Brooklyn, New York. Presto was a cabdriver, Socks worked in a local clothing store and was the fashion plate of the group, Figgy worked at a supermarket delivering groceries on his bike, Joey was an apprentice plumber studying at night to become a lawyer, and Turtle worked in his family's restaurant. Together, as the Flatbush Fungos, their local club/gang, they wandered the neighborhood in search of innocent fun and excitement. The ethnic stereotypes that appeared in this series so offended the real-life Brooklyn borough president that he publicly demanded the series be taken off the air, before it gave Brooklyn a bad name. CBS beat him to it and canceled it after three episodes, before it gave *them* a bad name.

FLESH 'N' BLOOD (*Situation Comedy*)

FIRST TELECAST: *September 19, 1991*
LAST TELECAST: *November 15, 1991*
BROADCAST HISTORY:
Sep 1991, NBC Thu 10:00–10:30
Sep 1991–Oct 1991, NBC Fri 9:30–10:00
Oct 1991–Nov 1991, NBC Fri 9:00–9:30
CAST:
D.A. Rachel Brennan .... Lisa Darr
Arlo Weed .... David Keith
King Weed (age 16) .... Chris Stacy
Beauty Weed (11) .... Meghan Andrews
Marty Travers .... Perry Anzilotti
Irene .... Peri Gilpin
THEME:
Written and performed by Leon Russell and David Keith

A career-obsessed Baltimore District Attorney found herself the reluctant host to cornpone kin in this variation of the *Beverly Hillbillies*. Rachel was a prototypical career woman of the '90s: young, single, attractive, and on the fast track to high political office. The one thing missing in her life was the chance to find her natural mother, who had placed her up for adoption when she was a baby. Up popped Arlo Weed, a brash but endearing Southern con man and widower who proved to be the brother she never knew she had—along with his kids, precious Beauty and overall-clad yokel King. They moved in and became an instant and meddlesome family for "Aunt Rachel."

City slick collided with country crude as Rachel tried to smooth Arlo's rough edges, and enthusiastic Arlo tried to marry off his sis ("the li'l filly"). It was almost as if Gomer Pyle had showed up on Mary Tyler Moore's doorstep. Rachel's eager-beaver chief investigator, the very short and very cynical Marty, had an unrequited crush on her; he also wanted her to run for governor. Irene, Rachel's secretary and best friend, had designs on Arlo.

FLIGHT #7 (*Travelogue*)

FIRST TELECAST: *June 14, 1954*
LAST TELECAST: *August 31, 1957*
BROADCAST HISTORY:
Jun 1954–Aug 1954, ABC Mon 7:30–7:45
Aug 1954–Feb 1955, ABC Sun 8:00–8:30
Jun 1955–Sep 1955, ABC Sat 7:00–7:30
Jun 1957–Aug 1957, ABC Sat 7:30–8:00

This summer series presented travel films, generally of areas outside the continental United States.

FLIGHT TO RHYTHM (*Music*)

FIRST TELECAST: *May 15, 1949*
LAST TELECAST: *September 22, 1949*
BROADCAST HISTORY:
May 1949–Jul 1949, DUM Sun 6:30–7:00
Aug 1949–Sep 1949, DUM Thu 8:00–8:30
REGULARS:
Delora Bueno
Miguelito Valdez Orchestra
Larry Carr

This 1949 summer series featured Latin music, with vocalist Delora Bueno. It was set in "Club Rio," a Brazilian nightclub.

FLINTSTONES, THE (*Cartoon*)

FIRST TELECAST: *September 30, 1960*
LAST TELECAST: *September 2, 1966*
BROADCAST HISTORY:
Sep 1960–Sep 1963, ABC Fri 8:30–9:00
Sep 1963–Dec 1964, ABC Thu 7:30–8:00
Dec 1964–Sep 1966, ABC Fri 7:30–8:00
VOICES:
Fred Flintstone .... Alan Reed
Wilma Flintstone .... Jean Vander Pyl
Barney Rubble .... Mel Blanc
Betty Rubble (1960–1964) .... Bea Benaderet
Betty Rubble (1964–1966) .... Gerry Johnson
Dino the Dinosaur .... Mel Blanc
Pebbles (1963–1966) .... Jean Vander Pyl
Bamm Bamm (1963–1966) .... Don Messick
CO-PRODUCERS:
Bill Hanna, Joe Barbera

The Flintstones was a parody on modern suburban life, set in the Stone Age. The characters in the cartoon series all behaved and spoke in a contemporary manner, though they lived in the prehistoric city of Bedrock. Fred worked as operator of a dinosaur-powered crane at the Rock Head & Quarry Cave Construction Co. (slogan: "Own Your Own Cave and Be Secure"). Around their split-level cave the Flintstones enjoyed such conveniences as Wilma's Stoneway piano, a hi-fi on which Fred could play his "rock" music (it consisted of a turntable and a bird with a long beak to serve as the needle), a vacuum cleaner (a baby elephant with a long trunk), and an automatic garbage-disposal unit (a famished buzzard stashed under the sink). Their car, which sported tail fins, also came equipped with steamroller wheels—to smooth out the rocky road.

At first the Flintstones had only Dino, their pet dinosaur, around the cave to play with. Then one day in 1963 they were blessed with a baby daughter, whom they named Pebbles. Not to be outdone, their neighbors the Rubbles adopted an orphan boy named Bamm Bamm. (The two kids later had a Saturday morning cartoon series of their own, *Pebbles and Bamm Bamm.*)

The Flintstones was always as much adult satire as children's fun. In many respects it resembled Jackie Gleason's popular *Honeymooners*, especially in the relationships of the principals. A wide range of caricatures passed through the stories: Lollobrickida, a pretty cook; Ann-Margrock, whose voice was supplied by Ann-Margret; attorney Perry Masonry (he never lost a case); Ed Sullystone, a TV host; Eppy Brianstone, a teenage impresario; and Weirdly and Creepella Gruesome, the strange couple who with their son Goblin moved into a cave nearby (this was a parody on *The Addams Family* and *The Munsters*, then popular). The Gruesomes thought that they were normal, and everyone *else* in Bedrock was odd.

The Flintstones and its spin-offs had a highly successful run on Saturday mornings—on NBC from January 1967–September 1970, on CBS from September 1972–January 1974, back on NBC from February 1979–September 1984, and on ABC with *The Flintstone Kids* from September 1986–September 1989.

FLIP WILSON SHOW, THE (*Comedy/Variety*)

FIRST TELECAST: *September 17, 1970*
LAST TELECAST: *June 27, 1974*
BROADCAST HISTORY:
Sep 1970–Jun 1971, NBC Thu 7:30–8:30
Sep 1971–Jun 1974, NBC Thu 8:00–9:00 (OS)
REGULARS:
Flip Wilson
The Jack Regas Dancers
The George Wyle Orchestra

Comic Flip Wilson was the first black performer to achieve major popularity as host of his own variety hour. *The Flip Wilson Show* was an enormous hit, placing number two among all programs on television during its first two seasons. Although music and guests were an important part of the format, Flip's comedy was the real focal point of the series. In various skits he played a collection of stock characters, which included: Geraldine Jones, sassy, swinging, liberated woman with a very jealous boyfriend named "Killer"; Reverend LeRoy of the Church of What's Happening Now, a gospel preacher who seemed to be slightly less than honest and just a touch lecherous; Danny Danger, private detective; and Herbie, the Good Time Ice Cream Man. Flip's best-known expression was a wide-eyed "The Devil made me do it!"

FLIPPED (*Documentary*)

BROADCAST HISTORY:
MTV
30 minutes
Original episodes: *2001*
Premiered: *August 6, 2001*

In this slyly instructive series two people exchanged lives for 24 hours, and each got to see firsthand how the other lived. Friends, classmates and colleagues were in on the "flip," which made it all the more realistic. When a mom and her resentful daughter flipped, the mom got a ponytail, was hit on by boys in the schoolyard, and got called to the principal's office; her daughter (as Mom) learned the true meaning of housework, grocery shopping, and being chewed out by the boss when she arrived late for work. Other flips involved the class wallflower and a popular classmate; a gay and a straight guy; and a cop and a civilian.

FLIPPER (*Adventure*)

FIRST TELECAST: *September 19, 1964*
LAST TELECAST: *September 1, 1968*
BROADCAST HISTORY:
Sep 1964–Sep 1967, NBC Sat 7:30–8:00
Jan 1968–Jun 1968, NBC Sun 6:30–7:00
Jun 1968–Sep 1968, NBC Sun 7:00–7:30
CAST:
Porter Ricks .... Brian Kelly
Sandy Ricks .... Luke Halpin
Bud Ricks .... Tommy Norden
Hap Gorman (1964–1965) .... Andy Devine
Ulla Norstrand (1965–1966) .... Ulla Stromstedt

Porter "Po" Ricks was the chief ranger of Coral Key Park, Florida, responsible for protecting both the game fish and the skin divers in the park. A widower, he lived with his two children, 15-year-old Sandy and 10-year-old Bud, in a cottage near the shore. The real star of the series was the boys' pet dolphin, Flipper, who was both friend and helper in their weekly adventures. The stories generally revolved around Flipper and his two young companions, with Bud involved more often than Sandy. Also regularly seen during the first season was Hap Gorman, an old marine carpenter with endless numbers of stories about sea life and adventures. During the second season Ulla Norstrand, an attractive oceanographer, was a regular character.

The role of Flipper was played by a dolphin named Suzy.

FLIPPER (*Adventure*)

SYNDICATION HISTORY:
60 minutes
Produced: *1995–1997* (44 episodes)
Released: *October 1995*
NETWORK HISTORY:
FIRST TELECAST: *September 5, 1998*
LAST TELECAST: *August 19, 2000*
Sep 1998–Oct 1998, PAX Sat 8:00–9:00
Nov 1998–Aug 1999, PAX Sat 9:00–10:00
Aug 1999–Sep 1999, PAX Sat 8:00–9:00
Sep 1999–Aug 2000, PAX Sat 7:00–8:00
CAST:
Dr. Keith Ricks (1995–1996) .... Brian Wimmer
Dr. Pamela Blondel (1995–1996) .... Colleen Flynn
Mike Blondel (age 14) (1995–1996) .... Payton Haas

Maya Graham (15) (1995–1997)
. . . . . Jessica Marie Alba
Alexis (1995–1996) . . . . . Lisa Lackey
Sheriff Tom Hampton (1996–2000) . . Whip Hubley
Jennifer "Jenn" Daulton (1996–1997)
. . . . . Elizabeth Morehead
Dep. Sheriff Quinn Garnett (1996–1997)
. . . . . Wren T. Brown
Dean Gregson (1996–1997) . . . . . Scott Michaelson
Holly Myers (1996–2000) . . . . . Anja Coleby
Cap Daulton (1996–2000) . . . . . Gus Mercurio
Dep. Mark Delany (1998–2000) . . . . . Darrin Klimek
Lt. Cmdr. Alexandra "Alex" Parker Hampton (1998–2000) . . . . . Tiffany Lamb
Chris Parker (1998– 2000) . . . . . Craig Marriott
Jackie Parker (1998–2000) . . . . . Laura Donaldson
Courtney Gordon (1999–2000) . . . . . Skye Patch

CLOSING THEME:

"My Bonnie," performed by Wendell Thomas

Keith Ricks, who had been the 10-year-old Bud on the original *Flipper* series in the 1960s, was now running the Bal Harbor Research Institute in Florida. He worked with Pam, a single mother and civilian scientist on assignment with the navy. In the series premiere her teen dream son Mike, after hearing Keith's tales of the Flipper of his youth, gave the name to a friendly, and incredibly intelligent, male dolphin his mother was working with. Aphrodite was the female research dolphin at the institute with whom Flipper had a baby dolphin at mid-season. Living near the institute was Maya, a cute young girl who became Mike's friend. Some episodes focused on the work of the institute and the relationships of the regulars, particularly the friendship between Mike and Maya, while others dealt with more serious—and sometimes violent—subjects like poachers, smugglers and polluters. The '90s *Flipper* was somewhat edgier than the gentle family show of the '60s.

In the spring of 1996 Mike and the others found out that Maya, who they thought had been living with her sister on a houseboat, was in fact a runaway from a child-care facility and living alone. Pam, not wanting to see the girl returned to state custody, took her in and started adoption procedures.

When *Flipper* returned for its second season there were major changes. Cap, a grizzled old character with a small salvage boat, had taken Flipper up the coast to Bal Harbor Key where his daughter, Jennifer, ran the relocated Bal Harbor Research Institute. Jenn was a marine biologist whose facility was adjacent to the Monroe County Search and Rescue Substation on the beach north of Bal Harbor. Dean and Holly were attractive young interns on her staff. Tom, with whom Jenn had a friendly rivalry, ran the substation with Quinn, who was also an experienced diver. The series' one silly gimmick was Jenn's use in her lab of a talking computer named Simon. Maya was the only holdover from the first season's cast—Pam had been transferred to the Naval Base at Pearl Harbor, and Keith, who had started dating her, had taken a position at a research facility in Hawaii.

A year after its syndicated run had ended, the series returned as *Flipper: The New Adventures* on the new Pax Network. Jenn and Maya were now gone, doing marine research in the Red Sea, and Tom had a new deputy, Mark. In the season premiere he married Alex, a widowed navy marine biologist who had moved to Florida from California to start a new life. She had two children, perky Jackie and moody Chris, who had not gotten over his father's death trying to save some people from drowning. After a while Chris came out of his shell and developed a loving relationship with his stepfather.

In the fall of 1999 Courtney, Tom's niece, arrived and moved in with the family. Her divorced mother, Tom's sister, was an attorney in Washington, and the two of them had been having problems.

Filmed in Queensland, Australia.

FLIX (Network), see *Showtime*

FLO (*Situation Comedy*)

FIRST TELECAST: *March 24, 1980*
LAST TELECAST: *July 21, 1981*
BROADCAST HISTORY:

Mar 1980–Apr 1980, CBS Mon 9:30–10:00
Jul 1980–Jan 1981, CBS Mon 8:00–8:30
Feb 1981, CBS Sat 9:00–9:30
Mar 1981–May 1981, CBS Sat 8:30–9:00
Jun 1981–Jul 1981, CBS Tue 8:30–9:00

CAST:

Florence Jean (Flo) Castleberry . . . . . Polly Holliday
Earl Tucker . . . . . Geoffrey Lewis
Farley Waters . . . . . Jim B. Baker
Mama Velma Castleberry . . . . . Sudie Bond
Fran Castleberry . . . . . Lucy Lee Flippin
Miriam Willoughby . . . . . Joyce Bulifant
Randy Stumphill . . . . . Leo Burmester
Les Kincaid . . . . . Stephen Keep
Wendell Tubbs (1980) . . . . . Terry Wills
Chester . . . . . Mickey Jones

THEME:

"Flo's Yellow Rose," sung by Hoyt Axton

After four seasons as the feisty, hot-blooded waitress at Mel's Diner on *Alice*, Flo "Kiss My Grits" Castleberry got her own place to run. While passing through her hometown of Cowtown, Texas, on her way to a hostess job in Houston, Flo impulsively bought a run-down old roadhouse she remembered from her rambunctious youth, and determined to make it a viable business. Not used to being the boss, Flo had her troubles running the place, renamed Flo's Yellow Rose. Earl, the bartender, hated the idea of working for a woman, and Farley was the obnoxious skinflint who held the mortgage. Les was the resident piano player and Randy the mechanic who worked at the garage located next door. Being back home meant spending time with Mama, in whose raucous image Flo was molded, and with an introverted, clutzy sister, Fran; and long-lost best friend Miriam. Wendell was Fran's fiancé, the owner of a feed supply business, and Chester was a regular customer at the Yellow Rose.

FLOOR SHOW, THE, see *Eddie Condon's Floor Show*

FLY BY NIGHT (*Adventure*)

FIRST TELECAST: *April 4, 1991*
LAST TELECAST: *January 3, 1995*
BROADCAST HISTORY:

Apr 1991–Oct 1991, CBS Thu 11:30–12:30 A.M.
Jan 1993–Aug 1993, CBS Wed 12:30–1:30 A.M.
Aug 1994–Sep 1994, CBS Tue 1:05–2:05 A.M.

Sep 1994–Dec 1994, CBS Tue 12:35–1:35 A.M.
Dec 1994–Jan 1995, CBS Tue 1:05–2:05 A.M.

CAST:

Sally "Slick" Monroe .... Shannon Tweed
Mack Sheppard .... David James Elliott
Jean-Phillippe Pasteur .... Francois Guetary

Sally Monroe was the owner of Slick Air, a small (one 727 jet), financially strapped charter airline flying out of Ellis Field in Vancouver. Sally, a wheeler-dealer entrepreneur who spent almost as much time avoiding creditors as she did finding clients, ran Slick Air with a single crew—pilot Mack Sheppard, a former Air Force pilot who commuted to work from Seattle, and co-pilot Jean-Phillippe Pasteur, a suave native of Martinique. Although most of her clients seemed to be in trouble with the police, organized crime, or others, Sally somehow managed to keep Slick afloat without getting herself or her crew killed. Despite a heavy dose of violence and sexual innuendo, *Fly by Night* managed to maintain a lighthearted quality.

Filmed on location in Vancouver and on the French Riviera. CBS aired reruns of *Fly by Night* from 1993 to 1995.

FLYING BLIND (*Situation Comedy*)

FIRST TELECAST: *September 13, 1992*
LAST TELECAST: *July 18, 1993*
BROADCAST HISTORY:

Sep 1992–Jul 1993, FOX Sun 10:00–10:30

CAST:

Neil Barash .... Corey Parker
Alicia .... Tea Leoni
Jeremy Barash .... Michael Tucci
Jordan .... Robert Bauer
Megan .... Clea Lewis
Ted Sharperson .... Marcus Giamatti
Ellen Barash (1992) .... Cristine Rose
Dennis Lake (1993) .... Charles Rocket

THEME:

"And She Was," by David Byrne, performed by Talking Heads

Another in a long line of urban comedies on Fox, *Flying Blind* was about a rather dull young man whose life was turned upside down by an unlikely affair with a beautiful, free-spirited woman. Neil was a marketing assistant at Hochman Foods, the company where his neurotic father, Jeremy, was a senior executive. His life was about as interesting as yesterday's dishwater until one night at a party he ran into Alicia, an incredibly sexy and uninhibited woman, and they fell madly in love. It was hard to understand what Alicia, who was almost totally preoccupied with sex, saw in boring Neil. But there was certainly something. Neil, who still lived at home, spent his days trying to look good at work and his nights having a torrid and exhausting affair with the insatiable Alicia. Ted was his unscrupulous officemate who would do almost anything to get ahead.

When he was laid off in February, during a downsizing at Hochman, Neil moved in with Alicia and her two Manhattan loft roommates—Jordan, a throwback to the hippies of the 1960s, and Megan, an arty neurotic with incredibly low self-esteem. Away from the watchful eye of his father, he tried to become more adventuresome by getting a job working for eccentric local film producer Dennis.

FLYING HIGH (*Adventure*)

FIRST TELECAST: *September 29, 1978*
LAST TELECAST: *January 23, 1979*
BROADCAST HISTORY:

Sep 1978–Dec 1978, CBS Fri 10:00–11:00
Jan 1979, CBS Tue 10:00–11:00

CAST:

Marcy Bowers .... Pat Klous
Lisa Benton .... Connie Sellecca
Pam Bellagio .... Kathryn Witt
Capt. Doug March .... Howard Platt
Raymond Strickman .... Ken Olfson

Marcy, Lisa, and Pam were three sexy young girls who had just graduated from flight attendant school. As stewardesses for Sunwest Airlines, they had romantic, interesting, and occasionally dangerous adventures. All three worked on the same jumbo jet, and reported to Captain Doug March. Sometimes episodes centered on the girls' working hours and sometimes on their active social lives. Doug, despite his constant efforts, was never quite the ladies' man he thought he was. His romantic interludes always seemed to fall apart, or get him into trouble with somebody. Raymond was the passenger relations agent who worked ground crew in Los Angeles, where Sunwest was based.

The three actresses who played the leads in this series were all former New York City–based models, with little previous acting experience. In an effort to make their roles more believable, they met with groups of real flight attendants prior to starting production on the series, to hear about actual incidents that had taken place on real flights and the manner in which the stewardesses had handled them. It didn't help—*Flying High* barely got off the ground before it was canceled.

FLYING NUN, THE (*Situation Comedy*)

FIRST TELECAST: *September 7, 1967*
LAST TELECAST: *September 18, 1970*
BROADCAST HISTORY:

Sep 1967–Jan 1969, ABC Thu 8:00–8:30
Feb 1969–Sep 1969, ABC Thu 7:30–8:00
Sep 1969–Jan 1970, ABC Wed 7:30–8:00
Jan 1970–Sep 1970, ABC Fri 7:30–8:00

CAST:

Sister Bertrille .... Sally Field
Sister Jacqueline .... Marge Redmond
Mother Superior .... Madeleine Sherwood
Carlos Ramirez .... Alejandro Rey
Sister Sixto .... Shelley Morrison
Sister Ana .... Linda Dangcil
Police Capt. Gaspar Formento (1968–1969)
.... Vito Scotti
Marcello, the orphan boy (1969–1970)
.... Manuel Padilla, Jr.

The subject of this comedy was Sister Bertrille, a bright, effusive young novice—the former Elsie Ethington—who brightened the lives of all at the ancient Convent San Tanco, situated on a hilltop near San Juan, Puerto Rico. Not the least of Sister Bertrille's attributes was that she could fly. How? Well, "when lift plus thrust is greater than load plus drag," any object can fly, including Sister Bertrille, who weighed only 90 pounds. Whenever a stiff wind caught the starched cornette worn by her order, off she went.

These aerodynamics were not always pleasant. Occasionally Sister Bertrille would get dunked in the ocean or be thrust in the midst of unlikely goings-on, and once she was almost shot down as an enemy aircraft (a pelican once fell in love with her, too). Least impressed was her staid, conservative Mother Superior. But Sister Bertrille got along well with the wise and humorous Sister Jacqueline, and with Sister Sixto, the Puerto Rican nun who fought a running battle with the English language. Sister Bertrille was also admired—from a distance—by Carlos Ramirez, the rich, handsome playboy owner of a discotheque in town who was a patron of the convent.

Believe it or not, *The Flying Nun* was commended by some religious orders—for "humanizing" nuns and their work. It was based on the book *The Fifteenth Pelican*, by Tere Rios.

FLYING TIGERS, THE, see *Major Dell Conway of the Flying Tigers*

FOCUS (*Documentary*)

FIRST TELECAST: *March 18, 1952*
LAST TELECAST: *October 10, 1957*

This was a blanket title for documentary films carried by ABC in various 15-minute and half-hour time slots, usually for short periods of time, between 1952 and 1957.

FOCUS ON AMERICA (*Documentary*)

FIRST TELECAST: *June 27, 1961*
LAST TELECAST: *September 10, 1963*
BROADCAST HISTORY:

Jun 1961–Sep 1961, ABC Tue 7:00–7:30
Jul 1962–Sep 1962, ABC Wed 8:00–8:30
Jul 1963–Sep 1963, ABC Tue 10:30–11:00

HOST:

Bill Shadel (1962)
Don Goddard (1963)

Documentaries that had originally been produced and aired by local ABC affiliates were telecast over the entire ABC network during three summers in the early 1960s. They were selected by members of the ABC News Department as examples of the best of locally originated informational programming, and ranged from "Clipper Ships and Paddle Wheelers" (KGO-TV, San Francisco) to "Cows, Cowboys and Cow Country" (KOCO-TV, Oklahoma City) to "To The Moon and Beyond" (WTVN-TV, Columbus).

FOLEY SQUARE (*Situation Comedy*)

FIRST TELECAST: *December 11, 1985*
LAST TELECAST: *July 23, 1986*
BROADCAST HISTORY:

Dec 1985–Feb 1986, CBS Wed 8:30–9:00
Mar 1986–Apr 1986, CBS Tue 9:30–10:00
Jun 1986–Jul 1986, CBS Wed 8:00–8:30

CAST:

Asst. D.A. Alex Harrigan .... Margaret Colin
D.A. Jesse Steinberg .... Hector Elizondo
Denise Willums .... Vernee Watson-Johnson
Peter Newman .... Michael Lembeck
Asst. D.A. Molly Dobbs .... Cathy Silvers
Asst. D.A. Carter DeVries .... Sanford Jensen
Angel Gomez .... Israel Juarbe
Mole .... Jon Lovitz
Spiro Papadopolis .... Richard C. Serafian

Foley Square was the location of the Manhattan District Attorney's office, the setting for this short-lived legal comedy. Jesse was an old-timer, a career public servant who had seen it all and was now in charge of a bureau with three assistant D.A.s. They were: Alex, who was perky, dedicated and single; Carter, ambitious and overbearing; and Molly, the neophyte just out of law school. Helping out was Denise, Alex's secretary; Angel, a young office messenger who was an ex-con; and—in the first several episodes—Mole, an investigator for the D.A.'s office. Mr. Papadopolis ran the neighborhood coffee shop where they all hung out.

On the personal side, Peter was a schoolteacher who lived in Alex's Upper West Side apartment building, and was her good friend. Although many of the episodes dealt with criminal cases at the office, nearly as much time was spent on Alex's uneven social life.

FOLLOW THAT MAN, syndicated title for *Man Against Crime*

FOLLOW THE LEADER (*Quiz/Audience Participation*)

FIRST TELECAST: *July 7, 1953*
LAST TELECAST: *August 4, 1953*
BROADCAST HISTORY:

Jul 1953–Aug 1953, CBS Tue 9:00–9:30

HOSTESS:

Vera Vague

This live show, which was telecast from Hollywood, gave members of the studio audience the opportunity to see how well they could imitate a scene pantomimed by actress Vera Vague (whose real name was Barbara Jo Allen).

FOLLOW THE SUN (*Adventure*)

FIRST TELECAST: *September 17, 1961*
LAST TELECAST: *September 9, 1962*
BROADCAST HISTORY:

Sep 1961–Sep 1962, ABC Sun 7:30–8:30

CAST:

Ben Gregory .... Barry Coe
Paul Templin .... Brett Halsey
Eric Jason .... Gary Lockwood
Katherine Ann Richards .... Gigi Perreau
Lt. Frank Roper .... Jay Lanin

This adventure series focused on the exploits of two footloose, handsome, freelance magazine writers living in Hawaii. Ben and Paul's bachelor pad was a plush penthouse in Honolulu, and they both led active social lives when not facing danger in pursuit of a story (their articles were not intended for the faint of heart). Helping them was Eric Jason, who did much of the legwork for their articles; Kathy Richards, who was a part-time secretary and full-time student at the University of Honolulu; and Lt. Roper of the Honolulu Police, who bailed them out whenever they got in over their heads.

FOOD NETWORK (Network) (*General Entertainment Cable Network*)

LAUNCHED:

November 23, 1993

SUBSCRIBERS (MAY 2003):

78.8 million (74% U.S.)

One of the tastier niche networks of the '90s was this

one, which offered cooking shows and related programming dealing with the one thing everybody has in common: food. Among its better known series have been *Emeril Live* (1997), with New Orleans chef Emeril Lagasse ("the engagin' Cajun"); *Two Fat Ladies,* with Jennifer Paterson and Clarissa Dickson Wright searching England for recipes in a motorcycle and a sidecar; *Ready, Set, Cook!,* a lively cook-off hosted by Sissy Biggers; *Cooking Live!,* a call-in show hosted by Sara Moulton; *East Meets West with Ming Tsai; Molto Mario,* with Italian chef Mario Batali; *Bill Boggs's Corner Table,* in which Boggs interviewed celebrity guests at their favorite restaurants; *Gourmet Getaways* with Robin Leach; and for the cooking-challenged, *How to Boil Water,* with Sean Donnellan. In its early days the network also aired vintage shows by such icons of the kitchen as Julia Child, Graham Kerr, and, from TV's earliest days, Dione Lucas.

The network was first known as the TV Food Network, shortened to Food Network in the mid-'90s.

FOOT IN THE DOOR (*Situation Comedy*)

FIRST TELECAST: *March 28, 1983*
LAST TELECAST: *May 2, 1983*
BROADCAST HISTORY:
Mar 1983–May 1983, CBS Mon 8:30–9:00
CAST:
Jonah Foot .... Harold Gould
Jim Foot .... Kenneth Gilman
Harriet Foot .... Diana Canova
Mrs. Griffin .... Marian Mercer

Following the death of his abstemious wife after 40 years of marriage, widower Jonah Foot moved from Pitts Valley, N.H., to the New York City co-op apartment of his son Jim and daughter-in-law Harriet and proceeded to become a liberated, skirt-chasing swinger. This created no end of problems for conservative Jim, an advertising agency copywriter, and sweet Harriet, a buyer for a Manhattan department store. It also failed to endear him to Mrs. Griffin, the cynical president of the board of directors of the building in which the Foots lived.

Adapted from the British comedy *Tom, Dick & Harriet.*

FOOTBALL (*Sports*)

FIRST TELECAST: *October 3, 1950*
LAST TELECAST:
BROADCAST HISTORY:
Oct 1950–Jan 1951, ABC Tue 8:00–8:30
Sep 1953–Dec 1953, ABC Sun 7:45–9:00
Oct 1953–Nov 1953, DUM Sat 8:00–Conclusion
Oct 1954–Nov 1954, DUM Sat 8:00–Conclusion
Oct 1957–Nov 1957, ABC Sun 10:00–10:30
Nov 1957–Dec 1957, ABC Sun 9:30–10:00
Aug 1959–Oct 1959, ABC Sat 11:00–Conclusion
Sep 1970–Dec 1987, ABC Mon 9:00–Conclusion (Sep–Dec each year)
Sep 1988, ABC Mon 8:00–Conclusion
Oct 1988–Dec 1988, ABC Mon 9:00–Conclusion
Aug 1989–Sep 1989, ABC Mon 8:00–Conclusion
Sep 1989–Dec 1989, ABC Mon 9:00–Conclusion
Aug 1990–Aug 1997, ABC Mon 8:00–Conclusion (August each year)
Sep 1990–Dec 1992, ABC Mon 9:00–Conclusion (Sept–Dec each year)
Sep 1993–Jan 1994, ABC Mon 9:00–Conclusion
Sep 1994–Dec 1997, ABC Mon 9:00–Conclusion (Sep–Dec each year)
Aug 1998–Dec 1998, ABC Mon 8:00–Conclusion
Aug 1999– , ABC Mon 8:00–Conclusion (August each year)
Sep 1999– , ABC Mon 9:00–Conclusion (Sep–Jan each year)
Feb 2001–Apr 2001, NBC Sat 8:00–Conclusion (XFL)
Feb 2001–Apr 2001, UPN Sun 7:00–Conclusion (XFL)
ANNOUNCER:
Bill Fisher (1950–1951)
Harry Wismer (1953)
Ford Bond (1953)
Chuck Thompson (1954, 1959)
Chick Hearn (1957)
Howard Cosell (1959, 1970–1983)
Keith Jackson (1970)
Don Meredith (1970–1973, 1977–1984)
Frank Gifford (1971–1997)
Fred Williamson (1974)
Alex Karras (1974–1976)
Fran Tarkenton (1979–1982)
O. J. Simpson (1983–1985)
Joe Namath (1985)
Al Michaels (1986–)
Dan Dierdorf (1987–1998)
Boomer Esiason (1998–1999)
Dan Fouts (2000–2001)
Dennis Miller (2000–2001)
John Madden (2002–)
Jim Ross (XFL, 2001)
Matt Vasgersian (XFL, 2001)
Jesse Ventura (XFL, 2001)

The 1950–1951 season brought a weekly highlight film of a major college football game to ABC. Titled *The Game of the Week,* it was narrated by Bill Fisher. Three years later, ABC was back with a nighttime football series featuring the most popular college team in football history. *Notre Dame Football,* with Harry Wismer and Ford Bond doing the play-by-play, was still a highlight film, but a more extensive one than the half-hour series aired in 1950. It was edited to 75 minutes in length, leaving out only dull and uneventful plays. Wismer did double duty that fall, also announcing the weekly *Pro Football* game carried live by DuMont on Saturday nights. This was the same Harry Wismer who, a decade later, was the original owner of the New York Titans of the fledgling American Football League (later to become the New York Jets). DuMont was back with *Pro Football* in 1954, but Chuck Thompson had replaced Wismer at the mike. The year 1957 saw the revival of ABC's first football series, as *The All-American Football Game of the Week,* which highlighted a major college game of the weekend, this time narrated by Chick Hearn.

Professional football made its first appearance on ABC in the fall of 1959, but it wasn't until a decade later that it really became successful as a prime-time series. The 1959 series, which ran at 11:00 P.M. on Saturday nights, consisted of a full-length videotape replay of a game that had been played earlier that day. Commentators were Chuck Thompson and Howard Cosell. When, in the spring of 1970, ABC secured the rights from the National Football League to carry a regularly scheduled *Monday Night Football* game that fall, it was around Cosell's caustic personality that the announcing team was organized. Whereas the traditional way of covering football was with two people, a play-by-play announcer and a color man to add insights and observations, ABC decided to put three people in the booth. Keith Jackson did the play-by-play during the first season, with Frank Gifford assuming that role in 1971. The other two commentators, Cosell and Don Meredith, were there to inform, observe, and entertain. It was this last aspect of their work that offended sports traditionalists. At times, especially during boring games, the men in the booth seemed to lose touch completely with what was happening on the field. They were accused of turning a sport into an entertainment show, but as long as the ratings were high enough (which they always were), they received full support from ABC's management.

Later years saw periodic changes in the broadcast booth, as new faces (usually former athletes) were brought in to do color. Easygoing Frank Gifford was for many years the play-by-play announcer, switching to color in 1986. Howard "The Mouth" Cosell got most of the press, however, and it marked the end of an era when he retired in 1983. ABC briefly tried a two-man team in 1986 (Gifford and Al Michaels), reverting to the former three-person arrangement the following year. The 1987 season saw the addition of cable TV, with ESPN's package of Sunday night prime-time NFL telecasts. Starting in 1990, TNT was added to the mix, airing the Sunday night games during the first half of the season, with ESPN taking over for the second half. In 1998 ESPN took over the entire Sunday night schedule.

Starting in 1988 ABC also telecast several preseason games on Monday, beginning at 8:00 P.M. rather than the regular season's 9:00 P.M. start. From 1989 onward, the first of these games was seen in August. In 1998, the telecasts began at 8:00 P.M., starting with a pre-game show hosted by veteran Frank Gifford, who had been demoted from the broadcast booth, but this only lasted for a year. In 2000 comedian Dennis Miller joined the team for two years.

The most talked-about development of 2001 was the launch of a new league, the XFL, by wrestling mogul Vince McMahon. It was billed as "smash mouth football," with much rougher competition and sexier cheerleaders on the sidelines. The most notable commentator was Jesse "The Body" Ventura, an ex-wrestler who had been elected governor of Minnesota the previous year. He was probably the only sitting governor to ever regularly announce professional sports on national television. XFL games also appeared on UPN and TNN, but after some initial curiosity viewing audiences dropped off sharply, and the league was discontinued after one season.

FOOTBALL NEWS, see *New York Giants Quarterback Huddle*

FOOTBALL SIDELINES (*Sports*)
FIRST TELECAST: *October 6, 1952*
LAST TELECAST: *December 29, 1952*
BROADCAST HISTORY:
Oct 1952–Dec 1952, DUM Mon 9:30–9:45
HOST:
Harry Wismer

Football Sidelines filled half of a 30-minute sports block that preceded the Monday night fights on DuMont in 1952. (The second half consisted of film clips of *Famous Fights.*) Here Wismer commented on filmed highlights from the previous weekend's football action.

FOOTBALL THIS WEEK (*Sports*)
FIRST TELECAST: *October 11, 1951*
LAST TELECAST: *December 6, 1951*
BROADCAST HISTORY:
Oct 1951–Dec 1951, DUM Thu 10:45–11:00

This program featured filmed highlights of the major college football games of the preceding weekend.

FOOTLIGHTS THEATER (*Dramatic Anthology*)
FIRST TELECAST: *July 4, 1952*
LAST TELECAST: *September 11, 1953*
BROADCAST HISTORY:
Jul 1952–Sep 1952, CBS Fri 9:30–10:00
Jul 1953–Sep 1953, CBS Fri 9:30–10:00

For two summers this anthology series aired on CBS, presenting adaptations of plays and novels as well as original stories. The 1952 version was broadcast live from New York, while 1953 saw filmed dramas presented under the same title. Lesser-known and predominantly younger actors and actresses were featured in the plays, with various episodes starring Victor Jory, Gig Young, Lloyd Bridges, Gale Storm, Barbara Hale, and Lynn Bari.

FOR LOVE AND HONOR (*Drama*)
FIRST TELECAST: *September 23, 1983*
LAST TELECAST: *December 27, 1983*
BROADCAST HISTORY:
Sep 1983–Nov 1983, NBC Fri 10:00–11:00
Dec 1983, NBC Tue 10:00–11:00
CAST:
First Sgt. Eugene Allard .... Cliff Potts
Platoon Sgt. James "China" Bell .... Yaphet Kotto
Capt. Carolyn Engel .... Shelley Smith
Capt. Stephen Wiecek .... Gary Grubbs
Cpl. Grace Pavlik .... Rachel Ticotin
Pvt. Chris Dolan .... Pete Kowanko
Pvt. Duke Johnson .... Keenen Ivory Wayans
Pvt. Dominick Petrizzo .... John Mengatti
Pvt. Utah Wilson .... Tony Becker
Sharon .... Amy Steel
Mary Lee .... Kelly Preston
Phyllis Wiecek .... Shanna Reed

For Love and Honor was a cross between the highly successful film *An Officer and a Gentleman* and the nighttime soap operas so popular in the early 1980s. The setting was the U.S. Army's Fort Geller, Texas, headquarters for the 88th Airborne Division, where paratroopers were trained for possible combat duty. In command of the unit around which most of the stories centered was bigoted Captain Stephen Wiecek, whose adulterous wife Phyllis was an alcoholic. Sgt. Allard was a compassionate drill instructor who was having a secret affair with Carolyn Engel, the base medical officer. The other drill instructor, China Bell, was an embittered former boxer and Vietnam veteran. Among their new recruits were con man Chris Dolan, who dated Sharon, a pretty local civilian; Duke Johnson, a young black who wanted China to help him become a professional boxer; Utah, a willing and gullible country boy; Utah's roommate, buddy, and protector, Dominick Petrizzo; and the unit's only female recruit, pretty but tough Puerto Rican Grace Pavlik. The base commander's adopted daughter Mary Lee was an oversexed teenager who flirted with most of the guys.

FOR THE PEOPLE (*Police Drama*)

FIRST TELECAST: *January 31, 1965*

LAST TELECAST: *May 9, 1965*

BROADCAST HISTORY:

Jan 1965–May 1965, CBS Sun 9:00–10:00

CAST:

David Koster .... William Shatner
Anthony Celese .... Howard Da Silva
Frank Malloy .... Lonny Chapman
Phyllis Koster .... Jessica Walter

William Shatner played David Koster, a strong-willed New York City assistant district attorney. David's passion for justice often brought him more trouble than he could handle, both from his superiors and from members of the criminal underground, who had little love for his obsessive dedication. Trying to keep David under tight rein, despite his admiration for the young prosecutor's zeal, was bureau chief Anthony Celese, his immediate boss. Helping David to ferret out criminals was detective Frank Malloy. David's wife, Phyllis, was a viola player in a classical string quartet, and had a life and priorities of her own that sometimes conflicted with his.

FOR THE PEOPLE (*Legal Drama*)

BROADCAST HISTORY:

Lifetime
60 minutes
Original episodes: *2002–2003* (18 episodes)
Premiered: *July 21, 2002*

CAST:

District Attorney Lora Gibson .... Debbi Morgan
Chief Deputy Asst. D.A. Camille Paris .... Lea Thompson
Prosecuting attorney Anita Lopez ... Cecilia Suarez
Michael Olivas .... A Martinez
Thomas Gibson .... Derek Morgan
Zach Paris (age 15) .... Matthew Richards
J. C. Hunter .... Frank Grillo
Scott Wilson .... Julian Bailey

A determined black conservative took over the Los Angeles D.A.'s office on a "get tough on crime" platform and immediately butted heads with her liberal chief deputy in this female-oriented drama. Intense Lora and emotional Camille had more in common than their politics might suggest, however, and they worked together to prosecute cases ranging from murder to child abuse to a gay-bashing talk-show host who had incited a killing. Gung-ho Chief Prosecutor Anita was Lora's ally, and public defender Michael was Camille's ex (to whom she was still close). On the home front was Lora's erudite professor husband, Thomas, and their two daughters; living with Camille was teenager Zach, the son of her drug-addicted sister Erica.

FOR YOUR LOVE (*Situation Comedy*)

FIRST TELECAST: *March 17, 1998*

LAST TELECAST: *August 11, 2002*

BROADCAST HISTORY:

Mar 1998–May 1998, NBC Tue 8:30–9:00
Sep 1998–Sep 1999, WB Thu 9:30–10:00
Jul 1999–Aug 1999, WB Mon 9:30–10:00
Sep 1999–Jul 2000, WB Fri 9:30–10:00
Jun 2000–Sep 2000, WB Sun 8:30–9:00
Jul 2000–Sep 2000, WB Sun 9:30–10:00
Oct 2000, WB Sun 7:30–8:00
Mar 2001–Aug 2001, WB Sun 9:30–10:00
Mar 2001, WB Sun 8:30–9:00
Jun 2001–Sep 2001, WB Sun 8:30–9:00
Jan 2002–Mar 2002, WB Sun 9:30–10:00
Jun 2002–Aug 2002, WB Sun 7:00–8:00

CAST:

Mel Ellis .... James Lesure
Malena Ellis .... Holly Robinson Peete
Reggie Ellis .... Edafe Blackmon
Bobbi Seawright .... Tamala Jones
Dean Winston .... D. W. Moffett
Sheri Winston .... Dedee Pfeiffer
Uncle Omar Ellis (2002) .... Eugene Byrd

THEME:

"For Your Love," by Ed Townsend, sung by Chaka Khan and Michael McDonald

The creator of *Living Single*, producer Yvette Lee Bowser, also produced this counterpart series, which might have been called "Living Together." It revolved around three couples in different stages of togetherness in the integrated, upscale Chicago suburb of Oak Park, Illinois. The "Veterans" were Dean and Sheri, a white architect (who had been a placekicker for the Tampa Bay Buccaneers) and a facialist, high school sweethearts who had been blissfully married for four years. Moving in next door were the "Newlyweds," Mel and Malena, an attorney and his psychiatrist wife, buppies (black, upwardly mobile professionals) who were very much in love. Then there was the "Not-Yet-Married," Mel's goofy, commitment-phobic brother Reggie, a restaurateur who could not bring himself to give a set of keys to his swank downtown apartment to girlfriend Bobbi, a divorced elementary school teacher. The three couples chattered about life, love, and lust amid numerous bed scenes, tub scenes, and couch cuddles.

When *For Your Love* moved to the WB for the 1998–1999 season, Reggie had opened a new Cajun restaurant, Soulstice, in Chicago. Dean and Sheri were trying to have a baby, but in the spring it was Malena who found out she was pregnant. In the fall of 1999 Bobbi moved in with Reggie, Malena was expecting a boy, and Mel was about to be made partner in his law firm. They wanted him to commit for 10 years, however, so instead he left to strike out on his own, setting up his practice in the same building in which Dean worked. Bobbi and Reggie almost broke up but, when the series returned in March 2001 after a five-month hiatus, Reggie proposed; in mid-April they were married, in a spur-of-the-moment ceremony. Dean and Sheri split up because she felt unfulfilled, and in the season finale Malena went into labor—after a two-year pregnancy!

After another hiatus *For Your Love* returned in January 2002, with Malena leaving the hospital with her new baby boy, Evan. Dean and Sheri had wild sex in the hospital while Malena was in labor, but they remained separated. Reggie saw a therapist and admitted he had misgivings about having gotten married. The following week he had an opportunity to become part owner of a resort in the Caribbean and, when

Bobbi told him she didn't want to go, he went without her. Mel's uncle Omar was hired to run the restaurant, where he locked horns with Bobbi, who had been managing the place since Reggie's departure. At the end of February Malena returned to work and Dean and Sheri reconciled. When Uncle Omar threw a party at Bobbi's apartment while she was away, he got her evicted. In mid-March Bobbi received her divorce papers from commitment-averse Reggie. This gave Omar the chance to make his move on her, but she wasn't interested despite having little success dating other guys.

FOR YOUR PLEASURE (*Music*)
FIRST TELECAST: *April 15, 1948*
LAST TELECAST: *September 10, 1949*
BROADCAST HISTORY:
Apr 1948–Jun 1948, NBC Thu 8:00–8:15
Jul 1948–Sep 1948, NBC Wed 8:00–8:15
Jul 1949–Sep 1949, NBC Sat 8:30–9:00
REGULARS:
Kyle MacDonnell
Norman Paris Trio
DANCERS:
Jack and Jill (Apr–Jun 1948)
Blaire and Deane (Jun–Sep 1948)
ORCHESTRA:
Earl Shelton (1949)

This live studio musical program featured Kyle MacDonnell, the pretty singing star of Broadway's *Make Mine Manhattan* and one of the most frequently seen "personalities" on early TV screens. The program was set in a nightclub with Kyle strolling among the tables, chatting with guests and singing a song or two. TV-set owners in 1948 had to put up with a lot of inconveniences to watch the winsome Miss MacDonnell, however. A *New York Times* reviewer complained that "the lighting has been particularly erratic, at times almost blotting out Miss MacDonnell and the other artists in a haze of whiteness, and at other moments reflecting both skill and thought. More rehearsal . . . should correct such defects."

See *Girl About Town* for the continuation of this program in similar format.

FORD FESTIVAL (*Musical Variety*)
FIRST TELECAST: *April 5, 1951*
LAST TELECAST: *June 26, 1952*
BROADCAST HISTORY:
Apr 1951–Dec 1951, NBC Thu 9:00–10:00
Jan 1952–Jun 1952, NBC Thu 9:30–10:30
REGULARS:
James Melton
Dorothy Warrenskjold
Vera Vague
The Wiere Brothers (1951)
Billy Barty

Ford Festival was originally a loosely structured "book" show in which a simple plot served to tie together performances by the singing star of the show, James Melton, and his semi-regulars, singer Dorothy Warrenskjold, comedienne Vera Vague (Barbara Jo Allen), and comedy singers The Wiere Brothers. On June 7, 1951, the format was changed to that of a straight revue, and all pretense of plot was dropped. Billy Barty was added to the cast of regulars the following week and The Wiere Brothers were dropped.

FORD SHOW, THE (*Musical Variety*)
FIRST TELECAST: *October 4, 1956*
LAST TELECAST: *June 29, 1961*
BROADCAST HISTORY:
Oct 1956–Jun 1961, NBC Thu 9:30–10:00 (OS)
REGULARS:
Tennessee Ernie Ford
The Voices of Walter Schumann (1956–1957)
The Top Twenty (1957–1961)
The Harry Geller Orchestra

Tennessee Ernie Ford was host, singer, comedian, and star of this variety show, whose title referred not to him, but to its sponsor, the Ford Motor Company. Ernie's informal, friendly quality set the tone for the program, which included his reminiscences about growing up in Bristol, Tennessee, and his homespun catchphrases ("Bless your pea-pickin' hearts!"). The musical portion of the program consisted mostly of country and western and gospel music, for which Ernie was famous, and the show generally ended with a hymn. The choral group "The Voices of Walter Schumann" backed Ernie during his first season; "The Top Twenty," a more contemporary mixed singing group, performed those duties for the remainder of the show's run.

FORD STAR JUBILEE (*Various*)
FIRST TELECAST: *September 24, 1955*
LAST TELECAST: *November 3, 1956*
BROADCAST HISTORY:
Sep 1955–Nov 1956, CBS Sat 9:30–11:00 (OS)

This series of "spectaculars," which aired roughly once per month, was CBS' "class" series for the 1955–1956 season. The material and the stars were all first-rate. Judy Garland (in her first network TV starring vehicle) hosted the premiere telecast "The Judy Garland Show," and other musical telecasts in the series included Mary Martin and Noel Coward in "Together with Music"; Eddie Fisher, Debbie Reynolds, Nat "King" Cole, Bobby Van, Ella Fitzgerald, and Red Skelton in "I Hear America Singing"; and Louis Armstrong, Dorothy Dandridge, and Shirley Jones in a tribute to Cole Porter titled "You're the Top." There was also drama—Lloyd Nolan, Barry Sullivan, and Frank Lovejoy in *The Caine Mutiny Court-Martial*; Jack Lemmon, Raymond Massey, Lillian Gish, and Charles Laughton in *The Day Lincoln Was Shot*; and Orson Welles, Betty Grable, and Keenan Wynn in *Twentieth Century*. The last telecast of *Ford Star Jubilee*, however, was really something special. It was the first airing of what later became a television tradition—Judy Garland's classic 1939 film *The Wizard of Oz*, with Judy's 10-year-old daughter Liza Minnelli and Bert Lahr (the cowardly lion from the film) on hand to introduce it.

FORD STAR REVUE (*Comedy/Variety*)
FIRST TELECAST: *July 6, 1950*
LAST TELECAST: *March 29, 1951*
BROADCAST HISTORY:
Jul 1950–Sep 1950, NBC Thu 9:00–10:00
Jan 1951–Mar 1951, NBC Thu 9:00–10:00
REGULARS:
Jack Haley
Havel Brothers (Jul–Sep 1950)

Dr. Roy K. Marshall
Mindy Carson (Jan–Mar 1951)
Carl Hoff Orchestra (Jan–Mar 1951)
Ted Adolphus Dancers (Jan–Mar 1951)

This musical comedy-variety series began as a summer replacement for *Kay Kyser's Kollege of Musical Knowledge*, then was given its own regular season slot (briefly) in early 1951. Many famous guest stars and semi-regular performers came and went during the life of the show. Haley, who was perhaps best known for his role as the Tin Woodsman in the 1939 movie classic *The Wizard of Oz*, failed to catch on as a TV host and the program was soon canceled.

Among the writers for the 1951 edition was Norman Lear.

FORD STARTIME, see *Startime*

FORD THEATRE (*Dramatic Anthology*)
FIRST TELECAST: *October 7, 1949*
LAST TELECAST: *July 10, 1957*
BROADCAST HISTORY:
Oct 1949–Jun 1951, CBS Fri 9:00–10:00 (OS)
Oct 1952–Sep 1956, NBC Thu 9:30–10:00
Oct 1956–Jul 1957, ABC Wed 9:30–10:00

Ford Theatre began as a monthly series of live hour-long dramatic plays on CBS on October 17, 1948. It became a regular series a year later, airing on alternate Friday nights with other dramatic shows. The live CBS edition used New York-based actors and actresses, primarily those working on Broadway. Among the plays aired during this period were an adaptation of *Little Women*, with Peggy Ann Garner, Kim Hunter, and June Lockhart; *Twentieth Century,* with Fredric March and Lilli Palmer; and *One Sunday Afternoon*, with Hume Cronyn and Burgess Meredith.

After a season's absence, *Ford Theatre* returned to the air on NBC in October 1952, as a filmed series of half-hour plays. This version of the show remained on NBC for four years and then moved to ABC for a final season. With the shift to film, the production moved to Hollywood and the episodes starred motion-picture performers. The scope ranged from light comedy to heavy drama and consisted of adaptations of plays and novels as well as original stories. Such familiar names as Charles Coburn, Barry Sullivan, Peter Lawford, Thomas Mitchell, Ann Sheridan, Claudette Colbert, Ida Lupino, and Teresa Wright starred in these shows. Ronald Reagan and his wife Nancy Davis made their first professional appearance together in this series, on February 5, 1953, in a teleplay titled "First Born."

FOREIGN INTRIGUE (*Intrigue*)
BROADCAST HISTORY:
Syndicated only
30 minutes
Produced: *1951–1955* (156 episodes)
Released: *Fall 1951*
CAST:
Robert Cannon (1951–1953) .... Jerome Thor
Helen Davis (1951–1953) .... Synda Scott
Michael Powers (1953–1954) .... James Daly
Patricia Bennett (1953–1954) .... Anne Preville
Christopher Storm (1954–1955) ...... Gerald Mohr

This syndicated mystery, filmed in Europe, owed its popularity more to its authentic locations and European flavor than to its stars (of whom it had five in four years). When it began, Jerome Thor played a trench-coated European correspondent for an American wire service whose assignments took him across the Continent, and involved him with political provocateurs, old war criminals, and neo-Nazis. There was a heavily political flavor to many of the episodes. His friendly rival was reporter Helen Davis, and their base of operations, Stockholm.

Thor was replaced after two seasons by James Daly, whose pipe-smoking correspondent for Associated News was a rougher yet less serious hero. Anne Preville, who played a correspondent for Consolidated Press, became his female foil, and production moved to Paris. Both Thor and Daly took "vacations" from time to time, Thor being spelled in some episodes by another correspondent (played by Bernard Farrel) and Daly by Miss Preville.

In 1954 the lead and location changed again. This time Gerald Mohr starred as the American owner of a hotel in Vienna, and a fast man both with a gun and with his fists. In the opening episodes he was involved in smashing a counterfeiting ring dealing in American currency.

Foreign Intrigue was created, produced, directed, and sometimes written by an ambitious young New Yorker named Sheldon Reynolds. It was repeated in later years under a variety of titles: *Dateline Europe* for the Thor episodes, *Overseas Adven-ture* for the Daly episodes, and *Cross Current* for the Mohr episodes. Also known as *Foreign Assignment*.

FOREIGN LEGION, see *Assignment: Foreign Legion*

FORENSIC FILES, THE (*Documentary*)
CABLE HISTORY:
Court TV
60 minutes
Produced: *2000–*
Premiered: *September 23, 2000*
NETWORK HISTORY:
FIRST TELECAST: *August 25, 2002*
LAST TELECAST: *October 19, 2002*
Aug 2002–Sep 2002, NBC Sun 8:00–9:00
Oct 2002, NBC Sat 8:00–9:00
NARRATOR:
Peter Thomas

This documentary series traced the work of forensic scientists as they meticulously followed the clues in heinous crimes. A model was murdered; a San Francisco pornographic filmmaker was mysteriously killed (was it by his brother?); hundreds became ill from food poisoning in Oregon (was a religious cult plotting germ warfare?). Most of the cases involved murders, rapes and other violent crimes, some celebrated (e.g., the Madalyn Murray O'Hair murder), but most not. Re-creations were used to dramatize the events. The series became a hit on cable and was the documentary version of the trend toward "forensics" dramas such as *CSI,* which debuted a few days later. *Forensic Files* was so popular that reruns were seen on NBC in 2002.

FOREVER FERNWOOD, see *Mary Hartman, Mary Hartman*

FOREVER KNIGHT (*Police/Supernatural Drama*)
FIRST TELECAST: *May 7, 1992*
LAST TELECAST: *August 23, 1994*
BROADCAST HISTORY:
May 1992–Aug 1993, CBS Tue 11:30–12:30 A.M.
Aug 1993, CBS Fri 12:30–1:30 A.M.
Nov 1993–Aug 1994, CBS Tue 12:35–1:35 A.M.
(In first-run syndication Sep 1994–Sep 1996, and on USA Network Sep 1995–Sep 1996)
CAST:
Det. Nicholas "Nick" Knight . . . Geraint Wyn Davies
Det. Don Schanke (1992–1995) . . . . John Kapelos
Natalie Lambert . . . . Catherine Disher
Capt. Joe Stonetree (1992–1993) . . . . . . Gary Farmer
Lacroix . . . . Nigel Bennett
Janette (1992–1995) . . . . Deborah Duchene
Capt. Amanda Cohen (1994–1995)
. . . . Natsuko Ohama
Javier Vachon (1995–1996) . . . . Ben Bass
Det. Tracy Vetter (1995–1996) . . . . Lisa Ryder
Capt. Joe Reese (1995–1996) . . . . Blu Mankuma

Nick Knight was a good-looking young homicide detective who worked the night shift out of necessity, not by choice. He could not work during the day because he was an almost 800-year-old vampire. It was while fighting in the Crusades that Nicholas had been lured by Janette, a vampire, into becoming a disciple of the immortal Lacroix, who had made him a vampire in Paris in the year 1228. Now Nick worked on a modern big-city police force while trying to find a way to end the curse of the undead. There were a couple of advantages to his condition—he had infrared vision, could fly (although he didn't turn into a bat), and was inhumanly strong. Nick drove a 1962 Cadillac with a big trunk in which he used to hide from the sun in emergencies. Unwilling to drain others of blood, he kept several bottles of cow's blood chilled in his refrigerator. The only person who knew Nick's secret was his friend, Natalie, the medical examiner who was trying to formulate something that would return him to human form. Det. Schanke was Nick's corpulent partner, and Capt. Stonetree was their boss. His old friend Janette ran The Raven, a club where other local vampires hung out, and his nemesis Lacroix kept turning up to torment him. In fact, while working on cases Nick would have flashbacks to incidents that had occurred during his eight centuries as a vampire.

Forever Knight originally aired on CBS during the 1992–1993 season and was rerun the following year. When it moved into first-run syndication, with new episodes, Nick and Schanke had been transferred to a different precinct and were now reporting to Capt. Cohen. Lacroix was working as a late-night radio personality, and, early in the season, Schanke found out Nick was a benign vampire.

In the fall of 1995, Nick was temporarily partnered with young detective Vetter, who was touchy because her father was the police commissioner and she was insecure about what people thought about her. Their partnership became permanent when a plane on which Schanke and Capt. Cohen were traveling was blown up by a bomb. Janette had left Toronto, and Lacroix was now running The Raven. New to the cast were Vachon, another vampire with a mission to do good who was in love with Tracy, and Capt. Reese, who had replaced Cohen.

The final original episode brought closure in a number of ways. Tracy died after a crazed gunman's bullet went through Nick's body and fatally wounded her. Natalie wanted him to bring her over to the world of the undead, but after he started to, he couldn't finish, and she died. As the episode ended, he had convinced Lacroix to end his eternal suffering by driving a stake through his heart.

Produced in Toronto, Canada.

FORTUNE DANE (*Police Drama*)
FIRST TELECAST: *February 15, 1986*
LAST TELECAST: *March 27, 1986*
BROADCAST HISTORY:
Feb 1986–Mar 1986, ABC Sat 9:00–10:00
CAST:
Fortune Dane . . . . Carl Weathers
Mayor Amanda Harding . . . . Penny Fuller
Kathy "Speed" Davenport . . . . Daphne Ashbrook
Perfect Tommy . . . . Joe Dallesandro

This rather violent series centered on an imposing black police detective who turned in his badge when the gangland killing he was investigating revealed a connection between his banker father, whom he idolized, and the mob. Following the hit man to a West Coast metropolis called Bay City, Dane solved the case and then became a troubleshooter for that city's lady mayor, who was almost as tough as he was.

FORTUNE HUNTER (*Adventure*)
FIRST TELECAST: *September 4, 1994*
LAST TELECAST: *October 2, 1994*
BROADCAST HISTORY:
Sep 1994–Oct 1994, FOX Sun 7:00–8:00
CAST:
Carlton Dial . . . . Mark Frankel
Harry Flack . . . . John Robert Hoffman
Yvonne . . . . Kim Faze

In this tongue-in-cheek spoof of James Bond, Carlton Dial was a debonair former spy for British counterintelligence who worked as a handsomely paid agent for Intercept Corporation, a recovery firm based in San Francisco. Intercept had clients all over the world and generated most of its revenue retrieving stolen valuables and/or top-secret military equipment. Harry was the nerdy computer whiz who monitored Carlton's activities using high-tech telemetry equipment that the agent wore—a miniaturized camera in a contact lens and a transceiver in a tiny ear implant, with a watch that amplified and transmitted for both. Carlton could have some privacy by taking off the watch, which had to be on his wrist to transmit effectively. As the monitoring partner Harry saw everything Carlton saw, heard everything he heard and provided him with useful information via the ear implant. Carlton's gun was a tranquilizer pistol that fired six high-potency darts (Intercept had been hit with lawsuits over excessive use of violence) instead of bullets. Yvonne was the sexy Intercept employee who, via a special video link, gave Carlton his assignments.

48 HOURS (*Documentary*)
FIRST TELECAST: *January 19, 1988*
LAST TELECAST:
BROADCAST HISTORY:
Jan 1988–Feb 1988, CBS Tue 8:00–9:00
Mar 1988–Sep 1990, CBS Thu 8:00–9:00
Sep 1990, CBS Sat 10:00–11:00
Oct 1990–Mar 1991, CBS Wed 8:00–9:00
Apr 1991–Dec 1994, CBS Wed 10:00–11:00
Jan 1995–Sep 2000, CBS Thu 10:00–11:00
Jul 1997–Sep 1997, CBS Wed 10:00–11:00
Mar 1998–Apr 1998, CBS Tue 10:00–11:00
Jun 1998–Sep 1998, CBS Mon 10:00–11:00
Jun 1999–Sep 1999, CBS Mon 10:00–11:00
Jul 1999–Sep 1999, CBS Tue 10:00–11:00
May 2000–Jul 2000, CBS Mon 10:00–11:00
Jun 2000, CBS Sat 8:00–9:00
Oct 2000–Dec 2000, CBS Thu 8:00–9:00
Dec 2000–Feb 2001, CBS Thu 10:00–11:00
May 2001–Aug 2001, CBS Thu 10:00–11:00
May 2001–Jul 2001, CBS Mon 10:00–11:00
Jul 2001–Jun 2002, CBS Fri 10:00–11:00
Aug 2001–Sep 2001, CBS Thu 8:00–9:00
Mar 2002–May 2002, CBS Wed 10:00–11:00
Apr 2002–Aug 2002, CBS Mon 10:00–11:00
Jun 2002–Jan 2003, CBS Fri 8:00–9:00
Jul 2002–Sep 2002, CBS Wed 10:00–11:00
Aug 2002–Sep 2002, CBS Fri 10:00–11:00
Jan 2003–Jun 2003, CBS Wed 10:00–11:00
Feb 2003– , CBS Fri 10:00–11:00
Jul 2003– , CBS Sat 8:00–9:00
ANCHOR:
Dan Rather (1988–2002)
Lesley Stahl (2002–)
CORRESPONDENTS:
Bernard Goldberg (1990–1992, 1998–2000)
Phil Jones (1988–1999)
Harold Dow
Erin Moriarity
Richard Schlesinger
Susan Spencer (1993–)
Roberta Baskin (1995–1998)
Bill Lagattuta (1995–)
Troy Roberts (1999–)
Peter Van Sant (1999–)

Not since the *CBS News Hour* left the air in 1971 had any network aired a regularly scheduled prime-time news series that focused on a single topic each week. The premise of *48 Hours* was to give viewers a *cinéma vérité* look at a news story, following correspondents and crews as each story was developed and filmed over a two-day period. Although the series often dealt with issues of topical interest, it did not necessarily focus on the hottest current news story. The first three episodes, for instance, covered Miami's struggle to overcome its image as a center for drug trafficking, the congestion at Denver's busy Stapleton Airport over New Year's weekend, and the work of the doctors, nurses, and staff at Dallas's Parkland Memorial Hospital. Dan Rather was the series' in-studio anchorman and Bernard Goldberg was its principal correspondent. Various CBS reporters contributed each week.

In addition to those listed above as correspondents, Deborah Potter, Doug Tunnell, Victoria Corderi, James Hattori, Betsy Aaron, Faith Daniels, Edie Magnus, and Peter Van Sant, who officially became a regular in 1999, were frequent contributors. In October 2002 Lesley Stahl replaced Dan Rather and the series was retitled *48 Hours Investigates.*

FOUL PLAY (*Detective*)
FIRST TELECAST: *January 26, 1981*
LAST TELECAST: *August 23, 1981*
BROADCAST HISTORY:
Jan 1981–Feb 1981, ABC Mon 10:00–11:00
Aug 1981, ABC Sun 8:00–8:30
CAST:
Gloria Munday .... Deborah Raffin
Det. Tucker Pendleton .... Barry Bostwick
Capt. Vito Lombardi .... Richard Romanus
Stella .... Mary Jo Catlett
Ben .... Greg Rice
Beau .... John Rice

Based on the movie of the same name starring Chevy Chase and Goldie Hawn, *Foul Play* concerned a TV talk-show hostess (Gloria) and a concert-violinist-turned-cop (Tucker) who teamed up to solve crimes in San Francisco. Capt. Lombardi was Tucker's boss, and Ben and Beau a couple of helpful midgets. The series had none of the raucous comedy of the movie, and was soon canceled.

FOUL-UPS, BLEEPS & BLUNDERS (*Comedy*)
FIRST TELECAST: *January 10, 1984*
LAST TELECAST: *August 11, 1985*
BROADCAST HISTORY:
Jan 1984–Oct 1984, ABC Tue 8:00–8:30
Nov 1984–Mar 1985, ABC various (occasional)
Apr 1985–Jul 1985, ABC Tue 8:30–9:00
Aug 1985, ABC Sun 10:30–11:00
HOSTS:
Don Rickles
Steve Lawrence
FOREIGN CORRESPONDENT:
Noel Edmunds

ABC seemed to be one step behind in the TV-outtakes craze. NBC started it all with its highly successful "Bloopers" specials, and ABC followed with its "Life's Most Embarrassing Moments" specials. Then NBC discovered that a special made up of commercials could be funny, and ABC copied that with its own "great commercials" specials. Finally NBC turned its good thing into a weekly Monday night series called *TV's Bloopers & Practical Jokes*, and ABC followed suit a day later with the practically identical *Foul-Ups, Bleeps & Blunders.*

The format was simply to string together outtakes from movies, TV shows, local newscasts, commercials, and elsewhere that showed supposed professionals—many of them major stars—fluffing their lines, falling over props, breaking up, etc. Interspersed were some *Candid Camera*–style segments in which ordinary citizens were given equal time to make fools of themselves.

NBC had the last laugh in all this, however. Running against NBC's super hit *The A-Team, Foul-Ups* barely survived, while the Monday night NBC version attracted large audiences.

FOUR CORNERS (*Drama*)
FIRST TELECAST: *February 24, 1998*
LAST TELECAST: *March 3, 1998*
BROADCAST HISTORY:
Feb 1998–Mar 1998, CBS Tue 10:00–11:00

CAST:

Amanda "Maggie" Wyatt .... Ann-Margret
Alex Wyatt .... Douglas Wert
Kate Wyatt .... Megan Ward
Carlotta Alvarez .... Sonia Braga
Tomas Alvarez .... Kamar de los Reyes
Eva Alvarez .... Dahlia Waingort
Sam Haskell .... Raymond J. Barry
Caleb Haskell .... Justin Chambers
Sheriff .... Tim Carhart
Dan .... Brian McNamara
Linda .... Yolanda Lloyd Delgado

Amanda Wyatt was the matriarch of a California ranching family going through unsettling changes. What had once been fertile farm country had seen the rise of expensive ski resorts and high-priced suburban housing developments. Following her husband's death in a plane crash, Amanda was trying to keep her sprawling Homestead Ranch out of the hands of land developers—not made any easier by her son, Alex's, desire to work with them and bail out with lots of cash. Her friend Carlotta, whose husband had died in the same plane crash as Amanda's, represented the migrant workers who depended on farming for their survival. Carlotta's son, Tomas, had been in love with Amanda's feisty daughter, Kate, but had given up the secular life to become a priest. Kate still wanted him. Sam, the ranch foreman, was trying to rebuild a relationship with his son, Caleb, who had just been released from prison.

Film star Ann-Margret's series television debut was not auspicious. One of the disasters of the 1997–1998 season, *Four Corners* aired only twice before being yanked from the CBS schedule.

FOUR IN ONE (*Drama*)

FIRST TELECAST: *September 16, 1970*
LAST TELECAST: *September 8, 1971*
BROADCAST HISTORY:

Sep 1970–Sep 1971, NBC Wed 10:00–11:00

Four in One was the umbrella title for a group of four mini-series, each of which was aired for a period of six consecutive weeks and then was rerun on a rotating basis. See *McCloud, San Francisco International Airport, Night Gallery,* and *The Psychiatrist.*

FOUR SEASONS, THE (*Situation Comedy*)

FIRST TELECAST: *January 29, 1984*
LAST TELECAST: *July 29, 1984*
BROADCAST HISTORY:

Jan 1984–Feb 1984, CBS Sun 8:00–8:30
Mar 1984–Jul 1984, CBS Sun 8:30–9:00

CAST:

Danny Zimmer .... Jack Weston
Ted Bolen .... Tony Roberts
Claudia Zimmer .... Marcia Rodd
Lorraine Elliot .... Barbara Babcock
Boris Elliot .... Alan Arbus
Pat Devon .... Joanna Kerns
Lisa Callan .... Beatrice Alda
Beth Burroughs .... Elizabeth Alda
Sharon Hogan .... Lori Carrell

EXECUTIVE PRODUCERS:

Alan Alda and Martin Bregman

Danny Zimmer was a born-and-bred New Yorker, a dentist, and a hypochondriac. He worried about almost everything, including the decision to move to California and establish a new practice in Los Angeles. Danny dreaded change of any kind, and the adjustment was traumatic although it was eased by the new friends he made in Los Angeles. Ted Bolen was his aggressive real-estate-salesman pal, who lived the "California" lifestyle and had a live-in relationship with stuntwoman Pat Devon. Danny's other close friend was Boris Elliot, a successful attorney who had given up the practice of law for the less pressured life of a bicycle-shop owner after suffering a heart attack. Boris's wife, Lorraine, was a professor of orthopedics at the UCLA School of Medicine and a good sport, despite a rather stuffy exterior. Also seen regularly were Beth Burroughs, the daughter of Danny's best friend from New York, and Beth's friend Lisa, who moved to California to find fame and fortune. Sharon was the girl with whom Beth and Lisa shared an apartment. They all shared little middle-class adventures, often involving Danny's beloved Mercedes automobile, and counterpointed by the music of Vivaldi—*The Four Seasons,* of course.

The Four Seasons was based on the Alan Alda movie of the same name, with Jack Weston and Alda's daughters Beatrice and Elizabeth re-creating the roles they had played in the movie.

FOUR SQUARE COURT (*Discussion*)

FIRST TELECAST: *March 16, 1952*
LAST TELECAST: *June 29, 1952*
BROADCAST HISTORY:

Mar 1952–May 1952, ABC Sun 7:30–8:00
May 1952–Jun 1952, ABC Sun 9:00–9:30

MODERATOR:

Norman Brokenshire

Many TV entertainment series have dealt with criminals of various types. This was probably the only network series ever to star the real thing: masked ex-convicts out on parole, who appeared each week to discuss their crimes and rehabilitation. No doubt the parolees watched their language on this live, coast-to-coast show, as state parole board officials appeared on the panel with them. The program emanated from New York.

FOUR STAR PLAYHOUSE (*Dramatic Anthology*)

FIRST TELECAST: *September 25, 1952*
LAST TELECAST: *September 27, 1956*
BROADCAST HISTORY:

Sep 1952–Sep 1954, CBS Thu 8:30–9:00
Oct 1954–Sep 1956, CBS Thu 9:30–10:00

REGULARS:

David Niven
Charles Boyer
Dick Powell
Ida Lupino

When *Four Star Playhouse* was announced, the four stars who were supposed to appear on a rotating basis were Charles Boyer, Dick Powell, Rosalind Russell, and Joel McCrea. Russell and McCrea never made it and were replaced by David Niven and Ida Lupino. Although *Four Star Playhouse* was essentially an anthology, one continuing character did make numerous appearances. That was nightclub owner Willie Dante, portrayed by Dick Powell. A later series based on Powell's characterization, *Dante,* appeared on NBC in 1960 with Howard Duff in the title role.

The format of the individual episodes varied greatly, with the content ranging from comedy to drama. The four stars were not the only headliners, especially during the first two seasons. Others who were featured over the years were Ronald Colman, Merle Oberon, Joan Fontaine, Teresa Wright, and Frank Lovejoy.

Four Star Playhouse was originally an alternate-week series, expanding to a weekly basis in September 1953.

FOUR STAR REVUE, see *All Star Revue*

413 HOPE STREET (*Drama*)
FIRST TELECAST: *September 11, 1997*
LAST TELECAST: *January 1, 1998*
BROADCAST HISTORY:
Sep 1997–Oct 1997, FOX Thu 9:00–10:00
Dec 1997–Jan 1998, FOX Thu 9:00–10:00
CAST:
Phil Thomas .... Richard Roundtree
Juanita Harris .... Shari Headley
Antonio Collins .... Jesse L. Martin
Sylvia Jennings .... Kelly Coffield
Nick Carrington .... Michael Easton
Quentin Jefferson .... Stephen Berra
Angelica Collins .... Dawn Stern
Carlos Martinez .... Vincent Laresca
Melvin Todd .... Karim Prince
Morgan Washington .... Rosey Brown

The address 413 Hope Street was a teen crisis center in a poor section of Manhattan that provided health services and rehab programs for the indigent. Attorney Phil Thomas was the unpaid chief administrator of the center; he was doing penance for being late picking up his teenage son after basketball and arriving just in time to see him murdered by a kid who wanted his basketball shoes. Among the others at the center were Antonio, a volunteer counselor married to Angelica; Juanita, a paid counselor; Sylvia, the center's eager attorney, who was always looking for other ways to contribute; Nick, the gym instructor who arrived about a month after the series premiere; and Morgan, the beefy receptionist. In the premiere, Juanita started adoption proceedings for Raimie, an infant girl whose drug-addicted mother had been murdered. Also seen were Quentin, a sometimes suicidal young man who had contracted HIV from his abusive father; Raimie's father, Carlos, who went through drug rehab and, when he finished, wanted to help raise her; and Melvin, a gay HIV-positive teenager who masked his fears with jokes. In the series' last episode, Angelica joined the center as the new dance instructor.

Despite glowing reviews from critics and praise from civic organizations, the generally depressing tone of *413 Hope Street* mitigated against its attracting a large audience and it was canceled after less than four months on the air. The series was created and co-executive-produced by actor Damon Wayans.

FOX FAMILY CHANNEL, THE (Network), see *ABC Family Channel*

FOX FILES (*News Magazine*)
FIRST TELECAST: *July 16, 1998*
LAST TELECAST: *August 31, 1999*
BROADCAST HISTORY:
Jul 1998–Jun 1999, FOX Thu 9:00–10:00
Jun 1999–Aug 1999, FOX Tue 9:00–10:00
ANCHORS:
Catherine Crier
Jon Scott
CORRESPONDENTS:
Catherine Herridge
Chris Cuomo
Amy Holmes (1998)
Eric Shawn
Arthel Neville
Kit Hoover (1999)

Each episode of this newsmagazine was designed to feature four stories, although the series premiere was a full-hour profile of the late Princess Diana. Subsequent episodes included a visit to a pro wrestling training camp, Internet gambling addiction, the escape of six convicted murderers from a private prison in Youngstown, Ohio, backstage with the Spice Girls on tour, gang members in search of "respect" on the streets, serial rapists, and the high rate of car theft in Newark, New Jersey.

Two regular features were commentary by Internet "citizen reporter" Matt Drudge (dropped after a couple of months) and "Heroes and Zeros," short takes on people doing good things and bad. Original correspondent Amy Holmes was replaced by Arthel Neville in December.

FOX MOVIE CHANNEL (Network) (*Cable Movie Network*)
LAUNCHED:
October 31, 1994
SUBSCRIBERS (FEB. 2003):
24.4 million (23% U.S.)

A noncommercial 24-hour classic-movie channel featuring films from the 1930s to the 1980s, many of them from the 20th Century Fox vaults. Also shown were short subjects, including old Fox Movietone News clips. The network was launched as fXM: Movies from Fox, with the name being changed to Fox Movie Channel in 2000.

FOX NEWS CHANNEL (Network) (*News and Talk Cable Network*)
LAUNCHED:
October 7, 1996
SUBSCRIBERS (MAY 2003):
82.0 million (77% U.S.)

"We report. You decide," was the slogan of this rather loud, tabloidish news channel launched in 1996 by Rupert Murdoch's News Corporation, which operated many newspapers as well as the Fox television network. It certainly raised the decibel level in TV news reporting. The daytime schedule consisted of reports and features on current breaking stories, while the evenings were filled with interview and analysis shows, almost all of them loud and contentious. Among the channel's evening standbys were Brit Hume, Bill O'Reilly, Judith Regan, Catherine Crier, the team of Sean Hannity and Alan Colmes, and business reporter Neil Cavuto. The network even made room on weekends for "underground" reporter Matt Drudge ("I'm Matt Drudge, keeping my eye on all the rascals")—the bane of serious reporters, due to his alleged reliance on rumor and innuendo.

Despite, or perhaps because of, its feisty approach to news, by the early 2000s the channel was giving the older news networks a run for their money, attracting large audiences and luring away top talent such as Geraldo Rivera from CNBC (2001) and Greta Van Susteren from CNN (2002).

FRANK LEAHY SHOW, THE (*Sports Commentary*)
FIRST TELECAST: *September 27, 1953*
LAST TELECAST: *December 6, 1953*
BROADCAST HISTORY:
Sep 1953–Dec 1953, ABC Sun 7:45–8:00
HOST:
Frank Leahy

The Frank Leahy Show was the pregame show leading up to *Notre Dame Football* in 1953. Notre Dame coach Frank Leahy would interview the coach of the team that Notre Dame had played the previous day. Following their discussion, the highlights of the game itself were shown on *Notre Dame Football.*

FRANK SINATRA SHOW, THE (*Musical Variety*)
FIRST TELECAST: *October 7, 1950*
LAST TELECAST: *April 1, 1952*
BROADCAST HISTORY:
Oct 1950–Jun 1951, CBS Sat 9:00–10:00
Oct 1951–Apr 1952, CBS Tue 8:00–9:00
REGULARS:
Frank Sinatra
Ben Blue (1950–1951)
Joey Walsh (1950–1951)
Axel Stordahl and His Orchestra
Sid Fields (1950–1951)
Roberta Lee (1950–1951)
Pat Gaye (1950–1951)

A good deal of publicity attended Frank Sinatra's initial plunge into television in 1950. He certainly had superstar credentials from music, radio, and films (though his greatest films were still to come); would he make it in the new medium of TV? The answer was no, although there was never a clear reason why Sinatra didn't, when such other singers as Perry Como and Dinah Shore did. *The Frank Sinatra Show* was telecast live from New York and featured top-line guest stars and plenty of Frankie's singing, assisted and backed by an assortment of female vocalists and backup groups. There was also, at least for the first three months, a regular supporting cast of comedians to help provide variety.

One factor that certainly didn't help was the competition. Sinatra was first scheduled opposite Sid Caesar's *Your Show of Shows,* then a red-hot sensation. For the second season he was moved to Tuesday, against *The Texaco Star Theater* with Milton Berle—the number-one show in television! Frank moved the show to Hollywood in November 1951, but it was hopeless.

There were no regulars other than host Sinatra during the second season.

FRANK SINATRA SHOW, THE (*Variety/Drama*)
FIRST TELECAST: *October 18, 1957*
LAST TELECAST: *June 27, 1958*
BROADCAST HISTORY:
Oct 1957–Jun 1958, ABC Fri 9:00–9:30
REGULARS:
Frank Sinatra
Nelson Riddle and His Orchestra

After his first, unsuccessful plunge into television in 1950–1952, singer-actor Frank Sinatra generally steered clear of the medium for several years. But despite the lack of success of his early variety show, he was considered a "hot property" and was actively sought for special appearances and another series of his own. His career in recording and movies had taken a considerable upturn in the mid-1950s, including his Academy Award for *From Here to Eternity.* Finally in 1957 he consented to do a regular weekly series for ABC, provided that he was given *carte blanche* to do it exactly as he wanted to. ABC paid $3 million for the honor of having him on its network.

What Sinatra had in mind was an unusual drama-plus-variety format, originally planned to include one-third variety shows, one-third dramas starring himself, and one-third dramas starring others, which he would host. Unfortunately he apparently approached the project with the attitude that all he had to do was appear, and TV success would be automatic. He rehearsed little, devoting most of his time to movies and other activities. The result was a disaster of the first magnitude, as *The Frank Sinatra Show* ran second or third in audience in its time period. Around December Sinatra buckled down to try to save the show. The number of musicals was increased, the show switched to filming before a live audience, and Sinatra himself began guesting on other shows to promote his program. Unfortunately it was too late.

Nelson Riddle, who had helped spark Sinatra's comeback on records with his imaginative arranging, was musical director on the variety episodes, whose guest stars included such names as Bob Hope, Peggy Lee, and the professional debut of Sinatra's daughter Nancy—aged 17—on November 1, 1957.

FRANK'S PLACE (*Situation Comedy*)
FIRST TELECAST: *September 14, 1987*
LAST TELECAST: *October 1, 1988*
BROADCAST HISTORY:
Sep 1987–Nov 1987, CBS Mon 8:00–8:30
Dec 1987–Feb 1988, CBS Mon 8:30–9:00
Feb 1988–Mar 1988, CBS Mon 9:30–10:00
Mar 1988, CBS Tue 8:00–8:30
Jul 1988–Oct 1988, CBS Sat 8:30–9:00
CAST:
Frank Parrish .... Tim Reid
Sy "Bubba" Weisburger .... Robert Harper
Hannah Griffin .... Daphne Maxwell Reid
Anna-May .... Francesca P. Roberts
Miss Marie .... Frances E. Williams
Mrs. Bertha Griffin-Lamour .... Virginia Capers
Big Arthur .... Tony Burton
Tiger Shepin .... Charles Lampkin
Reverend Deal .... Lincoln Kilpatrick
Cool Charles .... William Thomas, Jr.
Shorty La Roux .... Don Yesso
THEME:
"Do You Know What It Means to Miss New Orleans?," sung by Louis Armstrong.

One of the mellowest, most offbeat "comedies" of the 1980s, an easygoing mélange of eccentric characters set in a small Creole restaurant in New Orleans. Frank Parrish was not really cut out to run such a place. In fact, he had never been to New Orleans until he found out he had inherited Chez Louisiane from a father he had not seen since he was two years old. Raised in New England, and most recently a professor of Renaissance history in Boston, Frank had quite an adjustment to make—to New Orleans, to the restaurant business, and to a staff that at times resented him as an outsider and at other times tried to help him adjust to his new surroundings. The restaurant's staff included Big Arthur, the head chef; Shorty, the assistant chef; Tiger, the bartender; Anna-May, the head waitress; Miss Marie, the frail elderly "waitress emeritus"; and Cool Charles, the versatile handyman. The regulars at Chez Louisiane were Bubba Weisberger, a friendly lawyer; Reverend Deal, who appeared to be more con man than minister; Mrs. Griffin-Lamour, domineering owner of the neighborhood funeral parlor; and her beautiful daughter Hanna (played by star Tim Reid's real-life wife Daphne), a mortician and embalmer whose profession almost, but not quite, prevented Frank from becoming romantically involved with her.

Critics loved the rule-bending show, which offered no canned laughter, a slow, Dixieland-flavored musical background, and dramatic moments along with the comedy. Viewers were not so sure what to make of it.

FRANKIE LAINE TIME (*Musical Variety*)
FIRST TELECAST: *July 20, 1955*
LAST TELECAST: *September 19, 1956*
BROADCAST HISTORY:
Jul 1955–Sep 1955, CBS Wed 8:00–9:00
Aug 1956–Sep 1956, CBS Wed 8:00–9:00
REGULARS:
Frankie Laine
The Lynn Duddy Singers (1955)
The James Starbuck Dancers (1955)
The Jimmy Carroll Orchestra (1955)
The Mellolarks (1956)
The Edith Barstow Dancers (1956)
The Russ Case Orchestra (1956)

Popular singer Frankie Laine spent two summers on television as the replacement for *Arthur Godfrey and His Friends.* He sang, introduced, and performed with assorted guest stars, and acted in comedy sketches.

FRANNIE'S TURN (*Situation Comedy*)
FIRST TELECAST: *September 13, 1992*
LAST TELECAST: *October 10, 1992*
BROADCAST HISTORY:
Sep 1992, CBS Sun 8:00–8:30
Sep 1992–Oct 1992, CBS Sat 8:00–8:30
CAST:
Frannie Escobar .... Miriam Margolyes
Joseph Escobar .... Tomas Milian
Rosa Escobar .... Alice Drummond
Olivia Escobar (age 20) .... Phoebe Augustine
Eddie Escobar (18) .... Stivi Paskoski
Vivian .... LaTanya Richardson
Armando .... Taylor Negron
Father Anthony .... Dan Butler

Frannie Escobar was spunky and engaging but tired of being taken for granted by the men in her life—her husband, Joseph, a chauvinistic Cuban-American, and Armando, the insecure dress designer for whom she worked as a seamstress. The only person who seemed to understand her frustration was her mother-in-law, Rosa, not much of an endorsement since Rosa was on the border between eccentric and crazy. Adding to Frannie's anxiety was the fact that her daughter, Olivia, had fallen in love with a man who was as chauvinistic as her father. Eddie was Rosa's good-for-nothing high school son and Vivian a fellow seamstress and her best friend at work. Set on Staten Island, New York.

FRASIER (*Situation Comedy*)
FIRST TELECAST: *September 16, 1993*
LAST TELECAST:
BROADCAST HISTORY:
Sep 1993–Sep 1994, NBC Thu 9:30–10:00
Sep 1994–Sep 1998, NBC Tue 9:00–9:30
Jun 1998–Jul 1998, NBC Sun 9:00–9:30
Sep 1998–Jul 2000, NBC Thu 9:00–9:30
Jul 1999–Sep 1999, NBC Thu 9:30–10:00
Apr 2000–May 2000, NBC Thu 9:30–10:00
Jul 2000–Jul 2003, NBC Tue 9:00–9:30
May 2001–Jun 2001, NBC Tue 9:30–10:00
Jan 2002–May 2002, NBC Tue 8:00–8:30
May 2003– , NBC Thu 9:30–10:00
CAST:
Dr. Frasier Crane .... Kelsey Grammer
Dr. Niles Crane .... David Hyde Pierce
Martin Crane .... John Mahoney
Daphne Moon Crane .... Jane Leeves
Roz Doyle .... Peri Gilpin
Bob "Bulldog" Briscoe .... Dan Butler
**Gil Chesterton* .... Edward Hibbert
**Noel Shempsky* .... Patrick Kerr
**Kate Costas (1995–1996)* .... Mercedes Ruehl
**Sherry Dempsey (1996–1998)* ...... Marsha Mason
**Kenny Daly (1998–)* .... Tom McGowan
**Danny Douglas (1999–2000)* .... Saul Rubinek
**Dr. Melinda "Mel" Karnofsky Crane (1999–2000)*
.... Jane Adams

*Occasional

In this witty sequel to one of television's most famous shows, *Cheers'* neurotic psychiatrist Dr. Frasier Crane got off his Boston barstool, divorced his nagging wife, Lilith, and moved back to his hometown of Seattle to begin a new life, which turned out to be a lot like his old life, full of smart people who constantly deflated his pompousness. Frasier had a new job, hosting a radio advice show on KACL, and a striking, ultrachic apartment with a panoramic view of the Seattle skyline. Into this too orderly world came his psychiatrist brother, Niles, who was even fussier than he was, and his grumpy blue-collar dad, Martin, a retired cop. Martin was disabled (he had been shot in the line of duty) and came to live with Frasier, bringing his disgustingly tattered favorite chair and his small dog, Eddie, who simply sat and stared at Frasier. The three men argued constantly.

Smoothing the waters was Daphne, a cheerful—and seemingly psychic—English home-care worker and physical therapist who looked after Dad. Frasier's chief foils at the station were sensible Roz, his producer and call-screener (oh, those nutty calls!), and Bulldog, the macho sportscaster (*The Gonzo Sports Show*). Perhaps the funniest character in *Frasier* was not seen at all. Niles's rich, insufferable wife, Maris, was only spoken of or described as she moved off-camera, flaunting convention and sweeping lower classes of humanity before her. Niles, who lived with her in her family's preposterously ornate Gothic mansion, provided hilarious running commentary.

Others interacting with Frasier included Gil, the restaurant critic at the station, new station manager

Kate (with whom Fraser had an affair), and Martin's girlfriend Sherry, a barmaid at McGinty's Pub. Memorable guests included Frasier's conniving agent Bebe Glazer (Harriet Sansom Harris) and his school-age son Frederick (various actors). Several *Cheers* alumni dropped by: Shelley Long, Ted Danson, Woody Harrelson, and Bebe Neuwirth (Lilith). Real-life celebrities who did guest shots as callers to Frasier's show—literally phoning in their roles—included Mel Brooks (as a man who was traumatized because Santa left him a dead puppy), Art Garfunkel (who had so little to do that he agreed to stay on the line until tomorrow), Kevin Bacon (one of Roz's bad dates), Jane Pauley (who set someone's lawn on fire for not curbing their dog), Randy Travis (who couldn't fit into his evening gown), and Bob Costas (who asked a complicated basketball question).

Niles and Maris separated in early 1997, leading to a long estrangement and eventually a divorce, in which Niles's unseen skinnier-than-imaginable "ice princess" tried to bleed him dry. Niles longed for Daphne, who took his shy advances as friendly banter and didn't realize he truly loved her. All the principals actively dated, resulting in one calamity after another. In 1997, Roz became pregnant, giving birth in May 1998, just as Frasier cost the entire KACL crew their jobs by inadvertently convincing station management to switch to an all-Latin format (they were rehired after a few months).

Joining in later seasons were Kenny Daly, the new station manager, and Danny, Niles' scrappy lawyer. Mel was initially Frasier's girlfriend, but she subsequently eloped with Niles. Niles really loved Daphne, however, so he and Mel eventually divorced—though not until Mel had tormented him for months by making him engage in a "sham" marriage. Finally, during the 2000–2001 season, Niles and Daphne began dating and were engaged. The engagement was so long and complicated that in September 2002 they simply ran off to Reno and got married, to the dismay of parents and friends who wanted a formal wedding.

Frasier's and Niles' favorite hangout was the Café Nervosa. Eddie the dog was played by "Moose."

FRATERNITY LIFE (*Documentary*)

BROADCAST HISTORY:

MTV
30 minutes
Original episodes: *2003–*
Premiered: *February 26, 2003*

Another of MTV's many "reality" series snooping on teens and early twenty-somethings in their native habitats—this time a real college fraternity house. The first season followed the brothers of Sigma Chi Omega, a self-described "Animal House" at the State University of New York at Buffalo, as they judged rushees, sometimes brutally ("He comes off a little cocky"), consumed large amounts of beer, bonded and indulged petty jealousies. The show was in fact more about relationships than high jinks, and gave viewers a fairly realistic look at fraternity life. Spun off from MTV's *Sorority Life*.

FREAKS AND GEEKS (*Comedy/Drama*)

FIRST TELECAST: *September 25, 1999*
LAST TELECAST: *March 27, 2000*

BROADCAST HISTORY:

Sep 1999–Nov 1999, NBC Sat 8:00–9:00
Jan 2000–Mar 2000, NBC Mon 8:00–9:00

CAST:

Lindsay Weir .... Linda Cardellini
Sam Weir (age 14) .... John Daley
Neal Schweiber .... Samm Levine
Bill Haverchuck .... Martin Starr
Daniel Desario .... James Franco
Ken Miller .... Seth Rogen
Alan White .... Chauncey Leopardi
Nick Andopolis .... Jason Segel
Millie Kentner .... Sarah Hagan
Kim Kelly .... Busy Philipps
Cindy Sanders .... Natasha Melnick
Harris Trinsky .... Stephen Lee Sheppard
Gordon Crisp .... Jerry Messing
Harold Weir .... Joe Flaherty
Jean Weir .... Becky Ann Baker
Jeff Rosso .... Dave Allen
Mr. Kowchevski .... Steve Bannos

TV high school was never as painful, or as real, as in this acclaimed but low-rated series. The geeks at Michigan's William McKinley High School, circa 1980, were scrawny Sam, an undersized freshman runt who knew his place at the bottom of the social pecking order all too well, and pals Neal, a sci-fi fan who ran whenever trouble loomed, and Bill, a tall, intelligent-looking Bill Gates look-alike (with glasses) whose brain was actually mush. The bullying freaks, or school rebels, included rebellious Dan, sarcastic Ken, Sam's personal tormentor Alan, and Nick, a surprisingly good-hearted freak who was into drums and who sometimes actually listened to the geeks.

Lindsay was Sam's smart sister, a sophomore, who was caught between these two worlds. Uncertain about fitting in, she drifted away from her brainy friends, including childhood friend Millie, to hang with the cool crowd, especially Dan; Dan's snotty girlfriend Kim didn't like that one bit. Harold and Jean were Sam and Lindsay's overbearing parents, and there was a large cast of clueless and/or oppressive teachers, including laid-back guidance counselor Jeff and angry math teacher Mr. Kowchevski. In an inspired bit of stunt casting, also seen occasionally were *Mystery Science Theater 3000*'s Trace Beaulieu (as Mr. Hector Lacovara) and Joel Hodgson (in various roles). Although the series ended its regular run in March 2000, three additional original episodes were telecast on July 8.

FREAKYLINKS (*Supernatural*)

FIRST TELECAST: *October 6, 2000*
LAST TELECAST: *June 22, 2001*

BROADCAST HISTORY:

Oct 2000–Nov 2000, FOX Fri 9:00–10:00
Jan 2001, FOX Fri 9:00–10:00
Jun 2001, FOX Fri 9:00–10:00

CAST:

Derek Barnes .... Ethan Embry
Chloe Tanner .... Lisa Sheridan
Jason Tatum .... Karim Prince
Lan Williams .... Lizette Carrion
Vince Elsing .... Dennis Christopher

Adam Barnes had set up a Web site called occultresearch.com to post information about paranormal incidents, using his twin brother, Derek, a surfer-dude type, as his legman to track down information. One day Derek returned to his brother's big old Victorian house and found Adam drowned in the bathtub. Was it really suicide? Taking over the site, Derek renamed it FreakyLinks and, three years later, was still investigating the paranormal while trying to find out the truth about his brother's death. Lan, a computer-savvy chick with a master's in computer science from Berkeley, worked on the Web site, while Jason, a rather goofy cool cat who happened to have a Harvard law degree, was the cameraman. Also seen were Adam's fiancée, Chloe, a psychiatrist who reluctantly helped them, and Vince, a patient/prophet in a psychiatric hospital who may have held the answer to the mystery of Adam's death.

Derek told his Web site viewers, "The FreakyLinks team is determined to uncover the truth behind the strange and unusual. To answer the questions that have no answers and to take you with us." When they investigated stories they found in the media, or assisted people who came to them for help, they generally documented their activities with a video camera—cinema verité style—and posted it as streaming video on the Web site.

At the end of January, threatened with the loss of her license to practice, Chloe told the others she would have to quit working with them. *FreakyLinks* was then pulled from the schedule but, when it returned in the summer, Chloe had been fined almost $10,000 by the psychiatric board and was under investigation. With the aid of a client they had helped, the gang convinced the board to uphold her license—and the client paid her fine.

FRED ASTAIRE PREMIERE THEATER, syndicated title for *Alcoa Premiere*

FRED WARING SHOW, THE (*Musical Variety*)

FIRST TELECAST: *April 17, 1949*
LAST TELECAST: *May 30, 1954*
BROADCAST HISTORY:
Apr 1949–Jan 1952, CBS Sun 9:00–10:00 (OS)
Jan 1952–May 1954, CBS Sun 9:00–9:30 (OS)
REGULARS:
Fred Waring and His Pennsylvanians
THEME:
"Sleep" by Earl Lebieg

Fred Waring, and his orchestra and large chorus, had been an American institution for several decades when he first entered TV on a regular basis in 1949. Slotted right after the high-rated Ed Sullivan *Toast of the Town,* he quickly became a Sunday night standby. The entire Waring organization made up the regular TV cast of more than 60 members. In addition to standard instrumental and vocal numbers, the show included dancing (during the 1949–1950 season there was a dance contest titled "Video Ballroom" as a regular feature); sketch material that was musically related; and interpretations of fairy tales. Although all the members of the Pennsylvanians had solos at one time or another during the show's five-year run, those most frequently spotlighted were Jane Wilson, Joanna Wheatley, Joe Marine, Daisy Bernier, Keith and Sylvia Textor, Hugh "Uncle Lumpy" Brannum, Virginia Morley and Livingston Gearhart, and Poley McClintock (with whom Fred had founded his first band in 1915).

The Fred Waring Show was performed before a live studio audience during its first and last seasons, and without a live audience for the three seasons in between. In its last season it was cut back to alternate-week status, with *G.E. Theatre* airing on the alternate Sundays.

FREDDY MARTIN SHOW, THE (*Musical Variety*)

FIRST TELECAST: *July 12, 1951*
LAST TELECAST: *November 28, 1951*
BROADCAST HISTORY:
Jul 1951–Aug 1951, NBC Thu 10:00–10:30
Sep 1951–Nov 1951, NBC Wed 10:30–11:00
REGULARS:
Freddy Martin and His Orchestra
Merv Griffin
Murray Arnold
The Martin Men

Saxophone player and orchestra leader Freddy Martin was the star of this musical variety show, which featured, in addition to a guest female vocalist each week, the Freddy Martin Orchestra, a young male vocalist named Merv Griffin (later to have great success as a talk-show host), pianist Murray Arnold, and the Martin Men, a vocal quintet. Sponsored by Hazel Bishop cosmetics, this series was also known as *The Hazel Bishop Show.*

FREDDY'S NIGHTMARES (*Horror Anthology*)

BROADCAST HISTORY:
Syndicated only
60 minutes
Produced: *1988–1990* (44 episodes)
Released: *October 1988*
HOST:
Robert Englund (as *Freddy Krueger*)

The mythical town of Springwood was the setting for this anthology. Each episode featured people who, whether they were good or evil, were having nightmares—nightmares in which they died horrible and/or bizarre deaths. Unfortunately for them, all too often the nightmares came true. One thing which set *Freddy's Nightmares* apart from similar anthologies was that most of the episodes were structured like two-part stories, in which one of the survivors from the first part became a victim in the second part. During the first season, the featured performers were primarily young and unknown, with some more familiar faces—Tony Dow, Sheree North, David L. Lander, and Mary Crosby among them—showing up the following year.

Loosely based on the highly successful theatrical *Nightmare on Elm Street* movies and hosted by the star of the theatrical films, the maniacal Freddy Krueger.

FREE COUNTRY (*Situation Comedy*)

FIRST TELECAST: *June 24, 1978*
LAST TELECAST: *July 22, 1978*
BROADCAST HISTORY:
Jun 1978–Jul 1978, ABC Sat 8:00–8:30
CAST:
Joseph Bresner........................ Rob Reiner
Anna Bresner......................... Judy Kahan
Sidney Gewertzman.............. Fred McCarren
Ida Gewertzman.................... Renee Lippin
Leo Gold............................. Larry Gelman
Louis Peschi....................... Joe Pantoliano

Rob Reiner assumed the dual role of a young Lithuanian immigrant, and the same man at age 89, in this summer series. Reiner opened each episode as the elderly Joseph Bresner, reminiscing about the days when he was a young man newly arrived in the U.S.A. The scene then shifted to New York City's Lower East Side in the early 1900s, where Joseph and his bride Anna struggled to understand the customs of their adopted homeland. Ida and Sidney Gewertzman were their neighbors, Louis was a friend, and Leo Gold a boarder. Rob Reiner was co-writer and coproducer of this series, as well as its star.

FREE SPIRIT (*Situation Comedy*)
FIRST TELECAST: *September 22, 1989*
LAST TELECAST: *January 14, 1990*
BROADCAST HISTORY:
Sep 1989, ABC Fri 9:30–10:00
Sep 1989–Jan 1990, ABC Sun 8:00–8:30
Jan 1990, ABC Sun 8:30–9:00
CAST:
Winnie (The Witch) Goodwinn ..... Corinne Bohrer
Thomas J. Harper ..... Franc Luz
Robb Harper (age 16) ..... Paul Scherrer
Jessie Harper (13) ..... Alyson Hannigan
Gene Harper (10) ..... Edan Gross

Did you ever wish for a special friend? Feeling neglected by his busy father, 10-year-old Gene did—and up popped a young, pretty witch, assigned by the boss warlock in the sky. Winnie looked like a refugee from the '60s, with her long stringy hair and funky clothes, but she was just what the Harpers needed. To single dad Thomas, a divorced attorney who worked out of their Connecticut home, she was the slightly off-center housekeeper. Only the kids knew she had magical powers. Need an egg for breakfast? Poof—there's a bunch of hens cackling in the kitchen cabinet. Can't get tickets to a rock concert? Poof—two tickets pop up in the toaster. Does Jessie's date act like a cad? Poof—he's a monkey. Wow! Neat! Canceled!

FREEBIE AND THE BEAN (*Police*)
FIRST TELECAST: *December 6, 1980*
LAST TELECAST: *January 17, 1981*
BROADCAST HISTORY:
Dec 1980–Jan 1981, CBS Sat 9:00–10:00
CAST:
Det. Sgt. Tim Walker (Freebie) ..... Tom Mason
Det. Sgt. Dan Delgado (Bean) ..... Hector Elizondo
DA Walter W. Cruikshank ..... William Daniels
Rodney Blake ("Axle") ..... Mel Stewart

Freebie and the Bean were two plainclothes police officers working on special assignments for San Francisco District Attorney Walter Cruikshank. As a team, the two seemed totally mismatched. Freebie was a swinging single, always looking for angles and not above bending the law a little to help their investigations. Bean was introverted and serious, a family man with a wife and two children who believed in doing things more or less "by the book." They were often in conflict, with Freebie usually convincing the Bean that his way would work. It just seemed that every time Bean let himself get talked into one of Freebie's off-the-wall plans, *he* wound up on the short end. Their unorthodox methods, and history of destroying police property (mostly cars in wild chases), did not endear them to the DA, but they got results, and that's what counted. Axle was the mechanic at the police garage who had the unenviable task of trying to salvage the cars they used in the chases.

Unfortunately this series was such a mishmash of comedy and drama, slapstick and reality, that it soon sank without a trace. The fact that it was scheduled opposite ABC's *The Love Boat*—which had no trouble defining what *it* wanted to be—probably didn't help. *Freebie and the Bean* was based on the 1974 movie of the same name, starring James Caan and Alan Arkin.

FREEDOM (*Military Drama*)
FIRST TELECAST: *October 27, 2000*
LAST TELECAST: *January 5, 2001*
BROADCAST HISTORY:
Oct 2000–Jan 2001, UPN Fri 8:00–9:00
CAST:
Capt. Owen Decker ..... Holt McCallany
Lt. Becca Shaw ..... Scarlett Chorvat
Sgt. 1st Class Londo Pearl ..... Bodhi Elfman
Sgt. James Barrett ..... Darius McCrary
Col. Timothy Devon ..... James Morrison
Jin ..... Françoise Yip

As the voice-over introduction to *Freedom* intoned, "War broke out in the Middle East. Domestic terrorism got out of control. The president tirelessly toured the country, urging patience and calm. Then Air Force One went down, and the president was presumed dead. Martial law was declared, and the United States of America was turned, overnight, into a police state. Curfews were enforced. Identity papers were required for all. Penalties for unlawful behavior were harsh and certain. And it worked, too, for a time. The riots stopped. Everyone had food, water, and power. Stability and peace were returned to the country. But it was peace without freedom. And that was a price some of us would not pay."

Decker and three people he had befriended while jailed in the William Jefferson Clinton Federal Penitentiary—Shaw, Pearl and Barrett—were freed by The Resistance, a group fighting to overthrow the military junta that had effectively taken over the United States, and restore freedom to the nation. General Walter Young (Georg Stanford Brown), head of the Joint Chiefs of Staff, had wanted to return the country to its elected officials after things had stabilized, but the other members of the Joint Chiefs wouldn't let go. Somehow they had transformed U.S. troops into snarling, thuggish Nazis who maintained an iron grip on the country. Young became head of The Resistance and recruited Decker and the others to rescue his wife and two kids from the devious Colonel Devon. The team rescued them and Decker almost killed Devon, but restrained himself because Devon knew where Decker's own son was being held. The team then became full-time members of The Resistance, performing rescues and waging guerrilla warfare on the military government with ingenuity and flying high kicks. Jin was a member of The Resistance who sometimes worked with them.

FRESH PRINCE OF BEL AIR (*Situation Comedy*)
FIRST TELECAST: *September 10, 1990*
LAST TELECAST: *September 9, 1996*
BROADCAST HISTORY:
Sep 1990–Jun 1995, NBC Mon 8:00–8:30
Jun 1995–Jul 1995, NBC Mon 8:00–9:00

Jul 1995–May 1996, NBC Mon 8:00–8:30
May 1996–Sep 1996, NBC Mon 8:00–9:00

CAST:

Will Smith .... Will Smith
Philip Banks .... James Avery
Vivian Banks (1990–1993) ... Janet Hubert-Whitten
Vivian Banks (1993–1996) .. Daphne Maxwell Reid
Carlton Banks..................... Alfonso Ribeiro
Hilary Banks .... Karyn Parsons
Ashley Banks....................... Tatyana M. Ali
Nicholas "Nicky" Banks (1994–1996).. Ross Bagley
Geoffrey, the butler................ Joseph Marcell
**Jazz (1990–1994)*....... Jeff Townes (D.J. Jazzy Jeff)
**Jackie Ames (1993–1994)* .... Tyra Banks
**Lisa (1994–1995)* .... Nia Long

*Occasional

A black rapper from a tough neighborhood found himself deposited in a cartoonish sitcom in this rather funky comedy co-produced by musician Quincy Jones. Will was the kid from West Philadelphia who was sent west to live with wealthy relatives in Bel Air, California, when things got a little too dangerous in the 'hood. To groovin' Will, Uncle Philip and his stuck-up clan at first seemed like a travesty on upwardly mobile blacks. They lived in a preposterously ornate mansion, spoke in oh-so-refined language, and even had a liveried butler, Geoffrey. But the pompous Philip, an attorney, could tell Will a thing or two about the black experience when the occasion demanded; and Geoffrey, despite his imperious manner, was a surprising ally. Carlton was the preppy son, Hilary, the spoiled-brat teenage daughter, and Ashley, the youngest—with whom Will hit it off immediately. Sensible Aunt Vivian mediated as required.

Amid the comedy of clashing cultures, viewers were regularly offered morals, sometimes rather explicit, about the difficulties faced by blacks in a white society. Will's friend Jazz (among others) periodically brought a little soul to the Banks mansion, as well as to exclusive Bel Air Academy, where Will would never quite fit in.

Will Smith, who played the title role with infectious enthusiasm, was a real-life rap star. He and his partner Jeff Townes ("D.J. Jazzy Jeff and the Fresh Prince") won a Grammy Award for their 1988 hit "Parents Just Don't Understand." Mercifully the rap content in the series was confined to the credits, but a good deal of black music still found its way into episodes. Especially when Will wanted to loosen up those bros.

The 1993–1994 season brought a number of changes. Will and Carlton graduated from prep school and enrolled together at the University of Los Angeles while sharing the pool house as their bachelor pad. At the same time Jackie, Will's ex-girlfriend from Philadelphia, showed up to complicate his life. At home, Aunt Vivian gave birth to her fourth child, Nicky, who joined the cast full-time the following season (already five years old!). Also in 1994–1995 Ashley became a singer and Will found a new girlfriend, Lisa; after a whirlwind courtship they were nearly married in 1995.

In the series finale Uncle Philip put the mansion up for sale, and after showing it to several prospective buyers, including Mr. Drummond and Arnold of *Diff'rent Strokes* (Conrad Bain and Gary Coleman), sold it to George and Louise Jefferson of *The Jeffersons* (Sherman Hemsley and Isabel Sanford; Marla Gibbs also showed up as Florence). Everyone moved on to bigger things except Will, who seemed to be "stuck on the soft shoulder of life."

FRESHMAN DORM (*Drama*)

FIRST TELECAST: *August 11, 1992*
LAST TELECAST: *September 9, 1992*
BROADCAST HISTORY:

Aug 1992, CBS Tue 9:00–10:00
Aug 1992–Sep 1992, CBS Wed 8:00–9:00

CAST:

Danny Foley .... Matthew Fox
Molly Flynn .... Robyn Lively
K.C. Richards (nee Kamala Consuelo Ricardo)
.... Arlene Taylor
Lulu Abercrombie.................. Paige French
Zack Taylor .... Casper Van Dien
Alex Woods......................... Kevin Mambo
Joe Ellis............................ Justin Lazard
Cynthia .... Lisa Fuller
Neal............................... Richard Israel

This summer series focused on a group of beautiful young college freshmen living and loving in a coed dormitory at fictional Western Pacific University in Southern California. Molly, a theater major who wanted to become an actress, had enrolled to be with her boyfriend, Danny, who had gotten an athletic scholarship to WPU. After she moved in with him their relationship fell apart, and, though still friends, they went their separate ways. K.C., a lower-class Hispanic girl from Los Angeles on a financial aid scholarship, was ashamed of her modest background. She created a facade to get into the fancy Kappa sorority and was working as a waitress to pay some of the costs. Others in the dorm were Lulu, a pretty, spoiled rich girl from New York, used to getting anything she wanted; Zack, a free-spirited surfer with minimal interest in his studies; Alex, Zack's studious black roommate; and Joe, the new campus hunk.

Based on the *Freshman Dorm* books by Linda Alper Cooney and Kevin Cooney, which presumably had little more substance than this short-run series.

FRIDAY COMEDY SPECIAL, THE (*Comedy Anthology*)

FIRST TELECAST: *March 14, 1975*
LAST TELECAST: *May 23, 1975*
BROADCAST HISTORY:

Mar 1975–May 1975, CBS Fri 8:00–8:30

The situation comedies telecast in this series were a collection of unsold pilots for projected regular series.

FRIDAY NIGHT VIDEOS (*Music*)

FIRST TELECAST: *July 29, 1983*
LAST TELECAST: *December 29, 2000*
BROADCAST HISTORY:

Jul 1983–Jun 1987, NBC Fri 12:30–2:00 A.M.
Jun 1987–Aug 1991, NBC Fri 1:30–2:30 A.M.
Sep 1991–Dec 2000, NBC Fri 1:35–2:35 A.M.

ANNOUNCER (OFF CAMERA):

Nick Michaels (1983–1985)
Scott Muni (1985)
Frankie Crocker (1990–1995)

REGULARS:

Henry Cho (1994–1996)

Rita Sever (1994–2000)

This late-night series was NBC's (limited) answer to the considerable popularity of cable TV's MTV (Music Television) network. Like MTV, *Friday Night Videos* consisted primarily of the latest rock music videos, most of them by currently hot artists such as Culture Club, the Police, John Cougar Mellencamp, Styx, Quarterflash, and Paul McCartney. Mixed in were "Hall of Fame Videos" by stars of the 1960s and 1970s (the Beatles, Hollies, Doors, etc.); "Private Reel," a profile of a major star; and "Video Vote," in which viewers got to vote for one of two selected videos, using nationwide 900-numbers. On the series' premiere, Duran Duran's "Hungry Like the Wolf" trounced David Bowie's "Let's Dance" by 59,000 to 37,000 calls. On later telecasts the combined vote ran as high as 200,000 calls. A highlight of each show was a "World Premiere Video," the first network showing of a major artist's clip. The program got banner ratings in December 1983 when it premiered Michael Jackson's million-dollar "Thriller" video under this heading.

Initially there was no on-camera host or announcer for *Friday Night Videos*, with the songs being introduced by off-camera announcers. However a policy of on-camera celebrity guests was begun in the fall of 1985; among those hosting were stars of currently popular TV series (Phylicia Rashad, Lisa Bonet, Harry Anderson, Susan Saint James, Tony Danza, Michael Warren, etc.), movie actors, and some singers (Whitney Houston, Stevie Wonder).

Major changes took place in November 1990 as the series dramatically increased its comedy content. Five hip young comics were added doing weekly segments: Judy Tenuta ("Goddess of Gossip"), Richard Belzer ("Ask the Belz"), Kim Coles ("Girl Talk"), Tom Kenny ("Music News"), and James Stephens III ("Rapitorials"). Live musical performances were also added. Frankie Crocker, a well-known rhythm and blues disc jockey, became the regular announcer. During the 1990s various personalities served as host for multiple telecasts, sometimes remaining for several months. Among them were comic Tom Kenny, announcer Frankie Crocker (who also hosted "Frankie Crocker's Journal," about important dates in rock history), Darryl Bell, and Branford Marsalis. In 1994 the name of the series was shortened to *Friday Night*. Correspondent Henry Cho served as host in 1995–1996, succeeded by Rita Sever in the fall of 1996.

FRIDAY THE 13TH (*Horror/Drama*)

BROADCAST HISTORY:

Syndicated only

30 minutes

Produced: *1987–1990* (78 episodes)

Released: *October 1987*

CAST:

Micki Foster .... (Louise) Robey

Ryan Dallion (1987–1989).......... John D. Le May

Jack Marshak...................... Chris Wiggins

Johnny Ventura (1989–1990) .... Steven Monarque

Lewis Vendredi was an antiques dealer who had made a deal with the devil to sell cursed antiques in return for material wealth. When Lewis died, his niece Micki inherited the antique store, which she renamed "Curious Goods." With the help of her cousin Ryan and their partner, retired magician Jack Marshak, Micki attempted to recover the cursed antiques and seal them away in the basement under the store so that they could cause no more damage. The antiques they recovered always seemed to cause deaths—for example, a scalpel that could work miracles on the living, but only after it had been used to kill someone; and a cupid's statue that compelled women to fall in love with the owner but made him kill them after making love.

When *Friday the 13th* returned for the 1989–1990 season, Ryan was no longer around. He had been replaced by Johnny Ventura, a friend of Micki's who helped her and Jack recover the seemingly endless supply of cursed antiques.

Although this TV series used the title of a very popular series of horror movies—and was even advertised as "Friday the 13th—The Series"—it actually had nothing to do with the movies.

FRIDAYS (*Comedy/Variety*)

FIRST TELECAST: *April 11, 1980*

LAST TELECAST: *October 22, 1982*

BROADCAST HISTORY:

Apr 1980–Mar 1981, ABC Fri 11:30–12:40 A.M.

Apr 1981–Sep 1981, ABC Fri 12:00–1:10 A.M.

Sep 1981–Oct 1982, ABC Fri 12:00–1:40 A.M.

REGULARS:

Mark Blankfield

Maryedith Burrell

Melanie Chartoff

Larry David

Darrow Igus

Brandis Kemp

Bruce Mahler

Michael Richards

John Roarke

ABC's answer to NBC's *Saturday Night Live*—in fact, an out-and-out carbon copy of *Saturday Night Live*—was this live late-night program called *Fridays*. As on the prototype, there was a rambunctious cast of bright young comedians, heavy emphasis on satirical and sometimes raunchy humor, rock musicians as guests, and even a "Weekend Update"-style parody newscast. A guest host presided each week.

Some of the early sketches were so gross, in fact, that a number of network affiliates dropped the show. Among the offensive bits were a skit called "Diner of the Living Dead," in which the actors ate human flesh, and another entitled "Women Who Spit." Later things got a bit more sophisticated, with one of the highlights being an elaborate, 17-minute musical comedy satirizing the cult film *The Rocky Horror Show* (called "The Ronny Horror Show," and starring a mock President Reagan). John Roarke's Reagan was a regular feature, as was Mark Blankfield's speed-freak pharmacist, Larry David's rabbi, Bruce Mahler's Spanish announcer, and the "Rasta Chef" of Darrow Igus (the only black in the cast). A certain cynical commercialism remained, however, as when an apparently real on-camera fistfight between guest star Andy Kaufman and one of the show's producers turned out to have been staged to generate publicity.

The young repertory company was hardworking and inventive, and some of the writing (supervised by Jack Burns of *The Muppet Show*) was first-rate, but the program's reputation as a rip-off and its failure to provide an attention-getting new star (like Chevy Chase in *Saturday Night Live*'s first season) hindered its chances of becoming the breakthrough hit the earlier program had been.

FRIEND OR FOE (*Quiz*)

BROADCAST HISTORY:

Game Show Network
30 minutes
Original episodes: *2002–*
Premiered: *June 3, 2002*

EMCEE:

Kennedy

This game was designed to see how much a team of contestants trusted each other. In the first round three contestants picked three partners. The teams were then given four multiple-choice questions in fields such as popular culture, word definitions and geography, with each correct answer worth $500. The lowest-scoring team was eliminated. The second round was played similarly, with correct answers worth $1,000, while in the third round the last surviving team could win as much as $20,000.

The trust part came at the end of each round, as the two members of the eliminated team determined how to split their winnings. Each team member put his or her hands in a "trust box," which concealed a button. Not pushing the button indicated "friend," while pushing it meant "foe." If both indicated they were friends, they split the money; if one was a foe, the foe got everything; if both pushed foe, neither got anything.

The emcee, Kennedy (full name Lisa Kennedy Montgomery), was a curt, rather sarcastic young woman with long hair and glasses, formerly known for her appearances on MTV.

FRIENDS (*Comedy/Drama*)

FIRST TELECAST: *March 25, 1979*
LAST TELECAST: *April 22, 1979*

BROADCAST HISTORY:

Mar 1979–Apr 1979, ABC Sun 7:00–8:00

CAST:

Pete Richards .... Charles Aiken
Nancy Wilks .... Jill Whelan
Randy Summerfield .... Jarrod Johnson
Mr. Frank Richards .... Andy Romano
Mrs. Pamela Richards .... Karen Morrow
Cynthia Richards .... Alicia Fleer
Mr. Charley Wilks .... Dennis Redfield
Mr. Warren Summerfield .... Roger Robinson
Mrs. Jane Summerfield .... Janet MacLachlan

Supercute comedy-drama about life as seen through the eyes of three 11-year-olds from different backgrounds: Pete; Nancy, from a broken home; and Randy, a black youth and son of a lawyer. All about dating, learning to succeed, the meaning of friendship, etc.

FRIENDS (*Situation Comedy*)

FIRST TELECAST: *September 22, 1994*
LAST TELECAST:

BROADCAST HISTORY:

Sep 1994–Feb 1995, NBC Thu 8:30–9:00
Feb 1995–Aug 1995, NBC Thu 9:30–10:00
Aug 1995– , NBC Thu 8:00–8:30
Nov 1999, NBC Mon 8:00–8:30
Apr 2002–May 2002, NBC Thu 8:30–9:00

CAST:

Monica Geller Bing .... Courteney Cox
Rachel Green .... Jennifer Aniston
Ross Geller .... David Schwimmer
Chandler Bing .... Matthew Perry
Joey Tribbiani .... Matt LeBlanc
Phoebe Buffay .... Lisa Kudrow
**Jack Geller* .... Elliott Gould
**Judy Geller* .... Christina Pickles
**Carol Geller* .... Jane Sibbett
**Susan Bunch* .... Jessica Hecht
**Dr. Richard Burke (1996–1997)* .... Tom Selleck
**Emily Waltham Geller (1997–1998)* .... Helen Baxendale
**Gunther (1995–)* .... James Michael Tyler

*Occasional

THEME:

"I'll Be There for You"

This easygoing, unremarkable series about six bright, good-looking twenty-somethings in New York City simply hanging out and having a good time hit the spot with viewers in the stressed-out nineties. Monica was the unofficial den mother, a gorgeous young woman who just couldn't seem to find Mr. Right. She worked as an assistant chef but seemed to spend most of her time with the gang. Rachel, her best friend since high school, had dumped her fiancé at the altar (along with daddy's credit cards) and was now trying to make it on her own, starting as a waitress. Ross, a museum paleontologist, was Monica's goofy brother, whose pregnant wife Carol had left him when she decided she was a lesbian; struggling actor Joey, the cute Italian guy who lived across the hall; corporate number-cruncher Chandler, Joey's roommate and the group's resident clown; and Phoebe, a ditsy, waiflike folk singer who was into New Age "auras." They all hung out at Monica's apartment or at Greenwich Village's Central Perk coffeehouse and talked about love, sex, feelings, dates, lack of dates, the prospect of dates, and other matters of importance in their lives.

In 1995, Carol gave birth to a son, Ben, and Ross had to come to terms with his child being raised by Carol and her companion Susan. Ross then had an affair with Rachel (now a fashion buyer for a retail chain), for whom he had nursed a long-term crush, and when that ended disastrously he abruptly married British sourpuss Emily, in England in May 1998. Their wedding brought its own calamity, however, when Ross inadvertently blurted out Rachel's name during the ceremony, souring the newlyweds' relationship. They later divorced. Monica's most notable relationship during this period was with an older man, dentist Richard, but during Ross's wedding in 1998 she and affable Chandler became hot and heavy. They subsequently had a clandestine affair, which was discovered by their friends, one by one, during Fall 1998. Meanwhile, cheerful Phoebe agreed to become a surrogate mother for her half-brother Frank (Giovanni Ribisi) and his wife, and in October 1998 bore them triplets. She wanted to keep one—just one—but they declined.

At the end of the 1998–1999 season Ross and Rachel married during a reckless weekend in Las Vegas, but a few weeks into the next season decided it had been a drunken mistake and got a divorce. In May 2000 Chandler proposed to Monica, and a year later they were married. Rachel, who by this time was working for a fashion designer, restarted her off-and-on relationship with Ross and found herself pregnant with his baby. She gave birth to baby Emma in May 2002, and she and Ross moved in together to raise their child, although they decided not to remarry. Meanwhile actor Joey had found a regular role on the soap opera *Days of Our Lives*, where among other things he played a man with a woman's brain.

FRIENDS OF MAN (*Documentary*)

BROADCAST HISTORY:

Syndicated only
30 minutes
Produced: *1973–1974* (45 episodes)
Released: *Fall 1975*

NARRATOR:

Glenn Ford

This documentary series about animals as the "friends of man" was aimed primarily at younger viewers.

FRIENDS OR LOVERS (*Audience Participation*)

BROADCAST HISTORY:

USA Network
30 minutes
Original episodes: *2000*
Premiered: *March 27, 2000*

HOST:

Andi Matheny

Contestants had to choose between their best friend and their lover on this confrontational show. For example, a guy would appear with his best male friend, and the friend would tell him his girlfriend was ruining his life and cheating on him; the girlfriend would then join and rebut the friend's claims—or, if caught, confess on the "truth pillow" and ask forgiveness. At the end the guy would decide who to believe and take on an expense-paid vacation. There was a lot of yelling, gesturing and snarky jokes, along with some uncomfortable revelations; on one show a boyfriend was exposed as a recovering drug addict, but his girlfriend sobbed and agreed to stay with him. Presiding over this rowdy psychodrama was a suitably trampy Andi Matheny.

FRIGIDAIRE SUMMER THEATER (*Dramatic Anthology*)

FIRST TELECAST: *June 20, 1958*
LAST TELECAST: *August 1, 1958*
BROADCAST HISTORY:

Jun 1958–Aug 1958, ABC Fri 9:30–10:00

This program was a collection of filmed reruns of episodes from other anthology series.

FROM A BIRD'S EYE VIEW (*Situation Comedy*)

FIRST TELECAST: *March 29, 1971*
LAST TELECAST: *August 16, 1971*
BROADCAST HISTORY:

Mar 1971–Aug 1971, NBC Mon 7:30–8:00

CAST:

Millie Grover .... Millicent Martin
Maggie Ralston .... Pat Finley
Mr. Clive Beauchamp .... Peter Jones
Uncle Bert Quigley .... Robert Cawdron
Miss Fosdyke .... Noel Hood

The misadventures of two young stewardesses for an international airline based in London, England. Britisher Millie was so good-natured and well-meaning that she could never resist helping people. Every time she tried to help, however, something went wrong, and the more she tried to straighten things out, the more complicated they became. Maggie, her level-headed American friend, spent most of her time trying to get Millie out of her predicaments. Also featured was the girls' boss, Mr. Beauchamp, a harassed middle-management executive for the airline.

FROM HERE TO ETERNITY (*War Drama*)

FIRST TELECAST: *February 14, 1979*
LAST TELECAST: *August 16, 1980*
BROADCAST HISTORY:

Feb 1979, NBC Wed 9:00–11:00
Mar 1980–Apr 1980, NBC Wed 10:00–11:00
Aug 1980, NBC Various times

CAST:

Master Sgt. Milt Warden .... William Devane
Karen Holmes (1979) .... Natalie Wood
Karen Holmes (1980) .... Barbara Hershey
Pvt. Robert E. Lee Prewitt (1979) .... Steve Railsback
Capt./Maj. Dana Holmes .... Roy Thinnes
Pvt. Angelo Maggio (1979) .... Joe Pantoliano
Lorene Rogers .... Kim Basinger
Sgt. Cheney .... Will Sampson
Mrs. Kipfer (1979) .... Salome Jens
Lt./Capt. Ross .... David Spielberg
Fatso Judson (1979) .... Peter Boyle
Jefferson Davis Prewitt (1980) .... Don Johnson
Pfc. Ignacio Carmona (1980) ..... Rocky Echevarria
Emily Austin (1980) .... Lacey Neuhaus
Lt. Kenneth Barrett (1980) .... John Calvin
Mrs. Austin (1980) .... Priscilla Pointer
Mr. Austin (1980) .... Richard Roat
Dr. Anne Brewster (1980) .... Claire Malis
Aimee (1980) .... Joann Gordon
Kurt Von Nordlund (1980) .... Richard Erdman

James Jones's classic novel first came to television as a six-hour mini-series in the spring of 1979. *From Here to Eternity* was a story of World War II military life on Hawaii in 1941, prior to and just after the Japanese attack on Pearl Harbor. Sgt. Milt Warden was faced with two problems. He was having a torrid love affair with his commanding officer's wife, Karen Holmes; and he was trying to instill confidence in Pvt. Robert Prewitt, a sensitive young man in his unit, whose lack of aggression caused him to be ridiculed by the other men. The mini-series generally followed the lengthy Jones novel more accurately than did the 1953 theatrical movie version starring Burt Lancaster and Deborah Kerr.

The ratings success of the mini-series prompted NBC to introduce a regular weekly series that took up where the novel left off. It took place in Honolulu during 1942, with the city under martial law following the Japanese attack. Sgt. Warden was still having his affair with Karen, but now had to deal with Robert

Prewitt's brother Jefferson. (The AWOL Robert had been killed while trying to return to base on Warden's advice.) Jefferson Prewitt became romantically involved with Lorene Rogers, the prostitute who had been Robert's girlfriend, and eventually married her. Meanwhile Warden and Maj. Holmes had a showdown over Holmes's treatment of his wife, after which Warden suffered a minor heart attack. Karen Holmes thereupon left Honolulu to spend the duration of the war on the U.S. mainland.

This weekly soap opera drew few viewers, and was abruptly pulled from the schedule after less than a month. The resolution of the story, as described here, did not take place until August 1980, when the remaining original episodes were aired as specials.

FRONT PAGE (*Newsmagazine*)

FIRST TELECAST: *June 26, 1993*
LAST TELECAST: *April 26, 1994*
BROADCAST HISTORY:
Jun 1993–Jan 1994, FOX Sat 9:00–10:00
Feb 1994–Apr 1994, FOX Tue 9:00–10:00
CORRESPONDENTS:
Andria Hall
Tony Harris
Vicki Liviakis
Josh Mankiewicz
Ron Reagan

Front Page was a topical newsmagazine that featured three or four major stories on each weekly episode. Among the stories featured were a telemarketing scheme to bilk the elderly with phony production limited partnerships, teenagers getting plastic surgery, a man in Utah who couldn't develop his property because of a threat to an endangered species of snail, loggers affected by protection of spotted owls, the tough job market for college grads in a recessionary economy, and kids using spray cans to spread graffiti across major cities.

There were two things that distinguished *Front Page* from other magazines—the use of its five correspondents as weekly hosts on a rotating basis and the short commentaries that were aired before and after major stories. Among the most frequently seen commentators were Chris Matthews of the *San Francisco Examiner* and Norman Chad of *The Washington Post* on political issues, Mike Lupica with his "New York Minute," Joe Bob Briggs on "Family Values," and Lisa Birnbach.

FRONT PAGE, THE (*Newspaper Drama*)

FIRST TELECAST: *September, 29, 1949*
LAST TELECAST: *January 26, 1950*
BROADCAST HISTORY:
Sep 1949–Jan 1950, CBS Thu 8:00–8:30
CAST:
Walter Burns .... John Daly
Hildy Johnson .... Mark Roberts

Adapted from the famous Hecht-MacArthur play about a small-town newspaper editor and his star reporter, Hildy Johnson. The love-hate relationship between the two of them was the focal point of the story, as Hildy was always threatening to quit the *Center City Examiner* to find "a normal job." Despite what they said about each other, however, Walter and Hildy were loyal friends. The John Daly in this live series was the same person who worked for CBS and later ABC as a news correspondent. It was felt that his actual journalistic experience would give this dramatic role a sense of authenticity.

FRONT PAGE DETECTIVE (*Newspaper Drama*)

FIRST TELECAST: *July 6, 1951*
LAST TELECAST: *November 13, 1953*
BROADCAST HISTORY:
Jul 1951–Feb 1952, DUM Fri 9:30–10:00
Oct 1953–Nov 1953, DUM Fri 8:00–8:30
CAST:
David Chase .... Edmund Lowe
David's Girlfriend .... Paula Drew

Movie actor Edmund Lowe, known both for his matinee-idol roles and his portrayal of the grimy Sgt. Quirt in *What Price Glory?*, starred in this early filmed series as David Chase, a newspaper columnist who "couldn't be bought." David's stories usually involved murders, which he was unusually good at solving. Paula Drew played his girlfriend, a fashion designer.

Front Page Detective was primarily a syndicated series seen on local stations at various times, but it was carried on the DuMont network for two periods, as shown.

FRONT ROW CENTER (*Musical Variety*)

FIRST TELECAST: *March 25, 1949*
LAST TELECAST: *April 9, 1950*
BROADCAST HISTORY:
Mar 1949–Jun 1949, DUM Fri 9:00–9:30
Jun 1949–Sep 1949, DUM Fri 8:00–9:00
Oct 1949–Apr 1950, DUM Sun 7:00–8:00
REGULARS:
Phil Leeds
Monica Moore
Cass Franklin
Hal Loman
Bibi Osterwald
Joan Fields
Danny Shore
The Sammy Spear Orchestra

This was one of DuMont's early attempts to produce a big weekly variety show, and it starred numerous guests from Broadway and the nightclub circuit. Frank Fontaine hosted the first telecast, with special guest star Marilyn Maxwell in her TV debut. Various hosts appeared thereafter, along with a large and constantly changing supporting cast of regulars. Some of those with longer runs are listed above.

FRONT ROW CENTER (*Dramatic Anthology*)

FIRST TELECAST: *June 1, 1955*
LAST TELECAST: *September 21, 1955*
BROADCAST HISTORY:
Jun 1955–Sep 1955, CBS Wed 10:00–11:00

Live full-hour adaptations of Broadway plays were presented under the title *Front Row Center* on CBS during the summer of 1955, starting with the acclaimed *Dinner at Eight*. The series aired weekly throughout June and then became an alternate-week program when *The U.S. Steel Hour* moved in to share its time slot in July. It returned to the air the following January on Sunday afternoons, where it stayed until April.

FRONTIER (*Western Anthology*)
FIRST TELECAST: *September 25, 1955*
LAST TELECAST: *September 9, 1956*
BROADCAST HISTORY:
Sep 1955–Sep 1956, NBC Sun 7:30–8:00
NARRATOR:
Walter Coy

Walter Coy's opening and closing lines, the same for each episode, were descriptive of this anthology series about the West: "This is the West. This is the land of beginning again. This is the story of men and women facing the frontier. This is the way it happened." And finally, "It happened that way . . . moving west."

There was no glamour in *Frontier.* It depicted real people with real problems moving into, and coping with, a new territory. Indians were not the only villains; roving criminals, rustlers, and the sometimes harsh environment also beset the settlers. In addition to serving as narrator, Walter Coy acted in some of the episodes.

FRONTIER ADVENTURE, see *Death Valley Days*

FRONTIER CIRCUS (*Circus Drama*)
FIRST TELECAST: *October 5, 1961*
LAST TELECAST: *September 20, 1962*
BROADCAST HISTORY:
Oct 1961–Jan 1962, CBS Thu 7:30–8:30
Feb 1962–Sep 1962, CBS Thu 8:00–9:00
Sep 1962, CBS Thu 7:30–8:30
CAST:
Col. Casey Thompson .... Chill Wills
Ben Travis .... John Derek
Tony Gentry .... Richard Jaeckel

Set in the Southwest during the late 1800s, *Frontier Circus* was a cross between a circus drama and a traditional Western. The T&T Circus, operated by Col. Casey Thompson, traveled from town to town in a wagon train. Two handsome hunks of masculinity typical of the TV West were at the center of much of the action: Ben Travis, the straw boss, who supervised the workmen, and Tony Gentry, the advance man, who scouted likely stopping places for the circus. The stories involved the relationships between the performers and workmen of the circus, and their encounters with assorted frontier types. Where did the name T&T come from? From Thompson and Travis, who were actually partners, despite their divergent functions.

FRONTIER JUSTICE (*Western Anthology*)
FIRST TELECAST: *July 7, 1958*
LAST TELECAST: *September 28, 1961*
BROADCAST HISTORY:
Jul 1958–Sep 1958, CBS Mon 9:30–10:00
Jul 1959–Sep 1959, CBS Mon 9:00–9:30
Aug 1961–Sep 1961, CBS Thu 8:30–9:00
HOST:
Lew Ayres (1958)
Melvyn Douglas (1959)
Ralph Bellamy (1961)

For three summers, CBS aired reruns of episodes originally telecast on Dick Powell's *Zane Grey Theater*—in 1958 as the summer replacement for *December Bride,* in 1959 for *The Danny Thomas Show,* and in 1961 for the series from which they were taken, *Dick Powell's Zane Grey Theater.* Each season's host was a different actor.

FRONTIER THEATER, see *Movies—Prior to 1961*

FROSTY FROLICS (*Musical Variety*)
FIRST TELECAST: *September 19, 1951*
LAST TELECAST: *October 10, 1951*
BROADCAST HISTORY:
Sep 1951–Oct 1951, ABC Wed 8:00–9:00

This four-week series of musical variety shows on ice included the Ice Follies, Ice Capades, and Icelandia Skaters.

From Hollywood.

FU MANCHU, see *Adventures of Fu Manchu, The*

FUGITIVE, THE (*Drama*)
FIRST TELECAST: *September 17, 1963*
LAST TELECAST: *August 29, 1967*
BROADCAST HISTORY:
Sep 1963–Aug 1967, ABC Tue 10:00–11:00
CAST:
Dr. Richard Kimble .... David Janssen
Lt. Philip Gerard .... Barry Morse
**Donna Taft* .... Jacqueline Scott
**Fred Johnson, the One-Armed Man* ..... Bill Raisch
*Occasional
EXECUTIVE PRODUCER:
Quinn Martin

Dr. Richard Kimble had been accused, tried, convicted, and sentenced to die for a crime he did not commit—the murder of his wife. Kimble was being taken by Lt. Gerard to prison to be executed when the train in which they were riding was derailed and the lieutenant was knocked unconscious. Kimble escaped. For the next four highly successful seasons, while Gerard searched for Kimble, Kimble searched for the one-armed man he had seen actually murder his wife. Back and forth across the country, taking odd jobs and new identities, and constantly on the verge of being caught by the relentless Gerard, Kimble kept looking for the real killer. Only on rare occasions could the doctor return furtively to his former life (through contacts with his married sister Donna), and rarely did he glimpse his quarry, the one-armed man.

In a move unique among series of this type, *The Fugitive* actually resolved the situation that had sustained suspense throughout its run. In a special two-part story, aired on the last two Tuesdays that the show was seen on the network, Kimble found the one-armed man, Gerard found Kimble, and the doctor was exonerated of the crime—despite the death of the one-armed man. In a climactic chase scene, Kimble and the one-armed man cornered each other atop a tower. Lt. Gerard, in hot pursuit on the ground, realized he had been wrong about Kimble and shot the one-armed man to save the doctor's life. The one-armed man plunged to his death before he could be captured.

This final episode of *The Fugitive,* which aired on August 29, 1967, was seen by more people than any single episode of a regular series in the history of television until that time, and its 72 percent share of all television viewers that night set a regular series record which was not exceeded until the *Dallas* episode in which J.R.'s attacker was revealed, 13 years later.

The deep, resonant voice of the narrator on *The Fugitive,* who kept viewers apprised of Richard

Kimble's situation, belonged to rotund actor William Conrad.

Reruns of *The Fugitive* aired weekday afternoons on ABC from April 1967 to March 1968.

FUGITIVE, THE *(Drama)*
FIRST TELECAST: *October 6, 2000*
LAST TELECAST: *June 1, 2001*
BROADCAST HISTORY:
Oct 2000–Jan 2001, CBS Fri 8:00–9:00
Feb 2001–Jun 2001, CBS Fri 9:00–10:00
CAST:
Dr. Richard Kimble .... Tim Daly
Lt. Philip Gerard .... Mykelti Williamson
Fred Johnson, one-armed man .... Stephen Lang
Capt. Michael McLaren .... Bob Morrisey
Sara Gerard .... Gina Ravera
Det. Linda Westerschulte .... Cynthia Lauren Tewes
Abe Eisenberg .... Richard Brestoff
Matthew Ross .... John Aylward
Karl Vasick .... Rex Linn

In the premiere episode of this updated version of the classic 1960s series, Dr. Richard Kimble returned to his Chicago home to find his wife, Helen (Kelly Rutherford), bleeding to death. She had been beaten by a baseball-bat-wielding one-armed intruder who attacked Kimble and then disappeared. The saintly Kimble was arrested, tried, convicted and sentenced to death for her murder by an incredibly blind justice system. He escaped while being transported to prison by Lt. Gerard, who had testified at the trial, and began his search to find the real murderer, following up on clues that were in some cases provided by his attorney, Eisenberg. Going from city to city, he often helped the people he met, was nice to everyone, and gave his last crumbs of food to stray puppies. Nevertheless Gerard was blindly obsessed with recapturing Kimble because his own wife had been murdered by a man who had gotten out of prison by bribing judges and attorneys. Gerard usually seemed to be a few minutes late, and on the rare occasions when he actually caught Kimble, the fugitive somehow managed to escape again.

As if all this travail wasn't enough, Matthew Ross, Kimble's wealthy ex-father-in-law, wanted him dead. To that end he hired Gerard's boss, Capt. McLaren, to find a bounty hunter to track Kimble down and kill him—for $350,000. McLaren subsequently tried to convince Gerard to give up the hunt in the hope that Vasick, the bounty hunter, would finish the job and he would get his cut. In February Gerard discovered what was going on and shot Vasick before he could kill Kimble. He found incriminating evidence against McLaren, got himself promoted to captain and formed a new fugitive task force to search for Kimble.

As the season drew to a close Helen's sister Becca (Janet Gunn), who had always believed in his innocence, hired an expensive lawyer to take the case. They wanted Kimble to hide in Zurich while they worked to get him exonerated, but the plan fell apart when Gerard arrested her and had her assets frozen. With information from the attorney, Kimble caught the one-armed man in Las Cruces, New Mexico, and, after injecting him with a slow-acting poison to keep him under control, started back to Chicago. On the way he called Gerard to tell him they were coming and then, when they got to Chicago, arranged to meet him in a remote warehouse. Apparently things were more complicated than anyone had believed. Gerard and FBI Agent Gagomiros (Dennis Boutsikaris), who had recently been assigned to the case, took separate cars to the warehouse and, when they got there, Gagomiros shot Gerard. In the cliffhanger ending he caught up with Kimble and the one-armed man and fired another shot. Unfortunately, since *The Fugitive* had been canceled, nobody ever found out whom he had shot and whether or not Gerard had died.

FULL HOUSE (*Situation Comedy*)
FIRST TELECAST: *September 22, 1987*
LAST TELECAST: *August 29, 1995*
BROADCAST HISTORY:
Sep 1987, ABC Tue 8:30–9:00
Sep 1987–Feb 1988, ABC Fri 8:00–8:30
Mar 1988–Jul 1989, ABC Fri 8:30–9:00
Jul 1988–Sep 1988, ABC Tue 8:30–9:00
Aug 1989–Aug 1991, ABC Fri 8:00–8:30
Aug 1991–Aug 1995, ABC Tue 8:00–8:30
CAST:
Danny Tanner .... Bob Saget
Uncle Jesse Cochran/Katsopolis .... John Stamos
Joey Gladstone .... David Coulier
D.J. (Donna Jo) Tanner (age 10) .. Candace Cameron
Stephanie Tanner (5) .... Jodie Sweetin
Michele Tanner (6 mos.)
... Mary Kate & Ashley Fuller Olsen (alternating)
Kimmy Gibler .... Andrea Barber
Rebecca Donaldson (1988–1995) .... Lori Loughlin
**Nick Cochran/Katsopolis (1988–1991)*
.... John Aprea
**Irene Cochran/Katsopolis (1988–1991)*
.... Yvonne Wilder
Vicki Larson (1991–1994) .... Gail Edwards
Steve (1991–1993) .... Scott Weinger
Nicky Katsopolis (1992–1995)
.... Blake Tuomy-Wilhoit
Alex Katsopolis (1992–1995)
.... Dylan Tuomy-Wilhoit
**Teddy (1991–1995)* .... Tahj Mowry
**Denise Frazier (1992–1994)* .... Jurnee Smollett
**Terri (1993–1995)* .... Sara Moonves
**Derek (1993–1995)* .... Blake McIver Ewing
**Gia (1993–1995)* .... Marla Sokoloff
*Occasional

Three young men and three kids formed the latest of TV's unlikely "families" in this light comedy, set in San Francisco. The children belonged to TV sportscaster Danny, who was left with his hands full when his wife died suddenly. Moving in to help (?) were Danny's brother-in-law Jesse, a long-haired rock 'n' roller who wanted to PARTY!; and friend Joey, an aspiring standup comic given to loud jackets and nonsensical reactions to diapers.

Full House was an immediate hit on Friday, a night on which cute-kid shows seem to flourish (past hits on Friday have included *Webster, Diff'rent Strokes, The Brady Bunch, The Partridge Family,* and, years ago when Ricky was young, *The Adventures of Ozzie and Harriet*). The Tanner household evolved as seasons passed. Uncle Jesse left his family's exterminating business to pursue his dream of becoming a professional rock musician; later he wrote advertising jingles with Joey, whose own show business career was slowly growing (especially after he appeared on *Star Search*). Danny became co-host of a local TV morning talk show with the unpredictable Rebecca, who struck up a relationship with Jesse that eventually led to their marriage (in 1991). Rebecca and the newly domesticated Jesse didn't move out, however, but she moved in and had twin boys, Nicky and Alex, in late 1991, adding two new super-cute baby faces to the house (Michelle was by now five).

Danny had a long-term relationship with Vicki, another talk-show host, which didn't work out, so Rebecca remained the only wife in evidence. Various friends of the kids passed through, including D.J.'s friends Kimmy and Steve, Stephanie's classmate Gia, and Michelle's friends Teddy and Denise.

Jesse and his parents, Nick and Irene, abruptly changed their names to Katsopolis in the fall of 1990, after the visit of his grandparents from Greece, apparently in tribute to their roots. Actor John Stamos, whose own ancestral name was Stamotopoulos, was known to feel that his Greek heritage should be better represented on TV.

NBC aired repeats of this series weekday mornings from June–September 1991.

FUN FOR THE MONEY (*Quiz/Audience Participation*)
FIRST TELECAST: *June 17, 1949*
LAST TELECAST: *December 9, 1949*
BROADCAST HISTORY:
Jun 1949–Dec 1949, ABC Fri 9:30–10:00
EMCEE:
Johnny Olsen

This audience-participation quiz show was modeled along the lines of baseball, with stunts and games.

FUNNY FACE (*Situation Comedy*)
FIRST TELECAST: *September 18, 1971*
LAST TELECAST: *December 11, 1971*
BROADCAST HISTORY:
Sep 1971–Dec 1971, CBS Sat 8:30–9:00
CAST:
Sandy Stockton .... Sandy Duncan
Alice McRaven .... Valorie Armstrong
Kate Harwell .... Kathleen Freeman
Pat Harwell .... Henry Beckman

Sandy Duncan was considered one of the most promising new stars in television when this comedy series was launched in the fall of 1971. She was cast as Sandy Stockton, a pert young UCLA student majoring in education who made ends meet by working part-time as an actress in TV commercials. The big-city life of Los Angeles was a constant challenge for Sandy, who hailed from the small town of Taylorville, Illinois. Helping her cope were her next-door neighbor and best friend, Alice McRaven, and Mr. and Mrs. Harwell, the nosy landlords. *Funny Face* did not make the grade, but the character of Sandy Stockton was to return the following season in a similar venture called *The Sandy Duncan Show*.

FUNNY PEOPLE, see *George Schlatter's Funny People*

FUNNY SIDE, THE (*Comedy/Variety*)
FIRST TELECAST: *September 14, 1971*
LAST TELECAST: *December 7, 1971*
BROADCAST HISTORY:
Sep 1971–Nov 1971, NBC Tue 9:30–10:30
Nov 1971–Dec 1971, NBC Tue 8:30–9:30
REGULARS:
Gene Kelly
John Amos and Teresa Graves
Warren Berlinger and Pat Finley
Dick Clair and Jenna McMahon
Michael Lembeck and Cindy Williams
Burt Mustin and Queenie Smith

Comedy sketches, musical vignettes, and production numbers were the basic elements of this variety show, which each week looked at the funny side of a specific aspect of married life. Topics covered ranged from health to financial problems to sexual attitudes, and were seen from the perspectives of five married couples. John and Teresa were the minority couple, Warren and Pat represented blue-collar people, Dick and Jenna were wealthy, Michael and Cindy were counterculture teenagers, and Burt and Queenie were senior citizens. Gene Kelly was the regular host and participated in many of the sketches and production numbers.

FURTHER ADVENTURES OF ELLERY QUEEN, THE, see *Adventures of Ellery Queen, The*

FUSE (Network), see MuchMusic

FUTURAMA (*Cartoon Science Fiction*)
FIRST TELECAST: *March 28, 1999*
LAST TELECAST:
BROADCAST HISTORY:
Mar 1999–Apr 1999, FOX Sun 8:30–9:00
Apr 1999–May 1999, FOX Tue 8:30–9:00
Jun 1999–Dec 1999, FOX Sun 8:30–9:00
Feb 2000–Sep 2001, FOX Sun 7:00–7:30
Dec 2001–Apr 2002, FOX Sun 7:00–7:30
Feb 2002–Mar 2002, FOX Thu 9:30–10:00
Jun 2002–Aug 2002, FOX Sun 7:00–7:30
Nov 2002–Jan 2003, FOX Sun 7:00–7:30
Mar 2003–Apr 2003, FOX Sun 7:00–7:30
Jun 2003– , FOX Sun 7:00–7:30
VOICES:
Phillip Fry .... Billy West
Professor Hubert Farnsworth .... Billy West
Taronga Leela .... Katey Sagal
Bender .... John DiMaggio
Amy Wong .... Lauren Tom
Hermes Conrad .... Phil LaMarr
Dr. John Zoidberg .... Billy West

Fry was a somewhat dense, 25-year-old delivery boy for Panucci's Pizzas who took an order to Applied Cryogenics and accidentally fell into one of the company's capsules. One thousand years later he emerged to begin a new life in New York in the year 3000. He was befriended by Leela, a worker at the cryogenics company; Bender, a sarcastic robot who got his name from bending steel girders; and elderly Professor Farnsworth, Fry's frail, eccentric, great-great-great-etc. nephew. Together they traveled the Cosmos delivering merchandise for Planet Express, encountering all sorts of strange creatures. Leela, a sexy one-eyed alien martial-arts expert, served as their ship's captain, while Bender, who drank like a fish and smoked big cigars, was addicted to pornography. Amy, one of Farnsworth's engineering students, was an intern with the company and went on some of their delivery runs, and Hermes was one of their co-workers. On their much-changed Earth they were confronted by many reminders of "ancient times," including jars containing the preserved, talking heads of celebrities like Dick Clark, Leonard Nimoy, and Richard Nixon.

Created by Matt Groening, creator of *The Simpsons*, whose head was seen in one of those jars.

G

G.E. COLLEGE BOWL, THE, (*Quiz*)

FIRST TELECAST: *January 7, 1968*
LAST TELECAST: *June 14, 1970*
BROADCAST HISTORY:
Jan 1968–Jun 1968, NBC Sun 6:00–6:30
Jan 1969–Jun 1969, NBC Sun 6:00–6:30
Jan 1970–Jun 1970, NBC Sun 6:30–7:00
HOST/MODERATOR:
Robert Earle

G.E. College Bowl, one of the most intelligent of TV's many quiz shows, was seen through most of its long run as a Sunday afternoon program. However, on three occasions between 1968 and 1970 it was scheduled in the evening hours.

The format was simple, although the questions were not. Two teams of four scholars each, representing different colleges, were pitted against each other and the buzzer. Questions ranged across mathematics, science, engineering, literature, and philosophy and often sent viewers at home scurrying for their encyclopedias. The team amassing the most points won scholarship money for its college and the right to return the following week. A team winning for five consecutive weeks won a special trophy and was retired as an undefeated champion. Awards to a championship team could amount to as much as $19,500.

G.E. College Bowl premiered on Sunday afternoon, January 4, 1959, on CBS with Allen Ludden as host. He was succeeded by Robert Earle, who followed the program when it moved to NBC in 1963. In addition to this network series' 11-year run (1959–1970), the same format was used locally in many cities, with area high schools competing. The local high school version was usually titled *It's Academic.*

G.E. GUEST HOUSE (*Quiz/Panel*)

FIRST TELECAST: *July 1, 1951*
LAST TELECAST: *August 26, 1951*
BROADCAST HISTORY:
Jul 1951–Aug 1951, CBS Sun 9:00–10:00
EMCEE:
Oscar Levant
Durward Kirby

A different panel of four celebrities from four areas of show business—a critic, a writer, a performer, and a producer—appeared each week to answer assorted questions on this live summer game show. The object of the game was to determine which of the four areas produced people most knowledgeable about show business. Emcee Oscar Levant, a pianist, played a number of musical selections and conducted a musical quiz during each show. When he left the series, after its first three telecasts, Durward Kirby assumed the role of emcee.

GABRIELLE (*Music*)

FIRST TELECAST: *July 13, 1948*
LAST TELECAST: *August 12, 1948*
BROADCAST HISTORY:
July 1948–Aug 1948, ABC Tue/Thu 7:00–7:15
HOSTESS:
Gabrielle

This was a musical interlude with songs in the French style by Gabrielle.

GABRIEL'S FIRE (*Detective Drama*)

FIRST TELECAST: *September 12, 1990*
LAST TELECAST: *January 2, 1992*
BROADCAST HISTORY:
Sep 1990, ABC Wed 10:00–11:00
Sep 1990–Mar 1991 ABC Thu 9:00–10:00
Apr 1991–May 1991, ABC Wed 10:00–11:00
Jun 1991–July 1991, ABC Thu 9:00–10:00
Aug 1991–Jan 1992, ABC Thu 8:00–9:00
CAST:
Gabriel Bird .... James Earl Jones
Victoria Heller (1990–1991).......... Laila Robins
Louis Klein (1990–1991)............. Dylan Walsh
Jamil Duke (1990–1991) .... Brian K. Grant
"Empress" Josephine Austin .... Madge Sinclair
Mitch O'Hannon (1991–1992) ..... Richard Crenna

Gabriel Bird was a large, intelligent black man with a thundering voice and a cross to bear. He had once been a Chicago cop. One terrible day in 1969, he was involved in a botched raid during which he was forced to shoot his white partner rather than allow the latter to kill an innocent mother and child in cold blood. The jury considered this to be not an act of heroism but of murder, and sent him to prison for life.

After twenty years as a model prisoner, Bird came in contact with an aggressive attorney named Victoria, who was fascinated by his case and the many irregularities in his trial. Convinced he was innocent, she got him released, but the proud Bird found that life outside could be even tougher for an ex-con, especially since many on the police force still hated and distrusted him. Reluctantly, he agreed to become a private investigator for Victoria, using to good advantage the inside knowledge he had gained on the force and in prison. Louis was Victoria's assistant, and Empress Josephine was Bird's longtime friend and the proprietor of a café where Bird hung out—both for the food and for her company.

The downbeat premise of the series coupled with Bird's simmering anger at the injustices visited upon him drove away viewers during the first season, leading to major changes (and a new title) in the second. Returning in the fall of 1991 as *Pros and Cons,* the series was now about an upbeat Bird, who had almost magically shaken his anger and smiled continuously. Moving to Los Angeles, he teamed up with a colorful if somewhat over-the-hill private eye in their own agency, O'Hannon and Bird. The new, cheerful Gabriel and the mischievous, disorganized O'Hannon meshed perfectly. Adding to Bird's newfound happiness was his relationship with Josephine, which culminated in marriage in October 1991.

GALACTICA 1980, see *Battlestar Galactica*

GALAVISIÓN (Network) (*Spanish-Language Entertainment Cable Network*)

LAUNCHED:
October 1979
SUBSCRIBERS (SEP 2002):
34.0 million (32% U.S.)

A Spanish-language cable network run by Univision, the largest U.S. Spanish-language broadcaster, and featuring movies, novellas, sports, comedy and variety programming.

GALE STORM SHOW, THE (*Situation Comedy*)
FIRST TELECAST: *September 29, 1956*
LAST TELECAST: *March 24, 1960*
BROADCAST HISTORY:
Sep 1956–Apr 1959, CBS Sat 9:00–9:30
Oct 1959–Mar 1960, ABC Thu 7:30–8:00
CAST:
Susanna Pomeroy .... Gale Storm
Esmerelda Nugent .... ZaSu Pitts
Capt. Huxley .... Roy Roberts
Cedric (1956–1959) .... Jimmy Fairfax

Susanna Pomeroy was the social director of the luxury liner S.S. *Ocean Queen.* She spent much of her time in cahoots with her close friend Esmerelda "Nugey" Nugent, operator of the ship's beauty salon, and their alliance confounded the liner's rather stuffy Capt. Huxley. Adding to the captain's frustrations was the ship's steward, an impish little fellow named Cedric (who went overboard when the series moved to ABC). This filmed comedy was subtitled *Oh Susanna,* and that was the title it later adopted when it went into syndication.

Network reruns of this series appeared weekdays on ABC from April 1959 to September 1961.

GALEN DRAKE SHOW, THE (*Children's Variety*)
FIRST TELECAST: *January 12, 1957*
LAST TELECAST: *May 11, 1957*
BROADCAST HISTORY:
Jan 1957–May 1957, ABC Sat 7:00–7:30
REGULARS:
Galen Drake
Stuart Foster
Rita Ellis

This unusual variety show was aimed directly at children. Galen Drake was a popular radio personality who was known for the pleasant way in which he told stories. Here he sang a little, interviewed guests, and introduced songs by the show's regular singers, Stuart Foster and Rita Ellis. Guests on this live series were people presumably of interest to youngsters, such as puppeteer Bil Baird, the president of an art school, and a young girl who had run away from home because she was in love with Elvis Presley.

GALLANT MEN, THE (*War Drama*)
FIRST TELECAST: *October 5, 1962*
LAST TELECAST: *September 14, 1963*
BROADCAST HISTORY:
Oct 1962–Dec 1962, ABC Fri 7:30–8:30
Dec 1962–Sep 1963, ABC Sat 7:30–8:30
CAST:
Conley Wright .... Robert McQueeney
Capt. Jim Benedict .... William Reynolds
Lt. Frank Kimbro .... Robert Ridgely
1st Sgt. John McKenna .... Richard X. Slattery
PFC Pete D'Angelo .... Eddie Fontaine
Private Ernie Lucavich .... Roland LaStarza
Private Sam Hanson .... Robert Gothie
Private Roger Gibson .... Roger Davis

One of the TV trends of the early 1960s that never really got off the ground was the wartime action drama. ABC premiered two such shows in 1962, *Combat* and *The Gallant Men.*

The Gallant Men was set in Italy during World War II and followed the progress of a front-line infantry company, part of the 36th Infantry ("Texas") Division, as it fought its way up the peninsula. The company was led by a determined young captain named Jim Benedict, and the action was seen through the eyes of a war correspondent, Conley Wright. Other principals included free-swinging 1st Sergeant McKenna; handsome, guitar-playing ladies' man D'Angelo (the company's "operator"); the inseparable Lucavich and Hanson; and the callow young driver, Gibson.

The Gallant Men offered action, heroics, and a kind of gritty realism, plus plenty of sexy Italian girls along the way, but it failed to establish a beachhead against either *Rawhide* on Friday night or *Jackie Gleason* on Saturday, and soon disappeared.

GALLERY OF MME. LUI-TSONG, THE (*Crime Drama*)
FIRST TELECAST: *September 3, 1951*
LAST TELECAST: *November 21, 1951*
BROADCAST HISTORY:
Sep 1951–Oct 1951, DUM Mon 8:30–9:00
Oct 1951–Nov 1951, DUM Wed 9:00–9:30
CAST:
Mme. Lui-Tsong .... Anna May Wong

Chinese-American actress Anna May Wong (whose real name was Wong Lui-Tsong) portrayed the owner of a far-flung chain of art galleries who doubled as an exotic—and beautiful—sleuth in this short-lived series. Stolen treasure, international intrigue, and shady operators all provided material for the stories. Effective October 10, 1951, the program's title was shortened to *Mme. Lui-Tsong.*

GAMBLE ON LOVE (*Quiz/Audience Participation*)
FIRST TELECAST: *July 16, 1954*
LAST TELECAST: *August 6, 1954*
BROADCAST HISTORY:
Jul 1954–Aug 1954, DUM Fri 10:30–11:00
HOSTESS
Denise Darcel

In this short-lived summer quiz, three couples who were "married, about to be married, or just in love" were first interviewed on their "gamble on love." They then had a chance at the wheel of fortune, with one partner spinning the wheel and the other answering the questions. Top prize was a mink coat, or the like. Curvaceous actress Denise Darcel hosted. Ernie Kovacs replaced her in the same time period with a new format and title (see *Time Will Tell*).

GAME OF THE WEEK, THE see *Football*

GAME SHOW NETWORK (Network) (*Entertainment Cable Network*)
LAUNCHED:
December 1994
SUBSCRIBERS (MAY 2003):
51.3 million (48% U.S.)

TV's home for those endless hours of *Match Game, Pyramid, Family Feud, Newlywed Game, Password, Card Sharks, Joker's Wild, Wheel of Fortune* and all the rest that you thought had disappeared forever—

but hadn't. For the network's first half a dozen years its schedule consisted mostly of reruns of daytime game shows of the 1970s–1990s, leading to endless jokes about bell-bottoms, long sideburns and Day-Glo sets. Slowly the network began to increase original production, however, and by the early 2000s it sported an all-original prime time lineup consisting of such shows as *Whammy, Friend or Foe, Russian Roulette, Lingo* and *Wintuition*. Reruns of some contemporary games were also seen, such as *The Weakest Link* and *Greed*.

GAMES PEOPLE PLAY (*Sports*)
FIRST TELECAST: *August 21, 1980*
LAST TELECAST: *September 24, 1981*
BROADCAST HISTORY:
Aug 1980–Dec 1980, NBC Thu 8:00–9:00
Jun 1981–Aug 1981, NBC Sat 10:00–11:00
Sep 1981, NBC Thu 8:00–9:00
REGULARS:
Bryant Gumbel
Cyndy Garvey
Mike Adamle
Johnny Bench
Donna DeVarona
Gary Owens
Arte Johnson

These were not everyday sporting events. They were "games" played for novelty and amusement, often with an eye for the bizarre or ridiculous. Some of the "competitions" shown were for such titles or in such events as "America's Toughest Bouncer," "World's Bellyflopping Championship," "The Billiards Battle of the Generations," "Backwards Motor Racing," "Taxi Cab Demolition Derby," "Three-Ton Tug of War," and the "Disk Jockey Invitational Talk-Off." Bryant Gumble and Cyndy Garvey were co-hosts: Mike Adamle, Johnny Bench, Donna DeVarona, and Arte Johnson were regular field reporters at the locations around the country where the events had taken place; and Gary Owens was the announcer. In addition to the regulars, there were weekly guest stars serving as commentators, among them athletes such as Dorothy Hamill, Bruce Jenner, and Reggie Jackson, sports announcers such as Marv Albert and Joe Garagiola, and entertainment celebrities such as Darren McGavin, Tanya Tucker, Erik Estrada, and James Coburn.

GANGBUSTERS (*Police Anthology*)
FIRST TELECAST: *March 20, 1952*
LAST TELECAST: *December 25, 1952*
BROADCAST HISTORY:
Mar 1952–Dec 1952, NBC Thu 9:00–9:30
CREATOR/WRITER/NARRATOR:
Phillips H. Lord

Gangbusters was one of the all-time classics of radio, running for some 21 years (1936–1957) on various networks. However, its history on television was short, for unusual reasons.

The format was the same as in the radio version. Action-packed stories on the apprehension of major criminals, taken from "actual police and FBI files," were presented in semi-documentary style. There was no continuing cast, but Phillips H. Lord, creator and writer of the show, appeared each week as narrator. At the end of each telecast a photo of one of the nation's most-wanted criminals was shown, and anyone having knowledge of his whereabouts was asked to phone the local police, the FBI, or *Gangbusters*. (Over the years the "most-wanted" feature of the radio *Gangbusters* resulted in the apprehension of several hundred criminals.)

Gangbusters premiered on TV in March 1952, alternating on Thursday nights with *Dragnet*. Both shows were phenomenally successful, completely overwhelming their competition. (In fact the other three networks virtually gave up trying to compete, and scheduled political-discussion programs opposite them.) During the fall of 1952 *Gangbusters* averaged a 42 rating, garnering virtually all of the audience available in its time slot and ranking number eight among all programs on TV. Nevertheless, it left the air in December—making it probably the highest-rated program ever to be canceled in the history of television.

The reason for the cancellation appears to be that *Gangbusters* was never intended to be a full-time TV series, but merely a stopgap provided by the sponsor to fill in the weeks when *Dragnet* wasn't on. Jack Webb even appeared at the end of each telecast to plug the next week's *Dragnet* episode. Webb could not at first provide a new *Dragnet* film every week, but when he could, *Dragnet* (which was even more popular than *Gangbusters*) went weekly and *Gangbusters* had to make way.

GANGSTER CHRONICLES, THE (*Drama*)
FIRST TELECAST: *February 21, 1981*
LAST TELECAST: *May 8, 1981*
BROADCAST HISTORY:
Feb 1981–Mar 1981, NBC Sat 9:00–10:00
Apr 1981–May 1981, NBC Fri 10:00–11:00
CAST:
Charles "Lucky" Luciano .... Michael Nouri
Benjamin "Bugsy" Siegel .... Joe Penny
Michael Lasker..................... Brian Benben
Stella Siegel .... Kathleen Lloyd
Ruth Lasker .... Madeline Stowe
Joy Osler .... Chad Redding
Chris Brennan .... Markie Post
Goodman .... Alan Arbus
Al Capone...................... Louis Giambalvo
Frank Costello .... James Andronica
Vito Genovese .... Robert Davi
Salvatore Maranzano .... Joseph Mascolo
Vincent "Mad Dog" Coll .... David Wilson
Thomas E. Dewey.................. Kenneth Tigar
Giuseppe "Joe the Boss" Masseria
.... Richard Castellano
Thomas "Three Finger Brown" Lucchese . Jon Polito
Dutch Schultz.................... Jonathan Banks
NARRATOR:
E. G. Marshall

Dramatizations of the constant "warfare" between criminals and law-enforcement agencies are almost invariably shown from the perspective of the "good guys." However, the success of the two *Godfather* movies, both theatrically and on TV, inspired NBC to dramatize the Mafia from the inside, showing the relationships of gangland figures with each other and their families. *The Gangster Chronicles*, though based on historical fact, was a dramatization of the lives of three crime figures who had grown up together in

New York and worked together as bootleggers and racketeers during the Prohibition era. Lucky Luciano was the suave, cultured organizer; Bugsy Siegel, the violent, amoral enforcer; and Michael Lasker (a composite of several real people), the soft-spoken family man who was the brains of the operation. As with the *Godfather* movies, their personal lives were also explored. Unlike *The Untouchables* of 20 years before, which had drawn two-dimensional caricatures of Prohibition's gangsters, *The Gangster Chronicles* combined slam-bang action with a portrait of the hoods as real—though not necessarily very pleasant—people, and as products of their environment.

GARLUND TOUCH, THE, see *Mr. Garlund*

GARRISON'S GORILLAS (*War Drama*)

FIRST TELECAST: *September 5, 1967*
LAST TELECAST: *September 17, 1968*
BROADCAST HISTORY:
Sep 1967–Sep 1968, ABC Tue 7:30–8:30
CAST:
Lt. Craig Garrison .... Ron Harper
Actor .... Cesare Danova
Casino .... Rudy Solari
Goniff .... Christopher Cary
Chief .... Brendon Boone

This action series focused on a motley group of commandos recruited from stateside prisons to use their special skills against the Germans in World War II. They had been promised a presidential pardon at the end of the war if they worked out; if not, they could expect a firing squad. The four were Actor, a handsome, resonant-voiced con man; Casino, a tough, wiry safecracker; Goniff, a slender, likable cat burglar; and Chief, a rugged, somber American Indian proficient with a switchblade. Led by West Pointer Craig Garrison, and headquartered in a secluded spot in England, this slippery group ranged all over Europe in exploits that often took them behind enemy lines.

GARROWAY AT LARGE (*Variety*)

FIRST TELECAST: *April 16, 1949*
LAST TELECAST: *June 25, 1954*
BROADCAST HISTORY:
Apr 1949–Jul 1949, NBC Sat 10:00–10:30
Jul 1949–Jun 1951, NBC Sun 10:00–10:30 (OS)
Oct 1953–Jun 1954, NBC Fri 8:00–8:30
REGULARS:
Dave Garroway
Jack Haskell
Cliff Norton
Bette Chapel (1949–1951)
Carolyn Gilbert (1949)
Connie Russell (1949–1951)
Jill Corey (1953–1954)
Shirley Harmer (1953–1954)
Songsmiths Quartet (1949)
The Daydreamers (1950)
The Cheerleaders (1953–1954)
DANCERS:
Russell and Aura (1950–1951)
Ken Spaulding and Diane Sinclair (1953–1954)
ORCHESTRA:
Joseph Gallichio (1949–1951)
Skitch Henderson (1953–1954)
THEME:
"Sentimental Journey," by Bud Green, Les Brown, and Ben Homer

A former disc jockey and onetime NBC page, Dave Garroway first brought his relaxed brand of humor to network audiences in 1949, with this easygoing musical revue. The program, which was telecast live from Chicago, had Garroway chatting with guests and casually strolling from set to set, past cameras, props, and technicians. No attempt was made at elaborate production. Entertainment was provided by guest stars and a regular supporting cast of singers and musicians. Sometimes the guest or setting was unusual, as in the 1950 New Year's Eve show when Dave's guests were the cleaning women of NBC's Chicago studios, "who work on New Year's Eve while others play"; and a May 1950 telecast that moved up onto the roof of the studio building for a view of the Chicago skyline at night.

Perhaps most evocative of Dave's sincere, straightforward style was his regular closing, when he would turn to the camera, raise his hand, and bid farewell with a simple, "Peace."

In January 1952 Garroway began his long run as host of NBC's pioneering *Today Show*. He returned to prime time for the 1953–1954 season, with a revue similar to his 1949–1951 series but this time emanating from New York and titled simply *The Dave Garroway Show*. Singer Jack Haskell and comedian Cliff Norton returned from the earlier show, but otherwise the supporting cast was new. Unfortunately this second series was faced with overwhelming competition from *Mama* and *Ozzie & Harriet*, which were running opposite on CBS and ABC, and it lasted only a single season.

GARRY MOORE SHOW, THE (*Variety*)

FIRST TELECAST: *June 26, 1950*
LAST TELECAST: *December 27, 1951*
BROADCAST HISTORY:
June 1950–Jul 1950, CBS Mon–Fri 7:00–7:30
Jul 1950–Sep 1950, CBS Mon/Tue/Thu/Fri 7:00–7:30
Aug 1950–Sep 1950, CBS Wed 8:00–9:00
Oct 1951–Dec 1951, CBS Thu 8:00–8:30
REGULARS:
Garry Moore
Ken Carson
Denise Lor
Durward Kirby

The pace of the early, live *Garry Moore Show* was slow and relaxed, and very informal. Included were songs, poems, comedy sketches, chats with regulars and guests, and anything else that came to mind while the show was on the air. Ken Carson and Denise Lor were the featured vocalists while Durward Kirby doubled as announcer and comedian. The program was simulcast on television and radio, five days a week, during the summer of 1950. In August 1950 the Wednesday 7:00–7:30 P.M. telecast was moved (and expanded) to 8:00–9:00 P.M., to fill in for the vacationing Arthur Godfrey, who normally occupied that time slot.

The fall 1951 version of *The Garry Moore Show*, in the same format and with the same regulars, was aired once a week under the title *The Garry Moore Evening Show*, to distinguish it from Garry's highly successful daytime show on CBS.

GARRY MOORE SHOW, THE (*Variety*)
FIRST TELECAST: *September 30, 1958*
LAST TELECAST: *January 8, 1967*
BROADCAST HISTORY:
Sep 1958–Jun 1964, CBS Tue 10:00–11:00 (OS)
Sep 1966–Jan 1967, CBS Sun 9:00–10:00
REGULARS:
Garry Moore
Durward Kirby
Marion Lorne (1958–1962)
Carol Burnett (1959–1962)
Dorothy Loudon (1962–1964)
Allen Funt (1959–1960)
John Byner (1966–1967)
Jackie Vernon (1966–1967)
Chuck McCann (1966–1967)
Pete Barbutti (1966–1967)
Buster Davis Singers (1958–1959)
George Becker Singers (1959–1964)
Paul Godkin Dancers (1958–1959)
Ernest Flatt Dancers (1959–1963)
Carol Henry Dancers (1963–1964)
Bob Hamilton Dancers (1966–1967)
Howard Smith Orchestra (1958–1959)
Irwin Kostal Orchestra (1959–1964)
Bernie Green Orchestra (1966–1967)

This Garry Moore variety series ran very successfully for six seasons in the late 1950s and early 1960s. Among other things, it made a star out of Carol Burnett, brought back Allen Funt's Candid Camera (as a regular feature), and showcased many fine musical and comedic talents. And then there was, of course, the friendly humor of the bow-tied, crew-cut Moore himself. From 1958 to 1963 the highlight of the show was "That Wonderful Year," consisting of film clips, comedy sketches, and production numbers based on the events and styles of a given year. This often filled from one-third to one-half of the show.

The Garry Moore Show left the air in 1964, not because of low ratings but because Garry wanted to get away from the weekly grind and have some time to relax. After two years of well-earned rest (he had begun on network radio in 1939 and had been on television continuously since 1950) Garry returned in the fall of 1966 as host of a program featuring Durward Kirby and a rotating cast of comedians and guests. This was short-lived, however (partially due to the withering competition of *Bonanza*), and thereafter Garry was known primarily as a daytime TV personality.

GARY & MIKE (*Cartoon*)
FIRST TELECAST: *January 11, 2001*
LAST TELECAST: *April 13, 2001*
BROADCAST HISTORY:
Jan 2001, UPN Thu 9:30–10:00
Jan 2001–Mar 2001, UPN Fri 8:00–8:30
Mar 2001, UPN Fri 9:00–9:30
Mar 2001–Apr 2001, UPN Fri 9:00–10:00
VOICES:
Mike Bonner .... Harland Williams
Gary Newton .... Christopher Moynihan

In this Claymation buddy comedy Mike and Gary were two 21-year-olds who had just graduated from college. Mike, a womanizing slacker whose parents were alcoholics, had no idea what he wanted to do. Since he had no life goals, he hitched a ride with his serious, nerdy friend Gary, whose dad had given him the keys to his SUV and told him to take a three-month trip around the country following the trail of Lewis and Clark (supposedly, Clark was one of his ancestors) and come back a "man." Gary's dad also included cassettes, narrated by Charlton Heston, that described the trail. Gary meant well, but Mike's propensity for screwing things up constantly got them in trouble. Starting from St. Louis, they promptly picked up a hitchhiker who stole all their belongings—the SUV, the credit card Gary's dad had given him for emergencies, and even the clothes they were wearing. At episode's end Mike convinced Gary to continue the trip, and with Mike's limited money they bought a beat-up old Chevy convertible and headed off. In hot pursuit was the irate motorcycle-cop father of the girl Mike had slept with the night before their trip began. When the boys reached Chicago, they landed on *The Jerry Springer Show,* where they thought they were going to talk about their travels. The Springer staff set them up, however—bringing in Gary's dad, who heard what had happened to his SUV and went ballistic on the show. He demanded that Gary return home, take an accounting job at Northrup, and pay him back for everything—but Gary ultimately opted to stay on the road with Mike.

GAS COMPANY PLAYHOUSE (*Dramatic Anthology*)
FIRST TELECAST: *July 5, 1960*
LAST TELECAST: *September 13, 1960*
BROADCAST HISTORY:
Jul 1960–Sep 1960, NBC Tue 8:30–9:00
HOSTESS:
Julia Meade

This summer series was composed of reruns of *Goodyear TV Playhouse, The David Niven Show, Colgate Theatre,* and *Alcoa Theatre.* It was hosted by Julia Meade and alternated on Tuesday evenings with *NBC Playhouse.*

GAVILAN (*Adventure*)
FIRST TELECAST: *October 26, 1982*
LAST TELECAST: *March 18, 1983*
BROADCAST HISTORY:
Oct 1982–Dec 1982, NBC Tue 9:00–10:00
Mar 1983, NBC Fri 10:00–11:00
CAST:
Robert Gavilan .... Robert Urich
Milo Bentley .... Patrick Macnee
Marion Jaworski .... Kate Reid

His years as a CIA agent had made Robert Gavilan a little bit cynical, but not enough to stop him from fighting for what was right and just. In his current capacity, as inventor and consultant to California's DeWitt Institute of Oceanography, Gavilan helped rescue people in trouble, worked on underwater projects, and occasionally got involved with exactly the type of espionage activities that had caused him to leave the Agency. He shared his Malibu beach house with Milo Bentley, a suave, conniving travel agent who regularly helped Gavilan on his adventures. Mrs. Jaworski, Gavilan's boss at the Institute, was impressed by his talents but bothered by his tendency to get into dangerous situations. He did, it must be said, have to deal with more than his share of evil despots and foreign agents, as well as a never-ending stream of beautiful women, in this formula adventure.

GAY NINETIES REVUE, THE (*Musical Variety*)
FIRST TELECAST: *August 11, 1948*
LAST TELECAST: *January 14, 1949*
BROADCAST HISTORY:
Aug 1948–Oct 1948, ABC Wed 8:00–8:30
Nov 1948–Jan 1949, ABC Fri 8:30–9:00
REGULARS:
Joe Howard
Lulu Bates
The Florodora Girls
Ray Bloch Orchestra

Joe Howard was about as authentic an old-timer as TV could get for a show like this—and probably the oldest performer ever to headline a TV variety series. He had been in vaudeville since the 1890s, and, as a songwriter, his biggest hit had been "Hello Ma Baby," in 1899. At 81 years of age he was still a spry performer (he lived to be 93) and he emceed this old-fashioned variety show with period style. Lulu Bates added boisterous Gay Nineties vocals, and the Florodora Girls (named after the hit 1900 Broadway show) provided female harmonizing. The setting was an old gaslight nightclub. The program was adapted from the radio series of the same name that Howard had emceed in the early 1940s—when he was only in his 70s.

Joe Howard's trademark song, which he sang and used as a theme on all these programs, turned out to be one of the most durable cases of fraud in music-business history. For 40 years he had sung "I Wonder Who's Kissing Her Now," and regaled audiences with stories about how he had been inspired to write it by a chance remark he heard in 1909. Twentieth Century–Fox even called his 1947 screen biography *I Wonder Who's Kissing Her Now,* and played up the story of the song's composition in the film. That brought forth someone named Harold Orlob, who proved that he, when a young man, had written the song for Howard, who then appropriated credit for it and sang it for the next half-century. Howard died while singing "Let Me Call You Sweetheart" on the stage of a Chicago theater in 1961.

GEENA DAVIS SHOW, THE (*Situation Comedy*)
FIRST TELECAST: *October 10, 2000*
LAST TELECAST: *July 17, 2001*
BROADCAST HISTORY:
Oct 2000–Mar 2001, ABC Tue 9:30–10:00
May 2001–Jul 2001, ABC Tue 9:30–10:00
CAST:
Teddie Cochran .... Geena Davis
Max Ryan .... Peter Horton
Carter Ryan (age 13) .... John Francis Daley
Eliza Ryan (5) .... Makenzie Vega
Gladys .... Esther Scott
Hillary .... Mimi Rogers
Judy Owens .... Kim Coles
Alan .... Harland Williams

A high-powered Manhattan executive became an instant suburban mom in this manic, rather trite comedy. Teddie was a tall, fashionable (i.e., short skirts) event planner whose harried life consisted of Starbucks coffee in the morning and take-out Chinese at night. Judy and Hillary were her wisecracking best friends, and Alan, her whiny coworker. Everything changed when Teddie met Max, an easygoing writer and widower whose two kids, he thought, needed a mom. The kids weren't so sure, as Teddie found out when she and Max were engaged and she moved into their sprawling suburban home. Though she tried, in her own bumbling, hysterical way, she had no idea how to relate to nutty, curly-haired Carter and emotionally uncertain ("I-love-you-I-hate-you") kindergartner Eliza. Gladys was the standoffish black housekeeper. There were lots of sex jokes (Teddie's attempt to bake a cake in the shape of a baseball bat for Carter's bake sale was dubbed "the penis cake"), pratfalls, mugging and misunderstandings. Finally in an episode aired in June 2001, Teddie and Max were married in a chaotic city hall ceremony, but the series had by then been canceled.

GEMINI MAN (*Action/Adventure*)
FIRST TELECAST: *September 23, 1976*
LAST TELECAST: *October 28, 1976*
BROADCAST HISTORY:
Sep 1976–Oct 1976, NBC Thu 8:00–9:00
CAST:
Sam Casey .... Ben Murphy
Leonard Driscoll .... William Sylvester
Abby Lawrence .... Katherine Crawford

Sam Casey was an agent for INTERSECT, a government think tank and operations center specializing in missions requiring the utmost secrecy. While on a diving assignment, Sam was affected by the radiation from an underwater explosion. The radiation rendered him invisible, and it was only through the combined efforts of computer expert Abby Lawrence and Leonard Driscoll, Sam's boss at INTERSECT, that a way was devised to control his invisibility. Sam was fitted with a computerized watchlike contraption that kept him visible. He could, however, switch it off and become invisible again, for short periods. If he did this for more than 15 minutes in any 24-hour period, he would die. Needless to say, the ability to become invisible, despite the time limits, made Sam a very effective agent indeed.

Unfortunately, stiff competition from ABC and CBS rendered the ratings for this program almost invisible, and it did a fast fade-out after only one month on the air.

GENE AUTRY SHOW, THE (*Western*)
FIRST TELECAST: *July 23, 1950*
LAST TELECAST: *August 7, 1956*
BROADCAST HISTORY:
Jul 1950–Jul 1953, CBS Sun 7:00–7:30
Jul 1953–Sep 1954, CBS Tue 8:00–8:30
Sep 1954–Aug 1956, CBS Sat 7:00–7:30
REGULARS:
Gene Autry
Pat Buttram
THEME:
"Back in the Saddle Again," by Ray Whitley and Gene Autry

Gene Autry, the singing cowboy, made the transition from feature-length movies to half-hour TV films in the early 1950s and became very wealthy doing it. For six seasons he and his sidekick, Pat Buttram, rode from town to town in the Southwest helping maintain law and order. Each episode provided opportunities for Gene to sing, his sidekick Pat to get into some silly predicament, and his horse Champion to show off the training that made him a very talented hunk of horseflesh.

GENE RODDENBERRY'S ANDROMEDA (*Science Fiction*)

BROADCAST HISTORY:

Syndicated only
60 minutes
Produced: *2000–*
Released: *October 2000*

CAST:

Capt. Dylan Hunt .... Kevin Sorbo
Beka Valentine .... Lisa Ryder
Tyr Anasazi .... Keith Hamilton Cobb
Andromeda Ascendant "Rommie" .... Lexa Doig
Trance Gemini .... Laura Bertram
Seamus Harper .... Gordon Woolvett
Rev Bem (2000–2001) .... Brent Stait

Dylan was captain of the Commonwealth starship *Andromeda Ascendant* during a period in which the Commonwealth was at war with the Nietzcheans. When his vessel was severely damaged in battle he ordered his crew to abandon ship. Dylan stayed on, and the *Andromeda Ascendant* was swallowed up by a black hole. Three hundred years later a salvage ship, the *Eureka Maru*, commanded by Beka, recovered the *Andromeda* and Dylan. When he was revived the ship's computer (Rommie) informed him that he and the ship had been frozen in time and that the Commonwealth had lost the war and was no more. The idealistic Dylan convinced Beka and her crew to become his crew and help him form a New Commonwealth to restore law and order to a universe that had degenerated badly while he was in suspended animation. Beka's crew consisted of Harper, a brilliant but cynical young engineer; her pilot/medic Trance, a seemingly flighty alien with the ability to see the future, and Rev, a Magog who, unlike most of his bestial race, liked and got along well with humans. Tyr, the last addition to Dylan's crew, was an intellectual Nietzschean warrior and the last surviving member of his clan. In the series premiere, after Tyr and his fellow mercenaries failed in an attempt to invade the *Andromeda*, Dylan convinced him to join in his quest to build the New Commonwealth.

At the end of the third episode Harper succeeded in giving Rommie a physical body (and a very sexy one at that) and the ship's computer became a "member" of the crew. Tyr had his doubts about Dylan's ability to deal with a universe so vastly changed and tried to convince Beka to lead a mutiny—it didn't work out, and he eventually became less determined to oust Dylan. Much of their time was spent trying to convince the governments of the worlds they visited to join the New Commonwealth. In the season finale the *Andromeda* was attacked by the Magog who, after a bitter battle, captured Tyr and Harper, whom they injected with Magog larvae.

That fall Rev, who had faked allegiance to the other Magog, helped Dylan rescue Tyr and Harper, but eventually left the crew because he needed time alone to get his Magog instincts under control. Before he left the crew determined that they had two years to rebuild the New Commonwealth for an eventually confrontation with the Magog. Trance removed the Magog larvae from Tyr, but the procedure would have killed Harper so he took medication to keep them under control. In February Trance exchanged places with her older, more serious future self, after a device Harper had built to rid himself of the Magog larvae malfunctioned. The older Trance removed the larvae and took over her former self's position on the *Andromeda*, despite the misgivings of Dylan, who wasn't sure he trusted her.

GENE RODDENBERRY'S EARTH: FINAL CONFLICT (*Science Fiction*)

BROADCAST HISTORY:

Syndicated only
60 minutes
Produced: *1997–2002* (110 episodes)
Released: *October 1997*

CAST:

William Boone (1997–1998) .... Kevin Kilner
Capt. Lili Marquette (1997–2000) ..... Lisa Howard
Ronald Sandoval .... Von Flores
Da'an (1997–2001) .... Leni Parker
Jonathan Doors (1997–2000) ...... David Hemblen
Augur (1997–2001) .... Richard Chevolleau
Zo'or (1997–2001) .... Anita La Selva
**Dr. Julianne Belman (1997–1999)* ..... Majel Barrett
Liam Kincaid (1998–2002) .... Robert Leeshock
Renee Palmer (1999–2002) .... Jayne Heitmeyer
Juliet "J." Street (2000–2002) .... Melinda Deines
Howlyn (2001–2002) .... Alan Van Sprang
Juda (2001–2002) .... Guylaine St. Onge
**Joshua Doors (1998–2000)* .... William De Vry
**Maiya (1998–1999)* .... Montse Viader
**President Daniel Thompson (1998–2000)* .... Barry Flatman
**Sam Tate (1999–2002)* .... Richard Zeppieri
**Vorjak (2000–2001)* .... Dan R. Chameroy
**Director Hubbell Urich (1999–2002)* .... Frank Moore
**Ra'jel (2001–2002)* .... Helen Taylor
**Ryan Patrichio (2001–2002)* .... Noam Jennings
Capt. Brandon Michaels (2002) ... Dean McDermot

*Occasional

This series, developed from a never-produced script written by the late Gene Roddenberry, creator of *Star Trek*, described a more subtle and complex relationship between humans and aliens than was generally seen in TV science-fiction series.

The Taelons, who were referred to in the news media as the "Companions," were a race of serene and seemingly benevolent aliens who arrived on Earth in the mid-21st century. Most citizens believed there was no threat to Earth, due to the cagey newcomers' apparently benign intentions and the advanced technology they shared with humans. However some, led by the industrialist Doors, were more suspicious, forming an underground resistance movement of non-believers. One key agent for the Resistance was Lili, the chief pilot for the Taelons, who flew a helicopter-type craft that traveled inter-dimensionally both on Earth and to the orbiting Taelon mother ship; another was Augur, a computer hacker who, for a price, could break into almost any computer system. Lili recruited Boone, who had recently been hired by the Taelons to run their security operations, as a double agent. F.B.I. agent Sandoval was the primary human aide to Da'an, the head of the Taelon group on Earth.

In a February 1998 episode the Taelons, after evaluating the research of one of their own who had been on Earth 2,000 years earlier, concluded that their destiny as a race was tied to their relationship with humanity. It was discovered that this ancient Taelon had given ESP and psychic abilities to early man. Unfortunately, the Taelons had present-day problems. No sooner had Boone received psychic powers, with the help of Dr. Belman, than he was wounded in a confrontation with Ha'gel, a 10-million-year-old alien whose Jaridian race had once been part of the Taelons. At the end of the episode Boone was killed as the stasis tank in which he was healing was destroyed by Zo'or, a militant Taelon rival to Da'an.

That fall a new hero was introduced to try to figure out what the Taelons were really up to. He was the mysterious Liam Kincaid, born to a woman who had been impregnated by Ha'gel. Her pregnancy lasted nine hours, and Liam grew to adulthood in less than a day. At Boone's funeral Liam saved Da'an from a Jaridian replicant assassin and was given Boone's former job as his protector. The Jaridians and the Taelons had once been a single race but they diverged when the brainy Taelons created the "commonality" and lost both their emotional identity and their ability to reproduce. Zo'or and Da'an fought over control of the Taelon Synod on Earth and the way in which they would deal with humanity, whose unwitting assistance they needed to help them fight an impending war with the Jaridians. The more militant Zo'or won, but Da'an, who actually seemed to care about humanity, began to work quietly on behalf of the Resistance. Meanwhile Doors, who had been in hiding since the series premiere, emerged to run for President. In the season finale Doors' son Joshua despite being his father's campaign manager, worked to undermine the campaign and insure the re-election of Taelon pawn Daniel Thompson. When Thompson won he instituted a military state in which anyone associated with the resistance was arrested—including Da'an.

At the start of the 1999–2000 season Lili was captured by Sandoval's minions, who modified her physiology and sent her in an interdimensional shuttle to God knows where. President Thompson was under Zo'or's thumb and could do little; Doors appeared to have thrown in the towel, as he was working with Thompson's puppet government. Augur and Liam were saved from capture and exposure by Renee Palmer, a woman working for Doors who became their strongest ally. In December Lili resurfaced in a mind-controlled environment in which she provided the Jaridians with the information necessary for them to build ships that would enable them to attack Earth. Later that month it was revealed that Zo'or was the last Taelon conceived (over 1,000 years ago), that Da'an was his father, and that the Taelon race was doomed to extinction without the help of the humans. In May after Jonathan Doors died while saving his son's life, Joshua took over Doors Industries. Sandoval was also working with Da'an against Zo'or, but when Zo'or threatened to kill him for betrayal, he was forced to vow allegiance to Zo'or. In the season finale Lili returned with three Jaridians and survived when her ship was shot down in Antartica. Lili was carrying a Jaridian's baby because their own race was becoming barren and could continue only through human/Jaridian hybrids. Da'an showed up to provide an energy infusion to keep Lili from dying while she was being transformed into a hybrid herself. Liam and Renee arrived while she was in midconversion and found out that Da'an would have to sacrifice his own life to ensure the survival of Lili and her unborn baby.

Lili gave birth to a girl, Ariel, and Vorjak, her Jaridian husband, hoped she would help his race survive. Da'an's body had changed to a crystalline form, but he was actually in hibernation and recovered. Augur went on the run but left Street, a friend, to help Liam with information. Lili and her family left Earth to save themselves from dying in a now-hostile atmosphere. Doors was still alive, sort of, as an artificial intelligence program that gave his son, Joshua, instructions on how to run the family business and deal with the Taelons. Street developed a computer virus that forced the cyber-Jonathan to destroy itself; Joshua then destroyed the Taelon core energy vessel, forcing Da'an to share his core energy with Zo'or to keep him alive. In February 2001 dark matter struck the Taelon mother ship and put Zo'or in a state of suspended animation, leaving Sandoval in charge. Sandoval, seeking revenge for his wife's murder and other accumulated Taelon atrocities, planned to kill all of them to liberate Earth. Augur returned with plans to learn from a Taelon relic the means for synthesizing limitless core energy—the road to personal riches and a way to free humanity from the Taelons. He and Street were caught by Sandoval, but Liam and Renee helped them escape. Sandoval's wife, whom he thought had been killed but who had in reality deserted him, returned and betrayed his extracurricular activities to the Taelons.

In May the Taelons announced their plans to go into stasis because their core energy levels were running low. It was Da'an's plan, but Zo'or refused and took some of Zo'or's core energy reserves to enable him to function before pushing his father into stasis. Liam revived Da'an and started the sequence to revive the other Taelons in stasis. The revived Taelons took from Zo'or some of the core energy he had taken from Da'an, giving them roughly three months to live. An orbiting Jaridian energy source reprogrammed the CVIs in the protectors and forced them to attack the Taelons. It also took over Sandoval, who took the mother ship, with Liam and Renee on board, to the Jaridian home world, where Vorjak planned to kill all the Taelons and then exterminate humanity. Liam got through to Sandoval, who helped them get back to Earth. When they returned, the surviving Taelons were on the verge of death, and Liam and Renee convinced Street to help them find a source of energy that would keep the Taelons alive in stasis. Vorjak and a party of Jaridians were in pursuit and, when they arrived, struck a deal with Sandoval whereby he would rule Earth and help them kill all of the Taelons. They went to the regeneration chamber, where Liam convinced them that they had to be part of the regeneration process along with the Taelons. They entered the chambers, but as the episode ended the volcano in which they were housed exploded.

As the last season began, a badly burned Sandoval

was found alive on the abandoned Taelon mother ship. Renee and Street went in search of Liam and found an Atavus chamber embedded in volcanic rock. When their crew got into the chamber, they were attacked by Atavus—aliens resurrected when Liam merged the Taelon and Jaridian species. In a confrontation Renee hit an Atavus in the chest and released Ra'-jel, guardian of the collective consciousness of the Taelons, who had once resided on the mother ship. Ra'jel told her that the joining of the Taelons and Jaridians unleashed "the final conflict," and that Renee had been chosen to save humanity from the Atavus. Renee was then confronted by Howlyn, the head male Atavus, who told her that his race had been on Earth long before humans but had been forced underground by asteroids. Now revived, they needed to feed on human life force to survive and reclaim Earth. Renee escaped from Howlyn, but Sandoval arrived with the mother ship and took the Atavus chamber on board, where he negotiated a deal. Renee recovered in a military hospital and tried to convince Director Urich that the Atavus were a major threat. On the mother ship Ra'jel tried to reason, unsuccessfully, with Sandoval. Ra'jel ordered the mother ship into the atmosphere, which would destroy it and all on board, but Sandoval managed to right it.

Sandoval spirited Urich to the mother ship with the intention of altering him into an Atavus/human hybrid, but Renee saved him and returned him to Earth. He was in bad shape and went into a coma before he could tell Patrichio to order a strike on the mother ship. On the mother ship Sandoval revived Boone, the original leader of the human resistance movement, out of a state of suspended animation. Sandoval sent him to Earth hoping he would lead them to Renee and, after Boone joined Renee's crusade against the Atavus, Boone left because it was dangerous for him and Renee to be in the same place. In February Renee got Urich back to her hideout and they managed to revive him. Two weeks later he made a speech to the public warning of the Atavus threat. Juda, Howlyn's mate, died from wounds suffered during a raid (but remained in the opening credits for the rest of the season). In April Renee got emotionally involved with Howlyn's young son, Yulyn (Daniel Clark), who had a human-like soul. She felt obligated to protect Yulyn from his father. In the series finale Liam, set free by "the collective will of the universe," surfaced to give Renee guidance and solace. He helped her find the Atavus starship buried under the Siberian desert. They took Yulyn with them but he was caught by his father and Sandoval, who went after Renee and died in a failed attempt to kill her, while Howlyn revived the crew to run the ship. They rebelled and killed Howlyn, and Renee and Liam showed up with troops to defeat the remaining Atavus. They transported the ship's interdimensional drive along with the Atavus in stasis to the Taelon mother ship so that Yulyn could return to his home world. In the final scene Ra'jel convinced Renee to join Liam piloting the Taelon ship exploring the universe.

GENERAL ELECTRIC SUMMER ORIGINALS (*Dramatic Anthology*)

FIRST TELECAST: *July 3, 1956*
LAST TELECAST: *September 18, 1956*
BROADCAST HISTORY:
Jul 1956–Sep 1956, ABC Tue 9:00–9:30

This summer series consisted of 30-minute dramatic films never before seen on television, featuring such Hollywood standbys as Vivian Blaine, Joe E. Brown, Zachary Scott, and Ronald Reagan.

GENERAL ELECTRIC THEATER (*Dramatic Anthology*)

FIRST TELECAST: *February 1, 1953*
LAST TELECAST: *September 16, 1962*
BROADCAST HISTORY:
Feb 1953–Sep 1962, CBS Sun 9:00–9:30
HOST/STAR:
Ronald Reagan (1954–1962)

This long-running filmed anthology series premiered in February 1953 as an alternate-week program with *The Fred Waring Show.* There was no host when it first went on the air, Ronald Reagan taking over that role at the start of the 1954–1955 season. He occasionally added the role of episode star to his regular function as host and commercial spokesman. At first, not all of the dramas were filmed, but, as Mr. Reagan said many years later, the problems inherent in live drama on television gave the live episodes a less finished look than the filmed ones. Eventually all of the shows were filmed in advance.

The range of material covered was vast, with one week's story a contemporary adventure, like "Ride the River" with Broderick Crawford and Neville Brand, and the next week's a period biblical drama, like "The Stone" starring Tony Curtis. Everything from light bedroom comedy to heavy melodrama showed up on *General Electric Theater*, and when Westerns became very popular in the late 1950s they were well represented too—"Saddle Tramp in the Old West" starring James Stewart and "Too Good with a Gun" starring Robert Cummings and young Michael Landon (pre-*Bonanza*) among them.

Although most of the stories used on *General Electric Theater* were either original teleplays or adaptations from lesser-known authors, there were occasional exceptions. Phyllis Thaxter and Patric Knowles starred in "Nora," based on Henrik Ibsen's *A Doll's House*; Burgess Meredith starred in a condensed version of the motion picture *Edison, the Man*; Teresa Wright and Richard Boone had the leads in "Love Is Eternal," based on Irving Stone's novel of the same name; and Ronald Reagan and his wife Nancy Davis starred in "Money and the Minister," written by Charlotte Armstrong.

In its eight-plus years, however, *General Electric Theater*'s emphasis was primarily on simple dramas and diversionary entertainment. It was there to entertain, not to preach or educate, and most of the stories were not memorable. However, the list of famous performers appearing was formidable. In addition to those mentioned above, such people as Sir Cedric Hardwicke, Ward Bond, June Havoc, Alan Ladd, Barry Fitzgerald, Jane Wyman, Cornel Wilde, Myrna Loy, Jack Benny, Bette Davis, Anne Baxter, and Barbara Stanwyck starred at one time or another.

General Electric Theater was syndicated under the title *Star Showcase*, with new introductions by Edward Arnold.

GENERAL ELECTRIC TRUE (*Dramatic Anthology*)

FIRST TELECAST: *September 30, 1962*
LAST TELECAST: *September 22, 1963*
BROADCAST HISTORY:
Sep 1962–Sep 1963, CBS Sun 9:30–10:00
HOST/NARRATOR:
Jack Webb

The distinction between this series and its predecessor, *General Electric Theater,* was that all of the stories presented in this series were based on actual incidents and were dramatized with as much fidelity to the original as possible. The stories tended to be in the adventure-suspense vein, and many had military themes. All were taken from the files of *True* magazine.

Jack Webb, who was the host and narrator for the entire series, was the closest thing to a major star to appear in *General Electric True.* In "Code-Name Christopher," a two-part story which he also directed, Webb played an American agent planning the sabotage of a Nazi factory during World War II. Among the few other familiar names that appeared in these dramas were Jerry Van Dyke, Arte Johnson, Robert Vaughn, and Victor Buono.

GENERATION GAP, THE (*Quiz*)

FIRST TELECAST: *February 7, 1969*
LAST TELECAST: *May 23, 1969*
BROADCAST HISTORY:
Feb 1969–May 1969, ABC Fri 8:30–9:00
EMCEE:
Dennis Wholey (Feb–Apr)
Jack Barry (Apr–May)

Quiz in which two teams, one composed of three teenagers and the other of three adults, were each asked questions about the other generation's lifestyles and fads. The teenagers were quizzed about such things as the Edsel, Shirley Temple, Senator Claghorn, Carmen Miranda, and the like; the adults (all over 30) would have to answer questions about the boogaloo, current draft law, "hanging five," and so on. Film clips, photos, and recordings illustrated the questions. Celebrity parents and their offspring often appeared on opposing teams.

GENTLE BEN (*Adventure*)

FIRST TELECAST: *September 10, 1967*
LAST TELECAST: *August 31, 1969*
BROADCAST HISTORY:
Sep 1967–Aug 1969, CBS Sun 7:30–8:00
CAST:
Tom Wedloe .... Dennis Weaver
Mark Wedloe .... Clint Howard
Ellen Wedloe .... Beth Brickell
Henry Boomhauer .... Rance Howard
Willie (1968–1969) .... Angelo Rutherford

Ben was a 650-pound American black bear who, fortunately, was as friendly and lovable as he was large. He lived in the Everglades of Florida with his "family," the Wedloes. Ben's constant companion was eight-year-old Mark Wedloe, whose father, Tom, was a wildlife officer. Henry Boomhauer, portrayed by young star Clint Howard's real father Rance, was a backwoodsman who was both friend and advisor to the Wedloes.

GEOGRAPHICALLY SPEAKING (*Travelogue*)

FIRST TELECAST: *October 27, 1946*
LAST TELECAST: *December 1, 1946*
BROADCAST HISTORY:
Oct 1946–Dec 1946, NBC Sun 8:15–8:30
HOSTESS:
Mrs. Carveth Wells

This early series began locally on NBC's New York station on June 9, 1946, and was fed to the small NBC East Coast network in October, sponsored by Bristol-Myers. It consisted of travel films taken and narrated by Mrs. Carveth Wells, and it ended when she ran out of film.

GEORGE (*Situation Comedy*)

FIRST TELECAST: *November 5, 1993*
LAST TELECAST: *January 19, 1994*
BROADCAST HISTORY:
Nov 1993, ABC Fri 8:30–9:00
Nov 1993, ABC Sat 8:00–8:30
Dec 1993–Jan 1994, ABC Wed 8:30–9:00
CAST:
George Foster .... George Foreman
Maggie Foster .... Sheryl Lee Ralph
George "Bubba" Foster, Jr. .... Tony T. Johnson
Virginia Elizabeth "Vee" Foster ... Lauren Robinson
Juanita Holman .... Anne Haney
Lathan Basmore .... Larry Gilliard, Jr.
Daniel Hickok .... Cleandre Norman
Mauricio Butler .... Pablo Irlando
Shasta Roberta Rhodes .... Doniell Spencer
Vanessa Jasso .... LaCrystal Cooke
EXECUTIVE PRODUCER:
Tony Danza

Bald, burly ex-heavyweight champ George Foreman was the unlikely star of this short-lived sitcom, which was otherwise indistinguishable from dozens of others. At least he was cast to type, playing an ex-heavyweight champ who sat on his duff all day eating ice cream and watching TV, living off his earnings from the ring. George's high-energy wife, Maggie, on the other hand, was constantly in motion as a guidance counselor at inner-city Monroe High School. Intrigued by her stories of troubled kids, George decided to see if he could help by setting up an after-school boxing club called the TKO club. Disciplining these tough youngsters was not as easy as he thought. Tough guy Daniel, volatile Mauricio, sharp-tongued Shasta, motormouth Vanessa, and troubled Lathan were a handful for anyone, but George managed to pull it off with a mix of determination and unfailing good humor.

Bubba and Vee were George's kids and Juanita the sour housekeeper. Ex-boxer Tony Danza *(Who's the Boss?)* co-produced this series.

GEORGE & LEO (*Situation Comedy*)

FIRST TELECAST; *September 15, 1997*
LAST TELECAST: *June 22, 1998*
BROADCAST HISTORY:
Sep 1997–Dec 1998, CBS Mon 9:30–10:00
Jan 1998–Feb 1998, CBS Mon 9:00–9:30
Feb 1998–Mar 1998, CBS Mon 9:30–10:00
May 1998–Jun 1998, CBS Mon 9:30–10:00
CAST:
George Stoody .... Bob Newhart
Leo Wagonman .... Judd Hirsch
Ted Stoody .... Jason Bateman
Casey Wagonman Stoody (1997) .... Bess Meyer
Casey Wagonman Stoody (1997–1998)
.... Robyn Lively

Ambrose .... Darryl Theirse
**Officer Zajac* .... Paul Willson
Alice (1998) .... Julia Sweeney

*Occasional

Picturesque Martha's Vineyard was the setting for this comedy about two mismatched in-laws. George was a quiet, introspective New Englander who ran a small bookstore on the island. On the eve of his son Ted's wedding to an already pregnant Casey, George's orderly life was changed forever. Ted had invited Casey's father, Leo, to the wedding. Leo, who had not seen his daughter in 20 years (her choice), was a small-time hoodlum on the run from mobsters in Las Vegas, because he'd kept the last payoff he had collected. When he found out there was a spare room above George's bookstore, he moved right in—and George spent the season trying to get him to leave town. Leo was a piece of work, a loud, obnoxious, lusty con man whose every word and action caused shivers to run up and down George's spine. Whenever George let Leo talk him into anything, he got in trouble—offering a bribe to the Edgartown building inspector to avoid a zoning infraction caused by Leo's living above the bookstore landed George in jail. Ted and Casey ran a small restaurant, and Ambrose worked for George in the bookstore. After Casey gave birth in February, they hired Alice as the nanny for their baby.

GEORGE BURNS AND GRACIE ALLEN SHOW, THE (*Situation Comedy*)

FIRST TELECAST: *October 12, 1950*
LAST TELECAST: *September 22, 1958*
BROADCAST HISTORY:
Oct 1950–Mar 1953, CBS Thu 8:00–8:30
Mar 1953–Sep 1958, CBS Mon 8:00–8:30
CAST:
George Burns .... Himself
Gracie Allen .... Herself
Blanche Morton .... Bea Benaderet
Harry Morton (1950–1951) .... Hal March
Harry Morton (1951) .... John Brown
Harry Morton (1951–1953) .... Fred Clark
Harry Morton (1953–1958) .... Larry Keating
Bill Goodwin (1950–1951) .... Himself
Harry Von Zell (1951–1958) .... Himself
Mr. Beasley, the mailman .... Rolfe Sedan
Ronnie Burns (1955–1958) .... Himself
Bonnie Sue McAfee (1957–1958) .... Judi Meredith
THEME:
"Love Nest," by Louis A. Hirsch and Otto Harbach

George Burns and Gracie Allen had one of the most enduring acts in the history of show business. They were headliners in vaudeville in the 1920s, on radio in the 1930s and 1940s, and for almost a full decade on television in the 1950s. The factor which finally terminated the act was not loss of audience appeal, but Gracie's decision to retire in 1958.

The format of the TV Burns and Allen show was simple enough. It was set in the Burns home, and cast George in the dual role of on-screen narrator of the proceedings and straight man for Gracie's scatterbrained but delightful involvements with various people and situations. Gracie's cohort in many of her predicaments was neighbor Blanche Morton, whose long-suffering accountant husband Harry was as infuriated by the girls' escapades as George was tolerant. George was unflappable. He would simply turn to the camera, cigar in hand, and philosophize to the audience.

When it first came to television in 1950 *The George Burns and Gracie Allen Show* was produced live in New York and aired every other Thursday night. Members of the radio cast who followed the show to television were Bill Goodwin, the commercial announcer who doubled as George and Gracie's friend; Bea Benaderet, as neighbor Blanche Morton; Hal March as Blanche's husband Harry; and Rolfe Sedan as the mailman to whom Gracie gossiped. There was considerable turnover in the role of Harry Morton during the series' early years. March left the show in January 1951, to be replaced by John Brown. Brown lasted six months and was replaced in June by Fred Clark, who was in turn replaced in the fall of 1953 by Larry Keating. Harry Von Zell joined the cast at the start of the 1951–1952 season as replacement for Bill Goodwin, doing the commercials and playing a friend of the family. In the fall of 1952 the series became a weekly filmed feature originating from the West Coast.

GEORGE BURNS COMEDY WEEK (*Comedy Anthology*)

FIRST TELECAST: *September 18, 1985*
LAST TELECAST: *December 25, 1985*
BROADCAST HISTORY:
Sep 1985–Dec 1985, CBS Wed 9:30–10:00
HOST:
George Burns

Veteran funnyman George Burns, who was 89 years old when this series was on the air, served as both host and narrator of this comedy anthology series. Among the more familiar names appearing were Joe Piscopo, Robert Klein, Martin Mull, Don Rickles, Don Knotts, Fannie Flagg, Candy Clark, Howard Hesseman, Laraine Newman, James Whitmore, Roddy McDowall, and Samantha Eggar. One of the episodes, which had starred Harvey Korman and Valerie Perrine, surfaced as the series *Leo & Liz in Beverly Hills* four months after *George Burns Comedy Week* left the air.

GEORGE BURNS SHOW, THE (*Situation Comedy*)

FIRST TELECAST: *October 21, 1958*
LAST TELECAST: *April 14, 1959*
BROADCAST HISTORY:
Oct 1958–Apr 1959, NBC Tue 9:00–9:30
CAST:
George Burns .... Himself
Blanche Morton .... Bea Benaderet
Harry Morton .... Larry Keating
Harry Von Zell .... Himself
Ronnie Burns .... Himself
Judi Meredith .... Herself
Miss Jenkins .... Lisa Davis

Following his wife Gracie's retirement from show business, George Burns attempted a series of his own, including most of the regulars from the highly successful *Burns and Allen Show*. George played a theatrical producer beset with the usual problems of casting, booking, eccentric stars, and a complement of helpful friends who tended to create more problems than they solved. Blanche was George's secretary; Harry, her husband; and Harry Von Zell, a bumbling friend. George's real-life son Ronnie also appeared in the series, while Judi Meredith portrayed an aspiring actress who was Ronnie's steady girlfriend. Although Gracie Allen did not appear on this program, she was referred to. Blanche was a close friend of Gracie's, and as such was always trying to keep George from becoming involved with the attractive young starlets he constantly met—including a certain sexy secretary named Miss Jenkins.

Beginning in December and running through mid-February 1959, the format was altered to include a live variety show within almost every episode, featuring the regular cast and guest stars.

GEORGE CARLIN SHOW, THE (*Situation Comedy*)

FIRST TELECAST: *January 16, 1994*
LAST TELECAST: *September 3, 1995*
BROADCAST HISTORY:

Jan 1994–Aug 1994, FOX Sun 9:30–10:00
Oct 1994–Jan 1995, FOX Sun 9:30–10:00
Jul 1995–Sep 1995, FOX Sun 9:30–10:00

CAST:

George O'Grady .... George Carlin
Harry Rosetti .... Alex Rocco
Jack Donahue .... Anthony Starke
Sydney Paris .... Paige French
Dr. Neal Beck .... Christopher Rich
Kathleen Rachowski (1994) .... Susan Sullivan
Frank MacNamara .... Michael G. Hagerty
Larry Pinkerton .... Matt Landers
Bob Brown (1994) .... Phil LaMarr

George was a scruffy, ponytailed New York City cabbie who looked like an overage hippie from the 1960s. He spent most of his free time with a gang of other comic misfits at the Moylan Tavern, spouting philosophical observations and trading sarcastic complaints. Others 'round the bar were Jack, the slow-witted bartender who couldn't make drinks properly; Sydney the barmaid, an attractive, wise-cracking would-be model; Harry, the fast-talking bookie who had been George's friend for years; Neal, an out-of-his-element plastic surgeon; and Frank, a good-natured drinker with a beer belly to show for it. George, whose dating skills were marginal at best, developed a tenuous romance with Kathleen, owner of the pet shop where he got supplies for his new Yorkshire terrier, which he had named Miles, after jazz great Miles Davis. (He had won the dog from Neal in the premiere episode.) It was fortunate for Neal that he had a lucrative practice—a compulsive gambler, he lost not only his dog but thousands of dollars at a time to Harry. Toward the end of the series' run he was having an affair with Sydney. Larry and Bob were neighbors of George's who were often seen at the stoop of his Manhattan brownstone apartment.

GEORGE GOBEL SHOW, THE (*Comedy/Variety*)

FIRST TELECAST: *October 2, 1954*
LAST TELECAST: *June 5, 1960*
BROADCAST HISTORY:

Oct 1954–Jun 1957, NBC Sat 10:00–10:30 (OS)
Sep 1957–Mar 1959, NBC Tue 8:00–9:00 (OS)
Oct 1959–June 1960, CBS Sun 10:00–10:30

HOST:

George Gobel

REGULARS:

Alice (1954–1958) .... Jeff Donnell
Alice (1958–1959) .... Phyllis Avery
Peggy King (1954–1956)
Johnny Mann Singers (1957–1958)
Shirley Harmer (1957–1958)
John Scott Trotter Orchestra (1954–1958, 1959–1960)
Frank DeVol Orchestra (1958–1959)
Eddie Fisher (1957–1958)
The Kids Next Door (1958–1959)
Joe Flynn (1958–1959)
Anita Bryant (1959–1960)
The Modernaires (1959–1960)
Harry Von Zell (1959–1960)

THEME:

"Gobelues," by John Scott Trotter

Low-key comedian George Gobel, known affectionately as "Lonesome George," starred in his own live variety series for six years. It opened with George's monologue, included a sketch with or performance by the week's guest star, and always a sketch about George's family problems with his wife, Alice. Alice was his real-life wife's name, but on television she was portrayed first by Jeff Donnell and later by Phyllis Avery. (The Alice sketches were finally dropped when the series moved to CBS.)

For a time Gobel was one of TV's top hits, and his familiar sayings ("Well, I'll be a dirty bird!," "You don't hardly get those no more") became bywords. But then *Gunsmoke* came along, running opposite on CBS, and Gobel's star began to fade. During the two seasons that the show aired on Tuesday nights for a full hour, it alternated with *The Eddie Fisher Show*, and both stars were regular guests on each other's programs. When Gobel moved to CBS for a final season, he alternated with *The Jack Benny Show*.

GEORGE JESSEL SHOW, THE (*Variety*)

FIRST TELECAST: *September 13, 1953*
LAST TELECAST: *April 11, 1954*
BROADCAST HISTORY:

Sep 1953–Apr 1954, ABC Sun 6:30–7:00

HOST:

George Jessel

WRITERS:

George Jessel
Sam Carlton

George Jessel's most famous act, which he used throughout his long career, was that of the after-dinner speaker, and it was in that role that he appeared here. Each week Jessel, the self-proclaimed "Toastmaster General of the United States," was seen in a mock testimonial dinner, paying comic homage to the assembled guests of honor. In most cases these were personalities from the field of entertainment, such as Sophie Tucker, Mitzi Gaynor, and Margaret O'Brien. Live from New York.

GEORGE JONES SHOW, THE (*Interview*)

BROADCAST HISTORY:

The Nashville Network
60 minutes
Produced: *1999–2000*
Premiered: *January 19, 1999*

HOST:

George Jones

THEME:

"It Just Don't Get Any Better Than This"

Silver-haired George Jones (a.k.a. "The Possum"), looking very much the serene country legend behind his rose-colored glasses, presided like a hip elder statesman over this chatty hour that mixed stars of the past with hot, young, current artists. This being the country field, the latter were always deferential to the former, and everybody complimented everyone else's work. For the talk segments, George and his guests were seen in a living room set, chatting informally about their experiences performing. Periodically the scene would shift to a club setting, where George or his guests would perform. Sometimes George would amble through his picture gallery, spinning stories about ol' Hank Williams, Sr., or other greats he had known during his long career, which had begun in the '50s. Representing the older generation were such pals as Roy Clark and Johnny Paycheck; and the newer, Neal McCoy, Alan Jackson, and the Lynn Twins. *The George Jones Show* was first seen as a series of specials beginning on February 17, 1998.

GEORGE LOPEZ (*Situation Comedy*)

FIRST TELECAST: *March 27, 2002*
LAST TELECAST:
BROADCAST HISTORY:
Mar 2002–Apr 2002, ABC Wed 8:30–9:00
Oct 2002– , ABC Wed 8:30–9:00
CAST:
George Lopez .... George Lopez
Angie Lopez .... Constance Marie
Carmen Lopez (age 13)
.... Masiela Lusha (aka Stacey Haglund)
Max Lopez (9) .... Luis Armand Garcia
Benny .... Belita Moreno
Ernie .... Valente Rodriguez

For George, work life and home life were strangely intermixed. At Powers and Sons Aviation, a Los Angeles airplane parts manufacturer, he had been the first assembly-line worker ever to be promoted to manager. That put him in charge of his former pals—which could at times be a bit awkward—and worse yet in charge of his mother, Benny, who also worked on the line. Benny was cranky and sarcastic and gave him constant grief, laying on guilt with a trowel (not that it had much effect on good-natured George). She lived next door to George and hung out in his kitchen as well. Also at home were George's stylish wife, Angie, his whiny daughter, Carmen, and his happy young son, Max, who worshiped his dad. Together they dealt with little family crises and Benny's constant complaining, and there was also a recurring story line about George trying to find his father, whom Benny had falsely told him was dead. Despite the turmoil George maintained his sense of humor, one of his favorite little gags being a mechanical fish mounted on his office wall—which turned its head on cue and sang "Swanee River." Ernie was an assembly-line worker who was George's best friend.

The show was probably more distinctive for its Latino cast, a rarity in prime time, than for its content. One of the executive producers was actress Sandra Bullock, who appeared occasionally as disaster-prone factory worker "Accident Amy."

GEORGE MICHAEL SPORTS MACHINE, THE

(*Sports Highlights*)
FIRST TELECAST: *September 2, 1984*
LAST TELECAST: *September 8, 1991*
BROADCAST HISTORY:
Sep 1984–Sep 1991, NBC Sun 11:30–12:00
(In first-run syndication since September 1991)
HOST:
George Michael

A fast-paced, irreverent weekly wrap-up of major happenings in the world of sports, hosted by the sports reporter for NBC's Washington TV station, WRC-TV. Michael made extensive use of videotaped highlights from the week's games, along with player profiles, sports bloopers, and intentionally funny coverage of such non-mainstream "sports" as wrestling and rodeo.

When NBC dropped *Sports Machine* from its network lineup, it immediately went into syndication. Viewers on NBC affiliates that continued to carry the show probably didn't even know that anything had changed.

GEORGE SANDERS MYSTERY THEATER, THE

(*Dramatic Anthology*)
FIRST TELECAST: *June 22, 1957*
LAST TELECAST: *September 14, 1957*
BROADCAST HISTORY:
June 1957–Sep 1957, NBC Sat 9:00–9:30
HOST:
George Sanders

George Sanders served as host for all of these filmed dramas and appeared occasionally as an actor in them.

GEORGE SCHLATTER'S COMEDY CLUB

(*Comedy/Variety*)
BROADCAST HISTORY:
Syndicated only
30 minutes
Produced: *1987–1988* (26 episodes)
Released: *September 1987*
HOST:
George Schlatter

When he produced *Rowan & Martin's Laugh-In* two decades earlier, George Schlatter had altered the face of television comedy by making it hip and topical, and drastically increasing the pace. His 1987 series had no regular cast—each week a different group of young comics was featured—but the look was very reminiscent of his former hit. The individual monologues and sketches tended to be very short, with each change to a new performer or skit seeming to almost chop off the end of the previous one. The action took place on a large stage with different people doing different things, while the camera zoomed from one to another. There were background dancers and activities which never seemed to get any attention and the overall mood was one of frenzied confusion. Mr. Schlatter himself, who had not appeared on *Laugh-In,* opened and closed each episode from an on-camera "director's chair."

GEORGE SCHLATTER'S FUNNY PEOPLE

(*Comedy*)
FIRST TELECAST: *July 27, 1988*
LAST TELECAST: *September 7, 1988*

BROADCAST HISTORY:

Jul 1988–Aug 1988, NBC Wed 9:00–10:00
Aug 1988–Sep 1988, NBC Wed 8:00–9:00

HOSTS:

Leeza Gibbons
Scott Blakeman
Blake Clark
Rita Rudner
George Schlatter

REGULAR CONTRIBUTORS:

Dave Spector
Wayne Rostad

George Schlatter, the producer of *Real People*, recycled his Big Idea and featured himself prominently in the process (putting his name above the title and appearing on screen to "introduce the hosts") in this warmed-over version of the earlier show. Like *Real People*, *Funny People* featured clips of amusing people, places, and events around the United States and the world—from whistling midgets in Seattle to the San Diego jockey who claimed to weigh more than his horse. It also featured a similar group of studio comics to host the show. The principal difference was that it had a lot fewer viewers.

Also known as *Funny People*.

GEORGE WENDT SHOW, THE (*Situation Comedy*)

FIRST TELECAST: *March 8, 1995*
LAST TELECAST: *April 19, 1995*
BROADCAST HISTORY:

Mar 1995–Apr 1995, CBS Wed 8:00–8:30

CAST:

George Coleman .... George Wendt
Dan Coleman .... Pat Finn
Finnie .... Brian Doyle-Murray
Fletcher Williams ..... Mark Christopher Lawrence
Libby Schuster .... Kate Hodge

George and Dan Coleman were unmarried brothers who co-hosted a radio call-in show, "Points and Plugs," from the office of their auto repair shop in Madison, Wisconsin. Although they did provide useful information to callers, they also spent time musing about relationships, including what they considered the eternal triangle—a man, his woman, and his car. Dan, the impetuous younger brother, often got himself into situations that necessitated George's bailing him out, something that had been going on since they were kids. They had three other auto mechanics working for them—Finnie, Fletcher, and Libby.

GEORGETOWN UNIVERSITY FORUM (*Discussion*)

FIRST TELECAST: *July 3, 1951*
LAST TELECAST: *October 11, 1953*
BROADCAST HISTORY:

Jul 1951–Oct 1951, DUM Tue 8:00–8:30
Oct 1951–Nov 1951, DUM Thu 8:00–8:30
Dec 1951–Mar 1952, DUM Sun 6:30–7:00
Mar 1952–Oct 1953, DUM Sun 7:00–7:30

MODERATOR:

Frank Blair

Round-table discussions of topics of current interest, by members of the Georgetown University faculty and expert guests. At first the topics were political-social ("Is Our National Transportation Policy Outmoded?"), but later more popular subjects ("Flying Saucers") and descriptive programs on advances in medicine and daily living were featured as often as the debates. From Washington, D.C.

GEORGIA GIBBS AND HER MILLION RECORD SHOW (*Music*)

FIRST TELECAST: *July 1, 1957*
LAST TELECAST: *September 2, 1957*
BROADCAST HISTORY:

Jul 1957–Sep 1957, NBC Mon 7:30–7:45

REGULARS:

Georgia Gibbs
The Eddie Safranski Orchestra

"Her Nibs" Miss Georgia Gibbs (the nickname was given to her by Garry Moore) hosted this 15-minute summer show during 1957. In addition to introducing promising young singers, Georgia sang a number of popular songs, at least two of which were million sellers on record. Included, no doubt, were her own three gold records, "Kiss of Fire," "Tweedle Dee," and "Dance with Me, Henry." Occasionally, before doing her rendition of someone else's big hit, she would play an excerpt from the original recording, which had sold a million.

GERTRUDE BERG SHOW, THE (*Situation Comedy*)

FIRST TELECAST: *October 4, 1961*
LAST TELECAST: *April 5, 1962*
BROADCAST HISTORY:

Oct 1961–Jan 1962, CBS Wed 9:30–10:00
Jan 1962–Apr 1962, CBS Thu 9:30–10:00

CAST:

Sarah Green .... Gertrude Berg
Professor Crayton .... Sir Cedric Hardwicke
Maxfield .... May Wickes
Joe Caldwell .... Skip Ward
Susan Green (1961) .... Marion Ross
Jerry Green (1961) .... Leo Penn
George Howell .... Paul Smith
Irma Howell .... Aneta Corsaut
Carol .... Karyn Kupcinet

Gertrude Berg had become famous on radio and television in a series called *The Goldbergs*. Sarah Green, the character she played in this situation comedy, was in many ways an older version of her inimitable Molly Goldberg. Sarah was a matronly widow whose thirst for knowledge led her to enroll in college, despite her advancing years. Her English teacher, Professor Crayton, was an exchange teacher from Cambridge University. Maxfield ran the boardinghouse where Mrs. Green lived, and Joe Caldwell was an 18-year-old freshman in her class. The program was originally titled *Mrs. G. Goes to College*, but this was changed to *The Gertrude Berg Show*, in January 1962.

GET A LIFE (*Situation Comedy*)

FIRST TELECAST: *September 23, 1990*
LAST TELECAST: *June 14, 1992*
BROADCAST HISTORY:

Sep 1990–Aug 1991, FOX Sun 8:30–9:00
Nov 1991–Dec 1991, FOX Sat 9:30–10:00
Dec 1991–Mar 1992, FOX Sun 10:00–10:30
Apr 1992–Jun 1992, FOX Sun 10:30–11:00

CAST:

Chris Peterson .... Chris Elliott
Fred Peterson .... Bob Elliott

Gladys Peterson .... Elinor Donahue
Larry Potter (1990–1991) .... Sam Robards
Sharon Potter .... Robin Riker
**Amy Potter* .... Taylor Fry
**Bobby Potter* .... Zachary Benjamin
Gus Borden (1991–1992) ...... Brian Doyle-Murray

*Occasional

THEME:

"Stand," written and performed by R.E.M.

This offbeat comedy centered on the life of a 30-year-old paperboy who never quite grew up. Chris Peterson lived in an apartment over his folks' garage in the suburban community of Greenville. Making a living, such as it was, as a paperboy for the *Pioneer Press* was somehow appropriate for Chris, who acted more like a child than an adult. His best friend Larry, an uptight junior executive with a wife and two young children, lived next door. Larry's wife, Sharon, who disliked Chris intensely (especially when he crawled in their bedroom window), said it all when she told him "You're thirty. You still live with your parents. You're losing your hair, and you're stupid." None of this seemed to bother Chris, who floated through life with eternal optimism, incredible naivete, and a remarkable facility for avoiding any responsibility. At the start of the 1991–1992 season Chris moved into an "apartment" in the garage of retired Gus Borden, while Larry, unable to cope with the constant verbal abuse he received from his sharp-tongued wife, ran away from home.

The character Chris Elliot played in this series was a fleshed-out version of a character he had played on *Late Night with David Letterman*. Chris's real-life father, Bob Elliott of the comedy team of Bob and Ray, played his cynical, bathrobe-clad father on *Get a Life*.

GET CHRISTIE LOVE (*Police Drama*)

FIRST TELECAST: *September 11, 1974*
LAST TELECAST: *July 18, 1975*
BROADCAST HISTORY:

Sep 1974–Mar 1975, ABC Wed 10:00–11:00
Apr 1975–Jul 1975, ABC Fri 10:00–11:00

CAST:

Det. Christie Love .... Teresa Graves
Lt. Matt Reardon (1974) .... Charles Cioffi
Capt. Arthur P. Ryan (1975) .... Jack Kelly
Det. Joe Caruso .... Andy Romano
Det. Steve Belmont .... Dennis Rucker
Det. Valencia .... Scott Peters
Sgt. Pete Gallagher (1975) .... Michael Pataki

TECHNICAL ADVISOR/SOMETIME WRITER:

Det. Olga Ford, NYPD

Action series with black, sexy Teresa Graves as super-cop Christie Love of the Special Investigations Division, Los Angeles Police Department. Most of Christie's assignments were undercover jobs, giving her plenty of latitude for her slick, "with-it," rule-breaking style. Her hard-nosed boss was Lt. Matt Reardon, later replaced by Capt. Ryan, and her side-kick was Sgt. Pete Gallagher.

GET REAL (*Drama*)

FIRST TELECAST: *September 8, 1999*
LAST TELECAST: *April 12, 2000*
BROADCAST HISTORY:

Sep 1999–Apr 2000, FOX Wed 9:00–10:00
Sep 1999, FOX Mon 8:00–9:00

CAST:

Mitch Green .... Jon Tenney
Mary Green .... Debrah Farentino
Meghan Green (age 17) .... Anne Hathaway
Cameron Green (16) .... Eric Christian Olsen
Kenny Green (15) .... Jesse Eisenberg
Elizabeth Parker .... Christina Pickles
Victor Castillo .... Kyle Brent Gibson
Rebecca Peabody (1999) .... Taryn Manning
Clay Forman .... Scott Vickaryous
Jody Garrow .... Natalie Ramsey
Principal Bybee .... Scott Lawrence
Dr. Chris Carlyle (1999) .... Steven Gilborn
Amy Shepherd .... Alexandra Picatto

Mitch was a Jewish commercial real estate broker whose Catholic wife, Mary, ran a small party-planning and catering business in this drama about a troubled Los Angeles family. Their three rather smug kids, who provided narration, were all students at Truman High School. Meghan, the senior overachiever, had just decided not to go to college, much to her mother's dismay; Cameron was wasting his life bedding girls and skateboarding; and neurotic and insecure Kenny was infatuated with Rebecca, the new girl next door who, for some reason, actually seemed interested in him. Just when Kenny and Rebecca began to get serious, her dad—in the military—was reassigned and she moved away. Grandma Elizabeth, a widow, started dating her physician, Dr. Carlyle, but he dumped her for another woman. Victor was Kenny's best friend and Jody was Meghan's.

Mitch quit the brokerage business to convert an old firehouse into a restaurant and sell it. He had worked with his contractor dad in his youth, and had never lost his love for the sense of accomplishment obtained by actually building something. At Christmas Meghan was struggling with her attraction to Clay, her friend Amy's boyfriend; eventually they started to date, which destroyed Meghan's friendship with Amy. In late January Cameron, who had been in trouble before, was expelled from Truman for his involvement in a school prank that had gone disastrously wrong, and had to get a job. On his 16th birthday, in early March, Kenny collapsed at school from meningitis and almost died. Cameron was sent to a strict prison-like continuation school pending his reinstatement at Truman, but it was so rough his dad took him out and decided to home-school him instead. Eventually Cameron convinced Principal Bybee to reinstate him; once back at Truman he started dating Jody, who was less serious about their relationship than he was. Meanwhile Mitch struggled to make the payments on his firehouse project, and in the season finale, after tough negotiations with a developer who was hiding how desperately he needed the property, Mitch—with his dad's help—made a killing on the project. This was not the kind of series that could end happily, however; in the last scene Mitch found out he had a brain tumor.

Two episodes that never aired on Fox were seen in other countries.

GET SMART (*Situation Comedy*)

FIRST TELECAST: *September 18, 1965*
LAST TELECAST: *February 19, 1995*
BROADCAST HISTORY:

Sep 1965–Sep 1968, NBC Sat 8:30–9:00
Sep 1968–Sep 1969, NBC Sat 8:00–8:30

Sep 1969–Feb 1970, CBS Fri 7:30–8:00
Apr 1970–Sep 1970, CBS Fri 7:30–8:00
Jan 1995–Feb 1995, FOX Sun 7:30–8:00

CAST:

Maxwell Smart, Agent 86 .... Don Adams
Agent 99 .... Barbara Feldon
Thaddeus, the Chief (1965–1970)..... Edward Platt
Agent 13 (1966–1967) .... Dave Ketchum
Prof. Carlson (1966–1967)........ Stacy Keach (Sr.)
Conrad Siegfried (1966–1969) .... Bernie Kopell
Starker (1966–1969)................. King Moody
Hymie, the C.O.N.T.R.O.L. robot (1966–1969)
.... Dick Gautier
Agent 44 (1965–1970) .... Victor French
Larrabee (1967–1970)............ Robert Karvelas
99's Mother (1968–1969) .... Jane Dulo
Zach Smart (1995)..................... Andy Dick
Agent 66 (1995).................. Elaine Hendrix
Trudy (1995) .... Heather Morgan

DEVELOPERS/WRITERS:

Mel Brooks
Buck Henry

James Bond would have turned over in his grave. Here was secret agent Maxwell Smart, willing but inept, enthusiastic but confused, somehow stumbling through to defeat the evil agents of K.A.O.S. who, led by their mastermind Siegfried and his assistant Starker, planned to take over the world. Max worked for "The Chief," head of the Washington-based U.S. intelligence agency C.O.N.T.R.O.L. and had a beautiful and brilliant young partner known as Agent 99. Love blossomed and this mismatched pair married during the 1968–1969 season. During the next season, after the show had moved from NBC to CBS, 99 gave birth to twins, a boy and a girl.

Get Smart was a sophomoric, but highly successful, spoof of the secret-agent genre that had been spawned by James Bond movies in the 1960s, and was probably best typified by Max's pet expression "Would you believe?"—used whenever an agent of K.A.O.S. or someone on his own side didn't seem to accept one of his fabrications and he was trying to come up with a more acceptable alternative. That catchphrase became very popular with young people in the late 1960s.

When *Get Smart* was revived on Fox 25 years after the original series left the air, there were a number of changes. K.A.O.S. was now a corporation bent on world economic domination. Max was the new Chief of C.O.N.T.R.O.L., and 99 had been elected to Congress. The active agents were their son, Zach, a research nerd working for C.O.N.T.R.O.L. whom Max promoted to agent in the premiere episode, and 66, the sexy, intelligent, and totally in control agent with whom Zach was partnered. Trudy was Max's flighty secretary. The entrance to C.O.N.T.R.O.L. headquarters was now located through a hidden door in the soft-drink machine in the waiting room of a car wash. There were gimmicks reminiscent of the original series—Zach had a sneaker phone and 66 a bra that shot bullets—but the magic was long gone. Even guest appearances by Dave Ketchum and Bernie Kopell from the old *Get Smart* didn't help. After seven episodes, the new *Get Smart* was history.

One of the most frequently asked questions about the series was, "What was 99's real name?" In at least one episode she was referred to as Susan Hilton. However, elsewhere it was suggested that this was not her *real* name. Leave it to Mel Brooks and Buck Henry to keep us guessing!

GET THE PICTURE (*Quiz*)

BROADCAST HISTORY:

Nickelodeon
30 minutes
Produced: *1991* (115 episodes)
Premiered: *March 18, 1991*

HOST:

Mike O'Malley

A fast-paced and highly visual kids' quiz show played on a giant video monitor wall. Contestants had to use their knowledge and visual perception to uncover hidden pictures. Each episode culminated in a bonus round in which the winning team identified computer-controlled pictures.

GETTING BY (*Situation Comedy*)

FIRST TELECAST: *March 5, 1993*
LAST TELECAST: *June 18, 1994*
BROADCAST HISTORY:

Mar 1993–May 1993, ABC Fri 9:00–9:30
Sep 1993–Dec 1993, NBC Tue 8:30–9:00
Jan 1994–Feb 1994, NBC Sat 8:30–9:00
May 1994–Jun 1994, NBC Sat 8:30–9:00

CAST

Cathy Hale .... Cindy Williams
Nikki Hale (age 16)................ Nicki Vannice
Julie Hale (9) .... Ashleigh Blair Sterling
Dolores Dixon .... Telma Hopkins
Marcus Dixon (15)................ Merlin Santana
Darren Dixon (14) .... Deon Richmond

"We Are Family . . . Not!" might have been the title of this melting-pot sitcom in which terminally perky white mom Cathy and earthy black mom Dolores merged their broods to save a few bucks. Cathy's husband had run off with a bimbo, and Dolores was a widow. They shared an office as social workers, and decided to share a home, in the Chicago suburb of Oak Park, as well. Eyeing each other warily were their kids, blossoming Nikki and optimistic Julie on Cathy's side and girl-chasing schemer Marcus and trusting Darren on Dolores's. The laugh track roared as these opposites mixed and as cynical Dolores tried to teach her Goody Two-shoes partner the ways of the "real" world.

GETTING PERSONAL (*Situation Comedy*)

FIRST TELECAST: *April 6, 1998*
LAST TELECAST: *October 16, 1998*
BROADCAST HISTORY:

Apr 1998–Jun 1998, FOX Mon 8:30–9:00
Jul 1998–Sep 1998, FOX Fri 8:00–9:00
Sep 1998–Oct 1998, FOX Fri 8:30–9:00

CAST:

Robyn Buckley....................... Vivica A. Fox
Milo Doucette...................... Duane Martin
Sam Wagner............................ Jon Cryer
Jack Kacmarczyk.................... Elliott Gould
Shelly Tucci .... Nancy Cassaro
Leon Sykes Pettibone .... Reggie Hayes

Robyn was an administrative executive for Old Dog Productions, a small commercial production company in Chicago in this workplace comedy. She had been hired the morning after a disastrous blind date with Milo, the firm's talented but self-centered creative director, who now—surprise!—had to work for her. They found each other attractive but their egos wouldn't let them compromise enough to develop a viable working—or personal—relationship, and sarcastic sparks flew between them whenever they met. Sam, Milo's excitable best friend, was a film editor for the company who rode his bicycle to work and played bass with a jazz combo for recreation. The antithesis of Milo, he was very insecure and unsuccessful with women. Leon was the firm's pompous art director, and Shelly the cynical accountant who sided with Robyn on anything relating to men. Jack, the eccentric owner of Old Dog, had hired Robyn to run the business side of the company so he could go back to directing, or playing golf, or both.

GETTING TOGETHER (*Situation Comedy*)

FIRST TELECAST: *September 18, 1971*
LAST TELECAST: *January 8, 1972*
BROADCAST HISTORY:

Sep 1971–Jan 1972, ABC Sat 8:00–8:30

CAST:

Bobby Conway .... Bobby Sherman
Lionel Poindexter .... Wes Stern
Jennifer Conway .... Susan Neher
Officer Rudy Colcheck .... Jack Burns
Rita Simon .... Pat Carroll

THEME:

"Getting Together," by Helen Miller and Roger Atkins

Recording star Bobby Sherman played a young songwriter struggling to make it in the popular music business in this youth-oriented comedy. Bobby had the melodies, and his tone-deaf, offbeat friend Lionel wrote the lyrics. Bobby's mod-rock world was not without responsibilities, however, as he was legal guardian of his freckle-faced, 12-year-old sister Jennifer. The three of them, Bobby, Lionel, and Jennifer, lived in an antique shop (it was cheap—but occasionally the furniture got sold out from under them) while Bobby worked as a recording engineer, and the boys tried to peddle their songs. Rita was their motherly landlady, and Rudy her policeman-boyfriend.

Getting Together would seem to have been a perfect vehicle for Sherman to use in launching new hits, but in fact his real-life recording career went into something of a slump when the series went on the air. He did have one moderately popular disc derived from the program, however—titled "Jennifer"—and an album named after the show.

Getting Together was previewed on a March 1971 telecast of *The Partridge Family*, in which the Partridges introduced Bobby and Lionel to each other.

GHOST AND MRS. MUIR, THE (*Situation Comedy*)

FIRST TELECAST: *September 21, 1968*
LAST TELECAST: *September 18, 1970*
BROADCAST HISTORY:

Sep 1968–Sep 1969, NBC Sat 8:30–9:00
Sep 1969–Jan 1970, ABC Tue 7:30–8:00
Jan 1970–Sep 1970, ABC Fri 8:30–9:00

CAST:

Mrs. Carolyn Muir .... Hope Lange
Capt. Daniel Gregg .... Edward Mulhare
Martha Grant .... Reta Shaw
Candice Muir .... Kellie Flanagan
Jonathan Muir .... Harlen Carraher
Claymore Gregg .... Charles Nelson Reilly

Somewhere along a desolate stretch of New England coastline, overlooking Schooner Bay, sat a charming little house known as Gull Cottage. It was charming except for one slight problem—it was haunted by the ghost of a previous owner, Capt. Daniel Gregg, a 19th-century sea captain. Every time his nephew Claymore, the current owner, tried to rent the cottage to someone, the captain scared them off. Into Gull Cottage moved attractive widow Carolyn Muir with her two young children (aged 8 and 9), their pet dog Scruffy, and Martha, a housekeeper. The captain resented the invasion—Carolyn was sleeping in *his* bedroom—and he tried to scare them off. Eventually, however, they established a truce, and even developed a fondness for each other. *The Ghost and Mrs. Muir* was picked up by ABC for a second season after being canceled by NBC.

Based on the 1947 movie starring Gene Tierney and Rex Harrison.

GHOST STORIES (*Supernatural Anthology*)

BROADCAST HISTORY:

Syndicated only
60 minutes
Produced: *1997–1998* (22 episodes)
Released: *September 1997*

HOST:

Rip Torn

Tales of the supernatural hosted by actor Rip Torn. Each hour episode contained two separate horror stories adapted from newspaper accounts of supposedly real incidents, folk legends, and classic works of fiction. The performers were generally little-known actors.

In some cities the hour-long episodes were aired as two self-contained half-hour episodes.

GHOST STORY (*Supernatural Anthology*)

FIRST TELECAST: *September 15, 1972*
LAST TELECAST: *June 22, 1973*
BROADCAST HISTORY:

Sep 1972–Jun 1973, NBC Fri 9:00–10:00

HOST:

Sebastian Cabot (as *Winston Essex*, 1972)

When *Ghost Story* premiered in September 1972 it dealt exclusively with tales of ghosts, vampires, witches, and various other aspects of the supernatural. It was hosted by Sebastian Cabot in the role of Winston Essex. Essex would open the show by taking the audience to Essex House and introducing the story as something that could happen to anyone. As the story unfolded, however, it turned into a bizarre nightmare of one kind or another. On January 5, 1973, the title was changed to *Circle of Fear*. Under the new title stories of suspense could be included that did not have supernatural overtones. In addition, the narrator was no longer part of the program.

GIANT STEP (*Quiz*)

FIRST TELECAST: *November 7, 1956*
LAST TELECAST: *May 29, 1957*
BROADCAST HISTORY:

Nov 1956–May 1957, CBS Wed 7:30–8:00

EMCEE:

Bert Parks

Giant Step was somewhat different from the other big-money quiz shows of its time in that all of its contestants were students, mostly of high-school age, who competed for a free college education. The students picked their topic and then tried to answer enough questions successfully to win a four-year scholarship, and an all-expense-paid vacation to Europe after graduation. There were eight steps involved in reaching the final victory. As with *The $64,000 Question*, suspense was built by having the contestants—after their initial appearance—answer only one big question per week.

GIBBSVILLE (*Drama*)

FIRST TELECAST: *November 11, 1976*
LAST TELECAST: *December 30, 1976*
BROADCAST HISTORY:

Nov 1976–Dec 1976, NBC Thu 10:00–11:00

CAST:

Jim Malloy .... John Savage
Ray Whitehead .... Gig Young
Dr. Malloy .... Biff McGuire
Mrs. Malloy .... Peggy McCay
Pell .... Bert Remsen

This short-lived dramatic series centered around the activities of Jim Malloy in the small Pennsylvania town of Gibbsville, where he was cub reporter for the *Gibbsville Courier*, during the 1940s. Jim worked with senior reporter Ray Whitehead (both of them accountable to editor Pell) and made his home with his folks. Whitehead had started his career at the *Courier* and then moved on to more prestigious papers in larger cities. Unfortunately, he had lost a long bout with the bottle and was back in Gibbsville trying to salvage what was left of a once-promising career. Jim Malloy's father was the town physician. The stories and characters in this series were developed from the writings of John O'Hara.

GIDEON OLIVER (*Adventure*)

FIRST TELECAST: *February 20, 1989*
LAST TELECAST: *September 2, 1989*
BROADCAST HISTORY:

Feb 1989–May 1989, ABC Mon 9:00–11:00
Sep 1989, ABC Sat 9:00–11:00

CAST:

Prof. Gideon Oliver .... Louis Gossett, Jr.
Zina Oliver .... Shari Headley

Tall, bald Lou Gossett played a Columbia University anthropology professor who was fascinated with crime. No bookworm, this professor had a rather unbelievable collection of talents: kick-boxer, street-savvy tough guy, learned scholar, social reformer—and, did we mention, devoted father (his daughter, Zina, was occasionally seen)? When he was not helping the local New York constabulary, Gideon's amateur investigations took him to many exotic locales, including Central America, the Caribbean, Chinatown, and a desert cult community.

Gideon Oliver was one of the rotating elements of the *ABC Mystery Movie* and was seen every month or so.

GIDEON'S CROSSING (*Medical Drama*)

FIRST TELECAST: *October 3, 2000*
LAST TELECAST: *April 9, 2001*
BROADCAST HISTORY:

Oct 2000, ABC Tue 10:00–11:00
Oct 2000–Dec 2000, ABC Wed 10:00–11:00
Jan 2001–Apr 2001, ABC Mon 10:00–11:00

CAST:

Dr. Ben Gideon .... Andre Braugher
Dr. Max Cabranes .... Ruben Blades
Dr. Aaron Boies .... Russell Hornsby
Dr. Siddhartha "Sid" Shandar .... Ravi Kapoor
Dr. Wyatt Cooper .... Eric Dane
Dr. Maya Stiles .... Sophie Keller
Dr. Alejandra "Ollie" Klein .... Rhona Mitra
Dr. Bruce Cherry .... Hamish Linklater
Dr. Michael Pirandello .... Kevin J. O'Connor

Another of TV's heroic doctor shows, this one centering on intense, brilliant Dr. Ben Gideon, chief of experimental medicine at a big Boston teaching hospital. Cabranes was the sarcastic but understanding hospital head and Boies, the bossy chief resident who tormented the residents and interns, including ambitious worrywart Shandar and green young Cooper, Stiles and Klein. Skinny, nervous Cherry added a little comic relief, but only a little, as most stories were heavy-handed dramas filled with serious speeches about the meaning of life. Gideon was a widower with three seldom-seen kids (Rose, Eli and Charlie), and he still seethed about his wife's untimely death from cancer. He was in fact so noble he sometimes got on people's nerves. (Cabranes to Ben: "Be angry with God. Pick on someone your own size.") Though critics raved about the show, audiences generally avoided it, leading to a one-season run.

Based on the book *The Measure of Our Days* by Dr. Jerome Groopman.

GIDGET (*Situation Comedy*)

FIRST TELECAST: *September 15, 1965*
LAST TELECAST: *September 1, 1966*
BROADCAST HISTORY:

Sep 1965–Jan 1966, ABC Wed 8:30–9:00
Jan 1966–Sep 1966, ABC Thu 8:00–8:30

CAST:

Francine "Gidget" Lawrence .... Sally Field
Professor Russ Lawrence .... Don Porter
Anne Cooper .... Betty Conner
John Cooper .... Peter Deuel
Larue .... Lynette Winter
Peter Stone ("Siddo") .... Mike Nader

THEME:

sung by Johnny Tillotson

There was lots of California sun and surf in this frothy comedy about the adventures of a bright, winsome teenager. Gidget was age 15½, the daughter of Prof. Russ Lawrence, a widower. Despite the best efforts of her overly protective older sister, Anne, and Anne's husband John (a psychology student who practiced on the family), Gidget and her best friend Larue managed to find endless fun in the sun. Gidget's boyfriend Jeff (Stephen Mines) was "off to college" and seldom seen.

Sally Field was plucked from obscurity for the starring role in this series. Only 18 when the show began, she had enrolled in a Columbia Pictures actors' workshop as a summertime lark after completing high school and before beginning college. It proved to be a direct path to TV and, later, movie stardom.

Based on the *Gidget* series of movies, the first of which (1959) starred Sandra Dee in the title role. See *The New Gidget* for a 1980s sequel.

GILLETTE CAVALCADE OF SPORTS, see *Boxing*

GILLETTE SUMMER SPORTS REEL
(*Sports/Sports Commentary*)

FIRST TELECAST: *June 2, 1950*
LAST TELECAST: *August 19, 1955*
BROADCAST HISTORY:
Jun 1950–Aug 1955, NBC Fri 10:00–10:30 (summers only)
COMMENTATOR:
Don Dunphy (1950)
Jimmy Powers (1951)
Clem McCarthy (1953)
Ken Banghart (1953)
Ray Barrett (1953, 1955)
Jim Leaming (1954)
Bob Wilson (1953–1955)
Gene Kelly (1954)
Byrum Saam (1954)
Fred Caposella (1954–1955)
Lindsay Nelson (1955)
Radcliff Hall (1955)

For five years this series was the summer replacement for the Gillette *Cavalcade of Sports* Friday night boxing matches. There were very few live bouts scheduled during these summers, so the *Summer Sports Reel* used other sports programming to fill the time slot. The basic element of the show, and the one that was kept throughout its run, was the showing of newsreel highlights of major sports events from around the world.

In 1950, under the title *Cavalcade of Sports*, the show was hosted by Don Dunphy, who was the radio announcer for the boxing matches during the regular season. He made observations about the films shown as well as introducing the various events. This same format was used in 1951, under the title *Sports Newsreel*, when Jimmy Powers, the television announcer for winter boxing on Gillette *Cavalcade of Sports*, replaced Dunphy. In 1952 the stories stood on their own, with only the newsreel announcers providing explanations of the action and no commentary. The 1952 title was *Gillette Summer Sports Reel*, as it was the following summer when a regular group of commentators was used to discuss the various events shown on film. This same format with a group of commentators, not all of whom were seen every week, was used in 1954 and 1955 under the title *Sportsreel*.

GILLIGAN'S ISLAND (*Situation Comedy*)

FIRST TELECAST: *September 26. 1964*
LAST TELECAST: *September 4, 1967*
BROADCAST HISTORY:
Sep 1964–Sep 1965, CBS Sat 8:30–9:00
Sep 1965–Sep 1966, CBS Thu 8:00–8:30
Sep 1966–Sep 1967, CBS Mon 7:30–8:00
CAST:
Gilligan .... Bob Denver
Jonas Grumby (The Skipper) .... Alan Hale, Jr.
Thurston Howell III .... Jim Backus
Mrs. Lovey Howell .... Natalie Schafer
Ginger Grant .... Tina Louise
Roy Hinkley (The Professor) .... Russell Johnson
Mary Ann Summers .... Dawn Wells
THEME:
"The Ballad of Gilligan's Island," by George Wyle and Sherwood Schwartz

The small charter boat *Minnow* had been on a sightseeing party when it was caught in a storm and wrecked on the shore of an uncharted South Pacific island. Marooned together on the island were: the good-natured skipper; a somewhat blustery millionaire and his vacuous wife; a sexy movie star named Ginger; a high-school science teacher known as The Professor; a sweet, naive country girl named Mary Ann; and Gilligan. Gilligan was the boat's sole crew member, aside from the skipper. He was well-meaning but inept in his attempts to find a means of returning to civilization. As a result, and perhaps even more because this simple-minded farce became a top hit, the little band was stranded on that island for three full seasons. One question that never got answered, however, concerned the luggage. In the first episode, and in the theme song, it was pointed out that the cruise was only supposed to be for three hours. How, then, did the passengers have enough clothing to last three years?

Gilligan's biggest fans were kids, and when the series finally went into repeats on local stations they made it one of the biggest rerun hits of the 1960s and 1970s. An animated cartoon version called *The New Adventures of Gilligan* was produced for ABC, and ran on that network's weekend daytime schedule from 1974 to 1977. A second cartoon version, *Gilligan's Planet*, aired on CBS' weekend daytime lineup from 1982–1984.

Then in 1978 NBC had the bright idea of bringing the original cast back together for a reunion special, in which they were finally rescued. All agreed to appear except Tina Louise (who wanted too much money, and so was replaced by Judith Baldwin). "Rescue from Gilligan's Island" aired in October 1978 as a two-part special, and was a phenomenal hit. They did finally get off the island, and returned to a triumphant homecoming. But then they made the mistake of going on a reunion cruise on the *Minnow II*, only to wind up stranded back on the same island—the result of another freak storm! "Castaways on Gilligan's Island," a follow-up special aired in 1979, had them converting the island into a tourist resort. And in still another sequel in 1981, The Harlem Globetrotters dropped in. There was talk of reviving the series, but audiences for the 1979 and 1981 sequels were not very large, and the plans never materialized.

One of TV's great bits of trivia is Gilligan's first name. None was ever revealed on the show, but years later on a talk show Bob Denver claimed that he had talked the matter over with the show's creator/producer Sherwood Schwartz, and they had decided that if Gilligan ever *did* need a first name it would be "Willie."

GILMORE GIRLS (*Drama*)

FIRST TELECAST: October 5, 2000
LAST TELECAST:
BROADCAST HISTORY:
Oct 2000–Sep 2001, WB Thu 8:00–9:00
Mar 2001–Apr 2001, WB Mon 9:00–10:00

Aug 2001–   , WB Tue 8:00–9:00
Apr 2002, WB Thu 8:00–9:00
Sep 2002–   , WB Sun 7:00–8:00

CAST:

Lorelai Gilmore .... Lauren Graham
Rory Gilmore (age 16) .... Alexis Bledel
Sookie St. James .... Melissa McCarthy
Lane Kim .... Keiko Agena
Michel Gerard .... Yanic Truesdale
Luke Danes .... Scott Patterson
Emily Gilmore .... Kelly Bishop
Richard Gilmore .... Edward Herrmann
Miss Patty .... Liz Torres
Dean Forester .... Jared Padalecki
Paris Geller .... Liza Weil
**Madeline Lynn* .... Shelly Cole
**Louise Grant* .... Teal Redmann
Taylor Doose .... Michael Winters
Kirk .... Sean Gunn
Jackson Melville (2001–   ) .... Jackson Douglas
Jess Mariano (2001–   ) .... Milo Ventimiglia
Max Medina (2000–2001) .... Scott Cohen
Mrs. Kim .... Emily Kuroda
**Babette Dell* .... Sally Struthers
**Tristan Du Grey (2000–2001)*
.... Chad Michael Murray
**Morey Dell (2000–2002)* .... Ted Rooney
Rachel (2001) .... Lisa Ann Hadley
**Christopher Haden (2001–   )* ...... David Sutcliffe
**Dave Rygalsky (2002–   )* .... Adam Brody
**Nicole Leahy (2003–   )* .... Tricia O'Kelley

*Occasional

THEME:

"Where You Lead" performed by Carole King and Louise Goffin

Single mother Lorelai managed the Independence Inn in the rural Connecticut town of Stars Hollow, founded in 1779. Among her coworkers were Michel, the sarcastic concierge, and Sookie, the talented but accident-prone chef. Lorelai had gotten pregnant when she was 16 but never married Christopher, the father of her daughter, Rory. Her relationship with Rory was more sisterly than mother-daughter. Rory's best friend, Lane, was a typical teenager trying to deal with her very traditional Korean parents. When Rory was accepted to exclusive Chilton Prep, in nearby Hartford, Lorelai had to mend her estranged relationship with her stuffy and socially prominent parents, Emily and Richard, because she needed help paying the tuition—and that opened the door for her mother to gleefully start interfering in Rory's life. Also seen regularly were gruff Luke, who owned the café where Lorelai and Rory got their morning coffee; Miss Patty, the busybody dance teacher; Kirk, the eccentric handyman; and Taylor, who owned the local grocery store and thought he ran the town. Rory was attracted to Dean, who worked part time for Taylor, and by the end of the year they were dating. In January Rory got upset because Lorelai's relationship with Max, her English teacher, started to look more than casual. When they were seen kissing at parents' day, it created a furor that almost cost Max his job and they decided to put their relationship temporarily on hold. In February, while working on a debate, Rory and obnoxious Paris, the most competitive girl at Chilton, almost became friends.

That fall Lorelai accepted Max's proposal, but as the wedding day approached she got cold feet and they broke up. Afterward she and Sookie started making plans to open a small inn of their own. Luke took in his troublemaking 17-year-old nephew, Jess, and put him to work at the café. Rory, working on the Chilton school newspaper, had her problems with editor Paris, who still had it in for her, but as the season wore on they became friends and both were elected to the student council—Paris as president and Rory as vice president. Jess was attracted to Rory (who showed some interest) and alienated Dean in the process. In February Sookie got engaged to Jackson, the vegetable vendor. On the eve of Sookie's wedding, Rory's dad Christopher and Lorelai spent the night together, but talk of getting back together ended when he found out his former girlfriend was pregnant.

Early in the 2002–2003 season Rory applied to Harvard, which upset Dean, who was afraid her departure would end their relationship. Then he broke up with her after concluding she was more interested in Jess than in him. When Rory and Jess started to date, it upset Lorelai, who had never liked him. That winter Rory and Dean decided to be friends again, after which Jess told Dean he knew he was trying to get Rory back. In late February Paris, who had fallen out with Rory, had a mild breakdown when she found out she had not been accepted to Harvard. Rory was accepted but in April decided to go to Yale, her father's alma mater, instead. Both of Rory's boyfriends drifted away. Jess, who was working more than part time at Wal-Mart, cut school so often that he flunked his senior year. Luke tossed Jess out of the house because he refused to repeat his senior year, and the boy moved to Los Angeles to live with his father. Meanwhile Dean told Rory he was engaged to his new girlfriend. Lane's rock band—she played drums and was infatuated with its leader, Dave—had its debut. In the season finale the Independence Inn, which had suffered a fire earlier in the season, was shuttered. This gave Lorelai and Sookie, who were negotiating to buy another inn, the opportunity to concentrate on their new joint venture. Rory graduated from Chilton and, as class valedictorian, gave the commencement address.

GIMME A BREAK (*Situation Comedy*)

FIRST TELECAST: *October 29, 1981*
LAST TELECAST: *May 12, 1987*
BROADCAST HISTORY:

Oct 1981–Aug 1982, NBC Thu 9:30–10:00
Sep 1982, NBC Thu 9:00–9:30
Oct 1982–Dec 1982, NBC Sat 9:00–9:30
Jan 1983–Aug 1983, NBC Thu 9:00–9:30
Aug 1983–Sep 1984, NBC Thu 8:00–8:30
Sep 1984–Nov 1984, NBC Sat 8:30–9:00
Dec 1984–Aug 1985, NBC Sat 9:00–9:30
Sep 1985–Jun 1986, NBC Sat 8:00–8:30
Jun 1986–Mar 1987, NBC Wed 9:30–10:00
Mar 1987–May 1987, NBC Tue 9:00–9:30

CAST:

Nellie Ruth "Nell" Harper .... Nell Carter
Chief Carl Kanisky (1981–1985) .... Dolph Sweet
Katie Kanisky (1981–1986) .... Kari Michaelson
Julie Kanisky Maxwell (1981–1986) .. Lauri Hendler
Samantha "Sam" Kanisky .... Lara Jill Miller
Officer Ralph Simpson (1981–1986)
.... Howard Morton
Grandpa Stanley Kanisky (1982–1987) .. John Hoyt

Grandma Mildred Kanisky (1982–1983) . . Jane Dulo
Uncle Ed Kanisky (1982–1983) . . . . Pete Schrum
Joey Donovan (1983–1987) . . . . Joey Lawrence
Addy Wilson (1984–1987) . . . . Telma Hopkins
Jonathan Maxwell (1984–1986) Jonathan Silverman
Matthew Donovan (1986–1987) Matthew Lawrence
Marty/Esteban (1986–1987) . . . . Paul Sand
Maybelle Harper (1986–1987) . . . . . Rosetta LeNoire
Maggie O'Brien (1986–1987) . . . . . . Rosie O'Donnell

A rotund black housekeeper maintained order in the home of a portly white police chief in this old-fashioned comedy set in the fictional town of Glen Lawn, California. Policeman Carl's beloved wife Margaret had died only months before, leaving him with three winsome daughters, ranging in age from cute gradeschooler to troublesome teen. Wisecracks and fat jokes abounded, but there was a lot of love as Nell tried to be friend and surrogate mother to the clan. Officer Simpson was a dopey police officer who was frequently seen, and Joey was a six-year-old orphan and junior-grade hustler who joined the household in the third season.

As the 1985–1986 season opened the chief had passed away, and Nell became both mother and father to the Kanisky brood. The man of the house was now Jonathan, who had married Julie at the end of the previous season and moved in. By 1986, with the Kanisky girls grown and/or college-bound, Nell and her best friend Addy decided to leave Glen Lawn for New York City, with Grandpa and little Joe in tow. There they discovered Joey's irresponsible father Tim, who turned over Joey's younger brother Matthew (played by Joey Lawrence's real-life brother) and departed, adding a second child to the shifting household. Marty was Nell's nutty New York landlord, who also owned the restaurant El Gaspacho downstairs, where he put on a phony Spanish accent and called himself "Esteban."

GIRL ABOUT TOWN (*Music*)

FIRST TELECAST: *September 8, 1948*
LAST TELECAST: *June 11, 1949*
BROADCAST HISTORY:
Sep 1948–Jan 1949, NBC Wed 8:00–8:30
Feb 1949–Jun 1949, NBC Sun 10:00–10:30
REGULARS:
Kyle MacDonnell
Johnny Downs (1948)
Earl Wrightson (1948–1949)
Norman Paris Trio

Live musical program built around singer Kyle MacDonnell. The songs and chatter were interspersed with films of Kyle as a glamorous New Yorker, visiting chic night spots and attending Broadway shows, sailing on Long Island Sound, etc. Johnny Downs was her first co-host, replaced by baritone Earl Wrightson about a month after the program began. During its final three months the program was known as *Around the Town.*

GIRL ALONE, see *Dotty Mack Show, The*

GIRL FROM U.N.C.L.E., THE (*Spy Spoof*)

FIRST TELECAST: *September 13, 1966*
LAST TELECAST: *August 29, 1967*
BROADCAST HISTORY:
Sep 1966–Aug 1967, NBC Tue 7:30–8:30
CAST:
April Dancer . . . . Stefanie Powers
Mark Slate . . . . Noel Harrison
Alexander Waverly . . . . Leo G. Carroll
Randy Kovacs . . . . Randy Kirby

Following the success of *The Man from U.N.C.L.E.* (U.N.C.L.E. stood for the United Network Command for Law and Enforcement), NBC decided in the fall of 1966 to create *The Girl from U.N.C.L.E.*, a companion James Bond–type spy spoof. Organization head Alexander Waverly teamed American April Dancer, a young, attractive, and very resourceful agent, with Mark Slate, recently transferred from U.N.C.L.E.'s London office to its New York headquarters. In the fight against THRUSH and other enemies of the world community, this new team would add its skills and enthusiasm. If *The Man from U.N.C.L.E.* seemed rather far-fetched to fans of spy and espionage stories, *The Girl from U.N.C.L.E.* was even sillier and more implausible, and it soon disappeared.

GIRL OF THE WEEK, see *Sportswoman of the Week*

GIRL WITH SOMETHING EXTRA, THE (*Situation Comedy*)

FIRST TELECAST: *September 14, 1973*
LAST TELECAST: *May 24, 1974*
BROADCAST HISTORY:
Sep 1973–Dec 1973, NBC Fri 8:30–9:00
Jan 1974–May 1974, NBC Fri 9:00–9:30
CAST:
John Burton . . . . John Davidson
Sally Burton . . . . Sally Field
Anne . . . . Zohra Lampert
Jerry Burton . . . . Jack Sheldon
Owen Metcalf . . . . Henry Jones
Stuart Kline . . . . William Windom
Angela . . . . Stephanie Edwards
Amber . . . . Teri Garr

Marriages often have rocky starts, but *The Girl with Something Extra* posed an unusual dilemma for her new spouse. On their wedding night Sally informed her husband John that she possessed E.S.P. and could read his mind. After deciding that their love was more important than the problems her mind-reading might cause, John and Sally settled down to a decidedly abnormal marriage. Her ability to read minds, his as well as everyone else's, created embarrassing and amusing situations which formed the basis for most of the stories in this series. Featured were John's brother Jerry and Sally's friend Anne, both single, and platonic friends of each other. John was employed as an attorney with the firm of Metcalf, Kline, and Associates.

GIRLFRIENDS (*Situation Comedy*)

FIRST TELECAST: *September 11, 2000*
LAST TELECAST:
BROADCAST HISTORY:
Sep 2000–Sep 2002, UPN Mon 9:30–10:00
Aug 2002– , UPN Mon 9:00–9:30
Aug 2002–Sep 2002, UPN Mon 9:30–10:00
CAST:
Joan Clayton . . . . Tracee Ellis Ross
Maya Wilkes . . . . Golden Brooks
Toni Childs . . . . Jill Marie Jones
Lynn Searcy . . . . Persia White
William Dent . . . . Reggie Hayes
**Davis Hamilton (2000–2001)* . . . . Randy J. Goodwin
**Jabari Wilkes* . . . . Tanner Scott Richards

**Darnell Wilkes (2000–2001)* .... Flex Alexander
**Darnell Wilkes (2001–)* .... Khalil Kain
Yvonne Blackwell (2001–2002) .. Cee Cee Michaela
Sean Ellis (2001) .... Dondre T. Whitfield
Greg Sparks (2001)........... Chuma Hunter-Gault
**Charles Swedelson (2001–)*.......... Phil Reeves
**Stan Wright (2001–2002)* .... Don Franklin
**Ellis Carter (2002–)*................ Adrian Lester
Dr. Todd Garrett (2002–) .... Jason Pace
**Monica Charles Brooks (2002–2003)*
.... Keesha Sharp
Sharon Upton Farley (2003–)
.... Anne-Marie Johnson

*Occasional

Girlfriends was a somewhat raunchy comedy centering on the love lives of four thirty-something African American women and was, in some respects, a cross between the 1980s *Designing Women* and the 1990s *Sex and the City*. Joan, who commented to the viewing audience about herself and her friends, was an attorney at the Los Angeles law firm of Goldberg, Swedelson, McDonald and Lee. Her professional life was on track but not so her personal life—she constantly fretted about being unable to find "Mr. Right," and endured one dating disaster after another. Joan had three close friends with whom she shared her ups and downs and to whom she gave advice—Maya, her married assistant at work; her best friend, Toni, a self-centered, gold-digging real estate broker, and Lynn, a friend from college and perpetual student who lived with her. Joan's one male confidant was William, a fellow attorney at the firm, who made wisecracks about her social problems despite the fact that his own social life was, if anything, worse than hers.

For a while Joan dated Sean, a recovering sex addict, but was disappointed because he just had sex, he didn't make love. In February Lynn moved in with Toni, who wasn't happy about it—and Joan relished her newfound privacy. In May Toni accepted the proposal of Clay (Phil Morris), a rich doctor, even though she really loved Greg, another guy she had been dating. Because Joan convinced her to follow her heart, Toni gave the ring back only to have Greg dump her after he found out about the engagement and became convinced she was a gold digger. Meanwhile, William dated Yvonne, a feisty lady cop, and because he worried about her safety, he asked her to quit the force.

At the start of the 2001–2002 season Sean left for New York and William was engaged to Yvonne. Joan and Sean were having problems with a bicoastal relationship and broke up while William, finally committed to a Valentine's Day wedding, asked Joan to be his "best man." When the wedding day came Yvonne bailed out because she thought William was too controlling. Toni set up her own upscale real estate office—with Lynn as her assistant and William as her attorney. Lynn moved in with William, on a platonic level, although they did spend a little time as uncommitted "sex buddies." Maya and her husband, Darnell, had been having problems with their marriage, mostly about money. In the season finale he found out about Stan, a guy Maya had been flirting with, and kicked Maya and their son, Jabari, out.

When her visiting parents pressured her to pay off her student loans, Lynn took an office job, which she hated. Maya and Darnell's marriage counseling didn't help and she moved in with Joan while William began an affair with manipulative Monica, whom all the girls hated. In November Darnell told a distraught Maya that he wanted a divorce. When Mr. Swedelson brought Sharon into the firm as a new senior partner, William quit because he was convinced he should have been promoted. Unable to make a living on his own, he negotiated a return to the firm with a modest salary increase. In early February Maya and Jabari, who had been living with Joan for six months, finally moved into their own apartment. Toni got engaged to Todd, the successful plastic surgeon she had been dating, and during the spring she was making wedding arrangements. Her biggest concern, ironically, was not that he was white, but that he was shorter than she was. William's return to the firm created an awkward situation since he had been having an affair with Sharon and, even though they still had the hots for each other, they reluctantly broke it off. In the season finale Toni married Todd, whom she really did love, and Joan reconciled with Ellis, the actor with whom she had been having an on-again, off-again relationship for more than a year.

GIRLS, THE (*Situation Comedy*)
FIRST TELECAST: *January 1, 1950*
LAST TELECAST: *March 25, 1950*
BROADCAST HISTORY:
Jan 1950–Mar 1950, CBS Sun 7:00–7:30
CAST:
Cornelia Otis Skinner (Jan–Feb) .... Bethel Leslie
Cornelia Otis Skinner (Feb–Mar).... Gloria Stroock
Emily Kimbrough.................... Mary Malone
Todhunter Smith II................ Kenneth Forbes

Based on the autobiographical novel *Our Hearts Were Young and Gay* by Cornelia Otis Skinner and Emily Kimbrough, this early live comedy series followed the adventures of the two young Bryn Mawr graduates as they returned to New York in search of their careers, following a post-graduate fling in Europe. They moved to Greenwich Village at the height of the "Roaring 20s" and started looking for work, Miss Skinner as an actress and Miss Kimbrough as a writer. Bethel Leslie left the series in February to accept a role in a new play (that was considered far better work than television!), and was replaced by Gloria Stroock, the sister of actress Geraldine Brooks. The original title of this series was *Young and Gay*, changed to *The Girls* after the first two episodes had aired.

GIRLS' BASEBALL, see *Baseball*

GIRLS CLUB (*Legal Drama*)
FIRST TELECAST: *October 21, 2002*
LAST TELECAST: *October 28, 2002*
BROADCAST HISTORY:
Oct 2002, FOX Mon 9:00–10:00
CAST:
Lynne Camden..................... Gretchen Mol
Jeannie Falls .... Kathleen Robertson
Sarah Mickle....................... Chyler Leigh
Nicholas Hahn................ Giancarlo Esposito
Meredith Holt .... Lisa Banes
Rhanda Clifford .... Christina Chang
Kevin O'Neil.......................... Sam Jaeger
Michael Harrod .... Donovan Leitch
Spencer Lewis .... Brian Markinson

Mitchell Walton........................Eddie Shin
Meredith's assistant..................Shane Brown

Lynne, Jeannie and Sarah were three chattering, self-absorbed friends who had met while attending Stanford Law School. After graduation they decided to share an elegant Victorian loft apartment in the trendy North Beach section of San Francisco while trying to make their marks as associate attorneys at the prestigious law firm of Myers, Berry, Cherry & Fitch. Hahn was the no-nonsense senior partner who oversaw their training and was much more likely to criticize than to praise, which wasn't hard since "the girls" frequently seemed to screw up briefs and argue in court. (Lynne's petulant response to criticism: "You're not going to make me cry!") Ambitious Rhanda and friendly Mitchell were fellow associates; tough cookie Meredith (referred to behind her back as "the praying mantis") and lustful Spencer were partners in the firm. Kevin was Jeannie's boyfriend, and Michael was dating Sarah.

Girls Club was produced by David E. Kelley, who had had major successes with the legal series *The Practice* and *Ally McBeal*, the previous tenant of this time slot, but dismal ratings prompted Fox to cancel *Girls Club* after only two episodes.

GIRLS' NIGHT OUT (*Comedy*)

BROADCAST HISTORY:
Lifetime Network
60 minutes
Produced: *1994* (30 episodes)
Premiered: *April 2, 1994*

A Saturday-night standup comedy show featuring mostly (though not entirely) female comedians. Among the guest hosts were Judy Tenuta, Margaret Cho, Patti Davis, Geraldine Ferraro, and Dr. Joyce Brothers.

GISELE MACKENZIE SHOW, THE (*Musical Variety*)

FIRST TELECAST: *September 28, 1957*
LAST TELECAST: *March 29, 1958*
BROADCAST HISTORY:
Sep 1957–Mar 1958, NBC Sat 9:30–10:00
REGULARS:
Gisele MacKenzie
Jack Narz (1957–1958)
Tom Kennedy (1958)
The Curfew Boys
The Joe Pryor Group
The Axel Stordahl Orchestra

Canadian-born songstress Gisele MacKenzie made her starring debut in her own variety series in the fall of 1957, after being dropped from *Your Hit Parade* (along with the rest of the cast) in a "modernization" move. In addition to her singing and violin-playing, talents which she had regularly displayed in the past, she danced and acted with the guest stars who appeared each week. There was a small group of regular singers (The Joe Pryor Group) and dancers (The Curfew Boys) plus a regular announcer who was seen on camera. Initially the announcer was Jack Narz, who left the series on January 11, 1958, to be succeeded by his own brother, Tom Kennedy.

GLADYS KNIGHT & THE PIPS SHOW, THE (*Musical Variety*)

FIRST TELECAST: *July 10, 1975*
LAST TELECAST: *July 31, 1975*
BROADCAST HISTORY:
Jul 1975, NBC Thu 8:00–9:00
REGULARS:
Gladys Knight & the Pips
(Merald Knight, William Guest, Edward Pattern)
The George Wyle Orchestra

Gladys Knight and the Pips had been one of the top rock recording groups for nearly 15 years when they were chosen to headline this four-week summer variety series in 1975. Miss Knight, a onetime child prizewinner on *Ted Mack's Original Amateur Hour*, was joined by the Pips (all relatives of hers) as hosts and singing stars of the show. Each week they sang a number of their record hits and joined guest stars in musical and comedy routines.

GLAMOUR-GO-ROUND (*Interview*)

FIRST TELECAST: *February 16, 1950*
LAST TELECAST: *August 10, 1950*
BROADCAST HISTORY:
Feb 1950–Aug 1950, CBS Thu 9:30–9:45
HOSTS:
Ilka Chase
Durward Kirby
Bill Nalle

Ilka Chase, described in a CBS press release as a "recognized authority on style and beauty," hosted this informal talk show along with Durward Kirby. The setting was Miss Chase's drawing room where she and Durward, along with pianist Bill Nalle, welcomed distinguished visitors from New York's fashion world, show business, and various fields of cultural endeavor.

GLEN CAMPBELL GOODTIME HOUR, THE (*Musical Variety*)

FIRST TELECAST: *January 29, 1969*
LAST TELECAST: *June 13, 1972*
BROADCAST HISTORY:
Jan 1969–Dec 1969, CBS Wed 7:30–8:30 (OS)
Dec 1969–Jun 1971, CBS Sun 9:00–10:00 (OS)
Sep 1971–Jun 1972, CBS Tue 7:30–8:30
REGULARS:
Glen Campbell
Ron Poindexter Dancers (1969–1971)
Denny Vaughn Singers (1969–1970)
Marty Paich Orchestra
Larry McNeeley (1970–1972)
Jerry Reed (1970–1972)
Mike Curb Congregation (1971–1972)
Dom DeLuise (1971–1972)
THEME:
"Gentle on My Mind," by John Hartford

Country/popular singer Glen Campbell looked like a potential successor to Perry Como when this weekly variety hour was launched in 1969. He had a long string of enormously successful records in the late 1960s (including his theme, "Gentle on My Mind"), was popular with both teenagers and adults, and had an easy, ingratiating style which had won him a wide TV following during his frequent appearances on *The Smothers Brothers Show*. His own show was reminiscent of Como's, too, in a contemporary way—relaxed, informal, and down-home friendly. In addition to hosting, he sang many of his hits (two of which, "Wichita Lineman" and "Galveston," were on the charts about the time this series began) and did instrumental solos (he was a first-rate guitarist). Guests on the show tended to be country singers and sketch comedians. Although not usually credited as a regular, comedian Dom DeLuise appeared in more than half the show's telecasts during the final season. Composer-singer John Hartford, who had written Glen's theme song and was a close personal friend, was likewise not a regular but made frequent guest appearances throughout the show's run.

GLEN CAMPBELL MUSIC SHOW, THE (*Music*)
BROADCAST HISTORY:
Syndicated only
30 minutes
Produced: *1982–1983* (24 episodes)
Released: *Fall 1982*
HOST:
Glen Campbell

Pop singer Glen Campbell presided over this amiable half hour of songs with a minimum of chatter and a maximum of informality. He was joined by middle-of-the-road musical guests such as Willie Nelson, Chuck Mangione, and Leo Sayer.

GLENN MILLER TIME (*Music*)
FIRST TELECAST: *July 10, 1961*
LAST TELECAST: *September 11, 1961*
BROADCAST HISTORY:
Jul 1961–Sep 1961, CBS Mon 10:00–10:30
REGULARS:
Johnny Desmond
Ray McKinley
Patty Clark
The Castle Singers
THEME:
"Moonlight Serenade," by Glenn Miller and Mitchell Parish

Johnny Desmond and Ray McKinley were co-hosts of this summer music series that featured the style and sounds of the Glenn Miller Orchestra. Each telecast included a medley of "something old, something new, something borrowed, something blue," a regular feature of the band during the days when it had a regularly scheduled radio series during World War II. In addition to starring in this live series, Ray McKinley was then touring with "The Original Glenn Miller Orchestra" (Miller himself had died in 1944).

GLITTER (*Drama*)
FIRST TELECAST: *September 13, 1984*
LAST TELECAST: *December 27, 1985*
BROADCAST HISTORY:
Sep 1984, ABC Thu 9:00–10:00
Dec 1984, ABC Tue 9:00–10:00
Dec 1985, ABC Tue–Fri 12:00–1:00 A.M.
CAST:
Sam Dillon .... David Birney
Kate Simpson .... Morgan Brittany
Pete Bozak .... Christopher Mayer
Jennifer Douglas .... Dianne Kay
Chester "Chip" Craddock .... Timothy Patrick Murphy
Angela Timini .... Tracy Nelson
Shelley Sealy .... Barbara Sharma
Clive Richlin .... Arte Johnson
Earl Tobin .... Dorian Harewood
Terry Randolph .... Melinda Culea
Charles Hardwick .... Arthur Hill

Any resemblance between *People* magazine and the fictional *Glitter* magazine was purely intentional. As ABC's press department described it, "*Glitter*, the hottest magazine on the newsstands, sends its teams of reporters to probe the nation's most glamorous places and people." The series was flashy and unabashedly romantic, with happy endings in most of its subplots and a revolving door full of guest stars who seemed to be on their way to or from appearances on *The Love Boat*. Sam Dillon and Kate Simpson were the magazine's star reporters, covering the juiciest stories. Other reporters on the staff were Pete Bozak, Jennifer Douglas, Earl Tobin, and Terry Randolph. Shelley Sealy was the romance and health editor, Clive Richlin the chief photographer, and Charles Hardwick the magazine's publisher. Even the little people on the *Glitter* staff showed up on the air. Chip the mail clerk and pretty receptionist Angela Timini were madly in love with each other and their romance was a continuing thread amid the glamour of the stories featuring the weekly guest stars.

One of the first casualties of the 1984–1985 season, *Glitter* resurfaced briefly as part of ABC's late-night lineup a year later, airing seven original episodes not previously seen in prime time.

GLORIA (*Situation Comedy*)
FIRST TELECAST: *September 26, 1982*
LAST TELECAST: *September 21, 1983*
BROADCAST HISTORY:
Sep 1982–Apr 1983, CBS Sun 8:30–9:00
Jun 1983–Sep 1983, CBS Wed 8:30–9:00
CAST:
Gloria Bunker Stivic .... Sally Struthers
Dr. Willard Adams .... Burgess Meredith
Clark V. Uhley, Jr. .... Lou Richards
Dr. Maggie Lawrence .... Jo de Winter
Joey Stivic .... Christian Jacobs

Her marriage to Mike Stivic had crumbled when he left her to live on a commune with a flower child; she was back from California. Archie Bunker's little girl Gloria (see *All in the Family*) wanted to start a new life in fresh surroundings. Not wanting to be completely out of touch with her father, and hoping to become a vet, Gloria found a job as an assistant trainee to a couple of veterinarians in the rural upstate New York town of Foxridge. Crusty old Dr. Willard Adams was not only her boss but her landlord as well. Maggie Lawrence was Dr. Adams's partner at the clinic, a true liberated woman, and Clark Uhley was their other assistant. For Clark, becoming a vet seemed a ludicrous aim—he seemed to be feared or hated by almost every creature that came into the clinic.

The adjustments were not easy for Gloria, or for her eight-year-old son Joey. But her new friends—and all those cuddly animals—helped brighten things up for Archie's daughter, who never lost her little-girl innocence.

GLORY DAYS (*Drama*)
FIRST TELECAST: *July 25, 1990*
LAST TELECAST: *September 27, 1990*

BROADCAST HISTORY:

July 1990–Aug 1990, FOX Wed 8:00–9:00
Aug 1990–Sep 1990, FOX Thu 9:00–10:00

CAST:

Off. Dave Rutecki .... Spike Alexander
Walker Lovejoy .... Brad Pitt
Dominic Fopiano .... Evan Mirand
Peter "T-Bone" Trigg .... Nicholas Kallsen
Sheila Jackson .... Beth Broderick
Lt. V. T. Krantz .... Robert Costanzo

For the four recent graduates of Kensington High School who were featured in *Glory Days*, this was a time for change. Only Dominic was still in school, a commuting freshman at a local college. Dave was a rookie on the local police force, quickly losing the idealism of his youth; Walker, a former star high school quarterback, was a novice reporter for *The Century Post*, working for tough editor Sheila Jackson; and Trigg, the fast-talking dreamer, spent most of his time moving from one failed get-rich-quick scheme to another. Still good friends, they often got together at a local hangout to talk about what was going on in their lives—their jobs, personal lives, and romances—and to seek advice and help from each other.

GLORY DAYS (*Serial Drama*)

FIRST TELECAST: *January 16, 2002*
LAST TELECAST: *March 25, 2002*
BROADCAST HISTORY:

Jan 2002–Mar 2002, WB Wed 9:00–10:00
Mar 2002, WB Mon 9:00–10:00

CAST:

Mike Dolan .... Eddie Cahill
Sheriff Rudy Dunlop .... Jay R. Ferguson
Ellie Sparks .... Poppy Montgomery
Sam Dolan (age 16) .... Emily VanCamp
Sara Dolan .... Amy Stewart
Mitzi Dolan .... Frances Fisher
Hazel Walker .... Theresa Russell
Zane Walker .... Ben Crowley
Officer Tim .... David Kopp
Cal .... Erin Karpluk

When he was 21, Mike Dolan had written a best-selling mystery novel that was loosely based on the strange events surrounding his father's "accidental" death. Now, after four years of writer's block, he returned to Glory Island, the picturesque little town near Seattle where he had grown up. Mike wanted to reestablish broken relationships and recharge his creative battery, but his return was not met with much enthusiasm by the residents of Glory, whom he had caricatured in less-than-flattering terms in his novel. At the top of his list was boyhood friend Rudy, now the sheriff. Despite its small size, Glory had more than its share of bizarre happenings and murders and Mike, the amateur detective, was committed to helping Rudy, who had never forgiven him for depicting him in the novel as a gay idiot, solve them. Ellie, Glory's coroner and forensic expert, analyzed clues and worked with them to track down the murderers. Since she had not grown up in Glory, and had not appeared in Mike's novel, she had nothing against him and actually found him attractive. In late March, after the sexual tension between them had reached a fever pitch, Mike and Ellie, who had been verbally sparring since his return to Glory, finally shared a passionate kiss.

Mike's family included Mitzi, his slightly off-kilter mother; older sister Sara, who ran the local newspaper and grudgingly gave him a job as a reporter; and younger sister Sam, whose exuberant attitude and sense of style seemed out of place in Glory. Zane was Sam's lifelong best friend whose mother, Hazel, ran the town diner. In Mike's novel Hazel, who in real life had had a scandalous affair with his father, was the murderer. Tim and Cal worked with Rudy.

GLYNIS (*Situation Comedy*)

FIRST TELECAST: *September 25, 1963*
LAST TELECAST: *September 6, 1965*
BROADCAST HISTORY:

Sep 1963–Dec 1963, CBS Wed 8:30–9:00
Jul 1965–Sep 1965, CBS Mon 9:00–9:30

CAST:

Glynis Granville .... Glynis Johns
Keith Granville .... Keith Andes
Chick Rogers .... George Mathews

Keith Granville was a very successful attorney who had two problems, a scatterbrained wife and a penchant for getting involved in criminal cases as an amateur detective. With his wife joining him, they made a rather wacky pair of semi-pro sleuths who always managed to stumble onto the solution of whatever crime they were investigating. His wife's background as a mystery-story writer may have been of some help, but it was their incredible luck more than anything else that saved the day. Reruns of this series were aired by CBS during the summer of 1965.

GO FISH (*Situation Comedy*)

FIRST TELECAST: *June 19, 2001*
LAST TELECAST: *July 10, 2001*
BROADCAST HISTORY:

Jun 2001–Jul 2001, NBC Tue 8:30–9:00

CAST:

Andy "Fish" Troutner .... Kieran Culkin
Pete Troutner .... Will Friedle
Dr. Frank Troutner .... Joe Flaherty
Mrs. Troutner .... Molly Cheek
Henry "Krak" Krakowski .... Kyle Sabihy
Hazard .... Taylor Handley
Jess Riley .... Katherine Ellis
Mr. Ernie Hopkins .... Andy Dick
Miss Laura Eastwood .... Kristin Lehman

Fish had a plan. A new freshman at Westlake High, the teen schemer carefully plotted in his basement "war room" a four-point campaign to become the most popular kid in school, in part by winning the affections of the school's most popular girl, sweet sophomore Jess. Fish's pals Krak, a big lug with surprising smarts, and Hazard, a happy, oblivious pretty boy, helped out, but somehow every plan went awry. In part that was because of the boyish new teacher at Fish's school, none other than his older brother Pete, who knew him too well. Pete had a plan, too—to inspire the kids by acting like "one of them" (that didn't work too well), and to make out with sexy English teacher Miss Eastwood. Ernie was the wildly eccentric drama teacher who wore tie-dye shirts and offered generally good advice. Dr. Troutner was Pete's harried dad, and Mrs. Troutner, his smothering mom.

GO LUCKY (*Quiz/Audience Participation*)

FIRST TELECAST: *July 15, 1951*
LAST TELECAST: *September 2, 1951*

BROADCAST HISTORY:

Jul 1951–Sep 1951, CBS Sun 7:30–8:00

EMCEE:

Jan Murray

This comedy game show, the summer replacement in 1951 for *This is Show Business,* gave contestants the challenge of identifying an activity—fishing, bowling, burping a baby, etc.—by asking questions of the host. The studio and home audience had seen what the activity was, and the host would only answer yes or no to the questions. Each contestant worked with a team of two celebrities, the three of them trying to narrow the subject down until they could identify the activity. Small prizes were awarded for guessing correctly within a short time limit.

GOD, THE DEVIL AND BOB (*Cartoon*)

FIRST TELECAST: *March 9, 2000*

LAST TELECAST: *March 28, 2000*

BROADCAST HISTORY:

Mar 2000, NBC Thu 8:30–9:00

Mar 2000, NBC Tue 8:30–9:00

VOICES:

God .... James Garner

The Devil .... Alan Cumming

Bob Alman .... French Stewart

Donna Alman .... Laurie Metcalf

Megan Alman (age 13) .... Nancy Cartwright

Andy Alman (6) .... Kath Soucie

Mike .... Chi McBride

Smeck .... Jeff Doucette

A 32-year-old auto worker at Detroit's Associated Motors was picked by the devil to settle a bet with God in this offbeat, somewhat controversial cartoon. The bet was that if Bob succumbed to evil, via the devil's blandishments, God would give up on humankind and destroy the world. Bob was no perfect specimen. He drank, partied and visited strip clubs with his buddies from the auto plant, including big Mike. At home he dealt only moderately well with sensible wife Donna, whiny seventh-grader Megan and cute but selfish little Andy, who mostly ignored him. The devil appeared in a black cape, with little horns and a British accent, scratching cars and popping little kids' balloons for fun. He also showed up in other guises, often with his faithful henchman Smeck, a bumbling toadlike creature, to lead Bob astray. God visited in the guise of a mellow, white-bearded hippie (he looked a lot like Jerry Garcia), talking calmly in epigrams and seen only by Bob and little Andy. Bob wavered, but being a basically decent guy, did not give in. There were jokes about heaven and hell ("Every night, Guy Lombardo in concert"), as well as some interesting theological asides. In one conversation God remarked, "The trick is to inspire wonder without being heavy-handed, so that the atheists won't feel left out." Asked why he allowed evil in the world, he replied, "That's the big one, isn't it?" He then went on to give an answer that was drowned out by a passing train.

Some viewers thought the show was blasphemous, and more than a dozen NBC affiliates refused to carry it. They needn't have worried, as it was gone in less than a month.

GOING MY WAY (*Situation Comedy*)

FIRST TELECAST: *October 3, 1962*

LAST TELECAST: *September 11, 1963*

BROADCAST HISTORY:

Oct 1962–Sep 1963, ABC Wed 8:30–9:30

CAST:

Father Chuck O'Malley .... Gene Kelly

Father Fitzgibbon .... Leo G. Carroll

Tom Colwell .... Dick York

Mrs. Featherstone .... Nydia Westman

Clerical comedy-drama based on the 1944 movie, with Gene Kelly assuming the role created in the film by Bing Crosby. Father O'Malley, a lighthearted, progressive young priest, was assigned to a parish in a lower-class New York City neighborhood to aid the crusty old pastor, Father Fitzgibbon. There he encountered boyhood friend Tom Colwell (who ran the local community center), humor, and a great deal of warmth. Mrs. Featherstone was the housekeeper at the rectory.

GOING PLACES (*Situation Comedy*)

FIRST TELECAST: *September 21, 1990*

LAST TELECAST: *July 5, 1991*

BROADCAST HISTORY:

Sep 1990–Mar 1991, ABC Fri 9:30–10:00

May 1991–Jul 1991, ABC Fri 9:30–10:00

CAST:

Charlie Davis .... Alan Ruck

Jack Davis .... Jerry Levine

Alexandra (Alex) Burton .... Heather Locklear

Kate Griffin .... Hallie Todd

Dawn St. Claire .... Holland Taylor

Lindsay Bowen .... Staci Keanan

Dick Roberts (1991) .... Steve Vinovich

Arnie Ross (1991) .... Philip Charles MacKenzie

Nick Griffin (1991) .... J. D. Daniels

Sam Roberts (1991) .... Christopher Castile

This frothy comedy was the ultimate in navel-staring, TV comedy writers writing about the funny world of TV comedy writers. A team of four bright young neophytes had been put together to write gags for a *Candid Camera*–type series called *Here's Looking at You*: conservative Chicago ad man Charlie, his frisky, insecure brother Jack, sexy and slightly naive Alex from Denver, and abrasive New Yorker Kate. They all lived together and played pranks on one another in a sunny Los Angeles beachhouse—except when they were facing their alternately tyrannical/neurotic producer Dawn in her plush offices. Lindsay was the bouncy teenager who lived next door.

All this cheer failed to draw an audience, so in January *Going Places* was completely revamped. *Here's Looking at You* was canceled, and the foursome became the production team for a maniacal talk-show host named Dick Roberts and his frazzled producer Arnie. Dawn disappeared, but joining the show were Kate's troublemaking nephew Nick, who came to live with them, and (toward the end of the run) Dick's son Sam, who became Nick's best pal.

GOING PLACES WITH BETTY BETZ (*Discussion*)

FIRST TELECAST: *February 20, 1951*

LAST TELECAST: *May 15, 1951*

BROADCAST HISTORY:

Feb 1951–May 1951, ABC Tue 7:15–7:30

MODERATOR:

Betty Betz

Teenage panel show in which panelists and guests discussed career opportunities and other topics of interest to young people. Betty Betz was a nationally syndicated columnist for the Hearst newspapers, and an "authority" on teenagers.

GOING TO EXTREMES (*Comedy/Drama*)
FIRST TELECAST: *September 1, 1992*
LAST TELECAST: *January 27, 1993*
BROADCAST HISTORY:
Sep 1992–Jan 1993, ABC Tue 10:00–11:00
Jan 1993, ABC Wed 10:00–11:00
CAST:
Alex Lauren .... Daniel Jenkins
Colin Mitford .... Robert Duncan McNeill
Cheryl Carter .... Erika Alexander
Kathleen McDermott .... Joanna Going
Kim Selby .... Camilo Gallardo
Charlie Moran .... Andrew Lauer
Dr. Henry Croft .... Roy Dotrice
Dr. Michael Norris .... Carl Lumbly
Dr. Alice Davis .... June Chadwick
Dr. Jack Van DeWeghe .... Charles Keating
Nurse Sarah .... Pauline Stone
Solomon .... Stafford Ashani

"Welcome to Jantique, One Happy Island!" read the airport sign in the opening credits, to a background of reggae music, in this odd mix of medical drama and fun in the sun. Produced by the creators of *Northern Exposure*, it was in a sense *Northern Exposure*–South, with eccentric characters everywhere. Dr. Henry Croft was a barrel-chested, maverick doctor who had made $55 million from the invention of a revolutionary new joint-replacement system. Rebuffed by the stuffy U.S. medical establishment, he used the money to found Croft University Medical School on the sunny Caribbean island, where he could train other "mavericks" like himself. Among his young students were fun-loving Alex, dedicated Midwesterner Kathleen, metaphysical loner Kim, materialistic Cheryl, insecure Charlie, and arrogant Colin. Henry's sidekick and chief administrator was serious Dr. Norris, a Jantiquan native, who oversaw a staff that included seductive Dr. Davis (after whom Alex lusted), libidinous Dr. Van DeWeghe, and Nurse Sarah.

Anguish alternated with frolic on the beaches, in bed, and in the sunny classrooms, as Henry's enemies in the States tried to close him down. Filmed on location in Jamaica.

GOLD SEAL PLAYHOUSE (*Dramatic Anthology*)
FIRST TELECAST: *September 17, 1953*
LAST TELECAST: *October 8, 1953*
BROADCAST HISTORY:
Sep 1953–Oct 1953, ABC Thu 10:00–10:30

This was a short series of filmed dramas.

GOLDBERGS, THE (*Situation Comedy*)
FIRST TELECAST: *January 10, 1949*
LAST TELECAST: *October 19, 1954*
BROADCAST HISTORY:
Jan 1949–Feb 1949, CBS Mon 8:00–8:30
Mar 1949–Apr 1949, CBS Mon 9:00–9:30
Apr 1949–Jun 1951, CBS Mon 9:30–10:00
Feb 1952–Jul 1952, NBC Mon/Wed/Fri 7:15–7:30
Jul 1953–Sep 1953, NBC Fri 8:00–8:30
Apr 1954–Oct 1954, DUM Tue 8:00–8:30
(In first-run syndication during the 1955–1956 season)
CAST:
Molly Goldberg .... Gertrude Berg
Jake Goldberg (1949–1951) .... Philip Loeb
Jake Goldberg (1952) .... Harold J. Stone
Jake Goldberg (1953–1956) .... Robert H. Harris
Sammy Goldberg (1949–1952) ..... Larry Robinson
Sammy Goldberg (1954–1956) .... Tom Taylor
Rosalie Goldberg .... Arlene McQuade
Uncle David .... Eli Mintz
Mrs. Bloom (1953) .... Olga Fabian
Dora Barnett (1955–1956) .... Betty Bendyke
Carrie Barnett (1955–1956) .... Ruth Yorke
Daisy Carey (1955–1956) .... Susan Steel
Henry Carey (1955–1956) .... Jon Lormer

Gertrude Berg had conceived the role of Molly Goldberg and made her a popular radio character for almost 20 years. In January 1949 the entire Goldberg clan moved to television. Living in Apartment 3B at 1030 East Tremont Avenue in the Bronx, they were a middle-class Jewish family with middle-class problems. Molly's husband Jake was in the clothing business, and their two children, Sammy and Rosalie, were active teenagers. Molly was a housewife, prone to gossip with her neighbors across the inside courtyard of the apartment building. Her call to her favorite cohort in gossip—"Yoo-hoo, Mrs. Bloom"—came whenever she had something juicy to spread, which was quite regularly. Also living with the family was the educated and philosophical Uncle David, patriarch of the family. Molly was a good soul and was constantly involved in trying to help everybody in the neighborhood solve their problems.

The Goldbergs was a live series during the years it ran on CBS, NBC, and DuMont. In the fall of 1955 a filmed version was produced for syndication to local stations, using the same cast as had appeared on DuMont in 1954. In this last version, Molly and the family moved from the Bronx to the suburban community of Haverville. It lasted for one season. New to the cast were Sammy's fiancée, and later wife, Dora; Dora's mother, Carrie; and Molly's new neighbors, Daisy and Henry Carey.

The program ended its CBS run in 1951 under a cloud of controversy. Principal Philip Loeb had been blacklisted for alleged left-wing sympathies, causing sponsor General Foods to drop the series. Mrs. Berg fought to keep him, but to no avail—nervous sponsor and network executives said that either Loeb went or *The Goldbergs* would never be seen again. Thus when the series reappeared in 1952, it was without Loeb.

The charges against Loeb were never proven—indeed, he declared under oath that he was not a Communist Party member—but his career went into a sharp decline. He had become "controversial," and advertisers steered clear of him. He appealed to his union for help, with no result. His career in a shambles, Loeb became increasingly depressed and embittered. In 1955, alone in a hotel room, he took a fatal overdose of sleeping pills. Four years after he had been driven from TV, Philip Loeb was dead, a suicide.

GOLDDIGGERS, THE, see *Dean Martin Presents The Golddiggers*

GOLDEN GAME, THE (*Religion*)
FIRST TELECAST: *April 9, 1950*
LAST TELECAST: *May 7, 1950*
BROADCAST HISTORY:
Apr 1950–May 1950, ABC Sun 6:30–7:00
Biblical charades. Two teams of laymen representing different nationalities and creeds acted out charades based on biblical stories or proverbs. At the end they explained why they picked their subjects, and what these subjects meant to their lives.

GOLDEN GIRLS, THE (*Situation Comedy*)
FIRST TELECAST: *September 14, 1985*
LAST TELECAST: *September 14, 1992*
BROADCAST HISTORY:
Sep 1985–Jul 1991, NBC Sat 9:00–9:30
Aug 1991–Sep 1991, NBC Sat 8:00–8:30
Sep 1991–Sep 1992, NBC Sat 8:30–9:00
CAST:
Dorothy Zbornak .... Bea Arthur
Rose Nylund .... Betty White
Blanche Devereaux .... Rue McClanahan
Sophia Petrillo .... Estelle Getty
**Stanley Zbornak* .... Herb Edelman
**Miles Webber* .... Harold Gould
*Occasional
THEME:
"Thank You for Being a Friend," by Andrew Gold, sung by Cynthia Fee
For those who thought NBC's drug-drenched crime show *Miami Vice* was giving Miami a bad name, the network launched this equally popular comedy—nicknamed "Miami Nice." It centered on four mature, single women living together in the sunny city of retirees, and enjoying their "golden years" to the hilt. Dorothy was the outspoken divorcée, a substitute teacher whose strong personality often seemed to overpower her housemates. Rose was a flaky, naive, soft-spoken widow given to hilarious misinterpretations of almost everything that was said in her presence. She worked, believe it or not, as a grief counselor. Blanche, who owned the house, was also a widow, but of a different stripe. She was lusty, man-hungry, and dripping with charm, a Southern belle who never aged—in her own mind, at least. All in their 50s and 60s, the three were joined by Dorothy's elderly mother Sophia, who moved in when her retirement home, Shady Pines, burned to the ground. Sophia had the saltiest mouth in the house. She had had a stroke, it was said, that destroyed the "tact" cells in her brain.

Herb Edelman was seen occasionally as Dorothy's no-good ex-husband Stan, who had dumped her for a young bimbo but who now seemed to want Dorothy back. Scatterbrained Rose, for a time, had a boyfriend named Miles, who unfortunately turned out to be a former mob accountant in the Witness Relocation Program who had to leave town temporarily when his cover was blown.

In the final episode, wedding bells broke up the old gang as Dorothy married Blanche's visiting uncle Lucas (Leslie Nielsen). The following fall Blanche sold the house and with Rose and Sophia moved into a new series, *The Golden Palace* (q.v.).

Golden Girls was a smash hit and highly regarded in the industry. It won ten Emmy awards, including best comedy (twice), and each of its four leads individually won the best actress or supporting actress award—probably the first time in TV history that *all* the regulars in a "gang" series won Emmies. *Golden Girls* was rerun on NBC weekday mornings from July 1989 to August 1990.

GOLDEN PALACE, THE (*Situation Comedy*)
FIRST TELECAST: *September 18, 1992*
LAST TELECAST: *August 6, 1993*
BROADCAST HISTORY:
Sep 1992–Aug 1993, CBS Fri 8:00–8:30
CAST:
Rose Nylund .... Betty White
Blanche Deveraux .... Rue McClanahan
Sophia Petrillo .... Estelle Getty
Chuy Castillos .... Cheech Marin
Roland Wilson .... Don Cheadle
Oliver Webb .... Billy L. Sullivan
Looking for a good investment, Rose, Blanche, and Sophia, three of the original Golden Girls, decided to pool their money and purchase a small Art Deco hotel in the trendy South Bay section of Miami Beach. What they didn't realize was that the hotel, The Golden Palace, had almost no staff and was not generating any profits. So instead of moving in and living comfortably off the profits, they became live-in full-time staff helping to run the place. The rest of the staff was made up of Chuy, the recently divorced Mexican chef; Roland, the competent black manager/desk clerk; and Oliver, the street-smart young boy who did odd jobs for Roland. Roland was Oliver's unofficial foster father (the boy's mother had deserted him, and his father was in jail). Stories revolved around the problems the three new owners had keeping The Golden Palace afloat and the assorted loony guests who drifted in and out.

GOLDEN TOUCH OF FRANKIE CARLE, THE (*Music*)
FIRST TELECAST: *August 7, 1956*
LAST TELECAST: *October 29, 1956*
BROADCAST HISTORY:
Aug 1956, NBC Tue 7:30–7:45
Sep 1956, NBC Mon/Tue 7:30–7:45
Oct 1956, NBC Mon 7:30–7:45
REGULAR:
Frankie Carle
Pianist Frankie Carle starred in this live music show, originating from Hollywood, that filled the remainder of the half hour in which NBC aired its network news program during the summer of 1956. Guest vocalists appeared on a regular basis and the selections of songs, both instrumental and vocal, ranged from standards to currently popular numbers.

GOLDEN YEARS, see *Stephen King's Golden Years*

GOLDIE, see *Betty Hutton Show, The*

GOLF CHANNEL, THE (Network) (*Sports Cable Network*)
LAUNCHED:
January 17, 1995

SUBSCRIBERS (May 2003):

54.1 million (51% U.S.)

This specialty channel swung and putted to life in 1995, during a period when cable was offering a plethora of new special-interest channels. Co-founded by golf legend Arnold Palmer, it provided coverage of dozens of events including the PGA Tour, LPGA, USGA, Nike Tour, the European Tour, and ANZ Tour of Australasia. Among its evening series were *Golf Channel Academy* (instruction), *Golf Talk Live* (call-in, hosted by Peter Kessler), and *Profiles of a Pro* (biography). *Golf Central* was the daily roundup of scores and highlights from the major tours.

GOMER PYLE, U.S.M.C. (*Situation Comedy*)

FIRST TELECAST: *September 25, 1964*
LAST TELECAST: *September 9, 1970*
BROADCAST HISTORY:

Sep 1964–Jun 1965, CBS Fri 9:30–10:00
Sep 1965–Sep 1966, CBS Fri 9:00–9:30
Sep 1966–Aug 1967, CBS Wed 9:30–10:00
Sep 1967–Sep 1969, CBS Fri 8:30–9:00
Jul 1970–Sep 1970, CBS Wed 8:00–8:30

CAST:

Pvt. Gomer Pyle .... Jim Nabors
Sgt. Vince Carter .... Frank Sutton
Pvt. Gilbert "Duke" Slater .... Ronnie Schell
Corp. Chuck Boyle (1965–1968) .... Roy Stuart
Pvt. Frankie Lombardi (1965–1966) .... Ted Bessell
Bunny .... Barbara Stuart
Pvt. Lester Hummel (1965–1968)
.... William Christopher
Col. Edward Gray .... Forrest Compton
Sgt. Charlie Hacker (1965–1969) ...... Allan Melvin
Cpl. Nick Cuccinello (1964–1965) . Tommy Leonetti
Larry (1964–1965) .... Larry Hovis
Lou Ann Poovie (1967–1969) .... Elizabeth MacRae

After little more than a season playing Gomer Pyle on *The Andy Griffith Show*, Jim Nabors got his own series built around the same character. Gomer was a likable, naive, bumbling rural character who gave up his job as a gas station attendant in Mayberry to join the peacetime Marine Corps, which stationed him at Camp Henderson, California. His nemesis in the Marine Corps was his immediate superior, Sgt. Carter, who tried hard to be a cynical, tough leatherneck, but was constantly confounded by Gomer's wide-eyed innocence and trust in practically everyone. At first Carter believed that Gomer was trying to make a fool out of him, but he later realized that it was just Gomer's nature to be the way he was. Sgt. Carter eventually became Gomer's friend and protector, a role belying his gruff exterior. That is not to say, however, that Gomer did not continue to drive him crazy on a relatively regular basis. Bunny was Sgt. Carter's girlfriend, although the writers could never get her last name straight—it was Harper in one episode, Olsen in another, Wilson in another. Perhaps she was a fugitive!

The episodes that aired during the summer of 1970 in prime time and later in daytime were all reruns. The CBS daytime run began in August 1969 and ended in March 1972.

GONG SHOW, THE (*Comedy/Audience Participation*)

BROADCAST HISTORY:

Syndicated and network daytime
30 minutes
Produced: *1976–1980, 1988–1989*
Released: *Fall 1976*

HOST:

Gary Owens (1976–1977)
Chuck Barris (1977–1980)
Don Bleu (1988–1989)

PANELISTS:

Jaye P. Morgan
Jamie Farr
Rex Reed
Phyllis Diller
Arte Johnson
Rip Taylor
Steve Garvey
Ken Norton
Dr. Joyce Brothers

REGULAR:

Milton Delugg Orchestra (1976–1980)
Joey Carbone Orchestra (1988–1989)

Possibly the most bizarre program to air on American television in years, *The Gong Show* was a wild and sometimes raunchy parody of amateur programs. It consisted, simply enough, of a succession of amateurs demonstrating their dubious talents. Anyone could audition, but sometimes it seemed that only certifiable crazies need apply. Typical of the acts was a girl who whistled through her nose, a dentist who played "Stars and Stripes Forever" with his drill, a man who played lighted bulbs that blinked on and off, a dancer with four arms, a comedian who performed inside a barrel, a musician who blew a trumpet through his navel, another who meowed to the tune "Alley Cat," an endless parade of fat ladies who did unlikely things (tap-dancing, playing the tuba, belching to music, singing "On the Good Ship Lollipop"), and someone who broke eggs on his head while making faces through a distorting glass. And of course there was the lady in the tutu who stood on her head on a cup and spun slowly around, while playing "Old Folks at Home" on the mandolin.

Looking on during all this insanity, and sometimes joining in, was a rowdy panel of three celebrities who were supposed to rate each act on a scale of one to ten, or, if it was bad enough, gong it off the stage. (Some acts were gonged so fast there was eventually a minimum time limit imposed.) The act with the highest score got a prize of $712.05 ($516.32 on the daytime version), and a golden gong. About one-third of the acts were gonged, and on some shows they all were, leaving no winners at all.

There were also interludes with regulars, such as Gene-Gene the Dancing Machine (a big, black stagehand who came on dancing frantically, and was usually pelted with assorted objects thrown by the panel), and the Unknown Comic, who wore a paper bag over his head, the better to avoid responsibility for his corny jokes (he was later unmasked—or debagged—on *Real People* as one Murray Langston). It was, as one of the writers put it, "a cuckoo's nest without walls."

Jaye P. Morgan and Jamie Farr were virtually regular panelists, joined frequently by Arte Johnson, Rex Reed, Rip Taylor, Steve Garvey, Phyllis Diller, and others at home with this kind of mayhem. The show was created by Chris Bearde and Chuck Barris, and premiered on the NBC daytime lineup in June 1976, remaining there until July 1978. A syndicated nighttime version was added in the fall of 1976. Curly-headed Chuck "Chuckie Baby" Barris, one of the most successful game-show producers in Hollywood *(Dating Game, Newlywed Game)*, was the host of the daytime version throughout its run, and replaced Gary Owens on the syndicated version after its first year. When *The Gong Show* was revived in 1988, Don Bleu was the new host.

GOOD ADVICE (*Situation Comedy*)
FIRST TELECAST: *April 2, 1993*
LAST TELECAST: *August 10, 1994*
BROADCAST HISTORY:
Apr 1993–May 1993, CBS Fri 9:30–10:00
May 1994–Jun 1994, CBS Mon 9:30–10:00
Jun 1994–Aug 1994, CBS Wed 8:30–9:00
CAST:
Susan DeRuzza, Ph.D. .... Shelley Long
Jack Harold .... Treat Williams
Artie Cohen .... George Wyner
Ronnie Cohen (1993) .... Estelle Harris
Michael DeRuzza (age 9) .... Ross Malinger
Sean .... Lightfield Lewis
Paige Turner (1994) .... Teri Garr
Henriette Campbell (1994)........ Henriette Mantel

Susan DeRuzza was a very successful Los Angeles marriage counselor with a string of best-selling books on the subject, even though she seemed to know nothing about it. Her own marriage had fallen apart when she found her "loving" husband, Joey, in the middle of one of his apparently numerous affairs. She threw him out of the house and began rebuilding her life, ineptly. Susan shared an office suite with Jack, a womanizing, fast-talking divorce attorney who sometimes hovered like a vulture, hoping to get new clients when her patients failed to work out their marital problems. Others in the office were Artie, the building owner and a chiropractor who also shared the suite and who acted like an adopted "Jewish uncle"; Artie's mother, Ronnie, their receptionist; and Sean, the eccentric son of a wealthy family from Bel Air who sought refuge from the elitist world of his upbringing by doing odd jobs around the office. Michael was Susan's young son.

Good Advice had even more problems than Susan's patients. Originally scheduled to premiere in the fall of 1992, it was delayed first by health problems of its star, Shelley Long, and then because of extensive changes in the concept and story lines. After a short unsuccessful run the following spring it was supposed to be reworked and return in the fall. The producers kept tinkering with it, and then Long came down with the flu and its return was delayed until the following spring. When it did return there were two new cast members—Paige, Susan's flighty, self-centered older sister, who had just moved to L.A. and become the new inept receptionist, and Henriette, Susan's outspoken new housekeeper. The changes didn't help and the "new" *Good Advice* soon disappeared.

The series was based on a character created by Long.

GOOD AND EVIL (*Situation Comedy*)
FIRST TELECAST: *September 25, 1991*
LAST TELECAST: *October 30, 1991*
BROADCAST HISTORY:
Sep 1991–Oct 1991, ABC Wed 10:30–11:00
CAST:
Denise Sandler .... Teri Garr
Genevieve ("Genny")........... Margaret Whitton
George .... Mark Blankfield
Dr. Eric Haan .... Lane Davies
Mary.................................. Mary Gillis
David .... Seth Green
Roger......................... Sherman Howard
Charlotte Sandler................... Marian Seldes
Harlan Shell........................... Lane Smith
Caroline......................... Brooke Theiss
Ronald .... Marius Weyers
Sonny .... William Shockley

An off-the-wall comedy from Susan Harris, the creator of *Soap*, in many ways patterned on that hit series. In *Soap* the opposites were the uptown Tates and the blue-collar Campbells. Here they were two sisters: impossibly pure, idealistic Genny ("good"), and ruthless, conniving Denise ("evil"), the latter so mean she was determined to steal both her mother's cosmetics empire and her sister's boyfriend (Dr. Eric). Every character was a cartoon: Charlotte, the imperious mother, not about to be conned by anyone; Harlan, her feisty Southern boyfriend; Eric, the stiff but handsome heart surgeon with a sordid past; George, the blundering, blind psychiatrist also in love with sweet Genny; Caroline, Genny's daughter who had been mute since her father's death; Roger, Denise's dumb assistant; and Ronald, Denise's adventurer-husband, thought lost on the slopes of Mount Everest. Did he fall or was he pushed? Ronald was found frozen stiff in the opening episode, thawed out, and returned with revenge on his mind.

Stories included Denise's pursuit of a new face cream that could make the company's fortune—if it didn't peel faces first; her attempts to blackmail Eric; and her teenage son David's search for his real father, Sonny.

Like *Soap*, *Good and Evil* engendered some controversy, particularly for its wild parody of the blind (klutzy George tended to demolish everything in his path with his cane; interestingly, comedian Mark Blankfield had played a similar character on *Nutt House* in 1989). Members of the National Federation of the Blind picketed the network. ABC responded that "the show is a parody done to the extremes, and there is not a single character in the show intended to be believable."

GOOD COMPANY (*Interview*)
FIRST TELECAST: *September 7, 1967*
LAST TELECAST: *December 21, 1967*
BROADCAST HISTORY:
Sep 1967–Dec 1967, ABC Thu 10:00–10:30
HOST:
F. Lee Bailey
EXECUTIVE PRODUCER:
David Susskind

In a style reminiscent of Edward R. Murrow's *Person to Person*, famed criminal lawyer F. (for Francis) Lee Bailey visited the home of a different celebrity each week and chatted about his host's life and career. The principal difference was that Bailey was filmed at the home of the interviewee, rather than talking long-distance from the studio, as Murrow had done on his live program. Among those Bailey interviewed were actor Tony Curtis, publisher Hugh Hefner (at his million-dollar Chicago mansion), Senator Everett

Dirksen, and Jack Paar (who was such a good talker that he required two telecasts).

GOOD COMPANY (*Situation Comedy*)
FIRST TELECAST: *March 4, 1996*
LAST TELECAST: *April 15, 1996*
BROADCAST HISTORY:
Mar 1996–Apr 1996, CBS Mon 9:30–10:00
CAST:
Zoe Hellstrom .... Wendie Malick
Will Hennesy .... Jon Tenney
Jack .... Seymour Cassel
Jody .... Timothy Fall
Ron .... Jason Beghe
Liz .... Lauren Graham
Dale .... Elizabeth Anne Smith
Bobby .... Terry Kiser
Comedy set at a Manhattan ad agency. Zoe was the manipulative newly appointed creative director of the Blanton, Booker & Hayden Agency. Having just had a baby, and with a reputation around the agency for being a real bitch, Zoe found her life in turmoil. Working with her were Will, the art director who wanted to be an artist; Jack, the gruff but talented senior copywriter; Jody, Jack's airheaded assistant; Ron, the backstabbing account executive; Liz, an ambitious young copywriter; and Dale, a neurotic junior art director. Bobby, BB&H's president and CEO, didn't say much—and never smiled—but his mere presence struck terror into his staff. Problems with clients and advertising campaigns and office politics were the primary focus of the series, while it lasted.

GOOD GRIEF! (*Situation Comedy*)
FIRST TELECAST: *September 30, 1990*
LAST TELECAST: *March 17, 1991*
BROADCAST HISTORY:
Sep 1990–Mar 1991, FOX Sun 9:30–10:00
CAST:
Ernie Lapidus .... Howie Mandel
Warren Pepper .... Joel Brooks
Debbie Pepper Lapidus .... Wendy Schaal
Raoul .... Sheldon Feldner
Ringo Prowley .... Tom Poston
Comedian Howie Mandel starred in this absurd comedy as a former con artist who had married into a family of morticians and was now running roughshod over the business—The Sincerity Mortuary in Dacron, Ohio, the 63rd-largest city in the state. His straitlaced brother-in-law Warren, who had run the business prior to Ernie's arrival, found it difficult to deal with the high-profile promotional approach Ernie used to drum up business, including tasteless commercials on local TV. Debbie, Ernie's wife and Warren's sister, who played the organ at funerals, spent considerable time trying to keep peace between the men. Also on hand were Raoul, the mortuary's silent handyman, who was Ernie's mother before she/he had undergone a sex change operation, and Ringo, Ernie's father and former partner, whose scams around the funeral home drove poor Warren to distraction.

GOOD GUYS, THE (*Situation Comedy*)
FIRST TELECAST: *September 25, 1968*
LAST TELECAST: *January 23, 1970*
BROADCAST HISTORY:
Sep 1968–Sep 1969, CBS Wed 8:30–9:00
Sep 1969–Jan 1970, CBS Fri 8:00–8:30
CAST:
Rufus Butterworth .... Bob Denver
Bert Gramus .... Herb Edelman
Claudia Gramus .... Joyce Van Patten
Andy Gardner (1968) .... Ron Masak
Hal Dawson (1968–1969) .... George Furth
Big Tom (1969) .... Alan Hale, Jr.
Gertie (1969) .... Toni Gilman
Fresh from his success in *Gilligan's Island*, Bob Denver moved into the role of Rufus Butterworth in this 1968 comedy series. Rufus and Bert Gramus had been friends since they were children. Bert was married and ran a diner, "Bert's Place," while Rufus was single and worked as a cabdriver. Rufus also helped his friend out around the diner, and was constantly coming up with moneymaking schemes, none of which ever seemed to pan out—but all of which got the two of them into endless predicaments. Rufus gave up his cabdriving at the start of the second season to become a full-time partner in the diner, which closed its doors forever with the cancellation of the series in January 1970.

GOOD HEAVENS (*Situation Comedy*)
FIRST TELECAST: *March 8, 1976*
LAST TELECAST: *June 26, 1976*
BROADCAST HISTORY:
Mar 1976–Apr 1976, ABC Mon 8:30–9:00
May 1976–Jun 1976, ABC Sat 8:00–8:30
CAST:
Mr. Angel .... Carl Reiner
EXECUTIVE PRODUCER:
Carl Reiner
Gentle comedy starring Carl Reiner as a warm and witty business-suited angel who descended to earth to bestow one wish on a different mortal each week—any wish except money. Thanks to Mr. Angel, and to themselves, a sporting-goods salesman got his long-dreamt-of tryout in the big leagues; a young woman who couldn't decide between two suitors got a new beau who combined the best qualities of each; and an unsuccessful author got an adventure to which everyone wanted the literary rights.

GOOD LIFE, THE (*Situation Comedy*)
FIRST TELECAST: *September 18, 1971*
LAST TELECAST: *January 8, 1972*
BROADCAST HISTORY:
Sep 1971–Jan 1972, NBC Sat 8:30–9:00
CAST:
Albert Miller .... Larry Hagman
Jane Miller .... Donna Mills
Charles Dutton .... David Wayne
Grace Dutton .... Hermione Baddeley
Nick Dutton .... Danny Goldman
Albert and Jane Miller were a middle-class American couple who decided that the dull routine of their lives needed a change. Instead of dropping out, however, they contrived to "drop up"—obtaining work as butler and cook, respectively, for an extremely wealthy family. Amid the opulence of a millionaire's mansion, they hoped to share at least some of the benefits of "the good life." Their new employer, industrialist Charles Dutton, was unaware of their middle-class background.

He recognized their inexperience but found them pleasant enough company. His stuck-up sister Grace was upset with their lack of proper training, however, and constantly looked for ways to get them fired. Dutton's teenage son Nick was the only member of the household who discovered the truth about the Millers, but he thought that their charade was great fun and helped them through the many catastrophes caused by their unfamiliarity with social etiquette among the wealthy.

GOOD LIFE, THE (*Situation Comedy*)
FIRST TELECAST: *January 3, 1994*
LAST TELECAST: *April 12, 1994*
BROADCAST HISTORY:
Jan 1994, NBC Mon 8:30–9:00
Jan 1994–Feb 1994, NBC Tue 8:30–9:00
Mar 1994–Apr 1994, NBC Tue 8:00–8:30
CAST:
John Bowman .... John Caponera
Maureen Bowman .... Eve Bowman
Paul Bowman (age 15) .... Jake Patellis
Melissa Bowman (12) .... Shay Astar
Bob Bowman (6) .... Justin Berfield
Drew Clark .... Drew Carey
Tommy Bartlett .... Monty Hoffman

This rather pedestrian home-and-workplace comedy revolved around John Bowman, an amiable dad living with his family in the Chicago suburbs. On the home front there was Maureen, his somewhat dippy wife, a grade-school tutor; happy-go-lucky, long-haired teenager Paul; worldly-wise teen Melissa; and cute little Bob, who worshiped his dad. Over at Honest Abe Security Products, a lock-distribution business where John managed the loading dock, the main characters were dumpy, crew-cut bachelor Drew, co-manager of the loading dock and John's best friend, and Tommy, a rather dumb, Dunkin' Donuts–obsessed worker. Among the continuing stories was Maureen's ambition to become an avant-garde playwright and her incomprehensible plays.

GOOD MORNING, MIAMI (*Situation Comedy*)
FIRST TELECAST: *September 26, 2002*
LAST TELECAST:
BROADCAST HISTORY:
Sep 2002– , NBC Thu 9:30–10:00
CAST:
Jake Silver .... Mark Feuerstein
Dylan Messinger .... Ashley Williams
Frank Alfano .... Jere Burns
Gavin Stone .... Matt Letscher
Lucia Rojas-Klein (2002) .... Tessie Santiago
Sister Brenda Trogman (2002) ..... Brooke Dillman
Penny .... Constance Zimmer
Robby .... Stephon Fuller
Claire Arnold .... Suzanne Pleshette

Jake was a young hotshot TV producer from Boston who never really intended to take a job directing the lowest-rated morning talk show in the country, *Good Morning, Miami*—until he met the show's pretty young hairdresser, Dylan. He was stiff and dorky, she was flirty and cute as a button, and it was love at first sight—for him, at least. She was dating the show's pompous cohost Gavin, and didn't notice at first, but Jake was determined to win her so he stayed. Others on the loony set were Frank, the jittery station manager, Lucia, Gavin's trampy Hispanic cohost, Penny the wisecracking assistant and Robby the stage manager. Sister Brenda was the wacky weathercaster, a nun in full habit who made wisecracks about the "guy up there." Giving Jake advice was his stylish but salty grandmother, Claire, who lived nearby.

What started as a slapstick sitcom soon turned toward more romantic stories, with Lucia and Sister Brenda dropped from the cast and Jake alternating between Dylan and Penny. Even Jake's fun-loving grandma had her dalliances, with boyfriend Lenny (Tom Poston) among others.

GOOD MORNING, WORLD (*Situation Comedy*)
FIRST TELECAST: *September 5, 1967*
LAST TELECAST: *September 17, 1968*
BROADCAST HISTORY:
Sep 1967–Sep 1968, CBS Tue 9:30–10:00
CAST:
Dave Lewis .... Joby Baker
Larry Clarke .... Ronnie Schell
Roland B. Hutton, Jr. .... Billy DeWolf
Linda Lewis .... Julie Parrish
Sandy Kramer .... Goldie Hawn

Comedy about "Lewis and Clarke," two early-morning radio disc jockeys who worked together as a team at a small Los Angeles station owned by the overbearing Roland B. Hutton, Jr. Their adventures both on and off the air were the subjects of stories in this series. Dave was happily married, while Larry, a single, fancied himself quite a swinger. Goldie Hawn, in her pre–*Laugh-In* days, played the Lewises' gossiping neighbor Sandy.

GOOD NEWS (*Situation Comedy*)
FIRST TELECAST: *August 25, 1997*
LAST TELECAST: *August 31, 1998*
BROADCAST HISTORY:
Aug 1997–Mar 1998, UPN Mon 9:00–9:30
Apr 1998–Jul 1998, UPN Tue 9:30–10:00
Jul 1998–Aug 1998, UPN Mon 9:00–9:30
CAST:
Pastor David Randolph .... David Ramsey
Hattie Dixon .... Roz Ryan
Mona Phillips .... Alexia Robinson
Cassie Coleman .... Tracey Cherelle Jones
Little T .... Guy Torry
Vonita Stansberry .... Jazsmin Lewis
Billy .... Billy Preston

In this amiable comedy, Randolph was the new acting pastor at the Church of Life in Compton, California. When he arrived, he was greeted by a staff announcing they were leaving the church to start their own congregation. He took over as choir director and tried to rebuild things with the help of a few devoted congregants. Among them were Mrs. Dixon, the battle-axe volunteer church cook; Little T, the hip young hustler who took over as janitor; Cassie, Little T's sexy outspoken girlfriend; and Mona, the church's youth director, with her sights on the eligible but apparently disinterested new pastor. A few weeks after the series premiered, she got competition from Vonita, the newly hired church secretary, but Pastor Randolph was preoccupied with his congregation and didn't date anyone during the run of the series. There was rousing gospel music in most episodes, with real-life musician Billy Preston portraying the church organist.

GOOD SPORTS (*Situation Comedy*)

FIRST TELECAST: *January 10, 1991*
LAST TELECAST: *July 13, 1991*
BROADCAST HISTORY:

Jan 1991–Feb 1991, CBS Thu 9:30–10:00
Feb 1991, CBS Mon 10:30–11:00
Mar 1991, CBS Mon 10:00–10:30
May 1991–Jun 1991, CBS Mon 10:00–10:30
Jun 1991–Jul 1991, CBS Sat 10:30–11:00

CAST:

Gayle Roberts .... Farrah Fawcett
Bobby Tannen .... Ryan O'Neal
R. J. Rappaport .... Lane Smith
John "Mac" MacKinney .... Brian Doyle-Murray
Jeff Mussberger .... Cleavant Derricks
Missy Van Johnson .... Christine Dunford
Leash .... Paul Feig
Nick Calder .... William Katt

THEME:

"Good Sports," written by Andy Goldmark and performed by Al Green

Gayle Roberts was totally unprepared for the shock of Bobby Tannen entering her life for the second time, twenty years after a weekend fling in college that she had never forgotten and he couldn't remember. Over the intervening years, she had gone from being a supermodel to carving out a career for herself as a talented, hardworking sports journalist. Bobby, a star football player in college and later with the Green Bay Packers, had not been so fortunate. Relying on his football skills and good looks could only take him so far, especially since he wasn't too bright and had a temper that constantly got him into trouble. Bobby was desperate for a job when blustery, egocentric R. J. Rappaport (Ted Turner with a Texas drawl), the cable television magnate, gave him an on-air tryout co-anchoring "Sports Central" on his cable network ASCN (All Sports Cable Network). Rappaport liked having the ex-jock around and liked the sparks that flew between Bobby and Gayle on the air—caused by her resentment of Bobby's obvious lack of reportorial skills and the fact that he had totally forgotten their college relationship. Bobby really wanted to make good and sought her help, eventually falling in love with and proposing to her.

Others seen regularly in this spoof of TV sports programming were Jeff Mussberger and Missy Van Johnson, ASCN's other featured reporters; Mac MacKinney, the harried producer who agreed with everything Rappaport said; Leash, the watchdog hired by Bobby's mother to try to keep him out of trouble; and Nick Calder, Gayle's boyfriend who went nuts after she dumped him and started to show real interest in Bobby. Additionally, a number of real sports personalities showed up, primarily as comic interview guests on ASCN's "Sports Chat." Among them were Kareem Abdul-Jabbar, Lyle Alzado, Jim Brown, Bruce Jenner, George Steinbrenner, George Foreman, and Pete Rose.

Besides its big-name stars, *Good Sports* offered lots of sly little spoofs of television and celebrity. In the opening each week, an elegant Bobby swept glamorous Gayle away in a dance sequence worthy of Astaire and Rogers—then absentmindedly left her hanging from a chandelier; during the episode itself, characters would wander over to the nearby set of R. J.'s comedy network (like Ted Turner, R. J. ran lots of cable networks)—the Rap-HA-port Network—where a standup comic would pitch one-liners at them from the stage as they tried to sort out their problems.

GOOD TIME HARRY (*Situation Comedy*)

FIRST TELECAST: *July 19, 1980*
LAST TELECAST: *September 13, 1980*
BROADCAST HISTORY:

Jul 1980, NBC Sat 10:00–11:00
Aug 1980–Sep 1980, NBC Sat 10:30–11:00

CAST:

Harry Jenkins .... Ted Bessell
Jimmy Hughes .... Eugene Roche
Carol Younger .... Marcia Strassman
Billie Howard .... Jesse Welles
Stan .... Barry Gordon
Sally .... Ruth Manning
Martin Springer .... Steven Peterman
Lenny the bartender .... Richard Karron

Harry Jenkins was a sportswriter for the San Francisco *Sentinel*, whose dates with beautiful women tended to get in the way of his assignments for the paper. His extracurricular activities did not endear him to his editor, Jimmy Hughes, who had once fired him because of it. Harry's skill at his craft got him his job back, but his continuing playboy escapades made for an adversary relationship between him and his boss. Sally was Hughes's secretary; Carol, a sympathetic fellow reporter; Martin, the enthusiastic young copy boy; and Billie, a cocktail waitress. Living next door to Harry, and jealous of his success with beautiful women, was Stan, a rather bland insurance salesman who was always trying to get Harry to fix him up with dates. One of Harry's favorite haunts was Danny's Bar, a watering hole very popular with San Francisco writers.

GOOD TIMES (*Situation Comedy*)

FIRST TELECAST: *February 1, 1974*
LAST TELECAST: *August 1, 1979*
BROADCAST HISTORY:

Feb 1974–Sept 1974, CBS Fri 8:30–9:00
Sep 1974–Mar 1976, CBS Tue 8:00–8:30
Mar 1976–Aug 1976, CBS Tue 8:30–9:00
Sep 1976–Jan 1978, CBS Wed 8:00–8:30
Jan 1978–May 1978, CBS Mon 8:00–8:30
Jun 1978–Sep 1978, CBS Mon 8:30–9:00
Sep 1978–Dec 1978, CBS Sat 8:30–9:00
May 1979–Aug 1979, CBS Wed 8:30–9:00

CAST:

Florida Evans (1974–1977, 1978–1979) Esther Rolle
James Evans (1974–1976).............. John Amos
James Evans, Jr. (J.J.) .... Jimmie Walker
Willona Woods .... Ja'net DuBois
Michael Evans .... Ralph Carter
Thelma Evans Anderson .... BernNadette Stanis
Carl Dixon (1977).................... Moses Gunn
Nathan Bookman (1977–1979)...... Johnny Brown
Penny Gordon Woods (1977–1979) ... Janet Jackson
Keith Anderson (1978–1979) .... Ben Powers
Sweet Daddy (1978–1979) .... Theodore Wilson

PRODUCER:

Norman Lear

Good Times was a spin-off from *Maude*, which in turn was a spin-off from *All in the Family*. Florida

Evans was originally Maude Findlay's maid until, in the spring of 1974, she got a show of her own. Florida and James Evans were lower-middle-class blacks living with their three children in a high-rise ghetto on the South Side of Chicago. J.J. was the oldest (17 when the series started), Thelma was a year younger than he, and Michael was 10. Trying to make ends meet on the erratic income provided by James, who was always in and out of jobs, made life difficult, but there was plenty of love in the family. J.J. was an accomplished amateur painter who, though going to trade school, was always looking for some get-rich-quick scheme that would help get him and his family out of the ghetto. He formed a rock group, managed a young comic, and tried various other moneymaking ideas after he got out of school. He did manage to earn money with his painting and was also quite popular with the girls, something his mother viewed with mixed emotions. His catchphrase "Dy-No-Mite" became very popular in the mid-1970s. Florida's neighbor and best friend was Willona Woods.

At the start of the 1976–1977 season there was a major change in the cast. James had found a job working as a partner in a garage in Mississippi when he was killed in an auto accident. The entire family, which had been planning to move to their new home and start a new life, was now fatherless. J.J. became the man of the house and was even more determined to find a way out of the ghetto for his family, whether by means that were entirely legal or not. Some of his schemes became decidedly shady. Meanwhile Florida found a new man in her life in the spring of 1977, in the person of Carl Dixon, the owner of a small appliance repair shop. They were married during the summer of 1977 (though the wedding was not seen), and in the fall were referred to on the show as being "on their honeymoon."

Series star Esther Rolle had become disenchanted with the role model for young blacks provided by J.J.'s "jive-talking," woman-chasing, less-than-honest character and, on the pretense of illness, left the series prior to the start of the 1977–1978 season. In the story line, Carl had developed lung cancer and he and Florida were living in a Southern location that was better for his health. Friend and neighbor Willona became a surrogate mother to the Evans household. Little Penny Gordon, a victim of child abuse, became Willona's adopted daughter. J.J. was working full-time at a small ad agency, a job he had gotten during the 1976–1977 season, and Bookman, the building superintendent, became a more prominent member of the cast.

The following fall Esther Rolle returned to the cast (sans Carl or any explanation of what had happened to him), with the promise that J.J. would be a more respectable character, and daughter Thelma married football star Keith Anderson. J.J., who was paying for the wedding, had lost his job at the advertising agency when a business slowdown forced them to lay him off. He had to borrow money from loan shark Sweet Daddy to pay for the wedding and, to make matters worse, accidentally tripped Keith during the ceremony, resulting in a leg injury that jeopardized Keith's million-dollar pro-football contract. Money was hard to come by, and the newlyweds were living in the Evans apartment while Keith recuperated. Though depressed by his physical problems, Keith drove a taxi to help out, while Florida got a job as a school-bus driver and J.J. taught art at home.

With falling ratings, *Good Times* was pulled from the CBS schedule in December. It returned in the spring and, in the last original episode (there were no reruns aired in the last season), everything worked out for the series principals. Keith got his big contract as a running back and moved into his own place with Thelma, who was expecting their first child; J.J. sold the comic strip he had developed to a syndicate for a healthy advance; and neighbor Willona got promoted to head buyer at the clothing boutique where she worked.

GOOD VS. EVIL (*Occult*)

BROADCAST HISTORY:

USA Network, Sci-Fi Channel
60 minutes
Original episodes: *1999–2000* (22 episodes)
Premiered: *July 18, 1999*

CAST:

Chandler Smythe .... Clayton Rohner
Henry McNeil .... Richard Brooks
Ford Plasko .... Marshall Bell
Decker Benbow .... Googy Gress
Walker Rothenberg .... Susie Park
Corps Narrator .... Deacon Jones
Ben Smythe .... Tony Denman

Scruffy, sarcastic reporter Chandler Smythe was murdered one night as he emerged from a bar by a demonic-looking thug. Instead of finding eternal rest, Chandler was recruited by a pair of otherworldly bureaucrats to become an agent for The Corp, a shadowy organization dedicated to finding mortals who had made Faustian bargains, persuading them to renounce their deals with the Devil—and destroying those who had died unrepentant and become Morlocks. Chandler was assigned to Hollywood (The epicenter of demonic activity, of course), where the Corp's office was run out of Geraldo's Casa de Tires by pill-popping Chief Ford and his assistant Decker, and partnered with Henry, a black man with a tight Afro who looked straight out of the 1970s. Chandler and Henry had no special powers, and could themselves be killed (again), but they went about tracking down backsliders and killing Morlocks, who looked normal until they were attacked, whereupon they turned into monsters. (One most-wanted-Morlock poster depicted Don King, Senator Orrin Hatch, country songbird Leann Rimes, and *Love Boat*'s Gavin MacLeod.) Among the many rules they had to follow were no intimate contact (e.g., sex) with humans and no contact with people from their previous lives. The latter was particularly hard on Chandler, who longed to establish contact with his resentful teenage son, Ben; eventually he did, despite the rules.

All of this nonsense was narrated by NFL Hall of Famer Deacon Jones. The series was first called simply *GvsE*, with the title being expanded to *Good vs. Evil* when it moved to the Sci-Fi Channel in March 2000.

GOODE BEHAVIOR (*Situation Comedy*)

FIRST TELECAST: *August 26, 1996*
LAST TELECAST: *August 4, 1997*

BROADCAST HISTORY:

Aug 1996–Dec 1996, UPN Mon 9:00–9:30
Jan 1997–Aug 1997, UPN Mon 9:30–10:00

CAST:

Willie Goode .... Sherman Hemsley
Franklin Goode .... Dorien Wilson
Barbara Goode.......................Alex Datcher
Bianca Goode .... Bianca Lawson
Garth Shoup.......................... Scott Grimes
Chancellor Willoughby.............. Joseph Maher
Raquel DeLarosa (1997) .... Justina Machado

Willie was a paroled con artist whose freedom was contingent on his living with Franklin, the son he had not seen in fifteen years. They had not been particularly close prior to Willie's incarceration for insider trading, but were trying to make a go of it. Stuck-up Franklin had just been promoted to Dean of Humanities at Henshaw State University in Chapel Hill, North Carolina, and was concerned about his image, not materially improved by the presence of his conniving father. Willie moved in under house arrest—complete with ankle bracelet—and forced a reluctant Franklin to convert his cherished and newly refurbished study into a bedroom for his dad. Also in the house were Franklin's stylish wife Barbara, a local television news anchor; and Bianca, their clotheshorse teenage daughter. Garth was Franklin's fawning, gullible teaching assistant who somehow got caught up in most of Willie's marginally larcenous schemes. In the spring, the family took over a local restaurant and renamed it Willie's Chili, with Willie in charge. Raquel was one of the waitresses.

GOODNIGHT, BEANTOWN (*Situation Comedy*)

FIRST TELECAST: *April 3, 1983*
LAST TELECAST: *September 2, 1984*
BROADCAST HISTORY:

Apr 1983–May 1983, CBS Sun 8:00–8:30
Aug 1983–Jan 1984, CBS Sun 9:30–10:00
Jul 1984, CBS Sun 8:00–8:30
Aug 1984–Sep 1984, CBS Sun 8:30–9:00

CAST:

Matt Cassidy............................. Bill Bixby
Jennifer Barnes.................. Mariette Hartley
Susan Barnes......................... Tracey Gold
Dick Novak (1983).................... George Coe
Sam Holliday (1983)................ Charles Levin
Albert Addelson .... G. W. Bailey
Valerie Wood................... Stephanie Faracy
Frank Fletcher.......................... Jim Staahl
Augie Kleindab .... Todd Susman

Although infrequently used as the setting for a TV series, Boston was the setting of three shows that ran concurrently in the early 1980s: *St. Elsewhere, Cheers,* and *Goodnight, Beantown.* Much like *The Mary Tyler Moore Show, Goodnight, Beantown* dealt with the staff of a local television newsroom. Matt Cassidy and Jenny Barnes were co-anchors on the WYN evening news show, somewhat antagonistic but friendly competitors on the job, and sometimes lovers in private life. Amazingly, their professional rivalry seemed to have little negative impact on their romance. Others on the WYN staff were news director Dick Novak (replaced in the fall by anxiety-ridden Albert Addelson), news producer Sam Holliday, sexy feature reporter Valerie Wood, obnoxious sports reporter Frank Fletcher, and cameraman Augie Kleindab. The only regular away from the newsroom was the divorced Jenny's young daughter, Susan.

GOODRICH CELEBRITY TIME, see *Celebrity Times*

GOODTIME GIRLS (*Situation Comedy*)

FIRST TELECAST: *January 22, 1980*
LAST TELECAST: *August 29, 1980*
BROADCAST HISTORY:

Jan 1980–Feb 1980, ABC Tue 8:30–9:00
Apr 1980, ABC Sat 8:30–9:00
Aug 1980, ABC Fri 8:30–9:00

CAST:

Edith Bedelmeyer .... Annie Potts
Betty Crandall .... Lorna Patterson
Loretta Smoot .... Georgia Engel
Camille Rittenhouse .... Francine Tacker
Irma Coolidge .... Marcia Lewis
George Coolidge .... Merwin Goldsmith
Benny Loman .... Peter Scolari
Frankie Millardo .... Adrian Zmed
Skeeter............................ Sparky Marcus

Comedy set in Washington, D.C., during World War II (1942), where three young women (Edith, Betty, Loretta) descended on the same scarce one-room apartment. Snobbish Camille, doing a magazine story on the apartment shortage, was much amused until she found out that she'd lost hers and had to move in with them, making it four in the cramped attic room.

Edith, employed at the Office of Price Administration, was the group's unofficial leader; Betty, from Sioux City, Iowa, worked in a Baltimore defense plant; and shy Loretta, a war bride, worked for Gen. Culpepper, a Pentagon bureaucrat. The Coolidge House boarding facility where they lived was tightly run by George and Irma Coolidge. Frankie was the hustling cabbie who brought the girls there—because he lived downstairs.

Ration stamps, big bands, and the jitterbug provided the social backdrop.

GOODYEAR SUMMERTIME REVUE, see *Paul Whiteman's Goodyear Revue*

GOODYEAR TV PLAYHOUSE (*Dramatic Anthology*)

FIRST TELECAST: *October 14, 1951*
LAST TELECAST: *September 12, 1960*
BROADCAST HISTORY:

Oct 1951–Sep 1957, NBC Sun 9:00–10:00
Sep 1957–Sep 1960, NBC Mon 9:30–10:00

PRODUCER:

Fred Coe (1951–1955)

For six years, from the fall of 1951 through the fall of 1957, *Goodyear TV Playhouse* presented full-hour live dramas, originating from New York, on Sunday evenings. Some were original plays for television and some were adapted from other media. The series ran on alternate weeks with *Philco Television Playhouse.* In the fall of 1955, the title was shortened to *Goodyear Playhouse* and a new sponsor took the alternate Sundays with *The Alcoa Hour.*

Young playwright Paddy Chayefsky wrote several original dramas for this series, two of which were later made into feature films. "The Catered Affair" appeared in 1955 as a TV drama with Thelma Ritter, Pat Henning, and J. Pat O'Malley. The following year it was made into a movie with Bette Davis, Debbie Reynolds, and Ernest Borgnine. Chayefsky's other effort that became a successful theatrical feature was probably the single most acclaimed live drama in the history of television. It aired on May 24, 1953, with Rod Steiger in the title role of "Marty." There were no Emmy awards in 1953 for performances in a single telecast, only for series, so "Marty," ironically, won no TV awards. However, the 1955 movie version won Oscars for best picture and best performance by an actor (Ernest Borgnine). In addition to Rod Steiger, performers who starred in at least two *Goodyear TV Playhouse* productions during these live years included Roddy McDowall, Walter Matthau, Cyril Ritchard, Kim Stanley, Eva Marie Saint, Martin Balsam, Eli Wallach, Ralph Bellamy, Philip Abbott, and Tony Randall. Julie Harris, Paul Newman, Grace Kelly, Veronica Lake, and the Gish sisters (Lillian and Dorothy in separate but consecutive telecasts in 1953) also appeared.

In the fall of 1957, the series moved to Monday nights, was reduced to half an hour, and was on film rather than live. It was still alternating with Alcoa and, although the title of the Goodyear episodes was *Goodyear Theater*, the overall title for the series was *A Turn of Fate*, a designation that was dropped in February 1958. Initially there was to be a rotating roster of regular stars (David Niven, Robert Ryan, Jane Powell, Jack Lemmon, and Charles Boyer), but that concept petered out by the end of the first season. Stars featured during the last two seasons were Paul Douglas, Eddie Albert, Gig Young, Jackie Cooper, Ray Milland, James Mason, Edward G. Robinson, Peter Lawford, Errol Flynn, and Thomas Mitchell. In the spring of each of the last two seasons several of the episodes were pilots for proposed series. One of these was "Christobel" starring Arthur O'Connell as John Monroe, author James Thurber's harried hero. More than a decade later, the Thurber-based John Monroe character reappeared in the weekly series *My World and Welcome to It* starring William Windom.

GORDON MACRAE SHOW, THE (*Music*)
FIRST TELECAST: *March 5, 1956*
LAST TELECAST: *August 27, 1956*
BROADCAST HISTORY:
Mar 1956–Aug 1956, NBC Mon 7:30–7:45
REGULARS:
Gordon MacRae
The Cheerleaders
The Van Alexander Orchestra

The set used for this live musical program was a replica of Gordon MacRae's living room, with a large picture window looking out on a scene appropriate for the songs being performed on a given evening. Backing up MacRae, and occasionally with a featured number of their own, was a vocal group called the Cheerleaders. This show originated from Hollywood and was used to fill the remainder of the half hour in which NBC aired its network news.

GOSPEL JUBILEE (*Music*)
BROADCAST HISTORY:
The Nashville Network
30 minutes
Produced: *1990–1991* (30 episodes)
Premiered: *March 31, 1990*

Concert series originating from Opryland in Nashville, featuring Southern gospel music.

GOVERNOR & J.J, THE (*Situation Comedy*)
FIRST TELECAST: *September 23, 1969*
LAST TELECAST: *August 11, 1972*
BROADCAST HISTORY:
Sep 1969–Sep 1970, CBS Tue 9:30–10:00
Sep 1970–Dec 1970, CBS Wed 8:30–9:00
Jun 1972–Aug 1972, CBS Fri 10:30–11:00
CAST:
Gov. William Drinkwater .... Dan Dailey
Jennifer Jo ("J.J.") Drinkwater .... Julie Sommars
Maggie McLeod .... Neva Patterson
George Callison .... James Callahan
Sara Andrews .... Nora Marlowe

One of the needs of any man in high political office is someone to organize social functions and serve as first lady. For Governor William Drinkwater, the chief executive of a small Midwestern state, and a widower, that someone was his attractive young daughter Jennifer Jo. Despite the problems caused by their generation gap (J.J. was in her early 20s), J.J. served her father as a charming and efficient first lady. Bright and opinionated, she was always ready to debate issues with him, too. J.J. also had a regular job as assistant curator at a zoo, which presented a nice counterpoint to politics. It may also explain her fondness for the stray basset hound she brought into the family in January 1970 and named, appropriately, Guv. Around the executive mansion she sought and received assistance from the governor's secretary Maggie, his press secretary George, and the housekeeper, Sara. During the summer of the 1972 presidential election year, CBS aired reruns of this series.

GRACE UNDER FIRE (*Situation Comedy*)
FIRST TELECAST: *September 29, 1993*
LAST TELECAST: *February 17, 1998*
BROADCAST HISTORY:
Sep 1993–Mar 1994, ABC Wed 9:30–10:00
May 1994–Sep 1994, ABC Wed 9:30–10:00
Sep 1994–Mar 1995, ABC Tue 9:30–10:00
Mar 1995–Nov 1996, ABC Wed 9:00–9:30
Aug 1995–Sep 1995, ABC Wed 8:00–8:30
Dec 1996–Jul 1997, ABC Wed 8:00–8:30
Aug 1997–Sep 1997, ABC Tue 8:30–9:00
Nov 1997–Dec 1997, ABC Tue 8:00–8:30
Jan 1998–Feb 1998, ABC Tue 9:30–10:00
CAST:
Grace Kelly .... Brett Butler
Quentin Kelly (age 8) (1993–1996) .. Jon Paul Steuer
Quentin Kelly (1996–1998) .... Sam Horrigan
Elizabeth Louise "Libby" Kelly (5) ... Kaitlin Cullum
Patrick Kelly (8 months) ... Dylan and Cole Sprouse
Russell Norton .... Dave Thomas
Nadine Swoboda (1993–1997) .... Julie White
Wade Swoboda .... Casey Sander
**Jimmy Kelly* .... Geoff Pierson
Faith Burdette (1993–1995) .... Valri Bromfield
Bill Davis (1993–1994) .... Charles Hallahan
Dougie (1993–1996) .... Walter Olkewicz
Vic (1993–1997) .... Dave Florek
Carl (1993–1994) .... Louis Mandylor
Ryan Sparks (1994) .... William Fichtner
John Shirley (1994–1996) .... Paul Dooley
Rick Bradshaw (1995–1996) .... Alan Autry

Jean Kelly (1995–1998) .... Peggy Rea
Floyd Norton (1995–1998) .... Tom Poston
D.C. (1997–1998) .... Don "D.C." Curry
Dot (1997–1998) .... Lauren Tom
Bev Henderson (1998) .... Julia Duffy

*Occasional

THEME:

"Lady Madonna," by John Lennon and Paul McCartney (1968), sung by Aretha Franklin

Many critics called Brett Butler the successor to Roseanne—one tough, independent lady for the nineties. Her character, Grace, was certainly tough on men in the early episodes of this blue-collar comedy, and with some reason. She had just broken up with her physically abusive, "knuckle-dragging, cousin-loving, beer-sucking redneck husband" after eight years, convinced it was better to try and raise her three kids alone—whatever the sacrifices. Under an affirmative action program Grace got a job at an oil refinery (she called herself a "quota babe"), where she traded jibes with her Neanderthal male co-workers. Providing moral support were best friend Nadine and her husband, Wade, and mellow pharmacist Russell, who had just divorced *his* greedy wife.

In fact, a lot of people in this series had troublesome ex's. Grace's smooth-talking ex-husband, Jimmy, reappeared from time to time, trying to woo Grace and the kids (when that didn't work he got drunk and found another girlfriend); Russell fought comic running battles with his ex, Barbara; and Nadine was on her fourth husband with Wade. Grace's three kids, troublemaker (like his dad) Quentin, cute Libby, and baby Patrick added to the chaos at home. Also seen from time to time were Grace's loose-living sister, Faith; her huffy bosses at the refinery, Bill and later John; boyfriend (for a time) Ryan; and Jimmy's oddly named kin (Emmett Kelly, Jean Kelly, De Forest Kelly, etc.).

In the 1995–1996 season Grace was promoted at the oil refinery and gained a steady boyfriend in plant executive Rick. They broke up after a season and Grace reentered the dating scene, while attending night school to better herself. In 1996–1997 her ex, Jimmy, started turning up more regularly, apparently trying to clean up his act. Also showing up was Grace's fourth child, Matthew, whom she had given up for adoption when she was young, and who now was in trouble. In early 1997, Wade and Nadine had a baby, but within a few months they divorced and Nadine disappeared from the cast. By the truncated final season, Grace had left the oil refinery and went to work first for a St. Louis ad agency and then a local construction company, where D.C. was her boss. Her former mother-in-law, Jean, was more frequently seen, and a new friend was Dot, who ran the local hair salon. In early 1998, Bev, a rich friend, moved in with Grace to "get in touch with her roots," but the new relationship was short-lived as the series was abruptly canceled in mid-February.

GRADY (*Situation Comedy*)

FIRST TELECAST: *December 4, 1975*
LAST TELECAST: *March 4, 1976*
BROADCAST HISTORY:

Dec 1975, NBC Thu 8:00–8:30
Jan 1976–Mar 1976, NBC Thu 8:30–9:00

CAST:

Grady Wilson .... Whitman Mayo
Ellie Wilson Marshall .... Carol Cole
Hal Marshall .... Joe Morton
Laurie Marshall .... Roseanne Katan
Haywood Marshall .... Haywood Nelson
Mr. Pratt .... Jack Fletcher
Rose Kosinski .... Alix Elias

In this short-lived spin-off from *Sanford and Son*, Grady Wilson, one of Fred Sanford's friends, moved out of Watts and into a racially mixed middle-class neighborhood in Los Angeles to be with his daughter and her family. His daughter Ellie was married and had two children, Laurie and Haywood. Mr. Pratt was their landlord and Rose was one of their neighbors.

GRAND (*Situation Comedy*)

FIRST TELECAST: *January 18, 1990*
LAST TELECAST: *December 27, 1990*
BROADCAST HISTORY:

Jan 1990–Apr 1990, NBC Thu 9:30–10:00
Jul 1990–Aug 1990, NBC Thu 9:30–10:00
Oct 1990–Dec 1990, NBC Thu 9:30–10:00

CAST:

Harris Weldon .... John Randolph
Norris Weldon .... Joel Murray
Desmond .... John Neville
Janice Pasetti .... Pamela Reed
Edda Pasetti .... Sara Rue
Carol Anne Smithson .... Bonnie Hunt
Tom Smithson .... Michael McKean
Off. Wayne Kasmurski .... Andrew Lauer
Dylan .... Jackie Vinson
Richard Peyton .... Mark Moses

Three families from different social levels clashed comically in this sendup of soap operas. Seventy-year-old Harris Weldon was the patriarch of the town of Grand, Pennsylvania, where his piano factory was the leading (though declining) industry. Those blasted Japanese imports! Rattling around the mansion with him were his idiot son Norris and acerbic butler Desmond—whom Harris couldn't let go, despite the insults, because he had once saved his life. Also working for Harris was housekeeper Janice, a divorcée who lived in a trailer park with her overweight young daughter Edda.

Between these extremes of wealth was Harris's niece Carol Anne and her ambitious yuppie husband Tom, who hoped to get a job with the old man's piano company. Wayne was the grinning motorcycle cop who was trying to make time with sensible Janice.

At the end of the spring run, a hurricane struck Grand and blew away the middle social layer (Tom), along with Janice's trailer. It didn't help much. As a soap opera spoof, *Grand* was rather tame compared to the fabled *Soap*, and it expired before the end of the year.

GRAND OLE OPRY (*Country Music*)

NETWORK HISTORY:

FIRST TELECAST: *October 15, 1955*
LAST TELECAST: *September 15, 1956*

Oct 1955–Sep 1956, ABC Sat 8:00–9:00

REGULARS (1955–1956):

Carl Smith
Ernest and Justin Tubb
Hank Snow
Minnie Pearl
Chet Atkins

Goldie Hill
Marty Robbins
Rod Brasfield
Cousin Jody
Roy Acuff
June Carter
Jimmy Dickens
Louvin Brothers

CABLE HISTORY:

The Nashville Network / CMT
30/60 minutes
Produced: *1985–*
Premiered: *April 20, 1985* (TNN); *August 2001* (CMT)

HOST:

Keith Bilbrey (1985–late 1990s)
Bill Anderson (late 1990s–)

In the world of country music an appearance on the *Grand Ole Opry* has long been considered a symbol of ultimate success. Oddly enough, the *Opry* never became a regular feature on national TV until cable came along, although other, "lesser" country music shows had long runs (see, for example, *Ozark Jubilee*). During 1955–1956 ABC carried an hour of the *Opry* (it goes on all night) on a monthly basis, live from its longtime home in Nashville, Tennessee. The *Opry* troupe numbers in the dozens, and is constantly changing, and only those members most frequently seen during the ABC run are listed above.

The program's history has been primarily in syndication and cable, enabling it to maximize its availability in areas where country music is popular. Over the years there have been numerous syndicated country music shows using the Grand Ole Opry as a backdrop, some original and others just repackaged episodes from other shows. Among the most successful series were *Billy Walker's Country Carnival, Classic Country Featuring Stars of the Grand Ole Opry, Country Carnival, Country Music Caravan, Country Music Memories, The Country Show,* and *Hayride*.

Finally, in 1985, fans of classic country saw their fondest wish fulfilled when the *Opry* came to network television to stay, appropriately enough on cable's Nashville Network. At first the 8:00–8:30 P.M. half hour of the all-night Saturday show was carried live. Then, in April 1987, an introductory half hour called *Opry Backstage* was added, consisting of backstage interviews that took place while the show was in progress, and the onstage coverage moved to 8:30–9:00 P.M.

The *Opry* began on radio in Nashville in 1925, was first heard on network radio in 1939, and is still going strong today. It will probably continue forever, with or without network TV.

GRAND SLAM (*Adventure*)

FIRST TELECAST: *January 28, 1990*
LAST TELECAST: *March 14, 1990*
BROADCAST HISTORY:

Jan 1990, CBS Sun 9:30–11:00
Jan 1990–Mar 1990, CBS Wed 8:00–9:00

CAST:

Dennis "Hardball" Bakelenoff...... John Schneider
Pedro N. Gomez.................. Paul Rodriguez
Irv Schlosser......................... Larry Gelman
Al Ramirez.............................. Abel Franco
Grandma Gomez.................. Lupe Ontiveros

Hardball was working for Irv Schlosser at Bluebird Bail Bonds, and Gomez was working for Al Ramirez at Aztec Bail Bonds when they discovered that they were more effective as a team than working independently. The two San Diego bounty hunters decided to open their own office. *Grand Slam* had lots of action and car chases, much like Schneider's previous hit *The Dukes of Hazzard*, but never found much of an audience.

GRANDPA GOES TO WASHINGTON (*Situation Comedy*)

FIRST TELECAST: *September 7, 1978*
LAST TELECAST: *January 16, 1979*
BROADCAST HISTORY:

Sep 1978–Jan 1979, NBC Tue 8:00–9:00

CAST:

Senator Joe Kelley.................. Jack Albertson
Major General Kevin Kelley......... Larry Linville
Rosie Kelley..................... Sue Ane Langdon
Kathleen Kelley.................... Michele Tobin
Kevin Kelley, Jr...................... Sparky Marcus
Madge............................ Madge Sinclair
Tony De Luca.......................... Tom Mason

Jack Albertson portrayed a maverick freshman senator in this hour-long comedy series. Joe Kelley was a former political science professor who had been forcibly retired at age 66, and who promptly got himself elected to the U.S. Senate when the regular candidates were both exposed as crooks. Kelley's style was certainly unusual for Washington. He drove around in a Volkswagen, played drums for relaxation, and his campaign pledge was honesty in government (and he meant it!). His chief political asset was a network of "friends in low places," former students of his who regularly fed him inside political information. Kelley lived with his son, a bland, empty-headed Air Force general ("My son the fathead,") and his son's family, consisting of wife Rosie, daughter Kathleen, and son Kevin, Jr. Madge was the senator's trusty secretary, and Tony his aide.

GRAPEVINE (*Situation Comedy*)

FIRST TELECAST: *June 15, 1992*
LAST TELECAST: *March 27, 2000*
BROADCAST HISTORY:

Jun 1992–Aug 1992, CBS Mon 9:30–10:00
Feb 2000, CBS Mon 9:30–10:00
Mar 2000, CBS Mon 8:30–9:00

CAST:

David (1992)..................... Jonathan Penner
Susan (1992).......................... Lynn Clark
Thumper (1992).................. Steven Eckholdt
Susan Crawford (2000)........... Kristy Swanson
David Klein (2000)............... Steven Eckholdt
Thumper Klein (2000).............. George Eads
Matt Brewer (2000)................ David Sutcliffe

Set in Miami, *Grapevine* was an unusual variation on the *Love, American Style* sitcom format. The three continuing characters were David, who owned a small restaurant; his girlfriend, Susan, an executive with a cruise line; and his brother, Thumper, a local Miami sportscaster. In each episode they would make short comments to the camera about the relationship of a couple they knew. Key events in the couple's life, including some involving David, Susan, and/or Thumper, were shown in flashbacks interspersed with their running commentary. Some episodes dealt with couples who dated and eventually got married, some with couples whose relationships didn't work out, and others with married couples in which one spouse was having an affair. It was all very disjointed and soon left the air.

Eight years after *Grapevine*'s original short run, CBS brought it back, possibly because the setting, Miami's South Beach, had become very trendy. The three original characters were back, with Steven Eckholdt, who had played Thumper in the original run, now playing his older brother, David. New to the show was Matt, the recently divorced manager of a South Beach hotel. The second time was not the charm for *Grapevine.* The 2000 series lasted for five episodes, one less than the 1992 version.

GRAY GHOST, THE (*Adventure*)
BROADCAST HISTORY:
Syndicated only
30 minutes
Produced: *1957* (39 episodes)
Released: *October 1957*
CAST:
Maj. John Singleton Mosby .... Tod Andrews
Lt. St. Clair .... Phil Chambers

Civil War action series focusing on the true exploits of John Singleton Mosby, one of the South's most colorful heroes. A young lawyer who originally supported the Union, Mosby changed his mind when the South seceded, joined the 43rd Battalion of the 1st Virginia Cavalry, and began a series of lightning-swift raids on Union positions. So elusive was he that he became known as the "Gray Ghost."

Although this was basically an adventure series, with lots of galloping horses, gunplay, and derring-do, advertisers were extremely nervous about portraying a Confederate hero at a time of civil-rights strife, when Federal troops were in Little Rock. The series was originally intended for the CBS-TV network, but three times potential sponsors backed out. Finally CBS decided to syndicate it to local stations, and to everyone's surprise it both failed to stir up regional animosities and was a big hit in all parts of the country, especially with younger viewers. Tod Andrews, a New Yorker, was received as a hero when he toured the South.

The series was based on the book *Gray Ghosts and Rebel Raiders* by Virgil Carrington Jones, and Jones himself served as technical advisor.

GREAT ADVENTURE, THE (*Dramatic Anthology*)
FIRST TELECAST: *September 27, 1963*
LAST TELECAST: *April 23, 1965*
BROADCAST HISTORY:
Sep 1963–Sep 1964, CBS Fri 7:30–8:30
Mar 1965–Apr 1965, CBS Fri 8:30–9:30
NARRATOR:
Van Heflin

A great moment in American history was dramatized each week in this series. Careful attention was paid to the historical accuracy of each play, and all of them were produced with the cooperation and assistance of the National Education Association. Many well-known performers participated in the dramas—Joseph Cotten and Ricardo Montalban in "The Massacre at Wounded Knee," Lloyd Bridges in "Wild Bill Hickok—The Legend and the Man," Victor Jory and Robert Culp in "The Testing of Sam Houston," Jackie Cooper in "The Hunley" (the first submarine to sink an enemy warship), and Robert Cummings and Ron Howard in "The Plague" (about the discovery of anti-smallpox vaccine).

GREAT AMERICAN COUNTRY (GAC) (Network)
(*Music Cable Network*)
LAUNCHED:
December 31, 1995
SUBSCRIBERS (MAY 2003):
24.5 million (23% U.S.)

A full-time country music videos network, in competition with the larger CMT. Programming blocks included *CRL* (Country Request Live), *Top 20, Edge of Country* and *GAC Classic* (older videos).

GREAT AMERICAN TV POLL (*Information*)
BROADCAST HISTORY:
Lifetime Network
30 minutes
Produced: *1991* (65 episodes)
Premiered: *March 4, 1991*
REGULARS:
David Birney
Eleanor Mondale

A weeknight entertainment series built around results from an ongoing national poll in which Americans were asked questions about news events, social issues, and lifestyle preferences. Poll results were interspersed with man-on-the-street interviews and background reports.

GREAT CIRCUSES OF THE WORLD (*Variety*)
FIRST TELECAST: *February 26, 1989*
LAST TELECAST: *April 16, 1989*
BROADCAST HISTORY:
Feb 1989–Apr 1989, ABC Sun 7:00–8:00
HOSTESS:
Mary Hart

Dancing elephants, custard pie–throwing clowns, death-defying high-wire acts, a human cannonball, an animal trainer gingerly placing his head in the lion's mouth—all the sights of the big-time circus were featured on this fast-paced ABC filler program. Circuses from the United States, Mexico, Brazil, Poland, France, Sweden, Luxembourg, and Japan (among others) were seen, as were clips of great acts of the past. Two additional episodes of the series were aired after its regular run, on July 2 and September 2, 1989.

GREAT DEFENDER, THE (*Legal Drama*)
FIRST TELECAST: *March 5, 1995*
LAST TELECAST: *July 31, 1995*
BROADCAST HISTORY:
Mar 1995, FOX Sun 7:00–8:00
Jul 1995, FOX Mon 9:00–10:00
CAST:
Lou Frischetti .... Michael Rispoli
Pearl Frischetti .... Rhoda Gemignani
Frankie Collett .... Kelly Rutherford
Crosby Caufield III .... Peter Krause
Jason DeWitt .... Richard Kiley
Asst. D.A. Jerry Perez .... Carlos Sanz

Lou Frischetti was an ebullient, street-smart attorney in Boston who got many of his clients through crass, hard-sell TV commercials that featured testimonials from his blue-collar clients. His colorful style attracted the attention of Jason DeWitt, senior partner in the prestigious Beacon Hill law firm of Osbourne, Merritt & DeWitt. DeWitt was hoping the unorthodox Frischetti could breathe new life into the stodgy firm and teach his snooty grandson Crosby, an ambitious young associate, how to practice law effectively. Pearl, Lou's mother, was his outspoken receptionist and Frankie his sexy investigator. Dreadfully low ratings prompted Fox to pull the plug on *The Great Defender* after a single episode had aired.

Lou used a variation on the 1956 pop song "The Great Pretender" in his TV ads; hence the show's title.

GREAT GHOST TALES (*Occult Anthology*)

FIRST TELECAST: *July 6, 1961*
LAST TELECAST: *September 21, 1961*
BROADCAST HISTORY:
Jul 1961–Sep 1961, NBC Thu 9:30–10:00

This series of ghost stories was the 1961 summer replacement for *The Ford Show Starring Tennessee Ernie Ford.* Each of the plays was produced live in New York, something of a rarity for a dramatic show in the early 1960s. Among the actors who appeared were Robert Duvall, Arthur Hill, Lois Nettleton, Lee Grant, and a young Richard Thomas.

GREAT SCOTT! (*Situation Comedy*)

FIRST TELECAST: *October 4, 1992*
LAST TELECAST: *November 29, 1992*
BROADCAST HISTORY:
Oct 1992–Nov 1992, FOX Sun 7:00–7:30
CAST:
Scott Melrod (age 15)............... Tobey Maguire
Beverly Melrod.................... Nancy Lenehan
Walter Melrod .... Ray Baker
Nina Melrod (17).................. Sarah Koskoff
Larry O'Donnell (16).............. Kevin Connolly

Gentle comedy about a daydreaming teenager. Scott, a freshman at Taft High School, daydreamed to overcome his insecurity. He wanted desperately to be accepted by his peers, and his life was full of Walter Mittyesque fantasies in which he turned his bland suburban existence into a series of imaginatively weird encounters. Of course, they always ended when he was jarred back to reality. In gym class he would see himself winning the state wrestling championship just before being pinned by his opponent, or he would envision himself impressing his ideal dream date just before in real life she dumped him. Others in Scott's bland family were his dad, Walter, a successful civic-minded businessman who saw Scott as a chip off the old block; his overly protective mom, Beverly; Nina, his prissy, neurotic older sister; and Larry, the cousin who was everything at school that Scott fantasized about being—adventuresome, popular, athletic, and outgoing. Scott's parents considered Larry a role model for their son, repeatedly telling him that he could be like Larry if only he would "come out of his shell."

What's that you said, Mom?

GREATEST AMERICAN HERO, THE (*Adventure*)

FIRST TELECAST: *March 18, 1981*
LAST TELECAST: *February 3, 1983*
BROADCAST HISTORY:
Mar 1981–May 1981, ABC Wed 8:00–9:00
Aug 1981–Aug 1982, ABC Wed 8:00–9:00
Sep 1982–Nov 1982, ABC Fri 9:00–10:00
Jan 1983–Feb 1983, ABC Thu 8:00–9:00
CAST:
Ralph Hinkley (Hanley)................ William Katt
Bill Maxwell .... Robert Culp
Pam Davidson .... Connie Sellecca
Tony Villicana........................ Michael Pare
Rhonda Blake............................ Faye Grant
Cyler Johnson...................... Jesse D. Goins
Rodriguez.......................... Don Cervantes
Kevin Hinkley (1981)........... Brandon Williams

THEME:
"The Greatest American Hero (Believe It Or Not)," by Mike Post and Stephen Geyer, sung by Joey Scarbury

This superhero parody was beset by trouble practically from the time it premiered. First, the owners of the Superman copyright threatened to sue, charging that the program had stolen their character. Then a man with the same last name as the hero made a real-life assassination attempt on the President of the United States, causing scripts to be hurriedly rewritten. Then the ratings started to fall.

Superman advocates may have cried "Thief!," but others suggested that the program was more of a steal from *Mr. Terrific* and *Captain Nice,* two bumbling superhero shows of the mid-1960s. Ralph Hinkley was a curly-haired young high-school teacher in Los Angeles, who was set upon by extraterrestrial beings while on a field trip into the desert. The aliens presented him with an incredible red flying suit, which, when donned, gave him (and only him) the ability to fly. A neurotic FBI agent, Maxwell, convinced Ralph to use the suit to help him fight crime. Unfortunately Ralph promptly lost the instruction book for the suit, and had to spend succeeding episodes flailing about in the air trying to master aerodynamics while crashing into walls and plummeting into bushes. He also discovered other powers of the suit—often at inopportune times—such as the power to become invisible, and the power to see at great distances and through solid walls.

The only adult besides Ralph and Maxwell who knew of the suit's powers was Ralph's girlfriend, attorney Pam Davidson (kids knew, but who would believe them?). Anybody else who came upon Ralph while he was trying to jump off a roof in his red jammies just naturally assumed he was crazy.

Kevin was Ralph's young son by a former marriage; Tony, Rhonda, Cyler, and Rodriguez were street-tough students in Ralph's remedial education class. The students shared many of Ralph's adventures during the 1981–1982 season, but were phased out the following season, as Ralph and Pam were finally married. As for Ralph's last name, it was abruptly changed to "Mr. H" (sometimes "Mr. Hanley") for a time after John Hinckley (with a "c") made an attempt on the life of President Reagan on March 30, 1981. Eventually it reverted back to Hinkley.

The theme song of this series was a major record hit during the summer of 1981.

GREATEST FIGHTS OF THE CENTURY (*Sports*)

FIRST TELECAST: *October 15, 1948*
LAST TELECAST: *July 23, 1954*

BROADCAST HISTORY:

Oct 1948–Jan 1949, NBC Fri 10:45–11:00
Apr 1949–Jun 1950, NBC Fri 10:45–11:00 (OS)
Sep 1950–Jul 1954, NBC Fri 10:45–11:00

NARRATOR:

Jim Stevenson

This program was used to fill the time between the conclusion of the boxing match on *Gillette Cavalcade of Sports* and the start of the 11:00 P.M. local news. Jim Stevenson narrated newsreel films of some of the major boxing matches of the 20th century.

GREATEST MAN ON EARTH, THE (*Quiz/Audience Participation*)

FIRST TELECAST: *December 3, 1952*
LAST TELECAST: *February 19, 1953*
BROADCAST HISTORY:

Dec 1952–Feb 1953, ABC Thu 8:00–8:30

EMCEE:

Ted Brown (Dec–Jan)
Vera Vague (Jan–Feb)

ASSISTANT:

Miss Pat Conway

Five men chosen from the studio audience competed for the title of *The Greatest Man on Earth* by performing stunts and answering questions, in this live, New York–based quiz show. Finalists and their wives were eligible for a new car, a trip to Europe, or other prizes. Ted Brown was the original emcee, replaced on January 22 by comedienne Vera Vague.

GREATEST MOMENTS IN SPORTS, THE (*Sports Commentary*)

FIRST TELECAST: *July 30, 1954*
LAST TELECAST: *February 4, 1955*
BROADCAST HISTORY:

Jul 1954–Sep 1954, NBC Fri 10:30–10:45
Sep 1954–Feb 1955, NBC Fri 10:45–11:00

HOST:

Walter Kiernan

Greatest Moments in Sports was a 15-minute program comprised of interviews with famous sports personalities and film clips of memorable events in the world of sports. Walter Kiernan was the host to the various guests and served as narrator for the filmed portions of the program. It premiered on a regular basis at 10:30 P.M. and when the Gillette *Cavalcade of Sports* boxing bouts resumed in September was used to fill the time between the conclusion of the bout and 11:00 P.M.

GREATEST SHOW ON EARTH, THE (*Circus Drama*)

FIRST TELECAST: *September 17, 1963*
LAST TELECAST: *September 8, 1964*
BROADCAST HISTORY:

Sep 1963–Sep 1964, ABC Tue 9:00–10:00

CAST:

Johnny Slate .... Jack Palance
Otto King .... Stu Erwin

THEME:

"March of the Clowns," by Richard Rodgers

The Ringling Brothers Barnum & Bailey Circus—"The Greatest Show on Earth"—provided the background for this behind-the-scenes drama of circus performers. Hard-driving Johnny Slate was the working boss of the circus, whose job included, among other things, maintaining peace among a large group of individualistic performers. Otto King was the circus moneyman. Each week's story centered around the problems of a specific group—clowns, strongmen, aerialists, animal trainers, etc. Actual Ringling Brothers Barnum & Bailey performers were seen regularly in this series.

GREATEST SPORT THRILLS (*Sports*)

FIRST TELECAST: *January 23, 1954*
LAST TELECAST: *September 27, 1956*
BROADCAST HISTORY:

Jan 1954–Sep 1954, ABC Sat 8:30–9:00
Jun 1955–Sep 1955, ABC Mon 7:30–8:00
Jul 1955–Sep 1955, ABC Thu 9:30–10:00
Jul 1955–Sep 1955, ABC Fri 8:00–8:30
Jul 1955–Aug 1955, ABC Fri 9:00–9:30
Jul 1955, ABC Sun 7:30–8:00
Nov 1955–Jan 1956, ABC Thu 10:00–10:30
Jun 1956–Sep 1956, ABC Thu 9:30–10:00

HOSTS:

Marty Glickman
Stan Lomax

Filmed highlights of sports events that had taken place at Madison Square Garden in New York City over the years were narrated and discussed by Marty Glickman and Stan Lomax on *Greatest Sport Thrills.* Used primarily as a filler program, during the summer of 1955 it was being offered as often as five times per week on the ABC network—often with the same episodes repeated on different days. Many ABC stations, including the one in New York, often chose to carry other syndicated or local programming in its place.

GREED: THE MULTI-MILLION DOLLAR CHALLENGE (*Quiz*)

FIRST TELECAST: *November 4, 1999*
LAST TELECAST: *July 14, 2000*
BROADCAST HISTORY:

Nov 1999–Jan 2000, FOX Thu 9:00–10:00
Jan 2000–Jul 2000, FOX Fri 9:00–10:00

EMCEE:

Chuck Woolery

On this quiz show teams of people attempted to work together—and sometimes at cross purposes—to win large sums of money answering pop-culture questions. Initially six people were asked an elimination question, with the five closest to the right answer forming the team, and the one closest designated captain. The captain had the power to stop the game, whereupon team members would share their accumulated winnings (an incorrect answer at any point would send the team away with nothing). Host Chuck Woolery played up the greed theme by waving large wads of cash ("Smell it!") and asking, "Do you feel the need for greed?"

In the early rounds ($25K, $50K, $75K, and $100K) team members attempted to answer the question, and the captain had the option to either accept an answer or substitute one of his or her own. Once past the $100K level ($200K, $500K, $1 million, and the jackpot of $2 million, which rose by $100K after each episode) a new wrinkle, the eliminator, was added. Prior to being asked the question, one of the team members was randomly selected and given the opportunity to challenge one of the others to answer a single question, potentially grabbing his or her share of the winnings and knocking the teammate out of the game. Before it was revealed whether the team's answer was correct, the captain was given the option of splitting 10 percent of the value of the question with teammates and not taking a chance on losing.

When a team reached the last question, the rules changed again and the captain no longer had control. All of the surviving members of the team controlled their own fates. Each pushed a green button to continue, or a red button to quit and keep what he or she had already won. The first time this happened, there were three players left; the two who had successfully challenged other members decided to leave with their $400K each while the captain, who had $200K in his account, went for the jackpot—and lost.

Greed had originally aired as a series of specials in November but its popularity prompted Fox to make it a weekly series. On December 9 the title was changed to *Greed: The Series*, and the jackpot was fixed at a flat $2,000,000.

GREEN ACRES (*Situation Comedy*)

FIRST TELECAST: *September 15, 1965*

LAST TELECAST: *September 7, 1971*

BROADCAST HISTORY:

Sep 1965–Sep 1968, CBS Wed 9:00–9:30
Sep 1968–Sep 1969, CBS Wed 9:30–10:00
Sep 1969–Sep 1970, CBS Sat 9:00–9:30
Sep 1970–Sep 1971, CBS Tue 8:00–8:30

CAST:

Oliver Wendell Douglas .... Eddie Albert
Lisa Douglas .... Eva Gabor
Mr. Haney .... Pat Buttram
Eb Dawson .... Tom Lester
Hank Kimball .... Alvy Moore
Fred Ziffel .... Hank Patterson
Doris Ziffel (1965–1969) .... Barbara Pepper
Doris Ziffel (1969–1970) .... Fran Ryan
Sam Drucker .... Frank Cady
Newt Kiley (1965–1970) .... Kay E. Kuter
Alf Monroe (1966–1969) .... Sid Melton
Ralph Monroe (1966–1971) ... Mary Grace Canfield
Darlene Wheeler (1970–1971) ..... Judy McConnell

One of the most successful of CBS' rural situation comedies of the 1960s, *Green Acres* was closely intertwined with *Petticoat Junction*, another show produced by the same people. Oliver Wendell Douglas was a highly successful Manhattan lawyer who, despite his good life in New York City, longed to get closer to nature. Ignoring the objections of his socialite wife Lisa, Oliver bought a 160-acre farm, sight unseen, from Mr. Haney. The farm was located outside the town of Hooterville (the setting for *Petticoat Junction*). It was in horrible shape. It had not been worked in years, and the house was run-down, unfurnished, and in desperate need of major repairs.

Lisa wanted to turn right around and go back to their Park Avenue penthouse, but Oliver persisted in his determination to give it a chance. They found a shy, gawky handyman named Eb Dawson to help them get the place back into shape, and utilized the services of the Monroes, a sister-and-brother carpenter team, to rebuild the house and barn. Lisa never quite adjusted to the rural life. She kept applying the standards of sophisticated socialites to the ingenuous populace of Hooterville. Even her wardrobe, long flowing gowns and lots of jewelry, seemed out of place on Oliver's Green Acres. She did, however, grow quite fond of the animals they owned, giving names to all the chickens, cows, etc., on the farm. During the second season a pig, though not theirs, became a featured member of the cast. One of the Douglases' neighbors, pig farmer Fred Ziffel, had a pet pig named Arnold who watched television, could do various tricks on cue, and was so intelligent that Fred treated him like a son.

Until *Petticoat Junction* left the air in the fall of 1970, there was always a certain amount of interplay between it and *Green Acres*, with characters from one series making guest appearances on the other. *Green Acres* itself, though still successful, was canceled in 1971 as part of CBS' general purging of rural comedies from its schedule.

GREEN HORNET, THE (*Crime Drama*)

FIRST TELECAST: *September 9, 1966*

LAST TELECAST: *July 14, 1967*

BROADCAST HISTORY:

Sep 1966–Jul 1967, ABC Fri 7:30–8:00

CAST:

Britt Reid/The Green Hornet .... Van Williams
Kato .... Bruce Lee
Lenore "Casey" Case .... Wende Wagner
Mike Axford .... Lloyd Gough
District Attorney F. P. Scanlon .... Walter Brooke

CREATED BY:

George W. Trendle (on radio, in 1936)

THEME:

An updated arrangement of Rimsky-Korsakov's "Flight of the Bumble Bee," played by Al Hirt

"Faster, Kato!" Then, with a roar of Black Beauty's mighty engine, and the squeal of tires, *The Green Hornet* strikes again!

The TV version of this radio favorite of the 1930s and 1940s was launched close on the flying heels of *Batman*, in 1966, and was produced by the same production team. The plot outline was familiar: Britt Reid, crusading editor and publisher of *The Daily Sentinel*, fought crime in the secret guise of The Green Hornet. Only his faithful manservant Kato, his admiring secretary Casey, and the D.A. knew that Reid and the Hornet were one and the same. Others, including hard-nosed crime reporter Mike, never made the connection.

Some changes were made in adapting *The Green Hornet* to television, and to the 1960s. In addition to *The Daily Sentinel*, Britt owned a TV station. The evil he fought often involved organized crime (not the bizarre villains of *Batman*), and of course the crime-fighting gadgetry was brought up-to-date.

The chief piece of hardware was the Hornet's souped-up car, the Black Beauty (actually a 1966 Chrysler Imperial, rebuilt, at a cost of $50,000, by Hollywood customizer Dean Jeffries). Among its features were a built-in TV camera which could "see" four miles ahead, a kind of exhaust apparatus which spread ice over the road to foil pursuers, and brushes behind the rear wheels which lowered to sweep away tire tracks. For face-to-face combat, the Hornet had a special nonlethal gas gun which immobilized adversaries, and a sting gun which penetrated steel.

It is not generally known that *The Green Hornet* was directly related to George Trendle's other major hit, *The Lone Ranger*, whose plot line it closely paralleled. In fact, Britt Reid was originally introduced to radio audiences as the son of Dan Reid, the Lone Ranger's nephew.

GREETINGS FROM TUCSON (*Situation Comedy*)
FIRST TELECAST: *September 20, 2002*
LAST TELECAST: *May 30, 2003*
BROADCAST HISTORY:
Sep 2002–Feb 2003, WB Fri 9:30–10:00
Apr 2003–May 2003, WB Fri 8:30–9:00
CAST:
Joaquin Tiant .... Julio Oscar Mechoso
Elizabeth Tiant .... Rebecca Creskoff
Ernesto Tiant .... Jacob Vargas
David Tiant (age 15) .... Pablo Santos
Maria Tiant (17) .... Aimee Garcia
Sarah Tobin .... Sara Paxton
Magdalena Tiant .... Lupe Ontiveros
Daniel Tiant (9) .... Bobby Chavez
THEME:
performed by Los Lobos

Teenager David was the central focus of this comedy about growing up in an ethnically mixed household. His father, Joaquin, was a conservative Mexican American with very traditional values, who had recently moved the family into a new house in a nicer neighborhood in Tucson after getting a promotion. Elizabeth, his mother, was a feisty Irish American whose attitudes were much more liberal than her husband's. Maria, David's sexy older sister, was a petulant, status-conscious bitch who had told all her friends she was Spanish, not Mexican, and spent much of her time trying to manipulate her parents. Young David was particularly close to his uncle Ernesto, a thirty-something swinger who lived with them. Ernesto, a dog catcher with three ex-wives and a young son, Daniel, was always willing to give David advice—unfortunately not always good advice. Also seen were Magdalena, David's doting grandmother, and perky Sarah, the pretty next-door neighbor who became his best friend and fledgling love interest. The relationship between David and his father was very complex. They loved each other and Joaquin was proud of his son, but he found it easier to criticize than to praise and was convinced that without his direction David would make a mess of his life.

The autobiographical series was based on the life of series producer Peter Murrieta.

GREG THE BUNNY (*Situation Comedy*)
FIRST TELECAST: *March 27, 2002*
LAST TELECAST: *August 11, 2002*
BROADCAST HISTORY:
Mar 2002–Apr 2002, FOX Wed 9:30–10:00
Apr 2002, FOX Thu 8:30–9:00
May 2002–Jun 2002, FOX Wed 9:30–10:00
Jul 2002–Aug 2002, FOX Sun 7:30–8:00
CAST:
Greg the Bunny (voice) .... Dan Milano
Jimmy Bender .... Seth Green
Gil Bender .... Eugene Levy
Alison Kaiser .... Sarah Silverman
Junction Jack Mars .... Bob Gunton
Dottie Sunshine .... Dina Waters
Warren "the Ape" Demontague (voice)
.... Dan Milano
Count Blah (voice) .... Drew Massey

In this fantasy all of the puppets were really alive and happy Greg, who lived with his human roommate and best friend, Jimmy, was looking for a job. Jimmy got him an interview, with his father, Gil, the insecure and marginally competent producer/director of the struggling children's TV series *Sweetknuckle Junction*. Gil and pushy network executive Alison were so taken by Greg's charm and natural comedic skills that they gave him a job—as the show's new star. Then Gil found out that Greg, who had been looking for an office job, had never acted in his life. Much to his surprise and chagrin, Greg realized that he was responsible for the future of the cast and crew. The other regulars on *Sweetknuckle Junction* were foul-mouthed Junction Jack and sexpot Dottie, both humans, and puppets Warren and Count Blah (who looked and sounded like The Count on *Sesame Street*). Jimmy also got a job as a production assistant on the show.

Greg the Bunny began as a New York cable access show called *JunkTape*. In 1998 Greg became the host of the Independent Film Channel's Saturday Night Movie, which included comic sketches, parodies, and movie trivia. The show was created by Spencer Chinoy and Dan Milano (who voiced all of the puppets in the cable versions).

GREGORY HINES SHOW, THE (*Situation Comedy*)
FIRST TELECAST: *September 15, 1997*
LAST TELECAST: *March 6, 1998*
BROADCAST HISTORY:
Sep 1997, CBS Mon 8:30–9:00
Sep 1997–Oct 1997, CBS Fri 9:00–9:30
Dec 1997–Jan 1998, CBS Fri 8:30–9:00
Feb 1998–Mar 1998, CBS Fri 9:00–9:30
CAST:
Ben Stevenson .... Gregory Hines
Matty Stevenson (age 12) ...... Brandon Hammond
Carl Stevenson .... Wendell Pierce
James Stevenson .... Bill Cobbs
Alex Butler .... Mark Tymchyshyn
Nicole Moran .... Robin Riker
Angela Rice .... Judith Shelton

Widower Ben Stevenson had been father, mother, and buddy to his young son Matty since his wife's passing 18 months ago. Ben worked as a book editor for Oak Park Press, a small Chicago publishing house run by a formerly married couple, Alex and Nicole, who never passed on an opportunity to put each other down. His doddering father, James, and his pushy brother, Carl, offered him well-intentioned advice on everything, including dating, with mixed results. Also providing encouragement was Angela, Ben's administrative assistant. Episodes focused both on Ben's work and social life and on his loving and evolving relationship with his son. Matty's social life was definitely more active than his father's.

GRIFF (*Detective Drama*)
FIRST TELECAST: *September 29, 1973*
LAST TELECAST: *January 5, 1974*
BROADCAST HISTORY:
Sep 1973–Jan 1974, ABC Sat 10:00–11:00
CAST:
Wade Griffin .... Lorne Greene
S. Michael (Mike) Murdoch .... Ben Murphy

Gracie Newcombe .... Patricia Stich
Capt. Barney Marcus.................. Vic Tayback

Lorne Greene tried to discard his *Bonanza* image and shift to a more contemporary role in this short-lived detective series. He played Wade Griffin, a veteran police captain who had resigned from the force after 30 years—over a matter of principle—and gone into business on his own, as Wade Griffin Investigations. His home base was the swinging, youth-oriented Westwood section of Los Angeles, and his assistant was a young man named Mike Murdoch. Aided by their secretary Gracie, and Wade's many contacts in officialdom and on the streets, they tackled the usual array of murders, kidnappings, extortion schemes, etc.

GRIM & EVIL (*Cartoon*)

BROADCAST HISTORY:

Cartoon Network
30 minutes
Original episodes: *2001–*
Premiered: *August 24, 2001*

VOICES:

Death, the Grim Reaper ("Grim")....... Greg Eagles
Billy, Harold............... Richard Steven Horvitz
Mandy, Maj. Dr. Ghastly............. Grey DeLisle
Gladys .... Jennifer Hale
Hector Con Carne..................... Phil LaMarr
Boskov the Bear, Commando........... Jesse Corti
Boskov the Bear ....Frank Welker
Gen. Skarr .... Armin Shimerman

Grim & Evil was actually two separate cartoons. In *The Grim Adventures of Billy and Mandy* a cheerful but rather dense little boy (Billy) and his smarter but obnoxious playmate Mandy won a bet with the Grim Reaper over a sick hamster, forcing the deep-voiced, skeletal Reaper to become their playmate. The hyperactive kids drove him crazy. Harold was Billy's dad and Gladys, his mom. In the even stranger *Evil Con Carne* a bombastic megalomaniac named Hector was blown up, but his brain and stomach survived and were implanted in a dim-witted bear named Boskov. From its perch in a jar on top of Boskov, Hector's brain plotted to conquer the world, but he was constantly foiled by the amiable, bumbling bear on whom he had to depend. Gen. Skarr and Maj. Dr. Ghastly were Hector's incompetent apprentices.

GRINDL (*Situation Comedy*)

FIRST TELECAST: *September 15, 1963*
LAST TELECAST: *September 13, 1964*
BROADCAST HISTORY:

Sep 1963–Sep 1964, NBC Sun 8:30–9:00

CAST:

Grindl............................. Imogene Coca
Anson Foster.................... James Millhollin

In this single-season comedy series Imogene Coca played Grindl, a highly efficient, well-organized domestic worker who was constantly put upon by a world that seemed determined to make life difficult for her. Grindl worked for Foster's Temporary Employment Service, and each week she found herself in a different job. She was, at one time or another, a maid, a laundress, a ticket-taker at a theater, a babysitter, a cook, or anything else that Anson Foster could find for her to do.

GRIZZLY ADAMS, see *Life and Times of Grizzly Adams, The*

GROSSE POINTE (*Situation Comedy*)

FIRST TELECAST: *September 22, 2000*
LAST TELECAST: *February 18, 2001*
BROADCAST HISTORY:

Sep 2000–Oct 2000, WB Fri 8:30–9:00
Nov 2000–Feb 2001, WB Sun 9:30–10:00

CAST:

Hunter Fallow (Becky Johnson) .... Irene Malloy
Courtney Scott (Laura Johnson)
.... Bonnie Somerville
Marcy Sternfeld (Kim/Lynn Peterson)
.... Lindsay Sloane
Quentin King (Stone Anders)........ Kohl Sudduth
Johnny Bishop (Brad Johnson) .... Al Santos
Dave May, "The Stand-In"............ Kyle Howard
Rob Fields .... William Ragsdale
Kevin, the P.A .... Nat Faxon
Hope Lustig (2000)..................... Joely Fisher
**Richard Towers (Ted Johnson)*
.... Michael Hitchcock
Mary Engle (Mary Johnson) (2000)
.... Michele Dalcin
**Joan from the Network*............ Merrin Dungey
The Director (2000) .... David Gautreaux

*Occasional

This wild, satirical sitcom followed the behind-the-scenes activities of the youthful cast and crew of the fictional prime time serial drama *Grosse Pointe*. Hunter was the bitchy young star of the show and Courtney, newly hired to play her weird cousin. There were two male leads on *Grosse Pointe*—Quentin, who was hiding the fact that he was losing his hair, and Johnny, a gorgeous hunk who was obsessed with his own body and never studied his lines. Neurotic Marcy, whose father was president of the network, was Hunter's sidekick; she had the hots for Johnny, but he was attracted to newcomer Courtney. Hunter had a penchant for shoplifting, which the network had trouble keeping quiet, and Courtney had been hired as a possible replacement for her if she got into serious trouble. After producers Rob and Hope broke this news to her, Hunter conspired with Marcy to get rid of Courtney. Cash-strapped Dave had a crush on Marcy but didn't have the nerve to tell her, so he took a $15-per-hour job as Hunter's personal assistant to make a little extra money, ending up in the sack with her. In February the producers killed off Marcy's character, Kim, but the network demanded they bring her back because her TVQ ratings had gone sky-high. She returned at episode's end as Kim's identical twin sister, Lynn, from whom she had been separated at birth. In the last episode Hunter, on a whim, married gold digger Dweezil Zappa, whom she barely knew, and Marcy realized she loved honest Dave.

The creator and executive producer of *Grosse Pointe* was Darren Star, who had produced both *Beverly Hills 90210* and *Melrose Place*. Any similarity between the over-the-top characters on *Grosse Pointe* and actors from his previous shows was totally intentional.

GROUCHO SHOW, THE, see *You Bet Your Life*

GROUNDED FOR LIFE (*Situation Comedy*)
FIRST TELECAST: *January 10, 2001*
LAST TELECAST:
BROADCAST HISTORY:
Jan 2001–Jul 2002, FOX Wed 8:30–9:00
Jul 2002–Sep 2002, FOX Tue 8:30–9:00
Feb 2003– , WB Fri 9:30–10:00
CAST:
Sean Finnerty .... Donal Logue
Claudia Finnerty .... Megyn Price
Walt Finnerty (2001–2002) .... Richard Riehle
Eddie Finnerty .... Kevin Fitzgerald Corrigan
Lily Finnerty (age 14) .... Lynsey Bartilson
Jimmy Finnerty (11) .... Griffin Frazen
Henry Finnerty (9) .... Jake Burbage
Brad O'Keefe .... Bret Harrison
Dean .... Mike Vogel
**Sister Helen (2002–)* .... Miriam Flynn
*Occasional

Sean and Claudia were a married couple in their early thirties trying to raise their three kids on Staten Island, New York, while holding on to their youth. They had married when Sean got Claudia pregnant during the summer after they had graduated from high school. Over the years she had matured while, unfortunately, he had never grown up. Chunky, gross Sean, a subway worker, meant well but wasn't very reliable, a trait that irritated Claudia and frequently got him in trouble. The kids, all of whom went to St. Finnian's school, were insecure: Lily, just starting to date boys and prone to overreact to almost anything; quiet Jimmy, the good student, and energetic Henry, who had a devilish streak. Adding to their problems were Sean's opinionated father, Walt, the supervisor of a garbage landfill, and Sean's ne'er-do-well kid brother, Eddie, who was not above bending the law if he could make money doing it. Brad, the boy next door, had a crush on the totally disinterested Lily. She was more interested in Dean, a hot guy from a nearby public school.

At the start of the 2002–2003 season Sean quit his job and, with Eddie, bought the Red Boot Pub, an old Irish bar on Staten Island. Claudia wasn't thrilled that he had given up his union job to work with Eddie, but she was willing to give it a try.

GROWING PAINS (*Situation Comedy*)
FIRST TELECAST: *September 24, 1985*
LAST TELECAST: *August 27, 1992*
BROADCAST HISTORY:
Sep 1985–Mar 1986, ABC Tue 8:30–9:00
May 1986–Mar 1988, ABC Tue 8:30–9:00
Mar 1988–Aug 1990, ABC Wed 8:00–8:30
Aug 1990–Aug 1991, ABC Wed 8:30–9:00
Aug 1991–Sep 1991, ABC Fri 9:30–10:00
Sep 1991–Jan 1992, ABC Sat 8:30–9:00
Feb 1992–Apr 1992, ABC Sat 9:30–10:00
May 1992–Jul 1992, ABC Wed 8:30–9:00
Jul 1992–Aug 1992, ABC Thu 8:30–9:00
CAST:
Dr. Jason Seaver .... Alan Thicke
Maggie Seaver .... Joanna Kerns
Mike Seaver (age 15) .... Kirk Cameron
Carol Seaver (14) .... Tracey Gold
Ben Seaver (9) .... Jeremy Miller
Chrissy Seaver (1988–1990)
.... Kristen & Kelsey Dohring
Chrissy Seaver (age 6) (1990–1992) Ashley Johnson
**Richard Stabone ("Boner") (1985–1989)*
.... Josh Andrew Koenig
**Eddie* .... K.C. Martel
**Debbie (1987–1988)* .... Lisa Capps
**Shelley (1987–1988)* .... Rachael Jacobs
**Coach Graham Lubbock (1987–1988)*
.... Bill Kirchenbauer
**Irma (1988–1990)* .... Jane Powell
**Wally (1988–1990)* .... Robert Rockwell
**Ed Malone (1989–1991)* .... Gordon Jump
**Kate Malone (1989–1991)* .... Betty McGuire
Julie Costello (1989–1990) .... Julie McCullough
**Kate MacDonald (1989–1992)* .... Chelsea Noble
**Stinky Sullivan (1989–1991)* .... Jamie Abbot
Luke Brower (1991–1992) ...... Leonardo DiCaprio
*Occasional
THEME:
"As Long As We Got Each Other," sung by B.J. Thomas & Jennifer Warnes

If *Father Knows Best* had been revived in the 1980s, it would have been called *Growing Pains*. As amiable and wise as Jim Anderson had been, Jason Seaver was more so—and a little hipper to boot. This father was a psychiatrist (who better to deal with teenage traumas?) who had moved his office into his suburban New York home when his wife Maggie went back to work, in order to keep an eye on the kids. The young Seavers were Mike, a gangly teenager who was more interested in having a good time than in responsibility ("a hormone with feet," his mother called him); shy Carol, his brainy sister; and their cute little brother Ben, no slouch himself at getting into scrapes. Dad was always available with sage advice, while Mom, who had become a reporter for the *Long Island Herald* (later a TV reporter, as "Maggie Malone"), rushed off to work. Mike and Carol attended school at Thomas E. Dewey High.

The characters evolved as years went by. In 1988 Maggie had another child, which didn't stop her from quickly resuming her career. Baby Chrissy grew remarkably fast, turning six only two years later. Hormonal Mike graduated from high school and enrolled in a local college, while working odd jobs. His parade of girlfriends was truly awesome, the most notable being Julie (Chrissy's nanny, whom he almost married, but who dumped him at the altar) and later Kate. Boner and Eddie were his best pals. In later seasons Mike dabbled in acting and taught remedial education, for credit, at an inner-city school, where homeless boy Luke was his star student. Luke moved in with the Seavers, while Mike now had his own "pad"—over the family garage.

Studious Carol had a tougher time on the dating scene, but soared academically; following graduation she worked for several months, and then entered Columbia University. Ben, on the other hand, seemed to develop into a junior version of Mike, with mostly girls on his mind. Other kin seen in recurring appearances were Jason's vivacious, widowed mother Irma and her new husband Wally, and Maggie's parents Ed and Kate Malone.

In addition to the safe little stories of dates, first

jobs, and fun around the house, *Growing Pains* periodically tackled more serious issues than *Father Knows Best* ever imagined, including drunk driving, teen suicide, racism, and peer pressure on Mike to use cocaine. As in the earlier series, however, a wise dad and mom saw their basically decent kids through it all. In the final original episode, Maggie was offered a chance-of-a-lifetime job as media relations director for a senator in Washington, so the family moved there—minus Mike, who by now had become an actor(!), and Carol, who was in college. The following fall the Seaver house was occupied by none other than *Hangin' with Mr. Cooper.*

Fourteen-year-old Kirk Cameron, formerly unnoticed as a regular on *Two Marriages*, became something of a teenage heartthrob on this hit series, receiving 10,000 letters a month. "I'm still nervous and shy when I meet girls," he told a reporter. "The only thing that's changed is that I've gotten the chance to *meet* more girls because they introduce themselves to me."

In 1991, over his shyness, he married actress Chelsea Noble, who played Kate.

ABC aired reruns of *Growing Pains* on weekday mornings from July 1988 to August 1989.

GROWING PAYNES, THE (*Situation Comedy*)

FIRST TELECAST: *October 20, 1948*
LAST TELECAST: *August 3, 1949*
BROADCAST HISTORY:
Oct 1948–Aug 1949, DUM Wed 8:30–9:00
CAST:
Mr. Payne (1948–1949) .... John Harvey*
Mr. Payne (1949) .... Ed Holmes
Mrs. Payne (1948–1949) .... Judy Parrish
Mrs. Payne (1949) .... Elaine Stritch
ALSO:
David Anderson
Warren Parker
Lester Lonergan, Jr.
Ann Sullivan
ORIGINAL MUSIC:
Bill Wirges
*Also given as John Henry

This was an early live domestic comedy about the trials of an insurance salesman (John Harvey), his screwball wife (Judy Parrish), and young kids. Often it was Birdie, the maid, who saved the day. The setting was the family's apartment. Plugs for the sponsor, Wanamaker's Department Store, were worked into the early stories, as was the custom at the time.

GROWN UPS (*Situation Comedy*)

FIRST TELECAST: *August 23, 1999*
LAST TELECAST: *September 12, 2000*
BROADCAST HISTORY:
Aug 1999, UPN Mon 8:30–9:00
Aug 1999–Aug 2000, UPN Mon 9:00–9:30
Sep 2000, UPN Tue 8:30–9:00
CAST:
J. Calvin Frazier .... Jaleel White
Gordon Hammill......................... Dave Ruby
Shari Hammill........................ Marissa Ribisi
Marcus Wentworth .... Bumper Robinson
Melissa Daniels .... Tammy Townsend
Logan Thomas (2000)................ Derek Hughes
Rodney Carruthers (2000).......... Patrick Bristow

This Chicago-based comedy centered on Calvin, a young marketing executive who left his boring job with a corrugated box company to try his hand at Intergetters, a small Internet company. A daydreamer who was looking for a new image, he changed his first name to Jay because it sounded cooler than Calvin. Jay's chunky best friend, Gordon, an associate with a law firm, lived in the same apartment building. Other featured cast members were Shari, Gordon's perky wife; Marcus, an arrogant attorney who worked with Gordon; and Melissa, Jay's new girlfriend. When she returned from a business trip just before Thanksgiving their relationship had deteriorated and they broke up—but vowed to remain friends. In February Jay quit his job to become marketing director for Celuron, a maker of computer games. Logan, the eccentric, child-like genius who had started the company, liked him—which could not be said for Carruthers, the obnoxious business type who did all the administrative work and resented Jay's arrival.

In the series finale Jay ran into Melissa and mistakenly thought she was getting married the following Saturday. Afraid to lose her, he proposed, but after she accepted he found out that she wasn't the one engaged. As the scene ended, TO BE CONTINUED flashed on the screen—but, since the show had been canceled, there was no resolution.

GRUDGE MATCH, THE (*Audience Participation*)

BROADCAST HISTORY:
Syndicated only
60 minutes
Produced: *1991–1992* (26 episodes)
Released: *September 1991*
HOSTS:
Steve Albert
Jesse "The Body" Ventura
REGULARS:
Paula McClure
Andy Steinfeld
Pete Steinfeld
Theresa Ring
John Pinette
Michael Buffer

This series resembled a competitive version of *The People's Court.* The premise was that two people who had some form of festering disagreement could resolve their frustrations through nonsensical physical combat. Each match—there were usually three in each episode—consisted of three one-minute rounds. In the first round the combatants fought with oversized boxing gloves or something similar chosen by the show's production staff. In the second and third rounds the weapons were chosen by the participants. These might include fire extinguishers filled with glop and dust, fruit pies, rotten tomatoes, buckets of sludge, plastic trash cans, cream pies, chocolate syrup, and goose feathers, or even a tug-of-war over a glop-filled pool. At the end of the match, the studio audience voted for the winner, who won a prize chosen before the start of the match. The prize might be anything from furniture to stereo equipment to cash, with a value generally under $1,000.

Sports announcer Steve Albert co-hosted *The Grudge Match* with former professional wrestler Jesse "The Body" Ventura. Other regulars were hostess Paula

McClure, cornermen/trainers Andy and Pete Steinfeld, sexy ring-girl Theresa Ring, referee John Pinette, and ring announcer Michael Buffer. There was also a paramedic on hand in case anyone actually got hurt.

GRUEN GUILD THEATER, see *ABC Dramatic Shorts—1952–1953*

GRUEN PLAYHOUSE (*Dramatic Anthology*)
FIRST TELECAST: *January 17, 1952*
LAST TELECAST: *July 3, 1952*
BROADCAST HISTORY:
Jan 1952–Jul 1952, DUM Thu 9:00–9:30

Filmed dramas featuring such talent as Patrick O'Neal, Elisabeth Fraser, and Bobby Jordan. At least some of these films also appeared on ABC at about the same time on the various series listed under *ABC Dramatic Shorts.* Seen on alternate weeks.

GUARDIAN, THE (*Legal Drama*)
FIRST TELECAST: *September 25, 2001*
LAST TELECAST:
BROADCAST HISTORY:
Sep 2001– , CBS Tue 9:00–10:00
CAST:
Nick Fallin .... Simon Baker
Burton Fallin .... Dabney Coleman
Alvin Masterson .... Alan Rosenberg
Amanda Bowles (2000–2001) .... Erica Leerhsen
Jake Straka .... Raphael Sbarge
James Mooney .... Charles Malik Whitfield
Laurie Solt .... Kathleen Chalfont
Luise "Lulu" Archer .... Wendy Moniz
Judge Rebecca F. Damsen .... Denise Dowse
Gretchen, the receptionist (2002–)
.... Dorothea Harahan
Barbara Ludzinski .... Rusty Schwimmer
Brian Olsen (2002–) .... Johnny Sneed
Kate Shaw (2002–2003) .... Courtney Stevens
Shannon Gressler (2002–) .... Amanda Michalka

Handsome Nick was a successful corporate attorney, an associate in his father's Pittsburgh law firm, Fallin & Associates. His bright future was suddenly altered when he was convicted of drug use and, to avoid being disbarred, sentenced to 1,500 hours of community service working as a legal advocate for a struggling nonprofit organization, Children's Legal Services (CLS). Nick now alternated between servicing wealthy clients at the law firm and abused and disadvantaged children at CLS, and juggling his hours was not always easy. His constant need to shift from one job to the other irritated both his father, patrician Burton, and earthy Alvin, his dedicated boss at CLS, since both wanted more of his time than he could give them. At first Nick resented being at CLS, but after a while he started to care about the plight of its young clients and did his best to help them. Amanda was his assistant at the law firm and Jake, an ambitious fellow associate. Working with Nick at CLS were fellow advocates James and Lulu, to whom he was immediately attracted, and Laurie, a social worker.

When CLS lost its funding, the only way it could stay in business was to take on cases of adults as well as children, and it was renamed Legal Services of Pittsburgh (LSP). As the season wound down Burton landed an appointment as a federal judge and gave control of the firm to former senator Nathan Caldwell (John Rubinstein). Nick was so upset that he and Jake quit to start their own firm. After Caldwell, about to be investigated by the FBI, committed suicide in the office, Burton returned to helm the firm, convinced Nick and Jake to return, made Nick a partner (later Jake was also made partner) and renamed it Fallin & Fallin. Lulu married Brian, her physician boyfriend, but they had a rocky marriage that fell apart at the end of the year when he left town after it was revealed that he had epilepsy. A couple of months later Lulu and Nick were on the verge of having an affair when she was injured in a car accident. By the spring they were hot and heavy, however, and after Alvin caught them making love in the office at night, the word went out to everyone that they were involved. Meanwhile Burton had met Mary (Farrah Fawcett) and her young granddaughter Shannon during a case in which Nick was implicated in the death of Mary's daughter—Mary's testimony had exonerated the younger Fallin. Burton was attracted to Mary and very fond of Shannon and, when Mary died, he initiated efforts to become Shannon's foster father. In the season finale Lulu accepted a job in California, which upset Nick; James was shot, and Shannon decided she would rather be with her father.

GUESS AGAIN (*Quiz/Audience Participation*)
FIRST TELECAST: *June 14, 1951*
LAST TELECAST: *June 21, 1951*
BROADCAST HISTORY:
June 1951, CBS, Thu 8:30–9:00
MODERATOR:
Mike Wallace
ACTORS:
Joey Faye
Mandy Kaye
Bobby Martin

This short-lived game show—it only aired for two weeks—had a panel of three celebrities, each of whom was paired with a studio-audience contestant. Together the teams attempted to answer questions about a series of vignettes done by three actors, with each correct answer giving them the chance to tackle the next question and "guess again." The first correct answer was worth $10 and each succeeding answer was worth $5 more than the last, up to four questions worth a total of $70. Contestants kept their winnings and celebrity panelists donated theirs to their favorite charities.

GUESS WHAT (*Quiz/Panel*)
FIRST TELECAST: *July 8, 1952*
LAST TELECAST: *August 26, 1952*
BROADCAST HISTORY:
Jul 1952–Aug 1952, DUM Tue 9:00–9:30
EMCEE:
Dick Kollmar
PANELISTS:
Quentin Reynolds
Virginia Peine
Mark Hanna
Audrey Christie

Summer quiz show in which a panel of celebrities was given a series of cryptic quotations and asked to guess: "What is it?" Numerous personalities appeared on the panel during the short run of this show, of whom the above four were most frequently seen.

GUESS WHAT HAPPENED, see *What Happened*

GUESTWARD HO! (*Situation Comedy*)
FIRST TELECAST: *September 29, 1960*
LAST TELECAST: *September 21, 1961*
BROADCAST HISTORY:
Sep 1960–Sep 1961, ABC Thu 7:30–8:00
CAST:
Babs Hooten .... Joanne Dru
Hawkeye .... J. Carrol Naish
Bill Hooten .... Mark Miller
Brook Hooten .... Flip Mark
Lonesome .... Earle Hodgins
Pink Cloud .... Jolene Brand
Rocky .... Tony Montenaro, Jr.

Fed up with the hustle and bustle of New York City, the Hootens decided to look for someplace else to live and work. Their dream house proved to be *Guestward Ho,* a dude ranch in New Mexico. They bought it, sight unseen, and moved west, only to find a rather run-down establishment in need of much work. The only source of supplies in the area was a store run by an Indian named Hawkeye. Hawkeye read the *Wall Street Journal,* sold Indian trinkets that had been made in Japan, and was bound and determined to find a way to return the country to its rightful owners, *his* people. He was not really militant, just industrious and conniving, and his relationship with the Hootens, including their young son Brook, provided the basis for many amusing situations.

GUIDE RIGHT (*Variety*)
FIRST TELECAST: *February 25, 1952*
LAST TELECAST: *October 30, 1953*
BROADCAST HISTORY:
Feb 1952–Dec 1952, DUM Mon 9:00–9:30
Dec 1952–Jul 1953, DUM Thu 8:00–8:30
Jul 1953–Oct 1953, DUM Fri 8:30–9:00
EMCEE:
Don Russell
CONDUCTOR:
Elliot Lawrence

Korean War–era variety show designed to aid enlistments, and featuring both military and civilian talent. Some telecasts originated from military bases. Many of the Army and Air Force bands seen on *Guide Right* were unaccustomed to studio performances, and conductor Elliot Lawrence recalls that he was brought in after the first few telecasts specifically to rehearse the military musicians and direct them on the air. Among the civilian talent "doing their bit" for enlistments were Teresa Brewer, Denise Lor, Morey Amsterdam, Steve Lawrence and Eydie Gorme, Tony Bennett, and Chandu the Magician. Perhaps the hottest popular singer of the day came from the ranks, however—PFC Eddie Fisher, then serving his own enlistment, appeared in October 1952. Military talent such as The Airmen of Note and The Singing Sergeants were also seen.

GUINNESS GAME, THE (*Quiz/Audience Participation*)
BROADCAST HISTORY:
Syndicated only
30 minutes
Produced: *1979* (24 episodes)
Released: *September 1979*
HOST:
Don Galloway

This was another of those noisy early-evening game shows, but with a twist. Each telecast featured four live, onstage attempts to break a world's record in some specialty, and thus qualify the record-breaker for inclusion in *The Guinness Book of World Records.*

At the start of the program three contestants won money by answering a series of questions based on *Guinness.* They then used the money to bet, pro or con, on whether the attempts to break a world's record would succeed. The records challenged were often pretty bizarre. One man had to eat 17 bananas in less than two minutes; another, to jump rope 50 times on a wire suspended 33 feet above the stage; another, to make 256 five-foot-long noodles in under 63 seconds; and four burly men attempted to change all four tires on a sedan in less than two minutes. The race against the clock was followed as in a sports competition, and if it was successful the audience would erupt in great tumult as the screen flashed on and off, "New World's Record—Tire Changing—1:48.8!"

The producers insisted that *Guinness* was not intended to be a freak show, and the record challengers certainly seemed serious. On hand to authenticate new records was David Boehm, American editor of the book. Also on hand were giant nets, paramedics, and two husky "catchers" who tried to stop anyone falling or prevent other kinds of live, onstage disaster.

GUINNESS WORLD RECORDS; PRIMETIME (*Audience Participation*)
FIRST TELECAST: *July 28, 1998*
LAST TELECAST: *September 20, 2001*
BROADCAST HISTORY:
Jul 1998–Mar 1999, FOX Tue 9:00–10:00
Mar 1999–Jun 1999, FOX Fri 8:00–9:00
Jun 1999–Aug 1999, FOX Tue 8:00–9:00
Dec 1999, FOX Thu 8:00–9:00
Jul 2000, FOX Wed 9:00–10:00
Aug 2000, FOX Fri 9:00–10:00
Sep 2000, FOX Wed 9:00–10:00
Jul 2001–Sep 2001, FOX Thu 8:00–9:00
HOST:
Cris Collinsworth (1998–1999)
Mark Thompson (1999–2001)
ASSISTANT:
Mark Thompson (1998–1999)
CORRESPONDENT:
John Salley (1998–1999)

The famous *Guinness Book of World Records* was the inspiration for this TV freak show, which provided reports on bizarre record holders, coverage of attempts to set new records, and a voice-over announcer giving startling statistics to home viewers. The first telecast included the world's biggest (300 pounds) ovarian tumor, a tightrope walker on a beam between two hot-air balloons floating four miles high, a sword swallower who managed to put eight swords down his throat at one time, a woman who set the record for protruding eyeballs, and a man who set a record for balancing 62 glasses. Thompson was the in-studio host, with people attempting to set new records in front of a live audience.

Later episodes included a four-mile free fall, the

world's largest woman (at her peak, she weighed 1,200 pounds), a bubble-blowing tarantula eater, the man with the world's longest fingernails, a rubber man contortionist, the world's largest mouse plague (more than 100 million in Australia), and 18 college students who managed to stuff themselves into a 1998 New Beetle. Believe it, or not.

When Cris Collinsworth left the show in 1999, he was replaced by former assistant Mark Thompson.

GULF PLAYHOUSE, 1ST PERSON (*Dramatic Anthology*)

FIRST TELECAST: *October 3, 1952*
LAST TELECAST: *September 11, 1953*
BROADCAST HISTORY:
Oct 1952–Dec 1952, NBC Fri 8:30–9:00
Jul 1953–Sep 1953, NBC Fri 8:30–9:00

When *Gulf Playhouse* was originally aired in the fall of 1952 it was a conventional live dramatic anthology. It was replaced by *The Life of Riley* and was back again in the summer of 1953 as *Riley*'s summer replacement. The format had changed, however. Although it was still a live anthology series, under the new title *Gulf Playhouse: 1st Person* the camera itself became one of the actors, through whose "eyes" all of the action was seen. It had a voice, and could have been a person or an object or an animal. The other actors addressed the camera as if it were a live member of the cast and gave the viewer a sense of participation in these plays.

GULF ROAD SHOW STARRING BOB SMITH, THE (*Variety/Talent*)

FIRST TELECAST: *September 2, 1948*
LAST TELECAST: *June 30, 1949*
BROADCAST HISTORY:
Sep 1948–Jun 1949, NBC Thu 9:00–9:30
REGULARS:
Bob Smith
Eve Young (1949)
Heathertones (1949)
ORCHESTRA:
Enoch Light (1948)
Johnny Guarnieri (1948–1949)
Bobby Wren (1949)

Bob Smith, originator (in 1947) of TV's long-running *Howdy Doody Show*, hosted this prime-time talent/variety series during the 1948–1949 season. The program was notable for its frequent changes of format. There were three such changes during the first month alone, and five in all. In order, viewers were treated to a straight musical variety revue (first two weeks), a musical quiz show (one week), a series subtitled *What's New* featuring new talent, inventions, movies, books, etc. (three months), a straight talent show (four and a half months), and finally back to the original musical revue, with guest stars and the audience-participation segment (last two months).

Howdy Doody made a couple of appearances on the show, singing "All I Want for Christmas Is My Two Front Teeth" on the Christmas show, and the new talent included such notable attractions as young songstress Patti Page and "Miss Television Tube of 1949" (comedienne Patricia Bright).

GUN (*Dramatic Anthology*)

FIRST TELECAST: *April 12, 1997*
LAST TELECAST: *May 31, 1997*
BROADCAST HISTORY:
Apr 1997–May 1997, ABC Sat 10:00–11:00
THEME:
"Happiness Is a Warm Gun" (Lennon-McCartney), performed by U2

This arty anthology from film director Robert Altman ricocheted on and off the ABC schedule like a speeding bullet, which is unfortunate, since it had a point to make. The titular "star" was a pearl-handled, semi-automatic pistol that passed from owner to owner, usually bringing misery and pain to those whose lives it touched. The stories were not all downbeat, but often they ended with a twist. For example, in the premiere an obnoxious, failed actor's life was turned around when he foiled a convenience store robbery by thugs wielding the Gun. An overnight celebrity, he soon landed a movie deal portraying himself as the crime-stopping hero, with the two young thugs as his very realistic co-stars! The story then turned into a wild parody of Hollywood mythmaking, as he dickered with obtuse producers and tried to convince his on-screen "wife," Kathy Ireland, to do a love scene. Only at the end of the hour did viewers realize that it was all a momentary fantasy—the actor had actually been shot to death in the holdup, imagining the rest in his dying moments.

Some notable stars appeared during the series' short run, including Kathy Baker, Carrie Fisher, Daryl Hannah, Randy Quaid, and Martin Sheen. There were no regulars.

GUN SHY (*Situation Comedy*)

FIRST TELECAST: *March 15, 1983*
LAST TELECAST: *April 19, 1983*
BROADCAST HISTORY:
Mar 1983–Apr 1983, CBS Tue 8:30–9:00
Apr 1983, CBS Tue 8:00–8:30
CAST:
Russell Donovan .... Barry Van Dyke
Theodore Ogilvie .... Tim Thomerson
Amos Tucker .... Geoffrey Lewis
Clovis .... Keith Mitchell
Clovis .... Adam Rich
Celia .... Bridgette Anderson
Homer McCoy .... Henry Jones
Nettie McCoy .... Janis Paige
Colonel Mound .... Pat McCormick

Set in the small California town of Quake City in 1869, this comedy Western revolved around the lives of a good-natured gambler, the two young children he won in a card game, and the townsfolk in Quake City. Russell Donovan was the gambler, caring for his two young wards, Celia and Clovis (the latter played by Keith Mitchell in the first four episodes of this limited series and by Adam Rich in the last two). Theodore and Amos were two bumbling would-be desperadoes, vainly attempting to build reputations as outlaws, and Homer McCoy was Quake City's barber, sheriff, and justice of the peace. Homer's ex-wife Nettie ran the only hotel in town, and Col. Mound was the owner of the local stagecoach line. Russell's attempts to bring up two precocious children, and the hapless antics of Theodore and Amos, provided the focus of this series.

Based on the Walt Disney films *The Apple Dumpling Gang* and *The Apple Dumpling Gang Rides Again*, in which Bill Bixby played Donovan and Don Knotts and Tim Conway played Theodore and Amos.

GUNG HO (*Situation Comedy*)

FIRST TELECAST: *December 5, 1986*
LAST TELECAST: *June 27, 1987*
BROADCAST HISTORY:

Dec 1986–Jan 1987, ABC Fri 9:30–10:00
Jan 1987–Feb 1987, ABC Fri 9:00–9:30
Jun 1987, ABC Sat 9:00–9:30

CAST:

Hunt Stevenson .... Scott Bakula
Kaz Kazuhiro .... Gedde Watanabe
Buster .... Stephen Lee
Mr. Saito .... Sab Shimono
Googie .... Clint Howard
Ito .... Rodney Kageyama
Randi .... Heidi Banks
Umeki Kazuhiro .... Patti Yasutake
Yukiko Saito .... Emily K. Kuroda
Kenji .... Scott Atari

East and West comically clashed in a Hadleyville, Pennsylvania, auto plant in this short-lived comedy. Assan Motors of Japan had reopened the closed plant, and the workers were thankful for that, but problems were inevitable. Kaz was the newly installed plant manager, trying to balance his country's traditions, the unfamiliar customs of the U.S.A., and the demands of his management back in Japan; Saito was his conservative Japanese assistant, who didn't want to adapt at all. Kaz's wife Umeki, though properly subservient to her husband, sometimes flirted with the freedom accorded American women, while Saito's Yukiko was much more conservative. Hunt was the freewheeling go-between with the plant's American workers, who gave the new managers an introduction to America they would never forget.

Based on the 1986 movie of the same name, in which Gedde Watanabe also played the role of Kaz.

GUNS OF PARADISE, see *Paradise*

GUNS OF WILL SONNETT, THE (*Western*)

FIRST TELECAST: *September 8, 1967*
LAST TELECAST: *September 15, 1969*
BROADCAST HISTORY:

Sep 1967–May 1969, ABC Fri 9:30–10:00
Jun 1969–Sep 1969, ABC Mon 8:30–9:00

CAST:

Will Sonnett .... Walter Brennan
Jeff Sonnett .... Dack Rambo

A grizzled old ex-cavalry scout and his grandson searched the West for the boy's father in this unusual Western, set in the 1870s. James Sonnett had disappeared 19 years before, leaving the infant Jeff in Will's care. As the years passed the boy had grown into manhood determined to find his father, who had meanwhile become a notorious, but elusive, gunfighter. The old man (played by character actor Walter Brennan, then 73) and his grandson followed James's trail, finding many who knew of him, some with bitterness and hatred, others with gratitude and awe. James Sonnett (played by Jason Evers) was seen fleetingly in a few episodes, and Will and Jeff finally caught up with him at the end of the second season. They convinced him to stop running and begin a new career with them in a frontier town as lawmen! Unfortunately ABC did not renew the show, so their new careers were brief. *Sic transit* gunfighters.

GUNSLINGER (*Western*)

FIRST TELECAST: *February 9, 1961*
LAST TELECAST: *September 14, 1961*
BROADCAST HISTORY:

Feb 1961–Sep 1961, CBS Thu 9:00–10:00

CAST:

Cord .... Tony Young
Capt. Zachary Wingate .... Preston Foster
Pico McGuire .... Charles Gray
Billy Urchin .... Dee Pollock
Amby Hollister .... Midge Ware
Sgt. Major Murdock .... John Picard

THEME:

Sung by Frankie Laine

Set in the Southwest in the decade following the conclusion of the Civil War, *Gunslinger* was the story of Cord, a fast gun who worked on undercover assignments for Capt. Zachary Wingate, the commandant of Fort Scott, New Mexico. Pico and Billy were Cord's two close friends, who often went with him on assignments, and Amby Hollister ran the general store at the fort.

GUNSMOKE (*Western*)

FIRST TELECAST: *September 10, 1955*
LAST TELECAST: *September 1, 1975*
BROADCAST HISTORY:

Sep 1955–Sep 1961, CBS Sat 10:00–10:30
Sep 1961–Sep 1967, CBS Sat 10:00–11:00
Oct 1961–Oct 1964, CBS Tue 7:30–8:00
Sep 1967–Sep 1971, CBS Mon 7:30–8:30
Sep 1971–Sep 1975, CBS Mon 8:00–9:00

CAST:

Marshal Matt Dillon .... James Arness
Dr. Galen (Doc) Adams .... Milburn Stone
Kitty Russell (1955–1974) .... Amanda Blake
Chester Goode (1955–1964) .... Dennis Weaver
Festus Haggen (1964–1975) .... Ken Curtis
Quint Asper (1962–1965) .... Burt Reynolds
Sam, the bartender (1961–1974) .... Glenn Strange
Clayton Thaddeus (Thad) Greenwood (1965–1967) .... Roger Ewing
Newly O'Brien (1967–1975) .... Buck Taylor
Moss Grimmick (1955–1963) .... George Selk
Mr. Jonus (1955–1960) .... Dabbs Greer
Louie Pheeters .... James Nusser
Barney Danches .... Charles Seel
Howie Culver .... Howard Culver
Ed O'Connor .... Tom Brown
Percy Crump .... John Harper
Hank Miller (1957–1975) .... Hank Patterson
Ma Smalley (1962–1975) .... Sarah Selby
Nathan Burke (1963–1975) .... Ted Jordan
Mr. Bodkin (1965–1975) .... Roy Roberts
Mr. Lathrop (1966–1975) .... Woody Chamblis
Halligan (1967–1975) .... Charles Wagenheim
Dr. John Chapman (1971) .... Pat Hingle
Miss Hannah (1974–1975) .... Fran Ryan

MUSICAL THEME:

"Gunsmoke" (also known as "Old Trail"), by Glenn Spencer and Rex Koury

The few Westerns seen on television during the early 1950s starred old-style movie heroes such as the Lone Ranger and Hopalong Cassidy, and had little to do with the real West. Westerns were considered another form of obvious fantasy, strictly for the kids. Two shows, *Gunsmoke* and *The Life and Legend of Wyatt Earp*, changed all that. These two programs, which premiered during the same week in 1955, introduced the "adult Western" to TV, and began an enormous wave of Westerns on TV over the next ten years.

Gunsmoke had its genesis on CBS radio in the spring of 1952, with William Conrad in the role of the resolute, determined Marshal Matt Dillon. Conrad, who later became TV's *Cannon* in the 1970s, remained the radio voice of Matt Dillon for a total of nine years, but when CBS decided to add a video version of the series the first choice for the role was John Wayne. Wayne would probably have done very well in the role, but he did not want to commit himself to the rigors of a weekly television series and suggested James Arness, a young, relatively unknown actor friend of his. Wayne even offered to introduce the program's first episode, an offer which was quickly accepted by the CBS brass. James Arness, six feet seven inches in height, was even bigger physically than John Wayne, and he proved to be perfect casting for the role of the heroic marshal.

Gunsmoke was set in Dodge City, Kansas; the year, arbitrarily, was 1873 (according to producer John Mantley). Crusty old Doc Adams, the only cast member besides Arness to stay with the show for its entire run, was the town's kindly, sympathetic physician. Doc spent most of his spare time, as did many of Dodge City's residents, at the Long Branch Saloon, which was owned and operated by Kitty Russell. Kitty was extremely softhearted, beneath what could be a very businesslike exterior, and would have willingly become romantically involved with Matt. In the radio version the implication was that she was a prostitute, but on TV Matt and Kitty exchanged no more than smiles. Matt's loyal, well-meaning deputy was Chester Goode, who walked with a pronounced limp, talked with a twang ("Mister Dillon!"), and brewed a mean pot of coffee—which was often seen behind the closing credits.

Gunsmoke was not an immediate hit. It premiered on Saturday night against the established *George Gobel Show* and did not make TV's top 15 during its first season. In its second year it jumped to No. 8, however, and for the next four years—1957 to 1961—it was the top-rated program in all of TV. *Gunsmoke* precipitated a deluge of Westerns in the late 1950s (at one time there were more than 30 prime-time network Westerns on in the same season), but it outlived them all. It went into a considerable decline in the mid-1960s, after being expanded to an hour, and was about to leave the air when CBS gave it one more chance, moving it to Monday night in 1967. The result was a stunning comeback that put the show in the top ten once again, where it stayed well into the 1970s. It is ironic that when it finally did leave the air in 1975, it was the last Western left on network television at that time. In all, *Gunsmoke* ran for 20 years, longer than any other prime-time series with continuing characters in the history of the medium.

Over the years there were changes in the supporting cast. Chester (Dennis Weaver) left in 1964 to be replaced by Festus Haggen, the scruffy, illiterate hillbilly deputy who remained for the rest of the run. Half-breed Indian Quint Asper was featured for a while as the town blacksmith, as were gunsmith Newly O'Brien and Matt's young friend Thad Greenwood.

In addition to the principal cast members, there was an extensive supporting cast of Dodge City residents who appeared from time to time. Miss Hannah ran the Long Branch Saloon after Kitty's departure. Jones and Lathrop were storekeepers; Halligan and O'Connor, local ranchers; Louie, the town drunk; Barney, the telegraph agent; Howie, the hotel clerk; Percy, the Dodge City undertaker; Hank, the stableman; Nathan, the freight agent; Mr. Bodkin, the banker, and Ma Smalley, the boardinghouse owner. For a couple of months in 1971, John Chapman served as the town physician (while actor Milburn Stone was recovering from a heart attack).

As the years passed, less and less was seen of Matt. Stories often revolved around other members of the cast while he was out of town, and, to some extent, *Gunsmoke* frequently resembled an anthology as stories often came to center on guest stars, using Dodge City simply as a background. "Hard" social issues of the 1960s, such as the rights of minorities, social protest, and crimes such as rape, began to be tackled in stories adapted to the Dodge City setting.

Matt Dillon set the tone of the show throughout its long life, however, standing for justice, sincerity, and truth. The opening of the show (during its early seasons) said it all. There was Matt in a fast-draw showdown in the main street of Dodge City. The other man fired a fraction of a second faster, but missed completely, while Matt's aim was true. Matt could be beaten up, shot, and ambushed, but that indomitable will would never be defeated.

For the first three seasons following the expansion of *Gunsmoke* from half an hour to a full hour on Saturday nights, CBS aired reruns of the original half-hour version on Tuesdays under the title *Marshal Dillon*.

GUY LOMBARDO'S DIAMOND JUBILEE (*Musical Variety*)

FIRST TELECAST: *March 20, 1956*
LAST TELECAST: *June 19, 1956*
BROADCAST HISTORY:
Mar 1956–Jun 1956, CBS Tue 9:00–9:30
REGULAR:
Guy Lombardo and His Royal Canadians

Viewers of this series were asked to send in letters describing how a specific song had played an important role in their lives. Each week four of the people who had written in were selected to appear on the live show as Guy's guests and watch as their stories were dramatized. In addition to the viewer guests there was one celebrity guest who appeared on the show in connection with "the song of his life." The viewers who appeared on the show won, in addition to the free trip to New York, diamond jewelry and other gifts.

For the two years prior to this network exposure, Guy Lombardo had starred in a syndicated half-hour show titled *Guy Lombardo and His Royal Canadians*, playing "the sweetest music this side of heaven."

GUY MITCHELL SHOW, THE (*Musical Variety*)

FIRST TELECAST: *October 7, 1957*
LAST TELECAST: *January 13, 1958*
BROADCAST HISTORY:
Oct 1957–Jan 1958, ABC Mon 8:00–8:30
REGULARS:
Guy Mitchell
Dolores Hawkins
The Guy Mitchell Singers

The Ted Cappy Dancers
The Van Alexander Orchestra

THEME:
"Singing the Blues"

Singer Guy Mitchell hosted and starred in this short-lived musical variety series. Dolores Hawkins, not originally a cast regular, became one during the middle of the show's four-month run. Guest stars were featured and the focus of the show was on singing, which worked much better than the contrived comedy sketches that were also part of the format.

GUYS LIKE US (*Situation Comedy*)
FIRST TELECAST: *October 5, 1998*
LAST TELECAST: *January 11, 1999*
BROADCAST HISTORY:
Oct 1998, UPN Mon 8:00–8:30
Nov 1998–Jan 1999, UPN Mon 8:30–9:00
CAST:
Jared Harris .... Bumper Robinson
Sean Barker .... Chris Hardwick
Maestro Harris (age 6) .... Maestro Harrell
Jude .... Linda Cardellini
Vance .... Andy Berman
Nikki .... Courtney Mun
Kim .... Karen Maruyama
Bridget Cole .... Tammy Townsend

Jared and Sean were roommates sharing a bachelor pad apartment in Chicago. Jared was a rather stiff marketing executive for a sporting goods manufacturer, and Sean a free-spirited musician who worked in a music store and had a band. Life was just the way they wanted it until Maestro, Jared's kid brother, moved in when his widowed father got a 14-month job heading up an engineering team building a dam in Venezuela. Hyperactive Maestro tried to be helpful, including setting up both guys with dates, but his presence did cramp their social style. Jude and Vance, who booked Sean's band at high school and other dances, worked with him at the music store. Kim, a single mother who lived in their building, had a cute daughter, Nikki, who was in Maestro's class. Jared was attracted to their teacher, Miss Cole, but the show was canceled before they made it to their first date.

HBO (Network), see *Home Box Office*

H.E.L.P. (*Adventure*)
FIRST TELECAST: *March 3, 1990*
LAST TELECAST: *April 14, 1990*
BROADCAST HISTORY:
Mar 1990–Apr 1990, ABC Sat 8:00–9:00
CAST:
Chief Patrick Meacham............John Mahoney
Off. Lou Barton....................Wesley Snipes
Off. Larry Alba.........................Joe Urla
Mike Pappas.....................Lance Edwards
Suki Rodriguez.....................Kim Flowers
Jimmy Ryan......................Tom Breznahan
E. Jean Ballantry.............Marjorie Monaghan
Kathleen Meacham............Fionnula Flanagan
A fast-paced, standard-issue action series, whose chief attraction was the gritty backdrop of New York City, where the show was filmed. Leading the *H*arlem *E*astside *L*ifesaving *P*rogram, a combined team of police officers, firefighters, and medics, was fearless Battalion Chief Meacham. Rushing around the city coaxing jumpers off bridges, escaped cougars out of tenements, terrified residents out of burning buildings, and mad bombers out of subway tunnels were his earnest team members: police officers Barton and Alba, paramedics Pappas and Rodriguez, and firefighters Ryan and Ballantry. Kathleen was the Chief's understandably worried wife.

HA! (Network), see *Comedy Central*

HACK (*Adventure*)
FIRST TELECAST: *September 27, 2002*
LAST TELECAST:
BROADCAST HISTORY:
Sep 2002–Jun 2003, CBS Fri 9:00–10:00
Jul 2003– , CBS Sat 9:00–10:00
CAST:
Mike Olshansky.....................David Morse
Marcellus Washington............Andre Braugher
Father Tom "Grizz" Grzelak.......George Dzundza
Heather Olshansky................Donna Murphy
Michael Olshansky Jr............Matthew Borish
Faith O'Connor (2003–).........Bebe Neuwirth
Mike Olshansky was a former Philadelphia cop who had been kicked off the force for taking money from a crime scene. He regretted his mistake, but now he was going to pay for it. With his career in law enforcement up in flames Mike had turned to driving a cab to make a living—and found that his need to help people persisted regardless of whether or not he was wearing a badge. He helped a mother and daughter hide from her abusive husband, tracked down the identity of a homeless man who died in his cab, helped a john get his wedding band back from the hooker who had stolen it, protected a woman from a stalker and helped clear a man wrongfully arrested for murder. When he needed help or information, he often turned to his ex-partner, Marcellus, who was still on the force and indebted to Mike for not revealing the fact that he had taken some of the money, too. Grizz was Mike's best friend, drinking buddy, and confidant—providing both spiritual counsel and sound advice. Although his hours made it difficult, Mike tried hard to maintain relationships with his young son, Michael, and his ex-wife, Heather, who still had feelings for him. In the spring he started dating Faith, his high school girlfriend.

At the end of the season Mike, facing criminal charges for taking the money, found out that Marcellus had in fact been skimming money from drug busts for years. Internal Affairs suspected Marcellus and was pressuring Mike to testify against him, and Mike was tempted to do so. But Marcellus got his hands on evidence that the prosecuting attorney was himself involved in illegal activities and blackmailed him into dropping the investigation against him and reducing the charges against Mike to a misdemeanor with no jail time. Now agonized Mike was indebted to his crooked "friend." Mike told Marcellus that, despite his help, he couldn't deal with his unethical tactics and didn't want to be friends anymore. Meanwhile girlfriend Faith broke up with Mike, and ex-wife Heather moved in with the doctor she had been dating.

HAGEN (*Detective Drama*)
FIRST TELECAST: *March 1, 1980*
LAST TELECAST: *April 24, 1980*
BROADCAST HISTORY:
Mar 1980–Apr 1980, CBS Sat 10:00–11:00
Apr 1980, CBS Thu 9:00–10:00
CAST:
Paul Hagen..........................Chad Everett
Carl Palmer............................Arthur Hill
Jody..................................Aldine King
Mrs. Chavez......................Carmen Zapata
Paul Hagen and Carl Palmer made an interesting, if somewhat mismatched, team. Paul was a lover of the great outdoors, a hunter, and an accomplished tracker. Carl was a well-known San Francisco attorney, cosmopolitan, and attuned to all the subtle nuances of the legal system. Merging their respective skills, they teamed to solve difficult criminal cases, Paul doing most of the legwork and Carl handling the legal complications. Jody was Carl's secretary and Mrs. Chavez his housekeeper.

HAGGIS BAGGIS (*Quiz*)
FIRST TELECAST: *June 30, 1958*
LAST TELECAST: *September 29, 1958*
BROADCAST HISTORY:
Jun 1958–Sep 1958, NBC Mon 7:30–8:00
EMCEE:
Jack Linkletter
Contestants on *Haggis Baggis* faced a large game board consisting of 25 squares. The object was to guess the identity of the celebrity whose picture was revealed, bit by bit, as the squares were uncovered. The contestants picked questions corresponding to different squares, and upon answering correctly got to see what was behind that square. The winner (first to name the celebrity) had his choice of either of two groups of prizes, one labeled haggis (luxury items) and the other, baggis (utilitarian items). If the runner-up could guess which group the winner had taken, he got the other.

Haggis Baggis was also seen on NBC daytime, where it continued until June 1959.

HAIL THE CHAMP (*Children's*)
FIRST TELECAST: *September 22, 1951*
LAST TELECAST: *June 14, 1952*
BROADCAST HISTORY:
Sep 1951–Dec 1951, ABC Sat 6:30–7:00
Dec 1951–Jun 1952, ABC Sat 6:00–6:30
EMCEE:
Herb Allen

Children's program in which six youngsters competed for prizes in games and stunts. Also seen on Saturday daytime from 1952–1953. From Chicago.

HAIL TO THE CHIEF (*Situation Comedy*)
FIRST TELECAST: *April 9, 1985*
LAST TELECAST: *July 30, 1985*
BROADCAST HISTORY:
Apr 1985–Jul 1985, ABC Tue 9:30–10:00
CAST:
President Julia Mansfield.............. Patty Duke
Gen. Oliver Mansfield................. Ted Bessell
Premier Dmitri Zolotov/Ivan Zolotov ... Dick Shawn
Sec. of State LaRue Hawkes......... Glynn Turman
Helmut Luger.................. Herschel Bernardi
Gen. Hannibal Stryker................ John Vernon
Sen. Sam Cotton .... Murray Hamilton
Doug Mansfield................ Ricky Paul Goldin
Lucy Mansfield .... Quinn Cummings
Willy Mansfield .... Taliesin Jaffe
Lenore .... Maxine Stuart
Rev. Billy Joe Bickerstaff............. Richard Paul
Darlene the spy .... Alexa Hamilton
Randy................................ Joel Brooks
Raoul, the butler .... Chick Vennera

The President of the United States was surrounded by a cabinet of crazies in this comedy about life in the White House under the first woman chief executive. Created by the creator of *Soap* (Susan Harris), it used the same type of semi-serialized story lines as the earlier hit, and even some similar plots. Madame President was confronted by such ongoing crises as her husband Oliver's inability to make love; a lunatic major threatening to start World War III; an equally lunatic Russian Premier Zolotov on the hot line; the blackmailing of her husband by KGB head Ivan (the Premier's twin brother) after Oliver was caught in a compromising position with sexy spy Darlene; son Doug's impregnating of General Stryker's daughter; and an attempt to impeach her by ranting Rev. Billy Joe, who maintained that Satan had put this woman in the White House.

Hawkes was the sensible black Secretary of State, who was often outshouted by National Security Advisor Luger and Gen. Stryker. The President's three children were tennis pro Doug, Lucy (who had the hots for Raoul the butler), and little Willy; Lenore was Julia's bedazzled mom, and Randy her chief Secret Service agent. The whole ensemble was voted out of TV office after only seven episodes.

HAL IN HOLLYWOOD, see *Sawyer Views Hollywood*

HALF & HALF (*Situation Comedy*)
FIRST TELECAST: *September 23, 2002*
LAST TELECAST:
BROADCAST HISTORY:
Sep 2002– , UPN Mon 9:30–10:00
CAST:
Dee Dee Thorne.................... Essence Atkins
Mona Thorne......................... Rachel True
Phyllis Thorne.................... Telma Hopkins
Big Dee Dee Thorne............... Valarie Pettiford
Spencer Williams........ Theron "Chico" Benymon
**Charles Thorne* .... Obba Babatunde
**Adam Benet* .... Alec Mapa

*Occasional

Mona and Dee Dee were half sisters living in San Francisco who had never known each other when they were growing up in this opposites-attract comedy. Mona's mother, Phyllis, had divorced her father, Charles, when Mona was a little girl. Since feisty outspoken Phyllis and Charles' second wife, bitchy status-conscious Big Dee Dee, hated each other, there was little opportunity for their daughters to meet. All that changed as Mona prepared to moved into a penthouse apartment that wealthy Charles had been promising her for years. While she was settling in, Dee Dee showed up with her pushy mother who wanted the apartment for her—Dee Dee got the penthouse and Mona, to make peace, took another apartment in the building. Living in the same building gave them plenty of time to get to know each other. Mona, who worked for a record company, was supporting herself, while spoiled Dee Dee was in law school. Mona was practical, had a self-deprecating sense of humor and not much of a social life, while perky Dee Dee, the eternal optimist, had no idea what it meant to be on a budget and was a social butterfly. Despite their differences they found they liked each other—which certainly couldn't be said for their mothers—and they became fast friends. Mona's best friend and confidant, Spencer, was a fellow A&R executive at Delicious Records, where overtly gay Adam was the receptionist.

HALF HOUR COMEDY HOUR (*Comedy*)
BROADCAST HISTORY:
MTV
30 minutes
Produced: *1988–1993*
Premiered: *August 2, 1988*
HOST:
Mario Joyner (1989–1993)

Standup comedy taped at the Catch a Rising Star comedy club in New York City. Richard Belzer hosted the premiere episode, which featured comedians Kevin Meaney, Ken Ober, and Mario Joyner. Various hosts presided until 1989, when Joyner was named the regular host.

½ HOUR COMEDY HOUR, THE (*Comedy/Variety*)
FIRST TELECAST: *July 5, 1983*
LAST TELECAST: *August 9, 1983*
BROADCAST HISTORY:
Jul 1983–Aug 1983, ABC Tue 8:00–8:30
HOSTS:
Thom Sharp
Arsenio Hall
REGULARS:
John Moschitta
Peter Isacksen
John Paragon
Vic Dunlop
Jan Hooks

Victoria Jackson
Barry Diamond
Diane Stilwell

Sight gags, one-liners, and skits were packed into this frantic summer comedy show, which was on and off the schedule faster than one of John Moschitta's motor-mouthed monologues. (Moschitta was known at the time for his incredibly fast-talking commercials.) Routines on the premiere included "Bonan the Barbarian," "Jennifer Holiday-In," and "In Search of the Ridiculous." Besides the repertory company of comics, there was an assortment of guest stars including Henny Youngman—who must have felt right at home, since he had practically invented the TV one-liner years before.

HALF HOUR THEATRE, see *ABC Dramatic Shorts—1952–1953*

HALF NELSON (*Detective Comedy/Drama*)

FIRST TELECAST: *March 24, 1985*
LAST TELECAST: *May 10, 1985*
BROADCAST HISTORY:
Mar 1985, NBC Sun 9:00–11:00
Mar 1985–May 1985, NBC Fri 9:00–10:00
CAST:
Rocky Nelson .... Joe Pesci
Chester Long .... Fred Williamson
Annie O'Hara .... Victoria Jackson
Kurt .... Dick Butkus
Beau .... Bubba Smith
Det. Hamill .... Gary Grubbs
Dean Martin .... Himself

"Why doesn't someone standup to all the corruption in Beverly Hills?" read the ad. Next page: "He *is* standing up!" Rocky Nelson was a short detective, a former New York City undercover cop who moved to Beverly Hills, where he got a job with an expensive private security service for the rich and famous, while trying to break into acting. His police experience certainly came in handy, though it did not endear him to either his boss, Chester Long, or Det. Hamill of the Beverly Hills Police. Rocky was supposed to guard bejeweled poodles and manicured lawns, not solve crimes. However, he found that his short stature allowed him to sneak into secret places and obtain clues, simply because nobody took such a "little guy" seriously. Kurt and Beau were two of his fellow guards at the Patrol—all muscle and no brains—and Annie was the slightly daffy secretary at the office. Rocky liked the job mostly for the contact it gave him with celebrities, including client and confidant Dean Martin. Maybe one of them would give the little guy his big break?

HALLMARK CHANNEL(Network) (*General Entertainment Cable Network*)

LAUNCHED:
September 1988
SUBSCRIBERS (MAY 2003):
51.9 million (49% U.S.)

Originally a religious channel, this network went through many changes as it was taken over by commercial interests and switched to entertainment programming. The network was launched in 1988 as VISN (Vision Interfaith Satellite Network) by the National Interfaith Cable Coalition, a consortium of nearly eighty Protestant, Jewish, Catholic, and other organizations. In October 1992 it merged with ACTS (American Christian Television Service, launched on cable by the Southern Baptist Convention in June 1984), and was renamed VISN/ACTS. In 1994 it became the Faith & Values Channel. The channel was interdenominational and emphasized that it did not proselytize, favor any faith, or indulge in on-air fundraising (it carried advertising to defray expenses). Programming included discussion programs (*Catch the Spirit, Common Sense Religion, The God Squad*), documentaries (*Jewish Chronicles, World of Ideas*), youth programs (*Sunshine Factory, Straight Talk from Teens*), music (*Homeland Harmony, CCM-TV, Solid Rock V.O.D.*), and dramas illustrating family values (*The Campbells, Family Theater*).

In September 1996 the name was changed again, to the Odyssey Channel, and the schedule began to feature reruns of well-known network series that embodied family values, such as *Our House, Father Murphy,* and *Brooklyn Bridge.* Purely religious programs were for the most part relegated to daytime and weekends, although some inspirational series (*Quiet Triumphs,* a celebrity interview show) and music programs (CeCe Wynan's show, *Bobby Jones Gospel Hour*) could still be seen in prime-time. Then in 1998, Hallmark Entertainment and the Jim Henson Co. took control, and the channel moved even further away from religion. Daytime became a mix of religious programs, children's programs, and family movies, while the evening consisted of Hallmark-produced mini-series (*Gulliver's Travels, Lonesome Dove*), reruns of *The Hallmark Hall of Fame,* and other films. Film historian Leonard Maltin hosted a showcase of old Hal Roach films.

By the early 2000s the name had been changed again—to The Hallmark Channel (August 2001)—and the children's programming had been dumped. Daytime consisted of a sea of elderly reruns (*Perry Mason, The Beverly Hillbillies, Bonanza, The Rifleman*) while prime-time held Hallmark movies and reruns of *Touched by an Angel.* There was also occasional original programming such as the documentary series *Adoption* (2002) and the TV movies *Straight from the Heart* and *Love Comes Softly* (both 2003). Long gone were *The God Squad* and most of the religious programming. So much for diversity in American media.

HALLMARK SUMMER THEATRE (*Dramatic Anthology*)

FIRST TELECAST: *July 6, 1952*
LAST TELECAST: *August 31, 1952*
BROADCAST HISTORY:
Jul 1952–Aug 1952, NBC Sun 10:00–10:30
PRODUCER/DIRECTOR:
Albert McCleery

The individual was the focus of this live summer drama series, which was sponsored by Hallmark Cards. The plays were produced using the theater-in-the-round technique, with a minimum of props to suggest time periods ranging from the American Revolution to the present day. Stories usually involved a crisis or act of courage in one person's life. The actors appearing were generally lesser-known performers from the Broadway stage.

HALLS OF IVY, THE (*Situation Comedy*)

FIRST TELECAST: *October 19, 1954*

LAST TELECAST: *September 29, 1955*
BROADCAST HISTORY:
Oct 1954–Jul 1955, CBS Tue 8:30–9:00
Jul 1955–Sep 1955, CBS Thu 10:30–11:00
CAST:
Dr. William Todhunter Hall .... Ronald Colman
Vicky Hall .... Benita Hume
Alice .... Mary Wickes
Clarence Wellman .... Herb Butterfield
Dr. Merriweather (1954) .... Ray Collins
Dr. Merriweather (1954–1955) .... James Todd
THEME:
"Halls of Ivy," by Henry Russell and Vick Knight

Dr. William Todhunter Hall was president of scenic Ivy College, somewhere in the Midwest, in this filmed comedy about a literate, witty college administrator. The school's students, its faculty, and its board of governors all figured in the stories, as did Dr. Hall's wife Vicky ("a former actress"), their housekeeper, Alice, and Chairman of the Board of Governors Clarence Wellman. *The Halls of Ivy* was adapted from the radio series of the same name (1950–1952), with Ronald Colman and his wife Benita Hume re-creating their radio roles. However, its very literacy and lack of physical action militated against it in the video medium, and it soon disappeared.

One of the more memorable elements of the series was its theme ("We love the Halls of Ivy/That surround us here today . . ."), rendered in suitably collegiate fashion by a male chorus. The song achieved some popularity on records during the early 1950s.

HAMPTONS, THE (*Drama*)
FIRST TELECAST: *July 27, 1983*
LAST TELECAST: *August 24, 1983*
BROADCAST HISTORY:
Jul 1983–Aug 1983, ABC Wed 9:00–10:00
CAST:
Peter Chadway .... Michael Goodwin
Lee Chadway .... Leigh Taylor-Young
Brian Chadway .... Craig Sheffer
Jay Mortimer .... John Reilly
Adrienne Duncan Mortimer .... Bibi Besch
Tracy Mortimer .... Holly Roberts
Cheryl Ashcroft .... Kate Dezina
David Landau .... Philip Casnoff
Nick Atwater .... Daniel Pilon
Karen Harper .... Kathleen Buse
Penny Drake .... Jada Rowland
Ada .... Fran Carlon

Daytime soap-opera maven Gloria Monty produced this prime-time serial, which had a short run during the summer of 1983. As in other prime-time soaps, the principal characters were rich and miserable, but at least the setting was different: New York City and the fashionable nearby resort, the Hamptons. Two old-line families, the Chadways and the Duncan Mortimers, were linked both by romance and co-ownership of the chic Duncan-Chadway department store chain. Corporate intrigue and sexual scandal swirled through the short summer run, and by the fifth and final episode "good guy" Peter Chadway stood accused of murdering Penny Drake during his battle to retain control of Duncan-Chadway; conniving Jay Mortimer, who was trying to take the company away from him, was exposed as having an incestuous relationship with his stepdaughter Tracy (Jay: "You know I'd do anything for you." Tracy: "Then stay out of my bedroom, Daddy!"); Jay's drunken wife Adrienne was enraged; and suave mogul Nick Atwater was making a strong play for Peter's loyal wife, Lee.

HANDLE WITH CARE, see *Mail Story, The*

HANDS OF MYSTERY (*Suspense Anthology*)
FIRST TELECAST: *September 30, 1949*
LAST TELECAST: *December 11, 1951*
BROADCAST HISTORY:
Sep 1949–Jul 1950, DUM Fri 8:00–8:30
Jul 1950–Sep 1951, DUM Fri 9:00–9:30
Sep 1951–Dec 1951, DUM Tue 10:00–10:30

The TV plays in this live series generally revolved around a theme of murder or suspense, with episode titles such as "Don't Go Out Alone" and "Vulture of the Waterfront." Included were some stories of the supernatural and others based on true incidents, such as "The Man Who Killed Hitler." A novel aspect of the series, no doubt suggested to producer Larry Menkin by DuMont's minimal budget, was the almost complete absence of props and sets, with inventive camera angles and lighting used instead to suggest the locale. Lesser-known actors and actresses were featured.

The title of this series was changed twice, from the original *Hands of Murder* to *Hands of Destiny* in April 1950 and finally to *Hands of Mystery* in August 1950.

HANGIN' WITH MR. COOPER (*Situation Comedy*)
FIRST TELECAST: *September 22, 1992*
LAST TELECAST: *August 30, 1997*
BROADCAST HISTORY:
Sep 1992–Jul 1993, ABC Tue 8:30–9:00
Aug 1993–Sep 1993, ABC Fri 8:30–9:30
Sep 1993–Mar 1994, ABC Fri 9:30–10:00
May 1994–Aug 1996, ABC Fri 9:30–10:00
Jun 1997–Aug 1997, ABC Sat 8:30–9:00
Aug 1997, ABC Fri 9:30–10:00
CAST:
Mark Cooper .... Mark Curry
Vanessa Russell .... Holly Robinson
Robin Dumars (1992–1993) .... Dawnn Lewis
Earvin .... Omar Gooding
Coach Ricketts (1992–1993) ...... Roger E. Mosley
Isaac (1992–1993) .... George Lemore
Andre Bailis (1992–1994) ...... Christopher Carter
Tyler Foster (1993–1997) .... Marquise Wilson
Geneva Lee (1993–1997) ..... Saundra Quarterman
Nicole Lee (age 7) (1993–1997) .... Raven-Symone
Ms. P. J. Moore (1993–1994) .... Nell Carter
Thaddeus Jamison White (1993–1994)
.... Dominic Hoffman
Steve Warner (1994–1995) .... Steve White
Coach Corley (1994–1995) .... Ron Canada
THEME:
by En Vogue

Tall, gangly Mark Curry starred in this black, nineties variation on *Three's Company*. Mark Cooper was a former NBA player who, when his career faltered, moved back to his old high school in Oakland, California, to become a coach. Sharing his house (and the rent) were two beautiful women, old friend Robin, a music teacher, and sexy Vanessa, who worked for a brokerage firm. Their relationship was platonic, so stories revolved around their dating misadventures as well as Mark's experiences in his new career as a teacher. A loose, easygoing prankster, he created trouble everywhere. A suitable foil arrived in the second season in the person of formidable principal P. J. Moore. Adding to the fun at the house (which Mark and Vanessa had just bought) was cousin Geneva, who moved in (replacing Robin) with her forthright little daughter, Nicole.

Others who moved through the light, bright little stories included fun-loving neighborhood kid Tyler, rival coaches Ricketts and Corley, college buddy Steve, and assorted students.

In the fall of 1995, Geneva became principal at Oakbridge High School, making her Mark's boss as well as his housemate. Mark was increasingly attracted to Vanessa (as were most of the rest of Oakland's eligible males), and proposed more than once, but it took her a while to warm up to him. When the series did not return in Fall 1996, it appeared that viewers would never find out if they got together, but in an unusual series of original episodes run during the summer of 1997 they were engaged. The last episode, on August 30, 1997, was supposed to be their wedding day—but at the end they merely waved goodbye to viewers, without having taken their vows.

An interesting bit of trivia is that the house in which Mr. Cooper "hung" was originally that of the East Coast Seavers on *Growing Pains*; in the first episode, Jason Seaver (Alan Thicke) himself showed up to wish them well! Subsequently, the set was changed without explanation.

HANGING IN (*Situation Comedy*)

FIRST TELECAST: *August 8, 1979*
LAST TELECAST: *August 29, 1979*
BROADCAST HISTORY:
Aug 1979, CBS Wed 8:30–9:00

CAST:
Louis Harper .... Bill Macy
Maggie Gallagher .... Barbara Rhoades
Sam Dickey .... Dennis Burkley
Pinky Nolan .... Nedra Volz
Rita Zefferelli .... Darian Mathias

EXECUTIVE PRODUCER:
Norman Lear

Even educators have to cope with politics, or so this summer comedy series seemed to say. Lou Harper was a former pro football star who had subsequently devoted himself to helping the poor and underprivileged through various community projects. When he was offered the presidency of Braddock University, he brought his humanitarian attitudes with him, not realizing the problems this could create with the University board, prominent fund-raisers, and the university staff. Helping Harper, and often providing a practical solution to the problems he created, were Maggie Gallagher, Dean of Faculty; Sam Dickey, Director of Development and the university's highly manipulative public-relations man; and Pinky Nolan, Harper's diminutive but outspoken housekeeper.

The story of how this series got on the air is even more interesting than the program itself. The original concept was not about college politics, but about government politics in Washington, D.C. Early in 1978, when it became apparent that the long-running comedy *Maude* was getting stale, that series' producers decided to liven things up by moving their star to Washington. Maude was appointed to fill out the term of a congressman who had recently died, moved to Washington with her husband Walter (Bill Macy), and began to confront her inherited staff with her liberal outlook. After only two episodes in this new setting, however, Beatrice Arthur decided that she did not want to continue as Maude, and the series abruptly left the air.

The production company still believed the idea was workable and they filmed another series pilot, titled *Onward and Upward,* using essentially the same script and supporting cast. The only difference was that the Maude character had become a black former pro football star, played by John Amos. Creative differences between Mr. Amos and the producers led to his departure and a new series lead was sought. During this period the title was changed to *Mr. Dooley* and then to *Mr. Dugan.* Cleavon Little was hired to star and a third pilot was filmed, still with the same supporting cast. *Mr. Dugan* was scheduled to premiere on CBS in March of 1979—it even had on-air promotion—but was pulled at the last minute, when the producers received a generally negative reaction from a number of real-life black politicians who had been given a preview of the first episode. The politicians felt that the show's comic portrayal of a black politician was demeaning to all blacks.

Undaunted, the producers reworked the project again, finally coming up with *Hanging In.* The premise was the same, but now the setting had been changed to a college. Ironically, *Maude*'s Bill Macy resurfaced as the star of the version that finally did air. The supporting cast, except for Darian Mathias, had been in all four versions of the pilot and must have known their lines pretty well by the time they got to *Hanging In.*

After all this travail, *Hanging In* lasted just four weeks.

HANK (*Situation Comedy*)

FIRST TELECAST: *September 17, 1965*
LAST TELECAST: *September 2, 1966*
BROADCAST HISTORY:
Sep 1965–Sep 1966, NBC Fri 8:00–8:30

CAST:
Hank Dearborn .... Dick Kallman
Doris Royal .... Linda Foster
Dr. Lewis Royal .... Howard St. John
Prof. McKillup .... Lloyd Corrigan
Tina Dearborn .... Katie Sweet
Franny .... Kelly Jean Peters
Ossie Weiss .... Dabbs Greer
Mrs. Ethel Weiss .... Sheila Bromley
Miss Mittleman .... Dorothy Neumann
Asst. Coach Gazzari .... Lou Wills, Jr.

Dick Kallman, a promising young Broadway and Hollywood comic of the 1950s and 1960s who never quite made it to major stardom, was showcased in this single-season campus comedy. He played Hank Dearborn, a resourceful young man determined to get a college education despite his lack of funds or family support (his parents had been killed in a car accident when he was 15, leaving him to support his baby sister, Tina). Hank simply "dropped in" to classes at Western State University, filling the seats of students he knew would be absent, and wearing a variety of ingenious disguises.

To support himself and Tina, he engaged in a number of moneymaking schemes, including running a campus laundry service, a watch and shoe repair shop, a dating agency, etc. He was always one step ahead of Dr. Royal, the registrar, who was bent on tracking down the campus phantom. Just about everyone else was in on the secret, however, including Doris, Hank's girlfriend and Dr. Royal's daughter; Prof. McKillup; and Franny, Tina's baby-sitter. The track coach, Ossie Weiss, after seeing Hank sprint to classes, wanted him to join the track team.

HANK MCCUNE SHOW, THE (*Situation Comedy*)

FIRST TELECAST: *September 9, 1950*
LAST TELECAST: *December 2, 1950*
BROADCAST HISTORY:
Sep 1950–Dec 1950, NBC Sat 7:00–7:30
CAST:
Hank McCune .... himself
ALSO:
Larry Keating — Hanley Stafford
Arthur Q. Bryan — George Cleveland
Sara Berner — Florence Bates
Frank Nelson
Tammy Kiper

This early filmed situation comedy starred "likable blunderer" Hank McCune, who was constantly getting himself into comic predicaments of his own making. For example, on the first telecast Hank attended a convention held by his sponsor, Peter Paul candy bars, in Atlantic City, where he proceeded to foul up the hotel reservations, infuriate lifeguards, and disrupt the neighboring convention of a mystic fraternal order. Larry Keating played Hank's sidekick. The program was filmed in Hollywood and first ran as a local series in 1949.

The comedy on *The Hank McCune Show* was slapstick, and the show quickly disappeared from the air. However, one aspect of it has remained with us, with a vengeance. Toward the end of its review of the first telecast, *Variety* noted, almost incidentally, that the program

> . . . has an innovation in a sound track that contains audience laughter. Although the show is lensed on film without a studio audience, there are chuckles and yocks dubbed in. Whether this induces a jovial mood in home viewers is still to be determined, but the practice may have unlimited possibilities if it's spread to include canned peals of hilarity, thunderous ovations and gasps of sympathy.

This is the earliest documented use of a laugh track on TV.

A syndicated version of *The Hank McCune Show*, with a different supporting cast, was seen briefly in 1953–1954.

HANNA-BARBERA HAPPY HOUR, THE (*Comedy/Variety*)

FIRST TELECAST: *April 13, 1978*
LAST TELECAST: *May 4, 1978*
BROADCAST HISTORY:
Apr 1978–May 1978, NBC Thu 8:00–9:00
REGULARS:
Honey and Sis (puppets)
The Rudy Baga Band
PUPPETRY BY:
Iwao Takamoto
EXECUTIVE PRODUCER:
Joseph Barbera

William Hanna and Joseph Barbera, famous for such cartoon creations as the Flintstones and Yogi Bear, tried their hands at a prime-time variety hour with this short-lived series. The program was certainly unusual. Instead of a live host, it had as emcees two life-sized puppets, Honey (the flashy blonde) and Sis (the insecure redhead), who participated in skits and songs with such live guests as Tony Randall, Dan Haggerty, Twiggy, and Leif Garrett. Regular features were "The Disco of Life," where puppets and stars swapped gags, and "The Truth Tub," where guests could confess their comic problems.

The appearance of the show was that of a normal, slickly produced, live comedy-variety hour, and Honey and Sis appeared remarkably lifelike. (They were animated by a team of six men who stood behind them but who could not be seen on screen, due to an electronic masking technique called chroma-key.) However, TV viewers apparently preferred human hosts, for this series attracted a small audience and was canceled after four weeks.

HAPPILY EVER AFTER, see *With This Ring*

HAPPY (*Situation Comedy*)

FIRST TELECAST: *June 8, 1960*
LAST TELECAST: *September 8, 1961*
BROADCAST HISTORY:
Jun 1960–Sep 1960, NBC Wed 9:00–9:30
Jan 1961–Sep 1961, NBC Fri 7:30–8:00
CAST:
Happy .... David and Steven Born
Sally Day .... Yvonne Lime
Chris Day .... Ronnie Burns
Charlie Dooley .... Lloyd Corrigan
Clara Mason .... Doris Packer

Sally and Chris Day were a young married couple who were managers and part-owners (with Clara Mason) of the Desert Palm Motel, a very posh resort. Their efforts to keep the hotel running smoothly were often complicated by the well-meaning but not always useful assistance of Uncle Charlie. The most novel aspect of this show revolved around the Days' infant son, Happy, who was played by the Born twins. All of the goings-on at the hotel, business and personal, were observed by Happy, who regularly voiced his reactions through facial expressions and an off-screen voice—a variation on the observer-speaking-to-the-camera device used by George Burns in the *Burns and Allen Show*, and elsewhere.

HAPPY DAYS (*Variety*)

FIRST TELECAST: *June 25, 1970*
LAST TELECAST: *August 27, 1970*
BROADCAST HISTORY:
Jun 1970–Aug 1970, CBS Thu 8:00–9:00
REGULARS:
Louis Nye
Bob Elliott
Ray Goulding
Chuck McCann
Julie McWhirter

Alan Copeland
The Happy Days Singers
The Wisa D'Orso Dancers
The Happy Days Band with Jack Elliott and Allyn Ferguson
Laara Lacey
Clive Clerk
Bill O'Berlin
Jim McGeorge
Jerry Dexter

Songs, dance numbers, and comedy blackouts and sketches were all part of this summer variety series hosted by comedian Louis Nye. All of the material, comedic and musical, was based on the 1930s and 1940s, the period referred to in the title as the "happy days." Sounds of the big bands—including appearances by Duke Ellington—Bob and Ray satirizing old radio shows, as well as real excerpts from actual shows of the era and parties hosted by such comic strip characters as Mandrake the Magician and Little Orphan Annie were all woven into the show. There were even filmed interviews with major motion picture stars George Raft, Edward G. Robinson, and Charles Laughton talking about their memories of the period. Louis Nye had a regular spot as a song tester, trying to pick big potential hits; and Chuck McCann performed as The Great Voodini, the world's worst, and clumsiest, escape artist.

HAPPY DAYS (*Situation Comedy*)
FIRST TELECAST: *January 15, 1974*
LAST TELECAST: *July 12, 1984*
BROADCAST HISTORY:
Jan 1974–Sep 1983, ABC Tue 8:00–8:30
Sep 1983–Jan 1984, ABC Tue 8:30–9:00
Apr 1984–May 1984, ABC Tue 8:30–9:00
Jun 1984–Jul 1984, ABC Thu 8:00–8:30
CAST:
Richie Cunningham (1974–1980) ..... Ron Howard
Arthur "Fonzie" Fonzarelli .... Henry Winkler
Howard Cunningham .... Tom Bosley
Marion Cunningham .... Marion Ross
Warren "Potsie" Weber (1974–1983) .... Anson Williams
Ralph Malph (1974–1980)............. Donny Most
Joanie Cunningham .... Erin Moran
Chuck Cunningham (1974) .... Gavan O'Herlihy
Chuck Cunningham (1974–1975) .... Randolph Roberts
Bag Zombroski (1974–1975) .... Neil J. Schwartz
Marsha Simms (1974–1976)......... Beatrice Colen
Gloria (1974–1975) .... Linda Purl
Wendy (1974–1975) .... Misty Rowe
Trudy (1974–1975) .... Tita Bell
Arnold (Matsuo Takahashi) (1975–1976, 1982–1983) .... Pat Morita
Alfred Delvecchio (1976–1982) .... Al Molinaro
Charles "Chachi" Arcola (1977–1984) ... Scott Baio
Lori Beth Allen Cunningham (1977–1982) .... Lynda Goodfriend
**Eugene Belvin (1980–1982)* .... Denis Mandel
**Bobby (1980–1984)* .... Harris Kal
Jenny Piccalo (1980–1983) .... Cathy Silvers
Roger Phillips (1980–1984)........... Ted McGinley
Flip Phillips (1982–1983) .... Billy Warlock
K. C. Cunningham (1982–1983).... Crystal Bernard
Ashley Pfister (1982–1983) .... Linda Purl
Heather Pfister (1982–1983)..... Heather O'Rourke
**Officer Kirk* .... Ed Peck

*Occasional

MUSIC:
"Rock Around the Clock" (original recording by Bill Haley & His Comets); "Happy Days" (Gimbel-Fox); and recordings by Fats Domino, Connie Francis, Johnnie Ray, Kay Starr, and other stars of the 1950s and 1960s

Nostalgia for the 1950s became big business in the mid-1970s, and leading the wave was this updated version of teenage life in the mid-1950s. It started modestly and built in popularity until in the 1976–1977 season *Happy Days* was the number-one program in all of television. Along the way it made a major star out of one of its supporting actors.

Happy Days changed dramatically from the series that premiered in 1974. Originally it was the story of two high-school kids, Richie Cunningham and his pal Potsie Weber, at Jefferson High in Milwaukee, Wisconsin. Howard Cunningham, Richie's father, ran a hardware store while Chuck was Richie's college-bound older brother and Joanie his 13-year-old kid sister. Richie and most of his friends hung out at Arnold's Drive-In, a malt shop near the school.

Richie was supposed to be the innocent teenager and Potsie his more worldly pal. So as not to make the show too much like *Ozzie & Harriet*, however, the producers added some slightly more extreme counterpoint in the person of the greasy-haired motorcycle kid, Fonzie. That was the move that made the show a hit. Instead of the fairly hackneyed Richie-Potsie relationship, the show came to center on the relationship between the "cool" dropout Fonz, and the "straight" kids represented by Richie. Henry Winkler made the character of Fonzie three-dimensional, vulnerable as well as hip. One of the classic episodes, which ran traditionally every Christmas, was the one that first showed the Fonz's own pad, a dingy, cluttered room with his motorcycle in the middle of the floor—and only a tiny, pathetic tree to indicate that it was Christmas. Too proud to admit to being alone for the holiday, the Fonz—whose father had deserted him at the age of three—nevertheless allowed himself to be brought into the Cunninghams' home to share in their celebration.

As Fonzie's popularity spread (his thumbs-up gesture and "aaayyh!" became trademarks), the show became a bigger and bigger hit. Winkler moved from his original fifth billing to third, then second behind Ron Howard and finally first when Howard left in 1980. But ABC claimed that there would be no spin-off series, because without the Richie-Fonzie contrast there would be no *Happy Days*. Not only did Fonzie's billing change as the series grew, but so did his residence. During the 1975–1976 season he moved into a small apartment over the Cunningham garage. He was thus always available to give Richie advice about life and girls (the Fonz made every girl in Milwaukee swoon).

Changes in the cast were fairly minor in the early years. Dozens of high-school kids came and went, and Richie's older brother disappeared from the family early on, never to be referred to again. Arnold, the Japanese who owned Arnold's, first showed his face in 1975 but was replaced by a new owner, Alfred, in 1976. (Pat Morita had gotten his own series that fall, *Mr. T. and*

Tina. He returned for occasional episodes beginning in 1982.) Two lower-middle-class girls who turned up briefly in late 1975—on a double date with Richie and Fonzie—quickly went on to a series of their own, *Laverne & Shirley.* Chachi arrived in 1977, as Fonzie's young cousin, the same season that Richie began going steady with Lori Beth, with the performers who played both roles turning up together on an NBC series, *Who's Watching the Kids,* the following fall as well.

One of the most popular characters passing through was Pinky Tuscadero (played by Roz Kelly), the sexy motorcycle queen who wrapped the Fonz around her little finger—as "cool" as he was, she was "cooler." An old girlfriend of his, she roared into town in September 1976 with her Pinkettes (Tina and Lola, played by Doris Hess and Kelly Sanders) to join the Fonz in a demolition derby. A season later her sister Leather Tuscadero (played by rock star Suzi Quatro) turned up on a couple of episodes with her rock group, the Suedes. More nostalgic guests on the show ranged from Buffalo Bob Smith *(Howdy Doody)* to John Hart *(The Lone Ranger),* Frankie Avalon, and Jack Smith, onetime emcee of *You Asked For It.* Jack played the host of the mythical *You Wanted to See It* show in an episode where Fonzie set a new world's record by leaping his motorcycle over 14 garbage cans behind Arnold's Drive-In, on live TV.

As the 1976–1977 season ended, Richie and the gang graduated from high school and it seemed that Fonzie, the dropout, might be left behind. But at the last minute it turned out that the Fonz, while working days at various garages, had been going to night school and would get his diploma too. Richie, Potsie, and Ralph enrolled at the University of Wisconsin at Milwaukee, with Fonzie still around (though not enrolled) to advise them on love and life. Richie enrolled as a journalism student and Potsie as a psychology major, while Ralph followed in his father's footsteps to become an eye doctor—though he really wanted to be a comedian.

In 1980 major changes began to take place in both the cast and story line of *Happy Days.* Richie and Ralph graduated from college, joined the army, and were shipped off to Greenland (Ron Howard and Donny Most had left the show). From there the unseen Richie corresponded with and eventually married Lori Beth—by telephone, with Fonz as his stand-in. Lori Beth visited him from time to time and in 1981 gave birth to a son, Richie, Jr. Back in Milwaukee the Fonz had become so straight that he was now a co-owner of Arnold's, a shop teacher at Jefferson High, and operator of Bronco's Garage. "Mr. Cool" had a close brush with serious romance in 1982–83 when he fell for divorcée Ashley Pfister and her cute daughter Heather, but it didn't last. In 1983 he joined Marion's nephew Roger Phillips, an English teacher and basketball coach at Jefferson High, in a new career. Roger had just been appointed principal of the rowdy George S. Patton Vocational High School, and Fonz joined him there as Dean of Boys!

Potsie, the perennial college student, went to work for Mr. C. at Cunningham Hardware. But by this time it was the 1960s and the focus of the program turned increasingly to the next generation, particularly the rocky teenage love of Joanie and Chachi. They did their own spin-off show, *Joanie Loves Chachi,* for a time in 1982, but they never left *Happy Days* entirely. After a try at a singing career, Joanie enrolled in college and signed on as a trainee teacher at Roger's vocational school. Others of the '60s generation were Joanie's independent, boy-crazy friend Jenny Piccalo, who was finally seen after years of only being referred to; Roger's rambunctious younger brother Flip; and Howard's teenage niece K.C., who lived with the Cunninghams for a year.

The final season was a time of reunions and farewells. Richie and Lori Beth returned in the fall for a visit, with Richie, Jr., in tow, and another baby on the way. Then Richie headed for Hollywood to pursue his dream of becoming a screenwriter. In the series' final episode Richie and other former regulars returned one last time as Fonzie bought a home and adopted a young orphan named Danny, and Joanie and Chachi were finally married—by Al's look-alike brother, Father Delvecchio. With "both" their children now married (even *they* had forgotten Chuck), Howard and Marion thanked the audience for being part of their family, and made a tearful farewell.

In its later years *Happy Days* became something of an institution. In 1980 it was announced that the Fonz's leather jacket was being enshrined in the Smithsonian Institution. Three years later the *Happy Days* cast visited the real-life city of Milwaukee, and some 150,000 residents lined the streets to welcome them "home." Mr. C. got the key to the city, and the Fonz said "Aaayyh!"

The origin of this immensely successful series was a skit that appeared on *Love, American Style* in February 1972, titled "Love and the Happy Days," and starring Ron Howard and Anson Williams. The original theme song for the series was Bill Haley's famous 1955 hit record "Rock Around the Clock," which promptly became a best-seller all over again in 1974 as a result of its exposure on the show. It was later superseded as the theme by an original composition, "Happy Days," which was itself on the hit parade in 1976.

ABC aired reruns of *Happy Days* on its daytime lineup from September 1975 to March 1979, and an animated Saturday morning version from November 1980 to September 1983.

HAPPY HOUR (*Variety*)

BROADCAST HISTORY:

USA Network
60 minutes
Produced: *1999*
Premiered: *April 3, 1999*

REGULARS:

Dweezil Zappa
Ahmet Zappa
Leland Sklar & the Werewolves (band)

The very hip Zappa brothers, sons of rock legend Frank Zappa, hosted this noisy Saturday night hour of fun and games. Dweezil was the somewhat restrained, foxy one, Ahmet the tall, bald, life-of-the-party. The fun consisted of rock song sing-alongs, wild routines by a chorus of scantily clad female dancers called "The Bombshells" (who wiggled various parts of their anatomies as close to the camera lens as possible), and music by guests such as Lisa Loeb, Berlin, and Reel Big Fish. The games were played by a celebrity panel, usually five gals and five guys, consisting of offbeat names such as Chuck Woolery, Kathy Najimy, Lou Rawls, Cobi Jones, Danny Bonaduce, Christopher Darden, and WWF wrestling sexpot Sable. Among the games were Matchmakers (match the celebrity with their habits or strange jobs they've held), Star Struck (a star is pitted against their "number-one fan" to see who knows more about the star's life—that one could be scary), and Rocker or Rodent? (guess whether an extreme close-up is a picture of a rock star or a rodent), all randomly scored by Dweezil and Ahmet.

Based on the French variety show *La Fièvre* (*The Fever*).

HARBOR COMMAND (*Police Drama*)

BROADCAST HISTORY:

Syndicated only
30 minutes
Produced: *1957–1958* (39 episodes)
Released: *September 1957*

CAST:

Capt. Ralph Baxter .... Wendell Corey

Harbor Command was a straight police-action show, set in the harbor of a large city. Capt. Baxter was the plainclothes chief of the Harbor Command, fighting dope smugglers, murderers, and other assorted villains with the help of his uniformed officers.

HARBOURMASTER (*Adventure*)

FIRST TELECAST: *September 26, 1957*
LAST TELECAST: *June 29, 1958*
BROADCAST HISTORY:

Sep 1957–Dec 1957, CBS Thu 8:00–8:30
Jan 1958–Jun 1958, ABC Sun 8:30–9:00

CAST:

Capt. David Scott .... Barry Sullivan
Jeff Kittridge .... Paul Burke
Anna Morrison .... Nina Wilcox
Cap'n Dan .... Michael Keens
Danny .... Evan Elliott

Off the New England coast lay Scott Island, an idyllic little place far removed from the hustle and bustle of the mainland. David Scott's family had settled the island generations ago and had lived there ever since. A bachelor, David was the "Harbourmaster" for the island, arranging dock space for boats, anchorages, and serving as a one-man rescue squad and police force.

His hobby, which he pursued between storms, fires, and other problems, was running a boatyard. Here, with the help of young Jeff Kittridge, David repaired and rented small boats. Nearby was the Dolphin Restaurant, run by winsome Anna, a young woman whose interest in David was obvious to all but him. When the series moved to ABC in the middle of its one-season run, the title was changed to *Adventures at Scott Island*.

HARD COPY (*Newspaper Drama*)

FIRST TELECAST: *February 1, 1987*
LAST TELECAST: *July 3, 1987*
BROADCAST HISTORY:

Feb 1987, CBS Sun 10:00–11:00
May 1987–Jul 1987, CBS Fri 10:00–11:00

CAST:

Andy Omart .... Michael Murphy
David Del Valle .... Dean Devlin
Blake Calisher .... Wendy Crewson
William Boot .... Charles Cooper
Lt. Guyla Cook .... Fionnula Flanagan
Scoop Webster .... George O. Petrie
John Freed .... Jeffrey Kramer
Lt. Brian Packer .... Erich Anderson
Larry Coverson .... Jim McDonnell

The *Morning Post* was a Los Angeles newspaper with a reputation for hard-hitting journalism and a highly competitive staff of crime reporters. The lead reporter was veteran Andy Omart, who had seen just about everything in his years with the paper. A recent addition to the staff, fresh out of journalism school, was young David Del Valle, an eager beaver who found it difficult to compete with ambitious Blake Calisher, William Boot, Scoop Webster, and the other, more experienced reporters on the paper. Local TV anchorman Larry Coverson was forever trying to break major stories before the print reporters, but almost never succeeded.

HARD COPY (*Magazine*)

BROADCAST HISTORY:

Syndicated only
30 minutes
Produced: *1989–1999*
Released: *September 1989*

HOSTS:

Alan Frio (1989–1991)
Teri Murphy (1989–1998)
Barry Nolan (1990–1998)
Diane Dimond (1995)
Doug Bruckner (1997–1998)
Jerry Penacoli (1997–1998)
Kyle Kraska (1998–1999)

This was one of the more successful tabloid news series that sprouted after the success of *A Current Affair*. Each episode featured two or three segments, with an emphasis on celebrity interviews and revelations and investigative reports on sensational stories in the headlines. During its first season, *Hard Copy* provided a 900 telephone number for viewers to call with comments about stories they had seen on the show. Selected comments were played during the closing credits. In the fall of 1990 senior correspondent Barry Nolan started appearing semi-regularly as a New York–based, on-camera host (the series originated from Los Angeles). When Alan Frio left the series the following fall, Nolan moved to Los Angeles to take over as Teri Murphy's full-time co-host. In 1994 the 900 telephone number for viewer comments was revived.

In May 1995 the weekend edition was retitled *HCTV*, with its entire focus on celebrity gossip and Diane Dimond serving as host. The gossipy *HCTV* only lasted a few months. That fall the weekend edition of *Hard Copy* returned. In Fall 1997, Doug Bruckner, the show's New York–based correspondent, was formally made *Hard Copy*'s third host and Jerry Penacoli took over as host of the weekend edition, which had previously been hosted by the weekday regulars.

At the start of the 1998–1999 season *Hard Copy* was given a major overhaul. Kyle Kraska was the new host, the weekend edition was dropped, Penacoli stayed on as a correspondent, and the producers promised that the show would feature longer, more in-depth stories than in previous seasons.

HARD TIME ON PLANET EARTH (*Science Fiction*)
FIRST TELECAST: *March 1, 1989*
LAST TELECAST: *July 5, 1989*
BROADCAST HISTORY:
Mar 1989–Jul 1989, CBS Wed 8:00–9:00
CAST:
Jesse .... Martin Kove
Control (voice) .... Danny Mann

He was an intergalactic warrior who had been bred and conditioned from birth to be a fighter. It was all he knew—and that was the problem. Convicted by his society of being incorrigibly violent, he was transformed into human form and exiled to Earth to serve "Hard Time" until he learned compassion and tenderness, and managed to get his antisocial behavior under control. His experiences and progress were monitored by Control, a rookie cybernaut parole officer (which looked like a mobile, bread box–sized disembodied eye) that offered him advice (usually bad) and occasional assistance (generally ineffectual). He took the name Jesse—it was the name tag on the work uniform he had found for clothing when he first arrived—and proceeded to wreak havoc throughout Southern California.

Although he tried to do good deeds, Jesse, who bore a passing resemblance to Arnold Schwarzenegger, knew nothing of human customs, was as strong as ten men, and tended to take everything literally. This made for confusing, frequently dangerous, and sometimes funny or poignant situations. With Jesse traveling from place to place, taking odd jobs, and trying to help people, *Hard Time on Planet Earth* looked like *The Fugitive* with a warped sense of humor. In addition to dealing with humans, Jesse had periodic confrontations with other aliens, similarly transformed into human form, from his home and other planets.

HARDBALL (*Police Drama*)
FIRST TELECAST: *September 21, 1989*
LAST TELECAST: *June 29, 1990*
BROADCAST HISTORY:
Sep 1989, NBC Thu 9:30–11:00
Oct 1989–Dec 1989, NBC Fri 9:00–10:00
Apr 1990–Jun 1990, NBC Fri 10:00–11:00
Jun 1990, NBC Fri 9:00–10:00
CAST:
Charlie Battles .... John Ashton
Joe "Kaz" Kaczierowski .... Richard Tyson
THEME:
"Roll It Over," by Eddie Money, Sylvester LeVay, and Mark Spiro, performed by Eddie Money

A standard-issue, hard-action series about two L.A. cops who were total opposites, but paired to work together anyway. Charlie was the 45-year-old senior partner, tough as nails, sour disposition, who'd "rather go through a wall than around it." Kaz, his scruffy young partner, loved rock 'n' roll, rode a Harley, had very long hair, and wore a Mexican Day of the Dead earring. Everything about the rebellious Kaz, Charlie hated. As for Kaz, he thought hey, the old guy's a little paunchy but not so bad. Viewers were less generous.

HARDBALL (*Situation Comedy*)
FIRST TELECAST: *September 4, 1994*
LAST TELECAST: *October 23, 1994*
BROADCAST HISTORY:
Sep 1994–Oct 1994, FOX Sun 8:30–9:00
CAST:
Dave Logan .... Bruce Greenwood
Mike Widmer .... Mike Starr
Frank Valente .... Joe Rogan
Arnold Nixon .... Phill Lewis
Lloyd LaCombe .... Chris Browning
Ernest "Happy" Talbot .... Dann Florek
Brad Coolidge .... Steve Hytner
Lee Emory .... Alexandra Wentworth
Mitzi Balzer .... Rose Marie
Nelson .... Adam Hendershott
Announcer/Reporter/TV News Anchor
.... Dave Sebastian Williams

This short-lived baseball comedy spent much of its time in the locker room of the Pioneers, an inept American League baseball team, and quickly struck out. Dave, the intelligent, wise-cracking team leader, was a veteran pitcher. Mike, the team's starting catcher and Dave's best friend, was a former all-star who had put on so much weight he could barely squat behind home plate. Frank, the team's overpaid 25-year-old superstar, had a big ego, a big mouth, and no tact. Others around the lockers were Arnold, the stylish second baseman; Lloyd, a naive rookie pitcher with a strong arm but limited control; and Happy, the new manager, a disciplinarian who terrorized them all. Brad, the Pioneers' general manager, was a manipulating conniver, while Lee, the nervous young publicity manager, had her work cut out keeping Frank and his teammates from getting bad press for their verbal and social indiscretions. Mitzi, the widowed owner of the team, hated finishing in last place and yelled at the team with language worthy of a truck driver. Nelson, Mitzi's grandson, was the team's batboy, and Hardball, the team mascot, was a guy in a pioneer uniform with a giant baseball head and a bad attitude.

HARDBALL WITH CHRIS MATTHEWS (*Talk*)
BROADCAST HISTORY:
CNBC, MSNBC
30 minutes
Produced: *1996–*
Premiered: *c. February 5, 1996*
REGULARS:
Chris Matthews

Intense, close-cropped newsman Chris Matthews interrogated America's "power players" on this nightly talk show that focused on Washington and the board rooms of big business. Matthews was first seen on sister network America's Talking. He moved to CNBC in 1996 with a show called *Politics with Chris Matthews*, which was later changed to *Hardball*; the latter program aired on both CNBC and MSNBC from 1999 to 2002, and on MSNBC after that.

HARDCASTLE & MCCORMICK (*Detective/Adventure*)
FIRST TELECAST: *September 18, 1983*
LAST TELECAST: *July 23, 1986*
BROADCAST HISTORY:
Sep 1983–Dec 1984, ABC Sun 8:00–9:00
Dec 1984–May 1985, ABC Mon 8:00–9:00
Aug 1985–May 1986, ABC Mon 8:00–9:00
Jun 1986–Jul 1986, ABC Wed 9:00–10:00

CAST:

Judge Milton G. Hardcastle .... Brian Keith
Mark "Skid" McCormick .... Daniel Hugh-Kelly
Sarah Wicks (1983) .... Mary Jackson
Lt. Michael Delaney (1984–1985) .... John Hancock
Lt. Frank Harper (1985–1986) .... Joe Santos

Vigilante justice reached new extremes in this action series, in which an athletic retired judge decided to track down "the ones that got away"—presumed criminals who had beaten the rap in his courtroom over the previous 30 years thanks to smart lawyers, lack of evidence, and other "legal loopholes." Although Judge Hardcastle was still remarkably fit at 65, he needed some help in this crusade, so he recruited a handsome, young two-time loser named Mark, who just happened to be a hotshot racing driver. The deal was that Hardcastle would get the lad off the hook for his latest conviction (auto theft), if Mark would help the judge track down his quarry. "I figure it takes one to catch one," growled Hardcastle.

Mark agreed, partially just to be around such a colorful character. Hardcastle, who used to wear loud shirts and tennis shorts under his robes while on the bench, was now given to wearing T-shirts and slogans like NO PLEA BARGAINING IN HEAVEN and FIND 'EM AND HANG 'EM. He raced around in a macho red sports car (macho because you had to crawl in through the windows) with license plates reading DE JUDGE. Amid a steady stream of wisecracks and car crashes, he still knew how to lean on his many contacts in the judiciary and on the streets to help him crack cases. Home base for the series was the judge's palatial estate (he had evidently invested well). Presided over by housekeeper Sarah, it was the scene of his weekly poker game.

Of course there were a few "buts," presumably to keep the ACLU off his back. Mark hadn't really committed that crime, and Hardcastle only went after offenders for their current offenses. Once he even took on a trio of fellow judges who had decided simply to kill ex-cons as they were released from prison. But the criminal element presumably got the message: watch out for judges wearing T-shirts reading BLAST 'EM, TONTO!

HARDY BOYS, THE (*Adventure*)

BROADCAST HISTORY:

Syndicated only
30 minutes
Produced: *1995–1996*
Released: *September 1995*

CAST:

Joe Hardy .... Paul Popowich
Frank Hardy .... Colin Gray
Kate Craigen .... Fiona Highet

In this syndicated series the Hardy boys were somewhat older than in their network TV days. Frank was a 22-year-old investigative reporter for the *Bayport Eagle*, and his younger brother, Joe, was an undergraduate with a strong interest in computers who also freelanced as a photographer. Together they solved the assorted mysteries that seemed to surface every week in otherwise quiet, residential Bayport. Kate was Joe's editor at the *Eagle*.

Sold with the syndicated *Nancy Drew* series and aired with it as a back-to-back hour on most stations.

HARDY BOYS MYSTERIES, THE (*Adventure*)

FIRST TELECAST: *January 30, 1977*
LAST TELECAST: *August 26, 1979*
BROADCAST HISTORY:

Jan 1977–Jan 1979, ABC Sun 7:00–8:00
Jun 1979–Aug 1979, ABC Sun 7:00–8:00

CAST:

Joe Hardy .... Shaun Cassidy
Frank Hardy .... Parker Stevenson
Fenton Hardy .... Edmund Gilbert
Callie Shaw (1977) .... Lisa Eilbacher
Aunt Gertrude (1977–1978) .... Edith Atwater
Nancy Drew (1977–1978) .... Pamela Sue Martin
Nancy Drew (1978) .... Janet Louise Johnson
Carson Drew (1977–1978) .... William Schallert
George Fayne (1977–1978) .... Susan Buckner
Bess (1977–1978) .... Ruth Cox
Harry Gibbon (1978–1979) .... Phillip R. Allen
Harry Hammond (1978–1979) .... Jack Kelly

The adventures of 16-year-old Joe and 18-year-old Frank Hardy, the teenage detective sons of world-famous investigator Fenton Hardy, were the basis of this series. Their exploits were usually on the nonviolent side, involving ghosts, missing persons, smugglers, and other "mysteries" rather than violent action. Often they had a contemporary youth orientation, to appeal to the teenagers who made up much of the audience to this show, as when the boys traveled to Europe to Transylvania to attend a rock concert at Dracula's Castle, where they encountered strange goings-on. Helping out were Callie, who worked part-time in Fenton Hardy's detective agency, and Aunt Gertrude. Added in 1978 were federal agent Harry Gibbon and CIA operative Harry Hammond.

At first the series alternated on Sunday nights with *The Nancy Drew Mysteries*, which starred Pamela Sue Martin in the title role. In the fall of 1977 the Hardy Boys and Nancy Drew appeared jointly in some episodes, and then in February 1978, the two programs were combined into one, with all three leads appearing together regularly. Unhappy with the elimination of her separate series, Pamela Sue Martin left the program and was briefly replaced by 18-year-old Janet Louise Johnson. The character of Nancy Drew was dropped altogether in the fall of 1978, and the title was shortened to *The Hardy Boys*.

In addition to his adventures, Shaun Cassidy found time to launch a singing career while on this program, much as his older brother David Cassidy had done while on another TV series, *The Partridge Family*, seven years earlier. Shaun sang "Da Do Ron Ron" on an April 1977 telecast, and saw it become a number-one record hit.

The Hardy Boys mystery books, on which this series was based, were supposedly written by "Franklin W. Dixon," but in fact there was no such person. They were actually the product of a remarkable "writing factory" founded in the early 1900s by Edward Stratemeyer, which was also responsible for the Nancy Drew, Tom Swift, Rover Boys, and Bobbsey Twins series, and hundreds of other juvenile adventure best-sellers. Stratemeyer and his daughter Harriet Adams wrote or oversaw the writing of all of them, using more than 60 pseudonyms. "Franklin W. Dixon" was used for the Hardy novels, and "Carolyn Keene" for Nancy Drew. Several Nancy Drew movies were made in the late 1930s, and early television producers were also interested in using the stories. However, Harriet Adams insisted on script approval, and not until 1977 did Universal Studios agree to this condition, resulting in the ABC series.

HARNESS RACING (*Sports*)
FIRST TELECAST: *May 27, 1949*
LAST TELECAST: *August 19, 1958*
BROADCAST HISTORY:
May 1949–Sep 1949, NBC Fri 10:00–Conclusion
Jul 1949–Sep 1949, NBC Tue 9:30–Conclusion
Jun 1950–Aug 1950, NBC Thu 10:00–Conclusion
Jun 1950–Sep 1950, NBC Sat 10:00–Conclusion
Sep 1951–Nov 1951, ABC Sat Various times (9:00, 9:30, 10:00 starts)
Jun 1958–Aug 1958, ABC Fri 10:00–10:30
Aug 1958, ABC Tue 10:00–10:30

Back in the relatively early days of network television, NBC aired live coverage of races from New York's Roosevelt Raceway, usually two or three races each night. Veteran horse-race announcer Clem McCarthy called the races, described them prior to the start of each race, and talked about various horse owners and trainers. To keep viewers from being bored, there was a quiz game conducted between races with contestants from a studio audience. The quiz was conducted by Ray Barrett and Bill Stern, and was only used by NBC in the 1950 edition of *Trotting Races*, not the original in 1949.

ABC covered the trotters in 1951 and 1958 under the title *Harness Racing*. Races aired in 1951 originated from Maywood Park in Chicago until late October, and then shifted to Yonkers Raceway near New York City. The 1958 series, on ABC, originated only from the New York area, with individual telecasts aired from either Roosevelt Raceway or Yonkers Raceway.

HAROLD ROBBINS' "THE SURVIVORS," see *Survivors, The*

HARPER VALLEY P.T.A. (*Situation Comedy*)
FIRST TELECAST: *January 16, 1981*
LAST TELECAST: *August 14, 1982*
BROADCAST HISTORY:
Jan 1981–Aug 1981, NBC Fri 8:00–8:30
Oct 1981–Nov 1981, NBC Thu 8:00–8:30
Dec 1981–Jan 1982, NBC Sat 8:00–8:30
Jan 1982–Feb 1982, NBC Sat 8:30–9:00
Apr 1982–Jun 1982, NBC Sat 8:00–8:30
Jul 1982–Aug 1982, NBC Sat 8:30–9:00

CAST:
Stella Johnson .... Barbara Eden
Dee Johnson .... Jenn Thompson
Flora Simpson Reilly .... Anne Francine
Cassie Bowman .... Fannie Flagg
Mayor Otis Harper, Jr. .... George Gobel
Wanda Reilly Taylor .... Bridget Hanley
Scarlett Taylor .... Suzi Dean
Bobby Taylor .... Rod McCary
Tom Meechum .... Christopher Stone
Norman Clayton (1981) .... Gary Allen
Vivian Washburn (1981) .... Mari Gorman
Willamae Jones (1981) .... Edie McClurg
Cliff Willoughby (1981) .... Robert Gray
George Kelly (1981) .... Vic Dunlop
Coach Burt Powell (1981) .... Kevin Scannell
Winslow Homer (Uncle Buster) Smith (1981–1982)
.... Mills Watson

THEME:
"Harper Valley P.T.A.," written by Tom T. Hall

This was only the second series in network television history to be based on a phonograph record (the first: *The Alvin Show*). Jeannie C. Riley's huge 1968 record hit "Harper Valley P.T.A." told of the struggles of a liberated woman fighting hypocrisy in a small Southern town. The song served as the basis for a 1978 theatrical movie starring Barbara Eden as the outspoken Stella Johnson. The film was only a modest success in theaters, but it attracted a large audience when aired on television. This prompted NBC to develop it into a weekly situation comedy with Miss Eden re-creating her movie role.

Stella was a very attractive widow with a 13-year-old daughter (Dee) living in sleepy little Harper Valley, Ohio—a very staid and proper community on the surface, but actually full of miscreants, adulterers, and cheerful alcoholics. Stella was a real individual who did what she pleased, regardless of what anybody thought. Independent but principled, her approach to life endlessly distressed the self-righteous members of the P.T.A. board, to which she had been elected. Her short skirts, flirting, and "radical" ideas convinced the other board members that she made a disgusting role model for their children, not to mention a temptation for their husbands (who thought Stella was jus' fine). The stuffy matrons waged a constant struggle to have her removed from the board, while Stella fought back with a succession of hilarious put-downs that got them every time. Stella's principal adversary was wealthy Flora Simpson Reilly, the leader of Harper Valley "society." The entire Reilly family, in fact, shared Flora's pompous attitudes, including daughter Wanda; son-in-law Bobby, the town's leading attorney; and granddaughter Scarlett, a classmate of Dee's. Stella's one ally was beauty-parlor operator Cassie, who helped her with her schemes. In order to make a living, Stella sold Angelglow cosmetics door-to-door.

When the series returned in the fall of 1981 there were several changes. Since the P.T.A. meetings and involvement had been dropped, the title of the show was shortened to *Harper Valley*. Stella's relationship with Dee became more prominent, and a new character, Stella's uncle Buster, a bumbling, eccentric inventor, came to town and moved in with his niece. Buster's "inventions" never seemed to work the way they were supposed to; the results were usually catastrophic and hilarious.

HARRIGAN AND SON (*Situation Comedy*)
FIRST TELECAST: *October 14, 1960*
LAST TELECAST: *September 29, 1961*
BROADCAST HISTORY:
Oct 1960–Sep 1961, ABC Fri 8:00–8:30

CAST:
James Harrigan, Sr. .... Pat O'Brien
James Harrigan, Jr. .... Roger Perry
Gypsy .... Georgine Darcy
Miss Claridge .... Helen Kleeb

James Harrigan, Sr., had been practicing law, as a criminal attorney, since before his son was born. Now his boy had just graduated from Harvard Law School and joined the firm as a junior partner. Junior's problem was that he tried to do everything by the book and was constantly at odds with his father who was not above playing angles that would help his case. The two lawyers had secretaries that matched their styles completely. Senior had fiery, flip, effervescent Gypsy and Junior had sedate, efficient Miss Claridge.

HARRIS AGAINST THE WORLD (*Situation Comedy*)

FIRST TELECAST: *October 5, 1964*
LAST TELECAST: *January 4, 1965*
BROADCAST HISTORY:
Oct 1964–Jan 1965, NBC Mon 8:00–8:30
CAST:
Alan Harris .... Jack Klugman
Kate Harris .... Patricia Barry
Deedee Harris .... Claire Wilcox
Billy Harris .... David Macklin
Helen Miller .... Fay DeWitt
Norm Miller .... Sheldon Allman

Jack Klugman played Alan Harris, a plant superintendent at a huge movie studio who lived at 90 Bristol Court with his wife, Kate, and his two children, Deedee and Billy. Coping with life was a full-time job for Alan. His bosses, debts, taxes, and people in general always seemed to be one up on him. His wife was a champion spender who always managed to find him part-time jobs to work at in the spare time he didn't really have. But much as he complained about almost everything and everybody, Alan was really an old softie at heart.

Harris Against the World was the middle component of a series of three comedies that ran from 7:30–9:00 P.M. on Monday evenings under the blanket title *90 Bristol Court*, which referred to the fashionable apartment block where all three shows were set. *Karen* ran from 7:30–8:00 and *Tom, Dick and Mary* from 8:30–9:00.

HARRIS AND COMPANY (*Family Drama*)

FIRST TELECAST: *March 15, 1979*
LAST TELECAST: *April 5, 1979*
BROADCAST HISTORY:
Mar 1979–Apr 1979, NBC Thu 8:00–9:00
CAST:
Mike Harris .... Bernie Casey
David Harris .... David Hubbard
Liz Harris .... Renee Brown
Juanita Priscilla (J.P.) Harris .... Lia Jackson
Tommy Harris .... Eddie Singleton
Richard Allen Harris .... Dain Turner
Harry Foreman .... James Luisi
Louise Foreman .... Lois Walden
Charlie Adams .... Stu Gilliam
Angie Adams .... C. Tillery Banks

Following the death of his wife, black assembly-line worker Mike Harris and his five children decided to move from Detroit to Los Angeles and build a new life. As with every decision in the Harris household, all family members were consulted and it was put to a vote (hence the "company" in the series title). In L.A. Mike went into partnership with Harry Foreman running a garage. Stories revolved around problems with work and the comic difficulties of a single parent raising a family. The Harris children ranged in age from college-student Liz to 6-year-old Richard. Charlie and Angie Adams were cousins who helped Mike with the kids.

Harris and Company was an unusual attempt to build a dramatic series around a loving, caring black family. It attracted a small audience and had a short run.

HARRY (*Situation Comedy*)

FIRST TELECAST: *March 4, 1987*
LAST TELECAST: *March 25, 1987*
BROADCAST HISTORY:
Mar 1987, ABC Wed 8:30–9:00
CAST:
Harry Porschak .... Alan Arkin
Richard Breskin .... Richard Lewis
Bobby Kratz .... Matt Craven
Dr. Sandy Clifton .... Barbara Dana
Nurse Ina Duckett .... Holland Taylor
Wyatt Lockhart .... Kurt Knudson
Lawrence Pendelton .... Thom Bray

Alan Arkin starred as a wheeler-dealer supply clerk in a large hospital in this short-lived comedy. Kidney-stone pools and outpatient poker were the order of the day in Harry's basement domain at County General Hospital; overbearing Nurse Duckett and her meek, bow-tied toady Lawrence were his chief nemeses, and Wyatt Lockhart the bemused hospital administrator.

HARRY AND THE HENDERSONS (*Situation Comedy*)

BROADCAST HISTORY:
Syndicated only
30 minutes
Produced: *1990–1993* (72 episodes)
Released: *January 1991*
CAST:
Harry (1990–1991) .... Kevin Peter Hall
Harry (1991–1992) .... Dawan Scott
Harry (1992–1993) .... Brian Steele
George Henderson .... Bruce Davison
Nancy Henderson .... Molly Cheek
Ernie Henderson (age 10) .... Zachary Bostrom
Sara Henderson (17) .... Carol-Ann Plante
Samantha Glick (1990–1991) .... Gigi Rice
Tiffany Glick (1990–1991) .... Cassie Cole
Walter Potter (1990–1991) .... David Coburn
Bret Douglas (1991–1993) .... Noah Blake
Darcy Payne (1991–1992) .... Courtney Peldon
Hilton Woods, Jr. (1992–1993)
.... Mark Dakota Robinson
THEME:
"Your Feets Too Big," written and performed by Leon Redbone

Lots of families have pets, but this was ridiculous. The Hendersons had been driving on vacation in the forests of the Pacific Northwest when they accidentally hit a seven-foot-tall creature that ran in front of their car. They took the creature, a Sasquatch (also known as Bigfoot) home to Seattle to nurse it back to health. Their young son, Ernie, quickly became attached to the bright, gentle, but clumsy Sasquatch, whom he named Harry. Despite the misgivings of his parents, George and Nancy, Ernie convinced them to keep Harry, which presented all sorts of problems since they couldn't let everyone know that a Sasquatch was living with them. The only others who did know were Walter, a young biologist working for the department of animal control, and their next-door neighbor, Samantha, a divorced TV reporter with a young daughter. Both of them were sworn to secrecy, to protect Harry from being taken by the authorities. In the fall of 1991 Walter and Samantha were dropped from the cast, and Nancy's younger brother Bret, who moved in with the Hendersons, and obnoxious little Darcy, who was infatuated with a disinterested Ernie, were added. Later that season George quit his job with a sporting goods company to start *The Better Life*, a magazine dealing with ecological issues. Bret, who had helped finance the magazine, worked on it with George. In the fall of 1992 all of Seattle found out about Harry's existence when he was in the Mercer Island Animal Control Center. He became a local celebrity, and Bret was forever looking for ways to capitalize on Harry's fame. Hilton, whose father was the local police chief, was a neighborhood kid who had become Ernie's good friend.

Adapted from the 1987 movie of the same name, with Kevin Peter Hall reprising his role as Harry, the huge hairy, apelike star of the show. When Hall passed away in the spring of 1991, the role of Harry was taken over by Dawan Scott. Brian Steele, who had doubled for Harry earlier in 1992, took over the role at the start of the 1992–1993 season.

HARRY'S GIRLS (*Situation Comedy*)
FIRST TELECAST: *September 13, 1963*
LAST TELECAST: *January 3, 1964*
BROADCAST HISTORY:
Sep 1963–Jan 1964, NBC Fri 9:30–10:00
CAST:
Harry Burns .... Larry Blyden
Rusty .... Susan Silo
Lois.............................. Dawn Nickerson
Terry .... Diahn Williams

Harry Burns was a vaudeville entertainer with an act that featured three beautiful girl dancers, Rusty, Lois, and Terry. Although his act was much too old-fashioned to be successful in the United States, it was reasonably popular in Europe. Harry, in addition to being the star of the act, had to do the booking, handle finances, and try to keep tabs on the girls. The last was not always easy. Rusty was incredibly gullible and constantly falling in love, Lois was distressingly naive and often acted like a country girl on her first trip to the big city, and Terry was too sophisticated for her own good. Filmed on location throughout Europe, this series followed the travels of *Harry's Girls* as the act played in various continental cities. Occasional excerpts from the act were shown, but only as they fit into the story.

HARRY-O (*Detective Drama*)
FIRST TELECAST: *September 12, 1974*
LAST TELECAST: *August 12, 1976*
BROADCAST HISTORY:
Sep 1974–Aug 1976, ABC Thu 10:00–11:00
CAST:
Harry Orwell .... David Janssen
Det. Lt. Manuel (Manny) Quinlan (1974–1975)
.... Henry Darrow
Lt. K. C. Trench (1975–1976)........ Anthony Zerbe
Sgt. Don Roberts (1975–1976) .... Paul Tulley
Lester Hodges (1975–1976)............ Les Lannom
Dr. Fong (1976) .... Keye Luke

Harry Orwell was one of TV's more bohemian private eyes, living in a beachfront cottage near San Diego and often using the city bus for transportation (his car didn't work). An ex-Marine and ex-cop pensioned from the force after being injured in the line of duty, he augmented his income by taking cases that especially interested him. These usually involved luscious girls—none of whom seemed to matter much to Harry, however.

Harry's sometime nemesis, sometime ally, was Lt. Manny Quinlan of the San Diego Police Department. Manny was killed off in a February 1975 telecast, after which Harry moved his base of operations to Santa Monica. There, he inherited a new official nemesis, Lt. Trench, plus occasional unsolicited help with his cases from amateur criminologists Lester Hodges and Dr. Fong.

Infrequently seen, but highly visible on those occasions when she did appear, was Harry's girl-next-door, Farrah Fawcett.

HARSH REALM (*Science Fiction*)
FIRST TELECAST: *October 8, 1999*
LAST TELECAST: *October 22, 1999*
BROADCAST HISTORY:
Oct 1999, FOX Fri 9:00–10:00
CAST:
Lt. Thomas Hobbes .... Scott Bairstow
Mike Pinocchio...................... D. B. Sweeney
Sgt. Maj. Omar Santiago............ Terry O'Quinn
Sophie Green .... Samantha Mathis
Lt. Mel Waters................. Maximilian Martini
Florence .... Rachel Hayward
Inga Fossa.................. Sarah-Jane Redmond

Lt. Hobbes was about to leave the army and marry his live-in girlfriend, Sophie, when he was caught up in a bizarre experiment. In 1995 the Pentagon had developed a virtual-reality world called project Harsh Realm—a simulated war game designed to teach situational strategy. In it terrorists had destroyed New York City in a nuclear attack. Hobbes was recruited to "play" the game and compete against the current high scorer, a highly decorated combat veteran named Santiago. What Hobbes didn't know was that once he was in the game there was no getting out, unless he got to Santiago. Santiago had disappeared into this virtual world and been reborn there as a ruthless dictator—living in gleaming, heavily fortified Santiago City—and he alone held the key to releasing players who were sent in after him. The government in the real world couldn't catch him because he had hijacked the program and was in complete control of the game.

Once Hobbes was wired with electrodes and started the game, he was swallowed up into Harsh Realm—which was, in effect, a parallel world in which things were not always what they seemed. His allies were a group of rebels who lived outside the electrified fence that surrounded Santiago City. The most vociferous was Pinocchio, who had failed to outscore Santiago and was fed up with trying to help newcomers. Waters, who had also failed to beat Santiago in the game, was now living in Santiago City and working for him.

Hobbes provided narration in a dull monotone. While he was in the game his real body, along with the bodies of uncounted others who had been forced into the game before him, was in a coma-like state monitored by the military folks. In the real world his superiors told Sophie that Hobbes had been killed in action, and they even held a funeral for him. However, Sophie was tipped off that Hobbes was still alive by Inga, a mysterious woman who had the ability to move between Harsh Realm and the real world through a hidden portal.

Low ratings prompted Fox to drop *Harsh Realm* from its lineup after only three episodes. In the spring of 2000 these were repeated on sister cable network FX, along with six more episodes that had not run on Fox. In these Hobbes continued the battle in Harsh Realm, and after he and Pinocchio were partially blown up in a minefield they were revived by Florence, a soldier with the gift of healing, along with the help of another healer. They could not, however, escape Harsh Realm.

The series was inspired by the Harsh Realm comic-book series created by James D. Hudnall and Andrew Paquette.

HART TO HART (*Adventure*)

FIRST TELECAST: *August 25, 1979*
LAST TELECAST: *July 31, 1984*
BROADCAST HISTORY:
Aug 1979–Oct 1979, ABC Sat 10:00–11:00
Oct 1979–Jul 1984, ABC Tue 10:00–11:00
CAST:
Jonathan Hart .... Robert Wagner
Jennifer Hart .... Stefanie Powers
Max .... Lionel Stander

Jonathan and Jennifer Hart were rich, stylish, and supersleuths. He was a self-made millionaire, head of the huge Hart Industries conglomerate (which never seemed to require his attention); she was an internationally known freelance journalist. From their mansion in Beverly Hills, they rekindled their continuing love affair by setting out each week on a new adventure. They roamed the glamour spots of the world in their private jet, hobnobbed with the rich, famous, and not-so-famous, and along the way solved crimes that baffled more pedestrian souls. Gravel-voiced Max was their chauffeur and confidant; Freeway, their dog.

The series was created by best-selling novelist Sidney Sheldon.

HARTMANS, THE (*Situation Comedy*)

FIRST TELECAST: *February 27, 1949*
LAST TELECAST: *May 22, 1949*
BROADCAST HISTORY:
Feb 1949–May 1949, NBC Sun 7:30–8:00
CAST:
Grace Hartman .... Herself
Paul Hartman .... Himself
The handyman .... Harold J. Stone
Their brother-in-law .... Loring Smith
Their nephew .... Bob Shawley
The man next door .... Gage Clark
Grace's sister .... Valerie Cossart

Grace and Paul Hartman, the famous dance satirists, played straight comedy in this early live series about the trials of a young married couple living in a suburb called Forest Heights.

HARTS OF THE WEST (*Western Comedy*)

FIRST TELECAST: *September 25, 1993*
LAST TELECAST: *June 18, 1994*
BROADCAST HISTORY:
Sep 1993–Jan 1994, CBS Sat 9:00–10:00
Jun 1994, CBS Sat 9:00–10:00
CAST:
Dave Hart .... Beau Bridges
Alison Hart .... Harley Jane Kozak
Jake Tyrell .... Lloyd Bridges
L'Amour Hart (age 15) .... Meghann Haldeman
Zane Grey Hart (17) .... Sean Murray
John Wayne "Duke" Hart (11) .... Nathan Watt
Auggie Velasquez .... Saginaw Grant
Rose McLaughlin .... O-Lan Jones
R.O. Moon .... Stephen Root
Marcus St. Cloud .... Sterling Macer, Jr.
Cassie Velasquez .... Talisa Soto
Garral .... Dennis Fimple
THEME:
"In a Laid Back Way," written and performed by Clint Black

After suffering a mild heart attack while plying his trade in Bloomingdale's, lingerie salesman Dave Hart concluded that selling underwear in Chicago was not what life was all about. So he decided to follow his dream and become a cowboy, moving his less than enthusiastic family to the Flying Tumbleweed Ranch in Sholo, Nevada. He purchased it, sight unseen, from a now deceased real estate agent using a sales brochure printed in 1957 and ended up with a major reclamation project. The place was in total disrepair. Featured as the crusty, cantankerous ranch foreman was series star Beau Bridges's father, Lloyd. Others were Auggie, the Native American who ran the general store where son Zane worked part-time; Rose, the waitress at the only restaurant in Sholo; R.O., the town sheriff, who was living with Rose; Marcus, a manipulative young black ex-con who worked on the ranch; and Cassie, Auggie's granddaughter, on whom horny teenager Zane had a crush. For Dave, who was obsessed with the West (he had named his three kids after John Wayne and authors Zane Grey and Louis L'Amour), it was a dream come true, but for the rest of the family it was a dream of another kind.

HAT SQUAD, THE (*Police Drama*)

FIRST TELECAST: *September 16, 1992*
LAST TELECAST: *January 23, 1993*
BROADCAST HISTORY:
Sep 1992–Nov 1992, CBS Wed 8:00–9:00
Jan 1993, CBS Sat 10:00–11:00
CAST:
Rafael (Raffi) Martinez .... Nestor Serrano
Buddy Capatosa .... Don Michael Paul
Matt Matheson .... Billy Warlock
Capt. Mike Ragland .... James Tolkan
Kitty Ragland .... Shirley Douglas
Darnell Johnson .... Bruce Robbins

Violent cop show with an odd gimmick—the young retro-cool heroes all wore hats. Capt. Mike Ragland was a career cop in Los Angeles who had taken in three foster children as youngsters. Raised by Mike and his wife, Kitty, all three had joined the L.A.P.D., where their commander was none other than Capt. Mike. The oldest was Raffi, an impulsive, hot-blooded Hispanic who often needed Mike or Buddy to calm him down. Buddy was very competitive with Raffi, especially with women, but had more common sense, and Matt, the youngest, looked to the others for guidance. Together they were The Hat Squad, an updated version of a real L.A.P.D. special crimes unit from the

1940s. Incorruptible and dedicated to tracking down the most dangerous criminals, they wore distinctive fedoras and long coats, as had their predecessors half a century earlier.

HATHAWAYS, THE (*Situation Comedy*)
FIRST TELECAST: *October 6, 1961*
LAST TELECAST: *August 31, 1962*
BROADCAST HISTORY:
Oct 1961–Aug 1962, ABC Fri 8:00–8:30
CAST:
Elinore Hathaway.................... Peggy Cass
Walter Hathaway.................... Jack Weston
Jerry Roper.................... Harvey Lembeck
Thelma Brockwood................ Barbara Perry
Amanda Allison............. Mary Grace Canfield
Mrs. Harrison.................... Belle Montrose

The Hathaways were a family of five, all of them wearing normal clothes and eating together at the same table, but only two of them were people. Walter Hathaway was a real-estate agent and Elinore was his wife. Charlie, Enoch, and Cindy were chimps—the Marquis Chimps—and very bright chimps at that. Elinore, besides treating them like her children, was booking agent for their show-business act, which included riding bicycles and making faces. (They also had a formal talent agent named Jerry Roper.) Walter had mixed emotions about the whole arrangement, wondering if the chimps meant more to his wife than he did, and their suburban neighbors also had some difficulty adjusting to "the kids next door." One of the neighbors was played by Belle Montrose, the mother of comedian Steve Allen.

HAUNTED (*Supernatural Drama*)
FIRST TELECAST: *September 24, 2002*
LAST TELECAST: *November 5, 2002*
BROADCAST HISTORY:
Sep 2002–Nov 2002, UPN Tue 9:00–10:00
CAST:
Frank Taylor......................... Matthew Fox
Marcus Bradshaw............... Russell Hornsby
Jessica Manning..................... Lynn Collins
Simon Dunn......................... John F. Mann
Dante.............................. Michael Irby

Police detective Frank Taylor's life was turned upside down following the kidnapping of his young son, Kevin, in the middle of the night. His marriage crumbled and he left the force to become a private detective, hoping to get leads that would help him find his son. While working on the case of another abducted child he had a shootout with a pedophile named Simon, whom he killed in self-defense. Frank almost died from his wounds and after his recovery found himself haunted by a random collection of ghosts. Some helped him with cases while others, including the evil spirit of his assailant, Simon, gave him only aggravation. Among the living who helped, willingly or reluctantly, were his former partner Marcus, who had been promoted to detective; his ex-wife Jessica, who was an assistant D.A.; and Dante, a friend who had knowledge of the supernatural and tried to help Frank understand what he was going through. Frank's dog Gus sensed things, too.

This dark, brooding series never found much of an audience and was one of the first casualties of the 2002–2003 season.

HAVE FAITH (*Situation Comedy*)
FIRST TELECAST: *April 18, 1989*
LAST TELECAST: *July 23, 1989*
BROADCAST HISTORY:
Apr 1989–Jun 1989, ABC Tue 9:30–10:00
Jun 1989–Jul 1989, ABC Wed 8:00–8:30
CAST:
Monsignor Joseph ("Mac") MacKenzie
.... Joel Higgins
Father Vincent Paglia.................... Ron Carey
Father Gabriel ("Gabe") Podmaninski
.... Stephen Furst
Father Edgar Tuttle............... Frank Hamilton
Sally Coleman................. Francesca Roberts
Arthur Glass......................... Todd Susman

A short-lived clerical comedy about four offbeat priests in St. Catherine's, an inner-city Chicago church. Most of the action took place in the cozy, wood-paneled rectory. Mac was the slightly irreverent, nontraditional leader; Father Tuttle, the older and *very* reverent traditionalist; Father Paglia, the cherubic, penny-pinching parish accountant; and Gabe, the uncertain new priest, a former football player. Sally was their sardonic, non-Catholic secretary. Stories revolved around nutty parishioners, alarming confessions, nervous Gabe's first big sermon, and the like.

HAVE GUN WILL TRAVEL (*Western*)
FIRST TELECAST: *September 14, 1957*
LAST TELECAST: *September 21, 1963*
BROADCAST HISTORY:
Sep 1957–Sep 1963, CBS Sat 9:30–10:00
CAST:
Paladin.......................... Richard Boone
Hey Boy (1957–1960; 1961–1963)........ Kam Tong
Hey Girl (1960–1961)...................... Lisa Lu
THEME:
"The Ballad of Paladin," by Johnny Western, Richard Boone, and Sam Rolfe, sung on the sound track by Johnny Western

Have Gun Will Travel was one of the most popular programs of the late 1950s, and the chief prototype of a rash of dapper heroes invented by TV to populate the Old West. Paladin was certainly not your normal, everyday illiterate gunslinger. He was college-educated, having attended West Point in pursuit of a military career. Instead, after serving in the Civil War, he headed west to become a high-priced "gun for hire," a kind of Old West troubleshooter. He was based at the fancy Hotel Carlton in San Francisco and his calling card bore the figure of a paladin (the white chess knight) and the inscription, "Have Gun, Will Travel . . . Wire Paladin, San Francisco."

Paladin was a man of culture, enjoying the finest clothes, epicurean meals, and literate company—except when he was on assignment. Then, dressed all in black, he became a very intimidating figure indeed. Despite his somewhat violent profession, he had a sense of ethics that dictated what he would and would not do; it occasionally led him to seek out the very people who had hired him if they in fact were the guilty parties. Hey Boy, the Oriental working at the Hotel Carlton, was seen at the beginning of most episodes bringing a message to Paladin from a prospective client. (During the 1960–1961 season, while Kam Tong was involved in a more substantial role in another series, *The Garlund Touch*, he was replaced by Lisa Lu. He returned to *Have Gun Will Travel* after his new venture was canceled.)

Have Gun Will Travel was an overnight hit, ranking among the top five programs during its first season on the air. From 1958–1961 it was the number-three program on television, behind two other Westerns—*Gunsmoke* and *Wagon Train*. Its theme song, "The Ballad of Paladin," was a hit single in the early 1960s.

HAVING BABIES (*Medical Drama*)

FIRST TELECAST: *March 7, 1978*
LAST TELECAST: *June 26, 1979*
BROADCAST HISTORY:

Mar 1978–Apr 1978, ABC Tue 10:00–11:00
June 1979, ABC Tue 10:00–11:00

CAST:

Dr. Julie Farr .... Susan Sullivan
Dr. Blake Simmons .... Mitchell Ryan
Dr. Ron Danvers .... Dennis Howard
Kelly .... Beverly Todd

This medical drama was one of several new programs which got short-run tryouts during the spring of 1978 to test their potential as regular fall series. Dr. Julie Farr was a dedicated physician at Lake General Hospital whose practice brought her into contact with couples from all walks of life, many of whom had one thing in common: the joy and pain of childbirth. Several stories were usually seen in each episode, at least one of which always dealt with childbirth: for example, the illegal alien who wanted her baby to be born in the United States, even though she was suffering from malaria; the "storybook marriage" that threatened to crumble with the prospect of pregnancy; the wealthy father who had never learned to enjoy his success.

Dr. Simmons was the experienced older doctor, and Dr. Danvers the eager intern.

Having Babies was first seen as a series of movie specials from 1976–1978. Effective with the March 28, 1978, episode its title was changed to *Julie Farr, M.D.* The series was canceled with the April 18, 1978, telecast, but three additional original episodes were aired in June 1979.

HAWAII FIVE-O (*Police Drama*)

FIRST TELECAST: *September 26, 1968*
LAST TELECAST: *April 26, 1980*
BROADCAST HISTORY:

Sep 1968–Dec 1968, CBS Thu 8:00–9:00
Dec 1968–Sep 1971, CBS Wed 10:00–11:00
Sep 1971–Sep 1974, CBS Tue 8:30–9:30
Sep 1974–Sep 1975, CBS Tue 9:00–10:00
Sep 1975–Nov 1975, CBS Fri 9:00–10:00
Dec 1975–Nov 1979, CBS Thu 9:00–10:00
Dec 1979–Jan 1980, CBS Tue 9:00–10:00
Mar 1980–Apr 1980, CBS Sat 9:00–10:00

CAST:

Det. Steve McGarrett .... Jack Lord
Det. Danny Williams (1968–1979) .... James MacArthur
Det. Chin Ho Kelly (1968–1978) .... Kam Fong
Det. Kono Kalakaua (1968–1972) .... Zulu
Governor Philip Grey .... Richard Denning
Det. Ben Kokua (1972–1974) .... Al Harrington
Che Fong (1970–1977) .... Harry Endo
Doc Bergman (1970–1976) .... Al Eben
May (1968–1969) .... Maggi Parker
Jenny Sherman (1969–1976) .... Peggy Ryan
Luana (1978–1980) .... Laura Sode
Duke Lukela (1972–1980) .... Herman Wedemeyer
Att. Gen. Walter Stewart (1968–1969) .... Morgan White
Att. Gen. John Manicote (1972–1977) .... Glenn Cannon
James "Kimo" Carew (1979–1980) .... William Smith
Truck Kealoha (1979–1980) .... Moe Keale
Lori Wilson (1979–1980) .... Sharon Farrell

Though based in the Iolani Palace in downtown Honolulu, the men of Hawaii's Five-O group were not members of the Honolulu Police Department. They worked instead as part of the Hawaiian State Police and were accountable directly to the governor. Stolid, unemotional Steve McGarrett was the head of Five-O, and worked with his own men and the local police in solving various individual crimes and fighting the organized forces of the Hawaiian underworld. Most hated of all the evil men in the islands was the criminal genius Wo Fat (played by Khigh Dhiegh). He would pop up periodically to make life difficult for McGarrett, who was bound and determined to put him in jail. Though Steve did manage to interfere with Wo Fat's illegal operations, he couldn't piece together sufficient evidence to bring him to court.

Hawaii Five-O was filmed entirely on location and it may well have been the beautiful scenery as well as the action and adventure that made it so popular. Whatever the causes, *Hawaii Five-O* was immensely successful. It was the longest continuously running police show in the history of television. Surprisingly, there was very little turnover among the leads. Steve did have several secretaries—May being replaced by Jenny, with Luana turning up later, and one of his assistants, Kono, left after four seasons, but for most of the cast the working conditions in Hawaii were too pleasant to give up. After ten seasons, however, Kam Fong tired of the role of Chin Ho Kelly and was written out of the show by having his character killed in the final episode of the 1977–1978 season.

At the end of the following season, James MacArthur decided he had enough of playing McGarrett's top assistant, Danny "Danno" Williams, and he too left *Hawaii Five-O*. That fall three new members were added to the Five-O team, including former policewoman Lori Wilson. The ratings were falling, and the infusion of new people didn't help. It became obvious to all that this would be *Hawaii Five-O*'s last season. Near the end of the run, on April 5, 1980, McGarrett's most bitter enemy was finally brought to justice. Disguised as a scientist, McGarrett sprung a trap that sent Wo Fat, seen for the first time in five years, to jail.

The Iolani Palace, which in this series was the seat of the Hawaiian government, had at one time housed the Hawaiian Legislature. That time was long gone, however, as it had been a museum for many years prior to the start of *Hawaii Five-O*.

Reruns from the last season's episodes aired under the title *McGarrett* on *CBS Late Night*.

HAWAIIAN EYE (*Detective Drama*)

FIRST TELECAST: *October 7, 1959*
LAST TELECAST: *September 10, 1963*
BROADCAST HISTORY:

Oct 1959–Sep 1962, ABC Wed 9:00–10:00
Oct 1962–Sep 1963, ABC Tue 8:30–9:30

CAST:

Tom Lopaka .... Bob Conrad
Tracy Stele (1959–1962) .... Anthony Eisley
Cricket Blake .... Connie Stevens
Kazuo Kim .... Poncie Ponce
Greg MacKenzie (1960–1963) ...... Grant Williams
Quon (1960–1963) .... Mel Prestidge
Moke (1960–1963) .... Doug Mossman
Philip Barton (1962–1963) .... Troy Donahue

Hawaiian Eye has been called "*77 Sunset Strip* played in Hawaii." There certainly were similarities. Both shows were produced by the same studio (Warner Bros.), both featured two handsome, free-swinging young detectives as alternate leads, both had simple melodramatic plots set against glamorous backgrounds, and both made use of nutty sidekicks for comic relief.

Base of operations for Tom Lopaka and Tracy Stele was a swank, poolside office at the Hawaiian Village Hotel. Their sidekicks were a pert, somewhat addled young singer-photographer named Cricket, and a colorful cabbie named Kim. Kim, the operator of a one-man taxi service, was especially helpful as he had seemingly dozens of relatives scattered around the islands ready to help out if one of his employers needed some local assistance. Kim's trademarks were his *pupule* ("crazy") straw hat, dumb jokes, and ukulele.

A new detective named Greg MacKenzie arrived in December 1960, while Philip Barton joined the cast of characters in 1962 as the hotel's social director. Quon was the contact on the Honolulu police force. Fellow gumshoe Stu Bailey of *77 Sunset Strip* made an occasional visit from the mainland, possibly to get a closer look at some of the beautiful girls who peopled every *Hawaiian Eye* plot. But then he had beautiful girls in his series, too.

HAWAIIAN HEAT (*Police Drama*)

FIRST TELECAST: *September 14, 1984*
LAST TELECAST: *December 21, 1984*
BROADCAST HISTORY:
Sep 1984–Dec 1984, ABC Fri 9:00–10:00

CAST:

Andy Senkowski .... Jeff McCracken
Mac Riley .... Robert Ginty
Irene Gorley .... Tracy Scoggins
Maj. Taro Oshira .... Mako
Harker .... Branscombe Richmond

Talk about a change of scenery! Andy and Mac were two street cops from Chicago who, fed up with the weather and the frustrations of their jobs, moved to sun-drenched Hawaii—no more snow, no more city grime, no more sleazy street criminals to chase. And what did they get with the move? Sand, surf, beaches full of well-filled bikinis, and jobs working as undercover detectives for the friendly Honolulu police.

The two cops were a study in contrasts. Mac was brash, impulsive, and pugnacious, while Andy was introspective and cautious. They were assigned to cases ranging from murder, to smuggling, to underworld drug trafficking. Their boss, police Maj. Oshira, had his misgivings about the two young *haoles* (mainlanders), but they did seem to get the job done. The living arrangements weren't too bad either, as they shared a beach house with a number of bikini-clad beauties, including sexy helicopter pilot Irene Gorley.

HAWK (*Police Drama*)

FIRST TELECAST: *September 8, 1966*
LAST TELECAST: *August 11, 1976*
BROADCAST HISTORY:
Sep 1966–Dec 1966, ABC Thu 10:00–11:00
Apr 1976–Aug 1976, NBC Wed 10:00–11:00

CAST:

Lt. John Hawk .... Burt Reynolds
Det. Dan Carter .... Wayne Grice
Asst. D.A. Murray Slaken .... Bruce Glover
Asst. D.A. Ed Gorton .... Leon Janney

Hawk was a police story with a twist. John Hawk was a full-blooded Iroquois Indian working the night beat for the New York District Attorney's Office with his partner Det. Carter. Filmed on location in and around New York City at night, the cases in which he was involved sent him to the rich and the poor, from the exclusive penthouses along Park Avenue to the run-down tenements of the West Side. The star of this series, Burt Reynolds, was himself part Indian. *Hawk* was originally aired by ABC in the fall of 1966. Almost a decade later, hoping to capitalize on Burt Reynolds's later development into a celebrity, NBC aired reruns of the ABC series during the summer of 1976 (as CBS had done with *Dan August*, another ABC series in which Reynolds had starred).

HAWKEYE (*Adventure*)

BROADCAST HISTORY:
Syndicated only
60 minutes
Produced: *1994–1995* (22 episodes)
Released: *September 1994*

CAST:

Nathaniel Bumppo ("Hawkeye") .... Lee Horsley
Elizabeth Shields .... Lynda Carter
Chingachgook .... Rodney A. Grant
McKinney .... Lochlyn Munro
Peevey .... Jed Rees
Capt. Taylor Shields .... Garwin Sanford
**Col. Munro* .... Duncan Fraser

*Occasional

Another of TV's periodic travesties of American history, this series was set in 1755 in New York's Hudson Valley during the French and Indian Wars. Hawkeye was an incredibly noble woodsman, hunter, and pathfinder and Chingachgook, a Delaware Indian, his loyal companion. Hawkeye worked occasionally for the English soldiers stationed at Fort Bennington. William and Elizabeth Shields were merchants from Virginia planning to set up a trading post at the fort. On their way there, they were saved from hostile Huron Indians by Hawkeye and Chingachgook, but William was later set up by his brother, Taylor, the corrupt second in command at Fort Bennington, and taken by Indians, who tortured and may have killed him. Elizabeth stayed on at the fort to run the trading post and search for her husband. McKinney and Peevey were two teenagers who worked for her. Stories revolved around the war between the French and British, the problems with the thuggish Huron Indians, the machinations of the arrogant Taylor, and the developing relationship between Hawkeye and Elizabeth.

Adapted from James Fenimore Cooper's *Leatherstocking Tales*.

HAWKINS (*Law Drama*)

FIRST TELECAST: *October 2, 1973*
LAST TELECAST: *September 3, 1974*
BROADCAST HISTORY:
Oct 1973–Sep 1974, CBS Tue 9:30–11:00
CAST:
Billy Jim Hawkins .... James Stewart
R. J. Hawkins .... Strother Martin

Billy Jim Hawkins had given up his position as a deputy district attorney to enter private legal practice in rural West Virginia. His small-town location did not keep fancy clients away, however, as his fame as a specialist in murder cases attracted clients from far and wide. His pleasant, slow-talking, homespun qualities belied the shrewd, determined attorney that he really was, and he often traveled great distances with his cousin and investigative assistant R.J. in search of evidence that would clear his clients and lead to the apprehension of the real culprits.

Hawkins was one of the three rotating elements that filled the 9:30–11 P.M. time slot on Tuesday nights for CBS during the 1973–1974 season. The other two were *Shaft* and *The New CBS Tuesday Night Movies*.

HAWKINS FALLS, POPULATION 6,200 (*Comedy/Drama*)

FIRST TELECAST: *June 17, 1950*
LAST TELECAST: *October 12, 1950*
BROADCAST HISTORY:
Jun 1950–Aug 1950, NBC Sat 8:00–9:00
Aug 1950–Oct 1950, NBC Thu 8:30–9:00
CAST:
Clate Weathers .... Frank Dane
The Judge .... Phil Lord
Laif Flaigle .... Win Stracke
Mrs. Catherwood .... Hope Summers

This series, which later became a straightforward daytime soap opera, began as a prime-time summer replacement show containing an odd mixture of situation comedy, light drama, and musical entertainment. The setting was the "typical" small town of Hawkins Falls, U.S.A. (patterned after real-life Woodstock, Illinois). The format called for the local newspaper editor, Clate Weathers, to describe the latest events in town, which were then dramatized. Each weekly episode was complete in itself; for example, the uproar when the town loafer (Laif) was put forward as a candidate for mayor, and the events surrounding a typical country auction. Mrs. Catherwood was the president of the garden club.

Hawkins Falls returned to the air in April 1951, as a Monday–Friday daytime serial, retaining many of the same cast members. The daytime version lasted until July 1955.

HAYLOFT HOEDOWN (*Country Music*)

FIRST TELECAST: *July 10, 1948*
LAST TELECAST: *September 18, 1948*
BROADCAST HISTORY:
Jul 1948–Sep 1948, ABC Sat 9:30–10:00
REGULARS:
Elmer Newman
Jack Day
Murray Sisters
Jesse Rogers
Stuff Jumpers
Wesley Tuttle
Ranch Square Dancers
The Sleepy Hollow Gang (instrumental)

One of the earliest examples of country music on network television, and one of ABC's first series, was this bush-league production from Town Hall in Philadelphia, telecast on Saturday nights during the summer of 1948. The talent was little known even in the country field, but everyone pitched in with enthusiasm with square dancing, yodeling, comedy routines, and the like. Emcee Elmer Newman doubled as "Pancake Pete."

The program had been a radio favorite for several years, beginning on Philadelphia's WFIL in December 1944, and moving to the ABC radio network in 1945.

HAYRIDE, see *Grand Ole Opry*

HAYWIRE (*Comedy*)

FIRST TELECAST: *September 1, 1990*
LAST TELECAST: *January 26, 1991*
BROADCAST HISTORY:
Sep 1990–Jan 1991, FOX Sat 8:30–9:00
REGULARS:
John Keister
David Hirsch
Bob Perlow
Alan Hunter
Craig Copeland
Billy Quon

This series was a loosely structured collection of unrelated comedy segments. Among the recurring features were video clips of people on the street with silly voice-over dialogue; spoofs of commercials and movie trailers; clips from old black-and-white films with funny new dialogue; videos of people telling bad jokes to the camera; "The Persuaders," in which Perlow and Hirsch (later replaced by Hunter) competed to see who could con the most people on the street into doing things; "Mind Your Manners with Billy Quon," a weekly depiction of Kung Fu etiquette; and "Thrillseekers," which used the introduction to the old Chuck Connors syndicated series to show people with mundane jobs or in silly, nonthreatening situations.

HAZEL (*Situation Comedy*)

FIRST TELECAST: *September 28, 1961*
LAST TELECAST: *September 5, 1966*
BROADCAST HISTORY:
Sep 1961–Jul 1964, NBC Thu 9:30–10:00 (OS)
Sep 1964–Sep 1965, NBC Thu 9:30–10:00
Sep 1965–Sep 1966, CBS Mon 9:30–10:00
CAST:
Hazel Burke .... Shirley Booth
George Baxter (1961–1965) .... Don DeFore
Dorothy Baxter (1961–1965) .... Whitney Blake
Rosie .... Maudie Prickett
Harvey Griffin .... Howard Smith
Harold Baxter .... Bobby Buntrock
Harriet Johnson (1961–1965) .... Norma Varden
Herbert Johnson (1961–1965) .... Donald Foster
Deidre Thompson (1961–1965) .... Cathy Lewis
Harry Thompson (1961–1965) .... Robert P. Lieb
Mona Williams (1965–1966) .... Mala Powers
Millie Ballard (1965–1966) .... Ann Jillian
Steve Baxter (1965–1966) .... Ray Fulmer

Barbara Baxter (1965–1966).......... Lynn Borden
Susie Baxter (1965–1966) .... Julia Benjamin

George Baxter was a highly successful corporation lawyer who was always in control of everything at the office, but of almost nothing at home. When he returned from the office at day's end, to his wife, Dorothy, and his young son, Harold, he entered the world of Hazel. Hazel was the maid/housekeeper who ran the Baxter household more efficiently than George ran his office. She was always right, knew exactly what needed doing, and preempted his authority with alarming, though justified, regularity. The Johnsons were the Baxters' nutty neighbors.

When this series moved to CBS in 1965, Hazel changed families. George and Dorothy had been "transferred" to the Middle East on an assignment, leaving Hazel and son Harold to live with George's brother's family—which consisted of brother Steve, his wife Barbara, and daughter Susie. Steve Baxter was a real-estate agent who had never understood why George had let Hazel take over his home. He soon found out.

Hazel was based on the *Saturday Evening Post* cartoons of Ted Key.

HAZEL BISHOP SHOW, THE, see *Freddy Martin Show, The*

HAZEL SCOTT (*Music*)

FIRST TELECAST: *July 3, 1950*
LAST TELECAST: *September 29, 1950*
BROADCAST HISTORY:

Jul 1950–Sep 1950, DUM Mon/Wed/Fri 7:45–8:00

HOSTESS:

Hazel Scott

This summer music show was hosted by Trinidad-born singer and pianist Hazel Scott, who performed café favorites and show tunes. Miss Scott, a striking beauty who had appeared in nightclubs, on radio, and in a few movies and Broadway shows, was in private life the wife of New York Congressman Adam Clayton Powell, Jr. She also appeared on local television in New York for a time.

HE & SHE (*Situation Comedy*)

FIRST TELECAST: *September 6, 1967*
LAST TELECAST: *September 11, 1970*
BROADCAST HISTORY:

Sep 1967–Sep 1968, CBS Wed 9:30–10:00
Jun 1970–Sep 1970, CBS Fri 8:00–8:30

CAST:

Paula Hollister...................... Paula Prentiss
Dick Hollister................... Richard Benjamin
Oscar North.......................... Jack Cassidy
Harry Zarakardos.................. Kenneth Mars
Andrew Hummel .... Hamilton Camp
Norman Nugent..................... Harold Gould

Dick Hollister was a successful cartoonist whose creation, "Jetman," had been turned into a TV show starring Oscar North in the title role. Oscar was a bit on the arrogant, smug, egocentric side, and was constantly disagreeing with Dick about the proper interpretation of "Jetman." Paula, Dick's scatterbrained, social-worker wife, had problems of her own which always seemed to end up being shared by the two of them. Andrew Hummel was the fumbling superintendent of the New York apartment building in which Dick and Paula lived, and Harry was their fireman friend.

Paula Prentiss and Richard Benjamin were husband and wife in real life. Reruns of this series, which bore more than a passing resemblance to the classic *Dick Van Dyke Show*, were aired by CBS in the summer of 1970.

HEAD OF THE CLASS (*Situation Comedy*)

FIRST TELECAST: *September 17, 1986*
LAST TELECAST: *June 25, 1991*
BROADCAST HISTORY:

Sep 1986–Feb 1987, ABC Wed 8:30–9:00
Apr 1987–Jun 1989, ABC Wed 8:30–9:00
Aug 1989–Aug 1990, ABC Wed 8:30–9:00
Sep 1990–Jan 1991, ABC Tue 8:30–9:00
May 1991–Jun 1991, ABC Tue 8:30–9:00

CAST:

Charlie Moore (1986–1990) .... Howard Hesseman
Billy MacGregor (1990–1991) .... Billy Connolly
Dr. Harold Samuels........... William G. Schilling
Bernadette Meara............... Jeannetta Arnette
Arvid Engen....................... Dan Frischman
Maria Borges (1986–1989) .... Leslie Bega
Simone Foster..................... Khrystyne Haje
Jawaharlal Choudhury (1986–1989) ... Jory Husain
Eric Mardian .... Brian Robbins
Janice Lazarotto (1986–1989) .... Tannis Vallely
Alan Pinkard .... Tony O'Dell
Darlene Merriman.................. Robin Givens
Dennis Blunden .... Daniel J. Schneider
Sarah Nevins...................... Kimberly Russell
**Lori Applebaum (1986–1988)*...... Marcia Christie
T. J. Jones (1988–1991)................. Rain Pryor
Aristotle McKenzie (1989–1991)... De Voreaux White
Alex Torres (1989–1991)....... Michael DeLorenzo
Viki Amory (1989–1991) .... Lara Piper
Jasper Kwong (1990–1991) ...... Jonathan Ke Quan

*Occasional

This popular comedy was the flip side of *Welcome Back, Kotter*. Instead of underachieving "sweathogs," its focus was the overachieving honors students at Manhattan's Monroe High School. They were so brainy, in fact, that most of their former teachers had just read books while they taught themselves. Enter substitute teacher Charlie Moore, who realized that while these kids were long on facts, they were painfully short on maturity, and could use a few lessons from "the Book of Life" before they faced the real world.

Dr. Samuels was the principal, wary of Charlie's disruption of academic routine but generally supportive; and Bernadette, the energetic assistant principal. The class included Arvid, the classic nerd with glasses, pocket slide rule, and polyester pants; Maria, so driven that when she got a "B" she grounded herself; Simone, the poet; Jawaharlal, the word-mangling exchange student; Eric, the "cool dude" who hated being so smart that he was put with the geeks; Janice, a 12-year-old genius who hadn't had time to grow up; Alan the proto-yuppie; Darlene, the uptown rich girl; and Dennis, the chunky chemistry whiz who was overly fond of pizza.

Turnover in the cast was gradual, and many of these fast-track students stayed in class for the full five-year run. Oddly, Mr. Moore left before they did, moving on in 1990 to pursue his dream of an acting career. He was replaced by free-spirited Scotsman Billy MacGregor, who was more of a standup comic than the sometimes grumpy Moore. Another notable addition was T. J., a remedial-ed "problem student," whose slow learning had more to do with attitude than intelligence, and who ultimately fought her way into the IHP.

Highlights of later seasons included a trip to Moscow (*Class* was apparently the first American entertainment series ever to film an episode there, although some news programs and specials—such as *Candid Camera* in 1961—had preceded it), and another to the Johnson Space Center in Houston, where Arvid and Dennis placed an experiment on the Shuttle. The class also mounted full-scale musical productions of *Little Shop of Horrors* (1989) and *Hair* (1990). They all finally graduated in 1991 as the school, which had been renamed Millard Fillmore High School, was about to be torn down.

HEAD OVER HEELS (*Situation Comedy*)
FIRST TELECAST: *August 26, 1997*
LAST TELECAST: *December 30, 1997*
BROADCAST HISTORY:
Aug 1997–Oct 1997, UPN Tue 9:30–10:00
Dec 1997, UPN Tue 9:30–10:00
CAST:
Jack Baldwin .... Peter Dobson
Warren Baldwin .... Mitchell Whitfield
Ian .... Patrick Bristow
Carmen Montaglio .... Eva LaRue
Valentina .... Cindy Ambuehl
Nikki .... Heidi Mark
Fred Morehead .... Kevin Farley

Head Over Heels was a video dating service in the trendy South Beach section of Miami Beach. It was owned and operated by the Baldwin brothers. Jack, the free-spirited womanizer, was certainly not a poster boy for a service that purported to promote true romance (he regularly hit on the more attractive lonely women who came to Head Over Heels in search of love). Warren, the serious businessman, was recovering from the latest in a long line of failed relationships. Working for them were Ian, a neurotic romance advisor who had taken a vow of celibacy; Carmen, a fellow advisor working on a Ph.D. in human behavior and sexuality; and Valentina, the bimbo who happened to be a computer whiz hired as their office manager. Also seen were Nikki, Warren's sexy new girlfriend, and Fred, a fat client who had little success with women.

HEADLINE, syndicated title for *Big Town*

HEADLINE CLUES, see *Broadway to Hollywood—Headline Clues*

HEADLINE NEWS (Network), see *CNN*

HEADLINERS WITH DAVID FROST
(*Talk/Interview*)
FIRST TELECAST: *May 31, 1978*
LAST TELECAST: *July 5, 1978*
BROADCAST HISTORY:
May 1978–Jul 1978, NBC Wed 9:00–10:00
REGULARS:
David Frost
Liz Smith
Kelly Garrett

Celebrity interviewer David Frost hosted this 1978 summer series, which originated live from the NBC studios in New York. Those interviewed were generally show-business stars, with a few political figures thrown in, making the format an odd combination of superficial and serious subjects. Guests on the first show, for example, were the rock group the Bee Gees, actor John Travolta, and former C.I.A. chief Richard Helms. An additional feature was Headliners Forum, where Frost would pose a question such as "What is the secret of a happy marriage," and a succession of show-business, literary, and political figures would be seen (on tape) giving short, humorous answers. Liz Smith contributed a weekly gossip segment and Kelly Garrett sang of recent events in a "That Was the Week That Was" segment.

HEADMASTER, THE (*Drama*)
FIRST TELECAST: *September 18, 1970*
LAST TELECAST: *September 10, 1971*
BROADCAST HISTORY:
Sep 1970–Jan 1971, CBS Fri 8:30–9:00
Jun 1971–Sep 1971, CBS Fri 8:30–9:00
CAST:
Andy Thompson .... Andy Griffith
Jerry Brownell .... Jerry Van Dyke
Mr. Purdy .... Parker Fennelly
Margaret Thompson .... Claudette Nevins
Judy .... Lani O'Grady
THEME:
"Only a Man," by Gordon and Williams, sung by Linda Ronstadt

Andy Thompson was the headmaster of the Concord School, a private high school with high academic standards. His wife was one of the school's English teachers and his best friend, Jerry Brownell, was the physical-education teacher and coach. Andy's professional life at the school, dealing with the problems of teachers and students, provided the central focus of this folksy series.

Andy Griffith's past television success had been in a very different, country-boy role, and the viewing public did not accept him in this more dignified dramatic setting. In January 1971 he tried to revert to his earlier type of portrayal on a series called *The New Andy Griffith Show*, but that too proved unsuccessful and reruns of *The Headmaster* returned to the time slot in June.

HEALTH NETWORK, THE (Network)
(*Informational Cable Network*)
LAUNCHED:
December 1993
SUBSCRIBERS (MAY 2003):
30.3 million (28% U.S.)

A 24-hour health and fitness channel, not to be confused with the Discovery Health Channel (which it often is). Programming included workouts, medical instruction shows and some documentaries.

The network was launched in 1993 as Fit TV, a physical fitness channel, by the Family Channel and bodybuilder Jake Steinfeld (who at one time served as its CEO). In the late 1990s it merged with on-line medical site WebMD and was renamed The Health Network/Web MD. In 2001 the network was sold to Discovery, which operated its chief competitor Discovery Health Channel. Instead of immediately shutting it down, Discovery continued to operate it as a separate network, albeit with minimal publicity and no known Web site.

HEART OF THE CITY (*Police Drama*)
FIRST TELECAST: *September 20, 1986*
LAST TELECAST: *July 2, 1987*
BROADCAST HISTORY:
Sep 1986–Jan 1987, ABC Sat 9:00–10:00
Jun 1987–Jul 1987, ABC Thu 9:00–10:00
CAST:
Det. Wes Kennedy .... Robert Desiderio
Robin Kennedy (age 15) .... Christina Applegate
Kevin Kennedy (16) .... Jonathan Ward
Lt. Ed Van Duzer........... Dick Anthony Williams
Det. Rick Arno .... Kario Salem
Sgt. Luke Halui .... Branscombe Richmond
Det. Stanley .... Robert Alan Browne

Det. Wes Kennedy was a cop with problems. His wife had been murdered by a crazed killer, leaving Wes with recurrent flashbacks of the grisly event as well as with two teenagers to raise—Robin, a sullen, rebellious girl who blamed him for her mother's death, and Kevin, a better-adjusted youth who was mostly interested in girls. Wes had transferred from the L.A.P.D.'s S.W.A.T. team to the night shift in order to have more time for his son and daughter, but his co-workers—especially Lt. Van Duzer—sometimes had little patience for his family problems, like bailing the kids out of jail.

HEART OF THE CITY, syndicated title for *Big Town*

HEARTBEAT (*Medical Drama*)
FIRST TELECAST: *March 23, 1988*
LAST TELECAST: *April 6, 1989*
BROADCAST HISTORY:
Mar 1988–Apr 1988, ABC Wed 10:00–11:00
Apr 1988, ABC Thu 10:00–11:00
Jan 1989–Apr 1989, ABC Thu 10:00–11:00
CAST:
Dr. Joanne Springsteen/Halloran .... Kate Mulgrew
Dr. Eve Autrey/Calvert............. Laura Johnson
Dr. Leo Rosetti .... Ben Masters
Dr. Stan Gorshalk (1988) .... Ray Baker
Priscilla Gorshalk (1988) .... Katherine Cannon
Dr. Cory Banks..................... Lynn Whitfield
Nurse Marilyn McGrath .... Gail Strickland
Dr. Paul Jared...................... Darrell Larson
Receptionist Robin Flowers (1988)
.... Claudette Sutherland
Caroline Petrie (1988) .... Shanna Reed
Nurse Alice Swanson (1989) .... Julie Ronnie
Dr. Nathan Solt (1989) .... Carmen Argenziano
Dixon Banks (1989)................ Robert Gossett
Lyle Freedlander (1989) .... Allan Miller

Feminism met the TV doctor show met soap opera in this 1988 series. Women's Medical Arts was a new clinic founded by Doctors Joanne and Eve, who believed that women should chart their own direction in the traditionally male-dominated world of medicine. They emphasized women treating women (though there were men on their staff), and an unintimidating relationship between patient and doctor. At WMA, patients were encouraged to call physicians by their first names ("Don't I call her 'doctor'?" "Not around here . . . it's too much of a barrier between patient and doctor").

Dr. Springsteen . . . er, Joanne . . . was a gynecologist and the driving force behind WMA; Eve, a surgeon; Leo, a handsome pediatrician and Joanne's love interest; Stan, a worried psychiatrist; Cory, a young black doctor and mother of two; and Paul, the group's fertility specialist. Their battles were fought in the clinic, at male-dominated Bay General Hospital, with which they were affiliated, and sometimes in the bedroom.

Heartbeat returned in early 1989 with a few more episodes, and a few cast and name changes, but it was no more successful. For reasons that were not explained, Eve's last name was now Calvert, and Joanne's was Halloran.

HEARTLAND (*Situation Comedy*)
FIRST TELECAST: *March 20, 1989*
LAST TELECAST: *July 31, 1989*
BROADCAST HISTORY:
Mar 1989–Jul 1989, CBS Mon 8:30–9:00
CAST:
B. L. McCutcheon...................... Brian Keith
Tom Stafford.................. Richard Gilliland
Casey McCutcheon Stafford ..... Kathleen Layman
Johnny Stafford (age 16)........... Jason Kristofer
Gus Stafford (12)..................... Devin Ratray
Kim Stafford (14) .... Daisy Keith
THEME:
sung by Dion DiMucci

B. L. McCutcheon was the Nebraska cornfields version of Archie Bunker—a cranky, opinionated, but somehow lovable bigot—in this labored 1980s version of *All in the Family* meets *The Real McCoys.* A widower whose farm had been taken over by the bank when he couldn't keep up the payments, B. L. had moved in with his daughter, Casey, and her family. Although he loved Casey and doted on his grandchildren, B. L. just couldn't seem to get along with his son-in-law, Tom. The oldest of the Stafford children, Johnny, was a TV addict who wanted desperately to move to Southern California; Gus was a stereotypical, if incredibly clumsy, young farm boy; and Kim was their intellectual, adopted Asian daughter.

HEARTS AFIRE (*Situation Comedy*)
FIRST TELECAST: *September 14, 1992*
LAST TELECAST: *February 1, 1995*
BROADCAST HISTORY:
Sep 1992–Mar 1993, CBS Mon 8:30–9:00
Oct 1993–Dec 1993, CBS Wed 8:00–8:30
Dec 1993–Feb 1994, CBS Wed 8:30–9:00
Mar 1994–Apr 1994, CBS Mon 9:30–10:00
Jul 1994–Dec 1994, CBS Sat 9:30–10:00
Jan 1995–Feb 1995, CBS Wed 8:30–9:00
CAST:
John Hartman......................... John Ritter
Georgie Anne Lahti Hartman .... Markie Post
Ben Hartman (1992–1994) .... Justin Burnette
Ben Hartman (1994–1995) .... J. Skylar Testa
Elliot Hartman......................... Clark Duke
Billy Bob Davis................ Billy Bob Thornton
Mavis Davis (1992–1993) .... Wendie Jo Sperber
Carson Lee Davis .... Doren Fein
Dee Dee Starr (1992–1993) .... Beth Broderick
Senator Strobe Smithers (1992–1993)
.... George Gaynes
George Lahti (1992–1993)........... Edward Asner

Miss Lula (1992) .... Beah Richards
Adam Carlson (1992–1993)............. Adam Carl
Dr. Madeline Stoessinger (1993–1995)
.... Conchata Ferrell
Lonnie Garr (1993–1995)............. Leslie Jordan
Vickie Bumpers (1993–1994)...... Debbie Gregory

When *Hearts Afire* premiered in 1992 it was described by CBS as a "politically topical comedy series." Set in Washington, it focused on the professional and personal relationship of John Hartman, the legislative assistant to aging, conservative Southern senator Strobe Smithers, and Georgie Anne Lahti, the once globe-trotting but now out-of-work liberal journalist whom John hired as the senator's press secretary. John, the divorced father of two young sons, Ben and Elliot, offered to let Georgie Anne and her "mammy," Miss Lula, live in his home until they could find housing. There was an ulterior motive because, although they were on opposite sides of the political fence and constantly sparred about almost everything, they were physically attracted to one another. Within weeks they were having a steamy affair.

Others on Senator Smithers's staff were Billy Bob, a childhood friend of John's; Dee Dee, the sexy but simpleminded receptionist with whom the married Smithers was having an affair; Mavis, Billy Bob's efficient wife, who considered Dee Dee "the last bimbo in Congress"; and Adam, the incompetent office assistant. Things got even more crowded in the Hartman house when Georgie Anne's cantankerous father, George, recently released from prison, also moved in. Possibly because viewers were not enthralled by a couple effectively "living in sin" in a home with children, John proposed to Georgie Anne in February.

The 1993–1994 season brought major changes to *Hearts Afire*. John and Georgie Anne, now newlyweds, moved back to the small Southern town (never named) where he and Billy Bob had grown up to get a new start away from the political jungle of Washington. Billy Bob, recently divorced, returned home too, along with his young daughter, Carson Lee. They bought the financially troubled local paper, *The Daily Beacon*, and set to work to revive it. The only surviving member of the *Beacon*'s staff was Lonnie, the big-talking but insecure printer. Sharing space in the small building that housed the *Beacon* was Madeline, a cynical, sharp-tongued psychiatrist whom they convinced to write an advice column for the paper. The editorial approach of the *Beacon* was always a bone of contention between conservative John and liberal Georgie Anne, now abetted by Madeline, her new friend and progressive soul mate. In the fall 1994 season premiere Georgie Anne gave birth to a daughter, Amelia.

HEARTS ARE WILD (*Drama*)

FIRST TELECAST: *January 10, 1992*
LAST TELECAST: *March 13, 1992*
BROADCAST HISTORY:
Jan 1992–Mar 1992, CBS Fri 10:00–11:00
CAST:
Jack Thorpe........................ David Beecroft
Leon "Pepe" Pepperman.................. Jon Polito
Kyle Hubbard .... Catherine Mary Stewart
THEME:
"Viva Las Vegas"

Hearts Are Wild was a short-lived variation on the formula set by previous series like *The Love Boat* and *Hotel*. Set in and around the glamorous world of Caesar's Palace casino hotel in Las Vegas, it focused on the activities of guests and employees, especially the former. The only regulars were three of the hotel's staff—Jack Thorpe, the handsome owner; Pepe Pepperman, the gruff casino manager, who had been a trusted friend and associate of Jack's for many years; and Kyle Hubbard, the perky head of guest relations. Among the familiar guest stars passing through were Dick Van Patten, Mickey Rooney, John Astin, Alice Ghostley, Tom Bosley, Ricardo Montalban (whose *Fantasy Island* had used the same formula), Bonnie Franklin, Isabel Sanford, Sally Struthers, and Gene Barry.

Filmed on location in Las Vegas.

HEAVEN FOR BETSY (*Situation Comedy*)

FIRST TELECAST: *September 30, 1952*
LAST TELECAST: *December 23, 1952*
BROADCAST HISTORY:
Sep 1952–Dec 1952, CBS Tue/Thu 7:45–8:00
CAST:
Pete Bell .... Jack Lemmon
Betsy Bell........................... Cynthia Stone

This early live domestic comedy starred real-life newlyweds Jack Lemmon and Cynthia Stone as Pete and Betsy Bell, newlyweds who were adjusting to married life. Pete was assistant buyer in the toy department of a suburban New York department store. His biggest problem was a tendency to jump into a situation before realizing its ramifications. His wife, Betsy, a secretary turned full-time homemaker, was not really occupied maintaining their two-room apartment, but had plenty to do getting Pete out of various scrapes. Lemmon and Stone worked together in several TV series in the early 1950s, before he began his highly successful movie career in 1954.

HEAVEN HELP US (*Fantasy/Adventure*)

BROADCAST HISTORY:
Syndicated only
60 minutes
Produced: *1994*
Released: *August 1994*
CAST:
Mr. Shepherd................. Ricardo Montalban
Doug Monroe...................... John Schneider
Lexy Monroe .... Melinda Clarke

Doug was an egotistical pitcher for the Florida Marlins who was newly married to sexy Lexy Kitteridge in this lighter-than-air fantasy. Taking off in Doug's small private plane immediately after the wedding, they indulged in a little sex in the sky and, thus distracted, unfortunately crashed into the side of the San Antonio Marriott and were killed. That should have been the end of it, but not with Ricardo Montalban around. Before they could get into Heaven they had to earn their wings, so to speak, by helping people on earth, and he would be their guide.

Doug and Lexy were not too enthusiastic about this but, given the alternatives, decided to go along. The ghostly lovebirds "lived" in a luxury suite on the phantom thirteenth floor of the hotel into which they had crashed. They influenced people mostly by a sort of emotional osmosis; at times they might be visible, but only when they were angry and not pure of heart.

HEC RAMSEY (*Western*)

FIRST TELECAST: *October 8, 1972*
LAST TELECAST: *August 25, 1974*
BROADCAST HISTORY:
Oct 1972–Aug 1974, NBC Sun 8:30–10:00
CAST:
Hec Ramsey .... Richard Boone
Sheriff Oliver B. Stamp .... Richard Lenz
Doc Amos Coogan .... Harry Morgan
Arne Tornquist .... Dennis Rucker

Hec Ramsey was a grizzled old gunfighter, living around the turn of the century, who had become interested in the "newfangled" science of criminology and spent years learning all he could about it. He still carried a gun, but had come to rely on a trunk full of paraphernalia that included fingerprinting equipment, magnifying glasses, scales, and other odds and ends to track down culprits. As the series began Hec arrived in New Prospect, Oklahoma, to take a job as deputy sheriff. He soon discovered that the sheriff, Oliver B. Stamp, was very young and inexperienced. Stamp, fearing that Hec's legendary "fast gun" would attract trouble, was uncertain about his new partner, but young sheriff and old deputy eventually learned to make good use of Hec's novel methods.

Hec Ramsey spent two seasons as one of the four rotating elements of the *NBC Sunday Mystery Movie*. The other three elements were *Columbo*, *McCloud*, and *McMillan and Wife*.

HEE HAW (*Variety*)

FIRST TELECAST: *June 15, 1969*
LAST TELECAST: *July 13, 1971*
BROADCAST HISTORY:
Jun 1969–Sep 1969, CBS Sun 9:00–10:00
Dec 1969–Jun 1970, CBS Wed 7:30–8:30
Sep 1970–Jul 1971, CBS Tue 8:30–9:30
(In first-run syndication from 1971–1993)
HOSTS:
Roy Clark
Alvis Edgar "Buck" Owens (1969–1986)
ORIGINAL REGULARS (1969):
Cathy Baker (1969–1991)
Jennifer Bishop (1969–1971)
Archie Campbell (1969–1987)
Jim Hager (1969–1986)
Jon Hager (1969–1986)
Don Harron (1969–1986)
Gunilla Hutton (1969–1991)
Louis M. "Grandpa" Jones
Claude "Jackie" Phelps (1969–1986)
Don Rich (1969–1975)
Jimmy Riddle (1969–1983)
Jeannine Riley (1969–1971)
Alvin "Junior" Samples (1969–1984)
Diana Scott (1969–1970)
Lulu Roman
Stringbean (a.k.a. David Akeman) (1969–1974)
Gordie Tapp
Mary Taylor (1969–1970)
Sheb Wooley (1969)
The Buckaroos (1969–1986)
The Hee Haw Band
The Nashville Edition (1969–1991)
LATER REGULARS (IN ORDER THEY JOINED):
Minnie Pearl (1970–1991)
Lisa Todd (1970–1986)
Barbi Benton (1971–1976)
Sherry Miles (1971–1972)
Ray Sanders (1971–1972)
Harry Cole (1972–1976)
George Lindsey (1972–1992)
Ann Randall (1972–1973)
Marianne Gordon Rogers (1972–1991)
Misty Rowe (1972–1991)
Gailard Sartain (1972–1992)
Roni Stoneman (1973–1991)
Kenny Price (1974–1988)
John Henry Faulk (1975–1982)
Buck Trent (1975–1982)
Charlie McCoy (1976–1992)
Linda Thompson (1977–1992)
Mackenzie Colt (1978–1982)
Rev. Grady Nutt (1979–1983)
Roy Acuff (1980–1985)
Victoria Hallman (1980–1990)
Rodney Lay (1980–1987)
The Wild West & Fanci (1980–1989)
Diana Goodman (1981–1985)
Slim Pickens (1981–1983)
Chase Randolph (1981–1982)
Nancy Taylor (1981–1982)
Jonathan Winters (1983–1984)
Kelly Billingsley (1984–1987)
Irlene Mandrell (1984–1992)
Jeff Smith (1984–1991)
Jackie Waddell (1984–1987)
Patricia McKinnon (1985–1986)
Dub Taylor (1985–1991)
Mike Snyder (1987–1991)
Vicki Bird (1989–1991)
Terry Sanders (1989–1991)
Bruce Williams and Terry Ree (1989–1991)
Phil Campbell (1990–1992)
Donna Stokes (1992)
Becky Norris (1992)
Lindy Norris (1992)
Dawn McKinley (1992)
Alice Hathaway Ripley (1992)
Dennis Stone (1992)
Gary Mule Deer (1992)
Billy Baker (1992)
Pedro Tomas (1992)
The Hee Haw Singers (1992)

Hee Haw was country music's answer to *Rowan & Martin's Laugh-In*. Blackouts, nutty running gags, cameos by assorted guest stars, and some of the worst "corny" one-liners imaginable, appropriately delivered from a cornfield, all contributed to the mix. An animated donkey was used on a regular basis to react to the humor, and to provide the "hee haw" of the title.

Although the humor was purposely cornball, the music on *Hee Haw* was first-rate country material. Cohosts Buck Owens and Roy Clark were both major country stars, Clark being one of the best banjoist-guitarists in the business. Other big names from the country field, both current and long-established, were also featured regularly. *Hee Haw* was in the top 20 nationally when it was dropped from the network in 1971, a victim of CBS' decision to "de-ruralize" its programming (national advertisers want only young, urban audiences). Like Lawrence Welk, which was dropped by ABC for similar reasons, it promptly went into syndication with all-new shows and became a major hit on a non-network basis. When co-host Buck Owens left the show after the 1985–1986 season he was not replaced. Instead, a policy of having Roy Clark joined by weekly guest co-hosts was instituted.

In an effort to attract a more contemporary audience *Hee Haw* was given a complete overhaul in late 1991, and the results showed up in January 1992. The cornfield was gone, and the primary sets were now a city street and a shopping mall. Many of the longtime regulars had been replaced by a whole new crew of young unknowns to attract a younger audience. The changes didn't attract new viewers and, in fact, resulted in the loss of many loyal viewers of the venerable show who weren't interested in the new look or the unfamiliar faces. That summer *Hee Haw* went out of production, although host Roy Clark did provide new introductions for *Hee Haw Silver*, the selected reruns of earlier shows that were syndicated during the 1992–1993 season to commemorate the series' quarter century on the air.

HEE HAW HONEYS (*Comedy/Variety*)

BROADCAST HISTORY:

Syndicated only
30 minutes
Produced: *1978–1979* (26 episodes)
Released: *September 1978*

CAST:

Kathie Honey .... Kathie Lee Johnson
Misty Honey .... Misty Rowe
Willie Billie Honey .... Gailard Sartain
Lulu Honey .... Lulu Roman
Kenny Honey .... Kenny Price

In this spin-off from *Hee Haw*, five members of that show's cast appeared as operators of the Hee Haw Honeys Club, a Nashville nightspot. Lulu and Kenny Honey were the parents of good ole boy Willie, sexy Misty, and cute Kathie. The setting was little more than an excuse for a cornball variety show, along the lines of *Hee Haw* itself, with rustic jokes and country music performed by such guests as Loretta Lynn, the Oak Ridge Boys, Conway Twitty, and the Statler Brothers.

HEIGHTS, THE (*Drama*)

FIRST TELECAST: *August 27, 1992*
LAST TELECAST: *November 26, 1992*
BROADCAST HISTORY:

Aug 1992–Nov 1992, FOX Thu 9:00–10:00

CAST:

Mr. Mike .... Ray Aranha
Stan Lee .... Alex Desert
Arthur "Dizzy" Mazelli .... Ken Garito
Rita MacDougal .... Cheryl Pollak
Hope Linden .... Charlotte Ross
J. T. Banks .... Shawn David Thompson
Lenny Wieckowski .... Zachary Throne
Alex O'Brien .... Jamie Walters
Jodie Abramowitz .... Tasia Valenza
Harry Abramowitz .... Donnelly Rhodes
Shelley Abramowitz .... Camille Saviola

THEME:

"How Do You Talk to an Angel," by Stephanie Tyrell, Barry Coffing, and Steve Tyrell, performed by The Heights; "Children of the Night," by David Palmer and Steve Tyrell

The Heights was a rock and roll band made up of a group of ambitious, young, mostly blue-collar kids hoping to ride success out of their middle-class lives. The members of the group were Stan (guitar), who worked for his father, Mr. Mike, owner of the bar/pool hall where the group hung out; Dizzy (drums), a plumber's assistant; Rita (saxophone), a dispatcher for a beer distributor; Hope (guitar), whose wealthy family supported her while she played with the band; J.T. (guitar), the lead singer, an auto mechanic with a long-standing love/hate relationship with Hope; Lenny (keyboard), who worked at the Seven Seas restaurant; and Alex, the newest member of the group, a sensitive poet/songwriter who worked in a grocery store. Alex, who was in love with Rita, also sang leads, and his presence caused friction with J.T., who didn't like anybody else singing lead. When Dizzy married his pregnant girlfriend, Jodie, a nurses' aide whose father was his boss, Lenny moved in with his former roommate, Stan.

The series chronicled the ups and downs of the band members as well as their evolving relationships. At least one new song, filmed as a video montage, was performed each week. Ironically, the single version of the series theme, featuring Jamie Walters as lead singer, hit #1 on the *Billboard* charts in early November, one week before *The Heights* was canceled.

HELEN O'CONNELL SHOW, THE (*Music*)

FIRST TELECAST: *May 29, 1957*
LAST TELECAST: *September 6, 1957*
BROADCAST HISTORY:

May 1957–Sep 1957, NBC Wed/Fri 7:30–7:45

REGULAR:

Helen O'Connell

Big-band singer Helen O'Connell was on the air twice a week with this live musical show that occupied the remainder of the half hour in which NBC telecast its network news program. The show originated from New York and gave Miss O'Connell the opportunity to sing several songs, occasionally with a guest star but more often without.

HELEN REDDY SHOW, THE (*Musical Variety*)

FIRST TELECAST: *June 28, 1973*
LAST TELECAST: *August 16, 1973*
BROADCAST HISTORY:

Jun 1973–Aug 1973, NBC Thu 8:00–9:00

REGULARS:

Helen Reddy
The Jaime Rogers Dancers
Nelson Riddle and His Orchestra

THEME:

"I Am Woman," by Helen Reddy (lyrics) and Ray Burton (music)

Australian singer Helen Reddy, who became something of a symbol of the Women's Liberation movement through her best-selling recording "I Am Woman" ("I am strong, I am invincible . . ."), was the star of this 1973 summer series. The format of the show included comedy skits and musical numbers with guest stars. Each show closed with a question-and-answer session, with the questions coming from members of the studio audience.

HELL TOWN (*Drama*)

FIRST TELECAST: *September 4, 1985*

LAST TELECAST: *December 25, 1985*

BROADCAST HISTORY:

Sep 1985–Dec 1985, NBC Wed 9:00–10:00

CAST:

Father Noah "Hardstep" Rivers .... Robert Blake
One Ball .... Whitman Mayo
Lawyer Sam .... Jeff Corey
Mother Maggie .... Natalie Core
Sister Indigo .... Vonetta McGee
Sister Angel Cake .... Isabel Grandin
Stump .... Tony Longo
Sister Daisy .... Rhonda Dodson
Crazy Horse .... Zitto Kazann
Poco Loco .... Eddie Quillan

THEME:

sung by Sammy Davis, Jr.

"If I ever catch you down here sellin' garbage," the burly priest shouted at the startled drug dealer, "I'll tear your arms out." Ahem. "Are you really a priest?" he was later asked. "Why, soitanly. On Sunday, I even wear a dress. Come inta'da church and see."

Father Hardstep was *Baretta* as a priest. Sleeves rolled up, shooting pool, mangling the English language, he was surely the most unusual clergyman seen on TV, but one dedicated to bringing a little hope into the impoverished East Los Angeles parish of St. Dominic's. Hardstep was an ex-con, and a perfect choice for such a tough neighborhood. He had grown up there and knew all of the petty crooks, gangs, and others who preyed on the honest parishioners. Helping out with legal matters (Hardstep was often short of funds, or trying to bend the rules a bit) was Sam, a retired lawyer. One Ball, Stump, and Crazy Horse aided him when more physical assistance was needed. But it was "Father Brassknuckles" himself who laid down the law: "In Hell Town, nobody kills nobody for no reason. Nobody dies in Hell Town, unless it's from old age."

HELLO, LARRY (*Situation Comedy*)

FIRST TELECAST: *January 26, 1979*

LAST TELECAST: *April 30, 1980*

BROADCAST HISTORY:

Jan 1979–Feb 1979, NBC Fri 9:30–10:00
Feb 1979–Aug 1979, NBC Fri 8:30–9:00
Oct 1979, NBC Fri 8:30–9:00
Oct 1979–Apr 1980, NBC Wed 9:30–10:00

CAST:

Larry Alder .... McLean Stevenson
Diane Alder (1979) .... Donna Wilkes
Diane Alder (1979–1980) .... Krista Errickson
Ruthie Alder .... Kim Richards
Morgan Winslow .... Joanna Gleason
Earl .... George Memmoli
Meadowlark Lemon .... Himself
Tommy Roscini .... John Femia
Henry Alder (1980) .... Fred Stuthman
Leona Wilson .... Ruth Brown

Following the breakup of his marriage, radio talk-show host Larry Alder moved from Los Angeles to Portland, Oregon, to get a fresh start. He landed a job at radio station KLOW, where Morgan Winslow became the producer of his phone-in talk show. Earl was Larry's obese engineer. Larry had been given custody of his two daughters, 13-year-old Ruthie and 16-year-old Diane. Glib and in total control on the air, he was much less sure of himself at home as the single parent of two maturing girls. Leona, a schoolteacher and neighbor, tried to bring a little of the woman's touch to this chaotic household. Larry's ex-wife Marion (Shelley Fabares) also turned up occasionally. Added to the regular cast in the fall of 1979 were former Harlem Globetrotters basketball star Meadowlark Lemon, playing himself as owner of a sporting goods store, and Tommy, a 14-year-old neighbor. In February 1980 Larry's retired father, Henry, also moved in.

Hello, Larry's time slot on the NBC schedule was right after the much more popular *Diff'rent Strokes*. Since both shows were produced by Tandem Productions, and *Larry* needed a boost, it was established that Larry Alder and *Diff'rent Strokes*' Philip Drummond were old army buddies, and that Drummond's company had purchased the radio station where Larry worked. The producers hoped that by having the casts of the two shows appear together in crossover episodes the much larger *Diff'rent Strokes* audience would be attracted to *Hello, Larry*. It never happened.

HE-MAN AND THE MASTERS OF THE UNIVERSE (*Cartoon*)

BROADCAST HISTORY:

Cartoon Network
30 minutes
Original episodes: *2002–*
Premiered: *August 31, 2002*

VOICES:

He-Man/Prince Adam .... Cam Clarke
Teela .... Lisa Ann Beley
Queen Marlena/Sorceress .... Nicole Oliver
King Randor .... Michael Donovan
Keldor/Skeletor, Buzz-Off .... Brian Dobson
Man-At-Arms, Whiplash .... Gary Chalk
Mekaneck, Orko .... Gabe Khouth
Evil-Lyn .... Kathleen Barr
Man-E-Faces, Trap Jaw, Tri-Klops ..... Paul Dobson
Beast Man, Clawful, Mer-Man, Ram Man, Stratos .... Scott McNeil

Mythic adventure set in ancient times, featuring a buff, blond hero called He-Man. He-Man had been called upon to defend King Randor's Eternia against the attacks of Randor's evil brother Keldor (aka Skeletor, due to his skeletal face), who lived amid fire and flame in the Dark Hemisphere. He-Man was in fact teenage Prince Adam, guided and advised by the Sorceress and aided by his friends Teela, Man-At-Arms, Orko, Ram Man and others. Cringer was his pet green tiger/battle cat. Skeletor's henchmen included Beast Man, Evil-Lyn and Mer-Man. There were huge battles with swords, magic and cackling villains ("The power of Eternia will finally be mine—heh heh!"), but He-Man shouted, "By the power of Greyskull!" and prevailed.

Based on the 1983 syndicated cartoon and Mattel toy line of the same name.

HENNESEY (*Comedy/Drama*)

FIRST TELECAST: *September 28, 1959*

LAST TELECAST: *September 17, 1962*

BROADCAST HISTORY:

Sep 1959–Sep 1962, CBS Mon 10:00–10:30 (OS)

CAST:

Charles J. "Chick" Hennesey .... Jackie Cooper
Martha Hale .... Abby Dalton
Capt. Walter Shafer .... Roscoe Karns
Max Bronski .... Henry Kulky
Harvey Spencer Blair III .... James Komack
Seaman Shatz .... Arte Johnson
Dr. Dan Wagner (1960–1962) .... Herb Ellis
Dr. Owen King (1960) .... Robert Gist
Pulaski (1960–1962) .... Norman Alden
Mrs. Shafer .... Meg Wyllie

Stationed at a naval base in San Diego, Lt. Chick Hennesey was a young medical officer who treated the base personnel and their families. He worked for crusty Capt. Shafer (who during the course of the series would be promoted to admiral), and had attractive Martha Hale for an understanding and romantically interested nurse. Their romance blossomed and they became engaged, with the wedding taking place in the episode that aired on May 7, 1962. The biggest "character" in the entire medical department was Harvey Spencer Blair III, a young naval dentist whose society background and financial independence grated on all concerned. Blair was always looking for angles and gimmicks, much in the style of Ernie Bilko in *The Phil Silvers Show* but, unlike Bilko, fancied himself a real ladies' man.

HENNY AND ROCKY SHOW, THE (*Comedy/Variety*)

FIRST TELECAST: *June 1, 1955*
LAST TELECAST: *August 10, 1955*
BROADCAST HISTORY:
Jun 1955–Aug 1955, ABC Wed 10:45–11:00

REGULARS:
Rocky Graziano
Henny Youngman
Marion Colby
Bobby Hackett
Buddy Weed

Designed to fill the time slot between the end of *The Wednesday Night Fights* and the start of the eleven o'clock local news, *The Henny and Rocky Show* provided the singing of Marion Colby and the playing of a jazz combo featuring Bobby Hackett on trumpet and Buddy Weed on piano. Comedy was supplied by Henny Youngman and ex-middleweight boxing champion Rocky Graziano. Featured in the show was a recap of the night's fight and "Ribber's Digest" in which Henny satirized the current news. Henny left the show following the June 29 telecast and it was retitled *Rocky's Corner*.

HENRY MORGAN'S GREAT TALENT HUNT (*Comedy/Variety*)

FIRST TELECAST: *January 26, 1951*
LAST TELECAST: *June 1, 1951*
BROADCAST HISTORY:
Jan 1951–Mar 1951, NBC Fri 9:00–9:30
Mar 1951–Jun 1951, NBC Fri 9:30–10:00

REGULARS:
Henry Morgan
Dorothy Claire
Kaye Ballard
Dorothy Jarnac
Arnold Stang (as "Gerard")
Art Carney
Pert Kelton

This program started as a satire on the *Original Amateur Hour*–type program with Henry Morgan introducing people with offbeat "talents"—a man who played the violin by picking the strings with his teeth, a girl who tap-danced while playing an instrument, a woman who had taught her dog to talk, etc. Arnold Stang was Henry's helper, supposedly tracking down all of the "talented" guests on the show. Morgan opened the show with a monologue and, after the acts had performed, the winner was chosen by the applause level of the studio audience. On April 20, 1951, the title of this live program was shortened to *The Henry Morgan Show* and the format changed. It became a comedy-variety show with the emphasis on satiric comedy skits. Singer Dorothy Claire and dancer Dorothy Jarnac provided musical numbers between the skits.

HERALD PLAYHOUSE, syndicated title for *Schlitz Playhouse of Stars*

HERB SHRINER SHOW, THE (*Comedy/Variety*)

FIRST TELECAST: *November 7, 1949*
LAST TELECAST: *December 4, 1956*
BROADCAST HISTORY:
Nov 1949–Feb 1950, CBS Mon/Tue/Thu/Fri/Sat 7:55–8:00
Oct 1951–Apr 1952, ABC Thu 9:00–9:30
Oct 1956–Dec 1956, CBS Tue 9:00–9:30

REGULAR:
Herb Shriner

Herb Shriner was a humorist who had become famous on radio in the late 1940s with his folksy monologues on rural life back home in Indiana, interspersed with harmonica solos. His homespun philosophy, and his disarming, ingenuous personality often led to comparisons with the late Will Rogers. During the 1948–1949 season Shriner had a Monday–Friday daytime show on CBS and in the fall of 1949 he moved into nighttime television with a five-a-week series of short monologues called *The Herb Shriner Show*. ABC brought him back in 1951 as the host of an evening half hour entitled *Herb Shriner Time*. The longer format gave him a chance to play his harmonica and work in skits with guest stars, as well as deliver his tall tales. It was essentially this same format that was tried again in the fall of 1956 on CBS in *The Herb Shriner Show*.

HERBIE, THE LOVE BUG (*Situation Comedy*)

FIRST TELECAST: *March 17, 1982*
LAST TELECAST: *April 14, 1982*
BROADCAST HISTORY:
Mar 1982–Apr 1982, CBS Wed 8:00–9:00

CAST:

Jim Douglas .... Dean Jones
Susan MacLane .... Patricia Harty
Bo Phillips .... Richard Paul
Julie MacLane .... Claudia Wells
Robbie MacLane .... Douglas Emerson
Matthew MacLane .... Nicky Katt
Jason .... Bryan Utman
Randy Bigelow .... Larry Linville
Mrs. Bigelow .... Natalie Core

Herbie, a Volkswagen Beetle with a mind of its own, was the star of this lighthearted comedy series. Herbie had "adopted" its owner, Jim Douglas, and spent much of its time looking out for his welfare, including finding him an attractive young wife. Julie MacLane, a divorcée with three young children, was the chosen bride, discovered by Herbie and Jim when they thwarted a bank robbery in which she was being held hostage. Despite the efforts of her former boyfriend, Randy Bigelow, to disrupt her new romance, Jim prevailed and the two were married in the April 7 episode. Jim ran a driving school with help from easy-going Bo Phillips, but his limited income from this venture forced him also to teach driver education at a local high school.

Based on the *Love Bug* movies produced by Walt Disney Productions from 1969 to 1980, with Dean Jones reprising the role he had played in two of them—*The Love Bug* (1969) and *Herbie Goes to Monte Carlo* (1977).

HERCULES: THE LEGENDARY JOURNEYS

(*Adventure*)

BROADCAST HISTORY:

Syndicated only
60 minutes
Produced: *1994–1999* (111 episodes)
Released: *January 1995*

CAST:

Hercules .... Kevin Sorbo
Iolaus .... Michael Hurst
**Salmoneus* .... Robert Trebor
**Autolycus* .... Bruce Campbell
**Ares (1995)* .... Mark Newham
**Ares (1996–1999)* .... Kevin Smith
**Strife (1997–1998)* .... Joel Tobeck
**Aphrodite (1996–1999)* .... Alexandra Tydings
**Morrigan (1998–1999)* .... Tamara Gorsky

*Occasional

Greek and Roman mythology provided the basis for this beefcake adventure series that was spun off from several made-for-TV movies aired during 1994. Hercules was half man and half god, with greater strength than any mortal. His father, Zeus, was king of the gods and his mother, Alcmene, a beautiful woman. At the beginning of the first episode Hercules' wife, Deianira (played by Tawny Kitaen in the made-for-TV films), and his children were killed by his evil stepmother, Hera. Hercules, trying to cope with his loss, traveled from place to place helping people and battling the terrifying creations of Hera and the other rogue gods. In addition to other humans, he fought hydra-headed monsters, dragons, demons, and even a giant Cyclops. On occasion he used techniques that looked suspiciously like contemporary martial arts. Despite all the violence, there was plenty of time for romance and fun, and the series had a pronounced tongue-in-cheek quality about it.

Iolaus, Hercules' best friend since they were children, traveled with him and reveled in the many fights they got into. Among the recurring characters were Salmoneus, a talkative but cowardly peddler forever looking for his big score; Autolycus, "the prince of thieves," a likable crook who was almost as cowardly as Salmoneus; Ares the God of War, Hercules' malevolent half brother, who was obsessed with seeing Hercules dead; Strife, Ares' aide; and Aphrodite, the playful goddess of love.

In May 1998, Hercules' mother died and he decided to join his father Zeus on Olympus to rule the other gods, but he changed his mind and returned to Earth. Late that year Iolaus' body was taken over by Dahak, an ancient demon, and several episodes were spent with Hercules trying to exorcise the evil spirit. In January he succeeded, with the help of Nebula (Gina Torres) and Morrigan, with whom he had fallen in love, destroying Dahak and releasing Iolaus' spirit so that it could go to heaven. A few weeks later another Iolaus, who had been a jester on an alternative Earth, returned with Hercules to our Earth to replace the hero's dead friend. The new Iolaus was very timid and really didn't want to fight—but he adjusted. Hercules and Morrigan, who had gone their separate ways, got back together on a trip to Cyprus, reminiscing about their romance. In May Iolaus II and his beloved Nautica (Angela Dotchin), daughter of Triton, god of the sea, left to live in the ocean. The following week the gods allowed the original Iolaus to return to Earth to travel with his buddy.

The last eight original episodes of Hercules were telecast in the fall of 1999, with the series finale airing on Thanksgiving weekend. In it Zeus (Charles Keating), attempting to reconcile with Hera (Meg Foster), released her from the Abyss of Tartarus and accidentally released the two titans who, with the help of Atlas, attempted to destroy Olympus and Earth. Hercules prevented it. In the last scene, he and Iolaus walked off into the sunset wondering whether or not Zeus and Hera would really reconcile.

An early spin-off series was *Xena: Warrior Princess* (1995). Two other *Hercules* series surfaced on network television in September 1998. On weekday afternoons Fox aired *Young Hercules*, starring Ryan Gosling as Hercules and Dean O'Gorman as Iolaus, produced by the same people responsible for the grown-up Hercules, and ABC premiered the animated *Disney's Hercules* on Saturday mornings. *Young Hercules* ran until May 1999 and *Disney's Hercules* left the air four months later.

Both *Hercules: The Legendary Journeys* and *Young Hercules* were filmed in New Zealand.

HERE AND NOW (*Documentary*)

FIRST TELECAST: *September 29, 1961*
LAST TELECAST: *December 29, 1961*

BROADCAST HISTORY:

Sep 1961–Dec 1961, NBC Fri 10:30–11:00

HOST:

Frank McGee

Frank McGee narrated the three or four stories that were covered in each telecast of this magazine-format news program. The subjects were people involved in major news stories in varied areas ranging from politics to medicine to the arts. Emphasis was placed on how the people involved were affected by the news events, not simply upon the events themselves.

HERE AND NOW (*Situation Comedy*)

FIRST TELECAST: *September 19, 1992*
LAST TELECAST: *January 2, 1993*

BROADCAST HISTORY:

Sep 1992–Jan 1993, NBC Sat 8:00–8:30

CAST:

Alexander James (A.J.) ..... Malcolm-Jamal Warner
"Uncle" Sydney .... Charles Brown
Danielle .... Rachael Crawford
"T" .... Daryl "Chill" Mitchell

Randall Freeman .... Pee Wee Love
William .... Shaun Weiss
Ms. St. Marth .... S. Epatha Merkerson
Amy .... Jessica Stone

THEME:

"Tennessee," written and performed by Arrested Development

Bill Cosby was executive producer of this rather hard-edged, inner-city sitcom, which was as downscale black as *The Cosby Show* was upper-middle-class "white." A.J. (played by *The Cosby Show*'s Malcolm-Jamal Warner) was a young graduate student in psychology who volunteered to work at the Upper Manhattan Youth Center, a hotbed of smart-alecky and sometimes troubled kids. Reformed delinquent "T" was his sidekick and the class clown; Randall, the tough guy; William, a street-smart 13-year-old; Amy, a fellow student and co-worker at the center; and Ms. St. Marth the center's director. A.J. lived with his "uncle" (not really) Sydney, a doorman and his dad's old war buddy, and had designs on Sydney's cute daughter, his "cousin" (not really) Danielle.

Although the series strove to reflect black culture (every line seemed to include "yo" or "hey, man"), it could never quite decide whether it was drama or comedy. One episode might contain a truly frightening standoff between A.J. and a vicious drug dealer, another a warm, friendly comedy-with-a-moral. *Here and Now* was then-and-gone by January.

HERE COME THE BRIDES (*Comedy/Adventure*)

FIRST TELECAST: *September 25, 1968*
LAST TELECAST: *September 18, 1970*
BROADCAST HISTORY:

Sep 1968–Sep 1969, ABC Wed 7:30–8:30
Sep 1969–Sep 1970, ABC Fri 9:00–10:00

CAST:

Jason Bolt .... Robert Brown
Jeremy Bolt .... Bobby Sherman
Joshua Bolt .... David Soul
Lottie Hatfield .... Joan Blondell
Candy Pruitt .... Bridget Hanley
Aaron Stempel .... Mark Lenard
Big Swede .... Bo Svensen
Biddie Cloom .... Susan Tolsky
Capt. Charley Clancey .... Henry Beckman
Miss Essie Gillis .... Mitzi Hoag
Ben Jenkins .... Hoke Howell
Christopher Pruitt (1969–1970) .... Eric Chase
Molly Pruitt (1969–1970) .... Patti Cohoon

THEME:

"Seattle," by Jack Keller, Hugo Montenegro, and Ernie Sheldon

Comedy-adventure set in boomtown Seattle (pop. 152) in the 1870s. Logging camp operator Jason Bolt and his young brothers Jeremy and Joshua were in danger of losing their timberland, at Bridal Veil Mountain, because their men were in near revolt—over the lack of women in Seattle. Jason contrived an ingenious scheme. Using funds borrowed from rival sawmill operator Aaron Stempel, he sailed back to New Bedford, Massachusetts, and persuaded 100 prospective brides to return with him to the frontier. The girls, led by "straw boss" Candy Pruitt, returned with Jason aboard Capt. Clancey's decrepit ship, and Seattle was never the same again.

There was a catch, however. If any of the 100 girls left before a year was up, Jason would forfeit his land to Stempel. It was quite a year, but Jason won his wager.

Bobby Sherman and David Soul were both looked on as promising young singers when *Brides* was cast. Boosted by exposure on the series, Sherman went on to become a highly popular recording star beginning in 1969, and subsequently appeared in other TV series (see Index). Blond-haired David Soul, who had his first regular TV exposure as the hooded "mystery singer" on *The Merv Griffin Show* from 1966 to 1967, later became Hutch on the enormously popular *Starsky and Hutch*. He also married (in real life) one of the "brides" he met on this series' set, actress Karen Carlson.

HERE WE GO AGAIN (*Situation Comedy*)

FIRST TELECAST: *January 20, 1973*
LAST TELECAST: *June 16, 1973*
BROADCAST HISTORY:

Jan 1973–Jun 1973, ABC Sat 8:00–8:30

CAST:

Richard Evans .... Larry Hagman
Susan Evans .... Diane Baker
Jerry Standish .... Dick Gautier
Judy Evans .... Nita Talbot
Jeff .... Chris Beaumont
Cindy .... Leslie Graves
Jan .... Kim Richards

Divorce-as-comedy; the trials of a newly married couple whose former mates lived nearby, and kept intruding on their connubial bliss. Susan's first husband was Jerry Standish, a free-swinging restaurateur, owner of Jerry's Polynesian Paradise. Richard's ex-wife was Judy, a rather domineering magazine editor. Adding to the general confusion were the children, Susan's two little girls, Cindy and Jan (who lived with the Evanses), and Richard's teenage son, Jeff (who lived with his mother, Judy).

HERE'S BOOMER (*Adventure*)

FIRST TELECAST: *March 14, 1980*
LAST TELECAST: *August 14, 1982*
BROADCAST HISTORY:

Mar 1980–Aug 1980, NBC Fri 8:00–8:30
Sep 1981–Nov 1981, NBC Sun 7:30–8:00
Jul 1982–Aug 1982, NBC Sat 8:00–8:30

BOOMER'S TRAINERS:

Bryan Renfro and Ray Berwick

Boomer was television's answer to Benji. He was a mixed-breed little stray who had no owner, and who spent much of his time scrounging for food as he wandered from place to place. Boomer never stayed long in any one spot, but before he left he usually managed to solve somebody's problem. He saved two young campers from harm, helped a young aspiring jockey win his first race, broke up a ring of dognappers, and helped a little girl prove to adults that she was not mentally retarded, but simply suffering from a hearing impairment. Like Lassie and Rin Tin Tin before him, Boomer was an uncommonly intelligent dog.

Boomer was supposed to return in the fall of 1980 with a new wrinkle—viewers could hear what he was thinking via an off-screen voice. (Not so new, actually, as viewers in the 1950s could hear Jackie Cooper's basset hound on *The People's Choice* musing in much the same way.) Unfortunately Boomer couldn't talk network executives into renewing his series on a regular basis, and he was heard on only one episode, aired as a special on December 7, 1980. When more new episodes of *Here's Boomer* did surface on NBC during the 1981–1982 season, Boomer's thoughts were all his own again. You could watch him, but had no idea what he was thinking.

HERE'S EDIE, see *Edie Adams Show, The*

HERE'S LUCY, see *Lucy Show, The*

HERITAGE (*Music and Art*)
FIRST TELECAST: *August 1, 1951*
LAST TELECAST: *September 5, 1951*
BROADCAST HISTORY:
Aug 1951–Sep 1951, NBC Wed 8:00–9:00
HOST:
Frank Blair

The National Gallery of Art in Washington, D.C., was the setting for this cultural series telecast live during the summer of 1951. The program consisted primarily of classical selections played by the 30-piece National Gallery Orchestra, with commentary by one of its members, pianist Rose d'Amore. During the first intermission, chief curator of the museum John Walker or a member of his staff discussed the paintings currently on exhibit, while the camera gave viewers a chance to see them. During the second intermission Miss d'Amore interviewed one of the composers whose work was being performed that night.

HERMAN HICKMAN SHOW, THE (*Sports Commentary*)
FIRST TELECAST: *October 3, 1952*
LAST TELECAST: *March 27, 1953*
BROADCAST HISTORY:
Oct 1952–Mar 1953, NBC Fri 7:00–7:15
REGULARS:
Herman Hickman
Rex Marshall

Herman Hickman was the star of this program which featured football predictions, reminiscences of his days as head football coach at Yale University, other stories in the sports vein, and an occasional poetic recitation. Actor Rex Marshall was a regular on the show and helped in its presentation. Sports and entertainment personalities served as guests, chatting with Herman on sports and other topics.

HERMAN'S HEAD (*Situation Comedy*)
FIRST TELECAST: *September 8, 1991*
LAST TELECAST: *June 16, 1994*
BROADCAST HISTORY:
Sep 1991–Aug 1993, FOX Sun 9:30–10:00
Aug 1993–Jun 1994, FOX Thu 9:30–10:00
CAST:
Herman Brooks .... William Ragsdale
Jay Nichols .... Hank Azaria
Heddy Thompson .... Jane Sibbett
Louise Fitzer .... Yeardley Smith
Angel .... Molly Hagan
Animal .... Ken Hudson Campbell
Wimp .... Rick Lawless
Genius .... Peter Mackenzie
Mr. Paul Bracken .... Jason Bernard
**Mr. Crawford* .... Edward Winter

*Occasional

Herman Brooks was a wavy-haired young guy working as a fact checker in the research department of the Waterton Publishing Company in New York. To all outward appearances, he seemed perfectly normal but, whenever he was faced with making a decision, viewers were shown the workings inside the room in his brain. It was there that the four conflicting aspects of his personality—compassion (Angel), lust (Animal), anxiety (Wimp), and reason (Genius)—debated, argued, and sometimes fought over what course of action Herman should take. Working with Herman were his boss Mr. Bracken, a humorless man with encyclopedic knowledge and total commitment to accuracy; Louise, Bracken's sardonic secretary; and Heddy, an obnoxious, ambitious fellow researcher who took great pleasure in putting Herman down. Also working for the publisher was Herman's best friend Jay, a womanizer whose dalliances somehow always seemed to get Herman into trouble.

Seen from time to time was Mr. Crawford, an inept executive at Waterton who, despite taking constant advantage of Herman, had a penchant for forgetting his first name. Over the years Herman had a number of romantic relationships, including a short-lived affair with Heddy, who ultimately rejected him because his financial prospects weren't up to her standards. Even Jay, despite his attraction to flashy women, developed an on-again, off-again relationship with Louise.

HERO, THE (*Situation Comedy*)
FIRST TELECAST: *September 8, 1966*
LAST TELECAST: *January 5, 1967*
BROADCAST HISTORY:
Sep 1966–Jan 1967, NBC Thu 9:30–10:00
CAST:
Sam Garret .... Richard Mulligan
Ruth Garret .... Mariette Hartley
Paul Garret .... Bobby Horan
Fred Gilman .... Victor French
Burton Gilman .... Joey Baio
Dewey .... Marc London

The real world and the make-believe world of television are two completely different things. That was the message of this unusual TV self-satire. Sam Garret was a hugely popular TV star with his own (fictional) Western series, *Jed Clayton—U.S. Marshal.* The real Sam differed somewhat from the coolly imperturbable hero of the TV screen, however. To his wife Ruth and his son Paul, as well as to their neighbors, the Gilmans, Sam was a nice guy who, among other things, was afraid of horses, allergic to sagebrush, and all thumbs when it came to any activity requiring coordination.

HE'S THE MAYOR (*Situation Comedy*)
FIRST TELECAST: *January 10, 1986*
LAST TELECAST: *March 21, 1986*
BROADCAST HISTORY:
Jan 1986–Mar 1986, ABC Fri 9:30–10:00
CAST:
Mayor Carl Burke .... Kevin Hooks
Alvin Burke .... Al Fann
Wardell Halsey .... Wesley Thompson
Kelly Enright .... Margot Rose
Councilman Nash .... David Graff
Ivan Bronski .... Stanley Brock

Chief Walter Padget .... Pat Corley
Paula Hendricks .... Mari Gorman

Fun and games at City Hall was the premise of this 1986 comedy. Mayor Carl Burke, a black, had been elected at age 25 and found running things a little more difficult than criticizing from the outside. His "kitchen cabinet" consisted of his father Alvin, who was the City Hall janitor, and best friend Wardell, hizzoner's chauffeur.

HEY ARNOLD! (*Cartoon*)

BROADCAST HISTORY:

Nickelodeon
30 minutes
Produced: *1996–*
Premiered: *October 7, 1996*

VOICES:

Arnold (1996) .... Toran Caudell
Arnold (1997–1998) .... Phillip Van Dyke
Arnold (1998–) .... Spencer Klein
Helga Pataki .... Francesca Marie Smith
Gerald Johanssen .... Jamil W. Smith
Eugene Horowitz (1996) ...... Christopher J. Castile
Eugene Horowitz (1996–1997) ...... Jarrett Lennon
Eugene Horowitz (1997–2000) .... Ben Diskin
Eugene Horowitz (2001–) ... Blake McIver Ewing
Harold Berman, Iggy .... Justin Shenkarow
Phoebe Heyerdahl .... Anndi L. McAfee
Brainy .... Craig Bartlett
Stinky Peterson .... Christopher Walberg
Rhonda Willington .... Olivia Hack
Sid .... Sam Gifaldi
Grandpa "Steely" Phil, Willie "The Jolly Olly Man," Earl, Dr. Murray Steiglitz, Nick Vermicelli .... Dan Castellaneta
Grandma Gertie "Pookie," Miss Slovak .... Tress MacNeille

This whimsical, *Peanuts*-like cartoon centered on the world of 9-year-old Arnold, an irrepressibly happy city kid with blond hair and a football-shaped head. He lived in a boardinghouse run by his grandparents and inhabited by a melting pot of eccentric immigrants from Southeast Asia and Eastern Europe. In fact, the tone of the show was decidedly multicultural. Arnold's fourth-grade pals included Gerald, a black kid with a cylindrical Afro; Helga, a pigtailed little terror who showed her secret love for Arnold by constantly belittling him; and Eugene, an accident-prone geek. Harold was the school bully, and Phoebe was Helga's brainy friend. Arnold also interacted with numerous other kids in well-meaning little adventures that usually resulted in a trail of chaos across the city, or in the corridors of P.S. 118. The mood was enhanced by the gentle, jazzy score by Jim Lang.

HEY DUDE (*Situation Comedy*)

BROADCAST HISTORY:

Nickelodeon
30 minutes
Produced: *1989–1991* (65 episodes)
Premiered: *July 14, 1989*

CAST:

Ted .... David Lascher
Bradley ("Brad") Taylor .... Kelly Brown
Melody .... Christine Taylor
Danny .... Joe Torres
Mr. Benjamin Ernst .... David Brisbin
Buddy Ernst .... Josh Tygiel
Lucy .... Debrah Kalman
Jake (1991) .... Jonathan Galkin
Kyle (1991) .... Geoffrey Coy

Cheerful little comedy set at the Bar None Ranch, where a group of teenage staffers sometimes helped guests but mostly interacted with each other. Crew members included Ted, the handsome schemer; cheery Melody, the swimming instructor; Brad, the self-absorbed riding instructor; and Danny, the earnest Native American. Mr. Ernst was the goofball boss, Lucy his adult assistant, Buddy his young son, and Cassie was Buddy's dog. Shot on location in Tucson, Arizona.

HEY JEANNIE (*Situation Comedy*)

FIRST TELECAST: *September 8, 1956*
LAST TELECAST: *September 30, 1960*
BROADCAST HISTORY:

Sep 1956–May 1957, CBS Sat 9:30–10:00
Jun 1960–Sep 1960, ABC Thu 9:00–9:30

CAST:

Jeannie MacLennan .... Jeannie Carson
Al Murray .... Allen Jenkins
Liz Murray .... Jane Dulo

Jeannie MacLennan was a sweet, naive young Scottish lass who had arrived in the United States with no job and no place to live. After clearing immigration (which evidently didn't mind her lack of employment) she went on a tour of New York with cab driver Al Murray. For reasons he never fully understood, he offered to become her sponsor. Jeannie moved in with Al and his sister Liz, and then set about learning about her adopted country, its strange customs, and stranger people.

Three years after this filmed series ended its run on CBS it was brought back, in reruns, as an ABC summer series, under the title *The Jeannie Carson Show*.

HEY LANDLORD (*Situation Comedy*)

FIRST TELECAST: *September 11, 1966*
LAST TELECAST: *May 14, 1967*
BROADCAST HISTORY:

Sep 1966–May 1967, NBC Sun 8:30–9:00

CAST:

Woody Banner .... Will Hutchins
Chuck Hookstratten .... Sandy Baron
Timothy Morgan .... Pamela Rodgers
Kyoko Mitsui .... Miko Mayama
Jack Ellenhorn .... Michael Constantine

Woody, the landlord in this comedy series, was not the usual bumbling old codger but a young, trusting Ohio lad fresh out of college, who had come to New York to find out more about life. His building, inherited from an uncle, was a brownstone in Manhattan's East Thirties which was peopled with the usual assortment of lunatics generally found on TV comedies. Woody shared his own apartment with Chuck Hookstratten, an aspiring young comic who was born and raised in the city, and who was constantly amazed at Woody's blind faith in people. Woody planned to manage the building while living off the proceeds. Far from supporting him, however, he found that he had to go to work to support the brownstone—its condition and age caused constant and costly problems. Meanwhile his tenants, including photographer

Jack, glamorous Timothy, and her roommate Kyoko, yelled, "Hey, landlord!"

HEY MULLIGAN, see *Mickey Rooney Show, The*

HI HONEY, I'M HOME (*Situation Comedy*)

FIRST TELECAST: *July 19, 1991*
LAST TELECAST: *August 23, 1991*
BROADCAST HISTORY:
Jul 1991–Aug 1991, ABC Fri 9:30–10:00
(Also on Nickelodeon cable network)
CAST:
Honey Nielsen .... Charlotte Booker
Lloyd Nielsen .... Stephen Bradbury
Babs Nielsen .... Julie Benz
Chucky Nielsen .... Danny Gura
Elaine Duff .... Susan Cella
Mike Duff .... Pete Benson
Skunk Duff .... Eric Kushnick
THEME:
"Hi Honey, I'm Home," by Rupert Holmes

Ever wonder what *really* happened to those wholesome, vacuous sitcom families of the 1950s, the ones where mom stayed in the kitchen, the kids did what they were told, and to whom nothing worse ever happened than a stuck garage door? This oddball series suggested that they were in hiding, scattered around the country in ordinary communities waiting for their chance to return to the air—all part of the "Sitcom Relocation Program." One such family was the Nielsens of the fictional 1950s series *Hi Honey, I'm Home* who, in 1991, were secretly living in a New Jersey suburb. Honey was the unbelievably cheerful wife (she served everyone fudge and exclaimed "Oh, pooh" if anything was amiss), Lloyd, her bland white-collar husband, demure teenager Babs and chubby Chucky, the obedient kids. Living next door were the decidedly contemporary Duffs: sarcastic Elaine, a divorced mom, and her sons, horny teenager Mike and punkish youngster Skunk. It was Mike who discovered that his favorite sitcom family (from reruns) was living next door; he promised to keep their secret, while his puzzled mom and kid brother helped educate the out-of-touch Nielsens in such '90s facts of life as credit cards, microwave ovens, and homeless persons. When things got too much for the Nielsens to bear, they sometimes snapped back into their black-and-white world right before Mike's eyes.

Every episode featured an appearance by at least one famous actor of bygone TV times, in character, to meet the Nielsens. Among them were Gale Gordon (Mr. Mooney from *The Lucy Show*), Barbara Billingsley (June Cleaver from *Leave It to Beaver*), Audrey Meadows and Joyce Randolph (Alice and Trixie from *The Honeymooners*), Jim Nabors (*Gomer Pyle*), Al Lewis (Grandpa from *The Munsters*), and Ann B. Davis (Alice from *The Brady Bunch*). A more contemporary first for this series was its unique scheduling. The program was produced by the Nickelodeon cable channel, aired first on ABC each week and then repeated two nights later on Nickelodeon's Nick at Night. It was the first such cooperative venture ever between network and cable, which are traditional rivals, but it was not likely to be the last.

Additional original episodes aired on Nick during the summer of 1992.

HIDDEN HILLS (*Situation Comedy*)

FIRST TELECAST: *September 24, 2002*
LAST TELECAST: *January 21, 2003*
BROADCAST HISTORY:
Sep 2002–Jan 2003, NBC Tue 9:30–10:00
CAST:
Doug Barber .... Justin Louis
Dr. Janine Barber .... Paula Marshall
Emily Barber .... Alexa Nikolas
Derek Barber .... Sean Marquette
Zack Timmerman .... Dondré T. Whitfield
Sarah Timmerman .... Tamara Taylor
Belinda Slypich .... Kristin Bauer
Pam Asher .... Stacy Galina
THEME:
"Pleasant Valley Sunday"

A bland little sitcom about life in the generic suburb of Hidden Hills. It was narrated by Doug, a dutiful if somewhat sex-starved dad, who balanced his career as a construction manager with taking care of his kids, hyperactive tween Emily and chubby younger son Derek. Mom was a busy doctor, so most of the work ferrying the kids around, chaperoning parties and coaching the softball team fell to Doug. Serving as a constant reminder of a life he didn't have, best friend Zack and his stylish wife Sarah, a successful black couple, had sex constantly and easily, even while effortlessly raising their two little kids. Another distraction was the sexy new mom in the neighborhood, Belinda, who ran a pornographic Web site while not assistant-coaching Doug's softball team. Pam was Janine's friend, with her own marital problems.

There were numerous little digs at suburbia, from the Monkees' song "Pleasant Valley Sunday" to the omnipresent cell phones, SUVs, and the fact that all the girls on the soccer team were named Caitlin.

HIDDEN ROOM, THE (*Drama Anthology*)

BROADCAST HISTORY:
Lifetime Network
30 minutes
Produced: *1991–1993* (33 episodes)
Premiered: *July 23, 1991*

Moody, half-hour dramas about women's "fears, secrets and desires" from the creators of *The Hitchhiker*. Among the themes were miscarriage, incest, eating disorders, lost youth, the life-and-death decisions of a lady police officer, and the terrors of a haunted house. Guest stars included Amanda Plummer, Ally Sheedy, Adam Arkin, Dana Ashbrook, Linda Purl, John Glover, and Mariel Hemingway.

HIGH ADVENTURE WITH LOWELL THOMAS (*Adventure/Travelogue*)

FIRST TELECAST: *June 16, 1964*
LAST TELECAST: *September 15, 1964*
BROADCAST HISTORY:
Jun 1964–Sep 1964, CBS Tue 8:00–9:00
HOST:
Lowell Thomas

This summer series was a collection of reruns of selected specials, telecast under the same title, that had originally aired in the late 1950s. Lowell Thomas—newsman, adventurer, and explorer—had led these filmed expeditions to remote and exotic locations around the world. Among them were a visit to the capital of Tibet, a tour through the casbah of Morocco, and an expedition to the Australian Outback.

HIGH CHAPARRAL, THE (*Western*)

FIRST TELECAST: *September 10, 1967*
LAST TELECAST: *September 10, 1971*
BROADCAST HISTORY:

Sep 1967–Sep 1968, NBC Sun 10:00–11:00
Sep 1968–Dec 1970, NBC Fri 7:30–8:30
Feb 1971–Sep 1971, NBC Fri 7:30–8:30

CAST:

Big John Cannon .... Leif Erickson
Buck Cannon .... Cameron Mitchell
Billy Blue Cannon (1967–1970) .... Mark Slade
Manolito Montoya .... Henry Darrow
Victoria Cannon .... Linda Cristal
Don Sebastian Montoya (1967–1970). Frank Silvera
Sam Butler .... Don Collier
Reno (1967–1970) .... Ted Markland
Pedro (1967–1970) .... Roberto Contreras
Joe .... Robert Hoy
Wind (1970–1971) .... Rudy Ramos

High Chaparral was the name given to the ranch owned and operated by the Cannon family in the Arizona Territory during the 1870s. Stubborn, determined Big John Cannon was the patriarch of the family, and his driving ambition to establish a flourishing cattle empire in the rugged, Indian-infested Arizona Territory was the thrust of the entire show. His younger brother Buck was a good-natured carouser who could outdrink, outshoot, outfight, and when properly motivated outwork any man alive—with the possible exception of his brother. John's son, Billy Blue, was a young man in his 20s whose mother was killed by an Apache arrow in the first episode of the series. After his first wife's death, Big John married Victoria, daughter of Don Sebastian Montoya and heiress to his extensive cattle holdings. Her brother Manolito accompanied her to the Cannon ranch and became a permanent member of the household. Sam was the foreman, while Reno, Pedro, and Joe were ranch hands.

The marriage of John and Victoria also united the Cannons and the Montoyas in their efforts to tame the land. Family differences, the conflicts between the Mexicans and the Americans, and the ever-present threats from rustlers and renegade Indians all provided material for the stories in this series.

A number of cast changes occurred in the program's last season. The character of Billy Blue Cannon was dropped. Frank Silvera, who played Victoria's father, had died and his character was written out of the show by having Don Sebastian also pass away. Added to the cast was Wind, a half-breed youth who became a member of the Cannon household after helping Big John avoid a major disaster during a roundup.

HIGH FINANCE (*Quiz/Audience Participation*)

FIRST TELECAST: *July 7, 1956*
LAST TELECAST: *December 15, 1956*
BROADCAST HISTORY:

Jul 1956–Dec 1956, CBS Sat 10:30–11:00

EMCEE:

Dennis James

Contestants on *High Finance* were asked questions based on news items that had appeared in their local papers during the preceding week. Each contestant was given a cash stake to start with and then invested part of it on the assumption that he could answer the questions correctly. Correct answers yielded high returns and the money could be invested again and again until the contestant had achieved his desired objective. There were pitfalls involved and contestants could lose everything by not "investing" wisely. There were prizes available as well as cash, and the ultimate amount that any one contestant could win was set at $110,000. Nobody ever came within $50,000 of the upper limit, but there were many winners in the $10,000–$25,000 range.

HIGH INCIDENT (*Police Drama*)

FIRST TELECAST: *March 4, 1996*
LAST TELECAST: *September 4, 1997*
BROADCAST HISTORY:

Mar 1996–Apr 1996, ABC Mon 9:00–10:00
Jul 1996–Sep 1997, ABC Thu 8:00–9:00

CAST:

Sgt. Jim Marsh .... David Keith
Off. Randy Willitz .... Cole Hauser
Off. Gayle Van Camp (1996) ..... Catherine Kellner
Off. Len Gayer .... Matt Craven
Off. Leslie Joyner .... Aunjanue Ellis
Off. Richie Fernandez (1996) ... Julio Oscar Mechoso
Off. Terry Hagar .... Matthew Beck
Off. Russell Topps .... Louis Mustillo
Lynette White .... Wendy Davis
Off. Michael Rhoades .... Blair Underwood
Off. Jessica Helgado .... Lisa Vidal
Sgt. Helen Sullivan .... Lindsay Frost
Off. Anne Bonner .... Lucinda Jenney
Sgt. Crispo .... Titus Welliver

ABC had high hopes for this show about suburban cops, which was co-created by Steven Spielberg, but it proved to be surprisingly ordinary considering its auspices. Perhaps there were just too many cops patrolling the relatively quiet streets of El Camino, California. Marsh was the grim, surly tough guy, seemingly ready to shoot a driver for picking his nose; Willitz the rookie son of a cop, who drew the unfortunate assignment of being Marsh's partner; Van Camp the female trying to prove herself; Gayer and Hagar family men; Joyner an ambitious officer; Topps the pudgy, friendly fatherly type; and White a policeman's widow who remained emotionally tied to the force. Still more officers arrived in Fall 1996, including Rhoades, a recent arrival from the mean streets of South Central L.A., and Helgado, a cocky streetwise officer, but the routine of domestic violence, drunk driving, drugs, and child abandonment—not to mention keeping all those faces straight—failed to rivet viewers, and the series petered out at the end of its first full season.

HIGH MOUNTAIN RANGERS (*Adventure*)

FIRST TELECAST: *January 2, 1988*
LAST TELECAST: *July 9, 1988*
BROADCAST HISTORY:

Jan 1988–July 1988, CBS Sat 8:00–9:00

CAST:

Jesse Hawkes .... Robert Conrad
Matt Hawkes .... Christian Conrad
Cody Hawkes .... Shane Conrad
Frank Avila (White Eagle) .... Tony Acierto

Robin Kelly .... P. A. Christian
Cutler .... Russell Todd
Hart........................ Eric Eugene Williams
Izzy Flowers .... Timothy Erwin
Jackie Hawkes .... Robyn Peterson
Sheriff McBride .... Med Flory

Three decades ago, Jesse Hawkes had formed a mountain rescue/service team called the High Mountain Rangers. Based in the foothills of the Sierra Nevada mountains near Lake Tahoe, the rangers used the latest in high-tech equipment, along with their knowledge of mountaineering and survival techniques, to protect the human residents and visitors, as well as the animal life that lived in the mountains.

Jesse was now semiretired, living with his teenaged son Cody in a cabin high in the mountains. His older son Matt was running the operation, along with fellow rangers Robin, Cutler, Hart, full-blooded Shoshone Frank Avila, and Izzy the young apprentice. Matt kept in close contact with his dad by shortwave radio—there were no phone lines that far up the mountains—and sought Jesse's advice and help when needed, which seemed to be every week. Jesse and his wife Jackie, a blackjack dealer at one of the casinos in South Lake Tahoe, had been separated for years, primarily because she was not interested in living the relatively isolated lifestyle that appealed to her husband.

High Mountain Rangers was a real family affair for star Robert Conrad. His two sons on the series were his real-life sons, his daughter Joan was the series' executive producer, and her husband, Timothy Erwin, had a featured role. Filmed on location in the Sierra Nevada mountains near Lake Tahoe.

HIGH PERFORMANCE (*Adventure*)

FIRST TELECAST: *March 2, 1983*
LAST TELECAST: *March 23, 1983*
BROADCAST HISTORY:
Mar 1983, ABC Wed 8:00–9:00
CAST:
Brennan Flannery .... Mitchell Ryan
Kate Flannery .... Lisa Hartman
Shane Adams...................... Rick Edwards
Blue Stratton......................... Jack Scalia
Fletch .... Jason Bernard

A trio of athletic young instructors at a school for chauffeur/bodyguards hired out for freelance security and rescue missions in this action series. Using the Flannery School as their base, martial arts expert Kate, stunt driver Shane, and ex-military intelligence man Blue raced, parachuted, and helicoptered into adventures around the world. Their assignments came from Kate's father Brennan Flannery, and their high-tech gadgets from mechanical wizard Fletch.

HIGH RISK (*Magazine*)

FIRST TELECAST: *October 4, 1988*
LAST TELECAST: *November 15, 1988*
BROADCAST HISTORY:
Oct 1988–Nov 1988, CBS Tue 8:00–9:00
Nov 1988, CBS Tue 10:00–11:00
HOST:
Wayne Rogers

Daredevils of all sorts were profiled on this short-lived series, thrown together by CBS on short notice to fill time until the shows affected by the 1988 writers' strike could get into full production. Included were features on professional stuntmen at work, roller-coaster inspectors, a paraplegic water skier, forest firefighters, the work of U.S. Border Patrol agents along the Mexican border, cave explorers, and the dangers encountered by a family of car and truck repossessors.

HIGH ROAD, THE, see *John Gunther's High Road*

HIGH SCHOOL REUNION (*Reality*)

FIRST TELECAST: *January 5, 2003*
LAST TELECAST: *February 20, 2003*
BROADCAST HISTORY:
Jan 2003–Feb 2003, WB Sun 9:00–10:00
Jan 2003–Feb 2003, WB Thu 8:00–9:00
HOST:
Mike Richards

This reality series took 17 classmates from the Oak Park and River Forest, Illinois, high school class of 1992 to the island of Maui for an exotic two-week ten-year reunion. The reunion gave the participants opportunities to try to kindle or rekindle romances, get even with former classmates or show off. As categorized by the producers, the former classmates included Patricia (The Gossip), Dan B. (The Player), Amy (The Chubby Cheerleader), Sarah (The Bitchy Girl), Natasha (The Popular Girl), Chris (The Misfit), Dave (The Bully), Tim (The Artist), Maurice (The Loner), Jason (The Pipsqueak), Holly (The Shy Girl), Jeff (The Class Clown), Maya (The Homecoming Queen), Dan P. (The Jock), Ben (The Nerd), Nicole (The Tall Girl) and Summer (The Flirt).

There were assorted attempts at romance, confrontations between people who just didn't like each other, gossip about the way people had been in high school and plenty of skin, as onetime high school cliques reestablished themselves. The producers designed activities to stir things up. When a boxing ring was set up Dave beat the crap out of Ben, but they came out of the fight as friends. Each week two randomly chosen participants were given "Hall Passes" allowing them to ask anyone they wanted to go on a date. The last episode culminated in a "senior prom," which included a performance by the band Naughty By Nature. Those who had made love connections—however short term—were Dan B. and Natasha, Ben and Maya, Dave and Holly and Sarah and Jeff.

High School Reunion was produced by the same team responsible for *The Bachelor.* The Thursday telecasts were reruns of the episodes that had originally aired the preceding Sundays.

HIGH SIERRA SEARCH AND RESCUE (*Adventure*)

FIRST TELECAST: *June 11, 1995*
LAST TELECAST: *July 26, 1995*
BROADCAST HISTORY:
Jun 1995, NBC Sun 10:20–11:20
Jun 1995–Jul 1995, NBC Wed 8:00–9:00
CAST:
Griffin "Tooter" Campbell .... Robert Conrad
Morgan Duffy .... Dee Wallace Stone
Lisa Peterson......................... LaVelda Fann
Enrique Cruz....................... Ramon Franco
Dep. Sheriff Ty Cooper........ Alistair MacDougall
Kaja Wilson .... Brittney Powell
Flynn Norstedt....................... Jason Lewis

"Let's move, the fire jumped the ridge!" yelled somebody, and the brave volunteers of the Bear Valley Search & Rescue squad were off once again, in this adrenaline-filled summer series set in California's picturesque High Sierra mountains. Tooter Campbell was the fatherly leader, an experienced pilot who roared to the scene in his shiny black helicopter (a Bell 206B3, for those who keep track of such things). Morgan was Tooter's hyper friend, who ran the general store; Lisa (played by series star Robert Conrad's real-life wife) ran the gas station; Cruz was the handsome young schoolteacher; Ty, a young cop; Kaja, a clerk at the store; and Flynn, a long-haired young ski instructor. After a day filled with wilderness accidents, lost kids, and raging forest fires, they gathered in the local woods and relaxed by forming an Irish band, with Tooter on bagpipes (out of earshot of passing tourists, presumably).

Based on a television movie that aired on March 27, 1994.

HIGH SOCIETY (*Situation Comedy*)

FIRST TELECAST: *October 30, 1995*

LAST TELECAST: *February 26, 1996*

BROADCAST HISTORY:

Oct 1995–Feb 1996, CBS Mon 9:30–10:00

CAST:

Ellie Walker .... Jean Smart
Dorothy "Dott" Emerson .... Mary McDonnell
Valerie Brumberg .... Faith Prince
Brendan Emerson (age 17) .... Dan O'Donahue
Peter Thomas .... David Rasche
Alice Morgan .... Jayne Meadows
Stephano .... Luigi Amodeo

THEME:

"The Lady Is a Tramp," by Rodgers and Hart, sung by Chaka Khan

Ellie was an earthy, uninhibited, highly successful romance novelist—she had just finished her tenth novel—living the good life in Manhattan's literary world and café society. Dott, her best friend since college, was both her publisher and her drinking buddy. Dott had taken control of the publishing firm as part of her divorce settlement and depended on her partner, Peter, and her chic gay Italian assistant, Stephano, to keep the business running smoothly. Dott's son, Brendan, a Young Republican, was so conservative that he just about drove her crazy—she was forever trying to get him to do something, *anything,* spontaneous or unconventional. Also living in Dott's swank penthouse was her mother, Alice, who criticized almost everything she did. Into their lives came former college classmate Val, who moved in with Dott after separating from her husband. Val, who was pregnant, was the antithesis of Dott's friends. She didn't care about status and society trappings, and was so unpretentious that it made Dott uncomfortable and Ellie sick.

HIGH TIDE (*Adventure*)

BROADCAST HISTORY:

Syndicated only
60 minutes
Produced: *1994–1997* (66 episodes)
Released: *September 1994*

CAST:

Mick Barrett .... Rick Springfield
Joey Barrett .... Yannick Bisson
Gordon (1994–1995) .... George Segal
Fritz Boller (1994) .... Cay Helmich
Fritz Boller (1994–1995) .... Diana Frank
Annie (1995) .... Julie Cialini
**Lt. Samantha Harrold (1995–1996)* .... Paula Trickey
**Grace Warner (1996–1997)* .... Deborah Shelton
**Lt. Luis Ortega (1996–1997)* .... Julian Reyes

*Occasional

Gordon was a whiny retired CIA agent and restaurateur who ran a Los Angeles–based detective agency for which brothers Mick and Joey worked when they weren't surfing and chasing women. Mick, a former policeman, was more introspective and had his misgivings about Gordon, while Joey, his kid brother, was a free-spirited surfer whose impulsiveness tended to get both of them in trouble. Assignments took them everywhere from Bali to Maui, with emphasis on beautiful scenery and sexy women in skimpy outfits. In fact, this series seemed to specialize in shots of bikinis and bare-chested men, including the series' stars. Fritz, Gordon's sexy assistant who sometimes went on assignment to help Mick and Joey, was originally played by Cay Helmich. When she found out she was pregnant after having filmed only a few episodes, Diana Frank took over the role.

Filmed on location, mostly in the South Pacific, including New Zealand, Australia, and Fiji.

When *High Tide* returned for its second season, production moved to San Diego and the brothers now owned the High Tide Surf Shop on the beach in Venice, California. They still worked as P.I.'s in their spare time, and Annie (former *Playboy* Playmate of the Year Julie Cialini) helped them run the shop. She was gone by mid-season, replaced by a succession of attractive, temporary employees. Sam was their sexy contact at the North Shores Sheriff Station.

The following fall Mick and Joey sold the struggling surf shop and moved to Ventura, California, to try their luck as full-time P.I.'s. A friend of theirs, working as a bail bondsman and real estate agent, got them accommodations in the guest house of the beachfront estate of sexy, wealthy widow Grace Warner. A number of their cases involved helping Grace and/or her affluent friends.

HIGHCLIFFE MANOR (*Situation Comedy*)

FIRST TELECAST: *April 12, 1979*

LAST TELECAST: *May 3, 1979*

BROADCAST HISTORY:

Apr 1979–May 1979, NBC Tue 8:30–9:00

CAST:

Helen Blacke .... Shelley Fabares
Rev. Ian Glenville .... Stephen McHattie
Frances Kiskadden .... Eugenie Ross-Leming
Dr. Felix Morger .... Gerald Gordon
Wendy Sparkes .... Audrey Landers
Rebecca .... Jenny O'Hara
Bram Shelley .... Christian Marlowe
Dr. Lester .... David Byrd
Dr. Sanchez .... Luis Avalos
Smythe .... Ernie Hudson
Cheng .... Harold Sakata

This short-lived comedy was a sendup of the old, Gothic horror tales. The setting was Highcliffe Manor, a huge stone mansion located on an island off the coast of Massachusetts. Helen Blacke had inherited the place, and controlling interest in the Blacke Foundation, when her husband died in an explosion in his laboratory. Despite the fact that everyone there seemed to be plotting her demise, Helen cheerily went about running Highcliffe, oblivious to all that was going on around her. Populating the manor was a collection of eccentrics, including Rev. Glenville, a girl-chasing clergyman from South Africa; Frances, a mad scientist working her evil magic on freshly stolen corpses; Felix, the former assistant to Helen's husband; Bram, an attractive Frankenstein monster created by Frances, with limbs lifted from an Erector Set and a virtually nonexistent memory; Cheng, Frances's gigantic servant; and Dr. Lester and Dr. Sanchez, two evil men trying to take over the Foundation. Wendy was the girl-next-door secretary who was romantically attracted to Rev. Glenville, and Rebecca was the eerie maid.

HIGHER GROUND (*Drama*)

BROADCAST HISTORY:

Fox Family Channel
60 minutes
Original episodes: *2000* (22 episodes)
Premiered: *January 14, 2000*

CAST:

Peter Scarbrow .... Joe Lando
Sophie Becker .... Anne Marie Loder
Frank Markasian .... Jim Byrnes
Scott Barringer .... Hayden Christensen
Shelby Merrick .... A. J. Cook
Ezra Friedkin .... Kyle J. Downes
Katherine Ann "Kat" Cabot ...... Kandyse McClure
Juliette "Jules" Waybourne .... Meghan Ory
Daisy Lipenowski .... Jewel Staite
Augusto "Auggie" Ciceros .... Jorgito Vargas

This earnest drama was set at Mount Horizon High School, a wilderness camp for troubled teens, in the stunningly beautiful Pacific Northwest wilderness. Although they could not bring many personal belongings, everyone arrived at the remote camp with a ton of emotional baggage. Peter, the ruggedly handsome headmaster, was a former Wall Street executive and recovering drug addict; Sophie, his concerned assistant director (they met in rehab); and Frank, the fatherly, white-bearded founder of Mount Horizon, who had opened the camp after his own son died of a heroin overdose.

The teens were a handsome group (think *Dawson's Creek* in the woods), but similarly troubled. Scott was a rebellious 16-year-old hunk haunted by dark secrets at home (his young stepmother had seduced him); Shelby, a selfish blond princess who had flirted with drugs and prostitution after her stepfather abused her; curly-haired Ezra, the foolhardy risk taker, also with a drug problem; Kat, a black girl raised by a white family, who had self-esteem problems; Jules, a sexy young girl whose demanding family had driven her to bulimia and self-mutilation; Daisy, another abuse victim who had turned sullen and angry; and Auggie, a cute, spunky Latino who had been in trouble with the law due to a brush with barrio gangs.

Peter and the other counselors tried mightily to reach these troubled souls, sometimes with success, sometimes not. Hikes in the wilderness (someone was always falling into a ravine), rock climbing (Peter's favorite method of letting off steam), runaways, and visiting kin (who were often the problem) filled the story lines. There was also romantic tension between Peter and Sophie, and in the last original episode they decided to get married.

HIGHLANDER (*Adventure*)

BROADCAST HISTORY:

Syndicated only
60 minutes
Produced: *1992–1998* (119 episodes)
Released: *September 1992*

CAST:

Duncan MacLeod .... Adrian Paul
Tessa Noel (1992–1993) .... Alexandra Vandernoot
Richie Ryan (1992–1997) .... Stan Kirsch
Randi McFarland (1992–1993) ...... Amanda Wyss
Joe Dawson (1993–1998) .... Jim Byrnes
Charlie DeSalvo (1993–1994) .... Philip Akin
Maurice (1994–1995) .... Michel Modo
Dr. Anne Lindsey (1994–1996) .... Lisa Howard
Amanda Darieux (1994–1998) ... Elizabeth Gracen
Adam Pierson/Methos (1994–1998)
.... Peter Wingfield

THEME:

"Princes of the Universe," composed and performed by Queen

"I am Duncan MacLeod, born 400 years ago in the Highlands of Scotland. I am immortal, and I am not alone. For centuries we have waited for the time of the Gathering, when the stroke of a sword and the fall of a head will release the power of the Quickening. In the end, there can be only one." So began each episode of this popular series. The only way for an immortal to die was to be beheaded in a sword fight by a fellow immortal. Any other injuries—from falls, knife wounds, bullets, or anything else—would miraculously heal in a matter of hours. When one immortal killed another, the beheaded unleashed a tremendous energy surge (usually depicted by the destructive pyrotechnics of lightning, high winds, and implosions of glass) that was absorbed by the survivor. Eventually, when all the immortals had fought until there was only one left, that immortal would have the combined powers of all the immortals that ever lived and would rule the world. The only place where they didn't fight was on holy ground, such as a church. All immortals had a sixth sense that enabled them to know when another immortal was nearby.

The contemporary MacLeod was a Vancouver antique dealer (what better profession for a 400-year-old man!) who wore his hair in a ponytail. Tessa, his lover, knew he was immortal and would remain young as she aged; and Richie was a youthful burglar who was caught in the act by MacLeod and went to work for him in the antique shop. Randi, a reporter for KCLA-TV, kept running into him and had a feeling that something about him wasn't normal. Each episode brought other immortals into MacLeod's life, some friendly and others seeking to behead him and absorb his energy. As the plots developed there were flashbacks to his involvement over the centuries with the immortals with whom he was now in combat.

Originally located in Vancouver, MacLeod, Tessa, and Richie moved to Paris in the spring of 1993. That fall they moved back to Vancouver and met Joe Dawson, a bookstore owner who headed "The Watchers," a secret group that had been observing immortals for hundreds of years and was dedicated to tracking down and helping eliminate evil immortals. In October 1993 Tessa and Richie were shot by a mugger. She died, but Richie's latent immortality was triggered by his violent death. Later that season Duncan bought a martial arts business run by Charlie DeSalvo but asked Charlie to stay on and run it. When he moved back to Paris in the spring of 1994 he gave the business back to Charlie.

In the last episode of the 1993–1994 season MacLeod sold his houseboat and went off to wander with Richie. That fall they were back in Vancouver. In an October episode Charlie left to fight in a revolution in a foreign country and gave the martial arts business back to MacLeod. New to the cast was Dr. Anne Lindsey, a hospital emergency room surgeon who became his new love interest. In March 1995, after Anne had seen MacLeod "die" in a horrible fall while fighting another immortal, he returned to Paris and eventually let her know the truth about his immortality. She came to Paris to be with him but, unable to adjust to his immortality, she broke up with him and returned to Vancouver.

In September, MacLeod returned to Vancouver, and Anne, pregnant with his child, showed up occasionally during the 1995–1996 season, giving birth to a daughter, Mary, in February 1996. MacLeod gave her the house that he had been rebuilding for months. It was one of the few episodes in which no immortal was beheaded. A few months later he was back in Paris, where Joe was running Le Blues Bar. Amanda (who would later star in the spin-off series *Highlander: The Raven*), a cat burglar before becoming immortal, was having an affair with MacLeod in the spring of 1996. During the 1996–1997 season it was revealed that Methos (the world's oldest man), during his early centuries as an immortal, had been a member of the murderous "Four Horsemen," but over the centuries had reformed. He and MacLeod beheaded Kronos and the other two horsemen. In May 1997, fooled by Ahriman, an evil demon from the dawn of time, MacLeod was tricked into beheading Richie.

That fall Methos and Amanda, seen on an infrequent basis since 1994, became regulars in the credits—but still only showed up occasionally. It was one year since Richie's accidental beheading, and MacLeod returned to Paris to fight the evil demon, Ahriman. He abandoned his sword during his fight with the demon, not wanting to accidentally kill anyone else after the Richie debacle. Duncan defeated the demon through meditation and the realization that it fed off hatred and violent emotions. In the series-ending two-parter, he and Amanda were back together, but she and Joe were kidnapped by an immortal seeking revenge on MacLeod. Just as the immortal was about to behead MacLeod, Methos turned up and saved him. Duncan was shot in the gunfight that followed and awoke to see his old friend Hugh Fitzcairn (Roger Daltrey). As violence-weary Duncan despaired that "nothing ever changes," Hugh, now an angel, showed him how much worse his friends' lives would have been if he had never existed (shades of *It's a Wonderful Life*). When the sequence was over and MacLeod was revived, he defeated his antagonist and, after the traditional pyrotechnics following the beheading, told his friends—Methos, Joe, and Amanda—"never again." In the final scene a pensive MacLeod reflected on his long life and the people and immortals he had befriended and fought over the centuries. After saying goodbye to Methos, Joe, and Amanda, he just disappeared into the shadows.

Based on the 1986 theatrical film *Highlander* starring Christopher Lambert and Sean Connery. Lambert reprised his role as mentor Connor MacLeod in the pilot episode of the TV series.

HIGHLANDER: THE RAVEN (*Adventure*)

BROADCAST HISTORY:

Syndicated only
60 minutes
Produced: *1998–1999* (22 episodes)
Released: *September 1998*

CAST:

Amanda Darieux/Montrose ...... Elizabeth Gracen
Det. Nick Wolfe .... Paul Johansson
Lucy Becker .... Patricia Gage
Lt. Carl Magnus .... Michael Copeman
Bert Myers .... Hannes Jaenicke
Father Liam Riley (1999) .... Robert Cavanah

This spin-off from *Highlander* featured Duncan McLeod's friend and sometimes lover, the beautiful 1,200-year-old immortal Amanda, continuing her centuries-old career as a cat burglar with a penchant for expensive jewelry. In the premiere one of her fences was killed by a crooked detective who tried to frame her. At the episode's end, Amanda and a cop were killed by the crooked detective, who was then killed by the dead cop's partner, Nick. Amanda came back to life and split, which certainly confused Nick. Nick quit the force when his superior hushed up the crooked cop's activities, and decided to fight injustice as a private detective. He tracked down Amanda and found out the truth about her immortality. Although there was considerable initial distrust, and she had difficulty dealing with her newfound desire to assist Nick in his fight against evil, they helped each other and started to develop a relationship. Lucy was Amanda's 50-something companion, a scam artist in her own right, who knew Amanda was immortal. Bert, a former federal agent who ran a private security firm, often hired Nick to do his dirty work.

In February, Nick went to Paris after an immortal whom he thought had killed Amanda. Amanda, undead, followed him. After she killed the immortal, she and Bert bought a building together—the upstairs for Nick to run Bert's European operations and the downstairs for Amanda's living quarters. They were cohabiting—platonically. Liam, an immortal serving as a local priest, was an old friend of Amanda's.

As with its predecessor series, most episodes of *The Raven* included confrontations with other immortals, flashbacks to Amanda's involvement with them over the centuries, and spectacular pyrotechnics when an immortal was beheaded and all his life force and knowledge was transferred to his slayer. In the May 1999 series finale Amanda activated Nick's latent immortality by shooting him (immortality was triggered by violent death). When he found out he was an immortal he had decidedly mixed feelings about his altered existence.

Filmed on location in Toronto, Canada, and Paris, France.

HIGH-LOW (*Quiz/Audience Participation*)
FIRST TELECAST: *July 4, 1957*
LAST TELECAST: *September 19, 1957*
BROADCAST HISTORY:
Jul 1957–Sep 1957, NBC Thu 9:30–10:00
EMCEE:
Jack Barry
SEMI-REGULARS:
Burl Ives
John Van Doren
Patricia Medina
Walter Slezak
Hank Bloomgarden

This live quiz show was the 1957 summer replacement for *The Ford Show.* Contestants pitted their knowledge against that of the members of the panel, which consisted of three celebrities each week. The contestant was in an isolation booth and both he and the panelists were asked the same multi-part question. First the panelists each indicated how many parts of the question they could answer. Then the contestant could either attempt to answer as many parts as the "high" panelist, and triple his money, or answer as many parts as the "low" panelist, and double his money. If he failed to answer as many parts as the chosen panel member, however, he lost all but 10 percent of his previous winnings.

HIGHWAY PATROL (*Police Drama*)
BROADCAST HISTORY:
Syndicated only
30 minutes
Produced: *1955–1959* (156 episodes)
Released: *September 1955*
CAST:
Chief Dan Mathews .... Broderick Crawford
NARRATOR:
Art Gilmore

Beefy, gravel-voiced Broderick Crawford was the no-nonsense chief of the Highway Patrol in this action series, which was one of the most popular syndicated programs in television history (156 episodes were made, run, and rerun endlessly for years). The stories were straight crime dramas, with the chief and his uniformed officers nailing hijackers, smugglers, and robbers. In a typical episode a young newlywed couple were witnesses to a café holdup in which the proprietor was murdered. The Highway Patrol was at first stymied by their chief suspect's airtight alibi, but Mathews managed to get him in the end in a suspenseful chase, when the crook went after the couple who were the only witnesses to the crime. In another episode, a bank messenger absconded with $50,000 and took it home to his wife, only to have her slug him and make off with the loot herself. Chief Mathews put out an all-points bulletin and eventually nabbed them both.

Most of *Highway Patrol*'s action took place outdoors, on the sprawling highway system of an unidentified Western state (those official-looking emblems on the police cars read simply "Highway Patrol"). There was lots of hardware—patrol cars, motorcycles, and occasional helicopters—and Chief Mathews was always leaning on the side of a car, microphone in hand, bellowing orders ("Ten-four, ten-four!"). There were no other regular characters in the long-running series, although actor William Boyett, later a regular on *Adam-12,* was seen frequently in various supporting roles.

HIGHWAY TO HEAVEN (*Drama*)
FIRST TELECAST: *September 19, 1984*
LAST TELECAST: *August 4, 1989*
BROADCAST HISTORY:
Sep 1984–Mar 1988, NBC Wed 8:00–9:00
Mar 1988–May 1988, NBC Wed 9:00–10:00
Jun 1988, NBC Wed 8:00–9:00
Jun 1989–Aug 1989, NBC Fri 8:00–9:00
CAST:
Jonathan Smith .... Michael Landon
Mark Gordon......................... Victor French
EXECUTIVE PRODUCER/WRITER:
Michael Landon

Jonathan was a probationary angel with a very unusual mission on earth—to bring a little love and understanding into the lives of people who were in trouble. Although he had angelic powers he seldom used them, preferring to rely on persuasion and example as he slipped into and out of the lives of children and old folks, rich people and poor. It might be a mother whose child was dying of cancer, a young black boxer being pressured to throw a fight, or a Vietnamese child facing prejudice in her new American hometown. Each of them learned a little about coping with life through love.

Jonathan traveled around the country as an itinerant laborer. His only companion was a burly ex-cop named Mark, who had been a bitter, defeated man until Jonathan helped turn him around. Now he wanted to help his newfound friend in his heavenly mission. Tender, emotional stories about the value of kindness in life dominated this series created by Michael Landon, but there was also room for a twinkle in the eye. A notable example of the latter was an October 1987 Halloween episode lampooning Landon's first, famous movie role in *I Was a Teenage Werewolf* (1957)—called, what else, "I Was a Middle-Aged Werewolf."

HIGHWAYMAN, THE (*Adventure*)
FIRST TELECAST: *March 4, 1988*
LAST TELECAST: *May 6, 1988*
BROADCAST HISTORY:
Mar 1988–Apr 1988, NBC Fri 8:00–9:00
Apr 1988–May 1988, NBC Fri 9:00–10:00
CAST:
The Highwayman .... Sam Jones
Jetto .... Jacko
D.C. Montana .... Tim Russ
Tania Winthrop .... Jane Badler

Fantasy-action series starring a big, high-tech truck. The giant 18-wheeler, which looked a bit like a misshapen hot dog, was heavily armed, virtually impregnable, and equipped with such niceties as a cab that converted into a helicopter, allowing nifty escapes from danger. (In the 1987 TV movie on which this series was based the truck could also become invisible, but that was dispensed with.) Piloting this monster rig along the highways of America was a muscular, leather-clad crime fighter called only The Highwayman, one of a team of special federal marshals ("Highwaymen") empowered to right wrongs "where ordinary laws do not reach"—and to haul sensitive government cargo. Jetto was his growling, break-down-the-doors Australian partner, and Ms. Winthrop the beautiful but tough "controller" who gave him his rolling orders. D.C. was the hip, black electronics wizard who kept all the toys working.

Produced by Glen A. Larson, who also brought us—couldn't you guess?—*Knight Rider*.

HILL STREET BLUES (*Police Drama*)
FIRST TELECAST: *January 15, 1981*
LAST TELECAST: *May 19, 1987*
BROADCAST HISTORY:
Jan 1981, NBC Thu/Sat 10:00–11:00
Jan 1981–Apr 1981, NBC Sat 10:00–11:00
Apr 1981–Aug 1981, NBC Tue 9:00–10:00
Oct 1981–Nov 1986, NBC Thu 10:00–11:00
Dec 1986–Feb 1987, NBC Tue 9:00–10:00
Mar 1987–May 1987, NBC Tue 10:00–11:00
CAST:
Capt. Frank Furillo .... Daniel J. Travanti
Sgt. Phil Esterhaus (1981–1984) ... Michael Conrad
Officer Bobby Hill .... Michael Warren
Officer Andy Renko .... Charles Haid
Joyce Davenport .... Veronica Hamel
Det. Mick Belker .... Bruce Weitz
Lt. Ray Calletano .... Rene Enriquez
Det. Johnny (J.D.) LaRue .... Kiel Martin
Det. Neal Washington .... Taurean Blacque
Lt. Howard Hunter .... James Sikking
Sgt./Lt. Henry Goldblume .... Joe Spano
Officer/Sgt. Lucille Bates .... Betty Thomas
Grace Gardner (1981–1985) ...... Barbara Babcock
Fay Furillo (1981–1986) .... Barbara Bosson
**Capt. Jerry Fuchs (1981–1984)* ... Vincent Lucchesi
Det./Lt. Alf Chesley (1981–1982) .... Gerry Black
Officer Leo Schnitz (1981–1985)
.... Robert Hirschfield
Officer Joe Coffey (1981–1986) .... Ed Marinaro
Chief Fletcher P. Daniels .... Jon Cypher
Officer Robin Tataglia (1983–1987)..... Lisa Sutton
Asst. D.A. Irwin Bernstein (1982–1987)
.... George Wyner
**Jesus Martinez*..................... Trinidad Silva
**Judge Alan Wachtel* .... Jeffrey Tambor
Det. Harry Garibaldi (1984–1985)......... Ken Olin
Det. Patricia Mayo (1984–1985) .... Mimi Kuzyk
Mayor Ozzie Cleveland (1982–1985) ... J.A. Preston
Sgt. Stanislaus Jablonski (1984–1987)
.... Robert Prosky
Lt. Norman Buntz (1985–1987)....... Dennis Franz
Celeste Patterson (1985–1986) ...... Judith Hansen
Sidney (Sid the Snitch) Thurston (1985–1987)
.... Peter Jurasik
Officer Patrick Flaherty (1986–1987)
.... Robert Clohessy
Officer Tina Russo (1986–1987) .. Megan Gallagher
Officer Raymond (1987) .... David Selburg
*Occasional
THEME:
"Hill Street Blues," by Mike Post

This critically acclaimed series focused on the officers of Hill Street Station, located in the blighted ghetto area of a large, unnamed Eastern city. In command was Capt. Frank Furillo, a quiet yet forceful man with the patience of Job. Every day and long into the night, he dealt with the sleazy characters living in his precinct, which was rife with drugs, prostitution, burglary, murder, and the decay of a rotting neighborhood. As if that weren't enough, Frank had to cope with police bureaucracy and a chaotic personal life—an ex-wife (Fay) who constantly badgered him for more alimony, and a contentious public defender (Joyce) who was also his secret lover. The crazy assortment of cops under his command included the vaguely maniacal Belker, a scruffy little undercover officer who sometimes bit offenders and barked at startled dogs—but who regularly got calls from his mom at home. To surly criminals he was a terror ("Would you like to sit down, hair-ball, or would you prefer internal bleeding?"). Henry Goldblume was the dedicated and idealistic community affairs officer, who sometimes took the brutality he saw around him too much to heart; Howard Hunter was the trigger-happy leader of the precinct's SWAT team, ready to blast away at any excuse; Ray Calletano was the second-in-command at the precinct; and J.D. LaRue a cash-poor vice cop who was frequently in trouble. Hill and Renko were two young partners—one black, one white—who were shot in the first episode and had difficulty adjusting to life on the streets after that. There was also an assortment of cocky street-gang leaders, notably the pushy Jesus Martinez, with whom Furillo had to deal almost as an equal. Only tall, fatherly Phil Esterhaus, the head sergeant, provided a haven of calm in the storm. He ended each roll call with the same words, "And, hey—let's be careful out there."

Viewers followed dramatic turns in the lives of their favorite characters as stories unfolded from episode to episode in semiserial fashion. Chesley and Goldblume were promoted to lieutenant, with Chesley moving on after the first full season. Frank and Joyce finally went public with their relationship, and were married in the 1983–1984 season—in a quickie, lunch-hour ceremony. The manipulative Chief Daniels, to whom Furillo reported, ran for mayor that same season, but lost in a bitter contest, to everyone's relief. In another story in early 1984, a despondent Hunter attempted suicide, only to survive when it turned out that his co-workers had removed the bullets from his service revolver. In one of the most famous episodes, in 1982, the normally quiet Ray Calletano, who was proud and sensitive about his Colombian heritage and unhappy about the status of Hispanics in American society, was honored as the department's "Hispanic Officer of the Year." At his testimonial banquet, after being misidentified as Puerto Rican and served Mexican food, he threw away his acceptance speech and told his stunned audience: "Why is it . . . that I look around this room—full of ranking officers—and the only other Hispanics I see are waiters and busboys?"

Probably the most dramatic development was the sudden death of kindly Sgt. Esterhaus in the middle of the 1983–1984 season (following the death of actor Michael Conrad). He had been having a passionate affair with Grace Gardner, the middle-aged widow of a fellow officer, and according to the story he suffered a heart attack while making love to her. "The Blues" were deeply touched by his passing.

Hill Street Blues was a most unusual mixture of drama and comedy, fast-paced and deliberately choppy, as was life at the station house (each episode began with 7 A.M. roll call and ended late at night, with several stories interwoven). Although conceptually similar to ABC's *Barney Miller*, its rough texture and hard reality gave it a greater sense of honesty. The humor in it was the nervous humor of frustration and life in the streets. If *Barney Miller* was a police comedy with occasional dramatic overtones, *Hill Street Blues* was a police drama with occasional comedic moments.

Although the city in which the series took place was never mentioned, the real-life station house seen in exterior shots was the Maxwell Street Precinct in Chicago. The theme song from the series was on the record charts in late 1981.

HILLER AND DILLER (*Situation Comedy*)
FIRST TELECAST: *September 23, 1997*
LAST TELECAST: *March 27, 1998*
BROADCAST HISTORY:
Sep 1997–Dec 1997, ABC Tue 9:30–10:00
Mar 1998, ABC Fri 9:30–10:00
CAST:
Ted Hiller .... Kevin Nealon
Jeanne Hiller .... Jordan Baker
Lizzie Hiller .... Faryn Einhorn
Josh Hiller .... Jonathan Osser
Allison Hiller .... Jill Berard
Neil Diller .... Richard Lewis
Zane Diller .... Kyle Sabihy
Brooke Diller .... Allison Mack
Gordon Schermerhorn .... Eugene Levy

A mismatched pair of comedy writers mixed work and home life in this short-lived sitcom which was co-produced by Ron Howard. Ted and Neil had been writing partners for fifteen years, longer than either of them had been married, but they could not have been more different. Ted was the goofy but dedicated dad, devoted to his wife Jeanne and their three kids: brainy tween Lizzie, spunky Josh, and cute little Allison. Neil, on the other hand, was a self-centered, world-class neurotic whose second marriage was on the rocks. For some reason, he got custody of his two troublemaking kids, chubby teen operator Zane and sexpot Brooke, and boy, did he need help. With Ted's guidance and Jeanne's reluctant help, somehow he got along. Gordon was the loud, sarcastic boss who tried to get some work out of the pair at the office.

HIPPODROME (*Circus Variety*)
FIRST TELECAST: *July 5, 1966*
LAST TELECAST: *September 6, 1966*
BROADCAST HISTORY:
Jul 1966–Sep 1966, CBS Tue 8:30–9:30

Filmed in England, this summer replacement for *The Red Skelton Hour* featured a different celebrity host each week who introduced an assortment of acts that included many circus stalwarts (animal acts, aerialists, clowns, etc.) as well as the more traditional variety-show staples (singers, dancers, and comedians). Hosts included Allan Sherman, Woody Allen, and Merv Griffin.

HIRAM HOLIDAY, see *Adventures of Hiram Holiday, The*

HIS & HERS (*Situation Comedy*)
FIRST TELECAST: *March 5, 1990*
LAST TELECAST: *August 22, 1990*
BROADCAST HISTORY:
Mar 1990–Apr 1990, CBS Mon 10:30–11:00
Jul 1990, CBS Mon 10:30–11:00
Aug 1990, CBS Wed 8:30–9:00
CAST:
Dr. Doug Lambert .... Martin Mull
Dr. Regina "Reggie" Hewitt .... Stephanie Faracy
Jeff Spencer .... Richard Kline
Debbie .... Blair Tefkin
Noah Lambert .... Blake Soper
Mandy Lambert .... Lisa Picotte
Mr. Buckley .... Jim Doughan
Mrs. Buckley .... Jane Morris

Doug and Reggie were newly married marriage counselors who often seemed better at giving good advice to their clients than of taking it themselves. Reggie, who had never been married before, suffered tremendous anxiety over her seeming inability to get pregnant. Living with them were Noah and Mandy, the teenaged children from Doug's first marriage. Jeff was Doug's best friend, an unscrupulous divorce attorney who lined his pockets with the fallout from his buddy's counseling practice. Debbie was Doug and Reggie's spaced-out receptionist and the Buckleys were members of Doug's therapy group.

HISTORY CHANNEL, THE (Network) (*Documentary Cable Network*)
LAUNCHED:
January 1, 1995
SUBSCRIBERS (MAY 2003):
82.9 million (78% U.S.)

A spin-off from A&E, the History Channel presented straightforward documentaries on various aspects of world history. Some sample subjects were "Tales of the FBI," "Mount Rushmore," "The U.S. Mint," "Spy Gadgets," "Iran and Iraq," "Curse of the Pharaohs," "Assassinations That Changed the World," and "History's Greatest Hoaxes." Among the more frequently seen hosts have been Roger Mudd, Mike Wallace, Sander Vanocur, and Arthur Kent. Appropriately themed movies and mini-series (e.g., *Roots*) were also shown from time to time.

HITCHHIKER, THE (*Dramatic Anthology*)
BROADCAST HISTORY:
HBO and USA Network
30 minutes
Produced: *1983–1988* (HBO, 39 episodes); *1989–1990* (USA, 46 episodes)
Premiered: *November 23, 1983* (HBO); *January 6, 1989* (USA)
CAST:
The Hitchhiker (1983–1984) .... Nicholas Campbell
The Hitchhiker (1984–1990) .... Page Fletcher

Greed, lust, murder, and mysterious strangers filled this moody and graphic suspense anthology, which on HBO included female nudity as well. The most mysterious stranger was The Hitchhiker himself, a young drifter in tight jeans who introduced each story, interacted a bit with the principals, and then faded into the background as they proceeded to murder or maim each other. Some fairly notable actors appeared in the stories, including Harry Hamlin, Tom Skerritt, Barry Bostwick, and Margot Kidder.

HITZ (*Situation Comedy*)

FIRST TELECAST: *August 26, 1997*

LAST TELECAST: *December 30, 1997*

BROADCAST HISTORY:

Aug 1997–Oct 1997, UPN Tue 9:00–9:30
Nov 1997, UPN Tue 9:30–10:00
Dec 1997, UPN Tue 9:00–9:30

CAST:

Busby Evans .... Claude Brooks
Robert Moore .... Rick Gomez
Jimmy Esposito .... Andrew Dice Clay
Tommy Stans .... Spencer Garrett
April Beane .... Rosa Blasi
Neil, the bartender .... Reno Wilson
Angela .... Kristin Dattilo-Hayward

Busby and Robert were a young A&R (Artists and Repertoire) team working for Hitower Records in Los Angeles in this hip comedy. Busby was an operator with great ideas and a velvet tongue who needed the more responsible Robert to smooth things over when he alienated performers they were trying to sign. They were barely surviving in the cutthroat music business. Jimmy was the tyrannical owner of Hitower who dressed all in black, and Tommy was Hitower's sleazy head of promotion, who reveled in other people's problems but was always careful to kiss Jimmy's ass. Also seen were April, a beautiful fellow A&R executive who was trying to steal their clients; Angela, a Stanford Law School graduate and the firm's head of business affairs, who was constantly belittled by Jimmy; and Neil, the bartender at Riffs, a club where the guys hung out and negotiated deals.

HIZZONNER (*Situation Comedy*)

FIRST TELECAST: *May 10, 1979*

LAST TELECAST: *June 14, 1979*

BROADCAST HISTORY:

May 1979–June 1979, NBC Thu 8:00–8:30

CAST:

Mayor Cooper .... David Huddleston
James Cooper .... Will Seltzer
Annie Cooper .... Kathy Cronkite
Timmons .... Don Galloway
Ginny .... Diana Muldaur
Melanie .... Gina Hecht
Nails .... Mickey Deems

Mayor Cooper was a widower with two grown children: Annie, a feminist civil-rights attorney, and James, a hippie affiliated with a communal organization called the Wilderness Cult. As the well-loved chief executive of a small Midwestern city, Cooper was basically honest, but not above doing things that were politically to his advantage. Timmons was his chief of staff; Ginny, his personal secretary; Melanie, one of the other secretaries at city hall; and Nails, the childhood friend who served as both bodyguard and chauffeur. When things started to get out of hand, Mayor Cooper would break into song, and there was one musical number in each episode of this short-lived series. Actress Kathy Cronkite, who played Annie, was the daughter of CBS News's Walter Cronkite.

HOBBY LOBBY (*Comedy*)

FIRST TELECAST: *September 30, 1959*

LAST TELECAST: *March 23, 1960*

BROADCAST HISTORY:

Sep 1959–Mar 1960, ABC Wed 8:00–8:30

STAR:

Cliff Arquette (as *Charley Weaver*)

Hobby Lobby gave Charley Weaver the opportunity to chat each week with two people, one a celebrity and one not, about their interesting or amusing hobbies. Zsa Zsa Gabor discussed her love of fencing on one telecast and Gypsy Rose Lee sang the praises of sport fishing on another. Charley also made joking references to the hobbies of residents of his fictional hometown of Mount Idy, Ohio. The jokes were more interesting than the hobbies and the hobbies were eventually dropped. Effective with the November 25, 1959, telecast the title was changed to *The Charley Weaver Show.* Each week Charley had one or two guest celebrities come to visit with him in Mount Idy and chat about the activities of such local residents as Elsie Krack, Birdie Rudd, Wallace Swine, Clara Kimball Moots, and Grandpa Snider.

HOGAN FAMILY, THE (*Situation Comedy*)

FIRST TELECAST: *March 1, 1986*

LAST TELECAST: *July 20, 1991*

BROADCAST HISTORY:

Mar 1986, NBC Sat 8:30–9:00
Mar 1986–Jun 1986, NBC Mon 8:30–9:00
Jun 1986–Sep 1986, NBC Mon 8:00–8:30
Sep 1986–Nov 1986, NBC Sun 8:30–9:00
Nov 1986–Jan 1987, NBC Sun 8:00–8:30
Jan 1987–Mar 1987, NBC Sun 8:30–9:00
Mar 1987–Jun 1990, NBC Mon 8:30–9:00
Sep 1990–Dec 1990, CBS Sat 8:30–9:00
Jul 1991, CBS Wed 8:00–8:30
Jul 1991, CBS Sat 8:00–9:00

CAST:

Valerie Hogan (1986–1987) .... Valerie Harper
Sandy Hogan (1987–1991) .... Sandy Duncan
David Hogan (age 16) .... Jason Bateman
Willie Hogan (12) .... Danny Ponce
Mark Hogan (12) .... Jeremy Licht
Michael Hogan .... Josh Taylor
Barbara Goodwin (1986) .... Christine Ebersole
Annie Steck (1986–1987) .... Judith Kahan
Mrs. Patty Poole .... Edie McClurg
**Peter Poole (1987–1989)* .... Willard Scott
Rich (1986–1989) .... Tom Hodges
**Burt (1987–1991)* .... Steve Witting
**Cara (1990–1991)* .... Josie Bissett
**Brenda (1990–1991)* .... Angela Lee
Lloyd Hogan (1990–1991) .... John Hillerman

*Occasional

THEME:

"Together Through the Years," by Charles Fox and Stephen Geyer, performed by Roberta Flack

Uproar on and off the screen marked this family sitcom, originally called *Valerie.* The premise was straightforward enough—take one harried mom (Valerie), juggling part-time career and full-time responsibility for running a household due to the frequent absence of her husband (Michael), an international airline pilot; add one rambunctious teenager (David) and two super-cute fraternal twins (Willie and Mark). All that was missing was a dog, or a feisty maid.

Valerie did have a career of sorts, first as the manager

of an auction house and later as a graphic artist. However, most of the action took place in her suburban Oak Park, Illinois, home (near Chicago), where girl-hungry David (the "man of the house"), fun-loving Willie, and brainy Mark could always be counted on to stir things up. Barbara was Valerie's understanding friend, and Mrs. Poole the busybody neighbor.

In the fall of 1987 Valerie Harper abruptly left the show in a well-publicized dispute with the producers. NBC decided to continue without her, retitling the series *Valerie's Family* (some suggested "Where's Valerie?" or "Who's Valerie?" might be more appropriate). Later, in June 1988, it became *The Hogan Family*. Valerie was written out of the series as having died, and Michael's divorced sister Sandy, a high school counselor, moved in to serve as a sort of surrogate mom. Stories began to focus more on the kids, especially teenager David, who the producers hoped would become the next TV heartthrob. Others joining the cast included David's pals Rich and Burt, and Mrs. Poole's jovial husband Peter, played on an infrequent basis by *Today* show weatherman Willard Scott.

By the fall of 1988 everyone in the house had entered the dating scene, including Sandy and Michael (who was now home more often). David enrolled at nearby Northwestern University; later, the twins began working at a local fast-food establishment, Bossy Burger. Dates came and went like side orders of fries, but toward the end of the run Cara was Mark's steady girlfriend, while Brenda was Willie's. In the fall of 1990 Grandpa Lloyd Hogan (Sandy and Michael's father) joined the household, moving from Los Angeles after his own divorce.

In addition to dating and fun around the kitchen, *The Hogan Family* sometimes tackled more serious subjects, as when David nearly ended his friendship with Rich by stopping the latter from driving home from a party while drunk or when David and Burt discovered something more shocking—that their buddy Rich had AIDS.

HOGAN'S HEROES (*Situation Comedy*)

FIRST TELECAST: *September 17, 1965*
LAST TELECAST: *July 4, 1971*
BROADCAST HISTORY:
Sep 1965–Sep 1967, CBS Fri 8:30–9:00
Sep 1967–Sep 1969, CBS Sat 9:00–9:30
Sep 1969–Sep 1970, CBS Fri 8:30–9:00
Sep 1970–Jul 1971, CBS Sun 7:30–8:00
CAST:
Col. Robert Hogan .... Bob Crane
Col. Wilhelm Klink .... Werner Klemperer
Sgt. Hans Schultz .... John Banner
Cpl. Louis LeBeau .... Robert Clary
Cpl. Peter Newkirk .... Richard Dawson
Sgt. James Kinchloe (1965–1970) .... Ivan Dixon
Sgt. Richard Baker (1970–1971)
.... Kenneth Washington
Sgt. Andrew Carter .... Larry Hovis
Helga (1965–1966) .... Cynthia Lynn
Hilda (1966–1970) .... Sigrid Valdis

Hogan's Heroes set out to prove that, at least in the world of televised situation comedies, life in a Nazi POW camp during World War II could be fun. Commandant of the camp was the incompetent, monocled Col. Klink, and guarding Stalag 13, where the American-led resistance forces were housed, was the equally inept Sgt. Schultz. Under the direction of Col. Robert Hogan, the prisoners were actually in complete control of the camp. They had rigged the barbed-wire fence so that it could be opened and closed like a garage door. They fed classified information to the Allied forces on the outside, helped fugitives escape from Germany, printed counterfeit money, and did anything else imaginable to confound the Germans. Their living conditions were more reminiscent of a fancy hotel than a POW camp. They had a French chef, a steam room, a barbershop, and more comforts than they would have had at home. Since they were more important to the Allied cause in the camp than out of it, they had no desire to escape, especially considering the fun and comforts they had there.

HOLD IT PLEASE (*Quiz/Audience Participation*)

FIRST TELECAST: *May 8, 1949*
LAST TELECAST: *May 22, 1949*
BROADCAST HISTORY:
May 1949, CBS Sat 7:00–7:30
EMCEE:
Gil Fates
REGULARS:
Bill McGraw
Mort Marshall
Cloris Leachman

Contestants on this short-lived quiz program—it only lasted three weeks—were asked to answer questions that were acted out by the show's regulars. The questions might relate to events in history or be fictional in nature. The regulars often danced and sang, as well as acted, to illustrate the questions. The contestant who successfully answered the basic quiz questions won an opportunity to go for the $1,000 jackpot, as well as the prizes already won. If a contestant won the jackpot, he remained on the program as assistant emcee until there was a new jackpot winner.

HOLD THAT CAMERA (*Game/Variety*)

FIRST TELECAST: *August 27, 1950*
LAST TELECAST: *December 15, 1950*
BROADCAST HISTORY:
Aug 1950–Sep 1950, DUM Sun 7:30–8:00
Sep 1950–Dec 1950, DUM Fri 8:30–9:00
EMCEE:
Jimmy Blaine
Kyle MacDonnell
ORCHESTRA:
Ving Merlin

Hold That Camera began as a game show in which viewers at home played an important role. A home viewer, contacted by telephone, would give directions over the phone to an on-camera contestant who performed stunts for prizes. The contestant completing the stunts in the least amount of time won for both himself and his telephone "partner." Interspersed with the games were songs by host Jimmy Blaine.

After only about a month, both Blaine and the game-show format were scrapped and *Hold That Camera* became a straight variety show, hosted by songstress Kyle MacDonnell. The setting was a nightclub called "The Camera Room," in which Miss MacDonnell and visiting guest stars performed.

HOLD THAT NOTE (*Quiz/Audience Participation*)
FIRST TELECAST: *January 22, 1957*
LAST TELECAST: *April 2, 1957*
BROADCAST HISTORY:
Jan 1957–Apr 1957, NBC Tue 10:30–11:00
EMCEE:
Bert Parks
ANNOUNCER/HOST:
Johnny Olsen

Hold That Note appeared rather suddenly on January 22, 1957, as an unannounced and unexplained replacement for *Break the $250,000 Bank,* which had aired in the same time slot on the previous Tuesday. Bert Parks was the emcee of both programs, and informed viewers of the first telecast of *Hold That Note* that the contestants who were still on from last week's edition of *Break the $250,000 Bank* had been paid their winnings and given the opportunity to become contestants on the new show, which two of them did. There was really no mystery surrounding the sudden departure of *Break the $250,000 Bank.* It had been doing poorly in the ratings and seemed not to be working too well, so the producers decided to try another giveaway show in its place.

The object of *Hold That Note,* much like that of the somewhat similar but longer-lasting *Name That Tune,* was for the contestants to recognize a particular tune as soon as possible. The fewer notes played, the more the tune was worth. The first person to correctly identify three tunes was the winner of the round and the accumulated money in that round. There was a jackpot as an inducement for a winning contestant to keep playing, but also the possibility that he could lose some of his accumulated winnings. Bert Parks sang a song during each show and questions about the song he sang were worth extra money to the contestants.

HOLDING THE BABY (*Situation Comedy*)
FIRST TELECAST: *August 23, 1998*
LAST TELECAST: *December 15, 1998*
BROADCAST HISTORY:
Aug 1998–Oct 1998, FOX Sun 7:30–8:00
Dec 1998, FOX Sun 8:30–9:00
CAST:
Gordon Stiles .... Jon Patrick Walker
Kelly O'Malley .... Jennifer Westfeldt
Jimmy Stiles .... Eddie McClintock
Miss Boggs .... Sherri Shepherd
Daniel Stiles (pilot only)
.... Brendan and Kyle McRoberts
Daniel Stiles .... Carter and Jordan Kemp
Stan Peterson .... Ron Leibman

Gordon was a workaholic account executive at Los Angeles Consulting Group, whose wife, Michelle, had run off to Tibet with another man at the same time that their nanny quit—literally leaving him "holding the baby" (his infant son Daniel). Thinking that Kelly, a pretty young U.C.L.A. grad student who had applied for a receptionist job at his company, would make a perfect nanny, he offered her twice as much as that job paid ($12 an hour) to become Daniel's nanny. Despite misgivings, Kelly took the gig. Jimmy was Gordon's womanizing brother, an unemployed actor who lived with him. Miss Boggs was Gordon's sassy secretary, and Stan his demanding boss. Stories revolved around Gordon's problems balancing his responsibilities at work with the needs of his infant son and the complications that arose when he started dating again.

HOLIDAY HANDBOOK (*Travelogue*)
FIRST TELECAST: *April 4, 1958*
LAST TELECAST: *June 20, 1958*
BROADCAST HISTORY:
Apr 1958–Jun 1958, ABC Fri 10:00–10:30

Travel films, mostly of Western Europe, and keyed to what a visitor might find in local entertainment and culture.

HOLIDAY HOTEL (*Musical Variety*)
FIRST TELECAST: *March 23, 1950*
LAST TELECAST: *October 4, 1951*
BROADCAST HISTORY:
Mar 1950–Jun 1950, ABC Thu 9:30–10:00
Sep 1950–Oct 1951, ABC Thu 9:00–9:30
REGULARS:
Edward Everett Horton (1950)
Don Ameche (1950–1951)
Leonore Lonergan (1950)
Betty Brewer
Bill Harrington (1950)
Walter Dare Wahl (1950)
Don Saddler (1950)
Dorothy Greener (1951)
Florence Halop (1951)
Joshua Shelley (1951)
June Graham Dancers
Charles Tate Dancers (1951)
Bernie Green Orchestra
Don Craig's Chorus

Holiday Hotel premiered in the spring of 1950 as a musical variety show set in a Park Avenue hotel. Edward Everett Horton was the beleaguered manager of the hotel, running things for the absent Mr. Holiday, and trying to keep the bizarre tenants and guests under control. Leonore Lonergan provided comic counterpoint as the hotel's switchboard operator. After a comic sketch by the regulars the scene would shift to the ballroom for entertainment by the week's guest stars, and musical production numbers staged by Gordon Jenkins. Even the sponsor (Packard Motors) got into the act, with a Packard showroom conveniently located on the ground floor of the hotel.

Despite a big budget, the program received poor reviews, and for the fall Edward Everett Horton was replaced by Don Ameche as manager of the hotel. In July 1951 the hotel motif was dropped and the title changed to *Don Ameche's Musical Playhouse.* The setting became a playhouse run by "manager" Ameche, but otherwise format and cast were the same as for *Holiday Hotel.*

HOLIDAY LODGE (*Situation Comedy*)
FIRST TELECAST: *June 25, 1961*
LAST TELECAST: *October 8, 1961*
BROADCAST HISTORY:
Jun 1961–Oct 1961, CBS Sun 9:30–10:00
CAST:
Johnny Miller .... Johnny Wayne
Frank Boone .... Frank Shuster
Dorothy Jackson .... Maureen Arthur
Woodrow .... Charles Smith
J. W. Harrington .... Justice Watson

The Canadian comedy team of Johnny Wayne and Frank Shuster starred as Johnny Miller and Frank Boone in this situation comedy about the adventures of two men working as social directors at a posh summer resort. All of the regulars in this series were employees of the hotel, with Dorothy Jackson the girlfriend of Johnny Miller as well. The stories revolved around the wealthy, not-so-wealthy, and suspicious guests of the resort and the ways in which their activities involved them with the social directors.

HOLLYWOOD ADVENTURE TIME, see *Movies—Prior to 1961*

HOLLYWOOD AND THE STARS (*Documentary*)
FIRST TELECAST: *September 30, 1963*
LAST TELECAST: *September 28, 1964*
BROADCAST HISTORY:
Sep 1963–Sep 1964, NBC Mon 9:30–10:00
HOST:
Joseph Cotten

Hollywood and the Stars looked at all aspects of the motion-picture industry, in documentary form. Each telecast surveyed a particular theme or subject, such as biographies of famous stars, specific types of films and film cycles, the people behind the scenes, and depictions of movies actually being made. Among the stars whose lives and careers were profiled were Rita Hayworth, Paul Newman, Natalie Wood, Bette Davis, and Humphrey Bogart. Other individual telecasts treated Westerns, musicals, gangster movies, war movies, teenage idols, great comedians, movie lovers, and glamour girls. One entire program was spent on location with Elizabeth Taylor and Richard Burton as Burton filmed *The Night of the Iguana*.

HOLLYWOOD BABYLON (*Documentary*)
BROADCAST HISTORY:
Syndicated only
30 minutes
Produced: *1992* (26 episodes)
Released: *September 1992*
HOST:
Tony Curtis
NARRATOR:
Don Francks

Loosely based on the notorious book of the same name, *Hollywood Babylon* documented scandals and generally unknown truths about famous film-land celebrities, in some cases using actors to recreate situations, in others using file footage. Normally there were two featured stories per episode plus short bits of celebrity gossip and, at the end of each episode, "A Moment with Tony Curtis," in which the show's host reminisced about his career. Among the topics covered were Lucille Ball and Desi Arnaz's troubled marriage, the Fatty Arbuckle rape trial, Jayne Mansfield's tragic story, and the mysterious death of movie director Thomas Ince.

HOLLYWOOD BACKSTAGE (*Beauty Tips*)
FIRST TELECAST: *August 7, 1955*
LAST TELECAST: *September 11, 1955*
BROADCAST HISTORY:
Aug 1955–Sep 1955, ABC Sun 7:30–8:00
HOST:
Ern Westmore

Ern Westmore, dean of Hollywood makeup artists, gave demonstrations and advice to women in this series, which was also seen in daytime at various times during the mid-1950s. A regular feature of the show called for a woman from the studio audience to be glamorized with the full Westmore Treatment. Ern would also demonstrate how a screen star was made up for a famous role.

The program was known in daytime as *The Ern Westmore Show*.

HOLLYWOOD BEAT (*Police Drama*)
FIRST TELECAST: *September 21, 1985*
LAST TELECAST: *November 23, 1985*
BROADCAST HISTORY:
Sep 1985–Nov 1985, ABC Sat 8:00–9:00
CAST:
Det. Nick McCarren .... Jack Scalia
Det. Jack Rado .... Jay Acavone
George Grinsky .... John Matuszak
Capt. Wes Biddle .... Edward Winter

Nick and Jack were undercover cops working the seedy side of Hollywood with fast cars and to the sound of loud rock music, in this knock off of *Miami Vice*. Using sometimes bizarre disguises, they operated out of a business run by George Grinsky, a hulking brute who was openly gay, but so big that no one dared say anything about it. Bag ladies, pimps, and winos were their street contacts, and Capt. Biddle the usual tough superior.

HOLLYWOOD FILM THEATRE, see *Movies—Prior to 1961*

HOLLYWOOD GAME, THE (*Quiz/Game*)
FIRST TELECAST: *June 19, 1992*
LAST TELECAST: *July 10, 1992*
BROADCAST HISTORY:
Jun 1992–Jul 1992, CBS Fri 8:00–8:30
EMCEE:
Bob Goen

Summer game show that tested contestants' knowledge of movie and TV trivia. Each episode featured two teams of two contestants each. There were three preliminary rounds with the value of correct answers rising from $100 to $2,000. In the first each team chose a category from nine available—one for each letter of Hollywood—with many of the questions involving clips from TV series and movies. In the second and third rounds the other team could steal the value of a question by answering it correctly if the first team missed it. After the preliminary rounds the teams played the "Double Feature" round, in which they were shown two film clips and then asked a question about either the films or someone in them. Teams could wager all, half, or none of their accumulated winnings. The losers still got to keep their money.

The winners went on to the fast-picture round with a chance at $25,000. They chose one of two new categories and won $1,000 for each correct identification, and, if they identified all nine, they won $25,000. One contestant got 15 seconds to identify as many as possible, then the partner, who had been isolated offstage, got 15 seconds to try to identify the rest.

HOLLYWOOD HOUSE (*Variety*)
FIRST TELECAST: *December 4, 1949*
LAST TELECAST: *March 5, 1950*

BROADCAST HISTORY:

Dec 1949–Jan 1950, ABC Sun 7:30–8:00
Jan 1950–Mar 1950, ABC Sun 6:30–7:00

REGULARS:

Dick Wesson
Jim Backus
Gale Robbins

Comedy variety show set in a medium-sized Hollywood hotel, where anyone could wander in and anything could happen. Evidently not enough did, as the show was dropped after three months.

HOLLYWOOD INSIDER (*Entertainment News*)

BROADCAST HISTORY:

USA Network
30 minutes
Produced: *1985–1995* (464 episodes)
Premiered: *May 6, 1985*

HOST:

Sandy Newton (1985–1990)
Shawn Southwick (1990–1995)

A long-running weekly entertainment magazine along the lines of *Entertainment Tonight* but a little more features-oriented. *Hollywood Insider* was the successor to a similar program called *Seeing Stars,* hosted by Jim Finnerty, which ran on USA from June 1984 until early 1985 and then was seen briefly in syndication.

HOLLYWOOD MOVIE TIME, see *Movies—Prior to 1961*

HOLLYWOOD MYSTERY TIME, see *Movies—Prior to 1961*

HOLLYWOOD OFF BEAT, see *Steve Randall*

HOLLYWOOD OFF RAMP (*Dramatic Anthology*)

BROADCAST HISTORY:

E! Entertainment
30 minutes
Original episodes: *2000* (26 episodes)
Premiered: *June 4, 2000*

HOST:

Brian Unger

A short-lived dramatic anthology, billed as "a dark detour on the road to fame," in which denizens of Hollywood were caught up in murder, madness and mysterious happenings. Some of the stories were straight murder mysteries, while others were supernatural yarns involving curses and spells. Generally lesser-known actors appeared.

HOLLYWOOD OPENING NIGHT (*Dramatic Anthology*)

FIRST TELECAST: *July 20, 1951*
LAST TELECAST: *March 23, 1953*

BROADCAST HISTORY:

Jul 1951–Mar 1952, CBS Fri 10:30–11:00
Oct 1952–Mar 1953, NBC Mon 9:00–9:30

HOST:

Jimmy Fidler (1952–1953)

The dramas aired in this CBS series during the 1951–1952 season were half-hour films made especially for television. For the second season, however, the sponsor moved the show to NBC and the dramas became live productions. This was in fact the first live dramatic show to originate from the West Coast and the first program to make use of NBC's recently completed Burbank studios. Hollywood columnist Jimmy Fidler opened each show in a "theater" lobby and invited the television audience to join him inside to see the play. At the end of each week's performance he gave a brief preview of the next week's offering.

The fare was quite varied, ranging from serious dramas such as "Delaying Action" starring John Hodiak, John Agar, and Tab Hunter, and "The Pattern" starring Gloria Swanson, to light comedies like "Uncle Fred Flits By" with David Niven and "Legal Affairs" with Franchot Tone. With the Hollywood talent pool to draw from, the casts in this series were generally quite impressive.

HOLLYWOOD PALACE, THE (*Variety*)

FIRST TELECAST: *January 4, 1964*
LAST TELECAST: *February 7, 1970*

BROADCAST HISTORY:

Jan 1964–May 1967, ABC Sat 9:30–10:30
Sep 1967–Jan 1968, ABC Mon 10:00–11:00
Jan 1968–Feb 1970, ABC Sat 9:30–10:30 (OS)

ORCHESTRA:

Les Brown (1964)
Mitchell Ayres (1964–1969)

EXECUTIVE PRODUCER:

Nick Vanoff

The Hollywood Palace was a lavish, big-budget, big-name variety show of the 1960s which attempted to become to Saturday night what *The Ed Sullivan Show* was to Sunday. It premiered amid much hoopla in January 1964, live from the recently rebuilt ABC Palace Theater (formerly the El Capitan) in Hollywood. The first telecast headlined Bing Crosby as host, with Mickey Rooney, Bobby Van, Nancy Wilson, Bob Newhart, and Gary Crosby, as well as singers, dancers, magicians, balancing acts, and even clowns.

A different host topped the bill each week, but some returned more often than others. Bing Crosby was most frequently seen (30-plus appearances), while Fred Astaire, Milton Berle, Jimmy Durante, Sid Caesar and Imogene Coca, Sammy Davis, Jr., and Don Adams also made multiple appearances as host. Other acts on the *Palace* bill ranged from old-timers Groucho Marx and Ed Wynn to Frank Sinatra with the Basie band, to Judy Garland, to the Rolling Stones. The strictly vaudeville acts (acrobats, etc.) were seen less often during later years, as the show became more of a straight musical-comedy variety hour. A highlight of every season was the Christmas holiday show, usually presided over by Bing Crosby (sometimes with his family), and also the glamorous billboard girls (at one time including the then-unknown Raquel Welch).

Though *The Hollywood Palace* featured top-line talent, and attracted a substantial audience, it never developed the loyal following of the other great variety hours, probably because of the lack of a central figure as continuing host.

The show was known during its first few weeks as *The Saturday Night Hollywood Palace.* Attempts were made in both 1973 and 1977 to revive this series with syndicated versions. Each time the revivals lasted but a single season.

HOLLYWOOD PREMIERE (*Variety*)

FIRST TELECAST: *September 22, 1949*
LAST TELECAST: *November 17, 1949*

BROADCAST HISTORY:

Sep 1949–Nov 1949, NBC Thu 8:00–8:30

A short-lived series of half-hour programs showcasing established talent in comedic and dramatic material. There was no continuing cast. Among those appearing were Pinky Lee, Howard Da Silva, and Sterling Holloway. The programs were produced in Hollywood and shown via kinescope on the Eastern and Midwestern NBC networks.

HOLLYWOOD PREMIERE THEATRE, see *Hollywood Theatre Time*

HOLLYWOOD SCREEN TEST (*Talent*)

FIRST TELECAST: *April 15, 1948*

LAST TELECAST: *May 18, 1953*

BROADCAST HISTORY:

Apr 1948–May 1948, ABC Thu 8:00–8:30
May 1948–Jun 1948, ABC Sun 6:30–7:00
Aug 1948–Sep 1948, ABC Sun 7:30–8:00
Oct 1948–May 1949, ABC Sun 8:00–8:30
May 1949–Sep 1950, ABC Sat 7:30–8:00
Sep 1950–May 1953, ABC Mon 7:30–8:00 (OS)

HOST:

Bert Lytell (1948)
Neil Hamilton (1948–1953)

ASSISTANT:

Robert Quarry (1949)

"You, the public, make the stars" was the oft-repeated slogan of this long-running talent show of TV's early years. Unlike many TV talent shows, the production values here were commendably high. The young talent appearing on *Hollywood Screen Test* all had previous professional experience, and were looking for the "big break" that would bring them stardom. They were paired with established stars in dramatic sketches and comedy skits written especially for the program, as well as scenes adapted from famous plays and novels. The behind-the-scenes ambience of the show was heightened by the setting, an imitation Hollywood soundstage, with silent film actor Bert Lytell as the original "producer" and Neil Hamilton as his assistant. (Lytell left after a few months and Hamilton took over the show.)

Several newcomers got the break they were looking for, landing Hollywood contracts as a result of their appearance on the show. Among the program's Hollywood-bound alumni were Grace Kelly, Jack Klugman, Gene Barry, Pernell Roberts, Jack Lemmon, Betsy Palmer, Martin Balsam, Susan Cabot, and Robert Quarry (who also served as assistant on the show). Better known (at the time) were the guest stars with whom they played their scenes, including Mercedes McCambridge, Jeff Morrow, Edward Everett Horton, and others.

Hollywood Screen Test was created by Young & Rubicam advertising executive David Levy, and initially produced in the studios of ABC's Philadelphia affiliate WFIL. It was networked to at least one other ABC station (WMAL, Washington) from the start, making it—apparently—the first regular series on the "ABC Television Network." When ABC launched its New York flagship station, WJZ-TV, in August 1948, production moved there.

HOLLYWOOD SHOWDOWN (*Quiz*)

FIRST TELECAST: *January 24, 2000*

LAST TELECAST: *July 13, 2000*

BROADCAST HISTORY:

Jan 2000–Mar 2000, PAX Mon–Fri 7:00–7:30
Apr 2000–Jul 2000, PAX Mon–Fri 7:30–8:00

EMCEE:

Tom Newton

The questions on this quiz show were all about movies, television and music. At the start of each episode a randomly chosen contestant hoped to guess which of the six other potential contestants in the "gallery" was holding the "box office" card. He picked one of the members of the gallery, and the value of her card (between $100 and $1,000) was added to the "box office" jackpot, which had started at $10,000. The picked member then competed with the person who had chosen her. The first one to correctly answer three questions won the "showdown" and the right to continue the search. When the picked member of the gallery had the box office card, the winner of their showdown went on to the bonus round where she was asked five more questions (each worth $500) and, if she got all five correct, won the box office jackpot. Before each question, she could pick which of two categories it came from. A wrong answer forfeited all accumulated winnings. If, after hearing the categories, the contestant decided to stop, she kept the accumulated winnings and retained control in the search for another box office card with the previous competitors back in the gallery, and another chance at the ever-growing jackpot. After a contestant won the jackpot, and left the show, it was reset to $10,000.

HOLLYWOOD SQUARES (*Quiz/Game*)

FIRST TELECAST: *January 12, 1968*

LAST TELECAST: *September 13, 1968*

BROADCAST HISTORY:

Jan 1968–Sep 1968, NBC Fri 9:30–10:00

EMCEE:

Peter Marshall

REGULARS:

Cliff Arquette (*Charley Weaver*)
Wally Cox

This nighttime version of the highly popular NBC daytime game show (which premiered in October 1966) was seen on the network in 1968. The host, as in the daytime version, was Peter Marshall.

The *Hollywood Squares* set resembled a huge tic-tac-toe board, with a different celebrity in each of the nine squares. Two contestants took turns choosing celebrities. The chosen celebrity would be asked a question—sometimes serious, sometimes strange, often ridiculous—by emcee Marshall, and would give an answer. The contestant would then have to state whether the answer given was right or wrong. If the contestant guessed correctly, he won that square. If not, his opponent won it, unless that square would give the opponent three squares in a row and a victory. The first contestant to win three squares in a row won the round. Often, however, nobody noticed who won, as the quiz element in *Hollywood Squares* was distinctly secondary to the quips and jokes of the celebrities. Paul Lynde, who was to become the star "center square" regular of the daytime version of *Hollywood Squares,* was not yet a regular when the nighttime version was on. He appeared only six times during its run and became a regular on the daytime show roughly one month after the nighttime show left the air.

In addition to the daytime version, a syndicated once-a-week nighttime edition was begun in the fall of 1971. The daytime *Hollywood Squares* finally left the air in June 1980—after a 14-year run—but the syndicated nighttime edition continued, expanded to five nights a week, until the fall of 1982. A year later *Hollywood Squares* returned to the NBC weekday daytime lineup as part of *The Match Game–Hollywood Squares Hour*. The host of this version was Jon Bauman, formerly of the singing group Sha Na Na. He was the first person other than Peter Marshall—who had hosted all previous versions of the series—to emcee *Hollywood Squares. The Match Game–Hollywood Squares Hour* left the air in July of 1984.

A new syndicated version of *Hollywood Squares* premiered in the fall of 1986 with John Davidson as emcee. Regulars in this version included JM J. Bullock, who also filled in for Davidson as substitute emcee; Joan Rivers, who became the permanent "center square" in 1987; and the show's announcer, Shadoe Stevens, who took over as "center square" in 1988. This version left the air at the end of the 1988–1989 season.

The venerable series surfaced again in the fall of 1998 with Tom Bergeron as the emcee and comedienne Whoopi Goldberg, who was the show's executive producer, receiving star billing in the center square. She left the show at the end of the 2001–2002 season.

HOLLYWOOD SUMMER THEATRE (*Dramatic Anthology*)

FIRST TELECAST: *August 3, 1956*
LAST TELECAST: *September 28, 1956*
BROADCAST HISTORY:
Aug 1956–Sep 1956, CBS Fri 8:00–8:30
HOST:
Gene Raymond

This filmed summer anthology series was made up of original dramas, never before seen on television, and was hosted by Gene Raymond. Appearing were such performers as Merle Oberon, Laraine Day, Joanne Dru, Rod Cameron, Ricardo Montalban, and Preston Foster.

HOLLYWOOD TALENT SCOUTS (*Variety*)

FIRST TELECAST: *June 22, 1965*
LAST TELECAST: *September 5, 1966*
BROADCAST HISTORY:
Jun 1965–Sep 1965, CBS Tue 8:30–9:30
Dec 1965–Sep 1966, CBS Mon 10:00–11:00
HOST:
Art Linkletter

The performers in this variety series were young unknowns who had been seen by celebrities and brought by those celebrities to *Hollywood Talent Scouts* to get their first national television exposure. Each week there were four or five guest celebrities who chatted briefly with host Art Linkletter and then introduced their discoveries.

During its initial summer run there were a few discoveries who actually became successful in future years, but not always doing what they did on this show. Tom Smothers brought a young comic named Pat Paulsen (later to work on the Smothers Brothers' variety show), actor Bob Crane presented a young singer named Marilyn McCoo (later the lead singer with The Fifth Dimension), and Carl Reiner brought one of the writers from his *Dick Van Dyke Show*, Garry Marshall. Marshall, who went on the show to try his luck as a comedian, later became the producer of *Happy Days* and *Laverne & Shirley*. Most of the young talents never made it, though, and some were not so young. Cliff Arquette, as Charley Weaver, introduced the Frivolous Five, a Dixieland jazz group composed entirely of women over sixty.

When this series returned in December, the title had been altered to *Art Linkletter's Hollywood Talent Scouts* and on-location interviews with celebrities were included in the format. Singer Donna Theodore was the most notable talent presented in this run. Virtually the same program, with different hosts, aired under the title *Celebrity Talent Scouts*.

HOLLYWOOD THEATRE TIME (*Various*)

FIRST TELECAST: *October 8, 1950*
LAST TELECAST: *October 20, 1951*
BROADCAST HISTORY:
Oct 1950–Dec 1950, ABC Sun 8:00–8:30
Dec 1950–Oct 1951, ABC Sat 7:00–7:30

This series was a showcase for an assortment of variety shows, dramatic presentations, scenes from famous plays, and situation comedies, all produced in Hollywood. Frequently seen during the first few months was "The Gil Lamb Show," a half-hour musical variety show hosted by the screen comedian. Other presentations included "Mr. and Mrs. Detective" starring Gale Storm and Don DeFore, and "The Spectre" starring Marjorie Reynolds.

During its first two months the series was known as *Hollywood Premiere Theatre*.

HOLMES AND YOYO (*Situation Comedy*)

FIRST TELECAST: *September 25, 1976*
LAST TELECAST: *December 11, 1976*
BROADCAST HISTORY:
Sep 1976–Dec 1976, ABC Sat 8:00–8:30
CAST:
Det. Alexander Holmes .... Richard B. Shull
Gregory "Yoyo" Yoyonovich .... John Schuck
Capt. Harry Sedford .... Bruce Kirby
Officer Maxine Moon .... Andrea Howard

This was billed as the revival of the classic two-man comedy team. Said producer Leonard Stern, "For over thirty years we had the marvelous antics of Laurel & Hardy, Abbott & Costello, Hope & Crosby, Martin & Lewis, Gleason & Carney, and then suddenly came an unexplainable gap. But now, hopefully, Schuck & Shull will fill the comedy void."

Schuck & Shull did not become another Laurel & Hardy; their series *Holmes and Yoyo* lasted a brief three months. Holmes was an accident-prone cop who never got hurt himself, but kept sending partners to the hospital. So the department decided to try its latest development, a lifelike robot "computer-person" named Yoyo (after its inventor, Dr. Yoyonovich). Holmes was not supposed to know that his new partner was a robot. He did, secretly, but few others were aware of it, certainly not Officer Maxine Moon who kept making amorous advances to Yoyo. Yoyo did have his strong points, including a photographic memory, an independent power source, a silent trash compressor which permitted him to digest anything, and the ability to produce color prints. But there were drawbacks, too. Nobody could lift him because he weighed 427 pounds. And although he was uninjurable, an assailant's bullet once shorted out his rhythm system, causing him to tap-dance out of control during a chase.

HOME & GARDEN TELEVISION (Network) (*Informational Cable Network*)

LAUNCHED:
December 30, 1994

SUBSCRIBERS (MAY 2003):
80.6 million (76% U.S.)

Another of those delightful cable channels that does one thing only, but does it well. HGTV's "thing" is, of course, instructional programming about home maintenance and repair. Programs covered five main areas: building and remodeling (*Fix It Up!, The House Doctor, Dream House*), decorating and interior design (*Awesome Interiors, The Furniture Show, Kitchen Design*), gardening and landscaping (*Grow It!, The Gardener's Journal, The Great Indoors*), crafts and hobbies (*Great Antiques Hunt, What's Your Hobby?*), and special interests (*Party at Home, Appraise It, How's That Made?*). Most programs were newly produced, although reruns of a few classics such as Bob Vila's *This Old House* were seen.

HOME BOX OFFICE (HBO) (Network) (*General Entertainment Cable Network*)

LAUNCHED:
December 1975

SUBSCRIBERS (MAY 2003):
35.1 million (33% U.S.)

Though not the most watched cable network, and certainly not the most widely distributed (due to its premium price), HBO is perhaps the best-known name in cable and the reason why many people subscribed to "the wire" in the first place.

Its schedule consists primarily of the latest Hollywood movies, shown uncut and without commercial interruption. Some are telecast only a few months after they played in the theaters, and most were made within the past five years. HBO has also been active in original movie production, offering its first original film, *The Terry Fox Story,* in May 1983. Subsequent originals have been big-budget (for television) and featured top-name stars, among them *And the Band Played On, Barbarians at the Gate, Stalin,* and *The Josephine Baker Story.*

HBO carries some sports coverage (Wimbledon Tennis, title boxing matches) and specials, including the HBO-initiated *Comic Relief* (1986), a benefit for the homeless. It has also produced critically acclaimed regular series, some of which have tested the boundaries of good taste with explicit nudity and profanity. Among its notable series (which are often irregularly scheduled) have been the following:

Arli$$ (sitcom starring Robert Wuhl as a sports agent with no ethics), 1996–2002
Curb Your Enthusiasm (comedy starring Larry David), 2000–
Da Ali G Show (comedy starring hip British comic Sacha Baron Cohen), 2003–
Dennis Miller Live (talk), 1994–2002
*Dream On** (sitcom starring Brian Benben), 1990–1996
Encyclopedia (children's variety), 1988–1989
First & Ten (football sitcom starring Delta Burke, O. J. Simpson), 1984–1991
Fraggle Rock (puppet show produced by Jim Henson), 1983–1988
*Hitchhiker, The** (drama anthology), 1983–1988
Larry Sanders Show, The (sitcom starring Garry Shandling), 1992–1998
Mind of the Married Man, The (comedy about three married men), 2001–2002
Not Necessarily the News (satire with Rich Hall, others), 1982–1988
Oz (an extremely brutal prison drama starring Ernie Hudson as Warden Leo Glynn and Harold Perrineau, Jr., as the wheelchair-bound narrator), 1997–2003
*Ray Bradbury Theater** (science-fiction anthology), 1985–1987
Real Time with Bill Maher (talk), 2003–
Russell Simmons' Def Comedy Jam (black standup comedy, produced by rap impresario Simmons; the original host was Martin Lawrence), 1992–1997
Sessions (drama starring Michael McKean and Elliott Gould), 1991
*Sex and the City** (comedy), 1998–
Six Feet Under (comedy/drama set in a family-owned funeral parlor, starring Peter Krause and Michael C. Hall), 2001–
*Sopranos, The** (crime/drama) 1999–
Spawn (animated action series based on the dark, violent comics), 1997–1999
Spicy City (animated mix of sci-fi and sex, voice of Michelle Phillips), 1997
*Tales from the Crypt** (horror anthology), 1989–1995
Tanner '88 (political sitcom starring Michael Murphy), 1988
The Wire (crime drama starring Dominic West), 2002–

*See separate alphabetical entry.

HBO began as a local pay-television station in Wilkes-Barre, Pennsylvania. Its first film telecast, on November 8, 1972, was *Sometimes a Great Notion.* The service went national in December 1975 when its signal was beamed to cable systems around the country via the Satcom satellite. A second channel, Cinemax, showing older films, was launched in 1980 and currently has about 20 million subscribers. Other subsidiary networks include HBO2 (same shows, different schedule, 1998), HBO Family (family-friendly, including kids' shows, 1998), HBO Signature (female-themed, 1998), HBO Zone (cutting-edge films, series and videos, 1999), HBO Comedy (1999) and HBO Latino (2000).

HOME COURT, THE (*Situation Comedy*)

FIRST TELECAST: *September 30, 1995*
LAST TELECAST: *June 29, 1996*

BROADCAST HISTORY:
Sep 1995–Apr 1996, NBC Sat 9:30–10:00
Jun 1996, NBC Sat 9:30–10:00

CAST:
Judge Sydney J. Solomon .... Pamela Reed
Mike Solomon (age 19) .... Breckin Meyer
Neal Solomon (16).......... Meghann Haldeman
Marshall Solomon (13)............. Robert Gorman

Ellis Solomon (11) .... Phillip Glenn Van Dyke
Judge Gil Fitzgerald .... Charles Rocket
Greer .... Meagan Fay

Hey, kids, how would you like to have a tough-cookie family-court judge as your mom? That's what the Solomon siblings had, and were they frustrated! Sydney was the judge, a single mom who was hard-bitten in her Chicago courtroom and only slightly more lenient at home. Mike was her slacker eldest, a reluctant college student trying to "find himself"; Neal her self-centered teenage daughter; Marshall a computer nerd oblivious to the rest of the world; and Ellis a hyper 11-year-old. Greer was Sydney's wealthy sister, a trophy wife content to grow herbs, and Gil a wisecracking, single fellow judge.

HOME FIRES (*Situation Comedy*)
FIRST TELECAST: *June 24, 1992*
LAST TELECAST: *July 18, 1992*
BROADCAST HISTORY:
Jun 1992, NBC Wed 9:30–10:00
Jun 1992, NBC Thu 9:30–10:00
Jun 1992–Jul 1992, NBC Sat 8:30–9:00
CAST:
Teddy Kramer .... Michael Brandon
Anne Kramer .... Kate Burton
Libby Kramer (age 18)............... Nicole Eggert
Jesse Kramer (14) .... Jarrad Paul
Nana .... Alice Hirson
Mike .... Tyagi Schwartz
Dr. Frederick Marcus .... Norman Lloyd

This family "worry-com" from the producers of *St. Elsewhere* opened each episode with its family, appropriately, in therapy. Not that the Kramers really had much to worry about, with their nice, pleasant life in a nice pleasant suburb. But Dad fretted about his inability to bond with his kids, Mom pined for her lost youth as a social activist, boy-crazy Libby wanted her independence, and Jesse wanted nothing more from life than a new Ferrari. Anne's busybody mother, Nana, drove everyone crazy. Mike was Libby's current boyfriend, whose dad dropped dead in the fourth episode, putting the Kramers' complaints in some perspective.

NBC ran three episodes of this summer entry in one week and three more over the following three weeks. Then it was gone.

HOME FREE (*Situation Comedy*)
FIRST TELECAST: *March 31, 1993*
LAST TELECAST: *July 2, 1993*
BROADCAST HISTORY:
Mar 1993–Apr 1993, ABC Wed 8:30–9:00
May 1993–Jul 1993, ABC Fri 9:30–10:00
CAST:
Grace Bailey .... Marian Mercer
Matt Bailey .... Matthew Perry
Vanessa .... Diana Canova
Abby (age 13) .... Anndi McAfee
Lucas .... Scott McAfee
Walter Peters .... Dan Schneider
Laura .... Brooke Theiss
Ben Brookstone .... Alan Oppenheimer
THEME:
performed by Christopher Cross

A lazy, freeloading 22-year-old had his comfortable world disrupted in this lightweight sitcom. Bachelor Matt enjoyed a life of ease living at home with his indulgent mom, Grace, while playing the dating field, until his divorced older sister, Vanessa, moved in with her kids, Abby and Lucas. Wiseguy Matt and conservative Vanessa immediately began sparring, and with two kids around Matt began to learn unaccustomed lessons in responsibility.

Matt worked as a cub reporter at a newspaper where Ben was the gruff editor, Walter a dim-witted reporter, and Laura a foxy photographer whom Matt would have liked to bed.

HOME IMPROVEMENT (*Situation Comedy*)
FIRST TELECAST: *September 17, 1991*
LAST TELECAST: *September 17, 1999*
BROADCAST HISTORY:
Sep 1991–Aug 1992, ABC Tue 8:30–9:00
Aug 1992–Sep 1994, ABC Wed 9:00–9:30
Mar 1994–May 1994, ABC Wed 8:00–8:30
Sep 1994–Jul 1998, ABC Tue 9:00–9:30
Apr 1997–May 1997, ABC Tue 8:00–8:30
Sep 1997–Oct 1997, ABC Tue 8:00–8:30
Feb 1998–May 1998, ABC Tue 8:00–8:30
Jul 1998–May 1999, ABC Tue 8:00–8:30
Apr 1999–May 1999, ABC Fri 8:00–8:30
Jul 1999–Sep 1999, ABC Fri 8:00–8:30
CAST:
Tim Taylor .... Tim Allen
Jill Taylor .... Patricia Richardson
Brad Taylor (age 10) .... Zachery Ty Bryan
Randy Taylor (9) (1991–1998)
.... Jonathan Taylor Thomas
Mark Taylor (6) .... Taran Noah Smith
Wilson Wilson .... Earl Hindman
Al Borland .... Richard Karn
Lisa (1991–1993) .... Pamela Anderson
Heidi (1993–1999) .... Debbe Dunning
**Ilene Martin (1995–1997)* .... Sherry Hursey
**Lauren (1996–1999)* .... Courtney Peldon
*Occasional

Standup comic Tim Allen, who specialized in macho humor, brought his act to television in this comic saga of a man and his tool belt. Tim "The Tool Man" Taylor was a local celebrity in Detroit with his cable TV show *Tool Time*, a cheerful mix of fix-it advice and humor sponsored by Binford Tools. His answer to every problem: more power! At home he was a bit of a klutz, however, and when he strapped on his tool belt and whipped out his drill like a six-shooter, the kids cleared out. Frustrated wife Jill tried to keep him away from the appliances but to no avail; sons Brad, Randy, and winsome little Mark offered varying degrees of help; and neighbor Wilson, never clearly seen over the backyard fence, philosophized about the meaning of everything. Al was Tim's knowing helper on *Tool Time*, along with Lisa, the buxom "tool girl" (succeeded by Heidi in 1993).

Stories revolved mostly around the normal evolution of Tim's stable, nuclear family, especially the friends and dating habits of his growing boys. Brad was the first son to enter high school (1995), where he became a big man on the soccer team. Serious Randy and his girlfriend Lauren became involved in environmental and social issues, at one time boycotting Tim's employer Binford Tools, a major polluter. As for

Mark, he spent a season dressed in black, obsessed with heavy metal music; fortunately, he grew out of it. There were developments involving the adults as well. Jill pursued a master's degree in psychology, which had her out of the house at times, and doing practice counseling when she was home. Al became engaged to Ilene, but after a long relationship they broke up. *Tool Time* girl Heidi, on the other hand, married and became pregnant (as was actress Debbe Dunning at the time). In a typical comedy of errors, Tim delivered her baby in November 1996.

The first of the boys to leave the nest was Randy, in late 1998, when actor Jonathan Taylor Thomas decided he should devote himself full-time to his real-life college studies. On the show, Randy and Lauren left to save the rain forest in Costa Rica. In the highly rated series finale, Tim quit *Tool Time* after a fight with Binford Tools; Al married his new love, chubby Trudy, in the Taylors' backyard; and Jill accepted a position at a clinic in Bloomington. When she wavered over leaving their beloved home, Tim came up with an ingenious solution: they jacked up the house, and took it with them! The biggest surprise, however, came at the close of the show, as the cast took their bows and viewers, at last, got to see Wilson's face.

HOME MOVIES (*Animated Situation Comedy*)
NETWORK HISTORY:
FIRST TELECAST: *April 26, 1999*
LAST TELECAST: *June 7, 1999*
BROADCAST HISTORY:
Apr 1999–Jun 1999, UPN Mon 8:30–9:00
CABLE HISTORY:
Cartoon Network
30 minutes
Produced: *2001–*
Premiered: *September 2, 2001*
VOICES:
Paula Small.................... Paula Poundstone
Brendon Small (age 8).............. Brendon Small
Coach McGuirk.................. H. Jon Benjamin
Jason............................ H. Jon Benjamin
Melissa.................... Melissa Bardin Galsky

Eight-year-old Brendon was the central focus of this cartoon series that could just as easily have been done with live actors. An insecure, would-be filmmaker, his autobiographical short video movies probed the angst of an asthmatic underachiever. The rest of the Small household consisted of Brendon's dumpy divorced mother, Paula, who was almost as neurotic as he was, and his bespectacled baby sister, Josie. Other regulars were Melissa, Brendon's best friend; "snot-nosed" Jason, the obnoxious kid who lived down the block; and Coach McGuirk, his militaristic soccer coach.

Since they were produced by the same people, *Home Movies*' squiggly animation style and overlapping dialogue were very reminiscent of the style of Comedy Central's *Dr. Katz, Professional Therapist*. Brendon Small, one of the series' creators, provided the voice of his namesake.

Two years after its brief run on UPN, *Home Movies* resurfaced on the Cartoon Network.

HOME SHOPPING NETWORK (Network) (*Home Shopping Cable Network*)
LAUNCHED:
July 1985
SUBSCRIBERS (MAR 2003):
78.7 million (74% U.S.)

The network that made cubic zirconium famous, HSN is one of two major channels that continuously display merchandise and offer viewers the opportunity to purchase it by phone (the other is QVC). HSN launched a second network, HSN II, in September 1986 to handle premium merchandise; its second channel is now known as America's Store. Both are immensely profitable.

HSN got its start by accident in 1977 when a Clearwater, Florida, radio station accepted 112 electric can openers in lieu of cash from an advertiser who could not pay his bill. The station owner decided to auction them off over the air, and to his surprise, sold out immediately, leading to a regular radio series called "Suncoast Bargaineers." In 1981 this became a Tampa-area local cable channel called "Home Shopping Channel," and in 1985 it went national as HSN.

HOMEBOYS IN OUTER SPACE (*Situation Comedy*)
FIRST TELECAST: *August 27, 1996*
LAST TELECAST: *June 24, 1997*
BROADCAST HISTORY:
Aug 1996–Feb 1997, UPN Tue 8:30–9:00
Apr 1997–Jun 1997, UPN Tue 8:30–9:00
CAST:
Tyberius "Ty" Walker .... Flex Alexander
Morris "Mo" Clay.................... Darryl M. Bell
Loquatia .... Rhona L. Bennett
Vashti .... Kevin Michael Richardson
Amma .... Paulette Braxton
Android Lloyd Wellington III...... Peter Mackenzie

Ty and Morris were a pair of 23rd-century black guys who traveled from planet to planet across the galaxy in their Space Hoopty—a small spaceship which, from the outside, looked like an oversized beat-up car—seeking work. As they "traveled the Cosmos in search of fame and fortune," they took assorted odd jobs to pay the bills. Morris, the more serious of the two, had aspirations of becoming a starship commander, but Ty, his fun-loving friend with raging hormones and outrageous hair, had gotten both of them expelled from Starship Commander Community College. Loquatia, the onboard computer babe who controlled their obsolete ship, was seen as an impudent talking female head on a TV monitor. She liked Morris but barely tolerated Ty. The guys set up an office in Jupiter Too, a bar run by Ty's grumpy brother-in-law, Vashti. Working for Vashti was the arrogant Android Lloyd Wellington III. A constant thorn in their side was sexy, arrogant Amma, who got most of the good jobs while they got stuck with everything from mundane cargo runs to baby-sitting for aliens. Despite their best, but usually inept, efforts, they rarely did anything right in this nutty sci-fi parody filled with sight gags (the Planet Carvel appeared as a floating ice cream cone) and one-liners ("How many times have you looked up at the stars, and asked the age-old question: 'Are there any women up there?' ").

HOMEFRONT (*Drama*)
FIRST TELECAST: *September 24, 1991*
LAST TELECAST: *April 26, 1993*
BROADCAST HISTORY:
Sep 1991–Feb 1992, ABC Tue 10:00–11:00
Mar 1992–Apr 1992, ABC Wed 10:00–11:00

Jul 1992–Dec 1992, ABC Thu 9:00–10:00
Mar 1993–Apr 1993, ABC Tue 10:00–11:00
Apr 1993, ABC Mon 9:00–11:00

CAST:

Anne Metcalf .... Wendy Phillips
Lt. Hank Metcalf (1991–1992) ...... David Newsom
Linda Metcalf .... Jessica Steen
Jeff Metcalf .... Kyle Chandler
Sarah Brewer (1991–1992) ...... Alexandra Wilson
Sgt. Charlie Hailey .... Harry O'Reilly
Caroline Hailey .... Sammi Davis-Voss
Ginger Szabo .... Tammy Lauren
Mike Sloan, Sr. .... Ken Jenkins
Ruth Sloan .... Mimi Kennedy
Gina Sloan .... Giuliana Santini
Abe Davis .... Dick Anthony Williams
Gloria Davis .... Hattie Winston
Cpl. Robert Davis (1991–1992) ... Sterling Macer, Jr.
Judy Owen .... Kelly Rutherford
Al Kahn .... John Slattery
Sam Schenkkan .... John DiSantini
Grandmother Davis .... Montrose Hagins
Arthur Schillhab (1992–1993) .... Brian McNamara

THEME:

"Ac-cent-tchu-ate the Positive," sung by Jack Sheldon

Television series in the 1980s and early 1990s were highly contemporary, seldom dealing with periods prior to the 1950s. In this era, *Homefront* was an anomaly; the theme was GIs returning from World War II. The atmosphere may have been that of 1945 (Andrews Sisters and all), but the plot was pure soap opera. Lt. Hank had returned to middle-America River Run, Ohio, eager to wed his Sarah, unaware that in his absence she had fallen in love with his kid brother Jeff. Their hardworking widowed mother Anne and highly independent middle sister Linda faced a crisis of a different kind: having worked at the local factory while the men were away, they were both fired to make way for the returning GIs (every one of whom was guaranteed a job).

Hank's rambunctious buddy Charlie returned with a British war bride Caroline, much to the dismay of his childhood sweetheart Ginger, who thought he was coming back to *her*. Mike, the son of the wealthy, arrogant Sloans (who owned the factory), did not come home at all. A last-minute telegram devastated both them and his girlfriend Linda with the news of his death. They now had to decide what to do with his surprise legacy: his frightened and pregnant Italian war bride, Gina, who had arrived ahead of him.

Robert had another problem. As a black man he hoped his service in the war would help erase some of the prejudice he had known back home, but it didn't. He was offered a job all right, but it was as a janitor. His optimistic father Abe, the chauffeur for the Sloans, had to pull strings to get him upgraded to the assembly line. His mother Gloria was the Sloans' maid.

Hank married Sarah, but she was killed and he left River Run at the end of the first season. Kid brother Jeff moved on to a career as a rookie right fielder for the Cleveland Indians, and—after a fling with barmaid Judy—settled into a tumultuous long-term relationship with ambitious Ginger, who finally got her big break as the "Lemo Tomato Juice Girl" on network radio. Their buddy Charlie split up with scheming Caroline and fell in love with willowy Gina (who had given birth to her late husband's baby, Emma). Independent Linda, displaced from the factory, found work as a newspaper columnist.

Mike Sloan was the picture of an exploitative postwar industrialist, adamantly opposing unionization at Sloan Industries, which led to a lockout and violence. The Sloans also caused poor Gina, and their servants, the Davises, constant grief, leading the Davises to strike out on their own in the second season and open their own struggling business, Rupert's Diner. By year two the Sloans were exploiting the postwar housing boom. Organizer Al Kahn arrived during the labor turmoil and married Anne; they had a baby in late 1992. By 1993, however, Al had become the target of a Communist witch hunt.

HOMEROOM (*Situation Comedy*)

FIRST TELECAST: *September 24, 1989*
LAST TELECAST: *December 17, 1989*
BROADCAST HISTORY:

Sep 1989–Dec 1989, ABC Sun 8:30–9:00

CAST:

Darryl Harper .... Darryl Sivad
Virginia "Vicki" Harper .... Penny Johnson
Phil Drexler .... Bill Cobbs
Anthony Harper .... Claude Brooks
Sam .... Trent Cameron
Devon .... Jahary Bennett
Donald .... Billy Dee Willis
Lisa .... Daphne Lyn Jones
Tritia .... Tritia Setoguchi

A mild-mannered writer of advertising jingles became a mild-mannered fourth-grade teacher in this gentle comedy filled with kids. Darryl's change of career was supported by his loving bride Vicki, a medical student, but not by her caustic father Phil, who never failed to remind his son-in-law how much more he could be making in the ad world—or driving a bus (as Phil had). Phil got to give his opinion a lot; he owned the brownstone in which Darryl and Vicki lived, rent-free, and he lived upstairs. Down at P.S. 391, the inner-city school where Darryl taught, the kids were bright and cheerful. Anthony was Darryl's younger brother.

HOMETOWN (*Comedy/Drama*)

FIRST TELECAST: *August 22, 1985*
LAST TELECAST: *October 15, 1985*
BROADCAST HISTORY:

Aug 1985–Sep 1985, CBS Thu 10:00–11:00
Sep 1985–Oct 1985, CBS Tue 8:00–9:00

CAST:

Mary Newell Abbott .... Jane Kaczmarek
Ben Abbott .... Franc Luz
Christopher Springer .... Andrew Rubin
Barbara Donnelly .... Margaret Whitton
Peter Kincaid .... John Bedford-Lloyd
Jane Parnell .... Christine Estabrook
Joey Nathan .... Daniel Stern
Jennifer Abbott .... Erin Leigh Peck
Tess Abbott .... Donna Vivino
Dylan Nathan .... Mikey Viso

Hometown was an obvious, and unsuccessful, attempt to bring the feel of the highly successful 1983 movie *The Big Chill* to television. It was the story of seven close friends, who had been practically inseparable during their college days in the 1960s, trying to cope with the realities of their maturing lives in the 1980s. Mary and Ben got married in the series' premiere episode, after having lived together since their college days and raising two daughters. He was a successful businessman, while she wanted to renew her long-abandoned dancing career. Christopher was a wealthy rock star with an unhappy personal life; Barbara, an insecure divorcée trying to start a new life; Peter and Jane, both college professors and, in her case, a Presidential advisor as well; and Joey, a single parent and restaurant cook who was more content with his modest means than any of his materially more successful friends.

HOMICIDE: LIFE ON THE STREET (*Police Drama*)

FIRST TELECAST: *January 31, 1993*
LAST TELECAST: *August 13, 1999*
BROADCAST HISTORY:

Jan 1993, NBC Sun 10:25–11:25
Feb 1993–Mar 1993, NBC Wed 9:00–10:00
Jan 1994, NBC Thu 10:00–11:00
Oct 1994–May 1998, NBC Fri 10:00–11:00
Sep 1998–Aug 1999, NBC Fri 10:00–11:00

CAST:

Det. Stanley Bolander ("The Big Man") (1993–1995) .... Ned Beatty
Det. John Munch .... Richard Belzer
Det. Beau Felton (1993–1995) .... Daniel Baldwin
Det./Sgt. Kay Howard (1993–1997) .... Melissa Leo
Det. Meldrick Lewis .... Clark Johnson
Det. Steve Crosetti (1993–1994) .... Jon Polito
Det. Frank Pembleton (1993–1998) .... Andre Braugher
Det. Tim Bayliss .... Kyle Secor
Lt. Al Giardello .... Yaphet Kotto
Officer Chris Thormann (1993) .... Lee Tergesen
Dr. Carol Blythe (1993–1994) .... Wendy Hughes
Lt./Capt. Megan Russert (1994–1996) .... Isabella Hofmann
Det. Mike Kellerman (1995–1998) .... Reed Diamond
J. H. Brodie (1995–1997) .... Max Perlich
Dr. Julianna Cox (1996–1998) .... Michelle Forbes
Det. Paul Falsone (1997–1999) .... Jon Seda
Det. Laura Ballard (1997–1999) .... Callie Thorne
Det. Stuart Gharty (1997–1999) .... Peter Gerety
Det. Terri Stivers (1997–1999) .... Toni Lewis
**Mary Whelan-Pembleton (1997–1999)* .... Ami Brabson
**Col. Barnfather (1997–1999)* .... Clayton LeBouef
**Capt. Gaffney (1997–1999)* .... Walt MacPherson
Agent Mike Giardello (1998–1999) .... Giancarlo Esposito
Det. Rene Sheppard (1998–1999) .... Michael Michele
**Ed Danvers (1998–1999)* .... Zeljko Ivanek

*Occasional

Grit replaced glitz in this hard-edged series about homicide detectives working the very tough streets of inner-city Baltimore. The four original teams were Bolander, a hefty, fatherly old-timer, and cynical, seen-it-all Munch; wise guy Felton and ambitious female Howard; frustrated Lewis and his slacker-partner Crosetti; and rookie Bayliss who gradually gained the respect of his tough partner, flamboyant loner Pembleton. Giardello was the imposing superior who moved around like a tank, barking orders and taking no guff. Russert joined as another shift commander in 1994.

Homicide had few car chases or shoot-outs, though there were plenty of dead bodies and mean streets. The complex characters and realistic, serialized stories made the show a favorite of critics, although viewers took some time getting used to it. The cases were all listed on a big board in the squad room—red ink for those still open, black for those that were closed—and some were never solved. Among the continuing stories were the shooting and blinding of Officer Thormann in 1993, the murder of little Adena Watson in 1993, the death of Crosetti in December 1994, and the shooting of Felton, Howard, and Bolander during a bust gone awry in January 1995. There were lighter stories as well, including Bolander's on-again, off-again romance with medical examiner Carol and Munch and Lewis's plans to open a bar.

Homicide showed a remarkable ability to maintain its dramatic momentum despite a large and constantly changing cast. Bolander and Felton left in 1995, suspended from the force after running amok in a hotel during a national police convention. Two years later detectives discovered Felton's headless body during an investigation. Also in 1995–1996, Russert was promoted to captain, becoming the first female shift commander, but by the end of the season had been busted back to detective, and resigned. Breezy Det. Kellerman joined the squad, as did videographer Brodie. In May 1996 the intense Pembleton suffered a stroke, returning to full capacity only gradually during the following season.

The 1996–1997 season saw the arrival of Chief Medical Examiner Cox, a tough critic of the detectives' work. The following season began with the arrival of three new members: rough-hewn car-theft expert Falsone; strong-willed, media savvy Ballard; and veteran Gharty. It concluded with a complex story triggered by Kellerman's killing of a drug dealer, which ended in a wild shootout in the station house that left several officers and a judge dead. In the aftermath of the debacle, Kellerman and Pembleton angrily resigned (Kellerman later turned up as a private detective). Joining the team in 1998 were the driven Stivers (previously a recurring character), former beauty queen Sheppard, and Lt. Giardello's estranged son Mike, an F.B.I. agent.

In the May 1999 series finale, Giardello was promoted to captain, but turned it down; Munch married girlfriend Billie Lou McCoy (Ellen McElduff); and it was strongly suggested that Munch had killed the criminal who was responsible for the shooting of Felton, Howard, and Bolander.

Based on the book *Homicide: A Year on the Killing Streets* by David Simon.

HONDO (*Western*)

FIRST TELECAST: *September 8, 1967*
LAST TELECAST: *December 29, 1967*
BROADCAST HISTORY:

Sep 1967–Dec 1967, ABC Fri 8:30–9:30

CAST:

Hondo Lane .... Ralph Taeger
Angie Dow .... Kathie Browne
Johnny Dow .... Buddy Foster

Buffalo Baker .... Noah Beery, Jr.
Capt. Richards .... Gary Clarke
Chief Vittoro .... Michael Pate
Col. Crook .... William Bryant

Ralph Taeger played the title role of a cavalry scout in the Arizona Territory, c. 1870, in this Western adventure. Hondo was an embittered loner. He had once been a Confederate Cavalry captain, and had lived with the Apaches for a time under the aegis of Chief Vittoro, only to see his Indian bride—Vittoro's daughter—slain by the army in a massacre. Now he traveled with a dog named Sam, troubleshooting for the army and trying to avert further bloodshed in the campaign against renegade Indians, land grabbers, gunmen, and bandits around Fort Lowell. Capt. Richards was the young martinet commander of the fort; Buffalo Baker, a colorful scout; Angie Dow, Hondo's romantic interest, and Johnny, her nine-year-old son.

Based on Louis L'Amour's story, and the 1953 John Wayne movie derived from it.

HONESTLY CELESTE (*Situation Comedy*)
FIRST TELECAST: *October 10, 1954*
LAST TELECAST: *December 5, 1954*
BROADCAST HISTORY:
Oct 1954–Dec 1954, CBS Sun 9:30–10:00
CAST:
Celeste Anders .... Celeste Holm
Bob Wallace .... Scott McKay
Marty Gordon .... Mike Kellin
Mr. Wallace .... Geoffrey Lumb
Mr. Wallace's Secretary .... Mary Finney

Vivacious Celeste Anders had given up her position teaching journalism in the Midwest to come to New York and take a job as a reporter for *The New York Express*, to get some "real" experience. What she found was a new boyfriend (Bob Wallace, the publisher's son), a friendly cabbie named Marty who took her to many of her reporting assignments, and all sorts of predicaments. Despite the attraction of film star Celeste Holm and much favorable pretelecast publicity, this filmed comedy series lasted less than three months.

HONEY, I SHRUNK THE KIDS, see *Disney's Honey, I Shrunk the Kids*

HONEY WEST (*Detective Drama*)
FIRST TELECAST: *September 17, 1965*
LAST TELECAST: *September 2, 1966*
BROADCAST HISTORY:
Sep 1965–Sep 1966, ABC Fri 9:00–9:30
CAST:
Honey West .... Anne Francis
Sam Bolt .... John Ericson
Aunt Meg .... Irene Hervey

Honey West was a true rarity in 1965, a female private detective. She had inherited the family detective business and partner Sam Bolt from her late father, and she made quite a fetching female James Bond. Honey was skilled at judo, proficient at karate, owned a weapons arsenal full of the most amazing devices, and used a specially modified lipstick that contained a radio transmitter. Her traveling office was a specially equipped spy van labeled "H.W. Bolt & Co., TV Service." She had everything necessary to track down the bad guys—even a trench coat. The love of her life was her pet ocelot, Bruce, much to the consternation of partner Sam, who would willingly have married her.

Honey West was introduced to TV audiences in an April 1965 episode of *Burke's Law*, in which the sexy sleuth outwitted even that dapper investigator.

HONEYMOONERS, THE (*Situation Comedy*)
FIRST TELECAST: *October 1, 1955*
LAST TELECAST: *May 9, 1971*
BROADCAST HISTORY:
Oct 1955–Feb 1956, CBS Sat 8:30–9:00
Feb 1956–Sep 1956, CBS Sat 8:00–8:30
Jan 1971–May 1971, CBS Sun 10:00–11:00
CAST:
Ralph Kramden .... Jackie Gleason
Ed Norton .... Art Carney
Alice Kramden (1955–1956) ..... Audrey Meadows
Trixie Norton (1955–1956) .... Joyce Randolph
Alice Kramden (1971) .... Sheila MacRae
Trixie Norton (1971) .... Jane Kean

Although *The Honeymooners* is one of the best-remembered comedy highlights of TV's golden age, it was seen for most of its history as a segment within other programs. Oddly enough, on the few occasions when it was presented as an independent series, it was not successful. Yet practically anyone who has ever sat in front of a TV set has seen a bit of the saga of Ralph and Alice Kramden, the not-so-newlyweds living in a run-down apartment in Brooklyn. The surroundings were grimy and spartan, quite unlike the happy middle-class homes of most TV situation comedies. Ralph, a portly New York City bus driver, was one of life's colorful losers—blustery, ambitious, avaricious, and constantly searching for the one great moneymaking scheme that would make him rich. Always willing to help was his best friend Ed Norton, who lived upstairs. Norton was no better off than "Ralphie-boy"—he worked in the city's sewers—but he was a veritable fountain of cheer and encouragement. Unfortunately Norton negated through incompetence and naivete the benefits of his blind enthusiasm, and he was a constant source of grief and aggravation to Ralph. Their schemes never worked out, usually causing friction between Ralph and his more practical wife, Alice. Ralph's reaction, whenever Alice proved him wrong or disapproved of one of his great ideas, was to threaten to belt her, with such lines as "To the moon, Alice," or "One of these days, Alice, *one of these days* . . . Pow! Right in the kisser!" But Alice understood Ralph, and in the end, at the final curtain, he would beam and admit, "Alice . . . you're the greatest."

The Honeymooners was first seen in 1951 as a sketch within DuMont's *Cavalcade of Stars*, with Pert Kelton originating the role of Alice and Art Carney as Ed Norton. When the show moved to CBS as *The Jackie Gleason Show* Audrey Meadows assumed the role of Alice. *The Honeymooners* finally became a series in its own right in 1955. Jackie Gleason wanted a respite from the rigors of a full-hour live weekly variety show and was also interested in becoming a packager of other programs. It was decided to film a full season (39 episodes) of half-hour *Honeymooners* shows and fill the other half of what had been Gleason's regular hour in the CBS schedule with *Stage Show*, a program owned by Jackie. All of *The Honeymooners* episodes were filmed before a live audience, two episodes per week, using an advanced filming system called the Electronicam. This was one of the first examples of live-audience, single-set filmed situation comedy, so prevalent today (though it was not the first—see *I Love Lucy*). In 1956, with the failure of *Stage Show*, the less-than-anticipated response to *The Honeymooners*, and the strong competition from *The Perry Como Show* on NBC, Gleason returned to a regular variety format.

In 1966 *The Honeymooners*, which had only been seen on a very occasional basis since Art Carney's departure as a regular on *The Jackie Gleason Show* in 1957, was revived in the form of full-hour episodes of Gleason's then-current variety series. Carney was back, with Sheila MacRae and Jane Kean playing the wives. These episodes, in which the Kramdens and the Nortons traveled together in addition to getting into trouble at home in New York, were done on a grander scale than the 1955–1956 series, complete with songs and production numbers. They accounted for roughly half the total output of *The Jackie Gleason Show* during its last four years on the air. A collection of reruns of these hour episodes was aired as another *Honeymooners* series in 1971. In addition, reruns of the original 39 half-hour episodes from the 1955–1956 season continue to be shown, and will probably run forever, on local stations.

Those 39 episodes got a lot of company in the 1980s when "The Lost Episodes" of *The Honeymooners* surfaced on Showtime's pay-cable network. The episodes weren't really lost at all. They were actually Honeymooners sketches that had aired on *The Jackie Gleason Show* in the 1950s. Gleason had kinescopes of the sketches and released the material to Viacom, Showtime's parent company, in 1984. Although as sketches they varied in length from a few minutes to almost a full half hour, they were edited together to produce 68 new *Honeymooners* half hours. After airing on Showtime in 1984 and 1985, these "new" episodes subsequently went into syndication along with the original 39.

HONG KONG (*Adventure*)

FIRST TELECAST: *September 28, 1960*
LAST TELECAST: *September 20, 1961*
BROADCAST HISTORY:
Sep 1960–Sep 1961, ABC Wed 7:30–8:30
CAST:
Glenn Evans .... Rod Taylor
Neil Campbell .... Lloyd Bochner
Tully .... Jack Kruschen
Fong (1960) .... Harold Fong
Ling (1960–1961) .... Gerald Jann
Ching Mei .... Mai Tai Sing

The British Crown Colony of Hong Kong was the locale for the adventures of Glenn Evans, an American journalist living and working amid the intrigue of that exotic city. His search for stories led him into encounters with smugglers, murderers, dope peddlers, and slinky women disappearing behind beaded curtains. A source of stories, as well as a friend, was Neil Campbell, chief of the Hong Kong police. Tully ran the swank nightclub where Glenn spent much of his free time. Glenn's original houseboy was Fong, who was replaced by Ling within a month after the series premiered. By the end of the year Ching Mei had joined the cast as the hostess at the Golden Dragon, Tully's nightclub.

HOOPERMAN (*Police*)

FIRST TELECAST: *September 23, 1987*
LAST TELECAST: *September 6, 1989*
BROADCAST HISTORY:
Sep 1987–Sep 1988, ABC Wed 9:00–9:30
Nov 1988–Mar 1989, ABC Wed 9:30–10:00
Jun 1989–Sep 1989, ABC Wed 9:00–9:30
CAST:
Det. Harry Hooperman .... John Ritter
Susan Smith (1987–1988) .... Debrah Farentino
Capt. Celeste (C.Z.) Stern .... Barbara Bosson
Off. Boris "Bobo" Pritzger .... Clarence Felder
Off. Maureen "Mo" DeMott .... Sydney Walsh
Off. Rick Silardi .... Joseph Gian
Insp. Clarence McNeil .... Felton Perry
Betty Bushkin .... Alix Elias
T. J. (1988–1989) .... Paul Linke
Rudy (1988–1989) .... Rod Gist

The mid-1980s vogue for "dramedies" (half-hour comedy/dramas) was perhaps best exemplified by this odd cross between *Hill Street Blues* and *Barney Miller*, which combined humorous moments with hard action. Hooperman was a little like Lt. Goldblume of *Hill Street*, a thoughtful cop who hated to use his gun. His superior on the San Francisco P.D. was Capt. Stern, whose demanding manner masked basic insecurities, especially about her failed marriage. Mo was a female officer dedicated to "saving" her handsome-but-gay partner Rick, Bobo was the office redneck, and Betty the cheerful dispatcher.

Hooperman's private life was just as colorful. His landlady had been murdered, leaving him her broken-down apartment building and her yapping little terrier Bijoux—so he also had rebellious tenants to placate. Susan was the building handyman and aspiring writer with whom he had a somewhat rocky romantic relationship, but who, by early 1988, was about to bear his child. Unfortunately, she suffered a miscarriage and left him in the fall.

HOOTENANNY (*Music*)

FIRST TELECAST: *April 6, 1963*
LAST TELECAST: *September 12, 1964*
BROADCAST HISTORY:
Apr 1963–Sept 1963, ABC Sat 8:30–9:00
Sep 1963–Sep 1964, ABC Sat 7:30–8:30
HOST:
Jack Linkletter
THEME:
"Hootenanny Saturday Night," by Alfred Uhry and Richard Lewine, sung by Chad Mitchell

A traveling musical jamboree, taped before a live audience at a different college campus each week, and featuring the popularized "folk music" of the early 1960s. Artists were generally commercial pop-folk groups such as the Limeliters, the Chad Mitchell Trio, and the Smothers Brothers, but also included some traditional performers such as Josh White and the Carter Family.

Interestingly, several major stars refused to appear on this program because it continued the 1950s practice of "blacklisting" certain performers with alleged left-wing views (such as Pete Seeger and the Weavers). This, it was said, was due to sponsor pressure. Among those who refused to appear were the Kingston Trio, Joan Baez, and Peter, Paul and Mary.

HOPALONG CASSIDY (*Western*)
FIRST TELECAST: *June 24, 1949*
LAST TELECAST: *December 23, 1951*
BROADCAST HISTORY:
Jun 1949–Oct 1949, NBC Fri 8:00–9:00 (some telecasts local)
Apr 1950–Dec 1951, NBC Sun 6:00–7:00
(In first-run syndication 1952–1953)
CAST:
Hopalong Cassidy.................. William Boyd
Red Connors (1952–1953) .... Edgar Buchanan

Theatrical films of the adventures of Hopalong Cassidy had been shown on New York television at least as early as 1945, and became a regular local series in November 1948, later moving to NBC. The first films seen on TV were edited versions of his old "B" features, with Boyd adding narration and occasionally even a new scene or two (it is remarkable that a man of 50 could match scenes that he had filmed 15 years before, and look no different!). His sidekick in these old theatrical films was usually either Gabby Hayes or Andy Clyde. In 1952–1953, Boyd made a new series of original TV films, with Edgar Buchanan as his sidekick, which ran in syndication for many years thereafter.

The plots were the same as in the old "B" films, with Hoppy, silver-haired and dressed all in black, chasing villains to their doom on his faithful horse Topper. He was a true Knight of the West—and a far cry from the profane, unwashed, gimpy-legged cowpoke originally created in the stories of Clarence E. Mulford.

William Boyd had been wise enough to buy the TV rights to his theatrical films during the 1940s, and it was television—not Hollywood features—that made him a millionaire. He died in 1972.

HOPE & GLORIA (*Situation Comedy*)
FIRST TELECAST: *March 9, 1995*
LAST TELECAST: *June 28, 1996*
BROADCAST HISTORY:
Mar 1995–Sep 1995, NBC Thu 8:30–9:00
Sep 1995–Dec 1995, NBC Sun 8:30–9:00
Jan 1996–Apr 1996, NBC Sat 9:00–9:30
Jun 1996, NBC Sat 8:00–8:30
CAST:
Hope Davidson .... Cynthia Stevenson
Gloria Utz........................... Jessica Lundy
Sonny Utz (age 5).................. Robert Garrova
Louis Utz .... Enrico Colantoni
Dennis Dupree........................ Alan Thicke
Gwillem Blatt...................... Taylor Negron

Two single women shared a Pittsburgh brownstone, and their complicated lives, in this girl-buddy sitcom. In some ways they were complete opposites. Hope was a perky, ever-optimistic associate producer of a local TV talk show who couldn't believe that her darling husband, Jeffrey (Jeff Orlandt)—unbeknownst to her, a world-class philanderer—had left her after ten years. Gloria was a brassy, cynical hairdresser who knew all too well what a no-goodski her gross, carpet-salesman ex-husband Louis was. She ought to; she had married and divorced him twice.

Despite the fact that Gloria and Louis yelled at each other constantly, they still saw each other and shared the raising of their young son, Sonny; for all the wisecracks, Louis was a pretty good dad. Dennis was the vain, egocentric host of *The Dennis Dupree Show* on WPNN-TV, Channel 5—"the host who cares the most"—and Gwillem a high-strung program executive.

HOPE ISLAND (*Drama*)
FIRST TELECAST: *September 12, 1999*
LAST TELECAST: *April 17, 2000*
BROADCAST HISTORY:
Sep 1999–Jan 2000, PAX Sun 9:00–10:00
Oct 1999–Nov 1999, PAX Tue 11:00–midnight
Oct 1999–Apr 2000, PAX Mon 8:00–9:00
CAST:
Daniel Cooper.................... Cameron Daddo
Alex Stone .... Suki Kaiser
Brian Brewster .... Duncan Fraser
Nub Flanders.................... Haig Sutherland
Bonita Vasquez.................. Beverley Elliott
Ruby Vasquez .... Gina Stockdale
Molly Brewster................... Allison Hossack
Sheriff Kevin Mitchell................ David Lewis
Callie Pender.......................... Veena Sood
Father MacAnnally.............. Matthew Walker
Dylan Stone .... Max Peters
Boris Obolenski .... Brian Jensen

In this feel-good drama the son of a famous and wealthy televangelist tried to get away from his past by starting a new life as a minister in the Pacific Northwest seafaring community of Hope Island. A pleasant, guitar-strumming young man, Daniel soon found the picturesque small town to be a nest of tangled relationships. Brewster was the dictatorial local real estate developer/con man who had recruited him as part of a scheme to make Hope Island respectable. His daughter, Molly, had been dating sheriff Kevin for three years. Nub was Brewster's gofer, and widow Alex, an attractive, anti-religious woman, owned Widow's Walk, the local tavern where Molly worked as a waitress and Boris was the cook. Alex's fatherless young son, Dylan, immediately bonded with Daniel. Callie ran the local newspaper; Ruby and her daughter Bonita ran the Islander General Store but hadn't spoken to each other in 17 years—they communicated only by writing on blackboards. At first the townspeople were resentful of the new minister ("if and when we need a church we'll let you know"), but by the end of the first episode they were all singing "Amazing Grace."

Ruby's late sister Margaret had dated a black man (who had been killed in Vietnam) and given birth to his son—whom she gave up for adoption. The boy, Marcus (Dion Johnstone), showed up on Hope Island looking for his natural mother, staying to become the new sixth-grade teacher. Kevin and Molly's relationship progressed, and at the end of March they were married.

HOPKINS 24/7 (*Medical Documentary*)
FIRST TELECAST: *August 30, 2000*
LAST TELECAST: *September 28, 2000*
BROADCAST HISTORY:
Aug 2000–Sep 2000, ABC Wed 10:00–11:00
Sep 2000, ABC Thu 10:00–11:00

Verité-style documentary series about the inner workings of Johns Hopkins Hospital in Baltimore, Maryland, focusing on various doctors, their cases and their crises.

HORACE HEIDT SHOW, THE (*Talent*)
FIRST TELECAST: *October 2, 1950*
LAST TELECAST: *September 24, 1951*

BROADCAST HISTORY:

Oct 1950–Sep 1951, CBS Mon 9:00–9:30

HOST:

Horace Heidt

This series begun by the veteran bandleader on radio in 1947 as *Horace Heidt's Youth Opportunity Program,* added a television version in 1950. As with *The Original Amateur Hour,* the emphasis of the show was on finding young talent and exposing it to a national audience. At the end of each live show, the acts were voted upon by the studio audience, and the winner, as measured by applause meter, came back the following week to defend his championship.

HORIZONS (*Discussion*)

FIRST TELECAST: *December 2, 1951*
LAST TELECAST: *March 6, 1955*
BROADCAST HISTORY:

Dec 1951, ABC Sun 6:00–6:30
May 1952–Jun 1952, ABC Sun 7:30–8:00
Dec 1954–Mar 1955, ABC Sun 9:15–9:30

HOST:

Dr. Louis H. Bauer (1954–1955)

PRODUCERS:

Erik Barnouw and Jack Pacey (1951–1952)

DIRECTOR:

Leslie Gorall (1951–1952)

Live lecture series in which prominent professors from Columbia University and occasional outside experts spoke on likely future developments in their specialties. Included during the 1951–1952 season were Prof. Mark Van Doren on "The Future of Poetry," anthropologist Margaret Mead on "The Future of the Family," and Dr. Philip E. Mosley on "The Future of Soviet Diplomacy." For part of its run the 1951–1952 series aired on Sunday afternoons.

The title *Horizons* was revived in 1954 for a similarly erudite series of short talks on advances in medicine, presided over by Dr. Louis H. Bauer, past president of the American Medical Association and Secretary General of the World Medical Association.

HOT COUNTRY NIGHTS (*Musical Variety*)

FIRST TELECAST: *November 24, 1991*
LAST TELECAST: *March 8, 1992*
BROADCAST HISTORY:

Nov 1991–Mar 1992, NBC Sun 8:00–9:00

Country-music showcase, plugged into the NBC Sunday night schedule when the two sitcoms that began the season in the time slot (*Man of the People* and *Pacific Station*) failed. The first telecast featured Clint Black, K. T. Oslin, Doug Stone, Alabama, Kenny Rogers, and Pam Tillis.

Needless to say, country fans didn't miss the sitcoms.

HOT L BALTIMORE (*Situation Comedy*)

FIRST TELECAST: *January 24, 1975*
LAST TELECAST: *June 6, 1975*
BROADCAST HISTORY:

Jan 1975–Jun 1975, ABC Fri 9:00–9:30

CAST:

Bill Lewis .... James Cromwell
Clifford Ainsley .... Richard Masur
April Green .... Conchata Ferrell
Charles Bingham .... Al Freeman, Jr.
Suzy Marta Rocket .... Jeannie Linero
Millie .... Gloria Le Roy
Jackie .... Robin Wilson
Mr. Morse .... Stan Gottlieb
George .... Lee Bergere
Gordon .... Henry Calvert
Mrs. Bellotti .... Charlotte Rae

Hot L Baltimore was one of the most controversial comedies of the 1970s. Based on the award-winning off-Broadway play of the same name, and produced for TV by trendsetter Norman Lear (of *All in the Family* fame), it brought sexual innuendo and racy dialogue to the home screen. The setting was the lobby of the once-grand but now dilapidated Hotel Baltimore (the "e" in the sign had burned out and had never been replaced). Among its denizens were desk clerk Bill and his love, April; the harried manager, Clifford; the philosophical Charles; Suzy Marta Rocket, the Colombian prostitute; Millie, the unemployed waitress; Jackie, the tomboy; Mr. Morse, the septuagenarian always on the brink of expiring; George and Gordon, the homosexual couple; and eccentric Mrs. Bellotti. Often heard but never seen on-screen was Mrs. Bellotti's 26-year-old prankster son Moose, who delighted in such escapades as buttering the hallways, staging *The Poseidon Adventure* in the bathtub, and collecting unlikely pets. Once when the lobby habitués protested a rent increase, Moose glued himself to the ceiling of his room in sympathy.

HOT PURSUIT (*Drama*)

FIRST TELECAST: *September 22, 1984*
LAST TELECAST: *December 28, 1984*
BROADCAST HISTORY:

Sep 1984–Nov 1984, NBC Sat 10:00–11:00
Dec 1984, NBC Fri 10:00–11:00

CAST:

Kate Wyler/Cathy Ladd .... Kerrie Keane
Jim Wyler .... Eric Pierpoint
Estelle Modrian .... Dina Merrill
Alec Shaw .... Mike Preston

Love on the run was the theme of this 1984 adventure series. Kate and Jim were the young couple, very much in love, who seemed to have it all—he was a veterinarian, she was a top auto engineer developing a new, high-performance car. Then, in a sudden nightmare, Kate was accused and convicted of the murder of her avaricious employer, auto magnate Victor Modrian.

Jim then learned that Kate had been framed by Modrian's devious widow, Estelle, using an exact look-alike named Cathy Ladd. As Kate was being taken to prison, Jim staged a daring ambush to free her from custody, and the two of them set out on a cross-country pursuit to find the double—the one person who could prove Kate's innocence. As they followed their quarry from one city to another, they often became involved in the lives of people they met. But they could not stay long, because hot on their heels were not only the police but a vicious, one-eyed assassin named Shaw, who had been hired by the widow Modrian.

Although the series was admittedly reminiscent of *The Fugitive,* its emphasis on the close relationship between the leads gave it a somewhat different flavor from the earlier program.

HOT SEAT, THE (*Interview*)

FIRST TELECAST: *April 18, 1952*
LAST TELECAST: *December 29, 1952*

BROADCAST HISTORY:

Apr 1952–Jul 1952, ABC Fri 8:00–8:30
Oct 1952–Nov 1952, ABC Sun 7:30–8:00
Nov 1952–Dec 1952, ABC Mon 8:30–9:00

HOST:

Stuart Scheftel

Lively interview show in which public figures were grilled by ABC newsman Stuart Scheftel and a guest. Subjects ranged from radio-TV personality Tex McCrary to Senator Joseph McCarthy.

HOT SHOTS (*Magazine Drama*)

FIRST TELECAST: *September 23, 1986*
LAST TELECAST: *September 9, 1987*
BROADCAST HISTORY:

Sep 1986–Dec 1986, CBS Tue 11:30–12:40 A.M.
Jul 1987–Sep 1987, CBS Wed 11:30–12:40 A.M.

CAST:

Amanda Reed .... Dorothy Parke
Jason West .... Booth Savage
Nicholas Broderick .... Paul Burke
Al Pendleton .... Clark Johnson
Cleo .... Heather Smith
Receptionist .... Mung Ling

Amanda and Jason were two young, ambitious reporters for *CrimeWorld* magazine. In their quest for titillating stories they were often teamed together. Despite their competitive bickering and complaints about having to work together, they did respect each other's abilities and, though they would never admit it, were sexually attracted to each other. Nicholas Broderick was the editor and publisher of *CrimeWorld* magazine, Al his talented researcher, and Cleo his secretary.

Produced in Toronto.

HOTEL (*Drama*)

FIRST TELECAST: *September 21, 1983*
LAST TELECAST: *August 6, 1988*
BROADCAST HISTORY:

Sep 1983–May 1984, ABC Wed 10:00–11:00
Jun 1984–Jul 1984, ABC Tue 9:00–10:00
Aug 1984–Mar 1987, ABC Wed 10:00–11:00
May 1987–Sep 1987, ABC Wed 10:00–11:00
Sep 1987–Jan 1988, ABC Sat 10:00–11:00
Mar 1988–May 1988, ABC Thu 9:00–10:00
Jun 1988–Aug 1988, ABC Sat 10:00–11:00

CAST:

Peter McDermott .... James Brolin
Christine Francis .... Connie Sellecca
Mark Danning (1983–1986) .... Shea Farrell
Billy Griffin .... Nathan Cook
Dave Kendall (1983–1987) .... Michael Spound
Megan Kendall (1983–1987) .... Heidi Bohay
Julie Gillette .... Shari Belafonte-Harper
Victoria Cabot (1983–1986) .... Anne Baxter
Kei (1984–1988) .... Michael Yama
Harry, the bartender (1984–1988)
.... Harry George Phillips
Charles Cabot (1986) .... Efrem Zimbalist, Jr.
Elizabeth Bradshaw Cabot (1986)
.... Michelle Phillips
Cheryl Dolan (1987–1988) ...... Valerie Landsburg
Ryan Thomas (1987–1988) .... Susan Walters
Eric Lloyd (1987–1988) .... Ty Miller

THEME:

by Henry Mancini

San Francisco's St. Gregory was an elegant hostelry indeed. Its marble columns rose up over a cavernous lobby and elegant restaurants; above lay plush suites serviced by an attentive staff. This was the setting for romance, drama, and occasional comedy in the weekly series *Hotel*. Produced by the same people responsible for *Love Boat*, *Hotel* bore a certain resemblance to that seagoing series. There were different guests each week, usually in gentle stories of the heart, almost all with happy endings. Sometimes the drama was a little heavier, as when a prostitute was brought into the hotel and then gang-raped by some students; or lighter, as when the kindly old gentleman died in the dining room but was left propped up until after lunch so as not to disturb the other patrons.

The staff included Victoria Cabot, a wealthy aristocrat who oversaw the operations on behalf of her sister-in-law, Laura Trent; Peter McDermott, the suave, bearded general manager; Christine, his beautiful assistant and later lover; Mark, the handsome and likable public-relations director; and Billy Griffin, a black ex-con who had gone straight and now served as the hotel's security director. Julie was in charge of the information center, while cheerful newlyweds Dave and Megan were a bellhop and a desk clerk, respectively, who left the series when, after a long struggle, he graduated from law school.

Among the familiar faces appearing as guests were Morgan Fairchild, Shirley Jones, Pernell Roberts, Arte Johnson, Liberace, Donald O'Connor, McLean Stevenson, Stewart Granger, Connie Stevens, Peter Marshall, and Lynn Redgrave. Prior to the series' debut there was much publicity about the signing of Bette Davis for the recurring role of Laura Trent; however, due to illness she was seen only on the premiere and then departed on an "extended trip," leaving Victoria in charge.

When *grande dame* Victoria died in the middle of the 1985–1986 season it was revealed that she had left her half interest in the St. Gregory to her loyal assistant Peter. He promptly made *his* loyal assistant—and growing love interest—Christine the new general manager, while eager Megan became the new assistant manager. All this happiness was temporarily interrupted by a battle for control of the hotel waged by members of the Cabot family who owned the other half—Charles (played by Efrem Zimbalist, Jr.), Jessica (Dina Merrill), and Jake (Ralph Bellamy)—but in the end Peter managed to buy them out.

The series was based, more or less, on Arthur Hailey's best-selling novel of sex and scandal, and was also known as *Arthur Hailey's "Hotel."* The real hotel that served as its model was the regal Fairmont Hotel on Nob Hill in San Francisco, whose imposing façade was seen in exterior shots and whose giant lobby was re-created on a Hollywood soundstage.

HOTEL BROADWAY (*Variety*)

FIRST TELECAST: *January 20, 1949*
LAST TELECAST: *March 17, 1949*
BROADCAST HISTORY:

Jan 1949–Mar 1949, DUM Thu 8:30–9:00

REGULARS:

The Striders

Low-budget musical variety program featuring different singers and comedians each week, generally of less-than-top-name caliber. Among those who appeared were Johnny Desmond, Jean Darling, and Harry Ranch's Orchestra. There was no host, but a quartet called The Striders was used to introduce each act.

HOTEL DE PAREE (*Western*)
FIRST TELECAST: *October 2, 1959*
LAST TELECAST: *September 23, 1960*
BROADCAST HISTORY:
Oct 1959–Sep 1960, CBS Fri 8:30–9:00
CAST:
Sundance .... Earl Holliman
Monique............................. Judi Meredith
Annette Deveraux.................. Jeanette Nolan
Aaron Donager.................... Strother Martin

Western centered in the Hotel de Paree, the fanciest (and only) lodging in Georgetown, Colorado, and its chief hero-in-residence, Sundance. Sundance had come to Georgetown via a rather circuitous route. After accidentally killing a man there, he had spent 17 years in prison. He nevertheless returned to the town upon his release, c. 1870, to find the Hotel de Paree being operated by two rather attractive relatives of the dead man, Annette Deveraux and her niece, Monique. Their hotel was a little bit of European dignity in the midst of the Old West. They needed a strong arm (and fast gun) to keep things quiet, and Sundance was their man. Among his trademarks was a string of polished silver discs in the hatband of his black stetson, with which to blind his adversaries.

HOTEL MALIBU (*Serial Drama*)
FIRST TELECAST: *August 4, 1994*
LAST TELECAST: *September 8, 1994*
BROADCAST HISTORY:
Aug 1994–Sep 1994, CBS Thu 10:00–11:00
CAST:
Eleanor "Ellie" Mayfield........... Joanna Cassidy
Stephanie "Stevie" Mayfield .... Cheryl Pollak
Jack Mayfield.............................. John Dye
Harry Radzimski................... Harry O'Reilly
Nancy Radzimski Salvucci......... Romy Walthall
Melinda Lopez .... Jennifer Lopez
Salvatore Lopez.......................... Pepe Serna
George Bennett .... Scott Paulin
Mark Whitsett .... Paul Satterfield

Summer soap opera about the Mayfield family, who owned the Hotel Malibu on the coast of Southern California. For widow Ellie, running it was a labor of love. The same could not be said for her "devoted" son, Jack, an opportunistic womanizer who had been siphoning money off to make the hotel look unprofitable and convince his mother to sell it so that he could get his inheritance early. His plans went awry when his younger sister, Stevie, returned home and started snooping around. After righteous Stevie found out that her no-good brother had been stealing from the hotel, she forced him to use most of the money to pay off the second mortgage and help get Hotel Malibu back on its feet. Meanwhile Mom had no idea anything was going on. Others featured in the cast were Harry, the honest bartender working his way through college who became romantically involved with Stevie; Nancy, Harry's gold-digging sexpot sister, who worked as a maid while trying to snare a rich husband (including Stevie's former fiancé, Mark, to whom Nancy was briefly married); Melinda, a pretty, hardworking Mexican girl whom Jack had forced Harry to hire as a bartender even though she knew nothing about mixing drinks; and Sal, Melinda's overly protective father, a parole officer and former boyfriend of Ellie's. Sal, whose wife had died from cancer, provided emotional support to Ellie when she went into the hospital for breast-cancer surgery and, as the short run of *Hotel Malibu* ended, they were planning to get married.

Actors Lopez and Serna had played the same characters in *Second Chances*, a serial drama that had aired on CBS earlier that season.

HOTHOUSE (*Medical Drama*)
FIRST TELECAST: *June 30, 1988*
LAST TELECAST: *August 25, 1988*
BROADCAST HISTORY:
Jun 1988–Aug 1988, ABC Thu 10:00–11:00
CAST:
Dr. Sam Garrison.................... Josef Sommer
Lily Garrison Shannon .... Alexis Smith
Dr. Ved Lahari............................ Art Malik
Dr. Marie Teller .... Michael Learned
Louise Dougherty .... Louise Latham
Issy Garrison Schrader .... Katherine Borowitz
Leonard Schrader .... Bob Gunton
Matt Garrison .... Tony Soper
Claudia Garrison........................ Susan Diol
Dr. Art Makter .... Michael Jeter
Lucy Cox .... Maureen Moore

A serene country setting masked emotional turmoil in this medical drama-*cum*-soap opera set at the Garrison Center, a family-run psychiatric hospital outside of Boston. The director and family patriarch was Dr. Sam, whose ex-wife Lily (now married to a millionaire) caused him considerable anxiety. His dedicated staff included daughter Issy, a psychiatrist, and youngest son Matt, the center's worried business manager—worried because they were always short of cash. London-educated therapist Ved and mature psychiatrist Marie were having a May–December romance, while Art developed an emotional attachment to a teenage patient. Internist Leonard was Issy's husband, and Claudia was Matt's whiny wife. Louise was Sam's longtime, trusted secretary.

HOUR GLASS, see *ABC Dramatic Shorts—1952–1953*

HOUR GLASS, see *Movies—Prior to 1961*

HOUR GLASS (*Variety*)
FIRST TELECAST: *May 9, 1946*
LAST TELECAST: *March 6, 1947*
BROADCAST HISTORY:
May 1946–Mar 1947, NBC Thu 8:00–9:00
EMCEE:
Helen Parrish (1946)
Eddie Mayehoff
PRODUCER:
Howard Reilly
DIRECTOR:
Ed Sobel

Hour Glass was one of the most important pioneers in the early history of television. Yet its very existence, much less its place in the development of the medium, has scarcely been acknowledged anywhere until now. It was the first hour-long entertainment series of any kind produced for network television, the first show to develop its own star, the first big variety series, and the most ambitious production by far ever attempted up to its time. Milton Berle, Ed Sullivan, *Your Show of Shows,* Carol Burnett, and dozens of others are all its lineal descendants, as is, in a sense, the whole concept of "big-time" television.

To understand the breakthrough that *Hour Glass* represented we might first remember the other shows on the air in 1946. Commercial television was still in its infancy, with only a few thousand sets in use, mostly in New York and a few other large cities. New York was the only city with more than one station, and was the nation's TV "capital." The week in which *Hour Glass* premiered looked like this, in New York. Monday: one station on the air for one hour, with a 30-minute fashion show and a 30-minute excerpt from a grade-B Western film (*The Fighting Deputy* with Fred Scott). Tuesday: one station on for 90 minutes, 30 minutes of informal skits, 30 minutes of travel films, and 30 minutes of a disc-jockey show called *King's Record Shop.* Wednesday: two stations on, one with film shorts and the other with 90 minutes of mixed films and studio chatter. Thursday: the other two channels offered a cartoonist, a newscast, and an adaptation of the radio show *Famous Jury Trials.* Friday: three stations on, with some very obscure grade-B films, a short studio game show, and boxing from St. Nicholas Arena. This, pretty much, had been typical of TV programing up to that time.

Hour Glass was sponsored by a major company, Standard Brands (Chase & Sanborn Coffee, Tender Leaf Tea), which poured more money into it than TV had ever seen before—reportedly $200,000 over the show's ten-month run. For the first time there was money for elaborate sets, specially-made films, and reasonably respectable talent. Of course everything they tried was an experiment, since no one had attempted such a show before. The premiere telecast, on May 9, 1946, opened with a song by recording star Evelyn Knight, followed by a seriocomic sketch starring actor Paul Douglas, set in a cabin. Next came a live commercial for Chase and Sanborn coffee—two and a half minutes long! Comedian Joe Besser then appeared with several supporting players in a hilarious take-off on the military entitled "The Rookie," followed in quick succession by a ballroom-dancing sequence, a brief talk about TV and a booklet available on the subject from NBC, another song by Evelyn Knight, a monologue by fast-talking comic Doodles Weaver (a well-known personality in the 1940s), and finally a film of South American dancing. The end commercial, which included film of coffee-growing country, ran for four and a half minutes.

Subsequent shows tightened up the commercials quite a bit, and also brought on such acts as Bert Lahr, the singing Merry Macs, Dennis Day, Jerry Colonna, Joey Faye, and Peggy Lee. In November the show added TV's first regular chorus line, a group of leggy beauties. Compared to the nightclub rejects generally seen on TV in the late 1940s this was big talent indeed. Perhaps the biggest coup was the TV debut, on November 14, 1946, of ventriloquist Edgar Bergen (and Charlie McCarthy). This was one of the earliest instances of a top radio star bringing his act to television, a practice which was to become quite prevalent in the years to come, until TV developed its own galaxy of stars.

The hostess on the first *Hour Glass* telecast was Evelyn Eaton, and guest hosts appeared thereafter until a pretty young actress named Helen Parrish was signed as permanent "femcee." She was bright, pixieish, and as fresh as the medium itself, and she made quite a hit with TV viewers of 1946 (just about all of whom watched *Hour Glass* on Thursday night). The sponsor gave her a substantial publicity buildup, and it was said that she became as well known, at least in the cities which had TV, as the top radio stars of the day. She left the show in November to have a baby, after which her co-host Eddie Mayehoff took over.

Standard Brands was well aware that the limited viewership of television at this time did not justify such a large investment on a purely financial basis. But they, and NBC, wanted to see what could be done with the new medium, and the lessons they learned have influenced what we see today. They learned, for example, not to let single commercials run for four to five minutes; that money is better spent on obtaining "star" talent than on fancy, highly visual sets; that viewers liked the idea of a regular host (or hostess) providing continuity from week to week; and that TV in general was a medium which demanded staging and pacing far different from movies, the stage, or radio.

The network history of *Hour Glass* is sketchy, due to incomplete records for this very early period. NBC's network consisted of three stations at the time, in New York, Philadelphia, and Schenectady, and while it is not known whether *Hour Glass* was being fed to all three at the start (it originated in New York) it definitely was on the network by early November at the latest.

More than a year was to pass after the demise of *Hour Glass* before another sponsor could be induced to put similar amounts of money into television for a big-time variety hour. That one, drawing on the lessons learned here, brought TV out of its infancy and produced its first superstar: Milton Berle. And what became of Helen Parrish? She returned to Hollywood, where she had been a child star in the 1930s, and made a few more films. She died in 1959 at the age of 35.

HOUR OF DECISION (*Religion*)

FIRST TELECAST: *September 30, 1951*
LAST TELECAST: *February 28, 1954*
BROADCAST HISTORY:

Sep 1951–Mar 1952, ABC Sun 10:00–10:30
Jul 1952–Sep 1953, ABC Sun 10:00–10:15
Sep 1953–Feb 1954, ABC Sun 10:30–10:45

HOST:

Rev. Billy Graham

Almost from its inception as a mass medium, evangelist Billy Graham made frequent use of television to publicize his religious crusades. During 1951–1954 the Billy Graham Evangelical Association sponsored regular weekly Sunday night talks by Dr. Graham on the ABC network.

HOUR OF STARS, syndicated title for *20th Century-Fox Hour, The*

HOUSE CALLS (*Situation Comedy*)
FIRST TELECAST: *December 17, 1979*
LAST TELECAST: *September 13, 1982*
BROADCAST HISTORY:
Dec 1979–Mar 1980, CBS Mon 9:30–10:00
May 1980–Sep 1982, CBS Mon 9:30–10:00
CAST:
Dr. Charley Michaels................ Wayne Rogers
Ann Anderson (1979–1981)........ Lynn Redgrave
Jane Jeffries (1982).................. Sharon Gless
Dr. Norman Solomon............... Ray Buktenica
Dr. Amos Weatherby................ David Wayne
Conrad Peckler (1980–1982)........ Mark L. Taylor
Mrs. Phipps.......................... Deedy Peters
Head Nurse Bradley................. Aneta Corsaut
Nurse Sally Bowman (1979–1980).... Diane Lander
Nurse Nancy (1980–1982)............. Beth Jacobs
Nurse Shirley Bryan (1980–1982) ... Suzanne Hunt

Dating someone with whom you work can create problems, as Charley Michaels and Ann Anderson learned. He was a surgeon at Kensington General Hospital in San Francisco, a good doctor but less than enthusiastic about conforming to hospital rules and regulations. She was the hospital's new administrative assistant, an English lady with a commitment to keeping the hospital running efficiently. They were romantically involved but often at odds when Charley's concern for his patients conflicted with Ann's concern for the business side of Kensington. Others in the cast were Norman Solomon, a neurotic young obstetrician; Amos Weatherby, the brilliant but absentminded (some would say senile) chief of surgery; Ann's stuffy boss, Conrad Peckler; and Mrs. Phipps, a flighty hospital volunteer who provided patients with books, candy, and other inexpensive odds and ends.

A contract dispute between series co-star Lynn Redgrave and *House Calls*' producers prompted her departure in 1981. In the series' story line Ann Anderson suddenly disappeared from Kensington General but sent the staff a letter indicating that she had returned to England and her former husband. Ann's replacement, Jane Jeffries, turned out to be one of Charley's former love interests. Conveniently, his relationship with Jane was not noticeably different than the one he had had with Ann.

Based on the motion picture starring Walter Matthau and Glenda Jackson.

HOUSE OF BUGGIN' (*Comedy/Variety*)
FIRST TELECAST: *January 8, 1995*
LAST TELECAST: *April 23, 1995*
BROADCAST HISTORY:
Jan 1995–Feb 1995, FOX Sun 8:30–9:00
Apr 1995, FOX Sun 8:30–9:00
Apr 1995, FOX Sun 9:30–10:00
REGULARS:
John Leguizamo
Jorge Luis Abreu
Tammi Cubilettte
Yelba Osorio
David Herman
Luis Guzman

Antic, baby-faced comedian John Leguizamo, born in Colombia and raised in Queens, New York, was the star of this sketch comedy series that looked like a Hispanic version of *In Living Color*. Leguizamo played a variety of ethnic types and even appeared in drag. Among his recurring characters were Kogi Ono, host of a cheap Asian TV talk show, and Reuben Martinez, host of *Pass the Buck*, a TV game show. Another recurring sketch featured Leguizamo and his supporting cast as a group of Hispanic guys in a movie theater making cracks about the films on the screen.

As for that strange title, the producers defined "buggin' " as follows: "the state of truly free insanity where the rules of life have been temporarily suspended and all behavior, no matter how outrageous, is deemed appropriate."

HOUSE RULES (*Situation Comedy*)
FIRST TELECAST: *March 9, 1998*
LAST TELECAST: *April 20, 1998*
BROADCAST HISTORY:
Mar 1998–Apr 1998, NBC Mon 8:30–9:00
CAST:
Casey Farrell......................... Maria Pitillo
William McCusky................. David Newsom
Thomas Riley III..................... Bradley White

Three best friends since childhood roomed together in this short-lived buddy comedy, set in Denver. Casey was the smart one, a newly minted deputy District Attorney who attracted handsome, dense boyfriends like bees to honey. Riley and McCusky were her two goofball roommates, the former a reporter and the latter a tall, shaggy-haired medical student. They all lived in a big old Victorian house near a college campus.

HOUSTON KNIGHTS (*Police Drama*)
FIRST TELECAST: *March 12, 1987*
LAST TELECAST: *June 6, 1988*
BROADCAST HISTORY:
Mar 1987–Apr 1987, CBS Wed 10:00–11:00
Jul 1987–Sep 1987, CBS Tue 9:00–10:00
Sep 1987–Dec 1987, CBS Tue 8:00–9:00
Jan 1988–Feb 1988, CBS Sat 9:00–10:00
Apr 1988–Jun 1988, CBS Tue 8:00–9:00
CAST:
Sgt. Joey La Fiamma................. Michael Pare
Sgt. Levon Lundy..................... Michael Beck
Clarence ("Chicken").............. John Hancock
Lt. Joanne Beaumont............ Robyn Douglass
Sgt. Joe-Bill McCandless.......... James Crittenden
Annie.................................. Madlyn Rhue
Carol ("Legs")....................... Nancy Everhard
Sgt. Nat Holliday.................. Brian Mitchell
Sgt. Estaban Gutierrez........... Efrain Figuerroa
Jamie Kincaid...................... D. Franki Horner
Eric Kincaid.......................... Dana Young

A youth-oriented police-action series, in the *Starsky & Hutch* mold. Following the murder of his partner in an organized crime hit, high-strung, aggressive Chicago cop Joey La Fiamma transferred to the Houston Police Department to get away from the hoods who were still after him. La Fiamma's partner on the Houston force, and the person assigned to help the short-tempered Chicagoan adjust to Houston, was his opposite in temperament, laid-back Levon Lundy. Although neither of these young men was particularly fond of the other's methods, they were intensely loyal to each other. Others who worked out of their precinct were their boss, Lt. Beaumont; male officers McCandless, Holliday, and

Gutierrez; and two female officers, sexy Carol and Annie, who had been confined to a wheelchair since being shot while on duty several years earlier. Chicken, who ran the rib joint where La Fiamma and Lundy hung out on their off hours, was their most reliable tipster. Lundy was dating Jamie Kincaid, a widow with a 12-year-old son, who had misgivings about dating another cop since her first husband had been killed while on duty.

HOUSTON MEDICAL (*Medical Documentary*)
FIRST TELECAST: *June 18, 2002*
LAST TELECAST: *July 23, 2002*
BROADCAST HISTORY:
Jun 2002–Jul 2002, ABC Tue 10:00–11:00

A six-week documentary series, done cinema verité style and set at Memorial Hermann Hospital in Houston, Texas. Loud music, fast cuts and high drama were the keynotes of this attempt to craft a "real-life *ER*." Among the continuing stores were those of Dr. Marnie Rose, a 27-year-old pediatrician just beginning her career and diagnosed with brain cancer, and hunky Dr. Mark Henry, a microsurgeon trying to balance his career with a shaky marriage. Among his more innovative treatments was replacing an accident victim's lost finger by transplanting one of her toes to her hand.

HOW DID THEY GET THAT WAY? (*Discussion*)
FIRST TELECAST: *July 24, 1951*
LAST TELECAST: *March 10, 1952*
BROADCAST HISTORY
Jul 1951–Sep 1951, ABC Tue 8:00–8:30
Sep 1951–Jan 1952, ABC Tue 8:30–9:00
Feb 1952–Mar 1952, ABC Mon 9:30–10:00
MODERATOR:
Isabelle Leighton

Public-service program dealing with emotional problems, utilizing medical films and discussions by psychiatrists and guests. Among the topics covered were "Gossip," "Hostility," "Feelings of Rejection," and "Why Tommy Won't Eat." During its first few months the program was known as *What's on Your Mind?*

HOW THE WEST WAS WON (*Western*)
FIRST TELECAST: *February 12, 1978*
LAST TELECAST: *April 23, 1979*
BROADCAST HISTORY:
Feb 1978–May 1978, ABC Sun 8:00–9:00
Jul 1978–Aug 1978, ABC Sun 8:00–9:00
Jan 1979–Apr 1979, ABC Mon 9:00–11:00
CAST:
Zeb Macahan .... James Arness
Aunt Molly Culhane .... Fionnula Flanagan
Luke Macahan .... Bruce Boxleitner
Laura Macahan .... Kathryn Holcomb
Josh Macahan .... William Kirby Cullen
Jessie Macahan .... Vicki Schreck

James Arness, Marshal Dillon of the long-running *Gunsmoke* series, returned to TV screens in 1978 in this mixture of Western adventure and soap opera. Zeb Macahan was a rugged mountain man who had spent ten years in the Dakota Territory before returning to Virginia, where his brother's family was preparing to make the long trek west. No sooner had they set out than the Civil War broke out. Zeb's brother Timothy returned east and his wife Kate was subsequently killed in an accident, leaving the four Macahan children in Zeb's care. Luke, the eldest, had killed three men in self-defense, and was a fugitive from the law; Laura was pretty and ready for womanhood; Jessie was the tomboyish 12-year-old; and teenager Josh was exuberant and anxious to become the man of the family. Aunt Molly, Kate's widowed sister, came from Boston to help them on the long journey, through dangers and hardships caused by Indians, renegades, nature, and the other perils of an untamed West. After an initial run in 1978, the series returned in early 1979 with 11 new two-hour episodes depicting the Macahans as they homesteaded a ranch in the Tetons, and began to raise Appaloosa horses.

Adding to the epic scope of the series was the spectacular setting; the program was filmed on location in Utah, Colorado, Arizona, and Southern California. The executive producer was John Mantley, who had also been the producer of *Gunsmoke*. The series was loosely based on the 1963 motion picture of the same name, which was directed by John Ford and featured an all-star cast, including John Wayne.

HOW TO (*Informational*)
FIRST TELECAST: *July 10, 1951*
LAST TELECAST: *September 11, 1951*
BROADCAST HISTORY:
Jul 1951–Sep 1951, CBS Tue 9:00–9:30
MODERATOR:
Roger Price
PANEL:
Leonard Stern
Stanley Adams
Anita Martell

The solutions that moderator Roger Price and his panel of experts had for the various questions that were asked of them were not the most sensible in the world. To the person who asked "How to" open a beer can with a thumbtack the response was "place the tack on top of the can and hit it with a large ax." The obvious way to keep a faucet from leaking was to turn it on. Such pearls of wisdom were dispensed weekly on both radio and television (though not simulcast) during the summer of 1951.

HOW TO MARRY A MILLIONAIRE (*Situation Comedy*)
BROADCAST HISTORY:
Syndicated only
30 minutes
Produced: *1957–1959* (52 episodes)
Released: *October 1958*
CAST:
"Mike" McCall .... Merry Anders
Loco Jones .... Barbara Eden
Greta (1957–1958) .... Lori Nelson
Gwen Kirby (1958–1959) .... Lisa Gaye

Cheerful comedy about three sexy New York career girls living in a swank penthouse apartment they can barely afford, and out to snare rich husbands by any scheme they can concoct. The series was based on the hit 1953 movie of the same name, with Barbara Eden as Loco, the dim-witted blonde who was so nearsighted she kept walking into walls (the Marilyn Monroe role); Lori Nelson as Greta, the breezy manhunter (Betty Grable); and Merry Anders as Mike, the ringleader of the group (Lauren Bacall). The names of the girls were somewhat different in the film (Pola, Loco, and Schatz), but the glamorous gold-digging theme was the same.

Lori Nelson, upset that her role wasn't bigger, quit after the first season to do "heavier" stuff, and was written out as having married and moved away; she was replaced by Lisa Gaye. Miss Nelson was never heard from again (she was married for a time to musician Johnny Mann, but never did another TV series or movie). Lisa and Merry—who had a bit part in the 1953 movie—didn't fare much better after this series, making a few B-pictures in the 1960s and then disappearing (Anders's last film was *Women of the Prehistoric Planet* in 1966). However, Barbara Eden went on to TV stardom in the long-running *I Dream of Jeannie*, and later returned to TV on *Harper Valley P.T.A.*

HOWARD K. SMITH—NEWS AND COMMENT (*News Commentary*)

FIRST TELECAST: *February 14, 1962*
LAST TELECAST: *June 16, 1963*
BROADCAST HISTORY:
Feb 1962–Sep 1962, ABC Wed 7:30–8:00
Sep 1962–Jun 1963, ABC Sun 10:30–11:00
NEWSMAN:
Howard K. Smith

In his first regular television assignment for ABC, after severing a 20-year relationship with CBS News, Howard K. Smith presented this weekly news and commentary program. It featured a summary of the week's major news events, commentary and analysis by Mr. Smith, and interviews with prominent people in the news.

HOWARD STERN RADIO SHOW, THE (*Talk*)

BROADCAST HISTORY:
Syndicated only
60 minutes
Produced: *1998–2001*
Released: *August 22, 1998*
REGULARS:
Howard Stern
Robin Quivers
Jackie Martling
Gary Dell'Abate
Fred Norris
John Melendez

Television didn't get any grosser than this. Done in the style of his series on cable's E! Entertainment network, most of *The Howard Stern Radio Show* was shot in a dingy, cluttered radio studio during broadcasts of Howard's widely syndicated radio show. The self-proclaimed "king of all media" featured interviews with transsexuals, strippers, and gays. The premiere showcased a 225-pound body-building transsexual who displayed his/her breasts (obscured electronically for TV), an animated Jon-Benet Ramsey telling the audience to stay tuned for her announcement of who killed her, a guy who had participated in a Howard Stern look-alike contest, a couple of bisexual women—one of whom did a strip and lap dance for Howard—a satirical commentary on footage of O.J. Simpson being interviewed on a golf course, and the first annual Howard Stern Frankenstein make-over contest.

For variety, some episodes included taped coverage of Stern's production meetings, discussions with prospective show guests, and other out-of-studio activities that took place during the week. After the October 17, 1998, episode, in which Stern shaved the pubic hair of one of his female guests, five stations dropped the program. Other tasteless features included "Handicapped Star Search," "The Lesbian Dating Game," a kid who farted 217 times in five minutes, and the first annual "Howard Stern Small Penis Invitational."

The show limped along for more than three years but, in mid-November 2001 the distributor pulled the plug.

HOWARD STERN SHOW, THE (*Comedy/Talk*)

BROADCAST HISTORY:
Syndicated only
60 minutes
Produced: *1990–1992*
Released: *July 1990*
REGULARS:
Howard Stern
Robin Quivers
John Melendez ("Stuttering John")
Jackie Martling ("The Joke Man")
Billy West
Gary Dell'Abate ("Babbabooey")
Fred Norris ("Frightening Fred")

Morning radio personality Howard Stern, notorious for his sexist, raunchy, and otherwise offensive material, surfaced on television with a weekly late-night series guaranteed to offend almost everyone. Stern's appearance fitted his material perfectly—he was skinny, leather-jacketed, with scraggly long hair and a perpetual sneer. In other words, every parent's nightmare as a date for their daughter. From a set resembling a radio studio, he introduced video versions of his radio routines, including the notorious "Lesbian Love Connection" (in which two lesbians reported on their date). There were parodies of people or events in the news, lots of voluptuous "spokesmodels" in skimpy bikinis (which Howard sometimes tried to peel off), and videotaped on-location celebrity interviews conducted by "Stuttering John," who asked such insulting questions he often got thrown out for his troubles. Howard and his cool lady sidekick Robin Quivers (who had been with him on radio for years) also chatted with in-studio celebrities, including Elliott Gould, Joe Piscopo, Richard Simmons, Joan Rivers, and Siskel and Ebert. Some of them could be embarrassed, some could not.

The Howard Stern Show had premiered as a local show on a nervous WWOR-TV in New York, in July 1990. Though sponsors were few, at least no one burned the station down and it went into somewhat limited national syndication the following year.

HOW'D THEY DO THAT? (*Information*)

FIRST TELECAST: *March 10, 1993*
LAST TELECAST: *June 30, 1994*
BROADCAST HISTORY:
Mar 1993–May 1993, CBS Wed 8:00–9:00
Aug 1993, CBS Wed 8:00–9:00
Aug 1993–Sep 1993, CBS Fri 8:00–9:00
Jan 1994, CBS Thu 8:00–9:00
Jun 1994, CBS Thu 8:00–9:00

HOSTS:
Pat O'Brien
Dorothy Lucey

Segments aired on *How'd They Do That?* ran the gamut from the frivolous to the serious. They demonstrated how special effects were created for movies, TV shows, and commercials; chronicled scientific breakthroughs in medicine and physics; covered techniques in criminal investigation; and showed some of the unexplored wonders of nature. All the segments featured real people demonstrating their skills, eccentricities, and determination. A single episode covered such topics as how Las Vegas casinos identified cheating gamblers, how Olympic skaters spun on the ice without getting dizzy, how computer technology was used to make magazine cover girls look more attractive, how people needing organ transplants found donors, how people rebuilt their town after it was devastated by Hurricane Andrew, and how a sheriff collected more than $2 million per week in parking fines. Hosts Pat O'Brien and Dorothy Lucey provided wide-eyed, gee-whiz introductions.

HOWIE (*Comedy*)
FIRST TELECAST: *July 1, 1992*
LAST TELECAST: *July 22, 1992*
BROADCAST HISTORY:
Jul 1992, CBS Wed 8:00–8:30
REGULARS:
Howie Mandel
Shirley Green
Paul Ebejer
Gilbert Gottfried
Clarence Clemons
Lita Ford

Summer comedy series starring frenetic standup comedian/actor Howie Mandel. Each episode included footage from Mandel's stage performances at the Celebrity Theater in Anaheim, California, as well as taped comedy sketches. Featured were comedians Paul Ebejer, Gilbert Gottried, and Shirley Green (as Howie's mom), and musicians Clarence Clemons and Lita Ford. Guest stars included Robert Goulet, Billy Joel, Jackie Mason, Little Richard, Gary Busey, and Judy Tenuta.

HUCK FINN, see *New Adventures of Huck Finn, The*

HUDSON BROTHERS SHOW, THE (*Variety*)
FIRST TELECAST: *July 31, 1974*
LAST TELECAST: *August 28, 1974*
BROADCAST HISTORY:
Jul 1974–Aug 1974, CBS Wed 8:00–9:00
REGULARS:
The Hudson Brothers (Bill, Brett, and Mark)
Ronny Graham
Gary Owens
Stephanie Edwards
Ron Hull
The Jaime Rogers Dancers
The Jack Eskew Orchestra
Katee McClure

The Hudson Brothers were, according to series producer Alan Blye, "a cross between the Marx Brothers and the Beatles." They sang reasonably well and did sketch and monologue comedy in this short-lived summer variety series. They were all in their 20s and much of their material was aimed at the under-35 audience.

HUDSON STREET (*Situation Comedy*)
FIRST TELECAST: *September 19,1995*
LAST TELECAST: *June 19, 1996*
BROADCAST HISTORY:
Sep 1995–Jan 1996, ABC Tue 8:30–9:00
Feb 1996, ABC Sat 8:00–8:30
May 1996–Jun 1996, ABC Wed 8:30–9:00
CAST:
Det. Tony Canetti .... Tony Danza
Mickey Canetti (age 10) .... Frankie J. Galasso
Lucy Canetti .... Shareen Mitchell
Melanie Clifford .... Lori Loughlin
Lt. Al Teischer .... Jerry Adler
Det. Kirby McIntire .... Christine Dunford
Off. R. Regelski .... Tom Gallop
Winston Silvera .... Jeffrey Anderson-Gunter

A conservative cop and a liberal police reporter found themselves romantically attracted to one another in this gentle comedy, which was co-produced by star Tony Danza. Tony Canetti, a detective with the Hoboken, New Jersey, police department, was recently divorced from his onetime high school sweetheart, Lucy. They were still on good terms, and although he had custody of his adoring son Mickey, she visited often and still liked the lug. Reporter Melanie, an opinionated, impulsive woman who was quite sure of herself, didn't think much of Tony when they first met, but his cheerful demeanor and snappy banter won her over and they were soon dating—his first date "since the Carter administration." Winston was the cynical waiter at the restaurant where they met. Seen down at the station house were old-timer Al, rabid feminist Kirby, and oddball Regelski.

THE HUGHLEYS, THE (*Situation Comedy*)
FIRST TELECAST: *September 22, 1998*
LAST TELECAST: *August 6, 2002*
BROADCAST HISTORY:
Sep 1998–Jul 1999, ABC Tue 8:30–9:00
Jul 1999–Sep 1999, ABC Fri 8:30–9:00
Sep 1999–Oct 1999, ABC Fri 8:00–8:30
Oct 1999–Mar 2000, ABC Fri 9:30–10:00
Apr 2000, ABC Fri 8:30–9:00
Sep 2000–Feb 2001, UPN Tue 9:00–9:30
Mar 2001–Aug 2001, UPN Tue 8:30–9:00
Mar 2001–Apr 2001, UPN Fri 8:30–9:00
Sep 2001–Jul 2002, UPN Mon 8:00–8:30
Jun 2002, UPN Tue 9:30–10:00
Jul 2002–Aug 2002, UPN Tue 9:00–9:30
CAST:
Darryl Hughley .... D.L. Hughley
Yvonne Hughley .... Elise Neal
Sydney Hughley .... Ashley Monique Clark
Michael Hughley (age 8) .... Dee Jay Daniels
Dave Rogers .... Eric Allan Kramer
Sally Rogers .... Marietta DePrima
Seth Milsap .... John Henton
Shari (2001–2002) .... Adele Givens

An upwardly mobile black man worried about losing his "blackness" in this family comedy, a sort of '90s version of *The Jeffersons.* Darryl Hughley (pronounced "Hugh-glee") had made his money as "the vending machine king," and spent it on a nice home for his family in the white Los Angeles suburbs. What was worse, his new WASPy neighbors, Dave and Sally, were really *nice*, his adorable daughter Sydney had begun playing with a white doll, and his 8-year-old,

Michael, rejected Motown for—ugh—Hanson! Black best friend and employee Milsap, a shaved-head type from the inner city, played on his fears, but wise, tart-tongued wife Yvonne was there to bring Darryl down to earth.

At the end of the third season the whole gang went on a cruise and, after Darryl set off a false alarm, found themselves stranded in a lifeboat in the middle of the ocean. In a cliffhanger ending, they feared the end was near and confessed their sins to each other. As the 2001–2002 season opened, however, there was no mention of what had happened; instead, at the end of the first fall episode, a short clip announced that the cliffhanger was a bad idea and that viewers should forget it! During the final season Yvonne's outspoken sister Shari moved into the apartment over the Rogerses' garage, and in February D.L.'s niece Carly (Kelly Rowland), an aspiring singer who was estranged from her father, moved in with the family. Michael, who was having trouble at school, was diagnosed with dyslexia. In the two-part series finale Darryl and Milsap attended their 20th high school reunion and Milsap found out he had become a father after the 15th reunion. He decided to be a father to his four-year-old daughter, Adriana.

HULL HIGH (*Musical Drama*)

FIRST TELECAST: *August 20, 1990*
LAST TELECAST: *December 30, 1990*
BROADCAST HISTORY:
Aug 1990, NBC Mon 8:00–9:00
Sep 1990, NBC Sat 8:00–9:00
Sep 1990–Oct 1990, NBC Sun 7:00–8:00
Dec 1990, NBC Sun 7:00–8:00
CAST:
John Deerborn .... Will Lyman
Donna Breedlove .... Nancy Valen
Camilla .... Cheryl Pollak
Mark Fuller (age 16) .... Mark Ballou
Cody Rome .... Harold Pruett
D. J. Serkin .... Kristin Dattilo
Mr. Jim Fancher .... Marshall Bell
Louis Plumb .... Marty Belafsky
Emery Dobosh .... George Martin
Rapper #1 .... Trey Parker
Rapper #2 .... Phillip DeMarks
Rapper #3 .... Carl Anthony Payne II
Rapper #4 .... Bryan Anthony

Television executives, who like to consider themselves eternally young and hip, dubbed this musical drama "hip hop high" after a fleetingly popular musical style which lasted about as long as the series. Cordell Hull High School was home to the usual mixed bag of teachers and students: Mr. Deerborn, the teen-sensitive and popular history teacher, Miss Breedlove, the very sexy but naive English teacher ("why aren't students paying attention to my lectures?"), Camilla, the mature new girl on campus (was she a narc?), Mark, the 16-year-old All-American, Cody, the dark, dangerous one ("too cool for any school"), and D. J., the school radical who wanted a nerdy fellow student to take a picture of her in the boys' locker room—naked. The lives and loves of all of them were played out, in semi–soap opera fashion.

Commenting on the action were "The Hull High Devils," a sort of Greek Chorus of rappers (this *was* the '90s!). Periodically, the entire student body would break out in singing and dancing. Welcome to the school with a beat.

HULLABALOO (*Music*)

FIRST TELECAST: *January 12, 1965*
LAST TELECAST: *August 29, 1966*
BROADCAST HISTORY:
Jan 1965–May 1965, NBC Tue 8:30–9:30
Jun 1965–Aug 1965, NBC Tue 10:00–11:00
Sep 1965–Aug 1966, NBC Mon 7:30–8:00
REGULARS:
The Hullabaloo Dancers (6 girls, 4 boys)
MUSIC DIRECTOR:
Peter Matz
PRODUCER:
Gary Smith

Hullabaloo was one of TV's few attempts to give rock 'n' roll a big-budget, top-quality showcase all its own in prime time. (Another, seen at about the same time, was *Shindig.*) Each week top popular recording artists performed their current hits, backed by elaborate production and the frenetic, mini-skirted Hullabaloo Dancers. The whole affair was very youth-oriented, with a great deal of noise and motion, and the general atmosphere was that of a discotheque in full swing—in fact, one segment was called "Hullabaloo A-Go-Go." (Just for the record, "the girl in the cage" doing a perpetual frug was Lada Edmund, Jr.) A different host presided each week, including Paul Anka, Jack Jones, Frankie Avalon and Annette Funicello, and Jerry Lewis (with his rock-star son, Gary). Performing were such acts as the Supremes, the Ronettes, Sonny and Cher, and many others. A special feature during the first three months was a weekly segment taped in London, hosted by rock impresario Brian Epstein and presenting top English acts such as Gerry and the Pacemakers, Marianne Faithful, Herman's Hermits, and the Moody Blues. Brian never brought on the biggest English superstars of all, however—his own protégés, the Beatles. (They finally did appear after Brian had left the show, in a January 1966 telecast.)

HUMAN FACTOR, THE (*Medical Drama*)

FIRST TELECAST: *April 16, 1992*
LAST TELECAST: *May 28, 1992*
BROADCAST HISTORY:
Apr 1992–May 1992, CBS Thu 10:00–11:00
CAST:
Dr. Alec McMurtry .... John Mahoney
Joan McMurtry .... Jan Lucas
Matt Robbins .... Kurt Deutsch
Michael Stoven .... Eriq LaSalle
Rebecca Travis .... Melinda McGraw
Joe Murphy .... Matthew Ryan
George Teitlich .... Robert McNeill
Dr. Walter Burke .... Allan Miller

Alec McMurtry was a compassionate physician at U.C.I., an inner-city teaching hospital in this preachy drama. He had left a highly successful private practice because he felt it was his duty to teach students that there was more to medicine than diagnosis, treatment, and billing. He wanted them to learn to treat patients and their families with kindness and sympathy, to help them through the emotional trauma of injury and disease and deal with human mortality. Not only did he send them on house calls, he even encouraged them to get involved with their patients' nonmedical problems. Joan was his loving wife and Matt, Michael, Rebecca, Joe, and George five of the interns under his tutelage.

HUMAN TARGET (*Drama*)
FIRST TELECAST: *July 20, 1992*
LAST TELECAST: *August 29, 1992*
BROADCAST HISTORY:
Jul 1992, ABC Mon 10:00–11:00
Jul 1992–Aug 1992, ABC Sat 9:00–10:00
CAST:
Christopher Chance .... Rick Springfield
Philo Marsden .... Kirk Baltz
Jeff Carlyle .... SaMi Chester
Libby Page......................... Signy Coleman

Action-adventure series about Christopher Chance, a decoy-for-hire who impersonated people in danger while solving the mystery of who was out to kill them. Based on the DC Comics character.

HUMBLE REPORT, THE (*Documentary*)
FIRST TELECAST: *March 1, 1964*
LAST TELECAST: *September 15, 1964*
BROADCAST HISTORY:
Mar 1964–May 1964, NBC Sun 10:00–11:00
Jun 1964–Sep 1964, NBC Tue 10:00–11:00

This series of full-hour documentaries on various subjects, ranging from political issues to a profile of baseball player Willie Mays, aired on alternate weeks during the spring and summer of 1964. It was sponsored by the Humble Oil Company.

HUNTER (*Foreign Intrigue*)
FIRST TELECAST: *February 18, 1977*
LAST TELECAST: *May 27, 1977*
BROADCAST HISTORY:
Feb 1977–May 1977, Fri 10:00–11:00
CAST:
James Hunter.................... James Franciscus
Marty Shaw .... Linda Evans
Gen. Baker......................... Ralph Bellamy

Working for top Federal intelligence chief General Baker, James Hunter and his partner Marty Shaw were called upon to fight a multitude of international foes in their jobs as undercover counterespionage agents. Sometimes they fought with Communists, sometimes with underworld organizations, and occasionally with other U.S. intelligence agencies. Their assignments took them all over the world.

HUNTER (*Police Drama*)
FIRST TELECAST: *September 18, 1984*
LAST TELECAST: *August 30, 1991*
BROADCAST HISTORY:
Sep 1984, NBC Tue 9:00–10:00
Sep 1984–Jan 1985, NBC Fri 9:00–10:00
Mar 1985–Feb 1986, NBC Sat 10:00–11:00
Mar 1986–Aug 1986, NBC Tue 9:00–10:00
Aug 1986–Dec 1987, NBC Sat 10:00–11:00
Dec 1987–Mar 1988, NBC Tue 9:00–10:00
Mar 1988–Apr 1990, NBC Sat 10:00–11:00
Apr 1990–May 1990, NBC Mon 9:00–10:00
Jun 1990–Aug 1990, NBC Sat 10:00–11:00
Aug 1990–Feb 1991, NBC Wed 10:00–11:00
Mar 1991–Apr 1991, NBC Fri 9:00–10:00
May 1991–Jun 1991, NBC Fri 8:00–9:00
Aug 1991, NBC Fri 10:00–11:00
CAST:
Det. Sgt. Rick Hunter .... Fred Dryer
Det. Sgt. Dee Dee McCall (1984–1990)
.... Stepfanie Kramer
Off. Joanne Molenski (1990–1991)
.... Darlanne Fluegel
Sgt. Chris Novak (1991) .... Lauren Lane
Sgt. Bernie Terwilliger (1984–1986)
.... James Whitmore, Jr.
Capt. Lester Cain (pilot) .... Michael Cavanaugh
Capt. Lester Cain (1984) .... Arthur Rosenberg
Capt. Dolan (1984–1985).............. John Amos
Capt. Wyler (1985–1986)........... Bruce Davison
Capt. Charlie Devane (1986–1991)
.... Charles Hallahan
Lt. Ambrose Finn (1985–1988)........ John Shearin
**Carlos (1985–1987)*........... Richard Beauchamp
Arnold "Sporty" James (1986–1989)
.... Garrett Morris
**Barney (1987–1988)* .... Perry Cook
Reuben Garcia (1987–1988)
.... Rudy Ramos

*Occasional

One of the biggest box-office draws of the 1970s and 1980s was Clint Eastwood in his characterization of the violent, give-'em-no-quarter cop, Dirty Harry. Perhaps it was inevitable that television would produce its own version of this popular character, only slightly softened for the home screen. "Make my day," growled Harry as he aimed his pistol at a felon about to flee; "works for me" was Hunter's catchphrase. Both had Magnum revolvers big enough to send speeding cars into spectacular crashes. Hunter's was called Simon ("Says who?" scowled the crook; "Simon says," replied Hunter, brandishing the weapon). Both were saddled with the incompetent superiors who didn't understand their forceful ways and were constantly after their badges.

There were some differences. Hunter had a partner, a beautiful but rather tough lady cop named Dee Dee—otherwise known as "the brass cupcake." He also had an unusual family, most of them mobsters, who sometimes gave him grief. Another source of aggravation was Bernie, the inept senior detective to whom he was occasionally assigned. At least our hero had the satisfaction of knowing that his fatuous superiors in the L.A.P.D. came and went; three different actors portrayed Hunter's captain in the first six episodes.

Providing information to help crack cases were Carlos, an assistant at the morgue, and street hustler Sporty James.

In 1990, after six years in homicide, Hunter was transferred to the L.A.P.D.'s elite Metro Division, where he could strong-arm his way through a wider range of high-priority cases. Capt. Devane moved too, but Dee Dee had left the force to get married, so Hunter got a new partner, former street cop Joanne. She was killed off only three months later, after which Hunter did not have a regular partner. He did, however, gain a love interest in Chris, a fellow officer, a former girlfriend, and now a divorcée with a young daughter and plenty of family problems.

HUNTER (*Police Drama*)
FIRST TELECAST: *April 12, 2003*
LAST TELECAST: *May 10, 2003*
BROADCAST HISTORY:
Apr 2003, NBC Sat 9:00–11:00
Apr 2003–May 2003, NBC Sat 8:00–9:00
CAST:
Lt. Rick Hunter .... Fred Dryer
Lt. Dee Dee McCall .... Stepfanie Kramer
Capt. Roberto Gallardo .... Mike Gomez
Off. Sid Keyes .... Sid Sham
Off. Cynthia Monetti .... Michelle Gold
Det. Anthony Santiago .... Alex Mendoza

Tough cop Hunter and his partner Dee Dee McCall returned in this rather literal revival of the 1980s action series. Both had moved from L.A. to San Diego, where they were now detectives in that city's robbery homicide division. San Diego had plenty of snarling villains, underworld conspiracies and wild shootouts to keep them busy. First seen as a TV movie on November 16, 2002.

HUNTER, THE (*International Intrigue*)
FIRST TELECAST: *July 3, 1952*
LAST TELECAST: *December 26, 1954*
BROADCAST HISTORY:
Jul 1952, CBS Thu 9:00–9:30
Jul 1952–Sep 1952, CBS Wed 9:30–10:00
Jul 1954–Dec 1954, NBC Sun 10:30–11:00
CAST:
Bart Adams (1952–1954) .... Barry Nelson
Bart Adams (1954) .... Keith Larsen

Bart Adams was a wealthy, attractive young American businessman whose interests caused him to become involved in suspenseful adventures in exotic places all over the world. In order to move about unnoticed, he was a master of disguise, changing his appearance for each show. Most of the episodes in the series had Bart rescue someone who was in the clutches of Communist agents or thwart some evil plan that Communist agents had concocted to cause trouble for the Free World. The way he identified himself to friends in the European underground was by whistling "Frère Jacques," and ending it with a wolf whistle.

This filmed series was originally a CBS summer show, but films continued to be produced for syndication after the end of its network run. The episodes aired on NBC during the summer of 1954 were drawn from these syndicated films. Some new episodes were aired on NBC in the fall of 1954, with Keith Larsen replacing Barry Nelson in the role of Bart Adams.

HUNTRESS, THE (*Adventure*)
BROADCAST HISTORY:
USA Network
60 minutes
Original episodes: *2000–2001* (28 episodes)
Premiered: *July 26, 2000*
CAST:
Dorothy "Dottie" Thorson .... Annette O'Toole
Brandi Thorson (age 18) .... Jordana Spiro
Ricky Guzman .... Luis Antonio Ramos
Warren "Tiny" Bellows .... James Remar

Dottie Thorson was a housewife who had taken over her husband Ralph's bounty-hunting business by necessity after he was killed and left her broke. Worried but resilient, Dottie enlisted her bitchy but wise-beyond-her-years daughter Brandi to help, and the pair squabbled endlessly while tracking down thugs in order to keep the fridge from being repossessed. Ricky was Ralph's chief client, a sleazy bail bondsman who was skeptical of the ladies' abilities but tolerated them when they began to bring in the big fish. Their first catch was murderer Tiny Bellows, who proved to be a surprising friend and ally from behind bars, giving Dottie calm advice and helping her navigate the underworld. Romantic sparks flew, but Brandi reminded her, "You know he's not the only murderer in the world, Mom. You'll meet others."

The Huntress was first seen as a TV movie on March 7, 2000, with Craig T. Nelson in a cameo role as Ralph.

HUSBANDS, WIVES & LOVERS (*Situation Comedy*)
FIRST TELECAST: *March 10, 1978*
LAST TELECAST: *June 30, 1978*
BROADCAST HISTORY:
Mar 1978–Jun 1978, CBS Fri 10:00–11:00
CAST:
Helene Willis .... Jesse Welles
Ron Willis .... Ron Rifkin
Murray Zuckerman .... Stephen Pearlman
Paula Zuckerman .... Cynthia Harris
Harry Bellini .... Eddie Barth
Joy Bellini .... Lynne Marie Stewart
Lennie Bellini .... Mark Lonow
Rita DeLatorre .... Randee Heller
Dixon Carter Fielding .... Charles Siebert
Courtney Fielding .... Claudette Nevins

One format that has rarely worked in television, despite numerous attempts, has been the hour-long situation comedy. This one followed the lives of five couples, all friends, who lived in the San Fernando Valley suburbs outside of Los Angeles. Murray Zuckerman was a traveling salesman for a pharmaceutical firm and spent much of his time out of town; Harry Bellini was a rough-hewn, self-taught garbage truck tycoon with a young, naive second wife; Lennie was Harry's younger brother who was living with Rita DeLatorre, with whom he ran a stylish jean boutique; Ron Willis was a dentist who had an amicable relationship with his wife Helene, from whom he was separated; and Dixon Carter Fielding was Ron's best friend, a corporate attorney who was also representing Helene in the separation proceedings. Carter's wife, Courtney, was a spendthrift who managed to go through even more money than his substantial income provided.

The series was created by comedienne Joan Rivers.

HYPE (*Comedy*)
FIRST TELECAST: *October 8, 2000*
LAST TELECAST: *February 4, 2001*
BROADCAST HISTORY:
Oct 2000, WB Sun 9:00–9:30
Nov 2000–Feb 2001, WB Sun 8:30–9:00
REGULARS:
Michael Roof
Jennifer Elise Cox
Gavin Crawford
Daniele Gaither
Nadya Ginsburg
Stephen E. Kramer
Christen Nelson

Shayma Tash
Chris Williams
Frank Caliendo

"We're not celebrities but we play them on TV," declared the young comics on this sketch comedy series, which in the tradition of *Saturday Night Live* and *Mad TV* satirized everything in pop culture—movies, TV series, commercials, sports, rock music, politics, celebrities and the Internet. Each episode opened with the fast-paced "Hype Report" by Shayma Tash, followed by imitations of Martha Stewart, Whitney Houston, George W. Bush, a droning Kurt Loder (of MTV) and William Shatner selling whores on priceline.com. President Clinton, unable to see the real Monica Lewinsky anymore, had sex with a poster of her.

HYPERION BAY (*Drama*)

FIRST TELECAST: *September 21, 1998*
LAST TELECAST: *March 8, 1999*
BROADCAST HISTORY:

Sep 1998–Mar 1999, WB Mon 9:00–10:00

CAST:

Dennis Sweeney .... Mark-Paul Gosselaar
Nick Sweeney .... Dylan Neal
Amy Sweeney .... Christina Moore
Trudy Carson Tucker .... Cassidy Rae
Nelson Tucker .... Bart Johnson
Frank Sweeney .... Raymond J. Barry
Marjorie Sweeney (1998) .... Cindy Pickett
Jennifer Worth .... Sydney Penny
Marcus Fox .... Chaka Forman
Bordon Hicks .... Victor Slezak
Brian Stewart .... Colby French
Bart Corber .... Art LaFleur
Sarah Hicks (1999) .... Carmen Electra
Martin Hicks (1999) .... Guy Boyd

THEME:

"Hard Times Come Easy," by Richie Sambora and Richie Supa

High school computer nerd Dennis had left the small town of Hyperion Bay, on the California coast, and made a fortune writing software for Muse Prime, a high-tech computer company. Now he was back in an expensive sports car with a beautiful babe on his arm. Although he was heading a development project for Muse that might save the dying town from economic devastation, there was, to put it mildly, resentment over his success. Resenter number-one was Dennis's blue-collar older brother, Nick, who worked in the family construction business with their dad, and was separating from his wife Amy. Frank, the father, was a little uptight as well, since the business was failing and it failed to get a contract from Dennis's company. Then there was Nelson, the handsome dumb lug who used to beat the crap out of Dennis when they were in high school. Nelson, who now owned a gas station, was married to slutty Trudy, who immediately set her sights on the much more successful Dennis; she was in competition with the software geek's current babe, Jennifer, a classy art gallery employee. Marcus was a talented programmer who was Dennis's number two at Muse's Hyperion Bay facility, the Cannery.

Dennis was a purist, but his wealthy boss, Bordon, was more interested in the bottom line. In January, Bordon brought his sexy daughter, Sarah, to Hyperion Bay and installed her as Vice-President of Operations at Muse Prime, much to Dennis's chagrin. He also purchased a plot of land to develop into a condominium complex. Sarah, who hated her father for the way he had treated her mother, promptly conspired with Dennis in a boardroom showdown, ousting her father from control of Muse. Sarah then gave Nick a job working as facilities manager at the Cannery and on the condo project, and eventually they began an affair. In February, Nelson was killed at the condo construction site when Corber, the corrupt town supervisor looking for payoffs, shut off its power. After his death Trudy conspired with Corber and Bordon to sue Muse Prime for wrongful death, so that Bordon could regain control of the company. The plan failed and Amy replaced Corber as town supervisor.

In the series finale Jennifer got a job at a computer hardware firm that was setting up operations in Hyperion Bay. Dennis and Amy were on the verge of acknowledging their growing love for each other, and Nick and Sarah, after having broken up, were back together.

I

I AM WEASEL (*Cartoon*)

BROADCAST HISTORY:

Cartoon Network
30 minutes
Original episodes: *1997–1999* (79 episodes)
Premiered: *July 22, 1997*

VOICES:

I. M. Weasel .... Michael Dorn
I. R. Baboon/The Red Guy .... Charlie Adler

A loud, colorful cartoon of the frantic *Road Runner* type, featuring a deep-voiced, perpetually frustrated weasel and his friend, a big, dumb baboon. Together they got into many implausible adventures, such as a mission to the sun and becoming gladiators in ancient times. Nothing made much sense: in one episode they had a Ping-Pong match in the middle of the ocean; in another I. R. destroyed the law of gravity, so they had to go to the lawyers (the only ones who understood the law) to get it back. The series was spun off from, and shared many characters with, *Cow and Chicken*, including manic villain The Red Guy.

ICU: ARKANSAS CHILDREN'S HOSPITAL (*Documentary*)

FIRST TELECAST: *August 7, 2002*
LAST TELECAST: *August 28, 2002*
BROADCAST HISTORY:

Aug 2002, ABC Tue 10:00–11:00

Another of ABC's attempts to extract *ER*-style drama from a cinema verité documentary about life in a real hospital (for others, see *Hopkins 24/7* and *Houston Medical*). The setting this time was Arkansas Children's Hospital, where Chief Cardiac Surgeon Dr. Jonathan Drummond-Webb and his pediatric cardiologists struggled to save a succession of sick young kids, some of whom made it and some of whom did not. Urgent narration was provided by the principals, and by narrator Elizabeth Vargas.

I CAN'T BELIEVE YOU SAID THAT! (*Quiz/Audience Participation*)

BROADCAST HISTORY:

Fox Family Channel
30 minutes
Produced: *1998*
Premiered: *August 15, 1998*

REGULARS:

John Salley, host
Marc Summers, announcer (off-camera)

Few television quiz shows have had a host as distinctive as this early evening entry's. NBA star John Salley, a towering African-American with a shaven head and earring, refereed as two families competed to see who knew the most about their own family members. The members of each family had to guess what their spouses and siblings had said about them, and then reveal each other's "secrets" to win points.

I COVER TIMES SQUARE (*Newspaper Drama*)

FIRST TELECAST: *October 5, 1950*
LAST TELECAST: *January 11, 1951*
BROADCAST HISTORY:

Oct 1950–Jan 1951, ABC Thu 10:00–10:30

CAST:

Johnny Warren .... Harold Huber

PRODUCER:

Harold Huber

Harold Huber, a veteran actor who had portrayed dozens of squint-eyed, scheming villains on radio and in films (including the Charlie Chan pictures), was cast as a crusading Broadway columnist in this early series. His favorite hangout was the out-of-town newspaper stand in Times Square, and his beat, the seamy side of show business. In the first episode, for example, he was out to break up a gambling syndicate that controlled the boxing business in New York. The real-life prototype for Huber's role was said to be Walter Winchell.

After its prime-time run *I Cover Times Square* moved to Saturday afternoon, where it continued until late 1951.

I DARE YOU! THE ULTIMATE CHALLENGE (*Documentary*)

FIRST TELECAST: *January 18, 2000*
LAST TELECAST: *August 15, 2000*
BROADCAST HISTORY:

Jan 2000–Feb 2000, UPN Tue 8:00–9:00
Mar 2000, UPN Tue 9:00–10:00
May 2000–Aug 2000, UPN Tue 9:00–10:00

HOST:

Lee Reherman

FIELD REPORTERS:

Traci Melchor
Tyler Harcott
Connie Willis

Professional stunt people and daredevils performed spectacular and dangerous stunts in the various segments of this series. On the premiere telecast legendary daredevil Evel Knievel provided commentary in the Las Vegas studio with host Reherman. The two featured stunts were the monster truck "BigFoot" attempting a jump over seven trucks and a 75-foot long tractor trailer—a total distance of more than 175 feet—as well as a stuntman skydiving from a plane 5,000 feet over the Mojave Desert to land on top of a hot-air balloon and then work his way into the balloon's gondola. There was coverage of the preparations, background on and interviews with the participants, footage of some of their previous stunts and poststunt interviews. The monster truck easily cleared the vehicles—with 25 feet to spare—but lost one of its huge tires when it landed. The skydiver landed on the balloon but couldn't make it into the gondola. He used his reserve parachute to enable him to land safely in the desert. He did, however, take the challenge to try it again in a later episode.

In later episodes a daredevil motorcycle rider sped through a 202-foot-long tunnel of flame—he didn't make it all the way through; a stuntman used a ramp to fly his car in a narrow opening between the boxcars of a train moving at 25 m.p.h.; a plane flew into the back of a semi traveling at 40 m.p.h. in the desert; and a daredevil on a ski board sped across the surface of a flaming lake. There were also features on ordinary people who had survived life-threatening accidents and become active adventurers.

I DREAM OF JEANNIE (*Situation Comedy*)

FIRST TELECAST: *September 18, 1965*
LAST TELECAST: *September 1, 1970*

BROADCAST HISTORY:

Sep 1965–Sep 1966, NBC Sat 8:00–8:30
Sep 1966–Aug 1967, NBC Mon 8:00–8:30
Sep 1967–Aug 1968, NBC Tue 7:30–8:00
Sep 1968–Aug 1969, NBC Mon 7:30–8:00
Sep 1969–Sep 1970, NBC Tue 7:30–8:00

CAST:

Jeannie .... Barbara Eden
Capt. Tony Nelson .... Larry Hagman
Capt. Roger Healey .... Bill Daily
Dr. Alfred Bellows .... Hayden Rorke
Gen. Martin Peterson (1965–1969) .... Barton MacLane
Amanda Bellows (1966–1970) .... Emmaline Henry
Gen. Winfield Schaeffer (1969–1970) .... Vinton Hayworth
Tina (1969–1970) .... Farrah Fawcett

Astronaut Tony Nelson was on a space mission that aborted, forcing him to parachute onto a desert island. While waiting for a rescue team he came across an old bottle that had apparently washed ashore. When he opened the bottle, out popped a 2,000-year-old (but remarkably well-preserved) genie, who promptly accepted him as her master, since he had set her free.

Returning to Cocoa Beach, Florida, with the rescue team, Tony found that nobody would believe that he had found a luscious, sexy genie. The base psychiatrist, Dr. Bellows, was convinced that Tony had suffered delusions caused by exposure. Complicating the matter, the genie, appropriately named Jeannie, refused to perform magic or ever appear for anyone but Tony. Her efforts to serve him often resulted in rather confusing situations, caused in part by her lack of familiarity with 20th-century American customs.

Jeannie was in love with Tony, although their relationship was platonic during the first couple of seasons. She did not take kindly to any of the women he attempted to date, including Melissa (Karen Sharpe), the general's daughter to whom he was engaged when the series premiered. Jeannie used her powers to motivate Melissa's old boyfriend to propose to her. Roger, Tony's girl-crazy buddy and fellow astronaut, was the only person other than Tony who knew that Jeannie existed and had magical powers (he found out in Spring 1966). Roger was constantly getting Tony into situations that aggravated the very jealous Jeannie, who disrupted any of her master's romances. She finally convinced Tony that he loved her enough to marry her, and they were wed in the episode telecast on December 1, 1969.

Tony and Roger, originally captains, were both promoted to major in February 1966. During the show's run there were occasional appearances by Jeannie's magical and mostly invisible dog Djinn-Djinn, assorted crazy relatives, and, during the last three seasons, her wicked twin sister, Jeannie (played by Ms. Eden in a dark wig). During the last season Roger's sexy girlfriend Tina, who seldom spoke, appeared in a number of episodes.

An animated version of this series, simply titled *Jeannie,* aired Saturday mornings on CBS from September 1973 to August 1975.

I HAD THREE WIVES (*Detective Comedy/Drama*)

FIRST TELECAST: *August 14, 1985*
LAST TELECAST: *September 13, 1985*

BROADCAST HISTORY:

Aug 1985–Sep 1985, CBS Wed 8:00–9:00
Sep 1985, CBS Fri 8:00–9:00

CAST:

Jackson Beaudine .... Victor Garb
Mary Parker .... Maggie Coop
Liz .... Shanna Ree
Samantha .... Teri Copley
Andrew Beaudine .... David Faustino
Lt. Gomez .... Luis Avalos

This short-lived summer detective series, set in Los Angeles, followed the cases of Jackson Beaudine, a private investigator who made the most of his extended family. A three-time loser in the marital wars, Jackson was on very good terms with his ex-wives. Mary, his first wife and the only one who had remarried, was an attorney and had custody of their 10-year-old son, Andrew. Her legal advice always proved helpful. Sam—wife number two—was an actress, master of disguise, and martial arts expert, and loved to help Jackson out whenever he needed her assistance; and third wife Liz, a newspaper reporter with keen analytical skills and a host of useful contacts, also came in handy. The three of them, all too chummy to believe, seemed more than willing to work individually or together to assist Jackson in his investigations on this rather lighthearted show.

I LED THREE LIVES (*Intrigue*)

BROADCAST HISTORY:

Syndicated only
30 minutes
Produced: *May 1953–mid-1956* (117 episodes)
Released: *September 1953*

CAST:

Herbert Philbrick .... Richard Carlson
Eva Philbrick .... Virginia Stefan
Special Agent Jerry Dressler .... John Zaremba
Special Agent Henderson .... Ed Hinton
**Constance Philbrick* .... Patricia Morrow
**Special Agent Steve Daniels* .... John Beradino
**Special Agent Mike Andrews* ..... William Hudson
**Special Agent Joe Carey* .... Charles Maxwell

*Occasional

This product of the McCarthy era contained what was perhaps the most explicit political propaganda ever found in a popular dramatic series on American television. Today it stands as a genuine period piece, reflecting the stereotypes that were all too prevalent during the Red Scare of the 1940s and early 1950s. In this show, Communist spies really were behind every bush, and anyone with liberal views was indeed suspect.

The program had a documentary flavor, opening with an announcer booming, "This is the fantastically true story of Herbert A. Philbrick, who for nine frightening years did lead three lives—average citizen, member of the Communist Party, and counterspy for the FBI. For obvious reasons the names, dates, and places have been changed, but the story is based on fact."

Philbrick was a pipe-smoking Boston advertising executive who infiltrated the local CP organization in order to provide information to the U.S. government. He was constantly called upon to take part in nefarious plots against the U.S., and always ran the risk of discovery and perhaps elimination as a traitor.

...st schemes included sabotage of ...s, stealing government secrets, dope- ... (to poison the nation's youth), and ... the party line through infiltration of orga- ... such as labor unions, university faculties, ... en churches. Sometimes Philbrick was or- ... to carry out the plans himself, perhaps using ... position in the advertising agency; sometimes he ... as just a courier. Schemes were constantly being smashed and party members arrested wherever he went, but the party hierarchy—a rather thick lot—never seemed to catch on. Still, there was constant danger, to himself, his wife Eva, and their children. Dark alleyways and secret cell meetings in basements were part of every episode. So was suspicion. Any indication of left-wing views would cause a raised eyebrow, and the whispered comment "Maybe he is . . . a Communist."

In one episode a mother reported her daughter's boyfriend, Paul, because she thought he had caused her daughter to start talking about how she hated bombing and wars and such. "Where did my daughter get the outrageous ideas she's been expressing?" the mother worried. Philbrick tracked down the real Commie—an art dealer the daughter knew—and at the end noted with relief that the girl was "not only safe and sound, but cured of her Communist infection, a real dividend for her mother and Paul."

To heighten the dramatic impact, Philbrick was also the narrator, referring to himself in the third person. Even though there was little violence seen, he always emphasized the danger ("This could be a trap, Philbrick."). Politics aside, it was fascinating melodrama, tensely scripted and realistically staged, with many outdoor scenes on busy streets and on lonely highways. Occasionally Philbrick would even be sent to Europe or South America.

The only regulars besides Philbrick and his wife were the FBI agents with whom he rendezvoused, played most frequently by John Zaremba (a regular after the first few episodes) and Ed Hinton. The Reds got arrested so regularly that none of them lasted long.

Observers today might wonder how viewers in the 1950s could take so seriously the idea that "your best friend may be a traitor" (as opposed to the dangers of international Communism). The series got much of its impact from the fact that it was based on a true story, as told by the real Herbert A. Philbrick in his best-selling book *I Led Three Lives*. Philbrick himself served as technical consultant. The program even had the approval of J. Edgar Hoover and the FBI, which reviewed all scripts. In later episodes, as the writers began to run out of material, the stories strayed further and further from actual events. One episode even had the Commies plotting to undermine the U.S. guided-missile program by converting vacuum cleaners into bomb launchers.

This type of topical politico-drama was by no means new. Several popular radio series during World War II depicted scheming Nazis infiltrating the U.S., and there had already been a movie (1951) and a radio series (1952) titled *I Was A Communist for the F.B.I.*, based on a story similar to Philbrick's. Then too, many viewers, especially younger ones (including this writer), saw it as simply a good detective yarn with lots of suspense and no real political overtones at all. The very fact that it was on television, surrounded by all kinds of adventure fantasies, encouraged this attitude.

As for those involved in the series, they saw the program primarily as a profit-maker. "We're not trying to deliver a message," stated the production company, Ziv. "That's not our field. Our chief purpose is to find good story properties, turn them into good films, and sell them." Richard Carlson, when queried, invariably rattled off the financial advantages (he got a piece of the profits) and the benefits of a filmed series in allowing him time for other pursuits. "I'm just an actor," he insisted. "Philbrick is the guy who made the contribution, not me." Still, he admitted, he did see it as a "public service." Virginia Stefan expressed amazement at the seriousness with which some viewers took the show. "It's hard to believe, but people actually write us and ask us to investigate Communists in their neighborhood." The letters were turned over to the FBI.

Most politically motivated was author Philbrick, whose new career as a lecturer and writer on the Communist menace was boosted no end by this hit series. Philbrick continued to lecture for many years, and put out a newsletter from Washington, D.C.

Whatever the motives of those involved, *I Led Three Lives* was one of the major syndicated hits of television history. Breweries were its most frequent sponsors, but oil and steel companies, banks and utilities felt that it was an excellent public-service program for their patriotic "image" advertising and continued to sponsor reruns well into the 1960s. Today, however, *I Led Three Lives* is simply an especially interesting reflection of a very different time.

I LOVE LUCY (*Situation Comedy*)
FIRST TELECAST: *October 15, 1951*
LAST TELECAST: *September 24, 1961*
BROADCAST HISTORY:

Oct 1951–Jun 1957, CBS Mon 9:00–9:30 (OS)
Apr 1955–Oct 1955, CBS Sun 6:00–630
Oct 1955–Apr 1956, CBS Sat 6:30–7:00
Sep 1957–May 1958, CBS Wed 7:30–8:00
Jul 1958–Sep 1958, CBS Mon 9:00–9:30
Oct 1958–May 1959, CBS Thu 7:30–8:00
Jul 1959–Sep 1959, CBS Fri 8:30–9:00
Sep 1961, CBS Sun 6:30–7:00

CAST:

Lucy Ricardo .... Lucille Ball
Ricky Ricardo .... Desi Arnaz
Ethel Mertz .... Vivian Vance
Fred Mertz .... William Frawley
Little Ricky Ricardo (1956–1957) .... Richard Keith
**Jerry, the agent (1951–1954)* .... Jerry Hausner
**Mrs. Mathilda Trumbull (1953–1956)*
.... Elizabeth Patterson
**Caroline Appleby (1953–1957)* ..... Doris Singleton
**Mrs. MacGillicuddy (1955–1956)* ..... Kathryn Card
Betty Ramsey (1957) .... Mary Jane Croft
Ralph Ramsey (1957) .... Frank Nelson

*Occasional

THEME:

"I Love Lucy," by Harold Adamson and Eliot Daniel

Lucille Ball had spent three seasons on CBS radio as the female lead in the situation comedy *My Favorite Husband* when she decided to give the new medium, television, a try. In her radio role as Liz Cooper, she perfected many of the mannerisms that she would use in *I Love Lucy*, including the scatterbrained quality and the loud crying fits when things weren't going her way. CBS was enthusiastic about the concept of the show, but the network nabobs had two major objections—they were positive nobody would believe Desi was her husband (despite the fact that they were married in real life), and they wanted the show done live from New York, like most of the other early television comedies. Lucy was determined to use Desi and had no desire to commute from Hollywood to New York for the show. In the summer of 1950 the two of them went on tour performing before live audiences to prove that Desi was believable as her husband, and early in 1951 they produced a film pilot for the series with $5,000 of their own money. The pilot convinced the CBS brass that they had something special and *I Love Lucy* was given a berth on the fall schedule.

The premise of *I Love Lucy* was not that much different from that of other family situation comedies on television and radio—a wacky wife making life difficult for a loving but perpetually irritated husband—but the people involved made it something very special. Lucy Ricardo was an American of Scottish ancestry (maiden name MacGillicuddy) married to a Cuban bandleader. Husband Ricky was employed at the Tropicana Club and since she was constantly trying to prove to him that she could be in show business too, he spent much of his time trying to keep Lucy off the nightclub's stage. Ricky just wanted her to be a simple housewife. Whenever he became particularly exasperated with one of her schemes, Ricky's already broken English would degenerate into a stream of Spanish epithets. The Tropicana Club was in Manhattan, and so was the Ricardo apartment, in a middle-class building in the East Sixties where their neighbors, best friends, and landlords were Fred and Ethel Mertz. Lucy's partner in mischief was Ethel, and both Ricky and Fred had to endure the foolishness perpetrated by their wives.

I Love Lucy was an immediate smash hit and, during its six years in originals, never ranked lower than third in popularity among all television programs. The plots, by series creator and producer Jess Oppenheimer and writers Madelyn Pugh and Bob Carroll, Jr., were superb, the gags were inventive, and Lucy's clowning the *pièce de résistance* that took *I Love Lucy* beyond the realm of other contemporary comedies. As wacky as she was, audiences could emphathize with and adore her. Watching *I Love Lucy* in the early 1950s became as much a part of life as watching Milton Berle's *Texaco Star Theater* had been in the late 1940s. It was a national event when, on January 19, 1953, Lucy Ricardo gave birth to little Ricky on the air, the same night that Lucille Ball gave birth to her second child, Desiderio Alberto Arnaz IV.

Over the years, within the context of the show, Ricky became more successful. He got a movie offer that prompted a cross-country trip by car, with the Mertzes, during the 1954–1955 season. During the 1955–1956 season they took a trip to Europe, also with the Mertzes, and at the start of the 1956–1957 season Ricky opened his own club, the Ricky Ricardo Babaloo Club. He had also gotten a TV show and, with his good fortune, bought a country home in Connecticut early in 1957. (See *Lucy in Connecticut* for complete description.) It was also during the 1956–1957 season that Little Ricky was added to the regular cast. He had been played on a very occasional basis in the previous seasons by a pair of infant twins, Joseph David Mayer and Michael Lee Mayer. Also seen on an irregular basis over the years were Ricky's agent Jerry, the Ricardos' elderly neighbor Mrs Trumbull, Lucy's snooty friend Caroline Appleby, and Mrs. MacGillicuddy, Lucy's mother.

Everyone has certain favorite episodes of *I Love Lucy*, and there were so many memorable ones that trying to cite the "best" is particularly difficult. Even CBS executives had problems doing it. During the summer of 1958 there was a collection of reruns titled *The Top Ten Lucy Shows*—there were 13 different episodes in that "top 10." There was the show in which Lucy maneuvered her way onto Ricky's TV show to do a health-tonic commercial, and got drunk sampling the high-alcohol-content product. There was the time she tried to bake her own bread, and was pinned to the far wall in her kitchen when the loaf—into which she had thrown two entire packages of yeast—was released from the oven. While looking for souvenirs to take back to New York from their trip to Hollywood, Lucy and Ethel tried to pry loose the block of cement with John Wayne's footprints from in front of Grauman's Chinese Theatre. There was the time Lucy tried to get into Ricky's nightclub show by impersonating a clown. When they were going to be interviewed on the TV show *Face to Face* they almost got into a fight with the Mertzes because Ricky's new agent wanted them to move into a classier apartment. The messiest episode, however, had to be one that was part of their trip to Europe. Lucy had been offered a minor role in a film by an Italian producer and, in an effort to absorb atmosphere, ended up in a vat of unpressed grapes fighting with a professional grape stomper.

The success of *I Love Lucy* is unparalleled in the history of television. The decision to film it, rather than do it live, made it possible to have a high-quality print of each episode available for endless rebroadcasts, as opposed to the poor-quality kinescopes of live shows. The reruns, sold to independent stations after *I Love Lucy* left the network, and translated into virtually every language for foreign distribution, made millions. This set the pattern for all of television. The appeal of reusable filmed programs, all started by *I Love Lucy*, eventually resulted in the shift of television production from New York, where it had all started, to Hollywood, where the film facilities were. *I Love Lucy* was practically unique in that it was filmed before a live audience, something that did not become widespread in the situation comedy world until the 1970s, and the technique of simultaneously using three cameras during the filming to allow for editing of the finished product was also a *Lucy* first.

By the end of the 1956–1957 season, despite the fact it was still the number-one program in all of television, *I Love Lucy* ceased production as a weekly series. For the two years prior to the suspension of production, both Lucy and Desi had been seeking to cut down on their workload. They finally succeeded. After the fall of 1957 there was no *I Love Lucy*, but there were a number of *Lucille Ball–Desi Arnaz Shows*, full-hour specials about the continuing travels and tribulations of the Ricardos and the Mertzes. Reruns of *I Love Lucy* had aired during the summer of 1955 as *The Sunday Lucy Show* and during the

1955–1956 season on Saturdays as *The Lucy Show.* With the original show out of production, prime-time reruns of *I Love Lucy* were aired for another two years on CBS, showed up briefly in 1961, and ran in daytime on CBS until 1967. The syndicated reruns have been running continuously ever since, and there is no end in sight.

I LOVE TO EAT (*Cooking*)

FIRST TELECAST: *August 30, 1946*

LAST TELECAST: *May 18, 1947*

BROADCAST HISTORY:

Aug 1946–Oct 1946, NBC Fri 8:15–8:30 (approximately)
Nov 1946–Mar 1947, NBC Fri 8:30–8:45
Apr 1947–May 1947, NBC Thu 8:30–9:00

HOST:

James Beard

This Borden-sponsored program opened with a sketch of Elsie, the famed Borden cow. Then James Beard took over to demonstrate the preparation of some of his unique dishes for the television audience. Beard's cooking demonstrations were seen earlier as a segment of NBC-TV's *Radio City Matinee.*

I MARRIED DORA (*Situation Comedy*)

FIRST TELECAST: *September 22, 1987*

LAST TELECAST: *August 19, 1988*

BROADCAST HISTORY:

Sep 1987, ABC Tue 9:30–10:00
Sep 1987–Jan 1988, ABC Fri 8:30–9:00
May 1988–Aug 1988, ABC Fri 9:30–10:00

CAST:

Peter Farrell .... Daniel Hugh-Kelly
Dora Calderon .... Elizabeth Pena
Kate Farrell (age 13) .... Juliette Lewis
Will Farrell (11) .... Jason Horst
Hughes Whitney Lennox .... Henry Jones
Dolf Menninger .... Sanford Jensen
Marisol Calderon .... Evelyn Guerrero

This short-lived sitcom wins the Trivia Award both for the most outrageous premise of 1987, and for the most bizarre final episode. The idea, you see, was that busy Los Angeles architect and single dad Peter was faced with the loss of his efficient young housekeeper, a Central American refugee named Dora. The feds had discovered that she was an illegal alien and were about to deport her. So Peter, ever the practical type, married her—so that she could continue to be his maid. "No love," he kept reassuring her, "this is just a formality." Dora, a feisty young woman who assumed she would be shot if she were sent back to her native country, went along.

When it was pointed out to ABC that marrying an alien for the purpose of avoiding deportation was a direct violation of U.S. law, the network nonchalantly inserted a full-screen announcement in the premiere episode; it stated that what the series was depicting constituted a federal offense, and then helpfully added "You should not try this in your own home"! Peter (who apparently did not see the notice) then proceeded to marry Dora, while the laugh track roared. So much for love and legality.

Looking on were Peter's young kids Kate and Will, who really liked Dora and thought it was all a neat idea, legal or not. Mr. Lennox was Peter's doddering boss at the office, and Marisol was Dora's occasionally seen sister.

I Married Dora had a short run, and one of TV history's most surprising final episodes. In the last original telecast Peter received a lucrative offer for a two-year job in Bahrein, packed his bags, and prepared to leave Dora and the family. Dora pleaded with him not to go and couldn't believe he'd actually get on the plane, but he did. Then, to everyone's surprise, he got off again.

Peter: "It's been canceled."

Dora: "The flight?"

Peter: "No, our series!"

The camera then pulled back, revealing the stage and crew as everyone waved goodbye to the few remaining viewers. Now that's how a failed sitcom *should* end!

I MARRIED JOAN (*Situation Comedy*)

FIRST TELECAST: *October 15, 1952*

LAST TELECAST: *April 6, 1955*

BROADCAST HISTORY:

Oct 1952–Apr 1955, NBC Wed 8:00–8:30

CAST:

Joan Stevens .... Joan Davis
Judge Bradley Stevens .... Jim Backus
Minerva Parker (1952–1953) .... Hope Emerson
Beverly (1953–1955) .... Beverly Wills
Mabel (1953–1954) .... Geraldine Carr
Janet Tobin (1954–1955) .... Sheila Bromley
Kerwin Tobin (1954–1955) .... Dan Tobin

Bradley Stevens served as a judge in domestic court. Each episode opened with Judge Stevens on the bench. In the course of trying to resolve the problems of those who came before him, he would explain to them how he had dealt with a similar type of problem with his own beloved but slightly wacky wife, Joan. As he started to tell the story, the courtroom scene would fade into his home and the situation would be enacted. During the first season, Joan's next-door neighbor and partner-in-mischief was Minerva Parker. The following two seasons Joan Davis's real daughter was the only other regular in the cast, playing the part of Joan Stevens's much younger college-student sister, Beverly. Mabel and Janet, two of Joan's friends, also turned up frequently during the next two years.

I REMEMBER MAMA, see *Mama*

I SPY (*Adventure/Espionage*)

FIRST TELECAST: *September 15, 1965*

LAST TELECAST: *September 2, 1968*

BROADCAST HISTORY:

Sep 1965–Sep 1967, NBC Wed 10:00–11:00
Sep 1967–Sep 1968, NBC Mon 10:00–11:00

CAST:

Kelly Robinson .... Robert Culp
Alexander Scott .... Bill Cosby

I Spy was a departure from the traditional type of show about espionage. Both of its leads were realistically conceived characters and could see the humor in situations, enabling them to have fun with their work. It had its share of cloak-and-dagger action, but never took itself too seriously. Comedian Bill Cosby, who provided much of the subtle humor in the show, proved he was an accomplished serious actor and had the added distinction of being the first black performer to have a starring role in a regular dramatic series on American television.

Kelly Robinson and Alexander Scott were a team of American agents. The cover used by Kelly was that of a top-seeded tennis player traveling around the world for tournaments. A former law student at Princeton, he had played on two Davis Cup teams. Alexander Scott's cover was as trainer and traveling companion to Robinson. A graduate of Temple and a Rhodes scholar, his knowledge of languages was often useful in dealing with people all over the world. Both of them were dedicated to government service and America, but their dedication did not stop them from often questioning the motives and purposes behind some of the maneuvers in which they were involved. Their casual approach to life, and job, was a very refreshing contrast to the nature of their work.

Filmed on location in such cities as Hong Kong, Acapulco, Las Vegas, Marrakesh, Rome, and Tokyo, among others.

I WITNESS VIDEO (*Audience Participation*)
FIRST TELECAST: *August 16, 1992*
LAST TELECAST: *July 10, 1994*
BROADCAST HISTORY:
Aug 1992–Sep 1993, NBC Sun 8:00–9:00
Sep 1993–Mar 1994, NBC Sun 7:00–8:00
May 1994–Jul 1994, NBC Sun 7:00–8:00
HOST:
Patrick Van Horn (1992–1993)
John Forsythe (1993–1994)

"Reality" show focusing on real-life violence, disaster, and calamities, using home videotapes submitted by viewers and interviews with those involved. Among the shaky tapes lovingly played, and replayed, were those of hostage situations, thievery, brutal baby-sitters, tidal waves, earthquakes, firestorms, and a circus elephant gone berserk. *I Witness Video* was first seen as a series of six specials between February and May 1992. NBC received a certain amount of criticism at the time for the show's obsessive violence but nevertheless scheduled it as a regular series in Sunday "family viewing time"—opposite the decidedly lighter *America's Funniest Home Videos* on ABC—for the next two years.

ICE PALACE (*Musical Variety*)
FIRST TELECAST: *May 23, 1971*
LAST TELECAST: *July 25, 1971*
BROADCAST HISTORY:
May 1971–Jul 1971, CBS Sun 10:00–11:00

Each week the cast was different but the format remained the same: a guest celebrity host, one or two featured musical or comedy acts, and a selection of performers from the Ice Capades. Everything was tied to and revolved around the skating acts, which made this variety series somewhat different from most.

ICHABOD AND ME (*Situation Comedy*)
FIRST TELECAST: *September 26, 1961*
LAST TELECAST: *September 18, 1962*
BROADCAST HISTORY:
Sep 1961–Sep 1962, CBS Tue 9:30–10:00
CAST:
Robert Major .... Robert Sterling
Ichabod Adams .... George Chandler
Abigail Adams .... Christine White
Benjie Major .... Jimmy Mathers
Aunt Lavinia .... Reta Shaw
Jonathan Baylor .... Jimmy Hawkins
Martin Perkins .... Guy Raymond
Olaf .... Burt Mustin
Colby .... Forrest Lewis

Tiring of the rat race of newspaper work in New York City, reporter Bob Major bought the only paper in a small rural town called Phippsboro, and moved there with his six-year-old son, Benjie. The man from whom Bob had purchased the paper, and who still owned most of the town, was Ichabod Adams. Ichabod still kept his finger in the operation of the paper, while his attractive young daughter Abigail kept her eye on the highly eligible Mr. Major. Bob, a widower, spent most of his time winding down to the snail's pace of Phippsboro and of the small *Phippsboro Bulletin*.

I'D LIKE TO SEE (*Demonstration*)
FIRST TELECAST: *November 5, 1948*
LAST TELECAST: *March 29, 1949*
BROADCAST HISTORY:
Nov 1948–Dec 1948, NBC Fri 9:00–9:30
Dec 1948–Mar 1949, NBC Tue 9:00–9:30
HOST:
Ray Morgan
REGULAR:
Kuda Bux (Jan–Mar)

Viewer-participation program, which was the prototype for the long-running DuMont/ABC series *You Asked for It* (1950–1959). Viewers were asked to write in suggestions for unusual places or things they would like to see, and these were then presented via a combination of films and live studio demonstrations. The first show, for example, included scenes of the United Nations building, an Edgar Bergar–Charlie McCarthy routine, and film clips of presidents of the U.S. from McKinley to Truman. In January Indian performer Kuda Bux, "the man with the X-ray vision," was added as a regular and viewers were asked what feats they would like to see him perform blindfolded.

IDENTIFY (*Quiz*)
FIRST TELECAST: *February 14, 1949*
LAST TELECAST: *May 9, 1949*
BROADCAST HISTORY:
Feb 1949–May 1949, ABC Mon 9:00–9:15
HOST:
Bob Elson

This short-lived sports picture quiz originated in Chicago. Each week three contestants attempted to identify scenes from the sports world, through films, drawings, and photographs.

IDIOT BOX, THE (*Comedy*)
BROADCAST HISTORY:
MTV
30 minutes
Produced: *1991*
Premiered: *March 23, 1991*
HOST:
Alex Winter

An offbeat, late-night sketch comedy series in which Winter and his cohorts depicted a range of characters, such as a rock accountant and an electronic announcer.

IDIOT SAVANTS (*Quiz/Audience Participation*)
BROADCAST HISTORY:
MTV
30 minutes
Produced: *1996–1997*
Premiered: *December 9, 1996*
HOST:
Greg Fitzsimmons
Early-evening quiz show in which four college-age contestants were asked pop culture questions by a wiseguy host. The questions could be tough or goofy. The best, perhaps, was when a current rock video was played and contestants were challenged to actually understand the lyrics.

IF NOT FOR YOU (*Situation Comedy*)
FIRST TELECAST: *September 18, 1995*
LAST TELECAST: *October 9, 1995*
BROADCAST HISTORY:
Sep 1995–Oct 1995, CBS Mon 9:30–10:00
CAST:
Jessie Kent .... Elizabeth McGovern
Craig Schaeffer .... Hank Azaria
Eileen .... Debra Jo Rupp
Cal .... Jim Turner
Bobby Beaumont .... Reno Wilson
Elliot .... Peter Krause
Melanie .... Jane Sibbett
Love is not always easy to understand. Audio-book producer Jessie was engaged to Elliot, a brooding architect. Record producer Craig was engaged to neurotic singer Melanie. When Jessie and Craig first saw each other at a Chinese restaurant while with their respective fiancés, there was an instant attraction. The next day they found they were working in the same Minneapolis recording studio, Gopher Records, and they began to wonder whether they were engaged to the right people. Also working at the studio were Eileen, who did voices for airport warnings, and Cal, a flaky sound engineer. Bobby, a friend of Craig's, was an aspiring singer and composer who turned everything into a song.

By the fourth episode Jessie and Craig had told their fiancés that they were in love with each other, but the series was canceled before their romance had a chance to develop.

IF YOU HAD A MILLION, syndicated title for *The Millionaire*

IGOR CASSINI SHOW, THE (*Interview*)
FIRST TELECAST: *October 25, 1953*
LAST TELECAST: *March 3, 1954*
BROADCAST HISTORY:
Oct 1953–Jan 1954, DUM Sun 6:00–6:30
Jan 1954–Mar 1954, DUM Sun 6:15–6:30
HOST:
Igor Cassini
Igor Cassini, who as Cholly Knickerbocker wrote a society gossip column for the Hearst papers, hosted this interview program which was filmed in the homes of the guests. Typical of Cassini's guests was his first, Mrs. Gwen Cafritz, Washington's leading hostess. Society and literary types made up the bulk of the interviews. Cassini also reviewed current films and plays. The program was also known as *Exclusively Yours.*

I'LL FLY AWAY (*Legal Drama*)
FIRST TELECAST: *October 7, 1991*
LAST TELECAST: *February 5, 1993*
BROADCAST HISTORY:
Oct 1991, NBC Mon 8:00–10:00
Oct 1991–Jan 1992, NBC Tue 8:00–9:00
Feb 1992–May 1992, NBC Fri 9:00–10:00
Aug 1992–Feb 1993, NBC Fri 10:00–11:00
CAST:
D. A. Forrest Bedford .... Sam Waterston
Nathan Bedford (age 16) .... Jeremy London
Francie Bedford (13) .... Ashlee Levitch
John Morgan Bedford (6) .... John Aaron Bennett
Lilly Harper .... Regina Taylor
Christina LeKatzis .... Kathryn Harrold
Paul Slocum .... Peter Simmons
Coach Zollicofer Weed .... Brad Sullivan
Judge Lake Stevens (Uncle Lake) (1991–1992)
.... Ed Grady
Lewis Coleman .... Bill Cobbs
Tucker Anderson .... Scott Paulin
Parkie Sasser (1992) .... Amy Ryan
Critics cooed on cue over this well-meaning, but languid, drama about race relations in the South during the late 1950s. Forrest Bedford was the conservative, gentlemanly prosecuting attorney in the town of Bryland, perplexed by the changes going on around him as blacks began to seek their rights after generations of denial. He also had problems at home. His wife was in a mental institution, leaving him to care for three kids: moody teenage hunk Nathan; spirited, studious Francie; and lonely little John Morgan. Then Lilly arrived to become their new black housekeeper. In her quiet, yet intelligent, way she began to open their eyes to the people they didn't quite understand. While no revolutionary, Lilly quietly joined the sit-in on Forrest's courthouse steps and worked for voter registration. She was also a surrogate mom of sorts for the Bedford children, especially John Morgan, who asked wide-eyed questions about why the black people were different. Forrest, meanwhile, put his angst aside long enough to begin a campaign for State Attorney General.

Despite the fury of the times, the confrontations in Bryland were generally low-key, and everything moved very slowly. (Even a rave reviewer admitted that watching Waterston act was "like watching water drip.") Adding a little energy were Christina, the attractive local defense attorney with eyes for Forrest, and Zollicofer, Nathan's maniacal wrestling coach. Slocum was Nathan's wrong-side-of-the-tracks best friend and Lewis was Lilly's father, a former player in the Negro Baseball League. Stories included the death of Forrest's wife, Gwen; his appointment as U.S. Attorney; the pregnancy of Slocum's girlfriend, Parkie, which ended in his trial when she accused him of rape, and several racially motivated murder cases.

Despite the critical praise, and vocal fans, *I'll Fly Away* drew small audiences and was eventually canceled by NBC. In an unusual development PBS then produced a two-hour movie wrapping up many of the story lines, which aired on the public network on October 11, 1993. In it, 60-year-old Lilly, now a successful author, thumbed through her scrapbook, recalling for her grandson the tumultuous years of the early 1960s. She then returned to Bryland to visit doddering old Forrest and learn the fate of her former friends and employers.

Filmed on location in and around Atlanta.

ILONA MASSEY SHOW, THE (*Music*)

FIRST TELECAST: *November 1, 1954*
LAST TELECAST: *January 3, 1955*
BROADCAST HISTORY:
Nov 1954–Jan 1955, DUM Mon 8:00–8:30
REGULARS:
Ilona Massey
Irving Fields Trio

Hungarian-born movie actress Ilona Massey sang sultry ballads in a nightclub atmosphere in this short-lived musical show. The Irving Fields Trio provided instrumental backing to her intimate song styling.

I'M A BIG GIRL NOW (*Situation Comedy*)

FIRST TELECAST: *October 31, 1980*
LAST TELECAST: *July 24, 1981*
BROADCAST HISTORY:
Oct 1980–Jul 1981, ABC Fri 8:30–9:00
CAST:
Diana Cassidy .... Diana Canova
Dr. Benjamin Douglass .... Danny Thomas
Rebecca "Becky" Cassidy .... Rori King
Walter Douglass .... Michael Durrell
Neal Stryker .... Martin Short
Karen Hawks .... Deborah Baltzell
Edie McKendrick .... Sheree North
THEME:
"I'm a Big Girl Now," by George Aliceson Tipton and Leslie Bricusse, sung by Diana Canova

Danny Thomas returned to television in this gentle father-daughter comedy. He was Dr. Benjamin Douglass, a cantankerous dentist made all the more so by the fact that his wife had just run off to Spain with his partner, Ira. At the same time his pretty daughter, Diana, divorced her husband. Both a bit shell-shocked, father and daughter decided to live under the same roof for a while, for mutual support. The problem was for *her* to convince *him* she wasn't his little girl anymore, and to stop trying to run her life. Since they were both dating from time to time, she had some ammunition. With them was Diana's cute little scene-stealing seven-year-old daughter, Becky. Walter was Benjamin's neurotic son; and Edie, the hyper-tense boss at the research institute where Diana worked, in downtown Washington, D.C.

I'M DICKENS—HE'S FENSTER (*Situation Comedy*)

FIRST TELECAST: *September 28, 1962*
LAST TELECAST: *September 13, 1963*
BROADCAST HISTORY:
Sep 1962–Sep 1963, ABC Fri 9:00–9:30
CAST:
Arch Fenster .... Marty Ingels
Harry Dickens .... John Astin
Kate Dickens .... Emmaline Henry
Mel Warshaw .... Dave Ketchum
Mulligan .... Henry Beckman
Myron Bannister .... Frank DeVol

Comedy bordering on the slapstick with Dickens and Fenster, two carpenter–construction workers who were constantly getting into dangerous situations on and off the job. Single Arch Fenster was the more scatterbrained of the two, married Harry Dickens the responsible one. Warshaw and Mulligan were friends on the job. Bandleader Frank DeVol portrayed the balding building contractor in this series.

I'M THE LAW (*Police Drama*)

BROADCAST HISTORY:
Syndicated only
30 minutes
Produced: *1952–1953* (26 episodes)
Released: Early 1953
CAST:
Lt. George Kirby .... George Raft

Movie tough guy George Raft, who portrayed criminals in most of his screen roles, was a tough New York City police lieutenant in this syndicated series. There were a lot of fistfights and shoot-outs as he tracked down murderers and thieves all over the city, from the waterfront to Central Park. Raft also served as narrator.

Also known (incorrectly) as *I Am the Law*.

IMAGINE THAT (*Situation Comedy*)

FIRST TELECAST: *January 8, 2002*
LAST TELECAST: *January 15, 2002*
BROADCAST HISTORY:
Jan 2002, NBC Tue 8:00–8:30
CAST:
Josh Miller .... Hank Azaria
Wendy Miller .... Jayne Brook
Kenny Fleck .... Joshua Malina
Rina Oh .... Suzy Nakamura
Tabitha Applethorpe .... Julia Schultz
Barb Thompson .... Katey Sagal
Dr. Jule Berman .... Max Baker

Television looked to itself for comedy, and canceled what it saw almost immediately, in this "insider" sitcom. Josh was a comedy writer for an unnamed TV show who was having marital problems with his high-powered lawyer wife, so he reflected them in his skits. His best ideas, unfortunately, were promptly stolen by his megalomaniac boss, Barb. Others at work were his hyper young writing partner, Kenny, sarcastic Asian Rina and bossy Tabitha. Dr. Berman was Josh and Wendy's marriage counselor.

IMMORTAL, THE (*Adventure*)

FIRST TELECAST: *September 24, 1970*
LAST TELECAST: *September 8, 1971*
BROADCAST HISTORY:
Sep 1970–Jan 1971, ABC Thu 10:00–11:00
May 1971–Sep 1971, ABC Wed 9:30–10:30
CAST:
Ben Richards .... Christopher George
Fletcher .... Don Knight
Arthur Maitland .... David Brian
Sylvia Cartwright .... Carol Lynley

Handsome racing driver Ben Richards seemed to have everything in this adventure series, youth, health—and immortality. That last attribute was due to some peculiar antibodies in his blood which made him immune to disease or aging. Immortality was something that a lot of people wanted for their own purposes, however, so Richards was constantly pursued, principally by ruthless billionaire Arthur Maitland and his henchman Fletcher. Like *The Fugitive*, this was essentially a "chase" show, as Richards kept one step ahead of his relentless pursuers while living the life of a footloose young racing driver. Maitland and Ben's fiancée, Sylvia, were seen only occasionally in this series.

The Immortal was based on a TV movie aired in 1969, starring George.

IMMORTAL, THE (*Science Fiction*)

BROADCAST HISTORY:

Syndicated only
60 minutes
Produced: *2000–2001* (22 episodes)
Released: *October 2000*

CAST:

Raphael "Rafe" Cain .... Lorenzo Lamas
Dr. Sara Beckman .... April Telek
Goodwin .... Steve Braun
**Yashiro* .... Robert Ito
**Mallos* .... Dominic Keating
**Vashista* .... Kira Clavell

*Occasional

Sara was a paranormal physicist specializing in psychokinetic exploration who had invented a sonic transmitter that attracted demons—and an immortal demon hunter named Rafe. Rafe and his partner, Goodwin, traveled around the country in a large bus, which served as their office and home, and, after their first encounter, Sara became a member of Rafe's team. Demons had killed Rafe's wife and stolen his child, and his destiny as "the chosen one" was to hunt them down and destroy them. When he "killed" a demon, it lay twitching and was swallowed into a vortex to Hell. Goodwin had also been made an immortal with Rafe when they were given their mission by Rafe's mentor, Yashiro, in 1638. As with *Highlander* and *Forever Knight*, there were flashbacks to earlier times, most often to the period immediately after his wife's murder when Yashiro was giving him guidance. Also, as with *Highlander*, Rafe could sense when demons were nearby. Mallos was the evil demon leader who showed up periodically, and Vashista was his sexy lover/assistant.

In the series finale Rafe, Sara, and Goodwin came upon Rafe's now-teenage daughter Kiyomi (Melia McClure) lying on the sand. She couldn't remember anything that had happened to her since her disappearance three centuries earlier when she had been a child. Mallos needed to marry Kiyomi in order to carry out his plan for world domination. Vashista had raised Kiyomi in the Beyond, and still cared about her. She made a deal with Rafe to kill Mallos so that she and Kiyomi could be together. Kiyomi was lured to the building where the wedding was to take place, and Rafe, who followed, was captured by Mallos. Sara and Goodwin came to the rescue, and Vashista freed Rafe, who sent Mallos back to Hell and recovered his daughter. At the episode's end, however, Vashista appeared to Kiyomi and told her that her reunion with her father was only temporary.

IMOGENE COCA SHOW, THE (*Comedy/Variety*)

FIRST TELECAST: *October 2, 1954*
LAST TELECAST: *June 25, 1955*
BROADCAST HISTORY:

Oct 1954–Jun 1955, NBC Sat 9:00–9:30

REGULARS:

Betty Crane .... Imogene Coca
Helen Milliken (1955) .... Bibi Osterwald
Jerry Crane (1955) .... Hal March
Harry Milliken (1955) .... David Burns

MUSIC:

The Carl Hoff Orchestra

The Imogene Coca Show never quite figured out what it wanted to be. Initially it went on the air as a situation comedy with Miss Coca essentially playing herself as an actress whose comic adventures in "real life," away from the TV cameras, formed the basis for stories. After only two weeks in this format, the show was altered to become a comedy-variety show with sketches, production numbers, and guest stars. On February 19, 1955, the format was overhauled again. It was now a situation comedy about a newlywed couple, the Cranes, and the adventures they had with their neighbors, the Millikens. All the changes and tinkering with format never gave the show a solid audience and it was canceled at the end of its first season.

IN A HEARTBEAT (*Drama*)

BROADCAST HISTORY:

Disney Channel
30 minutes
Original episodes: *2000–2001* (21 episodes)
Premiered: *August 26, 2000*

CAST:

Hank Beecham .... Danso Gordon
Tyler Connell .... Shawn Ashmore
Val Lanier .... Reagan Pasternak
Jamie Waite .... Christopher Ralph
Caitie Roth .... Jackie Rosenbaum
Brooke Lanier (age 12) .... Lauren Collins
Dr. Alex Freeman .... Kevin Hicks

Four teens trained to become E.M.T.'s (emergency medical technicians) in this rather edgy drama, which was based on a true story. Members of the squad were Hank, the oldest and most responsible; easygoing dreamboat Tyler, a football player; black cheerleader Val, who had a crush on Tyler; and trouble-prone rebel Jamie, who was on probation for larceny and serving his time with the E.M.T. squad. Dr. Alex, their hard-driving boss, wanted to be rid of him. Brooke was Val's super-organized little sister, who helped Dr. Alex with his paperwork; Caitie was Val's slothful friend, dressed all in black (Tyler referred to her as "the Goth Sloth"). The setting was the town of Kingsport.

In addition to the usual angst of high school puppy loves and jealousies, these teen super-achievers had to deal with home problems (divorced or squabbling parents, siblings in trouble), plus beepers going off calling them to the next medical emergency.

IN CONCERT, see *ABC Late Night* and *ABC In Concert*

IN-FISHERMAN TELEVISION (*Fishing*)

BROADCAST HISTORY:

The Nashville Network
30 minutes
Produced: *1995–*
Premiered: *January 7, 1996*

HOST:

Al Lindner

In-Fisherman magazine, "the journal of freshwater fishing," produced this Sunday night instructional program seen on TNN.

IN-LAWS (*Situation Comedy*)
FIRST TELECAST: *September 24, 2002*
LAST TELECAST: *January 28, 2003*
BROADCAST HISTORY:
Sep 2002–Oct 2002, NBC Tue 8:00–8:30
Nov 2002–Jan 2003, NBC Tue 8:30–9:00
CAST:
Victor Pellet .... Dennis Farina
Marlene Pellet.......................... Jean Smart
Matt Landis............................ Elon Gold
Alex Pellet Landis .... Bonnie Somerville

Victor was a self-made man, the gruff owner of a security business who now lived in a palatial home in the suburbs. Life was just the way he wanted it—he didn't have to work much, and he even got to use his uniformed guards as gofers. Then his beloved daughter Alex moved back in with her new husband, Matt, a nerdy cooking school student, so they could save money while he completed his education. What Matt got was an education in dealing with in-laws. Bossy Victor sniped at him constantly, periodically demanding "private convo time" to straighten out his new son-in-law. Stylish mom-in-law Marlene was pretty much occupied with her own life, which alternated between shopping and starting a new career as a real estate agent. Perky Alex was the chief peacemaker between the two men in the household, playing the "daddy's little girl" card to get Victor to calm down.

Supposedly "based on the comedy of Elon Gold," *In-Laws* was coproduced by Kelsey Grammer.

IN LIVING COLOR (*Comedy/Variety*)
FIRST TELECAST: *April 15, 1990*
LAST TELECAST: *August 25, 1994*
BROADCAST HISTORY:
Apr 1990, FOX Sun 9:30–10:00
Apr 1990–May 1990, FOX Sat 9:00–9:30
May 1990–Aug 1990, FOX Sun 9:30–10:00
Sep 1990–Mar 1992, FOX Sun 8:00–8:30
Mar 1992–Apr 1992, FOX Sun 8:30–9:00
Apr 1992–Aug 1993, FOX Sun 8:00–8:30
Dec 1992–Aug 1994, FOX Thu 9:00–9:30
Oct 1993, FOX Mon–Fri 11:00–12:00 A.M.
Nov 1993–Jan 1994, FOX Mon–Fri 11:30–12:00 A.M.
REGULARS:
Keenen Ivory Wayans (1990–1992)
James Carrey
Kelly Coffield (1990–1993)
Kim Coles (1990)
Tommy Davidson
David Alan Grier
T'Keyah "Crystal" Keymah
Damon Wayans (1990–1992)
Kim Wayans (1990–1993)
S. W. Wayans (Shawn) (1990–1993)
Steve Park (1991–1992)
Jamie Foxx (1991–1994)
Marlon Wayans (1992–1993)
Alexandra Wentworth (1992–1994)
Twist (Leroy Casey) (1992–1994)
Anne-Marie Johnson(1993–1994)
Jay Leggett (1993–1994)
Chris Rock (1993–1994)
Carol Rosenthal (1993–1994)
Marc Wilmore (1993–1994)
Reggie McFadden (1993–1994)
The Fly Girls
CHOREOGRAPHER
Carla Earle (1990)
Rosie Perez (1990–1993)
Arthur Rainer (1993–1994)

The multitalented Keenen Ivory Wayans—writer, producer, actor, comedian—was the driving force behind this comedy-variety series that was, in many respects, a mostly black *Saturday Night Live.* The show featured biting satirical parodies of movies, TV series, commercials, celebrities, people in the news, and black stereotypes. Among the recurring sketches were "Men on Film," gay movie critics Blaine Edwards and Antoine Mayweather ("Two snaps up!"); "Hey Mon," the trials and tribulations of the Hedleys, a hard-working West Indian family in which everyone had at least six jobs; "The Buttmans," a family with buttocks instead of foreheads (you can imagine the jokes); "The Home Boys," Wiz and Ice, two young black scam artist/thieves ("Mo' money, mo' money, mo' money!"); Homey, the cynical nasty clown ("Homey don't play that!"); Anton Jackson, the spaced-out wino; Handi-Man, the handicapped superhero (with Debbie Lee Carrington as The Tiny Avenger in later sketches); and caricatures of Arsenio Hall and Oprah Winfrey.

In Living Color was a fast-paced show featuring a versatile repertory cast—including four of Keenen's nine siblings—and an energetic group of five dancers known as The Fly Girls (one of whom was actress Jennifer Lopez). Jim Carrey was the WASPy young white guy who sometimes played the stooge. Most episodes ended with a live song performed by a guest rap singer or group. Keenen's kid brother Shawn, whose previous role was as the show's DJ, SW-1, became a regular member of the repertory group in the fall of 1991.

Over the years there were changes. Starting in 1992 most episodes opened with spoofs of popular music videos. That fall Twist replaced S.W. as the show's DJ. By the end of the year Keenen Ivory Wayans, who was upset by Fox's overexposure of *In Living Color* because he felt it would reduce its later value in syndication, had left the show, and within a year all of his siblings had also departed. In the fall of 1993, with the entire Wayans family gone, Jim Carrey had become the star of the show and Jamie Foxx, as incredibly ugly, horny Wanda Wayne, the most popular supporting character. No longer did guest rap musicians close each episode, and almost half of the regular cast was white.

IN PERSON FROM THE PALACE (*Variety*)
FIRST TELECAST: *June 12, 1987*
LAST TELECAST: *August 21, 1987*
BROADCAST HISTORY:
Jun 1987–Aug 1987, CBS Fri 11:30–12:40 A.M.
HOST:
Bobby Colomby
EXECUTIVE PRODUCER:
Dick Clark

Each week a number of singers and rock bands performed in a taped concert setting from the Palace Theater in Hollywood. Bobby Colomby, a former rock star himself with the group Blood, Sweat & Tears, served as host and interviewed the performers. Among those appearing were Jody Watley, Anita Baker, the Heaters, Level 42, the Charlie Daniels Band, the Beastie Boys, the Nylons, Eddie Money, and Smokey Robinson.

IN RECORD TIME, see *Art Ford Show, The*

IN SEARCH OF . . . (*Documentary*)

BROADCAST HISTORY:

Syndicated only
30 minutes
Produced: *1976–1982* (144 episodes)
Release: *Fall 1976*

HOST/NARRATOR:

Leonard Nimoy

This documentary series dealt with bizarre phenomena on the fringes of science, such as ghosts and witchcraft. UFOs and ESP, the Lost City of Atlantis, and the Loch Ness Monster. It was presented in perfectly straightforward fashion with film clips, interviews, and occasional dramatizations. Host Leonard Nimoy appeared on camera at the end to explain that there were many possible explanations for what you had just seen, and we couldn't be sure which one was right, could we? Maybe Bigfoot, Amelia Earhart, and Count Dracula are out there, after all.

IN THE BEGINNING (*Situation Comedy*)

FIRST TELECAST: *September 20, 1978*
LAST TELECAST: *October 18, 1978*

BROADCAST HISTORY:

Sep 1978–Oct 1978, CBS Wed 8:30–9:00

CAST:

Father Daniel M. Cleary .... McLean Stevenson
Sister Agnes .... Priscilla Lopez
Sister Lillian .... Priscilla Morrill
Willie .... Olivia Barash
Jerome Rockefeller .... Bobby Ellerbee
Msgr. Francis X. Barlow .... Jack Dodson

This comedy was a kind of updated *Going My Way*, focusing on the conflict between the pompous, traditionalist, and continually exasperated Father Cleary and the streetwise nun assigned to him, Sister Agnes. They worked in a storefront of Baltimore. It was Sister Aggie's home neighborhood, and she loved the assignment, but Father Cleary found both her and the neighborhood hookers, hustlers, and winos more than he could stand. He kept trying to get reassigned, hoping to get as far away as possible from the Sister he called "Attila the Nun."

IN THE FIRST PERSON (*Interview*)

FIRST TELECAST: *January 29, 1949*
LAST TELECAST: *October 10, 1950*

BROADCAST HISTORY:

Jan 1949–Dec 1949, CBS Sat 7:30–7:45
Feb 1950–Mar 1950, CBS Sat 7:15–7:30
Mar 1950–Jun 1950, CBS Thu 10:30–10:45
Jun 1950–Jul 1950, CBS Sun 9:45–10:00
Jul 1950–Aug 1950, CBS Sun 9:15–9:30
Sep 1950–Oct 1950, CBS Tue 10:45–11:00

HOST:

Quincy Howe
Ned Calmer (1950)

Each week *In the First Person*'s host introduced and chatted informally with a celebrity or someone in the news. Entertainers, politicians, corporation heads, and others appeared on this live 15-minute program. Quincy Howe was the host from its inception through August 1950. He was replaced by Ned Calmer during the program's six-week run that fall.

IN THE HEAT OF THE NIGHT (*Police Drama*)

FIRST TELECAST: *March 6, 1988*
LAST TELECAST: *July 28, 1994*

BROADCAST HISTORY:

Mar 1988, NBC Sun 9:00–11:00
Mar 1988–May 1988, NBC Tue 9:00–10:00
Jul 1988–Sep 1988, NBC Tue 9:00–10:00
Dec 1988–Jan 1992, NBC Tue 9:00–10:00
Jan 1992–Jun 1992, NBC Tue 8:00–9:00
Jun 1992–Jul 1992, NBC Sun 8:00–9:00
Oct 1992–Aug 1993, CBS Wed 9:00–10:00
Aug 1993–Jan 1994, CBS Thu 8:00–9:00
Jan 1994–May 1994, CBS Wed 9:00–10:00
Jul 1994, CBS Thu 8:00–9:00

CAST:

Chief/Sheriff Bill Gillespie .... Carroll O'Connor
Chief of Det. Virgil Tibbs (1988–1993)
.... Howard Rollins
Althea Tibbs (1988–1993) .... Anne-Marie Johnson
Sgt./Capt. Bubba Skinner .... Alan Autry
Dep./Sgt. Parker Williams .... David Hart
Dep. Junior Abernathy (1988) ... Christian Le Blanc
Dep. Horace Goode (1988).............. Peter Gabb
Dep./Lt. Lonnie Jamison .... Hugh O'Connor
Mayor Findley (1988) .... Dennis Lipscomb
Off. Randy Goode (1988–1993)...... Randall Franks
Dep./Sgt. Willson Sweet (1988–1993)
.... Geoffrey Thorne
Joann St. John (1988–1989).......... Lois Nettleton
Sgt. LuAnn Corbin (1989–1994) .... Crystal Fox
Harriet DeLong (1989–1994) ...... Denise Nicholas
**Dr. Robb (1989–1994)*................. Dan Biggers
**D.A. Gerard Darnell (1990–1994)*
.... Wilbur Fitzgerald
Sgt. Dee Sheppard (1992–1994).......... Dee Shaw
Aunt Etta (1992–1994) .... Tonea Stewart
Off. Ken Covey (1992–1994) ...... Harvey E. Lee, Jr.
Off. Luke Everett (1992–1994) .... Mark Johnson
**Off. Peake (1992–1994)* .... C. C. Taylor
**Ted Marcus (1992–1993)* .... Thom Gossom, Jr.
Dr. Winona Day (1992–1994) .... Jen Harper
Chief Hampton Forbes (1993–1994)
.... Carl Weathers
Dep. Christine Surillo (1993–1994)
.... Barbara Lee-Belmonte

*Occasional

THEME:

by Quincy Jones and Alan and Marilyn Bergman, performed by Bill Champlin

A white Southern police chief and his new, black Chief of Detectives—forced on him by a mayor seeking the black vote—found they had more in common than they imagined in this moody crime series. Chief Bill Gillespie was a gruff old-timer who knew the streets and people of Sparta, Mississippi, like the back of his weathered hand. Virgil Tibbs, though he had been born in Sparta, had learned the latest techniques in scientific criminology as a big-city cop in Philadelphia. Now Virgil was back, and he found that Sparta was still living in another era in terms of police work and race relations. But his sleepy hometown was evidently a hotbed of crime (a murder or major drug bust every week, it seemed), so Virgil and the Chief—a fair man—learned to work together and ignore the rednecks in the town and on the force. Althea was Virgil's worried wife.

The series maintained a small-town feeling, and many of the crimes seemed to involve relatives or acquaintances of the regulars (such as wayward cousins and present and former lovers). The second season introduced a sophisticated black city councilwoman—Harriet DeLong—who often became involved in Gillespie's cases. Despite their different backgrounds, the Chief found himself attracted to Harriet, and by 1991–1992 they were having a discreet affair. Gillespie's enemies on the City Council got wind of this and in the last episode of the season tried to get him fired.

In the Heat of the Night moved to CBS in the fall of 1992, and the affair blossomed, as DeLong became a regular (previously she had been seen only occasionally). In the premiere episode of the 1993–1994 season Gillespie's enemies finally caught up with him. The City Council decided not to renew his contract and hired black former FBI agent and Memphis police officer Hampton Forbes to replace him. Gillespie became sheriff of Newman County and continued to work with the Sparta police on cases that fell into their joint jurisdiction. Meanwhile Tibbs had left to get his law degree. His marriage was on the rocks, and he was seen only occasionally during the final season.

At the end of the final season, in the spring of 1994, Gillespie married DeLong.

Based on the novel by John Ball and the Academy Award–winning 1967 movie starring Sidney Poitier and Rod Steiger, and filmed in and around Hammond, La. (later, Covington, Georgia). The role of Jamison was played by Carroll O'Connor's son, Hugh.

IN THE HOUSE (*Situation Comedy*)

FIRST TELECAST: *April 10, 1995*
LAST TELECAST: *September 28, 1998*
BROADCAST HISTORY:

Apr 1995–May 1995, NBC Mon 8:30–9:00
Jul 1995–Feb 1996, NBC Mon 8:30–9:00
Apr 1996–May 1996, NBC Mon 8:30–9:00
Aug 1996–Mar 1998, UPN Mon 8:00–8:30
Jul 1997–Aug 1997, UPN Tue 9:00–10:00
Mar 1998–Apr 1998, UPN Tue 9:30–10:00
May 1998–Jul 1998, UPN Tue 8:30–9:00
Jul 1998–Sep 1998, UPN Mon 8:00–8:30
Jul 1998–Aug 1998, UPN Tue 9:00–9:30
Sep 1998, UPN Mon 9:00–9:30

CAST:

Marion Hill .... LL Cool J (James Todd Smith)
Jackie Warren (1995–1996) .... Debbie Allen
Tiffany Warren .... Maia Campbell
Austin Warren (1995–1996) .... Jeffrey Wood
**Heather Comstock (1995)* .... Lisa Arrindell
Tonia Harris (1996–1998) .... Kim Wayans
Dr. Maxwell Stanton (1996–1998) .. Alfonso Ribeiro
Rodney (1996) .... Dee Jay Daniels
**Coach Sam (1996–1997)* .... John Amos
Carl (1997–1998) .... Ken Lawson
Raynelle (1997–1998) .... Gabrielle Carmouche
Bernie (1997) .... Derek McGrath
Natalie Davis (1997–1998) .... Paulette Braxton
Mercedes Langford (1997–1998) .... Lark Voorhees

*Occasional

Rap star LL Cool J made his TV series debut in this comedy about an NFL star who shared a house with a harried single mom and served as nanny to her two cute kids. Unlikely, you say? Not in sitcomland. Marion, a cool, self-confident type, was on medical leave from the Oakland Raiders due to two injured knees (he ran into a goalpost), with little to do other than work out to stay in shape. In order to raise some extra cash he moved into an apartment over his garage and rented out his small house to Jackie, a recent divorcée. Jackie had been rich but was now forced to go to work, and her new job as legal secretary to demanding lawyer Heather left little time for the kids. Where to turn? Nannies were hard to find, self-centered teenager Tiffany and hyperactive little Austin really liked the superstar over the garage—and he *was* home all day. Egged on by the kids, Jackie reluctantly popped the question: Would you be the nanny?

With a little persuasion superjock agreed, and TV's latest unlikely "family" was born. Much of the comedy came from the conflict between reserved Jackie and go-for-it Marion. *In the House* was scheduled right after NBC's *Fresh Prince of Bel Air,* which it strongly resembled and which was from the same producer (Quincy Jones).

When the series moved to UPN, Jackie had moved back East to Nashville with son Austin, leaving daughter Tiffany in Marion's charge to finish her senior year in high school in Los Angeles. After he found out his injury would force him to retire from football, Marion, along with physical therapist Tonia and arrogant, bottom-line Dr. Stanton, purchased the sports injury clinic where his condition had been diagnosed. Marion wanted to employ holistic medicine techniques at the clinic, which was okay with arty Tonia but created conflict with Dr. Stanton, a "slice and dice" moneymaker. After working out their problems, they renamed it the Hill-Stanton Clinic, although Tonia and Max continued to spar. Rodney, a cute little boy, hung out at the clinic for a time.

At the beginning of the 1997–1998 season Tiffany enrolled at U.C.L.A. along with her friends Carl and Raynelle, and the clinic, severely damaged by an earthquake, had to be rebuilt. Natalie, a childhood acquaintance working on a master's in psychology at U.C.L.A., turned up that fall and moved in with Marion and Tiffany. By late January she and Marion were unsuccessfully fighting a strong sexual attraction. In late February, Max and classy Mercedes, whom he had been dating for months, got engaged, and in early March they were planning their wedding.

IN THE KELVINATOR KITCHEN (*Instruction*)

FIRST TELECAST: *May 21, 1947*
LAST TELECAST: *June 30, 1948*
BROADCAST HISTORY:

May 1947–Jun 1948, NBC Wed 8:30–8:45

HOSTESS:

Alma Kitchell

Cooking program seen during the very early days of network television.

IN THE MORGAN MANNER (*Musical Variety*)

FIRST TELECAST: *March 1, 1950*
LAST TELECAST: *July 30, 1950*
BROADCAST HISTORY:

Mar 1950–Apr 1950, ABC Sun 10:00–10:30
Jul 1950, ABC Sun 8:00–8:30

HOST:

Russ Morgan and His Orchestra

THEME:

"Does Your Heart Beat for Me," by Mitchell Parish and Russ Morgan

This low-budget musical variety show originated in Chicago and featured Russ Morgan, who led one of the more popular dance bands of the late 1940s. Morgan was extremely big on the popular record charts at the time (at one point during 1949 he had six of the top 10 tunes, including the million-seller "Cruising Down the River"). That plus his easygoing personality made him a natural for television. This show was also seen on Sunday afternoons for a time.

Morgan's slogan was "Music in the Morgan Manner"; hence the program's title.

IN THE NAME OF LOVE (*Documentary*)

BROADCAST HISTORY:

Lifetime Network
30 minutes
Produced: *1994* (13 episodes)
Premiered: *September 10, 1994*

HOST:

Rachel Ward

British actress Rachel Ward narrated this misty-eyed recounting of true-life love stories, most well known, a few not, using both archival and new footage. The first episode set the tone, with the oft-told story of King Edward VIII and Mrs. Simpson; later episodes included the building of the Taj Mahal by Shah Jahan for his beloved, rock star Simon LeBon's pursuit of supermodel Yasmin, and a New York postman who carried on a mailbox courtship with his intended. Ward introduced each show from the presumably romantic setting of drafty Luttrellstown Castle outside Dublin, Ireland.

INA RAY HUTTON SHOW, THE (*Musical Variety*)

FIRST TELECAST: *July 4, 1956*
LAST TELECAST: *September 5, 1956*
BROADCAST HISTORY:

Jul 1956–Sep 1956, NBC Wed 10:30–11:00

REGULARS:

Ina Ray Hutton and Her All-Girl Band
Diane Brewster
Mickey Anderson

This may have been the first "Women's Lib" program on television. Ina Ray Hutton and Her All-Girl Band were the stars and principal performers. Miss Hutton, in addition to leading the band, sang and danced with guest stars in production numbers. Not only were the regulars on this show all women, but so were all of the guest stars, including Judy Canova, the King Sisters, Gogi Grant, Rose Marie, and Yma Sumac. Even the announcer was a woman, actress Diane Brewster. It was no wonder that the program was subtitled "No Men Allowed."

The most prominent member of Miss Hutton's 13-piece band was Mickey Anderson who, in addition to playing saxophone, clarinet, and flute, also did comic vocals. The remaining dozen members of the group were Dee Dee Ball, piano and organ; Helen Smith, bass; Margaret Rinker, drums; Jane Davies, guitar; Harriet Blackburn, saxophone and conga drums; Judy Von Euer, saxophone and clarinet; Evie Howeth, saxophone and clarinet; Helen Wooley, saxophone and clarinet; Lois Cronin, trombone and vibraphone; and trumpet players Peggy Fairbanks, Helen Hammond, and Zoe Ann Willy.

INCREDIBLE HULK, THE (*Adventure/Drama*)

FIRST TELECAST: *March 10, 1978*
LAST TELECAST: *June 2, 1982*
BROADCAST HISTORY:

Mar 1978–Jan 1979, CBS Fri 9:00–10:00
Jan 1979, CBS Wed 8:00–9:00
Feb 1979–Nov 1981, CBS Fri 8:00–9:00
May 1982–Jun 1982, CBS Wed 8:00–8:00

CAST:

David Bruce Banner .... Bill Bixby
The Incredible Hulk .... Lou Ferrigno
Jack McGee .... Jack Colvin

David Banner was a research scientist who had been experimenting with various means of determining the effects of stress on physical strength. In a freak accident in his laboratory, David was exposed to a massive dosage of radiation that had a dramatic effect on his physiology. Normally a quiet, peaceful man, David now found that every time he became angered he turned into the Incredible Hulk, a huge, greenish, manlike monster of immense strength and primitive passions. David knew what was happening when the transformation started to take place but, when he calmed down and returned to normal, had no recollection of what he had done when he was the creature. Traveling around the country in search of a cure, and taking odd jobs to keep himself fed and clothed, David sought to avoid the pursuit of investigative reporter Jack McGee, who suspected his secret but who had no real proof.

The Incredible Hulk was based on the comic-book character created by Stan Lee in 1962. From September 1982 to September 1985, NBC aired an animated version of *The Incredible Hulk* as part of its Saturday morning lineup. A new animated *Incredible Hulk* aired on the UPN Sunday morning children's lineup from September 1996 to September 1999.

INCREDIBLE SUNDAY, see *That's Incredible*

INDEPENDENT FILM CHANNEL (Network) (*Cable Movie Network*)

LAUNCHED:

September 1, 1994

SUBSCRIBERS (FEB 2003):

26.2 million (25% U.S.)

A premium movie channel, specializing in nonmainstream, art house, and imported films. The place to find odd little gems like *Volere Volare* (Italian, 1991; about a sound-effects engineer who slowly turns into a cartoon character); and *Dead Pigeon on Beethoven Street* (German, 1972).

The channel also aired a few original films, documentaries and series, the latter including *Dinner for Five* (2002), a celebrity chat show.

INDUSTRIES FOR AMERICA (*Documentary*)

FIRST TELECAST: *May 31, 1951*
LAST TELECAST: *September 19, 1957*
BROADCAST HISTORY:

May 1951–Jul 1951, ABC Thu 10:00–10:30
Jul 1951–Sep 1951, ABC Sun 10:00–10:30
Oct 1951–Dec 1951, ABC Fri 10:30–11:00

Feb 1952, ABC Thu 10:15–10:30
Jun 1957–Sep 1957, ABC Thu 9:30–10:00

Documentary films which ABC ran during the early and mid-1950s, mostly, it seems, to fill time. The central theme was American industry on parade, with such provocative titles as "The Magic of Lumber," "Drama of Portland Cement," and "The Cranberry Story."

INFORMATION PLEASE (*Quiz/Panel*)
FIRST TELECAST: *June 29, 1952*
LAST TELECAST: *September 21, 1952*
BROADCAST HISTORY:
Jun 1952–Sep 1952, CBS Sun 9:00–9:30
EMCEE:
Clifton Fadiman
PANELISTS:
Franklin P. Adams
John Kieran

Information Please had had a long and successful run on radio, but its only appearance on television was as the 1952 summer replacement for *The Fred Waring Show.* Viewers submitted questions to be answered by the members of the panel, two permanent and one guest. The viewer received a $10 certificate good for the purchase of books or magazines if his question was used, and a $50 certificate if it stumped the panel. Emcee/moderator Clifton Fadiman had long been associated with the radio version of this literate series, as had panelists Adams and Kieran.

INK (*Situation Comedy*)
FIRST TELECAST: *October 21, 1996*
LAST TELECAST: *May 26, 1997*
BROADCAST HISTORY:
Oct 1996–Feb 1997, CBS Mon 8:30–9:00
Mar 1997–May 1997, CBS Mon 9:30–10:00
CAST:
Mike Logan .... Ted Danson
Kate Montgomery .... Mary Steenburgen
Abby Logan (age 14)................. Alana Austin
Belinda Carhardt.............. Christine Ebersole
Ernie Trainor................... Charlie Robinson
Alan Mesnick .... Saul Rubinek
Donna French .... Jenica Bergere
**Leo Druin*.......................... Jonathan Katz
*Occasional

Journalists Mike and Kate had had a whirlwind courtship that resulted in marriage three months after their first meeting on the White House lawn. The marriage didn't last—their natural competitiveness and big egos got in the way—but it had produced a daughter, Abby, whom they both adored. When Kate became the first female managing editor of the *New York Sun,* where Mike was the star columnist, sparks flew. Wisecracking, womanizing Mike had problems coping with her as his new boss, and Kate found it difficult dealing with his macho attitude and regular sniping at her—with almost nonstop arguments the result. Abby, who loved them both, continued her persistent but futile efforts to get them back together. Others on the *Sun*'s staff were Belinda, the over-the-hill society columnist with a drinking problem, who had outgrown her love affair with the city's rich and famous; Ernie, the unflappable police reporter who had seen it all; and Alan, the uptight, neurotic financial reporter. Donna, a free-spirited young editorial assistant, who seemed out of place working at a mainstream newspaper, idolized Kate and barely tolerated Mike, whom she considered a chauvinist pig. Which he was.

CBS had high hopes for *Ink*, Ted Danson's first TV series since he turned off the lights on NBC's long-running hit, *Cheers.* With the charismatic Danson and his new wife Mary Steenburgen starring, CBS was sure they had a hit. Unfortunately, it was not to be. Problems with the series pilot and the original producers prompted CBS to bring in *Murphy Brown* producer Diane English to take over the reins in late August, less than a month before the scheduled premiere. The premiere was delayed while Ms. English made cast changes, but the chemistry—and audience appeal—weren't there. *Ink* never caught on, and was canceled at the end of its first season.

INNOCENT AND THE DAMNED, THE (*Drama*)
FIRST TELECAST: *May 31, 1979*
LAST TELECAST: *June 28, 1979*
BROADCAST HISTORY:
May 1979–Jun 1979, NBC Thu 10:00–11:00
CAST:
Tom Keating.......................... Sam Elliott
Lee Bishop............................ Perry King
Carl Osborne .... Gene Barry
Gloria Osborne .... Michelle Phillips
Max Kendrick........................ Roger Davis
Abe Singer .... George DiCenzo
Alex Budde.................. Anthony Franciosa
Kit Pepe .... Jessica Harper
Jon Osborne .... Douglas Matthew Heyes
Budd Townsend .... Bo Hopkins
Owen Keating...................... John McIntire
Len Ralston .... Angus Duncan
Joseph Drummond............... John Houseman
Judge Kendrick .... William Prince
Angela Morelli .... Debi Richter
Joan Carolinian .... Martine Beswick
Sheriff Dinehart............... Lee Jones-deBroux

The central focus of this mini-series was the 1964 trial of Lee Bishop for the rape-murder of 15-year-old Angela Morelli, a crime he didn't commit. Bishop was nevertheless convicted and young lawyer Tom Keating spent eight years working behind the scenes to get him freed from Colorado's death row. Woven into the legal maneuvering was the secondary story of manipulation by entrenched real-estate interests, including tycoon Carl Osborne (with whose daughter, Gloria, Bishop had been having an affair), to transform the sleepy town of Aspen into a major ski resort.

Adapted from the novels *Aspen* by Bert Hirschfield and *The Adversary* by Bart Spicer, this mini-series originally aired November 5–7, 1977, under the title *Aspen.*

INSIDE AMERICA (*Magazine*)
FIRST TELECAST: *April 4, 1982*
LAST TELECAST: *April 25, 1982*
BROADCAST HISTORY:
Apr 1982, ABC Sun 7:00–8:00
HOST:
Dick Clark

Dick Clark produced and hosted this magazine show filled with "fluff" pieces on show business. Among the subjects were "Who's Sexier: Tom Selleck or Burt Reynolds?," Rex Reed on the Ten Worst Movies of

1981, "Inside Graceland," and "Where Are Joey Dee & the Starliters Now?"

INSIDE BUSINESS (*Interview*)
BROADCAST HISTORY:
CNN
30 minutes
Produced: *1980–1998*
Premiered: *June 7, 1980*
HOST:
Myron Kandel
Deborah Marchini

This long-running weekend series tackled a single business subject each week with a background report followed by in-studio interviews with one or more executives. Originally the interviewing was done by a panel of business editors. Myron Kandel was the first host; he was later replaced by Deborah Marchini.

INSIDE DETECTIVE, see *Rocky King—Inside Detective*

INSIDE EDITION (*News Magazine*)
BROADCAST HISTORY:
Syndicated only
30 minutes
Produced: *1989–*
Released: *January 9, 1989*
ANCHORS:
Weekday-David Frost (1989)
Bill O'Reilly (1989–1995)
Deborah Norville (1995–)
Weekend-Nancy Glass (1992–1993)
Rolanda Watts (1993–1994)
Don Criqui (1994–)
Madeline McFadden (1994–1997)
Stacey Sweet (1997–2002)
Trish Bergin (2002–)

Prior to the premiere of *Inside Edition*, anchorman David Frost, the erudite English interviewer and talk-show host, told the press that his new series would not pander to its audience in the same manner as the popular tabloid show *A Current Affair*. No sensationalizing, no gratuitous sex, this series would concentrate on solid investigative and informative reporting.

Though it was a bit more sober, *Inside Edition* covered much the same material as its checkout-counter predecessor, however. Frost lasted only three weeks as anchor, being replaced by Bill O'Reilly, whose on-camera presence was thought to be less stuffy and intimidating. Frost remained as "special interviewer" for a month, then disappeared entirely—with a reported $2 million contract settlement. Later in 1989, no-holds-barred political columnist Jack Anderson and consumer advocate Ralph Nader were signed as contributing correspondents, joined in 1990 by actor and retired football player Dick Butkus, with occasional sports features (Anderson left in 1991). The spring of 1990 also saw the addition of featured senior correspondent Nancy Glass, the former anchorwoman of *This Evening*, a similar show that had run both in limited syndication and on the Lifetime cable network. In 1992, when a weekend version of *Inside Edition* was added, Glass was the original anchor.

In the spring of 1995 former network news correspondent Deborah Norville replaced Bill O'Reilly.

INSIDE PHOTOPLAY, see *Wendy Barrie Show, The*

INSIDE SCHWARTZ (*Situation Comedy*)
FIRST TELECAST: *September 27, 2001*
LAST TELECAST: *January 3, 2002*
BROADCAST HISTORY:
Sep 2001–Jan 2002, NBC Thu 8:30–9:00
CAST:
Adam Schwartz.................... Breckin Meyer
Gene Schwartz.................... Richard Kline
Eve Morris.................... Maggie Lawson
Julie Hermann.................... Miriam Shor
David Cobert.................... Bryan Callen
Emily Cobert.................... Jennifer Irwin
William Morris.................... Dondré T. Whitfield
Van Earl Wright.................... Himself
Kevin Frazier.................... Himself

Young, mild-mannered Adam was the vice president of marketing for his dad's sandwich chain, The Pita Factory, but his passion was sports. He had an occasional gig as announcer for a minor-league baseball team but, ever optimistic, hoped for bigger things. Unfortunately it didn't look like he would get much help from his incompetent agent, a black dude named William Morris (get it?). Eve was his former girlfriend, who had dumped him, though he hoped to get back together; Julie, his smart, sardonic pal at Dad's offices; David, a sex-obsessed friend; and Emily, David's put-upon wife. Gene was Adam's clueless, gregarious father, who wanted Adam to stay in the sandwich biz.

Sports was such a passion for Adam that he imagined his entire life as a sports contest, complete with fantasy announcers "calling" the progress of his dates and other interactions, and plenty of sports lingo ("I took a few shots to the head this week, but I'm still in the game"). Each episode opened with real-life commentators Van Earl Wright and Kevin Frazier on a *Sportscenter*-style set, setting the scene; sometimes they would then walk into the middle of scenes (unseen by the participants) and "call the play" there as well. Guest sports celebrities like Dick Butkus, Mills Lane and Bill Walton also appeared to comment.

INSIDE U.S.A. WITH CHEVROLET (*Musical Variety*)
FIRST TELECAST: *September 29, 1949*
LAST TELECAST: *March 16, 1950*
BROADCAST HISTORY:
Sep 1949–Mar 1950, CBS Thu 8:30–9:00
REGULARS:
Peter Lind Hayes
Mary Healy
Mary Wickes
Sheila Bond
Jay Blackton Orchestra
PRODUCER:
Arthur Schwartz

Songwriter and producer Arthur Schwartz brought his hit musical *Inside U.S.A.* to network television in the fall of 1949, as an alternate-week series. The program was done in revue style, with Peter Lind Hayes hosting in the role of a contemporary American minstrel, and each telecast included songs, comedy sketches, dance, and lavish production numbers. As the minstrel, Hayes would travel across the country and provide background to the individual program elements as he observed the splendor of America's natural beauty and the diversity of its people. Featured in the regular cast was his wife, singer-actress Mary Healy. There was also a big-name "star of the week" for every show, with such varied talents as Lucille Ball, Boris Karloff, Ethel Merman, David Niven, and Oscar Levant starring in individual telecasts.

INSIDERS, THE (*Newspaper Drama*)
FIRST TELECAST: *September 25, 1985*
LAST TELECAST: *June 23, 1986*
BROADCAST HISTORY:
Sep 1985–Jan 1986, ABC Wed 8:00–9:00
Jun 1986, ABC Mon 8:00–9:00
CAST:
Nick Fox........................ Nicholas Campbell
James Mackey..................... Stoney Jackson
Alice West........................ Gail Strickland

The fast-paced adventures of a pair of hip investigative reporters for a national magazine; each week they wormed their way inside a target, usually the mob or some other criminal organization, using disguises and help from street contacts from their checkered pasts. Nick, who looked a lot like rock star Sting, was a rebellious product of the '60s; his partner Mackey, a cool, young black dude who resembled rock star Prince, was a "reformed" ex-con (although he made much use of the tricks of his former trade, like hot-wiring cars). All of this was accompanied by an ample dose of violence, car chases, and loud rock music.

INSOMNIAC WITH DAVE ATTELL (*Comedy/Documentary*)
BROADCAST HISTORY:
Comedy Central
30 minutes
Original episodes: *2001–*
Premiered: *August 5, 2001*
HOST:
Dave Attell

Attell, a loud, young stand-up comic, took viewers on an offbeat tour of some large American cities by night in this late-night series—beginning in New York, where he visited an S&M club, the Federation of Black Cowboys in Brooklyn, a strip club, some bars, a waste transfer station, a Wall Street training office (at 5:00 A.M.), and a fortune cookie factory. Other cities visited ranged from Boston to Boise, with additional stops in Canada (Montreal) and Mexico (Tijuana).

INSPECTOR MARK SABER—HOMICIDE SQUAD, see *Mark Saber*

INSPORT (*Sports Magazine*)
BROADCAST HISTORY:
Syndicated only
30 minutes
Produced: *1989–1991*
Released: *October 1989*
HOST:
Ahmad Rashad (1989–1990)
Robin Swoboda
Al Trautwig (1990–1991)

This weekly magazine series featured profiles of, and interviews with, a variety of sports personalities, ranging from players to owners to officials. Also included were investigative reports on issues of concern to viewers and occasional human interest features.

INTERLUDE, see *Summer Theater*

INTERNATIONAL PLAYHOUSE, see *Movies—Prior to 1961*

INTERNATIONAL SHOWTIME (*Variety*)
FIRST TELECAST: *September 15, 1961*
LAST TELECAST: *September 10, 1965*
BROADCAST HISTORY:
Sep 1961–Sep 1965, NBC Fri 7:30–8:30
HOST:
Don Ameche

Circuses, ice shows, magic shows, and other similar types of spectaculars, from all over Europe, were shown each week on *International Showtime.* Some episodes focused on a specific talent—clowns, daredevils, etc.—and compiled the best examples from different performers into a single show. Don Ameche was the host of the series throughout its four-season run. He would introduce each act and then sit back as part of the audience to enjoy it. He traveled around Europe with the production crew and was actually present when each act was taped.

INTERNS, THE (*Medical Drama*)
FIRST TELECAST: *September 18, 1970*
LAST TELECAST: *September 10, 1971*
BROADCAST HISTORY:
Sep 1970–Sep 1971, CBS Fri 7:30–8:30
CAST:
Dr. Peter Goldstone .... Broderick Crawford
Dr. Greg Pettit...................... Stephen Brooks
Dr. Pooch Hardin .... Christopher Stone
Dr. Cal Barrin .... Hal Frederick
Dr. Lydia Thorpe...................... Sandra Smith
Dr. Sam Marsh........................... Mike Farrell
Dr. Hugh Jacoby...................... Skip Homeier
Bobbe Marsh............................ Elaine Giftos

Broderick Crawford starred in this medical series as the father figure to a nicely mixed group of five young interns (one black, one woman, one young married man, two swingers). New North Hospital was the setting, and the personal and professional lives of the young doctors provided the stories.

INTIMATE PORTRAIT (*Biography*)
BROADCAST HISTORY:
Lifetime
60 minutes
Produced: *1995–*
Premiered: *March 29, 1996* (series)

Lifetime's answer to the "biography craze" of the mid-'90s was this series of documentaries on the lives of famous women. The early subjects were certainly varied, including Grace Kelly, Carly Simon, Rose Kennedy, Jackie Onassis, Jessica Savitch, Mary Magdalen, and Marla Maples. The narrators (for contemporary subjects) were generally celebrity friends of the subjects. *Intimate Portrait* was first telecast as a monthly special, beginning on January 29, 1995, and became a weekly series in 1996.

INTO THE NIGHT (*Comedy/Variety*)
FIRST TELECAST: *July 16, 1990*
LAST TELECAST: *November 14, 1991*
BROADCAST HISTORY:
Jul 1990–May 1991, ABC Mon–Fri 12:00 midnight–1:00 A.M.
Jun 1991–Nov 1991, ABC Mon–Thu 12:00 midnight–1:00 A.M.
REGULARS:
Rick Dees (1990–1991)
Lisa Canning, announcer (1990–1991)
Greg Binkley (as *Dep. Barney Fife, Jr.*) (1990–1991)
Bob Perlow (1990)
Eric Boardman (1991)
Scott LaRose (1991)
Caroline Schlitt (1991)
Paul Willson (1991)
HOUSE BAND:
Billy Vera and the Beaters (1990–1991)
The Master Mix (1991)

Los Angeles disc jockey Rick Dees, who gained infamy in the 1970s by producing what was widely regarded as the worst record of that decade ("Disco Duck"), was the original star of this late-night contemporary variety hour. The baby-faced Dees (he was 40) introduced rock bands and standup comics and interviewed such celebrities as Chuck Norris, Muhammad Ali, and Kirstie Alley. He also threw a plethora of radio-style gimmicks at viewers, including several contests—a mystery oldies contest worth up to $40,000 (more than 100,000 calls were received), a weird photos contest, and a $5,000 funniest monologue contest. A basset hound called The Great Houndini picked winning teams on upcoming *Monday Night Football* contests (his season record: 6–7) and *Deesville*, a satirical soap opera, ran in the spring. "Deputy Barney Fife, Jr." was the studio chief of security who brought in oddball talent, and Bob Perlow was the "correspondent of chaos."

None of this frenzied activity drew much of an audience, so in July 1991 Dees and most of the gimmicks were dropped and weekly guest hosts took over. The name of the series was changed from *Into the Night Starring Rick Dees* to simply *Into the Night* in July, and then to *Studio 59* in October. Among the guest hosts were Chris Lemmon (frequently), Brad Garrett, Suzanne Somers, and Richard Belzer.

INVADER ZIM (*Cartoon*)
BROADCAST HISTORY:
Nickelodeon
30 minutes
Original episodes: *2001–2003* (46 episodes)
Premiered: *March 30, 2001*
VOICES:
Invader ZIM .... Richard Steven Horvitz
GIR .... Rosearik Rikki Simons
Dib .... Andy Berman
Gaz .... Melissa Fahn
Professor Membrane .... Rodger Bumpass
Miss Bitters .... Lucille Bliss
Almighty Tallest Red .... Wally Wingert
Almighty Tallest Purple .... Kevin McDonald

ZIM was an inept alien soldier who almost destroyed his home planet of Irk during Operation Impending Doom in this wild parody on science-fiction shows. He pleaded for another chance, so frustrated supreme rulers Almighty Tallest Red and Purple sent him to one of the smallest, most insignificant planets in the universe—Earth—telling him it was his "secret mission" as part of Operation Impending Doom II. With him went a malfunctioning robot made out of scrap metal, dubbed GIR. The Irken rulers hoped ZIM would die or disappear along the way, but he made it to Earth and set up his spy base in the form of a suburban house, with huge caverns full of scientific gear underneath. He gave himself and GIR some ridiculous disguises and enrolled in the local "skool," where he could observe human kids in their natural habitat. No one seemed to notice except for Dib, an alien-hunter kid, who was determined to expose ZIM. Gaz was Dib's scary, goth sister, and Professor Membrane, his oblivious scientist dad. Miss Bitters was a cranky old teacher who kept insisting that everyone was doomed.

Loud, excitable ZIM ("I will rule the world!") and obsessed Dib battled each other endlessly, and ingeniously, with all sorts of wild contraptions, but to no avail.

INVADERS, THE (*Science Fiction*)
FIRST TELECAST: *January 10, 1967*
LAST TELECAST: *September 17, 1968*
BROADCAST HISTORY:
Jan 1967–Jan 1968, ABC Tue 8:30–9:30
Jan 1968–Sep 1968, ABC Tue 10:00–11:00
CAST:
David Vincent .... Roy Thinnes
Edgar Scoville .... Kent Smith
EXECUTIVE PRODUCER:
Quinn Martin

One of the most durable science-fiction ideas is the one that questions the very reality of what we see around us. Could there be aliens in our midst? Architect David Vincent certainly thought so. He had witnessed the landing of a flying saucer, and stumbled onto an incredible secret: that scattered throughout the world's population, disguised as humans, was an advance guard of alien creatures from a dying planet, who were preparing to conquer the earth!

Convincing his fellow citizens of this was of course no easy task, so Vincent went on a one-man crusade to obtain solid evidence and warn mankind of the dangers it faced—while trying not to fall into the clutches of the aliens. Identifying the enemy was tricky, but it could be done. Sometimes the invaders would have slightly mutated hands, such as a little finger jutting out awkwardly; sometimes, though rarely, they would begin to glow when they were in need of regeneration to retain their human form. And of course, they had no pulse or heartbeat—because they had no hearts.

For the first few months of the series Vincent fought a lonely, largely undercover battle. Eventually, feeling that he was a bit too lonely to be plausible, the producers gave him some allies, a group of seven others who also learned the secret and wanted to help. His chief confederate, who joined the show in December 1967, was Edgar Scoville, the head of an electronics firm.

Could it really happen? Well, you never know, but actor Roy Thinnes, in a bit of promotional hype released by the ABC press department, claimed that he had actually seen a UFO during the filming of the series. Then again, maybe *he* is one of *them*. . . .

INVASION AMERICA (*Animated Science Fiction*)
FIRST TELECAST: *June 8, 1998*
LAST TELECAST: *July 6, 1998*
BROADCAST HISTORY:
Jun 1998, WB Mon 9:00–10:00
Jun 1998, WB Tue 9:00–10:00
Jul 1998, WB Tue 8:00–9:30
VOICES:
David Carter.......................... Mikey Kelley
Cale Oosha .... Lorenzo Lamas
The Dragit .... Tony Jay
Rafe .... Edward Albert
Rita Carter.......................... Kath Soucie
General Konrad .... Leonard Nimoy
Simon.......................... Thom Adcox
Sonia.......................... Kath Soucie
Philip Stark.......................... Greg Eagles
Angie Romar.......................... Kristy McNichol
Doc.......................... Ronny Cox
Major Lomack .... Jim Cummings
General Gordon .... James B. Sikking
Jim Bailey.......................... Rider Strong

Steven Spielberg was executive producer of this unusual, action-packed animated series about a 17-year-old boy who was the key to stopping an alien invasion. David was a typical, rebellious suburban teen being raised by a single mom who only gradually learned who he really was. It seems that twenty years earlier the Dragit, military leader of the dying planet Tyrus, had sent representatives of his people to Earth, ostensibly to quietly establish interstellar trade between the two worlds. In reality they were an advance military guard laying the groundwork for an invasion. When Tyrus's young ruler, the Dragit's nephew Cale, learned the true purpose of the mission, he tried to stop it, and the Dragit ordered him assassinated. Escaping to Earth with assassins close on his heels, he was saved by Rita, an Earth woman with whom he fell in love and later had a child—David. Cale then returned to Tyrus to lead a rebellion against his uncle, leaving behind his bodyguard Rafe to watch over his infant son.

By the time David learned all this, many years later, the evil Dragit's men had finally realized who he was and were after *him*. The rest of the series was a succession of chases, battles, and narrow escapes as David attempted to elude his pursuers and thwart the invasion. Among the villains was Konrad, a ruthless U.S. Air Force general who was really a Tyrusian agent. Rafe and David led an attack on his Utah base that resulted in both Rafe's and Konrad's deaths—and now the fate of the Earth was in the hands of David alone. He found a new ally in Doc, a renegade Tyrusian who helped him stop the alternate invasion plan—the bombardment of Earth by meteors launched from the dark side of the moon. Other villains included Simon and Sonia, Tyrusian/human hybrids working for Dragit; General Gordon, another evil agent; and Lomack, Konrad's and later Gordon's henchman. Jim was David's high-school buddy, who helped out when he could. In the climactic battle, David and Doc, on the moon, succeeded in destroying the Tyrusian meteor base as his father Cale reappeared, at the helm of the interstellar fighter *Rita's Dream*, to help foil the Dragit's dastardly plan.

Invasion America was originally intended to air as a weekly half-hour series, but the WB network chose instead to air it as an extended mini-series in full-hour installments with a 90-minute finale. The last episode closed with "End of Book One," but there were no more episodes produced. WB reran the series on Saturday mornings from September to October 1998.

INVASION OF THE HIDDEN CAMERAS (*Humor*)
FIRST TELECAST: *July 12, 2002*
LAST TELECAST: *August 9, 2002*
BROADCAST HISTORY:
Jul 2002–Aug 2002, FOX Fri 8:00–9:00
HOST:
Doug Stanhope

Invasion of the Hidden Cameras was another mean-spirited variant on the *Candid Camera* genre—the producers stated, "This is not your parents' hidden camera show." Each episode featured comedians who were unfettered by anything resembling good taste and setups that often had cruel and/or nasty elements designed to thoroughly embarrass their unsuspecting victims. Among them were a clown and a magician informed at the last minute that they had been hired to cheer up the attendees at a funeral, customers at a deli who were told that they had been poisoned and had to do disgusting things to keep from getting sick and a terrified man who had been dealt a winning hand in a staged mob-style poker game.

Comedian Doug Stanhope, who hosted the series, appeared in many of the setups—as a patient recovering from an organ transplant asking for a cocktail to test his new liver, a customer looking for a service that would ship a dead cat to his ex-girlfriend and a man trying to get a taxidermist to have his live poodle stuffed.

INVESTIGATOR, THE (*Detective Drama*)
FIRST TELECAST: *June 3, 1958*
LAST TELECAST: *September 2, 1958*
BROADCAST HISTORY:
Jun 1958–Sep 1958, NBC Tue 8:00–9:00
CAST:
Jeff Prior .... Lonny Chapman
Lloyd Prior .... Howard St. John

Jeff Prior was a swinging private investigator in his early 30s whose ability to track down clues and resolve mysteries had made him very successful. He had learned his skills from his father, Lloyd, a retired newspaperman who had a reputation of his own for solving mysteries when he was a young reporter in the 1920s. Jeff dug up most of the facts in each case and, with his father's help, tied them all together to nail the culprits. This live detective series aired as a summer replacement in 1958.

INVESTIGATORS, THE (*Detective Drama*)
FIRST TELECAST: *October 5, 1961*
LAST TELECAST: *December 28, 1961*
BROADCAST HISTORY:
Oct 1961–Dec 1961, CBS Thu 9:00–10:00
CAST:
Russ Andrews .... James Franciscus
Steve Banks .... James Philbrook

Maggie Peters .... Mary Murphy
Bill Davis .... Al Austin

With offices on the fashionable East Side of New York, the firm of "Investigators, Inc." was a highly successful and highly specialized operation. The cases dealt with by its staff were all tied in to very large insurance claims. As a team of insurance investigators, Russ, Steve, and Bill became involved with the underworld, the police, and others as they tracked down clues to determine whether or not claims were legitimate. Helping back at the office, and occasionally as an undercover operative, was Maggie Peters, their girl Friday.

INVISIBLE MAN, THE (*International Intrigue*)

FIRST TELECAST: *November 4, 1958*
LAST TELECAST: *September 22, 1960*
BROADCAST HISTORY:

Nov 1958–May 1959, CBS Tue 8:00–8:30
May 1959–Jul 1959, CBS Thu 7:30–8:00
Jul 1960–Sep 1960, CBS Thu 7:30–8:00

CAST:

Dr. Peter Brady .... Anonymous
Diane Brady .... Lisa Daniely
Sally Brady .... Deborah Watling

Dr. Peter Brady was an English scientist working with the principles that govern the refraction of light when he discovered a means of making himself invisible. The only problem was that after becoming invisible, he could not make himself visible again. Having decided to make the best of his handicap, Peter became an adventurer/agent, working with British Intelligence to thwart the efforts of evil organizations and their agents throughout Europe (he had no trouble getting through customs). Seen regularly were his helpful sister Diane and his young niece Sally.

The actor playing Peter was never seen at all, being concealed in bandages or only heard offscreen. His identity was kept a close secret by the producers, who for years after steadfastly refused to reveal his name (not that very many were asking). He turned out to be an obscure actor named Johnny Scripps (the voice was provided by Tim Turner).

The episodes aired during the summer of 1960 were not repeats but an additional group of original episodes. The series was produced in England.

INVISIBLE MAN, THE (*Adventure*)

FIRST TELECAST: *September 8, 1975*
LAST TELECAST: *January 19, 1976*
BROADCAST HISTORY:

Sep 1975–Jan 1976, NBC Mon 8:00–9:00

CAST:

Dr. Daniel Westin .... David McCallum
Walter Carlson .... Craig Stevens
Dr. Kate Westin .... Melinda Fee

In an attempt to update the classic H. G. Wells story, this series brought us Dr. Daniel Westin, a scientist who had discovered a means of making any object invisible—including himself. When he found out that the government planned to use his technique for military purposes, he memorized his secret formula, destroyed his equipment, and turned himself invisible to escape. Unfortunately his method for becoming visible again failed to work, and he was temporarily stuck in invisibility. Seeking the aid of a scientist friend, he had a wig, highly realistic face mask, and plastic hands made to conceal his invisibility, enabling him to resume a somewhat normal public life.

Daniel and his wife Kate then went to work for the KLAE Corporation, where he continued his experiments in order to find his way back. He also undertook an assortment of dangerous security missions for his boss, Walter Carlson. Whenever the situation got tight Daniel could take off his mask and clothes and "disappear." This did not always prove to be as helpful as it might seem, however, as when he was trapped in the house of a blind man, extraordinarily sensitive to sound, who was out to kill him.

INVISIBLE MAN, THE (*Science Fiction*)

BROADCAST HISTORY:

Sci-Fi Channel
60 minutes
Original episodes: *2000–2002* (46 episodes)
Premiered: *June 9, 2000*

CAST:

Darien Fawkes .... Vincent Ventresca
Robert "Bobby" Hobbes .... Paul Ben-Victor
The Keeper (*Claire Keeply*) .... Shannon Kenny
The Official (*Charles Bowden*) .... Eddie Jones
Agent Alex Monroe (*2001–2002*)... Brandy Ledford
Albert Eberts .... Michael McCafferty

Despite many insider jokes ("*Invisible Man* fades from the schedule," "You can see right through the plots," etc.), this third TV version of the H. G. Wells classic had a humorous style all its own. Darien Fawkes was a con man/thief who was sprung from prison by his scientist brother Kevin after he promised to take part in an experiment his brother was conducting for the government. Unfortunately terrorists killed Kevin halfway through the experiment, and Darien was left with an invisibility gland implanted in his neck. The gland secreted quicksilver whenever Darien was frightened, reflecting light and rendering him invisible. It also gave him severe headaches and could lead to "quicksilver madness," resulting in extreme violence, if he went too long without being injected with a special antidote. Surly, selfish Darien didn't like any of this, demanding "I want it out now!"—but it couldn't be removed without killing him. In order to keep receiving the antidote, he did what most TV heroes in similar predicaments do, agreeing to use his powers to fight crime for a shadowy government agency—in this case "The Agency."

Darien was teamed with a sleazy, balding, junk-food-loving agent named Bobby; their boss was a fat, imperious man known only as The Official. Keeping him alive was The Keeper, an attractive scientist who calmed him down when he flew off the handle (which was often) and arrived at critical moments with his antidote. Albert was a short, fussy bureaucrat and Alex, a sexy agent who joined later. Together the team fought numerous villains, including Arnaud and Stark of the evil Chrysalis organization. Darien had to be careful because even while invisible he could be exposed by detecting his low temperature, or by a blast from a fire extinguisher. His usual reaction when caught: "Oh, crap!" Also, his bouts of quicksilver madness became progressively worse. There were numerous jokes about government bureaucracy (The Agency was successively under the Department of Fish and Game, the Bureau of Indian Affairs, the Department of Human Services and the Bureau of

Weights and Measures), and some of the capers were pretty silly.

In the last episode Darien was finally cured of the madness, while retaining his ability to become invisible. He quit The Agency in a huff and joined the F.B.I., but later came back when The Official promised him better hours and pay.

IRON HORSE, THE (*Western*)
FIRST TELECAST: *September 12, 1966*
LAST TELECAST: *January 6, 1968*
BROADCAST HISTORY:
Sep 1966–Sep 1967, ABC Mon 7:30–8:30
Sep 1967–Jan 1968, ABC Sat 9:30–10:30
CAST:
Ben Calhoun .... Dale Robertson
Dave Tarrant .... Gary Collins
Barnabas Rogers .... Bob Random
Nils Torvald (1966–1967) .... Roger Torrey
Julie Parsons (1967–1968) .... Ellen McRae (Burstyn)

Ben Calhoun was a hard-driving ladies' man who had the good fortune to win a railroad in a poker game. Unfortunately, the Buffalo Pass, Scalplock, and Defiance Line was only half built and on the brink of bankruptcy, so it was up to Ben to finish the job. Helping him push the line to completion through the wild, untamed West of the 1880s were Dave, his young construction engineer; Nils, the giant crewman; and Barnabas, a young orphan who idolized Ben and served as his clerk. Julie Parsons arrived in the second season as the freight station operator and proprietor of the Scalplock General Store.

There was plenty of action in this epic of a railroad moving west, with crooked financiers, rampaging Indians, and assorted desperadoes peopling the stories.

IRONSIDE (*Police Drama*)
FIRST TELECAST: *September 14, 1967*
LAST TELECAST: *January 16, 1975*
BROADCAST HISTORY:
Sep 1967–Sep 1971, NBC Thu 8:30–9:30
Sep 1971–Nov 1971, NBC Tue 7:30–8:30
Nov 1971–Jan 1975, NBC Thu 9:00–10:00
CAST:
Robert Ironside .... Raymond Burr
Det. Sgt. Ed Brown .... Don Galloway
Eve Whitfield (1967–1971) ...... Barbara Anderson
Mark Sanger .... Don Mitchell
Fran Belding (1971–1975) .... Elizabeth Baur
Commissioner Dennis Randall .... Gene Lyons
Lt. Carl Reese (1969–1975) .... Johnny Seven
Diana Sanger (1974–1975) .... Joan Pringle

Robert Ironside had been chief of detectives for the San Francisco Police Department for many years, and a member of the force for 25, when a would-be assassin's bullet grazed his spine and left him paralyzed from the waist down. Forced to leave the force as a regular member, he convinced Police Commissioner Randall to appoint him to a position as special consultant. Helping him wage his unrelenting war against crime were two former assistants, Sgt. Ed Brown and Policewoman Eve Whitfield, and an ex-delinquent (Mark Sanger) who became his aide and bodyguard. Confined to a wheelchair, Ironside made use of a specially equipped police van for transportation and some unused office space at police headquarters as a base of operations. When Barbara Anderson left the series at the end of the 1970–1971 season over a contract dispute, she was replaced by Elizabeth Baur as Policewoman Fran Belding. Mark, who had found time to go to law school while working for Chief Ironside, graduated at the start of the 1974–1975 season and got married.

ISLAND SON (*Medical Drama*)
FIRST TELECAST: *September 19, 1989*
LAST TELECAST: *March 29, 1990*
BROADCAST HISTORY:
Sep 1989–Nov 1989, CBS Tue 10:00–11:00
Dec 1989–Mar 1990, CBS Thu 9:00–10:00
CAST:
Dr. Daniel Kulani .... Richard Chamberlain
Dr. Anthony Metzger .... Timothy Carhart
Dr. Caitlin McGrath .... Carol Huston
Dr. Margaret Judd .... Brynn Thayer
Dr. Kenji Fushida .... Clyde Kusatsu
Tutu Kulani .... Kwan Hi Lim
Nana Kulani .... Betty Carvalho
James Kulani .... Ray Bumatai
Sam Kulani .... William McNamara
Nina Delaney (1990) .... Alberta Watson
Tess Delaney (1990) .... Ariana Richards
Paul Brody .... Michael Adamshick

Returning to weekly series television for the first time since *Dr. Kildare* in the 1960s, Richard Chamberlain was again cast as a dedicated physician. Dr. Daniel Kulani had had a successful career as an internist on the mainland but decided to return home and take a staff position at the Kamehameha Medical Center in Honolulu. It was here that he could be close to the family that had adopted him as a child and work with needy native Hawaiians. Working with Daniel at the medical center were the chief surgeon, Kenji Fushida; two talented young residents, Metzger and McGrath; and the cost-conscious chief of staff, Margaret Judd. Although the series centered on activities at the hospital, the divorced Dr. Kulani did spend time with his adoptive parents, Tutu and Nana; his stepbrother James; and his own son, 18-year-old Sam, who was unsure about whether he wanted to be in college or out on his own. In the spring of 1990 Daniel fell in love with high school drama teacher Nina Delaney, a divorcée with a 13-year-old daughter, but *Island Son* was canceled before the course of their relationship was determined.

ISLANDERS, THE (*Adventure*)
FIRST TELECAST: *October 2, 1960*
LAST TELECAST: *March 26, 1961*
BROADCAST HISTORY:
Oct 1960–Mar 1961, ABC Sun 9:30–10:30
CAST:
Sandy Wade .... William Reynolds
Zack Malloy .... James Philbrook
Wilhelmina Vandeveer .... Diane Brewster
Naja .... Daria Massey
Shipwreck Callahan .... Roy Wright

Sandy and Zack were pilots flying for their own one-plane airline, based in the Spice Islands of the East Indies. Part of the spice was Wilhelmina "Steamboat Willie" Vandeveer, their beautiful, blond, self-appointed business manager. Something of an operator herself, Willie was not above playing all the angles when it came to landing business for the boys. Unfortunately for Sandy and Zack, the results were designed more to benefit Willie than themselves. Whether flying passengers or cargo, the results were usually other than originally planned. Smugglers, escaped convicts, stolen goods, and mysterious, beautiful women were always keeping things busy.

IT COULD BE YOU, see *Bill Gwinn Show, The*

IT COULD BE YOU (*Audience Participation*)
FIRST TELECAST: *July 2, 1958*
LAST TELECAST: *September 27, 1961*
BROADCAST HISTORY:
Jul 1958–Sep 1958, NBC Wed 10:00–10:30
Nov 1958–Mar 1959, NBC Thu 8:30–9:00
Sep 1959–Jan 1960, NBC Sat 10:30–11:00
Jun 1961–Sep 1961, NBC Wed 10:00–10:30
EMCEE:
Bill Leyden
ASSISTANT:
Wendell Niles

Unsuspecting members of the studio audience were reunited with friends or relatives, called upon to perform stunts, or given the opportunity to meet guest celebrities on this program. As on *This Is Your Life*, research was done on the "victims" before the show, and anecdotes about their lives and pictures from their childhood were brought out. Being in the audience was always exciting, because you never knew when "It Could Be You." Bill Leyden was also the host of the daytime version of this show, which premiered in June 1956 and ran until December 1961.

IT HAD TO BE YOU (*Situation Comedy*)
FIRST TELECAST: *September 19, 1993*
LAST TELECAST: *October 15, 1993*
BROADCAST HISTORY:
Sep 1993, CBS Sun 8:00–8:30
Sep 1993–Oct 1993, CBS Fri 8:00–8:30
CAST:
Laura Scofield .... Faye Dunaway
Mitch Quinn .... Robert Urich
Eve Parkin .... Robin Bartlett
David Quinn (age 16) .... Justin Whalin
Christopher Quinn (13) .... Will Estes
Sebastian Quinn (8) .... Justin Jon Ross
THEME:
"It Had To Be You," by Gus Kahn and Isham Jones (1924 pop song)

Short-lived comedy about the sometimes awkward romance of an unlikely couple—Laura, a high-powered, socially prominent book publisher in Boston, and Mitch, the carpenter she had hired to build a bookshelf for her. Despite the obvious social gulf between the lady publisher and the surprisingly literate blue-collar carpenter, the chemistry between them was powerful stuff. Eve was Laura's outspoken longtime assistant—who was all for the relationship—and David, Christopher, and Sebastian were widower Mitch's three sons.

IT HAPPENED IN SPORTS (*Sports Commentary*)
FIRST TELECAST: *July 3, 1953*
LAST TELECAST: *January 19, 1954*
BROADCAST HISTORY:
Jul 1953–Aug 1953, NBC Fri 10:45–11:00
Sep 1953–Jan 1954, NBC Tue 10:45–11:00
HOST:
Bud Palmer

It Happened in Sports was used to fill the time between the conclusion of the boxing bout that started at 10 P.M. and the local news at 11 P.M. Bud Palmer was the host and presided over both live and filmed interviews with famous sports personalities as well as films of historic events in the world of sport.

IT PAYS TO BE IGNORANT (*Quiz/Audience Participation*)
FIRST TELECAST: *June 6, 1949*
LAST TELECAST: *September 27, 1951*
BROADCAST HISTORY:
Jun 1949–Sep 1949, CBS Mon 8:30–9:00
Jul 1951–Sep 1951, NBC Thu 8:00–8:30
EMCEE:
Tom Howard
PANELISTS:
Lulu McConnell
Harry McNaughton
George Shelton

It was appropriate that *It Pays to Be Ignorant* was the summer replacement for *You Bet Your Life* in 1951, for neither was really a quiz show—both were primarily vehicles for comedy. *It Pays to Be Ignorant* had started as a radio series in 1942 and aired on TV once before, in the summer of 1949. The four cheerful lunatics who comprised host and panel were the same on radio and TV. "Professor" Tom Howard, a spry, 65-year-old ex-vaudevillian, posed extremely simple questions to the panel and got replies that ranged from the ridiculous to the absurd. The frustrated emcee would watch as the "experts" stumbled through an improbable answer, interrupted each other, and found that they had changed the subject completely. Members of the studio audience were invited to pull questions out of a dunce cap for the experts. If the experts failed to answer the question correctly, and the studio contestant could squeeze the right answer into the mayhem, the contestant won a nominal award.

More than two decades after it left the air, *It Pays to Be Ignorant* returned in a syndicated version that lasted the 1973–1974 season. Joe Flynn was the emcee; Jo Anne Worley, Billy Baxter, and Charles Nelson Reilly were regular panelists. The format was somewhat modified from the original.

IT TAKES A THIEF (*International Intrigue*)
FIRST TELECAST: *January 9, 1968*
LAST TELECAST: *September 14, 1970*
BROADCAST HISTORY:
Jan 1968–Aug 1969, ABC Tue 8:30–9:30
Aug 1969–Jan 1970, ABC Thu 10:00–11:00
Jan 1970–Sep 1970, ABC Mon 7:30–8:30
CAST:
Alexander Mundy .... Robert Wagner
Noah Bain (1968–1969) .... Malachi Throne
Wallie Powers (1969–1970) .... Edward Binns
Alister Mundy (1969–1970) .... Fred Astaire

Alexander Mundy was a cat burglar and professional thief who had style, class, and great talent. He had made only one mistake—getting caught. While serving a sentence in San Jobel Prison, he was contacted by representatives of a U.S. Government spy agency, the SIA. They offered to get him out if he would put his talents to work stealing for the government. Accepting the offer, he worked closely with an SIA department head, Noah Bain, who was his boss, aide, associate, friend, and watchdog. Filmed throughout Europe, *It Takes a Thief* saw Al Mundy on various assignments as a master thief for the SIA, romancing beautiful women, and generally being his relaxed, handsome self.

At the start of the 1969–1970 season there were a few changes. Whereas previously Mundy had been under house confinement when not on an assignment, he was now a free agent. His SIA contact had become Wallie Powers, and his father, played by Fred Astaire, became a semi-regular. Al's father was the retired thief from whom he had learned all his skills, and who occasionally teamed with his son on special jobs.

IT TAKES TWO (*Situation Comedy*)
FIRST TELECAST: *October 14, 1982*
LAST TELECAST: *September 1, 1983*
BROADCAST HISTORY:
Oct 1982–Sep 1983, ABC Thu 9:30–10:00
CAST:
Dr. Sam Quinn .... Richard Crenna
Molly Quinn .... Patty Duke Astin
Lisa Quinn .... Helen Hunt
Andy Quinn .... Anthony Edwards
Mama .... Billie Bird
Walter Chaiken .... Richard McKenzie
Decker .... Randy Dreyfuss
Judge Caroline Phillips .... Della Reese
THEME:
"Where Love Spends the Night," sung by Crystal Gayle and Paul Williams

A pair of overachievers found that dual careers can get in the way of family life in this contemporary comedy. Dr. Sam Quinn was chief of surgery at a Chicago hospital, working long hours but able to come home to a devoted wife—until she got her law degree. Now that Molly had embarked on her own busy career as an assistant D.A., Sam found his dinners cold, his shirts unironed, and his love life decidedly wanting. In bed, his wife just fell asleep. To complain would be chauvinistic, so Sam coped as best he could, which is more than could be said for the couple's teenaged kids, shy Lisa and aspiring rock musician Andy.

New careers brought new opinions, too. While Sam remained a dedicated liberal, Molly's exposure to street criminals had turned her into something of a hard-liner. One psychopathic offender caused her to erupt, "Says it's because he comes from a broken home. Of course he comes from a broken home—he killed his father!" Surprisingly, the one island of calm in this disrupted household was Molly's dippy mama, whose nutty responses sometimes helped make everyone else forget their complaints.

IT WAS A VERY GOOD YEAR (*Documentary*)
FIRST TELECAST: *May 10, 1971*
LAST TELECAST: *August 30, 1971*
BROADCAST HISTORY:
May 1971–Aug 1971, ABC Mon 8:30–9:00
HOST:
Mel Tormé

An exercise in nostalgia. *It Was a Very Good Year* compiled old film clips, memorabilia, and interviews with famous personalities to provide a capsule summary of the news, fashions, and songs of a given year in the 20th century. Mel Tormé was the host and, in addition to providing narration for some of the material and singing a song or two, he chatted with people who had been prominent in the year being covered. The years treated ranged from 1919 to 1964, but were mostly of the pre–rock 'n' roll era, so the show appealed primarily to older adults.

IT'S A BUSINESS? (*Situation Comedy*)
FIRST TELECAST *March 19, 1952*
LAST TELECAST: *May 21, 1952*
BROADCAST HISTORY:
Mar 1952–May 1952, DUM Wed 9:00–9:30
CAST:
Bob Haymes
Leo DeLyon
Dorothy Loudon

This situation comedy with music was set at the turn of the century and concerned the activities of a couple of Broadway song publishers. They had plenty of opportunities to demonstrate their wares (grand old favorites like "After the Ball"), as well as to welcome visiting vaudevillians to their offices. Bob Haymes, the brother of big-band singer Dick Haymes, and Leo DeLyon played the song-publisher partners and Dorothy Loudon played their secretary.

IT'S A GREAT LIFE (*Situation Comedy*)
FIRST TELECAST: *September 7, 1954*
LAST TELECAST: *June 3, 1956*
BROADCAST HISTORY:
Sep 1954–Sep 1955, NBC Tue 10:30–11:00
Sep 1955–Jun 1956, NBC Sun 7:00–7:30
CAST:
Denny Davis .... Michael O'Shea
Steve Connors .... William Bishop
Uncle Earl .... James Dunn
Mrs. Amy Morgan .... Frances Bavier
Kathy Morgan .... Barbara Bates

Denny and Steve were two recently discharged GIs who decided to room together while trying to find civilian jobs. They headed for Southern California because Steve had been stationed there during World War II, and loved the weather. Once in California, they found lodgings in the home of widow Amy Morgan, whose household also included her daughter Kathy and her brother Earl. Stories revolved around Denny and Steve's problems in adjusting to civilian life, their problems with various jobs, and the trouble they got into by repeatedly letting the conniving Uncle Earl lure them into his moneymaking schemes.

IT'S A LIVING (*Situation Comedy*)
FIRST TELECAST: *October 30, 1980*
LAST TELECAST: *September 10, 1982*
BROADCAST HISTORY:
Oct 1980–Jan 1981, ABC Thu 9:30–10:00
Jul 1981–Aug 1981, ABC Tue 9:30–10:00
Sep 1981–Oct 1981, ABC Fri 8:30–9:00
Oct 1981–Jan 1982, ABC Sat 8:30–9:00
Feb 1982, ABC Fri 9:30–10:00
Jun 1982–Sep 1982, ABC Fri 8:30–9:00
(In first-run syndication from September 1985–September 1989)

CAST:

Nancy Beebe . . . . Marian Mercer
Lois Adams (1980–1981) . . . . Susan Sullivan
Dot Higgins . . . . Gail Edwards
Vicki Allen (1980–1981) . . . . Wendy Schaal
Cassie Cranston (1980–1986) . . . . Ann Jillian
Jan Hoffmeyer Gray . . . . Barrie Youngfellow
Sonny Mann (née Manishewitz) . . . . . . Paul Kreppel
Mario (1980–1981) . . . . Bert Remsen
Maggie McBurney (1981–1982) . . . . . . Louise Lasser
Dennis Hubner (1981–1982) . . . . Earl Boen
Amy Tompkins (1985–1989) . . . . Crystal Bernard
Howard Miller (1985–1989) . . . . Richard Stahl
Ginger St. James (1986–1989) . . . . Sheryl Lee Ralph

This sexy comedy was about five pretty waitresses working at a posh Los Angeles restaurant (so posh that in one scene an enraged customer received a bill for $540, for six people). Nancy was the disciplinarian supervisor, trying to get a day's work out of Lois, Dot, Vicki, Cassie (the brassy one), Jan, and Sonny, the self-absorbed lounge pianist. Along with battling customers and chattering about their home life, the girls all giggled a lot, paraded around in skimpy outfits, and made jokes about who had "done it" the previous night.

ABC evidently had faith in this show. Despite a shaky first season, it was renewed, given a new name *(Making a Living)* and two new cast members, and tried out in several time periods. It didn't help.

Three years after leaving ABC, with its original title and most of the original cast, *It's a Living* returned to the air with new episodes produced for the syndicated market. Added to the cast were Amy, a naive, new young waitress; a new chef named Howard who was the constant, and disinterested object of Nancy's amorous advances; and the infrequently seen Richie Gray (played by Richard Kline), an electrician who eventually married Jan. In the fall of 1986 an out-spoken, sexy black waitress named Ginger joined the other waitresses at Above the Top. Late in 1987, in a moment of weakness, sarcastic Howard finally started dating Nancy and, to the surprise of everyone on the staff including himself, the two of them got married in Las Vegas.

During the 1988–1989 season there were two more marriages—Ginger to successful physician Reggie St. Thomas (Julius Carry) and her roommate Amy to Bobby Lee Lord (Jay Baker), a devout young preacher. As the series wound down, Dot was still looking for her big break as an actress, Sonny was as obnoxious as ever, Jan and Richie were expecting a baby and, most remarkably, Howard and Nancy were still together.

IT'S A MAN'S WORLD (*Situation Comedy*)

FIRST TELECAST: *September 17, 1962*
LAST TELECAST: *January 28, 1963*
BROADCAST HISTORY:

Sep 1962–Jan 1963, NBC Mon 7:30–8:30

CAST:

Wes Macauley . . . . Glenn Corbett
Howie Macauley . . . . Mike Burns
Tom-Tom DeWitt . . . . Ted Bessell
Vern Hodges . . . . Randy Boone
Houghton Stott . . . . Harry Harvey
Irene Hoff . . . . Jan Norris
Mrs. Iona Dobson . . . . Kate Murtaugh
Virgil Dobson . . . . Scott White
Alma Jean Dobson . . . . Jeanine Cashell
Nora . . . . Ann Schuyler

Comedy set in a small Midwestern college town where two college students (Wes and Tom-Tom), one kid brother (Howie), and one footloose guitarist (Vern) lived together in a houseboat. The stories, which ranged from light comedy to drama, involved their problems with school, girls, jobs, and each other.

IT'S A MIRACLE (*Religious Magazine*)

FIRST TELECAST: *September 6, 1998*
LAST TELECAST:
BROADCAST HISTORY:

Sep 1998–Aug 1999, PAX Sun 9:00–10:00
Aug 1999– , PAX Thu 8:00–9:00
Aug 1999–Mar 2001, PAX Sun 8:00–9:00
Oct 1999–Mar 2000, PAX Wed 11:00–midnight
Nov 1999–Mar 2000, PAX Fri 11:00–midnight
Feb 2000–Aug 2000, PAX Fri 8:00–9:00
Apr 2000–Nov 2001, PAX Mon–Fri 11:00–11:30
Mar 2001–Sep 2001, PAX Sun 11:00–midnight
Nov 2001–Feb 2003, PAX Mon–Thu 11:00–11:30
Apr 2003– , PAX Mon 8:00–9:00

HOST:

Billy Dean (1998)
Nia Peeples
Richard Thomas

Each episode of this inspirational series presented several incidents in which miracles had changed or saved the lives of people. Most segments used recreations of the actual incidents, with the real people describing what had happened to them, and in some cases actually participating. After their stories had been told, some of them were introduced to the studio audience in the theater from which *It's a Miracle* originated. Among the topics were medical miracles, dreams and visions, guardian angels, premonitions, and warning voices. One segment told of a man who didn't understand why he been drawn to the Hermosa Beach Pier until meeting a fisherman with whom he became friendly. He found that his kidneys were a perfect match for the fisherman's, who needed a transplant to save his life. In another a man survived the crash of his small plane when he was guided by an angelic presence, and got out of the burning plane just before it exploded. Each episode also included a few "miraculous moments"—short man-on-the-street-type interviews with people who related what they believed to have been miracles in their lives.

After the first few weeks the hosts were seen outside the studio introducing segments. Co-host Dean was replaced in mid-October by actor Richard Thomas.

IT'S A SMALL WORLD (*Travelogue*)

FIRST TELECAST: *June 27, 1953*
LAST TELECAST: *July 27, 1953*
BROADCAST HISTORY:

Jun 1953–Jul 1953, DUM Sat 7:30–8:00
Jul 1953, DUM Mon 8:00–8:30

HOST:

Dick Noel

Travel films narrated by Dick Noel. The program became a local New York presentation for the remainder of the summer.

IT'S ABOUT TIME (*Quiz/Panel*)

FIRST TELECAST: *March 4, 1954*
LAST TELECAST: *May 2, 1954*
BROADCAST HISTORY:

Mar 1954, ABC Thu 8:00–8:30
Apr 1954–May 1954, ABC Sun 7:30–8:00

EMCEE:

Dr. Bergen Evans

PANELISTS:

Robert Pollack
Ruthie Duskin
Sherl Stern
Vim Gottschalk
Fran Allison

Panelists on this quiz show were asked to identify well-known events of the past. Clues were given in the form of scrambled headlines, dramatic vignettes, old phonograph records, etc. There was also a mystery guest.

IT'S ABOUT TIME (*Situation Comedy*)

FIRST TELECAST: *September 11, 1966*
LAST TELECAST: *August 27, 1967*
BROADCAST HISTORY:

Sep 1966–Aug 1967, CBS Sun 7:30–8:00

CAST:

Lt. Hector Canfield .... Jack Mullaney
Capt. "Mac" MacKenzie .... Frank Aletter
Shad .... Imogene Coca
Gronk .... Joe E. Ross
Boss .... Cliff Norton
Mrs. Boss .... Kathleen Freeman
Clon .... Mike Mazurki
Mlor .... Mary Grace
Breer .... Pat Cardi
Mr. Tyler (1967) .... Alan DeWitt
Gen. Morley (1967) .... Frank Wilcox

After their space capsule made a wrong turn somewhere, and cracked the time barrier, astronauts Hector and Mac discovered that they were headed back to a world quite different from the one they had left. They landed in a swamp smack in the middle of Earth's Stone Age, not far from a tribe of cave dwellers. Among their new prehistoric neighbors were a friendly couple, Shad and Gronk; their two children, Mlor and Breer; the tribal bully, Clon; and the suspicious chief, Boss. In the episode of January 22, the astronauts finally managed to repair their spaceship and return to the 20th century, bringing Shad, Gronk, and their children back with them. The cave people had even more trouble adjusting to modern-day Los Angeles than the astronauts did to the prehistoric world. Mr. Tyler was the superintendent of their apartment building.

IT'S ALEC TEMPLETON TIME (*Music*)

FIRST TELECAST: *June 10, 1955*
LAST TELECAST: *August 26, 1955*
BROADCAST HISTORY:

Jun 1955, DUM Fri 10:30–11:00
Jul 1955–Aug 1955, DUM Fri 10:00–10:30

HOST:

Alec Templeton

This summer musical series was hosted by Alec Templeton, the blind pianist-satirist, who introduced guest singers, dancers, and musicians, and chatted with them following their numbers.

IT'S ALWAYS JAN (*Situation Comedy*)

FIRST TELECAST: *September 10, 1955*
LAST TELECAST: *June 30, 1956*
BROADCAST HISTORY:

Sep 1955–Jun 1956, CBS Sat 9:30–10:00

CAST:

Janis Stewart .... Janis Paige
Pat Murphy .... Patricia Bright
Val Marlowe .... Merry Anders
Josie Stewart .... Jeri Lou James
Stanley Schreiber .... Arte Johnson
Harry Cooper .... Sid Melton

Musical-comedy star Janis Paige starred in this comedy series about the problems of a single parent. Nightclub singer Janis Stewart had lost her husband during the war and had a 10-year-old daughter (Josie) to raise. Not possessed of very much money, Jan and Josie lived in a small apartment with two of Jan's friends. Pat was secretary to a theatrical producer and Val was an aspiring actress and model. Stanley Schreiber was the son of the man who owned the neighborhood delicatessen. The format of this series allowed Miss Paige the opportunity to sing a song in most episodes.

IT'S GARRY SHANDLING'S SHOW (*Situation Comedy*)

FIRST TELECAST: *March 6, 1988*
LAST TELECAST: *March 18, 1990*
BROADCAST HISTORY:

Mar 1988–Jul 1989, FOX Sun 9:00–9:30
Jul 1989, FOX Sun 9:30–10:00
Jul 1989–Aug 1989, FOX Sun 10:00–10:30
Aug 1989–Mar 1990, FOX Sun 10:30–11:00
(Also Showtime Cable Network)

CAST:

Garry Shandling .... Garry Shandling
Mrs. Shandling .... Barbara Cason
Nancy Bancroft .... Molly Cheek
Pete Schumaker .... Michael Tucci
Jackie Schumaker .... Bernadette Birkett
Grant Schumaker .... Scott Nemes
Leonard Smith .... Paul Willson
Ian (1989–1990) .... Ian Buchanan
Phoebe Bass (1989–1990) .... Jessica Harper

In the 1970s and 1980s television saw an increasing number of shows that mocked TV's own conventions—*Saturday Night Live*, *Fernwood 2-Night*, *Late Night with David Letterman*, *Max Headroom*, and *Moonlighting*, among others. One of the most innovative was this slice-of-life comedy that was so unconventional it was reportedly rejected by all three major commercial networks, before premiering on the Showtime cable network in the fall of 1986.

The focus, more or less, was the fictionalized personal life of offbeat comic Garry Shandling. Garry played himself, a friendly, rather neurotic young single coping not too successfully with the outside world. His main problems were his general insecurity, his limited success with women, and a tendency to have things fall apart around him. Most of the action took place in a set that was a replica of Garry's real-life living room. His platonic friend Nancy, his mother, his best married friend Pete, and Pete's intellectual young son Grant came by to help Garry deal with his problems. Leonard was the nosy next-door neighbor.

What made *It's Garry Shandling's Show* so different was its point of view. Garry knew he was on television. As George Burns had done three decades before, he opened each show talking directly to the audience and, as the story progressed, regularly paused to make observations to the camera. Not only did Garry know, but so did all the others in the cast, and stories were written to take advantage of this awareness. If Garry was leaving home he might invite the studio audience to use his living room while he was away—and they did—until he came back and they returned to their seats. At times he would leave the set and go into the audience to get personal reactions to what was going on or "take a call from a viewer" (à la *Donahue*). Sometimes the other actors, in character, chided Garry for paying too much attention to the camera and not enough to the plot. Garry and his writers were all too familiar with the standard elements of traditional sitcoms—including the "fourth wall" (between fictional character and real life)—and went out of their way to make fun of them, while still presenting a reasonably coherent, and funny, story. This extended even to the show's self-mocking theme song; Garry's fictional neighbor might drop by to complain that it was being played too loud—again!

It's Garry Shandling's Show received rave reviews from critics bored with standard TV fare, and did reasonably well on the limited-distribution Showtime cable service. In early 1988, in an effort to bolster its Sunday night lineup, the new Fox network secured the rights to air reruns of the Showtime episodes not less than one month after they had aired on Showtime, and all America could see what the fuss was about.

In 1989 both Garry and his friend Nancy found love, he with Phoebe Bass and she with Ian. Early in 1990 Garry and Phoebe were married, and he was still adjusting to married life when Fox canceled the show. New episodes continued to air on Showtime for the next three months.

IT'S LIKE, YOU KNOW (*Situation Comedy*)
FIRST TELECAST: *March 24, 1999*
LAST TELECAST: *January 5, 2000*
BROADCAST HISTORY:
Mar 1999–May 1999, ABC Wed 8:30–9:00
Jul 1999–Nov 1999, ABC Tue 8:30–9:00
Dec 1999–Jan 2000, ABC Wed 8:30–9:00
CAST:
Arthur Garment .... Chris Eigeman
Robbie Graham .... Steven Eckholdt
Shrug .... Evan Handler
Jennifer Grey .... Herself
Lauren Woods .... A. J. Langer

Los Angeles, a.k.a. "La La Land," never looked sillier than in this engaging spoof of the city and its sometimes bizarre, self-obsessed ways. The city and its denizens were seen though the eyes of Arthur, a churlish, thirty-something New York journalist who despised all things L.A., so much so that he had come to town to write a book about hating the place. He was staying in the guest house of Robbie, a glib former college roommate and self-made millionaire who had made it big there (he invented a TV pay-per-view scheme that allowed Jewish citizens to watch High Holy Day services from the comfort of their own homes, called "Pay-Per-Jew"). Robbie's other best pal, and landlord, was Shrug, a spaced-out, totally bald little nerd who had never worked a day in his life, thanks to a trust fund from his fabulously rich family. Another friend was Lauren, a perky, pretty young woman with two occupations ("just because")—masseuse and process server. Sometimes she combined the two, serving papers while her clients were naked and facedown on the massage table. The most inspired bit of casting, however, was neighbor Jennifer Grey—*the* Jennifer Grey, of *Dirty Dancing* fame—who mocked her famous nose job and sagging career ("You recognize me!"). (Ms. Grey must have a great sense of humor.)

Stories revolved around the little idiocies of L.A. life, such as spotting stars in unlikely places, taking the day off to watch a live telecast of a high-speed car chase on the freeway, or how shocked everybody is when someone is simply *nice*. For not honking his horn in backed-up traffic, Robbie was given a party by strangers, and approached by a producer interested in making a film about his "good deed." He couldn't tell them that the horn just didn't work.

IT'S MAGIC (*Magic*)
FIRST TELECAST: *July 31, 1955*
LAST TELECAST *September 4, 1995*
BROADCAST HISTORY:
Jul 1955–Sep 1955, CBS Sun 7:00–7:30
HOST:
Paul Tripp

Each week on this summer series, three famous magicians appeared to perform some of their tricks before a studio audience. The host of the show, Paul Tripp, had been the producer and star of the popular children's program *Mr. I Magination.*

IT'S NEWS TO ME (*Quiz/Panel*)
FIRST TELECAST: *July 2, 1951*
LAST TELECAST: *August 27, 1954*
BROADCAST HISTORY:
Jul 1951–Mar 1952, CBS Mon 9:30–10:00
Apr 1952–Jun 1952, CBS Fri 9:30–10:00
Jul 1952–Aug 1952, CBS Sun 6:30–7:00
Sep 1952, CBS Fri 10:30–11:00
Sep 1952–Nov 1952, CBS Sat 6:30–7:00
Dec 1952–Sep 1953, CBS Sat 10:30–11:00
Jul 1954–Aug 1954, CBS Fri 10:30–11:00
MODERATOR:
John Daly (1951–1953)
Walter Cronkite (1954)
PANELISTS:
John Henry Faulk
Anna Lee
Quincy Howe (1951–1952)
Quentin Reynolds
Nina Foch (1954)

The object of this quiz show was for the celebrity panelists to describe what news story was represented by a visual or verbal clue. The stories were always current news items and members of the studio audience could win small amounts of money by determining whether or not the celebrity panelists were correct. John Daly was the original host/moderator and was succeeded by Walter Cronkite when the series was revived as a summer replacement for *Person to Person.*

IT'S NOT EASY (*Situation Comedy*)
FIRST TELECAST: *September 29, 1983*
LAST TELECAST: *October 27, 1983*
BROADCAST HISTORY:
Sep 1983–Oct 1983, ABC Thu 9:30–10:00
CAST:
Jack Long .... Ken Howard
Ruth Long .... Jayne Meadows

Carol Long .... Rachael Jacobs
Johnny Long .... Evan Cohen
Sharon Long Townsend .... Carlene Watkins
Neal Townsend .... Bert Convy
Matthew Townsend .... Billy Jacoby

Divorce with a laugh track was the premise of this short-lived comedy, which seemed to suggest that even the kids don't mind it when parents split. Jack and Sharon were the divorced couple who decided to live across the street from one another so they could share custody of their cute children, 8-year-old Johnny and 11-year-old Carol. Sharon had since remarried, and her stepson, Matthew, age 14, was also mixed into the stew. They all ran into and out of each other's kitchens—and lives—as did Sharon's new hubby, Neal (who wondered if his new family was really his) and Jack's meddling mother, Ruth. One of the favorite pursuits was trying to fix up the athletic Jack with someone new, so that everything would be symmetrical again.

IT'S POLKA TIME, see *Polka Time*

IT'S SHOWTIME AT THE APOLLO (*Musical Variety*)

BROADCAST HISTORY:

Syndicated only
60 minutes
Produced: *1987–*
Released: *September 1987*

REGULARS:

Howard "Sandman" Sims (1987–2000)
Rick Aviles (1987–1988)
Kiki Shepard (1988–)
Sinbad (1989–1991)
Mark Curry (1992–1993)
Step Exhibition (1993–1994)
Steve Harvey (1994–2000)
Rudy Rush (2000–)
C. P. Lacey (2000–)
The Apollo Dancers (1987–1994)
Frank Owens and the Band (1987–1994)
Ray Chew & the Crew (1994–2002)
Adam Syndicate (2002–)

Taped before a live audience at Harlem's famous Apollo Theatre, this variety series was a showcase primarily for black performers. Each telecast featured a celebrity guest host. Regulars included dancer Sandman Sims, comic Rick Aviles, and the long-stemmed Apollo Dancers. Among those appearing as guests and guest hosts were Melba Moore, The Beastie Boys, Natalie Cole, Exposé, Al Jarreau, Bill Cosby, James Brown, Stephen Bishop, Mary Wilson, Stephanie Mills, and Freddie Jackson. There was a regular amateur night segment and most episodes included an Apollo Kids segment (just as at the real Apollo) as well as tributes to great former Apollo stars like Billie Holiday, Sam Cooke, The Nicholas Brothers, Pearl Bailey, and Moms Mabley. Comedian/actor Sinbad served as regular host for two seasons. When he departed in the fall of 1991, *Showtime* went back to using celebrity guest hosts. In the fall of 1994 comedian Steve Harvey took over as permanent host and held that role for six years. When the 1998–1999 season started, Harvey and Kiki Shepard hosted a series of "Best of" shows until late October, because production had been delayed by a labor dispute.

In the fall of 2000 Rudy Rush replaced Steve Harvey as host and C. P. Lacey replaced original comic dancer Sandman Sims. Two years later, after a dispute with The Apollo Theatre Foundation, the original producers took most of the talent to a new venue, the Brooklyn Academy of Music, and retitled the series *Showtime in Harlem*. Regular features included Comedy TKO, Showtime Teens, Showtime Kids and Amateur Night.

A similar series, hosted by Willie Bryant and titled simply *Showtime at the Apollo*, had been syndicated briefly in 1954. This earlier series provided a rare showcase for black jazz and rhythm and blues talent in the pre–rock 'n' roll days, and footage from it—sometimes the only existing film of legendary performers—is often seen in documentaries.

IT'S YOUR CHANCE OF A LIFETIME (*Quiz/Game*)

FIRST TELECAST: *June 5, 2000*
LAST TELECAST: *June 21, 2000*
BROADCAST HISTORY:

Jun 2000, FOX Mon–Fri 8:00–9:00
Jun 2000, FOX Wed 8:00–9:00

EMCEE:

Gordon Elliott

In this close clone of the hit ABC series *Who Wants to Be a Millionaire*—big open stage, host in monochrome outfits, long dragged-out questions set to ominous music as the camera circled around—the opening gimmick was that contestants were all people with large credit card bills. The first contestant came with a statement indicating she owed $9,279. Correctly answering a simple question erased their credit card debt (their statement went into a shredder) and started them on a path toward possible riches. Then the regular game began. A correct answer to the first question won $5,000 and gave contestants a "bank" of money to gamble on future questions, with the wager for each succeeding question required to be at least 50 percent of their current winnings. The questions got progressively more difficult and if they had problems, contestants got two "second chances"—they could turn one question into a multiple-choice question, and they could replace one with a question from a category they had preselected as their favorite. There were nine questions, with potential winnings of $1,280,000. Contestants could quit at any time and keep the money in their bank—and could even decide to quit after being told the category of the next question.

IT'S YOUR MOVE (*Situation Comedy*)

FIRST TELECAST: *September 26, 1984*
LAST TELECAST: *August 10, 1985*
BROADCAST HISTORY:

Sep 1984–Jan 1985, NBC Wed 9:30–10:00
Jan 1985–Mar 1985, NBC Sat 9:30–10:00
Jun 1985–Aug 1985, NBC Sat 8:30–9:00

CAST:

Matthew Burton .... Jason Bateman
Norman Lamb .... David Garrison
Eileen Burton .... Caren Kaye
Julie Burton .... Tricia Cast
Eli .... Adam Sadowsky
Lou Donatelli .... Ernie Sabella
Principal Dwight Ellis .... Garrett Morris

Comedy about a smooth-talking, 14-year-old con

artist who met his match when an equally slick writer moved in next door. Matt always had a scam going—selling term papers, arranging dates, bugging his sister Julie's slumber party so he could sell the girls' secrets at school. He had his single mother Eileen in the palm of his hand. Then in moved Norman, a would-be writer, always broke, who began to date Matt's mother. Norman neatly countered every one of Matt's plans to break up the incipient romance. A steady stream of pranks, schemes, and counterschemes followed, as Matt and Norman tried to outmaneuver each other. Eli was Matt's chubby, dim-witted companion.

ITSY BITSY SPIDER (*Cartoon*)

BROADCAST HISTORY:

USA Network
30 minutes
Produced: *1993–1994* (26 episodes)
Premiered: *October 31, 1993*

VOICES:

Itsy Bitsy Spider, Langston.......... Frank Welker
The Exterminator.......... Matt Frewer
Adrienne Van Leydon.......... Charlotte Rae
Leslie McGroarty.......... Francesca Marie Smith
George.......... Jonathan Taylor Thomas

"The itsy bitsy spider,
crawled up the water spout,
down came the rain,
and washed the spider out!"

The unfortunate spider of the children's poem bore little resemblance to the resourceful title character in this cable cartoon. With four big eyes and an equally big grin, Itsy constantly tormented the portly, arachnophobic music teacher, Miss Adrienne, and her hapless cat, Langston, as she attempted to supervise the cheerful little girl, Leslie. Each time the spider appeared Adrienne would scream for The Exterminator, a half-man, half-robot Goliath who would proceed to destroy everything in sight (including, sometimes, himself) in his fruitless quest to catch the little bugger. *The Itsy Bitsy Spider* ran as part of USA Network's *Cartoon Express* in both the morning and early evening.

IVAN THE TERRIBLE (*Situation Comedy*)

FIRST TELECAST: *August 21, 1976*
LAST TELECAST: *September 18, 1976*
BROADCAST HISTORY:

Aug 1976–Sep 1976, CBS Sat 8:30–9:00

CAST:

Ivan.......... Lou Jacobi
Olga.......... Maria Karnilova
Vladimir.......... Phil Leeds
Tatiana.......... Despo
Federov.......... Christopher Hewett
Sascha.......... Matthew Barry
Nikolai.......... Alan Cauldwell
Sonya.......... Caroline Kava
Raoul.......... Manuel Martinez
Svetlana.......... Nana Tucker

Ivan was the head waiter at the Hotel Metropole in contemporary Moscow in this five-week summer mini-series. His biggest problem was the congestion in his 3½-room apartment, inhabited by nine people and a ferocious, but unseen, dog named Rasputin. Living with Ivan were his wife, Olga; their children, Sonya, Nikolai, and Sascha; Olga's first husband, Vladimir, and her mother, Tatiana. Also in the household were Nikolai's wife Svetlana and a Cuban named Raoul. All of them except young Sascha and Raoul had various jobs in Moscow.

I'VE GOT A SECRET (*Quiz/Panel*)

FIRST TELECAST: *June 19, 1952*
LAST TELECAST: *July 5, 1976*
BROADCAST HISTORY:

Jun 1952–Jun 1953, CBS Thu 10:30–11:00
Jul 1953–Sep 1961, CBS Wed 9:30–10:00
Sep 1961–Sep 1962, CBS Mon 10:30–11:00
Sep 1962–Sep 1966, CBS Mon 8:00–8:30
Sep 1966–Apr 1967, CBS Mon 10:30–11:00
Jun 1976–Jul 1976, CBS Tue 8:00–8:30

MODERATOR:

Garry Moore (1952–1964)
Steve Allen (1964–1967)
Bill Cullen (1976)

PANELISTS:

Louise Allbritton (1952)
Laura Hobson (1952)
Walter Kiernan (1952)
Orson Bean (1952)
Melville Cooper (1952)
Bill Cullen (1952–1967)
Kitty Carlisle (1952–1953)
Henry Morgan (1952–1976)
Laraine Day (1952)
Eddie Bracken (1952)
Faye Emerson (1952–1958)
Jayne Meadows (1952–1959)
Betsy Palmer (1957–1967)
Bess Myerson (1958–1967)
Pat Collins (1976)
Richard Dawson (1976)
Elaine Joyce (1976)

THEME:

"Plink, Plank, Plunk," by Leroy Anderson

PRODUCERS:

Mark Goodson and Bill Todman

ASSOCIATE PRODUCER:

Allan Sherman (1952–1958)

The format of *I've Got a Secret* was both simple and durable. Four panelists took turns questioning the person with the secret to determine what the secret was. A nominal financial award was given to a contestant whose secret (flashed on the TV screen for the viewing audience) could not be guessed by the panel. Each show gave three regular contestants an opportunity to stump the panel, and also had one celebrity guest with his own secret to hide.

The program had a rocky start—the premiere telecast used a courtroom set, with Garry Moore as the judge, the guest in a defendant's dock, and the panelists questioning like lawyers as they stood before the bench. This complicated setup was scrapped by the second telecast, when *Secret* adopted a standard panel-show set. The series went on to a 15-year network run, and was the most successful prime-time network quiz show in the history of the medium. It placed in the top ten for four consecutive years during the late 1950s, and remained quite popular during the following decade as well, a record that no other quiz program has approached. Almost a decade after the final telecast of its original run, it was brought back for a short summer run in 1976, with Bill Cullen, one of the earliest regular panelists, in the role of moderator. It was also seen in a syndicated version during the 1972–1973 season, hosted by Steve Allen.

As with any panel show, the secret of *Secret*'s success lay with the chemistry of its regulars. After considerable turnover in 1952, the show settled down to a well-balanced and familiar crew. Through the 1950s it was grinning Bill Cullen and acerbic Henry Morgan, balanced on the female side by Faye Emerson and Jayne Meadows. In the 1960s the two men remained, but the women were replaced by Betsy Palmer and Bess Myerson. The repartee was witty and spontaneous, although the unplanned quality was occasionally shattered, as on the occasion when Monty Woolley appeared as guest celebrity. His secret was that he slept with his beard inside the covers. When asked why, he replied, "As a matter of fact I don't. That's merely the secret they decided upon for me." Garry Moore, for once, was speechless.

J

J.J. STARBUCK (*Adventure*)

FIRST TELECAST: *September 26, 1987*
LAST TELECAST: *August 17, 1988*
BROADCAST HISTORY:

Sept 1987, NBC Sat 9:30–11:00
Sept 1987–Dec 1987, NBC Tue 9:00–10:00
Dec 1987–Feb 1988, NBC Sat 10:00–11:00
Jun 1988–Jul 1988, NBC Tue 9:00–10:00
Aug 1988, NBC Wed 8:00–9:00

CAST:

J.J. (Jerome Jeremiah) Starbuck..... Dale Robertson
E.L. "Tenspeed" Turner (1988).......... Ben Vereen
Charlie Bullets........................ Jimmy Dean
**Jill Starbuck* .... Shawn Weatherly

*Occasional

THEME

"Gone Again," sung by Ronnie Milsap

"I reckon a diamond is just a hunk of coal that stuck to the job. . . . If you want something done, find the busiest person to do it. . . . You look happier than a termite in a sawmill. . . ." Mumbling a constant stream of such homey aphorisms, eccentric Texas billionaire J.J. Starbuck set out to solve crimes using his natural charm, down-home manner, and, when necessary, his vast wealth and connections. J.J. was one of TV's outrageous characters. Apparently Marklee Industries, the San Antonio–based corporation that was the source of his wealth, ran itself, freeing J.J. to drive around the country alone in his 1961 Lincoln convertible, complete with steer horns on the hood and a horn that blared "The Eyes of Texas." Old J.J. never charged a fee, and usually helped those who had been framed or abandoned by the system. Local law enforcement officials were not sure what to make of this superrich meddler, but J.J. just charmed their badges off. After all, if they told him to move on, he'd just chew a bit and observe, "Well, sir, the Lord never closes one door without openin' another."

Early in 1988 J.J. picked up a sidekick in the person of "Tenspeed" Turner, a con man whose tricks and disguises came in handy at times (Ben Vereen had played the same character in the failed 1980 series *Tenspeed and Brown Shoe*, marking one of TV's more unusual character revivals). Jill was J.J.'s infrequently seen niece.

JACK & JILL (*Drama*)

FIRST TELECAST: *September 26, 1999*
LAST TELECAST: *April 11, 2001*
BROADCAST HISTORY:

Sep 1999–Mar 2000, WB Sun 9:00–10:00
Dec 1999–Jan 2000, WB Mon 9:00–10:00
May 2000–Jun 2000, WB Sun 8:00–9:00
Jan 2001–Apr 2001, WB Wed 9:00–10:00

CAST:

Jacqueline "Jack" Barrett............. Amanda Peet
David "Jill" Jillefsky..................... Ivan Sergei
Elisa Cronkite .... Sarah Paulson
Audrey Griffin....................... Jaime Pressly
Bartholomew "Bartow" Zane............ Justin Kirk
Mikey Russo .... Simon Rex
Eddie Naiman .... Gary Marks
Matt Profitt (1999–2000)............ Josh Hopkins
Jonathan Appel (2000)............... Chad Willett
Peter (2001) .... Ed Quinn
Emily Cantor (2001) .... Lindsay Price
Russell James (2001)............... Jeremy Garrett

THEME:

written by Jeff Cohen and performed by Pancho's Lament

Jack and Jill were two 20-somethings dealing with romance in this rather trite romantic drama—the kind where perfect strangers meet in corridors and pour out their feelings, and music soars as characters ruminate about their emotions. Jack (the girl) had fled to Manhattan to start a new life after dumping her cheating fiancé at the altar, moving in with her high school friend Audrey, a dancer. Jill (the guy) worked as a designer for Major Toys and was dating Elisa, an assistant assignment editor at TV station WNKW. He had two buddies, Bartow, his medical student roommate, and Mikey, who worked as bartender at The @ Bar. While looking for a job Jack ran into Elisa, and they became fast friends. Jack took an unpaid job as an intern at the station and was soon promoted to field producer. Bartow was intrigued by Audrey but she was oblivious to his interest, instead dating a director who gave her the lead role in a new play. Bartow was so supportive, helping her work on the role, that she eventually decided she wanted a relationship with him. In November Jill finally asked Jack to go out on a date, but it didn't work out, and she started dating hotshot reporter Matt Profitt. When Jill was offered a vice presidency in the toy company contingent on modifying his design to make it a violent war toy, he quit. Then, at episode's end, he told Jack that he had wanted her from the moment he met her. In the season finale Jack and Jill considered moving in together but decided they weren't ready. Bartow and Audrey were going their separate ways—he got a medical fellowship in North Carolina, and she had a movie role in L.A. Bartow slept with a fellow med student, and, when she was leaving in the morning, Audrey showed up—and was livid. She broke up with him, but in the last scene he turned up at the airport and proposed to her as she, with tears in her eyes, was boarding the plane.

When *Jack & Jill* returned the following January, Jill was struggling to make it as a professional photographer. Audrey returned from L.A. after finishing the movie but did not want to see Bartow. Eventually they tried to be friends again. Jill proposed to Jack and she accepted. Elisa started dating Peter, a psychiatrist she had had sex with on a plane trip to L.A. to see the premiere of Audrey's movie—which bombed—but ultimately split when he seemed to be analyzing her. Jill, reluctantly, went into partnership with Mikey, running the bar where Mikey had been working. Audrey dated the obnoxious Russell, while Bartow started dating Emily. In the series finale Elisa and Mikey realized they might be interested in each other and Audrey told Bartow that she wanted to give their relationship another chance. Jack and Jill were planning their wedding and, before the ceremony, Jack found out she was pregnant. In the last scene Jill, who didn't know about the pregnancy, told her he wanted to call the wedding off and give them time to make sure they really wanted to get married.

JACK AND MIKE (*Comedy/Drama*)

FIRST TELECAST: *September 16, 1986*
LAST TELECAST: *May 28, 1987*
BROADCAST HISTORY:

Sept 1986–Mar 1987, ABC Tue 10:00–11:00
Apr 1987–May 1987, ABC Thu 9:00–10:00

CAST:

Jackie Shea .... Shelley Hack
Mike Brennan .... Tom Mason
Carol .... Holly Fulger
Nora Adler .... Jacqueline Brookes
Anthony Kubecek .... Kevin Dunn
Rick Scotti .... Vincent Baggetta
Belinda .... Noelle Bou-Sliman

Jack and Mike was one of several attempts by ABC to produce another young, trendy, romantic drama to follow its established Tuesday night hit *Moonlighting*. Jackie was a glamorous, dynamic newspaper columnist for the *Chicago Mirror*, who was always after a hot lead for an exposé, or sometimes just a warm human-interest story; Mike was a successful restaurateur, who operated two of the city's trendiest watering holes and was about to open a third. Though they were married and very much in love, their high-energy careers (her tips, his hors d'oeuvres) kept getting in the way.

Nora was the city editor and Anthony a reporter at the *Mirror*, and Carol the head waitress at Mike's new "Brennan's Grill." Rick was an occasionally seen attorney friend. The series was filmed on location in Chicago.

JACK BENNY SHOW, THE (*Comedy*)

FIRST TELECAST: *October 28, 1950*
LAST TELECAST: *August 30, 1977*
BROADCAST HISTORY:

Oct 1950–Jun 1959, CBS Sun 7:30–8:00 (OS)
Oct 1959–Jun 1960, CBS Sun 10:00–10:30
Oct 1960–Jun 1962, CBS Sun 9:30–10:00 (OS)
Sep 1962–Jun 1963, CBS Tue 9:30–10:00
Sep 1963–Sep 1964, CBS Tue 9:30–10:00
Sep 1964–Sep 1965, NBC Fri 9:30–10:00
Aug 1977, CBS Tue 8:00–8:30

REGULARS:

Jack Benny
Eddie "Rochester" Anderson
Don Wilson
Dennis Day
Mary Livingstone
Frank Nelson
Artie Auerbach
Mel Blanc

THEME:

"Love in Bloom," by Leo Robin and Ralph Rainger

Jack Benny had been a regular network-radio personality since 1932. When he made his first tentative forays into television in 1950, it was with a series of specials that aired on an infrequent basis in what would eventually become his regular Sunday nighttime slot. Ten of them aired during the 1950–1951 and 1951–1952 seasons. From October 5, 1952, through the following January his show was televised once every four weeks, and when he returned again, on September 13, 1953, it was on an alternate-week basis that lasted through June of 1960. For his last five seasons, *The Jack Benny Show* aired every week.

The format of the show, and the personality of its star, so well honed in two decades on radio, made the transition to television almost intact. Jack's stinginess, vanity about his supposed age of 39, basement vault where he kept all his money, ancient Maxwell automobile, and feigned ineptness at playing the violin were all part of the act—and were, if anything, bolstered by their visibility on the TV show. Added to Jack's famous pregnant pause and exasperated "Well!" were a rather mincing walk, an affected hand to the cheek, and a pained look of disbelief when confronted by life's little tragedies.

The two regulars who were with Jack throughout his television run were Eddie "Rochester" Anderson as his valet and Don Wilson as his announcer and friend. Appearing on a more irregular basis were Dennis Day, Artie Auerbach, Frank Nelson, Mary Livingstone (Mrs. Benny), and Mel Blanc, all veterans from the radio show. Blanc, the master of a thousand voices (including Bugs Bunny), was both heard as the engine of Jack's Maxwell and seen as Prof. Le Blanc, his long-suffering violin teacher.

Jack's underplayed comedy was as popular on television as it had been on radio. After fifteen years as a more or less regular television performer, he cut back his schedule to an occasional special and continued to appear until the year of his death, 1974. CBS brought back four episodes from *The Jack Benny Show*, originally filmed in the early 1960s, for a limited run in August 1977.

CBS had also aired reruns of this series on weekday afternoons from October 1964 to September 1965 as *The Jack Benny Daytime Show* and on Sunday afternoons from October 1964 to March 1965 as *Sunday with Jack Benny*.

JACK CARTER SHOW, THE (*Variety*)

FIRST TELECAST: *February 15, 1950*
LAST TELECAST: *June 2, 1951*
BROADCAST HISTORY:

Feb 1950–Jun 1951, NBC Sat 8:00–9:00 (OS)

REGULARS

Jack Carter
Don Richards
Bill Callahan
Lou Breese Orchestra (1950)
Harry Sosnik Orchestra (1950–1951)

NBC's innovative Vice President of Programs Pat Weaver introduced several novel concepts to television in the early 1950s, perhaps the best-remembered of which are the *Today* and *Tonight* shows. Another was the *Saturday Night Revue*, a package of two big-name variety shows on a single evening, one originating live from Chicago and the other live from New York. Comedian Jack Carter hosted the Chicago element from 8:00–9:00 P.M., while Sid Caesar and Imogene Coca starred from 9:00–10:30 P.M. in the New York segment, titled *Your Show of Shows*.

Jack Carter was a fast-rising young talent in 1950, having appeared on several programs, including his own series of specials on ABC in 1949. His element of the *Saturday Night Revue* was a music-comedy-variety hour, opening with a standup routine by Jack followed by guest stars and skits by a constantly changing supporting cast. Among the longer-lasting regulars were baritone Don Richards and dancer Bill Callahan. Memorable routines included a satire of current TV stars (Garroway, Godfrey, Berle, *et al.*) and elaborate musical productions such as "Gravediggers of 1950: A Musical Extravagangster" starring Carter, Cesar Romero, and the whole cast.

Both segments of the *Saturday Night Revue* were quite popular at the outset, blitzing the competition, but gradually the Caesar-Coca portion began to dominate. Carter's segment moved to New York at the start of the 1950–1951 season, but by the following summer it was dropped in favor of *The All Star Revue*.

JACK DREES SPORTS SHOW, THE (*Sports News*)

FIRST TELECAST: *July 2, 1956*
LAST TELECAST: *August 24, 1956*
BROADCAST HISTORY:
Jul 1956–Aug 1956, ABC Mon–Fri 7:00–7:15
REPORTER
Jack Drees

Jack Drees, who was also the announcer for ABC's *Wednesday Night Fights*, brought audiences up to date on the latest sports news with this nightly report. He also interviewed sports celebrities when they were available.

JACK LEONARD (*Music*)

FIRST TELECAST: *March 10, 1949*
LAST TELECAST: *May 5, 1949*
BROADCAST HISTORY:
Mar 1949–May 1949, DUM Thu 7:15–7:30
REGULARS:
Jack Leonard
Virginia Oswald, vocals
Bob Curtis, piano

Songs by the former big-band singer.

JACK OF ALL TRADES (*Adventure*)

BROADCAST HISTORY:
Syndicated only
30 minutes
Produced: *1999–2000* (22 episodes)
Released: *January 2000*
CAST:
Jack Stiles .... Bruce Campbell
Emilia Rothschild .... Angela Dotchin
Gov. Croque .... Stuart Devenie
Capt. Brogard .... Stephen Papps
Jean-Claude (*voice*) .... Shemp Wooley
Napoleon Bonaparte .... Verne Troyer

Set in the year 1801, this wild farce resembled an earlier version of the 1960s Western series *The Wild, Wild West*. Jack Stiles, a big-grinning adventurer, was a secret agent for President Jefferson, on worldwide assignment working undercover to thwart the plans of Napoleon to conquer the world. Emilia was his sexy English partner, a tough cookie who combined proto-feminism and heaving breasts. She ran an export business on the French island of Palau Palau and had a secret soundproof laboratory on her estate; Jack's cover was as her attaché. His alternate persona (behind a bad mask) was as "The Daring Dragoon," a Zorro-like defender of the island's people. Other cast regulars were Croque, the pretentious but ineffectual French administrator running the island; Brogard, Croque's buffoonish aide; and Croque's brother Napoleon (played for laughs by midget Verne Troyer), who frequently showed up on the island. Jean-Claude was the talking carrier parrot, dressed in a military uniform, who provided Jack and Emilia with useful information.

Jack of All Trades was filled with fancy swordplay, bad puns, double entendres and historical nonsense. Did Thomas Jefferson ever really say, "Touch my niece and I'll have George Washington cut off your cherry tree"?

Packaged with *Cleopatra: 2525* as the "Back 2 Back Action" hour.

JACK PAAR PROGRAM, THE (*Variety*)

FIRST TELECAST: *September 21, 1962*
LAST TELECAST: *September 10, 1965*
BROADCAST HISTORY:
Sep 1962–Sep 1965, NBC Fri 10:00–11:00
REGULARS:
Jack Paar
Jose Melis Orchestra

This was, in many respects, a prime-time version of Jack's earlier late-night talk show (*The Tonight Show*), which he had hosted from 1957–1962. It was somewhat more diversified, however, including topical films and recorded interviews, comedy sketches, musical segments, and home movies of Jack's travels with his wife, Miriam, and his teenage daughter, Randy. Each telecast opened with a Paar monologue and then, depending on the guest stars, went to either sketches, songs, or chats. The films of the Paar family's various trips to Africa, Europe, and Russia were often shown, with daughter Randy present to help with the narration.

Among the more notable moments were Richard Nixon playing a composition of his own on the piano on March 8, 1963 (his first public appearance since losing the gubernatorial race in California in 1962); Barry Goldwater discussing his chances of defeating Lyndon Johnson in the 1964 presidential race, one month after having announced his candidacy; and a filmed interview in Africa with Dr. Albert Schweitzer. In a precursor of what would become one of the most popular television series of the 1970s, Paar presented a condensed 20-minute episode from the British comedy series *Steptoe and Son* on his April 24, 1964, telecast. That series was the basis for the American situation comedy *Sanford and Son*. Although not classified as a regular, Jonathan Winters was a frequent guest during *The Jack Paar Program*'s first two seasons.

JACK PAAR SHOW, THE, see *Tonight Show, The*

JACK PAAR SHOW, THE (*Variety*)

FIRST TELECAST: *July 17, 1954*
LAST TELECAST: *September 4, 1954*
BROADCAST HISTORY:
Jul 1954–Sep 1954, CBS Sat 9:30–10:00
REGULARS:
Jack Paar
Betty Clooney
Johnny Desmond
Pupi Campo's Orchestra
Jose Melis

In addition to hosting a regular daytime series, which had started in November 1953, comedian Jack Paar served as host for this live summer replacement for *My Favorite Husband*. Jose Melis, who was to spend many years with Jack when he became host of *The Tonight Show* later in the 1950s, had started with him on the daytime show and appeared on this series. The format included monologues by Jack, appearances by guest stars, and songs by his regular singers.

JACKASS (*Comedy/Reality*)

BROADCAST HISTORY:

MTV
30 minutes
Original episodes: *2000–2002* (25 episodes)
Premiered: *October 1, 2000*

REGULARS:

Johnny Knoxville
Jason "Wee Man" Acuña
Brandon Dicamillo
Ryan Dunn
Dimitry Elyashkevich
Dave England
Stephanie Hodge
Greg Iguchi
Rick Kosick
Preston Lacy
April Margera
Bam Margera
Jess Margera
Phil Margera
"Danger" Ehren McGhehey
Steve-O (Stephen Otis)
Chris Pontius
Manny Puig
Chris Raab
Trip Taylor
Jeff Tremaine
Rake Yohn

Arguably, the show that sparked a mini wave of "gross-out" TV (*Fear Factor,* et cetera.) was this surprise hit on MTV in late 2000. A bunch of guys (mostly) played gross pranks—some quite painful—on passersby and themselves, often in public settings such as sidewalks and malls. In the first episode chief prankster Johnny Knoxville positioned himself in a Porta-Potti, which was then turned upside down by a giant crane—giving him a "poo cocktail." He then stripped naked for the cameras and was hosed down. In other gags (there were 10 to 20 per show) a chubby guy ran down a street clad only in a G-string; a guy on a bicycle with a (fake) baby took a fall, alarming bystanders; a guy farted loudly and repeatedly in a yoga class; a guy stuffed a dildo in his shorts to make it appear to bystanders that he was having a giant erection; the guys dumped a casket out of a speeding hearse; Johnny dressed in a fireproof suit and was "roasted" over an open barbecue; and Santa Claus asked for a colonic. Each show began with a skull and crossbones and the warning, "Don't try this dangerous crap at home." Some did, and sustained serious injuries.

Knoxville (real name Phillip John Clapp—but he was born in Knoxville, Tennessee) came up with the "inspiration" for this show, which was coproduced by Hollywood bad boy Spike Jonze. In 2002 it was the basis of *Jackass—The Movie,* which was not nominated for any major awards but did "gross" over $60 million.

JACKIE CHAN ADVENTURES (*Cartoon*)

BROADCAST HISTORY:

WB Saturday morning and Cartoon Network
30 minutes
Original episodes: *2000–*
Premiered: *September 9, 2000*

VOICES:

Jackie Chan, Shendu, Chow .... James Sie
Jade Chan (age 11) .... Stacie Chan
Uncle Chan .... Sab Shimono
Tohru .... Noah Nelson
Mama Tohru........................... Amy Hill
Capt. Augustus Black, Ratso .... Clancy Brown
Valmont (2000–2001) .... Julian Sands
Valmont (2001–)...................... Greg Ellis
Finn............................ Adam Baldwin
Hak Foo (2001–)................ Jim Cummings

Martial-arts movie star Jackie Chan was transformed into a somewhat younger and handsomer cartoon character in this action cartoon. In the story line Jackie was a young archeologist who came to the aid of his friend Capt. Black to retrieve 12 magic talismans that held the power to unleash havoc upon the world. Helping, more or less, were Uncle, who ran an antiques store, fiesty young niece Jade, who ignored his admonitions to "stay with Uncle" and joined in the martial-arts battles, and Tohru, a sumo wrestler. Of course there were snarling bad guys after the talismans—principally The Dark Hand, consisting of Valmont and his henchmen Finn, Ratso, Chow and Hak Foo. Shendu was the mighty dragon the talismans would unleash, if combined. The real Jackie Chan appeared on camera at the end of episodes to answer questions from his fans.

Jackie Chan Adventures premiered on the WB Saturday-morning kids' lineup in 2000, and in 2003 began reruns in prime time on Cartoon Network.

JACKIE GLEASON SHOW, THE (*Comedy/Variety*)

FIRST TELECAST: *September 20, 1952*
LAST TELECAST: *September 12, 1970*

BROADCAST HISTORY:

Sep 1952–Jun 1955, CBS Sat 8:00–9:00 (OS)
Sep 1956–Jun 1957, CBS Sat 8:00–9:00
Oct 1958–Jan 1959, CBS Fri 8:30–9:00
Sep 1962–May 1968, CBS Sat 7:30–8:30 (OS)
Sep 1968–Sep 1970, CBS Sat 7:30–8:30

REGULARS:

Jackie Gleason
Art Carney (1952–1957; 1966–1970)
Joyce Randolph (1952–1957)
Audrey Meadows (1952–1957)
Buddy Hackett (1958–1959)
Frank Fontaine (1962–1966)
Sue Ane Langdon (1962–1963)
Barbara Heller (1963–1965)
Horace McMahon (1963–1964)
Alice Ghostley (1962–1964)
Helen Curtis (1964–1966)
Sid Fields (1964–1966)
Phil Bruns (1964–1966)
George Jessel (1965–1966)
Sheila MacRae (1966–1970)
Jane Kean (1966–1970)
The June Taylor Dancers
The Glea-Girls (1956–1970)
Ray Bloch & His Orchestra (1952–1959)
Sammy Spear & His Orchestra (1962–1970)

ANNOUNCERS:

Jack Lescoulie (1952–1959)
Johnny Olsen (1962–1970)

THEME:

"Melancholy Serenade," by Jackie Gleason (written in 1953)

The lure of money brought *The Jackie Gleason Show* to CBS in the fall of 1952. The rotund comic had been starring in *The Cavalcade of Stars* on DuMont since the summer of 1950 and had developed into one of the few genuine successes on that money-poor network. When CBS offered him a staggering increase in weekly pay—reportedly $8,000 compared to the $1,600 that DuMont could afford—coupled with the funding to make his show a much more elaborate production, he could scarcely refuse.

Jackie's original CBS variety hour, done live from New York, bore a strong similarity to his previous show on DuMont, albeit with a much larger budget. His second banana, Art Carney, made the move with him, as did the June Taylor Dancers and Ray ("the Flower of the Musical World") Bloch's Orchestra. Audrey Meadows and Joyce Randolph were added to the cast of regulars, primarily in "The Honeymooners" sketches (see separate entry for details of *The Honeymooners*), and most of the characters that Gleason had developed on DuMont were honed to perfection on CBS. Among them, in addition to "The Honeymooners" Ralph Kramden, were The Poor Soul, Joe the Bartender, The Loudmouth, Reggie Van Gleason III, Rudy the Repairman, and Fenwick Babbitt. The Great One, as Jackie was called, opened each telecast with a monologue and then led into the first sketch with "And awa-a-aay we go," as he left the stage. His other catchphrase, used in reaction to almost anything at all, was "How sweet it is!"

The original *Jackie Gleason Show* ran three seasons and was replaced, for the 1955–1956 season, with a half-hour situation comedy version of *The Honeymooners.* When the variety show returned the following fall, it was with the same basic cast and format, plus some decorative additions in "Glea-Girls," 16 young models who did little else than look beautiful and introduce various sketches. There was no Gleason variety series during the 1957–1958 season, but Jackie was back in the fall of 1958 with a modified half-hour format. Gone were all the regular cast members from previous seasons and Buddy Hackett was added as Jackie's second banana. The chemistry wasn't there and, after only three months on the air, this short version of *The Jackie Gleason Show* expired.

In the fall of 1962, following an abortive failure with a quiz show *(You're in the Picture)* and the talk show *(The Jackie Gleason Show)* that replaced it in 1961, Jackie was back with a lavish full-scale variety show—*The Jackie Gleason Show: The American Scene Magazine.* His new second banana was Frank Fontaine (as Crazy Guggenheim in Joe the Bartender sketches), who could sing quite well when not in character and released a number of moderately successful record albums during his tenure with Gleason. Not only were most of Jackie's standard characters in evidence, but a new "Agnes and Arthur" sketch about two lovelorn tenement residents (with Alice Ghostley as Agnes) was added as a semi-regular feature. The beautiful "Glea-Girls," including Barbara Heller as "Christine Clam," were still in evidence introducing the segments of each show, but there was a considerable turnover in the supporting cast. There was more topical satire in this show than in Jackie's previous efforts, and more appearances by name guest stars. In keeping with the title, there were entire episodes that were done as musical comedies with book, lyrics, songs, dances, and sketches reflecting "the American scene." At Jackie's insistence, the entire production moved from New York to Miami Beach before the start of the 1964–1965 season, and remained a Florida-based show throughout the remainder of its run. A feature added the following year was a nationwide talent hunt, in which George Jessel traveled around the country auditioning young performers who would get their first national exposure on Jackie's variety show.

The 1966–1967 season brought a basic change in format, a modified title, and a different supporting cast. The title was shortened to *The Jackie Gleason Show,* Art Carney was back with Gleason on a regular basis after a nine-year absence, and Sheila MacRae and Jane Kean were the only other cast regulars. "The Honeymooners" was brought back as the principal source of program material. There were still variety shows with sketches and guest stars, special shows devoted to single subjects like circuses or tributes to show-business greats, and book musicals, but throughout this last four-year run over half of the telecasts were full-hour "Honeymooners" episodes. Sometimes they were done without music and other times they were done as musical comedies with songs and production numbers. They took place in Brooklyn, around New York, and in different locations around the world. They were done with and without guest stars, but the constants were always there, the Kramdens (Jackie as Ralph and Sheila as Alice) and the Nortons (Art as Ed and Jane as Trixie), middle-class schlepps bumbling their way through life.

JACKIE GLEASON SHOW, THE (*Talk*)

FIRST TELECAST: *January 27, 1961*
LAST TELECAST: *March 24, 1961*
BROADCAST HISTORY:

Jan 1961–Mar 1961, CBS Fri 9:30–10:00

HOST

Jackie Gleason

Jackie Gleason had been absent from network television for slightly over two years when he premiered a quiz show titled *You're in the Picture* on January 20, 1961. The program was a total failure and, on the following Friday, *The Jackie Gleason Show* was on in its place. The first telecast was simply a chat between Gleason and his television audience. It was an apology for *You're in the Picture,* made before a nationwide audience. For the next two months Gleason conducted an informal talk show in the time slot. Each telecast was devoted to a single guest who reminisced with Jackie about past experiences, both professional and personal. Among the guests were Mickey Rooney, Art Carney, Bobby Darin, and Jayne Mansfield.

JACKIE THOMAS SHOW, THE (*Situation Comedy*)

FIRST TELECAST: *December 1, 1992*
LAST TELECAST: *March 30, 1993*
BROADCAST HISTORY:

Dec 1992–Mar 1993, ABC Tue 9:30–10:00

CAST:

Jackie Thomas .... Tom Arnold
Jerry Harper .... Dennis Boutsikaris

Laura Miller . . . . Alison LaPlaca
Bobby Wynn . . . . Paul Feig
Grant Watson . . . . Michael Boatman
Nancy Mincher . . . . Maryedith Burrell
Chas Walker . . . . Breckin Meyer
Doug Talbot . . . . Martin Mull
Sophia Ford . . . . Jeannetta Arnette
Stephanie . . . . Ann Cusack

EXECUTIVE PRODUCERS:
Tom and Roseanne Arnold

Life on the set of a hit TV sitcom was itself a sitcom in this boisterous comedy starring Tom Arnold, which followed his wife's hit series *Roseanne* on the ABC Tuesday-night schedule. Parallels with real life abounded: Jackie Thomas was a Midwestern slaughterhouse worker and standup comic (like Tom) who got his own series and proceeded to drive his network and staff crazy (like Roseanne). A big, grinning, egotistical, obnoxious oaf, he was as innocent as a child and just as self-centered. His harried staff included new head writer Jerry, a serious-minded man with impeccable credentials, as well as Laura and Grant.

The Jackie Thomas Show was developed by Roseanne Arnold to give Tom his big chance; unfortunately the real-life series was a flop. Tom tried again the following season on CBS with *Tom* (q.v.), which was no more successful.

JACKPOT BOWLING STARRING MILTON BERLE (*Sports*)

FIRST TELECAST: *January 9, 1959*
LAST TELECAST: *March 13, 1961*
BROADCAST HISTORY:
Jan 1959–Jun 1960, NBC Fri 10:45–11:00
Sep 1960–Mar 1961, NBC Mon 10:30–11:00

HOSTS
Leo Durocher (1959)
Mel Allen
Bud Palmer (1959)
Milton Berle (1960–1961)

Under its original title, *Phillies Jackpot Bowling,* this program was used to fill the time between the conclusion of the bout on *Cavalcade of Sports* and the start of the 11 P.M. local news. Top professional bowlers competed for a $1,000 weekly prize with a special bonus awarded to the bowler able to throw six strikes in a row. Leo Durocher was the host for the first two telecasts, and Mel Allen took over until April 10, 1959, when he was replaced by Bud Palmer. Palmer stayed through October 2, 1959, and Mel Allen returned the following week and continued as host throughout the remainder of its Friday night run, which ended on June 24, 1960.

On September 19, 1960, the program returned under the new title *Jackpot Bowling Starring Milton Berle,* essentially the same show moved to Monday nights. Funnyman Berle was the host and there were two matches each week instead of the single match played when the show had been on Friday nights. An added feature of the new version was the appearance of a show-business celebrity each week who bowled for his favorite charity between the two regular matches.

JACK'S PLACE (*Drama*)

FIRST TELECAST: *May 26, 1992*
LAST TELECAST: *July 13, 1993*
BROADCAST HISTORY:
May 1992–Jul 1992, ABC Tue 10:00–11:00
Jan 1993–Feb 1993, ABC Thu 9:00–10:00
Jun 1993–Jul 1993, ABC Tue 10:00–11:00

CAST
Jack Evans . . . . Hal Linden
Chelsea Duffy . . . . Finola Hughes
Greg Toback . . . . John Dye

Romance was on the menu at this restaurant, a sort of *Love Boat* on dry land where lost loves and loves-to-be found each other under the fatherly eye of owner and former jazzman Jack Evans. Helping out in the youth department were cocktail waitress Chelsea, a no-nonsense, transplanted Britisher, and bartender Greg, a hopeless optimist juggling a life as a premed student and single father.

JACKSONS, THE (*Musical Variety*)

FIRST TELECAST: *June 16, 1976*
LAST TELECAST: *March 9, 1977*
BROADCAST HISTORY:
Jun 1976–Jul 1976, CBS Wed 8:00–8:30
Jan 1977–Mar 1977, CBS Wed 8:30–9:00

REGULARS:
Michael Jackson
Jackie Jackson
Tito Jackson
Marlon Jackson
Randy Jackson
LaToya Jackson
Rebie (Maureen) Jackson
Janet Jackson
Jim Samuels (1976)
Marty Cohen (1976)
Emmett Ashford (1977)
Tom Biener (1977)
Johnny Dark (1977)
Biff Manard (1977)

Five male members of the Jackson Family (aged 16–24) formed a rock combo called The Jackson Five, which had had numerous hit records in the early 1970s. In 1976 the boys were joined by three of their sisters in a four-week summer variety show. The emphasis was on comedy and popular music, with guest stars each week participating in both aspects of the show. The program returned for an additional run in the spring of 1977 with a different group of supporting regulars appearing in comic sketches.

JACQUES FRAY MUSIC ROOM, THE (*Music/Talent*)

FIRST TELECAST: *February 19, 1949*
LAST TELECAST: *October 16, 1949*
BROADCAST HISTORY:
Feb 1949–Apr 1949, ABC Sat 8:00–8:30
May 1949–Aug 1949, ABC Sun 8:00–8:30
Sep 1949–Oct 1949, ABC Sun 9:30–10:00

REGULARS:
Jacques Fray
Charles Stark (Feb–Jul)
Conrad Thibault (Aug–Oct)
John Gart, organ

This unusual program was essentially a longhair vaudeville/talent show. Pianist Fray, who specialized in concert numbers and show tunes, would play a bit, but most of the program consisted of performances by aspiring "high-brow" talent, rated by two judges in the studio and one at home (by telephone). It was all very classy. In August Conrad Thibault was brought in as emcee, replacing Charles Stark. Among those guesting were Marguerite Piazza, Bess Myerson, and Russell & Aura.

Also known as *The Music Room.*

JAG (*Legal Drama*)
FIRST TELECAST: *September 23, 1995*
LAST TELECAST:
BROADCAST HISTORY:
Sep 1995–Feb 1996, NBC Sat 8:00–9:00
Mar 1996–Jul 1996, NBC Wed 8:00–9:00
Jul 1996, NBC Sat 8:00–9:00
Jan 1997–Mar 1997, CBS Fri 9:00–10:00
Mar 1997–Apr 1997, CBS Fri 8:00–9:00
May 1997–Sep 1997, CBS Fri 9:00–10:00
Aug 1997–Jul 2000, CBS Tue 8:00–9:00
Jul 2000–Sep 2000, CBS Fri 9:00–10:00
Oct 2000–Jun 2003, CBS Tue 8:00–9:00
Jun 2001, CBS Thu 8:00–9:00
Jan 2002–Mar 2002, CBS Fri 8:00–9:00
Jul 2003–   , CBS Fri 9:00–10:00
CAST:
Lt./Lt. Cmdr. Harmon "Harm" Rabb, Jr. .... David James Elliott
Lt. j.g. Meg Austin (1995–1996) ... Tracey Needham
*Cmdr. Teddy Lindsey (1995–1996, *1998–)* .... W.K. Stratton
Cmdr. Allison Krennick (1995–1996) .... Andrea Thompson
Lt. j.g./Lt. Bud Roberts .... Patrick Labyorteaux
Adm. A.J. (Albert Jethro) Chegwidden (1996–) .... John M. Jackson
**Agent Clayton Webb (1997–)* .... Steven Culp
Maj./Lt. Col. Sarah "Mac" MacKenzie (1997–) .... Catherine Bell
Ensign/Lt. j.g. Harriet Sims (1997–) .... Karri Turner
Petty Officer Jason Tiner (1997–) .... Chuck Carrington
**Secretary of the Navy Nelson (1997–2002)* .... Paul Collins
**Rep. Bobbi Larham (1997–2001)* .... Anne-Marie Johnson
**Adm. Stiles Morris (1997–2002)* ..... Harrison Page
**Lt. Cmdr. Mattoni (1997–2001)* .... Rif Hutton
**Lt. Cmdr. Mic Brumby (1998–2001)* .... Trevor Goddard
Capt. Matthew Pike (1999) .... Mark Metcalf
Gunnery Sgt. Victor Galindez (1999–2002) .... Randy Vasquez
**Lt. Alfred Aldridge (1999–2000)* .... A.J. Tannen
Lt. Loren Singer (1999–2003) ..... Nanci Chambers
**Judge Owen Sebring (1999–2000)* .. Corbin Bernsen
Renee Peterson (2000–2001)....... Cindy Ambuehl
Dr. Sydney Walden (2000–2001)..... Cynthia Sykes
Cmdr. Sturgis Turner (2001–).... Scott Lawrence
Petty Officer Jennifer Coates (2001–) .... Zoe McLellan
**A.J. Roberts (2002–)*............ Matthew Josten
**Secretary of the Navy Sheffield (2002–)* .... Dean Stockwell
Lt. Cmdr. Tracy Manetti (2002–).. Tamlyn Tomita
Meredith Cavanuagh (2002–) .... Isabella Hofmann

*Occasional

Lt. Harmon Rabb, an attorney with the Judge Advocate General (JAG) Corps of the U.S. navy, was the son of a decorated navy pilot who had been shot down during the Vietnam War and was still classified as M.I.A. A former navy pilot himself, Harm had given up his wings after losing his night vision following the crash of his Tomcat on the deck of a carrier in rough seas. Although this was a courtroom drama, Harm spent plenty of time in the field while accumulating evidence—in submarines, aircraft carriers, and jet fighters, as well as more conventional modes of transportation. Although most of his cases dealt with the military, he also handled an occasional civilian case. Sometimes he and/or one of his assistants even went undercover. Most of the stories on *JAG* involved investigations, although a good deal of time was also devoted to the characters' personal lives. An ongoing thread was Harm's continuing search for his father, who had been lost when he was only 6 years old. Meg was Harm's partner, and Cmdr. Lindsey worked with them. In the spring of 1996 Harm was promoted to lieutenant commander; Cmdr. Krennick, a tough prosecutor who had been in a couple of episodes early in the season, replaced Cmdr. Lindsey on the JAG team; and Adm. Chegwidden, a former Navy SEAL and the new head of JAG in Washington, D.C., was introduced. He was a tough but supportive superior.

Mac, Harm's new partner when the series moved to CBS, was a talented lawyer coping with the "good old boy" attitude still harbored by many in the military. Bud, his newly assigned aide and law clerk, who had been in a few of the NBC episodes as the public affairs officer on the USS *Seahawk*, was taking night courses in law school to become an attorney himself. He finished law school and passed the bar, taking on his own cases during the 1998–1999 season. Webb, an intelligence agent with ties to the CIA, helped them on some cases and sought their assistance on some of his own. Harriet, originally the public affairs officer who had replaced Bud on the *Seahawk*, transferred to JAG headquarters in 1997 and started a serious relationship with Bud. They were married in May 1998, and a year later she had a baby boy, A.J.

In the spring of 1999 Bud was promoted to lieutenant, and that fall Mac was promoted to lieutenant colonel. In November Lt. Singer, an ambitious—and not always ethical—new JAG lawyer (played by series star Elliott's wife) was added to the staff. A few months later Australian attorney Mic, whom Mac had been dating, pushed her to make a commitment and they got engaged. Later in the spring Harm began dating Hollywood producer Renee and Adm. Chegwidden was seeing Dr. Walden. That fall Harriet went into premature labor and lost the baby, a daughter she and Bud had named Sarah.

At the start of the 2001–2002, because he was unsure about how much she really loved him—he knew she also had feelings for Harm—Mic called off his wedding to Mac, shut down his law practice and moved back to Australia to rejoin the Australian Navy. Renee left town to attend her father's funeral and didn't return. Despite the opportunity afforded by these departures, Harm and Mac didn't date. New to the JAG staff was Sturgis, an old friend of Harm's, who was good-natured but very competetive. In March Bud was assigned to a six-month deployment on the USS *Seahawk*. At the end of the season, while on assignment, Bud was seriously injured by an Afghan mine and lay bleeding on the ground with one leg blown off.

Bud survived, but had a rough time adjusting to the loss of his leg. Coates, with whom he had worked on the *Seahawk*, had problems adjusting to obnoxious Singer, who had replaced him. In October, Sen. Sheffield, the newly appointed secretary of the Navy, assigned Manetti to JAG and Chegwidden started dating Meredith, a college professor. In November it was revealed that Singer was three months' pregnant. Harm thought the father was his Russian half brother, Sergei (Jade Carter), with whom she had had a fling just before taking her shipboard assignment. She told Harm she was having an abortion but later changed her mind. Just before Christmas Coates was reassigned to JAG headquarters, Tiner showed immediate interest in her, and on Christmas Eve Harriet found out she was pregnant again. In January Singer went on maternity leave while Bud was struggling to stay with JAG; he had been told that because of his disability he would be on limited duty and could not be promoted. In the spring Manetti helped gather the evidence that prevented Lindsey, who had held a grudge against the admiral for years, from ruining Chegwidden's career.

In April Singer's body was found and an investigation was held into her death. It turned out that in January Lindsey, who had been having an affair with her, had thrown her off a bridge into a river, where she had died. He was sentenced to eight years in prison for manslaughter, although DNA evidence proved that neither he nor Sergei was the father. The following week Chegwidden proposed to Meredith, who accepted.

JAKE AND THE FATMAN (*Legal Drama*)

FIRST TELECAST: *September 26, 1987*
LAST TELECAST: *September 12, 1992*
BROADCAST HISTORY:

Sep 1987, CBS Sat 10:00–11:00
Sep 1987–Feb 1988, CBS Tue 9:00–10:00
Mar 1988–May 1988, CBS Wed 9:00–10:00
Jun 1988–Sep 1988, CBS Wed 8:00–9:00
Mar 1989–Jun 1992, CBS Wed 9:00–10:00
Jun 1992–Sep 1992, CBS Sat 10:00–11:00

CAST

Jason Lochinvar "Fatman" McCabe .... William Conrad
Jake Styles .... Joe Penny
Derek Mitchell .... Alan Campbell
Gertrude (1987–1988) .... Lu Leonard
Judge Smithwood (1989–1990) .... Jack Hogan
Sgt. Rafferty (1989–1990) ..... George O'Hanlon, Jr.
Lisbeth Berkeley-Smythe (1989–1992) .... Olga Russell

J.L. "Fatman" McCabe was the tough district attorney in what CBS described as "a large Southern California city" (could they have meant Los Angeles?). A former cop who was noted for his earthy language, lack of tact, dogged persistence, and willingness to skirt strict legal procedures when it suited his purpose, the Fatman had a remarkable record of convictions and a long list of enemies. Jake Styles was his special investigator, a flashy, high-living young stud who often went undercover to get evidence for the cases they were working on. Also on McCabe's staff were Derek Mitchell, a novice, overly enthusiastic young assistant D.A.; and Gertrude, the Fatman's sassy secretary. McCabe's ancient pet bulldog, Max—who somewhat resembled his owner—was J.L.'s constant companion.

When *Jake and the Fatman* started its second season, early in 1989, J.L. had retired as D.A. and moved to Hawaii, working as an undercover investigator for the Honolulu prosecutor's office, with fun-loving Jake as his partner and young Derek doing the legwork. That fall he became Honolulu's prosecuting attorney. A year later J.L. and his team, including his Honolulu secretary Lisbeth and the indomitable Max, were back on the mainland. The mayor of Los Angeles had asked him to investigate corruption in the D.A.'s office and J.L.'s efforts led to the prosecution of the current D.A. At the mayor's urging he returned to his old job to help restore the credibility it had lost during his absence. As in the old days, Jake was his investigator and Derek was the assistant D.A.

JAMBOREE, see *Windy City Jamboree*

JAMES AT 15 (*Drama*)

FIRST TELECAST: *October 27, 1977*
LAST TELECAST: *July 27, 1978*
BROADCAST HISTORY:

Oct 1977–Mar 1978, NBC Thu 9:00–10:00
Jun 1978–Jul 1978, NBC Thu 9:00–10:00

CAST

James Hunter .... Lance Kerwin
Mr. Paul Hunter .... Linden Chiles
Mrs. Joan Hunter .... Lynn Carlin
Sandy Hunter .... Kim Richards
Kathy Hunter .... Deirdre Berthrong
Sly Hazeltine .... David Hubbard
Marlene Mahoney .... Susan Myers
Mr. Shamley .... Jack Knight

James at 15 was one of TV's most honest attempts to portray the pains and joys of growing up in the 1970s. Fifteen-year-old James Hunter was a bright, sensitive boy who found his world completely disrupted when his father, a college professor, moved the family from Oregon to Boston, Mass., in order to accept a new teaching position. At first James tried to run away; then he began to learn how to cope with life in a new, city environment. Among his new friends at Bunker Hill High were a hip black named Sly, who always had a little sage advice, or "slychology," when James needed it; and Marlene, a plain but very intelligent girl who always took the intellectual point of view. Sandy was James's teenage sister, and Kathy their older sister.

James was an avid photographer and also a daydreamer, One of the novel elements of the series was his periodic lapses into daydreaming of himself as he would like to be—heroic, suave, etc.—portrayed in special dreamlike sequences. Although there was comedy in *James at 15*, none of the main characters were caricatures, and likewise the subject matter was sometimes rather serious: a young friend who was dying of cancer, teenage alcoholism, venereal disease, the discovery that Kathy was having a premarital affair. Perhaps the most controversial episode was one in which James lost his own virginity in an affair with a Swedish exchange student, Christina Killberg (portrayed by Kirsten Baker). Although the subject matter in the series was tastefully handled, and NBC had high hopes for the show, it did not attract a large audience and was canceled after a single season.

Effective February 9, 1978, the episode dealing with James's affair, the series' title was changed to *James at 16*.

JAMES GARNER AS NICHOLS, see *Nichols*

JAMES MICHENER'S ADVENTURES IN PARADISE, see *Adventures in Paradise*

JAMIE (*Situation Comedy*)

FIRST TELECAST: *September 28, 1953*
LAST TELECAST: *October 4, 1954*
BROADCAST HISTORY:
Sep 1953–Oct 1954, ABC Mon 7:30–8:00 (OS)

CAST:
Jamison Francis McHummer (Jamie) .... Brandon De Wilde
Grandpa .... Ernest Truex
Aunt Laurie .... Polly Rowles
Cousin Liz .... Kathy Nolan
Annie Moakum .... Alice Pearce
**Aunt Ella* .... Kathleen Comegys

*Occasional

Brandon De Wilde was one of the child-star discoveries of the 1950s. A sensitive lad, and a natural actor, he was signed by ABC for his own series three years after his professional debut (at age 8) in the hit Broadway play *A Member of the Wedding*. *Jamie*, which had previewed to rave reviews as an episode of *ABC Album* during the previous season, looked like a surefire winner as a series. De Wilde was cast as a likable orphan who had been shunted from one uncaring relative to another, until he landed in Aunt Laurie's household. There he met a kindred spirit in Grandpa (played to perfection by 63-year-old character actor Ernest Truex), who was similarly ignored by his kin. Grandpa, twinkle-eyed and with a zest for life, became Jamie's bosom buddy, sharing escapades, and the joys of growing up and of growing old. Others in the cast included Liz, Jamie's teenage cousin, and Annie, Aunt Laurie's helper in the catering business.

Jamie was a live weekly series and there was some publicity at the time about the problems of a youngster, however gifted, being so deeply involved in an adult profession during his formative years. De Wilde's parents had a special contract which allowed him to drop out of the series on short notice if he wanted to, or if his parents felt it was impairing his emotional growth. *Jamie* did indeed end abruptly two weeks into its second season, but it was not due to concern over Master De Wilde, but rather to a fight between network and sponsor over mundane business matters. An attempt was made to locate the popular program in another time slot or on another network, but this did not transpire.

The ending was unhappy in the long run for the tow-headed young star, as well. Never able to sustain the success of his youth into adulthood, Brandon De Wilde died in 1972, at the age of 30, in a traffic accident.

JAMIE FOXX SHOW, THE (*Situation Comedy*)

FIRST TELECAST: *August 28, 1996*
LAST TELECAST: *September 23, 2001*
BROADCAST HISTORY:
Aug 1996–Mar 1997, WB Wed 9:30–10:00
Mar 1997–Aug 1997, WB Wed 9:00–9:30
Aug 1997, WB Sun 8:00–9:00
Sep 1997–Dec 1997, WB Sun 8:00–8:30
Jan 1998–Jun 1998, WB Sun 8:30–9:00
Jul 1998–Sep 1998, WB Wed 8:30–9:00
Sep 1998–Sep 1999, WB Thu 8:30–9:00
Sep 1999–Oct 1999, WB Fri 8:30–9:00
Oct 1999–Apr 2000, WB Fri 8:00–9:00
Apr 2000–Jul 2000, WB Fri 8:00–8:30
Jun 2000–Oct 2000, WB Sun 9:00–9:30
Oct 2000–May 2001, WB Sun 7:00–7:30
Aug 2001–Sep 2001, WB Sun 7:00–8:00

CAST:
Jamie King .... Jamie Foxx
Uncle Junior King .... Garrett Morris
Aunt Helen King .... Ellia English
Francesca "Fancy" Monroe .... Garcelle Beauvais
Braxton T. Hartnabrig .... Christopher B. Duncan
Dennis (1996–1997) .... Andy Berman
Tyrone Koppel (1996–1997) .... Jamie Foxx
Cameron Caldwell (1998–1999) .... Susan Wood
Bob Nelson (1999–2000) .... Blake Clark
Gloria (1999–2001) .... Karen Maruyama
Nicole Evans (1999–2000) .... Rhona Bennett
Phil (1999–2000) .... Alex Thomas
Dwayne "Mouse" Abercrombie (1999–2000) .... Suli McCullough
Curtis Davis (1999–2000) .... Chris Spencer

Jamie was an aspiring actor in Los Angeles, working, and living, at King's Tower, the small hotel owned by his uncle and aunt. On the staff were Fancy, the sexy woman who worked the front desk; Braxton, an accountant; and Dennis, the clumsy white bellboy. Jamie was infatuated with Fancy, who, after training him, told him she didn't believe in office romances. Uncle Junior was a compulsive gambler. In a February 1998 episode Fancy finally relented and slept with Jamie, but he was so nervous he couldn't perform—and he left her apartment totally embarrassed. At the beginning of March he moved in with Braxton and accidentally started a fire that forced both of them into King's Tower, Braxton in his own room, and Jamie with his aunt and uncle. A year later, in the season finale, Jamie got a gig with the rap group K-Ci and JoJo, and as the episode ended, was about to embark on a year-long tour—not realizing that Fancy was in love with him.

That fall Jamie had a falling out with the group and returned to L.A. broke. Fancy had been dating others and, although there was still chemistry between them, she and Jamie no longer dated. Braxton's social life, however, had picked up. He was dating Cameron, the attractive blond delivery person for GPS. In the May 1999 season finale Fancy was on the verge of marrying Dr. Silas Landry (Alan F. Smith) when Jamie told her he loved her and she admitted she loved him too.

In October 1999 Junior and Helen promoted Braxton to general manager and Fancy to director of sales. Jamie, whose acting/singing career was going nowhere, took a job with Jingles 2000, a small advertising agency that specialized in commercial jingles. Bob was his new boss; Phil, Mouse, Curtis and Nicole, his coworkers. Jamie and Fancy were having an affair, but he was still living at King's Tower. In January, out of guilt, he decided to start paying rent for his room, and at the end of the month he was promoted to supervisor at the jingle company. In May Jamie got fired for working on a demo tape for a recording contract at the company's studio.

He and Nicole performed as a duo in Vegas and she put the move on him—which created serious problems when Fancy showed up. Jamie was forced to choose between her and his singing career with Nicole.

At the start of the 2000–2001 season Jamie decided to pursue his singing career but not to tour with Nicole. Although he broke up with Fancy, they eventually got back together on a tentative basis, while still dating others. In December Jamie proposed and she accepted. Junior and Helen decided to retire and announced they were giving 75 percent ownership of the hotel to Jamie and his soon-to-be bride. This bent Braxton—he had assumed that he'd be in charge—out of shape. It also forced Fancy to tell everyone she had been offered a job as marketing director for a New York–based hotel chain, which was a surprise to everyone. In the last original episode, which aired in mid-January, Jamie and Fancy got married and he gave her the key to the apartment in New York where he had decided they would live, so she could take her big job. He also, with the Kings' approval, appointed Braxton to run the hotel and gave him 25 percent ownership.

During the show's first season, star Foxx also played the recurring role of Tyrone Koppel, an arrogant local TV news personality.

JAMIE KENNEDY EXPERIMENT, THE (*Comedy*)

FIRST TELECAST: *January 13, 2002*
LAST TELECAST:
BROADCAST HISTORY:

Jan 2002–Feb 2002, WB Sun 8:00–8:30
Mar 2002, WB Sun 8:00–9:00
Apr 2002, WB Sun 9:00–9:30
Apr 2002–May 2002, WB Sun 9:30–10:00
May 2002–Jun 2002, WB Thu 8:00–9:00
Jul 2002–Sep 2002, WB Thu 8:30–9:30
Sep 2002–Oct 2002, WB Thu 9:00–9:30
Nov 2002–Jan 2003, WB Thu 9:00–10:00
Jan 2003–Feb 2003, WB Thu 9:30–10:00
Feb 2003–Mar 2003, WB Thu 9:00–10:00
Mar 2003–Apr 2003, WB Thu 9:00–9:30
Apr 2003–May 2003, WB Thu 9:00–10:00
Jun 2003– , WB Wed 9:00–10:00

REGULARS:

Jamie Kennedy
Chris Tallman (2002)

Young comic Jamie Kennedy was the host and star of this variation on *Candid Camera.* Each episode included a number of pranks in which Jamie, often in elaborate disguises, played practical jokes on unsuspecting people with the help of their friends or relatives, or encountered random people in what the producers referred to as "on-the-street sneak attacks." There were a number of recurring characters, including Judge Jamie, whose personality ranged from senile to dirty old man, Virginia Hamm, who gave personal advice on "her" talk show, and Brad Gluckman, the spaced-out Malibu rapper. Other characters included Jamie as the host of an infomercial cooking show for the Instacooker (a real studio audience ooh'ed on cue at the preposterous device, and applauded when he agreed to sell it not for $200, but for five easy payments of $39.99), a job interviewer whose mouth was wired open due to jaw surgery, a confused pizza delivery guy and an office manager who hired a new temp and told him to fire current employees from the company.

During the first season Chris Tallman was featured in many of the pranks.

JAMMIN' (*Music/Interview*)

BROADCAST HISTORY:

Syndicated only
60 minutes
Produced: *1992–1993* (26 episodes)
Released: *September 1992*

HOST:

Byron Allen

Byron Allen hosted this weekly hour of music videos and interviews with performers. Although all types of contemporary music were included on the show, its primary focus was on black performers and rap music.

JAN MURRAY TIME (*Variety*)

FIRST TELECAST: *February 11, 1955*
LAST TELECAST: *May 6, 1955*
BROADCAST HISTORY:

Feb 1955–May 1955, NBC Fri 10:45–11:00

REGULARS:

Jan Murray
Tina Louise
The Novelties
Fletcher Peck

This short and short-lived variety series was used to fill the time between the conclusion of the bout on *Cavalcade of Sports* and the start of the local 11 P.M. news, in the spring of 1955. It starred comedian Jan Murray and featured singer Tina Louise, the singing and instrumental group The Novelties, and pianist Fletcher Peck. There was no set format for this live show, since the length varied depending on how long the fight took. There were occasional guest stars and, time permitting, comedy sketches, in addition to Jan Murray's shorter comedy bits and musical numbers by his supporting cast.

JANE FROMAN'S U.S.A. CANTEEN (*Musical Variety*)

FIRST TELECAST: *October 18, 1952*
LAST TELECAST: *June 23, 1955*
BROADCAST HISTORY:

Oct 1952–Dec 1952, CBS Sat 9:00–9:30
Dec 1952–Jan 1954, CBS Tue/Thu 7:45–8:00 (OS)
Jan 1954–Jun 1955, CBS Thu 7:45–8:00 (OS)

REGULARS:

Jane Froman
The Peter Birch Dancers
The Alfredo Antonini Orchestra (1952–1953)
The Hank Sylvern Orchestra (1953–1954)

Singer Jane Froman, who had worked long and hard entertaining the troops during the Second World War, featured men in uniform on her CBS network television series. In cooperation with the Department of Defense, the program sought out talented servicemen who competed for the opportunity to perform on this live program. The setting was a re-creation of a U.S.O. Canteen, and it was there that Miss Froman sang, chatted with her guests, and introduced young performing servicemen to the nation.

At the start of the 1953–1954 season the title of the program was shortened to *The Jane Froman Show,* the servicemen were dropped, and the emphasis shifted to a straight musical variety show.

Although Miss Froman was perhaps best known for her signature tune, "With a Song in My Heart" (which was also the title of her 1952 movie biography), this series was more notable for the introduction of another song—one of the first songs to be made a hit by the new medium of television. It was "I Believe," a semi-religious number written especially for this series and sung incessantly on it by Miss Froman, which went on to become one of the top hits of 1953.

JANE PICKENS SHOW, THE (*Music*)
FIRST TELECAST: *January 31, 1954*
LAST TELECAST: *September 12, 1954*
BROADCAST HISTORY:
Jan 1954–Apr 1954, ABC Sun 9:15–9:30
Apr 1954–Jul 1954, ABC Sun 6:30–6:45
Jul 1954–Sep 1954, ABC Sun 9:15–9:30
REGULARS:
Jane Pickens
The Vikings

Songstress Jane Pickens starred in this informal 15-minute musical show, backed by a male singing group called The Vikings.

JANE WYMAN SHOW, THE, see *Fireside Theater*

JANET DEAN, REGISTERED NURSE (*Medical Drama*)
BROADCAST HISTORY:
Syndicated only
30 minutes
Produced: *1953–1955* (39 episodes)
Released: *February 1954*
CAST:
Janet Dean............................Ella Raines

Medical drama about an earnest young nurse who believed in treating patients' hopes and fears as well as their broken bones. Recently discharged from the Air Force, Nurse Dean traveled around the country on private assignments, involving herself in all sorts of human dramas. At the end of each episode she also appeared in a little spot promoting the nursing profession.

The series was filmed in New York.

JAYE P. MORGAN SHOW, THE (*Music*)
FIRST TELECAST: *June 13, 1956*
LAST TELECAST: *August 24, 1956*
BROADCAST HISTORY:
Jun 1956–Aug 1956, NBC Wed/Fri 7:30–7:45
REGULARS:
Jaye P. Morgan
The Morgan Brothers
The Joel Herron Orchestra

Jaye P. Morgan starred in this 1956 summer replacement for *Coke Time*. The informal quarter hour was filled with popular songs sung by Miss Morgan and a vocal quartet made up of her four brothers.

JEAN ARTHUR SHOW, THE (*Situation Comedy*)
FIRST TELECAST: *September 12, 1966*
LAST TELECAST: *December 5, 1966*
BROADCAST HISTORY:
Sep 1966–Dec 1966, CBS Mon 10:00–10:30
CAST:
Patricia Marshall......................Jean Arthur
Paul Marshall........................Ron Harper
Morton.............................Leonard Stone
Richie Wells.......................Richard Conte

Attractive Patricia Marshall was the best defense attorney in town and, as a widow, one of the most eligible women as well. Her 25-year-old son Paul had recently graduated from law school and returned home to practice law with her. Patricia's comic involvements with her clients and family provided the stories in this series. An almost silent member of the cast was her chauffeur, Morton, who would probably have had more to say if his boss had ever stopped talking long enough for him to get a word in.

JEAN CARROLL SHOW, THE, see *Take It From Me*

JEANNIE CARSON SHOW, THE, see *Hey Jeannie*

JEFF FOXWORTHY SHOW, THE (*Situation Comedy*)
FIRST TELECAST: *September 16, 1995*
LAST TELECAST: *May 26, 1997*
BROADCAST HISTORY:
Sep 1995, ABC Tue 8:30–9:00
Sep 1995–Jan 1996, ABC Sat 8:00–8:30
Feb 1996, ABC Sat 8:30–9:00
Sep 1996–May 1997, NBC Mon 8:00–8:30
CAST:
Jeff Foxworthy....................Jeff Foxworthy
Karen Foxworthy (1995–1996)........Anita Barone
Karen Foxworthy (1996–1997).........Ann Cusack
Matt Foxworthy (age 7).........Haley Joel Osment
Justin Foxworthy (1996–1997)...Jonathan Lipnicki
Walt Bacon (1995).......................Matt Clark
Russ Francis (1995)................Matt Borlenghi
Craig Lesko (1995)..................Steve Hytner
Sandi (1995)........................Sue Murphy
Elliot (1995–1996)...............Dakin Matthews
Lois (1995–1996)......................Bibi Besch
Nettie (1996–1997)..............Kathryn Zaremba
Big Jim Foxworthy (1996–1997)........G.W. Bailey

Good ol' boy Jeff Foxworthy adapted his unique brand of Southern humor ("If somebody takes his dog for a walk and they both use the tree by the corner, he might be a redneck") to TV in this family sitcom. In the first season he owned a small heating and air-conditioning company in Indiana. At home he traded gentle jibes with his wife Karen, a nurse, and their bright 7-year-old, Matt. Walt and Russ were his two dim-witted workers on the job, Sandi was Karen's worldly co-worker, and Craig the Foxworthys' condescending neighbor at The Hunt Club at Avon housing development. Elliot, a college professor, and Lois were Karen's disdainful parents.

When the series moved to NBC for its second season, the entire cast changed, with the exception of Jeff and son Matt (who suddenly became 9, and was somewhat dumber than he had been in Indiana). The locale was now near Atlanta, where Jeff managed the loading dock of a shipping company. He and Karen now had two children, adding youngest Justin, and there was a wisecracking, Army-brat kid-next-door named Nettie. Perhaps the most colorful member of the second cast was Big Jim, Jeff's larger-than-life father, who was an unrepentant ladies' man.

JEFFERSON DRUM (*Western*)

FIRST TELECAST: *April 25, 1958*
LAST TELECAST: *April 23, 1959*
BROADCAST HISTORY:
Apr 1958–Sep 1958, NBC Fri 8:00–8:30
Sep 1958–Oct 1958, NBC Fri 7:30–8:00
Oct 1958–Apr 1959, NBC Thu 7:30–8:00
CAST:
Jefferson Drum .... Jeff Richards
Lucius Coin .... Cyril Delevanti
Joey Drum .... Eugene Martin
Big Ed .... Robert Stevenson

The lawless frontier town of Jubilee, a mining community somewhere in the West during the 1850s, was the setting for *Jefferson Drum*. Jefferson was the editor of the local newspaper who, although he believed that the pen was mightier than the sword, was quite a gunfighter when he had to be. A widower with a young son, Jefferson had a sense of great responsibility to his community and the law-abiding people who lived there. His efforts to maintain a decent town were aided by his printer, Lucius Coin, and by Big Ed, the bartender in the town saloon.

JEFFERSONS, THE (*Situation Comedy*)

FIRST TELECAST: *January 18, 1975*
LAST TELECAST: *July 23, 1985*
BROADCAST HISTORY:
Jan 1975–Aug 1975, CBS Sat 8:30–9:00
Sep 1975–Oct 1976, CBS Sat 8:00–8:30
Nov 1976–Jan 1977, CBS Wed 8:00–8:30
Jan 1977–Aug 1977, CBS Mon 8:00–8:30
Sep 1977–Mar 1978, CBS Sat 9:00–9:30
Apr 1978–May 1978, CBS Sat 8:00–8:30
Jun 1978–Sep 1978, CBS Mon 8:00–8:30
Sep 1978–Jan 1979, CBS Wed 8:00–8:30
Jan 1979–Mar 1979, CBS Wed 9:30–10:00
Mar 1979–Jun 1979, CBS Wed 8:00–8:30
Jun 1979–Sept 1982, CBS Sun 9:30–10:00
Sep 1982–Dec 1984, CBS Sun 9:00–9:30
Jan 1985–Mar 1985, CBS Tue 8:00–8:30
Apr 1985, CBS Tue 8:30–9:00
Jun 1985, CBS Tue 8:30–9:00
Jun 1985–Jul 1985, CBS Tue 8:00–8:30
CAST:
George Jefferson .... Sherman Hemsley
Louise Jefferson .... Isabel Sanford
Lionel Jefferson (1975, 1979–1981) ..... Mike Evans
Lionel Jefferson (1975–1978) .... Damon Evans
Helen Willis .... Roxie Roker
Tom Willis .... Franklin Cover
Jenny Willis Jefferson .... Berlinda Tolbert
Harry Bentley (1975–1981, 1983–1985)
.... Paul Benedict
Mother Olivia Jefferson (1975–1978) .... Zara Cully
Ralph, the doorman .... Ned Wertimer
Florence Johnston .... Marla Gibbs
Marcus Garvey (1977–1979) ..... Ernest Harden, Jr.
Allan Willis (1978–1979) .... Jay Hammer
Jessica Jefferson (1984–1985) .... Ebonie Smith
Charlie (1984–1985) .... Danny Wells
THEME:
"Moving on Up," by Jeff Barry and Ja'net DuBois
PRODUCER:
Norman Lear

George Jefferson was the black Archie Bunker. In fact, he had been Archie's next-door neighbor in Queens for several years, a situation that created quite a turmoil between the two opinionated, blustery, bigoted individuals. George had started a small dry-cleaning business and his success resulted in expansion to a small chain. It was at that point that this spin-off from *All in the Family* started, with George, his levelheaded wife Louise, and their college-student son Lionel moving into a luxury high-rise apartment on Manhattan's East Side.

One of the Jeffersons' neighbors was an erudite Englishman, Harry Bentley; another was Tom Willis, a white man with a black wife (Helen). Their daughter Jenny became Lionel's girlfriend, fiancée, and finally wife when they were married in the 1976 Christmas show. George's quickly acquired wealth enabled his natural snobbishness to assert itself, and he was often pretty intolerable. He resented Lionel's involvement with the child of a mixed marriage and was continually at odds with Tom and Helen. Adding to the general level of discord in the Jefferson apartment was their wisecracking maid, Florence.

Mike Evans, who had played the role of Lionel on *All in the Family* and stayed with it when *The Jeffersons* first went on the air, left the show in the fall of 1975. He was replaced by Damon Evans, another young black actor, to whom he was not related. Early in the 1977–1978 season a young, streetwise black named Marcus Garvey was added to the cast as an employee of the branch of George Jefferson's chain of cleaning stores that was located in the lobby of the building in which the Jeffersons lived. The following fall brought Allan Willis, Jenny's white brother, back from a commune to become a regular member of the cast and source of irritation to both his own father and George Jefferson. Damon Evans had left the cast and, although Lionel was occasionally referred to in various episodes, he was no longer seen until Mike Evans, the original Lionel, returned to the series in the fall of 1979. Lionel and Jenny had a baby girl, Jessica, the following spring. After graduation from college, Lionel found a job as an electrical engineer for Teletex Electronics. His career was moving along but his marriage was faltering, and in the fall of 1981 Lionel and Jenny separated. Although Lionel no longer appeared on *The Jeffersons*, Jenny, who had become a fashion designer, continued to show up periodically. Neighbor Bentley returned in late 1983, after a two-year stay in Russia, still his very proper self, and George's business, as well as *The Jeffersons'* ratings, continued to prosper. In 1984 George went into partnership, along with Tom Willis, in Charlie's Bar, a little place that became their leisure-time hangout, and the following January Lionel and Jenny filed for divorce. That summer, after a run of more than a decade, *The Jeffersons* finally faded from the CBS prime-time schedule.

CBS aired reruns of *The Jeffersons* as part of its weekday daytime lineup from February 1980 to September 1981.

JEFF'S COLLIE, syndicated title for *Lassie*.

JENNIFER SLEPT HERE (*Situation Comedy*)

FIRST TELECAST: *October 21, 1983*
LAST TELECAST: *September 5, 1984*

BROADCAST HISTORY:

Oct 1983–Dec 1983, NBC Fri 8:30–9:00
Apr 1984–May 1984, NBC Sat 8:30–9:00
Jul 1984–Sep 1984, NBC Wed 8:30–9:00

CAST:

Jennifer Farrell .... Ann Jillian
Joey Elliot .... John P. Navin, Jr.
Susan Elliot .... Georgia Engel
George Elliot .... Brandon Maggart
Marilyn Elliot .... Mya Akerling
Marc .... Glenn Scarpelli

Shades of *Topper.* When George Elliot, his wife Susan, and their two children moved from New York to Beverly Hills they had no idea that the sumptuous home they had bought was haunted. The resident ghost was not a sheet-shrouded apparition, however, but the beautiful and sexy former owner, deceased movie star Jennifer Farrell. Jennifer decided to take 14-year-old Joey Elliot under her wing and help him adjust to life in California. She also thought he could use some help with girls, especially if he wanted to keep up with his much more worldly next-door neighbor and new friend, Marc. Under normal circumstances, Joey was the only one who could see Jennifer, which meant that his habit of talking to the furniture confused and worried his family and friends. There was the requisite walking through walls and objects floating in midair, but the focus of the show was on Jennifer's relationship with Joey and the spectacular wardrobe worn by Ann Jillian.

JENNY (*Situation Comedy*)

FIRST TELECAST: *September 28, 1997*
LAST TELECAST: *January 12, 1998*
BROADCAST HISTORY:

Sep 1997–Nov 1997, NBC Sun 8:30–9:00
Dec 1997–Jan 1998, NBC Mon 8:30–9:00

CAST:

Jenny McMillan .... Jenny McCarthy
Maggie .... Heather Paige Kent
Guy Hathaway .... George Hamilton
Max .... Rafer Weigel
Cooper ("Coop") .... Dale Godboldo

Jenny McCarthy became a media sensation during 1996 as the sexy, aggressive co-host of MTV's popular game show *Singled Out.* After considerable exposure (including a *Playboy* centerfold), she turned up in this cheerful but short-lived NBC sitcom as a small-town girl from Utica, New York, who inherited a '70s-style bachelor pad in Hollywood from her late father and decided to "go Hollywood." Moving in with her equally adventurous best chum Maggie, she immediately encountered two young, goofy, wannabe filmmakers who were living in the guest house—Max, an inept womanizer, and Coop, his slightly more sensible partner in "Pendulum Films." Even more surprising were the tapes left behind by her dad, whom she had never known. Guy had been a colorful B-movie actor in the '70s, renowned for his huge ego and skirt-chasing ways, and the tapes were little video letters to Jenny about having fun in life. Bubbly Jenny and loyal Maggie took his advice and shared slapstick adventures as they learned their way around Tinseltown, looking for work and having a good time, in stories filled with wild parodies on Hollywood stereotypes.

The over-the-top "tapes" from Guy (actor George Hamilton, having the time of his life) were the best thing about the show, but U.S. viewers did not get to see what eventually happened. NBC pulled the plug on *Jenny* after only ten episodes had aired, but Paramount Studios continued production in anticipation of the series being picked up by UPN. In an unaired episode, seen only in foreign markets, Guy showed up, not dead but merely missing, and "Disco Dad" became a partner in the girls' escapades.

JENNY MCCARTHY SHOW, THE (*Comedy/Variety*)

BROADCAST HISTORY:

MTV
30 minutes
Produced: *1997*
Premiered: *March 5, 1997*

REGULARS

Jenny McCarthy
Paul Greenberg
Michael Loprete
Jack Plotnick
Lou Thornton

MTV whipped up this rather standard sketch-comedy show to exploit the sudden success of Jenny McCarthy, the sexy, pushy co-host of *Singled Out* (q.v.). The skits were full of broad physical comedy, combined with the gross-you-out humor typical of MTV. In one she repeatedly threw up, just to remember what she ate; another consisted of gross guys sitting around in their underwear. Some of the jokes were a bit more sly; for example, the perky opening which lampooned the opening credits of *That Girl, The Mary Tyler Moore Show,* and other famous "single girl" shows. Jenny also made frequent fun of her own overnight celebrity. However, tight sweaters and breast jokes were more the norm during the series' short run.

JEOPARDY! (*Quiz/Audience Participation*)

NETWORK HISTORY:
FIRST TELECAST: *June 16, 1990*
LAST TELECAST: *September 8, 1990*

June 1990–Sep 1990, ABC Sat 8:00–8:30

BROADCAST HISTORY (Other):

Syndicated and network daytime
30 minutes
Produced: *1974–1975, 1984–*
Released: *September 1974*

CABLE HISTORY:

VH1
30 minutes
Produced: *1998–2002*
Premiered: *August 8, 1998*

EMCEE:

Art Fleming (1974–1975)
Alex Trebek (1984–)
Jeff Probst (1998–2002)

Jeopardy! was a game-show classic based on the simple premise of guessing the question to go with a given answer. In the first round three contestants faced a game board containing six categories; each category had five different hidden answers, worth different dollar amounts. A contestant picked a category and dollar amount, the "answer" was revealed, and all three contestants had the opportunity to be the first to guess the question that went with it. A correct guess got the designated dollar amount added to the winner's score, while an incorrect one subtracted that amount. A contestant's winnings were always in jeopardy! The second round was "double Jeopardy," with six new categories and the dollar amounts doubled. Then came "final Jeopardy," in which contestants who had anything left at this point could wager all or part of their accumulated winnings on the question that went with a single answer in a category chosen by the emcee.

Unlike most game shows, *Jeopardy!* prided itself on the difficulty of its questions and the intelligence of its contestants. It was a favorite among college students and a fixture on NBC's weekday daytime lineup from March 1964–January 1975. Art Fleming emceed the NBC series and the prime-time syndicated version during the 1974–1975 season. He was still with the show when it returned briefly to NBC daytime as *The All New Jeopardy!* from October 1978–March 1979.

Five years later, in the fall of 1984, *Jeopardy!* returned to the syndication market with Alex Trebek as both executive producer and emcee. The new version followed the same format as the original, although the dollar amounts were now ten times what they had been two decades earlier. *Jeopardy!* has been a major hit ever since—second in popularity only to the mega-hit *Wheel of Fortune* among syndicated game shows. Ironically, both series were created by the same person, talk-show host Merv Griffin.

A special version of *Jeopardy!* appeared on ABC in prime time during the summer of 1990, entitled *Super Jeopardy!* The game was the same, but the contestants were all winners from the regular series, now playing against each other for a grand prize of $250,000. Alex Trebek was again the host.

Still another mutation of the popular show turned up on cable's VH1 in 1998, this time called *Rock 'n' Roll Jeopardy* (a.k.a. *VH1's Rock 'n' Roll Jeopardy*). The rules and staging were very similar to the familiar syndicated version, except that now all the categories were about rock music: Rock of the '80s, Philadelphia Soul, Guitar Legends, etc. Some video and audio clips were used. The host was Jeff Probst, and the announcer Loretta Fox.

JERICHO (*War Drama*)

FIRST TELECAST: *September 15, 1966*
LAST TELECAST: *January 19, 1967*
BROADCAST HISTORY:
Sep 1966–Jan 1967, CBS Thu 7:30–8:30
CAST:
Franklin Sheppard .... Don Francks
Jean-Gaston André .... Marino Mase
Nicholas Gage .... John Leyton

Three undercover agents representing three countries worked together as Allied troubleshooters during the Second World War in this series. Their code name: *Jericho.* Franklin Sheppard was a captain in the American Army Intelligence, Jean-Gaston André an officer in the Free French Air Force, and Nicholas Gage a lieutenant in the British Navy. Specially trained, and having worked together since early in the war, they tackled assignments that ranged from sabotage to espionage to intelligence-gathering.

JERRY COLONNA SHOW, THE (*Comedy/Variety*)

FIRST TELECAST: *May 28, 1951*
LAST TELECAST: *November 17, 1951*
BROADCAST HISTORY:
May 1951–Jun 1951, ABC Mon 8:00–8:30
Jun 1951–Aug 1951, ABC Fri 8:00–8:30
Aug 1951–Sep 1951, ABC Thu 10:00–10:30
Oct 1951–Nov 1951, ABC Sat 7:30–8:00
EMCEE:
Jerry Colonna
REGULARS:
Barbara Ruick
Gordon Polk
"Cookie" Fairchild's Band

A program of music, comedy, and variety hosted by the famous comedian with the booming voice and the walrus mustache. From Hollywood.

JERRY LEWIS SHOW, THE (*Talk/Variety*)

FIRST TELECAST: *September 21, 1963*
LAST TELECAST: *December 21, 1963*
BROADCAST HISTORY:
Sep 1963–Dec 1963, ABC Sat 9:30–11:30
REGULARS:
Jerry Lewis
Del Moore
Lou Brown Orchestra
THEME:
"Smile"

This two-hour weekly marathon was possibly the most spectacular attempt at big-name variety programming in TV history—and also the most colossal flop. It was preceded by a great deal of fanfare, including the revelation that ABC had committed $8,000,000 in production costs for the first year alone. Headlining was Jerry Lewis, long a TV series holdout, and guesting were all sorts of big names. The first telecast, live from Hollywood's El Capitan Theatre, costarred Mort Sahl, Kay Stevens, Jack Jones, and Harry James. Later telecasts featured Sammy Davis, Jr., the Count Basie Orchestra, heavyweight challenger Cassius Clay (discussing his upcoming title fight with the champ, Sonny Liston), and the all-star cast of the movie *It's a Mad, Mad, Mad, Mad World.*

Whether it was simply too big, whether the controversial Lewis grated on too many viewers, or whether the scheduling was bad (NBC and CBS viewers had to leave in the middle of *The Defenders* or the *Saturday Night Movie* to catch the beginning), the initial airings garnered terrible reviews and disastrously low ratings. A considerable uproar ensued, in which the president of ABC flew to the West Coast for intensive conferences with Lewis and his writers (who included the young Dick Cavett) on how to save the show. Subsequent telecasts improved, but the ratings did not and the colossus folded after 13 weeks.

Two weeks later, *The Hollywood Palace*, a similar show—but sans Lewis—took over the theater and the first half of the time slot, and ran for six years.

JERRY LEWIS SHOW, THE (*Comedy/Variety*)

FIRST TELECAST: *September 12, 1967*
LAST TELECAST: *May 27, 1969*
BROADCAST HISTORY:
Sep 1967–May 1968, NBC Tue 8:00–9:00
Sep 1968–May 1969, NBC Tue 7:30–8:30
REGULARS:
Jerry Lewis
Lou Brown & His Orchestra

The George Wyle Singers
The Nick Castle Dancers (1967–1968)

THEME:

"Smile"

Jerry Lewis starred in this comedy-variety series that featured guest stars with primary appeal to young adults, teens, and children. The Osmond Brothers made a number of appearances on the show during its two seasons on the air and many other groups and individual performers popular with young people were occasional guests. Jerry's collection of comic characters, originally seen in his movies, all made their presence felt in short vignettes and longer comedy sketches. Among them were The Nutty Professor, The Poor Soul, The Shoeshine Boy, and, new for the TV series, Ralph Rotten. During the first season individual numbers and routines were recorded separately and pieced together to produce the hour-long show. In an attempt to generate a more spontaneous feeling, all shows for the second season were taped continuously in front of a live studio audience.

JERRY REED WHEN YOU'RE HOT YOU'RE HOT HOUR, THE (*Comedy/Variety*)

FIRST TELECAST: *June 20, 1972*
LAST TELECAST: *July 25, 1972*
BROADCAST HISTORY:

Jun 1972–Jul 1972, CBS Tue 7:30–8:30

REGULARS:

Jerry Reed
Spencer Quinn
Cal Wilson
Norman J. Andrews
Merie Earle
John Twomey
The George Wyle Orchestra

This five-week summer variety series starred the versatile Jerry Reed—comedian, singer, and songwriter. His musical success had been primarily in country music and the entire show had a country flavor. Comedy skits, songs, and production numbers were all part of the format. The most unusual regular on the show was John Twomey, a Chicago attorney who made music with his bare hands.

JESSE (*Situation Comedy*)

FIRST TELECAST: *September 24, 1998*
LAST TELECAST: *March 16, 2000*
BROADCAST HISTORY:

Sep 1998–Mar 2000, NBC Thu 8:30–9:00

CAST:

Jesse Warner .... Christina Applegate
"Little John" Warner (age 10) .... Eric Lloyd
John Warner, Jr. (1998–1999) .... John Lehr
Darren Warner (1998–1999) .... David DeLuise
John Warner, Sr. (1998–1999) ..... George Dzundza
Diego Vasquez .... Bruno Campos
Carrie .... Jennifer Milmore
Linda .... Liza Snyder
Kurt Bemis (1999–2000) .... Darryl Theirse
Dr. Danny Kozak (1999–2000) .... Kevin Rahm

Jesse was a 26-year-old single mom in Buffalo, New York, juggling her job, her dreams, and the many men in her life in this romantic comedy. The men came in all shapes and ages. Little John was her adorable and supportive young son, who ran up to guys who were trying to hit on his mom, hugging them and shouting "Daddy!"—which was usually enough to make them flee in terror. John Sr. was her grouchy dad, who ran Der Biergarten, the German-themed restaurant and bar where Jesse worked as a waitress, dressed in a dirndl. Also hanging around were her brothers: eccentric, long-haired John Jr., who, as the series began, had been mute for a year because he was looking for a better way to communicate (not finding it, he later opened up); and Darren, an unemployed "entrepreneur" who always had a get-rich-quick scheme. The man who made Jesse's heart go pitter-patter, however, was Diego, a considerate, suavely handsome Chilean artist who had moved in next door. She fought the attraction, but it was undeniable. Stories revolved around their mating dance and Jesse's dreams of becoming a nurse.

Carrie and Linda were Jesse's friends and fellow waitresses at Der Biergarten.

In February 1999 John, Sr., left for Alaska, leaving the restaurant to Jesse and her brothers. As the season ended Diego faced deportation because his visa had run out, but at the last minute he accepted a position at UCLA that allowed him to stay. Before leaving he proposed to Jesse, who turned him down. The second season brought major changes. Both brothers disappeared from the cast, and Jesse enrolled in a nursing school, taking a job as a nurse's assistant at the University Medical Center to pay the bills. Her new foils were Kurt, the prissy and arrogant chief nurse ("You're taking my precious time!"), and Danny, a boyish, somewhat distracted doctor, and much of the action took place in the university infirmary. Diego was back from the West Coast, resuming his teaching position in Buffalo. He proposed again, and was turned down again. In the series finale he faced deportation again, proposed again, was turned down again, and married Linda instead. Afterward Jesse had second thoughts, but it was too late. Although the series ended its regular run in March 2000, two additional episodes, including the finale, were seen on May 25, 2000.

JESSE HAWKES (*Adventure*)

FIRST TELECAST: *April 22, 1989*
LAST TELECAST: *May 27, 1989*
BROADCAST HISTORY:

Apr 1989–May 1989, CBS Sat 9:00–10:00

CAST:

Jesse Hawkes .... Robert Conrad
Matt Hawkes .... Christian Conrad
Cody Hawkes .... Shane Conrad

Having spent most of their lives in the rugged and beautiful Sierra Nevada mountains (see *High Mountain Rangers*), Jesse Hawkes and his sons, Matt and Cody, had relocated to San Francisco. The move was prompted when Matt was taken to a hospital there to recover from serious injuries suffered during a drug bust in the mountains, and Jesse and Cody followed to be close to him and find the drug dealers who were responsible. After solving the case they stayed on, working as detective/bounty hunters, using the skills they had developed as rangers to help them track down criminals.

JESSE JACKSON SHOW, THE (*Discussion*)

BROADCAST HISTORY:

Syndicated only
60 minutes

Produced: *1990–1991* (40 episodes)
Released: *September 1990*

MODERATOR:
Jesse Jackson

Reverend Jesse Jackson moderated this weekly show that addressed issues of political and/or social significance. Each week he and a selected panel of experts would bring their knowledge to bear on a single topic, which was often introduced in a filmed report. The topics were largely, though not exclusively, those of particular concern to the minority community, such as housing discrimination, the welfare system, and police brutality.

JESSE JAMES, see *Legend of Jesse James, The*

JESSICA NOVAK (*Drama*)

FIRST TELECAST: *November 5, 1981*
LAST TELECAST: *December 3, 1981*
BROADCAST HISTORY:
Nov 1981–Dec 1981, CBS Thu 10:00–11:00

CAST:
Jessica Novak .... Helen Shaver
Max Kenyon .... David Spielberg
Phil Bonelli .... Andrew Rubin
Ricky Duran .... Eric Kilpatrick
Audrey Stiles .... Nina Wilcox
Vince Halloran .... Kenneth Gilman
Katie Robbins .... Lara Parker

KLA-TV news reporter Jessica Novak handled feature stories that ranged from gentle human-interest pieces to exposés on such topics as gambling addiction, the pressures that cause high school students to contemplate suicide, and the frustrations that prompt husbands separated from their families to kidnap their children. Her boss, news director Max Kenyon, usually sent her out on harmless little "fluff" pieces, but Jessica was determined to show that she was as good as the best of them and always managed to wind up with a Big Scoop instead. Respected by her associates for her persistence and dedication, Jessica worked with a crew consisting of cameraman Phil Bonelli, sound man Ricky Duran, and tape editor Audrey Stiles.

Between assignments she tried to maintain a semblance of a social life, in hopes of finding the right man. Katie was a friend of Jessica's, as was public defender Vince Halloran.

JESSIE (*Police Drama*)

FIRST TELECAST: *September 18, 1984*
LAST TELECAST: *November 13, 1984*
BROADCAST HISTORY:
Sep 1984–Nov 1984, ABC Tue 10:00–11:00

CAST:
Dr. Jessie Hayden .... Lindsay Wagner
Lt. Alex Ascoli .... Tony Lo Bianco
Molly Hayden .... Celeste Holm
Officer Hubbell .... Tom Nolan
Ellie .... Renee Jones
Phil .... James David Hinton
Sgt. Mac McClellan .... William Lucking
Officer Floyd Comstock .... Peter Isacksen

Jessie Hayden was staff psychiatrist for an unnamed Southern California police department. As such, she attempted to help the police deal with mentally unstable criminals, ranging from petty thieves to psychopathic killers, and assisted in counseling victims of crime. Jessie's faith in her understanding methods often put her at odds with Lt. Ascoli, particularly when it placed her in physical danger, as it often seemed to in this action series. Her mother, Molly, with whom she lived, was also outspoken and opinionated, particularly when it came to the dangers of Jessie's chosen profession.

Star Lindsay Wagner had wanted *Jessie* to be rather cerebral, exploring psychiatric and medical themes, but ABC's programming executives felt that the pilot was too talky and boring, forcing the producers to cram in more chases, fights, and gunplay, and make the show generally more like other police action series.

The series was based in part on the book *Psychologist with a Gun*, by Detective Harvey Schlossberg, Ph.D., and Lucy Freeman.

JETSONS, THE (*Cartoon*)

FIRST TELECAST: *September 23, 1962*
LAST TELECAST: *September 8, 1963*
BROADCAST HISTORY:
Sep 1962–Sep 1963, ABC Sun 7:30–8:00

VOICES:
George Jetson .... George O'Hanlon
Jane Jetson .... Penny Singleton
Judy Jetson .... Janet Waldo
Elroy Jetson .... Daws Butler
Astro .... Don Messick
Rosie the Robot .... Jean VanderPyl

ALSO:
Mel Blanc, Howard Morris, Herschel Bernardi, Howard McNear, and Frank Nelson

PRODUCERS:
William Hanna and Joseph Barbera

This cartoon series about a middle-class family of the future was the 21st-century equivalent of *The Flintstones*, and was produced by the same people. George Jetson worked for Spacely Space Sprockets, Inc., commuting to the job in an atomic-powered bubble. He lived with his wife, Jane, and their children in Skypad Apartments, which were raised and lowered on huge hydraulic lifts to stay clear of bad weather. A robot maid packed son, Elroy, off to school in a pneumatic tube each morning, while teenybopper daughter, Judy, spent her free time learning the latest dance, the Solar Swivel. Astro was the family dog. Appearing occasionally was George's boss, Cosmo G. Spacely, voiced by the versatile Mel Blanc.

After leaving prime time, *The Jetsons* proved to be remarkably durable as a Saturday morning children's show, despite the fact that only 24 episodes had been produced. Reruns aired on ABC (1963–1964), CBS (1964–1965 and 1969–1970), and NBC (1965–1967, 1971–1976, and 1979–1983). In 1985, to make the series more viable in the syndication marketplace, 41 new episodes of *The Jetsons* were produced, with ten more in 1987, bringing the total to 75.

JIGSAW (*Police Drama*)

FIRST TELECAST: *September 21, 1972*
LAST TELECAST: *August 11, 1973*
BROADCAST HISTORY:
Sep 1972–Dec 1972, ABC Thu 9:00–10:00
Feb 1973–Aug 1973, ABC Sat 10:00–11:00

CAST:
Lt. Frank Dain .... James Wainwright

Frank Dain was a special investigator for the California

State Police Department's Bureau of Missing Persons. A rebel who broke the rules when necessary, he was tough, dry, and sardonic. Naturally he got the most difficult and intriguing cases, and solved them all. *Jigsaw* was one of three rotating elements of *The Men*.

JIGSAW JOHN (*Police Drama*)
FIRST TELECAST: *February 2, 1976*
LAST TELECAST: *September 6, 1976*
BROADCAST HISTORY:
Feb 1976–Sep 1976, NBC Mon 10:00–11:00
CAST:
John St. John ("Jigsaw John") .... Jack Warden
Sam Donner .... Alan Feinstein
Maggie Hearn .... Pippa Scott
Frank Chen .... James Hong

Jigsaw John dealt with the cases tackled by Los Angeles Police Department Special Investigator John St. John. He had received the nickname Jigsaw John because of the way in which he slowly, methodically, and precisely fitted together each of the seemingly unrelated pieces that collectively led to the determination of guilt in his homicide investigations. The highly individualistic way in which he and his partner, Sam Donner, worked did not always sit well with the police department bureaucracy, but the results could not be faulted. John's commitment to his job always took priority over the other things in his life, most noticeably his long-running romance with nursery-school teacher Maggie Hearn.

JIM BOWIE, see *Adventures of Jim Bowie, The*

JIM HENSON HOUR, THE (*Variety*)
FIRST TELECAST: *April 14, 1989*
LAST TELECAST: *July 30, 1989*
BROADCAST HISTORY:
Apr 1989–May 1989, NBC Fri 8:00–9:00
Jul 1989, NBC Sun 7:00–8:00
REGULARS:
Jim Henson, host
John Hurt as The Storyteller
VOICES:
Fran Brill
Kevin Clash
Dave Goelz
Rob Mills
Jerry Nelson
Dan Redican
Gordon Robertson
Steve Whitmire

A frog, a pig, and a talking dog all played a part in this whimsical hour from Jim Henson, the creator of the Muppets. The first half of each program was generally a variety show, with Kermit, Miss Piggy, Fozzie Bear, and the other Muppet characters joining human guest stars in skits and offbeat songs. Some numbers were accompanied by Solid Foam, the all-Muppet house band. The second half belonged to "The Storyteller," an old man seated before a fire in a medieval cottage, with his talking dog, who spun a tale of magic, sorcery, and good that triumphed over evil. The story was then enacted by a combination of actors (often young) and wondrous, imaginative creatures from Henson's fertile brain.

Previous episodes of The Storyteller had aired on NBC as specials.

JIM NABORS HOUR, THE (*Comedy/Variety*)
FIRST TELECAST: *September 25, 1969*
LAST TELECAST: *May 20, 1971*
BROADCAST HISTORY:
Sep 1969–May 1971, CBS Thu 8:00–9:00 (OS)
REGULARS:
Jim Nabors
Frank Sutton
Ronnie Schell
Karen Morrow
The Nabors Kids
The Tony Mordente Dancers
Paul Weston & His Orchestra

Jim Nabors, the twangy, rural comedian of *The Andy Griffith Show* and *Gomer Pyle, U.S.M.C.*, surprised everyone when in the mid-1960s he opened his mouth and began to sing. His voice was a rich baritone, and he proceeded to make quite a splash in the record field with several best-selling LPs. After *Gomer Pyle* had run its course, his versatility earned him this Thursday night variety hour. With him were two of his former co-stars from *Gomer Pyle*, Frank Sutton and Ronnie Schell. There were also guest stars, comedy sketches, and musical numbers on the show. One continuing comedy sketch was "The Brother-in-Law," in which Karen Morrow played Jim's sister and Frank Sutton her husband. Frank's role was that of a self-centered, insecure neurotic trying to cope with what he perceived as a hostile world.

JIM ROCKFORD, PRIVATE INVESTIGATOR,
syndicated title for *Rockford Files, The*

JIM STAFFORD SHOW, THE (*Comedy/Variety*)
FIRST TELECAST: *July 30, 1975*
LAST TELECAST: *September 3, 1975*
BROADCAST HISTORY:
Jul 1975–Sep 1975, ABC Wed 10:00–11:00
REGULARS:
Jim Stafford
Valerie Curtin
Richard Stahl
Phil MacKenzie ("Adam")
Deborah Allen
Cyndi Wood
Jeanne Sheffield
Tom Biener
Jean Anne Chapman
Eddie Karam Orchestra

Jim Stafford, am amiable, ingratiating young singer-composer with hits about such unlikely subjects as "My Girl Bill" and "Spiders and Snakes," hosted this summer variety hour. "Some people think I'm weird," he remarked. "I'm not really weird—unless you're picky." Rodney the robot, an insulting bag of transistors, also appeared on the show.

JIMMIE RODGERS SHOW, THE (*Musical Variety*)
FIRST TELECAST: *March 31, 1959*
LAST TELECAST: *September 1, 1969*
BROADCAST HISTORY:
Mar 1959–Sep 1959, NBC Tue 8:30–9:00
Jun 1969–Sep 1969, CBS Mon 10:00–11:00

REGULARS:
Jimmie Rodgers
Connie Francis (1959)
Kirby Stone Four (1959)
The Clay Warnick Singers (1959)
Buddy Morrow Orchestra (1959)
Frank Comstock Orchestra (1969)
Burgundy Street Singers (1969)
Lyle Waggoner (1969)
Vicki Lawrence (1969)
Nancy Austin (1969)
Bill Fanning (1969)
Don Crichton (1969)

In 1959 folk-popular singer Jimmie Rodgers was riding the crest of a wave of success with a string of hit records, most notably "Honeycomb" and "Kisses Sweeter Than Wine." NBC signed him for a variety show in the hopes of making him a TV star as well, as ABC had done with Pat Boone. However, the show never caught on. By the summer, regulars Connie Francis and the Kirby Stone Four had abandoned ship, and the show was soon canceled.

A decade later, after recovering from a mysterious accident that almost cost him his life and which occasioned a long gap in his career, Rodgers returned to television as the summer replacement for Carol Burnett, with a new variety series called *Carol Burnett Presents the Jimmie Rodgers Show.* Two of the regulars from Carol's series, Lyle Waggoner and Vicki Lawrence, also served as regulars on the summer show.

JIMMY AND DOUG'S FARMCLUB.COM (*Music/Talent Competition*)

BROADCAST HISTORY:
USA Network
60 minutes
Original episodes: *2000–2001*
Premiered: *January 31, 2000*

REGULARS:
Ali Landry
Matt Pinfield

A late-night musical showcase featuring rap, punk, and other contemporary music in a loud club setting. The show was an early attempt to integrate television with the Internet. Viewers were invited to download performances from the show's Web site, and aspiring bands could also upload examples of their work to the site. These were evaluated, and the best got record deals and invitations to appear on the show. Many of the performers were newcomers, but among the established stars appearing were NWA (a reunion), Enrique Iglesias, Snoop Dogg and Smash Mouth. The founders of farmclub.com were Jimmy Iovine and Doug Morris.

JIMMY BLAINE'S JUNIOR EDITION (*Music*)

FIRST TELECAST: *January 1, 1951*
LAST TELECAST: *August 31, 1951*
BROADCAST HISTORY:
Jan 1951–Feb 1951, ABC Mon/Wed/Fri 6:15–6:30
Jan 1951–Feb 1951, ABC Tue/Thu 6:15–6:45
Feb 1951–Jun 1951, ABC Mon–Fri 6:45–7:00
Jul 1951–Aug 1951, ABC Mon/Wed/Fri 6:45–7:00

REGULARS:
Jimmy Blaine
Mary Crosby
Buddy Weed Trio

Jimmy Blaine, featured vocalist on *Stop the Music,* hosted this short music and talk program featuring songs for teenagers.

JIMMY BRESLIN'S PEOPLE (*Talk/Interview*)

FIRST TELECAST: *September 25, 1986*
LAST TELECAST: *January 2, 1987*
BROADCAST HISTORY:
Sep 1986–Jan 1987, ABC Thu/Fri 12:00 MID–1:00 A.M.

HOST:
Jimmy Breslin

This talkfest was part of an abortive ABC attempt to bring relevance to the late-night schedule, with *Nightline* at 11:30 P.M. followed by Dick Cavett on Tuesday and Wednesday and Jimmy Breslin on Thursday and Friday. Breslin, a gruff, gravelly voiced syndicated columnist who had long been part of the New York scene, did his part with hard-hitting shows on AIDS, the criminal justice system, the excesses of fandom, etc. Unfortunately many local stations delayed or preempted the show in favor of rock videos and old movies. In Breslin's hometown of New York it was not seen until as late as 2:00 A.M., or only one night a week. Disgusted, Jimmy announced he was "canceling the network" and ended the series after only three months.

JIMMY DEAN SHOW, THE (*Musical Variety*)

FIRST TELECAST: *June 22, 1957*
LAST TELECAST: *April 1, 1966*
BROADCAST HISTORY:
Jun 1957–Sep 1957, CBS Sat 10:30–11:00
Sep 1963–Mar 1964, ABC Thu 9:00–10:00
Mar 1964–Aug 1964, ABC Thu 9:30–10:30
Sep 1964–Sep 1965, ABC Thu 10:00–11:00
Sep 1965–Apr 1966, ABC Fri 10:00–11:00

REGULARS:
Jimmy Dean
Texas Wildcats (1957)
The Country Lads (1957)
Jo Davis (1957)
Jan Crockett (1957)
Mary Klick (1957)
Chuck Cassey Singers (1963–1966)
Doerr-Hutchinson Dancers (1964–1965)
Tony Mordente Dancers (1965–1966)
Peter Matz Orchestra (1963–1965)
Don Sebesky Orchestra (1965–1966)

Country singer Jimmy Dean was frequently seen on daytime and nighttime television in the late 1950s and 1960s. A lanky, drawling Texan, he is best known for a Nashville-pop sound typified by his own most famous hit, "Big Bad John" (1961). The first *Jimmy Dean Show* was a half-hour daytime variety series, based in Washington, D.C., which ran on CBS from April to December 1957, and from September 1958 to June 1959. In addition, Jimmy hosted a prime-time summer show in 1957, also from Washington. This was a low-budget affair which generally featured guest country acts such as Johnny Cash and Jim Reeves, plus some rather out-of-date popular talent (the Andrews Sisters, Gene Austin).

Then from 1963–1966 Dean fronted his own big-league variety hour on ABC. Guests on this series also included country-and-western standbys such as Eddy Arnold, Homer and Jethro, and Molly Bee, but were more frequently popular talent. His first ABC telecast headlined comic Dick Shawn and cartoon character Fred Flintstone. A continuing character on the ABC series was Jim Henson's muppet hound, Rowlf, with whom Dean joked and bantered ("My ol' buddy"). Other semi-regulars included Ron Martin, the accident-prone singer who never seemed to finish a song, Lud and Lester (Roger Price and Mort Marshall) doing a Lum and Abner–type spot, and the Jubilee Four gospel quartet. The Chuck Cassey Singers, with their stetsons and guitars, provided vocal support.

In an effort to "jazz up" the show during its final season, special telecasts originated from the stage of the Grand Ole Opry (September), Miami Beach (November), and Carnegie Hall (December), while an October 1965 telecast played host to the first annual Country Music Awards presentations.

A syndicated half-hour *Jimmy Dean Show* was produced from 1973 to 1975.

JIMMY DURANTE PRESENTS THE LENNON SISTERS (*Musical Variety*)

FIRST TELECAST: *September 26, 1969*
LAST TELECAST: *July 4, 1970*
BROADCAST HISTORY:
Sep 1969–Jan 1970, ABC Fri 10:00–11:00
Feb 1970–Jul 1970, ABC Sat 9:30–10:30
REGULARS:
Jimmy Durante
Dianne Lennon
Peggy Lennon
Kathy Lennon
Janet Lennon
Jack Regas Dancers
George Wyle Orchestra

The year after they ended their long association with Lawrence Welk the four Lennon Sisters co-starred with veteran comedian Jimmy Durante in this weekly musical variety hour. The show normally opened with Durante at the piano, leading into a segment of friendly chatter and songs with the Lennons. Some big-name guests appeared, including Jack Benny, Glen Campbell, Bob Hope, and Phyllis Diller, but it didn't help much. The combination of old trouper and sweet young talent never quite worked and the show was canceled at the end of its first season.

JIMMY DURANTE SHOW, THE (*Comedy/Variety*)

FIRST TELECAST: *October 2, 1954*
LAST TELECAST: *September 21, 1957*
BROADCAST HISTORY:
Oct 1954–Jun 1956, NBC Sat 9:30–10:00
Jun 1957–Sep 1957, CBS Sat 8:00–8:30
Sep 1957, CBS Sat 8:30–9:00
REGULARS:
Jimmy Durante
Eddie Jackson
Jules Buffano
Jack Roth
The Durante Girls
The Roy Bargy Orchestra

The basic setting of *The Jimmy Durante Show* was a small nightclub, owned and operated by Jimmy and appropriately called the Club Durant. In the role of club operator, Jimmy interviewed and auditioned talent, coped with the headaches involved in dealing with his employees, and occasionally performed himself. His raspy voice and large "schnozzola" (nose, to the uninitiated) were his trademarks. With him were his longtime friend and partner from vaudeville days, Eddie Jackson, and two actor-musicians, Jules Buffano (piano) and Jack Roth (drums), along with a chorus line composed of The Durante Girls. At the end of each show, Jimmy would be seen walking off the stage, through a series of spotlights, after saying his perennial closing line: "And good night, Mrs. Calabash, wherever you are."

During its first season *The Jimmy Durante Show* aired on alternate weeks with Donald O'Connor, under the umbrella title *Texaco Star Theatre.* Jimmy's shows were all live and Donald's were on film. The Durante show was seen weekly during 1955–1956. The CBS summer series in 1957 was made up of kinescopes from the live series on NBC.

JIMMY HUGHES, ROOKIE COP (*Police Drama*)

FIRST TELECAST: *May 8, 1953*
LAST TELECAST: *July 3, 1953*
BROADCAST HISTORY:
May 1953–Jul 1953, DUM Fri 8:30–9:00
CAST:
Officer Jimmy Hughes .... William Redfield
Officer Jimmy Hughes .... Conrad Janis
Inspector Ferguson .... Rusty Lane
Betty Hughes .... Wendy Drew

In the opening telecast of this crudely produced series Jimmy Hughes (William Redfield) was introduced as a young soldier just returned from Korea after his father, a policeman, was killed in a gun battle. Jimmy joined the police force to avenge his father's death, and won his father's badge. In the process of tracking down the killers he learned that teamwork is more important than individual action. In later episodes Jimmy tackled cases ranging from narcotics to teenage gangs to kidnapping. Rusty Lane played Inspector Ferguson, his hard-boiled mentor, and Wendy Drew played his sister.

Redfield was replaced by Conrad Janis in later episodes.

JIMMY KIMMEL LIVE (*Talk*)

FIRST TELECAST: *January 26, 2003*
LAST TELECAST:
BROADCAST HISTORY:
Jan 2003, ABC Sun 12:30–1:30 A.M.
Jan 2003– , ABC Mon–Fri 12:05–1:05 A.M.
REGULARS:
Jimmy Kimmel

Late-night desk-and-couch talk show featuring amiable young comic Jimmy Kimmel, previously best known as a cohost or sidekick on such cable favorites as *The Man Show* and *Win Ben Stein's Money.* Guests included the usual Hollywood celebrity parade, along with musical acts, comedians and guest cohosts such as Snoop Dogg, Kathy Griffin, Janeane Garofalo, Don King, Mike Tyson and David Alan Grier.

The show was telecast live from a big Hollywood theater and emphasized looseness and irreverence, leading to a fair number of bleeps. On the premiere Snoop Dogg made obscene gestures at the camera and guest George Clooney passed around a bottle of vodka. It was later revealed that the audience's looseness was fueled in part by an open bar provided in the studio. The bar was discontinued after an audience member threw up near a Disney executive (Disney owned ABC) and complaints that the show was encouraging public drunkenness.

JIMMY STEWART SHOW, THE (*Situation Comedy*)
FIRST TELECAST: *September 19, 1971*
LAST TELECAST: *August 27, 1972*
BROADCAST HISTORY:
Sep 1971–Aug 1972, NBC Sun 8:30–9:00
CAST:
Prof. James K. Howard............. Jimmy Stewart
Martha Howard....................... Julie Adams
Peter Howard......................... Jonathan Daly
Wendy Howard............................ Ellen Geer
Dr. Luther Quince................... John McGiver
Jake Howard .... Kirby Furlong
Teddy Howard .... Dennis Larson

Anthropology professor James Howard was a good-natured soul, but his home life became suddenly complicated when he offered to let his 29-year-old son Peter temporarily move his family in, after Peter's home had been destroyed by fire. Howard senior and junior coped as best they could with the conflicts arising in the somewhat overcrowded household, with three generations of the same family living under one roof. The fact that James and his wife, Martha, had a second son, Teddy, who was the same age (8) as their grandson Jake, only added to the complications. Teddy did, indeed, feel funny referring to Jake as his uncle.

The setting for *The Jimmy Stewart Show* was beautiful Easy Valley, California, home of Josiah Kessel College, founded by Prof. Howard's grandfather and the institution where both James and his good friend Dr. Quince taught.

JO STAFFORD SHOW, THE (*Music*)
FIRST TELECAST: *February 2, 1954*
LAST TELECAST: *June 28, 1955*
BROADCAST HISTORY:
Feb 1954–Jun 1955, CBS Tue 7:45–8:00 (OS)
REGULARS:
Jo Stafford
The Starlighters
Paul Weston & His Orchestra

Singer Jo Stafford starred in this live 15-minute show that filled the remainder of the half hour in which CBS aired its network news program. Miss Stafford sang, chatted with occasional guest stars, and performed with them. The orchestra was under the direction of her husband, Paul Weston.

JOAN EDWARDS SHOW, THE (*Music*)
FIRST TELECAST: *July 4, 1950*
LAST TELECAST: *October 26, 1950*
BROADCAST HISTORY:
Jul 1950–Oct 1950, DUM Tue/Thu 7:45–8:00
HOSTESS:
Joan Edwards

Singer-pianist Joan Edwards, a familiar voice on radio and records during the 1940s (she had a long stint on *Your Hit Parade*), entertained on this 1950 musical interlude. She was actually something of a TV veteran, having starred on a local version of *Girl About Town* on New York television in 1941 during TV's early experimental period.

JOANIE LOVES CHACHI (*Situation Comedy*)
FIRST TELECAST: *March 23, 1982*
LAST TELECAST: *September 13, 1983*
BROADCAST HISTORY:
Mar 1982–Apr 1982, ABC Tue 8:30–9:00
Sep 1982–Dec 1982, ABC Thu 8:00–8:30
May 1983–Sep 1983, ABC Tue 8:30–9:00
CAST:
Chachi Arcola .... Scott Baio
Joanie Cunningham .... Erin Moran
Al Delvecchio.......................... Al Molinaro
Louisa Delvecchio .... Ellen Travolta
Uncle Rico............................ Art Metrano
Bingo .... Robert Peirce
Mario .... Derrel Maury
Annette..................... Winifred Freedman
THEME:
"You Look at Me," by Pamela Phillips and James P. Dunne, sung by Erin Moran and Scott Baio

Teenage heartthrob Scott Baio starred in this short-lived spin-off from *Happy Days*, which saw Fonzie's young cousin move to Chicago with his mother, Louisa, and stepfather, Al, and try to start a singing career. With him were best girl Joanie, who shared the vocals, and his backup band: a spaced-out drummer named Bingo, a chubby cousin named Annette, and another cousin, Mario. Mario and Annette's father, Uncle Rico, was their agent. Joanie and Chachi sang several numbers in each episode, usually at Al and Louisa's newly opened restaurant. Though there were new songs introduced in each episode, and Chachi had girls in the audience swooning, neither the songs nor the show caught on. Most of the cast soon returned to Milwaukee and *Happy Days*.

JOB, THE (*Situation Comedy*)
FIRST TELECAST: *March 14, 2001*
LAST TELECAST: *April 24, 2002*
BROADCAST HISTORY:
Mar 2001–Apr 2001, ABC Wed 9:30–10:00
Aug 2001–Sep 2001, ABC Wed 9:30–10:00
Jan 2002–Apr 2002, ABC Wed 9:30–10:00
CAST:
Det. Mike McNeil........................ Denis Leary
Det. Terrence "Pip" Phillips............. Bill Nunn
Det. Frank Harrigan .... Lenny Clarke
Det. Jan Fendrich....................... Diane Farr
Det. Tommy Manetti .... Adam Ferrara
Det. Ruben Sommariba .... John Ortiz
Det. Al Rodriguez.................... Julian Acosta
Lt. Williams............................ Keith David
Toni .... Karyn Parsons

Critics raved but audiences were a little less sold on this offbeat cop comedy featuring a kind of anti-hero, New York Det. Mike McNeil. He was handsome and stylish in his dark glasses, but also a heavy-drinking, pill-popping, smart-mouthed womanizer who alternated between his estranged wife, Karen (Wendy McKenna), and their kid Mikey, and his black mistress Toni. His idea of police work was to coerce a perpetrator into confessing by pretending to beat up his grandmother; sent to anger management class after chewing someone out, he created a brawl in the classroom. He agonized a lot about his deficiencies (something the critics also loved), but was supportive of his hefty, grumbling partner Pip who was bossed around by his wife, Adinah. Fellow cops included fat, white-haired Frank, tough cookie single-mom Jan, youthful by-the-book Tommy, and naive rookies Ruben and Al. Presiding over them all was blustery Lt. Williams.

JOE & MABEL (*Situation Comedy*)
FIRST TELECAST: *June 26, 1956*
LAST TELECAST: *September 25, 1956*
BROADCAST HISTORY:
Jun 1956–Sep 1956, CBS Tue 9:00–9:30
CAST:
Joe Sparton .... Larry Blyden
Mabel Spooner .... Nita Talbot
Mrs. Spooner .... Luella Gear
Sherman Spooner .... Michael Mann
Mike the Cabbie .... Norman Fell
Dolly Armstrong .... Shirl Conway

The course of true love never quite ran smooth for Joe and Mabel. Joe was a big-city cabdriver and Mabel was his girlfriend. Although he eventually planned to marry her, Joe's idea of when did not seem soon enough for Mabel. She was always trying to trap him into proposing and setting a date for the wedding. Mabel lived at home with her mother and her little brother, who helped her scheme to trap Joe. Joe's best friend was Mike, another cabdriver, who thought Joe was better off preventing the inevitable as long as possible.

JOE AND SONS (*Situation Comedy*)
FIRST TELECAST: *September 9, 1975*
LAST TELECAST: *January 13, 1976*
BROADCAST HISTORY:
Sep 1975–Jan 1976, CBS Tue 8:30–9:00
CAST:
Joe Vitale .... Richard Castellano
Gus Duzik .... Jerry Stiller
Aunt Josephine .... Florence Stanley
Estelle .... Bobbi Jordan
Mark Vitale .... Barry Miller
Nick Vitale .... Jimmy Baio

Italian-American widower Joe Vitale lived in Hoboken, New Jersey, with two teenage sons. His best friend, Gus Duzik, worked with him at the Hoboken Sheet and Tube Company. As a typical middle-class factory worker, Joe did the best he could to raise his boys, hold his job, and conduct some semblance of a social life, though the latter was rather limited. Helping him with the boys, and cooking an occasional meal for the entire family, was Estelle, the cocktail waitress who lived in the apartment across the hall.

JOE & VALERIE (*Situation Comedy*)
FIRST TELECAST: *April 24, 1978*
LAST TELECAST: *January 19, 1979*
BROADCAST HISTORY:
Apr 1978–May 1978, NBC Mon 8:30–9:00
May 1978, NBC Wed 8:30–9:00
Jan 1979, NBC Fri 8:30–9:00
REGULARS:
Joe Pizo .... Paul Regina
Valerie Sweetzer .... Char Fontane
Frank Berganski (1978) .... Bill Beyers
Frank Berganski (1979) .... Lloyd Alann
Paulie Barone .... David Elliott
Thelma Medina .... Donna Ponterotto
Stella Sweetzer (1978) .... Pat Benson
Stella Sweetzer (1979) .... Arlene Golonka
Vincent Pizo .... Robert Costanzo

Young love and its pitfalls was the theme of this comedy series, which attempted to cash in on the disco craze of the late 1970s. Joe and Valerie had fallen in love at a New York City disco, but theirs was still a probing, tentative, teenage affair, which was constantly being upset by their nutty friends. Joe shared an apartment with the macho Frankie, who worked at a health spa, and simpleminded Paulie, who drove a hearse for a living. Valerie lived at home with her divorced mother, Stella. Thelma was Valerie's man-hungry best friend. By day Joe worked at his father Vincent Pizo's plumbing store, and Valerie was a clerk at a cosmetics counter, but by night, when they met on the disco's glittering dance floor, they were Cinderella and her Prince Charming.

This series aired briefly in the spring of 1978 and then returned with new episodes for a few weeks the following January. During the January 1979 run Joe and Valerie got married.

JOE BASH (*Situation Comedy*)
FIRST TELECAST: *March 28, 1986*
LAST TELECAST: *May 10, 1986*
BROADCAST HISTORY:
Mar 1986–May 1986, ABC Fri 9:30–10:00
May 1986, ABC Sat 8:30–9:00
CAST:
Off. Joe Bash .... Peter Boyle
Off. Willie Smith .... Andrew Rubin

This peculiar series didn't seem to know what it wanted to be—drama or comedy. Joe was a balding, older New York City street cop near the end of his career, who just wanted to go out peacefully and with a nice, safe pension. Cynical about the system, he wasn't above a little larceny; in one episode he tried to keep the bag of cash he found in a dead woman's ratty apartment. Willie was his enthusiastic young partner, who was supposed to learn from him, but spent most of his time keeping Joe more or less honest. Lorna (DeLane Matthews) was Joe's hooker-girlfriend. A gritty, "mean streets" look and unappealing characters kept this series from attracting much of an audience.

JOE FORRESTER (*Police Drama*)
FIRST TELECAST: *September 9, 1975*
LAST TELECAST: *August 30, 1976*
BROADCAST HISTORY:
Sep 1975–Jan 1976, NBC Tue 10:00–11:00
Feb 1976–Aug 1976, NBC Mon 9:00–10:00
CAST:
Joe Forrester .... Lloyd Bridges
Georgia Cameron .... Patricia Crowley
Sgt. Bernie Vincent .... Eddie Egan
Jolene Jackson .... Dwan Smith
Det. Will Carson .... Taylor Lacher

Unlike most of the police series on television, *Joe Forrester* looked at the life of a regular cop on the beat, a patrolman who had been working the same district for many years. Joe felt that the friendships and information sources he had cultivated were worth much more than the comfort of a patrol car or the status of detective. He occasionally overlooked minor infractions of the law, but was known, respected, and trusted by everyone on his beat. When something serious took place, he could count on them for help in providing information. He had a girlfriend, Georgia Cameron, a good buddy in watch commander Bernie Vincent (who was played by former New York policeman Eddie Egan), and had become friendly with members of the black community in his district, including young student Jolene Jackson. The locale of the series was never any more specific than "a large city in California."

JOE MILLIONAIRE (*Romance/Reality*)
FIRST TELECAST: *January 6, 2003*
LAST TELECAST: *February 27, 2003*
BROADCAST HISTORY:
Jan 2003–Feb 2003, FOX Mon 9:00–10:00
Jan 2003–Feb 2003, FOX Thu 8:00–9:00
HOST:
Alex McLeod
BUTLER:
Paul Hogan

In the first episode of this hit series 20 young women traveled to France for the opportunity to be romanced by a man they all thought had inherited $50 million and was looking for a wife. In reality the guy—hunky, curly-haired Evan Marriott—was a $19,000-a-year construction worker. The object of the show was to separate the gold diggers from the sincere women and, at the end, to see how his final choice would react when she found out that he wasn't rich. Would true love prevail or would she dump him? Throughout the show the women were given the opportunity to comment on developments, what they really thought about Evan and how they felt about the other women.

The first episode introduced viewers to Evan and showed how Paul Hogan, the chubby, ebullient butler, had trained him to act wealthy. Then the 20 women arrived at his French château and viewers were given information about each of them. After meeting Evan, they all attended a ball that evening. Evan danced with each woman and gave pearls to each of the 12 he wanted to stay, with the eight others leaving at the end of the episode. On the second episode Evan and the women went on group dates—picking grapes at a vineyard, taking a train ride and horseback riding—and another seven were eliminated, with the survivors given sapphire necklaces. The following week Evan and the five remaining women went on individual dates in Paris, with each of the four chosen ones receiving emerald necklaces. At the end of episode four, during which the social activities were all around the château, the three survivors received ruby necklaces; the following week the two finalists, Sarah and Zora, were given diamond pendants.

In order to drag things out the producers made the next episode a collection of clips from previous episodes that chronicled Evan's activities with Sarah and Zora but stopped before he made his final decision. There were hot tubs, sensual encounters (accompanied by "oohs" and "aahhs" as the camera looked away) and plenty of champagne to lubricate the proceedings. When it was time to make the decision, he told Zora that he had chosen her because, among other things, she cared about people and had a real zest for life. Then he told her he didn't have $50 million and, if she could accept him for what he really was, to meet him in the ballroom that evening. She showed up and said that she still wanted to spend time with him, despite the fact that she felt slightly betrayed and that all successful relationships were based on trust. Paul then arrived and told them that their romance was like a fairy tale and should have a happy ending, surprising them with a joint check for $1 million. As the episode ended Evan asked Zora to dance and they were alone in the ballroom.

The following week, in an "aftermath" special, Evan and Zora were reunited for the first time in the months since the show was filmed. They implied that they wanted to find out how life would be with each other away from the cameras but, in an interview after the taping of the "aftermath" episode, she said that she and Evan were just friends and weren't dating anymore.

Joe Millionaire was so popular that Fox aired reruns of the original Monday episodes on Thursdays.

JOE'S LIFE (*Situation Comedy*)
FIRST TELECAST: *September 29, 1993*
LAST TELECAST: *December 15, 1993*
BROADCAST HISTORY:
Sep 1993–Dec 1993, ABC Wed 8:30–9:00
CAST:
Joe Gennaro .... Peter Onorati
Sandy Gennaro .... Mary Page Keller
Amy Gennaro (age 14) .... Morgan Nagler
Paul Gennaro (12) .... Robert Hy Gorman
Scotty Gennaro (7) .... Spencer Klein
Stan Gennaro .... George DiCenzo
Barbara Gennaro .... Mimi Kennedy
Leo Gennaro (16) .... Danny Masterson
Ray Wharton .... John Marshall Jones
Frank Ruscio .... Al Ruscio

A blue-collar family faced hard times in the nineties in this rather bland sitcom. Joe was an aircraft plant worker who had just made it to management when he was laid off, so now he became Mr. Mom during the day while his perky wife, Sandy, worked as an office temp. At night the roles were reversed; Sandy stayed home and Joe worked as a chef at big brother Stan's restaurant. Squabbles alternated with hugs as stubborn Joe and understanding Sandy dealt with their three kids, self-absorbed Amy, smart-mouthed operator Paul, and cute little Scotty. A bigger problem was Stan's irresponsible son Leo, who idolized Uncle Joe. Barbara was Stan's earthy wife and Ray an effete black chef at the restaurant.

JOE'S WORLD (*Situation Comedy*)
FIRST TELECAST: *December 28, 1979*
LAST TELECAST: *July 26, 1980*
BROADCAST HISTORY:
Dec 1979, NBC Fri 10:00–11:00
Jan 1980, NBC Wed 9:30–10:00
May 1980–Jul 1980, NBC Sat 9:30–10:00
CAST:
Joe Wabash .... Ramon Bieri
Katie Wabash .... K Callan
Steve Wabash .... Christopher Knight
Maggie Wabash .... Melissa Sherman
Jimmy Wabash .... Michael Sharrett
Rick Wabash .... Ari Zeltner
Linda Wabash .... Missy Francis
Brad Hopkins .... Russ Banham
Judy Wilson .... Misty Rowe
Andy .... Frank Coppola

This family comedy centered around an old-fashioned

family man, a strict disciplinarian who was trying to cope with a changing world both at home and on the job. Joe Wabash was a Detroit housepainter. He and his wife, Katie, had five children. The oldest was Steve, an apprentice painter on Joe's crew whom Joe hoped would someday carry on the family tradition. Steve wasn't so sure. Maggie, an attractive 16-year-old, gave her folks some anxious moments with the guys she was dating, while the three younger children had all the normal sibling rivalries of a large family. At work, Joe's paint crew included Brad, self-proclaimed stud; Judy, a sexy, blond mother who nursed her baby during lunch breaks; and Joe's longtime friend, Andy.

JOEY & DAD (*Musical Variety*)
FIRST TELECAST: *July 6, 1975*
LAST TELECAST: *July 27, 1975*
BROADCAST HISTORY:
Jul 1975, CBS Sun 7:30–8:30
REGULARS:
Joey Heatherton
Ray Heatherton
Pat Paulsen
Henny Youngman
Pat Proft
Bob Einstein
The Lex de Azevedo Orchestra

Sexy singer-dancer Joey Heatherton teamed with her father Ray in this short-lived summer variety series. Ray, who had been *The Merry Mailman* on television in the 1950s, was by this time more commonly known to TV viewers as the commercial spokesman for Tropicana Orange Juice. Father and daughter sang, danced, and did comedy sketches with the other regulars on the show and with their guest stars.

JOEY BISHOP SHOW, THE (*Situation Comedy*)
FIRST TELECAST: *September 20, 1961*
LAST TELECAST: *September 7, 1965*
BROADCAST HISTORY:
Sep 1961–Jun 1962, NBC Wed 8:30–9:00
Sep 1962–Sep 1964, NBC Sat 8:30–9:00
Sep 1964–Dec 1964, CBS Sun 9:30–10:00
Dec 1964–Sep 1965, CBS Tue 8:00–8:30
CAST:
Joey Barnes .... Joey Bishop
J.P. Willoughby (1961) .... John Griggs
Mrs. Barnes (1961–1962) .... Madge Blake
Barbara Simpson (1961–1962) .... Nancy Hadley
Frank (1961–1962) .... Joe Flynn
Betty (1961–1962) .... Virginia Vincent
Larry Barnes (1961–1962) .... Warren Berlinger
Stella Barnes (1961–1962) .... Marlo Thomas
Ellie Barnes (1962–1965) .... Abby Dalton
Mr. Jillson (1962–1965) .... Joe Besser
Charles Raymond (1962) .... Bill Bixby
Freddie (1962) .... Guy Marks
Hilda (1962–1965) .... Mary Treen
Larry Corbett (1963–1965) .... Corbett Monica
Dr. Sam Nolan (1964–1965) .... Joey Forman

When it premiered in the fall of 1961, *The Joey Bishop Show* focused on Joey Barnes, a young assistant to Los Angeles press agent J. P. Willoughby. Barnes, as played by deadpan comic Joey Bishop, was a softhearted, nice guy who had tried to build up his importance in the eyes of his family. Unfortunately, the members of that family often tried to take advantage of Joey's nonexistent influence with the big names of show business, and Joey spent much of his time getting into trouble while trying to help out his family. The program seemed to have too many regular characters, and by the middle of the first season, four of them were gone; Joey's older sister Betty; her husband Frank, an unsuccessful salesman; Mr. Willoughby's secretary, Barbara; and Willoughby himself. Joey's mother, stagestruck sister Stella, and kid brother Larry remained to the end of the first season.

At the start of the second season both the format and the supporting cast were changed completely. Joey Barnes was now the host of a *Tonight Show*–type talk program that originated in New York. Stories revolved around his personal and professional life as a TV celebrity, and many guest stars appeared, playing themselves. Joey was now married to a Texas girl named Ellie, had a manager named Freddie (later Larry Corbett became his manager), and lived in a fancy Manhattan apartment. In 1963 Ellie gave birth to a baby boy, who later was seen on the show, played by Abby Dalton's real-life infant son, Matthew Smith. Dr. Sam Nolan, a pediatrician neighbor, was added to the cast in 1964.

JOEY BISHOP SHOW, THE (*Talk*)
FIRST TELECAST: *April 17, 1967*
LAST TELECAST: *December 26, 1969*
BROADCAST HISTORY:
Apr 1967–Dec 1969, ABC Mon–Fri 11:30–1:00 A.M.
REGULARS:
Joey Bishop
Regis Philbin
Johnny Mann, Musical Director

The Joey Bishop Show was one of several attempts by ABC to establish a strong late-night talk show. Joey had been quite successful as a substitute host for Johnny Carson on NBC, and it was hoped that perhaps he could lure some of Carson's audience away permanently.

The beginning was not auspicious. The program was originally done live and, on premiere night, guest Governor Ronald Reagan showed up 14 minutes late. Petite actress Debbie Reynolds, demonstrating how to help someone on fire, tackled announcer Regis Philbin and threw him to the floor (to smother the "flames"). On the second night Joey gave a big introduction to guest Buddy Greco, only to be left gesturing toward an empty curtain—seems Buddy was still in the dressing room. Worse than the first-week gaffes, however, was a series of events on NBC. Just as Joey premiered, Johnny Carson staged a dramatic walkout, garnering reams of publicity. A few weeks later he returned triumphantly, and of course all eyes were on NBC to see what would happen (nothing further did).

With his thunder thus stolen at the outset, Joey limped along for more than two years, never posing much of a threat to the mighty *Tonight Show*. In 1969 ABC finally gave up the ghost. For the last month guest hosts were used.

JOEY FAYE'S FROLICS (*Comedy/Variety*)
FIRST TELECAST: *April 5, 1950*
LAST TELECAST: *April 12, 1950*
BROADCAST HISTORY:
Apr 1950, CBS Wed 9:30–10:00

REGULARS:

Joey Faye
Audrey Christie
Mandy Kaye
Danny Dayton
Joe Silver

Comic Joey Faye starred in this comedy variety show that obviously did not work too well. It only lasted two weeks.

JOHN BYNER COMEDY HOUR, THE (*Comedy/ Variety*)

FIRST TELECAST: *August 1, 1972*
LAST TELECAST: *August 29, 1972*
BROADCAST HISTORY:
Aug 1972, CBS Tue 7:30–8:30

REGULARS:

John Byner
Patti Deutsch
R. G. Brown
Linda Sublette
Gary Miller
Dennis Flannigan
The Ray Charles Orchestra

Comedian John Byner was the host and star of this short-lived summer variety series. In order to utilize his ability as an impressionist, the majority of comedy sketches were of the spoof variety. A continuing feature was "The Bland Family," satirizing situation comedies, while individual telecasts included takeoffs on *The Godfather*, soap operas, Fred Astaire–Ginger Rogers musicals (with Michele Lee as Ginger), Frank Sinatra, and George C. Scott's characterization of *Patton* shifted to the presidency of a toy company.

JOHN CONTE'S LITTLE SHOW, see *Van Camp's Little Show*

JOHN DAVIDSON SHOW, THE (*Musical Variety*)

FIRST TELECAST: *May 30, 1969*
LAST TELECAST: *June 14, 1976*
BROADCAST HISTORY:
May 1969–Sep 1969, ABC Fri 8:00–9:00
May 1976–Jun 1976, NBC Mon 8:00–9:00

REGULARS:

John Davidson
Rich Little (1969)
Mireille Mathieu (1969)
Aimi MacDonald (1969)
Jack Parnell Orchestra (1969)
Pete Barbutti (1976)
Lenny Stark Orchestra (1976)

Handsome singer John Davidson starred in two summer variety series. The 1969 version originated in London and placed the accent on youth, with popular music stars and up-and-coming comedians as guests. In 1976, doing a four-week mini-series on NBC that originated from Los Angeles, Davidson added an element of audience participation to the traditional variety aspects of his show. He would wander into the audience and choose people at random to appear in small parts in comedy sketches and to help introduce his guest stars.

JOHN DOE (*Science Fiction*)

FIRST TELECAST: *September 20, 2002*
LAST TELECAST: *April 25, 2003*
BROADCAST HISTORY:
Sep 2002–Apr 2003, FOX Fri 9:00–10:00

CAST:

John Doe .... Dominic Purcell
Lt. Jamie Avery .... Jayne Brook
Digger .... William Forsythe
Karen Kawalski .... Sprague Grayden
Det. Frank Hayes .... John Marshall Jones
Stella .... Rekha Sharma
**Yellow Teeth* .... Grace Zabriskie
**Trenchcoat Man* .... Gary Werntz

*Occasional

He awoke naked on Horsehoe Island, off the coast of Seattle, his mind bursting with knowledge of everything—except who he was and how he had gotten there. After being rescued by the crew of an Asian fishing boat, "John Doe" began the quest to determine his identity and where he came from. Since he was color-blind he saw almost everything in shades of gray, but one way he got clues was when he suddenly would see a person or thing in color. John's analytic brilliance allowed him to make some money betting and in stocks, and he set himself up in Seattle. One of the first people he met there was Frank, a local cop. At first Frank was suspicious of this brilliant but often confused guy who periodically would spout obscure random facts (the population of Peru in 1853; the number of blue cars in the state of Washington), but John's analytical skills and insights helped him do his job and they became friends. Others in John's small circle included Karen, the sassy young art student he hired as his assistant (mostly to help him track his origins); Frank's boss, Lt. Avery, who was confounded by John's remarkable abilities but thankful that his forensic insights helped them solve their toughest cases; Stella, the police information clerk with whom John shared information, and his understanding confidant Digger, the scruffy and mysterious owner of the Sea, the bar on the ground floor of the building in which John lived.

Although helping the police was rewarding, John was obsessed with tracking his origins. Everything seemed to revolve around a secret organization he eventually learned was called Phoenix. John had periodic encounters with two of its members, the Trenchcoat Man, a killer who never spoke and who communicated using sign language, and Yellow Teeth, a strange woman who seemed to know all about John. In late February they kidnapped Karen and, right after she called John with a clue, killed her. At the end of the episode John visited the dying Yellow Teeth, who told him Phoenix was looking for a staff that was tied to his destiny and would not stop till they got it. In the season finale the NSA captured the Trenchcoat Man and invited John to his interrogation. After the agents proved that he could speak, Trenchcoat revealed that John had been "chosen" and, when it was time, would complete the Phoenix Group's destiny. Then Trenchcoat used his mind to unlock his handcuffs and escape. John was able to visualize the home base of the Phoenix Group and went with NSA agents and cops to rescue Teresa, a woman he believed was part of the answer to his origins. At episode's end he discovered that the head of the Phoenix Group was apparently his "friend," Digger.

JOHN FORSYTHE SHOW, THE (*Situation Comedy*)
FIRST TELECAST: *September 13, 1965*
LAST TELECAST: *August 29, 1966*
BROADCAST HISTORY:
Sep 1965–Aug 1966, NBC Mon 8:00–8:30
CAST:
Major John Foster .... John Forsythe
Miss Margaret Culver .... Elsa Lanchester
Miss Wilson .... Ann B. Davis
Ed Robbins .... Guy Marks
Joanna .... Peggy Lipton
Kathy .... Darleen Carr
Pamela .... Pamelyn Ferdin
Susan .... Tracy Stratford
Norma Jean .... Brooke Forsythe
Marcia .... Page Forsythe

Air Force Major John Foster had been a bachelor all his life and his dealings with women had been exclusively social. When he retired from the air force he became the headmaster of the Foster School, an exclusive San Francisco school for girls that he had recently inherited from his aunt Victoria. Helping him run the school was a former air force sergeant and friend, Ed Robbins. The clash of these two men with an alien environment produced unexpected results. Misunderstandings between them and Miss Culver, the school principal, were frequent and often hilarious. John Forsythe's two daughters, Brooke (aged 11) and Page (aged 14) were among the young actresses portraying students at the school.

In the spring of 1966 there was a change in format. The Foster School was no longer the center of attention as John and Ed became world-traveling undercover agents for the U.S. government using the school only as a base from which to start, or end, their adventures. Their missions were not heavy cloak-and-dagger stuff, but were definitely more serious, and romantic, than anything that had happened at the school. No matter, the series never made it to a second season.

JOHN GARY SHOW, THE (*Musical Variety*)
FIRST TELECAST: *June 22, 1966*
LAST TELECAST: *September 7, 1966*
BROADCAST HISTORY:
Jun 1966–Sep 1966, CBS Wed 10:00–11:00
REGULARS:
John Gary
Mitchell Ayres Orchestra
The Jimmy Joyce Singers
The Jack Regas Dancers

Singer John Gary was the star and host of this summer variety show that filled in for the vacationing Danny Kaye (who was Gary's special guest on both the first and last telecasts of this series). There was a pretty fair balance between music and comedy, with each week's guest stars encompassing both fields. The singers were generally middle-of-the-road (not rock 'n' roll), like Vikki Carr, Vic Damone, and Joanie Sommers, while several of the comedians were regulars in TV series of their own (Tim Conway, Bob Crane, and Morey Amsterdam).

JOHN GRISHAM'S THE CLIENT (*Legal drama*)
FIRST TELECAST: *September 17, 1995*
LAST TELECAST: *July 16, 1996*
BROADCAST HISTORY:
Sep 1995, CBS Sun 9:00–11:00
Sep 1995–Jul 1996, CBS Tue 8:00–9:00
CAST:
Reggie Love .... JoBeth Williams
D.A. Roy Foltrigg .... John Heard
Momma Love .... Polly Holliday
Clint McGuire .... David Barry Gray
Judge Harry Roosevelt .... Ossie Davis
**Dr. Gus Cardoni* .... William Converse-Roberts
*Occasional

Reggie was an attorney in Atlanta practicing family law while trying to get her life back together after a messy divorce. Her serious drinking problem had contributed to the collapse of her marriage, and now, as a recovering alcoholic, she was still fighting to get back custody of her children, currently living with her wealthy ex, Dr. Gus Cardoni. Clint was Reggie's jack-of-all-trades assistant—paralegal, process server, investigator, and anything else she might need. Her mother, with whom Reggie lived, provided emotional support and opened their home to clients needing a place to stay while their cases were being adjudicated. Most of Reggie's clients were young people in trouble—a boy who ran off with a bag full of stolen money after witnessing a murder, a teenager accused of murdering the boy who stood her up for her high school prom, a young black man expelled from a private school after setting the Atlanta state flag on fire, and a crack addict trying to get her son out of an abusive foster home. Roy was her principal adversary in court, but they liked and respected each other and, under the right circumstances, might even have dated. Judge Roosevelt, who specialized in juvenile cases, was her strongest supporter in the Atlanta court system.

Based on the Grisham novel *The Client* and the 1994 theatrical film of the same name starring Susan Sarandon and Tommy Lee Jones.

JOHN GUNTHER'S HIGH ROAD (*Travelogue*)
FIRST TELECAST: *September 7, 1959*
LAST TELECAST: *September 17, 1960*
BROADCAST HISTORY:
Sep 1959, ABC Mon 8:30–9:00
Sep 1959–Sep 1960, ABC Sat 8:00–8:30
HOST:
John Gunther

Noted author and world traveler John Gunther served as host and narrator for this series. The filmed trips to interesting places around the world were of two categories: those made specifically for the series and those that had been made by some other group but were purchased for use in the series. Gunther had been to many of the places shown, but very little of the film had been made on his own trips.

JOHN LARROQUETTE SHOW, THE (*Situation Comedy*)
FIRST TELECAST: *September 2, 1993*
LAST TELECAST: *October 30, 1996*
BROADCAST HISTORY:
Sep 1993, NBC Thu 9:30–10:00
Sep 1993–Mar 1994, NBC Tue 9:30–10:00
Mar 1994–Apr 1994, NBC Tue 9:00–10:00
Jun 1994, NBC Tue 9:00–10:00
Jul 1994–Aug 1994, NBC Tue 9:00–9:30

Sep 1994–Mar 1995, NBC Tue 9:30–10:00
May 1995–Sep 1995, NBC Tue 9:30–10:00
Jun 1995, NBC Sat 9:00–9:30
Jul 1995, NBC Sat 9:00–10:00
Jul 1995–Aug 1995, NBC Tue 8:30–9:00
Sep 1995–Nov 1995, NBC Sat 9:00–9:30
Dec 1995–Jun 1996, NBC Tue 9:30–10:00
Aug 1996–Oct 1996, NBC Wed 8:30–9:00

CAST:

John Hemingway................ John Larroquette
Mahalia Sanchez .... Liz Torres
Carly Watkins.......................... Gigi Rice
Dexter Wilson.............. Daryl "Chill" Mitchell
Officer Hampton .... Lenny Clarke
Officer Eggers .... Elizabeth Berridge
Heavy Gene......................... Chi McBride
Max Dumas (1993–1994)....... John F. O'Donohue
Oscar, the bum (1994–1996) .... Bill Morey
Catherine Merrick (1994–1996)..... Alison LaPlaca

THEME:

written and performed by David Cassidy

In a TV world full of bright, cheery sitcoms, *The John Larroquette Show* was an anomaly. It was so dark and seedy that *TV Guide* called it "sitcom *noir*," but its smart, character-driven humor earned it a loyal following on NBC's Tuesday-night lineup. John Hemingway was a well-educated man who had lost his family and career due to alcoholism. He was now firmly on the wagon, but the best job he could get was as night manager of what was possibly the world's seediest bus terminal—the Crossroads, located in a run-down and dangerous section of St. Louis (one wonders why any traveler would go near it). Mahalia was his loud, sarcastic assistant, who knew more about the place than he did and thought she should have his job; Dexter the young black man with a chip on his shoulder who operated the snack bar and resented *all* whites; Gene the large, surly janitor who didn't like to clean (the appalling condition of the unseen men's room was a running gag); and hefty Hampton and tiny Eggers the jaded cops who mooched donuts.

Lightening things up a bit was Carly, the hooker-with-a-heart-of-gold who befriended John (and eventually bought the terminal's bar, where he stopped by but never imbibed) and, in the second season, Catherine, a nurse who lived in the apartment across from John's and provided a love interest.

The 1995 season brought major changes, as NBC struggled to save the sinking show by lightening its tone. The sun came up, literally, as the entire cast moved to the day shift: Oscar got a job running the newsstand, and Carly, who had given up her career as a hooker, found her millionaire (Ted McGinley) and sold the bar to Catherine, who used it to indulge her lifelong dream of being a torch singer. Stories revolved around John and Catherine's on-and-off relationship, and reminders of his former life. In one episode, both of John's kids, Rachel (Mayim Bialik) and Tony (Omri Katz)—neither of whom knew about the other—showed up. In 1996, Carly broke up with her sugar daddy and she and John abruptly decided to marry. However, during the ceremony in September, John learned that Catherine was apparently pregnant with his child! The series was canceled only a few weeks into the 1996–1997 season, leaving the few viewers who were left little time to sort all this out.

JOHN WOO'S ONCE A THIEF (*Adventure*)

BROADCAST HISTORY:

Syndicated only
60 minutes
Produced: *1997–1998* (22 episodes)
Released: *October 2002*

CAST:

Mac Ramsey.......................... Ivan Sergei
Li Ann Tsei .... Sandrine Holt
Victor Mansfield.................... Nicholas Lea
The Director........................ Jennifer Dale
Agent Dobrinsky .... Howard Dell
Camier .... Greg Kramer
Murphy .... Julian Richings
Nathan Muckle .... James Allodi
Jackie Janczyk (1998) .... Victoria Pratt

Movie director John Woo brought his trademark martial-arts violence, explosions and tongue-in-cheek humor to TV in this cartoonish action series. Mac and Li Ann were thieves and lovers living in China when Mac was apparently killed in a building explosion. Li Ann moved to Canada, became an agent for a secret government agency and was partnered with Victor, a former cop, who became her new lover. Everything was going smoothly until cocky Mac turned up. To protect himself from the ruthless Chinese gang that had tried to kill him, Mac joined the Agency and was teamed with Li Ann and Victor. It was awkward because he still had feelings for Li Ann, who was determined to forget their past, while Victor was jealous of their former relationship. Amid the banter the team engaged in wild firefights with villains, blazing away in midair, with guns upside down, two guns at once, etc. They reported to The Director, a petty manipulative agency official who treated them like children. Also working for The Director were Dobrinksy, who acted as her gofer; Camier and Murphy, the group's resident assassins, and Muckle, the neurotic librarian. In January Jackie, the daughter of a recently deceased local mob boss, joined the agency and, much to everyone's surprise, beat out Li Ann for the Agency's "Rookie of the Year" award.

John Woo's Once a Thief aired on Canada's CTV network during the 1997–1998 season but didn't surface in the U.S. until four years later. In the series finale Mac, Li Ann and Victor were killed in an explosion. A TV movie version of the last two episodes, aired under the title *Once a Thief: Brother Against Brother,* altered the ending, with the team leaving the building alive.

JOHNNY BAGO (*Comedy/Drama*)

FIRST TELECAST: *June 25, 1993*
LAST TELECAST: *August 18, 1993*
BROADCAST HISTORY:

June 1993–Aug 1993, CBS Fri 10:00–11:00
June 1993–Aug 1993, CBS Wed 11:30–12:40 A.M.

CAST:

Johnny Bago (nee Tenuti) .... Peter Dobson
Beverly Florio........................ Rose Abdoo
Ma Tenuti........................... Anna Berger
Don Roselli .... Michael Gazzo
Vinnie......................... Richard Romanus

THEME:

written and performed by Jimmy Buffett

Cartoonish series about a man on the run—in a Winnebago. Johnny Tenuti was something of a dim bulb, a small-time hustler recently paroled from prison whose cousin Vinnie, who had been responsible for his imprisonment, set him up a second time—this time for the murder of Chico Roselli, son of Don Roselli, a local crime boss in New York's Staten Island. Johnny fled New York and hitched a ride from Hick, a grizzled old man traveling around the country in a beat-up recreational vehicle. To conceal his identity Johnny took his last name from the RV (a Winnebago), which became his when Hick expired during a fishing tournament. Johnny lumbered from trailer park to trailer park trying to keep one step ahead of the police, Don Roselli's men, and his parole officer, who just happened to be his shrewish ex-wife-from-Hell, Beverly. He was hoping to find evidence that would exonerate him before he was either caught by Beverly, or killed by Roselli's bumbling men. As he moved from place to place, Johnny sent letters to his mother to reassure her that he was still alive and to recount his adventures in Middle America.

CBS attempted to build an audience for this quirky series by rerunning the Friday-night prime-time episodes as part of its late-night lineup on the following Wednesdays. It didn't help.

JOHNNY BRAVO (*Cartoon*)

BROADCAST HISTORY:

Cartoon Network
30 minutes
Produced: *1997–*
Premiered: *July 1, 1997*

VOICES:

Johnny Bravo.......................... Jeff Bennett
Bunny Bravo.......................... Brenda Vaccaro
Suzy.......................... Mae Whitman
Carl (1997–1999).......................... Micky Dolenz
Carlos "Carl" Chryniszzswics (1999–2001)
.... Tom Kenny
Pops (1999–2001).......................... Larry Drake

Big, muscular Johnny had broad shoulders, a huge shock of blond hair, and a brain the size of a pea. Although he thought he was God's gift to women, girls mostly ignored him, but Johnny was too dense to realize it. Stories consisted of Johnny's exploits around town, and sometimes his encounters with villains, whom, in his bumbling, naive way, he would manage to defeat with his trademark karate chops. The one female with a crush on him was a little kid named Suzy. Bunny was Johnny's loving mama.

First seen on Cartoon Network's *World Premiere Toons.*

JOHNNY CARSON SHOW, THE, see *Tonight Show, The*

JOHNNY CARSON SHOW, THE (*Comedy/Variety*)

FIRST TELECAST: *June 30, 1955*
LAST TELECAST: *March 29, 1956*
BROADCAST HISTORY:

Jun 1955–Mar 1956, CBS Thu 10:00–10:30

REGULARS:

Johnny Carson
Virginia Gibson
Barbara Ruick
Jill Corey
Jack Prince
The Lud Gluskin Orchestra

In the mid-1950s the CBS Press Department was hailing Johnny Carson as "a bright young comic." He had begun his TV career in Omaha in 1948, then turned up in Los Angeles in 1951 with a well-received local show called *Carson's Cellar.* His big break came when he began writing monologues for Red Skelton. This led to a stint as host of the 1954 summer quiz show *Earn Your Vacation,* and a CBS daytime series titled *The Johnny Carson Show* early in 1955. By the spring of 1955 it was decided by the network that he was ready for prime time. The format of the nighttime *Johnny Carson Show* relied heavily on comedy sketches and singing, with more of the former than the latter. Johnny created many of the sketches himself and, in addition to his weekly guests, used comediennes Virginia Gibson and Barbara Ruick in them. Two sketches that kept popping up on a semi-regular basis were parodies of other successful TV shows (*You Are There, Person to Person,* and *What's My Line* among them) and his "catch up with the news" feature in which he acted as a roving reporter doing interviews. Whom did he interview? One week it was the inhabitants of a flying saucer, another week a man about to be shot out of a cannon, and yet a third such divergent subjects as a butcher trapped for two weeks in an icebox, a dentist trying to relieve a whale's toothache, and a dog being rescued from a 500-foot-deep well. Johnny's then wife Jody was seen as the female singer for a few weeks at the beginning of the series, but Jill Corey took over that role. Jack Prince provided male vocals.

JOHNNY CASH PRESENTS THE EVERLY BROTHERS SHOW (*Musical Variety*)

FIRST TELECAST: *July 8, 1970*
LAST TELECAST: *September 16, 1970*
BROADCAST HISTORY:

Jul 1970–Sep 1970, ABC Wed 9:00–10:00

REGULARS:

Don Everly
Phil Everly
Joe Higgins
Ruth McDevitt

Rock 'n' roll singers Don and Phil Everly spent the summer of 1970 as the replacement for *The Johnny Cash Show.* Although their songs were generally known as top-40 hits, the sources of much of their material were country and gospel music and many of their guest stars were performers from that idiom. The emphasis of the series was on currently popular recordings, with Joe Higgins and Ruth McDevitt providing regular comic relief.

JOHNNY CASH SHOW, THE (*Musical Variety*)

FIRST TELECAST: *June 7, 1969*
LAST TELECAST: *September 19, 1976*
BROADCAST HISTORY:

Jun 1969–Sep 1969, ABC Sat 9:30–10:30
Jan 1970–May 1971, ABC Wed 9:00–10:00 (OS)
Aug 1976–Sep 1976, CBS Sun 8:00–9:00

HOST:

Johnny Cash

REGULARS (1969–1971):

Mother Maybelle & The Carter Family (June, Helen, Anita)
Statler Brothers
Carl Perkins

The Tennessee Three (Marshall Grant, bass; W. S. Holland, drums; Bob Wooton, guitar)
Bill Walker Orchestra

REGULARS (1976):

June Carter Cash
Steve Martin
Jim Varney
Howard Mann
Bill Walker Orchestra

THEME:

"Folsom Prison Blues" (opening theme)
"I Walk the Line" (closing theme)

One of the major attempts to bridge the gap between country music and the mass audience was made by Johnny Cash in 1969–1971. Unlike such earlier efforts as *Ozark Jubilee* (strictly for the sticks) and *The Jimmy Dean Show* (more pop than country), *The Johnny Cash Show* was true to its roots, yet packaged in a manner acceptable to most urban viewers. Part of its success lay with Cash himself, one of the few true superstars of both country and popular music, and a dramatic figure in his Lincolnesque "man in black" outfit. His craggy-featured authenticity, honed in real-life hardship, made him believable in such segments as "Ride This Train." Backing him were the members of his regular road show, the Carter Family (one of the legendary groups in country music history; Cash was married to one of the daughters, June), the Statler Brothers, Carl "Blue Suede Shoes" Perkins, and the Tennessee Three. Guest stars included first-rate talent from almost every musical genre, ranging from Louis Armstrong to Arlo Guthrie, Jose Feliciano, Glen Campbell, Rod McKuen, Pete Seeger, Linda Ronstadt, Merle Haggard, James Taylor, and Minnie Pearl.

One of the highlights of the 1969–1971 series was a two-part telecast in January 1971 tracing the "Country Music Story." Practically everybody who was anybody in country music appeared in this music documentary, which included film clips of such stars of the past as the original Jimmie Rodgers, Hank Williams, and Jim Reeves, and live performances by others ranging across the generations from Roy Acuff to Tammy Wynette.

In 1976 Johnny returned with a four-week summer series which, like the 1969–1971 program, originated from Nashville. This time guest stars were almost exclusively from the country field.

JOHNNY JUPITER (*Children's*)

FIRST TELECAST: *March 21, 1953*
LAST TELECAST: *June 13, 1953*
BROADCAST HISTORY:

Mar 1953–Jun 1953, DUM Sat 7:30–8:00

REGULARS:

Ernest P. Duckweather............Vaughn Taylor
His Boss............Gilbert Mack

PUPPETEER:

Carl Harms

This imaginative puppet show was produced by the company responsible for *Howdy Doody*, but it had a much shorter run. Its premise was a satirical view of our civilization as seen through the eyes of another planet's residents.

The initial setting was a TV studio, where E. P. Duckweather, an inquisitive janitor who liked to fiddle with the equipment, accidentally brought in Jupiter on one of the control-room consoles. He then talked with Johnny Jupiter and his friend B-12 (the puppets) and discovered that both Jupiterians were quite mystified about Earthling civilization—based on what they had seen on Earth's TV shows. Later the tables were turned and Duckweather became something of a personality on Jupiterian TV.

JOHNNY MANN'S STAND UP AND CHEER

(*Music*)

BROADCAST HISTORY:

Syndicated only
30 minutes
Produced: *1971–1973* (48 episodes)
Released: *Fall 1971*

REGULARS:

Johnny Mann
The Johnny Mann Singers

The well-scrubbed and youthful Johnny Mann Singers had a minor career on records in the 1960s doing pleasant, inoffensive versions of pleasant, upbeat songs like "Up Up and Away." They brought their act to TV in 1971 in this musical half hour that featured a lot of patriotic flag-waving and middle-of-the-road guests such as Patti Page, Jack Jones, Bobby Goldsboro, and Andy Griffith. Sometimes a guest star would also do a recitation—like Milton Berle reading "Desiderata." As host, Johnny Mann leapt about the stage "like a man possessed" *(Variety)*, while the boys and girls in their collegiate sweaters sang "Yankee Doodle Dandy."

Mama don't want no rock 'n' roll around here!

JOHNNY RINGO (*Western*)

FIRST TELECAST: *October 1, 1959*
LAST TELECAST: *September 29, 1960*
BROADCAST HISTORY:

Oct 1959–Sep 1960, CBS Thu 8:30–9:00

CAST:

Johnny Ringo............Don Durant
Laura Thomas............Karen Sharpe
Cully............Mark Goddard
Case Thomas............Terence de Marney

Johnny Ringo was a gunfighter-turned-lawman. Folks around Velardi, Arizona, apparently didn't mind their sheriff's past, and in fact one of them—pretty young Laura—thought he was a right handsome hunk of man. Case Thomas, Laura's father, was an old drunk who also happened to own the general store. Helping Johnny protect the people of Velardi, and filling in for him when he was busy fending off Laura, was the young deputy, Cully.

There really was a gunfighter-turned-lawman named Johnny Ringo in the 1880s, though it is doubtful that his exploits resembled those portrayed in this series.

JOHNNY STACCATO (*Detective Drama*)

FIRST TELECAST: *September 10, 1959*
LAST TELECAST: *September 25, 1960*
BROADCAST HISTORY:

Sep 1959–Mar 1960, NBC Thu 8:30–9:00
Mar 1960–Sep 1960, ABC Sun 10:30–11:00

CAST:

Johnny Staccato............John Cassavetes
Waldo............Eduardo Ciannelli

THEME:

composed and performed by Elmer Bernstein

When this series premiered in September 1959 its title was simply *Staccato*. Set in New York City, it centered on jazz pianist Johnny Staccato, who supplemented his meager income as a musician by working as a private detective. An important background for many episodes was "Waldo's," a small jazz club in Greenwich Village where Johnny Staccato spent much of his spare time and met most of his clients. Working at the club, and often featured in musical numbers, was the jazz combo of Pete Candoli, which included Barney Kessel, Shelly Manne, Red Mitchell, Red Norvo, and Johnny Williams. After *Johnny Staccato* was canceled by NBC, ABC picked it up and aired reruns of the NBC episodes through September 1960.

JOHNS HOPKINS SCIENCE REVIEW, THE
(*Information*)

FIRST TELECAST: *December 31, 1948*
LAST TELECAST: *September 2, 1954*
BROADCAST HISTORY:
Dec 1948–May 1949, CBS Fri 9:00–9:30
Oct 1950–Oct 1951, DUM Tue 8:30–9:00
Oct 1951–Apr 1953, DUM Mon 8:30–9:00
Apr 1953–Apr 1954, DUM Wed 8:00–8:30
Apr 1954–Sep 1954, DUM Thu 9:00–9:30
HOST:
Lynn Poole (1948–1949)
Robert Cochrane (1949)

This half hour of learned scientific discussion and demonstrations was what is known in the trade as a "time-filler." During its long run on CBS and DuMont it was scheduled against such hit shows as *Break the Bank, Milton Berle, Arthur Godfrey,* and *Dragnet*, programs from which its network had little chance of luring away viewers.

Anyone who did happen to tune over from *Godfrey, et al.* was treated to a genuinely worthwhile program, however. Conducted by members of the Johns Hopkins University faculty and other experts, and using films as well as discussions, it ranged across such topics as snails, TV, polio, X rays, baby-feeding, cancer, human fear, transistors, sunburn, and "Electrons at Work in a Vacuum."

When it left prime time, *Johns Hopkins Science Review* moved to Sunday afternoons, where it remained on DuMont until March 1955. Twenty months later it was back on Sunday afternoons with a new title (*Johns Hopkins File 7*) on a new network (ABC). It left the air for good in September 1960.

JOHNSON'S WAX THEATRE (*Dramatic Anthology*)

FIRST TELECAST: *June 18, 1958*
LAST TELECAST: *September 17, 1958*
BROADCAST HISTORY:
Jun 1958–Sep 1958, CBS Wed 8:30–9:00

The filmed half-hour plays aired in this series were all repeats of episodes previously seen on *Schlitz Playhouse.*

JOKER'S WILD, THE (*Quiz*)

BROADCAST HISTORY:
Syndicated and network daytime
30 minutes
Produced: *1976–1986; 1990–1991*
Released: *Fall 1976; Fall 1990*
HOST:
Jack Barry (1976–1984)
Bill Cullen (1984–1986)
Pat Finn (1990–1991)

A giant mock-up of a Las Vegas slot machine dominated this quiz show's set. By pulling the lever the two competing contestants spun the wheel and determined a category, then got questions in that category worth $50 or more. A "joker" on the machine could double or triple the loot, or allow the contestant to choose a category not showing on the slot machine. The first contestant to reach $500 won the game and got to play a bonus round worth more money.

The Joker's Wild ran on the CBS daytime schedule from September 1972 until June 1975, also with Jack Barry as host. In 1979 a children's version called *Joker! Joker! Joker!* appeared in syndication. It ran until 1981. When Jack Barry (who, with his longtime partner Dan Enright, also produced *The Joker's Wild*) died suddenly in the spring of 1984, veteran game-show emcee Bill Cullen was chosen to take over *The Joker's Wild* when it resumed production that fall.

Pat Finn hosted the revival of *The Joker's Wild* that aired in syndication during the 1990–1991 season.

JON STEWART SHOW, THE (*Talk*)

CABLE HISTORY:
MTV
30 minutes
Produced: *1993–1994* (48 episodes)
Released: *October 25, 1993*
SYNDICATION HISTORY:
Syndicated
60 minutes
Produced: *1994–1995*
Released: *September 12, 1994*
REGULARS:
Jon Stewart
Howard Feller (1994–1995)

MTV's first talk show was hosted by young Jon Stewart. The half-hour weeknight series featured celebrity guests with particular appeal to MTV's audience (the first was Howard Stern), satirical takes on current events, and musical performances.

Six months after the MTV series left the air, Stewart surfaced in syndication. He remained informal (he usually appeared in jeans and a sweater) but seemed somewhat uncomfortable attempting to reach a broader audience than his previous cable series. He did an opening monologue followed by interviews with celebrity and noncelebrity guests, comedy sketches, and musical performances. Like David Letterman, whose show also aired from New York, Stewart brought in an eclectic mix of local folks, including a woman from a local health club and the chef from a local restaurant who served dinner to him and a guest during the show. He sponsored the North Yonkers, New York, Knights Pop Warner football team, showed them practicing and playing, and had them on his show. Howard was the show's balding, nerdy-looking announcer. There was no house band. David Letterman was the first guest on the final telecast of the show, which aired on June 23, 1995.

Produced by MTV for syndication by Paramount as the replacement for *The Arsenio Hall Show.*

JONATHAN WINTERS SHOW, THE
(*Comedy/Variety*)

FIRST TELECAST: *October 2, 1956*
LAST TELECAST: *June 25, 1957*

BROADCAST HISTORY:

Oct 1956–Jun 1957, NBC Tue 7:30–7:45

REGULARS:

Jonathan Winters
Don Pardo (1956–1957)
Wayne Howell (1957)
The Eddie Safranski Orchestra

Comedian Jonathan Winters starred in this 15-minute series that occupied the remainder of the half hour in which NBC aired its network news program. Assisting him in sketches and comedy blackouts was the announcer, Don Pardo, until March 1957, when Wayne Howell succeeded him. Jonathan also had guest stars, primarily singers and musicians, who both performed on their own and participated with him in assorted comedy bits. Most telecasts opened with a Winters monologue, contained a song by the evening's guest star, and closed with a sketch. Among the subjects that got the Winters treatment were Hollywood movie premieres, Robin Hood, and General Custer. Typical was an interview (in the *You Are There* tradition) between Edward R. Murrow and Napoleon, with Winters playing both parts.

JONATHAN WINTERS SHOW, THE (*Comedy/Variety*)

FIRST TELECAST: *December 27, 1967*
LAST TELECAST: *May 22, 1969*
BROADCAST HISTORY:

Dec 1967–Dec 1968, CBS Wed 10:00–11:00 (OS)
Dec 1968–May 1969, CBS Thu 8:00–9:00

REGULARS:

Jonathan Winters
Abby Dalton
Dick Curtis
Pamela Rodgers (1968)
Alice Ghostley (1968–1969)
Paul Lynde (1968–1969)
Georgene Barnes (1968–1969)
Jerry Rannow (1968–1969)
Cliff Arquette (1968–1969)
The Establishment (1968–1969)
Bob Banas Dancers (1967–1968)
Tony Charmoli Dancers (1968)
Wisa D'Orso Dancers (1968–1969)
Paul Weston Orchestra (1967–1968)
Earl Brown Orchestra (1968–1969)

Inventive sketch comedian Jonathan Winters was the star of his own one-hour variety show for two seasons. Regular characters portrayed by Jonathan included Maude Frickert, Willard (in the "Couple Up the Street" sketches with Abby Dalton as his wife Margaret), and various strange people he played in "Face the Folks" sketches. Another regular feature was a satire on a well-known movie. The addition of a new regular sketch in the second season, "Jack Armstrong—The All-American Boy," featuring Jonathan as Jack, brought three new regulars to the cast: Cliff Arquette as Uncle Charley Weaver, Jerry Rannow as Billy, and Georgene Barnes as Betty, in addition to the other regulars who participated in non-recurring sketches.

JOHNNY QUEST (*Cartoon*)

FIRST TELECAST: *September 18, 1964*
LAST TELECAST: *September 9, 1965*
BROADCAST HISTORY:

Sep 1964–Dec 1964, ABC Fri 7:30–8:00
Dec 1964–Sep 1965, ABC Thu 7:30–8:00

VOICES:

Johnny Quest .... Tim Matheson
Dr. Benton Quest (1964) .... John Stephenson
Dr. Benton Quest (1964–1965) .... Don Messick
Race Bannon .... Mike Road
Hadji .... Danny Bravo

PRODUCERS:

William Hanna and Joseph Barbera

This rather realistic cartoon-adventure series, which later ran successfully as a Saturday morning children's show, spent one full season as a prime-time entry. The hero was 11-year-old Johnny Quest, who traveled the world with his scientist father, Dr. Benton Quest, on various missions. With them were Roger "Race" Bannon, their personal bodyguard; Hadji, a young Indian friend of Jonny's; and Bandit, the Quests' miniature bulldog. The Saturday morning run was on CBS from 1967–1970, ABC from 1970 to 1972, and NBC from 1979 to 1980.

JOSEPH COTTEN SHOW, THE (*Dramatic Anthology*)

FIRST TELECAST: *September 14, 1956*
LAST TELECAST: *September 21, 1959*
BROADCAST HISTORY:

Sep 1956–Sep 1957, NBC Fri 9:00–9:30
Jun 1958–Aug 1958, NBC Sat 10:30–11:00
Jul 1959–Sep 1959, CBS Mon 9:30–10:00

HOST/STAR:

Joseph Cotten

The filmed half-hour plays in this anthology were all based on records of actual legal cases from various parts of the world, and various periods of history. The host and occasional star was Joseph Cotten. Others starring in individual episodes included Joan Fontaine, Keenan Wynn, Dane Clark, Kim Hunter, Hoagy Carmichael, June Lockhart, and MacDonald Carey.

When this series first aired in the fall of 1956 its title was *On Trial.* Joseph Cotten became so identified with the series that its title was changed, effective February 1, 1957, to *The Joseph Cotten Show—On Trial.* NBC reran episodes from the series in the summer of 1958 as *The Joseph Cotten Show,* and CBS used that title again during the summer of 1959 for an anthology that included reruns from this series, *General Electric Theater,* and *Schlitz Playhouse.*

JOSEPH SCHILDKRAUT PRESENTS (*Dramatic Anthology*)

FIRST TELECAST: *October 28, 1953*
LAST TELECAST: *January 21, 1954*
BROADCAST HISTORY:

Oct 1953–Dec 1953, DUM Wed 8:30–9:00
Jan 1954, DUM Thu 8:00–8:30

HOST/STAR:

Joseph Schildkraut

Joseph Schildkraut, an actor who had appeared in many prestigious Broadway and Hollywood productions over the years, hosted and sometimes starred in this dramatic anthology series during the fall of 1953. Schildkraut's stage and screen roles had ranged from comedy to romance to classical drama, and he displayed a fairly wide range of talents here as well. But

DuMont, evidently carried away with the very fact of his presence on its fledgling network (his name was always preceded by the glowing term "noted" or "distinguished"), failed to provide him with decent scripts, and the program folded after only three months.

Also known as *Personal Appearance Theatre*.

JOURNEY OF ALLEN STRANGE (*Adventure*)

BROADCAST HISTORY:

Nickelodeon
30 minutes
Produced: *1997–2000* (57 episodes)
Premiered: *November 8, 1997*

CAST:

Allen Strange .... Arjay Smith
Robbie Stevenson .... Erin J. Dean
Josh Stevenson (age 11).............. Shane Sweet
Ken Stevenson .... Jack Tate
Gail Stevenson .... Mary Chris Wall
Phil Berg .... Dee Bradley Baker
Manfred Strange .... Robert Crow

A happy, inquisitive young alien from Xela was left behind on Earth when the Xelan spacecraft on which he was a stowaway took off without him in this whimsical series. Wandering into the local high school in Delport, California, he morphed into a young black boy, but encountered problems when he couldn't understand the ways of the strange beings he encountered—i.e., American teenagers. So he revealed himself to one of them, Robbie, who agreed to serve as his guide. She dubbed him "Allen Strange." Robbie was a little skeptical at first, but her younger brother Josh was a true believer in extraterrestrials, and thrilled to have one in the house. Their amiable single dad, Ken, who worked in the city planner's office, just thought they had a new friend. Gail was Ken's estranged but friendly wife, a nurse, who stopped by. When Allen needed to produce a parent, he summoned up an animated mannequin dubbed "Manfred."

The kids hung out in Josh's attic science lab, and tried to protect Allen's secret until his fellow aliens could return for him. One minor nuisance was Phil Berg, a goofy "alien hunter" with a show on local cable TV. A total klutz, Phil was mostly a danger to himself. A more serious threat was Shaw, a government agent so shadowy that viewers never saw his face. His agency, the ARC, was determined to track down aliens in order to experiment on them. Also after Allen was an evil alien race, the Trykloids. He was forced to use his powers, including the ability to disappear, to evade them.

JOURNEY TO THE UNKNOWN (*Suspense Anthology*)

FIRST TELECAST: *September 26, 1968*
LAST TELECAST: *January 30, 1969*
BROADCAST HISTORY:

Sep 1968–Jan 1969, ABC Thu 9:30–10:30

EXECUTIVE PRODUCER:

Joan Harrison

This series of melodramas focused on the psychological horrors experienced by warped and twisted minds, and the terrors that can confront people in situations that are all too real. The executive producer was a former aide to Alfred Hitchcock, and the producer of the Hitchcock television series, and she obviously tried to invoke the master's touch in this series—with only middling success. Among the stories: a mannequin comes to life for its loving admirer, but leads him into a nightmare; a mysterious man is seen in the crowd just before several disasters; and tales of witches, hallucinations, and deserted islands.

Journey to the Unknown was produced in England.

JUBILEE U.S.A., see *Ozark Jubilee*

JUDD, FOR THE DEFENSE (*Law Drama*)

FIRST TELECAST: *September 8, 1967*
LAST TELECAST: *September 19, 1969*
BROADCAST HISTORY:

Sep 1967–May 1969, ABC Fri 10:00–11:00
May 1969–Sep 1969, ABC Fri 9:00–10:00

CAST:

Clinton Judd .... Carl Betz
Ben Caldwell .... Stephen Young

Clinton Judd was a high-priced, high-powered criminal attorney modeled along the lines of such real-life superstars as F. Lee Bailey and Percy Foreman. Based in Houston, Texas, he traveled all over the U.S. with his young assistant Ben, defending wealthy tycoons and flower children. The series had a highly contemporary ring, as Judd was often involved in cases which mirrored recent headlines, such as draft evasion, Mexican-American labor activism, and civil rights murders.

JUDGE FOR YOURSELF (*Quiz/Audience Participation*)

FIRST TELECAST: *August 18, 1953*
LAST TELECAST: *May 11, 1954*
BROADCAST HISTORY:

Aug 1953–May 1954, NBC Tue 10:00–10:30

EMCEE:

Fred Allen

ANNOUNCER:

Dennis James

REGULARS:

Bob Carroll (1954)
The Skylarks (1954)
Milton Delugg & His Orchestra
Kitty Kallen (1954)
Judy Johnson (1954)

Three professional acts—singers, dancers, musicians, comedians, etc.—performed on this show each week. The three acts were rated in 1-2-3 order by two panels of judges, one composed of three show-business personalities and the other made up of three members of the studio audience. If one of the amateur judges rated the acts in the same order as the professional (show-business) judges, he or she won $1,000. The only acts that performed on this show that also had some professional success were two instrumental jazz groups—vibraphonist Terry Gibbs and the Marian McPartland Trio.

On January 5, 1954, the format of the show was changed. Gone were the professional judges, and the amateur judges were now rating new songs to determine which would become big hits. The winning judge was determined by his or her agreement with applause voting by the studio audience. Songs were performed by a regular cast consisting of Bob Carroll, the Skylarks, and Kitty Kallen. Miss Kallen was only with the show for two weeks, leaving the female vocalist spot to guest singers until Judy Johnson joined the cast at the end of February.

JUDGING AMY (*Legal Drama*)

FIRST TELECAST: *September 19, 1999*

LAST TELECAST:

BROADCAST HISTORY:

Sep 1999, CBS Sun 8:00–9:00

Sep 1999– , CBS Tue 10:00–11:00

CAST:

Amy Gray .... Amy Brenneman
Maxine Gray .... Tyne Daly
Lauren Cassidy (age 6) .... Karle Warren
Vincent Gray (1999–2001) .... Dan Futterman
Bruce Van Exel .... Richard T. Jones
Gillian Gray .... Jessica Tuck
Peter Gray .... Marcus Giamatti
Donna Kozlowski-Pant .... Jillian Armenante
Susie Nixon (1999–2000) .... Wendy Makkena
Evie Martell (2000–2001) .... Samantha Shelton
Lisa Matthews (1999–2000) .... Jeana Lavardera
Sean Potter (2000–) .... Timothy Osmundson
Carole Tobey (2000–2001) .... Sara Mornell
**Jared Duff (2000–2003)* .... Richard Crenna
Stuart Collins (2001, 2003–) ...... Reed Diamond
**Kimberly Fallon (2001–)* .... Alice Dodd
Kyle McCarty (2001–) .... Kevin Rahm
Andrea Salamon (2001–2002) .... Nia Long
**Judge Barry Krumble (2002)* .... Chris Sarandon
Zola Knox (2002–) .... Kathryne Dora Brown
Dr. Lily Reddicker (2002–) .... Kristin Lehman
Dr. Heather Labonte (2002–)
.... Sarah Danielle Madison
**Robert Clifton (2002–)* .... Inny Clemons

*Occasional

Following the breakup of her ten-year marriage to husband Michael, high-powered New York corporate attorney Amy returned home to Hartford, Connecticut, to start a new career as a superior court judge working on family court cases—a career she had to learn on the job. She and her daughter, Lauren, moved back into the family home with Amy's strong-willed mother, Maxine, a social worker for the Department of Children and Families (DCF). Amy's sensitive younger brother, Vincent, made a living grooming dogs and working odd jobs while seeking success as a writer. At family meals Amy's attorney brother, Peter, showed up, along with his high-strung wife, Gillian, who was trying artificial means to have a baby. Bruce was the veteran black court services officer (CSO), who guided Amy through the protocol of her new job, and Donna was her flighty but well-meaning court clerk. Most episodes included Amy's trial work and the interactions of the family members.

In October Amy married Donna and Oscar (Brent Sexton), who was in prison. Vincent, who had taken a job teaching English, was shot in the abdomen while trying to stop a mugging and later dated Lisa, the woman he had saved. Struggling financially, he also took Donna in as his new roommate. In January Gillian and Peter decided to adopt and made arrangements with Evie, a pregnant teen, to care for her during her pregnancy and take the baby after it was born. When she gave birth to a boy, Ned, they found out he was half black. In February Vincent's book of poetry, *A Time of Luck and Kindness,* was published but he developed writer's block and took a job as a cub reporter for the *Hartford Examiner* to get his writing juices flowing again. Amy prepared for a custody fight with Michael. In March Maxine's boss Susie was accused of embezzling money from DCF and replaced by Sean. In April Maxine went out with Jared, whom she met in a diner, unaware of how rich he was, and in the season-ending cliffhanger Vincent was almost killed in a courtroom explosion.

Vincent recovered and helped Donna get through her pregnancy, and in December she gave birth to a daughter, Ariadne. In January Maxine tried to set up Sanctuary House, a facility to bring therapists, social workers and investigators together, unknowingly with financial support from Jared, but things didn't work out and she had to give up the project. Gillian and Peter adopted Ned, lost a custody battle with Evie, but got him back in May because she decided being a mother was too much work. As the season was winding down Vincent quit his job to work on a novel and, at the end of the season, he told the family he and Carole, a coworker at the paper whom he had been dating, were moving to San Francisco.

At the start of the 2001–2002 season Amy had a brief fling with attorney Stuart Collins, who had never agreed with her about legal issues, just before he moved to Sri Lanka. Vincent's first novel *A Fortunate Son* was published; he and Carole, who was fighting breast cancer, eloped to Las Vegas, and at the end of October they moved to San Francisco. A couple of weeks later Maxine's nephew Kyle showed up. A former med student, he was recovering from drug addiction and hoping to make a new start in Hartford. He moved in with the Grays and took a menial job at a burger joint. Later he went to work at Teen Harbor, a facility helping troubled kids. Maxine helped him get funding to reopen it after she had ordered it closed because his boss was allowing drug trafficking on the premises. In January Maxine took in troubled, gay teen Eric and eventually convinced Sean to be his foster father. Bruce was dating Andrea, an ex-junkie who was the mother of one of his daughter's classmates, and, when he punched her abusive ex-husband, was suspended. In the season finale Maxine put her house up for sale (after a falling-out, Amy had moved out), Jared returned and proposed to her, Bruce was sentenced to community service for his assault but lost his job as her CSO, and Amy's ex, Michael, initiated a suit for full custody of Lauren.

That fall Bruce was going to school and working part time to pay his bills, Amy and Michael were in the middle of their acrimonious custody battle and Maxine accepted Jared's proposal. With the help of Zola, an activist attorney, Bruce got his job back. Although he found her pushy and aggressive, they eventually started dating. In October Amy bought the family home from her mother, who became her tenant, and moved back with Lauren. Kyle took a position working for Lily as a medical resident at struggling St. Michael's Hospital. In November Gillian found out she was pregnant and Amy was coping with Jason, a guy who was stalking her. Later that month Eric stabbed Jason to death in the Grays' front yard. Michael dropped the custody suit in January because his wife had left him. Jared and Maxine were planning to move up their wedding date but problems with his Asian operations forced them to put it on hold while he put out the fire. In February Stuart returned from Sri Lanka and took on Eric's case as a favor to Amy. After the trial (Eric lied on the stand, and was acquitted) Stuart renewed his affair with Amy. When their doctor told Peter and Gillian that their unborn child might have severe birth defects, he was depressed and she went into denial. In April Maxine found out that Jared had died of a heart attack in China (actor Richard Crenna had passed away from cancer in January) and Amy found out that Kyle was drinking. He started dating Lily, his boss at the clinic. In the season finale Stuart proposed to Amy—she accepted—and Gillian gave birth to a healthy baby, but went into cardiac arrest after the delivery.

Based on the real-life story of Ms. Brenneman's mother, a superior court judge in Connecticut.

JUDY GARLAND SHOW, THE (*Musical Variety*)

FIRST TELECAST: *September 29, 1963*
LAST TELECAST: *March 29, 1964*
BROADCAST HISTORY:
Sep 1963–Mar 1964, CBS Sun 9:00–10:00
REGULARS:
Judy Garland
Jerry Van Dyke (1963)
Ken Murray (1964)
The Mort Lindsey Orchestra
The Ernie Flatt Dancers (1963)
The Nick Castle Dancers (1963)
The Peter Gennaro Dancers (1963–1964)
MUSICAL ADVISOR:
Mel Tormé

Throughout its short history, *The Judy Garland Show* was a series desperately looking for a format. When it first went into production under the guidance of young George Schlatter (who would later do *Rowan and Martin's Laugh-In*) it was to be modeled after Judy's highly successful special that had aired in the spring of 1963—glossy, full of big production numbers, with a brassy driving quality. Schlatter was relieved of the production responsibilities after five shows had been taped, and was replaced by Norman Jewison. His efforts were geared to make Judy's show more folksy, in the style of *The Garry Moore Show*, in the hope that that approach would attract some of the audience of its primary competition, NBC's top-rated *Bonanza*. By the time it left the air in March of 1964, *The Judy Garland Show* had gone through two more producers, still without making even a dent in *Bonanza*'s audience.

At the outset Judy was aided by comic Jerry Van Dyke, but he was gone by the end of 1963. For a while there was a regular "Tea for Two" segment in which Judy chatted with guest stars about show business and various personal experiences. Among the guests were her young daughter Liza Minnelli; her co-star from Andy Hardy days, Mickey Rooney; and Ray Bolger, who had played the scarecrow in *The Wizard of Oz*. Early in 1964 Ken Murray was a regular contributor, with his home movies of Hollywood stars. Nothing seemed to work. Judy was at her best just singing, and several of the shows during the last two months were just that—no guest stars, no regulars, but a full hour of Judy. That may have been the best format, but it was too little too late.

A fascinating behind-the-scenes account of this show, from its creation to its demise, is contained in the 1970 book *The Other Side of the Rainbow* by Judy's friend, fellow artist, and "musical advisor" Mel Tormé.

JUDY SPLINTERS (*Children's*)

FIRST TELECAST: *June 13, 1949*
LAST TELECAST: *August 5, 1949*
BROADCAST HISTORY:
Jun 1949–Aug 1949, NBC Mon–Fri 7:00–7:15
HOST:
Shirley Dinsdale

Pretty 21-year-old ventriloquist Shirley Dinsdale and her saucy, pigtailed dummy Judy Splinters hosted this live program, which served as the 1949 summer replacement for *Kukla, Fran & Ollie*. The program was first seen in 1947 as a local entry in Los Angeles, moved to Chicago for its summer network run, and then to New York for nine months as a late-afternoon show in 1949–1950.

JUKE BOX JURY, see *Peter Potter Show, The*

JULIA (*Situation Comedy*)

FIRST TELECAST: *September 17, 1968*
LAST TELECAST: *May 25, 1971*
BROADCAST HISTORY:
Sep 1968–Jan 1971, NBC Tue 8:30–9:00
Jan 1971–May 1971, NBC Tue 7:30–8:00
CAST:
Julia Baker .... Diahann Carroll
Dr. Morton Chegley .... Lloyd Nolan
Marie Waggedorn .... Betty Beaird
Corey Baker .... Marc Copage
Earl J. Waggedorn .... Michael Link
Melba Chegley .... Mary Wickes
Sol Cooper .... Ned Glass
Carol Deering (1968–1969) .... Allison Mills
Hannah Yarby (1968–1970) .... Lurene Tuttle
Eddie Edson .... Eddie Quillan
Paul Cameron (1968–1970) .... Paul Winfield
Len Waggedorn .... Hank Brandt
Steve Bruce (1970–1971) .... Fred Williamson
Roberta (1970–1971) .... Janear Hines
Richard (1970–1971) .... Richard Steele
Kim Bruce (1970–1971) .... Stephanie James

This comedy was more notable for its casting than its content. Singer Diahann Carroll became the first black female to star in her own comedy series in a "prestige" role (i.e., not as a domestic such as *Beulah*, or a second banana). Julia was an independent woman, a young, widowed nurse whose husband had been killed in Vietnam. After his death she moved to Los Angeles and found a job in the medical office of Astrospace Industries. There she met fellow nurse Hannah Yarby, and feisty Dr. Chegley, whose bark was much worse than his bite. Life at the office coupled with her home and social lives provided the material for the stories.

The show was thoroughly integrated, and after this attracted some initial attention as a novelty, it met with immediate acceptance—to the relief of nervous network executives. Julia lived in a modern, integrated apartment building with her little boy, Corey, whose best friend was white Earl J. Waggedorn, one of their neighbors. Paul Cameron was Julia's romantic interest for the first two seasons, and was replaced by Steve Bruce during the series' final year.

JULIE (*Situation Comedy*)
FIRST TELECAST: *May 30, 1992*
LAST TELECAST: *July 4, 1992*
BROADCAST HISTORY:
May 1992–Jul 1992, ABC Sat 8:30–9:00
CAST:
Julie Carlyle-McGuire .... Julie Andrews
Sam McGuire .... James Farentino
Alexandra "Allie" McGuire (age 14) ... Hayley Tyrie
Adam McGuire (12) .... Rider Strong
I.F. "Wooley" Woolstein .... Eugene Roche
Dickie Duncan .... Kevin Scannell
Joy Foy .... Alicia Brandt
Bernice "Bernie" Farrell .... Laurel Cronin

Sixties superstar Julie Andrews returned to television—very briefly—in this rather pedestrian family sitcom that, according to *TV Guide*, "looked like something that came out of a time capsule buried around 1972." Julie Carlyle was a fabulously successful TV variety show star (when is the last time you saw one of those?) who abruptly decided to give up her hectic celebrity lifestyle, marry the man of her dreams, veterinarian Sam, and move with him to Iowa to help quietly raise his two lovely children.

Julie's producer and best friend "Wooley" was aghast but reluctantly agreed to move the show from New York to Sioux City. Even greater adjustments were necessary by Sam's not-so-quiet kids, Allie and Adam, who now had a celebrity mom, and by Julie herself, who found the little adventures of family life just as hectic as her old world. Not for long, though.

JULIE ANDREWS HOUR, THE (*Musical Variety*)
FIRST TELECAST: *September 13, 1972*
LAST TELECAST: *April 28, 1973*
BROADCAST HISTORY:
Sep 1972–Jan 1973, ABC Wed 10:00–11:00
Jan 1973–Apr 1973, ABC Sat 9:00–10:00
REGULARS:
Julie Andrews
Rich Little
Alice Ghostley
Tony Charmoli Dancers
The Dick William Singers
Nelson Riddle Orchestra

British musical-comedy star Julie Andrews hosted this hour of sweetness and light which lasted for a single season on ABC. There were songs, skits, and blackouts, with Julie re-creating some of her famous roles such as Eliza Doolittle (from *My Fair Lady*) and Mary Poppins. Comedians Rich Little and Alice Ghostley constituted a semi-regular comedy repertory company. Little's career received quite a boost on this series. Jack Benny so liked Rich's impersonation of him on the show that he sent the young comic an 18-carat-gold money clip and the message, "With Bob Hope doing my walk and you doing my voice, I can be a star and do nothing."

JULIE FARR, M.D., see *Having Babies*

JULIUS LAROSA SHOW, THE (*Music*)
FIRST TELECAST: *June 27, 1955*
LAST TELECAST: *September 23, 1955*
BROADCAST HISTORY:
Jun 1955–Sep 1955, CBS Mon/Wed/Fri 7:45–8:00
REGULARS:
Julius LaRosa
The Debutones
The Russ Case Orchestra

Singer Julius LaRosa was the star of this thrice-weekly live summer music show that filled the remainder of the half hour in which CBS aired its network news program. He sang, as did the female quartet, the Debutones, and introduced his guest stars.

JULIUS LAROSA SHOW, THE (*Musical Variety*)
FIRST TELECAST: *July 14, 1956*
LAST TELECAST: *September 7, 1957*
BROADCAST HISTORY:
Jul 1956–Aug 1956, NBC Sat 8:00–9:00
Jun 1957–Sep 1957, NBC Sat 8:00–9:00
REGULARS:
Julius LaRosa
Frank Lewis Dancers (1956)
The Spellbinders (1956)
Carl Hoff & His Orchestra (1956)
Louis Da Pron Dancers (1957)
Artie Malvin Singers (1957)
Mitchell Ayres & His Orchestra (1957)

Julius LaRosa spent two summers filling in for the vacationing Perry Como. During the summer of 1956, LaRosa, Patti Page, and Tony Bennett each spent about one month headlining a musical variety hour with the same supporting cast: the Spellbinders, the Frank Lewis Dancers, and Carl Hoff & His Orchestra. During the summer of 1957, LaRosa was the sole star and had Como's regular dancers and orchestra as part of his supporting cast.

JUNE ALLYSON SHOW, THE, see *DuPont Show with June Allyson, The*

JUNIOR PRESS CONFERENCE (*Interview*)
FIRST TELECAST: *October 5, 1953*
LAST TELECAST: *December 13, 1954*
BROADCAST HISTORY:
Oct 1953–Dec 1954, ABC Mon 9:00–9:30
MODERATOR:
Ruth Geri Hagy

Public-service program in which politicians and other personalities in the news were interviewed by a panel of four college correspondents from various campus newspapers. *Junior Press Conference* was first seen in October 1952, as a Sunday daytime entry, and continued on Sundays after its prime-time run until November 1960. In October 1954 the title was changed to *College Press Conference*. From Philadelphia.

JUST CAUSE (*Legal Drama*)
FIRST TELECAST: *September 15, 2002*
LAST TELECAST:
BROADCAST HISTORY:
Sep 2002–Oct 2002, PAX Sun 9:00–10:00
Sep 2002–Oct 2002, PAX Tue 9:00–10:00
Oct 2002– , PAX Sun 10:00–11:00
Nov 2002–Dec 2002, PAX Mon 9:00–10:00
Jan 2003–Jun 2003, PAX Tue 9:00–10:00
CAST:
Hamilton Whitney III .... Richard Thomas
Alex DeMonaco .... Lisa Lackey
Patrick Heller .... Shaun Benson

Peggy Kawamura .... Khaira Ledeyo
Ted Kasselbaum .... Mark Hildreth
C. J. Leon .... Roger R. Cross
D.A. David Kaplan .... Jason Schombing

Alex had just spent five years in prison for a crime she had not committed. Her husband, Jason, had skipped town with their two-year-old daughter, Mia, to avoid being arrested for running an insurance scam. Since he was gone and she had unwittingly signed documents relating to the fraudulent operation, Alex was tried and convicted. While in prison she had studied law and now that she was out, she was determined to clear her name and get her daughter back. By showing how much she knew about the law, Alex impressed senior partner Hamilton Whitney and talked her way into a job at the prestigious San Francisco law firm of Burdick, Whitney & Morgan. Although he seemed a little stuffy, and had spent most of his career helping the rich hold on to their fortunes, Hamilton had a soft heart and frequently let Alex involve him and the firm in cases to help the poor and downtrodden. As a convicted felon, Alex couldn't practice law, but Whitney, a personal friend of the governor, was working on getting her a pardon. Patrick, a former police officer who was a little smitten with Alex, was an associate attorney at the firm, and Peggy was Hamilton's assistant.

Kasselbaum, the private detective Alex hired to find her husband and daughter, also helped out on some of the firm's cases. As a condition of her parole Alex lived in a halfway house run by her tough parole officer, C. J. Leon. In an early-November episode Jason (David Julian Hirsh) and Mia showed up in San Francisco and Alex had a confrontation with him. He was running a scam and made a deal with Whitney to give Alex their daughter for $100,000, but he evaded capture when things fell apart. To help with her expenses Alex moonlighted working for a cleaning service but, at Christmas, Whitney gave her a raise so that she could quit her night job.

JUST IN TIME (*Situation Comedy*)
FIRST TELECAST: *April 6, 1988*
LAST TELECAST: *May 18, 1988*
BROADCAST HISTORY:
Apr 1988–May 1988, ABC Wed 9:30–10:00
CAST:
Harry Stadlin .... Tim Matheson
Joanna G. Farrell .... Paticia Kalember
Jack Manning .... Kevin Scannell
Steven Birnbaum .... Alan Blumenfeld
Isabel Miller .... Nada Despotovich
Carly Hightower .... Ronnie Claire Edwards
Nick Thompson .... Patrick Breen

Romantic comedy about an aggressive, modish young editor who was hired to shake up sagging *West Coast Review* magazine by making it, well, a bit livelier. That put him directly at odds with his top political columnist, smart but oh-so-serious Joanna. The romantic sparring began almost immediately. Harry says he'll print anything of hers that's a little more sensational? She gives him an exposé of his own amorous exploits back in Chicago. And so on.

Also on the staff were fact-bending sportswriter Jack, experienced right-hand man Steve, and enthusiastic young assistant Isabel. Carly was the drawling Southern secretary, and Nick the scruffy photographer.

JUST OUR LUCK (*Situation Comedy*)
FIRST TELECAST: *September 20, 1983*
LAST TELECAST: *December 27, 1983*
BROADCAST HISTORY:
Sep 1983–Dec 1983, ABC Tue 8:00–8:30
CAST:
Shabu .... T.K. Carter
Keith Barrow .... Richard Gilliland
Meagan Huxley .... Ellen Maxted
Nelson Marriott .... Rod McCary
Chuck .... Richard Schaal
Professor Bob .... Hamilton Camp
Jim Dexter .... Leonard Simon

The genie-in-the-bottle story has seldom been done with as many twists as in this 1983 comedy. First of all, the genie—Shabu—was a hip black man disgusted at having fallen into the hands of a wishy-washy young TV reporter. Shabu's previous assignments had been much more glamorous, serving the likes of Cleopatra, Napoleon, and King Arthur. His new master, Keith, was not so keen on the arrangement, either, especially since the fun-loving Shabu was given to practical jokes and throwing spells around at all the wrong times. Keith was more interested in trying to save his job at KPOX-TV, where he had just been replaced as weatherman by Professor Bob. The officious program director, Meagan Huxley, thought Keith lacked charisma ("You just stick on the screen. Like old gum."), so Shabu gave him enough for ten people. When Keith needed to throw a party to impress the station manager, Mr. Marriott, Shabu conjured up a night none of them would forget.

There were lots of surprises on this show, including cameos by such people as Roy Orbison, Dr. Joyce Brothers, and Wink Martindale (doing a burlesque quiz show in which he couldn't seem to give away anything). Unfortunately, Shabu's magic didn't work against *The A-Team*, running opposite on NBC. Just his luck.

JUST SAY JULIE (*Comedy*)
BROADCAST HISTORY:
MTV
30 minutes
Produced: *1989–1992*
Premiered: *February 15, 1989*
HOST:
Julie Brown

A sitcom-cum-music clips show hosted by uninhibited comedienne "West Coast" Julie Brown, featuring quirky videos and celebrity guests.

JUST SHOOT ME (*Situation Comedy*)
FIRST TELECAST: *March 4, 1997*
LAST TELECAST: *January 14, 2003*
BROADCAST HISTORY:
Mar 1997, NBC Tue 9:30–10:00
Mar 1997, NBC Wed 9:30–10:00
Jul 1997–Mar 1998, NBC Tue 9:30–10:00
Feb 1998–May 1998, NBC Thu 8:30–9:00
May 1998–Jun 1998, NBC Tue 9:30–10:00
Jun 1998–Aug 1998, NBC Thu 9:30–10:00
Aug 1998–Sep 1998, NBC Tue 9:30–10:00
Sep 1998–Aug 1999, NBC Tue 9:00–9:30
Jul 1999–Feb 2000, NBC Tue 8:00–8:30
Nov 1999, NBC Tue 9:30–10:00
Feb 2000–Sep 2002, NBC Tue 9:30–10:00
Jun 2000–Sep 2000, NBC Thu 9:30–10:00

Oct 2002, NBC Tue 8:30–9:00
Nov 2002–Jan 2003, NBC Tue 8:00–8:30

CAST:

Maya Gallo .... Laura San Giacomo
Jack Gallo .... George Segal
Nina Van Horn .... Wendie Malick
Elliott DiMauro .... Enrico Colantoni
Dennis Finch .... David Spade
Wally (1997) .... Chris Hogan
Adrienne Louise Barker (1999–2000)
.... Rebecca Romijin-Stamos
Kevin (1999–2003) .... Brian Posehn
Vicki Costa (2002–2003) .... Rena Sofer

Pretentiousness met profits (and pretentiousness lost) in this cheerful workplace comedy. Maya was a high-minded "serious journalist" who got fired from her TV newswriting job for standing up for her ideals once too often, and wound up writing for *Blush,* the sleazy women's fashion magazine published by her father—a publication that represented everything she detested. Pride was swallowed, however, and Maya reached a detente with Jack, her colorful, womanizing dad. Others around the office were Nina, the bossy, scheming former model who served as fashion editor; Elliott, the balding, intense head photographer; and Dennis, Jack's backstabbing young executive assistant. It seems gruff Jack was really a softy—he hired each of them at a low point in their lives, helping them turn things around. Unseen but often referred to was Ally, Jack's fourth wife, a bimbo/cheerleader who was a former classmate of Maya's.

Most stories revolved around dating and office politics. In the 1998–1999 season finale Dennis abruptly married glamorous model Adrienne, and Maya married Elliot. In the fall, Maya and Elliot discovered they were not legally married, but they continued to date off and on. Dennis and Adrienne were eventually divorced. In 2000 Jack and Ally divorced, putting him in the dating scene as well. Joining the cast in 1999 was Kevin the mail guy, and in 2002 opinionated Brooklyn hairstylist Vicki, the magazine's new editorial consultant.

JUST THE TEN OF US (*Situation Comedy*)

FIRST TELECAST: *April 26, 1988*
LAST TELECAST: *July 27, 1990*
BROADCAST HISTORY:

Apr 1988–May 1988, ABC Tue 8:30–9:00
Sep 1988–Jun 1989, ABC Fri 9:30–10:00
Jul 1989, ABC Wed 8:30–9:00
Aug 1989–Jul 1990, ABC Fri 9:30–10:00

CAST:

Coach Graham T. Lubbock ...... Bill Kirchenbauer
Elizabeth Lubbock .... Deborah Harmon
Marie Lubbock .... Heather Langenkamp
Cindy Lubbock .... Jamie Luner
Wendy Lubbock .... Brooke Theiss
Constance Lubbock ("Connie") ..... JoAnn Willette
Sherry Lubbock .... Heidi Zeigler
Graham Lubbock, Jr. ("J.R.") .... Matt Shakman
**Harvey Lubbock* .... Jason and Jeremy Korstjens
Father Robert Hargis .... Frank Bonner
**Gavin Doosler* .... Evan Arnold
**Coach Duane Johnson (1988–1989)*
.... Dennis Haysbert
**Father Bud (1989–1990)* .... Lou Richards
**Sister Ethel (1989–1990)* .... Maxine Elliott

*Occasional

THEME:

"Doin' It the Best I Can," sung by Bill Medley

Five young girls found heaven in an all-boys school, to their doting father's alarm, in this appealing spin-off from *Growing Pains.* Coach Lubbock was introduced as Mike Seaver's favorite teacher on *Pains.* When he was abruptly fired he moved his burgeoning family to Eureka, California, to accept a position at St. Augustine's Academy, a Catholic boys' school where every one of the 600 students wanted a date with those lovely girls of his. The chubby, bald coach sputtered and fumed, but the kids were always up to something. The large brood included Elizabeth, Graham's credulous (and fertile) wife; studious, conservative Marie (the eldest); spacy Cindy; blond flirt Wendy; Connie (the "literary" one); eight-year-old "genius" Sherry; and young hustler J. R., who always seemed to be overshadowed by his sisters, the four oldest of whom even formed their own singing group ("The Lubbock Babes"). Toddler Harvey and baby Melissa rounded out the ten. Father Hargis was the absentminded head of the school, Sister Ethel, the scatterbrained little old nun, Duane, the head of athletics, and Boosler, a goofy boyfriend. Lots of heartfelt lessons on dating, saving money (nobody had any), and the importance of family and faith were learned by all.

JUSTICE (*Law Drama*)

FIRST TELECAST: *April 8, 1954*
LAST TELECAST: *March 25, 1956*
BROADCAST HISTORY:

Apr 1954–Jun 1955, NBC Thu 8:30–9:00
Oct 1955–Mar 1956, NBC Sun 10:30–11:00

CAST:

Jason Tyler (1954–1955) .... Gary Merrill
Richard Adams (1955–1956) .... William Prince

PRODUCER:

David Susskind

Taken from the files of the National Legal Aid Society, the dramas presented in this live series were the stories of poor people in need of legal help, either criminal or civil in nature, with the emphasis on the former. There were no regulars in the cast when the series began but Legal Aid attorney Jason Tyler became the permanent lawyer on the series in the fall of 1954. He was replaced for the 1955–1956 season by a new attorney, Richard Adams.

A 1955 episode about song sharks in the music business, starring *Your Hit Parade* star Gisele MacKenzie, had an unexpected by-product. The song used in the drama, "Hard to Get," became quite a big seller on the real-life hit parade.

JUSTICE LEAGUE (*Cartoon*)

BROADCAST HISTORY:

Cartoon Network
30 minutes
Original episodes: *2001–*
Premiered: *November 17, 2001*

VOICES:

Superman (Clark Kent) .... George Newbern
Batman (Bruce Wayne) .... Kevin Conroy
Martian Manhunter (J'onn J'onzz) ..... Carl Lumbly
Green Lantern (John Stewart) .... Phil LaMarr
Hawkgirl (Shayera Hol) .... Maria Canals
Wonder Woman (Diana) .... Susan Eisenberg
The Flash (Wally West) .... Michael Rosenbaum

Seven heroes of DC Comics united to protect the world from bad stuff in this amalgam of cartoon classics. In the premiere Sen. J. Alan Carter (Gary Cole) persuaded the World Assembly to declare world disarmament and entrust the security of Earth to Superman. Carter was in reality an alien traitor, and as soon as the plan went into effect a carefully plotted alien invasion began, which overwhelmed both Superman and his buddy Batman. Things looked bleak until the two were able to rally more superheroes with additional powers, in the form of Martian Manhunter, a telepathic green shapeshifter, Green Lantern, who could cast protective shields with his Power Ring, Hawkgirl, who slugged away with an ax, Wonder Woman, who roped 'em in, and The Flash, a sarcastic red guy who moved so fast nobody could see him work. After this formidable force had defeated the invaders they decided to stay together on Batman's space station, watching over Earth and protecting it from other aliens, sorcerers and supervillains. (Aren't you glad they're there?) Numerous villains tested Our Heroes' mettle, including The Joker (Mark Hamill), Lex Luthor (Clancy Brown), Mongul (Eric Roberts) and Grodd (Powers Boothe).

JUVENILE JURY (*Quiz/Audience Participation*)
FIRST TELECAST: *April 3, 1947*
LAST TELECAST: *September 14, 1954*
BROADCAST HISTORY:

Apr 1947–Jul 1947, NBC Thu 8:00–8:30
Jun 1951–Sep 1951, NBC Tue 8:30–9:00
Jun 1952–Oct 1952, NBC Wed 8:00–8:30
Jul 1953–Sep 1953, NBC Mon 9:00–9:30
Jun 1954–Sep 1954, CBS Tue 8:30–9:00

EMCEE:

Jack Barry

Juvenile Jury was created by radio announcer Jack Barry, who served as its emcee on both radio and television. The format was simple and highly effective. A panel of five children, ranging in age from 3 to 12, was presented with "problems" sent in by viewers and asked to comment, or think up solutions. The kids were utterly uninhibited, and their answers were sometimes serious, sometimes funny, and always totally unpredictable. A typical exchange went like this. A mother wrote in, "My little girl wakes up very early every morning so she won't be late for school. But school is only two blocks away and she awakens the whole family, then arrives at school so early she has to sit on the steps and wait for the doors to open." To which the "jury" replied:

Richard (10): "Well, there's one good thing about her getting up so early—the rest of the family won't have to get in line for the bathroom!"

Mai-Lan (7): "Instead of keeping everyone else awake, why doesn't she go out and walk around the block a few thousand times?"

Elberta (6½): "Her teacher must be Gregory Peck or something . . ."

David (6): "Maybe she gets ready fast and early now—but wait till she gets older. Wait till she starts putting lipstick on and wearing a girdle."

Barry picked his kids carefully, and the results were always entertaining. (A similar format was used for years by Art Linkletter on a segment of his *House Party* show.) Once a sweet young child told him that when she grew up she wanted to be a doctor. "Why?" asked Barry. "Because," she answered, full of sincerity, "I like to stick needles in people."

Perhaps the best exchange, though, came after Barry had just finished delivering a commercial for the sponsor's health tonic, in which he was obliged to take a couple of swigs of the stuff. As he walked over to the panel to begin his next interview, the young subject eyed him suspiciously, sniffed the air, and piped up accusingly, "Have you been drinking?"

Juvenile Jury began on radio in 1946 and had a brief run on NBC's early East Coast TV network in mid-1947. It was seen again on network television, this time nationwide, for four summers from 1951–1954. It continued as a Sunday afternoon show until March 27, 1955. Fifteen years later Jack Barry revived *Juvenile Jury* as a syndicated series during the 1970–1971 season.

KABLAM! (*Cartoon*)
BROADCAST HISTORY:
Nickelodeon
30 minutes
Produced: *1996–1999* (29 episodes)
Premiered: *October 11, 1996*
VOICES:
Henry .... Noah Segan
June .... Julia McIlvaine
Billed as an animated comic book, this collection of short cartoons was "hosted" by Henry and June, two animated, bug-eyed 'tweens who "turned the pages" to introduce each new feature. Among the regulars were "Sniz & Fondue," a pair of crabby cats; "Action League Now!", a team of well-intentioned Barbie doll action figures who were constantly getting mangled; and "Life with Loopy," about a young girl with an overactive imagination.

KAISER ALUMINUM HOUR, THE (*Dramatic Anthology*)
FIRST TELECAST: *July 3, 1956*
LAST TELECAST: *June 18, 1957*
BROADCAST HISTORY:
Jul 1956–Jun 1957, NBC Tue 9:30–10:30
Live hour-long dramas were presented every other week on *The Kaiser Aluminum Hour*. It alternated on Tuesday evenings with *The Armstrong Circle Theatre* prior to the latter program's move to CBS. The format was varied to include both serious and light subjects, with both well-known and lesser-known actors. The first production, "Army Game," was headlined by Paul Newman. Others who were featured in this series included Eli Wallach, Robert Culp, Natalie Wood, Forrest Tucker, Jack Warden, MacDonald Carey, Claude Rains, Henry Hull, Hume Cronyn, Franchot Tone, Geraldine Brooks, Kim Hunter, and Ralph Bellamy.

KALLIKAKS, THE (*Situation Comedy*)
FIRST TELECAST: *August 3, 1977*
LAST TELECAST: *August 31, 1977*
BROADCAST HISTORY:
Aug 1977, NBC Wed 9:30–10:00
CAST:
Jasper T. Kallikak .... David Huddleston
Venus Kallikak .... Edie McClurg
Bobbi Lou Kallikak .... Bonnie Ebsen
Junior Kallikak .... Patrick J. Peterson
Oscar Heinz .... Peter Palmer
THEME:
"Beat the System," by Stanley Ralph Ross, sung by Roy Clark
In the hopes of finding his fortune out West, Jasper T. Kallikak had moved his family from their native Appalachia, where he had worked as a coal miner, to the small town of Nowhere, California. He had inherited a small, two-pump gas station there and figured that, as his own boss, he would improve his lot. Conniving and avaricious, Jasper lived by the theme song of this mini-series, always looking for a way to beat the system. With his overly affectionate wife Venus, his social-climbing teenage daughter, and his mechanical genius preteen son, not to mention his German hired hand Oscar who could barely speak English, Jasper had quite a household. One member of the cast should have felt right at home with this hillbillies-move-west format. Bonnie Ebsen's father Buddy had spent most of the 1960s as Jed Clampett on *The Beverly Hillbillies*.

KAREN (*Situation Comedy*)
FIRST TELECAST: *October 5, 1964*
LAST TELECAST: *August 30, 1965*
BROADCAST HISTORY:
Oct 1964–Aug 1965, NBC Mon 7:30–8:00
CAST:
Karen Scott .... Debbie Watson
Steve Scott .... Richard Denning
Barbara Scott .... Mary LaRoche
Mimi Scott .... Gina Gillespie
Janis .... Bernadette Withers
Candy .... Trudi Ames
Peter .... Teddy Quinn
Spider Gibson .... Murray MacLeod
David Rowe III .... Richard Dreyfuss
THEME:
performed by The Beach Boys
Karen was one of the three half-hour situation comedies that comprised the 90-minute *90 Bristol Court* series in the fall of 1964. The concept of *90 Bristol Court* was to link together three separate families living in the same Southern California apartment complex, each with their own story and own half-hour show each week. *Karen* was the only one of the three that made it through the entire 1964–1965 season, however, the other two (*Harris Against the World* and *Tom, Dick and Mary*) being dropped in January.

Karen Scott was an energetic 16-year-old whose activities constantly confounded her tolerant parents, Steve and Barbara. Karen's tomboyish younger sister Mimi created a different set of problems for the elder Scotts, and the situations she became involved in functioned as counterpoint to those of her older sister. Handyman Cliff Murdock (Guy Raymond), the only character appearing in all three parts of *90 Bristol Court*, did not appear on *Karen* after the other two comedies were dropped.

KAREN (*Situation Comedy*)
FIRST TELECAST: *January 30, 1975*
LAST TELECAST: *June 19, 1975*
BROADCAST HISTORY:
Jan 1975–Jun 1975, ABC Thu 8:30–9:00
CAST:
Karen Angelo .... Karen Valentine
Dale Busch (first telecast) .... Denver Pyle
Dale Busch .... Charles Lane
Dena Madison .... Dena Dietrich
Cissy Peterson .... Aldine King
Adam Cooperman .... Will Seltzer
Jerry Siegel .... Oliver Clark
Cheryl Siegel .... Alix Elias
This contemporary situation comedy centered around Karen Angelo, a single, bright, involved young woman who worked for a citizens' action organization called Open America, headquartered in Washington, D.C. Helping Karen uncover crooked politicians and lobby for citizens' legislation were crusty Dale Busch,

founder of Open America; Dena, the group's cynical office manager; Adam, a young student working for the organization; and Cissy, Karen's roommate. Jerry and Cheryl were Karen's neighbors in Georgetown.

KAREN'S SONG (*Situation Comedy*)

FIRST TELECAST: *July 18, 1987*
LAST TELECAST: *September 12, 1987*
BROADCAST HISTORY:
Jul 1987–Sep 1987, FOX Sat 9:30–10:00
CAST:
Karen Matthews .... Patty Duke
Claire Steiner .... Lainie Kazan
Steven Foreman .... Lewis Smith
Laura Matthews (age 18) .... Teri Hatcher
Michael Brand .... Charles Levin
Zach Matthews .... Granville Van Dusen

Ten years after her divorce, Karen Matthews's life was pretty good. She had just been promoted to editor for a Los Angeles book publisher and her daughter, Laura, had started college at UCLA. Then she fell in love with Steve, the owner of a small catering service called A Catered Affair. He was bright, friendly, interesting, loving, and 28 years old—12 years younger than Karen. Daughter Laura thought dating a younger man disgusting and best friend Claire thought it was great. Karen's neighbor and former lover, real-estate salesman Michael, was supportive but thought she and Steve should get married. As for Karen herself, she was alternately content and confused, unsure of whether a relationship with a younger man made sense or had a future. The relationship might have, but the series failed after only two months.

KATE & ALLIE (*Situation Comedy*)

FIRST TELECAST: *March 19, 1984*
LAST TELECAST: *September 11, 1989*
BROADCAST HISTORY:
Mar 1984–May 1984, CBS Mon 9:30–10:00
Aug 1984–Sep 1986, CBS Mon 9:30–10:00
Sep 1986–Sep 1987, CBS Mon 8:00–8:30
Sep 1987–Nov 1987, CBS Mon 8:30–9:00
Dec 1987–Jun 1988, CBS Mon 8:00–8:30
July 1988–Aug 1988, CBS Sat 8:00–8:30
Aug 1988–Sep 1988, CBS Mon 9:00–9:30
Dec 1988–Mar 1989, CBS Mon 8:30–9:00
Mar 1989–Jun 1989, CBS Mon 10:30–11:00
Jun 1989–Sep 1989, CBS Mon 8:00–8:30
CAST:
Kate McArdle .... Susan Saint James
Allie Lowell .... Jane Curtin
Emma McArdle (1984–1988) .... Ari Meyers
Chip Lowell .... Frederick Koehler
Jennie Lowell .... Allison Smith
**Charles Lowell (1984–1986)* .... Paul Hecht
Ted Bartelo (1984–1985, 1987–1988)
.... Gregory Salata
Bob Barsky (1987–1989) .... Sam Freed
Lou Carello (1988–1989) .... Peter Onorati
*Occasional

Kate and Allie were two divorcées who had been friends since high school. In an effort to save money and provide mutual emotional support, they decided to share an apartment in New York's Greenwich Village. Of course, there were problems. Between them they had three young children who caused a certain amount of turmoil, and Kate and Allie themselves had decidedly different lifestyles. Kate was glamorous, contemporary, and a bit frivolous, while Allie was old-fashioned, proper, and industrious to a fault. Stories revolved around the problems of adjusting to communal life, raising children in the city, and Allie's rocky love life. She had never dated much, and now more than ever needed the help of her more worldly friend.

Allie's ex-husband Charles was seen occasionally, picking up the kids; later, he remarried. Kate did find romance in 1985, in the unlikely person of plumber Ted Bartelo. They actually got engaged that spring, but broke up after a short time.

Allie's hard-earned bachelor's degree proved of little help in getting her a good job, and Kate became bored with being a travel agent, so in the spring of 1987 they started their own catering business. That fall both of their daughters enrolled at Columbia University. Emma subsequently moved into a dormitory, giving her more freedom than her friend Jennie. Allie was forced to face the reality that her daughter was becoming a woman, and reluctantly gave Jennie some of the same freedom at home that Emma had at the dorm. Kate's old boyfriend Ted was back, and Allie was dating sportscaster Bob Barsky.

In the season premiere episode in December of 1988, Allie and Bob got married and proceeded to move into a new high-rise apartment. When Bob got a job as a sportscaster on a Washington, D.C., TV station and decided to commute to work from New York, Kate moved in to keep Allie and Chip company during the week while he was in Washington. The two women were trying to make money with their catering business, Jenny was a sophomore at Columbia, and Emma had transferred to U.C.L.A. to be close to her dad. Lou, the high-rise's super, was forever trying to make time with a totally disinterested Kate.

KATE BRASHER (*Drama*)

FIRST TELECAST: *February 24, 2001*
LAST TELECAST: *April 14, 2001*
BROADCAST HISTORY:
Feb 2001–Apr 2001, CBS Sat 9:00–10:00
CAST:
Kate Brasher .... Mary Stuart Masterson
Abbie Schaeffer .... Rhea Perlman
Joe Almeida .... Hector Elizondo
Daniel Brasher .... Gregory Smith
Elvis Brasher .... Mason Gamble
Mercedes .... Andi Chapman
Earl .... Roger Robinson

Kate was the struggling single mother of two teenage boys in Los Angeles. She worked multiple minimum-wage jobs to make a living; when one of her bosses refused to pay for her work, she went to Brothers Keepers, the local community and advocacy center, looking for legal advice. Not only did the center's feisty but inexperienced attorney, Abbie, help Kate and her coworkers get their money, but Joe, the center's harried director, offered her a full-time job. The money wasn't great, but being a trainee caseworker gave her the opportunity to help others in need find jobs and get their lives together. Mercedes and Earl also worked at Brothers Keepers. People who came to the center included an overweight woman denied a job as a receptionist at a health club, a hyperactive 9-year-old whose artistic talent would be suppressed if he was put on Ritalin as mandated by the school board and a recently released ex-con looking for housing and a job. Daniel and Elvis were Kate's supportive kids, who helped where they could.

KATE LOVES A MYSTERY (*Detective Drama*)
FIRST TELECAST: *February 26, 1979*
LAST TELECAST: *December 6, 1979*
BROADCAST HISTORY:
Feb 1979, NBC Mon 9:00–11:00
Mar 1979, NBC Thu 10:00–11:00
Aug 1979–Dec 1979, NBC Thu 10:00–11:00
CAST:
Kate Columbo/Callahan .... Kate Mulgrew
Jenny Columbo/Callahan.............. Lili Haydn
Josh Alden .... Henry Jones
Sgt. Mike Varrick..................... Don Stroud

One of the biggest hits of the early 1970s was *Columbo*, the disheveled detective who always got his man. He often mentioned his wife ("the missus"), but she was never seen. *Columbo* finally ran its course, but the producers, unwilling to let a good (and profitable) idea die, decided to concoct a Mrs. Columbo who was also a sleuth, on a show of her own. Kate Columbo was the mother of a seven-year-old daughter and, to avoid the monotony of housework, a reporter for *The Valley Advocate*, a suburban weekly newspaper edited by crusty old Josh Alden. It may seem a little farfetched, but working for the paper somehow got Kate involved in numerous murder mysteries, all of which she solved in much the same manner of her celebrated spouse.

After a mixed reception in early 1979, the series underwent two title changes, from the original *Kate Columbo*, to *Kate the Detective*, to *Kate Loves a Mystery*. The producers apparently felt that tying Kate to *Columbo* had been a mistake, so they gave her a new last name, Callahan, and all references to a husband were dropped. She still worked at the paper, and Sgt. Varrick was added to the cast as her contact on the police force. It didn't help, and the program was canceled by early December.

KATE MCSHANE (*Law Drama*)
FIRST TELECAST: *September 10, 1975*
LAST TELECAST: *November 12, 1975*
BROADCAST HISTORY:
Sep 1975–Nov 1975, CBS Wed 10:00–11:00
CAST:
Kate McShane .... Anne Meara
Pat McShane .... Sean McClory
Ed McShane .... Charles Haid

Kate McShane was the first network dramatic series to feature a woman lawyer in the lead role. As played by Anne Meara, Kate was single, independent, aggressive, and softhearted. She had a tendency to become emotionally involved with her clients, which was not always a good idea. When she encountered problems (which was every week) she could turn to her father, Pat, a former cop who served as her investigator, or to her brother Ed, a Jesuit priest and law professor who helped her with the stickier legal and moral questions.

Miss Meara was half of the husband-and-wife comedy team of Stiller and Meara, which appeared on many variety shows during the 1970s. This was her first dramatic series.

KATE SMITH EVENING HOUR, THE (*Musical Variety*)
FIRST TELECAST: *September 19, 1951*
LAST TELECAST: *June 11, 1952*
BROADCAST HISTORY:
Sep 1951–Jun 1952, NBC Wed 8:00–9:00
REGULARS:
Kate Smith
Ted Collins
The Jack Allison Singers
The Johnny Butler Dancers
The Jack Miller Orchestra

Kate Smith, one of radio's favorite and most familiar personalities, made only two brief excursions into a nighttime television series (she also had a daytime show from 1950 to 1954). *The Kate Smith Evening Hour* was a live weekly variety show which featured Broadway and Hollywood stars in excerpts from famous plays, as well as musical numbers, comedy sketches, and the other traditional components of a variety show. Ted Collins, who was Miss Smith's manager and producer of this show, served as the host of the program. The semi-regular feature "Ethel and Albert," starring Peg Lynch and Alan Bunce, later became a series in its own right and ran for several seasons.

Two of Kate's guests on this series were making their television debuts: singer Josephine Baker and the Tommy Dorsey Orchestra. In contrast to her daytime theme, "When the Moon Comes Over the Mountain," Miss Smith opened her prime-time show with her stirring and familiar rendition of "God Bless America."

KATE SMITH SHOW, THE (*Musical Variety*)
FIRST TELECAST: *January 25, 1960*
LAST TELECAST: *July 18, 1960*
BROADCAST HISTORY:
Jan 1960–Jul 1960, CBS Mon 7:30–8:00
REGULARS:
Kate Smith
Neal Hefti and His Orchestra
The Harry Simeone Chorus

Kate Smith returned to nighttime television, after an absence of almost a decade, with this musical variety show. She sang, introduced her guest stars, and participated with them in production numbers. Most of the guests were popular singers, dancers, or musicians.

KATIE JOPLIN (*Situation Comedy*)
FIRST TELECAST: *August 9, 1999*
LAST TELECAST: *September 6, 1999*
BROADCAST HISTORY:
Aug 1999–Sep 1999, WB Mon 9:30–10:00
CAST:
Katie Joplin .... Park Overall
Glen Shotz .... Jay Thomas
Mitchell Tuit............................ Jim Rash
Gray Joplin (age 14).................. Jesse Head
Liz Berlin .... Ana Reeder
Tiger French........................... Simon Rex
Sara Shotz .... Majandra Delfino

Plainspoken Katie and her teenage son, Gray, had just arrived in Philadelphia from her native Knoxville,

Tennessee, and moved in with her fashion-plate niece Liz, the only person in town they knew. Katie's outspoken nature landed her a job hosting a late-night radio call-in show on FM station WLBP (87.5) when Glen, the station's general manager to whom she was trying to sell a car, was impressed by her perception, Southern wit, and strong opinions. Although her own social life was in shambles, she provided callers and listeners with good advice on how to deal with the problems in their personal and social lives. Mitchell was the arrogant program director who was upset that Glen was forcing him to air a talk show on his otherwise all-rock-'n'-roll station. He wanted to see Katie flop and teamed her with Tiger, an eager but inexperienced young producer, hoping for the worst.

KAY KYSER'S KOLLEGE OF MUSICAL KNOWLEDGE (*Quiz/Audience Participation*)

FIRST TELECAST: *December 1, 1949*
LAST TELECAST: *September 12, 1954*
BROADCAST HISTORY:

Dec 1949–Dec 1950, NBC Thu 9:00–10:00 (OS)
Jul 1954–Sep 1954, NBC Sun 7:00–7:30

EMCEE:

Kay Kyser (1949–1950)
Tennessee Ernie Ford (1954)

REGULARS (1949–1950):

Ish Kabbible
Liza Palmer
Sue Bennett
Michael Douglas
Honeydreamers
Dr. Roy K. Marshall (announcer)
Ben Grauer (announcer)
Diane Sinclair
Ken Spaulding
Carl Hoff (orchestra director)

REGULARS (1954):

The Cheerleaders Quintet
Frank DeVol Orchestra
Jack Narz (announcer and "Dean")

THEME (1949–1950):

"Thinking of You," by Walter Donaldson and Paul Ash

Kay Kyser was one of several bandleaders who had developed an audience-involvement "gimmick" while touring dance halls across the country in the 1930s, and then brought his routine successfully to radio in the 1940s (another was Sammy Kaye with his *So You Want to Lead a Band* routine). When television came along, hungry for programming, the bandleaders were ready with their pretested and already successful entertainment packages.

The *Kollege of Musical Knowledge* was a musical quiz show. "Professor" Kay, garbed in cap and gown, recruited contestants from the studio audience and posed musical questions, which were performed or acted out by members of the band and special guests. Three bearded judges, dressed in tails and somewhat resembling the Smith Brothers, sat behind a long desk and comically "judged" the answers (all three speaking in perfect unison). The band was dressed in sweaters and beanies. Contestants were sometimes required to give a totally incorrect answer, upon which Kay would shout, "That's right, you're wrong," or "That's wrong, you're right," as might be the case. The whole atmosphere was somewhat antic, with Kay constantly mugging for the audience and comedy and musical routines interpolated.

Assisting with the musical questions were "dumb" comedian Ish Kabbible (real name: Merwyn Bogue) and several of the band's regular vocalists, including young Michael (Mike) Douglas—later of TV talk show fame.

After a year's run the program was involved in a dispute between sponsor and network, which resulted in its cancellation. It probably could have been revived in another time slot or on another network, but Kyser, tired of years of the showbiz grind, threw in the towel and retired not only from TV but from the entertainment world entirely. He pursued religious activities for the rest of his life.

The *Kollege of Musical Knowledge* idea was revived in 1954 as a summer show, with Tennessee Ernie Ford as host. Kay Kyser was listed as "consultant" for the 1954 revival, and even appeared as special guest on one telecast, but without the regular presence of Kay and his maniac crew the program had lost its spark, and was not renewed.

KAY O'BRIEN (*Medical Drama*)

FIRST TELECAST: *September 25, 1986*
LAST TELECAST: *November 13, 1986*
BROADCAST HISTORY:

Sep 1986–Nov 1986, CBS Thu 10:00–11:00

CAST:

Dr. Kay O'Brien ("Kayo")........ Patricia Kalember
Dr. Robert Moffitt........ Lane Smith
Dr. Josef Wallach........ Jan Rubes
Dr. Michael Kwan........ Keone Young
Dr. Mark Doyle........ Brian Benben
Dr. Cliff Margolis........ Tony Soper
Nurse Rosa Villanueva........ Priscilla Lopez
Sam........ Franc Luz
Nat........ Michael Rogers
Anesthesiologist........ Myra Fried
O.R. Nurse........ Arlene Duncan

Fictional Manhattan General Hospital was the setting for this medical drama. Kayo was a 28-year-old surgical resident at the hospital; her stress-filled professional life, and, to a lesser extent, her personal life, provided the focus of most episodes. Others on the staff included Dr. Moffitt, the attending surgeon and Kayo's teacher; Dr. Doyle, an obnoxious fellow surgical resident who felt women shouldn't be surgeons; Dr. Margolis, the intern working under Kayo; Dr. Kwan, the senior resident physician on staff; and Dr. Wallach, the imposing head of surgery. Chief Emergency Room nurse Rosa was Kayo's best friend and confidante; Sam, the former boyfriend who left her because he didn't like taking second place in her life after medicine; and Nat was a helpful black orderly.

KAZ (*Law/Detective Drama*)

FIRST TELECAST: *September 10, 1978*
LAST TELECAST: *August 19, 1979*
BROADCAST HISTORY:

Sep 1978–Oct 1978, CBS Sun 10:00–11:00
Oct 1978–Jan 1979, CBS Sun 9:00–10:00
Jan 1979–Apr 1979, CBS Wed 10:00–11:00
Jul 1979–Aug 1979, CBS Sun 10:00–11:00

CAST:

Martin "Kaz" Kazinsky........ Ron Leibman
Samuel Bennett........ Patrick O'Neal

Katie McKenna .... Linda Carlson
Mary Parnell .... Gloria Le Roy
Peter Colcourt..................... Mark Withers
Illsa Fogel.......................... Edith Atwater
D.A. Frank Revko.................. George Wyner
Malloy .... Dick O'Neill

Kaz had an unusual background for an attorney—he had earned his law degree while serving time in prison. Upon his release he had managed to secure a position as a junior partner with the prestigious Los Angeles law firm of Bennett, Rheinhart and Alquist. The pay wasn't very good (as he frequently reminded senior partner Samuel Bennett), but someone with his background and inexperience had little choice. Kaz did have one advantage, however. Having been on the other side of the law himself, he had an understanding of the criminal mind not usually found in attorneys. His girlfriend was court reporter Katie McKenna, and his pad a small apartment over the Starting Gate, a jazz music nightclub owned by his friend Mary Parnell. Kaz often hung out at the Starting Gate, and sat in with the band as a drummer. Working with him at the law firm was another young attorney, Peter Colcourt.

KEANE BROTHERS SHOW, THE (*Musical Variety*)

FIRST TELECAST: *August 12, 1977*
LAST TELECAST: *September 2, 1977*
BROADCAST HISTORY:
Aug 1977–Sep 1977, CBS Fri 8:30–9:00
REGULARS:
Tom Keane
John Keane
Jimmy Caesar
The Anita Mann Dancers
The Alan Copeland Orchestra

If ABC could make series stars out of teenagers Donny and Marie Osmond, CBS figured they could try a summer mini-series with two performers who were even younger. Probably the youngest co-stars ever on a network variety series, piano-playing Tom was 13, and his drummer brother John was only 12. They sang and played popular tunes and performed with assorted guest stars. Impressionist Jimmy Caesar provided comic relief.

KEEFE BRASSELLE SHOW, THE (*Musical Variety*)

FIRST TELECAST: *June 25, 1963*
LAST TELECAST: *September 17, 1963*
BROADCAST HISTORY:
Jun 1963–Sep 1963, CBS Tue 10:00–11:00
REGULARS:
Keefe Brasselle
Noelle Adam
Ann B. Davis
Sammy Kaye
Rocky Graziano
The Bill Foster Dancers
Charles Sanford Orchestra

Keefe Brasselle was pushed hard as a "coming star" on television in the 1960s, but he never did seem to make the big time. In addition to producing programs and appearing in dramatic presentations, he starred in this variety series which was the summer replacement for *The Garry Moore Show.* Probably the highlight of the series was the premiere, on which a young guest named Barbra Streisand belted out "Soon It's Gonna Rain" from *The Fantasticks.*

Brasselle, who also worked in an executive capacity for CBS, later turned novelist and wrote a sex-and-scandal best-seller focusing on an unnamed TV network. The book was entitled *The CanniBalS.*

KEENEN IVORY WAYANS SHOW, THE (*Talk*)

BROADCAST HISTORY:
Syndicated only
60 minutes
Produced: *1997–1998*
Released: *August 4, 1997*
HOST:
Keenen Ivory Wayans
BAND:
Ladies of the Night

This hip, urban talk show was hosted by the multi-talented Keenen Ivory Wayans, who had been the creative center of the Fox hit *In Living Color* earlier in the '90s. Each telecast opened in a large studio resembling a nightclub, amid a loud party atmosphere with a rocking, sexy, all-girl band. The tall, bald, and very handsome host would then come on and do his monologue, then rap with his always-hip guests in an informal setting resembling a living room. There was a strongly contemporary feel to the show, and the guests were a mix of mainstream stars and cult sensations; for example: Jada Pinkett, Samuel L. Jackson, Nicollette Sheridan, and rap group Bone Thugs-N-Harmony. Even if the questions were sometimes jarringly trite ("So, what is it like to be the new *Baywatch* star?"), this was meant to be the coolest place on the planet. There were also filmed spoofs of TV commercials, comedy bits, and musical performances by the guests, many of whom were African-Americans.

Cool or not, neither *The Keenen Ivory Wayans Show* nor *Vibe,* the other urban-oriented late-night talk show that premiered in the fall of 1997, survived. Wayans's was the first to go, canceled in March, with its last (rerun) episode airing in April.

KEEP IT IN THE FAMILY (*Quiz*)

FIRST TELECAST: *October 12, 1957*
LAST TELECAST: *February 8, 1958*
BROADCAST HISTORY:
Oct 1957–Feb 1958, ABC Sat 7:30–8:00
EMCEE:
Keefe Brasselle (1957)
Bill Nimmo
ANNOUNCER:
Johnny Olsen

This quiz show pitted two families against each other. Each team, which might comprise several generations within one family, was presented with a multi-part question. Each member of the family, starting with the youngest, then had to answer one part. Winning families continued on the program until defeated. Keefe Brasselle was the host on the first telecast of this show, but was replaced for the remainder of the run by Bill Nimmo.

KEEP ON CRUISIN' (*Variety*)

FIRST TELECAST: *January 9, 1987*
LAST TELECAST: *June 5, 1987*

BROADCAST HISTORY:

Jan 1987–Jun 1987, CBS Fri 11:30 P.M.–12:30 A.M.

HOSTS:

Stephen Bishop
Jimmy Aleck
Sinbad

EXECUTIVE PRODUCER:

Dick Clark

Musical and comedy performers were featured on this variety series aired from a different location in the Los Angeles area each week. Singer-songwriter Stephen Bishop co-hosted with young comic Sinbad. When the show returned in April after a brief hiatus, Bishop had been replaced by comic Jimmy Aleck. The locations included the Santa Monica pier, Hollywood Boulevard, Johnny Rocket's Hollywood Diner, Mann's Chinese Theater, and Knotts' Berry Farm. Appearing were musical guests like the New Edition, Little Anthony, Billy Vera and the Beaters, Eddie Money, Oingo Boingo, and Ronnie Spector, and hip young comedians Rick Overton, Frank Welker, Lois Bromfield, and Rick Ducommun.

KEEP ON TRUCKIN' (*Comedy/Variety*)

FIRST TELECAST: *July 12, 1975*
LAST TELECAST: *August 2, 1975*
BROADCAST HISTORY:

Jul 1975–Aug 1975, ABC Sat 8:00–9:00

CAST:

Franklyn Ajaye
Rhonda Bates
Kathrine Baumann
Jeannine Burnier
Didi Conn
Charles Fleischer
Wayland Flowers
Larry Ragland
Marion Ramsey
Rhilo Fahir
Jack Riley
Fred Travalena
Gailard Sartain
Richard Lee Sung

This four-week summer variety series featured a repertory company of 14 bright young comics, who did rapid-fire gags and satirical sketches, and indulged in general buffoonery. Each telecast was to be introduced by respected writer-actor Rod Serling, but Serling died two weeks before the premiere and his pretaped segments were omitted from the actual telecasts.

KEEP POSTED (*Public Affairs*)

FIRST TELECAST: *October 9, 1951*
LAST TELECAST: *March 31, 1953*
BROADCAST HISTORY:

Oct 1951–Mar 1953, DUM Tue 8:30–9:00

MODERATOR:

Martha Rountree

REGULAR PANELIST:

Lawrence Spivak

Martha Rountree moderated this public-affairs program in which a panel of citizens, chaired by Lawrence Spivak, questioned a leading public figure. Among the guests was Rep. Richard M. Nixon (R-Calif), whose topic was "Fighting Communism." The program originated from Washington, D.C.

KEEP TALKING (*Quiz/Audience Participation*)

FIRST TELECAST: *July 15, 1958*
LAST TELECAST: *May 3, 1960*
BROADCAST HISTORY:

Jul 1958–Sep 1958, CBS Tue 8:30–9:00
Sep 1958–Oct 1958, CBS Tue 8:00–8:30
Nov 1958–Feb 1959, CBS Sun 10:00–10:30
Feb 1959–Sep 1959, CBS Wed 8:00–8:30
Sep 1959–May 1960, ABC Tue 10:30–11:00

EMCEE:

Monty Hall (1958)
Carl Reiner (1958–1959)
Merv Griffin (1959–1960)

REGULARS:

Joey Bishop
Ilka Chase (1958–1959)
Audrey Meadows (1958–1959)
Elaine May (1958–1959)
Paul Winchell
Danny Dayton
Morey Amsterdam
Peggy Cass
Pat Carroll
Orson Bean (1959–1960)

The players on *Keep Talking* were divided into two teams of three each. The emcee gave each player a different secret phrase, which the player was then required to incorporate into a story. After the phrase had been used the emcee would stop the story and ask the other team what the phrase was. Guessing the phrase won the team a point and the team with the most points at the end of the show was the winner. The object, therefore, was to ad-lib so skillfully that the phrases were masked from the other team. Monty Hall was the original emcee but was replaced by Carl Reiner when the show moved to Sunday nights in November 1958. When the series moved to ABC in September 1959, Merv Griffin took over as emcee.

KELLY KELLY (*Situation Comedy*)

FIRST TELECAST: *April 20, 1998*
LAST TELECAST: *June 7, 1998*
BROADCAST HISTORY:

Apr 1998, WB Mon 9:00–9:30
May 1998–Jun 1998, WB Sun 7:30–8:00

CAST:

Kelly Novack .... Shelley Long
Doug Kelly.............................. Robert Hays
Sean Kelly (age 17) .... Will Estes
Maureen "Mo" Kelly (14).......... Ashley Johnson
Brian Kelly (13)............................ Bug Hall
Casey Kelly (6) .... Gemini Barnett

This comedy was set in the New Jersey suburbs outside of Philadelphia. Kelly was a fluttery, status-conscious college professor who, while trying to keep her suicidal teaching assistant from ending it all, fell (literally and figuratively) for the handsome fireman who was trying to rescue him. She was chairperson of the English department at an unnamed Ivy League college. Doug was a blue-collar widower with four kids, all of whom considered Kelly snooty and not what they were looking for in a new mother. At the end of the premiere episode he proposed, and in the third they got married. Mo, Doug's only daughter, was a tomboy starting to mature into a woman, and Kelly tried, in her well-meaning, meddling way, to help things along. Sean was a manipulator who spent too little time studying, and his grades suffered accordingly. In every episode Kelly and Doug had passionate moments inspired by innuendoes which led them to rush somewhere to make love.

KELLY MONTEITH SHOW, THE (*Comedy/Variety*)

FIRST TELECAST: *June 16, 1976*
LAST TELECAST: *July 7, 1976*
BROADCAST HISTORY:
Jun 1976–Jul 1976, CBS Wed 8:30–9:00
REGULARS:
Kelly Monteith
Nellie Bellflower
Henry Corden

Kelly Monteith's forte was the comic monologue, with which he opened each episode of this four-week summer mini-series. Nellie Bellflower and Henry Corden, and a weekly guest star, also assisted Kelly in assorted sketches.

KEN BERRY "WOW" SHOW, THE (*Musical Variety*)

FIRST TELECAST: *July 15, 1972*
LAST TELECAST: *August 12, 1972*
BROADCAST HISTORY:
Jul 1972–Aug 1972, ABC Sat 10:00–11:00
REGULARS:
Ken Berry
Teri Garr
Billy Van
Carl Gottlieb
Don Lane
Steve Martin
Barbara Joyce
Laara Lacey
Cheryl Stoppelmoor (Cheryl Ladd)
Gene Merlino
Tom Kenny
Ted Zeigler
The New Seekers
Jaime Rogers Dancers
Jimmy Dale Orchestra

Ken Berry's previous exposure to a national television audience was almost exclusively as an actor in situation comedies, most notably *The Andy Griffith Show, Mayberry R.F.D.*, and *F Troop*. This contemporary summer series gave him an opportunity to show off his skills as a dancer and singer as well. Satires and lampoons of movies and TV shows were frequent features.

KEN MURRAY SHOW, THE (*Variety*)

FIRST TELECAST: *January 7, 1950*
LAST TELECAST: *June 21, 1953*
BROADCAST HISTORY:
Jan 1950–Jun 1952, CBS Sat 8:00–9:00 (OS)
Feb 1953–Jun 1953, CBS Sun 9:30–10:00
REGULARS:
Ken Murray
Darla Hood (1950–1951)
Joe Wong (1950–1951)
Tony Labriola (1950–1951)
Jack Mulhall (1950–1951)
Betty Lou Walters (1950–1951)
The Enchanters (1950–1951)
Joe Besser (1950–1951)
Art Lund (1951–1952)
Laurie Anders
Pat Conway (1951–1952)
Jane Bergmeier (1951–1952)
Lillian Farmer (1951–1952)
Anita Gordon (1951–1953)
Johnny Johnston (1953)

Old trouper Ken Murray, who had begun his career in vaudeville in the teens and who appeared on the first commercial program on television, in 1930, hosted his own comedy-variety series on CBS from 1950–1953. Murray was also a producer of some note, and his show featured top-name guest stars and elaborate sets—including his trademark Hollywood and Vine backdrop. He had a large cast of regular singers and dancers, including cowgirl Laurie "Ah love the wide open spaces" Anders and a bevy of long-stemmed "Glamourlovelies." Ken bridged the various acts with informal chatter and humor. The series began as an alternate-week entry, switched to weekly in the fall of 1950, and then back to alternate weeks in 1953. During the 1953 run it alternated with *The Alan Young Show* under the umbrella title *Time to Smile.*

KENAN & KEL (*Situation Comedy*)

BROADCAST HISTORY:
Nickelodeon
30 minutes
Produced: *1996–1999* (61 episodes)
Premiered: *October 12, 1996*
CAST:
Kenan Rockmore................Kenan Thompson
Kel Kimble...........................Kel Mitchell
Roger Rockmore.......................Ken Foree
Sheryl Rockmore................Teal Marchande
Kyra Rockmore (age 9).............Vanessa Baden
Chris Potter......................Dan Frischman
Sharla Morrison (1998–1999).........Alexis Fields
Marc McCram (1998–1999)........Biagio Messina
THEME:
written and performed by Coolio

Two goofy black Chicago teens schemed and dreamed in this slapstick sitcom, which was reminiscent of the '70s hit *What's Happening!!* Kenan, the chubby one, was the chief schemer, and Kel his good-looking, tagalong buddy. Kenan worked part-time at Rigby's convenience store, where he caused endless problems for his nervous boss, Mr. Potter (who twitched a lot as a result). Roger was Kenan's stern dad, an air traffic controller; and Sheryl his businesslike mom. Kyra, his little sister, delighted in snitching on her older brother, but harbored a not-so-secret crush on clueless Kel.

Kenan and Kel were previously seen on Nickelodeon's variety show *All That*, and by 1997 they'd become so popular that they starred in their own summer feature film, *Good Burger.* They opened each episode of this sitcom doing a standup bit in front of a curtain, before introducing the night's story. Wonder if they realized how old *that* device was (shades of Jack Benny and George Burns)?

KENTUCKY JONES (*Comedy/Drama*)

FIRST TELECAST: *September 19, 1964*
LAST TELECAST: *September 11, 1965*
BROADCAST HISTORY:
Sep 1964–Dec 1964, NBC Sat 8:30–9:00
Jan 1965–Sep 1965, NBC Sat 8:00–8:30

CAST:

"Kentucky" Jones .... Dennis Weaver
Ike Wong .... Ricky Der
Seldom Jackson .... Harry Morgan
Annie Ng .... Cherylene Lee
Mr. Ng .... Arthur Wong
Thomas Wong .... Keye Luke
Edith Thorncroft .... Nancy Rennick

Kenneth Yarborough Jones was a veterinarian and owner of a 40-acre ranch in Southern California. He had acquired the nickname Kentucky because of the way he signed his name: "K. Y. Jones." His wife had applied to adopt a nine-year-old Chinese orphan who arrived shortly after her sudden death. Kentucky's situation as a widower made him have second thoughts about taking the orphan, Dwight Eisenhower "Ike" Wong, into his household. Although reluctant to accept the responsibility, Kentucky came to love Ike. Seldom Jackson was the handyman around the ranch, Edith Thorncroft, the social worker looking after Ike's welfare. The other regulars were members of the local Chinese community.

KEVIN SEAL: SPORTING FOOL (*Sports*)

BROADCAST HISTORY:

MTV
30 minutes
Produced: *1990–1991*
Premiered: *January 12, 1990*

HOST:

Kevin Seal

A weekly collection of odd and unusual sporting events.

KEY CLUB PLAYHOUSE (*Dramatic Anthology*)

FIRST TELECAST: *May 31, 1957*
LAST TELECAST: *August 23, 1957*
BROADCAST HISTORY:

May 1957–Aug 1957, ABC Fri 9:00–9:30

The filmed dramas presented in this series were selected reruns of episodes from *Ford Theatre*.

KEY TO THE AGES (*Discussion*)

FIRST TELECAST: *February 27, 1955*
LAST TELECAST: *May 22, 1955*
BROADCAST HISTORY:

Feb 1955–May 1955, ABC Sun 8:00–8:30

HOST:

Dr. Theodore Low

Ancient Greek poets, great novels, and other literary or cultural subjects were examined on this ABC program, which ran opposite Ed Sullivan for a few months in 1955. It originated from Baltimore and was produced in cooperation with the Enoch Pratt Free Library and the Walters Art Gallery.

KEY TO THE MISSING (*Interview*)

FIRST TELECAST: *August 8, 1948*
LAST TELECAST: *September 16, 1949*
BROADCAST HISTORY:

Aug 1948–Oct 1948, DUM Sun 6:30–7:00
Oct 1948–Mar 1949, DUM Fri 7:00–7:30
Mar 1949–Apr 1949, DUM Thu 8:30–9:00
May 1949–Jun 1949, DUM Fri 9:30–10:00
Jun 1949–Sep 1949, DUM Fri 9:00–9:30

HOST:

Archdale J. Jones

This was a kind of missing persons bureau of the air. Archdale Jones interviewed relatives and friends and showed pictures, handwriting specimens, etc., of missing persons, and then appealed to viewers to call in any information they might have on the vanished person's whereabouts. Although some of the cases went back generations, quite a few long-lost kin were reunited this way. The wartime radio program upon which the show was based (called *Where Are They Now?*) claimed a success rate of 68 percent.

KEY WEST (*Adventure*)

FIRST TELECAST: *January 19, 1993*
LAST TELECAST: *July 20, 1993*
BROADCAST HISTORY:

Jan 1993–Mar 1993, FOX Tue 9:00–10:00
Jun 1993–Jul 1993, FOX Tue 9:00–10:00

CAST:

Seamus O'Neill .... Fisher Stevens
Abednigo (JoJo) .... T. C. Carson
Gumbo (Paul Beausoleil) .... Leland Crooke
Chaucy Caldwell .... Denise Crosby
Savannah Sumner .... Jennifer Tilly
Roosevelt "King" Cole .... Ivory Ocean
Rikki .... Lara Piper
Hector Allegria .... Geno Silva
Sheriff Jeremiah Jefferson Cody ... Brian Thompson
Hunter Farmer .... Michael Covert
Dr. Reilly Clarke .... Kim Myers
Flame (Joyce) .... Jennifer Barlow
Fig .... Maria Canals

Picturesque Key West, Florida, was the setting for this slightly off-kilter comedy/drama. Seamus O'Neill was a disgruntled assembly-line worker in New Jersey who won $1 million in the state lottery and moved to Key West to follow his dream of being a reporter for *The Meteor*, the newspaper for which Hemingway had written. The money from his lottery winnings wasn't what he had expected—his first check was for $32.59 after deductions, back taxes, and penalties, and his $40,000 annual income wouldn't start until September 1998. With only his meager salary from *The Meteor* to live on, Seamus rented a trailer from Gumbo, the spaced-out owner of an open-air bar on the beach. With notepad in hand he sought out newsworthy stories while enjoying the laid-back lifestyle Key West offered.

Others in Seamus's Key West were Chaucy, the uptight, conservative, alcoholic mayor; JoJo, the Rastafarian illegal alien from Jamaica; Savannah, the hooker with a heart of gold; King Cole, the demanding blind publisher of *The Meteor*; Rikki, a sexy go-go dancer at Gumbo's who lived next to Seamus; Hector, a tough local businessman; Cody, the macho, off-center sheriff; Hunter, who ran boat tours around Key West; Reilly, a marine biologist working with dolphins; Flame, another of Gumbo's go-go girls who was Mayor Caldwell's sponsor at Alcoholics Anonymous; and Fig, King Cole's assistant at the paper.

KHAN (*Detective Drama*)

FIRST TELECAST: *February 7, 1975*
LAST TELECAST: *February 28, 1975*
BROADCAST HISTORY:

Feb 1975, CBS Fri 8:00–9:00

CAST:

Khan .... Khigh Dhiegh
Anna Khan .... Irene Yah-Ling Sun

Kim Khan .... Evan Kim
Lt. Gubbins .... Vic Tayback

Based in San Francisco's Chinatown, private detective Khan, with the help of his two children, unraveled mysterious crimes in a style that could best be described as contemporary Charlie Chan. Daughter Anna was finishing a Ph.D. in criminology and son Kim was also a college grad. Using their mix of modern and traditional techniques, the three Khans made a highly efficient team. Unfortunately, they did not attract an audience and the show was canceled after only four weeks on the air.

KID GLOVES (*Sports*)

FIRST TELECAST: *February 24, 1951*
LAST TELECAST: *August 4, 1951*
BROADCAST HISTORY:
Feb 1951–Mar 1951, CBS Sat 7:30–8:00
Mar 1951–Aug 1951, CBS Sat 6:30–7:00
REGULARS:
Frank Goodman
Bill Sears
John De Grosa

Originating live from Philadelphia, where it had been a successful local show for several months prior to its moving to the full CBS network, *Kid Gloves* gave young children an opportunity to display their skills as boxers. Contestants ranged in age from 3 to 12 and fought three-round matches. The length of each round was between 30 seconds and one minute, depending on the age of the contestants. Frank Goodman was the referee, the judge, and the matchmaker. Bill Sears was the ringside announcer, and John De Grosa of the Pennsylvania State Athletic Commission interviewed celebrities from the sports world between rounds.

KIDS IN THE HALL, THE (*Comedy/Variety*)

FIRST TELECAST: *September 18, 1992*
LAST TELECAST: *January 6, 1995*
BROADCAST HISTORY:
Sep 1992, CBS Fri 11:30–12:30 A.M.
Sep 1992–Aug 1993, CBS Fri 12:30–1:30 A.M.
Sep 1993–Dec 1993, CBS Fri 12:35–1:35 A.M.
Dec 1993–Feb 1994, CBS Thu 12:35–1:35 A.M.
Mar 1994–Dec 1994, CBS Fri 12:35–1:35 A.M.
Oct 1994–Nov 1994, CBS Thu 12:35–1:35 A.M.
Dec 1994–Jan 1995, CBS Thu/Fri 1:05–2:05 A.M.
(Also HBO Cable Network)
REGULARS:
David Foley
Bruce McCulloch
Kevin McDonald
Mark McKinney
Scott Thompson

The Kids in the Hall was an irreverent sketch-comedy series from Canada that featured five exuberant young male comics who played both male and female roles and who wrote much of their own material. There were a number of recurring routines—Scott Thompson as office worker Idiot Boy and the entire group as weight-obsessed ladies at lunch, overly aggressive police interrogators, hyperactive office managers, and tough street walkers. Much of the humor was pretty dark, and many of the sketches had gay themes or characters.

The Kids in the Hall originated as a club group in Toronto in 1984 and became a TV series in 1989, airing on the CBC in Canada and in a raunchier version on HBO in the U.S. It was added to CBS' late-night lineup in 1992. The early episodes on CBS were reruns, but eventually the network aired episodes new to American viewers. Lorne Michaels, who had created *Saturday Night Live*, was co-executive producer along with Jeff Ross. At the end of the last episode the stars said goodbye to the studio audience, went into a field, and were buried alive. The tombstone simply said, "The Kids In the Hall TV Show 1989–1995."

KIDS SAY THE DARNDEST THINGS (*Comedy*)

FIRST TELECAST: *January 9, 1998*
LAST TELECAST: *June 23, 2000*
BROADCAST HISTORY:
Jan 1998–Jun 2000, CBS Fri 8:00–8:30
HOST:
Bill Cosby
CONTRIBUTOR:
Art Linkletter

For almost two decades, from 1952 to 1970, *Art Linkletter's House Party* was a staple of the CBS weekday lineup. One of its most popular segments was "Kids Say the Darndest Things," in which Art talked with four youngsters about various topics. Their responses ranged from the insightful to the embarrassing to the hilarious. Bill Cosby's renowned rapport with children made him the obvious choice to host this reworking of a television classic.

Each episode included a segment in which Bill talked with a panel of preteens about such topics as falling in love, the importance of good food and candy bars, the meaning of New Year's resolutions, and what they would do with $1 million. Other recurring features were appearances by Linkletter showing vintage clips from the original *House Party* and a "Kids Explain" segment in which youngsters provided their unique insights on such things as bad manners, the "true" meaning of Good Friday, and their opinions about the Pledge of Allegiance. Cosby also showcased talented young musicians and singers, who performed on the show.

KIERAN'S KALEIDOSCOPE (*Documentary*)

BROADCAST HISTORY:
Syndicated only
15 minutes
Produced: *1949–1952* (104 episodes)
Released: *Early 1949*
HOST:
John Kieran

John Kieran, longtime sports columnist for the *New York Times*, gained national fame with his incredibly wide range of knowledge on radio's *Information Please* in the 1930s and 1940s. In this series of early TV films (the first widely seen syndicated series) he augmented his erudite and witty comments with still photographs and films of various subjects, from the solar system to wood-carving to the life of the beetle. One topic was discussed per program.

KIERNAN'S CORNER (*Interview*)

FIRST TELECAST: *August 16, 1948*
LAST TELECAST: *March 30, 1949*

BROADCAST HISTORY:

Aug 1948–Sep 1948, ABC Mon 8:00–8:30
Sep 1948–Jan 1949, ABC Mon 7:30–8:00
Jan 1949–Mar 1949, ABC Mon 8:00–8:30

HOST:

Walter Kiernan

Newspaperman and radio commentator Walter Kiernan, a familiar face on early television, conducted this talk show. He interviewed tourists in New York and visited interesting places around the city with the ABC cameras.

KIM POSSIBLE (*Cartoon*)

BROADCAST HISTORY:

Disney Channel
30 minutes
Original episodes: *2002–*
Premiered: *June 7, 2002*

VOICES:

Kim Possible .... Christy Carlson Romano
Ron Stoppable .... Will Friedle
Rufus .... Nancy Cartwright
Wade .... Tahj Mowry
Dr. Drakken .... John DiMaggio
Shego .... Nicole Sullivan
Dr. Possible (Dad) .... Gary Cole
Dr. Possible (Mom) .... Jean Smart
Jim and Tim Possible .... Shaun Fleming
Señor Senior, Sr. .... Ricardo Montalban
Señor Senior, Jr. .... Nestor Carbonell

This action cartoon had a marvelous sense of humor about itself. Kim was a red-haired, athletic high schooler, fetchingly dressed with a bare midriff, who regularly saved the world—between classes. Ron was her cheerful, goofy best bud who accompanied her on missions, where he often screwed up (Ron: "I helped with that avalanche." Kim: "You *started* the avalanche!"). At school he tried vainly to be cool, making him the target of regular put-downs by the girls, but he always bounced back with a friendly grin. Come to think of it, he *was* pretty cool. Kim talked in a kind of easygoing teen code ("So what's the sitch?"; "So not!") but had no problem defeating preposterous, cackling villains bent on world domination, like Dr. Drakken and his sexy sidekick Shego, or Señor Senior, Sr., and his apprentice-villain son Junior. As Kim would say, "No big."

Rufus was Ron's long-suffering bucktoothed naked mole rat, which he carried everywhere in a pouch, and Wade was their computer-geek friend and support, usually seen on a portable screen. The kids at school were oblivious to Kim's exploits, but in an unusual twist (for this kind of show) Mom and Dad—Dr. and Dr. Possible—were both in on the secret, as were her unimpressed, pesky young brothers, Jim and Tim.

KINDRED: THE EMBRACED
(*Police/Supernatural Drama*)

FIRST TELECAST: *April 2, 1996*
LAST TELECAST: *May 8, 1996*
BROADCAST HISTORY:

Apr 1996, FOX Tue 8:00–9:30
Apr 1996–May 1996, FOX Wed 9:00–10:00

CAST:

Julian Luna .... Mark Frankel
Det. Frank Kohanek .... C. Thomas Howell
Caitlin Byrne .... Kelly Rutherford
Daedalus .... Jeff Kober
Cash .... Channen Roe
Det. Sonny Toussaint .... Erik King
Sasha .... Brigid Walsh
Lillie Langtry .... Stacy Haiduk
Archon .... Patrick Bauchau
Eddie Fiori .... Brian Thompson
Lt. Kwan .... Yuji Okumoto

Wealthy vampires infested San Francisco in this rather bizarre cross between a cop show and a monster movie. They looked a lot like mobsters, operating out of palatial estates and riding around in long black limousines, with the rather significant difference that they could turn into wolves, and could be killed not by bullets but by shotgun shells filled with phosphorous. Police detective Frank Kohanek stumbled onto their evil empire after falling in love with one of them, a pale beauty named Alexandra, who revealed their secret and was killed for it in the premiere. Unbeknownst to him, before dying she made Julian, the brooding head of the Ventrue clan and "Prince" of S.F. vampires, promise to protect the mortal cop. The dapper Julian struggled to keep peace among the five vampire clans in the city, which mixed blood-sucking with organized crime, and which had members—"kindred"—in all walks of life. Eddie, leader of the warlike Brujah, was scheming to topple Julian. Frank's own black partner, Sonny, was seemingly Eddie's henchman, but he later turned out to be a double agent working for Julian. Lillie, the leader of the artistic Torreadors, ran The Haven, the club where the vampires often hung out. Daedalus headed the bald, violent Nosferatu, which sided with Julian, and Cash led the rebellious, motorcycle-riding Gangrels.

As the story unfolded, reporter Caitlin threatened to expose them all, so Julian bought her paper, the *San Francisco Times*, to silence her. Eddie was killed by Lillie (by beheading) after a failed attempt to destroy Julian. In the series finale Julian and Caitlin, who were dating, took a weekend trip to the Napa Valley, where they were ambushed by renegade Brujah vampires and Julian was mortally wounded. He told Caitlin the whole truth—how he became a vampire, served as an enforcer, and rose to power after renouncing the senseless violence. She saved his "life" by slitting her forearm and dripping some of her mortal blood into his mouth, and he went back to San Francisco to reclaim his leadership—after wiping the knowledge of his true nature from her mind.

Adapted from the book *Vampire: The Masquerade* by Mark Rein-Hagen.

KING COLE'S BIRTHDAY PARTY, see *Birthday Party*

KING FAMILY SHOW, THE (*Musical Variety*)

FIRST TELECAST: *January 23, 1965*
LAST TELECAST: *September 10, 1969*
BROADCAST HISTORY:

Jan 1965–Sep 1965, ABC Sat 7:30–8:30
Sep 1965–Jan 1966, ABC Sat 8:00–8:30
Mar 1969–Sep 1969, ABC Wed 8:30–9:00

CAST:

The King Sisters (Yvonne, Luise, Marilyn, Alyce, Maxine, Donna), *et al.*

ORCHESTRA:

Alvino Rey Orchestra directed by Mitchell Ayres (1965–1966)
Ralph Carmichael (1969)

EXECUTIVE PRODUCER:

Nick Vanoff (1965–1966)

Yvonne King Burch and Luise King Rey (1969)

THEME:

"The Sound of Music," by Richard Rodgers and Oscar Hammerstein II

Thirty-seven—count 'em—37 King family members all singing on one stage at one time! Or was it 36? Or 41? Whatever it was, there was a lot of kin in this wholesome family musical series, which was a spin-off from a special appearance the Kings had made on *The Hollywood Palace* in August 1964. That appearance had drawn a reported 53,000 letters and a King Family series was assured.

At the center of things were the six King Sisters, a singing group popular since the early 1940s, when they had been part of Alvino Rey's orchestra. (Alvino was in fact married to one of them, Luise.) Sisters, brothers, husbands, nephews, cousins, and masses of kids were featured on this series (each of the King Sisters had from two to five offspring). Ages ranged from seven months to 79 years. The oldster was William King Driggs, the father, an old-time vaudevillian who had begun the family's musical tradition in 1921. Music ranged from semi-classical to semi-rock, interspersed with lots of gentle family humor. Alvino Rey had a regular spot with his talking guitar. A "Family Circle" segment, exploring in verse and song the meaning of familial happiness, was a regular feature. Each telecast ended with the family *en masse* singing "Love at Home."

All this built up an intensely loyal following. One viewing family, knowing what would move a sponsor's cold heart, wrote in that "the King Family program was beautiful, talented, and completely entertaining. We are buying Clairol and Wisk tomorrow." Apparently not enough Clairol and Wisk was sold, however, for the show was canceled after only a year.

A brief revival in 1969 spotlighted a more contemporary sub-group, the King Cousins, along with the sisters, Alvino, and the rest of the family.

KING OF DIAMONDS (*Crime Drama*)

BROADCAST HISTORY:

Syndicated only

30 minutes

Produced: *1961–1962* (39 episodes)

Released: *September 1961*

CAST:

John King.................... Broderick Crawford

Al Casey.......................... Ray Hamilton

Broderick Crawford attempted to repeat his recent success on *Highway Patrol* with this bare-knuckles private-eye series, without much luck. He played John King, "Chief of Security for the diamond industry," traveling around the world solving crimes and taking on other dangerous assignments relating to the diamond trade. Casey was his young sidekick. Thieves, smugglers, and fences abounded, and King met them with a great deal of violence, even beating up some of the shadier women (while making passes at the others). His recurring enemy was something called, incredibly enough, the Illegal Diamond Buyers' Syndicate.

KING OF QUEENS, THE (*Situation Comedy*)

FIRST TELECAST: *September 21, 1998*

LAST TELECAST:

BROADCAST HISTORY:

Sep 1998–Jul 1999, CBS Mon 8:30–9:00

Jul 1999–Jul 2000, CBS Mon 8:00–8:30

May 2000–Sep 2000, CBS Mon 8:30–9:00

Oct 2000–Jun 2003, CBS Mon 8:00–8:30

Jun 2003– , CBS Mon 9:30–10:00

CAST:

Doug Heffernan .... Kevin James

Carrie Heffernan .... Leah Remini

Arthur Spooner .... Jerry Stiller

Deacon Palmer.................... Victor Williams

Spence Olchin .... Patton Oswalt

Richie Iannucci .... Larry Romano

Sara Spooner (1998) .... Lisa Rieffel

Kelly Palmer (1999–2001) .... Merrin Dungey

**Danny Heffernan (1999–)*........ Gary Valentine

**Stephanie Heffernan (2000–2001)* ...... Ricki Lake

**Kirby Palmer (2000–2002)* .... Marshaun Daniel

**Mr. Pruzan (2000–)*.................. Alex Skuby

Holly Shumpert (2001–)........ Nicole Sullivan

*Occasional

In this working-class comedy beefy Doug drove a truck for the IPS delivery service in his Queens, New York, neighborhood, and Carrie, his sexy wife, worked for a fancy Manhattan law firm. Deacon, Spence, and Richie were Doug's buddies, with whom he liked to hang out in the basement he had remodeled to look like a sports bar. All was well until Carrie's recently widowed dad Arthur, who had no desire to live in a retirement home, moved into the basement after accidentally burning down his house, displaçing da guys to da garage. As if that wasn't bad enough, Doug also had to put up with Carrie's sexy younger sister, Sara, an aspiring actress who moved in with them to save money. She didn't last long, disappearing, without explanation, by the end of October. Doug tried to befriend his outspoken father-in-law, but the old man's sarcasm and total lack of tact made him hard to take. Seen occasionally were Doug's incompetent cousin Danny (played by Kevin James' real-life brother) and Mr. Pruzan, Carrie's boss at the law firm.

Early in the 2000–2001 season Doug's kid sister, Stephanie, a high school teacher, returned to Queens to recover from a failed romance and showed up occasionally to complain. In February Doug found out that Deacon and his wife, Kelly, were having marital problems—a year later she moved out with their two boys, Kirby and Major, and by the start of the 2002–2003 season they were divorced. In the fall of 2001 Arthur's last friend from the senior center moved away and he spent his days sleeping and his nights driving Doug and Carrie crazy. In an effort to keep his nighttime energy level down Doug hired Spence's dog walker, Holly, to take Arthur on walks three times a week. Unsuspecting Arthur was under the impression that she was a student who wanted to hear about his experiences during World War II.

KING OF THE HILL (*Cartoon*)

FIRST TELECAST: *January 12, 1996*

LAST TELECAST:

BROADCAST HISTORY:

Jan 1997–Jul 1998, FOX Sun 8:30–9:00

Jul 1998–Sep 1998, FOX Tue 8:00–9:00

Sep 1998–Oct 1998, FOX Tue 8:00–8:30

Oct 1998–Nov 1998, FOX Tue 8:00–9:00

Nov 1998–Jun 1999, FOX Tue 8:00–8:30

Jun 1999–Jul 2002, FOX Sun 7:30–8:00
Jul 2000–Sep 2000, FOX Wed 8:00–8:30
Feb 2002–Apr 2002, FOX Thu 9:00–9:30
Jul 2002–Jan 2003, FOX Sun 8:30–9:00
Nov 2002– , FOX Sun 7:30–8:00
Apr 2003–May 2003, FOX Sun 7:00–7:30
Jun 2003, FOX Sun 8:30–9:00

VOICES:
Hank Hill.............................. Mike Judge
Peggy Hill.......................... Kathy Najimy
Bobby Hill (age 12) .... Pamela Segall Adlon
Luanne Platter .... Brittany Murphy
Dale Gribble .... Johnny Hardwick
Nancy Gribble .... Ashley Gardner
Joseph Gribble .... Brittany Murphy
Boomhauer .... Mike Judge
Bill Dauterive .... Stephen Root
Buckley (1997–1998) .... David Herman
Eustis.............................. David Herman
Kahn Souphanousinphone .... Toby Huss
Minh Souphanousinphone .... Lauren Tom
Kahn, Jr. (Connie).................... Lauren Tom
Cotton Hill .... Toby Huss
Buck Strickland .... Stephen Root

In this animated world of rednecks and "good old boys," Hank Hill was a conservative 40-year-old family man living in suburban Arlen, Texas. He made his living selling propane gas and accessories, hated liberals and politicians, and chugged beer with his buddies. The Hill household included his wife Peggy, a substitute Spanish teacher who didn't take guff from anyone; their chubby 12-year-old son Bobby, a student at Tom Landry Middle School; and Hank's niece Luanne, a refugee from a trailer park who was attending beauty school. Hank hoped Bobby would be a jock, as he had been, but the boy had neither the talent nor the interest to succeed. In one episode, clumsy, insecure Bobby became a model for husky boys' clothing, much to his father's embarrassment. Living next door were the Gribbles—Dale, one of Hank's buddies, who was preoccupied with conspiracy theories, and Nancy, his philandering wife. Hank's other buddies were Bill, a divorced slob; and Boomhauer, a ladies' man whose drawl was so thick he was almost unintelligible. Bobby became very friendly with Connie, a classmate and the daughter of a Laotian couple who moved into the neighborhood.

At the end of the 1997–1998 season Strickland Propane closed its Arlen office and Hank went to work at Mega Lo Mart, the big company that forced his former employer out of business. Even worse, his new boss, the free-spirited Buckley, was Luanne's boyfriend. Hank staged a protest against the big impersonal chain and was caught in an accidental explosion at the store in the season-ending cliff-hanger. Along with Luanne and Chuck Mangione, who were in the store with him, Hank survived, but Buckley didn't make it. With Mega Lo Mart out of business, Hank went back to work for Strickland, and Luanne, who lost her hair and eyebrows in the explosion, became sullen because she refused to admit how much she missed Buckley. That fall Bobby and Connie were in high school. The following May Buckley's angel appeared to Luanne and motivated her to quit beauty school and enroll at Arlen Community College.

In the fall of 1999 Peggy was skydiving, but her parachute failed to open. She survived because she landed flat in a field of mud but was in a body cast until she recovered from compression fractures in her back. A year later she became a substitute teacher at Arlen High School. Hank's father, Cotton, had a baby boy with his young wife DeeDee and named the boy Good Hank, which ticked off Hank. Early in 2002 Connie and Bobby, who had been dating, broke up. They remained friends, but he had hopes that they would eventually get back together.

Created by Mike Judge, the driving force behind the much raunchier *Beavis & Butt-head*, and Greg Daniels, a former writer for *The Simpsons*.

KING'S CROSSING (*Drama*)

FIRST TELECAST: *January 16, 1982*
LAST TELECAST: *February 27, 1982*
BROADCAST HISTORY:
Jan 1982–Feb 1982, ABC Sat 8:00–9:00

CAST:
Paul Hollister .... Bradford Dillman
Nan Hollister .... Mary Frann
Lauren Hollister.................. Linda Hamilton
Carey Hollister..................... Marilyn Jones
Billy McCall .... Daniel Zippi
Jillian .... Doran Clark
Louisa Beauchamp.............. Beatrice Straight
Willa Bristol .... Dorothy Meyer

Unlike most prime-time soap operas, *King's Crossing* focused on the travails of the young, principally teenagers Lauren and Carey Hollister. They were the daughters of Paul and Nan Hollister, a couple who had moved their family to the small town of King's Crossing, California, in an effort to make a fresh start. Paul was an alcoholic teacher and writer trying to set his life straight, and Nan his supportive wife. Problems came from 19-year-old Lauren, who was ambitious and impetuous, and 17-year-old Carey, wide-eyed and having her first affair, with fun-loving stableboy Billy McCall.

Entwined with their lives were wealthy Aunt Louisa, who resented her niece's return to King's Crossing to claim the family house; Louisa's housekeeper Willa; and the Hollister girls' beautiful but disturbed young cousin Jillian, crippled in body and mind but slowly making her way back to a normal life, despite the callousness of the local teens toward her.

KING'S CROSSROADS, see *Movies—Prior to 1961*

KINGS ROW (*Drama*)

FIRST TELECAST: *September 13, 1955*
LAST TELECAST: *January 17, 1956*
BROADCAST HISTORY:
Sep 1955–Jan 1956, ABC Tue 7:30–8:30

CAST:
Dr. Parris Mitchell....................... Jack Kelly
Randy Monaghan .... Nan Leslie
Drake McHugh .... Robert Horton
Dr. Tower .... Victor Jory
Grandma .... Lillian Bronson
Dr. Gordon .... Robert Burton

Romantic drama (soap opera, if you prefer) about young Dr. Parris Mitchell, who returned to his hometown at the turn of the century to set up a psychiatric practice. There he encountered considerable resistance to his new methods, due to the superstitious citizenry and the traditionbound medical practices of the day. Based on the Henry Bellamann novel and 1942 movie classic.

Kings Row was seen approximately every third week, being one of three rotating elements of *Warner Bros. Presents.*

KINGSTON: CONFIDENTIAL (*Newspaper Drama*)
FIRST TELECAST: *March 23, 1977*
LAST TELECAST: *August 10, 1977*
BROADCAST HISTORY:
Mar 1977–Aug 1977, NBC Wed 10:00–11:00
CAST:
R. B. Kingston .... Raymond Burr
Tony Marino .... Art Hindle
Beth Kelly .... Pamela Hensley
Jessica Frazier .... Nancy Olson

San Francisco was the home base of the Frazier Group, a communications conglomerate that owned and operated 26 newspapers and 9 radio and TV stations around the country. Jessica Frazier was the chief operating officer and R. B. Kingston was one of her top executives, with a long history as one of the finest investigative reporters in the country. Despite his high status, Kingston was more than willing to leave the office and do his own digging to help unearth a particularly difficult or juicy story. His two young assistants, Tony and Beth, often went undercover to help track down useful information.

KIRBY STONE QUINTET, THE, see *Strictly for Laughs*

KIRK (*Situation Comedy*)
FIRST TELECAST: *August 23, 1995*
LAST TELECAST: *November 10, 1996*
BROADCAST HISTORY:
Aug 1995, WB Wed 8:30–9:00
Sep 1995–Oct 1995, WB Sun 8:00–8:30
Oct 1995–Dec 1995, WB Sun 7:30–8:00
Dec 1995–Jul 1996, WB Sun 8:30–9:00
Aug 1996–Nov 1996, WB Sun 7:00–7:30
CAST:
Kirk Hartman .... Kirk Cameron
Phoebe Hartman (age 13) .... Taylor Fry
Corey Hartman (15) .... Will Estes
Russell Hartman (7) .... Courtland Mead
Elizabeth Waters .... Chelsea Noble
Eddie Balducci .... Louis Vanaria
Sally Franklin .... Debra Mooney

Kirk was a graphic illustrator just returned to New York City after graduating from college to take a job with a company that painted billboards, and to chase girls, and have a good time. But when his 75-year-old Aunt Zelda, who had raised the Hartman kids since the death of their parents five years earlier, decided to move to Florida and get married, she dropped his three younger siblings at his Greenwich Village apartment and took off. Corey, the oldest and dumbest, was a free spirit who wanted more independence than his now-surrogate father was willing to give him; Phoebe, the intellectual, was the best student; and Russell was the young troublemaker. Their presence put a serious crimp in Kirk's social life. His loopy college buddy Eddie, who almost always entered their first floor apartment by climbing in through the living room window, wanted to party and have fun, but Kirk tried to be a responsible "father." He was smitten with sexy Elizabeth, an intern at St. Brennan's Hospital who lived across the hall, and by midseason had convinced her to go out with him. Sally, their cynical landlady, offered occasional advice and sometimes helped Kirk out with the kids.

In the fall 1996 premiere Kirk went with Elizabeth to a medical conference in Paris and, under the influence of the "City of Love," proposed to her. They were married before they returned to New York. Elizabeth moved in with them and Phoebe got accepted to exclusive Blakemore Academy, where Elizabeth had gone, but tuition was $8,000 a year and Kirk needed more money to pay for it. He got a job with Shotz Comics, where he revived the classic *Mercury Man* comic that had originally been drawn by his boss, Mr. Shotz.

The series was abruptly canceled two months into its second season, before Elizabeth's adjustment to instant "motherhood" and Kirk's new job had much time to develop. Elizabeth was played by Kirk Cameron's real-life wife, Chelsea Noble.

KIT CARSON, see *Adventures of Kit Carson, The*

KLEENEX SUMMER THEATRE (*Dramatic Anthology*)
FIRST TELECAST: *July 5, 1955*
LAST TELECAST: *August 16, 1955*
BROADCAST HISTORY:
Jul 1955–Aug 1955, NBC Tue 9:00–9:30

Kleenex Summer Theatre alternated with *Clorets Summer Theatre* as a 1955 summer replacement series for *Fireside Theater.* The dramas shown were all reruns of episodes from *Four Star Playhouse.*

KLONDIKE (*Adventure*)
FIRST TELECAST: *October 10, 1960*
LAST TELECAST: *February 6, 1961*
BROADCAST HISTORY:
Oct 1960–Feb 1961, NBC Mon 9:00–9:30
CAST:
Mike Halliday .... Ralph Taeger
Jeff Durain .... James Coburn
Kathy O'Hara .... Mari Blanchard
Goldie .... Joi Lansing

Skagway, Alaska, at the turn of the century, was the setting of this action-adventure series. In Alaska in search of gold and excitement during the famous gold rush of 1897–1899, rugged Mike Halliday spent much of his time trying to outwit Jeff Durain, a gambler and scoundrel whose efforts to make money often put him on the wrong side of the law. Durain owned and ran a hotel in Skagway that provided miners with a place to lose their earnings in games of chance that were not always on the up-and-up. The town's honest hotel was run by Kathy O'Hara, who often worked with Mike to foil Durain's illegal schemes. Mike was not quite ready to settle down with a good woman and raise a family and was involved with a number of ladies, including Durain's girlfriend and accomplice in crime, the beautiful but greedy Goldie.

KNIGHT & DAYE (*Situation Comedy*)
FIRST TELECAST: *July 8, 1989*
LAST TELECAST: *August 14, 1989*
BROADCAST HISTORY:
Jul 1989, NBC Sat 9:30–10:00

Jul 1989–Aug 1989, NBC Wed 9:30–10:00
Aug 1989, NBC Mon 9:30–10:00

CAST:

Hank Knight .... Jack Warden
Everett Daye .... Mason Adams
Gloria Daye .... Hope Lange
Ellie Escobar .... Lela Ivey
Cito Escobar .... Joe Lala
Chris Escobar .... Emily Schulman
Amy Escobar .... Shiri Appleby
Dougie Escobar .... Glenn Walker Harris, Jr.
Laurie Escobar .... Brittany Thornton
Janet Glickman .... Julia Campbell

Comedy about two old-timers and the woman they had both wooed many years ago—sort of a rusty love triangle. Everett had won fair Gloria, causing a permanent estrangement with his friend Hank, but now after forty years the two squabbling broadcasters had reluctantly agreed to co-host a new radio show. Quips and put-downs flew, but despite the top-drawer talent involved, this series lasted less than a month.

Julia was the worried station manager, Ellie was Everett's daughter, Cito, his son-in-law, and the other Escobars, his grandchildren. Set in San Diego.

KNIGHT RIDER (*Adventure*)

FIRST TELECAST: *September 26, 1982*
LAST TELECAST: *August 8, 1986*
BROADCAST HISTORY:

Sep 1982, NBC Sun 8:00–10:00
Oct 1982–Aug 1983, NBC Fri 9:00–10:00
Aug 1983–Mar 1985, NBC Sun 8:00–9:00
Mar 1985–Apr 1985, NBC Fri 8:00–9:00
Apr 1985–Aug 1985, NBC Sun 8:00–9:00
Aug 1985–Dec 1985, NBC Fri 8:00–9:00
Jan 1986–Apr 1986, NBC Fri 9:00–10:00
May 1986–Aug 1986, NBC Fri 8:00–9:00

CAST:

Michael Knight .... David Hasselhoff
Devon Miles .... Edward Mulhare
Bonnie Barstow (1982–1983, 1984–1986)
.... Patricia McPherson
April Curtis (1983–1984) .... Rebecca Holden
Voice of KITT .... William Daniels
Reginald Cornelius III "RC3" (1985–1986)
.... Peter Parros

Brandon Tartikoff, youthful head of programming at NBC, once gave *California* magazine this version of the creation of *Knight Rider*: It seems he and one of his assistants were discussing the problems of casting handsome leading men in series, because many of them can't act. Why not have a series, they mused, called "The Man of Six Words," which would begin with the guy getting out of a woman's bed and saying "Thank you." Then he would chase down some villains and say "Freeze!" Finally the grateful almost-victims would thank him, and he would murmur, "You're welcome." End of show. In between, the car could do the talking.

The series that made it to the air as *Knight Rider* was scarcely less preposterous than that, but it was played with such a twinkle in the eye that viewers—especially kids—made it one of the hits of the 1982 season. The opening episode told the story of how a dying millionaire named Wilton Knight rescued a young undercover cop who had been shot in the face. After plastic surgery, officer Michael Young had a new face, a new identity (Michael Knight), and a new mission in life: to fight for law and justice in Knight's incredible supercar, the Knight Industries Two Thousand—or KITT, for short. It was love at first sight between Michael and KITT. The car, a sleek, black, customized Pontiac Trans-Am, was impervious to attack, could cruise at 300 mph, could leap up to 50 feet through the air, and was loaded with such armaments as flamethrowers, smoke bombs, and infrared sensing devices. Best of all, it could talk, and in fact had a personality all its own; peevish, a bit haughty, but totally protective of Michael. He could summon the car when in trouble, and it would come crashing through walls to get him.

Its deceased inventor had left behind a huge fortune to finance the crime-fighting, and a trusted associate, the suave Devon, to look after things. Based at a palatial estate, called somewhat grandly the Foundation for Law and Government, Michael (and often Devon) went forth each week, trailed by a large maintenance van that served as a sort of mobile command post. Rounding out the crew was a beautiful mechanic, variously Bonnie or April, and "RC3," a streetwise black mechanic who joined the team in the fall of 1985. (Behind the scenes, the same Hollywood customizers who built Batman's Batmobile and the Green Hornet's Black Beauty worked on KITT.)

Though the gimmick in the series was the car, much of the show's appeal was due to actor David Hasselhoff, a tall, handsome former soap-opera heartthrob (on *The Young and The Restless*) who joked and kidded with his computerized companion. While he had more to say than "The Man of Six Words," his tight jeans, wavy hair, and laid-back style (his favorite phrase was "You got it") made women melt.

Team Knight Rider, a sequel to this series, aired during the 1997–1998 season.

KNIGHTS AND WARRIORS (*Sports/Audience Participation*)

BROADCAST HISTORY:

Syndicated only
60 minutes
Produced: *1992–1993* (24 episodes)
Released: *September 1992*

HOSTS:

Joe Fowler
Lisa Canning

EVILDOERS:

Plague
Steel Maiden
Pyro
Lady Battleaxe
Knightmare
Princess Malice
Chaos
Venom

In this highly stylized but unsuccessful copy of *American Gladiators* two teams (each with one man and one woman) competed as modern-day knights against the show's resident combatants. The contestants were all amateur athletes who entered a medieval arena ("the Warrior Dome") to vie for the honor of knighthood against a team of "evildoers" in a series of tournaments. Among the events were Catapult, Battle Swords, Sorcerer's Wheel, The Volcano, Roller Joust, Tug-O-Warriors, The Pit, and Target Onslaught.

Joe Fowler was the play-by-play announcer, Lisa Canning did commentary and interviews with the participants, and the Lord of Rules and Discipline served as both announcer and judge. There were eight resident muscular "evildoers" against whom the contestants competed—four men (Plague, Pyro, Knightmare, and Chaos) and four women (Steel Maiden, Lady Battleaxe, Princess Malice, and Venom).

KNIGHTWATCH (*Drama*)

FIRST TELECAST: *November 10, 1988*

LAST TELECAST: *January 19, 1989*

BROADCAST HISTORY:

Nov 1988–Jan 1989, ABC Thu 8:00–9:00

CAST:

Tony Maldonado .... Benjamin Bratt
Calvin Garvey .... Don Franklin
Leslie Chambers .... Paris Vaughan
Jason "Condo" Snyder .... Joshua Cadman
Casey Mitchell .... Ava Haddad
Mark "Burn" Johnson .... Calvin Levels
Jake .... Samantha Mathis
Barbara ("Babs") .... Harley Kozak

Every crime-related headline seems to find its way into a television series, and New York's much-publicized Guardian Angels were no exception. In this thinly disguised dramatization of the real-life anti-crime patrols made up of inner-city youths, ex-gang member Tony Maldonado headed a group of volunteers called the "Knights of the City." Operating out of a donated church basement, where they could train in the martial arts (they carried no weapons), the Knights set out in teams of two and easily found enough murders, rapes, and robberies to keep them busy. Unfortunately, they also had to deal with police harassment, a sensation-seeking press, and renegades within their own ranks (one Knight threw a thug from a rooftop). At least they could find time for a little romantic involvement on the side: Calvin with Leslie, Mark with Jake, Tony with Babs.

KNOTS LANDING (*Drama*)

FIRST TELECAST: *December 20, 1979*

LAST TELECAST: *May 13, 1993*

BROADCAST HISTORY:

Dec 1979–Mar 1980, CBS Thu 10:00–11:00
Jun 1980–Mar 1981, CBS Thu 10:00–11:00
Jun 1981–Oct 1981, CBS Thu 10:00–11:00
Nov 1981–Mar 1982, CBS Thu 900–10:00
Mar 1982–Mar 1983, CBS Thu 10:00–11:00
Jun 1983–Jun 1986, CBS Thu 10:00–11:00
Sep 1986–Nov 1986, CBS Thu 9:00–10:00
Nov 1986–Mar 1993, CBS Thu 10:00–11:00 (OS)
May 1993, CBS Thu 9:00–11:00

CAST:

Gary Ewing .... Ted Shackelford
Valene Ewing Gibson Waleska (1979–1992)
.... Joan Van Ark
Sid Fairgate (1979–1981) .... Don Murray
Karen Fairgate MacKenzie .... Michele Lee
Richard Avery (1979–1983) .... John Pleshette
Laura Avery Sumner (1979–1987)
.... Constance McCashin
Kenny Ward (1979–1983) .... James Houghton
Ginger Ward (1979–1983) .... Kim Lankford
Diana Fairgate (1979–84, 1993) .... Claudia Lonow
Michael Fairgate (1979–1991) .... Pat Petersen
Eric Fairgate (1979–1987, 1989–1990) ... Steve Shaw
Jason Avery (1979–1980) .... Justin Dana
Jason Avery (1980–1982) .... Danny Gellis
Jason Avery (1983–1985) .... Danny Ponce
Jason Avery (1986–1987) ...... Matthew Newmark
Abby Cunningham Ewing Sumner (1980–1989)
.... Donna Mills
Brian Cunningham (1980–1985) ..... Bobby Jacoby
Brian Cunningham (1986–1989)
.... Brian Austin Green
Olivia Cunningham Dyer (1980–1990)
.... Tonya Crowe
Judy Trent (1980–1981) .... Jane Elliot
Earl Trent (1980–1981) .... Paul Rudd
Sylvie (1980–1981) .... Louise Vallance
Linda Striker (1980–1981) .... Denise Galik
Roy Lance (1980–1982) .... Steven Hirsch
Lilimae Clements (1981–1987) .... Julie Harris
Scooter Warren (1981–1982) .... Allan Miller
Joe Cooper (1982–1983) .... Stephen Macht
Amy (1981–1983) .... Jill Cohen
M. (Mack) Patrick MacKenzie (1982–1993)
.... Kevin Dobson
Wayne Harkness (1982) .... Harry Northup
Ciji Dunne (1982–1983) .... Lisa Hartman
Jeff Munson (1982–1983) .... Jon Cypher
Chip Roberts (1982–1982) .... Michael Sabatino
Janet Baines (1983) .... Joanna Pettet
Mitchell Casey (1983) .... Edward Bell
Ben Gibson (1983–1987) .... Douglas Sheehan
Nick Morrison (1983–1984) .... Steve Kahan
Jim Westmont (1983) .... Joseph Hacker
Gregory Sumner (1983–1993) ..... William Devane
Cathy Geary Rush (1983–1986) ...... Lisa Hartman
Mary-Frances Sumner (1983–1984)
.... Danielle Brisebois
Mary-Frances Sumner (1990) .... Stacy Galina
Jane Sumner (1983–1984) .... Millie Perkins
Ray Geary (1984) .... Bruce Fairbairn
Mark St. Claire (1984) .... Joseph Chapman
Joshua Rush (1984–1985) .... Alec Baldwin
Carol (1984) .... Gigi Vorgan
P.K. Kelly (1984–1985) .... Wendel Meldrum
Tom Jezik (1984–1985) .... Peter Fox
Rev. Kathrun (1984–1985) .... Sandy Kenyon
Mary Kathrun (1984) .... Whitney Kershaw
Paul Galveston (1984–1985) .... Howard Duff
Ruth Galveston (1985) .... Ava Gardner
John Coblentz (1985) .... Madison Mason
Harry Fisher (1985) .... Joe Regalbuto
Sheila Fisher (1985) .... Robin Ginsburg
Frank Elliot (1985) .... Jonathan Goldsmith
Peter Hollister (1985–1987) .... Hunt Block
Jill Bennett (1985–1989) .... Teri Austin
Linda Martin (1985–1986) .... Leslie Hope
Sylvia Lean (1986) .... Ruth Roman
Det. Behar (1986) .... Allen Williams
Paige Matheson (1986–1993) .. Nicollette Sheridan
Jean Hackney (1986–1987) .... Wendy Fulton
Tina (1986–1988) .... Tina Lifford
Peggy (1986–1993) .... Victoria Ann-Lewis
Marsha (1986–1988) .... Marcia Solomon
Anne W. Matheson (1987, 1990–1993)
.... Michelle Phillips
Al Baker (1987) .... Red Buttons
Bobby Gibson (1987–1993) .... Joseph Cousins
Bobby Gibson (1987–1990) ...... Christian Cousins

Betsy Gibson (1987–1990)
.... Kathryn & Tiffany Lubran
Betsy Gibson (1990–1993) .... Emily Ann Lloyd
Carlos (1987–1993) .... Carlos Cantu
Jody Campbell (1987–1988) .... Kristy Swanson
Charles Scott (1987–1988) .... Michael York
Barbara (1987–1988, 1990) .... Ronne Troup
Ana (1987–1989) .... Movita Castenada
Johnny Rourke (1988–1989) .... Peter Reckell
Patricia Williams (1988–1990) .... Lynne Moody
Frank Williams (1988–1992) .... Larry Riley
Julie Williams (1988–1991) ..... Kent Masters-King
Harold Dyer (1988–1990) .... Paul Carafotes
Manny Vasquez (1988) .... John Aprea
The Dealer (1988) .... Ray Wise
Ted Melcher (1988–1989) .... Robert Desiderio
Mrs. Straub (1988–1989) .... Anne Faulkner
Paula Vertosick (1989–1990) .... Melinda Culea
Virginia Bullock (1989–1990) .... Betsy Palmer
Meg (1989)
.... Morgan Corey White & Whitney Harper White
Meg (1989–1990) .... Kara & Kimberly Albright
Meg (1991–1993) .... Rhianna Janette
Bob Phillips (1989–1991) .... Zane Lasky
Mort Tubor (1989–1993) .... Mark Haining
Sharon (1989) .... Jasmine Gagnier
Harvey (1989–1990) .... Robert M. Koch
Danny Waleska (1989–1990) .... Sam Behrens
Amanda Michaels (1989–1990) ...... Penny Peyser
Linda Fairgate (1989–1991) ...... Lar Park-Lincoln
Tom Ryan (1989–1990, 1993) .... Joseph Gian
Floor Manager (1989–1990) .... Sue Bugden
Dianne Kirkwood (1990) .... Robin Strasser
Jeff Cameron (1990) .... Chris Lemmon
Dr. Carrol (1990) .... France Nuyen
Claudia Whittaker (1990–1993) .... Kathleen Noone
Kate Whittaker (1990–1993) .... Stacy Galina
Nick Schillace/Dimitri Pappas (1990–1993)
.... Lorenzo Caccialanza
Jason Lochner (1990–1991)
.... Thomas Wilson Brown
Dick Lochner (1990–1991) .... Guy Boyd
Charlotte Anderson (1990–1991) .... Tracy Reed
Steve Brewer (1991) .... Lance Guest
Victoria Broyard (1991–1992) .... Marcia Cross
Pierce Lawton (1991–1992) ...... Bruce Greenwood
Benny Appleman (1991) .... Stuart Pankin
Brian Johnston (1991) .... Philip Brown
Joseph Barringer (1991–1992) .... Mark Soper
Debbie Porter (1991) .... Halle Berry
Alex Barth (1992) .... Boyd Kestner
Vanessa Hunt (1992–1993) ..... Felicity Waterman
Mary Robeson (1992–1993) ...... Maree Cheatham
Toni Fields (1992–1993) .... Tara Marchant
Dr. Stern (1992–1993) .... Karen Ludwig
Joe Robeson (1992–1993) .... Norman Merrill
Cliff Templeton (1992–1993) ... William Allen Young
Det. Pete Reynolds (1992–1993) .... Shelly Kurtz
Deputy Mayor Lofton (1992–1993) .... Gregg Daniel

Hoping to ride the crest of its success with *Dallas*, CBS spun off this series featuring the black sheep of the Ewing family, Gary. Gary was a weak-willed reformed alcoholic who had deserted his wife, Val, and then remarried her and moved to Southern California to escape the formidable pressures of life with the Ewings in Dallas. All the principals in this series lived on the same cul-de-sac in the quiet little community of Knots Landing. In addition to being neighbors, their lives intertwined in other ways. Gary worked for Sid Fairgate, owner of Knots Landing Motors, the local classic car dealership. Sid and his wife Karen had three teenaged children. The other two couples on the cul-de-sac were young recording executive Kenny Ward and his attractive wife, Ginger, and Richard and Laura Avery. Richard was an obnoxious, aggressive unprincipled attorney who was always lusting after other women and resented Laura's success selling real estate. One of her customers, who arrived in the fall of 1980, was Sid Fairgate's recently divorced sister, Abby Cunningham. She moved onto the cul-de-sac with her two kids and immediately began undermining the relationships of her married neighbors, spreading gossip about affairs, both real and imagined, and setting her own sights on Richard Avery. Gary, a member of Alcoholics Anonymous, sponsored a new member, Earl Trent, and ended up having an affair with Judy, Earl's passionate wife.

In the fall of 1981 Sid Fairgate was paralyzed and later died as the result of an auto accident, leaving his wife Karen to run Knots Landing Motors with Abby Cunningham and Gary Ewing. Abby started to set her sights on Gary, while his wife Val wrote a novel, *Capricorn Crude,* that was a thinly disguised chronicle of the manipulations of his family in the oil business. Eventually Gary divorced Val, married Abby, and inherited part of Jock Ewing's fortune. Val became quite a celebrity with her book and began dating reporter Ben Gibson.

Another plot involved Chip Roberts, who worked for Val's press agent and who was simultaneously having affairs with Diana Fairgate and Ciji Dunne, a pretty singer. When Ciji got pregnant, Chip killed her, but because of circumstantial evidence Gary Ewing was indicted for the crime. Diana and Chip skipped town together; later she returned alone and moved in with Abby. Chip was subsequently caught and convicted of Ciji's murder, escaped from prison, and died in a freak accident at Gary Ewing's ranch where he was hiding out with Diana.

Meanwhile, Richard Avery's marriage and career were falling apart. His wife Laura wanted to leave him but held off due to her pregnancy and his nervous breakdown. Richard's attempt to open a restaurant, "Daniel's," financed by Gary and Abby, was unsuccessful and his philandering with Abby finally caused Laura to divorce him. Abby, on the other hand, continued to build her power base. She had part of Knots Landing Motors, was married into Gary Ewing Enterprises (although living on Gary's ranch was something she could barely tolerate), was heavily into the Lotus Point real estate development, and was having another affair—this one with powerful, underworld-connected State Senator Gregory Sumner. Sumner was an old friend of Attorney Mack MacKenzie (Karen Fairgate's new husband); not anticipating honesty from a *Knots Landing* regular, he offered Mack a job as crime commissioner. When he realized that his friend could be a serious roadblock to his own schemes, Sumner sought to discredit Mack.

The 1984–1985 season brought problems for three of *Knots Landing*'s leading women. Karen was shot with a bullet meant for Gary, and was paralyzed for a period; Abby was taken hostage by St. Claire, who was eventually killed by Sumner; and Val gave birth to twins (by her ex, Gary). The babies were stolen from the hospital and sold in a black market scheme that took an entire season to unravel. Sen. Sumner continued his political machinations, pressuring Mack to drop his investigation of unscrupulous tycoon Paul Galveston (Sumner's father) and trying to force Gary out of the Empire Valley development project. The Senator also made a play for Laura, and they were married.

Handsome Joshua Rush (son of Lilimae, half brother of Val) entered the scene as a preacher turned successful local TV personality, wooing Cathy and proposing to her on the air. However, when she got more fan mail than he did he had a mental breakdown and then committed suicide (or was it murder?). That's showbiz. Other main stories in 1985–1986 involved young Olivia's bout with drugs; Val's rocky marriage to Ben; Cathy's flirtation with Ben; and more dirty doings at the Empire Valley project. Abby's latest conquest was Peter, an up-and-coming politico who claimed to be Sen. Sumner's brother.

Politics was a major focus in 1986–1987, as Gary ran against Peter for the Senate and lost both the campaign and his wife Abby to his opponent. Karen was kidnapped by Phil, who wanted to get even with her crimebusting husband Mack; and sexy young Paige, Mack and Anne's illegitimate daughter, caused problems for all. The young generation, in fact, was being seen more often on *Knots Landing*. Paige had affairs with Michael (Karen's son) and Peter, and there was a continuing story about Olivia's drug problem. Peter also tried to seduce Olivia, before he met a violent end at the close of the season.

The investigation of Peter's murder dominated the fall of 1987, with Abby confessing to cover for her daughter Olivia. (Actually, Paige did it.) Abby had by this time divorced Gary, receiving $2 million in the settlement, and had rekindled a romance with a long-ago lover named Charles Scott. Gary took up with unstable Jill, though viewers knew that Val would always be his true love. In the end-of-season cliffhanger, jealous Jill attempted to kill her pesky rival and make it look like suicide by forcing Val to swallow an overdose of sleeping pills. The other major story of the spring had Gary, Abby, and Karen involved in the Lotus Point luxury resort development with shady Manny Vasquez, who turned out to be an international drug lord planning to use the marina for his shipments; Vasquez almost had the entire cast killed for interfering in his operations. The following fall Vasquez was killed by nephew Harold in a kidnapping shoot-out in Mexico.

Older cast members were gradually phased out. Ben disappeared in South America in early 1987, and Laura died of a brain tumor. She was mourned in unusual "improvised" episodes. Her home on the cul-de-sac was then occupied by black couple Patricia and Frank Williams and their young daughter Julie—all hiding out in the federal Witness Protection Program! Youngsters Michael, Johnny, Paige, and Olivia played increasingly prominent roles.

By 1988 none of the original four couples who lived on the cul-de-sac when *Knots Landing* premiered were still together; only three of the eight spouses even remained with the show (Gary, Val, and Karen, all in new relationships). This willingness of *Knots Landing* to evolve, combined with first-rate writing and an emphasis on characters as real, relatable people, contributed to a growing perception in the late 1980s that this serial had become the best of the nighttime soaps.

As the 1988–1989 season began, Val survived but Jill continued to plot against her. When Jill was finally exposed, and all turned against her, she took her revenge in a most unlikely manner: she bound and gagged herself, hopped into Gary's trunk and expired there, so that he would be accused of her murder! Other main stories of 1988–1989 included Abby's plot to swindle her partners out of Lotus Point and illegally drill for oil, using the phony Japanese "Murakame Corporation" as a front; several murders resulting from the cover-up; mogul Greg's relationship with the much younger Paige; his marriage of convenience to Abby as he vainly tried to restart his political career with the help of PR man Ted; and a computer theft story involving younger cast members Ellen, Michael, and Johnny. As the season ended, Abby narrowly avoided exposure for her illegal dealings, was appointed to the U.S. Trade Representative job that Greg had been angling for, and left for Japan.

Dirty deals in business also dominated 1989–1990. Ted was accused of murder in the Lotus Point scandal and left for Japan, close on Abby's heels. Pension fund fraud at Oakman Industries (one of Greg's companies) grew into a series of murders involving crooked cop Tom, investigator Mack, Greg's estranged daughter Mary Frances (killed by her righteous boyfriend Robert), and Greg, himself, who was shot and then poisoned in the hospital with tainted pesticide from his own company. Karen cheerily began a TV talk show "Open Mike," only to be undercut by producer Dianne and stalked by two maniacal fans, one of whom turned out to be producer Jeff. Brothers Eric and Michael fought over Eric's wife Linda, Anne tried to steal her daughter Paige's inheritance, and poor Val married charming but violent Danny, who raped his former wife Amanda, terrorized Val's twins Betsy and Bobby, tried to kill Gary, ran over Pat Williams while drunk, and eventually fell into a pool and drowned while trying to rape Pat's daughter Julie. Nice guy.

In 1990–1991 Greg, dying from toxic poisoning, was saved by a liver transplant diverted from its intended recipient, then took up again with young schemer Paige. Paige's perpetual loser mother, Anne, tried raising cash by sending herself blackmail notes and asking a former lover for the payoff money, leading to an affair with shady Nick (a.k.a. Dimitri); the plan didn't work and by the end of the season Anne was homeless and on the streets. Greg's estranged sister Claudia showed up with her daughter Kate and rejected ex-con son Steve (happy family, they); good-guy Mack got into trouble trying to protect abused teenager Jason from his violent dad Dick; and widower Frank had problems with his wayward daughter Julie. The season ended with Gary and Val, who had been having bouts of temporary insanity, suddenly getting remarried, "before something else happens."

The 1991–1992 season saw Gary teaming up with Joseph Barringer and others in Tidal Energy, a grandiose plan to harness the ocean tides as an energy source. It failed, and Gary sustained such heavy losses he wound up as a worker on his own ranch. Val began researching a book on Greg Sumner, to the discomfiture of many; Linda's murder led to a long search for Brian Johnston, who terrorized a number of characters; homeless Anne worked her way off the streets by posing nude for a men's magazine (via Benny) and eventually launched a successful radio career; and Pierce, who had also lost his shirt in the Tidal Energy debacle, stalked Greg and other characters in revenge. At season's end Greg startled everyone by giving up the Sumner Group and retiring to a cabin in Montana.

As the final season began Gary searched desperately for his beloved Val, who had disappeared while researching that dangerous book. Despairing of ever finding her (as well he might—Joan Van Ark had left the series), he sought solace in Kate's arms. After much in-fighting, the Sumner Group was divided up among Claudia, Paige, and Meg, but not for long as Greg returned from the woods (pursued by Anne, who was trying to use the old false-pregnancy trick to get him to marry her) and plotted to regain control. Another major story had Mary Robeson trying to take little Meg away from adoptive parents Mack and Karen; this so unhinged good-guy Mack that he attempted to frame Mary for extortion, then was accused of her murder.

In the final episode familiar faces returned to bid farewell to the series that had outlasted all the other 1980s soaps. A mysterious and murderous man named Nigel Treadwell (Daniel Gerroll) was trying to wrest control of the Sumner Group; one of his cohorts was none other than Abby, who had been run out of town in 1989. Val, who had been captured by Treadwell, also made her way back in time to witness him shoot Greg, then try to blow up his plane. Didn't he know that Greg was indestructible (bullet deflected by a bulletproof vest, bomb defused at the last second)? Treadwell was shot by his hostage, Vanessa, just as he shot Nick. As the show closed Abby bought departing Claudia's house on the cul-de-sac and moved in. Seeing her, Val and Karen grabbed their husbands and turned away!

There was a certain interplay between *Knots Landing* and *Dallas* in the early years, with Gary's brothers turning up occasionally in Knots Landing, while he and Val made infrequent visits to Southfork, the Ewing ranch near Dallas, to see their daughter Lucy.

KNOWLEDGE TV (Network) (*Instructional Cable Network*)

LAUNCHED:
November, 1987

CEASED OPERATION:
c. 2000/2001

SUBSCRIBERS (JAN. 1999):
26.0 million (26% U.S.)

A cable channel devoted to adult education. Programming emphasized four general areas: health and wellness (*Healthy Women 2000, RxTV*), computers and technology (*New Media News, Disk Doctors, Home Computing*), careers and finance (*Women at the Top, Investment Club*), and culture and language (*Writer's Block, Great Museums*). Some programs even offered college credit courses through affiliation with various universities.

The network was launched in 1987 as Mind Extension University, the brainchild of cable mogul Glenn Jones. Originally dedicated to almost purely instructional programs, many concerned with computers, it was renamed Knowledge TV in October 1996 and began focusing on more general informational programming. Due to the difficulty of obtaining cable distribution, the channel shut down in 2000, although the owners continued to provide courses via the Internet (www.jonesinternational.edu).

KOBB'S KORNER (*Musical Variety*)

FIRST TELECAST: *September 29, 1948*
LAST TELECAST: *June 15, 1949*
BROADCAST HISTORY:
Sep 1948–Jan 1949, CBS Wed 8:00–8:30
Jan 1949–Feb 1949, CBS Thu 8:00–8:30
Feb 1949, CBS Wed 9:00–9:30
Mar 1949–Jun 1949, CBS Wed 9:30–10:00

REGULARS:
Stan Fritts and His Korn Kobblers
Hope Emerson
Jo Hurt
Betty Garde (1949)

This live series originated from New York but, if you could believe it, was supposed to come from Shufflebottom's General Store, U.S.A. The Korn Kobblers were a group of accomplished musicians who, in addition to playing straight music, used mouth harps, whistles, sirens, cowbells, jugs, washboards, and anything else that would make a noise. Actress Hope Emerson played Maw Shufflebottom, the owner of the general store, and Jo Hurt played her daughter Josiebelle. It was a little bit like a cross between *Hee Haw* and *Spike Jones* although it preceded them both, at least on television.

KODAK REQUEST PERFORMANCE (*Dramatic Anthology*)

FIRST TELECAST: *April 13, 1955*
LAST TELECAST: *September 28, 1955*
BROADCAST HISTORY:
Apr 1955–Sep 1955, NBC Wed 8:00–8:30

HOST:
Jack Clark

The dramas presented on *Kodak Request Performance* were all reruns of episodes of dramatic series that had aired originally during the 1954–1955 television season, primarily on *Ford Theatre* and *Fireside Theater*. Jack Clark provided live introductions to the filmed dramas.

KODIAK (*Police Drama*)

FIRST TELECAST: *September 13, 1974*
LAST TELECAST: *October 11, 1974*
BROADCAST HISTORY:
Sep 1974–Oct 1974, ABC Fri 8:00–8:30

CAST:
Cal "Kodiak" McKay .... Clint Walker
Abraham Lincoln Imhook .... Abner Biberman
Mandy .... Maggie Blye

Clint Walker was a cop with an unusual beat in this short-lived series. Kodiak was a member of the Alaska State Patrol, responsible for 50,000 square miles of rugged country and all the criminals, avalanche victims, and squabbling miners contained therein. He worked alone most of the time, traveling by four-wheel-drive truck, snowmobile, on skis, or snowshoes, as appropriate. Abraham Lincoln Imhook was his Eskimo friend and confidant. Filmed on location in Alaska.

KOJAK (*Police Drama*)
FIRST TELECAST: *October 24, 1973*
LAST TELECAST: *June 30, 1990*
BROADCAST HISTORY:
Oct 1973–Sep 1974, CBS Wed 10:00–11:00
Sep 1974–Sep 1975, CBS Sun 8:30–9:30
Sep 1975–Jan 1977, CBS Sun 9:00–10:00
Jan 1977–Sep 1977, CBS Mon 10:00–11:00
Sep 1977–Dec 1977, CBS Sun 10:00–11:00
Dec 1977–Apr 1978, CBS Sat 10:00–11:00
Nov 1989–Jun 1990, ABC Sat 9:00–11:00
CAST (1973–1978):
Lt. Theo Kojak .... Telly Savalas
Frank McNeil .... Dan Frazer
Lt. Bobby Crocker .... Kevin Dobson
Det. Stavros .... George Savalas
Det. Rizzo (1974–1977) .... Vince Conti
Det. Saperstein (1974–1977) .... Mark Russell
CAST (1989–1990):
Inspector Theo Kojak .... Telly Savalas
Det. Winston Blake .... Andre Braugher
Det. Paco Montana .... Kario Salem
Pamela .... Candace Savalas
Chief George "Fitz" Morris .... Charles Cioffi

When they started out together in the New York Police Department, Theo Kojak and Frank McNeil had worked closely together and, for a number of years, been partners. Over the years Frank had worked his way up the hierarchy to the point where he was now chief of detectives for the 13th Precinct in the Manhattan South district. Kojak, who had a cynical sense of humor and was determined to do things his way regardless of what his bosses thought, was now working for him. Kojak was outspoken and streetwise, and was not above stretching the literal interpretation of the law if it would help him crack a case. Working closely with him was plainclothes detective Bobby Crocker, as close to a regular partner as he had.

The supporting role of Detective Stavros was played by Telly Savalas's brother George who, during the first two seasons the show was on the air, was billed as Demosthenes in the credits rather than by his real name. Starting with the 1976–1977 season, considerable location filming was done in New York with Kojak seen all over the city licking his trademark lollipops. *Kojak* received much favorable publicity from police departments around the country for its realistic portrayal of police work.

In 1989, years after the original series ended, 65-year-old Telly Savalas returned to the mean streets of New York to make some new *Kojak* films for the *ABC Mystery Movie*. Kojak was now an Inspector, with a bright, young assistant named Winston Blake. Paco was Blake's regular partner, and Pamela was Kojak's secretary. Lollipops and "who loves ya, baby" were once again the order of the day, and in one episode a character from the old series even turned up: Crocker (played by Kevin Dobson), now a hotshot assistant D.A., was out to prosecute his successor Blake for murder.

KOLCHAK: THE NIGHT STALKER (*Occult*)
FIRST TELECAST: *September 13, 1974*
LAST TELECAST: *August 30, 1975*
BROADCAST HISTORY:
Sep 1974–Dec 1974, ABC Fri 10:00–11:00
Jan 1975–Jul 1975, ABC Fri 8:00–9:00
Aug 1975, ABC Sat 8:00–9:00
CAST:
Carl Kolchak .... Darren McGavin
Tony Vincenzo .... Simon Oakland
Ron Updyke .... Jack Grinnage
Emily Cowles .... Ruth McDevitt
Gordy Spangler .... John Fiedler
Monique Marmelstein .... Carol Ann Susi

Stories of the bizarre and supernatural, seen through the eyes of Carl Kolchak, crime reporter for Chicago's Independent News Service. The series was an odd mixture of reality and fantasy, with wisecracking reporter Kolchak and his commonsense investigations juxtaposed with inexplicable happenings. Instead of the usual hoods, Kolchak kept running into vampires, werewolves, zombies, and other esoteric phenomena. If he was sent to cover a crooked politician, he would find that the man had sold his soul to the Devil—literally. If he was covering a museum opening, a 500-year-old Aztec mummy would come to life. Kolchak's main trouble was convincing his skeptical editor, Tony Vincenzo, to print his incredible revelations.

Kolchak was based on the highly successful TV movie of the same name. It premiered, appropriately enough, on Friday the 13th, but lasted for only a single season.

KOLLEGE OF MUSICAL KNOWLEDGE, THE, see *Kay Kyser's Kollege of Musical Knowledge*

KOPYCATS, THE, see *ABC Comedy Hour*

KOVACS UNLIMITED, see *Ernie Kovacs Show, The*

KRAFT MUSIC HALL, THE (*Musical Variety*)
FIRST TELECAST: *September 13, 1967*
LAST TELECAST: *May 12, 1971*
BROADCAST HISTORY:
Sep 1967–May 1969, NBC Wed 9:00–10:00
Sep 1969–May 1971, NBC Wed 9:00–10:00
ANNOUNCER:
Ed Herlihy
ORCHESTRA:
Peter Matz
CHOREOGRAPHY:
Peter Gennaro

From 1933 to 1949 *The Kraft Music Hall* was one of the most popular variety shows on radio. Bing Crosby was probably its most famous host, at the helm from 1936–1946. When Kraft moved into television in 1947, it switched to weekly dramatic productions as *Kraft Television Theatre*. The music-hall format first appeared on television in the 1958–1959 season as *Milton Berle Starring in the Kraft Music Hall* and *Kraft Music Hall Presents: The Dave King Show*. *Perry Como's Kraft Music Hall* filled the Wednesday 9:00–10:00 P.M. hour for the next four seasons and there was a *Kraft Summer Music Hall* in 1966.

All of the above variations of *The Kraft Music Hall* had regular hosts, but beginning in the fall of 1967 each program became self-contained and featured a different host. During its first season there were a number of "theme" programs. Rock Hudson narrated "The Hollywood Musical," Lorne Greene hosted the musical potpourri "How the West Was Swung," George Burns did "Tin Pan Alley Today," and Dinah Shore did "The Nashville Sound." Although the title emphasized music, there were telecasts that were all comedy—"Woody Allen Looks at 1967" and Groucho Marx hosting "A Taste of Funny." In the spring and summer of 1968 there were periods when the same host appeared for a number of weeks—Eddy Arnold with the series subtitled "Country Fair" from April 24–June 5; John Davidson for the next three weeks; and Ed McMahon from July 3–September 4. While Eddy Arnold was hosting there was one regular along with him, comic John Byner.

Several performers who starred during the series' first season appeared during each of the succeeding seasons. In addition to Eddy Arnold, Don Rickles, and Alan King—the three stars who would appear most often throughout *The Kraft Music Hall*'s run—Steve Lawrence and Eydie Gorme were annual visitors. Others with multiple telecasts were Mitzi Gaynor, Bobby Darin, Roy Rogers and Dale Evans, Wayne Newton, and Johnny Cash. The Country Music Association Awards were telecast each year on *The Kraft Music Hall* and it was on this series that the Friars Club Roasts (later to become a semi-regular series of specials as "The Dean Martin Celebrity Roasts") first had national exposure. Johnny Carson, Milton Berle, Jack Benny, Don Rickles, and Jerry Lewis were all "roasted" over the years. During the last season there were two appearances by the Kopycats, talented impressionists who were later featured on *The ABC Comedy Hour*.

Summer replacements for the 1967–1971 versions of the *Kraft Music Hall* were Sandler and Young, and Don Ho in 1969, and English star Des O'Connor in 1970 and 1971.

KRAFT MUSIC HALL PRESENTS SANDLER & YOUNG (*Variety*)

FIRST TELECAST: *May 14, 1969*
LAST TELECAST: *August 13, 1969*
BROADCAST HISTORY:
May 1969–Aug 1969, NBC Wed 9:00–10:00
REGULARS:
Tony Sandler
Ralph Young
Jack Parnell and His Orchestra
Judy Carne
Norman Wisdom

The 1969 summer replacement for *The Kraft Music Hall* was this taped variety show from London, hosted by singers Tony Sandler and Ralph Young. A regular feature of the series was "Hands Across the Sea," a combination of messages to America from London and a salute to a foreign country. Des O'Connor was originally slated to host this series. He got his chance in a London-originated summer series of his own during the following two summers (see *Kraft Music Hall Presents the Des O'Connor Show*).

KRAFT MUSIC HALL PRESENTS: THE DAVE KING SHOW (*Variety*)

FIRST TELECAST: *May 20, 1959*
LAST TELECAST: *September 23, 1959*
BROADCAST HISTORY:
May 1959–Sep 1959, NBC Wed 9:00–9:30
REGULARS:
Dave King
Sid Greene
Dick Hills
Alan MacAteer
Jim Boles
Barney Martin
Bobby Gale
The Jerry Packer Singers
The Bill Foster Dancers
Vic Schoen Orchestra

English comedian/singer Dave King made his American television debut in this summer variety series. The format varied from music to skits, comic monologues, and pantomime, depending on the talents of his weekly guest stars. The variety was reflected in the show's theme song—"Anything Goes." One unusual aspect of this series was that its two writers, Sid Greene and Dick Hills, were also regular members of the on-air cast.

KRAFT MUSIC HALL PRESENTS THE DES O'CONNOR SHOW (*Variety*)

FIRST TELECAST: *May 20, 1970*
LAST TELECAST: *September 1, 1971*
BROADCAST HISTORY:
May 1970–Sep 1970, NBC Wed 9:00–10:00
Jun 1971–Sep 1971, NBC Wed 9:00–10:00
REGULARS:
Des O'Connor
Jack D. Douglas
The MacGregor Brothers (1970)
Jim Coulton and Rex (1970)
Patrick Newell (1970)
The Mike Sammes Singers
Jack Parnell and His Orchestra
Joe Baker (1971)
Connie Stevens (1971)
The New Faces (1971)

British TV personality Des O'Connor was the host and star of this London-originated summer replacement for *The Kraft Music Hall*. With Des was his longtime partner, Jack D. Douglas, whose regular role on the series was that of Alf Ippittimus, a stagestruck buffoon. When the series returned for its second summer run in 1971, the title was shortened to *The Des O'Connor Show* and included two new recurring weekly features—"Dandy Sandy" and "I Say I Say." The former was a satire on a children's television show and the latter a situation in which members of the cast would interrupt Des's attempt to recite something with snappy one-line jokes.

KRAFT MYSTERY THEATER (*Dramatic Anthology*)

FIRST TELECAST: *June 14, 1961*
LAST TELECAST: *September 25, 1963*
BROADCAST HISTORY:
Jun 1961–Sep 1961, NBC Wed 9:00–10:00
Jun 1962–Sep 1962, NBC Wed 9:00–10:00
Jun 1963–Sep 1963, NBC Wed. 9:00–10:00
HOST:
Frank Gallop (1961)

Filmed dramatic-anthology series, which served as summer replacement for *Perry Como's Kraft Music Hall*. The 1961 version consisted of mystery-suspense dramas, most of them filmed in England, originally for English television and theatrical distribution. Frank Gallop was host for the series. In 1962 American films shot at the Desilu Studios in Hollywood were used, some of them originals and some having already been seen on CBS' *Westinghouse Desilu*

Playhouse from 1958–1960. Many top Hollywood actors were seen. In 1963 the films were provided by Hollywood's Revue Studios, some of them having been aired previously on *Alcoa Playhouse* from 1961–1963.

KRAFT MYSTERY THEATRE, see *Kraft Television Theatre* for 1958 series

KRAFT SUMMER MUSIC HALL, THE (*Variety*)
FIRST TELECAST: *June 6, 1966*
LAST TELECAST: *August 29, 1966*
BROADCAST HISTORY:
Jun 1966–Aug 1966, NBC Mon 9:00–10:00
REGULARS:
John Davidson
George Carlin
Jackie and Gayle
The Five King Cousins
The Lively Set
Jimmie Haskell Orchestra

Handsome young singer John Davidson was the host and star of this summer variety series which placed its emphasis on youth. Most of the guest stars, as well as the series regulars, were performers in their 20s. Comedian George Carlin, in addition to performing on the show himself, wrote all of the comedy material. The Five King Cousins were members of the huge King family, which had had its own series on ABC.

KRAFT SUSPENSE THEATER (*Dramatic Anthology*)
FIRST TELECAST: *October 10, 1963*
LAST TELECAST: *September 9, 1965*
BROADCAST HISTORY:
Oct 1963–Sep 1965, NBC Thu 10:00–11:00

Kraft, which had used both dramatic and musical offerings to promote its products on TV over the years, mixed the two formulas in the 1963 and 1964 seasons. The emphasis was on drama, preempted by a Perry Como *Kraft Music Hall* special approximately once a month, all in the Thursday 10:00–11:00 P.M. time period (this in itself was a major change, as Kraft had "owned" the Wednesday 9:00–10:00 P.M. hour on NBC for the previous 15 years).

The dramas, which were filmed in Hollywood, employed top-name talent, with Lee Marvin, Gig Young, and Lloyd Bridges headlining during the first month that the series was on the air. Most of the plots concerned murder, psychological terror, or other stories of danger and mystery. Among these was "Rapture at Two Forty," presented in April 1965, the pilot for the later series *Run For Your Life.*

KRAFT TELEVISION THEATRE (*Dramatic Anthology*)
FIRST TELECAST: *May 7, 1947*
LAST TELECAST: *October 1, 1958*
BROADCAST HISTORY:
May 1947–Dec 1947, NBC Wed 7:30–8:30
Jan 1948–Oct 1958, NBC Wed 9:00–10:00 (OS)
Oct 1953–Jan 1955, ABC Thu 9:30–10:30
ANNOUNCER:
Ed Herlihy (1947–1955)
Charles Stark (1955)
REGULAR PRODUCERS/DIRECTORS:
Stanley Quinn
Maury Holland
Harry Hermann
Richard Dunlap
Fielder Cook
William Graham
Norman Morgan
David Susskind
Robert Herridge
Alex March
George Roy Hill
Buzz Kulik

Kraft Foods Co. was one of the major supporters of live television drama during the 1950s, before switching to musical offerings in 1958. The *Kraft Television Theatre* was one of television's most prestigious showcases, winning top ratings and many awards, and becoming a Wednesday night institution. By the end of its run, more than 650 plays, drama and comedy, both originals and adaptations for TV, had been presented. At one time *two* Kraft Theatre series were airing simultaneously on NBC and ABC. All of these plays were live (although kinescopes and a very few videotapes were made for delayed transmission purposes), so most of these dramatic presentations are lost to us today.

Kraft skimped on nothing. The casts were large, the sets often elaborate, and the playwrights and producers first-rate. One "event" production in 1956 about the sinking of the *Titanic* almost seemed to have an actor for each of the 1,502 souls who went down with that ill-fated ship! (Actually there were 107 in the cast.) A brief sampling of the actors and actresses who starred over the years would include E. G. Marshall (frequently), Jack Lemmon, Cyril Ritchard (his first U.S. TV appearance, in 1951), Rod Steiger, James Dean, Lee Remick, Art Carney, Joanne Woodward, Grace Kelly, Anthony Perkins—and many, many more. A number of performers who would later become film and TV stars gained early exposure on *Kraft*, including Cloris Leachman (1949), Martin Milner (1949), and Paul Newman (1952).

Scripts ranged from the classics (Shakespeare, Ibsen) to Tennessee Williams, Agatha Christie, and Rod Serling. Many new or unknown writers were given exposure too, and during the 1955–1956 season Kraft offered a $50,000 prize for the best original play presented during the year. Judges were Helen Hayes, Walter Kerr, and Maxwell Anderson. The prize went to William Noble for "Snap Finger Creek," telecast on February 22, 1956.

During the mid-1950s quite a few youth-oriented episodes were presented, mostly dramas revolving around popular music. Among the popular singers playing dramatic (and singing) roles were Gisele MacKenzie (1955), Ferlin Husky (1957), and Julius LaRosa (1957). Even more rock-oriented were actor-singer Tommy Sands, who starred in an Elvis Presley-type role in "The Singing Idol" in January 1957 (the featured song on this telecast, "Teenage Crush," went on to become a million-selling record); and Sal Mineo, who introduced his biggest hit, "Start Movin'," on the Kraft dramatic presentation "Drummer Man" in May 1957.

Another notable landmark in the series' history was the use of color, which began intermittently in April 1954 and became permanent in July 1956.

In April 1958 *Kraft Television Theatre* was taken over by a new production company and its title was shortened to *Kraft Theatre*. In June 1958 the title was changed again to *Kraft Mystery Theatre* (not to be confused with the filmed series of the same name in the early 1960s).

At the end of Kraft's long run in live TV drama, *TV Guide* summoned up a few statistics. In 11½ years *Kraft* had presented 650 plays culled from 18,845 scripts, starred or featured 3,955 actors and actresses in 6,750 roles, used up 26,000 hours of rehearsal time and employed 5,236 sets. Costs had risen from $3,000 for the first production on May 7, 1947 (a play called "Double Door" starring John Baragrey) to $165,000 by 1958. Ed Rice, the script editor for *Kraft* throughout the program's run, observed that the entire studio facilities used in 1947 were half the size of the space used just to produce the commercials in 1958.

But *Kraft*'s contribution to television is not measured in statistics alone. Quite simply, the series presented superlative live drama throughout television's "Golden Age."

KREISLER BANDSTAND (*Music*)
FIRST TELECAST: *March 21, 1951*
LAST TELECAST: *June 13, 1951*
BROADCAST HISTORY:
Mar 1951–Jun 1951, ABC Wed 8:30–9:00
EMCEE:
Fred Robbins

Big-name dance bands were featured each week on this program, hosted by New York disc jockey Fred Robbins. Among those appearing were Ralph Flanagan, Sammy Kaye, Duke Ellington, Benny Goodman, Art Mooney, and Cab Calloway, as well as such singers as Patti Page, Ella Fitzgerald, and Margaret Whiting.

KRISTIN (*Situation Comedy*)
FIRST TELECAST: *June 5, 2001*
LAST TELECAST: *July 10, 2001*
BROADCAST HISTORY:
Jun 2001, NBC Tue 8:30–9:00
Jun 2001–Jul 2001, NBC Tue 9:30–10:00
CAST:
Kristin Yancey .... Kristin Chenoweth
Tommy Ballantine .... Jon Tenney
Aldo Bonnadonna .... Larry Romano
Tyrique Kimbrough .... Dale Godboldo
Santa Clemente .... Ana Ortiz
Reverend Thornhill .... Christopher Durang

Pint-sized (4'11") dynamo Kristin arrived in New York from Broken Arrow, Oklahoma, full of spunk and optimism, looking for her big break on Broadway, but after a couple of disastrous auditions decided to find some paying work to tide her over. Her spiritual adviser, the Reverend Thornhill of a small Lower East Side chapel, got her a job with Tommy Ballantine, a powerful and handsome real estate developer who was having some image problems. Her clean-cut, superhonest, midwestern morality might be just the thing to "reform" this morally bankrupt, self-centered tycoon. It turned out that Tommy wasn't such a bad guy underneath, but the clash of their styles was the centerpiece of this comedy. Every time he tried to slip some underhanded deal by her, he discovered she was not as naive as he thought. Others in the swank offices of Ballantine Enterprises included Aldo, his slick, Brooklyn-accented right-hand man; Tyrique, the hip, dreadlocked messenger who could get *anything* done; and Santa Clemente, the Latin sexpot who was Tommy's director of sales, and jealous of Kristin's new influence over him.

All these city slickers learned a little from the newly arrived hick. As Tommy remarked, "You are one savvy Christian."

KRYPTON FACTOR, THE (*Quiz/Audience Participation*)
FIRST TELECAST: *August 7, 1981*
LAST TELECAST: *September 4, 1981*
BROADCAST HISTORY:
Aug 1981–Sep 1981, ABC Fri 8:30–9:00
HOST:
Dick Clark

Four contestants really worked for their prizes on this summer quiz show. First the four faced a memory test: after seeing clips from a current movie, they had to recall specific dialogue and identify one of the actors in a lineup with impostors. Then their reflexes were challenged by a difficult video or computer game; their physical stamina by a race through an obstacle course in speedboats, dune buggies, or motortrikes; their mental agility through brainteaser problems and general-knowledge questions. If they survived all that, they had a shot at the $50,000 grand prize in the championship finals held on the last telecast.

A contestant's score was called his or her "Krypton Factor."

KUDA BUX, HINDU MYSTIC (*Magic*)
FIRST TELECAST: *March 25, 1950*
LAST TELECAST: *June 17, 1950*
BROADCAST HISTORY:
Mar 1950–Jun 1950, CBS Sat 6:30–6:45
REGULARS:
Kuda Bux (real name: Khudah Bukhsh)
Rex Marshall
Janet Tyler

Kuda Bux, "the man with the X-ray eyes," was one of the favorite novelty acts on early television. After appearing as a regular on several series (including the appropriately named *I'd Like to See*), he had his own 15-minute network show in the spring of 1950. Feats of magic, mind reading, and other illusions were performed weekly by the man from Kashmir, India (who had been plying his trade in Europe for years before coming to the U.S.). The highlight always came when Kuda Bux's eyes were wrapped in bandages, tinfoil, lead, and just about anything one might conceive of. On one show, sponsored by a bakery, he had his eyes covered with baker's dough. He would then proceed to "see" through it all to thread needles, hit bull's-eyes, and perform other feats.

Every viewer had a theory about how he did it. One lad said it was obvious that Kuda saw through his nose. A lady said Kuda marked off places on the floor just before he was blindfolded, and then just felt his way around. A little boy wrote in to say he believed Kuda swiveled his head completely around, and then saw out the back. Kuda Bux just laughed, and looked mystifying.

Rex Marshall served as announcer and interpreter on this series, and Janet Tyler was Kuda's helper and assistant.

KUKLA, FRAN & OLLIE (*Children's*)

FIRST TELECAST: *November 29, 1948*

LAST TELECAST: *August 31, 1957*

BROADCAST HISTORY:

Nov 1948–Nov 1951, NBC Mon–Fri 7:00–7:30 (OS)
Nov 1951–Jun 1952, NBC Mon–Fri 7:00–7:15
Sep 1954–Aug 1957, ABC Mon–Fri 7:00–7:15 (OS)

HOSTESS:

Fran Allison

PUPPETEER:

Burr Tillstrom

MUSICAL DIRECTOR:

Jack Fascinato

PUPPETS:

Kukla
Ollie (Oliver J. Dragon)
Fletcher Rabbit
Mme. Ophelia Oglepuss
Buelah Witch
Cecil Bill
Col. Crackie
Mercedes
Dolores Dragon (1950–1957)
Olivia Dragon (1952–1957)

This whimsical puppet show was one of television's longest-running and most loved children's programs. It was always done live, and the dialogue was unscripted, with Fran and her little friends reacting to each other in an entirely spontaneous manner.

Burr Tillstrom created Kukla, the first of his "Kuklapolitan Players," in 1936. The name Kukla was supposedly bestowed by the famous Russian ballerina Tamara Toumanova when she first saw the puppet perform (it means "doll" in Russian). The Kuklapolitan troupe was seen on experimental television as early as 1939, and the *Kukla, Fran & Ollie* series (originally known as *Junior Jamboree*) began locally on Chicago's WBKB-TV on October 13, 1947. It was fed to NBC's newly established Midwest network beginning in November 1948, and as soon as coaxial cables were opened to the East Coast (1949) and West Coast (1951) it was seen live in those regions as well.

The members of the Kuklapolitan Players were as follows: Kukla, a solemn, bulb-nosed little fellow with a perpetually worried expression, who knew nothing of his own past; Fran, a Chicago actress and singer, and the only live character seen (the puppets performed on a miniature stage, with Fran standing in front of it); Oliver J. Dragon, a carefree, extroverted, one-toothed dragon who was born in Vermont, where his parents ran Dragon Retreat (there had been no fire-breathing dragons in Ollie's family since his great-great-great-great-grandfather swam the Hellespont, gulped some water, and doused the flame); Fletcher Rabbit, the mailman, whose ears drooped so badly they had to be starched for formal occasions; Ophelia Oglepuss, a haughty ex-opera star; Buelah Witch, who had studied electronics and who patrolled the coaxial cable, while not buzzing around on her jet-propelled broomstick; Cecil Bill, the stage manager who spoke a language all his own; Col. Crackie, the long-winded Southern-Gentleman emcee of the company, and Mme. Oglepuss's escort; Mercedes, the troupe's little girl; Dolores Dragon, infant daughter of Ollie's long-lost Uncle Dorchester (Ollie considered her a horrible little monster); and Olivia Dragon, Ollie's elderly mother, who had hair 75 yards long, *two* fine teeth, and a sharp New England accent.

In addition to episodes focusing on day-to-day experiences and songs, the Players sometimes presented full-dress productions, ranging from mild satires ("Martin Dragon, Private Tooth") to established operettas. *The Mikado,* with Kukla as Nanki Poo, Fran as Yum Yum, and Ollie as the Lord High Executioner, was an annual event for several years. There were also original musical plays, such as *St. George and the Dragon*, presented in June 1953, complete with musical accompaniment by Arthur Fiedler and the Boston Pops and Boston Mayor John B. Hines as special guest. This show was repeated in August 1953 as one of the first experimental telecasts in compatible color.

In addition to its prime-time telecasts, listed above, *Kukla, Fran & Ollie* appeared Sunday afternoons on NBC from August 1952 to June 1954; in a five-minute weekday spot on NBC from September 1961 to June 1962; on PBS (Public Television) from 1969–1971; and in a syndicated version during the 1975–1976 season.

KUNG FU (*Western*)

FIRST TELECAST: *October 14, 1972*

LAST TELECAST: *June 28, 1975*

BROADCAST HISTORY:

Oct 1972–Nov 1972, ABC Sat 8:00–9:00
Jan 1973–Aug 1974, ABC Thu 9:00–10:00
Sep 1974–Oct 1974, ABC Sat 9:00–10:00
Nov 1974–Jan 1975, ABC Fri 8:00–9:00
Jan 1975–Jun 1975, ABC Sat 8:00–9:00

CAST:

Kwai Chang Caine .... David Carradine
Master Po .... Keye Luke
Master Kan .... Philip Ahn
Caine (as a youth) .... Radames Pera
**Margit McLean* .... Season Hubley

*Occasional

Kung Fu could probably best be classified as a philosophical Western. It attracted quite a bit of notoriety and a cult following in the early 1970s, due to its unusual protagonist. Caine was a shaven-headed Buddhist monk, and a hunted man. He had been born in China in the mid-1800s of Chinese and American parents, and was raised as an orphan by the monks of Shaolin Temple. They tutored him in a mystic philosophy of internal harmony and the "oneness of all things," and a code of nonviolence. They also taught him the martial arts of kung fu—just in case.

Then one day young Caine was involved in an incident in which he was forced to kill a member of the Chinese royal family. Fleeing China, he landed in the American West where he began a search for a long-lost brother—while he himself was pursued by Chinese imperial agents and American bounty hunters.

Besides his background, there were many other unusual things about this particular Western hero. He spoke very little, uttering occasional cryptic statements about the nature of being and universal harmony ("Remember," his teachers had said, "the wise man walks always with his head bowed, humble, like the dust."); his use, when cornered, of the ancient Chinese martial arts instead of a gun; his pariah status—a Chinaman, as well as a hunted man. *Kung Fu* used many gimmicks to lend it a surreal aspect, such as slow-motion photography, and included frequent flashbacks to Caine's days as a youth in China (in which his teachers, Master Po and Master Kan, appeared, as well as Caine as a young boy). Caine was usually a loner, although in the final season an American cousin, Margit, began to make occasional appearances.

The star, David Carradine, was responsible for much of the publicity surrounding this show. A member of a respected theatrical family (his father, John Carradine, had appeared in many famous movies of the 1930s and 1940s), David dropped out of Hollywood's glittering world and lived a decidedly unconventional life in a ramshackle old house in the hills, reflecting the same philosophy of mysticism and "oneness with nature" that Caine represented.

Kung Fu, incidentally, translates roughly as "accomplishment technique," and is China's ancient science of personal combat, from which karate and judo are derived. It enjoyed quite a vogue in the U.S. during the late 1960s and early 1970s as a result of the movies of Chinese-American actor Bruce Lee.

KUNG FU—THE LEGEND CONTINUES

(*Adventure*)

BROADCAST HISTORY:

Syndicated only
60 minutes
Produced: *1992–1996* (88 episodes)
Released: *January 1993*

CAST:

Kwai Chang Caine .... David Carradine
Det. Peter Caine .... Chris Potter
Lo Si (The Ancient) .... Kim Chan
Young Peter (1993–1995)........ Nathaniel Moreau
**Capt. Paul Blaisdell (1993–1994)* ... Robert Lansing
Chief Frank Strenlich .... William Dunlop
Det. Jody Blakemore Powell (1994–1996)
.... Belinda Metz
Det. Mary Margaret Skalany (1994–1996)
.... Victoria Snow
**Capt. Karen Simms (1995–1996)*....... Kate Trotter
Det. Kermit Griffin (1994–1996)... Scott Wentworth
M. E. Nick Elder (1993–1996)........ David Hewlett
Det. Blake (1994–1996) .... Robert Nicholson

*Occasional

Kwai Chang Caine was the grandson of the character in the original *Kung Fu* series from the 1970s. He had trained his son, Peter, at a Shaolin Temple destroyed by an evil fellow teacher who became the leader of a criminal underground. Caine and Peter had each believed that the other had died. Then, 15 years later they were reunited. Peter was now a cop, and Caine helped him on cases. During their years apart Peter had been raised by Capt. Blaisdell and his wife. Peter's original partner was killed in a 1993 episode, and, in the spring of 1994 her sister, Jody, became his new partner.

There were flashbacks to Caine and Peter's years at the temple in most episodes, usually to illustrate some philosophical truth. The series had heavy supernatural overtones in addition to an abundance of martial arts by both Caine and Peter, despite Peter's protestations ("I don't do Kung Fu. I'm a cop"). Caine fought evil spirits and demons, traveled back in time, and managed to summon up assorted mystical powers whenever they were needed to get him, or Peter, out of trouble. Also seen regularly was The Ancient, a friend of Caine's and fellow resident of Chinatown who was also versed in martial arts skills and mystical powers.

In a December 1994 episode Blaisdell retired from the force to resolve personal problems from his C.I.A. days. The episode, which aired less than a month after Robert Lansing's death from cancer, was dedicated to his memory.

In the last original episode, which aired in December 1996, Peter quit the force to fulfill his destiny as a Shaolin priest, and at the episode's end his father left to search for Peter's mother, who he had just found out might still be alive.

L

L.A. DOCTORS (*Medical Drama*)

FIRST TELECAST: *September 21, 1998*
LAST TELECAST: *May 10, 1999*
BROADCAST HISTORY:

Sep 1998–May 1999, CBS Mon 10:00–11:00

CAST:

Dr. Roger Cattan .... Ken Olin
Dr. Tim Lonner .... Matt Craven
Dr. Evan Newman.......................... Rick Roberts
Dr. Sarah Church.......................... Sheryl Lee
Nick Newman.......................... Joseph Ashton
Kelly Newman.......................... Rebecca Rigg
Susann Blum.......................... Deirdre O'Connell
Felicity.......................... Melora Walters
Nina Morris.......................... Judith Scott
Patrick Owen .... Coby Bell
Eleanor Riggs .... Patricia Wettig
Julie Lonner.......................... Talia Balsam
Eva (1998) .... Erica Jimenez-Alvarado
Christine (1998) .... Vanessa Jimenez-Alvarado

Roger, Tim, and Evan were three well-meaning idealistic doctors in Los Angeles who set up their own private medical corporation—Lonner, Newman, and Cattan—to treat patients as people, not simply as a source of income. In the premiere they recruited a fourth doctor, Sarah, into their joint practice. Roger, the businessman of the group with the playboy lifestyle, was somewhat more concerned about turning a reasonable profit than his altruistic partners—at times alienating both them and some of his patients. Tim was often at odds with the medical insurance bureaucracy over issues of patient care. He and his wife Julie, unable to have children of their own, were struggling to maintain custody of foster twin girls (Eva and Christine). Eventually they had to give them up to the girls' recovering-drug-addict mother. Evan was divorced but maintained a reasonably good relationship with Kelly, his ex-wife, and tried to be a good father to his son, Nick. Sarah's marriage was falling apart, and Steven, her screenwriter husband, was cheating on her. In December she found out she was pregnant. Roger learned that the medical corporation's business manager had skipped town with their investment funds and married his former lover, Eleanor (played by star Olin's real-life wife). Felicity and Susann were two nurses working for the doctors, Patrick was a lab technician, and Nina was their office manager. In the spring Evan and Sarah began an affair but, sadly, she died from internal injuries suffered in a car crash in the series' final episode.

L.A. FIREFIGHTERS (*Adventure*)

FIRST TELECAST: *June 3, 1996*
LAST TELECAST: *July 8, 1996*
BROADCAST HISTORY:

Jun 1996–Jul 1996, FOX Mon 9:00–10:00

CAST:

Capt. Jack Malloy .... Jarrod Emick
Erin Coffey .... Christine Elise
Bernie Ramirez .... Miguel Sandoval
Capt. Dick Coffey .... Brian Smiar
Ray Grimes.......................... Carlton Wilborn
Kay Rizzo .... Alexandra Hedison
J. B. Baker .... Brian Leckner
Lenny Rose.......................... Michael Gallagher
Laura Malloy .... Elizabeth Mitchell
Flame.......................... China Kantner
Bobby Grimes .... Vicellous Reon Shannon
Norman.......................... Peter Crombie
Mike .... John Bradley
Helen Regan .... Kathryn Morris
Michelle Goldstein .... Meredith Salenger
Cerone .... Carmen Argenziano

This short-lived serial followed the working and personal lives of the firefighters at Station 132 in Los Angeles, commanded by Battalion Chief Dick Coffey. Erin and Kay coped with prejudice against women firefighters. Ray had a kid brother, Bobby, who was a crack addict with an attitude, got arrested on a drug charge, and caused Ray problems. Jack's marriage to Laura was in trouble, and she moved out. Erin was having problems with her firefighter dad, who had a drinking problem, and she and religious J.B. got caught under falling debris after thinking a fire was under control. In the euphoric adrenaline rush after rescuing J.B. and Erin, Jack and Kay ended up in the sack—and later both Erin and Jack's estranged wife Laura showed signs of jealousy. Further complicating the tangled relationships, Jack filed charges with the department because of Dick's drinking problem, forcing the latter into retirement.

L.A. Firefighters was taken off the air for retooling barely a month after its premiere, but never returned.

L.A. LAW (*Legal Drama*)

FIRST TELECAST: *October 3, 1986*
LAST TELECAST: *May 19, 1994*
BROADCAST HISTORY:

Oct 1986–Nov 1986, NBC Fri 10:00–11:00
Dec 1986–Aug 1990, NBC Thu 10:00–11:00
Oct 1990–Feb 1993, NBC Thu 10:00–11:00
Apr 1993–Dec 1993, NBC Thu 10:00–11:00 (OS)
Feb 1994–May 1994, NBC Thu 10:00–11:00

CAST:

Leland McKenzie .... Richard Dysart
Douglas Brackman, Jr.......................... Alan Rachins
Michael Kuzak (1986–1991) .... Harry Hamlin
Grace Van Owen (1986–1992).......... Susan Dey
Ann Kelsey.......................... Jill Eikenberry
Arnie Becker.......................... Corbin Bernsen
Stuart Markowitz.......................... Michael Tucker
Victor Sifuentes (1986–1991) .... Jimmy Smits
Abby Perkins (1986–1991)......... Michele Greene
Roxanne Melman (1986–1993)....... Susan Ruttan
**Elizabeth Brand (1986–1988)*......... Ellen Drake
**Sheila Brackman (1986–1988)* .... Joanna Frank
**Hilda Brunschweiger (1986–1987)*
.... Patricia Huston
**Iris Hubbard (1986–1987)* .... Cynthia Harris
Benny Stulwicz (1987–1994) .... Larry Drake
Jonathan Rollins (1987–1994).... Blair Underwood
**Alison Gottlieb (1988–1989)* .... Joyce Hyser
**David Meyer (1988–1990)*............ Dann Florek
Dorothy Wyler (1989)............... Nancy Vawter
Rosalind Shays (1989–1991) .... Diana Muldaur
Corrine Hammond (1989–1991) ... Jennifer Hetrick
Diane Moses (1989–1990) .... Renee Jones
**Murray Melman (1990)* .... Vincent Gardenia
**Gwen Taylor (1990–1993)*............ Sheila Kelley

Tommy Mullaney (1990–1994) .... John Spencer
Cara Jean (C. J.) Lamb (1990–1992)
.... Amanda Donohoe
Zoey Clemmons (1991–1992) ...... Cecil Hoffmann
Billy Castroverti (1991–1992)........... Tom Verica
Susan Bloom (1991–1992) .... Conchata Ferrell
Frank Kittredge (1991–1992)..... Michael Cumpsty
Daniel Morales (1992–1994)............ A Martinez
Eli Levinson (1993–1994).......... Alan Rosenberg
Denise Ianello (1993–1994) .... Debi Mazar
Jane Halliday (1993–1994) ...... Alexandra Powers
Melinda Paros (1993–1994) .... Liza Jane
**Rosalie (1993–1994)* .... Kathleen Wilhoite

*Occasional

This critically acclaimed ensemble drama was one of the hits of the 1986 season. Created by Steven Bochco (creator of *Hill Street Blues*) and Terry Louise Fisher (producer of *Cagney and Lacey*, and a former Deputy D.A. herself), it looked like *Hill Street* in a fancy law office, with many characters and stories intertwined in each episode. The high-powered Los Angeles law firm of McKenzie, Brackman, Chaney and Kuzak took on cases of all types, criminal and civil, usually for high fees (though they also did some "pro bono" work for the poor). Leland McKenzie was the esteemed, fatherly senior partner; Brackman, the vain, insufferable, balding partner struggling to fill his late father's formidable shoes; Kuzak, the savvy but compassionate younger partner; Van Owen, the idealistic Deputy D.A. who was Kuzak's lover and sometime courtroom opponent; Ann, another idealistic attorney; Stuart, the firm's nebbishy little tax attorney, who had a heart of gold and also had the hots for Ann; Arnie, the sleazy, womanizing divorce lawyer (whose object was often to create discord in order to produce a more profitable case); Victor, the uptight young Hispanic brought into the firm to meet racial quotas, and he knew it; Abby, the unsure-of-herself young intern; and Roxanne, the motherly receptionist. Added in 1987 were Jonathan, a young black lawyer, and Benny, a retarded office worker—one of the few continuing portrayals in TV series' history of a retarded person.

Plenty of office politics and sexual adventures were mixed in with the cases (Markowitz and Kelsey angling to become partners, Kuzak lusting after Van Owen, Markowitz after Kelsey, Becker after everybody). Perhaps the series' most publicized early episode was the one in which a bigamist-client taught Stuart a secret sexual maneuver guaranteed to melt down any woman—the "Venus Butterfly." Viewers never learned what it was, but Ann was his.

Other continuing stories unfolded soap-opera style. Abby left the firm to set up her own shaky practice, but eventually returned. Van Owen was named a judge, then resigned to join McKenzie, Brackman. Arnie produced a bestselling do-it-yourself divorce video in partnership with Roxanne's incredibly boring husband David, a direct-mail entrepreneur. He soon had use for it himself. After years of seducing rich, beautiful women, Arnie finally "settled down" and married Corrine, only to fall off the sexual wagon with, among others, of all people, his loyal, plain-Jane secretary Roxanne.

The most famous storyline began in 1989 with the arrival of hard-driving Rosalind Shays, a super-successful but unlikable litigator who was brought in as a partner to rejuvenate sagging revenues. Roz took over with a vengeance, wooing Leland in the process, but was eventually forced out in a battle royal that almost destroyed the firm. (Her subsequent lawsuit cost the remaining partners $2.1 million.) She met an abrupt end in March 1991 when she accidentally stepped into an empty elevator shaft and plunged to her death.

Besides its soap-opera entanglements, *L.A. Law* emphasized outrageous situations and trendy cases. Cases touched on such diverse subjects as the "outing" of prominent homosexuals, dwarf tossing, anti-American discrimination in Japanese firms, insurance companies that refused to cover AIDS medication, and a case involving a businessman with Tourette's syndrome—causing him to involuntarily blurt out obscenities at the most inopportune moments.

Major cast changes occurred in 1990. Kuzak angrily left to set up his own firm, causing yet another change in the company's name to McKenzie, Brackman, Chaney, and Becker. (Chaney, by the way, had died at his desk in the premiere episode.) Arriving were three very different attorneys: Tommy Mullaney, an anti-establishment maverick who worked on commission because he couldn't stand "suit and tie shops" like McKenzie, Brackman; Zoey, his ex-wife, an assistant D.A.; and C. J., a feisty, hot-shot litigator with an English accent, who happened to be bisexual.

Despite the turmoil, the practice of law did have its rewards. The opening titles showed the words "LA LAW" on a California license plate—resting securely on a Jaguar XJ6.

Later seasons brought brash entertainment lawyer Susan Bloom, charged with drumming up new business for the troubled firm; her associate Frank; Grace's departure for New York; C.J.'s departure to join a golf tour; Rollins' campaign for city council; the arrival of sexy single-dad Morales; Markowitz's slow emotional recovery from a beating; Benny's marriage to Rosalie; and the arrival in the last season of Eli and Denise from ABC's canceled *Civil Wars*—a rare instance of characters from one series moving to another. By this time the firm was called McKenzie, Brackman, Kelsey, Markowitz and Morales. In the May 1994 final episode, father figure Leland McKenzie announced his retirement, effectively closing the doors on *L.A. Law*.

L.A.P.D.: LIFE ON THE BEAT (*Police Documentary*)

BROADCAST HISTORY:

Syndicated only
30 minutes
Produced: *1995–1999*
Released: *September 1995*

NARRATOR:

Andrew Geller (1995–1996)
Hank Brandt (1996–1999)

Lovers of *cinéma verité* coverage of the police in action who didn't get enough from Fox's long-running *Cops* could tune in to this series for a half hour of similar fare Mondays through Fridays. The major difference was that *Cops* moved from city to city while *L.A.P.D.* explored the sprawling environs of greater Los Angeles, "from the glitter to the gutter." There were features on beat cops, cops in patrol cars, and officers working from helicopters. Segments also showcased S.W.A.T. teams, bomb squads, and the dogs of the K-9 units. Officers were also shown working on missing persons cases, performing rescues, and giving citizens advice on how to avoid becoming victims of crimes.

LA FEMME NIKITA (*Adventure/Espionage*)

BROADCAST HISTORY:

USA Network
60 minutes
Original episodes: *1997–2001* (96 episodes)
Premiered: *January 13, 1997*

CAST:

Nikita .... Peta Wilson
Michael Samuelle .... Roy Dupuis
Paul L. Wolfe ("Operations") .... Eugene Robert Glazer
Madeline .... Alberta Watson
Seymour Birkoff/Jason Crawford (1996–2000) .... Matthew Ferguson
Walter .... Don Francks
Kate Quinn (2000–2001) .... Cindy Dolenc

She was smart, sexy, and athletic. They had given her high-tech weapons and a license to kill. Yet Nikita felt like a caged animal. Framed for killing a cop, a crime she didn't commit, she had been sentenced to life in prison, only to be released into the clutches of a super-secret government antiterrorist organization known as Section One. The deal: the Section would train her as a covert agent, and she would follow its every command without question. If she ever wavered, she would be immediately "canceled" (killed).

Nikita reluctantly accepted the Faustian bargain, and was soon one of the Section's most effective operatives, battling terrorists and international criminals with all the considerable resources at its disposal. The Section's tactics were as ruthless as those of its adversaries, and abduction, assassination, and torture were the order of the day. Her mentor and immediate superior was Michael, a quiet, mysterious man to whom she was romantically attracted. The sexual tension between the two was central to the series, even though it was never entirely clear whether his feelings were genuine or he was using her. No one in Section One was to be completely trusted. "Operations" was the intense Section Chief, a man with connections to the highest levels of government and the power to determine who would live or die—including Nikita. Madeline was his master strategist, a chess player with human lives; Birkoff the brilliant young computer expert; and Walter the gruff, grizzled weapons specialist.

There were many twists and turns during the series' run, with Operations and Madeline plotting against each other and their agents, and Nikita sometimes on the run from her supervisors; Michael helped her stay alive. It turned out that he was secretly married to Elena and had a young son named Adam. Nikita allied with Center, an even more mysterious organization run by Mr. Jones (Carlo Rota) that oversaw Section One. Birkoff was killed and replaced by Kate, and Madeline committed suicide but was reconstituted as a holographic replica of herself. In the finale Adam was kidnapped by terrorists and Operations was shot trying to rescue him; Jones, who turned out to be Nikita's father, gave his own life in order to free the boy, and Nikita became the new head of Section One. Michael and Adam left a tearful Nikita ("I love you") to go "far away."

Based on the French film *La Femme Nikita* (1990), which was remade in the U.S. as *Point of No Return* (1993).

LADIES BE SEATED (*Quiz/Audience Participation*)

FIRST TELECAST: *April 22, 1949*
LAST TELECAST: *June 10, 1949*
BROADCAST HISTORY:

Apr 1949–Jun 1949, ABC Fri 8:30–9:00

EMCEE:

Tom Moore

ASSISTANT:

Phil Patton

This TV version of the long-running radio show featured a quiz and penalty stunts for members of the studio audience. The stunts were similar to those generally found on such shows, such as a blindfolded couple after an apple on a string, a man racing to put on women's clothes, etc. From Chicago.

LADIES MAN (*Situation Comedy*)

FIRST TELECAST: *September 20, 1999*
LAST TELECAST: *June 27, 2001*
BROADCAST HISTORY:

Sep 1999–Feb 2000, CBS Mon 8:30–9:00
Apr 2000–May 2000, CBS Mon 8:30–9:00
Jul 2000–Sep 2000, CBS Mon 8:30–9:00
Jun 2001, CBS Wed 8:00–9:00

CAST:

Jimmy Stiles .... Alfred Molina
Donna Stiles .... Sharon Lawrence
Mitzi Stiles .... Betty White
Peaches (1999–2000) .... Dixie Carter
Claire Stiles (1999–2000) .... Park Overall
Bonnie Stiles (age 15) (pilot only) .... Mariam Parris
Bonnie Stiles (1999–2000) .... Shawna Waldron
Bonnie Stiles (2001) .... Kaley Cuoco
Wendy Stiles (10) (pilot only) .... Katie Volding
Wendy Stiles .... Alexa Vega
Gene .... Stephen Root
Sabrina (2001) .... Elizabeth Beckwith
Alex Trebek (voice) (2001) .... Himself
Terry (2001) .... Kathleen McClellan
Chester Stiles (2001) ..... Nicholas and Noah Hight

Jimmy made furniture for a living and worked out of his Los Angeles home. A big, happy guy who bumbled a lot ("What'd I do?") he was surrounded by women. Living with him were Donna, his very pregnant second wife; their tomboy daughter, Wendy; Bonnie, his blossoming daughter by first wife, Claire, and Mitzi, his sarcastic mother. As if that was not enough, Peaches, his wealthy mother-in-law, showed up periodically to spoil her granddaughter and step-granddaughter. Gene, a Jaguar salesman who had been married four times, was Jimmy's best friend and regular golf partner. In the premiere Donna gave birth to—surprise—a son. Despite Jimmy's misgivings, they named him Chester, after Donna's late father.

A year after being canceled, *Ladies Man* returned to the CBS schedule with new episodes. Jimmy was hired as a contractor remodeling a house owned by game-show host Alex Trebek, and Sabrina was the insecure young architect with whom he was working. Jimmy's neurotic buddy Gene was dating Terry, a sexy but somewhat spaced-out young divorcée.

LADIES' MAN (*Situation Comedy*)

FIRST TELECAST: *October 27, 1980*

LAST TELECAST: *February 21, 1981*

BROADCAST HISTORY:

Oct 1980–Jan 1981, CBS Mon 8:30–9:00
Feb 1981, CBS Sat 9:30–10:00

CAST:

Alan Thackeray .... Lawrence Pressman
Amy Thackeray..................... Natasha Ryan
Elaine Holstein....................... Louise Sorel
Betty Brill.......................... Karen Morrow
Gretchen .... Simone Griffeth
Susan................................ Allison Argo
Andrea Gibbons.................... Betty Kennedy
Reggie .... Herb Edelman

It seemed as if everyone in Alan Thackeray's life was a woman. He was a single parent, raising a precocious eight-year-old daughter (Amy), and often had to seek the advice of Betty, a friendly housewife who lived in his apartment building. His job was that of a feature writer for *Women's Life* magazine, where his boss was sophisticated, dominant Elaine Holstein, and his co-workers, all extremely attractive, were serious Gretchen, militant feminist Susan, and romantic Andrea. His first assignment there was to write an article called "Sexual Harassment and the Working Woman," a subject for which firsthand research was a little difficult. The only other male around was *Women's Life*'s harried bookkeeper, Reggie.

LADY BLUE (*Police Drama*)

FIRST TELECAST: *September 15, 1985*

LAST TELECAST: *January 25, 1986*

BROADCAST HISTORY:

Sep 1985, ABC Sun 9:00–11:00
Sep 1985–Oct 1985, ABC Thu 9:00–10:00
Nov 1985–Jan 1986, ABC Sat 9:00–10:00

CAST:

Det. Katy Mahoney..................... Jamie Rose
Chief Det. Terry McNichols.......... Danny Aiello
Sgt. Gino Gianelli .... Ron Dean
Cassady.......................... Bruce A. Young
Capt. Flynn .... Ralph Foody

This tough lady detective reminded a lot of critics of someone else ("Skirty Harry"? "Dirty Harriet"?). Working the seedier side of Chicago, she tracked down drug pushers, money launderers, rapists, and other slime, blasting away with her .357 magnum more often than Internal Affairs would have liked (but, of course, those she blew away were always guilty). Though she could be reasonably sexy, the violence in her life tended to get in the way of any truly sensitive relationships. Terry was her worried-but-supportive boss, and Gino a fellow officer.

Filmed on location in Chicago.

LAMB'S GAMBOL, THE (*Musical Variety*)

FIRST TELECAST: *February 27, 1949*

LAST TELECAST: *May 22, 1949*

BROADCAST HISTORY:

Feb 1949–Mar 1949, NBC Sun 8:30–9:00
Mar 1949–May 1949, NBC Sun 8:00–8:30

Musical variety program using the resources of New York's famed theatrical association, the Lamb's Club. Broadway stars, old vaudevillians, and newcomers appeared each week to do their turns, or to reverse roles (such as a tragedian doing a song-and-dance routine). A different host presided each week, and there were no regulars.

LANCER (*Western*)

FIRST TELECAST: *September 24, 1968*

LAST TELECAST: *September 9, 1971*

BROADCAST HISTORY:

Sep 1968–Jun 1970, CBS Tue 7:30–8:30
May 1971–Sep 1971, CBS Thu 8:00–9:00

CAST:

Johnny Madrid Lancer .... James Stacy
Scott Lancer .... Wayne Maunder
Murdoch Lancer................... Andrew Duggan
Teresa O'Brien .... Elizabeth Baur
Jelly Hoskins (1969–1970) .... Paul Brinegar

Set in California during the 1870s, *Lancer* was the story of the struggles of a landowner against locals who were trying to take over his property by force. Old Murdoch Lancer was no longer able to defend his cattle and sheep ranch in the San Joaquin Valley by himself, and even trying to run it with only the help of his attractive young ward, Teresa, had become difficult. At his behest his two sons (from different marriages) came to the ranch to help their father. The half brothers had never met each other and had widely divergent backgrounds. Johnny was a drifter/gunfighter who had spent most of his life wandering around the border towns of the Southwest. Scott was a sophisticated college graduate who had been living in Boston. Despite their differences, they learned to respect each other and help their father manage his vast real estate holdings. Jelly Hoskins, a crochety old ranch hand, became a regular member of the cast for the second season. Yet another Lancer, hillbilly Chad Lancer (John Beck), was introduced in the spring of 1970 in anticipation of a third season, which did not materialize. The episodes telecast during the summer of 1971 were all reruns.

LAND OF THE GIANTS (*Science Fiction*)

FIRST TELECAST: *September 22, 1968*

LAST TELECAST: *September 6, 1970*

BROADCAST HISTORY:

Sep 1968–Sep 1970, ABC Sun 7:00–8:00

CAST:

Capt. Steve Burton .... Gary Conway
Mark Wilson .... Don Matheson
Barry Lockridge .... Stefen Arngrim
Dan Erikson......................... Don Marshall
Valerie Scott .... Deanna Lund
Betty Hamilton.................... Heather Young
Cdr. Alexander Fitzhugh............. Kurt Kasznar
Inspector Kobrick .... Kevin Hagen

CREATOR/PRODUCER:

Irwin Allen

This science-fiction fantasy concerned seven very small people in a very large world. Seven Earthlings had been on a suborbital flight from the U.S. to London in the mid–1980s when their craft was drawn into a "space warp." They landed in a strange world, much like Earth but with inhabitants 12 times their size. As the space castaways attempted to repair their rocketship in order to try and get home, they were continually menaced by giant children, huge pets and insects, and inhabitants who would exhibit them as freaks or experiment on them.

Capt. Steve Burton, his co-pilot Dan Erikson, and stewardess Betty Hamilton made up the crew of the lost craft, while on the passenger roster were engineer-tycoon Mark Wilson, jet-set (rocket-set?) heiress Valerie Scott, 12-year-old Barry and his dog Chipper, and mystery passenger Cdr. Fitzhugh. Tracking the Earth people down in the giant world was the responsibility of Inspector Kobrick of S.I.B., a security agency.

LAND'S END (*Detective*)

BROADCAST HISTORY:

Syndicated only
60 minutes
Produced: *1995–1996* (22 episodes)
Released: *September 1995*

CAST:

Mike Land .... Fred Dryer
Willis P. Dunleevy .... Geoffrey Lewis
Dave "Thunder" Thornton .... Tim Thomerson
Courtney Saunders .... Pamela Bowen
Chief Raoul Ruiz .... William Marquez

Sun, surf, bikinis, and gunfire mixed in this action series. Mike Land was a veteran L.A.P.D. cop who left the force after a case that had taken months to bring to trial resulted in the acquittal of a drug lord. He moved to sunny Cabo San Lucas, where he worked as a free-lance P.I. with the help of his hustler-buddy Willis, and also served as director of security for the Westin Regina Resort in town. Courtney was his sexy boss at the hotel, and Dave his friend who ran a charter fishing boat, *Solmar VI*.

Filmed on location in Cabo San Lucas, Mexico.

LANIGAN'S RABBI (*Police Drama*)

FIRST TELECAST: *January 30, 1977*
LAST TELECAST: *July 3, 1977*
BROADCAST HISTORY:

Jan 1977–Jul 1977, NBC Sun Various times

CAST:

Chief Paul Lanigan .... Art Carney
Rabbi David Small .... Bruce Solomon
Kate Lanigan .... Janis Paige
Miriam Small .... Janet Margolin
Bobbie Whittaker .... Barbara Carney
Lt. Osgood .... Robert Doyle

Paul Lanigan was the police chief of the small town of Cameron, California. A local rabbi and close personal friend of his was David Small. David was an amateur criminologist who had become quite good at analyzing clues and deducing the perpetrator of a crime. He had become so good, in fact, that his friend Paul had become somewhat dependent on his assistance in cracking tough cases. Not only did they work together, they spent many evenings socializing with their wives, who tended to get rather aggravated when the conversation inevitably turned to the latest case. The role of the persistent local reporter, Bobbie Whittaker, was played by Art Carney's daughter Barbara.

Lanigan's Rabbi was based on a series of novels by Harry Kemelman, the first of which was *Friday the Rabbi Slept Late.* In 1977 it aired in rotation with *Columbo, McCloud,* and *McMillan* under the umbrella title *The NBC Sunday Mystery Movie.*

LANNY ROSS SHOW, THE, see *Swift Show, The*

LARAMIE (*Western*)

FIRST TELECAST: *September 15, 1959*
LAST TELECAST: *September 17, 1963*
BROADCAST HISTORY:

Sep 1959–Sep 1963, NBC Tue 7:30–8:30

CAST:

Slim Sherman .... John Smith
Jess Harper .... Robert Fuller
Jonesy (1959–1960) .... Hoagy Carmichael
Andy Sherman (1959–1961) ... Bobby Crawford, Jr.
Mike Williams (1961–1963) .... Dennis Holmes
Daisy Cooper (1961–1963) .... Spring Byington
Mort Corey (1960–1963) .... Stuart Randall

Two brothers determined to maintain the family ranch after the death of their father were the central characters in this Western, which was set in the Wyoming Territory of the 1870s. After their father had been shot by a land-grabber, the responsibility of running the ranch had fallen to Slim and his 14-year-old brother Andy. Although possessed of great potential, the ranch had been barely able to provide a living for the Shermans before their father's death. Only Jonesy, a friend of their father who had helped raise them, was around to help run the ranch. In the first episode, however, a drifter named Jess Harper wandered in and was persuaded to settle down and throw in his lot with them. In addition to raising cattle, the Shermans used their ranch as a relay station for stagecoach traffic into and out of nearby Laramie, which accounted for many a desperado passing through.

There were cast changes. Jonesy, played by veteran singer-composer Hoagy Carmichael, left the show at the start of the second season, while Sheriff Mort Corey of Laramie became a regular. Young Andy, who had previously left the ranch and appeared only occasionally, was gone entirely by 1961, at the same time that two new members were added to the household. Mike Williams, an orphan whose parents had been killed by Indians, joined the family, and Daisy Cooper took over the job of housekeeper and surrogate mother in the previously all-male household.

LAREDO (*Western*)

FIRST TELECAST: *September 16, 1965*
LAST TELECAST: *September 1, 1967*
BROADCAST HISTORY:

Sep 1965–Sep 1966, NBC Thu 8:30–9:30
Sep 1966–Sep 1967, NBC Fri 10:00–11:00

CAST:

Reese Bennett .... Neville Brand
Chad Cooper .... Peter Brown
Joe Riley .... William Smith
Capt. Edward Parmalee .... Philip Carey
Erik Hunter (1966–1967) .... Robert Wolders

Stories of the Texas Rangers in the post–Civil War era were told with humor as well as action in this series. The stories centered around three members of Company B and their senior officer, Capt. Parmalee. Former Union Army officer Reese Bennett was already in his 40s when he joined the Rangers, and his age was quite a source of amusement to the two much younger rangers who were his partners. Riley had been a gunfighter whose activities were not always completely legal, and he had joined the Rangers because he liked action but wanted sanctuary from lawmen in other territories who were after him. Cooper, a Boston native and wartime member of the Border Patrol, joined the Rangers after the war to continue his hunt for the American gunrunners who had sold arms to the Mexicans who had wiped out most of his comrades. All three retained a sense of humor about life, however, and Capt. Parmalee, a stern man who assigned them their missions, sometimes found their jokes and horseplay rather frustrating. Erik Hunter was added to the cast in the second season as a new Ranger.

LARRY KING LIVE (*Discussion/Call-In*)

BROADCAST HISTORY:

CNN
60 minutes
Produced: *1985–*
Premiered: *June 3, 1985*

HOST:

Larry King

Larry King brought his Washington-based radio call-in show to television more or less intact—thick-rimmed glasses, hunched shoulders, shirtsleeves and all. It obviously wasn't his appearance, or slick production, that made *Larry King Live* one of the best-known programs on cable. Solid interviews with leading newsmakers and an intelligent audience characterized the series, which aired five nights a week in prime time. Perhaps its high point, at least to date, came during the 1992 presidential election campaign, when *Larry King Live* became the forum of choice for all the major candidates. Maverick Ross Perot announced his candidacy on the show. The following year it was the site of a formal debate between Perot and Vice President Al Gore on the NAFTA trade bill.

In 1993 the program expanded to six nights a week by adding Saturday.

LARRY STORCH SHOW, THE (*Comedy/Variety*)

FIRST TELECAST: *July 11, 1953*
LAST TELECAST: *September 12, 1953*
BROADCAST HISTORY:

Jul 1953–Sep 1953, CBS Sat 8:00–9:00

REGULARS:

Larry Storch
Ray Bloch and His Orchestra

Young nightclub comic Larry Storch was the star of this live 1953 summer replacement for *The Jackie Gleason Show*. Guest stars were featured along with Larry's odd assortment of sketch characters, built up from his club act. Among the characters were Victor, a 10-year-old troublemaking monster; Smilie Higgins, a TV cowboy; and Railroad Jack, a philosophical hobo.

LASH OF THE WEST (*Western*)

FIRST TELECAST: *January 4, 1953*
LAST TELECAST: *April 26, 1953*
BROADCAST HISTORY:

Jan 1953–Apr 1953, ABC Sun 6:30–6:45

CAST:

Marshal Lash La Rue .... Lash La Rue
Deputy Fuzzy Q. Jones .... Al "Fuzzy" St. John
Flapjack .... Cliff Taylor
Stratton .... John Martin

Cowboy star Lash La Rue recycled his B-grade Western movies of the late 1940s via this early, 15-minute TV series. Lash appeared at the opening of each show in his modern-day U.S. marshal's office and related a story about his grandfather—who looked just like him, was also a marshal, and was also named Lash La Rue. The scene then shifted to clips from Lash's old Westerns, in which his black-garbed "granddad" tracked down villains with the help of his bullwhip and his faithful, bewhiskered sidekick, Fuzzy Q. Jones.

The cheaply made 15-minute films were originally put together for syndication in 1952, but turned up on the ABC network on Sundays in early 1953, and on ABC's Saturday morning schedule from March to May 1953.

LASSIE (*Adventure*)

FIRST TELECAST: *September 12, 1954*
LAST TELECAST: *September 12, 1971*
BROADCAST HISTORY:

Sep 1954–Jun 1955, CBS Sun 7:00–7:30
Sep 1955–Sep 1971, CBS Sun 7:00–7:30
(In first-run syndication from fall 1971–fall 1974)

CAST:

Jeff Miller (1954–1957) .... Tommy Rettig
Ellen Miller (1954–1957) .... Jan Clayton
"Gramps" Miller (1954–1957) .... George Cleveland
Sylvester "Porky" Brockway (1954–1957) .... Donald Keeler
Matt Brockway (1954–1957) .... Paul Maxey
Timmy (1957–1964) .... Jon Provost
Doc Weaver (1954–1964) .... Arthur Space
Ruth Martin (1957–1958) .... Cloris Leachman
Paul Martin (1957–1958) .... Jon Shepodd
Uncle Petrie Martin (1958–1959) ... George Chandler
Ruth Martin (1958–1964) .... June Lockhart
Paul Martin (1958–1964) .... Hugh Reilly
Boomer Bates (1958–1959) .... Todd Ferrell
Cully Wilson (1958–1964) .... Andy Clyde
Corey Stuart (1964–1969) .... Robert Bray
Scott Turner (1968–1970) .... Jed Allan
Bob Erickson (1968–1970) .... Jack De Mave
Garth Holden (1972–1973) .... Ron Hayes
Ron Holden (1972–1974) .... Skip Burton
Mike Holden (1972–1974) .... Joshua Albee
Dale Mitchell (1972–1974) .... Larry Wilcox
Keith Holden (1973–1974) .... Larry Pennell
Lucy Baker (1973–1974) .... Pamelyn Ferdin
Sue Lambert (1973–1974) .... Sherry Boucher

LASSIE'S TRAINER:

Rudd Weatherwax

The one constant in this favorite long-running children's adventure series was Lassie, a brave, loyal, and remarkably intelligent collie. Lassie was always alert, ready to help her masters and protect them from evil and adversity. In fact, her heroics were often incredible—leading lost persons to safety, warning of all sorts of impending disasters, tending the sick and manipulating various human devices with ease. Fortunately Lassie was able to shift her allegiances periodically, for she was required to go through several sets of owners during her long career.

As originally conceived, *Lassie* was the story of a young boy and his companion collie. The boy was Jeff Miller, who lived on a small modern farm outside the town of Calverton with his widowed mother and his grandfather. In the spring of 1957 a runaway orphan boy named Timmy was brought in by Lassie and joined the Miller household. That fall Gramps died suddenly (actor George Cleveland in fact died soon after the start of the season). Ellen Miller found that she and Jeff could not work the farm alone, so she sold it to the Martins and moved to the city. Lassie and the orphan Timmy remained behind in the care of the Martins, who were childless, and Timmy became Lassie's new companion in weekly adventures.

By 1964 the Martins decided to leave the farm, responding to an advertisement for free land in Australia. Timmy went with them but Lassie could not go—due to animal quarantine regulations. The collie was left for a time in the care of an elderly friend of the family, Cully Wilson, but he subsequently suffered a heart attack. Lassie trotted off to get help from forest ranger Corey Stuart, and soon found herself with a new master. By this time Lassie was beginning to get the feeling that human masters are a temporary thing. In her adventures with ranger Corey, the scope of her exploits widened considerably, as she traveled with him to various parts of the country and situations far more exotic than those encountered around the farm. The premise of a small boy and his dog was gone completely.

In the fall of 1968 Corey was seriously hurt fighting a forest fire, and the Forest Service chief assigned two other rangers, Scott Turner and Bob Erickson, to watch over Lassie. By this time, however, her exploits were often independent of human help, and her contact with the two new rangers was not as frequent as it had been with Corey. By the start of the final season Lassie had become a wanderer without any human companionship at all. The ultimate step in her progression to independence came in a special seven-part story that began the 1970–1971 season. Lassie met a male collie, fell in love, and bore him a litter of puppies. In reality that would have been quite a trick, for all of the many collies that had portrayed Lassie over the years were male.

Although no longer on CBS, *Lassie* remained in production as a syndicated series for three more seasons—during the first as a wanderer similar to her final network season, and in the last two with a new family on the Holden ranch in Solvang, California. Garth Holden ran the ranch with the help of his sons, Ron and Mike, and his assistant Dale Mitchell. When Garth left to start up another ranch, at the start of the 1973–1974 season, his brother Keith arrived to watch over the ranch and his nephews. Lucy Baker was the little deaf girl who lived nearby and Sue Lambert was the local veterinarian. ABC brought Lassie back in an animated version, *Lassie's Rescue Rangers,* which ran on weekend mornings from September 1973 to August 1975. See *The New Lassie* for a 1980s sequel that revealed, at last, Timmy's real name!

Lassie originated in *Lassie Come Home*, a best-selling 1940 novel by Eric Knight which told the story of a poor family forced to sell its beloved collie, who then managed to make her way back to them against all odds. The book was made into a very successful 1943 movie starring a young Roddy McDowall and Elizabeth Taylor, among others, and this was followed by more *Lassie* movies and a radio series from 1947 to 1950.

LASSIE AND TIMMY, syndicated title for *Lassie*

LAST CALL (*Discussion*)

BROADCAST HISTORY:

Syndicated only
30 minutes
Produced: *1994–1995*
Released: *September 1994*

PANELISTS:

Sue Ellicott
Brianne Leary
Tad Low (1994)
Terry McDonell (1994)
Elvis Mitchell (1994)
"Stuttering John" Melendez (1995)
Herman Williams (1995)

"We're a news show, sort of" was host Terry McDonell's description of this youthful, late-night discussion/bull session. *Last Call* did cover stories and issues in the current day's news. Some were serious, some were gags, and some had elements of both. The five panelists were Sue Ellicott, the vérry English former North American correspondent for *The Sunday Times* of London; actress Brianne Leary; hip Tad Low, from *MTV News*; slightly more formal Terry McDonell, editor and publisher of *Sports Afield*; and Elvis "No Elvis jokes!" Mitchell, black showbiz reporter for *Spin* magazine and movie critic for National Public Radio. The set resembled a living room with a pool table and a huge big-screen TV that was used for out-of-studio segments. Low was the most irreverent and silly of the group, and Leary, who spent much of her time on location, was also on the lighter side. There were in-studio guests and semiregular contributors like *Washington Post* TV critic Tom Shales and ESPN Radio's Fabulous Sports Babe. Guitarist/composer Mike Errico appeared each Friday to sing the "News Jam," his summary of the week's news.

At the end of the initial 13-week run McDonell and Low decided they had had enough, and Mitchell, after a few January appearances, threw in the towel too. When new episodes started airing in January, Ellicott was back as the host and the format had been modified to focus on a single topic each night. "Stuttering John" Melendez, sidekick of radio shock jock Howard Stern and later Herman Williams, were featured as semiregular panelists, and each night's show featured guest panelists. Former pro football player Nick Lowery showed up a number of times, and Brianne Leary was still seen very occasionally as the show's "special correspondent." Topics included sexism, body piercing, racism, the O. J. Simpson murder trial (for a time comedienne Mother Love was providing nightly updates on the trial), young people who murdered homosexual men, ESP, and the effectiveness of Congress. The changes didn't help, and by the end of March, *Last Call* was history.

LAST CALL WITH CARSON DALY (*Talk*)

FIRST TELECAST: *January 8, 2002*
LAST TELECAST:
BROADCAST HISTORY:

Jan 2002–Aug 2002, NBC Mon–Thu 1:35–2:35 A.M.
Sep 2002– , NBC Mon–Fri 1:35–2:35 A.M.

HOST:

Carson Daly

Carson Daly, the young, very hip host of MTV's *Total Request Live*, hosted this late-night talk show that replaced the long-running *Later* on NBC's wee-hours schedule. The set was extremely simple (two big chairs in a warehouselike room), and the guests were mostly the young and the hip, including many from the music and movie industries such as record mogul/thug "Suge" Knight, Sean "P. Diddy" Combs, Katie Holmes, Andy Dick, Kid Rock and Chris Rock, with a few oddballs such as supermodel Heidi Klum and conservative news commentator Bill O'Reilly thrown in.

LAST CONVERTIBLE, THE (*Drama*)
FIRST TELECAST: *June 28, 1981*
LAST TELECAST: *July 20, 1981*
BROADCAST HISTORY:
Jun 1981, NBC Sun 9:00–11:00
Jun 1981–Jul 1981, NBC Mon 10:00–11:00
CAST:
Russ Currier .... Perry King
George Virdon .... Bruce Boxleitner
Chris Farris .... Deborah Raffin
Ron "Dal" Dalrymple .... Edward Albert
Terry Garrigan .... John Shea
Nancy Van Breymer .... Caroline Smith
Ann Rowan .... Kim Darby
Kay Haddon .... Sharon Gless
Liz Baynor .... Tracy Brooks Swope
Paul McCreed .... Fred McCarren
Sheilah Garrigan .... Stacey Nelin
Rob Dalrymple .... Shawn Stevens
Jean R. G. R. desBarres .... Michael Nouri

The Last Convertible was an adaptation of Anton Myrer's romantic novel following the loves and lives of five Harvard University roommates from their arrival on campus in 1940 through their 25th reunion in 1969. Calling themselves "The Five Fusiliers," the young men shared good times, a luxurious Packard convertible dubbed "The Empress," and the love of a beautiful Radcliffe student named Chris. Jean, the original owner of the car, died while fighting with the Free French during World War II, but roommates Russ, George, Terry, and Dal (who married Chris during the war) all survived. During the years that followed their lives continued to intertwine, with Chris at the center of much of the jealousy and passion, and the car as the symbol of their lost youth.

The Last Convertible originally aired as a three-part mini-series in September 1979, and was rerun in weekly installments in 1981.

LAST FRONTIER, THE (*Situation Comedy*)
FIRST TELECAST: *June 3, 1996*
LAST TELECAST: *July 8, 1996*
BROADCAST HISTORY:
Jun 1996–Jul 1996, FOX Mon 8:30–9:00
CAST:
Billy McPherson .... Anthony Starke
Reed Garfield .... John Terlesky
Andy .... Patrick Labyorteaux
Matt Garfield .... David Kriegel
Kate .... Jessica Tuck
Joy Garfield .... Leigh-Allyn Baker

Kate was the personnel director for Ridley International, a conglomerate building a tourist resort in Anchorage in this buddy comedy notable mostly for its location. Looking to rent a guest cottage, she ended up with three rather immature twenty-something male roommates. They were Reed, who ran an outdoor adventure company; Andy, a horny, obnoxious Air Force intelligence officer obsessed with flying saucers; and Billy, a conservative architect/builder. Matt was Reed's shaggy-haired younger brother, who had moved out when he married perky Joy six weeks earlier. Matt and Joy ran the Brew Pub, the rustic bar where Joy was a waitress and everybody hung out in their spare time.

LAST OF THE WILD, see *Lorne Greene's Last of the Wild*

LAST PRECINCT, THE (*Situation Comedy*)
FIRST TELECAST: *April 11, 1986*
LAST TELECAST: *May 30, 1986*
BROADCAST HISTORY:
Apr 1986–May 1986, NBC Fri 9:00–10:00
CAST:
Captain Rick Wright .... Adam West
Sgt. Price Pascall .... Jonathan Perpich
Off. William Raider ("Raid") .... Rick Ducommun
Det. Sgt. Tremaine "Night Train" Lane .... Ernie Hudson
Off. Mel Brubaker .... Randi Brooks
Alphabet (Shivaramanbhai Poonchwalla) .... Vijay Amritraj
King .... Pete Willcox
Butch .... Keenan Wynn
Sundance .... Hank Rolike
Off. Rina Starland .... Lucy Lee Flippin
Lt. Ronald Hobbs .... Wings Hauser
Sgt. Martha Haggerty .... Yana Nirvana
Justin Dial .... Geoffrey Elliott
Chief Bludhorn .... James Cromwell

Adam 12 was never like this. The title *The Last Precinct* referred to both the location of Los Angeles' 56th precinct (on the jurisdictional border between the L.A.P.D. and the county sheriff's office) and the fact that it was the dumping ground for all the eccentrics and misfits of the L.A.P.D. In charge of the precinct, more or less, was straight-arrow Capt. Rick Wright, who often seemed oblivious to the goings-on around him. His officers included handsome Price Pascall, the closest the 56th had to an effective, relatively normal policeman; Raid, a bumbling, overweight motorcycle cop; Rina, the records clerk with the hots for Raid; Night Train, a black plainclothes officer who dressed like a pimp; Mel Brubaker, a sexy, mini-skirted officer who had been a man before his/her sex-change operation; King, an Elvis Presley impersonator; Alphabet, a stereotypically polite Indian exchange officer; and over-the-hill veterans Butch and Sundance. The 56th was always in competition with the nearby county sheriff's office, run by Lt. Hobbs and his Nazi-like assistant Sgt. Haggerty.

LAST RESORT, THE (*Situation Comedy*)
FIRST TELECAST: *September 19, 1979*
LAST TELECAST: *March 17, 1980*
BROADCAST HISTORY:
Sep 1979–Oct 1979, CBS Wed 8:00–8:30
Dec 1979–Mar 1980, CBS Mon 8:30–9:00
CAST:
Michael Lerner .... Larry Breeding
Gail Collins .... Stephanie Faracy
Duane Kaminsky .... Zane Lasky
Zach Comstock .... Walter Olkewicz
Jeffrey Barron .... Ray Underwood
Mrs. Trilling .... Dorothy Konrad
Kevin .... John Fujioka
Murray .... Robert Costanzo

Summer resorts in the Catskill Mountains of upstate New York have always depended on college students as a source of cheap, unskilled labor, and the Last Resort was no exception. Four of the college students working there for the summer were bright, romantic premed Michael Lerner; bookish Duane Kaminsky; bumbling, overweight Zach Comstock; and snobbish Jeffrey Barron. Also on the staff were Gail Collins, a young woman who had run away from her wealthy husband and become the pastry chef despite a minimal knowledge of baking; Kevin, the Japanese chef who pretended not to understand English when it suited him; and Murray the maitre d', who ran the kitchen staff like an army unit, criticizing everybody and screaming continuously. Fortunately for the rest of the staff, Murray was not very bright and could easily be tricked by almost anyone.

A ratings failure when it premiered, *The Last Resort* was pulled from the CBS schedule after only three episodes. It returned two months later on a different night, but never found an audience and was permanently canceled in the spring.

LAST WORD, THE (*Informational/Panel*)

FIRST TELECAST: *June 2, 1957*
LAST TELECAST: *May 25, 1958*
BROADCAST HISTORY:
Jun 1957–Sep 1957, CBS Sun 6:00–6:30
Mar 1958–May 1958, CBS Sun 6:00–6:30
HOST:
Dr. Bergen Evans

The wonderful world of grammar and language was explored each week in this series which requested viewers to send in questions to be discussed by Dr. Evans and a rotating panel of linguistic experts. As the CBS press release announcing its premiere said, "the series would cover . . . such things as euphemisms, regional dialects, occupational lingo, metaphors and similes, pronunciation, British versus American words and usage, clichés, figures of speech, slang, secret languages (like pig Latin), journalese . . ." The series premiered in January as a Sunday afternoon entry but moved into evening hours for the summer of 1957 and the spring of 1958. *The Last Word*'s final Sunday afternoon telecast took place in October 1959.

LAST WORD, THE (*News*)

FIRST TELECAST: *October 26, 1982*
LAST TELECAST: *April 22, 1983*
BROADCAST HISTORY:
Oct 1982–Apr 1983, ABC Mon–Fri 12:00–1:00 A.M.
REGULARS:
Greg Jackson
Phil Donahue

This late-night informational series was telecast live from New York, and hosted by newsman Greg Jackson, who interviewed notables from politics, sports, and other fields, and invited viewers' opinions via toll-free national telephone lines. Phil Donahue contributed a taped interview segment from Chicago.

LATE FRIDAY (*Comedy Variety*)

FIRST TELECAST: *January 5, 2001*
LAST TELECAST: *August 30, 2002*
BROADCAST HISTORY:
Jan 2001–Aug 2002, NBC Fri 1:35–2:35 A.M.

A late-night showcase for up-and-coming young stand-up comics, set in a club atmosphere. Among the guest hosts were Kevin Nealon, Bobcat Goldthwait, Joe Rogan and Jeff Garlin; at times the performing acts would introduce each other.

LATE LATE SHOW, THE (*Talk*)

FIRST TELECAST: *January 9, 1995*
LAST TELECAST:
BROADCAST HISTORY:
Jan 1995– , CBS Mon–Fri 12:35–1:35 A.M.
HOST:
Tom Snyder (1995–1999)
Craig Kilborn (1999–)

In the 13 years after *The Tomorrow Show* left the air, Tom Snyder kept himself busy. From 1982 to 1985 he was a local TV news anchor in New York and later Los Angeles, from 1987 to 1992 he hosted a nighttime radio call-in show on one of the ABC radio networks, and from early 1993 to late 1994 he hosted the *Tom Snyder* call-in talk show on cable's CNBC. The critical acclaim for the latter attracted CBS' attention and Snyder was wooed back to network TV.

The format for *The Late Late Show* with Tom Snyder was very similar to his CNBC program. Each night Snyder chatted with one or two in-studio guests—generally show business celebrities, politicians, and other people in the news—and took calls from viewers. Although he could still ask probing questions, and occasionally be a little testy, Tom had mellowed over the years from the brash fellow he had been in his earlier network appearances.

Aired live from CBS' Television City in Los Angeles, *The Late Late Show* was simulcast on the CBS Radio Network, and the call-in segments included both TV viewers and radio listeners. Over time, the number of CBS affiliates airing the simulcast dwindled, but there were still a few diehards carrying it until the last telecast of *The Late Late Show with Tom Snyder* on March 27, 1999.

When Snyder departed, the show was renamed and overhauled to suit the personality and skills of sarcastic new host Craig Kilborn, who had previously hosted *The Daily Show* on cable's Comedy Central. *The Late Late Show with Craig Kilborn* replaced the more serious discussions that had been staples during the Snyder era with casual chatter, comedy bits, and occasional musical guests. Two regular features, brought over from *The Daily Show*, were "In the News," a satirical parody of the headline stories of the day, and "Five Questions," to test the intelligence of one of his guests.

LATE NIGHT WITH CONAN O'BRIEN (*Talk*)

FIRST TELECAST: *September 13, 1993*
LAST TELECAST:
BROADCAST HISTORY:
Sep 1993– , NBC Mon–Fri 12:35–1:35 A.M.
HOST:
Conan O'Brien
REGULARS:
Andy Richter (1993–2000)
Max Weinberg Seven

Thirty-year-old comedy writer Conan O'Brien got his big break on NBC's late-late show when David Letterman moved to CBS, and he seemed as startled by that as was the audience. (Previously he had been seen on-camera fleetingly on Fox's abortive *Wilton North Report.*) His youthful, offhanded manner wore well with viewers, however, as he interviewed the usual parade of celebrity guests and musical acts. Andy was his rather dense sidekick. The writing staff for the program was drawn mostly from Chicago's improv community and such Eastern bastions of youthful humor as *The Harvard Lampoon*, for which Conan himself had once been a writer.

Among the recurring comic bits were "Triumph the Insult Comic Dog," "If They Mated," "Clutch Cargo," "Pimpbot 5000" and "The Lips," in which photos of politicians and celebrities appeared with someone else's lips superimposed doing the talking.

LATE NIGHT WITH DAVID LETTERMAN (*Talk*)
FIRST TELECAST: *February 2, 1982*
LAST TELECAST: *September 10, 1993*
BROADCAST HISTORY:
Feb 1982–May 1987, NBC Mon–Thu 12:30–1:30 A.M.
Jun 1987–Aug 1991, NBC Mon–Fri 12:30–1:30 A.M.
Sep 1991–Sep 1993, NBC Mon–Fri 12:35–1:35 A.M.
HOST:
David Letterman
BANDLEADER:
Paul Shaffer
WITH:
Calvert DeForest as Larry "Bud" Melman

Late Night with David Letterman was to TV talk shows as Salvador Dali was to traditional painting. It was a real talk show, the elements were all there, but something was a bit off. The pleasant-looking young host would come out each evening, in sports jacket and tie, tell a joke, banter meaninglessly with his spaced-out bandleader, and sit down at his desk to welcome the night's first guest. Then, with mock-serious demeanor, Letterman might interview a mechanic about "celebrities and their auto repairs," or solicit movie reviews from unlikely "experts"—a dentist, for example, about the movie *Reds.* He might present "Small Town News," an ironic perusal of unintentionally funny items from local newspapers; "Stupid Pet Tricks," a demonstration of nonsensical tricks which ordinary people had tried (often unsuccessfully) to teach their pets; "Brush with Greatness" (who was that?); or "Nightcap Theater," one minute's worth of campy clips from old, bad movies, which viewers were presumably missing by watching this show. There were elevator races in the studio building, and walking tours of the streets of New York City (where the show was produced). Many of the bits poked fun at TV's fascination with new technology, in the best tradition of Ernie Kovacs; for example, the "Monkey-cam" (a live camera strapped to the back of a chimpanzee set loose in the studio), and "the 360 degree show" (in which the home picture made one complete rotation in the hour, so that halfway through David and his guests appeared upside down—NBC received a lot of calls about that one).

Letterman also had straight celebrity guests, who were often quite at sea when faced with the host's non-interview style; the guest did all the work. The introductions could be unnerving, too. Sir Alec Guinness was introduced just after the host tossed a carton of eggs into a giant electric fan.

The show had an unstructured, rambling quality. One evening Letterman let the studio audience vote on what it wanted to do that night; another time, he brought a woman up from the audience and let her take over the show—for real—while he disappeared for a lengthy time "to find my false tooth."

Regulars on the show were bandleader Paul Shaffer and a rotund little man with thick-framed glasses named Larry "Bud" Melman, who performed various chores—at the city's main bus terminal handing out hot towels to incoming passengers, or outside the Soviet Consulate distributing pamphlets urging defection and offering American appliances and pornography.

Others seen periodically included Jay Leno, Richard Lewis, Pee-wee Herman, Rita Rudner, Elayne Boosler, Brother Theodore, Carol Leifer, George Muller, and Sandra Bernhard. Appearing in skits from time to time were several of the show's writers, especially Chris Elliott ("guy under the seats," "the fugitive," etc.). Other writers seen included Gerard Mulligan, Larry Jacobson, and Steve O'Donnell.

Late Night with David Letterman in some ways resembled *Fernwood 2-Night*, but instead of being make-believe, it was the real thing. The show *The New York Times* called "an absurdist parody of mass culture" went over the heads of many viewers—who simply didn't find it funny—but a loyal core of fans made it a cult favorite on the late-night schedule.

In 1992 Letterman was passed over for the coveted host spot on *The Tonight Show* in a highly publicized battle with Jay Leno; the following year he left for CBS, where, for a time, he exacted sweet revenge by beating NBC at its own late-night game (see *Late Show with David Letterman*). His last original telecast on NBC was on June 25, 1993, with guest Tom Hanks. The network then aired repeats until September.

LATE SHOW, THE (*Talk*)
FIRST TELECAST: *October 9, 1986*
LAST TELECAST: *October 28, 1988*
BROADCAST HISTORY:
Oct 1986–Dec 1987, FOX Mon–Fri 11:00–12:00 midnight
Jan 1988–Feb 1988, FOX Mon–Fri 11:00–12:00 midnight
Feb 1988–Oct 1988, FOX Mon–Fri 11:30–12:30 A.M.
HOST:
Joan Rivers (1986–1987)
Arsenio Hall (1987)
Ross Shafer (1988)
REGULARS:
Clint Holmes (1986–1987)
Mark Hudson and the Party Boys (1986–1987)
Daniel Rosen (1988)
Mark Campbell (1988)
Jack Mack & the Heart Attack (1988)

This was the inaugural series in Fox Broadcasting's effort to start a fourth national television network and, initially at least, it was a ratings disaster.

The original star was caustic comedienne Joan Rivers, whose career had skyrocketed when she became the "permanent" guest host on *The Tonight Show Starring Johnny Carson* in 1983. The announcement in the spring of 1986 that Joan was leaving *Tonight* to become Johnny's competition that fall was a major media event, providing Fox with much desired publicity—including a heavily promoted feud between Joan and her mentor Carson.

Unfortunately for both Fox and Joan, after the initial curiosity about her show (which looked like a carbon copy of *Tonight* despite claims that it would be different), the audience departed. *The Late Show Starring Joan Rivers* never proved to be serious competition for Carson, and Joan left after the May 15, 1987, telecast. The title was shortened to *The Late Show* and an assortment of rotating guest hosts—most frequently Suzanne Somers and young, black comics Robert Townsend and Arsenio Hall—took over. By the end of the summer Hall had effectively become the regular host, staying until *The Late Show* was replaced by *The Wilton North Report* at the end of the year. Announcer Clint Holmes and orchestra leader Mark Hudson were with the series for its entire 14-month run.

When *The Wilton North Report* was yanked from the Fox schedule after only four weeks on the air, selected reruns of *The Late Show* (primarily with Rivers and Hall) returned until it could be revived with new regulars. Two months later, with virtually no publicity, the revamped *Late Show* premiered on March 10, 1988, with a new announcer (Daniel Rosen), a new band (Jack Mack & the Heart Attack), and a redesigned set. Although there was no permanent host, comedians Jeff Joseph and John Mulrooney were given most of the on-air tryouts early on, until Ross Shafer became the regular host later that spring. He remained with the show until it faded from view.

LATE SHOW WITH DAVID LETTERMAN (*Talk*)
FIRST TELECAST: *August 30, 1993*
LAST TELECAST:
BROADCAST HISTORY:
Aug 1993– , CBS 11:35 P.M.–12:35 A.M.
REGULARS:
David Letterman
Paul Shaffer and the CBS Orchestra
Leonard Tepper (1994–1998)

David Letterman had hosted *Late Night with David Letterman* for more than a decade following Johnny Carson's *Tonight Show*, and when Carson retired there were those, including Dave, who had assumed that when the king retired Prince David would inherit the throne. Unfortunately, those people did not include the NBC programming bosses, who gave *The Tonight Show* to Jay Leno, the show's regular guest host. Snubbed, Letterman jumped at CBS' offer of $42 million to appear on CBS opposite Leno's *Tonight Show* when his contract with NBC ran out in 1993. NBC did not take kindly to Dave's defection. For a time it even threatened legal action if he attempted to use comic bits like "Stupid Pet Tricks" and the "Top 10 List" on another network because, according to them, having been developed while he was on NBC, those bits remained the "intellectual property" of NBC. Dave laughed at their threats and used them anyway.

Late Show with David Letterman looked pretty much like the *Late Night* show Dave had done on NBC, with a few changes. The Ed Sullivan Theater, where it was housed (the same theater used for the long-running variety show that left the air in 1971), was considerably larger than his old studio at NBC and had room for a much larger audience. Paul Shaffer's band, rechristened the CBS Orchestra, had a few more players than the NBC version, and Dave dressed a little more conservatively. Bumbling Calvert DeForest still showed up once in a while (by the late 1990s only once or twice a year), but as himself, not using his Larry "Bud" Melman alias from NBC days. Another occasional character was Leonard Tepper as the bald guy who did stupid things. Isolated as it was from the other CBS facilities, Dave couldn't wander into other shows in progess as he had at NBC. He did, however, take cameras into a number of the small stores in a new "Meet Our Neighbors" segment and made minor celebrities out of novelty store clerks Sirajul Islam and Mujibar Rahman and deli owner Rupert Jee. In February 1994 he even sent his mother, Dorothy, to Lillehammer, Norway, as the *Late Show*'s special correspondent to the Winter Olympics, which were being covered by CBS, and that summer he sent Sirajul and Mujibar across the country on a promotional tour for *Late Show*. Since the neighborhood did not have as much traffic as his NBC location, he frequently got the local police to close the side street so he could use it for everything from a tennis court, to a human cannonball, to a test of the power of a New York City firehose.

When *Late Show* premiered there was only one television market in which it was not carried—Sioux City, Iowa. Dave made a running joke of the fact, naming Sioux City the "Home Office" of the *Late Show* Top 10 List. The people of Sioux City, in response, put a sign on the old vacated city hall proclaiming it the official *Late Show* "Home Office." One year after the show's premiere, KMEG-TV, the CBS affiliate in Sioux City, in response to local complaints and in recognition of the fact that Letterman had had higher ratings than Leno for every single week of the past year, relented and started carrying the show. As far as Dave was concerned, however, it was still the "Home Office." Although there were occasional references to other cities being the "Home Office," it was officially moved to Grand Rapids, Michigan, in June 1995, and to Wahoo, Nebraska, in May 1996.

Dave, who regularly made fun of his new employers at CBS, added a few new features to keep the show fresh—"Dave Talks to Kids," "Stupid Human Tricks," and "The CBS Mailbag" among them—but in 1995 the glow started to fade. Ratings slipped somewhat, and by the end of the year Letterman was running second to Leno's *Tonight Show*.

LATE SUMMER EARLY FALL BERT CONVY SHOW, THE (*Musical Variety*)
FIRST TELECAST: *August 25, 1976*
LAST TELECAST: *September 15, 1976*
BROADCAST HISTORY:
Aug 1976–Sep 1976, CBS Wed 8:00–8:30
REGULARS:
Bert Convy
Henry Polic II
Sallie Janes
Marty Barris
Donna Ponterotto
Lenny Schultz
Perry Botkin Orchestra

Bert Convy, who was the host of the CBS daytime game show *Tattletales*, was the singing and comedy star of this four-week summer mini-series. The only guest star to appear on the show was Don Knotts, on the premiere telecast. Bert and his comedy troupe, featuring Lenny Schultz as Lenny the Bionic Chicken, performed all of the musical and comedy numbers.

LATE WORLD WITH ZACH (*Talk/Variety*)

BROADCAST HISTORY:
VH1
30 minutes
Original episodes: *2002*
Premiered: *March 4, 2002*

HOST:
Zach Galifianakis

Offbeat comedy/variety show hosted by scruffy little actor/comedian Zach Galifianakis. There were short comic films, such as Zach going shopping with Carmen Electra, visiting a penile enlargement clinic, interviewing Ice Cube in the back of a car, and doing his monologue on a city bus. Musical guests included such trendy acts as the Foo Fighters. The show lasted for only about two months, but Zach certainly had a sense of humor about it all. On the final episode he had a soprano sing "It's Time to Say Good-Bye" while a large screen behind her flashed sarcastic comments from VH1 such as "We should have listened to the focus group," "You weren't that funny," and "Your guests were funnier than you." He then walked out of the studio on to the street and crawled into a Dumpster, which was hydraulically raised and dumped into a truck that drove off.

LATELINE (*Situation Comedy*)

FIRST TELECAST: *March 17, 1998*
LAST TELECAST: *March 16, 1999*
BROADCAST HISTORY:
Mar 1998–Apr 1998, NBC Tue 9:30–10:00
Jan 1999–Feb 1999, NBC Wed 9:00–9:30
Mar 1999, NBC Tue 8:30–9:00

CAST:
Al Freundlich .... Al Franken
Gale Ingersoll .... Megyn Price
Vic Karp .... Miguel Ferrer
Pearce McKenzie .... Robert Foxworth
Mona .... Catherine Lloyd Burns
Briana .... Sanaa Lathan
Raji .... Ajay Naidu

Newsroom comedy set behind the scenes at a Washington, D.C., nightly newscast resembling ABC's *Nightline*. If this is how *Nightline* was produced, however, it is a wonder it ever got on the air. Al Freundlich was the nerdy, clueless correspondent in horn-rimmed glasses who in his own mind represented the torch of journalistic integrity, while everyone around him considered him an idiot. Others in the newsroom included Gale, Al's savvy producer; Vic, the intense, sometimes sadistic boss; Pearce, the dapper, vain anchorman; Mona, Pearce's sycophantic assistant; Briana, the wisecracking show booker; and Raji, the unbelievably eager-to-please news intern. Lending an air of reality (or unreality?) were appearances by real Washington politicians as themselves, among them former presidential candidate Michael Dukakis, gay rights proponent Candace Gingrich, consumer activist Ralph Nader, and the entire fractious McLaughlin Group.

LATER (*Talk*)

FIRST TELECAST: *August 22, 1988*
LAST TELECAST: *February 1, 2001*
BROADCAST HISTORY:
Aug 1988–Aug 1991, NBC Mon–Thu 1:30–2:00 A.M.
Sep 1991–Feb 2001, NBC Mon–Thu 1:35–2:05 A.M.

HOST:
Bob Costas (1988–1994)
Greg Kinnear (1994–1996)
Cynthia Garrett (2000–2001)

Looking for an inexpensive way to program late-late night, NBC launched this simple but engaging interview show hosted by youthful-looking (he was 39) sportscaster Bob Costas. Each telecast was devoted to a single guest, whose life was profiled with film clips and who then joined Bob in *Later*'s overstuffed chairs. Guests were mostly TV celebrities and sports stars, with a few newsmen and politicians thrown in. Among them: Kareem Abdul-Jabbar, Steve Allen, Chevy Chase, Billy Crystal, New York governor Mario Cuomo, Wayne Gretzky, Valerie Harper (during her battle with NBC over *Valerie's Family*), Rob Lowe, Joan Rivers, Susan Saint James, Siskel and Ebert, Gene Wilder, and news anchors Tom Brokaw, Peter Jennings, and Dan Rather. The series was originally produced, appropriately enough, by "No Sleep Productions."

Costas was replaced in February 1994 by young comic Greg Kinnear, previously best known as the host of *Talk Soup* on the small E! Entertainment cable network. Greg opened each show with a "videologue" in which he commented on the day's events and also featured short comedy bits and a letter from the previous night's guest in addition to interviewing his single guest of the evening. After Kinnear left in 1996 various hosts appeared until January 2000, when the spot was assumed by VH1 VJ Cynthia Garrett—a vision of "hip" with her quirky clothes, nose ring and long, crinkly hair. She was the first African American female to host a late-night network talk show.

During Costas's tenure the show was called *Later with Bob Costas*; with the arrival of Kinnear, it became *Later with Greg Kinnear*. After his departure it was called simply *Later*.

LAUGH-IN, see *Rowan & Martin's Laugh-In*

LAUGH-IN (*Comedy/Variety*)

FIRST TELECAST: *June 6, 1979*
LAST TELECAST: *July 4, 1979*
BROADCAST HISTORY:
Jun 1979–Jul 1979, NBC Wed 8:00–9:00

REGULARS:
Nancy Bleiweiss
Ed Bluestone
Kim Braden
Claire Faulkonbridge
Wayland Flowers and Madam
June Gable
Jim Giovanni
Ben Powers
Bill Rafferty
Michael Sklar
Lenny Schultz
Antoinette (Toad) Atell
Robin Williams
Sergio Aragones

Producer George Schlatter had struck gold with the original *Rowan & Martin's Laugh-In* in the late 1960s (see separate listing). Its irreverent humor, fast pacing, and resident cast of nuts made it a huge success—the highest-rated program on television at the time.

Hoping that lightning would strike twice in the same format, Schlatter assembled a new cast of relatively obscure comics and revived *Laugh-In* as a series of specials aired by NBC during the 1977–1978 season. What had been fresh in the original seemed stale in the revival, and *Laugh-In* was not a significant audience attraction in its second incarnation. One of the comics, however, was a fellow named Robin Williams. He went on to star in the comedy smash of the 1978–1979 season, *Mork & Mindy,* which may well have prompted NBC to rerun the specials as a series during the summer of 1979. It was hardly accidental that the promotion for these repeat telecasts seemed to suggest that Robin Williams was the star of the show, even though his contribution had in fact been rather minor.

LAUGH LINE (*Quiz/Audience Participation*)
FIRST TELECAST: *April 16, 1959*
LAST TELECAST: *June 11, 1959*
BROADCAST HISTORY:
Apr 1959–Jun 1959, NBC Thu 9:00–9:30
EMCEE:
Dick Van Dyke
REGULAR:
Dorothy Loudon

A changing group of comedians enacted a silent comedy routine submitted by a viewer in this short-lived show. The celebrity panel would then suggest punch lines for the routine. Prizes for the person submitting the routine were determined by which punch line was funnier, the one submitted with the sketch or the one supplied by the pros. The panelists were generally comedians or comedy writers, with Dorothy Loudon the only regular. The young comedy team of Mike Nichols and Elaine May, though not regulars, made several appearances.

LAUGHS FOR SALE (*Comedy*)
FIRST TELECAST: *October 20, 1963*
LAST TELECAST: *December 22, 1963*
BROADCAST HISTORY:
Oct 1963–Dec 1963, ABC Sun 10:00–10:30
EMCEE:
Hal March

Each week a panel composed of prominent comics and comediennes participated in this series which sought to give young comedy writers exposure and help. The material that the writers submitted—sketches, monologues, routines, etc.—was performed by the members of the panel, who then discussed the strong and weak points they perceived in it. Panel members changed each week, but Shecky Greene, Mickey Rooney, and Phil Foster appeared frequently.

LAUREN HUTTON AND . . . (*Interview*)
BROADCAST HISTORY:
Syndicated only
30 minutes
Produced: *1995–1996* (195 episodes)
Released: *September 1995*
HOST:
Lauren Hutton

This interview show, in which model/actress Hutton chatted with one guest each night, was aired Mondays through Fridays after the late evening local news on most of the stations carrying it. Among Ms. Hutton's early guests were Kathleen Turner, Joy Behar, LL Cool J, Maury Povich, and Melvin Van Peebles. The only thing that distinguished this show from other interview shows was the placement of black-and-white TV monitors next to Ms. Hutton and her guest, which showed the person listening as well as the one talking.

LAURIE HILL (*Situation Comedy*)
FIRST TELECAST: *September 30, 1992*
LAST TELECAST: *October 28, 1992*
BROADCAST HISTORY:
Sep 1992–Oct 1992, ABC Wed 9:30–10:00
CAST:
Dr. Laurie Hill .... DeLane Matthews
Jeff Hill .... Robert Clohessy
Leo Hill (age 5) .... Eric Lloyd
Nancy MacIntyre .... Ellen DeGeneres
Dr. Spencer Kramer .... Kurt Fuller
Dr. Walter Wiseman .... Joseph Maher
Beverly Fielder .... Doris Belack

A brilliant, sensitive woman put up with boorish, self-centered men in this short-lived and rather stereotyped comedy/drama. Dr. Laurie Hill nearly glowed with nobility as she juggled her hectic roles as pediatrician and mother, while hubby Jeff, a freelance writer, sat around the house all day poking at his computer and spoiling their young son Leo. Noisy but lovable Leo just wanted to know why Mom didn't stay home and pay attention to *him.* At work, Drs. Spencer and Walter were hardly less demanding, but at least there were soul sisters in Nurse Nancy and receptionist Beverly.

LAVERNE & SHIRLEY (*Situation Comedy*)
FIRST TELECAST: *January 27, 1976*
LAST TELECAST: *May 10, 1983*
BROADCAST HISTORY:
Jan 1976–Jul 1979, ABC Tue 8:30–9:00
Aug 1979–Dec 1979, ABC Thu 8:00–8:30
Dec 1979–Feb 1980, ABC Mon 8:00–8:30
Feb 1980–May 1983, ABC Tue 8:30–9:00
CAST:
Laverne De Fazio .... Penny Marshall
Shirley Feeney (1976–1982) .... Cindy Williams
Carmine Ragusa .... Eddie Mekka
Frank De Fazio .... Phil Foster
Andrew "Squiggy" Squiggman .... David L. Lander
*Lenny Kosnowski** .... Michael McKean
Mrs. Edna Babish De Fazio (1976–1981)
.... Betty Garrett
Rosie Greenbaum (1976–1977) .... Carole Ita White
Sonny St. Jacques (1980–1981) .... Ed Marinaro
Rhonda Lee (1980–1983) .... Leslie Easterbrook

*Called "Kolowski" in earlier episodes

THEME:
"Making Our Dreams Come True," by Norman Gimbel and Charles Fox; sung by Cyndi Grecco

This slapstick 1950s-era comedy was about two spunky girls from lower-class backgrounds, without much education, with no money, but with the determination to get ahead. They worked on an assembly line in the bottle-cap division of the Shotz Brewery in Milwaukee. Laverne was the quick-tempered, defensive one, always afraid of getting hurt (which she usually did)—a glib realist. Shirley was naive and trusting, a sucker for a sad story. Others in the cast included Lenny and Squiggy, the girls' screwball neighbors and truck drivers at the plant; amorous Carmine, "The Big Ragu"; Laverne's father, Frank, owner of the Pizza Bowl, a local hangout; Mrs. Babish, the sardonic landlady who was first seen in the fall of 1976 (replacing the original landlady, Mrs. Havenwurst, played by Helen Page Camp, seen in only a couple of episodes); and Rosie, an uppity friend.

Laverne & Shirley was a spin-off of sorts from *Happy Days*, in which the girls appeared only briefly. It was set in the same city and period, and the girls' friend Fonzie sometimes stopped by to say hello. With friends like that *Laverne & Shirley* shot to the top of the ratings. Critics called it TV junk food; ABC program chief Fred Silverman responded by comparing it to the classic satire of the 17th-century French playwright Molière. No matter what anyone said, the public loved it. During the 1977–1978 season it was the number-one program on television.

With the 1978–1979 season, the program moved into the 1960s. Frank De Fazio and Mrs. Babish, both single, began dating, and in the fall of 1979 they were married. Then, in the fall of 1980, the whole crew picked up and moved to Burbank, California, all seeking to better their lot in a new environment. The girls began trying to get into the movies. Frank and Edna opened a restaurant, Cowboy Bill's. Carmine just wanted to be near his best girl, Shirley. New neighbors included Rhonda, a caustic dancer and model, and Sonny, a stuntman, and their apartment building manager.

Life behind the scenes on *Laverne & Shirley* had always been tumultuous, due to an intense rivalry between its two stars. Demands were made, writers fired, feuds erupted. Finally in 1982 Cindy Williams, who was pregnant, left the series. Her character, Shirley, married an army medic named Walter Meany who was assigned overseas. Laverne tried to go it alone, but, faced with withering competition from *The A-Team* on NBC, *Laverne & Shirley* quietly expired the following spring.

The theme song of this series was on the hit parade in 1976 in a recording by Cyndi Grecco, who was also heard on the show. Reruns of *Laverne & Shirley* were on ABC's daytime lineup from April 1979 to June 1980, and a Saturday morning cartoon version was seen from October 1981 to September 1983.

LAW AND HARRY MCGRAW, THE (*Detective*)

FIRST TELECAST: *September 27, 1987*
LAST TELECAST: *February 10, 1988*
BROADCAST HISTORY:

Sep 1987, CBS Sun 9:00–11:00
Sep 1987–Dec 1987, CBS Tue 10:00–11:00
Jan 1988–Feb 1988, CBS Wed 8:00–9:00

CAST:

Harry McGraw .... Jerry Orbach
Ellie Maginnis .... Barbara Babcock
Steve Lacey .... Shea Farrell
E. J. Brunson .... Juli Donald
Deputy D.A. Tyler Chase .... Peter Haskell
Howard .... Earl Boen
Cookie, the bartender .... Marty Davis

Harry McGraw was not the classiest private detective in Boston. He was disorganized, disheveled, irritable, and surly. On the other hand, he was a bright guy with good analytical skills and a dogged determination to stick with a case until he found what he was looking for. The best thing Harry had going for himself, however, was his friendship with attorney Ellie Maginnis, whose office was across the hall from his. There was a certain nepotism here—Harry's niece E.J. worked as his assistant/secretary and Ellie's nephew Steve was the junior partner in her legal office. Gilhooley's was the saloon where Harry spent much of his free time.

Harry McGraw had appeared a few times on *Murder, She Wrote* before getting a series of his own.

LAW AND MR. JONES, THE (*Legal Drama*)

FIRST TELECAST: *October 7, 1960*
LAST TELECAST: *October 4, 1962*
BROADCAST HISTORY:

Oct 1960–Sep 1961, ABC Fri 10:30–11:00
Apr 1962–Oct 1962, ABC Thu 9:30–10:00

CAST:

Abraham Lincoln Jones .... James Whitmore
Marsha Spear .... Janet De Gore
C. E. Carruthers .... Conlan Carter

That a man with a name like Abraham Lincoln Jones was honest was a foregone conclusion. This particular Abe was an attorney with great compassion for people, and a willingness to fight both literally and figuratively for his clients. His penchant for quoting Oliver Wendell Holmes did nothing to lessen his appeal. His cases rarely involved violence, however. Fraud, embezzlement, and jurisdictional disputes were the issues he most frequently addressed. Abe's law clerk was young C. E. Carruthers, and his winsome secretary was Marsha Spear.

ABC canceled this series after its initial season, but viewer response, in the form of thousands of angry letters, was so strong that it was brought back the following April. Alas, the size of its audience did not increase and it was canceled again in October.

LAW & ORDER (*Police/Legal Drama*)

FIRST TELECAST: *September 13, 1990*
LAST TELECAST:
BROADCAST HISTORY:

Sep 1990–Oct 1990, NBC Thu 10:00–11:00
Oct 1990–Apr 1991, NBC Tue 10:00–11:00
Jun 1991–Jan 1992, NBC Tue 10:00–11:00
Jan 1992–Jun 1992, NBC Tue 9:00–10:00
Jun 1992–Jul 1992, NBC Fri 10:00–11:00
Aug 1992–Feb 1997, NBC Wed 10:00–11:00
Jun 1995–Jul 1995, NBC Sat 10:00–11:00
Aug 1996, NBC Fri 10:00–11:00
Mar 1997, NBC Thu 10:00–11:00
Apr 1997– , NBC Wed 10:00–11:00
Jun 1998–Jul 1998, NBC Sun 10:00–11:00
Mar 1999–Apr 1999, NBC Mon 9:00–10:00
May 1999–Jul 1999, NBC Fri 10:00–11:00
Jul 1999–Sep 1999, NBC Mon 9:00–10:00
Nov 1999–Dec 1999, NBC Fri 10:00–11:00
May 2000–Sep 2000, NBC Mon 9:00–10:00
Nov 2000, NBC Mon 9:00–10:00
Mar 2003–Apr 2003, NBC Sat 8:00–9:00
Apr 2003–May 2003, NBC Sat 9:00–10:00
May 2003–Jul 2003, NBC Wed 9:00–10:00

CAST:

Det. Mike Logan (1990–1995) .... Christopher Noth
Det. Sgt. Max Greevey (1990–1991)
.... George Dzundza
Capt. Donald Cragen (1990–1993) ..... Dann Florek
Asst. D.A. Paul Robinette (1990–1993)
.... Richard Brooks

Asst. D.A. Ben Stone (1990–1994)
................................Michael Moriarty
D.A. Adam Schiff (1990–2000) ....Steven Hill
**Det. Tony Profaci (1990–1998)* ....John Fiore
Det. Phil Cerreta (1991–1992).........Paul Sorvino
**Dr. Elizabeth Olivet (1991–1998)*
.............................Carolyn McCormick
Det. Lennie Briscoe (1992–) ....Jerry Orbach
**Dr. Elizabeth Rodgers (1992–)* .... Leslie Hendrix
Lt. Anita Van Buren (1993–)..S. Epatha Merkerson
Asst. D.A. Claire Kincaid (1993–1996)
....................................Jill Hennessy
Exec. Asst. D.A. Jack McCoy (1994–)
.................................Sam Waterston
Det. Reynaldo "Rey" Curtis (1995–1999)
.................................Benjamin Bratt
Asst. D.A. Jamie Ross (1996–1998).... Carey Lowell
**Dr. Emil Skoda (1997–)* ....J. K. Simmons
**Det. Morris LaMotte (1998–2000)* ..... Larry Clarke
Asst. D.A. Abbie Carmichael (1998–2001)
.................................Angie Harmon
Det. Edward Green (1999–) .... Jesse L. Martin
D.A. Nora Lewin (2000–2002)........ Dianne Wiest
Asst. D.A. Serena Southerlyn (2001–)
................................Elisabeth Rohm
Det. Ann Cordova (2001–)....... Andrea Navedo
D.A. Arthur Branch (2002–)..... Fred Thompson

*Occasional

A gritty, straightforward crime show marked by first-rate acting (by an ensemble cast consisting mostly of stage and film character actors) and realistic stories. The hand-held camera shots and intense, low-key style looked so real that one critic commented that the series "starts to look like a local news report."

The "star," if there was one, was New York City, and the crimes mostly violent, high-profile cases of murder, rape, or the mob, sometimes complicated by social issues such as racism or the right of self-defense. The first half of each episode traced the investigation of the crime by Sgt. Greevey, a heavyset, no-nonsense type, and his young partner, Mike Logan. In the second half viewers saw the case prosecuted by equally dedicated assistant D.A.'s Stone and Robinette. Both teams found their jobs complicated by the constraints of the modern criminal justice system, with its deals and politics, but worked within the system to see that the guilty were brought to justice (which in this series, at least, they usually were). The stories were often "torn from the headlines" and included thinly disguised versions of such media events as the Anita Hill affair and the Mike Tyson rape trial. Unlike such series as *Homicide: Life on the Street* and *NYPD Blue*, *Law & Order* focused on the story, not the personal lives of its characters.

There was a good deal of cast turnover on this series. Logan's partner Greevey was killed while on duty and replaced by Cerreta and then Briscoe. At the end of the 1994–1995 season it was announced that Logan was being written out as well. Their boss, Capt. Cragen, was ousted in favor of Lt. Anita Van Buren, and in the D.A.'s office Robinette was replaced with Claire Kincaid (NBC, which reportedly wanted to give the show more female appeal, had imposed its own version of affirmative action). Dr. Olivet, the police psychiatrist who counseled and advised, also left.

Probably the most publicized departure was that of actor Michael Moriarty (Stone), who got into a very public spat with producer Dick Wolf over the issue of television censorship and quit at the end of the fourth season. He was replaced with respected actor Sam Waterston, who played Jack McCoy, a motorcycle-riding prosecutor who was decidedly looser than the buttoned-up Stone. In 1995, Det. Logan left, leaving the highly political D. A. Adam Schiff—appropriately—as the only character remaining from the first season. There were several crossover episodes with *Homicide* over the years, with characters from each series appearing on the other in a common story line.

Despite the cast turnover, two characters provided a degree of continuity from the mid-'90s on. On the investigative side, Det. Briscoe, who joined in late 1992, was partnered successively with Logan, Curtis (1995) and Green (1999). As for the prosecutors, McCoy, who took over from Stone in 1994, was teamed with Kincaid, Ross (1996), Carmichael (1998) and Southerlyn (2001). D.A. Schiff was finally replaced in 2000 by newly elected Lewin, but she lasted only two years before being ousted by hard-liner Branch, who was swept into office following the terrorist attacks of September 11, 2001.

LAW & ORDER: CRIMINAL INTENT (*Police Drama*)

FIRST TELECAST: *September 30, 2001*
LAST TELECAST:
BROADCAST HISTORY:
Sep 2001– , NBC Sun 9:00–10:00
Mar 2003, NBC Sat 9:00–10:00
Apr 2003–May 2003, NBC Sun 10:00–11:00
CAST:
Det. Robert Goren.............. Vincent D'Onofrio
Det. Alexandra Eames .... Kathryn Erbe
Capt. James Deakins .... Jamey Sheridan
Asst. D.A. Ron Carver........... Courtney B. Vance

This second spin-off from the immensely popular *Law & Order* was billed as looking at crimes from the criminal's perspective. It was certainly more introspective in approach, and more personality-driven, than its predecessors. Whereas *L&O* was an ensemble show, this one centered on Det. Goren, a brilliant and somewhat eccentric investigator who carefully pieced together clues and deduced their meaning in the style of a modern-day Sherlock Holmes. Often he would cock his head, ponder, and ask a question seemingly unrelated to the crime—but there was always a reason. Eames was his assertive partner, in awe of his deductive abilities, and Deakins, his politically savvy captain. Carver was the calm, determined representative of the D.A.'s office.

The *Law & Order* production devices were all here, from the businesslike efficiency of the investigators to the short, just-the-facts scenes with witnesses, the sharp musical punctuation and white-on-black title slides between scenes. The crimes were generally brutal murders, committed by clever (and often rich) criminals who hid their tracks well—but not well enough to escape the analytic power of Goren.

LAW & ORDER: SPECIAL VICTIMS UNIT (*Police/Legal Drama*)

FIRST TELECAST: *September 20, 1999*
LAST TELECAST:
BROADCAST HISTORY:
Sep 1999–Dec 1999, NBC Mon 9:00–10:00
Jan 2000– , NBC Fri 10:00–11:00
Mar 2002–Apr 2002, NBC Sun 10:00–11:00

Aug 2002–Sep 2002, NBC Fri 9:00–10:00
Jan 2003–Feb 2003, NBC Sat 9:00–10:00
Mar 2003–May 2003, NBC Sat 10:00–11:00

CAST:

Det. Elliot Stabler .... Christopher Meloni
Det. Olivia Benson .... Mariska Hargitay
Det. John Munch .... Richard Belzer
Det. Brian Cassidy (1999–2000) ...... Dean Winters
Det. Monique Jeffries (1999–2000) .. Michelle Hurd
Capt. Donald Cragen .... Dann Florek
Ken Briscoe (1999–2000) .... Chris Orbach
**Medical Examiner Warner (2000–)*
.... Tamara Tunie
Det. Odafin "Fin" Tutuola (2000–) .... Ice-T
Asst. D.A. Alexandra Cabot (2000–)
.... Stephanie March
Dr. George Huang (2001–) .... B. D. Wong
**Bureau Chief Elizabeth Donnelly (2002–)*
.... Judith Light

*Occasional

Special Victims was a euphemism for victims of sex crimes in this titillating spin-off from *Law & Order*. The New York Police Department's S.V.U. investigated all manner of rapes, mutilations and sex-based murders with the same efficiency as its counterparts on the other *L&O* shows. The detectives here included calm, experienced Stabler; his partner, hotheaded, emotionally involved Benson (a child of rape herself); acerbic Munch (a transfer from the Baltimore P.D. and *Homicide: Life on the Street*); Munch's partner, enthusiastic newcomer Cassidy, and street-savvy Jeffries. Their smart, tough boss was Captain Cragen, who had been a regular during the first three seasons of *Law & Order*. There was much emphasis on analyzing the perpetrators' motives and unraveling clues, and less on the prosecution, than on the other *L&O* shows.

Joining the unit in later seasons was Tutuola, whose wit and experience made him a match for Munch, with whom he was partnered (replacing Cassidy); Cabot, representing the D.A.'s office; and Dr. Huang, a forensic psychiatrist who helped the detectives gain insight into the criminal mind.

LAW OF THE PLAINSMAN (*Western*)

FIRST TELECAST: *October 1, 1959*
LAST TELECAST: *September 24, 1962*
BROADCAST HISTORY:

Oct 1959–Sep 1960, NBC Thu 7:30–8:00
Jul 1962–Sep 1962, ABC Mon 8:30–9:00

CAST:

Deputy U.S. Marshal Sam Buckhart
.... Michael Ansara
Marshal Andy Morrison .... Dayton Lummis
Tess Logan .... Gina Gillespie
Martha Commager .... Nora Marlowe

The struggle to reconcile Indian and white man in the wild New Mexico Territory of the 1880s was the subject of this series. The plainsman was Deputy U.S. Marshal Sam Buckhart, a lawman with a unique past. Born an Apache Indian, and known among the Indians as Buck Heart, he had befriended and nursed back to health a cavalry captain who had been wounded in an Indian ambush. When the captain died two years later, he left the youth money for an education at private schools and Harvard University.

Having acquired tremendous respect for the white man's laws and the U.S. Constitution, Sam returned to the troubled territory where he had spent his youth, determined to become a marshal. He served under Marshal Andy Morrison in Santa Fe, while living in a rooming house run by Martha Commager. The only other female in his life was eight-year-old Tess Logan, an orphan he had rescued from a stagecoach mishap. Martha served as a kind of surrogate mother for both Sam and his young ward.

Reruns of this NBC series were aired on ABC during the summer of 1962. Its pilot had aired on *The Rifleman* early in 1959.

LAWLESS (*Detective Drama*)

FIRST TELECAST: *March 22, 1997*
LAST TELECAST: *March 22, 1997*
BROADCAST HISTORY:

Mar 1997, FOX Sat 9:00–10:00

CAST:

John Lawless .... Brian Bosworth
Reggie Hayes .... Glenn Plummer
Esther Hayes .... Janet Hubert

Beefy former pro football player Brian Bosworth starred in this ill-fated action series that attracted so few viewers to its premiere that it was canceled after a single telecast. John Lawless was a swaggering ex-Special Forces operative working as a motorcycle-riding tough-guy private detective in Miami. Reggie, who ran a charter helicopter service, was his "hey, mon" Jamaican partner. Reggie's stylish mother, Esther, ran a café where they hung out . . . briefly.

LAWLESS YEARS, THE (*Police Drama*)

FIRST TELECAST: *April 16, 1959*
LAST TELECAST: *September 22, 1961*
BROADCAST HISTORY:

Apr 1959–Jun 1959, NBC Thu 8:00–8:30
Jul 1959–Sep 1959, NBC Thu 8:30–9:00
Oct 1959–Mar 1960, NBC Thu 10:30–11:00
May 1961–Sep 1961, NBC Fri 9:00–9:30

CAST:

Barney Ruditsky .... James Gregory
Max .... Robert Karnes

The setting of this police drama was wide-open New York City in the Roaring Twenties, city of speakeasies, gangsters, bathtub gin, and flappers. The exploits of Police Detective Barney Ruditsky in his fight against organized crime were portrayed. *The Lawless Years* had a certain claim to authenticity, both in its meticulous attention to period detail and in the fact that it was based (loosely) on actual cases of a real-life New York cop named Barney Ruditsky. The careers of real gangsters of the period were depicted, although with fictitious names.

Six months after *The Lawless Years* premiered, *The Untouchables*, treating the same subject but with Chicago rather than New York as the background, began on ABC. *The Lawless Years* folded soon after, but the success of *The Untouchables* inspired a revival with new episodes in the summer of 1961.

The real Barney Ruditsky, who had retired from police work in 1941 and was running a West Coast detective agency, was the technical advisor for *The Lawless Years*.

LAWMAN, THE (*Western*)

FIRST TELECAST: *October 5, 1958*
LAST TELECAST: *October 2, 1962*

BROADCAST HISTORY:

Oct 1958–Apr 1962, ABC Sun 8:30–9:00
Apr 1962–Oct 1962, ABC Sun 10:30–11:00

CAST:

Marshal Dan Troop .... John Russell
Deputy Johnny McKay .... Peter Brown
Dru Lemp (1958–1959) .... Bek Nelson
Lily Merrill (1959–1962) .... Peggy Castle
Jake (1961–1962) .... Dan Sheridan

The "lawman" in this straightforward Western was Marshal Dan Troop of Laramie, a granite-jawed, taciturn type. With his string tie and fatherly mustache, John Russell looked the part. There were no tricks or gimmicks in *Lawman*, just simple stories of desperadoes brought to justice by the long, stern arm of the law. Playing off Troop's fatherly image was his young deputy, Johnny McKay. Lily Merrill arrived in town during the second season to open the Birdcage Saloon and help the righteous marshal unbend a bit.

LAWRENCE WELK SHOW, THE (*Music*)

FIRST TELECAST: *July 2, 1955*
LAST TELECAST: *September 4, 1971*

BROADCAST HISTORY:

Jul 1955–Sep 1963, ABC Sat 9:00–10:00
Sep 1963–Jan 1971, ABC Sat 8:30–9:30
Jan 1971–Sep 1971, ABC Sat 7:30–8:30
(New episodes syndicated from 1971–1982)

HOST:

Lawrence Welk

MUSICAL DIRECTOR:

George Cates

CHAMPAGNE LADY:

Alice Lon (1955–1959)
Norma Zimmer (1960–1982)

ORIGINAL REGULARS (1955):

Aladdin, violin (1955–1967)
Jerry Burke, piano-organ (1955–1965)
Dick Dale, saxophone, vocals (1955–1982)
Myron Floren, accordion (1955–1982)
Larry Hooper, piano, bass vocals (1955–1982)
Dick Kesner, violin (1955–1959)
Bob Lido, violin (1955–1982)
Tiny Little, Jr., piano (1955–1959)
Buddy Merrill, guitar (1955–1974)
Jim Roberts, vocals (1955–1982)
Rocky Rockwell, trumpet, gravel-voiced vocals (1955–1962)
Sparklers Quartet (1955–1957)

LATER REGULARS (in order they joined):

Lennon Sisters (Dianne, Peggy, Kathy, Janet) (1955–1968)
Larry Dean, vocals (1957–1960)
Frank Scott, piano, arranger (1956–1969)
Maurice Pearson, vocals (1957–1960)
Joe Feeney, Irish tenor (1957–1982)
Jack Imel, tap dancer (1957–1982)
Alvan Ashby, hymn singer (1957–1959)
Pete Fountain, Dixieland clarinet (1957–1959)
Jo Ann Castle, ragtime piano (1959–1969)
Jimmy Getzoff, violin (1960–1962)
Bobby Burgess and Barbara Boylan, dancers (1961–1967)
(Boylan replaced by Cissy King (1967–1978) then by Elaine Niverson (1979–1982))
Joe Livoti, violin (1962–1982)
Bob Ralston, piano-organ (1963–1982)
Art Duncan, dancer (1964–1982)
Steve Smith, vocals (1965–1969)
Natalie Nevins, vocals (1965–1969)
The Blenders, vocal quartet (1965–1967)
Lynn Anderson, vocals (1967–1968)
Andra Willis, vocals (1967–1969)
Tanya Falan Welk, vocals (1968–1977)
Sandi Jensen, vocals (1968–1980)
Salli Flynn, vocals (1968–1972)
Hotsy Totsy Boys (1969–1980)
Clay Hart, vocals (1969–1975)
Ralna English Hovis (1969–1982)
Mary Lou Metzger (1970–1982)
Guy Hovis (1970–1982)
Peanuts Hucko (1970–1972)
Anacani (1972–1982)
Tom Netherton (1973–1981)
Ava Barber (1974–1982)
Kathy Sullivan (1976–1982)
Sheila & Sherry Aldridge (1977–1982)
David & Roger Otwell (1977–1982)
Jim Turner (1979–1982)

THEME:

"Bubbles in the Wine" (1955–1970), by Lawrence Welk, Frank Loesser, and Bob Calame; "Champagne Fanfare" (1971–1982), by George Cates

Lawrence Welk's Champagne Music was first heard on network television as a summer replacement program in 1955. The critics were not impressed. Reviewing the program at the end of the summer, *TV Guide* remarked smugly: "The program lacks the necessary sparkle and verve to give it a chance against any really strong competition. But it has been a satisfactory summertime entry. . . ." That proved to be the misjudgment of the year. Welk went on to a phenomenal 16-year network run on Saturday nights, and became one of the major musical success stories in all of TV history. From 1956 to 1959 he had *two* weekly hours on ABC, and he maintained good ratings throughout his run. In fact, when his program was finally canceled by ABC in 1971 it was primarily because his audience was "too old"—not too small. Welk then assembled a syndicated network of his own and continued to produce new programs that attracted bigger audiences than many network shows.

The Welk formula was good, old-fashioned, melodic music, unadorned and straightforwardly presented. Old folks loved it. This was the one place on TV—probably in all of modern media—where "I Love You Truly" could be heard sung completely straight. Moreover, everyone on the show was completely good, clean, and wholesome (or else they were fired). Welk himself had about as much stage presence as Ed Sullivan, but that did not stop either of them. The maestro read stiffly through the brief introductions, and his thick accent was the butt of endless jokes. But when he played his accordion (which was rarely) or danced with one of the ladies in the audience, viewers loved it.

Much of the appeal of the program lay with its close-knit family of performers. Practically every player in the band was given a chance to solo from time to time, though some (listed above) were seen more often than others. Welk, who was highly sensitive to viewers' letters, kept a "fever chart" on which each comment on a performer, pro or con, was carefully tallied. Performers with a lot of favorable comments were featured more, and those in disfavor with the letter-writing public tended to disappear from view. The viewer, too, was part of the "family."

Probably the most famous of Welk's alumni were "da lovely Lennon Sisters," who were first brought to his attention in 1955 by his son, Lawrence, Jr., who was dating Dianne Lennon at the time. Lawrence, Sr., signed them immediately. They first appeared on his Christmas Eve 1955 broadcast, and stayed for more than 12 years. Dianne left to get married in 1960, and the quartet was only a trio until her return in 1964.

Other favorites included accordionist Myron Floren, who was also the assistant conductor; deep-voiced singer-pianist Larry Hooper (who was off the show from 1967–1971 due to heart trouble; he died in 1983); dancers Bobby Burgess and Barbara Boylan; and Aladdin (real name: Aladdin Abdullah Achmed Anthony Pallante), the mustachioed violinist who also did dramatic readings. High point of the season was the annual Christmas show, when all the band members brought their children and Larry Hooper dressed up as Santa Claus for fun and gifts.

Most of Welk's musical family stayed with him for years, but there were a few highly publicized walkouts. Welk has always been a very straitlaced individual, and his moral as well as musical regimentation grated on some performers. Perhaps the most traumatic incident for Welk was his firing of Champagne Lady Alice Lon in July 1959, because she showed "too much knee" on camera. "Cheesecake does not fit our show," charged an angry Welk. "All I did was sit on a desk and cross my legs," replied Miss Lon. "That is the way a lady sits down." Welk got thousands of angry letters for his action, which evidently caused him second thoughts. He tried to get Alice back, but to no avail. After a year and a half of guest Champagne Ladies, soprano Norma Zimmer was hired on a permanent basis.

Hardly less painful was the departure of the Lennon sisters in 1968, to build a career of their own. Dixieland clarinetist Pete Fountain, one of the most jazz-oriented musicians ever to star with Welk, quit when the maestro refused to let him jive up a carol on a Christmas show. He later built a successful career on his own, as did Jo Ann Castle and country singer Lynn Anderson.

During his later years Lawrence Welk made a conscious effort to add younger, reasonably contemporary performers to his troupe. The success of his record "Calcutta" in 1960 evidently convinced him that good music and something remotely resembling a contemporary beat were not necessarily incompatible. Dancers Burgess and Boylan joined after winning a "Calcutta" dance contest in 1961, and added later were Sandi and Salli, Tanya Falan (who married Welk's son), and tap dancer Art Duncan, the only black face in the crowd.

After leaving the network *The Lawrence Welk Show* continued in production for 11 more years, remaining one of the top-rated programs on American television—a tribute to the unwavering maestro of the "uh-one, uh-two" and his continued popularity with millions of viewers. The last original episode was produced in February 1982. In later years early programs were repackaged with new introductions by Welk, and aired under the title *Memories With Lawrence Welk*.

The Lawrence Welk Show was seen on local television in Los Angeles for two years before going on the network in 1955. It was known for a time in 1958 as *The Dodge Dancing Party*.

LAWRENCE WELK'S TOP TUNES AND NEW TALENT (*Talent*)
FIRST TELECAST: *October 8, 1956*
LAST TELECAST: *May 27, 1959*
BROADCAST HISTORY:
Oct 1956–Jun 1958, ABC Mon 9:30–10:30
Sep 1958–May 1959, ABC Wed 7:30–8:30

REGULARS:
Lawrence Welk
The Lawrence Welk Orchestra
Lawrence Welk's Little Band (1958–1959)

In addition to his familiar Saturday night show, Lawrence Welk had a second hour on ABC between 1956 and 1959, featuring "top tunes and new talent." Some of the performers discovered in the talent-show portion of the series later became Welk regulars, among them Joe Feeney, Jack Imel, and Maurice Pearson. Also featured were Welk's regular orchestra and soloists.

In 1958 the title of the show was changed to *The Plymouth Show*, and the Lawrence Welk "Little Band" was added as a regular feature. This second band was composed of talented youngsters ranging in age from 12 to 20, and included such solo talent as drummer Cubby O'Brien (12), a former *Mickey Mouse Club* Mousketeer.

LAWYERS, THE (*Legal Drama*)
FIRST TELECAST: *September 21, 1969*
LAST TELECAST: *August 20, 1972*
BROADCAST HISTORY:
Sep 1969–Aug 1972, NBC Sun 10:00–11:00
CAST:
Walter Nichols .... Burl Ives
Brian Darrell .... Joseph Campanella
Neil Darrell .... James Farentino

Three attorneys with different skills, interests, and approaches joined forces to form the law firm of Nichols, Darrell and Darrell. Walter Nichols had been practicing law since before either of his two young partners was born. His vast experience gave him a perspective and patience that neither of the Darrell brothers had. Shrewd and effective, Walter functioned as a stabilizing influence, consultant, and sometimes father figure to his partners. Brian, the older of the Darrell brothers, was a superb researcher and detail man who did everything by the book. Neil, the younger brother, was more sympathetic to unpopular causes and more unorthodox than either of his partners. He was not above stretching the law to achieve a desired end. The blending of these three diverse personalities caused occasional conflict among the attorneys but resulted in a very effective team. *The Lawyers* was one of the rotating elements that comprised *The Bold Ones*.

LAYTONS, THE (*Situation Comedy*)
FIRST TELECAST: *August 11, 1948*
LAST TELECAST: *October 13, 1948*
BROADCAST HISTORY:
Aug 1948–Oct 1948, DUM Wed 8:30–9:00
CAST:
Amanda Randolph
Vera Tatum

Black actress Amanda Randolph, better known as Sapphire's mama on both the radio and TV versions of *Amos 'n' Andy*, stared in this short-lived domestic comedy/drama on DuMont. It had been previously seen as a local program in New York, in May–June 1948.

Little is known about the content of this early series, but judging by the presence of Randolph this may have been the first network series to feature a black actor or actress in a continuing role.

LAZARUS MAN, THE (*Western*)

BROADCAST HISTORY:

Syndicated and TNT Cable Network
60 minutes
Produced: *1995–1996* (22 episodes)
Released: *January 1996*

CAST:

Lazarus (James Cathcart)............ Robert Urich
Major Gafney......................... Wayne Grace
**Claire Cathcart*................ Isabelle Townsend

*Occasional

This was the story of a man who, in the fall of 1865, woke up in a shallow grave in the town of San Sebastian, Texas, with a bad case of amnesia. With no idea who he was or what had caused his memory loss, he took the name Lazarus and set out to discover what had happened. Flashbacks revealed that he had been one of President Lincoln's bodyguards who was ordered away from the box at Ford's Theatre just before the President was assassinated. Lazarus had been beaten and left to die in an open grave. He kept a diary of his experiences as he tried to regain his memory, find out who he really was, and unravel the plot that had led to Lincoln's murder. The leader of the conspiracy was the Major, a mysterious man in a derby hat with a handlebar mustache, who spent most of the season coordinating efforts to find Lazarus and finish the job that his men had failed to accomplish when the series began.

In the 21st episode, after undergoing hypnosis, Lazarus was able to remember much more, including the realizations that he had been an Army intelligence officer and who all the conspirators were. In the last episode the Major set a trap, with Lazarus's wife Claire as bait. Although Lazarus, with the help of his younger brother, was able to rescue her and kill the Major in the process, she was killed by one of the Major's wounded men as Lazarus prepared to search for his son and daughter, who had been taken by members of the conspiracy.

There were plans for a second season, but when series star Robert Urich was diagnosed with a rare form of cancer, the production company, fearing he would not be able to continue, pulled the plug on *The Lazarus Man*.

LAZARUS SYNDROME, THE (*Medical Drama*)

FIRST TELECAST: *September 4, 1979*
LAST TELECAST: *October 9, 1979*

BROADCAST HISTORY:

Sep 1979–Oct 1979, ABC Tue 10:00–11:00

CAST:

Dr. MacArthur St. Clair........... Louis Gossett, Jr.
Joe Hamill......................... Ronald Hunter
Gloria St. Clair...................... Sheila Frazier
Virginia Hamill.................... Peggy Walker
Stacy............................... Peggy McKay

This rather grim medical drama was one of the earliest casualties of the 1979–1980 season. Dr. MacArthur St. Clair, a tall, bald, black man with a somewhat ominous demeanor, was Chief of Cardiology at Webster Memorial Hospital. His life seemed to be a series of conflicts, both with the idealistic hospital administrator, Joe Hamill, who had signed on to help him fight the bureaucracy, and with his wife, Gloria, who wanted him to have a little more home life.

The term "Lazarus Syndrome" refers to a belief that doctors are omnipotent beings who can work miracles.

LEAGUE OF GENTLEMEN, THE (*Situation Comedy*)

BROADCAST HISTORY:

Comedy Central
30 minutes
Original episodes: *2000–*
Premiered: *June 19, 2000*

CAST:

Al, Hilary Briss, Dr. Matthew Chinnery, Val Denton, Iris Krell, Mama Lazarou, Martin Lee, Frau Lipp, Lance Longthorne, Mick McNamara, Les McQueen, Mickey M. Michaels, Brian Morgan, Phill Proctor, David Tattsyrup, Andrew Wood
.... Mark Gatiss

Pop, Pauline Campbell-Jones, Harvey Denton, Barbara Dickson (voice), Maurice Evans, Mike Harris, Charlie Hull, Herr Lipp, Dave Parkes, Tulip "Tubbs" Tattsyrup, Jed Tinsel, Ally Welles
.... Steve Pemberton

Richie, Cathy Carter-Smith, Samuel Chignell, Benjamin Denton, Pamela Doove, Ross Gaines, Stella Hull, Patch Lafayette, Papa Lazarou, Judee Levinson, Oliver Plimsoles, Henry Portrait, Edward Tattsyrup, Geoff Tipps, Reverend Bernice Woodall
.... Reece Shearsmith

This sex-laden English comedy was set in the small, and isolated, northern English village of Royston Vasey, a town filled with eccentrics. As the series began Benjamin Denton arrived to stay for the night with his uncle Harvey and auntie Val, a creepy couple obsessed with cleanliness, masturbation, and toads—apparently unaware that once in Royston Vasey, you could never leave. Also prominently seen were loony shopkeepers Tubbs and Edward Tattsyrup, who loathed strangers so much ("Are you local?") they apparently killed them; Pauline Campbell-Jones, the government job training officer obsessed with her pens and procedures (Mickey was her pet, and Ross the class troublemaker); Dr. Chinnery, the deadly veterinarian; butcher Hilary Briss, whose sausages contained a mysterious "special ingredient"; and talkative transsexual cab driver Barbara Dixon. Later stories included a long-running nosebleed epidemic, assorted murders, and bizarre performances by Ollie Plimsoles' Legz Akimbo theater company.

Perhaps the most remarkable fact about *League of Gentlemen* was that all of the principal roles—more than 60 of them (only a sampling are shown above)—were played by three male actors, Gatiss, Pemberton, and Shearsmith, who with Jeremy Dyson created the series. It originated as their stage act, becoming a radio series in 1997 and a cult hit on British TV in 1999. Episodes were filmed in Hadfield, High Peak, Derbyshire, in England.

LEAGUE OF THEIR OWN, A (*Situation Comedy*)
FIRST TELECAST: *April 10, 1993*
LAST TELECAST: *April 24, 1993*
BROADCAST HISTORY:
Apr 1993, CBS Sat 9:00–9:30
CAST:
Jimmy Dugan .... Sam McMurray
Dorothy "Dottie" Hinson .... Carey Lowell
Kit Keller .... Christine Elise
Betty "Spaghetti" Horn .... Tracy Reiner
Marla Hooch .... Megan Cavanagh
Mae Mordabito .... Wendy Makkena
Doris Murphy .... Katie Rich
Evelyn Gardner .... Tracy Nelson
Mr. Harvey .... Garry Marshall
Umpire .... Doug Harvey

Period comedy about the Rockford Peaches, one of the teams in the women's professional baseball league formed during World War II when the male players were serving overseas. Jimmy Dugan, a former major-league baseball player, was the manager. Among the women of the Peaches were Dottie, the star catcher; Kit, Dottie's younger sister and one of the team's pitchers; Betty, a pitcher whose husband had been killed in combat; Marla, the slugger who had almost been overlooked because she wasn't pretty; Mae, the sultry, man-hungry outfielder; and Doris, the outspoken but funny infielder. Mr. Harvey, the demanding owner of the league, was played by Garry Marshall, whose sister Penny Marshall was one of the producers of the series.

As sometimes happens with hitters in real baseball, *A League of Their Own* struck out after only three episodes had aired. On August 13 CBS ran the other two episodes that had been completed prior to the series' quick cancelation earlier that year.

Based on the 1992 theatrical movie of the same name starring Tom Hanks, Geena Davis, and Madonna. Reprising their film roles were Tracy Reiner and Megan Cavanagh.

LEAP OF FAITH (*Situation Comedy*)
FIRST TELECAST: *February 28, 2002*
LAST TELECAST: *April 4, 2002*
BROADCAST HISTORY:
Feb 2002–Apr 2002, NBC Thu 8:30–9:00
CAST:
Faith Wardwell .... Sarah Paulson
Patty .... Lisa Edelstein
Cynthia .... Regina King
Andy .... Ken Marino
Cricket Wardwell .... Jill Clayburgh
Lucas .... Tim Meadows
Dan Murphy .... Brad Rowe

NBC described this *Sex and the City* knockoff as depicting "what it's like when you stop doing what you should do, and start doing what makes you happy." The four principals, all young good-looking Manhattanites, certainly were self-absorbed. Faith was the winsome, neurotic ad executive, who dumped her fiancé two weeks before their wedding when she ran into hunky actor Dan and decided to jump into the sack with him instead. Of course she immediately told *everybody,* starting with flaky, frizzy-haired friend Patty, an art director; opinionated but sensible Cynthia (who was actually married!); and fun-loving Andy, a reporter for *Rolling Stone.* Patty, trying to keep up, immediately bedded the coffee guy. The four friends all laughed a lot, talked endlessly about their feelings and chased casual sex. Faith's elegant, socialite mother Cricket offered advice, while Faith's boss, Lucas, tried to keep her mind at least a little bit focused on work.

Created by *Sex and the City* writer-producer Jenny Bicks.

LEARNING CHANNEL, THE (Network)
(*Documentary/Instructional Cable Network*)
LAUNCHED:
1972
SUBSCRIBERS (MAY 2003):
84.7 million (79% U.S.)

This cable network has evolved over time from a purely instructional channel to one somewhat resembling Discovery, the History Channel, and other documentary channels. Its wide-ranging schedule included instructional programs for children in the morning (under the umbrella title, *Ready, Set, Learn!*), adult human-interest and how-to programs in the afternoon (*A Wedding Story*, Bob Vila home repair shows), and straight documentaries at night (*Savage Earth, Medical Detectives, Trauma: Life and Death in the ER, The Secret World of Professional Wrestling*). The documentaries generally have to do with people and the human experience as opposed to history or the world of nature, but there is some overlap with other channels.

Programs in the early and mid-'90s included children's shows (*Zoobilee Zoo, Beakman's World*) and programming dealing with adult education (*Learn to Read*), cuisine (*Cooking with the Urban Peasant*), how-to (*Furniture on the Mend*), science (*Amazing Space*), history (*Battles That Changed the World*), and "fine living" (*Romantic Escapes, Death by Chocolate*). In the late '90s the network began to target women with "real women" documentary series in the afternoon, including *A Dating Story, A Wedding Story, A Baby Story, A Makeover Story* and *A Personal Story.* A clever afternoon home improvement show, *Trading Spaces* (q.v.), proved so popular that it began airing in prime time in late 2001 and was a phenomenal hit. This led to similar "fun" how-to shows including *While Your Were Out* and *What Not to Wear.*

TLC is one of the oldest networks on cable, having been founded in 1972 by the U.S. Department of Health, Education and Welfare and NASA, and distributed free via a NASA satellite. It became privately owned in 1980, at first called the Appalachian Community Service Network, but was quickly renamed the Learning Channel. In February 1991 it was acquired by the Discovery Channel which, through heavy marketing, has expanded its reach considerably. In recent years the new owners have downplayed the name the Learning Channel, utilizing instead the initials TLC.

LEARNING THE ROPES (*Situation Comedy*)
BROADCAST HISTORY:
Syndicated only
30 minutes
Produced: *1988–1989* (26 episodes)
Released: *October 1988*
CAST:
Robert Randall .... Lyle Alzado
The Masked Maniac .... Steve "Dr. Death" Williams

Mark Randall (age 17) .... Yannick Bisson
Ellen Randall (15) .... Nicole Stoffman
Carol Dixon .... Cheryl Wilson
Principal Whitcomb Mallory .... Richard Farrell
**Dr. Jerry Larson* .... Barry Stevens
Beth .... Jacqueline Mahon
**Brad* .... Gordon Woolvett
Bertie Baxter .... Grant Cowan
Cheetah .... Jefferson Mappin
**Cue Ball* .... Kevin Rushton

*Occasional

Robert Randall led a most unusual double life in this cross between a sitcom and a wrestling show (a wrestlecom?). During the day he was a history teacher and assistant principal at the Ridgedale Valley preparatory school, the private school where his two children, Mark and Ellen, were students. At night, however, in an effort to earn some extra money for his family, Robert moonlighted as a professional wrestler called "The Masked Maniac." Although his children and all of his cronies at the arena knew what was going on, he worked diligently to keep his school colleagues and friends from finding out—wrestling just didn't seem like the sort of thing a Ph.D. would do. Robert's ex-wife was in law school in London, and trying to hold down two jobs and raise his kids kept him pretty busy. Carol, one of Ridgedale's English teachers, whose uncle was the school's principal, was forever trying to get Robert to go out with her. Also seen were Beth, Ellen's boy-crazy best friend; Jerry Larson, the psychologist who lived next door; and Brad, Mark's shy friend. Bertie was the ring announcer and play-by-play man at the arena, and Cheetah and Cue Ball, other wrestlers.

The Masked Maniac was not particularly successful, regularly being beaten by an assortment of NWA wrestlers—Ric Flair, Gorgeous Jimmy Garvin, Tully Blanchard, Lex Luger, and Rickey Morton among them—all of whom appeared as themselves on the show. Doubling for actor Lyle Alzado behind the mask in wrestling sequences was professional wrestler Steve "Dr. Death" Williams.

Produced in Canada and aired on the CTV network.

LEAVE IT TO BEAVER (*Situation Comedy*)

FIRST TELECAST: *October 4, 1957*
LAST TELECAST: *September 12, 1963*
BROADCAST HISTORY:

Oct 1957–Mar 1958, CBS Fri 7:30–8:00
Mar 1958–Sep 1958, CBS Wed 8:00–8:30
Oct 1958–Jun 1959, ABC Thu 7:30–8:00
Jul 1959–Sep 1959, ABC Thu 9:00–9:30
Oct 1959–Sep 1962, ABC Sat 8:30–9:00
Sep 1962–Sep 1963, ABC Thu 8:30–9:00

CAST:

June Cleaver .... Barbara Billingsley
Ward Cleaver .... Hugh Beaumont
Beaver (Theodore) Cleaver .... Jerry Mathers
Wally Cleaver .... Tony Dow
Eddie Haskell .... Ken Osmond
Miss Canfield (1957–1958) .... Diane Brewster
Miss Landers (1958–1962) .... Sue Randall
Larry Mondello (1958–1960) .... Rusty Stevens
Whitey Whitney .... Stanley Fafara
Clarence "Lumpy" Rutherford (1958–1963)
.... Frank Bank
Mr. Fred Rutherford .... Richard Deacon
Gilbert Bates (1959–1963) .... Stephen Talbot
Richard (1960–1963) .... Richard Correll

This family comedy focused on life through the eyes of a young boy. Beaver Cleaver was 7 when the series began, and his brother Wally, 12. Beaver was a typically rambunctious youth, more interested in pet frogs than in girls, but Wally, just entering his teens, was beginning to discover other things in life. The counterpoint between the two, plus some good writing and acting, lent the series its charm. The boys' parents, June and Ward Cleaver, were one of those nice, middle-class couples so often seen in this kind of program. Larry, Whitey, and Gilbert (among others) were Beaver's pals, Eddie and Lumpy were Wally's buddies. Eddie was one of the more memorable characters, unctuous and oily to adults ("Good evening, Mr. and Mrs. Cleaver"), but a bully to little kids—a thoroughgoing rat. Miss Canfield and Miss Landers were Beaver's schoolteachers. The locale was the suburban town of Mayfield where Ward worked for Mr. Rutherford (Lumpy's father) as an accountant.

As the years passed and Beaver got older, the stories naturally moved away from the little-boy premise until, in the final season, Beaver was about to enter his teens and Wally was ready for college.

In 1987, in the midst of a *Leave it to Beaver* revival, the original 1957 pilot episode for the series surfaced, containing a somewhat different cast than most people remembered. Billingsley and Mathers were there, but Ward Cleaver was played by Casey Adams, Wally by Paul Sullivan, and "Frankie"—the Eddie Haskell-type character—by Harry Shearer, who years later would become a regular on *Saturday Night Live*. For the further adventures of the Cleaver clan in the '80s, see *The New Leave It to Beaver*.

LEAVE IT TO LARRY (*Situation Comedy*)

FIRST TELECAST: *October 14, 1952*
LAST TELECAST: *December 23, 1952*
BROADCAST HISTORY:

Oct 1952–Dec 1952, CBS Tue 8:00–8:30

CAST:

Larry Tucker .... Eddie Albert
Mr. Koppel .... Ed Begley
Amy Tucker .... Betty Kean
Stevie Tucker .... Glenn Walken
Harriet Tucker .... Lydia Schaeffer

The problems of a young man working for his father-in-law formed the basis of this comedy. Larry Tucker, a pleasant enough fellow with a wife (Amy) and two children, faced Amy's father every morning in the shoe store where he worked. He faced Mr. Koppel every night, too, since Amy's father also owned and lived in the two-family house where Larry and his family lived. Too much family, all of the time, made Larry's life a bit hectic. Someone in the family always had it in for someone else, and he was always in the middle.

Leave It to Larry had premiered with a different cast supporting Albert and Begley—Katherine Bard (as Amy), Olive Templeton, Bradley Houston, Gene Lee, and Patsy Bruder. These were replaced almost immediately by the cast listed above.

LEAVE IT TO THE GIRLS (*Discussion*)

FIRST TELECAST: *April 27, 1949*
LAST TELECAST: *March 27, 1954*

BROADCAST HISTORY:

Apr 1949–May 1949, NBC Wed 8:00–8:30
May 1949–Aug 1949, NBC Sun 8:00–8:30
Aug 1949–Oct 1949, NBC Sun 8:30–9:00
Oct 1949–Sep 1951, NBC Sun 7:00–7:30
Oct 1951–Dec 1951, NBC Sun 10:30–11:00
Oct 1953–Mar 1954, ABC Sat 7:30–8:00

MODERATOR:

Maggi McNellis

PANELISTS:

Eloise ("The Mouth") McElhone
Vanessa Brown
Florence Pritchett
Lisa Ferraday
Ann Rutherford
Harriet Van Horne
Janet Blair
John Henry Faulk (1954)

CREATOR/PRODUCER:

Martha Rountree

This bit of piffle was created by Martha Rountree, the same woman responsible for *Meet the Press* and other deadly serious public-affairs shows. Indeed, when it was first heard on radio in 1945, *Leave It to the Girls* was conceived as a serious discussion of male-female problems by career women. However, it soon degenerated into a one-sided battle of the sexes, and by the time it got to TV the subject matter was mostly what was wrong with men, how to marry them, and clever jokes about their foibles. A lone male was generally present to "defend the honor of his sex," and he was given a toy horn with which to signal his intention to speak (which was often the only way to break in on the chatterbox panel).

The female panelists changed frequently. All were "of the Stork Club ilk," as *TV Guide* put it—glamorous, well-dressed, showbiz types. Eloise McElhone was the most constant panel member over the years, with Vanessa Brown and Florence Pritchett also closely associated with the show. Male guests were generally panel-show types, such as Henry Morgan, Morey Amsterdam, and George Jessel. A "permanent" male defender, John Henry Faulk, was added during the last months.

Leave It to the Girls was first seen on local television in New York in 1947, and moved to the network in 1949. Oddly enough, it was sponsored through part of its run by a tobacco company. Almost a decade later, during the 1962–1963 season, Miss McNellis returned to moderate a syndicated weekday daytime version of *Leave It to the Girls.* Regular panelists were Sue Oakland and Rita Hayes.

LEAVING L.A. (*Police Drama*)

FIRST TELECAST: *April 12, 1997*
LAST TELECAST: *June 14, 1997*
BROADCAST HISTORY:

Apr 1997–Jun 1997, ABC Sat 9:00–10:00

CAST:

Dr. Neil Bernstein .... Ron Rifkin
Reed Simms .... Chris Meloni
Libby Gallante .... Melina Kanakaredes
Dr. Claudia Chan .... Lorraine Toussaint
Tiffany Roebuck .... Hilary Swank
Manny Byrd .... Billie Worley
Dudley Adams .... Cress Williams
Martha Hayes .... Anne Haney

"Leaving L.A." was meant with a bit of black humor in this offbeat series about the world of the Los Angeles Coroner's Office. Helping the recently departed depart were Neil, the eccentric Chief Medical Examiner, who cooked gourmet meals in his office and maintained a garden on the roof outside; Reed, an experienced criminal investigator with a crush on Libby, his new, super-serious trainee; Claudia, the sarcastic medical examiner with a surprising taste for practical jokes; Tiffany, the sweet, spiritual lab technician who spoke to the corpses; Manny, a goofy attendant ("Wanna see the bodies in the refrigerator?"); Dudley, the hip photographer who listened to Vivaldi on his Walkman while snapping nude corpses; and Martha, the white-haired, psychic property clerk, whose predictions were eerily accurate. Much of their work was at crime scenes, where they found clues the police had missed, while trading photos of celebrity corpses, and they often became personally involved in the cases.

LEG WORK (*Detective*)

FIRST TELECAST: *October 3, 1987*
LAST TELECAST: *November 7, 1987*
BROADCAST HISTORY:

Oct 1987–Nov 1987, CBS Sat 9:00–10:00

CAST:

Claire McCarron .... Margaret Colin
Willie Pipal .... Frances McDormand
Lt. Fred McCarron .... Patrick James Clarke

This series was an odd cross between *Designing Women* and *Miami Vice,* about a young, single woman in the big city who spent her time chattering with her girlfriends about love and life, in between high-speed chases and shootouts. Claire was a former assistant district attorney who had decided to become a private detective. She was much better at tracking down people and uncovering information for her clients than she was at managing her own finances. Claire's expensive Manhattan apartment, fancy (and too often in the shop) Porsche, and tendency to overspend on her credit cards, kept her busy juggling creditors. Willie was her best friend and confidante and Fred her loving brother, conveniently placed in the public information office of the N.Y.P.D. Although the title of this series was supposed to refer to the tedious part of detective work, it could just as well have referred, as many reviewers pointed out, to the attractive mini-skirted legs of star Margaret Colin.

LEGACY (*Serial Drama*)

FIRST TELECAST: *October 9, 1998*
LAST TELECAST : *July 30, 1999*
BROADCAST HISTORY:

Oct 1998–Feb 1999, UPN Fri 8:00–9:00
Jul 1999, UPN Fri 8:00–9:00

CAST:

Ned Logan .... Brett Cullen
Clay Logan .... Jeremy Garrett
Sean Logan .... Grayson McCouch
Jeremy Bradford (age 17) .... Ron Melendez
Alice Logan (16) .... Lea Moreno
Lexy Logan (10) .... Sarah Rayne
Vivian Winters .... Lisa Sheridan
William Winters .... Sean Bridgers
Isaac .... Steven Williams
Marita .... Sharon Leal
John Hayden Turner .... Casey Biggs
Col. Harry Griffith .... Mark Joy

Molly McGuire (1999)............. Brigid Brannagh
Charlotte Bentley (1999)...... Gabrielle Fitzpatrick

THEME:

"The Mummer's Dance," performed by Loreena McKennitt

Lexington, Kentucky, in the 1880s was the setting for this serial drama about an Irish family running a horse farm. Widower Ned Logan was the patriarch who had just taken in troubled 17-year-old Jeremy, an orphan from New York. Sean, Ned's eldest, had been engaged to Vivian, the banker's daughter, but broke it off because he was secretly in love with Marita, the family's black housekeeper. Clay, Sean's impulsive, hot-tempered younger brother, often felt his father was more concerned about everyone else than about him. Alice was just blossoming into womanhood but lacked the self-confidence of Lexy, her precocious younger sister. Vivian's conniving and vengeful brother William tried to ruin the Logans, and his efforts were abetted by Turner, the manipulative administrator Vivian had hired to manage the family plantation when her father was incapacitated after being shot during a run on the bank. In December, Sean was appointed by the county's newly elected state assemblyman to the post of Deputy Director in Lexington. Sean was to keep him apprised of local problems that needed his attention, much to the chagrin of the devious Turner, who was trying to take things over on behalf of the Winters family. In February, Jeremy and Alice started to show romantic interest in each other. When the last episodes aired in July, Clay started to date Vivian, and Ned, after a whirlwind courtship, married Charlotte, a woman he had rescued after a buggy accident. She turned out to be a con woman and schemed with town tramp Molly and Turner, who knew her real identity, to undermine Ned's relationship with his sons and gain control of the farm.

LEGEND (*Western*)

FIRST TELECAST: *April 18, 1995*
LAST TELECAST: *August 22, 1995*
BROADCAST HISTORY:

Apr 1995–Aug 1995, UPN Tue 8:00–9:00
Jul 1995–Aug 1995, UPN Mon 9:00–10:00

CAST:

Ernest Pratt/Nicodemus Legend
.... Richard Dean Anderson
Prof. Janos Bartok.................. John de Lancie
Ramos............................ Mark Adair Rios
Skeeter............................... Jarrad Paul
Chamberlain Brown................ Robert Donner
Grady............................ Robert Shelton

Ernest Pratt was a hard-drinking San Francisco dime novelist in 1876 who assumed the identity of his literary creation, heroic Nicodemus Legend, "The Knight of the Prairie," in this series that looked like *The Wild Wild West* with its gadgets and tongue-in-cheek attitude. Pratt wasn't really all that interested in helping people, but he was prodded into it by Professor Bartok, an eccentric genius who lured him to Sheridan, Colorado, and supplied him with a wide range of wondrous, ahead-of-their-time devices. Among Bartok's inventions were electrical zappers, a steam-powered car, a gasoline-powered balloon, a bullet-proof vest, and a miniature surveillance camera mounted in a small, motorized, remote-controlled balloon. Others around Sheridan were Ramos, Bartok's brilliant Mexican assistant; Skeeter, the enthusiastic young man with the wild hair who was the bellboy at the local hotel; Chamberlain, Sheridan's mayor and undertaker, who hoped to exploit the town's association with the famous Nicodemus Legend; and Grady, the bartender who served Pratt tea-cups full of hard liquor (since the fictitious Legend was a teetotaler).

LEGEND OF CUSTER, see *Custer*

LEGEND OF JESSE JAMES, THE (*Western*)

FIRST TELECAST: *September 13, 1965*
LAST TELECAST: *September 5, 1966*
BROADCAST HISTORY:

Sep 1965–Sep 1966, ABC Mon 8:30–9:00

CAST:

Jesse James..................... Christopher Jones
Frank James.............................. Allen Case
Cole Younger........................ John Milford
Bob Younger.......................... Tim McIntire
Marshal Sam Corbett............... Robert Wilke
Mrs. James............................. Ann Doran

Television is apparently capable of making a hero out of anyone. This Western sympathetically portrayed the murderous James brothers, notorious in the Old West as robbers and desperadoes, as latter-day Robin Hoods driven to violence against their will. Christopher Jones played young, handsome, romantic Jesse, while Allen Case played his steadier older brother Frank. Occasionally featured in stories were Cole and Bob Younger, another pleasant pair drawn from Western history, and Marshal Sam Corbett. The Jameses' adventures, and attempts to show that they weren't all that bad, lasted for a single season on ABC.

LEGEND OF PRINCE VALIANT, THE (*Cartoon*)

BROADCAST HISTORY:

The Family Channel
30 minutes
Produced: *1991–1994* (65 episodes)
Premiered: *September 3, 1991*

VOICES:

Prince Valiant........................ Robby Benson
King Arthur.................... Efrem Zimbalist, Jr.
Queen Guinevere................. Samantha Eggar
Sir Gawain............................... Tim Curry
Merlin......................... Alan Oppenheimer
Arn.................................. Michael Horton
Rowanne............................... Noelle North

A world of castles, kings, and pageantry was the setting of this action cartoon, adapted from the long-running comic strip. Valiant, son of King Willem and aspiring knight of the round table at King Arthur's Camelot, was the teenage hero who fought dastardly foes across England with the help of his brave companions and the wise counsel of Merlin.

LEGENDS (*Documentary*)

BROADCAST HISTORY:

VH1
60 minutes
Original episodes: *1996–*
Premiered: *c. December 1, 1996*

Biography series about rock "legends," ranging from Johnny Cash to The Clash.

LEGENDS OF THE HIDDEN TEMPLE (*Quiz/Audience Participation*)

BROADCAST HISTORY:

Nickelodeon
30 minutes
Produced: *1993–1995* (120 episodes)
Premiered: *September 11, 1993*

REGULARS:

Kirk Fogg, host
Dee Baker, voice of Olmec

An action-packed kids' game show combining questions and physical challenges. The young contestants competed for the chance to retrieve an object from a giant Mayan temple, for example, the stolen royal pendant of King Kamehameha or the treasure map of Blackbeard. The show was co-hosted by Olmec, the temple's talking granite wall, who in rumbling tones revealed the legend of the day and explained the rules.

LEGMEN (*Detective Drama*)

FIRST TELECAST: *January 20, 1984*
LAST TELECAST: *March 16, 1984*
BROADCAST HISTORY:

Jan 1984–Feb 1984, NBC Fri 8:00–9:00
Feb 1984–Mar 1984, NBC Fri 9:00–10:00

CAST:

Jack Gage .... Bruce Greenwood
David Taylor .... J. T. Terlesky
Oscar Armismendi .... Don Calfa
Tom Bannon .... Claude Akins

Take two Southern California college students looking for a little extra income and a good time, and a seedy private eye who needed someone to do his legwork cheap, and you have the plot for *Legmen*. Jack and David usually started out on simple car-repossession or process-serving errands, but ended up involved in dangerous cases with flying bullets and beautiful women. Oscar was their original employer, replaced after a few episodes by the more demanding Tom Bannon.

LENNY (*Situation Comedy*)

FIRST TELECAST: *September 10, 1990*
LAST TELECAST: *March 9, 1991*
BROADCAST HISTORY:

Sep 1990, CBS Mon 8:30–9:00
Sep 1990–Oct 1990, CBS Wed 8:00–8:30
Dec 1990–Mar 1991, CBS Sat 8:30–9:00

CAST:

Lenny Callahan .... Lenny Clarke
Shelly Callahan .... Lee Garlington
Kelly Callahan (age 13) .... Jenna Von Oy
Tracy Callahan (10) .... Alexis Caldwell
Elizabeth Callahan .... The Farmer Twins
Eddie Callahan .... Peter Dobson
Pat Callahan .... Eugene Roche
Mary Callahan .... Alice Drummond

Lenny Callahan was a good-natured, philosophical, working-class husband holding down two jobs to try and make a better life for his family in this blue-collar comedy. By day he was a laborer for the Boston electric company and in the evenings he moonlighted as a doorman at a fancy hotel. His devoted wife, Shelly, was a full-time homemaker raising their three children—Kelly, a teenager more interested in her social life than her schoolwork; Tracy, a precocious if cynical 10-year-old; and Elizabeth, a cute little toddler. Also seen regularly were his younger brother, Eddie, an unemployed fast-buck artist who spent most of his time dreaming up get-rich-quick schemes that invariably ended up costing Lenny money; and his aging parents, Pat and Mary. Lenny loved them all, but their problems became his problems and their financial woes always seemed to be pushing him deeper into debt.

LEO & LIZ IN BEVERLY HILLS (*Situation Comedy*)

FIRST TELECAST: *April 25, 1986*
LAST TELECAST: *June 6, 1986*
BROADCAST HISTORY:

Apr 1986–Jun 1986, CBS Fri 8:30–9:00

CAST:

Leo Green .... Harvey Korman
Liz Green .... Valerie Perrine
Diane Fedderson .... Deborah Harmon
Jerry Fedderson .... Kenneth Kimmins
Mitzi Green .... Sue Ball
Lucille Trumbley .... Julie Payne
Leonard .... Michael J. Pollard

Leo & Liz in Beverly Hills had a certain family resemblance to *The Beverly Hillbillies*. Both series dealt with the comedic problems of folks from back East adjusting to the lifestyle in affluent Beverly Hills. Unlike the Clampetts of *Hillbillies* fame, however, who were oblivious to what they were doing wrong, the Greens wanted desperately to fit in. Having worked hard to make something of their lives in their native New Jersey, nouveau riche Leo and Liz moved to Beverly Hills to enjoy the fruits of their labors. Along with the normal problems of moving into a new place with a different social structure, they had to deal with the pretentious family into which their daughter Mitzi had married and two batty servants, Lucille the maid and Leonard the handyman. The Feddersons were their next-door neighbors.

Created, written, co-produced, and directed by veteran comedian Steve Martin, *Leo & Liz in Beverly Hills* was first seen as an episode of *George Burns Comedy Week* in the fall of 1985.

LES CRANE SHOW, THE, see *ABC's Nightlife*

LESLIE UGGAMS SHOW, THE (*Musical Variety*)

FIRST TELECAST: *September 28, 1969*
LAST TELECAST: *December 14, 1969*
BROADCAST HISTORY:

Sep 1969–Dec 1969, CBS Sun 9:00–10:00

REGULARS:

Leslie Uggams
Dennis Allen
Lillian Hayman
Lincoln Kilpatrick
Allison Mills
Johnny Brown
The Howard Roberts Singers
The Donald McKayle Dancers
Nelson Riddle and His Orchestra

Singer Leslie Uggams was the star of this musical-variety series. In addition to her singing and dancing, and turns by weekly guest stars, a regular feature of the program was a continuing comedy sketch called "Sugar Hill." It dealt with the lives of a middle-class black family in a large city. The family consisted of Henrietta (Leslie Uggams), her husband B.J. (Lincoln Kilpatrick), her mother (Lillian Hayman), her brother

Lamar (Johnny Brown), and her sister Oletha (Allison Mills). The only white regular on the show was sketch comedian Dennis Allen.

LESS THAN PERFECT (*Situation Comedy*)
FIRST TELECAST: *October 1, 2002*
LAST TELECAST:
BROADCAST HISTORY:
Oct 2002–, ABC Tue 9:30–10:00
CAST:
Claudia "Claude" Casey .... Sara Rue
Ramona Platt .... Sherri Shepherd
Owen Kronsky .... Andy Dick
Kipp Steadman .... Zachary Levi
Lydia Weston .... Andrea Parker
Will Butler .... Eric Roberts

Office temp Claude may have been a little "less than perfect" on the outside, with her chubby figure and low self-esteem, but she still managed to brighten the office at New York's GBN television network. She had worked for two years as a floater in the "middle earth" of obscure administrative departments before being promoted to the twenty-second floor and the coveted position of assistant to suave, egotistical anchorman Will. There she faced pompous backstabber Kipp, an assistant producer, and arrogant (and skinny) Lydia, who wanted Claude's job for herself. Every day Claude brought cheerfulness, and sometimes freshly baked brownies, to the office, and every day Kipp and Lydia plotted to sabotage her, to no avail. Chubby, tart Ramona and flaky Owen were Claude's pals from the lower floors.

LESSON IN SAFETY (*Instruction*)
FIRST TELECAST: *September 8, 1951*
LAST TELECAST: *October 20, 1951*
BROADCAST HISTORY:
Sep 1951–Oct 1951, ABC Sat 9:00–9:30

Accident-prevention films, covering such subjects as fire safety, driving, bicycling, and freight handling.

LET THERE BE STARS (*Musical Variety*)
FIRST TELECAST: *October 16, 1949*
LAST TELECAST: *November 27, 1949*
BROADCAST HISTORY:
Oct 1949–Nov 1949, ABC Sun 9:00–10:00

The premiere telecast of this hour-long musical revue was a producer's dream: big budget, cast of bright, talented young newcomers, top-notch production, and a rave review in the next morning's issue of *Variety* ("Here's a show to make the detractors of Hollywood's video entries eat their words."). The talent was rounded up by a Rodgers and Hammerstein talent scout in the process of casting R&H shows, and included Patti Brill, Jane Harvey, Tom Noonan, and Peter Marshall. One of the novel (for the time) production devices used on the program was "Teleparencies," a projected background effect that moved, dissolved, and faded in and out with the action.

Subsequent shows apparently did not live up to the premiere, and the series folded after a few weeks. It was seen in the East via kinescope, having premiered on West Coast television on September 21, 1949.

LET'S BOWL (*Situation Comedy*)
BROADCAST HISTORY:
Comedy Central
30 minutes
Original episodes: *2001* (10 episodes)
Premiered: *August 19, 2001*
CAST:
Steve "Chopper" Sedahl .... Himself
Wally Hotvedt .... Rich Kronfeld
William Nathan Beauregard Manassas "Ernie" Jansen .... Drew Jansen
Queen Pin Amanda Brewer .... Herself
Queen Pin Lisa Bartholomew .... Herself

Having found one hit series on a local station in Minnesota (*Mystery Science Theater 3000*), Comedy Central tried another in 2001, with less success. In this over-the-top parody of local bowling shows, two people with some kind of minor beef (an office employee who felt a coworker had "embarrassed" him, a wife who wanted her husband to get rid of his ugly haircut) competed for an apology, plus dubious prizes such as 500 pounds of Polish sausage, a used snowmobile, or lunch in Duluth. Covering the play-by-play in matching blue polyester blazers, yellow ties and huge headsets were Wally and Chopper. Both were terminally cheery, although Wally was prone to sudden outbursts of insults and bitterness. Ernie Jansen ("on the Mega-Jam") was the low-rent musical accompanist, and Amanda and Lisa the "Queen Pins" in red sequined dresses who performed synchronized dances during the competition.

Let's Bowl originated on a local Minneapolis station in 1995. Presumably it returned there after its short run on Comedy Central.

LET'S DANCE (*Music*)
FIRST TELECAST: *September 11, 1954*
LAST TELECAST: *October 16, 1954*
BROADCAST HISTORY:
Sep 1954–Oct 1954, ABC Sat 8:00–9:00
REGULARS:
(New York):
Ralph Flanagan Orchestra
Julius LaRosa
Martha Wright
(Chicago):
Art Mooney Orchestra
June Valli
Fran Allison

Short-lived dance-music series originating from both New York and Chicago. Featured bands were Ralph Flanagan from New York's Hotel New Yorker and Art Mooney from Chicago's Aragon Ballroom, with vocalists and guest celebrities. Celebrities, seated at a "VIP table" near the bandstand, were interviewed by Martha Wright in New York and Fran Allison (of *Kukla, Fran & Ollie* fame) in Chicago. Added features were a "Sing a Song for TV" segment in New York and a "Dance for TV" interlude in Chicago, in which a member of the audience was caught in the spotlight and invited to perform on live nationwide television. For the final telecast, Art Mooney was replaced on the Chicago end by Billy May's Orchestra.

LET'S MAKE A DEAL (*Quiz/Audience Participation*)
FIRST TELECAST: *May 21, 1967*
LAST TELECAST: *March 18, 2003*
BROADCAST HISTORY:
May 1967–Sep 1967, NBC Sun 8:30–9:00
Feb 1969–May 1969, ABC Fri 9:00–9:30

May 1969–Jan 1970, ABC Fri 7:30–8:00
Jan 1970–Jan 1971, ABC Sat 7:30–8:00
Jan 1971–Aug 1971, ABC Mon 7:30–8:00
Mar 2003, NBC Tue 8:00–9:00

EMCEE:
Monty Hall (1967–1971)
Billy Bush (2003)

ANNOUNCER:
Jay Stewart (1967–1971)

Let's Make a Deal premiered on the NBC daytime lineup in December 1963, and first moved to nighttime in 1967. The basic format had emcee Monty Hall open the show by choosing contestants from among members of the studio audience—who came dressed in outrageous costumes to attract his attention. The contestants chosen could trade something that they had brought with them for a first prize. They then had the opportunity to trade this first modest prize for objects hidden in boxes or behind curtains on the stage.

The hidden prizes could be trips, money, expensive jewelry, or other valuable merchandise—or they could be "zonks," worthless nonsense prizes. Many of the contestants were offered multiple options to test their greed in "trading" what they had already won for something possibly more expensive—or possibly a "zonk." At the end of the show the "Big Deal of the Day" gave two of the biggest winners the chance to trade their loot for whatever was behind one of three curtains. Although there was rarely a "zonk" at this point, a big winner could end up trading his current prizes for something worth much less.

In addition to its 13-year daytime run (1963–1968 on NBC, 1968–1976 on ABC), *Let's Make a Deal* appeared in prime time as a summer-replacement series in 1967 and as a regular series from 1969 to 1971. There was also a syndicated evening series from 1971 to 1976, a Vancouver-based revival in 1980, and another revival that premiered in the fall of 1984 and ran for two seasons. When *Let's Make a Deal* returned to the NBC daytime lineup in July of 1990, originating from the Disney/MGM Studios Theme Park in Orlando, Florida, there was one major change: for the first time Monty Hall was not the emcee. Hall, one of the creators and producers of *Let's Make a Deal*, had given the reins to a younger man, Bob Hilton. Low ratings prompted Hall to return after a few weeks but the series was dropped from the NBC lineup in January 1991.

Yet another revival aired in prime time on NBC in 2003, produced by Hall and hosted by young Billy Bush, an entertainment reporter for *Access Hollywood* and *The Today Show*, and nephew of President George W. Bush.

LET'S PLAY THE GAME, see *Play the Game*

LET'S RHUMBA (*Dance Instruction*)

FIRST TELECAST: *November 15, 1946*
LAST TELECAST: *January 17, 1947*
BROADCAST HISTORY:
Nov 1946–Jan 1947, NBC Fri 8:15–8:30 (approx.)

HOST:
D'Avalos

Dance-instruction program by D'Avalos, whose accent and oily good looks added a distinct Latin flavor to this early series. The featured dance was the "Ranchero."

LET'S SEE (*Quiz*)

FIRST TELECAST: *July 14, 1955*
LAST TELECAST: *August 25, 1955*
BROADCAST HISTORY:
Jul 1955–Aug 1955, ABC Thu 10:00–10:30

EMCEE:
John Reed King

A short-lived, oddly formatted quiz show filmed at Convention Hall in Atlantic City, New Jersey. Panelists attempted to discover through indirect questions what attractions contestants had seen in Atlantic City. Sponsored by the Atlantic City Chamber of Commerce.

LETTER TO LORETTA, A, see *Loretta Young Show, The*

LEVEL 9 (*Police Drama*)

FIRST TELECAST: *October 27, 2000*
LAST TELECAST: *January 26, 2001*
BROADCAST HISTORY:
Oct 2000–Jan 2001, UPN Fri 9:00–10:00

CAST:
Annie Price .... Kate Hodge
Jerry Hooten .... Romany Malco
Wilbert "Tibbs" Thibodeaux .. Michael Joseph Kelly
Jargon .... Esteban Powell
Margaret "Sosh" Perkins .... Kim Murphy
Joss Nakano .... Susie Park
Roland Travis .... Fabrizio Filippo
Jack Wiley .... Max Martini

"Geeks with guns" was the premise of this high-intensity action series. Annie was the tightly wound former F.B.I. agent who had founded Level 9, a top-secret cybercrime unit. From their high-tech computer operations center in Seattle they could tap into any electronic system, using its monitoring cameras or running its traffic control systems. They used all the latest computer and high-tech equipment to combat everything from the theft of high-security files the attempted destruction of a communications satellite, hackers selling a top-secret chemical formula to terrorists, or a criminal plotting his escape from a maximum-security prison.

Members of the team included Jerry, the tough surveillance specialist; Tibbs, a former Secret Service operative who coordinated mission activities; Joss, the best tracker in the group; Roland, a young hacker who had joined the group as an alternative to being sent to prison; Jack, who provides muscle; and Jargon and Sosh, two technicians with the computer skills to hack into any system as well as fight off the cyberterrorists (such as "CrayZhorse") who targeted them.

LEWIS & CLARK (*Situation Comedy*)

FIRST TELECAST: *October 29, 1981*
LAST TELECAST: *July 30, 1982*
BROADCAST HISTORY:
Oct 1981–Nov 1981, NBC Thu 8:30–9:00
Dec 1981–Jan 1982, NBC Sat 8:30–9:00
Jul 1982, NBC Fri 8:00–8:30

CAST:
Stewart Lewis .... Gabe Kaplan
Roscoe Clark .... Guich Koock
Alicia Lewis .... Ilene Graff
John, the bartender .... Michael McManus
Wendy, the waitress .... Wendy Holcombe

Silas Jones.......................... Clifton James
Kelly Lewis............................ Amy Linker
Keith Lewis .... David Hollander
Lester............................. Aaron Fletcher

Stu Lewis had a dream. Even though he was a city kid, he was fed up with the hustle and bustle of New York, so he packed up his wife Alicia and their two children and moved to sleepy Luckenback, in the Texas Panhandle. The wife and kids hated the idea, but no matter, Stu could at last realize his dream: owning a country-and-western club. He named it the Nassau County Café, after his former home in the New York suburbs. The place had been through so many owners that it sported a sign reading ALWAYS UNDER NEW MANAGEMENT, and the big night of the week was when they had armadillo races. That was just fine with Stu, who had finally found a place where even his weak one-liners could draw a laugh.

Adjusting to the slower pace and the wide-open spaces took some doing for all the Lewises, but they did grow to appreciate the place. Along with the café came a manager, Roscoe Clark—the hick with the dopey grin on his face who was really a mite smarter than he looked. Then there was John, the bartender; Wendy, the goofy waitress; Silas Jones, the local beer distributor; and Lester, the town drunk. They all went out of their way to make the transplanted Easterners feel at home, whatever they thought of those jokes.

LEWISOHN STADIUM CONCERT (*Music*)
FIRST TELECAST: *June 26, 1950*
LAST TELECAST: *August 7, 1950*
BROADCAST HISTORY:
Jun 1950–Aug 1950, NBC Mon 9:30–10:30

Live concerts from New York's Lewisohn Stadium, featuring the New York Philharmonic Orchestra with various conductors and soloists.

LEXX (*Science Fiction*)
BROADCAST HISTORY:
Sci-Fi Channel
60 minutes
Original episodes: *2000–2002* (61 episodes)
Premiered: *January 7, 2000*
CAST:
Stanley H. Tweedle .... Brian Downey
Zev Bellringer (2000).............. Eva Habermann
Xev Bellringer .... Xenia Seeberg
Kai .... Michael McManus
790 .... Jeffrey Hirschfield
Lexx (voice) .... Tom Gallant

A group of misfits traveled through space in a living spaceship resembling a giant dragonfly in this strange, rather gross sci-fi series that was filled with black humor. Lexx was a Manhattan-sized bug, genetically altered to serve as a spacecraft that provided such amenities as pulsing walls and toilets that licked you. Its accidental captain was Stanley Tweedle, a low-level security guard whose right hand happened to be the only object to which the ship's control panel would respond. A weak-willed, self-serving coward, Stanley nevertheless used his newfound power with some responsibility. Also on board were Xev (formerly Zev), a sultry sex slave looking for fulfillment, just not from weasely Stan; Kai, a hunky, pompadoured assassin from the extinct Brunnen-G civilization who had been cyrogenically frozen for 2,000 years and was technically dead; and 790, a decapitated robot of which only the head was left. Despite 790's reduced state, it possessed impressive analytic capabilities that were useful in a crisis. Unfortunately it spent much of its time lusting for Xev and refused to take orders from anyone but the dead Kai.

The motley crew traveled around the universe stopping at such unlikely destinations as the planet Potatohole and the Luvliner sex satellite (a kind of floating whorehouse). They traveled outside Lexx in small crafts called moths. As season two ended, the forces of evil Mantrid (Dieter Laser) were eating up the universe at exponential speed, and nearly got Lexx before it slipped away through a portal. As season three began, the crew emerged 4,000 years later in the Dark Zone, where they met the mysterious and cruel Prince (Nigel Bennett) and became involved in a war between the planets Fire and Water. In season four they orbited Earth, interacted with the milquetoast Earth president Reginald J. Priest and his bimbo companion Bunny, visited Las Vegas, fought off killer carrots, and tried to stop evil Lyekka (Louise Wischermann) from devouring Tokyo. As the series came to a close, Prince visited Lexx and warned of "Earth's date with destiny."

LIAR'S CLUB (*Quiz/Audience Participation*)
BROADCAST HISTORY:
Syndicated only
30 minutes
Produced: *1969; 1976–1978; 1988*
Released: *1969; September 1976; September 1988*
HOST:
Rod Serling (1969)
Bill Armstrong (1976–1977)
Allen Ludden (1977–1978)
Eric Boardman (1988–1989)
PANELISTS (1976–1978):
Larry Hovis
Betty White
Dick Gautier
Fannie Flagg
Norm Crosby
Joey Bishop
Dody Goodman

Contestants on this game show were shown an unusual-looking object, then each of a panel of four celebrities gave an outlandish but plausible explanation as to its use. The contestant then had to wager all or part of an initial $100 on which panelist was telling the truth.

Rod Serling hosted an early and rather obscure version of the show. It returned in 1976 with Bill Armstrong and then Allen Ludden as host. Larry Hovis was the regular panelist on the later show, joined frequently by Betty White, Dick Gautier, and others.

Another revival, titled *The New Liar's Club,* aired during the 1988–1989 season.

LIBERACE SHOW, THE (*Musical Variety*)
FIRST TELECAST: *July 1, 1952*
LAST TELECAST: *September 16, 1969*
BROADCAST HISTORY:
Jul 1952–Aug 1952, NBC Tue/Thu 7:30–7:45
Jul 1969–Sep 1969, CBS Tue 8:30–9:30
REGULARS:
Liberace
George Liberace and Orchestra (1952)

Richard Wattis (1969)
Georgina Moon (1969)
Jack Parnell Orchestra (1969)

Flamboyant pianist "Lee" Liberace (real name: Wladziu Valentino Liberace) appeared frequently on television during the 1950s and 1960s. His trademarks were always the same, and always the butt of innumerable jokes: the outlandish and very expensive wardrobe, the curly hair and pearly-tooth smile, and a florid piano style. Atop his Steinway was always perched an ornate candelabra (imitation Louis XIV). Women, especially older ones, loved it. The critics were not kind, but Liberace did not mind. "I cried," he remarked in one of show business's more memorable quotes, "all the way to the bank."

Liberace's first television exposure was on a local program in Los Angeles in 1951, followed by a 15-minute network summer series in 1952. The following year he began a syndicated series (filmed 1953–1955) that received extremely wide circulation and made him a great deal of money. These films were rerun for years and are said to have aired on more stations than any network or syndicated program up to that time. Later programs included an ABC daytime series in 1958–1959, and a network summer show in 1969, the latter a full hour in length. With him in the early years was violinist brother George, who led the orchestra. The 1969 variety show, which originated in London, featured guest stars and two regulars, Richard Wattis and Georgina Moon, who portrayed Liberace's butler and maid in a regular sketch sequence each week.

In later years Liberace concentrated on personal appearances, especially in Las Vegas, where he entertained a loyal, if aging, following.

LIBRARY OF COMEDY FILMS, see *Movies—Prior to 1961*

LIE DETECTOR (*Discussion*)

BROADCAST HISTORY:
Syndicated only
30 minutes
Produced: *1983* (5 per week; 170 episodes total)
Released: *January 1983*

HOST:
F. Lee Bailey

Famed criminal lawyer and showman F. Lee Bailey hosted this rather peculiar series, in which guests were allowed to substantiate their claims by taking an on-camera polygraph test. Guests were generally people who had been in the news, or on its fringes, due to claims of UFO sightings, reincarnation, involvement in scandals, etc.

LIEUTENANT, THE (*Drama*)

FIRST TELECAST: *September 14, 1963*
LAST TELECAST: *September 5, 1964*
BROADCAST HISTORY:
Sep 1963–Sep 1964, NBC Sat 7:30–8:30

CAST:
Lt. William (Bill) Rice .... Gary Lockwood
Capt. Ray Rambridge .... Robert Vaughn
Lt. Samwell (Sanpan) Panosian (1963) .... Steve Franken
Lt. Harris .... Don Penny
Lily .... Carmen Phillips
Various roles .... Chris Noel
Sgt. Kagey .... John Milford
Maj. Barker .... Henry Beckman
Col. Hiland .... Richard Anderson

The Lieutenant sought to convey what life was like for a newly commissioned officer in the peacetime Marine Corps. Bill Rice had graduated from Annapolis and gone through Marine Officers' Training School at Quantico, Virginia. After leaving Quantico, he was stationed as a second lieutenant at Camp Pendleton, California. Bill's friendly, easygoing manner made him popular with the recruits at Camp Pendleton and with the many girls he dated in an active off-duty social life. Bill's immediate superior was Capt. Ray Rambridge, who was harshly critical not because he disliked Bill, but because he wanted to make a good officer out of him. Also seen regularly was Lily, the owner of the nightclub frequented by Bill when he was off duty. Steve Franken was originally cast as one of Bill's fellow lieutenants, but left the show after five episodes were filmed and was replaced by Don Penny. Actress Chris Noel kept popping up as a recurring regular, but in a different role each time. In one episode she would be a nurse, in another a lady Marine, and in a third one of Bill's girlfriends. Sometimes her role was substantial and sometimes she was only peripherally involved in the story.

LIFE AND LEGEND OF WYATT EARP, THE (*Western*)

FIRST TELECAST: *September 6, 1955*
LAST TELECAST: *September 16, 1961*
BROADCAST HISTORY:
Sep 1955–Sep 1961, ABC Tue 8:30–9:00

CAST:
Wyatt Earp .... Hugh O'Brian
Bat Masterson (1955–1957) .... Mason Alan Dinehart III
Ben Thompson (1955–1956) .... Denver Pyle
Bill Thompson (1955–1956) .... Hal Baylor
Abbie Crandall (1955–1956) .... Gloria Talbot
Marsh Murdock (1955–1956) .... Don Haggerty
Doc Fabrique (1955–1956) .... Douglas Fowley
**Ned Buntline* .... Lloyd Corrigan
Jim "Dog" Kelly (1956–1958) .... Paul Brinegar
Jim "Dog" Kelly (1958–1959) .... Ralph Sanford
Mayor Hoover (1956–1957) .... Selmer Jackson
Deputy Hal Norton (1957–1958) ... William Tannen
Doc Holliday (1957–1961) .... Douglas Fowley
Doc Holliday (temporary; 1959) ...... Myron Healy
Kate Holliday (1957–1959) .... Carol Stone
Shotgun Gibbs (1958–1961) .... Morgan Woodward
Morgan Earp (1959–1961) .... Dirk London
Virgil Earp (1959–1961) .... John Anderson
Nellie Cashman (1959–1960) .... Randy Stuart
Old Man Clanton (1959–1961) ..... Trevor Bardette
Emma Clanton (1959–1960) .... Carol Thurston
Sheriff Johnny Behan (1959) .... Lash La Rue
Sheriff Johnny Behan (1959–1961) .... Steve Brodie
Curley Bill Brocius (1959–1961) .... William Phipps
Johnny Ringo (1960–1961) .... Britt Lomond
Mayor Clum (1960–1961) .... Stacy Harris
Doc Goodfellow (1959–1961) ..... Damian O'Flynn

*Occasional

In the make-believe world of TV Westerns, *Wyatt Earp* was unique. Not only was it based on fact (more or less—there was a real Marshal Wyatt Earp, and he did have a very colorful life), but it developed its characters over a period of six years in a continuing story involving politics and family relationships as well as standard Western action. It was in many respects a serial drama. Part of the reason for this orientation was no doubt author-playwright Frederick Hazlitt Brennan, who wrote the scripts from the start.

The series began in 1955 with an episode titled "Mr. Earp Becomes a Marshal," in which Wyatt's friend, Marshal Whitney of Ellsworth, Kansas, was killed by a gunman. Wyatt accepted his badge and avenged his death. Wyatt's friend, famed showman and writer Ned Buntline, then provided him with his trademark, two "Buntline Special" pistols—.45s with extra-long barrels—with which to keep the peace. (The first time Wyatt saw them he locked Buntline in the pokey for carrying "over-sized pistols.") Their recoil was pretty ferocious, but their extra range allowed the marshal to drop an opponent from the other side of town. They proved handy, for during the rest of the first season Wyatt faced an array of foes in and around Ellsworth, including the murderous John Wesley Hardin and—most frequently—the outlaw Thompson brothers.

But Ellsworth was too small for Wyatt's talents, and for the second season he moved on to Dodge City to become marshal there (with no reference made to the fact that Matt Dillon already had that job, at least on Saturday nights). Young Bat Masterson joined him as deputy for a while, before becoming a county sheriff in his own right. Wyatt then tried out Bat's brother Ed Masterson as a sidekick, but finally settled on Hal Norton as his deputy. Another character introduced in the 1956–1957 season was Wyatt's pal Jim "Dog" Kelly, who eventually got himself elected mayor of Dodge City, replacing Mayor Hoover. The 1957–1958 season brought an even more colorful real-life character to Dodge, the notorious Doc Holliday, a physician turned gambler and schemer (played by the same actor who had previously been Ellsworth's Doc Fabrique). Wyatt's brothers Virgil and Morgan Earp began to turn up in occasional episodes, usually requiring a steadying hand from their older brother.

In the 1959–1960 season Wyatt moved again, this time to Tombstone, Arizona, and the greatest battle of his career. Tombstone was a rough-and-ready town run by Old Man Clanton, leader of the "Ten Percent Gang." Clanton ruled the territory with an iron hand, exacting tribute from citizens and masterminding gunrunning schemes across the Mexican border. Johnny Behan was his hand-picked sheriff in Tombstone, and he had a private army of gunslingers to enforce his will. For two years, Earp, as marshal, battled the Clanton gang through political and legal means. Shotgun Gibbs, a peace-loving frontiersman, followed Wyatt from Dodge City to Tombstone to become his deputy. Some of Dodge's less respectable citizens showed up too, including Doc Holliday and gunslinger Curley Bill Brocius. Nellie Cashman provided some love interest for a season (Wyatt was always handy with the womenfolk) as the operator of the Birdcage Saloon.

The final showdown, again based on fact, came at the end of the last season, in 1961. In a five-part story that concluded *Wyatt Earp*'s original run, Wyatt discovered that the Clanton gang was using the O.K. corral as a center and fortress for their illegal activities. Wyatt tried to prevent bloodshed, but events moved rapidly toward a climactic shootout in which Wyatt, his brothers Morgan and Virgil, and Doc Holliday broke the power of the Clanton gang in the famous gunfight at the O.K. corral.

LIFE . . . AND STUFF (*Situation Comedy*)
FIRST TELECAST: *June 6, 1997*
LAST TELECAST: *June 27, 1997*
BROADCAST HISTORY:
Jun 1997, CBS Fri 8:30–9:00
CAST:
Rick Boswell . . . . Rick Reynolds
Ronnie Boswell . . . . Pam Dawber
Andy Boswell . . . . David Bowe
Bernie Skabinsky . . . . Fred Applegate
Jordan Emory . . . . Anita Barone
Jerry Boswell . . . . Tanner Lee Prairie
Shawn Boswell (pilot only) . . . . Brandon Allen
Shawn Boswell . . . . Kevin Keckeisen
Christine . . . . Andrea Martin

Short-lived summer comedy about a very loud marriage. Rick and Ronnie had been married for ten years and the wear and tear was showing. With his high-stress job as an advertising executive and her long hours running the household and caring for their two boys, Jerry and Shawn, there wasn't much time for romance—or even meaningful talk. So they yelled a lot. Jordan and Bernie, who they tried to fix up with Ronnie's friend Christine, worked with Rick. Andy, Rick's unemployed, slightly spaced-out brother, lived in a trailer parked in the family's suburban driveway.

Comedian Reynolds had adapted his rather dark standup material for this cynical series—this was no *Father Knows Best*—and the depressing mood didn't attract much of an audience. Six episodes had been produced, but CBS pulled the plug after only four had aired.

LIFE AND TIMES OF . . . (*Biography*)
BROADCAST HISTORY:
The Nashville Network
60 minutes
Produced: *1995–2001*
Premiered: *January 4, 1996* (series)

TNN's version of the venerable *Biography*, focusing on country stars past and present. Among the early subjects were Marty Robbins, Dottie West, Roy Acuff, and Gary Cooper. Some installments appear to have been recycled from earlier documentary series, such as *Yesterday & Today*. Previously seen as specials.

LIFE AND TIMES OF GRIZZLY ADAMS, THE (*Adventure*)
FIRST TELECAST: *February 9, 1977*
LAST TELECAST: *July 26, 1978*
BROADCAST HISTORY:
Feb 1977–Jul 1978, NBC Wed 8:00–9:00
CAST:
James "Grizzly" Adams . . . . Dan Haggerty
Mad Jack . . . . Denver Pyle
Nakuma . . . . Don Shanks
Robbie Cartman . . . . John Bishop

Set in the western United States during the late 1800s, *The Life and Times of Grizzly Adams* was the story of a man accused of a crime he had not committed, who sought refuge in the wilderness and discovered that life there suited him better than life in the city. With the help of a friend named Mad Jack and an Indian blood brother, Nakuma, Grizzly built a sturdy cabin and determined to live in harmony with nature. A grizzly bear cub that he had rescued from a ledge became his roommate. The bear was christened Ben, and though he grew to be an imposing animal weighing several hundred pounds, he remained as friendly as a child. With Ben as his constant companion, the bearded Grizzly Adams found wilderness adventure in dealing with nature, the elements, and strangers passing through. A frequent visitor was young Robbie Cartman, the son of a farmer living in the area, who loved to listen to Grizzly's tales.

Dan Haggerty, who starred in this series, played the same role in the movie *The Life and Times of Grizzly Adams*, and a similar role in another film, *The Adventures of Frontier Freemont*. Haggerty was originally an animal trainer rather than an actor, and was chosen for the film roles partly because of his remarkable rapport with bears. Denver Pyle appeared as his co-star in both films.

There was a real Grizzly Adams, upon whom this series was loosely based. He was born in Massachusetts in 1812, and spent many years in the Sierra Nevadas after having gone bankrupt through a series of unfortunate business deals. The real Grizzly was a bit less altruistic than his TV counterpart. Having deserted his wife and children, he spent much of his time hunting and killing animals and capturing others for zoos (a few of the larger beasts almost killed *him* on one occasion or another). The real Ben died in a zoo that Adams himself opened in San Francisco in the 1850s. But Adams also loved animals and cared for many of them throughout his wilderness days. He died while on tour with P. T. Barnum in 1860.

LIFE BEGINS AT EIGHTY (*Discussion*)
FIRST TELECAST: *January 13, 1950*
LAST TELECAST: *February 25, 1956*
BROADCAST HISTORY:
Jan 1950–Mar 1950, NBC Fri 9:30–10:00
Apr 1950–Jul 1950, NBC Sat 7:30–8:00
Jul 1950–Aug 1950, NBC Fri 9:00–9:30
Oct 1950–Dec 1950, ABC Tue 10:00–10:30
Dec 1950–Sep 1951, ABC Tue 9:30–10:00
Oct 1951–Mar 1952, ABC Mon 8:30–9:00
Mar 1952–Jun 1952, DUM Fri 8:30–9:00
Jul 1952–Jun 1954, DUM Fri 9:00–9:30
Sep 1954–Jul 1955, DUM Sun 9:30–10:00
Aug 1955–Oct 1955, ABC Sun 9:30–10:00
Oct 1955–Dec 1955, ABC Sun 10:00–10:30
Jan 1956–Feb 1956, ABC Sat 10:00–10:30
EMCEE:
Jack Barry
REGULAR PANELISTS:
Mrs. Georgiana Carhart
Fred Stein

Jack Barry created a radio version of *Life Begins at 80* in 1948, as a copy of his successful *Juvenile Jury*—substituting octogenarians for the youngsters. A panel of oldsters was posed questions submitted by viewers, and given the opportunity to expound on life from the vantage point of their years. They often provided hilarious quips and insights, and needed little prompting from Barry. An additional highlight of the show, which became more prominent toward the later years of the TV run, was the "Footlight Favorite." This was a show-business personality who performed for the audience. Some of these guests were themselves old-timers, like vaudevillians Joe Howard and Smith & Dale, singer Morton Downey and cornetist Vincent Buono (who performed with other original members of the Sousa Band); others, such as Lanny Ross and Faye Emerson, were younger.

Much of the appeal of *Life Begins at 80* lay in the chemistry of its panelists, the most delightful of whom were Mrs. Georgiana Carhart, an engaging flirt who told stories with an Irish brogue ("Why worry," she quipped, "you'll never get out of life alive anyway."), and Fred Stein, an active realtor who viewed life with similar enthusiasm. The two of them were with the show throughout its history, though both were nearing 90 by the end of the run. (The ages given for individual panelists vary somewhat, according to the source!) Oddly enough, continuity of panel members was less a problem on this show than on those with younger panels. The panelists might eventually die off, but none seemed to give up voluntarily. Among those appearing for extended periods were Joseph Rosenthal (85), John Draney (89), pianist Paolo Gallico (82), vaudevillian Lorna Standish (80), and Thomas Clark (81).

Emcee Barry (32) sometimes closed the show with a quote from Julia Ward Howe, who said of old age that "all the sugar is at the bottom of the cup."

LIFE, CAMERA, ACTION (*Comedy*)
BROADCAST HISTORY:
Fox Family Channel
30 minutes
Produced: *1998*
Premiered: *August 17, 1998*
HOST:
Kristen Eykel

Another home videos show, patterned after *America's Funniest Home Videos*.

LIFE GOES ON (*Drama*)
FIRST TELECAST: *September 12, 1989*
LAST TELECAST: *August 29, 1993*
BROADCAST HISTORY:
Sep 1989, ABC Tue 10:00–11:00
Sep 1989, ABC Fri 9:00–10:00
Sep 1989–Mar 1993, ABC Sun 7:00–8:00
May 1993–Aug 1993, ABC Sun 7:00–8:00
CAST:
Drew Thatcher .... Bill Smitrovich
Libby Thatcher .... Patti LuPone
Charles "Corky" Thatcher (age 18)
.... Christopher Burke
Rebecca "Becca" Thatcher (14) .... Kellie Martin
Paige Thatcher (1989–1990) .... Monique Lanier
Paige Thatcher (1990–1993) ...... Tracey Needham
Tyler Benchfield (1989–1991) .... Tommy Puett
Maxie (1989–1991) .... Tanya Fenmore
**Rona Lieberman (1989–1990)* .... Michele Matheson
Jerry Berkson (1990–1992) .... Ray Buktenica
Gina (1990–1991) .... Mary Page Keller
Zoe (1990–1991) .... Leigh Ann Orsi
Hans (1990–1991) .... David Byrd
Jesse McKenna (1991–1993) .... Chad Lowe
**Artie McDonald (1991–1993)* .... Troy Evans
Amanda Swanson (1992–1993) ... Andrea Friedman
Goodman (1992–1993) .... Kiersten Warren
**Michael Romanov (1992–1993)* .... Lance Guest

*Occasional
THEME:
"Ob-La-Di, Ob-La-Da," by John Lennon–Paul McCartney, sung by Patti LuPone and the cast

This gentle family drama was a television breakthrough, the first series built around a character who was mentally handicapped (although earlier series, such as *L.A. Law*, had such characters in the cast). Corky Thatcher was certainly intelligent, but because of his affliction with Down syndrome, he was just entering Marshall High School at age 18, "mainstreaming" after years of special education classes. There he would be a classmate of his younger sister Becca, who was torn between her sense of responsibility for her brother and her own need to fit in. Corky's loving parents were Drew, a former construction foreman who opened his own restaurant, the Glenbrook Grill; and Libby, a former singer (Broadway actress LuPone sometimes sang on the series) who alternated between a career in advertising and raising a family. In 1991 Libby, at age 40, had a third child, a baby boy. Paige was Drew's troubled daughter from a previous marriage, a college dropout who returned to live with him when her relationship failed.

Among the family's friends and relatives in Glenbrook were Becca's sometimes beau, Tyler; her archrival at school, Rona; Libby's sister Gina and her daughter Zoe, who also came to live in the crowded house; and Jerry, Libby's boss at the ad agency. The family "semi-wonder dog" was Arnold. Stories revolved around the ever-optimistic Corky's progress fitting in, his first date, etc., as well as Becca's growing pains and the travails of the family business.

The later seasons brought increasingly serious stories. Becca found a new love in handsome Jesse, who was HIV positive, leading to several AIDS-related stories. Corky fell in love with Amanda, who also had Down syndrome; they eloped in the fall of 1992. Paige married and became pregnant by Michael.

The final episode, in May 1993, described the characters' later lives. Becca and Jesse broke up but two years later reunited and were married. She wanted to have his baby, but they were married only a short time before he died; when she later married someone else, she named their son "Jessie." Corky finally completed high school but at the last minute was told he would not graduate because he had not met "all the requirements." Bitterly disappointed, he declared, "I'll be back." Paige, older, wiser, and once again single, went into the construction business with older partner Artie. Life goes on.

LIFE IS WORTH LIVING (*Religious Talk*)
FIRST TELECAST: *February 12, 1952*
LAST TELECAST: *April 8, 1957*
BROADCAST HISTORY:
Feb 1952–Apr 1955, DUM Tue 8:00–8:30 (OS)
Oct 1955–Apr 1956, ABC Thu 8:00–8:30
Oct 1956–Apr 1957, ABC Mon 9:00–9:30
HOST:
Bishop Fulton J. Sheen

There was a time when anything was possible in prime-time television, even a weekly half hour featuring a charming, well-spoken Catholic bishop offering anecdotes and little lessons in morality ("sermons" would be too stuffy a word) for a large and devoted following. *Life Is Worth Living* was probably the most widely viewed religious series in TV history, and sponsors often paid a premium to have their commercials next to it (since they couldn't get *in* it). Its "star" and only "regular" was the Most Reverend Fulton J. Sheen, Auxiliary Bishop of New York, a modest, middle-level cleric who had long been heard on radio. On TV he was seen in a simulated study, punctuating his points with drawings scrawled on a blackboard. (One of his "angels," his TV crew, would slip in when he moved away, to clean off the board; the identity of this unseen hand was a great source of speculation among viewers). The bishop's famous sign-off: "God love you."

Many of Bishop Sheen's talks revolved around the evils of world communism, and perhaps the series' most dramatic incident came in early 1953 when he delivered a hair-raising reading of the burial scene from *Julius Caesar*, with the names of Caesar, Cassius, Marc Antony, and Brutus replaced by Stalin, Beria, Malenkov, and Vishinsky. "Stalin," Sheen intoned, with hypnotic forcefulness, "must one day meet his judgment." A few days later the Russian dictator suffered a sudden stroke, and a week later he was dead. There was never any comment from Sheen's office on this remarkable coincidence, which was widely reported in the press.

Four years after leaving ABC, Bishop Sheen returned with a half-hour syndicated series, *The Bishop Sheen Program,* which ran from 1961 to 1968. Despite the name change, it was virtually indistinguishable in format from *Life Is Worth Living.*

LIFE OF LEONARDO DA VINCI, THE (*Historical Drama*)
FIRST TELECAST: *August 13, 1972*
LAST TELECAST: *September 10, 1972*
BROADCAST HISTORY:
Aug 1972–Sep 1972, CBS Sun 9:30–10:30
CAST:
Leonardo Da Vinci .... Philippe Leroy

This five-part dramatization of the life, achievements, and explorations of one of the greatest geniuses the world has ever known was originally produced in Italy. It was the Grand Prize winner at the 1972 Monte Carlo International Television Festival and was brought to American television by CBS in the summer of 1972.

LIFE OF RILEY, THE (*Situation Comedy*)
FIRST TELECAST: *October 4, 1949*
LAST TELECAST: *August 22, 1958*
BROADCAST HISTORY:
Oct 1949–Mar 1950, NBC Tue 9:30–10:00
Jan 1953–Sep 1956, NBC Fri 8:30–9:00 (OS)
Oct 1956–Dec 1956, NBC Fri 8:00–8:30
Jan 1957–Aug 1958, NBC Fri 8:30–9:00
CAST (1949–1950):
Chester A. Riley .... Jackie Gleason
Peg Riley .... Rosemary DeCamp
Junior .... Lanny Rees
Babs .... Gloria Winters
Jim Gillis .... Sid Tomack
Digby "Digger" O'Dell .... John Brown
CAST (1953–1958):
Chester A. Riley .... William Bendix
Peg Riley .... Marjorie Reynolds
Junior .... Wesley Morgan
Babs Riley Marshall .... Lugene Sanders
Jim Gillis (1953–1955, 1956–1958) ... Tom D'Andrea
Honeybee Gillis (1953–1955, 1956–1958)
.... Gloria Blondell

Egbert Gillis (1953–1955) .... Gregory Marshall
Cunningham .... Douglas Dumbrille
Dangle .... Robert Sweeney
Hank Hawkins .... Emory Parnell
Waldo Binney .... Sterling Holloway
Otto Schmidlap .... Henry Kulky
Calvin Dudley (1955–1956) ...... George O'Hanlon
Belle Dudley (1955–1956) ..... Florence Sundstrom
Don Marshall (1957–1958) .... Martin Milner

Television's original lovable bumbler was Chester A. Riley, a hardhat with a soft heart and a genius for unwittingly turning order into chaos. The role had been created on radio in 1943 by William Bendix. However, when the time came for the move to television, Bendix was tied up with movie commitments, and the opportunity went to young Jackie Gleason—his first TV series.

Riley worked in an aircraft plant in California, but viewers usually saw him at home, cheerfully disrupting life with his malapropisms and ill-timed intervention into minor problems. His stock answer to every turn of fate became a catchphrase: "What a revoltin' development this is!" Riley's long-suffering wife, Peg, and their children, Babs and Junior, somehow saw that it always came out all right in the end. Others seen were Gillis, Riley's sarcastic friend, and "Digger" O'Dell, the smiling undertaker ("Guess I'd better be shoveling off . . ."), played by John Brown, the only member of the radio cast to make the transition to TV.

Jackie Gleason's bug-eyed portrayal of Riley did not catch on, and the program was canceled after only one season. Three years later it returned with an entirely new cast, headed by William Bendix, and ran for five years. The cast was relatively stable through the second run, although a few neighbors came and went and Babs eventually left to get married and Junior to go to college. Both kids returned occasionally to visit.

The show was filmed in Hollywood.

LIFE WITH BONNIE (*Situation Comedy*)

FIRST TELECAST: *September 17, 2002*
LAST TELECAST:
BROADCAST HISTORY:
Sep 2002, ABC Tue 8:30–9:00
Oct 2002–Mar 2003, ABC Tue 9:00–9:30
Jul 2003– , ABC Tue 8:30–9:00

CAST:
Bonnie Molloy .... Bonnie Hunt
Dr. Mark Molloy .... Mark Derwin
Samantha Molloy ...... Samantha Browne-Walters
Charlie Molloy .... Charlie Stewart
Gloria .... Marianne Muellerleile
David Bellows .... David Alan Grier
Tony Russo .... Anthony Russell
Holly .... Holly Wortell
Marv .... Chris Barnes
Frankie .... Frankie Ryan

Bonnie was a happy, harried talk-show host and mom in this fast-paced sitcom set in Chicago. On the home front were her busy husband, Dr. Mark; young daughter Samantha; supercute, red-haired son Charlie, and gurgling baby Hunter, all of whom were seemingly in constant motion. Gloria was the dumpy, smart-aleck maid, and Frankie was Charlie's pint-sized friend. Bonnie's other family was found on the set of her show, *Morning Chicago*—fussy producer David, jazzy pianist Tony, and wisecracking stagehands Holly and Marv. One of the features of *Life with Bonnie* was Ms. Hunt's improvised segments with guests, who included such stars as David Duchovny, Jonathan Winters, Tom Hanks, Robin Williams and Carl Reiner (as station owner Mr. Portinbody).

LIFE WITH ELIZABETH (*Situation Comedy*)

BROADCAST HISTORY:
Syndicated only
30 minutes
Produced: *1953–1955* (65 episodes)
Released: *October 1953*

CAST:
Elizabeth .... Betty White
Alvin .... Del Moore
Mrs. Chlorine "Chloe" Skinridge .... Lois Bridge
Richard .... Dick Garton
Mr. Fuddy .... Ray Erlenborn

ANNOUNCER:
Jack Narz

This domestic comedy was the first starring vehicle for Betty White. Each program consisted of three separate episodes in the life of a married couple, with the emphasis placed on gentle comedy and more talk than action. Alvin was the husband, a junior executive; Chloe, their neighbor; Richard, Alvin's not-too-bright friend; and Mr. Fuddy, Alvin's boss. Stormy was the couple's 185-pound St. Bernard, and Bandie, their Pekinese.

Betty White was fresh from local TV in Los Angeles, where she had originated *Life With Elizabeth* on KLAC-TV a year earlier. Hailed for her girl-next-door good looks (*TV Guide* called her a candidate for "America's Sweetheart"), she soon had her own daytime show on NBC, then graduated to several nighttime series (see Index).

LIFE WITH FATHER (*Situation Comedy*)

FIRST TELECAST: *November 22, 1953*
LAST TELECAST: *July 5, 1955*
BROADCAST HISTORY:
Nov 1953–May 1954, CBS Sun 7:00–7:30
Aug 1954–Dec 1954, CBS Tue 10:00–10:30
Jan 1955–Jul 1955, CBS Tue 8:00–8:30

CAST:
Clarence Day, Sr. .... Leon Ames
Vinnie Day .... Lurene Tuttle
Clarence Day, Jr. (1953–1954) .... Ralph Reed
Clarence Day, Jr. (1954–1955) .... Steven Terrell
Whitney Day (1953–1954) .... Ronald Keith
Whitney Day (1954–1955) .... B. G. Norman
Whitney Day (1955) .... Freddy Ridgeway
Harlan Day .... Harvey Grant
John Day (1953–1954) .... Freddie Leiston
John Day (1954–1955) .... Malcolm Cassell
Margaret .... Dorothy Bernard
Nora .... Marion Ross

Clarence Day, Jr.'s nostalgic autobiographical articles in *The New Yorker* were very successful in the 1920s. They later led to a best-selling novel, hit play, Hollywood movie, and in 1953 to this live television series. Set in New York City in the 1880s, *Life with Father* was the story of Clarence Day, Sr., a stern but loving Victorian father, his wife Vinnie, and their four red-headed sons. Despite the fact that he ruled with an iron hand, and was a staunch traditionalist, Father Day dealt fairly with his family and earned their lifelong respect.

The turnover in actors playing the Day children in this series was rather high, although the adult members of the cast lasted longer. This was the first live color series for network TV originating in Hollywood.

LIFE WITH LINKLETTER (*Variety/Audience Participation*)

FIRST TELECAST: *October 6, 1950*
LAST TELECAST: *April 25, 1952*
BROADCAST HISTORY:
Oct 1950–Apr 1952, ABC Fri 7:30–8:00 (OS)
EMCEE:
Art Linkletter
REGULAR:
Muzzy Marcellino Orchestra

This was a nighttime version of Linkletter's long-running *House Party* show, a daytime standby on radio and television from 1945 until 1970. All of the familiar Linkletter elements were present, including the mad stunts performed by members of the studio audience for prizes, and the interviews with children. Guest stars also appeared, but the center of attraction was always Art himself, one of broadcasting's all-time favorite personalities. The program originated in Hollywood, and for a time in 1951–1952 alternated with *Say It with Acting.*

LIFE WITH LUCY (*Situation Comedy*)

FIRST TELECAST: *September 20, 1986*
LAST TELECAST: *November 15, 1986*
BROADCAST HISTORY:
Sep 1986–Nov 1986, ABC Sat 8:00–8:30
CAST:
Lucy Barker .... Lucille Ball
Curtis McGibbon .... Gale Gordon
Margo Barker McGibbon .... Ann Dusenberry
Ted McGibbon .... Larry Anderson
Becky McGibbon .... Jenny Lewis
Kevin McGibbon .... Philip J. Amelio II
Leonard Stoner .... Donovan Scott
THEME:
sung by Eydie Gorme

Probably the most widely anticipated new series—and most embarrassing flop—of the 1986 season was this ill-conceived comedy that marked the return of Lucille Ball to series television after 12 years. In order to get her, ABC had to promise a huge salary, complete creative control, no pilot or testing before preview audiences, and a guaranteed time slot on the fall schedule. What it got was an unimaginative rehash of the Lucy shows of many years before, only this time with a 75-year-old star.

Lucy was cast as a free-spirited grandmother whose husband Sam had died, leaving her half interest in M&B Hardware in South Pasadena, Calif. Lucy decided to move in and help run the place, but her idea of "help"—like arranging all the merchandise in alphabetical order on the shelves—was not appreciated by her late husband's partner, blustery old Curtis McGibbon (played by Ms. Ball's longtime foil Gale Gordon, then 80). To further complicate matters Lucy's daughter Margo was married to Curtis's son Ted, a law student, and all of them, plus Lucy's young grandchildren Becky and Kevin, lived in the building together. With one bathroom. Leonard was an employee at the store.

There was plenty of slapstick, sight gags, and Lucy celebrity chasing, as in days of old; Ms. Ball was in fine shape, but unfortunately the scripts were not. The series disappeared abruptly after less than two months, never to be seen again.

LIFE WITH LUIGI (*Situation Comedy*)

FIRST TELECAST: *September 22, 1952*
LAST TELECAST: *June 4, 1953*
BROADCAST HISTORY:
Sep 1952–Dec 1952, CBS Mon 9:30–10:00
Apr 1953–Jun 1953, CBS Thu 8:00–8:30
CAST:
Luigi Basco (1952) .... J. Carrol Naish
Luigi Basco (1953) .... Vito Scotti
Pasquale (1952) .... Alan Reed
Pasquale (1953) .... Thomas Gomez
Rosa (1952) .... Jody Gilbert
Rosa (1953) .... Muriel Landers
Miss Spalding .... Mary Shipp
Schultz .... Sig Ruman
Olson .... Ken Peters
Horwitz .... Joe Forte

Irish-American actor J. Carrol Naish became typecast as an Italian after playing the role of Luigi Basco for several years, first on CBS radio starting in 1948, and for a short period on a live TV series in 1952. Luigi was a newly arrived Italian immigrant who was learning to love his new homeland. He did not always understand what everything meant, and often took things too literally, but his sweet, gentle nature won everyone over. The setting alternated between Luigi's antique shop and his friend Pasquale's restaurant. Pasquale, a fellow immigrant who had been in this country for several years, had paid Luigi's boat fare to America in hopes that he might be able to marry off his fat daughter Rosa to his impressionable countryman. When *Life with Luigi* returned for a brief second run in the spring of 1953 all three principal parts were being played by different actors.

Despite its popularity on radio, *Life with Luigi* had only a short career on TV. Its extreme ethnic stereotyping was found offensive by some, and sponsor troubles provided the *coup de grâce.*

LIFE WITH ROGER (*Situation Comedy*)

FIRST TELECAST: *August 25, 1996*
LAST TELECAST: *June 15, 1997*
BROADCAST HISTORY:
Aug 1996–Jan 1997, WB Sun 9:30–10:00
Mar 1997–Jun 1997, WB Sun 9:30–10:00
CAST:
Roger Hoyt .... Mike O'Malley
Jason Fuller .... Maurice Godin
Lanie Fuller .... Hallie Todd
Myra Copeland .... Meredith Scott Lynn

A very odd couple shared a Manhattan apartment in this comedy. Roger and Jason had met on a bridge when Jason's car stalled out in the wee small hours of his wedding day and Roger, who was on the railing contemplating suicide, fixed it and then let Jason talk him out of jumping. Homeless Roger, an uninhibited free spirit, talked Jason out of the wedding—at the altar—and became his roommate, trying to loosen him up. Jason, an orthopedic surgeon, was responsible but neurotic, and Lanie, his sexy but insecure sister who lived across the hall, was taking acting classes.

She liked unpredictable Roger. Duffy's was the bar where Roger hung out and tried to find women for Jason to go out with. Myra, Jason's pushy ex-fiancée, who had been seen occasionally earlier in the season, became a regular in January when her father bought their building and made her manager—so she could drive everybody crazy.

LIFE WITH SNARKY PARKER (*Children's*)

FIRST TELECAST: *January 9, 1950*
LAST TELECAST: *August 30, 1950*
BROADCAST HISTORY:
Jan 1950–Mar 1950, CBS Mon/Tue/Thu/Fri 7:45–8:00
Apr 1950–Aug 1950, CBS Mon–Fri 6:15–6:30
PUPPETEERS:
Bil Baird
Cora Baird
PRODUCER/DIRECTOR:
Yul Brynner

The marionettes of puppeteers Bil and Cora Baird performed in this "saga" of life in the Old West. Snarky Parker was the deputy sheriff of the town of Hot Rock. He was in love with the local schoolteacher, rode a horse named Heathcliffe, and fought with Ronald Rodent, the local villain. Also seen regularly in this live series were Slugger, the piano player in the Bent Elbow Saloon, and Paw, the father of the schoolteacher. Yul Brynner, later more successful as a performer, was the producer and director of this show. After leaving evening hours in August, it remained on the air for another month as a late-afternoon weekday entry.

LIFE WITH THE ERWINS, see *Stu Erwin Show, The*

LIFEGAME (*Comedy/Variety*)

BROADCAST HISTORY:
TNN
60 minutes
Original episodes: *2001* (9 episodes)
Premiered: *August 23, 2001*
REGULARS:
Brian Lohmann, Host
Carson Elrod
Adrianne Frost
Nyima Funk
Rebecca Harris
Ben Hersey
Canedy Knowles
Dan O'Connor

Improvisational comedy show in which an audience member or guest star related a true story from his or her life—a perfect day, the worst boss, experiences with a childhood pet—and the cast improvised a scene based on that story. Only six of the nine episodes produced were aired. Based on the off-Broadway play of the same name.

LIFELINE (*Medical Documentary*)

FIRST TELECAST: *September 9, 1978*
LAST TELECAST: *December 30, 1978*
BROADCAST HISTORY:
Sep 1978, NBC Thu 10:00–11:00
Oct 1978–Nov 1978, NBC Sun 10:00–11:00
Dec 1978, NBC Sun 9:00–10:00
PRODUCER:
Alfred Kelman
DIRECTOR OF PHOTOGRAPHY:
Robert Elfstrom
NARRATOR:
Jackson Beck

This unusual program used no actors. It was essentially a medical documentary, focusing on a different real-life doctor in a different city each week, as he met one medical emergency after another. To produce the programs a camera crew followed each doctor for several months, filming him with his family and at work, including actual operating room and emergency room scenes where lives often hung in the balance. Viewers got to know the doctor and his patients, heightening the sense of real-life drama. The hard realities of medical life apparently depressed viewers to the point where they simply would not watch *Lifeline.* Acclaimed for its quality, that same dedication to gruesome detail led to *Lifeline*'s cancellation by year's end. The series was produced by the company that had produced the highly acclaimed "Body Human" specials during the 1977–1978 season.

LIFE'S MOST EMBARRASSING MOMENTS (*Comedy*)

FIRST TELECAST: *August 2, 1985*
LAST TELECAST: *September 10, 1985*
BROADCAST HISTORY:
Aug 1985–Sep 1985, ABC Fri 10:00–11:00
Sep 1985, ABC Tue 10:00–11:00
HOST:
Steve Allen

ABC's *Life's Most Embarrassing Moments* specials, which originally aired on an irregular basis beginning in 1983, were rerun as a weekly series during the summer of 1985. Hosted by veteran comic Steve Allen, each episode consisted primarily of celebrity outtakes, much in the manner of NBC's *TV's Bloopers & Practical Jokes* and ABC's less successful *Foul-Ups, Bleeps & Blunders.*

During the 1988–1989 season, there was a syndicated version of *Life's Most Embarrassing Moments* hosted by sportscaster/interviewer Roy Firestone.

LIFE'S WORK (*Situation Comedy*)

FIRST TELECAST: *September 17, 1996*
LAST TELECAST: *July 29, 1997*
BROADCAST HISTORY:
Sep 1996–Feb 1997, ABC Tue 8:30–9:00
May 1997–Jul 1997, ABC Tue 8:30–9:00
CAST:
Lisa Hunter .... Lisa Ann Walter
Kevin Hunter .... Michael O'Keefe
Tess Hunter (age 8) .... Alexa Vega
Griffin Hunter (2) .... Luca and Cameron Weibel
DeeDee Lucas .... Molly Hagen
Lyndon Knox .... Andrew Lowery
Jerome Nash .... Larry Miller
Matt Youngster .... Lightfield Lewis
Coach Brick .... Shashawnee Hall
Connie Minardi (1996) .... Lainie Kazan
Connie Minardi (1996–1997) .... Jenny O'Hara

Lisa was a 33-year-old woman who wanted to "have it all" in this very '90s career comedy. She had gotten married, had two kids, and simultaneously attended law school; now, with her degree in hand, she was starting work as an assistant state's attorney in Baltimore. A loud, abrasive superachiever, she struck some of those around her as a little over-the-top; others just got out of her way. Her easygoing husband Kevin, a college basketball coach, whined a bit but was supportive, helping take care of youngsters Tess and Griffin. At the office the chief skeptic was smarmy, sexist, politically ambitious Lyndon, who never failed to put her down. Jerome was the prickly division chief, DeeDee a perky associate, and Matt the bald, eccentric office helper. Connie was her worry-wart mom.

LIFESTORIES (*Dramatic Anthology*)

FIRST TELECAST: *August 20, 1990*
LAST TELECAST: *December 18, 1990*
BROADCAST HISTORY:
Aug 1990, NBC Mon 10:00–11:00
Sep 1990–Dec 1990, NBC Sun 8:00–9:00
Dec 1990, NBC Tue 10:00–11:00
NARRATOR:
Robert Prosky

TV's trend toward reality went over the top in this chillingly realistic hour that was evidently too much for most viewers. The theme was relatable medical stories dramatized in *cinéma vérité* style. Would you like to see the first 45 minutes of a heart attack reenacted as it happened? How about the emotional agony of a man when he is told he has colon cancer? Or that of a childless couple desperately trying to conceive by in-vitro fertilization? Well, neither did most other people; *Lifestories* was one of the lowest-rated series of the 1990 season.

The series did provide much information on detection and treatment of illness, and the cancer episode ended with a toll-free information number from the American Cancer Society. But the downbeat stories hit a little too close to home right after dinner on Sunday night, leading to the series' early demise.

LIFESTYLES OF THE RICH AND FAMOUS (*Magazine*)

FIRST TELECAST: *July 21, 1986*
LAST TELECAST: *September 19, 1986*
BROADCAST HISTORY:
Jul 1986–Aug 1986, ABC Mon–Fri 12:00 MID–12:30 A.M.
Sep 1986, ABC Tue–Fri 12:00 MID–12:30 A.M.
(In first-run syndication from January 1984 to September 1996)
HOST/NARRATOR:
Robin Leach
Shari Belafonte (1994–1995)
Katie Wagner (1995–1996)
Mary Major (1995–1996)
NARRATOR:
David Perry (1984–1994)

Some people have built an entire life's career out of One Big Idea—for example, Allen Funt's *Candid Camera*, or Ross Bagdasarian's squeaky-voiced *Alvin & the Chipmunks*. Celebrity reporter Robin Leach's Big Idea may not prove as durable as that, but it certainly received a lot of exposure in the mid-1980s. It consisted simply of documentary-style tours of the most opulent homes in the world, especially those of show-biz celebrities, accompanied by gushing narrative and endless paeans to the glories of wealth. Everything seen on this show was "elegant," "glamorous," "luxurious," "exclusive," or all of the above. As *TV Guide* remarked, "If you're into envy at all, it's a fudge sundae."

Leach, a British expatriate who was formerly a celebrity-chaser for *Entertainment Tonight*, *People* magazine, and the Cable News Network, narrated this hymn to avarice with such outrageous enthusiasm that he resembled a human press release. *Lifestyles of the Rich and Famous* began as a syndicated series in 1984, and aired concurrently on the ABC network in daytime from April to September 1986 and in late night from July to September 1986. A modified version continued in ABC daytime from September 1986 to May 1987 under the title *Fame, Fortune and Romance.* Still another variation was syndicated in early 1987 with the title *Runaway with the Rich and Famous.*

In the fall of 1994 the title of the show was changed to *Lifestyles with Robin Leach and Shari Belafonte* to reflect the new co-host and inclusion of some not-so-rich and famous people in the profiles. Also added as field reporters were supermodel Niki Taylor on fashion and Katie Wagner, Robert's daughter, interviewing aspiring show-business newcomers. Ms. Belafonte left the show after one season, and in fall 1995 it was retitled again to *Lifestyles.* Ms. Wagner was promoted to co-host, along with newcomer Mary Major.

LIFETIME MAGAZINE (*Newsmagazine*)

BROADCAST HISTORY:
Lifetime Network
60 minutes
Produced: *1994* (36 episodes)
Premiered: *January 2, 1994*
HOST:
Lisa McRee

Sunday-night magazine show examining women's issues such as women and AIDS, battered women, sexual harassment, and "Why Tomboys Succeed." Nonconformists were celebrated in a segment called "Digging In Your Heels," and viewers were invited to contribute via videos and recorded calls to an 800 number. The series was produced by the news division of ABC, which is a co-owner of Lifetime

LIFETIME TELEVISION (Network) (*General Entertainment Cable Network*)

LAUNCHED:
February 1, 1984
SUBSCRIBERS (MAY 2003):
85.8 million (80% U.S.)

The Lifetime cable network offers programming of special interest to women. Under that broad parasol has fallen a wide range of programming, from daytime service and game shows to sitcoms, dramas, and movies.

Lifetime has produced a substantial number of original programs, some of the recent ones becoming quite popular. During the mid-1980s it featured several evening shows hosted by sex therapist Dr. Ruth Westheimer. An early breakthrough was the production of new episodes of the highly regarded sitcom *The Days and Nights of Molly Dodd* (1989), which had been canceled by NBC after a short run. This was followed in the early 1990s by original early-evening game shows *(Shop 'Til You Drop, Supermarket Sweep)*, dramas *(Veronica Clare, The Hidden Room)*, magazine shows *(The Great American TV Poll, Lifetime Magazine)*, and talk shows *(Clapprood Live)*. More recent successes have included *Intimate Portrait* (1996), *New Attitudes* (1998), *Any Day Now* (1998), *Strong Medicine* (2000) and *The Division* (2001).

Lifetime produces several original movies each year, among the more successful to date being *Sudie and Simpson* (1990) with Lou Gossett, *Shame* (1992) with Amanda Donohoe, *Stolen Babies* (1993) starring Mary Tyler Moore, *Almost Golden: The Jessica Savitch Story* (1995) starring Sela Ward, several *Spenser* detective movies starring Robert Urich, *Dangerous Child* (2001) with Delta Burke, *Video Voyeur: The Susan Wilson Story* (2002) with Angie Harmon and *Homeless to Harvard: The Liz Murray Story* (2003) with Thora Birch. The network is also quite active in promoting women's causes, among other things sponsoring an annual *Women Rock! Girls and Guitars* concert to support the fight against breast cancer.

Lifetime was created in 1984 by the merger of two small cable channels, Daytime (launched in 1982 to provide self-help and female interest programs during the daytime) and the Cable Health Network (also launched in 1982, carrying health and fitness programs). Until 1993 its entire Sunday lineup consisted of instructional programming for medical doctors. The network first reached more than half of all U.S. television homes in November 1989, and its principal original prime-time series after that date are listed in this book under their individual titles.

Subsidiary networks include Lifetime Movie Network (all movies, launched July 1998) and Lifetime Real Women (reality programs, August 2001).

LIGHTNING FORCE *(Adventure)*

BROADCAST HISTORY:

Syndicated only
30 minutes
Produced: *1991–1992* (22 episodes)
Released: *October 1991*

CAST:

Lt. Col. Matthew Alan Coltrane ("Trane") .... Wings Hauser
Col. Zaid Abdul-Rahmad ("Zeke") .... Marc Gomes
Marie Joan Jacquard ("Joan") .... Guylaine St. Onge
Lt. Winston Churchill Staples ("Church") .... David Stratton
Maj. Gen. Bill McHugh .... Matthew Walker

Lightning Force was an elite paramilitary team assembled by the members of the International Oversight Committee for Anti-Terrorism. Each of the four members of the team had specific skills—Zeke, from Egyptian military intelligence, was an experienced negotiator and field cook; Joan, from French security services, was a pilot, computer expert, and cryptologist; Church, from the Canadian army, was a demolitions expert, engineer, and medic; and Trane, from U.S. Army Special Forces, was the team leader with expertise in operations and mission planning. Major General Bill McHugh, chairman of the Oversight Committee, was the man from whom they received most of their assignments. The original team leader, Mike "Lightning" Rodney, had died at the hands of terrorists during their first mission. Trane, who had trained Rodney in Special Forces, took his place as team leader and, in Rodney's memory, they decided to call themselves the "Lightning Force."

Filmed in Vancouver, British Columbia.

LIGHTS, CAMERA, ACTION *(Talent)*

FIRST TELECAST: *July 4, 1950*
LAST TELECAST: *August 20, 1950*
BROADCAST HISTORY:

Jul 1950–Aug 1950, NBC 10:00–10:30

EMCEE:

Walter Woolf King

Summer talent show originating in Hollywood and shown via kinescope over the NBC East and Midwest networks. Professional young talent and a panel of "name" judges were featured. Walter Woolf King, a matinee idol of the 1930s, emceed.

LIGHTS OUT *(Suspense Anthology)*

FIRST TELECAST: *July 19, 1949*
LAST TELECAST: *September 28, 1952*
BROADCAST HISTORY:

Jul 1949–Aug 1949, NBC Tue 9:00–9:30
Nov 1949–Sep 1952, NBC Mon 9:00–9:30

NARRATOR:

Jack LaRue (1949–1950)
Frank Gallop (1950–1952)

SPECIAL MUSIC EFFECTS:

Paul Lipman, theremin (1949)
Arlo Hults, organ (1949–1952)
Doris Johnson, harp (1950–1952)

Live dramatic show featuring stories of mystery, suspense, and the supernatural. At the beginning of each episode viewers would see only a close shot of a pair of eyes, then a bloody hand reaching to turn out the lights, followed by an eerie laugh and the words, "Lights out, everybody . . ."

The plays themselves were a combination of adaptations and dramas written especially for TV. Spooky houses, loved ones returned from the dead, and lonely country roads were frequent elements of *Lights Out*. At first lesser-known actors and actresses were featured, but beginning in 1950 a "guest star" policy brought in such names as Boris Karloff, Burgess Meredith, Billie Burke, Leslie Nielsen, Basil Rathbone, Eddie Albert, Raymond Massey, and Yvonne DeCarlo.

Lights Out began on radio in 1934 and had been seen on television in 1946 as a series of four specials produced by Fred Coe.

LIKE WE CARE *(Magazine)*

BROADCAST HISTORY:

MTV
30 minutes
Produced: *1992–1993*
Premiered: February 3, 1992

A daily prime-time youth magazine with features of interest to MTV's young viewers. Subjects included music, fashion, and sports as well as harder-edged topics like the environment, racism, violence in high schools, and birth control.

LIKELY SUSPECTS *(Police Drama)*

FIRST TELECAST: *September 13, 1992*
LAST TELECAST: *January 29, 1993*
BROADCAST HISTORY:

Sep 1992–Jan 1993, FOX Sun 9:30–10:00

CAST:

Det. Marshak .... Sam McMurray
Det. Harry Spinoza .... Jason Schombing

The gimmick in this unsuccessful whodunit show was that the home viewer was one of its stars. Everything was seen through the eyes of the rookie partner (the home viewer) of Marshak, a wisecracking veteran homicide detective. As he worked his way through the evidence at the crime scene, interrogating witnesses and suspects and, inevitably, solving the case, Marshak would discuss what he had found and the thinking process he was going through with his rookie partner by talking directly to the camera. Assisting Marshak and you, and doing most of the legwork, was Det. Spinoza.

LIME STREET (*Adventure/Detective*)

FIRST TELECAST: *September 21, 1985*
LAST TELECAST: *October 26, 1985*
BROADCAST HISTORY:

Sep 1985–Oct 1985, ABC Sat 9:00–10:00

CAST:

James Greyson Culver .... Robert Wagner
Edward Wingate .... John Standing
Henry Wade Culver .... Lew Ayres
Elizabeth Culver .... Samantha Smith
Margaret Ann Culver .... Maia Brewton
Celia Wesphal .... Julie Fulton
Evelyn Camp .... Anne Haney

A year after *Hart to Hart* left the air, Robert Wagner returned playing another glamorous, globe-trotting investigator in this short-lived series. Like Jonathan Hart, James Greyson Culver was very rich, and very fond of adventure. Operating out of his sprawling ranch in Virginia, where he bred horses, Culver was half of a team investigating international cases of insurance fraud for a large, London-based insurance company. His partner was Edward Wingate, a British aristocrat who lived in a castle outside London and who had been James' roommate at Oxford. Elizabeth and Margaret Ann were widower James' two adorable children; Henry, his dapper father; Celia, his private secretary; and Evelyn, the family housekeeper and surrogate mom.

Limited audiences and an off-screen tragedy contributed to the early demise of this series. Samantha Smith, a Maine schoolgirl who had become famous when she wrote to Soviet leader Yuri Andropov urging peace and then was invited to visit the U.S.S.R., was signed to play Elizabeth; however, the 13-year-old was killed in a plane crash after only a few episodes were filmed.

LINEUP, THE (*Police Drama*)

FIRST TELECAST: *October 1, 1954*
LAST TELECAST: *January 20, 1960*
BROADCAST HISTORY:

Oct 1954–Jun 1958, CBS Fri 10:00–10:30 (OS)
Sep 1958–Sep 1959, CBS Fri 10:00–10:30
Sep 1959–Jan 1960, CBS Wed 7:30–8:30

CAST:

Det. Lt. Ben Guthrie .... Warner Anderson
Inspector Matt Grebb (1954–1959) .... Tom Tully
Inspector Fred Asher (1954–1959) .. Marshall Reed
Inspector Dan Delaney (1959–1960)
.... William Leslie
Inspector Charlie Summers (1959–1960)
.... Tod Barton
Officer Pete Larkin (1959–1960) .... Skip Ward
Policewoman Sandy McAllister (1959–1960)
.... Rachel Ames

Produced in cooperation with the San Francisco Police Department, *The Lineup* sought to give realistic semi-documentary portrayals of the work of law officers in the beautiful Bay City. Ben Guthrie and Matt Grebb were the officers who tracked down criminals throughout most of the series' run. The stories were all based on actual cases from the files of the S.F.P.D., and generally included a police lineup where the victims of the crime attempted to pick out the perpetrators.

When the series expanded to an hour in the fall of 1959, there were a number of changes in the cast. Matt Grebb and Fred Asher were gone, replaced by two new inspectors. In addition, Officer Pete Larkin and Policewoman Sandy McAllister became regulars.

LINGO (*Quiz*)

BROADCAST HISTORY:

Game Show Network
30 minutes
Original episodes: *2002–*
Premiered: *August 5, 2002*

EMCEE:

Chuck Woolery

This game was a cross between a word game and bingo. Two teams of two contestants each stood facing a large board with five rows and five columns, similar to a crossword puzzle. Some boxes were already filled in, and the object was to guess a five-letter mystery word. Complications included letters out of their correct position, and time limits. Guessing the word correctly allowed a team to draw for numbers to fill out their own Lingo card. The maximum prize was $15,000.

Lingo was seen in the U.S. as a syndicated daytime series in 1987 (with Michael Reagan as emcee), and was popular on European television in the 1990s.

LIP SERVICE (*Talent*)

BROADCAST HISTORY:

MTV
30 minutes
Produced: *1992–1994* (187 episodes)
Premiered: *February 22, 1992*

HOST:

Jay Mohr (1992–1993)
John Ales (1993–1994)

A game show in which two teams competed to see who was best at lip-synching to prerecorded music. The series was generally seen in the late afternoon, although it also had some prime-time runs.

LIQUID TV (*Cartoons*)

BROADCAST HISTORY:

MTV
30 minutes
Produced: *1991–1993*
Premiered: *June 2, 1991*

MTV's showcase for offbeat, experimental animation, usually seen in short clips lasting five minutes or so. Among other things, it spawned *Beavis & Butthead* (q.v.).

LIST, THE (*Discussion*)

BROADCAST HISTORY:

VH1

30 minutes
Original episodes: *1999–2001*
Premiered: *October 4, 1999*

On this simple show four celebrities picked their top three choices on a musical topic—for example, "Best Rock Band," "Band or Artist Who Made the Most Influential Fashion Statement," "Best Hellraiser," "Best Feel Good Song," "Sexiest Male Artist," and so on. They explained their choices (sometimes with video clips) to the noisy, kibitzing studio audience, who then voted for their choices; viewers at home could also vote, via the Internet. Among those appearing were Ashton Kutcher (multiple times), Danny Bonaduce, Debrah Farentino, Kevin Bacon, Alice Cooper, Rick Springfield, Tara Lipinski, and a surprisingly hip Jane Seymour. Various celebrities hosted.

LITTLE HOUSE ON THE PRAIRIE
(*Adventure/Drama*)

FIRST TELECAST: *September 11, 1974*
LAST TELECAST: *March 21, 1983*
BROADCAST HISTORY:
Sep 1974–Sep 1976, NBC Wed 8:00–9:00
Sep 1976–Mar 1983, NBC Mon 8:00–9:00

CAST:
Charles Ingalls (1974–1982) .... Michael Landon
Caroline Ingalls (1974–1982) .... Karen Grassle
Laura Ingalls Wilder .... Melissa Gilbert
Mary Ingalls Kendall (1974–1981)
.... Melissa Sue Anderson
Carrie Ingalls (alternating; 1974–1982)
.... Lindsay Greenbush
Carrie Ingalls (alternating; 1974–1982)
.... Sidney Greenbush
Lars Hanson (1974–1978) .... Karl Swenson
Nels Oleson .... Richard Bull
Harriet Oleson .... Katherine MacGregor
Nellie Oleson Dalton (1974–1981) .. Alison Arngrim
Willie Oleson (1975–1983) .... Jonathan Gilbert
Dr. Baker .... Kevin Hagen
Rev. Robert Alden .... Dabbs Greer
Eva Beadle Simms (1974–1978)
.... Charlotte Stewart
Mr. Isaiah Edwards (1974–1977, 1982–1983)
.... Victor French
Ebenezer Sprague (1975–1976) .... Ted Gehring
Grace Edwards (1976–1977)........ Bonnie Bartlett
Jonathan Garvey (1977–1981) .... Merlin Olson
Andy Garvey (1977–1981) ...... Patrick Laborteaux
Alice Garvey (1977–1980) .... Hersha Parady
Albert Ingalls (1978–1982).... Matthew Laborteaux
Adam Kendall (1978–1981) ...... Linwood Boomer
Grace Ingalls (alternating; 1978–1982)
.... Wendy Turnbeaugh
Grace Ingalls (alternating; 1978–1982)
.... Brenda Turnbeaugh
Larrabee (1978–1979) .... Don "Red" Baker
Hester Sue Terhune (1978–1983) ...... Ketty Lester
Almanzo Wilder (1979–1983).......... Dean Butler
Eliza Jane Wilder (1979–1982) .... Lucy Lee Flippin
Percival Dalton (1980–1981) .... Steve Tracy
James Cooper (1981–1982) .... Jason Bateman
Cassandra Cooper (1981–1982)...... Missy Francis
Nancy Oleson (1981–1983) .... Allison Balson
Jenny Wilder (1982–1983) .... Shannen Doherty
John Carter (1982–1982) .... Stan Ivar
Sarah Carter (1982–1983) .... Pamela Roylance
Jeb Carter (1982–1983) .... Lindsay Kennedy
Jason Carter (1982–1983) .... David Friedman
Etta Plum (1982–1983).............. Leslie Landon

The time was the late 1870s, and the locale was the American West, but *Little House on the Prairie* was not a Western in the usual sense. There were no cowboys, Indians, or cow town saloons in this version of frontier life—it was more like *The Waltons* in a different setting, the story of a loving family in trying times.

Charles Ingalls was a homesteader struggling to make a living for his family on a small farm near the town of Walnut Grove, Plum Creek, Minnesota. The Ingalls had moved from the great plains of Kansas to Walnut Grove in search of a future in a young and growing community. With Charles were his wife, Caroline, and their three daughters, teenagers Mary and Laura, and little Carrie (played alternately by a pair of identical twins). Stories related the experiences of family life and growing children, the constant struggle against natural disasters and ruined crops, and the dealings with other members of the little community in which they lived. Among the Ingalls's new friends were Mr. Hanson, the mill owner; Nels Oleson, the proprietor of the general store; and Mr. Edwards, a nearby farmer who became a good friend, despite his rather harsh exterior.

A lot happened on *Little House* after that simple beginning, as the program came to resemble a serial. First, Mr. Edwards left in 1977 (Victor French got his own series, *Carter Country*), and was replaced by Jonathan Garvey (played by former Los Angeles Rams star Merlin Olsen). Garvey had a wife named Alice and a young son, Andy. In 1978 Caroline gave birth to a fourth daughter, Grace, but oldest daughter Mary lost her sight and was sent to a school for the blind. Mary promptly fell in love with her instructor, Adam Kendall, and they moved off to the Dakotas.

No sooner were they gone than the town of Walnut Grove fell on hard times, and Charles and his family (along with some other regulars) had to pack up and move to the bustling frontier city of Winoka, where their household was enlarged again by the addition of Albert, a young orphan they adopted. City life didn't sit well with the family, however, so they all moved back to Walnut Grove, which had miraculously recovered from its problems. Mary and Adam moved back too, and had a baby boy, who unfortunately perished (along with Alice Garvey) when the school for the blind where Mary was teaching burned down.

Feeling left out amid all this travail, daughter Laura decided to become a teacher, and was courted by and eventually married Almanzo Wilder, in the fall of 1980. Even nasty Nellie Oleson got married, although problems arose when it was discovered that her husband, Percival, was really Jewish (Isaac Cohen) and a decision had to be made about how to raise their children. Since Nellie had twins, everything was resolved by deciding they raise the son as a Jew and the daughter as a Christian!

Jonathan Garvey, now a widower, moved to nearby Sleepy Eye to manage a warehouse, and convinced Charles to set up a freight business between there and Walnut Grove. Meanwhile, over in the Adam and Mary subplot, Adam regained his sight in a freak accident, and was accepted to law school.

In the fall of 1981, Adam's father offered him a job with his law firm in New York, and Adam and Mary left Walnut Grove forever. Nellie and Percival were also in New York, where he had taken over his late father's business. Jonathan and Andy Garvey were no longer seen, while Hester Sue Terhune, who had worked at the Sleepy Eye school for the blind, moved to Walnut Grove to work, along with Caroline Ingalls, at Mrs. Oleson's restaurant.

There were more adoptions in the 1991–1982 season, with Charles and Caroline adding recently orphaned James and Cassandra Cooper to their household, and lonely Mrs. Oleson taking in an orphan named Nancy—who bore a striking resemblance to her departed Nellie, in both looks and nastiness. Mr. Edwards, whose problems with drinking had cost him his marriage, returned to Walnut Grove the following spring, and Laura gave birth to a daughter, Rose.

Michael Landon's decision to leave *Little House* prompted a number of changes in the fall of 1982. The title was changed to *Little House: A New Beginning* and Laura and Almanzo became the principal stars. Economic problems forced Charles to sell the "little house" and move to Burr Oak, Iowa, where he had found a job. Moving into the former Ingalls home were John and Sarah Carter, who ran the town newspaper, and their sons Jeb and Jason. Laura gave up her teaching job to raise both Rose and Jenny, who was orphaned when Almanzo's brother Royal died. Laura's replacement at the school, Etta Plum, was portrayed by Michael Landon's daughter Leslie.

The series' audience had been declining for several years, and the revised version lasted only a single season.

The stories told on *Little House* were originally based on the "Little House" books by Laura Ingalls Wilder, which contained her recollections of growing up on the American frontier. On the TV series, the actress playing Laura functioned as the narrator. Michael Landon, who starred in this series, was also its executive producer.

LITTLE MEN (*Drama*)

FIRST TELECAST: *November 7, 1998*
LAST TELECAST: *February 12, 2000*
BROADCAST HISTORY:

Nov 1998–Apr 1999, PAX Sat 8:00–9:00
Apr 1999–May 1999, PAX Sat 9:00–10:00
May 1999–Jul 1999, PAX Sat 8:00–9:00
Jul 1999–Dec 1999, PAX Fri 8:00–9:00
Aug 1999–Oct 1999, PAX Sat 9:00–10:00
Dec 1999–Feb 2000, PAX Sat 9:00–10:00

CAST:

Jo Bhaer .... Michelle Rene Thomas
Nick Riley .... Spencer Rochfort
Dan .... Corey Sevier
Nat Blake .... Trevor Blumas
Cynthia "Nan" Harding .... Brittney Irvin
Bess Lawrence .... Rachel Skarsten
Jack Ford .... Dov Tiefenbach
Tommy Bangs .... Matt Robinson
Emil .... Alex Campbell
Margret "Meg" Brooks .... Jennifer Wigmore
Isaac .... Michael Oliphant
Asia .... Sandra Caldwell
Franz Bhaer .... Robin Dunne
Theodore "Laurie" Lawrence (1999) .... Dan R. Chameroy
Amy Lawrence (1999) .... Amy Price-Francis
Isabelle McGregor (1999) .... Heidi Noelle Lenhart

Plumfield School, a private boarding school for children located in rural Massachusetts in 1871, was the setting for this squeaky-clean period drama. Headmistress Jo was having a difficult time keeping the school open since the unexpected death of her husband, Fritz. Jo's older sister, Meg, herself a widow, visited often to help out, and Jo's nephew Franz was the school's young teacher. There were only two girls attending Plumfield: younger sister Amy's snooty, pampered daughter Bess, and tomboyish Nan. Most of the students were male—Dan, Nat, Jack, Tommy, Emil, and Isaac among them. Needing a male role model for them, Jo hired Nick, an ex-merchant marine, as handyman and to help her maintain discipline. An adventurous free spirit, Nick didn't always agree with Jo's methods, but they usually managed to work things out. Asia was the black housekeeper.

During the second season, Jo expressed some romantic interest in Nick, Amy and Laurie were having marital problems, and Meg was dating an attorney with a Boston law firm. Franz started dating Isabelle, who worked in the general store in town; when she moved to Arizona to help her brother run the cattle ranch he was developing, Jo convinced Franz, who loved her, to follow after her. In his absence, Jo took over teaching the children. Although *Little Men* took place in the 19th century, it dealt with issues that were timeless: peer pressure, maturation, friendship, loyalty, the stress of studies, bigotry, etc.

Adapted from the books of Louisa May Alcott. Jo was the grown-up Jo March from Alcott's classic *Little Women*.

LITTLE PEOPLE, THE, see *Brian Keith Show, The*

LITTLE REVUE, THE (*Music*)

FIRST TELECAST: *September 4, 1949*
LAST TELECAST: *April 21, 1950*
BROADCAST HISTORY:

Sep 1949–Mar 1950, ABC Sun 8:30–9:00
Mar 1950–Apr 1950, ABC Fri 9:30–10:00

REGULARS:

Nancy Evans
Dick Larkin
Bill Sherry
Gloria Van
Billy Johnson
Nancy Doran and Dick France, dancers
Bill Weber Marionettes
Rex Maupin's Orchestra

A program of smooth, relaxed music and assorted variety-show elements from Chicago.

LITTLE SHOW, THE, see *Van Camp's Little Show*

LITTLE THEATRE, see *ABC Dramatic Shorts—1951–1953*

LITTLE WOMEN (*Drama*)

FIRST TELECAST: *February 8, 1979*
LAST TELECAST: *March 8, 1979*
BROADCAST HISTORY:

Feb 1979–Mar 1979, NBC Thu 8:00–9:00

CAST:

Marmee March .... Dorothy McGuire
Rev. John March .... William Schallert
Jo March .... Jessica Harper
Meg March Brooke .... Susan Walden
Amy March Laurence .... Ann Dusenberry
John Brooke .... Cliff Potts
Theodore Laurie Laurence .... Richard Gilliland
Prof. Friedrich Bhaer .... David Ackroyd
Aunt Kathryn March .... Mildred Natwick
Melissa Jane Driscoll ("Lissa") .... Eve Plumb
Hannah .... Virginia Gregg
James Laurence .... Robert Young
Amanda .... Maggie Malooly

In October 1978 NBC had aired a two-part movie adaptation of the Louisa May Alcott novel *Little Women*. The following spring this short-lived series, with most of the original movie cast, continued the saga of the March family where Miss Alcott's novel left off. Two of the three March daughters were married, Meg to John Brooke and Amy to the grandson of Rev. March's wealthy neighbor, Mr. Laurence. Headstrong aspiring writer Jo was engaged to the German-born Friedrich Bhaer, and a new member was added to the March household, in the person of young cousin Lissa, who was an eerie look-alike for the deceased daughter, Beth. The others living in the 19th-century New England home were old maid Aunt March and the housekeeper, Hannah.

LIVE! DICK CLARK PRESENTS (*Variety*)

FIRST TELECAST: *September 14, 1988*
LAST TELECAST: *October 22, 1988*
BROADCAST HISTORY:

Sep 1988, CBS Wed 8:00–9:00
Oct 1988, CBS Sat 8:00–9:00

HOST:

Dick Clark

Producer/host Dick Clark threw this variety series together on short notice to help CBS fill time until its scheduled fall series, delayed by the 1988 writers' strike, could get into full production. Clark's guest list consisted primarily of vintage rock music performers (The Four Tops, Paul Revere and the Raiders, Frankie Valli and the Four Seasons, Chubby Checker, Tony Orlando and Dawn, the Association, and The Captain and Tennille) and contemporary comedians (Yakov Smirnoff, David Brenner, Elayne Boosler, Steve Landesberg, and Byron Allen), along with an assortment of magicians, stunt people, and other novelty acts.

LIVE FROM THE HOUSE OF BLUES (*Music*)

BROADCAST HISTORY:

TBS
60 minutes
Produced: *1995–1996*
Premiered: *January 28, 1995*

Friday midnight rock concerts from the trendy House of Blues music clubs that were co-founded by "Blues Brother" Dan Aykroyd and located in several cities. Early guests included Sheryl Crow, the Neville Brothers, Doctor John, and Hootie and the Blowfish.

LIVE LIKE A MILLIONAIRE (*Talent/Variety*)

FIRST TELECAST: *January 5, 1951*
LAST TELECAST: *February 7, 1953*
BROADCAST HISTORY:

Jan 1951–Apr 1951, CBS Fri 9:30–10:00
Apr 1951–Jun 1951, CBS Fri 9:00–9:30
Jul 1951–Mar 1952, CBS Fri 10:00–10:30
Oct 1952–Feb 1953, ABC Sat 7:30–8:00

EMCEE:

Jack McCoy (1951)
John Nelson

ASSISTANT:

Michael O'Halloran (1951)
Connie Clawson (1951–1952)

The format of *Live Like a Millionaire* was a variation on Arthur Godfrey's *Talent Scouts*. Each week three or four sets of talented parents performed on the show, after being introduced by their children. The winning parent or parents won the chance to "live like a millionaire" for an entire week. They were waited on, sent on trips, provided with expensive cars, or whatever else they might desire.

Jack McCoy was the original emcee and, when he left at the end of March 1951, he was replaced by the show's announcer, John Nelson. At the outset, Michael O'Halloran played Merton the Butler, waiting on the winners, but he was soon replaced by hostess Connie Clawson. When ABC picked up *Live Like a Millionaire* in the fall of 1952, only emcee Nelson was with the show. The basic format was retained but the prize became purely monetary. The winning parents received one week's interest on $1,000,000, plus an all-expenses-paid vacation.

LIVE SHOT (*Drama*)

FIRST TELECAST: *August 29, 1995*
LAST TELECAST: *January 9, 1996*
BROADCAST HISTORY:

Aug 1995–Jan 1996, UPN Tue 9:00–10:00

CAST:

Marvin Seaborn .... Sam Anderson
Harry Chandler Moore .... David Birney
Liz Vega .... Wanda de Jesus
"Fast" Eddie Santini .... Michael Watson
Joe Vitale .... Bruce McGill
Nancy Lockridge .... Cheryl Pollak
Sherry Beck .... Rebecca Staab
Ricardo Sandoval .... Eddie Velez
Tommy .... Hill Harper
Alex Rydell .... Jeff Yagher
Shawn Rydell .... Spencer Klein
Lou Waller .... Tom Byrd
Peggy .... Antonia Jones
Helen Forbes .... Karen Austin
Rick Evers .... David Coburn
Ramona .... Nia Long

Behind the scenes at Channel 3's *Re-Action News* in L.A. was the setting for this news drama-cum-soap opera. Alex, the station's new news director, had just moved to L.A. with his son and found out that his wife, who had been having an affair, was filing for divorce. The on-air personalities included: pushy Sherry and egocentric Harry (the "Beacon of Truth"), feuding co-anchors who ended up having a steamy affair until she broke it off when she found out she had cervical cancer; Lou, the sports anchor who came out of the closet in November; Marvin, the self-righteous commentator; Liz, the field reporter with a conscience; and Ricardo, the ambitious noon news anchorman. Tommy, the black sound man, separated from his wife, and Eddie, his white cameraman partner, began having an affair with her. Marvin had a brief affair with new GM Helen Forbes, who didn't take it or him seriously—until he publicly sued her for sexual harassment and she was suspended; her lawyer, Hal, took over as temporary GM. On the production staff were Rick, the assignment editor; Joe, producer of the early evening news; and Nancy, producer of the eleven P.M. news. She and Alex eventually got involved when he realized he and his wife weren't going to be able to work things out. And you thought they were all there just to bring you the news!

LIVE THROUGH THIS (*Music/Drama*)

BROADCAST HISTORY:

MTV
60 minutes
Original episodes: *2000–2001* (13 episodes)
Premiered: *August 9, 2000*

CAST:

Annie Baker .... Jennifer Dale
Tallulah "Lu" Baker (age 22) ...... Sarah Manninen
Drake Taylor.............................. Ron Lea
Travis Williams (21)............... Matthew Carey
Keith Rooney...................... David Nerman
Chase Rooney (23) .... Tom Lock
Olivia Rooney (18).................. Jessica Welch
Rick Parsons .... Bruce Dinsmore
Darby Parsons (17)................ Jane McGregor

MTV's first hour-long drama series was, in the words of one of the younger characters, about "parents who suck and the children who love them." The Jackson Decker Band, one of the top bands of the 1980s, had broken up years ago after a long sex-drug-and booze-filled run. Annie was the temperamental lead singer, afflicted with stage fright and barely staying on the wagon with the help of her devoted daughter, Lu. Guitarist Drake was self-centered and irresponsible, and had played no part in the raising of his son, Travis. Bassist Keith was another lousy dad, with two kids, overachiever Chase and wild child Olivia. Drummer Rick, once the wildest member of the band, had become just the opposite, a dedicated father determined to protect his shy daughter, Darby, from the dangers of show business.

It was businesslike Chase, recently graduated with an M.B.A. from Stanford, who got the band back together for a reunion tour, serving as its road manager. The band members were joined on the road by their five offspring, but it was an emotional roller coaster for both generations. Lu struggled to keep her mercurial mother functioning, Travis tried to make emotional contact with his neglectful dad, Darby made her first stabs at independence from her overprotective father, and Chase had to deal with both his father and his trouble-prone younger sister.

LIVE-IN (*Situation Comedy*)

FIRST TELECAST: *March 20, 1989*
LAST TELECAST: *June 5, 1989*
BROADCAST HISTORY:

Mar 1989–Jun 1989, CBS Mon 8:00–8:30

CAST:

Danny Mathews (age 17) .... Chris Young
Lisa Wells .... Lisa Patrick
Ed Mathews....................... Hugh Maguire
Sarah Mathews.................... Kimberly Farr
Peter Mathews (14)................ David Moscow
Melissa Mathews........ Allison & Melissa Lindsay
Gator.......................... Lightfield Lewis
Muriel Spiegelman .... Jenny O'Hara

THEME:

"Happy Together"

Set in suburban New Jersey, not far from New York City, this light comedy was about the impact of an attractive, young, Australian live-in housekeeper (Lisa) on the family for whom she worked. Ed and Sarah Mathews both worked full time, he operating a sporting-goods store and she as the clothing buyer for a department store. They had hired Lisa to care for newborn Melissa, so that Sarah could go back to work. Perky Lisa got along with everyone, although Mrs. Mathews had occasional misgivings about how much more time Lisa spent with Melissa than she could. Danny, the older Mathews son, was forever fantasizing about becoming Lisa's boyfriend, and found it difficult to accept her as just a friend. Gator was his best buddy at school, and Muriel was a good friend of Sarah's.

LIVELY ONES, THE (*Musical Variety*)

FIRST TELECAST: *July 26, 1962*
LAST TELECAST: *September 12, 1963*
BROADCAST HISTORY:

Jul 1962–Sep 1962, NBC Thu 9:30–10:00
Jul 1963–Sep 1963, NBC Thu 9:30–10:00

REGULARS:

Vic Damone
Joan Staley ("Tiger," 1962)
Shirley Yelm ("Charley," 1962)
Quinn O'Hara ("Smitty," 1963)
Gloria Neil ("Melvin," 1963)
Jerry Fielding Orchestra

Vic Damone was host of this big, brash, swinging musical variety show which aired during the summers of 1962 and 1963. Each show presented established stars and new talent, appearing in different, often offbeat locations around the country. The only regulars on the series, other than Vic Damone, were his two "dates," Tiger and Charley in 1962 and Smitty and Melvin in 1963.

LIVIN' LARGE (*Magazine*)

BROADCAST HISTORY:

Syndicated only
60 minutes
Produced: *2002–*
Released: *September 2002*

HOSTS:

Carmen Electra
Kadeem Hardison

Each episode of this variation on *Lifestyles of the Rich and Famous* opened with a statement that said it all: "From the craziest mansions and the people who own them to the hottest gadgets and trends. People who are living life beyond all bounds, following their passions and living their dreams." A sample episode included features on the man who started Millionaire's Concierge, providing cars, yachts, mansions and other baubles to the wealthy; Cedric the Entertainer's CTE Charitable Foundation, providing help and motivation for young African Americans; a fancy beauty salon and boutique for pets in Manhattan; a woman who designed clothing for pregnant women, including major celebrities; Buster Keaton's Beverly Hills mansion, restored and on the market for $21,000,000, and a celebrity stylist specializing in clothes, jewelry and other opulent accessories.

LIVING DOLLS (*Situation Comedy*)
FIRST TELECAST: *September 26, 1989*
LAST TELECAST: *December 30, 1989*
BROADCAST HISTORY:
Sep 1989, ABC Tue 8:30–9:00
Sep 1989–Dec 1989, ABC Sat 8:30–9:00
CAST:
Trish Carlin .... Michael Learned
Charlie Brisco .... Leah Remini
Emily Franklin .... Halle Berry
Martha Lambert .... Alison Elliott
Caroline Weldon .... Deborah Tucker
Rick Carlin .... David Moscow

A lightweight comedy about four beautiful teenagers aspiring to become models under the tutelage of Trish Carlin, head of New York's small but influential Carlin Agency. The girls were innocent Martha, serious Emily (who wanted to use her earnings to become a doctor), self-centered Caroline, and tough-talking Charlie, a former street kid with a chip on her shoulder. The four lived with breezy Trish, who served as their mentor, teacher, and surrogate mother. Trish's other challenge was trying to control the overactive hormones of her 16-year-old son, Rick, who thought he was in heaven.

Living Dolls was a spin-off of sorts from *Who's the Boss?*, whose stars Tony Danza and Alyssa Milano sometimes dropped by. Also visiting was Trish's sister Marion (played by Marion Ross), who filled in as den mother when Trish was out of town.

LIVING IN CAPTIVITY (*Situation Comedy*)
FIRST TELECAST: *September 11, 1998*
LAST TELECAST: *October 16, 1998*
BROADCAST HISTORY:
Sep 1998–Oct 1998, FOX Fri 8:00–8:30
CAST:
Becca Merrick .... Melinda McGraw
Will Merrick .... Matt Letscher
Carmine Santucci .... Lenny Venito
Lisa Santucci .... Mia Cottet
Curtis Cooke .... Dondre T. Whitfield
Tamara Cooke .... Kira Arne
Vito Santucci .... Michael Bacall
Gordon, the security guard .... Terry Rhoades
Les .... Fred Stoller
Charlie .... George Wyner

Set in the exclusive gated suburban community of Woodland Heights, California, this comedy focused on the relationships and friendships of three couples. Will was a neurotic Christian novelist, and Becca a ball-busting Jewish attorney; Carmine a boorish auto-parts mogul (the "King of Mufflers") and Lisa his ditzy trophy wife; Curtis a successful black disc jockey, and Tamara his very pregnant spouse. Ethnic jokes abounded, cued by the arrival of the Cookes in the previously all-white enclave. Shortly after the premiere a baby, Louis, was born to the Cookes, and Carmine's horny young nephew, Vito, moved in with the Santuccis. Carmine got Vito a job as a bag boy at the local supermarket where everybody, including fellow residents Les and Charlie, seemed to hang out and gossip. Gordon was the gay security guard—look out, more stereotype jokes!

LIVING SINGLE (*Situation Comedy*)
FIRST TELECAST: *August 22, 1993*
LAST TELECAST: *January 1, 1998*
BROADCAST HISTORY:
Aug 1993–Jul 1994, FOX Sun 8:30–9:00
Aug 1994–Jul 1995, FOX Thu 8:30–9:00
Aug 1995–May 1996, FOX Thu 8:00–8:30
Aug 1995, FOX Sun 8:30–9:00
Jun 1996–Aug 1997, FOX Thu 8:30–9:00
Sep 1997–Jan 1998, FOX Thu 8:00–8:30
CAST:
Khadijah James ... Queen Latifah (née Dana Owens)
Synclaire James .... Kim Coles
Regine Hunter .... Kim Fields Freeman
Maxine Shaw ("Max") .... Erika Alexander
Kyle Barker .... T. C. Carson
Overton Jones .... John Henton
**Terrence "Scooter" (1994)* .... Cress Williams
**Ivan (1995–1997)* .... Bumper Robinson
**Russell Montego (1995–1998)* .... Shaun Baker
Ira Lee Williams III ("Tripp") (1997–1998)
.... Mel Jackson

*Occasional

THEME:
"Living Single," written and performed by Queen Latifah

Khadijah was the editor of *Flavor*, a magazine for black women in this black clone of *Designing Women*. She lived in an apartment in a Brooklyn brownstone with her cousin Synclaire, a perpetually perky but not too bright woman who was her secretary at *Flavor*, and gold-digging sexpot Regine, a childhood friend who worked at a fancy women's clothing boutique. Max, Khadijah's college roommate, a man-eating divorce attorney with an acid tongue, seemed to spend almost all her free time at their apartment. Living in the apartment upstairs were Synclaire's boyfriend, Overton, the building's dumb, happy handyman, and Kyle, a conceited financial planner who dished it out pretty well in his ongoing verbal exchanges with Max.

Khadijah's old boyfriend Terrence surfaced in the spring of 1994, and they started dating again. He got a job in the fall in public relations for a record company, and at Thanksgiving left to go on a six-month-long world tour managing a rock group. In the last original episode of the 1993–1994 season Max lost her job at the law firm, got drunk, and ended up spending the night in bed with Kyle. Despite their hostility they discovered they liked each other, which affected their relationship until they reverted to form. A month after the firing Max got her job back but, because her bosses effectively demoted her, she quit. After several months sponging off Khadijah and her roommates, she got a job with the Public Defender's office.

In fall 1995, Kyle and Max were secretly dating, but their mutual belittling of each other caused them to break up. Regine had a new job working behind the scenes on a soap opera, and Ivan, a sophomore at NYU, was working as a gofer at *Flavor*. Also on the *Flavor* staff was Russell, a Jamaican with the hots for a disinterested Regine. In 1996, a busy year, Maxine ran for alderman and, despite having her entire racy past exposed on local TV news, she won the election. She and Kyle resumed their clandestine affair. Overton and Synclaire got engaged. In November, Regine's soap opera, *Palo Alto,* was canceled, leaving her without a job, so she started organizing parties. At the end of the 1996–1997 season Overton and Synclaire got married and Kyle's firm offered him a chance to run its London office. He and Max broke up—but at the wedding Max told Kyle she loved him.

That fall Tripp, who wrote commercial jingles, moved into Synclaire's room. Max and Kyle fought over whether he was staying or she was moving to London with him (he left at the end of the season's second episode), and Synclaire and Overton were stranded on a deserted island when they missed getting back on their honeymoon cruise ship after a luau. In December, Regine found her millionaire, Dexter Knight (Don Franklin) and Khadijah reunited with Scooter. When the series aired its last two episodes on New Year's night, Max was artificially inseminated and became pregnant—with Kyle's sperm. She and Kyle got back together, and Synclaire, whose acting ambitions and work had landed her a role in a sitcom, moved to Hollywood with Overton.

LIZZIE MCGUIRE (*Situation Comedy*)

BROADCAST HISTORY:

Disney Channel
30 minutes
Original episodes: *2001–*
Premiered: *January 12, 2001*

CAST:

Lizzie McGuire (age 13) .... Hilary Duff
Matt McGuire .... Jake Thomas
Sam McGuire .... Robert Carradine
Jo McGuire .... Hallie Todd
Miranda Sanchez .... Lalaine
David "Gordo" Gordon .... Adam Lamberg
Kate Sanders (14) .... Ashlie Brillault
Ethan Craft (13) .... Clayton Snyder
**Larry Tudgeman* .... Kyle J. Downes
**Lanny Onasis* .... Christian Copelin

*Occasional

Popular teen-com in the tradition of *Clarissa Explains It All,* in which bright young middle-schooler Lizzie navigated her way through school, popularity, boys, parents and the inevitable bratty little brother—in this case named Matt. Sam and Jo were her understanding parents (who, annoyingly, still called her "sweet potato"), and sarcastic Miranda and eccentric Gordo, her two best friends. Together they shared many adventures in and around Hillridge Middle School, apparently (though not identified) located somewhere in California. Often they "talked" on the computer. An unusual twist was Lizzie's animated alter ego, which popped up to express her worries and fantasies—like what she was thinking about that hunky dreamboat Ethan.

Kate was a snotty cheerleader and frequent rival, Tudgeman was the class oddball and Lanny was Matt's silent friend.

LLOYD BRIDGES SHOW, THE (*Dramatic Anthology*)

FIRST TELECAST: *September 11, 1962*
LAST TELECAST: *August 27, 1963*
BROADCAST HISTORY:

Sep 1962–Aug 1963, CBS Tue 8:00–8:30

CAST:

Adam Shepherd and various others .... Lloyd Bridges

Lloyd Bridges narrated and starred in this dramatic-anthology series. Each episode began with freelance journalist Adam Shepherd digging into a story, sometimes current and sometimes historical. Shepherd then imagined himself as the primary protagonist (also played by Bridges), and the drama unfolded.

LOBO (*Police Comedy*)

FIRST TELECAST: *September 18, 1979*
LAST TELECAST: *August 25, 1981*
BROADCAST HISTORY:

Sep 1979–Mar 1980, NBC Tue 8:00–9:00
Dec 1980–Aug 1981, NBC Tue 8:00–9:00

CAST:

Sheriff Elroy P. Lobo .... Claude Akins
Deputy Perkins .... Mills Watson
Deputy Birdwell "Birdie" Hawkins .... Brian Kerwin
Sarah Cumberland (1979–1980) ..... Leann Hunley
Rose Lobo Perkins (1979–1980) . Cydney Crampton
Margaret Ellen (1979–1980) ...... Janet Lynn Curtis
Chief J. C. Carson (1980–1981) ...... Nicolas Coster
Sgt. Hildy Jones (1980–1981) .... Nell Carter
Peaches (1980–1981) .... Amy Botwinick
Brandy (1980–1981) .... Tara Buckman

THEME:

sung by Frankie Laine (1979–1980)

Lobo was a slapstick parody on police shows. Sheriff Elroy P. Lobo of Orly County, Georgia, was not really a crook. He might be a bit larcenous in intent, but somehow he always wound up doing the right thing, in spite of himself. Time and time again, he set off on a money-making scheme and wound up catching crooks and recovering loot—which he never got to keep. Of dubious help was his bumbling, idiot brother-in-law, Deputy Perkins. A bit brighter was the handsome, college-educated mayor's son, Deputy Birdie Hawkins, though he too was on the naive side. He somehow managed to believe in the integrity of his boss, despite mounting evidence to the contrary. Birdie dated pretty Sarah Cumberland, who ran the Orly Hotel. Sexy Margaret Ellen was a waitress who showed up regularly at the sheriff's office stuffed into one skimpy costume or another, bringing meals for prisoners and staff. As with *B.J. and the Bear,* from which it was spun off, *Lobo* had wild car chases and sexy women populating almost every episode.

When *Lobo* returned late in 1980 to start its second season there were a number of changes. The title, which had been *The Misadventures of Sheriff Lobo* during the first season, was shortened to *Lobo.* Elroy and his two deputies had moved to Atlanta, where they were appointed to a special police task force. In true *Lobo* fashion, they were there because the governor had been impressed by the low crime rate in Orly County under Lobo's regime, a misunderstanding caused by Lobo's neglecting to send crime statistics to the state capital. In Atlanta their presence was resented by Chief of Detectives Carson, who couldn't understand how the hicks from Orly were going to help his overworked force. Nevertheless Lobo and his boys bumbled their way to success fighting urban crime. Most of the Atlanta cops, including Carson's aide, sarcastic Sgt. Hildy Jones, didn't get along too well with the country bumpkins. About the only exceptions were Peaches and Brandy, two sexy undercover cops who worked with Lobo and his men on special assignments.

LOCAL HEROES (*Situation Comedy*)

FIRST TELECAST: *March 17, 1996*

LAST TELECAST: *April 14, 1996*

BROADCAST HISTORY:

Mar 1996–Apr 1996, FOX Sun 9:30–10:00

CAST:

Eddie Trakacs............. Ken Hudson Campbell
Jake.................................. Jay Mohr
Mert (Richard Mertola)............... Justin Louis
"Stosh" Stoskolowski.............. Jason Kristofer
Gloria.............................. Paula K. Cale
Bonnie................. Kristin Dattilo-Hayward
Mrs. Trakacs................... Rhoda Gemignani
Nikki Trakacs...................... Tricia Vessey

THEME:

sung by Southside Johnny

This blue-collar ripoff of *Friends* was about four twenty-something guys in Pittsburgh who had been buddies since high school. Mert, who worked with Eddie on an assembly line, was semi-engaged to Bonnie, while his three buddies were adamantly single. Chunky Eddie lived at home with his widowed mother and slutty 16-year-old younger sister, Nikki. Stosh was a glib cab driver and Jake was a salesman at an audio/video store. Gloria was the waitress/barmaid with an attitude at Blue Lou's, their local hangout. She and Mert's frustrated girlfriend Bonnie were best friends.

LOCK UP (*Police Drama*)

BROADCAST HISTORY:

Syndicated only
30 minutes
Produced: *1959–1961* (78 episodes)
Released: *August 1959*

CAST:

Herbert L. Maris................. Macdonald Carey
Casey................................. Olive Carey
Jim Weston...................... John Doucette

This rather straightforward lawyer series starred Macdonald Carey as Herbert L. Maris, a real-life corporation lawyer whose passion was defending those he believed had been unjustly convicted of crimes. Typically the program opened with the accused, or a friend of the accused, approaching Maris with a last-ditch appeal for help, whereupon the attorney set about obtaining evidence of his innocence.

Casey was Maris's middle-aged secretary, who was always trying to match him up with a "nice young girl" (actress Olive Carey was no relation to the show's star, but was the wife of Western star Harry Carey). The real Maris, 79 years old and semiretired when the series was made, opined that it was "well enough done that it won't—shall we say—do me any harm."

LOGAN'S RUN (*Science Fiction*)

FIRST TELECAST: *September 16, 1977*

LAST TELECAST: *January 16, 1978*

BROADCAST HISTORY:

Sep 1977, CBS Fri 9:00–10:00
Oct 1977–Jan 1978, CBS Mon 8:00–9:00

CAST:

Logan......................... Gregory Harrison
Jessica......................... Heather Menzies
Rem............................. Donald Moffat
Francis........................... Randy Powell

The Earth of 2319 was radically different from that of the 20th century. There had been a nuclear holocaust that had devastated much of the planet. The remnants of civilization were living in isolated cities, each with its own lifestyle, separated from each other by vast stretches of wasteland and ruins. One of the surviving communities was the City of Domes, where all residents lived entirely for their own pleasure. It would have been idyllic were it not mandated that nobody could live past his 30th birthday. Logan was one of the city's citizens, a Sandman (elite policeman) who had fled as his 30th birthday approached. Together with a young girl named Jessica, who had helped him escape from the city, and an android (humanlike robot) named Rem, Logan searched for a purported utopia called Sanctuary. Pursuing them was a dedicated Sandman (Francis) who wanted to take them back to the City of Domes to die in the ritual ceremony known as Carousel. The chase of the fugitives by their pursuer, and their encounters with the diverse and strange remnants of human civilization, both in modern cities and in the wilds between them, provided the subject matter for this series.

It was based on a novel by William F. Nolan and George Clayton Johnson and a feature-length movie, both also titled *Logan's Run*.

LOIS & CLARK—THE NEW ADVENTURES OF SUPERMAN (*Science Fiction*)

FIRST TELECAST: *September 12, 1993*

LAST TELECAST: *June 14, 1997*

BROADCAST HISTORY:

Sep 1993–Dec 1996, ABC Sun 8:00–9:00
Jan 1997, ABC Sun 7:00–8:00
Mar 1997, ABC Sun 7:00–8:00
Apr 1997–Jun 1997, ABC Sat 8:00–9:00

CAST:

Superman/Clark Kent................. Dean Cain
Lois Lane............................ Teri Hatcher
Perry White.......................... Lane Smith
Jimmy Olsen (1993–1994)........ Michael Landes
Jimmy Olsen (1994–1997).......... Justin Whalin
Catherine "Cat" Grant (1993–1994)
.... Tracy Scoggins
Lex Luthor............................ John Shea
Jonathan Kent....................... Eddie Jones
Martha Kent............................ K Callan

The Superman legend received a nineties makeover in this unusual version of the classic story. Although there was some action, the emphasis was on romance, with a strong dose of humor. Clark Kent was, as ever, the incredibly handsome, incredibly pure country boy who came to Metropolis to work at *The Daily Planet*, managed by blustery editor Perry White. He was paired with Lois, a cool, capable, career-obsessed take-charge type who paid little attention to his polite advances. Instead she pined for Superman, not realizing that he and Clark were one and the same. Jimmy was the eager cub reporter/photojournalist and "Cat" the catty society columnist who oozed sexuality and would have taken hunky Clark in a flash. Jonathan and Martha were Clark's American-Gothic adoptive parents.

Unable to snare Superman, Lois fell for the charms of dashing Lex Luthor, apparently unaware that he was the evil mastermind behind almost every calamity that befell Metropolis. At the end of the first season Lex had virtually destroyed *The Daily Planet* and was about to wed dear Lois, when she dumped him at the altar. He was then "killed," only to rise from the dead in early 1995 to seek revenge yet again against the Man of Steel.

Eventually Lois figured out that Clark and her Man of Steel were one and the same, and in 1995 he proposed. The course of true love did not go easily, however. First she had to forgive him for not telling her his secret. Then there was a botched wedding in early 1996; a detour to the planet Krypton, where a predesignated bride, Zara (Justine Bateman), was waiting for him; and finally, in October 1996, the actual ceremony, which came off despite the meddling of guest star Delta Burke. In the last original episode, on June 14, 1997, Lois and Clark decided to have a superbaby—although that would prove difficult since they were of different species, and therefore "biologically incompatible."

LONE GUNMEN, THE (*Comedy/Detective*)
FIRST TELECAST: *March 4, 2001*
LAST TELECAST: *June 22, 2001*
BROADCAST HISTORY:
Mar 2001, FOX Sun 9:00–10:00
Mar 2001–May 2001, FOX Fri 9:00–10:00
Jun 2001, FOX Fri 8:00–9:00
CAST:
John Byers .... Bruce Harwood
Melvin Frohike .... Tom Braidwood
Ringo Langly .... Dean Haglund
Yves Adele Harlow .... Zuleikha Robinson
Jimmy Bond .... Stephen Snedden

Seven years after their initial appearance on *The X-Files,* the nerdy, computer-hacking, conspiracy-exposing addicted Lone Gunmen got their own series. Humorless straight arrow Byers, diminuitive, bumbling Frohike, and stringy-haired hippie-ish Langly ran their low-circulation (2,800 subscribers) newsletter, *The Lone Gunman,* from a small office in Takoma Park, Maryland, outside Washington, and traveled in a beat-up old Volkswagen bus.

The Lone Gunmen had sometimes provided comic relief on *The X-Files*, and their own show was played more for laughs than serious drama. They had flashes of brilliance, but none of their operations ever worked out the way they had planned. Never strong on social skills and incapable of working effectively undercover, they had considerable difficulty coping with their principal competition in the "information business," the sexy, resourceful Yves Adele Harlow.

In the second episode they met enthusiastic but ineffectual Jimmy Bond, an idealistic young man whose money helped keep them solvent amid shaky finances. He went to work for them but was of little help. In the season finale, the guys, along with Yves, were caught by a government agent and TO BE CONTINUED flashed on the screen. Unfortunately, since *The Lone Gunmen* was not renewed for the fall, there was no resolution of the story.

In an *X-Files* episode that aired on April 21, 2002, the Lone Gunmen met their end. They were killed by a fast-acting virus created by an evil professor but managed to save Jimmy's life. As they were dying, they told him to fight the good fight and to never give up. Skinner pulled strings to get them buried in Arlington National Cemetery. He, Doggett, Reyes and Scully attended the ceremony, along with Jimmy and Yves.

LONE RANGER, THE (*Western*)
FIRST TELECAST: *September 15, 1949*
LAST TELECAST: *September 12, 1957*
BROADCAST HISTORY:
Sep 1949–Sep 1957, ABC Thu 7:30–8:00
Jun 1950–Sep 1950, ABC Fri 10:00–10:30
CAST:
The Lone Ranger (1949–1952, 1954–1957)
.... Clayton Moore
The Lone Ranger (1952–1954) .... John Hart
Tonto .... Jay Silverheels
THEME:
"William Tell Overture," by G. Rossini (composed in 1829)

The Lone Ranger was typical of the first wave of Westerns to hit TV in the early 1950s. Characters and plots were simple—good guys vs. bad guys—and there was none of the character development that marked the later "adult" Westerns.

The Lone Ranger had begun as a local radio show in 1933, and had quickly spread to a nationwide hookup (it was, in fact, the cornerstone of the then new Mutual Radio Network). In 1949 it was brought to TV in a series of half-hour films, made in Hollywood especially for the new medium. The opening episode, on September 15, 1949, told the familiar story of how the Lone Ranger got his name and his mission in life. He had been one of a posse of six Texas Rangers tracking a gang of desperadoes. The Rangers were lured into an ambush in a canyon, and five of them were slaughtered. The sixth, young John Reid, was left for dead. But Reid managed to crawl to safety near a water hole, where he was found and nursed back to health by a friendly Indian named Tonto. Reid had once helped Tonto and the Indian now vowed to stay with him as the "lone" Ranger sought to avenge the deaths of his comrades. "You kemo sabe," said Tonto; "it mean 'trusty scout.' " Avenge they did, cornering the outlaw Butch Cavendish in a dramatic battle.

Reid buried his past at the graves of the five dead Rangers, donned a mask, and set out with Tonto to avenge wrongs throughout the Old West. He had no visible means of support (he never accepted payment for his good deeds), but subsisted on the income from a silver mine that he and his brother—who was one of the deceased Rangers—had discovered. Periodically he returned to the mine, which was run for him by an honest old man, to collect the proceeds and stock up on silver bullets. Then, with a hearty "Heigh-ho Silver, away!" he would sally forth once again, like some idealized Don Quixote, with faithful Tonto at his side and their faithful mounts Silver and Scout.

Although the Lone Ranger never killed anyone (sometimes his adversaries killed themselves and each other), there was plenty of action, and the show was a great favorite with the younger audience. Parents liked it too, because of the lack of overt killing and the hero's faultless grammar—which in itself was unique for the Old West. *The Lone Ranger* was in fact the biggest hit ABC had in its early years, and when the A. C. Nielsen Company first began compiling national ratings for network programs in 1950 it was the only ABC program to rank in the top 15. Everything else was on NBC or CBS. Reruns of *The Lone Ranger* aired during the day on Saturdays from June 1953 to September 1960 on CBS and then on NBC for another year, as well as on ABC late afternoons for four years ending in September 1961 (the first three on Sunday and the last year on Wednesday). An animated version of *The Lone Ranger* aired Saturday mornings on CBS for three years ending in September 1969, and was revived in 1980 as part of *The Tarzan/Lone Ranger Hour.*

The Lone Ranger was created by George W. Trendle and Fran Striker, who were also responsible for *The Green Hornet*, and there was an unusual link between the two programs. John Reid's nephew Dan was supposed to be the father of Britt Reid, who became the avenger of crime in another era as *The Green Hornet.*

Clayton Moore was the best-known TV Lone Ranger (he also filled the role in two feature films made in the late 1950s), but the character was also played by veteran actor John Hart for a couple of seasons. Tonto was always played to poker-faced perfection by Jay Silverheels, a mixed-blood Mohawk Indian who in later years became quite successful as a horse breeder and racer. Asked once if he would consider racing Scout, he smiled and replied, "Heck, I can beat Scout."

LONER, THE (*Western*)

FIRST TELECAST: *September 18, 1965*
LAST TELECAST: *April 30, 1966*
BROADCAST HISTORY:
Sep 1965–Apr 1966, CBS Sat 9:30–10:00
CAST:
William Colton .... Lloyd Bridges

At the conclusion of the Civil War, ex-Union cavalry officer William Colton decided to head west in search of adventure and a new life. As he wandered the frontier, looking for something that would give his life meaning, his encounters with people both honest and dishonest, hardworking and fast-buck, gave him an expanded understanding of himself and of human beings in general.

LONESOME DOVE: THE SERIES (*Western*)

BROADCAST HISTORY:
Syndicated only
60 minutes
Produced: *1994–1996* (44 episodes)
Released: *September 1994*
CAST:
Newt Call .... Scott Bairstow
Hannah Peale Call (1994–1995) ... Christianne Hirt
Col. Francis Clay Mosby .... Eric McCormack
Josiah Peale .... Paul Le Mat
Austin Peale .... Paul Johansson
Ida Grayson (1994–1995) .... Diahann Carroll
Sheriff Owen Kearney (1995) .... Denny Miller
Mattie Shaw (1995–1996) .... Kelly Rowan
Amanda Carpenter (1995–1996) ..... Tracy Scoggins
UnBob Finch (1995–1996) .... Frank C. Turner
**Luther (1995–1996)* .... Bret Hart
**Dr. Cleese (1995–1996)* .... Sam Khouth
*Occasional

Set in the Dakota Territory during the 1870s, this old-fashioned "movie" Western featured majestic scenes of sweeping plains and soaring *Bonanza*-style music behind every climactic moment. It concerned the adventures of handsome young Newt Call in and around the town of Curtis Wells, Montana. At the beginning of each episode the elderly Newt would open the leather-bound book he had authored, *Lonesome Dove—Tales of the Plains,* and recall the story that was about to unfold. As the series opened Newt arrived in Curtis Wells and fell in love with Hannah, daughter of Josiah Peale, publisher of the *Montana Statesman.* When Newt proposed to Hannah, Josiah had his misgivings, but she eventually convinced him she loved Newt and he reluctantly agreed. The other major character in *Lonesome Dove* was Col. Mosby, a former officer in the Confederate Army, dressed all in black, who was quick on the draw and sometimes good and sometimes bad—he had once worked behind the scenes with a gang of other ex-Confederate soldiers to rob the bank. Although he had lost Hannah to Newt, Mosby still had a crush on her. A gambler, he won the Pigseye Saloon in a poker game and reopened it as the fancy Ambrosia Club. Also seen regularly were Hannah's brother, Austin, and Mrs. Grayson, a black settler, who took Newt as her partner to buy the Unity Hotel because the banker wouldn't sell it to a black. They renamed it "Lonesome Dove" in honor of Newt's home. Newt worked at the livery, and he and Hannah lived in The Lonesome Dove Hotel until he finished building their home on land outside of town. He became deputy sheriff in the spring of 1995.

When the series returned in the fall of 1995 it had a new title—*Lonesome Dove: The Outlaw Years*—and a much more somber tone. Newt was making a living as a bounty hunter, Mosby was running Curtis Wells, which looked much grimier than in the first season, Josiah had been elected mayor, and Austin was the deputy sheriff. In the opening episode Newt returned to town for the first time in the two years since Hannah had been killed by an explosion and fire at their home in the 1994–1995 season finale. The corrupt new sheriff was killed and Austin became sheriff, but the following spring he was relieved of the post. New to the cast were Mattie, a lady gunsmith who took over as undertaker; Amanda, a former grifter who arrived in town that fall and bought the Lonesome Dove Hotel at auction (Mrs. Grayson had left town and authorized the sale); UnBob, a gentle semi-derelict who worked for Mattie; and Luther, the stagecoach driver who was a friend of Newt's. In March 1996, Amanda lost her hotel in a poker game and was forced to operate an outdoor bar in the tent town outside of Curtis Wells. In the same episode Mattie, having given up on the prospects of developing a relationship with Newt, left town.

Adapted from the novel *Lonesome Dove*, written by Larry McMurtry and spun off from the two miniseries, *Lonesome Dove* and *Return to Lonesome Dove,* that had aired on CBS. Produced in conjunction with CTV network in Canada and filmed on the sweeping plains of Alberta, Canada.

LONG, HOT SUMMER, THE (*Drama*)

FIRST TELECAST: *September 16, 1965*
LAST TELECAST: *July 13, 1966*
BROADCAST HISTORY:
Sep 1965–Jan 1966, ABC Thu 10:00–11:00
Jan 1966–Jul 1966, ABC Wed 10:00–11:00
CAST:
"Boss" Will Varner (1965) .... Edmond O'Brien
"Boss" Will Varner (1966) .... Dan O'Herlihy
Ben Quick .... Roy Thinnes
Clara Varner .... Nancy Malone

Jody Varner .... Paul Geary
Minnie Littlejohn .... Ruth Roman
Eula Harker .... Lana Wood

Adult drama set in the small, Deep South community of Frenchman's Bend, dominated by aging, tyrannical Will Varner, who owned the town, and young Ben Quick, who had returned after 13 years to reclaim his father's farm and challenge Varner's absolute authority. Ben's father had been "destroyed" by Varner, but Ben was determined to settle the fight from which his father ran. Also featured were Varner's troubled, sensitive daughter Clara, his weak, immature son Jody, his mistress Minnie, and Eula, the sexy young daughter of the local postmaster.

The Long, Hot Summer was based on material by William Faulkner, primarily the novel *The Hamlet* and the short story "Barn Burning," which were adapted for a hit movie in 1958.

LONGSTREET (*Detective Drama*)

FIRST TELECAST: *September 9, 1971*
LAST TELECAST: *August 10, 1972*
BROADCAST HISTORY:
Sep 1971–Aug 1972, ABC Thu 9:00–10:00
CAST:
Mike Longstreet .... James Franciscus
Nikki Bell .... Marlyn Mason
Duke Paige .... Peter Mark Richman
Mrs. Kingston .... Ann Doran

Mike Longstreet was a New Orleans insurance-company investigator. While on a case he had the double misfortune of having his wife killed and his eyesight destroyed by people determined that he not solve the case. Despite his injury, Mike refused to quit the business. With his German shepherd guide dog Pax to help him get around, and an electronic cane to judge distances, Longstreet remained a remarkably successful investigator. If anything, blindness sharpened his other senses and analytical skills. Mike's girl Friday, Nikki, was his biggest booster; his insurance-company friend Duke Paige worked with him on many cases.

Kung Fu expert Bruce Lee appeared in this series as Longstreet's self-defense instructor.

LOOK MA, I'M ACTING, see *Say It With Acting*

LOOK PHOTOCRIME, see *Photocrime*

LOOKING BEYOND (*Supernatural Magazine*)

BROADCAST HISTORY:
Syndicated only
60 minutes
Produced: *1997–1998* (26 episodes)
Released: *September 1997*
HOSTESS:
Linda Bonnell

Produced by the same people responsible for *Sightings, Encounters: The Hidden Truth,* and *The Paranormal Borderline,* this series presented interviews with people relating their actual experiences with the supernatural, alien encounters, and mystical visions. In addition to the interviews, segments included film coverage of the actual events and/or re-creations. Viewers were asked to contact the producers if they had "an unusual story, rare photographs or videotape evidence of a paranormal nature." Series co-executive producer Linda Bonnell hosted the show.

LOOKING FOR LOVE: BACHELORETTES IN ALASKA (*Romance/Reality*)

FIRST TELECAST: *June 2, 2002*
LAST TELECAST: *July 7, 2002*
BROADCAST HISTORY:
Jun 2002–Jul 2002, FOX Sun 9:00–10:00
HOST:
Steve Santagati

In this chilly variation on the reality/romance theme, five single women between the ages of 26 and 36—Karen, Rebekah, Andrea, Cecile and Sissie—were flown to Alaska, where they silently picked 5 handsome bachelors from about 40 waiting for them on a glacier ("What drew me to him was his smile"). The five and their "Men on Ice" then moved into the rustic Northern Lights Wilderness Lodge on remote Promise Lake, where they got to know each other better. Days were spent on outdoor activities—snowshoeing, dogsledding and hiking—while nighttime dating included candlelight dinners and late-night frolics in the Jacuzzi. There were group dates in which all of the women and their Men on Ice took a cruise to a glacier or went to the Alaska Sealife Center.

In each episode four new men arrived and competed in such activities as ax throwing, skeet shooting, and wood chopping to determine which one could choose one of the women for his first date. The other women secretly chose among the remaining three new men; if two women picked the same man, he chose between them. The woman not chosen had to spend the day alone in her cabin. There was also the Reality Check, a game in which all of the participants answered questions about life, love, marriage, and morality. At the end of each episode everyone met at Proposal Point, where each new man made his plea, including a "dowry" contribution, to the woman of his choice to become her new Man on Ice and send her current Man on Ice home—if unsuccessful, he had to leave.

When the dust settled in the final episode, Karen and Rebekah, whose $23,000 dowry winnings were by far the largest, were both stood up by the men they had chosen. Andrea picked Kristian who, surprisingly, showed up and said he wanted to see more of her. Cecile chose Will, who turned her down, but was surprised by Tim, who pleaded with her. She agreed to give him a second chance. Lastly, Sissie chose Brent, who had been with her since the first day on the glacier. He agreed, asked if he could meet her parents, and tentatively proposed.

A postscript indicated that Tim had subsequently visited Cecile in California, but it didn't work out. Kristian and Andrea were trying to maintain a long-distance relationship, and Sissie had moved to Alaska to be with Brent.

LORETTA YOUNG SHOW, THE (*Dramatic Anthology*)

FIRST TELECAST: *September 20, 1953*
LAST TELECAST: *September 10, 1961*
BROADCAST HISTORY:
Sep 1953–Jun 1958, NBC Sun 10:00–10:30 (OS)
Oct 1958–Sep 1961, NBC Sun 10:00–10:30
HOSTESS/STAR:
Loretta Young

The Loretta Young Show's trademark, one that was often lampooned by comedians, was the dramatic entrance

Miss Young made at the beginning of each episode. She would come sweeping through a doorway with her full-skirted dress swirling around her and move into the center of the room to introduce the evening's play. Equally distinctive was the program's close, when she would return and read a few lines of poetry or a passage from the Bible that amplified or restated the message of the play just telecast. Miss Young starred in over half the plays aired during this filmed series' eight-season run, playing everything from nuns to housewives. The periods and locations varied, the story may have been serious, amusing, or touching, but all of the tales told on *The Loretta Young Show* were uplifting. They portrayed the nobler side of the human spirit and were designed to teach as well as entertain. Episodes in which Miss Young had not starred were rerun under various titles as summer series with other performers functioning as host. When *The Loretta Young Show* went into syndication, the introductions were deleted in compliance with Miss Young's wishes. She was concerned that the dresses she had worn for them had become dated with the passage of time.

When this series premiered in September 1953 it was titled *Letter to Loretta*. All of the stories were done as responses to letters that she had received from her fans during the years she had been a motion-picture star. She would read a letter at the beginning of each show and then star in the dramatized answer. Although the title was changed to *The Loretta Young Show* on February 14, 1954, this format was retained through the first two seasons of the series, with Miss Young starring in every episode. At the start of the 1955–1956 season there were a number of changes. The series became a straight dramatic show and the letter concept was dropped. Miss Young, who was recovering from an operation when filming had started in June, was replaced by a succession of guest hosts and stars until her return on Christmas night. After her return, however, she cut back her starring appearances to roughly half of each year's episodes.

Over the years many performers starred, with or without Miss Young, in episodes of this series. Those who had the leads in at least three stories were Eddie Albert, George Nader, Hugh O'Brian, Beverly Washburn, Jock Mahoney, Craig Stevens, Ralph Meeker, James Daly, James Philbrook, Stephen McNally, Pat Crowley, Claude Akins, Barry Atwater, Regis Toomey, Everett Sloane, Ricardo Montalban, and John Newland. The latter two deserve special mention. Ricardo Montalban starred on nine different occasions and John Newland on thirteen. Mr. Newland, in addition to being Loretta's most frequent co-star, from 1957 to 1959 directed numerous episodes in which he was not acting.

NBC aired reruns of this show on weekday afternoons from February 1960 to December 1964 under the title *The Loretta Young Theatre*.

LORNE GREENE'S LAST OF THE WILD

(*Wildlife/Nature*)

BROADCAST HISTORY:

Syndicated only
30 minutes
Produced: *1974–1979* (104 episodes)
Released: *Fall 1974*

HOST/NARRATOR:

Lorne Greene

A wildlife documentary series devoted to endangered series.

LORNE GREENE'S NEW WILDERNESS

(*Wildlife/Nature*)

BROADCAST HISTORY:

Syndicated only
30 minutes
Produced: *1982–1986* (104 episodes)
Released: *Fall 1982*

HOST/NARRATOR:

Lorne Green

A wildlife documentary series, similar to *Lorne Green's Last of the Wild*, hosted by the former star of *Bonanza*. Mr. Greene passed away in the fall of 1987.

LOST (*Adventure/Reality*)

FIRST TELECAST: *September 5, 2001*
LAST TELECAST: *October 3, 2001*
BROADCAST HISTORY:

Sep 2001–Oct 2001, NBC Wed 8:00–9:00

NARRATOR:

Al Trautwig

Lost might better have been called *Get Back*. The premise of this reality show was simple. Three teams of two strangers each were blindfolded and airlifted to a remote location somewhere around the globe, where they had to figure out where they were then make their way to the Statue of Liberty in New York. They were given only a little money and basic survival gear, which they carried on their backs—no maps, no credit cards, no cell phones (although they did have a closed-circuit radio connecting them to the production office in case of emergency). A cameraman, who offered no help, tagged along. Basically they had to panhandle and sweet-talk their way back to America. Each contest lasted three weeks.

In the first contest the three teams were dropped in the Mongolian desert, a fact they quickly figured out by the language on the back of the cigarette packs. They then set off in different directions, but excitement soon turned to despair as language and money-related hurdles arose. As the overwrought narrator put it, "Frustration and anger is coming at them in waves." Gay graphics designer Joe and morose Courtland squabbled constantly and, finding themselves sleeping on the streets in Moscow, gave up. Tammi and Celeste made their way through Vladivostok but, despite charming every male they encountered, kept getting delayed. Flirty makeup artist Carla and determined singer Lando, the black couple, convinced a cruise ship company to take them from Russia to Hawaii in return for Lando performing on board, then got an airline employee to "comp" them tickets on a flight to New York. They got to New York first and won the first grand prize of $200,000 and a new SUV for each.

Lost premiered a week before the terrorist attacks of September 11, 2001, and was shelved after one episode; subsequent episodes aired on September 26 and October 3, and December 23 and 30, 2001.

LOST AT HOME (*Situation Comedy*)

FIRST TELECAST: *April 1, 2003*
LAST TELECAST: *April 22, 2003*
BROADCAST HISTORY:

Apr 2003, ABC Tue 9:30–10:00

CAST:

Michael Davis .... Mitch Rouse
Rachel Davis .... Connie Britton
Will Davis .... Stark Sands
Sara Davis (age 13) .... Leah Pipes
Joshua Davis (7) .... Gavin Fink
Tucker .... Aaron Hill
Jordan King .... Gregory Hines

Michael was a successful Manhattan advertising executive whose workaholic ways had earned a comfortable lifestyle for his family but were causing him to completely miss his kids' growing-up years. He came to this revelation when his wife, Rachel, announced she was considering a divorce and, deciding that late was better than never, he started trying to reconnect. Amiable and befuddled around the big suburban farmhouse that he'd bought for them—but never paid much attention to—Michael fumbled in the kitchen, blundered into his kids' social lives, and was generally a klutz. But a klutz they knew was better than the dad they never saw. Oldest son Will was a high school jock, tentatively trying to find his way with the girls; Sara, the bright and somewhat shy 13-year-old, who turned to hefty best friend Tucker for advice when her dad wasn't there, and Joshua, the cute seven-year-old, who tried so hard to be the "good son" that counselors said it might lead to psychological problems. They were all good kids, and Michael's friend and boss at work, Jordan, agreed to cut him some slack so he could spend more time with them.

LOST CIVILIZATIONS (*Documentary*)

FIRST TELECAST: *June 25, 1995*
LAST TELECAST: *December 31, 1995*
BROADCAST HISTORY:

Jun 1995–Aug 1995, NBC Sun 7:00–8:00
Dec 1995, NBC Sun 7:00–8:00

NARRATOR:

Sam Waterston

An Emmy Award–winning series of documentaries on ancient cultures, utilizing reenactments and special effects as well as documentary footage. Among the subjects were Egypt, the Aegean, Mesopotamia, China, Tibet, and the Incas. Also known as *Time-Life's Lost Civilizations*.

LOST IN SPACE (*Science Fiction*)

FIRST TELECAST: *September 15, 1965*
LAST TELECAST: *September 11, 1968*
BROADCAST HISTORY:

Sep 1965–Sep 1968, CBS Wed 7:30–8:30

CAST:

Prof. John Robinson .... Guy Williams
Maureen Robinson .... June Lockhart
Don West .... Mark Goddard
Judy Robinson .... Marta Kristen
Will Robinson .... Billy Mumy
Penny Robinson .... Angela Cartwright
Dr. Zachary Smith .... Jonathan Harris
The Robot .... Bob May
The Robot's voice .... Dick Tufeld

The spaceship *Jupiter II* was supposed to take the Robinson family—Professor John, wife Maureen, and their three children—on a five-year voyage of exploration to a planet in the Alpha Centauri star system. It was, that is, until Dr. Zachary Smith sabotaged the control system so that it could not function properly. The control system was tied into the programming of the robot that went along as part of the exploration team, a friendly, logical, ambulatory machine that was strongly reminiscent of Robby the Robot in the movie *Forbidden Planet*. Smith, apparently in the employ of some foreign government, found himself trapped aboard the ship when it took off, leaving him hopelessly "lost in space" with the Robinsons and the ship's pilot, Major Donald West. An uneasy truce was made among all parties, for none of the scheduled passengers particularly trusted Dr. Smith, knowing what he had done. For three seasons the Robinsons and their unwanted guest wandered from planet to planet, trying to find their way home. The stories were fanciful and rather childish, full of monsters and strange intelligent life-forms that were a constant threat, and an endless series of cliff-hanger endings designed to bring viewers back the following week. Dr. Smith was always trying to make a deal with some form of extraterrestrial intelligence to get him back without the others, but his plans never worked out. If he wasn't thwarted by the adults in the party, resourceful little Will Robinson, or the Robot, he managed to botch it up all by himself. He was a rather pompous, cowardly, and inept character.

LOST ON EARTH (*Situation Comedy*)

BROADCAST HISTORY:

USA Network
30 minutes
Produced: *1996–1997* (13 episodes)
Premiered: January 4, 1997

CAST:

David Rudy .... Tim Conlon
Sherry Greckin .... Stacy Galina
George Greckin .... Paul Gleason
Nick .... Victor Togunde

VOICES OF ALIENS:

Ahab .... Kevin Carlson
Angela .... Terri N. Hardin
Bram .... Sandey Grinn
Cubby .... Carl Johnson
Philippe .... Peter McCowatt
Raleigh .... Drew Massey

Aliens landed on earth once again, only to get stuck in another dumb sitcom in this short-lived Saturday night entry. David was a failed newscaster on station KTEE-TV who had been demoted to hosting a kids' puppet show by tyrannical station manager George Greckin. Taken aback when the grotesque puppets began talking to him—and only him—he soon discovered that they were irritable aliens from an unpronounceable planet, who had mistakenly morphed into puppet form while watching the Muppets. Now they wanted to get home. Smarmy, self-centered David, thinking they might help jump-start his career, agreed to keep their secret. Sherry was Greckin's uptight daughter and second-in-command, who bossed David around but secretly wanted to undress him, and Nick was David's addlebrained pal. The gross, foul-mouthed puppets were grouchy, armless Ahab, sexy Angela, horny Bram, corpulent Cubby, homesick Raleigh, and cross-eyed Philippe, the ostensible leader.

LOT, THE (*Comedy*)

BROADCAST HISTORY:

American Movie Classics
30 minutes

Original episodes: *2001* (17 episodes)
Premiered: *January 7, 2001*

CAST:

Leo Sylver .... Victor Raider-Wexler
Harry Sylver .... Allen Garfield
Myron Sylver .... Jeffrey Tambor
June Parker .... Linda Cardellini
Rachel Lipton .... Kim Rhodes
Victor Mansfield .... Victor Webster
Jack Sweeney .... Perry Stephens
Charlie Patterson .... Steven Petrarca
Roland White .... Jonathan Frakes
Mary Parker .... Stephanie Faracy
Norma St. Claire .... Sara Botsford
Fabian .... François Giroday
Director Weller .... Eric Stoltz
Letitia DeVine .... Holland Taylor

The Hollywood star system of the 1930s took a ribbing in this period comedy, which appropriately ran on AMC, the modern home of many films of that era. Each episode opened with "gossip of the day" from boozy columnist Letitia DeVine, then segued into the behind-the-scene story at Sylver Screen Pictures. The original boss of the studio was Harry Sylver, ousted by playboy/mogul Roland after a few too many flops and replaced with his brother Leo. Leo and scheming publicist Jack had their hands full covering up the real-life peccadillos of their stars—June, a fresh-faced 17-year-old hopeful who turned into a diva overnight; Rachel, her rival; and Victor, a former stuntman with a secret morphine addiction. Stories included Rachel's romantic triangle with Victor and screenwriter Charlie; June's distress when she discovered that her father was legendary swashbuckler and Hollywood Lothario Colin Rhome (Michael York), a fact hidden from her by her protective stage mom, Mary; and the studio's efforts to make a hit film, including one portraying Oscar Wilde as a lusty heterosexual. "Hollywood," observed seen-it-all Mary, "is a sunny place filled with shady people where stars twinkle until they wrinkle."

A special four-episode preview of *The Lot* was telecast on AMC on August 19–20, 1999, more than a year before the launch of the series, which then lasted for only 13 additional episodes.

LOTSA LUCK (*Situation Comedy*)

FIRST TELECAST: *September 10, 1973*
LAST TELECAST: *May 24, 1974*
BROADCAST HISTORY:

Sep 1973–Jan 1974, NBC Mon 8:00–8:30
Jan 1974–May 1974, NBC Fri 8:30–9:00

CAST:

Stanley Belmont .... Dom DeLuise
Mrs. Belmont .... Kathleen Freeman
Arthur Swann .... Wynn Irwin
Olive Swann .... Beverly Sanders
Bummy .... Jack Knight

Bachelor Stanley Belmont was the custodian of the New York City bus company's lost-and-found department. But it was his home life and not his job that was the source of most of his problems and aggravations. Living with him was his bossy, autocratic mother, his klutzy sister, Olive, and Olive's unemployed husband, Arthur. The fact that Arthur was perfectly content to live off Stanley's earnings, and did not seem particularly interested in finding a job and moving out of Stanley's home, did not endear him to his brother-in-law. One of Stanley's co-workers, his good friend Bummy, was the only other regular in the cast. Based on the British series *On the Busses.*

LOTTERY (*Dramatic Anthology*)

FIRST TELECAST: *September 9, 1983*
LAST TELECAST: *July 12, 1984*
BROADCAST HISTORY:

Sep 1983–Dec 1983, ABC Fri 9:00–10:00
Mar 1984, ABC Thu 9:00–10:00
Jun 1984–Jul 1984, ABC Thu 9:00–10:00

CAST:

Patrick Sean Flaherty .... Ben Murphy
Eric Rush .... Marshall Colt

Television is a medium of fantasy, and this program offered the favorite fantasy of all: "What if I had a million dollars . . . ?" *Lottery* told two or three stories each week about ordinary people, often struggling to make ends meet, each of whom suddenly won two to four million dollars. The bearer of the good news was Patrick Flaherty, representative of Ireland's Intersweep Lottery, who first had to find the winner, then hand him an envelope containing $5,000 in cash and a check worth millions. With Flaherty was his smiling partner, handsome Eric Rush of the Internal Revenue Service.

No one seemed to mind the presence of the IRS at the joyous moment. Instead, stories centered around the little guy who now could give the big guys their comeuppance, life's losers who were winners at last, various moral dilemmas, and those frantic folks who had lost their all-important Sweepstakes ticket—without which they wouldn't get the money. In all, more than $133 million in make-believe winnings were given away during the short run of this series.

LOU GRANT (*Newspaper Drama*)

FIRST TELECAST: *September 20, 1977*
LAST TELECAST: *September 13, 1982*
BROADCAST HISTORY:

Sep 1977–Jan 1978, CBS Tue 10:00–11:00
Jan 1978–Sep 1982, CBS Mon 10:00–11:00

CAST:

Lou Grant .... Edward Asner
Charlie Hume .... Mason Adams
Joe Rossi .... Robert Walden
Billie Newman McCovey .... Linda Kelsey
Margaret Pynchon .... Nancy Marchand
Art Donovan .... Jack Bannon
Dennis "Animal" Price .... Daryl Anderson
National Editor (1977–1979) .... Sidney Clute
National Editor (1979–1982) .... Emilio Delgado
Foreign Editor (1977–1980) .... Laurence Haddon
Financial Editor (1978–1979) .... Gary Pagett
Adam Wilson (1978–1982) .... Allen Williams
Photo Editor (1979–1981) .... Billy Beck
Carla Mardigian (1977) .... Rebecca Balding
Ted McCovey (1981–1982) .... Cliff Potts
Linda (1981–1982) .... Barbara Jane Edelman
Lance (1981–1982) .... Lance Guest

In the final episode of *The Mary Tyler Moore Show,* Lou Grant and most of the news staff of WJM-TV in Minneapolis were all fired. Fifty years old, and out of work, Lou moved to Los Angeles, where, next season, he got a new job. No longer involved with television news, he became city editor of the *Los Angeles Trib-*

une, a crusading newspaper under the autocratic rule of its owner-publisher, Margaret Pynchon. Though he officially worked for managing editor Charlie Hume, an old friend, Lou often found himself in a battle of wills with the widowed Mrs. Pynchon, a woman with personality traits—stubbornness, toughness, and determination—very similar to his own. Despite the fireworks that usually erupted when they disagreed, there was an underlying mutual respect between them. Other principals included Joe Rossi, the hotshot, talented young investigative reporter; Carla Mardigian, an ambitious young girl reporter (who lasted only a few weeks, to be replaced by Billie Newman, another young reporter with similar aspirations); Art Donovan, the assistant city editor; and Animal, the staff photographer. Although essentially a dramatic series, *Lou Grant* did have its lighter moments, usually revolving around the interplay between the members of the paper's staff.

The personal life of reporter Billie Newman was the focus of the 1981–1982 season premiere episode of *Lou Grant*, as Billie wed baseball scout Ted McCovey. The series concluded its run the following spring, amid a controversy not radically different from the type that had served as story material for *Lou Grant*. Despite CBS' statement that *Lou Grant* was canceled because of declining ratings, there were many who felt that the political statements of series star Edward Asner were the real reason. Asner himself accused CBS of dropping the show because of his unpopular and highly publicized condemnation of U.S. involvement in Central America.

LOUIE SHOW, THE (*Situation Comedy*)
FIRST TELECAST: *January 31, 1996*
LAST TELECAST: *March 6, 1996*
BROADCAST HISTORY:
Jan 1996–Mar 1996, CBS Wed 8:30–9:00
CAST:
Dr. Louie Lundgren .... Louie Anderson
Det. Curt Sincic .... Bryan Cranston
Gretchen Lafayette .... Kate Hodge
Dr. Jake Reinhardt .... Paul Feig
Sandy Sincic .... Laura Innes
Helen .... Nancy Becker Kennedy
Kimmy .... Kimmy Robertson

Comedian Louie Anderson starred in this short-lived comedy as a psychotherapist in Duluth, Minnesota, whose honesty with both patients and friends often got him into trouble. Fortunately for him, he was such an endearing guy with a wonderful, self-deprecating sense of humor that almost nobody could remain upset with him for long. Louie's best friend, Curt, was a no-nonsense detective on the Duluth police department who was having marital problems, and he and his wife, Sandy, were getting counseling from Louie. Working with Louie at a local HMO were Helen, his upbeat, wheelchair-bound assistant; Jake, a talented but socially immature physician; and Kimmy, a loopy waitress in the HMO's coffee shop. Gretchen, a chatterbox free spirit recently arrived from Los Angeles in search of a simpler life, became his platonic housemate.

LOVE, AMERICAN STYLE (*Comedy Anthology*)
FIRST TELECAST: *September 29, 1969*
LAST TELECAST: *January 11, 1974*
BROADCAST HISTORY:
Sep 1969–Jan 1970, ABC Mon 10:00–11:00
Jan 1970–Sep 1970, ABC Fri 10:00–11:00
Sep 1970–Jan 1971, ABC Fri 9:30–10:00
Jan 1971–Jan 1974, ABC Fri 10:00–11:00
REPORTORY COMPANY:
Mary Grover (1969–1970)
Stuart Margolin (1969–1973)
Buzz Cooper (1969–1970)
Barbara Minkus
Bill Callaway (1969–1971)
Lynne Marta (1969–1970)
Tracy Reed (1969–1970, 1972–1974)
Phyllis Davis (1970–1974)
Jaki De Mar (1970–1972)
Richard Williams (1970–1972)
Jim Hampton (1971–1974)
Clifton Davis (1971)
James A. Watson, Jr. (1972–1974)
Jed Allan (1973–1974)

This imaginative anthology was a collection of short comedy playlets, starring all sorts of big names, and dealing with the all-important subject of love. Love was seen from all sides, young and old, rich and poor, unmarried, just married, long married, and multi-married. Generally three or four playlets were presented on each episode, interspersed with short comic "blackouts" by a repertory company of six or seven young performers. In 1972 a tasteful "Lovemate of the Week" centerfold was also added, featuring a different girl each week.

A short list of those appearing in *Love, American Style* reads like a Who's Who of Hollywood: Phyllis Diller, Nanette Fabray, Tammy Grimes, Ann Sothern, Paul Ford, Pat Paulsen, Milton Berle, Sonny & Cher, the Lennon Sisters, George Gobel, Dorothy Lamour, Wally Cox, Tony Randall, Paul Lynde, Burt Reynolds, Harry Morgan, Rich Little, Ozzie & Harriet, Tiny Tim (as a suspected vampire), Sid Caesar, Imogene Coca, Jacqueline Susann, and Martha Raye. Ronny Howard and Anson Williams appeared in a skit entitled "Love and the Happy Days," which served as the pilot for the hit series *Happy Days*.

The first telecast, on September 29, 1969, was typical of the show's format. Act I, "Love and a Couple of Couples": Michael Callan is a suitor about to propose when his ex-wife turns up, spies the ring, tries it on—and can't get it off. Act II, "Love and the Hustler": Flip Wilson is pool shark "Big Red," who undertakes to instruct a young lady in the fine points of the game. Act III, "Love and the Pill": Bob Cummings and Jane Wyatt are parents worried about their daughter's plans to embark on a "swinger's tour" of Europe with her boyfriend.

Love, American Style reruns were seen in ABC daytime from June 1971 to May 1974.

An updated series of romantic vignettes, titled *New Love, American Style*, was produced for ABC's weekday daytime lineup more than a decade later, running from December 1985 to August 1986.

LOVE & MARRIAGE (*Situation Comedy*)
FIRST TELECAST: *September 21, 1959*
LAST TELECAST: *January 25, 1960*
BROADCAST HISTORY:
Sep 1959–Jan 1960, NBC Mon 8:00–8:30
CAST:
William Harris .... William Demarest
Pat Baker .... Jeanne Bal

Steve Baker .... Murray Hamilton
Sophie .... Kay Armen
Stubby Wilson .... Stubby Kaye
Susan Baker.......................... Susan Reilly
Jennie Baker.......................... Jennie Lynn

William Harris was an old-time music publisher whose hatred for the currently popular rock 'n' roll music was hurting his business and his health. He loved melodious music and refused to deal with most of the popular songs submitted to him. His progressive son-in-law Steve was a constant source of irritation and his daughter Pat was often left in the role of mediator between her father and her husband. Pat had inveigled herself into partnership with her father so that she could keep an eye on him. Featured in the show were William Harris's secretary, Sophie, and song-plugger Stubby Wilson, who performed many of the songs submitted to the publisher and spent a lot of time reminiscing about the "good old days" in the music-publishing business.

LOVE AND MARRIAGE (*Situation Comedy*)

FIRST TELECAST: *September 28, 1996*
LAST TELECAST: *October 5, 1996*
BROADCAST HISTORY:
Sep 1996–Oct 1996, FOX Sat 9:30–10:00
CAST:
April Nardini .... Patricia Healy
Jack Nardini .... Anthony Denison
Christopher Nardini (age 11) .... Adam Zolotin
Gemmy Nardini (16)................ Alicia Bergman
Michael Nardini (17)................ Erik Palladino
Trudy Begg .... Meagan Fay
Louis Begg .... Michael Mantell
Max Begg (11) .... Adam Wylie

April worked nights as a waitress at the trendy New York restaurant Grill on the Park, and her husband Jack ran Drake's Parking Garage during the day in this failed comedy that only aired twice before it was canceled. High school sweethearts who still loved each other after seventeen years of marriage, they struggled to support their family and find time to see each other, clinking champagne glasses on the fire escape outside their apartment when they had a few minutes together. The three Nardini children were Christopher, the would-be tough guy with a penchant for cutting classes; Gemmy, the rebellious teen into outlandish fashions, dyed hair, and body piercing; and Michael, working five part-time jobs while in his first year in junior college in the hope of getting enough money together to move out. Their new neighbors, the Beggs, provided quite a contrast. Trudy didn't work, was obsessive about housework, and was smotheringly overprotective of her son, Max.

LOVE & MONEY (*Situation Comedy*)

FIRST TELECAST: *October 8, 1999*
LAST TELECAST: *July 18, 2000*
BROADCAST HISTORY:
Oct 1999, CBS Fri 8:30–9:00
Jul 2000, CBS Tue 8:30–9:00
CAST:
Eamon McBride .... Brian Van Holt
Allison Conklin .... Paget Brewster
Nicholas Conklin .... David Ogden Stiers
Effie Conklin .... Swoosie Kurtz
Puff Conklin .... Judy Greer
Nicky Conklin .... John Livingston
Finn McBride................ Brian Doyle-Murray

This short-lived comedy was set in a fancy Manhattan high-rise in which the building's hunky young superintendent was in love with the daughter of one of its wealthy residents. Eamon lived in a spartan basement apartment with his dad, Finn, the building's gruff doorman. He had had a summer fling several years earlier with sweet Allison, a kindergarten teacher, and their romance rekindled in the series premiere when she locked herself in the bathroom on her wedding day to avoid marrying a socially prominent guy she didn't love. Allison's family consisted of Nicholas, her stuffy billionaire father, who was appalled by her involvement with Eamon; Effie, her boozy mother, who secretly found the romance appealing; Puff, her spoiled, vacuous sister; and Nicky, her lazy brother, who preferred to live off the family fortune rather than find a real job. Nicholas was forever trying to break up the romance, while Effie looked for ways to help the lovebirds.

Pulled from the CBS lineup after four episodes had aired, it returned the following July and lasted only two more weeks.

LOVE & WAR (*Situation Comedy*)

FIRST TELECAST: *September 21, 1992*
LAST TELECAST: *February 1, 1995*
BROADCAST HISTORY:
Sep 1992, CBS Mon 10:00–11:00
Sep 1992–Mar 1994, CBS Mon 9:30–10:00
May 1994–Dec 1994, CBS Mon 9:30–10:00
Jan 1995–Feb 1995, CBS Wed 9:30–10:00
CAST:
Jack Stein............................ Jay Thomas
Wallis "Wally" Porter (1992–1993)....... Susan Dey
Ike Johnson (1992) .... John Hancock
Abe Johnson .... Charlie Robinson
Ray Litvak .... Joel Murray
Kip Zakaris .... Michael Nouri
Meg Tynan .... Suzie Plakson
Nadine Berkus .... Joanna Gleason
Dana Palladino (1993–1995) .... Annie Potts

It was certainly true that opposites attracted in this comedy—but twice in a row? Jack was a cynical, rather insecure columnist for the *New York Post.* Opinionated and aggressive, he was a regular at the seedy Blue Shamrock, a restaurant/bar where he hung out with his buddies and let off steam. Into his life, and the Blue Shamrock, walked Wally, recently divorced from egocentric would-be actor Kip. She was a classy uptown woman with champagne tastes. After exchanging heated words with Jack and downing one too many vodkas, Wally impulsively bought a share of the bar from Ike, its bartender and owner, and declared she would turn the "joint" into a chic restaurant. Jack was both aghast and excited. He loved the grubby familiarity of the Shamrock and hated what Wally was doing to it, but, at the same time, he was falling madly in lust with her. The other regulars, similarly disturbed by the proposed conversion, were Ray, a shy sanitation worker, and Meg, an outspoken sports reporter.

Needing a waitress, Wally hired Nadine, a suburban housewife with two kids in college and a husband in jail for stock fraud, who needed the job to make ends meet while she worked on a degree of her own.

After Ike died from a heart attack (as had actor John Hancock), his surly brother Abe, an out-of-work auto worker from Detroit, showed up to claim his inheritance—Ike's share of the Blue Shamrock. He stayed on and took over as bartender, mellowing ever so slightly over time. As the love affair between Jack and Wally got more serious ("your condom or mine?"), they kept questioning what was developing between them, musing directly to the viewing audience.

As the 1993–1994 season opened Jack was moping over being dumped by Wally, who had left for Paris (Dey had been fired by the producers because there was "no chemistry" between her and co-star Thomas). Into the Blue Shamrock, and his life, walked his new love. Dana was a gourmet chef who had quit her job at a fancy French restaurant when the executive chef position had been given to a man. She became the new chef at the Shamrock and, more outspoken and less tolerant than Wally, became Jack's new verbal sparring partner. Although there was an undercurrent of growing sexual tension, it was a full year before they ended up in bed together. Having been burned by Wally, Jack took everything much more slowly the second time around.

On August 18, 1995, more than six months after the show had left the air, a single original episode was telecast.

LOVE BOAT, THE (*Situation Comedy*)

FIRST TELECAST: *September 24, 1977*
LAST TELECAST: *September 5, 1986*
BROADCAST HISTORY:

Sep 1977–Jan 1978, ABC Sat 10:00–11:00
Jan 1978–Sep 1985, ABC Sat 9:00–10:00
Sep 1985–May 1986, ABC Sat 10:00–11:00
Jun 1986–Sep 1986, ABC Fri 10:00–11:00

CAST:

Captain Merrill Stubing .... Gavin MacLeod
Ship's Doctor Adam Bricker .... Bernie Kopell
Yeoman-Purser Burl "Gopher" Smith ... Fred Grandy
Bartender Isaac Washington .... Ted Lange
Cruise Director Julie McCoy (1977–1984) .... Lauren Tewes
Vicki Stubing (1979–1986) .... Jill Whelan
Cruise Director Judy McCoy (1984–1986).. Pat Klous
Photographer Ashley Covington Evans (Ace) (1984–1986)..................... Ted McGinley

THE LOVE BOAT MERMAIDS (1985–1986):

Susie............................ Deborah Bartlett
Maria.................................. Tori Brenno
Jane .... Nanci Lynn Hammond
Amy .... Teri Hatcher
Patti.............................. Debra Johnson
Sheila .... Macarena
Starlight .... Andrea Moen
Mary Beth .... Beth Myatt

THEME:

"The Love Boat," by Paul Williams and Charles Fox, sung by Jack Jones (1977–1985) and Dionne Warwick (1985–1986)

The Love Boat was closely patterned after ABC's hit series *Love, American Style,* which ran from 1969 to 1974. Both programs consisted each week of several short comic sketches dealing with love of all types, young and old, married and unmarried, and both featured famous guest stars in the sketches. The difference was that all of *Love Boat*'s stories were set aboard the *Pacific Princess*, a luxury cruise ship which embarked each week on a romantic, sentimental, and often hilarious voyage across tropic seas. The three or four stories told on each telecast were thus interwoven and often involved the ship's crew, who were seen on the show every week.

Famous movie and TV stars of the past and present were delighted to accept guest roles on *The Love Boat*'s floating soundstage, combining work with travel to exotic locations. Among the many famous names appearing were Raymond Burr, Pearl Bailey, Steve Allen, Janet Gaynor, Greer Garson, Jane Wyman, Don Adams, Helen Hayes, Mildred Natwick, Dick Van Patten, and Charo (in the recurring role of singer-guitarist April Lopez). Some stories revolved around the crew, with Capt. Stubing's womanizing brother Marshall (played by MacLeod wearing a toupée) showing up on occasion, and Vicki, Stubing's 12-year-old daughter by a past girlfriend, becoming a regular cast member in 1979.

Most of *Love Boat*'s episodes were filmed on two real cruise ships, the *Pacific Princess* and the *Island Princess*, during their regular voyages from the Virgin Islands to Alaska. Paying passengers were invited to participate as extras, getting a raffle ticket for each day they "worked." Most passengers were delighted to take part, and cruises on which filming was planned were always booked solid long in advance.

Among the highlights of later seasons were voyages to ever more exotic locations—Australia in 1981, the Mediterranean in 1982, and China in 1983. February 1982 saw the first "Love Boat Follies," a shipboard musical extravaganza featuring the regular cast plus Cab Calloway, Carol Channing, Van Johnson, Ethel Merman, Ann Miller, and Della Reese.

A number of changes were made in the fall of 1985, in an attempt to buoy the slowly sinking series. In addition to a new time period and a new theme singer, a group of eight beautiful singer/dancers (The Love Boat Mermaids) were added to the crew, appearing in a weekly musical number and working in the casino that had been added to the *Pacific Princess.* It didn't help. In the spring of 1986, at the end of the original series run, Capt. Stubing romanced and married Emily Heywood, played by Marion Ross. (A number of new two-hour *Love Boat* specials were aired during the following season.)

The series was based on Jeraldine Saunders's novel *The Love Boats* (drawn from her experiences as a cruise hostess), and first aired as a series of specials during the 1976–1977 season. ABC aired reruns of *The Love Boat* on weekday mornings from June 1980 to June 1983.

LOVE BOAT: THE NEXT WAVE (*Situation Comedy*)

FIRST TELECAST: *April 13, 1998*
LAST TELECAST: *July 30, 1999*
BROADCAST HISTORY:

Apr 1998–Jul 1998, UPN Mon 8:00–9:00
Oct 1998– Jul 1999, UPN Fri 9:00–10:00

CAST:

Captain Jim Kennedy III.............. Robert Urich
Security Chief Camille Hunter...... Joan Severance
Ship's Doctor John Morgan........... Corey Parker
Bar Manager Paolo Kaire........... Randy Vasquez
Chief Purser Will Sanders.............. Phil Morris

Cruise Director Suzanne Zimmerman (1998)
.... Stacey Travis
Cruise Director Nicole Jordan .... Heidi Mark
Danny Kennedy (age 15) .... Kyle Howard

In this fluffy updated version of the 1970s series *The Love Boat*, the setting had shifted from the West Coast to the East Coast. The new ship, the *Sun Princess*, sailed from Florida to the Caribbean rather than from Los Angeles to Mexico. In the premiere Jim Kennedy arrived as the stuffy new captain, divorced and recently retired from the Navy. He had taken the job in order to build a relationship with his troubled, juvenile delinquent son, Danny, who moved in with him on the ship. It took Jim a little while to adjust to the laid-back attitude on the ship—quite a change from the strict discipline of his military life—but he did loosen up. The principal crew members were Camille, the proper security chief; John, the insecure doctor who suffered from seasickness; Paolo, the friendly bartender; Will, the chief purser; and Suzanne, the perky cruise director. Danny turned 16 on the May 1998 season finale.

When *Love Boat* returned in the fall of 1998, Suzanne had been replaced by Nicole, a new, and sexier, cruise director. She arrived to share duties with Camille, who had thought she was shifting jobs without competition. They never quite got along. The last October episode included a reunion with the crew of the original *Love Boat* series (except Gopher), who were on board for Vicki's wedding. At the end of the episode it appeared that Julie and Doc were going to get it on.

Among the more familiar faces taking cruises on the show were Julia Duffy, Christine Ebersole, David Birney, Julie Hagerty, Wil Wheaton, Marion Ross, Dick Van Patten, Vicki Lawrence, and Ricardo Montalban. Although each episode opened with a newly arranged version of the venerable *Love Boat* theme, the producers did not credit the performers, classifying them simply as studio musicians.

LOVE CONNECTION (*Audience Participation*)

BROADCAST HISTORY:

Syndicated only
30 minutes
Produced: *1983–1995, 1998–1999*
Released: *September 1983*

HOST:

Chuck Woolery (1983–1995)
Pat Bullard (1998–1999)

In this highly successful variation on *The Dating Game*, participants were shown videos of three prospective blind dates and went on a date with the one of their choice. After the date they appeared on the show, along with their dates, to talk about what had transpired. Sometimes there were no sparks, sometimes the date was a disaster, and sometimes they really hit it off. The studio audience, which saw excerpts from the original videos, voted on which choice they thought was the best date before the date was described. The show would then pay for another date with whomever the audience had picked. Sometimes participants let the audience choose their date up front and then reported back to tell how things went.

The original *Love Connection* ran for twelve years, primarily as a weekday daytime series, with some stations airing reruns late at night. Three years after it left the air it returned, paired on most stations with another relationship program, *Change of Heart*.

LOVE CRUISE: THE MAIDEN VOYAGE

(*Adventure/Romance/Reality*)

FIRST TELECAST: *September 25, 2001*
LAST TELECAST: *October 16, 2001*
BROADCAST HISTORY:

Sep 2001–Oct 2001, FOX Tue 9:00–10:00
Oct 2001, FOX Mon 9:00–10:00

HOST:

Justin Gunn

Love Cruise gave 16 attractive singles—eight men and eight women—the opportunity to make love connections and win cash. Each episode included physical challenges and relationship games and ended with the men voting a woman off the ship and the women voting a man off. Those who were voted off were sent to "Loser Island" (Aruba). At the conclusion of the final episode one couple won the grand prize of $100,000 each and a trip around the world. Initially the women picked the men with whom they wanted to spend time, but the participants could choose to change partners every two days; some looked forward to their new love interests, while others didn't want to let go.

Every other night, the participants individually went to The Booth (a lower-deck cabin) and offered questions for one of the other men and one of the other women. The contestants who had the most questions asked of them had to take "The Hot Seat" and answer the questions. If their shipmates thought they were lying, they had to complete a dare chosen randomly from a group of dares that had been submitted by the participants prior to the start of the trip.

Starting with the second episode, couples competed for the opportunity to have voting power. One of the winners of the competitions—which ranged from a dance contest to mud wrestling—received an envelope that contained a "Switch Card." The possessor of the Switch Card could change the vote during the Elimination Ceremony at the end of the episode. This contestant could prevent him- or herself from being voted off, "switch" the gender vote to protect someone else or do nothing and let the will of the majority rule.

Some of the shipmates were more popular than others, causing much friction, and there was considerable political infighting among the participants as they maneuvered to protect themselves and undermine others they considered potential threats. From week to week there were numerous alliances that shifted and ultimately fell apart. On the fifth episode the surviving shipmates were given the opportunity to switch their current partners for someone who had been sent to Loser Island. Michael, the only one who took the option (he brought back Jeanette), alienated all his shipmates.

When there were only three couples left, the next elimination was done through a contest, not a vote. Each couple was given a bag full of fruit; the two couples who squeezed the most juice out of their bag survived. For the finale all the people who had been voted off returned for a barbecue party and the announcement of the winners. Justin gave the eliminated couples a chance to get back into the game and one couple, Gina and Adrian, was reinstated. The ten eliminated participants did the final voting among the three couples. Darin and Melissa won.

LOVE ON A ROOFTOP (*Situation Comedy*)
FIRST TELECAST: *September 6, 1966*
LAST TELECAST: *September 8, 1971*
BROADCAST HISTORY:
Sep 1966–Jan 1967, ABC Tue 9:30–10:00
Jan 1967–Apr 1967, ABC Thu 9:00–9:30
Apr 1967–Aug 1967, ABC Thu 9:30–10:00
May 1971–Sep 1971, ABC Wed 9:00–9:30
CAST:
David Willis .... Peter Deuel
Julie Willis .... Judy Carne
Stan Parker .... Rich Little
Carol Parker .... Barbara Bostock
Phyllis Hammond .... Edith Atwater
Fred Hammond .... Herb Voland
Jim Lucas .... Sandy Kenyon

The joys of young love between a married couple from different social backgrounds was the theme of this comedy. Art student Julie came from a wealthy family, but when she met $85-a-week apprentice architect David it was love at first sight. They married and moved into a small, windowless, top-floor walkup apartment. Its only asset was an adjacent stairway which led to the roof, and a spectacular view of the San Francisco Bay Area. Also seen were the neighbors, the Parkers (Stan was an "idea" man who composed menus for a living), Julie's unsympathetic parents, the Hammonds, and David's coworker, Jim.

Reruns of the 1966–1967 series were aired during the summer of 1971.

LOVE, SIDNEY (*Situation Comedy*)
FIRST TELECAST: *October 28, 1981*
LAST TELECAST: *August 29, 1983*
BROADCAST HISTORY:
Oct 1981–Sep 1982, NBC Wed 9:30–10:00
Oct 1982–Dec 1982, NBC Sat 9:30–10:00
Mar 1983–Aug 1983, NBC Mon 8:00–8:30
CAST:
Sidney Shorr .... Tony Randall
Laurie Morgan .... Swoosie Kurtz
Patti Morgan .... Kaleena Kiff
Judge Mort Harris (1981–1982) .... Alan North
Jason Stoller .... Chip Zien
Mrs. Gaffney (1982–1983) .... Barbara Bryne
Nancy (1982–1983) .... Lynne Thigpen

Series star Tony Randall's role of Sidney Shorr bore a certain resemblance to both Felix Unger from *The Odd Couple* and Judge Walter Franklin from *The Tony Randall Show.* They were all prim, proper, and meticulous to a fault. However, in the made-for-television film on which this series was based Sidney did have one distinctive trait. In that film, *Sidney Shorr,* which aired a few weeks before the series premiered, Sidney was a homosexual. In the series, although homosexuality could have been inferred, it was never mentioned.

Sidney was a middle-aged commercial artist who had been living alone for years. Into his bachelor life had come a perky young actress, Laurie Morgan, who was pregnant and unmarried. Laurie had considered an abortion until Sidney talked her out of it. Now, a few years later, a grateful Laurie and her cute young daughter Patti had moved into Sidney's eight-room Manhattan apartment, and Sidney was in seventh heaven. Into his lonely life, scarred by memories of a domineering mother, had come someone he could love. The relationship between Sidney and Laurie was that of a close brother and sister, and he doted on the precocious Patti like an indulgent uncle. To those who saw Laurie as the nymphomaniac Gloria Trenell on the inane daytime soap opera *As Thus We Are,* her real-life role of loving mother would have come as a surprise.

Jason Stoller was the art director for the Graham and Ludwig Advertising Agency, Sidney's biggest account. Nancy was Jason's secretary, Judge Harris was one of Sidney's neighbors, and Mrs. Gaffney his superintendent's nosy wife, who was romantically attracted to an uninterested and unresponsive Sidney.

LOVE STORY (*Anthology*)
FIRST TELECAST: *April 20, 1954*
LAST TELECAST: *June 29, 1954*
BROADCAST HISTORY:
Apr 1954–Jun 1954, DUM Tue 8:30–9:00

The teleplays that were aired in this live anthology were all stories that showed the better side of human nature—the affection and concern people could have for one another. Lesser-known actors and actresses were starred.

LOVE STORY (*Dramatic Anthology*)
FIRST TELECAST: *October 3, 1973*
LAST TELECAST: *January 2, 1974*
BROADCAST HISTORY:
Oct 1973–Jan 1974, NBC Wed 10:00–11:00
THEME:
"Love Story (Where Do I Begin)," by Francis Lai

In the wake of the best-selling novel and smash hit 1970 movie starring Ryan O'Neal and Ali MacGraw, NBC felt that *Love Story* was just what was needed for prime time. Unfortunately, the TV series had nothing to do with the book or the movie, sharing only the name and that pretty theme song. That may have accounted for its short tenure on the air.

The stories were about people in love, young and old, rich and poor, married and single, and were set in various locations across the U.S. Generally, lesser-known actors and actresses appeared.

LOVE THAT BOB, syndicated title for *Bob Cummings Show, The*

LOVE THAT JILL (*Situation Comedy*)
FIRST TELECAST: *January 20, 1958*
LAST TELECAST: *April 28, 1958*
BROADCAST HISTORY:
Jan 1958–Apr 1958, ABC Mon 8:00–8:30
CAST:
Jill Johnson .... Anne Jeffreys
Jack Gibson .... Robert Sterling
Richard .... James Lydon
Pearl .... Betty Lynn
Myrtle .... Polly Rose
Ginger .... Barbara Nichols
Melody .... Nancy Hadley
Peaches .... Kay Elhardt

Real-life husband-and-wife team Robert Sterling and Anne Jeffreys played the heads of rival Manhattan model agencies in this short-lived comedy. Jill was always after one of Jack's clients or models, and vice versa, and Jack would not have minded landing Jill as well. Also seen regularly were Jill's male secretary, Richard, Jack's secretary, Pearl, and a bevy of beautiful models with names such as Melody, Ginger, and Peaches.

LOVE THY NEIGHBOR (*Situation Comedy*)
FIRST TELECAST: *June 15, 1973*
LAST TELECAST: *September 19, 1973*
BROADCAST HISTORY:
Jun 1973–Jul 1973, ABC Fri 9:30–10:00
Aug 1973–Sep 1973, ABC Wed 8:00–8:30
CAST:
Ferguson Bruce .... Harrison Page
Jackie Bruce .... Janet MacLachlan
Charlie Wilson .... Ron Masak
Peggy Wilson .... Joyce Bulifant
Murray Bronson .... Milt Kamen
Harry Mulligan .... Herbie Faye
This integrated comedy revolved around the friendship between a Caucasian family and a young black couple who had just moved into their previously all-white neighborhood. Charlie Wilson was somewhat nonplussed when he first discovered that his new neighbor on Friar Tuck Lane in suburban Sherwood Forest Estates (near Los Angeles) was not only black, but was the new efficiency expert at Turner Electronics, the company where he was a union shop steward.

Based on the English TV hit, *Love Thy Neighbor.*

LOVELINE (*Advice*)
BROADCAST HISTORY:
MTV
30 minutes
Produced: *1996–2000* (369 episodes)
Premiered: *November 25, 1996*
REGULARS:
Adam Carolla
Dr. Drew Pinsky
Diane Farr
Late night call-in show, in which twenty-something guys and gals asked frank questions about sex, relationships, and sex. Typical for an evening were a girl distressed over her boyfriend's foot fetish; another with one breast too large; and a guy with testicles that hung low. Dealing with the problems were comic Adam, who cracked a few jokes; Dr. Drew, a really cool M.D., who would offer some sensible advice; actress Diane Farr (the woman's view); and a frequently embarrassed celebrity guest. The series was a spin-off of Carolla and Pinsky's syndicated radio show.

LOVES ME, LOVES ME NOT (*Situation Comedy*)
FIRST TELECAST: *March 20, 1977*
LAST TELECAST: *April 27, 1977*
BROADCAST HISTORY:
Mar 1977, CBS Sun 10:30–11:00
Mar 1977–Apr 1977, CBS Wed 8:30–9:00
CAST:
Jane .... Susan Dey
Dick .... Kenneth Gilman
Tom .... Art Metrano
Sue .... Phyllis Glick
This short romantic-comedy mini-series was about two young single people who were dating each other. Dick and Jane had their ups and their downs and, since their relationship was just getting off the ground, were unsure of their feelings for each other. He was a newspaper reporter and she was a teacher. Tom was Dick's best friend and his editor at the newspaper, and Sue was Tom's wife.

LUCAN (*Adventure*)
FIRST TELECAST: *December 26, 1977*
LAST TELECAST: *December 4, 1978*
BROADCAST HISTORY:
Dec 1977–Jan 1978, ABC Mon 8:00–9:00
Jun 1978–Jul 1978, ABC Sun 8:00–9:00
Nov 1978–Dec 1978, ABC Mon 8:00–8:00
CAST:
Lucan .... Kevin Brophy
Dr. Hoagland .... John Randolph
Prentiss .... Don Gordon
Lucan was the story of a young man of 20 who had been raised in the forest, by wolves. For his first ten years he had never known another human being, and now, though acclimated to the ways of civilization, he still found himself ill at ease in cities. His search for his parents and for his own identity formed the basis for most of the stories.

LUCAS TANNER (*School Drama*)
FIRST TELECAST: *September 11, 1974*
LAST TELECAST: *August 20, 1975*
BROADCAST HISTORY:
Sep 1974–Aug 1975, NBC Wed 9:00–10:00
CAST:
Lucas Tanner .... David Hartman
Margaret Blumenthal .... Rosemary Murphy
Glendon Farrell .... Robbie Rist
Jaytee Drumm .... Alan Abelew
Cindy Damon .... Trish Soodik
Terry Klitsner .... Kimberly Beck
Wally Moore .... Michael Dwight-Smith
John Hamilton (1975) .... John Randolph
Lucas Tanner had been both a baseball player and a sportswriter but had given up both after the death of his wife and son in an auto accident. Wanting to start a new life, he moved to St. Louis and obtained a job as an English teacher at Harry S. Truman Memorial High School in suburban Webster Groves, Mo. There he encountered frustrating resistance to his down-to-earth teaching style, primarily from the more tradition-bound teachers. The support of principal Margaret Blumenthal, who was replaced in January by John Hamilton, and the gratitude of his students were often the only things that kept him from "throwing in the towel." Lucas's warm and understanding nature made him a favorite of the students, who appreciated his ability to treat them as individuals. A special friend was little Glendon, a small boy who was one of Lucas's neighbors and who would often come over to visit and talk.

LUCIE ARNAZ SHOW, THE (*Situation Comedy*)
FIRST TELECAST: *April 2, 1985*
LAST TELECAST: *June 11, 1985*
BROADCAST HISTORY:
Apr 1985, CBS Tue 8:00–8:30
Jun 1985, CBS Tue 8:00–8:30

CAST:

Dr. Jane Lucas .... Lucie Arnaz
Jim Gordon .... Tony Roberts
Loretta .... Karen Jablons-Alexander
Jill .... Lee Bryant
Larry Love .... Todd Waring

Psychologist Jane Lucas had a work schedule that would make most people shudder. Not only did she maintain a private practice in New York City, but Jane also wrote a regular advice column for *Gotham Magazine* and was co-host, with egocentric Larry Love, of radio station WPLE's popular call-in program, the "Love and Lucas Show." It made for a hectic professional life, and didn't leave her with much time for herself, but Jane loved it—at least most of the time. Giving other people advice about their love lives was rewarding, but there were occasions when she would rather have been working on her own love life. The other principal people in Jane's life were Jim Gordon, WPLE's demanding and conniving station manager; Loretta, Jane's secretary at the office; and Jill, her older sister who, in her meddlesome way, was looking out for Jane's best interests.

LUCILLE BALL SHOW, THE, see *Lucy Show, The*

LUCKY (*Situation Comedy*)

BROADCAST HISTORY:

FX
30 minutes
Original episodes: *2003* (13 episodes)
Premiered: *April 8, 2003*

CAST:

Michael "Lucky" Linkletter .... John Corbett
Vinny Sticcarelli .... Billy Gardell
Buddy "Mutha" LeGendre .... Craig Robinson
Theresa Phillips .... Ever Carradine

"Lucky" was a suave, charming gambler whose vocation had practically ruined his life—but who couldn't kick the habit—in this dark comedy set in Las Vegas. A former World Poker Champion who had won and quickly lost $1 million and his new bride (who died), he tried Gamblers Anonymous but slid back into his old ways. His less talented sidekicks were Vinny, a chunky guy who raised money by various scams (like faking auto accidents), and Mutha, a black dude and sometime confidence man with a kind heart. Theresa was a perky Realtor with a gambling addiction who met Lucky at a GA meeting and adopted him as her "sponsor"—despite the fact that he couldn't stay away from the casinos. A variety of lovable junkies, loan sharks and crooks also passed through.

LUCKY PUP (*Children's*)

FIRST TELECAST: *August 23, 1948*
LAST TELECAST: *June 23, 1951*

BROADCAST HISTORY:

Aug 1948–Sep 1948, CBS Mon/Wed/Fri Various times
Sep 1948–Sep 1950, CBS Mon–Fri 6:30–6:45
Jan 1949–Jun 1951, CBS Sat Various half hours between 6:00–7:15

HOSTESS:

Doris Brown

PUPPETEERS:

Hope and Morey Bunin

Lucky Pup was one of the more popular puppet shows on early television. It was first previewed between 8:00 P.M. and 9:00 P.M. on two consecutive weeks in 1948 to let parents see what their children would have available to them at an earlier hour, and then began a three-year run in the early evening.

With the exception of hostess and narrator Doris Brown, all of the characters on *Lucky Pup* were puppets. Lucky Pup was a little dog that had inherited $5 million from a recently deceased circus queen. Foodini was the magician who was trying to use his black arts to steal the treasure, Pinhead was Foodini's dumb but friendly stooge, and Jolo was the resident clown. All of the action took place in a circus setting. Gradually Foodini and Pinhead came to dominate the stories, and Lucky Pup himself was seldom seen.

The series ended in June 1951, when Doris Brown married and left television. A charming, modest woman, she later recalled of those early days: "I can't honestly say I miss performing. I never was a real professional at it; just enjoyed myself and often wondered why they ever let me get away with it." The Bunins later returned with a spin-off series called *Foodini the Great.*

LUCY-DESI COMEDY HOUR, THE (*Situation Comedy*)

FIRST TELECAST: *July 2, 1962*
LAST TELECAST: *August 31, 1967*

BROADCAST HISTORY:

Jul 1962–Sep 1962, CBS Mon 9:00–10:00
Jun 1963–Sep 1963, CBS Sat 7:30–8:30
Jun 1964–Sep 1964, CBS Sat 7:30–8:30
Jun 1965–Sep 1965, CBS Wed 10:00–11:00
Jun 1967–Aug 1967, CBS Thu 7:30–8:30

CAST:

Lucy Ricardo .... Lucille Ball
Ricky Ricardo .... Desi Arnaz
Ethel Mertz .... Vivian Vance
Fred Mertz .... William Frawley
Little Ricky .... Richard Keith

At the end of the 1956–1957 season of *I Love Lucy*, the show's stars decided that they wanted to experiment with a longer form of program. Starting on November 15, 1957, and over the course of the next few seasons, all of the *I Love Lucy* regulars starred in a number of full-hour specials. In the specials they traveled to different places and became involved with various guest stars. Collections of these specials were aired as summer series for five years by CBS under the title *The Lucy-Desi Comedy Hour.*

LUCY IN CONNECTICUT (*Situation Comedy*)

FIRST TELECAST: *July 3, 1960*
LAST TELECAST: *September 25, 1960*

BROADCAST HISTORY:

Jul 1960–Sep 1960, CBS Sun 10:00–10:30

CAST:

Lucy Ricardo .... Lucille Ball
Ricky Ricardo .... Desi Arnaz
Ethel Mertz .... Vivian Vance
Fred Mertz .... William Frawley
Betty Ramsey .... Mary Jane Croft
Ralph Ramsey .... Frank Nelson

The episodes that made up this summer series were all reruns of episodes of *I Love Lucy* that covered the period in which Lucy had convinced Ricky that it would be a great idea to move to the country. She got him to make a large down payment on a big home in

Westport, Connecticut, and they spent the next several weeks learning about the advantages and disadvantages of suburban living. Mary Jane Croft, who would later replace Vivian Vance as Lucy's friend and companion in mischief on *The Lucy Show*, was showcased here as the Ricardos' next-door neighbor in Westport.

LUCY SHOW, THE, see *I Love Lucy*

LUCY SHOW, THE (*Situation Comedy*)
FIRST TELECAST: *October 1, 1962*
LAST TELECAST: *September 2, 1974*
BROADCAST HISTORY:
Oct 1962–Jun 1964, CBS Mon 8:30–9:00 (OS)
Sep 1964–Jul 1965, CBS Mon 9:00–9:30
Sep 1965–Jun 1967, CBS Mon 8:30–9:00 (OS)
Sep 1967–Sep 1971, CBS Mon 8:30–9:00
Sep 1971–Sep 1974, CBS Mon 9:00–9:30
CAST:
Lucy Carmichael/Carter .... Lucille Ball
Vivian Bagley (1962–1965) .... Vivian Vance
Mr. Barnsdahl (1962–1963)........... Charles Lane
Theodore J. Mooney/Harrison Otis Carter (1963–1974) .... Gale Gordon
Harry Conners (1962–1964) .... Dick Martin
Chris Carmichael (1962–1965)....... Candy Moore
Jerry Carmichael (1962–1966)....... Jimmy Garrett
Sherman Bagley (1962–1965)........... Ralph Hart
Harrison Cheever (1965–1968) .... Roy Roberts
Mary Jane Lewis (1965–1974) ...... Mary Jane Croft
Kim Carter (1968–1974) .... Lucie Arnaz
Craig Carter (1968–1971)............ Desi Arnaz, Jr.

Tackling a series on her own, without husband Desi Arnaz, Lucille Ball firmly established herself as the first lady of American television with this long-running series. With one exception, the supporting cast underwent numerous changes over the years, and at one time included both of Miss Ball's real-life children. The one exception was Gale Gordon, who provided Lucy with a stubborn, stuffy foil for most of the show's run. The real constant, however, was Lucy and her special brand of slapstick humor, played off of all sorts of guests and regulars. Such was her fame by this time that she could attract Richard Burton and Elizabeth Taylor (and their well-publicized diamond ring) as special guests to open one season (1971), as well as many other stars who normally shunned television.

When it appeared in the fall of 1962, *The Lucy Show* cast its star as a widow with two children, Chris and Jerry, living in suburban Danfield, Connecticut, and sharing her home with a divorced friend, Vivian Bagley, and Vivian's son, Sherman. Both women were desperately looking to snag new husbands and Lucy, in an effort to keep busy and meet eligible men, eventually went to work part-time for Mr. Mooney at the Danfield First National Bank. In September 1965, Lucy moved to San Francisco, as coincidentally did banker Mooney, and again she was working as his secretary, this time at the Westland Bank. Mooney, who had been president of the bank in Connecticut, was a vice-president at the bank in San Francisco, which was run by Harrison Cheever. Lucy's daughter Chris was no longer with the cast and Vivian Bagley, no longer a series regular, appeared only occasionally as a visitor from the East. Lucy's new cohort was friend Mary Jane Lewis. The last episode under this title aired on September 16, 1968.

In September 1968 the show returned with a new title *(Here's Lucy)*, a couple of major cast changes, and a modified story line. Lucy had moved to Los Angeles and her last name was now Carter. She was still a widow with two children, but they were now named Kim and Craig (played by her real-life children, Lucie and Desi). She worked for the Unique Employment Agency, which was owned by her brother-in-law, Harrison "Uncle Harry" Carter. Gale Gordon was thus retained as her blustery, ever-suffering foil. During the summers of 1968–1971 reruns of the earlier *Lucy Shows* were aired (prior to 1968 the series was replaced by various other programs during the summer months).

The program was initially titled *The Lucille Ball Show* when it went on the air in 1962, shortened to *The Lucy Show* after only one month, and then retitled *Here's Lucy* in the fall of 1968.

CBS aired weekday daytime reruns of *The Lucy Show* from September 1968 to September 1972, and of *Here's Lucy* from May to November 1977.

LUSH LIFE (*Situation Comedy*)
FIRST TELECAST: *September 9, 1996*
LAST TELECAST: *September 30, 1996*
BROADCAST HISTORY:
Sep 1996, FOX Mon 9:30–10:00
CAST:
Georgette "George" Sanders............. Lori Petty
Margot Hines...................... Karyn Parsons
Hal Gardner .... Sullivan Walker
Lance Battista .... Khalil Kain
Nelson "Margarita" Marquez........... John Ortiz
Hamilton Ford Foster................. Fab Filippo
Ann Hines-Davis-Wilson-Jefferson-Ali .... Concetta Tomei
Rene .... Paxton Whitehead
Jean-Michel Basquiat .... B'Nard Allen
Michelangelo .... Thomas MacGreevy
Leonardo da Vinci................ Ronny Graham

George, an eccentric struggling artist with a punk hairdo, was working as a waitress at Hooters to pay her bills while living in artsy Venice, California. Margot, her best friend and roommate, was a onetime actress who had left her wealthy philandering husband. Together they sought fun and romance on a very limited budget. Hal was the sarcastic owner of the restaurant where they hung out, and Nelson the flashy gay bartender. Among their neighbors were youthful Hamilton, who thought George was wonderful, and Lance, an ambitious restaurant manager and social climber. Margot's much-married mother, Ann, tried to get her daughter to move back home because she believed that George had always been a bad influence.

Star Lori Petty was one of the creators, producers, and writers of this flop that was the first casualty of the 1996–1997 season.

LUX PLAYHOUSE (*Dramatic Anthology*)
FIRST TELECAST: *October 3, 1958*
LAST TELECAST: *September 18, 1959*
BROADCAST HISTORY:
Oct 1958–Sep 1959, CBS Fri 9:30–10:00

This filmed dramatic-anthology series aired on alternate Fridays with *Schlitz Playhouse*. Content ranged from light comedies, to romance, to melodrama. Generally, better-known performers participated, with Polly Bergen and Rod Taylor in "The Best House in the Valley," Barry Nelson and Audrey Totter in "Drive a Desert Road," Jan Sterling in "Stand-in for Murder," and Gisele Mackenzie and John Forsythe in "The Miss and Missiles" among the presentations.

LUX SHOW STARRING ROSEMARY CLOONEY, THE (*Musical Variety*)

FIRST TELECAST: *September 26, 1957*
LAST TELECAST: *June 19, 1958*
BROADCAST HISTORY:
Sep 1957–Jun 1958, NBC Thu 10:00–10:30
REGULARS:
Rosemary Clooney
Paula Kelly & the Modernaires
Frank DeVol and His Orchestra
The Jones Boys (1958)

Rosemary Clooney starred in this variety series that included comedy skits as well as musical numbers. Regulars on the series were the vocal group of Paula Kelly & the Modernaires, who left in March 1958 and were replaced by an all-male group, the Jones Boys.

LUX VIDEO THEATRE (*Dramatic Anthology*)

FIRST TELECAST: *October 2, 1950*
LAST TELECAST: *September 12, 1957*
BROADCAST HISTORY:
Oct 1950–Jun 1951, CBS Mon 8:00–8:30
Aug 1951–Mar 1953, CBS Mon 8:00–8:30
Apr 1953–Jun 1954, CBS Thu 9:00–9:30
Aug 1954–Sep 1957, NBC Thu 10:00–11:00
HOST:
James Mason (1954–1955)
Otto Kruger (1955–1956)
Gordon MacRae (1956–1957)
Ken Carpenter (summers 1955–1957)

After 16 years on radio as a weekly dramatic series, *Lux Radio Theatre* became *Lux Video Theatre* on October 2, 1950. The first live play, from New York, was an adaptation of Maxwell Anderson's *Saturday's Children,* starring Joan Caulfield. For three seasons this live dramatic series originated from New York, finally moving to Hollywood with the September 2, 1953, telecast. Major motion-picture stars and Broadway actors performed on the show. Some of the names to appear during this period were Veronica Lake, Zachary Scott, Franchot Tone, Nina Foch, Celeste Holm, Broderick Crawford, Dennis O'Keefe, and young Charlton Heston. The subject matter ranged from contemporary to period, serious to light. On the more literary side, William Faulkner adapted two of his short stories—"The Brooch" and "Shall Not Perish"—for presentation on *Lux Video Theatre* in 1953 and 1954.

When the series moved to NBC in the fall of 1954, there were a number of changes in the format. The length of each telecast was expanded to a full hour, a regular host was added to the program, and adaptations of theatrical films became the principal type of material presented. The host introduced each act and, at the end of the show, conducted short interviews with the stars (female stars always gave plugs for their "Lux Complexion"). When the show had been adapted from a movie, the host also interviewed a principal from the studio whose film had been adapted to plug a current film from that studio. Film clips from the current film were shown as part of the interview.

A preview of this adaptation of feature films had actually occurred in 1954 while *Lux Video Theatre* was still on CBS. On January 28, 1954, John Derek, Ann Blyth, and Marilyn Erskine had starred in a television version of *A Place in the Sun,* with Ronald Reagan hosting. The first NBC telecast was an abridgement of *To Each His Own,* starring Dorothy Malone and Gene Barry. At the end of the show, Alfred Hitchcock was interviewed about his current film, *Rear Window.* Popular movies that aired in abbreviated versions over the years were *Double Indemnity,* with Laraine Day and Frank Lovejoy; *Sunset Boulevard,* with Miriam Hopkins and James Daly; *Casablanca,* with Paul Douglas, Arlene Dahl, and Hoagy Carmichael; *Mildred Pierce,* with Virginia Bruce and Zachary Scott; *Jezebel,* with Martha Hyer, Charles Drake, and Jack Lord; and *To Have and Have Not,* with Edmond O'Brien and Beverly Garland.

During the summers Ken Carpenter, the regular announcer for the series, doubled as host and the plays presented were short versions of scripts that were under consideration by the studios as possible full-length features. None of them were subsequently produced as feature films.

LYRICIST LOUNGE SHOW, THE (*Comedy*)

BROADCAST HISTORY:
MTV
30 minutes
Original episodes: *2000*
Premiered: *February 8, 2000*
REGULARS:
Wordsworth
Master Fũol
Michael "Baby Power" Viera
Tracee Ellis Ross
Heather McDonald
Mike Ricca
Marty Belafsky
Dartanyan Edmonds
Jordan Black

Sketch-comedy show done mostly in rhyme by rappers Wordsworth, Master Fũol, and Baby Power, assisted by a cast of young black and white comedians. Many of the short skits revolved around the youth scene, such as a black and white blind date (they trashed each other), catty girls at a party, "Annie Anal" at her grade school career day, and a wacko guidance counselor. Some went farther afield—for example, a rapping sheriff in the Old West and a super-cool rapper waiting in line at the Pearly Gates.

The show was a spin-off from New York City's underground Lyricist Lounge, a kind of floating open-audition talent show for up-and-coming rappers. Founded in 1991 by teenagers Danny Castro and Anthony Marshall, it was staged in various clubs and halls and provided a springboard for such well-known rappers as the Notorious B.I.G., Sean "P. Diddy" Combs, Eminem, Mos Def and Foxy Brown. The composer and music supervisor for the TV series was Def Jef.

M.A.N.T.I.S. (*Science Fiction*)
FIRST TELECAST: *August 26, 1994*
LAST TELECAST: *March 3, 1995*
BROADCAST HISTORY:

Aug 1994–Mar 1995, FOX Fri 8:00–9:00

CAST:

Dr. Miles Hawkins .... Carl Lumbly
John Stonebrake .... Roger Rees
Taylor Savidge .... Christopher Russell Gartin
Lt. Leora Maxwell...................... Galyn Gorg
**Capt. Ken Hetrick* .... Gary Graham
**Chief Grant*......................... Blu Mankuma

*Occasional

Miles Hawkins was an angry, somber, but brilliant black scientist and owner of Hawkins Technology, Inc. He had been shot by a corrupt cop working for an evil industrialist and was left paralyzed from the waist down. With the aid of his close friend and associate John, he had developed an exoskeletonlike suit that enabled him to walk. In fact, while wearing the M.A.N.T.I.S. suit (short for Mechanically Automated NeuroTransmitter Interactive System) he had superhuman strength and speed. When he was in the suit Miles looked like a praying mantis superhero.

Miles had a secret lab/headquarters located deep underneath his isolated home on the coast outside Port Columbia from which he launched the Chrysalis, a craft that looked like a car and could hover like a helicopter. The only people who knew he was the Mantis were John and Taylor, a bicycle delivery boy who had become his legman. As the Mantis, he fought crime and corruption, using a weapon that fired special darts that left those hit by them in temporary paralytic shock. Because the police considered the Mantis a vigilante, they established a task force to track him down. Beautiful Leora Maxwell was a member of the task force, but when she eventually found out that Miles was the Mantis, she decided to work with him rather than arrest him.

Carl Lumbly was the only returning member of the cast from the pilot for *M.A.N.T.I.S.*, which had aired early in 1994. The mostly black supporting cast from the pilot was completely replaced.

M*A*S*H (*Situation Comedy*)
FIRST TELECAST: *September 17, 1972*
LAST TELECAST: *September 19, 1983*
BROADCAST HISTORY:

Sep 1972–Sep 1973, CBS Sun 8:00–8:30
Sep 1973–Sep 1974, CBS Sat 8:30–9:00
Sep 1974–Sep 1975, CBS Tue 8:30–9:00
Sep 1975–Nov 1975, CBS Fri 8:30–9:00
Dec 1975–Jan 1978, CBS Tue 9:00–9:30
Jan 1978–Sep 1983, CBS Mon 9:00–9:30

CAST:

Capt. Benjamin Franklin Pierce (Hawkeye) .... Alan Alda
Capt. John McIntyre (Trapper John) (1972–1975) .... Wayne Rogers
Maj. Margaret Houlihan (Hot Lips) .... Loretta Swit
Maj. Frank Burns (1972–1977)....... Larry Linville
Cpl. Walter O'Reilly (Radar) (1972–1979) .... Gary Burghoff
Lt. Col. Henry Blake (1972–1975) .... McLean Stevenson
Father John Mulcahy (pilot only)... George Morgan
Father Francis Mulcahy ...... William Christopher
Cpl. Maxwell Klinger (1973–1983)....... Jamie Farr
Col. Sherman Potter (1975–1983).... Harry Morgan
Capt. B. J. Hunnicut (1975–1983)...... Mike Farrell
Maj. Charles Emerson Winchester (1977–1983) .... David Ogden Stiers
Lt. Maggie Dish (1972).............. Karen Philipp
Spearchucker Jones (1972) .... Timothy Brown
Ho-John (1972).................... Patrick Adiarte
Ugly John (1972–1973) .... John Orchard
Lt. Leslie Scorch (1972–1973).... Linda Meiklejohn
Gen. Brandon Clayton (1972–1973) ... Herb Voland
Lt. Ginger Ballis (1972–1974)..... Odessa Cleveland
Nurse Margie Cutler (1972–1973) .... Marcia Strassman
Nurse Louise Anderson (1973) .... Kelly Jean Peters
Lt. Nancy Griffin (1973) .... Lynette Mettey
Various Nurses (1973–1977)....... Bobbie Mitchell
Gen. Mitchell (1973–1974)......... Robert F. Simon
Nurse Kellye (1974–1983)......... Kellye Nakahara
Various Nurses (1974–1978)....... Patricia Stevens
Various Nurses (1976–1983).......... Judy Farrell
Igor (1976–1983) .... Jeff Maxwell
Nurse Bigelow (1977–1979).............. Enid Kent
Sgt. Zale (1977–1979) .... Johnny Haymer
Various Nurses (1978–1983) .... Jan Jordan
Various Nurses (1979–1983) .... Gwen Farrell
Various Nurses (1979–1981)........... Connie Izay
Various Nurses (1979–1980) .... Jennifer Davis
Various Nurses (1980–1983)............ Shari Sabo
Sgt. Luther Rizzo (1981–1983)......... G. W. Bailey
Roy (1981–1983) .... Roy Goldman
Soon-Lee (1983)..................... Rosalind Chao
Various Nurses (1981–1983) ..... Joann Thompson
Various Nurses (1982–1983) ..... Deborah Harmon

THEME:

"Suicide Is Painless," by Johnny Mandel

In 1972 America was still embroiled in a lingering war in Vietnam, a war that had polarized the population. The climate created by an unpopular war was the perfect environment for an antiwar comedy like *M*A*S*H*. The setting was different, Korea in the early 1950s, but the stories and situations could just as easily have been from Vietnam in the 1970s.

The cast of characters in *M*A*S*H* were all members of the 4077th Mobile Army Surgical Hospital, stationed behind the lines during the Korean War. Their job was to treat the wounded being sent to them from the front lines and to try to save as many lives as possible. The environment was depressing; many of the doctors (who had all been drafted) could not really believe they were living under the conditions to which they were being subjected. There was an overwhelming sense of the futility and insanity of war that permeated their daily lives. A certain sense of humor was necessary for survival.

Most of the senior members of the M.A.S.H. unit had wives and families back home, but that never stopped them from propositioning every good-looking nurse they could con into their quarters. After all, they did need something to alleviate the depression that resulted from contact with a constant stream of maimed and dying young GIs. Two of the surgeons were Hawkeye Pierce and Trapper John McIntyre.

Like virtually everyone else, they were always breaking regulations. Hawkeye, despite his escapades, was probably the most intellectual of the doctors and was sometimes seen musing on the dehumanizing nature of war and questioning its moral validity.

Among others who were featured was Frank Burns, who was possibly the worst doctor in the unit, and the constant butt of practical jokes perpetrated by Hawkeye and Trapper because of his arrogance and his feigned adherence to military regulations. Hot Lips Houlihan was the head nurse who, despite her admonitions to both her nurses and the doctors about fooling around with each other, had been having an affair with Frank Burns for an extended period. Henry Blake, the commanding officer whose prime concern was the work of the doctors in the operating room, couldn't care less about what they did during their free time. Radar O'Reilly was the extremely shy and bumbling young aide to Col. Blake. There were also numerous nurses who came and went, with the same actress being referred to in different episodes by different names—a large number of actresses were collectively called Nurse Able and Nurse Baker. Dr. Sidney Freeman (Alan Arbus), an army psychiatrist, made sporadic visits to the 4077th M.A.S.H. to check on the mental condition of the staff.

There were changes in the cast over the years. The first significant addition was that of Cpl. Maxwell Klinger, an aide to the doctors in the operating room. There was nothing really wrong with him: it was just that he always dressed in women's clothing in a desperate, though futile, attempt to get himself discharged as mentally unfit. McLean Stevenson left the series in the spring of 1975, to sign a long-term contract with NBC, and his character, Col. Blake, was written out of the show in the last episode of the 1974–1975 season (he was discharged and on his way home, only to have the plane in which he was flying go down in the Sea of Japan). He was replaced by Col. Potter, who was somewhat more sardonic and definitely less silly than his predecessor. In the summer of 1975 Wayne Rogers also left the series, in a contract dispute; his character, Trapper, got a discharge and returned home at the beginning of the 1975–1976 season. B. J. Hunnicut replaced Trapper as Hawkeye's tentmate and co-conspirator.

At the beginning of the 1977–1978 season Larry Linville left, and so Major Burns was written out of the series. Having seen his love affair with Hot Lips end when she married Lt. Col. Donald Penobscott, Frank abruptly went AWOL and was permanently transferred. Replacing him was an aristocratic Bostonian, Maj. Charles Emerson Winchester. Hot Lips's marriage to Col. Penobscott, who was not stationed with the 4077th and who was virtually never seen with his wife after the honeymoon, ended in divorce during the 1978–1979 season. Gary Burghoff, the only member of the cast who had played the same role in the movie version of *M*A*S*H,* departed in the fall of 1979. His character, clairvoyant company clerk Radar O'Reilly, received his discharge and returned to the States. Cpl. Klinger, after a rocky start, settled in as the new company clerk.

On February 28, 1983, the last original episode of *M*A*S*H* aired as a two-and-a-half-hour special. Highly publicized in both print and broadcast media, with TV tributes airing at the local and network level for several days before, this special *M*A*S*H* was a national event, and was seen by the largest audience ever to watch a single television program. The finale brought a dramatic ending to the series regarded by many as one of the finest in television history. In it, the war finally ended, but not before the long years of pressure pushed Hawkeye over the edge and into a chillingly portrayed nervous breakdown. He recovered, but Major Winchester never would recover from his experience with a group of P.O.W. musicians who had brought a bit of cherished civility to the front—before they were suddenly and senselessly killed. Klinger, on the eve of his long-anticipated departure for home, met and married a beautiful Korean woman named Soon-Lee. As the program came to a close, the men and women of the 4077th departed, one by one, for civilian life. Some of them—Col. Potter, Klinger, Father Mulcahy—would meet again in a sequel the following fall, called *AfterMASH.*

*M*A*S*H* was based on the hit motion picture of the same name, which in turn was taken from the novel. The novel was written by a doctor who had actually served in one of the Korean War M.A.S.H. units, but who used a pseudonym—Richard Hooker—in writing, so as not to compromise his medical standing by his revelations. Reruns of *M*A*S*H* aired on CBS' weekday lineup from September 1978 to September 1979.

MDs (*Medical Drama*)

FIRST TELECAST: *September 25, 2002*
LAST TELECAST: *December 18, 2002*
BROADCAST HISTORY:

Sep 2002–Dec 2002, ABC Wed 10:00–11:00

CAST:

Dr. Robert Dalgety .... John Hannah
Dr. Bruce Kellerman.............. William Fichtner
Shelly Pangborn .... Leslie Stefanson
Frank Coones .... Robert Joy
Dr. Quinn Joyner .... Aunjanue Ellis
Nurse "Doctor" Poole.................. Jane Lynch
Dr. Maggie Yang .... Michaela Conlin

*M*A*S*H* on the home front was the theme of this comedy/drama about two rebellious doctors at San Francisco's Mission General Hospital. Here the rebellion was not against war but against the big, heartless Sutro HMO that seemed to care more about profits than patients. Dalgety was the suave loose cannon, a brilliant surgeon who loved to buck the system while having sex with the female staff in supply closets; Kellerman was a little more serious, the head of cardiothoracic surgery, hounded by an angry ex-wife who was trying to get sole custody of their son. Together they twisted rules, stole supplies, and pulled fast ones on the system on behalf of their patients. For example, when the HMO denied surgery to a patient whose insurance was about to run out, they declared her dead and performed the procedure in the morgue, calling it an autopsy, and brought her "back to life."

The HMO officials they battled were virtual caricatures, obsessed with rules, constantly snooping, declaring patients "the enemy" and trying to throw truly sick people out of the hospital as soon as possible (unless they had lots of insurance). Shelly was the new hospital director, a high-powered administrator with no prior medical experience who passed out at the sight of blood; nevertheless she could on occasion be a surprising ally for Dalgety and Kellerman. Frank was her assistant, an officious toady who fortunately was clueless; and Poole, the "Utilization Review Nurse," a Ph.D. in management who was grim, snotty and totally uncaring. Quinn was the hard-ass head of residents, whose penchant for following the rules did not dissuade Kellerman from secretly lusting for her, and Yang, the naive young intern who was a nervous ally of the cowboy doctors.

MGM PARADE (*Documentary*)
FIRST TELECAST: *September 14, 1955*
LAST TELECAST: *May 2, 1956*
BROADCAST HISTORY:
Sep 1955–May 1956, ABC Wed 8:30–9:00
HOST:
George Murphy (1955–1956)
Walter Pidgeon (1956)

Originally conceived as an opportunity for the viewer to see the workings of a major motion-picture studio, this series was hosted by actor (eventually to become Senator) George Murphy. Segments included interviews with stars, explanations and demonstrations of technical aspects of production, excerpts from current and past MGM productions, and special entertainment featurettes produced specifically for this series by Pete Smith and others. Due to weak ratings, in the spring of 1956 the format was revised to serialize classic MGM films. Walter Pidgeon took over as host to present *Captains Courageous*, highlights of the work of Greta Garbo, and *The Pirate*.

MSNBC (Network) (*News and Talk Cable Network*)
LAUNCHED:
July 15, 1996
SUBSCRIBERS (MAY 2003):
78.8 million (74% U.S.)

A general news channel, launched by NBC and Microsoft Corp. (the MS in MSNBC), to compete with CNN. The daytime schedule consisted of news features and coverage of breaking news, while in the evening there was news analysis and discussion (usually loud and contentious). Among the network's signature series have been *Equal Time* (political debate), *Time and Again* (historical news footage), and *The McLaughlin Special Report* (discussion). Nighttime personalities have included Keith Olbermann, John Gibson, Charles Grodin, and John Hockenberry (who, despite confinement to a wheelchair, reported from the war zone in Albania). An unusual feature of the network has been extensive use of top NBC reporters, including Tom Brokaw, Katie Couric, Jane Pauley, Brian Williams, and Stone Phillips. In fact, viewers of NBC News are frequently directed to tune to MSNBC for continuing coverage of news events, and vice versa, blurring the line between broadcasting and cable. The network is also quite active on-line, as befits its Microsoft co-parentage.

MSNBC took over the channels previously occupied by America's Talking, NBC's failed all-talk cable network, which operated from 1994 to 1996.

M SQUAD (*Police Drama*)
FIRST TELECAST: *September 20, 1957*
LAST TELECAST: *September 13, 1960*
BROADCAST HISTORY:
Sep 1957–Sep 1959, NBC Fri 9:00–9:30
Sep 1959–Jan 1960, NBC Fri 9:30–10:00
Jan 1960–Sep 1960, NBC Tue 10:00–10:30
CAST:
Lt. Frank Ballinger.................... Lee Marvin
Capt. Grey.......................... Paul Newlan

The M Squad was an elite group of plainclothes detectives working to fight organized crime in Chicago. Lt. Frank Ballinger was one of these top detectives who worked, as did most of the other members of M Squad, by himself. Ballinger was a hard-nosed cop with no romantic interests. His commanding officer, and the man who assigned him to most of his cases, was Capt. Grey. Lee Marvin starred as Ballinger and also served as narrator of the series.

The original *M Squad* theme had been composed by the show's music director, Stanley Wilson. At the start of *M Squad*'s second season, however, the original theme was replaced by a more jazz-oriented tune composed by Count Basie, which was also known as the "Theme from *M Squad*."

MTV CRIBS (*Documentary*)
BROADCAST HISTORY:
MTV
30 minutes
Original episodes: *2000–2003* (57 episodes)
Premiered: *October 5, 2000*

In this droll documentary series, MTV cameras toured the sometimes bizarre homes ("cribs") of rock musicians and other stars. Subjects ranged from Mariah Carey (who had an entire room for her shoes) to Wu-Tang Clan and Melissa Joan Hart. Many episodes seemed to feature suddenly rich inner-city rappers hangin' with their homeboys in their shiny new Beverly Hills mansions; in one, pint-sized rapper Lil' Romeo (or was it Lil' Bow Wow?) was so young that he couldn't drive the fancy cars parked in his new multi-vehicle garage. Another, featuring Ozzy Osbourne and his nutty family, was so entertaining that MTV turned it into a spin-off series called *The Osbournes*.

MTV: MUSIC TELEVISION (Network)
(*Contemporary Music Cable Network*)
LAUNCHED:
August 1, 1981
SUBSCRIBERS (MAY 2003):
84.9 million (80% U.S.)

MTV seemed like one of the more unlikely ideas in the early days of cable, a 24-hour TV network programmed almost entirely with continuous rock music videos. It was the right idea at the right time, however, and backed by an ingenious and omnipresent promotion campaign it became one of the great success stories of the 1980s. Teenagers in cableless homes across America echoed the campaign's refrain, "I want my MTV!"—and they got it.

Today less of the schedule consists of videos, introduced by hip, youthful "veejays." The original five, in 1981, were Martha Quinn, Nina Blackwood, Mark Goodman, J.J. Jackson, and Alan Hunter. Among the better-known since then have been "Downtown" Julie Brown, "West Coast" Julie Brown, Daisy Fuentes, Adam Curry, and Carson Daly. The remainder of the schedule includes specials and series that fit the network's rock 'n' roll image. Perhaps the most successful special has been the annual *MTV Video Music Awards*, first telecast in October 1984. Other special programming includes *MTV Movie Awards* (1992) and live remotes during Spring Break and the summer months, the latter from an MTV beach house or similar locale. The network is also quite proud of its "Rock the Vote" campaign introduced during the 1992 presidential election, which encouraged young adults to get involved in the political process.

MTV original series in the late '80s and early/mid-'90s included *The Week in Rock* (music news, with Kurt Loder), *Unplugged* (acoustic concerts), *Half Hour Comedy Hour* (standup), *The Real World* (reality), *Dead at 21* (adventure), *Remote Control* (quiz), *Singled Out* (dating game), *Loveline* (advice), and *Liquid TV* (experimental cartoons). The last-named spun off some successful cutting-edge characters, notably *Beavis & Butt-head.* Hits of the late '90s and early '00s included *The Tom Green Show, Jackass* and *The Osbournes.* The channel has also occasionally aired reruns of broadcast series with a rock music angle, such as *The Monkees* (in 1986) and *Catwalk* (in 1994).

MTV's success has not come without controversy, both from parents (who dislike its gross-you-out attitude and the sexism and violence of some of the videos) and its own generation (who complained about the lack of black videos during its early years). Undeniably, it has been extremely influential, however, molding attitudes among youth and profoundly changing the music business. The first video ever telecast was, prophetically, "Video Killed the Radio Star" by the Buggles.

A sister channel, VH-1 (q.v.), was launched on January 1, 1985. MTV has also spread around the world, with customized feeds to almost every corner of the globe. In America, MTV first reached more than half of all U.S. television homes in January 1989; its principal original prime-time series after that date are listed in this book under their individual titles.

Subsidiary U.S. channels, which change periodically, have included MTV2 (all videos, 1996), MTV Español (Latin pop, 1998), MTVX (hard rock, c. 2000), MTV Jams (hip-hop, 2002) and MTV Hits (teen rock, 2002).

MTV ODDITIES (*Cartoon*)
BROADCAST HISTORY:
MTV
30 minutes
Produced: *1994–1995*
Premiered: *December 19, 1994*

A showcase for offbeat, serialized cartoons produced by MTV, most of them with the network's trademark kids-against-the-world point of view. The first entry was the multipart story *The Head,* about a teen named Jim who had an alien living in his oversized head; the second was *The Maxx,* based on the comic book about a homeless superhero who lived in a cardboard box.

MTV SPORTS (*Sports Magazine*)
BROADCAST HISTORY:
MTV
30 minutes
Produced: *1992–1996*
Premiered: *January 25, 1992*
HOST:
Dan Cortese

A fast-paced weekend sports magazine covering such sports as water skiing and mud wrestling.

MTV UNPLUGGED (*Music*)
BROADCAST HISTORY:
MTV
30 minutes
Produced: *1990–* (54 episodes)
Premiered: *January 21, 1990*
HOST:
Jules Shear (1990)

MTV, the network of head-bangers and heavy metal, attracted attention with this back-to-basics showcase of contemporary artists performing acoustically. A wide range of top stars were eager to show off their real stuff, including Aerosmith, Mariah Carey, Eric Clapton, Elvis Costello, Sinead O'Connor, Sting, LL Cool J, Pearl Jam, the Indigo Girls, and Paul McCartney (who forgot the words to his own "We Can Work It Out"). One of the more surprising appearances was by old-time but newly hip crooner Tony Bennett, who remarked, "I've always been unplugged." The performances were taped in clubs from London to Los Angeles and aired on Sunday nights. Jules Shear was host for the early episodes, after which there was no host.

M.Y.O.B. (*Situation Comedy*)
FIRST TELECAST: *June 6, 2000*
LAST TELECAST: *June 27, 2000*
BROADCAST HISTORY:
Jun 2000, NBC Tue 9:30–10:00
CAST:
Riley Veatch (age 16) .... Katherine Towne
Aunt Opal Brown .... Lauren Graham
Mitch Levitt .... Paul Fitzgerald
Lisa Overbeck .... Amanda Detmer
A. J. Swartz .... Colin Mortensen
Evan................................. Steve Moreno
Reuben .... Dan Bucatinsky

Riley was a sarcastic, worldly teenager, raised in a foster home in Ohio, who made her way to Gossett, California, 20 miles south of the Oregon border, in search of her long-lost birth parents. Enrolling in Gossett High, she immediately dumped herself on the doorstep of assistant principal Opal, whom she announced was her aunt. Opal, a lonely, arrogant woman, didn't believe her at first, but it appeared to be true. There were some laughs and a lot of heartfelt emotion as persistent Riley moved in with the reluctant Opal and got her to help, while using her street smarts to track down clues. Was her mother, Opal's sister, a psycho who got pregnant in high school and then moved to Finland? Maybe, maybe not. Clever Riley also helped Opal break out of her shell, getting her promoted to principal and helping her open up. Mitch was the hunky assistant principal and object of Opal's unrequited affection; Lisa, a sexy teacher who was dating Mitch, and A. J., the dumb office assistant.

The title, by the way, stood for "mind your own business."

MAC DAVIS SHOW, THE (*Musical Variety*)
FIRST TELECAST: *July 11, 1974*
LAST TELECAST: *June 17, 1976*
BROADCAST HISTORY:
July 1974–Aug 1974, NBC Thu 8:00–9:00
Dec 1974–Feb 1975, NBC Thu 8:00–9:00
Mar 1975–May 1975, NBC Thu 9:00–10:00
Mar 1976–Jun 1976, NBC Thu 8:00–9:00

REGULARS:

Mac Davis
Robert Shields and Lorene Yarnell (1976)
Strutt (1976)
Ron Silver (1976)
George Wyle Dancers (1974)
Tony Mordente Dancers (1974–1975)
Jim Bates Dancers (1976)
Mike Post Orchestra (1974–1976)

Country-oriented singer and composer Mac Davis had three tries as host of his own variety series, in the summer of 1974, early 1975, and the spring of 1976. None of the three attempts attracted sufficient audience to stay on the schedule more than a few months. Regular features on all three shows were Mac's singing of his own songs, reminiscing about his growing-up years in Texas, and informal chats with the audience. In fact, he was often seen seated with the audience during part of the show, while he answered questions or sang and played his guitar. He would also improvise songs from title suggestions submitted by the audience. The 1976 edition had, in addition to Mac and his guest star, three regulars: the mime team of Shields and Yarnell, comedian Ron Silver, and a group of singers and dancers known collectively as Strutt.

MACGRUDER & LOUD (*Police Drama*)

FIRST TELECAST: *January 20, 1985*
LAST TELECAST: *September 3, 1985*
BROADCAST HISTORY:

Jan 1985, ABC Sun 10:05–11:50
Jan 1985–Apr 1985, ABC Tue 9:00–10:00
Apr 1985, ABC Tue 10:00–11:00
Jun 1985–Sep 1985, ABC Tue 10:00–11:00

CAST:

Det. Malcolm MacGruder .... John Getz
Det. Jenny Loud MacGruder ...... Kathryn Harrold
Sgt. Myhrum .... Frank McCarthy
Det. Sgt. Debbin .... Ted Ross
Naomi .... Gail Grate
Zacharias .... Charles Boswell
Sgt. Hanson .... Lee de Broux
Geller .... Rick Rossovich

Police Officers in Love could have been the title of this unusual action series. MacGruder and Loud were uniformed officers who shared a patrol car by day, and a passionate love by night. They had secretly married despite department regulations, and now had to hide that fact to stay on the force. There were plenty of high-speed chases, shootouts, and other dangerous assignments in between stolen kisses during the day, but the brass never seemed to catch on to their little secret.

MACGYVER (*Adventure*)

FIRST TELECAST: *September 29, 1985*
LAST TELECAST: *August 8, 1992*
BROADCAST HISTORY:

Sep 1985–Jan 1986, ABC Sun 8:00–9:00
Jan 1986–Jul 1986, ABC Wed 8:00–9:00
Aug 1986, ABC Wed 9:00–10:00
Sep 1986–May 1987, ABC Mon 8:00–9:00
Jun 1987–Sep 1987, ABC Wed 9:00–10:00
Sep 1987–May 1988, ABC Mon 8:00–9:00
Jun 1988–Sep 1988, ABC Sun 8:00–9:00
Oct 1988–Aug 1989, ABC Mon 8:00–9:00
Aug 1989–Sep 1989, ABC Sun 8:00–9:00
Sep 1989–Dec 1991, ABC Mon 8:00–9:00
May 1992–Jun 1992, ABC Thu 9:00–10:00
Jul 1992–Aug 1992, ABC Sat 8:00–9:00

CAST:

MacGyver .... Richard Dean Anderson
Peter Thornton .... Dana Elcar
**Jack Dalton (1987–1992)* .... Bruce McGill
**Nikki Carpenter (1987–1988)* .... Elyssa Davalos

*Occasional

Actor Henry Winkler was co-producer of this action-adventure series about a rugged, handsome hero who preferred to use paper clips and candy bars rather than more conventional weapons. MacGyver was a former Special Forces agent now working for the Phoenix Foundation, a "think tank" dedicated to righting wrongs and defeating bad guys around the world. A clever fellow, he often slipped past the enemy's defenses and undermined their foul plans with ingenuity rather than brute force, using tidbits of scientific knowledge and ordinary items that happened to be lying around; for example, the paper clip might be used to short-circuit a nuclear missile, the candy bar to stop an acid leak, or a cold capsule to ignite a makeshift bomb, all just in the nick of time. MacGyver could work wonders with the contents of a lady's handbag! His assignments came from Peter Thornton, the Director of Field Operations for the Foundation.

In later seasons the series became increasingly issue-oriented, tackling such subjects as Thornton's blindness, the environment, and teenage runaways. Introducing Mac to the latter subject was his teenage friend Lisa, played by Mayim Bialik on a few occasions. Another infrequently seen but memorable character was MacGyver's nemesis, the evil Murdoc (played by Michael Des Barres). Nikki was MacGyver's brief romantic interest, and Dalton his ne'er-do-well friend.

Like many TV heroes (Columbo, Quincy, etc.), MacGyver had no first name—until the last season when, in a dream sequence, he was transported back to medieval times to find his ancestors. There, written in flame on a castle wall, was his name: Angus! "Oh," cooed a maiden, "it's a beautiful name." "Maybe in your time," he replied ruefully, "but where I come from . . ."

In the last regular episode, MacGyver discovered the son he never knew he had—a young man named Sean "Sam" Malloy (Dalton James)—and the two got on their motorcycles and rode off into the sunset to bond.

MACKENZIES OF PARADISE COVE, THE (*Adventure*)

FIRST TELECAST: *March 27, 1979*
LAST TELECAST: *May 18, 1979*
BROADCAST HISTORY:

Mar 1979, ABC Tue 8:30–9:30
Apr 1979, ABC Wed 8:00–9:00
Apr 1979–May 1979, ABC Fri 8:00–9:00

CAST:

Cuda Weber .... Clu Gulager
Kevin Mackenzie .... Shawn Stevens
Bridget Mackenzie .... Lory Walsh
Michael Mackenzie .... Sean Marshall
Celia Mackenzie .... Randi Kiger

Timothy Mackenzie .... Keith Mitchell
Big Ben Kalikini .... Moe Keale
Mrs. Kalikini .... Leinaala Heine
Little Ben Kalikini .... Sean Tyler Hall
Barney .... Harry Chang

Cuda Weber, a crusty old fishing-boat operator in Hawaii, found himself unofficial father to a pack of spirited orphans in this short-lived series. The Mackenzie kids ranged in age from 7-year-old Timothy to 17-year-old twins Kevin and Bridget. Their parents had been lost at sea in a sailing accident, and in an effort to foil the authorities and stay together they persuaded Cuda to pose as their uncle and guardian. From there on in, it was a sort of *Brady Bunch* beneath the palms, with all the little scrapes and adventures of growing kids.

MACKENZIE'S RAIDERS (*Western*)

BROADCAST HISTORY:

Syndicated only
30 minutes
Produced: *1958–1959* (39 episodes)
Released: *October 1958*

CAST:

Col. Ranald S. Mackenzie .... Richard Carlson

Richard Carlson, who sneaked around looking for Communists in the long-running *I Led Three Lives*, became a dashing cavalry officer chasing Mexican banditos in this rousing horse opera.

The story was based on historical fact. Col. Ranald Mackenzie was commander of the U.S. Fourth Cavalry stationed at Ft. Clark, Texas, in 1873. Mexican bandits were terrorizing the local settlers, and Mackenzie's secret order from President Grant and General Sheridan was to stop the marauders by pursuing them across the Rio Grande into Mexico if necessary. This had to be done in secret, to avoid an international incident; if Mackenzie was caught inside Mexico, the U.S. would have to disown him. If he succeeded, there would be no glory. Needless to say, the colonel and his troops galloped forth without hesitation, for a season of stealthy attacks and flashing swords.

Mackenzie was one of the most colorful figures in U.S. Army history, and has been written about widely. This series was based primarily on the book *The Mackenzie Raid* by Col. Russell Reeder.

MAD ABOUT YOU (*Situation Comedy*)

FIRST TELECAST: *September 23, 1992*
LAST TELECAST: *August 5, 1999*
BROADCAST HISTORY:

Sep 1992–Jan 1993, NBC Wed 9:30–10:00
Feb 1993–Jul 1993, NBC Sat 9:30–10:00
Jul 1993–Aug 1995, NBC Thu 8:00–8:30
Aug 1995, NBC Thu 8:30–9:00
Sep 1995–Jul 1996, NBC Sun 8:00–8:30
Aug 1996–Dec 1998, NBC Tue 8:00–8:30
Dec 1998–Jan 1999, NBC Mon 9:00–9:30
Feb 1999–May 1999, NBC Mon 8:30–9:00
May 1999–Jul 1999, NBC Mon 9:00–10:00
Aug 1999, NBC Thu 10:30–11:00

CAST:

Paul Buchman .... Paul Reiser
Jamie Buchman .... Helen Hunt
Lisa Stemple .... Anne Elizabeth Ramsay
Jay Selby (1992–1993) .... Tommy Hinkley
Fran Devanow (1992–1998) .... Leila Kenzle
Dr. Mark David Devanow (1992–1993)
.... Richard Kind
Ira Buchman (1993–1999) .... John Pankow
**Maggie (1993–1999)* .... Judy Geeson
**Hal (1993–1999)* .... Paxton Whitehead
**Marvin* .... Jeff Garlin
**Sylvia Buchman* .... Cynthia Harris
**Burt Buchman* .... Louis Zorich
**Debbie Buchman* .... Robin Bartlett
**Dr. Joan Herman (1996–1999)* .... Suzie Plakson
**Dr. Sheila Kleinman (1997–1999)* ...... Mo Gaffney

*Occasional

CREATED BY:

Paul Reiser and Danny Jacobson

In a TV world of single parents, fractured families, and divorce-as-comedy, *Mad About You* was a surprise—a sexy hit show about a husband and wife simply in love that explored what it meant to be newly married. Paul was a neurotic, excitable documentary filmmaker and Jamie a smart and impulsive public relations executive. Living in a Manhattan high-rise, they bickered constantly, but lovingly, sharing both the big events and the trivia that make marriage its own sitcom. "The feeling of this show should be like a couple's car ride home after a party, when you can finally say what you've been thinking all night," said co-creator Reiser. "It's what the world is like behind closed doors."

Sharing their world were Lisa, Jamie's luckless single sister; Jay, Paul's bachelor-slob friend; and married couple Fran and Mark, a gynecologist. Fran and Mark divorced after the first season (oops, it *was* the nineties), but Fran stayed on to dodge Paul and Jamie's one-liners. Ira was Paul's self-confident cousin, and Murray (played by Maui) was the Buchmans' indolent dog.

Stories followed the progress of the Buchmans' marriage, through a near breakup (1996) to the birth of a child, Mabel, in May 1997. Dr. Kleinman was their therapist during the rough times, while Paul's parents Sylvia and Burt offered well-meaning advice, as did Jamie's less frequently seen folks Theresa and Gus Stemple (Carol Burnett and Carroll O'Connor in later episodes). Maggie and Hal were their British neighbors, and Marvin the stock boy at Ira's store. Paul's sister Debbie turned up occasionally with her "life partner" Joan.

The series finale, in May 1999, was narrated by a grown-up Mabel (Janeane Garofalo), a filmmaker, who produced a film about her parents' later life. In 1999 Paul and Jamie discovered they were not legally married, causing a number of complications; in 2005 Jamie became pregnant again (she thought Paul had had a vasectomy), but lost the baby; and in 2021 they broke up. Fran and Mark remarried; Ira married and had eight kids; Burt died and Sylvia moved into the Buchmans' apartment building, still offering advice; Maggie and Hal turned out to be British spies; Marvin became an international wrestling champion (as "Angry Tina"); and Debbie and Joan were married in Hawaii. And lovebirds Paul and Jamie? They reunited, and "lived happily ever after."

MAD TV (*Comedy*)

FIRST TELECAST: *October 14, 1995*
LAST TELECAST:

BROADCAST HISTORY:

Oct 1995– , FOX Sat 11:00–12:00 mid
Jun 1997–Jul 1997, FOX Mon 8:00–8:30
Jun 1999– , FOX Fri 9:00–10:00

REGULARS:

Bryan Callen (1995–1997)
David Herman (1995–1997)
Orlando Jones (1995–1997)
Phil LaMarr (1995–2000)
Artie Lange (1995–1997)
Mary Scheer (1995–1998)
Nicole Sullivan (1995–2001)
Debra Wilson
Will Sasso (1997–2002)
Aries Spears (1997–)
Alex Borstein (1997–2002)
Chris Hogan (1997–1998)
Pat Kilbane (1997–2000)
Lisa Kushell (1997–1998)
Craig Anton (1997–1998)
Andrew Bowen (1998–1999)
Mo Collins (1998–)
Michael McDonald (1998–)
Nelson Ascencio (2000–2001)
Christian Duguay (2000–2001)
Andrew Daly (2000–2002)
Stephnie Weir (2000–)
Frank Caliendo (2001–)
Kathryn Fiore (2001–2002)
Taran Killam (2001–2002)
Bobby Lee (2001–)
Jill-Michelle Melean (2002–)
Ike Barinholtz (2002–)
Josh Meyers (2002–)
Ron Pederson (2002–)

Fox launched this sketch comedy series as direct competition for NBC's long-running *Saturday Night Live.* As with the venerable NBC series, *Mad TV* offered commercial spoofs, music video parodies, movie satires, TV series spoofs, political satire, and social commentary. Most episodes included a segment in which some or all of the cast were in a living room, out of character, chatting with the studio and/or home audience.

Among the wilder sketches were a takeoff on *Felicity* ("Intensity"), about a wacko college freshman stalking her dreamboat; a claymation version of *Cops* ("Clops"); a porn version of *Saving Private Ryan* ("Saving Ryan's Privates"); "The Eracists"; and an edition of *The Love Connection* on which Rosie O'-Donnell tried to get a lesbian date. Recurring characters included Sullivan's country singer Darlene McBride ("He May Be Trailer Trash to You, But He's a Trailer Treasure to Me") and heavily made-up, perpetually unemployed Vancome Lady; LaMarr's Desperation Lee, host of the '70s talk show *Funky Walker, Dirty Talker,* and intense deliveryman Jaq; chubby Sasso's President Clinton and Kenny Rogers (killed by Michael Jackson in a *Scream 2* parody); Borstein's Monica Lewinski and dim-witted manicurist Miss Swan; Kilbane's the Coffee Guy; Wilson's Miss Cleo; McDonald's Dr. Phil; Weir's Anna Nicole Smith; Collins' Martha Stewart; and Anton's the Hate Guy.

Mad TV also included short animated segments that were adapted directly from *Mad* magazine—"Spy vs. Spy" and "Mad's Maddest Artist Don Martin" (the latter dropped after the third season).

On the series premiere Kato Kaelin (the notorious houseguest from the O.J. Simpson trial) appeared to admit he had cheated in school as a child and to make other observations that were equally pointless and irrelevant. Other guest hosts included Rodney Dangerfield, Queen Latifah, Neve Campbell, Jack Wagner, French Stewart, Pauly Shore, Sandra Bernhard, Pam Grier, Robert Englund, Jennifer Love Hewitt, Halle Berry, Lou Diamond Phillips, and LL Cool J.

MME LIU TSONG, see *Gallery of Madame Liu Tsong, The*

MADAME'S PLACE (*Situation Comedy*)

BROADCAST HISTORY:

Syndicated only
30 minutes
Produced: *1982* (150 episodes)
Released: *September 1982*

PUPPETEER:

Wayland Flowers

CAST:

Sara Joy .... Judy Landers
Bernadette .... Susan Tolsky
Pinkerton........................... Johnny Haymer
Buzzy .... Corey Feldman

Puppeteer Wayland Flowers had created the character of Madame, a craggy, cackling, slightly off-color old hussy, and toured with her for many years on the cabaret and TV guest circuit. She was supposed to be an old show-business trouper who had started in vaudeville and then made more than 30 movies, and who still acted very much the glamorous star—despite her appearance. In 1982 the aging queen showed up surrounded by human supporting actors, in this five-night-a-week syndicated comedy, playing the host of a talk show originating from her palatial mansion in Hollywood. There was constant bickering with her neighbors, her network, and her staff, as well as an abundance of lecherous jokes and put-downs of anyone who wandered by.

Despite a large number of bizarre characters passing through (many of them parodies on show-business types), some guest celebrities such as William Shatner and Debbie Reynolds, and very clever puppet work by Flowers (who manipulated his creation with rods rather than strings), *Madame's Place* folded after a short run.

MADE IN AMERICA (*Quiz/Audience Participation*)

FIRST TELECAST: *April 5, 1964*
LAST TELECAST: *May 3, 1964*
BROADCAST HISTORY:

Apr 1964–May 1964, CBS Sun 9:30–10:00

EMCEE:

Hans Conried

PANELISTS:

Jan Sterling
Walter Slezak
Don Murray

The goal of the panel on this show was to guess in what manner each of the contestants had made their fortunes. All of the contestants were millionaires and they donated their winnings to charity. The amount they won, up to $600, was dependent on how long it took the panel to identify the source of their incomes. Three contestants appeared on each show.

MADELINE (*Cartoon*)
BROADCAST HISTORY:
The Family Channel
30 minutes
Produced: *1993* (33 episodes)
Premiered: *September 12, 1993*
VOICES:
Madeline .... Tracey-Lee Smyth
Pepito .... A. J. Bond
Miss Clavel, Genevieve .... Louise Vallance
Lord Cucuface .... French Tickner
Nicole .... Kristin Fairlie
Chloe .... Vanessa King
Narrator .... Christopher Plummer

"In an old house in Paris that was covered with vines, lived twelve little girls in two straight lines," begins the charming children's story that served as the basis of this gentle cartoon. Madeline was an adventurous little red-haired French girl with a round face; she lived with eleven others in a boardinghouse run by a nun, Miss Clavel. Pepito was Madeline's best friend and Genevieve their happy dog. Lord Cucuface was the starched trustee of the home.

The show was presented much like a children's book, drawn simply with rhyming narration read elegantly by Christopher Plummer. Each episode ended with a little lesson as the children were tucked into bed and the words "That's all there is, there isn't any more . . ." Based on the characters of Ludwig Bemelman's and first seen as a series of six specials in 1990–1991.

MADIGAN (*Police Drama*)
FIRST TELECAST: *September 20, 1972*
LAST TELECAST: *August 22, 1973*
BROADCAST HISTORY:
Sep 1972–Aug 1973, NBC Wed 8:30–10:00
CAST:
Sgt. Dan Madigan .... Richard Widmark

Dan Madigan was a New York City police detective, and a loner. Superficially abrasive and cool, he had a soft streak that he worked hard to conceal. Although some aspects of his job were unappealing, police work was the only life he knew. His social life was virtually nonexistent and his home was a spartan one-room apartment. At least he got to travel a bit, as cases sometimes took him as far away as London.

Madigan was one of three elements in the 1972–1973 version of *NBC Wednesday Mystery Movie*, along with *Banacek* and *Cool Million*.

MADIGAN MEN (*Situation Comedy*)
FIRST TELECAST: *October 6, 2000*
LAST TELECAST: *December 22, 2000*
BROADCAST HISTORY:
Oct 2000–Dec 2000, ABC Fri 9:30–10:00
CAST:
Benjamin Madigan .... Gabriel Byrne
Luke Madigan (age 17) .... John C. Hensley
Seamus Madigan .... Roy Dotrice
Alex Rosetti .... Grant Shaud
Wendy Lipton (pilot only) .... Clea Lewis
Wendy Lipton .... Sabrina Lloyd

A father and son were both looking for a little "luck of the Irish" with women in this multigenerational sitcom. Ben was a successful Manhattan architect whose wife of 18 years had left him for their nutritionist. Back in the dating scene, he was at a loss as to how to proceed. Despite his good looks and "Irish Spring" accent, his low-key, contemplative style (he even looked over his glasses) didn't exactly attract females. His skirt-chasing teenage son, Luke, offered some advice, but it was his colorful dad Seamus, recently arrived from Ireland to live with them, who was a bottomless fount of sage proverbs, usually delivered in a thick brogue. Together the three "Madigan men" helped each other, tossed wisecracks back and forth, and did some serious male bonding. Alex was Ben's partner at the firm of Madigan and Rosetti, and Wendy their perky secretary. Bailey was Ben's lazy dog.

MADISON SQUARE GARDEN, see *Saturday Night at the Garden*

MADISON SQUARE GARDEN HIGHLIGHTS (*Sports Commentary*)
FIRST TELECAST: *June 25, 1953*
LAST TELECAST: *April 15, 1954*
BROADCAST HISTORY:
Jun 1953–Sep 1953, ABC Thu 9:00–9:30
Sep 1953–Oct 1953, ABC Sat 8:30–9:00
Oct 1953–Dec 1953, ABC Sat 10:00–10:30
Jan 1954, ABC Sat 8:30–9:00
Feb 1954–Apr 1954, DUM Thu 8:00–8:30
HOSTS:
Marty Glickman
Stan Lomax

Sportscasters Marty Glickman and Stan Lomax narrated this weekly collection of filmed highlights of sports events that had taken place the previous week at Madison Square Garden in New York. There was some analysis and commentary mixed in with their narration of the events.

MADMAN OF THE PEOPLE (*Situation Comedy*)
FIRST TELECAST: *September 22, 1994*
LAST TELECAST: *June 24, 1995*
BROADCAST HISTORY:
Sep 1994–Jan 1995, NBC Thu 9:30–10:00
Jun 1995, NBC Sat 9:30–10:00
CAST:
Jack Buckner .... Dabney Coleman
Delia Buckner .... Concetta Tomei
Meg Buckner .... Cynthia Gibb
Dylan Buckner .... John Ales
B. J. Cooper .... Craig Bierko
Sasha Danziger .... Amy Aquino

Dabney Coleman brought his patented comic curmudgeon act back to television with little more success than he had in prior attempts (*Buffalo Bill, The Slap Maxwell Story,* for instance). Here he was an irreverent New York columnist who hated authority and used his "Madman of the People" column in *Your Times* magazine as his principal soapbox. The magazine was struggling, and who should take over as its new editor, determined to revive it, but his own daughter, Meg. That of course made her his boss (authority!), and the sparks flew. Also around the office were B.J., an ambitious investigative reporter with eyes for Meg, and Sasha, whose constant optimism irritated Jack. At home, irresponsible, 24-year-old son Dylan provided further irritation ("he has a sofa attached to his butt!" fumed dad), while wife Delia mediated as necessary.

MAGGIE (*Situation Comedy*)

FIRST TELECAST: *October 24, 1981*
LAST TELECAST: *May 21, 1982*
BROADCAST HISTORY:

Oct 1981–Nov 1981, ABC Sat 8:00–8:30
Apr 1982–May 1982, ABC Fri 8:30–9:00

CAST:

Maggie Weston .... Miriam Flynn
Len Weston .... James Hampton
Mark Weston .... Billy Jacoby
Bruce Weston .... Christian Jacobs
Loretta .... Doris Roberts
Chris .... Margie Impert
Buffy Croft .... Judith-Marie Bergan

CREATOR/EXECUTIVE PRODUCER:

Erma Bombeck

Maggie was the television version of the harried suburban housewife made famous in the books of Erma Bombeck. Husband Len was vice principal of schools in Dayton, Ohio, and a perfectly pleasant guy. The children were 8-year-old Bruce, 12-year-old Mark, and 16-year-old L.J., who was never seen because he was always in the bathroom. Their little adventures revolved around clogged drains, notes from the teacher, and Mark's braces, things Maggie liked to chat about during her weekly visits to Loretta's House of Coiffures. It was all very witty and true-to-life in Miss Bombeck's writings, but somehow fell flat on the screen, leading to an early cancellation for this series.

MAGGIE (*Situation Comedy*)

BROADCAST HISTORY:

Lifetime
30 minutes
Produced: *1998–1999*
Premiered: *August 18, 1998*

CAST:

Maggie Day .... Ann Cusack
Dr. Arthur Day .... John Getz
Amanda Day (age 17) .... Morgan Nagler
Dr. Richard Myers .... John Slattery
Amy Sherwood .... Melissa Samuels
**Reg* .... Todd Giebenhain
**Kimberly* .... Francesca Roberts

*Occasional

Maggie, age 39, was in the midst of a mid-life crisis. She had been married for eighteen years, and lived in a beautiful home in suburban Portland, Oregon. But husband Art, a successful cardiologist, was totally absorbed in his career and oblivious to her needs; rebellious daughter Amanda dressed like a slut and ignored her; and Maggie's dreams of a career of her own seemed to be fading fast as the big 4-0 approached. So she began studying to become a veterinarian, signing on as an intern at Dr. Myers's clinic. But her "crisis" only escalated as she developed an instant crush on the goofy, practical-joking vet. Richard, who was divorced, was just the man she had been looking for, and, unbeknownst to her, he had a secret crush on her as well.

What to do? See a shrink, of course. Dr. Kimberly tried to help Maggie work through her feelings, but the attraction between Maggie and Richard just grew, leading to one agonizing crisis after another for the guilt-ridden mom. Amy was Richard's dippy receptionist and Maggie's confidante at the veterinary office, and Reg was Amanda's nutty boyfriend, who pretended to be gay because he wanted to be an artist and "all the best artists are gay!" By the end of the season Maggie had received her veterinarian's degree, and she and Richard had acknowledged their mutual attraction, but a true relationship still seemed distant.

MAGGIE WINTERS (*Situation Comedy*)

FIRST TELECAST: *September 30, 1998*
LAST TELECAST: *February 3, 1999*
BROADCAST HISTORY:

Sep 1998–Feb 1999, CBS Wed 8:30–9:00

CAST:

Maggie Winters .... Faith Ford
Estelle Winters .... Shirley Knight
Robin Foster .... Jenny Robertson
Lisa Harte .... Alex Kapp Horner
Tom Vanderhulst .... Brian Haley
Rachel Tomlinson .... Clea Lewis
Jeff Foster (1998) .... Robert Romanus

An eternally optimistic wife, after being dumped by her dentist husband for his hygienist, returned to her hometown for a little emotional support in this single-girl comedy. Having divorced the louse, Maggie left Chicago and moved in with her dumpy, doting mom Estelle in Shelbyville, Indiana, determined to get back on her feet, both emotionally and financially. It was like opening a dusty school yearbook. She immediately connected with chattery high school pals Robin (now happily married with three kids) and Lisa, the bossy owner of a small boutique. Tom, the macho football star of their high school years, was now the bartender at Sonny's, where they hung out and were treated to stories of his glory days. Needing a job, Maggie went to work at Hanley's, a local department store, where her boss turned out to be none other than Rachel, another high school classmate who had resented Maggie's popularity then, and was ready to take it out on her now.

What was that about "you can't go home again"?

MAGGI'S PRIVATE WIRE (*Interview*)

FIRST TELECAST: *April 12, 1949*
LAST TELECAST: *July 2, 1949*
BROADCAST HISTORY:

Apr 1949, NBC Tue 7:30–7:45
May 1949–Jul 1949, NBC Sat 7:30–7:45

HOSTESS:

Maggi McNellis

Radio and TV personality Maggi McNellis hosted this weekly talk show, interviewing celebrities from show business and other fields.

MAGIC COTTAGE (*Children's*)

FIRST TELECAST: *July 18, 1949*
LAST TELECAST: *February 9, 1951*
BROADCAST HISTORY:

Jul 1949–Feb 1951, DUM Mon–Fri 6:30–7:00

HOSTESS:

Pat Meikle

Pat Meikle, who earlier had a daytime program billed as *The TV Babysitter*, hosted this storytelling session in 1949–1951. Her cottage had a drawing board, and from the board stepped children's characters from "Jack and the Beanstalk" and "Goldilocks," among other sources, to relate their famous tales, much to the delight of the youthful studio audience. Original stories such as "Oogie the Ogre's Christmas" and the continuing adventures of Wilmer the Pigeon were also presented, and there were games and contests for the kids. *Magic Cottage* was also seen as a daytime program and as a local series in New York.

MAGIC HOUR, THE (*Talk*)

BROADCAST HISTORY:

Syndicated only
60 minutes
Produced: *1998*
Released: *June 8, 1998*

REGULARS:

Earvin "Magic" Johnson
Sheila E.
Craig Shoemaker
Peter Michael
Tommy Davidson

Former NBA basketball superstar Magic Johnson fronted this ill-conceived late-night talk show. Johnson, whose charismatic personality and geniality had helped to make him a successful businessman, commercial spokesperson, and celebrity, was embarrassingly uncomfortable in the role of talk show host. When chatting with guests, more often than not, he seemed more like the interviewee than the interviewer. Writer/comedian Craig Shoemaker, the show's announcer and Magic's sidekick, was so disappointed with what he had gotten himself into that he left the show three weeks after its premiere, with Peter Michael taking over his role. In mid-July, Tommy Davidson, who had previously appeared occasionally doing remote comedy skits, became a regular, but it didn't help. Ironically, the highest ratings the show ever received came when shock jock Howard Stern, who had crucified *The Magic Hour* almost daily on his own radio show, accepted an invitation to make fun of Magic in person. Buxom percussionist Sheila E., who fronted the house band, stuck it out till the end, which, mercifully, came two months after *The Magic Hour*'s premiere. Canceled on August 7, the show continued in reruns for another month before leaving the air for good.

MAGIC SLATE, THE (*Children's*)

FIRST TELECAST: *June 2, 1950*
LAST TELECAST: *August 25, 1950*
BROADCAST HISTORY:

Jun 1950–Aug 1950, NBC Fri 8:00–8:30

PRODUCER:

Norman Gant

These dramatizations of classic and original children's stories were produced under the supervision of Charlotte Chorpenning of the Goodman Children's Theater in Chicago. *The Magic Slate* alternated with *Quiz Kids* on Friday nights in 1950, and then returned in January 1951 as a Sunday afternoon series, which it remained until July. Telecast from Chicago.

MAGICAL WORLD OF DISNEY, THE, see *Walt Disney*

MAGICIAN, THE (*Adventure*)

FIRST TELECAST: *October 2, 1973*
LAST TELECAST: *May 20, 1974*
BROADCAST HISTORY:

Oct 1973–Jan 1974, NBC Tue 9:00–10:00
Jan 1974–May 1974, NBC Mon 8:00–9:00

CAST:

Anthony Blake .... Bill Bixby
Max Pomeroy .... Keene Curtis
Dennis Pomeroy .... Todd Crespi
Jerry Wallace .... Jim Watkins
Dominick .... Joseph Sirola

Earlier in his life, stage magician Tony Blake had spent time in prison for a crime he had not committed. Prison had been a particularly distasteful experience for a man of his background, and had left him with a strong sense of concern for personal freedom and individual rights. Once he got out, he put his talents as an illusionist and escape artist to use helping people in danger and preventing crimes. Syndicated columnist and novelist Max Pomeroy was a close friend of Tony's and was often responsible for bringing him cases. Max's paraplegic son, Dennis, although confined to a wheelchair, also became involved in the cases, as did Jerry Wallace, the pilot of Tony's private airliner, *The Spirit.*

When this series moved to Monday nights in January 1974, Tony had taken up residence at Hollywood's famous Magic Castle, where many of the most renowned magicians in the world performed, and some of them were seen on this show. The magic acts performed by Blake were also genuine: Bill Bixby was himself an amateur magician.

MAGNAVOX THEATER (*Dramatic Anthology*)

FIRST TELECAST: *September 15, 1950*
LAST TELECAST: *December 8, 1950*
BROADCAST HISTORY:

Sep 1950–Dec 1950, CBS Fri 9:00–10:00

The first few dramas presented on this series were produced live in New York and aired on alternate Fridays with *Ford Theatre.* Content ranged from serious dramas starring Dane Clark and Geraldine Brooks, to light comedy with Edward Everett Horton. The most notable telecast in *Magnavox Theater*'s short run aired on November 24, 1950. There was nothing spectacular about Magnavox's adaptation of *The Three Musketeers*—which starred "fast-rising" young movie actor Robert Clarke (he had been trying to crash the big time since 1944) and such obscure supporting players as Mel Archer and Marjorie Lord. But this was, according to CBS, the first hour-long film made in Hollywood especially for television. It took just four and a half days to film, and was produced at the Hal Roach Studios, as were the two films which were aired as the last two telecasts of *Magnavox Theater.*

MAGNIFICENT SEVEN: THE SERIES, THE (*Western*)

FIRST TELECAST: *January 3, 1998*
LAST TELECAST: *July 30, 1999*
BROADCAST HISTORY:

Jan 1998, CBS Sat 8:00–9:00
Feb 1998–Mar 1998, CBS Sat 9:00–10:00
Jul 1998–Sep 1998, CBS Sat 9:00–10:00
Jan 1999–Mar 1999, CBS Fri 9:00–10:00
Jul 1999, CBS Fri 9:00–10:00

CAST:

Chris Larrabee .... Michael Biehn
Vin Tanner .... Eric Close
John "J.D." Dunne .... Andrew Kavovit
Buck Wilmington .... Dale Midkiff
Josiah Sanchez .... Ron Perlman

Ezra Standish .... Anthony Starke
Nathan Jackson .... Rick Worthy
Mary Travis .... Laurie Holden
**Judge Orin Travis* .... Robert Vaughn
Casey .... Dana Barron

*Occasional

THEME:

"The Magnificent Seven," by Elmer Bernstein

The Magnificent Seven began just after the end of the Civil War when a group of gunfighters helped a Seminole Indian tribe fight off a vengeful ex-Confederate colonel. When the confrontation was over, the group stayed together in Four Corners, the small nearby town, where they helped the townspeople fight criminals and other troublemakers. Chris, the leader, was the strong silent type—with the look and demeanor of Clint Eastwood's "Man with No Name" character from a series of 1970s Italian Westerns. Vin, his friend, was a bounty hunter and expert marksman. The five they had rounded up to fight the colonel were Buck, an easygoing ladies' man; Josiah, a former priest; Ezra, a smooth-talking gambler and con man; J.D., a bumbling young man in search of adventure who had recently arrived from back East; and Nathan, a former slave they had saved from a lynching in the series premiere. He had been a stretcher bearer in the Union Army, and served as a makeshift doctor in Four Corners. Mary, the widowed editor of the town's newspaper, *The Daily Clarion*, was a little sweet on Chris. Her late husband's father, Orin, was a federal judge who showed up periodically to dispense justice.

When the series returned in 1999 a federal marshal arrived to provide law enforcement in Four Corners, and Judge Travis disbanded the Seven, but they stayed in Four Corners and assorted situations kept getting them back together to help people out. J.D. started courting Casey, one of the town's attractive young women.

Adapted from the 1960 feature film starring Yul Brynner, Steve McQueen, Charles Bronson, James Coburn, and Robert Vaughn (in a different role than his recurring character in the TV series).

MAGNUM, P.I. (*Detective Drama*)

FIRST TELECAST: *December 11, 1980*
LAST TELECAST: *September 12, 1988*
BROADCAST HISTORY:

Dec 1980–Aug 1981, CBS Thu 9:00–10:00
Sep 1981–Apr 1986, CBS Thu 8:00–9:00
Apr 1986–Jun 1986, CBS Sat 10:00–11:00
Jun 1986–Aug 1986, CBS Tue 9:00–10:00
Sep 1986–May 1987, CBS Wed 9:00–10:00
Jul 1987–Feb 1988, CBS Wed 9:00–10:00
Jun 1988–Sep 1988, CBS Mon 10:00–11:00

CAST:

Thomas Sullivan Magnum .... Tom Selleck
Jonathan Quayle Higgins III .... John Hillerman
T.C. (Theodore Calvin) .... Roger E. Mosley
Rick (Orville Wright) .... Larry Manetti
**Robin Masters (voice only)(1981–1985)*
.... Orson Welles
**Mac Reynolds (1981–1982, 1984–1985, 1987–1988)*
.... Jeff MacKay
**Lt. Tanaka (1982–1988)* .... Kwan Hi Lim
**Lt. Maggie Poole (1982–1984, 1986–1988)*
.... Jean Bruce Scott
Agatha Chumley (1982–1988) .... Gillian Dobb
**Asst. D.A. Carol Baldwin (1983–1988)*
.... Kathleen Lloyd
**Francis Hofstetler "Ice Pick" (1983–1988)*
.... Elisha Cook, Jr.

*Occasional

For 12 years CBS viewers had been treated to the beautiful Hawaiian scenery on *Hawaii Five-O*. When Steve McGarrett and his special police finally wore out their welcome, *Magnum, P.I.* replaced them on the CBS schedule. It was in the same time period, had the same beautiful backdrop and hard-knuckles action, and it allowed CBS to continue to use the expensive production facilities it had constructed in the mid-1970s for *Hawaii Five-O*. Characters on *Magnum* even referred to McGarrett and his Five-O unit on occasion, as if the older series were still around.

Magnum was a private investigator with an enviable arrangement. In return for helping with the security arrangements for guarding the estate of wealthy writer Robin Masters (never seen on the show), he was provided with free living quarters at the rambling beachfront property on Oahu's north shore. Masters was always away, leaving his stuffy British manservant, Higgins, to run the estate. The laid-back lifestyle of Magnum was in direct opposition to the strict military discipline that ruled Higgins's life, and there was constant bickering between the two—though there was clearly, underneath, a deep-seated mutual affection.

When Magnum was not romancing the ladies or tooling around the island in Masters's $50,000 Ferrari, he functioned as a traditional detective. A former Vietnam naval intelligence veteran, Tom utilized the services of two of his wartime buddies when he needed help. T.C. was the owner/pilot of Island Hoppers, a helicopter charter service, and Rick (who hated his real name, Orville) ran a Honolulu nightclub patterned after the club run by Humphrey Bogart in *Casablanca*. Early on he sold the club and became the managing partner, with Robin Masters, of the exclusive King Kamehameha Beach Club. Both of them did legwork for Magnum, with Rick's underworld connections, including his relationship with the quasi-legal businessman Ice Pick, coming in handy. Asst. D.A. Carol Baldwin, a friend of Magnum's, who talked him into taking cases that never seemed to generate any fees, showed up once in a while, as did Higgins's English friend, Agatha.

The most unusual semiregular was Magnum's navy buddy Mac Reynolds. Early in the show's run Mac was a lieutenant, stationed at a local navy installation, who provided Magnum with information, until he was killed in a 1982 episode. Two years later a con man who was the spitting image of Mac turned up (initially impersonating the dead officer) to get Magnum into occasional trouble. Colonel Buck Greene (Lance LeGault), an old navy nemesis of Magnum's, turned up about once a season to cause him some kind of trouble. Zeus and Apollo were the two Doberman pinschers who helped Higgins provide security for the Masters estate, often by taking bites out of Magnum's hide.

The producers of *Magnum, P.I.* had anticipated its cancellation in the spring of 1987 and filmed a dramatic and somewhat surrealistic two-part finale, using almost all the occasional players, in which Magnum was shot, died from the wound, and went to heaven. When the series was unexpectedly renewed for a last season, it was explained that he had not died but had instead dreamed of going to heaven in his delirium. The series' real finale aired as a movie in May 1988 and was one of that season's highest-rated individual programs, but it still left some loose ends. Magnum was reunited with his long-lost young daughter, quit the private eye business, and rejoined the navy, while buddy Rick was married (or was he?), and Higgins was finally revealed to be Robin Masters (or was he?). Fans will have to wait until the *Magnum* reunion to find out.

MAIL STORY, THE (*Dramatic Anthology*)
FIRST TELECAST: *October 7, 1954*
LAST TELECAST: *December 30, 1954*
BROADCAST HISTORY:
Oct 1954–Dec 1954, ABC Thu 8:00–8:30
There were two completely different types of stories presented on *The Mail Story*: those that dealt with the good and varied services provided by the U.S. Postal Service, which were often in quasi-documentary form; and those that were dramas of people attempting to misuse the postal system and the efforts made by postal authorities to apprehend them. The latter were all based on actual case histories from the Postal Service's files and ranged from stagecoach robbing in the middle 1850s to contemporary mail fraud. This series was subtitled *Handle With Care*.

MAJOR ADAMS, TRAILMASTER, syndicated title for *Wagon Train*

MAJOR DAD (*Situation Comedy*)
FIRST TELECAST: *September 17, 1989*
LAST TELECAST: *September 13, 1993*
BROADCAST HISTORY:
Sep 1989, CBS Sun 8:30–9:00
Sep 1989–Sep 1990, CBS Mon 8:00–8:30
Sep 1990–Jun 1991, CBS Mon 8:30–9:00
Jun 1991–Jul 1991, CBS Mon 8:00–8:30
Jul 1991–Sep 1992, CBS Mon 8:30–9:00
Aug 1992–Apr 1993, CBS Fri 8:30–9:00
May 1993–Sep 1993, CBS Mon 8:30–9:00
CAST:
Major John D. "Mac" MacGillis.... Gerald McRaney
Polly Cooper MacGillis............... Shanna Reed
Elizabeth Cooper (age 15)............ Marisa Ryan
Robin Cooper (11).................. Nicole Dubuc
Casey Cooper (6)................. Chelsea Hertford
2nd Lt. Gene Holowachuk........... Matt Mulhern
Sgt. Byron James (1989–1990)...... Marlon Archey
Merilee Gunderson (1989–1990)
.... Whitney Kershaw
Chip Russell (16)(1989–1990).......... Rod Brogan
Gunnery Sgt. Alva Lucille Bricker (1990–1993)
.... Beverly Archer
Maj. Gen. Marcus Craig (1990–1993) ... Jon Cypher
John MacGillis was a dedicated career Marine officer stationed at Camp Singleton in San Diego, California, whose well-ordered life was turned upside down when he fell in love with Polly Cooper, a liberal reporter who had interviewed him for a local paper. Within weeks of their meeting John and Polly, a widow with three young daughters, were married and he had moved into her home. A man of discipline, John had a hard time adjusting to being father to three girls—Elizabeth, into rock music and boys; Robin, intellectual and sensitive; and Casey, just too cute for words. The contrast between his conservative views and Polly's liberal convictions were a constant source of conflict but, fortunately, they all learned to adjust and compromise. At the base, his staff included eager-to-please Lt. Holowachuk, bright Sgt. James, and his perpetually perky secretary Merilee Gunderson, daughter of the base commander. Chip was Elizabeth's boyfriend.

At the start of the second season, John and his family relocated to Camp Hollister, in Farlow, Virginia, near Washington, D.C., where he was now staff secretary to the base's gruff, eccentric commanding officer, Gen. Marcus Craig. Lt. Holowachuk had also been transferred to Camp Hollister, becoming his aide-de-camp, and "Gunny" Bricker was his new secretary. Polly's new job was feature editor of *The Bulldog*, Camp Hollister's newspaper. Some episodes dealt with the real-life military buildup and war that took place in Kuwait and Iraq during the winter of 1990–1991. At the end of the season, John started formal adoption proceedings for the girls.

That fall, again reflecting real-world situations, Camp Hollister was faced with possible closure as part of the government's efforts to reduce military expenditures. Gen. Craig was determined to save as much money as possible to keep Congress from shutting it down, so he promoted Polly to editor of *The Bulldog*, at a 10% salary cut.

MAJOR DELL CONWAY OF THE FLYING TIGERS (*Adventure*)
FIRST TELECAST: *April 7, 1951*
LAST TELECAST: *May 26, 1951*
BROADCAST HISTORY:
Apr 1951–May 1951, DUM Sat 6:30–7:00
CAST:
Major Dell Conway.................. Eric Fleming
Major Dell Conway....................... Ed Peck
ALSO:
Luis Van Rooten
Fran Lee (as *Ma Wong*)
David Anderson
Joe Graham
Harry Kingston
Bern Hoffman
This live action-adventure series traced the exploits of Major Dell Conway, a heroic pilot who had served with the famous "Flying Tigers" squadron in China during World War II. After the war Conway and some of his buddies, including sidekick Caribou Jones, founded Flying Tiger Airlines on the West Coast. In the series they fought Cold War spies and saboteurs, as well as international criminals.

Flying Tigers was an extremely low-budget production, and it underwent considerable cast and scheduling turmoil during its short run. The original lead, Hollywood B-movie actor Eric Fleming, was replaced almost immediately by Ed Peck, and the supporting cast evidently changed as well (all those who are known to have been regulars are listed above, although their roles have been lost over the years). The program went off for two months after May 26, then returned in late July on Sunday afternoon, where it continued until March 1952. There was a real Flying Tigers, both wartime squadron and postwar airline, which served—

loosely—as the basis for this series. The producer was "Gen" Genovese, who himself had been a pilot in China during the war.

MAJORITY RULES (*Quiz/Panel*)
FIRST TELECAST: *September 2, 1949*
LAST TELECAST: *July 30, 1950*
BROADCAST HISTORY:
Sep 1949–Jan 1950, ABC Fri 8:00–8:30
Feb 1950–Mar 1950, ABC Fri 9:30–10:00
Mar 1950–Jul 1950, ABC Sun 8:30–9:00
EMCEE:
Ed Prentiss
Tom Moore
Myron Wallace

A panel of three contestants was posed questions in this Chicago-originated quiz show, with the "right" answer being determined by the majority of two. Several hosts came and went during the run of the series, and a telephone gimmick involving celebrities was also introduced. One of the hosts would himself become a television celebrity in later years. But by then Myron Wallace would have changed his first name to Mike.

MAKE ME LAUGH (*Audience Participation*)
FIRST TELECAST: *March 20, 1958*
LAST TELECAST: *June 12, 1958*
BROADCAST HISTORY:
Mar 1958–Jun 1958, ABC Thu 10:00–10:30
EMCEE:
Robert Q. Lewis

The object of this game show was for contestants to refrain from laughing. Each week three different comedians participated in trying to make contestants laugh. One minute was allotted to each comedian. The contestants could win up to $180, one dollar for every second they refrained from laughter.

More than 20 years later, in 1979, a syndicated version of *Make Me Laugh* appeared, hosted by Bobby Van. Another version, hosted by Ken Ober and featuring hip young comics of the '90s, premiered on the Comedy Central cable network in June 1997.

MAKE MINE MUSIC, see *Face the Music*

MAKE ROOM FOR DADDY, see *Danny Thomas Show, The*

MAKE ROOM FOR GRANDDADDY, see *Danny Thomas Show, The*

MAKE THAT SPARE (*Sports*)
FIRST TELECAST: *October 8, 1960*
LAST TELECAST: *September 11, 1964*
BROADCAST HISTORY:
Oct 1960–Sep 1963, ABC Sat 10:45–11:00 (OS)
Sep 1963–Sep 1964, ABC Fri 10:45–11:00
COMMENTATOR:
Johnny Johnston (1960–1961, 1962–1964)
Win Elliot (1961–1962)

In this post-fight feature, a top professional bowler, or amateur, had the chance to win up to $5,000 with one roll of the ball by making a hard spare (two or more pins separated in such a way as to require great precision if all were to be knocked down with a single ball). The winner returned the following week—there were usually two bowlers competing each night—to defend his title of "King of the Hill," and individual champions collected as much as $38,000 competing on this show. *Make That Spare* was telecast live from Paramus, New Jersey.

MAKE THE CONNECTION (*Quiz*)
FIRST TELECAST: *July 7, 1955*
LAST TELECAST: *September 29, 1955*
BROADCAST HISTORY:
July 1955–Sep 1955, NBC Thu 8:30–9:00
MODERATOR:
Jim McKay
Gene Rayburn
PANELISTS:
Betty White
Gloria DeHaven
Gene Klavan
Eddie Bracken

The object of this live summer game show was for the panelists to guess the circumstances (when, where, how, and why) that caused the paths of the guests on the program to cross. They tried to *Make the Connection* between the guests. It was a variation on the successful formats of *What's My Line* and *I've Got a Secret*. Jim McKay was the moderator of the show until early in September, when he was replaced by Gene Rayburn.

MAKE THE GRADE (*Quiz/Audience Participation*)
BROADCAST HISTORY:
Nickelodeon
30 minutes
Produced: *1989–1990* (160 episodes)
Premiered: *October 2, 1989*
HOST:
Lew Schneider (1989–1990)
Mike O'Malley (1990–1991)

A game show in which kids alternated between answering fun questions (so they could "graduate") and performing offbeat physical stunts ("fire drills"). The series ran nightly in the early evening on Nickelodeon.

MAKE YOUR OWN KIND OF MUSIC (*Musical Variety*)
FIRST TELECAST: *July 20, 1971*
LAST TELECAST: *September 7, 1971*
BROADCAST HISTORY:
Jul 1971–Sep 1971, NBC Tue 8:00–9:00
REGULARS:
The Carpenters
Al Hirt
Mark Lindsay
The New Doodletown Pipers
Tom Patchett and Jay Tarses
Allyn Ferguson & the Jack Elliott Orchestra

This summer musical variety series featured popular singers Richard and Karen Carpenter, trumpet player Al Hirt, singer Mark Lindsay (formerly lead singer of the rock group Paul Revere and the Raiders), the New Doodletown Pipers (16-person singing group), and the comedy team of Patchett and Tarses.

The title for this show was taken from a popular song of 1969.

MAKIN' IT (*Adventure*)

FIRST TELECAST: *February 1, 1979*

LAST TELECAST: *March 23, 1979*

BROADCAST HISTORY:

Feb 1979, ABC Thu 8:30–9:00

Feb 1979–Mar 1979, ABC Fri 8:00–8:30

CAST:

Billy Manucci .... David Naughton
Tony Manucci .... Greg Antonacci
Tina Manucci .... Denise Miller
Dorothy Manucci .... Ellen Travolta
Joseph Manucci .... Lou Antonio
Al "Kingfish" Sorrentino .... Ralph Seymour
Bernard Fusco .... Gary Prendergast
Corky Crandall .... Rebecca Balding
Suzanne .... Wendy Hoffman
Felice .... Diane Robin
Ivy Papastegios .... Jennifer Perito

THEME:

"Makin' It," by Dino Fekaris and Freddie Perren, sung by David Naughton

This short-lived series was a thinly disguised TV adaptation of the hot movie *Saturday Night Fever*. The "disco freak" here was young college student Billy Manucci, who was torn between the glittering life of a big man on the dance floor and his more practical desire to complete his education and become a teacher. On the side of the night life were his pals, Bernard and Kingfish, and his laid-back brother, Tony, star dancer at the local disco; urging sober responsibility were his working-class parents, Joseph and Dorothy. Corky was Billy's girlfriend, and Tina his little sister.

To make the connection with the movie as close as possible, the producers used the music of the Bee Gees in the dance sequences, snared Ellen Travolta for one of the roles (since they couldn't get John), and even titled the premiere episode "Stayin' Alive." Robert Stigwood, who produced the movie, was involved with this series as well. None of this helped much, although David Naughton did have a real-life hit record with the show's theme song, in mid-1979.

MAKING A LIVING, see *It's a Living*

MAKING THE BAND (*Rock Music Documentary*)

NETWORK HISTORY:

FIRST TELECAST: *March 24, 2000*

LAST TELECAST: *July 13, 2001*

Mar 2000–May 2000, ABC Fri 9:30–10:00

May 2000–Sep 2000, ABC Fri 9:00–10:00

Apr 2001, ABC Fri 8:00–9:00

Jun 2001–Jul 2001, ABC Fri 8:00–9:00

CABLE HISTORY:

MTV

30 minutes

Original episodes: *2002*

Premiered: *January 19, 2002*

REGULARS:

Lou Pearlman (2000–2001)
Ashley Parker Angel
Erik-Michael Estrada
Dan Miller
Trevor Penick
Jacob Underwood
Ikaika Kahoano (2000)

It took more than 30 years, but it finally occurred to someone that if a band like the Monkees could be manufactured off screen and then put on television, why not manufacture the band on screen in the first place? Thus *Making the Band*, a combination talent show and look inside the contemporary music business that showed just how fraught with problems assembling a boy band—even one that only has to *look* good—can be.

The band's Svengali was real-life record mogul Lou Pearlman, the smiling, chubby president of Transcontinental Records, and the man responsible for creating 'NSYNC and The Backstreet Boys. The opening episode showed auditions being held in eight cities across the U.S. Out of 1,700 hunky young hopefuls who tried out, 25 made it to the semi-finals, and eight were invited to Orlando to live and work together for three months. At the end five would be chosen for the band. Once in Orlando the problems began. Lou's choreographers and vocal coaches worked intensively with the boys, but there were constant clashes and crises of confidence. The boys partied, talked individually to the camera and called their lonely girlfriends back home, making this look at times like MTV's *The Real World*.

About halfway through the training period one of the eight, Paul Martin, dropped out. Two more (Bryan Chan and Mike Miller) were eliminated, leaving the five chosen for the band, which was dubbed O-Town (for "Orlando"). They were Trevor Penick, an energetic black guy with a great attitude; Ikaika Kahoano, a tall, handsome Hawaiian filled with self-doubts; Ashley Parker Angel, with cute, youthful good looks; Jacob Underwood, who resembled Justin Timberlake of 'NSYNC; and Erik-Michael Estrada, a baby-faced Puerto Rican with an angelic voice. No sooner did the boys arrive in Los Angeles for an important photo shoot and to cut their first single than Ikaika, under pressure from his family to return to Hawaii, also dropped out. That left O-Town short a member, so the four remaining voted to ask Lou to bring back semi-finalist Dan Miller. The reconstituted group then left for Germany to record an album, signed a contract with Clive Davis' J Records and in December placed their first single, "Liquid Dreams," on the *Billboard* chart, peaking at number ten, followed by their self-titled album, which reached number five.

Season two opened in April 2002 with the band on tour, including a botched performance of "Liquid Dreams" at the Miss America pageant. ABC pulled the show after two telecasts due to low ratings, with the remaining episodes airing during the summer. The band split from Lou Pearlman and placed another single, "All or Nothing," on the charts, and Erik reunited with his estranged biological father. Season three, on MTV, followed the band as it toured, opening for Britney Spears, fighting off fans and making a second CD.

MAKING THE GRADE (*Situation Comedy*)

FIRST TELECAST: *April 5, 1982*

LAST TELECAST: *May 10, 1982*

BROADCAST HISTORY:

Apr 1982–May 1982, CBS Mon 9:30–10:00

CAST:

Harry Barnes .... James Naughton
Jack Felspar .... Graham Jarvis

Sara Conover .... Alley Mills
Jeff Kelton .... Steve Peterman
Anton Zemeckis .... Zane Lasky
Gus Bertoia .... George Wendt
David Wasserman .... Philip Charles MacKenzie
Janice Reeves .... Veronica Redd

Franklin High, a rambling, 4,500-student St. Louis school, was the setting for this short-lived comedy. Harry Barnes was the dedicated Dean of Boys, whose biggest problem was dull, pompous, assistant principal Jack Felspar. Felspar's unwillingness to deal with reality was typified by his definition of the "Lord of Death" gang that terrorized students and faculty alike as a "social club." Sara Conover was the beautiful young drama teacher who had to fend off the insistent and unwanted attentions of English teacher David Wasserman, a self-styled ladykiller. Jeff Kelton was an idealistic young English teacher, Anton Zemeckis a Latin teacher who made money on the side as a travel agent, and Gus Bertoia a superjock physical-education instructor.

MALCOLM & EDDIE (*Situation Comedy*)

FIRST TELECAST: *August 26, 1996*
LAST TELECAST: *September 12, 2000*
BROADCAST HISTORY:

Aug 1996–Mar 1998, UPN Mon 8:30–9:00
Jul 1997, UPN Tue 8:30–9:00
Nov 1997–Dec 1997, UPN Tue 9:00–9:30
Mar 1998–Jul 1998, UPN Tue 9:00–9:30
Jul 1998–Sep 1998, UPN Mon 8:30–9:00
Sep 1998–Oct 1998, UPN Mon 9:30–10:00
Oct 1998–Jan 1999, UPN Mon 9:00–9:30
Nov 1998–Jan 1999, UPN Mon 8:00–8:30
Jan 1999–Aug 1999, UPN Tue 9:00–9:30
Aug 1999–Aug 2000, UPN Mon 9:30–10:00
Sep 2000, UPN Tue 9:00–10:00

CAST:

Malcolm McGee .... Malcolm-Jamal Warner
Eddie Sherman .... Eddie Griffin
Kelly (1996–1997) .... Miriam Flynn
Tim Kirkley (1996–1998) .... Jamie Cardriche
Nicolette Vandross .... Karen Malina White
Holly (1996–1997) .... Angelle Brooks
Hector (1997–1998) .... Freez Luv
Simone Lewis (1997–1998) .... Michelle Hurd
Theodore Roosevelt (T. R.) Hawkins (1998–1999)
.... Tucker Smallwood
Doug Rickets (1998–2000) .... Ron Pearson
Leonard Rickets (1998–2000)
.... Christopher Daniel Barnes

Because their mothers were best friends, Malcolm and Eddie, who had nothing else in common, had become roommates. They lived in a shabby apartment above Kelly's Sports Bar in Kansas City and spent most of their spare time down at the bar. Malcolm was serious and wanted a career as a sports commentator, while the free-spirited, forever optimistic Eddie repaired cars and ran a towing service, Lancaster Auto. Against his better judgment, Malcolm was often sucked into Eddie's assorted get-rich-quick schemes. One of the regulars at Kelly's was Tim, a huge, beefy, perpetual student with hopes of becoming a successful poet. A few weeks after the series premiered, Malcolm and Eddie used $40,000 in lottery winnings to buy the building in which they lived from their landlord, Kelly, who was moving to Hawaii, and renamed the sports bar Malcolm McGee's. Nicolette was a cute, squeaky-voiced, meter maid tenant with the hots for Eddie, who wasn't interested; and Malcolm had designs on Holly, a barmaid at the sports bar, but she was more interested in work. In mid-May, while stranded on a camping retreat, Eddie and Nicolette, and Malcolm and Holly, made love while keeping warm in sleeping bags.

That fall Nicolette enrolled in the police academy. Tim was officially made a male nurse at the hospital where he had been working as an orderly, and Eddie hired Hector to work as a mechanic in his garage. Eddie and Nicolette were having an affair (it didn't work out), and Malcolm hired sexy Simone, who had the hots for him, as the chef. With her gourmet tastes, she had problems adjusting to the bar's cuisine. In the season finale Eddie got a job offer in Pittsburgh for three times what he was making in Kansas City and they sold the building.

At the beginning of the 1998–1999 season, Eddie returned from Pittsburgh and the guys decided to open a hot jazz club in Kansas City called The Fifty/Fifty Club. They rented back the space they had previously owned, at an inflated rate, from tough businessman T. R. Hawkins. Nicolette had quit the police force and took a job as a waitress at their jazz club. Also working for them were two cousins—Doug, a bartender, and Leonard, a waiter.

In the fall of 1999 Club Misdemeanor, a dance club down the street from the Fifty/Fifty Club, opened and provided serious competition. The following February T. R. died from a heart attack and willed everything to his daughter, Ashley (Alexia Robinson)—if she married Eddie (T. R. had liked his aggressive style) within 30 days. It almost happened, but she found a second will that left it all to her without any strings attached. In the series finale an out-of-control truck crashed through the front of the club. Unfortunately, their insurance company had gone bankrupt and they had only half the $100,000 they needed to rebuild. They were bailed out when Nicolette offered to invest the $50,000 they needed (she had done well trading stocks on-line) in exchange for a full partnership.

MALCOLM IN THE MIDDLE (*Situation Comedy*)

FIRST TELECAST: *January 9, 2000*
LAST TELECAST:
BROADCAST HISTORY:

Jan 2000–Jun 2002, FOX Sun 8:30–9:00
Jan 2000, FOX Tue 8:30–9:00
Nov 2000, FOX Wed 8:00–8:30
Jul 2002–Sep 2002, FOX Sun 9:00–10:00
Nov 2002, FOX Sun 9:00–10:00
Dec 2002– , FOX Sun 9:00–9:30

CAST:

Lois Wilkerson .... Jane Kaczmarek
Hal Wilkerson .... Bryan Cranston
Malcolm Wilkerson (age 11) .... Frankie Muniz
Francis Wilkerson (16)
.... Christopher Kennedy Masterson
Reese Wilkerson (13) .... Justin Berfield
Dewey Wilkerson (6) .... Erik Per Sullivan
Stevie Kenarban .... Craig Lamar Traylor
**Craig Feldspar* .... David Anthony Higgins
Cmdt. Edwin Spangler (2000–2001)
.... Daniel von Bargen

Cadet Stanley (2000) .... Karim Prince
**Cadet Drew (2000–2001)* .... Drew Powell
**Cadet Finley (2000–2001)* .... Arjay Smith
Cadet Eric Hansen (2000–2002) .... Eric Nenninger
Cadet Joe (2000–2001) .... Kasan Butcher
Caroline Miller (2000) ...... Catherine Lloyd Burns
**Lloyd* .... Evan Matthew Cohen
**Dabney* .... Kyle Sullivan
Pete (2001–2002) .... Sandy Ward
Artie (2002) .... John Ennis
Piama Tananahaakna (2002–) .... Emy Coligado
Otto (2002–) .... Kenneth Mars
**Gretchen (2002–)* .... Meagan Fay

*Occasional

In the premiere of this dysfunctional family sitcom, 11-year-old Malcolm scored 165 on an IQ test and, despite his objections, was put in a program for gifted children at school. His parents were thrilled but Malcolm, who just wanted to be one of the guys, didn't want to be stigmatized as a nerd. Lois, his mom, one of the loudest, strictest and most exasperated moms in TV history, reveled in exacting punishment on her squabbling sons. Outspoken and independent, she worked at a local Lucky Aide supermarket, where fellow worker Craig had the hots for her, even though he knew she was married. Hal, Malcolm's bumbling, ineffectual dad, meant well but never seemed to get anything right. Hal was subservient to his overbearing wife, but they did have a great sex life. He had a job, though what it was was never mentioned. Malcolm had three brothers. Francis, the oldest, had been sent away to Marlin Academy, a military school in Alabama, after destroying the family car. Reese was a lazy scam artist who was always getting into trouble and fought constantly with Malcolm, while wide-eyed younger brother Dewey was the quietest of the bunch. Malcolm's best friend, asthmatic, wheelchair-bound Stevie, was in the gifted program, as were Lloyd and Dabney.

Malcolm provided an overview of what was going on, frequently talking directly to the viewing audience, and most episodes alternated between what was going on at home and what was happening to Francis, wherever he was. In the fall of 2000 he found a lawyer who got him legally emancipated so he could drop out of military school and get a job in Alaska. He thought his friend Eric had a logging job for him but, when he got there, Francis was relegated to being a busboy at a restaurant run by tough Lavernia (Brenda Wehle). While in Alaska Francis married Piama, a no-nonsense Native American, and, after the restaurant went out of business, they took a cross-country trip in search of their fortune.

At the start of the 2002–2003 season Malcolm started high school and was determined to cast off the nerdy curse, but with little success. Francis secured the unlikely job as foreman for a dude ranch owned by Otto, a cheery ingenuous German who knew even less about horses and running a ranch than he did. To keep busy Piama got a job at an art gallery. In February Lois announced she was pregnant, which both thrilled and terrified Hal, and she gave birth in May.

MALIBU RUN, see *Aquanauts, The*

MALIBU SHORES (*Serial Drama*)

FIRST TELECAST: *March 9, 1996*
LAST TELECAST: *June 1, 1996*
BROADCAST HISTORY:
Mar 1996–Jun 1996, NBC Sat 8:00–9:00
CAST:
Chloe Walker .... Keri Russell
Josh Walker .... Greg Vaughan
Zack Morrison .... Tony Lucca
Nina Gerard .... Katie Wright
Julie Tate .... Essence Atkins
Teddy Delacourt .... Christian Campbell
Marc Delacourt .... Ian Ogilvy
Ashley Green .... Charisma Carpenter
Flipper Gage .... Randy Spelling
Suki Walker .... Michelle Phillips
Casey .... Tia Texada
Benny .... Jacob Vargas

A youth-oriented soap opera from producer Aaron Spelling, set at snobbish Pacific Coast High School, in the elite community of Malibu, California. A group of lower-class students from the San Fernando Valley had been transferred to the school when their own school was destroyed by an earthquake, leading to friction between the newcomers (largely ethnic) and the locals. The star-crossed lovers of the piece were rich Chloe and blue-collar Zack, a rebellious yet sensitive type from the Valley who wanted to be an artist. Their attraction for each other was immediate, even though their social positions were vastly different. Josh was Chloe's surly, violent brother, who hated Zack, and Suki her disapproving attorney-mom. Nina was Chloe's slutty friend, Teddy a nerdy young Malibu student who lusted for Chloe, and Casey was Zack's jealous ex-girlfriend back in the Valley. The anguish and backstabbing among these beautiful young people lasted only three months; in the final episode Chloe ran off with Zack in his convertible, heading up the Pacific Coast Highway for parts unknown.

MALIBU U (*Music*)

FIRST TELECAST: *July 21, 1967*
LAST TELECAST: *September 1, 1967*
BROADCAST HISTORY:
Jul 1967–Sep 1967, ABC Fri 8:30–9:00
REGULARS:
Rick Nelson
Robie Porter
The Bob Banas Dancers

Popular singer Rick Nelson was the host of this summer music show which originated from the famous Malibu Beach area in Southern California. As "Dean of the Drop-Ins" at this mythical college, Rick invited guest professors—all popular singers—to lecture (sing their hits) to the student body. There was a lot of body to lecture, mostly bikini-clad young girls ("Malibeauties"), and the curriculum for the summer school included such subjects as surfing, sunbathing, girl-watching, and a field trip to a bikini factory (not much going on there). Australian singer Robie Porter was a featured regular.

MAMA (*Comedy/Drama*)

FIRST TELECAST: *July 1, 1949*
LAST TELECAST: *July 27, 1956*
BROADCAST HISTORY:
Jul 1949–Jul 1956, CBS Fri 8:00–8:30 (OS)
CAST:
"Mama" Marta Hansen .... Peggy Wood
"Papa" Lars Hansen .... Judson Laire

Nels .... Dick Van Patten
Katrin .... Rosemary Rice
Dagmar (1949) .... Iris Mann
Dagmar (1950–1956) .... Robin Morgan
Aunt Jenny .... Ruth Gates
T. R. Ryan (1952–1956) .... Kevin Coughlin
Uncle Chris (1949–1951) .... Malcolm Keen
Uncle Chris (1951–1952) .... Roland Winters
Uncle Gunnar Gunnerson .... Carl Frank
Aunt Trina Gunnerson .... Alice Frost
Ingeborg (1953–1956) .... Patty McCormack

THEME:

"Holberg Suite" (open), "The Last Spring" (close), by Edvard Grieg

Mama was one of the best-loved of the early family comedies, and was in many ways the prototype of the "growing family" series which later proliferated on television (Ozzie & Harriet, Danny Thomas, et al.). There were no cheap gags or bumbling parents in *Mama*, but rather a warmhearted, humorous, true-to-life account of a Norwegian-American family of five making their way in turn-of-the-century San Francisco.

The opening each week was in the style of a reminiscence by Katrin, leafing through the pages of the family album, past the pictures she knew so well—"I remember my brother Nels . . . and my little sister Dagmar . . . and of course, Papa. But most of all, I remember Mama."

Mama herself was played to perfection by the noted stage actress, Peggy Wood. Strict yet loving, she epitomized the gentleness which endeared the series to viewers for so many years. Papa was a carpenter who made just enough money to support his family decently, if not richly. Nels, Katrin, and Dagmar were the children. Any member of the family might be the subject of a week's story—Papa's new invention, Dagmar's braces, Mama's attempts to brighten the household—but all shared in the resolution. Each week's episode ended with the family seated around a pot of the sponsor's Maxwell House coffee, sharing the lessons learned.

One of the classic stories, presented each year, was the Christmas episode in which Papa told Dagmar how the animals were given the gift of speech for a few hours each Christmas Eve, as a reward for their protection of the Christ child in Bethlehem. When the rest of the family was asleep, Dagmar slipped out to the stable, to await the special moment.

Other regulars who passed through the Hansens' proper Victorian household on Steiner Street were Aunt Jenny ("Yenny" to all), T. R. Ryan, and Willie, the family dog.

So popular was *Mama* that when CBS announced that it was finally cancelling the show, in 1956, the outcry was sufficient to bring the program back for a short additional run on Sunday afternoons. These episodes, aired from December 1956 through March 1957, were on film and featured the same cast as the prime-time series, except that Toni Campbell took over the role of Dagmar.

Mama was based on a book, *Mama's Bank Account*, which was written by a real-life Kathryn (Forbes). The book had subsequently become a highly successful play (1944) and movie (1948), both of which were titled *I Remember Mama*. Unlike some other early TV comedies such as *The Life of Riley* and *I Love Lucy*, *Mama* was telecast live rather than filmed. So while Lucy will be with us forever, the weekly dramas of life in the big white house on Steiner Street are, for the most part, gone forever. Like Katrin turning the pages of the album, we can only remember.

MAMA MALONE (*Situation Comedy*)

FIRST TELECAST: *March 7, 1984*
LAST TELECAST: *July 21, 1984*
BROADCAST HISTORY:

Mar 1984–Apr 1984, CBS Wed 8:30–9:00
Jun 1984–Jul 1984, CBS Sat 8:00–8:30

CAST:

Mama Renate Malone .... Lila Kaye
Connie Karamakopoulos .... Randee Heller
Frankie Karamakopoulos .... Evan Richards
Dino Forresti .... Don Amendolia
Austin .... Raymond Singer
Padre Guardiano .... Ralph Manza
Father Jose Silva .... Richard Yniguez
Ken .... Pendleton Brown
Harry .... Mitchell Group
Stanley .... Sam Anderson
Jackie .... Joey Jupiter

Graham Kerr and Julia Child would never have conducted a cooking show the way Mama Malone did. Not only was it aired live from her fourth-floor walk-up apartment in Brooklyn, but most of her family wandered in regularly while she was on the air and the show would degenerate into a discussion of moral values, social problems, and family happenings—a far cry from the recipes for lasagna, veal scallopini, and fish stew. "Cooking with Mama Malone" was carried by a local TV station in New York and the unplanned visits by family and friends drove her director, Austin, up the wall. Mama, the very Italian widow of an Irish policeman, fussed constantly over her daughter Connie (who was divorced from a Greek), her beloved grandson, Frankie, and her younger brother, Dino, a lounge singer who fancied himself as something of a swinger. Padre Guardiano was the elderly parish priest and Father Silva his handsome young assistant. Stanley was the announcer on the cooking show, and Ken, Harry, and Stanley the production crew.

MAMA ROSA (*Situation Comedy*)

FIRST TELECAST: *May 21, 1950*
LAST TELECAST: *June 11, 1950*
BROADCAST HISTORY:

May 1950–Jun 1950, ABC Sun 9:30–10:00

CAST:

Mama Rosa .... Anna Demetrio
Her daughter .... Beverly Garland
Her son .... Richard Anderson
Nikolai .... Vito Scotti

This obscure early comedy, which was produced live in Hollywood, was seen briefly on the ABC network in 1950. It was set in a theatrical boardinghouse run by Mama Rosa and located in Hollywood. An assortment of showbiz types passed through, including Nikolai, a violin instructor.

MAMA'S FAMILY (*Situation Comedy*)

FIRST TELECAST: *January 22, 1983*
LAST TELECAST: *August 17, 1985*

BROADCAST HISTORY:

Jan 1983–Jun 1983, NBC Sat 9:00–9:30
Aug 1983–Dec 1983, NBC Thu 8:30–9:00
Jan 1984–May 1984, NBC Sat 9:30–10:00
Jun 1984–Jul 1984, NBC Sat 9:00–9:30
Jul 1984–Sep 1984, NBC Sat 9:30–10:00
Jun 1985–Aug 1985, NBC Sat 9:30–10:00
(In first-run syndication from September 1986–September 1990)

CAST:

Mama (Thelma) Harper............ Vicki Lawrence
Aunt Fran Crowley (1983–1985).. Rue McClanahan
Vinton Harper......................... Ken Berry
Naomi Oates Harper............. Dorothy Lyman
Vinton "Buzz" Harper, Jr. (1983–1985) ... Eric Brown
Sonja Harper (1983–1985)........... Karin Argoud
**Ellen Jackson (1983–1985)*............ Betty White
**Eunice Higgins (1983–1985)* .... Carol Burnett
**Ed Higgins (1983–1985)*........... Harvey Korman
Alistair Quince (1983–1985) ...... Harvey Korman
Bubba Higgins (1986–1990) .... Allan Kayser
Iola Boylen (1986–1990) .... Beverly Archer

*Occasional

Mama's Family mined comedy from a squabbling family in the Midwestern blue-collar suburb of Raytown. The noisy clan was headed by Mama, a buxom, gray-haired widow with sharp opinions and a sharper tongue who shared her small house with her high-strung sister, Fran, a journalist for a local paper. Mama's lazy, dim-witted son, Vint, a locksmith by trade, moved in at the start of the series with his troublesome teenage children, Buzz and Sonja, after his wife ran off to become a Las Vegas showgirl. Much to Mama's disgust, Vint soon took up with the flirtatious neighbor, Naomi ("that floozy!"). The two were married in early 1983, and Naomi moved in too. Further uproar was caused by the periodic visits of Mama's two married daughters, the foulmouthed Eunice and the snobbish Ellen. Ed was Eunice's dolt of a husband.

The program was based on a series of sketches originally seen on *The Carol Burnett Show* and later made into the high-rated special "Eunice" in 1982. Each episode began with a short, pompous introduction by "your host" Alistair Quince, seen seated in his armchair. NBC aired reruns of *Mama's Family* during the summer of 1985.

In the fall of 1986 *Mama's Family* returned to TV in first-run syndication. Fran had recently passed away and Ed and Eunice had moved to Florida. They had neglected to mention this to their delinquent son Bubba who, after serving a term in juvenile hall for car theft, ended up living with Mama in Fran's old room, much to the consternation of Naomi and Vint, who thought they were getting it. Iola was the prissy neighbor who barely concealed her romantic designs on Vinton.

The biggest event in the run of *Mama's Family* occurred in the spring of 1990 when Naomi, who had seemingly been pregnant for an eternity, presented Vint with a bouncing baby girl named after his mama—Tiffany Thelma. They had moved out of the house but not out of her shadow, as they were now in a trailer on her property.

MAN AGAINST CRIME (*Detective Drama*)

FIRST TELECAST: *October 7, 1949*
LAST TELECAST: *August 19, 1956*
BROADCAST HISTORY:

Oct 1949–Mar 1952, CBS Fri 8:30–9:00 (OS)
Apr 1952–Jun 1952, CBS Thu 9:00–9:30
Oct 1952–Jun 1953, CBS Wed 9:30–10:00
Jul 1953–Oct 1953, CBS Fri 8:30–9:00
Oct 1953–Apr 1954, DUM Sun 10:30–11:00
Oct 1953–Jul 1954, NBC Sun 10:30–11:00
Jul 1956–Aug 1956, NBC Sun 10:00–10:30

CAST:

Mike Barnett (1949–1954).......... Ralph Bellamy
Mike Barnett (1956)................ Frank Lovejoy
Pat Barnett (1951)................. Robert Preston

The "man" was hard-boiled private detective Mike Barnett, who made his first appearance on CBS in the fall of 1949. Mike was a loner who used his brains and especially his fists to solve crimes in this rather violent show. The setting was the New York City area. The show was done live until the fall of 1952, when it went to film. The filmed episodes were all made at the Thomas A. Edison Studios in the Bronx and on location around New York.

When it left CBS in 1953 *Man Against Crime* did something almost unique—it became a regularly scheduled series on two different networks, NBC and DuMont, airing at the same time on both (Sun, 10:30 P.M.). The program left the air in 1954 but returned in the summer of 1956 as a live program, with Frank Lovejoy in the lead role.

During the summer of 1951, while Ralph Bellamy was on his vacation from the show, Robert Preston filled in for him in the role of Barnett's brother, Pat.

MAN AND THE CHALLENGE (*Adventure*)

FIRST TELECAST: *September 12, 1959*
LAST TELECAST: *September 3, 1960*
BROADCAST HISTORY:

Sep 1959–Sep 1960, NBC Sat 8:30–9:00

CAST:

Dr. Glenn Barton.................... George Nader

Dr. Glenn Barton was an athlete, doctor, and research scientist who worked for the government. Each week he was assigned to help others test the limits of their equipment and themselves under conditions of extreme stress. Barton's curiosity about his varied subjects and the fields with which he became involved occasionally resulted in his subjecting himself to the stresses in question before he would test their effects on others. He helped explorers test advanced jungle-survival techniques, he subjected two volunteers to an extended period in a small capsule to simulate the period in which astronauts await retrieval after returning from space, and he subjected other volunteers to the psychological torture and stress of brainwashing. In many of the episodes an emergency occurred, and Dr. Barton would have to push his own or others' endurance to limits not previously reached to try to save the situation—not always with positive results.

MAN AND THE CITY, THE (*Drama*)

FIRST TELECAST: *September 15, 1971*
LAST TELECAST: *January 5, 1972*
BROADCAST HISTORY:

Sep 1971–Jan 1972, ABC Wed 10:00–11:00

CAST:

Mayor Thomas Jefferson Alcala.... Anthony Quinn
Andy Hays........................... Mike Farrell

Marian Crane .... Mala Powers
Josefina .... Carmen Zapata

Academy Award winner Anthony Quinn starred as the ruggedly independent mayor of a fast-growing contemporary city in the Southwest. Mayor Alcala was no youngster, having been in office for 16 years. His longevity was assured by a constant and personal attention to the needs of individual constituents, whose stories made up this series. The mayor's sensible, button-down aide Andy tried to keep Hizzoner from becoming completely engrossed in individual people's problems, to the detriment of citywide affairs. Marian was the mayor's secretary.

Although the locale of *Man and the City* was not explicitly identified, the program was filmed on location in Albuquerque, New Mexico.

MAN BEHIND THE BADGE, THE (*Police Anthology*)

FIRST TELECAST: *October 11, 1953*
LAST TELECAST: *October 3, 1954*
BROADCAST HISTORY:
Oct 1953–Oct 1954, CBS Sun 9:30–10:00
HOST/NARRATOR:
Norman Rose

Each of the stories told in this live semidocumentary anthology series was a reenactment of an actual case from the files of a law enforcement agency. Although many of the stories were about police officers, they were not the only persons who fell into the category of "man behind the badge." Parole officers, park rangers, public defenders, U.S. Army MPs in Europe, and judges also appeared as leading characters in stories. Crime was not always the theme, either, as rehabilitation, life in a home for boys, and divorce were all touched upon at one time or another. On occasion the "man" behind the badge turned out to be a woman, such as a lady judge or a policewoman in a large city. Lesser-known talent was featured, although some of the actors (Jack Warden, Joey Faye, Bruce Gordon, and young Leslie Nielsen among them) later became well known.

A syndicated film version of *The Man Behind the Badge* was produced after the series had been canceled by CBS. The narrator of the filmed series, which was first seen in January 1955, was Charles Bickford.

MAN CALLED HAWK, A (*Drama*)

FIRST TELECAST: *January 28, 1989*
LAST TELECAST: *August 31, 1989*
BROADCAST HISTORY:
Jan 1989–May 1989, ABC Sat 9:00–10:00
Jul 1989, ABC Sat 10:00–11:00
Aug 1989, ABC Thu 8:00–9:00
CASTS:
Hawk .... Avery Brooks
Old Man .... Moses Gunn

Spenser's menacing "enforcer" on *Spenser: For Hire* got his own series (probably by threatening ABC executives) in this somber, violent crime show. Hawk was an enigmatic character. A tall, powerful black man who said little and scowled often, he wore expensive black clothes, drove a BMW, packed a huge silver .357 Magnum, and could explode into sudden violence; yet he was also highly literate, a connoisseur of fine foods, and an accomplished jazz pianist. Hawk had moved from Boston back to his hometown of Washington, D.C., where he held no position or official status but where people always seemed to know where to find him when they needed wrongs righted—forcefully, if not legally.

The character of Hawk was created by writer Robert B. Parker in his *Spenser* novels. In keeping with Parker's economy with names, Hawk (like Spenser) had no full name; and his single confidant, the even more mysterious "Old Man" (who uttered epigrams about life and meaning whenever Hawk needed a philosophical fix), apparently had no name at all.

Filmed on location in Washington.

MAN CALLED SHENANDOAH, A (*Western*)

FIRST TELECAST: *September 13, 1965*
LAST TELECAST: *September 5, 1966*
BROADCAST HISTORY:
Sep 1965–Sep 1966, ABC Mon 9:00–9:30
CAST:
Shenandoah .... Robert Horton

In the opening episode of this series two buffalo hunters out on the prairie stumbled upon a stranger who had been shot in a gunfight and left to die. Assuming that he might be an outlaw with a price on his head, they hauled the half-dead man into the nearest town. It turned out that he wasn't wanted, but when he recovered from the wound he couldn't remember who he was or why he had been shot. Taking the name Shenandoah, the stranger spent the rest of the season wandering from town to town in search of clues to his real identity. Robert Horton had left *Wagon Train* with the vow never to do another Western, but he relented long enough to play the lead in this single-season series.

MAN CALLED SLOANE, A (*International Intrigue*)

FIRST TELECAST: *September 22, 1979*
LAST TELECAST: *September 12, 1980*
BROADCAST HISTORY:
Sep 1979–Dec 1979, NBC Sat 10:00–11:00
Jun 1980–Jul 1980, NBC Fri 10:00–11:00
Sep 1980, NBC Fri 10:00–11:00
CAST:
Thomas Remington Sloane III ...... Robert Conrad
Torque .... Ji-Tu Cumbuka
The Director .... Dan O'Herlihy
Kelly .... Karen Purcill
Effie (voice only) .... Michele Carey

In his successful late 1960s series *The Wild, Wild West*, Robert Conrad played a 19th-century horse-opera version of James Bond. A decade later, he returned with a series in which he played a contemporary James Bond. Thomas Remington Sloane III was the top agent for UNIT, an American counterintelligence team committed to destroying the international criminal organization KARTEL. Suave, romantic, and brilliant, Sloane traveled all over the world to thwart the plans of KARTEL. With him was his trusted aide Torque, a six-foot, five-inch agent with a stainless steel hand that could be adapted to use a myriad of detachable gadgets. Running UNIT headquarters, located behind a toy boutique, was The Director. His only accountability was to the President. At headquarters was a special lab that provided Sloane and Torque with all sorts of devices to help them in emergencies. Lab assistant Kelly, who usually demonstrated the latest devices, occasionally got involved with them on missions. Also at headquarters was the E.F.I. series 3000 multifunction computer ("Effie") that assimilated data and gave its readouts not in print, but over a loudspeaker in a very sexy, very feminine voice.

MAN CALLED X, THE (*Intrigue*)

BROADCAST HISTORY:

Syndicated only
30 minutes
Produced: *1955–1956* (39 episodes)
Released: *January 1956*

CAST:

Agent Ken Thurston .... Barry Sullivan

Barry Sullivan portrayed a U.S. secret agent in this rather standard spy thriller. Thurston (code name "X") trotted off on missions around the world, from Prague to Teheran to Nepal, outwitting enemy agents and rescuing brilliant scientists and beautiful women. There was a certain note of authenticity, however, as the cases were based on real government files and technical supervision was by Ladislas Farago, a former agent of the U.S. Office of Naval Intelligence.

A radio version of *The Man Called X*, starring Herbert Marshall, aired from 1944 to 1952.

MAN FROM ATLANTIS (*Adventure*)

FIRST TELECAST: *September 22, 1977*
LAST TELECAST: *July 25, 1978*

BROADCAST HISTORY:

Sep 1977, NBC Thu 9:00–10:00
Oct 1977–Jan 1978, NBC Tue 8:00–9:00
Apr 1978–Jul 1978, NBC Tue 8:00–9:00

CAST:

Mark Harris .... Patrick Duffy
Dr. Elizabeth Merrill .... Belinda Montgomery
C. W. Crawford .... Alan Fudge
Mr. Schubert .... Victor Buono
Brent .... Robert Lussier
Jomo .... Richard Williams
Chuey .... J. Victor Lopez
Jane .... Jean Marie Hon
Allen .... Anson Downes

Mark Harris may have been the last survivor of the lost continent of Atlantis. Though he appeared to be human, there were distinct differences between Mark and his air-breathing brethren. Having grown up under the sea, Mark possessed gill tissue rather than lungs, which meant that he could survive for only about 12 hours before he had to return to the sea to "breathe." His hands and feet were webbed, he could swim faster than a dolphin, and he had superhuman strength and super-acute senses.

Despite his powers Mark had been washed ashore unconscious, where he was discovered by Dr. Elizabeth Merrill, who nursed him back to health. He then agreed to join her and a team of scientists from the Foundation for Oceanic Research in a project to learn more about life undersea. They traveled about in the "Cetacean," a special submersible vehicle, and their adventures included confrontations with extraterrestrial life and numerous evil scientists, notably the diabolical Mr. Schubert and his assistant, Brent. The foundation's director, preoccupied with budget problems, was C. W. Crawford.

Man from Atlantis was first seen in a series of four pilots that aired during the spring and summer of 1977 on varying days of the week. The first of these was telecast on March 4, 1977.

MAN FROM BLACKHAWK, THE (*Western*)

FIRST TELECAST: *October 9, 1959*
LAST TELECAST: *September 23, 1960*

BROADCAST HISTORY:

Oct 1959–Sep 1960, ABC Fri 8:30–9:00

CAST:

Sam Logan .... Robert Rockwell

This was a Western with a twist. Its hero was neither a gunfighter nor a lawman; he was an insurance investigator. Sam Logan, Chicago-based investigator for the Blackhawk Insurance Company, wore a city-slicker outfit complete with string tie and briefcase. He almost never used a gun but often had to resort to his fists as he traveled from place to place investigating attempts to defraud the company and settling claims. In addition to visiting many typical Western frontier towns, Logan also frequently turned up in cities like New Orleans and San Francisco.

MAN FROM INTERPOL (*Police Drama*)

FIRST TELECAST: *January 30, 1960*
LAST TELECAST: *October 22, 1960*

BROADCAST HISTORY:

Jan 1960–Oct 1960, NBC Sat 10:30–11:00

CAST:

Anthony Smith .... Richard Wyler
Superintendent Mercer .... John Longden

Filmed in England, *Man from Interpol* told of the adventures of Anthony Smith, a special agent for the Scotland Yard division of "Interpol," the International Police Force. The crimes he investigated were therefore generally international in scope, sending him trotting around Europe in pursuit of smugglers, counterfeiters, and other border-crossing culprits.

MAN FROM U.N.C.L.E., THE (*Spy Spoof*)

FIRST TELECAST: *September 22, 1964*
LAST TELECAST: *January 15, 1968*

BROADCAST HISTORY:

Sep 1964–Dec 1964, NBC Tue 8:30–9:30
Jan 1965–Sep 1965, NBC Mon 8:00–9:00
Sep 1965–Sep 1966, NBC Fri 10:00–11:00
Sep 1966–Sep 1967, NBC Fri 8:30–9:30
Sep 1967–Jan 1968, NBC Mon 8:00–9:00

CAST:

Napoleon Solo .... Robert Vaughn
Illya Kuryakin .... David McCallum
Mr. Alexander Waverly .... Leo G. Carroll
Lisa Rogers (1967–1968) .... Barbara Moore

The Man from U.N.C.L.E. was American television's answer to the very popular James Bond movies. Two superagents, Napoleon Solo and Illya Kuryakin, were teamed to fight the international crime syndicate THRUSH. U.N.C.L.E. (which stood for United Network Command for Law and Enforcement) had its secret American headquarters in New York. Running the office was Mr. Waverly, whose function was to assign agents to cases and coordinate their efforts. The suave, urbane American Solo and the blond, introverted Russian Kuryakin spent most of their time saving the world from THRUSH and, as the series wore on, the plots became more and more farfetched. The pinnacle of silliness was reached in the 1966–1967 season when *The Girl from U.N.C.L.E.* was created, bringing to television two hours of U.N.C.L.E. per week, with plots that were closer to ABC's *Batman* than to any sort of believable spy thriller.

At the end of the 1966–1967 season, *The Girl from U.N.C.L.E.* was dead and *The Man from U.N.C.L.E.* was dying. A transfusion of reality was tried at the start of the 1967–1968 season, with new sets for U.N.C.L.E.'s New York offices and stories that were more traditionally suspenseful, with danger that no longer seemed as if it had just come off the comic-book pages, and with a new regular cast member in Mr. Waverly's secretary Lisa Rogers. Unfortunately it was too late, and the series ended on the evening of January 15, 1968, to be replaced by the biggest hit of the late 1960s, *Rowan & Martin's Laugh-In*.

MAN IN A SUITCASE (*Detective Drama*)
FIRST TELECAST: *May 3, 1968*
LAST TELECAST: *September 20, 1968*
BROADCAST HISTORY:
May 1968–Sep 1968, ABC Fri 8:30–9:30
CAST:
McGill .... Richard Bradford

Filmed in England, as were most of the series about "loners" in the 1960s, *Man in a Suitcase* was the story of a private detective who had once been an American intelligence agent. McGill had been falsely accused of failing to prevent a noted scientist from defecting to Russia, a treasonous offense. The series followed McGill through the European underworld as he searched for the evidence and people that could prove his innocence.

MAN IN THE FAMILY (*Situation Comedy*)
FIRST TELECAST: *June 19, 1991*
LAST TELECAST: *July 31, 1991*
BROADCAST HISTORY:
Jun 1991–Jul 1991, ABC Wed 9:30–10:00
CAST:
Sal Bavasso .... Ray Sharkey
Angie Bavasso .... Julie Bovasso
Tina Bavasso .... Leah Remini
Annie .... Anne De Salvo
Robby .... Billy L. Sullivan
Uncle Bennie .... Louis Guss
Cha Cha .... Don Stark
THEME:
"When You're Smiling," sung by Louis Prima

A ne'er-do-well son reluctantly returned home to fulfill his father's dying wish and run the family's Brooklyn grocery store in this ethnic comedy. Sal wanted nothing in life but fast-buck schemes and womanizing, but now found that he had to deal with family: sarcastic mom Angie, rebellious teenaged sister Tina, cranky Uncle Bennie, skeptical divorced sister Annie, and Annie's young son Robby (who, unfortunately, idolized sleazy Uncle Sal). At least Sal could promote a scam now and then with his pal Cha Cha—or try to, until the women hauled him in.

MAN OF THE PEOPLE (*Situation Comedy*)
FIRST TELECAST: *September 15, 1991*
LAST TELECAST: *October 27, 1991*
BROADCAST HISTORY:
Sep 1991–Oct 1991, NBC Sun 8:00–8:30
CAST:
Councilman Jim Doyle .... James Garner
Constance Leroy .... Corinne Bohrer
Mayor Lisbeth Chardin .... Kate Mulgrew
Richard Lawrence .... Taylor Nichols
Councilman Art Lurie .... George Wyner
Rita .... Romy Walthall

James Garner, who built a career playing lovable rogues, tried another variation on the theme here without success. Jim Doyle, a small-time scam artist and gambler, found himself suddenly appointed to the city council of Long View, California, to fill out the term of his recently deceased wife, a popular councilwoman. He wasn't the pushover that unscrupulous Mayor Chardin thought he'd be, however. Jim alternated between scams, dubious ethics, the race track, and actually helping his constituents (usually for the wrong reasons, but with the right results). Watching him like a hawk was Constance, his late wife's humorless, straight-arrow assistant. Others hanging around city hall were Art, the mayor's obsequious ally, aspiring politico Richard, and Rita, a perky former prostitute hired by Jim as soon as he took office—to be his secretary. A single leftover hour-long episode of this series was aired on December 6, 1991.

MAN OF THE WEEK (*Interview*)
FIRST TELECAST: *April 20, 1952*
LAST TELECAST: *August 22, 1954*
BROADCAST HISTORY:
Apr 1952–Jan 1953, CBS Sun 6:00–6:30
Jul 1954–Aug 1954, CBS Sun 6:30–7:00
MODERATOR:
Walter Cronkite (1952–1953)
Ron Cochran (1954)

Each week on *Man of the Week*, a prominent public figure was interviewed about subjects of general interest. The program premiered as a Sunday afternoon entry in August 1951, and ran continuously until October 1954, alternating between nighttime and afternoon time slots. The nighttime telecasts are indicated above. This series was the forerunner of *Face the Nation*.

MAN SHOW, THE (*Discussion/Comedy*)
BROADCAST HISTORY:
Comedy Central
30 minutes
Original episodes: *1999–*
Premiered: *June 19, 1999*
REGULARS:
Jimmy Kimmel (1999–2003)
Adam Carolla (1999–2003)
Bill Foster (*The Fox*) (1999–2000)
Arturo Gil
Michael Zwiener
Aaron Hamill (2002–)
"THE JUGGIES"
Julie Costello
Shawnie Costello
Angelique Gorges
Paula Harrison
Vanessa Kay
Patti Kim
Joanna Krupa
Dani Lee (1999–2002)
Nicole Pulliam
Tiffany Richardson (2001)
Arlene Nicole Rodriguez (1999–2002)
Rachel Sterling
Suzanne Talhouk
Svetlana "Lana" Warren

Men—at least a certain kind of men—found revenge for

the "Oprah-ization of America" in this self-proclaimed joyous celebration of chauvinism. Smirking hosts Jimmy Kimmel and Adam Carolla presided over talk, interviews, skits and films about all things male, especially those things having to do with sex, sex, sex and . . . well, you get the idea. Typical features included comic discussions of penile enlargements, underwear and "Casual Sex Fridays," how to make a wedding "man-friendly," and movies men don't want to see. There were also filmed street gags, such as a petition to "end suffrage" (most people didn't know what it meant), rating passing women, and asking them, "Can I unhook your bra?" In the Wheel of Destiny game, the winner might get a wheelbarrow full of pornography, and the loser had to wear the host's underwear as a face mask. Another segment showed the opening of a topless carwash.

Regulars included Bill Foster as old, obscene piano player "The Fox," three-and-a-half-foot tall Arturo in a variety of predicaments, and young Michael and Aaron as "The Man Show Boy," there to learn the fine art of being gross. Beautiful women in bikinis abounded on the show, of course, dubbed "The Juggy Squad." Those most frequently seen are listed above. Perhaps the show's trademark was the shot of well-endowed young women bouncing on a trampoline as the credits rolled. Take *that*, Oprah!

The Man Show premiered at about the same time as the similar *X Show* on FX.

MAN WHO NEVER WAS, THE (*International Intrigue*)

FIRST TELECAST: *September 7, 1966*
LAST TELECAST: *January 4, 1967*
BROADCAST HISTORY:
Sep 1966–Jan 1967, ABC Wed 9:00–9:30
CAST:
Peter Murphy/Mark Wainwright .... Robert Lansing
Eva Wainwright .... Dana Wynter
Col. Jack Forbes .... Murray Hamilton
Roger Barry .... Alex Davion
Paul Grant .... Paul Stewart

This spy thriller starred Robert Lansing as an American espionage agent who took another man's identity—and wife, fortune, and lifestyle. As the series opened Peter Murphy was fleeing from East Berlin with enemy agents in hot pursuit. Taking refuge in a bar, he came upon his exact look-alike, millionaire playboy Mark Wainwright, who was later mistaken for him by the enemy and killed. Sensing an opportunity, Peter assumed Wainwright's identity, his wealth, and his aristocratic wife as a perfect cover for his undercover activities in the glamorous capitals of Europe.

Wainwright's wife Eva knew that Murphy was an impostor, but she went along with him to keep the family fortune, which would have otherwise fallen into the hands of grasping half brother Roger. Eva even taught Murphy her late husband's habits, so the "cover" would be perfect. Eventually Eva fell in love with her new "husband"—but Peter remained wary. The only other person who knew Murphy's new identity was his boss, Chief of Intelligence Col. Forbes.

Filmed on location in Berlin, Munich, London, Athens, and other cities in Europe.

MAN WITH A CAMERA (*Drama*)

FIRST TELECAST: *October 10, 1958*
LAST TELECAST: *February 29, 1960*
BROADCAST HISTORY:
Oct 1958–Mar 1959, ABC Fri 9:00–9:30
Oct 1959–Feb 1960, ABC Mon 10:30–11:00
CAST:
Mike Kovac .... Charles Bronson
Anton Kovac .... Ludwig Stossel
Lt. Donovan (1959–1960) .... James Flavin

During World War II Mike Kovac had been a combat photographer. Now he was making his living as a freelance professional lensman. At times it seemed as if he were still in combat. Mike took assignments from newspapers, insurance companies, the police, private individuals, and anyone else who wanted a filmed record of an event. The nature of his assignments often made Mike more private detective than photographer, a situation which was most likely planned by the producers of this series to capitalize on the popularity of detective shows at the time. Occasionally, when he needed advice or help, Mike sought out his father, Anton.

MAN WITHOUT A GUN (*Western*)

BROADCAST HISTORY:
Syndicated only
30 minutes
Produced: *Oct 1957–1959* (52 episodes)
Released: *Fall 1958*
CAST:
Adam MacLean .... Rex Reason
Marshal Frank Tallman .... Mort Mills
Mayor George Dixon .... Harry Harvey, Sr.
Doc Brannon .... Forrest Taylor

In this syndicated series handsome, brawny Rex Reason starred as a crusading newspaper editor in the Dakota Territory of the 1880s. Bandits, landgrabbers, and miscellaneous troublemakers were all around the town of Yellowstone, but editor MacLean preferred to use persuasion and the columns of *The Yellowstone Sentinel* rather than guns in his campaign for law and order—although a good fistfight now and then helped things along. MacLean also used his office as a schoolroom for the town's youngsters.

MANCUSO, FBI (*Police Drama*)

FIRST TELECAST: *October 13, 1989*
LAST TELECAST: *August 13, 1993*
BROADCAST HISTORY:
Oct 1989–Apr 1990, NBC Fri 10:00–11:00
Apr 1990–May 1990, NBC Fri 8:00–9:00
Jul 1993–Aug 1993, NBC Fri 8:00–9:00
CAST:
Agent Nick Mancuso .... Robert Loggia
Kristen Carter .... Lindsay Frost
Eddie McMasters .... Fredric Lehne
Jean St. John .... Randi Brazen
Dr. Paul Summers .... Charles Siebert

TV crime fighters seem to be either young and handsome or old and grumpy. Robert Loggia, who once played the former (*T.H.E. Cat,* 1966), here became the latter. Nick Mancuso was introduced to viewers in the 1988 mini-series *Favorite Son* as a cynical, seen-it-all veteran F.B.I. agent who nevertheless still believed in his job. As the press releases put it, he had "a passionate love affair with the United States Constitution." His politically oriented superiors dismissed him as "a lonely misanthrope with no respect for authority," but it's not easy to get rid of FBI agents so he got to continue his one-man crusade against corruption and murder in high government places in this action-filled series.

Assistant Special Agent in Charge Eddie McMasters was his button-down young superior, who constantly gave him grief, but others understood him better, including Justice Department lawyer Kristen (who sometimes joined him for the busts), forensics expert Dr. Summers, and loyal secretary Jean.

Set in Washington, D.C. NBC ran repeats of the series during the summer of 1993.

MANHATTAN, AZ (*Situation Comedy*)

BROADCAST HISTORY:

USA Network
30 minutes
Original episodes: *2000* (13 episodes)
Premiered: *July 23, 2000*

CAST:

Sheriff Daniel Henderson .... Brian McNamara
Atticus Finch Henderson (age 12).... Vincent Barry
Mayor Jake Manhattan .... Chad Everett
Sgt. Jane Pentowski.................... Kate Hodge
Miss Vega .... Jill-Michelle Melean

Slapstick comedy about a straight-arrow Los Angeles cop who took a job as sheriff of the small town of Manhattan, Arizona, after his Greenpeace activist wife was killed during a dolphin rescue. This Manhattan was dusty and God-forsaken; Daniel's chubby son, Atticus, hated it ("Life sucks!") and spent most of his time surfing the Internet for pornography. Daniel's new boss, and the man who owned Manhattan, was narcissistic 1970s TV star Jake Manhattan, who was apparently unaware that nobody remembered him. Sgt. Jane was the frustrated guard at the gate of the local U.S. Air Force compound, who came on to Daniel. There were dumb jokes about three-legged dogs, killer cacti, dressing in women's clothing, and guntoting, sex-obsessed locals, but not much of an audience. The buzzards that circled over Manhattan swooped in for the kill after only eight episodes, leaving five additional episodes made but not aired.

MANHATTAN MAHARAJA (*Variety*)

FIRST TELECAST: *October 4, 1950*
LAST TELECAST: *February 26, 1951*
BROADCAST HISTORY:

Oct 1950–Nov 1950, ABC Wed 9:30–10:00
Nov 1950–Feb 1951, ABC Mon 9:15–9:30

REGULARS:

George Ansbro
Joseph Biviano
Ralph Norman

In this odd series, George Ansbro donned the guise of a maharaja in the Arabian Nights vein and in tongue-in-cheek verse touched upon modern topics as they would be seen through the eyes of an Eastern potentate. "Pasha" Joseph Biviano and his Snake Charmers provided upbeat music, while "Sahib" Ralph Norman and his string group played for the maharaja's favorite dancing girls. Seen only on a limited number of ABC network stations during its prime-time run, *Manhattan Maharaja* continued in daytime until 1952.

MANHATTAN SHOWCASE (*Musical Variety*)

FIRST TELECAST: *February 28, 1949*
LAST TELECAST: *June 16, 1949*
BROADCAST HISTORY:

Feb 1949–Apr 1949, CBS Various, 7:15–7:30
Apr 1949–May 1949, CBS Mon/Tue/Thu/Fri 7:45–8:00
May 1949–Jun 1949, CBS Mon/Wed/Thu 7:15–7:30

REGULARS:

Johnny Downs
Helen Gallagher
Virginia Gorski
Evelyn Ward
The Tony Mottola Trio

Manhattan Showcase provided young entertainers with the opportunity to perform before a nationwide audience in the early days of live television. Johnny Downs was the one host who stayed with the show from beginning to end. His female helper was originally Helen Gallagher, who was joined by Virginia Gorski in April; the two of them left in June, to be replaced by Evelyn Ward. The series was initially aired on Mondays, Wednesdays, and Fridays, but later shifted to various combinations of weeknights.

MANHATTAN SPOTLIGHT (*Interview*)

FIRST TELECAST: *January 24, 1949*
LAST TELECAST: *April 20, 1951*
BROADCAST HISTORY:

Jan 1949–Apr 1951, DUM Mon–Fri Various 15-minute spots
Apr 1950–May 1950, DUM Wed 10:00–10:15
May 1950–Jun 1950, DUM Wed 10:30–10:45

HOST:

Chuck Tranum

DuMont Chief Announcer Chuck Tranum was primarily responsible for the station breaks and other announcements made over the fledgling network from its flagship station in New York. He also hosted this nightly 15-minute interview program, which featured ordinary citizens and smalltime entertainers with interesting hobbies and talents. Among those appearing were a Mr. Bimstein, who sculpted the Empire State Building in ice, the city's leading umbrella collector, a custom shoe manufacturer, a team of calypso dancers, the head of a lonely hearts club, and a man with a collection of electric eels.

Manhattan Spotlight began in daytime before moving to the nighttime schedule, where it was seen between 7:30 and 8:00 P.M. on various weeknights. There was also a late-night run during April–June 1950. During some periods the show was only seen locally in New York.

MANHATTAN TRANSFER (*Variety*)

FIRST TELECAST: *August 10, 1975*
LAST TELECAST: *August 31, 1975*
BROADCAST HISTORY:

Aug 1975, CBS Sun 7:30–8:30

REGULARS:

Manhattan Transfer
(Laurel Masse, Tim Hauser, Janis Siegel, Alan Paul)
Archie Hahn
Leland Palmer
Fayette Hauser
Laraine Newman
The Ira Newborn Orchestra

The Manhattan Transfer was a popular recording group whose material was impossible to type. Their routines, both musical and comic, spanned the entire

20th century and ran the gamut from semiclassical to rock. This potpourri of songs and humor aired for four weeks in the summer of 1975. Archie Hahn was the most prominent member of their supporting cast, portraying the character Doughie Duck in various comedy sketches.

MANHUNT (*Dramatic Anthology*)
FIRST TELECAST: *July 14, 1951*
LAST TELECAST: *August 23, 1952*
BROADCAST HISTORY:
Jul 1951–Sep 1951, NBC Sat 10:30–11:00
Jul 1952–Aug 1952, NBC Sat 10:30–11:00

Also known as *Assignment Manhunt,* this live dramatic series spent two years as the summer replacement for *Your Hit Parade.* The plays were all adaptations of suspense and adventure stories that had appeared previously in magazines or as books or movies.

MANHUNT (*Police Drama*)
BROADCAST HISTORY:
Syndicated only
30 minutes
Produced: *1959–1961* (78 episodes)
Released: *September 1959*
CAST:
Det. Lt. Howard Finucane .... Victor Jory
Ben Andrews .... Patrick McVey
Det. George Peters (episodes #1–13) .... Charles Bateman
Det. Bruce Hanna (#14–23) .... Rian Garrick
Det. Dan Kramer (#24–39) .... Chuck Henderson
Det. Paul Kirk (#40–52) .... Michael Steffany
Det. Phil Burns (#53–65) .... Robert Crawford
Det. Carl Spencer (#66–78) .... Todd Armstrong

Well-acted, straightforward, cops-and-robbers show starring two veteran actors, Victor Jory and Patrick McVey. Jory portrayed a hard-nosed detective with the San Diego Police Dept., and McVey an equally hard-nosed police reporter with the *Chronicle* (similar to his earlier role in *Big Town*). Their easy camaraderie helped lift the series out of the melodramatic rut of murder, mobs, and arson.

Supporting these two old-timers was an up-to-date jazz score and a succession of young police sidekicks for Jory, each of whom appeared in 10 or 15 of the 78 episodes filmed. The producer, Screen Gems, wanted to use this series to expose new talent, but none of the young actors who "tried out" here went on to particularly notable careers.

MANHUNT (*Adventure/Reality*)
FIRST TELECAST: *August 3, 2001*
LAST TELECAST: *September 7, 2001*
BROADCAST HISTORY:
Aug 2001–Sep 2001, UPN Fri 8:00–9:00
HUNTERS:
Big Tim Kingman .... John Cena
Rain .... Raye Hollitt
Koa .... Kala'i Miller

In this military-style reality series, which took place on the Hawaiian island of Kauai, contestants were tracked and attacked by three professional hunters. Big Tim's expertise was in tactics and marksmanship, Rain's in explosives and traps, and Koa's in tracking. They were armed with air-powered paint marker rifles, pyrotechnic grenades, tripwires, night-vision scopes, and climbing gear.

The game began with 13 contestants, all in their 20s and 30s. Each day they were given a map and as a group had to navigate across the island to a Safe Zone, the only place on the island where they could rest for the night without being hunted. While they were on the move, the hunters staged attacks with ambushes and "explosions," using their marker rifles (three paint marker rounds per attack) to eliminate contestants. Three hits and a contestant was out of the game. A cornered contestant could avoid elimination by surrendering, but only once in the game. At the end of each day, the contestants picked one of their group for the Gauntlet. That person had to run a 50-yard course while being fired at by the hunters, and bring back a flag, in order to remain in the game; if the runner was hit once, he or she was eliminated from the game. When a contestant was eliminated, the hunters shaved his or her hair as a trophy. Amid the action, contestants talked to the camera about their feelings regarding the game, and each other.

By the final episode only 4 of the original 13 contestants were left. They were given paintball guns so that, at last, they could fight back, and the hunters got some of their own medicine. Rain was hit first, then Big Tim, the blustery leader, followed by Koa and Big Tim again. All four of the contestants made it to the finish line without being eliminated, but 23-year-old Nicole Gordillo (in real life a live-event promoter) was the first across and won the $250,000 grand prize.

It turned out that this "reality show" was in some ways not so real. The day before the third episode aired, there were published reports that Bob Jaffe, an original coproducer, had said that some of the scenes were reshot in Los Angeles' Griffith Park, with scripted material inserted to make the show more exciting. Subsequently both Hash Shaalan, the judge who had trained the hunters and contestants, and Jacqueline Kelly, the first contestant eliminated, confirmed the charges. After fraud charges were filed with the FCC, the following disclaimer was added to each episode: "This program includes dramatic scenes intended for entertainment purposes only."

MANHUNTER, THE (*Detective Drama*)
FIRST TELECAST: *September 11, 1974*
LAST TELECAST: *April 9, 1975*
BROADCAST HISTORY:
Sep 1974–Apr 1975, CBS Wed 10:00–11:00
CAST:
Dave Barrett .... Ken Howard
Sheriff Paul Tate .... Robert Hogan
Lizabeth Barrett .... Hilary Thompson
James Barrett .... Ford Rainey
Mary Barrett .... Claudia Bryar
PRODUCER:
Quinn Martin

The Manhunter was a detective series set in the United States during the depression years of the 1930s. Dave Barrett was an ex-marine whose best friend had been killed by bank robbers during a holdup. Following his friend's death, Dave gave up his Idaho farm and became a private investigator with a mission: to bring to justice as many gangsters of the type that had killed his friend as possible. Tracking down these criminals sent him back and forth across the country, never staying in one place for long, except when he returned home to see his sister Liz and his folks.

MANIAC MANSION (*Situation Comedy*)

BROADCAST HISTORY:

The Family Channel
30 minutes
Produced: *1990–1993* (66 episodes)
Premiered: *September 14, 1990*

CAST:

Fred Edison .... Joe Flaherty
Casey Edison .... Deborah Theaker
Tina Edison (age 15) .... Kathleen Robertson
Ike Edison (10) .... Avi Phillips
Turner Edison (4) .... George Buza
Idella Orkin .... Mary Charlotte Wilcox
Harry Orkin, the fly .... John Hemphill

Loony sitcom about an inventor, Fred, who had accidentally turned his brother-in-law, Harry, into a fly and his four-year-old son, Turner, into a six-foot, 250-pound giant. Unfortunately Fred was not able to undo his mistake, so they all lived together in sitcomland with Harry buzzing around discontentedly and his wife, Idella, complaining that she couldn't hug her husband anymore without squashing him. Turner simply acted like a four-year-old, despite his size. Casey was Fred's wife and Ike and Tina *(sic)*, their other two children.

Based on a computer game distributed by moviemaker George Lucas' LucasFilm.

MANIMAL (*Police Drama/Fantasy*)

FIRST TELECAST: *September 30, 1983*
LAST TELECAST: *December 31, 1983*
BROADCAST HISTORY:

Sep 1983–Nov 1983, NBC Fri 9:00–10:00
Dec 1983, NBC Sat 9:00–10:00

CAST:

Jonathan Chase .... Simon MacCorkindale
Brooke McKenzie .... Melody Anderson
Ty Earle (pilot only) .... Glynn Turman
Ty Earle .... Michael D. Roberts
Capt. Nick Rivera .... Reni Santoni

TV superheroes have had many tricks up their sleeves over the years, but Jonathan Chase was really different. He had the ability, inherited from his late father in some faraway jungle, to turn himself into animals—all sorts of animals, from a pussycat to a black panther. To most people he appeared as a wealthy, cultured young professor who taught "animal behavioral sciences" at New York University. To the police, he was a valued consultant on the use of animals in criminology. But to criminals, he was a snarl in the night, the sudden hiss of a cobra, the cry of an observant hawk.

The transformations were at will, and dramatic: his breathing grew heavy, his hands began to show ripples and contractions, his nose grew snouty, and whiskers and fangs began to emerge. All of this was seen in intriguing, unconnected close-ups.

Only two mortals knew of Chase's secret powers: his hip black helper, Ty Earle, with whom he had shared a few scrapes in Vietnam, and a pretty police detective named Brooke. Brooke had stumbled on his secret by accident, and now worked with him on cases. She also found he had a certain—well, animal magnetism, but nothing much came of their budding romance during the short run of this series. Instead, viewers were treated to a steady diet of coy remarks ("I was a real pussycat," "He's probably out catting around"), while the heavy breathing was reserved strictly for business.

MANN & MACHINE (*Science Fiction*)

FIRST TELECAST: *April 5, 1992*
LAST TELECAST: *July 14, 1992*
BROADCAST HISTORY:

Apr 1992, NBC Sun 8:00–9:00
Jun 1992–Jul 1992, NBC Tue 8:00–9:00

CAST:

Det. Bobby Mann .... David Andrews
Sgt. Eve Edison .... Yancy Butler
Margaret Claghorn .... S. Epatha Merkerson

A familiar sci-fi premise was combined with standard cop-show in this hybrid series, set in Los Angeles in the early twenty-first century. Homicide detective Bobby Mann, a guy so unmechanical he couldn't even get the soft-drink dispenser to work, found himself partnered with "Eve," a beautiful, highly competent cyborg—the department's latest gizmo in the war against crime. Eve had strength and superhuman capabilities that were certainly handy in a pinch, and of course crooks could blow her up and she could still be put back together again. But she lacked Bobby's street smarts and ability to deal with surprises ("not programmed . . . not programmed!"). Most of the series dealt with his efforts to make her a little more human and a little less coldly rational.

MANNIX (*Detective Drama*)

FIRST TELECAST: *September 16, 1967*
LAST TELECAST: *August 27, 1975*
BROADCAST HISTORY:

Sep 1967–Sep 1971, CBS Sat 10:00–11:00
Sep 1971–Sep 1972, CBS Wed 10:00–11:00
Sep 1972–Dec 1972, CBS Sun 9:30–10:30
Jan 1973–Sep 1974, CBS Sun 8:30–9:30
Sep 1974–Jun 1975, CBS Sun 9:30–10:30
Jul 1975–Aug 1975, CBS Wed 10:00–11:00

CAST:

Joe Mannix .... Mike Connors
Lou Wickersham (1967–1968) ... Joseph Campanella
Peggy Fair (1968–1975) .... Gail Fisher
**Lt. Adam Tobias (1969–1975)* .... Robert Reed
Lt. Art Malcolm (1969–1975) .... Ward Wood

*Occasional

Mannix was one of the most violent detective shows of its time, and also one of the longest-running. The original format had Joe Mannix, a Los Angeles–based private detective, employed by a sophisticated detective firm called Intertect. Despite the fact that the company was dedicated to the use of computers and other advanced scientific detection aids, Mannix seemed happiest when working with no implements other than his own intuition and fists. At the start of the second season he had struck out on his own, taking a small office on the first floor of the building in which he lived. Helping him in his new role as an independent investigator was his secretary and girl Friday, Peggy Fair. Her husband, a friend of Mannix's and a former police officer, had been killed in the line of duty. Lou Wickersham, Joe's old boss from Intertect, was also seen occasionally during the second season.

Tobias and Malcolm were Joe's contacts on the police force beginning in 1969.

The high point of every episode seemed to be a wild brawl, and the body count even in the first few minutes of the show was sometimes appalling. On their radio show, Bob and Ray ran a continuing parody on the series called *Blimmix*, in which the hero always held a polite conversation with some suspect, calmly agreed that mayhem was the only answer, and then was invariably beaten to a pulp.

MANTOVANI (*Music*)

BROADCAST HISTORY:

Syndicated only
30 minutes
Produced: *1958–1959* (39 episodes)
Released: *January 1959*

HOST:

John Conte

WITH:

Mantovani and His Orchestra

English orchestra leader Mantovani was very popular in the U.S. in the 1950s, with a long succession of best-selling albums and even a couple of hit singles ("Charmaine," "Cara Mia") before rock 'n' roll took over the charts. His music was characterized by old favorites, lush arrangements, and a huge string section, all calculated to appeal to the old folks (it put the younger set to sleep). After many concert tours the maestro appeared in this widely seen syndicated TV series, produced in England, with his full 46-piece orchestra. Guest artists trying not to be drowned in all those cascading strings included Connie Francis, Vic Damone, Joni James, Dorothy Collins, the Hi-Lo's, and the Boscoe Holder West Indian Dancers.

Mantovani's real name was Annunzio Paolo Mantovani.

MANY HAPPY RETURNS (*Situation Comedy*)

FIRST TELECAST: *September 21, 1964*
LAST TELECAST: *April 12, 1965*

BROADCAST HISTORY:

Sep 1964–Apr 1965, CBS Mon 9:30–10:00

CAST:

Walter Burnley .... John McGiver
Harry Price .... Richard Collier
Joan Randall .... Elinor Donahue
Wilma Fritter .... Jesslyn Fax
Bob Randall .... Mark Goddard
Joe Foley .... Mickey Manners
Laurie Randall .... Andrea Sacino
Lynn Hall .... Elena Verdugo

Life was not peaceful for Walter Burnley. He had one of the most thankless jobs in the world, managing the complaint desk at Krockmeyer's department store. Working with him was a staff of four harried souls (Harry, Wilma, Joe, and Lynn), not all of whom managed to maintain their composure under the constant abuse of irate shoppers. Walter was a widower who made his home with his daughter Joan, Joan's husband Bob, and his four-year-old granddaughter Laurie.

MANY LOVES OF DOBIE GILLIS, THE (*Situation Comedy*)

FIRST TELECAST: *September 29, 1959*
LAST TELECAST: *September 18, 1963*

BROADCAST HISTORY:

Sep 1959–Sep 1962, CBS Tue 8:30–9:00
Sep 1962–Sep 1963, CBS Wed 8:30–9:00

CAST:

Dobie Gillis .... Dwayne Hickman
Maynard G. Krebs .... Bob Denver
Herbert T. Gillis .... Frank Faylen
Winifred (Winnie) Gillis .... Florida Friebus
Zelda Gilroy .... Sheila James
Thalia Menninger (1959–1960) .... Tuesday Weld
Milton Armitage (1959–1960) .... Warren Beatty
Riff Ryan (1959–1960) .... Tommy Farrell
Melissa Frome (1959–1960) .... Yvonne Lime
Davey Gillis (1959–1960) .... Darryl Hickman
Mr. Leander Pomfritt .... William Schallert
Clarice Armitage (1959–1960) .... Doris Packer
Mrs. Blossom Kennedy (1959–1961) .... Marjorie Bennett
Mrs. Chatsworth Osborne, Sr. (1960–1963) .... Doris Packer
Chatsworth Osborne, Jr. (1960–1963) Steve Franken
Mrs. Ruth Adams (1959–1960) .... Jean Byron
Dr. Burkhart (1961–1963) .... Jean Byron
Lt. Merriweather (1961) .... Richard Clair
Dean Magruder (1961–1963) .... Raymond Bailey
Duncan Gillis (1962–1963) .... Bobby Diamond

Dobie Gillis was a "typical" American teenager, with three primary interests in life: beautiful women, fancy cars, and money. Unfortunately he was the son of a grocer and not the most attractive of boys, which put a certain crimp in his aspirations. Dobie and his beatnik buddy Maynard—to whom work was a dirty word—did their best to get by with a minimum of effort. Dobie had two real nemeses in his life. The first was intelligent but unattractive Zelda Gilroy, who was constantly trying to get herself married to Dobie. The second, through most of the series, was millionaire Chatsworth Osborne, Jr., a spoiled young man who flaunted his social status, not to mention his money, to snare the attractive girls who eluded Dobie.

When the series premiered in 1959, Dobie had to contend with handsome Milton Armitage for the attention of his favorite girl, the aristocratic (despite her rather modest means) and mercenary Thalia Menninger. She was interested mostly in acquiring "oodles and oodles" of money. To this end she was constantly looking to better Dobie's prospects for supporting her in the style to which she would like to become accustomed. Dobie was also much concerned about his future, and was seen at the beginning and end of each episode in Central City's park next to a statue of *The Thinker*, assuming the same pose while pondering his fate.

In February 1960, Milton Armitage was replaced by Chatsworth Osborne, Jr., with Doris Packer assuming the role of his snobbish, overbearing mother, essentially the same part she had played as Milton's mother when the series began. In March 1961, Dobie and Maynard enlisted in the army, thinking that would help them find themselves. The army hitch lasted only until the first episode of the 1961–1962 season, when they resigned from the service and enrolled in St. Peter Prior Junior College. It was there that they remained, Maynard still fighting the system in his nonconformist way and his "good buddy" Dobie chasing women and trying to find himself, for the last two seasons that *The Many Loves of Dobie Gillis* was on the air.

On May 10, 1977, nearly 15 years after *Dobie Gillis* ended its run, CBS aired the pilot episode for a proposed revival series titled *Whatever Happened to Dobie Gillis?* What had happened was that Dobie had finally been snared by Zelda, become a partner in his family's grocery store, and had a teenage son, Georgie (played by Stephen Paul). Maynard, now fortyish but still unconventional, came back to visit. The new series never materialized. Another reunion took place in February 1988.

Based on characters created by author Max Shulman.

MARBLEHEAD MANOR (*Situation Comedy*)

BROADCAST HISTORY:

Syndicated only
30 minutes
Produced: *1987–1988* (24 episodes)
Released: *September 1987*

CAST:

Albert Dudley .... Paxton Whitehead
Hilary Stonehill .... Linda Thorson
Randolph Stonehill .... Bob Fraser
Jerry Stockton .... Phil Morris
Dwayne Stockton .... Rodney Scott
Lupe .... Dyana Ortelli
Elvis .... Humberto Ortiz
Rick .... Michael Richards

Randolph Stonehill had made his fortune in the vegetable oil business—a fortune large enough to provide him and his elegant wife, Hilary, with a large, fully staffed estate in this slapstick comedy. The staff was anything but efficient. The butler, Albert Dudley, was a stuffy, uptight Englishman who found it hard to deal with his unbelievably inept subordinates. Handyman Dwayne was always cooking up get-rich-quick schemes that got both him and the others in trouble. He was nothing like his hard-working brother, Jerry, the Stonehill chauffeur, who was going to night school to get his college degree. Others on the staff were Lupe, the well-meaning, if accident prone, household cook; Elvis, her precocious eight-year-old son; and Rick, the klutzy gardner.

Whenever things got out of control—which was often—it was the cool Mrs. Stonehill who kept her short-tempered husband and the staff from coming to blows.

In addition to playing the volatile Randolph Stonehill, Bob Fraser was one of the producers and writers of *Marblehead Manor*.

MARCH OF MEDICINE, THE (*Documentary*)

FIRST TELECAST: *July 8, 1958*
LAST TELECAST: *July 29, 1958*

BROADCAST HISTORY:

July 1958, ABC Tue 10:00–10:30

NARRATORS:

Ben Grauer
Eric Sevareid

Public-service films about the mental-health field made up this series.

MARCUS WELBY, M.D. (*Medical Drama*)

FIRST TELECAST: *September 23, 1969*
LAST TELECAST: *May 11, 1976*

BROADCAST HISTORY:

Sep 1969–May 1976, ABC Tue 10:00–11:00

CAST:

Dr. Marcus Welby .... Robert Young
Dr. Steven Kiley .... James Brolin
Consuelo Lopez .... Elena Verdugo
Myra Sherwood (1969–1970) .... Anne Baxter
Kathleen Faverty (1974–1976) .... Sharon Gless
Sandy Porter (1975–1976) .... Anne Schedeen
Phil Porter (1975–1976) .... Gavin Brendan
Janet Blake (1975–1976) .... Pamela Hensley

MEDICAL ADVISOR:

Dr. Robert Forten

CREATOR/PRODUCER:

David Victor

Robert Young was one of the few actors in television history to be closely identified with two highly successful and long-running roles—that of kindly family man Jim Anderson on *Father Knows Best* in the 1950s (8 years) and that of kindly Dr. Marcus Welby in the 1970s (7 years). The 62-year-old Young came out of a seven-year retirement to originate the role of Welby.

Marcus Welby, M.D. portrayed the cases of a veteran general practitioner in Santa Monica, California, whose thoroughness and dedication involved him in the lives of all sorts of patients. Assisting him was young Dr. Steven Kiley, who during the first season contracted to work with Welby for one year before resuming his training as a neurologist (he stayed). Thus the inevitable tension between youth and experience was established, but in this case Welby tended to be the more unorthodox of the two, often confounding the dedicated but textbook-oriented Kiley with his psychiatric approach to medicine. Welby treated the whole patient, his temperament, fears, and family environment, as well as his physical ailments. The ailments were certainly varied for a suburban GP: during the first season alone there were tumors, autistic children, strokes, pernicious anemia, blindness, emphysema, LSD side effects, leukemia, diabetes, Huntington's Chorea, faith healing, dope addiction, an overweight racing jockey, and a diver who kept getting the bends.

A love interest was provided for Dr. Welby during the first season by Myra Sherwood, but this role was soon dropped. The only other suggestion that Welby might have a life of his own came in the last season, when his married daughter (Sandy) and six-year-old grandson (Phil) were occasionally seen. There was no Mrs. Welby. The only other regulars over the years, in fact, were nurses Consuelo Lopez and Kathleen Faverty.

Although romance eluded Dr. Welby it did finally come to young Dr. Kiley, in the person of Janet Blake, public relations director of Hope Memorial Hospital. They were married on the telecast of October 21, 1975.

Marcus Welby premiered in 1969 and soon became the biggest hit in the history of the ABC network up to that time—it was the first ABC series ever to rank number one among all TV programs for a full season (1970–1971). Part of its success, truth to tell, was in scheduling; for its first two years it ran against a CBS news documentary hour and frequently against documentaries on NBC as well *(First Tuesday)*. The limited appeal of these shows practically forfeited the audience to ABC. But once viewers had gotten used to Welby they stayed, against competition soft and strong. The program also won an Emmy and was held in very high esteem by medical groups, with Young serving offscreen as honorary chairman of numerous fund drives and observances.

MARGE AND GOWER CHAMPION SHOW, THE
(*Situation Comedy*)

FIRST TELECAST: *March 31, 1957*
LAST TELECAST: *June 9, 1957*
BROADCAST HISTORY:
Mar 1957–Jun 1957, CBS Sun 7:30–8:00
CAST:
Marge Champion .... Herself
Gower Champion .... Himself
Marge's Father .... Jack Whiting
Cozy .... Buddy Rich
Amanda .... Peg La Centra
Miss Weatherly .... Barbara Perry
ORCHESTRA:
Richard Pribor

The format of this comedy series was designed to give the Champions at least one opportunity to dance each week. Gower played a choreographer and Marge his dancing partner, as they were in real life, and the situations used in the series were based on their actual experiences. Drummer Buddy Rich, appropriately, played their drummer and accompanist, and actress-singer Peg La Centra was cast as Marge's close friend and interior decorator. The program aired on alternate Sundays with *The Jack Benny Show.*

MARGE AND JEFF (*Situation Comedy*)

FIRST TELECAST: *September 21, 1953*
LAST TELECAST: *September 24, 1954*
BROADCAST HISTORY:
Sep 1953–Sep 1954, DUM Mon–Fri 7:15–7:30
CAST:
Marge .... Marge Greene
Jeff .... Jess/Jeff Cain

This pleasant 15-minute domestic comedy, presented five nights a week, concerned the day-to-day life of newlyweds Marge and Jeff, starting life together in a big-city apartment. Sharing in their little adventures were occasional neighbors and their cocker spaniel, Paisley. The program was written by Miss Greene, who previously produced a similar local program (called *Marge and Fred*) in Philadelphia.

Because of the confusing similarity of actor Jess Cain's name to that of his character Jeff, the actor had his name legally changed to Jeff shortly after the series began.

MARGIE (*Situation Comedy*)

FIRST TELECAST: *October 12, 1961*
LAST TELECAST: *August 31, 1962*
BROADCAST HISTORY:
Oct 1961–Apr 1962, ABC Thu 9:30–10:00
Apr 1962–Aug 1962, ABC Fri 7:30–8:00
CAST:
Margie Clayton .... Cynthia Pepper
Maybelle Jackson .... Penney Parker
Nora Clayton .... Wesley Tackitt
Aunt Phoebe .... Hollis Irving
Harvey Clayton .... Dave Willock
Heywood Botts .... Tommy Ivo
Johnny Green .... Richard Gering
Cornell Clayton .... Johnny Bangert

Growing up in the Roaring Twenties didn't seem to be radically different from growing up in the 1960s, as this series pointed out. The superficial things were different: flappers, bathtub gin, rumble seats, prohibition, raccoon coats, and the Charleston. The real issues were the same: conflicts with parents, troubled love affairs, the hassle of school, and maintaining "true" friends. Margie lived with her parents, her little brother, Cornell, and her aunt Phoebe. Her best friend, Maybelle Jackson, was a flapper, and Heywood and Johnny were the two boys fighting for her affection. To add to the period flavor of the show, *Margie*'s producers intermixed silent movie slides that told the audience "Please Pay Attention," "The Plot Thickens," etc., at critical points in the action.

Based on the 1946 theatrical film starring Jeanne Crain.

MARIAH (*Police Drama*)

FIRST TELECAST: *April 1, 1987*
LAST TELECAST: *May 13, 1987*
BROADCAST HISTORY:
Apr 1987–May 1987, ABC Wed 10:00–11:00
CAST:
Superintendent James Malone ... Philip Baker Hall
Dep. Superintendent Ned Sheffield ...... John Getz
Dr. Deena Hertz .... Tovah Feldshuh
Chaplain Timothy Quinlan .... Chris Wiggins
Brandis LaSalle .... Kathleen Layman
Leda Cervantes .... Wanda de Jesus
Rev. Howard Bouchard .... William Allen Young
Linda Grincato .... Renee Lippin

This earnest but rather grim drama concerned life—and death—at Mariah State Penitentiary. The focus was primarily on the staff, including tough, politically savvy Superintendent Malone and his hardworking young deputy, Sheffield; prison psychiatrist Deena, generally seen running from one suicide attempt to the next, with Father Quinlan close behind; and Brandis, the rich, idealistic activist who worked as a prison volunteer—and also wanted to set up a National Union of Prisoners' Wives and Families headquartered outside the gate. Stories concerned the travails of the staff, political infighting, and sometimes inmates' stories (e.g., a woman prisoner worried about losing her children).

MARIE (*Musical Variety*)

FIRST TELECAST: *December 12, 1980*
LAST TELECAST: *September 26, 1981*
BROADCAST HISTORY:
Dec 1980–Jan 1981, NBC Fri 8:00–9:00
Sep 1981, NBC Sat 9:00–10:00
REGULARS:
Marie Osmond
Howard Itzkowitz
Jeffrey Baron
Jamie Mizada
John Bates
Hennen Chambers
The Lester Wilson Dancers
Doris Hess
Jim Hudson
Greg Norberg
Charlie Gray
Kathe Flinders
Debi Ing
The Bob Rozario Orchestra

At age 21, Marie Osmond was already a veteran performer. She had begun singing with her family, the Osmond Brothers, before entering school and had her first hit record at the age of 14 ("Paper Roses" in 1973). Three years later Marie was starring with her brother Donny in a variety series on ABC *(Donny and Marie)*. This limited-run variety series was Marie's first attempt to go it alone as a single, even if it was produced by Osmond Productions. *Marie* was a mix of music and humor, and was billed as a more sophisticated show than the ABC series had been. Miss Osmond sang songs that ranged from standards to current pop tunes and participated in comedy sketches with a large supporting cast. There were numerous comedy blackouts on each telecast and, reminiscent of *The Carol Burnett Show*, weekly question-and-answer sessions with the studio audience. There were also guests, including Andy Williams, who had given the Osmonds their first TV exposure in the 1960s.

MARILYN MCCOO AND BILLY DAVIS, JR. SHOW, THE (*Musical Variety*)

FIRST TELECAST: *June 15, 1977*
LAST TELECAST: *July 20, 1977*
BROADCAST HISTORY:
Jun 1977–Jul 1977, CBS Wed 8:30–9:00
REGULARS:
Marilyn McCoo
Billy Davis, Jr.
Jay Leno
Lewis Arquette
Tim Reid
The John Myles Orchestra

Summer variety series featuring the husband-and-wife team of McCoo and Davis, who were members of the original Fifth Dimension pop group. This series, with music, comedy, and guest stars, came on the heels of their Grammy Award–winning record "You Don't Have to Be a Star to Be in My Show."

MARK SABER (*Detective Drama*)

FIRST TELECAST: *October 5, 1951*
LAST TELECAST: *May 15, 1960*
BROADCAST HISTORY:
Oct 1951–Apr 1952, ABC Fri 8:00–8:30
Apr 1952–Jun 1952, ABC Wed 9:30–10:00
Oct 1952–Jun 1953, ABC Mon 8:00–8:30
Oct 1953–Jun 1954, ABC Wed 7:30–8:00
Dec 1955–Jun 1957, ABC Fri 9:30–10:00
Sep 1957–Dec 1957, NBC Fri 7:30–8:00
Oct 1958–May 1959, NBC Sun 7:00–7:30
Oct 1959–May 1960, NBC Sun 6:30–7:00
CAST:
Mark Saber (1951–1954) .... Tom Conway
Mark Saber (1955–1960)............ Donald Gray
Sgt. Tim Maloney (1951–1954) .... James Burke
Barney O'Keefe (1955–1956) ...... Michael Balfour
Judy (1956) .... Teresa Thorne
Stephanie Ames (1956–1957)....... Diana Decker
Pete Paulson (1957–1958) .... Neil McCallum
Pete Paulson (1958) .... Gordon Tanner
Bob Page (1958–1960) .... Robert Arden
Inspector Parker (1957–1960)........ Colin Tapley

Mark Saber was an American cop show with an international flavor. Saber was British, though he worked on the homicide squad of a big-city American police department. Dapper in appearance (with pencil-thin mustache and pinstriped suits) and elegant in speech, he tracked down villains by leaps of brilliant deduction as much as by routine police work. His assistant was a more familiar TV type, the loyal but somewhat thick-headed Sgt. Maloney.

After a three-year run Saber left the air in June 1954, only to return a year and a half later in a series called *The Vise*. This time he was cast as a one-armed private detective in London. The settings were exclusively European, as Saber tracked assorted blackmailers, murderers, and other crooks through London, Paris, along the Riviera, and in other glamorous locales. The cast was all new, with Donald Gray taking the role of Saber and a succession of actors playing his sidekicks, Barney O'Keefe, Judy, Stephanie Ames, Pete Paulson, and Bob Page. Numerous Scotland Yard inspectors came and went as his "official" foil, with Colin Tapley, as Inspector Parker, seen most often.

When first seen in 1951, the program was known as *Mystery Theater*. It was later retitled *Inspector Mark Saber—Homicide Squad* in 1952, *The Vise* in December 1955 (see also under that title for another series by the same name), and *Saber of London* in 1957. It was called *Detective's Diary* in syndication and on NBC from March 1957 to September 1961, when it was rerun on Saturday afternoons.

MARKER (*Adventure*)

FIRST TELECAST: *January 17, 1995*
LAST TELECAST: *August 15, 1995*
BROADCAST HISTORY:
Jan 1995–Apr 1995, UPN Tue 8:00–9:00
Apr 1995–Aug 1995, UPN Tue 9:00–10:00
CAST:
Richard DeMorra .... Richard Grieco
Kimba Hills Rose .... Gates McFadden
Danny "Pipeline" Kahala .... Andy Bumatai
Taki Mochadomi "Moch" .... Keone Young

Richard DeMorra was a carpenter from New Jersey who had gone to Hawaii for the funeral of his father, the late Joe Rose. Joe had deserted him and his mother when Richard was a child and had become a wealthy and successful industrialist in Hawaii. Most of Richard's memories of his father were of the ruthless, ambitious man who had abandoned his family. He was surprised to find that his father had been respected and loved by many of the islanders whose lives he had touched. Over the years Joe had given out hundreds of poker-chip-sized numbered markers that could be redeemed when the recipients needed help or a favor. Now that he was gone, it was Richard's responsibility to honor them. It was through his interaction with the marker holders that Richard began to understand the man his father had become.

When he wasn't helping people who redeemed markers, Richard was building his own home on property left to him on the coast adjacent to the Rose estate where his stepmother, Kimba, with whom he had a tenuous relationship, was still living. The other two regulars were Pipeline, the fun-loving Hawaiian con man who lived on the property that Richard had inherited and helped him out on occasion, and Moch, the Rose family's attorney, who provided sound advice to the sometimes impetuous Richard.

Filmed on location in Hawaii.

MARKHAM (*Detective Drama*)
FIRST TELECAST: *May 2, 1959*
LAST TELECAST: *September 22, 1960*
BROADCAST HISTORY:
May 1959–Jan 1960, CBS Sat 10:30–11:00
Jan 1960–Sep 1960, CBS Thu 9:30–10:00
CAST:
Roy Markham .... Ray Milland
John Riggs (1959) .... Simon Scott

Movie star Ray Milland turned private eye for this series. Roy Markham was wealthy, well educated, and a very successful attorney. After spending many years trying cases, he had decided to attempt unraveling them, becoming a private investigator mainly for the excitement of it. Although he was based in New York, his cases took him all over the world on assignments ranging from murder to corporate fraud. Since he had other sources of income, Roy's fees were flexible, sometimes exorbitant and sometimes free, depending on the client. When this series first went on the air, Markham had an assistant named John Riggs who traveled with him and did much of the legwork, but less than two months after the show's premiere, Markham was doing it all by himself.

MARRIAGE, THE (*Situation Comedy*)
FIRST TELECAST: *July 8, 1954*
LAST TELECAST: *August 19, 1954*
BROADCAST HISTORY:
Jul 1954–Aug 1954, NBC Thu 10:00–10:30
CAST:
Ben Marriott .... Hume Cronyn
Liz Marriott .... Jessica Tandy
Pete Marriott .... Malcolm Broderick
Emily Marriott .... Susan Strasberg
Bobby Logan .... William Redfield

To this obscure comedy belongs the distinction of having been the first network series to be regularly telecast in color. *The Marriage* was a live comedy dealing with the home life of New York lawyer Ben Marriott. Ben's practice was moderately successful, allowing his wife Liz, who had been employed previously as a buyer for a department store, to stay home and run the household. Liz's need to keep occupied got her involved in all sorts of community, organizational, and personal projects. The Marriotts had two children, Pete, aged 10, and Emily, aged 15. Cronyn and Tandy had starred in the NBC radio version of this series, which had left the air in the spring of 1954.

MARRIED BY AMERICA (*Reality/Romance*)
FIRST TELECAST: *March 3, 2003*
LAST TELECAST: *April 14, 2003*
BROADCAST HISTORY:
Mar 2003–Apr 2003, FOX Mon 9:00–10:00
Mar 2003–Apr 2003, FOX Thu 8:00–9:00
HOST:
Sean Valentine

This series proposed to set a new "standard" for arranged marriages as five singles had their prospective mates chosen by friends, families and viewers at home—with unexpected results. The rules of *Married by America* stipulated that if any of the couples married they would be given $100,000, a fancy car and, if the marriage lasted, a new house. The five singles in search of spouses were Jill, a 25-year-old hostess for the New York Islanders hockey team; Stephen, a 35-year-old Manhattan restaurateur; Billie Jeanne, a 28-year-old Manhattan bartender; Jennifer, a 27-year-old Atlanta real estate agent, and Matt, a 26-year-old actor from Atlanta.

In the first two episodes viewers met the singles and their prospective mates, five for each of them. They were interviewed by family and friends of the singles, who reduced the possible choices from five to two, after which each of the two finalists was assigned a phone number and viewers at home voted for the one they thought should get "engaged" to each of the singles.

Episode three was the "engagement" episode, in which the singles met the persons viewers had chosen as their ideal mates. After each of the chosen spouses was announced, the women were given engagement rings by the men. Jill seemed unsure when she met Kevin; Matt and Cortez really hit it off; Billie Jeanne appeared to be more playful than her chosen, Tony, was expecting; Jennifer and Xavier were pretty nervous, and Stephen was pleasantly surprised by Denise.

For the next few weeks, with cameras taping all the action, the couples lived on Copper North Ranch, a 300-acre spread several hundred miles from Los Angeles. Each couple had been given an SUV for the drive to the ranch, which gave them a chance to learn about each other during the eight-hour drive. After arrival they were assigned their bedrooms (later they were given individual villas), went on dates, got romantic (or didn't) and continued to explore their budding relationships. Host Valentine introduced the panel of relationship experts who evaluated how well the couples were getting along and, at the end of each episode, eliminated the least compatible couple. First to get the ax were Matt and Cortez, both of whom admitted they really didn't like each other.

After the first elimination the remaining couples expressed anxiety about ways in which they weren't getting along, except for Jill and Kevin, who were having a wonderful time. Over the next few days they were visited by friends and family members and had counseling sessions with a sex therapist. Jennifer and Xavier were the second couple eliminated, primarily because she never seemed to loosen up and had remained rather distant. The three remaining couples then took trips to visit their future in-laws, with mixed results. When they got back to the ranch it was time for the next elimination and the panel chose Stephen and Denise. He certainly seemed relieved that, at least for him, it was over.

The two remaining couples started making preparations for their weddings. Their respective best men and maids of honor arrived to help with the shopping, and it was obvious that for Billie Jeanne it was a fantasy come true while Jill's approach was more matter-of-fact. Then it was off to Las Vegas for bachelor and bachelorette parties. After the parties it was apparent that Kevin and Jill were more realistic about their marriage prospects than Billie Jeanne and Tony.

Early in the final episode they went to get their marriage licenses, and viewers could see that all was not well—Tony was beginning to look terrified, he couldn't tell Billie Jeanne he loved her, and Jill was starting to have misgivings and was squabbling with Kevin.

When their respective families arrived for the weddings, there was considerable debate among them about the imminent nuptials. Unfortunately, neither couple made it through the ceremony. Jill said, "I don't," because she couldn't rush into marriage after such a short courtship and believed Kevin hadn't really found himself. He took it well and they decided to keep on dating in the hope that eventually it would work out. On the other hand, when Tony said, "I don't," because he realized he didn't really love her enough and she deserved someone who did, Billie Jeanne broke down in hysterical tears and Dwayne, one of her outraged friends, created an ugly scene. In the postscript the producers noted that the couple had subsequently talked by phone but were unsure if they would continue dating—although she was considering moving to Los Angeles.

Nobody won the wedding prizes.

MARRIED PEOPLE (*Situation Comedy*)

FIRST TELECAST: *September 18, 1990*
LAST TELECAST: *September 11, 1991*
BROADCAST HISTORY:

Sep 1990, ABC Tue 9:30–10:00
Sep 1990–Jan 1991, ABC Wed 9:30–10:00
Aug 1991–Sep 1991, ABC Wed 10:30–11:00

CAST:

Nick Williams .... Ray Aranha
Olivia Williams .... Barbara Montgomery
Russell Meyers .... Jay Thomas
Elizabeth Meyers .... Bess Armstrong
Baby Max Meyers ...... Jonathan & Matthew Lester
Allen Campbell .... Chris Young
Cindy Campbell .... Megan Gallivan

Three couples, at three stages of marriage, populated a New York brownstone in this easygoing comedy. On the ground floor were landlords Nick and Olivia, a sixtyish black couple who had raised their own children in the house and now found it possible to rent out the upper two floors as their Harlem neighborhood gentrified. Nick was a little cranky and Olivia very sensible, but both were traditionalists. On the second floor were the decidedly non-traditional Meyerses: Russell, a sensitive freelance writer who worked at home, and Elizabeth, an ambitious attorney for a midtown law firm, angling to become a partner. "Why doesn't he get out and work?" harrumphed Nick. In the third-floor attic apartment were the Campbells, cute teenage newlyweds just arrived in New York and oh-so-much in love. Gosh-golly Allen was a freshman at Columbia University, while his perky sweetness, Cindy, a midwestern cheerleader, supported them both as a waitress. "That's the whitest boy I've ever seen!" grumped Nick. "Even for a white boy, he's just too white."

Early in the season overachiever Elizabeth had her first child, Baby Max, turning Russell into a complete house-husband.

MARRIED: THE FIRST YEAR (*Drama*)

FIRST TELECAST: *February 28, 1979*
LAST TELECAST: *March 21, 1979*
BROADCAST HISTORY:

Feb 1979–Mar 1979, CBS Wed 8:00–9:00

CAST:

Billy Baker .... Leigh McCloskey
Joanna Huffman Baker .... Cindy Grover
Barbara Huffman .... Claudette Nevins
Cathy Baker .... K Callan
Bert Baker .... Stanley Grover
Cookie Levin .... Gigi Vorgan
Sharon Kelly .... Stepfanie Kramer
Tom Liberatore .... Gary Epp
Donny Baker .... Stephen Manley
Millie Baker .... Jennifer McAllister
Emily Gorey .... Christine Belford

Billy and Joanna were young newlyweds trying to make a life for themselves despite families that did not approve of their marrying so young. Joanna had just graduated from high school when she and Billy, only a couple of years older, were wed. They came from different backgrounds, he from a close-knit, blue-collar family, and she from a socially prominent, upper-middle-class one. Joanna's family had a history of divorces and acrimony, which did not help matters.

MARRIED . . . WITH CHILDREN (*Situation Comedy*)

FIRST TELECAST: *April 5, 1987*
LAST TELECAST: *July 7, 1997*
BROADCAST HISTORY:

Apr 1987–Oct 1987, FOX Sun 8:00–8:30
Oct 1987–Jul 1989, FOX Sun 8:30–9:00
Jul 1989–Nov 1993, FOX Sun 9:00–9:30
Nov 1993–Jan 1994, FOX Sun 9:00–10:00
Jan 1994–Apr 1995, FOX Sun 9:00–9:30
Apr 1995–May 1995, FOX Sun 9:00–10:00
May 1995–Jan 1996, FOX Sun 9:00–9:30
Jan 1996–Feb 1996, FOX Sun 9:00–10:00
Mar 1996–Apr 1996, FOX Sun 9:00–9:30
Apr 1996–May 1996, FOX Sun 9:00–10:00
May 1996–Jul 1996, FOX Sun 9:00–9:30
Jul 1996–Aug 1996, FOX Sun 8:30–9:00
Sep 1996–Oct 1996, FOX Sat 9:00–9:30
Nov 1996–Dec 1996, FOX Sun 7:00–8:00
Jan 1997, FOX Mon 9:30–10:00
Feb 1997–May 1997, FOX Mon 9:00–9:30
Jun 1997–Jul 1997, FOX Mon 9:00–10:00

CAST:

Al Bundy .... Ed O'Neill
Peggy Bundy .... Katey Sagal
Kelly Bundy (age 15) .... Christina Applegate
Bud Bundy (11) .... David Faustino
Steve Rhoades (1987–1990) .... David Garrison
Marcy Rhoades D'Arcy .... Amanda Bearse
Jefferson D'Arcy (1991–1997) .... Ted McGinley
**Voice of Buck (1991–1995)* .... Kevin Curran
**Seven Bundy (1992–1993)* .... Shane Sweet
**Officer Dan (1993–1997)* .... Dan Tullis, Jr.
Griff (1994–1997) .... Harold Sylvester
**Ike (1994–1997)* .... Tom McCleister
**Sticky (1994–1995)* .... Pat Millicano
**Bob Rooney (1994–1997)* .... E. E. Bell
**Voice of Lucky (1995–1996)* .... Kevin Curran
Voice of Mrs. Wanker (1995) .... Kathleen Freeman
**Efrem Wanker (1995–1996)* .... Tim Conway
**Gary (1995–1997)* .... Janet Carroll

*Occasional

THEME:

"Love and Marriage," by Sammy Cahn and Jimmy Van Heusen, sung by Frank Sinatra (1955 recording)

Suburban Chicago was the setting for this domestic comedy that had all the warmth of a boa constrictor. The Bundys were not your typical family. Although they occasionally let it slip that they cared for each other, every member of the household seemed intent on belittling and putting down the others. Al was a lowly but chauvinistic shoe salesman who had been married for 15 years. His wife, Peg, was a lazy housewife who almost never cleaned or cooked, and their semi-delinquent kids, Kelly and Bud, were forever at each other's throats. Al's bedroom prowess, or lack thereof, was a frequent topic of conversation, and there was constant bickering about money, the kids' activities, and SEX. Their newlywed neighbors, accountants Steve and Marcy Rhoades, were young and gloriously in love until Al started explaining the real world to Steve and Peg did likewise to Marcy. Buck was the Bundy dog.

The most successful series on the fledgling Fox network, *Married . . . with Children* drew the wrath of many for its unabashed raunchiness. During the 1988–1989 season, letter writers, led by Michigan housewife Terry Rakolta, encouraged viewers and advertisers to boycott the show, but to no avail. The audience grew even more and, as long as the ratings were high, there were plenty of sponsors. During that season Marcy's husband Steve authorized a loan to finance one of Al's get-rich-quick schemes and, when Al couldn't repay it, Steve lost his job at the bank. After months of unemployment he left Marcy to become a park ranger at Yosemite. Kelly, the blond sexpot with an IQ as low as her hemlines were high, somehow managed to graduate from high school in the spring but, despite making a little money as a model, continued to live at home. A year later Marcy found herself married to Jefferson D'Arcy, a guy she had met during a drinking binge at a bankers convention. Jefferson never had a job. He just lived off his wife's earnings as a banker.

In the fall of 1991, with star Katey Sagal expecting a child, the producers decided to have both Peg and Marcy pregnant, much to the consternation of their spouses and, in Peg's case, her other children. Ms. Sagal miscarried in October, and to minimize what would have been an awkward situation no matter how it was handled, the entire pregnancy story line was revealed to have been Al's horrible nightmare. Shades of *Dallas*.

The following year brought the arrival of Seven, the six-year-old son of one of Peg's cousins, who moved in with the Bundys. The writers apparently couldn't integrate his character into the series because he disappeared from the show a few months later with no mention of what had happened to him. Kelly actually got a job in 1992, as a waitress at a cheap diner. Waitressing didn't work out for Kelly, who tried TV commercials, first for Pest Boys exterminating company as "The Verminator," and later as the commercial spokesperson for Ice Hole Beer. Bud had begun college around the time Kelly started slinging hash, but finances, or lack thereof, kept both the Bundy kids at home, much to Al's chagrin. By 1994 Bud was working part time as a driving tester for the Illinois Bureau of Motor Vehicles and, that fall, finally lost his virginity to Marcy's young, sexually aggressive niece Amber (Juliet Tablak), who had moved in with the D'Arcys. Added to the cast was Griff, a shoe salesman working with Al at Gary's Shoe Emporium, who also liked to hang out with the guys—including Ike, Sticky, and Bob—at their favorite place, the nudie bar. Al had also started the anti-feminist group NO MA'AM (National Organization of Men Against Amazonian Masterhood), which was preoccupied with preserving their right to drink excessively, act like slobs, and lust over sexually explicit material.

In the fall of 1995, Bud moved out of his room and into the basement, and Peg's obese mother (heard but never seen) arrived to move into his room after she left her husband, Efrem. On the October 1, 1995, episode Buck died and was reincarnated, much to his chagrin, as the Bundys' new puppy, Lucky. He had wanted to come back as an eagle. The following spring Bud graduated from Trumaine University and, when *Married . . . with Children* began its final season, was trying to make it as a talent agent, with Kelly as his principal client. Showing up occasionally, during the last two seasons, was "Gary," the verbally abusive woman who owned the shoe store in which Al and Griff worked. In the series finale, in April 1997, Kelly almost got married to the unwitting accomplice of a lady con who tried to rob the Bundys after she had escaped from prison. Al objected until he found out the dumb hunk's family owned a huge meat by-product company, but in the end, stopped the wedding when he found out that the guy, and his wealthy father, had long histories of philandering.

MARSHAL, THE (*Police Drama*)

FIRST TELECAST: *January 31, 1995*
LAST TELECAST: *July 15, 1996*
BROADCAST HISTORY:

Jan 1995, ABC Tue 10:00–11:00
Feb 1995–Apr 1995, ABC Sat 10:00–11:00
Apr 1995–Dec 1995, ABC Mon 8:00–9:00
Jun 1996–Jul 1996, ABC Mon 8:00–9:00

CAST:

Deputy Marshal Winston MacBride ...... Jeff Fahey
Mrs. MacBride .... Patricia Harras

Winston MacBride was a loner, a deputy U.S. Marshal who tracked fugitives across the U.S. in this odd, moody series. With sheer determination, clever deduction, and an uncanny ability to get the drop on the bad guys (he might pop out of a snowdrift or rise from the water, gun in hand), he nearly always got his prey. The fugitives were part of the appeal of this series. They were not your ordinary felons but eccentric people with strange stories who were often not what they seemed; some episodes, in fact, resembled *Twin Peaks* or *The X-Files*.

There was another side to the quiet, relentless marshal. Seen fleetingly at the beginning or end of each episode were his beloved wife and children at their plain tract house in the suburbs.

MARSHAL DILLON, see *Gunsmoke*

MARSHAL OF GUNSIGHT PASS, THE (*Western*)

FIRST TELECAST: *March 12, 1950*
LAST TELECAST: *September 30, 1950*
BROADCAST HISTORY:

Mar 1950–Sep 1950, ABC Sat 6:30–7:00

CAST:

Marshal (Mar) .... Russell "Lucky" Hayden
Marshal Eddie Dean (Mar-Sep) .... Eddie Dean
Deputy Roscoe .... Roscoe Ates
Ruth .... Jane Adrian

MUSIC:

Andy Parker and the Plainsmen

Two veterans of Hollywood's Western B-movie factories appeared in this obscure oater, which was probably the only network Western action series produced live from a studio. Russell Hayden, best known for his Hopalong Cassidy films, was the original Marshal, replaced after a few weeks by singing cowboy Eddie Dean. (Riley Hill appeared as Marshal Riley Roberts in some episodes.) The real star was Roscoe Ates as the marshal's dopey, bug-eyed sidekick; Ruth was Roscoe's pretty niece. Andy Parker's Western string band provided musical interludes and backup for Eddie's occasional songs.

The series originated from Los Angeles and was seen live on the West Coast, and via kinescope in the rest of the country. The horses and stagecoaches moving (carefully) around an obvious stage setting, the awkwardly staged fight scenes, and the cheap "outdoor" backdrops looked so phony compared to filmed Westerns that the series was considered primitive even for 1950, and soon disappeared from the air.

MARSHALL CHRONICLES, THE (*Situation Comedy*)

FIRST TELECAST: *April 4, 1990*
LAST TELECAST: *May 2, 1990*
BROADCAST HISTORY:
Apr 1990–May 1990, ABC Wed 9:30–10:00
CAST:
Marshall Brightman................Joshua Rifkind
Melissa Sandler......................Nile Lanning
Johnny Parmetko................Gabriel Bologna
Sean Bickoff........................Bradley Gregg
Leslie Barash................Meredith Scott Lynn
Cynthia Brightman..................Jennifer Salt
Michael Brightman................Steve Anderson
Ira......................................Brad Bradley
THEME:
"Fallin' in Love," written and performed by Randy Newman

The perplexities of life as seen through the wire-rimmed glasses of an intelligent but gawky teenager. Marshall, who looked and sounded a little like a younger version of Woody Allen, was a curly haired Manhattan teen whose main goal was to outflank his rival Johnny for the affections of sweet Melissa (the girl in the fuzzy pink sweater). He didn't have much time to do it, as his daydreams were canceled after only five episodes. A leftover episode of this series aired on July 22, 1990.

MARSHALL PLAN IN ACTION, THE (*Documentary*)

FIRST TELECAST: *June 24, 1950*
LAST TELECAST: *February 22, 1953*
BROADCAST HISTORY:
Jun 1950–Jul 1950, ABC Sat 9:00–9:30
Jul 1950–Oct 1950, ABC Sun 10:00–10:30
Oct 1950–Mar 1952, ABC Sun 9:30–10:00
Jan 1951–Jun 1951, ABC Fri 10:00–10:30 (reruns)
Jul 1951–Oct 1951, ABC Mon 8:30–9:00 (reruns)
Apr 1952–Jun 1952, ABC Tue 8:00–8:30
Jul 1952–Aug 1952, ABC Thu 9:00–9:30
Sep 1952–Feb 1953, ABC Sun 6:00–6:30

Documentary films prepared by the U.S. government showing the results of Marshall Plan aid to war-ravaged Europe. Each film opened with a statement from Federal Administrator Paul G. Hoffman describing the films as "the story of one successful battle in the series of struggles now going on that have become known as the Cold War."

Impoverished ABC (which could have used some economic aid itself at this time) was sufficiently desperate for inexpensive programming to schedule two showings a week of these films during much of 1951. Effective December 30, 1951, the series' title was changed to *Strength for a Free World.*

MARTHA RAYE SHOW, THE (*Comedy/Variety*)

FIRST TELECAST: *September 20, 1955*
LAST TELECAST: *May 29, 1956*
BROADCAST HISTORY:
Sep 1955–May 1956, NBC Tue 8:00–9:00
REGULARS:
Martha Raye
Rocky Graziano
Carl Hoff and His Orchestra
The Danny Daniels Dancers

Loud-voiced comedienne and singer Martha Raye first brought her slapstick comedy to TV as one of the stars of NBC's *All Star Revue* in 1951. Between 1953 and 1955 she was seen in a series of specials entitled *The Martha Raye Show*, which served as a periodic replacement for *Your Show of Shows* and *The Milton Berle Show.* Finally, in 1955, she got her own weekly series.

The earlier specials had been relatively unstructured variety shows, with Rocky Graziano regularly appearing as her boyfriend in comedy skits. The 1955–1956 series attempted to tell a complete story each week, in musical variety format. Rocky was once again her boyfriend in each story, and the night's theme was developed in integrated comedy, singing, and musical production numbers. Guest stars also appeared.

MARTHA WRIGHT SHOW, THE (*Music*)

FIRST TELECAST: *April 18, 1954*
LAST TELECAST: *December 5, 1954*
BROADCAST HISTORY:
Apr 1954–Dec 1954, ABC Sun 9:15–9:30 (OS)
REGULARS:
Martha Wright
Norman Paris
Bobby Hackett and His Band

Songstress Martha Wright was the star of this live music show. Featured with her were pianist Norman Paris and trumpet player Bobby Hackett and his band. Miss Wright, whose show was the replacement for *The Jane Pickens Show* in April, was herself replaced on Miss Pickens's return in July, and replaced Miss Pickens again in September. Also known as *The Packard Showroom.*

MARTIAL LAW (*Police Comedy/Drama*)

FIRST TELECAST: *September 26, 1998*
LAST TELECAST: *June 3, 2000*
BROADCAST HISTORY:
Sep 1998–Jun 2000, CBS Sat 9:00–10:00
CAST:
Sammo Law........................Sammo Hung
Det. Dana Doyle (1998).............Tammy Lauren
Det. Louis Malone (1998–1999)....Louis Mandylor
Capt. Benjamin Winship (1998–1999)
....Tom Wright
Chen Pei Pei (Grace Chen)...............Kelly Hu
Terrell Parker........................Arsenio Hall

Capt. Amy Dylan (1999–2000) . . . . . . Gretchen Egolf
Ivana Bock (2000) . . . . Natalie Raitano

Portly Hong Kong martial-arts movie star Sammo Hung starred in this send-up of action/adventure movies. Sammo was a Chinese detective on temporary assignment with the L.A.P.D., working with detectives Doyle (who disappeared from the cast after five episodes) and Malone. Law's chubby physical appearance, inscrutably serious attitude, and butchering of the English language could have made him a laughingstock except for one thing: despite his bulk, he could dispatch the bad guys with incredibly quick moves and devastatingly well-placed karate chops and kicks. The fight scenes were so campy and absurd they looked like they could have been from the 1960s *Batman* series (but without the cartoon pop-up "Bams" and "Pows" to punctuate the action). Law's analytical and fighting skills quickly won over the skeptics, including his new partners and their boss, Capt. Winship.

When *Martial Law* premiered, Chen Pei Pei, Law's sexy protegée from the Shanghai Police Department, was undercover infiltrating the L.A.-based operations of international criminal Lee Hei (Tzi Ma). After Lee Hei's activities were exposed, Chen was made a member of the L.A.P.D. and started using her American name, Grace Chen. In late November, Sammo's team got a new member, Terrell Parker, an L.A.P.D. press spokesman. He helped them investigate the shooting of his nephew and convinced Winship to let him become a permanent member of the team. Terrell used his street smarts to catch the bad guys and was adept at talking his way out of potentially dangerous situations. He might not have had Sammo's martial-arts skills, but he loved a good fight, and the fast-talking African-American and the inscrutable Asian made quite a team.

There were major cast changes for the second season. Gone were Malone, who had transferred to the N.Y.P.D., and Captain Winship, who had retired. The latter was replaced by Law's new superior, Captain Dylan, the head of an anti-terrorist team in the season premiere who, by episode's end, took over as head of the Major Crimes Unit (M.C.U.). Unfortunately, Dylan and Grace, who were supposed to work together, almost never saw eye to eye. In 2000 a recurring target of the M.C.U. was Scorpio, an international crime cartel that wreaked havoc on a worldwide scale. Ivana Bock was the Scorpio operative who seemed to be involved in all of the nefarious schemes. In the two-part series finale the M.C.U. had a major confrontation with Scorpio, which had developed a computer that caused commercial airliners to crash. As part of the resolution Sammo convinced his son, Shain (Sung Kang), who had been recruited by Scorpio, to change sides.

MARTIN (*Situation Comedy*)
FIRST TELECAST: *August 27, 1992*
LAST TELECAST: *August 28, 1997*
BROADCAST HISTORY:
Aug 1992–Aug 1993, FOX Thu 8:30–9:00
Aug 1993–Jul 1994, FOX Sun 8:00–8:30
Aug 1994–Jul 1995, FOX Thu 8:00–8:30
Aug 1995, FOX Thu 8:30–9:00
Sep 1995–Oct 1995, FOX Sat 8:00–8:30
Nov 1995–Feb 1996, FOX Sun 8:30–9:00
Feb 1996–May 1996, FOX Thu 8:30–9:00
May 1996–Aug 1997, FOX Thu 8:00–8:30
CAST:
Martin Payne . . . . Martin Lawrence
Gina Waters . . . . Tisha Campbell
Cole Brown . . . . Carl Anthony Payne II
Tommy Strong . . . . Thomas Mikal Ford
Pam James . . . . Tichina Arnold
Stan Winters (1992–1994) . . . . Garrett Morris
Shawn (1992–1994) . . . . Jonathan Gries
Sheneneh Jenkins . . . . Martin Lawrence
Gloria Rodriguez (1994) . . . . Angelina Estrada
**Bernice (1994–1995)* . . . . Kymberly S. Newberry
**Nipsey (1994–1997)* . . . . Sean Lampkin
**Tracy (1994–1995)* . . . . Kellita Smith
**Sharice (1994–1995)* . . . . Trish Penix
**Shanise McGillicuddy (1996–1997)*
. . . . Maura McDade
*Occasional

Standup comic Martin Lawrence starred in this comedy that was adapted from a character he did in his act. Martin Payne was a sexist, wisecracking talk-show host on Detroit radio station WZUP. Gina, his girlfriend, was a marketing executive who put up with his attitude because she loved him, although, at times, he could be pretty hard to take. Other series regulars were Pam, Gina's sarcastic secretary, who despised Martin (the feeling was mutual); Cole and Tommy, Martin's buddies, who always seemed to be hanging out at his apartment; Stan, the stylish but arrogant owner of WZUP; Shawn, the station's handyman (and only white character on the show); and Sheneneh, the flashy, loudmouthed bimbo who had the apartment across the hall from Martin's.

In the fall of 1993 Gina moved in with Martin, and in early 1994, despite some problems they were having with each other, they got engaged. At the end of the season the station was sold to a group that changed the format to country music and Martin was fired by the new owner. Despondent, he left Detroit to find himself but returned in the fall and, with Gina's help, got a job as associate producer of "Speak Out," a TV talk show on Channel 51. His new boss was program director Gloria Rodriguez, and Bernice, who found Martin pretty obnoxious, was one of the other producers. Gina had temporarily moved in with Pam, who was getting some romantic attention from Tommy, so Martin could have the apartment to himself until he got back on his financial feet. When he took over as host of the show (retitled "Word on the Street"), she moved back in with him. Early in 1995 both Martin and Tommy got engaged to their girlfriends and in the season finale, Martin was married.

During the 1995–1996 season Pam and Tommy eased back on their involvement and started dating other people, while Martin and Gina adjusted to married life. Campbell bolted the show late in 1996, claiming sexual harassment by Lawrence—in the story line, she was out of town visiting her parents and setting up the West Coast office of her company. Campbell settled her case out of court and appeared in the series' final original episode—although never in the same scene with Lawrence. In the finale, Gina was made executive vice president of the L.A. office, Martin got an offer to host a talk show in L.A., and Cole proposed to his ditsy girlfriend, Shanise.

In April 1997 an episode aired that was actually the

pilot for a proposed spin-off series. Pam, out of work after she was downsized out of her job at Gina's advertising agency, got an A&R job with Keep It Real Records even though she had no experience in the music business. The spin-off series never went into production.

In addition to Martin and Sheneneh, Lawrence also played, among other characters, his mother, Emma; Otis, the security guard; and Jerome, a hippie neighborhood friend.

MARTIN KANE, PRIVATE EYE (*Detective Drama*)

FIRST TELECAST: *September 1, 1949*
LAST TELECAST: *June 17, 1954*
BROADCAST HISTORY:

Sep 1949–Jun 1954, NBC Thu 10:00–10:30 (OS)

CAST:

Martin Kane (1949–1951).......... William Gargan
Martin Kane (1951–1952).............. Lloyd Nolan
Martin Kane (1952–1953)................ Lee Tracy
Martin Kane (1953–1954)............ Mark Stevens
Happy McMann.................... Walter Kinsella
Don Morrow (1954)........................ Himself
Lt. Bender (1949–1950) .... Fred Hillebrand
Capt. Willis (1950–1951) .... Horace McMahon
Sgt. Ross (1950–1952).......... Nicholas Saunders
Capt. Leonard (1951)................ Walter Greaza
Capt. Burke (1951–1952)............ Frank Thomas
Lt. Grey (1952–1954) .... King Calder

This popular, live detective series, which was also heard on radio for several years, underwent several changes of emphasis as well as of cast during its run. William Gargan's original Martin Kane was a smooth, wisecracking operator who worked in close cooperation with the police, an unusual arrangement for TV sleuths. His base of operation was New York, and the crime was usually murder. Later Kanes projected more of a tough-guy image and got less cooperation from the cops, as Lt. Bender gave way to other, more antagonistic officers. In August 1953 the title of the series was shortened to *Martin Kane* and the emphasis shifted to greater mystery and suspense, with less reliance on the somewhat stereotyped situations of earlier seasons.

Throughout most of the run Happy McMann's tobacco shop served as Kane's hangout, and gave him the opportunity to slip in plugs for the sponsor's tobacco products (which included Sano and Encore cigarettes, and Old Briar pipe tobacco). After August 1953 Kane no longer frequented the store, but it remained the setting for the commercials, first by Happy and later (January 1954) by "new owner" Don Morrow.

There was in fact a real Martin Kane. The man who lent his name for use in the show was no sleuth, but an executive with J. Walter Thompson & Co., the advertising agency which produced this series. The real-life Kane later became a senior editor of *Sports Illustrated* magazine and died at the age of 70, in 1977.

Three years after it left the network *Martin Kane* was revived in a syndicated series called *The New Adventures of Martin Kane,* which was sold individually to local stations. In this version Kane was doing his sleuthing in London and sometimes Paris. The title role, ironically enough, was played by William Gargan—the original 1949 Martin Kane.

MARTIN SHORT SHOW, THE (*Situation Comedy*)

FIRST TELECAST: *September 15, 1994*
LAST TELECAST: *September 27, 1994*
BROADCAST HISTORY:

Sep 1994, NBC Thu 8:30–9:00
Sep 1994, NBC Tue 8:30–9:00

CAST:

Marty Short......................... Martin Short
Meg Harper Short...................... Jan Hooks
Caroline Short .... Noley Thornton
Charlie Short .... Zack Duhame
Alice Manoogian.................. Andrea Martin
Gary .... Brian Doyle-Murray

EXECUTIVE PRODUCER:

Martin Short

Sketch comedian Martin Short created this odd combination of character sketches, satire, and standard cute-kids sitcom. Like the old *Jack Benny Show,* it was a show-within-a-show. Marty was seen as the star of his own television comedy/variety hour (where he performed the sketches), lived in a world full of bizarre parodies of famous people, such as Elizabeth Taylor and Sally Jessy Raphael (the satire), and had a raucous home life with wife Meg and youngsters Caroline and Charlie (the cute kids). Alice was an old friend who appeared on his show. Viewers, critics, and NBC did not know what to make of this mishmash, and it had a very short run.

MARTY FELDMAN COMEDY MACHINE, THE (*Comedy/Variety*)

FIRST TELECAST: *April 12, 1972*
LAST TELECAST: *August 16, 1972*
BROADCAST HISTORY:

Apr 1972–Aug 1972, ABC Wed 9:00–9:30

REGULARS:

Marty Feldman
Barbara Feldon
Spike Milligan
Lenny Schultz
Fred Smoot
Thelma Houston
Orson Welles (frequent guest)

Bug-eyed, shaggy-haired British comedian Marty Feldman starred in this fast-paced half-hour of comedy sketches, blackouts, and music.

MARY (*Comedy/Variety*)

FIRST TELECAST: *September 24, 1978*
LAST TELECAST: *October 8, 1978*
BROADCAST HISTORY:

Sep 1978–Oct 1978, CBS Sun 8:00–9:00

REGULARS:

Mary Tyler Moore
Dick Shawn
James Hampton
Swoosie Kurtz
David Letterman
Judy Kahan
Michael Keaton
Tony Stevens Dancers
Alf Clausen Orchestra

After starring in two highly successful situation comedies, *The Dick Van Dyke Show* in the 1960s and *The Mary Tyler Moore Show* in the 1970s, Miss Moore tried unsuccessfully to launch this comedy/variety hour. Relying primarily on a group of repertory players rather than guest stars, much in the manner of the highly successful *Carol Burnett Show, Mary* placed strong emphasis on topical sketch comedy. Frequently referred to, but not seen, was Mary's husband, Grant Tinker, who was also the producer of this show.

The program attracted few viewers and was canceled after only three telecasts; Ms. Moore tried again the following spring with *The Mary Tyler Moore Hour*.

MARY (*Situation Comedy*)
FIRST TELECAST: *December 11, 1985*
LAST TELECAST: *April 8, 1986*
BROADCAST HISTORY:
Dec 1985–Feb 1986, CBS Wed 8:00–8:30
Mar 1986–Apr 1986, CBS Tue 9:00–9:30
CAST:
Mary Brenner.................. Mary Tyler Moore
Frank DeMarco.................. James Farentino
Jo Tucker.......................... Katey Sagal
Ed LaSalle.......................... John Astin
Susan Wilcox.................... Carlene Watkins
Lester Mintz...................... James Tolkan
Vincent Tully........................ David Byrd
Harry Dresden.................. Harold Sylvester
Ronnie Dicker.................. Derek McGrath

More than eight years after the tearful parting of the news staff of WJM-TV in the final episode of *The Mary Tyler Moore Show*, Miss Moore returned to the world of TV sitcoms, again in a news setting. This time she was working for a somewhat sleazy tabloid newspaper, *The Chicago Eagle*. Her character was a divorcée in her 40s who had taken the job at the *Eagle* when the high-fashion magazine for which she worked went out of business. Her "Helpline" column served as a consumer advocate, assisting readers in resolving problems with business and government, often by using the power of the press to cut through red tape. Mary's boss, managing editor Frank DeMarco, emphasized the more exploitive and sensational aspects of the *Eagle*, since that was what sold papers. He was also quite a ladies' man who had an undeniable appeal to Mary, though she was not sure how to deal with that.

Others on the *Eagle* staff included Jo Tucker, the cynical, chain-smoking columnist who sat across from Mary at the office; Ed LaSalle, the rather pompous theater critic; and Tully, the almost-blind copy editor whose job (and he never let you forget it) was protected by the union. On the home front Mary's friend and neighbor was Susan, whose new fiancé, Lester, seemed to have underworld connections.

Mary had its problems. The newspaper was supposed to be called the *Post*, but a lawsuit by the real *Chicago Post*—a small circulation weekly—forced the last-minute name change to the *Eagle*. Despite some positive reviews from columnists, the series did poorly and both its format and time slot were tinkered with. Mary's home life was minimized, and Susan and Lester were dropped from the cast. The changes didn't help, however, and *Mary* failed to survive its first season.

MARY HARTMAN, MARY HARTMAN (*Soap Opera*)
BROADCAST HISTORY:
Syndicated and network late night
30 minutes
Produced: *1975–1978* (325 episodes)
Released: *January 1976*
CAST:
Mary Hartman (1976–1977)......... Louise Lasser
Tom Hartman...................... Greg Mullavey
Martha Shumway................ Dody Goodman
George Shumway (1976–1977)........ Philip Bruns
George Shumway (1977–1978)......... Tab Hunter
Cathy Shumway.................... Debralee Scott
Heather Hartman.................. Claudia Lamb
Raymond Larkin...................... Victor Kilian
Sgt. Dennis Foley (1976–1977)..... Bruce Solomon
Loretta Haggers................... Mary Kay Place
Charlie Haggers..................... Graham Jarvis
Jimmy Joe Jeeter (1976–1977)....... Sparky Marcus
Merle Jeeter...................... Dabney Coleman
Wanda Jeeter....................... Marian Mercer
Garth Gimble (1976–1977)............ Martin Mull
Pat Gimble (1976–1977).......... Susan Browning
Eleanor Major (1977–1978)........ Shelley Fabares
Mac Slattery (1977–1978).......... Dennis Burkley
Harmon Farinella (1977–1978)...... Richard Hatch
Penny Major (1977–1978).............. Judy Kahan
Popesco (1977–1978)............... Severn Darden
Jeffrey DeVito (1977–1978)......... Randall Carver
Mel Beach (1977–1978)............ Shelley Berman
Annabelle (1977–1978)............... Renee Taylor
Reverend Brim (1977–1978)........... Orson Bean
Dr. Szymon (1977–1978).............. James Staley

This was the classic soap opera to satirize all soap operas. Mary Hartman was a "typical American housewife" living in the small town of Fernwood, Ohio. She was totally impressionable and rather slow-witted, with the most significant things in her life coming from television commercials, which she believed totally. One of her early concerns was the prospect of "waxy yellow buildup" on her kitchen floor and how to avoid it. Pigtailed and plain, her life was full of one crisis after another—her father (George Shumway) disappeared, her daughter (Heather) was held hostage by a mass murderer, her husband (Tom) was impotent, and her best friend (aspiring country music singer Loretta Haggers) was paralyzed. Eventually Mary's implacable calm collapsed and she had a nervous breakdown, as well as an affair with local cop Dennis Foley. Mary's grandfather, Raymond Larkin, was known to all as the Fernwood Flasher for his penchant for exposing himself in public; her sister, Cathy, was a local swinger; and her mother, Martha, was decidedly flaky. Tom Hartman was an assembly-line worker at the local automobile plant where he worked with Loretta's husband, Charlie. Jimmy Joe Jeeter was an eight-year-old evangelist whose career was cut short when he was electrocuted by a television set that fell into his bathtub. His father, Merle, was Fernwood's mayor.

Mary Hartman, Mary Hartman was the creation of producer Norman Lear and had been offered to the major networks, all of which rejected it as too controversial. Lear then sold the series to local stations as a syndicated entry in 1976 and had a much-publicized success with it. The novelty of a satirical soap opera attracted many viewers (*Mary Hartman, Mary Hartman* ran after the late local news in most cities). When star Louise Lasser left the show in 1977, it continued for another six months under the title *Forever Fernwood* with most of the original cast intact. However, Tab Hunter took over the role of Martha Shumway's husband George (with the explanation that George had fallen into a chemical vat and been restored with plastic surgery); and new characters included Eleanor Major, Tom Hartman's new love interest; Harmon Farinella, who sought an affair with Loretta Haggers; and Mac, the truck driver. CBS, the network that had first rejected it, aired selected reruns of *Mary Hartman, Mary Hartman* as part of its late-night lineup for a few months in 1980. For details of the late-night network run see *The CBS Late Movie*.

MARY KAY AND JOHNNY (*Situation Comedy*)
FIRST TELECAST: *November 18, 1947*
LAST TELECAST: *March 11, 1950*
BROADCAST HISTORY:
Nov 1947–Dec 1947, DUM Tues 9:00–9:15
Jan 1948–Aug 1948, DUM Tue 7:15–7:30
Oct 1948–Feb 1949, NBC Sun 7:00–7:30
Mar 1949–Jun 1949, CBS Wed 9:00–9:30
Jun 1949–Aug 1949, NBC Mon–Fri 7:15–7:30
Aug 1949–Dec 1949, NBC Thu 8:30–9:00
Jan 1950–Feb 1950, NBC Sat 9:00–9:30
Feb 1950–Mar 1950, NBC Sat 7:30–8:00
CAST:
Mary Kay Stearns .... Herself
Johnny Stearns .... Himself
Howie .... Howard Thomas
Mary Kay's mother .... Nydia Westman
Christopher William Stearns (1949–1950) .. Himself
WRITER:
Johnny Stearns

Live domestic comedy, revolving around young New York newlyweds Mary Kay and Johnny Stearns. She was pretty, pert, and something of a screwball, while he was more serious and always getting her out of various dilemmas. Johnny worked in a bank, but the setting for the action was usually the couple's apartment in Greenwich Village. The Stearns, who were also married in real life, had a baby boy in December 1948, whom they named Christopher. The blessed event was worked into the script and infant Chris was added to the cast less than a month after his birth, appearing in his bassinet. He was surely one of the youngest regular cast members on any show in TV history. Howie was Johnny's best friend, while Nydia Westman played Mary Kay's mother.

In addition to being one of the earliest network situation comedies, the series was notable for its longtime sponsor, Anacin, which even in 1948 was using an outline chart of a human figure with flashing lights to show the product bringing fast, fast relief to every corner of the body.

That sponsors were quite uncertain of the effectiveness of TV at this early stage, however, is illustrated by the following. A few weeks after the program premiered, the sponsor, who had no way of knowing whether anyone was watching (there were no audience ratings), decided to conduct a test by offering a free mirror to the first 200 viewers who wrote in their comments on the program. Just to be safe, the company ordered an extra 200 mirrors so as not to disappoint anyone; 8,960 letters were received!

MARY MARGARET MCBRIDE (*Interview*)
FIRST TELECAST: *September 21, 1948*
LAST TELECAST: *December 14, 1948*
BROADCAST HISTORY:
Sep 1948–Dec 1948, NBC Tue 9:00–9:30
HOSTESS:
Mary Margaret McBride

Interview program featuring the popular radio personality.

MARY TYLER MOORE HOUR, THE (*Comedy/Variety*)
FIRST TELECAST: *March 4, 1979*
LAST TELECAST: *June 10, 1979*
BROADCAST HISTORY:
Mar 1979–Jun 1979, CBS Sun 10:00–11:00
CAST:
Mary McKinnon .... Mary Tyler Moore
Iris Chapman .... Joyce Van Patten
Harry Sinclair .... Michael Lombard
Kenneth Christy .... Michael Keaton
Ruby Bell .... Dody Goodman
Mort Zimmick .... Bobby Ramsen

After the disastrous reception given her initial venture into comedy/variety (see *Mary*), Mary Tyler Moore returned in the spring of 1979 with this program, a hybrid that was part variety show and part situation comedy, using a show-within-a-show format.

Mary McKinnon was the star of a fictional network variety series called *The Mary McKinnon Show*. A versatile singer, dancer, and light comedienne, she had a well-established reputation and a large following. Iris was her personal secretary and companion; Harry, the producer of her show; Mort, its head writer; Kenneth, the ambitious young page; and, Ruby, her maid. Stories revolved around the problems encountered in putting a variety show together, including rehearsals and actual numbers from the show itself. Among her "guest stars," all of whom played themselves, were former CBS series stars Lucille Ball, Beatrice Arthur, Nancy Walker, and Dick Van Dyke, and current series stars Linda Lavin, Bonnie Franklin, and Ken Howard. Mike Douglas, Gene Kelly, and Johnny Mathis also showed up to help.

Unfortunately, despite all these friends, *The Mary Tyler Moore Hour* was no more successful than *Mary* had been, and Miss Moore acknowledged that her forte was, indeed, straight situation comedy. She promised to return to CBS in the fall of 1980 with a new situation comedy, to salvage her by now somewhat tarnished reputation. But instead, she tried Broadway, starring in the play *Who's Life Is It, Anyway?*, for which she won a special Tony Award in 1980, and feature films, winning accolades for her performance in *Ordinary People*.

MARY TYLER MOORE SHOW, THE (*Situation Comedy*)
FIRST TELECAST: *September 19, 1970*
LAST TELECAST: *September 3, 1977*
BROADCAST HISTORY:
Sep 1970–Dec 1971, CBS Sat 9:30–10:00
Dec 1971–Sep 1972, CBS Sat 8:30–9:00
Sep 1972–Oct 1976, CBS Sat 9:00–9:30
Nov 1976–Sep 1977, CBS Sat 8:00–8:30
CAST:
Mary Richards .... Mary Tyler Moore
Lou Grant .... Edward Asner
Ted Baxter .... Ted Knight
Murray Slaughter .... Gavin MacLeod
Rhoda Morgenstern (1970–1974) .... Valerie Harper

Phyllis Lindstrom (1970–1975) . . . Cloris Leachman
Bess Lindstrom (1970–1975) . . . . Lisa Gerritsen
Gordon (Gordy) Howard (1970–1973). . . John Amos
Georgette Franklin Baxter (1973–1977)
. . . . Georgia Engel
Sue Ann Nivens (1973–1977) . . . . Betty White
Marie Slaughter (1971–1977) . . . . Joyce Bulifant
Edie Grant (1973–1974) . . . . Priscilla Morrill
David Baxter (1976–1977) . . . . Robbie Rist

THEME:

"Love Is All Around," sung by Sonny Curtis

The Mary Tyler Moore Show was one of the most literate, realistic, and enduring situation comedies of the 1970s. Unlike the efforts generated by producer Norman Lear, typified by *All in the Family* and *Maude*, there was never a conscious attempt to humiliate or ridicule. Mary Richards was the idealized single career woman. She had come to Minneapolis after breaking up with a man she had been dating for four years. Ambitious, and looking for new friends, she moved into an older apartment building and went to work as an assistant producer of the local news show on television station WJM-TV. In her early 30s, Mary symbolized the independent woman of the 1970s. She would like to find a man and settle down to raise a family, but was not desperately grabbing at any chance for marriage. She would get married, but only if it was the right man. She was warm, loving, and vulnerable, and although it was never bluntly thrown out at the audience, could spend the night with a man she was not madly in love with.

Mary worked for WJM-TV News producer Lou Grant, an irascible, cantankerous, blustery man whose bark was much worse than his bite. Underneath that harsh exterior beat the heart of a pussycat. Lou had problems with his home life as well as his job. During the 1973–1974 season he separated from his wife Edie and they were later divorced. Though it never developed, there was an underlying feeling that he and Mary might have had a serious relationship, if they could have ever really gotten together.

Murray Slaughter was the head newswriter at the station. He was happily married, had a positive outlook no matter what happened, and was a good friend to all. Anchorman on the WJM-TV News was Ted Baxter, not too bright, prone to put his foot in his mouth both on and off the air, and possessor of such a misplaced sense of his own wonderfulness that he was the butt of everyone's jokes. Ted's long courtship of bland, empty-headed, but well-meaning Georgette Franklin culminated in a marriage he was not quite ready to commit himself to in November 1975. The following spring he and Georgette adopted 8-year-old David, and in the fall of 1976 had a baby of their own.

Mary's closest friend was one of her neighbors, Rhoda Morgenstern, a window dresser for a local department store who, like Mary, was still single though in her 30s. Unlike Mary, however, Rhoda was desperately looking for a husband. Unable to find one in Minneapolis, she moved back home to New York City, and to her own series, *Rhoda*, in the fall of 1974. The other neighbor seen frequently in Mary's apartment was Phyllis Lindstrom. Phyllis was the building's resident busybody, and though it took quite a while to find out, also its landlady (her husband Lars, who was talked about but never seen, actually owned the building). Phyllis was oblivious to everyone else's feelings and had an extremely flaky personality. She, too, got her own series when, following Lars's death, she and her daughter Bess moved to San Francisco in the fall of 1975 (see *Phyllis*), and Mary moved into a more luxurious apartment in a high-rise.

As some of the regulars left the series, including WJM-TV's weatherman Gordy Howard, others took up the slack. Sue Ann Nivens arrived at the station in 1973 with her "Happy Homemaker Show," and Georgette's role was expanded. Sue Ann was in her late 40s and extremely man-hungry. She was constantly trying to get every male in sight into the sack, but primarily Lou Grant. Mary was eventually promoted from associate producer to producer as Lou moved to the job of executive producer.

Mary Tyler Moore, who, with her husband Grant Tinker, produced *The Mary Tyler Moore Show*, decided that the series would end in 1977, despite its still-large audience. In the last episode new management took over the station and, in an effort to bolster its weak news ratings, fired virtually the entire staff. Ironically, the one survivor was anchorman Ted Baxter, probably the primary cause for the news' low ratings. There were tearful farewells and everyone went their separate ways.

MASK, THE (*Crime Drama*)

FIRST TELECAST: *January 10, 1954*
LAST TELECAST: *May 16, 1954*
BROADCAST HISTORY:

Jan 1954–May 1954, ABC Sun 8:00–9:00
Mar 1954–Apr 1954, ABC Tue/Wed 8:00–9:00

CAST:

Walter Guilfoyle . . . . Gary Merrill
Peter Guilfoyle . . . . William Prince

Though short-lived, this program was a pioneer in several ways. It was the first hour-long mystery series to feature a continuing cast of characters—and as such was the father of one of the predominant forms on TV today. It was also, during part of its run, repeated twice a week in prime time, in order that viewers who had missed the original live telecast on Sunday night might see the kinescope repeat on Tuesday or Wednesday (at least on those stations which carried all three).

Unfortunately, the content was not as innovative as the format and scheduling. *The Mask* was a routine crime show centering on two brothers who were attorneys and partners in the firm of Guilfoyle & Guilfoyle. Each week they tackled another case, somewhat in the manner of modern Robin Hoods, unmasking assorted gangsters and rescuing helpless victims. Unable to find a sponsor, and quite expensive to produce, *The Mask* was canceled after four months.

MASLAND AT HOME PARTY, see *Earl Wrightson Show, The*

MASQUERADE (*Foreign Intrigue*)

FIRST TELECAST: *December 15, 1983*
LAST TELECAST: *April 27, 1984*
BROADCAST HISTORY:

Dec 1983–Jan 1984, ABC Thu 9:00–10:00
Mar 1984–Apr 1984, ABC Fri 9:00–10:00

CAST:

Lavender . . . . Rod Taylor
Casey Collins . . . . Kirstie Alley
Danny Doyle . . . . Greg Evigan

THEME:

"Masquerade," by Stu Phillips and Marcia Waldorf, sung by Crystal Gayle

The National Intelligence Agency had a problem. Most of its top agents had suddenly been "neutralized" by the KGB, and NIA chief Lavender needed new recruits quickly, with skills as varied as those of a plumber, a diamond expert, a safecracker, and an electronics wizard. So, naturally enough, he recruited a plumber, a diamond dealer, a safecracker, and an electronics wizard—ordinary citizens whom he persuaded to serve their country as spies-for-a-week. Lavender's superiors thought this a bit irregular, but they had little choice, so each week a new group of Americans with diverse skills was pressed into service chasing foreign agents around the globe; this week they might include a dog trainer or race-car driver, next week a baseball star.

Casey and Danny were Lavender's young assistants who helped keep this unusual package tour together and get everyone home safe and sound after their little adventures with poison darts and stilettos in dark alleyways.

MASQUERADE PARTY (*Quiz/Panel*)

FIRST TELECAST: *July 14, 1952*
LAST TELECAST: *September 16, 1960*
BROADCAST HISTORY:

Jul 1952–Aug 1952, NBC Mon 8:00–8:30
Jun 1953–Sep 1953, CBS Mon 9:30–10:00
Jun 1954–Sep 1954, CBS Mon 9:30–10:00
Sep 1954–Jun 1956, ABC Wed 9:00–9:30
Jun 1956–Dec 1956, ABC Sat 10:00–10:30
Mar 1957–Sep 1957, NBC Wed 8:00–8:30
Aug 1958–Sep 1958, CBS Mon 8:30–9:00
Oct 1958–Sep 1959, NBC Thu 10:30–11:00
Oct 1959–Jan 1960, CBS Mon 7:30–8:00
Jan 1960–Sep 1960, NBC Fri 9:30–10:00

MODERATOR:

Bud Collyer (1952)
Douglas Edwards (1953)
Peter Donald (1954–1956)
Eddie Bracken (1957)
Robert Q. Lewis (1958)
Bert Parks (1958–1960)

PANELISTS:

Peter Donald (1952–1953)
Ilka Chase (1952–1957)
John S. Young (1952)
Madge Evans (1952)
Buff Cobb (1953–1955)
Ogden Nash (1953–1957)
Bobby Sherwood (1954–1957)
Dagmar (1955–1956)
Mary Healy (1955–1956)
Betsy Palmer (1956–1957)
Frank Parker (1957)
Johnny Johnston (1957–1958)
Jonathan Winters (1958)
Jinx Falkenburg (1958)
Pat Carroll (1958)
Audrey Meadows (1958–1960)
Lee Bowman (1958–1960)
Faye Emerson (1958–1960)
Sam Levenson (1958–1960)

Well-known celebrities were disguised in elaborate costumes and makeup when they appeared as contestants on *Masquerade Party*. The costume was designed to serve as a clue to the panelists, who questioned the contestants in an attempt to determine their real identities. Any prize money won by contestants was donated to their favorite charities. When contestants answered the panelists' questions, they did so through a special microphone which also disguised their voices. On the air through nine seasons, *Masquerade Party* went through six moderators and a total of 19 regular panelists.

Richard Dawson moderated a syndicated revival of *Masquerade Party* during the 1974–1975 season. Regular panelists were Bill Bixby, Lee Meriwether, and Nipsey Russell.

MASTER, THE (*Adventure/Drama*)

FIRST TELECAST: *January 20, 1984*
LAST TELECAST: *August 31, 1984*
BROADCAST HISTORY:

Jan 1984–Feb 1984, NBC Fri 9:00–10:00
Mar 1984–Aug 1984, NBC Fri 8:00–9:00

CAST:

John Peter McAllister .... Lee Van Cleef
Max Keller .... Timothy Van Patten
Okasa .... Sho Kosugi

Stealth and hand-to-hand violence were the hallmarks of this short-lived series. While stationed in Japan as an air force colonel after World War II, John Peter McAllister had become fascinated with the Ninja—a secret and now outlawed society of warriors trained in the martial arts. He entered the sect, and in time became a Ninja Master, the only Westerner ever to do so. When younger members of the sect began to use their deadly skills for evil ends, McAllister left for America, violating his sacred oath never to leave the Ninja. Here he met young Max Keller, a footloose adventurer, and the two of them set out in Max's van, searching for McAllister's long-lost daughter and righting wrongs they encountered along the way. Hard on their heels were deadly Ninja assassins, led by Okasa, after McAllister; but the aging Master, who had trained many of them, dispatched them all with cunning, swift blows, and a variety of exotic weapons such as razor-sharp little wheels that were thrown at the assailant, tiny smoke bombs, and a hand device to ward off blows.

MASTER OF THE GAME (*Drama*)

FIRST TELECAST: *June 6, 1987*
LAST TELECAST: *June 27, 1987*
BROADCAST HISTORY:

Jun 1987, CBS Sat 8:00–10:00

CAST:

Kate Blackwell .... Dyan Cannon
Tony Blackwell .... Harry Hamlin
Jamie McGregor .... Ian Charleson
Brad Rogers .... Cliff DeYoung
George Mellis .... Fernando Allende
David Blackwell .... David Birney
Eve/Alexandra Blackwell .... Liane Langland
Salomon Van der Merwe .... Donald Pleasence
Margaret Van der Merwe .... Cherie Lunghi
Mrs. Talley .... Jean Marsh
Dr. Harley .... Barry Morse
Banda .... Johnny Sekka
Marianne .... Angharad Rees

Dominique .... Maryam d'Abo
D'Usseau .... David Suchet
Solange .... Leslie Caron
McMillan .... Alan Dobie

Adapted from author Sidney Sheldon's best-selling novel of the same name, *Master of the Game* originally aired as a nine-hour mini-series in February 1984. CBS reran it as a weekly series in the summer of 1987.

The central figure of *Master of the Game* was Kate Blackwell, the matriarch who had been a young girl when her father, Jamie McGregor, moved the family to South Africa in the 1880s to seek his fortune in the diamond mines. His success, overcoming the machinations of greedy Boer merchant Salomon Van der Merwe, provided the foundation for what became Kruger-Brent, Ltd. Over the next 70 years, under Jamie's and then Kate's dynamic leadership, the company grew prosperous and powerful. Despite her financial success, Kate's failure to establish a family dynasty made her life incomplete. The disagreements, hostilities, and catastrophes that befell her husband, David, her son, Tony, her beautiful twin granddaughters, Eve and Alexandra, her valued assistant, Brad Rogers, and their assorted friends, enemies, lovers, and associates, were all chronicled in this sprawling dramatization that moved from the dirty diamond mines of South Africa to the artsy sections of Paris in the 1940s to the contemporary corporate splendor of Manhattan.

MASTERPIECE PLAYHOUSE (*Dramatic Anthology*)

FIRST TELECAST: *July 23, 1950*
LAST TELECAST: *September 3, 1950*
BROADCAST HISTORY:
Jul 1950–Sep 1950, NBC Sun 9:00–10:00

Live productions of seven great classics (Ibsen's *Hedda Gabler*, Shakespeare's *Richard III*, etc.), telecast during the summer of 1950. The plays were immaculately produced and used the top talent available to television in those days. Among those appearing were Jessica Tandy, William Windom, and Boris Karloff.

MASTERS OF ILLUSION (*Magic*)

FIRST TELECAST: *October 2, 2000*
LAST TELECAST: *October 28, 2000*
BROADCAST HISTORY:
Oct 2000, PAX Mon 8:00–9:00
Oct 2000, PAX Sat 8:00–9:00
HOST:
Franz Harary

Structured like a variety series, with most of the acts taped before a live studio audience, *Masters of Illusion* provided viewers a weekly potpourri of magic. There were escape artists, disappearances, card magicians, mentalists, hand tricks, etc. A regular feature was the "slow motion challenge" in which a trick was replayed in slow motion and the audience still couldn't figure out how it was done.

MASTERS OF MAGIC (*Magic*)

FIRST TELECAST: *February 16, 1949*
LAST TELECAST: *May 11, 1949*
BROADCAST HISTORY:
Feb 1949–May 1949, CBS Wed 7:45–8:00
HOST:
André Baruch

This live series, which filled the remainder of the half hour in which CBS aired its network news program, gave famous magicians the opportunity to dazzle the viewing audience, and host André Baruch, with their feats of magic.

MATCH GAME P.M. (*Quiz/Panel*)

BROADCAST HISTORY:
Syndicated and network daytime
30 minutes
Produced: *1975–1982*
Released: *September 1975*
EMCEE:
Gene Rayburn
PANELISTS:
Richard Dawson (1975–1978)
Brett Somers
Charles Nelson Reilly
Betty White
Fannie Flagg
Dick Martin
Richard Paul

This popular game show featured a heavy dose of celebrities and double-entendre questions. A panel of six (count 'em!) celebrities appeared along with two contestants, who won if their answers to the leering questions asked by emcee Gene Rayburn matched those of the panel. Richard Dawson, Brett Somers, and Charles Nelson Reilly were virtual regulars on the panel, joined frequently by the others listed above.

Match Game aired as a daytime series on NBC from 1962 to 1969, and on CBS from 1973 to 1979. It was revived again as part of *The Match Game–Hollywood Squares Hour* on NBC from October 1983 to July 1984. Gene Rayburn was the emcee on all versions.

When ABC resurrected *The Match Game* as part of its weekday daytime lineup in July 1990, Ross Shafer was the emcee. The ABC version ran for exactly one year. It was revived again, in syndication, for the 1998–1999 season with Michael Berger as the emcee.

MATLOCK (*Legal Drama*)

FIRST TELECAST: *September 20, 1986*
LAST TELECAST: *September 7, 1995*
BROADCAST HISTORY:
Sep 1986, NBC Sat 10:00–11:00
Sep 1986–Sep 1991, NBC Tue 8:00–9:00
Oct 1991–Aug 1992, NBC Fri 8:00–9:00
Jan 1993–Feb 1993, ABC Thu 8:00–9:00
Feb 1993–May 1993, ABC Thu 8:00–10:00
May 1993–Jul 1993, ABC Thu 8:00–9:00
Jul 1993–Jun 1994, ABC Thu 9:00–10:00
Jul 1994, ABC Thu 8:00–10:00
Aug 1994, ABC Thu 8:00–9:00
Oct 1994–Jan 1995, ABC Thu 9:00–10:00
Feb 1995, ABC Thu 8:00–9:00
Apr 1995, ABC Thu 8:00–9:00
Jul 1995–Sep 1995, ABC Thu 8:00–9:00
CAST:
Benjamin L. Matlock .... Andy Griffith
Charlene Matlock (1986–1987) .... Linda Purl
Tyler Hudson (1986–1989) .... Kene Holliday
Michelle Thomas (1987–1992) ..... Nancy Stafford
Cassie Phillips (1987–1988) .... Kari Lizer
Asst. D.A. Julie March (1987–1992) ... Julie Sommars
**D.A. Lloyd Burgess (1986–1990)* ... Michael Durrell
Lt. Bob Brooks (1986–1990) .... David Froman

**Judge Irene Sawyer (1986–1989)* .... Lucille Meredith
**Judge Richard Cooksey (1986–1990)*
.... Richard Newton
**Les Calhoun (1988–1990)* .... Don Knotts
Conrad McMaster (1989–1993)
.... Clarence Gilyard, Jr.
Leanne McIntyre (1993–1995) .... Brynn Thayer
Cliff Lewis (1993–1995) .... Daniel Roebuck
**Billy Lewis (1993–1995)* .... Warren Frost
Jerri Stone (1994–1995) .... Carol Huston

*Occasional

Andy Griffith brought his patented "cagey Southerner" portrayal back to TV in this murder-mystery series about an unassuming, but very canny, Harvard-educated lawyer. Ben Matlock was one of the top defense attorneys in Atlanta, and for good reason; like Perry Mason, he always seemed to prove his client innocent, often with some Mason-esque last-minute courtroom revelation. Helping out were his daughter, Charlene, a lawyer, and Tyler, a black stock market whiz whom Matlock kept luring away to do his legwork. When a case bogged down Ben would repair to his handsome, 100-year-old stone house in Willow Springs, Georgia, where he would strum his banjo and ponder clues. Mayberry was not far away, in spirit at least.

Ben Matlock proved to have long-term popularity with older viewers, running for six seasons on NBC and then moving to ABC. Ben's supporting characters were not so lucky, as they showed considerable turnover. Charlene was replaced by Michelle, who gave way to Leanne (who also was Ben's daughter). Ben's legmen were Tyler, then Conrad, then Cliff. Others seen for varying periods during later seasons were eager law clerk Cassie, pesky neighbor Les (played by Don Knotts, Andy's old friend from *The Andy Griffith Show*), Cliff's eccentric dad Billy, investigator Jerri, and an assortment of judges and officials. A number of episodes were made in a two-hour format.

MATRIX (*Supernatural Drama*)

BROADCAST HISTORY:
USA Network
60 minutes
Produced: *1992–1993* (13 episodes)
Premiered: *March 1, 1993*

CAST:
Steven Matrix .... Nick Mancuso
Billy Hicks .... Phil Jarrett
Liz Teel .... Carrie-Anne Moss

Steven Matrix was a steely-eyed professional hit man who took a bullet in the head one day, died, and went to . . . no, not there, but to a eerie Kafkaesque place called The City In-Between. There he was given an interesting choice: eternal damnation or returning to Earth to help others in deadly jams. Grudgingly he chose the latter, and with the help of black sidekick Billy and the occasionally seen Liz, who managed his gym, the Silver Flex, he became a sort of dark and violent version of Michael Landon in *Highway to Heaven*. Mysterious "guides" from the City provided him with cryptic clues along the way. Although Matrix did manage to right wrongs, including some of his own making, he did not find much of an audience, and after 13 episodes he reverted (presumably) to choice number one.

MATT DENNIS SHOW, THE (*Music*)

FIRST TELECAST: *June 27, 1955*
LAST TELECAST: *August 29, 1955*
BROADCAST HISTORY:
Jun 1955–Aug 1955, NBC Mon/Wed/Fri 7:30–7:45

REGULAR:
Matt Dennis

Versatile singer, composer, and pianist Matt Dennis was the host and star of this summertime musical interlude. Backing Dennis on many of his own hits ("Let's Get Away From It All," "Angel Eyes") was a small, jazz-flavored combo. Guest stars were featured occasionally.

MATT HELM (*Detective Drama*)

FIRST TELECAST: *September 20, 1975*
LAST TELECAST: *January 3, 1976*
BROADCAST HISTORY:
Sep 1975–Jan 1976, ABC Sat 10:00–11:00

CAST:
Matt Helm .... Anthony Franciosa
Claire Kronski .... Laraine Stephens
Sgt. Hanrahan .... Gene Evans
Ethel .... Jeff Donnell

Matt Helm was another of the swinging, wisecracking detectives who proliferated during TV's second and third decades. This one was based in Los Angeles (where else?), lived the good life with a fancy foreign sports car and a sexy girlfriend—attorney (Claire)—and took on only "high-level" cases around the world. The series certainly had an opulent look, with a posh bachelor pad provided for Matt and much of the outside filming done at private estates around Southern California. Sgt. Hanrahan was the somewhat less highly paid police contact (who nevertheless dined with Matt at the best restaurants), and Ethel the answering-service operator. It was, according to the producer, pure escapist fare.

Based on an extensive collection of detective novels by Donald Hamilton and several movies with Dean Martin in the title role.

MATT HOUSTON (*Detective Drama*)

FIRST TELECAST: *September 26, 1982*
LAST TELECAST: *July 19, 1985*
BROADCAST HISTORY:
Sep 1982–Aug 1983, ABC Sun 8:00–9:00
Sep 1983–Jun 1984, ABC Fri 10:00–11:00
Aug 1984–Mar 1985, ABC Fri 10:00–11:00
May 1985–Jul 1985, ABC Fri 10:00–11:00

CAST:
Matlock (Matt) Houston .... Lee Horsley
C. J. Parsons .... Pamela Hensley
**Murray Chase* .... George Wyner
Lt. Vince Novelli (1982–1983) .... John Aprea
Mama Novelli (1982–1983) .... Penny Santon
Bo (1982–1983) .... Dennis Fimple
Lamar Pettybone (1982–1983) .... Paul Brinegar
Chris (1982–1984) .... Cis Rundle
Det. Lt. Michael Hoyt (1983–1985)
.... Lincoln Kilpatrick
Roy Houston (1984–1985)............ Buddy Ebsen

*Occasional

ABC described *Matt Houston* as a "stylish, glamorous action/adventure series packed with beautiful women, stunning sets, and freewheeling adventure . . ." In other words, your standard TV adventure show. In this case the handsome private eye was a millionaire's son who had managed his father's oil business in Texas, then moved to California to handle the family's off-shore drilling operations. They didn't seem to require much attention, so Matt spent his time on his favorite hobby: detective work. Murray, his business partner, complained that Matt's sleuthing didn't make enough money to cover the $500 license fee, but super-rich Matt didn't care. Constantly surrounded by beautiful women, including his gorgeous Harvard-trained lawyer C.J., piloting his own private helicopter to and from his opulent penthouse, or racing around in sexy cars like his cream-colored Excalibur (later a more sedate Mercedes 380SL convertible), Matt evidently found other rewards in the work.

A slightly more down-to-earth flavor was added during the first season by friendly Lt. Novelli and his mom, who never failed to invite Matt in to sample her Italian cooking, as well as Bo and Lamar, two quarreling cowboys who came along from Matt's Texas ranch to help Matt out. Matt's father, Bill, even showed up a couple of times (played by David Wayne). Hominess was out in the second season, however, as Matt turned over his fabulously successful business enterprises to Murray and devoted himself full time to detective work, this time with Lt. Hoyt as his much less cooperative police adversary. Matt's cases usually involved the rich and famous, sometimes with a bizarre twist such as the murdered gourmet found encased in a mold of orange gelatin, or the killer robot, or the beautiful female lifeguards being killed off by a shark.

In the fall of 1984 Matt's uncle Roy, a successful detective in his day, came out of retirement to work with his nephew, C.J., and "Baby" (the nickname for the high-tech computer C.J. accessed to locate information needed in their cases).

MATT LINCOLN (*Medical Drama*)
FIRST TELECAST: *September 24, 1970*
LAST TELECAST: *January 14, 1971*
BROADCAST HISTORY:
Sep 1970–Jan 1971, ABC Thu 7:30–8:30
CAST:
Dr. Matt Lincoln .... Vince Edwards
Tag .... Chelsea Brown
Kevin .... Michael Larrain
Jimmy .... Felton Perry
Ann .... June Harding

Matt Lincoln was one of the youthful "relevance" dramas of the early 1970s. Vince Edwards (ex-*Ben Casey*) starred as a hip young psychiatrist who founded and ran a center-city telephone-assistance service for troubled teenagers. His helpers at Hotline were Tag and Jimmy, two equally hip young blacks; Ann; and Kevin, a cynical cop. As if Hotline didn't get him enough points, Matt also headed a walk-in clinic for those too poor to pay. His own life completed the picture: sports car, bachelor pad at the beach, and a small sailboat. The stories of these beautiful young people, and those they tried to help, formed the plots.

MATT WATERS (*High School Drama*)
FIRST TELECAST: *January 3, 1996*
LAST TELECAST: *February 7, 1996*
BROADCAST HISTORY:
Jan 1996–Feb 1996, CBS Wed 9:00–10:00
CAST:
Matt Waters .... Montel Williams
Nicole Moore .... Kristen Wilson
Charlie Sweet .... Sam McMurray
Flea Decker .... Richard Chevolleau
Angela Perez .... Cyndi Cartagena
Russ Achoa .... Felix A. Pire
Jack Tisdale .... Nathaniel Marston
Chloe Drescher .... Amy Hargreaves
Bob Prysybilski .... Glenn Fitzgerald
T .... Yancey Arias

Matt Waters had just retired after a twenty-year career in the navy to take a job as a science teacher at Bayview High School in Bayonne, New Jersey, the school he had attended 25 years before. Returning home after his brother had been killed in a gang-related murder, Matt found things far different than he remembered them. The armed security guards and metal detectors in the school were a constant reminder of how tough things had become. Matt believed in discipline and respect and took an aggressive approach to teaching—in the premiere, he hung one of his students out the window of the classroom by his ankles to make a point. As he was learning to deal with contemporary students, he got useful advice from his old friend Charlie, one of Bayview's gym teachers, and Nicole, a pretty African studies teacher who was the younger sister of a woman he had dated in his youth. Among his students were Flea, a bright kid tempted to join a local gang; Jack, a football player being abused by his parents at home; Angela, who worked after school to help her family and tried to hide her illiteracy; Russ, Angela's gay best friend; and Chloe, whose wealthy parents were too preoccupied with their own lives to get involved with their daughter's.

Matt Waters was filmed on location in New Jersey so that star Montel Williams could maintain the production schedule of his New York–based syndicated talk show *The Montel Williams Show*.

MATTY'S FUNDAY FUNNIES (*Cartoon*)
FIRST TELECAST: *September 30, 1960*
LAST TELECAST: *December 29, 1962*
BROADCAST HISTORY:
Sep 1960–Sep 1961, ABC Fri 7:30–8:00
Oct 1961–Dec 1962, ABC Sat 7:00–7:30
CARTOONIST:
Bob Clampett (for *Beany and Cecil*)

Matty's Funday Funnies was first seen on Sunday afternoons in October 1959, sponsored by the Mattel Toy Co. and "hosted" by cartoon characters Matty and Sisterbelle. The cartoons most frequently seen were those featuring Casper the Friendly Ghost, Little Audrey, Herman the Mouse, Catnip, Tommy the Tortoise, and Buzzy the Crow. Generally two or three cartoons were seen in each half-hour program.

In 1960 the series moved to nighttime television. Then in January 1962 the early characters were dropped and the series became *Matty's Funnies with Beany and Cecil*, starring the familiar characters of Bob Clampett's *Time for Beany* puppet show (which had been in syndication since the early 1950s). This time Beany and his friends were in cartoon form. Beany was the little boy with a big grin and a cap with a propeller on top. He sailed the seven seas with Capt. Huffenpuff on the *Leakin' Lena*, and his best friend was Cecil the Seasick Sea Serpent. Together they had adventures all over the world (and sometimes out of it), encountering such characters as the villainous Dishonest John, Homer the Octopus, Tear-a-Long the Dotted Lion (get it?), Careless the Mexican Hairless, and many others. Cartoonist Clampett always was fond of puns! He also developed his characters with an intelligence and wit that had made *Beany and Cecil* a favorite of many adults, including such diverse fans as Lionel Barrymore and Groucho Marx.

After the first three months the program's title was shortened to simply *Beany and Cecil*. Following its prime-time run during 1962 the show continued on ABC at other times of the day until 1967. *Beany and Cecil* returned to ABC's Saturday morning lineup for the first two months of the 1988–1989 season.

MAUDE (*Situation Comedy*)

FIRST TELECAST: *September 12, 1972*
LAST TELECAST: *April 29, 1978*
BROADCAST HISTORY:

Sep 1972–Sep 1974, CBS Tue 8:00–8:30
Sep 1974–Sep 1975, CBS Mon 9:00–9:30
Sep 1975–Sep 1976, CBS Mon 9:30–10:00
Sep 1976–Sep 1977, CBS Mon 9:00–9:30
Sep 1977–Nov 1977, CBS Mon 9:30–10:00
Dec 1977–Jan 1978, CBS Mon 9:00–9:30
Jan 1978–Apr 1978, CBS Sat 9:30–10:00

CAST:

Maude Findlay .... Beatrice Arthur
Walter Findlay .... Bill Macy
Carol .... Adrienne Barbeau
Phillip (1972–1977) .... Brian Morrison
Phillip (1977–1978) .... Kraig Metzinger
Dr. Arthur Harmon .... Conrad Bain
Vivian Cavender Harmon .... Rue McClanahan
Florida Evans (1972–1974) .... Esther Rolle
Henry Evans (1973–1974) .... John Amos
Chris (1973–1974) .... Fred Grandy
Mrs. Nell Naugatuck (1974–1977) .... Hermoine Baddeley
Bert Beasley (1975–1977) .... J. Pat O'Malley
Victoria Butterfield (1977–1978) . Marlene Warfield

PRODUCER:

Norman Lear

Maude was the first spin-off from producer Norman Lear's enormously successful comedy, *All in the Family*. Edith Bunker's cousin Maude was upper-middle-class, liberal, and extremely outspoken—a perfect counterpoint to Archie Bunker's blustering, hard-hat bigotry. The character became so popular that in the fall of 1972 Maude was given a series of her own—and it soon became almost as big a hit as *All in the Family* itself.

Maude lived in suburban Tuckahoe, New York, with her fourth husband, Walter, owner of Findlay's Friendly Appliances. Living with them was Carol, Maude's divorced, 27-year-old daughter, and Carol's 9-year-old son, Phillip.

Even though much of the comedy centered on Maude's determination to represent the independent, even dominant, woman, she herself always had a female servant in the house. In fact, during the course of the series, she ran through three of them. Maude's first maid was Florida, a bright, witty black woman who left early in 1974 to star in her own program, *Good Times*. (Her husband, Henry, was renamed James in *Good Times*, even though the same actor continued in the role.) Florida was succeeded by a cynical, hard-drinking Englishwoman, Mrs. Naugatuck. Mrs. Naugatuck was never as popular with viewers as Florida had been, and after marrying Bert Beasley in November 1976 she left the show, ostensibly to return to the British Isles. Her replacement was Victoria Butterfield, who joined the Findlay household in the fall of 1977.

The Findlays' next-door neighbor, and Walter's best friend, was Dr. Arthur Harmon. When the series began Arthur was a widower, but he subsequently began dating Maude's best friend, Vivian (who had just been divorced), and in February 1974 they were married. Everyone on this show seemed to be either married or getting married, except for Maude's daughter Carol. She came close with boyfriend Chris in 1974, but that didn't work out and he soon disappeared from the cast.

Although this was a comedy show, the subject matter was often on the serious side. During the run, Maude became involved in politics, had a face lift, had an abortion (which drew heavy viewer protest mail), and went through menopause. Walter went through a severe bout with alcoholism, saw his store go bankrupt, and had a nervous breakdown. *Maude* could be very funny, but in its efforts to be realistic, it could also be controversial and sometimes depressing. Yet for several seasons viewers made it one of the top programs on television.

Finally in 1977–1978 the audience began to decline, and some major cast changes were planned for the next season. The Harmons and Carol were to move out of town, and Walter was to retire from the appliance business. Maude would begin a career in politics, with a new supporting cast. But early in 1978 Bea Arthur announced that she was leaving the series. The producers candidly admitted that no one else could play the role as she had, and so after six years *Maude* ended its run.

The political career that had been planned for Maude was used as the basis for another proposed series—one that had a very rocky history. See *Hanging In* for details.

MAVERICK (*Western*)

FIRST TELECAST: *September 22, 1957*
LAST TELECAST: *July 8, 1962*
BROADCAST HISTORY:

Sep 1957–Sep 1961, ABC Sun 7:30–8:30
Sep 1961–Jul 1962, ABC Sun 6:30–7:30

CAST:

Bret Maverick (1957–1960) .... James Garner
Bart Maverick .... Jack Kelly
Samantha Crawford (1958–1959) .. Diane Brewster
Cousin Beauregard Maverick (1960–1961) .... Roger Moore
Brent Maverick (1961) .... Robert Colbert

In the days when dozens of staunch TV heroes were chasing lawbreakers in every corner of the Old West, this program was indeed a maverick—a Western with a sense of humor. It didn't start out that way. For the first few episodes *Maverick* was a fairly straight series about a dapper cardsharp and his adventures on the frontier. Then a bored scriptwriter slipped in some stage directions for star James Garner to look at someone "with his beady little eyes." Garner thought this great fun, and played the scene for laughs. It worked, and soon the whole series was moving toward a satirical orientation. Wisecracking ladies' man Bret was joined by a fairly straight brother, Bart, in November 1957, to keep the series from straying too far from the traditional Western mold (and indeed the series could always be enjoyed as a straight Western). But neither of the Brothers Maverick was really a hero in the usual sense. They would just as soon slip quietly out of town as face a gunman in an impending showdown; they were usually honest in poker (unless they were dealing); and Bret, in particular, handled a gun rather ineptly.

Bret and Bart alternated as leads, and sometimes appeared together, but Bret clearly had the juicier role and was more visible. Their exploits took them to frontier towns like Hounddog, Apocalypse, and Oblivion, and sometimes out of the country entirely, as when Bret sailed to the South Pacific to inspect an island. Occasionally appearing were Bart's friends Dandy Jim Buckley (played by Efrem Zimbalist, Jr.) and Gentleman Jack Darby (Richard Long). During the second season Bret had a running feud with Samantha Crawford, a pretty slick operator in her own right, to see who could out-con whom. And he would always remind listeners of the advice given him by his "pappy," who said that in the face of overwhelming odds, run. (Pappy, often referred to, actually showed up in one episode, played by Garner!)

Among the high points of *Maverick* were the periodic satires of other TV shows, Western and non-Western alike, such as a takeoff on *Gunsmoke* and another on *Dragnet* (in which Bret intoned a narration in deadpan Joe Friday style). Perhaps the best was a wild parody on *Bonanza*, in which Bart encountered a ranching baron named Joe Wheelwright (played by Jim Backus), owner of the vast Subrosa Ranch, who was trying to marry off his three idiot sons Moose (Hoss), Henry (Adam), and Small Paul (Little Joe). On still another show Bart, in trouble as usual, ran into Clint *(Cheyenne)* Walker, John Russell and his deputy Peter Brown *(Lawman)*, Will *(Sugarfoot)* Hutchins, Ty *(Bronco)* Hardin, and Edd "Kookie" Byrnes, all in one episode. None of them were of any help whatever!

James Garner was a maverick offscreen as well as on. In 1960 he walked out on Warner Bros. Studios, demanding a better contract. In a virtual replay of the confrontation between Warner Bros. and Clint Walker two years before (see *Cheyenne*), the studio refused to give in, and instead hired a new actor to replace him. Enter Cousin Beau Maverick, who was introduced as an expatriate Texan who had fought with valor in the Civil War (unusual behavior for a Maverick), then moved to England, and now returned as a cultured Englishman to further the family fortunes in America.

Unlike the situation in *Cheyenne*, James Garner never did return to *Maverick*. In December 1960 a court ruled that he could not be held to his contract, and he left Warner Bros. Cousin Beau and Bart alternated for the rest of the 1960–1961 season, and in the spring of 1961 still another brother, Brent Maverick, was tried out to see if he could fill Garner's shoes. None of this worked out very well, so in 1961–1962, the final season, Bart was seen alone, together with a healthy quantity of reruns of earlier episodes starring Bret and the two brothers together.

MAX HEADROOM (*Science Fiction*)

FIRST TELECAST: *March 31, 1987*
LAST TELECAST: *October 16, 1987*
BROADCAST HISTORY:

Mar 1987–May 1987, ABC Tue 10:00–11:00
Aug 1987–Oct 1987, ABC Fri 9:00–10:00

CAST:

Edison Carter/Max Headroom .... Matt Frewer
Theora Jones .... Amanda Pays
Ben Cheviot .... George Coe
Bryce Lynch .... Chris Young
Murray .... Jeffrey Tambor
Blank Reg .... William Morgan Sheppard
Dominique .... Concetta Tomei
Ashwell .... Hank Garrett
Edwards .... Lee Wilkof
Lauren .... Sharon Barr
Ms. Formby .... Virginia Kiser

While this unusual series was not a hit, it certainly showed that TV in the '80s had not lost its ability to innovate—or to make fun of itself. The setting was a rather grim futuristic era where television was everywhere, even built into the sides of trash cans in the slums. In fact, it was illegal to turn it off. There were thousands of stations, all vying for viewers; this was the ultimate consumerist society, and advertisers (mostly Japanese, it seemed) ruled the airwaves. "Ratings" were everything, and were reported every second. Any program that started to slip was canceled immediately!

Max Headroom was the ultimate star of this video age, a computer-generated character who popped on to screens at the oddest times, making sarcastic comments about his human creators' foibles. He belonged to top-rated Channel 23, and was created by its brilliant research head Bryce (a young boy!), who had modeled him after ace reporter Edison Carter. Unfortunately Bryce had not yet worked out all the kinks—Max looked a little angular, moved with jerky motions, and spoke with a distinct stutter. But, like Edison, Max had a mind of his own.

Most episodes had Edison chasing around the cold, cruel city to expose the corruption and crime that was evidently rampant. Armed with a powerful minicam (hand-held TV camera) he could uplink into the network from anywhere and go live nationwide, in between (or during) shootouts, druggings, and explosions. Back at the control room his beautiful assistant, Theora, monitored his movements from a computer console, while Bryce tried to work out bugs in the all-pervasive computer system, and keep butt-in Max out of the way. Ben Cheviot was the generally supportive head of Channel 23, who sat with the other bosses around a huge oak table in a darkened room staring at a giant screen, on which an advertiser would sometimes appear saying "your ratings have started to slip in the last few minutes . . . get them back up or else, Mr. Cheviot." Then Murray, the newsroom director (do we detect a hint of *The Mary Tyler Moore Show*'s newsroom here?), would fight to get Edison just a little more time to crack the latest scandal wide open.

Edison's chief rivals and sometime allies in the field were Blank Reg and his partner, Dominique, who ran a scruffy underground channel which lacked the power and money of Channel 23, but made up for that with ruthless aggressiveness.

The character of Max Headroom was originally

conceived by producer Peter Wagg for a 1984 British TV movie starring actor Frewer, and spread to the U.S. via the Cinemax cable network (doing an interview show) and heavy use in Coca-Cola commercials.

MAX LIEBMAN PRESENTS (*Musical Variety*)

FIRST TELECAST: *September 12, 1954*

LAST TELECAST: *June 6, 1956*

BROADCAST HISTORY:

Sep 1954–Jun 1956, NBC Sat 9:00–10:30 (OS)
Sep 1954–Jun 1955, NBC Sun 7:30–9:00

In the early 1950s Max Liebman had produced *Your Show of Shows*, one of the most popular variety shows on television. When that series left the air in 1954, Liebman continued to produce lavish variety programming for NBC. His specials aired roughly once every four weeks—for two seasons on Saturday nights in the same time period previously occupied by *Your Show of Shows* and, during 1954–1955, on Sunday nights as well. The Saturday editions of *Max Liebman Presents* were primarily musical comedies. Included among them were *Lady in the Dark* starring Ann Sothern and Paul McGrath; *Best Foot Forward* starring Jeannie Carson, Robert Cummings, and Marilyn Maxwell; *Babes in Toyland* starring Dave Garroway, Dennis Day, Jack E. Leonard, and Wally Cox; *The Merry Widow* starring Anne Jeffreys, Brian Sullivan, Edward Everett Horton, and John Conte; and *Heidi* starring Jeannie Carson, Wally Cox, Elsa Lanchester, and Natalie Wood. The Sunday episodes of *Max Liebman Presents* were musical revues. Among the performers starring in the revues were Judy Holliday, Steve Allen, Dick Shawn, Jimmy Durante, Perry Como, Pat Carroll, Buddy Hackett, Milton Berle, Martha Raye, Ray Bolger, and Frank Sinatra. The dance team of Bambi Linn and Rod Alexander, which had been featured on *Your Show of Shows*, appeared regularly on *Max Liebman Presents*, and Charles Sanford's Orchestra, which had provided the music on Liebman's earlier series, was also used often.

MAX MONROE: LOOSE CANNON (*Police Drama*)

FIRST TELECAST: *January 5, 1990*

LAST TELECAST: *April 19, 1990*

BROADCAST HISTORY:

Jan 1990, CBS Fri 8:00–9:00
Apr 1990, CBS Thu 9:00–10:00

CAST:

Det. Max Monroe .... Shadoe Stevens
Det. Charlie Ivers .... Bruce A. Young

Short-lived series about an unconventional but naturally effective Los Angeles police detective. Max was a brilliant but eccentric cop who was always in trouble with his superiors on the force. He was not above stretching the letter of the law to get his man, went undercover as everything from a sleazy lawyer to a monk, and was famous for the bills he had run up for destroying police cars and other property. Working with him was his long-suffering but loyal partner, Charlie Ivers. Conservative Charlie may not have approved of Max's methods, which often got him in almost as much trouble as his partner, but he had no complaints about the results.

MAXIMUM BOB (*Legal Comedy/Drama*)

FIRST TELECAST: *August 6, 1998*

LAST TELECAST: *September 15, 1998*

BROADCAST HISTORY:

Aug 1998–Sep 1998, ABC Thu 10:00–11:00

CAST:

Judge Bob Gibbs .... Beau Bridges
Leanne Lancaster .... Kiersten Warren
Kathy Baker .... Liz Vassey
Sheriff Gary Hammond .... Sam Robards
Wanda Grace (age 12) .... RaeVen Larrymore-Kelly
Elvin Crowe .... Brent Briscoe
Inez Crowe .... Beth Grant
Dirk Crowe .... Peter Allen Vogt
Bogart Crowe .... Paul Vogt
Dicky Crowe .... William Sanderson
Hector Finch .... T. Scott Cunningham
Sonny Dupree .... Sam Trammell
Dep. Dawson Hayes .... Garrett Dillahunt

Eccentricity abounded in the backwoods town of Deepwater, Florida, in this offbeat series that critics loved but viewers mostly ignored. Presiding over the town (pop. 30,000) like a benevolent despot was bear-like Judge Bob Gibbs, nicknamed "Maximum Bob" for his tendency to run his courtroom like a revival preacher, lecturing, cajoling, and doling out outrageous sentences for minor infractions when he thought the accused deserved it. His wife was a weirdo named Leanne, a former mermaid at a local aquarium who, after a mystical underwater experience, began "channeling" and now was inhabited by the spirit of a black slave girl (Wanda Grace) from the 1850s. Others in his world were Sheriff Gary, a level-headed sort with a penchant for tango lessons, lecherous Deputy Hayes, and dunderheaded criminal Sonny. Then there was the truly strange, possibly inbred, Crowe clan, who lived out in the swamps: Elvin, a pistol-packin' pizza man; Inez, the beady-eyed mother; and Dirk and Bogart, the dim-witted, heavy-set twins who were both incredibly strong and virtually indestructible.

In the premiere Bob met his match in Kathy Baker, a spunky Miami public defender who came to town because her parolee client had been given the death sentence for drinking beer in public. When she resisted the judge's advances, he threw her in the pokey for (or out of) contempt, but when she got out she decided to stay, alternately foiling his schemes and helping him catch the bad guys who infested Okeechobee County.

Based on the novel by Elmore Leonard.

MAXIMUM EXPOSURE (*Adventure/Reality*)

BROADCAST HISTORY:

Syndicated only
60 minutes
Produced: *2000–*
Released: *October 2000*

NARRATOR:

Cam Brainard

Maximum Exposure provided viewers with fast-paced video coverage of people engaged in dangerous activities with somewhat sarcastic voice-over commentary. The sources included home videos, surveillance camera coverage, stock footage from news agencies and videos from assorted law enforcement agencies. Individual segments covered everything from botched stunts to crimes in progress, natural disasters and sporting events that went horribly wrong. To increase the shock value, some of the clips were replayed in slow motion and extreme close-up.

MAXINE BARRAT, see *And Everything Nice*

MAYA (*Adventure*)
FIRST TELECAST: *September 16, 1967*
LAST TELECAST: *February 10, 1968*
BROADCAST HISTORY:
Sep 1967–Feb 1968, NBC Sat 7:30–8:30
CAST:
Terry Bowen .... Jay North
Raji .... Sajid Khan

Filmed in India, *Maya* was the story of two teenage boys who traveled around that country on the back of an elephant. American Terry Bowen had come to India to be with his father, a professional hunter, only to learn that his father was missing and presumed dead following an attack by a man-eating tiger. Terry refused to accept his father's death and, with the help of Raji, an orphan about his own age, set out to look for the missing man. Raji's faithful elephant Maya was their source of transportation and of much help during their jungle adventures in search of Mr. Bowen, whom the boys never found.

MAYBE IT'S ME (*Situation Comedy*)
FIRST TELECAST: *October 5, 2001*
LAST TELECAST: *July 26, 2002*
BROADCAST HISTORY:
Oct 2001–Jan 2002, WB Fri 8:30–9:00
Dec 2001, WB Thu 8:30–9:00
Jan 2002–Jun 2002, WB Fri 9:30–10:00
Jun 2002–Jul 2002, WB Fri 8:30–9:00
CAST:
Jerry Stage .... Fred Willard
Mary Stage .... Julia Sweeney
Molly Stage (age 15) .... Reagan Dale Neis
Mia Lieber .... Vicki Davis
Rick Stage (18) .... Andrew W. Walker
Grant Stage (17) .... Patrick Levis
**Nick Gibson* .... Shaun Sipos
Grandpa Fred Stage (pilot only) .... Walter Marsh
Grandpa Fred Stage .... Dabbs Greer
Mindy Stage .... Daniella Cantermen
Cindy Stage .... Deanna Cantermen
Grandma Harriet Krupp .... Ellen Albertini Dow
**Ben* .... Noah Bastian

*Occasional

This quirky comedy, set in fictional Wickettstown, Rhode Island, centered on Molly, a teenager who had lost a lot of weight over the summer, traded in her glasses for contacts, and had her braces removed. Now she was adjusting to her new svelte, and more popular, image while trying to overcome typical teenage self-consciousness and insecurity. Molly's biggest problem was her family, a collection of strange and offbeat characters. Father Jerry was a loony optometrist obsessed with the high school girls' soccer team he coached, and mother Mary was a perpetually late penny pincher who was oblivious to the eccentricities of the family. Molly's siblings were Grant, who wanted to be a Christian rock star; bad boy Rick, who was always in trouble with the cops; and Mindy and Cindy, younger, troublemaking identical twin sisters whom even her dad couldn't tell apart. Rounding out the household were Mary's mother, Harriet, who hid food whenever she got upset, and Jerry's father, Fred, who was always in a bad mood. Mia, Molly's best friend and confidante, had the hots for an oblivious Rick, and Molly was infatuated with Nick, a senior and star on the high school football team.

In February, at her request, the family staged a funeral for Harriet. At the end of the episode her niece Tillie, who had come for the funeral, married Grandpa Fred, who ceased to be a member of the cast. In the spring Molly developed feelings for her friend Ben and considered asking him to the prom. Meanwhile, Rick lost the family home in a card game with a gangster and Molly agreed to go to the prom with the gangster's nerdy son so they could keep the home. She double-dated with brother Grant, whose date was her best friend Mia. Things didn't work out with the nerd, but her dad won the house back playing poker with the mobster.

Molly, who recorded her daily travails in a computer journal, provided voice-over narration for the show.

MAYBE THIS TIME (*Situation Comedy*)
FIRST TELECAST: *September 16, 1995*
LAST TELECAST: *February 17, 1996*
BROADCAST HISTORY:
Sep 1995–Jan 1996, ABC Sat 8:30–9:00
Feb 1996, ABC Sat 8:30–9:00
CAST:
Julia Wallace .... Marie Osmond
Gracie Wallace (age 11) .... Ashley Johnson
Shirley .... Betty White
Logan .... Craig Ferguson
K. Ohara .... Amy Hill
Henry Witherspoon .... Elliot Reid

Julia was a recent divorcée trying hard to substitute a business career for love, in this bright single-woman comedy. Swearing off men, she plunged into managing the family's small-town coffee shop, unfortunately with more enthusiasm than ability. Her worldly mother Shirley, who had been married five times, was having none of her "modern business-woman" act, nagging Julia to get back into the dating scene and give love another chance. Watching the two generations spar were Julia's manipulative daughter Gracie, her unscrupulous British cook Logan, and Ohara, who ran the pawnshop down the street and was always cooking up business-building schemes. Henry was the courtly landlord.

MAYBERRY R.F.D. (*Situation Comedy*)
FIRST TELECAST: *September 23, 1968*
LAST TELECAST: *September 6, 1971*
BROADCAST HISTORY:
Sep 1968–Sep 1971, CBS Mon 9:00–9:30
CAST:
Sam Jones .... Ken Berry
Aunt Bee (1968–1970) .... Frances Bavier
Goober Pyle .... George Lindsey
Howard Sprague .... Jack Dodson
Emmett Clark .... Paul Hartman
Millie Swanson .... Arlene Golonka
Mike Jones .... Buddy Foster
Alice (1970–1971) .... Alice Ghostley

This was the successor to *The Andy Griffith Show,* in which Andy had starred for eight years as the sheriff of quiet, rural Mayberry, North Carolina. When Griffith decided to call it quits in 1968, CBS kept most of the rest of the cast together, added a new lead in the person of Ken Berry, and continued the show under the title *Mayberry R.F.D.*

Like Griffith's Andy, Berry's Sam Jones was a young widower with a small son, Mike. Sam was a gentleman farmer who had recently taken up residence near Mayberry. Not long after his arrival he found himself elected to the Mayberry Town Council, a position for which he had no prior experience. That hardly mattered in Mayberry, however, as in his friendly, bumbling way he attempted to perform his new duties and tend to the simple needs of the townsfolk. Aunt Bee moved in with him as his housekeeper for two years, then was replaced by Aunt Alice for the 1970–1971 season. Millie Swanson was Sam's romantic interest.

For a couple of years *Mayberry R.F.D.* was virtually as popular as *The Andy Griffith Show* had been. The new program was one of the top four shows on television during its first two years (*Andy Griffith* had reached number one in its final season). It was still in the top 20 when CBS canceled it in 1971, as part of an extensive cutback in "rural"-oriented programming.

MAYOR OF HOLLYWOOD (*Variety*)

FIRST TELECAST: *July 29, 1952*

LAST TELECAST: *September 18, 1952*

BROADCAST HISTORY:

Jul 1952–Sep 1952, NBC Tue/Thu 7:00–7:30

CAST:

Walter O'Keefe .... Himself
Secretary .... Jeanne Dyer
Campaign Manager .... Lou Crosby
Campaign Manager .... Bill Baldwin
Secretary .... Lina Romay

Walter O'Keefe, a well-known radio personality of the 1930s and 1940s, starred as himself in this live series. In his fictional quest to be elected mayor of Hollywood, he took viewers on a tour around the Hollywood area of Los Angeles while trying to drum up support for his campaign. As part of the "tour" he interviewed numerous famous personalities. His original secretary, Jeanne Dyer, was replaced by Lina Romay on August 14, and his campaign manager, Lou Crosby, who was also the show's announcer, was replaced by Bill Baldwin on August 7.

MCCLAIN'S LAW (*Police Drama*)

FIRST TELECAST: *November 20, 1981*

LAST TELECAST: *August 24, 1982*

BROADCAST HISTORY:

Nov 1981–Feb 1982, NBC Fri 9:00–10:00
Mar 1982–Apr 1982, NBC Sat 10:00–11:00
Apr 1982–Jul 1982, NBC Fri 10:00–11:00
Jul 1982–Aug 1982, NBC Tue 10:00–11:00

CAST:

Det. Jim McClain .... James Arness
Det. Harry Gates .... Marshall Colt
Lt. Edward DeNisco .... George DiCenzo
Det. Jerry Cross .... Carl Franklin
Vangie Cruise .... Conchata Ferrell

A leg injury had forced Jim McClain to retire from the San Pedro, California, police force 13 years ago, when he was 39. In the intervening years he had worked as a fisherman and lived in a houseboat on the waterfront. When his fishing partner was robbed and murdered, McClain fought to have himself reinstated, convinced that only he could find the killer. Despite the antagonism of his new boss, Lt. DeNisco, McClain proved himself quite effective in the modern, high-tech world of police work. He quickly gained the respect of most of his fellow officers, including young partner Harry Gates and fellow officer Jerry Gross. Fortunately for McClain, they tended to look the other way when he reverted to the old-fashioned, physical methods of apprehending criminals. Vangie Cruise ran the dockside cafe where McClain spent much of his spare time.

MCCLOUD (*Police Drama*)

FIRST TELECAST: *September 16, 1970*

LAST TELECAST: *August 28, 1977*

BROADCAST HISTORY:

Sep 1970–Oct 1970, NBC Wed 9:00–10:00
Mar 1971–Aug 1971, NBC Wed 9:00–10:00
Sep 1971–Aug 1972, NBC Wed 8:30–10:00
Sep 1972–Aug 1975, NBC Sun 8:30–10:00
Sep 1975–Aug 1976, NBC Sun 9:00–11:00
Oct 1976–Aug 1977, NBC Sun Various times

CAST:

Sam McCloud .... Dennis Weaver
Peter B. Clifford .... J. D. Cannon
Sgt. Joe Broadhurst .... Terry Carter
Chris Coughlin .... Diana Muldaur
Sgt. Grover .... Ken Lynch

McCloud was one of television's more tongue-in-cheek police series. Here was Deputy Marshal Sam McCloud from Taos, New Mexico, driving the New York City police crazy. He had originally arrived in New York to chase a prisoner who had escaped from him, and his direct, rather strong-arm methods were hard for the big-city police to cope with. After capturing his man, McCloud somehow found himself on temporary assignment in Manhattan's 27th Precinct under Chief Peter B. Clifford. Although he was ostensibly there to learn the methods employed by a large metropolitan police department, McCloud usually took things into his own hands and reverted to type, much to the chagrin and frustration of Chief Clifford. Whenever McCloud went on a case he dragged Sgt. Joe Broadhurst with him and, though they usually solved the crime and got along well with each other, Broadhurst's association with McCloud didn't seem to be doing him much good with their mutual superior Clifford. McCloud really looked out of place on the streets of New York, with his cowboy hat, sheepskin jacket, and matching accent. He was full of Western homilies and used the catchphrase "There you go" quite regularly. His romantic interest, not seen in every episode, was writer Chris Coughlin, who was working on a book that related to the fugitive he had chased to New York in the pilot for this series.

McCloud premiered in 1970 as the first of four miniseries aired under the collective title *Four-In-One*—the others being *San Francisco International Airport, Night Gallery,* and *The Psychiatrist.* The following fall it became, along with *Columbo* and *McMillan and Wife,* one of the three original elements in the *NBC Mystery Movie* rotation. It remained with that series throughout the rest of its run.

MCCOY (*Detective Drama*)

FIRST TELECAST: *October 5, 1975*

LAST TELECAST: *March 28, 1976*

BROADCAST HISTORY:

Oct 1975–Mar 1976, NBC Sun 9:00–11:00

CAST:

McCoy .... Tony Curtis
Gideon Gibbs................... Roscoe Lee Browne

The combination of an addiction to gambling, at which he was not particularly successful, and a very expensive lifestyle prompted McCoy to make a living as a sophisticated con man. He was something of a latter-day Robin Hood, finding ways to relieve wealthy criminals of their ill-gotten gains, then returning most of the loot to those who had been bilked of it, while retaining a healthy fee for his services. He would work elaborate cons on the con men themselves, and would usually take them for so much that after expenses, paying off the many accomplices who worked with him, and reimbursing the original victim, there was still a tidy sum left over for himself. McCoy's principal aide was a nightclub comedian named Gideon Gibbs.

McCoy was seen briefly as one of four rotating elements that made up the 1975–1976 edition of the *NBC Sunday Mystery Movie.* Its resemblance to the hit movie *The Sting* may or may not have been coincidental, but in any event did not help, as only four episodes of *McCoy* were actually telecast before the program was canceled.

MCCOYS, THE, syndicated title for *Real McCoys, The*

MCGARRETT, see *Hawaii Five-O*

MCGRAW, see *Meet McGraw*

MCHALE'S NAVY (*Situation Comedy*)
FIRST TELECAST: *October 11, 1962*
LAST TELECAST: *August 30, 1966*
BROADCAST HISTORY:

Oct 1962–Sep 1963, ABC Thu 9:30–10:00
Sep 1963–Aug 1966, ABC Tue 8:30–9:00

CAST:

Lt. Cdr. Quinton McHale .... Ernest Borgnine
Capt. Wallace B. Binghamton .... Joe Flynn
Ensign Charles Parker................ Tim Conway
Lester Gruber .... Carl Ballantine
George "Christy" Christopher .... Gary Vinson
Harrison "Tinker" Bell................. Billy Sands
Virgil Edwards .... Edson Stroll
Nurse Molly Turner (1962–1964)......... Jane Dulo
Joseph "Happy" Haines (1962–1964)
.... Gavin MacLeod
Willy Moss (1964–1966)............... John Wright
Fuji Kobiaji............................ Yoshio Yoda
Lt. Elroy Carpenter................... Bob Hastings
Col. Douglas Harrigan (1965–1966)... Henry Beckman
Gen. Bronson (1965–1966) .... Simon Scott
Dino Baroni (1965–1966) .... Dick Wilson
Mayor Mario Lugatto (1965–1966) ..... Jay Novello
Rosa Giovanni (1965–1966) .... Peggy Mondo

The U.S. Navy was never like this. Lt. Commander Quinton McHale was the commander of a World War II P.T. boat with one of the strangest, most outrageous crews ever assembled. The program was in many respects a copy of Phil Silvers's classic Sgt. Bilko show, its broad humor built on the conflict between the easy-going, regulation-ignoring, con-artist McHale and his long-suffering superior, Capt. Binghamton (known behind his back as "Old Lead Bottom"). The men loved McHale, Binghamton hated him, and the navy put up with him because, in the South Seas where P.T.73 was based at the island of Taratupa, McHale knew the territory "like the back of his hand."

At the start of *McHale's Navy*'s last season, the entire crew, including Capt. Binghamton, was transferred to Italy, where they helped maintain the occupation of the small town of Voltafiore against the possible incursion of German troops. Not only did Binghamton still have to deal with the incorrigible McHale, but he was now saddled with a conniving Italian mayor, Mario Lugatto, who was almost as adept a con man as McHale himself. Nothing changed but the environment. The gambling that had run rampant in the Pacific now included local residents as well as military personnel.

MCKEEVER & THE COLONEL (*Situation Comedy*)
FIRST TELECAST: *September 23, 1962*
LAST TELECAST: *June 16, 1963*
BROADCAST HISTORY:

Sep 1962–Jun 1963, NBC Sun 6:30–7:00

CAST:

Cadet Gary McKeever.................... Scott Lane
Col. Harvey Blackwell.................. Allyn Joslyn
Sgt. Barnes .... Jackie Coogan
Mrs. Warner .... Elisabeth Fraser
Tubby................................ Keith Taylor
Monk.............................. Johnny Eimen

Comedy about life in a military school. The cadets—McKeever abetted by his pals Tubby and Monk—were constantly getting into trouble and making it virtually impossible for Col. Blackwell to maintain any semblance of order, decorum, or discipline. Sgt. Barnes was the colonel's aide, Mrs. Warner the head of the school cafeteria.

MCKENNA (*Adventure*)
FIRST TELECAST: *September 15, 1994*
LAST TELECAST: *July 20, 1995*
BROADCAST HISTORY:

Sep 1994, ABC Thu 9:00–10:00
Jul 1995, ABC Thu 9:00–10:00

CAST:

Jack McKenna........................ Chad Everett
Brick McKenna .... Eric Close
Cassidy McKenna .... Jennifer Love Hewitt
Leigh McKenna .... Shawn Huff
Harry McKenna .... Jacob Loyst
Rose McKenna .... Ashlee Lauren
Dep. Sheriff Dale Goodwin .... Rick Peters
Walter Maddock...................... Jack Kehler

The spectacular mountain scenery of Bend, Oregon, provided the backdrop for this family drama. Jack, the rugged owner of McKenna Wilderness Outfitters, had been leading city slickers on wilderness adventures for 25 years, but began to let the business slip after his favorite son, Guy, was killed in a fall into a gorge. Enter estranged younger son Brick, who had run off two years earlier to try his luck on the auto racing circuit. Brick wanted to help get the family business back on track, and perhaps reconcile with his proud father, but mostly all they did was snap at each other. Looking on were Brick's rebellious sister, Cass, his sensible sister-in-law, Leigh (Guy's widow), who helped run the place, and Leigh's cute young kids, Harry and Rose. Dale was Brick's high school buddy, who hung around Leigh a lot, and Walter was the eccentric mountain man/hired hand, who provided comic relief (as did many of the inept visitors).

Romances, dark secrets, and surprising twists were promised for the first season, but the series only aired a few episodes before the entire McKenna clan fell into a deep Nielsen Ratings gorge and were never seen again.

MCLEAN STEVENSON SHOW, THE (*Situation Comedy*)

FIRST TELECAST: *December 1, 1976*
LAST TELECAST: *March 3, 1977*
BROADCAST HISTORY:
Dec 1976–Jan 1977, NBC Wed 8:30–9:00
Feb 1977–Mar 1977, NBC Wed 9:30–10:00
CAST:
Mac Ferguson.................McLean Stevenson
Peggy Ferguson....................Barbara Stuart
Grandma...........................Madge West
Janet..............................Ayn Ruymen
Chris...............................Steve Nevil
David.........................David Hollander
Jason............................Jason Whitney

Mac Ferguson was a typical middle-class family man, owner of a hardware store in his hometown of Evanston, Illinois. He and his wife had two grown children who, through circumstances that could not possibly have been anticipated by their parents, were living with them. Janet had separated from her husband and moved in along with her two young children, David and Jason. Chris, after several years of trying to "find" himself, principally spent bumming around in Hawaii, returned home to go back to college part-time, taking up residence in the basement and setting it up as a bachelor pad. If this didn't create enough congestion, Peggy's mother was also a member of the household.

MCMILLAN AND WIFE (*Police Drama*)

FIRST TELECAST: *September 29, 1971*
LAST TELECAST: *August 21, 1977*
BROADCAST HISTORY:
Sep 1971–Aug 1972, NBC Wed 8:30–10:00
Sep 1972–Jul 1974, NBC Sun 8:30–10:00
Sep 1974–Jul 1975, NBC Sun 8:30–10:30
Sep 1975–Aug 1976, NBC Sun 9:00–11:00
Dec 1976–Aug 1977, NBC Sun 8:00–9:30
CAST:
Commissioner Stewart McMillan....Rock Hudson
Sally McMillan (1971–1976).....Susan Saint James
Sgt. Charles Enright................John Schuck
Mildred (1971–1976)...............Nancy Walker
Agatha (1976–1977).................Martha Raye
Sgt. Steve DiMaggio (1976–1977). Richard Gilliland
Maggie (1976–1977)................Gloria Stroock

San Francisco Police Commissioner Stewart McMillan had a beautiful wife who had a penchant for getting both of them involved in criminal cases which she inadvertently stumbled upon. Mac was very supportive, though occasionally bewildered by the situations Sally got them into, and was often called upon to help solve the cases. This mystery/comedy police series was patterned after the relationship between Nick and Nora Charles in *The Thin Man* movies and TV series of the 1940s and 1950s. There were elements of romance and comedy thrown in with the actual case being solved. Mac's aide was plodding but enthusiastic Sgt. Enright, and Mildred was the McMillans' sarcastic, sharp-tongued maid.

McMillan and Wife was one of the three original rotating elements in the *NBC Mystery Movie*—the other two were *McCloud* and *Columbo*—and remained with the series throughout its long run. When Nancy Walker and Susan Saint James left the series at the end of the 1975–1976 season, the former to star in her own series on ABC and the latter in a contract dispute, the title was shortened to *McMillan* and cast changes were made. Sally was written out of the series by having her die in a plane crash, and Mac, now a widower, had a new maid/housekeeper named Agatha, who happened to be Mildred's sister. Mac also acquired a second assistant in Sgt. DiMaggio (the dim-witted Enright had been promoted to lieutenant) and a new secretary named Maggie.

ME AND MAXX (*Situation Comedy*)

FIRST TELECAST: *March 22, 1980*
LAST TELECAST: *September 12, 1980*
BROADCAST HISTORY:
Mar 1980–Apr 1980, NBC Sat 9:30–10:00
May 1980–Jul 1980, NBC Fri 8:30–9:00
Sep 1980, NBC Fri 8:30–9:00
CAST:
Norman Davis........................Joe Santos
Maxx Davis..................Melissa Michaelsen
Barbara..........................Jenny Sullivan
Mitch..............................Jim Weston
Gary..............................Denny Evans

In this awkward comedy dad was a heel, and his little daughter was a cute but unwanted child who could never get through to him. Norman Davis had walked out on his wife and child years earlier to take up the life of a swinging single. Now his ex-wife had decided that she too was going to "spread her wings," so, unannounced, 11-year-old Maxx showed up at Norman's bachelor pad looking for a home. Maxx was a precocious and sensitive youngster with an extensive vocabulary learned from watching soap operas. Although her initial attitude toward her father was understandably negative, with time, and a little love, she attempted to heal the old wounds. But Norman was irked at having to adjust his bachelor lifestyle to accommodate the presence of a young daughter. The tender "let's make up" scenes at the end of each episode were so cold as to be embarrassing, and the show quickly left the air.

Barbara was Norman's business partner (they brokered tickets to Broadway shows) and occasional girlfriend; Mitch, the swinging next-door neighbor with whom Normal hung out; and Gary, the inept elevator operator.

ME AND MOM (*Detective Comedy/Drama*)

FIRST TELECAST: *April 5, 1985*
LAST TELECAST: *May 17, 1985*
BROADCAST HISTORY:
Apr 1985–May 1985, ABC Fri 10:00–11:00
CAST:
Kate Morgan.........................Lisa Eilbacher
Zena Hunnicutt....................Holland Taylor
Lou Garfield....................James Earl Jones
Lt. Rojas..........................Henry Darrow

Mother and daughter private eyes. Kate was a beautiful, trained criminologist, and Zena her wealthy, socialite mom (you could tell by her ever-present mink coat); Zena was widowed, bored, and looking for a little excitement, so she routinely meddled in Kate's work. Kate's "official" partner, Lou, an ex-cop, helped keep the ladies from getting blown away in this action series. Rojas was their contact in the San Francisco Police Dept.

ME & MRS. C. (*Situation Comedy*)
FIRST TELECAST: *June 21, 1986*
LAST TELECAST: *July 4, 1987*
BROADCAST HISTORY:
Jun 1986–Jul 1986, NBC Sat 9:30–10:00
Apr 1987–May 1987, NBC Sat 9:30–10:00
Jun 1987–Jul 1987, NBC Sat 8:30–9:00
CAST:
Ethel Conklin (Mrs. C) .... Peg Murray
Gerri Kilgore .... Misha McK
Ethan Conklin .... Gary Bayer
Kathleen Conklin .... Ellen Regan

Mrs. C was a sixtyish white widow with a problem. She didn't have enough money to meet expenses, so in order to avoid losing her house she took in a boarder—which is when the fun really began. Gerri was a young black girl who was eager to work, but since she was just out of prison found it hard to land a job. In addition, Gerri's streetcorner ways clashed with Mrs. C's sedate, old-fashioned lifestyle, though the two genuinely liked each other. Mrs. C's cold-fish son, Ethan, an efficiency expert, and his snooty wife, Kathleen, were appalled at the arrangement, but did little to help mom out in this somewhat uncomfortable comedy.

ME AND THE BOYS (*Situation Comedy*)
FIRST TELECAST: *September 20, 1994*
LAST TELECAST: *August 2, 1995*
BROADCAST HISTORY:
Sep 1994–Feb 1995, ABC Tue 8:30–9:00
May 1995–Jun 1995, ABC Sat 8:00–8:30
Jun 1995–Aug 1995, ABC Wed 8:00–8:30
CAST:
Steve Tower .... Steve Harvey
Artis Tower (age 16) .... Chaz Lamar Shepherd
William Tower (13) .... Wayne Collins
Andrew Tower (10) .... Benjamin D. LeVert
Mary .... Madge Sinclair
Amelia .... Wendy Raquel Robinson

Gentle family comedy about a single black dad raising his three boys—Artis the slacker, William the schemer, and Andrew the cute ten-year-old who yearned to be older. Steve, a widower, ran a video store in their hometown of Dallas, but most of the action took place around the kitchen table, where they all laughed at each other's weak jokes and learned little lessons in life. Then father and son would bump fists and say "we cool."

Mary was Steve's sensible live-in mother-in-law and Amelia his equally sensible girlfriend.

ME AND THE CHIMP (*Situation Comedy*)
FIRST TELECAST: *January 13, 1972*
LAST TELECAST: *May 18, 1972*
BROADCAST HISTORY:
Jan 1972–May 1972, CBS Thu 8:00–8:30
CAST:
Mike Reynolds .... Ted Bessell
Liz Reynolds .... Anita Gillette
Scott Reynolds .... Scott Kolden
Kitty Reynolds .... Kami Cotler

Mike Reynolds was a happily married dentist living in the suburban Southern California community of San Pascal. He and his wife, Liz, had two young children and a small chimpanzee named Buttons. Buttons had been found in a local park by the two Reynolds children, Scott and Kitty, and been brought home as a pet. Despite Mike's objections, Buttons became a regular member of the household, having been given that name because of his infatuation with pushing any and all buttons he found on appliances, radios, cars, dental equipment, or anything else he got his little hands onto. Though very friendly and affectionate, Buttons caused all sorts of problems with his curiosity about almost everything and managed to get the entire household into difficult situations. It always seemed to be Mike's responsibility to get them out.

MEDALLION THEATER (*Dramatic Anthology*)
FIRST TELECAST: *July 11, 1953*
LAST TELECAST: *April 3, 1954*
BROADCAST HISTORY:
Jul 1953–Apr 1954, CBS Sat 10:00–10:30

This series of adaptations of plays and works from other media was aired live from New York with a different cast each week. The premiere telecast starred Henry Fonda in "The Decision of Arrowsmith," adapted from Sinclair Lewis's novel. Cast in the leads of other presentations were generally well-known performers, including Ronald Reagan, Jack Lemmon, Claude Rains, Robert Preston, Dane Clark, Martha Scott, and Jan Sterling.

MEDIC (*Medical Drama*)
FIRST TELECAST: *September 13, 1954*
LAST TELECAST: *November 19, 1956*
BROADCAST HISTORY:
Sep 1954–Nov 1956, NBC Mon 9:00–9:30
CAST:
Dr. Konrad Styner .... Richard Boone
THEME:
"Blue Star," by Edward Heyman and Victor Young

Case histories from the files of the Los Angeles County Medical Association were dramatized in this filmed series. In its efforts to present the practice of medicine realistically, *Medic* was shot at real hospitals and clinics, and often used real doctors and nurses as part of the cast. Dr. Styner was the host and narrator of the series, as well as a frequent participant in the cases. His introduction to each episode always included this description of the doctor: ". . . guardian of birth, healer of the sick, and comforter of the aged." The dramas generally centered around the struggle to preserve life, and the tragedies and triumphs that resulted.

Medic was a pioneer in TV realism, and was the first starring vehicle for actor Richard Boone. Its pretty theme song, "Blue Star," was quite popular during 1955.

MEDICAL CENTER (*Medical Drama*)
FIRST TELECAST: *September 24, 1969*
LAST TELECAST: *September 6, 1976*
BROADCAST HISTORY:
Sep 1969–May 1973, CBS Wed 9:00–10:00
May 1973–Sep 1976, CBS Mon 10:00–11:00

CAST:

Dr. Paul Lochner .... James Daly
Dr. Joe Gannon .... Chad Everett
Nurse Chambers (1969–1972) ..... Jayne Meadows
Dr. Jeanne Bartlett (1969–1971).... Corinne Camacho
Nurse Courtland..................... Chris Hutson
Nurse Wilcox (1972–1976)........... Audrey Totter
Dr. Barnes (1970–1971) .... Fred Holliday
Nurse Murphy (1971–1972).............. Jane Dulo
Nurse Holmby (1971–1976) ...... Barbara Baldavin
Nurse Canford .... Virginia Hawkins
Anesthesiologist (1969–1970) .... Daniel Silver
Dr. Weller (1970–1974)............ Eugene Peterson
Dr. Bricker (1970–1974)................... Ed Hall
Nurse Bascomb (1971–1973) .... Louise Fitch
Lt. Samuels (1971–1976).......... Martin E. Brooks

Located in the Los Angeles area, Medical Center was an otherwise unnamed hospital complex that was part of a large university campus. Dr. Paul Lochner was the chief of staff, an experienced, professional, compassionate man. Dr. Joe Gannon was a young associate professor of surgery and close friend and colleague of Dr. Lochner. At the start of the show's second season, Dr. Gannon took on the added responsibilities of director of the student health service, an appropriate post for a young physician who could identify closely with the students. A number of other doctors and nurses came and went in the cast; Miss Wilcox, the extremely efficient head nurse, achieved co-star billing in 1972.

The personal and medical stories of the doctors and their patients, as well as others with whom they came into contact, provided the drama in this series. Gannon and Lochner embodied the youth vs. experience tension which seems to be a necessary element of every medical show. The elements certainly worked here.

MEDICAL HORIZONS (*Public Affairs*)

FIRST TELECAST: *September 12, 1955*
LAST TELECAST: *March 5, 1956*
BROADCAST HISTORY:
Sep 1955–Mar 1956, ABC Mon 9:30–10:00
HOST:
Quincy Howe (1955)
Don Goddard (1955–1956)

During the 1955–1956 season ABC attempted to bring the television viewer an insight into the advances being made in medicine and an introduction to the people who were responsible for them. Quincy Howe was the original host/narrator, but other commitments forced him to leave this live series after a month. He was replaced by Don Goddard. Each week a different discovery, program of research, or branch of medicine was discussed, with interviews with doctors, technicians, researchers, etc., supplemented by actual scenes of the technique, equipment, or operation.

Medical Horizons returned to the air on Sunday afternoons in September of 1956 and continued until the following June.

MEDICAL STORY (*Medical Anthology*)

FIRST TELECAST: *September 4, 1975*
LAST TELECAST: *January 8, 1976*
BROADCAST HISTORY:
Sep 1975–Jan 1976, NBC Thu 10:00–11:00

Medical Story attempted to remove the mantle of sainthood from doctors. It dealt with the personal problems and human failings of members of the medical profession, as well as with their skills. Stories confronted many sensitive issues, most notably the mistakes made in hospitals and the selfishness and insensitivity of many doctors. Such a critical view of a profession whose practitioners people want to trust apparently did not sit well with viewers, and the program was dropped after a few months.

MEDICINE BALL (*Medical Drama*)

FIRST TELECAST: *March 13, 1995*
LAST TELECAST: *June 12, 1995*
BROADCAST HISTORY:
Mar 1995–Jun 1995, FOX Mon 9:00–10:00
CAST:

Dr. Katie Cooper..................... Jensen Daggett
Dr. Danny Macklin .... Donal Logue
Dr. Harley Spencer .... Harrison Pruett
Dr. Nia James...................... Kai Soremekun
Dr. Max Chang......................... Darryl Fong
Dr. Clate Baker.................... Jeffrey D. Sams
Dr. Tom Powell.................. Vincent Ventresca
Dr. Douglas McGill .... Sam McMurray
Patrick Yeats .... Timothy Omundson
Dr. Elizabeth Vasquez .... Terri Ivens

Fictional Bayview Medical Center in Seattle was the setting for this drama about the personal and professional lives of a group of first-year resident physicians at a teaching hospital. The work was hard, the hours were long, the stress level was high, and the frustrations were many as they learned that the real world of medicine was not as cut and dried as it had seemed in school. The young interns were Cooper, a talented surgeon who couldn't seem to get her home life under control; Macklin, a neurotic specialist in internal medicine who found it difficult to confront either patients or their loved ones with bad news when things didn't go well; earnest Spencer, who hated the protocol of hospital procedure and the politicization it represented; James, a pretty, outgoing psychiatrist; and Chang, who had the best bedside manner and most cynical sense of humor of the group. Working with the younger physicians were Dr. Baker, a second-year resident and single father with a young son; Dr. Powell, the hunky surgeon with the big ego who was Bayview's resident heartthrob; and Dr. McGill, the director of the residency program who offered sound advice and reprimanded when necessary. Yeats, an advocate of homeopathic medicine, had a medical degree (from "Croft University"—see ABC's *Going to Extremes*) but, because he hadn't been accepted into the residency program, was working as an orderly until he could convince McGill to find a slot for him.

In the sixth episode another first-year resident, Dr. Vasquez, died from injuries she had suffered when, leaving Bayview exhausted, she had fallen asleep at the wheel and had a bad car accident.

Actress Marilu Henner was one of the executive producers of *Medicine Ball*.

MEEGO (*Situation Comedy*)

FIRST TELECAST: *September 19, 1997*
LAST TELECAST: *October 24, 1997*
BROADCAST HISTORY:
Sep 1997–Oct 1997, CBS Fri 8:30–9:00
CAST:

Meego .... Bronson Pinchot
Dr. Edward Parker .... Ed Begley, Jr.

Trip Parker (pilot only) .... Erik von Detten
Trip Parker (age 15) .... Will Estes
Maggie Parker (11) .... Michelle Trachtenberg
Alex Parker (6) .... Jonathan Lipnicki

In this almost sickly sweet fantasy Meego was a goofy 9,000-year-old alien from the planet Marmazon 4.0 whose spaceship crashed in the backyard of Edward Parker, a widowed surgeon raising his three children. Originally intending to stay for only two days to repair his ship, Meego got attached to the kids, particularly wide-eyed young Alex, who laughed at all his jokes, and decided to stay on as their caretaker. He had all sorts of neat powers—he could change his shape into almost any living thing, was telekinetic (handy for doing the cleaning), could speed up or slow down the passage of time, could instantaneously move from one place to another, and could talk to Barkley, Alex's little dog. The kids knew he was an alien, but Dad, at least during the six weeks the show lasted, never found out.

MEET CORLISS ARCHER (*Situation Comedy*)
FIRST TELECAST: *July 12, 1951*
LAST TELECAST: *March 29, 1952*
BROADCAST HISTORY:
Jul 1951–Sep 1951, CBS Thu 9:00–9:30
Jul 1951–Sep 1951, CBS Fri 10:00–10:30
Jan 1952–Mar 1952, CBS Sat 6:30–7:00
(In first-run syndication during the 1954–1955 season)
CAST:
Corliss Archer (1951–1952) .... Lugene Sanders
Corliss Archer (1954–1955) .... Ann Baker
Mr. Harry Archer (1951–1952) .... Fred Shields
Mr. Harry Archer (1954–1955) ...... John Eldredge
Dexter Franklin .... Bobby Ellis
Mrs. Janet Archer (1951) .... Frieda Inescort
Mrs. Janet Archer (1952) .... Irene Tedrow
Mrs. Janet Archer (1954–1955) .... Mary Brian
Mr. Franklin (1954–1955) .... Ken Christy

Meet Corliss Archer had been on CBS radio since 1943 and was still being aired in the early 1950s when this television version was added in 1951. It was the story of a typical high school girl, her boyfriend, Dexter, and her parents. The stories revolved around the energetic and vivacious Corliss as she made the transition from little girl to young woman. Fred Shields, who had played Mr. Archer through most of the radio run, re-created his role for the new medium, as did Irene Tedrow as Mrs. Archer in part of the television run.

This series was fed to different parts of the country on different days during the summer of 1951. The Thursday shows were seen in the Midwest while the rest of the country was seeing *Your Esso Reporter*. On Friday nights *Meet Corliss Archer* was available to those stations that did not carry it on Thursdays. Since it was done live from Los Angeles, the cast did the same show on consecutive nights.

A syndicated film version of *Meet Corliss Archer* was produced for the 1954–1955 season. The only survivor from the network cast was Bobby Ellis as Dexter.

MEET MCGRAW (*Detective Drama*)
FIRST TELECAST: *July 2, 1957*
LAST TELECAST: *October 8, 1959*
BROADCAST HISTORY:
Jul 1957–Jun 1958, NBC Tue 9:00–9:30
Nov 1958–Dec 1958, ABC Sun 10:00–10:30
Jan 1959, ABC Sun 9:30–10:00
Feb 1959–Sep 1959, ABC Sun 10:30–11:00
Oct 1959, ABC Thu 9:00–9:30
CAST:
McGraw .... Frank Lovejoy

Although McGraw (that was the only name he used) was not officially a private detective, for all intents and purposes he might as well have been. Tough, willing to get into a fight, but never carrying a gun, he accepted all sorts of dangerous jobs for pay. In most of the episodes he regretfully had to leave a pretty woman behind but, as a loner, he just couldn't let himself get tied down. This series premiered on NBC, as *Meet McGraw*, on December 31, 1957, changed its title to *The Adventures of McGraw*, and was rerun on ABC in 1958–1959.

MEET MILLIE (*Situation Comedy*)
FIRST TELECAST: *October 25, 1952*
LAST TELECAST: *March 6, 1956*
BROADCAST HISTORY:
Oct 1952–Jun 1953, CBS Sat 9:30–10:00
Jun 1953–Aug 1953, CBS Sat 9:00–9:30
Aug 1953–Sep 1953, CBS Sat 9:30–10:00
Oct 1953–Feb 1954, CBS Sat 7:00–7:30
Mar 1954–Mar 1956, CBS Tue 9:00–9:30
CAST:
Millie Bronson .... Elena Verdugo
"Mama" Bronson .... Florence Halop
Mr. Boone (1952–1953) .... Earl Ross
Johnny Boone, Jr. (1952–1955) .... Ross Ford
Alfred Prinzmetal .... Marvin Kaplan
Mr. Boone (1953–1956) .... Roland Winters
Mrs. Boone (1953–1955) .... Isabel Randolph
Gladys (1956) .... Virginia Vincent

Millie Bronson was a young, attractive, middle-class secretary working in Manhattan. She lived in a brownstone apartment with her mother, who was always promoting Millie to eligible men as a potential spouse. Millie's boyfriend through most of the series' run was Johnny Boone, Jr., the son of her boss. A close friend of the Bronsons, who managed to get involved in most everything, was Alfred Prinzmetal. Alfred was an aspiring author-poet-composer.

Meet Millie had originated on CBS radio in July 1951 with Audrey Totter in the starring role. When her movie studio refused to let her do the TV version, Elena Verdugo took it over and eventually replaced Miss Totter in the radio edition before it expired in 1954. Earl Ross, as her boss, made the transition from radio to TV but was replaced by Roland Winters in June 1953.

MEET MR. MCNUTLEY, see *Ray Milland Show, The*

MEET MY FOLKS (*Romance/Reality*)
FIRST TELECAST: *July 22, 2002*
LAST TELECAST:
BROADCAST HISTORY:
Jul 2002–Aug 2002, NBC Mon 10:00–11:00
Jul 2002, NBC Wed 8:00–9:00
Aug 2002, NBC Sat 8:00–9:00
Sep 2002, NBC Sat 10:00–11:00
Jan 2003–Feb 2003, NBC Sat 10:00–11:00
Mar 2003, NBC Mon 9:30–11:00
Jun 2003– , NBC Mon 10:00–11:00

One of the more uncomfortable reality shows to watch was this one in which three horny young men spent a weekend together in the home of a sweet young girl, seeking a date—under the watchful eyes of her suspicious parents, who got to make the final decision. In the premiere the parents were the Blankenships of Dana Point, California: hard-ass high school football coach Randy; his wife, Rhoda, a nurse, and winsome daughter Senta. The guys were boyish, happy Kory, mature-looking boxer Christopher, and construction worker Jason, a deep-voiced Tom Cruise look-alike who played the bongos. They faced a weekend of questions, awkward dinners and physical challenges overseen by the parents (mostly Dad), along with surprises such as the arrival of ex-girlfriends who tattled on them, videotapes of their worst moments, and embarrassing questions that were faxed to the parents or arrived at the door by special delivery. It turned out that all three were pretty sleazy (cheated on dates, lied in school), and at one point tough-guy Randy said, "I think we should send all three of 'em back and get three more!" On the final day, however, the parents got to eliminate one, after which the other two took a lie detector test in the family garage with such questions as, "Did you bring condoms?" and "Do you think you're smarter than me?" Then the parents chose the "winner," who got an expense-paid trip to Hawaii—which Senta could take with him or not. There must be a better way to get a date.

MEET THE BOSS (*Interview*)
FIRST TELECAST: *June 10, 1952*
LAST TELECAST: *August 26, 1952*
BROADCAST HISTORY:
Jun 1952–Aug 1952, DUM Tue 10:30–11:00
HOST:
Bill Cunningham

Newsman Bill Cunningham interviewed top American executives on their careers and their industries in general, in this paean to big business.

MEET THE CHAMP, see *Boxing*

MEET THE CHAMPIONS (*Sports Interview*)
FIRST TELECAST: *July 21, 1956*
LAST TELECAST: *January 12, 1957*
BROADCAST HISTORY:
Jul 1956–Jan 1957, NBC Sat 6:45–7:00
HOST:
Jack Lescoulie

Each episode of this live program gave viewers the opportunity to see a sports celebrity interviewed by Jack Lescoulie, as well as a second sports-world figure (not necessarily an athlete) making predictions about the outcome of an upcoming athletic event.

MEET THE MARKS (*Audience Participation/ Comedy*)
FIRST TELECAST: *July 17, 2002*
LAST TELECAST: *July 31, 2002*
BROADCAST HISTORY:
Jul 2002, FOX Wed 8:30–9:00
CAST:
Joe Marks .... Joe O'Connor
Cathy Marks .... Cathy Shambley
Patrick Marks .... Patrick Cavanaugh
Kaitlin Marks .... Kaitlin Olson
Tara .... Tara Nulty

Meet the Marks was a sitcom with elements of *Candid Camera*. It centered on the Marks, a fictional family living in a real house in a real neighborhood. Joe was the father; Cathy, the mother, and Patrick and Kaitlin, their teenage children. Real people who were lured to their home became unsuspecting participants in scripted comedic situations. At the end of each segment the visitors were told they had been taped for a TV show.

Among the people who showed up were a hairdresser who caught Kaitlin's fiancé with another woman; a computer tutor hired to give Cathy lessons who caught Joe fooling around with his assistant, Tara, and was coerced into pretending to be her boyfriend; a clown hired to do a striptease at Kaitlin's bachelorette party, and a man hired to tutor Patrick, who had to pose as a family cousin to win 1,000 pies and appear in a commercial with Ed McMahon. Only three episodes aired before *Meet the Marks* was pulled from the Fox lineup.

MEET THE PRESS (*Interview*)
FIRST TELECAST: *November 20, 1947*
LAST TELECAST: *August 29, 1965*
BROADCAST HISTORY:
Nov 1947–Dec 1947, NBC Thu 8:00–8:30
Sep 1948–Feb 1949, NBC Sun 8:30–9:00
Feb 1949–Jul 1949, NBC Wed 10:00–10:30
Jul 1949–Sep 1949, NBC Mon 10:00–10:30
Sep 1949–Feb 1950, NBC Sat Various times
Oct 1950–May 1952, NBC Sun Various times
Jun 1951–Sep 1951, NBC Tue 8:00–8:30
May 1952–Sep 1952, NBC Sun 7:30–8:00
Oct 1952–Aug 1965, NBC Sun 6:00–6:30
REGULAR MODERATOR:
Martha Rountree (1947–1953)
Ned Brooks (1953–1965)
REGULAR PANELISTS:
Lawrence Spivak
Bill Monroe

This NBC public affairs program, which styles itself "America's Press Conference of the Air," is as of this writing the longest-running series on network television. Part of its career (as noted above) has been in prime time, while during other periods it has been telecast on Sunday afternoons.

Meet the Press usually originates from NBC's Washington, D.C., studios. It was created by Martha Rountree and Lawrence Spivak in 1945 as a radio promotion for the *American Mercury Magazine*, of which Spivak was then editor. It started on local television on November 6, 1947, and was first fed over the network (then consisting of two stations) on November 20 of that year. The format has always remained the same: a panel of reporters questions a leading public figure. Over the years virtually every major political figure in the United States has occupied the *Meet the Press* hot seat, and many foreign dignitaries as well. Martha Rountree was the original TV moderator. NBC newsman Ned Brooks took over in 1953, while Spivak remained a regular panelist and occasional moderator. Spivak became the regular moderator in 1965 and served in that capacity for a decade. He was subsequently replaced by Bill Monroe (1975–1984), Marvin Kalb (1984–1987), Chris Wallace (1987–1988), Garrick Utley (1988–1991), and Tim Russert since late in 1991. In September of 1992 *Meet the Press* expanded from 30 to 60 minutes.

During the summer of 1951, in a move unique to political interview shows of this type, *Meet the Press* aired two times per week, with different guests on each Sunday and Tuesday telecast. Following the end of its nighttime run, in August 1965, *Meet the Press* became a regular fixture on the NBC Sunday daytime lineup, where it remains to this day.

MEET THE VEEP (*Discussion*)
FIRST TELECAST: *June 30, 1953*
LAST TELECAST: *August 25, 1953*
BROADCAST HISTORY:
Jun 1953–Aug 1953, NBC Tue 10:45–11:00
REGULARS:
Alben W. Barkley
Earl Godwin

Originating live from Washington, D.C., this discussion show featured former Vice President Alben W. Barkley, who had acquired the affectionate nickname "The Veep" during his tenure with Truman, and NBC news commentator Earl Godwin. They would discuss various political issues, reminisce about Mr. Barkley's career, or chat about current nonpolitical issues. On occasion guests appeared on the show to discuss their points of view, be they similar to or different from Mr. Barkley's.

Meet the Veep had premiered as a Sunday afternoon series on NBC in February 1953. After a short spring run it left the air until showing up that June in prime time.

MEET YOUR CONGRESS (*Debate*)
FIRST TELECAST: *July 1, 1949*
LAST TELECAST: *July 4, 1954*
BROADCAST HISTORY:
Jul 1949–Aug 1949, NBC Fri 9:00–9:30
Aug 1949–Oct 1949, NBC Sat 8:00–8:30
Jul 1953–Sep 1953, DUM Wed 9:30–10:00
Oct 1953–Jul 1954, DUM Sun 6:30–7:00
MODERATOR:
Sen. Blair Moody

Public-affairs debate show, in which two Republicans and two Democratic Congressmen gave their views on an issue of national importance. The program originated in NBC's Washington, D.C., studios and was first seen as a Sunday afternoon program (March–June 1949). In 1953–1954, it turned up on DuMont. Former Senator Blair Moody of Michigan was the moderator.

MELBA (*Situation Comedy*)
FIRST TELECAST: *January 28, 1986*
LAST TELECAST: *September 13, 1986*
BROADCAST HISTORY:
Jan 1986, CBS Tue 8:00–8:30
Aug 1986–Sep 1986, CBS Sat 8:00–8:30
CAST:
Melba Patterson .... Melba Moore
Tracy Patterson .... Jamilla Perry
Susan Slater .... Gracie Harrison
Mama Rose .... Barbara Meek
Jack .... Lou Jacobi
Gil .... Evan Mirand

Melba was the unqualified disaster of the 1985–1986 TV season. A second-season comedy starring musical-comedy star Melba Moore, it was yanked from the CBS schedule after its premiere telecast and did not show up again until the last few episodes that had been produced were run off during the summer. The story line dealt with the work and home life of Melba Patterson, the director of New York's Manhattan Visitors' Center. Adapting to life after divorce, Melba was raising her 9-year-old daughter, Tracy, with the help of her mother, Rose, who lived with them. Melba's best friend was her white "sister," Susan—they had both been raised by Rose, who was the housekeeper in the Slater home when they were children. Jack and Gil worked for Melba at the Visitors' Center.

MELBA MOORE-CLIFTON DAVIS SHOW, THE (*Musical Variety*)
FIRST TELECAST: *June 7, 1972*
LAST TELECAST: *July 5, 1972*
BROADCAST HISTORY:
Jun 1972–Jul 1972, CBS Wed 8:00–9:00
REGULARS:
Melba Moore
Clifton Davis
Timmie Rogers
Ron Carey
Dick Libertini
Liz Torres
The Charles H. Coleman Orchestra

Young Broadway stars Melba Moore and Clifton Davis starred in this summer variety series. With the help of their regular supporting cast and special guest stars they performed skits and did musical numbers. The set for the show was designed to look like the side of an apartment building with the various acts taking place in different apartments.

MELODY, HARMONY & RHYTHM (*Music*)
FIRST TELECAST: *December 13, 1949*
LAST TELECAST: *February 16, 1950*
BROADCAST HISTORY:
Dec 1949–Feb 1950, NBC Tue/Thu 7:30–7:45
REGULARS:
Lynne Barrett
Carol Reed
Charlie Dobson
Tony DeSimone Trio

This musical interlude featured three vocalists and an instrumental trio. It originated from WPTZ, Philadelphia.

MELODY STREET (*Music*)
FIRST TELECAST: *September 23, 1953*
LAST TELECAST: *February 5, 1954*
BROADCAST HISTORY:
Sep 1953–Oct 1953, DUM Wed 8:30–9:00
Nov 1953–Feb 1954, DUM Fri 8:30–9:00
HOST:
Allan Brown (1953)
Elliot Lawrence (1953)
Tony Mottola (1954)
REGULARS:
Lyn Gibbs
Joe Buwen
Roberta McDonald

Another stop in DuMont's never-ending search for low-cost programming was this "musical stroll down Tin Pan Alley," in which a cast of regulars and guests lip-synched (mouthed) the words to a song while a phonograph record was played. The host for most of the run was noted orchestra leader Elliot Lawrence, who was seen sitting at a piano with a cigarette dangling from his mouth, Hoagy Carmichael-style, commenting on the music. "I was awful," he frankly admitted to the co-author of this book, "I don't even smoke!" Lawrence soon returned to what he did very well, conducting an orchestra, and guitarist Tony Mottola took over the host's spot for the show's last month.

MELODY TOUR (*Musical Variety*)
FIRST TELECAST: *July 8, 1954*
LAST TELECAST: *September 30, 1954*
BROADCAST HISTORY:
Jul 1954–Sep 1954, ABC Thu 8:00–9:00
REGULARS:
Stan Freeman
Norman Scott
Nellie Fisher
Jorie Remes
Nancy Kenyon
Peter Gladke
Jonathan Lucas
The Harry Sosnik Orchestra

Interesting summer musical series built around the concept of a vacation trip. The premiere took place mostly in a pier setting, as the cast prepared to embark, and subsequent programs highlighted various foreign ports of call. Guests were featured in addition to the regular cast.

MELROSE PLACE (*Drama*)
FIRST TELECAST: *July 8, 1992*
LAST TELECAST: *May 24, 1999*
BROADCAST HISTORY:
Jul 1992–Jun 1994, FOX Wed 9:00–10:00
Sep 1994–May 1999, FOX Mon 8:00–9:00 (OS)
CAST:
Jake Hanson (1992–1997) .... Grant Show
Alison Parker (1992–1997)
.... Courtney Thorne-Smith
Billy Campbell (1992–1998).......... Andrew Shue
Dr. Michael Mancini.............. Thomas Calabro
Jane Mancini (1992–1997, 1998–1999)
.... Josie Bissett
Rhonda Blair (1992–1993) .... Vanessa Williams
Matt Fielding (1992–1997)............ Doug Savant
Sandy Louise Harling (1992) .... Amy Locane
Lucy Cabot (1992–1993)........... Deborah Adair
Keith Gray (1992–1993)......... William R. Moses
Jo Beth Reynolds (1992–1996)...... Daphne Zuniga
**Kay Beacon (1992–1994)* .... Sydney Walsh
Terrence Haggard (1992–1993)
.... John Marshall Jones
Sydney Andrews (1993–1997)...... Laura Leighton
Amanda Woodward (1993–1999)
.... Heather Locklear
Dr. Kimberly Shaw (1992–1997) ...... Marcia Cross
**Nancy Donner (1993–1994)* .... Meg Wittner
Dr. Katya Petrova (1993)............ Beata Pozniak
Robert Wilson (1993–1994)........ Steven Eckholdt
Nikki Petrova (1993) .... Mara Wilson
Steve McMillan (1993) .... Parker Stevenson
**Palmer Woodward (1993–1994)* ...... Wayne Tippit
**Lauren Eskridge (1993–1994)* ..... Kristian Alfonso
Reed Carter (1994).................. James Wilder
Jeffrey Lindley (1994–1995) .... Jason Beghe
Dr. Stanley Levin (1994) .... Carmen Argenziano
Chas Russell (1994) .... Jeff Kaake
Hillary Michaels (1994) .... Linda Gray
Sarah Owens (1994)................... Cassidy Rae
Bruce Teller (1994) .... Stanley Kamel
Chris Marchette (1994) .... Andrew Williams
Dr. Peter Burns (1994–1999) .... Jack Wagner
Susan Madsen (1994)............... Cheryl Pollak
Brooke Armstrong (1995–1996)....... Kristin Davis
Jess Hanson (1995).................. Dan Cortese
Hayley Armstrong (1995) .... Perry King
Dr. Paul Graham (1995)............ David Beecroft
Richard Hart (1995–1996) .... Patrick Muldoon
Alycia Barnett (1995–1996)... Anne-Marie Johnson
Dr. Hobbs (1995)............. Francis X. McCarthy
Shelley Hanson (1995) .... Hudson Leick
Jack Parezi (1995) .... Antonio Sabato, Jr.
Nicholas Diamond (1995) .... Morgan Stevens
Bobby Parezi (1995–1996) .... John Enos III
Alan Ross (1995–1996) .... Lonnie Schuyler
David Johansen (1996) .... Rob Youngblood
Dr. Dominick O'Malley (1996)........ Brad Johnson
Det. Wylie (1996) .... Nigel Gibbs
Samantha "Sam" Reilly (1996–1998)
.... Brooke Langton
Kyle McBride (1996–1999)................ Rob Estes
Taylor McBride (1996–1998)............ Lisa Rinna
**Dr. Irene Shulman (1996–1999)*........ Dey Young
Craig Field (1996–1998) .... David Charvet
Arthur Field (1996–1997) ...... Michael Des Barres
Megan Lewis (1996–1999) .... Kelly Rutherford
Dr. Dan Hathaway (1996–1997) .... Greg Evigan
Walter (1996–1997)................... Phil Morris
Carter Gallavan (1996–1997)........... Chad Lowe
Nick Reardon (1997–1998)............ Scott Plank
Colleen (1997)........................ Stacy Haiduk
Chelsea Fielding (1997)............... Katie Wright
Harry Dean (1997)............... Markus Flanagan
Jim Reilly (1997)................ Anthony Denison
Denise Fielding (1997) .... Nancy Lee Grahn
Mark (1997) .... S.A. Griffin
Jennifer Mancini (1997–1998)....... Alyssa Milano
Dr. Brett Cooper (1997–1998)........ Linden Ashby
Lexi Sterling (1997–1999)............. Jamie Luner
Eric Baines (1997) .... Jeffrey Nordling
Connie Rexroth (1997–1998) .... Megan Ward
Christine Denton (1998)........... Susan Walters
Jeff Baylor (1998) .... Dan Gauthier
Jordan Arkin (1998).............. David Gautreaux
Rory Blake (1998)............ Anthony Tyler Quinn
Dr. Louis Visconti (1998–1999) ..... Mark L. Taylor
Ryan McBridge (1998–1999)... John Haymes Newton
Alex Bastian (1998) .... Steve Wilder
Eve Clery (1998–1999).................. Rena Sofer
Nurse Amy (1998–1999)............ Selma Archerd
Terry O'Brien (1999).............. Alexandra Paul
Sarah McBride (1999) .... Chea Courtney
Tony Marlin (1999) .... James Darren
*Occasional

This convoluted nighttime soap opera followed the intertwined lives of the twenty-something residents of 4616 Melrose Place, a garden apartment complex in Los Angeles. When the series premiered they were Jake, a motorcycle mechanic; Alison, a receptionist at D&D Advertising; Billy, an aspiring writer and Alison's platonic roommate; Michael, a resident at

Wilshire Memorial Hospital who was doing maintenance work around the complex to earn extra money, and his wife, Jane; Rhonda, a perky aerobics instructor who got involved with a wealthy restaurateur and was gone after the 1992–1993 season; Matt, a gay social worker; and Rhonda's roommate, Sandy, a waitress with a Southern accent who worked at Shooter's, where the gang hung out, and left in November when she got a role in a soap opera and moved to New York.

More probably happened to Alison than to anyone else on Melrose Place. She had an affair with married Keith and, after getting promoted to assistant account executive at D&D, quit her job and moved to Seattle to be with him after his divorce. Their relationship didn't work out, and Alison returned to L.A. and moved in with Billy, who became her lover. Unbalanced Keith showed up to stalk her before committing suicide that fall. She and Billy were to be married in the 1993–1994 season finale, but shaken by the realization that her father had molested her when she was a child, Alison left Billy at the altar. That fall he moved into his own apartment, though they still worked together at D&D, where Billy had been hired as a copy writer. When Billy started dating her friend Susan, Alison developed a drinking problem, which she eventually overcame. Her successful work culminated in the board's vote to make her president of D&D, replacing agency chief Amanda, who was suffering from cancer. Ironically, her new responsibilities and job pressures gave Alison the same "take no prisoners" attitude she had resented in Amanda.

Amanda had joined the show in 1993 as an ambitious art director at D&D. She got her father to finance her purchase of the Melrose Place apartment complex so that she could move in and be close to Billy. Ruthless and single-minded, she made life tough on Alison, since she wanted Billy. In the fall of 1994 she began a short affair with equally ruthless Peter Burns, chief of staff at Wilshire Memorial Hospital. They orchestrated a coup in which a group fronted by Peter won control of D&D and made her president, precipitating the suicide of her former boss, Bruce. Not long after, she was diagnosed with Hodgkin's disease, and while under treatment, was released from D&D. However, when Amanda recovered she took a low-level account executive position at D&D under Alison and plotted to get back into power, enlisting devious young Brooke, Alison's assistant, to spy for her. That May Amanda regained control of the agency.

Michael, who started out as a nice guy, became to *Melrose Place* what J.R. had been to *Dallas*: the man viewers love to hate. He was ambitious, unscrupulous, duplicitous, and unfaithful. He cheated on Jane with everyone, from fellow doctor Kimberly to Jane's sister Sydney, and would do anything to advance his medical career. When Jane threw him out, he proposed to Kimberly, but then got roaring drunk and almost killed her in a terrible car wreck. While she was in a coma he was conned into marriage by Sydney, who was almost as devious as he. In April 1994, Kimberly reappeared, but the accident had left her with a horrible scar (concealed by a wig) and affected her mental stability. She harassed Sydney, then allied with her to plot Michael's murder, running him down with Jane's stolen car to frame Jane. Michael survived, divorced Sydney, and ran off to Las Vegas to marry Kimberly, who alternately loved him and wanted to kill him. In spring 1995 he dumped her for Amanda, driving Kimberly to attempted suicide. Michael found her but would have let her die had Sydney not turned up and forced him to take her to the hospital. Nice guy.

Jane went to work at a women's clothing boutique and, after the store was sold, opened her own business, Jane Mancini Designs, but as part of her divorce settlement Michael retained half interest in it. After Kimberly framed her for the hit-and-run on Michael she went to prison, but got out by telling the cops she believed it was her sister Sydney who had run Michael down. Their father got Sydney committed to a sanitarium because he believed she was out of control, and she was eventually released into Jane's custody. Jane started dating Chris, her business partner, and he romanced her while lusting after Sydney. He absconded with the half million Jane had gotten to expand her business, kidnapped Sydney, took her to Vegas with him, and gambled away the money.

Sydney was both bad and good, but mostly bad. When she first arrived, after Michael and Jane had separated, she slept a few times with Michael, which ticked off her sister. She got a waitress job but, because the money was better, started turning tricks for Lauren, a Hollywood madam. Sydney was busted and went straight, only to take over the madam's business while Lauren was on trial, losing it when Lauren got off. Desperate for cash, she turned tricks for a while and then went to work for Jane after being released from the sanitarium. She got fired after complaining about Chris, Jane's sleazy new "partner" boyfriend, and convinced Jake to give her a job at Shooter's.

Jake bought the bike shop he worked at with financial help from his girlfriend, Jo, an aspiring photographer and summer 1992 arrival at the apartment complex. They had money troubles with the shop, and, after it was destroyed by a fire in September 1993, they broke up. Jake, who subsequently had an affair with Amanda, then got a job with Palmer, her crooked father, building Avanti replicas, almost getting arrested as part of the sting operation that resulted in Palmer's imprisonment. Then he ran the charter boat *Pretty Lady* with Jo's ex-con boyfriend, Reed, and took it over after she had killed Reed, who was using the boat to smuggle drugs. In the fall of 1994 Palmer, who had jumped bail, set Jake up to get even with him, using sexy Brittany (Kathy Ireland) to plant explosives on the *Pretty Lady*. She double-crossed Palmer, killing him before he could kill Jake, and then blew up the boat. Jake survived and bought Shooter's with reward money from the FBI for his contribution to Brittany's arrest. In the spring of 1995, following his mother's death, Jake's older brother, Jess, moved to L.A. and moved in with Jake, who gave him a job at Shooter's.

Jo's big break came when Amanda, who liked her portfolio, gave Jo photo assignments for D&D print ads. After Amanda broke up with Jake, she got involved with Reed. After killing him (in self-defense) on the *Pretty Lady* she found out she was pregnant with his child. When Reed's parents found out they took her to court and won sole custody of the unborn child. Kimberly worked out a deal with her to deliver the baby at her beach house and fake its being stillborn so Jo could keep it. When she came to get the baby boy (Austin), crazy Kimberly had taken him as her own. Jo eventually got the baby back but gave him up for adoption to keep Reed's parents from getting custody.

Matt worked at a halfway house for teens and when he was laid off in the fall of 1993 got an administrative job at Wilshire Memorial with Michael's help. Out of a sense of obligation to Michael, he changed the records of Michael's blood-alcohol level to keep him from losing his medical license and facing criminal charges from the accident in which Kimberly was hurt. Matt later got involved with Jeffrey, a gay navy officer, who came out of the closet and was forced out of the service. Eventually, Matt was accepted into medical school.

In the last episode of the 1994–1995 season, Billy married manipulative Brooke at her rich father's estate (despite Alison's last-minute attempt to stop the wedding), and Kimberly went completely off the deep end, plotting to blow up the entire Melrose Place complex with her enemies inside.

Kimberly's bombs damaged the complex on Melrose Place, killed the wife of Richard Hart (owner of the design firm Mackenzie Hart), and temporarily blinded Alison. Meanwhile Peter and Michael formed a joint medical practice, hiring Sydney as their receptionist. Peter got Kimberly, who had been sent to a mental hospital after the bombing, released into his custody, and Michael rekindled his romance with her. In February 1996 they got remarried, but soon after her emotional problems resurfaced, manifested by multiple personalities. Billy, finally fed up with Brooke, sued her for divorce but it turned out to be unnecessary—while drunk, she fell into the pool, hit her head, and drowned. Peter, who had lost Amanda to wheeler-dealer Bobby, schemed with attorney Alycia to ruin his rival. In a confrontation with Alycia, Bobby became violent, forcing her to hit him with a golf club that helped propel him through an office window to his death several flights below. Alycia died in a car accident before she could tell the police what happened, and Peter was arrested for Bobby's murder, but was later cleared. Jane, who was working for Richard, had affairs with Richard and Jake, and started her own design business, which she ran single-handedly out of a converted garage on the Melrose Place property. Jane and Richard got back together professionally, but after closing a big deal, Richard, who still had the hots for her, raped her at their hotel in New York. Jane convinced Sydney to help her murder Richard to avenge the rape. He then tried to kill *them*, but was himself killed in a shootout with a park ranger who came to their aid.

At the start of the 1996–1997 season Peter moved in with Amanda, who had married him while he was in prison. Eventually he went back to his practice. Kimberly gave up her medical license and went to work as the office manager for Michael and Peter. Arriving on the scene were Taylor and her husband Kyle, who moved to L.A. to open a restaurant; however, Taylor's real reason was to be close to her late sister's husband, Peter, with whom she was obsessed. They had an affair, causing Amanda to start divorce proceedings. Amanda went into partnership with Kyle, opening Upstairs, a jazz club, and the two of them left the country to get quickie divorces from their spouses. Troubled Kimberly, diagnosed with an inoperable brain tumor, set Michael up with Megan, started divorce proceedings, and planned her own suicide to look like an accidental death in order to provide Michael and Megan with financial security. After Michael married Megan, Kimberly died from a sudden stroke. Megan left Michael when she found out he had maneuvered Peter into resigning as chief of staff at Wilshire Memorial. Craig, the manipulative son of a D&D board member, arrived at the agency and, after much double dealing among himself, Amanda, and his father, took control. Forced out, Craig and Sydney formed a new agency, Sky High, and stole most of D&D's staff.

Following a robbery at her boutique, Jane went back to Chicago to rehab emotionally with her parents, leaving Sydney (who renamed the shop Sydney's) in charge. Sydney lost the boutique and, desperate for money, took a job as a waitress at Kyle's. Gay Matt's kid sister, Chelsea, turned up, and he was awarded legal guardianship by the courts. He later got a residency in San Francisco and moved there with Chelsea. Alison and Jake went away and got married by a local pastor, but she subsequently miscarried and started drinking again. Unable to be what she believed Jake needed, Alison divorced him and moved to Atlanta to start over. Craig and Sydney were married, but moments after the ceremony, Sydney was killed by a speeding car driven by Samantha's crazed dad, Jim, who had just held up the grocery store where Sam worked.

In fall 1997, Shooters was gone, replaced by the gang's new hangout, Upstairs, owned by Kyle and Amanda, who were now seriously involved. With Billy's help, Amanda started her own agency, Amanda Woodward Advertising, and raided back the unhappy staff working at Sky High. Craig, distraught over the failures of his business dealings, later committed suicide. In the spring, despite Taylor's plotting to disrupt things, Kyle and Amanda got married, but they had a rocky time of it. Taylor found out she was pregnant but didn't know who the father was (it was Michael, but he denied it). Bret "Coop" Cooper, who sought revenge for Kimberly's death, moved to L.A. and took a position at Wilshire Memorial, ingratiating himself with Michael. Megan got Michael and Peter to call a truce to save their joint practice, and Michael brought Coop in as a third partner, planning to push Peter out. Coop's sexy but shrewish ex-wife, Lexi, turned up to cause trouble, seducing Peter, much to Coop's chagrin. Billy and Sam, who was also working for Amanda, got married, but Sam became involved with pro baseball player Jeff, the pitchman in an ad campaign she was working on, opening the way for Billy to fall into the eager arms of Michael's sister Jennifer. Billy told Jennifer she was the only one he could trust and that he loved her.

As *Melrose Place*'s final season began, Amanda flew to the Dominican Republic, where she got divorced from Kyle and married sleazy Rory. Kyle arrived just in time to save her from Rory, who was planning to poison her on their honeymoon and get everything they owned. Rory died from a self-inflicted wound during the fight with Kyle, who then remarried Amanda, right there on the island. Kyle bought land to build a house, and he and Amanda decided to try to have a baby while she groomed Kyle's younger brother Ryan to take over the agency. Because of a lab mix-up, Kyle thought he was sterile, becoming moody and despondent and seeking solace in booze, which ultimately caused Amanda to toss him out. He went through alcohol rehab and they reunited.

Everything fell apart for Sam when Billy got a job in Rome and took Jennifer, to whom he proposed, with him. Sam then proposed to baseball player Jeff and he accepted. Lexi, in financial trouble, tried to arrange a sham marriage to Coop in order to take advantage of a codicil in her father's will that would net her $10 million. At Megan's urging, Coop went along, but eventually he got fed up with Lexi's scheming, told her lawyer about the sham marriage, and moved back East. Peter forced Michael to admit to Taylor that he was the father of her unborn baby, but after she gave birth to Michael, Jr., at the beach house, she moved back to Boston to raise him alone. Michael and Jane got back together after meeting at their tenth high school reunion, and she returned to L.A., going to work for Amanda. Michael married Jane but the marriage was broken up by her former lover Alex, who implied that she had had sex with him the night before the wedding. Peter married Eve, a childhood friend of Amanda's who had been working as a singer at Upstairs. Later in the season he fought with Dr. Shulman over his job, but when Eve presented him with the first $5 million check for leasing his late father's oil-laden land to a drilling company, Peter bought the hospital and turned it into a medical cooperative. Amanda sold the apartment complex and moved out when she found out the buyer was fronting for Lexi.

As the tangled series drew to a close, Megan and Ryan got married on the beach, and Amanda and Kyle broke up because she was more interested in the agency than in him. Kyle told pregnant Jane he wanted to marry her, even though the baby she was carrying was Michael's, while Peter left Eve for Amanda. In the series finale, things looked dark for Peter and Amanda. Amanda admitted that she had been responsible for the death, many years before, of a boy that Eve had spent 15 years in prison for killing, and Peter was about to be arraigned on charges related to one of Michael's hospital scams. Peter and Amanda faked their deaths in a cabin explosion and skipped the country, getting married on a tropical isle. Michael, who was now Chief of Staff at Wilshire Memorial, and who had been given $1 million for helping Peter and Amanda escape, was seen with a bimbo nurse on his lap, declaring that life is good.

MEMORIES . . . THEN AND NOW (*Magazine*)

BROADCAST HISTORY:

Syndicated only
30 minutes
Produced: *1990–1992* (52 episodes)
Released: *September 1990*

HOSTS:

Chuck Scarborough
Kathryn Kinley

Hosted by two news personalities from WNBC-TV in New York, this series was a weekly collection of nostalgia including newsreel clips from bygone years, old school yearbook photos of people who later became famous, a "Where Are They Now?" segment that showed what had happened to people who were once in the news, and childhood reminiscences of celebrities.

MEN (*Drama*)

FIRST TELECAST: *March 25, 1989*
LAST TELECAST: *April 22, 1989*
BROADCAST HISTORY:

Mar 1989–Apr 1989, ABC Sat 10:00–11:00

CAST:

Dr. Steven Ratajkowski .... Ted Wass
Paul Armas .... Saul Rubinek
Charlie Hazard .... Ving Rhames
Off. Danny McDaniel .... Tom O'Brien
Lisa Vaneti .... Kimberley Pistone
Margaret Hazard .... Candy Ann Brown

This series, which might have been called *Male Bonding* or *Guy Talk*, was about four Baltimore men bound by a weekly poker game and a deep friendship. Three of them, surgeon Steven, reporter Paul, and criminal lawyer Charlie, had been friends since high school. The original fourth member of the group had been policeman Tom McDaniel; his death in the first episode led the others to reach out to and include his hot-headed younger brother Danny (also a cop), whom they helped to deal with his loss. There was plenty of anguish to go around in subsequent episodes, too: longtime bachelor Steve's desire to become a dad, divorced Paul's longing for stability and for his children, and family man Charlie's turmoil when he was fired and had to set up his own practice. Lisa was young Danny's girlfriend.

MEN, THE (*Adventure*)

FIRST TELECAST: *September 21, 1972*
LAST TELECAST: *September 1, 1973*
BROADCAST HISTORY:

Sep 1972–Jan 1973, ABC Thu 9:00–10:00
Jan 1973–Sep 1973, ABC Sat 10:00–11:00

THEME MUSIC (OVERALL):

Isaac Hayes

This was the umbrella title for three rotating series, *Assignment Vienna, Delphi Bureau,* and *Jigsaw.* At first these elements rotated in normal fashion, each one appearing every third week. However, in January 1973, when *The Men* moved to Saturdays, the rotation scheme was changed and each element appeared for several weeks in a row, as follows:

Jan 13–Feb 10: *Assignment Vienna*
Feb 17–Mar 3: *Jigsaw*
Mar 17–Apr 7: *Delphi Bureau*
Apr 14–Jun 9: *Assignment Vienna*
Jun 16–Aug 11: *Jigsaw*
Aug 18–Sep 1: *Delphi Bureau*

See individual element titles for more complete program information.

MEN AT LAW, see *Storefront Lawyers*

MEN BEHAVING BADLY(*Situation Comedy*)

FIRST TELECAST: *September 18, 1996*
LAST TELECAST: *December 25, 1997*
BROADCAST HISTORY:

Sep 1996–Feb 1997, NBC Wed 9:30–10:00
Apr 1997–May 1997, NBC Wed 9:30–10:00
May 1997–Jun 1997, NBC Wed 8:30–9:00
Jun 1997–Sep 1997, NBC Thu 8:30–9:00

Aug 1997–Sep 1997, NBC Sun 8:30–9:00
Sep 1997–Nov 1997, NBC Sun 8:00–8:30
Dec 1997, NBC Thu 8:30–9:00

CAST:

Jamie Coleman .... Rob Schneider
Kevin Paterson/Murphy (1996–1997) ... Ron Eldard
Sarah Stretten/Mitchell (1996–1997) .. Justine Bateman
Cherie Miller (1996) .... Julia Campbell
Steve Cochran (1997) .... Ken Marino
Katie Hubble (1997) .... Jenica Bergere
Nurse Brenda Mikowski .... Dina Spybey

"Men are dogs . . . They just are" was the slogan displayed at the beginning of this gross sitcom, set in Indianapolis. Exhibit number one was unemployed photographer Jamie, a weasely, sexist slob who couldn't understand why he had no luck with women. His roommate Kevin, a manager at a security systems company, was only slightly smarter when it came to the opposite sex. Together they sat around guzzling beer, wolfing down dry cereal, and debating the merits of continued lovemaking if your girlfriend has fallen asleep. Sarah was a sensible nurse who loved Kevin despite his quirks, and Cherie the sexy next-door neighbor and target of many of the boys' pranks. NBC started tinkering with the show almost as soon as it premiered. About two months into the run Kevin and Sarah's last names were changed, for no apparent reason. At the beginning of the second season Kevin married Sarah and moved to Chicago; Cherie was also gone. Jamie's new roommate was Steve, who was coming off a long relationship and needed to get in touch with his hormones. His girlfriend Katie was a young art teacher with an unexpected wild streak, while Nurse Brenda (who had been seen occasionally during the previous season) was the boys' new target. Based on the British sitcom of the same name.

MEN FROM SHILOH, THE, see *Virginian, The*

MEN INTO SPACE (*Science Fiction*)

FIRST TELECAST: *September 30, 1959*
LAST TELECAST: *September 7, 1960*
BROADCAST HISTORY:

Sep 1959–Sep 1960, CBS Wed 8:30–9:00

CAST:

Col. Edward McCauley .... William Lundigan

On October 4, 1957, Russia launched the world's first man-made earth satellite. It was too late to get a show about it on television that season, or even the next, but in 1959 CBS was ready to capitalize on the high public interest in and concern about the "space race" with this realistic dramatization of space exploration. *Men into Space* was produced with the cooperation and assistance of the army, navy, air force, and numerous scientific organizations, and every attempt was made to present an accurate picture of man's likely experiences and problems away from Earth. Col. Edward McCauley was the only regular member of the cast. His adventures on the moon base, the space station, other planets within the solar system, and on rocketships in transit provided the stories. Problems with equipment, the environment, and the people involved in the space program all created crisis situations for the indomitable Col. McCauley.

MEN OF TOMORROW (*Documentary*)

FIRST TELECAST: *June 29, 1954*
LAST TELECAST: *September 21, 1954*
BROADCAST HISTORY:

Jun 1954–Sep 1954, ABC Tue 7:30–8:00

REGULARS:

Robert Mitchell Boys Choir

This filmed series was devoted to the Boy Scouts of America. Each episode explored some aspect of the Boy Scout movement, such as the training of young scouts and trips taken by them. Opening and closing music was provided by the Robert Mitchell Boys Choir of Hollywood.

MEN, WOMEN & DOGS (*Situation Comedy*)

FIRST TELECAST: *October 14, 2001*
LAST TELECAST: *December 30, 2001*
BROADCAST HISTORY:

Oct 2001–Nov 2001, WB Sun 8:30–9:00
Dec 2001, WB Sun 9:30–10:00

CAST:

Jeremiah .... Bill Bellamy
Clay .... Danny Pinn
Eric .... Niklaus Lange
Michelle .... Heather Stephens
Royce .... Mike Damus
Nina .... Tracey Cherelle Jones

This cheerfully sexist sitcom was about four guys who met every day with their pooches at an L.A. dog park. Jeremiah was the biggest womanizer of the group, a chef at The Strand restaurant who used his obscenely delicious chocolate cake as a seduction aid. He believed, apparently correctly, that if you could convince a woman to break her rule about not eating dessert, she would break her rules about having sex. Emotionally he was closer to his dog, Wolfgang, than he had ever been to a woman. Jeremiah's best friend, Clay, was the social antithesis of his buddy, a sensitive, almost wimpy, idealist with a new puppy who frowned on Jeremiah's aggressive attitude toward women. Eric, a hunky surfer, had just moved in with attorney Michelle, who was not comfortable sharing him with his beloved, aging, and very possessive bulldog, Betsy. Royce was the most recent addition to the group, a penny-pinching wannabe womanizer who didn't even own a dog but thought the dog park was a good place to pick up girls. In November he finally moved out of his mother's home. In the last episode Eric threw a surprise bar-exam-passing party for Michelle. Nina, initially seen as a food critic with whom Jeremiah had an affair, was, in this final episode, a lawyer friend of Michelle's who resisted his charms—and his "glorified brownie."

MENASHA THE MAGNIFICENT (*Situation Comedy*)

FIRST TELECAST: *July 3, 1950*
LAST TELECAST: *September 11, 1950*
BROADCAST HISTORY:

Jul 1950–Sep 1950, NBC Mon 8:00–8:30

CAST:

Menasha .... Menasha Skulnik
Mrs. Davis .... Zamah Cunningham

Short-lived situation comedy starring Yiddish comedian Menasha Skulnik, who began each day singing "Oh, What a Beautiful Morning," but usually wound up in trouble. Menasha, a little fellow with a hoplike walk and a tragicomic mien, was cast as the meek manager of a restaurant owned by the domineering, Amazon-like Mrs. Davis. His fate was to be pushed around constantly. Jean Cleveland appeared as Mrs. Davis in the first telecast, but was replaced by Zamah Cunningham the following week.

MEN'S ROOM, THE (*Discussion*)
BROADCAST HISTORY:
Lifetime
30 minutes
Produced: *1997*
Premiered: *June 6, 1997*

In this short-lived series, Lifetime, the cable channel for women, attempted to do what no one has been able to accomplish in five thousand years of civilization—explain men to women. Men (mostly handsome young studs) were shown in mini-documentaries bonding on an all-male ski trip, working together at a firehouse, getting all sweaty together on a basketball court. "I love being around guys," said one. "It's different with women around." That explains it.

There was no regular host.

There is no record that ESPN, the men's sports network, ever had a show that tried to explain women to men. Maybe they know better.

MERCY POINT (*Science Fiction/Medical Drama*)
FIRST TELECAST: *October 6, 1998*
LAST TELECAST: *October 20, 1998*
BROADCAST HISTORY:
Oct 1998, UPN Tue 9:00–10:00
CAST:
Dr. Grote Maxwell .... Joe Morton
Dr. Haylen Breslauer .... Maria Del Mar
Dr. Caleb "C. J." Jurado .... Brian McNamara
ANI .... Julia Pennington
Dr. Dru Breslauer .... Alexandra Wilson
Dr. Rema Cooke .... Gay Thomas
Dr. Batung .... Jordan Lund
Dr. Harris DeMilla .... Joe Spano
Lt. Kim Salisaw .... Salli Richardson
Nurse Molly Tobitt .... Christine Willes
Nurse Davies .... Kirstin Robek
Mednaut Cowan .... Leanne Adachi
Mednaut Thurston .... Rick Ravanello
Mednaut Westhusing .... Joe Pascual
Nagnom .... Haig Sutherland

Mercy Point was a space station hospital on the fringes of the galaxy, where doctors worked on both terrestrial and extraterrestrial patients. The year was 2249. Grote, an alien physiologist, was one of the top surgeons at the hospital, and Haylen was a senior surgeon whose young sister, Dru, with whom she didn't get along, had just arrived as a new resident physician. C.J. was the libidinous resident hunk, Rema a doctor concerned with patient rights, and DeMilla the Chief of Staff. ANI (Android Nursing Interface) was the extremely efficient and attractive synthetic life-form head nurse who was resented by her live subordinates, Dr. Batung the insensitive alien surgeon with the lousy bedside manner, and Hippocrates was the talking computer that monitored patient status. There were lots of medical crises in this extraterrestrial *ER*, but it went on life support after its premiere and expired two episodes later. UPN aired the four remaining completed episodes on consecutive Thursdays the following July.

MEREDITH WILLSON SHOW, THE (*Music*)
FIRST TELECAST: *July 31, 1949*
LAST TELECAST: *August 21, 1949*
BROADCAST HISTORY:
Jul 1949–Aug 1949, NBC Sun 8:30–9:00
REGULARS:
Meredith Willson
Norma Zimmer

Four-week summer musical series, hosted by famed composer and orchestra leader Meredith Willson. Norma Zimmer later became Lawrence Welk's "Champagne Lady."

MERV GRIFFIN SHOW, THE (*Talk*)
FIRST TELECAST: *August 18, 1969*
LAST TELECAST: *February 11, 1972*
BROADCAST HISTORY:
Aug 1969–Feb 1972, CBS Mon–Fri 11:30–1:00 A.M.
REGULARS:
Merv Griffin
Arthur Treacher
Mort Lindsey Orchestra

Merv Griffin had had a highly successful syndicated talk show for several years when CBS chose him to wage war on a network scale with Johnny Carson's *Tonight Show* in 1969. His arrival meant that there were competing late-night talk shows on all three networks, Joey Bishop having started one on ABC in the summer of 1967. A cherubic folksy individual, Merv was a former band singer and veteran of several network daytime talk and game shows, in addition to his syndicated show. His ingratiating manner and aversion to virtually anything that might be considered radical, offensive, or controversial made his show rather bland. It did force Joey Bishop off the air, to be replaced by the dry, intellectual wit of Dick Cavett, but it could never make a dent in Carson's late-night audience. As CBS' first regular late-night entry since *Chronoscope* in the mid-1950s, *The Merv Griffin Show* was never as big an audience-grabber as CBS had hoped and was canceled two and one-half years after its premiere. It was replaced by late-night movies, while Merv returned to the syndicated talk-show world.

Merv's first talk show had been a 55-minute daytime series on NBC from October 1962 to March 1963. Two years later he began the syndicated 90-minute talk show that attracted CBS' attention.

His last daily syndicated *Merv Griffin Show* ran from the summer of 1972 until September of 1986 and, along with a number of successful game shows he had created over the years (including *Jeopardy!* and *Wheel of Fortune*), made him a wealthy man.

METROPOLITAN OPERA AUDITIONS OF THE AIR (*Talent*)
FIRST TELECAST: *January 15, 1952*
LAST TELECAST: *April 1, 1952*
BROADCAST HISTORY:
Jan 1952–Apr 1952, ABC Tue 8:30–9:00
COMMENTATOR:
Milton J. Cross

This must have been one of the classiest talent shows in the history of network television, as newcomers competed for a place at the fabled "Met." Similar operatic auditions had been telecast by ABC on a specials basis as early as 1948.

MIAMI VICE (*Police Drama*)

FIRST TELECAST: *September 16, 1984*
LAST TELECAST: *July 26, 1989*
BROADCAST HISTORY:

Sep 1984, NBC Sun 9:00–11:00
Sep 1984–May 1986, NBC Fri 10:00–11:00
Jun 1986–Mar 1988, NBC Fri 9:00–10:00
Apr 1988–Jan 1989, NBC Fri 10:00–11:00
Feb 1989–May 1989, NBC Fri 9:00–10:00
Jun 1989–Jul 1989, NBC Wed 10:00–11:00

CAST:

Det. James "Sonny" Crockett .... Don Johnson
Det. Ricardo Tubbs .... Philip Michael Thomas
Lt. Martin Castillo .... Edward James Olmos
Det. Gina Navarro Calabrese..... Saundra Santiago
Det. Trudy Joplin .... Olivia Brown
Det. Stan Switek................... Michael Talbott
Det. Larry Zito (1984–1987)............ John Diehl
**Izzy Moreno*........................ Martin Ferrero
**Caitlin Davies (1987–1988)* .... Sheena Easton

*Occasional

The pulse and rhythm of a glamorous resort city was juxtaposed against the seamy haunts of the drug underworld in this gritty action series, which made heavy use of rock music backgrounds and music video effects. Sonny Crockett was a rough-edged Miami vice detective who lived on a sailboat called *St. Vitus' Dance* that was guarded by his dyspeptic pet alligator, Elvis. Ricardo Tubbs was a black ex-New York street cop who had come south to find the drug dealer who murdered his brother. They were an unlikely but effective team, working undercover on the flashy Gold Coast and down the seedy alleyways that made Miami such a city of contrasts. Often they sped around town in Sonny's black Ferrari Spider sports car (later upgraded to a state-of-the-art Ferrari Testarossa). Lt. Castillo was their moody superior, Gina and Trudy a hip, female undercover team, and Stan and Larry more conventional backup.

The stylish, MTV-influenced series (music by rock composer Jan Hammer) was a smash hit, and transformed struggling actor Don Johnson into a major sex symbol in the mid-1980s. His expensive pastel sports jackets worn over a T-shirt, with stubbly beard, no socks, and an angry scowl started a fashion trend for those into the macho/grubby look. Female characters on the show fawned over him—and usually got blown up or shot for their trouble. Sonny's estranged wife, Caroline (played by Belinda Montgomery), and his young son were rarely seen, and a later quickie bride played by rock singer Sheena Easton also appeared infrequently. A multipart story in 1988 had Sonny believing that he really was his drug-dealing undercover alter ego, Sonny Burnett, forcing partner Tubbs (who was "Rico Cooper" undercover) to bail him out. Sonny's coworkers weren't so lucky; his original partner in the pilot (played by a pre-*L.A. Law* Jimmy Smits) was killed, as were his backup Zito and his original superior Lt. Lou Rodriquez (Gregory Sierra). Even his original Ferrari was blown up accidentally at the beginning of the third season.

The hip series attracted many famous celebrities not normally seen in TV acting roles to do cameos (or more), including singers from the '50s (Little Richard, James Brown) to the '80s (Phil Collins, Ted Nugent, the Fat Boys). Watergate felon G. Gordon Liddy made quite an impression in the role of sneaky Capt. Real Estate; also seen fleetingly were such unlikely folks as boxing promoter Don King, boxing champ Roberto Duran, comic Tommy Chong, Chrysler chairman Lee Iacocca, and the President of NBC-TV (as a bartender!).

MICHAEL ESSANY SHOW (*Comedy*)

BROADCAST HISTORY:

E! Entertainment
30 minutes
Original episodes: *2003–*
Premiered: *March 2, 2003*

REGULARS:

Michael Essany
Ernie Essany
Tina Essany
Mike Randazzo

For those who might ask, "Michael who?," the eponymous star of this late-night series was a 19-year-old Valparaiso, Indiana, college freshman who had been producing a cable talk show from his parents' living room since the age of 14. This nationally televised version was about the production of that show, rather than the show itself. It followed Michael, a fresh-faced, deferential, yet confident young man, as he made calls to line up guests, wrote out his own cue cards and practiced his opening monologue. Helping out on the "set" (which Mom insisted be kept clean) were his dad Ernie as stage manager, mom Tina as director, and pal Mike Randazzo as his happy sidekick. Believe it or not real guest stars did show up, including Kelly Rowland of Destiny's Child (Mom fed her entourage in the kitchen), model Frederique (who dragged Michael off to the mall), Tom Green (who spit on Mom's carpet), David Brenner and Michael Ian Black.

MICHAEL HAYES (*Legal Drama*)

FIRST TELECAST: *September 15, 1997*
LAST TELECAST: *June 15, 1998*
BROADCAST HISTORY:

Sep 1997, CBS Mon 10:00–11:00
Sep 1997–Jan 1998, CBS Tue 9:00–10:00
Mar 1998–Apr 1998, CBS Wed 9:00–10:00
Jun 1998, CBS Mon 10:00–11:00

CAST:

Michael Hayes .... David Caruso
Eddie Diaz .... Ruben Santiago-Hudson
Caitlin Hayes .... Mary B. Ward
Danny Hayes, Jr. (age 5) .... Jimmy Galeota
Danny Hayes.......................... David Cubitt
Jenny Nevins .... Hillary Danner
Lindsay Straus .... Rebecca Rigg
John Henry Manning........... Peter Outerbridge
Joan .... Jodi Long

Michael Hayes was an intense, brooding, former New York City cop turned federal prosecutor who, in this series' premiere, was appointed acting U.S. Attorney for the Southern District of New York when his boss, the current U.S. Attorney, was almost killed. He was tough and idealistic, often pushing hard on cases that had the potential to get him into trouble. Michael didn't care if he offended politicians, his superiors, corporate power brokers, or anyone else. He wanted *justice*. Working on his team were Eddie, Michael's friend and chief investigator; Nevins, Strauss, and Manning, three hardworking assistant U.S. Attorneys; and his secretary, Joan.

A running subplot centered on Michael's relationship with his brother's family. Danny had had several run-ins with the law and spent time in prison. Although he was now out, he couldn't face his wife and son, so Michael served as surrogate father to Danny's son and tried to help out his sister-in-law, Caitlin. Unable to sever his underworld ties, Danny was being pursued by the authorities when, at season's end, he turned state's evidence and went into the witness protection program—alone. Michael's own lover, Rebecca, had died early in the series after being shot while on duty, and his social life during the season was rather limited, except for a short fling with a former girlfriend, Assistant D.A. Julie Siegel (Helen Slater).

MICHAEL NESMITH IN TELEVISION PARTS (*Variety*)

FIRST TELECAST: *June 14, 1985*
LAST TELECAST: *July 5, 1985*
BROADCAST HISTORY:
Jun 1985–Jul 1985, NBC Fri 8:00–8:30
REGULARS:
Michael Nesmith
John Hobbs, Musical Director
Donna Ruppert

Did you ever wonder what happened to the Monkees, the pre-fab rock group so popular in the 1960s? One of them, Michael "Wool Hat" Nesmith, was independently wealthy and later began producing avant-garde videos. One of these, *Elephant Parts,* attracted the attention of NBC, which decided—unwisely—to try to turn it into a TV series for the masses.

Television Parts was an offbeat mélange of music and comedy. Some of the music was done straight and some as absurdist satire; the comedy consisted largely of surrealistic special effects and incomprehensible bits of comic business. Guest comedians and musicians appeared, with Nesmith providing a degree of continuity both as host (often wandering off the set) and sometimes as participant. Musical Director John Hobbs also appeared on-screen, reworking two familiar songs into a new song each week. Viewers were mystified.

Originally aired as a special on March 7, 1985, *Television Parts* had a short regular run in the summer, with its last three original episodes combined into a 90-minute replacement for *Saturday Night Live* that aired on July 27, 1985.

MICHAEL RICHARDS SHOW, THE (*Situation Comedy*)

FIRST TELECAST: *October 24, 2000*
LAST TELECAST: *January 2, 2001*
BROADCAST HISTORY:
Oct 2000–Jan 2001, NBC Tue 8:00–8:30
CAST:
Vic Nardozza .... Michael Richards
Brady McKay .... William Devane
Stacey Devers .... Amy Farrington
Kevin Blakeley .... Tim Meadows
Jack .... Bill Cobbs

The first of the *Seinfeld* alumni to get his own show was Michael Richards, with this misbegotten sitcom (subsequently Jason Alexander's *Bob Patterson* and Julia Louis-Dreyfus' *Watching Ellie* did little better). Vic was a lanky, bumbling detective working for Brady McKay's small McKay Investigative Services. Although Vic usually got the job done, it was only after so many pratfalls, misunderstandings and screw-ups that everyone was left laughing rather than applauding. Brady was the cheerful, if curmudgeonly boss, while others in the streetside office were eager simpleton Stacey, the new hire; photographer Kevin, who had a Peeping Tom fetish; and grumpy old pro Jack, who sparred with Kevin constantly.

MICHAEL SHAYNE (*Detective Drama*)

FIRST TELECAST: *September 30, 1960*
LAST TELECAST: *September 22, 1961*
BROADCAST HISTORY:
Sep 1960–Sep 1961, NBC Fri 10:00–11:00
CAST:
Michael Shayne .... Richard Denning
Tim Rourke .... Jerry Paris
Lucy Hamilton (1960–1961) .... Patricia Donahue
Lucy Hamilton (1961) .... Margie Regan
Will Gentry .... Herbert Rudley
Dick Hamilton .... Gary Clarke

Michael Shayne was a suave, debonair Miami-based private detective whose cases tended to revolve around bizarre murders. Helping him solve the cases were Tim Rourke, a young newspaper-reporter friend; Will Gentry, the chief of the Miami police department; and Dick Hamilton, the younger brother of Shayne's secretary/girlfriend Lucy. Lucy was not the only love of his life, however, and his fondness for beautiful women often got him into sticky situations. The character of Michael Shayne had been established in a series of detective novels written by Brett Halliday, as well as in a radio series, a dozen movies, and a monthly mystery magazine. Mr. Halliday acted as technical consultant for the series.

MICHELOB PRESENTS NIGHT MUSIC, see *Sunday Night*

MICKEY (*Situation Comedy*)

FIRST TELECAST: *September 16, 1964*
LAST TELECAST: *January 13, 1965*
BROADCAST HISTORY:
Sep 1964–Jan 1965, ABC Wed 9:00–9:30
CAST:
Mickey Grady .... Mickey Rooney
Nora Grady .... Emmaline Henry
Sammy Ling .... Sammee Tong
Timmy Grady .... Tim Rooney
Buddy Grady .... Brian Nash
Mr. Swidler .... Alan Reed

At the outset of this comedy series Mickey Rooney was cast as a Coast Guard recruiter in landlocked Omaha, who dreamt of a life on the open sea. He got his wish—or at least got close to it—when he inherited a luxurious beachfront hotel in Newport Harbor, California. When the Gradys moved from Omaha to take over the Marina Palms, they thought their money worries and other troubles would be over. Little did they realize that Sammy Ling, the hotel's manager (with a "lifetime contract"), had let it go deeply into debt by letting too many of his relatives in on the operation. The legal work was being done by Ling's shyster cousin and the mortgage was held by the Ling Savings & Loan at an annual rate of 17 percent. Mickey and family set out to straighten things out, in their own comedic way. Mickey Rooney's real-life son, Tim, played his 16-year-old son Timmy, and Brian Nash played the 8-year-old, Buddy.

MICKEY ROONEY SHOW, THE (*Situation Comedy*)

FIRST TELECAST: *September 4, 1954*
LAST TELECAST: *June 4, 1955*
BROADCAST HISTORY:
Sep 1954–Jun 1955, NBC Sat 8:00–8:30
CAST:
Mickey Mulligan .... Mickey Rooney
Mrs. Mulligan .... Claire Carleton
Mr. Mulligan .... Regis Toomey
Pat .... Carla Balenda
Mr. Brown .... John Hubbard
Freddie .... Joey Forman
The Drama Instructor .... Alan Mowbray

Mickey Mulligan was a young man working as a page at the NBC Studios in Hollywood. His aspirations, however, went far beyond his lowly position. He really wanted to be a serious dramatic actor, and was only using the page job as a springboard to bigger things. At night Mickey attended dramatic school, with less-than-spectacular results. By day his thespian ambitions were not encouraged by either his peers or superiors at NBC. But there was no keeping Mickey down. The only people who did encourage him were his father and his girlfriend, Pat, who worked as a secretary at the studios. Mickey lived with his mother, a one-time star in burlesque, and his father, a lifelong cop.

Ironically, in real life the position of page at NBC is widely regarded as an excellent starting job in the broadcasting industry, and many former pages have gone on to become stars or top-level executives.

The official title of this series was *The Mickey Rooney Show*; however, it was also known by its subtitle, *Hey Mulligan*.

MICKEY SPILLANE'S MIKE HAMMER (*Detective Drama*)

BROADCAST HISTORY:
Syndicated only
30 minutes
Produced: *1957–1959* (78 episodes)
Released: *Late 1957*
CAST:
Mike Hammer .... Darren McGavin
Capt. Pat Chambers, N.Y.P.D. .... Bart Burns

This private-eye series was every bit as violent as the novels that made Mickey Spillane famous. *TV Guide* called it "easily the worst show on TV." *Variety* described it as a "mixture of blood, violence, and sex." A typical plot had a man and a woman thrown down a flight of stairs, a brutal fist fight, a knifing, and a shooting, plus Hammer making what appeared to be a highly successful pass at a married woman. Hammer was usually either kissing them or killing them (Angie Dickinson got bumped off in the premiere episode), while providing a steady stream of smart-alecky wisecracks. The setting was New York City, and episode titles were vintage Spillane, such as "Overdose of Lead" and "Music to Die By."

Spillane and McGavin both defended the showing of such violence on TV, but Spillane later admitted that his involvement with this series was minimal. "I just took the money and went home."

MICKEY SPILLANE'S MIKE HAMMER (*Detective Drama*)

FIRST TELECAST: *January 26, 1984*
LAST TELECAST: *September 9, 1987*
BROADCAST HISTORY:
Jan 1984, CBS Thu 9:00–11:00
Jan 1984–Apr 1984, CBS Sat 10:00–11:00
Aug 1984–Sep 1984, CBS Thu 10:00–11:00
Sep 1984–Jan 1985, CBS Sat 9:00–10:00
May 1985–Jul 1985, CBS Sat 10:00–11:00
Apr 1986–May 1986, CBS Tue 9:00–10:00
Sep 1986–Oct 1986, CBS Sat 9:00–10:00
Nov 1986–Sep 1987, CBS Wed 8:00–9:00
CAST:
Mike Hammer .... Stacy Keach
Velda .... Lindsay Bloom
Capt. Pat Chambers .... Don Stroud
Asst. D.A. Lawrence D. Barrington... Kent Williams
Ozzie the Answer (1984–1985).... Danny Goldman
Jenny the bartender .... Lee Benton
Moochie (1984–1985) .... Ben Powers
Ritchie (1984–1985) .... Eddie Barth
Hennessey (1984–1985) .... Eddie Egan
The Face .... Donna Denton
THEME:
"Harlem Nocturne," by Earle Hagen

When *Mickey Spillane's Mike Hammer* turned up on network television 25 years after the syndicated version was produced, things were little changed. It was still violent, sexist, and full of wisecracks. Mike's secretary, Velda, not seen in the syndicated version, was bustily present, as were a host of other beauties poured into tight, low-cut dresses to emphasize their obvious assets. There was also a regular coterie of street people and contacts, the most prominent of whom was Ozzie the Answer, Mike's most reliable source of information. Jenny was the sexy (what else?) bartender at the Light n' Easy, Mike's favorite hangout. His good buddy Pat, as well as Ritchie and Hennessey, were cops on the N.Y.P.D., and Barrington was the assistant D.A. with whom he never saw eye to eye. Mike's best friend, however, was not a person, but the powerful .45 caliber pistol he had nicknamed Betsy and carried with him almost all his waking hours.

Along with the typical cases of murder, extortion, kidnapping, and robbery were cases dealing with drug dealing and problems of the elderly. Regardless of the case, however, Mike always solved it, leaving a trail of bloodied bad guys and swooning women in his wake. There was one thing Mike never did quite solve. At some point in each episode he would catch a glimpse of the same strikingly beautiful brunette (practically the only attractive lady on the show whose assets were only on display from the neck up), but he never got close enough to actually meet her before she disappeared. The show's producers planned to build a 1985 episode around Mike's finally meeting "The Face," but by then star Stacy Keach was serving a six-month jail term in England for cocaine possession, and the 1984–1985 season had to be cut short before the episode was filmed. "Hammer in the Slammer," read the real-life newspaper headlines!

The following season CBS telecast a newly produced TV movie, *The Return of Mickey Spillane's Mike Hammer*, as well as reruns of the original series to test the waters for a possible revival. The series did return in the fall of 1986 as *The New Mike Hammer*. Some changes were made. In an attempt to attract female viewers who had heretofore been offended by the series' blatant sexism, the busty women billowing out of their clothes were gone. However, the violence was, if anything, increased. Claiming they wanted to be true to the original novels (which were *very* violent), the producers made their hero even more brutal than before. In one episode, a fight with a heavyset villain left the criminal clinging precariously to a high ledge; as he struggled to save himself he cried to Hammer, who stood just a few feet away, "For God's sake Hammer, give me a hand!" Our Hero just looked at him coldly—and began to slowly clap. The villain lost his grip and fell screaming to his death. Nice hero.

In the last original episode, which aired the following May, Mike finally met The Face and, after a rather convoluted plot, found out she was an author following him and watching his activities so that she could "fictionalize" his exploits in a series of detective novels. After one memorable romantic evening she disappeared from his life.

Ten years after this series left CBS, Keach returned to the role in the syndicated series *Mike Hammer: Private Eye (q.v.)*.

MICKIE FINN'S (*Musical Variety*)

FIRST TELECAST: *April 21, 1966*
LAST TELECAST: *September 1, 1966*
BROADCAST HISTORY:
Apr 1966–Sep 1966, NBC Thu 9:30–10:00
REGULARS:
Fred E. Finn
Mickie Finn
The Fred Finn Band
The Mickie Finn Dancers
The Dapper Dans
Harold "Hoot" Connors
Mickey Manners

The set on which this variety series was taped was a replica of the warehouse in San Diego that Fred and Mickie Finn had converted into a "Gay '90's" nightclub. The music played by the band ranged from current hits to ragtime and Dixieland jazz. In addition to the guest stars, the regular cast included Fred, as the proprietor who played piano and led the band, and his wife, Mickie, who played banjo. Harold Connors and Mickey Manners were the bartenders who often provided comic relief.

MIDDLE AGES (*Drama*)

FIRST TELECAST: *September 3, 1992*
LAST TELECAST: *October 1, 1992*
BROADCAST HISTORY:
Sep 1992–Oct 1992, CBS Thu 10:00–11:00
CAST:
Walter Cooper .... Peter Riegert
Cindy Nelson Cooper .... Ashley Crow
Terry Hannon .... William Russ
Ron Steffey .... Michael O'Keefe
Dave Nelson .... James Gammon
Blanche .... Amy Brenneman
Hillary Cooper .... Alex McKenna
Carson Cooper .... Ryan McWhorter
Brian Conover .... Kyle Secor
Robin .... Maria Pitillo

Short-lived summer drama about a group of middle-aged people in a Winnetka suburb of Chicago trying to make sense out of their lives. Walter, a 43-year-old traveling salesman with two teenager children, was going through a midlife crisis compounded by the fact that his wife, Cindy, had just landed an exciting job with a magazine. Terry, Walter's childhood friend, tackled his insecurities by quitting his job to perform in a band with Blanche, a dead ringer for a singer they had known in college. Ron was a public relations executive with a vivid fantasy life and a growing fear of impending baldness. Dave, Walter's divorced 60-year-old father-in-law, had a more substantial problem than these young worrywarts: he had to adjust to life as a cabdriver after being laid off from his job at the same company where Walter worked.

MIDNIGHT CALLER (*Drama*)

FIRST TELECAST: *October 25, 1988*
LAST TELECAST: *August 2, 1991*
BROADCAST HISTORY:
Oct 1988, NBC Tue 10:00–11:00
Dec 1988–Jul 1990, NBC Tue 10:00–11:00
Jul 1990–Aug 1991, NBC Fri 10:00–11:00
CAST:
Jack Killian .... Gary Cole
Devon King (1988–1990) .... Wendy Kilbourne
Billy Po .... Dennis Dun
Lt. Carl Zymack .... Arthur Taxier
Deacon Bridges (1989–1991) ... Mykel T. Williamson
**J.J. Killian (1989–1991)* .... Peter Boyle
Nicolette "Nicky" Molloy (1990–1991)
.... Lisa Eilbacher
**Inspector Martin Slocum (1990–1991)*
.... Steven Anthony Jones

*Occasional

The surrealistic world of late night radio call-in shows has seldom been more effectively portrayed than in this moody, involving series. Jack Killian was an ex-San Francisco police detective who had quit the force, devastated, after he had accidentally killed his partner during a shoot-out with criminals. Some of his former colleagues would not forgive him, and for a time Jack drowned his guilt in a bottle—until he received an unusual offer. Devon King, the wealthy, stylish, and savvy owner of radio station KJCM, persuaded the reluctant Jack to become "The Nighthawk," host of an all-night call-in show where he could talk to, and perhaps help, those whose troubles were even deeper than his own.

Jack related to the city's troubled, sleepless underworld of the night, and his show was a smash hit. The impulsive Jack did not confine his advice to the studio, often going into the streets and investigating crimes himself. Some were straightforward stories of murder and corruption (your basic TV serial killers and crooked politicians), but many touched on current social concerns such as AIDS (Jack's former girlfriend was infected), capital punishment, and child abuse. Jack even broadcast his show from such sites as a penitentiary during a riot, a kidnapper's hideout, and a homeless encampment. No wonder his ratings were high!

Jack's childhood had been an unhappy one, with a father who had abandoned the family. The errant dad, a colorful con man named J.J., turned up occasionally to renew an uneasy relationship with his son. Also seen once in a while were Jack's kid sister Kate (Terri Garber) and younger brother Frankie (Scott Valentine), both in trouble of one kind or another.

Billy was Jack's cheerful engineer/producer and link to San Franciso's large Asian community; Deacon, a black newspaper reporter; and Carl, his former boss and sometime ally on the S.F.P.D. Early in the third season the elegant Ms. King became pregnant (as was actress Kilbourne in real life), a result of her own troubled relationship; she eventually sold the station and Nicky Molloy took over as general manager and Jack's boss.

MIDNIGHT HOUR, THE (*Talk*)

FIRST TELECAST: *July 23, 1990*
LAST TELECAST: *September 14, 1990*
BROADCAST HISTORY:
Jul 1990–Sep 1990, CBS Mon–Fri 12:40 A.M.–1:40 A.M.
ANNOUNCER:
Jennifer Martin
MUSICAL DIRECTOR:
Patrice Rushen

In its continuing quest to develop a program to compete with NBC's *Tonight Show Starring Johnny Carson*, CBS used this series as a sort of on-air audition process for aspiring talk show hosts—similar to the way it had used the Friday telecasts of *The Pat Sajak Show* during its last couple of months early in 1990. Each "guest host" was on for a full week with a mix of talk, music, and comedy, with the emphasis on comedy. Among the aspiring hosts were comics Joy Behar, Warren Thomas, and Bill Maher; radio personalities Peter Tilden and the Chicago team of Steve Dahl and Garry Meier; and even Mark McEwan, the weatherman on *CBS This Morning*. Unfortunately, at 12:40 in the morning, they played to a mostly empty house.

MIDNIGHT SPECIAL, THE (*Music*)

FIRST TELECAST: *February 2, 1973*
LAST TELECAST: *May 1, 1981*
BROADCAST HISTORY:
Feb 1973–Sep 1980, NBC Fri 1:00–2:30 A.M.
Sep 1980–May 1981, NBC Fri 12:30–2:00 A.M.
HOSTESS:
Helen Reddy (1975–1976)
ANNOUNCER:
Wolfman Jack

For young people coming home from a Friday night date, or for those who were still up after *The Tonight Show, The Midnight Special* provided 90 minutes of taped in-concert popular music. The emphasis was on rock and, when the series first went on the air, everyone was a guest star—there was no regular host. Among the popular stars who hosted the show were Johnny Rivers, Mac Davis, Paul Anka, Lou Rawls, Ray Charles, Jerry Lee Lewis, Chubby Checker, Al Green, Curtis Mayfield, David Bowie, and Charlie Rich. It was Helen Reddy, the hostess of the premiere telecast, however, who finally became permanent host, two years later—in July 1975. Less than a year later she gave up that role and weekly guest hosts returned.

Beginning in the summer of 1975, a regular feature of *The Midnight Special* was "Rock Tribute," a segment that profiled a different rock star each week. Included were scenes of the star in concert, interviews, and various other insights into the star's life.

Another regular feature, added in the fall of 1979, was a weekly comedy segment in which a panel of comics and writers made fun of things that had happened on the previous week's telecast. The following April brought two other new features—"Golden Moments," highlighting clips of great performances from past telecasts of *The Midnight Special*, and "Top 10," a countdown of the week's top hits. The latter feature was dropped six months later.

MIDWESTERN HAYRIDE (*Musical Variety*)

FIRST TELECAST: *June 16, 1951*
LAST TELECAST: *September 6, 1959*
BROADCAST HISTORY:
Jun 1951–Sep 1951, NBC Sat 9:00–10:00
Jun 1952–Sep 1952, NBC Tue 8:00–9:00
Jun 1954–Sep 1954, NBC Tue 8:00–8:30
May 1955–Sep 1955, NBC Fri 8:00–8:30
Sep 1955–Jun 1956, NBC Wed 10:00–10:30
Jul 1957–Oct 1957, ABC Sun 9:30–10:00
Jun 1958–Sep 1958, ABC Sat 10:00–10:30
May 1959–Sep 1959, NBC Sun 7:00–7:30
EMCEE:
Bill Thall (1951–1954)
Bob Shrede (1951)
Hugh Cherry (1955–1956)
Paul Dixon (1957–1958)
Dean Richards (1959)
REGULARS:
The County Briar Hoppers (1951–1952)
Slim King & the Pine Mountain Boys
Zeke Turner
Bonnie Lou Ewins (1952–1959)
The Midwesterners (1954–1959)
The Hometowners (1957–1959)

This country music hoedown was a nighttime summer standby during the 1950s. Originating from the NBC affiliate in Dayton or Cincinnati, Ohio, it featured such talent as a square-dance ensemble (the County Briar Hoppers, later the Midwesterners), yodelers, guitarists, string bands, country comedy acts, etc. Many performers came and went over the years, among them guitarist Jerry Byrd, Ernie Lee, Charlie Gore & the Rangers, Lee Jones, Buddy Ross, the Kentucky Boys, Salty and Mattie (later Billy) Holmes, Freddy Langdon, Tommy Watson, Bobby Bobo, Penny West, Kenny Price, Helen and Billy Scott, and the Lucky Pennies.

Midwestern Hayride was also frequently seen on the network in non-evening hours during the regular season.

MIGHTY JUNGLE, THE (*Situation Comedy*)

BROADCAST HISTORY:
The Family Channel
30 minutes
Produced: *1993–1994* (26 episodes)
Premiered: *January 2, 1994*
CAST:
Dan Winfield .... Francis Guinan
Susan Winfield .... Charlene Fernetz
Alison Winfield .... Molly Atkinson

Andrew Winfield .... Noah Shebib
Vinnie, the alligator (voice)........... Tony Danza
Viola, the toucan (voice).............. Delta Burke
Winston, the orangutan (voice) ...... David Fowler
Jack, the sea lion (voice) .... P. J. Heslin
Kenneth Crisp .... Patrick McKenna
Sylvie .... Sylvie Loeillet

THEME:

"The Lion Sleeps Tonight (Wimoweh)," (1961 pop song)

Four exotic animals decided to break their "animal oath" and talk to a zookeeper—but only to him—in this fanciful comedy. Dan was a befuddled caretaker at the Cleveland Zoo who kept the talkative four in his junglelike backyard at the zoo. Vinnie was a wise-cracking Brooklyn sewer alligator, Winston a cultured British orangutan (who helped Dan learn chess), Viola a Southern belle toucan, and Jack a spaced-out sea lion. Naturally, nobody else had a clue about what was going on, not Dan's perky wife, Susan; his teenage kids, Alison and Andrew; the grinning zoo administrator, Kenneth; or the sexy French veterinarian, Sylvie.

MIKE HAMMER, see *Mickey Spillane's Mike Hammer*

MIKE HAMMER: PRIVATE EYE (*Detective Drama*)

BROADCAST HISTORY

Syndicated only
60 minutes
Produced: *1997–1998* (26 episodes)
Released: *September 1997*

CAST:

Mike Hammer .... Stacy Keach
Velda........................... Shannon Whirry
Nick Farrell......................... Shane Conrad
Capt. Skip Gleason..................... Peter Jason
Maya Ricci .... Malgossia Tomassi
**Deputy Mayor Barry Lawrence*....... Kent Williams
The Face .... Rebecca Chaney

*Occasional

A decade after Keach's last network episode of *Mickey Spillane's Mike Hammer* had aired on CBS, he returned to the role in this reworked syndicated version. He was still the hard-boiled private eye, albeit a little more grizzled and weathered by the passage of time. Velda, his loyal secretary, was still around, but none of the characters from the CBS *Hammer* series were present. In the premiere episode Mike hired Nick, the son of a murdered policeman friend, as a legman to help him on cases. Skip was Mike's buddy on the N.Y.P.D., and Maya (played by star Keach's real-life wife) the Swedish woman who ran the dance/yoga studio across the hall from his office. In February 1998 obnoxious Barry (played by Kent Williams, Mike's nemesis as a different character on the CBS series) was elected D.A. As with the CBS series, there was a mysterious, beautiful woman called "The Face" who showed up at some point in most episodes. In this series, however, Mike never did meet her. His hangout was a bar called Lou's.

MIKE, LU & OG (*Cartoon*)

BROADCAST HISTORY:

Cartoon Network
30 minutes
Original episodes: *1999–2000* (26 episodes)
Premiered: *May 7, 1999*

VOICES:

Michelene Ann "Mike" Mavinski .... Nika Frost
LuLu "Lu"........................ Nancy Cartwright
Og .... Dee Bradley Baker
Wendel .... S. Scott Bullock
Old Queeks........................... Corey Burton
Alfred............................. Martin Rayner
Margery .... Kath Soucie

A young New York girl with pigtails and attitude was stranded on a lush tropical island and had to learn to get along with the settlers and the natives in this cartoon. Glib, bossy Mike found her match in argumentative Lu, the island's "princess" and daughter of its amiable governor, Wendel. Og was a smart but naive native boy who liked to do scientific experiments and "invented" things Mike told him about from her past (television, in-line skates, etc.). These usually got everybody into trouble. Alfred was a lanky British hunter and Mr. Queeks, a wise, old seer who reminded everyone how the settlers had arrived on "The Good Ship *Betty Anne*." Lancelot was Lu's talking pet turtle, often the target of pirates who wanted to make it into turtle soup.

MIKE O'MALLEY SHOW, THE (*Situation Comedy*)

FIRST TELECAST: *September 21, 1999*
LAST TELECAST: *September 28, 1999*
BROADCAST HISTORY:

Sep 1999, NBC Tue 9:30–10:00

CAST:

Mike O'Malley .... Himself
Kerry O'Malley .... Herself
Weasel.......................... Mark Rosenthal
Dr. Jimmy Nilsson....................... Will Arnett
Marcia .... Kate Walsh
Shawna .... Missy Yager

Mike was a big, 30-year-old lug who didn't want to grow up. He worked as an EMS technician, but his free time was spent as a hockey nut and hanging out with scruffy slacker Weasel in the small house they shared in New Haven, Connecticut. Mike got a big slap upside the head when his friend Jimmy, known for his short relationships, decided to marry soul mate Marcia and invited Mike to be his best man. Realizing his own life was going nowhere, Mike tried to rekindle his relationship with perky, tight-jeaned ex-girlfriend Shawna, who was getting her second degree at Yale. Slobbish Mike should be just the kind of man she wanted! Mike's sister Kerry was played by series star Mike O'Malley's real-life sister. The show's other star was the big boat in Mike's driveway, belonging to Jimmy (who was forever "working on it"), in which Mike sometimes hung out.

MIKE WALLACE INTERVIEWS (*Interview*)

FIRST TELECAST: *April 28, 1957*
LAST TELECAST: *September 14, 1958*
BROADCAST HISTORY:

Apr 1957–Sep 1957, ABC Sun 10:00–10:30
Sep 1957–Apr 1958, ABC Sat 10:00–10:30
Apr 1958–Sep 1958, ABC Sun 10:00–10:30

HOST:

Mike Wallace

Newsman Mike Wallace conducted this ABC interview

program in the aggressive style for which he was to become famous. Among the guests undergoing his grilling were Gloria Swanson, the Imperial Wizard of the Ku Klux Klan, Mickey Cohen, Steve Allen, Arkansas Governor Faubus, stripper Lili St. Cyr, Tennessee Williams, and Major Donald Kehoe, an Air Force expert on Unidentified Flying Objects.

MILLENNIUM (*Police Drama*)
FIRST TELECAST: *October 25, 1996*
LAST TELECAST: *May 21, 1999*
BROADCAST HISTORY:
Oct 1996–May 1999, FOX Fri 9:00–10:00
CAST:
Frank Black..................... Lance Henriksen
Catherine Black (1996–1998) .... Megan Gallagher
Jordan Black .... Brittany Tiplady
Lt. Bob Bletcher (1996–1997)....... Bill Smitrovich
Peter Watts........................ Terry O'Quinn
Lara Means (1997–1998)............. Kristen Cloke
Det. Bob Geibelhouse (1998)... Stephen James Lang
Agent Emma Hollis (1998–1999)......... Klea Scott
Agent Barry Baldwin (1998–1999)
.... Peter Outerbridge
Asst. Dir. Andy MacLaren (1998–1999)
.... Stephen E. Miller

In this spooky, moody melodrama produced by the same people responsible for *The X-Files*, grim former F.B.I. man Frank Black had just moved back to Seattle with his wife, Catherine, and their young daughter, Jordan, after ten years in Washington, D.C. Frank worked with the Millennium Group, a shadowy organization ostensibly dedicated to fighting crime and preparing humanity for the battle between good and evil that was coming at the end of the millennium. He had a unique talent, the ability to "see" into the minds of disturbed violent criminals and anticipate their next moves. Frank also helped his old friend Bletcher, a homicide detective on the Seattle police force, solve grisly local crimes. Catherine counseled crime victims for the Seattle P.D. and worked with traumatized patients at a local hospital. Watts was Frank's primary contact with the Millennium Group and worked with him on cases that took them all over the country. In April, Frank was confronted with the supernatural when a "woman" that might have been a demon killed Bletcher, who was investigating a break-in at the Black home. Frank subsequently found out he would be involved in an ongoing struggle against the demonic forces of evil.

In fall 1997, Catherine separated from Frank to resolve conflicts over their relationship and his work. She and Jordan, who had inherited some of her father's psychic abilities, moved in with a friend, while Frank stayed in their house. Det. Geibelhouse was Frank's new contact on the Seattle P.D., and Lara another investigator with the Millennium Group. Frank's encounters with supernatural entities, including ghosts and demons, increased significantly. At the end of the season he left the Millennium Group, whose real purpose was never explained to him and whose goal, he had begun to believe, was world domination. He started studying a deadly biologically engineered virus while also trying to uncover the secrets behind the Millennium Group. The virus got out of control, and Frank (who had been vaccinated against it by the Group) moved his wife and daughter into a remote cabin to keep them away from infection. As the episode—which the producers thought would be the series finale—ended, apocalypse seemed to have arrived. Catherine had died from the virus, Frank was semi-comatose in shock with gray hair, and radio reports were chronicling the mounting crisis in the outside world.

But to everyone's surprise, *Millennium* was renewed. Next fall Frank was back in Washington, D.C., and, to explain away the previous season's finale, it was said that the ebola-like virus had been contained locally, only eighty people had been killed, and that much of what viewers had seen was part of Frank's delusional breakdown. Frank and Jordan were now living in suburban Falls Church, Virginia, removed from the Millennium Group. Frank worked on F.B.I. cases with his old friend Andy, and Hollis, a young F.B.I. agent. Baldwin, Hollis's previous partner, was in charge of the bureau's Critical Incidents Response Group. Frank was also investigating the Millennium Group, which had certainly proved to be malevolent, and he still had occasional contact with Watts. At the end of the season Barry was killed and Andy, who was retiring and had planned to promote Barry into his job, offered it to Emma. In the series finale Frank quit the F.B.I., discouraged because he felt Emma had sold out to the Millennium Group in exchange for a cure for her father's Alzheimer's disease, and he went off with Jordan to fight the battle alone.

MILLER & COMPANY (*Talk*)
BROADCAST HISTORY:
The Nashville Network
60 minutes
Produced: *1992–1993*
Premiered: *September 28, 1992*
HOST:
Dan Miller

Country-oriented late-night talk show hosted by Dan Miller, a former Nashville newsman and Pat Sajak's sidekick on *The Pat Sajak Show*. Miller was, alas, no more successful than his former boss; his show folded after less than a year.

MILLION DOLLAR MYSTERIES (*Public Service*)
FIRST TELECAST: *May 30, 2001*
LAST TELECAST: *June 27, 2001*
BROADCAST HISTORY:
May 2001–June 2001, FOX Wed 9:00–10:00
NARRATOR:
Donald Kobiela

This series presented real stories about missing treasures and unclaimed rewards. The show provided the background stories—including reenactments and interviews with the people involved—and clues that might enable viewers to solve the mysteries and reap big rewards. Among the stories were those of a bank president whose family had been held hostage while a thief stole millions ($50,000 reward), a U.C.L.A. college student who vanished without a trace ($100,000 reward), a flight attendant who was murdered ($115,000 reward), $200,000 in stolen antique jewelry ($50,000 reward), millions in unclaimed bank accounts, and a legendary stash of gold treasure supposedly buried in the Virginia hills. In addition, the International U.F.O. Research Center in Roswell, New Mexico, had a standing offer of $1,000,000 for a verifiable piece of an alien spacecraft.

Each episode included the following disclaimer—"*Million Dollar Mysteries* features stories about unsolved crimes. Reward money can be claimed by solving these mysteries. All rewards are paid by third parties and not by the producers of the show or Fox Broadcasting Company. But please do not take the law into your own hands. Contact your local authorities."

MILLIONAIRE, THE (*Dramatic Anthology*)

FIRST TELECAST: *January 19, 1955*

LAST TELECAST: *September 28, 1960*

BROADCAST HISTORY:

Jan 1955–Sep 1960, CBS Wed 9:00–9:30

CAST:

Michael Anthony .... Marvin Miller

Each week eccentric multibillionaire John Beresford Tipton (whose face was never seen on the series) would instruct his personal secretary, Michael Anthony, to present some unsuspecting individual with a cashier's check for one million dollars, tax free. The object was to see how this new-found wealth would change the lives of its recipients. The answers to the question "What would you do if you had a million dollars?" intrigued and entertained audiences for more than five years. Michael Anthony was the only regular member of the cast and functioned more as a host than as a participant in the dramas. The only stipulation that Mr. Anthony made when he presented the checks to their recipients was that they make no attempt to find out who their mysterious benefactor was, or reveal where they got the money to anybody but their spouse. If they did, they would have to forfeit the money.

Viewers never found out who he was, either. Each program opened with Tipton seated in the study of his huge estate, Silverstone, toying with his chessmen. He would call in his faithful secretary, deliver a few philosophical words of wisdom, and hand over the name of the latest recipient. Only the back of Tipton's head or his hand on the arm of a chair was ever seen on camera, and the files do not record who that hand or head belonged to (probably to several people over the years). The deep, authoritative voice of Mr. Tipton was that of a well-known Hollywood announcer, Paul Frees.

Reruns of *The Millionaire* were shown as part of the CBS daytime lineup from October 1959 to August 1963.

MILTON BERLE SHOW, THE (*Comedy/Variety*)

FIRST TELECAST: *June 8, 1948*

LAST TELECAST: *January 6, 1967*

BROADCAST HISTORY:

Jun 1948–Jun 1956, NBC Tue 8:00–9:00 (OS)
Oct 1958–May 1959, NBC Wed 9:00–9:30
Sep 1966–Jan 1967, ABC Fri 9:00–10:00

REGULARS:

Milton Berle
Fatso Marco (1948–1952; as *Marko Marcelle* from 1951)
Ruth Gilbert (1952–1955)
Bobby Sherwood (1952–1953)
Arnold Stang (1953–1955)
Jack Collins (1953–1955)
Milton Frome (1953–1955)
Irving Benson (*Sidney Sphritzer*; 1966–1967)

COMMERCIAL ANNOUNCER:

Sid Stone (1948–1951)
Jimmy Nelson (1952–1953)
Jack Lescoulie (1954–1955)

ORCHESTRA:

Alan Roth (1948–1955)
Victor Young (1955–1956)
Billy May (1958–1959)
Mitchell Ayres (1966–1967)

THEME:

"Near You," by Kermit Goell and Francis Craig

The most popular hour of the week during the early years of TV was Milton Berle's, on Tuesday night. Although Berle was the host on the very first telecast of *Texaco Star Theater*, June 8, 1948, he was not at that time considered the permanent emcee. During the summer of 1948 Harry Richman, Georgie Price, Henny Youngman, Morey Amsterdam, Jack Carter, and Peter Donald rotated in the host's spot. Berle won the "competition" and was made permanent emcee in September 1948.

Milton Berle was not unknown at the time, but he could hardly have been called a big name. He had been on radio since the 1930s, and even in a few films, but hadn't scored a big hit in either medium. On TV, however, he fast developed into something of a national institution—"Mr. Television"—and it is said that he sold more TV sets than any advertising campaign. People bought the newfangled thing just to *see* this crazy comedian everyone was talking about.

The original *Texaco Star Theater* was built along the lines of an old-fashioned vaudeville variety hour, with half a dozen guests each week, including singers, comedians, ventriloquists, acrobats—you name it. But the star was Berle, and he involved himself in many of the acts, adding comedy counterpoint. Soon the basic format was set. Each show opened with the four Texaco Service Men, singing the Texaco jingle ("Oh, we're the men of Texaco, we work from Maine to Mexico . . .") and then working into a musical introduction of Berle, who came on dressed in some outlandish costume. "And now the man with jokes from the Stone Age," and Berle came on dressed as a caveman. "The man who just paid his taxes. . . ," and Berle arrived wearing a barrel. For the sponsor's commercials, old-fashioned pitchman Sid Stone ("Awright, I'll tell ya what I'm gonna do!") would come on stage, set up his sample case, and launch into his spiel—until chased off by a whistle-blowing policeman. And each show would end with Berle singing his theme song, "Near You."

This format changed little during the first four seasons, although the accent was gradually placed more on Berle himself, his sight gags, outlandish costumes, and props. In 1952 young ventriloquist Jimmy Nelson and his dummy Danny O'Day replaced Sid Stone as the commercial announcer. In the fall of 1952 Berle returned with a somewhat different format. There were fewer guest acts, and each show was built around a central theme or comedy plot (often it was the rehearsal for the show itself), involving Berle, his guests, and several regulars. Ruth Gilbert joined the cast as Max, his secretary, and in 1953 Arnold Stang joined as Francis, an NBC stagehand and Max's secret love. In the fall of 1955 the regulars were dropped and an entirely new production staff was hired. The program's format was freer, alternating between straight variety hours, satires, and book musicals (including "State of Confusion" on October 18, 1955, a satirical comedy written for Berle by Gore Vidal). One of the guests during the last few months was Elvis Presley, making two appearances in early 1956.

Title and scheduling underwent several changes in the 1950s. After 1953 Texaco shifted its sponsorship to another night (see the *Jimmy Durante* and *Donald O'Connor* shows) and Berle's hour became the *Buick-Berle Show*. Then from 1954 to 1956 it was simply *The Milton Berle Show*, which alternated variously with Martha Raye, Bob Hope, and Steve Allen.

By 1956 the steam had run out for "Mr. Television." TV was by then becoming dominated by dramatic-anthology shows, Westerns, and private eyes, and the sight of a grinning comic jumping around in crazy costumes no longer had the appeal it did in 1948, when things were simpler.

Two years after his departure from the Tuesday lineup, Berle returned to prime time with a half-hour variety series on NBC, for Kraft (called *Milton Berle Starring in The Kraft Music Hall*). He was a more restrained performer this time—no slapstick or outrageous costumes—attempting to function more as a host than as the central focus of the show. Each telecast began with an opening monologue, often including informal patter with the evening's guest stars. Later, Berle might perform in skits with his guests. With the exception of the interplay between Milton and bandleader Billy May, the show was a somewhat refined version of *The Red Skelton Show*. Berle's new image did not, however, attract sufficient viewers to warrant renewal for a second season.

After his Kraft show was canceled Berle continued to show up as a guest on other programs, increasingly a nostalgic figure. Then in 1966 he was signed for a new variety hour of his own on ABC, and columnists made a great deal of his "comeback." "Can he grab the new generation?" headlined one. To give the show a youthful image singers Bobby Rydell and Donna Loren were signed as regulars (but they soon disappeared), while Irving Benson played the heckler in the audience. The producer was comic Bill Dana, who also appeared periodically as Jose Jiminez. Despite an infusion of top-name guests, Lucille Ball and Bob Hope among them, the program was massacred in the ratings by *The Man from U.N.C.L.E.* and was soon dropped.

MILTON BERLE STARRING IN THE KRAFT MUSIC HALL, see *Milton Berle Show, The*

MIND EXTENSION UNIVERSITY (Network), see *Knowledge TV*

MINOR ADJUSTMENTS (*Situation Comedy*)

FIRST TELECAST: *September 17, 1995*
LAST TELECAST: *August 20, 1996*
BROADCAST HISTORY:
Sep 1995–Nov 1995, NBC Sun 7:30–8:00
Jan 1996–Aug 1996, UPN Tue 8:30–9:00
Aug 1996, UPN Tue 9:30–10:00

CAST:
Dr. Ron Aimes .... Rondell Sheridan
Rachel Aimes .... Wendy Raquel Robinson
Trevor Aimes (age 10) .... Bobby E. McAdams II
Emma Aimes (4) .... Camille Winbush
Dr. Bruce Hampton .... Mitchell Whitfield
Dr. Francine Bailey .... Linda Kash
Darby Gladstone .... Sara Rue

Black standup comic Rondell Sheridan often cited Bill Cosby as one of his inspirations, and this gentle, Cosby-esque sitcom proved he meant it. Dr. Ron was a Philadelphia child psychologist who had a special way with youngsters, perhaps because he was basically an overgrown kid himself. Joking, mugging, winning their trust, he found ways to help them deal with their problems. Rachel was his savvy wife, Trevor his son (a "little operator" on whom Ron sometimes practiced), and Emma the adorable 4-year-old. Ron shared an office with fussy orthodontist Bruce, neurotic pediatrician Francine (recently divorced and reveling in her bitterness), and spaced-out receptionist Darby, who was Ron's niece.

Minor Adjustments was an unusual example of a series that switched networks in the middle of a season, moving from NBC to UPN. It fared no better on the smaller network, and was canceled at the end of its first year.

MIRACLE PETS (*Wildlife Magazine*)

FIRST TELECAST: *August 21, 2000*
LAST TELECAST:
BROADCAST HISTORY:
Aug 2000–Sep 2000, PAX Mon 8:00–9:00
Nov 2000–Jul 2001, PAX Sat 8:00–9:00
Nov 2000–Aug 2001, PAX Mon 8:00–9:00
Oct 2001–Jul 2002, PAX Mon 8:00–9:00
Sep 2002– , PAX Sun 6:00–7:00
Jan 2003– , PAX Sat 6:00–7:00

HOST:
Alan Thicke

Miracle Pets featured uplifting stories of pets who helped people. They included a dog that got help for its owner after his car had plunged into a ravine, leaving him with a neck injury and unable to move; a pig and a cow that had become friends and helped each other survive when a fire destroyed the shed in which they lived; a crow that had befriended a stray kitten and acted like its mother for several months, and an abandoned dog that was taken in by a woman with a young child and then saved the child from a possible rattlesnake bite.

Individual segments used actual footage, reenactments, home videos and interviews with the people involved.

MIRACLES (*Supernatural*)

FIRST TELECAST: *January 27, 2003*
LAST TELECAST: *March 31, 2003*
BROADCAST HISTORY:
Jan 2003–Mar 2003, ABC Mon 10:00–11:00

CAST:
Paul Callan .... Skeet Ulrich
Father Alva Keel .... Angus Macfadyen
Evelyn Santos .... Marisa Ramirez
Father "Poppi" Calero .... Hector Elizondo

In this strange and moody series, low-key, unassuming Paul Callan was a young seminarian who investigated claims of miracles for the Catholic Church. To the relief of authorities, he usually found logical explanations. When he began stumbling on occurrences that could *not* be so easily explained the church dismissed his findings, so Paul quit, joining forces with a former Harvard professor and full-time paranormal investigator named Alva. Alva, a rather creepy guy, headed a shadowy organization called Sodalitas Quaerito, or "brotherhood in search of truth," which operated out of a cluttered Boston loft. Both men feared that the rapidly growing number of strange and unexplained occurrences that were happening all over the world pointed to a frightening and deadly "large event" that was coming. Despite their fears they maintained a healthy skepticism about individual cases and were determined to sort out the merely coincidental from the truly miraculous. Cases included demonic possession, people who foretold disaster and death, and mysterious abductions. Paul's own life had been saved by a boy with healing powers who died by transferring his life to Paul. In the wake of this Paul had recurring visions involving the phrase "God Is Now Here," often written in blood, but he learned that there were others with the vision "God Is Nowhere." Which was it? Helping Paul and Alva sort all this out, along with various ghosts and voices from beyond, was former cop Evelyn, who brought a police investigator's training to their investigations.

MIRACLES AND OTHER WONDERS

(*Supernatural Anthology*)

FIRST TELECAST: *November 28, 1992*
LAST TELECAST: *March 6, 1993*
BROADCAST HISTORY:
Nov 1992–Dec 1992, CBS Sat 8:00–9:00
Mar 1993, CBS Sat 9:00–10:00
HOST:
Darren McGavin

Each episode of this series contained reenactments of stories of real people who had had their lives changed by experiences of a supernatural nature. Segments included a boy cured of lymphatic cancer when the religious pictures in his room were seen "weeping," a mother and her sick child helped by "guardian angels" when their car broke down in an isolated area, the dead grandfather of a young infant materializing to wake a dozing baby-sitter and warn her that his grandchild was choking on a locket, and a man who found a boy lost during a blizzard by searching an area he had seen in a dream.

MISADVENTURES OF SHERIFF LOBO, THE,

see *Lobo*

MISERY LOVES COMPANY (*Situation Comedy*)

FIRST TELECAST: *October 1, 1995*
LAST TELECAST: *October 22, 1995*
BROADCAST HISTORY:
Oct 1995, FOX Sun 9:30–10:00
CAST:
Joe DeMarco .... Dennis Boutsikaris
Perry .... Julius Carry
Lewis .... Stephen Furst
Mitch DeMarco .... Christopher Meloni
Connor .... Wesley Jonathan
Nicky St. Hubbins .... Kathe Mazur

This short-lived comedy focused on four men having relationship problems. Joe, a film professor at a local college, was having a tough time after divorcing his wife of twelve years. He had moved in with his brother, Mitch, a romantic swinger with little tolerance for his brother's neuroses. Joe's two best friends were Perry and Lewis, who hung out with him at Nicky St. Hubbins, the sports bar whose owner doubled as barmaid. Perry, the philosopher, had been divorced so many times that the other guys thought he was an expert on marriage—some expert! Lewis was the only one currently married, and he was in counseling trying to keep his troubled relationship from falling apart. Connor was Perry's teenage son.

MISFITS OF SCIENCE (*Adventure*)

FIRST TELECAST: *October 4, 1985*
LAST TELECAST: *February 21, 1986*
BROADCAST HISTORY:
Oct 1985–Dec 1985, NBC Fri 9:00–10:00
Dec 1985–Feb 1986, NBC Fri 8:00–9:00
CAST:
Dr. Billy Hayes .... Dean Paul Martin
Dr. Elvin "El" Lincoln .... Kevin Peter Hall
Johnny Bukowski ("Johnny B.")
.... Mark Thomas Miller
Gloria Dinallo .... Courteney Cox
Jane Miller .... Jennifer Holmes
Dick Stetmeyer .... Max Wright
Miss Nance .... Diane Civita

Misfits of Science was a teen-oriented fantasy adventure that set out to prove that outcasts and freaks could be TV heroes, too. The "freaks" in this case were all young people with bizarre physical abilities, who were being studied by Los Angeles' Humanidyne Institute. Not content to become living laboratory experiments, they formed a team to—what else—fight crime and save the world! Idealistic young scientist Billy Hayes of the Institute was the leader; others included his co-worker El Lincoln, a 7-foot, 4-inch black man who had the ability to shrink to just six inches in height by touching the back of his neck; Johnny B., a leather-jacketed rock musician who had once connected with 20,000 volts on stage and now could zap enough electricity from his fingertips to light the city; and reformed delinquent Gloria, whose telekinetic powers could levitate objects.

Dick Stetmeyer was the Institute's director, who wished these nice young people would spend more time on projects he could present to his board of directors. Miss Nance was the office receptionist/secretary who was forever filing her nails, and Jane Miller was Gloria's pregnant probation officer.

MISS WINSLOW AND SON (*Situation Comedy*)

FIRST TELECAST: *March 28, 1979*
LAST TELECAST: *May 2, 1979*
BROADCAST HISTORY:
Mar 1979–May 1979, CBS Wed 8:30–9:00
CAST:
Susan Winslow .... Darleen Carr
Harold Devore Neistadter ...... Roscoe Lee Browne
Warren Winslow .... Elliot Reid
Evelyn Winslow .... Sarah Marshall
Mr. Joseph X. Callahan .... William Bogert
Edmund Hillary Warren Winslow (pilot)
.... Benjamin Margolis
Edmund Hillary Warren Winslow
.... David Finger & Michael Finger
Rosa Vallone .... Ellen Sherman
Angelo Vallone .... Joe Rassulo

How times change! In 1952, when Lucille Ball was about to have a baby on *I Love Lucy,* the CBS censors would not even allow the word "pregnant" to be used in the scripts. That, they said, was too sexually suggestive (reluctantly, they used "expecting" instead). By 1979 the same network was ready for Miss Winslow, who was not only pregnant but unwed, having decided not to marry the father of her child.

In the first episode of this comedy she gave birth to a bouncing baby boy, whom she named Eddie. Daddy left for a job in Brazil and Susan, an attractive 23-year-old, set about raising the infant alone, making a living as a freelance art designer, and dealing with family and friends who did not approve of her decision. Susan sometimes sought the assistance of her neighbor, a rather arrogant and sarcastic author named Harold Neistadter, who grudgingly helped out with the baby when asked. Despite his gruff exterior, he was actually rather fond of Susan and Eddie. Susan's socially prominent parents were aghast at what she'd done and tried to keep the truth from their friends while scrambling to find her a husband. Little Eddie just cooed. Adapted from the British series, *Miss Jones & Son*.

MRS. COLUMBO, see *Kate Loves a Mystery*

MRS. G GOES TO COLLEGE, see *Gertrude Berg Show, The*

MISSING PERSONS (*Police Drama*)

FIRST TELECAST: *September 9, 1993*
LAST TELECAST: *February 17, 1994*
BROADCAST HISTORY:
Sep 1993–Feb 1994, ABC Thu 8:00–9:00
CAST:
Lt. Ray McAuliffe .... Daniel J. Travanti
Officer Johnny Sandowski .... Fred Weller
Officer Bobby Davison .... Erik King
Officer Carlos Marrone .... Juan Ramirez
Officer Connie Karadzic .... Jorjan Fox
Dan Manaher .... Bob Swan
Barbara McAuliffe .... Paty Lombard

A by-the-book cop show about the Missing Persons Squad of the Chicago Police Department, headed by low-key but earnest Lt. Ray McAuliffe. In fact everyone here was earnest: Johnny, the handsome young psychologist with a goofy smile; Bobby, the black officer; Carlos, the Hispanic with a young son; and Connie, the eager young officer who ran the office but wanted to be out on cases (and often got her wish). Barbara was Ray's longtime and long-suffering wife.

Distraught parents and disbelieving children ("Grandfather would never have wandered off like that!") filled their days, while Ray mostly charged around the squad room handing out files. About the only really surprising development was when Valerie Harper showed up in the last three episodes as Ray's former partner, Ellen Hartig, who still carried a torch for the stolid and now married lieutenant. Too late.

MISSING REWARD (*Public Service*)

BROADCAST HISTORY:
Syndicated only
30 minutes
Produced: *1989–1992* (72 episodes)
Released: *September 1989*
HOST:
Stacy Keach

Actor Stacy Keach hosted this series that dramatized cases of missing people and property, for which sometimes huge rewards had been offered. Information was provided on how viewers who had information that might help solve the cases could collect all or part of the reward.

MISSION HILL (*Cartoon*)

FIRST TELECAST: *September 21, 1999*
LAST TELECAST: *July 16, 2000*
BROADCAST HISTORY:
Sep 1999, WB Tue 9:00–9:30
Oct 1999, WB Fri 8:00–8:30
Jun 2000–Jul 2000, WB Sun 9:30–10:00
VOICES:
Andy French .... Wallace Langham
Posey Tyler .... Vicki Lewis
Jim Kuback .... Brian Posehn
Natalie Leibowitz-Hernandez .... Vicki Lewis
Kevin French .... Scott Menville
Gus/Mr. French/Stogie .... Nick Jameson
Wally .... Tom Kenny
Carlos Hernandez-Leibowitz ..... Herbert Siguenza
Gwen .... Jane Wiedlin
Mrs. French .... Tress MacNeille

Animated sitcom in Day-Glo colors about 20-somethings living in Mission Hill, the swinging section of the city of Cosmopolis. Andy was a wannabe cartoonist who worked as a salesman at Ron's Waterbed World. Sharing his cavernous loft apartment at 44 Bow Street were two roommates, the red-bearded, deep-voiced Jim and flower child Posey, an aspiring masseuse. Carlos, Natalie, and their baby lived across the hall, and aging gay roommates, Gus and Wally, were next door. In the premiere episode Andy was saddled with his annoying younger brother, Kevin, a super-smart but nerdy high school senior (he wore his S.A.T. scores on his T-shirt) who moved in when their parents moved to Wyoming. Stogie, the big, dumb family dog, arrived with Kevin. Gwen was Andy's sometime girlfriend. When the waterbed store was shut down by the government for nonpayment of taxes, Andy struggled to find another job. This episode, the first half of a two-part story, was the last one to air on the WB.

Dismal ratings prompted the WB to pull *Mission Hill* after only two episodes. Four more aired the following summer, and several that never aired on the WB surfaced on the Cartoon Network in the summer of 2002.

MISSION: IMPOSSIBLE (*International Intrigue*)

FIRST TELECAST: *September 17, 1966*
LAST TELECAST: *June 9, 1990*
BROADCAST HISTORY:
Sep 1966–Jan 1967, CBS Sat 9:00–10:00
Jan 1967–Sep 1967, CBS Sat 8:30–9:30
Sep 1967–Sep 1970, CBS Sun 10:00–11:00
Sep 1970–Sep 1971, CBS Sat 7:30–8:30
Sep 1971–Dec 1972, CBS Sat 10:00–11:00
Dec 1972–May 1973, CBS Fri 8:00–9:00
May 1973–Sep 1973, CBS Sat 10:00–11:00
Oct 1988–Jan 1989, ABC Sun 8:00–9:00
Jan 1989–Jul 1989, ABC Sat 8:00–9:00
Aug 1989, ABC Thu 9:00–10:00
Sep 1989–Dec 1989, ABC Thu 8:00–9:00
Jan 1990–Feb 1990, ABC Sat 8:00–9:00
May 1990–Jun 1990, ABC Sat 8:00–9:00

CAST (1966–1973):

Daniel Briggs (1966–1967) .... Steven Hill
James Phelps (1967–1973) .... Peter Graves
Cinnamon Carter (1966–1969) .... Barbara Bain
Rollin Hand (1966–1969).......... Martin Landau
Barney Collier .... Greg Morris
Willie Armitage .... Peter Lupus
Voice on Tape...................... Bob Johnson
Paris (1969–1971) .... Leonard Nimoy
Doug (1970–1971) .... Sam Elliott
Dana Lambert (1970–1971)..... Lesley Ann Warren
Lisa Casey (1971–1973)......... Lynda Day George
Mimi Davis (1972–1973) .... Barbara Anderson

CAST (1988–1990):

Jim Phelps .... Peter Graves
Nicholas Black.................... Thaao Penghis
Max Harte...................... Antony Hamilton
Grant Collier .... Phil Morris
Casey Randall (1988–1989)........ Terry Markwell
Shannon Reed (1989–1990)........... Jane Badler
Voice on Disc .... Bob Johnson

THEME:

"Mission: Impossible," by Lalo Schifrin

At the opening of each episode of *Mission: Impossible*, the leader of the Impossible Missions Force, a group of highly specialized government agents, would receive a tape-recorded message outlining instructions for an assignment he was to consider taking. The voice on the tape would give him some background information, usually tied to the pictures of adversaries that were included with the tape, and conclude with "Your mission, Dan, should you decide to accept it, is . . . As always, should you or any member of your I.M. Force be caught or killed, the secretary will disavow any knowledge of your actions. This tape will self-destruct in five seconds." On cue, five seconds later, the tape, and often the small portable recorder that had contained it, went up in a puff of smoke and flame. The leader would then leaf through the dossiers of the various operatives who might be utilized on the mission and pull out the appropriate ones. Except for an occasional guest star, however, he always picked out exactly the same team to work with, which made the entire selection process seem rather superfluous. This opening was so stylized that it was parodied on virtually every comedy show on the air during the period, from *The Carol Burnett Show* to *The Tonight Show*. Over the years it was modified and toward the end of the series' run the process of leafing through dossiers was dropped completely.

The top-secret assignments taken on by this elite group of agents usually involved disrupting the activities of various small foreign powers seeking to create problems for America or the Free World. By the last season the agents had begun to run out of little Communist countries and obscure principalities, so they concentrated their efforts more on dealing with organized crime within the United States. All of the plans executed by the Impossible Missions Force were incredibly complex and depended on split-second timing and an astounding array of sophisticated electronic gadgetry. The leader of the group, Daniel Briggs during the first season and Jim Phelps through the rest of *Mission: Impossible*'s run, devised the complex plans used to accomplish the team's missions. Barney Collier was the electronics expert and Willie Armitage provided muscle throughout the series' run. Rollin Hand was an expert at disguise and Cinnamon Carter was the versatile, beautiful female member of the team. Martin Landau and Barbara Bain, then husband and wife in real life, left the show at the end of the 1968–1969 season in a contract dispute and were replaced by other performers filling their respective functions.

The music for *Mission: Impossible* was written by Lalo Schifrin and had a pulsating, jazz-oriented urgency. The show's theme, which typified the music of the show, was released as a single and was on *Billboard*'s "Hot 100" chart for 14 weeks in 1968. There were also two albums of *Mission: Impossible* music released in the late 1960s.

In the rather literal 1988 revival of the series, a now white-haired Jim Phelps returned to head up the IMF when his protégé and successor was killed. Not much had changed. He got the same opening instructions ("Your mission, should you decide to accept it . . ."), read by the same voice, but now on a video disc player so he could see pictures of the bad guys. The disc then self destructed. His young team had new faces, but the same functions: master-of-disguises Nicholas, muscleman Max, seductress Casey, and electronics wizard Grant—the latter being the son, no less, of former electronics wizard Barney Collier (actor Phil Morris was also the son of Greg Morris, who played Barney). The female position was, as before, subject to turnover: Casey was replaced in early 1989 by Shannon Reed, who was not only beautiful but a former Olympic athlete, TV broadcaster, and cop.

The team still infiltrated small foreign countries to foil an assortment of petty tyrants, though there were now more non-political cases involving international arms dealers, terrorists, and drug lords. Ghosts of the past emerged too; in one episode the team sprung former IMF member Barney Collier from a Turkish prison, and in another rescued Lisa Casey from a death squad. The action even pulsed to the same music of Lalo Schifrin. It was as if your TV set had tuned in to 1966.

MISSISSIPPI, THE (*Legal Drama*)

FIRST TELECAST: *March 25, 1983*
LAST TELECAST: *March 13, 1984*
BROADCAST HISTORY:

Mar 1983–May 1983, CBS Fri 10:00–11:00
Sep 1983–Mar 1984, CBS Tue 8:00–9:00

CAST:

Ben Walker.......................... Ralph Waite
Stella McMullen .... Linda G. Miller
Lafayette "Lafe" Tate .... Stan Shaw

Filmed entirely on location, *The Mississippi* was the story of a highly successful, big-city criminal attorney who sought a more leisurely life. Ben Walker tried to get away from it all by purchasing a stern-wheel river tug and making a living with it up and down the Mississippi River. But his former life continued to get in the way as he became involved in criminal proceedings in almost every port. His clients often couldn't pay for his work, but Ben's sense of justice forced him to get involved. His "crew" consisted of Stella McMullen and Lafe Tate, both of whom were more interested in learning to become lawyers than in running the tug. Stella, one of Ben's former clients, was bright and argumentative, while Lafe, a Vietnam veteran who had had his fill of violence during the war, couldn't keep from getting into fights in civilian life. He did most of the maintenance on the boat, as well as the majority of the legwork on Ben's cases.

MR. ADAMS AND EVE (*Situation Comedy*)
FIRST TELECAST: *January 4, 1957*
LAST TELECAST: *September 23, 1958*
BROADCAST HISTORY:
Jan 1957–Feb 1958, CBS Fri 9:00–9:30
Feb 1958–Sep 1958, CBS Tue 8:00–8:30
CAST:
Eve Drake .... Ida Lupino
Howard Adams .... Howard Duff
Steve .... Hayden Rorke
Elsie .... Olive Carey
J. B. Hafter .... Alan Reed

Movie stars Howard Duff and Ida Lupino were married to each other in real life at the time they played husband-and-wife film stars in this series. Happenings at the studio, fights with studio boss J. B. Hafter, negotiations and dealings with their agent Steve, and the good and troublesome sides of their home life were all shown in *Mr. Adams and Eve.* Though exaggerated for comic effect, many of the stories were based on actual situations that had happened to Duff and Lupino.

MRS. & MRS. CARROLL, see *Most Important People, The*

MR. & MRS. NORTH (*Comedy/Mystery*)
FIRST TELECAST: *October 3, 1952*
LAST TELECAST: *July 20, 1954*
BROADCAST HISTORY:
Oct 1952–Sep 1953, CBS Fri 10:00–10:30
Jan 1954–Jul 1954, NBC Tue 10:30–11:00
CAST:
Pamela North .... Barbara Britton
Jerry North .... Richard Denning
Lt. Bill Weigand .... Francis De Sales

Jerry North was a publisher of mystery stories who fancied himself a fairly adept amateur detective. However, his wife, Pamela, an attractive, pleasant, rather naive woman, somehow always seemed to be one step ahead of both him and the police when it came to solving mysterious crimes. The Norths were supposed to be entirely normal Greenwich Village residents, but they seemed to stumble across bodies at every turn. *Mr. & Mrs. North* had long been a favorite on radio, and was also produced as a Broadway play and a movie. The characters were conceived by Richard and Frances Lockridge for a series of stories for *The New Yorker* magazine.

MR. & MRS. SMITH (*Foreign Intrigue*)
FIRST TELECAST: *September 20, 1996*
LAST TELECAST: *November 8, 1996*
BROADCAST HISTORY:
Sep 1996–Nov 1996, CBS Fri 9:00–10:00
CAST:
Mr. Smith .... Scott Bakula
Mrs. Smith .... Maria Bello
Mr. Big .... Roy Dotrice

Tongue-in-cheek espionage series with lots of high-tech equipment, exotic locations, and sexual innuendo. The "Smiths" were secretive spies whose real names were never revealed to anyone, especially each other. They worked for the Factory, a private security company specializing in industrial espionage, ostensibly "in the interest of protecting corporate America." Their boss, Mr. Big, had teamed them after steely Mrs. Smith, a freelance spy on assignment for one of the Factory's competitors, had helped amiable Mr. Smith save a scientist they were both searching for, and was fired by her employer for failing to deliver his formula for a pollution-free energy source to them. Their globe-trotting assignments included halting the leak of top secret military security codes, stopping the sale of Stinger missiles to terrorists, protecting a young singer from assassination, and preventing a saboteur from destroying the European wine industry. Although there was definitely sexual attraction between them, they were too professional and competitive to let it get in the way of their performance.

MR. ARSENIC (*Talk*)
FIRST TELECAST: *May 8, 1952*
LAST TELECAST: *June 26, 1952*
BROADCAST HISTORY:
May 1952–Jun 1952, ABC Thu 9:00–9:30
HOST:
Burton Turkus

Burton Turkus, co-author of *Murder, Incorporated* and prosecutor of Murder, Inc., during William O'Dwyer's terms of office as mayor of New York, hosted this program of factual information on current political personalities and gangsters. Mr. Turkus answered questions from an off-camera voice and gave detailed insights into headliners in crime and politics. Definitely not for the squeamish.

MR. BELVEDERE (*Situation Comedy*)
FIRST TELECAST: *March 15, 1985*
LAST TELECAST: *July 8, 1990*
BROADCAST HISTORY:
Mar 1985–Apr 1985, ABC Fri 8:30–9:00
Aug 1985–Mar 1987, ABC Fri 8:30–9:00
May 1987–Sep 1987, ABC Fri 8:30–9:00
Oct 1987–Jan 1988, ABC Fri 9:00–9:30
Jan 1988–Feb 1988, ABC Fri 8:30–9:00
Mar 1988–Jul 1989, ABC Fri 9:00–9:30
Aug 1989–Sep 1989, ABC Fri 8:30–9:00
Sep 1989–Dec 1989, ABC Sat 8:00–8:30
Jul 1990, ABC Sun 8:30–9:00
CAST:
Mr. Lynn Belvedere .... Christopher Hewett
George Owens .... Bob Uecker
Marsha Owens .... Ilene Graff
Kevin Owens (age 16) .... Rob Stone
Heather Owens (14) .... Tracy Wells
Wesley T. Owens (8) .... Brice Beckham
Angela (1986–1989) .... Michele Matheson
THEME:
by Judy Hart Angelo and Gary Portnoy, sung by Leon Redbone

Clifton Webb's memorably eccentric character from 1940s films was revived in this routine TV sitcom in the 1980s. Frumpy sportswriter George Owens and his wife, Marsha, a lawyer-to-be, were a two-career couple living in suburban Pittsburgh and having trouble finding time for their three rambunctious kids—especially "little operator" Wesley. Enter Mr. Belvedere, a witty, debonair, portly English housekeeper who had formerly served such gentry as Winston Churchill; to everyone's surprise he proved both a genius in the kitchen and an expert at solving all the little problems of growing up and getting along that fill "warm family comedies" such as this. Each episode ended with Belvedere writing the lessons of the day in his diary.

By the beginning of the 1987–1988 season Marsha had received her degree and begun her first job as a lawyer, and son Kevin had entered college. A notable occasional guest was singer Robert Goulet, who turned up for, among other things, Belvedere's wedding in the last original episode. The family dog was Spot.

The character of Mr. Belvedere was originally created by Gwen Davenport in the novel *Belvedere*; Clifton Webb played him in three popular movies, *Sitting Pretty* (1948), *Mr. Belvedere Goes to College* (1949), and *Mr. Belvedere Rings the Bell* (1951). Interestingly, there were at least three attempts to produce a series based on the character during the early days of television, with *Mr. Belvedere* pilots made in 1956 (starring Reginald Gardiner), 1959 (Hans Conried), and 1965 (Victor Buono). None were successful.

ABC aired reruns of *Mr. Belvedere* on weekday mornings from September 1987 to January 1988.

MR. BLACK (*Mystery Anthology*)

FIRST TELECAST: *September 19, 1949*
LAST TELECAST: *November 7, 1949*
BROADCAST HISTORY:
Sep 1949–Oct 1949, ABC Mon 9:30–10:00
Oct 1949–Nov 1949, ABC Mon 9:00–9:30
CAST:
Mr. Black .... Andy Christopher

This spooky series always saw that the bad guys got their due. That was taken care of by Mr. Black—Lucifer's representative on Earth—who appeared at the open and close of each show amid cobwebs and flickering lights. Stories were standard suspense yarns. From Chicago.

MR. BROADWAY (*Drama*)

FIRST TELECAST: *September 26, 1964*
LAST TELECAST: *December 26, 1964*
BROADCAST HISTORY:
Sep 1964–Dec 1964, CBS Sat 9:00–9:30
CAST:
Mike Bell........................... Craig Stevens
Hank McClure .... Horace McMahon
Toki................................ Lani Miyazaki

Michael Bell Associates–Public Relations was a highly successful venture that numbered among its clients movie stars, politicians, businessmen, philanthropists, and even phonies. All of them had one thing in common, a willingness to pay well for the creation and maintenance of their desired public image. That was Mike Bell's job and it got him into many an exciting, romantic, dangerous, and frequently amusing situation as he worked to protect his clients' images. Helping him were his assistant, ex-newspaperman Hank McClure, and his attractive and highly efficient girl Friday, Toki.

MR. CITIZEN (*Dramatic Anthology*)

FIRST TELECAST: *April 20, 1955*
LAST TELECAST: *July 13, 1955*
BROADCAST HISTORY:
Apr 1955–Jul 1955, ABC Wed 8:30–9:00
HOST:
Allyn Edwards

Dramatizations of acts of heroism by real people were presented each week in this series. Allyn Edwards introduced the show by providing background on the incident being dramatized. At the end of each episode, the person whose act of heroism had just been shown appeared in person to receive the "Mr. Citizen" award for the week. Each show had a different person in public life (senators, military personnel, etc.) present the award.

MR. DEEDS GOES TO TOWN (*Situation Comedy*)

FIRST TELECAST: *September 26, 1969*
LAST TELECAST: *January 16, 1970*
BROADCAST HISTORY:
Sep 1969–Jan 1970, ABC Fri 8:30–9:00
CAST:
Longfellow Deeds .... Monte Markham
Tony Lawrence .... Pat Harrington, Jr.
Henry Masterson...................... Herb Voland
George, the butler......................... Ivor Barry

Longfellow Deeds, a young newspaper editor in the small town of Mandrake Falls, suddenly inherited the multimillion-dollar corporation founded by his uncle, the unscrupulous Alonzo P. Deeds. Young Mr. Deeds promptly moved to New York to take over the corporation, and use the money to right the wrongs his uncle had perpetrated. His country naivete and extreme honesty almost brought him down in the cutthroat world of big business. Tony Lawrence was Uncle Alonzo's former public-relations man who became Longfellow Deeds's best friend and confidant, and Mr. Masterson was the continually infuriated chairman of the board of Deeds Enterprises.

Based rather loosely on the 1936 Gary Cooper movie of the same name.

MR. DISTRICT ATTORNEY (*Police Drama*)

FIRST TELECAST: *October 1, 1951*
LAST TELECAST: *June 23, 1952*
BROADCAST HISTORY:
Oct 1951–Jun 1952, ABC Mon 8:00–8:30
(In first-run syndication during the 1954–1955 season)
CAST:
District Attorney Paul Garrett (1951–1952)
.... Jay Jostyn
Harrington (1951–1952).................. Len Doyle
Miss Miller (1951–1952)................ Vicki Vola
District Attorney Paul Garrett (1954–1955)
.... David Brian
Miss Miller (1954–1955) .... Jackie Loughery

Mr. District Attorney was one of the most popular radio crime shows of the 1940s, largely because of its uncanny realism. It was often based on real headlines, and in some cases actually anticipated them. In addition, the lead character was based on a real, and very famous, D.A.—New York's crime-busting Thomas E. Dewey, who later became governor of the state and a two-time candidate for President of the U.S.

The leads in the TV version were the same as those through most of the radio run, Jay Jostyn as the relentless D.A., Len Doyle as an ex-cop who was his investigator, and Vicki Vola as his secretary. Producer Edward C. Byron, who had created the radio show in 1939, also supervised the TV series. The opening lines will be remembered by any fan of either the radio or TV show: "Mister District Attorney! Champion of the people! Guardian of our fundamental rights to life, liberty and the pursuit of happiness!"

Mr. District Attorney was produced live and alternated with *The Amazing Mr. Malone* during the 1951–1952 season. A syndicated version was produced in 1954, with David Brian in the lead role and Jackie Loughery as Miss Miller.

MISTER ED (*Situation Comedy*)
FIRST TELECAST: *October 1, 1961*
LAST TELECAST: *September 8, 1965*
BROADCAST HISTORY:
Oct 1961–Sep 1962, CBS Sun 6:30–7:00
Sep 1962–Mar 1963, CBS Thu 7:30–8:00
Mar 1963–Oct 1964, CBS Sun 6:30–7:00
Dec 1964–Sep 1965, CBS Wed 7:30–8:00
CAST:
Wilbur Post.......... Alan Young
Carol Post.......... Connie Hines
Roger Addison (1961–1963) .... Larry Keating
Kay Addison (1961–1964) .... Edna Skinner
Gordon Kirkwood (1963–1965).......... Leon Ames
Winnie Kirkwood (1963–1965)
.... Florence MacMichael
Voice of Mr. Ed .... Allan "Rocky" Lane

One of the more nonsensical TV comedies was this series about a talking horse. Ed belonged to Wilbur Post, a young architect who had decided to move out of the city and get a little closer to nature. The rambling country home Wilbur and his wife bought was everything they had imagined, except for one thing—with it came a palomino that could talk. Mr. Ed didn't talk to everybody; in fact he would only talk to Wilbur, because Wilbur was the first person worth talking to he had met. The confusion caused by a talking horse, and the situations Ed got Wilbur into, and occasionally out of, formed the stories. Larry Keating was featured as the Posts' next-door neighbor. Unfortunately he passed away shortly after the start of the 1963–64 season. Edna Skinner, as his wife, remained a while longer but was phased out as the Posts got new neighbors that December. After leaving the nighttime schedule in 1965, *Mister Ed* continued for one more season, airing on Sundays from 5:00 to 5:30 P.M. The only regular cast members during the 1965–1966 season were Ed and the Posts. Allan "Rocky" Lane, who provided the resonant, gravelly voice of Mr. Ed, was a retired actor who had starred in scores of low-budget Westerns in the 1940s.

Mister Ed had actually premiered as a syndicated series, with the same cast as the network version, in January 1961. It was one of the few series to begin in syndication and then be picked by a network for its prime-time lineup.

MR. GARLUND (*Adventure*)
FIRST TELECAST: *October 7, 1960*
LAST TELECAST: *January 13, 1961*
BROADCAST HISTORY:
Oct 1960–Jan 1961, CBS Fri 9:30–10:00
CAST:
Frank Garlund.......... Charles Quinlivan
Kam Chang.......... Kam Tong

At the age of 30, Frank Garlund had already amassed a considerable fortune. He was a financial wizard whose skill and conspicuous success had brought him into contact with a myriad of people, both honest and dishonest, none of whom were quite the same after their encounters with him. The young Mr. Garlund had a mysterious background and few close associates. The one person in whom he did confide, and from whom he sought counsel, was his foster brother, Kam Chang. Stories revolved around Garlund's rise in the world of international business and intrigue. The title of this series was changed to *The Garlund Touch* on November 11, 1960.

MR. I MAGINATION (*Children's*)
FIRST TELECAST: *May 29, 1949*
LAST TELECAST: *April 13, 1952*
BROADCAST HISTORY:
May 1949–Jul 1949, CBS Sun 7:00–7:30
Jul 1949, CBS Sun 7:30–8:00
Aug 1949–Sep 1949, CBS Sun 7:30–7:55
Oct 1949–Jun 1951, CBS Sun 6:30–7:00 (OS)
Jan 1952–Feb 1952, CBS Sun 6:30–7:00
Feb 1952–Apr 1952, CBS Sun 6:00–6:30
REGULARS:
Paul Tripp
Ruth Enders
Ted Tiller
Joe Silver

The title role of *Mr. I Magination* was played by the versatile Paul Tripp, author of *Tubby the Tuba* and other stories for children. Not only did he star in the show, but he created it and wrote many of the fantasies which were presented. Children who viewed this live series were asked to send in letters describing something that they wished could happen. Tripp and his fellow regulars would then transform the wishes into television playlets. Each show opened with Tripp in candy-striped overalls, as the engineer of a train carrying children to Imaginationland. The passengers got off at places like Ambitionville, Inventorsville, Seaport City, and "I Wish I Were" Town. That last stop was the point from which plays based on the life of various historical figures were done, with a young (9–12) actor as the historical figure. *Mr. I Magination* began as a local show in New York, and expanded to a four-station network on May 29, 1949, five weeks after its premiere.

MR. LUCKY (*Adventure*)
FIRST TELECAST: *October 24, 1959*
LAST TELECAST: *September 3, 1960*
BROADCAST HISTORY:
Oct 1959–Sep 1960, CBS Sat 9:00–9:30
CAST:
Mr. Lucky .... John Vivyan
Andamo.......... Ross Martin
Lt. Rovacs.......... Tom Brown
Maggie Shank-Rutherford .... Pippa Scott
Maitre'd .... Joe Scott
THEME:
"Mr. Lucky," by Henry Mancini

Mr. Lucky was an honest professional gambler who had won a plush floating casino, the ship *Fortuna*, and made it his base of operations. Staying beyond the 12-mile limit, where he could operate a gambling ship legally, Mr. Lucky played host to a wide variety of people, all of whom came to make use of his sumptuous facility. Helping him run the casino was his good friend Andamo. When he got into scrapes that required police assistance, Lt. Rovacs usually provided it. The music from this series, composed by

Henry Mancini, produced two successful albums, *The Music from Mr. Lucky* and *Mr. Lucky Goes Latin*. Based on the 1943 movie of the same name starring Cary Grant.

MR. MAGOO, see *Famous Adventures of Mr. Magoo, The*

MR. MERLIN (*Situation Comedy*)
FIRST TELECAST: *October 7, 1981*
LAST TELECAST: *August 18, 1982*
BROADCAST HISTORY:
Oct 1981–Jan 1982, CBS Wed 8:00–8:30
Jan 1982–Mar 1982, CBS Mon 8:00–8:30
Jul 1982–Aug 1982, CBS Wed 8:00–8:30
CAST:
Max Merlin........................Barnard Hughes
Zachary Rogers ....Clark Brandon
Leo Samuels......................Jonathan Prince
Alexandra...........................Elaine Joyce

What better cover for an ageless sorcerer than running a garage in a run-down section of San Francisco? Who would believe that crusty old Max Merlin in his greasy coveralls was the same Merlin renowned in the days of King Arthur's Court? Fifteen-year-old Zac Rogers certainly didn't take Max seriously when the old man offered him the opportunity to become an apprentice sorcerer. But when he found out that this was no joke, Zac figured that learning magic could solve all his problems—with girls, with money, with his grades at school, and with just about anything else. Max believed that Zac could become a responsible sorcerer, and spent an entire TV season trying to train him, despite the troubles that Zac got into—casting the wrong spells, partially casting spells that got out of control, misusing potions, alienating Max's superiors, almost revealing his newfound magical powers to normal people, etc. Leo was Zac's best friend, who often got caught up in the disasters caused by his buddy's imperfect magic, and Alexandra was the beautiful liaison between Max (and Zac) and the all-powerful sorcerers to whom he was responsible.

MR. NOVAK (*Drama*)
FIRST TELECAST: *September 24, 1963*
LAST TELECAST: *August 31, 1965*
BROADCAST HISTORY:
Sep 1963–Aug 1965, NBC Tue 7:30–8:30
CAST:
John Novak......................James Franciscus
Albert Vane..........................Dean Jagger
Jean Pagano (1963–1964)..............Jeanne Bal
Martin Woodridge (1964–1965)..Burgess Meredith
Larry Thor.........................Jim Hendriks
Nurse Bromfield (1963–1964)........Marion Ross
Mr. Jerry Allen (1963–1964) ....Steve Franken
Mr. Gallo (1963–1964) ....Donald Barry
Miss Marilyn Scott.................Marian Collier
Mr. Pete Butler....................Vince Howard
Mr. Everett Johns.................André Phillippe
Mr. Stan Peeples.................Stephen Roberts
Mrs. Ann Floyd ....Kathaleen Ellis
Miss Rosemary Dorsey (1964–1965)
.....................................Marjorie Corley
Ruth Wilkinson (1964–1965).........Phyllis Avery
Mr. Arthur Bradwell (1964–1965)...William Zuckert
Paul Webb (1964–1965).............David Sheiner
Mr. Parkson (1964–1965).............Peter Hansen
Mrs. Ring (1965).....................Irene Tedrow

The challenges, accomplishments, and frustrations of a young high school English teacher on his first job provided the stories in this series. John Novak started his career at Jefferson High School in Los Angeles under Principal Albert Vane, who, although not in complete agreement with Mr. Novak's approach to teaching, took a strong liking to him as a dedicated teacher. When Vane was elected to the post of state superintendent of schools, he chose Martin Woodridge, another English teacher at Jefferson High, to replace him as principal. A large number of teachers and other school staff members had recurring roles during the two years *Mr. Novak* was on the air.

MR. PEEPERS (*Situation Comedy*)
FIRST TELECAST: *July 3, 1952*
LAST TELECAST: *June 12, 1955*
BROADCAST HISTORY:
Jul 1952–Sep 1952, NBC Thu 9:30–10:00
Oct 1952–Jul 1953, NBC Sun 7:30–8:00
Sep 1953–Jun 1955, NBC Sun 7:30–8:00
CAST:
Robinson Peepers.........................Wally Cox
Rayola Dean (1952).................Norma Crane
Charlie Burr (1952) ....David Tyrell
Mr. Gabriel Gurney (1952–1953)......Joseph Foley
Mrs. Gurney ....Marion Lorne
Superintendent Bascom ....Gage Clark
Nancy Remington.................Patricia Benoit
Harvey Weskit.......................Tony Randall
Mr. Remington ....Ernest Treux
Marge Weskit ....Georgann Johnson
Mr. Hansen (1953–1954)........Arthur O'Connell
Mrs. Remington (1953–1955)..........Sylvia Field
Frank Whip (1953–1955) ....Jack Warden
Mom Peepers (1953–1955).........Ruth McDevitt
Agnes Peepers (1953–1955) ....Jenny Egan
Aunt Lil (1954) ....Reta Shaw

Jefferson High School, located in the small Midwestern town of Jefferson City, was the setting for this live situation comedy. The central character was Robinson Peepers, a shy, quiet, slow-moving science teacher whose efforts to do the right thing always seemed to backfire. He was such a nice guy that everyone on the staff tried to mother him and the students all thought he was great, despite being laughable at times. His best friend was history teacher Harvey Weskit, whose brash self-confidence contrasted with Robinson's low-key personality. Other regulars in the cast were the school nurse, Nancy Remington, English teacher Mrs. Gurney (whose husband was the principal for the first season), and their families.

Mr. Peepers went on the air in the summer of 1952 with a scheduled eight-week run and was slotted for oblivion when the regular fall season began. At the start of the season, however, an NBC filmed series called *Doc Corkle* met with such overwhelming critical and public castigation that it was canceled after only three episodes had been aired. *Mr. Peepers* was rushed back into production and returned on the last Sunday in October. The one major change was in Robinson's romantic interest. During the summer it had been music appreciation teacher Rayola Dean. Nurse Nancy Remington became his girlfriend that fall. Almost as quiet and unassuming as Robinson, she just seemed "right" for him. Their romance blossomed and at the end of the 1953–1954 season they were married on the air, an event that excited viewers at the time in much the same way that Rhoda's TV marriage would do more than 20 years later.

MR. PRESIDENT (*Situation Comedy*)

FIRST TELECAST: *May 3, 1987*
LAST TELECAST: *April 2, 1988*
BROADCAST HISTORY:

May 1987–Sep 1987, FOX Sun 9:00–9:30
Sep 1987–Oct 1987, FOX Sun 9:30–10:00
Oct 1987–Jan 1988, FOX Sat 8:00–8:30
Jan 1988–Apr 1988, FOX Sat 9:30–10:00

CAST:

President Samuel Arthur Tresch ... George C. Scott
Meg Tresch (1987) ... Carlin Glynn
Cynthia Tresch (age 16) ... Maddie Corman
Nick Tresch (12) ... André Gower
Charlie Ross ... Conrad Bain
Lois Gullickson ... Madeline Kahn
Daniel Cummings ... Allen Williams
Dave ... Earl Boen

The return to series television of renowned actor George C. Scott—the man who 23 years earlier, after the failure of his first series, said he would never do another, and the only actor *ever* to refuse an Emmy Award—was a media event in 1987. He was doing it, he said bluntly, for the money.

The series was about the home life of a U.S. President. Former Wisconsin Governor Sam Tresch was newly elected, and living in the White House was quite an adjustment for his entire family. Nobody had any privacy, reporters were always snooping for any sort of story, and the Secret Service was everywhere they looked. Sam was a gruff, somewhat grouchy, very determined man (Scott's patented Patton-esque character), and he could take it. However, his wife, Meg, couldn't, and in the fall of 1987 she left Sam "to find herself," leaving the President and the two rambunctious kids, Cynthia and Nick, to fend for themselves. (An older daughter, Jennifer, was married and rarely seen.) The role of First Lady was assumed by Meg's sister Lois, a flaky woman with delusions of grandeur who had the hots for Sam and thought this was her big chance.

Affable Charlie Ross, who had been with Sam since early in his political career, was the loyal Chief of Staff; Daniel and Dave were others on the squabbling White House staff.

MR. RHODES (*Situation Comedy*)

FIRST TELECAST: *September 23, 1996*
LAST TELECAST: *March 17, 1997*
BROADCAST HISTORY:

Sep 1996–Mar 1997, NBC Mon 8:30–9:00

CAST:

Tom Rhodes ... Tom Rhodes
Nikki Harkin ... Farrah Forke
Ray Heary ... Stephen Tobolowsky
Ronald Felcher ... Ron Glass
Amanda Reeves ... Jessica Stone
Jake Mandelleer ... Shaun Weiss
Zoey Miller ... Lindsay Sloane
Ethan Armstrong ... Travis Wester
Dani Swanson ... Alexandra Holden

Long-haired standup comic Tom Rhodes got to do his routine in front of a class of appreciative, laughing kids in this sitcom. Rhodes's character was an unsuccessful writer (critics liked his first novel, but it didn't sell) who returned home to New England to teach at Harkin Academy, a small-town prep school. There he found immediate chemistry with Nikki, a girl of his teenage fantasies who was now the high-strung guidance counselor. Headmaster Ray, a wannabe hipster, liked Tom's cool, leather-jacketed image but frowned on his casual teaching style; arrogant history teacher Ron didn't like anything about him; and freaky math teacher Amanda would sit astride his motorcycle any day. Jake, Zoey, Ethan, and Dani were among the more frequently seen students.

MR. ROBERTS (*Comedy/Adventure*)

FIRST TELECAST: *September 17, 1965*
LAST TELECAST: *September 2, 1966*
BROADCAST HISTORY:

Sep 1965–Sep 1966, NBC Fri 9:30–10:00

CAST:

Lt. (j.g.) Douglas Roberts ... Roger Smith
Ensign Frank Pulver ... Steve Harmon
Captain John Morton ... Richard X. Slattery
Doc ... George Ives
Seaman D'Angelo ... Richard Sinatra
Seaman Mannion ... Ronald Starr
Seaman Reber ... Roy Reese

The adventures of the crew of the U.S.S. *Reluctant*, a cargo ship operating far behind the lines in the South Pacific during World War II, provided the stories for this comedy. Life on board was incredibly dull and monotonous, especially for young Mr. Roberts. He wanted the opportunity to really participate in the war effort, not slosh around in the middle of nowhere on a mangy old tub, and was desperately trying to get transferred to another ship. Ensign Pulver was the crewman who was always scheming to find ways of livening up the otherwise boring existence of the crew—as long as no real work was involved. Stern old Captain Morton was the major concern of most of the crew—they were preoccupied with finding ways to drive him slowly out of his mind.

Based on the book by Thomas Heggen, which was subsequently made into a hit play (1948), and a movie (1955) starring Henry Fonda, Jack Lemmon, and James Cagney.

MR. SMITH (*Situation Comedy*)

FIRST TELECAST: *September 23, 1983*
LAST TELECAST: *December 16, 1983*
BROADCAST HISTORY:

Sep 1983–Dec 1983, NBC Fri 8:00–8:30

CAST:

Raymond Holyoke ... Leonard Frey
Tommy Atwood ... Tim Dunigan
Ellie Atwood ... Laura Jacoby
Dr. July Tyson ... Terri Garber
Cha Cha/Mr. Smith ... C.J. (voice: Ed Weinberger)
Dr. Klein ... Stuart Margolin

One of the most talked about but least viewed series of the 1983–1984 season was this light comedy about a talking orangutan. Cha Cha had been an ordinary circus orangutan until his inquisitiveness and thirst (he drank a whole bottle of experimental enzyme) transformed him into a talking primate genius with an I.Q. of 256. The government figured that made him smarter than anybody in Washington, and set him up as a special consultant on such things as nuclear energy and MX missile policy. He was renamed Mr. Smith, given a human wardrobe (except for shoes) and a pair of spectacles, and moved into a suburban Washington house along with his dim-witted former owner, Tommy, Tommy's smart-alecky kid sister, Ellie, and, eventually, his ordinary brother orangutan Bo Bo.

Attending to Mr. Smith's needs, and keeping a watchful eye on America's newest secret weapon, was prissy Raymond Holyoke, whose previous work had been as personal secretary to presidents and ambassadors. Dr. July Tyson was a research scientist from the Institute for Primate Studies who kept track of Mr. Smith's development, and Dr. Klein was her boss. Unfortunately the opportunity for political satire was never really exploited, as stories focused mostly on family contretemps and little misunderstandings, and the series was short-lived.

The orangutan who played Mr. Smith was already a star, having been featured in two Clint Eastwood movies, *Any Which Way You Can* and *Every Which Way But Loose*, and Bo Derek's version of *Tarzan*. Series co-executive producer Ed Weinberger provided his voice.

MR. SMITH GOES TO WASHINGTON (*Situation Comedy*)

FIRST TELECAST: *September 29, 1962*
LAST TELECAST: *March 30, 1963*
BROADCAST HISTORY:
Sep 1962–Mar 1963, ABC Sat 8:30–9:00
CAST:
Sen. Eugene Smith.................... Fess Parker
Pat Smith.......................... Sandra Warner
Uncle Cooter............................ Red Foley
Arnie .... Stan Irwin
Miss Kelly.............................. Rita Lynn

While starring as Davy Crockett in the mid-1950s, Fess Parker was at one point called upon to portray Crockett as a rustic representative to the United States Congress. In this series Parker once again headed for Washington, this time in contemporary garb, but with the same low-keyed, homespun approach to national—and family—politics and problems. Freshman Senator Eugene Smith and his wife Pat were from a small town, and they used the homilies of Middle America to cope with urban, political Washington. Arnie was Senator Smith's chauffeur, Uncle Cooter his philosophical, guitar-strumming uncle, and Miss Kelly his secretary.

Based on the 1939 movie starring James Stewart.

MISTER STERLING (*Political Drama*)

FIRST TELECAST: *January 10, 2003*
LAST TELECAST: *March 14, 2003*
BROADCAST HISTORY:
Jan 2003–Mar 2003, NBC Fri 8:00–9:00
CAST:
Sen. William Sterling, Jr. .... Josh Brolin
Jackie Brock..................... Audra McDonald
Tommy Doyle .... William Russ
Leon Montero....................... David Noroña
William Sterling, Sr. .... James Whitmore
Sen. Jackson .... Graham Greene
Laura Chandler.................... Chandra West

William Sterling, Jr., was an idealistic do-gooder and son of a former California governor who was donating his time to run a school for prison inmates when he was plucked out of obscurity to fill the unexpired term of one of the state's two senators. Washington, he found, was run by a clique of arrogant, unprincipled old men who cared about nothing put power—but despite his naïveté, he set out to fix things. He knew he needed help, so from his disgraced predecessor's staff he picked spunky former press secretary Jackie, a stylish black woman who spoke her mind, to be his new chief of staff; angry, distrustful Tommy to be his legislative director, because he knew the ropes better than anyone; and nerdy Leon to manage his computer databases (which told him where everyone stood on everything). Fellow senator Jackson was a confidant, while back home Sterling's crusty dad, the retired former governor, gave him sage political advice. Laura was a reporter who snooped around.

The pros who engineered his appointment assumed he would be an obedient Democrat like his famous father, but Sterling declared himself an independent because he didn't much like either party. In a closely divided Senate he had swing-vote power, and with Tommy's help he used it to push through all sorts of wonderful things (a tax on millionaires to fund an increase in the minimum wage, money for education, etc.). Sometimes his ignorance of the issues proved embarrassing—as when he didn't realize that his attempt to kill a "wasteful" military weapons program would cost thousands of people their jobs in his home state—but more often he was right. Lobbyists pursued him, reporters ambushed him and the Senate power brokers were livid, but with the help of his little staff he outsmarted them at almost every turn. Only on television.

MR. SUNSHINE (*Situation Comedy*)

FIRST TELECAST: *March 28, 1986*
LAST TELECAST: *September 3, 1986*
BROADCAST HISTORY:
Mar 1986–May 1986, ABC Fri 9:00–9:30
May 1986, ABC Sat 8:00–8:30
Jun 1986–Jul 1986, ABC Fri 9:00–9:30
Aug 1986–Sep 1986, ABC Wed 8:30–9:00
CAST:
Prof. Paul Stark .... Jeffrey Tambor
Grace D'Angelo .... Nan Martin
Mrs. June Swinford .... Barbara Babcock
Prof. Leon Walters .... Leonard Frey
Janice Hall............................ Cecilia Hart
Warren Leftwich .... David Knell
EXECUTIVE PRODUCERS:
John Rich and Henry Winkler

One of TV's rare attempts to deal with the subject of blindness in a series setting. Paul Stark was a tall, balding, and very acerbic English professor who had suffered two recent blows: he had been blinded in an accident, and divorced by his wife. He coped with his handicap fairly well, physically at least, continuing to teach and even reentering the singles scene (Janice was his chief romantic interest, though by their relationship you might not know it). Mrs. Swinford was his flightly landlady, Grace his caustic personal secretary, and Leon a drama professor. Paul neither asked for nor got pity; sometimes he helped his friends, in his domineering way, and sometimes they helped him.

MR. T. AND TINA (*Situation Comedy*)
FIRST TELECAST: *September 25, 1976*
LAST TELECAST: *October 30, 1976*
BROADCAST HISTORY:
Sep 1976–Oct 1976, ABC Sat 8:30–9:00
CAST:
Taro Takahashi ("Mr. T.") .... Pat Morita
Tina Kelly .... Susan Blanchard
Michi .... Pat Suzuki
Harvard .... Ted Lange
Miss Llewellyn .... Miriam Byrd-Nethery
Uncle Matsu .... "Jerry" Hatsuo Fujikawa
Sachi .... June Angela
Aki .... Gene Profanato

A comedy of clashing cultures. Mr. T. was a brilliant Japanese inventor who had been transferred by his firm from Tokyo to Chicago. There, he had to cope with the Americanization of his household by a nutty, effervescent, Nebraska-born housekeeper named Tina. Tina was well-intentioned but sometimes her ideas of a happy home were at fearful odds with the traditional, male-dominated society from which the Takahashis had so recently come. Michi was Mr. T.'s sister-in-law, Uncle Matsu the staunch traditionalist, and Sachi and Aki the two children. On the American side were Harvard, the hip handyman, and Miss Llewellyn, the landlady.

MR. TERRIFIC (*Situation Comedy*)
FIRST TELECAST: *January 9, 1967*
LAST TELECAST: *August 28, 1967*
BROADCAST HISTORY:
Jan 1967–Aug 1967, CBS Mon 8:00–8:30
CAST:
Stanley Beamish (Mr. Terrific) ... Stephen Strimpell
Barton J. Reed .... John McGiver
Hal Walters .... Dick Gautier
Harley Trent .... Paul Smith

Stanley Beamish was a young gas station operator whose partner in the service station, as well as his best friend and roommate, was Hal Walters. Stanley did have one secret that he kept from his buddy—with the aid of special top-secret power pills he could become that caped crime fighter, Mr. Terrific. The pills had been developed by the Bureau of Secret Projects, a special government agency. BSP chief Barton J. Reed sent Stanley on his missions and supplied him with the pills. A power pill would give him extraordinary abilities for only one hour. In emergencies he could take two booster pills, each good for an extra 20 minutes, but after that he reverted to normal. He was a nice, soft-spoken, naive guy who, unfortunately for the BSP, was the only person on whom the pills worked. His efforts to serve his government were noble, but not always what Mr. Reed would have liked. Stanley was too gullible, too considerate, and frequently too preoccupied to pay attention to the time limits of his powers. He had a disturbing propensity for returning to normal at the most inopportune times.

MR. WIZARD, see *Watch Mr. Wizard*

MIXED DOUBLES (*Drama*)
FIRST TELECAST: *August 5, 1949*
LAST TELECAST: *October 29, 1949*
BROADCAST HISTORY:
Aug 1949–Sep 1949, NBC Fri 9:00–9:30
Sep 1949–Oct 1949, NBC Sat 8:30–9:00
CAST:
Elaine Coleman (first 2 weeks) ..... Rhoda Williams
Elaine Coleman .... Bonnie Baken
Eddy Coleman .... Eddy Firestone
Ada Abbott .... Ada Friedman
Bill Abbott .... Billy Idelson

This early prime-time soap opera was about two newly married couples living side by side in one-room apartments, trying to build their lives on the husbands' meager incomes. Eddy and Bill were both copywriters at large advertising agencies. The program was created by Carleton E. Morse *(One Man's Family)* and first seen locally on the West Coast.

MOBILE ONE (*Adventure*)
FIRST TELECAST: *September 12, 1975*
LAST TELECAST: *December 29, 1975*
BROADCAST HISTORY:
Sep 1975–Oct 1975, ABC Fri 8:00–9:00
Oct 1975–Dec 1975, ABC Mon 8:00–9:00
CAST:
Peter Campbell .... Jackie Cooper
Maggie Spencer .... Julie Gregg
Doug McKnight .... Mark Wheeler
EXECUTIVE PRODUCER:
Jack Webb

Jackie Cooper, whose first acting experience was as a member of the *Our Gang* comedies in 1925 (at age 3), played a veteran TV news reporter in this 1975 series. Together with his producer Maggie, cameraman Doug, and the mobile unit from station KONE, he covered hard news and human-interest stories in a large city (not named, but the series was filmed in and around Los Angeles).

MOD SQUAD, THE (*Police Drama*)
FIRST TELECAST: *September 24, 1968*
LAST TELECAST: *August 23, 1973*
BROADCAST HISTORY:
Sep 1968–Aug 1972, ABC Tue 7:30–8:30
Sep 1972–Aug 1973, ABC Thu 8:00–9:00
CAST:
Pete Cochran .... Michael Cole
Linc Hayes .... Clarence Williams III
Julie Barnes .... Peggy Lipton
Capt. Adam Greer .... Tige Andrews
CREATOR:
Bud Ruskin

The Mod Squad was probably the ultimate example of the establishment co-opting the youth movement of the late 1960s. Its three members were "hippie cops," each of them a dropout from straight society who had had his own brush with the law. Pete was a longhaired youth who had been kicked out by his wealthy Beverly Hills parents and stolen a car; Linc was the Afroed son of a ghetto family of 13, raised in Watts and arrested in the Watts rioting; Julie was the daughter of a San Francisco prostitute who had run away from home and been arrested for vagrancy. All three were on probation and looking for some way to make sense out of their lives when they were approached by Capt. Adam Greer, who recruited them for a special "youth squad." Their purpose was to infiltrate the counterculture and ferret out the adult criminals who preyed upon the young in Southern California (no finking on their own generation, thank you).

A contentious trio, always questioning their own motives and their differing cultural backgrounds, the *Mod Squad* nevertheless proved an effective undercover task force against adult crime. For the first season they rattled around in a battered old 1960 station wagon named "Woody," but this was killed off early in the second season (driven over a cliff).

Strangely enough, *The Mod Squad* was based on the true experiences of creator Bud Ruskin, a former police officer and later private detective. While a member of the Los Angeles Sheriff's Department in the 1950s he was a member of an undercover narcotics squad composed of young officers, which served as the inspiration for *The Mod Squad*. He first wrote a pilot script for the series in 1960, but it took eight more years before it reached the air in this highly successful ABC program.

MODELS, INC. (*Drama*)
FIRST TELECAST: *June 29, 1994*
LAST TELECAST: *March 6, 1995*
BROADCAST HISTORY:
Jun 1994–Dec 1994, FOX Wed 9:00–10:00
Jan 1995–Mar 1995, FOX Mon 9:00–10:00
CAST:
Hillary Michaels .... Linda Gray
David Michaels (1994) .... Brian Gaskill
Sarah Owens .... Cassidy Rae
Carrie Spencer................... Carrie-Anne Moss
Teri Spencer (1994) .... Stephanie Romanov
Monique Duran................. Stephanie Romanov
Julie Dante.............................. Kylie Travis
Linda Holden .... Teresa Hill
Brian Peterson...................... Cameron Daddo
Eric Dearborn...................... David Goldsmith
Stephanie Smith (1994) .... Heather Medway
Cynthia Nichols................. Garcelle Beauvais
Lt. Louis Soto (1994) .... Robert Beltran
Kristy .... Kaela Dobkin
Kyle Carson (1994)................. Trenton Knight
Paul Carson (1994) .... William Katt
Marcia Carson (1994) .... Leann Hunley
Avery (1994) .... Nick Richert
Chris White (1994)................... Kurt Deutsch
Adam Louder .... James Wilder
Mark Warren................. John Haymes Newton
Craig Bowden .... Don Michael Paul
Ben Singer .... Lonnie Schuyler
Det. Towers (1994)................ Nancy Lee Grahn
Dr. Richard Heller (1994)............ Harley Venton
Grayson Louder .... Emma Samms
Joan .... Kim Zimmer
Daniel Louder (1995)...... Jared and Taylor Thorne
Anna Jacobs (1995)........................ Lisa Akey

This spin-off from *Melrose Place* focused on the lives of the people working for Models, Inc., a modeling agency in Los Angeles run by Hillary Michaels, the mother of *Melrose Place*'s Amanda Woodward. Hillary ran the agency with her son David, and a number of her top models lived together in a fancy beach house she owned on the Malibu coast.

In the premiere episode of *Models, Inc.* Teri Spencer, the agency's biggest and most ruthless star, was murdered at a farewell party celebrating her departure from the agency. For the next several months the murder investigation provided one of the major plotlines, with a number of people at the agency under suspicion at one time or another, including Hillary, who had a brief affair with Lt. Soto, the cop investigating Teri's death. After several months it was discovered that Hillary's emotionally disturbed assistant, Stephanie, infatuated with Teri's photographer boyfriend, Brian, had murdered Teri.

David had affairs with models Sarah and Julie. After his mother tried to break up the latter romance, he set up his own agency with Julie, called it J and D, and attempted to raid Hillary's models. Hillary foiled the attempt, and David stormed off to Europe, never to be heard from again.

Julie was one tough lady—cynical, nasty, and, most of all, extremely ambitious. After David left town she fell in love with surfer Craig. Unwilling to settle for someone without money she tried to dump him, unaware that he was really a wealthy romance novelist who used the pen name Blane Tudor. Julie went ballistic when his novel *Skin Deep*, a thinly veiled tell-all about the catty models at Models, Inc., became a best-seller and was made into a movie. As if that wasn't enough, the role of Julie in the film was to be played by Julie's conniving half sister Anna.

Brian had affairs with Sarah and Cynthia, the agency's only major black model, and endured with her a drawn-out stalker/kidnapping story. Carrie, Teri's older sister, was the most unstable of Hillary's models. At 27 she was fading as a model and afraid of losing her career. She had affairs with wealthy car dealer Paul (who, unbeknownst to her, had years earlier adopted her out-of-wedlock baby, Kyle), with a prospective investor in Models, Inc. (he thought she was Hillary), and with sleazy Dr. Keller, who had her committed to a psychiatric hospital to shut her up. She got out but ended up being drugged and shipped off to a Central American brothel.

Sarah, the talented newcomer, appeared to be a naive country bumpkin but was tougher than she looked. Into drinking and drugs, she dated David and then Mark, who left her to become a priest after impregnating her (but she miscarried). Linda was a waiflike model living with musician Eric, the boyfriend from Hell, at whose urging she had once done a porno movie. After he manipulated her once too often she dumped him for Chris, who wasn't much better.

Monique, a dead ringer for Teri, arrived soon after Teri's murder and was immediately signed to a contract by Hillary. She became a sort of surrogate sister to troubled Carrie and dated Adam, the owner of Stage 99, a club where the models hung out. Their relationship became complicated when Adam's long-missing wife, Grayson, returned. Grayson bought into Hillary's financially troubled agency and proceeded to cause trouble for everyone, setting up a call-girl service to finance her schemes. Eventually she hired a hit man to kill Adam at his wedding to Monique, but in the cliff-hanger series finale, it was uncertain who had been shot.

MODERN SCIENCE THEATER (*Documentary*)
FIRST TELECAST: *January 30, 1958*
LAST TELECAST: *March 13, 1958*
BROADCAST HISTORY:
Jan 1958–Mar 1958, ABC Thu 10:00–10:30
Documentary films on science and industry.

MOESHA (*Situation Comedy*)
FIRST TELECAST: *January 23, 1996*
LAST TELECAST: *August 27, 2001*
BROADCAST HISTORY:
Jan 1996–Sep 1997, UPN Tue 8:00–8:30
Aug 1997–Oct 1997, UPN Tue 8:30–9:00
Nov 1997–Aug 1999, UPN Tue 8:00–8:30
Aug 1998–Sep 1998, UPN Tue 9:00–9:30
Aug 1999–May 2001, UPN Mon 8:00–8:30
Apr 2000–May 2000, UPN Tue 830–9:00
Jul 2001–Aug 2001, UPN Mon 8:00–8:30
CAST:
Moesha "Mo" Mitchell (age 15). . Brandy (Norwood)
Frank Mitchell . . . . William Allen Young
Dee Mitchell . . . . Sheryl Lee Ralph
Myles Mitchell (9) . . . . Marcus T. Paulk
Hakeem Campbell . . . . Lamont Bentley
Andell Wilkerson (1996–2000). . . . . . . Yvette Wilson
Kim Parker (1996–1999) . . . . Countess Vaughn
Niecy Jackson . . . . Shar Jackson
Quenton "Q" Brooks (1996–1999). . . . . Fredro Starr
Dorian Long (1999–2001). . . . . Ray J. Norwood
Alicia (2000–2001). . . . . Alexis Fields
Barbara Lee Kennedy (2001) . . . . Olivia Brown
THEME:
written by Kurt Farquhar and Brandy, performed by Brandy

Pop music star Brandy was the star of this thoughtful but upbeat inner-city comedy set in Los Angeles. When the series premiered, Moesha was about to turn 16. Frank, her dad, sold cars for a local Saturn dealership; Dee, her new stepmother, taught at Moesha's school, Crenshaw High School; and Myles was her smart-mouthed kid brother. Mo's friends included Hakeem, a neighbor and classmate, who seemed to eat all his meals at the Mitchell home; Kim, her pudgy, outspoken best friend who had a crush on a disinterested Hakeem; and Niecy, a classmate who hung out with them and was the third member of the "Three Live Crew." Andell ran The Den restaurant where Mo and her friends hung out after school. In April, Dee became the faculty advisor for the school newspaper *Cry of the Cougar* and, less than a year later, was promoted to vice principal. During the 1996–1997 season Moesha was dating Q but unsure about how serious he was about her, and as a result, they broke up. Early in 1997, Frank, with help from some friends, bought his own Saturn dealership.

At the start of the 1997–1998 season Moesha was sent, despite her objections, to Bridgewood, a preppie private high school. In February she became co-editor of the school newspaper, the *Bridgewood Banner*, but few episodes actually dealt with the private school, concentrating instead on her family and her old friends. At the end of the season she went to a slumber party at which a couple of boys were planning to sleep over, and when she was dragged home by her irate father, they had an ugly confrontation. She left home and went to Andell's, where she lived for five months until she reconciled with her dad. The reconciliation took place when Myles got everybody to make up at Frank's birthday party and he let her go back to Crenshaw for her senior year. At the end of the season Kim and Hakeem were accepted to Santa Monica College and Moesha, who had been accepted to Northwestern University's School of Journalism, decided to postpone college to take a job at the magazine *Vibe*.

That fall Moesha was working at *Vibe* while Niecy was at California University and Hakeem was at Santa Monica College, as was Kim (in her own series, *The Parkers*). Frank took in his troubled teenage nephew, Dorian, who had arrived from Oakland, and tried to straighten him out. Early on Moesha was fired from *Vibe* and enrolled at California University. Dorian, the scam artist (who had given himself the rap name D Money), went too far and almost got sent back to Oakland before he showed real remorse. In February Hakeem was accepted to C.U. and a visiting aunt revealed that Frank was actually Dorian's father—he'd had an affair during a tough period in his first marriage and fathered him out of wedlock; Frank's sister had adopted the baby. The family didn't take this well, and Moesha moved into a crummy room at a C.U. dorm. She and her dad eventually made up, but Dorian still harbored resentment. In April Moesha and Hakeem started dating again. Dorian got involved with a lowlife but Frank bailed him out and, reluctantly, sent him to a juvenile boot camp. Moesha was offered a summer job touring as business manager for Q's rap group. She turned him down to stay with Hakeem, but due to a misunderstanding they broke up and Moesha wound up taking the job with Q.

In September Moesha was back from the tour and engaged to Q. Dorian had survived boot camp (and cleaned up his act) and was preparing to start his senior year in high school, and Dee was preparing to go back to Jamaica, where she had been offered a full-time education position. Moesha's new roommate at school was obnoxious Alicia—but she made up with Niecy and they became roommates. Hakeem was trying hard to get her back while Q was on tour in Japan. Frank wasn't pleased when Moesha finally told him she was engaged to Q, but they broke up at Thanksgiving. In February Dorian told Moesha he wanted to find his birth mother and she helped him track her down. The following week they found Barbara Lee, his mother, with whom he started to build a relationship. In May Dee came home in time for Dorian's high school graduation. He had gotten a recording contract, and in the season finale a guy who had been in jail with him tried to muscle in on his recording income. When Dorian refused, the guy kidnapped Myles. In the cliffhanger ending, as Moesha was about to tell Frank she was going to live with Hakeem, Dorian interrupted with the news about Myles, and Moesha fainted. Since the series was canceled, there was no resolution.

Each episode opened and closed with Moesha reflecting on how what happened affected her life and relationships.

MOHAWK SHOWROOM (*Music*)
FIRST TELECAST: *May 2, 1949*
LAST TELECAST: *November 23, 1951*
BROADCAST HISTORY:
May 1949–Dec 1949, NBC Mon–Fri 7:30–7:45
Dec 1949–Jul 1951, NBC Mon/Wed/Fri 7:30–7:45
Sep 1951–Nov 1951, NBC Mon/Wed/Fri 7:30–7:45
REGULARS:
Morton Downey (1949)
Trio (Carmen Mastren, Jim Ruhl, Trigger Alpert) (1949)
Roberta Quinlan
Harry Clark Trio
Bob Stanton

Live musical program with guest stars. For the first few months Morton Downey was featured on Monday, Wednesday, and Friday, while Roberta Quinlan appeared on Tuesday and Thursday. Beginning in December 1949 Miss Quinlan was the sole host. Sometimes announcer Bob Stanton also took part in the proceedings.

MOLE, THE (*Adventure/Game*)

FIRST TELECAST: *January 9, 2001*
LAST TELECAST: *February 12, 2003*
BROADCAST HISTORY:

Jan 2001–Feb 2001, ABC Tue 8:00–9:00
Feb 2001, ABC Wed 8:00–9:00
Sep 2001–Oct 2001, ABC Fri 8:00–9:00
May 2002–Aug 2002, ABC Tue 9:00–10:00
Jan 2003–Feb 2003, ABC Wed 10:00–11:00

HOST:

Anderson Cooper (2001–2002)
Ahmad Rashad (2003)

One of the many reality/competition shows that followed in the wake of CBS' megahit *Survivor, The Mole* emphasized mind games and sabotage. Approximately ten contestants were flown to various locations in the U.S. and Europe to complete team challenges, such as skydiving, bungee jumping, memory quizzes and following clues. When they succeeded money was added to the team's pot. However, one member of the team was a "mole," whose job it was to sabotage the team's efforts without detection. At the end of each episode the players were individually quizzed on facts about the mole—was it a man or a women, etc.—and whoever scored lowest was "executed," or expelled from the game. By the last episode only three were left, the mole plus two others. Whichever of the two correctly guessed the identity of the mole won the entire pot, which could potentially total as much as $1 million (reduced according to the effectiveness of the mole), and the mole was revealed. Twists along the way included bribes and buyouts, such as $50,000 to leave the game. The host was ominous, leather-clad Anderson Cooper.

Ten contestants competed in the original series, ranging in age from 23 to 63 and including helicopter pilot Jim, medical student Afi, undercover cop Steven, retired detective Charlie, folk-art dealer Wendi, event planner Manuel, grandma Kate, law school teacher Kathryn, sports enthusiast Jennifer and bartender Henry. Happy Manuel was the first to be "executed," while the eventual winner was Steven Cowles (who got $510,000). The mole was lawyer Kathryn Price. *Mole II: The Next Betrayal* premiered in September 2001 but was pulled after three episodes due to low ratings. It returned the following May to complete the game; one of its most ingenious challenges was having a contestant try to sleep in a room that constantly played "Tiny Bubbles" by Don Ho. In this edition 13 competed; the winner was 24-year-old musician Dorothy Hui (who got $636,000), and the mole was retired navy rear admiral Bill McDaniels.

The next edition, in early 2003, was *Celebrity Mole,* hosted by Ahmad Rashad and featuring as contestants actors Stephen Baldwin, Corbin Bernsen, Erik von Detten, Michael Boatman and Kim Coles, supermodel Frederique and comedian Kathy Griffin. This one was worth it just to see gangly young star von Detten and sarcastic earth-mom Griffin sparring. In the end Kathy won the pot ($233,000, for charity) and Frederique was revealed as the mole.

MOLLOY (*Situation Comedy*)

FIRST TELECAST: *July 25, 1990*
LAST TELECAST: *August 15, 1990*
BROADCAST HISTORY:

Jul 1990–Aug 1990, FOX Wed 9:00–9:30

CAST:

Molloy Martin (age 13) .... Mayim Bialik
Paul Martin .... Kevin Scannell
Lynn Martin .... Pamela Brull
Courtney .... Jennifer Aniston
Jason .... Luke Edwards
Simon .... I. M. Hobson
Sara .... Ashley Maw
Louis Duncan Jackson .... Bumper Robinson

Molloy was another of TV's endless stream of precocious, wise-beyond-their-years children. She and her widowed dad, Paul, lived in an exclusive section of Los Angeles with Paul's new wife, Lynn, and Lynn's two children—Courtney, an obnoxious, spoiled, status-conscious teenager, and Jason, a reasonably well-adjusted preteen. Lynn was a successful interior decorator, which may or may not have contributed to her daughter's—and her own—snobbishness. Although Molloy tolerated her stepmother and almost liked Jason, she and Courtney couldn't stand each other.

Paul, meanwhile, was the program director for TV station KQET, which led to a budding career for Molloy as well—as a regular cast member on *Wonderland,* a local children's show. Simon, Sara, and Louis were the other actors on *Wonderland.*

MOLONEY (*Police Drama*)

FIRST TELECAST: *September 19, 1996*
LAST TELECAST: *July 24, 1997*
BROADCAST HISTORY:

Sep 1996–Jul 1997, CBS Thu 9:00–10:00

CAST:

Dr. Nick Moloney .... Peter Strauss
Lt. Matty Navarro .... Nestor Sarrano
Asst. D.A. Calvin Patterson .... Wendell Pierce
Dr. Sarah Bateman .... Cherie Lunghi
Kate Moloney (age 11) .... Ashley Johnson
Off. Angela Vecchio .... Giuliana Santini
Det. Jimmy Wick .... Steve Rankin

Nick was both an L.A. cop and one of the department's psychiatrists—a rather unusual combination, and it had both advantages and disadvantages. His knowledge of the criminal mind and his psychiatric skills enabled him to talk his way into and out of almost any situation. Nick worked on all kinds of cases—hostages, serial killers, a rich young man who had accidentally killed his girlfriend, a religious fanatic who had kidnapped his own children, and cops with problems. At times he had to wrestle with the conflict between his responsibilities as a cop and the need to protect doctor/patient confidentiality. Matty was a friend on the force who was frequently at odds with Nick professionally, and Calvin, Nick's best friend, was an assistant D.A. who gave him help and advice. Nick's marriage to Sarah had failed, but he had a relatively good relationship with his ex-wife, and they both adored their daughter, Kate.

MOMENT OF DECISION (*Dramatic Anthology*)
FIRST TELECAST: *July 3, 1957*
LAST TELECAST: *September 25, 1957*
BROADCAST HISTORY:
Jul 1957–Sep 1957, ABC Wed 9:30–10:00
The dramas that made up this 1957 summer series consisted of reruns of episodes previously aired on *Ford Theatre.*

MOMENT OF FEAR (*Dramatic Anthology*)
FIRST TELECAST: *July 1, 1960*
LAST TELECAST: *August 10, 1965*
BROADCAST HISTORY:
Jul 1960–Sep 1960, NBC Fri 10:00–11:00
May 1964–Sep 1964, NBC Tue 8:30–9:00
May 1965–Aug 1965, NBC Tue 8:30–9:00
The 1960 version of *Moment of Fear* consisted of live dramas dealing with individuals who reached emotional crises in their lives. In the summers of 1964 and 1965 *Moment of Fear* was made up of filmed reruns of episodes from other anthology series. In 1964 the reruns were from *G.E. Theater, Schlitz Playhouse, Lux Video Theatre,* and *Studio 57.* In 1965 they came from the above four shows plus *Pepsi Cola Playhouse.*

MOMENTS OF MUSIC (*Music*)
FIRST TELECAST: *July 24, 1951*
LAST TELECAST: *September 11, 1951*
BROADCAST HISTORY:
Jul 1951–Sep 1951, ABC Tue 8:30–8:45
A short, and short-lived, filmed program of music.

MOMMIES, THE (*Situation Comedy*)
FIRST TELECAST: *September 18, 1993*
LAST TELECAST: *April 3, 1995*
BROADCAST HISTORY:
Sep 1993, NBC Sat 9:00–9:30
Sep 1993–Mar 1994, NBC Sat 8:00–8:30
Mar 1994–May 1994, NBC Sat 8:30–9:00
May 1994–Sep 1994, NBC Sat 8:00–8:30
Sep 1994, NBC Sat 8:30–9:00
Jan 1995–Mar 1995, NBC Sat 8:30–9:00
Apr 1995, NBC Mon 8:30–9:00
CAST:
Marilyn Larson .... Marilyn Kentz
Jack Larson .... David Dukes
Adam Larson (age 16) .... Shiloh Strong
Kasey Larson (7) .... Ashley Peldon
Caryl Kellogg .... Caryl Kristensen
Paul Kellogg (1993–1994) .... Robin Thomas
Paul Kellogg (1995) .... Lane Davies
Blake Kellogg (9) .... Ryan Merriman
Danny Kellogg (7) .... Sam Gifaldi
Tiffany (1993–1994) .... Jennifer Blanc
Barb Ballantine .... Julia Duffy
**Ken Ballantine* .... Peter Scolari
Tom Booker (1994–1995) .... Jere Burns
*Occasional
The Mommies began as the most white-bread of TV comedies, two cheerful suburban moms cracking girl jokes about periods, pregnancies, dumb husbands, and kids. The two were almost interchangeable. Marilyn was the brunette, married to accountant Jack and mom to dense teenager Adam and perky seven-year-old Kasey. Caryl was the blond, who was pregnant, married to easygoing computer technician Paul, and mom to little Blake and Danny. Tiffany was Adam's girlfriend.

Although *The Mommies* did not draw much of an audience, NBC continued to tinker with it, adding bits of spice as time went along. Barb joined the cast after a few months as a too-perfect neighbor, making the Mommies a little less so by comparison (she was married to Ken—as in "Barbie and Ken"). The role of Paul was recast with an actor with more of an edge, and sarcastic, stay-at-home dad Tom moved into the neighborhood. Then, in January 1995, Marilyn and Jack got divorced, leaving one mommy free to play the dating field. At the same time the name of the show was shortened to *Mommies.*

Based (at least originally) on the standup comedy act of the two stars, Marilyn Kentz and Caryl Kristensen.

MONA MCCLUSKEY (*Situation Comedy*)
FIRST TELECAST: *September 16, 1965*
LAST TELECAST: *April 14, 1966*
BROADCAST HISTORY:
Sep 1965–Apr 1966, NBC Thu 9:30–10:00
CAST:
Mona McCluskey .... Juliet Prowse
Mike McCluskey .... Denny (Scott) Miller
Gen. Crone .... Herb Rudley
Frank Caldwell .... Bartlett Robinson
Sgt. Gruzewsky .... Robert Strauss
Alice Henderson .... Elena Verdugo
Mona Carroll was a beautiful Hollywood star who made the astronomical salary of $5,000 per week. She was married to Mike McCluskey, a sergeant in the air force whose salary was $500 per month. In order to let her husband prove that he could support her, Mona lived with him in a two-room apartment and promised not to use any of her money to supplement his income. Her tastes, coupled with the knowledge that she really had much more money than she could spend, prompted Mona to try all sorts of schemes to improve her husband's financial situation.

MONDAY NIGHT SPECIAL (*Varied Format*)
FIRST TELECAST: *January 10, 1972*
LAST TELECAST: *August 14, 1972*
BROADCAST HISTORY:
Jan 1972–Aug 1972, ABC Mon 8:00–9:00
Throughout most of 1972, ABC set aside the 8:00–9:00 P.M. hour on Monday nights as a place for regular "specials." The programs telecast in this time slot varied greatly in format. Included were Jacques Cousteau nature programs, documentaries on athletics, an occasional circus, and Danny Kaye starring in "The Emperor's New Clothes."

MONDAY SPORTSNITE (*Sports News*)
FIRST TELECAST: *June 1, 1987*
LAST TELECAST: *August 31, 1987*
BROADCAST HISTORY:
Jun 1987–Aug 1987, ABC Mon 12:00–1:00 A.M.
HOST:
Al Trautwig
A 1986 summer series featuring interviews and offbeat moments in the week's sporting events.

MONDAY THEATRE (*Anthology*)
FIRST TELECAST: *July 21, 1969*
LAST TELECAST: *August 10, 1970*

BROADCAST HISTORY:

Jul 1969–Sep 1969, NBC Mon 8:00–8:30
Jul 1970–Aug 1970, NBC Mon 8:00–8:30

Monday Theatre spent two summers as a partial replacement for *Rowan & Martin's Laugh-In.* It was comprised of pilots for projected situation-comedy series in 1969 and projected adventure and drama series in 1970. None of them ever made the jump from pilot to regular series.

MONEYLINE (*News/Analysis*)

BROADCAST HISTORY:

CNN
30 minutes
Produced: *1980–*
Premiered: *June 1, 1980*

REGULARS:

Lou Dobbs (1980–1999, 2001–)
Willow Bay (1999–2001)
Stuart Varney (1999–2001)

A long-running nightly business news and analysis program that has been on the air literally since the day CNN was launched.

MONITOR (*newsmagazine*)

FIRST TELECAST: *March 12, 1983*
LAST TELECAST: *April 1, 1984*
BROADCAST HISTORY:

Mar 1983–Aug 1983, NBC Sat 10:00–11:00
Sep 1983–Apr 1984, NBC Sun 7:00–8:00

REGULARS:

Lloyd Dobyns
Steve Delaney
Rebecca Sobel

Lloyd Dobyns was the in-studio anchorman for this weekly newsmagazine series, with Steve Delaney and Rebecca Sobel filing weekly stories. Some of the stories were serious—"Children Don't Do That," on the problem of child suicide, and "Your Land Is My Land," about the dispute between Arabs and Jews over who had the right to live on the West Bank in Israel. Others were light—"King Pong," a profile of the inventor of Atari, and "The Survival of Peter O'Toole," with the actor reminiscing about his career.

In September 1983 the series changed its name to *First Camera* and moved to Sunday night, in a suicidal attempt to compete head-on with the number-one hit *60 Minutes.* A few months later, *First Camera* was no more.

MONK (*Detective Drama*)

CABLE HISTORY:

USA Network
60 minutes
Original episodes: *2002–*
Premiered: *July 12, 2002*

NETWORK HISTORY:

FIRST TELECAST: *August 13, 2002*
LAST TELECAST: *December 30, 2002*

Aug 2002–Sep 2002, ABC Tue 9:00–10:00
Sep 2002–Dec 2002, ABC Thu 8:00–9:00

CAST:

Adrian Monk .... Tony Shalhoub
Sharona Fleming .... Bitty Schram
Capt. Leland Stottlemeyer .... Ted Levine
Lt. Randall Disher .... Jason Gray-Stanford
Dr. Kroger .... Stanley Kamel
Benjy Fleming (pilot only) (age 11) .... Kane Ritchotte
Benjy Fleming .... Max Morrow

Viewers love eccentric detectives (remember *Columbo*?), and Adrian Monk was one of the quirkiest. A brilliant homicide detective with the San Francisco Police Department, he had gone off the deep end after his wife was killed three years earlier by a car bomb and been put on administrative leave. He had become obsessive-compulsive, afraid of everyday things like crowds, heights, dirt, germs, milk, the dark, and especially disorder. Despite the jokes about him ("the defective detective," "fraidy cop"), he noticed things at a crime scene—little things—that no one else saw. Nevertheless the SFPD refused to reinstate him until he was "cured," so he worked as a freelance consultant for skeptical Capt. Stottlemeyer and his wimpy deputy Lt. Disher, assisting on (and invariably solving) their toughest cases. Monk's phobias drove everyone crazy, including his nurse Sharona, who wouldn't let him go anywhere without her. Kroger was Monk's psychiatrist, and Benjy was Sharona's young son.

There was lots of humor in the series as the nervous Monk faced one fear after another, and seeing him take his first plane ride in years was a hoot. There were lots of gag cameos in this episode. For example, seated next to him on the airliner was Garry Marshall as a nutty extension cord salesman; the frustrated stewardess was played by Tony Shalhoub's real-life wife, Brooke Adams; and seated in first class was his onetime *Wings* costar Tim Daly.

MONKEES, THE (*Situation Comedy*)

FIRST TELECAST: *September 12, 1966*
LAST TELECAST: *August 19, 1968*
BROADCAST HISTORY:

Sep 1966–Aug 1968, NBC Mon 7:30–8:00

CAST:

Davy (guitar) .... David Jones
Peter (guitar) .... Peter Tork
Micky (drums) .... Micky Dolenz
Mike (guitar) .... Mike Nesmith ("Wool Hat")

MUSIC SUPERVISION:

Don Kirshner

This was a free-form youth-oriented comedy series, inspired by the Beatles' film *A Hard Day's Night* (1964). *The Monkees* was similarly unconventional, utilizing surrealistic film techniques (fast and slow motion, distorted focus, comic film inserts), one-liners, non sequiturs, etc., all delivered at a very fast pace. The Monkees played a rock quartet that got into all sorts of bizarre scrapes as they rescued maidens, ran afoul of dastardly villains, and generally played pranks on the world.

The Monkees simultaneously had a highly successful career on records, a fact which has driven some rock critics into paroxysms of fury since they were so obviously a "manufactured" group. The four members were carefully picked from among nearly 500 applicants in auditions held during the fall of 1965, then drilled and rehearsed until they could pass as reasonably competent musicians (Dolenz and Jones were actors, Tork and Nesmith had some previous musical experience). They were not allowed to play their instruments on their early records, supplying only the vocals, a fact which led to some embarrassment when they went on tour and could not re-create their recorded sound. It also led to dissension among the boys, some of whom had real musical ambitions. Nevertheless their discs, heavily promoted and carefully coordinated with the TV series, sold in the millions. (These included "Last Train to Clarksville," "I'm a Believer," and "Words.") Finally there was a showdown with the program's producers, following a rather remarkable 1967 press conference in which Nesmith bitterly complained that "we're being passed off as something we aren't." The boys were later allowed to "do their own thing" musically. Despite its commercial success, however, the group broke up shortly after the series left the air in 1968.

The Monkees was later seen on CBS in reruns on Saturday mornings, from September 1969 to September 1973. See also *New Monkees.*

MONOPOLY (*Quiz/Audience Patricipation*)

FIRST TELECAST: *June 16, 1990*
LAST TELECAST: *September 1, 1990*
BROADCAST HISTORY:
Jun 1990–Sep 1990, ABC Sat 8:30–9:00
EMCEE:
Michael Reilly
EXECUTIVE PRODUCER:
Merv Griffin

A glitzy, high-tech version of the famous real estate board game. Three contestants competed on a large illuminated board containing 22 property squares and 18 other spaces, via questions and rolls of the dice. The goal was to amass property, build monopolies, and stay out of jail. Prizes went as high as $50,000. The program was originally offered in syndication to local stations, but not finding enough takers wound up—briefly—on ABC instead.

MONROES, THE (*Western*)

FIRST TELECAST: *September 7, 1966*
LAST TELECAST: *August 30, 1967*
BROADCAST HISTORY:
Sep 1966–Aug 1967, ABC Wed 8:00–9:00
CAST:
Clayt Monroe................ Michael Anderson, Jr.
Kathy Monroe.................... Barbara Hershey
Jefferson Monroe .... Keith Schultz
Fennimore Monroe................... Kevin Schultz
Amy Monroe .... Tammy Locke
Major Mapoy .... Liam Sullivan
Dirty Jim .... Ron Soble
Sleeve .... Ben Johnson
Ruel Jaxon .... Jim Westmoreland
Barney Wales .... Robert Middleton
John Bradford ("Brad")................ Buck Taylor

The story of five orphaned youngsters, aged 6 to 18, who fought to establish a homestead in the rugged Wyoming Territory of 1876, after their parents had drowned. Leaders of the crew were Clayt (18) and Kathy (16), who looked after the 13-year-old twins Jeff ("Big Twin") and Fen ("Little Twin"), 6-year-old Amy, and a dog named Snow. Their ally was the renegade Indian Dirty Jim, and the villain in the piece was wicked British cattle baron Major Mapoy, who wanted their land (heh-heh!). Jaxon was one of Mapoy's cowboys.

Filmed on location in the rugged Grand Teton National Park area of Wyoming.

MONROES, THE (*Drama*)

FIRST TELECAST: *September 12, 1995*
LAST TELECAST: *October 19, 1995*
BROADCAST HISTORY:
Sep 1995, ABC Tue 10:00–11:00
Sep 1995–Oct 1995, ABC Thu 9:00–10:00
CAST:
John Monroe........................ William Devane
Kathryn Monroe .... Susan Sullivan
Congressman Billy Monroe .... David Andrews
Anne Monroe.......................... Lynn Clark
Greer Monroe .... Cecil Hoffmann
James Monroe .... Steve Eckholdt
Ruby Monroe......................... Tracy Griffith
Gabriel Monroe........................ Tristan Tait
Michael Bradley.................... Darryl Theirse

This sweeping saga of a large, powerful, Kennedy-esque political clan was swept off the ABC schedule only a few weeks after it debuted in 1995. The story read like an old-fashioned Washington insider's novel, filled with power, sex, politics, and ruthless people. John was the multimillionaire patriarch, foiled in his bid for governor when it was revealed that a woman he had an affair with twenty years earlier was a foreign spy. John certainly wasn't partial to spies, having had affairs with lots of women over the years, while his tightly wound, long-suffering wife Kathryn looked the other way. Womanizing son Billy, a liberal congressman, had picked up many of his dad's bad habits, although his wife Anne had a harder time dealing with it. Other Monroe siblings were Greer, a lawyer having an affair with a mysterious Washington "high official"; James, a famed, and rather self-righteous astronaut who hated politics and opposed his father's manipulative agenda; Ruby, a photographer and newlywed already on the brink of ending her marriage; and Gabriel, a rebellious young university student (you could tell, he rode a motorcycle) who felt he was not "good enough" for his illustrious family. Michael was the frequently needed family attorney.

MONSTER GARAGE (*Informational*)

BROADCAST HISTORY:
Discovery Channel
60 minutes
Original episodes: *2002–*
Premiered: *September 30, 2002*
REGULARS:
Jesse James

Garage warriors got their moment in the sun on this noisy show, in which professional mechanics used hammers, saws and torches to rebuild a standard vehicle into a completely different—and sometimes wacky—"monster machine." Leading the crew was Jesse James, a beefy, tattooed West Coast motorcycle builder who claimed he was a descendant of the famous outlaw. Each week Jesse and a guest team of five or so mechanics (most of them tough-looking guys like himself, but occasionally including a gal) were given one car, $3,000, and seven days to do the job—one day to design, five days to build, and the final day to show its stuff. A Porsche 944 was turned into a golf course golf-ball retriever that hurled balls back at the golfers with a cannon; a Geo Tracker became a hot-air balloon; a Volkswagen Beetle became a swamp boat, and a Chevy Impala morphed into a Zamboni. Interspersed with the hammering and torching were arguments, cameos of the participants, expeditions to forage for parts, and overheated narration ("He trims the excess metal like the fat on a slab of meat!"). If the rebuild was deemed successful, each guest mechanic got $3,400 in shop tools.

MONSTERS (*Horror Anthology*)

BROADCAST HISTORY:

Syndicated only
30 minutes
Produced: *1988–1990* (72 episodes)
Released: *October 1988*

Produced by the same people who had previously created *Tales from the Darkside*, this anthology series bore a strong resemblance to its predecessor. There were tales of witches, vampires, ghouls, zombies, prehistoric creatures, aliens, weird and eccentric people with bizarre and wondrous powers, and inanimate objects that weren't really inanimate. Although the performers were generally not well known, a few familiar actors were seen including David McCallum, Tempestt Bledsoe, Meatloaf, Laraine Newman, Alex Cord, Linda Blair, Robert Lansing, and Adrienne Barbeau.

MONTEFUSCOS, THE (*Situation Comedy*)

FIRST TELECAST: *September 4, 1975*
LAST TELECAST: *October 16, 1975*
BROADCAST HISTORY:

Sep 1975–Oct 1975, NBC Thu 8:00–8:30

CAST:

Tony Montefusco .... Joe Sirola
Rose Montefusco .... Naomi Stevens
Frank Montefusco .... Ron Carey
Joseph Montefusco .... John Aprea
Theresa Montefusco .... Phoebe Dorin
Angela Montefusco Cooney .... Linda Dano
Jim Cooney .... Bill Cort
Nunzio Montefusco .... Sal Viscuso
Anthony Carmine Montefusco .... Jeffrey Palladini
Jerome Montefusco .... Robby Paris
Gina Montefusco .... Dominique Pinassi
Anthony Patrick Cooney .... Damon Raskin

This short-lived series was about Tony Montefusco, a boisterous, middle-class Italian, living in Connecticut, who had his entire family over for dinner every Sunday night. The subjects that came up and situations that developed at, prior to, and following Sunday dinner provided the stories of the series. Tony's wife, Rose, his three sons and one daughter, and their families made up the entire cast. Frankie was a dentist, Joseph a priest, and Nunzio an unemployed actor, while Angela was married to Jim Cooney, the token WASP. Theresa was Frankie's wife.

Carmine, Jerome, and Gina were Frankie's children and Anthony Patrick was Angela's son.

MONTGOMERY'S SUMMER STOCK, see *Robert Montgomery Presents*

MONTY (*Situation Comedy*)

FIRST TELECAST: *January 11, 1994*
LAST TELECAST: *February 15, 1994*
BROADCAST HISTORY:

Jan 1994–Feb 1994, FOX Tue 8:00–8:30

CAST:

Monty Richardson .... Henry Winkler
Fran Richardson .... Kate Burton
Greg Richardson .... David Schwimmer
David Richardson .... David Krumholtz
Geena Campbell .... China Kantner
Clifford Walker .... Tom McGowan
Rita Simon .... Joyce Guy

EXECUTIVE PRODUCER:

Henry Winkler

The Fonz as Rush Limbaugh? That's what this sitcom, with former *Happy Days* star Winkler as both star and executive producer, wanted viewers to accept. Monty Richardson was the archconservative host of a TV talk show on Channel 35 on New York's Long Island. The title of his best-selling book summarized the way he dealt with anyone who didn't share his point of view—*I'm Right. I'm Right. I'm Right. Shut Up.* His viewers loved him, as did Clifford, his fawning yesman sidekick, while Rita, the cynical black producer of his show, despised everything for which he stood. Ironically Monty was happily married to Fran, a liberal grade-school teacher who was used to his unequivocal pontificating. His son Greg, a Yale lawschool dropout, had just returned from six months in Europe with a free-spirited girlfriend, Geena, and a new career goal—to become a vegetarian chef—just what his father wanted. For 14-year-old David, who wanted desperately to be accepted by his peers, having Monty for a father presented a major problem. Almost all of the kids he knew thought Monty was a pompous jerk. So did the audience.

MOON OVER MIAMI (*Detective Drama*)

FIRST TELECAST: *September 15, 1993*
LAST TELECAST: *December 15, 1993*
BROADCAST HISTORY:

Sep 1993–Dec 1993, ABC Wed 10:00–11:00

CAST:

Walter Tatum .... Bill Campbell
Gwen Cross .... Ally Walker
Billie .... Marlo Marron
Tito Savon .... Agustin Rodriguez

Detective series cum romantic comedy patterned after *Moonlighting*, set amid the surf, sand, and pastels of Miami Beach. Walter was the handsome, wisecracking young p.i.; into his life came Gwen, a glamorous heiress who had jumped off a yacht in her wedding dress to escape her family's stuffy idea of a perfect marriage. Now she wanted adventure, and she got it with an assortment of dangerous cases accompanied by hip banter and jazzy background music. Billie was Walter's electronics expert and Tito his young Cuban-American surveillance pro with contacts in Miami's ethnic subcultures. Elliott Gould appeared occasionally as Walter's world-weary mentor, Gavin Mills.

MOONLIGHTING (*Dectective Comedy/Drama*)

FIRST TELECAST: *March 3, 1985*
LAST TELECAST: *May 14, 1989*
BROADCAST HISTORY:

Mar 1985, ABC Sun 9:00–11:00
Mar 1985–Apr 1985, ABC Tue 10:00–11:00
Aug 1985–Sep 1988, ABC Tue 9:00–10:00
Dec 1988–Feb 1989, ABC Tue 9:00–10:00
Apr 1989–May 1989, ABC Sun 8:00–9:00

CAST:

Maddie Hayes .... Cybill Shepherd
David Addison .... Bruce Willis
Agnes Dipesto .... Allyce Beasley

Herbert Viola (1986–1989) .... Curtis Armstrong
Virginia Hayes (1987–1988) .... Eva Marie Saint
Alex Hayes (1987–1988)............ Robert Webber
MacGilicuddy (1988–1989) .... Jack Blessing

THEME:

by Lee Holdridge and Al Jarreau, sung by Al Jarreau

One of ABC's few major hits in the mid-1980s was this hip, romantic comedy, which was as much a TV "in-joke" as a normal detective show. Maddie was an extremely glamorous, and somewhat icy, top fashion model who had fallen on hard times when her manager had cheated her out of her accumulated fortune. Surveying her few remaining assets she found she owned the Blue Moon Detective Agency in Los Angeles, a notably unsuccessful venture which she was about to dump, until its principal employee, cocky David Addison, conned her out of doing so (to save his job). He then managed to get her involved in the business and the two of them—wisecracking David and reserved but strong-willed Maddie—became the city's latest unlikely detective team.

He also lusted for her, in his street-hip way (with wolf whistles and '60s "girl-watching" songs), but elegant Maddie resisted. Their uncommon courtship became a main theme of the show; by the end of the 1985–86 season he finally won a kiss in a parking garage, but not until the end of the following season did they finally make love. In the meantime their rocky relationship survived breakups, and, in early 1987, her wooing by handsome yuppie Sam Crawford (played by Mark Harmon). Maddie and David each got counseling, she from Dr. Joyce Brothers and he from Ray Charles. Eventually, in 1988, she became pregnant with David's baby, although she married (briefly) a twerp she met on a train named Walter Bishop (Dennis Dugan). The pregnancy ended in a miscarriage.

Moonlighting's constant production problems were widely publicized, particularly the running three-way battle between stars Shepherd and Willis and creator/executive producer Glenn Gordon Caron (who was forced off the show in the final season). Production delays resulted in numerous repeat episodes, although when they finally arrived they were often inventive—for example, the November 1986 takeoff on Shakespeare's *Taming of the Shrew* (a dream sequence), with David as Petruchio and Maddie as Kate. Many episodes began with the stars doing a little out-of-character skit, or commenting on the show itself, before the story began. Sometimes they would even turn to the camera and talk directly to viewers.

Seen from time to time were Maddie's mother and father, Virginia and Alex, David's dad, David Sr. (played by Paul Sorvino), and irresponsible brother, Richard (Charles Rocket). Agnes was the slightly daffy, rhyming receptionist, and Herbert the eager clerk-cum-junior-detective and object of Agnes's unrequited love.

MOREY AMSTERDAM SHOW, THE

(*Comedy/Variety*)

FIRST TELECAST: *December 17, 1948*
LAST TELECAST: *October 12, 1950*
BROADCAST HISTORY:

Dec 1948–Jan 1949, CBS Fri 8:30–9:00
Jan 1949–Mar 1949, CBS Mon Various
Apr 1949–Oct 1950, DUM Thu 9:00–9:30

REGULARS:

Morey Amsterdam
Art Carney
Jacqueline Susann
Johnny Guarnieri Orchestra

In June 1948 Morey Amsterdam premiered a series on the CBS radio network in which he was the emcee of a small fictional nightclub located in Times Square in New York City. The club was the Golden Goose Cafe and the only other regulars in the series were Art Carney as Charlie the Doorman (later as Newton the Waiter), and Jacqueline Susann as Lola, the wide-eyed cigarette girl. Morey told jokes, played his cello, and introduced guest acts on the show. In December 1948 the show moved to CBS television, while a separate radio version continued to be aired. The producer was Irving Mansfield—Miss Susann's husband.

Then in early 1949 CBS canceled the show, ostensibly not because of low ratings but because the network already had too many big names to promote. CBS' loss was DuMont's gain, because Morey was back a month later with his "yuk-a-puk" jokes on a Thursday night DuMont variety show, which ran for a year and a half. The setting changed to the Silver Swan Cafe, but Carney and Susann remained.

MORK & MINDY (*Situation Comedy*)

FIRST TELECAST: *September 14, 1978*
LAST TELECAST: *June 10, 1982*
BROADCAST HISTORY:

Sep 1978–Aug 1979, ABC Thu 8:00–8:30
Aug 1979–Dec 1979, ABC Sun 8:00–8:30
Jan 1980–Feb 1982, ABC Thu 8:00–8:30
Apr 1982–May 1982, ABC Thu 8:30–9:00
May 1982–Jun 1982, ABC Thu 8:00–8:30

CAST:

Mork............................. Robin Williams
Mindy Beth McConnell.............. Pam Dawber
Frederick McConnell (1978–1979, 1980–1982)
.... Conrad Janis
Cora Hudson (1978–1979, 1981–1982)
.... Elizabeth Kerr
Eugene (1978–1979)............... Jeffrey Jacquet
Orson (voice only)................... Ralph James
Franklin Delano Bickley.............. Tom Poston
Remo DaVinci (1979–1981)........... Jay Thomas
Jean DaVinci (1979–1981)............. Gina Hecht
Nelson Flavor (1979–1981)............. Jim Staahl
Exidor............................ Robert Donner
Glenda Faye "Crissy" Comstock (1980–1981)
.... Crissy Wilzak
Mr. Miles Sternhagen (1981) .... Foster Brooks
Mearth (1981–1982) .... Jonathan Winters

Mork & Mindy was a spin-off from an episode of *Happy Days* seen in February 1978, in which an alien from the planet Ork landed on Earth and attempted to kidnap Richie. So popular was the nutty character created by Robin Williams that Williams was given his own series in the fall of 1978, and it became an instant hit.

Mork was a misfit on his own planet because of his sense of humor (he was heard to call the Orkan leader, Orson, "cosmic breath"). So the humorless Orkans sent him off to study Earthlings, whose "crazy" customs they had never been able to understand. Mork landed, in a giant eggshell, near Boulder, Colorado. There he was befriended by pretty Mindy McConnell, a clerk at the music store run by her father, Frederick. Mork looked human, but his strange mixture of Orkan and Earthling customs—such as wearing a suit, but putting it on backwards, or sitting in a chair, but upside down—led most people to think of him as just some kind of nut. Mindy knew where he came from, and helped him adjust to Earth's strange ways. She also let him stay in the attic of her apartment house, which scandalized her conservative father, but not her swinging grandmother, Cora.

After a season of simple slapstick and big ratings, both the producers and the network unfortunately got a little cocky and violated one of television's cardinal rules: "Don't tamper with a hit." In the process of doing so, they almost destroyed the program. The producers decided to shift to more "meaningful" stories, opening the second season with a strange, surrealistic episode in which Mork shrunk away to nothing and dropped into a never-never world filled with caricatures of good and evil. At the same time practically the whole supporting cast was changed. Simultaneously ABC decided to move the series from its established Thursday time slot to Sunday, to prop up their sagging schedule on that night. Understandably confused, viewers deserted the show in droves and it lost nearly half its audience.

By December 1979 ABC and the producers were scrambling to undo their mistakes. Mork went back to Thursday, and stories got less complicated. Mindy's father, who had been dumped (along with the grandmother), returned for the third season. He was supposed to have sold the music store and gone on tour as an orchestra conductor, fulfilling a lifelong dream. Now he, but not Cora, was back full-time. Other changes in the second and third seasons included the addition of brother and sister Remo and Jean DaVinci, recently arrived from the Bronx. Remo ran the New York Deli and was helping put Jean through medical school. Nelson was Mindy's cousin, an uptight young social climber with grandiose political ambitions; Mr. Bickley was the grouchy downstairs neighbor (he had been on before, but his role was enlarged); and Mork's friend Exidor was a crazed prophet and leader of an invisible cult, the Friends of Venus. Mindy, a journalism student, got a job at local TV station KTNS, where her boss was Mr. Sternhagen.

All of this brought back some of the lost viewers, but *Mork & Mindy* never recaptured the enormous following it had during its first season.

The fall of 1981 brought the most surprising developments of all. Mork and Mindy were married, and honeymooned on Ork—which proved to be full of bizarre creatures. Shortly thereafter Mork gave birth, by ejecting a small egg from his navel. The egg grew and grew and finally cracked open to reveal a full-grown Jonathan Winters! Mearth, as they named their first child, weighed 225 pounds and looked middle-aged, but babbled like a baby, calling Mork "Mommy" and Mindy "Shoe." Since things work backwards on Ork, he would gradually grow younger (instead of older) and never want for affection in his waning years.

Despite some hilarious scenes between Robin Williams and his idol Jonathan Winters, the series was by this time losing audience rapidly and left the air at the end of the season. It had succeeded primarily because of the versatile talents of Williams, who mugged, mimicked, and delivered torrents of one-liners and Orkan gibberish. At the end of each episode he reported back to his leader Orson, on Ork, twisting his ears and signing off, "Na nu, na nu"—good-bye in Orkan.

MORNINGSTAR/EVENINGSTAR (*Drama*)

FIRST TELECAST: *March 25, 1986*
LAST TELECAST: *May 6, 1986*
BROADCAST HISTORY:
Mar 1986–May 1986, CBS Tue 8:00–9:00
CAST:
Debbie Flynn .... Sherry Hursey
Bob Lane .... Darrell Larson
Martha Cameron .... Kate Reid
Bill McGregor .... Jeff Corey
Binnie Byrd Baylor .... Sylvia Sidney
Kathy Kelly .... Elizabeth Wilson
Excell Dennis .... Scatman Crothers
Gordon Blair .... Mason Adams
Nora Blake .... Ketty Lester
Alan Bishop .... Fred Savage
Sarah Bishop .... Missy Francis
Kevin Murphy .... Chris Peters
Lisa Thurston .... Tammy Lauren
Martin Palmer .... David Goldsmith
Doug Roberts .... Leaf Phoenix
Eugenie Waters .... Ebonie Smith

The message of this warm, gentle drama was that there need not be a generation gap between old and young. When a fire destroyed the Morningstar Home, an orphanage administered by social worker Bob Lane, he sought temporary shelter for his waifs in the Eveningstar Home, a well-run senior citizens' facility managed by social worker Debbie Flynn. Bob and Debbie had been friends for a long time, and had mused over the potential advantages of getting the elderly together with the young, to their mutual benefit. The fire had made the experiment a necessity. The senior citizens—Martha, Bill, Binnie, Kathy, Excell, Gordon, and Nora—provided the children with the knowledge and skills acquired over their long lives, while the kids—Alan, Sarah, Kevin, Lisa, Martin, Doug, and Eugenie—provided their elders with a feeling of accomplishment and renewed vitality.

MORTAL KOMBAT: CONQUEST (*Fantasy*)

BROADCAST HISTORY:
Syndicated and TNT Network
60 minutes
Produced: *1998–1999* (22 episodes)
Released: *October 1998*
CAST:
Kung Lao .... Paulo Montalban
Siro .... Daniel Bernhardt
Taja .... Kristanna Loken
Shang Tsung .... Bruce Locke
Vorpax .... Tracy Douglas
Rayden the Thundergod .... Jeff Meek
Shao Kahn .... Jeff Meek

This incredibly violent fantasy took place at the crossroads of all civilizations, where Earth and other parallel realms converged. It was there that three warriors from Earth searched for a few others who could defend Earth from the dark forces of Outworld in a tournament called Mortal Kombat. The tournament had been created by the Elder Gods, at the behest of a group of wise men from the Far East, to provide an honorable way to battle for the realms. Previously, Shao Kahn, the masked evil emperor, had simply stolen realms and added them to his growing empire, Outworld. He wanted to conquer Earth because it was a young, energy-rich planet that was the gateway to other realms. The first Kombat had been won by Shang Tsung, Kahn's demon sorcerer, nearly 1,000 years ago, but fortunately for Earth realm, Tsung was subsequently defeated by Kung Lao, a noble warrior from China. While waiting for the next tournament to begin, Kung Lao sought out new warriors to help protect Earth realm.

In his quest, boyish Kung Lao had two companions: Siro, a surly, headstrong, fiercely loyal, exiled palace guard; and Taja, a sexy former thief who was always playing the angles and, more than once, threatened to abandon the other two when the going got tough. They ran a trading post in the city of Zhu Zin, from which they tried to recruit warriors worthy to train in the traditions of Mortal Kombat. Tsung, who had been banished to the Cobalt Mines of Outworld after his defeat and wanted revenge, was after Kung Lao, as were people from other worlds seeking to take over Earth. Even the city of Zhu Zin posed threats. It was a dangerous place where things were not always what they seemed, streets seemed to go on forever, and an innocent-looking doorway could transport you to another realm. Vorpax was Tsung's sexy, self-serving aide, and Rayden was the white-haired protector of Earth realm who showed up to provide Kung Lao and his friends with helpful advice. The hallmarks of the series were the frequent, almost cartoonish, martial-arts-style fights that broke out in every episode.

Adapted from the hit video game Mortal Kombat, created by Ed Boon and John Tobias and produced by Larry Kasanoff, who had also produced the theatrical films *Mortal Kombat* and *Mortal Kombat: Annihilation.* Each episode premiered in syndication on broadcast stations and was then aired the following week on the TNT cable network.

MORTON & HAYES (*Situation Comedy*)

FIRST TELECAST: *July 24, 1991*
LAST TELECAST: *August 28, 1991*
BROADCAST HISTORY:
Jul 1991–Aug 1991, CBS Wed 8:30–9:00
Aug 1991, CBS Wed 9:30–10:00
CAST:
Chick Morton .... Kevin Pollak
Eddie Hayes .... Bob Amaral
Rob Reiner .... Himself

This unusual series within a series was an attempt to pay loving homage to the classic comedy teams of the 1930s and 1940s—particularly Abbott & Costello and Laurel & Hardy. The premise was that there had been a great, but forgotten, comedy team—Chick Morton and Eddie Hayes—whose lost two-reel comedies had been found in the vault of their producer, Max King. Each week Rob Reiner, a great fan of the team, lovingly introduced viewers to a vintage black-and-white "film" starring Morton (the hefty, trusting, clumsy one) and Hayes (the cynical, conniving straight man). The situations and supporting casts changed from week to week with the team portraying everything from bumbling private eyes, to stowaways on a ship in the South Pacific, to surprised winners of $1,000,000 in a radio contest.

MORTON DOWNEY, JR. SHOW, THE
(*Talk/Debate*)

BROADCAST HISTORY:
Syndicated only
60 minutes
Produced: *1988–1989* (270 episodes)
Released: *May 1988*
HOST:
Morton Downey, Jr.

Caustic Morton Downey, Jr., former radio phone-in show host and son of the mellow-voiced tenor who had been an early TV star himself, hosted this confrontational show in which the studio audience spent most of its time baiting, hooting at, and arguing with the guests. Downey would take whatever side of the issue being discussed was likely to lead to verbal—and occasionally physical—confrontation. He was consciously abusive, often telling both guests and audience members with whom he disagreed to "zip it, pal," and sprinkling his language with such terms as slimeballs and scumbags. His studio audience, made up almost completely of raucous, blue-collar conservatives, was more than happy to get into the act. They could voice their support, or more likely, opposition to points of view expressed by Downey's guests from microphones set up at two podiums—"Loudmouth #1" and "Loudmouth #2."

The Morton Downey, Jr. Show had premiered as a local entry on New York City's WWOR-TV in the fall of 1987 and, after garnering reams of publicity for its host and style, went into national syndication the following May. The show always attracted more press than viewers and, because of its content, presented scheduling problems for the stations that carried it. Even WWOR, which had originally aired it at 9:00 P.M., moved it first to 11:30 P.M. and later, when *The Arsenio Hall Show* proved to be a bigger draw, to 12:30 A.M. Stations carrying the show received more negative than positive mail from their viewers and, after a much publicized incident in which Downey claimed to have been assaulted by neo-Nazi skinheads at the San Francisco International Airport, many of them decided they had had enough. Despite Downey's promise to cut down on the verbal violence and abusiveness, most of the stations carrying the show failed to renew it. The last episode aired on September 15, 1989.

Late in 1989 Downey surfaced on the CNBC cable network, initially as co-host of an interview show titled *Showdown* and later, in 1990, with a new *Morton Downey, Jr. Show.* Although he still dealt with sensitive issues, the Downey personality, so vitriolic during his broadcast days, was considerably muted on cable.

MORTON DOWNEY SHOW, THE, see *Mohawk Showroom, The*

MOSES—THE LAWGIVER (*Historical Drama*)

FIRST TELECAST: *June 21, 1975*
LAST TELECAST: *July 22, 1979*
BROADCAST HISTORY:
Jun 1975–Aug 1975, CBS Sat 10:00–11:00
Jun 1979–Jul 1979, CBS Sun 10:00–11:00
CAST:
Moses .... Burt Lancaster
Aaron .... Anthony Quayle
Miriam .... Ingrid Thulin

Zipporah .... Irene Papas
Pharaoh .... Laurent Terzieff

The story of the book of Exodus had been told twice by Cecil B. DeMille in spectacular feature films, in a silent and a sound version of *The Ten Commandments.* This series of six one-hour programs retold the story of the enslavement of the Jewish people at the hands of the Egyptians, their release by the pharaoh, and the long, arduous journey to the Promised Land. Filmed on location in Italy and Israel, this series was later reedited and released as a theatrical feature. CBS brought it back in the summer of 1979, four years after its original airing.

MOST DEADLY GAME, THE (*Detective Drama*)
FIRST TELECAST: *October 10, 1970*
LAST TELECAST: *January 16, 1971*
BROADCAST HISTORY:
Oct 1970–Jan 1971, ABC Sat 9:30–10:30
CAST:
Jonathan Croft .... George Maharis
Vanessa Smith .... Yvette Mimieux
Mr. Arcane .... Ralph Bellamy

A series in the classic whodunit tradition, involving a trio of highly trained criminologists who dealt only in unusual murders ("the most dangerous game"). This elite, and expensive, team was composed of Mr. Arcane, the urbane, cerebral leader; Jonathan, a ruggedly handsome, ex-military intelligence officer; and Vanessa, a beautiful, college-trained criminologist (formerly Mr. Arcane's ward).

MOST IMPORTANT PEOPLE, THE (*Musical Variety*)
FIRST TELECAST: *October 18, 1950*
LAST TELECAST: *April 13, 1951*
BROADCAST HISTORY:
Oct 1950–Apr 1951, DUM Wed/Fri 7:30–7:45
REGULARS:
Jimmy Carroll
Rita Carroll

This was a 15-minute program of songs and chatter by singer-pianist Jimmy Carroll and his wife Rita, plus guest performers.

The title *The Most Important People* referred to babies, who were indeed important to the sponsor, Gerber's baby food, but had little to do with this show. In December the title was changed to *Mr. and Mrs. Carroll.*

MOST WANTED (*Police Drama*)
FIRST TELECAST: *October 16, 1976*
LAST TELECAST: *April 25, 1977*
BROADCAST HISTORY:
Oct 1976–Feb 1977, ABC Sat 10:00–11:00
Mar 1977–Apr 1977, ABC Mon 9:00–10:00
CAST:
Capt. Linc Evers .... Robert Stack
Sgt. Charlie Benson .... Shelly Novack
Officer Kate Manners .... Jo Ann Harris
Mayor Dan Stoddard .... Hari Rhodes
PRODUCER:
Quinn Martin

The "Most Wanted" unit was an elite task force of the Los Angeles Police Department, concentrating exclusively on criminals on the mayor's most-wanted list. By taking on one case at a time, and cutting through normal red tape, Capt. Linc Evers and his two assistants were able to track down the city's most dangerous criminals, often by use of daring undercover work.

MOTHERS-IN-LAW, THE (*Situation Comedy*)
FIRST TELECAST: *September 10, 1967*
LAST TELECAST: *September 7, 1969*
BROADCAST HISTORY:
Sep 1967–Sep 1969, NBC Sun 8:30–9:00
CAST:
Eve Hubbard .... Eve Arden
Kaye Buell .... Kaye Ballard
Roger Buell (1967–1968) .... Roger Carmel
Roger Buell (1968–1969) .... Richard Deacon
Herb Hubbard .... Herbert Rudley
Jerry Buell .... Jerry Fogel
Susie Hubbard Buell .... Deborah Walley

The Hubbards and the Buells had been neighbors in suburban Los Angeles for 15 years. Herb Hubbard was a successful lawyer and a member of the board of trustees of his alma mater. His wife, Eve, was a great cook, former champion golfer, terrific gardener, and supporter of all the right causes. They were very straight. The Buells, on the other hand, were extremely unconventional. Roger Buell was a television writer who did most of his work at home and would test his scripts on anyone who happened to be available as a sounding board. His wife, Kaye, was not a particularly enthusiastic housekeeper and rather overbearing on occasion. Despite their differences, the Hubbards and the Buells were the best of friends and their children had gotten married to each other. The children, Jerry and Susie, were both in college and had to cope with in-laws who had very different ideas on how they should live. Roger Carmel left the series after the first season, in a contract dispute, and was replaced by Richard Deacon.

MOTOROLA TV THEATRE (*Dramatic Anthology*)
FIRST TELECAST: *December 1, 1953*
LAST TELECAST: *May 18, 1954*
BROADCAST HISTORY:
Dec 1953–May 1954, ABC Tue 9:30–10:30

Live dramas from New York featuring such first-rate talent as Jack Palance, Brian Donlevy, and Sir Cedric Hardwicke in the first three presentations. Later telecasts starred Helen Hayes, Charlie Ruggles, Walter Matthau, and many others. The program alternated with *The U.S. Steel Hour* in the Tuesday 9:30–10:30 P.M. time slot.

MOTOWN LIVE (*Musical Variety*)
BROADCAST HISTORY:
Syndicated only
60 minutes
Produced: *1998–2000* (52 episodes)
Released: *September 1998*
REGULARS:
Robert Townsend (1998–1999)
Montell Jordan (1999–2000)
The Motown Live Dancers
Rickey Minor and the Band

Motown Live premiered in the same year that Motown Records celebrated its fortieth anniversary. The show included veteran Motown performers from the 1960s and 1970s, along with current artists doing rap, hip hop, soul, and gospel music. The first telecast featured Earth Wind & Fire, the Temptations, and Wyclef Jean. Among the performers appearing in later telecasts were Al Green, Gloria Gaynor, Nu Nation, Destiny's Child, Brian McKnight, James Ingram, Patti LaBelle, and the Emotions. As part of the live format, the artists performed joint numbers in addition to their own material, and in addition to the music, there were short comedy bits used as bridges between the musical numbers. Each episode was taped before a live studio audience, with Robert Townsend serving as host. He was replaced by Montell Jordan at the start of the 1999–2000 season.

MOTOWN REVUE (*Musical Variety*)
FIRST TELECAST: *August 9, 1985*
LAST TELECAST: *September 13, 1985*
BROADCAST HISTORY:
Aug 1985–Sep 1985, NBC Fri 9:00–10:00
REGULARS:
Smokey Robinson
Arsenio Hall
Douglas Wood
Cheryl Rhoads
George Solomon
The Hitsville Gang Dancers

The "Motown Sound" was a slickly produced style of black rhythm & blues/rock music pioneered by recording mogul Berry Gordy, Jr., on his Detroit-based Motown and Tamla labels in the 1960s. Many an American teenager in the '60s danced to the music of Motown's artists: the Supremes, the Miracles, Stevie Wonder, the Four Tops, Marvin Gaye, the Jackson Five, and others. Nostalgia for this identifiable "sound of the '60s" erupted in 1983 with NBC's top-rated *Motown 25th Anniversary Special*, and two years later NBC decided to launch a weekly musical variety series based on the unique "sound." Smokey Robinson, onetime lead singer of the Miracles and latter-day solo artist, producer, and songwriter, was the host; guests included many old Motown favorites, newer artists such as Vanity, Chaka Khan, and Natalie Cole, and non-"Motown sound" acts including Weird Al Yankovic, Kim Carnes, Dean Martin, Rick Nelson, Linda Ronstadt, and Boy George. Four young comics were regular cast members.

MOUNTIES (*Police Documentary*)
BROADCAST HISTORY:
Syndicated only
30 minutes
Produced: *1997–2000*
Released: *September 1997*
HOSTS:
Constable Janice Armstrong
Sergeant Don Brown (1997–1998)

The full title of this series was *Mounties: True Stories of the Royal Canadian Mounted Police*. Hosted somewhat stiffly by two actual members of Canada's RCMP in uniform, the focus of the weekly episodes was *cinéma verité* footage of Mounties in action across Canada, from big cities to small rural towns. As with the similar syndicated series *Real Stories of the Highway Patrol* and *L.A.P.D.*, and Fox's long-running *Cops*, real officers discussed their work, the problems they faced, and how the Canadian law enforcement process worked. There were two or three separate incidents in each episode, generally less gritty and violent than those on the American series.

MOUSE FACTORY (*Children's*)
BROADCAST HISTORY:
Syndicated only
30 minutes
Produced: *1970–1973* (40 episodes)
Released: *January 1971*

The Walt Disney Studios attempted to crack the syndicated-program market with this mixture of animated film clips and live comedy. Mickey Mouse, Donald Duck, Goofy, Pluto, and all the other Disney characters appeared in clips from their films, interspersed with live segments featuring such guest comics as Pat Paulsen, Jonathan Winters, and Phyllis Diller. A different comedian hosted each week. The individual shows generally revolved around a theme, such as alligators or automobiles.

MOVIE CHANNEL, THE (Network), see *Showtime*

MOVIE STARS (*Situation Comedy*)
FIRST TELECAST: *July 11, 1999*
LAST TELECAST: *June 18, 2000*
BROADCAST HISTORY:
Jul 1999–Aug 1999, WB Sun 9:00–9:30
Jul 1999–Sep 1999, WB Mon 9:00–9:30
Apr 2000–Jun 2000, WB Sun 9:00–9:30
CAST:
Reese Hardin .... Harry Hamlin
Jacey Watts .... Jennifer Grant
Lori Lansford (pilot only) .... Shiri Appleby
Lori Lansford (age 16) .... Marnette Patterson
Apache Hardin (13) .... Zach Hopkins
Moonglow Hardin (6) .... Rachel David
Francine Hardin (1999) .... Anne Haney
Todd Hardin .... Mark Benninghoffen
Joey Travolta .... Himself
Don Swayze .... Himself
Frank Stallone .... Himself

Reese and Jacey were the movie stars in this series, a show-business couple living in a fancy home in Malibu and raising two children—Apache and Moonglow. Reese was a wooden star of over-the-top but huge-grossing action flicks, while Jacey was the oft-nominated star of classier dramatic films. Also in the house were Todd, Reese's notably less successful actor brother, who resented his brother's success but lived in the guest house and worked as Reese's personal assistant; and Lori, Reese's trashy daughter from his first marriage. Junior high schooler Apache was an aspiring mogul—forever coming up with marketing ideas for his folks and looking for "deals"—who resented the intrusion of obnoxious Lori into the family. He attended exclusive Buchanan Prep while Lori went to the local public high school. Reese's mother, Francine, was also a regular in 1999. Tom Hanks, never seen, lived next door. In the spring of 2000 he was working on a campaign to get Jacey, who had been nominated three times for the Academy Award but never won, the Oscar she so desperately wanted.

A running gag was Todd's three poker buddies, Joey, Don and Frank, real-life siblings of star actors who spent their time grousing about why they weren't as successful as their brothers.

MOVIELAND QUIZ (*Quiz/Audience Participation*)

FIRST TELECAST: *August 15, 1948*

LAST TELECAST: *November 9, 1948*

BROADCAST HISTORY:

Aug 1948–Nov 1948, ABC Tue 7:30–8:00

EMCEE:

Arthur Q. Bryan
Ralph Dumke
Patricia Bright

Studio contestants were asked to identify titles and stars of old-time movies from selected scenes shown on this 1948 quiz show, which was first seen locally in Philadelphia. The set depicted a theater front, with Patricia Bright as ticket seller and Arthur Q. Bryan (later replaced by Ralph Dumke) as emcee.

MOVIES—PRIOR TO 1961

The arrival of commercial television in the mid-1940s was not greeted with much enthusiasm by the major American movie studios. At first they considered television a passing fad that would have no long-range effects on their audience. Then, by the early 1950s, television had become their mortal enemy. Theater owners could not do what some had done in the heyday of radio—stop the film and let the audience listen to *Amos 'n' Andy* over the theater's sound system—all they could do was look at the dwindling attendance figures. On Mondays people stayed home to watch *I Love Lucy*, on Tuesday to watch Milton Berle, on Saturday to watch *The Jackie Gleason Show* and *Your Show of Shows*, and on Sunday to watch *The Toast of the Town*.

In this climate of life-and-death competition, it was no surprise that the motion-picture studios were not willing to provide television with recently released major films. Nor did they look favorably on actors who wanted to try the new medium. Many stars' contracts expressly forbade their appearance on television. Despite the efforts of the studios to restrict the availability of motion pictures for television, there were movies all over the home screen in the early days. They may not have been recent (most were made in the 1930s) or big hits (many were strictly "B" grade), but they filled time. Independent producers and suppliers of B films, such as Monogram, Republic, and RKO, provided television with many of its early movies.

Aged Westerns, including some that had been released as silent films but had sound tracks added, low-budget second features, and imported films (primarily from England) were seen locally, as network fillers, and as network series in the late 1940s and early 1950s. Some were so dreadful that in one city passersby seeing TV for the first time in a shop window were reportedly laughing out loud at the antique two-reelers being aired. One of the earliest network movies series was titled simply *Western Movie*, and aired on the fledgling DuMont network beginning in late 1946. Ironically, the first attempt to get quality films on TV was made not by a network but by an independent station, WPIX-TV in New York. In the spring of 1948 that station signed an agreement with Sir Alexander Korda, the English producer, for the rights to 24 major British films featuring such stars as Vivien Leigh, Laurence Olivier, and Charles Laughton.

Even when major films started becoming available to television, there was a tacit agreement among the producers to limit television films to features released no later than 1948. In this era of old and/or minor films, ABC's package during the summer of 1957, *Hollywood Film Theater*, was the most ambitious effort to date. Among the films aired in that series were *Gunga Din*, *Mr. Blandings Builds His Dream House*, and *Bringing Up Baby*, all with Cary Grant, *Top Hat* with Fred Astaire and Ginger Rogers, and the original 1933 version of *King Kong*. Most of television's early efforts at showing theatrical films were not nearly so memorable. It was not until the advent of *Saturday Night at the Movies* on NBC in 1961 that major contemporary films would become part of the television scene (see *Movies—1961 to Date*). Summarized below by title are most of the nighttime network movie series aired between 1948 and 1960. Some were full-length features, some were shorts, and some were serials, but they all had one thing in common—despite their age and/or quality they had all been released theatrically.

ABC FEATURE FILM

Oct 1949–Apr 1949, ABC Thu 9:00–10:00
May 1949–Jun 1949, ABC Fri 7:30–8:30
May 1949–Sep 1949, ABC Wed 8:00–9:00

ADMISSION FREE

May 1951–Aug 1951, ABC Mon 10:00–11:00
Aug 1951–Dec 1951, ABC Sun 8:00–9:00

ADVENTURE PLAYHOUSE

Apr 1950–May 1950, DUM Wed 8:00–9:00

BUDWEISER SUMMER THEATRE

Jun 1951–Sep 1951, CBS Sat 8:00–9:00

CINEMA-SCOPE

Apr 1952–May 1952, ABC Sun 9:30–10:30
Jun 1952, ABC Sun 10:00–11:00

CINEMA VARIETIES

Sep 1949–Nov 1949, DUM Sun 8:30–9:00

COMEDY PARADE

Apr 1951–May 1951, ABC Mon 8:00–8:30

CURTAIN UP

May 1951–Sep 1951, ABC Tue 10:00–11:00
Oct 1951–Dec 1951, ABC Mon 9:00–10:00
Nov 1951–Dec 1951, ABC Sat 9:00–10:00

ENCORE PLAYHOUSE

May 1952–Oct 1952, ABC Fri 8:30–9:00

FAMOUS FILM FESTIVAL

Sep 1955–Sep 1956, ABC Sun 7:30–9:00
Oct 1956–May 1957, ABC Sat 7:30–9:00
Jun 1957–Jul 1957, ABC Sat 7:30–8:00
Sep 1957, ABC Sat 7:30–8:30

FEATURE FILM

Oct 1950–Jan 1951, ABC Mon 10:00–11:00
Apr 1951, ABC Mon 10:00–11:00

FEATURE PLAYHOUSE

Jun 1952–Aug 1952, ABC Sat 8:30–10:30
Sep 1952–Jan 1953, ABC Sat 8:00–10:00
Feb 1953–Sep 1953, ABC Sat 8:00–9:00

FEATURE THEATRE

Mar 1949–Jun 1949, DUM Tue 8:00–9:00
Aug 1949–Jan 1950, DUM Tue 9:30–10:30
Jan 1950–Aug 1950, DUM Tue 10:00–11:00
Mar 1950–Apr 1950, DUM Thu 8:00–9:00

FILM SHORTS
Dec 1950–Jan 1951, ABC Sun 8:00–8:30
FILM FAIR
Mar 1956–Jul 1956, ABC Mon 9:00–11:00
Jul 1956–Oct 1956, ABC Mon 9:00–10:30
FILM THEATRE OF THE AIR
Mar 1949–Jul 1949, CBS Sat 8:00–9:30
Apr 1951–Oct 1951, CBS Tue 8:00–9:00
Apr 1953–Jun 1953, CBS Tue 8:00–9:00
FIRST NIGHTER
Oct 1950–Jan 1951, ABC Wed 8:00–9:00
FRONTIER THEATRE
May 1950–Sep 1950, DUM Sat 6:30–7:30
HOLLYWOOD ADVENTURE TIME
Jan 1951–Aug 1951, ABC Sun 8:00–9:00
HOLLYWOOD FILM THEATRE
Apr 1957–Sep 1957, ABC Sun 7:30–9:00
HOLLYWOOD MOVIE TIME
Jan 1951–May 1951, ABC Wed 8:00–9:00
Mar 1952–May 1952, ABC Sat 9:00–11:00
HOLLYWOOD MYSTERY TIME
Feb 1951–Jul 1951, ABC Tue 8:00–9:00
HOUR GLASS
Jun 1956–Sep 1956, ABC Thu 8:00–9:00
INTERNATIONAL PLAYHOUSE
Apr 1951–May 1951, DUM Mon 7:30–9:00
KING'S CROSSROADS
Oct 1951–Dec 1951, ABC Wed 10:00–11:00
Dec 1951–Oct 1952, ABC Sun 8:00–9:00
LIBRARY OF COMEDY FILMS
see *Comedy Parade*
MYSTERY THEATRE
Sep 1949–Mar 1950, DUM Thu 8:00–9:00
NBC CINEMA PLAYHOUSE
Jun 1950–Sep 1950, NBC Tue 8:00–9:00
NBC PRESENTS
Jun 1948–Aug 1948, NBC Tue 9:00–9:30
Sep 1948–Oct 1948, NBC Fri 8:00–8:30
Oct 1948–Dec 1948, NBC Thu 7:30–7:45
NORTHWEST PATROL
Jun 1951–Aug 1951, ABC Wed 8:00–9:00
PREMIERE PLAYHOUSE
Mar 1949–Jul 1949, CBS Fri 9:30–10:45
Jul 1949–Dec 1949, CBS Sat 9:00–10:00
May 1950–Jul 1950, CBS Sat 10:00–11:00
SADDLE PAL CLUB
Dec 1951–May 1952, ABC Sat 7:00–7:30
May 1952–Jun 1952, ABC Sat 6:30–7:30
Jun 1952–Aug 1952, ABC Sat 7:00–8:00
SCHLITZ FILM FIRSTS
Jul 1951–Sep 1951, CBS Fri 9:00–10:00
SCREEN MYSTERY
Apr 1950–Oct 1950, DUM Thu 8:00–9:00
SCREEN SHORTS
May 1951–Jul 1951, ABC Sun 10:30–11:00
SUMMER CINEMA
Jun 1952–Oct 1952, CBS Sat 8:00–Conclusion
WASHDAY THEATRE
Ap 1952–Aug 1952, ABC Mon 8:30–9:30
Sep 1952–Oct 1952, ABC Mon 9:00–10:00

MOVIES—1961 TO DATE

The evening of September 23, 1961, ushered in a new era in network-television programming. On that night NBC aired the movie *How to Marry a Millionaire* starring Marilyn Monroe, Lauren Bacall, and Betty Grable. It was the premiere telecast of a new series, *Saturday Night at the Movies,* the first movie series composed of films released by major studios after 1948. The war that had existed between the motion-picture community and the television community was finally over. The studios, which had initially feared that television would drive them out of business, were now thriving as the principal suppliers of filmed weekly TV series. It had been only a matter of time before they made the decision to release relatively current theatrical films for network showing.

Unlike previous efforts to program movies on television (ABC's *Hollywood Film Theatre* in 1957 had been the most recent), *Saturday Night at the Movies* was very successful. It did, admittedly, have certain advantages over earlier movie series. For one thing, *Saturday Night at the Movies* was the first movie series that could air color movies in color. But its primary advantage was that it had access to recent movies showcasing currently popular stars, not the poor grade-B films, imports, and dated films previously seen. The popularity of good-quality movies on TV was demonstrated by the rapid growth of such programming. Within a year of the premiere of *Saturday Night at the Movies,* ABC was carrying theatrical films on Sundays and NBC had added a Monday movie to its schedule. By the end of the decade there were as many as nine network movies on each week.

The increased demand for movies on television eventually led to another major development, the made-for-television film. Universal was the first major studio to attempt producing a film expressly for television, during the 1963–1964 season. Their first effort, however, was a brutal film called *The Killers* with Lee Marvin, Angie Dickinson, and Ronald Reagan (in his last film role before entering politics) that was deemed too violent for television and went into theatrical release instead.

The distinction of being the first made-for-television film aired goes to *See How They Run* starring John Forsythe and Senta Berger, originally telecast on October 7, 1964. Many of the early made-for-TV films (and a substantial quantity of those currently being made) were pilots for proposed TV series, one of the most successful being *Fame Is the Name of the Game,* which became the series *Name of the Game.* It was common practice for motion-picture companies to release these tele-features theatrically outside the U.S.

The acceptance of made-for-television films, which had originally been dropped into series that were made up primarily of theatrically released films, resulted in the first series of made-for-television films only, *The ABC Movie of the Week,* in the fall of 1969. The attraction was that every week would be a "world premiere" of a new motion picture. Over the years, a number of series relying on these new films appeared under titles such as *World Premiere Movie* and *Movie of the Week,* with later trends tending to minimize the distinction between theatrical and made-for-TV films. In fact, by the 1978–1979 season, with the available supply of theatrical films dwindling while demand for motion pictures on network television remained strong, a milestone was reached. Fifteen years after the first made-for-TV film aired on network television there were more of them aired during an entire season than there were theatrical features. In later seasons, as cable-television airings eroded the ability of theatrical films to generate large audiences when they were eventually run on the networks, all three networks became more dependent on made-for-TV films to fill their movie time slots.

By the 1986–1987 season the shift had reached the point that the networks aired barely more than 100 theatrical features and almost 300 made-for-TV films.

The highest-rated movies since the advent of *Saturday Night at the Movies* in 1961 are ranked below. Following the table is a chronology of network movie series by night of the week. In cases where a series consisted primarily of made-for-television films, and was so advertised to the viewing public, it has been indicated by (TV).

HIGHEST-RATED MOVIES ON TELEVISION

1.	*Gone With the Wind* (11/7–8/76)	47.6
2.	*The Day After* (TV) (11/20/83)	46.0
3.	*Airport* (11/11/73)	42.3
	Love Story (10/1/72)	42.3
5.	*Jaws* (11/4/79)	39.1
6.	*The Poseidon Adventure* (10/27/74)	39.0
7.	*True Grit* (11/12/72)	38.9
	The Birds (1/6/68)	38.9
9.	*Patton* (11/19/72)	38.5
10.	*The Bridge on the River Kwai* (9/25/66)	38.3
11.	*The Godfather* (11/16 & 18/74)	38.2
12.	*Jeremiah Johnson* (1/18/76)	37.5
13.	*Ben-Hur* (2/14/71)	37.1
	Rocky (2/4/79)	37.1
15.	*Little Ladies of the Night* (TV) (1/16/77)	36.9
16.	*Helter Skelter* (TV) (4/1–2/76)	36.5
17.	*The Burning Bed* (TV) (10/8/84)	36.2
18.	*The Wizard of Oz* (Rerun) (1/26/64)	35.9
19.	*Planet of the Apes* (9/14/73)	35.2
20.	*The Wizard of Oz* (Rerun) (1/17/65)	34.7
21.	*Born Free* (2/22/70)	34.2
22.	*The Sound of Music* (2/29/76)	33.6
23.	*Bonnie and Clyde* (9/20/73)	33.4
24.	*The Ten Commandments* (2/18/73)	33.2
	The Night Stalker (TV) (1/11/72)	33.2

In addition to the various prime-time movie series, in 1972 CBS premiered *The CBS Late Movie*, a Monday–Friday 11:30 P.M. collection of theatrical and made-for-television reruns; ABC incorporated a large number of made-for-television films in *ABC Late Night* beginning in 1973; and NBC added the *NBC Late Night Movie* on Sunday nights from September 1977 to August 1984.

MOVIETIME (Network), see *E! Entertainment Television*

MOVIN' ON (*Adventure*)

FIRST TELECAST: *September 12, 1974*
LAST TELECAST: *September 14, 1976*
BROADCAST HISTORY:

Sep 1974–May 1975, NBC Thu 10:00–11:00
Sep 1975–Sep 1976, NBC Tue 8:00–9:00

CAST:

Sonny Pruitt .... Claude Akins
Will Chandler .... Frank Converse
Moose (1975–1976).................. Rosey Grier
Benjy (1975–1976) .... Art Metrano

THEME:

"Movin' On," written and performed by Merle Haggard

Sonny and Will were two gypsy truck drivers who came from radically different backgrounds. Sonny was a burly veteran trucker, owner of the giant rig that they operated, and prone to settle most of his arguments with his fists. Will was much younger, a law school graduate who had turned to trucking as a means of learning more about himself. His legal training and quick mind often prevented disagreements from turning into brawls. They were good for each other; Sonny's outgoing gregariousness counterbalanced Will's quiet, reserved personality, while Will's rational approach to problems counteracted Sonny's sucker-prone willingness to help anyone at any time. Together they traveled back and forth across the country in search of adventure and freight to haul. During the second season another pair of truckers, Moose and Benjy, were seen frequently. Less than completely ethical, they were two of the most mobile con men ever seen on television. *Movin' On* was filmed on location in a different part of the country each week.

One of the fans of this program was President Gerald Ford. Once, when *Movin' On* was filming in Atlanta, Claude Akins happened to be staying at the same hotel as the President. Approached in the hotel dining room by a Secret Service agent, the actor was invited to the President's suite, where he and Ford chatted about the show for half an hour. "Now," remarked the President, "I can tell Betty I know more about *Movin' On* than she does."

MUCHMUSIC (Network) (*Contemporary Music Cable Network*)

LAUNCHED:

July 1994

SUBSCRIBERS (MAY 2003):

31.3 million (29% U.S.)

This competitor to MTV placed much more emphasis on music, and less on reality and lifestyle shows like *The Real World*. Interactivity with viewers was featured, via request shows and Internet comments and voting. There was even an interactive game *(IMX: Interactive Music Xchange)* in which viewers could "invest" in rock stars' new singles and win prizes if their picks became hits. Despite the concentration on music videos, a few alternative formats were seen, including the *MusicMusic Video Awards* and *Behind the Music That Sucks* (an animated parody of VH1's *Behind the Music*) and reruns of *Becoming* (formerly on MTV!) and *My Guide to Becoming a Rock Star*.

MuchMusic began in Canada in 1984, with the U.S. version launching in 1994. In early 2003 MuchMusic USA announced that it was changing its name to Fuse.

MUDDLING THROUGH (*Situation Comedy*)

FIRST TELECAST: *July 9, 1994*
LAST TELECAST: *September 7, 1994*
BROADCAST HISTORY:

Jul 1994–Aug 1994, CBS Sat 9:00–9:30
Aug 1994–Sep 1994, CBS Wed 8:30–9:00

CAST:

Connie Drego.................... Stephanie Hodge
Sonny Drego .... D. David Morin
Madeline Drego Cooper (age 18) ... Jennifer Aniston
Kerri Drego (16) .... Aimee Brooks
Officer Duane Cooper................ Scott Waara

Gidney .... Hal Landon, Jr.
Lyle .... Hank Underwood

Pistol-packin' Connie Drego had just been paroled from prison, where she had served three years for shooting her cheating husband, Sonny, in the butt, in this raucous comedy. She had returned home to go back to work at Drego's Oasis, the family's truck-stop diner/motel in rural Michigan. Now divorced, Connie hoped to get her life back to normal, but her family didn't help much. Her older daughter, Madeline, had married "Trooper Cooper," the dense but straight-arrow cop who had arrested Connie and whose testimony in court had been a major factor in her conviction. Her younger daughter, Kerri, had become a boy-crazy sexpot with little interest in schoolwork, and, to make things worse, no-good Sonny was still hanging around and living for free in one of the rental cabins behind the diner. Connie's hostility occasionally showed itself—mostly when dealing with Duane, unemployed Sonny, and the customers at Drego's, whose kidding about her past sometimes got under her skin. Gidney and Lyle were old-time regulars at the diner.

MULLIGAN'S STEW (*Comedy/Drama*)

FIRST TELECAST: *October 25, 1977*
LAST TELECAST: *December 13, 1977*
BROADCAST HISTORY:
Oct 1977–Dec 1977, NBC Tue 9:00–10:00
CAST:
Michael Mulligan .... Lawrence Pressman
Jane Mulligan .... Elinor Donahue
Mark Mulligan .... Johnny Doran
Melinda Mulligan .... Julie Anne Haddock
Jimmy Mulligan .... K. C. Martel
Adam Friedman .... Chris Ciampa
Stevie Friedman .... Suzanne Crough
Kimmy Friedman .... Sunshine Lee
Polly Friedman .... Lory Kochheim
Polo Polocheck .... Jaime Alba

Set in the fictitious Southern California suburban community of Birchfield, *Mulligan's Stew* was the story of Michael and Jane Mulligan and their extended family. The Mulligans had three children of their own, and were managing reasonably well, when Michael's sister and her husband were killed, leaving them with four more children, including a recently adopted five-year-old Vietnamese orphan named Kimmy. The Mulligan home, barely comfortable with its original family of five, was severely overcrowded with nine. The Mulligan children and the Friedman children had been raised with different lifestyles and had considerable problems adjusting to each other. Michael's income as a high school teacher/football coach was enough to get by on, but with nine mouths to feed very little was left for luxuries.

MUNSTERS, THE (*Situation Comedy*)

FIRST TELECAST: *September 24, 1964*
LAST TELECAST: *September 1, 1966*
BROADCAST HISTORY:
Sep 1964–Sep 1966, CBS Thu 7:30–8:00
(In first-run syndication from October 1988–September 1991)
CAST (1964–1966):
Herman Munster .... Fred Gwynne
Lily Munster .... Yvonne DeCarlo
Grandpa Munster .... Al Lewis
Edward Wolfgang (Eddie) Munster ... Butch Patrick
Marilyn Munster (1964) .... Beverly Owen
Marilyn Munster .... Pat Priest
CAST (1988–1991):
Herman Munster .... John Schuck
Lily Munster .... Lee Meriwether
Edward Wolfgang (Eddie) Munster ... Jason Marsden
Marilyn Munster .... Hilary Van Dyke
Vladimir Dracula (Grandpa) ...... Howard Morton

At 1313 Mockingbird Lane in Mockingbird Heights stood a musty, cobweb-covered gothic mansion. The residents considered themselves just a normal, everyday American family, but to neighbors—and viewers—they were a bit unusual. Herman, the man of the house, was seven feet tall and bore a striking resemblance to the Frankenstein monster. His wife, Lily, looked very much like a lady vampire; son Eddie looked like he was in the midst of changing from boy to wolf, or vice versa, take your pick; and Grandpa could have passed for an aging, 350-year-old Count Dracula. They all had their idiosyncracies. Grandpa was not above changing into a bat when the situation warranted it. Not only did this family look like monsters, they were monsters—albeit friendly, unassuming ones. They were concerned about their niece Marilyn, who looked somewhat strange to them (to an outsider she was the only normal-looking one of the lot). The effect their physical appearance had on the rest of the world was always predictable, often hilarious, and occasionally poignant. Herman, appropriately, worked in a menial capacity for the funeral home of Gateman, Goodbury & Graves, and was always on the lookout for a better job. Beverly Owen, who originated the role of Marilyn, left the series in December 1964 to get married, and was replaced by Pat Priest.

More than two decades after the original series had left the air, *The Munsters Today* surfaced in first-run syndication. An updated version of the original series (even to the point of mentioning a 20-year "sleep" in the title song during its first season), the show had a more contemporary look, while retaining much of the flavor of the original—including the family's pet dinosaur, Spot.

Oddly, rather than colorizing the old black-and-white episodes of *The Munsters* so that they would match the new ones, the new episodes were "decolorized"—i.e., the colors were toned down—so that the two series could run together.

MUPPET SHOW, THE (*Variety*)

BROADCAST HISTORY:
Syndicated only
30 minutes
Produced: *1976–1981* (120 episodes)
Released: *September 1976*
PUPPETEERS:
Jim Henson
Frank Oz
Richard Hunt
Dave Goelz
Jerry Nelson
Erin Ozker (1976–1977)
Louise Gold (1979–1981)
Kathryn Muller (1980–1981)
Steve Whitmire (1980–1981)

THE MUPPETS:
Kermit the Frog (Henson)
Miss Piggy (Oz)
Zoot (Goelz)
Fozzie Bear (Oz)
Gonzo (Goelz)
Sweetums (Hunt)
Sam the Eagle (Oz)
The Swedish Chef (Henson & Oz)
Dr. Teeth (Henson) & the Electric Mayhem
Floyd (Nelson)
Animal (Oz)
Capt. Link Heartthrob (Henson)
Dr. Strangepork (Nelson)
Wayne & Wanda (1976–1977)
Rowlf (Henson)
Dr. Bunsen Honeydew (Goelz)
Statler & Waldorf (Hunt & Henson)
Scooter (Hunt)
Beauregard (Goelz) (1980–1981)
Pops (Nelson) (1980–1981)
Lew Zealand (Nelson) (1980–1981)
Janice (Hunt)
Rizzo the Rat (Whitmire) (1980–1981)

MUSICAL DIRECTOR:
Jack Parnell

This whimsical mixture of puppets and people was probably the most widely viewed television program in the world during the late 1970s. Originated by an American and produced in England, it was seen in more than 100 countries by upward of 235 million people.

The host was a frog. Kermit presided over a half-hour of chaos each week as the desperate emcee and manager of a theatrical troupe of shaggy animals, monsters, and even humanoid screwballs who seemed to turn every big production number into a shambles. In the troupe was Miss Piggy, corpulent and very determined to be the star (anyone who disagreed got a karate chop); Rowlf, the shaggy, piano-playing dog; Fozzie Bear, with his peaked head and tiny hat; Dr. Teeth and the Electric Mayhem, the resident band, including spaced-out guitarist Floyd and drummer Animal; the maniacal Swedish Chef; Dr. Bunsen Honeydew, the short, balding, and quite mad scientist (modeled after the show's real-life backer, Sir Lew Grade); Gonzo, who always tried to open the show with a trumpet fanfare (but the trumpet would break, explode, emit butterflies, etc.); and a host of others. Observing the tumult with disdain from their box seats, and cracking awful jokes, were the two old geezers, Statler and Waldorf.

A running feature was "Pigs in Space," a soap opera with handsome Capt. Link Heartthrob of the starship *Swinetrek*, doing battle with the evil plots of Dr. Strangepork and the amorous advances of Miss Piggy (who went after almost every male in sight). Miss Piggy bullied her way from a supporting character in the early years of the show to second billing (but don't tell her that!) after Kermit. Guests on *The Muppet Show* ranged from George Burns, Zero Mostel, and Steve Martin to Rudolf Nureyev (dancing a *pas de deux* from "Swine Lake" with Miss Piggy), Elton John (doing "Crocodile Rock" to a chorus of crocodiles), Beverly Sills (in a battle of the sopranos in "Pigaletto"), and Peter Sellers (as a mad German chiropractor who tied a pig into knots, or a pompous actor reciting lines from *Richard III* while squeezing a clucking chicken under each arm).

The gags were often corny, and the skits bizarre to say the least, but what made the show such a hit with adults and children alike was the Muppets themselves, hilarious to look at yet invested with a warmth, wit, and fallibility that made them almost human.

Basically, of course, they *were* human, extensions of the warm and mischievous personality of creator Jim Henson and his associates. Henson was fascinated with puppetry from childhood, and followed *Kukla, Fran & Ollie* and the Baird puppets from the time he first saw a TV set. He had his first short-lived TV puppet show as a senior in high school, on a local station in Maryland. In 1955, as a freshman at the University of Maryland, he and his future wife, Jane Nebel, teamed to present a regular local show on WRC-TV, Washington, called *Sam and Friends.* Henson coined the label "Muppet" at about this time, to indicate the combination of "marionette" and "puppet." Soon he was doing commercials and then making national appearances on such network shows as *Tonight, Today, Ed Sullivan, Jimmy Dean* (where Rowlf was a regular), and *Perry Como.* On his first network appearance (Steve Allen's *Tonight Show* in 1957), a one-year-old Kermit (Henson) sang "I've Grown Accustomed to Your Face" to a purple monster (Nebel), which was so enchanted that it proceeded to eat its own face, and then attempted to devour Kermit, too.

The Muppets gained even greater fame with the debut of *Sesame Street*, on which they were featured, in 1969, but a network show of their own eluded them. Network officials saw the Muppets as strictly for kids, while Henson thought they had broader appeal. Finally English showman Sir Lew Grade offered to back this syndicated series, which became a bigger hit than many of the networks' own shows.

By the late 1970s there were more than 400 Muppet characters, of which those listed above were seen most often on *The Muppet Show.* Most were basically hand puppets, made of felt (like Kermit) or foam rubber (like Miss Piggy) and operated by either one or two men each.

In 1979 Henson's horizons expanded even further with the first *Muppet Movie.* There is all manner of Muppet merchandise available, including a famous parody on cheesecake posters featuring the inimitable Miss Piggy.

MUPPETS TONIGHT (*Situation Comedy*)

FIRST TELECAST: *March 8, 1996*
LAST TELECAST: *July 14, 1996*
BROADCAST HISTORY:
Mar 1996–Apr 1996, ABC Fri 8:30–9:00
Jun 1996–Jul 1996, ABC Sun 7:00–7:30

PUPPETEERS:
Bill Baretta
Kevin Clash
Dave Goelz
Brian Henson
Jerry Nelson
Steve Whitmire
Frank Oz

FEATURED MUPPETS:
Kermit the Frog
Miss Piggy

Gonzo the Great
Fozzie Bear
Rizzo the Rat
Clifford

The Muppets, those cute, foamy little creatures that won't go away, were back running a variety show on station KMUP-TV in this short-lived series. Rizzo was the stage manager and Clifford the harried Jamaican producer. Updated versions of some of the old Muppet sketches were seen ("Pigs in Space—Deep Dish Nine"), along with numerous good-natured guest stars ranging from Garth Brooks to Whoopi Goldberg.

MURDER IN SMALL TOWN X (*Detective/Reality*)
FIRST TELECAST: *July 24, 2001*
LAST TELECAST: *September 4, 2001*
BROADCAST HISTORY:
Jul 2001–Sep 2001, FOX Tue 9:00–10:00
HOST:
Gary Fredo

In this rather violent twist on the reality/game show format, 10 contestants, ranging in age from 21 to 45, acted as detectives trying to solve a murder. The setting was the picturesque coastal town of Sunrise, Maine, where, in the first episode, Nate Flint and his daughter Abby were brutally murdered by a mysterious intruder who kidnapped Nate's wife, Carmen, later killing her and dumping her body in the bay. The killer left a gory film of the murders and short clips of 15 suspects (including him- or herself)—among them the sheriff, the mayor, the pastor, the town attorney, a cabbie, a boyfriend, etc. Overseeing the investigation and training the contestants was real-life L.A.P.D. sergeant Gary Fredo, who helped the amateur sleuths follow up on clues and leads, while cameras followed them cinema verité style. They all strategized in a headquarters "war room." In addition to the actors portraying the suspects, the townspeople of Eastport, Maine, where *Murder* was filmed, served as extras, having been told that the producers were shooting a movie titled *Water's Edge.*

Every three days the killer sent two envelopes, one red and one black. The red one contained questions about the contestants' investigation which, if answered correctly, cleared 1 of the 15 suspects. The black one contained two scary locations. At one of them the killer left an important clue, but at the other the killer was waiting and would eliminate the contestant who was sent there. Every three days a "lifeguard" was chosen by the eliminated contestant via a taped "last will and testament." The lifeguard, based at headquarters and safe from the killer, coordinated the teams in the field and helped choose the teams. If a contestant chosen by the lifeguard to go to a black location returned, he or she usually harbored serious resentment.

The two-part finale of *Murder in Small Town X* began with eight suspects and four investigators remaining. The final explanation of the mystery began with a family, the Duchamps, who had supposedly been lost at sea but were actually smugglers working with a group called the O.S.L. Most of the family had been killed by the O.S.L. because the government was closing in on them, but one, a badly burned son, had survived and fathered the killer, William Lambert. Lambert was determined to kill anyone who was related to any of the members of the O.S.L. Contestant Angel Juarbe discovered Lambert's hiding place and won $250,000 and a new car.

Born and raised in the Bronx, Juarbe was a firefighter in the Chelsea district of New York City. In a sad irony, he died in the aftermath of the terrorist attack that destroyed New York's World Trade Center one week after the last episode of *Murder in Small Town X* aired.

MURDER ONE (*Legal Drama*)
FIRST TELECAST: *September 19, 1995*
LAST TELECAST: *January 23, 1997*
BROADCAST HISTORY:
Sep 1995, ABC Tue 10:00–11:00
Oct 1995–Nov 1995, ABC Thu 10:00–11:00
Jan 1996–Apr 1996, ABC Mon 10:00–11:00
Oct 1996–Jan 1997, ABC Thu 9:00–10:00
CAST:
Theodore Hoffman (1995–1996) .... Daniel Benzali
Ann Hoffman (1995–1996) .... Patricia Clarkson
Chris Docknovich .... Michael Hayden
Arnold Spivak .... J. C. MacKenzie
Justine Appleton .... Mary McCormack
Lisa Gillespie (1995–1996) .... Grace Phillips
Asst. D.A. Miriam Grasso .... Barbara Bosson
Det. Arthur Polson (1995–1996) .... Dylan Baker
David Blalock (1995–1996) .... Kevin Tighe
D.A. Roger Garfield .... Gregory Itzin
Neil Avedon (1995–1996) .... Jason Gedrick
Richard Cross (1995–1996) .... Stanley Tucci
Louis Heinsbergen .... John Fleck
Lila Marquette (1995–1996) ...... Vanessa Williams
James Wyler (1996–1997) .... Anthony LaPaglia
Aaron Mosely (1996–1997) ... David Bryan Woodside
Sharon Rooney (1996) .... Missy Crider
Malcolm Dietrich (1996–1997) .... Ralph Waite
Vince Biggio (1996–1997) .... Clayton Rohner
Rickey Latrell (1996–1997) .... Rick Worthy
Clifford Banks (1997) .... Pruitt Taylor Vince

Murder cases involving the rich and powerful, and the ruthless attorneys who defended them, were the principal theme of this intense legal drama that attracted much critical acclaim, but not enough viewers. At the center of the drama was Theodore Hoffman, a bald, very self-assured, very commanding attorney whose apparent willingness to make any moral compromise to win his case masked an absolute determination to get to the truth, no matter who it implicated. On his defense team—which he ruled with an iron hand—were young, ambitious lawyers Chris, Arnold, Justine, and Lisa. Louis was the fawning officer manager at their swank headquarters, Lila the receptionist, and Ann was Teddy's wife, who worried about how his cases consumed him. His principal adversaries were: Miriam Grasso, a tough assistant D.A. with whom he could nevertheless strike a deal when necessary; her ruthless, politically ambitious boss Garfield; determined police detective Polson; and Polson's mature investigator, Blalock.

An attention-getting aspect of the series was that it spent its entire first season unfolding a single byzantine case: that of an obnoxious young movie star, Neil Avedon, who was accused of the brutal murder of a young woman named Jessica, with whom he had shared drugs and sex. Also involved was Richard Cross, a fabulously wealthy businessman who owned the building in which the murder took place.

Episodes followed the case's twists and turns until, in the season finale, after Avedon had been convicted, the true murderer was unmasked. It turned out to be neither Avedon nor Cross, but rather a drug dealer named Roberto Portalegre, who had killed Jessica during a sexual encounter gone bad.

Although ratings were weak, ABC had sufficient faith in the show to bring it back for a second season, albeit with major changes. It moved into a new time slot; there would be three cases presented instead of one; and several cast changes were made, including the replacement of Hoffman with new lead attorney James Wyler. He was younger, had a full head of hair and a veneer of amiability, but underneath he was just as smart, driven, and cagey as his predecessor. Attorney Lisa was gone, replaced by an angry young lawyer named Aaron. The first case involved the sensational murder of California governor Van Allen and his mistress, during a tryst at a beach house. A troubled woman named Sharon was accused of the crime; Jimmy got her off the hook, only to have her commit suicide. Eventually it was revealed that the murder had been ordered by political power broker Dietrich, and that slimy D.A. Garfield—who had just been elected governor—was involved as well. In the second story, which was rather obviously based on the O.J. Simpson case, arrogant black basketball star Rickey Latrell was accused of murdering a despicable Las Vegas team owner named Sandy Fortas, who had ripped him off and had an affair with his wife. In the dramatic finale Jimmy coached Latrell to admit on the stand that he *had* committed the murder, whereupon the jury—impressed with his "honesty"—acquitted him. Returning to his old, arrogant ways, murderer Rickey then declared to the press that "justice was finally served for a black man."

Although *Murder One* ended its regular run in January 1997, the final story was presented as a three-part mini-series aired between May 25 and May 29, 1997. In this one Wyler defended serial killer Clifford Banks, who specialized in killing career criminals.

MURDER, SHE WROTE (*Detective Drama*)
FIRST TELECAST: *September 30, 1984*
LAST TELECAST: *August 4, 1996*
BROADCAST HISTORY:

Sep 1984–May 1991, CBS Sun 8:00–9:00
Jun 1991–Jul 1991, CBS Sun 9:00–10:00
Jul 1991–Sep 1995, CBS Sun 8:00–9:00
Aug 1995–Jun 1996, CBS Thu 8:00–9:00
Apr 1996–Aug 1996, CBS Sun 8:00–9:00

CAST:

Jessica Beatrice Fletcher .... Angela Lansbury
**Sheriff Amos Tupper (1984–1988)* ..... Tom Bosley
**Grady Fletcher (1985–1990)* .... Michael Horton
**Dr. Seth Hazlitt (1985–1996)* ..... William Windom
**Mayor Sam Booth (1986–1991)* .... Richard Paul
**Sheriff Mort Metzger (1989–1996)* ...... Ron Masak
**Dennis Stanton (1990–1991)* .... Keith Michell
**Robert Butler (1990–1991)* .... James Sloyan
**Lt. Perry Catalano (1990–1991)* ...... Ken Swofford
**Rhoda (1990–1991)*.................... Hallie Todd
**Deputy Andy Broom (1991–1996)*... Louis Herthum
*Occasional

Jessica Fletcher was a middle-aged widow living in quaint Cabot Cove on the coast of Maine. A former substitute teacher and PTA volunteer, she had attained celebrity late in life through the success of her mystery novels. Not only could Jessica write good stories, she was a talented amateur detective as well. Active and adventuresome, she took advantage of the money and opportunities that her writing had provided and traveled widely. Along the way she frequently got involved in convoluted real-life murder mysteries, which she diligently pursued by piecing together obscure clues to determine the culprit. As in *The Adventures of Ellery Queen*, an earlier television whodunit, viewers had to pay close attention to these clues if they hoped to figure out who the murderer was. The plots were complicated and the pacing brisk, and longtime stage actress Angela Lansbury seemed to be having the time of her life in this, her first television series.

Although Jessica was the series' only regular, there were a few others who turned up periodically—her good friend, and Cabot Cove's sheriff, Amos Tupper (replaced by Sheriff Metzger when actor Tom Bosley left the show to star in *The Father Dowling Mysteries*); its mayor, Sam Booth; her tax accountant nephew, Grady; and Dr. Seth Hazlitt, with whom she played a spirited game of chess. During the 1990–1991 season a number of episodes featured reformed jewel thief Dennis Stanton, a friend of Jessica's, who was working as an insurance investigator in San Francisco. Also seen in those episodes were his boss, Robert Butler; his secretary, Rhoda; and Lt. Catalano of the S.F.P.D. In the fall of 1991 Jessica, who had begun teaching a course in criminology at Manhattan University, moved into a Manhattan apartment. For a while she lived there during the week, returning home to Cabot Cove on weekends.

MURPHY BROWN (*Situation Comedy*)
FIRST TELECAST: *November 14, 1988*
LAST TELECAST: *August 10, 1998*
BROADCAST HISTORY:

Nov 1988–Feb 1997, CBS Mon 9:00–9:30
Apr 1997–May 1997, CBS Mon 8:30–9:00
Jun 1997–Sep 1997, CBS Mon 9:30–10:00
Jul 1997–Aug 1997, CBS Wed 8:30–9:00
Oct 1997–Jan 1998, CBS Wed 8:30–9:00
Apr 1998–May 1998, CBS Mon 9:30–10:00
Jul 1998–Aug 1998, CBS Mon 9:30–10:00

CAST:

Murphy Brown.................... Candice Bergen
Jim Dial...................... Charles Kimbrough
Frank Fontana .... Joe Regalbuto
Corky Sherwood......................... Faith Ford
Miles Silverberg (1988–1996) .... Grant Shaud
Phil (1988–1996)........................ Pat Corley
Eldin Bernecky (1988–1994) ...... Robert Pastorelli
Carl Wishnitski (1988–1997) .... Ritch Brinkley
John, the stage manager............ John Hostetter
**Gene Kinsella (1988–1992)*..... Alan Oppenheimer
**Peter Hunt (1993–1996)*............. Scott Bakula
**Avery Brown (1994–1995)*...... Dyllan Christopher
**Avery Brown (1996)* .... Jackson Buckley
**Avery Brown (1997–1998)* ...... Haley Joel Osment
**Stan Lansing (1994–1997)* .... Garry Marshall
**Miller Redfield (1995–1997)*...... Christopher Rich
**Andrew J. Lansing III (1995–1997)*.... Paul Reubens
McGovern (1995) .... Paula Korologos
Phil Jr. (1995–1998)....................... Pat Finn
**Matthew (1996–1997)*................ Matt Griesser
Kay Carter-Shepley (1996–1998)....... Lily Tomlin
*Occasional

This series was the classiest comedy about the world of broadcast news since the departure of *The Mary Tyler Moore Show* more than a decade earlier. The writing was crisp and witty, the characters were well crafted, and the chemistry among the actors was obvious even to the casual viewer.

Murphy Brown was the veteran star reporter of *F.Y.I.*, a highly successful CBS TV weekly magazine series originating from Washington, D.C. *F.Y.I.*, which aired on Wednesday nights, was in its twelfth season on the air when *Murphy Brown* premiered. Murphy was not the most lovable person in the world. She was opinionated, sarcastic, overbearing, and driven. She didn't know how to do anything in moderation—including the drinking and smoking for which she had spent a month at the Betty Ford Clinic. But, regardless of her faults, Murphy was a dedicated and tireless reporter with a great on-camera presence and an ethical sense not often seen on the air.

Jim Dial was *F.Y.I.*'s stuffy anchorman, a newsman for 25 years who had, remarkably, never developed any sense of humor. Frank Fontana was the show's investigative reporter and Murphy's longtime friend. His one concession to TV—and he hated it—was wearing an obvious toupee over his thinning hair when he was on camera. New to the *F.Y.I.* staff was Corky Sherwood, a perky former Miss America (she had taken over the title when the winner had been forced to relinquish it) whose primary assets were her looks and energy. She knew nothing about journalism and idolized Murphy, who found her cheerleader personality a bit hard to take. Corky married writer Will Forrest (Scott Bryce) at the end of the 1989–1990 season. Miles Silverberg was the executive producer of *F.Y.I.*, an enthusiastic but neurotic young man (somewhere around 25) who was not always comfortable or effective trying to control the program's staff, who considered both his age and lack of experience as liabilities. The local hangout for the team was Phil's, a neighborhood bar whose fatherly owner was always willing to listen to their problems and offer good advice.

There were a number of running gags on *Murphy Brown*. For the first two seasons there was no regular theme—each episode opened with a different Motown song (Murphy loved Motown music) whose title or lyrics related to the story line to follow. Murphy had a problem holding on to secretaries and they were referred to in the credits by number instead of name—she went through twenty during the first season and another twenty-six in the next two. And then there was Eldin, the eccentric house painter, who had been working on Murphy's town house from the time the series premiered. He was there at all hours of the day and night and, in some respects, offered the same kind of advice as Phil, if phrased a bit more cryptically. Even after he sold one of his paintings for $1,000,000 in January of 1991, Eldin continued to work on Murphy's place.

Mirroring changes in the real world of broadcasting, the network that aired *F.Y.I.* was bought in February 1991 by American Industrial Enterprises, resulting in anxiety for the staff, cutbacks, and assorted other problems for network president Gene Kinsella. Adding to his problems was 42-year-old Murphy's decision that fall to have the baby conceived during a brief fling with her ex-husband, Jake (Robin Thomas).

When the baby, a boy, was born in May 1992, it set off a national controversy perhaps unique in the history of American television. Murphy had her choice of two fathers, Jake and more recent boyfriend Jerry Gold, both of whom wanted to marry her. She rejected them both, saying she preferred to raise the child alone. The following day, real-life Vice President Dan Quayle, delivering a speech in San Francisco on the deterioration of family values in America, singled out the program for criticism. He said, "It doesn't help matters when prime-time TV has Murphy Brown, a character who supposedly epitomizes today's intelligent, highly paid professional woman, mocking the importance of fathers by bearing a child alone and calling it just another lifestyle choice."

The reaction was fast and predictable. Producer Diane English spit back, "If he believes that a woman cannot adequately raise a child without a father, then he'd better make sure abortion remains safe and legal." Other Hollywood producers insisted it was their free-speech right to show anything they wanted to, and creatively they had to be true to their characters. Others, however, supported the vice president, saying the episode was an unfortunate example of Hollywood's largely liberal agenda. CBS merely gloated that all the attention would raise its ratings (and make it money). As for English, she got her "revenge" the following fall with a highly hyped, rather mean-spirited hour-long episode that mocked the vice president's misspelling of the word "potato." Screamed the advertising, "Tonight, Murphy deals with some infantile behavior," evidently referring to Quayle. The episode got top ratings.

The baby was named Avery, after Murphy's late mother (played in earlier episodes by Colleen Dewhurst, who had also died). Murphy, however, was unable to find a suitable nanny until Eldin, her perennial painter, volunteered to take the job. Late that year Corky and Will Forrest separated, and eventually they got divorced.

Peter Hunt, a renowned globe-trotting reporter, was added to the *F.Y.I.* staff in the fall of 1993, but, after a few months confined to studio work, he got the wanderlust and went back to international reporting. During his tenure he began what became a tempestuous love affair with Murphy. Stan Lansing, the new network president, who was exasperated by Murphy's penchant for doing whatever was politically incorrect, began making occasional visits to *F.Y.I.* in 1994, and that November Eldin made the decision to leave Washington to study painting with a famous muralist in Spain. By the end of the year Corky and Miles had started dating. In the spring of 1995 Peter, on one of his visits back to Washington, proposed to Murphy . . . and she accepted, but they later called it off. By the end of the 1994–1995 season the number of secretaries who had gone through Murphy's revolving door was closing in on 80.

In spring 1995, Stan's obnoxious nephew Andrew first showed up when Stan forced Murphy to hire him as her secretary. His later executive positions caused the staff occasional grief. Pretty boy Miller Redfield got a job with *F.Y.I.* in 1995, much to the consternation of the rest of the team. That summer Corky and Miles eloped but, at the end of the 1995–1996 season, Miles was offered a job running a 24-hour news service and was moving to New York to take the job—with Corky staying behind in Washington. That fall Kay Carter-Shepley took over as executive producer of *F.Y.I.* with a take-charge attitude but virtually no experience in news—her most recent show was a daytime game show. Murphy, however, found she had met her match. In October, Phil passed away and the gang bought the place, but after arguing over how it should be run, sold it to his son.

In October 1997, Murphy was diagnosed with breast cancer, and the manner in which she dealt with the surgery and the follow-up treatment was a running story throughout much of the season. In the series' finale on May 18, 1998, there were a number of surprises. Murphy announced she was retiring. Sexy Julia Roberts came to visit *F.Y.I.* and had the hots for Frank, the social wallflower. Phil turned up at the bar—he had faked his death because he knew too much about Whitewater and the CIA had given him a new identity. He was whisked away again when it turned out he knew too much about the Monica Lewinsky situation. While Murphy was on the operating table for exploratory surgery checking out a possible cancer recurrence, her spirit was in heaven having a contentious interview with God (Alan King), who told her not to retire but to continue her work. When Murphy came out of the anesthesia the doctor told her it was only a cyst and she was in the clear. Murphy stayed with the show, and in the last scene at home, Eldin was back. He had returned from Spain after finding out from Avery what had happened to Murphy, and stayed to "touch up" her town house, including painting a mural depicting the breakup of the Soviet Union. Oh, and as for the revolving door at Murphy's secretarial desk, her 93rd and last secretary was played by Bette Midler.

A number of real-life news personalities made appearances, as themselves, on *Murphy Brown*, among them Linda Ellerbee, Connie Chung, Irving R. Levine, Walter Cronkite, Kathleen Sullivan, Larry King, and Paula Zahn.

MURPHY'S LAW (*Detective Drama*)

FIRST TELECAST: *November 2, 1988*

LAST TELECAST: *March 18, 1989*

BROADCAST HISTORY:

Nov 1988, ABC Wed 10:00–11:00
Dec 1988, ABC Sat 8:00–9:00
Jan 1989–Mar 1989, ABC Sat 10:00–11:00

CAST:

Daedelus Patrick Murphy .... George Segal
Kimiko Fannuchi .... Maggie Han
Wesley Harden .... Josh Mostel
Victor Beaudine .... Charles Rocket
Marissa Danforth .... Kim Lankford
Kathleen Danforth .... Sarah Sawataky
Ed .... Serge Houde

THEME:

performed by Al Jarreau

Disheveled, irresponsible insurance investigator D. P. Murphy had made a mess out of his life. He'd survived a bout with the bottle but his divorce had been bitter, and he longed to meet the 8-year-old daughter he'd never seen (he had been denied visitation rights). His job at First Fidelity Insurance was always on the line, and he was constantly harassed by his pompous but spineless boss Wes, who would give him the most rotten, bottom-of-the barrel cases. Murphy would almost blow them but then pull them out of the fire at the last minute, usually doing right in the process. At least he had Kimi, a beautiful Eurasian model whose loft he shared and with whose help he was trying to clean up his act. Victor was Murphy's conniving coworker, Marissa, the ex-wife who hated his guts, and Kathleen, the beloved daughter he finally got to see by the end of the series' brief run.

The series' philosophy was perhaps summed up in the title of one of the later episodes: "When You're Over the Hill, You Pick Up Speed."

MUSCLE (*Situation Comedy*)

FIRST TELECAST: *January 11, 1995*

LAST TELECAST: *May 24, 1995*

BROADCAST HISTORY:

Jan 1995–May 1995, WB Wed 9:30–10:00

CAST:

Jane Atkinson .... Shannon Kenny
Kent Atkinson .... Dan Gauthier
Bronwyn Jones .... Amy Pietz
Cleo (Lorna Louise) .... Wendy Benson
Garnet Hines .... Michael Boatman
Gianni .... Nestor Carbonell
Sam Pippin .... Steve Henneberry
Robert Bingham .... Jerry Levine
Dr. Marshall Gold .... Alan Ruck
Victor .... T. E. Russell
Angela .... Michole White
Dottie Shulman .... Maree Cheatham
Guy De Vore "The Carnivore" .... Brent Hinkley
Phil .... John Putch
Det. Paretti .... Francis X. McCarthy
Date .... Myra Turley
Karen Anders .... Carolyn Laurence
Sue .... Jill T. Klein

Manhattan's Survival Gym provided the setting for this rather mean-spirited spoof of soap operas. Jim Atkinson (Adam West), who had founded the Survival Gym chain of fitness centers, which had grown to 2,500 around the country, dropped dead in the premiere episode of *Muscle* after walking into the sauna and finding his wife, Jane, having sex with his fast-living son, Kent. It turned out Jim had been poisoned, but Kent, who was convinced his stepmother was responsible, was the first one arrested. The other prime suspects were Jane, the bitchy, horny, much younger wife who hoped to inherit Jim's fortune, and Victor, the hardworking gym manager who had been ill treated by his boss. The featured trainers at the gym were Cleo, an aspiring actress who looked and acted angelic but had a hidden past; Gianni, the resident gigolo; down-to-earth Angela, who loved Gianni but had to compete with rich Dottie for his affections; and Sam, the thickly muscled but naive and insecure star trainer.

Among the gym members were Kent's cousin Bronwyn, the beautiful lesbian local TV anchorwoman who, threatened with exposure, came out of the closet while on the air; Garnet, a sleazy grandstanding attorney with an insatiable appetite for publicity; Robert, a former financial manipulator on Wall Street recently released from prison, who hoped to make a new fortune marketing a line of exercise videos starring Sam; and Marshall, Jane's sex-obsessed psychiatrist, who told everyone what his patients had told him in confidence.

MUSEUM OF SCIENCE AND INDUSTRY (*Instruction*)

FIRST TELECAST: *July 30, 1948*
LAST TELECAST: *September 24, 1948*
BROADCAST HISTORY:
Jul 1948–Sep 1948, NBC Fri 8:00–8:30

A live and film program featuring exhibits at a New York City museum.

MUSIC AT THE MEADOWBROOK (*Musical Variety*)

FIRST TELECAST: *May 23, 1953*
LAST TELECAST: *April 19, 1956*
BROADCAST HISTORY:
May 1953–Sep 1953, ABC Sat 7:00–8:00
Oct 1953–Dec 1953, ABC Sat 8:00–9:00
Jan 1956–Apr 1956, ABC Thu 10:00–10:30
HOSTS:
Jimmy Blaine
Bill Williams
Walter Herlihy, and others
REGULAR:
Frank Dailey

This series of band remotes from Frank Dailey's famous Meadowbrook Night Club in Cedar Grove, New Jersey, was reminiscent of radio in the 1930s. In those days the Meadowbrook was one of the chief points of origination for live, nationwide broadcasts by the traveling big bands. In the TV era, however, it—and the big bands—were anachronisms and were televised only briefly, in the 1950s.

In addition to music by a different guest band each week (sometimes one stayed for several weeks), the 1953 series featured a regular college salute, in which students were interviewed and campus talent, such as the glee club, performed. Premiere-night guests in 1953 were Ralph Marterie and His Orchestra, Richard Hayman, and the Douglas Duke Trio. Seen later were such bands as those of Sauter-Finegan, Neal Hefti, Ray McKinley, the Korn Kobblers, Art Mooney, Ralph Flanagan, and King Guion and His Double Rhythm Orchestra, as well as assorted singers, dancers, and other acts.

Jimmy Blaine was the most frequent host in both 1953 and 1956, though others did appear and club owner Frank Dailey also wandered on and off the set.

MUSIC BINGO (*Quiz/Audience Participation*)

FIRST TELECAST: *May 29, 1958*
LAST TELECAST: *September 11, 1958*
BROADCAST HISTORY:
May 1958–Sep 1958, NBC Thu 10:30–11:00
EMCEE:
Johnny Gilbert

Music Bingo was a variation on the highly successful *Name That Tune.* Two contestants would listen to a tune being played and, when the tune was abruptly stopped, would run to an assigned place and push a buzzer. The first one to push the buzzer got the opportunity to identify the song. If correct, the contestant could place his mark—a musical sharp or flat symbol—anyplace on the music bingo board he chose. The first person to successfully complete a bingo, five in a line, was the winner of $500 and would keep facing new contestants until defeated. Three months after the prime-time version left the air, *Music Bingo* returned as an ABC daytime series. The daytime version lasted until January 1960.

MUSIC CITY TONIGHT (*Talk/Variety*)

BROADCAST HISTORY:
The Nashville Network
90 minutes
Produced: *1993–1996*
Premiered: *October 18, 1993*
REGULARS:
Lorianne Crook
Charlie Chase
Buddy Skipper (bandleader)

Lorianne Crook and Charlie Chase were so successful in their TNN talk show *Crook and Chase* (1986–1993) that when veteran host Ralph Emery retired in 1993, the network replaced his *Nashville Now* with this big, glossy, 90-minute nightly variety show starring the pair. C&C were decidedly more contemporary than the somewhat traditional Emery; appearing on their premiere telecast were Garth Brooks, Alan Jackson, and Pam Tillis. Combining glamour (Crook was a Mary Hart lookalike and Chase her suave, mustachioed partner) with undeniable down-home charm, they interviewed the greats of country music and introduced musical performances by a wide range of artists. The series originated live from Nashville, "Music City, U.S.A.," running until January 1996.

MUSIC COUNTRY, see *Dean Martin Presents Music Country*

MUSIC COUNTRY USA (*Musical Variety*)

FIRST TELECAST: *January 17, 1974*
LAST TELECAST: *May 16, 1974*
BROADCAST HISTORY:
Jan 1974–May 1974, NBC Thu 10:00–11:00

The concept of *Music Country USA* was essentially the same as that of *Dean Martin Presents Music Country,* a summer replacement for *The Dean Martin Show.* Country acts performed on the show, which was taped on location in various places around the U.S. There was a different host each week, including Jerry Reed, Lynn Anderson, Marty Robbins, Donna Fargo, Tom T. Hall, Mac Davis, Buck Owens, Wayne Newton, Dionne Warwick, Doug Kershaw, and Charlie Rich. All of them also made frequent appearances as performers on the show.

MUSIC 55 (*Music*)

FIRST TELECAST: *July 12, 1955*
LAST TELECAST: *September 13, 1955*
BROADCAST HISTORY:
Jul 1955–Sep 1955, CBS Tue 8:30–9:00
REGULAR:
Stan Kenton

This live weekly summer music series featured the sounds of Stan Kenton and his band. The repertoire included jazz, standards, and contemporary hits. Stan also played host to weekly guest stars.

MUSIC FOR A SUMMER NIGHT (*Music*)

FIRST TELECAST: *June 3, 1959*
LAST TELECAST: *September 21, 1960*
BROADCAST HISTORY:
Jun 1959–Aug 1959, ABC Wed 7:30–8:30

Feb 1960–Mar 1960, ABC Wed 7:30–8:00
Mar 1960–Sep 1960, ABC Wed 7:30–8:30

REGULAR:
Glenn Osser and His Orchestra

ABC salvaged a bit of the prestige it had lost by canceling the *Voice of Firestone* with this replacement program, produced by the same man (Fred Heidler) and containing approximately the same musical ingredients—but on a much lower budget. Like *Voice, Music for a Summer Night* ranged across the "better" musical idioms, principally Broadway show tunes and the classics. Good but not top-name singers were used, such as Betty Ann Grove, Bill Hayes, and Dorothy Collins. Complete productions of *Madame Butterfly, La Traviata,* and *Tosca* (set in Mussolini's Italy) were aired, along with lighter fare such as a visit to summer theaters and musical festivals around the country. A novel touch was the use of John Hoppe's Mobilux creations to introduce numbers.

When the program returned in February 1960, too early to be classified as a summer show, it was titled *Music for a Spring Night,* reverting to its original title in May. ABC documentary news specials preempted this series on an irregular but frequent basis.

MUSIC FROM CHICAGO (*Music*)

FIRST TELECAST: *April 15, 1951*
LAST TELECAST: *June 17, 1951*
BROADCAST HISTORY:
Apr 1951–Jun 1951, DUM Sun 9:30–10:00

A short-lived music series originating in Chicago, which at the time was a fairly important production center for network programs.

MUSIC FROM MANHATTAN, see *Sammy Kaye Show, The*

MUSIC FROM THE MEADOWBROOK, see *Music at the Meadowbrook*

MUSIC HALL (*Music*)

FIRST TELECAST: *July 1, 1952*
LAST TELECAST: *September 25, 1952*
BROADCAST HISTORY:
Jul 1952–Sep 1952, CBS Tue/Thu 7:45–8:00

REGULARS:
Patti Page
Carl Hoff and His Orchestra

Patti Page was the singing star of this twice-weekly 15-minute music show that filled the remainder of the half-hour in which CBS aired its nightly network news program. The show originated from New York and was telecast live.

MUSIC HALL AMERICA (*Music*)

BROADCAST HISTORY:
Syndicated only
60 minutes
Produced: *1976* (26 episodes)
Released: *Fall 1976*

REGULARS:
Dean Rutherford
Sandi Burnett

Country-flavored musical hour, taped at Opryland U.S.A., in Nashville. There was no regular host, but among those guest-starring were Ray Stevens, Jim Stafford, Pat Boone, Charley Pride, Lynn Anderson, and Bobby Goldsboro. The Statler Brothers and the Oak Ridge Boys made repeat appearances.

MUSIC IN VELVET (*Music*)

FIRST TELECAST: *January 16, 1949*
LAST TELECAST: *October 28, 1951*
BROADCAST HISTORY:
Jan 1949–Apr 1949, ABC Sun 9:30–10:00
Jul 1951–Oct 1951, ABC Sun 7:30–8:00

REGULARS:
Johnny Hill* (1949)
The Velveteers (1949)
Don Lindley Orchestra (1949)
Rex Maupin (1951)

*Also given as Johnny Holt

This was another of the easygoing song-and-dance programs that originated from Chicago during TV's early years, when that city was an important network production center. Baritone Johnny Hill was featured during the 1949 run, and Rex Maupin in 1951.

MUSIC ON ICE (*Musical Variety*)

FIRST TELECAST: *May 8, 1960*
LAST TELECAST: *September 11, 1960*
BROADCAST HISTORY:
May 1960–Sep 1960, NBC Sun 8:00–9:00

REGULARS:
Johnny Desmond
Jacqueline du Bief
Ben Dova
The Skip Jacks
The Dancing Blades
The Bob Boucher Orchestra

The melding of a musical variety hour with an ice show in a weekly series was unique. Not all of the numbers in the series were performed on ice, but there were a number of ice-skating features in each program. Johnny Desmond was the host, the Skip Jacks were the regular vocalists, and the Dancing Blades provided regular precision group skating. Guest singers and ice performers were on each show. Perfect for a warm summer's evening.

MUSIC ROOM, THE, see *Jacques Fray Music Room*

MUSIC SCENE, THE, (*Music*)

FIRST TELECAST: *September 22, 1969*
LAST TELECAST: *January 12, 1970*
BROADCAST HISTORY:
Sep 1969–Jan 1970, ABC Mon 7:30–8:15

HOSTS:
David Steinberg
Larry Hankin
Christopher Ross
Paul Reid Roman
Chris Bokeno
Lily Tomlin
Pat Williams Orchestra

A contemporary popular music program, at first utilizing six rotating hosts, but beginning in November hosted by David Steinberg (and guests) only. Practically every big name in rock music appeared on this short-lived show, with the first telecast alone featuring the Beatles, James Brown, Crosby, Stills, Nash & Young,

Buck Owens, Three Dog Night, Oliver, and Tom Jones. Seen in later telecasts were Janis Joplin, Bobby Sherman, Sly & the Family Stone, Isaac Hayes, Stevie Wonder, Mama Cass, and even Groucho Marx, among others. A special feature was performances of the latest hit songs in various fields, such as rock, rhythm & blues, country & western, and comedy, based on *Billboard* magazine's record popularity charts. An improvisational comedy group was also seen.

MUSIC SHOP, THE (*Musical Variety*)
FIRST TELECAST: *January 11, 1959*
LAST TELECAST: *March 8, 1959*
BROADCAST HISTORY:
Jan 1959–Mar 1959, NBC Sun 7:30–8:00
HOST:
Buddy Bregman

Most of the singers who appeared on this series had currently popular hit songs, with the emphasis on young performers on the way up. In addition to serving as host, Buddy Bregman accompanied on piano those who performed live. However, the majority lip-synched to their hit records. Among those who appeared were Bobby Darin, Ritchie Valens, the Platters, the Teddy Bears, and Annette Funicello, along with an established, older star each week (Milton Berle, Jerry Lewis, etc.) who would chat and perhaps perform. At the end of each show, Buddy announced the top five records of the week.

MUSIC SHOW, THE (*Music*)
FIRST TELECAST: *May 19, 1953*
LAST TELECAST: *October 17, 1954*
BROADCAST HISTORY:
May 1953–Jun 1953, DUM Tue 9:00–9:30
Jul 1953–Oct 1953, DUM Tue 8:30–9:00
Oct 1953–Jan 1954, DUM Wed 10:30–11:00
Jan 1954–Sep 1954, DUM Wed 10:00–10:30
Sep 1954–Oct 1954, DUM Sun 10:00–10:30
REGULARS:
Mike Douglas
Jackie Van
Henri Noel
Eleanor Warner (1953–1954)
Dolores Peterson (1954)
Robert Trendler Orchestra

This Chicago-originated program was exactly as billed—just music, with no frills, no fancy production, and no gimmicks. Four pleasant-voiced singers shared the vocal honors, with Mike Douglas and Jackie Van handling the more popular tunes and Henri Noel and Eleanor Warner (later replaced by Dolores Peterson) the meatier stuff. Repertoire was primarily standards, including medleys from *Carousel, South Pacific,* and other Broadway shows. Robert Trendler's 34-piece orchestra provided lush accompaniment.

MUSICAL ALMANAC (*Music*)
FIRST TELECAST: *May 10, 1948*
LAST TELECAST: *April 30, 1949*
BROADCAST HISTORY:
May 1948–Dec 1948, NBC Mon–Thu Various nights and times between 7:30–8:00
May 1948–Aug 1948, NBC Fri 9:00–9:15
Oct 1948–Dec 1948, NBC Fri 8:00–8:30
Feb 1949–Apr 1949, NBC Various nights 10:00–10:30
EMCEE:
Harvey Harding

For the first few weeks pianist-singer Harvey Harding "and his musical nostalgia" were featured exclusively on this 15–30-minute musical interlude, but later a variety of cabaret talent appeared from night to night. Among those seen were Ted Steele (from WPTZ, Philadelphia), Barbara Marshall, Verle Mills, and Roberta Quinlan. The program wandered all over the prime-time schedule for about a year in 1948–1949. The title was changed to *Musical Miniatures* in August 1948.

Harding was one of TV's pioneers, having had a similar regular weekly series on New York local television from July 1941 to May 1942.

MUSICAL CHAIRS (*Quiz/Audience Participation*)
FIRST TELECAST: *July 9, 1955*
LAST TELECAST: *September 17, 1955*
BROADCAST HISTORY:
Jul 1955–Sep 1955, NBC Sat 9:00–9:30
MODERATOR:
Bill Leyden
PANELISTS:
Mel Blanc
Johnny Mercer
Bobby Troup
SINGERS:
The Cheerleaders

After two years as a local show in Los Angeles, *Musical Chairs* moved to the NBC network for a summer run in 1955. Viewers of this musical quiz show were encouraged to send in questions to test the knowledge of the panel. Those who submitted questions that stumped the panel won a 21-inch RCA TV. There were four panel members: Mel Blanc, actor and impressionist who was most famous for his work as the voice of Bugs Bunny; composer Johnny Mercer; pianist-orchestra leader Bobby Troup (whose band, the Troup Group, provided the music for this series); and a guest panelist. The questions could have anything to do with music, from arranging, to composing, to performing. Members of the panel were often called on to imitate the singing or playing styles of well-known performers and occasionally collaborated on individual answers.

MUSICAL COMEDY TIME (*Musical Comedy*)
FIRST TELECAST: *October 2, 1950*
LAST TELECAST: *March 19, 1951*
BROADCAST HISTORY:
Oct 1950–Mar 1951, NBC Mon 9:30–10:30
REGULARS:
The Ken Christie Singers
The Kevin Jonson Dancers
Harry Sosnik Orchestra

Musical Comedy Time aired on alternate Monday evenings with *Robert Montgomery Presents.* Broadway musical comedies and standard operettas were adapted for presentation as live hour-long TV programs. Among the adaptations were such musical comedies as *Anything Goes* with Martha Raye and John Conte and *No No Nanette* with Jackie Gleason and Anne Crowley, and operettas like *The Merry Widow* with Irra Petina, Wilbur Evans, and Melville Cooper. The principal casts changed from show to show, but the same musical and dance groups were used for all.

MUSICAL MERRY-GO-ROUND (*Music*)
FIRST TELECAST: *July 25, 1947*
LAST TELECAST: *March 11, 1949*
BROADCAST HISTORY:
Jul 1947–Sep 1947, NBC Fri 8:00–8:30
Oct 1947–Jan 1948, NBC Thu 8:00–8:30
Jan 1948–Feb 1948, NBC Fri 7:45–8:00
Feb 1948–Mar 1949, NBC Fri 7:30–7:50
REGULARS:
Jack Kilty
Frederic (Fritz) DeWilde
Eve Young (1947)
Penny Gerard (1948–1949)

One of the earliest regular musical programs on network TV, this extremely simple series was at first called *Disc Magic* and was essentially a disc-jockey show. Viewers watched d.j. Kilty play popular records and occasionally introduce some live entertainment. In 1947, *anything* on the flickering screen seemed interesting to watch. Then in October 1947 the title was changed to *Musical Merry-Go-Round* and the format shifted to live entertainment exclusively, with songs by Kilty and Eve Young (and, later, Penny Gerard), bits by actor Fritz DeWilde, and guest performers. Most of the guests were unknown cabaret talent rather than established stars.

MUSICAL MINIATURES, see *Musical Almanac*

MUTANT X (*Science Fiction*)
BROADCAST HISTORY:
Syndicated only
60 minutes
Produced: *2001–*
Released: *October 2001*
CAST:
Adam Kane .... John Shea
Shalimar Fox "Shadowfox" .... Victoria Pratt
Brennan Mulwray "Fuse" .... Victor Webster
Jesse Kilmartin "Synergy" .... Forbes March
Emma deLauro "Rapport" .... Lauren Lee Smith
Mason Eckhart (2001–2002)........ Tom McCamus

Adam had worked for Genomex on a secret program to develop genetically enhanced humans. Because Mason Eckhart, who ran the company, wanted to control these "mutants" to serve his own purposes, Adam had left and started Mutant X, a group whose function was to help the human mutants—there may have been as many as 1,000 of them—who were the unfortunate results of genetic experimentation gone wrong. The group's base of operations was a hidden high-tech facility called Sanctuary. The mutants Adam recruited to help him were sexy Shalimar, whose cells included animal DNA that gave her abnormal strength, speed and cunning; Brennan, a streetwise hunk who could harness the power of electricity and hurl energy bolts from his hands; Jesse, a gentle guy who could alter his body density from rock hard to so tenuous that he could walk through walls, and Emma, an empath who could both receive and send emotional feelings. Eckhart, whose immune system had been destroyed by the research, had formed the Genetic Security Agency to track down the mutants and force them to serve him.

At the end of the first season Eckhart was captured and imprisoned in a security pod at Genomex, but the Mutant X team was then forced to deal with Gabriel Ashlocke (Michael Easton), a psychopathic supermutant whose powers were much stronger than any of the others. He had been in a security pod since childhood but was freed by another mutant and planned to take over the world. That fall Gabriel found a way to cure the destabilization of his body by his mutant genes, by going back in time and injecting an antidote into his younger self, but the Mutant X team defeated him and he blew up. Afterward the team helped good mutants and protected the unsuspecting public from bad mutants as well as other evil organizations and individuals. In April, however, they found out that Eckhart has escaped and was after them again.

MY ADVENTURES IN TELEVISION, see *Wednesday 9:30 (8:30 Central)*

MY BIG FAT GREEK LIFE (*Situation Comedy*)
FIRST TELECAST: *February 24, 2003*
LAST TELECAST: *April 13, 2003*
BROADCAST HISTORY:
Feb 2003, CBS Mon 9:30–10:00
Mar 2003–Apr 2003, CBS Sun 8:00–8:30
CAST:
Nia Portokalos Miller .... Nia Vardalos
Maria Portokalos .... Lainie Kazan
Gus Portokalos .... Michael Constantine
Thomas Miller .... Steven Eckholdt
Nick Portokalos .... Louis Mandylor
Cousin Nikki .... Gia Carides
Aunt Voula .... Andrea Martin
Little Nia .... Victoria Adams

When Nia returned home to Chicago after her honeymoon to start married life, she found out that her well-meaning but meddlesome family was convinced that she still needed their advice and supervision. Her husband, Thomas, an English teacher working on his dissertation, found them a little hard to take but adapted as best he could. Nia's father, Gus, owned a neighborhood restaurant, Dancing Zorba's, where Nia and most of her family worked. Incredibly patriotic to the land of his birth, Gus attributed everything good and/or important to the Greeks. Maria, her overprotective mother, had a good heart but seemed to worry about everything and laid on guilt with a trowel ("Nia, you're killing your father!"). Nia's marginally competent brother, Nick, worked as a cook at the restaurant and, despite his leather-jacketed macho appearance, was insecure and still living with his parents. Also seen were Nia's flamboyant aunt Voula, who had a solution for every problem, even those that didn't exist, and Nikki, her obnoxious and insensitive daughter, who found fault with everything Nia did. Most of the action took place at Dancing Zorba's, although there were frequent flashbacks showing how Nia's upbringing had affected her as an adult.

My Big Fat Greek Life took up where the 2002 theatrical film *My Big Fat Greek Wedding* left off and with the exception of John Corbett, who had played Thomas in the movie, the entire cast reprised their roles in the TV series.

MY BROTHER AND ME (*Situation Comedy*)
BROADCAST HISTORY:
Nickelodeon
30 minutes
Produced: *1994* (13 episodes)
Premiered: *October 15, 1994*

CAST:

Roger Parker .... Jim R. Coleman
Jennifer Parker .... Karen E. Fraction
Melanie Parker (age 13) .... Aisling Sistrunk
Alfie Parker (11) .... Arthur Reggie III
Dee Dee Parker (8) .... Ralph Woolfolk IV
Milton "Goo" Berry (11) .... Jimmy Lee Newman, Jr.
Harry .... Keith "Bubba" Naylor
Donnell Wilbur .... Stefan J. Wernli
Deonne Wilbur .... Amanda Seales
Mrs. Pinckney .... Kym Whitley

One of the few series on Nickelodeon featuring a black family, *My Brother and Me* depicted life through the eyes of an eight-year-old living in a pleasant suburb of Charlotte, North Carolina. Dee Dee was still at the impressionable "gee whiz!" stage. He worshipped his supercool older brother, Alfie, though both of them were disdained by self-absorbed sister Melanie. Dee Dee's best buddies were Harry and Donnell, while Alfie hung out with chubby Goo, a prankster who frequently got them into trouble while attempting to get himself off the hook by flattering adults. Deonne was Melanie's friend. Jennifer was the Parker kids' mom, a driver's ed teacher; Roger their sports-writer dad; and Mrs. Pinckney the operator of the local comics store, who was all too hip to the kids' tricks.

MY FAVORITE HUSBAND (*Situation Comedy*)

FIRST TELECAST: *September 12, 1953*
LAST TELECAST: *September 8, 1957*
BROADCAST HISTORY:

Sep 1953–Jun 1955, CBS Sat 9:30–10:00 (OS)
Oct 1955–Dec 1955, CBS Tue 10:30–11:00
Jun 1957–Sep 1957, CBS Sun 7:30–8:00

CAST:

George Cooper .... Barry Nelson
Liz Cooper (1953–1955) .... Joan Caulfield
Liz Cooper (1955) .... Vanessa Brown
Myra Cobb/Myra Shepard .... Alix Talton
Gillmore Cobb (1953–1955) .... Bob Sweeney
Oliver Shepard (1955) .... Dan Tobin
Uncle Norman Fildew (1955) .... David Burns

George Cooper was a successful bank executive with a fancy suburban home and a beautiful but scatter-brained wife. Living next door were the Cobbs, Gillmore, the peanut magnate, and Myra, the social snob. The Coopers, though wealthy, were rather unpretentious, and the Cobbs were always trying to get them to improve their social image.

Several changes took place at the start of the third season. Vanessa Brown replaced Joan Caulfield in the role of Liz, the next-door neighbors became the Shepards (with Alix Talton still playing the wife), and there was less emphasis on social status. Despite the changes, the program folded three months later. Reruns of this last group of episodes were aired during the summer of 1957.

My Favorite Husband was based on the 1948 radio series of the same name, which starred Lucille Ball as the nutty housewife Liz (the prototype for her long-running Lucy characterization on TV).

MY FAVORITE MARTIAN (*Situation Comedy*)

FIRST TELECAST: *September 29, 1963*
LAST TELECAST: *September 4, 1966*
BROADCAST HISTORY:

Sep 1963–Sep 1966, CBS Sun 7:30–8:00

CAST:

Uncle Martin (The Martian) .... Ray Walston
Tim O'Hara .... Bill Bixby
Mrs. Lorelei Brown .... Pamela Britton
Angela Brown (1963–1964) .... Ann Marshall
Mr. Harry Burns (1963–1964) .... J. Pat O'Malley
Det. Bill Brennan (1964–1966) .... Alan Hewitt
The Police Chief (1965–1966) .... Roy Engle

On the way to cover an assignment for his paper, *The Los Angeles Sun,* reporter Tim O'Hara stumbled upon a Martian whose one-man ship had crashed on Earth. Tim took the dazed Martian back to his rooming house to help him recuperate, while thinking of the fantastic story he would be able to present to his boss, Mr. Burns, about his find. The Martian, however, looked human, spoke English, and refused to admit to anyone but Tim what he was. Tim befriended him, passed him off as his uncle, and had many an interesting adventure with the stranded alien. Uncle Martin had little retractable antennae, could make himself invisible, was telepathic, could move objects just by pointing at them, and had a vast storehouse of advanced technological knowledge. While he was trying to fix his ship he stayed with Tim in Mrs. Brown's rooming house. During the first season, Mrs. Brown's teenage daughter Angela was a cast regular. The following year policeman Bill Brennan joined the cast as Mrs. Brown's boyfriend, a threat to Uncle Martin on two counts—not only was he always a potential discoverer of the Martian's true identity, but Uncle Martin had become romantically interested in Mrs. Brown himself and looked upon Brennan as a rival for her affections.

MY FRIEND FLICKA (*Adventure*)

FIRST TELECAST: *February 10, 1956*
LAST TELECAST: *May 18, 1958*
BROADCAST HISTORY:

Feb 1956–Feb 1957, CBS Fri 7:30–8:00
Mar 1957, CBS Sat 7:00–7:30
Apr 1957–May 1957, CBS Sun 6:00–6:30
Jun 1957–Aug 1957, CBS Wed 7:30–8:00
Sep 1957–Dec 1957, NBC Sun 6:30–7:00
Jan 1958–May 1958, NBC Sun 7:00–7:30

CAST:

Rob McLaughlin .... Gene Evans
Nell McLaughlin .... Anita Louise
Ken McLaughlin .... Johnny Washbrook
Gus Broeberg .... Frank Ferguson
Hildy Broeberg (1956) .... Pamela Beaird

Set in the ranchlands of Montana around the turn of the century, *My Friend Flicka* was the story of a boy and his horse. Young Ken McLaughlin's best friend was his beloved horse, Flicka. Ken, Flicka, Ken's parents, and ranch hand Gus encountered assorted adventures while struggling to make a living from the land and dealing with their neighbors and friends. Originally aired as a black-and-white series on CBS, this program, which had been filmed in color, was rerun as a color entry on NBC during the following season. *My Friend Flicka* made the complete circuit, with the reruns showing up on ABC as a late-afternoon entry weekdays during the 1959–1960 season. From the fall of 1961 to the fall of 1966 they were on Saturday afternoons; on CBS during the 1961–1962 season; on ABC from September 1962 to December 1963; and back on CBS for two years beginning in September 1964.

Based on the 1943 movie, which had been adapted from the stories of Mary O'Hara.

MY FRIEND IRMA (*Situation Comedy*)

FIRST TELECAST: *January 8, 1952*
LAST TELECAST: *June 25, 1954*
BROADCAST HISTORY:

Jan 1952–Mar 1952, CBS Tue 10:30–11:00
Apr 1952–Jun 1953, CBS Fri 8:30–9:00 (OS)
Oct 1953–Jun 1954, CBS Fri 10:00–10:30

CAST:

Irma Peterson .... Marie Wilson
Jane Stacy (1952–1953) .... Cathy Lewis
Mrs. O'Reilly .... Gloria Gordon
Professor Kropotkin (1952–1953) .... Sig Arno
Al (1952–1953)....................... Sid Tomack
Richard Rhinelander III (1952–1953).... Brooks West
Mrs. Rhinelander (1952–1953)... Margaret Dumont
Mr. Clyde........................... Don McBride
Joe Vance (1953–1954) .... Hal March
Bobby Peterson (1953–1954) .... Richard Eyer
Kay Foster (1953–1954) .... Mary Shipp
Mr. Corday (1953–1954)........... John Carradine

Marie Wilson was TV's—and radio's, and Hollywood's—favorite dumb blonde. She played many similar characters, but her most famous was the title role in *My Friend Irma,* which she created on radio in 1947. Irma Peterson was possibly the kookiest secretary in the entire world. She was friendly, enthusiastic, sexy—and very wacky. She just had no sense of logic. Her roommate was levelheaded Jane Stacy, whose affection for Irma usually overcame the frustrations she met coping with Irma's predicaments. Irma and Jane shared an apartment in Mrs. O'Reilly's run-down Manhattan boardinghouse, where much of the action took place in this live series. Jane's boyfriend was Richard Rhinelander III, her millionaire boss, while Irma's was an impoverished con artist named Al.

When the TV version was added to radio's *My Friend Irma* in 1952, the three female principals—Marie Wilson, Gloria Gordon, and Cathy Lewis—made the transition, with Miss Lewis talking to the audience in the manner of a narrator to set up the scenes as well as participating in them, as she had done on radio. However, the 1953–1954 season brought a number of cast changes. Irma had a new roommate in newspaper reporter Kay Foster (Jane had moved to Panama), her seven-year-old nephew Bobby had come to live with her, and she had a new boyfriend named Joe Vance. Her original nutty neighbor Professor Kropotkin, the violinist at the Paradise Burlesque, was also gone, replaced by an eccentric actor, Mr. Corday. The only original regulars left in the cast were Irma, her landlady Mrs. O'Reilly, and Mr. Clyde, the blustery, cranky attorney for whom she worked.

MY FRIEND TONY (*Detective Drama*)

FIRST TELECAST: *January 5, 1969*
LAST TELECAST: *September 31, 1969*
BROADCAST HISTORY:

Jan 1969–Sep 1969, NBC Sun 10:00–11:00

CAST:

Prof. John Woodruff .... James Whitmore
Tony Novello .... Enzo Cerusico

When he was in Italy shortly after the end of World War II, John Woodruff almost had his wallet stolen by a street urchin named Tony. Years later, a fully grown Tony arrived in America to join John as half of a private-investigation team. Professor Woodruff, whose academic career in criminology had given him the ability to analyze the most obscure clues to resolve cases, needed Tony to do his legwork and handle the physical side of the business. As they traveled around the country on various assignments, the contrast between Woodruff's stolid, conservative, analytical approach and Tony's carefree romanticism provided a contentious but productive relationship.

MY GENERATION (*Quiz/Audience Participation*)

BROADCAST HISTORY:

VH1
30 minutes
Produced: *1998* (48 episodes)
Premiered: *March 8, 1998*

HOST:

Craig Shoemaker

A music-trivia quiz, in which two teams of contestants from different generations, teenagers to forty-somethings, answered questions about their own and the other generation's music. Video clips were interspersed, and there were occasional "celebrity editions" with rock musicians from different eras playing the game.

MY GUIDE TO BECOMING A ROCK STAR (*Situation Comedy*)

FIRST TELECAST: *March 14, 2002*
LAST TELECAST: *March 21, 2002*
BROADCAST HISTORY:

Mar 2002, WB Thu 8:00–9:00

CAST:

Jason "Jace" Darnell .... Oliver Hudson
"Doc" Pike .... Kevin Rankin
Josephine "Joe" Delamo .... Lauren Hodges
Sarah Nelson .... Emmanuelle Vaugier
Eric Darnell................. Michael Des Barres
Gina Darnell..................... Shannon Tweed
Doyle Greyson .... Rick Overton
Danny Whitaker.................. James DeBello
Lucas Zank .... Kris Lemche

In this bizarre sitcom, which must have been inspired either by the movie *Spinal Tap* or by a bad dream, Jace Darnell was the tall, cocky lead singer of the struggling rock band SlipDog. Jace just knew he would become rich and famous in the music business, despite the band's troubles and the lack of support from his father, Eric, an over-the-hill former heavy-metal rock star who still sported shaggy hair and tight pants. (Actor Des Barres was an authentic former rocker, having been in bands including Silverfish and Detective in the 1970s and 1980s.) Other members of SlipDog were Doc, a spaced-out guitarist who made his living as a panhandling "blind" priest, punky bassist Joe, who worked as a guide at a local Seattle science museum, and dumb-jock drummer Danny. In the premiere episode Jace made a deal with thuggish junkyard owner Doyle to be their manager. Jace, who had been living on unemployment insurance for 18 months, also offered Sarah, the sexy lady from the unemployment office, a job with SlipDog as a D.J. and keyboard player. In the second episode Danny was killed in a bizarre touch-football accident—he drowned in a mud puddle—and was replaced with baby-faced, gay Lucas. Jace provided enthusiastic and frenetic narration.

Based on the popular British comedy created by Bryan Elsley. Although 12 half-hour episodes were produced, the WB pulled the plug after only five had aired.

MY GUYS (*Situation Comedy*)

FIRST TELECAST: *April 3, 1996*
LAST TELECAST: *April 10, 1996*
BROADCAST HISTORY:
Apr 1996, CBS Wed 8:30–9:00

CAST:
Sonny Demarco .... Michael Rispoli
Michael Demarco (age 15) .... Michael Damus
Francis Demarco (12) .... Francis Capra
Angela .... Marisol Nichols
Dori .... Sherie Scott
Harvey .... Peter Dobson

Sonny was a widower raising two sons in an apartment on Manhattan's middle-class Upper West Side in this laugh-challenged blue-collar comedy. He made his living running a fledgling limo company for which his greedy friend Harvey was one of the drivers. Inept schemer Michael was infatuated with Angela, the pretty 17-year-old living next door, and Francis, as was too often true of TV sitcom children his age, had more common sense than his father. Sonny got most of his advice on child-rearing from his dumb friend Dori, the waitress at a local diner who wanted to be an actress.

Dismally low ratings prompted CBS to yank *My Guys* from its schedule after only two episodes had aired.

MY HERO (*Situation Comedy*)

FIRST TELECAST: *November 8, 1952*
LAST TELECAST: *August 1, 1953*
BROADCAST HISTORY:
Nov 1952–Apr 1953, NBC Sat 7:30–8:00
Apr 1953–Aug 1953, NBC Sat 8:00–8:30

CAST:
Robert S. Beanblossom .... Robert Cummings
Julie Marshall .... Julie Bishop
Willis Thackery .... John Litel

Robert S. Beanblossom was a real estate salesman for the Thackery Realty Company. He was not a particularly good salesman, and his carefree attitude tended to create problems, but he was very lucky. In each episode of this filmed series he somehow managed to stumble through a proposed real-estate deal and come out a winner. His luck was helped along by the office secretary, Julie Marshall, who went out of her way to straighten out his mistakes and protect him from the wrath of the boss, Willis Thackery.

MY LIFE AND TIMES (*Drama*)

FIRST TELECAST: *April 24, 1991*
LAST TELECAST: *May 30, 1991*
BROADCAST HISTORY:
Apr 1991–May 1991, ABC Wed 9:30–10:00
May 1991, ABC Thu 9:00–10:00

CAST:
Ben Miller .... Tom Irwin
Rebecca Miller .... Helen Hunt
Susan .... Megan Mullally
Daniel Miller .... Tim Stack
Robert Miller .... Matt McGrath
Jessie (young) .... Claudia Christian
Jessie (old) .... Harriet Meden

In this wistful, offbeat series set in the year 2035, an 85-year-old man looked back on his life and loves from his rocker at the Briars Retirement Retreat. Ben had been a journalist, and his recollections (one of which was dramatized in each episode) served to comment rather pretentiously on events of the late twentieth century—the 1989 San Francisco earthquake, the 1976 Bicentennial, the stock market crash of 1987 (and the "greedy 1980s"), and the Great Depression of 1998, all seen from an ordinary person's point of view. Rebecca was his now-senile wife, Susan, a young aide at the retirement home ("now get your rest, Mr. Miller"), and Jessie, his lost love.

MY LIFE IS A SITCOM (*Comedy Reality*)

BROADCAST HISTORY:
ABC Family Channel
30 minutes
Original episodes: *2003–*
Premiered: *January 20, 2003*

JUDGES:
Dave Coulier
David Faustino
Maureen McCormick

The reality craze of the early 2000s produced some strange permutations, none stranger than this one in which real families auditioned to become the basis of a TV sitcom. Out of hundreds of audition tapes, the producers chose eight families to compete. A full episode was then devoted to each one, with a camera crew and a professional sitcom writer following the family members around during their daily lives, recording their interactions and exploits. The first episode featured the Mozian family of Greenwich, Connecticut, and centered mostly on chubby, goofball Dad, his adorable kids and his French mother-in-law. At the end of each episode a panel of three judges, all former sitcom stars, discussed the family's potential and decided whether they should stay in the competition. The eventual winners were the happy, chubby Zaccagnino sisters of Elmwood Park, Illinois, Diane (who was afraid of driving), Karen (the hairdresser) and Camille (who was obsessed with the dead). Their prize—they got to star in a professionally scripted sitcom pilot to be shot in front of a live studio audience, for possible network pickup.

MY LITTLE MARGIE (*Situation Comedy*)

FIRST TELECAST: *June 16, 1952*
LAST TELECAST: *August 24, 1955*
BROADCAST HISTORY:
Jun 1952–Sep 1952, CBS Mon 9:00–9:30
Oct 1952–Nov 1952, NBC Sat 7:30–8:00
Jan 1953–Jul 1953, CBS Thu 10:00–10:30
Sep 1953–Aug 1955, NBC Wed 8:30–9:00

CAST:
Margie Albright .... Gale Storm
Vernon Albright .... Charles Farrell
Roberta Townsend .... Hillary Brooke
Freddie Wilson .... Don Hayden
Mr. George Honeywell .... Clarence Kolb
Mrs. Odetts .... Gertrude W. Hoffman
Charlie .... Willie Best

Vern Albright was a very eligible widower whose 21-

year-old daughter was determined to save him from the machinations of various women. An executive with the investment-counseling firm of Honeywell and Todd, Vern was trimly athletic at age 50, and was most often romantically linked with Roberta Townsend. Margie, who shared her father's Fifth Avenue apartment, was always scheming with old Mrs. Odetts, the next-door neighbor, to make Dad more sedate, as well as to circumvent the parental control he vainly tried to maintain over her. Also recruited to help with various subterfuges were Margie's boyfriend, Freddie, and Charlie, the combination handyman and elevator operator in the Albrights' apartment building.

In a somewhat unusual move, *My Little Margie* went from TV to radio in December 1952, airing concurrently on the CBS radio network for the rest of its TV run (not in simulcasts, but in different original episodes). Gale Storm and Charles Farrell also played the leads in the radio version.

MY LIVING DOLL (*Situation Comedy*)

FIRST TELECAST: *September 27, 1964*
LAST TELECAST: *September 8, 1965*
BROADCAST HISTORY:

Sep 1964–Dec 1964, CBS Sun 9:00–9:30
Dec 1964–Sep 1965, CBS Wed 8:00–8:30

CAST:

Dr. Robert McDonald .... Robert Cummings
Rhoda Miller .... Julie Newmar
Peter Robinson .... Jack Mullaney
Irene Adams .... Doris Dowling

This comedy introduced the ultimate in male fantasy, a sexy, curvaceous, female robot programmed to do anything she was told—absolutely anything. AF 709 was the secret project number that designated this ultimate achievement in space-age technology, a robot that could think on its own and function like a man—well, like a woman. Statuesque Julie Newmar played the robot. She wandered into the office of base psychiatrist Robert McDonald one day and had a pleasant chat with him. Only later did he find out that she was a robot designed by Dr. Carl Miller. When Dr. Miller was called away on assignment to Pakistan he left the robot in Bob's care. Bob named her Rhoda and passed her off as Dr. Miller's niece. She moved into his home, where Bob took on the task of training her to be the "perfect" woman—one that only talked when spoken to, and did what was asked of her. To complicate things, Bob's neighbor Peter fell in love with Rhoda and had to be fended off lest he discover her secret.

Cummings abruptly left the show in January, with five episodes still to be filmed. In the story line, Dr. McDonald was transferred to Pakistan to join Dr. Miller, and Peter, who had accidentally discovered that Rhoda was a robot, took over as her caretaker.

MY MOTHER THE CAR (*Situation Comedy*)

FIRST TELECAST: *September 14, 1965*
LAST TELECAST: *September 6, 1966*
BROADCAST HISTORY:

Sep 1965–Sep 1966, NBC Tue 7:30–8:00

CAST:

Dave Crabtree .... Jerry Van Dyke
His Mother's Voice .... Ann Sothern
Barbara Crabtree .... Maggie Pierce
Cindy Crabtree .... Cindy Eilbacher
Randy Crabtree .... Randy Whipple
Capt. Manzini .... Avery Schreiber

In what was surely one of her more unusual roles, Ann Sothern played a talking car in this 1965 comedy. Dave Crabtree was a small-town lawyer of modest means with a wife (Barbara), two children (Cindy and Randy), and a small dog. On a visit to a used-car lot in search of an inexpensive secondhand car he found himself strangely attracted to an ancient 1928 Porter. When he got behind the wheel, the car talked to him, informing him that it was the reincarnation of his mother. Against the advice of family and friends he bought the car, because he didn't want to lose "Mother." Dave was the only one whom the car would talk to, or who could really hear what it had to say. The "villain" in the series was Capt. Manzini, an antique car collector who was constantly trying to find a way to get the Porter away from Dave.

MY SECRET IDENTITY (*Situation Comedy*)

BROADCAST HISTORY:

Syndicated only
30 minutes
Produced: *1988–1991* (72 episodes)
Released: *October 1988*

CAST:

Andrew Clements (age 14) .... Jerry O'Connell
Dr. Benjamin Jeffcoate .... Derek McGrath
Mrs. Stephanie Clements .... Wanda Cannon
Erin Clements .... Marsha Moreau
**Mrs. Ruth Shellenbach (1989–1991)* .... Elizabeth Leslie
Kirk Stevens (1989–1991) .... Christopher Bolton

*Occasional

This series was the ideal vehicle to attract a young audience of daydreamers. Andrew Clements was a teenager who had been exposed to radiation from an experiment conducted by his brilliant, but eccentric (is there any other kind?) scientist neighbor, Dr. Jeffcoate. The exposure left Andrew with a number of comic-book superhero powers—he was superfast, superstrong, impervious to injury, and able to fly (albeit slowly with the aid of a couple of aerosol cans). In his diary, Andrew dubbed his alter ego "Ultraman," although he had no costume and did his superdeeds in street clothes when nobody could see him. Only his buddy Dr. Jeffcoate, who was always working on some brilliant new invention, knew about Andrew's powers. Dr. Jeffcoate was constantly reminding Andrew to only use his powers for good and not to take advantage of them. Despite being a "normal" student at Briarwood High School, in Briarwood, North Dakota, Andrew did have occasion to thwart criminals, embarrass bullies, and bail out Dr. Jeffcoate whenever one of his inventions went haywire. Andrew's widowed mother, who sold real estate, and his kid sister Erin were unaware of his "secret identity."

Over time, the focus of the series shifted from Andrew's superpowers to more traditional personal relationships. High school life, and particularly Andrew's buddy Kirk, became more prominent, as did Dr. Jeffcoate's relationships with Mrs. Clements, to whom he was increasingly attracted, and his pushy neighbor Mrs. Shellenbach.

Filmed in Canada.

MY SISTER EILEEN (*Situation Comedy*)

FIRST TELECAST: *October 5, 1960*
LAST TELECAST: *April 12, 1961*
BROADCAST HISTORY:
Oct 1960–Apr 1961, CBS Wed 9:00–9:30
CAST:
Ruth Sherwood .... Elaine Stritch
Eileen Sherwood .... Shirley Bonne
Mr. Appopoplous .... Leon Belasco
Chick Adams .... Jack Weston
Bertha .... Rose Marie
Mr. Beaumont .... Raymond Bailey
Marty Scott .... Stubby Kaye

Ruth and Eileen Sherwood moved to New York from Ohio in order to further their careers, Ruth as a writer and her younger sister as an aspiring actress. They moved into a Manhattan brownstone, found an agent named Chuck Adams to help them get work, and tried to adjust to life in the big city. Ruth was more serious, more ambitious, and much more sensible than her beautiful younger sister. She got a job working for Mr. Beaumont, a publisher, and made a good friend of her co-worker Bertha. Eileen, on the other hand, was a sucker for every con man and would-be boyfriend who came along. Her life was full of all kinds of propositions, but few real jobs. Ruth spent much of her time trying to watch over her kid sister.

Based on a book by Ruth McKinley and two movies (1942 and 1955) derived from it.

MY SISTER SAM (*Situation Comedy*)

FIRST TELECAST: *October 6, 1986*
LAST TELECAST: *April 12, 1988*
BROADCAST HISTORY:
Oct 1986–Sep 1987, CBS Mon 8:30–9:00
Sep 1987–Nov 1987, CBS Sat 8:00–8:30
Mar 1986–Apr 1988, CBS Tue 9:00–9:30
CAST:
Samantha "Sam" Russell .... Pam Dawber
Patti Russell .... Rebecca Schaeffer
J.D. Lucas .... Joel Brooks
Dixie Randazzo .... Jenny O'Hara
Jack Kincaid .... David Naughton
THEME:
"Room Enough for Two," sung by Kim Carnes

Perky Samantha Russell was 29 years old and her career as a freelance commercial photographer in San Francisco was starting to jell. She had a committed, if somewhat fast-talking, agent in J.D. Lucas and a loyal assistant in outspoken Dixie Randazzo. Then her 16-year-old sister, Patti, arrived to take up residence with Sam in the apartment that doubled as her studio. Patti, who reminded Sam of the free spirit she had been as a teenager, was still in high school, and her presence created a number of problems for her older sister. It got in the way of Sam's social life and caused her to wonder about whether she should treat Patti like a sister, a friend, or a daughter—a conflict she never quite resolved. Living across the hall was Sam's good friend Jack Kincaid, a highly successful, globe-trotting photojournalist who provided emotional support when she needed it.

MY SO-CALLED LIFE (*Drama*)

FIRST TELECAST: *August 25, 1994*
LAST TELECAST: *January 26, 1995*
BROADCAST HISTORY:
Aug 1994–Jan 1995, ABC Thu 8:00–9:00
CAST:
Patty Chase .... Bess Armstrong
Graham Chase .... Tom Irwin
Angela Chase (age 15) .... Claire Danes
Danielle Chase (10) .... Lisa Wilhoit
Rayanne Graff .... A. J. Langer
Rickie Vasquez .... Wilson Cruz
Brian Krakow .... Devon Gummersall
Jordan Catalano .... Jared Leto
Sharon Cherski .... Devon Odessa

"School is a battlefield for your heart," narrated tormented teen Angela. "You are lucky to get out alive." Many adults found this teenage version of *Thirtysomething* (from the same producers) equally whiny and melodramatic, but teens and critics embraced it as one of the best new series of the 1994–1995 season. Angela's life had always been safe and predictable. Among its inhabitants were middle-class mom Patty, easygoing dad Graham, cheery little sis Danielle, best friend ("forever!") Sharon, goofy would-be boyfriend Brian (to whom she paid little attention), and dreamboat Jordan (who paid little attention to her). So far, *The Donna Reed Show.*

But this was the nineties, and Angela was just, you know, so *tormented.* She had to be "me." So she dumped "forever" friends and began walking the wild side with new best friend Rayanne (a drug-sampling, boy-sampling, counterculture type who even the producers admitted was "headed for serious trouble") and androgynous Rickie, a sweet boy from an abusive family who hung out in the girls' bathroom. With them she had close encounters with drugs, sex, violence, and the social underside, though she never quite went over the edge.

Needless to say, Angela's parents were distraught, especially uptight Patty, who snapped at her constantly. Nevertheless, Mom could come through in a pinch, as when only she had the presence of mind to save Rayanne's life when the latter OD'd. Fissures showed in the Chase marriage as well. Businesswoman Patty was noticeably more successful than failed-chef Graham, and Graham in turn was growing more distant from his rapidly maturing daughter ("My breasts have come between us," moaned Angela). Goofy Brian proved to have a sad home life, and Jordan—something was strange about him. *Donna Reed,* meet Kafka.

MY SON JEEP (*Situation Comedy*)

FIRST TELECAST: *July 4, 1953*
LAST TELECAST: *September 22, 1953*
BROADCAST HISTORY:
Jul 1953–Aug 1953, NBC Sat 7:30–8:00
Sep 1953, NBC Tue 8:00–8:30
CAST:
Dr. Robert Allison .... Jeffrey Lynn
Jeep Allison .... Martin Huston
Peggy Allison .... Betty Lou Keim
Barbara Miller .... Anne Sargent
Mrs. Bixby .... Leona Powers
Tommy Clifford .... William Lally
Boots .... Richard Wigginton

Grove Falls, U.S.A., was the setting for this live situation comedy that aired during the summer of 1953. "Jeep" Allison was 10 years old and lived with his 13-year-old sister Peggy and their widowed father, Robert. Robert, a physician, tried to be both mother and father to his two children but found them, particularly Jeep, almost too much to handle. The housekeeper, Mrs. Bixby, attempted to maintain some semblance of order at home while Dr. Allison was at the office. Beautiful Barbara Miller, a substitute teacher who also worked part-time as receptionist for Dr. Allison, was the romantic interest, primarily because Jeep liked her and tried to get his father interested in her in more than just a professional manner.

MY TALK SHOW (*Situation Comedy/Talk*)

BROADCAST HISTORY:

Syndicated only
30 minutes
Produced: *1990* (65 episodes)
Released: *September 1990*

CAST:

Jennifer Bass .... Cynthia Stevenson
Angela Davenport .... Stephanie Hodge
Marty Dissler .... David Packer
Mrs. Battle .... Josephine Hinds
Anne Marie Snelling............... Debra McGrath
Bucky Fergus.......................... Ron James
D. A. Young............................. Himself
Valerie .... Betsy Townsend

My Talk Show was a short-lived attempt to recreate the feel of one of the most bizarre shows of the 1970s, *Fernwood Tonight.* Set in fictional Derby, Wisconsin (the hat capital of the world), the series took place in the living room of Jennifer Bass, whose local cable TV talk show had just gone into national syndication. A live "living room audience" watched from bleacher-type benches.

Jennifer's co-hosts were her best friend and next door neighbor Angela, and her obnoxious brother-in-law Marty, who lived in a trailer parked in her driveway. Other regulars were Mrs. Battle, the organist whose feet were always killing her; Bucky, an opinionated paramedic who often wandered in during the middle of the show; and Anne Marie, the pretentious star and owner of the Top Hat Dinner Theater. Guests included real personalities such as Morton Downey, Jr., Jackie Collins, Jim Belushi, Nell Carter, Robert Goulet, Dr. Joyce Brothers, Jerry Mathers, and Mr. T, along with a parade of actors portraying local citizens and eccentrics.

Low ratings prompted ongoing changes. The original practice of having members of the studio audience serve as announcers at the opening of the show was dropped. Elderly Mrs. Battle was replaced by young hip D. A. Young (who had composed an upbeat replacement for the show's instrumental theme song), and even star Cynthia Stevenson was dumped. In the story line, Jennifer left the show when her estranged husband returned to Derby to take her away with him. Before leaving, Jennifer sold her house, furnishings, and TV show to Anne Marie (portrayed by series cocreator and writer Debra McGrath), who continued to broadcast *My Talk Show* from what was now her living room. The only surviving regular was Bucky, who was joined by Valerie, a young TV trainee with ambitions of replacing Anne Marie. None of the changes helped the show attract more viewers, and it was out of production before the end of the year.

MY THREE SONS (*Situation Comedy*)

FIRST TELECAST: *September 29, 1960*
LAST TELECAST: *August 24, 1972*

BROADCAST HISTORY:

Sep 1960–Sep 1963, ABC Thu 9:00–9:30
Sep 1963–Sep 1965, ABC Thu 8:30–9:00
Sep 1965–Aug 1967, CBS Thu 8:30–9:00
Sep 1967–Sep 1971, CBS Sat 8:30–9:00
Sep 1971–Dec 1971, CBS Mon 10:00–10:30
Jan 1972–Aug 1972, CBS Thu 8:30–9:00

CAST:

Steve Douglas .... Fred MacMurray
Mike Douglas (1960–1965) .... Tim Considine
Robbie Douglas (1960–1971) .... Don Grady
Chip Douglas .... Stanley Livingston
Michael Francis "Bub" O'Casey (1960–1965)
.... William Frawley
Uncle Charley O'Casey (1965–1972)
.... William Demarest
Jean Pearson (1960–1961) .... Cynthia Pepper
Mr. Henry Pearson (1960–1961)...... Robert P. Lieb
Mrs. Florence Pearson (1960–1961)
.... Florence MacMichael
Hank Ferguson (1961–1963) .... Peter Brooks
Sudsy Pfeiffer (1961–1963) .... Ricky Allen
Mrs. Pfeiffer (1961–1963) .... Olive Dunbar
Mr. Pfeiffer (1961–1963)................ Olan Soule
Sally Ann Morrison Douglas (1963–1965)
.... Meredith MacRae
Ernie Thompson Douglas (1963–1972)
.... Barry Livingston
Katie Miller Douglas (1967–1972) .... Tina Cole
Dave Welch (1965–1967)............... John Howard
Dodie Harper Douglas (1969–1972)...... Dawn Lyn
Barbara Harper Douglas (1969–1972)
.... Beverly Garland
Steve Douglas Jr. (1970–1972)........ Joseph Todd
Charley Douglas (1970–1972)....... Michael Todd
Robbie Douglas II (1970–1972) .... Daniel Todd
Fergus McBain Douglas (1971–1972)
.... Fred MacMurray
Terri Dowling (1971–1972)........... Anne Francis
Polly Williams Douglas (1970–1972)
.... Ronne Troup

THEME:

"Theme from *My Three Sons,*" by Frank DeVol

This long-running family comedy had a Disney flavor to it. Fred MacMurray and Tim Considine had starred together in the hit Disney movie *The Shaggy Dog,* and Don Grady was a former *Mickey Mouse Club* mouseketeer. Even little Stanley Livingston was a show-business veteran, having appeared in several episodes of *The Adventures of Ozzie & Harriet.*

The "family" in this case was all-male. Steve Douglas, a consulting aviation engineer, lived with his children at 837 Mill St. in a medium-sized Midwestern city. A widower, he seemed to spend more time raising his three sons than he did at his job, what with the usual growing pains of boys just beginning to date, going on camping trips, and the other "adventures" of middle-class suburbia. Steve also spent a good deal of time fending off attractive women, who wanted to marry him and take over that lovable, ready-made family. Steve's father-in-law was "Bub" O'Casey, a lovable old coot who lived with them and served as a kind of housekeeper to the clan. When he left after five seasons to take a trip to Ireland (William Frawley, seriously ill, left midway through the 1964–1965 season), he was replaced by his brother, Uncle Charley, a retired sailor whose crusty disposition masked a soft heart. Others joining the cast in the early years were Sally, Mike's girlfriend and later fiancée (the first serious romance he had had since his infatuation with the "girl next door," Jean Pearson); Robbie's friend Hank; and Chip's pals Sudsy Pfeiffer and Ernie Thompson. Tramp was the family dog.

When the series began in 1960, the boys were aged 18 (Mike), 14 (Robbie), and 7 (Chip). By the start of the 1965–1966 season when the show moved from ABC to CBS, Tim Considine had grown out of the role as oldest son and wanted out of the series. In the first CBS episode, Mike and Sally got married and moved east so that he might accept a job teaching psychology on the college level. To reestablish the "three sons," Steve subsequently adopted the orphaned Ernie. Things went along much as before for the next two seasons.

In the fall of 1967, Steve moved the family from the Midwest to North Hollywood, California, where his job had taken him. Although the adjustment was not completely pleasant—many of the Douglases' new acquaintances were not too friendly at first—there were good sides to the move. Robbie fell in love with Katie Miller, one of his fellow students at college, and their romance blossomed into marriage before the end of the season. (Katie was played by actress Tina Cole, who had been seen, over the previous few seasons, in a number of "high school girl" roles on *My Three Sons.*) In the fall of 1968, the newlyweds discovered that Katie was pregnant and during that season she gave birth to triplets, Steve, Jr., Charley, and Robbie II—three sons, of course. In 1969, new love finally came to father Steve in the person of widow Barbara Harper, one of Ernie's teachers. They were married during the season and Barbara's young daughter, Dodie, joined the family. Even Chip (who was by now 17) got into the act, eloping with his college girlfriend, Polly Williams, in the fall of 1970.

As if the sprawling family had not gotten big enough already, Steve's cousin, Fergus McBain Douglas, arrived in the fall of 1971 in search of a wife to take back home to Scotland. A nobleman in his native land, Lord Fergus fell in love with cocktail waitress Terri Dowling. She felt inadequate to go back to Scotland as royalty, but was eventually persuaded.

In its later years, as the size of the family on *My Three Sons* grew and separated into individual households, episodes could no longer include the entire group. More and more often, they dealt with the specific problems of only a part of the large cast of regulars, with different members taking the spotlight from week to week.

From December 1971 until a few weeks after the series ended its prime-time run, CBS ran repeat episodes in its daytime lineup.

MY TRUE STORY (*Dramatic Anthology*)

FIRST TELECAST: *May 5, 1950*
LAST TELECAST: *September 22, 1950*
BROADCAST HISTORY:

May 1950–Jun 1950, ABC Fri 8:30–9:00
Jun 1950–Sep 1950, ABC Fri 8:00–8:30

Early television, hungry for inexpensive material, tapped many sources. These romantic dramas were based on first-person stories from the pages of *My True Story* magazine. Examples: the conflict in a woman's mind when she must decide whether to marry for money or love; a forgotten actress makes a comeback and then dies; a man-hungry blonde's predicament.

MY TWO DADS (*Situation Comedy*)

FIRST TELECAST: *September 20, 1987*
LAST TELECAST: *June 16, 1990*
BROADCAST HISTORY:

Sep 1987–Feb 1988, NBC Sun 8:30–9:00
Jun 1988–Sep 1988, NBC Sun 8:30–9:00
Jan 1989–Jun 1989, NBC Wed 9:30–10:00
Jul 1989, NBC Sat 8:00–8:30
Aug 1989–Nov 1989, NBC Sun 8:30–9:00
Nov 1989–Jan 1990, NBC Wed 9:30–10:00
Mar 1990–Apr 1990, NBC Mon 8:00–8:30
Jun 1990, NBC Sat 8:00–8:30

CAST:

Michael Taylor .... Paul Reiser
Joey Harris .... Greg Evigan
Nicole Bradford .... Staci Keanan
Judge Margaret Wilbur .... Florence Stanley
Ed Klawicki (1987–1989) .... Dick Butkus
Cory Kupkus .... Vonni Ribisi
Zach Nichols (1989–1990) .... Chad Allen
Shelby Haskell (1989–1990) .... Amy Hathaway
Julian (1989–1990) .... Don Yesso

THEME:

composed and performed by Greg Evigan

Another of TV's ad-hoc families. This one had two young single men, uptight yuppie financial advisor Michael and free-spirited artist Joey, sharing a daughter. The two men had competed for the love of the same woman 13 years before, but had ultimately broken up with her—and parted enemies. Now, after years with no contact, they learned that their ex-flame had died and left them joint custody of her plucky 12-year-old daughter, Nicole. One of them was the father, but nobody knew which one. Putting their obvious lifestyle differences aside, they moved into Joey's artist's flat (filled with campy pop art) and set about child-rearing by comic compromise. Keeping an eye on things was Judge Wilbur, the sarcastic judge who had awarded them custody and who also happened to own the building. Awkward Cory and handsome Zack were Nicole's boyfriends, and Shelby her worldly best friend. Klawicki ran the local diner.

MY WIFE AND KIDS (*Situation Comedy*)

FIRST TELECAST: *March 28, 2001*
LAST TELECAST:
BROADCAST HISTORY:

Mar 2001–May 2001, ABC Wed 8:00–8:30
Jun 2001, ABC Tue 9:30–10:00
Jul 2001– , ABC Wed 8:00–8:30
Mar 2002, ABC Mon 8:00–8:30
Jul 2002–Sep 2002, ABC Wed 8:30–9:00

CAST:

Michael Kyle .... Damon Wayans
Janet Kyle .... Tisha Campbell-Martin
Michael Kyle, Jr. ("Junior") .... George O. Gore II
Claire Kyle (age 12) (2001) .... Jazz Raycole
Claire Kyle .... Jennifer Nicole Freeman
Kady Kyle (5) .... Parker McKenna Posey

Edgy comic Damon Wayans played the unlikely role of a "Mr. Mom" in this family sitcom, which was saved from terminal blandness both by him (a tall, shaven-headed Mr. Mom?) and the fact that this picture-perfect suburban family, with its neat colonial house and white picket fence, was black. Michael was the successful owner of a delivery service in the leafy suburb of Stamford, Connecticut, who apparently didn't have to work much and got to stay home with the kids while his businesslike wife Janet pursued her new career as a stockbroker. Truck fleets and stocks were one thing, but the kids were something else: rap-loving, rebellious but slightly dense teenager Junior ("Yo, Mom"), self-absorbed middle kid Claire ("Make him stop!") and wisecracking cutie Kady ("eeek!"). They all learned little lessons about growing up while Michael mugged, tried to deal with role reversal and tried to educate the kids about the things that mattered in life, like Michael Jackson and Marvin Gaye. They groaned.

MY WILDEST DREAMS (*Situation Comedy*)

FIRST TELECAST: *May 28, 1995*
LAST TELECAST: *June 25, 1995*
BROADCAST HISTORY:
May 1995–June 1995, FOX Sun 9:30–10:00

CAST:
Lisa McGinnis .... Lisa Ann Walter
Jack McGinnis .... John Posey
Danny McGinnis (age 7)............. Evan Bonifant
Gloria James .... Kelly Bishop
Stephanie James .... Mary Jo Keenen
Chandler Trapp............... Miquel A. Nunez, Jr.

Standup comedienne Lisa Ann Walter starred in this show about a working mother with stars in her eyes and an obsession with looking young and sexy. Loud Lisa worked at the Mound of Sound recording studio where Chandler was the owner/engineer doing dumb commercials. She had fantasies about being a rock star but had to deal with the unfortunate realities of life: she was unlikely to get that big break, and after eight years of marriage, had a family to take care of. She and Jack, who ran a struggling sporting goods store, had a son, Danny, and a 4-month-old infant daughter, Delilah. They lived in suburban New Jersey. Gloria was Lisa's crabby mother, and Stephanie her cheery younger sister.

MY WORLD AND WELCOME TO IT (*Situation Comedy*)

FIRST TELECAST: *September 15, 1969*
LAST TELECAST: *September 7, 1972*
BROADCAST HISTORY:
Sep 1969–Sep 1970, NBC Mon 7:30–8:00
Jun 1972–Sep 1972, CBS Thu 8:00–8:30

CAST:
John Monroe .... William Windom
Ellen Monroe .... Joan Hotchkis
Lydia Monroe........................ Lisa Gerritsen
Hamilton Greeley.................. Harold J. Stone
Philip Jensen........................ Henry Morgan

My World and Welcome To It was loosely based on the works of the late James Thurber. John Monroe was a writer and cartoonist whose overly active imagination was often as much of a problem as a blessing. As with most Thurber men, John was vaguely unsatisfied with his work, concerned about the direction his life was taking, and mortified by women. In his imaginary secret world he was king, but in real life he was somewhat dominated by his wife and terrified by his daughter. He would constantly muse about the predatory nature of women and was convinced that their sole function was to make his life miserable. Each episode opened with John making observations on a given situation before walking into an animated Thurberlike home in which his wife was reaching around to devour him. The use of Thurberlike cartoons to picture John's fears, as well as his dream world, gave this series a pleasant aspect of fantasy. Other than John's wife, Ellen, and daughter, Lydia, the only two regulars were his publisher, Hamilton Greeley, and cynical fellow writer Philip Jensen. In the summer of 1972 CBS reran episodes of the original NBC series.

MYSTERIES OF CHINATOWN (*Crime Drama*)

FIRST TELECAST: *December 4, 1949*
LAST TELECAST: *October 23, 1950*
BROADCAST HISTORY:
Dec 1949–May 1950, ABC Sun 9:30–10:00
May 1950–Sep 1950, ABC Sun 9:00–9:30
Sep 1950, ABC Tue 8:30–9:00
Oct 1950, ABC Mon 8:30–9:00

CAST:
Dr. Yat Fu............................. Marvin Miller

ALSO:
Robert Bice
Cy Kendall
Ed MacDonald

Marvin Miller portrayed Dr. Yat Fu, proprietor of an herb and curio shop in San Francisco's Chinatown, and an amateur sleuth of some note. The program originated in Hollywood and was seen in the East via kinescope.

MYSTERIOUS WAYS (*Supernatural*)

FIRST TELECAST: *July 24, 2000*
LAST TELECAST:
BROADCAST HISTORY:
Jul 2000–Sep 2000, NBC Mon 8:00–9:00
Aug 2000–Aug 2001, PAX Tue 8:00–9:00
Sep 2000–Jul 2001, PAX Sat 10:00–11:00
Jan 2001, NBC Mon 8:00–9:00
Jul 2001–Aug 2001, NBC Fri 8:00–9:00
Aug 2001–Dec 2001, PAX Tue 9:00–10:00
Sep 2001–Dec 2001, PAX Sun 10:00–11:00
Dec 2001–Sep 2002, PAX Tue 8:00–9:00
Dec 2001–Mar 2002, PAX Sun 11:00–Midnight
Mar 2002–Apr 2002, PAX Fri 9:00–10:00
May 2002–Sep 2002, PAX Sun 11:00–Midnight
Sep 2002–Dec 2002, PAX Sat 11:00–Midnight
Jul 2003– , PAX Tue 8:00–9:00

CAST:
Declan Dunn .... Adrian Pasdar
Peggy Fowler .... Rae Dawn Chong
Miranda Finkelstein .... Alisen Down

Declan was an earnest, quiet anthropologist whose hobby was investigating "miraculous phenomena"—which did not endear him to the dean of Northern Oregon University, where he taught. Several years earlier he had miraculously survived being buried in an avalanche, and that experience had motivated him to search for "proof" of other miracles. In the series premiere he investigated the case of a boy who had apparently been saved by a ghost after drowning under the ice in a frozen pond. Peggy, a nonbelieving psychiatrist affiliated with the hospital in which the boy had revived, subsequently worked with Declan on his investigations. Her skepticism came from the death of her husband, who had been hit by a drunk driver and died, despite her prayers for his recovery. Declan's graduate assistant, Miranda, helped with the research and legwork. Sometimes they found logical explanations for the miracles and sometimes they were left confounded.

Mysterious Ways was originally scheduled to premiere on Pax in August 2000, but NBC picked it up as a summer series and ran it for a month before the first Pax episode aired. Episodes that had been seen on Pax were later rerun on NBC in 2001.

MYSTERY FILES OF SHELBY WOO (*Adventure*)

BROADCAST HISTORY:

Nickelodeon
30 minutes
Produced: *1996–1999* (41 episodes)
Premiered: *March 17, 1996*

CAST:

Shelby Woo (age 17) .... Irene Ng
Mike Woo (Grandpa).................... Pat Morita
Cindi Ornette (1996–1999) ..... Preslaysa Edwards
Noah Allen (1996–1999).............. Adam Busch
Det. Whit Hineline (1996–1999) ..... Steve Purnick
Angie Burns (1999) .... Eleanor Noble
Vince Rosania (1999) .... Noah Klar
Det. Sharon Delancey (1999)........... Ellen David

Shelby Woo rhymes with Nancy Drew, and that was perhaps no accident in this imitative series about an inquisitive teenager who solved mysteries that stumped the police. Shelby had moved to America from China, where her parents still lived, to study. She stayed with her innkeeper grandfather, a retired San Francisco criminologist, and worked after school as an intern at Florida's Cocoa Beach Police Department. Grumpy Det. Hineline was skeptical but let her tag along on his generally nonviolent cases, perhaps because she always solved them before he did. Wisecracking Cindi and dumb Noah were her two best friends, who helped out.

In early 1999, Shelby and her grandfather moved from Florida to Wilton, Massachusetts, near Boston, where she promptly adopted a new police department, a new detective (Det. Delancey, who was notably sharper than Hineline), and two new teenage friends, Angie and Vince. Angie, a science student, was immediately struck by Shelby's ingenuity and persistence ("You just do stuff, don't you!"), while handyman Vince became a potential love interest. A novel feature of this series was Shelby's periodic recounting of the clues in the case, which popped up as if on a computer screen, so that viewers could solve the mystery along with her.

MYSTERY IS MY BUSINESS, syndicated title for *Ellery Queen* (1954 edition)

MYSTERY PLAYHOUSE, see *Danger*

MYSTERY PLAYHOUSE STARRING BORIS KARLOFF, see *Starring Boris Karloff*

MYSTERY SCIENCE THEATER 3000 (*Comedy*)

BROADCAST HISTORY:

Comedy Channel (1989–1991)
Comedy Central (1991–1996)
Sci-Fi Channel (1997–1999)
120 minutes
Produced: *1989–1999* (197 network episodes)
Premiered: *November 18, 1989*

CAST:

Joel Robinson (1989–1993)........... Joel Hodgson
Mike Nelson (1993–1999) .... Himself
Tom Servo .... Kevin Murphy
Crow T. Robot (1989–1996) .... Trace Beaulieu
Crow T. Robot (1997–1999)............. Bill Corbett
Dr. Clayton Forrester (1989–1996).... Trace Beaulieu
Dr. Larry Erhardt (1989–1990) ...... Josh Weinstein
TV's Frank (1990–1996)............. Frank Conniff
Pearl Forrester (1997–1999)........... Mary Jo Pehl
**Gypsy (robot) (1989–1997)* .... Jim Mallon
**Gypsy (robot) (1997–1999)* .... Patrick Brantseg

*Occasional

One of cable's favorite cult series, *Mystery Science Theater 3000* was essentially an old and awful B-movie "hosted" by a human and two robots who appeared in silhouette in the lower right-hand corner of the screen, offering sarcastic commentary as the flick unspooled. Seems the trio had been marooned in outer space, on the "Satellite of Love," by mad scientist Dr. Clayton Forrester. There, they were consigned to watch bad movies forever as part of a diabolical experiment to measure the effects of awful films on the human race.

The original host, a tormented lab technician abducted from the Gizmonics Institute, was portrayed by the show's creator, Joel Hodgson, in a red jump suit. After his departure in 1993 (his character escaped in a hidden pod called *Deus Ex Machina*), the host became head writer Mike Nelson. The two sarcastic 'bots were Tom Servo, who looked like a lightbulb, and bug-like Crow. Pearl was Forrester's equally mad mother, and Erhardt (who was succeeded by TV's Frank) his henchman. Among the films the stranded trio, and viewers, were forced to watch were such turkeys as *The Brain That Wouldn't Die*, *Teenage Strangler*, *Alien from L.A.*, and *Kitten with a Whip*. The series suffered in later years as executives at the studios that owned America's worst movies decided they didn't want them "demeaned" by *MST3K*'s wisecracks, and refused to allow many of them to be shown on the series.

MST3K debuted on Minneapolis UHF station KTMA on Thanksgiving Day, 1988, and went national on the newly launched Comedy Channel (which later became Comedy Central) in 1989. In 1996, Comedy Central announced its cancellation due to low ratings. Was this the end? "In science fiction, nobody dies forever," cracked Murphy, hopefully, and he was right. Following a noisy viewer campaign to save the show, it was picked up by the Sci-Fi Channel, which narrowed its focus to bad old sci-fi movies (plenty of those around), and by 1998 was piping it into more than fifty percent of U.S. television homes.

In the series finale the Satellite of Love landed on Earth, where Servo and Crow got an apartment with Mike, robot Gypsy started a Fortune 500 company and Pearl became the dictator of Qatar.

MYSTERY THEATER, see *Mark Saber*

MYSTERY THEATRE, see *Movies—Prior to 1961*

N

NBC ACTION PLAYHOUSE (*Dramatic Anthology*)
FIRST TELECAST: *June 24, 1971*
LAST TELECAST: *September 5, 1972*
BROADCAST HISTORY:
Jun 1971–Sep 1971, NBC Thu 7:30–8:30
May 1972–Sep 1972, NBC Tue 8:30–9:30
HOST:
Peter Marshall

The filmed dramas presented as *NBC Action Playhouse* were reruns of former episodes of *Bob Hope Presents the Chrysler Theatre.* Peter Marshall taped new introductions for the episodes, to replace the original introductions done by Hope. In 1971 this series was the summer replacement for *The Flip Wilson Show.* In 1972 some of the 1971 episodes were aired again with the same Peter Marshall introductions they had had the previous summer.

NBC ADVENTURE THEATRE (*Dramatic Anthology*)
FIRST TELECAST: *July 24, 1971*
LAST TELECAST: *September 7, 1972*
BROADCAST HISTORY:
Jul 1971–Sep 1971, NBC Sat 7:30–8:30
Jun 1972–Sep 1972, NBC Thu 8:00–9:00
HOST:
Art Fleming (1971)
Ed McMahon (1972)

NBC Adventure Theatre consisted of reruns of episodes of *Bob Hope Presents the Chrysler Theatre.* Art Fleming was the host in 1971 and Ed McMahon in 1972. The introductions that they provided to the filmed dramas replaced the original ones that had been done by Bob Hope. Some of the shows aired in 1972 were repeats of episodes aired in 1971.

NBC CINEMA PLAYHOUSE, see *Movies—Prior to 1961*

NBC COMEDY HOUR (*Comedy Variety*)
FIRST TELECAST: *January 8, 1956*
LAST TELECAST: *June 10, 1956*
BROADCAST HISTORY:
Jan 1956–Jun 1956, NBC Sun 8:00–9:00
REGULARS:
Jonathan Winters
Hy Averback
Gale Storm
Al White Dancers
Tony Charmoli Dancers
Gordon Jenkins Orchestra
Al Goodman Orchestra

When *NBC Comedy Hour* premiered in January of 1956, the network envisioned it as a showcase for new comedy talent. It was a rather unstructured vaudevillian collection of skits, monologues, song-and-dance numbers, one-liners, blackouts, pantomime, etc. There was to be no regular headliner and new young performers were to work with veterans. Initial reaction from both critics and viewers was extremely negative and the concept was altered drastically. The enormous writing staff was reduced substantially, musical production numbers were added, and each show was designed to have more of a sense of continuity than the disorganized, fragmented original. Gale Storm became the regular hostess at the start of February and remained for two months, to be replaced by a succession of weekly hosts. The only two other regular performers were comedian Jonathan Winters and actor-announcer Hy Averback.

NBC COMEDY PLAYHOUSE (*Comedy Anthology*)
FIRST TELECAST: *June 24, 1968*
LAST TELECAST: *September 5, 1970*
BROADCAST HISTORY:
Jun 1968–Aug 1968, NBC Mon 9:00–10:00
Aug 1970–Sep 1970, NBC Sat 7:30–8:30
HOST:
Monty Hall (1968)
Jack Kelly (1970)

The full-hour light comedies presented as *NBC Comedy Playhouse* were reruns of episodes of *Bob Hope Presents the Chrysler Theatre.* Monty Hall was the host of the 1968 edition and Jack Kelly was the host in 1970. They provided introductions to replace the originals that had been done by Bob Hope.

NBC COMEDY THEATER (*Comedy Anthology*)
FIRST TELECAST: *June 7, 1971*
LAST TELECAST: *September 2, 1972*
BROADCAST HISTORY:
Jun 1971–Aug 1971, NBC Mon 8:00–9:00
Jul 1972–Sep 1972, NBC Sat 8:00–9:00
HOST:
Jack Kelly

The light romantic comedies that comprised *NBC Comedy Theater* were filmed reruns of episodes of *Bob Hope Presents the Chrysler Theatre.* Jack Kelly was the host and provided introductions to replace the originals done by Hope. In 1971 this was the summer replacement for *Laugh-In* and in 1972 for *Emergency.*

NBC CONCERT HALL (*Music*)
FIRST TELECAST: *August 29, 1948*
LAST TELECAST: *September 26, 1948*
BROADCAST HISTORY:
Aug 1948–Sep 1948, NBC Sun 9:00–9:30

A brief summer series of excerpts from classical music and ballet, live and on film.

NBC FOLLIES (*Comedy Variety*)
FIRST TELECAST: *September 13, 1973*
LAST TELECAST: *December 27, 1973*
BROADCAST HISTORY:
Sep 1973–Dec 1973, NBC Thu 10:00–11:00
REGULARS:
Sammy Davis, Jr.
Mickey Rooney
Carl Jablonski Dancers
Harper MacKay Orchestra

Although there was no host on *NBC Follies,* Sammy Davis, Jr., and Mickey Rooney were two performers who appeared in virtually every episode. Without a host, the various acts—sketches, comedy monologues, musical numbers, etc.—were arranged to flow in much the same manner that a vaudeville show did, with one turn leading into the next. Guest talent was featured in each show.

NBC MAGAZINE WITH DAVID BRINKLEY (*Newsmagazine*)
FIRST TELECAST: *September 26, 1980*
LAST TELECAST: *July 31, 1982*
BROADCAST HISTORY:
Sep 1980–Apr 1981, NBC Fri 10:00–11:00
Apr 1981–Sep 1981, NBC Thu 8:00–9:00
Sep 1981–Apr 1982, NBC Fri 8:00–9:00
Apr 1982–Jul 1982, NBC Sat 10:00–11:00
REGULARS:
David Brinkley (1980–1981)
Jack Perkins
Garrick Utley
Douglas Kiker
Betsy Aaron

This series was NBC's third attempt to develop a newsmagazine that would attract the kind of audience obtained by CBS' highly successful *60 Minutes* (see *Weekend* and *Prime Time Sunday*). It was highly appropriate that NBC chose David Brinkley to anchor this series, for many people felt that he had originated the newsmagazine format with the critically acclaimed *David Brinkley's Journal* in 1961. Unlike *60 Minutes*, *NBC Magazine* aired stories that varied widely in length, some running only a few minutes and others as long as half an hour. The stories ranged from hard-news pieces on defective Titan missiles to light stories profiling ballet star Rudolf Nureyev and veteran actor James Cagney. Brinkley provided commentary on topics covered, as well as on other items in the week's news, and engaged in brief round-table discussion with one or more of the regular field reporters—Perkins, Utley, Kiker, and Aaron—following individual stories.

The original scheduling was not ideal, opposite CBS' red-hot soap opera *Dallas*, but as Brinkley wryly remarked on opening night, "This is a new television program for those of us who don't give a damn who shot J.R."

Brinkley's final appearance on the show was on September 18, 1981, prior to his leaving NBC after many years for rival ABC. The following week the series' title was shortened to *NBC Magazine*, with the remaining correspondents thereafter supplying their own commentary.

NBC MYSTERY MOVIE, THE (*Police/Detective Drama*)
FIRST TELECAST: *September 15, 1971*
LAST TELECAST: *September 4, 1977*
BROADCAST HISTORY:
Sep 1971–Jan 1974, NBC Wed 8:30–10:00
Sep 1972–Sep 1974, NBC Sun 8:30–10:00
Jan 1974–Sep 1974, NBC Tue 8:30–10:00
Sep 1974–Sep 1975, NBC Sun 8:30–10:30
Sep 1975–Sep 1976, NBC Sun 9:00–11:00
Oct 1976–Apr 1977, NBC Sun Various times
May 1977–Sep 1977, NBC Sun 8:00–9:30

The NBC Mystery Movie was an umbrella title used to cover a number of rotating series that appeared in the same time slot on different weeks. The first *Mystery Movie* series premiered in 1971 on Wednesday nights, and included *Columbo*, *McCloud*, and *McMillan and Wife*, three series that had considerable success over the years.

Due to the popularity of the *Mystery Movie* concept in the 1971–1972 season, NBC decided to try another one. The three original elements were moved to Sunday night (retitled *The NBC Sunday Mystery Movie*) and three new ones were introduced on Wednesday, under the new blanket title *The NBC Wednesday Mystery Movie*. However, *Madigan*, *Cool Million*, and *Banacek* were not as successful as their predecessors, nor were any of the elements that were subsequently tried. Following is a listing of all the various *Mystery Movie* elements aired over the years. Details on each will be found under their separate title headings.

1971–1972: *Mystery Movie* (Wed.): *Columbo, McCloud, McMillan and Wife*
1972–1973: *Sunday Mystery Movie: Columbo, McCloud, McMillan, Hec Ramsey*
Wednesday Mystery Movie: Madigan, Cool Million, Banacek
1973–1974: *Sunday Mystery Movie: Columbo, McCloud, McMillan, Hec Ramsey*
Wednesday Mystery Movie: Madigan, Tenafly, Faraday & Company, The Snoop Sisters. (Series moved to Tuesday effective January 1972, retitled *NBC Tuesday Mystery Movie.*)
1974–1975: *Sunday Mystery Movie: Columbo, McCloud, McMillan, Amy Prentiss*
1975–1976: *Sunday Mystery Movie: Columbo, McCloud, McMillan, McCoy*
1976–1977: *Sunday Mystery Movie: Columbo, McCloud, McMillan; Quincy, M.E.* (to December 1976); *Lanigan's Rabbi* (effective January 1977)

NBC NEWS ENCORE (*Documentary*)
FIRST TELECAST: *June 26, 1966*
LAST TELECAST: *August 21, 1966*
BROADCAST HISTORY:
Jun 1966–Aug 1966, NBC Sun 6:30–7:30
HOST:
Robert Abernethy

Host Robert Abernethy introduced and concluded each of the episodes of *NBC News Encore*, a series of rebroadcasts of selected NBC news documentaries, the bulk of which had originally aired as *NBC News Actuality Specials*.

NBC NOVELS FOR TELEVISION (*Drama*)
FIRST TELECAST: *February 14, 1979*
LAST TELECAST: *June 28, 1979*
BROADCAST HISTORY:
Feb 1979–Apr 1979, NBC Wed 9:00–11:00
May 1979–Jun 1979, NBC Thu 10:00–11:00

NBC Novels for Television was the umbrella title used to describe a collection of four mini-series that were serialized in consecutive weekly installments in 1979. In order of their showing they were: *From Here to Eternity* (February 14–February 28); *Studs Lonigan* (March 7–March 21); a repeat presentation of *Wheels* (April 4–April 18), which originally aired in May 1978; and a repeat presentation of *Aspen* under the title *The Innocent and the Damned* (May 31–June 28). See under individual titles for details.

NBC PLAYHOUSE, see *Variety*

NBC PLAYHOUSE (*Dramatic Anthology*)
FIRST TELECAST: *June 28, 1960*
LAST TELECAST: *September 6, 1960*

BROADCAST HISTORY:

Jun 1960–Sep 1960, NBC Tue 8:30–9:00

HOSTESS:

Jeanne Bal

Actress Jeanne Bal hosted this summer series composed of reruns of episodes of *The Loretta Young Show* in which Miss Young had not starred. *NBC Playhouse* alternated with *The Gas Company Playhouse.*

NBC PRESENTS, see *Movies—Prior to 1961*

NBC REPERTORY THEATRE (*Dramatic Anthology*)

FIRST TELECAST: *April 17, 1949*
LAST TELECAST: *July 10, 1949*
BROADCAST HISTORY:

Apr 1949–Jul 1949, NBC Sun 9:00–10:00

PRODUCER:

Owen Davis, Jr.

Early live dramatic program, presenting an original TV play or adaptation each week. Many noted stars appeared during the course of the series, which did not utilize a repertory company (despite the title) but had a new cast for each telecast. Perhaps the most notable single production was *Macbeth,* the annual Shakespearean production of The Players, a New York theatrical association. Among those appearing during the course of the series were Walter Hampden, Joyce Redman, Leo G. Carroll, Ralph Bellamy, John Carradine, David Wayne, and many others.

NBC REPORTS (*Documentary*)

FIRST TELECAST: *September 12, 1972*
LAST TELECAST: *September 4, 1973*
BROADCAST HISTORY:

Sep 1972–Sep 1973, NBC Tue 10:00–11:00

NBC Reports aired on a regular basis during the 1972–1973 season, presenting news documentaries on various subjects of current interest. It had no permanent host or narrator. Some of the subjects covered were "Pensions: The Broken Promise," "What Price Health," "And When the War Is Over . . . The American Military in the '70s," "The Meaning of Watergate" (on May 22, 1973, five days after the start of the hearings which ran all that summer), "American Communism Today," and, in a special three-hour final telecast, "The Energy Crisis—An American White Paper." The title *NBC Reports* was also frequently used for irregularly scheduled documentaries.

NBC SPORTS IN ACTION, (*Sports*)

FIRST TELECAST: *May 23, 1965*
LAST TELECAST: *September 5, 1965*
BROADCAST HISTORY:

May 1965–Sep 1965, NBC Sun 6:30–7:30

HOST:

Jim Simpson

NBC Sports in Action was an early attempt to compete with *ABC's Wide World of Sports.* Jim Simpson was the regular host and narrator of the series, which covered various types of sporting events in depth, with action footage of the event in progress, as well as interviews with and profiles of sports celebrities. Such sports as surfing, skiing, auto racing, rugby, sailing, and lacrosse—none of them seen on a regular basis on American TV—were featured in all or part of various episodes of this show. Although it aired in the evening only from May to August, *NBC Sports in Action* had actually premiered in January 1965 and ran until June 1966, usually airing on Sunday afternoons.

NBC SPORTS SPOT (*Sports Commentary*)

FIRST TELECAST: *January 10, 1958*
LAST TELECAST: *January 24, 1958*
BROADCAST HISTORY:

Jan 1958, NBC Fri 10:45–11:00

NBC Sports Spot replaced *Fight Beat* as the show filling the time between the end of the bout on *The Gillette Cavalcade of Sports* and the start of the 11:00 P.M. local news. Each week an outstanding nationally known sportswriter was to be host to a famous sports personality whom he would interview. Red Barber served as host for the first two weeks and Bud Palmer was the host on the third. After only three weeks on the air, however, *NBC Sports Spot* was replaced by *Phillies Jackpot Bowling.*

NBC SUNDAY MYSTERY MOVIE, THE, see *NBC Mystery Movie, The*

NBC TUESDAY MYSTERY MOVIE, THE, see *NBC Mystery Movie, The*

NBC WEDNESDAY MYSTERY MOVIE, THE, see *NBC Mystery Movie, The*

NBC'S BEST SELLERS (*Drama*)

FIRST TELECAST: *September 30, 1976*
LAST TELECAST: *April 25, 1977*
BROADCAST HISTORY:

Sep 1976–Jan 1977, NBC Thu 9:00–10:00
Jan 1977–Apr 1977, NBC Thu 9:00–11:00
Apr 1977, NBC Mon 9:00–11:00

NBC's Best Sellers was the umbrella title used to describe a collection of four novels which were serialized in consecutive installments. In order of their showing they were: *Captains and the Kings* (September 30–November 25), *Once an Eagle* (December 2–January 13), *Seventh Avenue* (February 10–24), and *The Rhinemann Exchange* (March 10–24). The first two were aired primarily in one-hour installments, except for the first and last chapters which ran two hours in length, while the latter two ran in two-hour segments. Of the four, only *Captains and the Kings* was repeated, all in two-hour segments, with its concluding chapter running on *NBC Monday Night at the Movies.* See under individual titles for specific details.

NBC'S SATURDAY NIGHT LIVE, see *Saturday Night Live*

NFL ACTION (*Sports*)

FIRST TELECAST: *May 12, 1971*
LAST TELECAST: *September 8, 1971*
BROADCAST HISTORY:

May 1971–Sep 1971, ABC Wed 10:30–11:00

NARRATOR:

John Facenda (and others)

Football films focusing on various players, teams, and big games.

N.Y.P.D. (*Police Drama*)

FIRST TELECAST: *September 5, 1967*
LAST TELECAST: *September 16, 1969*

BROADCAST HISTORY:

Sep 1967–Sep 1969, ABC Tue 9:30–10:00

CAST:

Det. Lt. Mike Haines .... Jack Warden
Det. Jeff Ward .... Robert Hooks
Det. Johnny Corso .... Frank Converse

New York City was the real star of this police series. Much of the filming was done on location there, and the city's underworld denizens were realistically portrayed. The three N.Y.P.D. plainclothes detectives were experienced Mike Haines, 18 years on the force, the younger Johnny Corso, and black officer Jeff Ward. Together they tracked murderers, extortionists, drug pushers, bombers, rapists, and other thugs around the bustling city. Locales varied from the Bowery to Wall Street, the Empire State Building to Shubert Alley, Greenwich Village to Times Square. The program was commended by real-life Mayor John Lindsay, who permitted filming of some scenes in City Hall. *N.Y.P.D.* was produced with the cooperation of the New York Police Department, with episodes based on actual cases.

N.Y.P.D. BLUE (*Police Drama*)

FIRST TELECAST: *September 21, 1993*

LAST TELECAST:

BROADCAST HISTORY:

Sep 1993–Aug 1994, ABC Tue 10:00–11:00
Oct 1994–Feb 1997, ABC Tue 10:00–11:00
Apr 1997–Jul 1998, ABC Tue 10:00–11:00
Oct 1998–Aug 1999, ABC Tue 10:00–11:00
Jan 2000–Sep 2000, ABC Tue 10:00–11:00
Jun 2000–Jul 2000, ABC Sat 10:00–11:00
Jan 2001–Sep 2001, ABC Tue 10:00–11:00
Nov 2001–Apr 2002, ABC Tue 9:00–10:00
Apr 2002–May 2002, ABC Tue 10:00–11:00
Sep 2002– , ABC Tue 10:00–11:00

CAST:

Det. Andy Sipowicz.................. Dennis Franz
Det. John Kelly (1993–1994).......... David Caruso
Lt. Arthur Fancy (1993–2001) ..... James McDaniel
Laura Hughes Kelly (1993–1994)
.... Sherry Stringfield
Officer Janice Licalsi (1993–1994)
.... Amy Brenneman
Officer/Det: James Martinez (1993–2000)
.... Nicholas Turturro
**Andy Sipowicz, Jr. (1993–1997)*... Michael DeLuise
Asst. D.A. Sylvia Costas (1994–1999)
.... Sharon Lawrence
Det. Greg Medavoy (1994–) .... Gordon Clapp
Donna Abandando (1994–1996) ..... Gail O'Grady
Det. Bobby Simone (1994–1998) ...... Jimmy Smits
Det. Adrienne Lesniak (1995–1996) .. Justine Miceli
Det. Diane Russell (1995–2001) .... Kim Delaney
Gina Colon (1996–1997)........ Lourdes Benedicto
Off. Abby Sullivan (1996–1997)........ Paige Turco
Det. Jill Kirkendall (1997–2000)
.... Andrea Thompson
Det. Danny Sorenson (1998–2001)... Rick Schroder
**Theo Sipowicz (1999–)*........... Austin Majors
John Irvin (1999–)................. Bill Brochtrup
Det. Baldwin Jones (2000–)...... Henry Simmons
A.D.A. Valerie Haywood (2001–)
.... Garcelle Beauvais-Nilon
Det. Connie McDowell (2001–) .... Charlotte Ross
Lt. Tony Rodriguez (2001–) .... Esai Morales
Det. John Clark, Jr. (2001–) .. Mark-Paul Gosselaar
Det. Rita Ortiz (2001–) ...... Jacqueline Obradors

*Occasional

This gritty police drama received notoriety at its premiere for minor amounts of nudity and language not normally heard on prime-time TV. It was, however, really just a well-crafted melodrama in the urgent *Hill Street Blues* style (from the same producers), mixing action with cops' tortured private lives. Kelly was a 15-year veteran of the force who somehow managed to retain his compassion in the face of the unremitting ugliness he saw. His partner at the fifteenth precinct, Sipowicz, reacted differently, turning to booze and hookers until he almost got killed, then slowly began to turn his life around. Laura was Kelly's ex, a lawyer, who still loved him; Officer Janice his new, tentative love interest; and Martinez an earnest rookie learning the ropes. Lt. Fancy was the hard-nosed precinct boss.

By the second season Sipowicz was involved with Sylvia from the D.A.'s office, while Medavoy, whose marriage was falling apart, was homing in on the precinct's voluptuous administrative assistant, Donna. Kelly departed in the second season (actor David Caruso left the series in a much-publicized bid for big-screen stardom), replaced by Simone, who was mourning the death of his wife. Amid all this anguish, the shootouts and drug busts continued unabated.

There were numerous station house relationships during the following seasons. Sipowicz married Sylvia, and in 1996 they had a baby, Theo—with whom he became obsessed after the death of his grown son. The gruff detective later fought a successful battle with prostate cancer (1998). Donut-chomping Medavoy had an affair with Donna, then fathered a son (as a sperm donor) by lesbian Abby, becoming a "surrogate parent" as she raised the child. After having affairs with troubled Adrienne and Gina, Martinez too eventually became a husband and father. But the most tortured path was that of sensitive Bobby Simone. After losing his beloved first wife, he began a secret relationship with alcoholic Diane. He was dropped from the force for a time in 1997, accused of being a dirty cop, but then reinstated. He finally married Diane in 1998, only to be stricken with a heart ailment in a dramatic story line that culminated with his death in November 1998 (actor Smits had decided to leave the show). Both viewers and his fellow officers were devastated by the loss of the popular Simone, whom many felt could never be replaced. However, the same thing had been said about Detective Kelly, who *he* had replaced, and now a new and very different officer took over his duties—the eager but slightly mysterious young narcotics detective Sorenson, who was partnered with the crusty, mistrustful Sipowicz.

The tragedies that stalked Sipowicz seemed to know no end. In 1999 Sylvia was shot in the courthouse, and with her dying breath told Andy to "take care of the baby." Now a single parent, Andy obsessed about his young son's safety, seeing him through a leukemia scare and numerous other threats. He got back together with ex-wife Katie for a period, and they even talked about remarrying, but eventually he bonded with new detective McDowell, who reached out to him, kept him on the wagon and helped him with parenting. After adopting her own dead sister's baby, Michelle, she moved in with Andy and Theo in 2002.

At the fifteenth precinct Lt. Fancy left in 2001 and was replaced by Rodriguez, and Andy's partner Sorenson disappeared during an undercover operation. His body was found months later buried in a vacant lot. Andy's new partner was John Clark, Jr., a young detective who was loyal and eager to work with him, despite the vehement opposition of his father, a veteran cop who was a longtime enemy of Andy's. Others joining the cast included Irvin, the gay office assistant, Haywood, a new A.D.A. who was tough on both criminals and cops, and Ortiz, a tough-talking Puerto Rican detective with a short fuse.

As the 2002–2003 season came to a close John Clark, Jr.'s, angry father committed suicide, and Andy and Connie were about to be quietly married—despite department policy against married detectives working in the same squad. However, the ceremony was postponed when Lt. Rodriguez was shot by a vengeful, drunken Internal Affairs captain who was after both him and Andy.

NAKED CITY (*Police Drama*)

FIRST TELECAST: *September 30, 1958*
LAST TELECAST: *September 11, 1963*
BROADCAST HISTORY:

Sep 1958–Sep 1959, ABC Tue 9:30–10:00
Oct 1960–Sep 1963, ABC Wed 10:00–11:00

CAST:

Det. Lt. Dan Muldoon (1958–1959) . . . John McIntire
Det. Jim Halloran (1958–1959) . . . James Franciscus
Janet Halloran (1958–1959) . . . . Suzanne Storrs
Ptlm./Sgt. Frank Arcaro . . . . Harry Bellaver
Lt. Mike Parker (1959–1963) . . . . . Horace McMahon
Det. Adam Flint (1960–1963) . . . . Paul Burke
Libby (1960–1963) . . . . Nancy Malone

THEME (1960–1963):

"Naked City Theme" ("Somewhere in the Night"), by Billy May and Milton Raskin

This popular series was shot on location all over the New York City metropolis, from the Staten Island Ferry to Times Square. A feeling of gritty reality pervaded the stories as veteran cop Dan Muldoon and his young sidekick Jim Halloran ran down the murderers and muggers, petty thieves and swindlers who inhabited the city's seamy side.

The program began undergoing cast changes even in its first season. Det. Muldoon was killed in a spectacular chase sequence seen in a March 1959 episode, when his squad car plowed into a gasoline tank truck (stuntmen were often used in *Naked City* for such effects). Lt. Mike Parker became the wizened old pro for the remainder of that season, and also returned when the series came back in hour-long form after a year's layoff. With him in the 1960–1963 run was a new young partner, Det. Adam Flint, Flint's girlfriend, Libby, and Sgt. Frank Arcaro (who had been a patrolman from 1958–1959).

Parker, portrayed by steely-eyed Horace McMahon, was the perfect hard-nosed cop for a hard city, and his portrayal helped make the series a success. Added, too, was some dramatic city-at-dawn theme music by Billy May. But the star was New York itself, where, as the narrator intoned, "There are eight million stories in the Naked City . . ."

Based on a story by Mark Hellinger, which was made into a 1948 movie titled *Naked City*.

NAKED TRUTH, THE (*Situation Comedy*)

FIRST TELECAST: *September 13, 1995*
LAST TELECAST: *June 1, 1998*
BROADCAST HISTORY:

Sep 1995–Feb 1996, ABC Wed 9:30–10:00
Jan 1997–Apr 1997, NBC Thu 9:30–10:00
Jul 1997, NBC Tue 8:30–9:00
Sep 1997–Mar 1998, NBC Mon 9:30–10:00
May 1998–Jun 1998, NBC Mon 9:30–10:00

CAST:

Nora Wilde . . . . Tea Leoni
Nick Columbus (1995–1997) . . . . . . Jonathan Penner
Camilla Dane . . . . Holland Taylor
Chloe Banks (1995–1996) . . . . Amy Ryan
Mr. Donner (1995–1996) . . . . Jack Blessing
Les Polonsky (1997) . . . . George Wendt
Dave Fontaine . . . . Mark Roberts
T.J. (1995–1997) . . . . Darryl Sivad
Bradley Crosby (1997–1998) . . . . Chris Elliott
Suji (1997–1998) . . . . Amy Hill
Harris Van Doren (1997–1998) . . . . Jim Rash
Jake Sullivan (1997–1998) . . . . Tom Verica

Nora was a highly principled political photojournalist, a woman of so many principles that when she found out her rich husband Leland was cheating on her, she turned down a seven-figure divorce settlement in order to start anew, on her own terms. He promptly blackballed her at every reputable newspaper in the country. Out of money and out of work, Nora was forced to become a celebrity-chaser for the sleazy tabloid *The Comet*. According to one coworker, it was the "fastest descent into the gutter" he'd ever seen. Her new colleagues were a rowdy bunch: Nicky was the worldly and experienced hunky photographer with no principles at all; Camilla the tyrannical editor; and Chloe her chatty new best friend. Bobo, T.J., Carmine, and Stupid Dave were fellow paparazzi. Despite her misgivings, Nora adapted, and there were celebrity gags galore.

In January 1997, *The Comet* changed hands, with chubby Les taking over as editor-in-chief. He knew nothing about publishing, having previously been in the family business, Polonsky Meats, but fancied himself the next Ben Bradlee. Nora switched to writing an advice column, "Nora Knows," while office oddball Dave was delighted to be covering pets and babies, dapper T.J. was made fashion editor, and Camilla—to her disgust—was demoted to reporter. In the fall, Camilla defected to the rival tabloid *The National Inquisitor* to become editor-in-chief, taking Nora and Dave with her. Dave (formerly "Stupid Dave") was made managing editor. Their new coworkers included eccentric photographer Bradley, photographer Suji, fastidious head of research Harris, and handsome reporter Jake, who was both a rival and potential love interest for Nora.

NAKIA (*Police Drama*)

FIRST TELECAST: *September 21, 1974*
LAST TELECAST: *December 28, 1974*
BROADCAST HISTORY:

Sep 1974–Dec 1974, ABC Sat 10:00–11:00

CAST:

Deputy Nakia Parker . . . . Robert Forster
Sheriff Sam Jericho . . . . Arthur Kennedy

Irene James .... Gloria DeHaven
Deputy Hubbel Martin .... Taylor Lacher
Half Cub .... John Tenorio, Jr.

This action series was about a modern-day deputy sheriff in a New Mexico city. Nakia was of Indian heritage, and he frequently found his loyalties divided between ancient tribal customs and modern police methods. Symbolic was his transportation, which alternated between pickup truck and horse rather than a squad car. His cases involved everything from violent demonstrations on the reservation to inflammatory political scheming on the town council. Irene James was the secretary in the sheriff's office.

Filmed in and around Albuquerque, New Mexico.

NAME OF THE GAME, THE (*Adventure*)
FIRST TELECAST: *September 20, 1968*
LAST TELECAST: *September 10, 1971*
BROADCAST HISTORY:
Sep 1968–Sep 1971, NBC Fri 8:30–10:00
CAST:
Glenn Howard .... Gene Barry
Jeff Dillon .... Tony Franciosa
Dan Farrell .... Robert Stack
Peggy Maxwell .... Susan Saint James
Joe Sample .... Ben Murphy
Andy Hill .... Cliff Potter
Ross Craig .... Mark Miller

The Name of the Game was actually three series under one title. Each of the three stars of the show, Robert Stack, Tony Franciosa, and Gene Barry, was featured in his own self-contained episodes. The connection between them was Howard Publications, a Los Angeles–based publishing empire that had been built up from scratch by its dynamic owner, Glenn Howard. Glenn's position of power, his confrontations with business and political enemies, and his own flamboyant lifestyle were portrayed in his portion of *The Name of the Game*. Within the Howard empire were investigative correspondent Jeff Dillon and editor Dan Farrell. Dillon was a superaggressive former newsboy who had clawed his way up to a position of power and respect working for Howard's *People Magazine*. Farrell was a former FBI agent (possibly type-casting for Robert Stack, Eliot Ness in *The Untouchables*) who had gone into the publishing business because it provided a position from which to make the public aware of the threats posed by organized crime. He was the senior editor of *Crime Magazine*. Common to all three elements of *The Name of the Game* was Peggy Maxwell, the bright, ambitious, and occasionally somewhat kooky editorial assistant to all three men. Joe, Andy, and Ross were reporters with recurring, but not weekly, roles. What was "The Name of the Game"? Well, the title of the 1966 TV-movie on which this series was based was more explicit. It was called *Fame Is the Name of the Game*.

NAME THAT TUNE (*Quiz/Audience Participation*)
FIRST TELECAST: *June 29, 1953*
LAST TELECAST: *October 19, 1959*
BROADCAST HISTORY:
Jun 1953–Jun 1954, NBC Mon 8:00–8:30
Sep 1954–Mar 1955, CBS Thu 10:30–11:00
Sep 1955–Sep 1958, CBS Tue 7:30–8:00
Sep 1958–Oct 1959, CBS Mon 7:30–8:00
EMCEE:
Red Benson (1953–1954)
Bill Cullen (1954–1955)
George De Witt (1955–1959)

Contestants on *Name That Tune* competed with each other to identify the title of a song being played by the Harry Salter Orchestra. When a contestant thought he knew the title, he would race his competitor to ring a bell that was 25 feet away to have the opportunity to guess the title. The biggest winner at the end of each show had the opportunity to win a $1,600 jackpot by correctly identifying seven songs in 30 seconds. Viewers submitted the songs used in this "Golden Medley" and won as much money as the contestants if their song list was used. As the era of the big-money quiz show arrived, a variation in this jackpot system was devised. People working in teams could return each week and try to build their winnings up to a possible $25,000 in the renamed "Golden Medley Marathon." They could win $5,000 per week for a maximum of five weeks.

During the 1970–1971 season a syndicated version of *Name That Tune* was produced with Richard Hayes as emcee. NBC revived it as a network daytime series for two short runs, July 1974 to January 1975, emceed by Dennis James, and January 1977 to June 1977, emceed by Tom Kennedy. Kennedy was also host of a separate weekly syndicated version that ran from 1974 to 1981. This syndicated version was retitled *The $100,000 Name That Tune* in 1976 when it instituted a means by which winning contestants could become really big winners. After 1977 the big winner was determined in a season-ending playoff.

This latter syndicated version of *The $100,000 Name That Tune* was revived for the 1984–1985 season, with Jim Lange as emcee.

NAME THAT VIDEO (*Quiz/Audience Participation*)
BROADCAST HISTORY:
VH1
30 minutes
Original episodes: *2001*
Premiered: *March 12, 2001*
EMCEE:
Karyn Bryant

A variation on the classic *Name That Tune*, in which three contestants attempted to answer questions about music videos. The first round included Rock & Rhyme (identify rewritten songs), Finish the Phrase (finish a line sung in a video), and Tainted Tunes (unscramble unintelligible lyrics). In round two the two highest scorers competed to name videos in the shortest time ("I can name that video in two seconds!"). In the rapid-fire third round the finalist had to name 10 videos and the artists' names in under 60 seconds. The grand prize was a new car.

NAME'S THE SAME, THE (*Quiz/Panel*)
FIRST TELECAST: *December 5, 1951*
LAST TELECAST: *October 7, 1955*
BROADCAST HISTORY:
Dec 1951–Nov 1952, ABC Wed 7:30–8:00
Dec 1952–Aug 1954, ABC Tue 10:30–11:00
Oct 1954–Jun 1955, ABC Mon 7:30–8:00
Jun 1955–Sep 1955, ABC Tue 10:00–10:30
Sep 1955–Oct 1955, ABC Fri 10:00–10:30

EMCEE:
Robert Q. Lewis (1951–1954)
Dennis James (1954–1955)
Bob Elliott and Ray Goulding (1955)
Clifton Fadiman (1955)

PANELISTS:
Abe Burrows (1951–1952)
Joan Alexander
Meredith Willson (1951–1953)
Bill Stern (1953–1954)
Gene Rayburn (1953–1955)
Bess Myerson (1954–1955)
Roger Price (1954–1955)
Audrey Meadows (1955)

PRODUCERS:
Mark Goodson and Bill Todman

This simple variation on *What's My Line* (produced by the same company) could well have been called *What's My Name*. The gimmick was that each of the contestants appearing on the show, whose names the panel had to guess, had the same name as a famous person or an object. Thus ordinary folks who happened to be named A. Garter, A. Beard, Abraham Lincoln, Mona Lisa, or Napoleon Bonaparte tried to stump the panel.

The regular panel was fairly stable during the program's first two years, but then considerable turnover began to take place. In addition to those listed above (who lasted six months or more), such celebrities as Jerry Lester, Carl Reiner, Basil Rathbone, and Mike Wallace appeared for shorter runs.

NANCY (*Situation Comedy*)

FIRST TELECAST: *September 17, 1970*
LAST TELECAST: *January 7, 1971*
BROADCAST HISTORY:
Sep 1970–Jan 1971, NBC Thu 9:30–10:00

CAST:
Nancy Smith .... Renne Jarrett
Dr. Adam Hudson .... John Fink
Uncle Everett .... Robert F. Simon
Abigail Townsend .... Celeste Holm
Turner .... William Bassett
Rodriguez .... Ernesto Macias
Willie .... Eddie Applegate
Tom Daily .... Frank Aletter

Nancy was the attractive young daughter of the President of the United States. She met a young veterinarian from Center City, Iowa, and they fell in love. Unfortunately, being under constant surveillance by secret service agents Turner and Rodriguez did nothing to promote the romance, and Nancy's chaperone, Abigail, and Adam's Uncle Everett also seemed constantly to get in the way, not to mention the press. The President was never shown on camera, but his aides were, and his voice was heard on occasion. The couple got married in the November 5, 1970, episode, but even that could not save the series from cancellation.

NANCY DREW (*Adventure*)

BROADCAST HISTORY:
Syndicated only
30 minutes
Produced: *1995–1996*
Released: *September 1995*

CAST:
Nancy Drew .... Tracy Ryan
Bess Marvin .... Jhene Erwin
George Fayne .... Joy Tanner
**Ned Nickerson* .... Scott Speedman

*Occasional

Nancy Drew resurfaced in this syndicated series as a 21-year-old sharing a Manhattan apartment with her good friends Bess and George. Bess wrote the "Ask Me Anything" advice column for *The Rag*, and Nancy was working for a temp agency to make spending money—and somehow almost every temporary job led to a mystery for her to solve. At mid-season the girls took a trip to Paris. Ned was her friend/boyfriend who, after several adventures, left to go to Africa for six months.

Sold with the syndicated *Hardy Boys* series, and aired with it as a back-to-back hour on most stations.

NANCY DREW MYSTERIES, THE (*Adventure*)

FIRST TELECAST: *February 6, 1977*
LAST TELECAST: *January 1, 1978*
BROADCAST HISTORY:
Feb 1977–Jan 1978, ABC Sun 7:00–8:00

CAST:
Nancy Drew .... Pamela Sue Martin
Carson Drew .... William Schallert
Ned Nickerson (1977) .... George O'Hanlon, Jr.
George Fayne (1977) .... Jean Rasey
George Fayne (1977–1978) .... Susan Buckner
Bess .... Ruth Cox

Nancy Drew was the girls' equivalent of *The Hardy Boys Mysteries*, with which it alternated on Sunday nights. Both programs featured teenage sleuths helping adults solve exciting (but not usually violent) mysteries, such as robberies, haunted houses, blackmail attempts on a college football star, etc.

Nancy was 18 and the daughter of famed criminal lawyer Carson Drew, a widower. George (a girl) was her buddy, not particularly brave but willing to stick by Nancy through thick and thin. Ned was her father's law-student assistant, always willing to help (later he became an investigator for the district attorney's office, and more anxious to keep Nancy out of cases than in them). The Drews' home base was River Heights, a suburb of New York, but the mysteries took them far and wide.

In the fall of 1977 Nancy Drew appeared in several joint episodes with the Hardy Boys. Then in February 1978 the two series were combined, at which time Pamela Sue Martin left the program. See *Hardy Boys Mysteries* for further details.

Based on the Nancy Drew books by "Carolyn Keene" (see *Hardy Boys* for true authorship).

NANCY WALKER SHOW, THE (*Situation Comedy*)

FIRST TELECAST: *September 30, 1976*
LAST TELECAST: *December 23, 1976*
BROADCAST HISTORY:
Sep 1976–Dec 1976, ABC Thu 9:30–10:00

CAST:
Nancy Kitteridge .... Nancy Walker
Lt. Cdr. Kenneth Kitteridge .... William Daniels
Terry Folson .... Ken Olfson
Lorraine .... Beverly Archer
Glen .... James Cromwell
Michael Futterman .... Sparky Marcus
Teddy Futterman .... William Schallert

EXECUTIVE PRODUCER:
Norman Lear

THEME:

"Nancy's Blues," by Marilyn & Alan Bergman and Marvin Hamlisch

Sarcastic, wisecracking Nancy Kitteridge had an ideal life. Ten months of the year she was an active career woman, head of the Nancy Kitteridge Talent Agency which she ran from her Hollywood apartment. Two months of the year, when her navy husband of 29 years returned for his annual shore leave, she was a newlywed, madly in love. Then disaster struck. Hubby came home to stay, and he seemed intent on both bringing navy-style order to her chaotic life and making up for 29 years of lost time romantically. Ken didn't see why that gay, unemployed actor named Terry should be kept around the house (Terry earned his room and board by serving as Nancy's secretary), and in fact he thought she should close down the talent agency entirely. Adding to the confusion was Nancy's handwringing, hypochondriac daughter, Lorraine, son-in-law Glen, and Michael, the precocious, six-year-old son of boy-wonder TV network executive Teddy Futterman.

NANETTE FABRAY SHOW, THE, see *Westinghouse Playhouse*

NANNY, THE (*Situation Comedy*)

FIRST TELECAST: *November 3, 1993*

LAST TELECAST: *June 23, 1999*

BROADCAST HISTORY:

Nov 1993–Dec 1993, CBS Wed 8:30–9:00
Dec 1993–Sep 1994, CBS Wed 8:00–8:30
Jun 1994, CBS Mon 8:30–9:00
Jul 1994–Sep 1996, CBS Mon 8:00–8:30
Aug 1995–Sep 1995, CBS Wed 8:00–9:00
Sep 1996–Feb 1999, CBS Wed 8:00–8:30
May 1999–Jun 1999, CBS Wed 8:00–9:00

CAST:

Fran Fine .... Fran Drescher
Maxwell Sheffield .... Charles Shaughnessy
Chastity Claire "C. C." Babcock .... Lauren Lane
Niles .... Daniel Davis
Maggie Sheffield (age 14) .... Nicholle Tom
Brighton Sheffield (10) .... Benjamin Salisbury
Grace Sheffield (6) .... Madeline Zima
Sylvia Fine .... Renee Taylor
Yetta .... Ann Morgan Guilbert
Val Toriello .... Rachel Chagall
**Dr. Jack Miller (1997–1998)* .... Spaulding Gray
**Dr. Reynolds (1998–1999)* .... Nora Dunn

*Occasional

THEME:

"The Nanny Named Fran," composed and performed by Ann Hampton Callaway

Fran was a caricature of a middle-class Jewish girl—nasal voice, loud clothes—who, purely by accident, stumbled into a job working as a nanny for the children of a successful British theatrical producer. Showing up at the door of the Sheffield town house in Manhattan selling cosmetics, she was mistaken for an applicant for the vacant nanny position. After talking her way into the job, for which she had no experience, Fran moved into the Sheffield mansion, quite a change from the modest Queens apartment in which she had been living with her parents. The Sheffield household included Maxwell's three children—Maggie, a shy teenager; Brighton, a budding promoter; and cute-as-a-button Grace—and Niles, the sarcastic but compassionate butler. Also seen regularly were Maxwell's patronizing business partner, C.C., who had romantic designs on her widowed boss and felt threatened by the sexy, if uncultured, Fran; Sylvia and Yetta, Fran's mother and grandmother, who couldn't believe how lucky she had been to fall into her current job; and Val, Fran's best friend. She may not have been formally trained, but Fran's common sense and middle-class values stood her in good stead when solving the children's problems and offering sound advice. As Fran became more a part of the Sheffield family C.C. got progressively more hostile, while Niles, who despised C.C., loved it all.

In spring 1996, Maxwell was starting to realize he had strong feelings for Fran, and at season's end, in Paris, they actually got romantic and he proposed marriage to her—but later took it back. Fran agonized over her on-again off-again romance with Maxwell, and early in 1997 she started seeing a therapist, Dr. Miller, to help her cope with her marriage obsession. That spring Maxwell's play, *The Widower*, won the Tony Award for Best Play.

In the 1997–1998 season finale, with lots of flashbacks covering the ups and downs of their relationship over the years, Fran and Maxwell finally got married, in a traditional Jewish ceremony. At episode's end they were on a honeymoon cruise, but all did not go well. Fran fell over the railing, Maxwell dived in to save her, and as a result, their honeymoon was spent on an uninhabited island. When they got back to New York, they worked at adjusting to married life and Fran adopted Maxwell's children. In November, Fran discovered she was pregnant. In the series' swan song, aired as a special on May 19, 1999, Fran gave birth to twins; Niles married C.C.; and, amid a series of sentimental flashbacks, Fran closed up the New York house in preparation for the family's move to California.

Star Fran Drescher and her husband, Peter Marc Jacobson, who was one of the executive producers of *The Nanny*, were the creators of the series.

NANNY AND THE PROFESSOR (*Situation Comedy*)

FIRST TELECAST: *January 21, 1970*

LAST TELECAST: *December 27, 1971*

BROADCAST HISTORY:

Jan 1970–Aug 1970, ABC Wed 7:30–8:00
Sep 1970–Sep 1971, ABC Fri 8:00–8:30
Sep 1971–Dec 1971, ABC Mon 8:00–8:30

CAST:

Phoebe Figalilly .... Juliet Mills
Prof. Howard Everett .... Richard Long
Hal Everett .... David Doremus
Butch Everett .... Trent Lehman
Prudence Everett .... Kim Richards
Aunt Henrietta (1971) .... Elsa Lanchester
Francine Fowler .... Eileen Baral
Mrs. Florence Fowler .... Patsy Garrett

Phoebe was an uncanny young nanny who breezed in unannounced from England and captivated the Everett household. She arrived just at the right time, as Miss Dunbar, Prof. Everett's fifth housekeeper in a year, had just quit in utter frustration at trying to keep order in the chaotic household. That left the widowed mathematics professor in charge of Hal, a 12-year-old with a fascination for scientific experiments; 8-year-old Butch, who was into everything; and 5-year-old Prudence, a musical prodigy who practiced the same piano piece incessantly; plus Waldo, the family sheep-dog, Myrtle, the guinea pig, and other pets. Nanny's sunny disposition and apparently psychic abilities (could she really talk to the animals?) won everybody's heart in this relentlessly cute comedy.

NARROW ESCAPES (*Magazine*)
FIRST TELECAST: *November 26, 2002*
LAST TELECAST: *December 31, 2002*
BROADCAST HISTORY:
Nov 2002–Dec 2002, PAX Tue 9:00–10:00

Narrow Escapes told stories of real people who had survived disasters. The actual participants recounted what had happened to them and how they had pulled through. Among the escapees were a small boy who fell into a gorilla pit at a zoo, a pilot who brought his plane down without landing gear, a man trapped in his car after the 1989 San Francisco earthquake, a Daytona International Speedway pit crew worker who was hit by a speeding race car, and a pregnant woman who survived a fall from a burning apartment building in Chicago without losing her baby. Lucky folks.

NASH AIRFLYTE THEATER (*Dramatic Anthology*)
FIRST TELECAST: *September 21, 1950*
LAST TELECAST: *March 15, 1951*
BROADCAST HISTORY:
Sep 1950–Mar 1951, CBS Thu 10:30–11:00
HOST:
William Gaxton

This live New York-originated anthology series aired during the 1950–1951 season and was hosted by William Gaxton. The range of material was extremely varied. John Payne starred in the premiere telecast, a Western adapted from the O. Henry story "A Double-Dyed Deceiver." Metropolitan Opera soprano Marguerite Piazza starred in an original musical comedy called "The Box Supper," and Patricia Morison was featured in an adaptation of the Gilbert and Sullivan operetta *Trial by Jury*. On the more serious dramatic side, Barbara Bel Geddes starred in the first televised adaptation of a John Steinbeck story, "Molly Morgan." Grace Kelly, Otto Kruger, Fredric March, and Lee Bowman also starred in straight plays on this series.

NASH BRIDGES (*Police Drama*)
FIRST TELECAST: *March 29, 1996*
LAST TELECAST: *July 13, 2001*
BROADCAST HISTORY:
Mar 1996–May 1996, CBS Fri 10:00–11:00
Jul 1996–Jul 2001, CBS Fri 10:00–11:00
CAST:
Insp. Nash Bridges .... Don Johnson
Insp. Joe Dominguez .... Cheech Marin
Insp. Evan Cortez (1996–2000) ..... Jaime P. Gomez
Lt. A. J. Shimamura (1996)
.... Cary-Hiroyuki Tagawa
Insp. Harvey Leek .... Jeff Perry
Lisa Bridges (1996–1997) .... Annette O'Toole
**Kelly Weld (1996)* .... Serena Scott Thomas
Cassidy Bridges (age 16) .... Jodi Lyn O'Keefe
Insp. Bryn Carson (1996–1997) .... Mary Mara
**Asst. D.A. Stacy Bridges (1996–1999)*
.... Angela Dohrmann
Nick Bridges .... James Gammon
**Rick Bettina (1996–2000)* .... Daniel Roebuck
**Inger Dominguez* .... Caroline Lagerfelt
Whitney Thomas (1996–1997) .... Kate Vernon
**Insp. Michelle Chan (1997–1998)* .... Kelly Hu
Officer Ronnie (1997–2001) .... Ronald Russell
**Pepe (1997–2001)* .... Patrick Fischler
Lynette Summers (1998) .... Suki Kaiser
Caitlin Cross (1998–2000) .... Yasmine Bleeth
Insp. Antwon Babcock (2000–2001)
.... Cress Williams
Officer Rachel McCabe (2000–2001)
.... Wendy Moniz
Betty Ann McCurry (2001) .... Suzanne Krull
Lt. Ray Urbanski (2001) .... Bill Smitrovich
*Occasional

Seven years after *Miami Vice* left the air, hunky Don Johnson returned to network TV playing a cop who was a more mature and likable version of his Sonny Crockett character from the former series. Wisecracking Nash Bridges was head of the elite Special Investigations Unit of the San Francisco Police Department. He was laid-back, self-effacing, and friendly (he called everybody "bubba"), likely to try to talk his way out of tight situations before resorting to violence. When the series premiered, he reported to Lt. Shimamura, a by-the-book superior who was confounded by Nash's methods and amazed by his success rate. Others on the team were Harvey, the technology specialist who hadn't completely outgrown his counter-culture youth in the 1960s; Evan, the ambitious young womanizer who idolized Nash; Rick, Nash's rival, whose incompetence got him fired; and Bryn, a sexy but tough cop who didn't take crap from anyone. Nash's former partner, Joe, had retired from the force to become a private detective but seemed to get involved in most of Nash's cases. By the start of the second season he was back on the force and an official member of the team, but he still had a penchant for working on get-rich-quick schemes in his spare time—often getting both himself and Nash into embarrassing situations. The S.I.U. headquarters was in a domed plaza during the first season, and relocated to a boat moored at the Hyde Street Pier at the start of the second. In addition to the normal robberies and murders, their cases, which often necessitated going undercover, ran the gamut from chasing down drug dealers, to retrieving weapons stolen from the army, to finding the antidote for a deadly virus contracted by Joe.

Nash may have been one of the Bay area's top cops, but his personal life was a shambles. He had two failed marriages. The first, with Lisa, a successful caterer who still harbored animosity (mixed with affection) over their breakup, had produced a child, headstrong Cassidy, who lived with her mother. Nash and Lisa kept trying to get back together but it never worked out. The second, with Kelly, whose family was socially prominent, had failed because he wouldn't leave the force and get a safer and more acceptable job. Other family members were Nick, Nash's retired longshoreman father, who shared his fancy apartment; and Stacy, Nash's short-tempered sister, who revealed she was a lesbian during the 1996–1997 season. Nash tooled around town in a classic canary yellow 1970 Plymouth Barracuda convertible.

In November 1996, Shimamura moved back to Hawaii after being passed over for a promotion, and Nash became the acting head of the S.I.U. During that season Nash had a hot affair with Whitney, who was not quite separated from her husband, and in the spring of 1997, Joe's wife, Inger, gave birth to a daughter, Lusia. In spring 1998, Evan started an affair with Cassidy. That fall Michelle, an ambitious rookie cop, replaced the departed Bryn on the S.I.U. team. In December, Rick, who had been a bounty hunter after getting fired early on, returned as Director of Police Investigations, not because of his skills, but because his mother had recently married the Chief of the S.F.P.D. With the S.I.U. reporting to him, he became a recurring thorn in Nash's side. Late in the season Nash found out that Cassidy, who had been living with Lisa's sister Lynette since her mother had gotten a job as a chef in Paris, was having an affair with Evan.

At the start of the 1998–1999 season Cassidy, still involved with Evan, went off to college at Berkeley, and Nash and Joe had started a detective agency and were moonlighting, trying to build up a clientele. In October, Michelle was killed by a stalker (actress Hu moved to a featured role on CBS's *Martial Law* that season). Two weeks later Caitlin joined the cast as a straight-arrow Internal Affairs investigator assigned to find evidence to exonerate Nash and Joe from murder charges arising from a drug bust that had blown up. She didn't like Nash but succeeded anyway, staying on to do a comprehensive investigation of the S.I.U. group and occasionally assist on Nash's cases. Over time she started to warm up to him and at the end of the season finale, after admitting they were in love with each other, they consummated their relationship.

That fall Nash and Caitlin were living together and she was still working undercover for his team. Harvey had returned to work after having lost his left testicle to an accidental self-inflicted gunshot wound. During the season Evan, suffering from drug addiction, was suspended but, after getting his act back together, was reinstated. In the last episode of the season Cassidy and Evan were planning to get married but, while on an undercover assignment, he was shot and killed by a crook. In the last scene Caitlin, whose relationship with Nash had gotten pretty rocky during the season, moved to Washington. As the 2000–2001 season began Cassidy, who had just graduated from the police academy, joined the S.F.P.D. and Nash hired Antwon Babcock as Harvey's new partner. The following week Cassidy and her new partner, Rachel, got themselves transferred to the S.I.U. In the spring Joe, recently promoted to lieutenant, hired Betty Ann—a nutcase Nash had fired as his housekeeper—to be the S.I.U.'s new office assistant. As the series wound down it was revealed that Rachel, with whom Nash had fallen in love, was a mole planted in the S.I.U. to get incriminating evidence against him. She didn't and, in fact, discovered that Lt. Urbanski, who had it in for Nash, had altered files to make the case. After she told Nash what was going on, Rachel helped get the evidence that saved him and resulted in Urbanski's arrest. At end of the series finale Cassidy quit the police force and was leaving on a trip to Paris.

NASHVILLE NETWORK, THE (Network), see TNN

NASHVILLE 99 (*Police Drama*)

FIRST TELECAST: *April 1, 1977*
LAST TELECAST: *April 22, 1977*
BROADCAST HISTORY:
Apr 1977, CBS Fri 8:00–9:00
CAST:
Det. Lt. Stonewall Jackson "Stoney" Huff .... Claude Akins
Det. Trace Mayne .... Jerry Reed
Birdie Huff .... Lucille Benson

Filmed on location in Nashville, and utilizing many country music performers as guest stars playing themselves, *Nashville 99* was the story of a Southern lawman fighting crime in the C&W capital of the world. Stoney Huff was a veteran cop who, with the aid of his partner Trace (played by country music star Jerry Reed), fought organized crime, chased down kidnappers, and performed other law-enforcement duties in this short-lived series.

NASHVILLE NOW (*Talk/Variety*)

BROADCAST HISTORY:
The Nashville Network
60/90 minutes
Produced; *1983–1993*
Premiered: *March 8, 1983*
HOST:
Ralph Emery

One of country music's best-known hosts and interviewers, Ralph Emery was in many ways the face of the Nashville Network during its first decade. His live, nightly, prime-time variety show premiered on the day after the network went on the air and continued for ten years thereafter. Always courtly, never slick, and always respectful of the music both he and his audience loved, he lent the new network an air of instant respectability and tradition—perhaps a little *too* much tradition for the younger generation. Nevertheless, everybody who was anybody in country music showed up here, making the show almost as much an institution in Nashville as the *Grand Ole Opry* itself.

When Emery retired in 1993 he was replaced by the more contemporary team of Crook and Chase in the similarly styled *Music City Tonight* (q.v.).

NASHVILLE ON THE ROAD (*Music*)

BROADCAST HISTORY:
Syndicated only
30 minutes
Produced: *1975–1983* (208 episodes)
Released: *1975*
HOST:
Jim Ed Brown (1975–1981)
Jim Stafford (1981–1983)
REGULARS:
Jerry Clower (1975–1981)
Wendy Holcombe (1975–1981)
The Cates Sisters (1975–1976)
The Fairchilds (1976–1977)
Helen Cornelius (1977–1981)
Rex Allen, Jr. (1981–1983)
Sue Powell (1981–1983)

This popular country music series was filmed at colorful outdoor locations from Florida to Hawaii to Prince Edward Island, Canada—hence the "on the road." Different guest stars were featured each week.

NASHVILLE PALACE, THE (*Musical Variety*)
FIRST TELECAST: *October 24, 1981*
LAST TELECAST: *August 7, 1982*
BROADCAST HISTORY:
Oct 1981–Nov 1981, NBC Sat 9:00–10:00
Jul 1982–Aug 1982, NBC Sat 9:00–10:00
REGULARS:
Slim Pickens
Lynn Hancock
Chuck Bulot
Terri Gardner
Harry Murphy
Kent Perkins
Donna Siegel
Wendy Suits
Hamilton Camp
The Dixie Dozen Dancers
The Charlie McCoy Band

Originating from Opryland U.S.A. in Nashville, and produced by the people responsible for *Hee Haw, The Nashville Palace* was a mix of country music, comedy skits, and big production numbers. Each week a guest host presided over the show, although resident announcer Slim Pickens was on hand to heckle. Lynn Hancock was featured in a weekly visit to the "Boots" honky-tonk, where she was the hostess, Miss Boots. A group of comedians, collectively known as the Nashville Palace Comedy Company, performed in the skits. Guest hosts included Roy Clark, Roy Rogers and Dale Evans, and Joe Namath, with country stars Hank Williams, Jr., Mickey Gilley, Tom T. Hall, and Larry Gatlin among the performers.

NASHVILLE STAR (*Talent*)
BROADCAST HISTORY:
USA Network
60 minutes
Original episodes: *2003*
Premiered: *March 8, 2003*
HOST:
Nancy O'Dell
JUDGES:
Tracy Gershon
Charlie Robison
Robert K. Oermann
CREATIVE CONSULTANT:
Clint Black

Country music got its own version of *American Idol* in this elaborate talent competition designed to find the next country star. It began with 8,000 auditions nationwide, conducted in conjunction with 50 country radio stations, leading to five regional finals in cities from Los Angeles to Baltimore. In addition to the five regional winners the judges picked seven more from the audition tapes, for a total of 12 finalists who were flown to Nashville to begin nine weeks of live telecasts. Some of the finalists were notified in their homes or on their farms as cameras caught the whoops and hugs of family and friends. Hee-haw!

Once in Nashville the 12 (six men, six women)—an interesting mix of young newcomers and old hands who had never quite made it in the music biz—lived in a big old brick house, where they practiced and got to know each other. On the weekly telecasts, from Opryland's BellSouth Acuff Theatre, they performed classic country songs, their own compositions, and pop songs in a country style. They were judged by a trio of experts who seemed to be aping *American Idol*'s "squabbling judges" format—Sony Music executive Tracy, sarcastic singer Charlie and seen-it-all author Robert. The judges could be pretty cutting, too. To a sexy female: "I loved the way you slapped your ass. Unfortunately ass-slapping is only a very small part of country music"; to a rocker: "Great—but I don't think there's a country bone in your body." In addition, guest stars appeared, including Clint Black, Wynonna Judd and Brad Paisley.

In the early rounds two finalists were eliminated each week, one by the judges and one by viewers at home (via phone and Internet vote), but starting with episode five only one was eliminated per week, by viewer vote. On the next-to-last episode the three remaining finalists (Buddy Jewell, Miranda Lambert and John Arthur Martinez) got to sing duets with real Nashville stars, and on the finale viewers chose the winner, who got a Sony recording contract and had his CD produced by country star Clint Black. The winner was 41-year-old Nashville demo singer Buddy Jewell, a former *Star Search* winner who had been trying to break into the big time for years. A commanding presence with his hefty appearance, black hat and "cry in the voice" vocal style, he showed considerable humility at his win but closed out the show with the ironic rhythm number, "I Just Want to Thank Everyone Who Ever Told Me 'No'—Down on Music Row."

NASTY BOYS (*Police Drama*)
FIRST TELECAST: *February 19, 1990*
LAST TELECAST: *July 22, 1990*
BROADCAST HISTORY:
Feb 1990, NBC Mon 9:00–11:00
Feb 1990–Jun 1990, NBC Fri 9:00–10:00
Jul 1990, NBC Sun 9:00–11:00
CAST:
Paul Morrissey .... Jeff Kaake
Eduardo Cruz .... Benjamin Bratt
Alex Wheeler .... Don Franklin
Danny Larsen .... Craig Hurley
Jimmy Kee .... James Pax
Lt. Stan Krieger .... Dennis Franz
Chief Bradley .... Sandy McPeak
Serena Cruz .... Nia Peeples

A routine action series about a team of young Las Vegas undercover vice cops who plied their violent trade wearing hoods and ninja-style black outfits. That's right, the cops wore hoods. (Their outfits were at least emblazoned with the word "POLICE" in big letters, so bystanders would have some idea which side they were on.) Their cases were the big league murders, drug deals, and arms trading that seemed to have made Las Vegas into Crime City, U.S.A. Paul (the hunk), Danny (the kid), Alex (the black), Eduardo (the Latino), and Jimmy (the Asian) made up the typically TV-mixed team, while Lt. Krieger was their hard-bitten superior and Serena was Eduardo's pregnant wife.

Surprisingly, *Nasty Boys* was based on a real-life police unit, the North Las Vegas Narcotics Bureau.

NAT "KING" COLE SHOW, THE (*Musical Variety*)

FIRST TELECAST: *November 5, 1956*

LAST TELECAST: *December 17, 1957*

BROADCAST HISTORY:

Nov 1956–Jun 1957, NBC Mon 7:30–7:45
Jul 1957–Sep 1957, NBC Tue 10:00–10:30
Sep 1957–Dec 1957, NBC Tue 7:30–8:00

REGULARS:

Nat "King" Cole
The Boataneers (1956)
The Herman McCoy Singers
The Randy Van Horne Singers (1957)
The Jerry Graff Singers (1957)
The Cheerleaders (1957)
Nelson Riddle and His Orchestra

Nat "King" Cole was a man ahead of his time, and that fact cost him his network series. When his 15-minute show premiered in 1956, he became the first major black performer to headline a network variety series. There had been previous attempts at black series, but they were either short-lived fill-ins with lesser-known talent such as *Sugar Hill Times* in 1949 and *Hazel Scott* in 1950, or rather degrading parodies such as *Beulah* or *Amos 'n' Andy*. Nat's short Monday evening show, which filled the remainder of the half hour in which NBC aired its nightly news program, allowed him little more than the opportunity to sing a couple of songs and occasionally welcome a guest vocalist. The following July, Nat moved to Tuesdays with an expanded half-hour show, allowing time for more variety and guests.

Throughout its run, however, *The Nat "King" Cole Show* was plagued with problems. It failed to attract a significant audience, and therefore sponsors were reluctant to underwrite the show. From 1956–1957 Nat averaged only 19 percent of the viewing audience, compared to the 50 percent who were watching *Robin Hood* on CBS. Nat even trailed a documentary-travelogue on ABC, called *Bold Journey*, which got 21 percent of the audience (the remaining 10 percent were watching non-network programs).

Despite widespread apathy on the part of viewers and sponsors, NBC did not give up on the show, keeping it on the air, at a loss, through the fall of 1957. The performing community was well aware of Nat's sponsor problems, and many stars appeared on the show for minimum fees as personal favors to him, in an effort to save the show. Virtually every black musical star showed up at one time or another, including Count Basie, Mahalia Jackson, Pearl Bailey, Billy Eckstine, Sammy Davis, Jr., the Mills Brothers, Cab Calloway, Ella Fitzgerald, and Harry Belafonte. Nat had his white supporters too, among them Stan Kenton, Frankie Laine, Mel Torme, Peggy Lee, Gogi Grant, Tony Martin, and Tony Bennett. But the effort was in vain. It would be another decade before black entertainers could begin to make a significant dent in the mass medium of television.

NATIONAL BARN DANCE, THE, see *ABC Barn Dance*

NATIONAL BOWLING CHAMPIONS (*Sports*)

FIRST TELECAST: *April 8, 1956*

LAST TELECAST: *December 29, 1957*

BROADCAST HISTORY:

Apr 1956–Dec 1956, NBC Sun 10:30–11:00
Sep 1957–Dec 1957, ABC Sun 8:30–9:00

COMMENTATOR:

"Whispering" Joe Wilson

In 1956 *National Bowling Champions* was telecast live from Chicago. Two professional bowlers competed in a three-game match, the last game and a half telecast on the air. The winner received $1 for every pin knocked down, $10 for every pin in excess of 700 for the series, and $10,000 for a perfect "300" game.

Essentially the same show, with some minor changes, returned on ABC in the fall of 1957, under the title *Bowling Stars*. Also originating from Chicago, the ABC show was filmed in advance, and the winner who, as on NBC, would return the following week to defend his "King of the Hill" title, won a minimum of $1,000. The bonuses for scores in excess of 700 applied to both bowlers, with the loser taking home $1 for every pin knocked down (instead of the flat $500 on NBC), and the $10,000 bonus for a "300" game was still in effect. The series moved to Sunday afternoons in 1958. It remained on Sundays, with the new title *Bowling Stars*, from January 1958 to March 1959 on ABC, and from October 1960 to May 1961 on NBC.

NATIONAL GEOGRAPHIC CHANNEL (Network)
(*Documentary Cable Network*)

LAUNCHED:

January 2001

SUBSCRIBERS (MAY 2003):

43.1 million (40% U.S.)

After years of watching *National Geographic Specials* and the *National Geographic Explorer* series, viewers finally got a whole channel from the famous exploration society in 2001. The schedule, not surprisingly, consisted of documentaries on the flora and fauna of the world, including the strange habits of *Homo sapiens*. Among them were *Phobia* (human phobias), *Taboo* (taboos worldwide), *Dogs with Jobs* and *Built for the Kill* (predators), along with such whimsical titles as *Croc Around the Clock, Animals of the NFL* and *Mummy Road Show*.

NATIONAL GEOGRAPHIC EXPLORER
(*Documentary*)

BROADCAST HISTORY:

Nickelodeon/TBS/CNBC/MSNBC
3 hours/2 hours
Produced: *1985–*
Premiered: *April 7, 1985* (NIK); *February 2, 1986* (TBS); *September 4, 1999* (CNBC); *2001* (MSNBC)

HOST:

David Greenman (1985–1986)
Tom Chapin (1986–1989)
Bob Ballard (1989–1991)
Robert Urich (1991–1994)
Boyd Matson (1994–)

A highly regarded magazine show produced by the National Geographic Society, exploring the natural wonders of the world. It began as a three-hour show late Sunday afternoon on Nickelodeon, which was then a daytime children's network. The first episode followed explorers down 128 miles of raging river in Iceland, then visited the wildlife of Mount McKinley and Brazil's Pantanal region. When the series moved to TBS in February 1986, it was scheduled for two hours on Sunday nights, where it remained for many years. It later moved to CNBC, and then MSNBC.

The Society is also well known for its *National Geographic Specials*, aired on CBS (1964–1973), ABC (1973–1975), and PBS (since 1975).

NATIONAL VELVET (*Adventure*)
FIRST TELECAST: *September 18, 1960*
LAST TELECAST: *September 10, 1962*
BROADCAST HISTORY:
Sep 1960–Sep 1961, NBC Sun 8:00–8:30
Sep 1961–Sep 1962, NBC Mon 8:00–8:30
CAST:
Velvet Brown .... Lori Martin
Martha Brown .... Ann Doran
Mi Taylor .... James McCallion
Herbert Brown .... Arthur Space
Edwina Brown .... Carole Wells
Donald Brown .... Joseph Scott
Teddy .... Carl Crow
John Hadley (1961–1962) .... Rickey Kelman

National Velvet, with its story of a girl and her dreams to run her horse in a championship race, is a classic young people's novel. The movie version (1944) had propelled child actress Elizabeth Taylor to stardom. For TV the setting was changed from England to a Midwestern American dairy farm. Twelve-year-old Velvet had a beautiful chestnut thoroughbred named King, and her greatest dream in the whole world was to train King well enough to run in the Grand National Steeplechase. Velvet's parents, Herbert and Martha, who ran the small dairy farm, shared her love and hopes. Helping her train King was Mi Taylor, an ex-jockey who worked around the farm as a handyman. Also in the cast were Velvet's teenage sister, Winna, her younger brother, Donald, Winna's boyfriend, Teddy, and Donald's friend John. The episodes dealt with the other members of the family on occasion, but centered mostly on Velvet and King.

NATION'S FUTURE, THE (*Debate*)
FIRST TELECAST: *November 12, 1960*
LAST TELECAST: *September 16, 1961*
BROADCAST HISTORY:
Nov 1960–Sep 1961, NBC Sat 9:30–10:30
MODERATOR:
John K. M. McCaffery (1960–1961)
Edwin Newman (1961)

The Nation's Future was a live weekly debate series in which two internationally known public figures, often politicians, expressed their opposing views on a specific issue of national interest. Topics covered ranged from foreign policy and social services to censorship and birth control. On occasion the first half hour of the show was national with local stations filling the second half hour with their own discussion of the issue being covered. John K. M. McCaffery was the moderator through May 27, 1961, and was replaced on June 10, 1961, by Edwin Newman.

NATURE OF THINGS, THE (*Instruction*)
FIRST TELECAST: *February 5, 1948*
LAST TELECAST: *August 29, 1952*
BROADCAST HISTORY:
Feb 1948–Mar 1948, NBC Thu 9:45–10:00
Apr 1948–Dec 1948, NBC Thu 8:15–8:30
Dec 1948–May 1949, NBC Mon Various 15-minute spots
Jul 1949–Aug 1949, NBC Mon 9:30–9:45
Sep 1949–Feb 1950, NBC Sat 7:30–7:45
Mar 1950–Jun 1950, NBC Sat 6:45–7:00
Jun 1950–Sep 1950, NBC Wed 8:15–8:30
Jun 1951–Aug 1951, NBC Fri 10:45–11:00
Jul 1952–Aug 1952, NBC Fri 10:45–11:00
HOST:
Dr. Roy K. Marshall

Dr. Roy K. Marshall of the Fels Planetarium was one of early TV's favorite scientists. His live science program, which was telecast from Philadelphia, featured illustrated talks and interviews on many subjects, including physics, astronomy, and the weather. One early 1948 telecast originated from an observatory, where the camera gave a live telescope's-eye view of the moon and Saturn. Such subjects as the possibility of future space travel were also discussed.

After two and a half years in prime time the program left the air in September 1950. It returned the following January as a Saturday afternoon show, and remained a Saturday/Sunday fixture (aside from some prime-time telecasts in the summers) until 1954.

NAVY LOG (*Military Anthology*)
FIRST TELECAST: *September 20, 1955*
LAST TELECAST: *September 25, 1958*
BROADCAST HISTORY:
Sep 1955–Oct 1955, CBS Tue 8:00–8:30
Nov 1955–Sep 1956, CBS Tue 8:30–9:00
Oct 1956–Oct 1957, ABC Wed 8:30–9:00
Oct 1957–Jan 1958, ABC Thu 10:00–10:30
Jan 1958–Sep 1958, ABC Thu 9:30–10:00

The filmed dramas aired in this series were all reenactments of incidents that had actually happened to U.S. Navy personnel.

The focus was on individual sailors and airmen, often in a battle setting but sometimes in their private lives, as in the story of a mentally disturbed veteran, or a romance disrupted by a sailor's transfer. Most of the subjects were ordinary servicemen, but some famous incidents were dramatized, such as the plan to ambush the plane carrying Admiral Yamamoto, the Japanese commander during World War II, and the sinking of John F. Kennedy's PT-109 in the South Pacific (Kennedy, then a senator, appeared as a special guest on this telecast). Lesser known actors and actresses were featured, although famous personalities sometimes served as host. The stories were all based on official navy files, and produced with the cooperation of the Navy Department.

NEARLY DEPARTED (*Situation Comedy*)
FIRST TELECAST: *April 10, 1989*
LAST TELECAST: *May 1, 1989*
BROADCAST HISTORY:
Apr 1989–May 1989, NBC Mon 8:30–9:00
CAST:
Grant Pritchard .... Eric Idle
Claire Pritchard .... Caroline McWilliams
Mike Dooley .... Stuart Pankin
Liz Dooley .... Wendy Schaal
Derek Dooley .... Jay Lambert
Jack Garrett .... Henderson Forsythe

Shades of *Topper! Monty Python* star Eric Idle headlined this ghostly comedy, which flashed on and off the NBC schedule like a fleeting apparition. Grant was a snobbish English professor who, with his wife, Claire, was killed in an auto accident. As if that wasn't enough to ruin their day, they were then forced to watch (as ghosts) while plumbing contractor Mike, his wife Liz, and obnoxious teenage son Derek moved into their elegant home and proceeded to "redecorate" the place. The irritable professor had only one contact with the world of the living; he was able to communicate with the Dooleys' Grandpa Jack, an old curmudgeon who gave him lip. It was enough to make one want to die.

NED AND STACEY (*Situation Comedy*)
FIRST TELECAST: *September 11, 1995*
LAST TELECAST: *January 27, 1997*
BROADCAST HISTORY:
Sep 1995–Dec 1995, FOX Mon 9:30–10:00
Dec 1995–Apr 1996, FOX Mon 9:00–9:30
Jun 1996–Jul 1996, FOX Mon 8:00–8:30
Nov 1996–Jan 1997, FOX Sun 8:30–9:00
Jan 1997, FOX Mon 9:00–9:30
CAST:
Ned Dorsey .... Thomas Haden Church
Stacey Colbert .... Debra Messing
Eric "Rico" Moyer .... Greg Germann
Amanda Moyer .... Nadia Dajani
**Saul Colbert (1995–1996)* .... Harry Goz
**Ellen Colbert (1995–1996)* .... Dori Brenner
**Les MacDowell (1995–1996)* .... John Getz
**Howard Moyer (age 8)* .... Andrew Arons
**Patrick Kirkland (1995–1996)* .... James Karen
Nate (1996–1997) .... Ford Rainey
*Occasional

This was certainly not a marriage made in heaven. Stacey, a writer for the *Village Voice*, was desperate for an apartment, and Ned was an arrogant, conniving executive who needed a wife to help his image at the Kirkland & Haywood Advertising Agency where he worked. In the first episode they were fixed up by her sister Amanda, whose neurotic husband, Eric, the accountant at Kirkland & Haywood, was Ned's best friend. Despite the fact that it was despise-at-first-sight, they got married the following week—she got the spare bedroom in his fancy apartment and he got the "perfect wife" to take to company functions. After she was let go at the *Voice*, Stacey got a job writing for *Skyward*, the in-flight magazine for Dollar Jet Airlines. Ned and Stacey feuded all the time, were both dating other people (although his were a succession of one-night stands), and yet, at times, almost seemed to be developing affection for each other. In the season finale Ned fixed Stacey up with a guy she fell in love with, and when that relationship created all sorts of problems for his sham married life, he tossed her out—despite a passionate kiss just before the final "get out."

Even though they were getting divorced at the start of the second season, Stacey moved back into Ned's apartment. Then Amanda convinced Ned to invest in a big real estate deal, and when it fell apart, they ended up as partners (his investment gave him 86 percent) in "Amanda's Muffins," a small store that gave them plenty of time to push each other's buttons. The focus of the series shifted to the Ned and Amanda relationship, with Stacey's role diminishing. Amanda ran the business with Ned, who was still at the ad agency but constantly butting in at the store where Nate was a regular customer.

NED BLESSING—THE STORY OF MY LIFE & TIMES (*Western*)
FIRST TELECAST: *August 18, 1993*
LAST TELECAST: *September 8, 1993*
BROADCAST HISTORY:
Aug 1993–Sep 1993, CBS Wed 9:00–10:00
CAST:
Ned Blessing .... Brad Johnson
One Horse .... Wes Studi
Crecencio .... Luis Avalos
Sticks Packwook .... Tim Scott
The Wren .... Brenda Bakke
Judge Longley .... Richard Riehle
Verlon Borgers .... Bill McKinney
Hugh Bell Borgers .... Jeremy Roberts
Roby Borgers .... Rob Campbell
Big Emma .... Rusty Schwimmer

Each episode of this supernatural Western opened with old Ned Blessing, a notorious bandit, in his jail cell writing his memoirs while waiting to be hanged for his crimes. Viewers may have wondered how bad those crimes really were since his memoirs—and the series—dealt mostly with his incredible heroics when he had been sheriff of the town of Plum Creek. Ned had returned to Plum Creek, his hometown, in search of his father, only to find it run by the maniacally ruthless Verlon Borgers and his three sons (the good, the bad, and the idiot). Borgers had killed the sheriff and put his head in a pickle jar, which he kept on display in Big Emma's saloon. Noble Ned took him on and was almost killed too when the dead sheriff's ghost materialized and struck Borgers deaf, dumb, and blind. Unfortunately Borger's youngest son, Roby, blamed Ned for this, as did Big Emma, who loved the now insensible lout, whom she led around on a rope. Treacherous Emma, a Swede built like a tank, and Roby looked for ways to kill Ned. Others in town were Crecencio, Ned's cautious sidekick; One Horse, an Indian who carried around a mysterious bag he would never open; Sticks, a cowardly local who idolized Ned, and The Wren, a sexy dance hall girl who fell in love with Ned.

NEEDLES AND PINS (*Situation Comedy*)
FIRST TELECAST: *September 21, 1973*
LAST TELECAST: *December 28, 1973*
BROADCAST HISTORY:
Sep 1973–Dec 1973, NBC Fri 9:00–9:30
CAST:
Nathan Davidson .... Norman Fell
Harry Karp .... Louis Nye
Wendy Nelson .... Deirdre Lenihan
Sonia Baker .... Sandra Deel
Charlie Miller .... Bernie Kopell
Max .... Larry Gelman
Myron Russo .... Alex Henteloff
Julius Singer .... Milton Selzer

New York City's famous garment district was the setting for this situation comedy about Nathan Davidson, owner of the Lorelei Fashion House, a manufacturer of women's clothing. Also prominent were Nathan's brother and partner, Harry, and his new designer, Wendy, a Nebraska girl adjusting both to life in the big city and the hectic pace of the fashion industry. Featured in the series were Sonia, the bookkeeper and secretary; Charlie, the firm's salesman; Max, the fabric cutter; Myron, the pattern maker; and Singer, Nathan's principal competitor.

NEON RIDER (*Drama*)

BROADCAST HISTORY:

Syndicated only
60 minutes
Produced: *1990–1994* (64 episodes)
Released: *October 1990*

CAST:

Dr. Michael Terry .... Winston Rekert
Vic .... Samuel Sarkar
C. C. Dechardon .... Alex Bruhanski
Fox Devlin .... Antoinette Bower
John Philip Reed .... William S. Taylor
Pin .... Peter Williams
Rachel Woods .... Suzanne Errett-Balcom

Michael Terry was a psychologist with a concern for the well-being and rehabilitation of troubled teenagers. He had given up his practice to purchase and run a ranch where young people with emotional and/or criminal problems were sent to try and get their lives back on track in an environment free from the stresses and temptations of city life. Working at the ranch were Vic, the Indian ranch hand; C. C., the cook; and Fox, the woman who had been running it for the previous owner. Also seen regularly were Pin, Michael's West Indian friend and contact on the streets of Vancouver; John Reed, the Vancouver cop who was responsible for remanding juvenile offenders to Michael's custody; and Rachel, who worked for the social service agency that placed young people with him.

Originally produced for the CTV television network in Canada. Only the first season's episodes were syndicated in the U. S.

NERO WOLFE (*Detective Drama*)

FIRST TELECAST: *January 16, 1981*
LAST TELECAST: *August 25, 1981*

BROADCAST HISTORY:

Jan 1981–Apr 1981, NBC Fri 9:00–10:00
Apr 1981–Aug 1981, NBC Tue 10:00–11:00

CAST:

Nero Wolfe .... William Conrad
Archie Goodwin .... Lee Horsley
Saul Panzer .... George Wyner
Theodore Horstman .... Robert Coote
Fritz Brenner .... George Voskovec
Inspector Cramer .... Allan Miller

Nero Wolfe was a reclusive, rotund crime-solving genius who rarely ventured out of his lavish New York City brownstone. A wealthy eccentric, Nero seemed most concerned with his prize-winning orchids, spending much of his time tending them in his private greenhouse. But he also had a nose for detective work. Since he rarely left his home, he depended on his trusted assistant, Archie Goodwin, to do most of the legwork and gather the clues. Nero then neatly provided the brilliant analysis and deduction that led to the solution. Others on Nero's staff were Saul Panzer, who helped Archie; Horstman, Nero's valued horticulturist; and Fritz, the gourmet cook.

Although adapted from the extensive series of novels by author Rex Stout, *Nero Wolfe* could actually have been an extension of the character played by star William Conrad in his previous series *Cannon*. Wolfe certainly looked like Cannon in semiretirement. Both men had expensive tastes, were lovers of gourmet food, and had similarly well-developed powers of analytical deduction.

NERO WOLFE (*Detective Drama*)

BROADCAST HISTORY:

Arts & Entertainment Network
60 minutes
Original episodes: *2001–2002* (29 episodes)
Premiered: *April 22, 2001*

CAST:

Nero Wolfe .... Maury Chaykin
Archie Goodwin .... Timothy Hutton
Saul Panzer .... Conrad Dunn (aka George Jenesky)
Fritz Brenner .... Colin Fox
Insp. Cramer .... Bill Smitrovich

This 2001 version of *Nero Wolfe* was a meticulous adaptation of the Rex Stout novels, right down to the layout of the sleuth's elegant 35th Street New York City brownstone—the one-way mirror panel in the front door (the better to see visitors before they see you), his private elevator, the leather chairs in his opulent office, and the greenhouse on the roof for his beloved orchids. As in the novels, Wolfe was gruff and arrogant, speaking in epigrams and lecturing the cigar-chomping, perpetually annoyed Inspector Cramer about the "obvious" clues he had missed in their latest murder mystery. Archie (who narrated) was Wolfe's nebbishy, wiseguy assistant; Saul, his security chief; and Fritz, the dignified old Swiss butler. The 1950s setting was reinforced by period music, two-tone shoes, fedoras, and stylized fights, but it all must have seemed rather musty in the high-tech 21st century. The series was spun off from a TV movie, *The Golden Spiders*, telecast on A&E on March 5, 2000.

NET, THE (*Drama*)

BROADCAST HISTORY:

USA Network
60 minutes
Produced: *1998* (22 episodes)
Premiered: *July 19, 1998*

CAST:

Angela Bennett .... Brooke Langton
Sorcerer (voice) .... Tim Curry
Trelawney .... Joseph Bottoms
Greg Hearney .... Mackenzie Gray
Jacob Resh .... Eric Szmanda

Angela was your typical, beautiful, computer geek, happily hacking away in her equipment-filled apartment when she suddenly got a strange e-mail that she was not supposed to see. Within minutes her best friend had been killed, her identity had been erased from all public records (no more credit cards), and men with guns were after her. *Delete, delete!* Too late. Soon Angela was on the run, battling the mysterious forces that had destroyed her life, and, as it turned out, perhaps her scientist father's as well. They were a secret and very ruthless organization called the Praetorian Guard, a well-funded cabal whose goal was to take over the world by staging natural, technological, economic, and other disasters, to disrupt society. Angela was in their way, and smug but ineffective agent Trelawney and his henchman Hearney were dispatched to eliminate her.

In addition to her own considerable resourcefulness,

Angela had an ally in the person—or at least, the voice—of the Sorcerer. Speaking through her high-tech, laptop computer, which seemed to work wherever she took it, he gave her directions, warnings, and the resources she needed to continue her fight. Sorcerer was connected somehow with her father's disappearance many years before, but his identity and motives remained unclear. Toward the end of the series' short run Angela and her friend Jacob finally did bring down the Praetorians, and she embarked on a new career as an agent for a federal agency called the C.I.C. Alas, it was a short career.

Based on the 1995 techno-thriller movie starring Sandra Bullock as the deleted damsel.

NEVER MIND THE BUZZCOCKS (*Quiz*)

BROADCAST HISTORY:

VH1
30 minutes
Original episodes: *2002* (5 episodes)
Premiered: *March 4, 2002*

REGULARS:

Marc Maron, Emcee
Daphne Brogdon
Matt Price

Music trivia quiz in which two teams of wisecracking "celebrities" competed to answer generally silly questions about music and music videos. Categories included Quotes ("Who said 'Saw myself on TV and threw up'—Neil Diamond or Carnie Wilson?"), Song Intros (two team members answered by performing them a capella), Dress You Up (identify signature duds), and Finish-the-Lyrics. Guests were mostly B-list and/or past their prime, including David Cross, Scott Thompson, Lisa Lisa, Coolio, and the inevitable Sebastian Bach. The show itself became trivia after only five episodes had aired.

Based on a more successful British show that began in 1996. The odd title was a nod to the Sex Pistols' groundbreaking 1977 album *Never Mind the Bollocks* and the 1980s punk-rock band the Buzzcocks.

NEW ADDAMS FAMILY, THE (*Situation Comedy*)

BROADCAST HISTORY:

Fox Family Channel
30 minutes
Produced: *1998–1999* (65 episodes)
Premiered: *October 19, 1998*

CAST (1998):

Morticia Addams .... Ellie Harvie
Gomez Addams .... Glenn Taranto
Uncle Fester .... Michael Roberds
Lurch .... John DeSantis
Grandmama .... Betty Phillips
Pugsley Addams .... Brodie Smith
Wednesday Addams .... Nicole Marie Fugere
**Grandpa Addams* .... John Astin

*Occasional

A new live-action version of the durable "ghoul comedy" *The Addams Family* (q.v.) was seen on cable beginning in 1998. This one was wilder and more effects-laden than its predecessors, influenced, apparently, by the *Addams Family* movies of the late '90s. John Astin was back, this time in a recurring role as Grandpa Addams.

NEW ADVENTURES OF BEANS BAXTER, THE (*Adventure/Espionage*)

FIRST TELECAST: *July 18, 1987*
LAST TELECAST: *April 9, 1988*
BROADCAST HISTORY:

Jul 1987–Oct 1987, FOX Sat 8:30–9:00
Oct 1987–Apr 1988, FOX Sat 9:00–9:30

CAST:

Benjamin "Beans" Baxter, Jr. .... Jonathan Ward
Number Two .... Jerry Wasserman
Cake Lase .... Karen Mistal
Woodshop .... Stuart Fratkin
Mrs. Susan Baxter .... Elinor Donahue
Scooter Baxter .... Scott Bremner
Mr. Sue .... Kurtwood Smith
Vlodia .... Bruce Wagner
Henry .... David Longworth

Teenager Beans Baxter led a double life in this very tongue-in-cheek espionage series. To the outside world he was just a student at Upper Georgetown High School in suburban Washington, D.C., living with his mother, Susan, who was oblivious to all that was going on around her, and his little brother, Scooter. Woodshop was Beans's off-beat best friend at school and Cake the beautiful girl who would have gone steady with him if only he wasn't so distracted.

Those distractions stemmed from Beans's other life as a courier-spy for an intelligence agency known as "The Network." His father, Benjamin, (played by Rick Lenz), had been a top courier for The Network—disguised as a mailman—until he was kidnapped by agents for U.G.L.I., the subversive Underground Government Liberation Intergroup. The minions of U.G.L.I., led by the diabolical Mr. Sue, were forever trying to capture Beans, hoping to use the threat of harming him to force his dad to reveal top-secret information. Meanwhile Beans, under the direction of The Network's second-in-command, Number Two, delivered top-secret messages by hiding in vending machines and riding his bicycle into secret hideouts, while trying to find a way to free his dad from the clutches of U.G.L.I.

NEW ADVENTURES OF CHARLIE CHAN, THE (*Mystery*)

BROADCAST HISTORY:

Syndicated only
30 minutes
Produced: *1956–1957* (39 episodes)
Released: *June 1957*

CAST:

Charlie Chan .... J. Carrol Naish
Barry Chan .... James Hong

Earl Derr Biggers's famous philosopher-sleuth came to television only briefly in the 1950s, in this British-made series. In previous productions Chan had been an inspector on the Honolulu Police Force, but here he operated out of London, unraveling complex mysteries with the patience and deduction for which he had become famous. As always, his manners were impeccable. His number-one son and trusted aide was Barry.

New York Irishman J. Carrol Naish was one of a long line of non-Orientals to play Chan. Among the others were Warner Oland, Sydney Toler, and Roland

Winters in the movies of the 1930s and 1940s; Walter Connolly, Ed Begley, and Santos Ortega on radio during the same period. There were also Charlie Chan comic strips and comic books. In 1971 there were plans for another TV series, and a pilot movie was made starring Ross Martin, but it was not successful. Even later, there was a somewhat ridiculous Charlie Chan cartoon on CBS' Saturday morning schedule (1972–1974) called *The Amazing Chan and the Chan Clan*.

Charlie Chan was originally modeled on a real person, detective Chang Apana of the Honolulu police.

NEW ADVENTURES OF HUCK FINN, THE (*Adventure*)

FIRST TELECAST: *September 15, 1968*
LAST TELECAST: *September 7, 1969*
BROADCAST HISTORY:
Sep 1968–Sep 1969, NBC Sun 7:00–7:30
CAST:
Huck Finn .... Michael Shea
Becky Thatcher .... Lu Ann Haslam
Tom Sawyer .... Kevin Schultz
Injun Joe .... Ted Cassidy

Much in the style of the highly successful Disney movie *Mary Poppins*, *The New Adventures of Huck Finn* combined live actors with animated settings. The three young principals, Huck, Becky, and Tom, were confronted with Injun Joe at the start of the first episode. He had sworn to get even with Huck for testifying against him in court and the three youngsters, fearing for their lives, ran away to escape him. As they ran, they began an adventure in which the villain was an animated version of Injun Joe. From episode to episode, the settings varied between contemporary and historical, domestic and foreign. The youngsters were always the only live characters in an otherwise animated adventure series.

NEW ADVENTURES OF MARTIN KANE, THE, see *Martin Kane, Private Eye*

NEW ADVENTURES OF ROBIN HOOD, THE (*Adventure*)

BROADCAST HISTORY:
TNT and Syndication
60 minutes
Produced: *1996–1997* (52 episodes)
Premiered: *January 13, 1997* (TNT); *September 1998* (Syndication)
CAST:
Robin Hood (1997–1998) .... Matthew Porretta
Robin Hood (1998–1999) .... John Bradley
Maid Marion Fitzwalter (1997) .... Anna Galvin
Maid Marion Fitzwalter (1997–1999) .... Barbara Griffin
Little John .... Richard Ashton
Friar Tuck .... Martyn Ellis
Kemal .... Hakim Alston
**Olwyn* .... Christopher Lee
Rowena (1998–1999) .... Christie Woods

*Occasional

An attempt to update the Robin Hood legend for the '90s. Robin was dapper and wisecracking; Maid Marion, clad in skimpy leather outfits, was into female empowerment, teaching self-defense to the village women; Little John was a big, blond lug—a little dense, but not stupid; and Friar Tuck was always eating. Together they fought villains in twelfth century England's Sherwood Forest, among them marauding Vikings, Mongols, and the local tyrant: pompous, cowardly Prince John. The series incorporated more fantasy elements than previous versions, with ghosts, demons, sorcerers, and black magic, but due to budget limitations the special effects were rather primitive—for example, the Prince's men being knocked off their horses by branches as they galloped through the forest. The dialogue was campy ("Let's go kick some butt!").

Due to low ratings, first Marion, and then Robin, were recast, and several new characters—previously unknown in Robin Hood lore—were added. Kemal was Robin's big, black karate-kicking ally; Olwyn, a mighty sorcerer; and Rowena, Olwyn's sexy but marginally competent Valley Girl apprentice.

The New Adventures of Robin Hood aired on TNT in 1997–1998, with new episodes appearing in syndication during the latter year. An animated *Robin Hood* was syndicated at the same time, by the same producers, but was equally unsuccessful.

NEW ADVENTURES OF WONDER WOMAN, THE, see *Wonder Woman*

NEW ANDY GRIFFITH SHOW, THE (*Situation Comedy*)

FIRST TELECAST: *January 8, 1971*
LAST TELECAST: *May 21, 1971*
BROADCAST HISTORY:
Jan 1971–May 1971, CBS Fri 8:30–9:00
CAST:
Andy Sawyer .... Andy Griffith
Lee Sawyer .... Lee Meriwether
Nora .... Ann Morgan Guilbert
Lori Sawyer .... Lori Rutherford
T. J. Sawyer .... Marty McCall
Buff MacKnight .... Glen Ash
Verline MacKnight .... Susan Davis

Andy Sawyer had been working in a government capacity in the state capital when he was informed that the mayor of his hometown of Greenwood was retiring and looking for someone to take over the unexpired portion of his current term. Andy moved home, with his wife, Lee, and his two children, to take the job. Greenwood was a small, rural Southern town and the role of mayor gave star Andy Griffith the opportunity to return to the type of gentle, homespun comedy that had made the original *Andy Griffith Show* so popular. This was on the heels of his failure in the much different title role in *The Headmaster*, but it lasted little longer.

NEW ATTITUDE (*Situation Comedy*)

FIRST TELECAST: *August 8, 1990*
LAST TELECAST: *September 7, 1990*
BROADCAST HISTORY:
Aug 1990, ABC Wed 9:30–10:00
Aug 1990–Sep 1990, ABC Fri 9:30–10:00
CAST:
Vicki St. James .... Sheryl Lee Ralph
Yvonne St. James .... Phyllis Yvonne Stickney
Lamarr .... Morris Day

Taylor .... Karen Bankhead
Leon .... Earl Billings
Chilly D .... Larenz Tate
Bebe .... Bebe Drake-Massey

The St. James sisters had sunk everything they could beg or borrow into their new business venture, the New Attitude beauty salon, where the gossip alone was worth a visit. The partnership was fifty-fifty: outrageous, try-anything Yvonne got them into trouble, and conservative, sensible Vicki got them out. Lamarr was their colorful top hairdresser, the "prince of perms"; Taylor, the ambitious but inept receptionist (she had flunked the beautician's exam eleven times); and Leon, the landlord.

Based on the play "Beauty Shop," by Shelly Garrett.

NEW ATTITUDES (*Magazine*)

BROADCAST HISTORY:
Lifetime
30 minutes
Produced: *1998–1999*
Premiered: *March 9, 1998*

HOSTS:
Leanza Cornett
Suzanne Whang

Perky former Miss America Leanza Cornett cohosted this nightly women's lifestyles magazine on cable. Included were features on beauty, fashion, fitness, finance, relationships, and health, all from a woman's point of view, along with celebrity interviews and humorous short takes by comedienne Mo Gaffney. The series was a revival of sorts of *Attitudes*, a daytime series hosted by soap opera diva Linda Dano, which aired on Lifetime from October 1986 to December 1992.

NEW BILL COSBY SHOW, THE (*Comedy Variety*)

FIRST TELECAST: *September 11, 1972*
LAST TELECAST: *May 7, 1973*
BROADCAST HISTORY:
Sep 1972–May 1973, CBS Mon 10:00–11:00

REGULARS:
Bill Cosby
Lola Falana
Susan Tolsky
Foster Brooks
Frank Shaw
Quincy Jones Orchestra
Oscar DeGruy
Pat McCormick
Mike Elias
Ronny Graham
Stan Ross
Ray Jessel

Comedian Bill Cosby was the star and host of this variety series that showcased guest stars in addition to its regulars. Each episode included a Cosby monologue, several comedy sketches, and one or two musical numbers. Two regular sketches were "The Wife of the Week" and vignettes about "The Dude," a character who was so cool that nothing fazed him. Dancer Lola Falana also functioned as the announcer on this series.

NEW BREED, THE (*Police Drama*)

FIRST TELECAST: *October 3, 1961*
LAST TELECAST: *September 25, 1962*
BROADCAST HISTORY:
Oct 1961–Nov 1961, ABC Tue 9:00–10:00
Nov 1961–Sep 1962, ABC Tue 8:30–9:30

CAST:
Lt. Price Adams .... Leslie Nielsen
Sgt. Vince Cavelli .... John Beradino
Ptlmn. Joe Huddleston .... John Clarke
Ptlmn. Pete Garcia .... Greg Roman
Capt. Keith Gregory .... Byron Morrow

These men were a "new breed" of policeman. They were trained in the use of sophisticated electronic gadgetry to track down criminals who were uncapturable by traditional police methods. As members of the elite Metropolitan Squad of the Los Angeles Police Department, they were under the immediate supervision of Lt. Price Adams. Price was both their superior and leader as they assaulted the underworld in the Southern California area.

NEW CHRISTY MINSTRELS, THE (*Musical Variety*)

FIRST TELECAST: *August 6, 1964*
LAST TELECAST: *September 10, 1964*
BROADCAST HISTORY:
Aug 1964–Sep 1964, NBC Thu 9:30–10:00

REGULARS:
The New Christy Minstrels

This five-week summer replacement for *Hazel* was actually titled *Ford Presents the New Christy Minstrels*, in deference to its sponsor. The nine-member folksinging group was led by Randy Sparks and was quite popular during the mid-1960s. Lead singer was Barry McGuire. Sparks and his group were joined each week by a guest comedian and the shows all had outdoor settings, including two from the New York World's Fair and three from locations in the Los Angeles area. The original Christy Minstrels was a famous minstrel troupe of the mid-1800s which popularized many of Stephen Foster's songs.

NEW COMEDY SHOWCASE (*Comedy Anthology*)

FIRST TELECAST: *August 1, 1960*
LAST TELECAST: *September 19, 1960*
BROADCAST HISTORY:
Aug 1960–Sep 1960, CBS Mon 10:00–10:30

The situation comedies that were aired in this anthology series were unsold pilots for projected regular series, including one starring Johnny Carson called *Johnny Come Lately* and another with Dick Van Dyke titled *The Trouble with Richard*.

NEW DICK VAN DYKE SHOW, THE (*Situation Comedy*)

FIRST TELECAST: *September 18, 1971*
LAST TELECAST: *September 2, 1974*
BROADCAST HISTORY:
Sep 1971–Sep 1972, CBS Sat 9:00–9:30
Sep 1972–Dec 1972, CBS Sun 9:00–9:30
Jan 1973–Sep 1973, CBS Sun 7:30–8:00
Sep 1973–Sep 1974, CBS Mon 9:30–10:00

CAST:
Dick Preston .... Dick Van Dyke
Jenny Preston .... Hope Lange
Bernie Davis (1971–1973) .... Marty Brill
"Mike" Preston (1971–1973) .... Fannie Flagg
Carol Davis (1971–1973) .... Nancy Dussault

Ted Atwater (1972–1973) .... David Doyle
Lucas Preston (1971–1973) .... Michael Shea
Lucas Preston (1973) .... Wendell Burton
Annie Preston (age 9) .... Angela Powell
Max Mathias (1973–1974) .... Dick Van Patten
Dennis Whitehead (1973–1974) ...... Barry Gordon
Alex Montenez (1973–1974) .... Henry Darrow
Richard Richardson (1973–1974) ... Richard Dawson
Connie Richardson (1973–1974) ...... Chita Rivera
Margot Brighton (1973–1974) .... Barbara Rush

During its first two seasons on the air, *The New Dick Van Dyke Show* was filmed on location at Carefree, Arizona. Dick Preston was the host of a local talk show on KXIV-TV, a mythical Phoenix, Arizona, television station. The series revolved around his personal life with his wife, Jenny, and their nine-year-old daughter, and his professional life with the talk show. His manager, Bernie, and Bernie's wife were personal friends and his sister Mike doubled as his secretary. Seen occasionally was Dick's son Lucas, who was away at a private boarding school.

For the third season, the setting of the show moved to Hollywood, and so did its production. Dick moved his family there so that he could take advantage of an opportunity to star in a daytime soap opera, *Those Who Care.* New series regulars were the soap opera's writer, Dennis Whitehead; its producer, Max Mathias; its stage manager, Alex Montenez; and the soap opera's star, Margot Brighton. In the soap Dick played Dr. Brad Fairmont. At home the Prestons had acquired new neighbors in Richard and Connie Richardson.

NEW DOCTORS, THE (*Medical Drama*)

FIRST TELECAST: *September 14, 1969*
LAST TELECAST: *June 23, 1973*
BROADCAST HISTORY:
Sep 1969–Sep 1972, NBC Sun 10:00–11:00
Sep 1972–Jan 1973, NBC Tue 9:00–10:00
May 1973–Jun 1973, NBC Fri 10:00–11:00

CAST:
Dr. David Craig .... E. G. Marshall
Dr. Paul Hunter .... David Hartman
Dr. Ted Stuart (1969–1972) .... John Saxon
Dr. Martin Cohen (1972–1973) ...... Robert Walden

The stories told on *The New Doctors* took place at the fictional David Craig Institute of New Medicine. The institute was a combination hospital and research center, founded, named after, and run by Dr. David Craig, and dedicated to perfecting new medical techniques. Dr. Craig's expertise in the field had earned him the respect of the profession and had made it possible for him to obtain the funding to pursue new medical breakthroughs. His chief of surgery was brilliant young heart-transplant specialist Dr. Ted Stuart, while Dr. Paul Hunter worked on nonsurgical techniques for treating disease. Dr. Martin Cohen became a regular at the start of the final season, replacing the departed Dr. Stuart. Incidents involving these dedicated men and their patients were dramatized on *The New Doctors.*

This program was an element of *The Bold Ones.* It was the only *Bold Ones* element to be aired throughout that series' entire four-season run, and was, in fact, the only element left in the series during the final season, all of the others having been dropped.

NEW GIDGET, THE (*Situation Comedy*)

BROADCAST HISTORY:
Syndicated only
30 minutes
Produced: *1986–1988* (44 episodes)
Released: *September 1986*

CAST:
Francine Lawrence Griffin (Gidget)*
.... Caryn Richman
Jeff Griffin (Moondoggie) .... Dean Butler
Danni Collins .... Sydney Penny
Russ Lawrence .... William Schallert
Larue Wilson (1986–1987) .... Jill Jacobson
Gayle Baker .... Lili Haydn
Murph the Surf (1987–1988) .... David Preston
***Wilton Parmenter (1986–1987)* .... Richard Paul

*Also given as Frances
**Occasional

Twenty years after TV's first *Gidget* series had left the air this equally sunny syndicated series surfaced. Gidget was now in her late 20s and she and her girlhood idol, Moondoggie, had been married for eight years. They still lived close to the beautiful beach in Santa Monica, but were now a modern working couple. Moondoggie was an architect with the city planning department and Gidget ran her own little travel agency. Working for her at Gidget Travel was her long-time friend Larue.

Most of the stories revolved around the exploits of Gidget's niece, Danni, who was living with the Griffins while her folks were overseas. Danni was the vivacious, impish sort of teenager Gidget herself had been in the earlier series—and like Gidget of yore, she and her best friend, Gayle, were forever getting in trouble. Gidget's dad, Russ, was around to offer sage advice and remind Gidget of how similar she had been to Danni.

The pilot for this series was *Gidget's Summer Reunion,* a 1985 made-for-television film starring Richman and Butler.

NEW KIND OF FAMILY, A (*Situation Comedy*)

FIRST TELECAST: *September 16, 1979*
LAST TELECAST: *January 5, 1980*
BROADCAST HISTORY:
Sep 1979–Oct 1979, ABC Sun 7:30–8:00
Dec 1979–Jan 1980, ABC Sat 8:30–9:00

CAST:
Kit Flanagan .... Eileen Brennan
Andy Flanagan .... David Hollander
Hillary Flanagan .... Lauri Hendler
Tony Flanagan .... Rob Lowe
Abby Stone (Sep–Oct) .... Gwynne Gilford
Jill Stone (Sep–Oct) .... Connie Ann Hearn
Jess Ashton (Dec–Jan) .... Telma Hopkins
Jojo Ashton (Dec–Jan) .... Janet Jackson
Harold Zimmerman .... Chuck McCann

In this comedy Kit Flanagan, recently widowed, decided to pack up her three children and move from her native New York to Los Angeles. They had rented a house sight unseen, but when they got there they found that someone else had rented it too: divorcée Abby Stone and her daughter Jill. Since neither the Flanagans nor the Stones could afford the place by themselves, they all moved in together—despite the very different lifestyles of cynical, free-swinging Kit and conservative, by-the-book (Dr. Spock) Abby. The kids loved the arrangement, especially early adolescents Hillary and Jill, who were the same age. Mr. Zimmerman was the landlord, who also had his own TV show, and Heinz was the family pooch (played by "O.J.").

The series was an instant flop and was pulled from the schedule after only a few weeks. It returned briefly in December–January with new episodes, in which the Stones had been replaced by Jess Ashton and her daughter Jojo.

NEW LAND, THE (*Adventure*)

FIRST TELECAST: *September 14, 1974*
LAST TELECAST: *October 19, 1974*
BROADCAST HISTORY:
Sep 1974–Oct 1974, ABC Sat 8:00–9:00
CAST:
Anna Larsen ...... Bonnie Bedelia
Christian Larsen ...... Scott Thomas
Tuliff Larsen ...... Todd Lookinland
Anneliese Larsen ...... Debbie Lytton
Bo ...... Kurt Russell
Rev. Lundstrom ...... Donald Moffat
Molly Lundstrom ...... Gwen Arner
Murdock ...... Lou Frizzel

The hardships and triumphs of a courageous family of young Scandinavian immigrants struggling to carve out a life in the hostile wilderness near Solna, Minnesota, in 1858. Anna and Christian were the parents, Tuliff (age nine) and Anneliese (eight) their children. Rev. Lundstrom and his wife and Murdock, the owner of the general store, also pitched in, but the Larsens' travails lasted for only six weeks before the series was canceled.

Filmed on location in Oregon and California, and based (loosely) on two Swedish movies, *The Emigrants* (1972) and *The New Land* (1973).

NEW LASSIE, THE (*Adventure*)

BROADCAST HISTORY:
Syndicated only
30 minutes
Produced: *1989–1991* (48 episodes)
Released: *September 1989*
CAST:
Will McCullough (age 10) ...... Will Nipper
Chris McCullough ...... Christopher Stone
Dee McCullough ...... Dee Wallace Stone
Megan McCullough (14) ...... Wendy Cox
**Steve McCullough* ...... Jon Provost
*Occasional

This low-budget update of the *Lassie* legend had the bright, resourceful, and lovable collie living with a middle-class family in suburban Glen Ridge, California. Lassie's master was young Will McCullough, whose parents (played by real-life married couple Christopher and Dee Wallace Stone) were Chris, a struggling building contractor, and Dee, a homemaker. Also seen were Will's teenage sister, Megan, and his uncle, Steve, a real estate agent. Jon Provost, who was in the opening credits of every episode but appeared in relatively few, had starred in the original *Lassie* series in the 1950s and 1960s. In fact, he played the same part. Although he had been called Timmy in the original series, it was explained that Timmy was the name he had taken as an orphan, prior to being reunited with his real family after he had grown up.

NEW LEAVE IT TO BEAVER, THE (*Situation Comedy*)

BROADCAST HISTORY
The Disney Channel (1985–1986)
WTBS (1986–1989)
30 minutes
Produced: *1985–1989* (105 episodes)
Released: *September 1985*
CAST:
June Cleaver ...... Barbara Billingsley
Theodore "Beaver" Cleaver ...... Jerry Mathers
Ward "Kip" Cleaver, Jr. ...... Kipp Marcus
Oliver Cleaver ...... John Snee
Wally Cleaver ...... Tony Dow
Mary Ellen Cleaver ...... Janice Kent
Kelly Cleaver ...... Kaleena Kiff
Eddie Haskell ...... Ken Osmond
**Freddie Haskell* ...... Eric Osmond
***Bomber Haskell* ...... Christian Osmond
Gert Haskell ...... Ellen Maxted
Clarence "Lumpy" Rutherford ...... Frank Bank
Kevin Cleaver (1987–1989) ...... Troy Davidson
*Eddie Haskell, Jr., during the 1985–1986 season
**Occasional

Twenty years after *Leave It to Beaver* ended its original run, viewers got a glimpse of what had become of the Cleavers in the March 1983 TV movie *Still the Beaver.* Unlike most TV reunions, this one was bittersweet. Beaver's eternal innocence had not served him well in adult life. At 33, he was out of work, had two young sons he couldn't communicate with, and was being divorced by his wife. Wally was a successful attorney—in fact he handled Beaver's divorce—but he had problems at home as well. Wally's sleazy friend Eddie Haskell had become a crooked contractor. Dad was no longer around to make things right with a few words of sage advice (actor Hugh Beaumont had passed away) and he was sorely missed, by his sons and by his wife, June, who sat by his grave and said "Ward, what would *you* do?"

Despite this dour picture, viewers apparently wanted more of the Cleaver clan, and so the movie led to a series *Still the Beaver* on the pay-cable Disney Channel in 1985–1986, and then *The New Leave It to Beaver* on cable superstation WTBS in 1986. Things got somewhat better as time went along. Beaver and his sons (he had custody) moved in with June, who provided some emotional support. He then went to work for Lumpy Rutherford's father and eventually he and Lumpy formed a highly successful business partnership, although it was never explained exactly what they did. Much of the action shifted to the younger generation—Beaver's boys, teenager Kip and preteen Oliver; Wally's kids, cute Kelly and little Kevin (his mother, Mary Ellen, was pregnant with him for 18 months on the series and three months after his birth he was three years old!); and Eddie's son Freddie, who was Kip's best friend. Although Freddie had picked up some of his father's obnoxious traits, underneath it all he was a pretty good guy. Freddie's brother, Bomber, had been sent off to military school for accidentally spilling grape juice on the white carpeting in the Haskell living room, but showed up periodically. The same gentle, homespun quality that had characterized the original series began to permeate *The New Leave It To Beaver.*

Eddie Haskell's sons were played by actor Ken Osmond's real-life sons.

NEW LORETTA YOUNG SHOW, THE (*Drama*)

FIRST TELECAST: *September 24, 1962*

LAST TELECAST: *March 18, 1963*

BROADCAST HISTORY:

Sep 1962–Mar 1963, CBS Mon 10:00–10:30

CAST:

Christine Massey.................... Loretta Young
Paul Belzer...................... James Philbrook
Marnie Massey.......................... Celia Kaye
Vickie Massey................. Beverly Washburn
Judy Massey...................... Sandy Descher
Binkie Massey....................... Carol Sydes
Dirk Massey......................... Dirk Rambo
Dack Massey........................ Dack Rambo
Maria Massey.................... Tracy Stratford

Christine Massey was a widowed mother of seven children, living in the suburban community of Ellendale, Connecticut. Her children ranged in age from 6 to 18 and were typical of other youngsters of their respective ages in terms of attitudes, wants, and conflicts with each other and with their mother. Christine made her living as a magazine writer, selling stories to various publications. One of those publications, *Belzer's Woman's Journal*, was edited and owned by Paul Belzer, the mature bachelor who was Christine's love interest. They met when she was working on her first assignment for his magazine and their romance continued throughout the six-month run of this series, culminating in marriage on the last telecast, March 18, 1963.

This was Miss Young's sole venture in a continuing role on television. Her previous series, *The Loretta Young Show*, gave her the freedom of playing different people on the occasions in which she starred in as well as hosted the show. On this show, she was the center of action in roughly every other episode, with stories centering around individuals in the family on alternate weeks.

NEW MIKE HAMMER, THE, see *Mickey Spillane's Mike Hammer*

NEW MONKEES (*Situation Comedy*)

BROADCAST HISTORY:

Syndicated only
30 minutes
Produced: *1987* (13 episodes)
Released: *September 1987*

CAST:

Larry................................. Larry Saltis
Dino................................. Dino Kovas
Jared............................. Jared Chandler
Marty................................ Marty Ross
Manford, the butler............. Gordon Oas-Heim
Rita, the waitress........................ Bess Motta
Helen, the lips.................... Lynnie Godfrey

The 1980s was an era of nostalgia, and perhaps the most surprising revival was that of the ultimate "manufactured" rock group of the '60s—the Monkees. Reruns of their '60s TV series on the MTV cable network, a highly publicized concert tour by original members of the group in the summer of 1986, and reissues of their LPs all led trend-conscious producers to think the time was right to bring the public a "new" Monkees. A heavily promoted nationwide talent hunt was staged to find four young men to star in a new version of the '60s series.

The result was this high-tech, special-effects-laden collection of music videos, comic blackouts, and offbeat plots. It was set in a huge gothic mansion in which the four new Monkees (Larry, Dino, Jared, and Marty) lived and frolicked. They had a stuffy butler named Manford and hung out at a diner attached to the mansion, but many of their adventures took place without even leaving home. Commenting on the proceedings was a sarcastic, bodiless pair of lips which appeared on television screens that seemed to be in every room.

The hype didn't work. The New Monkees' album didn't sell and the series didn't attract an audience; apparently the public was more interested in the old Monkees. *New Monkees* was in production for less time than the search for its stars had taken.

NEW ODD COUPLE, THE, see *Odd Couple, The*

NEW ORIGINAL AMATEUR HOUR, THE (*Talent*)

BROADCAST HISTORY:

The Family Channel
60 minutes
Produced: *1991–1992* (13 episodes)
Premiered: *January 26, 1992*

HOST:

Willard Scott

The classic talent show was revived by cable's Family Channel for a brief run in 1992, with effervescent *Today Show* weatherman Willard Scott as host.

NEW PEOPLE, THE (*Drama*)

FIRST TELECAST: *September 22, 1969*

LAST TELECAST: *January 12, 1970*

BROADCAST HISTORY:

Sep 1969–Jan 1970, ABC Mon 8:15–9:00

CAST:

Susan Bradley..................... Tiffany Bolling
Bob Lee.............................. Zooey Hall
Ginny Loomis.......................... Jill Jaress
Gene Washington.................. David Moses
Stanley Gabriel................... Dennis Olivieri
George Potter...................... Peter Ratray

CREATOR:

Rod Serling

This fantasy drama centered on a heterogeneous group of 40 young Americans stranded on a South Pacific atoll after a plane crash. The island just happened to be an abandoned U.S. atomic test site, which meant that, though safe, it came complete with buildings, provisions, and all the other physical appurtenances of a modern society—but no people. Inhabiting this eerie world, the young folks, with their different ethnic and social backgrounds (they were returning from a cultural exchange tour of Southeast Asia), set about organizing their own "new" society, sans adults. A few guest stars did wander on and off their "lost" island, however.

NEW PHIL SILVERS SHOW, THE (*Situation Comedy*)

FIRST TELECAST: *September 28, 1963*

LAST TELECAST: *June 27, 1964*

BROADCAST HISTORY:

Sep 1963–Nov 1963, CBS Sat 8:30–9:00
Nov 1963–Jun 1964, CBS Sat 9:30–10:00

CAST:

Harry Grafton........................ Phil Silvers
Brink............................ Stafford Repp

Waluska .... Herbie Faye
Roxy .... Pat Renella
Lester .... Jim Shane
Mr. Osborne .... Douglas Dumbrille
Fred Starkey .... Steve Mitchell
Bob .... Bob Williams
Nick .... Buddy Lester
Grabowski .... Norm Grabowski
Audrey (1964) .... Elena Verdugo
Susan (1964) .... Sandy Descher
Andy (1964) .... Ronnie Dapo

The character played by Phil Silvers in his second series was similar to Sgt. Ernie Bilko in the original *Phil Silvers Show*, with one exception—Harry was a civilian. He was the maintenance superintendent of Osborne Industries, a small manufacturing company whose products changed from episode to episode, to suit the plot. Harry was a small-time swindler and office con artist. He would do almost anything to avoid real work, and managed to find angles to provide himself with a little something extra from each job that he and his crew worked on. The boss, Mr. Brink, could only look on helplessly.

NEW SHOW, THE (*Comedy Variety*)
FIRST TELECAST: *January 6, 1984*
LAST TELECAST: *March 23, 1984*
BROADCAST HISTORY:
Jan 1984–Mar 1984, NBC Fri 10:00–11:00
REGULARS:
Buck Henry
Valri Bromfield
Dave Thomas
Maggie Jakobson
Maura Moynihan

The New Show was an hour of offbeat comedy sketches by a cast of regulars and guests. The humor was often topical, as in the regular "Weekend Tonight" mock newscast and in film clips of world leaders with new dialogue dubbed in. Other skits generally emphasized teen-oriented humor; one show opened at the "Restaurant of Revulsion," where a waiter (guest Raul Julia) ceremoniously unveiled for his customers the Catch of the Day, "Tête du Jour"—a severed head on a platter that exclaimed, "(Groan) . . . it's *The New Show*!" Among the guests making multiple appearances were John Candy and Catherine O'Hara, both alumni of SCTV, and actress Candice Bergen.

A musical spot each week featured rock acts such as the Pretenders and Rick James. *The New Show* was produced by Lorne Michaels, the man who created *Saturday Night Live*, but it failed to capture the novelty or the breakthrough talent of the earlier series, and was soon canceled.

NEW TEMPERATURES RISING SHOW, THE, see *Temperatures Rising*

NEW YORK DAZE, see *Too Something*

NEW YORK GIANTS QUARTERBACK HUDDLE (*Sports Commentary*)
FIRST TELECAST: *September 15, 1950*
LAST TELECAST: *November 12, 1953*
BROADCAST HISTORY:
Sep 1950–Dec 1950, ABC Fri 8:30–9:00
Sep 1952–Dec 1952, DUM Wed 7:30–8:00
Oct 1953–Nov 1953, DUM Thu 8:00–8:30
HOST:
Joe Hasel (1950)
Steve Owen (1952–1953)

Highlight films of the New York Giants' game of the previous week, interviews with players, and discussions of more general National Football League news and issues were all included in this weekly show. Sportscaster Joe Hasel hosted the ABC version in 1950, while Steve Owen, coach of the New York Giants team, hosted on DuMont. The 1953 DuMont version continued as a local show until the season ended. Also known as *Pro Football Highlights*, *Football News*, and *New York Giants Football Huddle*.

NEW YORK NEWS (*Newspaper Drama*)
FIRST TELECAST: *September 28, 1995*
LAST TELECAST: *November 30, 1995*
BROADCAST HISTORY:
Sep 1995–Nov 1995, CBS Thu 9:00–10:00
CAST:
Jack Reilly .... Gregory Harrison
Nan Chase .... Madeline Kahn
Louise Felcott .... Mary Tyler Moore
Angela Villanova .... Melina Kanakaredes
Mitch Cotter .... Joe Morton
Tony Amato .... Anthony DeSando
Ellie Milanski .... Kelli Williams
Victor .... Kevin Chamberlin
Benny .... Harold Perrineau, Jr.

The New York *Reporter* was a struggling tabloid in the nation's largest market. Running the paper was its autocratic Editor-in-Chief, Louise "the Dragon" Felcott, who made life difficult for the paper's managing editor, Mitch Cotter. Star columnists included Reilly, a grizzled veteran with great news instincts and dogged determination when he was on a hot story (he actually sneaked around back alleys in a trench coat!); Villanova, Reilly's young admirer, toughest competition, and sometimes lover; and Chase, the paper's obnoxious but highly successful gossip columnist. Others on the staff included Milanski, an eager young intern; Amato, the paper's top sports columnist; and Victor, the lovable, slow-witted office clerk. The *Reporter*'s owner was on the verge of selling the paper and instituted harsh cost controls that made everyone's life more difficult and contributed to Cotter's mild heart attack.

Ms. Moore, unhappy with the tough, unsympathetic character she was asked to portray, asked to be written out of *New York News*, but the series was canceled before the writers could do it.

NEW YORK TIMES YOUTH FORUM (*Discussion*)
FIRST TELECAST: *October 5, 1952*
LAST TELECAST: *June 21, 1953*
BROADCAST HISTORY:
Oct 1952–Jun 1953, DUM Sun 6:00–7:00

Discussion of topics of importance to young people, by politicians, scientists, and other authorities, including writers from the *New York Times*. Subjects included "Do We Learn Only at School?," "How Does Soviet Policy Affect Us?," "Music: Jazz *vs* Classics," and "Are Mothers Necessary?"

The series had started one month earlier on Sunday afternoons before shifting to a 6:00 P.M. start. Following the run listed above it returned to Sunday afternoons, where it remained until June 1954.

NEW YORK UNDERCOVER (*Police Drama*)

FIRST TELECAST: *September 8, 1994*
LAST TELECAST: *June 25, 1998*
BROADCAST HISTORY:

Sep 1994–Aug 1997, FOX Thu 9:00–10:00
Aug 1995, FOX Mon 9:00–10:00
Jul 1996–Aug 1996, FOX Sun 9:00–10:00
Jan 1998–Jun 1998, FOX Thu 9:00–10:00

CAST:

Det. Eddie Torres (1994–1997). Michael De Lorenzo
Det. James "J.C." Williams .... Malik Yoba
Lt. Virginia Cooper (1994–1997)
.... Patti D'Arbanville-Quinn
Det. Ricciarelli (1994–1995) ...... Frank Pellegrino
M. E. Wong (1994–1997) .... Lee Wong
**Sandra Gill (1994–1995)*.......... Michael Michele
**Chantal Tierney (1994–1997)*........ Fatima Faloye
**Gregory "G" Williams*............... George Gore II
**Mike Torres (1994–1995)* .... José Perez
**Carmen Torres (1994–1995)* .... Lisa Vidal
Det. Nina Moreno (1995–1998) .... Lauren Velez
Det. Tommy McNamara (1996–1997)
.... Jonathan LaPaglia
**Capt. Arthur O'Bryne (1996–1997)*
.... James McCaffrey
Nadine Jordan (1997–1998)......... Dana Eskelson
Lt. Malcolm Barker (1998) .... Tommy Ford
Det. Neil DeLaney (1998).............. Marisa Ryan
Det. Alec Stone (1998) .... Josh Hopkins
**Frankie Stone (1998)* .... Justin Theroux
**Gina Stone (1998)* .... Jennifer Esposito

*Occasional

Eddie and J.C. were two young undercover cops assigned to the fourth precinct in the Harlem section of Manhattan in this gritty cop show with a cinema verité style. Black J.C. had a son by former girlfriend Chantal and maintained a close relationship with her because he wanted "G" to grow up straight. Sandra, his current girlfriend, was a successful attorney. Baby-faced Puerto Rican Eddie had never been married and dated a lot of women. He and his sister, Carmen, tried to look out for their dad, Mike, a recovering drug addict and jazz saxophone player. Lt. Cooper was their tough boss at the precinct. There was lots of pulsating jazz and Hispanic and rap music for background as the cops and criminals went about their business, along with plenty of street language and slang. Each episode ended with performances by guest musical artists at Natalie's jazz club where Eddie and J.C. hung out when they weren't on duty.

In the May 1995 season finale, Sandra, pregnant with J.C.'s child, was murdered by a vengeful criminal on the day before she and J.C. were to be married. In the climactic scene her murderer (played by rap star Ice-T) was shot by Eddie to keep him from stabbing a wounded J.C. to death.

That fall, J.C. was having emotional problems dealing with his loss and took it out on criminals he was arresting. New to the precinct was Nina Moreno, a tough lady cop, who got involved with Eddie. J.C. eventually killed the hood who had murdered Sandra when the hood's plan to get even with him failed. In the 1995–1996 season finale Nina took a bullet meant for Eddie while trying to take down a drug dealer at a bank, and as the episode ended, was dying in the hospital with an emergency crew trying to save her life. She survived, temporarily paralyzed from the waist down.

In fall 1996, Tommy McNamara, a white detective, was transferred into their precinct, and Eddie and Nina had a rocky time after she recovered from the shooting. She was partnered with Tommy and almost resigned after freezing during a shootout. Eddie's dad found out he had developed AIDS from his years as an addict, and he died from a heroin overdose in November. Lt. Cooper, who was having marital problems, had an affair with Capt. O'Byrne but broke it off because of her family. Unfortunately, when her husband found out, he filed for divorce. The daughter Nina had had as a teenager and given up for adoption surfaced in spring 1997, and Nina waged an unsuccessful custody fight to get her back from her late adoptive mother's sister. In May, Eddie proposed to her, and in the season finale they got married. Their happiness was short-lived: McNamara was killed by a gang of bank robbers he was trying to infiltrate, and Eddie, about to change precincts, was killed by a car bomb set off by a vengeful lady bank robber whose lover had been mortally wounded by him during a failed heist.

When *New York Undercover* returned early in 1998 there were many changes. Dropped was the hip hop music of previous seasons. J.C. and Moreno were recruited into a special undercover unit tracking Nadine Jordan, the bank robber who had killed Eddie and McNamara in the 1996–1997 season finale. Barker was their new boss, and DeLaney and Stone the other members of the team. DeLaney, at age 22, was extremely cold-blooded, and Stone had problems dealing with his brother, Frankie, a Mafia soldier who abused his wife, Gina. When they separated in June, she moved in with Stone, because she had no source of income, and they got physically involved. Nina and J.C. finally caught Jordan in March and realized that they, too, were attracted to each other. The following week, while undercover in a local prison, Nina got into a fight with Jordan and killed her with her own knife. Afterward Nina and J.C. tentatively started to date.

NEWHART (*Situation Comedy*)

FIRST TELECAST: *October 25, 1982*
LAST TELECAST: *September 8, 1990*
BROADCAST HISTORY:

Oct 1982–Feb 1983, CBS Mon 9:30–10:00
Mar 1983–Apr 1983, CBS Sun 9:30–10:00
Apr 1983–May 1983, CBS Sun 8:30–9:00
Jun 1983–Aug 1983, CBS Sun 9:30–10:00
Aug 1983–Sep 1986, CBS Mon 9:30–10:00
Sep 1986–Aug 1988, CBS Mon 9:00–9:30
Aug 1988–Mar 1989, CBS Mon 8:00–8:30
Mar 1989–Aug 1989, CBS Mon 10:00–10:30
Aug 1989–Oct 1989, CBS Mon 10:30–11:00
Nov 1989–Apr 1990, CBS Mon 10:00–10:30
Apr 1990–May 1990, CBS Mon 8:30–9:00
May 1990–Jul 1990, CBS Mon 10:00–10:30
Jul 1990–Aug 1990, CBS Fri 9:00–9:30
Sep 1990, CBS Sat 9:00–9:30

CAST:

Dick Loudon........................... Bob Newhart
Joanna Loudon .... Mary Frann

Kirk Devane (1982–1984) ...... Steven Kampmann
George Utley .... Tom Poston
Leslie Vanderkellen (1982–1983) ... Jennifer Holmes
Stephanie Vanderkellen (1983–1990) ... Julia Duffy
Larry .... William Sanderson
First Darryl .... Tony Papenfuss
Second Darryl .... John Voldstad
**Jim Dixon* .... Thomas Hill
**Chester Wanamaker* .... William Lanteau
Cindy Parker Devane (1984) .... Rebecca York
Michael Harris (1984–1990) .... Peter Scolari
**Harley Estin (1984–1988)* .... Jeff Doucette
Elliot Gabler (1984–1985) .... Lee Wilkof
**Bev Dutton (1984–1988)* .... Linda Carlson
**Constable Shifflett (1985–1989)* ..... Todd Susman
**J.J. (1985–1987)* .... Fred Applegate
**Bud (1985–1990)* .... Ralph Manza
**Paul (1988–1990)* .... Cliff Bemis
**Prudence Goddard (1989–1990)* ..... Kathy Kinney
**Art Rusnak (1989–1990)* .... David Pressman

*Occasional

Four years after the highly successful *Bob Newhart Show* had ended its run, Bob Newhart brought his relaxed style, gentle humor, and immaculate comedy timing back to CBS in *Newhart*. Dick Loudon, a New York writer of "How To" books, decided to put his knowledge to practical use by renovating and reopening an authentic colonial inn in scenic Norwich, Vermont. Leaving city life behind, Dick and his somewhat skeptical wife, Joanna, arrived full of anticipation at their new home, the Stratford Inn, built in 1774. It had been shuttered for years and needed a good deal of work, but as a history buff Dick found the building and its past endlessly fascinating.

Dick and Joanna also found that Norwich did not lack eccentric characters. Helping run the inn was crusty and colorful George Utley, whose family had been caretakers there for more than 200 years. Kirk, who ran the Minuteman Cafe and Giftshop next door, was a guilt-ridden compulsive liar who was constantly apologizing for his fibs. After years of searching for the perfect woman, he was finally married in the spring of 1984—to Cindy, a professional clown. Leslie was a pretentious and wealthy student at nearby Dartmouth College, who had taken the part-time job of maid to find out what it was like to be "average." She left to continue her education in England at the end of the first season, and was replaced by her equally attractive cousin, Stephanie. Also seen were three weird brothers who were possibly the world's most inept handymen—Larry, Darryl, and Darryl. Larry was the spokesman for the group, since neither Darryl ever spoke at all.

In the fall of 1984, looking for a little diversity in his life, Dick became the host of "Vermont Today," a talk show on local TV station WPIV. Now, in addition to the folks at the inn, he had to cope with the guests on his TV show and its fast-talking young producer, Michael Harris. When Michael started dating Stephanie—they made the perfect pretentious yuppie couple—Dick had the dubious pleasure of seeing him at the inn almost as much as at the station. Larry, Darryl, and Darryl were around even more than before, since they had taken over the Minuteman Cafe when Kirk left the area.

In this sea of eccentrics, Dick and Joanna were a small island of normalcy, a situation not radically different from that of Newhart and his wife (played by Suzanne Pleshette) in his previous series.

Major changes occurred during the 1988–1989 season. Michael lost his job at the TV station and became a shoe clerk. After breaking up with status-conscious Stephanie, he had a nervous breakdown, spent two weeks in a sanitarium, then took a job as a bagboy at Menkey's grocery store. In the last episode of the season, after months of trying to find each other new loves, Michael and his "cupcake" (Stephanie) decided they were meant for each other and ran off and got married.

The following fall Michael and a very pregnant Stephanie returned from a six-month honeymoon cruise and took up residence at the Stratford Inn. Stephanie gave birth in January to baby Stephanie, and her wealthy parents, to provide for their daughter and granddaughter, bought WPIV and gave it to the baby, with Michael as its figurehead general manager.

The last original episode of *Newhart*, which aired in the spring of 1990, was a television classic. A Japanese businessman bought the entire town for $1,000,000 per house so he could convert it into a golf course, except for the Stratford Inn, which Dick refused to sell. Five years later, the inn had become a Japanese hotel on the 14th fairway of the Tagadachville Hotel and Country Club golf course. The townspeople returned for a visit and decided to move back. While they were arguing about the details, Dick went out the front door and was knocked unconscious by an errant golf ball—only to wake up in bed with Emily (Suzanne Pleshette) from *The Bob Newhart Show* and tell her about this strange dream he had about running an inn in Vermont!

NEWLYWED GAME, THE (*Quiz/Audience Participation*)

FIRST TELECAST: *January 7, 1967*
LAST TELECAST: *August 30, 1971*
BROADCAST HISTORY:
Jan 1967–Jan 1971, ABC Sat 8:00–8:30
Jan 1971–Aug 1971, ABC Mon 8:00–8:30
EMCEE:
Bob Eubanks
EXECUTIVE PRODUCER:
Chuck Barris

Each week on *The Newlywed Game* four couples, all married less than one year, competed with each other to win their own special "dream gift," usually appliances or furniture. The emcee asked the wives questions about their husbands, and the husbands questions about their wives, each while the other mate was out of earshot. The couple that correctly guessed the greatest number of each other's answers was the winner. Questions were usually designed to produce embarrassing situations and disagreements between husbands and wives, much to the delight of the audience. For example, "What animal would you compare your mother-in-law to?" or "Would your wife say she sleeps with her toes pointing toward the wall, the ceiling, or the floor?"

There was also a daytime version of the program on ABC from July 1966 to December 1974, and a syndicated version from 1977 until 1980. Bob Eubanks hosted them all. He was still with the show when it surfaced again as *The New Newlywed Game* in the fall of 1985. Despite the name change nothing much had changed, other than the freedom to be somewhat more explicit in the sexual innuendos, a function of the changing mores of American television.

In the fall of 1988, when yet another revival of *The Newlywed Game* surfaced, the emphasis had shifted to comedy, and longtime host Eubanks was replaced by Latin comic Paul Rodriguez. The Rodriguez version ran for a single season.

The Newlywed Game was resurrected again in fall 1996 with Gary Kroeger as emcee. The following fall the producers went back to the series' roots, replacing Kroeger with the original host, Bob Eubanks. It went off the air at the end of the 1999–2000 season.

NEWS—ABC

FIRST TELECAST: *August 11, 1948*
LAST TELECAST:
BROADCAST HISTORY:

Aug 1948–Oct 1952, ABC Mon–Sat 7:00–7:15
Oct 1952–Dec 1952, ABC Mon 9:00–10:00
Oct 1952–Dec 1952, ABC Wed 8:00–9:00
Oct 1952–Dec 1952, ABC Thu 8:00–8:30
Oct 1952–Jan 1953, ABC Fri 8:30–9:30
Oct 1952–Aug 1953, ABC Sun 8:00–9:00
Aug 1998–Sep 1998, ABC Thu 10:00–11:00 *(Nightline)*
Jul 1999–Sep 1999, ABC Thu 10:00–11:00 *(Nightline)*
Monday–Friday early evening:
Oct 1953–May 1959, ABC Mon–Fri 7:15–7:30
May 1959–Jan 1967, ABC Mon–Fri Various early evening (15 min.)
Jan 1967– , ABC Mon–Fri Various early evening (30 min.)
Monday–Friday late night:
Sep 1958–May 1959, ABC Mon–Fri 10:30–10:45
Oct 1961–Jan 1965, ABC Mon–Fri 11:00–11:10
Mar 1980–Jan 1981, ABC Mon–Thu 11:30–11:50
Jan 1981–Mar 1981, ABC Mon–Thu 11:30–Midnight
Mar 1981–Apr 1983, ABC Mon–Fri 11:30–Midnight
Apr 1983–Feb 1984, ABC Mon–Fri 11:30–12:30 A.M.
Feb 1984–Apr 1993, ABC Mon–Fri 11:30–Midnight
Jan 1992– , ABC Mon–Thu 2:00–6:00 A.M.
Apr 1993– , ABC Mon–Fri 11:35–12:05 A.M.
Weekends:
Jan 1965–Sep 1991, ABC Sat/Sun 11:00–11:15 (or later)
Feb 1973–Jan 1979, ABC Sat 6:30–7:00
Jan 1979– , ABC Sun 6:30–7:00
Jan 1985– , ABC Sat 6:30–7:00

ABC's first regularly scheduled nightly newscast was *News and Views,* which premiered in August 1948 with H. R. Baukhage and Jim Gibbons sharing the anchor position. Aired six nights each week, it lasted three years, and was succeeded by *After the Deadlines* in April 1951.

The program that succeeded *After the Deadlines* was the most ambitious news show in the early days of television. In an attempt to offer news as an alternative to prime-time entertainment, ABC introduced *All Star News* in October 1952. This offered four and one-half hours of national news coverage per week, a full hour on some nights, all running in the middle of the evening against NBC's and CBS' top entertainment shows. Featured were Bryson Rash, Pauline Frederick, Gordon Fraser, and Leo Cherne. In addition to straight headline reporting, *All Star News* provided analysis and interviews with newsmakers, and had a documentary quality to much of its coverage. It was a noble effort, but it attracted few viewers against *Ed Sullivan, Arthur Godfrey,* and *I Love Lucy,* and by early 1953 only the Sunday night edition remained on the air.

Smarting from this expensive disaster, ABC reverted to a 15-minute early evening news in October 1953. The anchor was veteran newsman John Daly, who was brought over from CBS. About the only distinctive feature of ABC News at this time was that Daly stood at a podium as he delivered the news, rather than being seated at a desk as were the other networks' anchormen. An interesting sidelight is that even while Daly was anchoring ABC's nightly news, he remained moderator of CBS' top-rated quiz show, *What's My Line.* Daly remained in the ABC anchor position for more than seven years, except for one short stint from 1958–1959 when he anchored a short-lived 10:30 P.M. newscast, and Don Goddard filled in at 7:15 P.M. When Daly left ABC in December 1960, a trio of anchormen took over the early news, Bill Lawrence, Al Mann, and former NBC anchorman John Cameron Swayze.

In the fall of 1961 ABC introduced its first 11:00 P.M. newscast, running from Monday to Friday. The first anchor was Ron Cochran, succeeded by Murphy Martin in 1963 and Bob Young in 1964. In January 1965 ABC dropped this newscast and substituted an 11 P.M. Saturday/Sunday news instead. Called *The ABC Weekend News,* it remained on the air until 1991, although after a short tenure by Bob Young (1965–1966) there was no regular anchor until the mid-1970s. On Saturday, Tom Jarriel was the principal anchor from 1977–1983, succeeded by Max Robinson (1983–1984), Jarriel again (1986–1987), and Britt Hume (1987–1991). On Sunday, it was Jarriel from 1975–1976, Bill Beutel (1976–1977), Jarriel and Sylvia Chase (1977–1979; she also joined him on Saturday during this period), and then it was Jarriel alone (1979–1991).

Weekends also saw the addition of an early evening news on Saturdays in 1973. At first called *The Reasoner Report,* this was taken over by Ted Koppel in the summer of 1975, followed by Tom Jarriel and Sylvia Chase in 1977, Sam Donaldson from 1979 (when the program moved to Sunday) to 1989, Forrest Sawyer (1989–1993), and Carole Simpson (1993 to date). A new early Saturday edition was begun in January 1985, with Kathleen Sullivan as anchor, later succeeded by Barry Serafin (1988) and Carole Simpson (1988–1993). When Simpson moved to Sunday in 1993, rotating anchors took over the Saturday newscast. Capitalizing on the heightened interest in news during the 1979 Iranian crisis, ABC also began regular "Iran reports," Monday through Thursday at 11:30 P.M., in November 1979. These were converted into a regular newscast called *Nightline* with Ted Koppel in March 1980. In addition to its long and successful run weeknights at 11:30 P.M., *Nightline* aired special prime-time editions *(Nightline in Primetime)* during the summers of 1998 and 1999. An overnight newsfeed from 2:00 to 6:00 A.M., called *ABC's World News Now,* was launched in January 1992 (stations could pick up whatever portion they wished). The original anchors were Aaron Brown and Lisa McRee, succeeded by Thalia Assuras and Boyd Matson (1993), Assuras and Kevin Newman (1994), Assuras and

Mark Mullen (1996), Mullen and Asha Blake (1997), Juju Chang (1999–2000), and in various combinations Alison Stewart (2000), Derek McGinty (2001) and Lizbeth Cho (2002).

There has been, over the years, considerable turnover in anchormen on ABC's early evening news. Ron Cochran took over in January 1963. He was replaced by youthful Peter Jennings in February 1965, and Jennings was still with the newscast when it expanded from 15 minutes to a half hour on January 9, 1967. Bob Young replaced Jennings in January 1968, and Frank Reynolds took over in May 1968. A year later ABC decided to try two anchors, and Howard K. Smith joined Reynolds. In December 1970 it became *The ABC Evening News with Howard K. Smith and Harry Reasoner*, Reasoner having been hired away from CBS (where, it seemed, he was never going to get the chance to succeed the venerable Walter Cronkite). The Smith-Reasoner team lasted almost five years, with Reasoner going it alone in September 1975. In October 1976 he was joined, amid a blaze of publicity, by former NBC newswoman Barbara Walters, who reportedly got an annual salary of $1,000,000 to make the switch. Reasoner and Walters did not work well together, however, and in the summer of 1978 the network decided to try a four-person arrangement called *World News Tonight*, originating from four different cities each night: Max Robinson from Chicago, Frank Reynolds from Washington, Peter Jennings (remember him?) from London, and Barbara Walters doing periodic features from New York.

The next major change took place in mid-1983, when Frank Reynolds died unexpectedly. The multicity approach was dropped and Peter Jennings became the sole anchor in August, resuming the position he had held more than 15 years before.

The changes made in the 1980s, together with the general momentum provided by ABC's improved position in prime time, made a difference as ABC's traditionally third-place news began to gain in audience and eventually surpassed both CBS and NBC. Peter Jennings, dismissed as "the kid" in the 1960s, had risen in stature to become America's leading anchorman in the 1990s.

NEWS—CBS

FIRST TELECAST: *May 3, 1948*
LAST TELECAST:
BROADCAST HISTORY:

Monday–Friday early evening:
May 1948–Sep 1955, CBS Mon–Fri 7:30–7:45
Sep 1955–Aug 1963, CBS Mon–Fri 7:15–7:30
Sep 1963– , CBS Mon–Fri Various times (30 min.) between 6:00–7:30
Sunday early evening:
Aug 1948–Dec 1948, CBS Sun Various times (15 min.) between 7:00–8:00
Jan 1970–Sep 1972, CBS Sun 6:00–6:30 (Jan–Sep each year)
Jan 1976– , CBS Sun 6:00–6:30
Sunday late evening
Jan 1949–Jun 1950, CBS Sun Various times (15 min.) between 10:00–11:00
Aug 1950–Sep 1950, CBS Sun 10:00–10:15
Jan 1951–Nov 1970, CBS Sun 11:00–11:15
Nov 1970–Sep 1997, CBS Sun 11:00–11:15 or 11:15–11:30
Saturday early evening:
Jan 1949–Mar 1950, CBS Sat 7:30–7:45
Jun 1950–Sep 1950, CBS Sat 6:15–6:30
Sep 1950–Jan 1951, CBS Sat 7:30–7:45
Oct 1951–Nov 1951, CBS Sat 6:30–6:45
Nov 1951–Jan 1952, CBS Sat 6:45–7:00
Jan 1966– , CBS Sat 6:30–7:00
Overnight:
Oct 1982– , CBS Sun 2:00–6:00 A.M.
Oct 1982–Oct 1989, CBS Mon–Thu 2:00–6:00 A.M.
Oct 1989–Sep 1990, CBS Mon–Thu 1:35–6:00 A.M.
Oct 1990–Mar 1991, CBS Mon–Thu 2:10–6:00 A.M.
Apr 1991– , CBS Mon–Thu 1:35–6:00 A.M.

Doug Edwards had been doing television news for the CBS station in New York since the mid-1940s and, when it was decided to produce a nightly network newscast, his local show became CBS' first network news show. Edwards remained with the weekday evening news until 1962. One month short of Edwards' 14th anniversary with the series Walter Cronkite took over, on April 16, 1962. Cronkite lasted even longer than Edwards. When he finally left the show, on March 6, 1981, he had spent almost two decades coming into our living rooms five nights a week. He had become an institution and a celebrity, whose soft-spoken manner and clear, concise delivery had also made him, according to at least one poll, the most trusted man in America. It was with a sad sense of passing that his audience heard him utter "and that's the way it is" at the end of his final newscast. The mantle passed to Dan Rather, who had the unenviable task of trying to replace a living legend in American broadcasting. For most of the next decade Rather did well, maintaining CBS' dominance of network weekday news ratings. By the nineties, however, he had slipped out of first place, and in June 1993, in an effort to boost sagging ratings, Connie Chung joined him at the anchor desk. She was dropped in 1995.

Compared to the extreme stability of the weekday news, CBS' weekend shows have gone through many more changes of personnel. The Saturday early news debuted in January 1949 with Quincy Howe reporting. *Quincy Howe with the News* lasted 15 months and was replaced in the summer of 1950 by *The Week in Review*, a filmed newsreel summary of the happenings of the past week. That September *The Saturday News Special*, anchored by Don Hollenbeck, replaced the newsreels for slightly over three months. *Up to the Minute* arrived in October 1951, with Edward P. Morgan anchoring for the first three weeks and Walter Cronkite for the last two months. After no Saturday news program for 14 years, *The CBS Saturday News* arrived on January 12, 1966. Roger Mudd was the original anchor of this show, replaced in July 1973 by Dan Rather, who was in turn replaced by Bob Schieffer in November 1976. Schieffer's tenure was three months short of twenty years when he stepped down for Paula Zahn in September 1996. She departed in January 1999 for a job with the Fox News Channel. That fall Thalia Assuras became the primary anchor, although other CBS correspondents filled in from time to time.

CBS' initial news offering on Sundays, running from August 1948 to June 1950, was the filmed newsreel *The Week in Review*. John Daly had a brief turn with a Sunday weekly news summary show that fall, but the long-lasting 11:00 P.M. Sunday news did not actually start until January 1951. Walter Cronkite was at the helm for more than 11 years, leaving to take over *The CBS Evening News* in April 1962. Cronkite, therefore, was on continuous view as a CBS anchorman from the time he began on *Up to the Minute* in 1951 until 1981. None of the Sunday anchormen who succeeded Cronkite had his endurance. Eric Sevareid was his initial replacement (lasting only nine months), followed by Harry Reasoner (February 1963–November 1970), Dan Rather (November 1970–July 1973), Bob Schieffer (July 1973–August 1974), Rather again (September 1974–December 1975), Morton Dean (December 1975–December 1976), Ed Bradley (December 1976–May 1981), Charles Osgood (June 1981–December 1987), Susan Spencer (December 1987–March 1988), Bill Plante (June 1988–July 1995) and Russ Mitchell from July 1995 until it was canceled in September 1997. In addition to the late Sunday news, there was an early evening version for parts of 1970 and 1971 with Roger Mudd anchoring, and in 1976 with Bob Schieffer. Schieffer departed in November of that year, with Morton Dean moving over from the late Sunday news to the earlier edition, where he remained until December 1984. Susan Spencer became a semiregular anchor on the *CBS Sunday News* in April 1985, alternating mostly with Bill Redeker and Bruce Morton in 1985, with Bob Schieffer and Forrest Sawyer in 1986, and almost exclusively with Sawyer until she became sole anchor in September of 1987. She was replaced in April of 1989 by Connie Chung. When she left to join Dan Rather on the weeknight anchor desk in June 1993, the Sunday early evening news continued without a regular anchor for almost two years until John Roberts took the reins in March of 1995.

In addition to these famous names, CBS News gave short-lived celebrity to another newscaster, albeit unintentionally. During a 13-day performers' union strike in March 1967, CBS and others were forced to put some of their office staff on the air to fill in for striking talent. The honor of sitting in for Walter Cronkite fell to a bespectacled young CBS lawyer named Arnold Zenker, who so caught the fancy of viewers (if not of the union) that he became something of a fad, with Arnold Zenker buttons and jokes abounding. He later tried to parlay this unexpected fame into a show-business career of his own, hosting local news and talk programs in Boston and Baltimore.

Concern about the impact of the 24-hour news service provided to cable television subscribers by Ted Turner's Cable News Network, coupled with expansion in the news programming of NBC and ABC, prompted CBS to add an overnight network news service in late 1982. Premiering in October of that year, and anchored by the team of Harold Dow, Felicia Jeter, Christopher Glenn, Karen Stone, and Mary Jo West, *CBS News Nightwatch* aired weeknights from 2:00 to 6:00 A.M. When the original anchor team departed in January 1984, Charlie Rose and Lark McCarthy took the reins, with McCarthy leaving in September 1985 and Rose staying on as the sole full-time anchor. When Rose departed for the syndicated series *Personalities* in June 1990, various CBS correspondents worked on the show with no one designated as full-time anchor. *Nightwatch* continued to air until it was replaced by a more hard-news-oriented series, *Up to the Minute*; in March 1992. Russ Mitchell and Monica Gayle were the original coanchors of *Up to the Minute*; Troy Roberts replaced Mitchell in July 1993. Two months later Sharyl Atkisson took over the distaff coanchor slot, where she remained until Nanette Hansen arrived in January 1995. Rick Jackson replaced Roberts that August, and Mika Brzezinski took over for Hansen in July 1997. When Jackson departed at the end of 1998, the coanchor format was dropped. Brzezinski held the anchor seat until the spring of 2000, when she was replaced by Melissa McDermott.

NEWS—DUMONT

FIRST TELECAST: *August 25, 1947*
LAST TELECAST: *April 1, 1955*
BROADCAST HISTORY:

Aug 1947–May 1948, DUM Mon–Fri 6:45–7:00
Jan 1948–Jan 1949, DUM Mon–Fri 7:30–7:45
Jan 1948–Jan 1949, DUM Tue 7:45–8:00
Nov 1948–Feb 1949, DUM Sun 6:30–7:00
Feb 1949–May 1950, DUM Mon 8:00–8:30
Sep 1954–Apr 1955, DUM Mon–Fri 7:15–7:30

DuMont never had the financial resources of the other television networks and, though it was second only to NBC with a regularly scheduled evening news program, the DuMont news never developed into the complex and comprehensive effort that its competitors were to become by the early 1950s. The first DuMont network news show, carried on a two-station network, was 1947's *Walter Compton News.* The first network news series to originate from Washington, D.C., where it had been seen since June 1947, *Walter Compton News* became a network program when it was seen simultaneously in New York starting in August. The production was minimal, with Compton reading from a script and only occasional slides being shown.

In January 1948 *Camera Headlines,* a filmed 15-minute newsreel, was added to the DuMont schedule at 7:30 P.M. Since *Camera Headlines* dealt only with domestic stories, *INS Telenews* followed it on Tuesday nights to provide world news coverage. The *INS Telenews* newsreel was a wrap-up of the major world news stories of the week, provided to DuMont by Hearst's *I*nternational *N*ews *S*ervice, essentially a print service similar to U.P.I. and A.P.

Not precisely a hard-news show, *Newsweek Analysis* premiered in November 1948. Moderated by senior *Newsweek* editor Ernest K. Lindley, it was an interview program in which various editors of the magazine chatted with personalities in the news. When the series moved from Sundays to Mondays the following February, the title was changed to *Newsweek Views the News.*

In the fall of 1954, after an absence of almost five years, regularly scheduled nightly news returned to the DuMont network. Anchored by Morgan Beatty, this show remained on the air until the crumbling DuMont network virtually ceased functioning the following April.

NEWS—NBC

FIRST TELECAST: *April 10, 1944*
LAST TELECAST:

BROADCAST HISTORY:

Apr 1944–Jul 1944, NBC Mon Various times (10 or 15 min. between 8:00–9:00 P.M.)
Aug 1944–Jul 1945, NBC Mon 8:00–8:10
Jul 1945–Jun 1946, NBC Sun 8:00–8:15
Jun 1946–Dec 1946, NBC Mon/Thu 7:50–8:00
Dec 1946–Oct 1947, NBC Mon 9:00–9:10
Dec 1946–Oct 1947, NBC Thu 7:50–8:00
Nov 1947–Dec 1947, NBC Wed 8:45–9:00
Feb 1948–Feb 1949, NBC Mon–Fri 7:50–8:00
Jun 1948–Sep 1948, NBC Sun 7:50–8:00
Sep 1948–Feb 1949, NBC Sun 7:20–7:30
Feb 1949–Sep 1957, NBC Mon–Fri 7:45–8:00
Apr 1949–Feb 1950, NBC Sat 7:45–8:00
Jul 1949–Oct 1949, NBC Sun 7:00–7:30
Sep 1957–Sep 1963, NBC Mon–Fri 6:45–7:00
Oct 1961–Oct 1965, NBC Sat 6:00–6:15
Sep 1963– , NBC Mon–Fri Various times (30 min.)
Sep 1965–Aug 1967, NBC Sun 6:00–6:30
Oct 1965– , NBC Sat 6:30–7:00
Sep 1967– , NBC Sun 6:30–7:00
Jul 1982–Dec 1983, NBC Mon–Thu 1:30–2:30 A.M.
Jul 1982–Dec 1983, NBC Fri 2:00–3:00 A.M.
Nov 1991–Sep 1998, NBC Mon–Sun 3:00–4:30 A.M. (approx.)

NBC, which pioneered television networking, was also the first to carry a regular network newscast. This was an outgrowth of the local newscasts that had begun on NBC's New York station almost as soon as the first regular TV service began in 1939 (see Introduction). Lowell Thomas, a nationally known radio commentator, had frequently simulcast his regular weeknight *Sunoco News* on radio and local TV between February and July 1940 (and occasionally thereafter); and there was also a weekly *Esso Television Reporter* from March until May 1940 (the NBC files indicate that "news photos, maps and graphic diagrams" were used, and that "an organ will supply a musical background"). William Spargrove was the reporter. From July 1941 to May 1942 Sam Cuff provided a weekly news commentary on *Face of the War.*

During late 1942 and 1943 television operations were curtailed drastically because of World War II, but February 21, 1944, saw the debut of a new weekly program called *The War As It Happens*—and NBC-TV news has been on the air more or less continuously ever since. At first *The War As It Happens* was a local telecast, like its predecessors, but the NBC files indicate that beginning in April 1944 it was fed to Philadelphia and Schenectady, thus becoming the first TV newscast regularly seen in multiple cities.

What viewers saw on their tiny screens in 1944 was far different from what we see today. Broadcasters did not then have film crews to send out to cover stories, and, in fact, the entire broadcast news apparatus—radio and television—was tiny compared to that maintained by newspapers, newsreels, and the wire services. The first breakthrough came in 1944 when John F. Royal, the first head of television at NBC, acquired rights to U.S. Army Signal Corps footage. Using this footage, *The War As It Happens* followed basically a newsreel format: several minutes of government-supplied film about the war effort, with background music and subtitles, interspersed with Ray Forrest in the studio explaining the latest developments with the help of maps on an easel. Narration for the film was provided by Paul Alley, a former newsreel man. Alley recalled signing off each telecast by saying, "This is the NBC Television Network—WNBT, New York; WPTZ, Philadelphia; and WRGB, Schenectady," after which he read the megacycle band on which each station was operating. Imagine an anchorman doing that today, with more than 200 stations on the network! (While this newscast was definitely seen on a three-city network from April 1944 until January 1945, the files are unclear as to whether it remained a network hookup or reverted to a local broadcast during 1945. NBC news was in any event being telecast over a network from early 1946 on.)

In August 1945, with the war over, the Sunday newscast was retitled *NBC Television Newsreel.* In mid-1946 it was rescheduled to two nights a week, Monday and Thursday, and gained a sponsor, becoming *The Esso Newsreel.*

November 1947 brought *Current Opinion* to the NBC Wednesday night schedule for a one-month run. Hosted by Robert McCormick from Washington, D.C., it was one of the earliest examples of a news commentary program, with opinions rather than facts taking the spotlight. In February 1948, NBC began a Monday–Friday evening news show called the *Camel Newsreel Theatre.* It was only 10 minutes long, and was not much different from *Esso Newsreel,* which it succeeded, but it was the genesis of the *Camel News Caravan* which took its place a year later. When that happened, John Cameron Swayze, one of the announcers behind the newsreels, moved in front of the camera and became an "anchorman." The sponsor was so nervous about this radical departure from the traditional newsreel concept of TV news that it insisted on including fashion shows and other light features to maintain visual interest and attract female viewers. These were soon phased out, but the background music—another holdover from newsreels—remained until the mid-1950s, as did the film narration by a second, newsreel-style announcer. Nevertheless John Cameron Swayze became America's best-known individual newscaster. His nightly sign-off, "Glad we could get together," was one of early television's most familiar phrases.

Swayze was essentially a newsreader, however. By the mid-1950s television had become a news-gathering force in its own right, and NBC (feeling pressure from CBS) felt it necessary to put someone with more field experience in front of the cameras. So in October 1956 Swayze was replaced by Chet Huntley and David Brinkley, both of whom had years of experience as reporters and who had proven a charismatic team covering the political conventions that summer. They were the first superstars of TV news: the stolid, sober Huntley providing a perfect counterpoint to the wry, sometimes caustic Brinkley. Their habitual closing, "Good Night, Chet . . . Good Night, David," became more famous than Swayze's. By 1965 a poll showed that they were recognized by more adults than Cary Grant, James Stewart, or the Beatles.

The Huntley-Brinkley Report became a national institution, running almost 14 years. It expanded to a half hour on September 9, 1963, (a week after CBS had done the same thing), and added a Saturday telecast in 1969. After Chet Huntley retired in July 1970, NBC experimented for a year with a system in which Brinkley, John Chancellor, and Frank McGee rotated as anchormen seven nights a week, under the blanket title *The NBC Nightly News*. In August 1971 Chancellor emerged as the sole Monday–Friday anchor, remaining in the anchor chair for the next 11 years (joined by Brinkley as coanchor from 1976 to 1979). He was succeeded in April 1982 by Tom Brokaw, who was at first paired with a recent arrival from CBS, Roger Mudd, but became sole anchor in late 1983.

Saturday newscasts have been more eratic on NBC. The first was *Leon Pearson and the News* in 1949–1950, followed by a hiatus of more than a decade. NBC returned to Saturday newscasting with Sander Vanocur in October 1961. Subsequent Saturday anchormen included Ray Scherer and Robert MacNeil (1965), Frank McGee (1967), Garrick Utley (1971), Tom Brokaw (1973), and John Hart (1976). Sunday newscasts resumed in 1965, with anchors including Frank McGee (1965), Garrick Utley (1971), Floyd Kalber (1973), Tom Snyder (1975), and John Hart (1976).

It was at the start of 1977 that women anchors began to be featured on NBC weekend news shows, beginning with Catherine Mackin and followed by Jessica Savitch (November 1977), Jane Pauley (1980), Connie Chung (1983), and Maria Shriver (1988). Chris Wallace (1982, 1986), John Palmer (1984), and Garrick Utley (1987) also had stints on the Sunday edition. Garrick Utley was the principal anchor on both Saturday and Sunday from 1989 to 1993, after which Brian Williams took over the Saturday edition and rotating anchors were used on Sunday. (Giselle Fernandez was regular anchor during 1995–1996.) John Seigenthaler was named anchor for both Saturday and Sunday in July 1999.

A short-lived addition to NBC's roster of regular newscasts was *NBC News Overnight*, which ran from 1:30 to 2:30 A.M. Monday–Thursday, and 2:00–3:00 A.M. on Friday, beginning July 1982—primarily as a response to the growing popularity of 24-hour cable news networks. Lloyd Dobyns and Linda Ellerbee were the original anchors, with Dobyns replaced by Bill Schechner in November 1982. It was a hip, unconventional newscast, but not enough people were viewing at that hour to make the expense worthwhile, and it faded from the air in December 1983. On November 4, 1991, NBC returned to the wee-hours news business with *NBC Nightside*, which was formatted in short segments that could be run by an affiliate in various patterns, generally between 3:00 A.M. and 4:30 A.M. The principal anchors were Kim Hindrew (1992), Tom Miller (1992), Tom Donovan (1993), Tonya Strong (1995), and Hillary Lane (1996).

NEWS IS THE NEWS, THE (*Comedy/Variety*)

FIRST TELECAST: *June 15, 1983*
LAST TELECAST: *July 13, 1983*
BROADCAST HISTORY:
Jun 1983–Jul 1983, NBC Wed 10:00–10:30
REGULARS:
Michael Davis
Simon Jones
Charlotte Moore
Lynn Thigpen
Trey Wilson

Mix a little bit of *Saturday Night Live*'s "Weekend Update" and a dash of the satiric weekly 1960s series *That Was the Week That Was* and you had *The News Is the News*. Like its predecessors, it was produced live from New York and satirized the current week's headlines with a team of "newspersons" doing most of the sendups, abetted by an occasional guest correspondent. It may have been topical, but it certainly wasn't very funny. The regulars often seemed uncomfortable with the material and the show had a depressingly unfinished look. It was abruptly canceled after only a month on the air.

NEWS SATURDAY/THURSDAY NIGHT

(*News Documentary*)
FIRST TELECAST: *January 24, 1998*
LAST TELECAST: *April 1, 1999*
BROADCAST HISTORY:
Jan 1998–Jun 1998, ABC Sat 10:00–11:00
Jun 1998–Jul 1998, ABC Thu 10:00–11:00—News Thursday Night
Aug 1998–Sep 1998, ABC Thu 9:00–10:00—ABC News Summer Thursday
Jan 1999–Apr 1999, ABC Thu 10:00–11:00—News Thursday Night
ANCHOR:
Forrest Sawyer

Yet another prime-time newsmagazine, distinguished primarily by the fact that it generally dealt with a single story per hour. Subjects ranged from the Pope's visit to Cuba to a night at the Academy Awards. Various ABC correspondents anchored from time to time, including Peter Jennings, Barbara Walters, and Hugh Downs. Originally titled *News Saturday Night*, it was known as *News Thursday Night* and *ABC News Summer Thursday* during various periods of its Thursday run.

NEWSRADIO (*Situation Comedy*)

FIRST TELECAST: *March 21, 1995*
LAST TELECAST: *July 13, 1999*
BROADCAST HISTORY:
Mar 1995–May 1995, NBC Tue 8:30–9:00
Aug 1995–Jan 1996, NBC Tue 8:30–9:00
Jan 1996–Jul 1996, NBC Sun 8:30–9:00
Jun 1996–Aug 1996, NBC Tue 8:30–9:00
Sep 1996–Feb 1997, NBC Wed 9:00–9:30
Mar 1997–Jun 1997, NBC Wed 8:00–8:30
Jun 1997–Aug 1997, NBC Sun 8:30–9:00
Jun 1997–Jul 1997, NBC Wed 8:00–9:00
Jul 1997–Mar 1998, NBC Tue 8:30–9:00
Mar 1998–May 1998, NBC Wed 8:00–8:30
May 1998–Aug 1998, NBC Tue 8:30–9:00
Sep 1998–Dec 1998, NBC Wed 9:30–10:00
Nov 1998–Jul 1999, NBC Tue 8:30–9:00
CAST:
Dave Nelson .... Dave Foley
Lisa Miller .... Maura Tierney
Bill McNeal (1995–1998) .... Phil Hartman
Catherine Duke (1995–1998) .... Khandi Alexander
Matthew Brock .... Andy Dick
Joe Garelli .... Joe Rogan
Beth .... Vicki Lewis
Jimmy James .... Stephen Root
Max Lewis (1998–1999) .... Jon Lovitz

All-news radio station WNYX in New York was the setting for this fast-paced slapstick comedy. Boyish, enthusiastic Dave Nelson had just been brought in from Wisconsin as the latest in a string of news directors by curt, overbearing station owner Jimmy James. Bewildered and somewhat inept, Dave was nevertheless determined to make the most of his big break. Watching warily, but mostly supportive, were self-important on-air anchors Bill and Catherine, inept, hypersensitive reporter Matthew, got-a-deal maintenance man Joe, and gumcracking—but surprisingly savvy—secretary Beth. More problematic was newswriter Lisa, who was smart, talented, and knew it and thought she should have gotten the news director's job. Despite an edgy relationship she and Dave found themselves attracted to one another with an off-and-on romance that became the talk of the office. Stories dealt with little incidents and jealousies around the office, with an occasional "fantasy" episode. In one, WNYX was blasted into space, in another, the cast did a takeoff on the hit movie *Titanic* (sweet Lisa was pursued by Dave, while Joe tried to use duct tape to plug holes in the sinking ship).

The tragic murder of actor Phil Hartman in May 1998 almost spelled the end of the show, but his character was replaced by pathologically insecure on-air personality Max Lewis—a man who had held 37 jobs in the past twenty years. Ironically, actor Jon Lovitz had appeared before in a 1997 episode as a man who threatened to jump from a ledge outside Dave's office unless he was allowed on the air. In a memorial episode, Bill McNeal was said to have died of a heart attack while watching TV. Everyone cried except for clueless Matthew, who thought he had gone to Afghanistan.

NEWSSTAND THEATRE (*Dramatic Anthology*)
FIRST TELECAST: *January 16, 1952*
LAST TELECAST: *February 6, 1952*
BROADCAST HISTORY:
Jan 1952–Feb 1952, ABC Wed 9:30–10:00

Four-week series of dramatizations of short stories from national magazines. Included was "Size 12 Tantrum," starring Jack Lemmon and his then wife, Cynthia Stone.

NEWZ, THE (*Comedy*)
BROADCAST HISTORY:
Syndicated only
30 minutes
Produced: *1994–1995*
Released: *September 1994*
REGULARS:
Tommy Blaze
Mystro Clark
Deborah Magdalena
Dan O'Connor
Stan Quash
Brad Sherwood
Nancy Sullivan
Shawn Alex Thompson
Lou Thornton

The Newz offered sketch comedy six nights a week with a regular group of young comics. It was done in front of a live studio audience à la *Saturday Night Live,* showing cameras and crew in between most of the sketches. Included were spoofs of commercials, classic movies, TV shows and celebrities, short films by Thompson, advice from "Ask Abby and Andy" (Sullivan and Blaze), Tommy Blaze and the News (a variation on *Saturday Night Live*'s "Weekend Update"), and other sketches, some of which were very topical. Each episode included an opening with one or two of the regulars seated on a couch doing a comic bit. Tim Watters was a frequent guest portraying president Bill Clinton.

Taped at Universal Studios Florida in Orlando.

NEXT STEP BEYOND, THE, see *Alcoa Presents*

NICHOLS (*Western*)
FIRST TELECAST: *September 16, 1971*
LAST TELECAST: *August 1, 1972*
BROADCAST HISTORY:
Sep 1971–Nov 1971, NBC Thu 9:00–10:00
Nov 1971–Aug 1972, NBC Tue 9:30–10:30
CAST:
Nichols .... James Garner
Ma Ketcham .... Neva Patterson
Ketcham .... John Beck
Mitch .... Stuart Margolin
Ruth .... Margot Kidder
Bertha .... Alice Ghostley

This was one TV series in which the hero really was shot because of low ratings—as in the movie *Network*. The setting was Nichols, Arizona, in 1914. Nichols (he never did have a first name) returned to the town his family had founded only to discover that it had been taken over by the powerful Ketcham family, dominated by matriarchal Ma Ketcham. He was promptly blackmailed by Ma into serving as sheriff, a powerless but hazardous position where she could keep an eye on him. Although Nichols had spent 18 years in the army, he really hated violence and didn't even carry a gun. His real aim in life was to find a means to get rich, and he concocted all sorts of schemes toward that end. Mitch was the town bully, Ma Ketcham's son, and Nichols's not-too-honest deputy; Ruth, the barmaid, was Nichols's girlfriend; and Bertha was the proprietor of the saloon where Ruth worked. The program had an interesting early-20th-century Western background, with Nichols using an auto and motorcycle rather than the traditional horse.

In the last episode Nichols was shot down, only to be avenged by his identical twin brother Jim Nichols (yes, *he* had a first name) also played by James Garner. At the time that the last episode was filmed it was assumed that, despite marginal ratings, the series would be renewed. By replacing the avaricious Nichols with his stronger, more traditionally heroic twin brother, it was felt that the next season's program would be more successful. By the time the episode actually aired, however, establishing a real hero for the series had become a moot point—*Nichols* had been given the ax.

Effective with the October 25, 1971, telecast, the official title of the series became *James Garner as Nichols*, in the hopes that the drawing power of its star would boost ratings.

NICK & HILLARY, see *Tattingers*

NICK ARCADE (*Quiz/Audience Participation*)
BROADCAST HISTORY:
Nickelodeon
30 minutes
Produced: *1991–1992* (84 episodes)
Premiered: *January 3, 1992*
HOST:
Phil Moore

Two teams of two kids each competed in this fast-paced quiz show set in a video arcade. In the preliminary rounds the teams played traditional video games and answered questions, while in the final round (the "Video Zone") the winning team was electronically inserted into a life-size video game in which they ran an obstacle course and scored points against the clock.

NICK CANNON SHOW, THE (*Comedy*)

BROADCAST HISTORY:

Nickelodeon
30 minutes
Original episodes: *2002–*
Premiered: *January 19, 2002*

REGULARS:

Nick Cannon

Nick Cannon, a hip, versatile, black comic formerly in the cast of *All That*, took his act on the road in this unusual on-location comedy series. The premise was that Nick would "take over" ordinary people's lives—those of a suburban family, a school full of kids, a military unit, a group of rodeo performers, beachgoers, or even residents of London—and fill them with his own type of insanity. For example, at the suburban home he set up a messy lemonade stand for the kids, did the dishes with a water gun, and dusted with a leaf blower, then invaded dad's office (boogying in the staff meeting), and visited Grandpa at the old folks' home (playing nonsensical games with the residents); the show ended back home with a backyard pool party featuring his pals real-life rap stars Master P and Lil' Romeo. The neighborhood kids loved that one! Other stars who joined him included Eddie Murphy, Britney Spears, Mary J. Blige, P. Diddy and Will Smith. Nick was also seen in character as Latayna, Francis Spunkle and Oswald Watkins.

NICK FRENO: LICENSED TEACHER (*Situation Comedy*)

FIRST TELECAST: *August 28, 1996*
LAST TELECAST: *July 5, 1998*

BROADCAST HISTORY:

Aug 1996–Feb 1997, WB Wed 8:30–9:00
Jan 1997–Jun 1997, WB Sun 7:30–8:00
Jun 1997–Jul 1998, WB Sun 7:00–7:30

CAST:

Nick Freno .... Mitch Mullany
Elana Lewis (1996–1997) .... Portia de Rossi
Mezz Crosby (pilot only) .... Reggie Hayes
Mezz Crosby .... Clinton Jackson
Tyler Hale (1996–1997) .... Ross Malinger
Orlando Diaz (1996–1997) .... Jonathan Hernandez
Sarah (1996–1997) .... Cara DeLizia
Jared (1996–1997) .... Arjay Smith
Davey Marcucci (1996–1997) .... Kyle Gibson
Al Yaroker .... Charles Cyphers
Kurt Fust (1996–1997) .... Stuart Pankin
Phil, the security guard .... Sid Newman
Dr. Katherine Emerson (1997–1998) .... Jane Sibbett
Sophia Del Bono (1997–1998) .... Christina Vidal
Miles Novacek (1997–1998) .... Giuseppe Andrews
Marco Romero (1997–1998) .... Andrew Levitas
Jordan Wells (1997–1998) .... Blake Heron
Tasha Morrison (1997–1998) .... Malinda Williams
Samantha (1998) .... Donna D'Errico

Nick was an aspiring young actor who worked as a substitute English teacher at the Gerald R. Ford Middle School to pay the bills until he got his big break. Among the kids in his fifth grade class were Orlando, the smart, shy boy; Tyler, the operator who rarely did his homework; Jared, Tyler's partner in crime; Sarah, the intellectual; and Davey, who liked to play the sax. Nick, whose frenetic teaching style included running question and answer sessions like game shows, was attracted to Elana, the perky, dedicated social studies teacher. Other teachers on staff were Mezz, his childhood friend, now a science teacher; Al, the cynical shop teacher who had seen it all; and Kurt, the obnoxious gym teacher who eventually became assistant principal. At the end of the first season, after having bailed out on a short-lived relationship with Nick earlier in the season, Elana rekindled their romance.

When the show returned for its second season there were major changes. Nick was a full-time teacher—at the same school that was now, magically, a high school—and Elana had dumped him and left town. He was stuck with a class full of misfits and had to deal with a new principal, Dr. Emerson, an intellectual who had trouble dealing with miscreant students and little patience for Nick's sense of humor. Among his new students were Sophia, a trashy sexpot who wasn't as worldly wise as she thought; Miles, the neurotic foil for most of his classmates; Marco, the overage hunk who was still in school because he hadn't graduated with his class; Jordan, an older operator along the lines of Tyler from the first season; and Tasha, an opinionated girl who didn't want her blue collar classmates to know that her father was an investment banker and her mother a real estate agent. In the spring Nick started dating Samantha, the sexy supervisor in his apartment building.

NICK HIT LIST, THE (*Kids' Magazine*)

BROADCAST HISTORY:

Nickelodeon
30 minutes
Produced: *1991–1992* (26 episodes)
Premiered: *November 1, 1991*

HOSTS:

Kenan Scott
Shondi Jones

An entertainment and lifestyles magazine show by and for kids. Fashion, music, hairstyles, slang, movies, and books were among the topics covered by the youthful reporters.

NICK KENNY SHOW, THE (*Talk/Music*)

FIRST TELECAST: *July 18, 1951*
LAST TELECAST: *January 1, 1952*

BROADCAST HISTORY:

Jul 1951–Aug 1951, NBC Wed 11:00–11:15
Aug 1951–Jan 1952, NBC Tue 11:00–11:15

REGULARS:

Nick Kenny
Irene Walsh
Don Tippen

Nick Kenny was a columnist for the *New York Daily Mirror* and this series was set in a replica of his newspaper office. Each week he read some of his original poetry, sang, chatted with guests from the worlds of theater and sports, and philosophized about life. Irene Walsh was his secretary and assistant while Don Tippen provided piano background and accompaniment for singers. The show returned for a couple of months in the spring of 1952 on Saturday afternoons.

NICK NEWS (*Kids' Newsmagazine*)
BROADCAST HISTORY:
Nickelodeon
30 minutes
Produced: *1992–*
Premiered: *April 18, 1992*
HOST:
Linda Ellerbee

A newsmagazine designed to educate kids about the important issues of the day. This was one of the few programs on Nickelodeon that tackled such serious issues as AIDS and child abduction.

NICKELODEON (Network) (*Kids' Cable Network*)
LAUNCHED:
April 1, 1979
SUBSCRIBERS (MAY 2003):
86.0 million (81% U.S.)

Nickelodeon—or "Nick" as it is known to its legions of young fans—is one of the great innovations of the cable age, an entire network devoted to kids. It has become enormously popular, attracting more child viewers than the broadcast networks, despite the fact that it is available only on cable.

Nick's success has come as a result of carefully building a schedule full of excitement and action, with plenty of kids on-screen. Here kids can play, be encouraged to stretch their minds and bodies, even see scary stories *(Are You Afraid of the Dark?)*. Conspicuously absent is the climate of fear so widely promoted by broadcast TV; on Nick kids are not constantly bombarded with violence, sex, child abduction, abuse, and the other terrors of modern life so frequently seen on news, reality shows, dramas, and even sitcoms.

Original series make up most of the Nickelodeon schedule. Daytime is for younger kids, including variety shows *(Eureeka's Castle)* and cartoons. Late afternoon switches to their older siblings, with everything from game shows *(Family Double Dare, Nickelodeon GUTS)* to magazines *(U to U)*, cartoons *(Doug, Rugrats, Ren & Stimpy)*, sitcoms *(Clarissa Explains It All)*, sketch comedy *(Roundhouse)*, and even science fiction *(Tomorrow People)*. The late '90s and early '00s brought a new wave of kids' favorites on Nick, including *The Wild Thornberrys, SpongeBob SquarePants, Rocket Power, The Fairly Oddparents* and *The Adventures of Jimmy Neutron*. In between the shows are short features like "Looking at Each Other," video letters from kids around the world.

Nickelodeon began as "Nick Flicks," a local program for children in Columbus, Ohio, in 1977, and went national via satellite in 1979. Originally it was noncommercial and daytime only. In July 1985 it expanded into the evening hours with reruns of old sitcoms, packaged as high camp for baby boomers and called "Nick at Nite." The combined network (Nickelodeon/Nick at Nite) first reached more than half of all U.S. television homes in April 1989, and its principal post–6:00 P.M. original series after that date (including those mentioned above) are listed in this book under their individual titles. Nickelodeon operates several others networks, including Nick Too (same shows at different times, 1999), Nickelodeon GAS (games and sports, 1999) and Noggin (a noncommercial network for younger kids, produced with the Children's Television Workshop, 1999).

NICKELODEON GUTS (*Sports/Audience Participation*)
BROADCAST HISTORY:
Nickelodeon
30 minutes
Produced: *1992–1995* (126 episodes)
Premiered: *September 19, 1992*
REGULARS:
Mike O'Malley, host
Moira Quirk, referee

Kids faced imaginative physical challenges in this fast-paced competition. The games, which took place in the "Extreme Arena," included performing various stunts while bouncing high into the air on the end of a bungee cord, roller-blading through an obstacle course, and racing across a swirling pool in a small rubber raft. The final round consisted of a mad scramble up "The Mega Crag," a huge, artificial, metal "mountain" that periodically erupted in snowstorms and clouds of smoke to drive the climbers back. Exhausted winners got trophies and the assurances that they had GUTS!

NICKELODEON WILD SIDE SHOW, THE (*Wildlife/Nature*)
BROADCAST HISTORY:
Nickelodeon
30 minutes
Produced: *1992–1993* (26 episodes)
Premiered: *August 22, 1992*
HOSTS:
Jessica Duarte (1992–1993)
Scott Tunnell (1992–1993)
Jillian Hirasawa (1993–1994)
Gordon Michael Woolvett (1993–1994)

Exhibitions of wildlife, at the zoo and in the wild, hosted by two intrepid youngsters.

NIGHT COURT (*Situation Comedy*)
FIRST TELECAST: *January 4, 1984*
LAST TELECAST: *July 1, 1992*
BROADCAST HISTORY:
Jan 1984–Mar 1984, NBC Wed 9:30–10:00
May 1984–Mar 1987, NBC Thu 9:30–10:00
Mar 1987–Jun 1987, NBC Wed 9:00–9:30
Jun 1987–Jul 1987, NBC Wed 9:30–10:00
Jul 1987–Aug 1987, NBC Wed 9:00–9:30
Aug 1987–Mar 1988, NBC Thu 9:30–10:00
Mar 1988–Apr 1988, NBC Fri 9:00–9:30
May 1988–Sep 1988, NBC Thu 9:30–10:00
Oct 1988–Aug 1990, NBC Wed 9:00–9:30
Sep 1990–Jan 1991, NBC Fri 9:00–9:30
Jan 1991–Nov 1991, NBC Wed 9:00–9:30
Dec 1991–May 1992, NBC Wed 9:30–10:00
May 1992–Jun 1992, NBC Sun 9:30–10:00
Jun 1992–Jul 1992, NBC Wed 9:30–10:00
CAST:
Judge Harry T. Stone .... Harry Anderson
Court Clerk Lana Wagner (1984) ...... Karen Austin
Selma Hacker (1984–1985)........ Selma Diamond
Bailiff Nostradamus "Bull" Shannon .... Richard Moll
Asst. D.A. Dan Fielding........... John Larroquette
Liz Williams (1984) .... Paula Kelly
Court Clerk Mac Robinson (1984–1992)
.... Charlie Robinson
Billie Young (1984–1985).............. Ellen Foley

**Al Craven (1984)* .... Terry Kiser
Christine Sullivan (1985–1992) .... Markie Post
Florence Kleiner (1985–1986) ...... Florence Halop
**Phil/Will Sanders (1985–1986, 1989–1992)*
.... William Utay
**Leon (1985–1986)* .... Bumper Robinson
**Art Fensterman (1986–1992)* .... Mike Finneran
Roz Russell (1986–1992) .... Marsha Warfield
**Quon Lee Robinson (1985–1990)* ... Denice Kumagai
**Buddy Ryan (1988–1990)* .... John Astin
Jack Griffin (1990–1991) .... S.Marc Jordan
Lisette Hocheiser (1990–1992) .... Joleen Lutz
**Margaret Turner (1990–1991)* ...... Mary Cadorette
*Occasional

This courtroom comedy revolved around Harry Stone, a boyish, blue-jeaned judge who had been appointed to New York's Manhattan Night Court almost by accident. His unconventional, flippant style dismayed his staff, but often produced unexpectedly positive results with the loonies who paraded through his nocturnal court. Lana was the perky clerk, secretly in love with the cute judge; Selma the caustic, chain-smoking matron; and Bull the bald, towering bailiff. Representing the state was nattily dressed, sex-starved Assistant D.A. Dan Fielding, and the defense, black legal-aid lawyer Liz Williams.

There was a good deal of turnover in the supporting cast, with Lana replaced by sensible Mac, Selma by Florence and then Roz, and Liz by Billie and then Christine (for whose sexy body Dan, and even Harry, lusted). A number of recurring characters were seen occasionally in the carnival-like courtroom, among them obnoxious newspaper reporter Al Craven, who snooped around for stories during the first season; runaway orphan Leon; and maintenance man Art. Quon Lee was seen a few times each season as Mac's Asian wife.

Others included Buddy, an eccentric former mental patient who turned out to be Harry's father; Margaret, an attractive reporter who Harry dated a few times; Jack, a cynical, blind newsstand operator; and Lisette, a ditsy court stenographer. A recurring guest star was Harry's musical idol, Mel Tormé.

In 1990 sexy Christine married undercover cop Tony Guiliano (Ray Abruzzo) and bore his child while he was off on a case, but they were divorced the following year. Shaken, she fell into Harry's arms—however, they finally decided that they made better friends than lovers. Another continuing story in 1991 involved Dan's lackey, Phil the derelict. When he died (crushed by a piano) he was revealed to be an eccentric Wall Street millionaire who left self-centered Dan in charge of his charitable "Phil Foundation," worth ten million dollars. It proved to be nothing but trouble—Phil's crooked twin brother Will showed up, stole the whole thing, and almost landed Dan in prison.

The final episode found everyone going to a suitable reward. Christine was elected to Congress in a squeaker election; Dan saw the error of his sleazy ways and resigned to pursue his one true love—Christine; Mac dropped out of law school and became a filmmaker; and Bull departed with midget aliens from the planet Jupiter. As for Harry, he received a string of offers, one more incredible than the next—superior court judge, top law firm, university professor, talk-show host, Nike spokesman, road manager on a Mel Tormé tour! In the end he elected to remain on the bench at night court.

NIGHT EDITOR (*Dramatic Anthology*)
FIRST TELECAST: *March 14, 1954*
LAST TELECAST: *September 8, 1954*
BROADCAST HISTORY:
Mar 1954–Jul 1954, DUM Sun 10:45–11:00
Jul 1954–Sep 1954, DUM Wed 10:30–10:45
HOST:
Hal Burdick

This was one of many attempts by DuMont to devise low-cost TV programming. In this case there was one actor and one set. Hal Burdick, the night editor of an unidentified newspaper, was seen in his office narrating a short crime or human interest story. As he spoke he would sit at his desk or walk around the room, changing his voice to differentiate between characters. The stories ranged across many periods and subjects, including an old policeman on school-crossing duty who had an adventure on his last day on the force; a Korean War veteran who got a medal undeservedly; and a Civil War sentry who fell asleep at his post.

Films of *Night Editor* had been seen locally and in late night for several years before this prime-time network run.

NIGHT GALLERY (*Supernatural Anthology*)
FIRST TELECAST: *December 16, 1970*
LAST TELECAST: *August 12, 1973*
BROADCAST HISTORY:
Dec 1970–Sep 1972, NBC Wed 10:00–11:00
Sep 1972–Jan 1973, NBC Sun 10:00–10:30
May 1973–Aug 1973, NBC Sun 10:00–10:30
HOST:
Rod Serling

Night Gallery was one of the original elements in the 1970–1971 NBC series *Four in One*. It aired for six weeks from December 16, 1970, to January 20, 1971, and was rerun on a rotating basis with the other three elements of the series—*McCloud*, *San Francisco International Airport*, and *The Psychiatrist*—from April through the end of the season. It remained in the Wednesday time slot by itself during the 1971–1972 season and was then moved to Sunday nights.

Night Gallery was a weekly collection of short, supernatural vignettes. Rod Serling introduced each one from a bizarre gallery, in which grotesque paintings foreshadowed the stories to follow. Not all of the stories were frightening, and many times humorous blackouts were used between more serious stories. In many respects, *Night Gallery* was the supernatural equivalent of *Love, American Style*.

NIGHT GAMES (*Quiz/Audience Participation*)
FIRST TELECAST: *October 14, 1991*
LAST TELECAST: *June 12, 1992*
BROADCAST HISTORY:
Oct 1991–Jun 1992, CBS Mon–Fri 1:00–1:30 A.M.
EMCEE:
Jeff Marder
ASSISTANT/ANNOUNCER:
Luann Lee

Insomniacs looking for a little titillation in the wee

small hours of the morning were the primary audience for this series, yet another trashy variation on *The Dating Game.* Three guys and three gals competed to win a romantic dinner date at a fancy restaurant in Los Angeles. Each player was asked questions in three areas: honesty, creativity, and sensuality. The responses—verbal for honesty and through demonstrations with a player of the opposite sex for creativity and sensuality—were scored by all of the other players, both male and female. Demonstrations might be "give the guy of your choice a sensually creative palm reading," "pick the girl with the sexiest feet and perform a pleasing foot massage," or "give the guy you choose an earful of unabashed sensuality on your personal 900 number." The contestant with the most points at the end of the show won the dinner date and his/her choice of a companion from among the other players. After a few weeks, the format was changed. The demonstration round was dropped, each contestant was simply scored by the opposite sex on the answers to dating questions, and the dinner date went to the male and female who had received the most points for their responses. The winners then participated in a "compatibility round" in which they could win a weekend trip by choosing the same answers to questions about things they found romantic. Emcee Jeff Marder was assisted by the show's sexy announcer Luann Lee.

NIGHT HEAT (*Police Drama*)
FIRST TELECAST: *January 31, 1985*
LAST TELECAST: *September 13, 1991*
BROADCAST HISTORY:
Jan 1985–Mar 1985, CBS Thu 11:30–12:40 A.M.
May 1985, CBS Thu 11:30–12:40 A.M.
Jun 1985–Jul 1985, CBS Wed 11:30–12:40 A.M.
Sep 1985–Jul 1987, CBS Thu 11:30–12:40 A.M.
Aug 1987–Sep 1987, CBS Tue 10:00–11:00
Sep 1987–Sep 1988, CBS Thu 11:30–12:40 A.M.
Sep 1988–Jan 1989, CBS Tue–Thu 11:30–12:40 A.M.
Jan 1989–Jun 1989, CBS Mon–Thu 1:00–2:00 A.M.
Jun 1989–Sep 1989, CBS Tue–Thu 1:00–2:00 A.M.
Sep 1989–Oct 1989, CBS Mon–Thu 1:00–2:00 A.M.
Oct 1989–Jan 1990, CBS Mon–Thu 12:30–1:35 A.M.
Feb 1990–Apr 1990, CBS Wed 12:30–1:35 A.M.
Apr 1990–Jun 1990, CBS Wed 12:40–1:45 A.M.
Jul 1990–Aug 1990, CBS Thu 11:30–12:40 A.M.
Sep 1990, CBS Mon 11:30–-12:40 A.M.
Sep 1990, CBS Wed 12:40–1:45 A.M.
Oct 1990–Nov 1990, CBS Wed 1:10–2:15 A.M.
Jan 1991–Mar 1991, CBS Mon–Fri 1:10–2:15 A.M.
Apr 1991–Sep 1991, CBS Mon–Fri 12:30–1:40 A.M.
CAST:
Det. Kevin O'Brien .... Scott Hylands
Tom Kirkwood .... Allan Royal
Det. Frank Giambone.................. Jeff Wincott
Nicole "Nickie" Rimbaud .... Susan Hogan
Prosecutor Dorothy Fredericks (1985)
.... Wendy Crewson
Det. Fleece Toland (1985) ..... Lynda Mason Green
Det. Freddie Carson .... Stephen Mendel
Det. Colby Burns..................... Eugene Clark
Lt. Jim Hogan .... Sean McCann
Whitey Low .... Tony Rosato
Prosecutor Elaine Jeffers .... Deborah Grover
Det. Stephanie "Stevie" Brody (1985–1986)
.... Louise Vallance
**Det. Dave Jefferson (1986–1988)*..... Clark Johnson
Det. Christine Meadows (1987–1989)
.... Laura Robinson
*Occasional

Filmed entirely on location in Toronto, Canada, *Night Heat* was a straightforward action series about the professional, and occasionally personal, lives of a group of police detectives working in a large metropolitan city—as seen through the eyes of their friend, newspaper columnist Tom Kirkwood. Tom's popular column, "Night Heat," was carried in the major newspaper in town, *The Eagle*. The series focused on two men: Kevin was the veteran, a divorced cop who had seen it all, while Frank was his hot-tempered skirt-chasing young partner. They worked out of the Mid South precinct and Lt. Hogan, once Kevin's partner, was their boss. Kevin's girlfriend, Nickie, the widow of another cop, was the owner of Nicole's, the lounge where most of the detectives hung out. Whitey was a street snitch who worked and lived in the sleazy neighborhood in which much of the criminal activity in this series took place.

In the fall of 1988 *Night Heat* expanded to three nights a week, with reruns airing on Tuesdays and Wednesdays, while new episodes continued to appear on Thursdays. In the last original episode, aired in January of 1989, the Mid-South precinct was about to be shut down, forcing the officers who had worked together for years to be scattered to other precincts.

Reruns of *Night Heat* continued to air as part of CBS' late-night lineup until September of 1991.

NIGHT MUSIC see *Sunday Night*

NIGHT STAND WITH DICK DIETRICK (*Comedy*)
BROADCAST HISTORY:
Syndicated only
60 minutes
Produced: *1995–1997* (48 episodes)
Released: *September 1995*
CAST:
Dick Dietrick....................... Timothy Stack
Mueller........................ Robert Alan Beuth

This weekly send-up of pandering daytime talk shows featured mousy, pompous host Dick Dietrick, his producer Mueller, a former L.A. cop, and Dick's guests and studio audience. Topics included sexaholics, reuniting lovers whose only encounters had been one night stands, teenage hardbody prostitutes, and "Fatsos: Meet Them, Know Them, and Chew the Fat with Them." In addition to the actors playing parts, a number of celebrities appeared on *Night Stand*, among them Rosie O'Donnell, Phil Hartman, Morgan Fairchild, Rodney Dangerfield, Garry Marshall, and Harry Anderson. Talk show host Jerry Springer showed up on three episodes—"Are Talk Shows Out of Control?" "Getting Even," and "Supernatural Sex."

As on many of the daytime talk shows *Night Stand* lampooned, there were several doctors who made return visits evaluating guests and offering "useful" advice. The most popular were psychologist Lonnie Lanier (Tim Silva), plastic surgeon Hamilton George (Andrew Prine), sex education specialist Edward Burns (John Paragon), and Doctor of Lesbian Studies Susan Sonspeen (Jordana Capra). There were also a number of recurring characters, including the lady in the audience with glasses and frumpy dresses (Lynne Marie Stewart), New Age priest Father Chip (Hal Sparks), angry black filmmaker Tupac Zemeckis (Steve White); Bob the nymphomaniac (Christopher Darga), rapper M. C. Carjak (Dwayne Barnes), and Astounding Andy, debunker of the supernatural (Steve Valentine).

Each episode of *Night Stand* consisted of two self-contained half-hour shows. During its second season the E! cable network aired reruns as a half hour series on Monday through Thursday evenings, appropriately between *Talk Soup* and *The Howard Stern Show*.

NIGHT VISIONS (*Supernatural Anthology*)

FIRST TELECAST: *July 12, 2001*
LAST TELECAST: *September 6, 2001*
BROADCAST HISTORY:
Jul 2001–Sep 2001, FOX Thu 9:00–10:00
HOST:
Henry Rollins

This weekly suspense anthology was modeled after Rod Serling's venerable *Twilight Zone*. Each episode presented two separate stories with psychological as well as supernatural elements. For example, a psychiatrist could draw diseases out of people and into himself, but it was killing him; a woman bought a car only to take on the personality of the dead woman who once owned it, then was killed by the car herself. Among the actors featured were Gil Bellows, Lou Diamond Phillips, Brian Dennehy, Luke Perry, Sherilyn Fenn and Randy Quaid.

Night Visions was hosted by brooding rock musician Henry Rollins.

NIGHTINGALES (*Medical Drama*)

FIRST TELECAST: *January 21, 1989*
LAST TELECAST: *April 26, 1989*
BROADCAST HISTORY:
Jan 1989, NBC 9:30–11:00
Jan 1989–Apr 1989, NBC Wed 10:00–11:00
CAST:
Christine Broderick .... Suzanne Pleshette
Dr. Garrett Braden .... Barry Newman
Bridget Loring .... Susan Walters
Samantha "Sam" Sullivan .... Chelsea Field
Rebecca "Becky" Granger .... Kristy Swanson
Yolanda "Yo" Elena Puente .... Roxann Biggs
Allyson Yates .... Kim Ulrich
Megan Sullivan .... Taylor Fry
Head Nurse Lenore Ritt .... Fran Bennett
Dr. Charlene Chasen .... Doran Clark
Dr. Paul Petrillo .... Gil Gerard
Effie Gardner .... Jennifer Rhodes

As if to see whether junk TV was really dead in the realism-obsessed 1990s, NBC tried this T&A throwback to the '70s from producer Aaron Spelling (*Charlie's Angels, The Love Boat*). The student nurses at Wilshire Memorial Hospital in Southern California were clearly more interested in their love lives and casual sex in the linen closet than in their patients. They all lived in Nightingale House, the student nurse quarters, where they were seen taking their clothes off a lot. Each had a soap-opera story to tell: Bridget was in the Federal Witness Protection Program, trying to start life over under a new name after testifying against a mobster; Sam was a recovering alcoholic who worked as a dancer on the side to support her little daughter, Megan; Becky was the innocent from Missouri; Allyson, the sexy blond (she was the one in the linen closet); and Yo, the token Latino. Chris, Director of Student Nurses, tried to keep a lid on things but carried her own torch for handsome Dr. Paul, her ex. Head Nurse Ritt kicked those pretty butts as necessary, while Dr. Braden, the dedicated Chief of Staff, did most of the life saving.

NIGHTLIFE (*Talk*)

BROADCAST HISTORY:
Syndicated only
30 minutes
Produced: *September 1986–May 1987*
Released: *September 8, 1986*
HOST:
David Brenner
MUSICAL DIRECTOR:
Billy Preston

Offbeat comedian David Brenner, who had been a frequent guest and occasional guest host on *The Tonight Show Starring Johnny Carson*, got the opportunity to host his own syndicated talk show—briefly—in 1986.

NIGHTLINE, see *News—ABC*

NIGHTMAN (*Adventure*)

BROADCAST HISTORY:
Syndicated only
60 minutes
Produced: *1997–1999* (44 episodes)
Released: *September 1997*
CAST:
Johnny Domino/NightMan .... Matt McColm
Frank Dominus (1997–1998) .... Earl Holliman
Rollie Jordan (1997–1998) .... Derek Webster
Rollie Jordan (1998–1999) .... Derwin Jordan
Jessica "Night Bird" Rogers (1997–1998) .... Felecia Bell
Lt. Charles Dann (1997–1998) .... Michael Woods
Lt. Briony Branca (1998–1999) .... Jayne Heitmeyer
Kieran Keyes (1998–1999) .... Kim Coates
Ali (1998–1999) .... Kiara Hunter
Jasmine, the singer (1998–1999) .... Saskia Garel

Johnny Domino was a jazz musician in a city that looked a lot like San Francisco (although it was called Bay City in the series); he moonlighted as the mysterious crime-fighting superhero NightMan. While preparing to perform at a party, he was struck by lightning and acquired the ability to sense evil thoughts—almost like listening in on a radio. Helping him was Rollie, who provided Johnny with an antigravity belt, a red eye-like device that gave him X-ray vision, a masked suit that was virtually bulletproof, a device that made him invisible, and another that allowed him to project a holographic image of himself. Rollie, an engineering genius, maintained NightMan's equipment and worked as an audio engineer at the House of Soul radio station run by Jessica, the owner of the club where Johnny starred as a sax player. She also sang at the club and was a disc jockey on the radio station. Frank, Johnny's retired cop father, managed to get involved in many of his son's cases. In addition to conventional criminals, NightMan fought demons, ghosts, other supernatural creatures, and assorted extraterrestrial visitors. Johnny tooled around in an exotic, open hot-rod car.

In its second season the tone of the series was darker and more serious, more like the comic book series on which it was based. Charlie was on vacation and Briony had taken his caseload. In the season premiere Frank died after getting involved with crazed, computer genius industrialist Kieran Keyes. Keyes and Ali, his sexy henchwoman, were recurring villains throughout the season. Two months later Jonathan Chase (played by Simon MacCorkindale, who had played the same character in *Manimal*) worked with Johnny to defeat Jack the Ripper, whom he had unleashed on the contemporary world when he had gone back in time and inadvertently given the demonic killer the secret of time travel.

Adapted from the NightMan comic book created by Steve Englehart.

NIGHTMARE CAFÉ (*Science Fiction/Horror*)
FIRST TELECAST: *January 29, 1992*
LAST TELECAST: *April 3, 1992*
BROADCAST HISTORY:
Jan 1992, NBC Wed 1000–11:00
Feb 1992–Apr 1992, NBC Fri 10:00–11:00
CAST:
Blackie .... Robert Englund
Frank .... Jack Coleman
Fay .... Lindsay Frost

Robert Englund of the *Nightmare on Elm Street* movies starred in this eerie tale of death and redemption that was produced by the director of those films, Wes Craven. Fay was a distraught woman and Frank a night watchman attacked by thugs who were then drawn inexplicably to an empty, waterfront café. Its lights glowed brightly in the night, but its only inhabitant was the gleefully cynical, enigmatic Blackie. Once inside Fay and Frank realized they had both been killed but now had the chance to stick around and help others who were about to make major mistakes in their lives—with the help of this strange café, where the TV showed the past and future and the doors led to other places and other times.

NIKKI (*Situation Comedy*)
FIRST TELECAST: *October 8, 2000*
LAST TELECAST: *January 27, 2002*
BROADCAST HISTORY:
Oct 2000, WB Sun 9:30–10:00
Nov 2000–Oct 2001, WB Sun 9:00–9:30
Sep 2001–Nov 2001, WB Sun 9:30–10:00
Nov 2001–Jan 2002, WB Sun 8:30–9:00
CAST:
Nikki White .... Nikki Cox
Dwight White .... Nick von Esmarch
Jupiter .... Toby Huss
Mary Campbell .... Susan Egan
Luna (2000–2001) .... Marina Benedict
Martine (2000–2001) .... Steve Valentine
**Marion White (2000–2001)* .... Christine Estabrook
**Thor (2000–2001)* .... Brad Henke
Ken Gillespie (2001) .... Todd Robert Anderson
Alice Gillespie (2001) .... Jacqueline Heinze

*Occasional

Beauty met brawn in this lightweight, young-love sitcom. Cheeky, cheerful Nikki and earnest Dwight were newlyweds trying to make a living in Las Vegas. She was a dancer at the struggling Golden Calf Casino. Shy, blond Luna and sarcastic, brunette Mary were two of her fellow showgirls; Martine was their effete choreographer. Each episode opened with a tacky production number at the Golden Calf. Husky Dwight was trying to become a professional wrestler in the CWF—to his dismay his sleazy manager, Jupiter, had given him the stage name The Crybaby. In November Dwight's obnoxious mom, Marion, broke the news that she had decided to stay in Vegas permanently. Marion was convinced that the marriage had prevented Dwight from getting a real job and had no love for Nikki. Luna was dropped from the cast early in 2001 but was back in the season finale and Mary, who was always competing with Nikki, started dating Jupiter. At the end of April the I.R.S. took over the Golden Calf for failure to pay millions in taxes. In the season finale Nikki's kid brother Scott (Aaron Paul) showed up in Vegas looking for a job.

Early in the 2001–2002 season the workers at the Golden Calf went on strike and the owners decided to close the place down. The loss of Nikki's income was tough on the Whites. Despite her job situation, the tacky opening production numbers were still used for a couple of months. In November Jupiter sold his wrestling operation to the WXL and Dwight almost lost his job, too. Ken and Alice, their incredibly straight and conservative neighbors, became the building's managers and evicted Nikki and Dwight. At the same time, Dwight and Jupiter started a new wrestling league, and Jupiter let the Whites "live" in the old beat-up bus on his property. Desperate for an income, Nikki took a job at a local auto parts store. They got their old apartment back when, at their first wrestling promotion event, Ken was almost killed wrestling Kevin Nash and Dwight saved him. In late January Nikki changed jobs and went to work as a dance instructor with a famous choreographer, but it didn't work out. Neither did the series. That was the last episode of *Nikki.*

NINE THIRTY CURTAIN (*Dramatic Anthology*)
FIRST TELECAST: *October 13, 1953*
LAST TELECAST: *January 1, 1954*
BROADCAST HISTORY:
Oct 1953–Jan 1954, DUM Fri 9:30–10:00

A series of 30-minute filmed dramas starring lesser-known actors and actresses. After its network run *Nine Thirty Curtain* was seen for a time as a local show in New York.

9 to 5 (*Situation Comedy*)
FIRST TELECAST: *March 25, 1982*
LAST TELECAST: *October 27, 1983*
BROADCAST HISTORY:
Mar 1982–Apr 1982, ABC Thu 9:00–9:30
Sep 1982–Sep 1983, ABC Tue 9:30–10:00
Sep 1983–Oct 1983, ABC Thu 9:00–9:30
(In first-run syndication from fall 1986–fall 1988)
CAST:
Violet Newstead (1982–1983) .... Rita Moreno
Doralee Rhodes Brooks .... Rachel Dennison
Judy Bernly .... Valerie Curtin
Franklin Hart (1982) .... Jeffrey Tambor
Franklin Hart (1982–1983) .... Peter Bonerz
Roz Keith (1982–1983) .... Jean Marsh
Harry Nussbaum (1982–1983) ...... Herb Edelman
Clair (1982–1983) .... Ann Weldon
Michael Henderson (1983) .... George Deloy

Linda Bowman (1983).................. Leah Ayres
Tommy (1983) .... Tony Latorra
Marsha McMurray Shrimpton (1986–1988)
.... Sally Struthers
William "Bud" Coleman (1986–1988)
.... Edward Winter
Charmin Cunningham (1986–1987)
.... Dorian Lopinto
Russ Merman (1986–1988) .... Peter Evans
Morgan (1986–1988) .... Art Evans
James (1986–1988) .... James Martinez
E. Nelson Felb (1987–1988) .... Fred Applegate

THEME:

"9 to 5," written by Dolly Parton, sung by Phoebe Snow (1982) and later by Dolly Parton

Three put-upon secretaries matched wits with their overbearing, sexist boss in this contemporary comedy. Franklin Hart, vice-president of Midwestern Sales for Consolidated Companies, was an inept executive who viewed the girls in the outer office as either sex objects or mere flunkies to use in his climb upward. Facing him every day were Violet, a fiery Latin, single (widowed) mother, and 12-year veteran of the company; Doralee, a good-hearted country girl with a fulsome figure; and Judy, an incredibly smart college graduate with no common sense. Roz, the office manager, was Mr. Hart's ally and in-house snoop, though she got little in return for her trouble.

There was a good deal of turnover onscreen and off during the run of this series. The actor playing Hart was replaced after the initial spring 1982 tryout run. Harry Nussbaum was added in the fall as the company's fatherly good-natured top salesman, always ready to cheer up the girls with a joke or bit of help in their schemes. When the second full season began in September 1983, Judy had been replaced by Linda, a free-spirited young woman in her 20s who also moved in to share an apartment with Violet and Doralee. At the same time, Violet's 12-year-old son, Tommy, joined the cast, Roz was gone, and good old Harry Nussbaum was replaced by a decidedly sexier young salesman named Michael. Somewhere along the way, the company changed its name to American House. Offscreen, actress/activist Jane Fonda, who was the initial coproducer, was replaced by veteran sitcom producer James Komack. The revised show lasted barely over a month before being canceled.

Three years later *9 to 5* resurfaced in first-run syndication. Only Doralee and Judy were back from the original cast, with the former now married and the latter still desperately trying to find a boyfriend. New to the secretarial group was Marsha, a sweet, lovable, but incredibly inept divorcée with two young children. The company they were working for was now Barkley Foods International and among the staff were Judy's boss, womanizing Russ Merman, Director of Foreign Acquisitions; Marsha's boss, ambitious young administrative executive Charmin Cunningham (and later obnoxious V.P. of Foreign Sales, Mr. Felb); and Doralee's boss, Vice-President Bud Coleman.

The series was based on the hit 1980 movie *9 to 5*, which starred Jane Fonda, Dolly Parton (Rachel Dennison's sister), and Lily Tomlin.

1986 (*Newsmagazine*)

FIRST TELECAST: *June 10, 1986*
LAST TELECAST: *December 30, 1986*
BROADCAST HISTORY:

Jun 1986–Dec 1986, NBC Tue 10:00–11:00

COANCHORS:

Roger Mudd
Connie Chung

PRINCIPAL CORRESPONDENTS:

Ed Rabel
Lucky Severson
Maria Shriver
Peter Kent

NBC's fifteenth attempt to launch a prime-time newsmagazine similar to CBS' top-rated *60 Minutes* was no more successful than the previous 14 tries. The format was standard, with NBC correspondents contributing filmed reports on various issues of the day.

90 BRISTOL COURT (*Situation Comedy*)

FIRST TELECAST: *October 5, 1964*
LAST TELECAST: *January 4, 1965*
BROADCAST HISTORY:

Oct 1964–Jan 1965, NBC Mon 7:30–9:00

90 Bristol Court was actually three situation comedies airing in consecutive half-hours. They were tied together by the fact that the principal characters in each lived in the same apartment complex at 90 Bristol Court. For specific information see the titles of the individual situation comedies—*Karen*, *Harris against the World*, and *Tom, Dick and Mary*. Although the overall series failed, one of the three parts—*Karen*—was successful enough to finish out the season after the other two elements were canceled in January. A thread of continuity among the three individual comedies was provided in the person of the complex's handyman, Cliff Murdoch, portrayed by Guy Raymond. He was generally seen greeting the residents of the three focal apartments and working around the complex.

NO BOUNDARIES (*Adventure/Reality*)

FIRST TELECAST: *March 3, 2002*
LAST TELECAST: *March 24, 2002*
BROADCAST HISTORY:

Mar 2002, WB Sun 7:00–8:00

HOST:

Troy Hartman

GUIDE:

Melanie McLaren

In this reality series 15 people between the ages of 19 and 53 journeyed through the Canadian wilderness from Vancouver Island, British Columbia, through the Yukon onward to the Arctic Circle. They traveled by everything from train to seaplane to llama and camped out at night. During the journey they participated in a number of dangerous sports, including rock climbing, kayaking and whitewater rafting. Every two days the group chose a new leader/guide who, at the end of his or her term, eliminated one of the group from the game. The choice was usually based on a combination of poor performance and political maneuvering. Each episode included two challenges—a Group Reward Event in which everyone shared if successful, and an Individual Reward Event in which the winner, or winners, won useful prizes like waterproof lighters, battery-operated spotlights, or walkie-talkies. At the end of the 30-day trek the winner won $100,000 and a new Ford Explorer Sport Trac (Ford was the primary sponsor of the series).

The WB abruptly canceled *No Boundaries* after

only four of the 13 episodes had aired, so American viewers had no idea who won. The entire series ran in Canada, however, and the three finalists were Kelly (age 26), an advertising account executive; Allen (25), a medical student; and Stephanie (30), a sales representative for a surfwear company. In the final contest they were sent to a large wooded area in which the producers had placed 20 flagpoles, each bearing a question relating to something that had happened during the trek. The first contestant to find all five flagpoles, walkie-talkie the correct answers back to host Troy, and then make it back to the finish line was Kelly. She was told that to complete the contest she had to drive her new SUV to the Arctic Circle, which she apparently did.

NO HOLDS BARRED (*Comedy/Variety*)
FIRST TELECAST: *September 12, 1980*
LAST TELECAST: *October 3, 1980*
BROADCAST HISTORY:
Sep 1980–Oct 1980, CBS Fri 11:30–12:40 A.M.
HOST:
Kelly Monteith

This short-lived series attempted to be a little bit like *60 Minutes,* a little bit like NBC's *Saturday Night Live,* and a little bit like *Fridays,* its direct competition on ABC. Hosted by comedian Kelly Monteith, *No Holds Barred* was a mixture of offbeat short documentary features, animated and filmed comedy sketches, rock music, and interviews. Segments covered such topics as young comedians at work, a cable TV show that served as a video dating service, the plight of a Deadwood, South Dakota, madam whose brothel had been closed, and a preacher who used magic in his services. None of the comics or musical groups who performed on *No Holds Barred* were well known, most of them being struggling performers looking for a break.

NO SOAP, RADIO (*Situation Comedy*)
FIRST TELECAST: *April 15, 1982*
LAST TELECAST: *May 13, 1982*
BROADCAST HISTORY:
Apr 1982–May 1982, ABC Thu 8:00–8:30
CAST:
Roger .... Steve Guttenberg
Karen .... Hillary Bailey
Mr. Plitzky .... Bill Dana
Mrs. Belmont .... Fran Ryan
Morris .... Jerry Maren
Tuttle .... Stuart Pankin
Marion .... Edie McClurg
Rico .... Phil Rubenstein

No Soap, Radio might best be described as the *Twilight Zone* of situation comedies. There was a story of sorts in each episode, but it was frequently interrupted by sight gags, blackouts, and surrealistic skits that might or might not have anything to do with anything else. The setting was the seedy Pelican Hotel in Atlantic City, where you might open the door to your room and find yourself standing in the woods, or pass a glass-enclosed fire station in the corridor and notice a live fireman inside. Riding in the elevator was always interesting, as you could never tell what would be revealed on each floor as the doors opened; Miami Beach, perhaps, or a coronation ball?

Presiding over this house of non sequiturs was the pleasant young manager, Roger, assisted by Karen and Tuttle, the house detective. They hardly batted an eye at such goings-on as they chase after a man-eating chair, the little old lady who was attacked by a submarine, the frustrations of a gunfighter whose opponent overslept, or the pause for a preview of the new science-fiction movie "The Day Everyone's Name Became Al." As for the series' title, *No Soap, Radio*—why should that make any more sense than anything else? (According to columnist William Safire in *You Could Look It Up,* the phrase originated many years ago as the punchline of the following gag: "A lion and a lioness were taking a bath together. The lion said, 'Please pass the soap,' and the lioness replied, 'No soap, radio.' " Doesn't make sense? That's the point; it isn't supposed to. If you laugh, you obviously don't get it.)

NO TIME FOR SERGEANTS (*Situation Comedy*)
FIRST TELECAST: *September 14, 1964*
LAST TELECAST: *September 6, 1965*
BROADCAST HISTORY:
Sep 1964–Sep 1965, ABC Mon 8:30–9:00
CAST:
Airman Will Stockdale .... Sammy Jackson
Sgt. King .... Harry Hickox
Airman Ben Whitledge .... Kevin O'Neal
Millie Anderson .... Laurie Sibbald
Capt. Martin .... Paul Smith
Col. Farnsworth .... Hayden Rorke
Grandpa Jim Anderson .... Andy Clyde
Pvt. Jack Langdon .... Michael McDonald
Capt. Krupnick .... George Murdock
Pvt. Blanchard .... Greg Benedict
Pvt. Mike Neddick .... Joey Tata

Comedy about a simpleminded but resourceful hillbilly who found new worlds to conquer in the air force. Airman Will Stockdale didn't have much in the way of rank, but he always seemed to be "improving" things around Oliver Air Force Base, usually to the exasperation of the brass. In the opening episode, for example, he was assigned to permanent K.P., whereupon the food in the mess hall improved so much that the officers began eating there along with the enlisted men. When the colonel inspected the kitchen he discovered that Will had been trading with the local farmers for choice meat and produce—but it was *what* Will had been trading away that upset the colonel when he discovered equipment missing. Sgt. King was Will's incredulous NCO, while Ben was his buddy and Millie his sexy girlfriend.

Based on the novel by Mac Hyman, which was subsequently made into a hit play (1955) and movie (1958), both starring Andy Griffith.

NO WARNING (*Dramatic Anthology*)
FIRST TELECAST: *April 6, 1958*
LAST TELECAST: *September 7, 1958*
BROADCAST HISTORY:
Apr 1958–Sep 1958, NBC Sun 7:30–8:00
NARRATOR:
Westbrook Van Voorhis

People involved in sudden, unanticipated crisis situations were the protagonists in *No Warning.* At the start of each story the focal character was established, along with the crisis that was thrust upon him. The remainder of the story presented the resolution of the crisis. All of the episodes dealt with personal and emotional crises, rather than with the threat of violence.

NOAH KNOWS BEST (*Situation Comedy*)

BROADCAST HISTORY:

Nickelodeon
30 minutes
Original episodes: *2000–2001* (13 episodes)
Premiered: *October 7, 2000*

CAST:

Noah Beznick .... Phillip Glenn Van Dyke
Megan Beznick .... Rachel Roth
Jeff Beznick .... Richard Kline
Martine Beznick .... Marcia Strassman
Alton Martin .... Willie G (Willie Green)
D. J Martin .... Stacy Meadows
Marcus Clay .... Dempsey Pappion
Alana Stern .... Stephanie Sesler
Zeke Allen .... Tyler Andrews
Camille Ruiz .... Cori Ann Yarckin

This innocuous teen-com centered on young operator Noah, who lived in a Manhattan apartment with his academically challenged sister, Megan; their savvy mom, Martine ("I saw that!"); and their playwright dad, Jeff, who was pretty much out of it. Although Noah tormented his older sis, she usually found ways to even the score, and they shared many little adventures together. Among their friends at nearby Hudson Prep School were Noah's jumpy best friend, Alton, and his domineering older brother D. J., Megan's pal Camille, and others listed above.

NOAH'S ARK (*Medical Drama*)

FIRST TELECAST: *September 18, 1956*
LAST TELECAST: *October 5, 1958*
BROADCAST HISTORY:

Sep 1956–Feb 1957, NBC Tue 8:30–9:00
Jun 1958–Oct 1958, NBC Sun 7:00–7:30

CAST:

Dr. Noah McCann .... Paul Burke
Dr. Sam Rinehart .... Vic Rodman
Liz Clark .... May Wynn

PRODUCER/DIRECTOR:

Jack Webb

Produced in cooperation with the Southern California Veterinary Medical Association and the American Humane Association, *Noah's Ark* was the story of two veterinarians, the veterinary hospital where they worked, and the animals they treated. Dr. Sam Rinehart was an older man confined to a wheelchair. His young assistant and partner was Dr. Noah McCann. Their secretary and all-purpose assistant was Liz Clark. The relationships that developed between the regulars were as much a part of the story as the collection of animals that they treated. Reruns of the series were aired in the summer of 1958.

NOBODY'S PERFECT (*Situation Comedy*)

FIRST TELECAST: *June 26, 1980*
LAST TELECAST: *August 28, 1980*
BROADCAST HISTORY:

June 1980–Aug 1980, ABC Thu 9:30–10:00

CAST:

Det. Inspector Roger Hart .... Ron Moody
Det. Jennifer Dempsey .... Cassie Yates
Lt. Vince de Gennaro .... Michael Durrell
Det. Jacobi .... Victor Brandt
Det. Grauer .... Tom Williams
Det. Ramsey .... Renny Roker

Roger Hart was an elegant anachronism, an urbane Scotland Yard detective on loan to the San Francisco Police Department, where he worked with decidedly earthier U.S. cops. Hart was a bit confusing to his hosts. On the one hand he seemed klutzy and accident-prone—objects in his vicinity tended to tip over, fall apart, spill, run dry, unravel, or burst into flames. But in a pinch, he could be a man of unexpected talents—bomb expert, pilot, swordsman, or master of disguise. His boss, Lt. Vince de Gennaro, teamed the tall, grinning Englishman with another problem person on the squad, Det. Jennifer Dempsey, and off they went to surprise San Franciscans. On their first assignment Hart so surprised a would-be suicide on the Golden Gate Bridge that the man did indeed jump. Bring up the laugh track.

Jacobi, Grauer, and Ramsey were other detectives on the squad.

NOGGIN (Network),
see Nickelodeon

NORBY (*Situation Comedy*)

FIRST TELECAST: *January 5, 1955*
LAST TELECAST: *April 6, 1955*
BROADCAST HISTORY:

Jan 1955–Apr 1955, NBC Wed 7:00–7:30

CAST:

Pearson Norby .... David Wayne
Helen Norby .... Joan Lorring
Diane Norby .... Susan Hallaran
Hank Norby .... Evan Elliott
Wahleen Johnson .... Janice Mars
Mr. Rudge .... Ralph Dunn
Mrs. Maude Endles .... Carol Veazie
Bobo .... Jack Warden
Maureen .... Maxine Stuart

Pearson Norby was vice-president in charge of small loans at the Pearl River First National Bank, in Pearl River, a small town in upstate New York. He lived there with his wife, Helen, and his two children, Diane and Hank. The problems Pearson had on the job and situations involving his wife and his children were subjects for episodes. Featured were three of the bank's employees, president Maud Endles, vice-president and efficiency expert Mr. Rudge, and switchboard operator Wahleen Johnson. Bobo and Maureen were their next-door neighbors. *Norby* was the first television series to be filmed in color and was, appropriately, sponsored by the Eastman Kodak Company.

NORM (*Situation Comedy*)

FIRST TELECAST: *March 24, 1999*
LAST TELECAST: *April 6, 2001*
BROADCAST HISTORY:

Mar 1999–May 1999, ABC Wed 9:30–10:00
Jul 1999–Nov 1999, ABC Wed 8:30–9:00
Nov 1999–Jan 2000, ABC Wed 9:30–10:00
Jan 2000–Mar 2000, ABC Wed 8:30–9:00
Jun 2000–Sep 2000, ABC Wed 8:30–9:00
Aug 2000–Sep 2000, ABC Tue 9:30–10:00
Sep 2000–Dec 2000, ABC Fri 9:00–9:30
Jan 2001, ABC Fri 9:30–10:00
Feb 2001–Apr 2001, ABC Fri 8:30–9:00

CAST:

Norm Henderson .... Norm Macdonald
Laurie Freeman .... Laurie Metcalf
Danny Sanchez .... Ian Gomez
Molly Carver (1999) .... Amy Wilson
Anthony Curtis (1999) .... Bruce Jarchow
Max Denby .... Max Wright
Shelley Kilmartin .... Faith Ford
Artie Henderson .... Artie Lange
Taylor Clayton (1999–2000) .... Nikki Cox

Big goofball Norm Henderson was a former professional hockey player who had been booted out of the league and sentenced to five years of community service after being caught cheating on his income tax. His service consisted of serving as a New York social worker—one reprobate counseling others, as it were. Norm wasn't very interested, but it was either that or go to jail, so he put in his time and somehow managed to wind up helping his clients, despite himself. Danny was his bald, nerdy friend at the agency, who was just as self-centered as Norm, and Laurie the exasperated coworker who was perpetually indignant at Norm's scams and schemes. As for Mr. Curtis, the officious boss, his attitude perhaps reflected what a lot of viewers were thinking, when he told Norm, "I can never tell if you're joking or you're just stupid." After a few weeks Curtis tried to kill Norm, and was replaced by Mr. Denby.

During the next two seasons Norm continued to get into trouble. In one episode he caused a prison riot, which resulted in a law being passed called "The Norm Law" requiring social workers to be better trained. There was also a good deal of romantic byplay, with Danny dating first office receptionist Taylor and then Shelley, who was attracted to Norm, and even Mr. Denby searching for dates. Norm's half brother Artie arrived, causing more uproar. At the end of the 2000–2001 season it appeared that Norm would be released from community service, and he and Shelley might get married, but the series was canceled so viewers never found out where this amiable slacker would cause trouble next.

The series was originally called *The Norm Show*, then changed in September 1999 to simply *Norm*.

NORMAL LIFE (*Situation Comedy*)

FIRST TELECAST: *March 21, 1990*
LAST TELECAST: *July 18, 1990*
BROADCAST HISTORY:

Mar 1990–Apr 1990, CBS Wed 8:00–8:30
Apr 1990–Jul 1990, CBS Wed 8:30–9:00

CAST:

Jake Harlow .... Dweezil Zappa
Tess Harlow .... Moon Unit Zappa
Anne Harlow .... Cindy Williams
Max Harlow .... Maxwell Gail
Simon Harlow .... Josh Williams
Prima .... Bess Meyer
Bob .... Jim Staahl

Real-life siblings Dweezil and Moon Unit Zappa starred in this family comedy that did such a good job living up to its title that it was too boring to attract much of an audience. Max Harlow was a successful freelance writer and his wife, Anne, worked for the school board. The Harlows lived in the Hollywood Hills with their three children—Jake, an aspiring rock guitarist who didn't want to go to college; Tess, recently graduated from college but unsure what she wanted to do with her life; and Simon, the quiet, insecure 13-year-old kid brother who was neither as popular or athletic as Jake had been. Also seen regularly were Tess's spaced-out best friend, Prima, and Bob, the wacky doctor who lived next door.

Viewers may have wondered what the oddly named children of eccentric rock musician Frank Zappa were doing in a comedy as pedestrian as this. Therein lies a tale. When originally proposed, the series was supposed to be based on the Zappa family's real-life, highly unconventional household, in which the activist, radical parents allowed their teenagers to do anything—drop out of school, experiment with drugs, alcohol, or cigarettes, sleep over with friends of the opposite sex. The kids called their parents by their first names, and rock music blared throughout the house. It was anarchy rooted in love. With nothing to rebel against, the kids became surprisingly responsible. A pilot was made, but the thought of such an unconventional family (a sort of *Abnormal Life*) on its schedule made CBS so uncomfortable that the concept was progressively watered down. In the end, the most radical thing anybody did was go on a date or adopt a dog.

NORMAL, OHIO (*Situation Comedy*)

FIRST TELECAST: *November 1, 2000*
LAST TELECAST: *December 13, 2000*
BROADCAST HISTORY:

Nov 2000–Dec 2000, FOX Wed 8:30–9:00

CAST:

William "Butch" Gamble, Jr. .... John Goodman
Charlie Gamble .... Greg Pitts
Pamela .... Joely Fisher
Bill Gamble .... Orson Bean
Joan Gamble .... Anita Gillette
Kimberly (age 15) .... Julia McIlvaine
Robbie (12) .... Cody Kasch
Elizabeth Gamble .... Mo Gaffney
Danny .... Charles Rocket

The setting for this short-lived sitcom was Normal, Ohio, a rural community near Cincinnati. In the series premiere big, friendly Butch, who four years earlier had announced he was gay and moved to Santa Monica, returned home for his son Charlie's off-to-med-school party. At the party Charlie, who had never forgiven his father for leaving, announced to the family that he really didn't want to be a doctor and wasn't going to medical school. Much to the chagrin of many in his conservative family, Butch decided to stay and try to rebuild a relationship with his son. He moved in with Pamela, his slutty single-mom sister, and her two kids—bookish, insecure Kimberly and worried Robbie ("Am I gay?"). Butch's rude ex-wife, Elizabeth, who had married boring but straight Danny, tossed in occasional insults. Butch's mom, Joan, tried to accept things but hoped he was only going through a phase, while his cranky dad, Bill, spewed a constant stream of dated gay jokes.

Although 12 episodes of *Normal, Ohio*, were produced, Fox pulled the plug after the seventh episode.

NORTH AND SOUTH, BOOK II (*Historical Drama*)

FIRST TELECAST: *May 13, 1989*
LAST TELECAST: *June 17, 1989*
BROADCAST HISTORY:

May 1989–Jun 1989, ABC Sat 9:00–11:00

CAST:

Orry Main .... Patrick Swayze
Brett Main Hazard .... Genie Francis
Ashton Main Huntoon .... Terri Garber
Charles Main .... Lewis Smith
Madeline Fabray LaMotte ...... Lesley-Anne Down
Justin LaMotte .... David Carradine
Elkanah Bent .... Philip Casnoff
James Huntoon .... Jim Metzler
George Hazard .... James Read
Constance Hazard .... Wendy Kilbourne
Billy Hazard .... Parker Stevenson
Virgilia Hazard Grady .... Kirstie Alley
Isabel Hazard .... Mary Crosby
Stanley Hazard .... Jonathan Frakes
Augusta Barclay .... Kate McNeil
Jefferson Davis .... Lloyd Bridges
Mrs. Neal .... Olivia de Havilland
Rose Sinclair .... Linda Evans
Burdetta Halloran .... Morgan Fairchild
Abraham Lincoln .... Hal Holbrook
Rafe Beaudeen .... Lee Horsley
Dorothea Dix .... Nancy Marchand
Captain Turner .... Wayne Newton
Clarissa Main .... Jean Simmons
Miles Colbert .... James Stewart
Congressman Sam Greene ..... David Ogden Stiers
Maude Hazard .... Inga Swenson
Ulysses S. Grant .... Anthony Zerbe

The sprawling 12-hour mini-series *North and South* in 1985 and its 12-hour sequel *North and South, Book II* in 1986 were both rating blockbusters. The original was repeated during a single week in October 1988 and *Book II* on six consecutive Saturdays in May–June 1989, qualifying the latter as a "series" for the purposes of this book.

Based on the novel by John Jakes, *North and South* was the story of the intertwined lives and loves of two proud families, the Hazards of Pennsylvania and the Mains of South Carolina, in the years preceding the Civil War. *Book II* (based on Jakes' sequel, *Love and War*) followed the families through the war itself as longtime friends George Hazard and Orry Main became officers in the opposing armies. Orry's great love, Madeline, was locked in a doomed marriage to the brutal Justin LaMotte, and his family was threatened by the duplicity of his scheming sister Ashton; George and his love, Constance, faced the treachery of their war-profiteering kin Stanley and Isabel. The families were linked by the enduring friendship of George and Orry, their common enemy Elkanah Bent (in cahoots with Ashton), and the love of George's kid brother Billy for Orry's youngest sister Brett. The exploits of George's spunky sister nurse Virgilia, tending to the wounded while fending off evil Congressman Greene, were another major story.

NORTHERN EXPOSURE (*Drama*)

FIRST TELECAST: *July 12, 1990*
LAST TELECAST: *August 9, 1995*
BROADCAST HISTORY:

Jul 1990–Aug 1990, CBS Thu 10:00–11:00
Apr 1991–Dec 1994, CBS Mon 10:00–11:00
Jan 1995–Mar 1995, CBS Wed 10:00–11:00
Jul 1995–Aug 1995, CBS Wed 9:00–10:00

CAST:

Dr. Joel Fleischman .... Rob Morrow
Maggie O'Connell .... Janine Turner
Maurice Minnifield .... Barry Corbin
Chris Stevens .... John Corbett
Ed Chigliak .... Darren E. Burrows
Holling Vincouer .... John Cullum
Shelly Tambo .... Cynthia Geary
Marilyn Whirlwind .... Elaine Miles
Ruth-Anne Miller .... Peg Phillips
**Rick Pederson (1990–1991)* .... Grant Goodeve
**Adam (1991–1995)* .... Adam Arkin
Dave the Cook (1991–1995) .... William J. White
**Leonard Quinhagak (1992–1993)* .. Graham Greene
**Bernard Stevens (1991–1995)*
.... Richard Cummings, Jr.
Mike Monroe (1992–1993) .... Anthony Edwards
Walt Kupfer (1993–1995) .... Moultrie Patten
Eugene (1994–1995) .... Earl Quewezance
Hayden Keyes (1994–1995) .... James L. Dunn
Dr. Phillip Capra (1994–1995) .... Paul Provenza
Michelle Schowdoski Capra (1994–1995) . Teri Polo

*Occasional

Joel Fleischman had just graduated from Columbia University Medical School and, at the age of 27, expected to spend four years working in Anchorage to repay the state of Alaska for financing his medical education. He was not prepared for being reassigned to the tiny town of Cicely (pop. 813) on the "Alaskan Riviera," following the death of its only doctor. Life in an isolated town in the scenic, but remote, Alaskan interior was not what this lifetime New Yorker had in mind. Joel spent much of his early time in Cicely trying to get out of his contract and back to his fiancé in New York.

The town was full of eccentrics. Joel was constantly at odds with Maurice Minnifield, a former astronaut and president of the Cicely Chamber of Commerce, who loved the great outdoors. The biggest incentive Joel had to stay, though neither of them was really willing to admit it, was his developing relationship with Maggie O'Connell, the feisty, independent, air taxi pilot who owned the cabin he was living in. Among the other offbeat townspeople were Holling, a retired adventurer who owned the local tavern, The Brick; Shelly, Holling's 18-year-old girlfriend; Chris Stevens, the sexy, quirky disc jockey on Cicely's only radio station, KBHR; Ed, Minnifield's young assistant who was fascinated by tales of big city life; Ruth-Anne, who ran the general store; and Marilyn, the imperturbable Eskimo receptionist/assistant in Joel's medical office. Rick Pederson, Maggie's boyfriend, was killed by a falling satellite in a freak accident in the spring of 1991, the fifth of her boyfriends to die under bizarre circumstances. She maintained a shrine to each of them on her mantel. Many of Cicely's citizens were convinced that Maggie had a love curse.

During the 1992–1993 season Mike Monroe, a former lawyer who suffered allergic reactions to toxic chemicals in the environment, moved to the outskirts of Cicely, where he lived in a huge plastic bubble, only leaving it in a protective surplus astronaut suit. He and Maggie developed a romance, but when Joel declared him cured in the spring, he left for Russia to work with Greenpeace. That spring Holling and Shelly, who was several months pregnant, got married. When her daughter Miranda ("Randy") was born in February 1994 she became Cicely's 844th citizen.

In the fall of 1994 Joel and Maggie, who had been

alternately sparring and shooting off sexual sparks for years, finally got serious. Joel proposed to her and they moved in together, but, despite her uncharacteristic warmth, they had problems cohabiting. When she couldn't deal with Joel's obsessiveness and told him to move out, he left Cicely and went native with the Eskimos to find himself. With Joel gone and his contract with Cicely about to expire, Maurice hired Dr. Phillip Capra to take his place. Dr. Capra and his wife, Michelle, a journalist, moved into the same house Joel had rented from Maggie, and she went to work for the local paper. In Joel's last appearance, in February 1995, he and Maggie went looking for the mythical city Keewaa Aani and it turned out to be, in true *Northern Exposure* fashion, Manhattan. He wanted her to go with him, but, since it was his fantasy, she left and returned to Cicely.

Filmed on location in Bellevue and Roslyn, Washington, not far from the locale of *Twin Peaks*.

NORTHWEST PASSAGE (*Adventure*)
FIRST TELECAST: *September 14, 1958*
LAST TELECAST: *September 8, 1959*
BROADCAST HISTORY:
Sep 1958–Jan 1959, NBC Sun 7:30–8:00
Jan 1959–Jul 1959, NBC Fri 7:30–8:00
Jul 1959–Sep 1959, NBC Tue 7:30–8:00
CAST:
Major Robert Rogers .... Keith Larsen
Sgt. Hunk Marriner .... Buddy Ebsen
Ensign Langdon Towne .... Don Burnett
Gen. Amherst .... Philip Tonge

The actual historical search for an inland waterway that would enable boat traffic to cross the breadth of America was the backdrop for *Northwest Passage*, which was set during the French and Indian War (1754–1759). Major Robert Rogers, an experienced explorer and Indian fighter, had organized Rogers' Rangers to help him search for that mythical route. The adventures of these men, exploring, fighting Indians, and battling the American wilderness, provided the stories. Chief among the troops were veteran Indian fighter and long-time friend Hunk Marriner, and Langdon Towne, a Harvard graduate from a well-to-do Eastern family who had become the company mapmaker. They never found the Northwest Passage, but did do a lot of fighting with both the French and the Indians in the course of helping settlers in the area now known as New York state and Eastern Canada.

NORTHWEST PATROL see *Movies—Prior to 1961*

NOT FOR PUBLICATION (*Newspaper Drama*)
FIRST TELECAST: *May 1, 1951*
LAST TELECAST: *May 27, 1952*
BROADCAST HISTORY:
May 1951–Sep 1951, DUM Mon/Thu 7:45–8:00
Dec 1951–Mar 1952, DUM Fri 8:30–9:00
Mar 1952–May 1952, DUM Tue 10:00–10:30
CAST:
Collins (May–Sep 1951) .... William Adler
Collins (Dec 1951–May 1952) .... Jerome Cowan
Luchek (1952) .... Jon Silo

Human-interest stories and adventures in the lives of ordinary people as seen through the eyes of kind-hearted reporter Collins of the big-city newspaper, *The Ledger*. Among the stories were those of an actor who agreed to impersonate an ambassador whose life was in danger; a baseball player who set out to clear his father's name; and a doctor who faced conflict in the operating room. Generally lesser-known actors and actresses appeared in these short dramas, although one February 1952 telecast was billed as the dramatic acting debut of Morey Amsterdam.

NOTHING BUT THE BEST (*Musical Variety*)
FIRST TELECAST: *July 7, 1953*
LAST TELECAST: *September 13, 1953*
BROADCAST HISTORY:
Jul 1953–Aug 1953, NBC Tue 9:00–9:30
Aug 1953–Sep 1953, NBC Sun 10:00–10:30
REGULARS:
Eddie Albert
Skitch Henderson & His Orchestra

Eddie Albert was the star and emcee of this live musical variety show that started out on Tuesday evenings as the summer replacement for *Fireside Theater* and then moved to Sundays.

The acts, each billed as the best in their field, were introduced by Mr. Albert, who chatted with the performers and then left them to perform. As he had said on his opening show: "I have the dream spot on TV this season for the sponsor told me to go out and get my favorite talent and to let them do on the show what they feel is the best of their career—for the show is *Nothing but the Best.*"

NOTHING BUT THE TRUTH see *To Tell the Truth*

NOTHING IN COMMON (*Situation Comedy*)
FIRST TELECAST: *April 2, 1987*
LAST TELECAST: *June 3, 1987*
BROADCAST HISTORY:
Apr 1987–May 1987, NBC Thu 9:30–10:00
Jun 1987, NBC Wed 9:30–10:00
CAST:
David Basner .... Todd Waring
Max Basner .... Bill Macy
Jacqueline North .... Wendy Kilbourne
Norma Starr .... Mona Lyden
Mark Glick .... Bill Applebaum
Victoria Upton-Smythe .... Elizabeth Bennett
Myron Nipper .... Patrick Richwood
Joey D. .... Billy Wirth
Wally .... Allan Kent
Autumn .... Julie Paris

Based on the 1986 movie of the same name, this frothy comedy followed the travails of nutty young ad-agency head David Basner and his irresponsible, unemployed father, Max, who mooched off him unmercifully. Stories concerned such burning questions as "should David cancel a long-planned fishing trip with his father to save a sausage account?" A typical cast of TV loonies inhabited David's agency, among them sexy new agency executive Jacqueline, neurotic copywriters Norma and Mark, and leather-jacketed young cameraman Joey D.

NOTHING IS EASY, see *Together We Stand*

NOTHING SACRED (*Religious Drama*)
FIRST TELECAST: *September 18, 1997*
LAST TELECAST: *March 14, 1998*

BROADCAST HISTORY:

Sep 1997–Dec 1997, ABC Thu 8:00–9:00
Jan 1998, ABC Sat 8:00–9:00
Mar 1998, ABC Sat 9:00–10:00

CAST:

Father Ray (Francis Xavier Rayneaux)
.... Kevin Anderson
Father Leo .... Brad Sullivan
Sister Maureen........................ Ann Dowd
Father Eric Gillen .... Scott Michael Campbell
Sidney Walters...................... Bruce Altman
J.A. Ortiz............................ Jose Zuniga
Rachel............................. Tamara Mello
Martin .... David Marshall Grant
Justin Madsen Judd .... Jennifer Beals

A rather earnest drama about a tousle-haired young Catholic priest wrestling with his parish, his beliefs, and his own all-too-human failings. Father Ray was not your typical cleric, playing blues CDs, sipping cocktails, and playing cards with his fellow priests after hours. But his passion for helping people was desperately needed at St. Thomas, a large urban church in a troubled inner-city neighborhood. Father Leo was the older, wise counselor, Father Eric the newly ordained, idealistic recruit, Sister Maureen the feminist nun who insisted that God was not a "He," Ortiz the youth minister, Rachel the 18-year-old receptionist, and Sidney the atheist business manager trying to keep the place afloat. Among the challenges faced by Father Ray were the developer who wanted to shut down the soup kitchen, the Bishop who had "zero tolerance" for deviation from Church doctrine, the old flame who returned and was sexually attracted to Ray, and the young woman wrestling with an abortion decision who surreptitiously taped his equivocal advice on the subject and got him into trouble. Arriving partway through the season to help the somewhat disorganized Father Ray run the parish were ambitious young "copastor" Martin and a new, and very smart, head of religious education, Justin.

There were some protests against *Nothing Sacred* due to its frank handling of sensitive religious issues, but in the end the series was done in not by protests but by that great god of commercial television, the Nielsen ratings.

NOW (*Documentary*)

FIRST TELECAST: *May 9, 1954*
LAST TELECAST: *September 14, 1970*
BROADCAST HISTORY:

May 1954–Jun 1954, ABC Sun 7:30–8:00
Mar 1970–Sep 1970, ABC Mon 10:30–11:00

EXECUTIVE PRODUCER:

Arthur Holch (1970)

Two unrelated summer documentary series were aired under the title *Now.* The 1954 version consisted of assorted documentary films. The 1970 series was produced by ABC News and hosted by a different ABC newsman each week. It covered such subjects as communes, Women's Liberation, and "A Black Mayor in Dixie."

NOW AND AGAIN (*Science Fiction*)

FIRST TELECAST: *September 24, 1999*
LAST TELECAST: *May 5, 2000*
BROADCAST HISTORY:

Sep 1999–May 2000, CBS Fri 9:00–10:00

CAST:

Michael Wiseman.......................... Eric Close
Dr. Theodore Morris............. Dennis Haysbert
Roger Bender........................ Gerrit Graham
Heather Wiseman.............. Heather Matarazzo
Lisa Wiseman...................... Margaret Colin

Frustrated, overweight Michael Wiseman (played in opening scenes by John Goodman) was waiting for a subway in New York when he was accidentally pushed off the platform into the path of an incoming train. His body died, and his family held his funeral, but humorless Dr. Morris, in charge of an experimental government research team, had removed his brain and kept it alive so that it could be placed into a perfect, genetically enhanced body (the biological equivalent of Steve Austin's body in the *Six Million Dollar Man* series). In return for saving his life and giving him a new body, he had to promise to "stay dead" and not let any of his family, friends, or loved ones know that he was, in a manner of speaking, still alive. That was difficult. Michael's wife, Lisa, was in dire straits, forced to fight for the $1 million settlement she was due from the ruthless insurance company for which he had worked. She even had to go on welfare for a time due to lack of funds. Eventually Michael, in his new body, convinced the company to settle because he knew things about its shady dealings that would prove extremely embarrassing if they were made public.

When he had adapted to his new body, Michael was moved to a fancy Manhattan apartment, at 63rd and Madison, where his activities could be monitored by the government. He was, after all, an experiment in which they had invested billions. Michael's first assignment was to catch the diabolical Egg Man (Kim Chan), an elderly Asian terrorist who had developed deadly biological agents that wreaked havoc on a Tokyo subway and later at the baggage claim area at Charles DeGaulle Airport in Paris. Michael eventually caught him in New York.

Despite constant admonitions and threats of reprisal from Dr. Morris, Michael continued to have limited contact with his family and with Roger, a former coworker. They thought he was a Mr. Newman (the name Dr. Morris used to refer to him when they were working on cases) from the I.R.S. In one episode he was outside the hospital room where his teenage daughter, Heather, was recovering after being struck by lightning; when she woke up and saw him she thought he was an angel.

In the season finale the Egg Man escaped from prison—after generating nerve gas that killed the prisoners and guards during a meal—bent on revenge against Michael. At the same time, Michael escaped and picked up his family, with Morris and the feds hot on his trail. Since the series had been canceled, there was no resolution.

NOW IT CAN BE TOLD (*Magazine*)

BROADCAST HISTORY:

Syndicated only
30 minutes
Produced: *1991–1992*
Released: *September 1991*

ANCHORMAN:

Geraldo Rivera

REPORTERS:

Gail Anderson
Roberta Baskin

Krista Bradford
Alexander Johnson
Craig Rivera
Richard Wiese

Geraldo Rivera, whose daytime talk show *Geraldo* was generally considered both harder hitting and sleazier than its principal competitors—*Donahue*, *Oprah*, and *Sally Jessy Raphael*—returned to his journalistic roots with this evening series. Airing five nights a week, *Now It Can Be Told* focused almost exclusively on investigative reporting. As Geraldo said on the opening telecast, nothing would be sacred and nobody would be untouchable. There were stories about the misuse of tax dollars, political and corporate corruption, the mob, scandals, and ripoffs. Geraldo's field reporters included Washington-based chief investigative reporter Roberta Baskin, senior correspondent Krista Bradford (formerly of *A Current Affair*), and his own younger brother Craig. In addition to the pre-taped stories, Geraldo often conducted interviews with principals in the stories.

With his daytime talk show still in production, Geraldo was on the air for 7½ hours a week in cities where both series were carried.

NOW WHAT (*Situation Comedy*)

BROADCAST HISTORY:

MTV
30 minutes
Original episodes: *2002* (13 episodes)
Premiered: *April 6, 2002*

CAST:

Zack Altman .... Adam Brody
Ted Ogilvy .... Adam Nicholas Frost
Gilby Van Horn .... Johnny K. Lewis
J. C. Climan .... Kenny Fisher
Lisa Holiday .... Andi Eystad
Nancy Winograd .... Kristen Renton

A goofy little sitcom about four buddies attending West Boulder High School. Zack had nursed a crush on Lisa since third grade, but every time he tried to get close to her he messed things up; Ted was the rich kid who couldn't score with his girlfriend, Nancy; Gilby was the geek from a trailer park who landed dates for his friends but never himself; and J. C. was the suave dude who seemed to attract older women. Off campus they hung out at the Down Hill Diner.

The series originated in Canada, where it was known as *The Sausage Factory.*

NOW WITH TOM BROKAW AND KATIE COURIC (*Newsmagazine*)

FIRST TELECAST: *August 18, 1993*
LAST TELECAST: *September 7, 1994*
BROADCAST HISTORY:

Aug 1993–Sep 1994, NBC Wed 9:00–10:00

HOSTS:

Tom Brokaw
Katie Couric

REGULAR CORRESPONDENTS:

Fred Francis, Senior Correspondent
Mike Boettcher
Chris Hansen
Elizabeth Vargas
Bob Costas (1994)

One of the parade of newsmagazines on television in the mid-1990s, pairing NBC's top anchorman and the perky cohost of *The Today Show*. Stories included the usual mix of screaming headlines from the present (*see* the last days of baby Jessica before she was torn from her adoptive parents!) and from the past (*relive* the 1968 Chicago Democratic Convention riots!) and celebrity profiles of such important Americans as Bette Midler, Jane Fonda (and her new husband, TV mogul Ted Turner), and Ann-Margaret (and her dead boyfriend, Elvis).

NOWHERE MAN (*Drama*)

FIRST TELECAST: *August 28, 1995*
LAST TELECAST: *August 19, 1996*
BROADCAST HISTORY:

Aug 1995–Aug 1996, UPN Mon 9:00–10:00

CAST:

Thomas Veil .... Bruce Greenwood
**Alison Veil* .... Megan Gallagher

*Occasional

Veil was a photojournalist living in Chicago who had taken a picture of a secret jungle execution, which he titled "Hidden Agenda." To keep him from making it public, and to extract information from him, highly placed people set him up. Veil went into the men's room of a restaurant after a successful exhibition of his work and came out as a non-person—a "Nowhere Man." Suddenly none of the people he used to know—his friends, his wife, even his mother—seemed to know who he was. His entire identity had been erased. Thrown into a sanitarium, Veil was "treated" by a psychiatrist working for those who had destroyed his identity. He escaped, retrieved the negatives he had hidden in his studio, and went on the run, trying to stay one step ahead of the men after him while trying to figure out who they were. Veil kept a diary to chronicle his experiences and provide himself with reassurance that what he was going through was real and not just in his mind.

In January an unseen member of the conspiracy, to further his own interests, provided Veil with a palm-top computer that contained information he could use against the people responsible for his plight. Subsequent episodes detailed his travels to places and people in the files in the palm-top computer, and his attempts to get revenge against them. In March, Veil was led to believe he had been brainwashed in 1994 and that the actual place where he had taken the "Hidden Agenda" photograph was just outside Washington, D.C.—not in Nicaragua, as he believed.

In the last episode Tom retrieved a folder full of information from a safe deposit box. In it was a variation of "Hidden Agenda" with the four hanged men showing their faces—they were U.S. senators on the Senate Intelligence Committee. The picture was either a composite used to pressure the senators into voting against an anti-terrorism bill supported by Senator Wallace (Hal Linden), or it proved that they had been killed and replaced by doubles who would do the bidding of "the organization." When Senator Wallace suspected the killings, his "buddy," the number two man at the F.B.I., had him killed and replaced. At the end Veil found out that even his "prior life" was a sham, a product of F.B.I. brainwashing that included his name, his wife, his photojournalism career, his friends, everything. He would have to start from scratch to figure out who he really was. Unfortunately, the series did not last long enough for him to do so.

NUMBER 96 (*Drama*)

FIRST TELECAST: *December 10, 1980*

LAST TELECAST: *January 2, 1981*

BROADCAST HISTORY:

Dec 1980, NBC Wed 10:00–11:00
Dec 1980, NBC Thu 10:00–11:00
Dec 1980–Jan 1981, NBC Fri 900–10:00

CAST:

Horace Batterson .... Barney Martin
Lisa Brendon .... Christine Jones
Mark Keaton .... Howard McGillin
Jill Keaton .... Sherry Hursey
Sharon St. Clair .... Hilary Thompson
Chick Walden .... John Reilly
Anthea Bryan .... Rosina Widdowson-Reynolds
Roger Busky .... James Murtaugh
Ginny Ramirez .... Maria O'Brien
Maureen Galloway .... Betsy Palmer
Sandy Galloway .... Jill Choder
Marion Quintzel .... Randee Heller
Max Quintzel .... Greg Mullavey
Dr. Robert Leon .... Brian Curran
Nathan Sugarman .... Todd Susman
Lou Sugarman .... Eddie Barth
Rita Sugarman .... Ellen Travolta
Lyle Bixler .... Charles Bloom

Life at Number 96 Pacific Way, a Southern California apartment complex, was full of sex, gossip, and all sorts of miscellaneous personal problems. The people who lived there had bizarre lives, though, in all fairness, a soap opera would be dull if its characters were normal. Among the residents were recently divorced Roger Busky, a salesman trying to become a swinging single; retired navy commander Horace Batterson, the resident voyeur; the Quintzels, a couple experimenting with "open marriage"; psychologist Robert Leon, also a transvestite; Nurse Sandy Galloway, living with her widowed, alcoholic mother; and professional con man Chick Walden. Everyone at 96 Pacific Way seemed to be involved with someone else there, either professionally, socially, or sexually, with the strongest emphasis on the latter.

Number 96 was adapted for American television from an Australian series of the same name. Although it tried to retain the flavor of the original, the American version was considerably tamer. The Australian *Number 96* created a sensation when it went on the air in 1972, dealing graphically with homosexuality, drug and alcohol addictions, ambitious and promiscuous people, insanity, rape, and sex—mostly sex. Perhaps its greatest notoriety came from its display of full frontal nudity, something American networks were not ready to attempt. NBC ran a huge promotional campaign for its version of *Number 96,* designed to titillate potential viewers, and premiered the series on three consecutive nights. Despite the hype, it lasted less than a month.

NURSE (*Medical Drama*)

FIRST TELECAST: *April 2, 1981*

LAST TELECAST: *May 21, 1982*

BROADCAST HISTORY:

Apr 1981–May 1981, CBS Thu 10:00–11:00
Sep 1981–Oct 1981, CBS Thu 9:00–10:00
Nov 1981–Dec 1981, CBS Wed 9:00–10:00
Dec 1981–Mar 1982, CBS Thu 10:00–11:00
Apr 1982–May 1982, CBS Fri 10:00–11:00

CAST:

Nurse Mary Benjamin .... Michael Learned
Dr. Adam Rose .... Robert Reed
Nurse Toni Gilette .... Hattie Winston
Nurse Penny Brooks .... Bonnie Hellman
Nurse Betty LaSada .... Hortensia Colorado
Nurse Bailey (1981) .... Clarice Taylor
Chip Benjamin (1981) ...... Christopher Marcantel
Joe Calvo .... Dennis Boutsikaris
Dr. Greg Manning .... Rex Robbins

Fictional Grant Memorial Hospital in New York City was the setting for this medical drama. It was there that former head nurse Mary Benjamin returned to work following the death of her husband, a physician on Grant Memorial's staff. As a supervising floor nurse, Mary was responsible for a considerable staff of nurses and orderlies. But the stories on *Nurse* dealt frequently with Mary's personal life, as she adjusted to life alone, as well as with medical crises at the hospital. A mature and somewhat motherly type, she offered wise counsel to those around her in meeting their problems, while she herself turned to good friend Dr. Adam Rose, a staff physician at the hospital, for help in making her own difficult adjustments. Mary's college student son, Chip, strong-willed and independent, was alternately a comfort and a trial to her. In the fall of 1981 Mary acquired a new neighbor, young lawyer Joe Calvo. He moved into the apartment next door and the two became quite friendly. While Mary dealt with the daily problems at the hospital, Joe got involved in assorted idealistic causes, trying to help the poor and disenfranchised.

NURSES (*Situation Comedy*)

FIRST TELECAST: *September 14, 1991*

LAST TELECAST: *June 18, 1994*

BROADCAST HISTORY:

Sep 1991–Jan 1993, NBC Sat 9:30–10:00
Jan 1993–Jul 1993, NBC Sat 8:30–9:00
Jul 1993–Jun 1994, NBC Sat 9:30–10:00

CAST:

Nurse Sandy Miller (1991–1993) ... Stephanie Hodge
Nurse Annie Roland .... Arnetia Walker
Nurse Julie Milbury .... Mary Jo Keenen
Greg Vincent (1991–1992) .... Jeff Altman
Gina Cuevas .... Ada Maris
Dr. Hank Kaplan .... Kip Gilman
Paco Ortiz .... Carlos LaCamara
Dr. Riskin (1991–1992) .... Florence Stanley
Luke Fitzgerald (1992–1993) ..... Markus Flanagan
Jack Trenton (1992–1994) .... David Rasche
Casey MacAfee (1993–1994) .... Loni Anderson

Miami's Community Medical Center, right around the corner from *Empty Nest* and *The Golden Girls* (both on NBC on the same night), was the setting for this rather standard medical sitcom. The center of the action—which was mostly talk—was the third floor nurses' station, manned by five harried, underpaid R.N.'s: working mom Annie, the nurse-in-charge; dedicated, cynical Sandy; neurotic newcomer Julie, who was deathly afraid of germs; worldly wise immigrant Gina; and flaky Greg, an anti-authority type with a penchant for physically attacking the doctors. Most of the incompetent M.D.'s deserved it, with the exception of financially strapped good-guy Dr. Hank. Paco was the sees-all-tells-all orderly.

Among those joining the cast in later years were Luke, a wacky loner; Jack, a crooked financier sentenced to perform community service at the hospital; and Casey, the new, ambitious administrator who arrived when the hospital was sold to a large HMO. In the final year Gina became pregnant with Dr. Hank's child.

NURSES, THE (*Medical Drama*)
FIRST TELECAST: *September 27, 1962*
LAST TELECAST: *September 7, 1965*
BROADCAST HISTORY:
Sep 1962–Dec 1962, CBS Thu 9:00–10:00
Jan 1963–Sep 1964, CBS Thu 10:00–11:00
Sep 1964–Sep 1965, CBS Tue 10:00–11:00
CAST:
Liz Thorpe .... Shirl Conway
Gail Lucas .... Zina Bethune
Dr. Anson Kiley (1962–1964) .... Edward Binns
Dr. Ned Lowry (1963–1964) .... Stephen Brooks
Dr. Alex Tazinski (1964–1965) ...... Michael Tolan
Dr. Ted Steffen (1964–1965) .... Joseph Campanella

Filmed on location in New York, *The Nurses* dealt primarily with the personal and professional lives of two nurses working in a large metropolitan hospital. Liz Thorpe was the older, more experienced head nurse and Gail Lucas (played by 17-year-old Zina Bethune) was the somewhat naive student nurse. Two doctors, one older (Steffen) and one a young resident (Tazinski), joined the program when it moved to Tuesday nights in the fall of 1964. They made efforts to help the nurses with their medical and moral problems and the series title was changed to *The Doctors and the Nurses* to include them.

The Nurses was seen as a daytime serial following its nighttime run. The cast changed but the setting (New York City's Alden General Hospital) remained the same. The daytime serial ran from September 1965 to March 1967.

NUTT HOUSE, THE (*Situation Comedy*)
FIRST TELECAST: *September 20, 1989*
LAST TELECAST: *October 25, 1989*
BROADCAST HISTORY:
Sep 1989–Oct 1989, NBC Wed 9:30–10:00
CAST:
Reginald J. Tarkington .... Harvey Korman
Ms. Frick .... Cloris Leachman
Mrs. Edwina Nutt .... Cloris Leachman
Freddy .... Mark Blankfield
Charles Nutt III .... Brian McNamara
Sally Lonnaneck .... Molly Hagan
Dennis .... Gregory Itzin
EXECUTIVE PRODUCERS:
Mel Brooks
Alan Spencer

Lunatics ran the asylum in this slapstick farce from the twisted mind of famed actor/producer Mel Brooks. The setting was Nutt House, a once elegant New York City hotel that had fallen on hard times, no doubt due in part to the hilariously incompetent staff. Reginald was the tall, supercilious manager; Ms. Frick, the overpadded, oversexed head housekeeper with a thick accent, who was constantly trying to bed Reginald; Freddy, the nearly blind elevator operator; and Charles, the handsome but vacuous playboy son of owner Edwina Nutt, who had put him in charge. Only Sally, Mrs. Nutt's pretty secretary, was almost normal. Add an assortment of senile doormen, bumbling bellboys, and babbling maids, plus pratfalls and sight gags galore, and you get the idea: *Hotel* gone mad. Would you like a room for the evening? Are you sure?

O

O.K. CRACKERBY (*Situation Comedy*)

FIRST TELECAST: *September 16, 1965*
LAST TELECAST: *January 6, 1966*
BROADCAST HISTORY:
Sep 1965–Jan 1966, ABC Thu 8:30–9:00
CAST:
O. K. Crackerby .... Burl Ives
St. John Quincy .... Hal Buckley
O. K., Jr. .... Brian Corcoran
Cynthia Crackerby .... Brooke Adams
Hobart Crackerby .... Joel Davison
Susan Wentworth .... Laraine Stephens
Slim .... Dick Foran
The Chauffeur .... John Indrisano
CREATED BY:
Cleveland Amory and Abe Burrows

Widower O. K. Crackerby was the richest man in the world, but he lacked the one thing he wanted above all else—acceptance in the world of high society. A rough-and-tumble Oklahoman, he lacked certain qualities that the refined snobs who controlled the Social Register deemed necessary. To help his kids "get into polite society," O. K. hired an unemployed Harvard graduate, St. John Quincy, as a tutor. Traveling from one society playground to another, the two men split their time fighting with each other on an intellectual level and banding together to battle the social snobs on a personal level. Susan was St. John's girlfriend, and Slim was O. K.'s business pal.

Although they would probably rather not have been reminded of it, this short-lived comedy was the creation of Cleveland Amory, who skewered many a TV series in print during his long tenure as *TV Guide*'s chief critic and reviewer, and noted playwright Abe Burrows.

O.S.S. (*War Drama*)

FIRST TELECAST: *September 26, 1957*
LAST TELECAST: *March 17, 1958*
BROADCAST HISTORY:
Sep 1957–Jan 1958, ABC Thu 9:30–10:00
Jan 1958–Mar 1958, ABC Mon 7:30–8:00
CAST:
Capt. Frank Hawthorn .... Ron Randell
The Chief .... Lionel Murton
Sgt. O'Brien .... Robert Gallico

After just about every police file in the country had been raided for "true stories," ABC came up with an obvious source of true-life high adventure: the Office of Strategic Services (OSS), America's World War II superspy agency. Since the OSS had been dissolved by executive order after the war, to be replaced by the CIA, its files were open to the public. Authenticity was insured by coproducer Colonel William Eliscu, who had been real-life aide to OSS Chief General "Wild Bill" Donovan during the war.

In this series, agent Frank Hawthorn engaged in considerable derring-do behind German lines, often in cahoots with the French Resistance. Sgt. O'Brien was his assistant. Filmed in England and France.

OAK RIDGE BOYS LIVE FROM LAS VEGAS
(*Variety*)

BROADCAST HISTORY:
The Nashville Network
60 minutes
Produced: *1998–1999*
Premiered: *April 7, 1998*
REGULARS:
The Oak Ridge Boys (Duane Allen, tenor; Joe Bonsall, tenor; William Lee Golden, baritone; Richard Sterban, bass)
The Mighty Oaks Band
The Clark Family Experience

This weekly variety hour, patterned after TNN's successful *Statler Brothers Show*, presented another highly popular country/pop quartet hosting musical acts, comedians, ventriloquists, jugglers, and even animal trainers. Duane was the spokesman for the group. The show was produced live at the Las Vegas Hilton, and was glitzier than most TNN productions, with show girls, flashing strobe lights, a huge audience, and the Oak's own rocking band. The quartet's signature song was their 1981 hit "Elvira," which bordered on rock 'n' roll, but they also showed their country roots (all had begun in gospel groups) with an occasional sacred number such as "Just a Closer Walk with Thee." The Clark Family was a string band consisting of six handsome teenagers and young men.

OBLIVIOUS (*Quiz/Audience Participation*)

BROADCAST HISTORY:
TNN
30 minutes
Original episodes: *2002–*
Premiered: *August 12, 2002*
REGULARS:
Regan Burns
Tom Binns
Davina McCall

This was a game show contestants didn't even know they were playing. Regan Burns and his confederates went on location in stores and public places, posing as clerks and customers, and struck up conversations with people they encountered, slipping in quiz-show-style questions. If the subject responded with a correct answer (and did not blow them off), he or she could win anywhere from $20 to $500. Sometimes they would recruit the winner of one question to ask a question of the next target.

OBLONGS, THE (*Cartoon*)

FIRST TELECAST: *April 1, 2001*
LAST TELECAST: *May 20, 2001*
BROADCAST HISTORY:
Apr 2001–May 2001, WB Sun 7:30–8:00
VOICES:
Bob Oblong .... Will Ferrell
Pickles Oblong .... Jean Smart
Milo Oblong, Jared Klimer, & the Debbies
.... Pamela Segall Adlon
Biff Oblong .... Randy Sklar
Chip Oblong .... Jason Sklar
Beth Oblong, Susie, & Mikey .... Jeannie Elias
Helga Fugley .... Lea DeLaria
Peggy, Pristine Klimer, & Debbie Klimer
.... Becky Thyre
George Klimer, James, & Anita Bidet ..... Billy West

The WB promoted the Oblongs as "an unusual nuclear family where physical challenges may have more to do with society's ills than we want to admit." They certainly looked the part. Cheerful family head Bob Oblong, who worked at Globocide on the production line in the Pesticides, Defoliant, & Infant Formula Division, had no arms or legs (he hopped). Bald wife Pickles was a heavy drinker who wore outrageous wigs. Their kids were Biff and Chip, Siamese twin sons joined at the hip, hyperactive young Milo, and four-year old Beth, who had a stalk growing out of her head. Even their cat smoked. The rich people, like the socially prominent Klimers, lived in the hills, while those who lived in the valley, like the Oblongs, had suffered the effects of toxic waste. Milo's friends, and fellow social outcasts, were fat Helga, tall, toothy Peggy, French Susie, and redheaded Mikey.

Adapted from the book *Creepy Susie* by Angus Oblong.

OBOLER COMEDY THEATRE (*Comedy Anthology*)
FIRST TELECAST: *October 11, 1949*
LAST TELECAST: *November 20, 1949*
BROADCAST HISTORY:
Oct 1949, ABC Tue 9:00–9:30
Nov 1949, ABC Sun 7:30–8:00

A live series of original stories by Arch Oboler, the noted radio writer, also known as *Arch Oboler's Comedy Theatre*. The series began a few weeks earlier on KECA, Los Angeles.

OCCASIONAL WIFE (*Situation Comedy*)
FIRST TELECAST: *September 13, 1966*
LAST TELECAST: *August 29, 1967*
BROADCAST HISTORY:
Sep 1966–Aug 1967, NBC Tue 8:30–9:00
CAST:
Peter Christopher .... Michael Callan
Greta Patterson .... Patricia Harty
Max Brahms .... Jack Collins
Mrs. Brahms .... Joan Tompkins
Mrs. Christopher .... Sara Seegar
Man-in-Middle .... Bryan O'Byrne
Bernie .... Stuart Margolin
Wally Frick .... Jack Riley
Vera .... Susan Silo
Marilyn .... Chris Noel

Peter Christopher was a young executive at the Brahms Baby Food Company whose single status had prevented him from getting numerous promotions. Due to the nature of its product, the Brahms Company was a strong believer in marriage and family. Peter hit upon the idea of having someone pose as his wife, whenever his boss was around, so that he could move up in the company and still retain his bachelor status. To that end, he convinced Greta Patterson, an aspiring young painter who was temporarily working as a hat-check girl, to take the "job" of his "occasional wife." In return, he set her up in an apartment two floors above his and agreed to pay for her art lessons and a pair of contact lenses. She had to be in his apartment whenever his boss dropped by and appear at his office from time to time, as well as attend company functions with him.

The problems caused by this arrangement, which often saw one or both of them on the fire escape between their apartments, provided most of the material for episodes. The poor man who lived in the apartment between them, and was often witness to the constant traffic on the fire escape, remained totally confused by the goings-on. Sportscaster Vin Scully served as narrator for the series, commenting on the increasingly complicated problems created by the arrangement between Peter and Greta.

OCEANQUEST (*Documentary*)
FIRST TELECAST: *August 18, 1985*
LAST TELECAST: *September 15, 1985*
BROADCAST HISTORY:
Aug 1985–Sep 1985, NBC Sun 8:00–9:00
REGULARS:
Shawn Weatherly
Al Giddings

Former Miss Universe Shawn Weatherly and underwater cinematographer Al Giddings were featured in this documentary mini-series which explored the flora and fauna of the six oceans of the world. Miss Weatherly had no experience as a diver before signing on for the around-the-world voyage (which took nearly a year), but she learned the equipment and techniques and dove and endured the elements along with the professionals, from the tropics to the icy Antarctic.

ODD COUPLE, THE (*Situation Comedy*)
FIRST TELECAST: *September 24, 1970*
LAST TELECAST: *June 16, 1983*
BROADCAST HISTORY:
Sep 1970–Jan 1971, ABC Thu 9:30–10:00
Jan 1971–Jun 1973, ABC Fri 9:30–10:00
Jun 1973–Jan 1974, ABC Fri 8:30–9:00
Jan 1974–Sep 1974, ABC Fri 9:30–10:00
Sep 1974–Jan 1975, ABC Thu 8:00–8:30
Jan 1975–Jul 1975, ABC Fri 9:30–10:00
Oct 1982–Feb 1983, ABC Fri 8:30–9:00
May 1983, ABC Fri 8:00–8:30
May 1983–Jun 1983, ABC Thu 8:30–9:00
CAST (1970–1975):
Felix Unger .... Tony Randall
Oscar Madison .... Jack Klugman
Murray Greshner .... Al Molinaro
Speed (1970–1974) .... Garry Walberg
Vinnie .... Larry Gelman
Roger (1973–1974) .... Archie Hahn
Roy (1970–1971) .... Ryan McDonald
Cecily Pigeon (1970–1971) .... Monica Evans
Gwendolyn Pigeon (1970–1971) .... Carol Shelly
Dr. Nancy Cunningham (1970–1972)
.... Joan Hotchkis
Gloria Unger (1971–1975) .... Janis Hansen
**Blanche Madison* .... Brett Somers
Myrna Turner (1971–1975) .... Penny Marshall
Miriam Welby (1972–1974) .... Elinor Donahue
CAST (1982–1983):
Felix Unger .... Ron Glass
Oscar Madison .... Demond Wilson
Murray .... John Schuck
Speed .... Christipher Joy
Roy .... Bart Braverman
Cecily Pigeon .... Sheila Anderson
Gwendolyn Pigeon .... Ronalda Douglas
Maria .... Liz Torres
Mona .... Jo Marie Payton-France

*Occasional

If comedy thrives on contrasts, *The Odd Couple* offered a perfect situation. Felix was a prim, fastidious photographer, a compulsive cleaner; Oscar was a gruff, sloppy sportswriter for the fictional *New York Herald*, to whom a floor was a place to toss things. Both were divorced, and only a mutual need for companionship and a place to stay brought them together to live in the same apartment. Well, coexist in the same apartment. The conflicts were obvious and endless, as each upset the other's way of life and attempted to mix with the other's friends. Frequently seen were Oscar's poker partners, notably Murray the cop, Speed the compulsive gambler, and meek Vinnie. Nancy Cunningham was Oscar's girlfriend during the first season, and Myrna his secretary. The Pigeon Sisters were two nutty English girls who lived upstairs, and Christopher Shea for a time played the obnoxious kid next door. Oscar's ex-wife, Blanche, was played by Jack Klugman's real-life wife, Brett Somers, in occasional appearances. Seen infrequently was Felix's daughter, Edna (played by Pamelyn Ferdin in the first few seasons and Doney Oatman later).

For a couple of seasons Miriam served as Felix's girlfriend, but by the final season he had reconciled with his ex-wife, Gloria. The situation on which the series had been built was neatly resolved in the final episode when Felix moved out to remarry Gloria. Oscar returned to the apartment alone, looked around, and exploded into noisy, messy celebration at the prospect of uninhibited chaos—at last!

Notwithstanding this clear-cut ending to the original *Odd Couple*'s run, the series returned to the ABC schedule seven years later as *The New Odd Couple*, with an all-new cast. This time the principals were black, with Ron Glass as fussy photographer Felix and Demond Wilson as sloppy sportswriter Oscar. The setting was the same, and many of the favorite supporting characters were back, although Felix's ex-wife was now called Frances (played in a couple of episodes by Telma Hopkins). It was no more successful than most other revivals of former hit series.

An animated spin-off of this series, titled *The Oddball Couple* and starring a neat cat and a sloppy dog, ran as a weekend daytime entry on ABC from September 1975 to September 1977.

The Odd Couple was based on Neil Simon's hit Broadway play (1965), which was made into a movie (1968) starring Walter Matthau and Jack Lemmon. *The New Odd Couple* marked ABC's second unsuccessful attempt to stage a Neil Simon comedy with black actors—the first being *Barefoot in the Park*.

ODD MAN OUT (*Situation Comedy*)
FIRST TELECAST: *September 24, 1999*
LAST TELECAST: *January 7, 2000*
BROADCAST HISTORY:
Sep 1999–Oct 1999, ABC Fri 9:30–10:00
Oct 1999–Jan 2000, ABC Fri 8:30–9:00
CAST:
Julia Whitney .... Markie Post
Andrew Whitney (age 15) .... Erik von Detten
Paige Whitney .... Natalia Cigliuti
Val Whitney (14) .... Agnes Bruckner
Elizabeth Whitney (12) .... Marina Malota
Aunt Jordan .... Jessica Capshaw
Keith Carlson .... Trevor Fehrman

Andrew Whitney was living what should have been a horny teenager's dream—growing up in a house full of beautiful women. Unfortunately the women were his mother, his aunt and his three sisters, all of whom were constantly snooping on his affairs and giving him advice. His glamorous mom Julia, a widow, was a busy Miami caterer; Aunt Jordan was a booker at a modeling agency (more beautiful women!). His sisters were self-absorbed aspiring model Paige, counterculture Val and prying little Elizabeth. The only male around to give tall, gawky Andrew some moral support was his fast-talking best bud Keith, whose own false sense of being cool collapsed whenever he was confronted with a real woman. There were lots of sex jokes and plenty of cleavage, even from the teens, but the show was short-lived.

ODDVILLE (*Comedy/Variety*)
BROADCAST HISTORY:
MTV
30 minutes
Produced: *1997*
Premiered: *June 16, 1997*
REGULARS:
Frank Hope .... Rich Brown
David Greene .... himself
Melissa Gabriel .... herself

MTV twisted the talk show format into something truly odd in this rather bent series, which featured a nerdy host (Frank), a silent, oblivious sidekick (David), and a buxom young announcer (Melissa), along with Joey the dancing monkey and puppets bouncing behind the couch. Among the guests were a perky female concertina player, a guy who smoked through his ear, and some truly terrible bands. There was usually one slightly bewildered celebrity guest on each show.

ODYSSEY CHANNEL (Network),
see Hallmark Channel

OF MANY THINGS (*Discussion*)
FIRST TELECAST: *October 5, 1953*
LAST TELECAST: *January 11, 1954*
BROADCAST HISTORY:
Oct 1953–Jan 1954, ABC Mon 8:30–9:00
HOST:
Dr. Bergen Evans

Discussion program that ranged over many subjects, from the capture of the German submarine *U-505* on the high seas during World War II (with a Navy admiral as guest), to American popular music (with Mitch Miller), to the art of practical joking. From WBKB-TV, Chicago.

OFF CENTRE (*Situation Comedy*)
FIRST TELECAST: *October 14, 2001*
LAST TELECAST: *October 31, 2002*
BROADCAST HISTORY:
Oct 2001, WB Sun 9:30–10:00
Oct 2001–Mar 2002, WB Sun 9:00–9:30
Mar 2002–Apr 2002, WB Sun 9:30–10:00
Jul 2002–Oct 2002, WB Thu 9:30–10:00
CAST:
Euan Pearce .... Sean Maguire
Mike Platt .... Eddie Kaye Thomas
Chau Presley .... John Cho
Liz .... Lauren Stamile
Status Quo (né Nathan Cole) .... Jason George

THEME
composed by Ben Vaughn and performed by Gordon Gano

They were two mismatched twenty-something roommates who had met while students at Oxford and now were living in a trendy section of Manhattan. British Euan was a suave, free-spirited womanizer while American Mike was incredibly neurotic and conservative. Euan was working as an investment banker while altruistic Mike was writing press releases for a nonprofit organization. The parade of sexy women with whom Euan had a succession of short-term relationships made Mike question his commitment to his girlfriend Liz, his supervisor at work. Also seen regularly were Chau, their smart-aleck friend who worked at a neighborhood Vietnamese restaurant, and Status Quo, a self-absorbed rap star who lived in the building and who alternated between his professional persona as an angry black man and his real personality as a savvy businessman.

In January, after a security camera caught Mike and Liz making love in the office, he quit and struggled to find a new job. At the start of the short-lived second season, Mike and Liz, concerned that their relationship had gone stale, broke up. They remained friends and occasionally still made love, which seemed to mean more to Mike than to Liz. When the charity for which they had worked lost its funding and shut down, Liz was also out of work.

OFF THE RACK (*Situation Comedy*)

FIRST TELECAST: *March 15, 1985*
LAST TELECAST: *September 6, 1985*
BROADCAST HISTORY:
Mar 1985–Apr 1985, ABC Fri 9:30–10:00
Aug 1985–Sep 1985, ABC Fri 9:30–10:00
CAST:
Sam Waltman .... Edward Asner
Kate Halloran .... Eileen Brennan
Shannon Halloran (age 16) .... Claudia Wells
Timothy Halloran (7)................. Corey Yothers
Brenda Patagorski .... Pamela Brull
Cletus Maxwell.................. Dennis Haysbert
Skip Wagner .... Sandy Simpson

Comedy set in a struggling, small-time Los Angeles garment factory. Sam, the gruff coowner, thought he would have to run the place alone when his long-time partner Dan died, but he was soon confronted with an even worse prospect: Dan's strong-willed widow Kate. Her husband had left her no money, so she was determined to work at the place, despite Sam's chauvinistic objections, to help keep it afloat. Lots of yelling ensued. Shannon and Timothy were Kate's children, to whom San became a sort of grouchy surrogate father.

OFF TO SEE THE WIZARD (*Children's Films*)

FIRST TELECAST: *September 8, 1967*
LAST TELECAST: *September 20, 1968*
BROADCAST HISTORY:
Sep 1967–Sep 1968, ABC Fri 7:30–8:30

This series was a collection of films, geared specifically to appeal to children. Among the movies aired, often in two parts if they were full-length theatrical features, were *Flipper, Clarence, the Cross-eyed Lion*, and *The Adventures of Huckleberry Finn*. In addition, a number of films were made especially for this series. Most of these were nature documentaries, but one was an engaging hour entitled "Who's Afraid of Mother Goose," featuring such stars as Frankie Avalon and Nancy Sinatra as Jack and Jill, Rowan & Martin as Simple Simon and the Pieman, the Three Stooges as Three Men in a Tub, and other major names in storybook roles.

The title *Off to See the Wizard* derived from the use of animated characters from *The Wizard of Oz* to host each telecast—Dorothy, the Tin Woodman, the Cowardly Lion, the Scarecrow, Toto, the Wicked Witch of the West, the Wizard, and others.

OFFICE, THE (*Situation Comedy*)

FIRST TELECAST: *March 11, 1995*
LAST TELECAST: *April 15, 1995*
BROADCAST HISTORY:
Mar 1995–Apr 1995, CBS Sat 9:00–9:30
CAST:
Rita Stone......................... Valerie Harper
Frank Gerard.................... Dakin Matthews
Beth Avery .... Debra Jo Rupp
Natalie Stanton........................... Lisa Darr
Deborah Beaumont .... Kristin Dattilo-Hayward
Steve Gilman .... Kevin Conroy
Mae D'arcy .... Andrea Abbate
Bobby Harold .... Gary Dourdan

The executive offices of Package Inc., a package design company in Chicago, provided the setting for this comedy about secretaries and their bosses. Rita, the veteran, a divorcée who had been with the firm for 19 years, was the glue that held things together, seeing that everything got done on time, mediating disputes, and trying to be a good listener to both job-related and personal problems. Her inept boss, Frank, the senior manager, was so dependent on her that he felt threatened by anything that might cause change, including an improvement in her social life. Others in the office were Natalie, the firm's only female executive, more than capable of dealing with the "boys" on their own terms; Natalie's secretary, Beth, a mother of four barely able to keep up with the demands of work and family; glib top salesman Steve, not above stretching the truth to close a deal; Steve's secretary, Deborah, an incredibly naive M.B.A. student who took everything literally; talented but temperamental graphic artist Bobby, who had brought the firm a lot of business but often had to be kept out of earshot of clients; and Bobby's free-spirited secretary, Mae, a three-time loser at marriage whose last job had been with Club Med.

OH BABY (*Situation Comedy*)

BROADCAST HISTORY:
Lifetime
30 minutes
Produced: *1998–2000* (44 episodes)
Premiered: *August 18, 1998*
CAST:
Tracy Calloway .... Cynthia Stevenson
Charlotte St. John .... Joanna Gleason
Celia Calloway.................... Jessica Walter
Ernie Calloway .... Matt Champagne
**Shelly Calloway*...................... Dina Spybey
Dr. Doug Bryan .... Doug Ballard
Rick .... Jack Coleman
Brad.................................. Patrick Kerr
Don Lewis .... Don McManus

*Occasional

Another of the me-first-coms so popular in the '90s, *Oh Baby* milked laughs from the decision of a fortyish professional woman to ignore her commitment-phobic boyfriend and have a baby on her own, via the wonders of modern science—artificial insemination. Tracy's boyfriend Grant (Daniel Hugh Kelly) was a little taken aback by this, but had only himself to blame since the most he could muster on their third anniversary of dating was a "friendship ring." Her bossy mom Celia was even more aghast, laying on guilt with a trowel, but at least she figured she'd get a grandchild out of it. More supportive was busybody best friend Charlotte, who also happened to be the office psychiatrist at the software firm where she worked. Ernie was Tracy's neurotic accountant-brother, quietly frustrated in his own kid-filled marriage, and Shelly was Ernie's fluttery wife. A novel aspect of the series was Tracy's tendency to address the camera directly, then with a remote control in her hand turn to a TV screen and "fast forward" through her life.

In the final episode of the first season, surrounded by squabbling friends, ex-boyfriends, and relatives, Tracy gave birth to a boy, Danny. Charlotte drove everybody in the hospital crazy until *her* boyfriend, Dr. Doug, proposed to her—and she accepted.

In the second season Tracy juggled child rearing and running her own start-up Internet business, trustmom.com.

OH, BOY (*Music*)

FIRST TELECAST: *July 16, 1959*
LAST TELECAST: *September 3, 1959*
BROADCAST HISTORY:
Jul 1959–Sep 1959, ABC Thu 7:30–8:00
HOST:
Tony Hall

Filmed in England, and featuring popular vocal groups from Great Britain plus American guest stars, this series of half-hour musical programs aired on ABC for an eight-week period during the summer of 1959. Among those most frequently featured were Cliff Richard and the Drifters, the Dallas Boys, Marty Wilde, Cherry Wainer, and Dickie Pride. Jimmy Henny was cohost of the program for the last few weeks.

OH, GROW UP (*Situation Comedy*)

FIRST TELECAST: *September 22, 1999*
LAST TELECAST: *December 28, 1999*
BROADCAST HISTORY:
Sep 1999–Nov 1999, ABC Wed 9:30–10:00
Dec 1999, ABC Tue 8:30–9:00
CAST:
Hunter Franklin .... Stephen Dunham
Norris Michelsky .... David Alan Basche
Ford Lowell .... John Ducey
Suzanne Vandermeer .... Rena Sofer
Chloe Sheffield (age 18) .... Niesha Trout

Hunter Franklin was a hunky, self-obsessed, successful construction executive with an unusual home life—he shared his New York City brownstone with two very different pals. Norris, his wisecracking best friend and college roommate, had quit his boring job "selling catheters" (medical supplies) and become a struggling artist, so he needed a place to crash. Yuppie friend Ford, a neat freak and paralegal, had ended his marriage rather abruptly when he realized he was gay. His wife, Suzanne, was not quite sure what to make of this, but they remained on good terms as Ford moved in with Hunter as well. One more arrival was Chloe, Hunter's long-lost daughter, who lived there while she attended New York University.

The three guys hit the dating scene (with lots of gay jokes in Ford's case), while Chloe added a little bit of "family matters" to the mix, forcing Hunter to learn to be a dad. "Mom" the dog commented via subtitles. In December Chloe's mom, Julie, visited and revealed that Hunter was not Chloe's real dad, but this new twist was not explored as the series was canceled shortly thereafter.

OH MADELINE (*Situation Comedy*)

FIRST TELECAST: *September 27, 1983*
LAST TELECAST: *May 15, 1984*
BROADCAST HISTORY:
Sep 1983–May 1984, ABC Tue 9:30–10:00
CAST:
Madeline Wayne .... Madeline Kahn
Charlie Wayne .... James Sloyan
Robert Leone .... Louis Giambalvo
Doris Leone .... Jesse Welles
Annie McIntyre .... Francine Tacker

After ten years of marriage, Madeline was bored. Not with husband Charlie, a sweet but square guy who made his living writing steamy romance novels under the name Crystal Love. Not with best friend Doris, a timid divorcée formerly married to Charlie's best friend, a middle-aged swinger named Bob. Just with her sedate, predictable existence in a middle-class suburb. Wanting to put some zip in her life, Madeline decided to try every trendy diversion that came along, whether it was health foods made of seaweed, exercise clubs that seemed intent on bodily destruction, or "ladies only" clubs featuring male strippers. There was plenty of slapstick comedy in this series, along with marital-misunderstanding plots reminiscent of *I Love Lucy.* Annie was Charlie's amorous editor, who seemed to want more than just his manuscripts.

Based on the British television series, *Pig in the Middle.*

OH, SUSANNA, syndicated title for *Gale Storm Show, The*

OH, THOSE BELLS (*Situation Comedy*)

FIRST TELECAST: *March 8, 1962*
LAST TELECAST: *May 31, 1962*
BROADCAST HISTORY:
Mar 1962–May 1962, CBS Thu 7:30–8:00
CAST:
Herbie Bell .... Herbert Wiere
Harry Bell .... Harry Wiere
Sylvie Bell .... Sylvester Wiere
Henry Slocum .... Henry Norell
Kitty Mathews .... Carol Byron
Mrs. Stanfield .... Reta Shaw

This series was a loosely structured attempt to bring contemporary slapstick humor to television. The Wiere Brothers, an internationally known trio of slapstick comedians, portrayed the last living members of a family with a long history as theatrical prop, costume, and wig makers. They worked in a Hollywood prop shop, run by irascible Henry Slocum with the help of his sweet, understanding secretary, Kitty.

Despite their gentle natures, the brothers managed to turn simple everyday situations into frenetic disasters. When things started to go wrong their world looked like it had been taken over by The Three Stooges in their prime.

OHARA (*Police/Detective Drama*)
FIRST TELECAST: *January 17, 1987*
LAST TELECAST: *August 6, 1988*
BROADCAST HISTORY:
Jan 1987–May 1987, ABC Sat 9:00–10:00
Oct 1987–Nov 1987, ABC Sat 9:00–10:00
Dec 1987–Jan 1988, ABC Sat 8:00–9:00
Jan 1988–Aug 1988, ABC Sat 9:00–10:00
CAST:
Lt. Ohara .... Pat Morita
Capt. Lloyd Hamilton (1987) .... Kevin Conroy
Capt. Ross (1987) .... Jon Polito
Gussie Lemmons (1987) .... Madge Sinclair
Lt. Jessie Guerrera (1987) .... Richard Yniguez
Lt. Cricket Sideris (1987) .... Catherine Keener
Sgt. Phil O'Brien (1987) .... Jack Wallace
Lt. George Shaver .... Robert Clohessy
Asst. U.S. Attorney Teresa Storm .... Rachel Ticotin
Roxy (1987) .... Meagan Fay

ABC really wanted this show to work—so much so that they kept changing its format trying to find *Ohara* an audience. When the series premiered its star was a cop unlike any seen on American television. Lt. Ohara (pronounced "Oh-Har-Ra") was a Japanese-American policeman in Los Angeles who almost never used a gun, preferred patience and persuasion to violence, and didn't even drive a car. A widower, he had a traditional shrine in his home, believed in daily meditation, and was always ready with a sage saying ("When the going gets tough, the wise get help"). His fellow officers were skeptical, but Ohara's patient methods worked most of the time—and when they didn't he could always resort to the martial arts. Ohara's friend Gussie ran the White Orchid restaurant where the lieutenant could often be found when not on duty.

In the fall of 1987 the format was changed and the entire cast, with the exception of star Pat Morita, was dropped. Ohara was assigned to a federal task force headed by determined lady D.A. Teresa Storm, and his new partner was a brash young officer named Shaver. Though still contemplative, Ohara had suddenly become a more conventional cop—he used his gun and drove his own car, though when on assignment Shaver usually did the driving in his aging convertible. The ratings still were lousy so, in February 1988, the format was changed yet again. After being frustrated by the law enforcement system's bureaucracy—resulting in the murder of a friend—the Lieutenant and his partner both resigned from the force, and short, thoughtful Ohara and tall, hunky Shaver became private eyes.

O'HARA, U.S. TREASURY (*Police Drama*)
FIRST TELECAST: *September 17, 1971*
LAST TELECAST: *September 8, 1972*
BROADCAST HISTORY:
Sep 1971–Dec 1971, CBS Fri 8:30–9:30
Jan 1972–Sep 1972, CBS 8:00–9:00
CAST:
Jim O'Hara .... David Janssen

Produced with the approval and cooperation of all of the various branches of the Department of the Treasury, this series followed the adventures of special agent Jim O'Hara. Working in pursuit of violators of federal laws, sometimes undercover, Jim served all five of the enforcement agencies of the department: Bureau of Customs, Secret Service, Internal Revenue Service Intelligence Division, Internal Revenue Service Inspection Division, and Internal Revenue Service, Alcohol, Tobacco, and Firearms Division.

OHH, NOOO! MR. BILL PRESENTS (*Comedy*)
BROADCAST HISTORY:
Fox Family Channel
30 minutes
Produced: *1998*
Premiered: *August 15, 1998*
VOICE:
Mr. Bill .... Walter Williams

Mr. Bill, the ill-fated little doughboy puppet who was always being squashed by Sluggo on the original *Saturday Night Live,* was back as host of this collection of British comedy sketches on the newly relaunched Family Channel. Back too, unfortunately, was Sluggo (a.k.a. Mr. Hand), the giant hand that regularly reached into the little fellow's world and practiced violence on him, as Mr. Bill squealed "Oh, noooo!" The sketches, from British TV, featured such performers as Rowan Atkinson (Mr. Bean), Hale and Pace, Freddie Star, and Russ Abbot.

OKY DOKY RANCH, see *Adventures of Oky Doky*

OLD AMERICAN BARN DANCE (*Music*)
FIRST TELECAST: *July 5, 1953*
LAST TELECAST: *August 9, 1953*
BROADCAST HISTORY:
Jul 1953–Aug 1953, DUM Sun 10:30–11:00
EMCEE:
Bill Bailey

Filmed summertime country music show, featuring Pee Wee King, Tennessee Ernie Ford, and others.

OLD FASHIONED MEETING (*Religion*)
FIRST TELECAST: *October 8, 1950*
LAST TELECAST: *April 1, 1951*
BROADCAST HISTORY:
Oct 1950–Apr 1951, ABC Sun 10:00–10:30

An old-fashioned religious revival hour, sponsored by the Gospel Broadcasting Association.

OLDEST ROOKIE, THE (*Police Drama*)
FIRST TELECAST: *September 16, 1987*
LAST TELECAST: *January 6, 1988*
BROADCAST HISTORY:
Sep 1987–Jan 1988, CBS Wed 8:00–9:00
CAST:
Det. Ike Porter .... Paul Sorvino
Det. Tony Jonas .... D. W. Moffett
Lt. Marco Zaga .... Raymond J. Barry
Det. Gordon Lane .... Marshall Bell
Chief Black .... Patrick Cronin

After 25 years on the administrative side of police work Ike Porter, Deputy Chief of Police in Charge of Public Affairs, decided to give up the cushy life and get back to the basics of law enforcement. Despite the misgivings of his friends and colleagues, Ike put himself through the rigors of training at the police academy and, much to the surprise of almost everyone, his 50-year-old body survived. Using his connections in the department he got himself and his young rookie partner, Tony Jonas, assigned to the detective division. Their new boss, grizzled veteran Lt. Zaga, wasn't thrilled about having the former P.R. head under his command, and neither was Zaga's second-in-command, Det. Lane, who had been a classmate of Ike's when he had originally joined the force. Despite the problem, Ike and Tony proved to be an effective team.

OLDSMOBILE MUSIC THEATRE (*Anthology with Music*)

FIRST TELECAST: *March 26, 1959*
LAST TELECAST: *May 7, 1959*
BROADCAST HISTORY:
Mar 1959–May 1959, NBC Thu 8:30–9:00
HOST:
Bill Hayes
Florence Henderson

This anthology series presented live plays in which a musical element was woven into the storyline, as in musical comedies or dramas with incidental songs. None of the music used was original, however. Hosts Bill Hayes and Florence Henderson appeared in some presentations, along with such stars as Carol Lawrence and Roddy McDowall. The series premiered as *Oldsmobile Music Theatre*, had a single telecast on April 16 as *Oldsmobile Theatre*, and on April 23 became *Oldsmobile Presents*.

OLIVER BEENE (*Situation Comedy*)

FIRST TELECAST: *March 9, 2003*
LAST TELECAST:
BROADCAST HISTORY:
Mar 2003–Apr 2003, FOX Sun 8:30–9:30
Apr 2003–Jun 2003, FOX Sun 9:30–10:00
CAST:
Oliver Beene (age 11) .... Grant Rosenmeyer
Dr. Jerry Beene .... Grant Shaud
Charlotte Beene .... Wendy Makkena
Ted Beene .... Andy Lawrence
Joyce .... Daveigh Chase
Michael .... Taylor Emerson
Susan Brotsky .... Amy Bruckner
Bonnie Smith (pilot) .... Amy Castle
Bonnie Smith .... Amanda Michalka
Adult Oliver (voice) .... David Cross

Oliver Beene was sort of a nerd version of *The Wonder Years*. It was 1962, and 11-year-old Oliver was just approaching puberty. A little on the chubby side, uncoordinated and decidedly neurotic, Oliver tried his best to deal with life at home and at school. His dentist father, Jerry, was hyperactive and destructively competitive, while his not-quite-happy homemaker mother, Charlotte, had visions of moving up from their middle-class life in Rego Park, Queens. Oliver's older brother Ted was totally wrapped up in sports and girls and tolerated his younger sibling but did little to help him. Oliver went to PS-206, where his best friends were intelligent Joyce, who frequently nagged him, and easygoing Michael. Susan was the smarty-pants teachers' pet who was hated by all the other students (and many of her teachers), and Bonnie was the unattainable girl of Oliver's dreams.

The series was narrated by the adult Oliver, and there were frequent flashbacks and flash-forwards to emphasize points.

OMNIBUS (*Culture*)

FIRST TELECAST: *October 4, 1953*
LAST TELECAST: *March 31, 1957*
BROADCAST HISTORY:
Oct 1953–Apr 1956, CBS Sun 5:00–6:30 (OS)
Oct 1956–Mar 1957, ABC Sun 9:00–10:30
HOST:
Alistair Cooke

Omnibus was the most outstanding and longest-running cultural series in the history of commercial network television. It premiered on November 9, 1952, as a late Sunday afternoon offering on CBS, running from 4:30–6:00 P.M. for its first season. That premiere telecast set the tone for the diversity that would make *Omnibus* a unique program throughout its run. William Saroyan narrated an adaptation of his short story "The Bad Men," there were excerpts from Gilbert and Sullivan's *The Mikado*, and Rex Harrison and his then wife, Lilli Palmer, starred in Maxwell Anderson's "The Trial of Anne Boleyn"—all in one 90-minute program.

As in that first telecast, the range of subject matter presented on *Omnibus* was quite impressive. Opera, symphony, ballet, dramatic plays, and true-life adventure films prepared by the New York Zoological Society and the American Museum of Natural History were but a few of the offerings of this award-winning show. The financing came from the Ford Foundation TV-Radio Workshop, and enabled the producers to devote the full 90 minutes of each show to program content—there were no commercials on *Omnibus*, a rarity in commercial television.

In the fall of 1953, the start time of *Omnibus* was moved up to 5:00 P.M. and, since it ran until 6:30 P.M., it is eligible for inclusion in this book as an evening program. That first evening season presented dramas based on the works of William Inge, James Thurber, Stephen Vincent Benét, Ernest Hemingway, Carson McCullers, John Steinbeck, and T. S. Eliot. Performing were such talents as Hume Cronyn, Jessica Tandy, Carol Channing, Yul Brynner, Walter Slezak, Elsa Lanchester, Anne Bancroft, Mel Ferrer, Helen Hayes, Claude Rains, E. G. Marshall, John Cassavetes, Susan Strasberg, and Thomas Mitchell. But there was much, much more that season. Orson Welles starred in *King Lear*, Jack Benny in a full 90-minute re-creation of his film role in *The Horn Blows at Midnight*, and Victor Borge in a solo segment showing his piano and comedic mastery. Jacques Cousteau, who would have many popular documentaries aired on television in the 1970s, had his first network exposure in January 1954 with "Undersea Archaeology." There were excerpts from the musical *Oklahoma!*, a performance by the Azumi Kabuki Dancers from Japan, a demonstration of the recording techniques used by popular performers Les Paul and Mary Ford, and the ballet *Billy the Kid* with music by Aaron Copland performed by the Ballet Theatre Company. Informational pieces included discussions of the medical uses of X-ray photography and new techniques for determining art forgeries.

Omnibus had a little bit of everything. In subsequent seasons Leonard Bernstein made his television debut with a technical explanation of Beethoven's

Fifth Symphony, George C. Scott played Robespierre, Peter Ustinov played Samuel Johnson, and Kim Stanley played Joan of Arc. When it left the evening hours in the spring of 1957, it was only to return on Sunday afternoons that fall on NBC, where it remained on an increasingly irregular schedule until its final telecast on April 16, 1961. When it left the air, something wonderful about television went with it, creating a void that was not to be filled until the emergence of network Public Television a decade later.

ABC made a half-hearted attempt at reviving *Omnibus* in 1981, with a few irregularly scheduled special telecasts in prime time.

ON BROADWAY TONIGHT (*Talent/Variety*)

FIRST TELECAST: *July 8, 1964*
LAST TELECAST: *March 12, 1965*
BROADCAST HISTORY:
Jul 1964–Sep 1964, CBS Wed 10:00–11:00
Jan 1965–Mar 1965, CBS Fri 8:30–9:30
EMCEE:
Rudy Vallee

Many talented young performers were given their first national television exposure on this show. Host Rudy Vallee would interview each of the six acts that were performing on a given week's telecast, and then let them do their routines. A special feature of each show was the appearance of a well-known celebrity who would chat with Mr. Vallee about his or her big break in show business. Interestingly, most of the young performers on this series who later became successful were comedians. Among them were Rich Little, Richard Pryor, Marilyn Michaels, Rodney Dangerfield, George Carlin, Jo Anne Worley, and Renee Taylor. Singer Adam Wade, however, made more appearances on the show than anyone else.

ON GUARD (*Documentary*)

FIRST TELECAST: *April 28, 1952*
LAST TELECAST: *May 29, 1954*
BROADCAST HISTORY:
Apr 1952–Aug 1952, ABC Mon 9:30–10:00
Sep 1952–Dec 1952, ABC Thu 9:30–10:00
Dec 1952–Apr 1953, ABC Sun 6:00–6:30
Dec 1953–May 1954, ABC Sat 10:00–10:30

This program consisted of documentary films about the military, produced by the army, navy, and air force.

ON OUR OWN (*Situation Comedy*)

FIRST TELECAST: *October 9, 1977*
LAST TELECAST: *August 20, 1978*
BROADCAST HISTORY:
Oct 1977–Aug 1978, CBS Sun 8:30–9:00
CAST:
Maria Teresa Bonino .... Lynnie Greene
Julia Peters .... Bess Armstrong
Toni McBain .... Gretchen Wyler
April Baxter .... Dixie Carter
Craig Boatwright .... Dan Resin
Eddie Barnes .... John Christopher Jones
J. M. Bedford .... Bob Randall

On Our Own, the story of two young women trying to make it in the New York advertising world, was the only prime-time series actually being produced in New York as of the start of the 1977–1978 season. Maria and Julia had both just been promoted from the secretarial positions they had previously held at the Bedford Advertising Agency, Maria to art director and Julia to copywriter. They were enthusiastic and energetic, if a bit naive and inexperienced, and wanted desperately to take full advantage of their first big step up the corporate ladder. Others in the agency were copywriter April Baxter, beautiful, sexy, and worldly wise with all sorts of advice about men; Eddie Barnes, creative producer of television commercials; and salesman Craig Boatwright. Running the whole operation was sophisticated, sloganmaking Toni McBain, the head of the agency. The only person she had to please was board chairman J. M. Bedford.

ON OUR OWN (*Situation Comedy*)

FIRST TELECAST: *September 13, 1994*
LAST TELECAST: *April 14, 1995*
BROADCAST HISTORY:
Sep 1994, ABC Tue 8:30–9:00
Sep 1994, ABC Fri 8:30–9:00
Sep 1994–Dec 1994, ABC Sun 7:30–8:00
Mar 1995–Apr 1995, ABC Fri 9:30–10:00
CAST:
Josh Jerrico/Aunt Jelcinda ...... Ralph Louis Harris
Jimi Jerrico .... JoJo Smollett
Jai Jerrico .... Jazz Smollett
Jesse Jerrico .... Jussie Smollett
Jordee Jerrico .... Jurnee Smollett
Joc Jerrico .... Jake Smollett
Jarreau Jerrico .... Jocqui Smollett
Alana Michaels (1994) .... Kimberly Kates
Gordon Ormsby (1994) .... Roger Aaron Brown
Scotti Decker (1995) ...... T'Keyah Crystal Keymah
Suki (1995) .... Karen Kim
Nails (1995) .... Laura Ponce

Slapstick "warmth-com" about seven middle-class black St. Louis youngsters, aged 20 years to 18 months, whose parents had been killed in a car crash and who went to unusual lengths to stay together. Josh, the oldest, took charge, working at a restaurant to help pay the bills. Then Mr. Ormsby and Miss Michaels from Family Services came snooping around, announcing that if a "responsible adult" were not found all the young'uns would be carted off to foster care (awwww!). Quicker than you can say *Mrs. Doubtfire*, Josh donned a wig, dress, and new identity as just that—"Aunt Jelcinda."

Incredibly dense Ormsby fell for it and even had a crush on "Mama J." Miss Michaels was not so easily fooled but was so smitten with the kids that she went along with the masquerade ("Somehow, this wonderful family has gotten to me!"). A loud laugh track alternated with reaction shots of cute kids and the family bulldog, Jinx.

When the series returned in the spring, Josh had been awarded custody of the family and could discard his dress. But money was tight, forcing the clan to take in Scotti as a border. A free-spirited but experienced young woman who worked as a freelance contractor, she became a sort of older sister/adviser to the kids. Stories increasingly revolved around hunky Jimi, usually seen in cutoffs with muscles bulging.

The six younger kids were played by real-life siblings, the Smolletts, a rap/R&B musical family from New York City.

ON PARADE (*Musical Variety*)
FIRST TELECAST: *July 17, 1964*
LAST TELECAST: *September 18, 1964*
BROADCAST HISTORY:
Jul 1964–Sep 1964, NBC Fri 9:30–10:00

On Parade was originally produced by the Canadian Broadcasting Company. Each telecast spotlighted a particular performer or group of performers from the American musical world such as Rosemary Clooney, Henry Mancini, Diahann Carroll, and the Limeliters. Production numbers, comedy sketches, and interviews were all part of the regular format.

ON SCENE—EMERGENCY RESPONSE
(*Documentary*)
BROADCAST HISTORY:
Syndicated only
30 minutes
Produced: *1990–1994* (104 episodes)
Released: *Fall 1990*
HOST:
Dave Forman

This weekly series showed the activities of paramedics, air rescue teams, and other municipal rescue services from cities all over the country. Each episode covered three or four specific examples of the groups at work. Series producer Dave Forman also served as host and Los Angeles correspondent.

ON STAGE (*Music*)
BROADCAST HISTORY:
The Nashville Network
30 minutes
Produced: *1989–1992*
Premiered: *July 31, 1989*

Contemporary country artists performed their latest releases, and greatest hits, in concert rather than via videos, in this TNN series.

ON STAGE AMERICA (*Variety/Magazine*)
BROADCAST HISTORY:
Syndicated only
120 minutes
Produced: *1984* (13 episodes)
Released: *April 1984*
HOSTS:
Susie Bono
Todd Christianson
Steve Edwards
Randi Oakes
REGULARS:
John Barbour
Minnie Pearl

This unusual variety series not only gave its weekly guests the opportunity to perform, but offered viewers in-depth profiles of many of them. Some of the profiles were informative and serious while others looked like fluff pieces from *Lifestyles of the Rich and Famous*, a series that had premiered only a couple of months earlier. Among the more notable personalities appearing were Dean Martin, Barbara Mandrell, Shelley Berman, Jackie Mason, Suzanne Somers, Neil Sedaka, Lisa Hartman, Sid Caesar, Tina Turner, Paul Anka, Diahann Carroll, and David Brenner.

ON THE AIR (*Situation Comedy*)
FIRST TELECAST: *June 20, 1992*
LAST TELECAST: *July 4, 1992*
BROADCAST HISTORY:
Jun 1992–Jul 1992, ABC Sat 9:30–10:00
CAST:
Lester Guy .... Ian Buchanan
Vladja Gochktch .... David L. Lander
Ruth Trueworthy .... Nancye Ferguson
Bert Schein .... Gary Grossman
Betty Hudson .... Marla Jeanette Rubinoff
Dwight McGonigle .... Marvin Kaplan
Mickey .... Mel Johnson, Jr.
"Blinky" Watts .... Tracey Walter
Bud Budwaller .... Miguel Ferrer
Nicole Thorn .... Kim McGuire
The Hurry Up Twins
.... Raleigh and Raymond Friend
Buddy Morris .... Buddy Douglas
Shorty .... Irwin Keyes

Every so often a series flashes by on the TV screen that is so strange even critics aren't sure what to make of it (remember *Quark*? *Police Squad*? *Eerie, Indiana*?). *On the Air*, from producer David Lynch (of *Twin Peaks* fame), fit the bill. It was set in 1957, behind the scenes at the Zoblotnick Broadcasting Corporation during the production of a big, brassy TV variety show called *The Lester Guy Show*. Lester was a young but fading star who hoped the show would revive his career; unfortunately he kept getting knocked unconscious by falling props. Others rushing about included Vladja, the show's incomprehensible director; stage manager Ruth, who translated for him; Bert, the nervous second banana; Betty, the ingenue who gave the phrase "dim bulb" new meaning; incompetent producer Dwight; Shorty the stagehand; and sound engineers Mickey and Blinky (who was blind and kept hitting the wrong buttons).

Tyrannizing them all was hot-tempered ZBC network head Budwaller, who stalked the stage with his ruthlessly ambitious assistant Nicole, frightening everyone, even Snaps, the little dog who performed in the commercials (and who hated the sponsor's dog food so much he had to be chained to the bowl).

ON THE BOARDWALK WITH PAUL WHITEMAN
(*Variety*)
FIRST TELECAST: *May 30, 1954*
LAST TELECAST: *August 1, 1954*
BROADCAST HISTORY:
May 1954–Aug 1954, ABC Sun 8:00–9:00
EMCEE:
Paul Whiteman
MUSICAL DIRECTOR:
Bernie Lowe

Telecast live from the famous Steel Pier in Atlantic City, New Jersey, this program was a variation on *The Original Amateur Hour*. During the first half hour of each show, eight young acts auditioned briefly and were rated by a panel of four people from show business. The four acts with the greatest potential would then return the following week to perform again after they had had a full week of professional coaching.

ON THE CORNER (*Variety*)
FIRST TELECAST: *April 18, 1948*
LAST TELECAST: *May 16, 1948*
BROADCAST HISTORY:
Apr 1948–May 1948, ABC Sun 6:30–7:00

HOST:

Henry Morgan

A modest variety program which is said by ABC to have been the first ABC network series. The network at the time consisted of four stations: WFIL in Philadelphia (where *On the Corner* originated); WMAR, Baltimore; WMAL, Washington; and WABD, New York. The last was a DuMont station, since ABC's own New York outlet was not yet on the air.

Henry Morgan was a major radio star in the 1940s, and was one of the first performers to try the new medium of television on a regular basis. *On the Corner* showed him thumbing the pages of *Variety*, turning up the names of his guests—who generally turned out to be little-known, and sometimes second-rate, nightclub performers. Appearing on the first telecast were George Guest with his marionettes, puppeteer Virginia Austin, impersonator Roy Davis, and the Clark Sisters singing quartet. Laced through it all was Morgan's sardonic wit, which included jibes at the sponsor's commercials. Apparently Admiral Corporation was not amused, as *On the Corner* was canceled after only five weeks of its projected 13-week run.

For another candidate for "First ABC Series," see *Hollywood Screen Test*.

ON THE LINE WITH CONSIDINE (*News Interview*)

FIRST TELECAST: *January 8, 1952*
LAST TELECAST: *August 29, 1954*
BROADCAST HISTORY:

Jan 1952–Jun 1953, NBC Tue 10:45–11:00
Jun 1953–Jan 1954, NBC Tue 10:30–10:45
Jul 1954–Aug 1954, ABC Sun 9:00–9:15

HOST:

Bob Considine

After a long career as a journalist, both in print and on radio, Bob Considine came to television. His show, *On the Line with Considine*, actually premiered on Saturday, January 20, 1951, at 5:45 P.M. After a year in that time slot, it moved to Tuesday evening where it remained on NBC for two years. After the show was canceled, it returned for the summer of 1954 on ABC. The format of the show consisted of Bob Considine reading the current news headlines, with occasional comment, and then conducting a short interview with a prominent figure about a pertinent issue of current interest.

ON THE ROAD WITH CHARLES KURALT (*Magazine*)

FIRST TELECAST: *June 26, 1983*
LAST TELECAST: *August 23, 1983*
BROADCAST HISTORY:

Jun 1983, CBS Sun 8:00–8:30
Jun 1983–Aug 1983, CBS Tue 8:00–8:30

HOST/CORRESPONDENT:

Charles Kuralt

For years CBS correspondent Charles Kuralt had contributed whimsical segments to the *CBS Evening News* and other news series such as 1977's *Who's Who*. These "On the Road" stories were vignettes about the people, places, and bits of history he had encountered while traveling around the country. In the summer of 1983 he got the opportunity to expand the "On the Road" feature with longer pieces in a weekly series of his own.

Much in the style of *Real People*, which may have stolen part of its concept from him, Kuralt had chats with, among others, a man who had traveled around the country for almost 12 years blowing bubbles of all sorts for anyone who cared to watch; the world's record holder in the art of domino-toppling; an Ohio man who had built everything from a Ferris wheel to a grandfather clock—out of toothpicks; a group of real-life cowboys describing what life on the range was truly like; and a man in Denver who collected junk mail by the bagful to use as fuel in his iron stove.

ON THE ROCKS (*Situation Comedy*)

FIRST TELECAST: *September 11, 1975*
LAST TELECAST: *May 17, 1976*
BROADCAST HISTORY:

Sep 1975–Jan 1976, ABC Thu 8:30–9:00
Jan 1976–May 1976, ABC Mon 8:00–8:30

CAST:

Hector Fuentes .... Jose Perez
DeMott .... Hal Williams
Cleaver .... Rick Hurst
Nicky Palik .... Bobby Sandler
Mr. Gibson .... Mel Stewart
Mr. Sullivan .... Tom Poston
Gabby .... Pat Cranshaw
Baxter .... Jack Grimes
Warden Wilbur Poindexter .... Logan Ramsey

Comedy centering on the inmates of Alamesa Minimum Security Prison, a "low-risk" institution apparently run as much by the prisoners as by the authorities. The usual setting was the cell containing Hector, the resourceful Latin; his friend DeMott; Cleaver, the eternal optimist; and Nicky, a juvenile offender. Nearby was Gabby, a toothless, elderly inmate. Mr. Gibson was the hard-nosed corrections officer, whose attempts at keeping the boys in line were often unintentionally thwarted by Mr. Sullivan, a mild-mannered guard.

Taped before a live audience and originally telecast immediately following TV's leading cop comedy, *Barney Miller*, which prompted ABC to promote the two shows together with the line "funny cops, and funny robbers." The series was based on the British show *Porridge*.

ON THE SPOT (*Comedy*)

FIRST TELECAST: *March 20, 2003*
LAST TELECAST: *April 17, 2003*
BROADCAST HISTORY:

Mar 2003–Apr 2003, WB Thu 9:30–10:00

CAST:

Mr. Henderson .... Tim Conway
Jeff Miller .... Jeff B. Davis
Brenda .... Erinn Carter
Caramel .... Arden Myrin
Monty .... Jordan Black
Fifi .... Mindy Sterling
The Professor .... Michael Hitchcock

VARIOUS CHARACTERS:

Lance Barber
Lindsey Stoddart

REGULARS:

Chip Esten
Dweezil Zappa, bandleader

The rundown Sun Spot Hotel in Malibu, California, was the setting for this series, an unusual mix of sitcom and improvisational comedy. Hyperactive Mr.

Henderson ran the company that owned the hotel, and when the Sun Spot's manager died unexpectedly, he gave the job to enthusiastic young Jeff, formerly the mail clerk. This did not sit well with Brenda, the ambitious assistant manager who was convinced she deserved the promotion. Others working at the Sun Spot were Caramel, the spaced-out maid; Monty, the bartender, and Fifi and the Professor, the hotel's weird and long-in-the-tooth but excessively amorous lounge act.

What made *On the Spot* unique was its improvisational component. Host Esten, who also provided narration to move the plot along, sat with the studio audience on bleacher-type seats adjacent to the set. At various points in the show the action would stop and he would ask the audience for suggestions on how the story line should proceed—which the actors would then incorporate. Among the familiar faces who showed up in guest appearances were Andy Dick, Robert Wagner, Drew Carey and Jack Black.

ON TRIAL, see *Joseph Cotten Show, The*

ON TRIAL (*Debate*)
FIRST TELECAST: *November 22, 1948*
LAST TELECAST: *August 12, 1952*
BROADCAST HISTORY:
Nov 1948–Feb 1950, ABC Various nights and times, 30 minutes
Mar 1950–Sep 1950, ABC Wed 8:00–8:30
Oct 1950–Sep 1951, ABC Mon 9:30–10:00
Oct 1951–Jun 1952, ABC Tue 9:30–10:00
Jun 1952–Aug 1952, ABC Tue 8:00–8:30
MODERATOR:
David Levitan

Public-affairs debate in the manner of a courtroom trial, with a real-life judge presiding; affirmative and negative counsel and expert witnesses (guest authorities) argued the various points of an issue. Later the format was altered slightly to provide for affirmative arguments one week followed by negative arguments the next. The first issue "on trial" in November 1948 was "Should Wiretapping Be Prohibited?"

For its first 15 months *On Trial* was shifted all over the ABC schedule, seldom spending more than two months in any one time slot. Beginning in early 1950 it settled down to longer runs on various weeknights.

ON YOUR WAY (*Quiz/Talent*)
FIRST TELECAST: *September 9, 1953*
LAST TELECAST: *April 17, 1954*
BROADCAST HISTORY:
Sep 1953–Jan 1954, DUM Wed 9:30–10:00
Jan 1954–Apr 1954, ABC Sat 7:00–7:30
EMCEE:
Bud Collyer (1953–1954)
Kathy Godfrey (1954)
John Reed King (1954)

On Your Way began as an audience-participation quiz show in which contestants were given the opportunity to win free transportation to a destination of their choice (thus sending them "on their way"). Bud Collyer was the original host. On January 23, 1954, the program moved to ABC, with new hosts and (two weeks later) a new format. Kathy Godfrey, Arthur Godfrey's younger sister, interviewed four aspiring young performers who then competed in a talent show, under the supervision of emcee John Reed King. In its talent-show format the program was supposed to send winners "on their way" in show business. Unfortunately, not many of them ever gained any sort of fame, although one contestant—a 16-year-old guitarist named Charlie Gracie—later became an important rock star in the late 1950s.

ONCE A HERO (*Fantasy/Adventure*)
FIRST TELECAST: *September 19, 1987*
LAST TELECAST: *October 3, 1987*
BROADCAST HISTORY:
Sep 1987–Oct 1987, ABC Sat 8:00–9:00
CAST:
Captain Justice/Brad Steele .... Jeff Lester
Abner Bevis .... Milo O'Shea
Emma Greely .... Caitlin Clarke
Woody Greely .... Josh Blake
Gumshoe .... Robert Forster
Eddie Kybo .... David Wohl
Rachel Kirk .... Dianne Kay
Gent .... William Griffis

The first cancellation of the 1987–1988 season was this fantasy-adventure about a cartoon superhero who crossed the "Forbidden Zone" into the real world because he feared his comic strip was about to be canceled. Captain Justice (and his alter ego, mild-mannered professor Brad Steele) hoped to revitalize his creator, legendary cartoonist Abner, with real-world adventures. However, he found that once he was here his super-powers didn't work; no crashing through walls, no deflected bullets, and no one awed by his bright red tights. Cartoon detective Gumshoe (that's right, floppy hat, Sam Spade sneer) also came from fictional Pleasantville into the real world to help Justice battle such adversaries as Max Mayhem and Lobsterman, but it was all uphill. Emma was a suspicious newspaper reporter, and Woody her 12-year-old son.

Once a Hero was canceled after only three weeks, before an already-filmed episode guest starring Adam West ("Batman") could even air. It's tough in the real world.

ONCE A THIEF, see *John Woo's Once a Thief*

ONCE AN EAGLE (*Military Drama*)
FIRST TELECAST: *December 2, 1976*
LAST TELECAST: *January 13, 1977*
BROADCAST HISTORY:
Dec 1976–Jan 1977, NBC Tue 9:00–10:00
CAST:
Sam Damon .... Sam Elliott
Courtney Massengale .... Cliff Potts
Tommy Caldwell Damon .... Darleen Carr
George Caldwell .... Glenn Ford
Lt. Merrick .... Clu Gulager
Emily Massengale .... Amy Irving
Jinny Massengale .... Melanie Griffith
Donny Damon .... Andrew Damon

Adapted from Anton Myrer's novel, *Once an Eagle* was the story of two men's careers in the military over a 30-year period. Sam Damon was a dedicated soldier who cared little for the comforts of home, prestige, power, and the other affectations of rank. Relishing front-line combat, he was a soldier who regarded the military life as a profession to be handled to the best of his ability. Courtney Massengale, on the other hand, was a conniver and maneuverer. More concerned about appearance than substance, he was always on the lookout for a contact to help boost him further up on the ladder to power and prestige. The two men had started out in similar situations as young officers in World War I and individual chapters of *Once an Eagle* showed how their respective lives changed and developed during the intervening period to, and through, World War II.

Once an Eagle was one of four novels dramatized under the collective title *NBC's Best Sellers*. Although individual chapters generally ran only one hour, as indicated in the broadcast history above, the first and last chapters ran from 9:00–11:00 P.M.

ONCE AND AGAIN (*Drama*)
FIRST TELECAST: *September 21, 1999*
LAST TELECAST: *April 15, 2002*
BROADCAST HISTORY:
Sep 1999–Dec 1999, ABC Tue 10:00–11:00
Jan 2000–Jul 2000, ABC Mon 10:00–11:00
Oct 2000–Dec 2000, ABC Mon 10:00–11:00
Jan 2001–May 2001, ABC Wed 10:00–11:00
Sep 2001–Dec 2001, ABC Fri 10:00–11:00
Jan 2002, ABC Fri 9:00–10:00
Mar 2002–Apr 2002, ABC Mon 10:00–11:00
CAST:
Lily Manning .... Sela Ward
Rick Sammler .... Billy Campbell
Grace Manning (age 14) .... Julia Whelan
Zoe Manning (9) .... Meredith Deane
Eli Sammler (16) .... Shane West
Jessie Sammler (12) .... Evan Rachel Wood
Jake Manning .... Jeffrey Nordling
Karen Sammler .... Susanna Thompson
David Casilli .... Todd Field
Judy Brooks .... Marin Hinkle
Tiffany Porter .... Ever Carradine
Jennifer (1999–2000) .... Kimberly McCullough
Carla (2000–2001) .... Audrey Anderson
Samuel Blue (2001–2002) .... Steven Weber
Katie Singer (2001–2002) .... Mischa Barton

This intense, emotional drama from the producers of *thirtysomething* explored the relationship between a divorced father and a soon-to-be divorced mother as they fell in love, combined their families and struggled against massive odds to begin a new life. Rick was a handsome and successful Chicago architect whose resentful ex-wife, Karen, blamed the divorce—and practically every other problem in the world—on him. Lily worked at an on-line company and was in the process of ending her own marriage to selfish restaurateur Jake, who likewise seemed to blame everything on her. With their similar situations Rick and Lily found a lot of comfort with each other, and soon fell in love. This did not sit well with either their exes or their kids. Rick's were Eli, a teen hunk afflicted with a learning disability, and younger Jessie. Lily's were insecure Grace, who had major self-esteem problems ("I'm not pretty Mom!"), and little Zoe, who more than anything wanted her parents back together. David was Rick's partner and Judy was Lily's sister, who ran a bookstore. Tiffany was Jake's new girlfriend.

The characters were carefully drawn, but the grief they faced over the next three years was almost unbearable. In the first season Lily worked through her rocky divorce proceedings with Jake. In the second season Rick was almost ruined when the Atlantor project, on which he was working for ruthless developer Miles Drentell (David Clennon)—yes, *that* Miles Drentell, from *thirtysomething*—collapsed in a sea of lawsuits and criminal investigations. Surprisingly, it was Rick's angry ex, Karen, who got him off the hook. Rick and Lily were finally married in May 2001. Carla was Eli's troubled friend, who eventually left town. As the third season opened the two families moved in together in Lily's house, causing even more strife. New characters included Samuel, Rick's coworker and Judy's boyfriend, and Katie, who was Jessie's girlfriend. Tiffany had Jake's baby, but Karen was struck by a car and endured a slow and painful recovery. Lily had to deal with her mentally challenged brother Aaron, as well as her mother's slow descent into Alzheimer's. In the series finale Rick was offered a big architectural job in Australia and alienated Lily by simply assuming she'd go with him; Lily's radio talk show was picked up for national syndication, and she learned she was pregnant; Karen fell in love with her physical therapist, a soft-spoken black man named Henry; and Tiffany and Jake were married.

Throughout the series the characters addressed the camera directly about their feelings in short black-and-white "confessionals." As if that navel-staring was not enough, they also got counseling from time to time from Dr. Edward Rosenfeld, played by series co-creator Edward Zwick. In the finale the actors stepped out of character and addressed the audience about the series itself, and how much it had meant to them.

ONCE UPON A FENCE (*Children's*)
FIRST TELECAST: *April 13, 1952*
LAST TELECAST: *July 20, 1952*
BROADCAST HISTORY:
Apr 1952–Jul 1952, NBC Sun 6:30–7:00
REGULARS:
Dave Kaigler
Katherine Heger

Music, stories, and magical adventures were all part of this live children's show that originated from Philadelphia during the summer of 1952. The show starred Dave Kaigler, a singer and guitar player who was aided by Eric the Bluebird, an imaginary pet, and Princess Katherine of Storyland, played by Katherine Heger. Miss Heger was a dancer and actress who told stories to the children by acting out all the parts.

ONCE UPON A TUNE (*Musical Anthology*)
FIRST TELECAST: *March 6, 1951*
LAST TELECAST: *May 15, 1951*
BROADCAST HISTORY:
Mar 1951–May 1951, DUM Tue 10:00–11:00
REGULARS:
Phil Hanna
Holly Harris
Reginald Beane
Bernice Parks
Ed Holmes

This bright, though somewhat amateurish, program presented a complete musical every week, usually a takeoff on a current Broadway show or a famous story (for instance, "Little Red Riding Hood"). Various young performers were seen, in addition to the regulars listed above. The program was previously seen locally in New York.

ONE BIG FAMILY (*Situation Comedy*)

BROADCAST HISTORY:

Syndicated only
30 minutes
Produced: *1986–1987* (22 episodes)
Released: *September 1986*

CAST:

Jake Hatton........................ Danny Thomas
Don Hatton .... Anthony Starke
Jan Hatton........................ Kim Gillingham
Marianne Hatton (age 19)....... Anastasia Fielding
Brian Hatton (17)................ Michael DeLuise
Kate Hatton (14).................. Alison McMillan
Roger Hatton (8) .... Gabriel Damon

This multigeneration family comedy brought Danny Thomas back to series TV—but not for long. Jake was a semiretired nightclub comedian (do they ever really retire?) who moved to Seattle to help out when his son and daughter-in-law were killed in an auto accident. Did we say help out? The five orphaned children ranged in age from eight to adult, and already had surrogate parents in eldest son Don, a policeman, and his new bride Jan. Though grandfather Jake was a peacemaker at times, he also sparked many an uproar, was generally cranky, and was not above running off for an occasional liaison with a mature lady friend.

ONE DAY AT A TIME (*Situation Comedy*)

FIRST TELECAST: *December 16, 1975*
LAST TELECAST: *September 2, 1984*

BROADCAST HISTORY:

Dec 1975–Jul 1976, CBS Tue 9:30–10:00
Sep 1976–Jan 1978, CBS Tue 9:30–10:00
Jan 1978–Jan 1979, CBS Mon 9:30–10:00
Jan 1979–Mar 1979, CBS Wed 9:00–9:30
Mar 1979–Sep 1982, CBS Sun 8:30–9:00
Sep 1982–Mar 1983, CBS Sun 9:30–10:00
Mar 1983–May 1983, CBS Mon 9:30–10:00
Jun 1983–Feb 1984, CBS Sun 8:30–9:00
Mar 1984–May 1984, CBS Wed 8:00–8:30
May 1984–Aug 1984, CBS Mon 9:00–9:30
Aug 1984–Sep 1984, CBS Sun 8:00–8:30

CAST:

Ann Romano Royer............... Bonnie Franklin
Julie Cooper Horvath (1975–1980, 1981–1983)
.... Mackenzie Phillips
Barbara Cooper Royer............ Valerie Bertinelli
Dwayne Schneider.............. Pat Harrington, Jr.
David Kane (1975–1976) .... Richard Masur
Ginny Wrobliki (1976–1977) .. Mary Louise Wilson
Mr. Jerry Davenport (1976–1979) ... Charles Siebert
Max Horvath (1979–1980, 1981–1984)
.... Michael Lembeck
Grandma Katherine Romano (1979–1984)
.... Nanette Fabray
Nick Handris (1980–1981)............. Ron Rifkin
Alex Handris (1980–1983)......... Glenn Scarpelli
Francine Webster (1981–1984)..... Shelley Fabares
Mark Royer (1981–1984).............. Boyd Gaines
Sam Royer (1982–1984)........ Howard Hesseman
Annie Horvath (1983–1984) Lauren/Paige Maloney

After 17 years of marriage, Ann Romano found herself divorced and living with her two teenage daughters in an apartment building in her hometown of Indianapolis. The problems of trying to keep a job and be an understanding mother to two headstrong girls provided the plots for most episodes of this series. Ann resumed use of her maiden name while both 17-year-old Julie and 15-year-old Barbara kept their father's. The building's super, who regarded himself as the Rudolph Valentino of Indianapolis, was Dwayne Schneider. His first name was virtually never used—all the tenants referred to him only as Schneider. David Kane was Ann's romantic interest during the first season, and at one point they did almost get married, but he departed early in the fall of 1976. Not long after his departure, Ann acquired an outspoken, brassy new neighbor in Ginny Wrobliki, but she only lasted one season in the cast. It was during that season, however, that Ann found herself a substantial job working as an account executive for the advertising agency of Connors and Davenport. Although not a regular in the series, Joseph Campanella made occasional appearances as Ann's ex-husband, Ed Cooper.

In 1979, while still in college, Julie married Max Horvath, an airline flight steward. No sooner did they get married than he got laid off from his job, forcing the newlyweds to move in temporarily with Ann and Barbara. Max did get back to work and, when he got promoted to a new position in Houston, he and Julie moved away from Indianapolis (series star Mackenzie Phillips had developed a serious drug problem during the 1979–1980 season and was written out of the show to allow her to rehabilitate herself). When Ann left the advertising agency in the fall of 1980 she started a new professional, and eventually personal, involvement with Nick Handris. They became partners doing free-lance advertising—Ann writing copy and Nick doing the art work—and despite initial hostility, romance did bloom. Nick was divorced with a young son, Alex. Ann's mother, Katherine, also became a frequent visitor to the Romano household, especially after her husband died and she moved to Indianapolis to be close to her daughter.

As the 1981–1982 season began, Ann was getting over the shock of Nick's tragic death in an auto accident. Since Nick's ex-wife, Felicia (guest star Elinor Donahue), had moved to Chicago and remarried, Ann was talked into letting Alex move in with her and Barbara until things settled down. Francine Webster, Ann's old nemesis from the days at Connors and Davenport, turned up and convinced her to go into a partnership similar to the one she had had with Nick. Julie and Max also returned to Indianapolis, where he got a job as a travel agent while trying to make extra money as a writer. Barbara and her new boyfriend, dental student Mark Royer, got married in the fall of 1982 and, soon thereafter, Julie gave birth to a daughter, Annie. The following spring, in an effort to economize, Barbara and Julie and their families decided to share a house.

Then, following a courtship that had begun several months earlier, Ann married Mark's divorced father, architect Sam Royer. With Alex moving to Chicago to be with his mother, and her daughters sharing their own house, Ann had no children at home for the first time in years. The only thing to mar her happiness was the sudden disappearance of Julie, who walked out of her home, leaving Max, Barbara, and Mark, now a practicing dentist, to care for little Annie. (Mackenzie Phillips, suffering severe weight loss and other physical problems, was written out of the show for the second time.)

Knowing that stars Bonnie Franklin and Valerie Bertinelli planned to leave the series at the end of the 1983–1984 season, the producers of *One Day at a Time* ended the show's run with a couple of dramatic changes. Ann, having received a fantastic job offer in London, moved overseas with her husband, Sam, and Schneider moved to Florida to raise his orphaned niece and nephew following the unexpected death of his brother.

Reruns of *One Day at a Time* were seen on the CBS daytime lineup from September 1979 to September 1982.

ONE HAPPY FAMILY (*Situation Comedy*)
FIRST TELECAST: *January 13, 1961*
LAST TELECAST: *September 8, 1961*
BROADCAST HISTORY:
Jan 1961–Mar 1961, NBC Fri 8:00–8:30
May 1961–Sep 1961, NBC Fri 8:00–8:30
CAST:
Dick Cooper .... Dick Sargent
Penny Cooper .... Jody Warner
Barney Hogan .... Chick Chandler
Mildred Hogan .... Elisabeth Fraser
Charlie Hackett .... Jack Kirkwood
Lovey Hackett .... Cheerio Meredith

Newlyweds Dick and Penny Cooper moved in with Penny's family for a night and somehow ended up as permanent residents. Also part of the household were Penny's grandparents, the Hacketts. Dick was a meteorologist whose good nature was often strained by the efforts of his assembled in-laws to be "helpful," despite their protestations that they would let the young couple lead their own lives. Penny's father, Barney Hogan, was a successful plumbing contractor with an extremely energetic wife, Mildred. Grandfather Charlie Hackett was a strong-willed old coot with a nutty, fun-loving wife named Lovey. The conflicts between the three generations making up *One Happy Family* generated most of the humor in this series.

100 CENTRE STREET (*Legal Drama*)
BROADCAST HISTORY:
Arts & Entertainment Network
60 minutes
Original episodes: *2001–2002* (31 episodes)
Premiered: *January 15, 2001*
CAST:
Judge Joe Rifkind .... Alan Arkin
Sarah Rifkind .... Phyllis Newman
Judge Attallah "Queenie" Sims
.... LaTanya Richardson
Asst. D.A. Cynthia Bennington .... Paula Devicq
Asst. D.A. Bobby Esposito .... Joseph Lyle Taylor
Asst. D.A. Jeremiah "J. J." Jellinek Bobby Cannavale
Ramon Rodriguez .... Manny Perez
Fatima Kelly .... Michole White
Michelle Grande .... Margo Martindale
Charlie the Bridgeman .... Chuck Cooper
Peter Davies .... Joel de la Fuente

The moral dilemmas as well as the intense politics of the criminal justice system were explored in this dark drama from acclaimed director Sidney Lumet, set in Manhattan's Centre Street courthouse. Judges Rifkind and Sims represented polar ends of the spectrum, Rifkind a bleeding-heart liberal known around the courthouse as "Let-'em-go Joe," Sims being such a hard-liner that she was nicknamed "Attallah the Hun." Nevertheless they were best friends. Idealistic, young A.D.A.'s Cynthia and Bobby were opposites as well. She came from a wealthy family that couldn't understand why she was slumming in the criminal courts prosecuting drug dealers and other scum, while he was from a Brooklyn mob family that seemed mostly interested in exploiting his insider status. Of course they were in love. Ramon was a skirt-chasing Legal Aid lawyer; Michelle, the A.D.A. supervisor; and Sarah, Joe's long-suffering wife.

Turmoil engulfed them all. Judge Joe was hounded throughout the first season by press and politicians for freeing a scumbag offender who promptly went out and shot a cop; Attallah was nearly forced off the bench herself, until she ran for mayor and cut a deal with the politicians; Bobby was forced out of the D.A.'s office and lost his law license after his family pressured him to alter the arrest record of his no-good drug-addict brother. He then set up a nonprofit Legal Aid business with Cynthia, serving as its investigator. New A.D.A. J. J. was ambitious and ruthless, but fell for Legal Aid lawyer Fatima, a closet addict. Then Joe's angry daughter (by a previous marriage) Rebecca turned up, causing uproar in the Rifkinds' tony uptown apartment.

100 DEEDS FOR EDDIE MCDOWD (*Situation Comedy*)
BROADCAST HISTORY:
Nickelodeon
30 minutes
Original episodes: *1999–2002* (40 episodes)
Premiered: *October 16, 1999*
CAST:
Justin Taylor (age 12) .... Brandon Gilberstadt
Eddie McDowd (voice) (1999–2000) .... Seth Green
Eddie McDowd (voice) (2001–2002) .. Jason Hervey
Gwen Taylor (15) (1999–2001) ...... Morgan Kibby
Doug Taylor .... William Francis McGuire
Lisa Taylor .... Catherine MacNeal
The Drifter .... Richard Moll
Sariffa Chung .... Brenda Song
Tori Sloan (2001–2002) .... Melanee Murray
Flaco .... Josh Hammond
Spike Cipriano .... Danny Tamberelli
Sally (voice) .... Joe Piscopo
Caesar (voice) .... David L. Lander
THEME:
"You Got Me," by The Hippos (1999–2000); "Who Let the Dogs Out," by Baha Men (2000–2002)

A school bully got an unusual comeuppance in this sitcom. Smug 17-year-old Eddie McDowd (played in the pilot by Jason Dohring) had just finished terrorizing his latest victim, new kid Justin, by running him up a flagpole when he met a mysterious Drifter who turned him into a dog. The only way he could get back to boyhood, he was told, was by completing good deeds. Worse yet, his family and buddies had lost all memory that he ever existed, and the only person who could hear him now was Justin! At first Justin wasn't much interested in helping Eddie escape his sentence, and Eddie wasn't even sure he could bring himself to do that much good, but Justin was a sweet kid and eventually they bonded, despite Eddie's continuing mean streak. Gwen was Justin's self-absorbed older sister; Doug, his mailman dad; and Lisa, his overachieving mom, an advertising executive. Sariffa was a very smart new kid in school who befriended Justin. Midway through the series' run, Gwen went to England on an exchange program and the Taylors took in her English counterpart Tori, who became Justin's new foil. Sally and Caesar were neighborhood dogs with whom Eddie commiserated. Unfortunately, the series was canceled after 40 episodes and only 72 deeds, so he is presumably still out there somewhere barking.

Eddie (the dog) was played by a mixed-breed Australian shepherd/Siberian husky named Rowdy.

100 GRAND (*Quiz/Audience Participation*)

FIRST TELECAST: *September 15, 1963*

LAST TELECAST: *September 29, 1963*

BROADCAST HISTORY:

Sep 1963, ABC Sun 10:00–10:30

EMCEE:

Jack Clark

Promoted by ABC as the return of the "big-money" quiz show (none had been aired since the 1958 quiz show scandals), this program offered contestants the chance to win up to $100,000. Each contestant challenged a panel of five professional authorities in his particular field of knowledge and, if successful, was to contend with five questions submitted by viewers to the show. The concept didn't work very well and the ratings were so low that the show was canceled after only three weeks on the air.

100 LIVES OF BLACK JACK SAVAGE, THE, see *Disney Presents the 100 Lives of Black Jack Savage*

$128,000 QUESTION, THE (*Quiz*)

BROADCAST HISTORY:

Syndicated only
30 minutes
Produced: *1976–1978* (81 episodes)
Released: *September 1976*

HOST:

Mike Darrow (1976–1977)
Alex Trebek (1977–1978)

This was a rather limp revival of the quiz-show sensation of the 1950s, *The $64,000 Question.* Besides adjusting the top prize upward for inflation, there was a new host (Hal March having passed away) and questions and answers were fed from a distant point—to lessen the chance of collusion. Otherwise the format was more or less unchanged, with contestants tackling difficult questions in a category of their choosing over a period of weeks, for continuously doubling amounts ($2,000, $4,000, $8,000, etc.). What was lacking was both novelty and suspense. The original had gone on live each week, and anything could happen right there in front of the whole country. The revival was pretaped weeks in advance and shipped around the country for different stations to play at different times.

ONE IN A MILLION (*Situation Comedy*)

FIRST TELECAST: *January 8, 1980*

LAST TELECAST: *June 23, 1980*

BROADCAST HISTORY:

Jan 1980, ABC Tue 8:30–9:00
Jan 1980–Mar 1980, ABC Sat 8:00–8:30
Jun 1980, ABC Mon 8:00–8:30

CAST:

Shirley Simmons .... Shirley Hemphill
Barton Stone .... Richard Paul
Mr. Cushing .... Keene Curtis
Max Kellerman .... Carl Ballantine
Nancy Boyer .... Dorothy Fielding
Duke .... Ralph Wilcox
Edna .... Ann Weldon
Raymond .... Mel Stewart
Dennis .... Billy Wallace

Shirley Hemphill, who played the overpowering black waitress on *What's Happening,* got her own comedy series in 1980. In *One in a Million* down-to-earth cabdriver Shirley Simmons happened to inherit Grayson Enterprises, a multi-million-dollar, white-run conglomerate, when one of her customers died. Bald, scowling Mr. Cushing found this quite inexplicable, as he had planned to take over himself, and he was doubly vexed when scrappy Shirley decided to teach the big "en-dustrialists" how to look out for the ordinary people. Barton Stone was the somewhat naive nephew of the late Mr. Grayson; Nancy, Grayson's secretary and Shirley's ally; Max, the owner of a deli where Shirley hung out; and Edna and Raymond, her parents.

ONE MAN'S FAMILY (*Serial Drama*)

FIRST TELECAST: *November 4, 1949*

LAST TELECAST: *June 21, 1952*

BROADCAST HISTORY:

Nov 1949–Jan 1950, NBC Fri 8:00–8:30
Jan 1950–May 1950, NBC Thu 8:30–9:00
Jul 1950–Jun 1952, NBC Sat 7:30–8:00 (OS)

CAST:

Henry Barbour .... Bert Lytell
Fanny Barbour .... Marjorie Gateson
Paul Barbour .... Russell Thorson
Hazel Barbour/Herbert .... Lillian Schaaf
Claudia Barbour (1949–1950) ...... Nancy Franklin
Claudia Barbour/Roberts (1950–1952)
.... Eva Marie Saint
Cliff Barbour (1949) .... Frank Thomas, Jr.
Cliff Barbour (1949) .... Billy Idelson
Cliff Barbour (1949–1952) .... James Lee
Jack Barbour (1949–1950) .... Arthur Cassell
Jack Barbour (1951–1952) ...... Richard Wigginton
Judge Hunter (1949) .... Calvin Thomas
Dr. Thompson (1949–1950) .... Luis Van Rooten
Johnny Roberts (1949–1951) ...... Michael Higgins
Beth Holly (1949–1950) ... Mercedes McCambridge
Beth Holly (1950–1952) .... Susan Shaw
Mrs. Roberts (1950–1951) .... Mona Bruns
Mr. Roberts (1950–1952) .... Ralph Locke
Betty Carter (1950) .... Norma Jean Marlowe
Judith Richardson (1950) .... Athena Lorde
Danny Frank (1950) .... John Newland
Mac (1950–1952) .... Tony Randall
Joe Yarbourogh (1950–1952) .... Jim Boles
Bill Herbert (1950) .... Les Tremayne
Bill Herbert (1950–1952) .... Walter Brooke
Teddy Lawton (1951–1952) ...... Madeline Belgard
Ann Waite (1951–1952) .... Nancy Franklin

Burton (1951–1952) .... Billy Greene
Capt. Nicholas Lacey (1952) .... Lloyd Bochner
Sgt. Tony Adams (1952) .... Michael McAloney
Sir Guy Vane (1952) .... Maurice Manson
Jo Collier (1952) .... Gina Holland

CREATOR/WRITER:
Carleton E. Morse

THEME:
"Deserted Mansion"

Television version of the favorite radio serial, which began in 1932. None of the radio cast initially carried over into the TV version, but the story remained essentially the same. It was the saga of San Francisco banker Henry Barbour and his clan, set at the Barbours' suburban home in Sea Cliff, overlooking the Golden Gate Bridge. Paul, the eldest son, was the philosophical member of the family, serving as confidant for the other children and the person they turned to when in trouble (which was often). He was single and a pilot by profession (he had been wounded in World War II). Hazel, the eldest daughter, was 28 when the TV series began and rather anxious to find a husband—which she finally did, in Bill Herbert. Claudia and Cliff were the twins, students at Stanford University, and somewhat rebellious against their father's old-fashioned ways. Jack was the youngest child, aged 10, mischievous and loved by all.

Among the central plot developments during the program's three-year run in prime time were the stormy marriages of Hazel and Claudia, Paul's adopting the orphan Teddy Lawson, Claudia's adventures in Paris where she met the sinister Sir Guy Vane, and assorted illnesses, family feuds, and intrigues. Longtime fans of the radio *One Man's Family* must have had the strange feeling that they were going back in time when watching the TV version—for the action was a full generation behind the continuing radio serial. Ten-year-old Jack was 32 years old on radio, and had six children; the college-age twins were 37 on radio, each having been through two marriages and endless traumas; Paul had been a pilot in World War I on radio—and so on.

The TV version was also seen as a daytime serial from 1954–1955. The program continued on radio until 1959.

ONE MINUTE PLEASE (*Quiz/Panel*)

FIRST TELECAST: *July 6, 1954*
LAST TELECAST: *February 17, 1955*
BROADCAST HISTORY:
Jul 1954–Oct 1954, DUM Tue 8:30–9:00
Oct 1954, DUM Tue 9:00–9:30
Nov 1954–Jan 1955, DUM Fri 9:30–10:00
Jan 1955–Feb 1955, DUM Thu 9:30–10:00

MODERATOR:
John K. M. McCaffery (1954)
Allyn Edwards

REGULAR PANELISTS:
Hermione Gingold
Alice Pearce
Cleveland Amory
Ernie Kovacs
Marc Connelly

The object of *One Minute Please* was to see how well the panelists could do at talking nonstop for a full minute on subjects of which they had little knowledge. Such topics as "How to Make Glue," "Breeding Guppies," "Whale Blubber," and "Why I Ride Sidesaddle" were representative of the nonsense talked about. The panelist who managed to say the most in one minute was the winner for the week. Effective November 19, 1954, Allyn Edwards replaced John K. M. McCaffery as permanent moderator.

ONE OF THE BOYS (*Situation Comedy*)

FIRST TELECAST: *January 23, 1982*
LAST TELECAST: *August 20, 1982*
BROADCAST HISTORY:
Jan 1982–Apr 1982, NBC Sat 8:00–8:30
Apr 1982–Jun 1982, NBC Sat 8:30–9:00
Aug 1982, NBC Fri 8:00–8:30

CAST:
Oliver Nugent .... Mickey Rooney
Adam Shields .... Dana Carvey
Jonathan Burns .... Nathan Lane
Mrs. Green .... Francine Beers
Bernard Solomon .... Scatman Crothers
Jane .... Meg Ryan

There was no generation gap here. Sixty-six-year-old Oliver Nugent was retired, energetic, and full of fun. His grandson, Adam, a student at Sheffield College in New Jersey, decided that Gramps was too young at heart to be cooped up at the nearby Bayview Acres retirement home, so he invited Oliver to move in with him and his roommate, Jonathan. He didn't have to ask twice. Coeds thought the old guy was cute, while Mrs. Green, the divorcée who owned their apartment building, found Oliver both attractive and eligible. Oliver's closest friend was Bernard, a retired entertainer with whom he performed occasionally at the local soda shop to entertain the kids. Adam's girlfriend Jane was one of Oliver's biggest fans.

ONE OF THE BOYS (*Situation Comedy*)

FIRST TELECAST: *April 15, 1989*
LAST TELECAST: *May 20, 1989*
BROADCAST HISTORY:
Apr 1989, NBC Sat 9:30–10:00
Apr 1989, NBC Sat 8:00–8:30
May 1989, NBC Sat 8:30–9:00

CAST:
Maria Conchita Navarro ... Maria Conchita Alonso
Mike Lukowski .... Robert Clohessy
Luke Lukowski .... Michael DeLuise
Steve Lukowski .... Billy Morrissette
Nick Lukowski .... Justin Whalin
Bernice DeSalvo .... Amy Aquino
Ernie .... Dan Hedaya

A lightweight comedy about a spunky woman in a man's world. Maria, tired of being pinched on her waitress job, decided to switch careers and take another shot at the American dream. Landing the job of bookkeeper for the small, family owned Lukowski Construction Co., she discovered that owner and single-dad Mike needed as much help in his personal as in his professional life. The opinionated, motorcycle-riding Venezuelan hit it off immediately with "the boys." By the third episode she and Mike were dating, and in the fifth they were married, but it didn't save the series.

Mike's three boys were beefy Luke, who worked with him on the job, and teenagers Steve and Nick, who were in school. Ernie was the foreman, and Bernice was Maria's best friend, a gum-snapping waitress.

ONE ON ONE (*Interview*)
FIRST TELECAST: *April 25, 1983*
LAST TELECAST: *July 29, 1983*
BROADCAST HISTORY:
Apr 1983–Jul 1983, ABC Mon–Fri 12:30–1:00 A.M.
HOST:
Greg Jackson

Following the demise of his late-night series *The Last Word*, Greg Jackson briefly hosted this half-hour series in which he interviewed current newsmakers. Only the guest was seen, with Jackson asking the questions from offscreen.

ONE ON ONE (*Situation Comedy*)
FIRST TELECAST: *September 3, 2001*
LAST TELECAST:
BROADCAST HISTORY:
Sep 2001– , UPN Mon 8:30–9:00
Aug 2002, UPN Mon 9:30–10:00
CAST:
Mark "Flex" Washington .... Flex Alexander
Breanna Barnes (age 14) .... Kyla Pratt
Duane O'Dell Knox .... Kelly Perine
Spirit Jones .... Sicily
Arnaz Ballard .... Robert Ri'Chard
**Nicole Barnes* .... Tichina Arnold
**Eunice Barnes* .... Joan Pringle
**Richard Barnes* .... Ron Canada
**Tonya (2001–2002)* .... Tamala Jones
**Stacy (2001–2002)* .... Holly Robinson Peete
Natalie Clark (2002–) .... Melissa De Sousa
**Josh McIntyre (2002–)* .... Josh Henderson
Malik (2002–) .... Omar Gooding
Candy (2002–) .... Shondrella Akesan
Walt (2002–) .... Rashaan Nall
*Occasional

Flex, a sportscaster for TV station WYNX in Baltimore, had been living the good life—junk food, strange hours and a lot of women—and then everything changed. When his ex-wife Nicole left Atlanta to study marine life in Nova Scotia, he became the custodial parent to their teenage daughter, Breanna. Flex was used to his bachelor life, and there had been few rules when she visited her dad. Now she chafed at the more restrictive environment he attempted to maintain as a responsible father. Since he was not always successful, Flex's parents, bossy Eunice and meek Richard, were concerned about the lack of control he had over Breanna. Duane, a fast-talking car salesman at Big Sal's Used Cars, was Flex's skirt-chasing buddy; Spirit was Breanna's confidante and best girlfriend, and Arnaz was a friend with ambitions to become a rap star. He was unaware that Breanna had a big crush on him. In November Flex's girlfriend Tonya broke up with him because he refused to commit, and the following spring—when he thought he was hitting it off with his boss, Stacy—he found out she was secretly dating Duane.

That fall Flex had a short-lived tryout with the NBA—he had once been a promising basketball star—but didn't make it as a 33-year-old rookie. When he returned to Baltimore he found out Nicole had decided to move back, too, to be close to Breanna. He went back to work at WYNX and Nicole moved in with them while she looked for a job and her own apartment. Since Arnaz, who now knew Breanna loved him, was involved with someone else, she dated Josh, who was white. Meanwhile, Flex went out with Breanna's art teacher, Natalie, and, despite his fear of commitment, got pretty serious. In February he took over his father's barbershop, initially causing some friction with Malik and Walt, two of the barbers with whom he had previously been very friendly. Duane, who had moved out of his mother's place and into an apartment across the hall from Flex, was dating Candy, the sharp-tongued manicurist at the barbershop.

Flex's real last name was Barnes, but he used Washington as his professional name.

ONE STEP BEYOND, syndicated title for *Alcoa Presents*

1, 2, 3 GO (*Educational Children's*)
FIRST TELECAST: *October 8, 1961*
LAST TELECAST: *May 27, 1962*
BROADCAST HISTORY:
Oct 1961–May 1962, NBC Sun 6:30–7:00
REGULARS:
Richard Thomas
Jack Lescoulie

Hosts of this educational program for children were 10-year-old Richard and his adult friend Jack, who traveled around the country learning about our society and the people who comprise it. Trips were taken to such diverse places as NASA headquarters in Houston, the Treasury Department in Washington, D.C., and an Eskimo village in Alaska. Although informative to viewers of all ages, the emphasis of the show was on professions, skills, and environments that would be of particular interest to young children. Young Richard later went on to fame as John-Boy on *The Waltons.*

ONE WEST WAIKIKI (*Police Drama*)
FIRST TELECAST: *August 4, 1994*
LAST TELECAST: *September 8, 1994*
BROADCAST HISTORY:
Aug 1994–Sep 1994, CBS Thu 8:00–9:00
(in first-run syndication from September 1995 to September 1996)
CAST:
Dr. Dawn "Holli" Holliday, M.E. .... Cheryl Ladd
Lt. Mack Wolfe .... Richard Burgi
Nui Shaw .... Elsie Sniffen
Capt. Dave Herzog .... Paul Gleason
Kimo .... Ogie Zulueta

Holli was a highly regarded Los Angeles forensics expert who, while attending a symposium in Hawaii, had helped solve the murder of a former boyfriend of hers. That had resulted in her taking a medical examiner's position with the Honolulu Police Department. Holli was forced to work with homicide detective Mack Wolfe, with whom she was constantly at odds. He was an impulsive, physical cop who had little use for the analytical side of police work. His refusal to do anything by the book drove Captain Herzog to distraction. He was constantly in trouble, both in his career and in his personal life. Although there was some sexual tension between Holli and Mack, their differences always seemed to get in the way of any budding romance.

Nui was Holli's assistant, a novice forensics examiner intent on making her mark in the field, and Kimo was Mack's eager young Polynesian helper.

Additional episodes of this series were filmed after the brief CBS run for sale in syndication, but it was not successful there either.

O'NEILLS, THE (*Drama*)
FIRST TELECAST: *September 6, 1949*
LAST TELECAST: *January 10, 1950*
BROADCAST HISTORY:
Sep 1949–Jan 1950, DUM Tue 9:00–9:30
CAST:
Peggy O'Neill .... Vera Allen
Janice O'Neill .... Janice Gilbert
Eddie O'Neill .... Michael Lawson
Uncle Bill .... Ian Martin
Mrs. Bailey .... Jane West
Morris Levy .... Ben Fishbein
Mrs. Levy .... Celia Budkin
The O'Neills was an attempt to re-create on television one of the most popular radio serials of the 1930s. Although the radio version had been off the air since 1943, TV brought back many of the characters, including dress designer Peggy O'Neill, who was struggling to raise two fatherless children, cantankerous Uncle Bill, nosy Mrs. Bailey, and the next-door neighbors, the Levys. Actresses Janice Gilbert and Jane West were veterans of the radio show, but their presence was not enough to save the video version of it, which folded after a few months.

ONLY IN HOLLYWOOD (*Magazine*)
BROADCAST HISTORY:
Syndicated only
30 minutes
Produced: *1992* (26 episodes)
Released: *September 1992*
HOST/NARRATOR:
Peter Jones
Each week series host Peter Jones showed viewers nonfamous people who worked in Hollywood. Among them were celebrity hairdressers, valets for fancy stars' cars, volunteers who cleaned stars on Hollywood's Walk of Fame, a shoemaker to the stars, tattoo artists, and tabloid photographers. Also included were tours of celebrity cemeteries and some of the odd buildings in Hollywood.

OOH LA LA (*Fashion*)
BROADCAST HISTORY:
Lifetime Network
30 minutes
Produced: *1994–1995*
Premiered: *September 10, 1994*
REGULARS:
Monika Deol
Laurie Pike
Veronica Webb
A lighthearted weekly look at the world of high fashion. Regular features included videos of the latest styles, brief moments with celebrities, comedians and their views on fashion, and "street fashions from real people."

OPEN ALL NIGHT (*Situation Comedy*)
FIRST TELECAST: *November 28, 1981*
LAST TELECAST: *March 5, 1982*
BROADCAST HISTORY:
Nov 1981–Jan 1982, ABC Sat 8:00–8:30
Feb 1982–Mar 1982, ABC Fri 8:30–9:00
CAST:
Gordon Feester .... George Dzundza
Gretchen Feester .... Susan Tyrrell
Terry Feester .... Sam Whipple
Robin .... Bubba Smith
Officer Steve .... Jay Tarses
Officer Edie .... Bever-Leigh Banfield
An all-night grocery store might not seem to be a natural setting for comedy, unless it's packed with loonies as this one was. Gordon Feester was the pudgy owner, a semi-failure at everything else he'd done and working on a repeat performance managing the local "364 Store" (closed Christmas). His wife Gretchen helped out, which is more than could be said for their addlebrained teenage son, Terry, who created havoc by just thinking about work. Robin was the towering, black night manager, and Officers Steve and Edie the local cops who were better at helping themselves to coffee and doughnuts than at catching shoplifters. Passing through was a parade of bumbling holdup men, scam artists, hostile midgets, and other assorted weirdos.

Whether in a fit of versatility or just to save money, the cocreator of this show, Jay Tarses, also produced and wrote episodes, coauthored the lyrics to the theme, and appeared on screen as Officer Steve. His creator partner, Tom Patchett, produced, wrote, and directed.

OPEN END, see *David Susskind Show, The*

OPEN HEARING (*Public Affairs*)
FIRST TELECAST: *February 1, 1954*
LAST TELECAST: *September 28, 1958*
BROADCAST HISTORY:
Feb 1954–Jul 1954, ABC Thu 9:00–9:30
Feb 1957–Mar 1957, ABC Sun 8:30–9:00
Nov 1957–Jan 1958, ABC Sun 9:00–9:30
Jan 1958–Mar 1958, ABC Sun 7:00–7:30
Jun 1958–Sep 1958, ABC Sun 9:30–10:00
HOST/MODERATOR:
John Daly (1954)
John Secondari (1957–1958)
The first ABC program called *Open Hearing* consisted of filmed documentaries and commentary on various topics of general interest, such as the Army-McCarthy controversy, corporate stockholders' meetings, and Alcoholics Anonymous. The 1957–1958 version was a live interview program in which public figures were either interviewed by ABC newsmen, or participated in debates on subjects of current interest. Among the non-politicians appearing were disc jockey Dick Clark, commenting on teenagers and rock 'n' roll, and academician Dr. Henry Kissinger on the state of the nation in 1958. In addition to the prime-time telecasts listed above, this latter version was frequently seen on Sunday afternoons, where it continued until 1960.

For an earlier series on CBS called *Open Hearing* see *The Facts We Face.*

OPEN HOUSE (*Situation Comedy*)
FIRST TELECAST: *August 27, 1989*
LAST TELECAST: *July 21, 1990*
BROADCAST HISTORY:
Aug 1989–May 1990, FOX Sun 9:30–10:00
Jun 1990, FOX Sat 9:00–9:30
Jul 1990, FOX Sat 9:30–10:00

CAST:

Linda Phillips .... Alison LaPlaca
Ted Nichols .... Philip Charles MacKenzie
Laura Kelly .... Mary Page Keller
Richard Phillips (1989) .... Chris Lemmon
Margo Van Meter .... Ellen DeGeneres
Scott Babylon .... Danny Gans
Roger McSwain .... Nick Tate
Dave Hayes .... Ray Buktenica

In this spin-off from *Duet*, aggressive yuppie Linda Phillips had the perfect job—selling expensive homes in greater Los Angeles to snobs like herself, for Juan Verde Real Estate. Working with her were Ted, who was her chief competition and almost as pushy and overbearing as she was; Scott, an agent who used his skill as an impressionist to help him sell; Linda's friend Laura, who had separated from her novelist husband and was working as an apprentice agent (she was much too nice to ever succeed); Margo, the marginally competent man-hungry receptionist with designs on her boss; and Roger, the demanding manager of the agency. Linda's husband, Richard, played piano at Jasper's, where she and her coworkers hung out after work, but he disappeared after their marriage floundered at mid-season. Also seen regularly was wealthy Dave Hayes, a client for whom Ted never seemed to find the right house.

Open House was perhaps unique as a spin-off in which the star and a supporting actor in the original series reversed roles—in *Duet*, Keller had been the star and LaPlaca the support.

OPENING NIGHT (*Dramatic Anthology*)
FIRST TELECAST: *June 14, 1958*
LAST TELECAST: *September 8, 1958*
BROADCAST HISTORY:
Jun 1958–Sep 1958, NBC Sat 9:00–9:30
HOSTESS:
Arlene Dahl

The filmed dramas presented on *Opening Night* were reruns of episodes of the ABC series *Ford Theatre*. Arlene Dahl introduced the plays, which aired on alternate Saturdays with *Club Oasis*.

OPERA CAMEOS (*Music*)
FIRST TELECAST: *January 10, 1954*
LAST TELECAST: *November 21, 1954*
BROADCAST HISTORY:
Jan 1954–Nov 1954, DUM Sun 7:30–8:00 (OS)
COMMENTATOR:
Giovanni Martinelli
CONDUCTOR:
Maestro Guiseppe Bamboschek (and others)

Grand opera has been a rare commodity on American television, but this program of excerpts from famous operas was a fixture on New York TV for many years beginning in 1950. For several months in 1954 (and perhaps for other short periods as well) it was also fed out on the DuMont network. The host, retired Metropolitan Opera star tenor Giovanni Martinelli, introduced the presentations, describing the plot and setting. A mixture of established and younger, lesser-known operatic talent was featured, including some who were billed as future superstars (whatever *did* happen to Gianni Iaia, "the next Caruso"?), some who later did have important careers (such as Beverly Sills), and some whose connection with grand opera was tenuous at best (such as movie vocalist Marni Nixon). Martinelli himself did not appear in the productions, which generally included standard repertoire such as *Tosca*, *Cavalleria Rusticana*, *Madame Butterfly*, *Carmen* and the like.

OPERA VS. JAZZ (*Music*)
FIRST TELECAST: *May 25, 1953*
LAST TELECAST: *September 21, 1953*
BROADCAST HISTORY:
May 1953–Sep 1953, ABC Mon 7:30–8:00
REGULARS:
Nancy Kenyon
ABC Piano Quartet

This was not really a competition, but simply a mixed presentation of popular tunes (not "jazz") and standard operatic arias, performed by a different pair of guests each week. Nancy Kenyon gave the musical introductions, and accompaniment was by the ABC Piano Quartet, four pianos on a revolving stage. Among those representing the popular field were Alan Dale, Don Cornell, Karen Chandler, and Jerry Vale; the operatic, Jan Peerce, Thomas Hayward, Robert Merrill, and Virginia MacWatters.

OPERATION: ENTERTAINMENT (*Variety*)
FIRST TELECAST: *January 5, 1968*
LAST TELECAST: *January 31, 1969*
BROADCAST HISTORY:
Jan 1968–Apr 1968, ABC Fri 8:30–9:30
Sep 1968–Jan 1969, ABC Fri 7:30–8:30
REGULARS:
The Operation Entertainment Girls
The Terry Gibbs Band
EXECUTIVE PRODUCER:
Chuck Barris

With a different guest host and new guest stars each week, this series of filmed variety shows traveled around the world to entertain U.S. military personnel at army, navy, and air force bases, much in the manner of the Bob Hope Christmas shows. Rich Little was host of the first telecast, from Camp Pendleton, California, and such stars as Tim Conway, Jimmy Dean, and Ed Ames appeared on subsequent telecasts.

OPERATION INFORMATION (*Instruction*)
FIRST TELECAST: *July 17, 1952*
LAST TELECAST: *September 18, 1952*
BROADCAST HISTORY:
Jul 1952–Sep 1952, DUM Thu 8:00–8:30

Korean War era informational program for veterans, designed to acquaint them with their benefit rights.

OPERATION NEPTUNE (*Science Fiction*)
FIRST TELECAST: *June 28, 1953*
LAST TELECAST: *August 16, 1953*
BROADCAST HISTORY:
Jun 1953–Aug 1953, NBC Sun 7:00–7:30
CAST:

Commander Bill Hollister .... Todd Griffin
Dink Saunders .... Richard Holland
Kebeda .... Harold Conklin
Mersennus .... Dehl Berti
Admiral Bigelow .... Rusty Lane
Thirza .... Margaret Stewart
Trychus .... Humphrey Davis

Operation Neptune was a live science-fiction series

with a strong children's orientation. After the disappearance of a number of ships, the navy concluded that certain evil forces were operating from under the seas to destroy the people living on the surface of Earth. Bill Hollister, who had the nickname "Captain Neptune" for his extensive undersea survey work, was called upon by the navy to track down the source of the trouble, which turned out to be the evil Kebeda and his henchman Mersennus. Helping Captain Neptune was his young assistant and protégé, Dink Saunders.

OPERATION PETTICOAT (*Situation Comedy*)

FIRST TELECAST: *September 17, 1977*

LAST TELECAST: *August 10, 1979*

BROADCAST HISTORY:

Sep 1977–May 1978, ABC Sat 8:30–9:00
May 1978–Jun 1978, ABC Thu 8:30–9:00
Jun 1978–Aug 1978, ABC Fri 8:30–9:00
Sep 1978–Oct 1978, ABC Mon 8:30–9:00
Jun 1979–Aug 1979, ABC Fri 8:00–8:30

CAST:

Lt. Cdr. Matthew Sherman (1977–1978) ... John Astin
Lt. Nick Holden (1977–1978) ..... Richard Gilliland
Major Edna Howard (1977–1978) ... Yvonne Wilder
Lt. Dolores Crandell .... Melinda Naud
Lt. Barbara Duran (1977–1978) .... Jamie Lee Curtis
Lt. Ruth Colfax (1977–1978) ...... Dorrie Thomson
Lt. Claire Reid (1977–1978) .... Bond Gideon
Yeoman Hunkle .... Richard Brestoff
Ensign Stovall (1977–1978) ... Christopher J. Brown
Seaman Dooley (1977–1978) .... Kraig Cassity
Ramon Gallardo (1977–1978) .... Jesse Dizon
Chief Herbert Molumphrey (1977–1978) .... Wayne Long
Pharmacist's Mate Williams (1977–1978) .... Richard Marion
Radioman Gossett (1977–1978) .... Michael Mazes
Chief Machinist's Mate Tostin (1977–1978) .... Jack Murdock
Seaman Horwich (1977–1978) .... Peter Schuck
Lt. Watson (1977–1978) .... Raymond Singer
Seaman Broom .... Jim Varney
Lt. Mike Bender (1978–1979) ... Randolph Mantooth
Lt. Comdr. Haller (1978–1979) .... Robert Hogan
Lt. Katherine O'Hara (1978–1979) ..... Jo Ann Pflug
Lt. Betty Wheeler (1978–1979) .... Hilary Thompson
Chief Engineer Dobritch (1978–1979) .... Warren Berlinger
Seaman Horner (1978–1979) .... Don Sparks
Doplos (1978–1979) .... Fred Kareman
Seaman Dixon (1978–1979) .... Scott McGinnis

This was a World War II comedy set in the Pacific. Lt. Cdr. Matthew Sherman was a navy career officer anxious to see action before the war was over. When he finally was assigned to command the submarine *Sea Tiger*, however, he arrived to find the craft sunk at dockside. No sooner did he get it patched up and half painted, with pink undercoating, than he had to put to sea quickly to avoid another air raid—hence the navy's first pink submarine. Compounding his problems on board were five army nurses, whom he had rescued, and a wheeler-dealer supply officer, Lt. Holden, who wanted to avoid combat as much as Sherman wanted to find it.

Operation Petticoat was as leaky in the ratings as it was at sea, and when it returned for a second season virtually the entire cast had been changed. Lt. Cdr. Haller was the new skipper, and Lt. Bender his wheeler-dealer executive officer. There were new nurses, led by Lt. O'Hara, new crew members, and also a new mission. The *Sea Tiger* was now assigned to patrol the Pacific for downed airmen and sailors. It didn't help. The series was canceled after only four episodes with the new crew. Repeats aired during the summer of 1979, along with the one new episode.

Based on the 1959 movie starring Cary Grant and Tony Curtis, whose daughter, Jamie Lee Curtis, played one of the nurses in this series during the 1977–1978 season.

OPERATION: RUNAWAY, see *Runaways, The*

OPERATION SUCCESS (*Information*)

FIRST TELECAST: *September 21, 1948*

LAST TELECAST: *June 23, 1949*

BROADCAST HISTORY:

Sep 1948–Oct 1948, DUM Tue 8:00–8:30
Jan 1949–Jun 1949, DUM Thu 8:00–8:30

HOST:

Bob Pfeiffer

Public-service program in which host Bob Pfeiffer and others interviewed disabled veterans, and then asked the audience to come forward with job offers. One-hundred-percent placement was claimed.

OPPOSITE SEX (*School Drama*)

FIRST TELECAST: *July 17, 2000*

LAST TELECAST: *August 21, 2000*

BROADCAST HISTORY:

Jul 2000–Aug 2000, FOX Mon 8:00–9:00

CAST:

Jed Perry .... Milo Ventimiglia
Phil Steffan .... Kyle Howard
Cary Baston .... Chris Evans
Miranda Mills .... Margot Finley
Stella .... Lindsey J. McKeon
Kate Jacobs .... Allison Mack
Rob Perry .... Chris L. McKenna
Will Perry .... Christopher Cousins
Mr. Oslo .... Chris Hogan
Beau .... Paul Fitzgerald
Ms. Maya Bradley .... Garcelle Beauvais

Jed, Phil, and Cary were 15-year-old sophomores at Evergreen Academy, an exclusive girls' prep school at which they were the first male students. Jed had just moved to Northern California with his widowed father, Will, and his older brother, Rob. He had been dumped by his girlfriend before he moved and had sworn off girls, which made his new all-girl surroundings awkward, at best. Phil, the geeky intellectual, just wanted to excel, while horny Cary, still a virgin, was in heaven. Artsy Miranda and cute Kate were both interested in Jed, though he really wasn't aware of it, while Stella, the junior class president, resented having boys in the school because they would destroy its "traditions." Jed occasionally saw Rob, at Stanford, to talk about the problems he was having adjusting. While in New York participating in a model U.N., Cary and Stella, who despised each other, almost had a passionate liaison. Also seen regularly were Mr. Oslo, the history teacher; Ms. Bradley, the sexy guidance counselor; and Beau, the custodian.

The series was abruptly pulled from the Fox schedule in mid-August, and the last two of the eight episodes produced aired only in Canada.

ORCHID AWARD, THE (*Musical Variety*)
FIRST TELECAST: *May 24, 1953*
LAST TELECAST: *January 24, 1954*
BROADCAST HISTORY:
May 1953–Jul 1953, ABC Sun 6:45–7:00
Jul 1953–Jan 1954, ABC Sun 9:15–9:30
EMCEE:
Bert Lytell (1953)
Ronald Reagan (1953–1954)
Donald Woods (1953–1954)
Paul Weston Orchestra

This musical variety show formed a half-hour block with Walter Winchell's news and gossip program. After Winchell had finished "throwing orchids" at leading entertainers in his commentary, *The Orchid Award* presented one with a real orchid and had him or her perform. Originally *The Orchid Award* presented a performer's biography in music, with Rosemary Clooney being the first guest. Later it became a straight (though short) variety show, with such guests as Rex Harrison, Teresa Brewer, Victor Borge, Lauritz Melchior, Eddie Fisher, and others. Bert Lytell was the original host, replaced in July by alternating hosts Ronald Reagan from Hollywood and Donald Woods from New York. Also known as *The Orchid Room.*

ORDINARY/EXTRAORDINARY (*Documentary*)
FIRST TELECAST: *August 1, 1997*
LAST TELECAST: *September 5, 1997*
BROADCAST HISTORY:
Aug 1997–Sep 1997, CBS Fri 8:00–9:00
HOSTS:
John Schneider
Leanza Cornett

This summer series showcased what CBS categorized as "amazing inspirational stories and astounding feats accomplished by ordinary people." Among the inspirational stories were those of a couple whose marriage was delayed seven years by an automobile accident that almost killed the bride and left her wheelchair-bound, a special summer camp for young victims of fires, a man who had become one of the fastest off-road truck drivers in the world despite being paralyzed from the chest down, and a brain surgeon who returned to the field of microsurgery less than three years after suffering severe brain damage himself in a car crash. On the extraordinary side were a 1,400-pound Kodiak bear taking acting lessons for movies, a 21-year-old man in Philadelphia living with a heart that remained outside his chest, a girl in Indiana who managed to roller skate underneath 22 cars with her body barely off the ground, and the world's greatest pool trick-shot artist.

OREGON TRAIL, THE (*Western*)
FIRST TELECAST: *September 21, 1977*
LAST TELECAST: *October 26, 1977*
BROADCAST HISTORY:
Sep 1977–Oct 1977, NBC Wed 9:00–10:00
CAST:
Evan Thorpe .... Rod Taylor
Margaret Devlin .... Darleen Carr
Luther Sprague .... Charles Napier
Andrew Thorpe .... Andrew Stevens
William Thorpe .... Tony Becker
Rachel Thorpe .... Gina Marie Smika

In 1842 widower Evan Thorpe decided to leave his native Illinois with his three children—Andy, age 17; William, age 12; and Rachel, age 10—in search of a new life in the Oregon Territory. He joined a wagon train heading west, was soon elected its captain when the original leader proved to be unreliable, and found a new romantic interest in fellow traveler Margaret Devlin. As the train moved west it was beset with all the traditional enemies—bad weather, unfriendly Indians, rough terrain, and dishonest con men. Luther Sprague was the hardened scout who had little tolerance for the citified travelers' lack of preparedness for the rigors of the trip.

ORIGINAL AMATEUR HOUR, THE (*Talent*)
FIRST TELECAST: *January 18, 1948*
LAST TELECAST: *September 26, 1960*
BROADCAST HISTORY:
Jan 1948–Sep 1949, DUM Sun 7:00–8:00
Oct 1949–Jan 1952, NBC Tue 10:00–11:00
Jan 1952–Sep 1952, NBC Tue 10:00–10:45
Apr 1953–Sep 1954, NBC Sat 8:30–9:00
Oct 1955–Dec 1955, ABC Sun 9:30–10:00
Jan 1956–Feb 1956, ABC Sun 9:30–10:30
Mar 1956–Sep 1956, ABC Sun 9:00–10:00
Oct 1956–Mar 1957, ABC Sun 7:30–8:30
Apr 1957–Jun 1957, ABC Sun 9:00–10:00
Jul 1957–Sep 1957, NBC Mon 10:00–10:30
Sep 1957–Dec 1957, NBC Sun 7:00–7:30
Feb 1958–Oct 1958, NBC Sat 10:00–10:30
May 1959–Jun 1959, CBS Fri 8:30–9:00
Jul 1959–Oct 1959, CBS Fri 10:30–11:00
Mar 1960–Sep 1960, ABC Mon 10:30–11:00
EMCEE:
Ted Mack
ANNOUNCER:
Dennis James

Ted Mack's durable talent show made the rounds of all four networks during its 22 sporadic years on television, including ten (1960–1970) on Sunday afternoons. It was first brought to television on the DuMont network in 1948, a year and a half after the original radio version had ended due to the death of Major Bowes, the founder and original host. It quickly became a Sunday night institution (the radio version was also revived, from 1948 to 1952). The *Amateur Hour* was DuMont's most popular program, and one of the few that was competitive with NBC and CBS—so it was soon stolen away by NBC, in 1949. (This was a pattern which was often repeated during the existence of the DuMont network—whenever a successful program was developed, one of the major networks lured it away with the promise of much more money.)

The format was taken directly from radio's *Major Bowes' Amateur Hour,* on which Mack had been an assistant. Mack, in fact, used the same booking staff and even the same Wheel of Fortune ("Round and round she goes, and where she stops, nobody knows"). He presided over the weekly parade of mimics, kazoo players, and one-man bands with genial good humor. Viewers voted for their favorites by telephone or postcard, and the finalists were awarded scholarships.

Although thousands of hopefuls appeared on the *Original Amateur Hour* over the years and hundreds were winners, surprisingly few ever went on to major or even minor stardom in show business. Probably the most famous "find" of radio days was Frank Sinatra, in 1937. On TV, seven-year-old Gladys Knight and 18-year-old college sophomore Pat Boone were among the grand prize winners. On August 10, 1954, the program celebrated its 1,001st broadcast with a lineup of all-time talent who had graduated from the show.

A familiar feature during the early TV days (1948–1952) was the dancing Old Gold cigarette pack and matchbook (with very shapely legs!) of sponsor P. Lorillard Tobacco Company. For a 1992 revival on cable's Family Channel, see *The New Original Amateur Hour.*

ORLEANS (*Legal Drama*)
FIRST TELECAST: *January 8, 1997*
LAST TELECAST: *April 11, 1997*
BROADCAST HISTORY:
Jan 1997, CBS Wed 10:00–11:00
Mar 1997–Apr 1997, CBS Fri 9:00–10:00
CAST:
Judge Luther Charbonnet .... Larry Hagman
Det. Clade Charbonnet .... Brett Cullen
Deputy D.A. Jesse Charbonnet
.... Michael Reily Burke
Paulette Charbonnet .... Colleen Flynn
Rene Doucette .... Lynette Walden
Rosalee Clark.............. Vanessa Bell Calloway
Gloria .... Lara Grice
D.A. Bill Brennecke................... Cotter Smith
Vincent Carraze................... Richard Fancy
Leon Gillenwater .... Jerry Hardin
Curtis Manzant .... O'Neal Compton
Frank Vitelli..................... Charles Durning
Gina Vitelli .... Melora Hardin

Luther Charbonnet was a respected New Orleans judge and the father of three successful but troubled children—Clade, a homicide detective on the N.O.P.D.; Jesse, an ambitious young Deputy D.A.; and Paulette, rebellious manager of the Lady Orleans riverboat casino. Clade and Jesse fought over how to deal with drug dealers and murderers, while the former tried to track down police corruption and the latter, recently returned to his hometown, tried to resolve his relationship with cousin Rene, with whom he had had an affair. Paulette was trying to hide her checkered past while watching many of the people she worked with carted off to jail. Others seen regularly were Rosalee, the young black defense attorney with whom Luther was having a clandestine affair; Gloria, his sexy legal secretary, who was the object of the affections of attorneys Gillenwater and Manzant; and mob boss Frank Vitelli.

Orleans was said to be inspired by the experiences of coexecutive producer Toni Graphia, who was the daughter of a prominent Louisiana judge.

OSBOURNES, THE (*Documentary*)
BROADCAST HISTORY:
MTV
30 minutes
Original episodes: *2002–*
Premiered: *March 5, 2002*
REGULARS:
Ozzy Osbourne
Sharon Osbourne
Kelly Osbourne (age 17)
Jack Osbourne (16)

The surprise sensation of the summer of 2002 was this witty look into the family life of one of rock music's legendary bad boys. It was too good to be true. Could it really be that the "Prince of Darkness" himself, the foulmouthed, heavily tattooed lead singer of '70s heavy-metal band Black Sabbath, known for such onstage antics as biting the heads off bats and offstage behavior like urinating on the Alamo, had become an addled dad with a wife and kids, trying to maintain order in a riotous household but unable to even operate his new wall-sized TV ("It's stuck on the Weather Channel")? While amiable Ozzy mumbled and cursed (every other word in this show seemed to be bleeped), sensible Sharon, his wife of 20 years, managed his life and career. Living with them were party girl Kelly, with her spiked Technicolor hair, and chubby Jack, who wore black-rimmed glasses and a camouflage helmet. (Eldest daughter Aimee, whom Sharon called "the normal one," declined to participate in the show.) They all rattled around their huge Beverly Hills mansion, where Sharon's menagerie of dogs and cats defecated on the carpets and Ozzy tried to figure out that [bleep!] remote.

OSMOND FAMILY SHOW, THE, see *Donny and Marie*

OTHER LANDS, OTHER PLACES (*Travelogue*)
FIRST TELECAST: *July 24, 1951*
LAST TELECAST: *May 17, 1953*
BROADCAST HISTORY:
Jul 1951–Sep 1951, ABC Tue 8:45–9:00
Nov 1951–Dec 1951, ABC Sun 9:00–9:30
Apr 1953–May 1953, ABC Sun 7:30–7:45

Documentary travel films. Also known as *Other Lands, Other People,* and also seen locally in New York at various times.

OTHERS, THE (*Horror/Supernatural*)
FIRST TELECAST: *February 5, 2000*
LAST TELECAST: *June 17, 2000*
BROADCAST HISTORY:
Feb 2000–May 2000, NBC Sat 9:00–10:00
May 2000–Jun 2000, NBC Sat 10:00–11:00
CAST:
Marian Kitt.................. Julianne Nicholson
Elmer Greentree .... Bill Cobbs
Mark Gabriel .... Gabriel Macht
Warren Day.................... Kevin J. O'Connor
Ellen "Satori" Pawlowski .... Melissa Crider
Prof. Miles Ballard .... John Billingsley
Albert McGonnagal .... John Aylward

Strange things were going on at the small New England college where Marian had enrolled. Startling visions of a young woman who had died in her dorm room drove her to go to a big old house off campus and meet with a group of eccentrics dubbed The Others—people who had extrasensory abilities to reach beyond this world and into other dimensions. Grizzled, 83-year-old Elmer was the founding father, a famous medium; Mark, a hunky resident at St. Joseph's Hospital who was an empath, able to detect people's feelings and even transfer life into them; Warren, a gaunt young psychic who yelled a lot; Satori, a New Age "sensitive" who used Tarot cards; Miles, a professor of folklore and mythology who was calm and businesslike, and Albert, a blind, grouchy old seer who had prophetic visions ("You'll die if you stay in that room!"). Together they helped people beset with ghosts and goblins. Fighting evil was no picnic, and some of their cases were quite dangerous, as when Marian was flung into eternity and Elmer had to reach down through swirling "other dimensions" to pull her back from death. Others were sweeter, as when the team helped a dead husband tell his wife where the money was hidden. The special effects were often gripping, as spooks jumped out of bathroom drains and faces appeared in the flames.

OTHERWORLD (*Science Fiction*)
FIRST TELECAST: *January 26, 1985*
LAST TELECAST: *March 16, 1985*
BROADCAST HISTORY:
Jan 1985–Mar 1985, CBS Sat 8:00–9:00
CAST:
Hal Sterling .... Sam Groom
June Sterling .... Gretchen Corbett
Trace Sterling .... Tony O'Dell
Gina Sterling .... Jonna Lee
Smith Sterling .... Brandon Crane
Kommander Nuveen Kroll .... Jonathan Banks

Hal and June Sterling were on a sightseeing trip with their three children—Trace (18), Gina (17), and Smith (11)—when their lives took a most bizarre twist. While touring the Great Pyramid of Cheops in Egypt they inadvertently passed through a portal to a strange parallel universe. The land in which they found themselves was full of radically different societies, each inhabiting its own area. There were, among others, a mining town run by human-appearing androids, a society in which families were against the law, and a pleasure resort that killed its guests to obtain from their bodies a substance that could give eternal youth to others. Each week the Sterlings found themselves in a new environment where they had to try to fit in, and keep their identities secret, as they searched for the capital city of Imar. There the Supreme Governors of Otherworld had the power to return them to their own world. Hot on their trail was the malevolent Kommander Kroll, whose mysterious "access crystal" they had stolen when they first stumbled into Otherworld.

OUR FAMILY HONOR (*Drama*)
FIRST TELECAST: *September 17, 1985*
LAST TELECAST: *January 3, 1986*
BROADCAST HISTORY:
Sep 1985–Oct 1985, ABC Tue 10:00–11:00
Nov 1985–Jan 1986, ABC Fri 10:00–11:00
CAST:
Commissioner Patrick McKay .... Kenneth McMillan
Vincent Danzig .... Eli Wallach
Det. Sgt. Frank McKay .... Tom Mason
Officer Liz McKay .... Daphne Ashbrook
Katherine McKay .... Georgann Johnson
Augie Danzig .... Michael Madsen
Marianne Danzig .... Barbara Stuart
Jerry Cole (Danzig) .... Michael Woods
Officer Ed Santini .... Ray Liotta
Rita Danzig .... Sheree J. Wilson
Jonas Jones .... Dick Anthony Williams
George Bennett .... Ron Karabatsos

One critic called it "a series you can't refuse," but viewers evidently felt otherwise about this soap opera about two families, one involved in organized crime and the other stalwarts of the New York City Police Department. The McKay clan was headed by Commissioner Patrick, whose hotheaded son, Frank, was a detective and niece, Liz, a recent graduate of the academy. Liz had been assigned to street patrol, where she was partnered with Off. Ed Santini. On the other side of the law were the Danzigs, headed by ruthless crime lord Vincent, whom Commissioner McKay had known since childhood. Augie was Vincent's inept but dangerous son and heir apparent, killing people to please his father. Among the worried wives were Katherine (Patrick's), Marianne (Vincent's), and Rita (Augie's).

Principal stories included Liz's star-crossed love affair with Jerry Cole, who proved to be Vincent's rebel son; the Danzigs' involvement in the death of a contractor whom Jerry tried to help; and Augie's death (in the last episode) in a struggle with Frank, who was trying to take him in for killing Rita's lover.

OUR HOUSE (*Drama*)
FIRST TELECAST: *September 11, 1986*
LAST TELECAST: *June 26, 1988*
BROADCAST HISTORY:
Sep 1986, NBC Thu 8:30–9:30
Sep 1986–May 1987, NBC Sun 7:00–8:00
May 1987–Jun 1987, NBC Sun 8:00–9:00
Jun 1987–Jun 1988, NBC Sun 7:00–8:00
CAST:
Gus Witherspoon .... Wilford Brimley
Jesse Witherspoon .... Deidre Hall
Kris Witherspoon (15) .... Shannen Doherty
David Witherspoon (12) .... Chad Allen
Molly Witherspoon (8) .... Keri Houlihan
Joe Kaplan .... Gerald S. O'Loughlin
Bertha .... Nicole Dubuc
**Crimshaw* .... Owen Bush
**Cliff* .... Bob Hoy
Mark (1987) .... Thomas Wilson Brown
J. R. Dutton (1987–1988) .... David Mendenhall

*Occasional

The Associated Press called this homey series "a family show suitable for framing." It was certainly warm and old-fashioned, a gentle story about getting along and growing up. Gus was a cantankerous 65-year-old grandpa with a walrus mustache who treasured his privacy living alone in his handsome, tree-shaded Victorian house. However, when his married son died, Gus was faced with the prospect of taking in his distraught widow Jesse—who had no funds—and her three rambunctious children. That was the end of serenity in Gus' house. It was now, as he told Jesse, "our house."

Jesse worked at various jobs, including that of freelance photographer. Granddaughter Kris had Gus' strong will, and aimed to become an air force test pilot someday; David was headstrong too, but unsure of himself at age 12; and Molly was just a sweet girl who wanted everyone to get along. Joe was Gus' long-time pal. Stories revolved around the compromises made by three generations living under one roof, and the lessons learned by all, including the grumpy, heart-of-gold granddad.

OUR MAN HIGGINS (*Situation Comedy*)
FIRST TELECAST: *October 3, 1962*
LAST TELECAST: *September 11, 1963*
BROADCAST HISTORY:
Oct 1962–Sep 1963, ABC Wed 9:30–10:00
CAST:
Higgins .... Stanley Holloway
Alice MacRoberts .... Audrey Totter
Duncan MacRoberts .... Frank Maxwell
Tommy MacRoberts .... Rickey Kelman
Dinghy MacRoberts .... K. C. Butts
Joanie MacRoberts .... Regina Groves

Stanley Holloway, the veteran British music-hall comic who achieved fame in America in the role of Eliza Doolittle's father in *My Fair Lady*, was the star of this comedy. He played Higgins, a gentleman butler from Scotland who found himself sent to America to serve a suburban couple, the MacRoberts. They had "inherited" him as part of an ancestral bequest. The couple and their three children, Tommy, Dinghy, and Joanie, were constantly being saved from various predicaments by the ever-resourceful Higgins.

OUR MISS BROOKS (*Situation Comedy*)
FIRST TELECAST: *October 3, 1952*
LAST TELECAST: *September 21, 1956*
BROADCAST HISTORY:
Oct 1952–Jun 1953, CBS Fri 9:30–10:00
Oct 1953–Jun 1955, CBS 9:30–10:00
Oct 1955–Sep 1956, CBS Fri 8:30–9:00
CAST:
Connie Brooks .... Eve Arden
Osgood Conklin .... Gale Gordon
Philip Boynton .... Robert Rockwell
Walter Denton (1952–1955) .... Richard Crenna
Mrs. Margaret Davis .... Jane Morgan
Harriet Conklin (1952–1955) ..... Gloria McMillan
Stretch Snodgrass (1952–1955) ..... Leonard Smith
Miss Daisy Enright (1952–1954) .... Mary Jane Croft
Mrs. Martha Conklin (1952–1953)
.... Virginia Gordon
Mrs. Martha Conklin (1953–1956)
.... Paula Winslowe
Superintendent Stone (1953–1955)
.... Joseph Kearns
Angela (1954–1956) .... Jesslyn Fax
Ricky Velasco (1954–1955) .... Ricky Vera
Mr. Oliver Munsey (1955–1956) ...... Bob Sweeney
Mrs. Nestor (1955) .... Nana Bryant
Mrs. Nestor (1955–1956) .... Isabel Randolph
Gene Talbot (1955–1956) .... Gene Barry
Clint Albright (1955–1956) .... William Ching
Benny Romero (1955–1956) .... Ricky Vera
Mr. Romero (1956) .... Hy Averback

Our Miss Brooks had originated on CBS radio in 1948, and was heard on both radio and TV throughout the mid-1950s with essentially the same cast. It was one of the period's most popular and loved comedies, and gave Eve Arden a role with which she will forever be identified. She played Connie Brooks, the wisecracking English teacher at Madison High. Her nemesis was crusty, blustery principal Osgood P. Conklin, who was constantly blowing his stack at her for something. Mr. Boynton, the handsome but incredibly shy biology teacher, was the potential husband she was always trying to snag—without success. Connie rented a room from kindly old Mrs. Davis and rode to school each morning with one of her students, the somewhat dimwitted Walter Denton. Her interaction with these varied regulars, played by an excellent supporting cast, comprised the stories. No one in *Our Miss Brooks* was an out-and-out lunatic, as is so often the case in TV comedies, but everyone had some pronounced but realistic idiosyncrasy that viewers could identify with, thus making the show's principals a perfect TV "family." Eve Arden herself was much in demand to speak to educational groups and at PTA meetings, and even received a dozen offers of positions as an English teacher at real high schools. They could hardly have afforded her, as she was by then making $200,000 per year!

By the start of the 1955–1956 season the ratings were beginning to slip and the setting was changed. Madison High was razed for a highway project and Miss Brooks found a new job at Mrs. Nestor's Private Elementary School nearby. For some reason, Mr. Conklin had acquired the job of principal there, and he and other cast members remained on the show to harass her. Connie's new love interest was the young physical education teacher, Gene Talbot, who was chasing her, quite a turnaround from Mr. Boynton's shy indifference. Somehow the revised format seemed to limp along and Mr. Boynton was brought back in the spring of 1956. His return did not help, however, and the show ended its run shortly thereafter.

Connie's long pursuit of Mr. Boynton did finally pay off, though not in the TV series. In a 1956 Warner Bros. movie based on the series, he finally proposed, and she became Mrs. Philip Boynton.

OUR NEIGHBORS TO THE NORTH (*Documentary*)
FIRST TELECAST: *June 15, 1952*
LAST TELECAST: *August 29, 1952*
BROADCAST HISTORY:
Jun 1952, ABC Sun 10:00–10:30
Aug 1952, ABC Fri 8:00–8:30

This was a series of film shorts about Canada, produced by the Canadian government.

OUR PLACE (*Musical Variety*)
FIRST TELECAST: *July 2, 1967*
LAST TELECAST: *September 3, 1967*
BROADCAST HISTORY:
Jul 1967–Sep 1967, CBS Sun 9:00–10:00
REGULARS:
The Doodletown Pipers
Jack Burns
Avery Schreiber
The George Wilkins Orchestra

Narrated by a huge puppet dog named Rowlf, one of Jim Henson's Muppets, this musical and comedy variety series was the 1967 summer replacement for *The Smothers Brothers Comedy Hour.* It featured the singing of the Doodletown Pipers and the comic antics of the team of Burns & Schreiber.

OUR PRIVATE WORLD (*Serial Drama*)
FIRST TELECAST: *May 5, 1965*
LAST TELECAST: *September 10, 1965*
BROADCAST HISTORY:
May 1965–Sep 1965, CBS Wed 9:30–10:00
May 1965–Sep 1965, CBS Fri 9:00–9:30

CAST:

Lisa Hughes .... Eileen Fulton
Helen Eldredge .... Geraldine Fitzgerald
John Eldredge .... Nicolas Coster
Eve Eldredge .... Julienne Marie
Tom Eldredge .... Sam Groom
Brad Robinson .... Robert Drivas
Dr. Tony Larson .... David O'Brien
Sandy Larson .... Sandy Smith
Franny Martin .... Pamela Murphy
Dick Robinson .... Ken Tobey
Pat .... Kathy Dunn

In the wake of ABC's great success with its prime-time soap opera *Peyton Place*, CBS decided to try its own version of the form during the summer of 1965. This series was a spin-off from the highly successful daytime serial *As the World Turns*, and focused on Lisa Hughes, one of *World*'s leading characters. Young divorcée Lisa decided to find a new life for herself by leaving her small hometown and moving to Chicago, where she found a job in the admitting room of a hospital. The two major plot lines involved her life and associations at the hospital and the machinations of the Eldredges, a socially prominent and extremely wealthy family living in the exclusive suburb of Lake Forest. The CBS experiment proved not to be very successful and the series was canceled at the end of the summer, leaving actress Eileen Fulton to her daytime role only.

OUR SECRET WEAPON—THE TRUTH (*Discussion*)

FIRST TELECAST: *February 6, 1951*
LAST TELECAST: *April 17, 1951*
BROADCAST HISTORY:

Feb 1951–Apr 1951, DUM Tue 7:30–8:00

PANELISTS:

Leo Cherne
Ralph de Toledano

This propaganda program had been presented on CBS radio during World War II as a forum for debunking Nazi claims against America. It was revived during the Korean War for use against a new enemy, with regulars Leo Cherne and Ralph de Toledano on hand each week to "answer Communist lies about us" with facts and testimony from special guests. Previously a local program in New York.

OUR TIME (*Variety*)

FIRST TELECAST: *July 27, 1985*
LAST TELECAST: *September 7, 1985*
BROADCAST HISTORY:

Jul 1985–Aug 1985, NBC Sat 8:00–8:30
Aug 1985, NBC Sat 8:30–9:00
Sep 1985, NBC Sat 9:30–10:00

REGULARS:

Karen Valentine
Tim Stack
Patti Lee
Zane Buzby
Phil Hartman
Denny Evans
Harry Anderson

Nostalgia for the 1960s was the theme of this lightweight summer series, hosted by actress Karen Valentine with a different cohost each week. Fads of the era were satirized in comedy sketches, and TV and music stars of the '60s paraded through the show, some as featured guests and others in cameos. Old film clips of guests in their TV series of the past were used in a regular "then and now" feature to show how they had aged. Among the "TV kids" of the '60s who received this treatment were Tim Considine, Don Grady, and Barry and Stanley Livingston (from *My Three Sons*), Dwayne Hickman and Sheila James (*The Many Loves of Dobie Gillis*), Jay North (*Dennis the Menace*), Jon Provost (*Lassie*), Ken Osmond and Frank Bank (*Leave It to Beaver*), Noreen Corcoran (*Bachelor Father*), Marc Copage (*Julia*), and Butch Patrick (*The Munsters*). Musical performers appearing included such moldy oldies as Frankie Avalon, The Coasters, Johnny Rivers, Leslie Gore, Mitch Ryder, and Paul Revere and the Raiders. Cohosts included Paul Petersen, Sonny Bono, and John Sebastian. No doubt they all appreciated the work.

OUR TIMES WITH BILL MOYERS (*Documentary*)

FIRST TELECAST: *June 26, 1983*
LAST TELECAST: *August 23, 1983*
BROADCAST HISTORY:

Jun 1983, CBS Sun 8:30–9:00
Jun 1983–Aug 1983, CBS Tue 8:30–9:00

HOST/CORRESPONDENT:

Bill Moyers

Each episode of this summer series featured CBS correspondent Bill Moyers talking with people about a social problem in modern-day America. Among them: residents of Gadsden, Alabama, discussed trying to get by in a community dependent on the depressed rubber and steel industries; a profile of Dina Rasor, who revealed information to the public about Pentagon waste and inefficiency; the search for a cure for A.I.D.S. (Acquired Immune Deficiency Syndrome); and the reflections of a number of people who heard Martin Luther King, Jr.'s "I Have a Dream" speech in Washington in 1963, about what the speech had meant to them.

OUR WORLD (*Documentary*)

FIRST TELECAST: *September 25, 1986*
LAST TELECAST: *September 3, 1987*
BROADCAST HISTORY:

Sep 1986–Jul 1987, ABC Thu 8:00–9:00
Jul 1987–Sep 1987, ABC Thu 9:00–10:00

HOSTS:

Linda Ellerbee
Ray Gandolf

ABC had a problem . . . how to compete against the red-hot *Cosby Show* and not lose a fortune in the process. The answer: raid the news division's vaults, string together old film footage from a specific period, and package it with some glitzy graphics and intelligent commentary. *Our World* was probably the cheapest hour on prime-time TV, yet it was the darling of critics (and a small but vociferous group of fans) who saw it as a worthwhile alternative to the escapist hits on NBC and CBS. In addition to news clips, the show featured first-hand "witness" commentary from people who were there, music, TV and radio entertainment of the era, and even some docudrama "re-creations" of famous events. Periods spotlighted ranged from October 1938 (approaching war in Europe, *The War of the Worlds* radio broadcast at home), to the summer of 1969 (Vietnam and the "Woodstock Generation"), and beyond.

OUT ALL NIGHT (*Situation Comedy*)

FIRST TELECAST: *September 19, 1992*

LAST TELECAST: *July 9, 1993*

BROADCAST HISTORY:

Sep 1992–Oct 1992, NBC Sat 8:30–9:00
Nov 1992–Jan 1993, NBC Thu 8:00–8:30
Feb 1993, NBC Fri 8:00–8:30
Jun 1993–Jul 1993, NBC Fri 8:30–9:00

CAST:

Chelsea Paige .... Patti LaBelle
Jeff Carswell .... Morris Chestnut
Vidal Thomas .... Duane Martin
Charisse Chamberlain .... Vivica A. Fox
Angus McEwen .... Simon O'Brien

Grammy winner Patti LaBelle starred as a former singing star and owner of a high-tech Los Angeles nightclub in this hip, music-oriented black sitcom. Club Chelsea was the trendiest spot around, with flashing lights, high-energy dancers, and a video wall. Jeff, a recent NYU graduate with dreams of becoming a music entrepreneur, smooth-talked Chelsea into making him manager-trainee. Chelsea also got Jeff and his buddy Vidal a luxurious apartment in a building she owned. Also in the building were Charisse, Chelsea's daughter and a successful fashion stylist, who had to deal with constant overtures from horny, happy-go-lucky Vidal, and Angus, a Scottish student who was the stereotypically nutty neighbor. Dance routines and songs by pop groups at the club enlivened this otherwise unlikely series.

OUT OF THE BLUE (*Situation Comedy*)

FIRST TELECAST: *September 9, 1979*

LAST TELECAST: *December 16, 1979*

BROADCAST HISTORY:

Sep 1979–Oct 1979, ABC Sun 7:00–7:30
Dec 1979, ABC Sun 7:30–8:00

CAST:

Random .... Jimmy Brogan
Aunt Marion .... Dixie Carter
Chris Richards (age 16) .... Clark Brandon
Laura Richards (13) .... Olivia Barash
Stacey Richards (10) .... Tammy Lauren
Jason Richards (8) .... Jason Keller
Shane Richards (8) .... Shane Keller
Gladys .... Hannah Dean
Boss Angel .... Elieen Heckart

Kiddie comedy in the style of *Bewitched* and *My Favorite Martian.* In this one, an inept angel was dispatched to help a harried Chicago woman cope with her five adorable nieces and nephews, after their parents had died in a plane crash. Aunt Marion decided to accept a boarder, to help meet expenses, so Random moved in. The fact that he was an angel, with magical powers, was the kids' secret. Random could move people and places around with a twinkle, and he used his powers to teach the kids little lessons about growing up. Gladys was the black housekeeper.

OUT OF THE FOG (*Drama*)

FIRST TELECAST: *April 7, 1952*

LAST TELECAST: *September 22, 1952*

BROADCAST HISTORY:

Apr 1952–Sep 1952, ABC Mon 8:00–8:30

This was a short-lived series of mystery films, which alternated with *Mr. District Attorney* from April through June, then was seen weekly.

OUT OF THIS WORLD (*Situation Comedy*)

BROADCAST HISTORY:

Syndicated only
30 minutes
Produced: *1987–1991* (96 episodes)
Released: *September 1987*

CAST:

Donna Garland .... Donna Pescow
Evie Garland (age 13) .... Maureen Flannigan
Mayor Kyle Applegate .... Doug McClure
Beano Froelich (1987–1990) .... Joe Alaskey
Buzz .... Buzz Belmondo
Troy (voice only) .... Burt Reynolds
Lindsay Selkirk .... Christina Nigra
**Phil (1987–1988)* .... John Roarke
**Quigley Handlesman (1987–1988)* ..... Carl Steven
Chris Fuller .... Steve Burton
**Jeffrey Cummings (1990)* .... Tony Crane
Peter (1990–1991) .... Peter Pitofsky
**Mick (1990–1991)* .... Tom Nolan

*Occasional

THEME:

"Swinging on a Star" (1944 pop song)

Donna Garland ran a private school for gifted children in the town of Marlowe, near Carmel, California, but none was more gifted than her daughter Evie. Evie was starting to develop powers she had inherited from her father Troy, an extraterrestrial visitor from the planet Antareus who had married her mother and then been called back to his home planet shortly after her birth. Evie's powers included the ability to stop time (freezing people in mid-sentence was a favorite trick) and to materialize things simply by willing them into existence. Whenever she had problems dealing with her powers she could communicate with her dad through a special cube that functioned as an interstellar phone. The only other person who knew about Troy was Donna's brother, Beano, the rotund owner of "Beano's Diet Clinic." Anyone else who happened to see Evie's remarkable powers at work simply thought that she—or they—were crazy.

Buzz was the eccentric character who ran the clinic for Beano, and Mayor Kyle an egocentric former TV star who had turned to politics.

After the first season there were numerous changes. The focus of the series shifted from the use of Evie's powers to the everyday problems of high school life, with her best friend Lindsay and her boyfriend Chris moving up from occasional to regular players. Troy's voice, which only Evie could hear during the first season, was audible to everyone starting in the fall of 1988. The third season saw Donna defeating Kyle for mayor, and subsequently appointing him police chief, and the fourth season brought Donna's brother Mick, a former rock musician, back to Marlowe. Also seen during the last season were Jeffrey, the new hunk in high school (Chris was a student at Marlowe Community College) and Peter, a klutzy alien who was working as a waiter at the Goodie Goodie, the restaurant where Evie and all her friends hung out.

OUT THERE (*Science Fiction Anthology*)

FIRST TELECAST: *October 28, 1951*

LAST TELECAST: *January 13, 1952*
BROADCAST HISTORY:
Oct 1951–Jan 1952, CBS Sun 6:00–6:30

A live anthology series which used filmed special effects, *Out There* sought to bridge the gap between serious drama and the juvenile science fiction of such shows as *Captain Video* and *Tom Corbet—Space Cadet.* All of the episodes were adapted from stories by prominent science-fiction writers and were presented in such a way as to attract an adult audience but still be exciting enough to hold the attention of children.

OUTCASTS, THE (*Western*)

FIRST TELECAST: *September 23, 1968*
LAST TELECAST: *September 15, 1969*
BROADCAST HISTORY:
Sep 1968–Sep 1969, ABC Mon 9:00–10:00
CAST:
Earl Corey .... Don Murray
Jemal David.............................. Otis Young

This violent Western teamed a Virginia aristocrat-turned-gunman-and-drifter with a freed slave-turned-bounty hunter, in the years after the Civil War. The two of them had an uneasy relationship at best, often erupting into fights and arguments, as they pursued a common goal of making money by tracking down wanted criminals. Corey was the white man, and David the black.

OUTDOOR LIFE NETWORK (Network)

(*Informational Cable Network*)
LAUNCHED:
July 1995
SUBSCRIBERS (MAY 2003):
51.7 million (48% U.S.)

For those who prefer to break a sweat from the comfort of their sofa, there is the Outdoor Life Network, presenting films of high-octane outdoor adventure sports and recreation. Typical documentary programs included *Wild Survival with Corbin Bernsen* (reenactments of close brushes with natural disasters and outdoor mishaps), *Danger Zone with Picabo Street* (extreme sports), *Adventure Quest* (adventurers), *Friends of the Forests* (ecology), *Killer Instinct* (wild animals), films by Jacques Cousteau, and *Hunting with Hank* (hunting with canine Hank and his owner Dez Young). Sports coverage included professional bull riding, the Tour de France bicycle race and World Cup Ski and Snowboarding events. A special event in 2003 was *Global Extremes: Mt. Everest,* in which 12 "everyday" people showed their stuff in the jungles of Central America, the sands of the Kalahari and the glaciers of Iceland in order to win a place on an expedition to the summit of Mt. Everest.

OLN is not to be confused with the smaller Outdoor Channel (launched in 1993 and currently in about 20 million homes), which emphasizes somewhat more accessible hunting, fishing and motor sports outdoor activities as opposed to the adventure orientation of OLN.

OUTER LIMITS, THE (*Science Fiction Anthology*)

NETWORK HISTORY:
FIRST TELECAST: *September 16, 1963*
LAST TELECAST: *January 16, 1965*
Sep 1963–Sep 1964, ABC Mon 7:30–8:30
Sep 1964–Jan 1965, ABC Sat 7:30–8:30
CABLE HISTORY:
Showtime (1995–2001); Sci-Fi Channel (2001–2002)
60 minutes
Produced: *1995–2001* (154 episodes)
Premiered: *March 26, 1995*
CONTROL VOICE:
Vic Perrin (1963–1965)
Kevin Conway (1995–2001)
CREATOR/EXECUTIVE PRODUCER:
Leslie Stevens (1963–1965)

At the opening of each episode in this anthology series the picture on the TV screen started to do funny things and the deep unemotional "control voice" intoned: "There is nothing wrong with your television set. Do not attempt to adjust the picture. We are controlling transmission. We will control the horizontal. We will control the vertical. We can change the focus to a soft blur—or sharpen it to crystal clarity. For the next hour sit quietly and we will control all that you see and hear. You are about to participate in a great adventure. You are about to experience the awe and mystery which reaches from the inner mind to . . . THE OUTER LIMITS."

The special effects were good, the alien costumes interesting, and the plots inventive, often leaving viewers with a sense of unease that was either relieved or exacerbated by the moral/commentary the control voice gave at the end of each episode just before returning control of your television set to you.

Among the actors starring in episodes of *The Outer Limits* were Robert Culp, Martin Sheen, Bruce Dern, Martin Landau, Sally Kellerman, Lloyd Nolan, Cliff Robertson, and William Shatner. In the episode in which Shatner starred, he played an astronaut on a fly-by mission to the planet Venus. The mission was called Project Vulcan. What would Mr. Spock have said about that coincidence?

Thirty years after *The Outer Limits* left the air, a new weekly version was produced for the Showtime cable network. After airing on Showtime the episodes were packaged for syndication to local stations. After six seasons on Showtime *The Outer Limits* moved to the Sci-Fi Channel for its last year.

OUTLAWS, (*Detective Drama*)

FIRST TELECAST: *December 28, 1986*
LAST TELECAST: *May 30, 1987*
BROADCAST HISTORY:
Dec 1986, CBS Sun 9:00–11:00
Jan 1987–May 1987, CBS Sat 8:00–9:00
CAST:
John Grail .... Rod Taylor
Harland Pike...................... William Lucking
Wolfson "Wolf" Lucas.............. Charles Napier
Isaiah "Ice" McAdams .... Richard Roundtree
Billy Pike .... Patrick Houser
Lt. Maggie Randall.............. Christine Belford

It was 1899 and Texas Sheriff John Grail was leading a posse after a gang of bank robbers led by Harland Pike—a gang he had been a member of before he had gone straight and become a peace officer. Caught in a freak electrical storm, Grail and the gang were catapulted through time to contemporary Texas, a totally alien world from the one they knew. Realizing what had happened, though having no idea how, they reconciled their differences, used the gold coins from the robbery to buy a ranch they named the Double Eagle, and attempted to adjust to the modern world. At Grail's urging they opened the Double Eagle Detective Agency, literally bringing old-fashioned justice to Houston and the Southwest. Their biggest problem was keeping Harland's hot-headed kid brother, Billy, under control. These guys were a little hard to take. They wore outfits that, though newly made, were replicas of the clothes they had worn at the turn of the century; they still used their dated weapons; and they never seemed to get shot by the bad guys despite their penchant for striding side-by-side into gunfights. Maggie Randall was the contemporary Houston police officer who befriended them, got them out of trouble, and had a soft spot for John Grail.

OUTLAWS, THE (*Western*)
FIRST TELECAST: *September 29, 1960*
LAST TELECAST: *September 13, 1962*
BROADCAST HISTORY:
Sep 1960–Sep 1962, NBC Thu 7:30–8:30
CAST:
U.S. Marshal Frank Caine (1960–1961) .... Barton MacLane
Deputy Marshal Will Forman .... Don Collier
Deputy Marshal Heck Martin (1960–1961) .... Jock Gaynor
Deputy Marshal Chalk Breeson (1961–1962) .... Bruce Yarnell
Slim (1961–1962) .... Slim Pickens
Connie Masters (1961–1962) .... Judy Lewis

In its first season, *The Outlaws* approached the struggle between law officers of the Old West and the desperadoes they chased from a novel point of view. Although Marshal Frank Caine and his two deputies, Will Forman and Heck Martin, were the series regulars, each episode was seen through the eyes of the outlaws they were pursuing. The setting for the series was the Oklahoma Territory in the 1890s, when the Dalton Boys, the Jennings Gang, and other outlaws made it one of the most lawless of all the West's frontiers.

When *The Outlaws* returned in the fall of 1961 there were a number of changes. Gone were Caine and Martin, and Will Forman was a full marshal with his own deputy. The perspective of the series was now from the side of the marshals and the honest citizens rather than the criminals. The action was based in the town of Stillwater, Oklahoma, where the marshals were headquartered. Connie Masters worked at the Wells Fargo office, and Slim was the town character.

OUTLOOK, see *Chet Huntley Reporting*

OUTRAGEOUS (*Audience Participation*)
BROADCAST HISTORY:
Fox Family Channel
30 minutes
Produced: *1998*
Premiered: *August 15, 1998*
HOST:
Idalis DeLeon

In this cross between *Truth or Consequences* and *Candid Camera,* teams of contestants were sent out into Los Angeles to try to get ordinary people to do silly things for the camera. For example, under the pretense that they would be in a commercial, passersby might be asked to cry on cue; jump into a pool (for "Splash" soft drink); or eat from a trough like a pig. The studio audience then voted for the best resulting video, with the winning team receiving a $1000 prize. The rather sexy host was an actress named Idalis.

OUTSIDE U.S.A. (*Documentary*)
FIRST TELECAST: *September 1, 1955*
LAST TELECAST: *June 3, 1956*
BROADCAST HISTORY:
Sep 1955–Oct 1955, ABC Thu 10:00–10:30
Nov 1955–Jan 1956, ABC Tue 10:00–10:30
Jan 1956–Mar 1956, ABC Mon 10:00–10:30
Apr 1956–Jun 1956, ABC Sun 10:00–10:30
NARRATOR/COMMENTATOR:
Quincy Howe

Each week Mr. Howe introduced filmed coverage of an event or issue in world politics. Following the film he would analyze or evaluate the situation being covered.

OUTSIDER, THE (*Detective Drama*)
FIRST TELECAST: *September 18, 1968*
LAST TELECAST: *September 3, 1969*
BROADCAST HISTORY:
Sep 1968–Sep 1969, NBC Wed 10:00–11:00
CAST:
David Ross .... Darren McGavin

David Ross was not the stereotyped glamorous private detective. He did not make much money, lived in a run-down Los Angeles apartment building, drove a beat-up 10-year-old car, and often got beat up himself while on cases. Ross was a loner who had never finished high school and had been orphaned when a small child. As an adult, he had served six years in prison on a trumped-up murder charge, before being pardoned. In short Ross had found the world a very unfriendly place—he was an "outsider." Nevertheless he turned private eye to tackle other people's problems, and proved an extremely thorough and productive investigator.

OUTSIDERS, THE (*Drama*)
FIRST TELECAST: *March 25, 1990*
LAST TELECAST: *August 26, 1990*
BROADCAST HISTORY
Mar 1990, FOX Sun 9:30–11:00
Apr 1990–Aug 1990, FOX Sun 7:00–8:00
CAST:
Ponyboy Curtis (age 15) .... Jay R. Ferguson
Sodapop Curtis (17) .... Rodney Harvey
Darrel Curtis (19) .... Boyd Kestner
Tim Shepard .... Robert Rusler
Two-Bit Matthews .... David Arquette
Steve Randle .... Harold Pruett
Belinda (Scout) Jenkins .... Heather McComb
Cherry Valance .... Kim Walker
Randy Adderson .... Scott Coffey
Greg .... Sean Kanan
Marcia .... Jennifer McComb
Buck Merrill .... Billy Bob Thornton

The Outsiders was the story of three orphaned brothers trying to keep their household together in Tulsa, Oklahoma, in 1966. The youngest, 15-year-old Ponyboy Curtis, who also served as the series' narrator, was a student at Walker Ridge High School. A sensitive, introspective youth, who wanted to become a writer, Ponyboy was caught up in the conflicts between the tough street kids ("Greasers") and the affluent jocks ("Socs"). There were constant fights, with Ponyboy being a favorite target of the Socs. The other Curtis brothers were Darrel, a carpenter trying to keep his family from being split up by the welfare authorities, and short-tempered Sodapop, who split his time between chasing girls and getting into fights. Other Greasers were tough Tim, wacky Two-Bit, and forthright Steve. The principal Socs, who lost most of the fights but still had all the money, were Randy and Greg. Two featured girls were underprivileged Scout, who had been befriended by Ponyboy, and beautiful Cherry, who was fascinated by the Greasers but attracted to the Socs' money.

Based on the S. E. Hinton novel and the 1983 movie, produced by Francis Ford Coppola, who also produced the series. The young stars of the film were Matt Dillon, Patrick Swayze, Rob Lowe, Ralph Macchio, Emilio Estevez, and Tom Cruise.

OVER MY DEAD BODY (*Detective Drama*)

FIRST TELECAST: *October 26, 1990*
LAST TELECAST: *June 20, 1991*
BROADCAST HISTORY:
Oct 1990–Dec 1990, CBS Fri 9:00–10:00
Jun 1991, CBS Thu 10:00–11:00
CAST:
Maxwell Beckett .... Edward Woodward
Nikki Page .... Jessica Lundy
Wendy .... Jill Tracy
Det. Mueller .... Peter Looney
Det. Ritter .... Rick Fitts

They were certainly an unlikely detective team. Maxwell Beckett was a cranky sixtyish English mystery writer suffering through a dry spell. His three bestselling novels had been followed by two bombs. Nikki Page wrote obituaries for *The San Francisco Union* while trying to move up to a job as a reporter. Because Maxwell was her favorite author, Nikki got him involved in a murder she had seen from her window and, after they solved the crime, they became friends and a team of amateur sleuths. All the action got Maxwell's creative juices flowing again. Wendy was Nikki's friend and coworker at the paper.

Produced by William Link, this series resembled Link's earlier hit *Murder, She Wrote*. In each series a middle-aged writer stumbled upon a new murder mystery to solve every week. And if Maxwell didn't, Nikki did.

OVER THE TOP (*Situation Comedy*)

FIRST TELECAST: *October 21, 1997*
LAST TELECAST: *November 4, 1997*
BROADCAST HISTORY:
Oct 1997–Nov 1997, ABC Tue 8:30–9:00
CAST:
Simon Ferguson .... Tim Curry
Hadley Martin .... Annie Potts
Gwen Martin .... Marla Sokoloff
Daniel Martin (age 7) .... Luke Tarsitano
Yorgo Galfanikos .... Steve Carell
Robert McSwain .... John O'Hurley
Rose .... Liz Torres

Hadley was the sensible owner of a small, struggling Manhattan hotel, and Simon her wildly flamboyant ex, in this slapstick sitcom that certainly lived up to its title, but lasted only three weeks on the ABC schedule. Thrice-divorced Hadley was trying to make a go of the genteel Metropolitan Hotel, along with feisty right-hand woman Rose, overemotional chef Yorgo, and her two kids, whiny teenager Gwen and jug-eared, enthusiastic 7-year-old Daniel. Then in blew Simon, her first husband (or "first mistake"—they had been married for twelve days, twenty years earlier). A larger-than-life British soap opera actor who had just been fired from his show, *Days to Remember*, he was out of cash and needed a new gig. Hadley was understandably suspicious, but could not resist his charms, not to mention the traffic he brought into the dowdy Metropolitan with his grand promotions, such as the colorful "theme nights" at the hotel bar. Robert was a silver-haired investor who wasn't sure what to make of him either.

OVERLAND TRAIL, THE (*Western*)

FIRST TELECAST: *February 7, 1960*
LAST TELECAST: *September 11, 1960*
BROADCAST HISTORY:
Feb 1960–Sep 1960, NBC Sun 7:00–8:00
CAST:
Frederick Thomas Kelly .... William Bendix
Frank "Flip" Flippen .... Doug McClure

The opening of the Overland Trail, one of the major stage routes to the West, and the effort to push that route all the way to the Pacific Ocean, served as the backdrop for this series. The two men charged with moving the stage line from Missouri, over the Rockies, and through to California were Frederick Thomas Kelly and Frank Flippen. Kelly was a crusty former civil engineer and Union Army guerrilla who found getting the Overland Stage Line into operation the most exciting challenge of his life. His young friend and aide, nicknamed Flip, had been brought up by Indians and was full of an adventurous enthusiasm that complemented Kelly's cautious nature. Their adventures and the adventures of their passengers provided the stories for this series.

OVERSEAS ADVENTURE, see *Foreign Intrigue*

OVERTIME . . . WITH PAT O'BRIEN (*Talk*)

FIRST TELECAST: *August 10, 1990*
LAST TELECAST: *August 24, 1990*
BROADCAST HISTORY:
Aug 1990, CBS Fri 11:30–12:30 A.M.
HOST:
Pat O'Brien

This short-lived talk show, hosted by CBS Sports analyst Pat O'Brien, featured interviews with personalities ranging from football's Joe Montana and John Madden to rock music performers MC Hammer and Glenn Frey.

OWEN MARSHALL, COUNSELOR AT LAW (*Legal Drama*)

FIRST TELECAST: *September 16, 1971*
LAST TELECAST: *August 24, 1974*
BROADCAST HISTORY:
Sep 1971–Jan 1973, ABC Thu 10:00–11:00
Jan 1973–Jan 1974, ABC Wed 10:00–11:00
Jan 1974–Aug 1974, ABC Sat 10:00–11:00

CAST:

Owen Marshall .... Arthur Hill
Jess Brandon .... Lee Majors
Danny Paterno (1973–1974) .... Reni Santoni
Ted Warrick (1974) .... David Soul
Melissa Marshall .... Christine Matchett
Frieda Krause .... Joan Darling

This popular lawyer drama depicted the life and trials of Owen Marshall, a compassionate defense attorney practicing in a small town in California. Marshall's cases ranged from civil suits to murder, but were always marked by a warmth and consideration for the accused. In a way, *Owen Marshall* was the courtroom equivalent of medicine's kindly *Marcus Welby*, and, in fact, the two series sometimes had joint episodes. In 1972 Marshall found himself defending the father of one of Dr. Welby's patients against a murder charge, and in 1974 he defended Dr. Kiley, Welby's associate, against a paternity suit.

Owen Marshall had several young law partners during his run, the first of whom was Jess Brandon. For a time in 1973–1974 Lee Majors, the actor portraying Brandon, was starring in two ABC series, this one and *The Six Million Dollar Man*. He was finally replaced in February 1974 by another future star, David Soul, in the role of Ted Warrick. In addition, Danny Paterno was seen as a partner during the final season. Melissa was widower Marshall's 12-year-old daughter, and Frieda his loyal law clerk.

Owen Marshall was well regarded by real-life legal associations, and won several public-service awards. It's cocreators were David Victor and University of Wisconsin law professor Jerry McNeely.

OXYGEN (Network) (*General Entertainment Cable Network*)

LAUNCHED:
February 2, 2000

SUBSCRIBERS (MAY 2003):
46.9 million (44% U.S.)

Oxygen is a women's network that was founded with a great deal of fanfare in 2000 to compete with long-time category leader Lifetime. The original positioning had a feisty, rather aggressively feminist tone (one famous advertisement showed baby girls in a maternity ward raising their fists), and there was a considerable amount of original, if somewhat low-budget, programming. Shows on the original schedule included *Pure Oxygen* (magazine), *Exhale with Candice Bergen* (interviews), *Ka-Ching* (financial advice), *X-Chromosome* (cartoons), *We Sweat* (women athletes) and *Pajama Party* (a late-night variety show set in an apartment with everyone in their PJs). The network was also closely intertwined with the Internet, and a small band along the bottom of the screen offered directions to related Web sites and miscellaneous information. Much was also made of the high-powered backers of the channel, including Oprah Winfrey (who contributed a show called *Oprah Goes Online*, in which she learned about the Internet), former Nickelodeon head Geraldine Laybourne and Hollywood power producers Marcy Carsey and Tom Werner (*Roseanne, Murphy Brown*, etc.).

Alas, none of this attracted much of an audience, so the Internet connection was subsequently downplayed and many of the original programs were replaced by rerun (but female-appropriate) fare such as *Xena: Warrior Princess, La Femme Nikita, Cybill* and *Absolutely Fabulous*. More time was also devoted to movies. There were still some original series, including *The Isaac Mizrahi Show* (interviews), *Girls Behaving Badly* (a female and somewhat sexy *Candid Camera*–style prank show) and *Conversations from the Edge with Carrie Fisher* (interviews). Oprah contributed a new series called *Oprah After the Show*, in which she talked to her studio audience after a taping of her syndicated daytime show.

Why is it called Oxygen? Founder Geraldine Laybourne said that the name came to her one night when she woke up gasping for breath.

OZARK JUBILEE (*Country Music*)

FIRST TELECAST: *January 22, 1955*
LAST TELECAST: *September 24, 1960*
BROADCAST HISTORY:

Jan 1955–Jun 1955, ABC Sat 9:00–10:00
Jul 1955–Sep 1956, ABC Sat 7:30–9:00
Oct 1956–Dec 1956, ABC Thu 10:00–11:00
Dec 1956–Jun 1957, ABC Sat 10:00–11:00
Jun 1957–Sep 1957, ABC Sat 10:00–10:30
Sep 1957–Sep 1959, ABC Sat 8:00–9:00
Sep 1958–Oct 1958, ABC Mon 7:30–8:30
Oct 1959–Sep 1960, ABC Sat 10:00–11:00

REGULARS:

Red Foley
Webb Pierce (occasional 1955–1956)
Jean Shepard (1955)
Hawkshaw Hawkins (1955)
Tommy Sosebee (1955)
Porter Wagoner (1955–1956)
Foggy River Boys/Marksmen (1955–1959)
Pete Stamper (1956)
Oklahoma Wranglers (1955)
Bud Isaac (1955)
Uncle Cyp & Aunt Sap Brasfield (1956–1960)
Flash & Whistler (1956–1957)
Tadpoles (1956)
Bill Wimberly's Country Rhythm Boys (1956–1957)
Bobby Lord (1957–1960)
Jim Wilson (1957)
Marvin Rainwater (1957)
Slim Wilson's Jubilee Band (1958–1960)
Wanda Jackson (1957–1960)
Billy Walker (1957)
Tall Timber Trio (1957–1960)
Bill McMain (1957)
Norma Jean (1958)
Leory Van Dyke (1958)
Suzi Arden (1958–1959)
Smiley Burnette (1959)
The Promenaders (1959–1960)
Shug Fisher (1960)
Lew Childre (1960)

THEME:

"Sugarfoot Rag," by Hank Garland

Country and western music had a major showcase on network television in the late 1950s in this weekly hoedown from Springfield, Missouri. The host was genial country singer Red Foley, a veteran of the *Grand Ole Opry*, who projected a good-natured warmth and sincerity which characterized the whole proceedings. Appearing on *Jubliee* were many of the top names in country music, including regulars Webb Pierce (who was once-a-month host for a time in 1955–1956), the

Foggy River Boys vocal quartet (renamed the Marksmen in 1957), comic Pete Stamper, and Porter Wagoner. Among the regular features were square dancing by the Tadpoles, a group of two-to-ten year olds, and the cornpone comedy act of Uncle Cyp and Aunt Sap, who portrayed an elderly married couple who were always throwing ancient jokes at one another. The "Junior Jubilee" portion of the show gave exposure to younger talent. Perhaps its biggest discovery was a sweet-as-peaches little 11-year-old with a booming voice, named Brenda Lee. She made her first appearance in March 1956, quickly became a *Jubliee* favorite, and later went on to stardom in both the country and popular music fields.

Julibee ran until 1960, when it was abruptly canceled by ABC. The official reason was that the network had acquired the Gillette fights and wanted to carry them in *Jubliee*'s time slot. The real reason, however, was that host Red Foley had been indicted for tax fraud and was about to stand trial—a situation hardly consonant with the down-home sincerity he projected on the show (Foley's first trial ended in a hung jury, and a second, in 1961, in acquittal).

Ozark Jubliee underwent two name changes during its run, becoming *Country Music Jubliee* in July 1957 and *Jubliee U.S.A.* in August 1958.

OZZIE AND HARRIET, see *Adventures of Ozzie & Harriet, The*

OZZIE'S GIRLS, see *Adventures of Ozzie & Harriet, The*

P

PJS, THE (*Cartoon Situation Comedy*)
FIRST TELECAST: *January 10, 1999*
LAST TELECAST: *June 17, 2001*
BROADCAST HISTORY:

Jan 1999, FOX Sun 8:30–9:00
Jan 1999–Mar 1999, FOX Tue 8:30–9:00
Apr 1999–Jun 1999, FOX Tue 9:00–9:30
Jun 1999–Sep 1999, FOX Thu 9:30–10:00
May 2000–Jul 2000, FOX Tue 8:30–9:00
May 2000–Sep 2000, FOX Tue 9:30–10:00
Sep 2000–Oct 2000, WB Sun 8:30–9:00
Nov 2000–May 2001, WB Sun 7:30–8:00
May 2001–Jun 2001, WB Sun 7:00–8:00

VOICES:

Thurgood Stubbs .... Eddie Murphy
Muriel Stubbs .... Loretta Devine
Mrs. Avery .... Ja'net DuBois
Calvin Banks .... Crystal Scales
Juicy Hudson .... Michele Morgan
Jimmy Ho .... Michael Paul Chan
Bebe Ho .... Jenifer Lewis
Sanchez .... Pepe Serna
Haiti Lady .... Cheryl Francis Harrington
Smokey .... Shawn Michael Howard
Tarnell .... James Black
HUD Woman .... Cassi Davis
Walter .... Marc Wilmore
Papa Hudson and *the Jamaican*
.... Kevin Michael Richardson

THEME:

written by Quincy Jones, George Clinton, LaRita Norman, and Marie Norman

Thurgood was the blustery building super in this visually unusual inner city sitcom whose characters were "foamation" puppets. The setting was the Hilton-Jacobs projects ("the PJs") of an unnamed city. Thurgood may have sounded like George Jefferson but he really cared about the building and its tenants, and he often let a couple of the tenant kids—Calvin, whom he treated like a son, and Juicy, the fat kid who could barely get through doorways—help him with maintenance around the building. Muriel, his loving wife, was the calming influence in his life, able to reason with him when he started on one of his tirades. The tenants included Mrs. Avery, a cranky old woman who hated Thurgood; Haiti Lady, the building's fortune-teller, who kept sticking pins in the Thurgood voodoo doll she had made; Muriel's sister Bebe and her Korean husband Jimmy; and Sanchez, Thurgood's chess-playing friend.

There were lots of stereotypical lines about welfare, medicare, drugs, and other aspects of slum living. Most of the tenants complained about their rent, the noise level from the boom boxes could be deafening, the neighborhood was filthy, and there were roaches everywhere. Even though a prominent black performer, Eddie Murphy, was the creator of *The PJs*, there were many in the black community, including filmmaker Spike Lee, who resented its negative portrayal of minorities and the poor.

PM MAGAZINE (*Magazine*)
BROADCAST HISTORY:

Syndicated only
30 minutes
Produced: *1978–1990*
Released: *September 1978*

PM Magazine was an unusual hybrid of local and national programming. Each city had its own version of the show, with local hosts who introduced short, entertaining pieces featuring tips for better living, interesting people, and unusual places. A typical week's stories might include a profile of Alan Alda, a man's reunion with girlfriends from his past, a recipe for gooseberry compote, and ways to reduce stress. Some features were produced locally, but many of them came from other cities and even foreign countries, giving *PM Magazine* a very cosmopolitan look for a locally originated show. The show also stressed mobility—stories were introduced outdoors and taped on location using small, portable "minicam" TV cameras that allowed maximum maneuverability. The viewer never saw the inside of a TV studio.

These rather expensive production techniques were made possible on local TV by a unique experiment in interstation cooperation. The idea for the series originated in August 1976 as a local show called *Evening Magazine* on KPIX in San Francisco, a station owned by the Westinghouse company. Four other stations owned by Westinghouse soon began their own versions, and in the fall of 1978 the company offered the idea to stations across the country, on the following basis: each station was to use two local cohosts (so that the show, not the host, would be the chief attraction), follow certain guidelines as to the show's format, and—most importantly—contribute at least one locally produced segment each week to a national pool. In return the station would get access to the best tapes other stations had contributed to the pool, the use of the *PM Magazine* name and graphics, and the help of an experienced national staff in producing its local version of the show. A station could thus concentrate on producing only a few good segments each week, and still have enough first-rate material to fill its own five-nights-a-week *PM Magazine*.

By the mid-1980s the number of stations carrying *PM Magazine* had started to dwindle, as stations sought out programming that came completely packaged and did not require local involvement. The trend accelerated with the emergence of the more sensational "Tabloid News" programs like *A Current Affair*, which attracted larger audiences than *PM Magazine*. By 1990, with fewer than two dozen stations still carrying the show, Westinghouse Broadcasting decided to put it out of its misery. *PM Magazine* went out of production that December.

P.S. I LUV U (*Detective Drama*)
FIRST TELECAST: *September 15, 1991*
LAST TELECAST: *January 4, 1992*
BROADCAST HISTORY:

Sep 1991, CBS Sun 9:00–11:00
Sep 1991–Jan 1992, CBS Sat 10:00–11:00

CAST:

Dani Powell (Wanda Talbert) ...... Connie Sellecca
Cody Powell (Joey Paciorek) .... Greg Evigan

Matthew Durning .... Earl Holliman
**Uncle Ray Bailey* .... Patrick Macnee
Fuji .... Rob Narita
Dori .... Lisa Canning
Jojo .... Jayne Frazer
Sheriff Hollings .... Jack Ging

*Occasional

THEME:

"P.S. I Luv U," written by Glen A. Larson and Matthew Delgado, sung by Greg Evigan and Suzanne Fountain

Wanda and Joey had been unlikely, and unenthusiastic, partners in an N.Y.P.D. sting operation that had gone sour. She was a con artist who, to keep out of prison, had agreed to set up a mobster, and he was the detective coordinating the operation. When it fell apart, she and Joey entered the witness protection program and were relocated to Palm Springs to hide from the vengeful mobster. Once there they assumed the identities of Dani and Cody Powell, a "married" couple working for Palm Security and Investigations, a local security and detective agency. Matthew Durning, who ran the agency, was the only one who knew who they really were. Cody and Dani spent most of their time working on cases for P.S.I. and fighting with each other. The combination of an honest, analytical cop and a creative con artist, even though they didn't like each other very much, made them a very effective team. Dani even managed to convince Durning to let them stay in a huge mansion, whose owner was almost never in Palm Springs, as live-in security guards. Others on the P.S.I. staff were Fuji the lab technician, Durning's secretary/receptionist Dori, and Jojo, who worked in its communications center. Seen occasionally were Dani's con man friend Ray Bailey and real-life Palm Springs Mayor Sonny Bono.

The title of the series was the phone number (774-5888 or PSI-LUVU) of Palm Security and Investigations.

PABST BLUE RIBBON BOUTS, see *Boxing*

PACIFIC BLUE (*Police Drama*)

BROADCAST HISTORY:

USA Network
60 minutes
Produced: *1996–2000* (101 episodes)
Premiered: *March 2, 1996*

CAST:

Lt. Anthony Palermo (1996–1998)
.... Rick Rossovich
Off./Sgt./Lt. Terence (T.C.) Callaway
.... Jim Davidson
Off. Chris Kelly (1996–1999) .... Darlene Vogel
Off./Sgt. Cory McNamara .... Paula Trickey
Off. Victor Del Toro (1996–1998) ... Marcos Ferraez
Elvis Kryzenski (1996) .... David L. Lander
Off. Bobby Cruz (1998–2000) .... Mario Lopez
Off. Russ Granger (1998–2000) .... Jeff Stearns
Off. Monica Harper (1998–2000) .. Shanna Moakler
Off. Jamie Strickland (1998–2000)
.... Amy Hunter-Cornelius

"Baywatch on bikes" was the shorthand description of this frothy but action-packed cop show airing on Saturday (later Sunday) nights on USA Network. Fatherly Lt. Palermo headed the Santa Monica Beach Bike Patrol, whose handsome young officers in tight shorts peddled furiously to run down the drug dealers, robbers, neo-Nazis, serial killers, and other lawbreakers who infested the sun-drenched (and skin-drenched) boardwalk. There were plenty of tense shootouts and hostage situations, but the action was also sometimes light, as when shapely Officer Cory chased an unlicensed street peddler into the middle of a wet T-shirt contest, where she was promptly thrown on the stage, drenched, and pronounced the winner!

T.C. was the intense, Zen-practicing second-in-command; Chris the rookie; Cory the ambitious daughter of an L.A. police family; Victor the street-smart Hispanic; and Elvis the eccentric bicycle repair technician (with all those wheelies and high-flying leaps, the squad's high-tech bikes needed a lot of repair). Appearing occasionally was ex-Monkee Mickey Dolenz as the indecisive mayor of Santa Monica. T.C. married Chris and replaced Palermo as boss in 1998, as Victor left (he was later killed) and four new hotshot officers joined the patrol: Bobby, Russ, Monica, and Jamie.

PACIFIC PALISADES (*Drama*)

FIRST TELECAST: *April 9, 1997*
LAST TELECAST: *July 30, 1997*
BROADCAST HISTORY:

Apr 1997–Jul 1997, FOX Wed 9:00–10:00

CAST:

Nick Hadley .... Jarrod Emick
Joanna Hadley .... Michelle Stafford
Robert Russo .... Greg Evigan
Kate Russo .... Finola Hughes
Jessica Mitchell .... Jocelyn Seagrave
Laura Sinclair .... Kimberley Davies
Matt Dunning .... Lucky Vanous
Rachel Whittaker .... Natalia Cigliuti
Beth Hooper .... Brittney Powell
Dr. Cory Robbins (early episodes) .... Joel Wyner
Dr. Cory Robbins (later episodes) .... Dylan Neal
Michael Caras .... Trevor Edmond
Ashley .... Jennifer Banko
Christina Hobson .... Joan Colllins
John Graham .... Paul Satterfield
Frank Nichols .... Gianni Russo

Hunks and hunkettes abounded in this Aaron Spelling soap opera about rich, beautiful people scheming and sleeping with each other in the yuppie enclave of Pacific Palisades, west of Los Angeles. Straight-arrow architect Nick and his "just a midwestern girl" wife Joanna were the newcomers, recently arrived from Michigan and reunited with their college friends, and new neighbors, Robert and Kate. Robert owned the architectural firm Russo & Associates, and had brought Nick in to work for him. Robert soon needed a new house himself when Kate tossed him out after he revealed he was in love with employee Jessica. Sultry Laura was a gold-digging real estate agent who slept with clients to make a sale. Beth, the receptionist at Russo & Associates, was sleeping with Cory, a young plastic surgeon who was also having recreational sex with Laura. Matt was an unscrupulous building contractor (always one of those around) whose use of substandard materials had caused a mall he had built for Robert to collapse, killing and injuring scores of people;

he then murdered a guy who knew the truth about what had happened.

Showing up after a few episodes was Laura's bitchy mother, Christina (Joan Collins!), who returned from England to buy the Sun Hills Real Estate Agency and chase other women's men. It then transpired that "farm girl" Joanna had been date-raped at age 14, and her "kid sister" Rachel, who was attending Pacific High School, was actually her daughter.

The last episode of *Pacific Palisades* did something rarely seen on short-lived soap operas—it tied up all the loose ends of the convoluted story lines. Teenager Rachel planted evidence meant to convince Joanna that she and Nick were having an affair, but when that cry for attention failed, Joanna and Nick proved they loved her by moving with her back to Ann Arbor. Robert filed for divorce, and Kate decided to go to work for her father, leaving Robert and Jessica to marry with her blessing. Cory and Beth, who had broken up, reunited. Crooked Matt was finally arrested for the mall collapse, and Laura and Christina called a truce in order to pursue a wealthy shipping magnate and his handsome son. And so the sun set on *Pacific Palisades.*

PACIFIC STATION (*Situation Comedy*)
FIRST TELECAST: *September 15, 1991*
LAST TELECAST: *January 3, 1992*
BROADCAST HISTORY:
Sep 1991–Oct 1991, NBC Sun 8:30–9:00
Dec 1991–Jan 1992, NBC Fri 9:00–9:30
CAST:
Det. Bob Ballard.................Robert Guillaume
Det. Richard Capparelli..........Richard Libertini
Capt. Ken Epstein.....................Joel Murray
Det. Al Burkhardt....................Ron Leibman
Det. Sandy Calloway.............Megan Gallagher
Dep. Commissioner Hank Bishop....John Hancock

Barney Miller seemed to be the inspiration for this police comedy about a sensible detective (Guillaume) surrounded by a squad room full of crazies. Among the targets for Bob's barbs were his newly assigned partner, Richard, a gangly, aging flower child just off psychiatric leave, who kept trying to get Bob in touch with his feelings; Capt. Kenny, the massively incompetent mama's boy who had just been promoted to the job Bob deserved; Al, the resident lech and sycophant; and Bishop, the hefty, black Deputy Commissioner who reveled in his own importance. Passing through were a parade of loony arrestees from the precinct's notoriously eccentric beach community of Venice, California.

Sound familiar?

PACKARD SHOWROOM, THE, see *Martha Wright Show, The*

PALACE GUARD (*Detective Comedy/Drama*)
FIRST TELECAST: *October 18, 1991*
LAST TELECAST: *November 1, 1991*
BROADCAST HISTORY:
Oct 1991–Nov 1991, CBS Fri 10:00–11:00
CAST:
Tommy Logan........................D. W. Moffett
Christy Cooper......................Marcy Walker
Arturo Taft.........................Tony Lo Bianco

After serving time for burglarizing one of the luxurious Palace hotels, master jewel thief Tommy Logan finally decided to go straight. He promptly got a surprising job offer: security chief for the entire Palace chain. Who better to protect the international chain, reasoned its president, Arturo Taft, than someone who had been so successful in ripping it off? Besides, Arturo wanted Tommy (his illegitimate son raised by nuns in an orphanage—only Arturo and the nuns knew of the relationship) to make an honest living. Tommy's immediate superior was beautiful Christy Cooper, a former B-movie actress who was the vice president of public relations for the chain. Together they traveled around the world investigating thefts and murders and dealing with other security issues. Tommy did most of the sleuthing while Christy, who often found it hard to resist his charms, scrambled to protect the company's image and smooth over the problems caused by Tommy's unconventional methods.

PALL MALL PLAYHOUSE (*Western Anthology*)
FIRST TELECAST: *July 20, 1955*
LAST TELECAST: *September 7, 1955*
BROADCAST HISTORY:
Jul 1955–Sep 1955, ABC Wed 8:30–9:00

This summer series was comprised of a collection of unsold pilots for dramatic Westerns. Among those starring were John Ireland, Carolyn Jones, and Will Rogers, Jr.

PALMERSTOWN, U.S.A. (*Drama*)
FIRST TELECAST: *March 20, 1980*
LAST TELECAST: *June 9, 1981*
BROADCAST HISTORY:
Mar 1980–May 1980, CBS Thu 8:00–9:00
Mar 1981–Jun 1981, CBS Tue 8:00–9:00
CAST:
Bessie Freeman.....................Jonelle Allen
Luther Freeman..........................Bill Duke
Diana Freeman............Star-Shemah Bobatoon
Booker T. Freeman........Jermain Hodge Johnson
W. D. Hall..........................Beeson Carroll
Coralee Hall........................Janice St. John
Willy-Joe Hall......................Michael J. Fox
David Hall..................Brian Godfrey Wilson
The Sheriff.........................Kenneth White
Widder Brown (1981)........................Iris Korn

Booker T. Freeman and David Hill were nine-year-old boys growing up together in the rural Southern community of Palmerstown during the Depression of the 1930s. They were best friends, despite the fact that Booker T. was black and David was white. Booker T.'s father, Luther, was the town blacksmith and David's father, W.D., was the local grocer. Diana was Booker T.'s older sister and Willy-Joe was David's older brother. Because of the fast friendship between the two boys their families had become quite close, despite the racial animosities prevalent at the time. In the middle of the South, in the middle of the Depression, they proved that blacks and whites could get along with each other. Most of what happened in Palmerstown was seen through the eyes of the two young friends.

Palmerstown, U.S.A. was coproduced by veteran TV producer Norman Lear and award-winning author Alex Haley, whose book and TV mini-series *Roots* were huge successes during the mid-1970s. For

Haley this series was somewhat autobiographical, since he had grown up with a close white friend in an integrated Southern town during the Depression.

In March 1981 the title of the program was shortened to *Palmerstown*.

PANDORA (*Astrology*)

BROADCAST HISTORY:

Lifetime
30 minutes
Produced: *1997*
Premiered: *January 24, 1997*

HOST:

Ellee Devers

On this unusual Friday night series bubbly Ellee Devers explored alternative ways of looking at life, including astrology, numerology, tarot cards, palm reading, and ritual candles. Unfortunately, the signs were not good for Ms. Devers, as the series was canceled after about three months.

PANIC (*Dramatic Anthology*)

FIRST TELECAST: *March 5, 1957*
LAST TELECAST: *September 17, 1957*
BROADCAST HISTORY:

Mar 1957–Sep 1957, NBC Tue 8:30–9:00

NARRATOR:

Westbrook Van Voorhis

At the outset of each episode of *Panic* an individual was put into a sudden crisis situation which posed threats of an emotional or physical nature to him. The remainder of each episode delineated how well he reacted to and coped with the crisis. For example, a young man found himself on the brink of suicide; a vaudeville dancer was stalked by a murderer; and a family was trapped in their home. Appearing were such stars as June Havoc, Darryl Hickman, and James and Pamela Mason.

PANTOMIME QUIZ (*Quiz/Audience Participation*)

FIRST TELECAST: *July 3, 1950*
LAST TELECAST: *September 16, 1963*
BROADCAST HISTORY:

Jul 1950, CBS Mon 9:30–10:00
Jul 1950–Sep 1950, CBS Mon 8:00–8:30
Jul 1951–Aug 1951, CBS Mon 8:00–8:30
Jan 1952, NBC Wed 10:30–11:00
Jan 1952–Mar 1952, NBC Wed 10:00–10:30
Jul 1952–Sep 1952, CBS Fri 8:30–9:00
Jul 1953–Aug 1953, CBS Fri 8:00–8:30
Oct 1953–Apr 1954, DUM Tue 8:30–9:00
Jul 1954–Aug 1954, CBS Fri 8:00–8:30
Jan 1955–Mar 1955, ABC Sun 9:30–10:00
Jul 1955–Sep 1955, CBS Fri 8:00–8:30
Jul 1956–Sep 1956, CBS Fri 10:30–11:00
Jul 1957–Sep 1957, CBS Fri 10:30–11:00
Apr 1958–Sep 1958, ABC Tue 9:30–10:00
Jun 1959–Sep 1959, ABC Mon 9:00–9:30
Sep 1962–Sep 1963, CBS Mon 10:30–11:00

HOST:

Mike Stokey
Pat Harrington, Jr. (1962)

REGULARS:

Hans Conried (1950–1952, 1955–1957, 1962–1963)
Vincent Price (1950–1952)
Adele Jergens (1950–1952)
Jackie Coogan (1950–1955)
John Barrymore, Jr. (1953–1954)
Dave Willock (1953–1954)
Rocky Graziano (1954–1956)
Dorothy Hart (1953–1958)
Robert Clary (1954–1957)
Peter Donald (1953–1955, 1957)
Carol Haney (1955–1956)
Milt Kamen (1957–1959)
Jan Clayton (1953–1954, 1962–1963)
Elaine Stritch (1953–1955, 1958)
Jerry Lester (1953–1955)
Carol Burnett (1958–1959)
Stubby Kaye (1958–1959, 1962–1963)
Dick Van Dyke (1958–1959)

Pantomime Quiz was the perennial summer-replacement series. Created by Mike Stokey, who was its producer and host, it had premiered as a local show in Los Angeles in 1947. The game itself was a variation on the parlor game of charades. Two teams of four members each, three regulars and one guest, competed with each other in attempting to act out famous phrases, mottos, literary quotes, etc. The team that took the least amount of time solving the total of four or five phrases that each team was given during a telecast was declared the winner. Home viewers were asked to send in suggestions for phrases to be used on the show and won cash if their submissions were used, and a bonus if the team trying to solve it could not do so within the two-minute time limit.

The durability of *Pantomime Quiz* is evident in its survival on network television for more than a decade, generally running during the summers. When it was revived for the last time, for a full-season run on CBS in 1962–1963, the title was changed to *Stump the Stars* and Pat Harrington, Jr., became the host. He lasted less than three months in that role, however, being replaced by program producer Mike Stokey on December 10, 1962.

The turnover among regular charaders on *Pantomime Quiz* was extremely high. The list of regulars shown above only includes those who were with the show for at least two different runs. Among the other personalities who were regulars for a single season were Fred Clark, Robert Stack, Angela Lansbury, Orson Bean, Rose Marie, John Carradine, Howard Morris, Tom Poston, Beverly Garland, Sebastian Cabot, Ross Martin, Diana Dors, Mickey Manners, and Ruta Lee.

PAPER CHASE, THE (*Drama*)

FIRST TELECAST: *September 9, 1978*
LAST TELECAST: *July 17, 1979*
BROADCAST HISTORY:

Sep 1978, CBS Sat 8:00–9:00
Sep 1978–Jan 1979, CBS Tue 8:00–9:00
Feb 1979, CBS Tue 10:00–11:00
Mar 1979–Jul 1979, CBS Tue 8:00–9:00
(New episodes produced for Showtime Cable Network 1983–1986)

CAST:

Professor Charles W. Kingsfield, Jr. .... John Houseman
James T. Hart .... James Stephens
Franklin Ford III .... Tom Fitzsimmons
Thomas Craig Anderson (1978–1979) .... Robert Ginty

Willis Bell .... James Keane
Jonathan Brooks (1978) .... Jonathan Segal
Elizabeth Logan (1978–1979) .... Francie Tacker
Asheley Brooks (1978) .... Deka Beaudine
Ernie (1978–1979) .... Charles Hallahan
Carol (1978–1979) .... Carole Goldman
Mrs. Nottingham .... Betty Harford
Dean Rutherford (1978–1979) .... Jack Manning
Mallison (1978–1979) .... Jessica Salem
Gagarian (1978–1979) .... Stanley De Santis
Connie Lehman (1983) .... Jane Kaczmarek
Gerald Golden (1983–1986) .... Michael Tucci
Rita Harriman (1984–1986) ..... Clare Kirkconnell
Laura (1984–1986) .... Andra Millian
Vivian (1984–1986) .... Penny Johnson
Rose Samuels (1985–1986) .... Lainie Kazan
Tom Ford (1985–1986) .... Peter Nelson
Professor Tyler (1985–1986) .... Diana Douglas

THEME:

"The First Years," by Charles Fox and Norman Gimbel, sung by Seals and Crofts

James T. Hart was a first-year law student whose upbringing in rural Iowa had not prepared him for the intensity and ruthlessness that he found at a highly competitive law school. His nemesis was Professor Charles Kingsfield, the world's leading authority on contract law, who inspired both awe and terror in his students with his imperious and authoritarian manner. To help cope with the heavy workload, Hart joined a study group consisting of other students who were working together sharing notes and assignments. The group had been organized by Franklin Ford III, a would-be third generation lawyer from a socially prominent family. Others in the group were Anderson, Bell, Logan, and Brooks. Brooks, the only married member of the group, left school after he got caught cheating.

Even with his heavy workload, Hart had to find time for a part-time job at Ernie's pizza joint. There he met Carol, a waitress who admired him but couldn't understand his dedication to his studies. Also seen occasionally was Mrs. Nottingham, Professor Kingsfield's secretary.

Despite being hailed by critics as the most praiseworthy new series of the 1978–1979 season, *The Paper Chase* never attracted a competitive audience and was canceled at the end of the year. PBS aired reruns of *The Paper Chase* for a few years following its departure from CBS and, in the first case of its kind, the pay-cable television service Showtime revived it in the spring of 1983. Under the title *The Paper Chase: The Second Year*, these new episodes introduced Hart's love interest, first-year law student Connie Lehman, as well as students Rita, Laura, Vivian, and Gerald Golden, who was editor of the *Law Review* for which Hart was writing. Nineteen eighty-five brought a title change—*The Paper Chase: The Third Year*—and two new first-year law students, Ford's younger brother Tom and older, former housewife Rose Samuels. When Hart finally graduated in 1986 (it had taken him eight years since the series' original premiere to complete three years of law school), he had hoped to get a teaching post at the law school. His appointment failed to materialize, however, and he joined a law firm in the last original episode.

The series was based on the movie of the same name, for which John Houseman (as Kingsfield) won a supporting-actor Academy Award. Although the movie took place at Harvard, no mention was made of a specific university in the television series.

PAPER DOLLS (*Drama*)

FIRST TELECAST: *September 23, 1984*
LAST TELECAST: *December 25, 1984*
BROADCAST HISTORY:

Sep 1984, ABC Sun 9:00–11:00
Sep 1984–Nov 1984, ABC Tue 9:00–10:00
Nov 1984–Dec 1984, ABC Tue 10:00–11:00

CAST:

Grant Harper .... Lloyd Bridges
Wesley Harper .... Dack Rambo
Blair Harper-Fenton .... Mimi Rogers
David Fenton .... Richard Beymer
Racine .... Morgan Fairchild
Taryn Blake .... Nicollette Sheridan
Julia Blake .... Brenda Vaccaro
Laurie Caswell .... Terry Farrell
Dinah Caswell .... Jennifer Warren
Michael Caswell .... John Bennett Perry
Marjorie Harper .... Nancy Olson
Sara Frank .... Anne Schedeen
Colette Ferrier .... Lauren Hutton
Steve .... Geoffrey Blake
Mark Bailey .... Roscoe Born
Chris York .... Don Bowren
Sandy Parris .... Jonathan Frakes
Dr. Van Adams .... Alan Fudge
Gabrielle .... Joyce Gittlin
Grayson Carr .... Larry Linville
Lewis Crosby .... Thom Matthews
Jenna .... Amy Resnick
Conrad .... Jeffrey Richman

Paper Dolls was another of television's sagas of power, lust, and family, this time set in the glamorous world of New York's modeling and cosmetics industry. Grant Harper was the mogul who manipulated all; his womanizing son, Wesley, was president of Harper Cosmetics, while his beautiful daughter, Blair, was a top model and the loving wife of hard-working young executive David Fenton, head of Tempus Sportswear. Wesley and David were bitter rivals, both looking for an exclusive fresh new face that would sell their products and free them from Grant's domination. Both were also clients of Racine, the powerful and shrewd head of a top modeling agency, whose hottest property, teenage superstar Taryn Blake, was on the verge of burnout. Although she was only 16, Taryn's frequent temper tantrums and the demands of her aggressive mother and manager, Julia, made the young starlet likely to be pushed aside when the next discovery came along.

That discovery arrived in the person of Laurie Caswell, also 16 and fresh from the suburbs, who projected an innocent beauty and enthusiasm. Laurie's mother and father, Dinah and Michael, worried about what the high pressure life of a model would do to their daughter, but soon they too were drawn into the high-stakes corporate and personal intrigues of Madison Avenue. Colette Ferrier, who ran Ferrier Cosmetics, was one of Harper Cosmetics' chief rivals.

Paper Dolls was based on the 1982 TV movie of the same name.

PARER MOON (*Situation Comedy*)
FIRST TELECAST: *September 12, 1974*
LAST TELECAST: *January 2, 1975*
BROADCAST HISTORY:
Sep 1974–Jan 1975, ABC Thu 8:30–9:00
CAST:
Moses (Moze) Pray .... Christopher Connelly
Addie Pray .... Jodie Foster
THEME:
"It's Only a Paper Moon," by Harold Arlen, Yip Harburg, and Billy Rose

This was a gentle comedy about an itinerant Bible salesman/con artist and his precocious 11-year-old daughter, traveling across Kansas during the Depression years. If Moze and Addie never had much money, it wasn't for lack of trying every fast-buck scheme in the book. Though they just "got by," and were often only one step ahead of the law, they at least had each other. Much period flavor was featured in this series, including an authentic 1933 theme song. The series was filmed on location in Kansas.

Based on the 1973 hit movie starring Ryan and Tatum O'Neal, which had in turn been taken from the novel *Addie Pray* by Joe David Brown.

PARADISE (*Western*)
FIRST TELECAST: *October 27, 1988*
LAST TELECAST: *June 14, 1991*
BROADCAST HISTORY:
Oct 1988–Mar 1989, CBS Thu 9:00–10:00
Apr 1989–Sep 1990, CBS Sat 8:00–9:00
Jan 1991–Jun 1991, CBS Fri 8:00–9:00
CAST:
Ethan Allen Cord .... Lee Horsley
Claire Carroll (age 13) .... Jenny Beck
Joseph Carroll (11) .... Matthew Newmark
Ben Carroll (9) .... Brian Lando
George Carroll (5) .... Michael Patrick Carter
John Taylor .... Dehl Berti
Amelia Lawson .... Sigrid Thornton
Scotty McBride (1988–1990) .... Mack Dryden
Tiny .... John Bloom
Deputy Charlie .... James Crittenden
Wade Stratton (1988–1990) .... Randy Crowder
Mr. Lee (1988–1990) .... Benjamin Lum
Carl (1989–1991) .... Will Hunt
Mr. Axelrod (1989–1991) .... Michael Ensign
Pearl (1989–1991) .... Gay Hagen
Mr. Dodd (1989–1991) .... F. William Parker
Toy Lien (1989–1990) .... Kenny Lao
Dakota (1991) .... John Terlesky

Ethan Cord was a grizzled professional gunfighter living in the frontier mining town of Paradise, California, during the 1890s. His outlook on life and responsibility were changed radically when his dying sister, Lucy Cord Carroll, a singer in a musical revue in St. Louis, sent her four children out West to live with their uncle. Although he wasn't convinced that he could adjust to the role of parent, Ethan rented a farmhouse from Amelia Lawson, owner of the Paradise Bank and eventually his love interest, and moved his new family in. Despite his efforts to become a peaceable rancher, a more suitable living for a man with a family, Ethan was still hired for his skills with a gun and called upon to protect the honest folk of Paradise from criminals. Indian medicine man John Taylor was his close friend, a quiet man who always was around when he was needed, particularly when a gunfight was imminent. Among the townspeople seen frequently were Scotty the bartender, Tiny the blacksmith, storekeepers Lee and Axelrod, and Mr. Dodd, who worked in the hotel.

When the series returned for its third-season early in 1991, there were a number of changes. It had been retitled *Guns of Paradise*; Ethan was in the process of becoming the town's new Marshal; he was building a new home for the children and his fiancé, Amelia; and he had acquired a new friend, a brash young gambler named Dakota, who came to Paradise to avenge his father's shooting and stayed in hopes of winning large sums of money from those working the mines.

PARANOIA (*Quiz/Audience Participation*)
BROADCAST HISTORY:
Fox Family Channel
60 minutes
Original episodes: *2000*
Premiered: *April 14, 2000*
EMCEE:
Peter Tomarken

The point of this complicated live quiz show seemed to be to make the contestant—and perhaps the audience—as paranoid as possible. For starters, the set looked like something out of *Star Wars.* Emcee Peter Tomarken was perched on a crane, facing a contestant standing on a kind of catwalk suspended above a cavernous abyss; above them loomed giant monitors. (This was in fact a "virtual set," created by computer simulation.) The studio contestant competed against three remote players who were beamed in from their homes or other locations via satellite. One remote player competed from underwater in full scuba gear! The studio contestant began with $10,000, and was asked 10 questions. The goal was to answer correctly while eliminating remote players by selectively challenging them to answer, and not lose all the money in the process (each wrong answer, or right answer by a challenged player, cost $1,000). Questions were generally of the popular-culture variety, such as "What series used the 'William Tell Overture' as its theme?"

If the studio contestant survived this round, he proceeded to the playoff, in which he chose a category and received a question in that category that could multiply his winnings by anywhere from 10 to 100. The maximum prize was $1.5 million. While pondering the question, the sound of his heartbeat was piped through the sound system. *Thump, thump, thump . . . !*

Viewers could play along with the game on the Internet, or by phone, and affect the size of the studio contestant's jackpot. Successful Internet/phone players were invited to become remote contestants, and remote contestants could become studio players on a future show. Though billed as a breakthrough in interactive "play along" television, it was all so complicated that viewers soon gave up, and the show fell into its own ratings abyss within a few weeks.

PARANORMAL BORDERLINE, THE (*Supernatural*)
FIRST TELECAST: *March 12, 1996*
LAST TELECAST: *August 6, 1996*
BROADCAST HISTORY:
Mar 1996–Aug 1996, UPN Tue 9:00–10:00

HOST:

Jonathan Frakes

This exploitive series dealt with people who had crossed the paranormal borderline into the world of the supernatural. The stories in each episode included interviews, dramatic re-creations, and documentary-style film, with the first episode featuring tales of alien abductions, psychic detectives trying to solve a missing person's case, a near-death experience, "exclusive videotape" of a Yeti (a "goat-sucker" monster) in Puerto Rico, and a fire-starting ghost. "Something," intoned bearded host Jonathan Frakes, "was very, very wrong."

PARENT GAME, THE (*Quiz*)

BROADCAST HISTORY:

Syndicated only
30 minutes
Produced: *1972–1974*
Released: *Fall 1972*

HOST:

Clark Race

EXECUTIVE PRODUCER:

Chuck Barris

Three pairs of young parents or parents-to-be competed in this game show. The questions all concerned how to handle familiar and funny situations that arise in raising children. Answers were matched with those of an expert on child care (University of Southern California child psychologist Dorothy Thompson), and the couple with the most "matches" won.

PARENT 'HOOD, THE (*Situation Comedy*)

FIRST TELECAST: *January 18, 1995*
LAST TELECAST: *July 25, 1999*

BROADCAST HISTORY:

Jan 1995–Jul 1996, WB Wed 8:30–9:00
Jul 1995–Aug 1995, WB Wed 8:00–8:30
Mar 1996–Jul 1996, WB Sun 7:30–8:00
Jul 1996, WB Wed 8:00–8:30
Aug 1996, WB Wed 8:30–9:00
Aug 1996–Jun 1997, WB Sun 8:00–8:30
Jun 1997–Jul 1997, WB Wed 8:30–9:00
Jul 1997–Dec 1997, WB Sun 7:30–8:00
Jan 1998–Mar 1998, WB Sun 8:00–8:30
Mar 1998–May 1998, WB Sun 7:30–8:00
May 1998–Jun 1998, WB Sun 7:00–7:30
Jun 1998–Jul 1998, WB Sun 7:30–8:00
Jul 1998–Aug 1998, WB Sun 7:00–8:00
May 1999–Jul 1999, WB Sun 7:00–8:00
Jul 1999, WB Sun 7:00–7:30

CAST:

Robert Peterson .... Robert Townsend
Jerri Peterson .... Suzzanne Douglas
Michael Peterson (age 15) (1995–1997)
.... Kenny Blank
Zaria Peterson (14) .... Reagan Gomez-Preston
Nicholas Peterson (7) .... Curtis Williams
Cece Peterson (3) .... Ashli Adams
Derek Sawyer (1995) .... Bobby McGee
Mrs. Wilcox (1995) .... Carol Woods
Wendell Wilcox (1995–1998) .... Faizon Love
Shakim (1996) .... Nigel Thatch
Theresa (1996–1997) .... Tasha Scott
T. K. Anderson (1997–1999)
.... Tyrone Dorzell Burton
Gordon (1997–1998) .... Cory King
Kelly Peterson (1999) .... Kelly Perine

For series star (and coexecutive producer) Robert Townsend, whose *Townsend Television* on Fox the previous season had attempted to stretch the envelope for variety series, this was a pretty pedestrian family sitcom. Robert Peterson was an outgoing professor of communications at N.Y.U. He and his wife, Jerri, who was in law school, lived in a Manhattan brownstone apartment with their four children. Michael, the prankster, and Zaria were more interested in friends and dating than in their schoolwork, while Nicholas was remarkably outspoken for his age and Cece was just so cute. Others seen around the Peterson household were Mrs. Wilcox, their sometimes belligerent housekeeper, who had been Robert's baby-sitter when he was a child; her son, Wendell, the handyman; and Derek, Robert's charming childhood friend who was struggling to succeed as an actor.

For a series with a title that implied it would show a "real" black family, there was very little difference between the Petersons and the Huxtables *(The Cosby Show)* of the nineties or, for that matter, the Cleavers *(Leave It to Beaver)* or the Stones *(The Donna Reed Show)* of the fifties and sixties.

During the 1996–1997 season Robert hosted a public access cable show, *Community Focus*, on which he and Wendell were the movie critics—"brothers in the balcony." Many of the episodes included Robert's daydreams, in which the regulars played other people or something prompted him to fantasize about how things might have been different. Michael started a band, and he and the band's singer, Zaria's friend Theresa, were dating. Zaria was dating Shakim, a politically active senior who rubbed her parents the wrong way. In May 1997, Jerri graduated from law school.

That fall Michael was away at college and T.K. joined the cast. He was a tough street kid who Jerri brought into the household, hoping to provide the young con artist an environment in which he could straighten out his life. Jerri was working at home trying to build a legal practice, and Zaria had a new boyfriend, Gordon. Early in 1998 Wendell was suddenly dropped from the cast. In the last original episode of the season Robert prevented T.K. from using a gun to get back his stuff from some thugs in his old neighborhood, but at the end, the thugs fired two shots at Robert and T.K. Viewers did not find out what happened until a year later, when *The Parent 'Hood* returned for an abbreviated run during the summer of 1999. Robert had suffered a gunshot wound, but recovered, and things were back to normal. New to the cast was his well-meaning but ineffectual brother, Kelly. The 1999 episodes were scheduled in an hour-long block, consisting of a rerun followed by an original episode.

PARENTHOOD (*Comedy/Drama*)

FIRST TELECAST: *August 20, 1990*
LAST TELECAST: *November 10, 1990*

BROADCAST HISTORY:

Aug 1990, NBC Mon 9:00–10:00
Sep 1990, NBC Thu 10:00–11:00
Sep 1990–Nov 1990, NBC Sat 8:00–8:30

CAST:

Gil Buckman .... Ed Begley, Jr.
Karen Buckman .... Jayne Atkinson
Kevin Buckman (age 10) .... Max Elliott Slade

Taylor Buckman (8) .... Thora
Justin Buckman (4) .... Zachary LaVoy
Helen Buckman .... Maryedith Burrell
Garry Buckman (13) .... Leonardo DiCaprio
Julie Buckman Hawks (18) .... Bess Meyer
Tod Hawks .... David Arquette
Susan Buckman-Merrick........... Susan Norman
Nathan Merrick .... Ken Ober
Patty Merrick (4) .... Ivyann Schwan
Frank Buckman .... William Windom
Marilyn Buckman................. Sheila MacRae
Great Grandma Greenwell........... Mary Jackson

EXECUTIVE PRODUCERS:
Ron Howard, et al.

It took six executive producers (including Ron Howard) to create this complicated series, based on the 1989 Steve Martin movie of the same name. The theme was raising kids—if you could keep track of everybody's peculiarities, and of who belonged to whom.

Mild-mannered financial analyst Gil and his wife Karen were the parents of angst-ridden Kevin, daddy's girl Taylor, and rambunctious Justin. Gil was determined to be a "quality dad," unlike his workaholic father Frank, though that often got him only ice cream in his ear. Gil's divorced sister Helen's kids were insecure Garry and rebellious Julie, the latter being married to quirky young house painter Tod. And sister Susan, a free-spirited high school teacher, supported her fastidious husband Nathan, who was working on his Ph.D. while exploring "alternative" parenting procedures for their gifted four-year-old, Patty.

Grandparents Frank and Marilyn looked on all of this with some dismay, while hard-of-hearing Great Grandma simply said "Eh? What?"

Leftover original episodes of this series were telecast on December 16, 1990, and August 11, 1991.

PARIS (*Police Drama*)

FIRST TELECAST: *September 29, 1979*
LAST TELECAST: *January 15, 1980*
BROADCAST HISTORY:
Sep 1979–Oct 1979, CBS Sat 10:00–11:00
Dec 1979–Jan 1980, CBS Tue 10:00–11:00

CAST:
Woody Paris..................... James Earl Jones
Barbara Paris.................... Lee Chamberlain
Deputy Chief Jerome Bench .... Hank Garrett
Stacey Erickson....................... Cecilia Hart
Charlie Bogart....................... Jake Mitchell
Willie Miller .... Mike Warren
Ernie Villas .... Frank Ramirez

Woody Paris was an erudite and highly principled black police captain whose interests went beyond simple law enforcement. By night he taught a course in criminology at a local university. He even had a home life—unlike most TV cops—shared with his understanding wife, Barbara. On the job, Paris reported to Deputy Chief Jerome Bench, a longtime friend, and ran a special Metro Squad assigned to break tough cases. Assigned to his squad were four young officers, Stacey, Charlie, Willie, and Ernie.

What Paris lacked, unfortunately, was a little bit of believability. James Earl Jones, a highly respected actor, strutted through this role speaking in booming, stentorian tones, as if it were *Richard III*. Despite good reviews from an awed press, *Paris* did not attract much of an audience, and was soon canceled.

PARIS CAVALCADE OF FASHIONS
(*Fashion Show*)

FIRST TELECAST: *November 11, 1948*
LAST TELECAST: *January 20, 1949*
BROADCAST HISTORY:
Nov 1948–Jan 1949, NBC Thu 7:15–7:30

NARRATOR:
Faye Emerson (Nov–Dec 1948)
Julie Gibson (Dec 1948–Jan 1949)

Films of the latest Paris creations. The series was formerly seen locally on WNBT, New York.

PARIS 7000 (*Adventure*)

FIRST TELECAST: *January 22, 1970*
LAST TELECAST: *June 4, 1970*
BROADCAST HISTORY:
Jan 1970–Jun 1970, ABC Thu 10:00–11:00

CAST:
Jack Brennan.................... George Hamilton
Robert Stevens .... Gene Raymond
Jules Maurois .... Jacques Aubuchon

Movie star George Hamilton starred in this series as a State Department employee attached to the U.S. Embassy in Paris, whose job it was to help Americans in trouble. The number to call for help: Paris 7000. Robert Stevens was his aide, and Maurois the contact on the local gendarmerie.

PARK PLACE (*Situation Comedy*)

FIRST TELECAST: *April 9, 1981*
LAST TELECAST: *April 30, 1981*
BROADCAST HISTORY:
Apr 1981, CBS Thu 8:00–9:00

CAST:
David Ross......................... Harold Gould
Jeff O'Neil .... David Clennon
Howard "Howie" Beech .... Don Calfa
Frances Heine.................. Alice Drummond
Ernie Rice .... Cal Gibson
Joel "Jo" Keene .... Mary Elaine Monti
Aaron "Mac" MacRae............... Lionel Smith
Brad Lincoln .... James Widdoes

Patterned after such successful urban "gang comedies" as *Barney Miller* and *Taxi*, *Park Place* was the story of a motley group of lawyers working at a New York City legal aid clinic. Into the Park Place Division of the New York City Legal Assistance Bureau came the poor, the ignorant, and the downright obnoxious—all seeking free legal help. In charge, more or less, was senior attorney David Ross. Five young attorneys made up his staff: Jeff O'Neill, the naive eager beaver; Howie Beech, the status-seeking opportunist; Jo Keene, the aggressive women's libber; Mac MacRae, the wheelchair-ridden black Vietnam veteran; and Brad Lincoln, the inexperienced young Harvard graduate trying to obtain some recognition from his peers. Frances, the efficient but spaced-out secretary, and Ernie, the hip receptionist, rounded out the cast.

PARKER LEWIS CAN'T LOSE (*Situation Comedy*)

FIRST TELECAST: *September 2, 1990*
LAST TELECAST: *August 22, 1993*
BROADCAST HISTORY:
Sep 1990, FOX Sun 9:30–10:00

Sep 1990, FOX Thu 8:30–9:00
Sep 1990–Jun 1992, FOX Sun 7:30–8:00
Jul 1992–Aug 1992, FOX Thu 8:30–9:00
Aug 1992–Sep 1992, FOX Sun 7:30–8:00
Mar 1993–Aug 1993, FOX Sun 7:00–7:30

CAST:

Parker Lewis .... Corin Nemec
Principal Grace Musso .... Melanie Chartoff
Mikey Randall .... Billy Jayne
Jerry Steiner .... Troy Slaten
Shelly Lewis .... Maia Brewton
Frank Lemmer (1990–1992) .... Taj Johnson
Francis Larry Kubiak .... Abraham Benrubi
**Mr. Martin Lewis* .... Timothy Stack
**Mrs. Judy Lewis (1990–1991)* .... Anne Bloom
**Mrs. Judy Lewis (1991–1993)* ... Mary Ellen Trainor
Nick Comstock (1991–1992) .... Paul Johansson
Annie Sloan (1992–1993) .... Jennifer Guthrie
Coach Hank Kohler (1992–1993) ...... John Pinette
Brad Penny (1992–1993) .... Harold Pruett

*Occasional

Suburban Santo Domingo High School was the setting for this youth-oriented comedy. Parker Lewis, a junior, was what every teen wishes he could be in school—bright, popular, resourceful, and cool. Despite his penchant for subverting the rules—usually with the help of his "best bud," Mikey, and Jerry, the nerdy sophomore genius who idolized him—Parker never seemed to get caught. No matter the situation, as he always said, it was "not a problem." He was a constant thorn in the side of autocratic principal Grace Musso, whose goal was to get him expelled. Helping Ms. Musso was student Frank Lemmer, her ominous "special obedience counselor." Also featured were Larry Kubiak, the giant, hulking dumb jock with the voracious appetite; Parker's bratty younger sister Shelly, who delighted in ratting on him; and Nick, the cool counterman at the Atlas Diner who dispensed sound advice. Parker's dad owned a video rental store.

When the series premiered on Fox it was considered a clone of NBC's *Ferris Bueller,* which had premiered ten days earlier. Both starred hip high school students who managed to get around all of the rules. But *Parker*'s extensive use of unusual camera angles and video special effects, as well as TV monitors everywhere at school and home, gave the series a unique, almost surrealistic cartoon look. It survived, while the all too realistic *Ferris* was gone from the NBC lineup before Christmas.

New episodes were aired during the summer of 1992, as was the case with *Beverly Hills 90210* during summer vacation. These new episodes heralded a number of changes. The title had been shortened to *Parker Lewis,* there was less emphasis on odd camera angles and surrealistic qualities, and several new characters were added—Annie Sloan, Parker's serious love interest; Coach Kohler, who was infatuated with Principal Musso; and Brad Penny, a tough dropout who was hostile to everyone, especially Parker. During the series' final run in 1993 Jerry had skipped from sophomore to senior and Mikey was working after school as a waiter at the Atlas Diner, which had been bought by Coach Kohler.

PARKERS, THE (*Situation Comedy*)

FIRST TELECAST: *August 30, 1999*
LAST TELECAST:

BROADCAST HISTORY:

Aug 1999–Feb 2001, UPN Mon 8:30–9:00
Apr 2000–May 2000, UPN Tue 8:00–8:30
Mar 2001–Jul 2002, UPN Mon 9:00–9:30
Mar 2001–Apr 2001, UPN Fri 8:00–8:30
May 2001–Jun 2001, UPN Mon 8:00–8:30
Jul 2002–Sep 2002, UPN Tue 9:30–10:00
Aug 2002– , UPN Mon 8:00–8:30

CAST:

Kim Parker .... Countess Vaughn James
Margaret "Nikki" Parker .... Mo'Nique
Professor Stanley Oglevee .... Dorien Wilson
Desiree Littlejohn (1999) .... Mari Morrow
Stevie Van Lowe .... Jenna Von Oy
Thaddeus Tyrell Radcliffe ("T") .... Ken Lawson
Andel Wilkerson .... Yvette Wilson
Veronica Cooper (1999–2001) ..... Paulette Braxton
**Regina Foster* .... Kara Brock
**Joe Woody* .... Dwight Woody
Dean Toni Ross (2001) .... Angelle Brooks

*Occasional

THEME:

written by Rodney "Darkchild" Jerkins and Countess Vaughn, performed by Countess Vaughn James

In this spin-off from *Moesha,* Mo's best friend, Kim, and her large, loud single mother, Nikki, were both enrolled as freshmen at Santa Monica College. Kim had the hots for fellow student T while her mother was obsessed with handsome but totally disinterested Professor Oglevee, who was mortified by her aggressiveness. Nikki's friend and neighbor Desiree was the receptionist for the Artistic Endeavors talent agency but her character was dropped before the end of the year. In November T formed a singing group, Free Style Unity, with Kim as lead singer and their white friend, Stevie, doing backup. After the first of the year Nikki's friend Andel, who owned a restaurant (she had previously been on *Moesha*), became a regular. In April Kim and Stevie got an apartment together, in Professor Oglevee's building. In the season finale Kim's boyfriend Jerel (Trent J. Cameron), who had been offered a job as a music producer in Paris, proposed and they went to Las Vegas to get married.

That fall the marriage was annulled because Jerel was underage. He still went to Paris and Kim had to put her life back together. Nikki's romantic designs on Oglevee perked up after Veronica, his longtime girlfriend, dumped him for another guy. Their proximity improved, at least, when she gave up her apartment and moved in with Kim (Stevie had moved out). In November Kim and Nikki ran for student body president, but both were disqualified for cheating and obnoxious sorority girl Regina won by default. In May Nikki was dating a friend of Oglevee's and the professor, who felt qualms about it, saw a psychologist who told him he was in love with Nikki.

As the 2001–2002 season began, Oglevee couldn't get Nikki out of his mind, despite Dean Ross' aggressive efforts to have an affair with him. When he found out the psychologist was actually a janitor, he tried to get back together with Toni but she had decided to take an extended leave of absence to get over him. In November Andel reopened her restaurant as an upscale club. In the season finale Oglevee, fired because of budget cutbacks, got drunk and ended up in the sack with Nikki. The next morning he woke up mortified that he had actually slept with her. Nikki did, however, help him by convincing the school's dean, whom she had caught in a compromising position, to reinstate Oglevee. In November T and Stevie started dating, which didn't last, and Nikki, after a stint as the chef at Andel's bistro, started a catering business.

PARTNERS (*Situation Comedy*)
FIRST TELECAST: *September 11, 1995*
LAST TELECAST: *April 1, 1996*
BROADCAST HISTORY:
Sep 1995–Dec 1995, FOX Mon 9:00–9:30
Dec 1995–Apr 1996, FOX Mon 9:30–10:00
CAST:
Owen .... Tate Donovan
Bob .... Jon Cryer
Alicia Sundergard .... Maria Pitillo
Heather Pond .... Catherine Lloyd Burns
Lolie (1996) .... Corinne Bohrer

Owen and Bob were architects and best friends working together at a San Francisco architectural firm. Their relationship underwent a major change when Owen, the creative one, proposed to Alicia, a sexy lawyer, in the series premiere. Obsessive Bob had always gotten along with Alicia, but now that she and Owen were engaged, he felt threatened, and for the next several months competed with her for Owen's attention. Early in 1996, Bob started dating Alicia's best friend, Lolie, and in March, after a falling out with their boss, Owen and Bob quit the firm to start their own architectural firm. Heather, their efficient but incredibly accident-prone secretary/assistant, went with them. In the season finale, as Owen and Alicia were about to get married, Bob proposed to Lolie—who turned him down because they hadn't been going out long enough. They decided to give it more time. At the end of the episode, on the morning of their wedding day, Owen and Alicia woke up after having spent the night stranded in his old car whose battery had died. As the credits rolled they were walking back to town to get married.

Since the series was not renewed, nobody will ever know if they made it to the church on time.

PARTNERS, THE (*Situation Comedy*)
FIRST TELECAST: *September 18, 1971*
LAST TELECAST: *September 8, 1972*
BROADCAST HISTORY:
Sep 1971–Jan 1972, NBC Sat 8:00–8:30
Jul 1972–Sep 1972, NBC Fri 8:00–8:30
CAST:
Det. Lennie Crooke .... Don Adams
Det. George Robinson .... Rupert Crosse
Capt. Andrews .... John Doucette
Sgt. Higgenbottom .... Dick Van Patten
Freddie Butler .... Robert Karvelas

Lennie Crooke and George Robinson were a pair of police detectives who were always getting into crazy situations while investigating crimes. In their enthusiasm, they would occasionally get themselves into more trouble than did the criminals they were after. Their boss, Captain Andrews, was constantly frustrated and confounded by their activities which, despite all, somehow resulted in their solving the crimes. Sgt. Higgenbottom, who was trying to ingratiate himself with the captain, spent much of his time belittling Lennie and George. A recurring nuisance was Freddie Butler, a compulsive confessor who claimed responsibility for everything from murder to shoplifting.

PARTNERS IN CRIME (*Detective Drama*)
FIRST TELECAST: *September 22, 1984*
LAST TELECAST: *December 29, 1984*
BROADCAST HISTORY:
Sep 1984–Nov 1984, NBC Sat 9:00–10:00
Nov 1984–Dec 1984, NBC Sat 10:00–11:00
CAST:
Carole Stanwyck .... Lynda Carter
Sydney Kovak .... Loni Anderson
Lt. Ed Vronsky .... Leo Rossi
Harmon Shain .... Walter Olkewicz
Jeanine .... Eileen Heckart

Two beautiful women—both ex-wives of the same man—joined forces to solve his murder in this light mystery series set in San Francisco. Carole was a professional photographer, a former heiress, and a rather proper brunette; Sydney was a jazz bass player, an amateur pickpocket, and a fun-loving blonde. Their ex-hubby, eccentric detective Raymond Caulfield, had left them, as a joint bequest, his fine old Victorian house and his thriving detective agency. After solving Raymond's last case, the girls decided to continue the business themselves. The series featured glamorous fashions, catty chatter about being married to the same man, and beautiful San Francisco locations. Lt. Vronsky, their contact on the S.F.P.D., was always after a date with Sydney; Shain was their dense helper; and Jeanine was Raymond's mother, an amateur sleuth and busybody who ran a mystery bookshop called—what else—"Partners In Crime."

PARTRIDGE FAMILY, THE (*Situation Comedy*)
FIRST TELECAST: *September 25, 1970*
LAST TELECAST: *August 31, 1974*
BROADCAST HISTORY:
Sep 1970–Jun 1973, ABC Fri 8:30–9:00
Jun 1973–Aug 1974, ABC Sat 8:00–8:30
CAST:
Shirley Partridge .... Shirley Jones
Keith Partridge .... David Cassidy
Laurie Partridge .... Susan Dey
Danny Partridge .... Danny Bonaduce
Christopher Partridge (1970–1971)
.... Jeremy Gelbwaks
Christopher Partridge (1971–1974) ... Brian Forster
Tracy Partridge .... Suzanne Crough
Reuben Kinkaid .... David Madden
**Ricky Stevens (1973–1974)* .... Ricky Segall
**Alan Kinkaid (1973–1974)* .... Alan Bursky
*Occasional
THEME
"When We're Singin'," music by Wes Farrell, lyrics by Diane Hilderbrand (1970); new lyrics and title "Come On, Get Happy," by Danny Janssen (1972)

Oscar-winner Shirley Jones and her stepson, David Cassidy, starred in this comedy about a family that hit the big time in the music business. Shirley Partridge was just another widowed suburban mother with a houseful of rambunctious kids, until one day the kids asked her to take part in an impromptu recording session they were holding in the garage. Seems they needed a vocalist. The song they were recording was "I Think I Love You," and to everyone's surprise they sold it to a record company, the record became a smash hit, and the Partridges were soon setting off in a wildly painted old school bus to perform around the country. They were authentic members of the rock generation. Stories depicted their exploits on the road, and in their California hometown.

Besides Shirley and 16-year-old Keith (Cassidy), the band included Laurie (15), Danny (10, and the freckle-faced con man of the family), Christopher (7), and Tracy (5). Reuben Kinkaid was their fast-talking, child-hating agent—and perpetual foil for Danny. During the 1973–1974 season a neighbor's son, 4-year-old Ricky, joined the cast, and he sang too. Simone was the family pooch.

The Partridges were heavily promoted in the real-life music business, and they caught on with several hit singles, including "I Think I Love You," which sold four million copies, as well as albums. David Cassidy became the hero of the subteen set and had considerable success as a single act. Unlike the Monkees, the Partridges had no artistic pretensions—none of them were professional musicians—and the backgrounds on their records were in fact done by professional studio musicians, with Shirley and David providing the vocals. Their success was as spectacular on the record charts as on TV, but it did not last long in either case.

An animated Saturday morning sequel, *The Partridge Family, 2200* A.D. ran on ABC from September 1974 to September 1975.

The Partridge Family was loosely based on the experiences of a real-life popular recording family, the Cowsills.

PARTY GIRL (*Situation Comedy*)
FIRST TELECAST: *September 9, 1996*
LAST TELECAST: *September 30, 1996*
BROADCAST HISTORY:
Sep 1996, FOX Mon 9:00–9:30
CAST:
Mary .... Christine Taylor
Judy Burkhard .... Swoosie Kurtz
Derrick .... John Cameron Mitchell
Wanda .... Merrin Dungey
Oneal .... Matt Borlenghi
THEME:
"It's My Life" by Carole Bayer Sager and Oliver Leiber

Lust in the library. Mary was a free-spirited young woman living the Manhattan social life to the hilt. At night she partied with her friends, but during the day she worked as a clerk at the New York Public Library for her late mother's uptight best friend, and her surrogate mother, Judy. Also working for Judy was Wanda, who found Mary's flower child attitude a bit hard to take and training her in the Dewey Decimal System almost impossible. Mary's artsy friends included Derrick, a cynical gay assistant fashion stylist who ogled Mary's dates, and Oneal, a rather dense one-time boxer working as a bartender at the neighborhood restaurant where Judy and her friend hung out.

Based on the 1995 feature film of the same name.

PARTY LINE (*Quiz/Audience Participation*)
FIRST TELECAST: *June 8, 1947*
LAST TELECAST: *August 31, 1947*
BROADCAST HISTORY:
Jun 1947–Aug 1947, NBC Sun 8:30–9:00
EMCEE:
Bert Parks

Bert Parks, one of the most familiar faces on early TV, hosted this primitive phone-in quiz show which occupied half of the Sunday 8:00–9:00 P.M. Bristol-Myers hour during the summer of 1947. (For the other half, see *Tex and Jinx*.) Bert would ask a question, sometimes illustrated with a short film or performed by actors in the studio, and then would call a number at random from among the cards sent in by viewers. If the person called was watching and could answer the question, he won a prize of $5 and a box of Bristol-Myers products.

The program was sponsored on a two-station network consisting of WNBT, New York, and WPTZ, Philadelphia.

PARTY MACHINE WITH NIA PEEPLES, THE
(*Music*)
BROADCAST HISTORY:
Syndicated only
30 minutes
Produced: *1991*
Released: *January 1991*
HOSTESS:
Nia Peeples

Produced by Arsenio Hall, this noisy, energetic series was designed to follow Hall's late-night talk show. Hosted by actress/singer/dancer Nia Peeples, *Party Machine* was a non-stop half hour of rock music in a setting that resembled a multilevel club with patrons dancing and partying throughout. Miss Peeples was seen moving about the "club" and talking to both the viewing audience and the celebrities who were there for the evening, some of whom performed. The focus was on the hippest contemporary popular music, with an emphasis on rap, and among those appearing were MC Hammer, Ice-T, Run-DMC, Howard Hewitt, L. L. Cool J., Sheena Easton, Al B. Sure!, and Color Me Badd. Miss Peeples also chatted with such non-musical guests as Mario Van Peebles, Dr. Ruth Westheimer, Jasmine Guy, and Sinbad.

Party Machine ran as a half-hour series on weekday evenings, with a re-edited full-hour version available for airing on Saturday or Sunday night. Never able to find an audience, it left the air in September, after an eight-month run.

PARTY OF FIVE (*Drama*)
FIRST TELECAST: *September 12, 1994*
LAST TELECAST: *May 3, 2000*
BROADCAST HISTORY:
Sep 1994–Dec 1994, FOX Mon 9:00–10:00
Dec 1994–Mar 1995, FOX Wed 9:00–10:00
Jun 1995–Apr 1997, FOX Wed 9:00–10:00
Aug 1997–May 1999, FOX Wed 9:00–10:00 (OS)
Oct 1999–Apr 2000, FOX Tue 9:00–10:00
Apr 2000–May 2000, FOX Wed 9:00–10:00
CAST:
Charlie Salinger (age 24) .... Matthew Fox
Bailey Salinger (16) .... Scott Wolf
Julia Salinger (15) .... Neve Campbell
Claudia Salinger (11) .... Lacey Chabert
Owen Salinger (1) (1995–1998)
.... Brandon & Taylor Porter
Owen Salinger (1998–2000) .... Jacob Smith
Kirsten Bennett .... Paula Devicq
Will McCorkle (1994–1998, 1999–2000)
.... Scott Grimes

Ross Werkman (1994–1997, 1999–2000) .... Mitchell Anderson
Nina (1994–1995) .... Cari Shayne
Justin Thompson (1994–1997, 1999–2000) .... Michael Goorjian
Kate Bishop (1994–1995) .... Jennifer Blanc
Joe Mangus .... Tom Mason
Artie (1994–1995) .... Michael Shulman
Bill (1994–1995) .... David Burke
Jill Holbrook (1994–1995) .... Megan Ward
Griffin Holbrook (1995–2000) ...... Jeremy London
Sarah Reeves (1995–1999) .... Jennifer Love Hewitt
Jody (1995–1996) .... Marla Sokoloff
Kathleen Eisely (1996) .... Brenda Strong
Jacob Gordon (1996–1997) .... Carroll O'Connor
Callie (1996–1997) .... Alexandra Lee
Grace Wilcox (1996–1997) .... Tamara Taylor
Sam Brody (1996–1997) .... Ben Browder
Coach Russ Petrocelli (1996–1997) ..... Dan Lauria
Mrs. Reeves (1997–1999) .... Alyson Reed
Reed (1997–1998) .... Andrew Keegan
Annie Mott (1997–1998) .... Paige Turco
Nina (1997) .... Jessica Lundy
Dr. Paul Thomas (1997–1999) .... Tim Dekay
Natalie Mott (1997–1998) .... Allison Bertolini
Dr. Rabin (1997–1999) .... Brenda Wehle
Rosalie (1998) .... Ever Carradine
Daphne Jablonski (1998–2000) ..... Jennifer Aspen
Jamie Burke (1998) .... Ross Malinger
Ned Grayson (1998–1999) .... Scott Bairstow
Maggie (1998–1999) .... Heather McComb
Josh (1998–1999) .... Adam Scott
Cody (1999) .... Chad Todhunter
Evan Stilman (1999) .... Kyle Secor
Alexa (1999) .... Maggie Lawson
Cameron Woolcott (1999) .... Andrew Levitas
Victor (1999–2000) .... Wilson Cruz
Myra Wringler (1999) .... Lauren Ambrose
Holly Baggens (1999–2000) .... Rhona Mitra
Gus (1999–2000) .... Charles Esten
Adam (2000) .... Sean Maher
Tod (2000) .... Thomas Ian Nicholas

*Occasional

THEME:

"Everybody Wants to Be Closer to Me"

Following the death of their parents in a tragic automobile accident, the five Salinger children were forced to be more than siblings as they tried to keep the family together. Appointed legal guardian of the others, oldest brother Charlie worked evenings as a bartender at Salinger's, the San Francisco restaurant his father had owned, and days as a carpenter. Trying to live his own life and be a surrogate father to the others was a constant source of frustration for the still immature young man. Helping him manage the family checkbook was brother Bailey, who found his new responsibilities were putting a crimp in his social life. Julia was having the most trouble adjusting to the loss of her parents, while her younger sister, Claudia, a gifted violinist, had the strangest bedroom, a tent set up in the dining room. All of them helped take care of their baby brother, Owen, who had only been a few months old at the time of the accident. Kirsten, their pretty young nanny, was in grad school at Berkeley majoring in child psychology, and Joe Mangus (Tom Mason), their late father's partner, was the current owner of Salinger's.

Kirsten started dating Charlie, which initially bothered Bailey, who had a crush on her. Eventually she moved into the house—not as a nanny, Bill had been hired to replace her—and, by the end of the 1994–1995 season, Kirsten and Charlie were engaged. Will was Bailey's best friend and confidante at Grant High School, where he met his first serious girlfriends. The first was Kate, who left town to go to a boarding school back east at midseason, and the second, emotionally troubled and sexually active Jill, who died from a cocaine overdose in the season finale. Julia, who spent much of the year trying to overcome her insecurities, was helped when she started dating Justin, a writer on the school's yearbook staff. Claudia continued to work on her music with the help of Ross, her violin teacher, and spent much of her free time with her best buddy, Artie.

During 1995–1996, Julia alternated between Justin and Griffin, a troubled youth. Charlie and Kirsten were to be married in December, but he got cold feet on their wedding day and they broke up. Bailey's main relationship was with Sarah, who had previously been dating his buddy Will. In January, Jacob, the Salingers' maternal grandfather, showed up and became part of the family. Charlie had an affair with Kathleen, and when he broke up with her, she put together an investment group to buy the building housing the restaurant and told him she wouldn't renew its lease. The restaurant was saved when Bailey convinced Grandfather Jacob to use his college fund money to buy the building.

That fall Bailey began college and Will went away to school. Kirsten lost a teaching job when her advisor found out that she had inadvertently plagiarized material in her doctoral dissertation, and she went into a major depression. Eventually, when she didn't improve, her parents arrived and took her back to Chicago. Bailey moved out of the house and was living with free spirit Callie, with whom he had an affair. He developed a serious drinking problem, and after a long battle, the family got him to join Alcoholics Anonymous. He finally moved back home in March. Grace, an ambitious African-American girl whom Charlie was dating, moved into the Salinger home after a fire destroyed her apartment and began a run for city council. In the season finale Charlie broke up with Grace on the eve of the city council election, which she won; and Julia and Griffin, who had been living together, got a quickie wedding in Nevada, making her the first of the "five" to be married. The others gave her their mother's wedding ring.

At the start of the 1997–1998 season Julia returned from two months in Europe and had problems adjusting to married life. She had forgone college and gone to work because Griffin's motorcycle repair business wasn't thriving; late in the year he sold out, and they moved into the Salinger attic. Bailey started to date Annie, a member of his AA group who was seven years older than he and who had a young daughter, Natalie. Kirsten, now married, returned to the Bay area with her physician husband, Paul. Then the entire family was shocked when Charlie was diagnosed with Hodgkin's disease. Bailey, overwhelmed by the stress of his schoolwork, helping care for sick Charlie, and running Salinger's, dropped out of college. In March, Annie, who had fallen off the wagon, went into a rehab center, leaving Natalie in Sarah's care. Late in

April, Charlie found out he was cured. Joe sold his half of Salinger's to the family, and Bailey, who loved the work, became the full-time manager. At season's end Julia got accepted to Stanford, and Charlie found out that Daphne, the woman he was currently dating, was pregnant. Bailey got back together with Sarah after Annie rejected his marriage proposal.

In fall 1998, Sarah and Bailey, who was now running the family restaurant, moved into a much nicer apartment. Julia started school and began an affair with her roommate Maggie's boyfriend Ned, but left him—after a time—when he proved to be abusive. Bailey and Sarah took Claudia to a boarding school near Boston, but when she came home at Thanksgiving, Claudia found excuses not to go back because she hated it. Daphne was living at the Salinger home (she gave birth to Diana in November) but couldn't adjust to motherhood, and in January she left. Charlie, working as a high school shop teacher, was left to raise Diana alone. He and Bailey got into a nasty custody battle over Owen, who was having learning problems; Charlie won, but then gave custody of the child to Bailey. Later that spring Bailey, Sarah, and Owen moved back into the Salinger home and Charlie, with a chance to get away from the family, moved in with Kirsten. He proposed to her in May (she accepted) as did Bailey to Sarah. Sarah's initial acceptance was short-lived and, at season's end, she was preparing to move to New York.

In the 1999–2000 season premiere Charlie and Kirsten finally got married and Sarah, who had rejected his proposal, was taking verbal abuse from Bailey. Julia left Stanford for the California School of Fine Arts to concentrate on her writing, Sarah went to New York in search of her birth father (and her own series, *Time of Your Life*) and Bailey had difficulty accepting her departure. Will had dropped out of college and was working as a gofer for a local pro wrestling operation; he later got an administrative job with the 49ers pro football team. Bailey hired Joe, his father's former partner, as a manager at Salinger's. Daphne was stripping at a club to make a living, and by Thanksgiving she and Griffin were having an affair. Charlie left teaching to work for a furniture maker and eventually took day-to-day control to produce higher-quality furniture than Gus, the owner, was used to. Claudia wanted to skip her senior year of high school and was applying for early admission to schools in the East. In late January Joe admitted to Bailey that he had embezzled money from the restaurant to gamble on the stock market to pay his divorce expenses—and had lost it all. Bailey, trying to deal with assorted financial pressures, fell off the wagon and decided to go into rehab. While he was in rehab, Charlie was stretched to the limit managing the furniture business and helping run the restaurant.

Bailey told Charlie he was tired of being the responsible problem solver in the family and was never really interested in running Salinger's. Charlie got a huge chair order from a hotel chain and needed to set up a second factory—with Bailey's help on the business end. Using the family restaurant as collateral, Charlie was able to finance his purchase of Gus' furniture business. In April Justin returned after having broken up with his bride, and he and Julia had an affair until he went back to Yale. Will decided to go back east to school, and Charlie wanted to scale back the furniture business after his foreman died from a heart attack. In the series finale Bailey was accepted to Wharton in Philadelphia, Claudia decided to go to Juilliard in New York, Julia got a job as an intern at N.O.W. (the National Organization for Women) in Washington, Justin decided to transfer from Yale to Georgetown so they could live together, and Kirsten's long-sought pregnancy was going well—she was carrying a boy. Charlie took back custody of Owen and gave Daphne's boyfriend Bailey's job with the furniture business. He sold the family home to provide money for Bailey and Claudia's education, Owen's future expenses, and to help out Julia and still leave enough for him to buy a smaller home for his family. In the closing scene, while they were packing stuff up, all of them were mentally reminiscing about their experiences in the family home.

The show's title referred to the five siblings having dinner at their late dad's restaurant as a "party of five."

PARTY TIME AT CLUB ROMA (*Variety*)

FIRST TELECAST: *October 14, 1950*
LAST TELECAST: *January 6, 1951*
BROADCAST HISTORY:
Oct 1950–Jan 1951, NBC Sat 11:00–11:30
REGULARS:
Ben Alexander
Pat Emery
Chris Emery
Camille Leong
Doodles and Spicer
The Cheerleaders

Set in the mythical Club Roma in San Francisco, where this series was actually filmed, *Party Time at Club Roma* started out as a variation on *Beat the Clock*, with emcee Alexander inviting guests at the club to join in attempting various stunts or playing games in which they might win small merchandise prizes. His assistants included a pair of identical twins (Pat and Chris), a beautiful girl from San Francisco's Chinatown (Camille), and the pantomime team of Doodles and Spicer. The format was soon changed to a talent contest with emcee Alexander picking acts out of the audience to perform for the crowd at the club. The winners were chosen by applause meter.

An interesting sidelight to this series is that it was also produced by Ben Alexander. A former child star in films, he was an account executive with Foote, Cone & Belding, the advertising agency for the sponsor, Roma Wines, and this was his first exposure to network television. He subsequently left the agency and played Jack Webb's partner on *Dragnet*.

PASADENA (*Serial Drama*)

FIRST TELECAST: *September 28, 2001*
LAST TELECAST: *November 2, 2001*
BROADCAST HISTORY:
Sep 2001–Nov 2001, FOX 9:00–10:00
CAST:
Lily Greeley McAllister .... Alison Lohman
George Reese Greeley .... Philip Baker Hall
Lillian Greeley .... Barbara Babcock
Robert Greeley .... Mark Valley
Catherine McAllister .... Dana Delany
Beth Greeley............ Natasha Gregson Wagner
Nate Greeley .... Balthazar Getty
Will McAllister .... Martin Donovan

Mason McAllister .... Chris Marquette
Jennie .... Nicole Paggi
Henry Bellows .... Alan Simpson
Jayleen Richards .... Christine Moore
Tom Bellows .... Derek Cecil
Pilar, the maid .... Lupe Ontiveros

This short-lived prime time soap opera was set in upscale Pasadena, California. Fifteen-year-old Lily McAllister, whose wealthy dysfunctional family was immersed in scandals, served as the show's narrator. Lily's great-grandfather had established the Pasadena Country Club and Pasadena Pavilion, where the family had a long tradition of entertaining the wealthy and politically connected. Her grandfather George Reese Greeley was a multibillionaire who served on the boards of more than 50 corporations. As chairman of Reese Corporation, which owned, among other things, the *Los Angeles Sun* newspaper, he presided over the family's fortune. George and his wife, Lillian, had four children—Robert, the firstborn and heir to the family business; neurotic Catherine, the only one to marry; independent Beth, a free spirit who had no interest in the family's social standing; and drug-addicted Nate, their youngest. Lillian and Catherine were socially prominent hostesses with a penchant for throwing lavish parties and contributing to cultural and charitable organizations. Catherine and her husband, Will, had two children, Lily and her younger brother Mason. Jennie was Lily's best friend.

As the series opened one of Lily's classmates at the Arroyo Alto Preparatory School, Henry, urged her to investigate the questionable dealings within her family. Both Catherine and Will, whose marriage was failing, were having affairs while Robert was trying to keep the family's dirty laundry from going public and waiting to be named chairman of Reese Corporation. When he found out his father was giving the position to Will, he was incensed and hired back Will's vindictive ex-lover, Jayleen, whom Will had fired. Then, before the backstabbing could really begin, *Pasadena* was abruptly canceled after four episodes.

PASSPORT TO DANGER (*Intrigue*)

BROADCAST HISTORY:

Syndicated only
30 minutes
Produced: *Apr 1954–1956* (39 episodes)
Released: *November 1954*

CAST:

Steve McQuinn .... Cesar Romero

The principal attraction of this foreign-adventure series was Cesar Romero, whose debonair good looks and sly sense of humor (he evidently didn't take the role too seriously) lifted it a bit above the ordinary. Otherwise it was the usual international-intrigue series. Glamorous locales, beautiful but mysterious women, and dangerous incidents swirled around diplomatic courier Steve McQuinn as he went about his appointed rounds delivering top-secret messages to U.S. embassies from Rome to Rangoon.

PASSWORD (*Quiz/Audience Participation*)

FIRST TELECAST: *January 2, 1962*
LAST TELECAST: *May 22, 1967*
BROADCAST HISTORY:

Jan 1962–Sep 1962, CBS Tue 8:00–8:30
Sep 1962–Mar 1963, CBS Sun 6:30–7:00
Mar 1963–Sep 1963, CBS Mon 10:00–10:30
Sep 1963–Sep 1964, CBS Thu 7:30–8:00
Sep 1964–Sep 1965, CBS Thu 9:00–9:30
Apr 1967–May 1967, CBS Mon 10:30–11:00

EMCEE:

Allen Ludden

Password was a word-association game. Two teams, each composed of one celebrity and one non-celebrity contestant, competed in trying to identify the "password" with the least number of clues. The "password," usually a common word, was handed to one member of each team and these two people would then take turns giving their partners one-word clues to make them guess the word. After the first clue a correct response was worth ten points, after the second clue, nine points, and so forth. The first team to accumulate 25 points won the round. In the "Lightning Round" one member of each team would have 60 seconds to get his partner to properly associate a total of five "passwords." Winners got cash prizes and the chance to return to face a new challenging team.

The daytime version of *Password* premiered in October 1961 and ran on CBS until 1967. It was syndicated from 1967 to 1969, ran on ABC from 1969 to 1975, and aired on NBC from January 1979 to March 1982. Allen Ludden hosted all versions until suffering a debilitating stroke in 1980 (he died in 1981). He was replaced by Tom Kennedy, who remained with the show until it was canceled. When NBC revived it in the fall of 1984, as a weekday daytime series titled *Super Password,* Bert Convy was the host. He remained with the series until it left the air in March of 1989.

PAT BOONE-CHEVY SHOWROOM, THE (*Musical Variety*)

FIRST TELECAST: *October 3,1957*
LAST TELECAST: *June 23, 1960*
BROADCAST HISTORY:

Oct 1957–Jun 1960, ABC Thu 9:00–9:30 (OS)

REGULARS:

Pat Boone
Louise O'Brien(1959)
Artie Malvin Chorus (1958–1960)
Mort Lindsey Orchestra

Pat Boone was one of the fastest-rising stars in show business when this series went on the air. He had just completed a long stint with Arthur Godfrey, his records were selling in the millions ("Love Letters in the Sand" was riding high on the charts just as the show premiered), and his movies were box-office hits. The publicity about him was enormous. Kids loved him and so did adults, for his smooth, super-wholesome appearance and that deep, rich voice. A somewhat jaded *TV Guide* reviewer called his new ABC show "about as exciting as a milk-shake with two straws," but that didn't matter to viewers. The show continued for three seasons, without the benefit of a large supporting cast or fancy production.

Guests tended to the "nicer" popular singers, such as the Four Lads, Johnny Mathis, Nat "King" Cole, and Gogi Grant (though Danny and the Juniors did slip in), together with such well-scrubbed acts as the Texas Boys' Choir. Most shows ended with an inspirational tune. In 1959 a regular was added in the person of singer Louise O'Brien, a former Miss Oklahoma, but Pat really needed no supporting cast and she soon became an occasional guest.

Believe it or not, one of the staff writers for this show was a young Woody Allen (Pat hardly ever used his material). The head writer was Larry Gelbart, who later created *M*A*S*H.*

PAT PAULSEN'S HALF A COMEDY HOUR (*Comedy/Variety*)
FIRST TELECAST: *January 22, 1970*
LAST TELECAST: *April 16, 1970*
BROADCAST HISTORY:
Jan 1970–Apr 1970, ABC Thu 7:30–8:00
REGULARS:
Pat Paulsen
Hal Smith
Bob Einstein
Sherry Miles
Jean Byron
George Spell
The Denny Vaughn Orchestra
Joan Gerber
Pepe Brown
Pedro Regas
Vanetta Rogers

Comedian Pat Paulsen's *Half a Comedy Hour* lasted for less than half a season in early 1970. Pat and his cast of mostly youthful comics were seen in skits such as "Children's Letters to the Devil," and with guest stars. Guesting on the first telecast were Debbie Reynolds, former Vice President Hubert H. Humphrey, and Daffy Duck.

PAT SAJAK SHOW, THE (*Talk*)
FIRST TELECAST: *January 9, 1989*
LAST TELECAST: *April 13, 1990*
BROADCAST HISTORY:
Jan 1989–Oct 1989, CBS Mon–Fri 11:30–1:00 A.M.
Oct 1989–Apr 1990, CBS Mon–Fri 11:30–12:30 A.M.
REGULARS:
Pat Sajak
Dan Miller
Tom Scott

Folksy, easygoing Pat Sajak, veteran emcee of the highly successful game show *Wheel of Fortune*, joined the late-night talk show wars in 1989. This was CBS' first attempt to go head-to-head with Johnny Carson since it had given up on *The Merv Griffin Show* almost 17 years earlier, and it was somewhat ironic that Sajak had become a television star on a show—*Wheel*—created and produced by Griffin. Sajak's announcer and second banana was Dan Miller, a personal friend who had been a local news anchorman at station WSMV-TV in Nashville where Sajak was the weatherman from 1972–1977. Saxophone player Tom Scott was the show's musical director.

Sajak never was able to build a substantial audience, generally attracting fewer viewers than the action/adventure series reruns he had replaced. His conservative series also suffered by comparison with the ultra-hip *Arsenio Hall Show* which had premiered at the same time but attracted both a larger audience and more favorable press. *The Pat Sajak Show* went through a number of changes in efforts to find a larger audience. Sajak's opening monologue, formal attire, and desk were dropped (too much like Johnny Carson), replaced by a more informal setting, with Sajak in a sweater rather than a jacket. The show was shortened from 90 minutes to 60 in the fall of 1989 and, the following February, Pat vacated Friday nights to guest hosts who the producers maintained were *not* getting on-air auditions as possible replacements. Among the guest hosts were comics John Mulrooney, Tom Parks, Elayne Boosler, and Paul Rodriguez; actors Jonathan Prince and Mario Van Peebles; talk radio personality Rush Limbaugh; and movie critics Gene Siskel and Roger Ebert.

Nothing helped. In April of 1990, despite the money spent on sets and production and the unexpired two-year contract with Sajak (at $60,000 per week), CBS replaced *The Pat Sajak Show* with reruns of *Wiseguy*.

PATH TO STARDOM (*Documentary*)
BROADCAST HISTORY:
The Nashville Network
30 minutes
Produced: *1993–1995*
Premiered: *April 3, 1993*

A weekly profile of new country artists, including concert footage.

PATRICE MUNSEL SHOW, THE (*Musical Variety*)
FIRST TELECAST: *October 18, 1957*
LAST TELECAST: *June 13, 1958*
BROADCAST HISTORY:
Oct 1957–Dec 1957, ABC Fri 8:30–9:00
Jan 1958–Jun 1958, ABC Fri 9:30–10:00
REGULARS:
Patrice Munsel
The Martins Quartet
The Charles Sanford Orchestra

Metropolitan Opera soprano Patrice Munsel demonstrated her versatility as a singer in this live variety show. Show tunes, popular songs, and operatic excerpts were all part of her repertoire in addition to comedy sketches with her weekly guest stars.

PATRICIA BOWMAN SHOW, THE (*Dance/Music*)
FIRST TELECAST: *August 11, 1951*
LAST TELECAST: *November 3, 1951*
BROADCAST HISTORY:
Aug 1951–Nov 1951, CBS Sat 6:45–7:00
REGULARS:
Patricia Bowman
Paul Shelley
The Norman Paris Trio

This live dance-and-music show was hosted by famous American ballerina Patricia Bowman. Each show featured Miss Bowman and her guest stars performing various types of dances, from ballroom, to jazz, to modern, to ballet.

PATTI PAGE OLDS SHOW, THE (*Musical Variety*)
FIRST TELECAST: *September 24, 1958*
LAST TELECAST: *March 16, 1959*
BROADCAST HISTORY:
Sep 1958–Nov 1958, ABC Wed 9:30–10:00
Dec 1958–Mar 1959, ABC Mon 10:00–10:30
REGULARS:
Patti Page
Rocky Cole
The Jerry Packer Singers
The Matt Mattox Dancers
The Vic Schoen Orchestra

Popular singer Patti Page was the hostess and star of this live musical variety show that featured her singing, regular guest stars, and the dance numbers of the Matt Mattox Dancers. When Patti sang ballads her pianist/accompanist Rocky Cole was featured.

PATTI PAGE SHOW, THE (*Musical Variety*)
FIRST TELECAST: *June 16, 1956*
LAST TELECAST: *July 7, 1956*
BROADCAST HISTORY:
Jun 1956–Jul 1956, NBC Sat 8:00–9:00
REGULARS:
Patti Page
The Frank Lewis Dancers
The Spellbinders
The Carl Hoff Orchestra

Patti Page was one of three stars who filled in for *The Perry Como Show* during the summer of 1956, the other two being Julius LaRosa and Tony Bennett. They shared the services of the Frank Lewis Dancers and the vocal group the Spellbinders. Each star had his/her own guest stars and the show included production numbers, songs by the star, and performances by each week's guests.

PATTY DUKE SHOW, THE (*Situation Comedy*)
FIRST TELECAST: *September 18, 1963*
LAST TELECAST: *August 31, 1966*
BROADCAST HISTORY:
Sep 1963–Aug 1966, ABC Wed 8:00–8:30
CAST:
Patty/Cathy Lane .... Patty Duke
Martin Lane .... William Schallert
Natalie Masters .... Jean Byron
Ross Lane .... Paul O'Keefe
Richard Harrison .... Eddie Applegate
J. R. Castle (1963–1964) .... John McGiver
Nicki Lee (1963–1964) .... Susan Melvin
Sue Ellen (1963–1965) .... Kitty Sullivan
Ted (1963–1965) .... Skip Hinnant
Maggie (1963–1965) .... Alberta Grant
Gloria (1964–1965) .... Kelly Wood
Eileen (1965–1966) .... Ann Alford
Roz (1965–1966) .... Robyn Miller

Teenage actress Patty Duke, fresh from her motion-picture triumph in *The Miracle Worker* (for which she won an Academy Award), starred in a dual role in this light family comedy. As Patty Lane she was a perky, bubble-gum-chewing teenager who dug Paul Anka records and "slumber parties" with her girlfriends. As Cathy, she was Patty's intellectual Scottish cousin, newly arrived from overseas to live with the Lanes, complete with bagpipes and burr. The girls confused everybody in their middle-class Brooklyn Heights, New York, neighborhood by mischievously switching personalities at critical moments. Since they were exact look-alikes, no one could tell them apart. Martin Lane was Patty's harried father, a newspaper editor; Natalie the mother; and 12-year-old Ross the younger brother, who was constantly at war with the girls. Richard was Patty's boyfriend, a part-time Western Union messenger (she liked men in uniform).

Guest appearances by popular singing stars such as Bobby Vinton, Chad and Jeremy, and Frankie Avalon helped boost this series' popularity among teenagers.

Having one actress play two parts did present certain problems, especially when both girls were in the same scene. The young woman who served as Patty/Cathy's double, and was seen from the back as one girl while Patty Duke faced the camera as the other, was Rita McLaughlin.

PAUL ARNOLD SHOW, THE (*Music*)
FIRST TELECAST: *October 24, 1949*
LAST TELECAST: *June 23, 1950*
BROADCAST HISTORY:
Oct 1949–Dec 1949, CBS Mon/Wed/Fri 7:15–7:30
Jan 1950, CBS Mon/Wed/Thu/Fri 7:15–7:30
Jan 1950–Jun 1950, CBS Mon–Fri 7:15–7:30
STAR:
Paul Arnold

This thrice-weekly 15-minute program gave Mr. Arnold an opportunity to sing a few country and western and rural songs, play his guitar, relate a little homespun philosophy, and chat with an occasional guest. Originating live from New York, it added a fourth day of the week the first week in January and became a five-day-a-week series three weeks later.

PAUL DIXON SHOW, THE (*Variety*)
FIRST TELECAST: *August 8, 1951*
LAST TELECAST: *September 24, 1952*
BROADCAST HISTORY:
Aug 1951–Sep 1951, ABC Wed 8:00–9:00
Sep 1951–Oct 1951, ABC Mon 9:00–10:00
Oct 1951–Jan 1952, ABC Thu 10:00–10:30
Oct 1951–Sep 1952, ABC Wed 8:00–9:00
REGULARS:
Paul Dixon
Dotty Mack
Wanda Lewis
Len Goorian

Paul Dixon, one of the most popular radio and TV personalities in the Midwest, was brought to network television by ABC for a prime-time run from 1951–1952. The program was similar in format to his long-running local variety show in Cincinnati, which began in 1949: fun and games with the audience, occasional guests, and his specialty, pantomiming to popular records. Paul contorted his face and mouthed the words as the top singers of the day sang their big hits, on record. Dotty Mack also did musical pantomimes (she later had her own network series doing this), and Wanda Lewis drew pictures as the records were played. Other features in this folksy show included "Visits for Interviews," both light and serious, and "People in Your Life"—the mailman, milkman, policeman, etc. At one time Paul was on two nights a week, for a total of 90 minutes with this potpourri.

In addition to the prime-time show, there was a weekday edition from February to May 1952 on ABC, and from October 1952 until April 1955 on DuMont. Nearly two decades later, in 1973, Dixon returned to the national scene with a similarly formatted syndicated show, which lasted only a year.

PAUL HARVEY NEWS (*News Commentary*)
FIRST TELECAST: *November 16, 1952*
LAST TELECAST: *August 9, 1953*
BROADCAST HISTORY:
Nov 1952–Aug 1953, ABC Sun 11:00–11:15
NEWSCASTER:
Paul Harvey

Famed radio commentator Paul Harvey presented news and his own highly individual opinions on current events in this 1952–1953 ABC series, which originated live from Chicago. Harvey always ended his newscasts with an upbeat "Good . . . day!"

PAUL LYNDE SHOW, THE (*Situation Comedy*)

FIRST TELECAST: *September 13, 1972*
LAST TELECAST: *September 8, 1973*
BROADCAST HISTORY:
Sep 1972–May 1973, ABC Wed 8:00–8:30
Jun 1973–Sep 1973, ABC Sat 8:30–9:00
CAST:
Paul Simms .... Paul Lynde
Martha Simms .... Elizabeth Allen
Sally Simms .... Pamelyn Ferdin
Barbara Simms Dickerson .... Jane Actman
Howie Dickerson .... John Calvin
Barney Dickerson .... Jerry Stiller
Grace Dickerson .... Anne Meara
T. J. McNish .... Herb Voland
T. R. Scott .... James Gregory
Alice .... Allison McKay

Comedian Paul Lynde, a familiar face on TV for many years in guest-star and supporting roles, starred in this situation comedy. He portrayed Paul Simms, a quiet, respectable attorney living with his wife, Martha, and two daughters in Ocean Grove, California. Quiet—until one day the household was invaded by Howie, a blond, shaggy-haired, blue-jeaned, eccentric university student with an IQ of 185—Paul's new son-in-law. Howie and his bride, Barbara, took up residence in the Simms home, for while the new family genius was a whiz at just about anything he tried—and he tried to offer advice on everything—he couldn't seem to hold a job. All of this drove Paul to distraction, and gave Mr. Lynde plenty of opportunities to do that slow burn for which he was so famous.

Jerry Stiller and Anne Meara were seen occasionally as Howie's parents, the Dickersons.

PAUL SAND IN FRIENDS AND LOVERS (*Situation Comedy*)

FIRST TELECAST: *September 14, 1974*
LAST TELECAST: *January 4, 1975*
BROADCAST HISTORY:
Sep 1974–Jan 1975, CBS Sat 8:30–9:00
CAST:
Robert Dreyfuss .... Paul Sand
Charlie Dreyfuss .... Michael Pataki
Janice Dreyfuss .... Penny Marshall
Jack Riordan .... Dick Wesson
Fred Meyerbach .... Steve Landesberg
Mason Woodruff .... Craig Richard Nelson
Ben Dreyfuss .... Jack Gilford

Robert Dreyfuss was a bass violinist with the Boston Symphony Orchestra. A young, unaggressive, incurable romantic whose shyness always made success with women difficult, Robert was nevertheless constantly falling in love with just about every pretty girl he met. His emotional opposite was his older brother Charlie—aggressive, loud, and overprotective of Robert. Charlie's wife Janice was forever making fun of Robert's girl problems.

PAUL WHITEMAN'S GOODYEAR REVUE (*Musical Variety*)

FIRST TELECAST: *November 6, 1949*
LAST TELECAST: *March 30, 1952*
BROADCAST HISTORY:
Nov 1949–Mar 1952, ABC Sun 7:00–7:30 (OS 1950)
REGULARS:
Paul Whiteman
Earl Wrightson (1950–1952)
Maureen Cannon (1951–1952)
Glenn Osser conducting the Paul Whiteman Orchestra (summer 1951)
THEME:
"Rhapsody In Blue," by George Gershwin

At the same time that *Paul Whiteman's TV Teen Club* was a Saturday night fixture during the early 1950s, the bandleader was also seen on Sunday nights with his *Goodyear Revue.* The format was that of a standard musical variety show, with guests such as Victor Borge, Jane Froman, Mel Torme, Charles Laughton, Mindy Carson, and numerous others. Eleven-year-old Junie Keegan of the *TV Teen Club* was a semiregular at the outset of the show, and vocalists Earl Wrightson and Maureen Cannon later became regulars. Dancers and choral groups were also featured.

During the summer of 1951, while Whiteman was on vacation, the program was hosted by regulars Earl Wrightson and Maureen Cannon and renamed *The Goodyear Summertime Revue.*

PAUL WHITEMAN'S TV TEEN CLUB (*Talent*)

FIRST TELECAST: *April 2, 1949*
LAST TELECAST: *March 28, 1954*
BROADCAST HISTORY:
Apr 1949–Aug 1949, ABC Sat 9:00–10:00
Sep 1949–Dec 1951, ABC Sat 8:00–9:00
Dec 1951–Aug 1952, ABC Sat 8:00–8:30
Sep 1952–Oct 1952, ABC Sat 7:30–8:00
Oct 1952–Dec 1953, ABC Sat 7:00–7:30 (OS)
Dec 1953–Mar 1954, ABC Sun 7:30–8:00
REGULARS:
Paul Whiteman
Margo Whiteman (1949–1950)
Nancy Lewis (1950–1953)
Junie Keegan (1949–1953)
Stanley Klet (1950–1953)
Andrea McLaughlin
Sonny Graham (1950)
Bobby Rydell (1951–1953)
MUSICAL DIRECTOR:
Bernie Lowe (1952)
PRODUCER/DIRECTOR:
Edmund "Skipper" Dawes

Paul Whiteman, one of the great innovators in American popular music, was something of a musical institution by the time television came along in the late 1940s. During the 1920s he had led a fabulously successful dance and concert band, which had been a veritable hotbed of new talent and musical innovation. He was dubbed, with some poetic license, "The King of Jazz." In the 1930s and 1940s he appeared regularly on radio and in films, and when TV came along he plunged enthusiastically into that medium too. From 1949 until the mid-1950s he was frequently seen on the new ABC-TV network, as host of several programs, and he was also ABC's vice president in charge of music.

Paul Whiteman's TV Teen Club provided a second childhood for the rotund, gregarious bandleader. The idea for a teenage talent contest had originated in an antidelinquency program he had begun in his hometown of Lambertville, New Jersey. In 1949 he moved the talent show to the ABC network, live from Philadelphia. Each week a series of youthful singers, tap dancers, and instrumentalists would perform, with the winners being given professional coaching and returning for subsequent appearances. Special contests were also held, such as a *TV Guide*—Paul Whiteman Talent Search in 1952 which brought in 1,500 applications.

Youngsters not only performed on the *TV Teen Club*, but helped run it as well. Whiteman's daughter Margo was the original coemcee, later replaced by 14-year-old Nancy Lewis. Singer Stan Klet (also 14) became a regular, as did "Pop's" youngest protégée, 4-year-old Andrea McLaughlin. Whiteman's most famous discovery in the 1920s had been young Bing Crosby, and while no one on the TV show equaled that "find" he did have one youngster of whom he was particularly proud: 11-year-old singer Junie Keegan. A notable moment in Junie's career came in June 1950 when she was honored on the show by the National Confectioners' Association as their "Crown Princess of Candyland." She received from Pops "a crown of gumdrops, an all-day sucker, and a giant peppermint-stick scepter" as the fitting symbols of her installation as "The Sweetest Girl in America"—an auspicious, if somewhat gooey, beginning to any girl's career. Junie later made guest appearances on other TV shows, had her own show in New York, and a Decca recording contract.

Better known in later years was a nine-year-old from South Philadelphia who joined the cast in 1951. Robert Ridarelli—who later changed his name to Bobby Rydell—went on to become one of the major pop singers of the late 1950s and early 1960s. The young staff announcer who read the show's Tootsie Roll commercials in 1952 also later became something of a force in rock 'n' roll. His name was Dick Clark.

The dynamo who kept things rolling on the *Teen Club*, however, was Pops himself. Dressed in a flamboyant shirt and an even louder sports jacket, he delighted in using the kids' own catchphrases ("Real gone!") and dispensing the sponsor's Tootsie Rolls and chewing gum from a paper bag. Since he couldn't remember all the kids' names, they variously became "Junior," "Brains," "Pardner," or "Squidgage." One day when he overdid it a bit, little Andrea shot back, "Oh Pops, how corny can we get!"

But Pops didn't mind. "The way to feel young," he confided to a reporter, "is to stay around young people."

During its last few months on the air the show's format was altered to include "at home" and "on camera" guest celebrities who judged the performances (previously this had been done by audience applause). The *TV Teen Club* finally left the air in early 1954, after a five-year run. The concept was revived during the following summer for Whiteman's *On the Boardwalk*.

PAUL WINCHELL—JERRY MAHONEY SHOW, THE (*Comedy/Variety*)

FIRST TELECAST: *September 18, 1950*
LAST TELECAST: *May 23, 1954*
BROADCAST HISTORY:
Sep 1950–Jun 1953, NBC Mon 8:00–8:30 (OS)
Aug 1953–May 1954, NBC Sun 7:00–7:30
REGULARS:
Paul Winchell
Dorothy Claire (1951–1952)
Diane Sinclair and Ken Spaulding (1951–1953)
Mary Ellen Terry (1953–1954)
Margaret Hamilton (1953–1954)
John Gart Orchestra
ANNOUNCER:
Jimmy Blaine (1950)
Ted Brown (1951–1954)

Ventriloquist Paul Winchell and his dummy Jerry Mahoney were the stars of this variety series, which mixed comedy, music, quiz show, and even dramatic elements during its four-year run. At first the program opened with a comedy routine by Winchell and Mahoney, followed by a quiz segment called "What's My Name?", which they emceed. The questions all had to do with famous personalities, and guest stars appeared to act out or sing the clues. Contestants were drawn from the studio audience and viewers could also be called at home if they had sent in their name and phone number.

Gradually the entertainment element took over an increasing portion of the show, and the quiz portion was dropped altogether by 1953. Featured in the variety segments were Winchell and his dummies Jerry, Knucklehead, Oswald, and others, plus vocalist Dorothy Claire, dancers Sinclair and Spaulding, other regulars, and guests.

During the fall of 1953 the program added a filmed dramatic vignette of approximately 10 minutes' duration, starring a well-known actor or actress in a serious short story (Winchell was often seen in a supporting role). This odd insertion lasted until November, when the show returned to a straight comedy-variety format for the rest of its run.

The annual *Look* Magazine TV Awards were presented on special telecasts of this series in December 1952 and December 1953, with many top names appearing.

The *Winchell-Mahoney* show was known as the *Speidel Show* during its first year and a half on the air (until December 1951), and was also sometimes referred to by the quiz element, *What's My Name?*

Following their departure from prime time, Winchell and Mahoney moved to weekend daytime where they could still entertain their primary audience—children. They were seen on CBS' Saturday lineup from November 1954 to June 1956 and then moved to ABC's Sunday lineup from September 1957 to April 1961.

PAULA POUNDSTONE SHOW, THE (*Comedy/Variety*)

FIRST TELECAST: *October 30, 1993*
LAST TELECAST: *November 6, 1993*
BROADCAST HISTORY:
Oct 1993, ABC Sat 10:00–11:00
Nov 1993, ABC Sat 9:00–10:00
REGULAR:
Paula Poundstone
MUSICAL DIRECTOR:
Nils Lofgren

Gangly, scratchy-voiced standup comic Paula Poundstone hosted this odd hour of mayhem that lasted for only two episodes at the start of the 1993–1994 season. Amid sketches, chats with audience members, and a satellite interview with a popcorn scooper at a theater in Boise, Idaho, Paula liked to poke fun at politics and big issues: For example, four economists riding spinning teacups at the Santa Cruz boardwalk answered questions such as "Should the government regulate private business?" Sam Donaldson read from children's author Maurice Sendak, and Senator Paul Simon mused on the workings of government while touring Wild World Amusement Park. Musical acts also appeared.

PAULINE FREDERICK'S GUESTBOOK
(*Interviews*)
FIRST TELECAST: *January 12, 1949*
LAST TELECAST: *April 13, 1949*
BROADCAST HISTORY:
Jan 1949–Apr 1949, ABC Wed 9:15–9:30
HOSTESS:
Pauline Frederick

Interviews with guests from business, political, and cultural life. The program had been seen locally in New York since August 1948.

PAULY SHORE SHOW, THE (*Situation Comedy*)
FIRST TELECAST: *March 3, 1997*
LAST TELECAST: *April 7, 1997*
BROADCAST HISTORY:
Mar 1997–Apr 1997, FOX Mon 9:30–10:00
CAST:
Pauly Sherman .... Pauly Shore
Edward Sherman .... David Dukes
Dawn .... Charlotte Ross
Sumi .... Amy Hill
Burger .... Kevin Weisman
Zach (age 10) .... Theo Greenly

Short-lived comedy about Pauly, the spoiled, unemployed son of a wealthy businessman. Goofball Pauly lived in the family mansion in the exclusive Brentwood section of Los Angeles with his father, Edward. Edward's fiancée, the sexy, much younger Dawn, had just moved in, along with her smart-mouthed son, Zach. Pauly was convinced she was the latest bimbo trying to make Edward her meal ticket, and was constantly trying to undermine their relationship. Sumi was the Shermans' bossy, tank-like housekeeper, and Burger was Pauly's best friend, a nerdy guy who worked at a video rental store.

PAYNE (*Situation Comedy*)
FIRST TELECAST: *March 15, 1999*
LAST TELECAST: *April 28, 1999*
BROADCAST HISTORY:
Mar 1999, CBS Mon 9:30–10:00
Mar 1999, CBS Wed 8:30–9:00
Mar 1999–Apr 1999, CBS Wed 8:00–8:30
Apr 1999, CBS Wed 8:30–9:00
CAST:
Royal Payne .... John Larroquette
Connie Payne .... JoBeth Williams
Breeze O'Rourke .... Julie Benz
Mohammed ("Mo") .... Rick Batalla
Flo .... Ellen Albertini Dow
Ethel .... Dona Hardy

No subtlety here. Royal Payne (yes, that was his name, and he sure was) was the sarcastic innkeeper who owned and ran Whispering Pines, a small hotel somewhere on the California coast. Royal was abusive to his staff and struggled to keep from verbally alienating his guests. Connie, his gossipy wife of nineteen years, tried to soften his rough edges but had minimal success. The hotel's small staff consisted of Breeze, the naive young chambermaid whom Royal belittled behind her back as the only virgin to set foot in Whispering Pines in years, and Mo, the aging bellboy who spoke broken English. Flo and Ethel were two elderly residents of the hotel who were taking marijuana for "medicinal" purposes. Royal was incredibly cheap: when he replaced the phone system, rather than buying a new one, he purchased one secondhand from the county mental institution.

This was CBS' second attempt to adapt John Cleese's classic 1975 British sitcom farce *Fawlty Towers* for American audiences. The first, never acknowledged as a *Fawlty Towers* adaptation, was 1983's short-lived *Amanda's*, starring Beatrice Arthur.

PEACEABLE KINGDOM, A (*Drama*)
FIRST TELECAST: *September 20, 1989*
LAST TELECAST: *November 15, 1989*
BROADCAST HISTORY:
Sep 1989–Nov 1989, CBS Wed 8:00–9:00
CAST:
Rebecca Cafferty .... Lindsay Wagner
Dr. Jed McFadden .... Tom Wopat
Dr. Bartholomew Langley .... David Ackroyd
Sequoya Ridge .... David Renan
Kate Galindo .... Conchata Ferrell
Dean Cafferty (age 16) .... Michael Manasseri
Courtney Cafferty (12) .... Melissa Clayton
Sam Cafferty (6) .... Victor DiMattia
Robin .... Kathryn Spitz

Rebecca Cafferty was the newly hired managing director of the Los Angeles County Zoo. Recently arrived from New York to start a new life after her husband had died from a heart attack, Rebecca and her three children took up residence in a house on the zoo's grounds close to the animals but far from any other children. Young Sam was the most content with the situation—he even had a pet seal named Rover, who sometimes flapped through the living room—but the older children had mixed feelings about being somewhat isolated from other kids. Moreover, Mom spent so much time dealing with the problems of running the zoo—maintenance, animal acquisition and health problems, funding, and staff—that she found it difficult to give her children the time they deserved. Others on the zoo's staff were her brother Jed, the curator of mammals; Dr. Langley, the sometimes insensitive director of animal research; Ridge, the Indian groundskeeper whose tribe had once lived on the land occupied by the zoo; and Rebecca's secretary, Kate.

Filmed on location at the San Diego Zoo and the Los Angeles City Zoo.

PEAK OF THE SPORTS NEWS, THE, see *Red Barber's Corner*

PEARL (*Situation Comedy*)
FIRST TELECAST: *September 16, 1996*

LAST TELECAST: *June 25, 1997*
BROADCAST HISTORY:
Sep 1996–Oct 1996, CBS Mon 8:30–9:00
Oct 1996–Feb 1997, CBS Wed 8:30–9:00
Jun 1997, CBS Wed 8:30–9:00
CAST:
Pearl Caraldo .... Rhea Perlman
Professor Stephen Pynchon ... Malcolm McDowell
Annie Carmen .... Carol Kane
Frankie Spivak .... Kevin Corrigan
Amy Li .... Lucy Alexis Liu
Joey Caraldo .... Dash Mihok
**Margaret Woodrow*..................... Nikki Cox
*Occasional

Pearl was a spunky blue collar working widow in her forties who wanted to better herself. By day she labored as loading dock manager for University Electronics. She was ecstatic when she was accepted to night classes at prestigious local Swindon University. Not so her doofus-like 20-year-old son Joey, a single dad who depended on his mother as a live-in babysitter for his infant daughter. Nor was Pearl's sister-in-law Annie, her best friend and coworker, who feared that Pearl would become "one of them intellectuals" and lose touch with her blue-collar friends. Then there was Professor Stephen Pynchon, a pompous, condescending elitist who taught Swindon's most difficult humanities course, "The Meaning of Life." He was convinced that uncultured Pearl had no business being in his class. Almost every week he did or said something to belittle or embarrass her, inevitably resulting, by episode's end, in some form of apology or reconciliation. Three of Pynchon's other students were seen regularly—Frankie, likable but socially inept; Ami, a driven perfectionist from San Francisco who was obsessed with her grades; and Margaret, a bright, sexy girl from Manhattan who had difficulty adjusting to the cultural world when there were, like, clothes to try on.

PEARL BAILEY SHOW, THE (*Musical Variety*)
FIRST TELECAST: *January 23, 1971*
LAST TELECAST: *May 8, 1971*
BROADCAST HISTORY:
Jan 1971–May 1971, ABC Sat 8:30–9:30
REGULARS:
Pearl Bailey
The Allan Davies Singers
The Robert Sidney Dancers
Louis Bellson & His Orchestra

Pearl Bailey's sole venture into series television was this musical variety series in which she starred during early 1971. Her husband, drummer Louis Bellson, directed the orchestra and Pearlie Mae entertained with an assortment of celebrity guest stars, including Bing Crosby, Louis Armstrong, Andy Williams, Kate Smith, and B.B. King.

PECK'S BAD GIRL (*Situation Comedy*)
FIRST TELECAST: *May 5, 1959*
LAST TELECAST: *September 29, 1960*
BROADCAST HISTORY:
May 1959–Aug 1959, CBS Tue 9:00–9:30
Jun 1960–Sep 1960, CBS Tue 8:00–8:30
Sep 1960, CBS Thu 9:30–10:00
CAST:
Steve Peck .... Wendell Corey
Jennifer Peck .... Marsha Hunt
Torey Peck .... Patty McCormack
Roger Peck .... Ray Ferrell
Francesca .... Reba Waters
Jeannie .... Bernadette Withers

Research physicist Steve Peck was a typical middle-class American with a typical middle-class family. He had a charming wife, two children, and a home in the suburbs. Torey, his 12-year-old, was at that awkward age. She wasn't quite sure whether she was going to become a young lady or stay an aggressive tomboy. Her indecision and inconsistency were very trying on her parents, who tried to understand and give useful advice, and completely mind-boggling to her little brother, who never quite figured out what was going on. The episodes telecast by CBS during the summer of 1960 were all reruns.

The title and format were a variation on the *Peck's Bad Boy* movies of the 1920s and 1930s starring Jackie Cooper.

PEE WEE KING SHOW (*Musical Variety*)
FIRST TELECAST: *May 23, 1955*
LAST TELECAST: *September 5, 1955*
BROADCAST HISTORY:
May 1955–Sep 1955, ABC Mon 9:00–10:30
REGULARS:
Pee Wee King and His Golden West Cowboys
Redd Stewart
Little Eller Long
Neal Burris

Ninety-minute country music-variety show from WEWS, Cleveland, Ohio, featuring best-selling country bandleader King ("Tennessee Waltz," "Slow Poke"), his vocalist Redd Stewart, six-foot-five comedienne Little Eller Long, "shuffling cowboy singer" Neal Burris, and a square-dance unit, among others.

PELSWICK (*Cartoon*)
BROADCAST HISTORY:
Nickelodeon
30 minutes
Original episodes: *2000–*
Premiered: *October 24, 2000*
VOICES:
Pelswick Eggert (age 13)............ Robert Tinkler
Kate Eggert.......................... Tracey Moore
Priscilla "Gram Gram" Eggert.. Ellen-Ray Hennessy
Quentin Eggert .... Tony Rosato
Ace Nakamura......................... Phil Guerrero
Goon Gunderson .... Peter Oldring
Sandra Scoddle .... Kim Kuhteubl
Julie Smockford..................... Julie Lemieux
Boyd Scullarzo.................. Chuck Campbell
Vice Principal Zeigler .... David Huband
Mr. Jimmy .... David Arquette

This entertaining cartoon delivered humor with a message. Pelswick Eggert was a hip, happy, sarcastic eighth-grader who tooled around with his cap on backward—in a wheelchair (he was paralyzed from the neck down). Despite his disability, he went to school, had adventures with his gang of pals, was into rock music and pop culture, and faced the usual challenges of growing up, including girls, parents and peer pressure. At home were his angelic little sister Kate and little brother Bobby (who hardly ever spoke), his fiercely protective and totally insane Gram

Gram (a wild old bag who raced around with her walker) and his uptight father, Quentin. At school his best buds were numbers-obsessed Ace, big dumb Goon, fashionable Sandra and bossy red-haired Julie, on whom Pelswick had a not-so-secret crush. His chief tormentor was bully Boyd and his not-so-bright sidekicks, but Pelswick always outsmarted them with a smile. Mr. Jimmy was Pelswick's guardian angel, a Jerry Garcia look-alike whom only he could see.

Pelswick was filled with cultural parody that even adults could enjoy. Pelswick lived in the Bayview section of San Francisco, the hilliest city in the U.S., of course; his dad got tied into knots trying to be politically correct ("nobody's wrong, they're just differently right!"); Boyd called his foe a cripple, which Pelswick laughed off with "I'm just permanently seated"; school elections were travesties; local politicians were a joke, and the Pokémon-like trading cards that were all the rage were called Brain Suckers.

Pelswick was originally created as a comic strip by John Callahan, who was himself paralyzed from the shoulders down.

PENDULUM, THE, syndicated title for *Vise, The*

PENNY TO A MILLION (*Quiz*)
FIRST TELECAST: *May 4, 1955*
LAST TELECAST: *October 5, 1955*
BROADCAST HISTORY:
May 1955–Oct 1955, ABC Wed 9:30–10:00
EMCEE:
Bill Goodwin

The first question in the play-off round of this summer quiz show was worthy exactly one cent. However, each subsequent question doubled in value until a contestant could win as much as a million pennies ($10,000). Contestants were chosen in a preliminary round from two teams drawn from the studio audience.

PENSACOLA: WINGS OF GOLD (*Military Drama*)
BROADCAST HISTORY:
Syndicated only
60 minutes
Produced: *1997–2000* (66 episodes)
Released: *September 1997*
CAST:
Lt. Col. Bill Kelly ("Raven") .... James Brolin
Lt. Annalisa Lindstrom ("Stinger") (1997–1998) .... Kathryn Morris
Lt. Bobby Griffin ("Chaser") (1997–1998) .... Rod Rowland
Lt. Wendell McCray ("Cipher") (1997–1998) .... Rodney Van Johnson
Lt. A. J. Conaway ("Buddha") (1997–1998) .... Salvator Xuereb
Janine Kelly (1997–1998) .... Kristanna Loken
Col. Rebecca Hodges (1997–1998) ... Brynn Thayer
Dr. Valerie West (1997–1998) .... Leslie Hardy
Lt. Butch Barnes ("Burner") (1998–2000) .... Kenny Johnson
Lt. Tucker Henry III ("Spoon") (1998–2000) .... Michael Trucco
Lt. Alexandra Jensen ("Ice") (1998–2000) .... Sandra Hess
Maj. MacArthur Lewis, Jr. ("Hammer") (1998–2000) .... Bobby Hosea
Kate Anderson (1998–2000) .... Barbara Niven
Lt. Ally Willis ("Breaker") (1998) .... Kim Flowers
Cpl. Martinez (1998–1999) .... Israel Juarbe
Capt. Edward Terrelli ("Capone") (1999–2000) .... David Quane
Lt. Abigail Hawling ("Mad Dog") (1999–2000) .... Felicity Waterman
Col. Doug Drayton (1999–2000) ... Marshall Teague

Hard-driving Col. Kelly led a team of young marine fighter pilots, the Sea Dragons, based in Pensacola, Florida, in this action series. Their missions included everything from rescuing stranded D.E.A. agents in Central America, to combating a team of criminals that had infiltrated a submarine factory, to saving the colonel from a crazed serial bomber. Kelly, whose wife had died after their divorce, was estranged from his daughter, Janine, who worked as a waitress at an outdoor beachfront restaurant. When Bobby, one of his charges, got involved with Janine, Kelly tried, unsuccessfully, to break them up even while he himself was dating Dr. West, one of the base physicians.

In the first-season finale Kelly was informed that budget cutbacks mandated his cutting one member of his team. However, when *Pensacola* returned in the fall, the entire Sea Dragon team had been deactivated because of the cuts. Col. Kelly was reassigned to train a new group of marine fighter pilots with the assistance of Major Lewis, who was even tougher on the recruits than he was. Their principal recruits, who shared a house on the beach, were Barnes, a hotshot pilot who had never outgrown the problems of being raised in foster homes; Tucker, a third generation officer who resented his rich, meddlesome dad; and Jensen, a tough but insecure perfectionist who could compete with anyone. Kate's Bucket was the local bar where the pilots hung out when they were off-duty. Its proprietress, a Navy widow, was everybody's friend, but had a particularly soft spot for Kelly. In October, Willis, the militant female pilot trainee, was killed when her jet crashed on the tarmac trying to land. Teri (Ali Landry), Tucker's father's fiancée, fell in love with Tucker in a two-parter in the fall and returned the following spring.

In the fall of 1999 Col. Kelly got into more serious action as leader of The Flying Bandits, the new name for his team of young fighter pilots. They were the aviation combat unit of the 18th Marine Expeditionary Unit and went on sometimes dangerous missions. New to the group were Capone, a New Yorker with romantic tendencies, and Mad Dog, a sexy helicopter pilot on loan from the British Royal Air Force. Hammer joined as the unit's operations officer. In October Burner, who was miraculously saved after he ran out of fuel during a storm at sea, turned in his wings and Capone moved into his room in the house he had shared with Spoon and Ice. Teri turned up to visit, but the chemistry developing between Spoon and Ice made things awkward. In February Ice turned down an offer to join NASA and train for the future Mars mission. In April Burner turned up—he had transferred into a marine community relations program and eventually transferred into Special Operations to get back into the action—but he missed flying. He helped them capture a South American drug lord and, although the mission succeeded, he was left behind. Col. Kelly led the rescue mission that got him out. In the series finale Kelly was being evaluated for his last chance to make full colonel, Spoon and Ice were trying to decide whether they wanted their relationship to get more serious, and Kate was preparing to get married and move away.

PENTAGON (*Interview*)
FIRST TELECAST: *May 13, 1951*
LAST TELECAST: *November 24, 1952*
BROADCAST HISTORY:
May 1951–Nov 1951, DUM Sun 8:30–9:00
Dec 1951–Nov 1952, DUM Mon 8:00–8:30

Korean War era interview program in which top Pentagon brass and other officials discussed the war effort with reporters.

PENTAGON U.S.A. (*Dramatic Anthology*)
FIRST TELECAST: *August 6, 1953*
LAST TELECAST: *September 24, 1953*
BROADCAST HISTORY:
Aug 1953–Sep 1953, CBS Thu 10:00–10:30
CAST:
The Colonel.................... Addison Richards

The dramas presented in this live summer anthology series were adaptations of cases from the criminal investigation files of the U.S. Army. At the beginning of each episode, the Colonel assigned the investigators who were to handle that week's case and gave them a rundown on what or who they were looking for. His office was located in the Pentagon, in Washington.

PENTHOUSE PARTY (*Variety*)
FIRST TELECAST: *September 15, 1950*
LAST TELECAST: *June 8, 1951*
BROADCAST HISTORY:
Sep 1950–Dec 1950, ABC Fri 10:00–10:30
Jan 1951–Jun 1951, ABC Fri 8:30–9:00
REGULARS:
Betty Furness
Don Cherry
Buddy Weed Trio

Betty Furness opened this weekly gathering with the words, "Come on inside and meet all the folks." The "folks," her guests, were generally celebrities from the New York music and theater world who, with little coaxing, would demonstrate unsuspected talents for the viewing audience. Matinee idol Hurd Hatfield did a Hindu dance, British actor Arthur Treacher sang "Ragtime Cowboy Joe," and actress Joan Blondell, famous for her wisecracking blonde chorine characterization in films, whipped up a casserole. It all took place in the style of a swell party in Betty's New York penthouse.

PEOPLE (*Newsmagazine*)
FIRST TELECAST: *September 18, 1978*
LAST TELECAST: *November 6, 1978*
BROADCAST HISTORY:
Sep 1978–Nov 1978, CBS Mon 8:30–9:00
REGULARS:
Phyllis George
Mark Shaw

People was a televised version of the magazine of the same name and, in fact, was produced by the television production arm of Time Inc., the publishers of the magazine. Hosted by former Miss America Phyllis George, *People* provided short interviews and profiles of people in the news, especially show-business personalities. Despite its half-hour length, *People* offered fleeting glimpses of many celebrities in each episode. One telecast included Jimmy Durante, Carroll O'Connor, Bette Midler, Francesco Scavullo, Cheryl Tiegs, Kristy McNichol, Bill Cosby, Merv Griffin, Rob Reiner, and several lesser-known folk. As with the magazine, the coverage here tended to be fast, flashy, and without much substance. Mark Shaw was a regular contributor, traveling around the country to visit interesting places and interview subjects.

PEOPLE ARE FUNNY (*Quiz/Audience Participation*)
FIRST TELECAST: *September 19, 1954*
LAST TELECAST: *July 21, 1984*
BROADCAST HISTORY:
Sep 1954–Sep 1955, NBC Sun 7:00–7:30
Sep 1955–Sep 1956, NBC Sat 9:00–9:30
Sep 1956–Sept 1959, NBC Sat 7:30–8:00
Sep 1959–Apr 1960, NBC Fri 7:30–8:00
Apr 1960–Sep 1960, NBC Wed 10:30–11:00
Sep 1960–Apr 1961, NBC Sun 6:30–7:00
Mar 1984–May 1984, NBC Sat 9:00–9:30
Jun 1984–Jul 1984, NBC Sat 9:30–10:00
EMCEE:
Art Linkletter (1954–1961)
Flip Wilson (1984)

Contestants on the original *People Are Funny* were picked from the studio audience by host Art Linkletter prior to the filming of each week's episode. On the air they would be interviewed by Art and then asked to get involved in some stunt that would prove that "people are funny." Some stunts, including tests of memory, greed, decision-making or some other trait, took place in the studio—and often ended in pie-throwing, water-dousing, or the like as the penalty. In others, contestants were given an assignment to complete before the next week's telecast, usually a trick on or test of unsuspecting outsiders—for example, trying to cash a check written on a 40-pound watermelon, or simply trying to give away money to passersby (that can be surprisingly hard). On the next show the contestant would report back with the often hilarious results.

People Are Funny began on radio in 1942. During its first three seasons of TV the radio broadcasts continued, consisting of the sound track from the TV version. Later the TV version was a film of the previously aired radio show. In the 1956–1957 season a computer-dating feature was added, in which a couple, matched by Univac computer, got to know each other while answering questions in a quiz-show segment of the program.

More than 20 years after the original *People Are Funny* ended its run, NBC aired a short-lived revival hosted by Flip Wilson. The stunts were similar, but this time conducted entirely outside the studio, mostly on the streets of Los Angeles. Among the gags were two men trying to get passersby to join them "fishing" in an open manhole, while they caught healthy-looking trout; a little girl in a restaurant who tried to get a patron to eat her "icky" vegetables for her, before her mother came back; and a woman who tried to persuade a delivery boy to disrobe before entering a "nudist condominium" to make a delivery.

PEOPLE DO THE CRAZIEST THINGS (*Humor/ Audience Participation*)
FIRST TELECAST: *September 20, 1984*
LAST TELECAST: *August 2, 1985*
BROADCAST HISTORY:
Sep 1984, ABC Thu 8:00–8:30
Dec 1984–May 1985, ABC Various (occasional)
May 1985–Aug 1985, ABC Fri 9:30–10:00
REGULARS:
Bert Convy
Bob Perlow
Wendy Cutler

Patterned after Allen Funt's long-running *Candid Camera, People Do the Craziest Things* attempted to show how easy it is to get people to make fools of themselves. Women got hysterical when they were weighed on a scale that registered absurdly high weights, motorists overreacted to parking lot gates that refused to open, and assorted other situations were contrived to confuse and embarrass "average folks." If anything, *People Do the Craziest Things* was more heartless than *Candid Camera*, lacking the inoffensive vignettes that appeared on the earlier show.

Bert Convy was the in-studio host of the series, assisted by Bob Perlow and Wendy Cutler, who were often seen on location setting up the situations. The series was pulled from the schedule only two weeks after its premiere, then run infrequently, to fill holes in the ABC schedule, for the rest of the 1984–1985 season.

PEOPLE NEXT DOOR, THE (*Situation Comedy*)
FIRST TELECAST: *September 18, 1989*
LAST TELECAST: *October 9, 1989*
BROADCAST HISTORY:
Sep 1989–Oct 1989, CBS Mon 8:30–9:00
CAST:
Walter Kellogg .... Jeffrey Jones
Abigail MacIntyre Kellogg .... Mary Gross
Matthew Kellogg (age 14) .... Chance Quinn
Aurora Kellogg (11) .... Jaclyn Bernstein
Cissy MacIntyre .... Christina Pickles
Truman Fipps .... Leslie Jordan

This absurd fantasy was one of the first casualties of the 1989–1990 season. Walter Kellogg was a successful cartoonist with two children who had fallen in love with small-town girl Abigail MacIntyre and, after a whirlwind courtship, moved from New York to her hometown of Covington, Ohio, to marry her. Walter had an imagination so vivid that things he imagined actually materialized in his presence. Despite his attempts to keep this "ability" under control, since Walter and his children feared Abby would never understand, all sorts of things he thought about came to life—a moosehead on the wall, his answering machine, a bikini model, Sigmund Freud, and real-life celebrities like Steve Allen, Dick Clark, and Dr. Joyce Brothers. Abby, a psychologist, had concluded that Walter was eccentric but lovable, while her cynical sister Cissy, who disapproved of their marriage, just thought he was weird. Truman Fipps was the nosy mailman who knew something strange was going on but couldn't figure out exactly what.

PEOPLE'S CHOICE, THE (*Situation Comedy*)
FIRST TELECAST: *October 6, 1955*
LAST TELECAST: *September 25, 1958*
BROADCAST HISTORY:
Oct 1955–Dec 1955, NBC Thu 8:30–9:00
Jan 1956–Sep 1958, NBC Thu 9:00–9:30
CAST:
Socrates "Sock" Miller .... Jackie Cooper
Amanda "Mandy" Peoples Miller .... Pat Breslin
Aunt Gus .... Margaret Irving
Mayor John Peoples .... Paul Maxey
Roger Crutcher (1955–1957) ...... John Stephenson
Pierre (1955–1956) .... Leonid Kinskey
Rollo (1956–1958) .... Dick Wesson
Cleo .... Herself (voice: Mary Jane Croft)

Socrates (Sock) Miller was a government naturalist who had been elected to the city council, a job he took with great seriousness. His interest in helping the community occasionally got him in trouble with Mayor Peoples, a problem that was compounded by the fact that the mayor's daughter, Mandy, was Sock's girlfriend. Making numerous observations to the audience, although no one in the cast could hear her, was Cleo, Sock's pet basset hound. At the end of the 1956–1957 season Sock and Mandy were secretly married. They made it public early in the 1957–1958 season, following his graduation from law school. He got a job selling homes in the neighboring community of Barkerville, for the developer Mr. Barker, and he and Mandy were given one of the homes to live in. Moving in with them was Sock's freeloading friend Rollo. After the move, neither the mayor nor Sock's Aunt Gus were seen on a weekly basis.

PEOPLE'S COURT, THE (*Courtroom*)
BROADCAST HISTORY:
Syndicated only
30 minutes
Produced: *1981–1993* (2,484 episodes)
Released: *September 1981*
REGULARS:
Judge Joseph A. Wapner (ret.)
Doug Llewelyn
Rusty Burrell, bailiff

One of television's oldest low-budget traditions was real-life courtroom drama, as featured in such 1950s series as *They Stand Accused, Famous Jury Trials,* and *Traffic Court.* It offered a perfect mix of TV's favorite elements: a focus on individuals, realism, high drama, and low production costs. *The People's Court* brought the format back in the 1980s, with an ingenious twist. The plaintiffs were ordinary people who had taken their grievances to Los Angeles area small claims courts, then agreed (along with the defendants) to have their cases heard by an arbitrator—retired Superior Court Judge Joseph Wapner. For their trouble they got speedy disposition of their claims, a moment on national TV, and reimbursement whatever the outcome.

Although strictly speaking this was a private arbitration proceeding, it was staged in a courtroom setting with Judge Wapner on the bench, a bailiff, and spectators in the gallery. As in small claims court, there was no legal counsel or jury. The citizen stated his case to the understanding but firm judge, who rendered a verdict immediately after the next commercial.

Cases revolved around such everyday contretemps as broken contracts, faulty merchandise, and arguments over who owned some shrubbery. Many had odd twists, however: the mother who refused to pay a clown she had hired to appear at her child's party as a Smurf (he had showed up as a towering purple monster and terrified the kiddies); the woman who wanted a stud fee after her poodle mated with a stranger's; the befuddled old gent who wanted his money back when the car he bought proved to have a tiller instead of a steering wheel. All cases were within the small claims court's $1,500 limit.

After each case—one or two per show—reporter Doug Llewelyn interviewed the opposing parties on their way out of the courtroom, and sometimes also reported the "people's verdict" based on a poll of the spectators. Then he closed the show with lines like these: "Remember, when you get mad, don't take the law into your own hands. Take 'em to court."

PEOPLE'S COURT, THE (*Courtroom*)

BROADCAST HISTORY:
Syndicated only
60 minutes
Produced: *1997–*
Released: *September 1997*

REGULARS:
Edward Koch (1997–1999)
Carol Martin (1997–1999)
Harvey Levin
Curt Chaplin
Josephine Ann Longobardi (1997–2001)
Jerry Sheindlin (1999–2001)
Marilyn Milian (2001–)
Davy Jones (2001–)
Douglas MacIntosh (2001–)

This updated version of the venerable courtroom series starred attorney and former New York City mayor Ed Koch as the judge. Carol Martin served as in-studio host, and attorney Harvey Levin got comments from people on the street who could watch the proceedings on a mobile monitor. Other regulars were Curt Chaplin, the in-court reporter, and Josephine Ann Longobardi, the court officer. There were three cases in each hour-long episode. Levin, coexecutive producer of the show, had been the behind-the-scenes legal consultant for the original series' twelve-year run, and he had written a book about the show titled *The People's Court: How to Tell It to the Judge*.

At the start of the 1999–2000 season Koch was replaced by Judge Jerry Sheindlin, husband of the star of *Judge Judy*, its primary competition in the daytime arena, and the in-studio closing observations were dropped. He departed in the spring of 2001 to be replaced by Marilyn Milian. That fall Davy Jones took over as the court officer and Douglas MacIntosh was added as the bailiff.

PEOPLE'S PLATFORM (*Discussion*)

FIRST TELECAST: *August 17, 1948*
LAST TELECAST: *August 11, 1950*

BROADCAST HISTORY:
Aug 1948–Dec 1948, CBS Tue 9:30–10:00
Jan 1949–Sep 1949, CBS Mon Various times
Oct 1949–Aug 1950, CBS Fri 10:00–10:30

MODERATOR:
Quincy Howe

This long-running public-affairs program was begun by the noted educator Dr. Lyman Bryson on CBS radio in 1938, and continued on radio until 1952. It was first seen on TV as a local New York program in May 1948, and moved to the network three months later.

The format was that of a simple debate between major political or other public figures on an important issue of the day. Each side stated its opening arguments, followed by rebuttals. The program was seen on Mondays during most of 1949, but the time varied from week to week (usually between 8:30 and 10:00 P.M.). It continued on TV as a Sunday afternoon feature until July 1951.

PEPSI-COLA PLAYHOUSE (*Dramatic Anthology*)

FIRST TELECAST: *October 2, 1953*
LAST TELECAST: *June 26, 1955*

BROADCAST HISTORY:
Oct 1953–Jun 1954, ABC Fri 8:30–9:00
Jul 1954–Jun 1955, ABC Sun 7:30–8:00

HOSTESS:
Arlene Dahl (1953–1954)
Anita Colby (1954)
Polly Bergen (1954–1955)

Arlene Dahl was the original hostess of this dramatic series which began as a live show and switched to film in the middle of its first season. Miss Colby took over the hostess function in April 1954 and was in turn succeeded by Polly Bergen in October 1954.

The stories ranged from melodrama to comedy, and generally featured lesser-known (and thus inexpensive) actors and actresses. Such stars as Craig Stevens, Lee Marvin, Vera Miles, Hans Conried, and Charles Bronson made early TV appearances here.

PERFECT CRIME, THE, see *Telltale Clue, The*

PERFECT SCORE, A (*Quiz/Audience Participation*)

FIRST TELECAST: *June 15, 1992*
LAST TELECAST: *December 9, 1992*

BROADCAST HISTORY:
Jun 1992–Jul 1992, CBS Mon–Fri 1:00–1:30 A.M.
Aug 1992–Sep 1992, CBS Mon–Fri 12:30–1:00 A.M.
Sep 1992–Dec 1992, CBS Mon–Thu 12:30–1:00 A.M.

EMCEE:
Jeff Marder

In this variation of *The Dating Game* and *Love Connection* three friends of a man or woman served as questioners to pick the perfect date for their friend. The show's staff had picked three potential dates based on information provided by the friends, and the dates were then interviewed by the friends while the man or woman was on the other side of a screen listening. The matched pair were then sent on a date paid for by the show, and, since everything was taped in advance, at the end of the show home viewers saw the reactions of the couple after the date. If the couple wanted to go out again on their own—a perfect score—the people who had selected the date each won a prize for making such a good choice. Home viewers were given a 900 number (at $2.95/minute) to leave messages for any of the people they had seen. Who knows, if the people on camera couldn't make "a perfect score" maybe some of the home viewers could.

PERFECT STRANGERS (*Situation Comedy*)

FIRST TELECAST: *March 25, 1986*
LAST TELECAST: *August 6, 1993*

BROADCAST HISTORY:

Mar 1986–Apr 1986, ABC Tue 8:30–9:00
Aug 1986–Feb 1988, ABC Wed 8:00–8:30
Mar 1988–Jul 1989, ABC Fri 8:00–8:30
May 1988–Jul 1988, ABC Tue 8:30–9:00
Aug 1989–Apr 1991, ABC Fri 9:00–9:30
Apr 1991–May 1991, ABC Fri 9:30–10:00
May 1991–Dec 1991, ABC Fri 9:00–9:30
Jan 1992, ABC Fri 9:30–10:00
Feb 1992–Apr 1992, ABC Sat 9:00–9:30
May 1992–Jun 1992, ABC Sat 9:30–10:00
Jun 1992–Jul 1992, ABC Sat 9:00–9:30
Jul 1992–Sep 1992, ABC Fri 9:30–10:00
Jul 1993–Aug 1993, ABC Fri 9:30–10:00

CAST:

Larry Appleton .... Mark Linn-Baker
Balki Bartokomous................ Bronson Pinchot
Mr. Donald Twinkacetti ("Twinkie") (1986–1987) .... Ernie Sabella
Edwina Twinkacetti (1986–1987) ... Belita Moreno
Susan Campbell (1986) .... Lise Cutter
Mary Anne .... Rebeca Arthur
Jennifer.......................... Melanie Wilson
Harriette Winslow (1987–1989) .... Jo Marie Payton-France
Lydia Markham (1987–1992)........ Belita Moreno
**Harry Burns (1987–1988)* .... Eugene Roche
Mr. Sam Gorpley (1987–1992) ...... Sam Anderson
**Mr. Wainright (1989–1992)*............. F. J. O'Neill
Tess Holland (1990) .... Alisan Porter

*Occasional

THEME:

"Nothing's Gonna Stop Me Now," by Jesse Frederick and Bennett Salvay, performed by David Pomeranz

A slapstick "buddy comedy" that explored the wonderment of a newly arrived immigrant at the ways of America—"The land of the Whopper." Balki was a young shepherd from the Mediterranean island of Mypos, who showed up unexpectedly at the Chicago apartment of his distant cousin, bachelor Larry. Balki's wide-eyed, fun-loving manner, his nutty Myposian customs, and his tendency to take everything Americans told him quite literally, promised considerable disruption for Larry's carefully organized life, but Larry took him in. After all, getting started as a shepherd in Chicago was not going to be easy.

Larry was just getting started himself, hoping to become a photojournalist. For the time being he worked downstairs at the Ritz Discount Shop, run by a greedy, insensitive man named "Twinkie" (Twinkie on blind people: "Give somebody a white cane, they think they own the streets"). Susan was Larry's friend, a nurse who lived upstairs. She was soon replaced by Mary Anne and Jennifer, two stewardesses who lived in the building.

Stories involved Balki's comic misadventures as he learned about America, studied citizenship at night school, and chased girls with Larry. His answer to every problem: "Don't be ridikalus!" At first Larry got crazy Balki a job in Twinkie's store, but in the fall of 1987 they both went to work for *The Chicago Chronicle,* Larry as a cub reporter and Balki in the mailroom. Harriette was the wisecracking elevator operator at the paper, Harry the occasionally seen editor, and Lydia—who looked a lot like Twinkie's wife of the previous season!—the neurotic advice columnist.

Before long Balki earned his high school diploma and began taking college courses at night; at the *Chronicle* his constant optimism tormented his snide, Scrooge-like mailroom boss, Mr. Gorpley. Larry was promoted to investigative reporter, and by 1990 he had also been assigned to write dialogue for a comic strip—which was drawn by none other than Balki, who turned out to have considerable artistic talents. The strip was about a sheep named Dimitri (and you wondered what kind of career the writers could concoct for a shepherd in Chicago!). Balki insisted that Larry's dialogue must reflect "a sheep's sensibility." Wainwright was the publisher of the paper, and Tess, a young girl who lived in Larry and Balki's apartment building for a time.

Advances were made on the romantic front too, with Larry dating Jennifer and Balki having a crush on Mary Anne. Larry and Jennifer were married in 1991 and moved into a big Victorian house—where they were joined, of course, by Balki and Mary Anne. In a sitcom, there is no escape.

Original episodes of the series ended rather abruptly in April 1992, with Balki about to marry Mary Anne. A few additional original episodes aired during the summer of 1993 in which he had married her, and both wives gave birth—Mary Anne in the driveway to Robespierre and Jennifer in a runaway balloon to Tucker. As the series finally expired for good, the two couples promised to stay close forever.

ABC aired reruns of *Perfect Strangers* in daytime from August 1989 until July 1990.

PERRY COMO SHOW, THE (*Musical Variety*)

FIRST TELECAST: *December 24, 1948*
LAST TELECAST: *June 12, 1963*

BROADCAST HISTORY:

Dec 1948–Jan 1949, NBC Fri 7:00–7:15
Jan 1949–Jun 1949, NBC Fri 11:00–11:15
Oct 1949–Jun 1950, NBC Sun 8:00–8:30
Oct 1950–Jun 1955, CBS Mon/Wed/Fri 7;45–8:00 (OS)
Sep 1955–Jun 1959, NBC Sat 8:00–9:00 (OS)
Sep 1959–Jun 1963, NBC Wed 9:00–10:00 (OS)

REGULARS:

Perry Como
Fontane Sisters (1948–1954)
Ray Charles Singers (1950–1963)
Louis Da Pron Dancers (1955–1960)
Peter Gennaro Dancers (1960–1963)
Mitchell Ayres Orchestra

KRAFT MUSIC HALL PLAYERS:

Kaye Ballard (1961–1963)
Don Adams (1961–1963)
Sandy Stewart (1961–1963)
Jack Duffy (1961–1963)
Paul Lynde (1961–1962)
Pierre Olaf (1962–1963)

ANNOUNCER:

Martin Block (1948–1950)
Durward Kirby (1950–1951)
Dick Stark (1951–1955)
Frank Gallop (1955–1963)
Ed Herlihy (1959–1963)

THEME (1955–1963):

"Dream Along with Me (I'm on My Way to a Star)," by Carl Sigman

Perry Como was one of the hottest properties in show

business, with a four-year string of hit records and an NBC radio series already to his credit, when his first TV series began in 1948. The *Chesterfield Supper Club* premiered in the Friday 7:00–7:15 P.M. time slot on December 24, 1948, but stayed there only three weeks before moving to 11:00 P.M. on January 14, 1949. It was at first a simulcast of Perry's popular radio show and made few concessions to the new medium. Cameras were simply brought into the radio studio and Como and his guests were seen in front of a radio microphone, with scripts and music stands in full view. In succeeding months this was gradually modified, with simple backdrops and props being added. The basic format remained Perry's easygoing crooning, often of his latest hit record, with interludes by regulars the Fontane Sisters (Marge, Bea, and Geri) and assorted guest stars. The guest on the very first show, Christmas Eve 1948, was a boys' choir, which included Perry's eight-year-old son, Ronnie. Subsequent guest spots tended also to be filled by singers, some headliners such as Nat "King" Cole, Burl Ives, Patti Page, etc., and some less well-known, including an early appearance by the black rhythm and blues group, the Ravens. Personalities from other areas of show business, such as comedians and actors, were also seen.

In 1950 Perry moved to CBS with a thrice weekly 15-minute program called *The Perry Como Show*. Then in 1955 he finally graduated to a full prime-time variety hour on Saturday nights, on NBC. The basic format remained unchanged for the next eight years. Perry opened with his new theme, "Dream along with me, I'm on my way to a star . . . ," there was a request spot introduced by girls singing "Letters, we get letters, we get stacks and stacks of letters!", and top-name guest stars engaging in easy banter with the relaxed Mr. C. The show would frequently close with Perry singing a religious or serious number, blending into the closing theme, "You are never far away from me . . ." When the show moved to Wednesday nights, Kraft took over sponsorship, and in 1961 a group of young players was added, backing Perry and his guests in regular comedy skits. Announcer Frank Gallop also assumed a regular role on the show over the years, as a comic foil to Perry. Gallop was generally heard off camera, his voice booming as if in an echo chamber.

Although Perry's regular weekly series ended in 1963, he remained popular with TV viewers and was seen every five or six weeks in Kraft Music Hall specials from 1963 to 1967. After that his specials were less frequent.

PERRY MASON (*Legal Drama*)

FIRST TELECAST: *September 21, 1957*
LAST TELECAST: *January 27, 1974*
BROADCAST HISTORY:

Sep 1957–Sep 1962, CBS Sat 7:30–8:30
Sep 1962–Sep 1963, CBS Thu 8:00–9:00
Sep 1963–Sep 1964, CBS Thu 9:00–10:00
Sep 1964–Sep 1965, CBS Thu 8:00–9:00
Sep 1965–Sep 1966, CBS Sun 9:00–10:00
Sep 1973–Jan 1974, CBS Sun 7:30–8:30

CAST (1957–1966):

Perry Mason . . . . Raymond Burr
Della Street . . . . Barbara Hale
Paul Drake . . . . William Hopper
Hamilton Burger . . . . William Talman
Lt. Arthur Tragg (1957–1965) . . . . Ray Collins
David Gideon (1961–1962) . . . . Karl Held
Lt. Anderson (1961–1965) . . . . Wesley Lau
Lt. Steve Drumm (1965–1966) . . . Richard Anderson
Sgt. Brice (1959–1966) . . . . Lee Miller
Terrence Clay (1965–1966) . . . . Dan Tobin

CAST (1973–1974):

Perry Mason . . . . Monte Markham
Della Street . . . . Sharon Acker
Paul Drake . . . . Albert Stratton
Lt. Arthur Tragg . . . . Dane Clark
Hamilton Burger . . . . Harry Guardino
Gertrude Lade . . . . Brett Somers

CREATED BY

Erle Stanley Gardner

Perry Mason was television's most successful lawyer series. For nine seasons during the 1950s and 1960s Erle Stanley Gardner's famous defense attorney solved murder mysteries in the courtroom. With the aid of his personal investigator Paul Drake and his devoted secretary Della Street, Perry always managed to piece together the puzzle just in time to thwart District Attorney Hamilton Burger, his perpetual adversary. The format was certainly predictable, which may have accounted for much of its appeal. Every case culminated in a courtroom trial, and every trial culminated in the guilty party taking the witness stand, only to break down in a dramatic confession under Mason's battering cross-examination ("But if you were at home on the night of the murder, Mr. Jones, then *how could you have known that* . . ." To which the shell-shocked culprit could only sob, "I didn't mean to kill her"). Judges never seemed to object to these histrionics, and in fact looked on with as much fascination as the viewing audience. Often the deciding clue would be rushed into the courtroom at the last moment by Paul Drake. At the end of every episode, Perry, Della, and Paul would gather to recap and explain what had led to the solution, a neat little coda which often sorted things out for confused viewers.

Mason never lost a case and it seemed that the accumulated frustrations made D.A. Burger determined to convict at least one of Perry's clients. Once actor Raymond Burr was confronted by a fan who demanded to know how it was that he won every case. "But madam," he replied smoothly, "you only see the cases I try on Saturday." Actually, Perry did lose one trial, in 1963, when his client refused to reveal the evidence that would save her. Mason found the real culprit anyway, and eventually exonerated his client, despite herself.

Perry Mason was revived in 1973 with an all-new cast (Burr was by that time sleuthing around in a wheelchair on *Ironside*). A new regular was his receptionist, Gertie (a character who had been played, on a very occasional basis, by Connie Cezon during the long run of the original *Perry Mason*). However, *The New Perry Mason* could not recapture the magic of the old, and the revival soon folded.

Twelve years later, in December 1985, NBC aired a reunion movie, *Perry Mason Returns*, starring Burr and Hale. Its success led to a series (two or three a year) of new feature-length *Perry Mason* cases until Burr passed away late in 1993.

The Perry Mason character has an interesting background. The fictional alter ego of lawyer-novelist Erle

Stanley Gardner, he first became famous in a series of best-selling novels, then in a CBS radio series which ran from 1943 to 1955. The radio series was part soap opera and part detective story (it ran five days a week), and when the time came to move to TV Gardner opted to shift the emphasis to pure sleuthing. The original format also went on TV, in 1956, as *The Edge of Night* (complete with the *Perry Mason* radio production staff and most of the cast, who were given new names). This continued in daytime until December 1984. The name Perry Mason was used for the Raymond Burr series, which had a whole new cast and which dropped the soap-opera elements.

PERRY PRESENTS (*Musical Variety*)
FIRST TELECAST: *June 13, 1959*
LAST TELECAST: *September 5, 1959*
BROADCAST HISTORY:
Jun 1959–Sep 1959, NBC Sat 8:00–9:00
REGULARS:
Teresa Brewer
Tony Bennett
The Four Lads
Jaye P. Morgan
The Modernaires
The Mel Pahl Chorus
The Louis Da Pron Dancers
Mitchell Ayres Orchestra

Following *The Perry Como Show*'s last season on Saturday nights, *Perry Presents* aired as the summer replacement. It was a musical variety show starring Teresa Brewer and Tony Bennett, who also acted as hosts, and the Four Lads. Miss Brewer left the show on July 4 and the Four Lads departed on July 25. On August 1, Jaye P. Morgan and the Modernaires were added to the regular cast. Each show attempted to treat events in history and issues of current interest musically, with songs and production numbers as well as comedy skits.

PERSON TO PERSON (*Interview*)
FIRST TELECAST: *October 2, 1953*
LAST TELECAST: *September 15, 1961*
BROADCAST HISTORY:
Oct 1953–Jun 1959, CBS Fri 10:30–11:00 (OS)
Oct 1959–Sep 1960, CBS Fri 10:30–11:00
Sep 1960–Dec 1960, CBS Thu 10:00–10:30
Jun 1961–Sep 1961, CBS Fri 10:30–11:00
HOST:
Edward R. Murrow (1953–1959)
Charles Collingwood (1959–1961)

Being chosen as one of Ed Murrow's subjects on *Person to Person* was both an honor and an ordeal. Each Friday night Ed would "visit" with two celebrities at their homes. The interviews were all done live, with Ed seated in a comfortable chair in the studio while the subject showed him around his or her home—via the immediacy of live television. At the midpoint of the show Ed would shift to a different personality, who could well be in a different part of the country entirely. TV cameras were bulky and inconvenient to move around those days, meaning that a technical crew virtually had to take over the home of the subject several days in advance, running heavy cables from room to room and carefully mapping out every movement to be used on the night of the broadcast, to avoid tangles and confusion.

Among the people who chatted informally with Murrow were Marilyn Monroe, Zsa Zsa Gabor, A. C. Nielsen of the ratings company, Fidel Castro, Margaret Mead, John Steinbeck, Sam Rayburn, Tom Dewey, and then-Senator John F. Kennedy. Actors and actresses, politicians, diplomats, heads of state, inventors, scientists, musicians, and high church officials were all "visited" on the series. When Charles Collingwood took over for Murrow at the start of the 1959–1960 season, enabling Ed to ease off on his busy schedule, the show did more world traveling and many of the interviews were filmed or taped on location.

PERSONAL APPEARANCE (*Dramatic Anthology*)
FIRST TELECAST: *July 4, 1958*
LAST TELECAST: *September 19, 1958*
BROADCAST HISTORY:
Jul 1958–Sep 1958, CBS Fri 10:30–11:00

The filmed dramas telecast in this summer replacement for *Person to Person* were all reruns of shows that had originally aired as episodes of *Schlitz Playhouse* and *Screen Director's Playhouse.*

PERSONAL APPEARANCE THEATER (*Dramatic Anthology*)
FIRST TELECAST: *October 27, 1951*
LAST TELECAST: *May 23, 1952*
BROADCAST HISTORY:
Oct 1951–Nov 1951, ABC Sat 7:00–7:30
Dec 1951–Jan 1952, ABC Fri 9:30–10:00
May 1952, ABC Fri 8:30–9:00

A collection of 30-minute comedy and mystery films starring lesser-known actors and actresses, such as Franklin Pangborn, Jane Darwell, Robert Clarke, and Anita Louise.

PERSONAL APPEARANCE THEATRE, see *Joseph Schildkraut Presents*

PERSONALITIES (*Interview*)
BROADCAST HISTORY:
Syndicated only
30 minutes
Produced: *1990–1991*
Released: *September 1990*
HOSTS:
Charlie Rose (1990)
Bill Sternoff (1990–1991)
Janet Zappala (1991)
Jim Moret (1991)

Personalities started as a weeknight magazine-style series in which Charlie Rose, who had spent the previous 6½ years as the primary anchor on *CBS News Nightwatch*, chatted with three or four celebrities, people in the news, or others. Rose departed the show a few weeks after the premiere, and was replaced by Bill Sternoff. Janet Zappala specialized in show business gossip but did other interviews and stories as well and, in early 1991, was promoted to cohost.

In July 1991 the series was retitled *E.D.J.* (Entertainment Daily Journal) and cohost Sternoff was replaced by Jim Moret. With the new title came a broader focus, including investigative pieces and other features designed to make the show more like the long-running *Entertainment Tonight.* As cohost Janet Zappala intoned on the premiere telecast of the retitled series, "It's not just about famous personalities anymore." Among the changes were the addition of several regular reporters including syndicated newspaper gossip columnist Liz Smith, *People* magazine's Mitchell Fink, and Bryn Freedman. The changes didn't help and three months after the change in format, *E.D.J.* had its last telecast on October 25, 1991.

PERSONALITY PUZZLE (*Quiz/Panel*)
FIRST TELECAST: *March 19, 1953*
LAST TELECAST: *June 25, 1953*
BROADCAST HISTORY:
Mar 1953–Jun 1953, ABC Thu 10:30–11:00
EMCEE:
Robert Alda
REGULAR PANELIST:
Lisa Ferraday

Quiz in which the panelists were given personal possessions of a famous celebrity, who was seated behind them, and then had to guess who the celebrity was. Various guests appeared on the panel from week to week along with regular Lisa Ferraday. The program alternated with the similar *Quick as a Flash.*

PERSONALS (*Audience Participation*)
FIRST TELECAST: *September 16, 1991*
LAST TELECAST: *December 23, 1992*
BROADCAST HISTORY:
Sep 1991–Jul 1992, CBS Mon–Fri 12:30–1:00 A.M.
Aug 1992–Sep 1992, CBS Mon–Fri 1:00–1:30 A.M.
Sep 1992–Dec 1992, CBS Mon–Thu 1:00–1:30 A.M.
Dec 1992, CBS Mon Thu 12:30–1:00 A.M.
HOST:
Michael Berger
ANNOUNCER:
Tim Jones

This contemporary update of *The Dating Game* scoured "personals" ads in magazines and newspapers, and solicited "video personals" from viewers to locate its contestants. Each contestant chosen was asked to pick three potential dates from other ads or videos, and all four people then met on the show. The game was straightforward. The contestant had been asked questions before the show, and the three potential dates had to guess the answers. The first one to get three answers correct won the date.

The contestant and his or her date then played another round to determine where their date would be. Competing with a previous day's couple, they were asked a rapid-fire series of "yes or no" questions; each time they answered the same way their destination improved (Lake Tahoe, Club Med, Switzerland), but each time they disagreed it got worse. At the bottom was a gag date to "Pink's Hot Dog Stand" on LaBrea in Hollywood.

Personals was played primarily for laughs, with comedian/host Michael Berger making fun of both the contestants and the show. Not surprisingly, there was plenty of sexual innuendo. Viewers were encouraged to send messages to anyone they saw on the show via a 900 number for $2.95 per minute or to send in videos for airing on the show and being seen by other viewers for possible dates. The show was taped at the Sheraton Los Angeles Airport Hotel.

PERSPECTIVE (*Discussion*)
FIRST TELECAST: *November 13, 1952*
LAST TELECAST: *April 6, 1953*
BROADCAST HISTORY:
Nov 1952–Jan 1953, ABC Thu 9:00–9:30
Jan 1953–Apr 1953, ABC Mon 9:00–9:30

Live public-affairs program produced in cooperation with the Bar Association of the City of New York, and featuring experts from politics, education, science, and industry discussing how their fields could benefit society.

PERSUADERS, THE (*Adventure*)
FIRST TELECAST: *September 18, 1971*
LAST TELECAST: *June 14, 1972*
BROADCAST HISTORY:
Sep 1971–Jan 1972, ABC Sat 10:00–11:00
Jan 1972–Jun 1972, ABC Wed 9:30–10:30
CAST:
Danny Wilde .... Tony Curtis
Lord Brett Sinclair .... Roger Moore
Judge Fulton .... Laurence Naismith
THEME:
"The Persuaders," by John Barry

Danny and Brett were two wealthy playboys who had attained their wealth in very different ways. Danny Wilde was an American, born and raised in Brooklyn, who was a self-made man. Although he had made a great deal of money in the stock market, he was still a "poor kid" underneath. As a member of the British aristocracy, Brett Sinclair was born to great wealth. They were brought together at a Riviera party by retired Judge Fulton, who persuaded them to tackle criminal cases which the legal authorities couldn't handle. So they set out, half seriously and half on a lark, traveling around Europe looking for romance, adventure, and wrongs to right. The contrast in their styles and backgrounds was always apparent, as when they went camping out. There was Danny, under the stars with nothing but a blanket for protection, while Brett had a deluxe tent, complete with bar and freezer.

The show was produced in England.

PET SHOP (*Animals*)
FIRST TELECAST: *December 1, 1951*
LAST TELECAST: *March 14, 1953*
BROADCAST HISTORY:
Dec 1951–Mar 1953, DUM Sat 7:30–8:00
REGULARS:
Gail Compton
Gay Compton
George Menard (1953)

This gentle pet show was presided over by Gail Compton and his young daughter, Gay. They exhibited a variety of domestic animals, welcomed guests with their performing pets, and encouraged adoptions (more than 3,000 homeless dogs were placed during the first nine months alone). Among the regulars were Sissie the poodle, Snooky the squirrel monkey, Mac the macaw, and Tin Can the goat.

George Menard was host for the show's last four weeks on the network. From Chicago.

PETE AND GLADYS (*Situation Comedy*)
FIRST TELECAST: *September 19, 1960*
LAST TELECAST: *September 10, 1962*
BROADCAST HISTORY:
Sep 1960–Sep 1962, CBS Mon 8:00–8:30
CAST:
Pete Porter .... Harry Morgan
Gladys Porter .... Cara Williams

Hilda Crocker (1960–1961) .... Verna Felton
Alice (1960–1961) .... Barbara Stuart
George Colton .... Peter Leeds
Janet Colton .... Shirley Mitchell
Pop (1961) .... Ernest Truex
Peggy Briggs (1961–1962) .... Mina Kolb
Ernie Briggs (1961–1962)............... Joe Mantell
Uncle Paul.......................... Gale Gordon
Nancy (1961–1962).............. Frances Rafferty
Bruce Carter (1961–1962) .... Bill Hinnant

During his years as the sardonic next-door neighbor on *December Bride*, Pete Porter was always complaining about his scatterbrained, ineffectual wife, Gladys. She was never seen on that series but became the costar, in the person of Cara Williams, in this successor to *December Bride*. Along from the original series was Hilda Crocker, the nosy older woman friend who had tried to defend Gladys when Pete made some nasty comment about his wife. Gladys' Uncle Paul was seen occasionally during the first season and became a regular the second, as did the Porters' next-door neighbors and Gladys' friend Nancy (played by *December Bride* regular Frances Rafferty, in a different role). Gladys' nephew Bruce, who was attending a nearby college, moved in with them in the fall of 1961. The conflict between the sincere, ingenuous, and often confused Gladys and sarcastic, deprecating Pete formed the crux of the stories in this series.

Reruns of *Pete and Gladys* were on CBS' daytime lineup from October 1962 to October 1964.

PETE KELLY'S BLUES (*Drama*)

FIRST TELECAST: *April 5, 1959*
LAST TELECAST: *September 4, 1959*
BROADCAST HISTORY:
Apr 1959–Jul 1959, NBC Sun 8:30–9:00
Jul 1959–Sep 1959, NBC Fri 7:30–8:00
CAST:
Pete Kelly...................... William Reynolds
Savannah Brown .... Connee Boswell
George Lupo .... Than Wyenn
Fred................................ Phil Gordon
Johnny Cassiano .... Fred (Anthony) Eisley
PRODUCER:
Jack Webb

Life in Kansas City during the Roaring Twenties, from the standpoint of a musician working in a speakeasy, was the subject of Pete Kelly's Blues. Pete was a trumpet player and the leader of Pete Kelly's Original Big Seven Band. His best friend was the band's pianist, Fred, and his closest female friend was Savannah Brown, a blues singer at another speakeasy. Pete worked for George Lupo, who was essentially a nice guy but had become rather jaded since opening his own place on Cherry Street. The stories revolved around the adventures Pete had as he ran into people who got him involved in murder, tracking down missing people, and other non-musical exploits.

Jack Webb, who produced this series, had been the original Pete Kelly in the radio series of the same name, which ran for six months in 1951, and also starred in the movie version which was released in 1955. The offscreen trumpet player who dubbed in Pete's solos was Dick Cathcart, a well-regarded jazz performer of the period. He had originally been picked by Webb for the radio series and also appeared with him in the movie.

PETER AND MARY SHOW, THE, see *Peter Lind Hayes Show, The*

PETER BENCHLEY'S AMAZON (*Adventure*)

BROADCAST HISTORY:
Syndicated only
60 minutes
Produced: *1999–2000* (22 episodes)
Released: *September 1999*
CAST:
Dr. Alex Kennedy .... C. Thomas Howell
Karen Oldham .... Carol Alt
Jimmy Stack................ Chris William Martin
Pia Claire......................... Fabiana Udenio
Will Bauer ....Tyler Hynes
Andrew Talbott...................... Rob Stewart
First Elder Cole.. .... John Neville
Falconer John .... Gabriel Hogan
Elder Balaam...................... Joseph Scoren
Korakal .... Pedro Salvin
Prudence................... Katie Emme McIninch
Elder Malakai .... Julian Richings
Kinchka .... Inga Breede
Hekka............................. Deborah Politt
Adam................................. Kyle Fairlie

When an electrical fire forced a Trans Rio Air airliner to crash deep in the Amazon jungle, the rescue team thought there were no survivors and left. They didn't know that a handful of people who had been in the broken-off tail section of the plane had survived to became castaways in the remote wilderness of South America. Those survivors met the Caucasian descendants of a group of people who had been shipwrecked in the jungle almost 400 years before.

The survivors were Alex, an American physician; Karen, a flight attendant; Will, a teenager whose injuries had been tended to by the natives; Pia, an arrogant opera diva; Andrew, a biology teacher who was suffering from leukemia; and Jimmy, a young mechanic. They had to contend with hostile natives, spiders, snakes, and crocodiles, and were unable to signal the rescue party that they were still alive. In October, after escaping from the warrior Spider Tribe, they were befriended by Falconer John, a mysterious white man (with an Irish accent) living with the natives. He took the survivors to the Village of the Chosen, where the locals—particularly Elders Cole (the kindly one) and Balaam (the manipulator)—were suspicious of them. Meanwhile, Will had been taken captive by the Spider People, was adopted by Korakal, their leader, and became one of them.

In November Will left the Spider People to join the other survivors with the Chosen, hoping that they would be able to escape and return to civilization. Falconer John had convinced the Elders that Will was their "Child of Promise" who could help them reconstruct lost aspects of their history and, despite indications to the contrary, it seemed Will might really be he. In February five of the survivors—Pia had bailed out—escaped from the Village of the Chosen. Will, during a treacherous time when it looked like everything was falling apart, was rescued by Falconer John, who left the others to die. They survived but were captured by cannibals. Fortunately, the Spider People, supposedly in negotiations with the cannibals, attacked them and saved the survivors. Andrew returned to the Chosen Village, while the others continued to search for a way to the outside world. Their ticket out was a seaplane that had brought geologists into the jungle. They had been killed by the cannibals who later killed the pilot as well. In the series' final scene Karen was flying out of the jungle in the seaplane while Alex had returned to the Village of the Chosen to get help for Jimmy, who had accidentally been shot in the stomach when they fought over a pistol.

PETER GUNN (*Detective Drama*)
FIRST TELECAST: *September 22, 1958*
LAST TELECAST: *September 25, 1961*
BROADCAST HISTORY:
Sep 1958–Sep 1960, NBC Mon 9:00–9:30
Oct 1960–Sep 1961, ABC Mon 10:30–11:00
CAST:
Peter Gunn .... Craig Stevens
Edie Hart .... Lola Albright
Lt. Jacoby .... Herschel Bernardi
"Mother" (1958–1959) .... Hope Emerson
"Mother" (1959–1961) .... Minerva Urecal
THEME:
"Peter Gunn," by Henry Mancini

Peter Gunn was one of the first suave, aggressive, lady-killer private detectives to be seen on television. Working to get his clients out of trouble, and to solve crimes, he often found himself on the short end of a fight but somehow managed to come out on top, often through the intervention of his friend, police lieutenant Jacoby. Gunn spent much of his free time at a jazz nightclub called "Mother's," where his girlfriend Edie was the featured singer.

Original jazz themes by Henry Mancini punctuated the action and conveyed mood in this detective series, setting a pattern that was followed by many of the other detective shows of the late 1950s and early 1960s. RCA released two very successful albums of music from this series, *The Music from Peter Gunn* and *More Music from Peter Gunn.*

PETER LIND HAYES SHOW, THE (*Situation Comedy*)
FIRST TELECAST: *November 23, 1950*
LAST TELECAST: *March 29, 1951*
BROADCAST HISTORY:
Nov 1950–Mar 1951, NBC Thu 8:30–9:00
REGULARS:
Peter Lind Hayes
Mary Healy
Mary Wickes (1950)
Claude Stroud (1950)

The set for this live series was a replica of the New Rochelle, New York, home of its stars, Peter Lind Hayes and Mary Healy. At the start of each episode, a guest star would be seen apologizing over the phone to someone with whom he could not have dinner that evening because of a previous commitment to have dinner with Peter and Mary. The guest star(s) then went to Peter and Mary's "house" for dinner where the talents they possessed—singing, dancing, comedy, etc.—were worked into the script. The series had actually premiered as *The Peter and Mary Show* but was changed to *The Peter Lind Hayes Show* on December 14. Mary Wickes was their housekeeper and Claude Stroud an unemployed comedian who had come for a visit and become a permanent member of the household. Both of them were last seen in the December 28 telecast.

PETER LOVES MARY (*Situation Comedy*)
FIRST TELECAST: *October 12, 1960*
LAST TELECAST: *May 31, 1961*
BROADCAST HISTORY:
Oct 1960–May 1961, NBC Wed 10:00–10:30
CAST:
Peter Lindsey .... Peter Lind Hayes
Mary Lindsey .... Mary Healy
Wilma .... Bea Benaderet
Leslie Lindsey .... Merry Martin
Steve Lindsey .... Gil Smith
Happy Richman .... Alan Reed
Horace Gibney .... Howard Smith
Charlie .... Arch Johnson

Peter Lind Hayes and Mary Healy, husband and wife in real life, here played a show-business couple adjusting to a move to the suburbs. The move from Manhattan to Oakdale affected the members of the household in different ways. Peter longed for the exciting life of the city, where all the show-business people with whom they were friendly congregated in such hangouts as Lindy's. Mary wanted to become involved in all the traditional suburban activities—local government, P.T.A., social causes, etc. The conflicts between their work in the city and their suburban life with housekeeper Wilma and their two children, Leslie and Steve, produced the material for the stories in this series.

PETER MARSHALL VARIETY SHOW, THE (*Talk/Variety*)
BROADCAST HISTORY:
Syndicated only
90 minutes
Produced: *1976* (19 episodes)
Released: *September 1976*
REGULARS:
Peter Marshall
Rod Gist & Denny Evans
Chapter 5
Alan Copeland Orchestra

Peter Marshall was best known as quizmaster on *The Hollywood Squares* when this big budget variety show was made. He still is. *The Peter Marshall Variety Show* debuted with nationwide coverage and made a big initial splash, then promptly sank after only 19 weeks. The format was standard-issue variety show (which may have been the problem): Peter chatting amiably and singing pleasantly; relentlessly middle-of-the-road guests such as Charles Nelson Reilly, John Byner, Patti Page, and Betty White; two bright young sketch comics who were never heard of again (Rod Gist and Denny Evans); and a forgettable singing group with the usual clever name, the Chapter 5. There were even home movies. The program was run in many cities on Saturday or Sunday night at 11:30 P.M., and viewers were evidently asleep by the time Peter said hello.

PETER POTTER SHOW, THE (*Music/Discussion*)
FIRST TELECAST: *September 13, 1953*
LAST TELECAST: *March 28, 1954*
BROADCAST HISTORY:
Sep 1953–Jan 1954, ABC Sun 9:30–10:30
Jan 1954–Mar 1954, ABC Sun 9:30–10:00
HOST:
Peter Potter

Hollywood disc jockey Peter Potter brought his *Juke Box Jury* to national television in 1953. It consisted of the playing of new records, with ensuing discussion by a panel of celebrities from movies, theater, TV, and the recording industry. The studio audience also participated in the voting on each new record—"Will it be a hit (bong!) . . . or a miss (clunk!)?" Some live performances were also included.

The program was known during its first month by the familiar title *Juke Box Jury*, then switched to *The Peter Potter Show*.

PETROCELLI (*Legal Drama*)

FIRST TELECAST: *September 11, 1974*

LAST TELECAST: *March 3, 1976*

BROADCAST HISTORY:

Sep 1974–Mar 1976, NBC Wed 10:00–11:00

CAST:

Tony Petrocelli .... Barry Newman
Maggie Petrocelli .... Susan Howard
Pete Ritter .... Albert Salmi
Lt. John Ponce .... David Huddleston

Set in the fictional Southwestern town of San Remo, *Petrocelli* was not quite a typical legal series. Harvard-educated Tony Petrocelli had decided to practice law in a part of the country that was not always receptive to big-city, Eastern ways. He and his wife moved to the Southwest, set up housekeeping in a camper-trailer, and opened up his law practice in the middle of wide-open cattle country. Tony hired Pete Ritter, a local cowboy, as his investigator. Tony's propensity for taking on cases whether or not his clients could really afford his services often made it rather hard for him and his wife to make ends meet. Lt. Ponce of the local police, a good friend of Tony's despite the fact that they found themselves in adversary positions in the courtroom, was often involved in investigating the cases Tony was working on. An interesting technique used in this series was showing the actual crime in flashbacks from the perspective of various people involved. The flashbacks, naturally, differed depending on whose recollections were being shown.

Barry Newman created the role of Petrocelli in a 1970 movie called *The Lawyer*, which was loosely based on the Sam Sheppard murder case.

PETTICOAT JUNCTION (*Situation Comedy*)

FIRST TELECAST: *September 24, 1963*

LAST TELECAST: *September 12, 1970*

BROADCAST HISTORY:

Sep 1963–Sep 1964, CBS Tue 9:00–9:30
Sep 1964–Aug 1967, CBS Tue 9:30–10:00
Sep 1967–Sep 1970, CBS Sat 9:30–10:00

CAST:

Kate Bradley (1963–1968) .... Bea Benadaret
Uncle Joe Carson .... Edgar Buchanan
Billie Jo Bradley (1963–1965) .... Jeannine Riley
Billie Jo Bradley (1965–1966) .... Gunilla Hutton
Billie Jo Bradley (1966–1970) .... Meredith MacRae
Bobbie Jo Bradley (1963–1965) .... Pat Woodell
Bobbie Jo Bradley (1965–1970) ...... Lori Saunders
Betty Jo Bradley Elliott ...... Linda Kaye (Henning)
Charlie Pratt (1963–1967) .... Smiley Burnette
Floyd Smoot (1963–1968) .... Rufe Davis
Homer Bedloe (1963–1968) .... Charles Lane
Sam Drucker .... Frank Cady
Norman Curtis (1963–1964) .... Roy Roberts
Newt Kiley (1964–1970) .... Kay E. Kuter
Selma Plout (1964–1965) .... Virginia Sale
Selma Plout (1965–1970) .... Elvia Allman
Henrietta Plout (1965–1966) .... Susan Walther
Henrietta Plout (1966–1970) .... Lynette Winter
Steve Elliott (1966–1970) .... Mike Minor
Eb Dawson (1966–1970) .... Tom Lester
Dr. Barton Stuart (1968–1969) .... Regis Toomey
Dr. Janet Craig (1968–1970) .... June Lockhart
Wendell Gibbs (1968–1970) .... Byron Foulger
Bert Smedley (1968–1969) .... Paul Hartman
Kathy Jo Elliott (1968–1970) .... Elna Hubbell
Jeff Powers (1968) .... Geoff Edwards
Orrin Pike (1969–1970) .... Jonathan Daly

The small farming community of Hooterville provided the setting for this highly successful rural situation comedy. Kate Bradley was the widowed owner of the only transient housing in town, the Shady Rest Hotel. Helping her run the hotel were her three beautiful daughters, Billie Jo, Bobbie Jo, and Betty Jo. Also assisting was the girls' Uncle Joe, who had assumed the title of manager. In addition to her involvement with the hotel, the romantic lives of her daughters, and her associations with the townspeople, Kate was constantly at odds with Homer Bedloe, vice-president of the C.&F.W. Railroad. Homer was determined to close down the steam-driven branch of the railroad that ran through Hooterville, scrap its lone engine (the Cannonball), and put its two engineers (Charlie Pratt and Floyd Smoot) out of jobs.

Two years after the premiere of *Petticoat Junction*, CBS added *Green Acres* to its lineup. This situation comedy was the story of a Manhattan lawyer who gave up big-city life and bought a farm near Hooterville. For the remainder of their existences there was a certain interplay between the characters of the two shows. The two characters from *Green Acres* who most frequently showed up on *Petticoat Junction* were farmer Newt Kiley and handyman Eb Dawson.

In the fall of 1966 pilot Steve Elliott crashed outside Hooterville and was nursed back to health by the Bradley girls. He later became romantically involved with Betty Jo and eventually married her. They set up housekeeping not far from the hotel, and had a daughter, Kathy Jo. This despite the efforts of Kate's hated adversary, Selma Plout, to get Steve interested in her daughter, Henrietta.

Bea Benaderet passed away soon after production began for the 1968–1969 season and her absence left the show without a unifying center of attention. To fill the void, the role of Dr. Janet Craig, a mature woman doctor who became the town physician when old Dr. Stuart retired, was added late in 1968. The chemistry was not there anymore, however, and the show was canceled in 1970.

One of the distinguishing aspects of *Petticoat Junction* was the turnover in its cast. In addition to those roles that were played by more than one performer as listed in the credits above, a number of actors had appeared, albeit infrequently, as Dr. Stuart and barber Bert Smedley. Not only that, but several people who eventually became regulars on the show—Elvia Allman, Mike Minor, and Byron Fougler—had shown up previously on *Petticoat Junction* in other roles. The one regular who was most likely to stay, however, was Linda Kay Henning. Her father, Paul Henning, was the producer of *Petticoat Junction* as well as *Green Acres*.

PEYTON PLACE (*Drama*)

FIRST TELECAST: *September 15, 1964*

LAST TELECAST: *June 2, 1969*

BROADCAST HISTORY:

Sep 1964–Jun 1965, ABC Tue/Thu 9:30–10:00
Jun 1965–Oct 1965, ABC Tue/Thu/Fri 9:30–10:00
Nov 1965–Aug 1966, ABC Mon/Tue/Thu 9:30–10:00
Sep 1966–Jan 1967, ABC Mon/Wed 9:30–10:00
Jan 1967–Aug 1967, ABC Mon/Tue 9:30–10:00
Sep 1967–Sep 1968, ABC Mon/Thu 9:30–10:00
Sep 1968–Jan 1969, ABC Mon 9:00–9:30 Wed 8:30–9:00
Feb 1969–Jun 1969, ABC Mon 9:00–9:30

CAST:

Constance Mackenzie/Carson(1964–1968) .... Dorothy Malone
Allison Mackenzie (1964–1966) .... Mia Farrow
Mr. Michael Rossi .... Ed Nelson
Matthew Swain, editor of The Clarion *(1964–1965)* .... Warner Anderson
Leslie Harrington (1964–1968) .... Paul Langton
Rodney Harrington, Leslie's oldest son .... Ryan O'Neal
Norman Harrington, Leslie's younger son .... Christopher Connelly
Betty Anderson/Harrington/Cord/Harrington .... Barbara Parkins
Julie Anderson, Betty's mother .... Kasey Rogers
George Anderson, her father (1964–1965) .... Henry Beckman
Dr. Robert Morton (1964–1965) .... Kent Smith
Steven Cord .... James Douglas
Hannah Cord, Steven's mother (1965–1967) .... Ruth Warrick
Paul Hanley (1965) .... Richard Evans
Elliott Carson (1965–1968) .... Tim O'Connor
Eli Carson, Elliott's father .... Frank Ferguson
Nurse Choate (1965–1968) .... Erin O'Brien-Moore
Dr. Claire Morton (1965) .... Mariette Hartley
Dr. Vincent Markham (1965) .... Leslie Nielsen
Rita Jacks/Harrington (1965–1969) .... Patricia Morrow
Ada Jacks, Rita's mother (1965–1969) .... Evelyn Scott
David Schuster (1965–1966) ..... William Smithers
Doris Schuster, his wife (1965) .... Gail Kobe
Kim Schuster, his deaf, 6-year-old child (1965) .... Kimberly Beck
Theodore Dowell, attorney (1965) ... Patrick Whyte
Stella Chernak (1965–1966) .... Lee Grant
Joe Chernak (1965) .... Don Quine
Gus Chernak (1965–1966) .... Bruce Gordon
Dr. Russ Gehring (1965–1966) .... David Canary
District Attorney John Fowler (1965–1966) .... John Kerr
Marian Fowler, his wife (1965–1966) .... Joan Blackman
Martin Peyton (1965–1968) ...... George Macready
Martin Peyton (temporary replacement, 1967) .... Wilfred Hyde-White
Sandy Webber (1966–1967) .... Lana Wood
Chris Webber (1966–1967) .... Gary Haynes
Lee Webber (1966–1968) .... Stephen Oliver
Ann Howard (1966) .... Susan Oliver
Rachel Welles (1966–1967) .... Leigh Taylor-Young
Jack Chandler (1966–1967) .... John Kellogg
Adrienne Van Leyden (1967) ...... Gena Rowlands
Eddie Jacks, Rita's father (1967–1968) .... Dan Duryea
Carolyn Russell (1968–1969) .... Elizabeth "Tippy" Walker
Fred Russell (1968–1969) .... Joe Maross
Marsha Russell (1968–1969) .... Barbara Rush
Rev. Tom Winter (1968–1969) .... Bob Hogan
Susan Winter, his wife (1968–1969) ... Diana Hyland
Dr. Harry Miles (1968–1969) ...... Percy Rodriguez
Alma Miles, Harry's wife (1968–1969) .... Ruby Dee
Lew Miles, Harry's teenage son (1968–1969) .... Glynn Turman
Jill Smith/Rossi (1968) .... Joyce Jillson
Joe Rossi, Dr. Rossi's brother (1968) .... Michael Christian

EXECUTIVE PRODUCER:

Paul Monash

Based on the novel *Peyton Place*, by Grace Metalious, this continuing romantic drama was set in the small New England town of Peyton Place, a community that was apparently seething with extramarital affairs, dark secrets, and assorted skulduggery. *Peyton Place* was the first soap opera to become a major hit in prime time. It aired up to three times per week, and every one of the 514 telecasts during its five-year run was an original episode.

Receiving top billing (though not necessarily the most prominent role) was Dorothy Malone as bookshop proprietress Constance Mackenzie, whose own dark secret involved the circumstances surrounding the birth of her daughter Allison 18 years earlier. In May 1965 Constance was finally able to marry Allison's real father, Elliott Carson, upon his release from prison. Meanwhile Allison experienced her own romantic entanglements, leading to a romance with wealthy Rodney Harrington in early 1966. But by August Allison had mysteriously "disappeared" (Mia Farrow had decided to leave the series). Her character was not soon forgotten. First a young girl named Rachael turned up with a clue to Allison's disappearance (a bracelet), setting off a long investigation. Then in 1968 another girl, Jill, arrived in town with what she claimed was Allison's baby.

Other major stories revolved around Rodney Harrington, who was tried for murder in an extended story from 1965–1966. Rodney's lawyer was Steven Cord, another young man with a past, who soon found himself embroiled in the town's active romantic life. So did Dr. Michael Rossi, a young physician who had arrived in Peyton Place on the first telecast in 1964, and who was facing his own murder trial when the series ended in 1969.

And there were many, many more: Betty Anderson, who was married successively to Rodney Harrington (October 1964), Steven Cord (April 1966), and then Rodney Harrington again (June 1968); tavernkeeper's daughter Rita Jacks, who married Norman Harrington (January 1966); David Schuster, who took over the management of the Peyton Mills when Leslie Harrington, Rodney and Norman's father, was sacked by owner Martin Peyton; Rev. Tom Winter, whose affairs were more than clerical; and, toward the end, in a bow to relevance, Dr. Harry Miles, a black neurosurgeon with *his* family and problems.

Aging Martin Peyton, the town's patriarch, was not seen at first. He first appeared in November 1965, as his grandson Rodney Harrington was about to go on trial for murder. Over the next two years Peyton was an important character. An extended story in late 1967 had newcomer Adrienne Van Leyden all set to marry the old codger and collect his loot, until she was killed during a confrontation with Betty (December 1967), resulting in an investigation with multiple consequences. Shortly thereafter Martin Peyton departed for a Boston clinic, where he died in November 1968, and was buried in a funeral attended by most of the town. (Notwithstanding this fact, he was brought back to life when *Peyton Place* was revived as a daytime serial from 1972 to 1974).

The regular cast of *Peyton Place* would fill a telephone book. One ABC cast credits card lists over 100 "regulars." Those shown above figured most prominently in the various continuing stories. At the outset of the series Dorothy Malone, in the role of Constance Mackenzie, received top billing. A year later, in September 1965, Miss Malone suddenly fell ill and the role was taken over temporarily by Lola Albright. Miss Malone returned in January 1966 and continued for another two and a half years. After she left in June 1968, Ed Nelson, as heartthrob Dr. Michael Rossi, was given top billing.

Probably the two most famous discoveries of *Peyton Place,* however, were Mia Farrow and Ryan O'Neal. Miss Farrow, as the alluring Allison, was seen only during the first two seasons, but O'Neal, as Rodney, continued for virtually the full run of the series.

PHENOM (*Situation Comedy*)

FIRST TELECAST: *September 14, 1993*
LAST TELECAST: *August 31, 1994*
BROADCAST HISTORY:

Sep 1993–Jun 1994, ABC Tue 8:30–9:00
Aug 1994, ABC Wed 8:30–9:00

CAST:

Dianne Doolan .... Judith Light
Angela Doolan (age 15) .... Angela Goethals
Brian Doolan .... Todd Louiso
Mary Margaret Doolan .... Ashley Johnson
Lou Del La Rosa .... William Devane
Roanne .... Jennifer Lien
Monica .... Sara Rue

THEME:

sung by Carly Simon

Bright sitcom about a teenage prodigy, Angela, who had the potential to become a top tennis star (a "phenom") if she would but follow the guidance of abrasive, egotistical coach Lou Del La Rosa. Angela's vacillating mom, Dianne, was not sure whether this was the right career choice for her daughter, but strong-willed Lou pulled her along, together with her neurotic older brother Brian and jealous younger sister Mary Margaret.

PHIL HANNA SINGS, see *Starlit Time*

PHIL SILVERS SHOW, THE (*Situation Comedy*)

FIRST TELECAST: *September 20, 1955*
LAST TELECAST: *September 11, 1959*
BROADCAST HISTORY:

Sep 1955–Oct 1955, CBS Tue 8:30–9:00
Nov 1955–Feb 1958, CBS Tue 8:00–8:30
Feb 1958–Sep 1959, CBS Fri 9:00–9:30

CAST:

M/Sgt. Ernie Bilko .... Phil Silvers
Cpt. Rocco Barbella .... Harvey Lembeck
Pvt. Sam Fender .... Herbie Faye
Col. John Hall .... Paul Ford
Pvt. Duane Doberman .... Maurice Gosfield
Sgt. Rupert Ritzik .... Joe E. Ross
Cpl. Henshaw .... Allan Melvin
Pvt. Dino Paparelli .... Billy Sands
Pvt. Zimmerman .... Mickey Freeman
Nell Hall .... Hope Sansberry
Sgt. Grover .... Jimmy Little
Sgt. Joan Hogan (1955–1958) ...... Elisabeth Fraser

Mythical Fort Baxter, Kansas, was the setting for this outrageous satire on military life. Master Sergeant Ernie Bilko was the biggest con man on the post. With little to do in the wilds of Middle America, Bilko spent most of his time gambling, conjuring up assorted money-making schemes, and outmaneuvering his immediate superior, Colonal Hall. Loud, brash, and highly resourceful, Ernie could talk his way out of almost any situation. His attitude and approach filtered down to most of the members of his platoon, and collectively they ran roughshod over the rest of the men stationed at Fort Baxter. WAC Joan Hogan, who worked in the base's office, was Bilko's mild romantic interest during the first three seasons, but was phased out. The original title of the series was *You'll Never Get Rich*, which remained as the subtitle when the series became *The Phil Silvers Show* less than two months after its premiere.

The name Bilko was supposedly taken from real-life baseball player Steve Bilko, a hero of series creator Nat Hiken.

PHILCO TV PLAYHOUSE (*Dramatic Anthology*)

FIRST TELECAST: *October 3, 1948*
LAST TELECAST: *October 2, 1955*
BROADCAST HISTORY:

Oct 1948–Oct 1955, NBC Sun 9:00–10:00

HOST:

Bert Lytell (1948–1949)

This live dramatic-anthology series featured top-name actors and actresses in original TV plays and adaptations of novels, short stories, and plays. The first season was produced under the aegis of the Actors' Equity Association, and concentrated on TV adaptations of Broadway dramas and musicals, often with original cast members appearing. Former Equity president Bert Lytell was the host. Perhaps the most elaborate production during the first season was an adaptation of *Cyrano de Bergerac* with Jose Ferrer and a large supporting cast, which used seven sets (including street scenes) to re-create 17th-century Paris. This, remember, was on *live* television. Other first-season productions included adaptations of *Dinner at Eight* with Peggy Wood and Dennis King, and *Counsellor at Law* starring Paul Muni (his TV debut, re-creating the role that had brought him fame on Broadway 17 years earlier).

During the second season Equity was no longer involved, but instead an arrangement was made with the Book-of-the-Month Club to present each week a dramatization of a different novel, usually one which was currently popular. After 1950 this theme was dropped and offerings ran the gamut between original and adapted plays, musicals, and occasional true-life documentaries, always meticulously produced. Among the many top stars who appeared on *Philco* were Anthony Quinn, Grace Kelly, young Brandon

De Wilde, Lillian Gish (narrating "The Birth of the Movies," a documentary), Walter Matthau, Julie Harris, Rod Steiger, Paul Newman (as Billy the Kid), and Charlton Heston. The last *Philco* telecast was a rough waterfront drama called "A Man Is Ten Feet Tall" with Sidney Poitier, one of the few instances of a black actor appearing in a starring role in a 1950s drama.

From 1951–1955 *Philco TV Playhouse* alternated with *Goodyear TV Playhouse* which presented similar productions.

PHILIP MARLOWE (*Detective Drama*)
FIRST TELECAST: *October 6, 1959*
LAST TELECAST: *March 29, 1960*
BROADCAST HISTORY:
Oct 1959–Mar 1960, ABC Tue 9:30–10:00
CAST:
Philip Marlowe .... Philip Carey

When author Raymond Chandler wrote his first Philip Marlowe stories in the late 1930s, the detective hero was a hard-bitten loner, rough around the edges, and particularly aggressive. When Philip Marlowe reached television in 1959 he had been laundered considerably. He was still a rather independent loner but had become a much more gentlemanly sort than on the printed page. Working to protect people, solve crimes, and track down missing persons, he moved freely from place to place without getting entangled in any lasting personal relationships.

PHILIP MORRIS PLAYHOUSE (*Dramatic Anthology*)
FIRST TELECAST: *October 8, 1953*
LAST TELECAST: *March 4, 1954*
BROADCAST HISTORY:
Oct 1953–Mar 1954, CBS Thu 10:00–10:30

This live dramatic series, with individual plays ranging in tone from comedies to melodramas, was aired from New York. Lorne Greene, Eddie Albert, and Constance Ford starred in the premiere telecast, titled "Journey to Nowhere," and Nina Foch, Franchot Tone, Sterling Hayden, Vincent Price, and Otto Kruger appeared in subsequent episodes.

PHILLIES JACKPOT BOWLING, see *Jackpot Bowling Starring Milton Berle*

PHILLY (*Legal Drama*)
FIRST TELECAST: *September 25, 2001*
LAST TELECAST: *April 23, 2002*
BROADCAST HISTORY:
Sep 2001–Apr 2002, ABC Tue 10:00–11:00
CAST:
Kathleen Maguire .... Kim Delaney
Will Froman .... Tom Everett Scott
Patrick Cavanaugh (age 10) ... Scotty Leavenworth
Asst. D.A. Daniel X. Cavanaugh .... Kyle Secor
Asst. D.A. Terry Loomis .... Rick Hoffman
Patricia .... Diana-Maria Riva
Lisa Walensky .... Kristanna Loken
Jerry Bingham .... Scott Alan Smith
Judge Augustus Ripley .... Jamie Denton
Judge Irwin Hawes .... Robert Harper
Judge Ellen Armstrong .... Dena Dietrich

Kathleen Maguire was a criminal attorney in Philadelphia whose life seemed to be filled with scheming men and sleazy clients in this fast-paced legal drama. First she had to deal with her vengeful ex-husband, Asst. D.A. Dan, who fought her in the courtroom and did his best to turn their young son, Patrick, against her as well. Suave and politically ambitious, he was a fast-rising star in the city. Will was Kathleen's new law partner (the last one having been shipped off to a sanitarium after suffering a breakdown in court), a boyish womanizer who made out with female A.D.A.'s in empty conference rooms, and who seemed to attract the very dregs of humanity for clients. Murderers, rapists, pornographers and wife beaters filled her day. Terry was another A.D.A. who had a love-hate relationship with Kathleen, and Lisa was Will's off-and-on girlfriend. Dyspeptic judges also dissed her from the bench. While she and Will fought for the innocent, all this travail gave Kathleen something of an edge, simply to survive (angry cop, passing her in the courthouse: "Bitch!" Kathleen: "Asshole!").

In the spring Dan was elected district attorney, but the series did not last long enough to allow him to use his new power to further torment Kathleen. A leftover episode of the series aired on May 28, 2002, more than a month after the regular run had ended.

PHOENIX, THE (*Science Fiction*)
FIRST TELECAST: *March 19, 1982*
LAST TELECAST: *September 15, 1982*
BROADCAST HISTORY:
Mar 1982–Apr 1982, ABC Fri 9:00–10:00
Aug 1982–Sep 1982, ABC Wed 8:00–9:00
CAST:
Bennu of the Golden Light .... Judson Scott
Preminger .... Richard Lynch

Though he looked like a rather concerned young beach bum (frequently bare-chested), Bennu was in fact a messenger from an alien world, far away and long ago. He had come to the earth 1,500 years before as a scout from a dying civilization, and had been entombed in a pre-Incan sarcophagus in the Andes. Centuries later, when modern scientists had stumbled upon him and revived him, his goal became finding Mira, his partner, now in some other ancient burial ground somewhere in North America. Along the way he lent his exceptional powers, vested in the amulet he wore around his neck, to people in distress, and talked frequently of his concern for the environment—which seemed to be in as much danger here as it had been on his home planet.

None of this impressed a hard-nosed government agent named Preminger, whose goal was to capture Bennu and control his special powers.

The Phoenix was first seen as a movie special on April 26, 1981, and returned for a short run as a series in early 1982.

PHOTOCRIME (*Crime Drama*)
FIRST TELECAST: *September 21, 1949*
LAST TELECAST: *December 14, 1949*
BROADCAST HISTORY:
Sep 1949–Dec 1949, ABC Wed 8:30–9:00
CAST:
Inspector Hannibal Cobb .... Chuck Webster
ALSO:
Diana Douglas
Joe DeSantis

Easygoing Inspector Hannibal Cobb was the long arm of the law in this mystery series, which was produced in cooperation with *Look* magazine. Also known as *Look Photocrime.*

PHOTOGRAPHIC HORIZONS (*Instruction*)
FIRST TELECAST: *January 12, 1949*
LAST TELECAST: *March 7, 1949*
BROADCAST HISTORY:
Jan 1949–Mar 1949, DUM Mon 8:00–8:30
REGULARS:
Joe Costa
Peggy Corday

Many unusual program formats were tried in the early days of television, including that of the TV camera club. It seemed like a natural for the new medium. Not only could expert photographers describe picture-taking techniques, home-darkroom procedures, etc., they could actually show the results. *Photographic Horizons* began as a local show on DuMont's New York station in December 1947, and was quite popular with early set owners. There were interviews and demonstrations, and a succession of lovely models didn't hurt viewership. The models posed before special backgrounds and viewers at home were encouraged to take pictures of them off the TV screen. Joe Costa, president of the National Press Photographers Association, was host, and 23-year-old Peggy Corday his chief model. Maxine Barrat also frequently modeled for home shutterbugs.

PHOTOPLAY TIME, see *Wendy Barrie Show, The*

PHYL & MIKHY (*Situation Comedy*)
FIRST TELECAST: *May 26, 1980*
LAST TELECAST: *June 30, 1980*
BROADCAST HISTORY:
May 1980–Jun 1980, CBS Mon 8:30–9:00
CAST:
Phyllis Wilson ("Phyl") .... Murphy Cross
Mikhail Orlov ("Mikhy") .... Rick Lohman
Max Wilson .... Larry Haines
Vladimir Gimenko .... Michael Pataki
Edgar "Truck" Morley .... Jack Dodson
Connie .... Deborah Pratt

Phyllis Wilson and Mikhail Orlov were two young track stars who fell in love and wanted to get married. There were complications. Mikhail was a Russian, so he had to defect to the United States. Since the newlyweds had no money, they moved in with Phyl's widowed father Max, who was somewhat dubious about his new Russian son-in-law. Mikhy, for his part, had to learn to cope with the strange American lifestyle—not to mention all the unfamiliar appliances in the kitchen. They all had to put up with Gimenko, a representative of the Russian government who kept trying to get Mikhy to return to Mother Russia. Truck Morley was Max's boss and Connie was a friend of Phyl's.

Phyl & Mikhy was originally intended as a topical series to be broadcast prior to coverage of the 1980 Summer Olympics from Moscow, on NBC. But when Russia invaded Afghanistan, the U.S. withdrew its team and Olympic coverage was canceled. CBS considered dropping this series (which it had already paid for), but finally decided to run the six episodes it had. It didn't get much of an audience.

Rick Lohman and Larry Haines had both been on the daytime soap opera *Search for Tomorrow,* where Lohman played Haines's grandson.

PHYLLIS (*Situation Comedy*)
FIRST TELECAST: *September 8, 1975*
LAST TELECAST: *August 30, 1977*
BROADCAST HISTORY:
Sep 1975–Jan 1977, CBS Mon 8:30–9:00
Jan 1977–Jul 1977, CBS Sun 8:30–9:00
Aug 1977, CBS Tue 8:30–9:00
CAST:
Phyllis Lindstrom .... Cloris Leachman
Bess Lindstrom .... Lisa Gerritsen
Julie Erskine (1975–1976) .... Liz Torres
Leo Heatherton (1975–1976) .... Richard Schaal
Audrey Dexter .... Jane Rose
Judge Jonathan Dexter .... Henry Jones
Sally "Mother" Dexter .... Judith Lowry
Leonard Marsh (1976–1977) .... John Lawlor
Harriet Hastings (1976–1977) .... Garn Stephens
Dan Valenti (1976–1977) .... Carmine Caridi
Arthur Lanson (1976) .... Burt Mustin
Mark Valenti (1977) .... Craig Wasson

After five years playing Mary Richards's neighbor, friend, and landlady on *The Mary Tyler Moore Show,* Cloris Leachman began her own spin-off series. Phyllis Lindstrom returned to her hometown of San Francisco following the death of her husband Lars. In her mid-40s, and with a teenage daughter to support, Phyllis moved in with Lars's scatterbrained mother, Audrey, and Audrey's second husband, Judge Jonathan Dexter. Though not a member of the household when the series started, Judge Dexter's mother was also living with them before the first season's end.

Phyllis found a job working as assistant to Julie Erskine at Erskine's Commercial Photography Studio. Also working as a photographer for Julie was Leo Heatherton. (Barbara Colby was the actress originally signed for the role of Julie Erskine but only appeared in the first episode of the series. Miss Colby was brutally murdered soon after production had started and was replaced by Liz Torres.) This job, with Phyllis being her busybody, self-centered, oblivious self, lasted only one season.

At the start of the 1976–1977 season, in an effort to improve upon the mediocre ratings of the first season, Phyllis was given a new job as administrative assistant to Dan Valenti, a member of the San Francisco Board of Supervisors. She worked in an office with another supervisor, Leonard Marsh, and his assistant Harriet. On the home front things were also changing. Witty, sharp-tongued Mother Dexter, far and away the best member of the family when it came to putting down Phyllis, had become involved with a man. She was 87 and Arthur was 92, but love flowered and they were married in December 1976. Ironically, elderly actress Judith Lowry had died while on vacation in New York during a break in production early in December, before the episode aired, and Burt Mustin, who was too ill to see it, died not long after. Bess also found a man, in the person of Phyllis's boss's nephew Mark. They sneaked off to Las Vegas and were married in the spring. The changes in cast and multiple marriages didn't help the ratings enough to save the series. It was canceled at the end of the 1976–1977 season.

PHYLLIS DILLER SHOW, THE, see *Pruitts of Southampton, The*

PICCADILLY PALACE, THE (*Musical Variety*)
FIRST TELECAST: *May 20, 1967*
LAST TELECAST: *September 9, 1967*
BROADCAST HISTORY:
May 1967–Sep 1967, ABC Sat 9:30–10:30
REGULARS:
Millicent Martin
Eric Morecambe
Ernie Wise
The Paddy Stone Dancers
The Michael Sammes Singers
The Jack Parnell Orchestra

The Piccadilly Palace was produced in London and was the 1967 summer replacement for *The Hollywood Palace.* It followed a similar format, but with regular hosts—who also performed—and with young popular singers (primarily) as guests. The hosts were singer Millicent Martin and the comedy team of Morecambe and Wise, who were seen each week introducing the guests, performing with them, and performing on their own.

PICK THE WINNER (*Political*)
FIRST TELECAST: *August 14, 1952*
LAST TELECAST: *October 31, 1956*
BROADCAST HISTORY:
Aug 1952–Oct 1952, CBS/DUM Thu 9:00–9:30
Nov 1952, CBS/DUM Mon 10:00–10:30
Sep 1956–Oct 1956, CBS Wed 7:30–8:00
HOST:
Walter Cronkite

In both the 1952 and 1956 Presidential election years, CBS newsman Walter Cronkite hosted a series of political telecasts that enabled the candidates and various spokesmen for the parties to discuss the issues and explain their respective positions. The 1952 edition, which was sponsored by Westinghouse Electric as a public service, was carried simultaneously on both the CBS and DuMont networks. After the conclusion of the regular 1956 series, a special telecast was aired from 10:45–11:00 P.M. on the night before the election in which CBS correspondents made analyses of various races and predicted winners.

PICKET FENCES (*Drama*)
FIRST TELECAST: *September 18, 1992*
LAST TELECAST: *June 26, 1996*
BROADCAST HISTORY:
Sep 1992–Mar 1993, CBS Fri 10:00–11:00
Apr 1993–Aug 1993, CBS Thu 10:00–11:00
Aug 1993–Jul 1995, CBS Fri 10:00–11:00
Dec 1993–Mar 1994, CBS Fri 12:35–1:45 A.M.
Jun 1994–Jul 1994, CBS Thu 10:00–11:00
Aug 1995–Sep 1995, CBS Fri 9:00–11:00
Sep 1995–Nov 1995, CBS Fri 9:00–10:00
Dec 1995–Feb 1996, CBS Fri 10:00–11:00
Jun 1996, CBS Wed 9:00–10:00
CAST:
Sheriff Jimmy Brock .... Tom Skerritt
Dr. Jill Brock .... Kathy Baker
Kimberly Brock (age 16) .... Holly Marie Combs
Matthew Brock (11) .... Justin Shenkarow
Zach Brock (8) .... Adam Wylie
Officer Kenny Lacos .... Costas Mandylor
Officer Maxine Stewart .... Lauren Holly
Ginny Weeden (1992–1994) ...... Zelda Rubinstein
Judge Henry Bone .... Ray Walston
Douglas Wambaugh .... Fyvush Finkel
M.E. Carter Pike .... Kelly Connell
Mayor Bill Pugen (1992–1993) ..... Michael Keenan
**Michael Oslo* .... Roy Brocksmith
**Minister Henry Novotny* .... Dabbs Greer
**Father Gary Barrett (1993–1996)* .... Roy Dotrice
**Cynthia Parks (1992–1993)* .... Elizabeth Moss
D.A. Jonathan Littleton (1993–1995)
.... Don Cheadle
**Rachel Harris (1993–1995)* ..... Leigh Taylor-Young
**Ed Lawson (1994–1995)* .... Richard Masur
**Laurie Bey (1994–1996)* .... Marlee Matlin
**Franklin Dell (1994–1996)* .... Denis Arndt
**Rebecca (1995–1996)* .... Lisa Chess
**Dr. Joanna "Joey" Diamond (1995–1996)*
.... Amy Aquino

*Occasional

The quaint little town of Rome, Wisconsin, was the setting for this quirky drama. On the surface everything in Rome seemed perfectly normal, but strange things happened there. The central focus was the Brock family—Jimmy, the level-headed sheriff; his compassionate wife, Jill, the town's doctor who was on staff at Thayer Hospital; Kimberly, the daughter from his first marriage who was starting to blossom into a woman; and their two sons, sensitive young Zack and borderline juvenile delinquent Matthew. Also featured were Kenny and Maxine, Jimmy's ambitious and frequently overly enthusiastic deputies; Ginny, their eavesdropping busybody receptionist who after retirement was found frozen solid in her freezer chest; Carter, the eccentric medical examiner; Wambaugh, the outlandish, bombastic defense attorney; and crusty old Judge Bone, in whose courtroom much of the action took place.

The tone was set in the first episode, when the Tin Man in a community theater production of *The Wizard of Oz* was murdered with a lethal injection of nicotine—not a normal poison, nicotine! There was the student who brought a severed hand to class for show-and-tell, the circus elephant ridden into town by a midget saving it from cruel handlers, the male victim of date rape; the serial bather who snuck into people's home and left rings in their bathtubs; the woman who ran her husband over with a steamroller and blamed it on menopause; the parents of a terminally ill son who were refused permission to have him cryogenically frozen before he died from leukemia; the obese woman who accidentally suffocated her husband by rolling over him when they were asleep; and the premiere episode of the second season in which Mayor Pugen killed an unarmed carjacker and was convicted of murder.

In spring 1995, Laurie Bey helped find missing Mayor Lawson, suspected of committing several freezer murders. When they found him, he too was dead in the freezer in his own home, and, unfortunately, was decapitated during the removal effort. His wife Marcia turned out to be the freezer murderer. Surprisingly, the person who succeeded Lawson as mayor was Laurie (previously seen occasionally as the "Dancing Bandit") herself. Considering the track records of previous mayors, many of whom had met tragic ends, she was taking a pretty risky job. That fall, Jill went into partnership with outspoken, overbearing radio talk show host Dr. Joana Diamond, a woman she could barely tolerate, because she needed the extra money the joint practice would bring in. In the series finale, which aired as a special in late April, it was revealed that Mayor Bey, who had given birth to a boy a few weeks earlier, had carried the baby for her gay brother and his lover. Judge Bone presided over a triple wedding ceremony: Kenny and Max, whose relationship had been rocky for almost a year, agreed to get married; Carter was married to plain Sue; and Wambaugh and his wife, who had been having marital problems, decided to renew their vows. In the last scene, Jill and Jimmy privately renewed their vows.

Despite running the series finale as a special in April, CBS aired a few more original episodes that June.

Episodes of *Picket Fences* almost always mixed serious topics with extraneous, often silly, subplots. The resolutions of the serious plotlines often ended up in the courtroom, where Judge Bone's impassioned verdicts shed light on moral and ethical issues that left viewers with much to ponder (series creator and executive producer David E. Kelley was himself a lawyer). The critics loved the series for the complexity and unpredictability of the stories and the quality of the performances, but it was an acquired taste for many viewers and the show struggled to build an audience. It ranked 80th among all prime-time series in its first season and 66th in the second.

PICTURE THIS (*Cartoons*)

FIRST TELECAST: *November 17, 1948*
LAST TELECAST: *February 9, 1949*
BROADCAST HISTORY:
Nov 1948–Feb 1949, NBC Wed 8:20–8:30
HOSTESS:
Wendy Barrie

This was a live program, each week featuring a different guest cartoonist who would draw sketches to accompany stories or jokes, some of them submitted by the viewing audience.

PICTURE THIS (*Quiz/Audience Participation*)

FIRST TELECAST: *June 25, 1963*
LAST TELECAST: *September 17, 1963*
BROADCAST HISTORY:
Jun 1963–Sep 1963, CBS Tue 9:30–10:00
EMCEE:
Jerry Van Dyke

This summer game show featured two teams, each composed of a celebrity and non-celebrity contestant. One member of each team was given a secret phrase, then had to direct the drawing of a picture which was supposed to provide his partner with a clue to the phrase. The first partner to guess the phrase won for his team, while the emerging picture and the byplay between contestants provided the laughs.

This was the first regular series for Jerry Van Dyke, who had previously appeared in a few episodes of his brother's popular series, *The Dick Van Dyke Show.*

PIG STY (*Situation Comedy*)

FIRST TELECAST: *January 23, 1995*
LAST TELECAST: *July 24, 1995*
BROADCAST HISTORY:
Jan 1995–Mar 1995, UPN Mon 9:30–10:00
Mar 1995–Jul 1995, UPN Mon 9:00–9:30
CAST:
Cal Evans .... David Arnott
Johnny Barzano .... Matt Borlenghi
P. J. Morris .... Timothy Fall
Randy Fitzgerald .... Brian McNamara
Joe "Iowa" Dantley .... Sean O'Bryan
Tess Galaway .... Liz Vassey

The setting of this grunge comedy was an Upper Westside Manhattan high-rise apartment shared by five single guys in their twenties. Johnny, an egotistical assistant district attorney, left to live with his girlfriend in the premiere episode but couldn't deal with commitment and ended up back with the guys. Iowa, an incredibly naive intern from the Corn Belt, worked in the emergency room at St. Victor's Hospital in a tough New York inner-city neighborhood. Randy, an unpublished writer, worked as a bartender at Mory's to make a living. His late grandmother had lived in the apartment, and they had moved in after she passed away. P.J., a neurotic, insecure long-haired guy, spent most of his time playing guitar and living off the $2,200 a month he got from his parents. Cal, a sleazy, manipulative, dumpy slob worked for an ad agency and got great pleasure stabbing his fellow employees in the back while clawing his way up the ladder of success. Johnny and Iowa were roommates, P.J. and Randy were roommates, and Cal was living in the walk-in closet with P.J.'s dog, Jimmy, all surrounded by half-eaten pizzas and dirty sox. Tess, the sexy young building superintendent who was trying to make it as an actress, was the disinterested object of Randy's affection.

PINK LADY (*Comedy/Variety*)

FIRST TELECAST: *March 1, 1980*
LAST TELECAST: *April 4, 1980*
BROADCAST HISTORY:
Mar 1980, NBC Sat 10:00–11:00
Mar 1980–Apr 1980, NBC Fri 9:00–10:00
REGULARS:
Pink Lady (Mie Nemoto and Kei Masuda)
Jeff Altman
Cheri Eichen
Anna Mathias
Jim Varney
Ed Nakamoto
The Peacock Dancers

Something must have been lost in the translation. Pink Lady was a Japanese rock duo that was a big hit in Japan and even had one moderately popular record in the U.S.A. ("Kiss in the Dark"). The singers were Mie and Kei ("Me" and "Kay"), two sexy young ladies who spoke very little English and who were depicted in comedy sketches as trying to learn about American customs. Helping them was young comic Jeff Altman, who acted as their guide and interpreter. The show had guest stars, songs, comedy sketches with a regular supporting cast, and a scene at the end of each program with Mie and Kei in bikinis in a hot tub. What it didn't have, unfortunately, was an audience.

PINKY AND THE BRAIN (*Cartoon*)

FIRST TELECAST: *September 10, 1995*
LAST TELECAST: *July 28, 1996*

BROADCAST HISTORY:

Sep 1995–Jul 1996, WB Sun 7:00–7:30

VOICES:

The Brain..................... Maurice LaMarche
Pinky .... Rob Paulsen

This frenetic spin-off from *Steven Spielberg Presents Animaniacs* was about two genetically altered laboratory mice bent on taking over the world. As the theme song intoned, "one is a genius, the other is insane." In each episode they escaped from their cage at ACME Labs in New York City with a new scheme to attain their goal of world domination. Among their abortive efforts were attempts to buy up all the night vision glasses in the world and then paint the entire planet black; starting a dance craze to literally tie people in knots; and putting heat-activated glue on the soles of everyone's shoes to render them immobile. Each plan seemed logical to the Brain, and Pinky went along with everything since he just wanted to make his cage-mate happy, but none of them ever quite worked out. After each failure they returned to ACME Labs to plot another, hopefully more successful, scheme.

Pinky and the Brain premiered on the WB on Saturday mornings the day before its first prime-time telecast and started airing weekday afternoons two years later. The Saturday morning telecasts ran until January 1999, and the weekday telecasts ended eight months later. The full title of the series was *Steven Spielberg Presents Pinky and the Brain.*

PINKY LEE SHOW, THE (*Situation Comedy*)

FIRST TELECAST: *April 5, 1950*
LAST TELECAST: *November 9, 1950*
BROADCAST HISTORY:

Apr 1950–May 1950, NBC Wed 8:30–9:00
Jun 1950–Aug 1950, NBC Wed 10:30–11:00
Sep 1950–Oct 1950, NBC Sat 6:30–7:00
Oct 1950–Nov 1950, NBC Thu 8:30–9:00

CAST:

The Stagehand............................ Pinky Lee
The Stage Manager............. William Bakewell

Pinky Lee (real name: Pincus Leff) first came to network TV in 1950. This series was a loosely structured situation comedy, set in a vaudeville theater. Pinky appeared as a stagehand, dressed in baggy clothes, who usually managed to fumble every assignment, but who was nevertheless called upon to fill in for singers and comedians who couldn't make it—thus giving him the opportunity to appear on stage in a variety of roles.

The program originated in Hollywood and was seen in the rest of the country via kinescope. Pinky later starred in the comedy *Those Two* from 1951 to 1953 and in various weekday afternoon and Saturday morning children's shows from 1954 to 1957.

PINNACLE (*Profile*)

BROADCAST HISTORY:

CNN
30 minutes
Produced: *1984–2003*
Premiered: *February 4, 1984*

HOST:

Tom Cassidy (1984–1988)
Beverly Schuch (1988–2001)
Willow Bay (2001–2003)

A Saturday-night program profiling a top business executive each week, including an interview with the subject.

PIONEERS, THE, see *Death Valley Days*

PIRATE TV (*Comedy*)

BROADCAST HISTORY:

MTV
60 minutes
Produced: *1990–1991*
Premiered: *January 26, 1990*

A weekly comedy hour including parodies of TV shows and commercials.

PISTOLS 'N' PETTICOATS (*Situation Comedy*)

FIRST TELECAST: *September 17, 1966*
LAST TELECAST: *August 19, 1967*
BROADCAST HISTORY:

Sep 1966–Jan 1967, CBS Sat 8:30–9:00
Jan 1967–Aug 1967, CBS Sat 9:30–10:00

CAST:

Henrietta Hanks .... Ann Sheridan
Grandpa .... Douglas Fowley
Grandma .... Ruth McDevitt
Lucy Hanks .... Carole Wells
Sheriff Harold Sikes .... Gary Vinson
Buss Courtney .... Robert Lowery
Chief Eagle Shadow................ Lon Chaney, Jr.
Gray Hawk .... Marc Cavell
Little Bear .... Alex Henteloff

Set in and around the town of Wretched, Colorado, in the 1870s, this Western situation comedy told the story of the Hanks family, three generations strong. Despite their respective ages and sex, all the members of the Hanks family, with the exception of Henrietta's city-bred daughter Lucy, were remarkably adept with guns. They could outdraw and outshoot any desperadoes and hotshot gunslingers within 500 miles of their home. It was extremely embarrassing for a reputedly dangerous outlaw to be subdued by an attractive woman and her grandparents, but that was a common occurrence around Wretched, especially since inept and bumbling young Sheriff Sikes offered little resistance. The Hanks family was so tough, in fact, that normal household pets were too tame for them. So what did they have for a pet? Would you believe, a wolf named Bowser?

PITTS, THE (*Situation Comedy*)

FIRST TELECAST: *March 30, 2003*
LAST TELECAST: *April 20, 2003*
BROADCAST HISTORY:

Mar 2003–Apr 2003, FOX Sun 9:30–10:00

CAST:

Bob Pitt .... Dylan Baker
Liz Pitt .... Kellie Waymire
Faith Pitt (age 16) .... Lizzy Caplan
Petey Pitt (12)..................... David Henrie

If the Pitts didn't have bad luck they wouldn't have had any luck at all. This family was truly cursed. When they took a walk through the woods the parents, Bob and Liz, were bitten by werewolves, became werewolves and were taken to an animal shelter. When Bob took a bus to fight a parking ticket, he got on the wrong bus and landed in prison. When their car became sentient it fell in love with daughter Faith and took her to Las Vegas to get married. You get the idea. Despite all the things that went wrong, Bob was an eternal optimist who always saw the bright side of things, even when it was almost impossible to find, and Liz, his adoring wife, just wished he were a little less trusting of others. Bob and Liz ran a Mail Boxes & More franchise store that made copies and other things but was not very profitable—at least for them. Faith was constantly embarrassed by the endless crises and disasters that befell her family and prayed for just one week when everything would be normal, while Petey, her kid brother, thought everything that happened to them was neat and great fun.

PLACE THE FACE (*Quiz/Audience Participation*)
FIRST TELECAST: *July 2, 1953*
LAST TELECAST: *September 13, 1955*
BROADCAST HISTORY:
Jul 1953–Aug 1953, NBC Tue 8:30–9:00
Aug 1953–Aug 1954, CBS Thu 10:30–11:00
Sep 1954–Dec 1954, NBC Sat 8:00–8:30
Jun 1955–Sep 1955, NBC Tue 8:00–8:30
EMCEE:
Jack Smith (1953)
Jack Bailey (1953–1954)
Bill Cullen (1954–1955)

Contestants on *Place the Face* were confronted with an individual from their past, who had encountered them in a specific situation, and asked to identify the face within a short time limit. The associations were such things as the person who had walked next to the contestant at his high school graduation, a policeman who had given him or her a ticket, a former teacher, etc. Clues were given by the emcee and the contestant could ask questions requiring only a yes or no answer of the individual. When Jack Smith was the emcee, the majority of the contestants were not celebrities and won prizes dependent on how quickly they made the identification. Jack Bailey took over as interim host in November 1953 and Bill Cullen became the permanent emcee the following February. By the time Cullen took over most of the contestants were celebrities, the prize aspect was minimized, and the emcee chatted at length with each contestant before the game began.

PLACES PLEASE (*Talent/Variety*)
FIRST TELECAST: *August 16, 1948*
LAST TELECAST: *February 25, 1949*
BROADCAST HISTORY:
Aug 1948–Feb 1949, CBS Mon/Wed/Fri 7:15–7:30
HOST:
Barry Wood

This live talent show was produced and emceed by Barry Wood. Each week he would introduce a number of young performers who were then given the opportunity to do their acts on network television. The show had originated as a local show in New York during early July 1948. It had three network telecasts at different times during the week of July 13–16 and then reverted to local status for another month before becoming a regular network feature.

PLAINCLOTHESMAN, THE (*Police Drama*)
FIRST TELECAST: *October 12, 1949*
LAST TELECAST: *September 19, 1954*
BROADCAST HISTORY:
Oct 1949–May 1950, DUM Wed 9:00–9:30
May 1950–May 1951, DUM Wed 9:30–10:00
Jun 1951–Sep 1954, DUM Sun 9:30–10:00
CAST:
The Lieutenant........................ Ken Lynch
Sgt. Brady........................... Jack Orrison
Annie, the waitress (1952).......... Helen Gillette

A number of series over the years have featured an unseen character—Bracken in *Bracken's World,* Charlie in *Charlie's Angels*—but this was one of the few series in which the lead role went to someone who was never seen on screen. The technique was camera-as-actor, in which the viewer saw everything exactly as the Lieutenant would. If he lit his cigar, a hand (his) came toward the camera with a lighted match (even the tip of his cigar could be seen jutting out at the bottom of the screen); if he was knocked down, the viewer looked up from floor level; if he got something in his eye, the camera blinked, flickered, and winked clear again. A punch in the nose provided the most spectacular effect for home viewers.

Aside from the novel effect, *The Plainclothesman* was a straightforward big-city crime drama, with the unnamed Lieutenant and his sidekick Sgt. Brady working out of homicide to solve assorted murders. Scientific crime-detection techniques were used.

Oh, yes, the unseen Lieutenant, in reality a handsome actor named Ken Lynch, *was* seen at least once—in a July 1952 episode which featured a series of flashbacks.

PLANET OF THE APES, THE (*Science Fiction*)
FIRST TELECAST: *September 13, 1974*
LAST TELECAST: *December 27, 1974*
BROADCAST HISTORY:
Sep 1974–Dec 1974, CBS Fri 8:00–9:00
CAST:
Galen........................... Roddy McDowall
Alan Virdon .... Ron Harper
Pete Burke .... James Naughton
Urko .... Mark Lenard
Zaius .... Booth Colman

Astronauts Alan Virdon and Pete Burke, hurled through the time barrier by some unexplained force, found themselves crash-landed on an Earth of the far future. This future Earth was ruled by apes who regarded humans as representatives of a destructive and dangerous past civilization. In the ape civilization, gorillas like Urko comprised the military class and orangutans like Zaius were the ruling class. Befriended by a curious chimpanzee named Galen, the astronauts sought to find acceptance in their strange new world. The threat they posed to the ape civilization made them hunted quarry and forced them into the life of fugitives. Roddy McDowall re-created the role he had played in a number of the highly successful *Planet of the Apes* theatrical films, upon which this rather less-successful television series was based. The movie, in turn, was adapted from a novel by Pierre Boulle.

An animated version of this series, titled *Beyond the Planet of the Apes,* aired Saturday mornings on NBC from September 1975 to September 1976.

PLATINUM (*Drama*)
FIRST TELECAST: *April 14, 2003*
LAST TELECAST: *May 13, 2003*

BROADCAST HISTORY:

Apr 2003, UPN Mon 9:00–10:00
Apr 2003–May 2003, UPN Tue 9:00–10:00

CAST:

Grady Rhames .... Sticky Fingaz
Jackson Rhames .... Jason George
Monica Rhames .... Lalanya Masters
Jade Rhames .... Davetta Sherwood
David Ross .... Steven Pasquale
VersIs .... Vishiss
Lady Bryce .... Kia Joy Goodwin
2Way .... Bishop
Nick Tashjian .... Tony Nardi
Olivia Ross .... Sarah Manninen
Max .... N'Bushe Wright
Gayle .... Patrice Goodwin
Rich .... Joel Keller
Walter .... Chris Collins
Kev .... Merwin Mondesir
Kari .... Karen LeBlanc
Sweets .... Shawn Singleton
Lisa .... Kira Clavell
Beth .... Charlotte Sullivan
Sharice .... Melyssa Ford

The highly competitive and sometimes violent hip-hop music scene was the backdrop for this serial drama. Brothers Jackson and Grady owned Sweetback Entertainment, a struggling independent record label in the cutthroat New York music business. Conservative Jackson, whose expertise was on the business side, was a family man whose supportive wife, Monica, was a successful attorney. Flamboyant single Grady was a jive-talking cool dude with an ear for talent and an eye for the ladies, who liked livin' large and being followed around by his "posse" (Grady: "I'm not tryin' to score no girl. I'm tryin' to score *acts*!"). Longtime white family friend David was Sweetback's legal counsel. After bad-ass white rapper VersIs jumped ship, Jackson refocused his energies on Lady Bryce, their most promising new artist. Max was a tough female executive who ran Conflict, a competitive label that was also having financial problems. The major threat to Sweetback's survival was Nick, who ran a conglomerate determined to either buy or destroy their record label. Grady and Jackson's younger sister Jade was a student at NYU who was more interested in guys, including Nick and VersIs, than in her studies.

PLATYPUS MAN (*Situation Comedy*)

FIRST TELECAST: *January 23, 1995*
LAST TELECAST: *July 24, 1995*
BROADCAST HISTORY:

Jan 1995–Mar 1995, UPN Mon 9:00–9:30
Mar 1995–Jul 1995, UPN Mon 9:30–10:00

CAST:

Richard Jeni .... Richard Jeni
Lou Golembiewski .... Ron Ohrbach
Paige McAllister .... Denise Miller
Tommy Jeni .... David Dundara

Standup comedian Richard Jeni adapted his stage material for this series. Richard was the host of the New York City-based TV cooking show *Cooking with the Platypus Man.* Each episode opened with him on the set of the show preparing some dish for his viewing audience and telling them about his assorted troubles with women. Richard, who wanted to find the perfect woman and settle down, had a lot of dates but couldn't sustain a long-term relationship. Lou, the producer of the cooking show and Richard's friend since childhood, was a happily married guy with ambitions of moving from local Channel 72 to network TV. Paige was Richard's next-door neighbor, a sportswriter for one of New York's papers who also had dating problems. But in her case the problem wasn't so much sustaining a relationship as finding someone to start one with. Tommy, Richard's dumb but hunky younger brother, a bartender at the neighborhood saloon where all of the series regulars hung out, had an active social life unencumbered by his older brother's need to find Ms. Right.

In the opening credits Platypus Man was defined as "an adult male human that attempts to mate frequently but spends most of its time alone."

PLAY THE GAME (*Charades*)

FIRST TELECAST: *September 24, 1946*
LAST TELECAST: *December 17, 1946*
BROADCAST HISTORY:

Sep 1946–Dec 1946, DUM Tue 8:00–8:30

HOST:

Dr. Harvey Zorbaugh

Dr. Harvey Zorbaugh, Professor of Educational Sociology at New York University, was something of a minor celebrity among the small band of TV-set owners during the early and mid-1940s. His charade show was seen locally on the NBC station in New York as early as 1941, had a 13-week run on DuMont in 1946, and was seen locally again on ABC in 1948. It was charades, pure and simple, with celebrity guests such as Ireene Wicker, Ray Knight, and Will Mullin performing. Viewers were invited to phone in their guesses to certain charades.

Although seen over DuMont's two-station network, this version was produced by ABC. That network did not yet have any stations of its own on the air, and so bought time on other stations in order to allow its production crews to gain experience against the day when ABC's own facilities would open.

Also known as *Let's Play the Game.*

PLAY YOUR HUNCH (*Quiz/Audience Participation*)

FIRST TELECAST: *April 15, 1960*
LAST TELECAST: *September 26, 1962*
BROADCAST HISTORY:

Apr 1960–Jun 1960, NBC Fri 7:30–8:00
Jun 1960–Sep 1960, NBC Fri 9:00–9:30
Jun 1962–Sep 1962, NBC Wed 10:00–10:30

EMCEE:

Merv Griffin

ANNOUNCER:

Johnny Olsen

Two teams of related contestants—father and son, husband and wife, etc.—competed in this game. Various problems were presented to them and they pooled their knowledge to try to come up with the solutions. Each correct solution was worth a point and the first team to score three points won the game. The winners kept playing until they lost a game. Each point was worth $100 and the losers kept whatever money they had won.

Play Your Hunch also ran in daytime, making a tour of all three networks between June 1958 and September 1963. Merv Griffin, Robert Q. Lewis, Richard

Hayes, and Gene Rayburn each had stints as emcee of the daytime version.

PLAYERS (*Police Drama*)

FIRST TELECAST: *October 17, 1997*
LAST TELECAST: *April 17, 1998*
BROADCAST HISTORY:
Oct 1997–Apr 1998, NBC Fri 8:00–9:00
CAST:
Isaac "Ice" Gregory .... Ice-T (née Tracy Morrow)
Alphonse Royo .... Costas Mandylor
Charlie O'Bannon .... Frank John Hughes
Special Agent Christine Kowalski .... Mia Korf

A trio of young misfits solved crimes to a rap beat in this cartoonish crime series. The three were convicted con artists who were paroled from prison on condition that they use their dubious skills against their own scummy kind for the FBI. The ostensible leader was Ice, a cool, black dude with brains. Ice's first rule of a con: always let the mark think he's in control. O'Bannon was the nerdy computer whiz with a basketload of phobias, and Royo the sticky-fingered ladies' man who had a 12-year-old son by his ex. They squabbled constantly while breaking into heavily guarded criminal fortresses and hacking into impenetrable computers. After a first assignment in New York, they worked out of the FBI office in Los Angeles, where their boss was supportive Special Agent Kowalski.

For a similar series the same season, see the WB's *Three.*

PLAYERS, THE, see *Variety*

PLAYHOUSE, THE, syndicated title for *Schlitz Playhouse of Stars*

PLAYHOUSE, THE (*Dramatic Anthology*)

FIRST TELECAST: *September 3, 1957*
LAST TELECAST: *September 24, 1959*
BROADCAST HISTORY:
Sep 1957, CBS Tue 10:30–11:00
Jul 1959–Sep 1959, CBS Wed/Thu 7:30–8:00

The films aired on this summer anthology series were all reruns of episodes previously seen on other anthology programs, primarily *Schlitz Playhouse of Stars.* The 1957 edition lasted only four weeks. When *The Playhouse* returned as a summer series two years later, it was aired on Wednesdays and Thursdays. To distinguish between the days, the Wednesday episodes were titled *Wednesday Playhouse* while the Thursday films went under the generic title *The Playhouse.*

PLAYHOUSE 90 (*Dramatic Anthology*)

FIRST TELECAST: *October 4, 1956*
LAST TELECAST: *September 19, 1961*
BROADCAST HISTORY:
Oct 1956–Jan 1960, CBS Thu 9:30–11:00
Jul 1961–Sep 1961, CBS Tue 9:30–11:00

Of all the fine dramatic-anthology series to grace television in the 1950s, *Playhouse 90* was the most ambitious and remains the standard against which all the others are judged. Each week this series aired a complete 90-minute drama. Blessed with a very high budget, *Playhouse 90* could afford to hire the best actors, producers, directors, and writers that money could buy. The logistics of doing such a long show every week—usually live—gave the series' principal director, John Frankenheimer, a task worthy of a military strategist. The sets, the camera movements, the action, the timing were all planned so precisely that even the slightest slip could mean disaster. Yet there were few disasters, and the very first season produced such classics as "Requiem for a Heavyweight" starring Jack Palance (the series' second telecast), "The Miracle Worker" with young Patty McCormack, "The Comedian" with Mickey Rooney, "Charley's Aunt" with Art Carney, and "The Helen Morgan Story" with Polly Bergen. Directors for these and later telecasts included Fred Coe, Franklin Schaffner, George Roy Hill, Alex Segal, and Robert Stevens. Plays included adaptations from Hemingway, Shaw, Faulkner, and Saroyan and originals by Rod Serling (who wrote "Requiem"), Reginald Rose, and others.

In succeeding seasons there were "Point of No Return," "Bitter Heritage," "The Plot to Kill Stalin," "The Days of Wine and Roses," "Judgment at Nuremberg," and a two-part "For Whom the Bell Tolls." Aired weekly for three seasons, *Playhouse 90* was cut back to alternate-week status in the fall of 1959, sharing the time period with *The Big Party.* Its last telecast as a regular series was on January 21, 1960. A total of eight more shows aired on an irregular basis in different time slots through May 18, 1960, and a series of reruns was presented weekly during the summer of 1961.

All of the first season's presentations were done live. During the 1957–1958 season, to give the production team an occasional breather, roughly one drama each month was filmed in advance, by different production teams, and during the third season many of the *Playhouse 90*s were done using the relatively new process of videotape. Even in later seasons some of the productions were done live, however, and *Playhouse 90* is still remembered as the pinnacle of live drama from TV's "Golden Age."

PLAYHOUSE #7, see *ABC Dramatic Shorts—1952–1953*

PLAYHOUSE OF MYSTERY, see *Johnson's Wax Theater*

PLAYHOUSE OF MYSTERY (*Dramatic Anthology*)

FIRST TELECAST: *February 10, 1959*
LAST TELECAST: *September 15, 1959*
BROADCAST HISTORY:
Feb 1959–Mar 1959, CBS Tue 8:00–8:30
May 1959–Sep 1959, CBS Tue 8:00–8:30

The dramas telecast in this filmed anthology series were all reruns of previously aired episodes from other anthology series. They all had one element in common—the plot was designed to keep viewers in suspense until the action resolved itself.

PLAYHOUSE OF STARS (*Dramatic Anthology*)

FIRST TELECAST: *July 21, 1960*
LAST TELECAST: *September 1, 1960*
BROADCAST HISTORY:
Jul 1960–Sep 1960, CBS Thu 8:00–8:30

The filmed episodes of this summer anthology series were made up of reruns of episodes from other series.

PLAYROOM (*Children's*)

FIRST TELECAST: *January 9, 1948*
LAST TELECAST: *May 28, 1948*
BROADCAST HISTORY:
Jan 1948–May 1948, DUM Fri 7:00–7:30

This was an early children's program, about which no specific information is available.

PLAY'S THE THING, THE, see *Actors Studio*

PLEASE DON'T EAT THE DAISIES (*Situation Comedy*)

FIRST TELECAST: *September 14, 1965*
LAST TELECAST: *September 2, 1967*
BROADCAST HISTORY:
Sep 1965–Aug 1966, NBC Tue 8:00–8:30
Sep 1966–Sep 1967, NBC Sat 8:00–8:30
CAST:
Joan Nash .... Patricia Crowley
James (Jim) Nash .... Mark Miller
Kyle Nash .... Kim Tyler
Joel Nash .... Brian Nash
Tracey Nash .... Joe Fithian
Trevor Nash .... Jeff Fithian
Marge Thornton .... Shirley Mitchell
Herb Thornton (1965–1966) .... Harry Hickox
Herb Thornton (1966–1967) .... King Donovan
Ed Hewley (1965–1966) .... Dub Taylor
Martha O'Reilly .... Ellen Corby
Dean Gerald Carter (1966–1967) .... Bill Quinn
Ethel Carter (1966–1967) .... Jean VanderPyl

Based on the best-selling book and popular Doris Day movie of the same title, *Please Don't Eat the Daisies* was author Jean Kerr's story of an unusual suburban family. Jim Nash was a professor of English at Ridgemont College in Ridgemont, New York, the community in which he lived with his family. Wife Joan was a newspaper columnist who hated housework, didn't like to cook, and was totally unconcerned about how her traditional suburban housewife neighbors felt about it. She got up at noon and did whatever moved her at the moment. Completing the household were the four Nash children, all boys, including mischievous seven-year-old twins; Martha, the family maid; and a huge 150-pound sheep dog named Ladadog. The Thorntons were next-door neighbors of the Nashes.

PLYMOUTH PLAYHOUSE (*Various*)

FIRST TELECAST: *April 12, 1953*
LAST TELECAST: *June 21, 1953*
BROADCAST HISTORY:
Apr 1953–Jun 1953, ABC Sun 7:30–8:00
HOST:
Donald Cook

This series of auditions for possible series was presented by ABC in hopes of attracting sponsor interest for the fall 1953 season. The productions used top-named talent and expensive budgets (ABC wanted to show that it could produce "big-time programming," just like CBS and NBC) and, indeed, three of the efforts became series. Unfortunately, only one of them aired on ABC—*Jamie*, starring child actor Brandon De Wilde. DuMont picked up *Colonel Humphrey Flack* with Alan Mowbray for its fall lineup, and *Justice*, based on the files of the Legal Aid Society and starring Paul Douglas and Lee Grant, turned up on NBC for a two-year run in the fall of 1954. (See those titles for details.)

Other productions included an elaborate, live, two-part adaptation of *A Tale of Two Cities* starring John Ireland, Wendell Corey, and Joanne Dru, with original music by Dmitri Tiomkin; "Mr. Glencannon Takes All," directed by Sir Cedric Hardwicke and starring Robert Newton; and a series of four classic short stories produced by Hardwicke. Other stars appearing included Robert Preston, Janis Paige, and Walter Matthau. Some productions were live, others on film.

The series was first known as *ABC Album*, but switched to *Plymouth Playhouse* when a sponsor came aboard beginning with the third telecast.

PLYMOUTH SHOW, THE, see *Lawrence Welk's Top Tunes and New Talent*

POINTMAN (*Adventure*)

BROADCAST HISTORY:
Syndicated only
60 minutes
Produced: *1994–1995* (22 episodes)
Released: *January 1995*
CAST:
Constantine "Connie" Harper .... Jack Scalia
**Jennifer Ellis* .... Kathy Trageser
**Vivian* .... Sandra Thigpen
*Occasional

Connie Harper was a wheeler-dealer in arbitrage on Wall Street who had been sent to prison for corporate fraud. As with most TV heroes, he was not really guilty but had been set up by one of his rivals. While in prison, Connie had learned skills that would later serve him well, and had eventually been cleared of the charges. With his release, after two-and-a-half years behind bars, had come a sizable settlement for false imprisonment with which he had purchased a nice beach club. Now he tooled around in his Mercedes convertible helping people in trouble. Because he had been caught up in the system and been unable to control his life while in prison, Connie felt obligated to help people who were in trouble through no fault of their own. He preferred to negotiate solutions rather than resort to violence. Jennifer was a pretty former model who worked at Connie's beach club and Vivian, the woman who managed it for him.

Filmed in Jacksonville, Florida.

POLICE ACADEMY: THE SERIES (*Situation Comedy*)

BROADCAST HISTORY:
Syndicated only
60 minutes
Produced: *1997–1998* (26 episodes)
Released: *September 1997*
CAST:
Chris Casey .... Matt Borlenghi
Sgt. Rusty Ledbetter .... Rod Crawford
Dirk Tackleberry .... Toby Proctor
Dana Tackleberry .... Jeremiah Birkett
Annie Medford .... Heather Campbell
Alicia Conchita Montoya Cervantes .... Christine Gonzales
Luke Kackley .... Tony Longo

Lester Shane .... P. J. Ochlan
Commandant Stuart Hefilfinger....... Joe Flaherty
Sgt. Larvelle Jones .... Michael Winslow
**Kendall Jackson* .... Larke Miller

*Occasional

No real police academy could have been like this—populated with incompetent officers and misfit recruits. Ledbetter, one of the trainers, was a pompous fool with a bad toupee that kept getting caught on things. He had it in for Casey, a recruit whose father had regularly outperformed him during their academy days two decades earlier. The Tackleberrys, despite their racial differences, were bumbling "twins." There were two female recruits: Alicia, a tough, street-smart former gang member, and Annie, a cute girl who was afraid of getting involved in relationships because every guy she had ever been sweet on had suffered horrible accidents. Despite this, she and Casey started dating—although they kept it a secret from their fellow recruits. Luke was a muscular lug with limited intelligence, and Lester the goofy recruit who did Ledbetter's bidding. Hefilfinger was the ineffectual head of the academy, and Kendall his sexy but ditsy secretary.

Adapted from the successful series of seven theatrical films, with Michael Winslow, who had been featured in all of them, reprising his role.

POLICE SQUAD (*Situation Comedy*)

FIRST TELECAST: *March 4, 1982*
LAST TELECAST: *September 4, 1991*
BROADCAST HISTORY:

Mar 1982, ABC Thu 8:00–8:30
Jul 1982–Aug 1982, ABC Thu 9:30–10:00
Sep 1982, ABC Thu 9:30–10:00
Jul 1991–Sep 1991, CBS Wed 8:00–8:30

CAST:

Det. Frank Drebin .... Leslie Nielsen
Capt. Ed Hocken .... Alan North
Ted Olson .... Ed Williams
Johnny the Snitch .... William Duell

The creators of the hit movie *Airplane!* brought their bent humor to television in this short-lived series, which, like the movie, starred Leslie Nielsen. The setting this time was a "large American city," where straight-faced Detective Frank Drebin and his loyal Captain Hocken investigated puzzling cases filled with sight-gags and non sequiturs. In the opening episode they arrived at the scene of a murder to find a chalk outline of the body with Egyptian hieroglyphics alongside, the police photographer taking a picture of a grinning policeman posing with the corpse, and a witness who had a hard time talking through her braces. Parked nearby was a police car, with big letters on the hood reading—of course—POLICE CAR.

Sometimes police scientist Ted Olson might offer dubious help, as when he identified the sounds in the background of a ransom tape as "a foghorn and a bell buoy"—they must be at the harbor! But en route to storm the waterfront with a small army of cops, Drebin stopped for gas and noticed an uncanny similarity between the "bell buoy" and the bell on the gas pump. And that foghorn, was it really a tuba? So they went off to find a tuba next to a gas station, to storm that instead.

Then there was the clue found in a note tied to a window, thrown into a pile of rocks. And so on. Johnny was the shoeshine boy and street snitch, who could give them incredible inside information—for a price.

Where did the creators of this odd program—two brothers named Zucker—get their offbeat approach to comedy? "A lot of our humor was developed as a self-defense for not being good in school," said one of them. "The only difference between then and now is that now we are getting paid for what used to get us kicked out of class."

Although *Police Squad* was not a success on television—there were those who claimed that there were so many sight gags you had to pay more attention to the show than people normally paid to TV—it fared much better in the movies. A feature film version titled *The Naked Gun: From the Files of Police Squad*, with Leslie Nielsen reprising his role as Det. Drebin, was a big hit in 1988 and, when its sequel *The Naked Gun 2½: The Smell of Fear*, was released in the summer of 1991, CBS reran the original TV series, but once again its ratings were low.

POLICE STORY (*Police Anthology*)

FIRST TELECAST: *April 4, 1952*
LAST TELECAST: *September 26, 1952*
BROADCAST HISTORY:

Apr 1952–Sep 1952, CBS Fri 10:00–10:30

NARRATOR:

Norman Rose

Case histories were drawn from the files of various law-enforcement agencies and adapted for television presentation in this live dramatic series that originated from New York. Not only were crime-detection stories presented but episodes devoted to crime prevention were included as well. The actors playing lead roles were chosen for their resemblance to the actual officers who had been involved in the cases and used the officers' real names. Settings were various big cities and rural areas around the country with both local and state police operations shown. Generally lesser-known performers participated, with James Gregory, Edward Binns, and E. G. Marshall the most familiar.

POLICE STORY (*Police Anthology*)

FIRST TELECAST: *September 25, 1973*
LAST TELECAST: *December 3, 1988*
BROADCAST HISTORY:

Sep 1973–Sep 1975, NBC Tue 10:00–11:00
Sep 1975–Oct 1975, NBC Tue 9:00–10:00
Nov 1975–Aug 1976, NBC Fri 10:00–11:00
Aug 1976–Aug 1977, NBC Tue 10:00–11:00
Oct 1988–Dec 1988, ABC Sat 9:00–11:00

CREATOR:

Joseph Wambaugh

One of the more realistic police series to be seen on television was *Police Story*, created by former Los Angeles policeman Joseph Wambaugh. After retiring from the force, Wambaugh had written two highly successful novels about police operations, *The New Centurions* and *The Blue Knight* (the latter also became a TV series in its own right). Wambaugh served as a consultant to this series, insuring that everything was treated with utmost authenticity. Stories covered the more mundane aspects of police work as well as the excitement. They probed the psychology of individual police officers and even dealt with their home lives, how their jobs affected their families, and personal problems such as drinking, injuries, and forced retirement.

Two episodes from *Police Story* went on to become series of their own. "The Gamble" was aired on March 26, 1974, with Angie Dickinson in the role of policewoman Lisa Beaumont. That fall, with her name changed to Pepper Anderson, she became *Police Woman.* "The Return of Joe Forrester," aired as a special 90-minute episode on May 6, 1975, became *Joe Forrester* that fall, with Lloyd Bridges re-creating his role. Although *Police Story* was an anthology, characters occasionally made return appearances. The most notable examples were Tony Lo Bianco (as Tony Calabrese) and Don Meredith (as Bert Jameson). During its first two seasons on the air, these two appeared four times as partners and once each separately as detectives on various cases. Despite the frequency of their visits, they never got a series of their own. NBC aired occasional two-hour *Police Story* specials after the series ceased weekly production.

More than a decade after the original series left NBC, ABC aired four new *Police Story* movies at the beginning of the 1988–1989 season, using scripts from the original run, to fill in for its strike-delayed *ABC Saturday Mystery Movie*. There were no recurring characters. The leads included Ken Olin (as a troubled cop), Robert Conrad (as an imprisoned cop), and Jack Warden (as a cop who didn't want to retire).

POLICE SURGEON, see *Dr. Simon Locke*

POLICE VIDEOS, see *World's Wildest Police Videos*

POLICE WOMAN (*Police Drama*)

FIRST TELECAST: *September 13, 1974*
LAST TELECAST: *August 30, 1978*
BROADCAST HISTORY:

Sep 1974–Oct 1975, NBC Fri 10:00–11:00
Nov 1975–Aug 1977, NBC Tue 9:00–10:00
Oct 1977–Dec 1977, NBC Tue 10:00–11:00
Dec 1977–Mar 1978, NBC Wed 10:00–11:00
Mar 1978–May 1978, NBC Thu 10:00–11:00
Jun 1978–Aug 1978, NBC Wed 10:00–11:00

CAST:

Sgt. Suzanne "Pepper" Anderson .. Angie Dickinson
Lt. Bill Crowley.................... Earl Holliman
Det. Joe Styles .... Ed Bernard
Det. Pete Royster................. Charles Dierkop
Lt. Paul Marsh (1974–1976)............ Val Bisoglio

Sexy Sgt. Pepper Anderson was an undercover agent for the criminal conspiracy department of the Los Angeles Police Department. Working on a vice-squad team that included Joe Styles and Pete Royster, two other undercover cops, she was called on to pose as everything from a prostitute to a gangster's girlfriend. The team reported directly to Lt. Bill Crowley, who was the coordinator of its operations. Although not seen on a regular basis, Pepper's autistic younger sister Cheryl, played by Nichole Kallis, was visited occasionally at the Austin School for the Handicapped during the first season of *Police Woman.* Her role was dropped in the fall of 1975.

The pilot for *Police Woman,* which starred Angie Dickinson and all of the series regulars except Earl Holliman, aired as an episode of *Police Story* titled "The Gamble."

POLITICALLY INCORRECT (*Comedy/Talk*)

CABLE HISTORY:

Comedy Central
30 minutes
Produced: *1993–1996*
Premiered: *July 25, 1993*

NETWORK HISTORY:

FIRST TELECAST: *January 6, 1997*
LAST TELECAST: *July 5, 2002*

Jan 1997–Jul 2002, ABC Mon–Fri 12:05–12:35 A.M.
Jul 1997, ABC Tue 10:00–11:00

HOST:

Bill Maher

An unusual example of a series that originated on cable, and moved successfully to broadcast television, *Politically Incorrect* was the brainchild of comic Bill Maher. Each night Maher put together a wildly diverse group of four panelists from the worlds of politics, media, and entertainment to discuss semi-serious issues such as "Reagan: Moron or Genius?" "Is the *National Enquirer* Always Right?" "Convenient Feminism," and "Since Vietman, We Only Fight the Easy Wars." Conservative and liberal shibboleths alike were skewered with wry observations by such disparate guests as Arianna Huffington, MeatLoaf, Chris Rock, Bishop John Spong, and Joe Queenan. The sight of G. Gordon Liddy arguing with rapper Coolio was by itself enough to get a laugh. Guests on the premiere telecast were Jerry Seinfield, Robin Quivers, Ed Rollins, and Larry Miller.

After a three year run on Comedy Central, ending in November 1996, *Politically Incorrect* moved to ABC late night on January 6, 1997.

POLITICS ON TRIAL (*Debate*)

FIRST TELECAST: *September 4, 1952*
LAST TELECAST: *October 30, 1952*
BROADCAST HISTORY:

Sep 1952–Oct 1952, ABC Thu 9:00–9:30

This was a public-affairs debate in the style of a courtroom trial, and was presented in the weeks leading up to the 1952 Presidential election. A prominent Republican or Democrat presented his party's position on a major issue, which was then attacked by "opposing counsel" and defended by his own "counsel." A real-life judge presided.

POLKA-GO-ROUND (*Music*)

FIRST TELECAST: *June 23, 1958*
LAST TELECAST: *September 28, 1959*
BROADCAST HISTORY:

Jun 1958–Sep 1958, ABC Mon 9:30–10:30
Oct 1958–Dec 1958, ABC Mon 7:30–8:30
Dec 1958–May 1959, ABC Mon 8:00–8:30
Jun 1959–Sep 1959, ABC Mon 7:30–8:30

REGULARS:

Bob Lewandowski
Carolyn DeZurik
Lou Prohut
The Polka Rounders
Caine Dancers
Tom "Stubby" Fouts
The Singer Waiters
Georgia Drake

A full hour of polka music in network prime time every week? That's what this program provided throughout most of its run. The colorfully costumed singers and dancers performed in an outdoor cafe setting. Telecast from Chicago.

POLKA TIME (*Music*)
FIRST TELECAST: *July 13, 1956*
LAST TELECAST: *September 24, 1957*
BROADCAST HISTORY:
Jul 1956–Oct 1956, ABC Fri 10:00–10:30
Oct 1956–Sep 1957, ABC Tue 10:00–10:30
REGULARS:
Bruno (Junior) Zielinski
Carolyn DeZurik
Richard (Hodyl) and Mildred (Lawnik)
Wally Moore and Chick Hurt
Rusty Gill
Stan Wolowic's Polka Chips

A half hour of authentic Polish music and dancing, telecast from Chicago. Also known as *It's Polka Time.*

POLLY BERGEN SHOW, THE (*Musical Variety*)
FIRST TELECAST: *September 21, 1957*
LAST TELECAST: *May 31, 1958*
BROADCAST HISTORY:
Sep 1957–May 1958, NBC Sat 9:00–9:30
REGULARS:
Polly Bergen
Peter Gennaro Dancers
Bill Bergen
The Luther Henderson, Jr., Orchestra

Singer Polly Bergen starred in this musical variety series which featured Peter Gennaro and his dancers, special guest stars, and, from November through February, her father Bill Bergen. Each show was tailored to the talents of the guest stars, be they singers, dancers, comedians, etc., but always included some songs by Miss Bergen.

POLTERGEIST: THE LEGACY (*Horror/Supernatural*)
BROADCAST HISTORY:
Showtime and Sci-Fi Channel
60 minutes
Produced: *1995–1999* (88 episodes)
Released: *September 1995* (Showtime):
March 18, 1999 (Sci-Fi Channel)
CAST:
Dr. Derek Rayne .... Derek de Lint
Dr. Rachel Corrigan .... Helen Shaver
Alexandra "Alex" Moreau .... Robbi Chong
Nick Boyle .... Martin Cummins
**Katherine "Kat" Corrigan (age 8)* .... Alexandra Purvis
***Father Philip Callaghan* .... Patrick Fitzgerald
William Sloan (1997) .... Daniel J. Travanti
Kristin Adams (1998–1999) .... Kristin Lehman

*Occasional
**Occasional; named Connolly in the pilot.

The Legacy was a secret society that had been formed in the sixth century as humanity's last line of defense against "those creatures that inhabit the shadows and the night," the unspeakable evil of the supernatural world. Over the centuries, its members, selected by invitation only, included Bram Stoker, Robert Louis Stevenson, John Milton, Sigmund Freud, Edgar Allan Poe, and H. P. Lovecraft. Currently working out of a castle on Angel Island in San Francisco Bay, the members of the society waged their never-ending war against demons, evil spirits, possessions, and other manifestations of supernatural evil, often on dark and stormy nights, amid thunder and lightning. The group included Derek, the precept of the San Francisco Legacy House, who had Ph.D.'s in both Anthropology and Theology and was their psychic leader; Rachel, a brilliant psychiatrist; Alex, a gifted psychic and their principal researcher; and Nick, a young, impetuous former Navy SEAL. Seen occasionally were Father Philip, their young spiritual guide, and Kat, Rachel's young daughter. Kat had emerging psychic powers, and encountered or was possessed by spirits with alarming frequency. Sloan, head of the ruling London House of the Legacy, worked with them in 1997, but in the next-to-last episode of the season, he was sucked into a gateway to hell, never to reappear. Kristin, a young anthropologist and member of the Legacy's Boston House, moved to San Francisco and joined the local group there in 1998. In the series finale Derek found out that the Apocalypse was about to happen and that the anti-Christ would arrive from hell using the portal that existed under the Legacy House. Anticipating that he wouldn't survive the imminent battle with evil, Derek hinted to Alex that he loved her; they had a passionate kiss. Nick and Derek set C4 explosives under the house, and Derek gave Nick his precepts ring and told him to take over after his death. Then he set off the explosives, which destroyed the house, the portal, his evil father who was about to open the portal, and himself. In the last scene Rachel, Alex and Nick reflected on what Derek had meant to them.

Poltergeist premiered on Showtime in the fall of 1995. A year later, while new episodes continued to premiere on the cable network, reruns from the previous season began airing in syndication. After three seasons on Showtime, *Poltergeist* moved to the Sci-Fi Channel with new episodes.

PONDEROSA, see *Bonanza*

PONDEROSA, THE (*Western*)
FIRST TELECAST: *September 9, 2001*
LAST TELECAST: *November 9, 2002*
BROADCAST HISTORY:
Sep 2001–Jul 2002, PAX Sun 9:00–10:00
Sep 2001–Dec 2001, PAX Sat 8:00–9:00
Mar 2002–Sep 2002, PAX Sat 7:00–8:00
Nov 2002, PAX Sat 7:00–8:00
CAST:
Ben Cartwright .... Daniel Hugh Kelly
Adam Cartwright (age 21) .... Matt Carmody
Eric "Hoss" Cartwright (17) .... Drew Powell
Little Joe Cartwright (12) .... Jared Daperis
Carlos Rivera De Vega .... Fernando Carillo
Shelby Sterrett .... Nicki Wendt
Eli Orowitz .... Petru Gheorghiu
Ruth Orowitz .... Abbe Holmes
Big Dan Larson .... Bruce Dickinson
Hop Sing .... Gareth Yuen
Tess Green .... Sara Gleeson
Jack Roberts (2001) .... Don Halbert
Margaret Green .... Josephine Byrnes
Maurice "Frenchy" Devereaux (2001) .... Brad Dourif
Isabella Maria Rivera De Vega (2001) .... Marcella Toro

Isabella Maria Rivera De Vega (2002)
.................................Jacqueline Aries
Jack Wolf (2002)...................Jim Knobeloch

This prequel to *Bonanza* followed the exploits of the Cartwrights during the years when they first established the Ponderosa ranch in the Nevada territory. As the series opened in 1849, Ben and Adam were working for Eli Orowitz, who ran the Trading Post in Eagle Station, Nevada. After the death of Ben's wife, Marie (Lisa Baumwol), Eli gave Ben a 180-acre parcel of land on which to start a ranch in her memory. Ben protested, "I don't know anything about ranching," but with his three rambunctious young sons he set about building the Ponderosa from the ground up. Hop Sing became the family cook after Ben paid savvy Shelby, who ran the local saloon, $50 to free him from indentured servitude. Helping Ben set up the ranch was Carlos, a Mexican whose family's land had been seized by Americans after the war with Mexico. It was now the neighboring ranch of tough but fair widower Margaret Green. When Carlos' sister, Isabella, showed up, she moved in with Margaret and her daughter, Tess, who was sweet on Adam. (Unlike *Bonanza*, this series featured a lot of strong women.)

Late in the year Frenchy, one of the town's more avaricious merchants, moved to New Orleans and left control of the Outpost to Big Dan, who had worked for him. In January Carlos was killed while rescuing Tess and Hoss from a kidnapper while Isabella, who also had been shot, recovered. The following week Jack Wolf arrived in Eagle Station, rented Frenchy's holdings from Big Dan and jacked up the prices. Corrupt and manipulative, he built a hotel and got the stage line to pass through town, all to line his pockets with profits. Adam, who had been dating Isabella, offered to marry her, and Hoss, who was dating Tess, at one point considered marriage in order to adopt an abandoned Indian baby. The series did not last long enough for either of these nuptials to take place—which was fortunate, as that would have greatly complicated the all-male successor series, *Bonanza*.

PONDS THEATER (*Dramatic Anthology*)

FIRST TELECAST: *January 13, 1955*
LAST TELECAST: *July 7, 1955*
BROADCAST HISTORY:
Jan 1955–Jul 1955, ABC Thu 9:30–10:30

For 15 months, the Kraft Corporation had been sponsoring two live plays a week, both titled *Kraft Television Theatre*. The NBC version, which aired on Wednesday nights at 9:00 P.M. and had been in that time period since the late 1940s, was by far the more successful. When Kraft decided to drop the Thursday night version on ABC, Ponds took over sponsorship and retitled the series *Ponds Theater*. The dramas continued to be produced live in New York, and included such leading talent as Joanne Woodward, E. G. Marshall, Ed Begley, Roddy McDowall, Eva Gabor, Lee Grant, and Ernest Truex.

PONTIAC PRESENTS PLAYWRIGHTS 56 (*Dramatic Anthology*)

FIRST TELECAST: *October 4, 1955*
LAST TELECAST: *June 19, 1956*
BROADCAST HISTORY:
Oct 1955–Jun 1956, NBC Tue 9:30–10:30

During the 1955–1956 season *Pontiac Presents Playwrights 56* aired live plays on alternate Tuesdays with *Armstrong Circle Theatre*. The plays in this series were all adapted from the works of such famous writers as Irwin Shaw, Ernest Hemingway, and F. Scott Fitzgerald, and were somewhat more traditional in form than the documentary-dramas presented on *Armstrong Circle Theatre*.

POP ACROSS AMERICA (*Comedy/Variety*)

BROADCAST HISTORY:
TNN
60 minutes
Original episodes: *2001*
Premiered: *August 24, 2001*
HOST:
Steve Marmel

This was possibly the lowest-budget variety hour ever seen on national television, taking place on the back of a flatbed truck and utilizing non-professional talent such as nutty collectors and a lint sculptor. The big truck rolled through various cities, where host Steve Marmel (a comedy writer for cartoons such as *Johnny Bravo* and *The Fairly OddParents*) interviewed local denizens and showed film clips of such entertaining fare as fat people dancing and a ketchup-drinking contest. Each episode culminated with an outdoor nighttime "show" from the back of the flatbed, usually with a small audience of curious locals looking on.

POP! GOES THE COUNTRY (*Music*)

BROADCAST HISTORY:
Syndicated only
30 minutes
Produced: *1974–1982* (234 episodes)
Released: *1974*
HOST:
Ralph Emery (1974–1980)
Tom T. Hall (1980–1982)
Jim Varney (1982)

One of the more widely circulated country music programs was *Pop! Goes the Country*, taped at the shrine of country music, Opryland U.S.A. in Nashville. It featured all the old Opry favorites—Ray Price, Loretta Lynn, Tammy Wynette and George Jones, Johnny Paycheck, Dolly Parton, Merle Haggard, Hank Williams, Jr., *et al.*

The original host was Ralph Emery, succeeded in 1980 by Tom T. Hall (the "Old Storyteller"). Rubber-faced comedian Jim Varney joined as a regular for the final season. Also in 1982 the setting was changed from a studio to Opryland's Gaslight Theatre, to give the show a more intimate "club" look, and the series' title was changed to *Tom T.'s Pop! Goes the Country Club*.

POPCORN KID, THE (*Situation Comedy*)

FIRST TELECAST: *March 23, 1987*
LAST TELECAST: *April 24, 1987*
BROADCAST HISTORY:
Mar 1987, CBS Mon 8:30–9:00
Mar 1987–Apr 1987, CBS Fri 8:30–9:00
CAST:
Scott Creasman........................Bruce Norris
Leonard Brown.............................Raye Birk
Willie Dawson.......................Jeffrey Joseph
Gwen Stottlemeyer...........Penelope Ann Miller

Marlin Bond .... John Christopher Jones
Lynn Holly Brickhouse .... Faith Ford

The venerable old Majestic movie house, a revival theater in Kansas City, was the setting for this comedy about teenagers. It was the Majestic's policy to hire local high school kids to man the concession stand, and they were a motley group. Scott loved movies and dreamt of becoming a star himself someday; Willie wanted people to see him as more than just a great athlete; Gwen was the "intellectual," a good student who had a secret crush on Scott; and Lynn Holly was the stereotypical dumb bombshell whose beauty was a turn-on for Scott, despite the fact that he was too shy to ask her out. Marlin was the Majestic's spaced-out projectionist and Leonard its married manager who had no kids of his own—which suited him just fine.

POPI (*Situation Comedy*)
FIRST TELECAST: *January 20, 1976*
LAST TELECAST: *August 24, 1976*
BROADCAST HISTORY:
Jan 1976–Feb 1976, CBS Tue 8:30–9:00
Jul 1976–Aug 1976, CBS Tue 8:00–8:30
CAST:
Abraham Rodriguez .... Hector Elizondo
Lupe .... Edith Diaz
Junior Rodriguez .... Anthony Perez
Luis Rodriguez .... Dennis Vasquez
Maggio .... Lou Criscuolo

Abraham Rodriguez was a poor Puerto Rican immigrant who held three part-time jobs to make enough money to support his family. A widower with two young sons, he lived in a small apartment. One of his neighbors in the building was Lupe, the woman he was dating. Life in New York City was not easy for him, but he managed somehow to survive and maintain his self-respect and dignity. The first five episodes of this series aired early in 1976 but did so poorly that the show was canceled. During the following summer the remaining original episodes were aired, along with a few reruns.

Adapted from the 1969 theatrical film starring Alan Arkin.

POPSICLE PARADE OF STARS, THE (*Variety*)
FIRST TELECAST: *May 15, 1950*
LAST TELECAST: *July 17, 1950*
BROADCAST HISTORY:
May 1950–Jul 1950, CBS Mon 7:45–8:00

A different guest star appeared every week on this short-lived, 15-minute variety show sponsored by the Popsicle company. Each star performed his own specialty, whether it was singing, dancing, playing an instrument, or doing comedy sketches, aiming his material at both adults and children—both, hopefully, being consumers of the sponsor's product.

POPSTARS (*Talent/Music*)
FIRST TELECAST: *January 12, 2001*
LAST TELECAST: *January 3, 2002*
BROADCAST HISTORY:
Jan 2001, WB Fri 9:00–10:00
Jan 2001–Apr 2001, WB Fri 8:30–900
May 2001–Jul 2001, WB Fri 9:00–10:00
Oct 2001–Jan 2002, WB Thu 8:00–8:30
Nov 2001, WB Thu 8:30–9:00
JUDGES:
Travis Payne (2001)
Jaymes Foster-Levy
Jennifer Greig-Costin (2001)
Tony Michaels
Brad "Riprock" Daymond
ANNOUNCER:
Matthew Porretta

Popstars, a talent contest with the goal of "manufacturing" a successful five-girl singing group, showed how unpredictable that manufacturing process can be. The three judges evaluating the first round of aspiring singers were choreographer Travis Payne, female record executive Jaymes Foster-Levy, and talent manager Jennifer Greig-Costin. The premiere episode showed auditions in New York, Chicago, Dallas, Los Angeles, Atlanta, and Miami. Some of the girls showed real talent, while others were painfully incompetent. An alarming number seemed to choose "I Will Always Love You" as their audition song. The short first-day auditions led to callbacks for a limited number, and at episode's end 239 women who had survived the open auditions were preparing for longer auditions and interviews that would eventually reduce their number to 26.

The 26 semi-finalists assembled in Los Angeles for an intense workshop week, overseen by vocal coach Roger Love and producer David Foster, at the end of which 10 finalists were chosen. Six weeks after the series began, five of these were chosen to be members of the group. Unfortunately, after the judges decided on the final five, two of the strongest singers decided they really didn't want to go through with it. Another candidate from the 10 finalists was substituted, but that still left the group short one member. Under extreme time pressure, the producers restarted auditions for the fifth member—a process that now had to be completed in one day. Hundreds showed up and, by late in the day, the group was complete: Nicole Scherzinger, Rosanna Tavarez, Ana Maria Lombo, Ivette Sosa, and, from the last-minute auditions, Maile Misajohn—who, ironically, had been the last person to audition.

The following week the girls moved into a house together and prepared to record their first single, "Get Over Yourself." They competed for lead singer on the single and worked on a name for the group, ultimately calling themselves Eden's Crush. Subsequently they filmed a music video and worked on choreographing their songs and creating a unique style and look. While they were preparing for their first major photo shoot, the girls bickered and seemed unsure about how successful they would be.

The series' 11th episode opened with an announcement that the "Get Over Yourself" single had gone to the top of the record charts (actually it reached number eight on the *Billboard* charts). The girls traveled to New York for promotional appearances, went on a shopping binge, were interviewed on TV and radio and in magazines, and had their first live performance on the syndicated TV series *Live with Regis & Kelly.* Afterward they returned to L.A. to record more songs for their debut CD.

When *Popstars 2* premiered in the fall of 2001, the big change was the addition of guys interviewing for what was going to be a mixed group. More than 6,000 people showed up for the open auditions in six cities. Jaymes Foster-Levy returned as a judge, joined by choreographer Tony Michaels and producer/songwriter Brad "Riprock" Daymond. After weeks of auditions and eliminations, the six chosen for the new group were Donavan Green, Dorothy Szamborska, Josh Henderson, Laurie Gidosh, Moi Juarez and Monika Christian.

Soon after the group moved to L.A. and into their house, the judges confronted Moi about violating the rules by seeing his friends outside and inviting people into the house. As a result, he was dismissed. The other five decided to name the group Scene 23 because they were two guys and three girls whose backgrounds were all from very different "scenes." Four months later, after their CD was finished, they went on a publicity tour including radio, TV, and Internet interviews and CD signings. They then went to Minnesota to perform their first live concert in front of 4,000 fans at the Mall of America, the largest mall in the United States.

On February 3, 2002, a month after the last original episode, the WB telecast a special three-hour recap showing the formation of Scene 23.

POPULAR (*School Drama*)
FIRST TELECAST: *September 29, 1999*
LAST TELECAST: *May 18, 2001*
BROADCAST HISTORY:
Sep 1999, WB Wed 9:00–10:00
Sep 1999–Aug 2000, WB Thu 8:00–9:00
Feb 2000–Mar 2000, WB Mon 9:00–10:00
Aug 2000–May 2001, WB Fri 9:00–10:00

CAST:
Sam McPherson .... Carly Pope
Brooke McQueen .... Leslie Bibb
Nicole Julian .... Tammy Lynn Michaels
Carmen Ferrara .... Sara Rue
Harrison John .... Christopher Gorham
Lily Esposito .... Tamara Mello
Josh Ford .... Bryce Johnson
Jane McPherson .... Lisa Darr
Mike McQueen .... Scott Bryce
Mary Cherry .... Leslie Grossman
Bobbi Glass/Nurse Jessie Glass .... Diane Delano
Principal Cecilia Hall (1999–2000) .. Diana Bellamy
Popita "Poppy" Fresh (1999–2000)
.... Anel Lopez Gorham
Emory Dick .... Hank Harris
Miss Ross (1999–2000) .... Arnetia Walker
Michael Sugar Daddy Bernadino .... Ron Lester
Lady T (1999–2000) .... Natasha Pearce
**Godfrey* .... Robert Clendenin
**Mrs. Cherry Cherry* .... Delta Burke
Calvin Krupps (2000–2001) .... Robert Gant
April Tuna (2000–2001) .... Adria Dawn
George Austin (2000–2001) ...... A.T. Montgomery
*Occasional

THEME:
performed by Kendall Payne

This biting satire of high school life centered on a group of sophomores at Jacqueline Kennedy High School. Intellectual Sam had just been named editor of the school newspaper, the *Zapruder Reporter.* Her personal nemesis was beautiful and popular Brooke, who was dating Josh, the star quarterback. Nicole was Brooke's bitchy, status-conscious friend with the fancy sports car; Mary Cherry was their spoiled rich friend from Dallas. Sam's anti-clique included Carmen, the overweight girl looking for acceptance; Harrison, who had a crush on Sam; and Lily, the social activist. Sam's widowed mother, Jane, and Brooke's divorced father, Mike, returned from a vacation trip together engaged. Since Sam and Brooke despised each other, the prospect of being stepsisters was totally repugnant to both. In November their parents decided they were all going to live together in Brooke's home. Sam and Brooke were appalled but had to make the best of an awkward situation. When Brooke and Josh finally made love in November, she didn't feel the closeness she had thought she would and broke up with him. In December Harrison's mom came out of the closet and her gay lover moved in with them, and in February Josh's mother left his dad and took Josh with her. Amazingly, Josh started dating chunky Carmen, but later decided he was uncertain about his feelings for both her and Brooke and decided to go it alone for a while.

When Mike asked Jane to marry him, Brooke and Sam decided to work together to prevent their families from being legally merged. Brooke eventually accepted the inevitable but Sam still fought it and, on the eve of the wedding, left home. She went to San Francisco to find Brooke's mother but came back and made peace with Brooke. In the season finale Nurse Jesse drugged her hated sister, biology teacher Bobbi, and almost succeeded in having her cremated. Sam and Brooke's folks were going to be married in a double wedding with Cherry Cherry and Erik Estrada. At the ceremony Brooke's mother, Kelly (Peggy Lipton), surfaced to announce that she and Mike were not divorced and Bobbi, who was in a casket, revived after having been given an antidote to the drugs.

Junior year started with Brooke and Sam recounting the summer events—Kelly had spent the summer in town trying to make things up to her daughter, which made everyone uncomfortable and, when it seemed like they might get back together, Jane moved into a motel with Sam—and then Kelly moved back to San Francisco. Former vice principal Krupps, who was the new principal, dropped Nicole from the Glamazon squad because she had a knee problem and gave her slot to a grateful Carmen. Jane found out she was pregnant and Carmen, whose parents had separated, moved in with Ms. Glass, but went back home to help her mother deal with a drinking problem. Josh was having problems dealing with George, a new arrival who took over as first-string quarterback on the football team and started dating Sam. When one of nasty Nicole's plans to embarrass many of her peers failed, Josh discovered he was attracted to Lily, and Harrison decided Mary Cherry was not as shallow as he had thought. In November, in a turnabout, Brooke ran for student council president and Sam for homecoming queen. Despite the best efforts of Nicole and Mary Cherry to undermine her campaign, Carmen was elected homecoming queen. Harrison withdrew from the race for student council president because he was suffering from leukemia and, by default, Brooke was declared the winner—but gave it to gawky April Tuna. In December Harrison was in the hospital, Brad and Lily were getting serious, and Carmen found out that Nicole's mother was also an alcoholic. When his leukemia went into remission, Harrison returned to school, having become much more assertive. In

March Nicole maneuvered April out of the class presidency and was, herself, sworn in by a reluctant Krupps. Over spring break Brooke and Harrison got together and made love. When Sam found out, she couldn't deal with it and told him she never wanted to see him again. The following week Brooke and Sam's barely civil relationship deteriorated. Josh's mother got a job in St. Paul and he moved in with his estranged father for his senior year. Lily offered him an alternative—getting married—which they did at city hall. In the series finale Brooke and Sam delivered Jane's baby—a girl—in the living room. The experience almost made them friends—they were going to the prom as a threesome with Harrison. Josh and Lily rented an apartment in Ms. Glass' home but were struggling financially. In the last scene, as Brooke ran from the restaurant where Harrison had just chosen between her and Sam, she was apparently hit by Nicole's speeding car.

PORTRAIT (*Interview*)

FIRST TELECAST: *August 9, 1963*

LAST TELECAST: *September 6, 1963*

BROADCAST HISTORY:

Aug 1963–Sep 1963, CBS Fri 10:30–11:00

HOST:

Charles Collingwood

Host Charles Collingwood interviewed guests from many walks of life in this series, including comedian Peter Sellers, commentator H. V. Kaltenborn, General Curtis E. LeMay, Oregon Governor Mark Hatfield, and actor Jimmy Stewart. The program was first seen in February 1963, and continued irregularly until the end of September. For five weeks during August and September, however, it was seen as a regular weekly feature.

PORTRAIT OF AMERICA (*Interview*)

FIRST TELECAST: *December 8, 1949*

LAST TELECAST: *December 29, 1949*

BROADCAST HISTORY:

Dec 1949, NBC Thu 8:00–8:30

HOST:

Norman Barry

Four-week documentary series in which NBC's cameras visited a different "typical American family" at home each week.

POST FIGHT BEAT, see *Fight Beat*

POWER OF WOMEN, THE (*Discussion*)

FIRST TELECAST: *July 1, 1952*

LAST TELECAST: *November 11, 1952*

BROADCAST HISTORY:

Jul 1952–Nov 1952, DUM Tue 8:00–8:30

Sep 1952–Oct 1952, DUM Mon 8:00–8:30

HOSTESS:

Vivien Kellems

Mrs. John G. Lee

Discussion of politics and social problems from the woman's point of view, by Vivien Kellems, president of the Liberty Belles. Sometimes guests appeared, sometimes it was a one-woman show. In October Mrs. John G. Lee, president of the League of Women Voters, took over as moderator. For the final telecast, on the week after the 1952 Presidential election, the topic was "Who Cares?"

POWER PLAY (*Drama*)

FIRST TELECAST: *June 14, 1999*

LAST TELECAST: *June 21, 1999*

BROADCAST HISTORY:

Jun 1999, UPN Mon 9:00–10:00

CAST:

Brett Parker .... Michael Riley
Colleen Blessed .... Kari Matchett
Duff McArdle .... Gordon Pinsent
Coach Lloyd Gorman .... Al Waxman
Mark Simpson .... Dean McDermott
Michelle Parker (age 17) .... Caterina Scorsone
Renate D'Alessandro .... Lori Alter
"Shakey" Al Tremblay .... Normand Bissonnette
Rose Thornton .... Krista Bridges
Coach Harry Strand .... Neil Crone
"Braniac" Jukka Branny-Acke .... Mark Lutz
"Terminal" Todd Maplethorpe .. Jonathan Rannells

Parker was a big-time New York–based sports agent who was involved in a shady deal to move the Hamilton Steelheads, the worst team in the NHL, to Houston. His deal would make him millions in under-the-table monies for parking and concession revenues. In order to get the league to approve the move, Parker and his cohorts, including Blessed, the team's bitchy president, had to show that there was no local fan support. Parker, though rotten to the core, surprisingly found himself caring about the team. Also featured were Duff, the crusty old team owner who hired Parker to replace the team's general manager; Michelle, Parker's wayward teenage daughter, who was put in his custody after attempting a little embezzlement; Simpson, the team's captain and most beloved player; Renate, the sarcastic administrative assistant to the general manager; and Thornton, the shy sports reporter from the *Hamilton Spectator*.

Power Play was produced in Toronto and ran for two seasons on Canada's CTV network. UPN picked it up after the first Canadian season but canceled it after only two episodes had aired.

POWERPUFF GIRLS, THE (*Cartoon*)

BROADCAST HISTORY:

Cartoon Network

30 minutes

Produced: *1998–*

Premiered: *November 18, 1998*

VOICES:

Blossom .... Catherine Cavadini
Bubbles .... Tara Charendoff Strong
Buttercup .... E. G. Daily
Prof. Utonium .... Tom Kane
Narrator, Mayor .... Tom Kenny

"Saving the world before bedtime" was the slogan of the three round, pixie-ish little girls with the big eyes who were the Powerpuff Girls. Created by fatherly Professor Utonium when he accidentally spilled some Chemical X into a vat of "sugar and spice and everything nice," they could fly, knock down doors, and crash through walls. They were frequently called out of their classes at Pokey Oaks kindergarten to fight the sneering villains who seemed to infest Townsville, including Mojo Jojo (a turbaned chimp), Fuzzy Lumpkins (a hillbilly monster), and "Him" (a crimson fiend)—which they did, with childish glee and innocent giggles. In 2002 a *Powerpuff Girls* feature film was released.

Originally seen on Cartoon Network's *World Premiere Toons.*

POWERS OF MATTHEW STAR, THE (*Science Fiction*)

FIRST TELECAST: *September 17, 1982*
LAST TELECAST: *September 11, 1983*
BROADCAST HISTORY:
Sep 1982–Aug 1983, NBC Fri 8:00–9:00
Aug 1983–Sep 1983, NBC Sun 7:00–8:00
CAST:
Matthew Star .... Peter Barton
Walt Shephard .... Louis Gossett, Jr.
Pam Elliott (1982) .... Amy Steel
Bob Alexander (1982) .... Chip Frye
Major Wymore (1983) .... James Karen

He may have looked just like any other student at Crestridge High, but he was not what he appeared to be. Matthew Star was actually a crown prince from the planet Quadris who, when his father was overthrown by tyrants, had been sent to Earth to allow his powers of telepathy and telekinesis to develop. Eventually, when he was ready, Matthew would return to fight the oppressors. In the meantime, he and his guardian, Walt Shephard, were forced to hide from their Quadrian foes, who might appear at any time in human, robot, or other form.

Despite the danger, Matthew tried to lead a normal life as a student. He excelled at sports and even had a cute girlfriend named Pam and friend named Bob. Walt was a science teacher and football coach at Crestridge and posed as Matthew's legal guardian. By midseason Matthew's powers were expanding—he had added astral projection (sending part of himself to another place, while his body did not move) and transmutation to his repertoire—and his activities were no longer based at the school. He now utilized his powers to help the government fight espionage and other crimes, on assignments from Maj. Wymore.

The Powers of Matthew Star was originally scheduled to premiere in the fall of 1981. It was delayed for a season when star Peter Barton was seriously burned during the filming of one of the early episodes.

POWERS THAT BE, THE (*Situation Comedy*)

FIRST TELECAST: *March 7, 1992*
LAST TELECAST: *June 19, 1993*
BROADCAST HISTORY:
Mar 1992–Apr 1992, NBC Sat 8:30–9:00
Aug 1992–Sep 1992, NBC Sat 8:30–9:00
Nov 1992–Jan 1993, NBC Sat 8:30–9:00
Jun 1993, NBC Sat 10:30–11:00
CAST:
Senator William Powers .... John Forsythe
Margaret Powers .... Holland Taylor
Caitlyn Van Horne .... Valerie Mahaffey
Rep. Theodore Van Horne ...... David Hyde Pierce
Pierce Van Horne .... Joseph Gordon-Levitt
Sophie Lipkin .... Robin Bartlett
Jordan Miller .... Eve Gordon
Bradley Grist .... Peter MacNicol
Charlotte .... Elizabeth Berridge
THEME:
"The Powers That Be," written by Marvin Hamlisch and Alan and Marilyn Bergman, sung by Stephen Bishop
EXECUTIVE PRODUCER:
Norman Lear

It is unclear whether Democratic setbacks in the 1994 congressional elections were related to this ribald parody of Washington insiders, featuring an idiotic Democratic senator and his dysfunctional family. But it couldn't have helped. Senator William Powers was a 26-year-veteran of Capitol Hill, a distinguished-looking, very charming, and totally vacuous ally of Bill Clinton (who was referred to but seldom seen). He was probably harmless by himself since he didn't have a clue as to what was going on, but his manipulative family and staff were something else. Margaret was his imperious, status-obsessed wife; Caitlyn his vain, neurotic daughter; Theodore his suicidal son-in-law, a little-noticed U.S. congressman; Jordan his scheming administrative assistant and mistress; Bradley his counter-scheming, incompetent press secretary; and Charlotte the skinny, bumbling maid.

The only remotely normal people around the Powers's elegant town house were Sophie, the senator's illegitimate daughter from a wartime tryst and a breath of fresh air with her forthright New Yawk opinions, and Pierce, Caitlyn and Theo's young son, whom they dressed like Little Lord Fauntleroy (in case there was a photo op) but who just wanted to go play.

Stories revolved mostly around family and staff's efforts to boost the senator's sagging image and/or trump each other, usually with disastrous results. The series did not last long enough for viewers to learn what happened to Powers and Van Horne in the 1994 elections, but one can almost guess.

After the series was abruptly canceled in early January 1993, several episodes not aired by NBC were telecast on the USA cable network on January 19, just before (the real) Bill Clinton's inauguration. A few more episodes turned up on NBC the following summer.

POZNER & DONAHUE (*Talk/Discussion*)

BROADCAST HISTORY:
Syndicated only
60 minutes
Produced: *1991–1992*
Released: *October 1991*
(Also CNBC Cable)
HOSTS:
Phil Donahue
Vladimir Pozner

Daytime talk show host Phil Donahue and his friend, American-born Soviet journalist Vladimir Pozner, cohosted this discussion series that focused on current issues of public concern. Each week they, and a panel of experts on the subject at hand, analyzed the topic and took phone calls from viewers. Although not successful in syndication, *Pozner & Donahue* moved to cable's CNBC network in the fall of 1992, where it remained until 1995.

PRACTICE, THE (*Situation Comedy*)

FIRST TELECAST: *January 30, 1976*
LAST TELECAST: *January 26, 1977*
BROADCAST HISTORY:
Jan 1976–Jul 1976, NBC Fri 8:30–9:00
Oct 1976–Nov 1976, NBC Wed 8:00–8:30
Dec 1976–Jan 1977, NBC Wed 9:30–10:00

CAST:

Dr. Jules Bedford.................... Danny Thomas
Molly Gibbons .... Dena Dietrich
Jenny Bedford..................... Shelley Fabares
Dr. David Bedford................. David Spielberg
Helen .... Didi Conn
Paul Bedford.......................... Allen Price
Tony Bedford .... Damon Raskin
Dr. Roland Caine .... John Byner
Nate...................................... Sam Laws
Lenny.................................. Mike Evans

There were two doctors in the Bedford family, but they had radically different approaches to the practice of medicine. The elder Bedford, Jules, was really from the old school. He was a little absentminded, could be grouchy and preoccupied, but was a warm, concerned individual with a love of people and a willingness to help, whether or not there was money to be made. Jules' office was on Manhattan's middle-class West Side. His nurse, Molly, had been with him for years and had an obvious crush on the widowed doctor; the outer office was "run" by a young, slightly daft receptionist named Helen. Son David Bedford, on the other hand, had set up practice on exclusive Park Avenue, was making money hand over fist, and was always after his dad to move in and share office space with him. Completing the cast were David's wife, Jenny, and his two young boys.

PRACTICE, THE (*Legal Drama*)

FIRST TELECAST: *March 4, 1997*
LAST TELECAST:
BROADCAST HISTORY:

Mar 1997–Apr 1997, ABC Tue 10:00–11:00
Jul 1997–Jan 1998, ABC Sat 10:00–11:00
Jan 1998–Aug 1998, ABC Mon 10:00–11:00
Aug 1998–Jan 2003, ABC Sun 10:00–11:00
Jan 2003–May 2003, ABC Mon 9:00–10:00
May 2003– , ABC Sun 10:00–11:00

CAST:

Bobby Donnell .... Dylan McDermott
Eugene Young .... Steve Harris
Ellenor Frutt..................... Camryn Manheim
Lindsay Dole .... Kelli Williams
Rebecca Washington .... Lisa Gay Hamilton
Jimmy Berluti.................. Michael Badalucco
Helen Gamble .... Lara Flynn Boyle
Lucy Hatcher (1998–)............ Marla Sokoloff
Asst. D.A. Richard Bay (1999–2001) .. Jason Kravits
Asst. D.A. Alan Lowe (2001–2002).. Ron Livingston
Asst. D.A. Kenneth Walsh (2001–)
.... Bill Smitrovich
Jamie Stringer (2002–).......... Jessica Capshaw

This acclaimed, Emmy-winning legal drama was the flip side of the stylish *L.A. Law.* Donnell and Associates, a low-rent Boston law firm specializing in criminal cases, was more often than not forced to defend the dregs of society in order to pay the bills. Trouble was, the dregs were often guilty, leading to much ethical agonizing. Success for these lawyers was sometimes getting a heinous murderer off the hook. Bobby was the handsome founder, his small staff consisting of Eugene, a bald, black, self-assured young attorney; Ellenor, a heavy-set, rather pushy attorney; Lindsay, a recent Harvard grad who was somewhat less sure of herself; and Rebecca, their ambitious paralegal and office manager. Joining shortly after the premiere was Jimmy, a pugnacious little guy who ran colorful TV ads for his own practice. Helen was the attractive, antagonistic D.A. who often fought the firm, while carrying on an intermittent affair with Bobby.

In an early story arc the firm won a big settlement against a tobacco firm represented by Lindsay's arrogant former law professor, Anderson Pearson (Edward Herrmann); Pearson was later charged with murdering a man who had stalked his family, and convicted despite being defended by the firm. In other notable cases, the firm fought off a huge libel suit, defended Ellenor's nerdy podiatrist friend who arrived in their offices with a severed head in his medical bag, defended a priest who accidentally killed someone during an exorcism, and fought a powerful Boston utility company, with Jimmy getting shot in the process. There were numerous romances, including Bobby and Helen, Bobby and Lindsay, and Ellenor and her insurance-scamming boyfriend, with occasional nude scenes.

In 1998, Rebecca passed her bar exam and Lucy joined the firm as its new secretary. With the staff agitating to become coowners, the firm was reconstituted as Donnell, Young, Dole & Frutt, but their cases didn't get any more prestigious. As a judge put it when ordering the firm to defend a man accused of brutally killing a nun and stuffing her remains in a closet: "You people fight for murderers better than anybody."

In 2000 Bobby and Lindsay eloped, and in 2001 she gave birth to a son, Bobby, Jr., on the courtroom floor. Ellenor also became pregnant that season, by sperm donor Michael Hale (Ted McGinley), and gave birth. Two of the firm's partners faced murder charges. In 2001 Bobby killed serial killer William Hinks and was acquitted, only to have his office blown up in reprisal; in 2002 Lindsay was tried for the fatal shooting of cannibal Lawrence O'Malley and convicted. The conviction was later overturned. A.D.A. Bay was shot and killed in 2001, and replaced by Lowe. Jamie, a young attorney fresh out of law school, joined the firm in 2002 as an associate.

PRACTICE TEE (*Golf Lesson*)

FIRST TELECAST: *August 5, 1949*
LAST TELECAST: *September 9, 1949*
BROADCAST HISTORY:

Aug 1949–Sep 1949, NBC Fri 7:30–7:45

HOST:

William P. Barbour

Fifteen-minute golf lesson, notable mostly for being the first regular network TV series to originate from Cleveland. Host William P. Barbour served as golf pro.

PREMIERE (*Dramatic Anthology*)

FIRST TELECAST: *July 1, 1968*
LAST TELECAST: *September 9, 1968*
BROADCAST HISTORY:

Jul 1968–Sep 1968, CBS Mon 10:00–11:00

The full-hour dramas that were aired in this summer replacement for *The Carol Burnett Show* were all pilots for dramatic series that had not been bought by any of the networks. Among the stars who did not make it, this time around, were Burt Reynolds in "Lassiter," Carl Betz and Susan Strasberg in "Crisis," and Sally Kellerman and John McMartin in "Higher and Higher." "Call to Danger," made some years earlier as the pilot film for *Mission: Impossible*, was also included.

PREMIERE PLAYHOUSE, see *Movies—Prior to 1961*

PRESENTING SUSAN ANTON (*Musical Variety*)
FIRST TELECAST: *April 26, 1979*
LAST TELECAST: *May 17, 1979*
BROADCAST HISTORY:
Apr 1979–May 1979, NBC Thu 10:00–11:00
REGULARS:
Susan Anton
Jack Fletcher (as *Robert Tibidas*)
Jack Knight
Dick Wilson
Terry McGovern (as *Bruce Larson*)
The Walter Painter Dancers
Jimmy Martinez
Buddy Powell
Donovan Scott

This limited-run variety series starred statuesque singer-dancer Susan Anton, who had first achieved notice as the successor to Edie Adams doing commercials for Muriel Cigars. There was an even mix of comedy and musical numbers, with a recurring sketch about the Disco Monks (Martinez, Powell, and Scott), three religious men attempting to modernize their order to make it more appealing to contemporary men. In the first episode they decided to offer two alternatives to the vow of silence—the vow of backgammon or the vow of jogging. Guest stars appeared with Miss Anton and her regulars on each telecast.

PRESIDENT EISENHOWER'S NEWS CONFERENCE (*News*)
FIRST TELECAST: *February 2, 1955*
LAST TELECAST: *September 11, 1955*
BROADCAST HISTORY:
Feb 1955–May 1955, ABC Wed 10:00–10:30
Feb 1955–Sep 1955, ABC Sun 8:30–9:00

Coverage of President Eisenhower's weekly news conferences was provided by ABC during most of 1955. On weeks when there was no news conference a half-hour filmed drama was presented. From the latter part of February through the end of May these filmed news conferences were offered on both Wednesdays and Sundays, after which they were telecast on Sundays only.

PRESIDENTIAL COUNTDOWN (*Political*)
FIRST TELECAST: *September 12, 1960*
LAST TELECAST: *October 31, 1960*
BROADCAST HISTORY:
Sep 1960–Oct 1960, CBS Mon 10:30–11:00
ANCHORMAN:
Walter Cronkite

As the 1960 Presidential campaign moved toward its conclusion, CBS aired a weekly summary program that covered candidates Nixon and Kennedy. Results of CBS News polls on the mood of the voters in various parts of the country were also part of the show. Walter Cronkite anchored the series with regular contributions from other CBS News correspondents. On Friday, November 4, a final telecast was aired in which the contributing reporters summed up what they had seen and felt throughout the campaign.

PRESIDENTIAL STRAWS IN THE WIND (*Political*)
FIRST TELECAST: *August 24, 1948*
LAST TELECAST: *October 5, 1948*
BROADCAST HISTORY:
Aug 1948–Oct 1948, CBS Tue 9:30–10:00
FEATURED:
Elmo Roper
HOST:
Lyman Bryson

Pollster Elmo Roper was the star of this pre-election series that broadcast the results of public-opinion polls his organization had taken on various issues, and on the popularity of the candidates themselves. Four members of the studio audience were brought on stage and asked the same questions that had been asked in the poll, so that viewers could see how the poll had been taken, and the results of the actual poll were then analyzed by Mr. Roper. The first telecast of this series had aired as a local program in New York on August 10, then it expanded to the full network for the four succeeding biweekly telecasts.

PRESIDENTIAL TIMBER (*Public Affairs*)
FIRST TELECAST: *May 27, 1948*
LAST TELECAST: *June 20, 1952*
BROADCAST HISTORY:
May 1948–Jul 1948, CBS Thu 9:00–9:30
Apr 1952–Jun 1952, CBS Fri 10:30–11:00
MODERATOR:
Robert Trout (1952)

Presidential Timber gave candidates for the nation's highest office, or their authorized representatives, the opportunity to present their platforms and programs to a nationwide television audience. This live program did not air each week, only when there was a candidate who wanted to speak. The series was patterned after the CBS radio program of the same name that had been aired during previous Presidential election years.

PRESIDIO MED (*Medical Drama*)
FIRST TELECAST: *September 24, 2002*
LAST TELECAST: *January 24, 2003*
BROADCAST HISTORY:
Sep 2002, CBS Tue 10:00–11:00
Sep 2002–Nov 2002, CBS Wed 10:00–11:00
Jan 2003, CBS Fri 8:00–9:00
CAST:
Dr. Harriet Lanning................ Blythe Danner
Dr. Rae Brennan .... Dana Delany
Dr. Letty Jordan............... Anna Deavere Smith
Dr. Jackie Colette................. Sasha Alexander
Dr. Jules Keating .... Julianne Nicholson
Dr. Nicholas Kokoris.................... Oded Fehr
Dr. Matt Slingerland .... Paul Blackthorne
Sean Brennan .... Robert Knepper
Norman Drum .... David Kaufman
Nurse Lynette .... Joceyln Rose
Dr. Tom Roback...................... Vyto Ruginis
Dr. David Eidenberg................. Stewart Bick

This medical drama focused on the professional and personal lives of a group of women doctors working at the Presidio Medical Group in San Francisco. Dr. Lanning, a caring obstetrician, was the effective matriarch of the group, offering sage advice to her younger cohorts. Dr. Brennan, an oncologist, had just returned from an overseas medical mission where she had had a passionate affair with Dr. Kokoris, a Greek surgeon who followed her back to San Francisco and hoped to resume their relationship. His presence on the hospital staff made her very uncomfortable—particularly since her marriage was troubled and she still had feelings for him. Other featured doctors were Dr. Jordan, a tough and often abrasive cardiologist whose husband, Dr. Roback, was also working at Presidio Med; Dr. Colette, a young and headstrong plastic surgeon; and Dr. Keating, an unmarried pediatrician who wanted to have her own baby. Dr. Slingerland, an attractive but arrogant internist, offered to provide the sperm to fertilize her eggs and, after the fertilization process succeeded, took her out to dinner to celebrate. In November Dr. Brennan admitted to her husband that she had had an affair, and by January they had separated.

PRESS CONFERENCE (*Interview*)
FIRST TELECAST: *July 4, 1956*
LAST TELECAST: *July 15, 1957*
BROADCAST HISTORY:
Jul 1956–Sep 1956, NBC Wed 8:00–8:30
Oct 1956–Dec 1956, ABC Sun 8:30–9:00
Apr 1957–Jul 1957, ABC Mon 9:00–9:30
MODERATOR:
Martha Rountree

In a format similar to that of *Meet the Press*, this series brought people in the news, generally the political news, to a weekly news conference. Some of them made opening statements and others simply began by asking for the first question. Martha Rountree was the moderator and called on various members of the press for questions. At the end of each program, she summed up the key points for the viewing audience. The series moved from NBC to ABC in the fall of 1956, moved from prime time to Sunday afternoons for three months at the beginning of 1957, and returned to prime time in April with the title changed to *Martha Rountree's Press Conference.*

PRESS CORRESPONDENTS PANEL (*Discussion*)
FIRST TELECAST: *April 10, 1949*
LAST TELECAST: *May 22, 1949*
BROADCAST HISTORY:
Apr 1949, CBS Sun 6:30–7:00
Apr 1949–May 1949, CBS Sun 6:00–6:30

This live weekly program gave news correspondents an opportunity to discuss the events of the week in a round-table discussion fashion.

PRESS YOUR LUCK, see *Whammy!*

PRESTON EPISODES, THE (*Situation Comedy*)
FIRST TELECAST: *September 9, 1995*
LAST TELECAST: *October 28, 1995*
BROADCAST HISTORY:
Sep 1995–Oct 1995, FOX Sat 8:30–9:00
CAST:
David Preston.................... David Alan Grier
Larry Dunhill.......................... Clive Revill
Kelly Freeman......................... Judith Scott
Derek .... Tommy Hinkley
Harlow .... Brent Hinkley
Adam Green .... Matthew Walker
Donald Preston .... Ron Canada
Penelope Preston .... Lynne Thigpen
Mary Ann .... Deborah Lacey

David was a 37-year-old divorced English professor who had moved from the womb-like security of his New Jersey college campus to the competitive bustle of Manhattan, where he could toss wisecracks and chase dates. Convinced he would became a Pulitzer Prize–winning writer, David was crestfallen when the only job he could find was as a photo caption writer for *Stuff* magazine, a weekly with content closer to the tabloids than *Time* or *Newsweek*. Neurotic David was constantly trying to convince himself, and others, that his job was more important than it was. Working with him at *Stuff* were Larry, the magazine's loutish editor, who liked the trashy tone of the magazine and had no interest in making it more literate; his reluctant confidante Kelly, who had burned out as an investigative reporter and preferred the puffery and reduced stress working at *Stuff*; Harlow, the weird fact checker who stared at the floor; and Adam, the writer who had hired him. Derek, the eccentric guy who lived across the hall from David, had no job but was forever trying to make his big score. Also seen were David's parents and his ex-wife, Mary Ann.

PRETENDER, THE (*Science Fiction*)
FIRST TELECAST: *September 19, 1996*
LAST TELECAST: *August 26, 2000*
BROADCAST HISTORY:
Sep 1996, NBC Thu 10:00–11:00
Sep 1996–May 1997, NBC Sat 9:00–10:00
Jun 1997–Sep 1997, NBC Sat 8:00–9:00
Nov 1997–Jan 1998, NBC Sat 8:00–9:00
Jan 1998–Apr 1998, NBC Sat 9:00–10:00
May 1998, NBC Sat 8:00–9:00
Jul 1998–Aug 1998, NBC Wed 8:00–9:00
Aug 1998–Sep 1998, NBC Sat 8:00–9:00
Oct 1998–Dec 1998, NBC Sat 9:00–10:00
Jan 1999–Feb 1999, NBC Sat 8:00–9:00
Feb 1999–May 1999, NBC Sat 9:00–10:00
Jun 1999–Aug 1999, NBC Sat 8:00–9:00
Sep 1999–Nov 1999, NBC Sat 9:00–10:00
Dec 1999–May 2000, NBC Sat 8:00–9:00
Jul 2000–Aug 2000, NBC Sat 10:00–11:00
CAST:
Jarod Russell..................... Michael T. Weiss
Dr. Sydney Green................. Patrick Bauchau
Miss Parker .... Andrea Parker
Mr. Parker .... Harve Presnell
Broots.................................. Jon Gries
Bobby Lyle .... Jamie Denton
Angelo .... Paul Dillon
Dr. William Raines .... Richard Marcus
**Jarod (as child)*................. Ryan Merriman
**Miss Parker (as child)* .... Ashley Peldon
Sydney (as child)...................... Alex Wexo
**Margaret (Jarod's mother)*............ Kim Myers
**Sam the sweeper* .... Sam Ayers
**Willie the sweeper*.................... Willie Gault
**Brigitte (1997–2000)*............... Pamela Gidley
*Occasional

"There are extraordinary individuals among us known as pretenders," began this series, "geniuses with the ability to insinuate themselves into any walk of life, to literally become anyone." Jarod was a pretender. A child prodigy, he had been taken from his parents at an early age and raised in a secret, fortress-like facility at Blue

Cove, Delaware, called the Centre by kindly psychiatrist Dr. Green, who honed his extraordinary mental capabilities so that, eventually, they could be sold to the highest bidder. But Jarod escaped (he *was* smart, after all). Now he was on the run from the Centre's heavily armed operatives, seeking to expose the Centre and find clues to his real background—he had been told his parents died in a plane crash, but had they? Melting into society, he used his abilities and his enormous bank of knowledge to become many things—a doctor, a sea captain, an airline pilot—helping those he met along the way.

Hot on his heels was Miss Parker, an alluring but totally ruthless Centre assassin who was determined to eliminate this threat to her employer. When she got close, she snarled, she hissed, she screamed "Kill him!"—but Jarod, smiling, always slipped away. In the second season, Miss Parker faced competition from another Centre team assigned to get Jarod—Brigitte and Mr. Lyle. As seasons passed, secrets of the Centre and its denizens began to be revealed, sometimes in flashbacks, and Miss Parker began to learn more about her own dark past. Lyle, it turned out, was her twin brother; her long-missing father, Mr. Parker, also turned up and in fact ran the Centre. Moreover it appeared that her mother had been killed by Jarod's father. Additional clues came from Angelo, who was mentally ill due to unfortunate medical experiments performed on him as the Centre was trying to make him into a pretender. Broots was the Centre's computer genius; Raines, the evil doctor behind many of the Centre's experiments (in later episodes, after an assassination attempt, he lurched around gasping air from a portable oxygen tank), and "sweepers," the ruthless operatives who "cleaned up" the Centre's dirty work in the field.

In the series finale Jarod and Miss Parker—who at times now worked together—learned new secrets about the intertwined lives of those in the Centre, many of whom seemed to be related, and Jarod was reunited with his father, Major Charles (George Lazenby). In a follow-up TV movie aired on TNT in January 2001, Parker and Sydney discovered that Jarod had not escaped the Centre alone, and that there were two other pretenders on the loose—Eddie (who was subsequently killed) and Alex (a psycho seeking vengeance on Jarod, who appeared to die at the end of the episode—although they never found his body). Another TV movie on TNT in December 2001 found Jarod and Miss Parker trapped on a strange island, learning even more about their pasts.

PREVIEW (*Magazine*)

BROADCAST HISTORY:

Syndicated only
30 minutes (60 minutes on weekends)
Produced: *1990*
Released: *September 1990*

REPORTERS:

Chuck Henry
Rona Elliot
Paula McClure
Marilyn McCoo
Robin Leach
Dana Hersey
Bobbie Brown

Subtitled "The Best of the New," this series gave viewers a daily dose of soft news features covering a wide range of media and lifestyle subjects. Chuck Henry, the Hollywood-based anchor of the show, specialized in stories about technological breakthroughs. The other regular reporters were Rona Elliot (celebrity news and gossip), Paula McClure (TV), Marilyn McCoo (music), Dana Hersey (movies), Bobbie Brown (fashion), and series creator/executive producer Robin Leach *(Lifestyles)*. Heavily promoted in the fall of 1990, *Preview* attracted small audiences and went off the air at the end of the year.

PREVIEW TONIGHT (*Dramatic Anthology*)

FIRST TELECAST: *August 14, 1966*
LAST TELECAST: *September 11, 1966*
BROADCAST HISTORY:

Aug 1966–Sep 1966, ABC Sun 8:00–9:00

This was a collection of unsold pilots for proposed series which never made the network's schedule. It was, in other words, a "preview" of series which never happened. Perhaps the most unusual was *Great Bible Adventures*, starring Hugh O'Brian as Joseph leading the Jews in Egypt.

PREY (*Science Fiction*)

FIRST TELECAST: *January 15, 1998*
LAST TELECAST: *July 9, 1998*
BROADCAST HISTORY:

Jan 1998–Mar 1998, ABC Thu 8:00–9:00
Jun 1998–Jul 1998, ABC Thu 9:00–10:00

CAST:

Dr. Sloan Parker .... Debra Messing
Tom Daniels .... Adam Storke
Dr. Ed Tate .... Vincent Ventresca
Dr. Walter Attwood .... Larry Drake
Det. Ray Peterson .... Frankie R. Faison

The invaders were among us once again in this sci-fi series, ready to take over the world and kill us all, but rather than being aliens from outer space, they were an advanced race of humans with DNA exactly 1.6 percent different from that of normal humans. Their development had been triggered, somehow, by global warming. Dr. Coulter, head of the bio-anthropology lab at Whitney University in Pasadena, California, had stumbled onto this terrible secret and been killed for her trouble (the DNA-enhanced murdered anyone who discovered what they were up to). Picking up the struggle to expose and defeat the rapidly multiplying enemy were Sloan Parker, an earnest young associate, Tate, her boyish coworker, and Attwood, the somewhat mysterious new head of the lab, who seemed to know more than he was letting on. They all sat in front of computer screens muttering "Oh, my god," while the brutal (but often handsome) mutants, when cornered, snarled, "You will all die!"

Parker and her friends were afraid to go public with their discovery, because the mutants had infiltrated government and could be anyone—it was impossible to identify them without a DNA sample. They did gain two allies in "Tom Daniels," a mutant who couldn't bring himself to kill and who turned against his kind, and Peterson, the police detective on the Coulter case, who learned the incredible truth.

PRICE IS RIGHT, THE (*Quiz/Audience Participation*)

FIRST TELECAST: *September 23, 1957*

LAST TELECAST: *July 5, 2003*
BROADCAST HISTORY:
Sep 1957–Jun 1958, NBC Mon 7:30–8:00
Jun 1958–Sep 1958, NBC Thu 10:00–10:30
Sep 1958–Sep 1961, NBC Wed 8:30–9:00
Sep 1961–Sep 1962, NBC Mon 8:30–9:00
Sep 1962–Jan 1963, NBC Mon 9:30–10:00
Feb 1963–Sep 1963, NBC Fri 9:30–10:00
Sep 1963–Nov 1963, ABC Wed 8:30–9:00
Dec 1963–Sep 1964, ABC Fri 9:30–10:00
Aug 1986–Sep 1986, CBS Thu 8:00–9:00
May 2002–Jul 2002, CBS Thu 8:00–9:00
Jul 2002, CBS Fri 9:00–10:00
May 2003–Jul 2003, CBS Sat 8:00–9:00
EMCEES:
Bill Cullen (1957–1964)
Bob Barker (1986, 2002)
PRODUCERS:
Mark Goodson and Bill Todman

Four contestants competed with each other on *The Price Is Right.* They tried to guess the retail price of merchandise prizes, which were displayed by two beautiful models. The contestant who came closest to the retail price, without going over it, won the merchandise. Most prizes were open to continuously rising price guesses until either the contestants decided to stop, or an undefined time limit forced them to make final bids. If a contestant wanted to hold at a final bid, he could "freeze" at that level and wait until the bidding was over to see if he had won. An added attraction was a home-viewer game in which TV watchers sent in their to-the-nearest-penny price estimates for a group of prizes, which they might then win.

The Price Is Right also ran in daytime on NBC from November 1956 until September 1965. It returned to daytime in the fall of 1972 with a modified format in which different kinds of pricing games were employed. This new version, emceed by Bob Barker, has been a fixture on the CBS daytime lineup ever since. In addition, a syndicated version was produced from 1972 to 1980, with Dennis James serving as emcee until 1977 and Bob Barker taking the reins for the last three seasons. A new syndicated version aired during the 1985–1986 season, emceed by Tom Kennedy. At the end of that season *The Price Is Right* was given a brief prime-time run on CBS, with daytime host Barker doing double duty.

The fall of 1994 brought yet another syndicated version of *The Price Is Right* to the airwaves. This one, designed to air on weekday evenings, featured bigger prizes than the CBS daytime version, as big winners were able to walk away with merchandise and cash worth more than $50,000. Doug Davidson, an actor on CBS's daytime soap opera *The Young & the Restless,* was emcee. It lasted less than six months.

Bob Barker brought the series back to prime time beginning in the summer of 2002, with some episodes featuring contestants from the armed forces.

PRIDE & JOY (*Situation Comedy*)
FIRST TELECAST: *March 21, 1995*
LAST TELECAST: *July 11, 1995*
BROADCAST HISTORY:
Mar 1995–May 1995, NBC Tue 9:30–10:00
Jun 1995–Jul 1995, NBC Tue 8:30–9:00
CAST:
Greg Sherman .... Craig Bierko
Amy Sherman .... Julie Warner
Nathan Green .... Jeremy Piven
Carol Green .... Caroline Rhea
Katya .... Natasha Pavlovic

Role reversal comedy in which two dads did diaper duty while their wives pursued the yuppie dream. Greg and Amy were a young couple living in a Manhattan high-rise and entranced with their newborn, Mel. Since Greg, a freelance magazine writer, worked at home he took care of the baby while Amy, an advertising agency art director, trooped off to work. Across the hall Nathan and Carol were in a slightly different situation. Neurotic Nathan was an unemployed stockbroker looking for a job, while outspoken, excitable Carol was a copywriter at Amy's agency. Six-month-old Mitchell was their second child; 12-year-old computer genius Steven was the first. Together Greg and Nathan learned the fine points of baby changing and cuddling, while their wives fretted about their lack of quality time.

Katya was the Sherman's perky Romanian housekeeper.

PRIDE OF THE FAMILY, THE (*Situation Comedy*)
FIRST TELECAST: *October 2, 1953*
LAST TELECAST: *July 10, 1955*
BROADCAST HISTORY:
Oct 1953–Sep 1954, ABC Fri 9:00–9:30
Jun 1955–Jul 1955, CBS Sun 7:00–7:30
CAST:
Albie Morrison .... Paul Hartman
Catherine Morrison .... Fay Wray
Ann Morrison .... Natalie Wood
Junior Morrison .... Bobby Hyatt

Albie Morrison worked in the advertising department of the newspaper in the small town in which he lived. He was married and had two teenage children, Ann and Junior. Despite the best of intentions, Albie somehow managed to ruin almost everything he tried to do, whether it was something industrious at the office or an attempt to prove how handy he was around the house. His wife still loved him and, except for the occasions when they resented his attempts to prevent them from being as independent as they would have liked, so did his children. Reruns of this filmed ABC series were aired on CBS for a short time during the summer of 1955.

PRIME SUSPECT (*Public Service*)
BROADCAST HISTORY:
Syndicated only
30 minutes
Produced: *1992–1994* (52 episodes)
Released: *September 1992*
HOST:
Mike Hegedus

Prime Suspect was *America's Most Wanted* without the reenactments. Originally produced locally on KNBC in Los Angeles as *Murder One,* it focused exclusively on unsolved murders. The series used only police, law enforcement officials, and relatives of and/or victims to provide information on the crimes. Each episode covered three or four cases.

PRIME TIME COUNTRY (*Variety*)
BROADCAST HISTORY:
The Nashville Network
90/60 minutes

Produced: *1996–1999*
Premiered: *January 15, 1996*
HOSTS:
Tom Wopat (1996)
Gary Chapman (1996–1999)
Nan Sumrall (1998–1999)
A big, noisy, prime-time variety show originating nightly from Opryland, U.S.A., outside Nashville. Musical acts and comedians from the field of county music guest-starred.

PRIME TIME PETS (*Comedy*)
FIRST TELECAST: *July 9, 1990*
LAST TELECAST: *September 4, 1991*
BROADCAST HISTORY:
Jul 1990, CBS Mon 8:30–9:00
Jul 1990–Aug 1990, CBS Fri 8:00–8:30
Apr 1991–May 1991, CBS Wed 8:30–9:00
Aug 1991, CBS Fri 8:30–9:00
Sep 1991, CBS Wed 8:30–9:00
REGULARS:
Wil Shriner
Dorothy Lucey
This low-budget summer series was a mix of *Those Amazing Animals*, *America's Funniest Home Videos*, and the "Stupid Pet Tricks" segment from *Late Night with David Letterman*. Hosted by humorist Wil Shriner, each episode contained stories on assorted pets with unusual talents, jobs, or skills. Most frequently shown were dogs—a bowling dog, a dog who ate corn on the cob, a dancing poodle, jogging dogs, seeing-eye dogs, and videos of frisbee-catching dogs, police dogs at work, and dogs who tapped their paws to the beat of rap music. Other features included a nursing home resident with his pet duck, a boy with his pet goose, a woman who supplied ants to ant farms, and Cheetah, the retired chimp from the "Tarzan" movies. Dorothy Lucey was the show's roving reporter, traveling around the country looking for interesting and unusual pets. Viewers were also encouraged to send in videos of their pets in action, which an alarming number of them did.

PRIME TIME SUNDAY (*Newsmagazine*)
FIRST TELECAST: *June 24, 1979*
LAST TELECAST: *July 5, 1980*
BROADCAST HISTORY:
Jun 1979–Dec 1979, NBC Sun 10:00–11:00
Dec 1979–Jul 1980, NBC Sat 10:00–11:00
REGULARS:
Tom Snyder
Jack Perkins
Jessica Savitch
Bob Dotson
John Dancy (1980)
Chris Wallace
Sandy Gilmour (1980)
Prime Time Sunday was another NBC attempt to produce a successful prime-time magazine series, replacing the departed *Weekend*. Unlike *Weekend*, which had a somewhat irreverent approach to its subject matter (see separate listing), *Prime Time* was a more traditional, hard-hitting news program. Tom Snyder, the sometimes abrasive anchorman, was seen in a control-room atmosphere, with the technical aspects of the show visible to viewers to heighten the sense of immediacy. Each telecast opened with the director counting down to the program start and cueing Snyder, and closed with a shot of a technician pulling the switch that faded the picture to black.

Each episode of *Prime Time Sunday* contained at least three feature stories, usually narrated by field reporters Jack Perkins and Chris Wallace (son of *60 Minutes*' Mike Wallace). Perkins' stories tended to be human interest and whimsical (profiles of commercial creators Dick Orkin and Bert Berdis, of former cowboy star and current owner of the California Angels baseball team Gene Autry, and of three rodeo cowboys; a piece on a Swedish law making it illegal to spank kids), while Wallace did investigative reporting (on parole-board policies, legal clinics that advertise, and safety problems with commuter airlines). There were also live in-studio panel discussions and updates on breaking news stories. Jessica Savitch became a frequent reporter in the fall of 1979, as did Bob Dotson. Chris Wallace left early in 1980 to be replaced by John Dancy and Sandy Gilmour. The title of the program was changed to *Prime Time Saturday* in December 1979.

PRIMETIME GLICK (*Comedy*)
BROADCAST HISTORY:
Comedy Central
30 minutes
Original episodes: *2001–*
Premiered: *June 20, 2001*
CAST:
Jiminy Glick .... Martin Short
Adrien Van Voorhees .... Michael McKean
Martin Short donned a fat suit to lampoon clueless, fawning celebrity interviewers in this improvised series. The outrageously overweight Glick wiggled and squirmed in his chair as he showered real celebrity guests with effusive compliments, frequent misunderstandings, and sometimes embarrassing questions. Often he would laugh and slap their knees with his rolled-up question sheet for emphasis. Submitting themselves to this surreal experience—and trying to maintain their composure—were such celebrities as Jerry Seinfeld, Regis Philbin, Kathie Lee Gifford, Tom Hanks, Rosie O'Donnell, and Ray Romano. Some, like Steve Martin, seemed a bit annoyed, but most played along with the gag. Adrien Van Voorhees was Jiminy's harp-playing orchestra leader. Numerous comics played walk-on roles, especially in the second season when Jiminy presented such features as LaLaWood Fables, Home Movies, and Steam Room. Among the more frequently seen characters seen were Jiminy's wife, Dixie (Jan Hooks), and audience member Ronette (Jackie Stevens). The show's tagline: "If you think you know Hollywood . . . You don't know GLICK!"

PRIMETIME LIVE (*Newsmagazine*)
FIRST TELECAST: *August 3, 1989*
LAST TELECAST:
BROADCAST HISTORY:
Aug 1989–Dec 1994, ABC Thu 10:00–11:00
Jan 1995–Sep 1998, ABC Wed 10:00–11:00
Oct 2000– , ABC Thu 10:00–11:00
ANCHORS:
Sam Donaldson (1989–1998)
Diane Sawyer
Charles Gibson (2000–)

PRINCIPAL CORRESPONDENTS:
Chris Wallace
Judd Rose (1989–1998)
Jay Schadler
Sylvia Chase (1989–1998)
John Quinones (1991–)
Nancy Collins (1993–1995)
Renée Poussaint (1993–1998)
Cynthia McFadden (1996–1998)
Brian Ross (1994–)
Chris Cuomo (2000–)
Dr. Nancy Snyderman (2000–)
Elizabeth Vargas (2002–)

ABC seems to have a history of disastrous launches for its newsmagazines, even those that ultimately go on to become successful; *20/20* has become the second most successful newsmagazine in history (after *60 Minutes*), but its first telecast was a disaster. Similarly, *Primetime Live* began amidst much criticism of the awkward, staged "banter" between stiff Sam Donaldson and Diane Sawyer, and their even hokier attempts to interact with a live studio audience, as if they were hosting some bush league imitation of the *Donahue* show. Within a few weeks the banter and the studio audience were dropped, and the series got down to doing what network news departments do best, thoroughly researched and vividly presented short documentaries on current political and social issues, and interviews with the hottest current newsmakers.

Highlights during the first two seasons included a live tour of the White House hosted by President Bush and Mrs. Bush, an extensive tour of the inner sanctums of the Kremlin in Moscow, an undercover exposé of patient abuse in a Cleveland VA hospital, and an investigation of the 1988 bombing of Pan Am Flight #103, which won several awards. Later notable stories included an interview with former Defense Secretary Robert McNamara, shortly before his death, in which he admitted mistakes of the Vietnam War; correspondent Jay Schadler hitchhiking across America; and an undercover investigation of the Food Lion grocery chain that revealed it was changing dates on old food and repackaging old meats for resale. The latter report, in 1992–1993, led to a landmark lawsuit over ABC's "hidden camera" tactics and a $5.5 million judgment against the network, which was overturned in 1999. In the wake of the charges, ABC aired a 1997 special report on the uses of hidden cameras and undercover reporting. By far the largest audience to a single telecast (60 million) was on June 14, 1995, for Diane Sawyer's live interview with Michael Jackson and Lisa Marie Presley, in which they spoke about allegations of child molestation by the singer and their recent (to be short-lived) marriage.

In September 1998, in an effort to consolidate its proliferating newsmagazines, *Primetime Live* was folded into the venerable *20/20* (q.v.), but in October 2000 it was relaunched as an independent series, now called *Primetime Thursday*.

PRIMUS (*Adventure*)

BROADCAST HISTORY:
Syndicated only
30 minutes
Produced: *1971* (26 episodes)
Released: *Fall 1971*

CAST:
Carter Primus........................Robert Brown
Charlie Kingman......................Will Kuluva
Toni Hayden..........................Eva Renzi

PRODUCER:
Ivan Tors

Producer Ivan Tors *(Sea Hunt, Flipper)* tried to revive the underwater-adventure genre with this 1971 syndicated series. Carter Primus was a global underwater troubleshooter, like *Sea Hunt*'s Mike Nelson, but he had a lot more gadgets—an underwater robot called Big Kate, a little exploration and photography sub called *Pegasus*, and a nifty little runabout sea sled. He also had a crusty, bewhiskered sidekick named Charlie, and a pretty assistant, Toni. Unfortunately the plots and acting were strictly kid stuff, and the show, though widely carried at first, lasted for only 26 episodes.

PRINCE STREET (*Police Drama*)

FIRST TELECAST: *March 6,1997*
LAST TELECAST: *March 12, 1997*
BROADCAST HISTORY:
Mar 1997, NBC Thu 10:00–11:00
Mar 1997, NBC Wed 10:00–11:00

CAST:
Lt. Tom Warner........................Joe Morton
Det. Alex Gage.....................Vincent Spano
Det. Nina Echeverria............Mariska Hargitay
Det. Jimmy Tasio.............Lawrence Monosan
Det. Tony Libretti..................Steven Martini
Det. Diane Hoffman...............Dana Eskelson

THEME:
by Jan Hammer

Unlikely as it might seem, this undercover-cop show was based on the exploits of a real New York City police unit, which was formed in 1971 and operated secretly for twenty years. Headquartered behind a print shop on Prince Street, in SoHo, its officers carried no badges, wore no uniforms, and frequently operated in disguise in order to break up some of the most impenetrable criminal organizations in the city. Lt. Warner was the boyish commander, with a squad including shaggy, suspicious-looking Gage, tough but *very* cool single-mom Echeverria, father-confessor Tasio, and cocky recruit Libretti. The show's presence on the NBC schedule was also evidently something of a secret, as it aired just twice, on two different nights, before being abruptly canceled.

PRINCESS SAGAPHI (*Travelogue*)

FIRST TELECAST: *September 6, 1948*
LAST TELECAST: *January 7, 1949*
BROADCAST HISTORY:
Sep 1948, NBC Mon 8:00–8:15
Sep 1948–Dec 1948, NBC Thu 8:00–8:15
Dec 1948–Jan 1949, NBC Mon 8:45–9:00

HOSTESS:
Princess Annette Sagaphi

Princess Sagaphi, an authority on the Far East, narrated these travelogue films of faraway places.

PRINCESSES (*Situation Comedy*)

FIRST TELECAST: *September 27, 1991*

LAST TELECAST: *October 25, 1991*
BROADCAST HISTORY:
Sep 1991–Oct 1991, CBS Fri 8:00–8:30
Oct 1991, CBS Fri 8:30–9:00
CAST:
Tracy Dillon .... Julie Hagerty
Princess Georgina De La Rue ("Georgy")
.... Twiggy Lawson
Melissa Kirshner .... Fran Drescher
Debra Kirshner-Kleckner .... Leila Kenzle
THEME:
"Some Day My Prince Will Come," sung by The Roaches

Three young, single women became roommates in a most unusual way. Tracy was a shy, trusting English teacher who left her fiancé at the altar when she found out he had been married twice before and that one of his ex-wives was his sexy business partner. What she salvaged, however, was a fabulous Manhattan penthouse apartment overlooking Central Park. Tony, the owner of the apartment, a globetrotting friend of her almost husband, had given it to them for a year, rent free, as a wedding present. Apparently he was a little forgetful, having also loaned the apartment to Georgy, a recently widowed English princess (and former showgirl) who had moved to the States while her late husband's children fought with her attorney over his will. Since Georgy had no friends in New York, she was more than happy to share the huge apartment with Tracy. The third "princess" was Tracy's longtime roommate and best friend Melissa, an outspoken, stereotypical Jewish American who sold cosmetics at a department store. She was thrilled to give up their little apartment for the glitz of Manhattan, and the price was certainly right. The conflict of personalities, as well as Georgy's adjustment to being on her own after years of being waited upon, provided the basis for the comedy. Also seen was Melissa's married younger sister, Debra, who sounded and acted exactly like her.

Julie Hagerty abruptly left the show after only a few episodes had been taped, and *Princesses* was put on hiatus while the producers hunted for a replacement. Low ratings and generally bad reviews for the series caused them to rethink their plans, and *Princesses* ceased to exist after the last Hagerty episode had been telecast.

PRISONER, THE (*Mystery/Adventure*)

FIRST TELECAST: *June 1, 1968*
LAST TELECAST: *September 11, 1969*
BROADCAST HISTORY:
Jun 1968–Sep 1968, CBS Sat 7:30–8:30
May 1969–Sep 1969, CBS Thu 8:00–9:00
CAST:
The Prisoner (Number 6) .... Patrick McGoohan
The Butler .... Angelo Muscat

The Prisoner was one of the most original dramas seen on U.S. television. Perhaps it was too original, for it lasted for only 17 episodes. Filmed in England, it was the story of a government agent who abruptly resigned his position, only to be abducted and imprisoned in a strange, Kafkaesque community. His mind held top-secret information which somebody obviously wanted—but who? Or was he simply being tested? His captors were seldom seen, and when they were, their faces were always different. The village itself was a beautiful little hamlet, set on a hilly peninsula, ringed by mountains, forest, and the sea. But there was no leaving. Anyone who got close to the perimeter was set upon by strange, glowing spheres ("rovers") that floated overhead and kept an eye on everyone in the village.

The inhabitants were enigmas too. Some, like the hero (who was known only as "Number 6"), were prisoners, resisting the brainwashing attempts of their captors. Others had already been brainwashed of their secrets and were condemned to spend the rest of their days in the comfortable and peaceful, but eerie, village. Others might be spies. Which was which? Standing alone in a clearing was the Castle, used both as a hospital and interrogation center by the mysterious "Number 1" and his chief agent (played by different actors in different episodes, but invariably designated "Number 2").

Number 6, though he could not escape, outwitted his captors at every turn. Finally, in the last episode, they not only admitted defeat but made an astonishing offer: they wanted him to be their leader. Skeptical, he was at last led into the Castle to meet Number 1—and into a trap. With his ally, the silent Butler (the only other regular in the series), and two other rebels, he managed to escape as the Castle and its inhabitants and their mysterious world were destroyed.

The Prisoner was created and produced by its star, Patrick McGoohan, who also wrote some episodes. Although it was not explicitly stated, the series was widely believed to be a sequel to McGoohan's earlier show *Secret Agent*, in which he played a character named Drake. (Many *Prisoner* fans believe that the hero here was actually addressed in one episode as "Drake"; however, others argue that what was said is "Classes will resume during the morning . . . *break*"!) The picturesque "village" used in the filming was actually a resort on Cardigan Bay in North Wales, called Portmeirion—a favorite retreat of such writers as Bertrand Russell, George Bernard Shaw, Noel Coward . . . and Patrick McGoohan. The series was rerun during the summer of 1969.

PRIVATE BENJAMIN (*Situation Comedy*)

FIRST TELECAST: *April 6, 1981*
LAST TELECAST: *September 5, 1983*
BROADCAST HISTORY:
Apr 1981, CBS Mon 8:00–8:30
Oct 1981–Jan 1982, CBS Mon 8:00–8:30
Jan 1982–Mar 1982, CBS Mon 8:30–9:00
Apr 1982–Sep 1982, CBS Mon 8:00–8:30
Sep 1982–Jan 1983, CBS Mon 8:30–9:00
May 1983–Sep 1983, CBS Mon 8:30–9:00
CAST:
Pvt. Judy Benjamin .... Lorna Patterson
Capt. Doreen Lewis .... Eileen Brennan
Sgt. Major Lucien C. (Ted) Ross .... Hal Williams
Pvt. Carol Winter (1981–1982) .... Ann Ryerson
Pvt. Barbara Ann Glass (1981) .... Joan Roberts
Pvt. Rayleen White (1981) .... Joyce Little
Pvt. Maria Gianelli .... Lisa Raggio
Pvt. Luanne Hubble (1981–1982) .... Lucy Webb
Pvt. Harriet Dorsey (1981) .... Francesca Roberts

Pvt. Jackie Sims (1981–1983) . . . Damita Jo Freeman
Col. Lawrence Fielding (1982–1983)
. . . . Robert Mandan
Lt. Billy Dean (1982) . . . . Joel Brooks
Pvt. Stacy Kouchalakas (1982–1983)
. . . . Wendie Jo Sperber

Practically every major movie hit seems to spawn TV imitations—either directly or in disguise—and Goldie Hawn's box office smash *Private Benjamin* was no exception. Goldie wasn't available for the TV counterpart, so a little-known actress named Lorna Patterson (previously of *Working Stiffs* and *Goodtime Girls*) assumed the role of the spoiled New York socialite who decided to tackle the U.S.Army. Trading in her designer clothes for olive drab, and giving up haute cuisine for such delicacies as chipped beef on toast, Judy found it difficult to adapt to life in "Today's Modern Army." Yet here she was, at Fort Bradley, outside Biloxi, Mississippi, determined to make it through basic training. The unfortunate task of trying to mold Judy into a soldier fell to her frustrated company commander, Capt. Doreen Lewis. Fellow recruits included street-wise Maria Gianelli, who chose the army as an alternative to jail; Rayleen White, a bright, ambitious child of the Detroit ghettos; Barbara Ann Glass, a hayseed who often felt compelled to sing obscure country songs; and Carol Winter, a brownnosing, obnoxious brat. Sgt. Ted Ross was their nononsense drill instructor.

Col. Fielding, the base commander, an unctuous, publicity-hungry officer of marginal competence, became a regular early in 1982. Capt. Lewis was promoted to Fort Bradley's public affairs officer, and Judy ended up working for her. Amazingly, Pvt. Gianelli became an MP.

Eileen Brennan and Hal Williams re-created their movie roles for this series. Brennan was seriously hurt in October 1982 when she was struck by a car, and Polly Holliday was added to the show's cast as a temporary replacement. She only appeared in a single episode before *Private Benjamin* was canceled.

PRIVATE EYE (*Detective Drama*)
FIRST TELECAST: *September 13, 1987*
LAST TELECAST: *January 8, 1988*
BROADCAST HISTORY:
Sep 1987, NBC Sun 9:15–11:15
Sep 1987–Jan 1988, NBC Fri 10:00–11:00
CAST:
Jack Cleary . . . . Michael Woods
Johnny Betts . . . . Josh Brolin
Lt. Charlie Fontana . . . . Bill Sadler
Dottie Dworski . . . . Lisa Jane Persky

Having successfully launched one stylish crime series set in the '80s *(Miami Vice)*, and another in the '60s *(Crime Story)*, NBC tried the '50s with this rather violent show. There was lots of period atmosphere: chrome-laden cars, primeval rock 'n' roll, ducktail haircuts, and everybody dragging on cigarettes. Jack Cleary was a moody, scruffy ex-cop, wrongfully busted from the Los Angeles police force, who inherited his brother's detective agency upon the latter's violent demise. Although he was later cleared and offered his badge back, he declined, preferring the fast life of a private eye. Johnny Betts was a greasy-haired, leather-jacketed rock 'n' roller who helped out with such necessities of the trade as hot-wiring cars and squealing on the younger generation. Fontana was Cleary's former police partner and contact, and Dottie his gumcracking secretary.

PRIVATE SECRETARY (*Situation Comedy*)
FIRST TELECAST: *February 1, 1953*
LAST TELECAST: *September 10, 1957*
BROADCAST HISTORY:
Feb 1953–Jun 1953, CBS Sun 7:30–8:00
Jun 1953–Sep 1953, NBC Sat 10:30–11:00
Sep 1953–Jun 1954, CBS Sun 7:30–8:00
Jun 1954–Sep 1954, NBC Sat 10:30–11:00
Sep 1954–Mar 1957, CBS Sun 7:30–8:00
Apr 1957–Sep 1957, CBS Tue 8:30–9:00
CAST:
Susie McNamera . . . . Ann Sothern
Peter Sands . . . . Don Porter
Vi Praskins . . . . Ann Tyrrell
Cagey Calhoun . . . . Jesse White
Sylvia . . . . Joan Banks

Susie McNamera was private secretary to Peter Sands, a very successful New York talent agent. She was attractive, efficient, and conscientious, but she also had one serious failing. Susie couldn't tell when her responsibilities to her boss ended, and, as a result, kept getting mixed up in his personal life. Her efforts to help him with personal problems usually led to confusion and misunderstanding, despite their good intent. Vi Praskins, the agency's receptionist/switchboard operator, was Susie's friend, as was Sylvia, although the latter was often vying with Susie for the affections of a particularly attractive man. Peter's chief competition in the talent business was fast-talking, loudmouthed, cigar-smoking Cagey Calhoun.

The CBS episodes aired during the winter season were rerun by NBC during the summers of 1953 and 1954. During the winter seasons from the fall of 1954 through the spring of 1957, *Private Secretary* aired on alternate Sundays with *The Jack Benny Show.* While Benny was on vacation during the summers, *Private Secretary* played every week.

PRIZE PERFORMANCE (*Talent/Variety*)
FIRST TELECAST: *July 3, 1950*
LAST TELECAST: *September 12, 1950*
BROADCAST HISTORY:
Jul 1950–Aug 1950, CBS Mon 8:30–9:00
Aug 1950–Sep 1950, CBS Tue 10:00–10:30
HOST:
Cedric Adams
PANELISTS:
Arlene Francis
Peter Donald

Each week four professional child entertainers competed on this live talent show. Arlene Francis and Peter Donald were the judges, evaluating the talent and picking the week's winner. Every five weeks a grand prize of a $500 scholarship was awarded after a special competition among the weekly winners from the four preceding weeks.

PRO FOOTBALL HIGHLIGHTS, see *New York Giants Quarterback Huddle*

PROBE (*Mystery*)
FIRST TELECAST: *March 7, 1988*
LAST TELECAST: *June 25, 1988*
BROADCAST HISTORY:
Mar 1988, ABC Mon 9:00–11:00
Mar 1988–May 1988, ABC Thu 8:00–9:00
Jun 1988, ABC Sat 8:00–9:00
CAST:
Austin James .... Parker Stevenson
Mickey Castle .... Ashley Crow

Famed science-fiction writer Isaac Asimov cocreated this literate series. Austin James was a brilliant young scientist who operated out of a warehouse laboratory nicknamed the "batcave"; his secretary and helper was the ever-amazed Mickey. With cocky self-confidence, the ability to analyze physical clues in his high-tech lab, and deductive reasoning worthy of Sherlock Holmes, Austin managed to unravel crimes perpetrated by the world's most clever criminals.

The most distinctive aspect of this series was the plots, all based on scientific principles—a computer whose artificial intelligence program had run amok, a murder plot utilizing genetic engineering, a super-intelligent ape accused of murder (in an episode titled "Metamorphic Anthropoidic Prototype Over You"). The police simply shook their heads and arrested whomever Austin fingered.

The series was created by Asimov and former *Hill Street Blues* story editor Michael Wagner.

PROBLEM CHILD (*Cartoon*)
BROADCAST HISTORY:
USA Network
30 minutes
Produced: *1993–1994* (26 episodes)
Premiered: *October 31, 1993*
VOICES:
Junior Healy .... Ben Diskin
Little Ben Healy .... Mark Taylor
Big Ben Healy .... Jonathan Harris
Mr. Peabody .... Gilbert Gottfried
Yoji, Murph .... John Kassir
Cyndi .... E. G. Daily
Betsy, Ross .... Nancy Cartwright
Spencer (1994) .... Cree Summer
Miss Hill .... Iona Morris

Red-haired terror Junior Healy wreaked havoc on the adult world in this cartoon based on the theatrical film comedies *Problem Child* (1990) and *Problem Child 2* (1991). Little Ben was Junior's policeman-dad and Big Ben his scheming grandpa, while pals his own age included best friend Cyndi, big Murph, siblings Betsy and Ross, and Asian girl Spencer. Yoji was his strange pet, which looked like a cross between a dog and a warthog. Gilbert Gottfried reprised his movie role as the harried principal at Toe Valley Elementary School.

PRODUCER'S CHOICE (*Dramatic Anthology*)
FIRST TELECAST: *March 31, 1960*
LAST TELECAST: *September 15, 1960*
BROADCAST HISTORY:
Mar 1960–Sep 1960, NBC Thu 8:30–9:00

The filmed dramas shown on this summer series consisted of reruns of former episodes of *G.E. Theater, Lux Playhouse, Schlitz Playhouse,* and *Lux Video Theatre.*

PRODUCERS' SHOWCASE (*Anthology*)
FIRST TELECAST: *October 18, 1954*
LAST TELECAST: *May 27, 1957*
BROADCAST HISTORY:
Oct 1954–May 1957, NBC Mon 8:00–9:30

Live 90-minute productions were aired under this title every fourth Monday on NBC for three seasons. The productions were lavish and included many memorable performances by top stars. *Peter Pan* was presented on March 7, 1955, with Mary Martin and Cyril Ritchard in the lead roles. So popular was this family show that it was repeated live on the same series less than a year later (January 9, 1956), with Miss Martin and Ritchard repeating their roles. Humphrey Bogart and Lauren Bacall made their TV dramatic debuts in an adaptation of *The Petrified Forest,* which also starred Henry Fonda. Bogie's role was the same one that had propelled him to stardom on Broadway more than twenty years previously, and one that he had played on the silver screen as well.

Thornton Wilder's *Our Town* had been adapted for television on *Robert Montgomery Presents* in 1950, but the musical version of the play that aired on *Producers' Showcase* in 1955 is the best-remembered TV version of this classic. It starred Paul Newman and Eva Marie Saint, with Frank Sinatra (as the stage manager) singing most of the songs, including "Love and Marriage," which became a major hit record for him.

The range of material was vast, Margot Fonteyn and Michael Somes starred in two ballets, *Sleeping Beauty* and *Cinderella. Romeo and Juliet* was presented with Claire Bloom, Paul Rogers, and John Neville heading the cast. Fredric March, Claire Trevor, and Geraldine Fitzgerald starred in an adaptation of *Dodsworth.* The most unusual telecast in the series, because of its contrast to the general tone of the show, was probably the premiere of *Wide Wide World.* The conceptualization of dynamic NBC President Pat Weaver, *Wide Wide World* sought to take full advantage of the technical marvel of live television. Hosted by Dave Garroway, who would remain with it during its run as a late Sunday afternoon series during the latter half of the 1950s, this premiere telecast of *Wide Wide World* enabled the audience to see live entertainment from three countries—the United States, Canada, and Mexico—on the same show, the first inter-American telecast in the history of television.

PRODUCTION FOR FREEDOM (*Documentary*)
FIRST TELECAST: *June 22, 1952*
LAST TELECAST: *September 21, 1952*
BROADCAST HISTORY:
Jun 1952–Jul 1952, ABC Sun 9:30–10:00
Jul 1952–Sep 1952, ABC Sun 10:30–11:00

Documentary films about leading power companies and industries of America.

PROFESSIONAL FATHER (*Situation Comedy*)
FIRST TELECAST: *January 8, 1955*
LAST TELECAST: *July 2, 1955*
BROADCAST HISTORY:
Jan 1955–Jul 1955, CBS Sat 10:00–10:30
CAST:
Thomas Wilson, M.D. .... Steve Dunne
Helen Wilson .... Barbara Billingsley

Thomas (Twig) Wilson, Jr. .... Ted Marc
Kathryn (Kit) Wilson .... Beverly Washburn
Nurse Madge Allen .... Phyllis Coates
Nana .... Ann O'Neal

Tom Wilson was a highly successful child psychologist. At the office he spoke with the wisdom of Solomon as he resolved family problems that were causing aggravation and suffering to the many parents who sought his services. At home, however, it was a completely different story. All the good judgment and analytical skills that had made him so proficient at his profession deserted him when he tried to cope with his own family.

PROFILER (*Police Drama*)

FIRST TELECAST: *September 21, 1996*
LAST TELECAST: *May 6, 2000*
BROADCAST HISTORY:

Sep 1996–May 1997, NBC Sat 10:00–11:00
May 1997–Jul 1997, NBC Fri 10:00–11:00
Nov 1997–Nov 1999, NBC Sat 10:00–11:00 (OS)
Dec 1999–Feb 2000, NBC Sat 9:00–10:00
Mar 2000–May 2000, NBC Sat 10:00–11:00

CAST:

Dr. Samantha "Sam" Waters (1996–1999)
.... Ally Walker
Cloe Waters (age 7)(1996–1998) ...... Caitlin Wachs
Cloe Waters (1998–1999) .... Evan Rachel Wood
Angel Brown (1996–1999) .... Erica Gimpel
Agent Bailey Malone .... Robert Davi
Det. John Grant .... Julian McMahon
Det. Nathan Brubaker (1996–1997)
.... Michael Whaley
Grace Alvarez .... Roma Maffia
George Fraley .... Peter Frechette
Jack of All Trades/Albert Newquay (1996–1999)
.... Dennis Christopher
Agent Nick "Coop" Cooper (1996–1997)
.... A Martinez
Det. Marcus Payton (1997–1998)
.... Shiek Mahmoud-Bey
Frances Malone (17)(1997–1998)
.... Heather McComb
Sharon Lesher (a.k.a. "Jill")(1997–1998)
.... Traci Lords
Rachel Burke (1999–2000) .... Jamie Luner

Sam was a forensic psychologist with an unusual and somewhat frightening skill. Simply by visiting the scene of a murder she could visualize what happened, through the eyes of both the victim and the killer. Her "visions," seen in black and white, were the cornerstone of this rather gory series. Sam's skills were of great value to the F.B.I., but after she got too close to serial killer Jack—who became obsessed with her, and killed her husband—she retired to the country with her young daughter Chloe and sensitive best friend Angel. She was not left alone for long. Old friend and mentor Bailey lured her back to work with his Violent Crimes Task Force, based in Atlanta, which sent her to the scenes of gruesome murders across the country to help track down serial killers, cannibals, and other maniacs (*Profiler* seemed to delight in finding new and innovative ways to kill people—decapitating them, setting them on fire, skewering them, mutilating them in numerous ways). On the VCTF team were Grant, a handsome, driven agent; Brubaker, an altruistic former attorney; Alvarez, a forensic pathologist; Payton, who was skeptical of Sam's methods; and Fraley, the teams's computer hacker (the Internet being a favorite playground for homicidal maniacs these days). Frances was Malone's wayward teen daughter.

Unfortunately, Jack, who styled himself "Jack of All Trades," had not forgotten Sam either. Even as he continued his killing spree he stalked her, taunted her, and threatened those around her, including innocent Chloe. In 1997 he even recruited an accomplice, a sicko named Jill, whom he trained in serial murdering. In May 1998, Jill was killed, and the following fall the VCTF finally closed in on Jack—but it proved to be a trap he had set, and he escaped once again. Some effort was made to lighten the very dark tone of the series, however, with Sam dating from time to time. One such relationship was with Coop, an ATF explosives expert who helped the team in 1996–1997.

As the fourth season began Bailey was shot and Sam was kidnapped by Jack, who played mind games with her and in a last, God-like gesture, tried to turn her into a serial killer like himself. A new profiler, Rachel, was brought in to find her, and stayed after Sam was rescued and left the team. Rachel, a former instructor at Quantico, had special senses, too, but also a very brusque take-charge manner that alienated some of the team members (another agent to Rachel: "We were just wondering if there was anything you weren't sure about"). As the series ended Rachel faced her own crisis when her brother was killed, and it appeared that the VCTF might be shut down by Congress.

NBC was at first coy about who played the shadowy "Jack," identifying him only as "?." But fans identified the actor as Dennis Christopher. Although the series ended its regular run in May 2000, an additional original episode aired on July 1, 2000.

PROFILES FROM THE FRONT LINE
(*Documentary*)

FIRST TELECAST: *February 27, 2003*
LAST TELECAST: *March 13, 2003*
BROADCAST HISTORY:

Feb 2003–Mar 2003, ABC Thu 8:00–9:00

This documentary series profiled members of the U.S. Special Forces in action in Afghanistan. Though scheduled to run for six episodes, it was pulled from the schedule abruptly when a new war broke out in Iraq in March 2003.

PROFILES IN COURAGE (*Biography*)

FIRST TELECAST: *November 8, 1964*
LAST TELECAST: *May 9, 1965*
BROADCAST HISTORY:

Nov 1964–May 1965, NBC Sun 6:30–7:30

This program marked the first time that a President of the United States was directly involved in the production of a television dramatic series. John F. Kennedy's Pulitzer Prize-winning book *Profiles in Courage* was first adapted for TV in 1956, in a special based on the chapter concerning the senator who cast the deciding vote against the impeachment of President Andrew Johnson. Kennedy, then a U.S. Senator, served as a consultant for the broadcast. Eight years later, after Kennedy's death, this anthology series dramatized additional chapters from the book, as well as the stories of other Americans who had also displayed extraordinary personal courage. Prior to his death, President Kennedy himself had stipulated that more biographies be added to those in his book so that the scope of the series would be broader than politics. He had approved of all the additions and read all of the scripts to make sure that they conformed to the Kennedy definition of a "Profile in Courage."

PROFIT (*Drama*)
FIRST TELECAST: *April 8, 1996*
LAST TELECAST: *April 29, 1996*
BROADCAST HISTORY:
Apr 1996, FOX Mon 9:00–10:00
CAST:
Jim Profit .... Adrian Pasdar
Joanne Meltzer .... Lisa Zane
Charles Henry "Chaz" Gracen .... Keith Szarabajka
Pete Gracen .... Jack Gwaltney
Nora Gracen .... Allison Hossack
Gail Koner .... Lisa Darr
Bobbi Stakowski .... Lisa Blount
Jeffrey Sykes .... Sherman Augustus
Jack Walters .... Scott Paulin
Elizabeth Gracen Walters .... Jennifer Hetrick

Jim Profit was an unscrupulous, ambitious, totally amoral 28-year-old executive who would do anything to get ahead in this incredibly dark drama. He had just been promoted to junior V.P. of acquisitions at Gracen & Gracen, a large multinational conglomerate. His boss, Jack, was president of acquisitions, and Jim had blackmailed Gail, Jack's secretary, to get access to Jack's computer files. Among other things, he tried to seduce Nora, whose husband, Pete, was the younger brother of Gracen's CEO. Joanne, head of West Coast security, was the only one who suspected how duplicitous Jim was. She and Jack, a former lover, were always one step behind Jim, trying to nail him for his nefarious activities.

Bobbi, Jim's white-trash stepmother, blackmailed him into putting her up in a fancy penthouse apartment to keep her quiet about his bizarre background. When he was still a teenager named Jim Stakowski, he had handcuffed his abusive father to a bed and set him on fire. The father had kept Jim in a Gracen & Gracen packing box as a child, where Jim learned everything about the world by watching TV through an opening cut in its side—since he never went to school. Psychopathic, demented Jim still spent time at night curled up nude in a large box in his fancy apartment. To keep Jack and Joanne off his trail, Jim framed Jack for the murder of his predecessor, who had died of natural causes. After Jack went to jail Joanne convinced him to agree to a plea bargain in order to buy time to get evidence on Jim. Jim then made the mistake of hiring Jeffrey Sykes, a lawyer in Business Affairs. Sykes proved to be a real threat to Jim, much to Joanne's satisfaction. Jim's next move was to blackmail Joanne's psychiatrist into first planting hypnotic suggestions in her mind and then getting her committed to a psychiatric hospital.

And that was as far as it got. After four weeks of *Profit,* both Fox and the viewing audience, which tuned out in droves, had enough.

PROGRAM PLAYHOUSE (*Various*)
FIRST TELECAST: *June 22, 1949*
LAST TELECAST: *September 14, 1949*
BROADCAST HISTORY:
Jun 1949–Sep 1949, DUM Wed 9:00–9:30

This was a series of tryouts for potential series on the DuMont network. At least one of them, *The Hands of Murder,* later became reasonably successful as an independent series. Among the others were "Trouble, Inc." starring Earl Hammond as an amateur private eye, Ernest Truex in a live comedy called "The Timid Soul," and Roscoe Karns in his first TV effort (before *Rocky King*), playing comedy in "Roscoe Karns and Inky Poo." This family comedy had Karns being followed around by his conscience, dressed in a clown suit and called "Inky Poo."

PROJECT: ADVENTURE, syndicated title for *Adventure Theater*

PROJECT U.F.O. (*Drama*)
FIRST TELECAST: *February 19, 1978*
LAST TELECAST: *August 30, 1979*
BROADCAST HISTORY:
Feb 1978–Sep 1978, NBC Sun 8:00–9:00
Sep 1978–Jan 1979, NBC Thu 8:00–9:00
Jul 1979–Aug 1979, NBC Thu 8:00–9:00
CAST:
Maj. Jake Gatlin (1978) .... William Jordan
Capt. Ben Ryan .... Edward Winter
Staff Sgt. Harry Fitz .... Caskey Swaim
Libby Virdon .... Aldine King
EXECUTIVE PRODUCER:
Jack Webb
PRODUCER:
Col. William T. Coleman

Jack Webb applied his highly successful drama-documentary technique to the unlikely subject of unidentified flying objects (i.e., flying saucers) in this 1978 series. To prepare the series Webb spent eight months poring over the files of the real-life U.S. Air Force investigation into U.F.O.'s, Project Blue Book, which had been disbanded in 1969. Many of the sightings had turned out to be mistaken or simply fraudulent, but about 30 percent remained unexplained—and it was those that Webb dramatized in this series.

Regulars were Maj. Jake Gatlin and S/Sgt. Harry Fitz, Project Blue Book's stolid investigators, who traveled around the country interviewing people who had reported seeing a U.F.O. Some of the stories verged on character studies of these people, but there was always a certain amount of hardware seen, including vivid re-creations of the flying saucers and spacemen that the people had claimed seeing. Offscreen narration reinforced the series' appearance of authenticity.

Maj. Gatlin was replaced in the fall of 1978 by Capt. Ben Ryan as Project Blue Book's chief. Libby was Gatlin's, and later Ryan's, secretary. Colonel William T. Coleman, who had headed the real-life Project Blue Book, was producer of the series.

PROMISED LAND (*Adventure*)
FIRST TELECAST: *September 17, 1996*
LAST TELECAST: *July 22, 1999*

BROADCAST HISTORY:

Sep 1996–Jul 1997, CBS Tue 8:00–9:00
Aug 1997–Jul 1999, CBS Thu 8:00–9:00

CAST:

Russell Greene .... Gerald McRaney
Claire Greene .... Wendy Phillips
Hattie Greene .... Celeste Holm
Joshua Greene (age 15) .... Austin O'Brien
Dinah Greene (13) .... Sarah Schaub
Nathaniel Greene (9) .... Eddie Karr
**Erasmus Jones (1996–1998)* .... Ossie Davis
Lawrence "L.T." Taggert (1998–1999)
.... Eugene Byrd
Shamaya Taggert (1998–1999)
.... Kathryne Dora Brown
Principal Vincent Peters (1998–1999)
.... Michael Flynn
Bobbie Wagner (1998–1999) .... Tinsley Grimes
Margot Notewirthy (1998–1999)
.... Ashleigh Norman

*Occasional

In this wholesome, uplifting adventure series Russell Greene was on a mission. On the premiere, which aired as a special episode of *Touched By an Angel*, angels Tess and Monica asked the recently laid-off factory worker to "redefine what it meant to be a good neighbor and recapture the American dream." To do this he and his family traveled around the country in a beat-up trailer, helping people in need, looking for work, and learning from their experiences. Russell's family included his wife, Claire, who was licensed to home-school the kids while they were on the road; his mother, Hattie, who updated a hand-embroidered map to show all the places they had visited; his two children, Joshua and Dinah; and his inquisitive young nephew, Nathaniel, who had been abandoned by Russell's troubled brother, Tom (Richard Thomas). Erasmus was an old friend of the family who lived in Chicory Creek, the small town where Russell and Tom had grown up. The family periodically returned to Chicory Creek to celebrate holidays and rest. Occasionally they were assisted by Tess or other angels while they tried to help people overcome their problems or rekindle their lapsed faith.

Early in the second season Claire found out she was pregnant, but, tragically, their daughter Grace died unexpectedly soon after her birth in May 1998. That November, the family decided it was time to settle down and moved into a run-down house in a poor neighborhood in Denver. Russell convinced the owner to let them live there rent free in exchange for the renovations he made and Claire got a job as a guidance counselor at the local high school, where Josh and Dinah were students. Russell volunteered at the Ridley Center, a neighborhood teen center. Living next door were Shamaya and her brother, L.T., a former gang member having problems going straight. Bobbie, an unwed mother with an infant son, was Josh's girlfriend, and Margot was a friend of Dinah's. In the series' finale Hattie married an old friend of the family and Russell was leaving the Ridley Center to become a policeman.

PROS AND CONS, see *Gabriel's Fire*

PROTECTORS, THE (*Police Drama*)

FIRST TELECAST: *September 28, 1969*
LAST TELECAST: *September 6, 1970*

BROADCAST HISTORY:

Sep 1969–Sep 1970, NBC Sun 10:00–11:00

CAST:

Sam Danforth .... Leslie Nielsen
William Washburn .... Hari Rhodes

Deputy Police Chief Sam Danforth and District Attorney William Washburn were both committed to enforcing the law, but approached that enforcement from very different positions. Chief Danforth followed the rules that had always worked in the past, though they were being sorely tested in the changing moral climate of a modern big city. D.A. Washburn, a black who had used his political savvy to reach his current post, dealt with issues on a more human basis, as objectively and honestly as he could. Each of these men believed that his way of handling situations was right, and they were often in conflict with each other. Each, in his own way, was a dedicated public servant attempting to protect the society he served.

The Protectors was one of three rotating elements that comprised *The Bold Ones* during the 1969–1970 season. The other two were *The New Doctors* and *The Lawyers.*

PROTECTORS, THE (*Adventure*)

BROADCAST HISTORY:

Syndicated only
30 minutes
Produced: *1972–1973* (52 episodes)
Released: *Fall 1972*

CAST:

Harry Rule .... Robert Vaughn
Contessa di Contini .... Nyree Dawn Porter
Paul Buchet .... Tony Anholt

This stylish adventure series brought back *The Man From U.N.C.L.E.*'s Robert Vaughn in the not dissimilar role of Harry Rule, one of a three-person team of "protectors" fighting high-level crime in Europe. There was also a dash of *The Avengers* in the Contessa di Contini's high-fashion wardrobe, and of James Bond in the breakneck pace of the stories, which mostly involved murders, espionage, drug rings, and the like. Harry's fellow protectors were the Contessa, a British noblewoman and widow of a wealthy Italian, and Paul Buchet, a Frenchman.

Clipped dialogue, fancy cars, and picturesque European locales added to the *élan*, but star Robert Vaughn complained that it was all rather thin stuff and he would not do another show like it again. But then, he had said after *The Man From U.N.C.L.E.* that he would never do another TV series, period.

Filmed in Europe.

PROUD FAMILY, THE (*Cartoon*)

BROADCAST HISTORY:

Disney Channel
30 minutes
Original episodes: *2001–*
Premiered: *September 15, 2001*

VOICES:

Penny Proud (age 14) .... Kyla Pratt
Zoey .... Soleil Moon Frye
Dijonay Jones .... Karen Malina White
Sticky Webb .... Orlando Brown

LaCienega Boulevardez .... Alisa Reyes
Oscar Proud .... Tommy Davidson
Trudy Proud .... Paula Jai Parker
Suga Mama .... Jo Marie Payton
Bebe Proud, Cece Proud, Puff the Poodle
.... Tara Strong
The Gross Sisters .... Raquel Lee

THEME:
performed by Destiny's Child

The Proud Family was a cheerful little comedy about the teenage daughter of a middle-class black family and her friends. Penny was upbeat and friendly; her pals at school were shy Zoey, who sported orange hair and braces, supercool Sticky, with his laptop and gadgets, and party-loving Dijonay. LaCienega was her new neighbor, sometimes a friend and sometimes a rival, who came from a family whose members all seemed to be named after streets in Los Angeles (Felix Boulevardez, Sunset Boulevardez, etc.). At home there was her goofy dad, Oscar, owner of Proud's Snacks, and her stylish mom, Trudy, a veterinarian. Suga Mama was her rude and crude grandma, obsessed with her poodle Puff, and Bebe and Cece, the infant twins who crawled around and giggled.

Stories revolved around family and school, such as dealing with the bullying Gross Sisters. There were also periodic lessons on black subjects, such as Black History Month and Kwanzaa (Oscar's initial reaction: "Kwa-who?").

PROVIDENCE (*Serial Drama*)

FIRST TELECAST: *January 8, 1999*
LAST TELECAST: *December 20, 2002*
BROADCAST HISTORY:
Jan 1999–May 2002, NBC Fri 8:00–9:00
Sep 2002–Dec 2002, NBC Fri 8:00–9:00

CAST:
Dr. Sydney Hansen .... Melina Kanakaredes
**Syd (young)* .... Rosario Gru
Dr. Jim Hansen .... Mike Farrell
Lynda Hansen .... Concetta Tomei
Joanie Hansen .... Paula Cale
Robbie Hansen .... Seth Peterson
Dr. Helen Reynolds (1999) .... Leslie Silva
Heather Tupperman .... Dana Daurey
Nurse Elizabeth "Izzy" Nunez .... Samaria Graham
Lily Gallagher (1999) .... Nicki Lynn Aycox
Kyle Morgan (1999) .... Tom Verica
**Doug Boyce (1999–2000)* .... Tom Cavanagh
**Andi Paulsen (2000)* .... Angela Featherstone
Burt Ridley (2000–2001) .... Jon Hamm
Hannah Hansen (2001–2002) .... Tessa Allen
Tina Calcatera Hansen (2001–2002) .. Maria Pitillo
Pete Calcatera (2001) .... Mickey Toft
Pete Calcatera (2001–2002) .... Alex D. Linz
**Owen Frank (2002)* .... George Newbern
**Dr. David Baylor (2002)* .... Jeffrey Nordling

*Occasional

Sydney was a successful plastic surgeon in Hollywood, tending to the conceits and vanities of the stars, who decided to bag it and return to her dysfunctional family in Providence, Rhode Island, in this whimsical, serialized drama. The event that triggered the decision was the sudden death of her controlling mother, Lynda, at the wedding of her all-too-pregnant sister, Joanie. With mom gone, sensible Sydney became the center of the family, looking after distracted dad Jim, an amiable veterinarian who related better to animals than to people, mixed-up Joanie, who now had a baby girl, Hannah (and no husband—the wedding was called off) to look after; and younger brother Robbie, a wannabe hustler who was really a good kid at heart. Meddlesome mom wasn't really gone either, appearing to Sydney in dreams to lecture her from the hereafter. Seeking a little more meaning in life, Sydney took a position at a downtown clinic helping the poor, run by committed Dr. Reynolds, who became her friend and confidante.

Providence was a surprise mid-season hit for NBC, its mixture of drama, eccentricity, and gently comic moments reminiscent of such past successes as *Northern Exposure* and *Picket Fences*. Stories revolved mostly around the romantic entanglements of the Hansen family members and their family crises. Joanie opened a trendy pet food store, and in the 2000–2001 season became pregnant again, this time by fireman Burt, but had a miscarriage and they broke up. Robbie was stalked by crazy Andi, and in the season finale Jim was shot in the head, taking most of the next season to recover. Robbie began dating Tina, and they became increasingly serious. They were married in November 2001, and had a baby, Nick, in 2002. Tina also had a young son, Pete, by a previous marriage, and when she ran off due to postpartum depression Robbie found himself taking care of both children. The one-time hustler was becoming increasingly responsible. Syd's life was a succession of disappointing affairs, including one with Congressman Joe (Steven Eckholt). When she was sued for malpractice in early 2002, her attorney was handsome Owen, who became her latest love. In December 2002 series finale they were married in a big church wedding, and she agreed to move with him to Chicago where he had a job offer.

Others passing through stories included Jim's squeaky assistant Heather, troubled teen Lily, outspoken nurse Izzy and Syd's colleague Dr. David.

PRUDENTIAL FAMILY PLAYHOUSE, THE (*Dramatic Anthology*)

FIRST TELECAST: *October 10, 1950*
LAST TELECAST: *March 27, 1951*
BROADCAST HISTORY:
Oct 1950–Mar 1951, CBS Tue 8:00–9:00

This live hour-long dramatic presentation aired on alternate Tuesdays with *Sure as Fate*. The policy was to present top stars in outstanding dramas. Among the stars who appeared were Gertrude Lawrence, Ruth Chatterton, Helen Hayes, Walter Abel, Bert Lahr, and Grace Kelly.

PRUITTS OF SOUTHAMPTON, THE (*Situation Comedy*)

FIRST TELECAST: *September 6, 1966*
LAST TELECAST: *September 1, 1967*
BROADCAST HISTORY:
Sep 1966–Jan 1967, ABC Tue 9:00–9:30
Jan 1967–Sep 1967, ABC Fri 9:30–10:00

CAST:
Phyllis (Mrs. Poindexter) Pruitt .... Phyllis Diller
Uncle Ned Pruitt .... Reginald Gardiner
Stephanie Pruitt .... Pam Freeman
Regina Wentworth .... Gypsy Rose Lee
Maxwell .... Charles Lane

Sturgis .... Grady Sutton
Rudy Pruitt (1967) .... John Astin
Norman Krump (1967)................ Marty Ingels
Harvey (1967) .... Paul Lynde
Mr. Baldwin (1967)................ Richard Deacon
Vernon Bradley (1967) .... Billy DeWolfe

Phyllis Diller, whose trademarks were a fright wig and an uproarious cackle, was cast as the widowed matriarch of a down-on-their-luck Long Island society family in this frantic comedy. The Pruitts could live life to the hilt in their 60-room Southampton mansion, despite the fact that they were $10 million in debt to the government, so long as they kept the secret. Seems an unusually understanding I.R.S. would rather let them maintain the fiction that they were fabulously wealthy than risk a stock-market tumble with news of the Pruitts' bankruptcy. Phyllis spent most of her time on harebrained schemes to keep the family afloat, and keep the secret. Ned was her octogenarian uncle, Regina Wentworth her nosy neighbor and archrival, Sturgis the butler, and Stephanie her 22-year-old daughter.

In January 1967 the program title was changed to *The Phyllis Diller Show*, and the mansion became an elegant boardinghouse in an attempt to raise money to pay off the government. Neighborhood Mr. Fixit Norman Krump was a boarder, while Harvey was introduced as Phyllis' ne'er-do-well brother. Occasional roles were star boarder Vernon Bradley, an author; Mr. Baldwin of the I.R.S.; and assorted relatives played by such guest stars as Louis Nye.

Based on the novel *House Party* by Patrick Dennis.

PSI FACTOR: CHRONICLES OF THE PARANORMAL (*Supernatural*)

BROADCAST HISTORY:

Syndicated only
60 minutes
Produced: *1996–2000* (88 episodes)
Released: *September 1996*

HOST:

Dan Aykroyd

CAST:

Professor Connor Doyle (1996–1997) ... Paul Miller
Lindsay Donner............ Nancy Anne Sakovich
Peter Axon .... Barclay Hope
Professor Anton Hendricks .... Colin Fox
Dr. Curtis Rollins (1996–1997, 1999–2000)
.... Maurice Dean Wint
Ray Donahue (1996–1999)......... Peter MacNeill
Frank Elsinger (1996–1999).......... Nigel Bennett
Lennox Cooper ("L. Q.") (1996–1999).... Peter Blais
Dr. Claire Davison .... Soo Garay
**Dr. Natasha Constantine (1996–1999)*
.... Lisa LaCroix
**Sandra Miles (1996–1999)* .... Lindsay Collins
**Michael Kelly (1997–1999)*....... Michael Moriarty
Matt Prager (1997–1999) .... Matt Frewer
Mia Stone (1999–2000) .... Joanne Vannicola

*Occasional

A sort of cluttered, low-rent version of Fox's cult hit *The X-Files*, this series followed the work of a scientific team investigating alleged paranormal incidents—hauntings, poltergeists, UFO encounters, miracles, reincarnations, telepathy, and near death experiences. The original O.S.I.R. (Office of Scientific Investigation and Research) team consisted of case managers Doyle and Rollins; savvy, sensitive Donner, a psycho-biologist; fatherly Chief of Medicine Hendricks, a psychiatrist; and headstrong Chief Science Analyst Axon, a physicist/statistician. Also seen were O.S.I.R. Director of Operations Elsinger, Security Coordinator Donahue, zoologist Cooper, and pathologist Davison. Seen occasionally were anthropologist Constantine and investigator Miles. The team spent a good deal of time sitting around conference tables discussing cases; while in the field they used all sorts of high-tech equipment and maintained contact with their command center via microphones and miniature video cameras. Each episode consisted of two rather crudely produced stories, with deadpan host Aykroyd (who was one of the show's producers) introducing and summarizing each one.

In the fall of 1997 there were several changes. The number of cases per episode was reduced to one, there was less reliance on the high-tech equipment, and more emphasis was placed on story exposition and weird elements, including occasional monsters and mutants. The new leader of the team was sarcastic Prager, who had to deal with initial hostility from the others. Doyle had died in an accident, and Donner, who knew that Elsinger had been responsible, was convinced Elsinger was keeping too many secrets. Donner provided information to Kelly, an eccentric recluse who lived in an isolated cabin in Canada (and who was a friend of Prager's), and he gave the team bits of information on some episodes. Kelly was seemingly murdered in the spring of 1998, but turned up in the season finale to tell an irate Prager to forgive and protect Donner, who he had just found out was leaking information.

During the 1998–1999 season Anton, in an experiment, went through a portal to the "Other Side" in an attempt to find his wife and daughter who had disappeared twelve years earlier. Two months later he was recovered, along with his wife Catherine (Catherine N. Blythe), but their daughter, Nicole, died after coming through. A few months later he concluded that Catherine, who had not aged during her time on the other side, was not his wife but some otherworldly replacement, a potentially demonic lost soul. He froze her body cryogenically, and when she was revived, the lost soul was gone and her real self was back—*MAYBE*.

In the fall of 1999 Anton had taken over as director of operations and was mostly seen on a large TV monitor from their high-tech command center—although he occasionally did on-site casework. Added to the team was Mia, a newly minted Ph.D. in parapsychology from the University of Edinburgh. In October, while trying to help a strange man, Matt's genetic makeup was altered so that he couldn't live on Earth. This was the work of a geneticist preparing humans to colonize another planet. At the end of the episode Matt was transported, along with other volunteers, to the new planet. Some of the episodes during the 1999–2000 season were played for laughs—including one in which a sexy producer from The Alien Channel, a cable channel that wanted to do a TV series based on the O.S.I.R. case files, hounded Peter and, after hostile discourse, had a one-night stand with him in the O.S.I.R. mobile lab. In April Connor Doyle turned up, three years after his death in a plant explosion while on assignment with Peter. He said the Russians, who had been monitoring the plant, had pulled him out before the explosion and kept him prisoner for nearly three years in a research facility. In reality he was a human/alien hybrid created by a former O.S.I.R. scientist and was killed to save Lindsay at the end of the episode. In the series finale Mia, who had been the subject of a secret project to measure the impact of O.S.I.R. cases on the investigators, appeared to have died from sensory overload.

According to the producers, there was a real Office of Scientific Investigation and Research on which this series was based. *MAYBE.*

PSYCHIATRIST, THE (*Medical Drama*)

FIRST TELECAST: *February 3, 1971*
LAST TELECAST: *September 1, 1971*
BROADCAST HISTORY:
Feb 1971–Sep 1971, NBC Wed 10:00–11:00
CAST:
Dr. James Whitman.................. Roy Thinnes
Dr. Bernard Altman .... Luther Adler

Jim Whitman was a young psychiatrist working in association with a Los Angeles-based institute. His use of modern techniques to help emotionally troubled people, through personal and group therapy, were explored in this series. His older colleague, Dr. Bernard Altman, worked with Jim in evaluating procedures and the progress of various patients. *The Psychiatrist* was one of the four elements that were all aired under the overall title *Four in One.*

PUBLIC DEFENDER, THE (*Legal Drama*)

FIRST TELECAST: *March 11, 1954*
LAST TELECAST: *June 23, 1955*
BROADCAST HISTORY:
Mar 1954–Jul 1954, CBS Thu 10:00–10:30
Jul 1954–Sep 1954, CBS Mon 9:00–9:30
Sep 1954–Jun 1955, CBS Thu 10:00–10:30
CAST:
Bart Matthews .... Reed Hadley

Actor Reed Hadley had most recently been seen in the role of a police officer who tracked down confidence men in *Racket Squad.* Here, he portrayed another side of the law—an attorney defending destitute individuals who had been charged with crimes and could not afford their own legal counsel. As a public defender he tried to help these people prove their innocence. The cases adapted for this series were all based on files from public-defender agencies throughout the country and a feature of each episode was a salute to a real public defender who had made some outstanding effort to exonerate a falsely accused person.

PUBLIC EYE WITH BRYANT GUMBEL (*Newsmagazine*)

FIRST TELECAST: *October 1, 1997*
LAST TELECAST: *September 16, 1998*
BROADCAST HISTORY:
Oct 1997–Jan 1998, CBS Wed 9:00–10:00
Mar 1998–Apr 1998, CBS Tue 9:00–10:00
Apr 1998–Sep 1998, CBS Wed 9:00–10:00
ANCHOR:
Bryant Gumbel
CORRESPONDENTS:
Bernard Goldberg
Alison Stewart
Peter Van Sant
Maggie Cooper
Derek McGinty
Rita Braver
Steve Hartman
Richard Schlesinger
Kristin Jeannette-Meyers

Following his departure as cohost of NBC's long-running *Today,* Bryant Gumbel was sought after by all of the broadcast networks. CBS, which won the bidding war, saw him as the centerpiece for a new magazine series, and *Public Eye* was the result. The show was a mix of traditional CBS investigative pieces and live interviews by Gumbel that, it was hoped, would add spontaneity and energy to the standard magazine format. Unfortunately, it came across as a rather generic newsmagazine show. The first episode featured a report on a horrible famine in North Korea, and subsequent stories about the problem of dogs attacking people, restaurant kitchens that failed to maintain sanitary conditions, and immigrant women forced into prostitution to make enough money to survive. Many CBS correspondents provided segments for the show, but the nine listed above were seen most regularly.

Gumbel's interviews, some in the studio and others with the subjects at home or at work—in the style of the 1950s CBS series *Person to Person*—included singer Celine Dion, actor Will Smith, singer-composer Paul Simon, Olympic skater Tara Lipinski, and, in one episode, Imelda Marcos, Defense Secretary William Cohen, and Hugh Hefner.

PUBLIC LIFE OF CLIFF NORTON, THE (*Comedy*)

FIRST TELECAST: *January 7, 1952*
LAST TELECAST: *February 29, 1952*
BROADCAST HISTORY:
Jan 1952–Feb 1952, NBC Mon–Fri 11:10–11:15
REGULAR:
Cliff Norton

Veteran comic Cliff Norton appeared five times per week, giving short, humorous talks about the problems of everyday life.

PUBLIC MORALS (*Situation Comedy*)

FIRST TELECAST: *October 30, 1996*
LAST TELECAST: *October 30, 1996*
BROADCAST HISTORY:
Oct 1996, CBS Wed 9:30–10:00
CAST:
Det. Ken Schuler .... Donal Logue
Det. Richie Biondi.................. Larry Romano
Det. Mickey Crawford .... Justin Louis
Off. Darnell "Shag" Ruggs......... Joseph Latimore
Det. Corinne O'Boyle .... Julianne Christie
Sgt. Val Vandergoodt............ Jana Marie Hupp
Lt. Neil Fogerty .... Peter Gerety
John Irvin .... Bill Brochtrup

A comedy about a vice squad unit of the N.Y.P.D.'s Public Morals Division, the cops who kept the hookers under control and underage drinkers from hanging out in bars. Schuler was a barely tolerable cop who favored loud Hawaiian shirts and whose only saving grace was his culinary skill; Biondi was a super-dumb young Italian ("Duh!") from a family full of career criminals. Crawford, handsome but obnoxious, had recently been added to the unit by headquarters to "beef" up the division, and Ruggs was the unbelievably square, butt-kissing rookie. The two women in the unit were sexy, streetwise O'Boyle and tough, ambitious Vandergoodt, who held their own while kidding the guys. They all reported to Lt. Fogerty, a bumbling career cop whose job was to hold the "sleaze patrol" together. Irvin was the very gay administrative assistant recently transferred to the department from uptown.

Producer Steven Bochco's track record with serious cop shows was impressive—*Hill Street Blues* and *N.Y.P.D. Blue*, for example—but comedy was another matter, and trying to make light of prostitution, and all those stereotypes, didn't work. The critics brutalized *Public Morals* from the day it was announced on the CBS schedule (at which time it was billed, tastefully, as "the pussy patrol"). When it finally aired, it was also a commercial disaster. Uncomfortable with the raunchy language and disappointed with minuscule ratings, CBS dropped the show after a single telecast. Thirteen episodes were reportedly filmed; will they ever be seen?

PUBLIC PROSECUTOR, see *Crawford Mystery Theatre*

PULITZER PRIZE PLAYHOUSE (*Dramatic Anthology*)

FIRST TELECAST: *October 6, 1950*
LAST TELECAST: *June 4, 1952*
BROADCAST HISTORY:
Oct 1950–Jun 1951, ABC Fri 9:00–10:00
Dec 1951–Jun 1952, ABC Wed 10:00–10:30

This was one of ABC's most prestigious programming efforts in the early 1950s, presenting top-quality dramas written or adapted for television and starring first-rate talent. Among those appearing were Helen Hayes in her TV debut, Melvyn Douglas, Raymond Massey, Edmond O'Brien, Peggy Wood, and Mildred Natwick. The first telecast was an adaptation of the Moss Hart-George S. Kaufman classic *You Can't Take It with You*. Equally famous writers (many of them Pulitzer Prize winners) such as Maxwell Anderson, Thornton Wilder, Marc Connelly, Edna Ferber, and James A. Michener were later represented. There were also original TV plays by Budd Schulberg and Lawrence Hazard, among others.

During its second season *Pulitzer Prize Playhouse* alternated with *Celanese Theatre* on Wednesday nights.

PULSE, THE (*Newsmagazine*)

FIRST TELECAST: *July 11, 2002*
LAST TELECAST:
BROADCAST HISTORY:
Jul 2002–Sep 2002, FOX Thu 9:00–10:00
Jan 2003– , FOX Thu 9:00–10:00

REGULARS:
Shepard Smith
Bill O'Reilly
Geraldo Rivera (2002)
Linda Vester (2002)
Catherine Herridge (2002)
Laurie Dhue (2002)
Juliet Huddy (2003–)

Fox News Channel anchorman Shepard Smith hosted this loud, tabloidish magazine series. Each episode included three or four longer segments and a collection of short stories titled the Pulse 8—silly and/or strange video clips from Fox News. Correspondents included Catherine Herridge, Geraldo Rivera, who focused on stories relating to terrorism, Laurie Dhue and Linda Vester. Bill O'Reilly did double duty as the resident debater ("Factor This") and the show's complainer—telling viewers what was going on that ticked him off ("Who's Annoying Me Now").

When *The Pulse* returned in January, O'Reilly was the only returning correspondent. One new addition was a weekly piece on *American Idol*, the network's hit talent show, hosted by Juliet Huddy.

PUNK'D (*Humor*)

BROADCAST HISTORY:
MTV
30 minutes
Original episodes: *2003–*
Premiered: *March 17, 2003*

HOST:
Ashton Kutcher

"FIELD AGENTS":
Al Shearer
Dax Shepard

In this raucous reality show Hollywood stars "punk'd" (staged pranks on) other stars, and sometimes civilians, while lanky young host Ashton Kutcher and his confederates watched from a high-tech control van. For example, in one routine Sharon Osbourne brought her punkish daughter Kelly to some wacko "image consultants" for a makeover (Kelly cursed and resisted until she found out it was all a gag); in another, a nebbishy locksmith was lured into the middle of a staged, but very real-looking, robbery. Most of the stars appearing were young MTV-generation types, or those who were older but hip, such as Christina Aguilera, Frankie Muniz, Justin Timberlake, Kid Rock, Oscar de la Hoya, Pamela Anderson, Pierce Brosnan, Seth Green, Tom Arnold and Tori Amos.

PUNKY BREWSTER (*Situation Comedy*)

FIRST TELECAST: *September 16, 1984*
LAST TELECAST: *September 7, 1986*
BROADCAST HISTORY:
Sep 1984–May 1985, NBC Sun 7:30–8:00
Jun 1985–Apr 1986, NBC Sun 7:00–7:30
May 1986–Sep 1986, NBC Sun 7:30–8:00
(In first-run syndication during 1988 and 1989)

CAST:
Penelope "Punky" Brewster ...... Soleil Moon Frye
Henry Warnimont .... George Gaynes
Eddie Malvin (1984) .... Eddie Deezen
Cherie Johnson .... Cherie Johnson
Mrs. Betty Johnson .... Susie Garrett
Margaux Kramer .... Ami Foster
**Mrs. Kramer (1984–1985)* .... Loyita Chapel
Allen Anderson .... Casey Ellison
**Mrs. Morton (1984–1985)* .... Dody Goodman
Mike Fulton (1985–1986) .... T. K. Carter

*Occasional

Punky was a cute seven-year-old Chicago girl with a lot of problems, but a sunny outlook on life. Abandoned by her parents, spunky Punky and her adorable puppy set up housekeeping in an empty apartment, where they were soon discovered by the building manager, Henry Warnimont, a dour old bachelor. He was about to turn them over to the authorities when—well, those big eyes, that winning smile, that loving heart, who could resist? Somehow he persuaded the skeptical authorities to let Punky stay with him for a while, and the little girl began to bring sunshine into Henry's world. Stories revolved around their adjustments to each other, and Henry's professional work as a photographer. Eddie was the kooky building maintenance man, Cherie was Punky's playmate, Margaux the stuck-up classmate at school, Allen another of Punky's friends, and Mrs. Morton her teacher. Punky got a new teacher, Mike Fulton, for the 1985–1986 season.

According to reports published when this series was announced, there was a real Punky Brewster, though not quite as depicted in the show. NBC programming head Brandon Tartikoff, while a youth, had had a crush on a tomboyish older girl by that name. Years later he nicknamed his own first child Punky. He also thought it would make a great name for a TV series, so when this show went into development, Punky it was—after NBC's lawyers tracked down the real Punky and got permission to use her name (she was married to a lawyer in Connecticut, received a royalty for the use of her name, and even appeared once in a cameo role as one of the teachers at Punky's school). And the puppy who followed Punky around on the show? It's name was "Brandon."

NBC aired an animated version of this series, titled *It's Punky Brewster*, on Saturday mornings from September 1985–September 1987 and from October 1988–September 1989.

PUREX SUMMER SPECIALS (*Anthology*)
FIRST TELECAST: *July 11, 1961*
LAST TELECAST: *September 12, 1963*
BROADCAST HISTORY:
Jul 1961–Sep 1961, NBC Tue 10:00–11:00
Jul 1962–Sep 1962, NBC Fri 9:30–10:30
Jun 1963–Sep 1963, NBC Thu 10:00–11:00

For three summers, NBC aired a series comprised of reruns of special programs that the Purex Corporation had originally sponsored. During 1961 and 1962 approximately half of the shows were reruns of various *Purex Special for Women* telecasts, and the remainder were profiles of famous people, some historical and some current show-business personalities. In 1963 the majority of the shows were profiles, and aired under the general title *The World of. . . .*

PURSUIT (*Dramatic Anthology*)
FIRST TELECAST: *October 22, 1958*
LAST TELECAST: *January 14, 1959*
BROADCAST HISTORY:
Oct 1958–Jan 1959, CBS Wed 8:00–9:00

The plays that were aired on this live dramatic series had one element in common—they all told in some way the story of a man, or group, being pursued. The circumstances varied from show to show, but the element of the hunter and the hunted was present in each episode. The casting was strong and several of the authors were well known. A Daphne duMaurier story, "Kiss Me Again, Stranger," featured Jeffrey Hunter, Margaret O'Brien, and Mort Sahl; a Ross Macdonald thriller entitled "Epitaph for a Golden Girl" starred Michael Rennie, Rick Jason, Rip Torn, Sally Forrest, and Joan Bennett; and Rod Serling provided "The Last Night of August" with Franchot Tone, Dennis Hopper, and Cameron Mitchell.

PURSUIT OF HAPPINESS (*Situation Comedy*)
FIRST TELECAST: *October 30, 1987*
LAST TELECAST: *January 8, 1988*
BROADCAST HISTORY:
Oct 1987–Jan 1988, ABC Fri 9:30–10:00
CAST:
Asst. Prof. David Hanley .... Paul Provenza
Prof. Roland G. Duncan .... Brian Keith
Sara Duncan .... Judie Aronson
Margaret Callahan .... Wendel Meldrum
Vernon Morris.................. Wesley Thompson
Prof. Stevens .... John Petlock
Earvin "Magic" Johnson.................. Himself
Thomas Jefferson .... Kevin Scannell
Mrs. Lopez .... Wanda de Jesus

A short-lived comedy about an idealistic young history teacher who, after years of wandering around the country searching for "meaning," decided to see if he could find it teaching history at a small Philadelphia college. David was especially anxious to meet his idol, noted historian and author Roland G. Duncan. Duncan was not what he expected, gruff and very practical ("They can't fire *me*—I've got tenure!") but he nevertheless became the older man's protégé. Other eccentrics inhabiting David's new world were Margaret, a brilliant Egyptian studies scholar unable to cope with everyday life; Duncan's sexy, not-too-bright teenage daughter, Sara; and David's college buddy Vernon. David had two other role models—the intellectual in him idolized President Thomas Jefferson and the sports lover idolized Los Angeles Laker basketball star Magic Johnson. Whenever he had a problem, both of his idols would "come to life" to offer David advice. Since their approaches were very different, Thomas and Magic would often disagree about which course of action he should take.

PURSUIT OF HAPPINESS, THE (*Situation Comedy*)
FIRST TELECAST: *September 19, 1995*
LAST TELECAST: *November 14, 1995*
BROADCAST HISTORY:
Sep 1995–Nov 1995, NBC Tue 9:30–10:00
CAST:
Steve Rutledge .... Tom Amandes
Macenzie "Mac" Rutledge .... Melinda McGraw
Larry................................ Larry Miller
Alex Chosek......................... Brad Garrett
Jean Mathias .... Meredith Scott Lynn
Eleanor "Gram" Rutledge .... Maxine Stuart

Despite its upbeat title, the producers said this sitcom was really about "the little roadblocks that get between us and nirvana." It must have seemed that way to Steve, an idealistic lawyer in his thirties who was forced to accept sleazy clients to help make ends meet. His career-obsessed wife Mac had lost her big advertising agency job and now hung around the house; his trouble-prone brother

Larry also lived with them, causing disasters wherever he went; and Grandmother was in a nursing home. At the office, Alex was his big, pushy, gay partner, who had no scruples at all; and Jean their surly secretary.

There were, of course, compensations. Mac wanted to have sex with him whenever she had bad news, and as for Alex's sexual orientation, "Who cares—people hate lawyers a lot more than they hate gays."

PUSH (*Drama*)

FIRST TELECAST: *April 6, 1998*
LAST TELECAST: *April 13, 1998*
BROADCAST HISTORY:
Apr 1998, ABC Mon 8:00–9:00
CAST:
Victor Yates........................... Adam Trese
Nikki Lang........................... Jaime Pressly
Cara Bradford........................ Laurie Fortier
Tyler Mifflin.......................... Scott Gurney
Dempsey Easton........................ Jason Behr
Gwen Sheridan................ Audrey Wasilewski
Scott Trysfan.......................... Eddie Mills
Erin Galway................... Maureen Flannigan
Milo Reynolds...................... Jacobi Wynne

The joy of victory, the agony of defeat—and of sex, treachery, lust, seduction, jealousy, and low ratings—were all part of this sudsy, short-lived drama about handsome young athletes training for the 2000 Olympics at fictional Cal Southern University, in California. Victor was the earnest young gymnast coach, whose assistant coach, and former girlfriend, Nikki, was plotting against him. Among the other pretty faces were Cara, a flirty gymnast and aspiring writer; Tyler, a freshman from the Midwest; Dempsey, a track star; Gwen, a redhead who dealt drugs; Scott, a gay party-guy who might be HIV-positive; Erin, a swimmer; and Milo, a gifted black freshman sprinter whom Dempsey was out to destroy.

No one had time to destroy anyone, however, as *Push* was pulled from the schedule after only two low-rated telecasts. ABC planned to restart the series during the summer, but after a single episode on August 6, 1998, it was canceled for good.

PUSH, NEVADA (*Drama*)

FIRST TELECAST: *September 17, 2002*
LAST TELECAST: *October 24, 2002*
BROADCAST HISTORY:
Sep 2002, ABC Tue 9:00–10:00
Sep 2002–Oct 2002, ABC Thu 9:00–10:00
CAST:
Agent Jim Prufrock.................... Derek Cecil
Mary............................ Scarlett Chorvat
Grace............................ Melora Walters
Martha.......................... Conchata Ferrell
Sheriff Gaines.................. Eric Allan Kramer
Deputy Dawn............................ Liz Vassey
Sloman........................ Raymond J. Barry

Push, Nevada was one of the most hyped, and certainly most unusual, new series of the 2002–2003 season, co-created by actor-writer Ben Affleck and bearing more than a passing resemblance to cult favorite *Twin Peaks*. This time the small-town-where-everything-was-strange was in the middle of the Nevada desert. Mousy, straitlaced Internal Revenue Service agent Jim Prufrock was drawn to Push after he received a mysterious fax indicating a possible tax-evasion scheme at the town's Versailles Casino, which paid out unusually large jackpots. The casino manager was killed shortly after Jim met him, and everyone warned Jim to get out of town before the same happened to him, but that, of course, only made him more determined. At Sloman's slow-dance bar he met Mary, a dancer who turned out to be the daughter of the owner, and who gave him enigmatic clues (the town's mysteries, she said, were "like all the best secrets, not quick in the telling"). Other characters passing in and out of the action (there was a very large unbilled cast) included Grace, Jim's loyal secretary back at the office with whom he talked by phone and laptop computer; Martha, the fat, sassy operator of the boardinghouse where he stayed; Gaines, the amiable sheriff who seemed to declare all murders "suicides," and Dawn, his unassuming deputy, who proved an unexpected ally.

While Jim investigated, driving around the area in his vintage Rambler, he was constantly monitored by shadowy men in a hidden, high-tech surveillance center. He learned that the casino, and indeed the town, was owned by Watermark LLC, a mysterious organization that had revived the local economy in 1985 and had some type of connection with state and possibly federal agencies. His room was bugged, and he was set up on a murder charge by Sheriff Gaines—but who was behind it all?

To make the series "interactive" ABC offered a $1-million-plus prize to the first person who could decipher the numerous clues in the stories and unravel the mystery. Due to low ratings the series was canceled prematurely, so ABC crammed all of the clues into the last of the seven episodes that did air. Within two minutes of the final clue being revealed, a 24-year-old viewer from New Jersey named Mark Nakamoto called a special number and won $1,045,000 (he wasn't the only one watching: ten thousand more called the number during the next 24 hours, but were too late).

PUTTIN' ON THE HITS (*Music/Competition*)

BROADCAST HISTORY:
Syndicated only
30 minutes
Produced: *1985–1988* (104 episodes)
Released: *Fall 1985*
HOST:
Allen Fawcett
EXECUTIVE PRODUCERS:
Dick Clark
Chris Bearde

Contestants on this series competed by doing elaborate pantomimes to songs by professional singers. There were celebrity judges to score each contestant on three factors—originality, appearance, and lip-sync. Weekly first-round winners won $1,000 and during the season-long competition could advance through several rounds to win the annual grand prize of $25,000.

Q.E.D. (*Quiz/Panel*)
FIRST TELECAST: *April 3, 1951*
LAST TELECAST: *October 9, 1951*
BROADCAST HISTORY:
Apr 1951–Sep 1951, ABC Tue 9:00–9:30
Oct 1951, ABC Tue 10:00–10:30
MODERATOR:
Doug Browning
Fred Uttal
REGULAR PANELISTS:
Hy Brown
Nina Foch
Harold Hoffman

This show presented its panel with a short mystery story, sketch, or playlet, submitted by a viewer, which stopped just before the solution to the mystery was revealed. The panel was then supposed to guess the outcome, based on the clues within the story and a limited number of questions which could be answered with a yes or no. *Q.E.D.* stands for *quod erat demonstrandum* in Latin, or, in English, "which was to be proved."

Doug Browning was moderator for the first telecast only, replaced on April 10 by Fred Uttal. The program was also known as *Mystery File.*

Q.E.D. (*Adventure*)
FIRST TELECAST: *March 23, 1982*
LAST TELECAST: *April 27, 1982*
BROADCAST HISTORY:
Mar 1982–Apr 1982, CBS Tue 8:00–9:00
CAST:
Quentin E. Deverill .... Sam Waterston
Phipps .... George Innes
Charlie Andrews .... A. C. Weary
Dr. Stefan Kilkiss .... Julian Glover
Jenny Martin .... Caroline Langrishe

Q.E.D. resembled the hit 1960s series *The Wild, Wild West*, only it was set in England in 1912. Like the earlier program, it was an adventure filled with scientific marvels which seemed far ahead of their time, and an evil genius—Dr. Kilkiss—bent on world domination. Fighting Kilkiss and other international villains was a brilliant American professor named Quentin E. Deverill, whose ability to construct incredible scientific gadgets was exceeded only by his analytical skills as an amateur sleuth. Helping out were: Phipps, his Cockney chauffeur and butler; Jenny, his beautiful and resourceful secretary; and a snooping American reporter named Charlie.

The series was produced in England by John Hawkesworth, who was also responsible for the acclaimed PBS series *Upstairs, Downstairs* and *The Duchess of Duke Street.*

QVC (Network) (*Home Shopping Cable Network*)
LAUNCHED:
November 1986
SUBSCRIBERS (JAN. 2003):
84.9 million (80% U.S.)

One of two major shop-at-home channels, displaying merchandise and urging viewers to order it by phone (the other: Home Shopping Network). Between them, they have probably sold more junk jewelry than Kmart and all its kin.

A subsidiary channel, Q2, was launched in September 1994.

QUADRANGLE, THE see *Campus Corner*

QUANTUM LEAP (*Science Fiction*)
FIRST TELECAST: *March 26, 1989*
LAST TELECAST: *August 15, 1993*
BROADCAST HISTORY:
Mar 1989, NBC Sun 9:00–11:00
Mar 1989–Apr 1989, NBC Fri 9:00–10:00
May 1989, NBC Wed 10:00–11:00
Sep 1989–Aug 1990, NBC Wed 10:00–11:00
Aug 1990–Jan 1991, NBC Fri 8:00–9:00
Mar 1991–Jul 1992, NBC Wed 10:00–11:00
Jun 1992–Jul 1992, NBC Tue 9:00–10:00
Aug 1992–Apr 1993, NBC Tue 8:00–9:00
Aug 1993, NBC Sun 7:00–8:00
CAST:
Dr. Sam Beckett .... Scott Bakula
Al Calavicci ("The Observer") ...... Dean Stockwell

What would it be like to be inside someone else's body? Dr. Sam Beckett got the chance to find out in this unusual series that captured viewers' imaginations by focusing on people, rather than on the sci-fi elements of time travel.

Beckett was a physicist sent bouncing around in time as the result of a flawed experiment. His "leaps" into strangers' bodies, in other times, followed certain rules, however. First, he traveled only within his own lifespan, roughly from the mid 1950s to the 1980s. Second, he could change events only to a degree. The course of ordinary people's lives could be altered, hopefully for the better, but major historical events, such as the assassination of President Kennedy, could not. Third, to the viewer he appeared as himself no matter whose body he occupied, but to those around him he was that person.

The people into whom he "leapt" were certainly a diverse lot—a gorgeous secretary subjected to sexual harassment, an elderly black man in the pre-civil rights South, a blind concert pianist, a nerdy teenage hot rodder, even a pregnant young girl about to give birth. Knowing nothing about these people until he "arrived," Sam often had to improvise. Finding himself suddenly in the body of a trapeze artist about to execute his most difficult stunt was challenging indeed!

Sam was accompanied in his leaps by Al, a holographic observer, who coached him (for better or worse), kibitzed, and used a small portable device linked to a computer named Ziggy to determine the odds and reasons for Sam's current situation. Al, who was actually a U.S. navy admiral (sometimes he appeared in a sparkling dress white uniform), could be seen only by Sam—and by animals and small children.

Social issues were tackled within this odd format, including racism, prejudice against the mentally handicapped, Vietnam, and the problems of single parents. Most of the stories, though, played on the theme of seeing life through someone else's eyes. As for Sam, as each leap took place, it was "Oh, boy!"

Quantum Leap ended its regular run on April 20, 1993 (with Sam leaping into the body of a young, unknown Elvis Presley!), but the final original episode aired as a special on the following May 5. In it Sam leapt into his own body in a 1953 mining town tavern where a mysterious bartender seemed to hold the answers about his strange fate. Other leapers appeared, as did ghostly echoes of Sam's later life and the Quantum Leap project itself. Desperately homesick, Sam pleaded for the answer he had so long sought: How could he leap home? The cryptic reply was that he had had the ability all along; leaping into others' lives was his own choice. When it came to the real decision, however, Sam could not do it. Instead he leaped ahead to the Vietnam War, at the moment when Al's wife was about to leave him, and saved her from ruining his best friend's life. At the end viewers were told that Sam never returned home.

NBC ran scattered repeats of the series between May and August 1993.

QUARK (*Situation Comedy*)

FIRST TELECAST: *February 24, 1978*

LAST TELECAST: *April 14, 1978*

BROADCAST HISTORY:

Feb 1978–Apr 1978, NBC Fri 8:00–8:30

CAST:

Adam Quark .... Richard Benjamin
Gene/Jean .... Tim Thomerson
Ficus .... Richard Kelton
Betty I .... Tricia Barnstable
Betty II .... Cyb Barnstable
Andy the Robot .... Bobby Porter
Otto Palindrome .... Conrad Janis
The Head .... Alan Caillou

Quark was a parody on space adventure epics, which were highly popular at this time due to the success of the movie *Star Wars.* The setting was the year A.D. 2222 on the giant space station Perma One, where Adam Quark had been given command of a vital, though not necessarily romantic, mission: to clean up the garbage in outer space. His assignments came from The Head, a disembodied head who governed the universe, and who was seen only on a TV screen; and from Otto Palindrome, the fussy chief architect of Perma One. Quark's crew included first officer Gene/Jean, a transmute with both male and female characteristics; science officer Ficus, a kind of humanoid vegetable; copilots Betty I and Betty II, two sexy and identical girls, one of whom was a clone of the other (nobody knew which was which); and Andy the Robot, a walking junkpile.

Though Quark was supposed to stick to his sanitation patrols, he often met adventure with such colorful space denizens as the evil High Gorgon, Zoltar the Magnificent, and Zorgon the Malevolent. A strange mixture of sex, intellectual jokes, and basic slapstick comedy, *Quark* failed to attract a substantial audience and was soon canceled.

QUEEN AND I, THE (*Situation Comedy*)

FIRST TELECAST: *January 16, 1969*

LAST TELECAST: *May 1, 1969*

BROADCAST HISTORY:

Jan 1969–May 1969, CBS Thu 7:30–8:00

CAST:

Charles Duffy .... Larry Storch
Oliver Nelson .... Billy DeWolfe
Becker .... Carl Ballantine
Barney .... Pat Morita
Wilma Winslow .... Barbara Stuart
Max Kowalski .... Dave Morick
Capt. Washburn .... Liam Dunn
Ozzie .... Dave Willock

The *Amsterdam Queen* was an aging ocean liner whose owners had decided to retire and sell her for scrap. Fighting the inevitable was the ship's purser, Charles Duffy, who was not above trying anything to save the boat and his job. The various ways in which he had been able to supplement his income with the ship—making it available for weddings and bar mitzvahs when it was in port, shaming the passengers into giving bigger tips, etc.—made him particularly desperate to save it. Most of the crew members were enthusiastic about his efforts, with the exception of First Mate Nelson, who had never been able to catch Charlie at any of his shenanigans but who would be happy to see him out of a job.

QUEEN OF SWORDS (*Adventure*)

BROADCAST HISTORY:

Syndicated only
60 minutes
Produced: *2000–2001* (22 episodes)
Released: *October 2000*

CAST:

Maria Teresa "Tessa" Alvarado .... Tessie Santiago
Capt. Marcus Grisham .... Anthony Lemke
Vera Hidalgo .... Elsa Pataki
Dr. Robert Helm .... Peter Wingfield
Marta .... Paulina Galvez
Col. Luis Ramirez Montoya .... Valentine Pelka
Don Gaspar Hidalgo .... Tacho Gonzalez

THEME:

"Behind the Mask," written by Spencer Proffer and Steve Plunkett, performed by Jose Feliciano

Queen of Swords was the distaff version of *Zorro* in this cartoonish adventure. Tessa was a Spanish aristocrat who traveled to California in 1817 to run the family hacienda after learning of her father's death. Tessa and her gypsy servant, Marta, arrived to find the hacienda in disrepair and Col. Montoya, a despotic military dictator, in control, taxing the residents so heavily they could barely survive. After she found out that her father had been murdered, Tessa vowed to avenge him and help the downtrodden people of old California. She donned a flimsy mask and, as the Queen of Swords (taken from a Tarot card), set about to right wrongs and protect the weak and infirm. Fat Don Hidalgo's sexy young wife, Vera, was having an affair with sadistic Capt. Grisham, Col. Montoya's right-hand man, who had murdered Tessa's father. Tessa and Marta found a hidden room behind the wine cellar in which her father had hidden gold (which enabled her to pay the colonel's taxes) and a family sword, which she used when she became the Queen of Swords, her father's avenging angel. In the second episode the mysterious and deadly Dr. Helm arrived from Texas, and later in the season Tessa started to have romantic feelings for him.

QUEENS SUPREME (*Legal Comedy/Drama*)

FIRST TELECAST: *January 10, 2003*

LAST TELECAST: *January 24, 2003*

BROADCAST HISTORY:

Jan 2003–Feb 2003, CBS Fri 10:00–11:00

CAST:

Judge Jack Moran .... Oliver Platt
Judge Thomas O'Neill .... Robert Loggia
Judge Kim Vicidomini .... Annabella Sciorra
Judge Rose Barnea .... L. Scott Caldwell
Carmen Hui .... Marcy Harriel
Mike Powell .... James Madio

Jack Moran was a brilliant but extremely unorthodox judge trying cases at the Queens County Courthouse in New York. His fellow jurists appreciated his knowledge and integrity but sometimes had difficulty tolerating his cynicism and outspoken behavior. O'Neill, the senior judge at the courthouse, assigned the cases and was a sort of father figure to the other judges—sometimes cajoling, sometimes serving as confidant and occasionally reprimanding them for their actions. Vicidomini was an attractive, ambitious, politically connected young judge who had recently been appointed to the courthouse and was still learning the ropes, while Barnea was a veteran judge who had seen it all, pulled no punches when she had an opinion and was suspicious of Vicidomini. Carmen and Mike were legal assistants working for the judges.

Queens Supreme seemed unable to decide whether it was a comedy or drama and attracted small audiences. CBS abruptly canceled it after only three episodes had aired. Filmed on location in Queens, New York.

QUEST, THE (*Western*)

FIRST TELECAST: *September 22, 1976*
LAST TELECAST: *December 29, 1976*
BROADCAST HISTORY:
Sep 1976–Dec 1976, NBC Wed 10:00–11:00

CAST:

Morgan Beaudine .... Kurt Russell
Quentin Beaudine .... Tim Matheson

Set in the West during the 1890s, *The Quest* was the story of two young brothers in search of their long-lost sister. Several years before, Morgan Beaudine and his sister Patricia had been captured by Cheyenne Indians and become separated. Morgan had been raised by the Cheyenne but was now living in the white man's world, though he actually trusted the Indians more than he did the whites. His brother Quentin, meanwhile, was educated in San Francisco and planned to be a doctor. Together these two young men set out in search of their sister. Morgan affected Indian dress, spoke fluent Cheyenne, and understood Indian customs well enough to get them out of dangerous situations when they encountered unfriendly red men. He even had an Indian name, Two Persons.

The time seemed ripe for a successful Western when this series premiered. The season before had seen not a single Western on prime-time network television, for the first time in more than 20 years. There was plenty of action and violence on *The Quest*, but it could not compete with the pulchritude on ABC's new entry opposite it, *Charlie's Angels*.

QUEST, THE (*Adventure*)

FIRST TELECAST: *October 22, 1982*
LAST TELECAST: *November 19, 1982*
BROADCAST HISTORY:
Oct 1982–Nov 1982, ABC Fri 10:00–11:00

CAST:

Dan Underwood .... Perry King
Art Henley .... Noah Beery
Cody Johnson .... Ray Vitte
Carrie Welby .... Karen Austin
Count Louis Dardinay .... Michael Billington
Sir Edward .... John Rhys-Davies
King Charles .... Ralph Michael

The tiny Mediterranean principality of Glendora was due to be absorbed by neighboring France when aging King Charles passed away. If, that is, he had no royal successors. So the king's advisor, Sir Edward, studied the family tree and discovered four Americans, each of whom was distantly related to His Majesty and could rightfully claim the throne—if they could pass a 13th-century test of skill and worthiness. Thus began the quest, in which four ordinary Americans each tried to prove himself and inherit a beautiful little seaside country.

Dan was a handsome international sports photographer, a veritable magnet for beautiful girls; Art a gruff, down-to-earth retired cop from Wilko, Kansas; Cody a slick, black con man and hustler with a heart of gold; and Carrie (can you hear the producers saying, "We need a bimbo!") a good-looking New York department store buyer. Sir Edward gave them their assignment each week, usually in cryptic verse, and off they went, sometimes racing, sometimes helping each other as well as the people they met. The quest, you see, was not only a race but a test of their valor and good deeds. Trying to foil them was the exiled and villainous Count Dardinay, who stood to regain his lands only if none of them won and the country *did* become part of France.

QUEST FOR ADVENTURE, see *ABC Presents*

QUICK AS A FLASH (*Quiz/Panel*)

FIRST TELECAST: *March 12, 1953*
LAST TELECAST: *February 25, 1954*
BROADCAST HISTORY:
Mar 1953–Jul 1953, ABC Thu 10:30–11:00
Sep 1953–Feb 1954, ABC Thu 8:00–8:30

MODERATOR:
Bobby Sherwood
Bud Collyer

REGULAR PANELISTS:
Jimmy Nelson
Faye Emerson

Quick as a Flash was designed to test the panel's speed in guessing the significance or outcome of a short, specially prepared film. The film might depict a person, event, or a mystery playlet. The program was based on the long-running (1944–1951) radio quiz of the same name, but unlike the radio version it utilized celebrity panelists. Many guest panelists appeared, in addition to the regulars shown above. Bud Collyer replaced Bobby Sherwood as host in May.

The program was telecast live from New York, and alternated with *Personality Puzzle*.

QUICK ON THE DRAW (*Quiz/Panel*)

FIRST TELECAST: *January 15, 1952*
LAST TELECAST: *December 9, 1952*
BROADCAST HISTORY:
Jan 1952–Dec 1952, DUM Tue 9:30–10:00

HOSTESS:
Robin Chandler

CARTOONIST:
Bob Dunn

This panel show used cartoons suggested by viewers and drawn by cartoonist Bob Dunn to provide pictorial clues to familiar words and phrases. The clues were usually in the form of puns or plays on words, for example a comedian on a stage taking off his clothes (representing "a newspaper term"); a baseball player about to swing a rolled-up venetian blind (for "a well-known expression"); or a man putting a tuxedo on a rabbit (for "an occupation"). (See below for the correct answers.) A different panel of celebrities appeared each week.

Quick on the Draw had been seen locally in New York since 1950.

Answers: (1) comic strip; (2) "blind as a bat"; (3) hair (hare) dresser.

QUINCY, M.E. (*Police Drama*)
FIRST TELECAST: *October 3, 1976*
LAST TELECAST: *September 5, 1983*
BROADCAST HISTORY:

Oct 1976–Nov 1976, NBC Sun 9:30–11:00
Feb 1977–May 1977, NBC Fri 10:00–11:00
Jun 1977–Jul 1977, NBC Fri 9:30–11:00
Jul 1977–Aug 1978, NBC Fri 10:00–11:00
Sep 1978–Apr 1980, NBC Thu 9:00–10:00
Apr 1980–Jun 1983, NBC Wed 10:00–11:00
Jun 1983–Sep 1983, NBC Sat 9:00–10:00
Sep 1983, NBC Mon 10:00–11:00

CAST:

Quincy, M.E. .... Jack Klugman
Lt. Frank Monahan .... Garry Walberg
Sam Fujiyama .... Robert Ito
Lee Potter (1976–1977) .... Lynette Mettey
Danny Tovo .... Val Bisoglio
Dr. Robert Astin .... John S. Ragin
Sgt. Brill .... Joseph Roman
Eddie .... Ed Garrett
Diane, the waitress (1980–1983) .... Diane Markoff
Marc (1978–1983) .... Marc Scott Taylor
Dr. Emily Hanover (1982–1983) ...... Anita Gillette

Quincy was a man with a strong sense of principle. He had given up a lucrative private medical practice to join the Los Angeles County Coroner's Office as a medical examiner ("M.E."). His understanding of forensic medicine led him to conclude that many of the supposed "normal" deaths that he was assigned to investigate were actually murders. Whenever this happened, Quincy tended to resemble a detective more than a pathologist, as he sought evidence to prove his contentions. These wanderings out of his field into the province of the police did not endear Quincy to Dr. Astin, his vacuous, pompous, and insecure superior in the coroner's office. It also alienated many of the police officers who were involved in the investigations and got in the way of his social life, much to the consternation of his girlfriend, Lee. None of this seemed to bother Quincy, however, as he and his young assistant Sam plugged away at solving the cases. Quincy lived on a boat and spent much of his free time at Danny's Place, the bar adjacent to the marina where the boat was docked.

Over the years some things changed. Dr. Astin became less obnoxious and, in fact, actually became almost likable. His problems with Quincy's tendency to play detective never ended, however, and much of his time was spent trying to defend his star pathologist's activities to the police, the local government, the medical board, and the press. He never could get Quincy to conform, and the exasperation showed. Quincy's love life, after Lee's departure, was quite active until he fell for Emily Hanover (played by the same actress who had portrayed his deceased first wife in a 1979 flashback episode), an attractive psychiatrist who provided him with help on some of his cases. They were married in the spring of 1983, after a courtship that suffered because of his preoccupation with his work.

Although Quincy's first name was never mentioned on the show, he did, apparently, have a first initial. His business card was seen briefly in one episode and it read "Dr. R. Quincy."

Quincy was one of the four rotating elements in the 1976–1977 edition of *The NBS Sunday Mystery Movie*—the others being *Columbo, McCloud,* and *McMillan.* It proved so popular during the fall of 1976, however, that after the first of the year it moved to Friday nights as a weekly series.

QUIZ KIDS (*Quiz/Panel*)
FIRST TELECAST: *March 1, 1949*
LAST TELECAST: *September 27, 1956*
BROADCAST HISTORY:

Mar 1949–May 1949, NBC Tue 8:00–8:30 (Midwest net only)
Jun 1949–Sep 1949, NBC Wed 8:00–8:30
Sep 1949–Jan 1950, NBC Mon 10:00–10:30
Jan 1950–Oct 1951, NBC Fri 8:00–8:30
Jul 1952–Sep 1952, NBC Mon 8:00–8:30
Jan 1953–Jul 1953, CBS Sat 10:00–10:30
Jul 1953–Nov 1953, CBS Sun 7:00–7:30
Jan 1956–Sep 1956, CBS Thu 10:30–11:00

EMCEE:

Joe Kelly (1949–1953)
Clifton Fadiman (1956)

This popular series had started on radio in 1940 and was brought intact to television, first as a local program on WNBQ, Chicago (January 1949) and later as a network entry (March 1949). The format was simple: a panel of four or five youngsters, chosen through a battery of tests, answered difficult questions requiring both general and specific knowledge. One youngster might be an "arithmetic expert," another a "music expert," etc. Panelists were as young as six, and a child could remain on the show as long as his answering rank remained high or until he or she reached 16. Celebrity guests sometimes appeared, and periodic contests were held for viewers (e.g., describe your "teacher of the year"). Viewers also submitted questions for the panel and received cash prizes if the young intellects failed to come up with the correct answers. *Quiz Kids* was sometimes scheduled in afternoon time slots during its long run; only the prime-time telecasts are reflected above.

One of the great ironies of the show was that Joe Kelly, who was quizmaster from the early 1940s until 1953, had only a third-grade education himself.

Possibly the most famous of the gifted children who appeared as panelists on *Quiz Kids* was young Robert Strom, who became a regular on the show in March 1956 when he was nine years old. His specialty on *Quiz Kids* was astronomy, but during the next two years his general knowledge of mathematics and physics won him huge sums of money on *The $64,000 Question, The $64,000 Challenge,* and other big-money quiz shows.

A syndicated version of *Quiz Kids* was produced in 1978, with Jim McKrell as emcee. Yet another syndicated version, *The Quiz Kids Challenge,* emceed by Jonathan Prince, was produced for the 1990–1991 season.

QUIZZING THE NEWS (*Quiz/Panel*)

FIRST TELECAST: *August 16, 1948*
LAST TELECAST: *March 5, 1949*
BROADCAST HISTORY:

Aug 1948–Sep 1948, ABC Mon 7:30–8:00
Sep 1948–Oct 1948, ABC Mon 8:00–8:30
Nov 1948–Jan 1949, ABC Wed 8:30–9:00
Jan 1949–Mar 1949, ABC Sat 8:30–9:00

EMCEE:

Allen Prescott

A panel of guest celebrities attempted to identify news events from cartoon clues in this early ABC quiz show. Viewers could also participate, and win prizes. *Quizzing the News* was one of the programs produced locally in New York by ABC production crews, using the facilities of an independent station, so that the ABC personnel could gain working experience in TV prior to the opening of ABC's own flagship station. As soon as ABC's own station opened on August 10, 1948, the program moved over intact and was fed to the newly established network.

R

RCA VICTOR SHOW, THE (*Various*)

FIRST TELECAST: *November 23, 1951*
LAST TELECAST: *August 2, 1954*
BROADCAST HISTORY:
Nov 1951–Jun 1953, NBC Fri 8:00–8:30 (OS)
Oct 1953–Aug 1954, NBC Mon 9:00–9:30
CAST:
Ezio Pinza (1951–1952) .... Himself
Dennis Day (1952–1954) .... Himself
Mrs. Day (1952) .... Verna Felton
Kathy (1952) .... Kathy Phillips
Charley Weaver (1952–1954) .... Cliff Arquette
Lois Sterling (1952–1953) .... Lois Butler
Mrs. Pratt (1952–1953) .... Minerva Urecal
Hal March (1952–1953) .... Himself
Susan Sterling (1952–1954) .... Jeri Lou James
Lavinia (1953–1954) .... Ida Moore
Marian (1953–1954) .... Carol Richards
Peggy (1953–1954) .... Barbara Ruick

When *The RCA Victor Show* premiered, its sole star was singer Ezio Pinza. Each episode of the loosely formatted show opened with urbane bachelor Pinza in his luxurious penthouse apartment, from which he would chat with the audience and sing a song or two. He would then leave the apartment, encounter the evening's guest star, and the two would return to his home. Pinza and guest would perform musical numbers separately and together, and the show closed with Mr. Pinza alone at home singing a last song.

On February 8, 1952, Dennis Day made his first appearance as the alternate-week star of *The RCA Victor Show*. His shows were more traditional situation comedies. Dennis played himself as a singer whose mother felt that he had been underpaid working on Jack Benny's radio program and should look for a career of his own. The only person who had real love for and faith in him was his girlfriend, Kathy.

On April 11, 1952, the format of the Ezio Pinza part of the show was changed. Each episode starred Mr. Pinza in a dramatic story with guest stars and appropriate songs woven into the general plot line. When *The RCA Victor Show* returned in the fall of 1952, after a summer hiatus, Dennis Day was its sole star, the Ezio Pinza episodes having been dropped.

The format for the Dennis Day situation comedy had also changed. He played himself again, but was a young bachelor living in a luxurious apartment building in Hollywood. He couldn't really afford it, but felt that it was necessary for his image in the quest to get ahead in show business. Charley Weaver was the janitor, Mrs. Pratt his landlady, Hal March a girl-crazy neighbor, and Lois Sterling his girlfriend who lived with her little sister.

In the fall of 1953, the show returned with essentially the same format under the new title *The Dennis Day Show*. Previously live, it was now filmed. Charley Weaver had acquired a girlfriend named Lavinia, and Dennis went through two new girlfriends, Marian and Peggy. Although Lois Sterling was gone, her little sister Susan was still in the cast as Dennis' youngest fan.

R.F.D. AMERICA (*Instruction*)

FIRST TELECAST: *May 26, 1949*
LAST TELECAST: *September 15, 1949*
BROADCAST HISTORY:
May 1949–Sep 1949, NBC Thu 8:00–8:30
EMCEE:
Bob Murphy

A "how to" program dealing with plants and animals, and originating from Chicago (where it began as a local show in January 1949). Host Murphy interviewed various guest experts on raising cattle, watering plants, carving meat, etc., and occasionally displayed live examples of the animal subject at hand. For example, the premiere telecast was said to be the first time in history that an entire herd of cattle was driven into a studio to be seen on live television.

RACHEL GUNN, R.N. (*Situation Comedy*)

FIRST TELECAST: *June 28, 1992*
LAST TELECAST: *September 4, 1992*
BROADCAST HISTORY:
Jun 1992–Aug 1992, FOX Sun 8:30–9:00
Aug 1992–Sep 1992, FOX Fri 9:30–10:00
CAST:
Rachel Gunn .... Christine Ebersole
Dr. David Dunkle .... Kevin Conroy
Nurse Becky Jo Woolbright .... Megan Mullally
Nurse Zac .... Bryan Brightcloud
Dane Grey .... Dan Tullis, Jr.
Sister Joan .... Kathleen Mitchell
Jeannette .... Lois Foraker
THEME:
"Workin' for a Living" by Mario Cipollina, Johnny Colla, Bill Gibson, Chris Hayes, Sean Hopper, and Huey Lewis; sung by Christine Ebersole

The elective surgery floor of Little Innocence Hospital in Nebraska was the setting for this medical comedy. Sarcastic Rachel Gunn was the unit's dedicated, hardworking, and underpaid head nurse. The prime target of her vitriol was arrogant young Dr. David Dunkle, a talented but selfish surgeon whose condescending attitude toward patients and staff was a constant thorn in her side. In an ironic twist, since he needed inexpensive housing following a costly divorce and she needed a tenant for the duplex apartment she owned, Rachel became his landlord. Other regulars were Becky, a young, naive, and overly enthusiastic new nurse on the floor; Zac, a Native American male nurse whose service in Vietnam had prepared him well for Rachel's disciplined unit; Dane, the black orderly whose aspiration to become a nurse was somewhat in doubt since he was afraid of blood; Sister Joan, the peppy black nun who ministered to both patients and staff; and Jeannette, the hospital's obnoxious fat dietitian.

RACKET SQUAD (*Police Drama*)

FIRST TELECAST: *June 7, 1951*
LAST TELECAST: *September 28, 1953*
BROADCAST HISTORY:
Jun 1951–Dec 1952, CBS Thu 10:00–10:30
Jan 1953–Jul 1953, CBS Thu 10:30–11:00
Jul 1953–Sep 1953, CBS Mon 9:00–9:30
CAST:
Capt. John Braddock .... Reed Hadley

Capt. John Braddock worked in the racket squad of a large metropolitan police department. He did not deal with crimes of violence but instead sought to protect the public from the various confidence rackets that were a more direct threat to them than outright robbery. The series was based on actual case records from police departments around the country and described in detail the means by which shady characters fleeced unsuspecting people of their money. Reed Hadley, in addition to his role as star, provided the narration for each episode. Hadley had previously been seen in a syndicated version of *Racket Squad* that was produced in 1950, a year before CBS decided to give the series network exposure.

RAFFERTY (*Medical Drama*)
FIRST TELECAST: *September 5, 1977*
LAST TELECAST: *November 28, 1977*
BROADCAST HISTORY:
Sep 1977–Nov 1977, CBS Mon 10:00–11:00
CAST:
Sid Rafferty, M.D. .... Patrick McGoohan
Nurse Vera Wales .... Millie Slavin
Daniel Gentry, M.D. .... John Getz
Dr. Calvin............................ David Clennon
Nurse Keynes......................... Joan Pringle
Nurse Koscinski .... Eddie Benton

After 23 years as a doctor in the U.S. Army, Sid Rafferty had retired from the service to open a private practice. Used to military discipline, and possessed of a very short temper, the idealistic and stubborn Rafferty was not the easiest person to get along with. He did things his way, resented the clubbiness of other doctors—particularly their tendency to cover up for each other's shortcomings and mistakes—and was often at odds with the staff of City General Hospital, where he performed surgery. Rafferty's young associate in his private practice was Daniel Gentry, whose freewheeling personal life was in marked contrast to Rafferty's more conservative approach. Their nurse/receptionist was Vera Wales, thoroughly professional in the office but also madly in love with widower Rafferty.

RAGS TO RICHES (*Comedy/Drama*)
FIRST TELECAST: *March 9, 1987*
LAST TELECAST: *September 11, 1988*
BROADCAST HISTORY:
Mar 1987, NBC Mon 8:00–10:00
Mar 1987–May 1987, NBC Sun 8:00–9:00
Jul 1987, NBC Sun 8:00–9:00
Aug 1987–Jan 1988, NBC Fri 8:00–9:00
Jul 1988–Sep 1988, NBC Sun 7:00–8:00
CAST:
Nick Foley .... Joseph Bologna
John Clapper, the butler............ Douglas Seale
Rose (16).......................... Kimiko Gelman
Marva (15) .... Tisha Campbell
Diane (15) .... Bridget Michele
Patty (13).......................... Bianca DeGarr
Mickey (7).......................... Heidi Zeigler
Nina (pilot only) .... Heather McAdam

The '60s were fun and games for a group of young orphans in this frothy TV version of a B-movie musical, set in 1961. Nick was the millionaire bachelor playboy-businessman who adopted them, in order to look more respectable (seems he could close more deals that way); and Clapper was the elderly Cockney butler who looked after them all in Nick's huge Los Angeles mansion. The five girls were strong-willed Rose, often the ringleader; charming Diane; wisecracking Marva, who wanted to follow in Nick's entrepreneurial footsteps; tomboy Patty; and insufferably cute little Mickey. They all engaged in lots of singing and dancing, often '60s tunes with new lyrics that commented on the story.

RAISING DAD (*Situation Comedy*)
FIRST TELECAST: *October 5, 2001*
LAST TELECAST: *August 30, 2002*
BROADCAST HISTORY:
Oct 2001–Jan 2002, WB Fri 9:30–10:00
Jan 2002–Jun 2002, WB Fri 8:30–9:00
Jun 2002–Aug 2002, WB Fri 9:30–10:00
CAST:
Matt Stewart.............................. Bob Saget
Sarah Stewart (age 15).............. Kat Dennings
Emily Stewart (10)...................... Brie Larson
Sam Stewart.............................. Jerry Adler
Katie .... Meagan Good
Mr. Stuart Travers................... Andy Kindler
Josh .... Ben Indra
Evan .... Beau Wirick
Olivia .... Camille Guaty
**Liz Taylor*............................ Tembi Locke
Jared Ashby (2002)..................... Riley Smith
*Occasional
THEME:
"Raising Dad"

Matt was a funny, friendly English teacher living in Boston with his two daughters and his retired dad, Sam, a former baseball player for the Red Sox. Matt's wife had passed away two years earlier, and he was trying hard to be father, mother, and friend to Sarah and Emily. He taught at the high school where Sarah was a sophomore, and was quite popular with the students, but his presence there sometimes caused awkward moments for Sarah. The other regulars were primarily students—Sarah's hip best friend Katie, nerdy classmate Josh, and dumb jock Evan, who had a rock band. Also seen were Matt's friend Stuart, a math teacher, and Liz, the vice principal. In January Jared, who had been in a juvenile facility for stealing a car, enrolled in the school, and Sarah was obviously attracted to him. The following month Katie disappeared from the show and Olivia, another classmate, replaced her in Sarah's circle of friends. In the spring Sarah and Jared started dating and, by the series finale, their relationship was getting pretty serious.

RAISING MIRANDA (*Situation Comedy*)
FIRST TELECAST: *November 5, 1988*
LAST TELECAST: *December 31, 1988*
BROADCAST HISTORY:
Nov 1988–Dec 1988, CBS Sat 8:30–9:00
CAST:
Donald Marshack .... James Naughton
Miranda Marshack.................. Royana Black
Joan Hoodenpyle .... Miriam Flynn
Bob Hoodenpyle .... Steve Vinovich
Jack Miller.................... Michael Manasseri
Russell............................ Bryan Cranston
Marcine Lundquist........................ Amy Lynne

Yet another of the myriad single-parent comedies so prevalent on TV in the 1980s, but one with a singularly unfunny premise. *Raising Miranda* was the story of a construction contractor in Racine, Wisconsin, Donald Marshack, raising his 15-year-old daughter after his wife, Bonnie, had deserted them to "find herself." Helping Donald adjust to his new role as both father and mother to a distressed Miranda were his good friends, Joan and Bob Hoodenpyle. Marcine was Miranda's lifelong best friend and confidante, Jack, the new transfer student at her high school whom she had befriended, and Russell, Donald's flaky brother-in-law who lived in a van permanently parked in the Marshack driveway.

RAMAR OF THE JUNGLE (*Adventure*)

BROADCAST HISTORY:

Syndicated only
30 minutes
Produced: *1952–1954* (52 episodes)
Released: *October 1952*

CAST:

Dr. Tom Reynolds (Ramar) .... Jon Hall
Professor Howard Ogden .... Ray Montgomery

ALSO:

James Fairfax
M'liss McClure
Nick Stewart

Adults shook their heads at this one, but kids thought it was *neat* and made *Ramar of the Jungle* one of the leading children's adventure shows of the 1950s. Dr. Tom Reynolds was the son of missionaries who returned to the jungle as head of a medical-research expedition. There he stayed, tending to the natives as if they were little children and fighting off at least one real bad guy every episode (poachers, crooks who wanted to steal the opals right off the natives' idol, etc.). Ramar, as any under-12-year-old could tell you, meant "White Medicine Man"... or "Great White Doctor," or something like that. Ray Montgomery played his companion.

The plots and dialogue were pretty primitive; for example:

NATIVE CHIEF: Gun make no boom-boom.
RAMAR: You mean it made no sound?
CHIEF: No boom-boom!
RAMAR: Hmmm . . . The gun must have been equipped with a silencer.

It was all good, clean fun, with lots of exciting animal shots. Hall, who knew his juvenile audience, insisted on historical and geographical accuracy (episodes were set in both Africa and India) and no sex. "Kids get smarter every day," he said. "You can't fool them . . . even our African dialects are genuine. As for sex, who needs it at their age?" The program was produced on a rock-bottom budget and, together with the merchandising of pith helmets, games, and other Ramar paraphernalia, made a lot of money for former B-movie actor Hall. Some of the *Ramar* TV films were also strung together and released theatrically in the late 1950s and early 1960s.

RANDOM PLAY (*Comedy*)

BROADCAST HISTORY:

VH1
30 minutes
Original episodes: *1999*
Premiered: *July 24, 1999*

REGULARS:

Craig Anton
Michael Ian Black
Jim Gaffigan
Jackie Harris
Stephen Hibbert
Bruce McCulloch
Jerry Minor
Jason Nash
Mark Rivers
Michael Showalter
David Wain
Nancy Walls

Comedy sketches with musical themes. Among them: a panhandling guitar player sings about a passerby's secrets; a lounge singer's songwriting chimp; an uptight female executive goes bonkers over David Cassidy; and John and Yoko's private moments around the house.

RANDOM YEARS, THE (*Situation Comedy*)

FIRST TELECAST: *March 5, 2002*
LAST TELECAST: *March 19, 2002*
BROADCAST HISTORY:

Mar 2002, UPN Tue 9:30–10:00

CAST:

Alex Barnes .... Will Friedle
Todd Mitchell .... Sean Murray
Wiseman .... Joshua Ackerman
Casey Parker .... Natalia Cigliuti
Steve .... Winston J. Rochas

In this short-lived buddy sitcom, three guys in their early 20s who had been friends since grade school were sharing a loft apartment in New York's Chinatown and trying to figure out what they were going to do with their lives. Alex, who wanted to be a music critic, was working as a researcher for a magazine; insecure Wiseman, whose mother had made all his decisions in the past, was a dental hygienist; and unemployed and unmotivated Todd spent most of his time watching TV in the apartment. Alex hired ambitious Casey, who was going to N.Y.U. Business School, to work on his Internet music Web site and, in the second episode, helped her get an apartment in their building. Steve, the building's shifty supervisor, had been using the space to store merchandise that his brother had stolen.

After only three weeks on the air, the UPN pulled the plug on *The Random Years.*

RANGE RIDER, THE (*Western*)

BROADCAST HISTORY:

Syndicated and network reruns
30 minutes
Produced: *1951–1952* (78 episodes)
Released: *Fall 1952*

CAST:

The Range Rider .... Jock Mahoney
Dick West .... Dick Jones

THEME:

"Home on the Range"

Six-foot four-inch former stuntman and cowboy star Jock Mahoney headed this early kids' Western. With his youthful sidekick Dick West, he ranged all over the old frontier, righting wrongs and helping out everyone from Arizona Navajos to Canadian Mounties. There was a lot of hard riding and flying tackles, but relatively little gunplay.

The Rider's trusty horse was Rawhide, while Dick's was Lucky. The series was produced by Gene Autry's Flying A Productions, which also sold buckskin shirts and other Range Rider gear in a merchandise tie-in.

Reruns of *Range Rider* appeared on the ABC network on Sunday afternoons from September to December 1965.

RANGO (*Situation Comedy*)

FIRST TELECAST: *January 13, 1967*
LAST TELECAST: *September 1, 1967*
BROADCAST HISTORY:
Jan 1967–Sep 1967, ABC Fri 9:00–9:30
CAST:
Rango .... Tim Conway
Pink Cloud .... Guy Marks
Capt. Horton .... Norman Alden
THEME:
"Rango," by Earle Hagen and Ben Raleigh, sung by Frankie Laine

Rango was a Western comedy about the Texas Ranger that legends don't talk about. He was an inept, bumbling lawman who had been assigned to Deep Wells Ranger Station, the quietest post in the state, in an attempt to keep him out of trouble. But trouble came with him. Criminal activity sprouted in a town which had been quiet for 20 years. Rango's assistant in the post supply room was Pink Cloud, a "chicken" Indian who had discovered that the white man's ways were much to his liking—an interesting book in a comfortable bed was much better than skulking around the plains. "Rango say him return when sun high over teepee," grunted the red man. "By that, I presume he meant he would be back by noon."

Rango's nemesis was Captain Horton, the post commander, who would have dearly loved to have him transferred, but couldn't, because Rango's father happened to be head of the Texas Rangers.

RANSOM SHERMAN SHOW, THE (*Comedy/Variety*)

FIRST TELECAST: *July 3, 1950*
LAST TELECAST: *August 25, 1950*
BROADCAST HISTORY:
Jul 1950–Aug 1950, NBC Mon–Fri 7:00–7:30
REGULARS:
Ransom Sherman
Nancy Wright
Johnny Bradford
Art Van Damme Quintet

Radio emcee and comic Ransom Sherman brought his wide-ranging monologues to television in 1950, as a summer replacement for *Kukla, Fran & Ollie.* A variety of vocalists provided musical entertainment, including Nancy Wright, Johnny Bradford, and four different vocal groups who rotated from night to night. One of these groups, the Four Lads, later became famous in their own right.

Sherman was later seen in an afternoon series on NBC from October 1950 to January 1951.

RAT PATROL, THE (*War Drama*)

FIRST TELECAST: *September 12, 1966*
LAST TELECAST: *September 16, 1968*
BROADCAST HISTORY:
Sep 1966–Sep 1968, ABC Mon 8:30–9:00
CAST:
Sgt. Sam Troy .... Chris George
Sgt. Jack Moffitt .... Gary Raymond
Pvt. Mark Hitchcock .... Lawrence Casey
Pvt. Tully Pettigrew .... Justin Tarr
Capt. Hauptman Hans Dietrich .... Hans Gudegast

"Leapin' jeeps!" *The Rat Patrol* came roaring onto TV screens in 1966 as a wartime action-adventure series with a touch of humor. The Rat Patrollers were four young commandos, three Americans and one Englishman, fighting General Rommel's elite Afrika Korps in the North African desert early in World War II. Sam Troy was the head rat, Jack Moffitt his very British demolitions expert (and there was a lot of demolition in *Rat Patrol*), Mark Hitchcock the young private trying to live down a "sissy" reputation, and Tully Pettigrew the charming con man of the group. They traveled over the burning sands in two machine-gun-mounted jeeps, working as an independent team because no organized unit could hold them. Capt. Dietrich, C.O. of a German armored unit, was their usual enemy, though sometimes the two sides had to join forces to fight off the Arabs.

The Rat Patrol was filmed in part on the deserts of Spain, where a great deal of war materiel left over from the filming of the movies *Battle of the Bulge* and *The Great Escape* was used for backdrop.

RAVEN (*Drama*)

FIRST TELECAST: *June 24, 1992*
LAST TELECAST: *April 17, 1993*
BROADCAST HISTORY:
Jun 1992–Aug 1992, CBS Wed 9:00–10:00
Sep 1992–Oct 1992, CBS Sat 9:00–10:00
Jan 1993, CBS Sat 9:00–10:00
Mar 1993–Apr 1993, CBS Sat 10:00–11:00
CAST:
Jonathan Raven .... Jeffrey Meek
Herman Jablonski ("Ski") .... Lee Majors
The Big Kahuna .... Andy Bumatai

Raven was a martial arts master who had infiltrated the Black Dragons, a dreaded group of Japanese assassin/terrorists, and become the only Westerner ever accepted into the secret organization. His purpose in joining was to avenge their murder of his parents; after he succeeded, the Dragons were determined to find and kill both him and his lost son. With the help of his buddy Ski, a grizzled, overweight private detective he had served with in the Green Berets, Raven attempted to find his son while thwarting repeated attempts by the Black Dragons to assassinate him. Along the way Raven and Ski helped other people in trouble and occasionally took on paying clients, although the authorities must have wondered about the trail of gunfire, explosions, and martial arts battles that followed them everywhere. Based in Honolulu, they traveled the world in search of Raven's son.

RAWHIDE (*Western*)

FIRST TELECAST: *January 9, 1959*
LAST TELECAST: *January 4, 1966*
BROADCAST HISTORY:
Jan 1959–Apr 1959, CBS Fri 8:00–9:00
May 1959–Sep 1963, CBS Fri 7:30–8:30
Sep 1963–Sep 1964, CBS Thu 8:00–9:00
Sep 1964–Sep 1965, CBS Fri 7:30–8:30
Sep 1965–Jan 1966, CBS Tue 7:30–8:30

CAST:

Rowdy Yates........................Clint Eastwood
Gil Favor (1959–1965)................Eric Fleming
Pete Nolan (1959–1963)..............Sheb Wooley
Wishbone.............................Paul Brinegar
Jim Quince............................Steve Raines
Joe Scarlett (1959–1964)............Rocky Shahan
Harkness "Mushy" Mushgrove (1959–1965)
..................................James Murdock
Hey Soos Patines (1961–1964)........Robert Cabal
Clay Forrester (1962–1963)..........Charles Gray
Ian Cabot (1965–1966)..............David Watson
Jed Colby (1965–1966)................John Ireland
Solomon King (1965–1966)... Raymond St. Jacques

THEME:

"Rawhide," by Ned Washington and Dmitri Tiomkin, sung over credits by Frankie Laine

Rawhide was the cattleman's answer to *Wagon Train*. Whereas *Wagon Train* told of the adventures of people traveling across the Great Plains in wagons, *Rawhide* took its regular performers back and forth across the country as organizers and runners of communal cattle drives. The constant traveling allowed both series to tell stories of people met along the way and those who joined the regulars in transit. Gil Favor was the trail boss, the supervisor of the entire cattle-drive operation. His right-hand man, and second-in-command, was Rowdy Yates. Other regulars were the cooks, drovers, and scouts who helped the cattle drive stay together and avoid possible dangers. In the fall of 1965 Rowdy Yates took over as trail boss and organized his own team to start another drive. This last one, however, only made it partway, or wherever it was when it was canceled in January 1966.

RAY ANTHONY SHOW, THE (*Musical Variety*)

FIRST TELECAST: *October 12, 1956*
LAST TELECAST: *May 3, 1957*
BROADCAST HISTORY:

Oct 1956–Apr 1957, ABC Fri 10:00–11:00
Apr 1957–May 1957, ABC Fri 10:00–10:30

REGULARS:

Ray Anthony and His Orchestra
Frank Leahy
The Four Freshmen
Don Durant
Med Flory
Gene Merlino
Belvederes
Leroy Anthony
The Savoys

ABC, which had struck gold with bandleader Lawrence Welk the previous summer, was reportedly trying to repeat its success by signing up Ray Anthony in 1956. Unfortunately Anthony did not possess quite the same magic, but he did provide a season's worth of pleasing entertainment with a somewhat more sophisticated brand of music than Welk's. A few guests were seen, but mostly it was just Anthony, his trumpet, orchestra, and regulars. Former Notre Dame coach Frank Leahy added an unusual touch with a regular sports feature. Live from Hollywood.

Ray Anthony was also seen in three syndicated series over the years, in the summer of 1956 (just before this network entry), in 1962, and in 1968. Vocalist Vikki Carr was featured on the last two.

RAY BOLGER SHOW, THE (*Situation Comedy*)

FIRST TELECAST: *October 8, 1953*
LAST TELECAST: *June 10, 1955*
BROADCAST HISTORY:

Oct 1953–Jul 1954, ABC Thu 8:30–9:00
Sep 1954–Jun 1955, ABC Fri 8:30–9:00

CAST:

Raymond Wallace.......................Ray Bolger
Jonathan (1953–1954)................Allyn Joslyn
Pete Morrisey.....................Richard Erdman
June (1953–1954).......................Betty Lynn
Susan (1954–1955)...................Marjie Millar
Katie Jones (1954–1955)..........Christine Nelson
Artie Herman (1954–1955).........Charlie Cantor
Ray's dancing partner.................Sylvia Lewis

Singer-dancer Ray Bolger tried two situation-comedy formats in two successive years in the mid-1950s, and had little luck with either. The 1953–1954 edition, called *Where's Raymond*, cast him as a musical-comedy star with a bright, infectious personality but an unfortunate tendency to arrive at the theater at the last possible moment before the show began—causing constant pandemonium. Jonathan was his meticulous agent (and brother), Pete his pal, and June a friend who ran a restaurant near the theater. This format was little more than an excuse to get Ray into one of his dance routines in each show, often employing one of his famous characterizations such as his role in the Broadway show *Where's Charley?* (where he introduced "Once in Love with Amy") or the scarecrow from *The Wizard of Oz*.

In the fall of 1954 the program became *The Ray Bolger Show*. It still had Ray cast as a Broadway star, but this time he was in love with a young lass from Iowa (Susan) who was trying to achieve fame in the big city as a writer. His attempts to help her inevitably backfired. Of the previous year's supporting cast, Pete returned, being joined by Susan, her roommate Katie, and Ray's new friend Artie. Sylvia Lewis, who served as Ray's dancing partner in the big production numbers, was the choreographer for Ray's show throughout its two-year run.

RAY BRADBURY THEATER, THE (*Science Fiction Anthology*)

BROADCAST HISTORY:

HBO and USA Network
30 minutes
Produced: *1985–1987* (HBO, 6 episodes), *1987–1992* (USA, 59 episodes)
Premiered: *June 16, 1985* (HBO); *October 31, 1987* (USA)

HOST:

Ray Bradbury

The famous and prolific science fiction author Ray Bradbury served as host for dramatizations of his own thoughtful short stories in this cable series. Among the guest stars who appeared were Nick Mancuso, Drew Barrymore, and Jeff Goldblum.

RAY MILLAND SHOW, THE (*Situation Comedy*)

FIRST TELECAST: *September 17, 1953*
LAST TELECAST: *September 30, 1955*
BROADCAST HISTORY:

Sep 1953–Jun 1955, CBS Thu 8:00–8:30 (OS)
Jul 1955–Sep 1955, CBS Fri 9:30–10:00

CAST:

Prof. Ray McNutley/McNulty .... Ray Milland
Peggy McNutley/McNulty .... Phyllis Avery
Dean Josephine Bradley (1953–1954) .... Minerva Urecal
Pete Thompson (1953–1954) .... Gordon Jones

During its first season the title of this series was *Meet Mr. McNutley*. Ray McNutley was the married, but very attractive, head of the English department of Lynnhaven College, an exclusive women's school. In fact, the only female on campus who was not distracted by his suave manners was stern, matronly Dean Bradley. Constantly getting McNutley into trouble was his hulking friend, Pete Thompson.

When the show returned in the fall of 1954, a number of changes had been made. Ray's last name was now McNulty, he was now teaching at coeducational Comstock University, and he was now a drama professor rather than an English teacher. The show's title had also been changed, to *The Ray Milland Show*. The basic plot, however, remained the same. He was still an attractive professor whose female acquaintances were somewhat infatuated with him, he still had the same loving and supportive wife, and still had his problems with other members of the faculty.

RAY SCHERER'S SUNDAY REPORT (*News/Documentary*)

FIRST TELECAST: *June 23, 1963*
LAST TELECAST: *August 25, 1963*
BROADCAST HISTORY:

Jun 1963–Aug 1963, NBC Sun 6:30–7:00

HOST:

Ray Scherer

NBC White House correspondent Ray Scherer opened each show with about five minutes of hard news and spent the rest of the half hour reviewing in detail the major event, or events, of the past week. Subject matter of these expanded stories ranged from politics to science to international affairs.

RAY STEVENS SHOW, THE, see *Andy Williams Presents Ray Stevens*

RAYMOND BURR SHOW, THE, syndicated title for *Ironside*

REAL LIFE WITH JANE PAULEY (*Magazine*)

FIRST TELECAST: *July 17, 1990*
LAST TELECAST: *November 1, 1991*
BROADCAST HISTORY:

Jul 1990–Sep 1990, NBC Tue 10:00–11:00
Jan 1991–Feb 1991, NBC Sun 8:00–8:30
Mar 1991–Sep 1991, NBC Sun 8:30–9:00
Sep 1991–Oct 1991, NBC Fri 8:00–8:30
Nov 1991, NBC Fri 9:30–10:00

HOST:

Jane Pauley

As if to provide counterbalance to the screaming headlines, exposés, and disasters that dominate the news, NBC launched this "kinder and gentler" newsmagazine hosted by the former sweetheart of the *Today* show, Jane Pauley. Subjects ranged from pedestrian (why life is so hurried, coping with the new school year) to quirky (why can't 80% of Americans program their VCRs?). A few celebrity profiles were included, but most of the reports were human interest stories or subjects likely to touch the lives of ordinary viewers. Boyd Matson contributed regular reports from small and interesting places around the United States.

REAL MCCOYS, THE (*Situation Comedy*)

FIRST TELECAST: *October 3, 1957*
LAST TELECAST: *September 22, 1963*
BROADCAST HISTORY:

Oct 1957–Sep 1962, ABC Thu 8:30–9:00
Sep 1962–Sep 1963, CBS Sun 9:00–9:30

CAST:

Grandpa Amos McCoy .... Walter Brennan
Luke McCoy .... Richard Crenna
Kate McCoy (1957–1962) .... Kathy Nolan
"Aunt" Hassie .... Lydia Reed
Little Luke (1957–1962) .... Michael Winkleman
Pepino Garcia .... Tony Martinez
George MacMichael .... Andy Clyde
Flora MacMichael .... Madge Blake
Aggie Larkin (1959–1960) .... Betty Garde
Louise Howard (1963) .... Janet De Gore
Greg Howard (1963) .... Butch Patrick
Winifred Jordan (1963) .... Joan Blondell

When this rural comedy was first proposed to the networks by writers Irving and Norman Pincus, the experts said it would never work. Okay for the sticks, maybe, but no good for city viewers. NBC, at first interested, finally turned the series down cold. Walter Brennan, their intended star, wanted nothing to do with it. But the Pincus brothers persevered. Brennan was finally won over, financing was obtained from Danny Thomas Productions, and a spot was found on ABC's impoverished schedule. The two New York-bred Pincuses had the last laugh, as *The Real McCoys* became one of the biggest hits on TV for the next six years, and started a major trend toward rural comedy shows which lasted through the 1960s. This was the inspiration for *The Andy Griffith Show*, *Beverly Hillbillies*, *Petticoat Junction*, *Green Acres*, and several others.

The premise was simple: a happy-go-lucky West Virginia mountain family picks up stakes and moves to a ranch in California's San Fernando Valley. Center of the action, and undisputed star of the show, was Grandpa, a porch-rockin', gol-darnin', consarnin' old codger with a wheezy voice who liked to meddle in practically everybody's affairs, neighbors and kin alike. Three-time Academy Award-winner Walter Brennan (who was 63 when the series began) played the role to perfection. His kin were grandson Luke and his new bride, Kate; Luke's teenage sister, "Aunt" Hassie; and Luke's 11-year-old brother, Little Luke (their parents were deceased). Completing the regular cast were Pepino, the musically inclined farm hand, and George MacMichael, their argumentative neighbor. George's spinster sister Flora had eyes for Grandpa, but she never did snare him.

In 1962, when the series moved to CBS, Luke became a widower and many of the plots began to revolve around Grandpa's attempts to match him up with a new wife. The series ended its run in 1963.

CBS aired reruns of this series, with the title shortened to *The McCoys*, from October 1962 to September 1966 on weekday mornings.

REAL PEOPLE (*Human Interest/Audience Participation*)

FIRST TELECAST: *April 18, 1979*

LAST TELECAST: *July 4, 1984*

BROADCAST HISTORY:

Apr 1979–Jul 1984, NBC Wed 8:00–9:00

REGULARS:

Fred Willard (1979, 1981–1983)
Sarah Purcell
John Barbour (1979–1982)
Mark Russell
Skip Stephenson
Bill Rafferty
Byron Allen
Kerry Millerick (1982–1983)
Peter Billingsley (1982–1984)

Producer George Schlatter was truly one of television's comic innovators. In 1968 he introduced *Rowan & Martin's Laugh-In*, a classic series that mixed burlesque with topical satire, and in 1979 he was responsible for this trend-setter. As the title implied, the stars of this series were not celebrities but "real people" with offbeat professions, hobbies, and interests. Each episode opened with the hosts roaming the studio audience soliciting comments and opinions (which led to a short-lived off-shoot series called *Speak Up, America*). Then a succession of "real people" were profiled in filmed reports, among them the world's fastest artist (more than 83,000 paintings), a man who ate soil, a man who went through life walking backward, and a shapely lady truck driver. There were features on a hollering convention, barbershop quartets, and a disco class for senior citizens. Some of the segments were heartwarming, others bizarre. The hosts, who went on location to film the stories, chatted about them in the studio and generally maintained a lighthearted pace. In between segments they read humorous letters from viewers, and showed photos of strange signs, unusual names, and funny typographical errors from newspapers and magazines—all submitted by viewers. Each one used won its sender a *Real People* T-shirt. On occasion, the subject of one of the stories would be present in the studio, presumably to prove that he *was* real.

Real People premiered as a limited series in the spring of 1979. When it returned that fall Fred Willard, one of the original hosts, had been replaced by Byron Allen. Allen, Sarah Purcell, John Barbour, and Skip Stephenson appeared regularly in the studio and on location in the filmed stories. Bill Rafferty was a roving reporter who did all of his commentary on film, never appearing in the studio, and political satirist Mark Russell made pungent comments on the federal bureaucracy, from Washington. Fred Willard returned to the show for two seasons, starting in 1981, and the following fall young Peter Billingsley was added to the roster to cover stories with particular emphasis on children. Kerry Millerick, another roving reporter, was also added in 1982, but appeared infrequently. When Kerry was added, former roving reporter Bill Rafferty began to appear in the studio, as well as on location. Only moderately successful when it began, *Real People* soon grew into one of the top hits on television, spawning a host of imitators—*That's Incredible, Those Amazing Animals,* and *That's My Line* among them.

REAL STORIES OF THE HIGHWAY PATROL (*Police Documentary*)

BROADCAST HISTORY:

Syndicated only
30 minutes
Produced: *1992–1996* (780 episodes)
Released: *April 1993*

HOST:

Maury Hannigan

Maury Hannigan, commissioner of the California Highway Patrol, hosted this series that told real stories of CHP officers and law-enforcement officers from around the country. Some stories used only cinema verité action footage, and some included reenactments, often with actual officers participating. Real officers talked about their work, the dangers they faced, and the law-enforcement process.

REAL WORLD, THE (*Documentary*)

BROADCAST HISTORY:

MTV
30 minutes
Produced: *1992–*
Premiered: *May 21, 1992*

The 1990s vogue for reality shows produced many variations, some rather exploitative, but one of the most compelling—and lauded—was this unusual series on cable's MTV. The premise was simply to recruit seven young strangers to live together in a large apartment for three months, at MTV's expense, while film crews followed their every move. These strangers were not randomly chosen. All were good-looking, articulate twenty-somethings, most seeking careers in glamorous fields such as music, acting, or modeling.

As viewers watched voyeuristically they went through the trials of job hunting, auditions, college applications, dating, lost dogs, and just living together. Sometimes one would talk directly to the camera about his or her hopes, fears, and dreams. According to producer Jonathan Murray, "We told them, 'The only time the cameras are not on is when you're about to score or in the bathroom.' " Tightly edited, the show often held high drama.

The first 13 episodes, in 1992, were set in an apartment in New York City's trendy SoHo district. The seven were Julie, a naive but engaging 19-year-old from Alabama getting her first taste of the Big Apple; Heather B., a hefty black rapper; Eric, a hunky, oft-undressed model with designs on Julie; Norman, a bearded young painter; André, a long-haired musician; Kevin; and Becky. Among the highlights were Julie's encounters with urban life ("they pee on the street!") and her worried father's reactions back home, Norman's declaration that he was bisexual, and a trip by the three girls to Jamaica, where they could bond and talk about the guys.

Interestingly enough, when the seven got together for a reunion the following year there was an undercurrent of jealousy. One of them, Eric Nies, had already hit the big time, as host of MTV's afternoon dance show, *The Grind*.

Real World II aired in mid-1993 and followed seven more young people, this time in a beach house in Venice, California. They were Tami (who became pregnant), Jon (from Kentucky), Dominic, Aaron,

Glen (a musician), Beth S., and Dave (a comedian). In the course of the run the first six ganged up on Dave and kicked him out of the house, whereupon he was replaced by a second Beth. There was also an Outward Bound excursion and a trip to Mexico.

Real World III (1994), set in San Francisco, was perhaps the most dramatic to date. This time there were eight, Rachel, Pam, Cory, Puck, Judd, Pedro, Mohammed, and Jo. Pedro Zamora, a handsome, likable young man, had been diagnosed earlier as HIV-positive, and several episodes dealt with his attempts to live a normal life under the cloud of AIDS. Viewers got to know him well, and when he died of the disease, in November 1994, the news saddened millions.

The most notorious member of the class of '94, however—and, perhaps, of any edition—was David "Puck" Rainey, whose disgustingly slovenly habits are remembered to this day.

Real World IV (1995) traveled to London, with wholesome Kat, whose passion was competitive fencing, British punk rocker Neil, Australian model Jacinda, boyish playwright Jay, goateed German Lars, hunky race-car driver Mike, and chatterbox Sharon. Dramatic moments included Neil nearly getting his tongue bitten off by an enraged fan during a loud, violent club performance, and Sharon's throat surgery to remove nodules on her vocal cords. *Real World V* (1996) was set at an opulent dockside house at Miami Beach. The lucky seven this time were slinky Sarah, gay Dan, brunette Melissa, goofy Joe, Cynthia, the obligatory black, loud, raspy Flora (who, with two boyfriends, preferred "chaos in relationships"), and Mike, da hunk. The sunsets were beautiful. *Real World VI* (1997) moved north to Boston, amid ice and snow, with the cast settling into a funky converted firehouse. They were Montana, fun guy Sean, moody Jason (the one with a nose ring, who wrote poetry), Kameelah (the black girl), Genesis (the blonde, from Mississippi), tall, bald and very hip Syrus, and conservative Elka.

A spacious waterfront loft in Seattle was the setting for *Real World VII* (1998). Amid the usual introductory pleasantries (Girl: "Are you gay?" Boy: "No, you lesbian?"), viewers met the seven: military school pals Nathan and David; happy Asian girl Janet, who bonded immediately with playful Lindsay; quiet, athletic Rebecca; curly-haired New Yorker Irene; and underage Stephen, who felt like an outsider when the others left him behind to go bar-hopping. The gang all went to work at a local radio station.

Real World VIII (1999) took viewers to beautiful Hawaii, for one of the "skin-iest" series to date. The housemates were hunky Colin, vivacious Amaya, clean-cut Matt, uncomfortable Justin (who quit the show partway through), happy lesbian Ruthie, topless Kaia and oft-naked Teck. In one of the more dramatic stories Ruthie, who had a drinking problem, was rushed by her friends to the hospital after lapsing into seizures. She subsequently left the show for 30 days to recover, but returned. *Real World IX* (2000) visited New Orleans, where the kids were put up in a palatial mansion called "Belfort." Viewing the stunning bathroom decor, one commented, "It's like Martha Stewart and Busta Rhymes got together and created a bathroom." The gang was perky Mormon Julie, bodybuilder David, chatterbox Melissa, sensitive gay Danny, spiked-hair Matt, take-charge Kelley and mature-looking Jamie.

For *Real World World X* (2001) the show returned to New York, in a spectacular Hudson Street loft that all agreed was "phat!" Buzz-cut Mike, touchy black girl Coral ("Once somebody gets on my bad side . . ."), flirty Lori, calm Malik, Nicole, BMOC Kevin and bubbly virgin Rachel were the housemates. The gang worked for Arista Records and took a quick trip to Morocco, although everything seemed to be overshadowed by Coral hissing at people, especially racially naive Mike (they eventually made up). Nudity returned in force in *Real World XI* (2002), set in an artsy loft in Chicago. Tall black Theo immediately ripped off his shirt and began lusting for Aneesa, who turned out to be gay; he pursued her anyway ("Maybe she's bi?"), and she teased back by jumping into the shower with him naked and showing him what he couldn't have. There was also hot babe Keri, movie-star-handsome Kyle, busty Tonya, sweet shy Chris (whose homosexuality seemed to make Theo uncomfortable) and Cara. Outside, real-life protesters lobbed paintballs at the building to protest "big business" (MTV) invading their neighborhood.

Real World XII (2002) moved to a 28th-floor penthouse overlooking Las Vegas, with country girl Trishelle, Steven, Irulan, Alton, Frank, Arissa and Brynn. *Real World XIII* is scheduled for Paris.

In 2000 MTV combined this and another of its most popular shows for the *Real World/Road Rules Extreme Challenge*, in which cast members from the two shows competed in various physical challenges.

REASONABLE DOUBTS (*Police Drama*)

FIRST TELECAST: *September 26, 1991*
LAST TELECAST: *July 31, 1993*
BROADCAST HISTORY:

Sep 1991, NBC Thu 10:00–11:00
Sep 1991–Jan 1992, NBC Fri 10:00–11:00
Feb 1992–Mar 1992, NBC Tue 10:00–11:00
Jun 1992–Jul 1992, NBC Fri 9:00–10:00
Aug 1992–Jan 1993, NBC Tue 9:00–10:00
Mar 1993–Apr 1993, NBC Sat 10:00–11:00
Apr 1993, NBC Tue 8:00–9:00
Jun 1993–Jul 1993, NBC Sat 10:00–11:00

CAST:

Assistant D.A. Tess Kaufman .... Marlee Matlin
Det. Dicky Cobb .... Mark Harmon
Arthur Gold .... William Converse-Roberts
Bruce Kaufman .... Tim Grimm
Kay Lockman (1991–1992) .... Nancy Everhard
Maggie Zombro (1992–1993) .... Kay Lenz
Sean Kelly (1991–1992) .... John Mese

An attorney worried about the rights of the accused paired with a bust-'em-at-all-costs cop would not normally be considered innovative television—but in this case there was a difference. The attorney was deaf. Oscar winner Marlee Matlin *(Children of a Lesser God)* played Tess, a crackerjack Chicago assistant D.A. assigned to the felony division, who had been paired with handsome but hard-edged Dicky Cobb by division chief Gold, mostly because Cobb understood sign language. That was just about the only thing Tess and Dicky had in common. Despite some inevitable attraction between them, each had their own rocky love life to contend with: Bruce was

Tess' philandering, estranged attorney husband, and Kay was Dicky's jealous, manipulative girlfriend (who died at the start of the second season). The other cops with whom Dicky had to work were mostly thick-headed louts. Maggie was a confrontational attorney.

Most of Tess's dialogue was in sign language, which Dicky summarized aloud (so the audience would know what was going on). Occasionally she would speak, albeit awkwardly.

REBA (*Situation Comedy*)
FIRST TELECAST: *October 5, 2001*
LAST TELECAST:
BROADCAST HISTORY:
Oct 2001– , WB Fri 9:00–9:30
Jul 2002–Sep 2002, WB Thu 8:00–8:30
Jun 2003– , WB Fri 8:00–8:30
CAST:
Reba Hart .... Reba McEntire
Cheyenne Hart (age 17) .... Joanna Garcia
Kyra Hart (13) .... Scarlett Pomers
Jake Hart (9) .... Mitch Holleman
Dr. Brock Hart .... Christopher Rich
Van Montgomery .... Steve Howey
Barbra Jean .... Melissa Peterman
Lori Ann (2001–2002) .... Park Overall
Elizabeth Hart (2002–)
.... Alena & Gabrielle Leberger
THEME:
"I'm a Survivor," written by Shelby Kennedy and Phillip White, performed by Reba McEntire

Life was not exactly going Reba's way as this sitcom premiered. She and Brock were in the midst of divorce proceedings when he told her he had to marry his girlfriend, perpetually perky Barbra Jean, the hygienist at his Houston dental office, because she was pregnant. Reba's somewhat spaced-out older daughter, Cheyenne, was also pregnant, by her boyfriend Van, the dim-witted star player on the Westchester High School football team. When his parents kicked him out, Van moved into the Hart home and he and Cheyenne got married. Reba and Brock had two other children, bright sarcastic Kyra, who had problems dealing with the divorce and thought both her older sister and Van were idiots (she wasn't far off), and mop-top Jake, who was much more adaptable and just wanted to play. Resilient Reba coped with all this, abetted by her sharp-tongued friend Lori Ann, taking verbal potshots at Brock and clueless Barbra Jean. In February Reba started working as a substitute teacher, her divorce became final and Brock and Barbra Jean got married. A couple of months later Barbra Jean had a son, Henry Charles Jesus Hart, and in the season finale Cheyenne went into labor during her graduation ceremony and was rushed to the hospital to give birth to a daughter, Elizabeth. Now it was grandma Reba.

At the start of the second season Cheyenne, Van and the baby had to move back in with Reba when he injured his knee in a car accident and lost his football scholarship at the University of Houston. This annoyed Kyra no end, as she was finally starting to get more attention from her mother. Cheyenne stayed in school but Van took the semester off to rehab his knee. Reba, needing additional cash, took a job in Brock's dental office, unhappily reporting to Barbra Jean. She couldn't take it and went work full time for Brock's rival, Dr. Fisher (Dan Castellaneta). In the spring Van was reinstated to the football team.

REBEL, THE (*Western*)
FIRST TELECAST: *October 4, 1959*
LAST TELECAST: *September 12, 1962*
BROADCAST HISTORY:
Oct 1959–Sep 1961, ABC Sun 9:00–9:30
Jun 1962–Sep 1962, NBC Wed 8:30–9:00
CAST:
Johnny Yuma .... Nick Adams
THEME:
"The Ballad of Johnny Yuma," by Andrew J. Fenady and Dick Markowitz

Johnny Yuma was an ex-Confederate soldier whose adventures on the Western frontier, following the end of the Civil War, were the basis of the stories in this series. As the only regular in the series, he traveled from town to town, getting involved with people and functioning, in an unofficial way, as an arbiter of justice. Not only did he get involved in criminal issues, but moral ones as well. The theme song was sung over the opening credits of each episode by popular singer Johnny Cash. In the summer of 1962, NBC aired reruns of episodes that had previously been seen on ABC.

REBOUND (*Dramatic Anthology*)
FIRST TELECAST: *February 8, 1952*
LAST TELECAST: *January 16, 1953*
BROADCAST HISTORY:
Feb 1952–Jun 1952, ABC Fri 9:00–9:30
Nov 1952–Jan 1953, DUM Fri 8:30–9:00

This filmed anthology series presented short stories of mystery and suspense, always with a trick O. Henry–type ending. The films were made in Hollywood by Bing Crosby Enterprises, and featured lesser-known (at the time) talent such as Onslow Stevens, Lee Marvin, John Doucette, and Rita Johnson.

RECKONING (*Dramatic Anthology*)
FIRST TELECAST: *July 11, 1959*
LAST TELECAST: *September 18, 1963*
BROADCAST HISTORY:
Jul 1959–Sep 1959, CBS Sat 7:30–8:30
Jun 1960–Aug 1960, CBS Wed 7:30–8:30
Jun 1963–Sep 1963, CBS Wed 10:00–11:00

The dramas presented in this summer series were all reruns of episodes previously shown on *Pursuit*, *Climax!*, and *Studio One in Hollywood*. All of the originals had aired in 1958.

RED BARBER'S CORNER (*Sports Commentary*)
FIRST TELECAST: *July 2, 1949*
LAST TELECAST: *January 3, 1958*
BROADCAST HISTORY:
Jul 1949–Feb 1950, CBS Sat 6:30–6:45
Sep 1950–Oct 1950, CBS Tue 10:30–10:45
Sep 1953–Dec 1953, CBS Sat 6:45–7:00
Dec 1954–May 1955, CBS Wed 10:45–11:00
May 1955–Jun 1955, NBC Fri 10:45–11:00
Sep 1955–Jan 1958, NBC Fri 10:45–11:00
REPORTER:
Red Barber

Sportscaster Red Barber, the "Old Redhead," was reporter, interviewer, and analyst on this weekly sports news program. In 1949 and 1950 it went under the title *Red Barber's Clubhouse*, and in the fall of 1953 it was *The Peak of the Sports News*. During that period Red was director of sports for CBS. From the fall of 1954 on CBS, then on NBC through the winter of 1958, under the title *Red Barber's Corner*, this series was used to fill the time between the conclusion of the boxing match and the start of the local 11:00 P.M. news. The format remained relatively constant. There were feature pieces on sports or individual athletes, interviews with sports figures, and bulletins on and scores of current contests.

RED BUTTONS SHOW, THE (*Comedy/Variety*)

FIRST TELECAST: *October 14, 1952*

LAST TELECAST: *May 13, 1955*

BROADCAST HISTORY:

Oct 1952–Dec 1952, CBS Tue 8:30–9:00
Dec 1952–Jan 1953, CBS Sat 9:00–9:30
Jan 1953–Jun 1954, CBS Mon 9:30–10:00 (OS)
Oct 1954–May 1955, NBC Fri 8:00–8:30

REGULARS:

Red Buttons
Dorothy Jolliffe (1952)
Pat Carroll (1952–1953)
Beverly Dennis (1952–1953)
Allan Walker (1952–1953)
Joe Silver
Betty Ann Grove (1953–1954)
Phyllis Kirk (1955)
Paul Lynde (1955)
Bobby Sherwood (1955)
The Elliot Lawrence Orchestra

The most memorable thing about *The Red Buttons Show* was an inane little song that Red sang called the "Ho-Ho" song. He would put his hands together in what appeared to be a gesture of supplication, lean his head against them at a funny angle, and hop around the stage singing "Ho! Ho! . . . He! He! . . . Ha! Ha! . . . Strange things are happening." For a time that song became a national craze that infected millions of children around the country. The show itself featured monologues and dance numbers by Red, and sketches with his regulars and any guest stars. Some of the recurring characters portrayed by Red were Rocky Buttons, a punchy boxer; the Kupke Kid, a lovable little boy; the Sad Sack; and Keeglefarven, a dumb, blundering German. There were also regular sketches about Red and his wife (in a style that was to be imitated by George Gobel later in the 1950s) with Dorothy Jolliffe as his wife when the show first started. She was replaced in October by Beverly Dennis, and Miss Dennis gave way to Betty Ann Grove at the start of the 1953–1954 season.

A smash hit in its first season, *The Red Buttons Show* began to fade in its second year on CBS and was picked up by NBC after it had been canceled. The NBC series started as a variety show with guests but no regulars other than Red. That didn't seem to work so the format was changed to a situation comedy at the end of January. Red played himself as a TV comic who was always getting into troubles of one sort or another. Phyllis Kirk was his new wife, Bobby Sherwood his pal and director of the TV show, and Paul Lynde played Mr. Standish, a network vice-president with whom Red had constant run-ins. Nothing seemed to help and Red, who had gone through literally dozens of writers in his quest to find a workable format, left the air that spring.

RED SKELTON SHOW, THE (*Comedy/Variety*)

FIRST TELECAST: *September 30, 1951*

LAST TELECAST: *August 29, 1971*

BROADCAST HISTORY:

Sep 1951–Jun 1952, NBC Sun 10:00–10:30
Sep 1952–Jun 1953, NBC Sun 7:00–7:30
Sep 1953–Jun 1954, CBS Tue 8:30–9:00
Jul 1954–Sep 1954, CBS Wed 8:00–9:00
Sep 1954–Dec 1954, CBS Tue 8:00–8:30
Jan 1955–Jun 1961, CBS Tue 9:30–10:00 (OS)
Sep 1961–Jun 1962, CBS Tue 9:00–9:30
Sep 1962–Jun 1963, CBS Tue 8:30–9:30
Sep 1963–Jun 1964, CBS Tue 8:00–9:00
Sep 1964–Jun 1970, CBS Tue 8:30–9:30 (OS)
Sep 1970–Mar 1971, NBC Mon 7:30–8:00
Jun 1971–Aug 1971, NBC Sun 8:30–9:00

REGULARS:

Red Skelton
David Rose and His Orchestra
Carol Worthington (1970–1971)
Chanin Hale (1970–1971)
Jan Arvan (1970–1971)
Bob Duggan (1970–1971)
Peggy Rea (1970–1971)
Brad Logan (1970–1971)
The Burgundy Street Singers (1970–1971)

THEMES:

"Holiday for Strings" (main); "Lovable Clown" (Freeloader skits); "Our Waltz" (intermittent), all by David Rose

Comedian Red Skelton, son of a circus clown, was one of the brightest young stars in radio during the 1940s. While many of radio's big names never fully made the transition to television, Red did. He had been essentially a visual comedian all along. In September 1951, almost ten years to the day after he had first appeared with his own show on network radio, he arrived on TV, and remained a TV superstar for the next 20 years.

Most of Red's repertoire of regular characters had been developed on radio, before a live audience, and they worked just as well on television. Among the best known were The Mean Widdle Kid, who left chaos wherever he went (his favorite expression: "I dood it!"); Clem Kadiddlehopper, the befuddled rustic; Sheriff Deadeye, the scourge of the West; boxer Cauliflower McPugg; Willie Lump-Lump, the drunk; San Fernando Red, the con man; and Bolivar Shagnasty. The one major addition to Red's character list for the TV show was Freddie the Freeloader, a hobo who never spoke. The sketches with Freddie were always pantomimed, and would, therefore, have been completely lost on a radio audience.

The format of the show consisted of an opening monologue by Red, performances by his guest stars, and comedy sketches with them. The only other regular on the show was orchestra leader David Rose, who had been with Red on radio and stayed with him throughout his 20 years on television. This finally changed for Red's last season on NBC, when he worked with a regular repertory cast. In general the humor was broad, but occasionally it could be touching and warm, particularly in the mime sketches with Freddie the Freeloader. These were often included in the completely pantomimed "Silent Spot," which for years was written for Red by Mort Greene.

Skelton was a warm, human performer who loved his audience as much as they loved him. His closing line was always a sincere, "God bless."

REDD FOXX (*Comedy/Variety*)
FIRST TELECAST: *September 15, 1977*
LAST TELECAST: *January 26, 1978*
BROADCAST HISTORY:
Sep 1977–Jan 1978, ABC Thu 10:00–11:00
REGULARS:
Redd Foxx
Gerald Wilson Orchestra

Old trouper Redd Foxx had been an obscure standup comic for decades before he got his first big break as the star of *Sanford and Son* in 1972. He had to clean up his act considerably for the television medium, as he had previously been known for his off-color humor and "party" albums, but the public loved his crotchety old Fred Sanford characterization and the show became a major hit.

In 1977 Foxx left that series and turned up on ABC in the kind of program he had wanted to do all along, his own comedy variety hour with a strong black orientation. Among the regular features were "Redd's Corner," in which he spotlighted old show-business friends who had not had much TV exposure (usually for good reason—they were awful) and "The History of the Black in America," Redd's view of how things *really* happened. Among Redd's semiregular guests were comedian Slappy White, songstress Damita Jo, and Redd's comic partner from *Sanford and Son*, LaWanda Page. Gravel-voiced Redd also frequently offered a song or two.

REDD FOXX SHOW, THE (*Situation Comedy*)
FIRST TELECAST: *January 18, 1986*
LAST TELECAST: *April 19, 1986*
BROADCAST HISTORY:
Jan 1986–Apr 1986, ABC Sat 8:00–8:30
CAST:
Al Hughes .... Redd Foxx
Toni Rutledge .... Pamela Segall
Diana Olmos .... Rosana DeSoto
Sgt. Dwight Stryker .... Barry Van Dyke
Jim-Jam .... Nathaniel Taylor
Jim-Jam (as of Feb 22) .... Theodore Wilson
Felicia Clemmons-Hughes .... Beverly Todd
Byron Lightfoot .... Sinbad
Duds .... Iron Jaw Wilson
THEME:
Sung by Kool & the Gang

Redd Foxx attempted a comeback in this funky little comedy about a small-time businessman in New York City. Al Hughes was a gruff old codger who ran a combination diner/newsstand in a black, inner-city neighborhood. Hanging around the counter were Toni, a white street kid he had adopted as a foster daughter; Diana, the waitress; Jim-Jam, a friend; and Dwight, a local cop. There was a lot of street life in the neighborhood, and early episodes were enlivened by a group of four young harmonizing black kids (played by Ron Jaxon, Phil Perry, Theo Forsett, and Oren Waters) who worked as movers and constituted the "Mulberry St. Du-Wop Moving Company."

Major cast changes were made in March in a vain attempt to improve the program's sagging ratings. Diana and Toni departed (the latter to boarding school), and Al was descended upon by his sharp-tongued ex-wife Felicia, who demanded a half-interest in the business in lieu of the alimony he had never paid her. Byron was a new foster son.

REDHANDED (*Audience Participation*)
FIRST TELECAST: *March 8, 1999*
LAST TELECAST: *September 28, 1999*
BROADCAST HISTORY:
Mar 1999–Apr 1999, UPN Mon 8:30–9:00
Jun 1999–Jul 1999, UPN Mon 9:00–10:00
Sep 1999, UPN Tue 8:30–9:00
COMMENTATOR:
Adam Carolla

Redhanded was *Candid Camera*'s evil twin. Unlike the venerable series which saw the humor in situations and used accomplices and hidden cameras to amuse and entertain, the mean-spirited *Redhanded* used the same techniques to embarrass and humiliate. The professional pranksters of this series set up unsuspecting people in situations that were sure to cause them problems. People caught "redhanded" included a guy who stole everything that wasn't nailed down from his hotel room; an engaged woman who couldn't resist flirting with an attractive man; a man who would say anything to pick up women; another who lied to his fiancée about what was going on at his stag party; customers shoplifting at a grocery store; and applicants cheating on an entrance exam for a job.

Adam Carolla provided smarmy running commentary—from pointing out why each victim had been chosen (usually explained by a "friend" of the victim who participated in the setup), through the perpetration of the "stings" (shown via hidden camera), to the moments when the poor saps were told that they had been had (Carolla: "What a schmuck!"). After getting caught, they suffered the additional indignity of trying to rationalize their actions on camera.

REDIGO (*Western*)
FIRST TELECAST: *September 24, 1963*
LAST TELECAST: *December 31, 1963*
BROADCAST HISTORY:
Sep 1963–Dec 1963, NBC Tue 8:30–9:00
CAST:
Jim Redigo .... Richard Egan
Mike .... Roger Davis
Frank Martinez .... Rudy Solari
Gerry .... Elena Verdugo
Linda Martinez .... Mina Martinez

Empire had failed during the 1962–1963 season but its focal character, Jim Redigo, survived to try it on his own. In *Empire* he had been the manager of the vast Garret ranch in the contemporary Southwest. Now he was the owner and operator of his own small ranch in the same area at roughly the same time. The problems of making the ranch profitable and the relationships between people on it provided the story material. The two most prominent employees on the Redigo ranch were Mike and Frank, and Jim's casual romantic interest (despite the fact that she was seriously in love with him) was Gerry, manager of the Gran Quivera

Hotel in the nearby town of Mesa. Frank's wife Linda was the ranch's cook.

REEL GAME, THE (*Quiz*)

FIRST TELECAST: *January 18, 1971*
LAST TELECAST: *May 3, 1971*
BROADCAST HISTORY:
Jan 1971–May 1971, ABC Mon 8:30–9:00
EMCEE:
Jack Barry

Each of the three contestants in this quiz show was given a sum of money and then asked to bet portions of it on his knowledge of famous people and events. The answers were then compared with newsreels or film clips of the right answers.

The program was created by Jack Barry, who was said to have been involved in the creation and production of 30 different quiz, game, and audience-participation shows up to this time.

REGGIE (*Situation Comedy*)

FIRST TELECAST: *August 2, 1983*
LAST TELECAST: *September 1, 1983*
BROADCAST HISTORY:
Aug 1983, ABC Tue 9:30–10:00
Aug 1983–Sep 1983, ABC Thu 9:00–9:30
CAST:
Reggie Potter .... Richard Mulligan
Elizabeth Potter .... Barbara Barrie
Mark Potter .... Timothy Busfield
Linda Potter Lockett .... Dianne Kay
Tom Lockett .... Timothy Stack
C. J. Wilcox .... Chip Zien
Joan Reynolds .... Jean Smart

Reggie was based on a British television series that had begun with an interesting premise: a frustrated, middle-aged executive, exhausted by the pressures and monotony of his life, faked his own suicide by walking into the ocean. He then came back in all manner of outrageous disguises to snoop on his family and friends (who were mourning him—sort of) and ended up romancing and marrying his own "widowed" wife, before the ruse was discovered. The American series never tried that innovative plot, but it did depict a frustrated Reggie trying to cope with his perpetual midlife crisis through daydream fantasies that viewers saw and that sometimes came true.

Reggie's job at the Funtime Ice Cream Company gave him the most woe, especially his incredibly overbearing young boss, C.J., and his luscious secretary, Joan, about whom he had been having sexual fantasies for years (unknown to Reggie, she had been having the same fantasies about him). He worried about his sexual prowess with his wife, Elizabeth, worried about his daughter, Linda, and her obnoxious husband, Tom, lusted for his son Mark's girlfriend, and confided his darkest secrets to Monty, a large stuffed toy fox attired in English hunting habit.

Based on the British series *The Fall and Rise of Reginald Perrin,* and David Nobbs' book of the same name.

REGULAR JOE (*Situation Comedy*)

FIRST TELECAST: *March 28, 2003*
LAST TELECAST: *April 18, 2003*
BROADCAST HISTORY:
Mar 2003–Apr 2003, ABC Fri 9:30–10:00
CAST:
Joe Binder .... Daniel Stern
Grant Binder .... John Francis Daley
Joanie Binder .... Kelly Karbacz
Baxter Binder .... Judd Hirsch
Sitvar .... Brian George

A well-meaning dad tried to hold his somewhat splintered family together in this bland sitcom set in New York. Since the death of his wife Angela, and the birth of a baby to his unwed daughter, Joanie, amiable Joe was both mom *and* dad to his bright and busy daughter, a freshman at Queens College, and his gawky son, Grant, who was still in high school. Joe spent a good deal of time taking care of Joanie's baby, Zoey, as well as fending off wisecracks from his own cranky father, Baxter, who lived with them. The family business was a neighborhood hardware store, where Joe and Baxter (and sometimes Grant) worked. Sitvar was their snide, neurotic employee at the store, a native of India.

REHEARSAL CALL (*Variety*)

FIRST TELECAST: *March 20, 1949*
LAST TELECAST: *April 24, 1949*
BROADCAST HISTORY:
Mar 1949–Apr 1949, ABC Sun 9:15–9:30
HOSTESS:
Dee Parker
REGULARS:
Leonard Stanley Trio

Short-lived 15-minute variety program originating from Detroit.

RELATIVITY (*Comedy/Drama*)

FIRST TELECAST: *September 24, 1996*
LAST TELECAST: *April 14, 1997*
BROADCAST HISTORY:
Sep 1996–Oct 1996, ABC Tue 10:00–11:00
Sep 1996–Jan 1997, ABC Sat 10:00–11:00
Mar 1997–Apr 1997, ABC Mon 8:00–9:00
CAST:
Isabel Lukens .... Kimberly Williams
Leo Roth .... David Conrad
David Lukens .... Cliff DeYoung
Eve Lukens .... Mary Ellen Trainor
Karen Lukens Nichols .... Jane Adams
Jennifer Lukens (age 21) .... Poppy Montgomery
Barry Roth .... Richard Schiff
Jake Roth (17) .... Devon Gummersall
Rhonda Roth .... Lisa Edelstein
Hal Roth .... Robert Katims
Doug Kroll .... Adam Goldberg

The producers of *thirtysomething* and *My So-Called Life* offered another tale of emotional angst in this romantic drama about two young lovers. Isabel, 24, met house painter Leo, 26, in a plaza in Rome, where she was agonizing over the marriage proposal of her boyfriend Everett and he was contemplating the death of his mother. They fell madly and passionately in love, but of course it could not be. Returning to Los Angeles, she prepared to marry her stiff and he went back to trying to pull together his dysfunctional family. However, their mutual attraction was too strong to be quenched ("I just keep picturing your face"), and complications quickly ensued. Isabel's distressed family included dad David, who ran *Epicenter* magazine, where she worked as an editorial assistant; mom Eve; older sister Karen, who was married to a workaholic husband; and younger sis Jennifer, who was arty, hip, and self-absorbed. Leo's family consisted of his dad Barry, emotionally distant since his wife's death; truant brother Jake, who badly needed a strong father figure; sister Rhonda, who had just been dumped by her lesbian lover; and Grandfather Hal. Doug was Leo's best friend and roommate.

RELIABLE SOURCES (*Discussion*)

BROADCAST HISTORY:

CNN
30 minutes
Produced: *1992–*
Premiered: *March 7, 1992*

REGULARS:

Bernard Kalb
Howard Kurtz (1998–)

A weekly panel discussion about the media, seen on the weekend.

RELIC HUNTER (*Adventure*)

BROADCAST HISTORY:

Syndicated only
60 minutes
Produced: *1999–2002* (66 episodes)
Released: *September 1999*

CAST:

Sydney Fox .... Tia Carrere
Nigel Bailey .... Christien Anholt
Claudia (1999–2001) .... Lindy Booth
Karen Petrusky (2001–2002) .... Tanja Reichert

This cheap *Indiana Jones* clone centered on Sydney, a remarkably sexy history professor at Trinity College who moonlighted as a hunter of the ancient and arcane. Each episode opened with a scene set in the past that provided background on the relic she was subsequently hired to find. Among the artifacts she retrieved were the decapitated body of a 400-year-old nun, Al Capone's diamond-encrusted pistol, Buddha's overflowing alms bowl and a guitar that Elvis Presley had given to a fellow GI in Germany in 1960. Nigel was Sydney's intellectual young teaching assistant, and Claudia, an airhead student who served as the Ancient History Department's secretary and had designs on an oblivious Nigel. Most of the hunts were disrupted by unscrupulous people in search of the same artifacts and Nigel's penchant for getting himself, and Sydney, in trouble. There were plenty of booby-trapped temples and shifty-eyed natives, and many of the artifacts had supernatural qualities.

During the second season Claudia started helping out, often getting herself into predicaments in the process. At the start of the third season she departed for a job in New York and was replaced by resourceful Karen, who had originally been hired as a temp but was quickly given a permanent job.

REMEMBER WENN (*Drama*)

BROADCAST HISTORY:

American Movie Classics
30 minutes
Produced: *1996–1998* (56 episodes)
Premiered: *January 13, 1996*

CAST:

Jeff Singer .... Hugh O'Gorman
Hilary Booth .... Melinda Mullins
Betty Roberts .... Amanda Naughton
Mackie Bloom .... Chris Murney
Thomas Eldridge .... George Hall
Mr. Foley .... Tom Beckett
Victor Comstock .... John Bedford Lloyd
Scott Sherwood .... Kevin O'Rourke
C. J. McHugh (1996–1997) .... C. J. Byrnes
Maple LaMarsh .... Carolee Carmello
Gertrude Reece .... Margaret Hall
Celia Mellon (1996) .... Dina Spybey
Eugenia Bremer .... Mary Stout

This curious little comedy-drama was the first original series produced by AMC, a channel principally known for its old—sometimes *very* old—movies. The setting was behind-the-scenes at Pittsburgh radio station WENN in 1939, an era when radio drama was being produced live on local stations around the country. WENN's diva was Hilary, a Broadway castoff who lorded it over her fellow players with her grandiose airs. Jeff was her handsome ex-husband, Mackie the mousy "man of a thousand voices" (this was radio, so who cared what they looked like?), Foley the sound effects man, and Betty the enthusiastic young intern. Plots were sometimes bizarre, as when station manager Victor Comstock was programmed by the Nazis to kill whenever he heard the phrase "buy barley futures."

REMINGTON STEELE (*Detective Drama*)

FIRST TELECAST: *October 1, 1982*
LAST TELECAST: *March 9, 1987*

BROADCAST HISTORY:

Oct 1982–Mar 1983, NBC Fri 10:00–11:00
Mar 1983–Dec 1983, NBC Tue 9:00–10:00
Jan 1984–Feb 1986, NBC Tue 10:00–11:00
Feb 1986–Aug 1986, NBC Sat 10:00–11:00
Feb 1987, NBC Tue 10:00–11:00
Mar 1987, NBC Mon 10:00–11:00

CAST:

Laura Holt .... Stephanie Zimbalist
Remington Steele .... Pierce Brosnan
Murphy Michaels (1982–1983) .... James Read
Bernice Foxe (1982–1983) .... Janet DeMay
Mildred Krebs (1983–1987) .... Doris Roberts

Laura Holt and Remington Steele had come together quite by accident, but they made a great pair of sleuths. She was smart, brassy, and attractive; he was cultured, handsome, and extremely charming. Together they solved complex murder mysteries in high society, while maintaining a relationship that bordered on the romantic. Actually, Remington had begun as a figment of Laura's imagination. Opening her own investigation agency, she found that a woman's name did not bring in assignments, so she invented an imaginary boss—Remington Steele—and business boomed. Trouble was, wealthy clients kept wanting to meet this supersleuth whose name was on the door. Along came an incredibly handsome chap with a suave manner and a mysterious background; just what she needed. Steele (his real name and background remained a mystery) bumbled a lot at first, but learned the private eye's trade quickly and soon was more than a front man for Laura. A fan of old Hollywood movies, he often pursued a case by playing out a scene from a classic film like *The Thin Man*, *Notorious*, or *Key Largo*. With easy banter and close teamwork, and occasional comic interludes, the stylish pair proved that romance and mystery did still mix.

There were changes in the supporting cast for the second season, as Bernice the secretary ran off with a saxophone player and was replaced by Mildred, an ex-I.R.S. agent who had lost her government job after letting Remington beat a tax-evasion charge; and Murphy, Laura's original partner, left to form his own agency.

Remington Steele's last regular season was 1985–1986. However, in early 1987 NBC aired two new two-hour movies in which Laura and Remington solved international mysteries, and finally consummated their relationship.

REMOTE CONTROL (*Quiz/Audience Participation*)

BROADCAST HISTORY:

MTV
30 minutes
Produced: *1987–1990*
Premiered: *December 7, 1987*
(Also first-run syndication, 1989)

REGULARS:

Ken Ober
Colin Quinn

A rapid-fire early-evening game show in which three college-age kids tried to gain control of the remote by answering questions on pop culture trivia. The funky setting was Ken Ober's parents' basement at 72 Whooping Cough Lane, complete with lounge chairs, a worn-out couch, refrigerator, bowls of popcorn, and a huge television set. Losers suffered the indignity of suddenly being whisked out of sight, chair and all.

After the show gained popularity on MTV, new episodes were produced for syndication.

REN & STIMPY SHOW, THE (*Cartoon*)

BROADCAST HISTORY:

Nickelodeon
30 minutes
Produced: *1991–1995* (52 episodes)
Premiered: *August 11, 1991*

VOICES:

Ren (1991–1992) .... John Kricfalusi
Ren (1992–1995) .... Billy West
Stimpy .... Billy West

A fast-paced "gross-out" cartoon that became a cult favorite in the early 1990s. Ren was a scrawny, temperamental Chihuahua who constantly demanded attention from his trusting feline housemate, Stimpy. Each episode was filled with explosions, squashing, mangling, nose-picking, regurgitating, underhanded tricks, and sight gags galore as the two interacted with each other and a menagerie of others. A jazzy score added to the avant-garde atmosphere of the show.

Ren & Stimpy was created by John Kricfalusi, who also originally provided the voice of the aggressive Ren. After a falling-out over creative matters, he was fired by Nickelodeon and Billy West took over both voices.

RENDEZ-VIEW (*Dating*)

BROADCAST HISTORY:

Syndicated only
30 minutes
Produced: *2001–2002*
Released: *September 2001*

HOST:

Greg Proops

ROMANCE EXPERT:

Ellen Ladowsky

Described by the producer as *Blind Date* meets *Politically Incorrect*, each episode of *Rendez-View* chronicled a blind date between two participants while the show's regulars and two celebrity guest hosts (one male and one female) commented on the proceedings. Host Proops was a stand-up comic and Ellen Ladowsky was a well-known relationship expert. The four evaluators provided analysis and rated everything each of the daters did. Among the celebrity hosts were Brad Sherwood, Stephanie Miller, Alfonso Ribeiro, Nicole Eggert, Traci Bingham, Debra Wilson, Soleil Moon Frye, Jerry Springer and Diedrich Bader.

RENDEZVOUS (*International Intrigue*)

FIRST TELECAST: *February 13, 1952*
LAST TELECAST: *March 5, 1952*

BROADCAST HISTORY:

Feb 1952–Mar 1952, ABC Wed 9:30–10:00

CAST:

Nikki Angell .... Ilona Massey

ALSO:

David McKay

This short-lived series starred gorgeous Hungarian-born film star Ilona Massey as the owner and chief attraction at Chez Nikki, a posh nightclub in Paris. She had been a French underground agent during World War II, and was now engaged in international espionage on the Continent, foiling Communist agents and incidentally romancing newspaperman David McKay. Miss Massey also had an opportunity to sing one or two songs in each episode, in her sultry style.

RENDEZVOUS WITH MUSIC (*Music*)

FIRST TELECAST: *July 11, 1950*
LAST TELECAST: *August 8, 1950*

BROADCAST HISTORY:

Jul 1950–Aug 1950, NBC Tue 9:00–9:30

REGULARS:

Carol Reed
Don Gallagher
Tony DeSimone Trio

This was a musical interlude, reflecting "the varied tempos of summertime." Emcee Carol Reed was also featured as a singer on the show.

RENEGADE (*Adventure*)

BROADCAST HISTORY:

Syndicated and USA Network
60 minutes
Produced: *1992–1997* (110 episodes)
Released: *September 1992*

CAST:

Reno Raines/Vince Black .... Lorenzo Lamas
Bobby Sixkiller .... Branscombe Richmond
Cheyenne Phillips (1992–1996)
.... Kathleen Kinmont
Lt./Marshal Donald "Dutch" Dixon
.... Stephen J. Cannell
**Sgt. Frank "Woody" Bickford* .... Ron Johnson
**Hound Adams (1993–1996)* .... Geoffrey Blake
Sandy Caruthers (1996–1997) .... Sandra Ferguson

*Occasional

Reno Raines was a young policeman in Bay City, California, who had testified about police corruption and gotten framed for the murder of a cop by bad cops. He had escaped before going to trial and was on the run trying to get evidence to prove his innocence. Using the name Vince Black, Reno worked as a bounty hunter for his buddy, Bobby Sixkiller, who frequently got him out of trouble. Reno sure didn't look like a cop with his shoulder-length hair and a beard (shaved off in the fall of 1993). A martial arts expert, he traveled on his powerful motorcycle and kept in touch with Bobby via cellular phone. Cheyenne, Bobby's half sister, was a computer whiz who worked with her brother, often accessing databases from the field on her laptop computer. Dutch Dixon (played by series creator/executive producer Stephen J. Cannell) was the corrupt cop hunting Reno down. It was he who had murdered the cop Reno had been framed for killing, and he had also been responsible for the fatal shooting of Reno's fiancée.

In the fall of 1994, Dixon caught up with Reno, who then went on trial for the murder Dixon had originally pinned on him at the start of the series. Sleazy Hound Adams was set to testify with evidence that would have exonerated Reno and pinned the crime on Dixon, but Adams doubled-crossed our hero and Reno was convicted of murder with special circumstances. While being transferred from one prison to another Reno escaped and resumed bounty hunting for Bobby and his search for Adams or other evidence to prove his innocence.

In the spring of 1994, Kathleen Kinmont, star Lorenzo Lamas' wife, filed for divorce. She remained on the show for two more years, but was abruptly dropped in early 1996 when she was quoted in the press making derogatory comments about Lamas' new love, Shauna Sand, who had begun making occasional appearances on the show as Bobby's personal trainer. In September 1996 the series moved to USA Network, which continued original production for a final season. Sandy joined the team as a new assistant, after completing the Sixkiller video correspondence course, Dutch was now a Federal Marshal, and Reno was once again sporting his long hair. Early in the season Dixon's wife, Melissa (Gloria Loring), fed up with her husband's murderous ways, approached Reno and Bobby and offered to help take him down. Dixon killed her before she could do so, pinning the murder on Reno. In the final episode Dixon's son Donnie (Steven Flynn) escaped from prison and sought revenge against Reno for his mother's murder. Dixon, seeing his schemes unraveling, offered Reno $500,000 to leave the country, but in a climactic confrontation, the evil lawman was finally killed, and Reno roared off into the sunset.

RENEGADES (*Police Drama*)

FIRST TELECAST: *March 4, 1983*
LAST TELECAST: *April 8, 1983*
BROADCAST HISTORY:
Mar 1983–Apr 1983, ABC Fri 9:00–10:00
CAST:
Bandit .... Patrick Swayze
Eagle .... Randy Brooks
J.T. .... Paul Mones
Tracy .... Tracy Scoggins
Dancer .... Robert Thaler
Dragon .... Brian Tochi
Gaucho .... Fausto Bara
Lt. Marciano .... James Luisi
Capt. Scanlon .... Kurtwood Smith

With a premise reminiscent of *The Mod Squad*, this short-run series brought together a group of seven tough young gang leaders and a hip cop named Lt. Marciano to fight crime in the big city. The incentive was to clear their records, and Marciano was a tough taskmaster. Their undercover operations often included finking on their own generation (infiltrating gangs, high schools, etc.), although there usually was a crooked adult behind it all. Capt. Scanlon was dubious about the whole idea, and was constantly on Marciano's back to give it up.

The Renegades was originally seen as a TV-movie on August 11, 1982.

REPORT CARD FOR PARENTS (*Discussion*)

FIRST TELECAST: *December 1, 1952*
LAST TELECAST: *February 2, 1953*
BROADCAST HISTORY:
Dec 1952–Feb 1953, DUM Mon 8:00–8:30

Panel-discussion program on the problems of bringing up children, with different guests each week.

REPORT FROM . . . (*News/Travelogue*)

FIRST TELECAST: *July 9, 1963*
LAST TELECAST: *September 10, 1963*
BROADCAST HISTORY:
Jul 1963–Sep 1963, NBC Tue 10:30–11:00

Film portraits of 11 cities around the world, hosted by the NBC News correspondent in each city.

REPORT ON . . . (*Documentary*)

FIRST TELECAST: *March 13, 1949*
LAST TELECAST: *April 3, 1949*
BROADCAST HISTORY:
Mar 1949–Apr 1949, CBS Sun 6:30–7:00
NARRATOR:
Charles Hodges

This four-week documentary series, hosted and narrated by CBS News correspondent Charles Hodges, analyzed the current world political situation. The reports were on Moscow, the North Atlantic Pact, Italy, and a United Nations press conference.

REPORT TO MURPHY (*Situation Comedy*)

FIRST TELECAST: *April 5, 1982*
LAST TELECAST: *May 31, 1982*
BROADCAST HISTORY:
Apr 1982–May 1982, CBS Mon 8:30–9:00
CAST:
Murphy .... Michael Keaton
Blanche .... Olivia Cole
Lucy .... Donna Ponterotto
Charlie .... Donnelly Rhodes
Baker .... Margot Rose
Big Walter .... Ken Foree

Short-lived comedy about the trials of an idealistic young parole officer. Murphy was new to the profession and was not yet as disillusioned as his fellow parole officers. His enthusiasm and willingness to try unorthodox approaches in dealing with parolees were ridiculed by veteran, by-the-book Charlie, the office sourpuss. Even his supervisor, Blanche, and his fellow parole officer, Lucy, sometimes found it hard to understand why Murphy got so personally involved with his "clients." Baker was a pretty young assistant district attorney with whom Murphy had an on-again/off-again relationship, depending on whether or not she was prosecuting one of his parolees, and Big Walter was a car thief who was one of Murphy's favorite "clients."

REPORTER, THE (*Newspaper Drama*)
FIRST TELECAST: *September 25, 1964*
LAST TELECAST: *December 18, 1964*
BROADCAST HISTORY:
Sep 1964–Dec 1964, CBS Fri 10:00–11:00
CAST:
Danny Taylor .... Harry Guardino
Lou Sheldon .... Gary Merrill
Artie Burns .... George O'Hanlon
Ike Dawson .... Remo Pisani

Danny Taylor was a reporter for *The New York Globe,* a Manhattan daily. He was young, tough, and determined, all qualities necessary for a newsman in "The Big Apple." City editor Lou Sheldon was Danny's boss. He was also the father figure who understood what made Danny tick and could use his knowledge of the workings of the younger man's mind to drive him to dig deeper and harder into a story. Artie Burns was the friendly cabbie who was always available to take Danny off on a story, and Ike Dawson ran the Press Box, a bar where newspaper people gathered in their off hours.

REPORTER COLLINS, see *Not for Publication*

REPORTERS, THE (*Newsmagazine*)
FIRST TELECAST: *July 30, 1988*
LAST TELECAST: *March 31, 1990*
BROADCAST HISTORY:
Jul 1988–May 1989, FOX Sat 8:00–9:00
Jul 1989–Dec 1989, FOX Sat 8:30–9:30
Dec 1989–Mar 1990, FOX Sat 9:00–10:00
REPORTERS:
Jim Paymar
Steve Dunleavy
Steve Dunlop (1988–1989)
Steve Wilson (1988–1989)
Rafael Abramovitz (1988–1989)
Krista Bradford
Kristin Altman (1989–1990)
Bob Drury (1989–1990)

One of the first major successes of Fox Broadcasting was the syndicated tabloid-style magazine series *A Current Affair.* In an effort to repeat its success on its fledgling network operation, Fox created *The Reporters.* Although the format was slightly different—the reporters introduced their own stories and there was no anchor/host—the content was virtually identical to *A Current Affair.* The same exploitive, sensational, and sexy stories that had provided fodder for *A Current Affair* turned up on *The Reporters.* To further blur the distinction, several of the reporters on this series were former and/or current reporters on *A Current Affair*—Rafael Abramovitz, Krista Bradford, and Steve Dunleavy. Although most of the reporters used a confrontational style, Steve Wilson was the show's designated "investigative reporter."

RERUN SHOW, THE (*Comedy Anthology*)
FIRST TELECAST: *August 1, 2002*
LAST TELECAST: *August 20, 2002*
BROADCAST HISTORY:
Aug 2002, NBC Thu 9:30–10:00
Aug 2002, NBC Tue 8:30–9:00
REGULARS:
Brian Beacock
Ashley Drane
Candy Ford
Daniele Gaither
Danielle Hoover
Don Reed
Mitch Silpa
Paul Vogt

Nostalgia ran amok on this summer series, which took actual scripts from classic sitcoms and reenacted them in a way that the creators never envisioned. At least it was unlikely that the creators of *Diff'rent Strokes* envisioned a mumbling Mr. Drummond, Arnold being handed around like a doll, a horny Willis ripping off his shirt and jumping into bed with his date, and Kimberly posing for sexy pictures taken by Mr. D. Everything was wildly overplayed, with lots of sex jokes, mugging, superimposed comments, and walk-ons by original stars like Gary Coleman and Danny Bonaduce. Among the other shows lampooned with their own scripts were *The Partridge Family* (with the family obviously faking their instruments), *Saved By the Bell* (a "very special episode" about drugs), *The Facts of Life* (the "shoplifting episode"), *The Jeffersons, What's Happening!, Married . . . With Children* and others.

RESCUE 8 (*Adventure*)
BROADCAST HISTORY:
Syndicated only
30 minutes
Produced: *1958–1959* (73 episodes)
Released: *September 1958*
CAST:
Wes Cameron .... Jim Davis
Skip Johnson .... Lang Jeffries
Patty Johnson .... Nancy Rennick

This predecessor of *Emergency, 240-Robert,* and other "rescue" shows was based on the files of the Los Angeles County Fire Department's rescue squads. Wes Cameron headed the two-man team that inched its way into all sorts of precarious situations to save people in awkward straits (scaffolds, Ferris wheels, cliffs, etc.). Skip was the junior member of the team, whose wife, Patty, wished he'd do something less dangerous for a living.

RESCUE 911 (*Informational*)
FIRST TELECAST: *September 5, 1989*
LAST TELECAST: *September 3, 1996*
BROADCAST HISTORY:
Sep 1989–Sep 1995, CBS Tue 8:00–9:00
Jan 1992–Feb 1992, CBS Fri 8:00–9:00
Feb 1996–Jun 1996, CBS Thu 9:00–10:00
Aug 1996–Sep 1996, CBS Tue 8:00–9:00
HOST:
William Shatner

Hosted by veteran actor William Shatner, *Rescue 911* was a reality-based series which straightforwardly documented the heroic efforts of police, paramedics, firefighters, and, in some cases, just plain citizens. Most, but not all, of the segments dealt with responses to 911 emergency line calls in cities around the country. Some included film of the real rescue efforts and most contained dramatic re-creations of the incidents with the actual participants providing narration. Among the stories were doctors and paramedics saving the life of a young football player who had suffered a heart attack during a game; the rescue of scuba divers lost in an underwater cave; the revival of a bear that had electrocuted itself on a transformer; and assorted confrontations with criminals. One recurring theme was the resourcefulness of the 911 dispatchers—tracing addresses when something prevented the caller from providing the information, calming down hysterical callers, and providing assistance over the phone until professional rescuers could reach the victim.

Originally aired as a series of specials that had premiered on April 18, 1989, *Rescue 911* was credited by law enforcement agencies with providing life-saving information that had helped many of its viewers respond to their own emergencies. It also struck a universal chord, and by 1991 was airing in 45 countries around the world, some of which produced special versions based on their own "911" (or similar) systems.

RESCUE 77 (*Medical Adventure*)
FIRST TELECAST: *March 15, 1999*
LAST TELECAST: *September 5, 1999*
BROADCAST HISTORY:
Mar 1999–Jul 1999, WB Mon 9:00–10:00
Aug 1999–Sep 1999, WB Sun 7:00–8:00
CAST:
Michael Bell .... Victor Browne
Wick Lobo .... Christian Kane
Kathleen Ryan .... Marjorie Monaghan
Capt. Durfee .... Richard Roundtree
Nurse Megan Cates .... Robia LaMorte
Dr. Griffith .... Terence Knox

This updated version of the 1970s series *Emergency* focused on the activities of three young paramedics working out of Fire Station #77 in Los Angeles—bull-headed Bell, whose impulsiveness sometimes got him in trouble; rich kid Wick, whose father had tried to get him to quit the department for an executive position in the family corporation; and conflicted Ryan, who had just returned from a leave of absence after getting burned out during her previous tour of duty with the L.A.F.D. Bell was starting to date Megan, an Emergency Room nurse at the hospital where they took the injured for treatment. She worked with Dr. Griffith, who gave the team medical instructions via cellular phone when they were working on injured people in the field. Captain Durfee was their tough but understanding superior. In *Rescue 77*'s first episode they got workers out of a building after a methane explosion, rescued a private pilot after his small plane crashed, and dealt with a domestic violence situation in which the wife died from injuries suffered at the hands of her abusive husband. A daily ritual was sitting at a meal table with the next shift and shaking hands at the shift change.

The series' executive producer was former firefighter Gregory Widen, who had written the screenplay for the theatrical film *Backdraft*. He also wrote several of the series' episodes.

RESTLESS GUN, THE (*Western*)
FIRST TELECAST: *September 23, 1957*
LAST TELECAST: *September 14, 1959*
BROADCAST HISTORY:
Sep 1957–Sep 1959, NBC Mon 8:00–8:30
CAST:
Vint Bonner .... John Payne

The adventures of a loner traveling through the post-Civil War Southwest provided the stories told in *The Restless Gun*. Vint Bonner was a cowboy who just couldn't seem to stay in one place too long. Although he was a very proficient gun-fighter, Vint was basically a quiet, idealistic individual who preferred not to fight if there was an acceptable alternative. Unfortunately, there often was no alternative.

ABC aired reruns of *The Restless Gun* weekdays from October 1959 to September 1960, and Saturday mornings from November 1959 to March 1960.

RETURN ENGAGEMENT, see *ABC Dramatic Shorts—1952–1953*

RETURN ENGAGEMENT, syndicated title for *Fireside Theatre*

RETURN OF THE SAINT, see *Saint, The*

REUNITED (*Situation Comedy*)
FIRST TELECAST: *October 28, 1998*
LAST TELECAST: *December 29, 1998*
BROADCAST HISTORY:
Oct 1998–Nov 1998, UPN Tue 9:30–10:00
Dec 1998, UPN Tue 9:00–9:30
Dec 1998, UPN Tue 9:30–10:00
CAST:
Nicki Beck .... Julie Hagerty
Joanne .... Kelly De Martino
Gary Beck .... Cliff Bemis
Ami Beck (age 7) .... Renee Olstead
Bo Bruener .... Fabrizio Filippo
THEME:
"Reunited" (1979 pop song)

There was serious culture clash when punk-rock, tattooed, and pierced, 21-year-old Joanne showed up on the doorstep of her very straight suburban biological mother. Raised by a wealthy couple, but knowing she was adopted, she had always felt out of place and decided to seek out her real mother. Joanne's perpetually perky birth mother, Nicki, who worked at Major Mart, a discount department store in Pittsburgh, had become pregnant by a drum major in high school and given the child up for adoption. Now she was a veritable Stepford wife, cloyingly sweet and obsessed with her Hummel figurines. Joanne was cynical, a total vegetarian, and found it difficult to live with the Catholic Becks, particularly with Nicki's grouchy husband Gary. In mid-November she tried to make peace with the family and got a job helping their young, amiable neighbor, Bo, stuffing envelopes for companies. Bo had the hots for Joanne, but she preferred to keep him as a friend in whom she could confide. Nicki's other daughter was sugary sweet little Ami, who, to her mom's dismay, picked up some of her half-sister's traits ("I want to be a pagan like Joanne.")

REVEALED WITH JULES ASNER (*Interview*)
BROADCAST HISTORY:
E! Entertainment
60 minutes

Original episodes: *2001–*
Premiered: *December 5, 2001*

HOST:
Jules Asner

Celebrity interviews by glamorous, raven-haired Jules Asner, who tried to draw out feelings as well as facts from her subjects as they talked about their struggles and careers. Guests were mostly A-list, beginning with George Clooney and Julia Roberts and later including Mel Gibson, Celine Dion, and The Rock.

REVLON MIRROR THEATRE (*Dramatic Anthology*)

FIRST TELECAST: *June 23, 1953*
LAST TELECAST: *December 12, 1953*
BROADCAST HISTORY:
Jun 1953–Sep 1953, NBC Tue 8:00–8:30
Sep 1953–Dec 1953, CBS Sat 10:30–11:00

HOSTESS:
Robin Chandler

During the summer of 1953, Revlon sponsored a series of live dramas that aired on NBC on Tuesday nights. When the series moved to CBS in September, the plays shown were on film. During the NBC run, Eddie Albert, Martha Scott, Jackie Cooper, and Peggy Ann Garner appeared. Joan Crawford made her TV dramatic debut in the first CBS episode, and subsequent telecasts featured such stars as Agnes Moorehead, Dana Clark, Angela Lansbury, and Charles Bickford. Hostess Robin Chandler was also the commercial spokeswoman for Revlon Cosmetics, the show's sponsor.

REVLON REVUE, THE (*Variety*)

FIRST TELECAST: *January 28, 1960*
LAST TELECAST: *June 16, 1960*
BROADCAST HISTORY:
Jan 1960–Jun 1960, CBS Thu 10:00–11:00

This series was a collection of variety specials, each of which starred different performers. It presented both comedy and music with the emphasis of a particular show depending on the makeup of its cast. Among the stars of individual telecasts were Mickey Rooney, Maurice Chevalier, Jackie Cooper, Gordon and Sheila MacRae, and Peggy Lee. Miss Lee starred in several shows, while the others were in only one each. On March 24 the show's title was changed to *Revlon Presents* and, effective May 12, when it began a series of musical specials, to *Revlon Spring Music Festival.*

RHINEMANN EXCHANGE, THE (*Foreign Intrigue*)

FIRST TELECAST: *March 10, 1977*
LAST TELECAST: *March 24, 1977*
BROADCAST HISTORY:
Mar 1977, NBC Tue 9:00–11:00

CAST:
David Spaulding .... Stephen Collins
Leslie Hawkewood .... Lauren Hutton
Bobby Ballard .... Roddy McDowall
Walter Kendall .... Claude Akins
Geoffrey Moore .... Jeremy Kemp
Ambassador Granville .... John Huston
Gen. Swanson .... Vince Edwards
Erich Rhinemann .... Jose Ferrer
Heinrik Stoltz .... Bo Brundin

Adapted from Robert Ludlum's best-selling novel of World War II espionage, *The Rhinemann Exchange* was the story of the exploits of David Spaulding, a young intelligence officer who had covered Europe on concert tours with his late father prior to the start of the war. His familiarity with the Continent and knowledge of many European tongues made him an invaluable wartime agent for the U.S. His biggest assignment developed when he was sent to Argentina to set up a deal between the Americans and certain dissident elements in Hitler's Germany for the exchange of material desperately needed to facilitate the successful conduct of the war by the Allies.

The Rhinemann Exchange was one of four novels dramatized under the collective title *NBC's Best Sellers.*

RHODA (*Situation Comedy*)

FIRST TELECAST: *September 9, 1974*
LAST TELECAST: *December 9, 1978*
BROADCAST HISTORY:
Sep 1974–Sep 1975, CBS Mon 9:30–10:00
Sep 1975–Jan 1977, CBS Mon 8:00–8:30
Jan 1977–Sep 1978, CBS Sun 8:00–8:30
Sep 1978–Dec 1978, CBS Sat 8:00–8:30

CAST:
Rhoda Morgenstern Gerard .... Valerie Harper
Brenda Morgenstern .... Julie Kavner
Joe Gerard (1974–1977) .... David Groh
Ida Morgenstern (1974–1976, 1977–1978)
.... Nancy Walker
Martin Morgenstern (1974–1976, 1977–1978)
.... Harold J. Gould
Carlton the Doorman (voice only) ... Lorenzo Music
Mae (1974–1975) .... Cara Williams
Alice Barth (1974–1975) .... Candy Azzara
Donny Gerard (1974) .... Todd Turquand
Myrna Morgenstern (1974–1976) ... Barbara Sharma
Justin Culp (1975–1976) .... Scoey Mitchlll
Gary Levy (1976–1978) .... Ron Silver
Sally Gallagher (1976–1977) .... Anne Meara
Johnny Venture (1977–1978) ...... Michael Delano
Benny Goodwin (1977–1978) .... Ray Buktenica
Jack Doyle (1977–1978) .... Ken McMillan
Ramón Diaz, Jr. (1977–1978) .... Rafael Campos
Tina Molinari (1978) .... Nancy Lane

As Mary Richards' friend and neighbor on *The Mary Tyler Moore Show,* Rhoda had been somewhat overweight, insecure in her relationships with men, and jealous of the trim Mary. Over the years, however, she had slimmed down, and when she returned home to New York for a visit at the start of *Rhoda* in the fall of 1974, she was a more attractive and self-confident person. The visit turned into a permanent change of residence when she met and fell in love with Joe Gerard. Joe was the owner of the New York Wrecking Company, divorced, and the father of a 10-year-old son. Rhoda moved in with her sister Brenda, since living with her parents Ida and Martin was just not working out, and got a job as a window dresser for a department store. The romance blossomed and, in a special full-hour telecast on October 28, 1974, Rhoda Morgenstern the husband-hunter became Rhoda Gerard.

The newlyweds moved into the same building in which Brenda and Rhoda had been living. Joe went off every day to the office to deal with his partner Justin while Rhoda was a relatively unoccupied housewife. Boredom precipitated her decision to start her own window-dressing business with a high school friend, shy Myrna, as a partner. With Rhoda happily married, the comedy shifted to her chubby sister, Brenda, a bank teller with constant problems trying to get a boyfriend, sort of a younger version of the Rhoda who started on *The Mary Tyler Moore Show* in 1970.

After two years of stories about wedded bliss the producers of *Rhoda* decided that a happily married couple was just not as funny as two single people trying to cope with the world. In order to create more flexibility in Rhoda's role, she and Joe separated soon after the start of the 1976–1977 season. Now they were able to make new friends, suffer the adjustments of living apart, and again deal with the world of the lonely "single." Joe was gradually phased out of the show, preparatory to the inevitable divorce, and Rhoda joined her sister at mixers and singles bars. She found a new friend in 39-year-old divorced airline stewardess Sally Gallagher, and both she and Brenda were frequently escorted by platonic friend Gary Levy. In the middle of that season Rhoda began an off-again, on-again romance with egocentric Las Vegas-based entertainer Johnny Venture.

The 1977–1978 season brought another raft of changes. Rhoda found a new job working at the Doyle Costume Company, a run-down business struggling to survive. Jack Doyle was the owner of the company and his assistant was Ramón. Brenda had a new boyfriend in Benny Goodwin (who replaced the infrequently seen Las Vegas musician Nick Lobo, played by Richard Masur, who had romanced her from 1975 to 1977), and mother Ida had just returned from a year's traveling around the country. By the start of the last season Ida too was single, having been deserted by Martin.

RHYTHM & BLUES (*Situation Comedy*)

FIRST TELECAST: *September 24, 1992*
LAST TELECAST: *October 22, 1992*
BROADCAST HISTORY:
Sep 1992–Oct 1992, NBC Thu 8:30–9:00
CAST:
Bobby Soul .... Roger Kabler
Veronica Washington .... Anna Maria Horsford
Don Philips .... Ron Glass
"The Love Man" .... Troy Curvey, Jr.
Colette Hawkins .... Vanessa Bell Calloway
Jammin .... Miguel A. Nunez, Jr.
Earl "Ziggy" Washington .... Christopher Babers

A hip white disc jockey turned an all-black Detroit radio station on its ear in this short-lived racial comedy. Mrs. Washington had inherited longtime soul station WBLZ from her late husband, but ratings were slipping and she had to do something fast. Enter Bobby Soul, whom she hired sight unseen based on a hilarious audition tape that included a send-up of Michael Jackson. When she found out he was white she tried to fire him, but the staff rallied behind him, and so did listeners. Besides the screechy, domineering Mrs. Washington (who regularly consulted her husband's ashes, kept in an urn behind her desk), the staff included sales manager Don, who eternally regretted abandoning his singing career years before as an original member of the Five Tops (after he left, they became the *Four* Tops!); The Love Man, a rotund deejay with babes hanging on his arms, who always referred to himself in the third person; Colette, the earnest program director; and Bobby's chief rival, Jammin. Ziggy was Mrs. W's young son, who fancied himself Jamaican.

Four months after the series was abruptly canceled, a single leftover episode aired on February 19, 1993.

RHYTHM RODEO (*Music*)

FIRST TELECAST: *August 6, 1950*
LAST TELECAST: *January 7, 1951*
BROADCAST HISTORY:
Aug 1950–Jan 1951, DUM Sun 8:00–8:30
REGULARS:
Art Jarrett
Paula Wray
The Star Noters

Art Jarrett, a band singer with a career stretching back into the 1920s, hosted this early, low-budget musical program from Chicago. Although the motif was supposed to be "Western," all types of songs were featured. Running opposite Ed Sullivan's *Toast of the Town*, it didn't really matter what they did.

RICH LITTLE SHOW, THE (*Comedy/Variety*)

FIRST TELECAST: *February 2, 1976*
LAST TELECAST: *July 19, 1976*
BROADCAST HISTORY:
Feb 1976–Jul 1976, NBC Mon 8:00–9:00
REGULARS:
Rich Little
Charlotte Rae
Julie McWhirter
R. G. Brown
Mel Bishop
Joe Baker
The Robert E. Hughes Orchestra

Impressionist Rich Little was the host and star of this comedy/variety series. Each episode contained a monologue, a number of comedy sketches, and performances by the week's guest stars. The one running character that appeared on each episode was Julie McWhirter's Family Hour Good Fairy (a satire on the TV networks' recently announced policy of reserving 8:00–9:00 P.M. each night for wholesome "family entertainment" rather than violence). For a four-week period in the middle of this show's run, from May 24 to June 14, it was replaced by a mini-series, *The John Davidson Show*.

RICH MAN, POOR MAN—BOOK I (*Drama*)

FIRST TELECAST: *February 1, 1976*
LAST TELECAST: *June 21, 1977*
BROADCAST HISTORY:
Feb 1976–Mar 1976, ABC Mon 10:00–11:00
May 1977–Jun 1977, ABC Tue 9:00–11:00
CAST:
Rudy Jordache .... Peter Strauss
Tom Jordache .... Nick Nolte
Julie Prescott Abbott Jordache .... Susan Blakely
Axel Jordache .... Edward Asner
Mary Jordache .... Dorothy McGuire
Willie Abbott .... Bill Bixby
Duncan Calderwood .... Ray Milland
Teddy Boylan .... Robert Reed
Virginia Calderwood .... Kim Darby
Sue Prescott .... Gloria Grahame
Asher Berg .... Craig Stevens

Joey Quales .... George Maharis
Linda Quales .... Lynda Day George
Nichols .... Steve Allen
Smitty .... Norman Fell
Teresa Sanjoro .... Talia Shire
Marsh Goodwin .... Van Johnson
Irene Goodwin .... Dorothy Malone
Kate Jordache .... Kay Lenz
Sid Gossett .... Murray Hamilton
Arnold Simms .... Mike Evans
Al Fanducci .... Dick Butkus
Clothilde .... Fionnula Flanagan
Brad Knight .... Tim McIntire
Bill Denton .... Lawrence Pressman
Claude Tinker .... Dennis Dugan
Gloria Bartley .... Jo Ann Harris
Pete Tierney .... Roy Jenson
Lou Martin .... Anthony Carbone
Papadakis .... Ed Barth
Ray Dwyer .... Herbert Jefferson, Jr.
Arthur Falconetti .... William Smith
Col. Deiner .... Andrew Duggan
Pinky .... Harvey Jason
Martha .... Helen Craig
Phil McGee .... Gavan O'Herlihy
Billy .... Leigh McCloskey
Wesley .... Michael Morgan

MUSIC:

Alex North

If it had not been overshadowed so quickly by *Roots*, *Rich Man, Poor Man* would probably be ranked today as the biggest dramatic spectacular in the history of television. It was an enormous hit, not only spawning a separate series the following season (see *Rich Man, Poor Man—Book II*) but also stimulating a rash of novels-for-television.

The source was Irwin Shaw's sprawling (720-page) 1970 best-seller about the divergent careers of two brothers in the years from 1945 to the 1960s. Rudy Jordache was the "rich man," the ambitious, educated entrepreneur who triumphed over his impoverished immigrant background to build a business and political empire. Tom was the "poor man," the trouble-prone rebel who turned boxer for a time, and was eventually murdered in the last episode by the vicious Falconetti. Axel and Mary were the parents, and Julie, Rudy's lifelong love. An enormous, all-star cast paraded through the 12-hour presentation as lovers, enemies, scoundrels, and friends. The entire 12 hours was repeated in May–June 1977.

RICH MAN, POOR MAN—BOOK II (*Drama*)

FIRST TELECAST: *September 21, 1976*

LAST TELECAST: *March 8, 1977*

BROADCAST HISTORY:

Sep 1976–Mar 1977, ABC Tue 9:00–10:00

CAST:

Senator Rudy Jordache .... Peter Strauss
Wesley Jordache .... Gregg Henry
Billy Abbott .... James Carroll Jordan
Maggie Porter .... Susan Sullivan
Arthur Falconetti .... William Smith
Marie Falconetti .... Dimitra Arliss
Ramona Scott .... Penny Peyser
Scotty .... John Anderson
Charles Estep .... Peter Haskell
Phil Greenberg .... Sorrell Booke
Annie Adams .... Cassie Yates
Diane Porter .... Kimberly Beck
Arthur Raymond .... Peter Donat
Claire Estep .... Laraine Stephens
Senator Paxton .... Barry Sullivan
Kate Jordache .... Kay Lenz
John Franklin .... Philip Abbott
Max Vincent .... George Gaynes
Al Barber .... Ken Swofford
Senator Dillon .... G. D. Spradlin

This sequel to the 1976 mini-series began in the year 1965, after the death of Tom Jordache, and followed brother Rudy's further career as a U.S. Senator. Rudy was now surrogate father to a family consisting of Wesley (Tom's boy) and Billy (Julie's boy, by one of her marriages), two young men ambitious for futures of their own. Much of the action in Book II involved their entanglements, and Senator Rudy's protracted battle against the greedy, power-hungry, and mysterious billionaire Estep, owner of Tricorp. Falconetti was back, apparently intent on killing off *all* the Jordaches. Backgrounds of Las Vegas, Aspen, and other haunts of the rich gave this melodrama a lavish appearance, but it was soap opera nevertheless.

In the last original episode, Rudy and Falconetti faced each other with guns in hand and shot it out, apparently leaving the two of them lying bleeding to death on a sidewalk.

RICHARD BOONE SHOW, THE (*Dramatic Anthology*)

FIRST TELECAST: *September 24, 1963*

LAST TELECAST: *September 15, 1964*

BROADCAST HISTORY:

Sep 1963–Sep 1964, NBC Tue 9:00–10:00

REGULARS:

Richard Boone
Robert Blake
Lloyd Bochner
Laura Devon
June Harding
Bethel Leslie
Harry Morgan
Jeanette Nolan
Ford Rainey
Warren Stevens
Guy Stockwell

The Richard Boone Show was television's equivalent of repertory theater. Although there were no continuing roles in this anthology series, the same group of actors and actresses played parts in almost all the plays. Richard Boone was the host for all episodes and starred in roughly half of the shows. Each of the regulars had an opportunity to star in at least one of the episodes, in addition to having supporting roles in many of them.

RICHARD DIAMOND, PRIVATE DETECTIVE

(*Detective Drama*)

FIRST TELECAST: *July 1, 1957*

LAST TELECAST: *September 6, 1960*

BROADCAST HISTORY:

Jul 1957–Sep 1957, CBS Mon 9:30–10:00
Jan 1958–Sep 1958, CBS Thu 8:00–8:30
Feb. 1959–Sep 1959, CBS Sun 10:00–10:30
Oct 1959–Jan 1960, NBC Mon 7:30–8:00
Jun 1960–Sep 1960, NBC Tue 9:00–9:30

CAST:

Richard Diamond.................... David Janssen
Lt. Dennis "Mac" McGough (1957–1958)
.... Regis Toomey
Karen Wells (1959) .... Barbara Bain
Lt. Pete Kile (1959–1960)............. Russ Conway
Sgt. Alden (1959–1960) .... Richard Devon
"Sam" (1959) .... Mary Tyler Moore
"Sam" (1959–1960)............... Roxanne Brooks

Richard Diamond was an ex-New York City policeman who had turned in his badge to go into private practice as a detective. His familiarity with the force and his friends on it, most notably Lt. McGough, gave him access to information and help not normally afforded private detectives. In February 1959 he relocated to Hollywood, acquired a semiregular girlfriend in Karen Wells, and began using an answering service to get his messages. His contact at the answering service was a sultry-voiced woman whom he called "Sam." Her voice was heard and her body was seen from the waist down, to show off her legs, but her identity was not revealed in the screen credits at the end of each episode. The first actress to play "Sam" was young Mary Tyler Moore, a fact that was revealed to readers of *TV Guide* when an article appeared in May 1959 in which she modeled the latest in women's hosiery. It was in the middle of that month that she left the series to be replaced by another unbilled leggy actress. "Sam" was important to Richard Diamond since she often reached him in his car, which had a built-in phone, to warn of impending danger. Although Diamond had a friend on the L.A.P.D. (Lt. Kile), he also had to deal with Sgt. Alden, who was out to get him.

Dick Powell, whose Four Star Productions produced this series, had starred as Richard Diamond on the radio from 1949–1952.

RICHARD PRYOR SHOW, THE (*Comedy/Variety*)

FIRST TELECAST: *September 13, 1977*
LAST TELECAST: *October 20, 1977*
BROADCAST HISTORY:

Sep 1977–Oct 1977, NBC Tue 8:00–9:00
Oct 1977, NBC Thu 9:00–10:00

REGULARS:

Richard Pryor
Allegra Allison
David Banks
Sandra Bernhard
Victor Dunlop
Argus Hamilton
Jimmy Martinez
Paul Mooney
Tim Reid
Marsha Warfield
Robin Williams
"Detroit" John Witherspoon

The career of young black comic Richard Pryor was definitely on the rise when production started on his first regular television series during the summer of 1977. He had become successful as a nightclub performer, was seen regularly on television's talk shows, and had begun a career in motion pictures. His original commitment had been to do a minimum of ten variety shows for the series but, with the demands for his time growing after the success of two 1977 films, *Silver Streak* and *Greased Lightning*, coupled with censorship problems he had with NBC management, it was mutually agreed that he would do only five shows.

Although considered one of the most inventive, offbeat, and satirical performers around, Pryor's background as a nightclub comic led him to try material that might be considered in questionable taste for television. There were constant disagreements on what material was acceptable, and the opening sequence from his first show—in which he was shown nude from the waist up commenting that he had lost nothing in his battles with the network censors, followed by a pan down his body in which he appeared to be both completely nude and emasculated (he was actually wearing a body stocking)—was censored before the show was aired. His feud with NBC was highly publicized in the press but did little to attract viewers from ABC's *Happy Days*, his prime competition, which had twice as large an audience as *The Richard Pryor Show*.

RICHIE BROCKELMAN, PRIVATE EYE (*Detective Drama*)

FIRST TELECAST: *March 17, 1978*
LAST TELECAST: *August 24, 1978*
BROADCAST HISTORY:

Mar 1978–Apr 1978, NBC Fri 9:00–10:00
Aug 1978, NBC Thu 9:00–10:00

CAST:

Richie Brockelman .... Dennis Dugan
Sgt. Ted Coopersmith .... Robert Hogan
Sharon Deterson .... Barbara Bosson

Richie Brockelman didn't look like a detective and that, as he put it, was his "trump card." Since almost no one, criminal or police, took the youthful-looking sleuth seriously, he was able to talk his way into and out of all sorts of dangerous situations in the course of his investigations. But Brockelman was indeed for real, a glib, 23-year-old, college-educated private investigator with his own, admittedly small, agency. Sharon was his trusted secretary and Sgt. Coopersmith his skeptical police contact.

The series was a spin-off of *The Rockford Files*, on which Brockelman had appeared on occasion to help out Jim Rockford.

RIDDLE ME THIS, see *Celebrity Time*

RIFLEMAN, THE (*Western*)

FIRST TELECAST: *September 30, 1958*
LAST TELECAST: *July 1, 1963*
BROADCAST HISTORY:

Sep 1958–Sep 1960, ABC Tue 9:00–9:30
Sep 1960–Sep 1961, ABC Tue 8:00–8:30
Oct 1961–Jul 1963, ABC Mon 8:30–9:00 (OS)

CAST:

Lucas McCain .... Chuck Connors
Mark McCain.................... Johnny Crawford
Marshal Micah Torrance .... Paul Fix
Miss Milly Scott (1960–1962)........... Joan Taylor
Lou Mallory (1962–1963)............ Patricia Blair
Sweeney, the bartender................. Bill Quinn
Hattie Denton (1958–1960) .... Hope Summers

The Rifleman was the saga of Lucas McCain, a homesteader in the Old West struggling to make a living off his ranch and make a man out of his motherless son, Mark. Chuck Connors, a former professional baseball player, won critical acclaim for his portrayal of Lucas, and young Johnny Crawford also started on a successful career with this series. The setting was the town of North Fork, New Mexico, whose marshal seemed incapable of handling any of the numerous desperadoes who infested the series (as they did all Western series) without the help of Lucas. Helpful, too, was the trick rifle that Lucas always carried, a modified Winchester with a large ring which cocked it as he drew. Supposedly, he could fire off his first round in three-tenths of a second, which certainly helped in a showdown.

Though quite successful at first, the series began to slip in its third season, due to a number of reasons including Lucas' rather righteous tone. To "humanize" him the producers brought Miss Milly to North Fork, to serve as storekeeper and McCain's love interest. In 1962 a somewhat pushier female arrived: Lou Mallory, a kind of con-artist-with-a-heart-of-gold hotel keeper who began buying up the property around town and took out a lease on Lucas as well. In addition, Mark began to experience problems associated with adolescence (he had been 12 when the series started).

RIKER (*Police Drama*)
FIRST TELECAST: *March 14, 1981*
LAST TELECAST: *April 11, 1981*
BROADCAST HISTORY:
Mar 1981–Apr 1981, CBS Sat 10:00–11:00
CAST:
Frank Riker .... Josh Taylor
Brice Landis .... Michael Shannon

To the general public, and to his former fellow officers on the Los Angeles Police Department, Frank Riker was a busted cop, expelled from the force for blatant disregard of rules and regulations. What they didn't know was that Frank had secretly been offered the chance to work undercover for California Deputy Attorney General Brice Landis—Frank's former partner. Landis gave him assignments, and was the only person besides the governor who knew of Frank's special status. Everyone else seemed to hate Riker, which didn't stop the two-fisted investigator from infiltrating smuggling operations, prostitution rings, and other unsavory activities.

RIN TIN TIN, see *Adventures of Rin Tin Tin, The*

RIN TIN TIN K-9 COP (*Adventure*)
BROADCAST HISTORY:
The Family Channel
30 minutes
Produced: *1988–1993* (106 episodes)
Premiered: *September 17, 1988*
CAST:
Officer Hank Katts .... Jesse Collins
Stevie Katts .... Andrew Bednarski
Maggie Davenport (1988–1989) ...... Cali Timmins
Officer Ron Nakamura .... Denis Akiyama
Capt. Murdoch (1988–1989) .... Ken Pogue
Officer Connie (1988–1989) .... Corrine Koslo
Officer Dennis Brian (1988–1992) .. Brian Kaulback
Sgt. Callaghan (1988–1990) .... Peter MacNeill
Officer/Sgt. Lou Adams (1988–1991) ... Dan Martin
Officer Renée Daumier (1989–1992)
.... Denise Virieux
Sgt. O. C. Phillips (1991–1993) .... Phil Jarrett
Lt. Logan (1991–1992) .... Chuck Shamata
Officer Leah McCray (1992–1993) .. Nancy Sakovich

Rin Tin Tin, the resourceful German shepherd who was last seen battling bad guys in the Old West, returned to TV in 1988 on the Family Channel as a police dog in modern times. Part of the K-9 corps in an unnamed big city, he faced just as much violence and danger as he had at old Fort Apache—but in an urban setting. Rinty's handlers were Officer Hank Katts and his teenage nephew, Stevie. Hank became Stevie's guardian when the boy's mother, Maggie, died in the first season; in the third season he adopted him as his son.

Numerous changes took place at the precinct house during the series' five-year run. Among the notable characters passing through were tough commanding officers Callaghan, Adams, and Phillips and Hank's partner, Renée, a French policewoman who was here on an exchange program. In fact the only supporting officer to last for the entire run was Nakamura, who was shot during the third season and thereafter worked from a wheelchair. Life was dangerous on the urban frontier.

The Rin Tin Tin seen on this series was a descendant of the original, who died in 1932.

RIPCORD (*Adventure*)
BROADCAST HISTORY:
Syndicated only
30 minutes
Produced: *1961–1963* (76 episodes)
Released: *September 1961*
CAST:
Ted McKeever .... Larry Pennell
Jim Buckley .... Ken Curtis
Chuck Lambert (1961–1962) .... Paul Comi
Charlie Kern (1962–1963) .... Shug Fisher

The youthful heroes of this series literally jumped into a new adventure every week. Ted and Jim ran Ripcord, Inc., which taught skydiving and also hired out for rescues, recovery work, and other situations where parachutists were needed. Often they landed right in the middle of a crime in progress, and solved that too—who would expect the good guys to come floating down out of the sky? Chuck was their original pilot, replaced midway through the first season by Charlie Kern.

The series featured a lot of spectacular skydiving scenes, including one involving a fistfight in midair (shot by a cameraman in free-fall with the actors). At one point, two planes accidentally crashed while filming scenes for the program. With a little script adjustment, the footage of the crash was later used in the series.

RIPLEY'S BELIEVE IT OR NOT (*Variety/Drama*)
NETWORK HISTORY:
FIRST TELECAST: *March 1, 1949*
LAST TELECAST: *December 16, 2001*
Mar 1949–Jun 1949, NBC Tue 9:30–10:00
Jul 1949–Sep 1949, NBC Wed 10:00–10:30
Oct 1949–Nov 1949, NBC Various times
Jan 1950–May 1950, NBC Wed 8:00–8:30
May 1950–Sep 1950, NBC Thu 8:00–8:30
Sep 1982–Jan 1986, ABC Sun 7:00–8:00
May 1985–Jun 1985, ABC Fri 8:30–9:00
Jan 1986–Sep 1986, ABC Thu 8:00–9:00
Oct 2001–Dec 2001, WB Sun 7:00–8:00

CABLE HISTORY:

TBS
60 minutes
Original episodes: *2000–*
Premiered: *January 12, 2000*

HOST:

Robert L. Ripley (Mar–May 1949)
Robert St. John (Jul–Nov 1949)
Jack Palance (1982–1986)
Dean Cain (2000–)

COHOST:

Catherine Shirriff (1982–1983)
Holly Palance (1983–1985)
Marie Osmond (1985–1986)
Kelly Packard, field correspondent (2002–)

This highly successful radio series moved to television in March 1949. Seen seated in a living room decorated with oriental antiques and mementoes of his worldwide travels, Ripley recounted for viewers a number of strange stories each week, sometimes with the aid of exhibits or dramatizations. At times the program had a freak-show atmosphere. Among the early guests were Kuda Bux, the Indian fakir with "X-ray vision"; a man who could thread a needle with one hand while balancing his body parallel to the floor with the other; and a four-eyed Mongolian. However, there were also stories of ordinary people who had triumphed over great adversity to lead normal, and even exceptional, lives.

On May 27, 1949, less than three months after the series began, Bob Ripley died suddenly. He had already prepared the next week's program and it was presented, along with a tribute to his long career. The series continued, hosted by "guest custodians" of Ripley's sketchbook until Robert St. John became permanent host in July 1949. The program left the air briefly at the end of the year and returned in January 1950 as a dramatic series loosely based on Ripley's stories. Each week a guest cast enacted one of his remarkable true tales, usually one involving murder, romance, or both.

Thirty-two years after the original television run of *Believe It or Not*, the series returned under the title *Ripley's Believe It or Not*, with Jack Palance as host. The show still used much original Ripley material, and had the full cooperation of the Ripley estate. Now, however, film crews scoured the world for new and up-to-date oddities, and Palance and his cohost, Catherine Shirriff (later replaced by Palance's daughter Holly), were seen on location marveling over the bizarre phenomena they uncovered. Palance loved to skulk about the ruins, and add a sinister tone to his narration of the stories. Among them: the skeleton of the queen of Portugal, albino gorillas, Mad King Ludwig of Bavaria, drive-in funerals, a museum of torture in Peru, secret weapons of World War II, strange rituals in various parts of the globe, and the Texas millionairess who specified in her will that she be buried in her Ferrari, wearing her sexiest nightgown. Some features were lighter, such as the first showing of a long-lost production number featuring young Judy Garland, Ray Bolger, Bert Lahr, and Jack Haley that had been cut from the 1939 movie classic *The Wizard of Oz*. Others were up-to-date, including wonders of outer space and zero-gravity life aboard the Skylab space station. Ripley's ghost has resurfaced several times since then. On November 26, 1993, TBS Superstation telecast a two-hour documentary entitled *The Incredible Life and Times of Robert Ripley, Believe It or Not!* Beginning in July 1999 the Fox Family Channel briefly ran a daytime cartoon called *Ripley's Believe It or Not* chronicling the adventures of teenager "Michael Ripley" and his pals. In January 2000 *Ripley's Believe It or Not* returned in its normal format on TBS, this time hosted by Dean Cain. In the fall of 2001 the WB network ran reruns of episodes that had previously aired on TBS.

The syndicated newspaper column on which all this was based was begun by Robert L. Ripley in 1918. Believe it or not.

RIPTIDE (*Detective Drama*)

FIRST TELECAST: *January 3, 1984*
LAST TELECAST: *April 18, 1986*

BROADCAST HISTORY:

Jan 1984–Feb 1986, NBC Tue 9:00–10:00
Mar 1986–Apr 1986, NBC Fri 8:00–9:00

CAST:

Cody Allen .... Perry King
Nick Ryder .... Joe Penny
Murray "Boz" Bozinsky .... Thom Bray
Mama Jo (occasional, 1984) .... Anne Francis
Lt. Ted Quinlan (1984–1985) .... Jack Ging
Kirk "The Dool" Dooley (1984–1985) ... Ken Olandt
Lt. Joanna Parisi (1985–1986) ...... June Chadwick

Nick and Cody were two Southern California beach bums who decided to go into the private-detective business. Working from Cody's cabin cruiser, the *Riptide*, docked at Pier 56 in King's Harbor, or from their hangout, the Straightaways Restaurant, they had at least two advantages over the competition: Cody's speedboat, the *Ebbtide*, and Nick's aging but serviceable helicopter, the *Screaming Mimi* (a bulky Sikorsky, painted pink with a gaping mouth on the front).

The boys knew that this was the high-tech era, so they recruited one more element, an army buddy named Boz, a mousy computer nerd who happened to be a genius with electronics. Well, almost; he never could get his computerized robot, Roboz, to work right. The three of them tackled cases that invariably involved high-speed chases, explosions, and beautiful girls in bikinis. Sometimes they enlisted the help of Mama Jo and the all-girl crew of her charter boat, the *Barefoot Contessa*, which was moored next to theirs. The Dool was a dockboy who occasionally did some of their legwork.

It was a tough job, but someone had to do it.

On August 22, 1986, four months after the series had been dropped from the lineup, a final repeat episode of *Riptide* was aired on NBC.

RITUALS (*Drama*)

BROADCAST HISTORY:

Syndicated only
30 minutes
Produced: *1984–1985*
Released: *September 1984*

CAST:

Patrick Chapin .... Dennis Patrick
Taylor Chapin Field Von Platen (1984)
.... Jo Ann Pflug
Taylor Chapin Field Von Platen (1984–1985)
.... Tina Louise

Julia Field .... Andrea Moar
Brady Chapin (1984) .... Marc Poppel
Brady Chapin (1984–1985) .... Jon Lindstrom
Carter Robertson .... Monte Markham
Christina Robertson .... Christine Jones
Jeff Robertson .... Tim Maier
Eddie Gallagher .... Greg Mullavey
Sara Gallagher (1984) .... Lorinne Vozoff
Sara Gallagher (1984–1985) .... Laurie Burton
Tom Gallagher .... Kevin Blair
Mike Gallagher .... Kin Shriner
Noel Gallagher .... Karen Kelly
Lacey Jarrett .... Philece Sampler
Dakota "Koty" Lane (1984) .... Claire Yarlett
Dakota "Koty" Lane (1984–1985) ... Mary Beth Evans
Cherry Lane .... Sharon Farrell
Logan Williams .... George Lazenby
Diandra Santiago Gallagher .... Gina Gallego
Marissa Mallory (1984) .... Patti Davis
Marissa Mallory (1984–1985) .... Janice Heiden
Bernhardt .... Cameron Smith
Patty Dupont .... Winifred Freedman
Clay Travis .... Michael Weldon
C.J. Field (1985) .... Peter Haskell
Lt. Lucas Gates (1985) .... Antony Ponzini
Lisa Thompson (1985) .... Wesley Ann Pfenning
Maddie Washington (1985) .... Lynn Hamilton
Lucky Washington (1985) ... Lawrence-Hilton Jacobs

Rituals was an expensive experiment that failed. In the wake of the success of prime-time network soap operas like *Dallas*, *Dynasty*, and *Knots Landing*, the producers of this series felt that the time was ripe for a syndicated nightly prime-time soap opera. *Rituals* represented an investment of tens of millions of dollars that attracted a minimal audience and limped through a single year on the air.

Set in fictional Wingfield, Virginia, outside of Washington, D.C., *Rituals* focused on three families—the wealthy Chapins; the middle-class Gallaghers, who ran a motel on the other side of town; and the Robertsons, whose head, Carter, was the conniving president of Haddon Hall, a local women's college that had been founded by the Chapin family.

The mortality rate was rather high among the early principals on this series. Patrick Chapin, the powerful patriarch who owned Wingfield Mills and Chapin Industries, had just been widowed as the series began; a few months later he died of heart disease, resulting in another round of bequests and in-fighting. None of Patrick's children had turned out well. His greedy, scheming daughter, Taylor, had gone through five husbands and had a daughter, Julia, who hated her. A principal troublemaker during *Rituals'* early months, Taylor departed for Paris midway through the run. Patrick's young son, Brady, was a spoiled playboy who had affairs with Noel Gallagher and actress Koty Lane. Then there was the inevitable son nobody knew about—none other than manipulative Carter Robertson, who turned out to be Patrick's illegitimate offspring—a Chapin! Even before this was revealed Carter had wormed his way into Chapin Industries.

Eddie Gallagher, a violent man involved with criminal elements, survived only until February, when his daughter, Noel, murdered him to get even for years of abuse. Other members of Eddie's family were Sara, his long-suffering wife, son Tom, a relatively honest cop, and half-brother Mike, a slightly flaky artist. Others prominently featured included Carter's wife, Christina (Sara's sister), another schemer, and their dishonest son, Jeff; Tom Gallagher's girlfriend and later wife, Diandra, the daughter of a Latin dictator, who was involved with revolutionaries; Lacey, the teacher who married Mike but couldn't have his baby (so Koty did); writer Logan, one of Taylor's former paramours; and another of Taylor's exes, billionaire C.J. Field. Much of the latter part of the series was consumed by the battle between C.J. and Carter for control of everybody and everything; as the series ended Carter got most of the booty, but C.J. had just been elected governor of Virginia.

RIVERA LIVE (*Talk*)

BROADCAST HISTORY:

CNBC
60 minutes
Produced: *1994–2001*
Premiered: *February 7, 1994*

REGULARS:

Geraldo Rivera

Newsman Geraldo Rivera brought his hard-driving, opinionated interviewing style to CNBC in 1994 with this nightly show. Not only did most shows have a single topic (usually news-related), sometimes it would stay on a single subject for weeks at a time. Rivera practically obsessed on the O.J. Simpson case, devoting the whole show to it for the duration of Simpson's long murder trial in 1994–1995.

RIVERBOAT (*Adventure*)

FIRST TELECAST: *September 13, 1959*
LAST TELECAST: *January 16, 1961*

BROADCAST HISTORY:

Sep 1959–Jan 1960, NBC Sun 7:00–8:00
Feb 1960–Jan 1961, NBC Mon 7:30–8:30

CAST:

Grey Holden .... Darren McGavin
Ben Frazer (1959–1960) .... Burt Reynolds
Travis (1959–1960) .... William D. Gordon
Carney .... Richard Wessell
Joshua .... Jack Lambert
Chip (1959–1960) .... Mike McGreevey
Pickalong (1959–1960) .... Jack Mitchum
Terry Blake (1959–1960) .... Bart Patten
Bill Blake (1960–1961) .... Noah Beery, Jr.

The *Enterprise* was a 100-foot-long stern-wheeler that churned up and down the Mississippi, Missouri, and Ohio rivers during the 1840s. The captain and owner of the boat was Grey Holden, a former fighter, rum-runner, swordsman, dock foreman, and soldier. A fun-loving romantic, he had won the boat in a poker game and was determined to make it a profitable venture, carrying passengers, hauling freight, and doing anything else it could to generate revenue. Boat pilot Ben Frazer was the colead when *Riverboat* first aired, an orphan whose entire life had been spent along the Mississippi. Both he and crew member Travis were written out of the series in the middle of its first season. When it returned in the fall of 1960, *Riverboat* had a new colead in Bill Blake, as a pilot who had bought 49 percent of the *Enterprise* and was constantly seeking to take controlling interest. First mate Joshua and crew member Carney were still in the cast, but gone were cabin boy Chip; Pickalong, the ballad-singing cook; and Terry Blake, the cub-pilot who had replaced Ben Frazer. Captain Holden spent more time away from the boat and got involved in more romantic entanglements than during the first season.

ROAD, THE (*Country Music*)

BROADCAST HISTORY:

Syndicated only
60 minutes
Produced: *1994–1995* (26 episodes)
Released: *September 1994*

NARRATORS:

Levon Helm
Mary Chapin Carpenter

Each week *The Road* showcased three or four country music performers or groups with excerpts from their stage performances as well as behind-the-scenes views of setting up and traveling around the country on tour. Included were impromptu jam sessions and commentary by the performers about their work, personal lives, and the good and bad aspects of touring. Among the artists featured were Travis Tritt, Shelby Lynne, Hal Ketchum, Patty Loveless, Sawyer Brown, and Kathy Mattea. The show was narrated by The Band's Levon Helm and singer Mary Chapin Carpenter.

Beginning in early 1996, the series aired in prime time on the Nashville Network.

ROAD HOME, THE (*Family Drama*)

FIRST TELECAST: *March 5, 1994*
LAST TELECAST: *April 16, 1994*
BROADCAST HISTORY:

Mar 1994–Apr 1994, CBS Sat 9:00–10:00

CAST:

Alison Matson .... Karen Allen
Jack Matson.......................... Terence Knox
Sawyer Matson .... Christopher Masterson
Darcy Matson .... Jessica Bowman
Calvin Matson .... Greg Perrelli
Jinx Matson .... Cecilly Carroll
Walter Babineaux...................... Ed Flanders
Charlotte Babineaux .... Frances Sternhagen
Dickie Babineaux................. Alex McArthur
Arthur Dumas......................... Bobby Fain
Webb .... Jeff Johnson

A warm family drama about Alison and Jack Matson and their children, who returned to the tidewaters of North Carolina for their annual summer vacation. They did not expect to stay as long as they did. The family shrimp boat business, run by Alison's brother, Dickie, was struggling and her mother, Charlotte, refused to seek treatment for her failing health. They extended their vacation so Jack could help Dickie try to get the shrimping business back on its feet while Alison spent time with her mom and dad. The teenage Matson children were not thrilled with the decision, Sawyer because he had no interest in, or skill as, a shrimper and Darcy because being in "the middle of nowhere" was boring and interfering with her social life back home in Detroit. The younger kids, Calvin and Jinx, saw the summer as an adventure and enjoyed being with their grandparents. Darcy's summer became a little more bearable after she started dating Arthur Dumas.

ROAD HOME, THE (*Documentary*)

BROADCAST HISTORY:

MTV
30 minutes
Original episodes: *2002–*
Premiered: *March 6, 2002*

A homey documentary series in which contemporary music stars such as the Goo Goo Dolls, Destiny's Child, Blink-182, Papa Roach, Nelly, and Lenny Kravitz traveled back to their hometowns and gave viewers a personal tour of the people and places that influenced their lives. Episodes ended with the stars giving a concert for their hometown fans.

ROAD RULES (*Documentary*)

BROADCAST HISTORY:

MTV
30 minutes
Produced: *1995–*
Premiered: *July 19, 1995*

Mary-Ellis Bunim and Jon Murray, creators of MTV's hit series *The Real World,* produced this spin-off in which five or six young adults were given an unusual challenge. After surrendering their money and credit cards, they were given the keys to an RV and a series of clues that led them from one location to another across the country. As a camera crew filmed their every move, they faced various tests en route to their final destination—for example, high-diving in a gorge, land sailing, assuming roles in a Gay Pride festival, or tracking down America's youngest mayor. It was *Real World* hits the road, with all the flirting, squabbling, and bonding of the earlier series, but with real physical and mental challenges.

In the first series Kit Hoover, Carlos "Los" Jackson, Mark Long, Shelly Spotted Horse, and Allison Jones explored the United States in a big white Winnebago, ending up in Malibu. Serious Allison and flirty Carlos will probably never speak to each other again. In *Road Rules 2* (1996) the gang was Christian, Devin, Effie, Emily, and Timmy. Devin and Emily were the "item" on this trip, an interracial relationship, while Timmy was the class clown. *Road Rules 3* (1997) traveled to Europe and featured an international cast—Antoine (Belgian), Belou (Dutch), Chris (American), Michelle (American), and Patrice (German). *Road Rules 4* (1997) was a Caribbean adventure, with the gang traveling both on boats and in the trusty Winnebago. They were Erika (the "mother" of the group), babyface Jake, Kalle, Oscar, and Vince.

Road Rules 5 (1998) followed a northern U.S. route, with Anne, Dan, Jon, Noah, Roni, and Tara. In *Road Rules 6* (1998) the crew was Chadwick, Christina, Kefla, Piggy, Shayne, and Susie; their jumping-off point was Hawaii, followed by an adventure in Australia. Moody Britisher Piggy bonded with Christina and Susie, but spent much of the trip hissing at bewildered "nice guys" Chad and Shayne. *Road Rules 7* (1999) headed south to Latin America. Abe, Brian, Gladys, Holly, Joshua, and Sarah met in a bull ring, and were told they would have to retrieve the key to their van from the neck of an enraged bull which was about to be set loose. Instead, they were set upon by fifty yapping Chihuahuas, with fifty keys around their necks.

Road Rules 8 (1999) took its six for a 100-day "Semester at Sea," stopping in Cuba, Brazil, South Africa, Kenya, India, Malaysia, Vietnam, China and Japan. The multicultural cast included Yes (a shaved-head male), Pua (a Hawaiian girl), Pawel (a Polish American from Brooklyn), Veronica (a busty Cuban), Ayanna (a black girl) and Shawn (da hunk). *Road Rules 9* (2000), with Msaada, Theo, Holly, James, Laterrian and Kathryn, was filled with competitions with a variety of guest teams who dropped in as the gang made its way across the southern United States and South Africa. They included the mtv.com team, the *Playboy* Extreme Team, the cast from *The Real World*, the boy band O-Town, and a team consisting of the *Road Rulers'* own parents!

Reflecting the vogue for *Survivor*-type prime time reality shows, *Road Rules 10* (2001), set in Morocco and Spain, introduced new rules that required the cast members to "vote someone off the bus" during the tour. The starting cast was Ellen, Blair, Sophia, Adam, Jisela and Steve, but halfway through Jisela (who failed a rock climbing mission) was voted off and replaced by Katie. *Road Rules 11* (2002) was "The Campus Crawl," a competition-filled tour of 15 campuses across the southern United States. Cast members were Darrell, Rachel, Eric, Kendal, Sarah and gay Shane (whom one of the girls remarked seemed to be "homosexual during the day but heterosexual at night"). This one included drunken revelry in New Orleans, and the entire cast was required to pose nude for an art class. Midway through Sarah was voted off and replaced by Raquel.

In 2000 MTV combined this series and another of its most popular shows for the *Real World/Road Rules Extreme Challenge*, in which cast members from the two shows competed in various physical challenges. In addition to the regular seasons to date, a special *Road Rules All Stars* tour (1998) was made up of cast members from five different seasons of *The Real World*—Cynthia (Miami), Eric (New York City), Jon (Los Angeles), Rachel (San Francisco), and Sean (Boston).

ROAD TEST MAGAZINE (*Information*)

BROADCAST HISTORY:

The Nashville Network
30 minutes
Produced: *1990–1995*
Premiered: *January 7, 1990*

HOST:

Don Garlits

Host "Big Daddy" Don Garlits tested new cars, pickups, sport utility vehicles, and vans on this weekend automotive series.

ROAD WEST, THE (*Western*)

FIRST TELECAST: *September 12, 1966*
LAST TELECAST: *August 28, 1967*
BROADCAST HISTORY:

Sep 1966–Aug 1967, NBC Mon 9:00–10:00

CAST:

Benjamin Pride .... Barry Sullivan
Timothy Pride .... Andrew Prine
Midge Pride .... Brenda Scott
Kip Pride .... Kelly Corcoran
Grandpa Pride .... Charles Seel
Chance Reynolds .... Glenn Corbett
Elizabeth Reynolds .... Kathryn Hays

Benjamin Pride was a widower who had taken his family from Springfield, Ohio, where they had lived for generations, and moved them to the Kansas Territory shortly after the end of the Civil War. The problems encountered by this pioneering family in the fertile but lawless West provided the stories in this series. Benjamin's family consisted of his 24-year-old son, Timothy, his daughter, Midge (18), and son, Kip (8), Elizabeth Reynolds, and her younger brother, Chance. Elizabeth, the daughter of a doctor, had become Benjamin's second wife just prior to his move to Kansas. Her brother had gone with the Prides in search of excitement and adventure.

ROAR (*Adventure*)

FIRST TELECAST: *July 14, 1997*
LAST TELECAST: *September 5, 1997*
BROADCAST HISTORY:

Jul 1997–Sep 1997, FOX Mon 9:00–10:00
Aug 1997–Sep 1997, FOX Fri 8:00–9:00

CAST:

Conor .... Heath Ledger
Fergus .... John Saint Ryan
Catlin .... Vera Farmiga
Tully .... Alonzo Greer
Longinus .... Sebastian Roche
Queen Diana .... Lisa Zane

EXECUTIVE PRODUCER:

Shaun Cassidy

Action adventure series set in fifth century Ireland, in the year 400 A.D., where a group of rebels were fighting the oppressive Romans who were ruling their land. Twenty-year-old Conor was a callow, tousle-haired Celtic prince who, after his family had been massacred by a rival tribe on his brother's wedding day, became the reluctant leader of the local tribes in their fight against the Romans. Conor led a group that included his mentor Fergus, a tall, bald warrior of great repute; Tully, a scrappy black teenage apprentice magician; and Catlin, a runaway slave who was a better fighter than most men. Their principal foe was Longinus, a hooded sorcerer who looked thirty but was actually a 400-year-old Roman centurion who had been cursed after piercing the side of Jesus on the cross with his spear. Longinus' lover, Diana, was a greedy, power-hungry Roman queen. Longinus wanted to die, but no matter how hard he tried, the curse kept him alive. In each episode, Conor was faced with a difficult situation that threatened the safety and unity of his people.

The series title came from the moment in the first episode in which Conor was told to "remember all we are and all that's come before and hear the roar . . . the voice that echoes in every living thing, the power that binds us together."

Filmed in Queensland, Australia.

ROAR OF THE RAILS, THE (*Adventure*)

FIRST TELECAST: *October 26, 1948*
LAST TELECAST: *December 12, 1949*
BROADCAST HISTORY:

Oct 1948–Dec 1948, CBS Tue 7:00–7:15
Oct 1949–Dec 1949, CBS Mon 7:00–7:15

The object of this live adventure/documentary series was to dramatize the events that had made railroad history.

Veteran railroad men appeared to explain what their jobs were like and the dramatizations were carried out with model trains and a miniature set that included mountains and tunnels. Not coincidentally, the program's sponsor was the A. C. Gilbert Company, manufacturer of American Flyer model trains. The sponsor had created the miniature set that was used in the series.

Rival trainmaker Lionel sponsored a similar program on ABC, called *Tales of the Red Caboose*.

ROARING TWENTIES, THE (*Newspaper Drama*)
FIRST TELECAST: *October 15, 1960*
LAST TELECAST: *September 21, 1962*
BROADCAST HISTORY:
Oct 1960–Jan 1962, ABC Sat 7:30–8:30
Sep 1962, ABC Fri 7:30–8:30
CAST:
Scott Norris .... Rex Reason
Pat Garrison .... Donald May
Pinky Pinkham .... Dorothy Provine
Chris Higbee .... Gary Vinson
Jim Duke Williams .... John Dehner
Lt. Joe Switolski .... Mike Road
Robert Howard .... James Flavin

This adventure series was set in New York City in the 1920s and, in an attempt at documentary-style authenticity, included newsreel footage of events that had actually happened during that period. Pat and Scott were investigative reporters for the *New York Record* who, with the assistance of their young copy boy and friend, Chris, sought big scoops by infiltrating the underworld and exposing the hoods who were controlling the city during the Prohibition era. They were often seen at the Charleston Club, a posh speakeasy where the leading attraction was beautiful songstress Pinky Pinkham. Working in a club that was frequented by mobsters, Pinky often had tips that would help the reporters break their cases. Whenever they got in over their heads, Lt. Switolski of the N.Y.P.D. would bail them out.

If this format sounds slightly familiar don't be surprised. Except for the fact that the leads in the series were reporters rather than detectives, *The Roaring Twenties* was interchangeable with any of the other formula series Warner Bros. produced for ABC in the late 1950s and early 1960s, the most successful of which were *77 Sunset Strip*, *Hawaiian Eye*, and *Surfside Six*. Canceled early in 1962, *The Roaring Twenties* returned for a few weeks that September with reruns.

ROBBERY HOMICIDE DIVISION (*Police Drama*)
FIRST TELECAST: *September 27, 2002*
LAST TELECAST: *December 7, 2002*
BROADCAST HISTORY:
Sep 2002–Dec 2002, CBS Fri 10:00–11:00
Dec 2002, CBS Sat 10:00–11:00
CAST:
Det. Sam Cole .... Tom Sizemore
Sgt. Alfred Simms .... Barry "Shabaka" Henley
Det. Sonia Robbins .... Klea Scott
Det. Ron Lu .... Michael Paul Chan
Det. Richard Barstow .... David Cubitt

This straightforward police drama followed the activities of a team working in the elite Robbery Homicide Division of the Los Angeles Police Department. Heading the team was Sam Cole, who had developed uncanny instincts during his many years in the department. Working with him were Simms, whose weapon of choice was a shotgun; Robbins, the pathology expert; and Lu and Barstow, who had transferred from the department's Asian and Hispanic gang units. Among the cases they worked on were the assassination of a local cop, the rescue of a kidnapped hip-hop star, the hunt for a white supremacist gang member on a rampage after his recent release from prison, and going undercover to break up an Asian gunrunning syndicate.

ROBBINS NEST, THE (*Comedy/Variety*)
FIRST TELECAST: *September 29, 1950*
LAST TELECAST: *December 22, 1950*
BROADCAST HISTORY:
Sep 1950–Dec 1950, ABC Fri 11:00–11:15
REGULARS:
Fred Robbins
Nate Cantor
Fran Gregory

New York disc jockey Fred Robbins, known for his hip slang, tried TV comedy in this late-night program. Robbins and his supporting players appeared in various skits, and he also sang (passably), but the humor was rather weak. A typical gag had Robbins telling his secretary Fran to file a letter, whereupon she pulled out a metal file and began honing away. The program lasted three months.

ROBERT GUILLAUME SHOW, THE (*Situation Comedy*)
FIRST TELECAST: *April 5, 1989*
LAST TELECAST: *August 9, 1989*
BROADCAST HISTORY:
Apr 1989–Aug 1989, ABC Wed 9:30–10:00
CAST:
Edward Sawyer .... Robert Guillaume
Ann Sherr .... Wendy Phillips
Henry Sawyer .... Hank Rolike
Pamela Sawyer .... Kelsey Scott
William Sawyer .... Marc Joseph

Robert Guillaume portrayed a black marriage counselor who could have used some counseling himself in this short-lived comedy. For one thing he was divorced, a fact he didn't mention to most of his nutty clients. Moreover, the woman he was dating, his new secretary Ann, was white, which caused continuing problems with his opinionated father Henry. Pamela and William were Edward's barely-under-control teenage children.

ROBERT KLEIN TIME (*Talk*)
BROADCAST HISTORY:
USA Network
60 minutes
Produced: *1986–1988* (49 episodes)
Premiered: *October 3, 1986*
REGULARS:
Robert Klein
Bob Stein (orchestra leader)
THEME:
"I Can't Stop My Leg"

Comedian Robert Klein hosted this low-budget prime-time talk show on cable's USA Network, welcoming well-known and up-and-coming guests, including Robin Williams, Billy Crystal, Lauren Bacall, Gilbert Gottfried, Brett Butler, and Jerry Seinfeld. Musical guests ranged from Marvin Hamlisch and Phoebe Snow to an all-dentist jazz band. Klein also did comedy sketches, including the recurring bit "What's Your Problem?" in which he portrayed the crabby host of a radio call-in show.

ROBERT MONTGOMERY PRESENTS (*Dramatic Anthology*)
FIRST TELECAST: *January 30, 1950*
LAST TELECAST: *June 24, 1957*
BROADCAST HISTORY:
Jan 1950–Jun 1957, NBC Mon 9:30–10:30
HOST/EXECUTIVE PRODUCER:
Robert Montgomery
SUMMER REPERTORY PLAYERS:
John Newland (1952–1954)
Vaughn Taylor (1952–1954)
Margaret Hayes (1952–1953)
Elizabeth Montgomery (1953–1954, 1956)
Jan Miner (1954–1956)
Anne Seymour (1954)
Cliff Robertson (1954)
Charles Drake (1955–1956)
Augusta Dabney (1955)
House Jameson (1955)
Dorothy Blackburn (1955)
Eric Sinclair (1955)
Mary K. Wells (1956)
John Gibson (1956)
Tom Middleton (1956)

One of the best-remembered big-budget live dramatic series of TV's golden age. Hollywood actor-director-producer Robert Montgomery introduced each telecast, sometimes interviewing one of the stars and sometimes appearing in the play himself. The series had a Hollywood flavor, with many familiar names from the screen appearing in leading roles. At first it presented adaptations of classic motion pictures, such as *Rebecca*, *A Star Is Born*, and *Dark Victory*, all of which were done within the first few months. Later original TV plays and adaptations of stage plays, books, and short stories were used due to copyright rules which prevented the kinescoping of any production based on a motion picture—these could be telecast on a live basis only. (Kinescopes were needed so that the program could be seen on some non-interconnected affiliates.)

The first telecast was an adaptation of W. Somerset Maugham's classic *The Letter*, and the quality of the scripts remained similarly high throughout the run of the series. The program won many awards. Jane Wyatt, Zachary Scott, and Montgomery's daughter, Elizabeth (later of *Bewitched* fame), made their TV debuts on this program. Claudette Colbert made one of her rare appearances in the medium, as did James Cagney. Helen Hayes and other famous stars, as well as newer talent, were also featured.

Some of the productions were truly spectacular for live television, such as a drama built around the destruction of the great dirigible *Hindenburg*, followed by interviews with some of the actual survivors.

Beginning in 1952, during the summers, *Robert Montgomery Presents* adopted a summer-stock format, with a repertory company of regulars appearing in starring or supporting roles in each production. Among these regulars were both newcomers such as Elizabeth Montgomery, Cliff Robertson, and John Newland, and some old-timers as well.

While the series was generally known as *Robert Montgomery Presents* the actual title varied from week to week according to the sponsor: *Robert Montgomery Presents Your Lucky Strike Theater, . . . the Johnson's Wax Program, . . . the Richard Hudnut Summer Theater*, etc. It alternated with various other programs during its first two years on the air, then became a weekly series in December 1951.

ROBERT Q. LEWIS SHOW, THE (*Comedy/Talk*)
FIRST TELECAST: *July 16, 1950*
LAST TELECAST: *January 7, 1951*
BROADCAST HISTORY:
Jul 1950–Sep 1950, CBS Sun 9:00–9:15
Sep 1950–Jan 1951, CBS Sun 11:00–11:15
HOST:
Robert Q. Lewis

While still functioning as emcee on *The Show Goes On*, comedian Robert Q. Lewis added this informal show to his list of television credits. The live 15-minute show gave him the opportunity to chat with guest stars and introduce the weekly "Breadwinner of the Week," an individual performing an unusual job somewhere in the New York City area.

ROBERT TAYLOR'S DETECTIVES, see *Detectives, Starring Robert Taylor, The*

ROBERT YOUNG, FAMILY DOCTOR, syndicated title for *Marcus Welby, M.D.*

ROBIN HOOD, see *Adventures of Robin Hood, New Adventures of Robin Hood*

ROBIN'S HOODS (*Adventure*)
BROADCAST HISTORY:
Syndicated only
60 minutes
Produced: *1994–1995* (22 episodes)
Released: *August 1994*
CAST:
Brett Robin .... Linda Purl
Annie Beckett .... Jennifer Campbell
Eddie Bartlett .... David Gail
Stacey Wright .... Julie McCullough
Maria Alvarez (1994) .... Mayte Vilan
Mackenzie Magnuson ("Mac") .... Claire Yarlett
**Det. Stephen DeCosta (1994)* .... Michael Beck
**Det. Chris Carpenter* .... Ramy Zada
K. T. Parker .... Gretchen Palmer
Nick Collins (1995) .... Rick Springfield
*Occasional

After her husband, police detective Jake Robin, was killed while on a case, assistant D.A. Brett Robin took over management of Robin's Nest, his harborside country and western nightclub. The place was staffed entirely by young convicted criminals who had been paroled to Jake in lieu of serving their time. They worked at the nightclub and lived in the rooms above it. Mac, from a wealthy family, had passed bad checks; Annie had been a burglar; Eddie, who had a short temper, had been convicted of aggravated assault, Maria had participated in an armed robbery; and Stacey had been set up for drug trafficking when marijuana had been planted in her car. Brett's first impulse was to send them all back to the slammer, but after they helped her track down Jake's killer and continued to help others in need, she grew very fond of them. Stephen was her late husband's partner.

In November Eddie and Annie, while working a stakeout, began an affair and Mac got involved with police detective Chris Carpenter. In December Maria had her parole commuted so she could go home to Miami and help her father recover from a heart attack. Tough K.T. took her place among the parolees. Soon after she took over the club Brett found out she was pregnant with her late husband's child. In February Brett gave birth to a son, and in the same episode Eddie and Annie broke up and Mac caught Chris cheating on her. While Brett was living with her in-laws after the birth of the baby, Nick Collins was brought in to manage Robin's Nest and protect the interests of the bank that carried her loan. Stacey, who had always been sweet on him, started dating Eddie after his breakup with Annie, but it didn't work out either.

Filmed on location in Vancouver, British Columbia.

ROBOCOP—THE SERIES (*Science Fiction*)

BROADCAST HISTORY:

Syndicated only
60 minutes
Produced: *1993–1994*
Released: *March 1994*

CAST:

Alex Murphy/Robocop .... Richard Eden
Det. Lisa Madigan .... Yvette Nipar
Sgt. Stanley Parks.................... Blu Mankuma
Diana Powers .... Andrea Roth
OCP Chairman........................ David Gardner
Gadget (nee Gertrude Modesto).... Sarah Campbell
Charlie Lippincott .... Ed Sahely
Bo Harlan................................. Dan Duran
Rocky Crenshaw.......................... Erica Ehm
**Nancy Murphy* .... Jennifer Griffin
**Jimmy Murphy (age 15)* .... Peter Costigan
**Little Jimmy Murphy* .... Jordan Hughes
**Pudface Morgan*...................... James Kidnie

*Occasional

Broad, cartoonish action and social satire marked this TV adaptation of the violent *RoboCop* movies. The setting was Delta City in the early 21st century. The city, and much of the surrounding area, seemed to be run by Omni Consumer Products (OCP). Not only did OCP have its hands in almost everything people bought, it also ran the local government and had taken over the police department. OCP's technological marvel was Robocop, a high-tech "security cyborg" that mated an almost indestructible body, complete with integrated weapons systems, to the head and brain of former cop Alex Murphy, who had almost died in a shootout. Others featured were Lisa, Murphy's former partner, one of the few people who knew he was Robocop (at least from the neck up); Sgt. Parks, their well-meaning superior officer; Diana, a former OCP secretary and Robocop ally, who "lived" in the electronic communications network after being killed off in the series pilot; the OCP Chairman, who often seemed ineffectual and too easily swayed by manipulative underlings; Gadget, a young orphan adopted by Parks who spent most of her time hanging out at the Metro South Precinct; and Charlie Lippincott, the OCP technician who did maintenance work on Robocop.

Much of the action took place in Old Detroit ("Dog Town"), the run-down section of the city where the poor lived and crime ran rampant. It was there that Murphy's wife, Nancy, lived with their son, Jimmy. Although Alex had had most of his human memories erased as part of his Robocop conversion, he was, on occasion, able to recall earlier times with his family.

The tongue-in-cheek quality of the show was always evident: Each episode opened with *Media Break*, a local newscast anchored by perpetually perky Bo Harlan and Rocky Crenshaw that used the slogan "Give us 3 minutes and we'll give you the world." Local TV was overloaded with commercials for OCP products featuring the animated superhero Commander Cash. Robocop seemed to have a stronger sense of duty and was more honest than any of the humans.

Adapted from the theatrical *RoboCop* films, the first two of which starred Peter Weller as Murphy. There were also two cartoon versions produced for syndication—*Robocop: The Animated Series* in 1994, and *Robocop: Alpha Commando* in1998.

ROBOT WARS: EXTREME WARRIORS (*Sports/Audience Participation*)

BROADCAST HISTORY:

TNN
60 minutes
Original episodes: *2001–*
Premiered: *August 20, 2001*

REGULARS:

Mick Foley, Host
Rebecca Grant, Pit Reporter (2001)
Carol Grow, Pit Reporter
Joanie Laurer, Pit Reporter (2002–)
Stefan Frank, Commentator

A high-tech demolition derby, modeled after Comedy Central's successful *Battlebots,* in which small, radio-controlled robots bashed each other to smithereens as a rowdy audience hooted and cheered. Six robots fought it out in each episode, with the winner going on to the season finale. In addition to an arena full of obstacles (fire, a pit, a spinning disk, various infernal machines), there were six powerful "House Robots" to add to the mayhem—Shunt, Dead Metal, Matilda, Sergeant Bash, Refbot, and the feared Sir Killalot with its hydraulic cutters and lance. A psycho host and bodacious "pit reporters" added to the color. A slightly less violent version of the show appeared on Nickelodeon. Based on a 1998 British series of the same name.

ROC (*Situation Comedy*)

FIRST TELECAST: *August 24, 1991*
LAST TELECAST: *August 30, 1994*

BROADCAST HISTORY:

Aug 1991, FOX Sun 7:30–8:00
Sep 1991–Mar 1992, FOX Sun 8:30–9:00
Mar 1992–Apr 1992, FOX Sun 8:00–8:30
Apr 1992–Aug 1993, FOX Sun 8:30–9:00
Aug 1993–Jan 1994, FOX Tue 8:00–8:30
Jan 1994–Feb 1994, FOX Tue 8:30–9:00
Apr 1994–Aug 1994, FOX Tue 8:00–8:30

CAST:

Roc Emerson .... Charles S. Dutton
Eleanor Emerson .... Ella Joyce
Joey Emerson .... Rocky Carroll
Andrew Emerson .... Carl Gordon
Wiz (1991–1992).................... Garrett Morris
**Miles Taylor (1992–1993)* .... Oscar Brown, Jr.
**Curtis Vincent (1992–1993)* .... Wally Taylor
**Helen (1992–1993)*................ Heidi Swedberg
**Jenise (1992–1993)* .... Natalie Belcon
**Charlaine (1992–1993)* .... Ann Weldon
**Charlaine (1993)*..................... Jenifer Lewis
Sheila Hendricks (1993–1994)........ Alexis Fields
**Crazy George Stevens (1993–1994)* ..... Jamie Foxx
**André Thompson (1993–1994)*...... Clifton Powell

*Occasional

THEME:

"God Bless the Child," original theme

Roc Emerson was a hard-working black garbage man in Baltimore, just trying to make enough money to provide for his family. He had a good heart and good instincts, even if he wasn't too bright—when confronted with something he didn't understand, his usual response was "I ain't worked that out yet." Living with Roc were his loving wife Eleanor, a nightshift nurse whose work schedule was not doing their love life much good; his freeloading kid brother Joey, an unemployed trumpet player with a penchant for gambling and other fast-buck schemes; and his opinionated father Andrew, who distrusted white people and attributed almost everything of consequence to blacks. Roc's buddy Wiz, so named because of a bladder problem, was a regular at the local bar where Roc hung out during his spare time.

After successfully airing an episode live in the spring of 1992, the producers of *Roc* decided that the entire 1992–1993 would be live rather than on tape. All the regulars, who were primarily stage actors, felt that performing live would give the show more energy. At the start of that season Joey, living in the fancy apartment of a musician friend who was on tour, formed a jazz trio with a bass player (Curtis) and pianist (Miles), both old-timers. When the friend for whom he was house sitting returned, Joey moved back into Roc's house and got free room and board for working as the superintendent for Roc's properties—an apartment house along with the adjoining row houses. Roc had gone into hock to buy them when his landlord decided to sell and move south. At the end of the season Eleanor got pregnant.

In the fall of 1993, with the series back on tape, 11-year-old Sheila Hendricks, whose father, Calvin, went to prison in the season premiere, moved in with the Emersons. Eleanor gave birth to Marcus Garvey Emerson in November (viewers were given a 900 number to call and pick the name for the baby). Joey, living in an adjacent apartment owned by Roc, still didn't have a job. With both a new baby and a young girl living in their home, Roc and Eleanor became more involved with quality-of-life issues in the inner city. During that season there were more serious themes, including Roc's unsuccessful run for city council (with Joey as his campaign manager) on a clean-up-the-crime-in-the-neighborhood platform and his periodic confrontations with local drug dealer André Thompson.

Star Charles Dutton, who had himself been in prison before becoming an actor, was very concerned about the types of role models presented on *Roc*. In 1993 he won an NAACP Image Award for Best Actor.

ROCK AND ROLL RECORD BREAKERS (*Music Documentary*)

BROADCAST HISTORY:

VH1
30 minutes
Original episodes: *2000*
Premiered: *January 28, 2000*

This fast-paced documentary series celebrated rock's twin spirits of rebellion and excess. The short (one- to five-minute) reports covered such topics as the band that did the most shows in one day (Jackyl, with 21 shows in 24 hours), the band banned for the longest time from a hotel chain (The Who, banned from Holiday Inn for 31 years), the biggest cover song of all time (Whitney Houston's "I Will Always Love You," originally by Dolly Parton), the most disturbing rock collectible (Elvis' wart), and the highest rooftop concert (a Nepalese Sherpa band performing atop the World Trade Center).

ROCK AND ROLL YEARS, THE, see *Dick Clark Presents the Rock and Roll Years*

ROCK CANDY (*Comedy*)

BROADCAST HISTORY:

VH1
30 minutes
Original episodes: *1999*
Premiered: *March 8, 1999*

A short-lived "comedy magazine," with filmed reports and skits. In the first episode a band called The Brian Jonestown Massacre visited a psychotherapist, and hidden cameras showed applicants interviewing for the job of personal assistant to a fictitious (and eccentric) rock star. Among the "correspondents" was Jim Gaffigan.

ROCK 'N' ROLL EVENING NEWS, THE (*News/Information*)

BROADCAST HISTORY:

Syndicated only
60 minutes
Produced: *Fall 1986–January 1987*
Released: *September 1986*

HOST/ANCHOR:

Steve Kmetko

CORRESPONDENTS:

Adrienne Meltzer
Eleanor Mondale
Nelson George
Richard Blade
Marjorie Wallace
Robert Hilburn
Marianne Rogers
Clarence

The Rock 'n' Roll Evening News was a weekly potpourri of interviews, gossipy news about the happenings in the rock music world, and performances by established and new rock groups. It had a large number of regular correspondents and an expensive high-tech look. To keep current, it was taped only a couple of days before airing (late on Saturday nights in most cities). What it didn't have was a large audience. An ambitious failure, it ceased production less than four months after its premiere.

ROCK N' ROLL JEOPARDY, see *Jeopardy!*

ROCK 'N' ROLL SUMMER ACTION (*Musical Variety*)

FIRST TELECAST: *July 17, 1985*
LAST TELECAST: *August 28, 1985*
BROADCAST HISTORY:
Jul 1985–Aug 1985, ABC Wed 8:00–9:00
HOST:
Christopher Atkins
REGULARS:
Paul Revere & the Raiders
The Action Kids '85 (dancers)
EXECUTIVE PRODUCER:
Dick Clark

Another of Dick Clark's innumerable lightweight rock 'n' roll series, this one set outdoors on California's Malibu Beach. There were plenty of bikinis, Frisbee-throwing, offbeat contests (e.g., the "bury-your-boyfriend-in-the-sand contest"), hip young standup comics, and clips of the kooky fashions and rock stars of yesteryear. Guests included Kim Carnes, Jan and Dean, the New Edition, Weird Al Yankovic, Stephanie Mills, and the Commodores.

For a similar series in 1967, see *Malibu U.*

ROCK OF AGES (*Discussion*)

BROADCAST HISTORY:
VH1
30 minutes
Produced: *1998–2000* (29 episodes)
Premiered: *June 15, 1998*
HOSTS:
Henry Alford
Emmy Laybourne
Phoebe Jonas
Michael Collins
Godfrey Danchimah

VH1 tried once again to bridge the generation gap—or perhaps illuminate it—with this clever show in which different generations gathered to comment on videos of each other's music. Surprisingly, some 40-year-olds actually liked gangsta rap, and teenagers could also find rock pioneers cool. But they split on Bob Dylan. "He sounds like a Muppet," said one mall rat.

ROCK THE HOUSE (*Informational*)

BROADCAST HISTORY:
VH1
30 minutes
Original episodes: *2002–*
Premiered: *October 28, 2002*
REGULARS:
Lisa Snowdon, Host
Kelly Van Patter, Designer
Paul Roome, Designer

In this droll take-off on TLC's hit *Trading Spaces,* a "huge fan" of a rock star was set up by a friend to have a room in his or her home redecorated by the star—unbeknownst to the fan. First the fan was lured out on a pretext and followed by a "spy cam"; then the star, the friend, and the show's design crew moved in and quickly remade the place in the star's personal style. The premiere episode had wild man Sammy Hagar redoing a fan's digs in the style of his bar in Cabo San Lucas, Mexico. At the end the fan returned and shrieked in delight as friends and family crowded around; then Sammy Hagar himself walked in. Other celebrities giving their fans the treatment included Paula Abdul, Snoop Dogg, the Goo Goo Dolls, and Weird Al Yankovic. The series was hosted by sexy Lisa Snowdon, with alternating designers Kelly and Paul.

ROCKET POWER (*Cartoon*)

BROADCAST HISTORY:
Nickelodeon
30 minutes
Original episodes: *1999–*
Premiered: *August 16, 1999*
VOICES:
Oswald "Otto" Rocket (age 9) .... Joseph Ashton
Regina "Reggie" Rocket (11) .... Shayna Fox
Maurice "Twister" Rodriguez (9) ... Ulysses Cuadra
Sam "The Squid" Dullard (9) (1999–2000) .... Sam Saletta
Sam "The Squid" Dullard (2000–) .... Gary Leroi Gray
Ray "Raymundo" Rocket .... John Kassir
Tito Makani, Jr. .... Ray Bumatai
Lars Rodriguez .... Lombardo Boyar
Paula Dullard .... Jennifer Hale
Sputz Piston .... Dominic Armato
Maori (2001) .... Stan Harrington
Trish, Sherry (1999) .... Lauren Tom
Eddie Valentine ("Prince of the Netherworld") .... Jordan Warkol
Merv Stimpleton .... Henry Gibson
Violet Stimpleton .... Edie McClurg

Four active kids in the California town of Ocean Shores were addicted to extreme sports in this fast-paced cartoon. Otto was the leader of the pack, a rather self-centered, highly competitive dude who excelled at skateboarding, surfing, hockey and other action sports. Reggie was his bossy older sister; Twister, his best friend who followed the gang around with a video camera; and Squid, the new kid in town and the brains of the gang. Otto and Reggie's single dad, Ray, worked at the Shore Shack and tried to keep his kids in line while his friend Tito, a native of Hawaii, offered them sage advice on surfing. Lars was Twister's older brother, who had his own competitive gang of friends; Eddie, a neighborhood kid who affected a villainous wardrobe but was really a mama's boy, and the Stimpletons, the sometimes annoyed next-door neighbors.

ROCKFORD FILES, THE (*Detective Drama*)

FIRST TELECAST: *September 13, 1974*
LAST TELECAST: *July 25, 1980*
BROADCAST HISTORY:
Sep 1974–May 1977, NBC Fri 9:00–10:00
Jun 1977, NBC Fri 8:30–9:30
Jul 1977–Jan 1979, NBC Fri 9:00–10:00
Feb 1979–Mar 1979, NBC Sat 10:00–11:00
Apr 1979–Dec 1979, NBC Fri 9:00–10:00
Mar 1980–Apr 1980, NBC Thu 10:00–11:00
Jun 1980–Jul 1980, NBC Fri 9:00–10:00
CAST:
Jim Rockford .... James Garner
Joseph "Rocky" Rockford (pilot only) .... Robert Donley
Joseph "Rocky" Rockford .... Noah Beery, Jr.
Det. Dennis Becker .... Joe Santos
Beth Davenport (1974–1978) ..... Gretchen Corbett

Evelyn "Angel" Martin............ Stuart Margolin
John Cooper (1978–1979)............. Bo Hopkins
Lt. Alex Diehl (1974–1976)............. Tom Atkins
Lt. Doug Chapman (1976–1980)....... James Luisi
**Lance White (1979–1980)*............ Tom Selleck

*Occasional

THEME:

"The Rockford Files," by Mike Post and Peter Carpenter

Jim Rockford was a private detective with a difference. He was an ex-convict. Once imprisoned for a crime he had not committed, but eventually exonerated when new evidence turned up, Jim had a penchant for taking cases that were closed—those the police were sure had been resolved. His knack for turning up information that might reverse the already established verdict did not endear him to the police, particularly to Det. Dennis Becker with whom he had a love-hate relationship. Jim was always getting Dennis involved in situations he would have preferred to avoid, aggravating the cop who, despite it all, had a personal affection for him. Jim lived in, and worked out of, a house trailer at the beach in the Los Angeles area and was not the cheapest detective available, charging $200 per day plus expenses. His father, a retired trucker, helped him on occasion and his girlfriend, attorney Beth Davenport, was always around to bail him out when he ran afoul of the law. Having been in prison, Jim had many ex-con friends. One of them, his former cellmate, Angel Martin, was constantly in need of Jim's help because of his tendency to get involved with his former criminal associates. Another friend was John Cooper, a disbarred lawyer whose ties to the Corporation for Legal Research proved useful.

Jim used all the seamier ploys for which detectives are known—impersonating others to get information, cheap disguises, petty bribery, eavesdropping—but his powers of reasoning and dogged hard work usually solved the case. If, along the way, he got beaten up, had his car damaged, and got shot at—well, he had a sense of humor. He resented fellow private investigator Lance White who, during *The Rockford Files'* last season, always seemed intuitively to know all the answers and have everything fall into his lap without effort. That final season was cut short when Garner, tired of the role and suffering from a variety of ailments, abruptly quit the show.

The theme song from this series was on the hit parade in mid-1975s.

ROCKLINE ON MTV (*Talk*)

BROADCAST HISTORY:

MTV
30 minutes
Produced: *1991–1992*
Premiered: *February 26, 1991*

HOST:

Martha Quinn

A weekly live call-in show that gave viewers the chance to talk to their favorite recording artists. The guest on opening night was MC Hammer.

ROCKO'S MODERN LIFE (*Cartoon*)

BROADCAST HISTORY:

Nickelodeon
30 minutes
Produced: *1993–1996* (53 episodes)
Premiered: *September 18, 1993*

VOICES:

Rocko.......................... Carlos Alazraqui
Heffer................................ Tom Kenny
Ed Bighead......................... Charlie Adler
Filburt..................... Mr. (Doug) Lawrence
Slippy (1993–1995).................. Dom Irrera

Despite its name and its home on the ultracontemporary Nickelodeon cable network, *Rocko's Modern Life* echoed the fantasy cartoons of the 1940s in which objects were exaggerated, characters demolished and put back together, and the action unfolded at a frantic pace. The principal character was Rocko, an Australian wallaby overwhelmed by the complexities of life. With him in various episodes were his friends Heffer the obese steer, Filburt the timid turtle, Slippy the conniving slug, and the Bigheads, loudmouth cane toads.

ROCKY AND HIS FRIENDS see *Bullwinkle Show, The*

ROCKY KING, INSIDE DETECTIVE (*Police Drama*)

FIRST TELECAST: *January 14, 1950*
LAST TELECAST: *December 26, 1954*

BROADCAST HISTORY:

Jan 1950–Jul 1950, DUM Sat 8:30–9:00
Jul 1950–Mar 1951, DUM Fri 9:30–10:00
Mar 1951–Dec 1954, DUM Sun 9:00–9:30

CAST:

Det. Rocky King.................... Roscoe Karns
Mabel King.......................... Grace Carney
Sgt. Lane (1950–1953)............ Earl Hammond
Det. Hart (1953–1954)................ Todd Karns

Rocky King was probably the most popular continuing dramatic show to come out of the DuMont network. It never had the opportunity to attain top nationwide ratings, due to DuMont's limited station lineup and severely restricted production budgets (you never saw a big-name guest star acting in a *Rocky King* episode!), but it did attract a loyal and enthusiastic following which kept it on the air for five years, nearly until the end of DuMont operations.

The program centered on hard-working Rocky King, a detective on the New York City Homicide Squad, and was in most respects a standard low-budget cops-and-robbers show. What set it apart were its lead, Roscoe Karns; its sense of believability; and its touches of humor. Those who think that *Dragnet* brought realism to TV cop shows obviously never saw *Rocky King*. Rocky had no flashes of brilliant deduction or unbelievably lucky breaks, nor did he tackle impossibly convoluted cases. He simply tracked down the facts, doggedly, and pieced them together until they made sense—and pointed to the culprit. There was plenty of action in *Rocky King* too, but it usually came after some good, hard work.

Rocky also had a family, which generated a good deal of interest, because they were heard but never seen on camera. This began as an economy measure (typical of DuMont), when an actress who was playing a role in a mystery was asked to double as Rocky's wife at home. Since there was no time to change clothes or makeup (the show was live), she spoke from offscreen. Viewers liked the touch and Grace Carney became a permanent feature, her off-camera presence always bringing Rocky back to earth with her problems around the house. For a time there was also an unseen son, named Junior.

Roscoe Karns, who had had a long career in Hollywood as a second banana, was appreciative of the opportunity to extend his career via TV (he frankly said that *Rocky King* had "rescued" him from enforced retirement) and stayed with the show until its demise. During the final year of its run, his son, Todd Karns, played his sidekick, Det. Hart. Roscoe Karns later had a leading role in *Hennessey*. He died in 1970.

ROCKY'S CORNER see *Henny & Rocky Show, The*

ROD SERLING'S NIGHT GALLERY see *Night Gallery*

RODEO DRIVE (*Quiz/Audience Participation*)

BROADCAST HISTORY:

Lifetime Network
30 minutes
Produced: *1990* (130 episodes)
Premiered: *February 5, 1990*

HOST:

Louise DuArt

This 1990 game show on Lifetime was a revival of a short-lived 1981 syndicated series that had been hosted by Peter Tomarken, but it was no more successful. Contestants answered questions about celebrity rumors, with the winner getting a shopping spree on a simulated Rodeo Drive—"the most fabulous shopping street in the World." Host/comedienne Louise DuArt added celebrity impersonations. The real Rodeo Drive is located in Beverly Hills, California.

RODMAN WORLD TOUR, THE (*Interview*)

BROADCAST HISTORY:

MTV
30 minutes
Produced: *1996–1997* (13 episodes)
Premiered: *December 8, 1996*

REGULAR:

Dennis Rodman

NBA bad boy Dennis Rodman hosted this unusual show in which the green-haired hoops star traveled around the world, hanging out with celebrities. In one segment he might go motorcycling with Jay Leno, in another play poker with Kelsey Grammer. Said Rodman, "I want people to see my world through my eyes"—or better, through those cool shades.

ROGER EBERT AND THE MOVIES, see *Siskel & Ebert*

ROGER MILLER SHOW, THE (*Musical Variety*)

FIRST TELECAST: *September 12, 1966*
LAST TELECAST: *December 26, 1966*
BROADCAST HISTORY:

Sep 1966–Dec 1966, NBC Mon 8:30–9:00

REGULARS:

Roger Miller
The Eddie Karam Orchestra

THEME:

"King of the Road"

Singer-composer Roger Miller, who had won five 1965 Grammy Awards for his recordings, starred in this short-lived variety show. In addition to singing popular songs and the country and western tunes which had made him so popular, he introduced and performed with one or two guest stars each week. There were no other regulars, but the Doodletown Pipers made a number of appearances during the less than four months the show was on the air.

ROGGIN'S HEROES (*Human Interest/Sports*)

BROADCAST HISTORY:

Syndicated only
30 minutes
Produced: *1990–1993* (102 episodes)
Released: *January 1991*

HOST:

Fred Roggin

REGULAR:

Officer Feldman

Los Angeles TV sports reporter Fred Roggin hosted this weekly collection of video clips from all over the world of people at their competitive worst and/or best. Most of the clips were sports related—amateur, high school, college, and professional. Each episode had its Hall of Shame feature of embarrassing clips, and viewers were encouraged to send in home video clips of people making fools of themselves. Also seen regularly was "Officer Feldman's Safety Tips" in which the stonefaced policeman showed viewers the comic consequences of not following proper "safety" precautions.

ROGUES, THE (*Comedy/Drama*)

FIRST TELECAST: *September 13, 1964*
LAST TELECAST: *September 5, 1965*
BROADCAST HISTORY:

Sep 1964–Sep 1965, NBC Sun 10:00–11:00

CAST:

Tony Fleming............................ Gig Young
Alec Fleming........................ David Niven
Marcel St. Clair.................. Charles Boyer
Timmy St. Clair..................... Robert Coote
Margaret St. Clair................ Gladys Cooper
Inspector Briscoe................. John Williams

"Honor before Honesty" was the credo of the Flemings and the St. Clairs, the two most successful families of scoundrels the civilized world had ever known. Their lines had been forever crossed when Sir Giles Fleming and la Comtesse Juliette St. Clair had met and fallen in love while both were independently trying to lift a jewel box from Marie Antoinette of France in 1789. The modern descendants of these aristocratic jewel thieves and con men, whose primary activity was relieving the rich of their wealth, were spread all over the world. Tony was the dashing young American member of the family, who worked out of New York and had been hand-picked to take over the family "throne" from his English cousin, Alec, when the latter went into semiretirement. Alec had moved to Montego Bay but was still active for special deals. Marcel was the head of the French branch of the family and Timmy, a master of disguises, was on hand to help each of the principals. His mother, Aunt Margaret, was the planner and coordinator of most of the heists and cons, all of which were finalized at her home across from Buckingham Palace.

ROLL OUT (*Situation Comedy*)
FIRST TELECAST: *October 5, 1973*
LAST TELECAST: *January 4, 1974*
BROADCAST HISTORY:
Oct 1973–Dec 1973, CBS Fri 8:30–9:00
Jan 1974, CBS Fri 8:00–8:30
CAST:
Cpl. "Sweet" Williams.................. Stu Gilliam
Pfc. Jed Brooks........................ Hilly Hicks
Sgt. B. J. Bryant .... Mel Stewart
Capt. Rocco Calvelli.................. Val Bisoglio
Lt. Robert W. Chapman.............. Ed Begley, Jr.
"Wheels".......................... Garrett Morris
Jersey .... Darrow Igus
Phone Booth .... Rod Gist
High Strung .... Theodore Wilson
Madam Delacort................... Penny Santon

Set in France during World War II, *Roll Out* was the story of the men of the 5050th Trucking Company, the "Red Ball Express," an army trucking unit that managed to get supplies through to troops at the front despite any and all problems. Military discipline meant little to these rowdy men, whose prime purpose was to move war supplies no matter how they did it. Capt. Calvelli was the leader of the unit, which was mostly black. Sweet and Jed were two of his best drivers, and Sgt. Bryant the tough, crusty career military man. When not on assignment, the men of the 5050th sought recreation at the nightclub adjacent to their base camp, run by Madam Delacort.

Based on the story of an actual World War II transportation unit.

ROLLER DERBY (*Sports*)
FIRST TELECAST: *March 24, 1949*
LAST TELECAST: *August 16, 1951*
BROADCAST HISTORY:
Mar 1949–Jun 1949, ABC Thu 10:00–11:15
Mar 1949–May 1949, ABC Sat 10:00–11:00
May 1949–Jun 1949, ABC Mon 9:30–Conclusion
May 1949–Jul 1949, ABC Fri 10:00–Conclusion
Sep 1949–Nov 1949, ABC Mon/Fri 10:00–Conclusion
Sep 1949–Sep 1950, ABC Thu 10:00–Conclusion
Nov 1949–May 1951, ABC Sat 9:00–Conclusion
Jun 1950–Sep 1950, ABC Fri 8:30–9:30
Sep 1950–May 1951, ABC Tue/Thu 10:00–11:15
Jul 1951–Aug 1951, ABC Thu 10:00–11:15
ANNOUNCER:
Ken Nydell
Joe Hasel (1949–1950)
Howard Myles (1950–1951)
Ed Begley (1951)

Roller Derby was at one time the most popular program on the ABC schedule, that is if amount of air time occupied is a measure of popularity. The sport, which sometimes seemed more like a head-bashing free-for-all than a test of athletic skill, combined elements of skating, football, rugby, and wrestling, aired as often as three times a week. The show originated from such exotic locations as the 14th Regiment Army in Brooklyn, and other similar places around New York City and adjacent areas of Long Island and New Jersey. The resident announcer was Ken Nydell, who did the play by play throughout the run, sometimes by himself and sometimes with an assistant. The New York Chiefs were always the home team, playing the San Francisco Bay Bombers, the Midwest Pioneers, and others.

ROLLER GIRLS, THE (*Situation Comedy*)
FIRST TELECAST: *April 24, 1978*
LAST TELECAST: *May 10, 1978*
BROADCAST HISTORY:
Apr 1978–May 1978, NBC Mon 8:00–8:30
May 1978, NBC Wed 8:00–8:30
CAST:
Don Mitchell.............................. Terry Kiser
Mongo Sue Lampert................... Rhonda Bates
J. B. Johnson...................... Candy Ann Brown
Selma "Books" Cassidy............. Joanna Cassidy
Honey Bee Novak .... Marcy Hanson
Shana "Pipeline" Akira .... Marilyn Tokuda
Howie Devine .... James Murtaugh

The Pittsburgh Pitts were an all-girl roller derby team, owned and managed by conniving Don Mitchell, who was constantly looking for ways to save the foundering team—and his investment. The Pitts were a sexy, but sometimes inept crew: towering Mongo, feisty J.B. (the token black), sophisticated "Books," dizzy blonde Honey Bee, and innocent "Pipeline," an Eskimo-American. Announcer for the team's raucous games was the snobbish Howie Devine, a down-on-his-luck former opera commentator who would do anything for a buck.

ROLLIN' ON THE RIVER (*Music*)
BROADCAST HISTORY:
Syndicated only
30 minutes
Produced: *1971–1973* (52 episodes)
Released: *Fall 1971*
REGULARS:
Kenny Rogers and the First Edition (Terry Williams, guitar; Kin Vassey, rhythm guitar; Mickey Jones, drums; Mary Arnold, vocals)

Kenny Rogers and the First Edition, a group formed by ex-members of the New Christy Minstrels, had several soft-rock hits during the late 1960s and early 1970s, including "Ruby, Don't Take Your Love to Town" and "Just Dropped In." After network appearances on *The Smothers Brothers Comedy Hour* and other series, they showed their versatility in this Canadian-produced syndicated program of their own. It included contemporary music, comedy bits, and guests of a generally youthful persuasion—Kris Kristofferson, B. J. Thomas, Mac Davis, Bill Withers, Gladys Knight and the Pips, etc. The program was shot in front of a bright riverboat set.

The title was based on a line from the 1969 Creedence Clearwater Revival hit, "Proud Mary." It was shortened in the second season to *Rollin'*.

The pressures of taping a weekly show led to problems for the group, and after four hitless years they disbanded in 1976. Kenny Rogers then went on to an even bigger solo career acting and singing ballads such as "The Gambler" and "Lady."

ROMANCE (*Dramatic Anthology*)
FIRST TELECAST: *November 3, 1949*
LAST TELECAST: *December 29, 1949*
BROADCAST HISTORY:
Nov 1949–Dec 1949, CBS Thu 8:30–9:00

Premiering with an updated version of *Camille*, this live anthology series presented television adaptations of famous love stories. *Romance* aired on alternate Thursdays with *Inside U.S.A. with Chevrolet.*

ROMANCE CLASSICS (Network),
see WE: Women's Entertainment

RON REAGAN SHOW, The (*Discussion*)

BROADCAST HISTORY:
Syndicated only
60 minutes
Produced: *1991*
Released: *August 1991*

HOST:
Ron Reagan

After pursuing careers as a ballet dancer and as a correspondent for *Good Morning, America*, Ron Reagan turned up in the summer of 1991 as the host of a rather intelligent, syndicated discussion show that looked like a cross between *Donahue* and *Nightline*. Each weeknight telecast focused on a single topic, ranging from the serious to the frivolous, with Mr. Reagan leading the discussion among a panel of experts. As with daytime talk shows, members of the studio audience posed questions to the members of the panel but, since the show was taped in advance, there was no live call-in segment.

ROOKIES, THE (*Police Drama*)

FIRST TELECAST: *September 11, 1972*
LAST TELECAST: *June 29, 1976*
BROADCAST HISTORY:
Sep 1972–Sep 1975, ABC Mon 8:00–9:00
Sep 1975–Apr 1976, ABC Tue 9:00–10:00
May 1976–Jun 1976, ABC Tue 10:00–11:00

CAST:
Officer Terry Webster .... Georg Stanford Brown
Officer Willie Gillis (1972–1974) ... Michael Ontkean
Officer Mike Danko .... Sam Melville
Jill Danko .... Kate Jackson
Lt. Eddie Ryker .... Gerald S. O'Loughlin
Officer Chris Owens (1974–1976) .. Bruce Fairbairn

Three wet-behind-the-ears rookie cops in a large Southern California city provided the focus of this series. The trio, variously fresh out of college, a government social program, and the army, were dedicated to the new, more humane methods of law enforcement, which often put them at odds with their hard-nosed mentor, Lt. Ryker. The combination of their youthful enthusiasm and Ryker's experienced guidance helped mold them into effective officers. The only married one of the three was Mike, whose wife, Jill, was a registered nurse. In 1974 a cast change occurred when Willie was replaced by Chris Owens, a new recruit.

ROOM FOR ONE MORE (*Situation Comedy*)

FIRST TELECAST: *January 27, 1962*
LAST TELECAST: *September 22, 1962*
BROADCAST HISTORY:
Jan 1962–Sep 1962, ABC Sat 8:00–8:30

CAST:
George Rose .... Andrew Duggan
Anna Rose .... Peggy McCay
Flip Rose .... Ronnie Dapo
Laurie Rose .... Carol Nicholson
Mary Rose .... Anna Carri
Jeff Rose .... Timmy Rooney
Walter Burton .... Jack Albertson
Ruth Burton .... Maxine Stuart

This family comedy was about a middle-class couple, George and Anna Rose, their two natural children, Flip and Laurie, and their adopted children, Mary and Jeff (the latter played by Mickey Rooney's son Timmy). The Roses' easygoing ways and sympathy for children in general kept bringing other homeless waifs in and out of the household as well—they always had "room for one more." Tramp was the family dog, and Ruth a family friend (Jack Albertson appeared briefly as her husband).

Adapted from the autobiography of Anna Perrott Rose, which was also made into a 1952 movie (originally titled *Room for One More*, later retitled *The Easy Way*) starring Cary Grant.

ROOM FOR ROMANCE (*Comedy/Drama Anthology*)

FIRST TELECAST: *July 27, 1990*
LAST TELECAST: *August 24, 1990*
BROADCAST HISTORY:
Jul 1990–Aug 1990, CBS Fri 10:00–11:00

CAST:
Roman Carciofi .... Dom Irrera
Caroline Gidot .... Rebecca Harrell
Vikram .... Sumant
Lola Fields .... Terri Ann Linn

An expensive apartment building on New York City's fashionable upper east side was the setting for this anthology series that resembled a landlocked *Love Boat*. Each episode consisted of three separate stories about residents of the building and jumped from one story to another over the course of the hour. Everything was seen through the eyes of Roman Carciofi, the building's cynical concierge, and his lonely young friend Caroline Gidot, who lived in one of the penthouses with her mother. Little that went on in the building got by them as they observed everyone's comings and goings. Stories tended to deal with the love lives and/or family problems of tenants.

ROOM FOR TWO (*Situation Comedy*)

FIRST TELECAST: *March 24, 1992*
LAST TELECAST: *July 6, 1993*
BROADCAST HISTORY:
Mar 1992–Apr 1992, ABC Tue 9:30–10:00
Apr 1992–May 1992, ABC Wed 9:00–9:30
Sep 1992–Dec 1992, ABC Thu 8:30–9:00
Jun 1993–Jul 1993, ABC Tue 9:30–10:00

CAST:
Edie Kurland .... Linda Lavin
Jill Kurland .... Patricia Heaton
Ken Kazurinsky .... Peter Michael Goetz
Naomi Dillon .... Bess Meyer
Reid Ellis .... Andrew Prine
Diahnn Boudreau .... Paula Kelly
Matt Draughon .... John Putch
Keith Wyman .... Jeff Yagher

A bossy, recently widowed Ohio mom descended on her upwardly mobile daughter in New York City in this mother-daughter comedy. Edie was looking for a new lease on life, and she got it with an apartment in the Big Apple, reentry into the dating scene, and—most surprisingly—a regular spot as lifestyle commentator on *Wake Up, New York*, the local TV show produced by her daughter. Sparks, of course, flew (Jill was now her mother's boss), but the two bonded by the end of each episode. Admiring the fireworks were Edie's neighbor and new best friend Ken, Jill's boyfriend Matt and her associate Naomi.

ROOM 222 (*School Drama*)

FIRST TELECAST: *September 17, 1969*
LAST TELECAST: *January 11, 1974*
BROADCAST HISTORY:
Sept 1969–Jan 1971, ABC Wed 8:30–9:00
Jan 1971–Sep 1971, ABC Wed 8:00–8:30
Sep 1971–Jan 1974, ABC Fri 9:00–9:30

CAST:
Pete Dixon .... Lloyd Haynes
Liz McIntyre .... Denise Nicholas
Seymour Kaufman .... Michael Constantine
Alice Johnson .... Karen Valentine
Richie Lane (1969–1971) .... Howard Rice
Helen Loomis .... Judy Strangis
Jason Allen .... Heshimu
Al Cowley (1969–1971) .... Pendrant Netherly
Bernie (1970–1974) .... David Jolliffe
Pam (1970–1972) .... Ta-Tanisha
Larry (1971–1973) .... Eric Laneuville

Schoolroom drama about Pete Dixon, a black history teacher in an integrated big-city high school. An idealist, Pete instilled his students at Walt Whitman High with gentle lessons in tolerance and understanding. The number of his home room was 222, but wherever he went he was surrounded by a cluster of kids. They loved him for his easygoing manner and willingness to side with them when he knew they were being short-changed by the system. Seymour Kaufman was the cool, slightly sarcastic principal, Liz McIntyre Pete's girlfriend and a school counselor, and Alice Johnson an exuberant student teacher (in the second season she was promoted to full-fledged English teacher). The rest of the regulars were students.

The program was highly regarded for tackling current problems relevant to today's youth (prejudice, drugs, dropping out, etc.) and it received many awards and commendations from educational and civil rights groups. Its sense of reality was heightened by the fact that it was based on, and partially filmed at, 3,000-student Los Angeles High School.

ROOMIES (*Situation Comedy*)

FIRST TELECAST: *March 19, 1987*
LAST TELECAST: *May 15, 1987*
BROADCAST HISTORY:
Mar 1987, NBC Thu 9:10–9:40
Mar 1987–May 1987, NBC Fri 8:00–8:30

CAST:
Nick Chase .... Burt Young
Matthew Wiggins .... Corey Haim
Ms. Adler .... Jane Daly
Sheldon .... Joshua Nelson
Carl .... Sean Gregory Sullivan
Singing Freshmen
.... Michael Lesco, Robert Rheames, Larry Wray

Two unlikely college freshmen shared a dorm room in this "odd couple" comedy. Nick was a burly, balding, 42-year-old former drill sergeant, who had retired after 20 years in the marine corps and entered Saginaw University a little late. Matthew was a 14-year-old genius who got there a little early. His main passion was rare fish. Both had adjustments to make—Nick to the unaccustomed chaos of dorm life, Matthew to the fact that almost everyone was older than he was, and brains alone do not a "cool guy" make. Among the dorm inhabitants were a nutty trio of "Singing Freshmen" who harmonized through the hallways.

NBC aired reruns of *Roomies* as part of its Saturday morning lineup during the summer of 1991.

ROOTS (*Drama*)

FIRST TELECAST: *January 23, 1977*
LAST TELECAST: *September 10, 1978*
BROADCAST HISTORY:
Jan 1977, ABC 9:00–11:00 or 10:00–11:00 each night for eight days
Sep 1978, ABC 8:00–11:00 or 9:00–11:00 each night for five days

CAST:
Kunta Kinte (as a boy) .... LeVar Burton
Kunta Kinte (Toby; adult) .... John Amos
Binta .... Cicely Tyson
Omoro .... Thalmus Rasulala
Nyo Boto .... Maya Angelou
Kadi Touray .... O. J. Simpson
The Wrestler .... Ji-Tu Cumbuka
Kintango .... Moses Gunn
Brima Cesay .... Hari Rhodes
Fanta .... Ren Woods
Fanta (later) .... Beverly Todd
Capt. Davies .... Edward Asner
Third Mate Slater .... Ralph Waite
Gardner .... William Watson
Fiddler .... Louis Gossett, Jr.
John Reynolds .... Lorne Greene
Mrs. Reynolds .... Lynda Day George
Ames .... Vic Morrow
Carrington .... Paul Shenar
Dr. William Reynolds .... Robert Reed
Bell .... Madge Sinclair
Grill .... Gary Collins
The Drummer .... Raymond St. Jacques
Tom Moore .... Chuck Connors
Missy Anne .... Sandy Duncan
Noah .... Lawrence-Hilton Jacobs
Ordell .... John Schuck
Kizzy .... Leslie Uggams
Squire James .... Macdonald Carey
Mathilda .... Olivia Cole
Mingo .... Scatman Crothers
Stephen Bennett .... George Hamilton
Mrs. Moore .... Carolyn Jones
Sir Eric Russell .... Ian McShane
Sister Sara .... Lillian Randolph
Sam Bennett .... Richard Roundtree
Chicken George .... Ben Vereen
Evan Brent .... Lloyd Bridges
Tom .... Georg Stanford Brown
Ol' George Johnson .... Brad Davis
Lewis .... Hilly Hicks
Jemmy Brent .... Doug McClure

Irene .... Lynne Moody
Martha .... Lane Binkley
Justin .... Burl Ives

PRODUCER:

Stan Margulies

ADAPTED FOR TV BY:

William Blinn

Under the usual definition of a "series," *Roots* would not be included in this book—it was really an extended special. But the fact that it was the most-watched dramatic show in TV history, and its considerable impact on viewers, warrant an exception.

Roots' success was unprecedented. Approximately 100 million viewers saw the concluding installment, and it must be considered an event of considerable magnitude when nearly half the entire population of the U.S. can be assembled in front of its TV sets to watch a single dramatic presentation. No one, not even ABC, was prepared for anything that big. In fact, one of the reasons given for scheduling *Roots* on eight consecutive nights was that if it were a flop it would be over with quickly.

Alex Haley's novel of his own roots was 12 years in the writing. Its story began in 1750 in Gambia, West Africa, with the birth of Kunta Kinte to Binta and Omoro. Kunta grew up free and happy until, at the age of 17, he was taken prisoner by white slave catchers and shipped to America on a vessel commanded by the conscience-stricken Capt. Davies and his cruel third mate, Slater. Kunta remained rebellious for the rest of his life, making several attempts to escape and eventually losing a foot in the process. Then his daughter, Kizzy, was born. She grew to womanhood and bore a son (after she was raped by her owner), later to be named Chicken George. Chicken George was sent into servitude in England in the 1820s, as rumors of slave rebellions swept the American South. Thirty years later he returned, an old but free man, only to find America on the brink of Civil War. George's son, Tom, a blacksmith, was recruited into the army, but after emancipation found that freedom meant little in a land of hooded nightriders and economic exploitation. As the series ended, Tom—the great-grandson of Kunta Kinte—struck out to start a new life in Tennessee, and sow the roots for a better life for his free descendants.

The TV *Roots* was daring in many ways, including its massive historical sweep, its often mature content (including bare breasts in the early African segments), and its scheduling over a full week. However, it was not for rape or nudity that *Roots* received most of its criticism, but for distortion of history, particularly its sensationalized version of black-white relations in the slave era (one critic called it ABC's "shackles, whips and lust" view of slavery). It was pointed out that much of the cruelty attributed to racism was in reality the cruelty of the 18th and 19th centuries, which affected whites fully as much as it did blacks; and that the slave trade rested largely on African blacks selling their own brothers into slavery, not on "white slave parties."

Whether or not the TV *Roots* was pseudo-history, it reached and affected an unprecedented audience, and its effect on future TV programming was profound. That kind of success is not ignored by TV's programmers.

Roots was repeated in September 1978, again as a one-week special.

ROOTS: THE NEXT GENERATIONS (*Drama*)

FIRST TELECAST: *February 18, 1979*

LAST TELECAST: *July 12, 1981*

BROADCAST HISTORY:

Feb 1979, ABC 8:00–10:00 or 9:00–10:00 each night for seven days

May 1981–Jul 1981, ABC Sun 7:00–9:00

CAST:

Tom Harvey .... Georg Stanford Brown
Irene Harvey .... Lynne Moody
Elizabeth Harvey .... Debbi Morgan
Cynthia Harvey Palmer ...... Bever-Leigh Banfield
Cynthia Harvey Palmer (old) .... Beah Richards
Col. Warner .... Henry Fonda
Mrs. Warner .... Olivia de Havilland
Jim Warner .... Richard Thomas
Andy Warner .... Marc Singer
Will Palmer .... Stan Shaw
Bertha Palmer Haley .... Irene Cara
Chicken George Moore .... Avon Long
Earl Crowther .... Paul Koslo
Lee Garnett .... Roger E. Mosley
Bob Campbell .... Harry Morgan
Simon Haley .... Dorian Harewood
Queen Haley .... Ruby Dee
Big Slew Johnson .... Rosey Grier
Dr. Horace Huguley .... Paul Winfield
Alex Haley (child) .... Christoff St. John
Alex Haley (young man) .... Damon Evans
Alex Haley (adult) .... James Earl Jones
Nan Branch Haley .... Debbie Allen
Malcolm X .... Al Freeman, Jr.
George Lincoln Rockwell .... Marlon Brando
Cousin Georgia .... Lynn Hamilton

PRODUCER:

Stan Margulies

Two years after *Roots* made television history, this sequel continued the saga, again attracting large audiences. The story resumed in 1882, by which time Tom Harvey, great-grandson of Kunta Kinte, had established a marginal existence as a blacksmith in Henning, Tennessee. Relations between the races were strained, and old prejudices survived. Tom forbade his daughter's marriage to a light-skinned Negro because he was "too white"; and town patriarch Col. Warner disowned his own son Jim when he dared to marry a black schoolteacher. Before long "literacy tests" were being used to deny blacks their recently won right to vote, and lynch law had reappeared.

Tom's younger daughter, Cynthia, married a hard-working young man named Will Palmer, who, despite the oppression, had risen to ownership of the local lumberyard. In time Will would succeed Tom as leader of the local black community, as Ku Klux Klan terror swept the South. Will and Cynthia's daughter, Bertha, became the first descendant of Kunta Kinte to enter college. There, in 1912, she met ambitious young Simon Haley, son of a sharecropper, whose education was being sponsored by a philanthropic white man. After serving in a segregated combat unit during World War I, Simon returned to wed Bertha and begin teaching agriculture at a black college in Alabama.

While Simon was organizing farmers during the New Deal, his son, Alex, soaked up family lore from the older generation.

As World War II approached, Alex enlisted in the Coast Guard, where he spent the next 20 years. When he retired in 1960 he turned to writing, interviewing such national figures as black activist Malcolm X, whose "autobiography" he helped write, and American Nazi leader George Lincoln Rockwell—who held a gun on him throughout their conversation. Then a visit to his boyhood home of Henning reignited his interest in his family's past, all the way back to the "Old African" Kunta Kinte, and started him on a journey to Africa to begin his greatest work.

Roots: The Next Generations was first shown during the eight-day period in February 1979, and was repeated as a weekly series from May to July 1981.

ROPERS, THE (*Situation Comedy*)

FIRST TELECAST: *March 13, 1979*

LAST TELECAST: *May 22, 1980*

BROADCAST HISTORY:

Mar 1979–Apr 1979, ABC Tue 10:00–10:30
Aug 1979–Sep 1979, ABC Sun 8:30–9:00
Sep 1979–Jan 1980, ABC Sat 8:00–8:30
Jan 1980–Mar 1980, ABC Sat 8:30–9:00
May 1980, ABC Thu 9:30–10:00

CAST:

Stanely Roper .... Norman Fell
Helen Roper .... Audra Lindley
Jeffrey P. Brookes III .... Jeffrey Tambor
Anne Brookes .... Patricia McCormack
David Brookes .... Evan Cohen
Ethel .... Dena Dietrich
Hubert .... Rod Colbin
Jenny Ballinger (1980) .... Louise Vallance

In this spin-off from *Three's Company*, landlord Stanley Roper sold his apartment building in Santa Monica and bought a condominium town house in posh Cheviot Hills. His new foil was balding realtor Jeffrey P. Brooks III, who felt that the earthy Roper was downgrading the neighborhood. Helen Roper, socially aspiring but ever frustrated by Stanley's crass ways, found a supportive friend in Jeffrey's wife, Anne, however. David was the Brookes' young son; Jenny, an attractive art student who rented a room; and Ethel, Helen's snobbish sister. Muffin was Helen's little dog.

Just as *Three's Company* was based on the English TV hit *Man About the House*, *The Ropers* was based on its spin-off, *George & Mildred*.

ROSCOE KARNS, INSIDE DETECTIVE see *Rocky King, Inside Detective*

ROSEANNE (*Situation Comedy*)

FIRST TELECAST: *October 18, 1988*

LAST TELECAST: *August 26, 1997*

BROADCAST HISTORY:

Oct 1988–Feb 1989, ABC Tue 8:30–9:00
Feb 1989–Sep 1994, ABC Tue 9:00–9:30
Sep 1994–Mar 1995, ABC Wed 9:00–9:30
Mar 1995–May 1995, ABC Wed 8:00–8:30
May 1995–Jul 1995, ABC Wed 9:30–10:00
Aug 1995–Sep 1995, ABC Tue 8:30–9:00
Sep 1995–Aug 1997, ABC Tue 8:00–8:30

CAST:

Roseanne Conner .... Roseanne**
Dan Conner .... John Goodman
Becky Conner (age 13) (1988–1992, 1995–1996)
.... Lecy Goranson***
Becky Conner Healy (1993–1997)
.... Sarah Chalke***
Darlene Conner (11) .... Sara Gilbert
D. J. (David Jacob) Connor (6) (pilot only)
.... Sal Barone
D. J. (David Jacob) Connor (6) .... Michael Fishman
Jackie Harris .... Laurie Metcalf
Crystal Anderson (1988–1992) .... Natalie West
Booker Brooks (1988–1989) .... George Clooney
**Pete Wilkins (1988–1989)* .... Ron Perkins
**Juanita Herrera (1988–1989)* .... Evelina Fernandez
**Sylvia Foster (1988–1989)* .... Anne Falkner
**Ed Conner (1989–1995)* .... Ned Beatty
**Bev Harris (1989–1997)* .... Estelle Parsons
**Arnie Merchant / Thomas (1989–1994)* .. Tom Arnold
Mark Healy (1990–1997) .... Glenn Quinn
David Healy (1992–1997) .... Johnny Galecki
Leon Carp (1991–1997) .... Martin Mull
Bonnie Watkins (1991–1992) ..... Bonnie Sheridan
**Nancy Bartlett (1991–1997)* ...... Sandra Bernhard
Fred (1993–1996) .... Michael O'Keefe

*Occasional
**Originally Roseanne Barr, later Roseanne Arnold
***Goranson alternated with Chalke as Becky during the 1995–1996 season.

Roseanne was the biggest new hit on TV during the late 1980s (an era with very few new hits). It was the lineal descendant of blue-collar TV families stretching back to *All in the Family* and *The Honeymooners*, but like all great hits it introduced new elements to reflect its times: mom, not dad, was the center of the household; both were hefty people (and always in the kitchen), not TV-handsome; both worked; and when mom got home, she never failed to have a foul word for her kids.

Kid: "Why are you so mean?"

Roseanne: " 'Cause I hate kids . . . and I'm not your real mom."

Kid: "I'm bored."

Roseanne: "Go play in traffic."

One thing that didn't change, however, was the basic element of a loving family. Mom didn't really mean it, and every put-down was accompanied by a big grin and a laugh. Chronically short of money, with employment precarious, the Conners needed to keep laughing. Dan was an intermittently employed small-time contractor, who eventually opened a motorcycle shop in their hometown of Lanford, Illinois. Roseanne and her younger sister, Jackie, at first worked at a plastics plant, where several coworkers were seen (Pete, Juanita, Sylvia). Later she had odd jobs and became a waitress at a local hangout, the Lobo Lounge. Jackie became a cop. Becky was the boy-crazy oldest child, Darlene, the tomboy, and D.J., the six-year-old who idolized his dad.

Stories included Jackie's relations with her lecherous foreman Booker, the marriage of Dan's father, Ed, to Roseanne's best friend Crystal, and lots of stories about "little people" against the system (the IRS, the school, etc.). Keeping up with the times, the series added Leon in early 1991 as Roseanne's gay boss at a restaurant. Roseanne Arnold's real-life husband Tom appeared periodically as Dan's buddy Arnie.

Later seasons dwelled on the Conners' economic travails and their daughters' rocky romances. In 1992 Dan's cycle shop went bust, putting new strains on the family. Becky's boyfriend, Mark, who had been working for Dad, eloped with 17-year-old Becky, making Roseanne the "mother-in-law from Hell." The newlyweds moved to Minneapolis, then returned, and Mark eventually wound up working for Dan once again. Darlene and her boyfriend, mixed-up David, had an on-again, off-again relationship until she left for art school in 1993. He then moved into the Conner household since his parents had broken up.

In 1992 Roseanne and Jackie launched their own business, the Lanford Lunch Box coffee shop, with help from their mother, Bev. It managed to survive, but soon the sisters had other things on their minds. Jackie had a baby in 1994, then married its father, Fred (who got the inspiration to propose watching *One Life to Live*). Then in the fall Roseanne too became pregnant. She gave birth in October 1995 to Jerry Garcia Conner, in a weird Halloween episode in which Roseanne was visited in the delivery room by the spirit of the late rock musician. Meanwhile, Jackie separated from her husband Fred, and they were eventually divorced, leaving her to raise baby Andy alone. Leon married a guy he had dumped years before, Scott.

The final year was a bit bizarre. In the May 1996 season finale, Dan suffered a heart attack at Darlene's wedding reception with David; he recovered, but after a fight, Dan and Roseanne separated (actor John Goodman wanted to reduce the number of episodes in which he appeared in 1996–1997). In September the Conners won $108 million in the Illinois State Lottery, ending their monetary worries, and reunited for a time, exploring the world of the rich and famous. Over the winter, Dan traveled to California alone, where he had a secret affair that Roseanne soon found out about, and they broke up again. In the series finale, after a difficult pregnancy, Darlene gave birth to Roseanne's first grandchild, Harris Conner Healy. The scene then flashed forward to a future date, with Roseanne musing about all that had happened to the Conner clan. She had lost Dan "last year" to another heart attack, but determined to move on, was now a writer. The episode ended with a T. E. Lawrence quote about dreamers, and Roseanne's trademark laugh.

ROSEMARY CLOONEY LUX SHOW, THE see *Lux Show Starring Rosemary Clooney, The*

ROSETTI AND RYAN (*Law Drama*)
FIRST TELECAST: *September 22, 1977*
LAST TELECAST: *November 10, 1977*
BROADCAST HISTORY:
Sep 1977–Nov 1977, NBC Thu 10:00–11:00
CAST:
Joseph Rosetti .... Tony Roberts
Frank Ryan .... Squire Fridell
Jessica Hornesby .... Jane Elliot
Judge Hardcastle .... Dick O'Neill
Judge Black .... William Marshall

They were both single and good-looking, they were both attorneys (in fact, partners), but they had very different personalities. Rosetti had been born to the comfortable life of an upper-middle-class family. He wore the finest clothes, considered himself a gourmet, and was a smooth operator around attractive women. He was also brash, arrogant, and egocentric. Ryan was a former cop who had worked his way through law school at night. He was introspective, modest, and a dogged, persistent researcher—the perfect complement to his glib, impulsive partner. The combination was highly successful, usually to the consternation of Assistant District Attorney Jessica Hornesby, their frequent opponent in the courtroom.

ROSWELL (*Science Fiction*)
FIRST TELECAST: *October 6, 1999*
LAST TELECAST: *May 14, 2002*
BROADCAST HISTORY:
Oct 1999–Mar 2000, WB Wed 9:00–10:00
Apr 2000–May 2001, WB Mon 9:00–10:00
Oct 2001–Feb 2002, UPN Tue 9:00–10:00
Apr 2002–May 2002, UPN Tue 9:00–10:00
CAST:
Max Evans .... Jason Behr
Isabel Evans .... Katherine Heigl
Michael Guerin .... Brendan Fehr
Liz Parker .... Shiri Appleby
Maria DeLuca .... Majandra Delfino
Kyle Valenti .... Nick Wechsler
Sheriff Jim Valenti .... William Sadler
Alex Whitman (1999–2001) .... Colin Hanks
**Dep./Sheriff Hanson* .... Jason Peck
**Geoffrey Parker* .... John Doe
Kathleen Topolsky (1999–2000) .... Julie Benz
**Diane Evans* .... Mary Ellen Trainor
Nancy Parker (1999–2001) .... Jo Anderson
**Milton Ross (1999–2000)* .... Steve Hytner
**Amy DeLuca (1999–2001)* .... Diane Farr
Tess Harding (2000–2001) .... Emilie de Ravin
Ed Harding (The Sato) (2000) .... Jim Ortlieb
**Philip Evans (2000–2002)* .... Garrett M. Brown
Agent Daniel Pierce (2000) .... David Conrad
**Grant Sorenson (2000–2001)* ..... Jeremy Davidson
Courtney Vance (2000) .... Sara Downing
Brody Davis (2000–2001) .... Desmond Askew
Jesse Ramirez (2001–2002) .... Adam Rodriguez
Sean DeLuca (2001) .... Devon Gummersall
*Occasional
THEME:
"Here with Me," performed by Dido

Roswell was a youth-oriented soap opera about three alien teenagers stranded on Earth and their tangled web of friends, pursuers and alien enemies. Max, Isabel and Michael had been in incubation pods from the time they had been left on Earth in 1959 until they emerged, looking like normal human six-year-olds, in 1989 in Roswell, New Mexico, a small town made famous by a 1947 UFO sighting. They could connect psychically with people, manipulate molecular structure and do other strange things (Isabel could listen to a CD by holding it to her ear). The three alien kids didn't know where they had come from or why they were on Earth, but were searching for the answers. Michael, in particular, wanted to go "Home" (wherever that was) and be with his own people. In the meantime they were attending Roswell High School. Michael lived with an insensitive foster father in a trailer, while Max and Isabel were living in a nice home with their adoptive parents.

In the premiere, local teenager Liz was accidentally shot and killed in the Crashdown Café, run by her dad, where she and her best friend, Maria, worked as waitresses. Max, who was sweet on Liz, surreptitiously used molecular manipulation to remove the bullet and all traces of the damage it had done. Liz's jock boyfriend was jealous Kyle, the son of Sheriff Jim, who had been hunting for proof of the aliens' existence for years. Jim figured out that Topolsky, a new teacher at the high school, was an FBI agent, and after he threatened to blow her cover, she offered to work with him to keep from being replaced on the case. In January there was another UFO sighting, which Jim tried to track down. Meanwhile Maria had become attracted to Michael, and Isabel told her friend Alex, who wanted to date her, that she and the others were aliens. Michael almost killed his drunken father (in the process revealing that he had telekinetic powers), sought refuge with Maria and, with the help of Mr. Evans, an attorney, obtained adult status so that he could live on his own.

In April Agent Topolsky, who had disappeared months earlier, returned to warn the kids that there was an alien hunter after them and that Max was its primary target. She had been sent back to Washington after her cover was blown, and found out about a special "alien hunters" unit within the agency run by the brutal Pierce. After telling the kids, she was caught by Pierce and died in a fire at a psychiatric hospital the next week. Max found himself strangely sexually attracted to Tess, the new student in school, who turned out to be a fellow alien who had been "born" with the rest of them back in 1979. She helped them find the cave where they had been born. Ed, her "father," was a shape shifter with whom she had been traveling for years.

The feds were closing in. Pierce's men caught Max and held him in a "white room" where they could conduct interrogation and medical tests. Isabel contacted him telepathically and Michael, Ed and Sheriff Jim rescued Max, but Ed was apparently killed when he stayed to deal with Pierce. In the season finale the kids admitted to Jim that they had powers but just wanted to survive; he proved surprisingly sympathetic. In a shoot-out Pierce attempted to kill Jim and his son Kyle, but was himself shot by Michael; Max revived Kyle the same way he had saved Liz in the premiere. The aliens then recovered Ed's body and revived it, after which Ed said Max was destined to be their leader. Max had Ed take the form of the late Pierce, so that they would be safe while he ran the operation supposedly tracking them down. A message from Max and Isabel's mother indicated that on their home world Tess had been Max's wife and Michael, his second in command. Their destiny was to deal with enemies from their home world, who had also come to Earth, and eventually return to their home world and free it. Liz left them because she would not interfere with their destiny.

At the start of the 2000–2001 season things were starting to heat up after a quiet summer. The Sato, in the guise of Agent Pierce, testified before a congressional subcommittee determining whether or not to disband the special unit. Sorenson, a geologist, came to the sheriff's office with the partial remains of Agent Pierce, and eager Deputy Hanson got in the way of Jim's efforts to quash the investigation. At end of the season premiere the Sato was killed by the "skins," evil aliens searching for Max and the others. Courtney, another waitress at the Crashdown, was a skin, as was Congresswoman Whitaker, who killed the Sato and was eventually destroyed by Isabel. In late October Michael met the guy who had, in 1947, rescued the pods in which he and the others had developed and found out that there were four more missing pods somewhere.

When Michael found out that Courtney was a skin, she revealed that their home planet had been on the brink of a golden age—which all fell apart because Max, on the throne, couldn't bring the warring factions together. Courtney was a member of a renegade skin group that wanted Michael to take the throne when they returned. Meanwhile Max and the others had gone to Copper Summit, Arizona, in search of the skins. They were saved when Isabel succeeded in destroying the place where the skins were growing new husks (their skins) to replace the ones that were about to die—they could not survive on Earth without them. They did, however, salvage one husk for Courtney—who later destroyed herself to keep the skin leader from finding out critical information.

The following week the aliens from the other four pods, who resembled punk-rock versions of Michael, Isabel and Tess (they had killed their Max), came to Roswell from New York to convince Max to attend a summit with leaders from other planets. He and Tess went, but it was a setup. The alternative punk Isabel was plotting with the skin leader and knew that Max would be killed by an opposing faction when he returned to his home world. When he refused to agree to the deal at the summit, the punk Michael and Isabel tried to kill him—but he was saved by a warning from an astral projection of Liz, who had acquired some extraterrestrial powers since he had saved her life. Back in Roswell Jim was suspended from the police force for failing to answer questions about Max and Isabel, and Hanson took over as sheriff.

In late April Alex, who had taken Isabel to the prom, was killed when his car hit a truck head-on. Max tried to revive him at the morgue, but it was too late. Later Max and Tess made love and she got pregnant while Isabel brooded over Alex's death. Liz was intent on proving that Alex had been killed by aliens and found out he had spent two months at the University of New Mexico computer center translating the book from Max's home planet that was the key to their getting home. There was a device that would teleport them, but was good for only one trip. Max activated the device, and they prepared to say good-bye to their Earthly friends. Liz and Maria realized that Tess had mind-warped Kyle, among others, and was responsible for Alex's death. They warned Max that Tess had made a deal with their enemies to bring back Max, Isabel and Michael to be imprisoned or killed. Max sent Tess back alone.

In the fall of 2001, following Tess' departure, Max and Liz restarted their relationship. Isabel, now in college, had been having a secret affair with Jesse, a young attorney working for her father's law firm. When they decided to get married, the reactions from both family and friends were decidedly negative. Liz's father banned her from spending time with Max and, when he found out they were secretly seeing each other, he told Max he would send Liz to a New England boarding school if he got close to her again. Jim, the former sheriff, was trying to make a living as lead singer with a country music group. In November, after Isabel and Jesse got married, she was stalked by an alien with whom she had had an affair on her home planet—but convinced him to return home. Meanwhile, Liz and Maria found out that Philip was investigating Max and the disappearance of Tess. In February Liz, who was beginning to exhibit alien-like powers, went to boarding school in Vermont. Michael uncovered a conspiracy at Meta-Chem, the place where he was working nights as a security guard, and convinced Max and Isabel to help him figure out what was going on. Meris Wheeler (Morgan Fairchild), the evil head of Meta-Chem, found out Max was a healer and forced him to try to rejuvenate her aged husband, Clayton. It seemed to be working but for Max, who aged quickly during the process, it proved fatal. Clayton Wheeler underwent a transformation and found himself with Max's body and Max's mind sharing space in his brain. He was drawn to Liz in Vermont and, when he went there, the Max portion of the brain helped Liz kill the Clayton part and bring Max back to life—after which both of them returned to Roswell.

Isabel revealed to Jesse that she, Max and Michael were aliens, and he had serious problems dealing with the knowledge. Michael witnessed a crash between a fighter jet and an alien ship and recovered an artifact from the alien ship. As high school graduation approached, Max's quest to find his son ended when Tess returned with the baby (who was completely human), and the whole gang found themselves in danger trying to protect the child. Tess eventually blew up herself and a military base to protect the others. Isabel and Max revealed their true origins to their parents, and the elder Evanses ensured their grandson's safety by giving him to an adoption attorney friend of theirs. In the series finale Max, Isabel, Michael and Liz were almost killed by government agents at the high school graduation ceremonies but, at the last minute, managed to escape. They went into hiding, along with Maria and Kyle, and Max and Liz got married.

Based on the *Roswell High* series of books.

ROTTEN TV (*Comedy*)
BROADCAST HISTORY:
VH1
30 minutes
Original episodes: *2000* (3 episodes)
Premiered: *January 23, 2000*
HOST:
Johnny Rotten (John Lydon)

Short-lived and bizarre series in which the lead singer of the notorious 1970s punk band the Sex Pistols ranted about various subjects and tweaked the entertainment biz. In one episode he tried to crash a taping of Roseanne Arnold's talk show (and was escorted out), then dressed in colorful garb and burned rock-'n'-roll memorabilia; in another he and his wife, Nora, visited the Sundance Film Festival and ambushed such stars as Danny DeVito and Kevin Spacey. Then, after only three episodes, he disappeared.

ROUGH RIDERS, THE (*Western*)
FIRST TELECAST: *October 2, 1958*
LAST TELECAST: *September 24, 1959*
BROADCAST HISTORY:
Oct 1958–Sep 1959, ABC Thu 9:30–10:00
CAST:
Capt. Jim Flagg .... Kent Taylor
Lt. Kirby .... Jan Merlin
Sgt. Buck Sinclair .... Peter Whitney

At the end of the Civil War three soldiers, each of whom planned to move west in search of a new life, joined forces for mutual companionship and protection on the trip. Jim Flagg and Buck Sinclair were veterans of the Union Army, and Lt. Kirby had served the Confederacy. As they crossed the country they encountered numerous bands of outlaws, renegade Indians, and deserters from both armies.

ROUND TABLE, THE (*Drama*)
FIRST TELECAST: *September 18, 1992*
LAST TELECAST: *October 16, 1992*
BROADCAST HISTORY:
Sep 1992–Oct 1992, NBC Fri 9:00–10:00
Oct 1992, NBC Fri 8:30–9:30
CAST:
Rhea McPherson .... Stacy Haiduk
Jennifer Clemente .... Roxann Biggs
Danny Burke .... David Gail
Mitchell Clark .... Thomas Breznahan
Agent Devereaux Jones .... Pepper Sweeney
Officer Wade Carter .... Erik King
Anne McPherson .... Jessica Walter
Sen. Jack Reed .... David Ackroyd
Kaitlin Cavanaugh .... Alexandra Wilson

Six horny young guys and gals hung out, killed people, and played football in this odd cross between *thirtysomething* and a violent TV cop show. All were law-enforcement, lawmaking, or related professionals in Washington, D.C.: Rhea, a spoiled, giggling reporter for her tyrannical mother Anne's newspaper who thought it would be neat to become an FBI agent; Jennifer, an earnest but incompetent prosecutor for the U.S. attorney's office; Danny, a hunky bartender and Jen's boyfriend, who was still "finding himself"; Mitchell, a sneaky Justice Department attorney who was constantly kissing up to his mentor, crooked Senator Jack; Devereaux, a big, grinning hick from Amarillo, Texas, who was a rookie FBI agent; and Wade, a sensitive black rookie D.C. cop. Between shootouts, career scheming, and exposés of the corrupt, they could all be found hanging out at The Round Table, a yuppie bar in Georgetown.

As if six self-absorbed young people weren't enough, the producers added a seventh in the second episode: Rhea's troublemaking cousin Kaitlin, who came to town intending to scheme her way to the top.

ROUNDERS, THE (*Comedy/Western*)
FIRST TELECAST: *September 6, 1966*
LAST TELECAST: *January 3, 1967*
BROADCAST HISTORY:
Sep 1966–Jan 1967, ABC Tue 8:30–9:00
CAST:
Ben Jones .... Ron Hayes
Howdy Lewis .... Patrick Wayne
Jim Ed Love .... Chill Wills
Ada .... Bobbi Jordan
Sally .... Janis Hansen
Shorty Dawes .... Jason Wingreen

Regan .... Walker Edmiston
Vince .... J. Pat O'Malley

Robust comedy, set in the contemporary West. Ben Jones and Howdy Lewis were two rowdy, fun-loving cowpokes who found themselves hog-tied and in debt to unscrupulous Jim Ed Love, owner of a vast ranch and reputedly the second richest man in Texas (Andy Devine made a single guest appearance as Honest John Denton, the first richest man). Jim Ed, a fast-talking wheeler-dealer, dressed in custom-tailored white cowboy suits and rode the range in a souped-up station wagon, while Ben and Howdy had to put up with a mean old roan named Old Fooler. They got some relief at the Longhorn Cafe in the nearby town of Hi Lo, which they tore up every Saturday night, with the assistance of their girlfriends, Ada and Sally.

Based on the novel by Max Evans, which was made into a 1965 movie costarring Chill Wills in the same role he played on TV.

ROUNDHOUSE (*Comedy/Variety*)

BROADCAST HISTORY:

Nickelodeon
30 minutes
Produced: *1992–1994* (52 episodes)
Premiered: *August 15, 1992*

CAST:

Alfred J. Carr, Jr.
John Crane
Mark David
Shawn Daywalt
Ivan Dudynsky
Micki Duran
(Seymour) Willis Green
Crystal Lewis (1992)
Dominic Lucero
Natalie Nucci
Julene Renee
David Sidoni
Amy Ehrlich (1992–1993)
Shawn Minoz (1992–1993)
Bryan Anthony (1993–1994)
Lisa Vale (1993–1994)
David Nicoll (1993–1994)
Natasha Pearce (1993–1994)

One of the fastest-paced shows ever seen on television, *Roundhouse* was a frantic sketch comedy show for kids of the nonstop nineties. Hand-held cameras followed the intricately choreographed action around a huge, open soundstage as one short scene blended into another. Props, such as a frame held up to simulate a TV screen or cardboard clouds waved over someone's head to evoke an "angelic" background, were minimal. Characters darted in and out of the action, and Mom and Dad scooted around the stage on a motorized easy chair. Periodically the youthful ensemble would break into a dance routine or turn into a rock band (Natasha was a notable lead vocalist during the last season). Definitely not for the faint of heart.

ROUSTERS, THE (*Adventure*)

FIRST TELECAST: *October 1, 1983*
LAST TELECAST: *July 21, 1984*
BROADCAST HISTORY:

Oct 1983, NBC Sat 9:00–10:00
Jun 1984–Jul 1984, NBC Sat 10:00–11:00

CAST:

Wyatt Earp III .... Chad Everett
Evan Earp .... Jim Varney
Amanda Earp .... Maxine Stuart
Michael Earp .... Timothy Gibbs
Cactus Jack Slade .... Hoyt Axton
Ellen Slade .... Mimi Rogers

It was a far cry from the life led by his famous great-grandfather, but Wyatt Earp III made a living working for a traveling carnival show in the modern-day Southwest. He served as a patch (combination bouncer, peacekeeper, and a second-in-command) for Cactus Jack's Sladetown Carnival. His lunatic family had other ideas about how to make a living, however, which constantly got the long-suffering Wyatt into trouble. Brother Evan fancied himself a mechanical genius, but always managed to "fix" things so they would never work again. Their feisty and eccentric mother, Amanda, couldn't fry an egg, but was determined to keep alive the "Earp legend" (which was mostly bunk) by chasing modern-day varmints—as a bounty hunter. Wyatt's girlfriend, Ellen Slade, was the boss's daughter as well as a lion tamer and schoolteacher for the children traveling with the carnival. Michael was Wyatt's semi-normal young son.

ROUTE 66 (*Adventure*)

FIRST TELECAST: *October 7, 1960*
LAST TELECAST: *September 18, 1964*
BROADCAST HISTORY:

Oct 1960–Sep 1964, CBS Fri 8:30–9:30

CAST:

Tod Stiles .... Martin Milner
Buz Murdock (1960–1963) .... George Maharis
Linc Case (1963–1964) .... Glenn Corbett

Tod Stiles and Buz Murdock were two young men who traveled around the country together in Tod's Corvette in search of adventure. They came from radically different backgrounds but had become good friends. Tod was born to wealth, but when his father had died unexpectedly, he discovered that most of the money was gone. Buz had grown up in the jungle of New York's Hell's Kitchen and had been employed by Tod's father prior to his death. The series was filmed on location as they crisscrossed the United States in their destinationless travels, meeting all sorts of people and getting into all kinds of situations: romantic, dangerous, amusing, etc. George Maharis left the series in November 1962, while production was still in progress for the 1962–1963 season, because of the lingering effects of a case of hepatitis. He was seen intermittently in episodes aired through March 1963. In the episode aired on March 22, 1963, Linc Case, who was to take over as Tod's traveling companion, was introduced. He was a Vietnam war hero from Houston who returned to the United States unsure of what he was looking for in life. He joined Tod while trying to find himself and stayed with him throughout the remainder of the series.

Nelson Riddle's recording of his theme music for the show, a driving jazz melody which sounded like the open road, was on the hit parade in 1962.

ROUTE 66 (*Adventure*)

FIRST TELECAST: *June 8, 1993*
LAST TELECAST: *July 6, 1993*

BROADCAST HISTORY:

Jun 1993–Jul 1993, NBC Tue 8:00–9:00

CAST:

Nick Lewis .... James Wilder
Arthur Clark .... Dan Cortese

MUSIC:

by Warren Zevon

Ever wonder what happens to the great old props from classic TV series of the past? Sometimes they roll them out of the garage for one more spin, as in this rather literal revival of the 1960s classic *Route 66*. Young Nick was the abandoned son of Buz Murdock, a father he never knew, who had left him one bequest: his perfectly preserved, gleaming red-and-white 1961 Corvette. Taking the bait, Nick hit the road too, along with a gregarious hitchhiker named Arthur. Like Tod and Buz three decades before, they found adventure helping people in little towns from coast to coast. Except for the heroes' long hair and shaggy clothes, it was 1961 all over again.

As you read this, producers are searching the warehouse for Lucy and Desi's old sofa, around which they hope to build a new series.

ROWAN AND MARTIN SHOW, THE see *Dean Martin Summer Show, The*

ROWAN & MARTIN'S LAUGH-IN (*Comedy Variety*)

FIRST TELECAST: *January 22, 1968*
LAST TELECAST: *May 14, 1973*

BROADCAST HISTORY:

Jan 1968–May 1973, NBC Mon 8:00–9:00 (OS)

REGULARS:

Dan Rowan
Dick Martin
Gary Owens
Ruth Buzzi
Judy Carne (1968–1970)
Eileen Brennan (1968)
Goldie Hawn (1968–1970)
Arte Johnson (1968–1971)
Henry Gibson (1968–1971)
Roddy-Maude Roxby (1968)
Jo Anne Worley (1968–1970)
Larry Hovis (1968, 1971–1972)
Pigmeat Markham (1968–1969)
Charlie Brill (1968–1969)
Dick Whittington (1968–1969)
Mitzi McCall (1968–1969)
Chelsea Brown (1968–1969)
Alan Sues (1968–1972)
Dave Madden (1968–1969)
Teresa Graves (1969–1970)
Jeremy Lloyd (1969–1970)
Pamela Rodgers (1969–1970)
Byron Gilliam (1969–1970)
Ann Elder (1970–1972)
Lily Tomlin (1970–1973)
Johnny Brown (1970–1972)
Dennis Allen (1970–1973)
Nancy Phillips (1970–1971)
Barbara Sharma (1970–1972)
Harvey Jason (1970–1971)
Richard Dawson (1971–1973)
Moosie Drier (1971–1973)
Patti Deutsch (1972–1973)
Jud Strunk (1972–1973)
Brian Bressler (1972–1973)
Sarah Kennedy (1972–1973)
Donna Jean Young (1972–1973)
Tod Bass (1972–1973)
Lisa Farringer (1972–1973)
Willie Tyler & Lester (1972–1973)

Rowan & Martin's Laugh-In was one of TV's classics, one of those rare programs which was not only an overnight sensation, but was highly innovative, created a raft of new stars, and started trends in comedy which other programs would follow. In some ways, it was not original at all, being a cross between Olsen & Johnson's *Helzapoppin'* (which in turn traced its lineage to the frantic, knockabout comedy of the Keystone Cops) and the highly topical satire of *That Was the Week That Was*. But *Laugh-In* crystallized a kind of contemporary, fast-paced, unstructured comedy "happening" that was exactly what an agitated America wanted in 1968.

Laugh-In was first seen as a one-time special on September 9, 1967. It was such an enormous hit that it inevitably led to a series premiering the following January. Its lightning-fast pace took full advantage of the technical capabilities of television and videotape. Blackouts, sketches, one-liners, and cameo appearances by famous show-business celebrities and even national politicians were all edited into a frenetic whole. The regular cast was large and the turnover high, and of the 40 regulars who appeared in the series only four were with it from beginning to end—the two hosts, announcer Gary Owens, and Ruth Buzzi.

The essence of *Laugh-In* was *shtick*, a comic routine or trademark repeated over and over until it was closely associated with a performer. People love it, come to expect it, and talk about it the next morning after the show. All great comedians have at least one, but what was remarkable about *Laugh-In* was that it developed a whole repertoire of sight gags and catchphrases using little-known talent exclusively (though some of them became quite famous later). Among the favorites: Arte Johnson as the German soldier, peering out from behind a potted palm and murmuring, "Verrry interesting!"; Ruth Buzzi as the little old lady with an umbrella, forever whacking the equally decrepit old man who snuggled up beside her on a park bench; Lily Tomlin as the sarcastic, nasal telephone operator (even the phone company wanted to hire her to do commercials using that routine—she wouldn't); Gary Owens as the outrageously overmodulated announcer, facing the microphone, hand cupped to ear; Alan Sues as the grinning moron of a sports announcer; Goldie Hawn as the giggling dumb blonde, and so on.

Some of the devices of the show were the Cocktail Party, Letters to Laugh-In, The Flying Fickle Finger of Fate Award, Laugh-In Looks at the News (of the past, present, and future), Hollywood News with Ruth Buzzi, the gags written on the undulating body of a girl in a bikini, and the joke wall at the close of each show, in which cast members kept popping out of windows to throw each other one-liners—or a bucket of water.

Many catchphrases came out of the sketches and blackouts on *Laugh-In*, and some became national bywords. It is said that a foreign delegate at the United Nations once approached an American member of that organization to ask, in all seriousness, "I have heard a phrase in your country that I do not understand. What is it you mean by 'bippy'?" Besides "You bet your bippy," there were: "Sock it to me" (splash!), "Look that up in your Funk and Wagnalls," "Beautiful Downtown Burbank," and even "Here come de judge!"

The pace never let up. If it wasn't a short clip of a raincoated adult falling off a tricycle, it was a shot of Richard M. Nixon solemnly declaring "Sock it to me." It didn't even end at the closing credits, as jokes kept flying and, finally, one pair of hands was heard clapping until a station break forcibly took over.

Laugh-In went straight to the top of the TV ratings and was the number-one program on the air for its first two full seasons, 1968–1970. It then began to drop off as the best talent left to pursue newfound careers, and finally ended its run in 1973.

ROXIE (*Situation Comedy*)

FIRST TELECAST: *April 1, 1987*
LAST TELECAST: *April 8, 1987*
BROADCAST HISTORY:
Apr 1987, CBS Wed 8:00–8:30
CAST:
Roxie Brinkerhoff .... Andrea Martin
Marcie McKinley .... Teresa Ganzel
Michael Brinkerhoff .... Mitchell Laurance
Vito Carteri .... Ernie Sabella
Randy Grant .... Jerry Pavlon
Leon Buchanan .... Jack Riley

Roxie was the program director for WNYU, a struggling UHF TV station in New York City. Working with her at the station were Marcie, the secretary and bookkeeper; Vito, the technical genius who operated and fixed all the broadcasting equipment; Randy, the impressionable young gofer; and Leon, the cynical, aging station manager who was also—ironically—the star of WNYU's afternoon children's show. Roxie's husband, Michael, was a schoolteacher.

Roxie was based on a similar character of a cable TV station manager that Martin had played in two episodes of *Kate & Allie* in December 1986.

Roxie and the program that followed it, *Take Five,* were the disasters of the 1986–1987 season. They were both canceled after only two weeks on the air, never to be seen again.

ROY ROGERS & DALE EVANS SHOW, THE (*Musical Variety*)

FIRST TELECAST: *September 29, 1962*
LAST TELECAST: *December 29, 1962*
BROADCAST HISTORY:
Sep 1962–Dec 1962, ABC Sat 7:30–8:30
REGULARS:
Roy Rogers & Dale Evans
Pat Brady
Sons of the Pioneers
Kirby Buchanon
Kathy Taylor
Cliff Arquette (as *Charley Weaver*)
Ralph Carmichael Orchestra

This short-lived series featured "The King of the Cowboys" with his wife, Dale Evans, plus regulars and guests in a very wholesome musical variety hour. Regulars included Roy's old sidekick, Pat Brady, rodeo-rider-turned-singer Kirby Buchanon, folk singer Kathy Taylor, and comic Cliff Arquette. Circus and horse-show acts were also included.

ROY ROGERS SHOW, THE (*Western*)

FIRST TELECAST: *December 30, 1951*
LAST TELECAST: *June 23, 1957*
BROADCAST HISTORY:
Dec 1951–Jun 1952, NBC Sun 6:00–6:30
Aug 1952–Jun 1957, NBC Sun 6:30–7:00
REGULARS:
Roy Rogers
Dale Evans
Pat Brady
THEME:
"Happy Trails to You," by Dale Evans

Singing Western movie actor Roy Rogers, who, ironically, was born and raised in Cincinnati, Ohio, struck gold as the most popular television cowboy of the early and mid-1950s. The "King of the Cowboys" was joined by his wife, Dale Evans, and bumbling sidekick, Pat Brady, in his fight for law and order in the contemporary West. In addition to the people, Roy's horse Trigger, Dale's horse Buttermilk, dog Bullet, and Pat's cantankerous jeep Nellybelle were regular members of the cast around the ol' Double R Bar Ranch.

Reruns of *The Roy Rogers Show* turned up on CBS' Saturday morning lineup in January 1961 and remained there until September 1964.

ROYAL FAMILY, THE (*Situation Comedy*)

FIRST TELECAST: *September 18, 1991*
LAST TELECAST: *May 13, 1992*
BROADCAST HISTORY:
Sep 1991–Oct 1991, CBS Wed 8:00–8:30
Nov 1991, CBS Wed 8:30–9:00
Apr 1992–May 1992, CBS Wed 8:00–8:30
CAST:
Alfonso Royal (1991) .... Redd Foxx
Victoria Royal .... Della Reese
Elizabeth .... Mariann Aaida
Kim (age 16) .... Sylver Gregory
Curtis (15) .... Larenz Tate
Hillary (4) .... Naya Rivera
Ruth (aka Coco) .... Jackee
Willis Tillis .... Shabaka

Redd Foxx returned to series television one last time as Al Royal, a cranky Atlanta mailman looking forward to an active retirement with his loving, if somewhat contentious, wife Victoria. Everything changed, however, when his daughter Elizabeth arrived with the news that she was getting divorced from her husband Dexter. Al, who had never liked Dexter, thought that was great news until he found out that Elizabeth was moving back home with her three children and wanted to go to medical school. The three grandchildren were almost more than Al could take—high schoolers Kim and Curtis, who were more interested in their social lives than in school, and adorable little Hillary.

Less than a month after *The Royal Family*'s premiere, star Redd Foxx collapsed and died from a massive heart attack during a rehearsal on October 11, 1991. His death was written into the show and actress Jackee was added to the cast as Victoria's half-sister Ruth, who returned to help her deal with Al's passing. When the series returned, briefly, in the spring of 1992, Jackee's character had been recast as Victoria's sexy older daughter.

The series was produced by comedian Eddie Murphy.

ROYAL PLAYHOUSE, see *DuMont Royal Theatre*

ROYAL PLAYHOUSE, syndicated title for *Fireside Theatre*

RUBY WAX (*Interview*)

BROADCAST HISTORY:

Lifetime
30 minutes
Original episodes: *1999*
Premiered: *August 21, 1999*

HOST:

Ruby Wax

The irrepressible Ruby Wax conducted more of her zany, on-location interviews in this short-lived Lifetime series. Among other things, she hung out backstage with Las Vegas showgirls (filling in, clumsily, for one of them onstage) and headed for Nevada with pal Carrie Fisher to find some "real men" to flirt with, on a cattle drive.

RUBY WAX SHOW, THE (*Interview*)

FIRST TELECAST: *June 9, 1997*
LAST TELECAST: *July 7, 1997*
BROADCAST HISTORY:

Jun 1997–Jul 1997, FOX Mon 8:30–9:00

HOSTESS:

Ruby Wax

Forty-something Chicago native Ruby Wax had been doing outrageous celebrity interviews on British TV for over a decade when Fox offered her the opportunity to do the same Stateside. Instead of doing the show in a studio, Ruby went to the stars. She was in a swimsuit at the beach with Pamela Anderson (on location with *Baywatch*); discussed sex with Goldie Hawn in the bed of Goldie's hotel suite in London; shopped with Bette Midler at the supermarket; hung out in a biker bar in West Hollywood talking with Brett Butler about her dating experiences; visited with Burt Reynolds at his ranch and museum in Florida; met with Imelda Marcos in her town house in Manila; and sat with Sarah Ferguson in her home in the English countryside.

RUGGLES, THE (*Situation Comedy*)

FIRST TELECAST: *November 3, 1949*
LAST TELECAST: *June 19, 1952*
BROADCAST HISTORY:

Nov 1949–Dec 1949, ABC Thu 9:30–10:00
Dec 1949–Mar 1950, ABC Fri 8:30–9:00
Apr 1950–Jun 1950, ABC Sun 10:00–10:30
Jun 1950–Aug 1950, ABC Thu 9:30–10:00
Sep 1950–Dec 1950, ABC Sun 6:30–7:00
Jan 1951–Mar 1951, ABC Mon 8:30–9:00
Mar 1951–Jun 1951, ABC Wed 8:00–8:30
Jun 1951–Sep 1951, ABC Fri 8:30–9:00
Oct 1951–Nov 1951, ABC Sat 7:00–7:30
Dec 1951–Jan 1952, ABC Sun 6:30–7:00
Jan 1952–Apr 1952, ABC Wed 9:00–9:30
Apr 1952–Jun 1952, ABC Thu 8:00–8:30

CAST:

Charlie Ruggles .... Himself
Margaret Ruggles (1949) .... Irene Tedrow
Margaret Ruggles (1950–1952) .... Erin O'Brien-Moore
Sharon Ruggles .... Margaret Kerry
Chuck Ruggles .... Tommy Bernard
Donna Ruggles .... Judy Nugent
Donald Ruggles .... Jimmy Hawkins

Veteran Hollywood character actor Charlie Ruggles portrayed an insurance salesman and harassed hubby in this early family comedy. The family, which was the source of Charlie's dilemmas around the house, consisted of his wife, Margaret, teenagers Sharon and Chuck, and the cute twins Donna and Donald. Stories revolved around such gentle subjects as who got to use the bathroom first in the morning, how the kids got dad to go square dancing, Sharon's and Chuck's first dates, etc.

The program was produced live at ABC's Hollywood station, KECA-TV, premiering on a seven-station West Coast network on Sunday, October 23, 1949. Shortly thereafter it began airing on ABC's East and Midwest network, using kinescopes of the live West Coast show. The poor quality of these dim kinescopes, and the constant movement of the series all over the ABC schedule, may have contributed to *The Ruggles'* failure to become a hit.

RUGRATS (*Cartoon*)

BROADCAST HISTORY:

Nickelodeon
30 minutes
Produced: *1991–*
Premiered: *August 11, 1991*

VOICES:

Tommy Pickles .... E. G. Daily
Angelica Pickles .... Cheryl Chase
Chuckie Finster, Jr. (1991–2001) .... Christine Cavanaugh
Chuckie Finster, Jr. (2001–) .... Nancy Cartwright
Phil, Lil and Betty DeVille .... Kath Soucie
Diane "Didi" Kerpacketer-Pickles .... Melanie Chartoff
Stu Pickles .... Jack Riley
Andrew "Drew" Pickles, Charles "Chaz" Finster, Sr. Boris Kerpacketer .... Michael Bell
Louis Kalhern "Grandpa" Pickles (1991–1998) .... David Doyle
Louis Kalhern "Grandpa" Pickles (1998–) .... Joe Alaskey
Charlotte Pickles (1992–) .... Tress MacNeille
Dylan Prescott "Dill" Pickles (1998–), Timmy McNulty (1997–) .... Tara Charendoff (Strong)
Lulu Pickles (2000–) .... Debbie Reynolds
Kira Wantabe-Finster (2000–) .... Julia Kato
Kimi Wantabe-Finster (2001–) .... Dionne Quan
Howie DeVille .... Philip Proctor
Susie Carmichael .... Cree Summer
Randy Carmichael .... Ron Glass

The world from a baby's point of view was the theme of this unusual animated series. Tommy, who was still in diapers, fuzzy-haired Chuckie, and twins Phil and Lil shared a playpen and endless adventures crawling around the house and neighborhood. Everything looked enormous to them, and the world was full of mysteries; such ordinary sights as a garbage truck chewing up refuse in the early morning might be a monster on the street outside. Angelica was Tommy's malevolent three-year-old cousin who terrorized the four tykes, and Didi and Stu were his misunderstanding parents.

RUN BUDDY RUN (*Situation Comedy*)
FIRST TELECAST: *September 12, 1966*
LAST TELECAST: *January 2, 1967*
BROADCAST HISTORY:
Sep 1966–Jan 1967, CBS Mon 8:00–8:30
CAST:
Buddy Overstreet .... Jack Sheldon
Devere (Mr. D.) .... Bruce Gordon
Junior .... Jim Connell
Wendell .... Nick Georgiade
Harry .... Gregg Palmer

Buddy Overstreet was a very average person. He had made one mistake, however, which altered his entire life. While relaxing at a Turkish bath he accidentally overheard syndicate gangsters discussing a proposed rub-out. They realized that he had heard their code phrase—"chicken little"—and spent the rest of the season trying to capture him because he knew too much. They were not particularly adept at this and kept fouling it up. The front for their organization was Devere Enterprises, where Mr. Devere's son, Junior, proved to be inept at running either the legitimate or criminal side of the business.

RUN FOR YOUR LIFE (*Adventure*)
FIRST TELECAST: *September 13, 1965*
LAST TELECAST: *September 11, 1968*
BROADCAST HISTORY:
Sep 1965–Sep 1967, NBC Mon 10:00–11:00
Sep 1967–Sep 1968, NBC Wed 10:00–11:00
CAST:
Paul Bryan .... Ben Gazzara

Paul Bryan was a very successful 35-year-old lawyer who had everything a man could want—intelligence, good looks, popularity, and money. He also had something that nobody wants—an incurable disease. Told by doctors that he had, at most, two years to live, Paul closed down his law practice and started traveling around the world in the hope of cramming a lifetime of adventure and excitement into the limited time he had left. With money no problem, he went from one exotic and fascinating place to another and encountered all sorts of people. He had come to terms with his problem and, rather than running away from life, he ran toward it. The show ran three years, even though he supposedly had only two years to live, and he was still running when it faded from the screen in 1968. The series was based on an episode of *Kraft Suspense Theater,* which was telecast in April 1965.

RUNAWAYS, THE (*Drama*)
FIRST TELECAST: *April 27, 1978*
LAST TELECAST: *September 4, 1979*
BROADCAST HISTORY:
Apr 1978–May 1978, NBC Thu 9:00–10:00
Aug 1978, NBC Thu 10:00–11:00
May 1979–Sep 1979, NBC Tue 8:00–9:00
CAST:
David McKay (1978) .... Robert Reed
Steve Arizzio (1979) .... Alan Feinstein
Karen Wingate .... Karen Machon
Mark Johnson .... Michael Biehn
Susan Donovan (1978) .... Ruth Cox
Debbie Shaw (1979) .... Patti Cohoon
Sgt. Hal Grady (1979) .... James Callahan

Each year in the U.S. between one and two million teenagers run away from home. This socially conscious program dramatized that phenomenon, through fictional stories of youngsters trying to escape from the demands of insensitive parents, broken homes, the shame of unwanted pregnancies, or other problems that were more than they could face.

The central character was David McKay, a psychologist who maintained an office on the campus of Westwood University in Los Angeles. His travels in search of runaway youngsters took him up and down the West Coast. David's girlfriend Karen Wingate, was Dean of Women at the college. Mark and Susan were his two wards, former runaways who had built lives of their own under David's care. Both were now college students nearing graduation.

The series began with a limited run in the spring of 1978, under the title *Operation: Runaway.* There were plans to bring it back as a regular series in the fall, but it was pulled at the last minute. It finally reappeared in the spring of 1979 retitled *The Runaways* and starring Alan Feinstein as psychologist Steve Arizzio. Unlike McKay, Arizzio was more concerned with tracking down the runaways than in discerning their psychological motivations. He had two former runaways living with him, Mark (who had been McKay's ward) and Debbie. Helping him trace the missing youngsters was Sgt. Grady of the Los Angeles Police Department.

RUPAUL SHOW, THE (*Talk*)
BROADCAST HISTORY:
VH1
30 minutes
Produced: *1996–1998* (99 episodes)
Premiered: *October 12, 1996*
HOST:
RuPaul

A nighttime interview show hosted by female impersonator RuPaul, the statuesque black woman who really wasn't. The first guest, appropriately, was NBA bad boy Dennis Rodman, a sometime cross-dresser himself.

RUSH LIMBAUGH (*Talk/Discussion*)
BROADCAST HISTORY:
Syndicated only
30 minutes
Produced: *1992–1996*
Released: *September 14, 1992*
HOST:
Rush Limbaugh

Portly, outspoken Rush Limbaugh added viewers of this nightly New York-based talk show to his already huge radio audience. Each night he spouted his opinions in front of a small studio audience that occasionally laughed and snickered at his diatribes against liberals, feminists, and Democrats, among others. Limbaugh, an archconservative, was in one sense delighted with Bill Clinton's win in the 1992 presidential election; the show was much more entertaining when he took the Democratic administration to task than when he had been defending the policies of George Bush. He was fond of saying that the people in the audience, who unequivocally supported his views, had to pass an intelligence test to be there.

Limbaugh, whose syndicated radio *Rush Limbaugh Show* had the largest audience of any radio show on the air in the early 1990s, used both the TV and radio versions to promote his *Limbaugh Letter* newsletter and his two best-selling books, *The Way Things Ought to Be* and *See, I Told You So*. He also read letters from his radio and televsion audience, who had developed into almost a cult following. His supporters were referred to and referred to themselves, as "ditto-heads," a testament to their almost reverential agreement with any position he took on any issue.

There was a tongue-in-cheek quality to it all. Limbaugh's show was "produced" by the E.I.B. (Excellence in Broadcasting) Network; his "lectures" came from The Limbaugh Institute for Advanced Conservative Studies, and, after the Clinton administration was in power, each episode of his radio show opened with a countdown of the number of days remaining during which America was being "held hostage" by the Democrats. Later, after the Republicans won control of Congress in the 1994 elections, each episode opened with the admonition that his program showed "America, the way it ought to be." Although his TV series went off the air in fall 1996, Rush's radio show was still going strong.

RUSS HODGES' SCOREBOARD (*Sports News*)

FIRST TELECAST: *April 14, 1948*

LAST TELECAST: *May 22, 1949*

BROADCAST HISTORY:

Apr 1948–Jan 1949, DUM Mon–Fri 6:30–6:45
Jan 1949–Mar 1949, DUM Mon–Fri 6:45–7:00
Mar 1949–May 1949, DUM Mon–Fri 7:45–8:00

REPORTER:

Russ Hodges

Latest news from the world of sports. Game scores, observation, and commentary by Russ Hodges, and his interviews with sports celebrities were all part of this nightly show.

RUSS MORGAN SHOW, THE (*Music*)

FIRST TELECAST: *July 7, 1956*

LAST TELECAST: *September 1, 1956*

BROADCAST HISTORY:

Jul 1956–Sep 1956, CBS Sat 9:30–10:00

REGULARS:

Russ Morgan
Helen O'Connell

Bandleader Russ Morgan was the host and star of this live summer music show that featured the singing of Helen O'Connell.

RUSSELL SIMMONS' ONEWORLD MUSIC BEAT (*Music/Interview*)

BROADCAST HISTORY:

Syndicated only
60 minutes
Produced: *1998–2000*
Released: *September 1998*

REGULARS:

Kimora Lee
Pierre Edwards (1998–1999)
Sky Nellor (1998–1999)
Yvonna (1998–1999)
Daphnee Duplaix (1999–2000)
Shang (1999–2000)
Ed Lover (2000)

Russell Simmons, cofounder of Def Jam Records, a rap label, produced this series that was formatted similarly to his music magazine *Oneworld* and targeted to an urban audience. Kimora Lee (Mrs. Simmons), the nominal host of the show, conducted interviews (or party coverage) with mostly black music celebrities that were done on location cinema verité style and broken up into segments interspersed throughout the show. Also contributing to the show were Pierre, with the Oneworld News and views about music (mostly rap); Sky, the only Caucasian host, who checked out the club scene in major cities; and Yvonna, with reviews of hot movies. Other regular features were rap videos, "hot release" reviews of new albums, and fashion coverage. Initially there was a weekly discussion segment with a diverse group of young people, but it was dropped after a few weeks.

When the 1999–2000 season started the series was billing itself as the hottest show in hip-hop. Kimora was a more traditional host and didn't do the chopped-up interviews she had done during the first season. Daphnee took over the show/lifestyle scene for Yvonna; Pierre's gossip segment was supposed to still be around, but he was replaced by Shang then, in January, by Ed Lover. When Kimora went on maternity leave in January, she was initially replaced by guest host T-Boz (Tionne Watkins), one-third of the musical group TLC. Later in the season other rap artists hosted individual episodes, along with series regular Ed Lover.

RUSSIAN ROULETTE (*Quiz*)

BROADCAST HISTORY:

Game Show Network
30 minutes
Original episodes: *2002–*
Premiered: *June 3, 2002*

EMCEE:

Mark L. Walberg

In this unusual game show losing contestants literally dropped out of sight. Round one began with four players on a circular stage standing in four out of six possible "drop zones" (circles on the stage that indicated a trapdoor underneath). Emcee Mark Walberg asked a multiple-choice question, and a predesignated contestant challenged another contestant to answer. A correct answer meant becoming the new challenger; a wrong answer meant losers had to give their winnings to the challenger and pull a lever to find out if they themselves were standing in an active drop zone. At first only one of the six zones was active, but with each additional question another was added; if unlucky contestants happened to be standing in one of the active zones, the trapdoor sprang open and they dropped through the floor—usually with alarmed looks on their faces! At the end of the round at least one contestant had dropped out of sight.

Rounds two and three were played similarly, with higher-value questions. In the final round the last surviving contestant was given more difficult questions and could win a maximum prize of $100,000, again with the risk of falling through the floor.

The multiple-choice questions were moderately difficult ("What does *NAFTA* stand for?"), but the real gimmick was seeing the trapdoors open. Each "drop" was replayed, in slow motion. What happened to the disappearing contestants? The fall was approximately three feet, onto deep, soft padding, and in the first season only one contestant was slightly injured (a twisted ankle). Needless to say everyone had to sign a lengthy waiver form before playing, but one wonders how a special edition featuring liability lawyers would have turned out!

RUTHIE ON THE TELEPHONE (*Comedy*)
FIRST TELECAST: *August 7, 1949*
LAST TELECAST: *November 5, 1949*
BROADCAST HISTORY:
Aug 1949–Sep 1949, CBS Mon/Tue/Thu/Sat/Sun 7:55–8:00
Sep 1949–Nov 1949, CBS Mon/Tue/Thu/Sat 7:55–8:00
CAST:
Ruthie .... Ruth Gilbert
Richard .... Philip Reed

Ruthie was a young lady much in love with Richard, a man she had never met and who was not interested in meeting her. Regardless, every night for five minutes she tried to inspire Richard over the phone while he tried to avoid her. Split-screen technique was used in this live show, enabling the viewer to see both Ruthie at home and Richard at his desk at the advertising agency where he worked. The idea for this series originated on the Robert Q. Lewis radio program, on which Ruthie's telephone adventures had been featured for about a year.

RYAN CAULFIELD: YEAR ONE (*Police Drama*)
FIRST TELECAST: *October 15, 1999*
LAST TELECAST: *October 22, 1999*
BROADCAST HISTORY:
Oct 1999, FOX Fri 8:00–9:00
CAST:
Officer Ryan Caulfield .... Sean Maher
Officer Vincent Susser .... Michael Rispoli
Officer Kim Veras .... Roselyn Sanchez
Sgt. Palermo .... Richard Portnow
Lt. Vaughn .... Clifton Powell
Vic Toback .... James Roday
Phil "H" Harkins .... Chad Lindberg

This odd cross between a coming-of-age drama and a cop show centered on a hunky 19-year-old rookie beat cop in the Philadelphia Police Department. Ryan worked out of the 13th district station house in the Badlands, one of the most violent sections of the city. Raised in the suburbs, he could have gone to college but wanted to contribute to society—possibly because of some guilt he felt about his father, a former cop serving time in prison. Susser was his veteran partner, who called Ryan "Mo," and Veras was an attractive 24-year-old fellow rookie who became his confidante and friend. They reported to tough Sgt. Palermo and savvy but cool Lt. Vaughn, who ran the precinct. Ryan's best friend, Vic, was a brilliant guy who could have gone to college but didn't want to be regimented by "the system," and worked as a night clerk at a gas station/convenience store. "H" was a nerdy pal who worked in his family's plumbing business. Ryan had problems dealing with the brutal reality of life and death in the inner city, and shared his angst in voice-over narration.

Fox had problems with the series' minuscule ratings, and its angst canceled the show after two episodes.

RYAN'S FOUR (*Medical Drama*)
FIRST TELECAST: *April 6, 1983*
LAST TELECAST: *April 27, 1983*
BROADCAST HISTORY:
Apr 1983, ABC Wed 9:00–10:00
CAST:
Dr. Thomas Ryan .... Tom Skerritt
Dr. Ingrid Sorenson .... Lisa Eilbacher
Dr. Edward Gillian .... Timothy Daly
Dr. Terry Wilson .... Albert Hall
Dr. Norman Rostov .... Dirk Blocker
Dr. Morris Whitford .... Nicolas Coster

Ryan's four were four young interns working under the supervision of experienced Dr. Thomas Ryan, who had two important goals: to make them the best doctors possible, and to make sure they did not suffer the fate of his son, an intern who had cracked under the incredible pressure of medical training and then committed suicide. The four were: Ingrid, a brilliant young doctor who needed to learn that compassion is as necessary as skill; Gillian, rich and spoiled; Terry, the black whose marriage was in jeopardy because of his long hours; and Norman, whose working-class background had given him a sense of inferiority. Dr. Whitford was the hospital's medical director, to whom Ryan, as director of interns, reported, and who wanted the interns to be shown no favors.

The series was coproduced by David Victor, who was also responsible for *Dr. Kildare* and *Marcus Welby, M.D.*, and actor-producer Henry Winkler.

S

SCTV NETWORK 90 (*Comedy*)
FIRST TELECAST: *May 15, 1981*
LAST TELECAST: *June 24, 1983*
BROADCAST HISTORY:
May 1981–Jun 1983, NBC Fri 12:30–2:00 A.M.
(New episodes on Cinemax 1983–1984)
REGULARS:
Joe Flaherty
Andrea Martin
John Candy
Eugene Levy
Rick Moranis (1981–1982)
Catherine O'Hara (1981–1982)
Dave Thomas (1981–1982)
Martin Short (1982–1983)
Mary Charlotte Wilcox (1982–1983)

In 1981 the syndicated series *Second City TV* moved to the NBC network, expanding from 30 to 90 minutes and changing its name to *SCTV Network 90* in the process. The length of skits, the number of features on each show, and the variety of roles played by each member of the *SCTV* repertory troupe increased significantly as a result. Weekly musical guests were also added, with their performance integrated into the skits.

Station president Guy Caballero (Joe) and station manager Edith Prickley (Andrea) were still around, along with "The Happy Wanderers," a polka variety show hosted by Stan (Eugene) and Yosh (John) Shmenge; Gil Fisher (John), the "Fishin' Musician"; "Great White North," a talk show with two beer-drinking Canadian bozos, Bob (Rick) and Doug (Dave) MacKenzie; "Mel's Rock Pile," a satire on *Don Kirshner's Rock Concert* hosted by Mel Slurp (Eugene); "The Sammy Maudlin Show," with star Sammy (Joe) and his announcer, William B. (John); a send-up of *The Merv Griffin Show* with Rick as Mr. Griffin; and the continuing soap opera "The Days of the Week" with the entire cast.

The series shortened its title to *SCTV Network* in the fall of 1981. In the fall of 1983, after being canceled by NBC, *SCTV* surfaced for one more season on the pay-cable television service Cinemax, with new episodes and some changes in the cast. The only regulars on the Cinemax version were Flaherty, Martin, Levy, and Short. All versions of the series, syndicated, network, and cable TV, were produced in Canada. Almost two decades later NBC brought back edited reruns of *SCTV* as a half-hour late-night filler series; these ran from February 2001 to January 2002.

SOF SPECIAL OPS FORCE, see *Soldier of Fortune, Inc.*

S.O.S. IN AMERICA (*Informational*)
BROADCAST HISTORY:
Syndicated only
30 minutes
Produced: *1999–2002*
Released: *September 1999*
HOSTS:
Carol Martin (1999–2000)
Sandra Pinckney (2000–2002)

This series billed itself as "the nation's new watchdog—watching out for you." A sample episode provided viewers with information about Internet pedophiles, gun control, and reckless school bus drivers. Other episodes featured stories on ministers combating gang violence in the inner city, a guy who had invented a personal flying machine, companies scamming people with hopeless work-at-home schemes, and whether herbs and pills could increase a woman's bust size.

Individual story segments were contributed by the news departments of local TV stations around the country that carried the show.

S.R.O. PLAYHOUSE (*Dramatic Anthology*)
FIRST TELECAST: *May 11, 1957*
LAST TELECAST: *September 7, 1957*
BROADCAST HISTORY:
May 1957–Sep 1957, CBS Sat 9:30–10:00

The dramas telecast in this summer series were all reruns of episodes that had originally aired on *Schlitz Playhouse.*

S.S. HOLIDAY, see *Starlit Time*

S.W.A.T. (*Police Drama*)
FIRST TELECAST: *February 24, 1975*
LAST TELECAST: *June 29, 1976*
BROADCAST HISTORY:
Feb 1975–Aug 1975, ABC Mon 9:00–10:00
Aug 1975–Apr 1976, ABC Sat 9:00–10:00
Apr 1976–Jun 1976, ABC Tue 9:00–10:00
CAST:
Lt. Dan "Hondo" Harrelson .... Steve Forrest
Sgt. David "Deacon" Kay .... Rod Perry
Officer Jim Street .... Robert Urich
Officer Dominic Luca .... Mark Shera
Officer T. J. McCabe .... James Coleman
Betty Harrelson .... Ellen Weston
Matt Harrelson .... Michael Harland
Kevin Harrelson .... David Adams
THEME:
"Theme from 'S.W.A.T.,' " by Barry DeVorzon

This series brought army-style warfare to big-city police work. S.W.A.T. stood for *S*pecial *W*eapons *A*nd *T*actics, whose job it was to tackle situations—usually violent ones—that line police couldn't handle, with whatever weaponry was necessary. Vietnam veterans all, the S.W.A.T. squad dressed in semimilitary attire, and were organized along the lines of a front-line patrol. Lt. Harrelson was the C.O., Sgt. Kay the observer and communicator, Jim the team scout, Dominic the marksman, and T.J. the backup. Often the young junior officers were a bit too eager to use their firepower, and Harrelson had to hold them back. But as often as not, it was blast away. The team traveled in a specially equipped van, since tanks don't work too well in urban locales.

Filmed in Southern California, and based, loosely at least, on real-life S.W.A.T. teams formed in several large American cities following the disturbances of the late 1960s.

SABER OF LONDON, see *Mark Saber*

SABLE (*Adventure*)
FIRST TELECAST: *November 7, 1987*
LAST TELECAST: *January 2, 1988*
BROADCAST HISTORY:
Nov 1987, ABC Sat 8:00–9:00
Dec 1987–Jan 1988, ABC Sat 9:00–10:00
CAST:
Jon Sable/Nicholas Flemming .... Lewis Van Bergen
Eden Kendall .... Rene Russo
Joe "Cheesecake" Tyson .... Ken Page
Myke Blackmon .... Holly Fulger
Cynthia .... Marge Kotlisky

What does one make of a slender, rather bookish man who wears stripes of black greasepaint on his face, a black jumpsuit and hood, and a perpetual scowl? Though in his nocturnal getup he looked like a nervous second-story man (or a dropout from army jungle training), this was actually two men—by day Nicholas Flemming, business-suited, successful author of children's books, by night Sable, black-clad crime-fighter and free-lance avenger of wrongs. Sable was unusual among TV heroes in that he worried a great deal. A trauma in his past (he had once *killed* a man!) left him with an aversion to violence, and that perpetual scowl. Mostly he was seen being attacked by others, clinging to window ledges, etc.

There were other problems. Whenever he would bed down with his supportive girlfriend and literary agent, Eden, after a hard night's work, that d****d greasepaint would rub off on everything! Cheesecake, a corpulent, blind computer hacker, was his main source of information and the only other person who knew Sable's true identity.

Myke was the illustrator of Flemming's stories, and Cynthia his secretary. The series was filmed on location in Chicago.

SABRINA THE TEENAGE WITCH (*Situation Comedy*)
FIRST TELECAST: *September 27, 1996*
LAST TELECAST: *June 5, 2003*
BROADCAST HISTORY:
Sep 1996–Oct 1996, ABC Fri 8:30–9:00
Oct 1996–Sep 1997, ABC Fri 9:00–9:30
Sep 1997–Sep 1998, ABC Fri 8:00–8:30
Dec 1998–May 1998, ABC Fri 9:00–9:30
Sep 1998–May 2000, ABC Fri 9:00–9:30
Jun 2000–Aug 2000, ABC Fri 8:00–8:30
Sep 2000–Oct 2000, WB Fri 8:00–8:30
Nov 2000–Dec 2000, WB Fri 8:00–9:00
Jan 2001–Sep 2002, WB Fri 8:00–8:30
Apr 2001–Sep 2001, WB Fri 8:30–9:00
Aug 2002–Feb 2003, WB Fri 8:30–9:00
Feb 2003–Jun 2003, WB Thu 8:00–8:30
CAST:
Sabrina Spellman (age 16) .... Melissa Joan Hart
Aunt Hilda Spellman (1996–2002) .. Caroline Rhea
Aunt Zelda Spellman (1996–2002)
.... Beth Broderick
Salem the cat (voice) .... Nick Bakay
Jenny Kelley (1996–1997) .... Michelle Beaudoin
Harvey Kinkle (1996–2000, 2001–2003)
.... Nate Richert
Libby Chessler (1996–1999) ..... Jenna Leigh Green
Mr. Eugene Pool (1996–1997) .... Paul Feig
Valerie Birckhead (1997–1999) ..... Lindsay Sloane
Willard Kraft (1997–2000) .... Martin Mull
Albert the Quizmaster (1997–1998) .. Alimi Ballard
Brad Alcerro (1999–2000) .... Jon Huertas
Dreama (1999–2000) .... China Jesusita Shavers
Morgan Cavanaugh (2000–2003) ... Elisa Donovan
Josh (1999–2002) .... David Lascher
Miles Goodman (2000–2002) ...... Trevor Lissauer
Roxie King (2000–2003) .... Soleil Moon Frye
Mike Shelby (2001–2002) .... George Wendt
Cole (2002–2003) .... Andrew W. Walker
Leonard (2002–2003) .... John Ducey
Annie Martos (2002–2003) ...... Diana-Maria Riva
James (2002–2003) .... Bumper Robinson
Aaron Jacobs (2003) .... Dylan Neal

This bright, frothy sitcom was a *Bewitched* for the '90s. Perky Sabrina was a pretty normal teenager in a new school who, on her sixteenth birthday, began to do strange things like levitate in her sleep and bring dead frogs in biology class back to life. Her two eccentric aunts, with whom she lived, then gave her a little cauldron for her birthday—happy birthday, you're a witch! Witchly powers seemed like a neat thing to have down at Westbridge High School in Boston, but Sabrina soon found out they were kind of hard to master, and could backfire if she wasn't careful. So, under the tutelage of sweet Aunt Hilda and acerbic Aunt Zelda, and with a little counseling from her absent dad, seen as a talking picture in an old book (he was in "another dimension"), she began to learn the ropes. Salem was a mischievous warlock doing penance as the Spellman's sarcastic black cat; Mr. Pool the nerdy biology teacher; Jenny her free-spirited best friend; Harvey a would-be love interest; and Libby the stuck-up cheerleader, who Sabrina could now turn into a pineapple. There was a lot of opening closet doors and walking into other dimensions, comic negotiations with the witches council, and turning people and things into unlikely objects.

The second season saw the arrival of new best friend Valerie, suspicious Vice Principal Kraft, and most importantly, the Quizmaster, who administered a series of tests allowing Sabrina to officially get her witch's license. No sooner had she done that, however, but she was presented with a new challenge in 1998: to discover the "family secret." It proved to be that she had an evil twin, Katrina, who was banished after a trial on a Hawaiian beach determined that Sabrina was the "nice witch."

In the fall of 1999 Sabrina entered her senior year at Westbridge and, although her nemesis Libby moved away, she was replaced by a new foil, Harvey's new friend Brad, who unbeknownst to Harvey was a witch hunter. That year Mr. Kraft was promoted to principal and Sabrina was stuck tutoring an accident-prone witch named Dreama. During the year she was dating both Harvey and Josh. At the end of the season, after the two of them had fought over her affections, Harvey found out she was a witch and they broke up.

That September there were many changes, including moving from ABC to the WB. Sabrina, now a freshman journalism major at Adams College, moved out of the family home and into an apartment close to campus. Roxie was her sexy, cynical roommate and Morgan, the ditsy RA (Resident Assistant) more interested in her social life than the students she was supposedly overseeing. Also living in the building was nerdy Miles, who believed in aliens. Zelda got a job as an associate professor of quantum physics at Adams; Hilda bought the coffee shop where Sabrina worked part time and Josh was the manager and renamed it Hilda's.

At the start of the 2001–2002 season Sabrina and Josh were dating seriously. He got a job as a photojournalist for the *Boston Citizen* newspaper and convinced Mike, his boss, to hire Sabrina as an intern. Morgan, who had been cut off by her father, became a waitress at Hilda's and started dating Harvey (they broke up in the spring), who was back and now a hockey player for Boston College. In May Hilda got married to her true love Will (Douglas Sills), Harvey professed his love for Sabrina and moved to California (he was back in the fall) and Josh left for a newspaper job in Prague. Sabrina, who had meddled, unsuccessfully, in Hilda's love life, paid the price and was turned to stone.

As the last season began Sabrina was brought back to life when Zelda gave up her adult years for her and became a child, and since both her aunts had returned to the witchly "Other Realm," Sabrina moved back into the family home with Roxie and Morgan as her roommates. She also got her first paying job in journalism as a writer for *Scorch*, an alternative music magazine. Annie was her demanding editor, and hunky Cole, versatile Jeff and "idea guy" Leonard were coworkers. Roxie was hosting a call-in radio show and Morgan was trying to make it as a fashion designer. In February Sabrina left *Scorch* because Annie didn't appreciate her work and decided to become a freelance writer. She also started dating Aaron, who owned a small music club. After a whirlwind courtship he proposed and she accepted. A couple of months later they were planning the wedding while Roxie and Morgan, whom she was going to let keep the house, were looking for a new roommate. In the series finale Sabrina was saying her vows at the altar when she realized that Harvey was her true love. She bid farewell to a remarkably understanding Aaron and, still in her wedding gown, departed on the back of Harvey's motorcycle.

A cartoon version, *Sabrina: The Animated Series,* ran on Saturday mornings on ABC from September 1999 to October 2001, on UPN Sunday mornings from December 2000 to September 2001 and on UPN weekday mornings from November 2000 to September 2002.

Based on the Archie comic book character.

SADDLE PAL CLUB, see *Movies—Prior to 1961*

SAFARI TO ADVENTURE (*Documentary*)

BROADCAST HISTORY:

Syndicated only
30 minutes
Produced: *1969–1975* (156 episodes)
Released: *1969*

NARRATOR:

Bill Burrud

This long-running wildlife documentary series was produced by Bill Burrud, who made a career out of such shows. Typical subjects were "Sea Otters and Brown Bears in Alaska," "Life Cycle of a Salmon," "Reindeer Roundup in Lapland," and "Pink Porpoises of the Amazon."

SAFE HARBOR (*Drama*)

FIRST TELECAST: *September 20, 1999*
LAST TELECAST: *January 17, 2000*
BROADCAST HISTORY:

Sep 1999–Nov 1999, WB Mon 9:00–10:00
Nov 1999–Jan 2000, WB Sun 7:00–8:00
Jan 2000, WB Mon 9:00–10:00

CAST:

Sheriff John Loring .... Gregory Harrison
Grandma Loring ("Betsy") .... Rue McClanahan
Hayden Loring (age 16)
.... Christopher Khaymen Lee
Turner Loring (14) .... Jeremy Lelliott
Jeff Loring (12) .... Jamie Williams
Chris .... Orlando Brown
Jamie Martin .... Chyler Leigh
Deputy Debbie "Stuckey" Lopez
.... Deborah Magdalena
Hayley .... Alison Lohman

John was a widower raising three sons in Magic Beach, Florida, where he was the local sheriff. His wife had been killed in a boat explosion meant for him by a crooked cop working with drug dealers and, in the series premiere, the cop was arrested for the crime. John and the boys lived with John's spunky mother, Betsy, in the Magic Beach Motel. Hayden, John's eldest son, was a long-haired teen dreamboat who was recovering from the breakup of his relationship with his longtime (since fourth grade) girlfriend. He subsequently started dating Hayley, who was almost a dead ringer for her. Turner was something of a rebellious free spirit, and little Jeff was into the military. Jeff's best friend and partner in crime, Chris, a black kid who practically lived with the Lorings, was the son of an assistant district attorney. Teenage Jamie, on the run from her sexually abusive dad, turned up in the second episode and moved into the motel. John pressured her wealthy father into granting her adult status, with John given custody until her 18th birthday.

SAINT, THE (*Mystery/Adventure*)

FIRST TELECAST: *May 21, 1967*
LAST TELECAST: *September 12, 1969*
BROADCAST HISTORY:

May 1967–Sep 1967, NBC Sun 10:00–11:00
Feb 1968–Sep 1968, NBC Sat 7:30–8:30
Apr 1969–Sep 1969, NBC Fri 10:00–11:00

CAST:

Simon Templar (1967–1969) .... Roger Moore
Simon Templar (1978) .... Ian Ogilvy
Inspector Claude Teal (1967–1969) ...... Ivor Dean

Simon Templar was a dashing figure, urbane, sophisticated, and independently wealthy. He was also a crook, but a gentlemanly, modern-day Robin Hood–type crook who took on the causes of those who had been robbed, swindled, or in other ways taken advantage of by their fellow man. He pursued his quest for adventure throughout Europe and the world. His calling card, a stick figure with a halo (representing a "saint"), was equally well known in society circles and among the police of six continents. The police generally regarded him as a mixed blessing, for although he was dedicated to justice, he often used extralegal means to achieve his ends.

The Saint had long been a popular character in fiction, first in the best-selling mystery novels of Leslie Charteris and later in a series of movies and a radio show in the 1930s and 1940s. This television version was produced in England and was first seen in syndication in the U.S. in the early 1960s. It made its network television debut, with all new episodes, in 1967. A decade after the Roger Moore version left the air, CBS added *Return of the Saint* to its *Late Movie* lineup. Ian Ogilvy replaced Moore in the title role (these episodes had been produced in England in 1978). CBS also aired reruns of the original Roger Moore episodes during the summer and fall of 1980 and, for a time, both series were running simultaneously (on different nights of the week) on *The CBS Late Movie*. See that series for specific schedule details.

Yet another version of *The Saint* surfaced during the 1989–1990 season, with Simon Dutton playing the role in a series of made-for-television movies.

ST. ELSEWHERE (*Medical Drama*)

FIRST TELECAST: *October 26, 1982*

LAST TELECAST: *August 10, 1988*

BROADCAST HISTORY:

Oct 1982–Aug 1983, NBC Tue 10:00–11:00
Aug 1983–May 1988, NBC Wed 10:00–11:00
Jul 1988–Aug 1988, NBC Wed 10:00–11:00

CAST:

Dr. Donald Westphall .... Ed Flanders
Dr. Mark Craig .... William Daniels
Dr. Ben Samuels (1982–1983) .... David Birney
Dr. Victor Ehrlich .... Ed Begley, Jr.
Dr. Jack Morrison .... David Morse
Dr. Annie Cavanero (1982–1985) .... Cynthia Sikes
Dr. Wayne Fiscus .... Howie Mandel
Dr. Cathy Martin (1982–1986)... Barbara Whinnery
Dr. Peter White (1982–1985) .... Terence Knox
Dr. Hugh Beale (1982–1983) .... G. W. Bailey
Nurse Helen Rosenthal .... Christina Pickles
Dr. Phillip Chandler .... Denzel Washington
Dr. V. J. Kochar (1982–1984) .... Kavi Raz
Dr. Wendy Armstrong (1982–1984) ..... Kim Miyori
Dr. Daniel Auschlander .... Norman Lloyd
Nurse Shirley Daniels (1982–1985) .... Ellen Bry
Orderly Luther Hawkins .... Eric Laneuville
Joan Halloran (1983–1984) .... Nancy Stafford
Dr. Robert Caldwell (1983–1986) .... Mark Harmon
Dr. Michael Ridley (1983–1984) .... Paul Sand
Mrs. Ellen Craig .... Bonnie Bartlett
Dr. Elliot Axelrod (1983–1988) .... Stephen Furst
Nurse Lucy Papandrao .... Jennifer Savidge
Dr. Jaqueline Wade (1983–1988) ...... Sagan Lewis
Orderly Warren Coolidge (1984–1988)
.... Byron Stewart
Dr. Emily Humes (1984–1985) .... Judith Hansen
Dr. Alan Poe (1984–1985) .... Brian Tochi
Nurse Peggy Shotwell (1984–1986) .. Saundra Sharp
Mrs. Hufnagel (1984–1985) .... Florence Halop
Dr. Roxanne Turner (1985–1987) .... Alfre Woodard
Ken Valere (1985–1986) .... George Deloy
Terri Valere (1985–1986) .... Deborah May
Dr. Seth Griffin (1986–1988) .... Bruce Greenwood
Dr. Paulette Kiem (1986–1988) ...... France Nuyen
Dr. Carol Novino (1986–1988) .... Cindy Pickett
Dr. John Gideon (1987–1988) .... Ronny Cox

St. Elsewhere was a hospital drama with a difference. There was high emotion, there were dedicated, caring physicians, but there were no miracles. Sometimes the patient made it, sometimes not. And they weren't always brave about it. As in real life.

St. Eligius was one of the seedier hospitals on TV, a big-city dumping ground for patients not wanted by the higher-class (and more expensive) medical facilities in Boston. In a typical day the staff might have to deal with a doctor being mugged in the emergency room, a mentally ill patient who wandered away, a drug addict trying to raid the pharmacy, and the wealthy, snobbish parents of an ill child who insisted that she be transferred immediately to a fancier hospital.

Whatever the reputation of St. Eligius, its staff was first-rate. Dr. Westphall was the chief of staff, a seasoned doctor and father figure to the young interns and residents completing their training there; Dr. Craig, an egotistical heart surgeon who was a brilliant doctor, but totally oblivious to his patients' feelings; and Dr. Auschlander, a veteran physician who found he must fight his own battle with cancer. Among the younger doctors, Samuels was a free spirit who had slept with practically every nurse in the hospital; Fiscus was having an affair with pathologist Cathy Martin, who insisted on making love on a slab in the morgue, among the sheet-draped corpses; Morrison was so dedicated to his work that he neglected his young wife, who died tragically in 1983; Cavanero tended to become too involved with her patients; Axelrod was constantly fighting obesity; and Chandler, the black resident, was always afraid he did not quite measure up to the high standards of medicine. A given episode might combine black comedy and tragedy. For example, in one well-remembered May 1984 episode, sexually active Caldwell decided to dispense with underwear, and promptly caught his most sensitive appendage in the zipper of his fly—whereupon it had to be surgically freed and stitched up by a female colleague while he tried not to become, er, excited; meanwhile, in a more somber story, young resident Armstrong, overwhelmed by the pressure and the rage of a woman whose baby was lost through her misdiagnosis, committed suicide. She left a pathetic note saying, "Why must life always begin tomorrow?"

Continuing stories included Auschlander's coming to terms with his own illness, Nurse Rosenthal and her breast surgery, and Ehrlich's gradual progression from a bright but inexperienced young graduate to a confident doctor and new husband (he was married in early 1984). Peter White was a particularly troubled young doctor who, after experiencing marriage difficulties, turned rapist—and was eventually shot to death by Nurse Daniels.

In the fall of 1987 St. Eligius was taken over by the huge, profit-oriented Ecumena Hospitals Corporation, subjecting the staff more than ever to the pressures of the "business" of medicine. The new Chief of Services, Dr. Gideon, orchestrated a showdown with Westphall, who responded by "mooning" him—and quitting. Craig, meanwhile, pursued an artificial heart project (the "Craig 9000"), but found his marriage to Ellen Craig collapsing. The series' final original episode, in May 1988, was bizarre. Auschlander saved the hospital from closing, then died of a stroke; Westphall returned; Craig moved to Cleveland; and in a final, surrealistic scene, the entire six-year saga of *St. Elsewhere* appeared to have been a figment of the imagination of Westphall's uncommunicative, autistic young son.

St. Elsewhere was produced by the same company responsible for *Hill Street Blues*, and it had much of the same gritty reality and *cinéma vérité* technique of the police series. Although never a top-ten hit, it had an exceptionally loyal audience and won several Emmy Awards.

SAINTS AND SINNERS (*Newspaper Drama*)
FIRST TELECAST: *September 17, 1962*
LAST TELECAST: *January 28, 1963*
BROADCAST HISTORY:
Sep 1962–Jan 1963, NBC Mon 8:30–9:30
CAST:
Nick Alexander........................ Nick Adams
Mark Grainger........................ John Larkin
Lizzie Hogan........................ Barbara Rush
Klugie........................ Richard Erdman
Dave Tabak........................ Robert F. Simon
Polly........................ Sharon Farrell
Charlie........................ Nicky Blair

Newspaper action-drama centering on Nick Alexander, crusading reporter for the *New York Bulletin*. Also seen were editor Mark Grainger, staff photographer Klugie, copy editor Dave Tabak, and Washington correspondent Lizzie Hogan.

SALLY (*Situation Comedy*)
FIRST TELECAST: *September 15, 1957*
LAST TELECAST: *March 30, 1958*
BROADCAST HISTORY:
Sep 1957–Mar 1958, NBC Sun 7:30–8:00
CAST:
Sally Truesdale........................ Joan Caulfield
Mrs. Myrtle Banford........................ Marion Lorne
Bascomb Bleacher (1958)............ Gale Gordon
Jim Kendall (1958)............... Johnny Desmond
Bascomb Bleacher, Jr. (1958)......... Arte Johnson

When this series premiered, Sally Truesdale was a former department store salesgirl who had become the traveling companion of a wealthy widow named Myrtle Banford. The matronly Mrs. Banford was slightly wacky and always getting into scrapes of one sort or another as she and Sally moved from city to city around the world. When they returned home, in the February 16, 1958, episode, the format changed. Sally and Mrs. Banford spent most of their time helping to run the Banford-Bleacher Department Store, of which Mrs. Banford was part owner. Added to the cast were Mr. Bleacher and his incompetent but lovable son, and Jim Kendall, an artist in the store's advertising department who became Sally's love interest.

SALUTE YOUR SHORTS (*Situation Comedy*)
BROADCAST HISTORY:
Nickelodeon
30 minutes
Produced: *1991–1992* (26 episodes)
Premiered: *July 6, 1991*
CAST:
Bobby Budnick........................ Danny Cooksey
Michael Stein (1991–1992).............. Ian Giatti
Ronald Foster Pinsky (1992–1993)..... Blake Soper
Donkey Lips........................ Michael Bower
Sponge Harris........................ Tim Eyster
Telly Radford........................ Venus De Milo
Dina Alexander........................ Heidi Lucas
Z. Z. Ziff........................ Megan Berwick
Kevin "Ug" Lee........................ Kirk Baily

Shades of *Camp Runamuck*! This slapstick comedy was set at Camp Annawanna, a summer camp for kids where seven lively teens enjoyed schemes and pratfalls at the expense of their extraordinarily dopey counselor, "Ug." Long-haired Bobby was the number-one schemer, abetted by athletic Michael, chubby Donkey Lips, and brainy little kid Sponge. Counterplotting were the girls, sensible Telly, Dina the princess, and Z.Z. the dreamer. Dr. Kahn was the unseen camp owner, heard only over the PA system. A real skinflint, his main interest was to cut costs. The series was filmed primarily at Griffith Park Boy's Camp.

SALVAGE I (*Adventure*)
FIRST TELECAST: *January 20, 1979*
LAST TELECAST: *November 11, 1979*
BROADCAST HISTORY:
Jan 1979, ABC Sat 9:00–11:00
Jan 1979–May 1979, ABC Mon 8:00–9:00
Jun 1979–Aug 1979, ABC Sun 8:00–9:00
Nov 1979, ABC Sun 7:00–8:00
CAST:
Harry Broderick........................ Andy Griffith
Skip Carmichael........................ Joel Higgins
Melanie Slozar........................ Trish Stewart
Mack........................ J. Jay Saunders
Klinger........................ Richard Jaeckel
Hank Beddoes........................ Lee De Broux

Harry Broderick was TV's first adventurer in search of junk. His Jettison Scrap and Salvage Company, headquartered in Southern California, specialized in such exotic missions as retrieving old B-52s from a jungle, oil from dried-out oil wells, diamonds from an active volcano, and icebergs from the polar ice cap (which he could steer to a drought-stricken island). His most spectacular forays were into outer space, however, using a Vulture rocket to lasso abandoned, gold-encased satellites and recover scientific "junk" on the moon. Harry's young partners were Skip, a former member of the NASA space team, and Melanie. Klinger was his FBI friend.

SAM (*Police Drama*)
FIRST TELECAST: *March 14, 1978*
LAST TELECAST: *April 18, 1978*
BROADCAST HISTORY:
Mar 1978–Apr 1978, CBS Tue 8:00–8:30
CAST:
Officer Mike Breen........................ Mark Harmon
Captain Tom Clagett........................ Len Wayland

An unusual variation on police series, *Sam* dealt with the exploits of a man-and-dog patrol car team of the Los Angeles Police Department. Mike Breen was the human half of the team and Sam was the yellow Labrador retriever police dog with which he was partnered. They patrolled in a police car designated Two-Henry-Six and made much use of Sam's uncommon skills in detection (his speed, maneuverability, and keen senses of smell and hearing) in their pursuit of criminals. Despite their record of performance, Mike's boss Capt. Clagett had his doubts about Sam's abilities as a crime fighter.

SAM BENEDICT (*Law Drama*)

FIRST TELECAST: *September 15, 1962*
LAST TELECAST: *September 7, 1963*
BROADCAST HISTORY:
Sep 1962–Sep 1963, NBC Sat 7:30–8:30
CAST:
Sam Benedict....................Edmond O'Brien
Hank Tabor........................Richard Rust
Trudy Wagner....................Joan Tompkins

Courtroom drama series loosely based on the career of famed real-life trial lawyer Jacob W. "Jake" Erlich. Set in San Francisco, the program was notable for its intermixing of human-interest and comic elements with the standard lawyer-as-sleuth format. Hank was Sam's assistant, and Trudy his secretary.

The real Erlich served as "technical consultant" for the show.

SAM LEVENSON SHOW, THE (*Comedy*)

FIRST TELECAST: *January 27, 1951*
LAST TELECAST: *June 10, 1952*
BROADCAST HISTORY:
Jan 1951–Jun 1951, CBS Sat 7:00–7:30
Feb 1952–Apr 1952, CBS Sun 6:30–7:00
Apr 1952–Jun 1952, CBS Tue 8:00–8:30
REGULAR:
Sam Levenson

Former schoolteacher Sam Levenson was the star and only regular performer in this informal comedy series aired live from New York. His gentle humor manifested itself in monologues about his growing up in New York, family life in general, and the experiences he had had as a teacher. A regular feature of the program was a visit by a guest celebrity and his or her child.

SAMMY (*Cartoon*)

FIRST TELECAST: *August 8, 2000*
LAST TELECAST: *August 15, 2000*
BROADCAST HISTORY:
Aug 2000, NBC Tue 8:30–9:00
VOICES:
James Blake, Sammy Blake..........David Spade
Todd Blake....................Harland Williams
Gary Blake........................Bob Odenkirk
Kathy Kelly........................Maura Tierney
Mark Jacobs..........................Andy Dick
ALSO:
David Cross

Actor David Spade used his own dysfunctional relationship with his father as the basis for this animated sitcom, and it wasn't pretty. James was a twenty-something Hollywood celebrity, the star of a silly sitcom called *Hey, Rebecca,* about a man pretending to be gay so he could share a Manhattan apartment with a supermodel. He had just finished his first movie, *Mongo Man,* which was about to open. Sharing James' life were his two brothers, Gary, his bland business manager, and Todd, a big dumb lug who worked as a handyman. What the Blake brothers did not anticipate was the arrival of their gross, philandering dad Sammy, an absentee father mostly interested in "reconnecting with" (leeching off?) his now famous son. Todd welcomed him back, Gary wanted him to get lost again, and James was somewhere in between. Kathy was James' sexy assistant and Mark, his weasely agent.

The characters were drawn stick-figure ugly, Sammy's voice grating ("hee-hee!"), and the whole premise rather uncomfortable. NBC ordered 13 episodes for the 1999–2000 season, delayed airing them until the summer, then canceled the series after two telecasts.

SAMMY AND COMPANY (*Talk/Variety*)

BROADCAST HISTORY:
Syndicated only
90 minutes
Produced: *1975–1977* (55 episodes)
Released: *Early 1975*
REGULARS:
Sammy Davis, Jr.
William B. Williams
Avery Schreiber
George Rhodes Orchestra

Sammy Davis, Jr., tried to get a foothold in the lucrative syndicated talk-show market with this Las Vegas-style series, which was run in the late evening on most stations. William B. Williams was his right-hand man and Avery Schreiber the resident comedian, but Sammy's high-energy imprint was on the whole enterprise—as it was in everything he did—and in the long run that may have proved too much for weary viewers (most successful talk/variety show hosts are fairly laid-back).

Guests were mostly performers, such as Sandy Duncan, Wayne Newton, Flip Wilson, Freddie Prinze, and Ray Charles. The program was taped in Las Vegas, Lake Tahoe, Acapulco, and other glamour spots.

SAMMY DAVIS JR. SHOW, THE (*Musical Variety*)

FIRST TELECAST: *January 7, 1966*
LAST TELECAST: *April 22, 1966*
BROADCAST HISTORY:
Jan 1966–Apr 1966, NBC Fri 8:30–9:30
REGULARS:
Sammy Davis, Jr.
The Lester Wilson Dancers
The George Rhodes Orchestra

The multitalented Sammy Davis, Jr., starred in this short-lived musical variety series. In addition to regular guest stars, the series was a showcase for Mr. Davis as singer, dancer, comedian, musician, and impressionist. An unusual situation occurred at the start of this series. Mr. Davis had a prior commitment to do a special on ABC with the stipulation that he could not appear on television during the three weeks preceding the special. For that reason, he was seen on the premiere of *The Sammy Davis Jr. Show,* had substitute hosts for the three succeeding telecasts, and returned to the show on February 11. The substitute hosts were Johnny Carson, Sean Connery, and Jerry Lewis.

SAMMY KAYE SHOW, THE (*Musical Variety*)

FIRST TELECAST: *June 11, 1950*
LAST TELECAST: *June 13, 1959*
BROADCAST HISTORY:
Jun 1950–Jul 1950, NBC Sun 8:00–8:30
Jul 1951–Jul 1952, CBS Sat 7:00–7:30
Aug 1953–Sep 1953, NBC Sat 8:00–8:30
Aug 1954–Jan 1955, ABC Thu 9:00–9:30
Sep 1958–Feb 1959, ABC Sat 10:00–10:30
Feb 1959–Apr 1959, ABC Thu 10:00–10:30
Apr 1959–Jun 1959, ABC Sat 10:00–10:30

REGULARS:

Sammy Kaye
Tony Alamo (1950–1955)
Judy Johnson (1950)
Barbara Benson (1951–1952)
Peggy Powers (1953)
Ray Michaels (1958–1959)
Lynn Roberts (1958–1959)
Susan Silo (1958–1959)
J. Blasingame Bond & the Dixieland Quartet (1958–1959)
Larry Ellis (1958–1959)
Hank Kanui (1958–1959)
Johnny McAfee (1958–1959)
Harry Reser (1958–1959)
The Kaydets
Sammy Kaye Choir

Bandleader Sammy Kaye first brought his swing-and-sway music to television in 1949, with two specials. He later appeared in several series during the 1950s, on various networks. Kaye's most famous trademark was his "So You Want to Lead a Band" audience-participation routine, which he had used for years in personal appearances and on radio, and it was also featured in most of his TV series. In it, Kaye chose half a dozen members of the studio audience to try their hands at band-leading. The band did exactly what the "leader's" baton indicated, sometimes to hilarious effect. The best bandleader was chosen by audience applause and awarded a prize. Kaye also provided straight entertainment with his orchestra, vocalists, and guests, and often led a community sing. He ended each program with an inspirational poem.

The various Sammy Kaye series, though essentially similar in format, went under a number of titles over the years. The 1950 edition was called *So You Want to Lead a Band*. In 1951–1952 it was *The Sammy Kaye Variety Show*, in 1953 *The Sammy Kaye Show*, and in 1954–1955 *So You Want to Lead a Band*. The 1958 series was first called *Sammy Kaye's Music from Manhattan* (the sponsor was Manhattan shirts), then in January 1959 switched to *The Sammy Kaye Show* and in April 1959 to *Music from Manhattan*. You would never have known the difference by watching them.

SAMURAI JACK (*Cartoon*)

BROADCAST HISTORY:

Cartoon Network
30 minutes
Original episodes: *2001–*
Premiered: *August 10, 2001*

VOICES:

Samurai Jack .... Phil LaMarr
Aku .... Mako

VARIOUS CHARACTERS:

Grey Delisle
Jeff Bennett
Kevin Michael Richardson

Yet another hero based on Japanese mythology reached American television in this colorful anime cartoon. It began in ancient Japan as the nation was attacked by the glowering, shapeshifting wizard Aku. As Japan, and the world, crumbled before his might, the climactic battle fell to the son of the emperor, who was endowed with a sacred sword capable of defeating Aku. Before he could land the fatal blow, however, the young warrior was flung far into the future, where he encountered an unfamiliar high-tech world ruled ruthlessly by Aku and his minions. Adopting the name Jack (because somebody sarcastically called him that), the young samurai made it his mission to get back to his own time and defeat Aku before these things could come to pass.

Jack was large and powerful, dressed in flowing robes, but with a quizzical look and frequent befuddlement at the strange futuristic worlds he encountered. He was often torn and bloodied in his battles with Aku and his armies of robotic monsters, but he always outwitted his cackling foe as they bounced around through history.

SAN FRANCISCO BEAT, syndicated title for *Lineup, The*

SAN FRANCISCO INTERNATIONAL AIRPORT (*Suspense Drama*)

FIRST TELECAST: *October 28, 1970*
LAST TELECAST: *August 25, 1971*
BROADCAST HISTORY:

Oct 1970–Dec 1970, NBC Wed 10:00–11:00
Mar 1971–Aug 1971, NBC Wed 10:00–11:00

CAST:

Jim Conrad .... Lloyd Bridges
Bob Hatten .... Clu Gulager
June .... Barbara Werle
Suzie Conrad .... Barbara Sigel

San Francisco International Airport attempted to portray the problems and challenges involved in running one of the larger airports in the nation, and probably the world. "SFX" employed 35,000 workers, and 15 million passengers used it annually. Jim Conrad was the airport manager, Bob Hatten its chief of security, and June was Mr. Conrad's secretary. Real problems in airport life were depicted—mechanical crises, demonstrations, security issues, etc. *San Francisco International Airport* was one of four elements in the NBC series *Four in One*. Each of the elements aired for a six-week period in the first part of the 1970–1971 TV season and the reruns were aired on a rotating basis.

SAN PEDRO BEACH BUMS, THE (*Situation Comedy*)

FIRST TELECAST: *September 19, 1977*
LAST TELECAST: *December 19, 1977*
BROADCAST HISTORY:

Sep 1977–Dec 1977, ABC Mon 8:00–9:00

CAST:

Buddy .... Christopher Murney
Stuf .... Stuart Pankin
Dancer .... John Mark Robinson
Moose .... Darryl McCullough
Boychick .... Chris De Rose
Louise .... Louise Hoven
Suzi .... Susan Mullen
Margie .... Lisa Reeves
Ralphie .... Christoff St. John
Julie .... Nancy Morgan

Knockabout comedy about five carefree young "beach bums" in sunny California, living on a houseboat called "Our Boat." The five boys, who had been buddies since their high school days, were the ever-confident Buddy, self-proclaimed leader of the group;

the shy and nervous Dancer (so named because he couldn't sit still); Stuf, a compulsive eater who believed that heavy is beautiful; the muscular but very gentle Moose; and Boychick, the beach bums' answer to Clark Gable.

SANDBLAST (*Sports Competition*)
BROADCAST HISTORY:
MTV
30 minutes
Produced: *1994–1996*
Premiered: *December 19. 1994*
HOSTS:
Summer Sanders
Peter King
Kari Wuhrer
One of MTV's numerous fun-in-the-sun competition shows, full of bare-chested guys and gals in skimpy swimsuits. Two-person teams competed in events including freestyle swimming, hose hockey, beach soccer, and sand bike races. Olympic gold medalist Summer Sanders and professional surfer Peter King were the original hosts, with Sanders later replaced by Kari Wuhrer. Taped at Walt Disney World.

SANDY DREAMS (*Children's Variety*)
FIRST TELECAST: *October 7, 1950*
LAST TELECAST: *December 2, 1950*
BROADCAST HISTORY:
Oct 1950–Dec 1950, ABC Sat 7:00–7:30
A musical fantasy in which Sandy, an eight-year-old girl, dreamt of adventure and travel. As she drifted off to sleep viewers were transported along with her to a program of sketches and songs and dances, performed by a changing cast of youngsters. Previously seen as a local program in Los Angeles.

SANDY DUNCAN SHOW, THE (*Situation Comedy*)
FIRST TELECAST: *September 17, 1972*
LAST TELECAST: *December 31, 1972*
BROADCAST HISTORY:
Sep 1972–Dec 1972, CBS Sun 8:30–9:00
CAST:
Sandy Stockton .... Sandy Duncan
Bert Quinn .... Tom Bosley
Kay Fox .... Marian Mercer
Alex Lembeck .... M. Emmet Walsh
Hilary .... Pam Zarit
Ben Hampton .... Eric Christmas
Sandy Stockton was a cute young woman working for Quinn & Cohen, a small advertising agency. She lived in an apartment building where two of her neighbors, Kay and Alex, were also close friends. Alex was a somewhat overprotective motorcycle cop who was worried about what could happen to a young single girl living alone. Sandy was always trying to help people out and frequently got into trouble because of it.

The character of Sandy Stockton had previously appeared in Miss Duncan's 1971 series *Funny Face*, which was no more successful than this attempt.

SANDY STRONG (*Children's*)
FIRST TELECAST: *September 25, 1950*
LAST TELECAST: *March 23, 1951*
BROADCAST HISTORY:
Sep 1950–Mar 1951, ABC Mon–Fri 6:15–6:30
CAST:
Sandy Strong and:
Mr. Mack (1950) .... Ray Suber
Mr. Mack (1950–1951) .... Forrest Lewis
Children's puppet program from Chicago.

SANFORD (*Situation Comedy*)
FIRST TELECAST: *March 15, 1980*
LAST TELECAST: *July 10, 1981*
BROADCAST HISTORY:
Mar 1980–Jul 1980, NBC Sat 9:00–9:30
Aug 1980–Sep 1980, NBC Wed 9:30–10:00
Jan 1981, NBC Fri 8:30–9:00
May 1981–Jul 1981, NBC Fri 8:30–9:00
CAST:
Fred Sanford .... Redd Foxx
Cal Pettie .... Dennis Burkley
Evelyn "Eve" Lewis .... Marguerite Ray
Rollo Larson .... Nathaniel Taylor
Cissy Lewis .... Suzanne Stone
Clara .... Cathy Cooper
Winston .... Percy Rodriguez
Cliff Anderson .... Clinton Derricks-Carroll
One of the most successful comedy series of the 1970s was *Sanford and Son*, the saga of Fred Sanford, a cantankerous, conniving Los Angeles junk dealer. Its run ended not because of failing ratings, but because star Redd Foxx left the series to star in a variety show on ABC. The variety show lasted less than a season and, three years after leaving the role, Redd attempted to revive *Sanford*. Fred was still running his Watts junkyard but, since son Lamont was away working on the Alaskan pipeline, he had two new partners, both friends of Lamont. Rollo was a holdover from the original *Sanford and Son*, and Cal was an obese white Southerner who invested $2,000 to become part owner of "The Sanford Empire." Fred also had an unlikely new girlfriend in Eve Lewis, a wealthy Beverly Hills widow. What she saw in Fred nobody could understand, especially her daughter, Cissy, her brother, Winston, and her outspoken maid, Clara. Fred's place got a little crowded as first Cal and then Aunt Esther's college-student son, Cliff, moved in to keep him company. Unfortunately for Fred, he had very little company among viewers at home and, after three short runs, *Sanford* quietly passed from view.

SANFORD AND SON (*Situation Comedy*)
FIRST TELECAST: *January 14, 1972*
LAST TELECAST: *September 2, 1977*
BROADCAST HISTORY:
Jan 1972–Sep 1977, NBC Fri 8:00–8:30
Apr 1976–Aug 1976, NBC Wed 9:00–9:30
CAST:
Fred Sanford .... Redd Foxx
Lamont Sanford .... Demond Wilson
Melvin (1972) .... Slappy White
Bubba Hoover .... Don Bexley
Officer Swanhauser (1972) .... Noam Pitlik
Officer Smith ("Smitty") (1972–1976)
.... Hal Williams
Aunt Ethel (1972) .... Beah Richards
Julio Fuentes (1972–1975) .... Gregory Sierra
Rollo Larson .... Nathaniel Taylor
Aunt Esther Anderson (1973–1977)
.... LaWanda Page
Grady Wilson (1973–1977) .... Whitman Mayo

Donna Harris .... Lynn Hamilton
Officer Hopkins ("Happy") (1972–1976) .... Howard Platt
Ah Chew (1974–1975) .... Pat Morita
Janet Lawson (1976–1977) .... Marlene Clark
Woody Anderson (1976–1977) .... Raymond Allen
Roger Lawson (1976–1977) .... Edward Crawford

PRODUCER:
Norman Lear

Fred Sanford was a 65-year-old Los Angeles junk dealer whose 34-year-old son, Lamont, was his partner, a situation that Lamont was not always happy with. At his advanced age, Fred was very happy with his little business and the marginal income it provided him. Lamont, on the other hand, was looking to better himself by getting out of the junk business and trying something more challenging and, hopefully, more lucrative. Fred, whose wife, Elizabeth, had died some years before, would do anything to keep his son from deserting him and the business. Every time Lamont threatened to leave, Fred would fake a heart attack and start moaning, "I'm coming, Elizabeth, I'm coming." Lamont wasn't really fooled by his father's machinations but he did love him and, despite what he said about his future, really wouldn't have left the old man or the business.

Sanford and Son was producer Norman Lear's second major hit (*All in the Family* was the first) and, like *All in the Family*, was based on a successful British TV comedy. *Sanford and Son*'s source was called *Steptoe and Son*. *Sanford and Son* was an instantaneous hit and ranked among the top ten programs throughout its run. Fred had a steady girlfriend in Nurse Donna Harris, whom he was always promising to marry, and was constantly at odds with Aunt Esther, who ran the Sanford Arms, a run-down rooming house that was located next to the junkyard. Early in 1976 Lamont found a serious romantic interest in Janet, a divorcée with a young son, and they became engaged at the end of the 1976–1977 season. The marriage never took place, however, as the series left the air in the fall of 1977. Redd Foxx had committed himself to do a variety show for ABC and costar Demond Wilson left the series in a dispute over his remuneration as the sole star of the series after Foxx's departure. With the two stars gone, NBC premiered *The Sanford Arms* (named after Aunt Esther's rooming house) in the fall of 1977, which featured most of the supporting players from *Sanford and Son*.

For a three-month period during the summer of 1976, a second episode of *Sanford and Son* was seen each week on Wednesday nights. The second episodes were reruns from previous seasons and titled *The Best of Sanford and Son*. Reruns were also telecast weekdays on NBC from June 1976 to July 1978.

SANFORD ARMS, THE (*Situation Comedy*)

FIRST TELECAST: *September 16, 1977*
LAST TELECAST: *October 14, 1977*
BROADCAST HISTORY:
Sep 1977–Oct 1977, NBC Fri 8:00–8:30

CAST:
Phil Wheeler .... Theodore Wilson
Esther Anderson .... LaWanda Page
Jeannie .... Bebe Drake-Hooks
Grady Wilson .... Whitman Mayo
Dolly Wilson .... Norma Miller
Bubba Hoover .... Don Bexley
Woody Anderson .... Raymond Allen
Angie Wheeler .... Tina Andrews
Nat Wheeler .... John Earl

In 1977 NBC's highly successful comedy *Sanford and Son* lost both of its stars—Redd Foxx to a variety series of his own on ABC, and Demond Wilson because the producers would not meet his salary demands. With most of the supporting players still around, however, *The Sanford Arms* took its place. The new lead character was Phil Wheeler, a widower with two teenage children. He had made a down payment on the entire Sanford property—house, junkyard, and rooming house—and attempted to turn the latter into a successful residential hotel. With Fred and Lamont Sanford having moved to Arizona, Fred's sister-in-law Esther was left to watch over the property and collect the monthly mortgage payments. Also carried over from the *Sanford and Son* cast of characters were Esther's husband, Woody, Fred's friend Grady (who had married Dolly), and Bubba, who worked at the Sanford Arms as both bellboy and maintenance man. Newcomers to the cast in addition to Phil Wheeler were his children Angie and Nat, and his girlfriend Jeannie.

If anything proved more dificult than getting customers for the hotel, it was finding an audience for the series. The attempt to salvage the series without its two departed stars was a total failure and it lasted less than a month.

SARA (*Western*)

FIRST TELECAST: *February 13, 1976*
LAST TELECAST: *July 30, 1976*
BROADCAST HISTORY:
Feb 1976–Jul 1976, CBS Fri 8:00–9:00

CAST:
Sara Yarnell .... Brenda Vaccaro
Emmet Ferguson .... Bert Kramer
Martin Pope .... Albert Stratton
Claude Barstow .... William Phipps
George Bailey .... William Wintersole
Julia Bailey .... Mariclare Costello
Martha Higgins .... Louise Latham
Georgie Bailey .... Kraig Metzinger
Debbie Higgins .... Debbie Lytton
Emma Higgins .... Hallie Morgan

Set in the frontier town of Independence, Colorado, in the 1870s, *Sara* was the story of a strong-willed young schoolteacher who had given up a dull, predictable existence in the East for the challenge of the West. A fighter, Sara battled ignorance and prejudice, to the horror of many of the more conservative townspeople who had expected a passive "schoolmarm" for their children. Her actions drew mixed reviews from the school board members, Emmett Ferguson, Claude Barstow, and George Bailey; the approval of newspaper editor Martin Pope and her friend Julia Bailey; and the disapproval of her landlady, Martha Higgins. Most important to Sara, however, was the fact that she had the endorsement and enthusiastic interest of her students in the one-room school where she was the only teacher.

SARA (*Situation Comedy*)

FIRST TELECAST: *January 23, 1985*
LAST TELECAST: *June 15, 1988*
BROADCAST HISTORY:
Jan 1985–May 1985, NBC Wed 9:30–10:00
Jun 1988, NBC Wed 9:30–10:00

CAST:

Sara McKenna .... Geena Davis
Rozalyn Dupree .... Alfre Woodard
Marty Lang .... Bill Maher
Dennis Kemper .... Bronson Pinchot
Stuart Webber .... Mark Hudson
Jesse Webber .... Matthew Lawrence
Helen Newcomb .... Ronnie Claire Edwards

Sara was a comedy about the professional and personal life of a young, attractive single woman in San Francisco. Sara was a lawyer who shared a storefront office with three other attorneys. One of them, Rozalyn, was also her best friend and full of advice on how Sara should run her social life. The other two were men—sleazy Marty, whose ambition often got in the way of his principles and, unfortunately, won; and Dennis, the obligatory gay (it was, after all, San Francisco), whose honesty and integrity often put him at odds with Marty. Helen was the office secretary and surrogate mother to them all. Stuart, who lived in Sara's apartment building, was a recently divorced single parent trying to get back into the single world while raising his four-year-old son, Jesse.

NBC aired reruns of Sara briefly in 1988.

SARGE (*Drama*)
FIRST TELECAST: *September 21, 1971*
LAST TELECAST: *January 11, 1972*
BROADCAST HISTORY:
Sep 1971–Nov 1971, NBC Tue 8:30–9:30
Nov 1971–Jan 1972, NBC Tue 7:30–8:30

CAST:

Father Samuel Cavanaugh (Sarge)
.... George Kennedy
Valerie .... Sallie Shockley
Kenji Takichi .... Harold Sakata
Barney Verick .... Ramon Bieri

Set in San Diego, *Sarge* was the story of Father Samuel Cavanaugh, a priest at St. Aloysius Parish. Father Cavanaugh had spent nine years as a member of the San Diego Police Department, part of the time as a homicide detective in the same area in which he was now a priest. He was known as "Sarge" because of his police background, which often helped him provide guidance to his parishioners in their struggle to cope with the problems of a metropolitan environment. The other members of the parish staff seen regularly were Kenji, the rectory cook, and Valerie, the parish secretary. Barney Verick, chief of detectives and long-time friend of Father Cavanaugh, often sought the priest's help when members of the parish were involved in criminal cases.

SATURDAY NIGHT AT THE GARDEN (*Sports*)
FIRST TELECAST: *October 7, 1950*
LAST TELECAST: *March 31, 1951*
BROADCAST HISTORY:
Oct 1950–Mar 1951, DUM Sat 8:30–11:00

Back when Saturday night viewing was dominated by Sid Caesar and Imogene Coca's *Your Show of Shows* on NBC, DuMont offered this weekly program as an alternative for those who preferred sports. Aired live from New York City's Madison Square Garden, *Saturday Night at the Garden* presented whatever event was being staged there, in its entirety. The first three telecasts consisted of a rodeo at which Gene Autry was the guest star, with Don Russell functioning as emcee, and there was one week devoted to a horse show, but most of the remaining telecasts were of more conventional sporting contests. The majority of the broadcasts were basketball games, both professional and college, including the then prestigious NIT College Basketball Tournament, with Curt Gowdy and Don Dunphy doing the commentary. Several track meets were also aired in the spring.

Originally titled *Madison Square Garden*, the series' name was changed to *Saturday Night at the Garden* in November.

SATURDAY NIGHT DANCE PARTY (*Variety*)
FIRST TELECAST: *June 7, 1952*
LAST TELECAST: *August 30, 1952*
BROADCAST HISTORY:
Jun 1952–Jul 1952, NBC Sat 9:30–10:30
Jul 1952–Aug 1952, NBC Sat 9:00–10:30

HOST:
Jerry Lester

This series was the 1952 summer replacement for *Your Show of Shows*. It was a comedy and music variety show that was hosted by comedian Jerry Lester. Each week his guests included a different name band and a number of variety acts.

SATURDAY NIGHT FIGHTS, THE, see *Boxing*

SATURDAY NIGHT HOLLYWOOD PALACE, THE,
see *Hollywood Palace, The*

SATURDAY NIGHT JAMBOREE (*Country Music*)
FIRST TELECAST: *December 4, 1948*
LAST TELECAST: *July 2, 1949*
BROADCAST HISTORY:
Dec 1948–Jan 1949, NBC Sat 8:00–9:00
Jan 1949–Apr 1949, NBC Sat 8:00–8:30
Apr 1949–Jul 1949, NBC Sat 9:30–10:00

EMCEE:
Elton Britt (1948)
Boyd Heath (1949)

REGULARS:
Chubby Chuck Roe, comic
Sophrony Garen, vocals
Ted Grant, violin
Eddie Howard, banjo
John Havens, guitar
Edwin Smith, accordion
Gabe Drake, bass

Country music program, with a heavy leavening of cornpone humor. Yodeler Elton Britt was the original host, but he skedaddled after three telecasts and no other major stars from the country field associated themselves with this New York–based program during its brief run.

SATURDAY NIGHT LIVE (*Comedy Variety*)
FIRST TELECAST: *October 11, 1975*
LAST TELECAST:
BROADCAST HISTORY:
Oct 1975– , NBC Sat 11:30–1:00 A.M.
Oct 1979–Mar 1980, NBC Wed 10:00–11:00
Mar 1980–Apr 1980, NBC Fri 10:00–11:00

REGULARS:
Chevy Chase (1975–1976)
John Belushi (1975–1979)
Dan Aykroyd (1975–1979)

Gilda Radner (1975–1980)
Garrett Morris (1975–1980)
Jane Curtin (1975–1980)
Laraine Newman (1975–1980)
Bill Murray (1977–1980)
Albert Brooks (1975–1976)
Gary Weis (1976–1977)
Jim Henson's Muppets (1975–1976)
Don Novello (1978–1980, 1985–1986)
Paul Shaffer (1978–1980)
Al Franken (1979–1980, 1988–1995)
Tom Davis (1979–1980, 1988–1995)
Denny Dillon (1980–1981)
Gilbert Gottfried (1980–1981)
Gail Matthius (1980–1981)
Joe Piscopo (1980–1984)
Ann Risley (1980–1981)
Charles Rocket (1980–1981)
Eddie Murphy (1981–1984)
Robin Duke (1981–1984)
Tim Kazurinsky (1981–1984)
Tony Rosato (1981–1982)
Christine Ebersole (1981–1982)
Brian Doyle-Murray (1981–1982)
Mary Gross (1981–1985)
Brad Hall (1982–1984)
Gary Kroeger (1982–1985)
Julia Louis-Dreyfus (1982–1985)
Jim Belushi (1983–1985)
Billy Crystal (1984–1985)
Christopher Guest (1984–1985)
Harry Shearer (1984–1985)
Rich Hall (1984–1985)
Martin Short (1984–1985)
Pamela Stephenson (1984–1985)
Anthony Michael Hall (1985–1986)
Randy Quaid (1985–1986)
Joan Cusack (1985–1986)
Robert Downey Jr. (1985–1986)
Nora Dunn (1985–1990)
Terry Sweeney (1985–1986)
Jon Lovitz (1985–1990)
Damon Wayans (1985–1986)
Danitra Vance (1985–1986)
Dennis Miller (1985–1990)
Dana Carvey (1986–1993)
Phil Hartman (1986–1994)
Jan Hooks (1986–1991)
Victoria Jackson (1986–1992)
A. Whitney Brown (1986–1991)
Kevin Nealon (1986–1991, 1993–1995)
Mike Myers (1989–1995)
G.E. Smith & the Saturday Night Live Band (1989–1995)
Chris Farley (1990–1995)
Chris Rock (1990–1993)
Julia Sweeney (1990–1994)
Ellen Cleghorne (1991–1995)
Siobhan Fallon (1991–1993)
Tim Meadows (1991–2000)
Adam Sandler (1991–1995)
David Spade (1991–1996)
Rob Schneider (1991–1994)
Melanie Hutsell (1991–1994)
Beth Cahill (1991–1993)
Sarah Silverman (1993–1994)
Norm Macdonald (1993–1998)
Jay Mohr (1993–1995)
Michael McKean (1994–1995)
Chris Elliott (1994–1995)
Janeane Garofalo (1994–1995)
Mark McKinney (1995–1997)
Laura Kightlinger (1994–1995)
Molly Shannon (1995–2001)
Morwenna Banks (1994–1995)
Jim Breuer (1995–1998)
Will Ferrell (1995–2002)
Darrell Hammond (1995–)
David Koechner (1995–1996)
Cheri Oteri (1995–2000)
Nancy Walls (1995–1996)
Ana Gasteyer (1996–2002)
Chris Kattan (1996–)
Tracy Morgan (1996–)
Colin Quinn (1995–2000)
Chris Parnell (1998–)
Horatio Sanz (1998–)
Jimmy Fallon (1998–)
Rachel Dratch (1999–)
Tina Fey (2000–)
Jerry Minor (2000–2001)
Maya Rudolph (2000–)
Dean Edwards (2001–)
Seth Meyers (2001–)
Amy Poehler (2001–)
Jeff Richards (2001–)
Fred Armisen (2002–)
Will Forte (2002–)

ANNOUNCER:

Don Pardo (1975–1981, 1982–)

Saturday Night Live was one of the landmark programs of the 1970s, an attempt to bring fresh, often outrageous comedy and the excitement of live TV (from New York) to late-night viewers. It featured "The Not Ready for Prime Time Players," a repertory company of wacky comics who presented 90 minutes of topical satire, straight comedy, and music every Saturday night. Each week a different guest star served as the host and the person around whom many of the sketches were written. Some of the more familiar guests were George Carlin (host of the first telecast), Candice Bergen, Buck Henry, Elliott Gould, Lily Tomlin, Dick Cavett, Steve Martin, Eric Idle, Richard Dreyfuss, and Paul Simon. Some hosts weren't from the entertainment world at all, such as New York Mayor Ed Koch, consumer advocate Ralph Nader, football star Fran Tarkenton, Georgia legislator Julian Bond, and even Presidential Press Secretary Ron Nessen (in a controversial but good-humored appearance). Perhaps most unusual was 80-year-old Mrs. Miskel Spillman, who happened to win an "Anyone Can Host" write-in contest during the 1977–1978 season.

Each week also had a musical guest, ranging from some truly offbeat and eccentric musicians to such major rock stars as Blondie and the Rolling Stones.

The chief "discovery" of *Saturday Night Live* during its initial season was comic Chevy Chase, famous for his opening pratfall and his role as the earnest young newsman reporting preposterous headlines on "Weekend Update." His trademark line was "Good evening. I'm Chevy Chase and you're not." Jane Curtin took over the role as newscaster after Chevy left the show in November 1976, and was later joined by Dan Aykroyd when an anchor team was instituted. Other frequent bits included Chevy as bumbling President Ford; Dan as candidate, and later President, Jimmy Carter; Gilda Radner as a lisping Barbara Walters (Ba Ba Wawa), a confused Emily Litella making editorial replies on Weekend Update, and later as rambling, loudmouthed newscaster Rosanne Rosanna-Dana; John Belushi as a Samurai warrior; Aykroyd and Belushi as the Blues Brothers; Don Novello as Father Guido Sarducci; and practically everyone in ridiculous costumes as the Bees or the alien Coneheads.

Originally Jim Henson's Muppets were a regular feature, as was a short, offbeat film produced each week by Albert Brooks (later the films were by Gary Weis). Still later came the "Mr. Bill" films, about the hapless little puppet made of dough who was always being squashed or dismembered by Sluggo. These evolved from a short film submitted by a young man named Walter Williams. And of course there were the ersatz "commercials," satirizing everything from the telephone company to milk.

Over the years *Saturday Night Live* developed a large and loyal audience, and by the 1977–1978 season it was by far the most popular program in late-night television, surpassing the longtime champ *The Tonight Show*. With the success of the show came success for its stars, and eventually the departure of the entire original cast. Chevy Chase left in the fall of 1976 to pursue a career in films and prime-time specials. Three years later Belushi (a major film star in *Animal House*) and Aykroyd left to make a large-screen production based on the Blues Brothers characters they had developed on *Saturday Night Live*. By the spring of 1980 producer Lorne Michaels decided to leave and the remainder of the original cast went with him. A new producer, Jean Doumanian, a new cast, and new writers took over in the fall of 1980, to generally poor reviews. Declining audiences resulted in considerable behind-the-scenes turmoil, with more cast changes and a new production team taking over in 1981. Michaels returned in 1985.

The major discovery of the recast *Saturday Night Live* was youthful black comic Eddie Murphy, whose career exploded with the success of his first feature film, *48 Hrs.*, in 1982. Later favorite characters included Billy Crystal's oily interviewer Fernando ("Mahvelous, mahvelous!"). A frequent musical guest in the mid-'80s was David Johansen as gravelly voiced singer Buster Poindexter.

After considerable turmoil during the early 1980s (42 regulars appears on the show between 1980 and 1985), things settled down in the late 1980s with a stable cast of nine players: Nora Dunn, Jon Lovitz, Dennis Miller, Dana Carvey, Phil Hartman, Jan Hooks, Victoria Jackson, Kevin Nealon, and A. Whitney Brown. Carvey's "Church Lady" and Lovitz's pathological liar Tommy Flanagan ("That's the ticket!") were favorite characters, as was newcomer Mike Myers' Wayne (spun off into the 1992 hit movie *Wayne's World*). While no program can be expected to recapture the magic of its youth (or of ours), many felt that *SNL* was once again one of television's best comedy showcases.

Among the notable comics to emerge from the constantly changing cast in later years were Chris Rock (1990), Adam Sandler (1991), David Spade (1991), Chris Elliott (1994), Janeane Garofalo (1994) and Molly Shannon (1995), the latter best known for her nervous Catholic schoolgirl Mary Katherine Gallagher.

Edited reruns of *Saturday Night Live* were telecast in prime time in 1979–1980, under the title *The Best of Saturday Night Live*.

SATURDAY NIGHT LIVE WITH HOWARD COSELL

(*Variety*)

FIRST TELECAST: *September 20, 1975*
LAST TELECAST: *January 17, 1976*
BROADCAST HISTORY:
Sep 1975–Jan 1976, ABC Sat 8:00–9:00
REGULARS:
Howard Cosell
Elliot Lawrence Orchestra
"EXECUTIVE IN CHARGE OF COMEDY":
Alan King

This is the kind of program ABC used to put on before it became a big-league network. Howard Cosell, the acerbic sportscaster who had been a regular for years on *Monday Night Football*, was chosen as host apparently on the dubious premise that familiarity equals popularity. Polls showed him to be one of the best-known personalities in all of television. More people also said that they couldn't stand him than practically anyone else in TV.

He presided over this variety hour with awkward unease and, despite the presence of all sorts of top-name talent, the whole affair had a very amateurish air to it. (Ed Sullivan, from whose old theater *Saturday Night Live* originated, was awkward too, but at least he sounded like he knew show business inside out—as indeed he did.) The program was produced by the head of ABC Sports, and was telecast live, which was highly unusual for TV at the time. This was supposed to give it a greater "immediacy," but apparently viewers didn't notice the difference.

The premiere featured the U.S. TV debut of one of the hottest groups in popular music, the Bay City Rollers, live via satellite, who drove a teeny-bopper audience to frenzy. Frank Sinatra, John Denver, and John Wayne showed up, as did such sports stars as Evel Knievel, Alex Karras, Jimmy Connors, and Muhammad Ali and Joe Frazier, live by satellite from Manila on the eve of their championship fight. Cosell even offered Shamu the 5,000-pound killer whale, in a pickup from San Diego's Seaworld Oceanarium.

Howard tried hard—he even sang on one telecast, coached by Andy Williams—but bad is not good, and the show folded after half a season.

SATURDAY NIGHT REVUE (*Variety*)

FIRST TELECAST: *June 6, 1953*
LAST TELECAST: *September 18, 1954*
BROADCAST HISTORY:
Jun 1953–Sep 1953, NBC Sat 9:00–10:30
Jun 1954–Sep 1954, NBC Sat 9:00–10:30
REGULARS:
Hoagy Carmichael (1953)
Eddie Albert (1954)
Ben Blue (1954)
Alan Young (1954)
Pat Carroll (1954)
The Sauter-Finegan Band (1954)

This live series was the summer replacement for *Your Show of Shows* in 1953 and 1954. The 1953 edition starred Hoagy Carmichael, who opened the show from his penthouse apartment (a set) where he informally entertained his friends. In the same building was a nightclub called the Sky Room, to which Hoagy invited his guests to see the dinner show. The locale then switched to the nightclub set where the various acts on the evening's program performed. Emphasis was on introducing and showcasing new talent.

The 1954 version starred Eddie Albert and was more of a straight revue. Albert would introduce the acts, sing, dance, and act in sketches himself. The guest artists, in addition to solo performances, also participated in sketches and production numbers with regular members of the cast. As in 1953, the focus was on showcasing new talent.

SATURDAY NIGHT REVUE, THE, see *Jack Carter Show, The* and *Your Show of Shows*

SATURDAY NIGHT SPECIAL (*Comedy Variety*)
FIRST TELECAST: *April 13, 1996*
LAST TELECAST: *May 18, 1996*
BROADCAST HISTORY:
Apr 1996–May 1996, FOX Sat 11:00–12:00
REGULARS:
Jennifer Coolidge
Kathy Griffin
Warren Hutcherson
Heath Hyche
Laura Kightlinger
C. D. LaBove
Bob Rubin
Jason Davis
EXECUTIVE PRODUCER:
Roseanne

This late-night series was a mix of comedy sketches, performances by musical guests, animation, short films, and novelty acts. Executive producer Roseanne hosted the first show (and showed up on each of the subsequent episodes), followed by Ben Stiller, John Goodman, Rosie Perez, Yasmine Bleeth, and Jenny McCarthy. Among the stars featured in sketches were Sharon Stone, Eric Idle, Ed McMahon, Rodney Dangerfield, Harvey Keitel, and the Smothers Brothers. Musical guests included Coolio, Melissa Etheridge, and D'Angelo. Although on the premiere Roseanne promised things "never before done on television," it all looked rather familiar. Kightlinger, in fact, had been a regular on *Saturday Night Live*, the series on which it was clearly modeled.

SATURDAY NIGHT WITH CONNIE CHUNG (*Newsmagazine*)
FIRST TELECAST: *September 23, 1989*
LAST TELECAST: *September 10, 1990*
BROADCAST HISTORY:
Sep 1989–Jun 1990, CBS Sat 10:00–11:00
Jul 1990–Sep 1990, CBS Mon 10:00–11:00
ANCHORWOMAN:
Connie Chung

When it premiered, *Saturday Night with Connie Chung* was a somewhat muddled mix of hard news stories, interviews, and dramatized reenactments of events pertinent to the stories being covered. The reenactments caused much initial controversy, with critics complaining about the docudrama aspect of what was billed as a serious news show. They were eventually dropped, and the series hit its stride with Ms. Chung focusing more on interviews with personalities ranging from actor Marlon Brando to comedian Jackie Mason and businessman Donald Trump. There were also features on political issues and stories on such controversial topics as fetal tissue transplantation, flag burning, and garbage recycling.

When the series moved to Monday nights in the summer of 1990, it was retitled *Face to Face with Connie Chung*, and the focus of the series shifted to celebrity and non-celebrity interviews, at which Ms. Chung seemed best. Although the show was on the CBS schedule for that fall, Ms. Chung's decision to cut back her workload and concentrate on trying to have a baby with husband Maury Povich resulted in it airing as a collection of irregularly scheduled specials, rather than as a weekly series.

SATURDAY ROUNDUP (*Western Anthology*)
FIRST TELECAST: *June 10, 1951*
LAST TELECAST: *September 1, 1951*
BROADCAST HISTORY:
Jun 1951–Sep 1951, NBC Sat 8:00–9:00
REGULAR:
Kermit Maynard

The stories of James Oliver Curwood were dramatized in this filmed Western anthology. Although Kermit Maynard starred in all of them, the character that he played varied from show to show.

Maynard was a onetime world's champion rodeo rider, and had appeared in many grade-B Westerns in the 1930s. He was the younger brother of cowboy star Ken Maynard.

SATURDAY SPORTS FINAL, THE (*Sports News*)
FIRST TELECAST: *July 7, 1962*
LAST TELECAST: *October 6, 1962*
BROADCAST HISTORY:
Jul 1962–Oct 1962, ABC Sat 10:45–11:00
SPORTSCASTER:
Merle Harmon

Weekly wrap-up of news from the world of sports, including filmed highlights of major events. Harmon also interviewed guest sports celebrities.

SATURDAY SPORTS MIRROR (*Sports News*)
FIRST TELECAST: *July 14, 1956*
LAST TELECAST: *September 15, 1956*
BROADCAST HISTORY:
Jul 1956–Sep 1956, CBS Sat 7:00–7:30
REGULARS:
Jack Drees
Bill Hickey

This summer sports series featured sportscasters Drees and Hickey with a summary of the week's sports news, interviews with sports celebrities, and occasional coverage of events in progress on the day of the telecast.

SATURDAY SQUARE (*Variety*)
FIRST TELECAST: *January 7, 1950*
LAST TELECAST: *February 18, 1950*
BROADCAST HISTORY:
Jan 1950–Feb 1950, NBC Sat 8:00–9:00

Short-lived musical variety program which originated from Chicago and incorporated elements from *Chicago Jazz* and *Stud's Place*, which it replaced. In

Saturday Square, a central figure, at first a policeman but in later telecasts a street-corner loafer, directed the viewer to different spots around the square where entertainment was being offered. The viewer was then transported to one of those spots: a musical rehearsal hall where a jam session was in progress, a stylish penthouse party, to Studs Terkel's pub, etc. Various talent appeared as guests.

SAVANNAH (*Serial Drama*)
FIRST TELECAST: *January 21, 1996*
LAST TELECAST: *February 24, 1997*
BROADCAST HISTORY:
Jan 1996–Jul 1996, WB Sun 9:00–10:00
Aug 1996–Feb 1997, WB Mon 9:00–10:00
CAST:
Reese Burton .... Shannon Sturges
Peyton Richards .... Jamie Luner
Lane MacKenzie .... Robyn Lively
Det. Dean Collins .... David Gail
Tom Massick .... Paul Satterfield
Edward Burton .... Ray Wise
Travis Peterson/Nick Corelli .... George Eads
Veronica Kozlowski .... Beth Toussaint Coleman
Lucille Richards (1996) .... Wendy Phillips
Det. Michael Wheeler .... Taurean Blacque
Jason Collins (age 5) .... Austin Cruce
Vincent Massick (1996) .... David Lee Smith
Brian Alexander (1996) ..... Scott Thompson Baker
Elinore Alexander .... Mimi Kennedy
Tom Alexander (1996) .... Ted Shackelford
Cassie Wheeler .... Alexia Robinson
Dave, the bartender .... Ron Clinton Smith
Det. Sam Lucas (1997) .... Russell Curry

Three Southern belles who had been best friends in high school—Reese, Peyton, and Lane—were the focal points of this steamy prime time soap opera. Reese Burton was wealthy, trusting, and naive; Peyton, the daughter of the Burton family housekeeper, was scheming and amoral; and Lane, just returned to Savannah from New York, was the sensible one, an aspiring newspaper writer. In the premiere episode virginal Reese married handsome Travis Peterson, an embezzling bank employee, who cheated on her—with Peyton—and stole Lane's savings. Travis was murdered shortly thereafter. Peyton thought she had killed him when she slugged him over the head with a bottle, but it turned out he had been poisoned by her mother, Lucille, to prevent him from revealing the fact that Lucille had had an illicit affair with Reese's powerful father, Edward, and that Peyton was in fact Edward's illegitimate daughter. Edward, the head of Burton Industries, rigged the trial to get Lucille off the hook.

Meanwhile, Lane got a job as a reporter for the *Savannah Dispatch* and began dating her old flame Dean, a local cop with a young son, Jason. The other major player in this soap opera was Tom Messick, a con man with a vendetta against Edward. He cheated in a poker game to win the S. S. *Savannah* from Edward, and turned the riverboat into a floating casino, in which Peyton gained half ownership. Tom's scam artist partner, Veronica, had an affair with Edward, but she proved an embarrassment when, during his campaign for state senate, it was revealed that she had been a hooker. In response, the ever-ingenious Edward set up a foundation to help wayward girls, with Veronica as its head, to show voters that she had reformed! Eventually he dumped her and quickly married Elinore, to prevent her from testifying against him in a trial resulting from their crooked business dealings. Veronica got even, though, scamming him out of a fortune in family jewelry and skipping town.

At the end of the first season Travis' identical twin brother Nick showed up (they had been adopted by different families). Nick, who was as good as Travis had been bad, started dating Reese and bought a share in the riverboat, where he became a thorn in crooked Tom's side. Lane, now engaged to Dean, lost her job when Elinore bought the *Dispatch* and fired her. Addicted to painkillers, she almost ruined her relationship with Dean, but in the final episode they tied the knot.

Filmed on location in Lilburn, Georgia, outside of Atlanta.

SAVE OUR STREETS (*Informational*)
BROADCAST HISTORY:
Syndicated only
60 minutes (1995–1997), 30 minutes (1997–1999)
Produced: *1995–1999*
Released: *September 1995*
HOST/NARRATOR:
Tim Reid

This series showed viewers the realities of crime in their neighborhoods and gave them information on how to improve things. Among the topics covered were street crime (muggings, car theft, vandalism, etc.), scams, and child molesters released in residential neighborhoods. *Save Our Streets* used actual filmed footage, dramatic re-creations, and interviews with victims and law enforcement professionals to show how crimes were committed, and gave viewers tips on how to avoid being victimized.

SAVED BY THE BELL: THE COLLEGE YEARS (*Situation Comedy*)
FIRST TELECAST: *September 14, 1993*
LAST TELECAST: *February 8, 1994*
BROADCAST HISTORY:
Sep 1993–Feb 1994, NBC Tue 8:00–8:30
CAST:
Zack Morris .... Mark-Paul Gosselaar
Kelly Kapowski .... Tiffani-Amber Thiessen
A. C. Slater .... Mario Lopez
Samuel "Screech" Powers .... Dustin Diamond
Leslie Burke .... Anne Tremko
Alex Tabor .... Kiersten Warren
Michael Rogers .... Bob Golic
Professor Lasky .... Patrick Fabian
Dean Susan McMann (1994) .... Holland Taylor

One of the most popular programs on television among teenagers during the early 1990s was the frothy teen sitcom *Saved by the Bell,* which premiered on NBC's Saturday-morning lineup on August 20, 1989, and was subsequently seen in syndication and as an occasional prime time special. The show concerned the escapades of a group of students at Bayside High School in California. In this prime time series, four of them graduated and enrolled as freshmen at California University.

Continuing from the earlier series were Zack, the ringleader, a handsome charmer whose schemes seldom worked out in the end; Kelly, his high school sweetheart; Slater, the good-natured muscleman who had enrolled on a wrestling scholarship; and their buddy Screech, a socially inept computer nerd who seemed to gain confidence in college. They shared a suite of rooms in a coed dormitory with Leslie, a rich girl from San Francisco who was wise to Zack, and Alex, a flighty theater arts major who wanted to become an actress. Limiting the gang's schemes were no-nonsense Resident Advisor Michael, a hulking former pro football player (played by former Los Angeles Raiders defensive tackle Bob Golic); anthropology professor Lasky; and, toward the end, imposing Dean McMann. Faced with all that firepower, the gang (or at least the series) never made it to their sophomore year.

Actress Tiffani-Amber Thiessen (Kelly) did stay in school, however. The following season she joined the cast of *Beverly Hills 90210* as a student at a different "California University."

Three days before this series premiered, a new group of students turned up at Bayside High School in *Saved By the Bell: The New Class*, the show that replaced the original *Saved by the Bell* on NBC's Saturday morning lineup. Screech even returned to his high school as a teacher. Production of *The New Class* continued through Fall 1998, with NBC airing the last original episodes during the 1999–2000 season.

SAWYER VIEWS HOLLYWOOD (*Musical Variety*)

FIRST TELECAST: *June 29, 1951*
LAST TELECAST: *August 31, 1951*
BROADCAST HISTORY:
Jun 1951–Aug 1951, ABC Fri 10:00–10:30
REGULARS:
Hal Sawyer
Gaylord Carter Trio

Musical variety program, featuring Hal Sawyer's interviews with Hollywood stars. Previously seen in daytime as *Hal in Hollywood* starting in April 1951.

SAY IT WITH ACTING (*Charades*)

FIRST TELECAST: *January 6, 1951*
LAST TELECAST: *February 22, 1952*
BROADCAST HISTORY:
Jan 1951–May 1951, NBC Sat 6:30–7:00
Aug 1951–Feb 1952, ABC Fri 7:30–8:00
TEAM CAPTAINS:
Maggi McNellis (1951)
Bud Collyer (1951)

Celebrity charades, featuring two teams of actors and actresses from current Broadway productions. Team captains for the NBC series were Maggi McNellis and Bud Collyer, while team members varied. Formerly a local program in New York, where it began in January 1949 under the title *Look Ma, I'm Acting*, then became *Act It Out*, and finally *Say It with Acting*.

SCARE TACTICS (*Humor*)

BROADCAST HISTORY:
Sci-Fi Channel
30 minutes
Original episodes: *2003–*
Premiered: *April 4, 2003*
HOST:
Shannen Doherty

In this *Candid Camera*-style show, pranks were staged on unsuspecting people with the intention of "scaring the hell out of them." For example two young people in a car on their way to a party were attacked along a lonely stretch of road by "monsters"; their driver (an actor) was dragged away screaming, while a friend (who was in on the stunt) ran for cover amid explosions and flashing lights. Hidden cameras and mikes recorded their screams—there were a lot of screams on this show. Other stunts included a job interview at a cemetery and a visit to a haunted camp in the forest. If all of this sounds a little extreme it was for at least one victim, who filed suit charging physical and emotional trauma. That prank wasn't shown.

SCARECROW AND MRS. KING (*Adventure/Espionage*)

FIRST TELECAST: *October 3, 1983*
LAST TELECAST: *September 10, 1987*
BROADCAST HISTORY:
Oct 1983–Sep 1986, CBS Mon 8:00–9:00
Sep 1986–Feb 1987, CBS Fri 8:00–9:00
May 1987–Sep 1987, CBS Thu 8:00–9:00
CAST:
Lee Stetson ("Scarecrow") .... Bruce Boxleitner
Amanda King .... Kate Jackson
Dotty West .... Beverly Garland
Billy Melrose .... Mel Stewart
Francine Desmond .... Martha Smith
Philip King .... Paul Stout
Jamie King .... Greg Morton
T. P. Aquinas (1986–1987) .... Raleigh Bond
Dr. Smyth (1986–1987) .... Myron Natwick

Amanda was just another bored, suburban divorcée and mother—until a handsome, mysterious man thrust a package into her hands at a train station and disappeared. It turned out he was "Scarecrow," an agent for a secret government organization called "The Agency," and he needed her help dodging Russian spies. She proved to be so good at it that he convinced her to become his partner, much to the skepticism of his boss, Melrose, and the confusion of Amanda's family, who were never quite sure what was going on (as she was sworn to secrecy).

Chasing foreign spies was certainly more exciting than vacuuming and P.T.A. meetings in the Washington, D.C., suburbs, and Amanda warmed to the challenge of her double life, as well as to the handsome Scarecrow himself. Their relationship was full of quips and the hint of mutual interest, which inspired much curiosity in her mother, Dotty. Were they friends? Lovers? What did this mysterious acquaintance do for a living? Francine was a wisecracking operative of "The Agency," and Philip and Jamie were Amanda's two young children. In order to deflect her friends' questions, Amanda got a part-time job at the International Federal Film Company—which happened to be the "cover" firm for The Agency office out of which Lee worked. Eventually she went through The Agency's training program and officially became Lee's partner.

In 1986 Lee's favorite and most reliable source of information, T. P. Aquinas, became a regular, and the head of The Agency, Dr. Smyth, also made several appearances. The romantic tension between Amanda and Lee finally reached its logical conclusion when, in February 1987, they were married. Unfortunately, in true spy fashion, no one could be told in order to protect Amanda's family from The Agency's many enemies.

SCENE OF THE CRIME (*Detective Anthology*)
FIRST TELECAST: *April 14, 1985*
LAST TELECAST: *May 26, 1985*
BROADCAST HISTORY:
Apr 1985, NBC Sun 10:00–11:00
May 1985, NBC Sun 8:00–9:00
HOST:
Orson Welles

NBC attempted to solve an unusual problem with this series. The network had two unrelated half-hour shows, neither of which was suitable for the schedule. So the programmers stitched the two together, added some continuity in the form of host Orson Welles, and tried to pass the result off as a new, one-hour series. The public didn't bite.

The first half hour was a standard whodunit, with the audience supposed to guess the perpetrator from in the story, before he or she was revealed. The story told in the second half hour (with a different cast) always ended with an O. Henry twist. Generally lesser-known performers were featured, with Barbara Rush, John Davidson, Michelle Phillips, and Dennis Dugan among the more familiar.

SCENE OF THE CRIME (*Dramatic Anthology*)
FIRST TELECAST: *April 3, 1991*
LAST TELECAST: *August 24, 1994*
BROADCAST HISTORY:
Apr 1991–Mar 1992, CBS Wed 11:30–12:30 A.M.
Mar 1992–Apr 1992, CBS Tue 11:30–12:30 A.M.
Jan 1993–Aug 1993, CBS Mon/Thu 12:30–1:30 A.M.
Mar 1994–Aug 1994, CBS Wed 12:35–1:35 A.M.
HOST:
Stephen J. Cannell
REPERTORY COMPANY:
Kim Coates (1991)
Lisa Houle
Maxine Miller
Francois Montagut
Sandra Nelson
Barbara Parkins (1991)
Olivier Pierre
George Touliatos
Teri Austin
Stephen McHattie
Robert Paisley

Successful producer/writer Stephen J. Cannell hosted this anthology series, which presented a murder mystery each week. Produced in Vancouver, British Columbia, *Scene of the Crime* relied primarily on a regular repertory cast, with each member having roles that ranged from starring to supporting to minor, depending the story. CBS aired reruns of *Scene of the Crime* in 1993 and 1994.

SCHLITZ FILM FIRSTS, see *Movies—Prior to 1961*

SCHLITZ PLAYHOUSE OF STARS (*Dramatic Anthology*)
FIRST TELECAST: *October 5, 1951*
LAST TELECAST: *March 27, 1959*
BROADCAST HISTORY:
Oct 1951–Mar 1952, CBS Fri 9:00–10:00
Apr 1952–Sep 1955, CBS Fri 9:00–9:30
Oct 1955–Mar 1959, CBS Fri 9:30–10:00
HOSTESS:
Irene Dunne (1952)

For eight seasons, the Schlitz Brewing Company sponsored a regular Friday night dramatic-anthology series on CBS. When it premiered in October 1951, under the title *Schlitz Playhouse of Stars*, it was an hour-long live drama from New York. The premiere telecast starred Helen Hayes and David Niven in "Not a Chance," and CBS heavily promoted the fact that Miss Hayes had signed an exclusive contract to perform only for this series. She did make two other appearances during 1951, but was never seen again on this show. The hour version produced some substantial dramas. Walter Hampden and Chester Morris starred in an adaptation of Herman Melville's *Billy Budd*, Dane Clark in Ernest Hemingway's "Fifty Grand," and Margaret Sullavan and Wendell Corey in a version of *Still Life*, the first Noel Coward play adapted for television.

In April 1952 the length of the plays presented was cut from an hour to 30 minutes and the literary merit of the material started to slip. There were still occasional plays like W. Somerset Maugham's "A String of Beads" starring Joan Caulfield and Tom Drake; and experiments like "Autumn in New York," a musical love story with Polly Bergen and Skip Homeier; but potboilers like "The Ordeal of Dr. Sutton" with Raymond Burr and Marilyn Erskine became progressively more common. For roughly six months, in the second half of 1952, Irene Dunne was on hand as a regular hostess, but that function was dropped in favor of letting one of the week's stars introduce the play, and then that too was phased out.

Although this was essentially a live series, filmed episodes started showing up in the summer of 1953, at first on an infrequent basis, then for the entire summer of 1954, and accounting for more than half of the telecasts during the 1954–1955 season. By the fall of 1956 there were no live episodes at all, and that November the title was shortened to *Schlitz Playhouse.* It remained weekly until the start of its last season, when it aired on an alternate-week basis with *Lux Playhouse.*

With a run of almost eight years, countless stars appeared on *Schlitz Playhouse of Stars.* Young James Dean made one of his rare television appearances as the star of "The Unlighted Road" in 1955, and in 1957 Gene Kelly made his television dramatic debut in "The Life You Save" with Agnes Moorehead and Janice Rule. Two episodes were turned into series—"The Restless Gun" starring John Payne and "A Tale of Wells Fargo" starring Dale Robertson—both Westerns aired during the 1956–1957 season. They turned up on NBC's lineup in the fall of 1957.

SCHOOL HOUSE (*Comedy Variety*)
FIRST TELECAST: *January 18, 1949*
LAST TELECAST: *April 19, 1949*
BROADCAST HISTORY:
Jan 1949–Apr 1949, DUM Tue 9:00–9:30
EMCEE ("TEACHER"):
Kenny Delmar
APPEARING:
Arnold Stang
Wally Cox
Tommy Dix
Betty Anne Nyman
Kenny Bowers

Maureen Cannon
Roger Price
Wendy Drew
Mary Ann Reeve
Aileen Stanley, Jr.
Russell Arms
Beverly Fite
Patty Adair
Buddy Hackett

Early television sometimes looked back into show-business history—*way* back—for material. Gus Edwards' "School Days" routine had been a sensation in vaudeville just after the turn of the century, producing such future stars as Georgie Jessel, Groucho Marx, Eleanor Powell, Ray Bolger, and Mae Murray. Evidently DuMont felt that it might be a hit all over again for video viewers in 1949. The format was a comedy variety show set in a schoolhouse, with a constantly beset "teacher" as emcee and a class full of talented youngsters as "students" (plus some older acts). Arnold Stang and Wally Cox were among the comical students on this TV version, and such notable performers as Buddy Hackett and Russell Arms also appeared. Except for "teacher" Kenny Delmar, the cast was constantly changing and those listed above are a sampling of the talent that performed.

Also seen as a local New York program during 1948, under the title *School Days*, with Happy Felton as "teacher."

SCIENCE CIRCUS (*Instruction*)

FIRST TELECAST: *July 4, 1949*
LAST TELECAST: *September 12, 1949*
BROADCAST HISTORY:
Jul 1949–Sep 1949, ABC Mon 8:30–9:00
HOST:
Bob Brown

Children's instructional program featuring Bob Brown in the role of an absentminded science professor presenting scientific stunts and experiments in front of a studio audience. From Chicago.

SCIENCE FICTION THEATRE (*Science Fiction Anthology*)

BROADCAST HISTORY:
Syndicated only
30 minutes
Produced: *1955–1957* (78 episodes)
Released: *April 1955*
NARRATOR:
Truman Bradley
PRODUCER:
Ivan Tors

This semidocumentary anthology series explored the "what ifs" of modern science. Each drama was based on scientific fact, dealing with such subjects as UFOs, mental telepathy, psychokinesis, robots, man's first flight into outer space, and the possibility of thawing out frozen prehistoric animals. Actors included such Hollywood standbys as Howard Duff, Gene Barry, Basil Rathbone, and William Lundigan, and the narrator was news commentator Truman Bradley.

The series was one of the first produced by Ivan Tors, a man with a healthy regard for science and nature. He later went on to create such hits as *Sea Hunt*, *Daktari*, *Flipper*, and *Gentle Ben*. Real-life scientific experts served as advisors to this series to insure authenticity.

SCI-FI CHANNEL, THE (Network) (*General Entertainment Cable Network*)

LAUNCHED:
September 24, 1992
SUBSCRIBERS (MAY 2003):
80.0 million (75% U.S.)

One of the most popular new cable networks of the 1990s, the Sci-Fi Channel offered 24 hours a day of science fiction, fantasy, and classic horror programs. Most of its schedule consisted of reruns, some well known (*Star Trek, Quantum Leap, The Twilight Zone*) and others less so (*Misfits of Science*, *Otherworld*). Among its early original series were the following. (Host names are in parentheses.)

C/Net Central (computer magazine, Richard Hart), 1995–1999
Inside Space (science magazine. In order, the hosts were *Star Trek*'s Nichelle Nichols, Laura Banks, ex-astronaut Mike Mullane, *Lost in Space*'s Bill Mumy, Julie Golden, and Geoff Fox), 1992–1998
Mission Genesis (space adventure, Kelli Taylor, Gordon Michael Woolvett), 1997–1998.
Mysteries from Beyond the Other Dominion (stories of the bizarre with the bizarre Dr. Franklin Reuhl), 1992–1994
Mysteries, Magic & Miracles (documentary, Patrick Macnee), 1994–1996
Sci-Fi Buzz (sci-fi newsmagazine, Mike Jerrick. Author Harlan Ellison was a frequent commentator, and Jeffrey Lyons became the show's "Virtual Critic" in 1994), 1992–1998
Sci-Fi Trader, The (merchandise sales, Darla Haun, Warren James, and young Joshua Miller), 1994–1997
Science Show, The (documentary. Lu Hanessian), 1992–1995

In the late '90s the channel began producing new episodes of former broadcast series *Sightings* and *Sliders* and cable series *Poltergeist: The Legacy* (formerly on Showtime) and *Mystery Science Theater 3000* (from Comedy Central). In 1999 it introduced a full night of original dramatic programming, including the new series *Farscape* and *First Wave*.

Sci-Fi has produced numerous specials and several original movies, among them *Homewrecker*, *Official Denial*, and *The Lifeforce Experiment*. A major hit in late 2002 was the two-week Steven Spielberg miniseries *Taken*. At one time it even had its own news division, which—appropriately—reported from 150 years in the future via futuristic "news updates" scattered throughout the schedule, called "FTL Newsfeed" (FTL is science fiction jargon for "Faster Than Light.")

The channel scheduled numerous theatrical movies in the sci-fi genre, including box-office hits such as *Star Wars* and *Close Encounters of the Third Kind*, avant-garde Japanese animation, and hilariously awful monster flicks of decades past. These old films, now largely phased out, were presented in marathons and theme weeks, such as "*The Phantom Creeps* Marathon" (Bela Lugosi), "Vampire Fest," "The Aroma from Troma" (Troma studio's toxic films), and "Bad Brains and Hideous Heads Week."

The Sci-Fi Channel first reached more than half of all U.S. television homes in April 1998 and its principal original prime time series after that date are listed in this book under their individual titles.

SCI-FI ENTERTAINMENT (*Magazine*)

BROADCAST HISTORY:

Sci-Fi Channel
30 minutes
Produced: *1998*
Premiered: *May 1, 1998*

HOSTS:

Chase Masterson
Scott Mantz

Weekly entertainment magazine focusing on the world of science fiction, hosted by a suitably odd couple: hip, leather-clad (Ms.) Chase Masterson and geeky Scott Mantz.

SCORCH (*Situation Comedy*)

FIRST TELECAST: *February 28, 1992*
LAST TELECAST: *March 13, 1992*
BROADCAST HISTORY:

Feb 1992–Mar 1992, CBS Fri 8:00–8:30

CAST:

Brian Stevens .... Jonathan Walker
Jessica Stevens (age 8) .... Rhea Silver-Smith
Jack Fletcher .... Todd Susman
Allison King .... Brenda Strong
Howard Gurman .... John O'Hurley
Robin .... Lauren Katz
Edna Bracken .... Rose Marie
Scorch .... trained by Ronn Lucas

Brian Stevens was a single parent and struggling actor in New Haven, Connecticut, whose world was turned upside down when Scorch entered his life. Scorch, a 1,300-year-old dragon with an attitude, had recently awakened from a long sleep to find that he seemed to be the only one of his kind alive, at least in New Haven. He flew into the window of Brian's apartment and immediately endeared himself to Brian's daughter, Jessica, but not to her father. When Brian took him along in a tote bag (don't ask why) to a job interview as weatherman on WWEN-TV's *News at Noon,* Scorch popped out of the bag and convinced station manager Jack Fletcher that he was Brian's ventriloquist's dummy. Fletcher thought the "ventriloquist" and his talking miniature dragon made a cute team and hired them for the job. Others working at the station were Howard, the stuffy news anchorman; Allison, the sexy coanchor; and Robin, who worked on the production team. Edna Bracken, Brian's landlady, was convinced he was hiding a pet in his apartment and kept barging in trying to find it.

The viewing audience apparently didn't find this fantasy to their liking, and neither did the programming executives at CBS. They yanked it from the schedule after only three episodes had aired.

SCOTLAND YARD (*Police Anthology*)

FIRST TELECAST: *November 17, 1957*
LAST TELECAST: *October 3, 1958*
BROADCAST HISTORY:

Nov 1957–Mar 1958, ABC Sun 10:00–10:30
May 1958–Jun 1958, ABC Wed 9:30–10:00
Aug 1958–Oct 1958, ABC Fri 10:00–10:30

HOST:

Edgar Lustgarten

Filmed in England, this series presented dramas based on actual cass from the files of Scotland Yard, Britain's world-renowned crime investigation unit. Series host Edgar Lustgarten was a noted English criminologist. No regular characters appeared in this series—there seemed to be a different superintendent, inspector, or sergeant on the case every week—but one role, that of Inspector Duggan (played by Russell Napier), did recur in about half a dozen episodes.

SCOTT ISLAND, see *Harbourmaster*

SCOTT MUSIC HALL (*Musical Variety*)

FIRST TELECAST: *October 8, 1952*
LAST TELECAST: *August 26, 1953*
BROADCAST HISTORY:

Oct 1952–Aug 1953, NBC Wed 8:30–9:00

REGULARS:

Patti Page
Frank Fontaine
Mary Ellen Terry
The Carl Hoff Orchestra

Patti Page had come to prominence in the late 1940s singing country-flavored tunes and employing an unusual recording technique which allowed her to sing in harmony with herself, or even in whole choruses of her own voice. Her biggest hit, from 1950–1951, was "The Tennessee Waltz." In this network variety program she initially costarred with Frank Fontaine, Fontaine providing the comedy and Miss Page ("The Singing Rage") the songs. Guests were also seen. In February 1953 Fontaine was phased out of the show and Miss Page became its sole star. The only other regular on the show was featured dancer Mary Ellen Terry.

SCRAPBOOK JUNIOR EDITION (*Children's*)

FIRST TELECAST: *June 27, 1948*
LAST TELECAST: *November 14, 1948*
BROADCAST HISTORY:

Jun 1948–Nov 1948, CBS Sun 6:00–6:30

HOSTS:

Jini Boyd O'Conner
Scotty MacGregor

This children's show invited viewers to send in information or examples of their hobbies and interests so that the TV audience could learn from them. The show started as a local program in October 1947 and remained on the air until May 1949 at an earlier time on Sunday afternoons. A feature which enabled viewers to win prizes was the puzzle tune contest. A child was called on the phone and asked to identify what was wrong with a picture that represented a nursery rhyme. If he or she identified the flaw it was worth anything from a pet dog, to a camping set, to a new bicycle.

SCRATCH + BURN (*Comedy*)

BROADCAST HISTORY:

MTV
30 minutes
Original episodes: *2002* (5 episodes)
Premiered: *October 19, 2002*

REGULARS:

GQ (Gregory Qaiyum)
J. A. Q. (Jeffrey Qaiyum)

Jordan (Jordan Allen-Dutton)
Dragon (Erik Weiner)

Sketch-comedy series set to rap music featuring four young guys from the off-Broadway play *The Bombitty of Errors*, a hip-hop version of Shakespeare's *Comedy of Errors*. Subjects ranged from Bill Gates' high school years, to learning to drive, to friends having sex with their ex-girlfriends. J. A. Q. was GQ's younger brother.

SCREEN DIRECTORS PLAYHOUSE (*Anthology*)
FIRST TELECAST: *October 5, 1955*
LAST TELECAST: *September 26, 1956*
BROADCAST HISTORY:
Oct 1955–Jun 1956, NBC Wed 8:00–8:30
Jul 1956–Sep 1956, ABC Wed 9:00–9:30

The one distinguishing characteristic of this filmed anthology series was that each of the dramatizations was directed by an outstanding director of Hollywood motion pictures. Among the participating directors were John Ford, Leo McCarey, Fred Zinnemann, Ida Lupino, and George Stevens. The scope of the series ranged from serious dramas to Westerns to comedies, and the players from relative newcomers such as Cloris Leachman, Alan Young, and Pat Hitchcock (Alfred's daughter) to such old-timers as Walter Brennan and Edgar Buchanan.

SCREEN MYSTERY, see *Movies—Prior to 1961*

SCREEN SHORTS, see *Movies—Prior to 1961*

SCRUBS (*Comedy/Drama*)
FIRST TELECAST: *October 2, 2001*
LAST TELECAST:
BROADCAST HISTORY:
Oct 2001–Aug 2002, NBC Tue 9:30–10:00
Jun 2002– , NBC Thu 8:30–9:00
CAST:
Dr. John "J. D." Dorian .... Zach Braff
Dr. Chris Turk .... Donald Faison
Dr. Elliott Reid .... Sarah Chalke
Dr. Bob Kelso .... Ken Jenkins
Dr. Perry Cox .... John C. McGinley
Nurse Carla Espinosa .... Judy Reyes
The Janitor .... Neil Flynn
Nurse Laverne Roberts .... Aloma Wright
Todd .... Robert Maschio

Life at Sacred Heart Hospital was seen through the eyes of three wide-eyed interns in this clever, and somewhat surreal, comedy. Amiable J. D. was so innocent, and cute, that the nurses nicknamed him Bambi; his friendly college buddy Chris was a surgical aide, and Elliott was a bubbly but somewhat indecisive blonde. Put on Earth to terrorize them was Kelso, the deceptively kind and fatherly chief of medicine whose eyes could glow flame-red (literally) when they made a mistake; and Cox, the loud, gruff and quirky doctor whom no one could figure out. Then there was The Janitor, a tall, ominous cleaning man who lurked in the corridors and silently tormented J. D. Carla was the sarcastic but knowledgeable Hispanic nurse.

There were numerous fantasy sequences (showing things as J. D. wished they were) and gross-out sight gags, but then the story would suddenly snap back to a sometimes dark reality, as when all three interns had to inform a different family about the death of a loved [illegible] *Scrubs* was filmed at a real-life hospital, the Hollywood Medical Center in Los Angeles.

SEA HUNT (*Adventure*)
BROADCAST HISTORY:
Syndicated only
30 minutes
Produced: *Feb 1957–1961* (156 episodes)
Released: *January 1958*
CAST:
Mike Nelson .... Lloyd Bridges
PRODUCER:
Ivan Tors

"*Sea Hunt*," said the *New York Times*, "may best be described as an adventure series in depth." *TV Guide* called it "an epic so watery that Lloyd Bridges' colleagues tell him they have to drain their TV sets after watching his show." Beyond the inevitable jokes, *Sea Hunt* was one of the best-remembered programs of the 1950s, and one of the most successful syndicated series of all time. The networks, in fact, had turned it down because they felt the possibilities of a weekly series set underwater were too limited. They let a big one get away.

The premise was simple. Mike Nelson was an ex-navy frogman who had become a free-lance undersea investigator. Traveling around the world on jobs, he rescued a trapped flyer in a sunken plane, brought up stolen goods, located hidden clues, and encountered an amazing number of underwater criminals (including one ingenious fellow who was going to blast his way into the vault of a seaside bank). His employers were insurance companies, salvage firms, a Hollywood moviemaker, and sometimes the U.S. government. During later seasons, in fact, when the plausible excuses for dangerous civilian assignments began to run out, he more and more frequently went on missions connected with national security, a job one might expect the navy to do. There was a good deal of action, including underwater fights and occasional chases on a sea scooter. But mostly, the attraction was simply the surreal world of the deep. When the series began perhaps 25 percent of the action took place there. "We weren't sure at first how much underwater stuff we could get by with," commented producer Ivan Tors. "But we soon found out that was what the audience wanted—water, water, and more water." Soon more than half the show took place beneath the waves, with much of the remainder aboard Mike Nelson's boat, the *Argonaut*.

Sea Hunt certainly presented some of Hollywood's more unusual production problems. Filming had to be moved around, from Southern California to Florida to the Caribbean, to follow the warm water. As a result, this was one of the more expensive half-hour series of its day, costing about $40,000 per episode, despite the small cast (Bridges was the only regular). Filming was normally done at depths of 20 to 40 feet—beyond that stuntmen were used—and only three crew members went down with the actors, cameraman, director, and producer. There were remarkably few close scrapes. Barracudas swam within camera range, but none took a bite (they usually attack only near the surface). Seasick actors were a greater problem. "Their faces get so green you can't shoot them," complained Tors. "It would be too ghastly to put on television" (although *Sea Hunt* was filmed in black-and-white).

Advising the program on matters of authenticity were a number of experts, including ex-navy frogman Jon Lindbergh, son of flyer Col. Charles Lindbergh.

Underwater photography was by Lamar Boren, one of the country's leading undersea cameramen. Nevertheless, authenticity was not always possible; the wrong kind of fish would swim by for the locale where the story was supposedly taking place—you just couldn't control what happened on the "set"—and, worst of all, Mike always dived alone, something professionals never do.

Such quibbles hardly mattered. Viewers made *Sea Hunt* a major hit during its four years of original production, and watched countless reruns throughout the 1960s. Actor Bridges thoroughly enjoyed making it, too. An all-around athlete in college, he took to skindiving like a fish. "Surefire way to escape Los Angeles smog . . . I love every minute of it." He even used his young son Beau Bridges in several episodes.

SEA HUNT (*Adventure*)

BROADCAST HISTORY:

Syndicated only
30 minutes
Produced: *1987–1988* (22 episodes)
Released: *September 1987*

CAST:

Mike Nelson .... Ron Ely
Jennifer Nelson.................... Kimber Sissons

More than 25 years after the original *Sea Hunt* had left the air, a new version bubbled to the surface with former TV Tarzan Ron Ely in the starring role. This time around Mike Nelson was a widower who used his boat, the *Sea Hunt* (hence the series title?) for assorted private and commercial uses—charters, research, salvage jobs, etc. His attractive daughter, Jennifer, who was a college student majoring in marine biology, somehow found time to take part in many of the adventures with her dad. The underwater scenes were filmed in the Bahamas, while the rest of the series was shot on location in British Columbia.

SEAQUEST DSV (*Science Fiction*)

FIRST TELECAST: *September 12, 1993*
LAST TELECAST: *December 27, 1995*

BROADCAST HISTORY:

Sep 1993–Aug 1995, NBC Sun 8:00–9:00
Sep 1995–Dec 1995, NBC Wed 8:00–9:00

CAST:

Capt. Nathan Hale Bridger.......... Roy Scheider
Cdr. Jonathan Ford .... Don Franklin
Dr. Kristin Westphalen (1993–1994)
.... Stephanie Beacham
Lt. Cdr. Katherine Hitchcock (1993–1994)
.... Stacy Haiduk
Lucas Wolenczak (age 16) .... Jonathan Brandis
Lt. (j.g.) Tim O'Neill.................... Ted Raimi
Sensor Chief Miguel Ortiz.......... Marco Sanchez
Chief Manilow Crocker (1993–1994)
.... Royce D. Applegate
Lt. Benjamin Krieg (1993–1994)..... John D'Aquino
Lt. James Brody (1994–1995) .... Edward Kerr
Dr. Wendy Smith (1994–1995) ...... Rosalind Allen
Tony Piccolo (1994–1995) .... Michael DeLuise
Dagwood (1994–1995).............. Peter DeLuise
Helmswoman Lonnie Henderson (1994–1995)
.... Kathy Evison
Capt. Oliver Hudson (1995)....... Michael Ironside
Lt. J. J. Fredericks (1995) .... Elise Neal

EXECUTIVE PRODUCERS:

Steven Spielberg
David J. Burke
Patrick Hasburgh

Movie magician Steven Spielberg must have watched *Voyage to the Bottom of the Sea* as a kid. *seaQuest DSV* was that classic series brought up to date, with all the technical wizardry of the 1990s. Roundly criticized by critics when it premiered ("the soggy *Supertrain*," "Voyage to the Bottom of the Ratings"), it nevertheless attracted a sufficient audience to stay afloat in the turbulent, competitive waters of Sunday night.

The time was 25 years in the future, and man had begun to populate the vast expanses of the oceans with undersea colonies and mines. A fragile peace was maintained by the United Earth/Oceans Organization, whose crown jewel was the highly advanced, 1,000-foot *seaQuest* Deep Submergence Vehicle. Captained by stolid Nathan Bridger, who had also designed it, it served both security and scientific purposes. In fact, the crew was divided between scientists and naval personnel, who were often at odds. Bridger's second in command was earnest Cdr. Ford; others included no-nonsense chief engineer Hitchcock, communications wizard O'Neill, sonarman Ortiz, crusty security chief Crocker, and conniving "appropriations expert" Krieg. Heading the scientific contingent, and giving Bridger as good as he gave, was determined pacifist Dr. Westphalen. The resident technogenius was a teenager, 16-year-old Lucas, who was discovering manhood and the next frontier of science at the same time. His best buddy was Ensign Darwin, a talking dolphin with a tank right inside the ship. (Well, even *Supertrain* had a swimming pool on board.)

Neat special effects abounded, such as the holographic "advisor" in Bridger's quarters. Still, at the end of the first season, the producers blew up the *seaQuest* (in "an oceanic catastrophe") in order to replace it with a redesigned and somewhat more intimate vessel. Several new crew members were added, including ESP-gifted Dr. Smith and genetically reengineered "gentle giant" Dagwood, the janitor. Lucas, who had become something of a teenage heartthrob to young viewers, was also prominently featured.

In the May 1995 season finale, the entire ship was transported to another planet and apparently destroyed, but in September it mysteriously reappeared on Earth ten years later, with its crew intact—they had not aged, and had no memory of their ordeal. The series was renamed *seaQuest 2032* to reflect the new setting. Captain Bridger retired to an island research post (although he kept in contact), and Captain Hudson assumed command of the mighty sub. His tour of duty was short, as the series was canceled at the end of the year. A few leftover original episodes aired as filler, seen on the West Coast only, during 1996.

SEARCH (*Adventure*)

FIRST TELECAST: *September 13, 1972*
LAST TELECAST: *August 29, 1973*

BROADCAST HISTORY:

Sep 1972–Aug 1973, NBC Wed 10:00–11:00

CAST:

Hugh Lockwood .... Hugh O'Bria
Nick Bianco.......................... Tony Francio

C. R. Grover .... Doug McClure
Cameron .... Burgess Meredith
Gloria Harding .... Angel Tompkins
Dr. Barnett (1972) .... Ford Rainey
Dr. Barnett (1973) .... Keith Andes
Miss Keach (1972) .... Ginny Golden
Ramos .... Tony De Costa
Kuroda .... Byron Chung
Griffin .... Albert Popwell
Carlos .... Ron Castro
Murdock .... Amy Farrell
Harris (1973) .... Tom Hallick
Miss James (1973) .... Pamela Jones

The Probe Division of World Securities had reached the ultimate in sophistication and technological development in equipping its agents as they traveled around the world on missions. Each agent had a transmitter and earphone implanted in one ear, enabling him to keep in constant contact with mission control. He also carried a miniaturized scanning device, in a ring or tie clip, that provided visual contact as well. The staff at mission control could maintain complete surveillance on whatever was happning to any of the agents. Hugh Lockwood, Nick Bianco, and C. R. Grover were the three agents whose exploits were shown, on a rotating basis, from week to week. Their assignments usually involved finding and/or protecting some valuable object or person, often with political implications. The control staff was headed by Cameron and included Gloria Harding, a telemetry specialist. Her function was to monitor the agents' vital signs. Mission control also provided the agents with computer support, status reports, warnings of impending danger, and the advice of the many experts on its permanent staff who were on hand to assist them.

SEARCH, THE (*Documentary*)

FIRST TELECAST: *July 12, 1955*
LAST TELECAST: *October 5, 1958*
BROADCAST HISTORY:
Jul 1955–Sep 1955, CBS Tue 10:30–11:00
Jun 1958–Oct 1958, CBS Sun 6:00–6:30
NARRATOR:
Charles Romine

Produced in cooperation with a number of American universities, this series spotlighted the research projects that were being carried out in such diverse fields as speech therapy, marriage counseling, automobile safety, and robotics. All of the episodes were filmed at the respective schools where the research was in progress. The series had actually premiered in October 1954 on Sunday afternoons before moving into prime time for the summer of 1955. All of the episodes aired in 1958 were reruns of the earlier series.

SEARCH FOR THE NILE, THE (*Historical Drama*)

FIRST TELECAST: *January 25, 1972*
LAST TELECAST: *February 29, 1972*
BROADCAST HISTORY:
Jan 1972–Feb 1972, NBC Tue 7:30–8:30
NARRATOR:
James Mason
[...]T:
Richard Burton .... Kenneth Haigh
[...]Hanning Speke .... John Quentin
[...]mes Grant .... Ian McCulloch
Dr. David Livingstone .... Michael Gough
Samuel Baker .... Norman Rossington
Florence Baker .... Catherine Schell
Henry Stanley .... Keith Buckley
Isabel Arundell Burton .... Barbara Leigh-Hunt
Sir Roderick Murchison ..... Andre van Gyseghem
Bombay .... Seth Adagala
King Mutesa .... Oliver Litonde

Filmed on location in Africa by the BBC, this miniseries chronicled the efforts of six mid-19th-century adventurers to trace the source of the Nile River. The six, all members of England's Royal Geographic Society, were explorer Sir Richard Burton; soldier-adventurer John Hanning Speke and his traveling companion, James Grant; missionary David Livingstone; sportsman Samuel Baker (who traveled with his wife); and American writer Henry Stanley. Most of the scenes were filmed as near as possible to the actual sites where the events had taken place and the scripts were adapted from the writings of the principal explorers.

SEARCHER, THE (*Comedy/Adventure*)

FIRST TELECAST: *July 11, 1993*
LAST TELECAST: *August 22, 1993*
BROADCAST HISTORY:
Jul 1993–Aug 1993, FOX Sun 7:30–7:45
CAST:
The Searcher .... Diedrich Bader

In this parody of wandering TV heroes, The Searcher traveled around the country attempting to help people being harassed or threatened. Dressed all in black and riding a powerful motorcycle, he looked cool but was unbelievably klutzy, constantly running into things on his motorcycle and miraculously staggering away unhurt. The Searcher got distracted by every beautiful woman he saw, and absurdly extreme close-ups were used to show his emotional reactions to everything. He narrated each episode in an incredibly deep voice. When he collected his fee at the end of each episode his phone number 1-800-SRCH-ME flashed on the screen.

The Searcher was one of the elements of FOX's *Danger Theatre*.

SECOND CHANCE (*Situation Comedy*)

FIRST TELECAST: *September 26, 1987*
LAST TELECAST: *July 2, 1988*
BROADCAST HISTORY:
Sep 1987–Oct 1987, FOX Sat 9:00–9:30
Oct 1987–Jan 1988, FOX Sat 9:30–10:00
Jan 1988–Apr 1988, FOX Sat 8:00–8:30
Apr 1988–Jul 1988, FOX Sat 8:30–9:00
CAST:
Charles Russell/Time (1987) .... Kiel Martin
Chazz Russell .... Matthew Perry
Helen Russell .... Randee Heller
Francis "Booch" Lottabucci .... William Gallo
Eugene Blooberman .... Demian Slade
St. Peter (1987) .... Joseph Maher
Debbie Miller (1988) .... Terri Ivens
Alex (1988) .... Adam Sadowsky

When *Second Chance* premiered it was a fantasy about a man caught between heaven and hell. Charles Russell died in the year 2011 in a hovercraft accident. When St. Peter attempted to determine where Charles's soul should be sent, he found that Mr. Russell was not good enough for heaven or bad enough for hell. To resolve the situation Charles was given a second chance—returning to earth 24 years earlier to provide moral guidance to his own younger self, under the watchful eye of St. Peter. Hopefully he could earn his way into heaven.

Charles assumed the last name Time (from the magazine), and rented the room over the garage at the Venice, California, home in which he had grown up. His divorced mother Helen, who thought he looked familiar, needed the money. The proximity to his younger self, Chazz, gave him plenty of opportunity to help the teenager become a more responsible adult than Charles had turned out to be. Chazz's best friends were Booch, a worldly wise, black-leather-jacketed womanizer reminiscent of *Happy Days*' Fonzie; and Eugene, an incredibly naive nerd.

Unhappy with the original format, the producers dropped the fantasy element and the original star, Kiel Martin. In January 1988 the series was retitled *Boys Will Be Boys* and the focus shifted to the escapades of the three teens—Chazz, Booch, and Eugene. Though still in high school, Chazz and Booch, whose alcoholic father had recently died, became roommates. They were living in that room over Mrs. Russell's garage (more shades of *Happy Days*) that Charles had lived in. Chazz also had a new girlfriend in perky, next-door neighbor Debbie Miller.

SECOND CHANCES (*Serial Drama*)

FIRST TELECAST: *December 2, 1993*
LAST TELECAST: *February 10, 1994*
BROADCAST HISTORY:
Dec 1993–Jan 1994, CBS Thu 10:00–11:00
Feb 1994, CBS Thu 12:35–1:45 A.M.

CAST:
Dianne Benedict .... Connie Sellecca
Mike Chulack .... Matt Salinger
Kate Benedict .... Megan Porter Follows
Melinda Lopez .... Jennifer Lopez
Salvador Lopez .... Pepe Serna
Cesar Lopez .... Daniel Gonzalez
Johnny Lopez .... John Chaidez
Pete Dyson (1994) .... John Schneider
Kevin Cook .... Justin Lazard
Felicity Cook .... Frances Lee McCain
George Cook .... Ronny Cox
Judge Jim Stinson .... Ray Wise
Joanna .... Michelle Phillips
Bruce Christianson (1993) .... Erich Anderson
Brian Christianson (age 8) .... Sean Fitzgerald
Det. Jerry Kuntz .... Ramy Zada
Officer Parker .... Chuck Bulot

THEME:
"Save the Last Dance for Me," sung by The Drifters (1960 recording)

The small California town of Santa Rita was the setting for this short-lived serial drama. In the opening episode public defender Dianne Benedict's husband, Bruce Christianson, was murdered in Parties Galore, the catering store owned and operated by Dianne's flighty younger sister, Kate. Dianne and Kate were only two of the suspects being investigated by Detective Jerry Kuntz. Also on the list were Joanna, Bruce's secretary, with whom he had been having an affair; Mike, Dianne's high school sweetheart who had just returned to Santa Rita to get his life back together after serving ten years in prison for manslaughter; and Judge Stinson, an unscrupulous local politician who was running for reelection against Dianne. In January it was discovered that Kuntz himself was the murderer. He had been involved in drug dealing, and Bruce had stolen drug money from his car. Secondary plots revolved around Melinda, a Mexican American coed with an overly protective father, whose marriage to socially prominent law student Kevin had been sabotaged by his father, George; the continuing social and business problems of Kate, who tooled around town in a vintage pink Cadillac; the evolving romance between Dianne and Mike; and the arrival of contractor Pete Dyson, who became partners with Dianne to try to save her late husband's construction business from going under and taking her home with it.

Second Chances was a series canceled by acts of God and nature. It was in production when the major Los Angeles earthquake in January 1994 destroyed most of its sets. By the time they could have been rebuilt two of its principal leads, Connie Sellecca and Megan Follows, would have been into the late stages of pregnancy. The timing was such that the producers decided to shut the show down for good. The last original episode aired as part of CBS' *Crimetime After Primetime* instead of in the series' regular Thursday-night time slot.

SECOND CITY TV (*Comedy*)

BROADCAST HISTORY:
Syndicated only
30 minutes
PRODUCED: *1977–1981* (78 episodes)
Released: *September 1977*

CAST:
Guy Caballero .... Joe Flaherty
Edith Prickly .... Andrea Martin
Moe Green (1977–1978) .... Harold Ramis
Johnny LaRue (1977–1979) .... John Candy
Earl Camembert .... Eugene Levy
Lola Heatherton/Lorna Minnelli (1977–1980)
.... Catherine O'Hara
Angus Crock/various famous stars .... Dave Thomas
Rabbi Karlov (1980–1981) .... Rick Moranis
Marcello (1980–1981) .... Tony Rosato
Molly Earl (1980–1981) .... Robin Duke

Second City TV was a TV parody on TV. Each program consisted of a group of sketches set at the "SCTV Studios," Channel 109, in which cast members did devastating takeoffs on quiz shows, farm reports, and anything else on the tube from *Ben Hur* to *Leave It to Beaver*, interspersed with commercials for sponsors such as "The Evelyn Wolf School of Speed Eating." Guy Caballero was the unlikely Argentinian station owner; Edith Prickly, the know-it-all manager (succeeding Moe Green, after the latter was kidnapped in 1978); Johnny LaRue, the inept features man; and Earl Camembert, the announcer-newscaster. Dave Thomas and Catherine O'Hara played an assortment of roles. For example, "Lee A. Iacocca's Rock Concert," a twin parody of *Don Kirshner's Rock Concert* and the financially troubled Chrysler Corp., featured Thomas as the host of a rock show which was three billion dollars over budget. Later additions to the cast included Marcello the cowboy star and Molly Earl with her crazy crafts.

The Second City troupe began as an improvisational-comedy theater company performing in a defunct Chinese laundry in Chicago in 1959 (it was so named because Chicago was America's "second city," after New York). A branch sprang up in Toronto, and it was the Toronto group that began the SCTV series in 1977. Second City alumni over the years have included such famous names as Valerie Harper, Alan Arkin, Joan Rivers, Mike Nichols and Elaine May, Robert Klein, David Steinberg, and *Saturday Night Live*'s Gilda Radner, John Belushi, and Dan Aykroyd.

Early in 1981 it was announced that SCTV was finally coming to network television, as part of NBC's late-night lineup—(see *SCTV Network 90*).

SECOND HALF (*Situation Comedy*)

FIRST TELECAST: *September 7, 1993*
LAST TELECAST: *April 12, 1994*
BROADCAST HISTORY:

Sep 1993–Dec 1993, NBC Tue 9:30–10:00
Mar 1994–Apr 1994, NBC Tue 8:30–9:00

CAST:

John Palmaro .... John Mendoza
Cathy Palmaro (age 14) .... Ellen Blain
Ruth Palmaro (9) .... Brooke Stanley
Robert Piccolo .... Wayne Knight
David Keller .... Joe Guzaldo
Denise Palmaro .... Jessica Lundy
Maureen .... Mindy Cohn

EXECUTIVE PRODUCER, COCREATOR:

John Mendoza

John Palmaro was a dumpy, absentminded sports columnist for *The Chicago Daily Post* who ambled through life issuing wisecracks. Newly divorced, he had reverted to his naturally slovenly ways and could often be found slouched in his sparsely furnished apartment watching TV, surrounded by empty pizza cartons. Though barely able to organize his new life, he nevertheless had weekend custody of his two daughters, self-absorbed Cathy and bright little Ruthie, which required at least a part-time show of parental responsibility. Fortunately his sensible sister Denise, a nurse, lived across the hall and helped out. Down at the office John pecked out his column, "The Second Half," and got plenty of free advice from self-assured editor Robert and bon vivant critic David. Maureen was John's chubby but eager assistant.

SECOND HUNDRED YEARS, THE (*Situation Comedy*)

FIRST TELECAST: *September 6, 1967*
LAST TELECAST: *September 19, 1968*
BROADCAST HISTORY:

Sep 1967–Feb 1968, ABC Wed 8:30–9:00
Mar 1968–Sep 1968, ABC Thu 7:30–8:00

CAST:

Luke Carpenter/Ken Carpenter ... Monte Markham
Edwin Carpenter .... Arthur O'Connell
Col. Garroway .... Frank Maxwell
Marcia Garroway .... Karen Black
Nurse Lucille Anderson .... Bridget Hanley

In the year 1900 Luke Carpenter, 33, bid farewell to his wife and his infant son Edwin and set out to prospect for gold in Alaska. He was lost in a glacier slide. Sixty-seven years later, by some freak of nature, Luke thawed out, revived, and was brought to the home of his now-aging son in Woodland Oaks, California. Chronologically Luke was 101, but he hadn't aged while in deep freeze and was physiologically still 33—younger than his own son.

In fact, he was younger in spirit, at least, than his 33-year-old grandson Ken, who was his exact look-alike (both parts were played by Monte Markham). Ken was stuffy and conservative, while Luke was ebullient, full of fun, and a rugged individualist.

The comedy centered both on the contrast between them and on Luke's problems in adapting to the modern world, while his origin was kept a military secret (Col. Garroway, an army doctor, was assigned to look after him). The first thing Luke had seen on awakening in Edwin's home was a 1967 TV set with what appeared to be little people aiming guns at him. He applied his simple, individualistic ways to the problems of the 20th century with some success, though he never could get used to a modern job.

SECOND NOAH (*Drama*)

FIRST TELECAST: *January 5, 1996*
LAST TELECAST: *August 10, 1997*
BROADCAST HISTORY:

Jan 1996–Apr 1996, ABC Mon 8:00–9:00
Jun 1996–Oct 1996, ABC Sat 8:00–9:00
May 1997–Aug 1997, ABC Sun 7:00–8:00

CAST:

Noah Beckett .... Daniel Hugh Kelly
Jesse Beckett .... Betsy Brantley
Ricky (age 17) .... James Marsden
Ben (Bing) .... Gemini
Danny (14) .... Jon Torgerson
Ranny (14) .... Jeremy Torgerson
Bethany (10) .... Zelda Harris
Hannah (10) .... Ashley Gorrell
Roxanna .... Erika Page
Luis .... Jeffrey Licon
Shirley Crockmeyer .... Deirdre O'Connell
Darby .... Joey Lauren Adams

THEME:

by Stephen Stills

Kids, animals, and love abounded in this gentle family drama, set in a big yellow house just outside Busch Gardens in Florida. Jesse was the chief veterinarian at the Busch animal park, and husband Noah a stay-at-home former basketball coach and writer. His first book had sold two million copies and he was now working on his second, to be called, appropriately, *The Ark*. Noah and Jesse loved to take in strays, animal or human, but particularly kids. They had eight adopted children, making househusband Noah a somewhat harried dad. Handsome Ricky was the oldest, already a single father to baby Ben; Danny and Ranny were the hell-raising twins; Bethany the uncertain young girl; and Hannah, Roxanna, and Luis the youngest. Shirley was the earthy, take-charge housekeeper, and Darby was Ricky's current girlfriend. Stories involved puppy loves, loose animals, growing up, and learning responsibility.

SECRET ADVENTURES OF JULES VERNE, THE (*Science Fiction*)

BROADCAST HISTORY:

Sci-Fi Channel and syndicated
60 minutes
Produced *1999–2000* (22 episodes)
Released: *January 5, 2001* (Sci-Fi); *October 2001* (syndication)

CAST:

Jules Verne .... Chris Demetral
Phileas Fogg .... Michael Praed

Rebecca Fogg .... Francesca Hunt
Passepartout .... Michael Courtemanche
Count Gregory..................... Rick Overton
Sir Jonathan Chatsworth............. Jonathan Coy

This stylish series assumed that the novels Jules Verne wrote later in life were based on the real-life adventures of his youth. When the series premiered, Jules was a boyish young dreamer studying law at La Sorbonne in Paris in the 1860s while seeking success as a writer. His visions of the future attracted the attention of the League of Darkness, a malevolent organization run by evil Count Gregory, an ancient being who had been given a mechanized form of immortality by a group of monks. The League kidnapped Jules but he was saved by Rebecca, a daring and athletic British Secret Service agent who had been sent to Paris in search of the machine the League was using to obtain information from Jules' mind. After the rescue, Jules and Rebecca joined forces—along with her often obnoxious cousin, retired secret agent Phileas Fogg—to fight vampires, ghosts, aliens, sorcerers and an Egyptian priestess who fed on human life energy. In one episode they even used a time machine to go back to the days of the Three Musketeers. Their principal mode of transportation was the airship *Aurora*, which Phileas had won in a game of cards. Passepartout, Phileas' manservant and the airship's navigator and engineer, could fix almost anything. The League of Darkness, despite being thwarted in its attempt to gain Jules' knowledge, was a constant menace, attempting to change the balance of power in the American Civil War, assassinate Queen Victoria, and pursuing Jules. Seen on a recurring basis was Sir Jonathan, Rebecca's superior in the Secret Service.

The Secret Adventures of Jules Verne originally aired in 2000 on Canada's CBC network.

SECRET AGENT (*International Intrigue*)

FIRST TELECAST: *April 3, 1965*
LAST TELECAST: *September 10, 1966*
BROADCAST HISTORY:
Apr 1965–Sep 1965, CBS Sat 9:00–10:00
Dec 1965–Sep 1966, CBS Sat 8:30–9:30
CAST:
John Drake..................... Patrick McGoohan
THEME:
"Secret Agent Man," by Phil Sloan and Steve Barri

John Drake was a special security agent working for the British government as a professional spy. He traveled throughout Europe on various cases and had the usual confrontations with enemy agents and beautiful women. His supposed function was to "preserve world peace and promote brotherhood and better understanding between people and nations." He was one of the more violent "peaceful" people seen on television during the 1960s. Somehow, preserving peace always demanded beating people up and shooting them. This series was produced in England and had been popular in Europe before its importation by CBS. Popular singer Johnny Rivers had a highly successful recording of "Secret Agent Man," the theme song which he sang over the opening titles of this series. *Secret Agent* was actually an expanded version of *Danger Man*, another British series. Patrick McGoohan played the same character in both.

SECRET AGENT MAN (*Foreign Intrigue*)

FIRST TELECAST: *March 7, 2000*
LAST TELECAST: *September 22, 2000*
BROADCAST HISTORY:
Mar 2000–Apr 2000, UPN Tue 8:00–9:00
May 2000–Sep 2000, UPN Fri 9:00–10:00
CAST:
Monk.......................... Costas Mandylor
Davis (Parker)................ Dondre T. Whitfield
Holiday.............................. Dina Meyer
Roan Brubeck .... Paul Guilfoyle
Helga Devereaux (Prima)......... Musetta Vander
THEME:
"Secret Agent Man," written by Phil Sloan and Steve Barri, performed by Supreme Beings of Leisure

Monk was a smart-alecky American secret agent in this rather lightweight update of the famous British series from the 1960s. He was a suave womanizer whose conquests always seemed to be interrupted by crises that called for his attention. Davis was Monk's nervous new partner, who described their employer, the Agency, as a secret arm of a covert organization that didn't exist. Holiday was a sexy but no-nonsense agent who frowned on Monk's sexual pursuits; Brubeck was their boss. Trinity was the evil organization, run by Jay, a brilliant young computer hacker, that Monk and his partners were constantly trying to thwart. Prima, a freelance spy who worked with Trinity, was a recurring villainess. She had once had an affair with Monk and still had a soft spot in her heart for him—almost.

Among the silly revelations in this tongue-in-cheek series were the fact that to help pay its bills, the Agency sold modified versions of its spy equipment on the Home Shopping Network, and that there were thousands of brainwashed Russian agents living in the U.S., all of whom were members of the Elks and thought they had been raised in Kansas.

SECRET DIARY OF DESMOND PFEIFFER, THE (*Situation Comedy*)

FIRST TELECAST: *October 5, 1998*
LAST TELECAST: *October 26, 1998*
BROADCAST HISTORY:
Oct 1998, UPN Mon 9:00–9:30
Oct 1998, UPN Mon 9:30–10:00
CAST:
Desmond Pfeiffer..................... Chi McBride
Abraham Lincoln..................... Dann Florek
Mary Todd Lincoln........... Christine Estabrook
Nibblet .... Max Baker
Ulysses S. Grant.................... Kelly Connell

Pfeiffer (the P was not silent) was the fictional butler in the Lincoln White House of the 1860s in this tasteless, bawdy comedy. Lincoln was played as a fool, his wife Mary Todd as a horny shrew. A drunken General Grant lurched about. The only person in the White House with any class was Desmond, a black nobleman from England who had fled to the States to avoid paying gambling debts and was working as butler/confidant to the President. His "diary" provided the material for the series. Nibblet was Desmond's ineffectual assistant, whom he had won at a county fair. The series seemed totally preoccupied with sex, and most of the jokes were loosely based on problems President Bill Clinton was having at the time over his extramarital dallying. In one episode Lincoln was having "telegraph sex" in the Oval Office (it turned out his secret lover was Mary) while paying little attention to the war effort. Desmond accused him of acting no better than a hillbilly from Arkansas (where are you, Mr. Clinton?).

Critics had crucified this series even before its premiere, and, living down to the horrible reviews and attracting a minuscule audience, it lasted less than a month on the air.

SECRET EMPIRE, THE (*Serial*)

FIRST TELECAST: *February 27, 1979*
LAST TELECAST: *May 1, 1979*
BROADCAST HISTORY:
Feb 1979–May 1979, NBC Tue 8:20–8:40
CAST:
Marshal Jim Donner .... Geoffrey Scott
Billy .... Tiger Williams
Millie .... Carlene Watkins
Jess Keller .... Peter Breck
Maya .... Pamela Brull
Princess Tara (Feb–Apr) .... Diane Markoff
Princess Tara (Apr–May) .... Stepfanie Kramer
Emperor Thorval .... Mark Lenard
Roe .... Peter Tomarken
Hator .... David Opatoshu
Yannuck .... Sean Garrison

This "cliff-hanger" serial was part science fiction and part Western. In the 1880s, Cheyenne Marshal Jim Donner was trying to track down a group of gold-shipment-stealing desperadoes known as the Phantom Riders, when he stumbled upon the entrance to the hidden underground city of Chimera. The people of Chimera were visitors from another planet, living in futuristic splendor marred only by the dictatorial rule of the evil Thorval. Thorval maintained control over his subjects with the use of the compliatron, a device that enslaved minds and was powered by the gold stolen by his soldiers. Thorval's daughter Tara was spoiled and self-indulgent, and his aide, Hator, almost as power-hungry as he. Struggling to free their people from the rule of Thorval was a group known as the Partisans, led by Roe and the beautiful Maya. Most of the folks around Cheyenne had no idea that they were neighbors of aliens. Only Donner's friends Millie and Billy knew, as did gold miner Jess Keller, who planned to provide Thorval with gold in exchange for an army of slaves with which to take over the surface world.

The daring marshal tried both to help the Partisans overthrow Thorval and to stop the gold robberies on the surface. In the last episode aired, in true cliff-hanger fashion, Donner was chased into the generator room in Chimera, where there was a power overload explosion. TO BE CONTINUED flashed on the screen but, since the series had been canceled, the audience never found out how or if he had survived.

The Secret Empire was one of three serials aired under the umbrella title *Cliff Hangers*. A nice touch, used only with *The Secret Empire*, was that all of the scenes around Cheyenne, on the surface of the Earth, were filmed in black-and-white, while in the futuristic world of Chimera everything was in color.

SECRET FILES OF CAPTAIN VIDEO, THE, see *Captain Video and His Video Rangers*

SECRET LIVES OF MEN, THE (*Situation Comedy*)

FIRST TELECAST: *September 30, 1998*
LAST TELECAST: *November 11, 1998*
BROADCAST HISTORY:
Sep 1998–Nov 1998, ABC Wed 9:30–10:00
CAST:
Phil .... Brad Whitford
Michael .... Peter Gallagher
Andy .... Mitch Rouse
Maria .... Sofia Milos

Three recently divorced Manhattan guys decided to deal with bachelorhood by doing a little serious male bonding in this sitcom. Phil was a sports manager, hard driving, sarcastic, and disdainful of "feelings"—or so he claimed; Michael was a straight arrow who renovated brownstones, but was constantly trying to live down the reputation of his shady contractor-father; and Andy was a rather dense, neurotic manufacturer of artificial fruits, a muscular black belt in martial arts who was deathly afraid of germs. On the golf course or at their favorite small midtown restaurant, run by understanding Maria, they whined about the unfairness of it all, the unreliability of women, how bad last night's date was, and how only guys understood. Yeah, yeah, said Maria.

SECRET SERVICE (*Docudrama*)

FIRST TELECAST: *August 16, 1992*
LAST TELECAST: *June 18, 1993*
BROADCAST HISTORY:
Aug 1992–Feb 1993, NBC Sun 7:00–8:00
Mar 1993–Jun 1993, NBC Fri 8:00–9:00
HOST:
Steven Ford

Re-creations of cases from the files of the government agency that is responsible not only for protecting government leaders but also for investigating other threats to the nation's security and economy. Host Steven Ford added recollections of his own experiences of being guarded by the Service when his father, Gerald Ford, was President.

SECRET WORLD OF ALEX MACK, THE (*Comedy/Adventure*)

BROADCAST HISTORY:
Nickelodeon
30 minutes
Produced: *1994–1998* (78 episodes)
Premiered: *October 8, 1994*
CAST:
Alexandra "Alex" Mack (age 13)..... Larisa Oleynik
Annie Mack...................... Meredith Bishop
George Mack .... Michael Blakely
Barbara Mack .... Dorian Lopinto
Raymond Alvarado (13) .... Darris Love
Danielle Atron..................... Louan Gideon
Vince Carter....................... John Marzilli
Dave Watt.......................... John Nielsen
Robyn Russo .... Natanya Ross
Nicole Wilson...................... Alexis Fields
Louis Driscoll (1995–1998) .... Benjamin Smith
Lars Fredrickson (1996–1998)....... Kevin Quigley

Fantasy comedy about a young girl living in the pleasant suburb of Paradise Valley who gained super powers when she was doused with a top-secret chemical in a freak accident. Bewildered Alex found herself able to levitate objects, set electrical appliances in operation by looking at them, even morph into a golden blob and escape through the pipes. Only two people knew of her powers: her brainy, bossy older sister, Annie, who constantly put Alex down but nevertheless looked after her and got her out of scrapes, and her best friend, Raymond, a saxophone-playing black classmate who was as immature as she was.

Super powers should have made junior high bearable, but Annie told her that if anyone found out about them she would be locked in a cage as a living experiment. So the powers had to be kept secret, which was not easy since Alex would sometimes glow or emit sparks when frightened. George was her amiable dad, who worked at the plant where the chemical was made, and Barbara her worrywart mom. Seen occasionally were Danielle Atron, the scheming plant executive responsible for the illegal chemical GC-161, and her henchman Vince, both of whom were determined to find the "mystery kid" who they knew had been doused.

In 1995, Alex gained a new friend in Louis, a wisecracking kid from Cincinnati, but did not immediately tell him about her powers. Robyn and Nicole were other pals. Annie became an intern at the chemical plant, looking for evidence to expose its illegal experiments, but Miss Atron and her flunky Vince (replaced by Lars in 1996) stayed one step ahead of her. Annie left for college in early 1997 and was seldom seen thereafter, leaving Alex, Ray, and Louis pretty much on their own. In the two-part finale, as the plant prepared to release the dangerous GC-161 to the public as a "weight loss drug," Alex's secret was discovered and she and her parents were taken prisoner in the fortified plant to prevent them from revealing the chemical's real effects. At the end Atron and Lars were exposed and arrested, and Alex had to decide whether to take an antidote to "cure" her of the effects of GC-161.

SECRETS OF MIDLAND HEIGHTS (*Drama*)

FIRST TELECAST: *December 6, 1980*

LAST TELECAST: *January 25, 1981*

BROADCAST HISTORY:

Dec 1980–Jan 1981, CBS Sat 10:00–11:00

CAST:

Dorothy Wheeler .... Bibi Besch
Guy Millington .... Jordan Christopher
Nathan Welsh .... Robert Hogan
Calvin Richardson .... Mark Pinter
Burt Carroll .... Lorenzo Lamas
Ann Dulles .... Doran Clark
Holly Wheeler .... Marilyn Jones
Lisa Rogers .... Linda Hamilton
John Grey .... Jim Youngs
Teddy Welsh .... Daniel Zippi
Danny Welsh .... Stephen Manley
Micki Carroll .... Melora Hardin
Margaret Millington .... Martha Scott
Lucy Dexter .... Jenny O'Hara
Mark Hudson .... Bill Thornbury
Eric Dexter .... Fred Weiss
Etta Bormann .... Bea Silvern
Max Bormann .... Gordon Clark
Serena Costin .... Erica Yohn
Sue .... Irene Arranga

Set in a sleepy Midwestern college town, this was another entry in the *Dallas*-inspired soap-opera boom of the early 1980s. The principal variation was an emphasis on the local teenage population, which led some to characterize this as the first "teenage soap." All the usual elements were there. Sex: rampant, with married people cheating on their spouses and the kids cheating on their boyfriends and girlfriends. Class struggle: the wealthy Millingtons ruthlessly maintained their power over the community. Power struggle: within the Millington family, devious Guy Millington manipulated people and events to make sure he would inherit the family fortune. Lack of an audience undid them all, as the series was canceled in less than two months.

SEE IT NOW (*Documentary*)

FIRST TELECAST: *April 20, 1952*

LAST TELECAST: *July 5, 1955*

BROADCAST HISTORY:

Apr 1952–Jun 1953, CBS Sun 6:30–7:00 (OS)
Sep 1953–Jul 1955, CBS Tue 10:30–11:00 (OS)

HOST:

Edward R. Murrow

See It Now was the prototype of the in-depth quality television documentary. It had started as a Sunday afternoon program on November 18, 1951. On that first telecast, Edward R. Murrow showed a live camera shot of the Atlantic Ocean, followed by a live shot of the Pacific Ocean, and then commented: "We are impressed by a medium through which a man sitting in his living room has been able for the first time to look at two oceans at once." The subject matter could be as serious as his famous essay on Senator Joe McCarthy or as light as an interview with painter Grandma Moses. Despite the fact that many of the personalities covered in this series could also have been on his other weekly series, *Person to Person*, the tone of *See It Now* was more serious and informative. The thing that distinguished *See It Now* was its penchant for taking controversial positions and dealing directly with major, and often unpopular, issues. In addition to his attacks on McCarthyism and the threat it posed in a free society, Murrow's documentaries detailed the recriminations of atomic scientist J. Robert Oppenheimer over the course of nuclear technology, and the relationship between cigarette smoking and cancer (despite the fact that Murrow himself was a chain smoker). His in-person visit to GIs on the front lines in Korea was a memorable telecast. Each broadcast ended with "Good night . . . and good luck."

Six months after its premiere, *See It Now* moved into the evening lineup, where it remained for more than three years. When it returned in the fall of 1955 it was no longer a weekly half-hour, but had become an irregularly scheduled hour. The longer format enabled more complete coverage of an issue. The last telecast of *See It Now* was on July 7, 1958. Murrow made occasional appearances on its successor, *CBS Reports.*

SEINFELD (*Situation Comedy*)

FIRST TELECAST: *May 31, 1990*

LAST TELECAST: *September 10, 1998*

BROADCAST HISTORY:

May 1990–Jul 1990, NBC Thu 9:30–10:00
Jan 1991–Feb 1991, NBC Wed 9:30–10:00
Apr 1991–Jun 1991, NBC Thu 9:30–10:00
Jun 1991–Dec 1991, NBC Wed 9:30–10:00
Dec 1991–Jan 1993, NBC Wed 9:00–9:30

Feb 1993–Aug 1993, NBC Thu 9:30–10:00
Aug 1993–Sep 1998, NBC Thu 9:00–9:30
Jan 1998–Sep 1998, NBC Wed 8:30–9:00

CAST:

Jerry Seinfeld .... Himself
Elaine Benes .... Julia Louis-Dreyfus
George Costanza .... Jason Alexander
Cosmo Kramer .... Michael Richards
**Helen Seinfeld* .... Liz Sheridan
Morty Seinfeld (1991–1998)* .... Barney Martin
**Uncle Leo (1991–1998)* .... Len Lesser
**Newman (1991–1998)*............... Wayne Knight
**Jack Klompus (1991–1997)* .... Sandy Baron
**Mr. Lippman (1991–1998)* .... Richard Fancy
**Russell Dalrimple (1992–1993)*........ Bob Balaban
**Susan Biddle Ross (1992–1997)* ... Heidi Swedberg
**"Crazy Joe" Davola (1992–1993)* ..... Peter Crombie
**Estelle Costanza (1992–1998)* .... Estelle Harris
**Frank Costanza (1993–1998)*........... Jerry Stiller
**Mickey Abbott (1994–1998)* ..... Danny Woodburn
**Justin Pitt (1994–1998)*........... Ian Abercrombie
**Kenny Bania (1994–1998)* .... Steve Hytner
**Dr. Tim Whatley (1994–1997)*...... Bryan Cranston
**Wilhelm (1995–1998)*................ Richard Herd
**David Puddy (1995–1998)* ...... Patrick Warburton
**J. Peterman (1995–1998)*............ John O'Hurley
**Jackie Chiles (1995–1998)*.............. Phil Morris

*Occasional
**Played by Phil Bruns in earliest episode

Standup comics were frequently cast in TV sitcoms in the 1990s; this one brought his regular stage act with him. Jerry Seinfeld portrayed himself as a young single comic in New York coping with dating, nutty friends, and the indignities of city life. Elaine was his ex-girlfriend and platonic pal, real estate agent George, his worrywart best friend, and eccentric entrepreneur Kramer, the next-door neighbor who wandered in and out of his apartment. Stories revolved around innocent little misadventures of love and life, which Jerry then commented on in his regular stage routine (which was seen in cutaways to a nightclub where Jerry was performing).

Seinfeld, the "show about nothing," gradually grew into an enormous hit on NBC and was the archetypal friends-hanging-out series of the 1990s. Although most of the stories were about life's trivia (waiting in line, forgetting where your car is parked, throwing out someone's prized *TV Guide*), there were occasional longer story arcs, such as George and Jerry's efforts in 1992–1993 to sell NBC a TV series based on . . . nothing. Others included George's job with the New York Yankees (1994–1997), in which Yankees owner George Steinbrenner was frequently heard but not seen; and his engagement to Susan (1995–1996), which ended, to his all-too-obvious relief, when she died after licking out-of-date cheap envelopes for their wedding invitations. Elaine originally worked as an editor at a publishing house; later (1995) she went to work as a copywriter for globetrotting catalog magnate J. Peterman.

Numerous recurring characters were seen, some quite memorable. Among them were Jerry's parents, Helen and Morty; George's folks, Estelle and Frank (who were as neurotic as he was); Newman, the malevolent postal worker; Elaine's bosses, Mr. Lippman and later Mr. Pitt; her hapless boyfriend, Puddy; her comical stalker, Crazy Joe; George's ill-fated girlfriend, Susan; his boss at the Yankees, Wilhelm; Jerry's ill-humored Uncle Leo; his pragmatic dentist, Tim; rival comedian Kenny; Kramer's pompous attorney Jackie Chiles; his short friend, Mickey; and the obsessed President of NBC, Russell, to whom Jerry and George pitched their pilot. The gang frequently hung out at Monk's diner. Memorable stories included "The Pez Dispenser"(1992); Elaine showing a bit too much of her breast on a Christmas card (1992); Jerry and the date (Susan Walters) whose name he could never remember—"it rhymes with a female body part" (1993); Jerry wearing a silly puffy pirate shirt on the *Today Show* (1993); the gang's experiences at a local soup restaurant run by the tyrannical "Soup Nazi" (1995); Kramer trying to smuggle in some "Cubans" (cigars), and instead getting a group of real Cubans—who turned out to actually be Dominicans (1997); and the "backwards episode" (1997), in which the scenes were shown in reverse order—first the final scene (a wedding in India!), then the scenes that led up to it, then the scenes that led up to that, and so on all the way back to thirteen years before the ceremony took place.

In December 1997, Jerry Seinfeld announced that he was quitting while he was on top—*Seinfeld* had been the number-one or number two program on TV for the previous four years. In the much-hyped final episode, on May 14, 1998, NBC was again interested in George and Jerry's fictional pilot. The network loaned them a private jet, and the gang was on the way to Paris for a quick holiday when the plane was forced to make an emergency landing in Latham, Massachusetts. While waiting for repairs, they witnessed a carjacking, which they of course made jokes about, resulting in their arrest under the town's new Good Samaritan Law because they "did nothing" to stop a crime. The incident quickly escalated into a *cause célèbre*, with Geraldo Rivera reporting live from the scene. Characters whom they had slighted over the past eight years came pouring into town, delighted to testify against them at their trial (particularly Newman, who could barely contain his glee). At the end they were convicted of crimes against common decency, and sentenced to a year in jail—where Jerry immediately began doing standup routines for the disinterested inmates. The self-centered protagonists on the "show about nothing" had received their comeuppance.

The pilot for the series was seen as a one time special on July 5, 1989, titled *The Seinfeld Chronicles.*

SEMINAR, see *Columbia University Seminar*

SEMI-TOUGH (*Situation Comedy*)

FIRST TELECAST: *May 29, 1980*
LAST TELECAST: *June 19, 1980*
BROADCAST HISTORY:

May 1980–Jun 1980, ABC Thu 9:30–10:00

CAST:

Billy Clyde Pucket .... Bruce McGill
Shake Tiller .... David Hasselhoff
Barbara Jane Bookman................ Markie Post
Big Ed Bookman .... Hugh Gillin
Big Barb .... Mary Jo Catlett
Burt Danby .... Jim McKrell
Coach Cooper............................ Ed Peck
Puddin............................ Bubba Smith
Story Time .... Freeman King

Billy Clyde and Shake were two hulking members of football's losingest team, the New York Bulls, who happened to share their apartment—platonically, of course—with a pretty young thing named Barbara Jane. This slapstick comedy was based on the novel by Dan Jenkins, which had previously been made into a hit movie starring Burt Reynolds.

SENATOR, THE (*Political Drama*)

FIRST TELECAST: *September 13, 1970*
LAST TELECAST: *August 22, 1971*
BROADCAST HISTORY:

Sep 1970–Aug 1971, NBC Sun 10:00–11:00

CAST:

Sen. Hayes Stowe .... Hal Holbrook
Jordan Boyle........................ Michael Tolan
Erin Stowe .... Sharon Acker
Norma Stowe..................... Cindy Eilbacher

Junior Senator Hayes Stowe was a very idealistic politician. His goals were the betterment of society and the environment in which we live. His affinity for getting involved with causes and issues of public concern did not endear him to the old-line professional politicians he had to deal with in Washington. In trying to resolve problems he often stepped on the toes of entrenched business interests with impressive political connections. With the help of Jordan Boyle, his administrative aide, and the support of his wife (Erin) and his daughter (Norma), Hayes relentlessly fought for what he believed was right and just.

The Senator was one of the three rotating elements that comprised *The Bold Ones* during the 1970–1971 season. The other two were *The New Doctors* and *The Lawyers.*

SENSELESS ACTS OF VIDEO (*Documentary*)

BROADCAST HISTORY:

MTV
30 minutes
Original episodes: *2000–2001*
Premiered: *January 27, 2000*

REGULARS:

Troy Hartman
Marisa Ramirez (2000)
Kimberly Pressler (2001)

Death-defying stunts seen in music videos, most of them computer-created special effects, were re-created in real life in this unusual series. Cars flipped, motorcycles leapt over barriers, people were set on fire or dived from airplanes, and a man was deprived of oxygen (that one from a Britney Spears video), among other things. All of this was quite dangerous, as chief stuntman Troy Hartman found out at the end of the first season when he flew a light plane close under a hovering helicopter, collided with it, and broke his neck. After many months in the hospital he returned for another season, but with new cohost Kimberly (original cohost Marisa, who had been with him in the plane, fled the show).

SENTINEL, THE (*Science Fiction/Police Drama*)

FIRST TELECAST: *March 20, 1996*
LAST TELECAST: *August 12, 1999*
BROADCAST HISTORY:

Mar 1996–Oct 1997, UPN Wed 8:00–9:00
Nov 1997–Mar 1998, UPN Wed 9:00–10:00
Apr 1998–Sep 1998, UPN Wed 8:00–9:00
Jan 1999–Jun 1999, UPN Mon 9:00–10:00
Jul 1999–Aug 1999, UPN Mon 8:00–9:00
Aug 1999, UPN Thu 8:00–10:00

CAST:

Det. Jim Ellison .... Richard Burgi
Blair Sandburg .... Garett Maggart
Capt. Simon Banks .... Bruce A. Young
**Capt. Joel Taggert* .... Ken Earl
**Det. Brown (1996–1998)*.............. Henri Brown
**Det. Rafe (1997–1998)*................. Ryf Van Rij
Megan Connor (1998–1999)........... Anna Galvin

*Occasional

Jim was a police detective working in Cascade, Washington. While serving as a captain in the army he had crashed in the Peruvian jungles, and come back to civilization eighteen months later as what the natives call a "sentinel." Jim had developed hypersensitive smell and hearing, precognition, and vision that enabled him to magnify things he was looking at. The drawback was that he had little control over when or where his hyperactive senses kicked in, and when they did, he ceased to be aware of his surroundings and was very vulnerable. From a police standpoint Jim's enhanced sensory awareness made him "a human crime lab with organic surveillance equipment." Blair, a shaggy-haired anthropology student interested in Jim's evolution into a sentinel, helped him adjust to his evolving senses. Capt. Banks gave Blair the title of "special consultant" to the police department so he could work with Jim. In November 1997, Cassie Wells (Lisa Akey), an enthusiastic young forensic specialist, joined the Cascade police. She only showed up a couple of times, and in late April 1998, Jim's new love interest was sexy Australian exchange detective, Megan Connor, with whom he was teamed.

In the last episode of the 1997–1998 season Jim was chasing down a professional thief (played by *Star Trek Voyager*'s Jeri Ryan) who, during a prison stretch in solitary confinement, had unleashed her own sentinel senses. But unlike Jim, she used them to further her illegal activities. At the end of the episode she had left Blair facedown in a pool near his office at the university, and the EMS people were unable to revive him. It was a cliffhanger finale, but since the show was not renewed by UPN, there was no immediate resolution. Viewer letters and a generally poor fall season motivated UPN to bring the show back in January 1999, and in the opener, Jim used his sentinel powers to bring Blair back to life. In the series finale Blair's mother accidentally gave his thesis on Jim's remarkable talents to a publisher friend and Jim became a public sensation. After too much publicity Blair held a press conference to announce that his thesis was fraudulent, to take the heat off Jim. Blair was tossed out of his graduate program but, in the last scene, was given the opportunity to become a real cop and Jim's fulltime partner.

SERENADE, see *Sing-Co-Pation*

SERGEANT BILKO, syndicated title for *Phil Silvers Show, The*

SERGEANT PRESTON OF THE YUKON (*Police Drama/Adventure*)

FIRST TELECAST: *September 29, 1955*

LAST TELECAST: *September 25, 1958*
BROADCAST HISTORY:
Sep 1955–Sep 1958, CBS Thu 7:30–8:00
CAST:
Sgt. Preston.................... Richard Simmons
THEME:
"Donna Diana Overture," by Emil Von Reznicek

"On, King! On, you huskies," he cried, and Sergeant Preston was off across the snow to single-handedly enforce law and order on Canada's frozen frontier. The time was the turn of the century, and the place was the Yukon Territory, where thieves and scoundrels preyed upon the gold miners and settlers who had come to open up the wilderness. Aided only by his remarkably intelligent malamute dog, Yukon King, and his black horse, Rex, Preston represented the long arm of the Royal Northwest Mounted Police. He cut a splendid figure in his smart red uniform (even in black-and-white!), his broad-brimmed hat, and his pencil-thin mustache.

The series was filmed in color in mountainous sections of California and Colorado, against a spectacularly scenic backdrop. It was widely seen in reruns, including a season on Saturday afternoons on the NBC network in 1963–1964.

Sergeant Preston had originated on radio in 1947, and was created by George W. Trendle and Fran Striker (who were also responsible for the Lone Ranger and the Green Hornet). It continued on radio until 1955.

SERPICO (*Police Drama*)
FIRST TELECAST: *September 24, 1976*
LAST TELECAST: *January 28, 1977*
BROADCAST HISTORY:
Sep 1976–Jan 1977, NBC Fri 10:00–11:00
CAST:
Frank Serpico .... David Birney
Tom Sullivan......................... Tom Atkins

Frank Serpico was a New York City cop who may have been too idealistic for the system through which he had to work. He often went undercover to track down drug dealers, break up numbers racket operations, and cut down the illegal traffic in weapons. He was also very involved in efforts to prove that various police officers and officials, some in very high places, were on the take from organized crime. Tom Sullivan was a full-time undercover agent who worked with Frank and was his contact with the police when he was on an undercover assignment.

There was a real Frank Serpico, on whose career this series was based. His search for, and exposure of, corruption in the New York City Police Department did not endear him to his fellow officers, many of whom expressed their hatred of him as a "troublemaker." On February 3, 1971, he was shot in the face by a dope pusher, and he subsequently retired from the force on a disability pension. He left with a profound sense of disillusionment and a permit to carry a gun for his own protection, possibly from other police personnel. He later was the subject of a book titled *Serpico* which was the story of his experiences as a police officer. The book was made into a movie of the same name, starring Al Pacino, and that, in turn, was the basis for this series.

SERVING THROUGH SCIENCE (*Instruction*)
FIRST TELECAST: *June 18, 1946*
LAST TELECAST: *May 27, 1947*
BROADCAST HISTORY:
Jun 1946–May 1947, DUM Tue 9:00–9:30 (approx.)
HOST:
Dr. Guthrie McClintock (also given as Dr. Miller McClintock)

This was an early experiment in educational programming, consisting of short films from the Encyclopedia Britannica with discussion by Dr. McClintock and guests. The setting was Dr. McClintock's study. Shortly after the program began, *Television* magazine conducted a poll of its readers that indicated that while everyone thought the presentation worthwhile, some found it to be rather boring. ("It made us very sleepy," wrote one respondent.) So the sponsor added a musical segment with performances by promising young artists, which had nothing whatever to do with the subject at hand but was supposed to "liven things up." This mishmash lasted only a few weeks before the program was finally dropped.

As with some other early programs, it is not known whether *Serving through Science* was fed over the network from the beginning, though it was on the network by the beginning of 1947 at the latest. Sponsor U.S. Rubber had presented similar educational TV shows locally in New York in 1945 and perhaps earlier.

SESSIONS, see *Chicago Jazz*

SEVEN AT ELEVEN (*Comedy/Variety*)
FIRST TELECAST: *May 28, 1951*
LAST TELECAST: *June 27, 1951*
BROADCAST HISTORY:
May 1951–Jun 1951, NBC Mon/Wed 11:00–Midnight
REGULARS:
George De Witt
Sid Gould
George Freems
Sammy Petrillo
Dorothy Keller
Jane Scott
Denise Lor
Betty Luster & Jack Stanton
Jackie Loughery
Herbie Faye
Milton Delugg & His Sextet

Short-lived live comedy variety series originating from New York.

SEVEN BRIDES FOR SEVEN BROTHERS (*Adventure*)
FIRST TELECAST: *September 19, 1982*
LAST TELECAST: *July 2, 1983*
BROADCAST HISTORY:
Sep 1982, CBS Sun 8:00–9:30
Sep 1982–Mar 1983, CBS Wed 8:00–9:00
Jun 1983–Jul 1983, CBS Sat 8:00–9:00
CAST:
Adam McFadden .... Richard Dean Anderson
Daniel McFadden (age 18) .... Roger Wilson
Crane McFadden (21) .... Peter Horton
Brian McFadden (25)............. Drake Hogestyn
Ford McFadden (15) .... Bryan Utman
Evan McFadden (16) .... Tim Topper

Guthrie McFadden (12) .... River Phoenix
Hannah McFadden...................... Terri Treas
Marie .... Joan Kjar

ORIGINAL MUSIC:
by Jimmy Webb

There was singing and dancing, hootin' and hollerin' in this lively, updated revival of the hit 1954 MGM movie classic. While the movie was set on the frontier, this series took place in contemporary times, as a parentless family of boys tried to go it alone on a ranch in northern California. Only the eldest brother, 27-year-old Adam, was married, and his new bride, Hannah, faced the unmanageable task of living with this rowdy, unkempt houseful of brothers. Fortunately, Hannah was high-spirited herself, and got their attention the first day by dumping an entire table full of food in their laps. Besides hijinks around the house, stories revolved around struggles to keep the ranch solvent, personal squabbles, and romances. Despite all the singing, dancing, and romancing, none of the other six McFadden brothers found a bride during the one season *Seven Brides for Seven Brothers* was on the air.

SEVEN DAYS (*Science Fiction*)

FIRST TELECAST: *October 7, 1998*
LAST TELECAST: *August 14, 2001*
BROADCAST HISTORY:
Oct 1998–Apr 2001, UPN Wed 8:00–9:00
Jul 1999–Aug 1999, UPN Mon 9:00–10:00
May 2001–Jun 2001, UPN Tue 8:00–9:00
Jun 2001–Aug 2001, UPN Tue 8:00–10:00

CAST:
Frank Parker .... Jonathan LaPaglia
Capt. Craig Donovan .... Don Franklin
Dr. Isaac Mentnor .... Norman Lloyd
Olga Vukavich.......................... Justina Vail
Dr. John Ballard (1998–2000) .... Sam Whipple
Nate Ramsey .... Nick Searcy
Bradley Talmadge .... Alan Scarfe
Andy "Hooter" Osley (2000–2001) ... Kevin Christy

Parker was a former C.I.A. agent who had had a breakdown after being tortured in Somalia by enemies of the U.S. He was in a psychiatric hospital on a remote island when he was recruited by a secret government agency to be the guinea pig in Operation Backstep, a top-secret project that potentially allowed people to travel back through time. Their device, harvested from UFO technology from a flying saucer that had landed at Roswell, New Mexico, in 1947, enabled him to go back seven days before a major event and undo it. Parker was bright, had a photographic memory, an incredibly high pain threshold, and, most important, was expendable. The process worked, but it was a decidedly unpleasant, jarring experience ("You may lose a thin layer of skin"). In the first episode, Parker surfaced on the fringes of Las Vegas due to temporal displacement, although he was supposed to be in Washington to prevent the assassination of the president (by late October they were working on a navigational system to control where his capsule landed). The following week he headed off a mutated ebola virus that would have otherwise wiped out 98 percent of Earth's population. The seven day limit in time travel was a function of the amount of power that could be generated with the reactor used to activate the machine.

Others regulars were Donovan, a friend of Parker's and his backup time traveler; Mentnor, the avuncular head of the Backstep team in Nevada; Vukavich, a Russian member of the team to whom Parker was attracted; Ballard, the wheelchair-bound genius technician who worked on the kinks in the system; Ramsey, the short-tempered government representative who hated Parker; and Talmadge, the project's wavering government coordinator. Conundrum was the code word Parker used when he called them after going back in time, to let them know a mission from the future was in progress. They then picked him up and started working with him to prevent the calamity he had been sent back to stop.

In February 2000 Parker was coping with "time burps" that enabled him to "rerun" and make changes in the time line that he failed to achieve the first time around. In this episode it was postulated that he was still in a mental hospital and that Backstep and its staff were all figments of his deranged imagination. By late spring Olga was softening up and showing a little romantic interest in him, but it never blossomed. That fall Mentnor was gone (he made a few guest appearances during the season) and Ballard was on the way out. In November Ballard videophoned from a South Pacific island that he had won in a poker game in Vegas. He was there with two sexy young women—he had gotten married while drunk and wasn't sure which of the two was his wife. Ballard had recommended Andy, a brilliant but eccentric young mathematician (I.Q. 240) and former student, as his temporary replacement.

700 CLUB, THE (*Newsmagazine/Religion*)

BROADCAST HISTORY:
Syndicated/CBN/The Family Channel
2 hours/90 minutes
Produced: *1972–*
Premiered: *1972* (syndicated); *1977* (CBN)

REGULARS:
Pat Robertson (1972–)
Ben Kinchlow (1975–1988, 1992–1996)
Danuta Rylko Soderman (1983–1987)
Tim Robertson (1987–1988)
Susan Howard (1987–1988)
Sheila Walsh (1989–1992)
Terry Meeuwsen (1993–)
Lee Webb (1994–)
Lisa Ryan (1997–)
Gordon Robertson (1999–)
Kristi Watts (1999–)

One of the most unique, and longest-running, programs in prime time, *The 700 Club* was essentially a cross between a newsmagazine and a talk show, with an underlying religious theme. Slickly produced, it began with news reports from reporters around the world, much like those on network newscasts. This was followed by commentary by the hosts (usually from a conservative point of view), interviews with prominent newsmakers, and inspirational features about people overcoming adversity. Sometimes there were entertainment features as well, such as talent competitions à la *Star Search*. Explicitly religious segments usually appeared toward the end; these included Bible readings, moments of prayer (during which the studio audience held hands), and even low-key "miraculous healings." Commercials consisted of appeals for membership and promotion of the show's free counseling line for those in distress ("Bringing hope to a hurting world").

During later years the program was telecast first during the morning, in a 90-minute version, then rerun in prime time and in the late night as an hour.

The 700 Club had a long and colorful history. It was begun by Marion G. "Pat" Robertson in 1966 as the outgrowth of a 1963 telethon on his small, struggling UHF religious station in Virginia. Robertson, the son of a U.S. senator, had turned to religion in the late 1950s and wanted to use the station to promote his fundamentalist views. Costs had risen to a (then) staggering $7,000 per month, so he went on the air and asked 700 viewers to pledge $10 per month to keep the station going. Although he only got half that, *The 700 Club* was born.

From 1966 to 1972 the daily show, seen locally, was hosted by evangelist Jim Bakker. In 1972 it was syndicated to other stations and Robertson himself took over as host. A new, much slicker format was instituted, patterned after *The Tonight Show*; Robertson interviewed guests before a backdrop of a city skyline at night, and there was even a band. The length was cut from two hours to 90 minutes in 1974. Viewers might not realize what they were watching until the host turned to prayer, exhorting people to kneel down in front of their TV sets and ask God to heal them!

In 1977 *The 700 Club* became the cornerstone of the new CBN cable network, fed to cable systems across the U.S. (while continuing on many broadcast stations). In 1980 it switched to a more news-oriented format, with a set resembling a comfortable den and the hosts in easy chairs. Determined to be more accessible than the usual "preacher and pulpit" religious shows, Robertson even threatened to sue *TV Guide* for categorizing his program as "religion" rather than "news" or "features." More than 300,000 viewers were now donating $15 per month.

Robertson cut back his appearances during 1987–1988 while campaigning for President, and his son Tim Robertson took over along with actress Susan Howard *(Dallas)*. Pat's longtime sidekick, a tall, distinguished-looking black preacher named Ben Kinchlow, also left for a time but returned in the early 1990s. In later years the principal cohost was former Miss America Terry Meeuwsen. In 1993 the first half hour of the show was turned over to news coverage and Pat became more and more the elder statesman and commentator, always with his trademark smile and friendly chuckle. Today *The 700 Club* airs on more than 200 broadcast stations as well as on CBN successor The Fox Family Channel.

704 HAUSER (*Situation Comedy*)
FIRST TELECAST: *April 11, 1994*
LAST TELECAST: *May 9, 1994*
BROADCAST HISTORY:
Apr 1994–May 1994, CBS Mon 8:30–9:00
CAST:
Ernie Cumberbatch .... John Amos
Rose Cumberbatch .... Lynnie Godfrey
Thurgood Marshall "Goodie" Cumberbatch
.... T. E. Russell
Cheryln Markowitz .... Maura Tierney

If the address sounded familiar it was for good reason. More than two decades after the premiere of *All in the Family* this ghostly echo of that trail-blazing show appeared on the CBS schedule. There was now a black family living in Archie Bunker's old home on Hauser Street in Queens, New York. Ernie Cumberbatch, an auto mechanic, was a blustery, outspoken liberal who had been actively involved in the civil rights movement of the 1960s. He had even named his only child, Goodie, after his idol, the first black member of the Supreme Court. Much to Ernie's chagrin, college student Goodie had turned out to be a politically active conservative. Not only that, but his girlfriend, Cheryln, was idealistic, outspoken, white, and Jewish. Ernie and Goodie disagreed about political and social issues as well as Goodie's inability to find a black girlfriend. Rose, Ernie's religious wife, was forever trying to keep them from coming to blows. Sound familiar? Joey Stivic, son of Gloria and Meathead, even showed up in the premiere episode.

For executive producer Norman Lear this was a return to his series roots. He took out ads in newspapers imploring viewers to watch the series and write CBS to keep it on the air, but low ratings resulted in cancellation after a five-week spring tryout.

SEVENTH AVENUE (*Drama*)
FIRST TELECAST: *February 10, 1977*
LAST TELECAST: *February 24, 1977*
BROADCAST HISTORY:
Feb 1977, NBC Thu 9:00–11:00
CAST:
Jay Blackman .... Steven Keats
Rhoda Gold .... Dori Brenner
Myrna Gold .... Anne Archer
Joe Vitelli .... Herschel Bernardi
Harry Lee .... Alan King
Marty Cass .... John Pleshette
Eva Meyers .... Jane Seymour
Al Blackman .... Kristoffer Tabori
Celia Blackman .... Anna Berger
Morris Blackman .... Mike Kellin
Frank Topo .... Richard Dimitri

Adapted from Norman Bogner's novel, *Seventh Avenue* was the story of Jay Blackman, a poor young man from New York's Lower East Side who succeeded in becoming a major force in the garment industry in the 1940s and 1950s. His rise to power from humble beginnings and involvements with organized crime as well as his marital problems and affairs were all chronicled.

Seventh Avenue was one of four novels dramatized under the collective title *NBC's Best Sellers*.

7TH HEAVEN (*Drama*)
FIRST TELECAST: *August 26, 1996*
LAST TELECAST:
BROADCAST HISTORY:
Aug 1996– , WB Mon 8:00–9:00
May 1998–Jun 1998, WB Mon 9:00–10:00
Aug 1998–May 1999, WB Sun 7:00–8:00
Sep 1999–Nov 1999, WB Sun 7:00–8:00
Nov 1999–Dec 1999, WB Mon 9:00–10:00
Jan 2000–Sep 2000, WB Sun 7:00–8:00
CAST:
Rev. Eric Camden .... Stephen Collins
Annie Jackson Camden .... Catherine Hicks

Matt Camden (age 16) (1996–2002) .. Barry Watson
Mary Camden (14) (1996–2002) .... Jessica Biel
Lucy Camden (12) .... Beverley Mitchell
Simon Camden (10)............... David Gallagher
Ruthie Camden (5) .... Mackenzie Rosman
Jimmy Moon (1996–1998)........ Matthew Linville
**Wilson West (1997–1999, 2001–2002)*
.... Andrew Keegan
**Grandpa (Charles Jackson) (1996–2003)*
.... Graham Jarvis
**Sgt./Det. Michaels*............ Christopher Michael
**Rev. Morgan Hamilton (1996–2001)*
.... Dorian Harewood
**Patricia Hamilton (1996–2000)* ...... Olivia Brown
**John Hamilton (1996–2001)*
.... Chaz Lamar Shepherd
**Keisha Hamilton (1996–1999)*..... Gabrielle Union
**Lynn Hamilton (1996–1999)* ..... Camille Winbush
**Nigel Hamilton (1996–1999)*.......... David Netter
Rod (1998–1999) .... Rick Scarry
Jordan (1998–1999)............... Wade Carpenter
Shauna (1998–2000).......... Maureen Flannigan
Deena Stewart (1998–2001) .. Nicole Cherie Saletta
Robbie Palmer (1999–2002)....... Adam LaVorgna
Sam and David Camden (1999)
.... Bryce and James Braxmeyer
Sam and David Camden (1999–2001)
.. Lorenzo, Myrinda, Nikolas and Zachary Brino
Sam and David Camden (2001–)
.... Nikolas and Lorenzo Brino
**Dr. Hank Hastings (1999–)*......... Ed Begley, Jr.
**Andrew Nayloss (1999–2000)* .... Will Estes
**Cheryl (2000–)* .... Barret Swatek
**Mike Pierce (2000–2002)*........... Jeremy Lelliott
**Priscilla Carter (2000–2001)*....... Andrea Pearson
Luke (2000–2001) .... Michael Canavan
**Jeremy (2001–2002)* .... David Lago
**Billy West, Jr. (2001–2002)* .... Mike Weinberg
**Joy Reyes (2001–2002)* .... Joy Enriquez
Ben Kinkirk (2001–)................. Geoff Stults
Kevin Kinkirk (2002–) .... George Stults
Sarah Glass (2002)........ Sarah Danielle Madison
Rabbi Richard Glass (2002) .... Richard Lewis
Rosina Glass (2002)............. Laraine Newman
Roxanne Richardson (2002–)
.... Rachel Blanchard
Cecilia (2002–) .... Ashlee Simpson
**George (2002–)* .... Brad Maule
Chandler Hampton (2002–) ..... Jeremy London
**Paris Petrowski (2002–)*......... Shannon Kenny
Peter Petrowski (2002–)..... Scotty Leavenworth

*Occasional

For producer Aaron Spelling, who had populated prime time with a succession of sexy serial dramas from *Dynasty* in the 1980s to *Melrose Place* in the 1990s, this wholesome drama about a loving family was quite a departure. It may have been a throwback to the 1950s, with a non-working housewife mother and children who actually liked and respected their siblings and parents, but for its loyal viewers it was an oasis of normalcy in a TV desert full of dysfunctional and ever more hostile families. Despite the occupation of its lead character, *7th Heaven* managed to deal with subjects like drugs, spousal abuse, teen pregnancy, personal morals, racial and ethnic prejudice, and family relationships, without being preachy.

Eric Camden, the minister of the Glen Oak Community Church in suburban Los Angeles, had a wife, Annie, and five children. Dreamboat Matt, the oldest, was a high school junior trying to assert his independence while suffering from raging hormones. His siblings were Mary, a sociable basketball jock just starting to date; Lucy, sensitive, adventurous, and adjusting to the onset of puberty; Simon, bright, good natured, and outgoing; and cute little Ruthie, who seemed willing to do whatever her brothers and sisters asked of her but later turned out to be a bit manipulative. Rounding out the household was Happy, a cute little mutt Annie got for Simon in the series premiere. Many of the episodes focused on the social lives of the Camden teenagers. During the first season Lucy spent a lot of time with classmate Jimmy Moon, but they broke up at the end of the school year; Matt got involved with a deaf girl, who went away to school and found another guy; and Mary was dating semi-geeky Wilson, an unwed father raising his young son at his parents' home.

That fall, Eric and Annie renewed their vows on their nineteenth wedding anniversary. In the spring Matt, a senior, convinced his folks to let him go to the University of Tennessee but changed his mind and decided to go to local Crawford University. At the end of the season Annie found out she was pregnant. As the 1998–1999 season began, Annie's doctor told her she was carrying twins. In November Grandpa married his girlfriend Ginger (Beverly Garland). The twins, David and Samuel, were born on Valentine's Day and their arrival seriously disrupted life for everyone in the Camden household. Lucy's boyfriends included Rod and Jordan, while Matt was dating Shauna, an old girlfriend who was back in his life.

In September 1999 Matt moved into an apartment with John Hamilton. He and John took part-time jobs working at a local hospital—Matt in the cafeteria and John running the AV department. In November Mary got into trouble when she and her basketball teammates trashed the gym after their coach suspended the season because their grades had fallen off. She was arrested, lost her scholarship and was put into a diversionary program with lots of counseling. After Thanksgiving Shauna was accepted to a pre-med program at N.Y.U.; she moved to New York in January. Robbie, a manipulative guy Mary had met in the diversionary program, professed his love but was actually two-timing her. In the spring Shauna found out from Mary that Matt had been seeing Heather, who was back in town and going to college, and broke up with him. Later Matt became an orderly at the hospital and gave up his job in the cafeteria. At season's end Mary decided to move in with Robbie (she didn't), Matt was torn between Heather and Shauna (but believed he loved Heather) and Deena decided she and Simon should see other people (which was a cover for the fact that she was moving back east).

At the start of the 2000–2001 season Lucy was starting her senior year, Simon was starting high school and Heather and Matt, who had almost gotten married, broke up. Mary, out of school and having problems holding on to a job, got into financial trouble. Her circumstances made her moody and belligerent, and she fought with her parents. Everything came to a head when her failure to pay bills, lies about her job status, drinking and stealing from the family to get money forced them to ship her off to Eric's parents in Buffalo to get her act together. In late November Robbie, the guy Mary had dated after rehab, became a regular. His parents had left town, and the Camdens took him in; in late January he got a job at a day-care center. When John's girlfriend Priscilla lost her apartment she moved in with him—and Matt moved back home. Mary came home for a weekend and made everyone uncomfortable, especially Robbie, who didn't want to be involved with her because he had gotten attached to the rest of the family. In May Mary returned home for the summer; Lucy proposed to her boyfriend, Jeremy, so that they could be together in the fall going to school in New York; Matt admitted to the family that he was dating Cheryl (Robbie's ex), and Robbie was trying to keep his distance from Mary. Wilson, whom Mary had been dating in Buffalo, showed up to profess his love for her, and John and Priscilla got married.

That fall Matt was laid off at the hospital, took a job at a local free clinic and decided he wanted to become a gynecologist. Lucy returned from New York after having broken up with Jeremy; and Mary, back in Buffalo and planning to marry Wilson (they broke up), started training to become a firefighter. Robbie rented the newly built room over the Camden garage and was in love with Joy, a professional singer with a wealthy father. Mary returned to Glen Oak, and when she started college, she and Lucy were taking some of the same courses. Matt and fellow clinic worker Sarah, both of whom had been accepted to Columbia Medical School, fell madly in love. Since she was Jewish, neither his nor her parents were happy about it, but they eloped anyway. They told the families they were engaged and, for the sake of the happy couple, as the wedding approached the Camdens and the Glasses tried to became friends. In the season finale Eric and Richard performed a joint wedding ceremony and the "newlyweds" headed off to New York. Meanwhile, Mary had decided to move back to Buffalo to become a flight attendant and date Ben, a firefighter she had met during her training, and Lucy went out with his brother, Kevin, a Buffalo cop. Kevin was so taken with her that he moved to Glen Oak and got a job on the local police department.

As the 2002–2003 season started, Robbie was no longer living with the Camdens; Kevin was renting the apartment over the Camden garage. He planned to marry Lucy, who was insanely jealous of his sexy rookie partner, Roxanne. Mary had moved to Ft. Lauderdale and was dating an older pilot, while Simon was becoming more involved with Cecilia, who had just been a friend. In October Eric had heart bypass surgery and, while he was recovering, the church hired young Chandler as a new associate pastor. Despite his apathy toward returning to the pulpit, Eric was convinced the church elders wanted to replace him permanently. In January Chandler started dating Roxanne, which gave Lucy some relief, and Eric was seeing a therapist. On Valentine's Day Kevin proposed to Lucy—who obviously accepted—and Chandler was close to proposing to Roxanne. With her wedding approaching, Lucy convinced Eric to return to the ministry so he could perform the service, which he did in April.

Reruns of the first season's episodes were aired on Sundays during the 1998–1999 season under the title *7th Heaven Beginnings*.

77 SUNSET STRIP (*Detective Drama*)

FIRST TELECAST: *October 10, 1958*
LAST TELECAST: *September 9, 1964*
BROADCAST HISTORY:

Oct 1958–Oct 1959, ABC Fri 9:30–10:30
Oct 1959–Sep 1962, ABC Fri 9:00–10:00
Sep 1962–Sep 1963, ABC Fri 9:30–10:30
Sep 1963–Feb 1964, ABC Fri 7:30–8:30
Apr 1964–Sep 1964, ABC Wed 10:00–11:00

CAST:

Stuart Bailey .... Efrem Zimbalist, Jr.
Jeff Spencer (1958–1963) .... Roger Smith
Gerald Lloyd Kookson III ("Kookie") (1958–1963) .... Edd Byrnes
Roscoe (1958–1963) .... Louis Quinn
Suzanne Fabray (1958–1963) ...... Jacqueline Beer
Lt. Gilmore (1958–1963) .... Byron Keith
Rex Randolph (1960–1961) .... Richard Long
J. R. Hale (1961–1963) .... Robert Logan
Hannah (1963–1964) .... Joan Staley

THEME:

"77 Sunset Strip," by Mack David and Jerry Livingston

77 Sunset Strip was the prototype for a rash of glamorous private-detective teams in the late 1950s and early 1960s. Half the team was Stu Bailey, a suave, cultured former OSS officer who was an expert in languages. An Ivy League Ph.D., he had intended to become a college professor but turned private investigator instead. The other half was Jeff Spencer, also a former government undercover agent, who had a degree in law. Both of them were judo experts. They worked out of an office at No. 77 Sunset Strip, in Hollywood, though their cases took them to glamour spots all over the world.

Next door to No. 77 was Dino's, a posh restaurant whose maître d', Mario, was seen occasionally in the series. Seen often was Dino's parking lot attendant, a gangling, jive-talking youth named Kookie, who longed to be a private detective himself and who often helped Stu and Jeff on their cases. Kookie provided comic relief for the series, and his "Kookie-isms" became a trademark. For example: "the ginchiest" (the greatest); "piling up the Z's" (sleeping); "keep the eyeballs rolling" (be on the lookout); "play like a pigeon" (deliver a message); "a dark seven" (a depressing week); and "headache grapplers" (aspirin).

Other regulars included Roscoe the racetrack tout and Suzanne the beautiful French switchboard operator. But it was Kookie who caught the public's fancy and propelled the show into the top ten. In the first telecast of the 1959–1960 season he helped Stu Bailey catch a jewel thief by staging a revue, in which he sang a novelty song called "Kookie, Kookie, Lend Me Your Comb" (after his habit of constantly combing his hair). The song was released on record as a duet between Byrnes and Connie Stevens, and became a smash hit. Byrnes soon began to overshadow the series' principals as a popular celebrity, a kind of "Fonzie" of the 1950s.

Unsatisfied with his secondary role in the show, the young actor demanded a bigger part and eventually walked out. Warner Bros. at first replaced him with Troy Donahue as a long-haired bookworm, about as far from the Kookie character as you could get. But Byrnes came back a few months later and was promoted to a full-fledged partner in the detective firm at the start of the 1961–1962 season. His permanent replacement at the parking lot was J. R. Hale. Previously, for a single season, Rex Randolph had been seen as a third partner in the firm.

Kookie was not the only one who tried parlaying the show's success into a hit record. Following his example, actor Roger Smith put out an album called *Beach Romance* (which bombed), and even Efrem Zimbalist, Jr., who was no singer but who had perhaps the best musical background of the lot (he was the son of a famous concert violinist and a famous opera singer), was lured into a studio to record "Adeste Fideles" in English and Latin. Also, the finger-snapping theme music from the series was made into a best-selling album.

By 1963 the novelty had worn off and the show was in decline. In an attempt to save it, Jack Webb was brought in as producer, and William Conrad as director, and drastic changes were made. The entire cast was dropped with the exception of Efrem Zimbalist, Jr., who became a free-lance investigator traveling around the world on cases. Lavish production values were featured. The season opened with a five-part chase-thriller featuring two dozen big-name guest stars and written by eight top writers. Stu Bailey was seen pursuing operatives of a gigantic smuggling ring across two continents. The rest of the season was spent on the road as well, with Stu acquiring a permanent secretary named Hannah, but it didn't help.

Reruns of *77 Sunset Strip* were seen during the summer of 1964.

77TH BENGAL LANCERS, THE, see *Tales of the 77th Bengal Lancers*

SEX AND THE CITY (*Situation Comedy*)

BROADCAST HISTORY:

Home Box Office
30 minutes
Original episodes: *1998–*
Premiered: *June 6, 1998*

CAST:

Carrie Bradshaw .... Sarah Jessica Parker
Samantha Jones .... Kim Cattrall
Charlotte York McDougal .... Kristin Davis
Miranda Hobbes .... Cynthia Nixon
Mr. Big .... Chris Noth
**Stanford Blatch* .... Willie Garson
**Steve Brady (1999–)* .... David Eigenberg
**Aidan Shaw (2000–)* .... John Corbett
**Dr. Trey McDougal (2000–)* .... Kyle MacLachlan
**Richard Wright (2001–)* .... James Remar

*Occasional

Four beautiful Manhattan women in their mid-30s found sex easy to come by, but love harder to find, in this adaptation of the best-selling book by Candace Bushnell. The ringleader, Carrie, was a svelte blonde with long, flowing locks who wrote a column for the *New York Star* on the late-night party and sex scene in New York. "Carrie Bradshaw knows good sex," the column read, so of course she did her research, which apparently meant sleeping with every eligible bachelor in the city. Her three best friends were Samantha, a public relations executive who preferred one-night stands to a lasting relationship, Charlotte, an art gallery curator looking for Mr. Right, and Miranda, a lawyer with a sometimes eccentric taste in men. All were catty, self-absorbed, and constantly gossiping about their latest conquests—and their worries that they might never find the "right one."

Carrie thought she had found the right one in the devastatingly charming Mr. Big, and their on-and-off romance was a thread that ran throughout the series. After too many letdowns from the emotionally unavailable Big, she took up with furniture designer Aidan, which led to an awkward triangle—even though Big had in the meantime married Natasha (Bridget Moynahan). Stanford was Carrie's gay pal and confidant. Samantha ran through a constant stream of men (Charlotte to Sam: "Is your vagina listed in New York guidebooks? It should be. Hottest spot in town! Always open!"), even trying lesbian Maria. Client Richard was her longest-standing relationship. Charlotte finally married Dr. Trey, only to discover he had impotence problems and a nutty mom (played by Frances Sternhagen). Miranda had a fling with Skipper, then conceived a baby by bartender Steve. She considered an abortion—babies did not fit these women's lifestyle—but instead gave birth, as a single mom, to baby Brady.

The emphasis on casual sex hardly fit the cautious 1990s, but the foursome's constant worries about fitting in, growing old, self-fulfilment, and female empowerment obviously struck a chord (Samantha: "The only place you can control a man is in bed. If we perpetually gave men blow jobs, we could run the world"). Although it appeared on the premium cable network HBO, seen in only about one-third of U.S. homes, *Sex and the City* was a major hit and trendsetter in the 1990s and early 2000s, and for that reason is included in this book.

SEX WARS (*Quiz*)

BROADCAST HISTORY:

Syndicated only
30 minutes
Produced: *2000–2001*
Released: *October 2000*

EMCEES:

J. D. Roth
Jennifer Cole

This noisy battle-of-the-sexes quiz show pitted a team of three women against a team of three men. The first round, Land Mine, consisted of asking the guys "girl questions," and the girls "guy questions." Each team was given two questions and four possible answers to each, three of which were correct. Picking a correct answer was worth five points, but picking the wrong answer gave points to the other team.

The next round, The List, consisted of two questions that had been asked of visitors to the show's Web site (For example, "What is your favorite daytime talk show?"). The goal here was to see how many of the top 10 answers they could name. The team with the highest number got 10 points for each correct answer, but if one team stumbled the other could steal points by coming up with one of the remaining answers (shades of *Family Feud*).

The nine questions for the third round were taken from statistics or public opinion polls—all with the answer "men" or "women." The first eight were each worth 10 points and the last one was worth 25. An incorrect answer gave the points to the other team. Each team gambled at least half its points on the final question.

There were three categories; a team got to pick the category for the other team's question. The winning team received $2,500.

SHA NA NA (*Musical Variety*)

BROADCAST HISTORY:

Syndicated only
30 minutes
Produced: *1977–1981* (97 episodes)
Released: *September 1977*

MEMBERS OF SHA NA NA:

Jon "Bowzer" Bauman
Lennie Baker
Johnny Contardo
Frederick "Dennis" Greene
"Dirty Dan" McBride (1977–1980)
John "Jocko" Marcellino
Dave "Chico" Ryan
"Screamin' Scott" Simon
Tony Santini (Scott Powell)
Donald "Donny" York

OTHER REGULARS:

Avery Schreiber (1977–1978)
Pam Myers
Kenneth Mars (1977–1978)
Phil Roth (1977–1978)
Jane Dulo
June Gable (1978–1981)
Soupy Sales (1978–1981)
Karen Hartman (1980–1981)
Michael Sklar (1978–1979)

This exuberant mixture of 1950s good-time rock 'n' roll and cornball comedy sketches was one of the surprise hits of the late 1970s. The setting was a city street, and the 10 members of Sha Na Na all played variations on the dumb-but-lovable 1950s "greaser"—like Fonzie on *Happy Days*—with ducktail haircuts, leather jackets, or hairy chests under cutaway undershirts. The emcee and unofficial leader was Bowzer, who would strike a pose and flex imaginary muscles in his skinny arm, while grinning with a mouthful of crooked teeth.

The jokes were awful and the comedy skits usually silly, but done with infectious enthusiasm. The boys performed energetically, and obviously didn't take anything or anybody too seriously, which helped make this a very appealing half hour. *TV Guide* said, "They seem like nothing so much as ten little boys—average age late 20s—having fun in Hollywood." Each had his own personality. Bowzer was the smarter-than-he-looks leader; Lennie, the jolly, bearded sax player; Johnny, the sexy, baby-faced Italian; Denny Greene, the only black; Dirty Dan, another youthful goodlooker; Jocko, chunky and a bit on the crazy side; Chico, a handsome, macho type; Screamin' Scott, the balding piano player who looked a bit like Elton John; Santini, also balding and on the heavy side (he used to be called Captain Outrageous, and before that Scott Powell); and Donny, the spaced-out guy in dark glasses.

When they launched into an upbeat oldie like "At the Hop" or "Book of Love," there might be cut-ups, but they were definitely not mocking the music. "They have a lot of fun," said singer Bobby Vee after doing the show, "but they're doing the music of the 50s in the spirit it was intended." And when sexy Johnny did a dreamy ballad like "Our Day Will Come"—well, girls in the audience just wet their pants.

Helping out were all sorts of guests, from Phyllis Diller and Ethel Merman to Dr. Joyce Brothers (who offered to give the boys psychiatric counseling). Many were authentic 1950s rock artists such as Chuck Berry, Bo Diddley, Freddy Cannon, the Shirelles, Chubby Checker, and Brenda Lee. A backup cast of comics, including Pam Myers, the gum-chewing dizzy blonde, was also seen.

Sha Na Na was founded in 1969 by 12 Columbia University students, who did a cappella oldies first on campus, and then in professional engagements. The group was first called the Kingsmen, then changed their name to avoid confusion with another group with the same name (the one that recorded "Louie, Louie"). Sha Na Na—the name came from the background chant in a 1950s hit by the Silhouettes, called "Get a Job"—was a surprise hit with the spaced-out, acid-rock generation, scoring a major triumph at Woodstock in the summer of 1969. However, since they did only other people's hits, the novelty soon began to wear off and they were in decline when their manager pushed them into television—and a whole new comedy/rock career. Only four of the group's original members remained by then—Greene, Marcellino, Santini, and York. Thorough professionals, but still kids at heart, they closed each week with the slogan, "Grease for peace!"

SHADETREE MECHANIC, THE (*Instruction*)

BROADCAST HISTORY:

The Nashville Network
30 minutes
Produced: *1992–2000*
Premiered: October 4, 1992

HOST:

Dave Bowman
Sam Memmolo

A weekend instructional series on TNN providing tips for the do-it-yourself automotive enthusiast.

SHADOW CHASERS (*Comedy/Fantasy*)

FIRST TELECAST: *November 14, 1985*
LAST TELECAST: *January 16, 1986*
BROADCAST HISTORY:

Nov 1985–Jan 1986, ABC Thu 8:00–9:00

CAST:

Prof. Jonathon MacKensie .... Trevor Eve
Edgar (Benny) Benedek .... Dennis Dugan
Dr. Juliana Moorhouse .... Nina Foch

Ghosts, zombies, graverobbers, and nutty curses filled this obvious but unacknowledged ripoff of the hit comedy movie *Ghostbusters*. The young parapsychology investigators in this case were Prof. MacKensie, an anthropologist with the Georgetown Institute of Science, and Benny, a wisecracking reporter for the tabloid *The National Register* (and you thought they made that stuff up!). Dictatorial Dr. Moorhouse, who worked in a dark, cluttered cave of an office, sent them off on their missions to neutralize the spirits among us.

SHADOW OF THE CLOAK (*International Intrigue*)

FIRST TELECAST: *June 6, 1951*
LAST TELECAST: *April 3, 1952*
BROADCAST HISTORY:

Jun 1951–Nov 1951, DUM Wed 9:30–10:00
Dec 1951–Apr 1952, DUM Thu 9:00–9:30

CAST:

Peter House......................Helmut Dantine

Helmut Dantine, who played the arrogant Nazi in many Hollywood films during the 1940s, starred as the chief agent of International Security Intelligence in this espionage series. He tangled with an assortment of spies, traitors, and other international villains. Despite scripts by a number of notable writers, including Mel London and a young Rod Serling, the series disappeared in less than a year. During its last three months it alternated with *Gruen Playhouse*.

SHADOW THEATER (*Documentary*)

BROADCAST HISTORY:

USA Network
30 minutes
Produced: *1990* (13 episodes)
Premiered: *April 1, 1990*

HOST:

Robert Englund

Interviews and clips from horror films, both classic and contemporary, hosted by Robert Englund, who was best known as murderous Freddy Krueger in the *Nightmare on Elm Street* movies.

SHAFT (*Detective Drama*)

FIRST TELECAST: *October 9, 1973*
LAST TELECAST: *August 20, 1974*
BROADCAST HISTORY:

Oct 1973–Aug 1974, CBS Tue 9:30–11:00

CAST:

John Shaft....................Richard Roundtree
Lt. Al Rossi..............................Ed Barth

THEME:

"Theme from 'Shaft,' " by Isaac Hayes

John Shaft was a flamboyant, streetwise black private detective working in New York City, although his cases often took him far from the "Big Apple." Smooth, imperturbable, and deadly efficient, he was sought out by all sorts of people when they needed help. His source of information, when he needed it, was police lieutenant Al Rossi, with whom he had a friendly working relationship.

Shaft was one of three elements that rotated in the Tuesday 9:30–11:00 P.M. time period on CBS during the 1973–1974 season. The other two were *Hawkins* and *The New CBS Tuesday Night Movies*. Richard Roundtree brought John Shaft to television after a series of highly successful theatrical features in which he had played the part. The theme for the television series was written for the first *Shaft* movie, and had won composer Hayes an Academy Award.

SHAKY GROUND (*Situation Comedy*)

FIRST TELECAST: *December 13, 1992*
LAST TELECAST: *July 4, 1993*
BROADCAST HISTORY:

Dec 1992–Jul 1993, FOX Sun 7:30–8:00

CAST:

Bob Moody..........................Matt Frewer
Helen Moody..........................Robin Riker
Carter Moody (14)...............Matthew Brooks
Bernadette Moody (13).......Jennifer Love Hewitt
Dylan Moody (7)...................Bradley Pierce
Russell..........................Harold Sylvester
Arthur Dannenberg....................Alex Nevil
Harry..................................Tony Longo

Bob Moody worked as a quality-control inspector for United General Technologies, a Los Angeles company in the aerospace business. Recently passed over for the supervisor's job, he had quit but was persuaded to come back by his new boss, obnoxious Arthur Dannenberg. Although he had to keep a low profile at work, which was often difficult since he knew more than the much younger Dannenberg, Bob let it all out when he got home. Fortunately his wife, Helen, was used to dealing with his sarcasm and frustrations and his three kids were too preoccupied with their own lives to pay much attention to Dad's grousing. Russell was an engineer who was Bob's primary confidant at work, and Harry was a beefy worker on the United General Technologies assembly line.

SHANE (*Western*)

FIRST TELECAST: *September 10, 1966*
LAST TELECAST: *December 31, 1966*
BROADCAST HISTORY:

Sep 1966–Dec 1966, ABC Sat 7:30–8:30

CAST:

Shane..........................David Carradine
Marian Starett..........................Jill Ireland
Tom Starett..............................Tom Tully
Joey Starett....................Christopher Shea
Rufe Ryker..............................Bert Freed
Sam Grafton..........................Sam Gilman

The 1953 Western movie *Shane* is considered one of the classics of the cinema. It was the story of a young boy's idolization of a wandering gunfighter who stops to help the boy's family but who must, in time, move on. In the poignant final scene he did, as the boy (played by Brandon De Wilde) cried out, "Shane . . . come back!"

Shane did come back, for a few months anyway, in this 1966 TV version starring David Carradine as the silent, brooding gunfighter and Christopher Shea as the eight-year-old rancher's son, Joey. Marian Starett was recently widowed and was having a difficult time protecting her homestead against the ravages of nature and of the vicious rancher Ryker. It was the classic confrontation between the cattle ranchers who first claimed the land (Ryker) and the homesteaders who followed (the Staretts). Though Shane was there to help them in their battle, the Staretts knew that he might at any time move on. Tom, Marian's father-in-law, and Sam Grafton, the saloonkeeper, were the only other regulars.

SHANNON (*Police Drama*)

FIRST TELECAST: *November 11, 1981*
LAST TELECAST: *April 7, 1982*
BROADCAST HISTORY:

Nov 1981–Dec 1981, CBS Wed 10:00–11:00
Mar 1982–Apr 1982, CBS Wed 10:00–11:00

CAST:

Det. Jack Shannon..................Kevin Dobson
Det. Norm White................William Lucking
Lt. Moraga........................Michael Durrell
Inspector Schmidt....................Bruce Kirby
Johnny Shannon....................Charlie Fields
Paul Locatelli..............................Al Ruscio
Irene Locatelli....................Karen Kondazian

Following the untimely death of his young wife, N.Y.P.D. plainclothes detective Jack Shannon moved to San Francisco with his ten-year-old son, Johnny. The move served two purposes—it provided a change of scene to help him get over his grief and, since his wife's parents (the Locatellis) lived there, it gave him some assistance in the raising of Johnny. With the help of some of his former superiors in New York (which fostered initial resentment) Jack obtained a position with the S.F.P.D. Special Squad of Investigators. Norm White was his partner and Lt. Moraga was their immediate superior.

SHANNON'S DEAL (*Legal Drama*)

FIRST TELECAST: *April 13, 1990*
LAST TELECAST: *May 21, 1991*
BROADCAST HISTORY:

Apr 1990, NBC Fri 9:00–11:00
Apr 1990–May 1990, NBC Mon 10:00–11:00
Aug 1990, NBC Fri 9:00–10:00
Apr 1991–May 1991, NBC Tue 10:00–11:00

CAST:

Jack Shannon .... Jamey Sheridan
Lucy Acosta .... Elizabeth Pena
Neala Shannon .... Jenny Lewis
Wilmer Slade .... Richard Edson
D.A. Todd Spurrier .... Miguel Ferrer
**Lou Gondolf* .... Martin Ferrero

*Occasional

THEME:

by Wynton Marsalis

Jack Shannon was a little less Perry Mason-esque than your average TV lawyer. His personal and professional lives were a mess. Once a high-profile partner in a prestigious Philadelphia law firm, he had dropped out, disillusioned, after years of litigating on behalf of undeserving corporate clients. His loss of income, combined with a compulsive gambling habit, had cost him his marriage. Now a "failure" by the standards of his former world, scraping by on small cases in his own small walkup practice, he was determined to pursue the law on his own, more ethical, terms.

Lucy was his pushy but protective secretary, working off the debt she had incurred when Jack defended her boyfriend; Neala was Jack's precocious teenage daughter, who mothered him mercilessly; and Wilmer, the classics-quoting "collector" sent around by the loan shark to whom Jack owed money. Lou was a shyster lawyer.

Some notable people worked on this series behind the scenes, which won the admiration of critics, if not of viewers. The series was created by film writer/director John Sayles; scripts were provided by leading film writers; the legal consultant was noted Harvard law professor and bestselling author Alan Dershowitz (*Reversal of Fortune*); and contributing to the score were a number of prominent jazz artists, including Wynton Marsalis (who wrote the theme), Dave Grusin, Chick Corea, and Lee Ritenour.

SHAPING UP (*Situation Comedy*)

FIRST TELECAST: *March 20, 1984*
LAST TELECAST: *April 17, 1984*
BROADCAST HISTORY:

Mar 1984–Apr 1984, ABC Tue 9:30–10:00

CAST:

Buddy Fox .... Leslie Nielsen
Ben Zachary .... Michael Fontaine
Shannon Winters .... Jennifer Tilly
Melissa McDonald .... Shawn Weatherly
Zoya Antonova .... Cathie Shirriff

Buddy Fox was a graying but physically fit health-club owner who served the sweat-band set with the help of an athletic young manager, Ben, and two curvaceous aerobics instructors, Shannon and Melissa. Despite ample displays of pulchritude in motion, the series quickly died.

SHASTA MCNASTY (*Situation Comedy*)

FIRST TELECAST: *September 30, 1999*
LAST TELECAST: *August 15, 2000*
BROADCAST HISTORY:

Sep 1999, UPN Thu 9:30–10:00
Oct 1999, UPN Tue 8:30–9:00
Nov 1999–Jan 2000, UPN Tue 8:00–8:30
Jan 2000–Feb 2000, UPN Tue 9:00–9:30
May 2000–Aug 2000, UPN Tue 8:00–8:30

CAST:

Scott .... Carmine Giovinazzo
Dennis .... Jake Busey
Ran .... Dale Godboldo
Diana (pilot only) .... Mary Lynn Rajskub
Diana .... Jolie Jenkins
Verne Valentine .... Verne Traylor

Semi-sensible Scott, very dumb Dennis, and goofball Ran were the members of the hip-hop music group Shasta McNasty in this offbeat series that used some of the same free-form film techniques and slapstick elements as the 1960s series *The Monkees*. They lived in an apartment at Venice Beach, California, and had been buddies since first grade. The guys were preoccupied with sex—there were lots of scenes with sexy girls in bikinis on the beach and their crude observations about them. Diana was their platonic friend and neighbor. Scott, the "thinker," talked directly to viewers about the action on the show.

When the show moved into its 9:00 P.M. time slot in January, the title had been shortened to *Shasta*, but nothing else had changed; they were still a band trying to get their big break. In February Verne, a midget occasionally seen (and frequently humiliated) in the fall, returned and bought the bar where the guys spent much of their free time, and renamed it Captain Vern's (yes, it was spelled differently from his name). When *Shasta* returned in late May with new episodes, the guys were working at the bar for Verne and playing there as well. In July Diana, who was about to leave for a new job in New York, kissed Scott good-bye, and they had a passionate revelation of their mutual affection for each other.

The last episode was done as a documentary episode of *Behind the Band 2010*. After their early success Scott had become a spaced-out existentialist and Diana, whom he had married, was pregnant, while Dennis went off the deep end, spending a fortune and doing drugs. When their third album flopped they switched to a new look and new sound, but it didn't help; they each tried solo careers, which didn't help, either. In 2004 they reunited, went back to their original sound, and were a hit all over again. The money from their successful tour gave them the freedom to pursue other interests. Dennis had gotten into puppetry (he was horrible); Ran, who had changed his professional name to DJ I Smoka, was still making music; and Scott and Diana, looking like aging hippies, were performing at clubs along the Las Vegas Strip.

SHE SPIES (*Espionage*)
NETWORK HISTORY:
FIRST TELECAST: *July 20, 2002*
LAST TELECAST: *August 3, 2002*
BROADCAST HISTORY:
60 minutes
Produced: *2002–*
Released: *September 2002*
Jul 2002, NBC Sat 10:00–11:00
Aug 2002, NBC Sat 8:00–9:00
CAST:
Cassie McBain .... Natasha Henstridge
Deedra "D. D." Cummings .... Kristen Miller
Shane Phillips.................. Natashia Williams
Jack Wilde .... Carlos Jacott

This was an unabashed send-up of the 1970s hit series *Charlie's Angels.* Three sexy ex-cons had been released from prison and recruited by a secret government agency to fight crime. Cassie, their tough leader, was as brilliant as she was beautiful, a career con artist who had slipped up once and been sent to prison because of it. Her partners were sweet, almost childlike D. D., a stunning high-tech nerd whose appearance belied her ability to hack into computers and crack code with the best of them, and street-smart Shane was the muscle of the group who, when given the choice, would much rather use force than guile. Bumbling, ineffectual Jack was supposed to be their boss, and he had his rules and policies, but regardless of how much he complained, they did pretty much as they pleased. As long as they got the bad guys nobody cared.

She Spies was not above making fun of itself. In one early episode the girls ran onto the set of a TV show about three beautiful girl spies who had been released from prison to work for a secret government agency—sound familiar? Cassie was even heard saying that they were "ex-cons working for a clandestine government organization trying to rid the world of evildoers." They crashed through windows without getting a scratch, engaged in big kick-'em-sock-'em fights and spouted all sorts of inside pop-culture jokes ("At the risk of more exposition, what are you doing here?"; "Shane, come back!"; and, after a particularly loud crash, "That's my Nielsen box, you cow!"). In addition, from time to time, in comic-book fashion, cynical text observations popped up on the screen. Even the promotional material for the show made fun of it. One of the ads said, "Every once in a while, an elite crime fighting team emerges—a highly sophisticated covert ops, specially trained in global intelligence maneuvers. This is not one of those teams."

She Spies was previewed on NBC before its syndicated run. Apparently viewers didn't get the joke; although it was supposed to run for a month, minuscule Nielsen ratings prompted NBC to pull it after only three weeks.

SHE TV (*Comedy/Variety*)
FIRST TELECAST: *August 16, 1994*
LAST TELECAST: *September 6, 1994*
BROADCAST HISTORY:
Aug 1994–Sep 1994, ABC Tue 10:00–11:00
REGULARS:
Nick Bakay
Carl Banks
Jennifer Coolidge
Elon Gold
Linda Kash
Simbi Khali
Becky Thyre
Linda Wallem

Sketch comedy, billed as "from the women's point of view." Subjects included the usual range of movies and celebrities, and the treatment was neither feminist nor male-bashing, which is perhaps why it all seemed rather routine.

SHEENA (*Adventure*)
BROADCAST HISTORY:
Syndicated only
60 minutes
Produced: *2000–2001* (35 episodes)
Released: *October 2000*
CAST:
Sheena............................ Gena Lee Nolin
Matt Cutter .... John Allen Nelson
Kali .... Margo Moorer
Mendelsohn........................ Kevin Quigley
Rasheed............................ Veryl Jones

This updated version of the campy 1950s series was, if possible, even sillier than the original. Sheena was a sexy, scantily clad, super-smart babe whose parents had been killed in the jungle when she was young, and who had lived with the animals and become one with them. When she grew up she dedicated herself to protecting the animals and native people of the jungle. Not only could she communicate with the animals, but she could morph into them as well. Kali, the shaman of the tribe with whom she lived, was Sheena's mentor.

New to Sheena's world was Matt, who ran an air taxi service that provided charter tours and shipped merchandise. Some guys he had taken into the remote jungle had tried to kill him, and sexy Sheena had morphed into a gorilla and scared them off. She and Matt became friends and she always seemed to be around when he needed her help, which was often. He fantasized about a more intimate relationship (as no doubt did some viewers), but had no more luck than Trader Bob in the 1950s. There were episodes about smugglers, poachers, an attempted corporate land takeover, illegal game hunting, tribal disputes, treasure hunting, and an infestation of killer ants. Mendelsohn, Matt's scruffy, cynical sidekick, had a pet white cockatoo and a vulture. Rasheed was the local constable. In a February 2001 episode Sheena found out from an adventurer that her real name was Cheryl Hamilton.

Ratings were as skimpy as Sheena's outfit, and production of the series was shut down halfway through the second season. Filmed in Florida.

SHEENA, QUEEN OF THE JUNGLE (*Adventure*)
BROADCAST HISTORY:
Syndicated only
30 minutes
Produced: 1955–1956 (26 episodes)
Released: 1955
CAST:
Sheena............................ Irish McCalla
Bob .... Christian Drake

Sheena had something for everyone. For kids, it was full of jungle excitement, with wild animals and brave heroes battling the bad guys. For adults, it was so trite it was absolutely hilarious, a cliché-ridden parody on *Tarzan*. For boys just entering adolescence—well, Sheena, with her voluptuous figure and skimpy leotard, was something else entirely.

The setting was Kenya, where statuesque Sheena played White Goddess and protector to the beasts and natives. Since she couldn't manage the Tarzan yell, she carried a hunting horn to ward off danger. Her pet chimpanzee was named Chim (played by Neal the Chimp), and Bob was her trader friend. Robbers and interlopers turned up regularly, often capturing Bob. Always, he would get rescued by Sheena. And that's all he got.

The series was shot in Mexico, where some of Sheena's tree-swinging stunts were actually done by men in wigs. The series was based on the popular comic strip created by S. M. Iger and Will Eisner in the late 1930s.

Whatever happened to Sheena? Irish McCalla made a few B-movies in the late 1950s and early 1960s, and then became a successful painter.

SHEEP IN THE BIG CITY (*Cartoon*)

BROADCAST HISTORY:
Cartoon Network
30 minutes
Original episodes: *2000–2002* (27 episodes)
Premiered: *November 17, 2000*

VOICES:
Sheep, Gen. Specific, Ranting Swede ... Kevin Seal
Farmer John, Pvt. Public .... James Godwin
Ben Plotz (The Narrator) .... Ken Schatz
Angry Scientist .... Mo Willems

In this absurdist cartoon a rather worried-looking sheep found himself on the lam (ahem) from a crazed general who wanted to use him as part of the firing mechanism of a new gun he was building. Sheep fled the idyllic farm of sensitive Farmer John (so sensitive he had therapy sessions for his herd) to hide in the big city. Bewildered and put-upon, he looked for an apartment and a job. Chasing him were broad-shouldered, blowhard Gen. Specific, leader of the Secret Military Organization, his right-hand man Pvt. Public, and Angry Scientist, the brains behind the SMO, who screamed a lot. The show was filled with puns and sight gags; for example, the "Attack of the 50 Foot Creature" featured a creature with 50 feet; a Complimentary Sandwich complimented people. Episodes ended, for no particular reason, with a ranting Swede. All of this nonsense was described in Gary Owens–like tones by The Narrator, who appeared both on and off screen and who complained about the writing of the episode.

SHEILAH GRAHAM IN HOLLYWOOD (*Talk*)

FIRST TELECAST: *January 20, 1951*
LAST TELECAST: *July 14, 1951*
BROADCAST HISTORY:
Jan 1951–Jul 1951, NBC Sat 11:00–11:15

HOSTESS:
Sheilah Graham

Syndicated Hollywood gossip columnist Sheilah Graham had been doing a weekly live show in Los Angeles for several months before NBC decided it would be interesting to give it a try on the network. The show combined straight movie news, gossip, fashion information, and chats with visiting stars. Aired live in Los Angeles on Tuesday evenings, with a kinescope made and flown to New York for telecast by NBC on the following Saturday at 11:00 P.M.

SHELL GAME (*Comedy Drama*)

FIRST TELECAST: *January 8, 1987*
LAST TELECAST: *June 17, 1987*
BROADCAST HISTORY:
Jan 1987–Feb 1987, CBS Thu 8:00–9:00
Jun 1987, CBS Wed 9:00–10:00

CAST:
Jennie Jerome .... Margot Kidder
John Reid .... James Read
Bert Luna .... Chip Zien
William Bauer .... Rod McCary
Natalie Thayer .... Marg Helgenberger
Vince Vanneman .... Fred McCarren

Jennie and John had worked together as husband-and-wife con artists but had gone their separate ways when their marriage broke up. He had gone straight and become the producer of *Solutions*, a *60 Minutes*–type series on a local TV station in Santa Ana, California. When Jennie, who was still running scams for personal gain, ran into John and his film crew, she wangled her way onto the team. Together again, they used their well-honed skills to expose corruption and collect information for exposé segments on the TV show. Jennie's presence did not sit well with John's fiancée, Natalie Thayer, the station owner's daughter who feared the two of them would get back together. Others at the office were station manager Bert Luna, *Solution*'s arrogant host William Bauer, and Vince Vanneman.

SHERIFF OF COCHISE, THE (*Police Drama*)

BROADCAST HISTORY:
Syndicated only
30 minutes
Produced: *1956–1960* (156 episodes)
Released: *Fall 1956*

CAST:
Sheriff/Marshal Frank Morgan ..... John Bromfield
Deputy Olson (1956–1958) .... Stan Jones
Deputy Blake (1958) .... Robert Brubaker
Deputy Tom Ferguson (1959–1960)
.... James Griffith

John Bromfield played a jut-jawed, no-nonsense lawman in this contemporary Western set in Cochise County, Arizona. The emphasis was on high-speed chases and fistfights rather than on gunplay, and the scripts were generally interchangeable with those of *Highway Patrol* or *State Trooper*. Actor-songwriter Stan Jones created the series and originally played the deputy, but left when Sheriff Morgan was promoted to U.S. Marshal and given the run of the whole state, in 1958. The series title was also changed to *U.S. Marshal* at this time.

Among the future stars playing supporting roles in episodes of this series were Gavin MacLeod, David Janssen, Michael Landon, Stacy Keach, Charles Bronson, Jack Lord, Doug McClure, Ross Martin, and Martin Milner.

SHE'S THE SHERIFF (*Situation Comedy*)

BROADCAST HISTORY:
Syndicated only
30 minutes

Produced: *1987–1989* (48 episodes)
Released: *September 1987*

CAST:

Sheriff Hildy Granger............ Suzanne Somers
Dep. Max Rubin.................... George Wyner
Gussie Holt............................ Pat Carroll
Allison Granger....................... Nicky Rose
Kenny Granger...................... Taliesin Jaffe
Dep. Dennis Putnam................ Lou Richards
Dep. Hugh Mulcahy................. Guich Koock
Dep. Alvin Wiggins .... Leonard Lightfoot

Following the death of her husband Jim, Hildy Granger succeeded him as sheriff of Lakes County, Nevada, in the beautiful mountain country near Lake Tahoe. As a widow with two young children (Allison and Kenny) to support, Hildy definitely needed the job. Unfortunately her second in command, obnoxious Max Rubin, was a constant thorn in her side. The other male deputies accepted her, but Max was constantly trying to undermine her authority and embarrass her, in a never-ending quest to get the job that was rightfully his. Helping out on the home front was Hildy's bubbly mother, Gussie, who moved to Lakes County to take care of her grandchildren while her daughter was at work.

SHIELD, THE (*Police Drama*)

BROADCAST HISTORY:

FX
60 minutes
Original Episodes: *2002–*
Premiered: *March 12, 2002*

CAST:

Det. Vic Mackey.................. Michael Chiklis
Det. Shane Vendrell.............. Walton Goggins
Det. Curtis "Lemonhead" Lemansky
.... Kenneth Johnson
Capt. David Aceveda............. Benito Martinez
Det. Claudette Wyms .... CCH Pounder
Det. Holland "Dutch" Wagenbach .... Jay Karnes
Officer Danielle "Danny" Sofer ..... Catherine Dent
Officer Julien Lowe.................... Michael Jace
Asst. Chief Ben Gilroy .... John Diehl
Corrine Mackey .... Cathy Cahlin Ryan
Matthew Mackey .... Joel Rosenthal

Television arguably broke new ground with this violent drama about cops operating on—and well beyond—the edge of the law in the battle against rampant street crime in the drug-infested barrio of Los Angeles. At the center of the action was Det. Vic Mackey, leader of the Farmington District Strike Force, a beefy, bald tough guy ready to use any means to nail the perps. That could include planting evidence, beating confessions out of prisoners, strip-searching gang leaders in front of their homies, and sometimes meting out "street justice." His violent tactics had earned him the respect of gang leaders: they often turned over evidence, or agreed to treaties, just to keep him from cracking their skulls. Key members of Mackey's team were Vendrell, a loose cannon who sometimes went too far even for Mackey, and Lemansky, a muscular enforcer.

Mackey's other major battle was with Capt. Aceveda, his nominal boss, who was determined to bring down this "Al Capone with a badge." They hated each other. Aceveda had his own demons, however. Arrogant, cocky and ambitious, he was using the Farmington District strictly for his own political ends (he wanted to run for mayor), so he often looked the other way while Mackey cleaned it up for him, then took the credit. Others in the station house were tough but sensible veteran Wyms and her wimpy partner, Wagenbach, and the experienced Sofer (an Aceveda ally) and her partner, gay black rookie Lowe. Assistant Chief Gilroy was Mackey's sometimes frustrated "protector" at headquarters. At home Mackey dealt with his worried wife Corrine and three children, including autistic son Matthew.

Violence (in the first episode Mackey shot an informer who had been sent to infiltrate his team), nudity and strong language, including racial epithets, permeated the show, though they hardly seemed out of place. Michael Chiklis won an Best Actor Emmy for his role as the tortured Det. Mackey, the first time the lead in a cable drama was ever so honored.

SHIELDS AND YARNELL (*Variety*)

FIRST TELECAST: *June 13, 1977*
LAST TELECAST: *March 28, 1978*
BROADCAST HISTORY:

Jun 1977–Jul 1977, CBS Mon 8:30–9:00
Jan 1978–Mar 1978, CBS Tue 8:30–9:00

REGULARS:

Robert Shields
Lorene Yarnell
Ted Zeigler (1977)
Joanna Cassidy (1977)
Gailard Sartain (1978)
Flip Reade (1978)
Norman Maney Orchestra

The talented young mime team of Shields and Yarnell first starred in a brief summer series which featured, in addition to mime, dancing and comedy sketches. A recurring sketch concerned the adventures of the Clinkers, a pair of clumsy robots adjusting to life in their new suburban home. The show was one of the major hits of the summer of 1977, and promised a bright future in TV for the young performers. That future dimmed when they returned in January 1978 opposite ABC's top-rated *Laverne & Shirley* and lasted only two months before being replaced.

SHINDIG (*Music*)

FIRST TELECAST: *September 16, 1964*
LAST TELECAST: *January 8, 1966*
BROADCAST HISTORY:

Sep 1964–Jan 1965, ABC Wed 8:30–9:00
Jan 1965–Sep 1965, ABC Wed 8:30–9:30
Sep 1965–Jan 1966, ABC Thu/Sat 7:30–8:00

REGULARS:

Jimmy O'Neill
The Shindig Dancers

FREQUENTLY SEEN:

Bobby Sherman
Righteous Brothers
The Wellingtons
Everly Brothers
Donna Loren
Glen Campbell
Sonny & Cher

Shindig was one of two rock 'n' roll shows seen in prime time during the mid-1960s (the other: NBC's *Hullabaloo*). It was a fast-paced, youthful program and, like its NBC counterpart, featured many of the top names in popular music performing their latest hits, while platoons of dancers staged elaborate production numbers. There was also a "disc pick of the week" feature.

The premiere telecast starred Sam Cooke and featured such acts as the Everly Brothers, the Righteous Brothers, the Wellingtons, Bobby Sherman (a *Shindig* "discovery"), and comic Alan Sues. The second season had an even bigger opening, as the show expanded to two nights a week and opened with the Rolling Stones. Although none of the rock stars seen on *Shindig* were weekly regulars, some (noted above) returned many times. Others appearing included such superstars as the Beatles, the Beach Boys, Chuck Berry, Neil Sedaka, and even old-timer Louis Armstrong. They couldn't get the biggest rock star of all, however—nobody could get Elvis—so in May 1965 *Shindig* devoted an entire telecast to his songs, as a tribute to Elvis' tenth anniversary in show business.

During the 1965–1966 season guest stars from other areas of show business also began to appear, such as Mickey Rooney, Zsa Zsa Gabor, Ed Wynn, and, on Halloween, Boris Karloff.

SHIPMATES (*Dating*)

BROADCAST HISTORY:

Syndicated only
30 minutes
Produced: *2001–*
Released: *August 2001*

HOST:

Chris Hardwick

Each episode of this dating show focused on a single couple—two strangers who spent three days and two nights together on a cruise ship and one day on an exotic island. Everything from their first meeting on the ship to their farewells at the end of the three days was caught on tape. Some of the couples hit it off right away, while others took an immediate dislike to each other. Viewers saw the participants' shared experiences, sexual tensions (or lack of them), emotional moments and, occasionally, confrontations. The "shipmates" were given cameras with which to keep video diaries of the date. At the end of the date each one viewed a video made by the other that contained his or her final thoughts about the experience. They ranged from romantic and sentimental to hostile and embarrassing.

Chris Hardwick, who had emceed the MTV game show *Singled Out*, served as the host of *Shipmates* and provided his own tongue-in-cheek observations. *Shipmates* was taped on a number of Carnival cruise ships sailing the Bahamas, the Caribbean, the Mexican Riviera and the Canadian Maritime Provinces.

SHIRLEY (*Comedy/Drama*)

FIRST TELECAST: *October 26, 1979*
LAST TELECAST: *January 25, 1980*
BROADCAST HISTORY:

Oct 1979–Jan 1980, NBC Fri 8:00–9:00

CAST:

Shirley Miller........................ Shirley Jones
Lew Armitage........................ Patrick Wayne
Bill Miller........................ Peter Barton
Debra Miller........................ Rosanna Arquette
Hemm Miller........................ Bret Shryer
Michelle Miller........................ Tracey Gold
Dutch McHenry........................ John McIntire
Charlotte McHenry........................ Ann Doran
Tracey McCord........................ Cindy Eilbacher

The Miller family had planned to move out of the congestion of New York City, and had gone so far as to put a down payment on a rambling old house at scenic Lake Tahoe, California, when Jack Miller died unexpectedly. His widow, Shirley, decided to make her late husband's dream come true, even if he could not be there to share it with her. There were adjustments for all of the Millers to make in moving from a large city to a small-town environment. Shirley, who had taught school in New York, could not get a full-time position at the local high school, and had to settle for odd jobs for income. Her stepson, Bill, was a high school senior, and still somewhat resentful of his stepmother. Shirley's own three children were Debra (16), Hemm (10), and Michelle (8). Debra's best new friend at school was Tracey, who had an instant crush on Bill. The Millers also discovered that their new home had a resident housekeeper named Charlotte, whose cranky ex-husband ran the local sandwich shop, owned a boat-rental business, and was an all-purpose repairman. Lew Armitage was Shirley's new romantic interest, and a friend to the entire family. A free spirit, he worked as a ski instructor in the winter and a rodeo rider in the summer. Oregano was the family dog.

SHIRLEY TEMPLE'S STORYBOOK (*Children's Anthology*)

FIRST TELECAST: *January 12, 1959*
LAST TELECAST: *September 10, 1961*
BROADCAST HISTORY:

Jan 1959–Dec 1959, ABC Mon 7:30–8:30 (OS)
Sep 1960–Sep 1961, NBC Sun 7:00–8:00

HOSTESS/OCCASIONAL STAR:

Shirley Temple

Shirley Temple, the popular child star of movies in the 1930s, came to television as narrator, hostess, and sometimes star of this series of dramatized fairy tales. Among the stories adapted (often in musical form) for this family entertainment program were "Winnie the Pooh," "The Prince and the Pauper," "Babes in Toyland," and "The Reluctant Dragon." Many famous stars appeared in the productions, including Claire Bloom, Charlton Heston, Jonathan Winters, and Agnes Moorehead.

The show was first seen as a series of 16 specials which aired on ABC on various nights between January and December 1958. In January 1959 the program began to run regularly every third Monday night, alternating with *Cheyenne*. When it moved to NBC in 1960 it was a weekly series and was renamed *The Shirley Temple Show*.

SHIRLEY'S WORLD (*Situation Comedy*)

FIRST TELECAST: *September 15, 1971*
LAST TELECAST: *January 5, 1972*
BROADCAST HISTORY:

Sep 1971–Jan 1972, ABC Wed 9:30–10:00

CAST:

Shirley Logan........................ Shirley MacLaine
Dennis Croft........................ John Gregson

Movie actress Shirley MacLaine starred as a mod young reporter-photographer in this, her first TV series. Shirley Logan was based in London, but her assignments for *World Illustrated* magazine took her all over the world. She was saucy, bubbly, and impulsive, and her knack for getting involved with her subjects, be they spies or movie queens, often led to hilarious results, much to the despair of her editor, Dennis Croft.

Filmed in England, Scotland, Tokyo, Hong Kong, and other locales.

SHOP 'TIL YOU DROP (*Quiz/Audience Participation*)

CABLE HISTORY:
Lifetime Network
30 minutes
Produced: *1991–1995 (390 episodes)*
Premiered: July 8, 1991

NETWORK HISTORY:
FIRST TELECAST: *April 5, 1999*
LAST TELECAST: *January 31, 2003*
Apr 1999–Aug 2001, PAX Mon–Fri 6:30–7:30
Oct 2000–Nov 2000, PAX Sat 7:30–8:00
Sep 2001–Sep 2002, PAX Mon–Fri 6:30–7:30
Sep 2002–Jan 2003, PAX Mon–Fri 7:00–7:30

EMCEE:
Pat Finn

ANNOUNCER/ASSISTANT:
Mark Walberg (1991–1995)
Dee Bradley Baker (1999–2003)

In this fast-paced early-evening game show, two two-person teams answered humorous product-related questions. For example, a wife had to decide which of several types of underwear her husband might wear, a husband had to pick the dresses he thought his wife had previously chosen and then model them for her, a girlfriend had to figure out what product slogan her partner was saying through a mouthful of marshmallows. Whoever got the most right answers won a $1,000, a 90-second mad-dash shopping spree in the show's bright, mock shopping mall—and the chance to win an expense-paid shopping trip to Paris, Hong Kong, or New York.

Four years after it left Lifetime *Shop 'Til You Drop* resurfaced on Pax. In this version two married couples competed to win prizes. They had to perform stunts—like stuffing each other's oversized shorts with 15 items in 45 seconds. The selected team could pass the stunt to its competitors. The winning team in each preliminary round won points (100 for round one, 200 for round two), picked one of the stores in the mall and won the mystery prize associated with that store. In the Shoppers Challenge round they competed to answer questions in 90 seconds, getting 50 points for each correct answer. The losing team kept whatever they had won in the preliminary rounds, and the winning team had 90 seconds to keep six merchandise items or exchange each of them for something else from other stores in the mall. If the retail value of the six items they kept exceeded $2,500, they won a luxury vacation in addition to the all the prizes they had selected.

SHOPNBC (Network) (*Home Shopping Cable Network*)

LAUNCHED:
October 1991

SUBSCRIBERS (JAN 2003):
49.1 million (46% U.S.)

This home shopping network was founded as ValueVision in 1991 to compete with the better-known QVC and Home Shopping Network. In June 2001, following a substantial investment by NBC, it was renamed ShopNBC.

SHORT SHORT DRAMAS (*Dramatic Anthology*)

FIRST TELECAST: *September 30, 1952*
LAST TELECAST: *April 9, 1953*
BROADCAST HISTORY:
Sep 1952–Apr 1953, NBC Tue/Thu 7:15–7:30

HOSTESS:
Ruth Woods

Model and cover girl Ruth Woods hosted this filmed series of one-act plays that aired twice weekly during the 1952–1953 season. At the start of each episode she would introduce a different storyteller, who would set the scene for the play to follow. By establishing the background in this way the producer hoped to compress into a short time period a story that would otherwise require at least half an hour to do. Once the background had been set the storyteller, who was one of the stars in the short drama, joined the rest of the cast and the play began. Some of the stories were serious and others light, but none of them particularly memorable. Among the stars performing in this series were Leslie Nielsen, Neva Patterson, E. G. Marshall, Cliff Robertson, Tony Randall, and Bethel Leslie.

SHORT STORY PLAYHOUSE (*Dramatic Anthology*)

FIRST TELECAST: *July 5, 1951*
LAST TELECAST: *August 23, 1951*
BROADCAST HISTORY:
Jul 1951–Aug 1951, NBC Thu 10:30–11:00

NARRATOR:
Robert Breen

Originating live from Chicago, this was aired only on the NBC Midwest network, as a summer replacement for *The Wayne King Show.* The off-screen voice of Robert Breen was heard throughout the productions, serving to add story elements and to tie together loose ends. The performers were not well known, but many of the stories were adapted from works by major authors—Sinclair Lewis's "The Good Sport," James Thurber's "My Life and Hard Times," and Pearl Buck's "Ransom" being the most noteworthy.

SHOTGUN SLADE (*Western*)

BROADCAST HISTORY:
Syndicated only
30 minutes
Produced: *1959–1961* (78 episodes)
Released: *November 1959*

CAST:
Shotgun Slade .... Scott Brady

Shotgun Slade was an odd mixture of swinging private eye and Western hero. Slade was a detective in the Old West, in fact, working on horseback for clients like Wells Fargo, insurance companies, banks, saloon owners, and others who wanted crimes solved. His weapon was a unique two-in-one shotgun.

A pulsating jazz score, and Slade's way with women, gave the series overtones of *77 Sunset Strip.* Still, there was plenty of Western-style action; one single episode had an ambush, a mine explosion, a knock-down fight in a saloon, a hanging, and lots of gunfire. Another oddity about the series was its casting of unlikely people in supporting roles. Ernie

Kovacs played a bewhiskered desert rat in the first episode; others included football star Elroy "Crazylegs" Hirsch as a saloonkeeper, World War II ace Gregory "Pappy" Boyington as a wealthy rancher, recording stars Johnny Cash, Tex Ritter, and Jimmy Wakely as sheriffs, and golfer Paul Hahn, baseball players Chuck Essegian and Wally Moon, and heavyweight boxer Lou Nova in other roles.

SHOW, THE (*Situation Comedy*)
FIRST TELECAST: *March 17, 1996*
LAST TELECAST: *June 6, 1996*
BROADCAST HISTORY:
Mar 1996–Apr 1996, FOX Sun 8:30–9:00
May 1996–Jun 1996, FOX Thu 8:30–9:00
CAST:
Tom Delaney.......................... Sam Seder
Wilson Lee.......................... Mystro Clark
Denise Everett............ T'Keyah Crystal Keymah
Allison Delaney...................... Eliza Coyle
George Hart...................... Tom McGowan
Devo Griffin........................ Shaun Baker
Trent Vance...................... Chris Spencer
Terrence Thorpe.................... Keith Amos
Marvin "Big Chewy"............ Reginald Ballard
Chocolate Walt.................. Marcello Thedford
Chris................ Mark Christopher Lawrence

In this clash-of-cultures comedy, Tom was the newly hired white head writer for *The Wilson Lee Show*, a Los Angeles–based comedy variety TV series with an all black cast. Wilson, the tyrannical star of the show, wanted to attract a bigger white male audience, but there were problems. The things that Tom thought were funny did not always fit in with the star's sense of what was right for his show, particularly when Tom came up with a sketch that was too "white." Others working on the show were Denise, Devo, and Trent, black writers who were slow to accept a white supervisor; Terrence, the beefy receptionist with a crush on Whitney Houston; Big Chewy, Chocolate Walt, and Chris, members of the stage crew; and George, the white comedy writer that Tom brought in to work with him. There was a lot of black street talk among the cast and crew and adjustment problems on both sides, but for the most part they all tried to make things work. Allison was Tom's supportive wife.

SHOW BUSINESS, INC. (*Variety*)
FIRST TELECAST: *March 20, 1947*
LAST TELECAST: *May 4, 1947*
BROADCAST HISTORY:
Mar 1947, NBC Thu 8:00–8:30
Apr 1947–May 1947, NBC Sun 8:00–8:30
REGULARS:
Helen V. Parrish
John Graham

Early music and variety show, telecast only four times in early 1947 over NBC's fledgling East Coast network. There was apparently no regular host, but the performers listed above appeared on all four telecasts.

The title was also used briefly for a series hosted by columnist Danton Walker in 1949 (see *Broadway Spotlight*).

SHOW FOR A SUMMER EVENING (*Dramatic Anthology*)
FIRST TELECAST: *July 16, 1957*
LAST TELECAST: *September 10, 1957*
BROADCAST HISTORY:
Jul 1957–Sep 1957, NBC Tue 9:30–10:00

Show for a Summer Evening alternated with *Armstrong Summer Playhouse* on Tuesday nights during the summer of 1957. All of the dramas shown on it were filmed reruns of episodes from a syndicated series, *Heinz Playhouse.*

SHOW GOES ON, THE (*Variety*)
FIRST TELECAST: *January 19, 1950*
LAST TELECAST: *February 16, 1952*
BROADCAST HISTORY:
Jan 1950–Mar 1950, CBS Thu Various times
Mar 1950–Nov 1950, CBS Thu 8:00–9:00
Nov 1950–Jun 1951, CBS Thu 8:30–9:00
Jun 1951–Feb 1952, CBS Sat 9:30–10:00
HOST:
Robert Q. Lewis

The format of this talent show had young hopefuls performing their acts for a group of interested talented "buyers," who were on hand to appraise the acts and sign up the best ones for actual theater and nightclub bookings. Impresario Max Gordon and bandleader Guy Lombardo were among those who appeared on the show in that capacity. Talent ranged from acrobats, to singers, to comics.

Robert Q. Lewis, who had substituted for Arthur Godfrey on *Arthur Godfrey's Talent Scouts* during the summertime, had his own first starring role with this series. When it first went on the air in January 1950, *The Show Goes On* wandered all over the CBS Thursday night schedule in 30- and 60-minute versions. It finally stabilized in March at a full hour from 8:00 P.M. to 9:00 P.M., and was cut back to a half hour the following fall.

SHOW ME THE FUNNY (*Comedy*)
BROADCAST HISTORY:
Fox Family Channel
30 minutes
Produced: *1998–1999* (80 episodes)
Premiered: *August 15, 1998*
HOST:
Stephanie Miller

A clone of *America's Funniest Home Videos*, featuring funny home videos and some staged gags. Standup comic Stephanie Miller provided the suitably corny introductions.

SHOWBIZ TODAY (*Newsmagazine*)
BROADCAST HISTORY:
CNN
30 minutes
Produced: *1984–2001*
Premiered: *October 29, 1984*
HOSTS:
Liz Wickersham (1984–1989)
Bill Tush (1984–1985, 1988–1989, 1990's–2001)
Lee Leonard (1985–1988)
Bella Shaw (1989–1992)
Laurin Sydney (1989–2001)
Jim Moret (1992–2001)

This nightly wrap-up of show business news, with interviews and features, was CNN's answer to *Entertainment Tonight.* The two anchors originated from New York and Hollywood. In 1989 the show was moved from the early evening to a late-afternoon time slot (with a late-night repeat). There was also a weekend version called *Showbiz This Week*.

SHOWCASE '68 (*Variety*)
FIRST TELECAST: *June 11, 1968*
LAST TELECAST: *September 3, 1968*
BROADCAST HISTORY:
Jun 1968–Sep 1968, NBC Tue 8:00–8:30
HOST:
Lloyd Thaxton

Each week *Showcase '68* originated from a different city in the United States, introducing talented young performers to the viewing audience. All of them were under 22 years of age and made their television debuts on the show. In addition to the young performers, an established star appeared on each telecast. At the end of each show a panel of judges selected the performer with the greatest potential for success. On its last telecast *Showcase '68* expanded to a full hour (8:00–9:00 P.M.) and the ten weekly winners competed for a final $10,000 prize. The winner of the grand prize was rock group Sly and the Family Stone (which already had its first hit on the record charts while this show was on the air). Among the runners-up were Julie Budd, the Chambers Brothers, and the American Breed.

SHOWCASE THEATER (*Dramatic Anthology*)
FIRST TELECAST: *September 12, 1953*
LAST TELECAST: *November 20, 1953*
BROADCAST HISTORY:
Sep 1953–Oct 1953, ABC Sat 8:00–8:30
Oct 1953–Nov 1953, ABC Fri 10:00–10:30

This was a filmed anthology series.

SHOWER OF STARS (*Musical Variety*)
FIRST TELECAST: *September 30, 1954*
LAST TELECAST: *April 17, 1958*
BROADCAST HISTORY:
Sep 1954–Apr 1958, CBS Thu 8:30–9:30 (OS)
HOST:
William Lundigan

This live musical series aired approximately once per month in the time period normally occupied by the dramatic anthology series *Climax!* Both series were sponsored by Chrysler Corporation and shared the same host, William Lundigan. In contrast to the heavy dramas seen on *Climax!, Shower of Stars* offered viewers light entertainment featuring some of the biggest names in comedy and music. Although there were occasional plays—*Lend an Ear* with Edgar Bergen, Sheree North, and Mario Lanza; and *A Christmas Carol* with Fredric March and Basil Rathbone (which was broadcast live three straight years)—most of the telecasts were musical-comedy revues. Among the performers who made multiple appearances in these were Betty Grable and her husband Harry James, Ed Wynn, Ethel Merman, Red Skelton, Shirley MacLaine, Frankie Laine, Van Johnson, and Bob Crosby. The most familiar face on *Shower of Stars*, however, belonged to Jack Benny. He first appeared on the show as the star of *Time Out for Ginger*, the play that opened the 1955–1956 season, and after that turned up as one of the principal stars of virtually every telecast of *Shower of Stars* until it left the air in 1958.

SHOWTIME (*Variety*)
FIRST TELECAST: *June 11, 1968*
LAST TELECAST: *September 17, 1968*
BROADCAST HISTORY:
Jun 1968–Sep 1968, CBS Tue 8:30–9:30
REGULARS:
The Mike Sammes Singers
The London Line Dancers
Jack Parnell and His Orchestra

This 1968 summer replacement for *The Red Skelton Hour* was produced in London and featured a different roster of guest performers each week. Most of the headliners, with the exceptions of Englishmen Terry-Thomas and Dave Allen and South African-born Juliet Prowse, were Americans. Of the Americans, most were comics—Don Knotts, Phyllis Diller, Godfrey Cambridge, Steve Allen, and George Gobel among them.

SHOWTIME (Network) (*General Entertainment Cable Network*
LAUNCHED:
March 7, 1978
SUBSCRIBERS (MAY 2003):
23.0 million (22% U.S.)

A premium channel that shows recent Hollywood films uncut and without commercial interruption. Its programming is similar to that of HBO, which it has consistently trailed in audience. Like its larger rival, Showtime produces its own original movies, airs occasional specials (especially standup comedy), and has produced a number of original series, some of which have been rather adult in content. The network made news—and alarmed broadcasters—in 1983 when it became the first cable network to produce new episodes of a canceled network series, the critically acclaimed *The Paper Chase*.

The long-running *Showtime Comedy Club Network* has showcased more than 500 comics in 100 comedy clubs nationwide. One of its major discoveries was Tim Allen in May 1988. Most of Showtime's original evening series are irregularly scheduled. Among them are the following:

Beggars and Choosers (comedy set at a TV network, Brian Kerwin), 1999–2001
Bizarre (sketch comedy, hosted by John Byner), 1980–1985
Boys, The (sitcom starring Normal Fell and Norm Crosby), 1988
Brothers (sitcom featuring gay characters, starring Robert Walden and Paul Reiser), 1984–1989
Chris Isaak Show (situation comedy), 2001–
Dead Man's Gun (western anthology), 1997–1999
Directed By (anthology), 1994
Faerie Tale Theater (children's anthology, hosted by Shelley Duvall), 1982–1987
Fallen Angels (anthology in film noir style), 1993
Hunger, The (erotic anthology hosted by Terence Stamp), 1997
*It's Garry Shandling's Show** (sitcom), 1986–1990
Jeremiah (science-fiction drama, Luke Perry, Malcolm-Jamal Warner), 2002–
Linc's (political comedy, Pam Grier, Tim Reid), 1998
Odyssey 5 (science-fiction drama, Peter Weller), 2002
*Outer Limits, The** (sci-fi anthology), 1995–2001

*Paper Chase, The** (drama), 1983–1986
*Poltergeist: The Legacy** (sci-fi), 1996–1998
Queer as Folk (gay drama, Gale Harold, Hal Sparks, Sharon Gless), 2000–
Red Shoe Diaries ("erotic anthology" hosted by David Duchovny), 1992–1998
Resurrection Blvd. (Hispanic drama, Michael DeLorenzo, Elizabeth Pena), 2000–
Robin of Sherwood (the Robin Hood legend, first season starring Michael Praed, second season Jason Connery), 1984–1986
Rude Awakening (sitcom, Sherilyn Fenn, Lynn Redgrave), 1998–2001
Shelley Duvall's Bedtime Stories (animated), 1992
Shelley Duvall's Tall Tales & Legends (children), 1985–1988
Showtime Comedy Club Network (standup), 1987–1994
Soul Food (black drama, Vanessa Williams, Nicole Ari Parker), 2000–
*Stargate SG-1** (sci-fi, Richard Dean Anderson), 1997–2002
Street Time (crime drama, Scott Cohen, Rob Morrow), 2002–
*Super Dave** (sitcom starring Bob Einstein), 1987–1994
*Showtime 30-Minute Movie** (anthology of short films by first-time directors, originally hosted by Rob Reiner), 1990–1997
Total Recall 2070 (sci-fi, Michael Easton), 1999

*See separate alphabetical entry

Showtime began operation on July 1, 1976, on a group of cable systems in Northern California and went national, via satellite, in 1978. In 1983 it acquired The Movie Channel, which it operates as a second service (TMC began life in 1973 as The Star Channel, a regional pay service, and had gone national in 1979 as The Movie Channel). On August 1, 1992, Showtime launched a third channel, Flix, featuring older movies.

Other networks launched in later years were Showtime Extreme (action flicks, 1998), Showtime Beyond (science fiction, 1999), Showtime Family Zone (family films, 2001), Showtime Next (young adult films, 2001), Showtime Showcase (same shows, different times, 2001), Showtime Too (all movies, 2001) and Showtime Women (women's films, 2001).

SHOWTIME AT THE APOLLO (*Musical Variety*)

BROADCAST HISTORY:
Syndicated only
60 minutes
Produced: *2002–*
Released: *October 2002*

REGULARS:
Mo'Nique
Angie Martinez
Chuck Jackson
Christopher "Kid" Reid
Rickey Minor Band

The owners of Harlem's Apollo Theatre started this series after a falling-out with the producers of *It's Showtime at the Apollo* (the original producers took most of the regulars and started a competing program called *Showtime in Harlem*). The new Apollo-based version, with the *It's* removed from the title, was hosted by comedienne Mo'Nique. Other regulars included singers Angie Martinez and Chuck Jackson, and comic Christopher "Kid" Reid, who oversaw a children's talent segment. Regular features includes The Original Apollo Amateur Night and The Apollo Star of Tomorrow. Ray Chew, who had led the band for many years on *It's Showtime at the Apollo*, was a member of the Rickey Minor Band.

SHOWTIME AT THE APOLLO, see *It's Showtime at the Apollo*

SHOWTIME IN HARLEM, see *It's Showtime at the Apollo*

SHOWTIME, U.S.A. (*Variety*)

FIRST TELECAST: *October 1, 1950*
LAST TELECAST: *June 24, 1951*
BROADCAST HISTORY:
Oct 1950–Jun 1951, ABC Sun 7:30–8:00
PRODUCER/EMCEE:
Vinton Freedley

This weekly variety show was a plug for Broadway. Produced and cohosted by Vinton Freedley, president of the American National Theatre Academy, it featured scenes from top (and usually current) Broadway productions performed by the original stars. One of the stars would serve as cohost each week. The first telecast had Helen Hayes, Carol Channing, Alec Templeton, Grace and Paul Hartman, Henry Fonda, and the chorus from the currently running *Kiss Me Kate*. Later shows presented Gertrude Lawrence in scenes from *Susan and God*, Fonda in *Mr. Roberts*, and a host of others.

SIBS (*Situation Comedy*)

FIRST TELECAST: *September 17, 1991*
LAST TELECAST: *May 6, 1992*
BROADCAST HISTORY:
Sep 1991, ABC Tue 9:30–10:00
Sep 1991–Oct 1991, ABC Wed 9:30–10:00
Apr 1992–May 1992, ABC Wed 9:30–10:00

CAST:
Nora Ruscio .... Marsha Mason
Howie Ruscio .... Alex Rocco
Audie .... Margaret Colin
Lily .... Jami Gertz
Warren Morris .... Dan Castellaneta

The relationship between three sisters, one happily married and two miserably single, was explored in this character comedy. Nora was the oldest and most stable of the "sibs," a successful accounting executive who provided a shoulder for neurotic Audie (a real estate agent in a collapsing market), and vulnerable youngest sister Lily (just dumped by her heel of a boyfriend), to whine on. Nora's wisecracking schoolteacher husband Howie put up with it all, though not gladly. Warren was Nora's ex-boss, an egotistical wimp who had inherited his uncle's firm, promptly fired Nora, then discovered that all his best customers went with her when she set up her own firm. He later came crawling to her for a job.

SID CAESAR INVITES YOU (*Comedy/Variety*)

FIRST TELECAST: *January 26, 1958*
LAST TELECAST: *May 25, 1958*
BROADCAST HISTORY:
Jan 1958–May 1958, ABC Sun 9:00–9:30

REGULARS:

Sid Caesar
Imogene Coca
Carl Reiner
Paul Reed
Milt Kamen
Bernie Green Orchestra

Sid Caesar and Imogene Coca had become two of the most famous comedians in America, thanks to *Your Show of Shows* in the early 1950s. When that series ended its run in 1954 Caesar and Coca went their separate ways, hoping to build independent careers with separate series. But alone, neither one could capture the magic they had created together, and so in 1958 they were briefly reunited in this live comedy program. As in the days of old, they appeared in sketches and pantomime, with excellent support from regulars, including Carl Reiner, and writers, including Neil Simon and Mel Brooks. But classic comedy is a fragile commodity which cannot easily be revived, and this attempt ended in failure after only a four-month run.

SID CAESAR SHOW, THE, see *Caesar's Hour*

SID CAESAR SHOW, THE (*Comedy/Variety*)

FIRST TELECAST: *October 3, 1963*
LAST TELECAST: *March 12, 1964*
BROADCAST HISTORY:
Oct 1963–Mar 1964, ABC Thu 10:00–10:30

REGULARS:

Sid Caesar
Joey Forman
Gisele MacKenzie
Marilyn Hanold

Sid Caesar's inventive sketch comedy filled this Thursday night half hour on alternate weeks during the 1963–1964 TV season. Singer Edie Adams starred in a musical variety half-hour on the alternate weeks. To start the season they both starred together in a full-hour variety special that ran from 10:00–11:00 P.M. on September 19. Sid's regulars included comic Joey Forman and singer Gisele MacKenzie, with frequent visits by a gorgeous lass named Marilyn Hanold—who never spoke, only looked beautiful. Although the production team was first-rate (including head writer Goodman Ace and producer-director Greg Garrison), the program failed to catch on and ended after a single season.

SIDEKICKS (*Police Drama*)

FIRST TELECAST: *September 19, 1986*
LAST TELECAST: *June 27, 1987*
BROADCAST HISTORY:
Sep 1986–Nov 1986, ABC Fri 9:00–9:30
Nov 1986–Mar 1987, ABC Sat 8:00–8:30
Jun 1987, ABC Sat 8:30–9:00

CAST:

Sgt. Jake Rizzo .... Gil Gerard
Ernie Lee .... Ernie Reyes, Jr.
Patricia Blake .... Nancy Stafford
Det. R. T. Mooney .... Frank Bonner
Sabasan .... Keye Luke
Capt. Blanks .... Vinny Argiro

Jake Rizzo was your typical bachelor cop—dedicated and hard-working, personal life empty, apartment a mess. Into his rather routine existence came a most unusual bundle of energy, a polite but determined ten-year-old named Ernie, who was deposited on his doorstep by Ernie's dying grandfather. Granddad had spied Jake through a window and thought he'd make a good foster father for the parentless child. An unusual situation? Just wait. Pint-sized Ernie happened to be a karate expert, able to mow down a whole crowd of burly bad guys with his flying feet; moreover, he was endowed with mystical powers by grandfather "Sabasan," who, before he died, passed on to him the Patasani title of "The Last Electric Knight."

All of this seemed rather dubious to grumpy Jake, not to mention social worker Patricia, who was all set to place Ernie in an orphanage. But one doesn't argue with Electric Knights, so Jake became a foster dad, coping with Ernie's enthusiasm for a new life as well as with his occasional loneliness for his Sabasan and his Asian cultural heritage. Ernie constantly got involved in Jake's cases, where the kid's martial arts expertise, and those powers, often saved the day. Patricia stayed around to help, providing some much-needed female companionship for Jake.

Young actor Ernie Reyes, Jr., was in real life a juvenile black belt and a veteran of martial arts competitions. The karate sequences in the series were choreographed by his father, Ernie Reyes, Sr.

SIERRA (*Dramatic Adventure*)

FIRST TELECAST: *September 12, 1974*
LAST TELECAST: *December 12, 1974*
BROADCAST HISTORY:
Sep 1974–Dec 1974, NBC Thu 8:00–9:00

CAST:

Ranger Tim Cassidy .... James G. Richardson
Ranger Matt Harper .... Ernest Thompson
Chief Ranger Jack Moore .... Jack Hogan
Ranger P. J. Lewis .... Mike Warren
Ranger Julie Beck .... Susan Foster

The work of rangers employed by the National Park Service at fictitious Sierra National Park was dramatized in this series. The problems and satisfactions of supervisor Jack Moore and his staff, consisting of rangers Cassidy, Harper, Lewis, and Beck, were shown. Their problems stemmed from the conflict between trying to preserve the natural beauty of the wilderness and accommodating the flood of tourists wanting to utilize the resources of the park. The campers, skiers, hikers, and climbers came in all shapes and sizes. Some were friendly, some stubborn, and some nasty and cruel. Tracking people who had gotten lost, coping with the visitor who got into a situation he couldn't really handle, and enforcing park regulations were all part of the job. *Sierra* was filmed on location, primarily at Yosemite National Park, in cooperation with the National Park Service. Cruncher was the park's troublemaking bear.

SIFL & OLLY SHOW (*Comedy*)

BROADCAST HISTORY:
MTV
Produced: *1998–1999*
Premiered: *July 14, 1998*

VOICES:

Sifl, Chester, Precious Roy .... Matt Crocco
Olly .... Liam Lynch

Possibly one of the cheapest-to-produce series ever on

a national network, *Sifl & Olly* featured sock puppets in front of a microphone, against a plain background, horsing around, cracking bad jokes, and singing silly songs. Sifl was the dark sock, Olly the light-colored (and generally smarter) one, and Chester their sidekick. Among the recurring bits were interviews with other socks, bogus rock facts, and "The Precious Roy Home Shopping Network" (peddling bizarre junk). It all seemed okay to stoned viewers at 12:30 A.M. in the morning, where it was originally scheduled, although MTV later tried the socks in prime time, hosting videos. Created by Crocco and Lynch.

SIGHTINGS (*Supernatural*)
FIRST TELECAST: *April 17, 1992*
LAST TELECAST: *July 23, 1993*
BROADCAST HISTORY:
Apr 1992–Jan 1993, FOX Fri 9:00–9:30
Feb 1993–Jun 1993, FOX Fri 9:00–10:00
Jun 1993–Jul 1993, FOX Fri 9:00–9:30
(In first run syndication September 1994–September 1996; on the Sci-Fi Channel October 1996–September 1997)
HOST/NARRATOR:
Tim White
CORRESPONDENT:
Carla Wohl (1995–1996)

This weekly series was an updated version of the 1970s syndicated series *In Search Of* . . . Each week Tim White served as host/narrator for an investigation of some type of unexplained phenomena. ESP, near death experiences, psychic abilities, ghosts, vampires, reincarnation, monsters, curses, and UFOs were all fodder for this show. Episodes included eyewitness accounts, discussions with experts, and dramatic reenactments.

When *Sightings* returned to the airwaves as a syndicated series in the fall of 1994, it had expanded from a half hour to a full hour. Original production continued for the Sci-Fi Channel in 1996–1997. One of its executive producers was Henry Winkler.

First seen as a series of specials on Fox.

SIGNIFICANT OTHERS (*Drama*)
FIRST TELECAST: *March 11, 1998*
LAST TELECAST: *March 25, 1998*
BROADCAST HISTORY:
Mar 1998, FOX Wed 9:00–10:00
CAST:
Campbell Chasen....................Eion Bailey
Nell....................Jennifer Garner
Henry....................Scott Bairstow
Ben Chasen....................Michael Weatherly
Jane Chasen....................Elizabeth Mitchell
Charotte Lerner....................Gigi Rice
Leonard Chasen....................Richard Masur
Bev Chasen....................Jennifer Savidge

Short-lived show about a group of self-centered, twentysomething friends living and working in L.A. Campbell, Nell, and Henry had been friends since they were kids. Campbell was something of a dreamer, looking for the get-rich-quick scheme that would set him up for life; Nell, who worked for an advertising agency, was terrified of committing to anything or anyone—she couldn't hold onto either jobs or relationships; and Henry made a living writing porn for an Internet website. Campbell's older brother Ben, who was working in the family brassiere business, married Campbell's ex-girlfriend, Jane, in the premiere. Charlotte was Henry's married boss, with whom he was having a steamy affair that his friends found unacceptable. In the premiere Campbell found out that Henry and Nell had been having an affair for several months without telling him, but by episode's end they had broken up because of her fear of commitment. Campbell, in order to fund the children's video he was producing, went to work for his domineering father, Leonard, in the family business.

All this angst in three weeks, and then the show was pulled from the Fox schedule, never to be seen again.

SILENT FORCE, THE (*Police Drama*)
FIRST TELECAST: *September 21, 1970*
LAST TELECAST: *January 11, 1971*
BROADCAST HISTORY:
Sep 1970–Jan 1971, ABC Mon 8:30–9:00
CAST:
Ward Fuller....................Ed Nelson
Jason Hart....................Percy Rodriguez
Amelia Cole....................Lynda Day

The Silent Force was a strike force of government agents assigned to fight organized crime. Ward, Jason, and Amelia were the agents, working mostly undercover to infiltrate "the mob" and expose its operations which preyed on innocent citizens. On several occasions they became involved with companies or individuals who were being pressured by the syndicate, and in the first telecast they exposed a candidate for governor who was actually a member of the syndicate.

Set in Southern California.

SILENT SERVICE, THE (*Dramatic Anthology*)
BROADCAST HISTORY:
Syndicated only
30 minutes
Produced: *1956–1958* (78 episodes)
Released: *March 1957*
HOST/NARRATOR:
Rear Adm. (ret.) Thomas M. Dykers

This series consisted of documentary-style dramas about the exploits of the U.S. Navy's submarine fleet. All were based on fact, and the realism was heightened by the use of actual combat footage from the Navy's files. Most of the stories took place in the South Pacific during World War II, but some were from the Korean War or had a peacetime context. There were no continuing characters, and in fact the acting was pretty much limited to terse commands ("Up periscope" . . . "All secure, sir") and worried looks at dangerous moments.

The series was the brainchild of Rear Adm. Thomas M. Dykers, who retired from the Navy in 1949 after 22 years of service, most of it in the submarine service. After serving as technical advisor for several Hollywood movies, he produced this syndicated show himself, with the full cooperation of the Navy (which loaned him the U.S.S. *Sawfish* for filming).

SILENTS PLEASE (*Silent Movies*)
FIRST TELECAST: *August 4, 1960*
LAST TELECAST: *October 5, 1961*
BROADCAST HISTORY:
Aug 1960–Oct 1960, ABC Thu 10:30–11:00
Mar 1961–Oct 1961, ABC Thu 10:30–11:00

HOST:

Ernie Kovacs (1961)

Classic silent films, some in their entirety, some condensed to fit the confines of a half-hour time slot, were aired in this series. The films included the work of Buster Keaton, Charlie Chaplin, Laurel and Hardy, Lillian Gish, and Douglas Fairbanks, Sr. When it was first telecast in the summer of 1960 there was no host. Ernie Kovacs, whose show *Take a Good Look* had aired in this time slot from October 1960 until *Silents Please* returned the following March, became the host of the show during its second run.

SILK STALKINGS (*Police Drama*)

NETWORK HISTORY:

FIRST TELECAST: *November 7, 1991*

LAST TELECAST: *November 4, 1993*

Nov 1991–Nov 1993, CBS Thu 11:30–12:30 A.M.

CABLE HISTORY:

USA Network

60 minutes

Produced: *1991–1999*

Premiered: November 10, 1991

CAST:

Sgt. Chris Lorenzo (1991–1995) .... Rob Estes

Sgt. Rita Lee Lance ("Sam") (1991–1995) .... Mitzi Kapture

Capt. Hutchinson (1991–1993) .... Ben Vereen

Capt. Harry Lipschitz (1993–1999) .... Charlie Brill

**Assistant D.A. George Donnovan (1991–1996)* .... William Anton

**Melissa Cassidy (1991–1992)* ... Kim Morgan Greene

**Roger (1991–1992)*.................... Danny Gans

**Fran Lipschitz (1993–1999)* .... Mitzi McCall

**Cotton Dunn (1992–1994)*.............. John Byner

**Donnie "Dogs" DiBarto (1993–1994)* .... Dennis Paladino

Det. Michael Price (1995–1996) .... Nick Kokotakis

Det. Holly Rawlins (1995–1996) .... Tyler Layton

Det. Sgt. Tom Ryan (1996–1999) .... Chris Potter

Det. Sgt. Cassandra (Cassy) St. John (1996–1999) .... Janet Gunn

*Occasional

Glamour, murder, and sex—especially sex—were the focus of this entry in CBS' *Crimetime After Primetime* late night program lineup. The setting was fabulously wealthy Palm Beach, Florida, where young, handsome Chris and sexy Rita were the police department's leading experts on "crimes of passion" among the rich and famous. They certainly had plenty to do, as kinkiness and homicide seemed to be the resort's leading sports. Rita narrated each episode with a world-weary tone, and bantered with Chris in a sort of hip code ("silk stalkings" was their term for society murders). She relished the excitement of operating on the edge in a world of power and psychopaths, since her own life was on the line in an unusual way—she had an inoperable brain aneurysm that might "pop" and kill her at any time. Chris, her "best pal" (no romance on the job), worried about this constantly, to no avail. Hutch was their grumpy captain, who complained about the ultra-stylish station house the citizenry gave him to work out of.

Numerous recurring characters were seen, including politically ambitious Assistant D.A. Donovan, radio talk-show shrink Melissa (who bedded Chris), and morgue attendant Roger (who had the hots for Rita). Later characters tended to add comic relief; among them were hypochondriac Capt. Lipschitz, his bossy wife, Fran, playboy con man Cotton Dunn, and cheerful mobster Donnie "Dogs."

Chris was shot in 1994 and almost died, later falling in love with, and almost marrying, the doctor who attended him. The sexual chemistry between Chris and Rita finally began to heat up in Fall 1995, and in November they were married, only a week before he was killed in a shootout. Rita, devastated, left the force (both stars had decided to leave the series). A new team then took over—Michael, a former Chicago cop, and Holly, a Southern-born officer haunted by her sister's death from an overdose. Fans of *Silk Stalkings* sometimes refer to them as the "lost cast," since they lasted only a few months, disappearing without a trace in the spring. In the fall a new team was introduced (with no explanation of what had happened to the previous one). Tom and Cassy had once been married, for seven stormy months, but they didn't let their divorce get in the way of their new working relationship. However, the jibes flew thick and fast, and their former intimacy left neither with any secrets from the other. In the last original episode Tom was framed for murder by a new girlfriend, and in the course of trying to clear him, Cassy was suspended from the force and Capt. Lipschitz forced to resign. In the final scene, with vengeful Internal Affairs officers on their way to arrest him, Tom revealed to Cassy that he loved her, adding, "So where do we go from here?" She responded, "I don't know." Fade to black.

Silk Stalkings was at first jointly produced by CBS and USA Network and ran concurrently on both, a most unusual arrangement for those traditional rivals. After the cancellation of CBS' *Crimetime After Primetime* late-night lineup in 1993 it continued with new episodes seen exclusively on USA.

SILVER SPOONS (*Situation Comedy*)

FIRST TELECAST: *September 25, 1982*

LAST TELECAST: *September 7, 1986*

BROADCAST HISTORY:

Sep 1982–Sep 1984, NBC Sat 8:30–9:00

Sep 1984–May 1985, NBC Sun 7:00–7:30

Jun 1985–Mar 1986, NBC Sun 7:30–8:00

May 1986–Sep 1986, NBC Sun 7:00–7:30

(In first-run syndication during the 1986–1987 season)

CAST:

Ricky Stratton..................... Ricky Schroder

Edward Stratton III .... Joel Higgins

Kate Summers Stratton................. Erin Gray

Leonard Rollins (1982–1983) .... Leonard Lightfoot

Dexter Stuffins................... Franklyn Seales

Derek Taylor (1982–1984) .... Jason Bateman

Freddy Lippincottleman (1983–1985) .... Corky Pigeon

Alfonso Spears (1984–1987)....... Alfonso Ribeiro

**J. T. Martin (1983–1984)*............... Bobby Fite

**Grandfather Edward Stratton II* ... John Houseman

Uncle Harry Summers (1985) .... Ray Walston

**Brad (1985–1986)*..................... Billy Jacoby

*Occasional

A mature 12-year-old and his childlike father found that they could learn from each other in this comedy. Ricky was an uncommonly bright, attractive youngster who had been brought up by his divorced mother, then dumped in a military school. Finagling an invitation to move in with his wealthy father, whom he had never known, he discovered that his 35-year-old dad was more of a child than he was. Stratton's palatial home was filled with video games, stuffed animals, and a miniature railroad on which he rode through the rooms. They had a lot of love to give each other, and Ricky soon helped Edward learn to be a father, while Edward taught his son a little about enjoying life.

Kate was Edward's amorous secretary (who did, finally, become Mrs. Stratton in February 1985), Leonard his lawyer, and Dexter his fussy business manager and a family friend. Stopping in periodically was the formidable Grandfather Stratton, a stuffy tycoon who had been estranged from his immature son but now found better communication with the help of Ricky. Derek was Ricky's conniving school chum, and Freddie and J.T. were also friends. Dexter's nephew, Alfonso, arrived in 1984, and became Ricky's new best friend.

NBC aired reruns of *Silver Spoons* on weekday mornings during the summer of 1985.

SILVER THEATER, THE (*Dramatic Anthology*)

FIRST TELECAST: *October 3, 1949*
LAST TELECAST: *June 26, 1950*
BROADCAST HISTORY:
Oct 1949–Jun 1950, CBS Mon 8:00–8:30
HOST:
Conrad Nagel

The teleplays in this series, most of which were aired live, emphasized romance—the humorous, silly, frustrating, futile, and rewarding aspects of it. Famous stars such as Burgess Meredith, Paul Lucas, Glenda Farrell, and Geraldine Brooks appeared in the dramas and Conrad Nagel was the host. The sponsor, the International Silver Company, whence came the title, had also sponsored a radio version of this show during the 1930s and 1940s. A special feature of this program was the monthly "Silver Award" presented to the most deserving supporting performer in the dramas aired in the series during the month. A panel of drama critics determined the monthly winner.

SIMON (*Situation Comedy*)

FIRST TELECAST: *September 10, 1995*
LAST TELECAST: *March 3, 1996*
BROADCAST HISTORY:
Sep 1995–Oct 1995, WB Sun 8:30–9:00
Oct 1995–Dec 1995, WB Sun 9:30–10:00
Jan 1996–Mar 1996, WB Sun 7:30–8:00
CAST:
Simon Hemphill .... Harland Williams
Carl Hemphill .... Jason Bateman
Libby Keeler .... Andrea Bendewald
Mitch Lowen .... Patrick Breen
Duke Stone .... Paxton Whitehead
Franz .... David Byrd

This offbeat comedy centered on the lives of two mismatched brothers living together in a ratty tenement apartment in the Harlem section of Manhattan. Slow-witted Simon was trusting and earnest, while his recently divorced brother, Carl, was more worldly, decidedly more obnoxious, and tolerated the living arrangement because he had lost his corporate job. When simple Simon fell into a job as a programming executive at Vintage Television, a cable network featuring reruns of dated series—apparently because he babbled lines from old TV shows—his brother couldn't believe it. Neither could Mitch, the arrogant nephew of Vintage's eccentric owner, Duke Stone. Mitch spent most of his time trying to undermine the oblivious Simon while currying favor with his wealthy uncle. Also working in Vintage's programming department was Libby, who liked Simon and foiled Mitch's efforts to get rid of him. When Simon subsequently got Carl a job at Vintage that was more menial than his, it was quite a comedown for his ambitious brother, who desperately wanted to regain the executive perks he had once had. Franz was Duke's long suffering butler.

At the end of each episode, as the closing credits rolled, there was a short "Ask Simon" segment in which he answered viewer questions with Forrest Gump–like innocence and wisdom.

SIMON & SIMON (*Detective Drama*)

FIRST TELECAST: *November 24, 1981*
LAST TELECAST: *December 31, 1988*
BROADCAST HISTORY:
Nov 1981–Mar 1982, CBS Tue 8:00–9:00
Apr 1982, CBS Thu 9:00–10:00
Jul 1982–Apr 1986, CBS Thu 9:00–10:00
Apr 1986–Jun 1986, CBS Thu 8:00–9:00
Jun 1986–Sep 1986, CBS Tue 8:00–9:00
Sep 1986–Nov 1986, CBS Thu 8:00–9:00
Dec 1986–Jan 1987, CBS Thu 8:30–9:30
Jan 1987–May 1987, CBS Thu 9:00–10:00
Jul 1987–Sep 1987, CBS Tue 8:00–9:00
Dec 1987–Aug 1988, CBS Thu 9:00–10:00
Oct 1988–Dec 1988, CBS Sat 9:00–10:00
CAST:
Andrew Jackson (A.J.) Simon ...... Jameson Parker
Rick Simon .... Gerald McRaney
Cecilia Simon .... Mary Carver
Janet Fowler (1981–1983) .... Jeannie Wilson
Myron Fowler (1981–1983) .... Eddie Barth
Det. Marcel "Downtown" Brown (1983–1987)
.... Tim Reid
Officer Nixon (1986–1988) .... Scott Murphy
Lt. Abigail Marsh (1987–1988) .... Joan McMurtrey
Officer Susie (1988) .... Donna Jepsen

A.J. and Rick were brothers, but you'd never have known it by looking at them. A.J. was conservative, dedicated, clean-cut, and ambitious. Rick was eccentric, grubby, and laid-back to the point of being lazy. A.J. drove an immaculate convertible and kept his apartment (located behind their office) in spotless condition. Rick bummed around San Diego in a beat-up pickup truck, lived like a slob on a houseboat, and was more interested in pickin' on his guitar than working. Despite their different lifestyles, A.J. and Rick were partners in a small, struggling detective agency, with A.J. spending much of his time trying, however hopelessly, to get Rick into a more "corporate" mold. There was much sibling rivalry—Rick tended to exasperate his younger brother—as well as occasional disapproval from their mother, Cecilia, who wasn't thrilled when they took cases that didn't pay them much.

Across the street from their office was a rival agency run by crabby Myron Fowler. Myron's daughter, Janet, who worked for her dad as a secretary, got an occasional chance to play detective by helping Rick and A.J. on some of their cases, much to Myron's consternation. After graduating from law school Janet became a local assistant district attorney, which strained her relationship with the Simons when she was prosecuting one of their clients. Myron, meanwhile, had closed his detective agency and retired, only to show up as a part-time legman for Rick and A.J. when he got bored with inactivity. Undercover police detective Downtown, whose unorthodox techniques for dealing with criminals and obtaining information appealed to Rick and appalled A.J., was around to help out—as long as he got something out of it. As he told them, "You do for me, and I'll do for you."

When Downtown departed in the fall of 1987 (Tim Reid had moved on to star in his own series, *Frank's Place*), he was replaced on the force by the much less friendly, by-the-book Lt. Abby Marsh.

SIMPLE LIFE, THE (*Situation Comedy*)

FIRST TELECAST: *June 3, 1998*

LAST TELECAST: *July 15, 1998*

BROADCAST HISTORY:

Jun 1998–Jul 1998, CBS Wed 8:30–9:00

CAST:

Sara Campbell (née Lipschitz) .... Judith Light
Muriel Lipschitz .... Florence Stanley
Luke Barton .... Brett Cullen
Greg Champlain .... James Patrick Stuart
Frederica "Freddi" Campbell .... Ashlee Levitch
Will .... Ross Malinger
Charlotte .... Eliza Dean
Melanie .... Sara Rue
Jeff .... Jeff Blumenkrantz
Nick, the Stage Manager .... Vasili Bogazianos

Sara Campbell had built a financial empire around her reputation as America's foremost authority on living a relaxed country lifestyle—this despite growing up in Queens and living most of her adult life in a fancy Manhattan townhouse. Now she had decided to take her own advice, and moved her family and TV show, *The Simple Life*, to a small farm in upstate New York. With her were her acerbic mother, Muriel, who didn't believe Sara could survive in the country, and her slacker daughter, Freddi, who hated being away from the big city. She turned the farm's barn into a TV studio, to the consternation of Luke, the farm's hunky foreman, who was raising his late sister's two kids, Will and Charlotte. He was bemused by how ignorant Sara was about real country living and found her alternately irritating and appealingly vulnerable. Greg was Sara's obnoxious British producer, and Melanie, Jeff, and Nick worked on the TV show.

This was CBS' second attempt to parody Martha Stewart (whose own series *Martha Stewart Living* was distributed by CBS) during the 1997–1998 season. The first, *Style & Substance*, had aired briefly early in 1998 and returned in the time period vacated by *The Simply Life* after its cancellation.

SIMPSONS, THE (*Cartoon*)

FIRST TELECAST: *December 17, 1989*

LAST TELECAST:

BROADCAST HISTORY:

Dec 1989–Aug 1990, FOX Sun 8:30–9:00
Aug 1990–Apr 1994, FOX Thu 8:00–8:30
Apr 1994–May 1994, FOX Thu 8:00–9:00
May 1994–July 1994, FOX Thu 8:00–8:30
Aug 1994, FOX Sun 8:00–9:00
Sep 1994–Oct 1994, FOX Sun 8:00–8:30
Oct 1994–Dec 1994, FOX Sun 8:00–9:00
Dec 1994–Apr 1996, FOX Sun 8:00–8:30
Jan 1995–Feb 1995, FOX Sun 7:00–7:30
Apr 1996–May 1996, FOX Sun 8:00–9:00
May 1996–Aug 1996, FOX Sun 8:00–8:30
Oct 1996–Jul 1998, FOX Sun 8:00–8:30
Aug 1998, FOX Sun 8:00–9:00
Aug 1998– , FOX Sun 8:00–8:30

VOICES:

Homer J. Simpson, Barney Gumble, Grandpa Simpson, Mayor Joe Quimby, Krusty the Klown & others .... Dan Castellaneta
Marjorie Bouvier Simpson, Patty Bouvier, Selma Bouvier, Grandma Jackie Bouvier ... Julie Kavner
Bartholomew Jo-Jo "Bart" Simpson (age 10) .... Nancy Cartwright
Lisa Marie Simpson (8) .... Yeardley Smith
Mrs. Edna Krabappel .... Marcia Wallace
Charles Montgomery Burns, Waylon Smithers, Principal Seymour Skinner, Ned Flanders, Otto Mann, Scratchy & others ..... Harry Shearer
Moe Szyslak, Apu Nahasapeemapetilon, Chief Clancy Wiggum, Dr. Nick Riviera & others .... Hank Azaria
Milhouse van Houten, Janey Hagstrom, Jimbo Jones, Dolph .... Pamela Hayden
Agnes Skinner, Ms. Albright, Mrs. Glick .... Tress MacNeille
Maude Flanders, Luanne van Houten, Helen Lovejoy, Elizabeth Hoover .... Maggie Roswell (to 2000)
Lionel Hutz, Troy McClure .... Phil Hartman (to 1998)

Certain series defined how much 1990s television had changed (for better or worse, depending on your point of view) from the squeaky-clean days of the 1950s and 1960s. *Roseanne* was one, *Married . . . with Children* another. Arguably, *The Simpsons* was the most subversive of them all. It got away with its anarchic message largely because it was a cartoon, the first hit animated series since the very different *Flintstones* in the 1960s.

The seemingly idyllic town of Springfield had all the important things a city should have—a mall, a prison, a dump site, a mountain of burning tires, toxic waste, and a nuclear power plant. The safety inspector at the plant was Homer Simpson, a lazy, balding slob of a man. Homer, who wasn't too bright (his boss, Mr. Burns, referred to him as "bonehead"), spent his spare time guzzling beer at Moe's Tavern and bowling at Barney's New Bowlerama. Although Homer and his wife Marge had their disagreements, they did love each other and their three kids. Marge was the family peacemaker, a gentle, caring woman with an enormous blue beehive hairdo held together by a single bobby pin. Maggie, the youngest child, an infant who had just started walking, was never seen without a pacifier in her mouth. A silent observer of all around her, she communicated through sign language. Her older sister Lisa, an eternally optimistic second grader and baritone saxophone prodigy, was the smartest one in the family, but nobody seemed to notice she was a straight A student.

And then there was Bart, television's most popular underachiever. An obnoxious misfit with spiked hair who masked his intelligence with sarcasm, he tore around town on a skateboard, grossed out his friends at every opportunity, and drove his fourth-grade teacher, Mrs. Krabappel, crazy. He was preoccupied with only one thing—being cool. Bart, whose name is an anagram for brat, was the consummate preteen wiseguy, forever getting in trouble but somehow managing to maneuver his way out before real catastrophe struck. His two most popular catch phrases during the series' early years—"Don't have a cow, man!" and "Ay, caramba!"—were immortalized on *Simpsons* T-shirts, along with many others ("Smooth move, man!," "Underachiever, and proud of it, man!," "I'm Bart Simpson! Who the hell are you?" "Eat my shorts," and "Make sure there are plenty of escape routes") that he probably never said—but certainly were in character.

In addition to the central family, *The Simpsons* had a huge cast of semi-regular and recurring characters—family, friends, coworkers, city officials, and local personalities. Among the most popular were Homer's father, Abraham, who lived at the retirement home; Marge's twin older sisters, Patty and Selma; their next-door neighbors the Flanders; Mr. Burns, Homer's despicable boss; Moe, who ran Homer's favorite tavern; Apu, the Kwik-E-Mart clerk; Milhouse, Bart's best friend; and Bart's favorite TV personality, Krusty the Klown. The real "cartoon violence" on *The Simpsons* took place on episodes of "The Itchy and Scratchy Show," a cat (Scratchy) and mouse (Itchy) cartoon on Krusty's show in which the mouse routinely mangled, disemboweled, or blew up the cat. In February 2000 Maude Flanders was killed off (Maggie Roswell, who had done the voice, had left the series) when she was hit by a balled-up T-shirt at the new racetrack, lost her balance and fell over the railing to her death.

Occasionally there were serious moments on *The Simpsons.* Bart had an epiphany when he realized he had really hurt Lisa's feelings, Homer and Bart brought home the sorriest dog from the dog track and made it the family pet, Lisa uncovered political corruption in Washington, D.C., and Marge exposed Mr. Burns as Springfield's worst polluter. In certain areas the show's continuity was lacking—perhaps on purpose. The Simpsons' home address, usually on Evergreen Terrace, varied from episode to episode, as did their home and business phone numbers, and the profusion of characters who were left-handed (as was creator Groening) in early episodes were not always left-handed in later episodes. The Halloween episode, which each year parodied classic science fiction and/or horror movies, may well have been the most-anticipated *Simpsons* event of the season.

The Simpsons was virtually unnoticed when it began as a series of short vignettes on *The Tracey Ullman Show* in 1987, but it became a sensation as a regular series two years later. In a TV world where most of the people were attractive and the kids too good to be true, Homer and his unruly brood were a welcome contrast. Children loved the show and, to the surprise of some, so did many adults who appreciated its satirical content. The result was a ratings and merchandising bonanza. There were *Simpsons* air fresheners, dolls, beach towels, toothbrushes, posters, hats, watches, bed linens, and scores of other products. Celebrities vied for the opportunity to do guest voices, much as they had competed to be guest villains on *Batman* 25 years earlier. Among those heard were Penny Marshall, Albert Brooks, Ringo Starr, Tony Bennett, Danny DeVito, Larry King, Cloris Leachman, Elizabeth Taylor, Dustin Hoffman, Michael Jackson, and Johnny Carson.

Creator Matt Groening swore the series was not autobiographical, despite the fact that his parents and two sisters had the same names as the Simpsons. A cartoonist who had been drawing the "Life In Hell" comic strip since 1977, Groening was both gratified and amazed by the success of his animated blue-collar family. It was his decision for the Simpsons, unlike real people, never to age. Although there were flashbacks and flash-forwards in some episodes, in general time stood still for them—Bart was doomed to spend his entire animated existence in fourth grade.

SINBAD SHOW, THE (*Situation Comedy*)
FIRST TELECAST: *September 16, 1993*
LAST TELECAST: *July 28, 1994*
BROADCAST HISTORY:
Sep 1993–Jul 1994, FOX Thu 8:30–9:00
CAST:
David Bryan .... Sinbad
Clarence Hull .... T. K. Carter
Zana Beckley (age 5) .... Erin Davis
Little John ("L.J.") Beckley (13) ..... Willie Norwood
Louise Bryan .... Nancy Wilson
Rudy Bryan .... Hal Williams
Gloria Contreras (1993) .... Salma Hayek

Comedy about a multigenerational, black extended family. Big guy David Bryan was a struggling young computer video game designer living in the Silicon Valley area south of San Francisco who took in two foster children, lovable Zana and her smartass older brother L.J. Setting a good example for the two youngsters did put a crimp in his swinging bachelor lifestyle, but the love he got from them made it all worthwhile. David's parents, Rudy and Louise, were frequent visitors who adored the kids and helped out. Less enthusiastic about the situation was Clarence, David's best friend and former roommate, who had to move out when the kids moved in. A born hustler and womanizer, he found it much more difficult to get David to party now that he was responsible for two children. At midseason David got a job as host of the local children's TV show *It's Science Time*, in which he used funny demonstrations to explain scientific principles to the audience.

When *The Sinbad Show* premiered, one of the regulars was Gloria, the daughter of David's landlady. Her character was dropped barely a month later.

SING ALONG (*Music*)
FIRST TELECAST: *June 4, 1958*
LAST TELECAST: *July 9, 1958*
BROADCAST HISTORY:
Jun 1958–Jul 1958, CBS Wed 7:30–8:00
REGULARS:
Jim Lowe
Tina Robin
Florence Henderson
Somethin' Smith
The Redheads
Harry Sosnik Orchestra

Jim Lowe, a radio personality whose one hit record was a novelty item called "The Green Door," was the host of this live weekly music show. The regular singers were joined by guest stars and the studio and home audience was invited to "sing along." The lyrics were provided by various forms of cue cards so that everyone would know what to sing. Apparently Lowe was a few years ahead of his time. This show had a mere six-week run and then disappeared forever, but while it was on the air an obscure Columbia record album by Mitch Miller called "Sing Along with Mitch" first began attracting attention. Three years and several million records later, Miller brought the idea back to television, and was a national sensation.

SING ALONG WITH MITCH (*Musical Variety*)
FIRST TELECAST: *January 27, 1961*
LAST TELECAST: *September 2, 1966*
BROADCAST HISTORY:
Jan 1961–Apr 1961, NBC Fri 9:00–10:00
Sep 1961–Sep 1962, NBC Thu 10:00–11:00
Sep 1962–Sep 1963, NBC Fri 8:30–9:30
Sep 1963–Sep 1964, NBC Mon 10:00–11:00
Apr 1966–Sep 1966, NBC Fri 8:30–9:30
REGULARS:
Mitch Miller
The Sing Along Gang
The Sing Along Kids
Leslie Uggams
Diana Trask (1961–1962)
Carolyn Conway (1962–1963)
Gloria Lambert
Louise O'Brien
Sandy Stewart (1963–1964)
The James Starbuck Dancers
THEME:
"Sing Along," by Robert Allen

Bearded record producer Mitch Miller was responsible for a large proportion of America's popular music during the 1950s. As head of recording for mighty Columbia Records, he launched literally dozens of stars and trends in music, and even had a choral hit under his own name ("The Yellow Rose of Texas" in 1955). But Mitch didn't like rock 'n' roll, and when the teen beat began swamping the business in the late 1950s *his* kind of music—melodic and stylish—went into a severe decline. In 1958 he conceived the idea of packaging "Sing-along" LPs consisting of old favorites with the words printed on the album cover so the listener could sing along with the chorus. This ran contrary to everything that was happening in popular music, but it found a large, obviously frustrated audience, and the albums became enormous sellers. In 1961 Miller tried the idea on television. Overnight, Mitch Miller, who had for decades been a behind-the-scenes man, became a national celebrity. During the first season his show alternated with *The Bell Telephone Hour.* It became such a large ratings success that when it returned in the fall of 1961 it was a weekly show. Old favorites and some currently popular songs were sung by Mitch's Sing Along Gang, the preteenage Sing Along Kids, and by featured vocalists doing solos. Mitch himself said very little, simply standing there waving his baton. For all the group songs, the lyrics would be flashed on the screen so that the home audience could also sing along. In addition to the regulars, occasional guest stars and lavish production numbers were a part of the show. Three of Mitch's "discoveries," Leslie Uggams, Diana Trask, and Sandy Stewart, went on to considerable success in the music business.

The 1966 summer series was made up entirely of reruns.

SING-CO-PATION (*Music*)
FIRST TELECAST: *January 23, 1949*
LAST TELECAST: *October 30, 1949*
BROADCAST HISTORY:
Jan 1949–Mar 1949, ABC Sun 7:45–8:00
Mar 1949–Aug 1949, ABC Sun 9:00–9:15
Sep 1949–Oct 1949, ABC Sun 6:45–7:00
HOST:
Jack Brand
REGULARS:
Dolores Marshall
George Barnes Trio
Jack Fascinato Trio

Musical interlude from Chicago, featuring vocalist Dolores Marshall. During the program's final month the title was changed to *Serenade.*

SING IT AGAIN (*Quiz/Audience Participation*)
FIRST TELECAST: *September 2, 1950*
LAST TELECAST: *June 23, 1951*
BROADCAST HISTORY:
Sep 1950, CBS Sat 10:00–10:30
Oct 1950–Jun 1951, CBS Sat 10:00–11:00
EMCEE:
Dan Seymour (1950–1951)
Jan Murray (1951)
REGULARS:
Alan Dale
Judy Lynn
Bob Howard
Ray Bloch Orchestra
The Riddlers
Betty Luster
Jack Stanton

This musical quiz show was simulcast on the CBS Radio and Television networks. Dan Seymour was the host when the radio show expanded to both media and was replaced in February by Jan Murray. The regulars, both singers and dancers, stayed with the show throughout most of its TV run. Musical questions were asked of studio audience members and viewers at home. A special feature was the Phantom Voice, in which home viewers attempted to guess the identity of a celebrity, not known as a singer, when they were called. Correct identification could be worth a $15,000 jackpot. Each week a new clue to the identity of the Phantom Voice was given by the emcee.

SINGER & SONS (*Situation Comedy*)
FIRST TELECAST: *June 9, 1990*
LAST TELECAST: *June 27, 1990*
BROADCAST HISTORY:
Jun 1990, NBC Sat 9:30–10:00
Jun 1990, NBC Wed 9:00–9:30
CAST:
Nathan Singer .... Harold Gould
Sarah Patterson .... Esther Rolle
Mitchell Patterson .... Bobby Hosea
Reggie Patterson .... Tommy Ford
Deanna Patterson (age 5) .... Brooke Fontaine

Sheldon Singer .... Fred Stoller
Claudia James .... Arnetia Walker
Mrs. Tarkasian .... Anne Berger
Lou Gold .... Phil Leeds

Nathan's problem: what to do when you're the third generation of Singers to run a Jewish deli in uptown New York City, and you're getting on in years, and you've got no sons to take the place over? Sarah's solution: why not hire mine? The catch: Sarah, who had been Nathan's housekeeper since his wife had died, was black, providing the basis for this clash-of-cultures, bagels-and-soul-food sitcom. Mature Mitchell and streetwise Reggie, Sarah's very different sons, did the best they could for grouchy old Nathan. Other regulars included Sheldon, Singer's timid nephew, Claudia, a beautiful waitress, and an assortment of loyal but eccentric customers.

SINGING LADY, THE (*Children's*)

FIRST TELECAST: *November 7, 1948*
LAST TELECAST: *August 6, 1950*
BROADCAST HISTORY:

Nov 1948–Sep 1949, ABC Sun 6:30–7:00
Oct 1949–Aug 1950, ABC Sun 6:00–6:30

HOSTESS:

Ireene Wicker

ANNOUNCER:

Bob Dixon (in costume) (1949)
Dick Collier (1949)
John Griggs (1950)

REGULARS:

The Suzari Marionettes

Ireene Wicker was one of the most famous—and least likely—victims of the political blacklisting which disgraced television in the early 1950s. She had been a radio favorite for nearly 20 years with her gentle children's stories and lessons in good behavior when she first appeared on the ABC-TV network in 1948. Her program, as on radio, consisted of songs and fairy tales, acted out with the aid of the Suzari Marionettes. Some were true stories of American history, such as Betsy Ross and the flag.

In February 1950 her program was renewed for another year. Then in June a right-wing publication called *Red Channels* listed her among a large group of actors and actresses who had allegedly been associated with left-wing causes. In August, her program was abruptly canceled.

The principal charge, that she had in 1945 signed a petition for the election of Communist candidate Benjamin J. Davis to the New York City Council, turned out to be totally erroneous. An investigation was made of the 30,000 signatures on his petitions and her name was not there (Miss Wicker herself said that she had never heard of Benjamin Davis). Another citation, that she had sided with leftist causes in the Spanish Civil War, turned out to refer to her support of a fund-raising drive for Spanish refugee children. In Miss Wicker's defense, it was pointed out that she had performed playlets emphasizing good citizenship, had conducted an "I'm glad I'm an American because . . ." contest for children, and even recorded a series of records based on American history. Her accusers reluctantly admitted that *perhaps* a mistake had been made.

But the damage had been done. Advertisers and their agencies did not want to be associated with anyone "controversial." No network could find a spot for her. Her only work in this period was at a small radio station in western Massachusetts, and a couple of guest appearances. Finally from 1953–1954 ABC found a sponsor for a Sunday morning show for her, which lasted a single year. A bright and worthwhile career, built laboriously over two decades, had been destroyed by innuendo.

SINGLE GUY, THE (*Situation Comedy*)

FIRST TELECAST: *September 21, 1995*
LAST TELECAST: *April 16, 1997*
BROADCAST HISTORY:

Sep 1995–Mar 1996, NBC Thu 8:30–9:00
May 1996–Feb 1997, NBC Thu 8:30–9:00
Mar 1997–Apr 1997, NBC Wed 8:30–9:00

CAST:

Johnny Eliot .... Jonathan Silverman
Sam Sloane .... Joey Slotnick
Trudy Sloane .... Ming-Na Wen
Matt Parker (1995–1996) .... Mark Moses
Janeane Percy-Parker (1995–1996) ... Jessica Hecht
Manny .... Ernest Borgnine
Marie (1996–1997) .... Olivia d'Abo
Russell (1996–1997) ...... Shawn Michael Howard

EXECUTIVE PRODUCER/CREATOR:

Brad Hall

This urban comedy centered around the last "single guy" in a circle of young friends. Johnny was a fledgling Manhattan novelist who had no trouble finding dates, but no luck at all when it came to finding the woman of his dreams. His married friends, who were constantly trying to fix him up, were Sam, a loony studio engineer, and Trudy, his Asian wife, who ran a gallery; and Matt, a big, smiling lug who worked as a financial advisor, and his chatty wife Janeane. The latter couple were discovering the joys of parenthood with their baby Sebastian. The voice of experience was provided by Manny, the ebullient doorman at Johnny's apartment building, who had been married for fifty years.

In the second season Matt and Janeane left (Matt got a job with the Dole campaign), and Johnny got a couple of single friends—Marie, an English divorcée who moved into Johnny's apartment building, and Russell, a law student who worked at The Bagel Café, where the gang hung out.

SINGLED OUT (*Quiz/Audience Participation*)

BROADCAST HISTORY:

MTV
30 minutes
Produced: *1995–1997*
Premiered: *June 5, 1995*

REGULARS:

Chris Hardwick
Jenny McCarthy
Carmen Electra (1997)

MTV's raucous '90s take on the old *Dating Game* made a star out of its cohost. The format was typically MTV: fifty howling, horny guys in jeans and sweats lined up behind a young woman; those who matched her answers to a series of personal questions ("chest hair: like 'em bare, or like a bear?") moved forward one square, until only one wound up next to her in the winner's circle. Then she turned around to see what (er, who) she had "won" for a date. In the next round the game was reversed, with a guy in the chair and fifty howling chicks behind him. A veritable teenager's dream.

A dream, too, was the female cohost, blond bombshell Jenny McCarthy, who hooted and jeered at the losers, grabbed contestants by the arm, and generally dominated the proceedings. Her sexy, aggressive manner made her a media sensation during the first season, leading to a show of her own on MTV (*Jenny McCarthy*) and then a sitcom on NBC (*Jenny*). Poor Chris Hardwick, her funky cohost, could hardly get noticed until she left in February 1997, replaced by *Baywatch* babe Carmen Electra.

SINS OF THE CITY (*Detective Drama*)

BROADCAST HISTORY:

USA Network
60 minutes
Produced: *1998* (13 episodes)
Premiered: *July 19, 1998*

CAST:

Vince Karol .... Marcus Graham
Det. Freddie Corillo .... Jose Zuniga
Samantha (Sam) Richardson .... Barbara Williams

TV detectives are not generally known for their compassion and understanding—it's usually blow away the bad guys and move on—but Vince Karol was an exception. He knew what it was like to screw up, having done it himself, big-time, when he was a Miami Beach cop, by sleeping with his captain's wife. That ended his police career, so he became a private detective with a special interest in lawbreakers who had "made a mistake" but were redeemable. The unredeemable ones, of course, he blew away. At least that was the premise of this series, although it was sometimes hard to tell from the muddled stories.

Freddie was Vince's moralizing best friend on the force, a sensitive guy who had once studied to become a priest, and Sam his tough-as-nails friend in the District Attorney's office.

SIR ARTHUR CONAN DOYLE'S THE LOST WORLD (*Adventure*)

BROADCAST HISTORY:

Syndicated only
60 minutes
Produced: *1999–2002* (66 episodes)
Released: *October 1999*

CAST:

Prof. George Challenger .... Peter McCauley
Marguerite Krux .... Rachel Blakely
Lord John Roxton........................ Will Snow
John Malone (pilot only)........... William de Vry
Ned Malone .... David Orth
Veronica (Layton)................. Jennifer O'Dell
Dr. Arthur Summerlee (1999–2000)
.... Michael Sinelnikoff
Finn (2002) .... Lara Cox

Professor Challenger was an English explorer who, in 1920, returned from the Amazon with a diary and a photograph of dinosaurs taken by another explorer who had died in the jungle. After he failed to convince the London Zoological Society to fund an expedition to verify the existence of living prehistoric animals, he was approached by Marguerite, a rich amoral heiress, who offered to provide all the necessary resources—as long as she went along. Challenger assembled a team that included Malone, a young reporter for the *International Herald Tribune* (his first name was John in the film that preceded the series, but when it was rerun as part of the series *Ned* had been dubbed in); Roxton, an arrogant adventurer, and elderly Dr. Summerlee, a skeptical member of the Society.

When they arrived, the porters carrying their supplies were killed by cannibals, but they were able to use a hydrogen-filled balloon to carry them onto the plateau where the prehistoric animals resided. Once there they met Veronica, a beautiful girl who saved Roxton from a man-eating plant. She lived in a tree house built by her explorer parents, who had disappeared eleven years earlier. Veronica agreed to help them on their quest for knowledge, although she told them getting off the plateau was almost impossible, and let them use the tree house as their base of operations. In addition to the dinosaurs and other prehistoric animals and plants, they encountered a wide variety of people, ranging from contemporaries to apemen, cavemen and scaly nonhuman lizardmen. Roxton and bitchy Marguerite had a sexual attraction that she constantly tried to deny (by the third season she was much less adamant), while Malone was smitten with a more receptive Veronica.

In the first season finale, in a confrontation with primitives aligned with the lizardmen, Summerlee was shot in the stomach with an arrow while Challenger, Roxton and Malone apparently fell to their death from a great height into a swollen river. They survived the fall but Summerlee died from his wound. The second-season finale saw them attempting to leave the plateau in a dirigible. Unfortunately, after they discovered it was a ghost ship, Malone and the captain fell out clutching a single parachute; the rest of the explorers were still in the airship as it crashed into the side of a mountain and exploded. This time they survived because of time distortion caused by the ghost ship, and everyone was okay except Malone, who was floating in a temporal limbo. In November they managed to get him back into the real world, but a few months later he wandered off (although still in the credits, he did not appear in any more episodes).

In the spring Challenger's experiments with an energy source enabled him, Marguerite and Roxton to travel through time to the year 2033, when Earth had been devastated by war. When they returned they brought Finn, a woman from the future, back with them and vowed to change history to prevent the apocalyptic future from happening. Veronica and Finn didn't get along too well. Through a pendant with mysterious powers Veronica discovered it was her legacy to be the protector of the plateau, and that the power that infused the plateau could control all life on Earth. During the last episode temporal distortions were tossing everyone into different times and planes of reality, and Veronica attempted to save the others by sacrificing herself to the plateau, with no idea of the impact of the powers she was releasing. Nobody will ever know what happened. There was supposed to be a fourth season of *Lost World*, but the producers ran into financial problems that prevented its continuing in production.

Adapted from the novel *The Lost World* by Sir

Arthur Conan Doyle and filmed in Australia. The pilot for *Sir Arthur Conan Doyle's The Lost World* aired as a made-for-television movie on April 3, 1999, on TNT.

SIR FRANCIS DRAKE, see *Adventures of Sir Francis Drake, The*

SIR LANCELOT, see *Adventures of Sir Lancelot, The*

SIRENS (*Police Drama*)
FIRST TELECAST: *March 10, 1993*
LAST TELECAST: *August 18, 1993*
BROADCAST HISTORY:
Mar 1993–Apr 1993, ABC Wed 10:00–11:00
Jun 1993–Aug 1993, ABC Wed 10:00–11:00
(In first-run syndication September 1994–September 1995)
CAST:
Off. Sarah Berkezchuk (1993) .... Jayne Brook
Off. Lynn Stanton .... Adrienne-Joi Johnson
Off. Molly Whelan.................... Liza Snyder
Off./Sgt. James "Buddy" Zunder (1993–1995)
.... Tim Thomerson
Off. Heidi Schiller (1993)........ Deirdre O'Connell
Off. Dan Kelly (1993)................ John Terlesky
Off. Dan Kelly (1994–1995).......... Claude Genest
Cary Berkezchuk (1993) .... John Speredakos
Off./Sgt. Amy Shapiro (1994–1995) ... Ellen Cohen
Off. Richard Stiles (1994–1995)
.... D. Christopher Judge
Off. Jessie Jaworski (1994–1995) ... Jayne Heitmeyer
Det. Lyle Springer (1994–1995) .... Joel Wyner
Lt. Ray Gonzales (1994–1995) .... Don Jordan

Three rookie policewomen found action on the streets of Pittsburgh in this police show distinguished by its female point of view. The original three were Sarah, recently married and partnered with Dan; Lynn, a black single parent partnered with older cop Buddy; and Molly, single, looking, and paired with Heidi. Shootouts alternated with family and romantic entanglements, as Sarah and Cary's marriage almost broke up, Lynn dealt with her young son and daughter, and Molly found dates reluctant to share their beds with a police officer.

When new episodes of *Sirens* were produced for syndication in the fall of 1994, after its short run on ABC the year before, there were a number of changes. Sarah was replaced by Jessie, whose fellow officer husband, Chris, was murdered in the premiere episode. She was partnered with Dan (played by a different actor), and both Lynn and Molly were assigned new training partners (Amy and Richard, respectively). Buddy had been shifted to desk sergeant because of an irregular heartbeat. In a February 1995 episode he and Dan were caught off duty at the scene of a liquor store robbery and taken hostage by the thieves, who eventually shot them both. Dan survived, but Buddy didn't make it. The following week Amy was promoted to desk sergeant, Lynn and Jessie became partners, and Molly started working with Detective Springer.

Filmed in Montreal and Pittsburgh.

SIROTA'S COURT (*Situation Comedy*)
FIRST TELECAST: *December 1, 1976*
LAST TELECAST: *April 13, 1977*
BROADCAST HISTORY:
Dec 1976–Jan 1977, NBC Wed 9:00–9:30
Apr 1977, NBC Wed 9:30–10:00
CAST:
Matthew J. Sirota............. Michael Constantine
Maureen O'Connor................ Cynthia Harris
Gail Goodman .... Kathleen Miller
Bud Nugent.......................... Fred Willard
Sawyer Dabney .... Ted Ross
Bailiff John Bellson .... Owen Bush

Matthew J. Sirota was a night-court judge in a large metropolitan city, and far from the traditional serious, austere justices of most TV series. He had a sense of humor, was often more concerned with the practical rather than strictly legal resolution of cases, and was considered a character by many of his associates. For years he had been having an on-again, off-again affair with court clerk Maureen O'Connor, and periodically seemed on the verge of marriage. Others seen regularly in his court were super-liberal public defender Gail Goodman, forever the idealist but lacking the skills to be really successful; District Attorney Bud Nugent, whose incredible ambition and vanity blinded him to his own incompetence; Sawyer Dabney, an attorney who would handle any case if the price were right; and John, Sirota's bailiff, who treated the judge with the adoration of one who believed him to be Solomon.

SISKEL & EBERT (*Commentary*)
BROADCAST HISTORY:
Syndicated only
30 minutes
Produced: *1986–*
Released: *September 1986*
HOSTS:
Gene Siskel (1986–1999)
Roger Ebert
Richard Roeper (2000–)

For more than two decades Siskel (the tall thin one with the receding hair line) and Ebert (the hefty one with the glasses) shared a movie balcony exchanging barbs and debating the relative merits of theatrical movies. Their weekly series made them, arguably, the most influential movie critics in the world.

Siskel and Ebert's movie review series started on PBS as *Sneak Previews* in 1977 and went to commercial television in 1982 as *At the Movies*. A dispute with the series' original syndicator in 1986 prompted them to leave and start *Siskel & Ebert & the Movies*, whose title was shortened to *Siskel & Ebert* a few years later. Over the years there were some changes in the format. They added reviews of films on video and video equipment in addition to reviewing current films. Some episodes were done as theme shows on genres or the works of individual producers, directors, or actors. Without doubt the most popular show every year was their Oscar special, in which they made their personal picks for the Academy Awards.

Production companies, directors, producers, and actors put tremendous stock in Siskel and Ebert's "thumbs up/thumbs down" evaluations of their films, and when a movie received a "two thumbs up" review, its ads were sure to tout the fact. Over the years these print rivals—Siskel's reviews appeared in the *Chicago Tribune* and Ebert's in the *Chicago Sun-Times*—had become good friends despite their sometimes acrimonious disagreements on the show. When Siskel passed away in February 1999, nine months after surgery to remove a brain tumor, it was a sad day for movie fans everywhere. Ebert vowed to continue the show, using rotating guest cohosts, as had been done during the six weeks when Siskel was recovering from the surgery. During this period the title was changed to *Roger Ebert and the Movies.*

In the fall of 2000, after more than a year of rotating cohosts, the producers hired *Chicago Sun-Times* columnist Richard Roeper as Ebert's new permanent cohost, and the show was rechristened *Ebert & Roeper and the Movies.*

SISTER KATE (*Situation Comedy*)

FIRST TELECAST: *September 16, 1989*
LAST TELECAST: *July 30, 1990*
BROADCAST HISTORY:

Sep 1989, NBC Sat 9:30–10:00
Sep 1989–Nov 1989, NBC Sun 8:00–8:30
Dec 1989–Jan 1990, NBC Sun 8:30–9:00
Jul 1990, NBC Mon 8:00–8:30

CAST:

Sister Katherine Lambert (Kate) .... Stephanie Beacham
Todd Mahaffey (age 16) .... Jason Priestley
April Newberry (16) .... Erin Reed
Frederika Marasco (16) .... Hannah Cutrona
Hilary Logan (12) .... Penina Segall
Eugene Colodner (11) .... Harley Cross
Violet Johnson (9) .... Alexaundria Simmons
Neville Williams (7) .... Joel Robinson
**Lucas Underwood* .... Gordon Jump

*Occasional

THEME:

"Maybe An Angel," sung by Amy Grant

In one of 1989's more intriguing bits of casting, Stephanie Beacham, most recently seen as the scheming vixen Sable on *The Colbys,* donned a nun's habit and confronted a bunch of scheming orphans in this cutesy comedy. The unruly kids of Redemption House had already driven out three kindly old priests, but they proved to be no match for "Sister Mary Rambo." She had been transferred to the orphanage from an archeological dig, a move she had not requested. ("Sifting through the bones of ancient skeletons . . . is my preferred way of dealing with people.") But Sister Kate managed to outwit the little plotters at every turn.

There were plenty of the moral lessons one expects from a show like this, and an ample supply of heartwarming moments, as when some possible adoptive parents came to look over the kids. Out came young Hilary wearing a sign reading "Low Mileage," and Eugene with one that said "$500 Rebate." Awwww.

SISTER, SISTER (*Situation Comedy*)

FIRST TELECAST: *April 1, 1994*
LAST TELECAST: *September 19, 1999*
BROADCAST HISTORY:

Apr 1994–May 1994, ABC Fri 9:30–10:00
Jun 1994–Sep 1994, ABC Tue 8:30–9:00
Nov 1994–Mar 1995, ABC Wed 8:00–8:30
Mar 1995–Apr 1995, ABC Fri 8:30–9:00
May 1995–Jun 1995, ABC Wed 8:00–8:30
Aug 1995–Jul 1996, WB Wed 8:00–8:30
Sep 1995–Oct 1995, WB Sun 7:30–8:00
Oct 1995–Jul 1996, WB Sun 8:00–8:30
Jul 1996, WB Wed 8:30–9:00
Aug 1996–Feb 1997, WB Wed 8:00–8:30
Aug 1996–Sep 1996, WB Sun 8:30–9:00
Mar 1997, WB Wed 8:00–9:00
Apr 1997–Mar 1998, WB Wed 8:00–8:30
Mar 1998–Sep 1999, WB Sun 8:00–8:30
Mar 1998–May 1998, WB Wed 8:30–9:00

CAST:

Ray Campbell .... Tim Reid
Tamera Campbell (age 14) .... Tamera Mowry
Lisa Landry .... Jackee Harry
Tia Landry (14) .... Tia Mowry
Roger Evans (1995–1998) .... Marques Houston
**Terrence Winninham (1995–1996)* ... Dorien Wilson
**Denise Mondello (1995)* .... Anna Slotky
**Principal Mitushka (1995–1997)* ...... Fred Willard
Tyreke Scott (1997–1999) .... RonReaco Lee
**Viveca Sinclair Shaw (1997–1999)* ... Rolanda Watts
Diavian Johnson (1997–1999) .... Alexis Fields
Jordan Bennett (1997–1999) ...... Deon Richmond
Simone Flasser (1998) .... Rachel Harris

*Occasional

A light, cheerful sitcom about twin girls, separated at birth, who suddenly found each other after 14 years. They had been adopted by different parents, Tia growing up in downtown Detroit, where her mom, Lisa (now a widow), worked intermittently as a seamstress, and Tamera raised in the suburbs, where her affluent dad, Ray (now a widower), owned a limousine service. Encountering each other in a department store, the girls took to each other immediately, vowing never to be separated again. Their single parents were another story. Brash, pushy, working-girl Lisa clashed immediately with quiet, conservative Ray, a sort of black yuppie. Stories revolved around the girls' escapades and Ray and Lisa's gradual, grudging attraction to one another. Roger was a younger boy with a crush on disdainful Tia. Or was that Tamera?

When *Sister, Sister* was added to the WB lineup in the fall of 1995, it was shown twice a week. Newly produced episodes aired Wednesdays, while reruns of the "classic" (according to the WB press department) ABC episodes aired on Sundays. In the first new episode on the WB, Tamera and Tia were starting their sophomore year at Roosevelt High School. Seen occasionally were Denise, a bright classmate; Terrence, who was dating Lisa; and Principal Mitushka. A year later fawning Roger had matured into someone both girls found—surprise!—attractive. Ray and Lisa started dating, and by the spring of 1997 they were getting serious—but it fizzled out. Early in their senior year Tia, the more studious of the twins, got a job working in a bookstore in the neighborhood mall. Even though *The Smart Guy* was set in Washington, D.C., T.J. (played by the Mowry twins' real-life kid brother) showed up as an S.A.T. tutor in October 1997. Tia started dating Tyreke, a 19-year-old reformed street kid working as a mechanic for Ray, and Jordan became Tamera's steady guy. In February the twins were both accepted at the University of Michigan.

That fall they went off to Ann Arbor, 35 miles from Detroit, but because they couldn't get housing, commuted from an apartment over their parents' garage. Also with them at school were Tyreke, who had a part-time job working for campus security; Jordan; and their girlfriend Diavian. Diavian's roommate, Simone, was an obnoxious, pretentious white girl repeating her senior year because she had flunked a couple of courses the previous year. Ray ran for state senate (he lost a close race) and Lisa's dress business flourished. In February the girls met their birth father, famous photojournalist Matt Sullivan (Tony Carreiro). In the last episode Lisa married Victor Sims (Richard Lawson), Ray took a job working for the governor in Lansing, Tia was preparing to spend the summer in New York as an intern with the WNBA and Tamera was on her way to Africa for a summer with her birth father.

SISTERS (*Serial Drama*)
FIRST TELECAST: *May 11, 1991*
LAST TELECAST: *May 4, 1996*
BROADCAST HISTORY:

May 1991–Jun 1991, NBC Sat 10:00–11:00
Aug 1991–May 1993, NBC Sat 10:00–11:00
Jun 1993–Jul 1993, NBC Thu 10:00–11:00
Aug 1993–Apr 1995, NBC Sat 10:00–11:00
Sep 1995–May 1996, NBC Sat 10:00–11:00

CAST:

Alex Reed Halsey Barker .... Swoosie Kurtz
Teddy Reed .... Sela Ward
Georgie Reed Whitsig .... Patricia Kalember
Frankie Reed (1991–1995) .... Julianne Phillips
Beatrice Reed .... Elizabeth Hoffman
*Dr. Wade Halsey (1991**)* .... David Dukes
Reed Halsey (1991) .... Kathy Wagner
Reed Halsey (1991–1994) .... Ashley Judd
Reed Halsey (1995–1996) .... Noelle Parker
John Whitsig .... Garrett M. Brown
Evan Whitsig (age 9) .... Dustin Berkovitz
Trevor Whitsig .... Ryan Francis
Mitch Margolis (1991–1994) .... Ed Marinaro
Cat Margolis (15) .... Heather McAdam
**Victor Runkle (1991–1992)* .... David Gianopoulos
**Judge Truman Ventnor (1991–1995)* .. Philip Sterling
**Simon Bolt (1992–1993)* .... Mark Frankel
**Kirby Philby (1992–1994)* .... Paul S. Rudd
Big Al Barker (1993–1996) .... Robert Klein
Norma Lear (1993–1996) .... Nora Dunn
Det. James Falconer (1993–1994) ... George Clooney
Dr. Charlotte "Charley" Bennett (1994–1995) .... Jo Anderson
Dr. Charlotte "Charley" Bennett (1995–1996) .... Sheila Kelley
Dr. David Caspian (1994–1995) ..... Daniel Gerroll
Lucky (1994–1995) .... John Wesley Shipp
**Roxie (1994–1995)* .... Kathryn Zaremba
Daniel Albright (1994–1995) ..... Gregory Harrison
Off. Billy Griffin (1995–1996) .... Eric Close
Brian Kohler-Voss (1995–1996) .... Joe Flanigan
Dr. Gabriel Sorenson (1995–1996)... Stephen Collins

*Occasional
**Occasional thereafter

Set in deceptively peaceful Winnetka, Illinois, *Sisters* explored the emotional entanglements of the four Reed sisters as they came together to help their mother after the death of their father. Alex, the eldest, was a wealthy, WASP-ish plastic surgeon's wife who didn't realize that her marriage was in trouble (doc was a cross-dresser!); Frankie, the youngest, a high-powered young marketing analyst in love with Mitch; Georgie, a part-time real estate agent and the wife of flaky, out-of-work John; and Teddy, a free-spirited artist and on-and-off alcoholic, who breezed into town after "searching for herself" in California and promptly began trying to win Mitch, her ex, back from Frankie. Mother Beatrice was hitting the bottle a bit hard herself, leaving level-headed Georgie to play the role of family mediator. Kids included Alex's overachieving daughter Reed, Teddy's teenager Cat, and Georgie's sons Evan and Trevor.

Each episode opened with the sisters chattering about their lives in a steam room. They had a lot to talk about: Alex and Wade's acrimonious separation, Frankie and Mitch's wedding (invaded by Teddy with a shotgun), Teddy's pregnancy, Evan's leukemia. Another unique feature of the series was the inclusion of nostalgic "thinkbacks" to the sisters' childhood in Winnetka, in which the characters' younger and adult selves interacted.

Stories unfolded in soap-opera fashion over the years. Alex divorced Dr. Wade, had an affair with plumber Victor, battled breast cancer (1993), and finally began a new career as a talk-show host. Norma was her gay producer. In February 1994, Alex married Big Al, who proposed to her on the air. Shortly thereafter he was imprisoned on a tax fraud charge, only to be released and elected mayor, making her a first lady! Meanwhile Reed eloped with Kirby (1992), had a baby (1994), and moved to Los Angeles.

Teddy began a new career as a fashion designer, had an affair with millionaire Simon, and in May 1994 married police detective Falconer (who had been investigating Cat's rape) on a plane when they thought it was about to crash. Falconer was killed by a drug dealer the following year. Georgie, having weathered Evan's leukemia and troubled son Trevor's problems, agreed to be a surrogate mother for her sister Frankie. In November 1992, she was in an auto accident and went into labor while trapped in the car, with everyone looking on, unable to reach her. This story was so bizarre that Hollywood approached her about making it into a movie. Subsequently she went into therapy with unscrupulous Dr. Caspian.

As for Frankie, she left the corporate world to run the Sweet Sixteen malt shop, where her sibs often hung out. She married Mitch in the fall of 1991. Unable to conceive, the couple used sister Georgie as a surrogate; the baby was named Thomas George. The marriage was nevertheless unstable, and eventually they broke up. In 1994–1995 Frankie began managing a prizefighter named Lucky.

Mother Bea found romance as well, marrying retired Judge Ventnor in 1992. He developed Alzheimer's disease and died in early 1995, and Alex was accused of his murder via assisted suicide.

The four sisters were joined by a fifth in April 1993, when it was revealed that their late father had still another daughter as a result of a long-term affair with his nurse. They were at first wary of their new half sister, Charley, but she eventually became one of the family, adding her woes to their own.

In the final season Frankie left to pursue her business career; Georgie, divorced, had an affair with Brian; Cat became a police officer; and Teddy, shot during a car jacking, fell in love with the surgeon who saved her life, Gabriel, and became pregnant. In the final episode, Georgie got her degree with a thesis based on the lives of her sisters, but when she received an offer from Random House to publish it, the siblings were furious. Then mother Bea had a stroke and died, leaving Charley—the newest sister—as her executor. Super-sucessful businesswoman Frankie flew in from the Orient at the last minute, and the five sisters, together one last time, with Alex now the matriarch, scattered Bea's ashes in her beloved rose garden.

SIT OR MISS (*Quiz/Audience Participation*)
FIRST TELECAST: *August 6, 1950*
LAST TELECAST: *October 29, 1950*
BROADCAST HISTORY:
Aug 1950–Oct 1950, ABC Sun 8:30–9:00
EMCEE:
Kay Westfall
George Sotos
MUSICAL ACCOMPANIMENT:
Porter Heaps

This was a TV variation on the old parlor game of musical chairs. Five contestants competed. Each time one of them missed a chair, he was faced with a question, and if he missed the question he had to perform a stunt to win a $10 prize. At the end of the game all five contestants had a chance at a $75 jackpot by guessing, from a verbal clue, the contents of a mystery box. From Chicago.

SIX MILLION DOLLAR MAN, THE (*Adventure*)
FIRST TELECAST: *January 18, 1974*
LAST TELECAST: *March 6, 1978*
BROADCAST HISTORY:
Jan 1974–Oct 1974, ABC Fri 8:30–9:30
Nov 1974–Jan 1975, ABC Fri 9:00–10:00
Jan 1975–Aug 1975, ABC Sun 7:30–8:30
Sep 1975–Jan 1978, ABC Sun 8:00–9:00
Jan 1978–Mar 1978, ABC Mon 8:00–9:00
CAST:
Col. Steve Austin....................... Lee Majors
Oscar Goldman................. Richard Anderson
Dr. Rudy Wells (1974–1975) .... Alan Oppenheimer
Dr. Rudy Wells (1975–1978)....... Martin E. Brooks

The Six Million Dollar Man touched off a wave of superheroes on TV in the mid-1970s. It was first seen as a series of 90-minute movies run on ABC in March, October, and November 1973 (part of the *ABC Suspense Movie* package), then became a regular weekly series in January 1974. At first the ratings were mediocre, but the program grew steadily until by 1975 it was one of TV's biggest hits.

Handsome, athletic Steve Austin was a U.S. astronaut who had been critically injured when the moon-landing craft he was testing over a Southwestern desert crashed to the ground. Fighting to save his life, government doctors decided to try a new type of operation devised by Dr. Rudy Wells—the replacement of certain human parts by atomic-powered electromechanical devices, capable of superhuman performance. Steve lived and became a cyborg—part human, part machine, endowed with powerful legs that permitted him great speed, a right arm of incredible strength, and a left eye of penetrating vision (it even had a built-in grid screen!). Armed with these weapons, Steve set out on dangerous missions for the Office of Scientific Information, battling international villains, mad scientists, and even a few alien monsters such as Bigfoot.

Early in the series Steve learned that he was not the only bionic wonder around. It seemed that Dr. Wells had built a *seven*-million-dollar man as backup for Steve, using an injured race-car driver named Barney Miller (played by Monte Markham). Unfortunately, the other superman ran amok, and Steve had to find a way to dispatch him, in a battle of the bionic men. A few months later, in January 1975, Jaime Sommers (Lindsay Wagner) was introduced as Steve's love interest and a former tennis pro who had been grievously injured in a sky-diving accident. She was reconstructed into the Bionic Woman. Unfortunately her body rejected its bionic parts, and she died—at least Steve (and viewers) thought she did, until she was brought back ("out of a coma") for several more episodes in the fall. Then she got her own spin-off series called *The Bionic Woman*.

Steve and Jaime's romance seemed destined never to be fulfilled, but nevertheless in November 1976 the series did produce a bionic boy—not theirs, but 16-year-old athlete Andy Sheffield (played by Vincent Van Patten), whose paralyzed legs were replaced by Dr. Wells. Using his new powers the boy promptly set out on a crusade to clear his dead father's name.

Oscar Goldman appeared as Steve's government boss, and Peggy Callahan (Jennifer Darling) was seen occasionally as his secretary. The role of Dr. Rudy Wells was played by a number of actors, including Martin Balsam in the movie pilot and Alan Oppenheimer and Martin E. Brooks in the series.

Based on the novel *Cyborg,* by Martin Caidin.

SIX WIVES OF HENRY VIII, THE (*Historical Drama*)
FIRST TELECAST: *August 1, 1971*
LAST TELECAST: *September 5, 1971*
BROADCAST HISTORY:
Aug 1971–Sep 1971, CBS Sun 9:30–11:00
CAST:
Henry VIII .... Keith Michell
Catherine of Aragon (divorced).... Annette Crosbie
Anne Boleyn (beheaded) .... Dorothy Tutin
Jane Seymour (natural death) .... Anne Stallybrass
Anne of Cleves (divorced) .... Elvi Hale
Catherine Howard (beheaded) ... Angela Pleasence
Catherine Parr (outlived him).... Rosalie Crutchley
Duke of Norfolk................ Patrick Troughton
Oliver Cromwell .... Wolfe Morris
Archbishop Cranmer .... Bernard Hepton
NARRATOR:
Anthony Quayle

This series of six 90-minute programs had been produced in England by the BBC and won the British equivalent of the Emmy award in five categories. CBS brought it to American television in the summer of 1971. The one addition to the American version was narrator Anthony Quayle. He introduced and concluded each telecast and provided historical background. During his reign as English monarch, Henry VIII had two wives beheaded for adultery, saw one die of natural causes, was divorced from two others, and, when he died in 1547 at the age of 56, was survived by his sixth, Catherine Parr.

SIXTH SENSE, THE (*Occult*)
FIRST TELECAST: *January 15, 1972*
LAST TELECAST: *December 30, 1972*
BROADCAST HISTORY:
Jan 1972–Dec 1972, ABC Sat 10:00–11:00 (OS)

CAST:

Dr. Michael Rhodes.................... Gary Collins
Nancy Murphy (Jan–May) .... Catherine Ferrar

"You enter a strange room for the first time, yet you know you've been there before. You dream about an event that happens some days later. Someone begins to talk, and you already know what they're going to say. A coincidence? Maybe. But more than likely it's extrasensory perception, a sixth sense that many scientists believe we all possess, but rarely use."

That quotation from a press release pretty well sums up the kind of stories told on *The Sixth Sense*. Dr. Michael Rhodes' studies in parapsychology at a major university took him into the uncharted world of ESP, telepathy, and other psychic phenomena every week, sometimes leading to eerie adventures. Perhaps his most useful exploit was communicating an escape plan to an American prisoner of war in Vietnam, by thought transference. Nancy Murphy was his research assistant during the series' first few months.

$64,000 CHALLENGE, THE (*Quiz/Audience Participation*)

FIRST TELECAST: *April 8, 1956*
LAST TELECAST: *September 7, 1958*
BROADCAST HISTORY:

Apr 1956–Sep 1958, CBS Sun 10:00–10:30

EMCEE:

Sonny Fox (1956)
Ralph Story (1956–1958)

This was a highly successful spin-off of CBS' popular big-money quiz show *The $64,000 Question*. Any of the winners from the original show whose earnings had been at least $8,000 were eligible to be challenged on this series, in the field of knowledge in which they had already demonstrated their skill. The same questions were asked of champion and challenger, each in a separate isolation booth. If one of them missed a question at any level, and the other answered it correctly, the loser was then eliminated. The contestant who had answered correctly continued alone until he also missed a question, quit, or reached the $64,000 question. In any event, he was guaranteed no less than the amount at which he had defeated his opponent. A successful challenger could be challenged by others. On occasion a defeated champion returned as a challenger and won. Through this format, contestants could multiply their winnings from a prior round several times over.

The biggest winner in the era of big-money quiz shows became a regular on this show. Teddy Nadler was a $70-per-week civil service clerk from St. Louis who happened to have a photographic memory. He had, apparently, memorized a complete encyclopedia and could dredge up the most obscure information. By the time *The $64,000 Challenge* left the air in 1958, he had won $252,000 and was still going strong. He became such a celebrity on the show that he was often competing with two or three different people, on totally unrelated topics, all at the same time.

$64,000 QUESTION, THE (*Quiz/Audience Participation*)

FIRST TELECAST: *June 7, 1955*
LAST TELECAST: *November 2, 1958*
BROADCAST HISTORY:

Jun 1955–Jun 1958, CBS Tue 10:00–10:30
Sep 1958–Nov 1958, CBS Sun 10:00–10:30

EMCEE:

Hal March

ASSISTANT:

Lynn Dollar

QUESTION AUTHORITY:

Dr. Bergen Evans

The era of the big-money quiz show arrived during the summer of 1955 in the form of *The $64,000 Question*. A much-inflated variation on radio's *$64 Question*, it offered contestants the opportunity to win vast sums of money by answering extremely complex questions on whatever subject they professed to be experts. A contestant first went through preliminary rounds up to the $4,000 level, with each question, starting at $64, worth twice as much as the preceding question. At that point the contestant would go home and return to answer one question a week until missing or reaching $64,000. The consolation prize for missing after reaching the $8,000 plateau was a new Cadillac. Contestants could quit at any time and leave with their winnings. In order to enable the contestants to concentrate completely, and to avoid any possible answers shouted from the studio audience, all questions from $8,000 on up were asked while contestants were sealed inside a Revlon isolation booth (named for the sponsor).

The appeal of seeing ordinary people sweating through complex questions to win huge sums of money was enormous, and *The $64,000 Question* became an overnight sensation. It shot to number-one among all programs on TV in its first season on the air, displacing *I Love Lucy*, and it spawned many imitators in the big-money sweepstakes. Among them were *Twenty-One* and, from Louis G. Cowan, the man who had started it all here, *The Big Surprise* and *The $64,000 Challenge*.

Many of the contestants were interesting people and generated tremendous empathy from the audience. One of the early winners was New York City policeman Redmond O'Hanlon, an expert on Shakespeare, who took home $16,000. Gino Prato, a shoemaker from the Bronx, took home $32,000 for his knowledge of opera. Catherine Kreitzer was a housewife who won $32,000 on the subject of the Bible, and was then signed to do a series of Bible readings on *The Ed Sullivan Show*. Jockey Billy Pearson was an early winner of $64,000—his subject was art. Many of the winners on *The $64,000 Question* went on to make extra money on its companion show, *The $64,000 Challenge*. One of those was a young psychologist, Dr. Joyce Brothers, who parlayed her knowledge of boxing to the grand prize $64,000 here, another $70,000 on *Challenge*, and a long and successful career as a radio and television personality. The biggest winner on *The $64,000 Question*, however, was young Robert Strom, an 11-year-old genius who amassed $192,000 during a period when, in order to hold onto its audience amid the competing shows, three new plateaus were added to *The $64,000 Question* making the maximum possible winnings $256,000. Strom's total quiz-show winnings, $224,000 including money won on other shows, made him the second biggest winner of the big-money quiz-show era. Only Teddy Nadler's $252,000 on *The $64,000 Challenge* was higher.

The money angle was a magic attraction, especially during the early days of the giant giveaway shows. *TV Guide* kept a running total of the amount given away on this show—$750,000 and 10 Cadillacs in the first year and $1,000,000 by November 1956—and published numerous articles about the show and its contestants. There were always rumors that the series was rigged, that the desire to put interesting personalities on the air, rather than brilliant but dull geniuses, resulted in the producers providing answers in advance to some, but not all, of the contestants. As early as September 1956 there was a lengthy article in *TV Guide* in which the producers of *Question, Challenge*, and *The Big Surprise* adamantly denied that there was anything misleading or dishonest about the shows, but in the fall of 1958 the bubble burst. A disgruntled loser on *Dotto*, another giveaway show, announced that the show was rigged, and precipitated the quiz-show scandal that eventually forced all of them off the air. No longer would contestants sweat and ponder in the "isolation booths" that kept them from hearing what was going on in the outside world while searching for answers to incredibly complicated questions.

For a syndicated revival of this program in the 1970s, see *The $128,000 Question*.

60 MINUTES (*Newsmagazine*)
FIRST TELECAST: *September 24, 1968*
LAST TELECAST:
BROADCAST HISTORY:
Sep 1968–Jun 1971, CBS Tue 10:00–11:00 (OS)
Jan 1972–Jun 1972, CBS Sun 6:00–7:00
Jan 1973–Jun 1973, CBS Sun 6:00–7:00
Jun 1973–Sep 1973, CBS Fri 8:00–9:00
Jan 1974–Jun 1974, CBS Sun 6:00–7:00
Jul 1974–Sep 1974, CBS Sun 9:30–10:30
Sep 1974–Jun 1975, CBS Sun 6:00–7:00
Jul 1975–Sep 1975, CBS Sun 9:30–10:30
Dec 1975– , CBS Sun 7:00–8:00
CORRESPONDENTS:
Mike Wallace
Harry Reasoner (1968–1970, 1978–1991)
Morley Safer (1970–)
Dan Rather (1975–1981)
Andrew Rooney (1978–)
Ed Bradley (1981–)
Diane Sawyer (1984–1989)
Meredith Vieira (1989–1991)
Steve Kroft (1989–)
Lesley Stahl (1991–)
DEBATERS:
James J. Kilpatrick (1971–1979)
Nicholas Von Hoffman (1971–1974)
Shana Alexander (1975–1979)

60 Minutes was the *Time* magazine of the air. Each telecast opened with a "table of contents" (brief excerpts from the three or more stories that would be covered on that episode) superimposed on what appeared to be a magazine cover. Also superimposed at various times, usually between stories, was a moving stopwatch letting viewers know precisely how much of that night's "60 Minutes" was left. Within the magazine trappings lay a documentary series with remarkable scope. There were pieces on politics and politicians; the workings of governments, both domestic and foreign; personality profiles on artists, athletes, and citizens whose stories had mass appeal; and light feature pieces on everything from trade shows, to new inventions, to the shopping phenomenon that was Bloomingdale's department store. Indeed, *60 Minutes* was sufficiently diversified that, like each issue of a successful magazine, it had something to appeal to, concern, or interest almost everybody.

Among the more provocative stories featured in segments of *60 Minutes* were numerous items on politics in the Middle East; a 1971 feature on the situation in the Gulf of Tonkin; "The Poppy Fields of Turkey—The Heroin Labs of Marseilles—The N.Y. Connection" (1972); "The Selling of Colonel Herbert" (1973); "The End of a Salesman" (1974); "Local News and the Ratings War" (1974); several items on, and interviews with, participants in the Watergate scandal during 1974–1976; a controversial story on the plight of Jordanian Jews (1976); a feature on the brain damage suffered by workers in a chemical plant manufacturing Kepone (1976); and a dramatic report by Dan Rather from inside the sealed borders of Afghanistan, reporting on resistance to the Soviet invasion (1980).

60 Minutes spent its first three seasons on an alternate-week schedule with *CBS New Hour*. It was during this period that one of the original two correspondents, Harry Reasoner, left the show to join ABC News. His last appearance was on November 24, 1970. Two weeks later, Morley Safer joined Mike Wallace. When it moved into its own weekly time slot on Sunday evenings, a new regular feature called "Point Counterpoint" was added. Each week two columnists at opposite ends of the ideological spectrum—conservative James J. Kilpatrick and liberal Nicholas Von Hoffman (replaced by Shana Alexander in 1975)—would debate a current issue. They never agreed about anything. Dan Rather joined the show in December 1975, when it moved into the prime 7:00–8:00 P.M. hour, expanding the correspondent team from a duet to a trio. It was here that *60 Minutes* became a major hit, violating the traditional rule that documentary programs are marginal audience attractions. The summer of 1978 saw the addition of "Three Minutes or So with Andy Rooney" as a weekly feature filling in for the vacationing debaters from "Point Counterpoint." At the start of the 1978–1979 season Mr. Rooney's musings shared time with "Point Counterpoint," each feature airing on alternate weeks. It was also that fall that Harry Reasoner returned to *60 Minutes*, bringing the number of correspondents to four.

In the spring of 1979 Shana Alexander decided to leave *60 Minutes* and, although there was an attempt to find a new liberal to debate James Kilpatrick, the "Point Counterpoint" feature was dropped from the show (last telecast May 29, 1979) and Andy Rooney's observations became a weekly feature. The 1979–1980 season was a milestone for *60 Minutes* as it became the highest-rated series in all of prime time. It was in the spring of 1980 that CBS announced Dan Rather would leave. Despite leaving *60 Minutes* to anchor the CBS News in the spring of 1981, Rather had already recorded enough features to remain a *60 Minutes* regular through the end of the 1980–1981 season. Ed Bradley replaced Rather in 1982 and Diane Sawyer joined in late 1984.

When Ms. Sawyer left *60 Minutes* in 1989 to become cohost of ABC's *PrimeTime Live*, Meredith Vieira and Steve Kroft were added to the roster of correspondents. Vieira's departure in early 1991, reportedly due to a dispute with *60 Minutes* executive producer Don

Hewitt, brought Lesley Stahl to the show. Longtime correspondent Harry Reasoner retired that May, with a nostalgic collection of excerpts from stories he had done for the show over the years. In failing health, he passed away less than two months later.

In May 1996, as part of an effort to freshen the 28-year-old series, the producers revived the old "Point Counterpoint" debate segment featuring three commentators—outspoken syndicated newspaper columnists Molly Ivins and Stanley Crouch and author P. J. O'Rourke. Negative critical and viewer response prompted them to drop the segment less than two months after it premiered. The segment returned again, in March 2003, with former president Bill Clinton "debating" former senator Bob Dole, the man he had defeated in the 1996 presidential election. However, since the two were never seen together on the same set (their segments were taped separately) and did not directly respond to each other, it was hardly a debate.

The conclusion of *60 Minutes* telecasts, in true magazine fashion, consisted of one of the correspondents reading a collection of letters to the editors, followed by that ever-moving stopwatch signaling the end of the hour while the closing credits rolled.

SIXTY MINUTES II (*Newsmagazine*)

FIRST TELECAST: *January 13, 1999*

LAST TELECAST:

BROADCAST HISTORY:

Jan 1999–Jun 1999, CBS Wed 9:00–10:00
Jun 1999–Jul 2001, CBS Tue 9:00–10:00
Jul 2001–Jan 2003, CBS Wed 8:00–9:00
Jan 2003–Jun 2003, CBS Wed 9:00–10:00
Jun 2003– , CBS Wed 8:00–9:00

CORRESPONDENTS:

Dan Rather
Bob Simon
Charlie Rose
Vicki Mabrey
Scott Pelley
Lara Logan (2002–)

COMMENTATOR:

Jimmy Tingle (1999–2000)
Charles Grodin (2000–2003)

As the cost of entertainment programming skyrocketed in the '90s, cheap-to-produce newsmagazines proliferated on ABC and NBC. CBS pressured Don Hewitt, executive producer of its hit series *60 Minutes*—the granddaddy of TV newsmagazines—to produce multiple editions, but he and the show's correspondents fought against it for months, feeling it would water down the original. Eventually a compromise was reached. Hewitt would oversee the new show, but unlike newsmagazines on other networks, whose correspondents were seen on multiple nights, CBS left the original series intact and staffed *60 Minutes II* with a new roster of correspondents.

CBS anchorman Dan Rather, himself an alumnus of *60 Minutes*, was the lead correspondent. Simon and Mabrey had been contributors to other CBS news programs, and Rose was a former CBS newsman who continued to host his *Charlie Rose* interview show on PBS. Hewitt did make one concession to the new show. In addition to the stories by its own correspondents, each episode repeated a segment that had first aired on *60 Minutes*, introduced and updated by the original correspondent. Humorist Tingle was *60 Minutes II*'s Andy Rooney, providing offbeat commentary. He categorized his perspective on life's little absurdities as "uncommon sense." Tingle was replaced by Charles Grodin, but when Grodin departed in March 2003, the position of commentator was dropped from the show.

SK8 TV (*Kids' Magazine*)

BROADCAST HISTORY:

Nickelodeon
30 minutes
Produced: *1990* (13 episodes)
Premiered: *July 4, 1990*

HOSTS:

Skatemaster Tate
Matthew Lyn

Always ready to catch a wave, Nickelodeon, the kids' network, launched this skateboarding show in the summer of 1990 as the skateboarding craze swept America. The "clubhouse" was the bottom of an empty swimming pool in California, and topics were the dress, the gear, the language, and of course exhibitions of daredevil skateboarding. *SK8 TV* was first seen as a Nickelodeon special in January 1990.

SKAG (*Drama*)

FIRST TELECAST: *January 6, 1980*

LAST TELECAST: *February 21, 1980*

BROADCAST HISTORY:

Jan 1980–Feb 1980, NBC Thu 10:00–11:00

CAST:

Pete "Skag" Skagska .... Karl Malden
Jo Skagska .... Piper Laurie
David Skagska .... Craig Wasson
John Skagska .... Peter Gallagher
Patricia Skagska .... Kathryn Holcomb
Barbara Skagska .... Leslie Ackerman
Petar Skagska .... George Voskovec
Whalen .... Powers Boothe
Paczka .... Frank Campanella
Dottie Jessup .... Shirley Stoler

Pete Skagska was a 56-year-old union foreman at a steel mill in Pittsburgh. It was a hard life, but the only one he knew, until he almost lost it when a crippling stroke temporarily forced him to stay home and try to put his life back together. He did have problems. He was concerned about his second wife, Jo, the only Jewish member of an otherwise staunchly Serbian Orthodox Catholic household, and 12 years his junior. His relationships with his children were troubled. The eldest, David, worked with him at the mill but felt uncomfortable about it; 24-year-old John was in medical school and more concerned with making money than with his family; 18-year-old Patricia was extremely shy and insecure; and 15-year-old Barbara was sleeping around to make herself popular despite her obesity. Skag's elderly father, Petar, left speechless and partially incapacitated by a major stroke of his own, also lived in the Skagska household. Whalen was the young steelworker who had taken over Skag's crew while he recovered from the stroke and coveted the job on a permanent basis. All the while, Skag, the stubborn traditionalist, was trying to adjust to a changing world whose values he did not fully understand.

The issues dramatized on *Skag* made for heavy viewing: impotence, senility, prostitution, labor problems, jealousy, family discord, and the conflicts caused by different value structures. The critics loved the show. They called it the season's most thought-provoking, realistic depiction of contemporary life. Boosted by tremendous advance publicity, the special Sunday three-hour premiere of *Skag* attracted a large audience. Unfortunately, the viewers did not stay with it when it moved to its regular Thursday time slot. Maybe it was too depressing to see that much hard reality. The producers of the show took out full-page newspaper ads in major cities beseeching the public to save *Skag*, but it didn't help. After its original limited run, *Skag* expired, rejected by the viewing public.

SKIP FARRELL SHOW, THE (*Music*)
FIRST TELECAST: *January 17, 1949*
LAST TELECAST: *August 28, 1949*
BROADCAST HISTORY:
Jan 1949–Feb 1949, ABC Mon 9:00–9:30
Feb 1949–May 1949, ABC Mon 9:15–9:30
May 1949–Jun 1949, ABC Mon 9:00–9:30
Jul 1949–Aug 1949, ABC Sun 9:30–10:00
REGULARS:
Skip Farrell
The Honeydreamers
Adele Scott Trio
Bill Moss Orchestra
George Barnes Trio
Joanelle James

Musical program from Chicago, starring singer Skip Farrell.

SKY KING (*Western*)
FIRST TELECAST: *September 21, 1953*
LAST TELECAST: *September 12, 1954*
BROADCAST HISTORY:
Sep 1953–Sep 1954, ABC Mon 8:00–8:30
Aug 1954–Sep 1954, ABC Sun 6:00–6:30
CAST:
Sky King .... Kirby Grant
Penny .... Gloria Winters
Clipper .... Ron Hagerthy

Sky King was a contemporary Western, starring Kirby Grant as an Arizona pilot-rancher who used an airplane instead of a horse to fight wrongdoers. With him on the Flying Crown Ranch were his teenage niece Penny and nephew Clipper. Sky's twin-engine Cessna was called *The Songbird*.

Sky King wandered all over the weekend daytime schedule before touching down in prime time in 1953. It was seen Sunday afternoons on NBC from 1951–1952 and Saturday afternoons on ABC in 1952–1953. Later, from 1959–1966, the same films showed up Saturday afternoons on CBS. The program was also heard on radio from 1946–1954.

SLAP MAXWELL STORY, THE (*Situation Comedy*)
FIRST TELECAST: *September 23, 1987*
LAST TELECAST: *September 14, 1988*
BROADCAST HISTORY:
Sep 1987–Mar 1988, ABC Wed 9:30–10:00
Jun 1988–Sep 1988, ABC Wed 9:30–10:00
CAST:
Slap Maxwell .... Dabney Coleman
Judy Ralston .... Megan Gallagher
Annie Maxwell .... Susan Anspach
Nelson Kruger .... Brian Smiar
The Dutchman .... Bill Cobbs
Charlie Wilson .... Bill Calvert

Dabney Coleman made a career of playing interesting reprobates (e.g., *Buffalo Bill*), and he essayed another in this 1987 comedy. "Slap" Maxwell was an unbelievably egocentric sportswriter working for a second-rate newspaper, *The Ledger*, located in the Southwest. His column "Slap Shots" was pecked out on an old typewriter (*The Ledger* refused to modernize), and it was certainly lively; however, its rumors and innuendo tended to draw lawsuits, giving editor Nelson Kruger fits. That often got Slap fired, though he'd always come crawling back. Despite his monumental insensitivity to everyone around him, Slap had an on-again, off-again girlfriend in Judy, the newspaper's secretary. Annie, who knew better, was his estranged wife, and Dutchman was the friendly bartender at the local tavern. They all managed to put up with Slap's bluster and bravado, which in the end, of course, got him nowhere.

In case the point of the series was not clear enough, each episode opened with shots of Slap getting slapped around—by (in producer Jay Tarses' words) "An athlete, a nun, or someone hurling a salami in anger."

SLATTERY'S PEOPLE (*Political Drama*)
FIRST TELECAST: *September 21, 1964*
LAST TELECAST: *November 26, 1965*
BROADCAST HISTORY:
Sep 1964–Dec 1964, CBS Mon 10:00–11:00
Dec 1964–Nov 1965, CBS Fri 10:00–11:00
CAST:
James Slattery .... Richard Crenna
Frank Radcliff .... Edward Asner
Johnny Ramos .... Paul Geary
B. J. Clawson .... Maxine Stuart
Speaker Bert Metcalf .... Tol Avery
Liz Andrews (1965) .... Kathie Browne
Mike Valera (1965) .... Alejandro Rey
Wendy Wendkowski (1965) .... Francine York

The professional and personal conflicts and activities of the minority leader in a fictional state legislature were depicted in *Slattery's People*. James Slattery was an idealistic, concerned state representative who was very interested in governmental reforms and constantly found himself involved in causes. With the help of his aide, Johnny Ramos, and his secretary, B.J., he attempted to push legislation that would better the lot of his constituents. House Speaker Bert Metcalf of the stronger opposition party, was his friendly enemy. When this series returned for an abbreviated second season, Slattery had a new aide (Mike Valera), a new secretary (Wendy Wendkowski), and a regular girlfriend in Liz Andrews.

SLEDGE HAMMER! (*Situation Comedy*)
FIRST TELECAST: *September 23, 1986*
LAST TELECAST: *June 30, 1988*
BROADCAST HISTORY:
Sep 1986, ABC Tue 8:30–9:00
Sep 1986–Nov 1986, ABC Fri 9:30–10:00
Nov 1986–Mar 1987, ABC Sat 8:30–9:00
Apr 1987, ABC Tue 8:30–9:00
Jun 1987–Jul 1987, ABC Fri 8:00–8:30
Aug 1987–Jan 1988, ABC Thu 8:00–8:30
Jan 1988–Feb 1988, ABC Fri 9:30–10:00
Mar 1988, ABC Thu 8:30–9:00
Jun 1988, ABC Thu 8:00–8:30

CAST:

Det. Insp. Sledge Hammer .... David Rasche
Off. Dori Doreau .... Anne-Marie Martin
Capt. Trunk .... Harrison Page
Off. Mayjoy .... Leslie Morris
Off. Daley (1987–1988) .... Patti Tippo
Norman Blates (1986–1987) .... Kurt Paul

Satire, they say in theatrical circles, is what closes on Saturday night. Nevertheless, this wild burlesque on tough-cop shows (particularly the *Dirty Harry* type) managed to hang on the ABC schedule for an extended period. Sledge was the ultimate tough cop: square-jawed, totally self-confident, with no mercy for the wimps and scum who infested his fair city. That included jaywalkers and litterers, who deserved to be shot like all the rest. In one episode he forced a miscreant, at gunpoint, to punch *himself* silly. Sledge's appearance was distinctive, with his reflecting sunglasses, striped shirts, and loud, mismatched ties. But his one true love was his giant, pearl-handled .44 Magnum—named "Gun." Each episode opened with the camera caressing this gleaming weapon, while ominous music thundered in the background. Sledge even talked to it. To others he would say, "Trust me . . . I know what I'm doing."

Though he was often suspended from the force, Sledge was always reinstated and got his man—although it was usually his savvy partner, Off. Dori Doreau (a woman!), who actually solved the case. Capt. Trunk was their migraine-ridden, bellowing superior.

What did all this mean? Creator/producer Alan Spencer said that much as *Get Smart* poked fun at the spy mania of its day, this show did the same for the current crop of rebel police reactionary movies and TV shows. "Ultimately," he said, "what the show is about . . . is a half hour."

SLEEPWALKERS (*Science Fiction*)

FIRST TELECAST: *November 1, 1997*
LAST TELECAST: *November 8, 1997*
BROADCAST HISTORY:

Nov 1997, NBC Sat 9:00–10:00

CAST:

Dr. Nathan Bradford .... Bruce Greenwood
Gail Bradford .... Kathrin Nicholson
Vince Konefke .... Abraham Benrubi
Kate Russell .... Naomi Watts
Ben Costigan .... Jeffrey D. Sams

Scientists in jammies were at the center of this imaginative Saturday night drama. Dr. Bradford, a driven neurophysiologist, had founded the Morpheus Institute to study dreams and their mysterious link to the waking world. By entering a sleep chamber and wiring electrodes to their temples and those of their subjects, he and his associates could actually enter other people's dreams, where they could help them battle the demons tormenting them. Unfortunately, the dream world could be a terrifying and dangerous place—those demons could really kill!—and Bradford had many a narrow escape. Vince was the institute's burly, efficient polysomnograph technician; Kate a sexy, adventurous dream interpreter; and Ben, a muscular former fighter pilot who joined the team after having had his own demons exorcized in the first episode. Gail was Bradford's wife, comatose since being injured in an accident, with whom he communicated through dreams.

For NBC, the dream ended rather quickly, as the series was canceled after only two telecasts.

SLEEPY JOE (*Children's*)

FIRST TELECAST: *October 3, 1949*
LAST TELECAST: *October 28, 1949*
BROADCAST HISTORY:

Oct 1949, ABC Mon–Fri 6:45–7:00

HOST:

Jimmy Scribner

Jimmy Scribner—a white man—had a long career on radio in the 1930s and 1940s playing comic Southern darkies. On his long-running series *The Johnson Family* (a kind of rural *Amos 'n' Andy*) he portrayed a whole townful, switching voices as necessary. Scribner appeared on television in the late 1940s with a short-lived puppet show on the ABC network, telling Uncle Remus–type stories for the kids. Later he had a syndicated puppet show built around similar Southern stories for which he did all the character voices.

SLIDERS (*Science Fiction*)

FIRST TELECAST: *March 22, 1995*
LAST TELECAST: *August 8, 1997*
BROADCAST HISTORY:

Mar 1995–May 1995, FOX Wed 9:00–10:00
Jun 1995–Aug 1995, FOX Sun 7:00–8:00
Mar 1996–Aug 1997, FOX Fri 8:00–9:00
(First-run on the Sci-Fi Channel from June 1998 to February 2000)

CAST:

Quinn Mallory (1995–1999) .... Jerry O'Connell
Rembrandt "Crying Man" Brown .... Cleavant Derricks
Prof. Maximilian Arturo (1995–1997) .... John Rhys-Davies
Wade Wells (1995–1997) .... Sabrina Lloyd
Maggie Beckett (1997–2000) .... Kari Wuhrer
Colin Mallory (1998–1999) ...... Charlie O'Connell
Quinn 2 (1999–2000) .... Robert Floyd
Dr. Diana Davis (1999–2000) .... Tembi Locke

In the basement of his home in San Francisco, brilliant college grad student Quinn Mallory accidentally created a device that opened a wormhole to an infinite number of parallel universes where history had taken different paths, some subtly different from ours and others radically different. The device used a timing mechanism resembling a TV remote that would always return him to the San Francisco from which he had come. But when Quinn took Arturo, his blustery physics professor, and Wade, a friend from the computer store where he worked part-time, on a test trip—along with Rembrandt, a washed-up soul singer who happened to be driving by when the field of the device swallowed him up along with the others—something went terribly wrong. Materializing in a San Francisco that was a frozen wasteland and threatened by a giant tornado, they transported before the timer was ready. Instead of returning to their own San Francisco, they landed in one in which the cold war had been won by the Communists.

Thus began an odyssey in which they continued to transport (slide) from one alternate universe to another, hoping to find their way home. Some of the San Franciscos they slid to were subtly different from home, and others were totally unrecognizable. In many of them they encountered other versions of themselves, some good and some bad, with whom they became involved. Wry humor characterized the stories, with scenes such as Judge Wapner presiding over a Communist "People's Court" and Rembrandt in his former life as anguished vocalist for the soul group The Spinning Tops. There was even one ironic episode in which they slid briefly back to their home dimension, but when reading in the paper that the Cleveland Indians were in the World Series and that O.J. Simpson had been on trial for murder, didn't believe it was their San Francisco and slid on.

Early in the 1996–1997 season they landed in an alternate San Francisco in which their sliding device was modified so that future slides might land them not just in the Bay area, but anywhere within a 400 mile radius of it (hopefully not in the middle of the Pacific Ocean). In the spring Prof. Arturo died after being wounded in an alternate California where evil Col. Angus Rickman (played by Roger Daltrey in two episodes and Neil Dickson in four), suffering from a fungus that destroyed brains, drained brain tissue from innocents to keep himself alive. Rickman escaped by sliding, and the original sliders, along with new slider Maggie, whose husband Rickman had murdered, went after him. In the season finale Wade and Rembrandt returned to their home world and Rickman was killed diving off a cliff when the timer's vortex closed before he could reach it. Quinn and Maggie used Rickman's tracking timer to escape, but it had been damaged and they slid into the future, rather than to Quinn's original Earth.

When *Sliders* returned in 1998 with new episodes on the Sci-Fi Channel, Quinn and Maggie reached his home Earth to discover that the Kromaggs, a warrior race of Nazi-like sliders from whom Quinn had barely escaped in a previous encounter, had found his home Earth and enslaved its people. They found Rembrandt, but Wade had been taken to a breeding camp on another Earth. Quinn's mother told him that his real parents were sliders from a different Earth who had left him in her custody when he was just a baby, while they fought the Kromaggs. She revealed that he had a microdot implant that contained information from them, including the coordinates for the parallel world where they had left his brother, Colin. Quinn was now on a quest to find his brother, his parents, and the weapon his parent had developed that had forced the Kromaggs off their Earth. He was unaware that during his first encounter with the Kromaggs they had implanted a tracking device on him to enable them to follow him when he found the weapon, and destroy it. Quinn, Rembrandt, and Maggie slid to the Earth where Quinn's brother Colin lived, and he joined them in their pursuit of the weapon that would save all the alternate Earths from the Kromaggs. Along the way they fought Kromaggs and numerous other enemies, as they slid from one Earth to another.

In 1999, Quinn and Colin were lost during a slide gone bad (actors Jerry and Charlie O'Connell had decided to leave the series). Colin was blasted into thousands of pieces (which, it was implied, might be reassembled someday), while Quinn's essence was incorporated into another person whose slide had collided with theirs. Thus, Quinn 2 looked different, but had Quinn's knowledge and soul within him—a novel way to change actors! On a new Earth, Rembrandt and Maggie linked up with Quinn 2 and black scientist Diana to become the new *Sliders* team.

In the series finale the gang slid to an Earth on which their exploits had become a popular TV show, and later a religion called Slidology, started by The Seer, a psychic who had written down his visions of their real adventures and used them as the basis for the series. His people had developed a Kromagg-specific virus that had allowed them to defeat the aliens on their Earth, and the sliders wanted to take the virus to Rembrandt's Earth (he was the only slider left from the original group) to free it. When their timer was destroyed, they found a Kromagg sliding machine that could transport one person to Rembrandt's home world, and after he injected himself with blood containing the virus, he made the slide. The other sliders went to The Seer to find out what happened, but he had died from a heart attack; Rembrandt's fate was unresolved.

SMALL & FRYE (*Situation Comedy*)

FIRST TELECAST: *March 7, 1983*
LAST TELECAST: *June 15, 1983*
BROADCAST HISTORY:

Mar 1983, CBS Mon 8:30–9:00
Jun 1983, CBS Wed 8:00–8:30

CAST:

Nick Small .... Darren McGavin
Chip Frye .... Jack Blessing
Phoebe Small .... Debbie Zipp
Dr. Hanratty .... Bill Daily
Eddie .... Warren Berlinger
Vicki, the waitress .... Victoria Carroll
The drunken bar fly .... Dick Wilson

Nick Small was an old-line private eye who had never adjusted to the modern world. He was right out of the 1930s, hard-nosed, trench-coated, and patterned after the likes of Mike Hammer and Sam Spade. His eager young partner, Chip Frye, was more contemporary, and also brought something else to the partnership. As a result of a freak laboratory accident, Chip could shrink to a height of only six inches by using a special ring device. This gave Small & Frye the ability to get into places their competition couldn't. There was one minor glitch: outside factors like lightning, minerals in certain foods, and his own hiccups could cause Chip to shrink at the most inopportune times.

Phoebe, Nick's young daughter, served as the office receptionist and was Chip's girlfriend. Dr. Hanratty was the eccentric head of the Police Criminal Lab and Eddie was the proprietor of Nick's favorite local hangout, Eddie's Bar and Grill.

SMALL FRY CLUB (*Children's*)

FIRST TELECAST: *March 11, 1947*
LAST TELECAST: *June 15, 1951*
BROADCAST HISTORY:

Mar 1947–Apr 1947, DUM Tue 7:00–8:00
Apr 1947–Jan 1948, DUM Mon–Fri 7:00–7:30
Jan 1948–Apr 1948, DUM Mon–Fri 6:15–6:45
Apr 1948–Jun 1951, DUM Mon–Fri 6:00–6:30

HOST:

Bob Emery

DuMont's *Small Fry Club* was one of the gentlest and most widely lauded children's shows of TV's early days. To an adult viewer it might be pure corn: letters from the little tykes read over the air, with their pictures shown; lessons on good behavior, safety, drinking more milk, etc.; and sketches by a studio cast of actors representing different animals. For the kindergarten set, however, it was *their* show. Its host, a remarkable man who went by the name of "Big Brother" Bob Emery, had spent his whole life entertaining youngsters while imparting lessons of good behavior. From the time he began his "club" on a radio station in Medford, Massachusetts, in 1921, he stressed involvement rather than one-way entertainment, and his young listeners flocked to obtain official membership cards, wrote him letters, sent in pictures and drawings, and joined in contests.

Emery (he then spelled it Emory) later came to New York and got into television on the ground floor, as announcer and producer at DuMont's WABD. He assumed his radio role of "Big Brother" on the station's Christmas show in 1946, and in March 1947 began his first video series, called *Movies for Small Fry*. At first it was just that, cartoons and other children's films, with voiceover narration by Bob—he was not even seen. But soon the program expanded to five days a week (possibly the first ever to do so) and a regular studio setting was developed. Membership cards were offered and letters came pouring in. If anyone doubted the effectiveness of the new medium in reaching an audience, they had only to look at the figures for the *Small Fry Club*: 1,200 cards sent out by May 1947, 15,000 by January 1948, 150,000 "active" members by 1950. Some of these were children of parents who had themselves been *Small Fry Club* members in the 1920s. Contests drew enormous responses, including 150 returns a week for a jingle contest in 1947, 10,000 drawings by 1948 (these were regularly shown on the air), and 24,000 letters to name a new member of the cast in 1951. (She became Trina the Kitten.)

Other regulars with Bob were Honey the Bunny, Mr. Mischief the Panda, Willy the Wiz, and Peggy the Penguin. Big Brother himself always appeared in a business suit, with heavy, dark-rimmed glasses—the picture of a kindly uncle. In addition to skits such as "Columbus and Isabella" and "Washington at Mt. Vernon," educational films and advice for kids were offered.

As with some other early shows, it is not known whether the *Small Fry Club* was fed over the network from the start; in any event, it was on the network (i.e, two stations) by late 1947. Bob Emery left DuMont in 1951 to return to Boston, where he later was seen in a series of local programs.

SMALL SHOTS (*Audience Participation*)

BROADCAST HISTORY:

TNN
30 minutes
Original episodes: *2001* (10 episodes)
Premiered: *August 22, 2001*

REGULARS:

Chris Cox
Matt Sloan

In this gag series two cheeky young guys claiming to be Hollywood filmmakers traveled across America stopping in small towns and recruiting the locals with flyers and a bullhorn to appear in their next on-location epic. The films they claimed to be making were so preposterous (*Silence of the Yams, Jurassic Dog Park, Charlie's Middle Aged Angels, The Amish Matrix, The Great Great Godfather, The 2 Commandments*) that someone should have caught on, but the lust for stardom is apparently so great that many were duped. Real film was shot, and at the end of each episode the guys revealed the scam and showed everyone their finished short film, which was generally hilarious.

SMALL TALK (*Comedy*)

FIRST TELECAST: *May 4, 1990*
LAST TELECAST: *May 25, 1990*
BROADCAST HISTORY:

May 1990, CBS Fri 8:00–8:30

HOST:

Roger Rose

This series had its roots in the "kids say the darndest things" segment from *People Are Funny* and similar segments from *Candid Camera*. There were interviews with youngsters responding to questions about pet fish, dating, President Bush, good manners and posture, and how to walk and dress "cool." Hidden cameras observed them practicing dancing, reacting to strangely colored foods, and serving ice cream to the studio audience. There were also features on a four-year-old Elvis Presley impersonator, a six-year-old violinist, and a bubble gum blowing contest for preschoolers. Actor/comedian Roger Rose was the series' constantly upstaged host.

SMALL WONDER (*Situation Comedy*)

BROADCAST HISTORY:

Syndicated only
30 minutes
Produced: *1985–1989* (96 episodes)
Released: *September 1985*

CAST:

Ted Lawson .... Dick Christie
Joan Lawson .... Marla Pennington
Jamie Lawson .... Jerry Supiran
Vicki .... Tiffany Brissette
Reggie Williams .... Paul C. Scott
Harriet Brindle .... Emily Schulman
**Bonnie Brindle (1985–1986)* .... Edie McClurg
**Warren (1986–1987)* .... Daryl T. Bartley
**Jessica (1986–1988)* .... Lihann Jones
Brandon Brindle (1986–1989) .... William Bogert
**Ida Mae Brindle (1988–1989)* .... Alice Ghostley
**Debbie Barnhill (1988–1989)* .... Devon Odessa

*Occasional

Ted Lawson was a research engineer with United Robotronics. He had secretly developed a robot that, superficially, looked exactly like a cute little 10-year-old girl. Ted took the robot, a "Voice Input Child Identicon" which he had nicknamed Vicki, home to his wife and young son Jamie, so that he could get the kinks out of its programming. Vicki generally talked in a monotone, was totally logical, and given to taking anything that was said quite literally—resulting in confusion and embarrassment for Ted and his family when others were around. She was extremely strong, a quality that endeared her to "brother" Jamie when he had to deal with the neighborhood bully. She was also given to repeating things that others had said, much like a parrot. Only Ted's family knew she was not human and they were hard-pressed to keep others from finding out. Reggie was Jamie's friend and Harriet the obnoxious girl next door who was almost as nosy as her mother. Harriet's father, Brandon, was Ted's overbearing boss at United Robotronics.

In the second season Jamie went to junior high school and Vicki went too, creating problems for the other students who didn't have her perfect memory. His life at school was also complicated by having his mom show up frequently as a substitute teacher, falling in puppy-love with gold-digging Jessica (age 11), and coping with another kid in his class, obnoxious Warren. During the 1988–1989 season, Jamie's romantic focus had shifted to a new girl, Debbie Barnhill.

SMALL WORLD (*Discussion*)

FIRST TELECAST: *October 12, 1958*

LAST TELECAST: *May 29, 1960*

BROADCAST HISTORY:

Oct 1958–May 1960, CBS Sun 6:00–6:30 (OS)

MODERATOR:

Edward R. Murrow

Each week on this filmed series, moderator Edward R. Murrow conducted an informal, unrehearsed discussion with three or four world celebrities. The celebrities were located at widely divergent places around the world and it was only through the use of advanced electronic technology that these people could get together "face to face." Serious discussions on world politics might include Thomas E. Dewey, Jawaharlal Nehru, and writer Aldous Huxley, as on the premiere telecast. Lighter shows might involve actress Ingrid Bergman, *New York Times* film critic Bosley Crowther, and producer Darryl F. Zanuck chatting about the state of the motion-picture industry.

SMALLVILLE (*Adventure*)

FIRST TELECAST: *October 16, 2001*

LAST TELECAST:

BROADCAST HISTORY:

Oct 2001– , WB Tue 9:00–10:00
Jul 2002–Sep 2002, WB Mon 9:00–10:00

CAST:

Clark Kent .... Tom Welling
Lana Lang .... Kristin Kreuk
Alexander "Lex" Luthor ..... Michael Rosenbaum
Jonathan Kent .... John Schneider
Martha Kent .... Annette O'Toole
Pete Ross .... Sam Jones III
Chloe Sullivan .... Allison Mack
Lionel Luthor .... John Glover
Whitney Fordman (2001–2002) .... Eric Johnson
**Nell Lang (2001–2002)* .... Sarah-Jane Redmond
Dr. Helen Bryce (2002–) .. Emmanuelle Vaughier

*Occasional

THEME:

"Save Me" written and performed by Remy Zero

Before he became Superman, Clark Kent had grown up in the town of Smallville, Kansas, "The Creamed Corn Capital of the World." This story of his high school years began with the 1989 arrival of the baby Kal-El from Krypton in a small spaceship, in the midst of a meteor shower that rained glowing green rocks (kryptonite) all over Smallville. Farmer Jonathan Kent and his wife, Martha, found the baby, took him in as their own child, and named him Clark. Now a teenager, Clark was trying to escape his "loser" status at school while hiding his superstrength, superspeed and other developing powers from everyone but his parents. He was sweet on pretty Lana Lang, a cheerleader who was living with her aunt Nell because her parents had been killed during the meteor shower. Others at school included Pete, Clark's best friend; Chloe, the editor of the school newspaper, who was barely able to hide her infatuation with Clark, and Lana's boyfriend Whitney, the star quarterback on the Smallville football team. Rich young Lex Luthor, who had lost his hair during the meteor shower, was running a Smallville fertilizer plant for his manipulative father, Lionel, the corrupt head of Luthor Corp., and had yet to become the archvillain of his later years. Lex was more ethical than his father and often disagreed with his tactics. After Clark saved him from drowning when his car plunged into a river, Lex and Clark became friends of sorts, although Lex suspected that there was something special about Clark and started to compile information about him.

The radiation from the kryptonite rocks around Smallville, in addition to being potentially lethal to Clark, caused problems for many of the residents of the area, which Clark had to deal with. Among those affected were a student, bitten by kryptonite-radiated bugs, who took on the characteristics of the bugs and killed other students; another who developed the ability to morph into duplicates of other people and commit crimes; a girl who went on a diet of kryptonite-infected vegetables that made her beautiful but left her with the need to absorb the body fat of others, killing them in the process; and a guy who fell into a lake with kryptonite at the bottom, turned into a heat-absorbing battery and survived by absorbing the body heat from others. After the first of the year Lana convinced Lex to invest in the Talon movie theater so she could convert it into a coffee bar. In May Whitney, whose father had died, joined the Marine Corps and later died while on a mission in Indonesia. In the season finale a tornado hit Smallville, nearly killing Lionel.

The tornado also ripped Clark's spaceship from its hiding place and left it exposed in a field, where Lex's agents found it. In order to get the spaceship back Clark had to reveal his alien origins to Pete, who helped him retrieve it. Late in the year Aunt Nell moved to Metropolis with her fiancé and Lana moved in with Chloe and her father, an awkward situation for Chloe, who knew Clark was in love with Lana, not her. Because the farm was struggling, Martha took a job as Lionel's executive assistant, which displeased Jonathan until he realized she could spy on Lionel, whom he didn't trust. Lex began dating Helen, the doctor from whom he had taken anger management classes, and, when their relationship got serious, he showed her the room containing the evidence of his suspicions about Clark. She didn't tell him that while treating Clark and Martha, who was pregnant, in the hospital for exposure to kryptonite spores, she had discovered that Clark had alien blood.

In April Lex and Helen got engaged; Clark was to be Lex's best man. At the end of the season Chloe found out that Lana and Clark had become romantically involved and, feeling hurt and betrayed, agreed to investigate Clark for Lionel. Clark learned that it was time to leave Smallville and "fulfill his destiny" to rule the Earth, and on the day of Lex's wedding he tried to alter his fate by destroying the spaceship. Unfortunately the resulting shock wave flipped over the truck in which his parents were riding; Jonathan was unhurt, but Martha lost her baby. A distraught Clark told Pete he was leaving and said a sad farewell to a confused Lana. Under the influence of a red kryptonite ring, which gave him the feeling of power but robbed him of his moral focus, he then rode off on a red motorcycle.

SMART GUY (*Situation Comedy*)
FIRST TELECAST: *April 2, 1997*
LAST TELECAST: *September 19, 1999*
BROADCAST HISTORY:
Apr 1997–May 1997, WB Wed 8:30–9:00
Aug 1997–Mar 1998, WB Wed 8:30–9:00
Mar 1998–Jun 1998, WB Wed 8:00–8:30
Jun 1998–Jul 1998, WB Wed 8:00–9:00
Jul 1998–Jul 1999, WB Sun 8:30–9:00
Apr 1999, WB Thu 8:00–8:30
Jul 1999, WB Sun 7:30–8:00
Aug 1999–Sep 1999, WB Sun 8:30–9:00
CAST:
T. J. Henderson (age 10) .... Tahj Mowry
Floyd Henderson .... John Marshall Jones
Marcus Henderson (16) .... Jason Weaver
Yvette Henderson (15).............. Essence Atkins
Morris L. Tibbs ("Mo").............. Omar Gooding

Smart Guy was set in Washington, D.C., where cute 10-year-old genius T.J. was a sophomore at Piedmont High School. He had skipped six grades and was trying to fit in at the school where both his older brother Marcus and his sister Yvette were students. Marcus, a mediocre student who was more concerned with girls than with grades, resented T.J.'s presence, while sexy Yvette, who was more studious, didn't seem to mind. Mo was Marcus' trouble-prone best friend. In the fall T.J. got a job as the school's team mascot because he was small enough to fit into the penguin costume. Floyd, their dad, was a widowed roofing contractor. Late in 1998 the guys formed a band—Mackadocious—with T.J. on keyboard, Marcus as lead singer, and Mo on bass.

SMASH HITS (*Music Videos*)
BROADCAST HISTORY:
Syndicated only
30 minutes
Produced: *1989–1991* (104 episodes)
Released: *September 1989*
HOST:
Scott Shannon

Popular radio disc jockey Scott Shannon hosted this weekly music video showcase. The gimmick that distinguished this series from a myriad of other music video shows was that the videos aired each week were determined by *Smash Hits'* viewers, who were encouraged to call a toll-free phone number (1-800-COCA-COLA) to vote for their favorite video. The ten videos receiving the most votes comprised the following week's "top 10."

SMILIN' ED MCCONNELL AND HIS BUSTER BROWN GANG (*Children's*)
FIRST TELECAST: *August 26, 1950*
LAST TELECAST: *May 19, 1951*
BROADCAST HISTORY:
Aug 1950–May 1951, NBC Sat 6:30–7:00
HOST:
Ed McConnell

Childen's program, based on McConnell's radio show, which featured him playing the piano, singing and telling stories from his storybook—sometimes in the form of films, always with a moral. In the cast were Midnight the tabby cat, Squeaky the mouse, Old Grandie the talking piano, and Uncle Fishface, the world's greatest storyteller. After its prime-time run the series returned to television on Saturday mornings, on CBS, August 1951–April 1953, and on ABC, August 1953–April 1955. Since McConnell had passed away in 1954, the episodes aired during the 1954–1955 season were all reruns.

Andy Devine took over as host when the series went into syndication in Fall 1955 under the new title *Andy's Gang.* For the next five years, from August 1955 to December 1960, it ran in syndication, with the exception of the period November 1957–June 1958, when it aired on NBC's Saturday morning lineup.

SMITH & JONES (*Comedy/Variety*)
FIRST TELECAST: *September 16, 1991*
LAST TELECAST: *October 10, 1991*
BROADCAST HISTORY:
Sept 1991–Oct 1991, CBS Mon–Fri 1:00–1:30 A.M.
REGULARS:
Mel Smith
Griff Rhys Jones

In a style reminiscent of Benny Hill, without the scantily clad girls and sexual innuendo, fellow Brits Mel Smith and Griff Rhys Jones brought viewers a loosely structured collection of comedy sketches parodying movies, TV shows, news coverage, English mores, and anything else that struck their fancy. Although not regulars, Robin Driscoll, Chris Langham, and Peter McCarthy made frequent appearances in individual sketches. Langham and McCarthy, in addition to performing, were on the writing staff of the show.

Originally produced for BBC television in England.

SMITH FAMILY, THE (*Drama*)
FIRST TELECAST: *January 20, 1971*
LAST TELECAST: *June 14, 1972*
BROADCAST HISTORY:
Jan 1971–Sep 1971, ABC Wed 8:30–9:00
Sep 1971–Jan 1972, ABC Wed 9:00–9:30
Apr 1972–Jun 1972, ABC Wed 8:30–9:00
CAST:
Det. Sgt. Chad Smith .... Henry Fonda
Betty Smith .... Janet Blair
Cindy Smith .... Darleen Carr
Bob Smith......................... Ronny Howard
Brian Smith............... Michael-James Wixted
Capt. Hughes .... Charles McGraw
Sgt. Ray Martin....................... John Carter
THEME:
"Primrose Lane," by W. Shanklin and G. Callendar, sung by Mike Minor

Henry Fonda starred in this family drama about the home life of a big-city cop. Det. Sgt. Chad Smith was a Los Angeles plainclothesman, 25 years on the force, who worked on burglaries, drug busts, runaway children, bomb threats, and, occasionally, homicides. His suburban family consisted of wife Betty; 18-year-old daughter Cindy, an L.A. City College student with marriage on her mind; 15-year-old son Bob; and 7-year-old son Brian. Stories touched on the generation gap and the problems of youth as much as on Chad's police work, which did include some dangerous situations but not really much hard action. His captain and partner, Sgt. Martin, were only seen occasionally.

SMITHSONIAN, THE (*Documentary*)

FIRST TELECAST: *June 25, 1967*
LAST TELECAST: *August 27, 1967*
BROADCAST HISTORY:
Jun 1967–Aug 1967, NBC Sun 6:30–7:00
HOST:
Bill Ryan

The vast Smithsonian Museum complex in Washington, D.C., was the starting point for this series. Each week a specific exhibit in one of the Smithsonian buildings opened a filmed exploratory journey into history or some field of scientific endeavor. NBC newsman Bill Ryan narrated the background material with on-location film footage, stills, and animation. The series had originally aired from October 1966 to April 1967 on Saturdays at 12:30 P.M. The episodes seen on Sunday evenings during the summer of 1967 were all reruns.

SMOTHERS BROTHERS COMEDY HOUR, THE (*Comedy/Variety*)

FIRST TELECAST: *February 5, 1967*
LAST TELECAST: *May 26, 1975*
BROADCAST HISTORY:
Feb 1967–Jun 1969, CBS Sun 9:00–10:00 (OS)
Jul 1970–Sep 1970, ABC Wed 10:00–11:00
Jan 1975–May 1975, NBC Mon 8:00–9:00
REGULARS:
Tom Smothers
Dick Smothers
Pat Paulsen
Leigh French (1967–1969, 1975)
Bob Einstein (as *Officer Judy*; 1967–1969, 1975)
The Louis Da Pron Dancers (1967–1968)
The Ron Poindexter Dancers (1968–1969)
The Anita Kerr Singers (1967)
The Jimmy Joyce Singers (1967–1969)
Nelson Riddle and His Orchestra (1967–1969)
The Denny Vaughn Orchestra (1970)
Mason Williams (1967–1969)
Jennifer Warnes (Warren) (1967–1969)
John Hartford (1968–1969)
Sally Struthers (1970)
Spencer Quinn (1970)
Betty Aberlin (1975)
Don Novello (1975)
Steve Martin (1975)
Nino Senporty (1975)
The Marty Paich Orchestra (1975)

Tom and Dick Smothers had been a very popular comedy/singing team in the early and mid-1960s with a number of successful, offbeat comedy albums. Tom, who played the guitar, acted the role of the dullard, unable to think logically, making all sorts of inane remarks, and being generally impossible to deal with. Dick, who played bass, was, by contrast, calm, reasonable, and hard pressed to retain his composure when confronted by his brother's stupidity and silliness. Extremely popular with young people, they were an immediate hit with their irreverent variety series on CBS in 1967. Abetted by Pat Paulsen's low-keyed "editorials" and other material, which at times rivaled Tom for the evening's silliest moments, and a large supporting cast, *The Smothers Brothers Comedy Hour* poked fun at virtually all the hallowed institutions of American society—motherhood, church, politics, government, etc. It was topical, it was funny, and occasionally it was in bad taste.

There were always problems getting program material cleared with the CBS censors, and the adamant position taken by the show's stars over what they considered was acceptable did not endear them to CBS management. First there were minor skirmishes. Pat Paulsen had started a campaign for President on their summer series in 1968 (*The Summer Brothers Smothers Show*) with the slogan "If nominated I will not run, and if elected I will not serve." It was a joke but CBS, fearing demands for equal time from real candidates, kept him off the show until after the election. Pete Seeger, a controversial folk singer long blacklisted on television, made several appearances on the show and got them into trouble with his Vietnam protest song "Waist Deep in the Big Muddy." Early in 1969 they did a comedy sketch making fun of religion that outraged the clergy and forced an on-air apology.

CBS had had enough. The ratings were still high, but CBS management finally concluded that *The Smothers Brothers Comedy Hour* was just not worth the trouble. The brothers' choice of guests, predominantly antiwar, left-wing, and outspoken; their fights over material; and their repeated failure to deliver finished programs early enough in the week for the censors to get them edited by air time on Sunday were all advanced as reasons when the series was abruptly canceled. There was a good deal of furor over freedom of speech and the like, but the CBS decision stuck. The Smothers Brothers were replaced by *Hee Haw*.

Thirteen months later, *The Smothers Brothers Summer Show* turned up on ABC. Apparently their time had passed, and the show (which included three repeats of episodes from the original CBS series) did not make it to the ABC fall schedule. The following fall Tom turned up by himself as the star of a syndicated half-hour comedy series titled *Tom Smothers' Organic Prime Time Space Ride*. It tried to be irreverent and satirical, but did not attract much of an audience and was not renewed. In 1975 NBC gave Tom and Dick yet another chance, with a new variety series simply titled *The Smothers Brothers Show*. There were no real problems with the NBC censors, probably because the biting edge was gone from their material. The closest they came to anything controversial on the premiere telecast was when Tom announced that they had an "iron-clad" 13-week contract. It got off to a strong start, due more to audience curiosity about what had happened to Tom and Dick in the five years since they had last been on network television than to the merits of the program, but quickly sank into obscurity.

SMOTHERS BROTHERS COMEDY HOUR, THE (*Comedy/Variety*)

FIRST TELECAST: *March 30, 1988*
LAST TELECAST: *August 23, 1989*
BROADCAST HISTORY:
Mar 1988–May 1988, CBS Wed 8:00–9:00
Jan 1989–Feb 1989, CBS Sat 9:00–10:00
Aug 1989, CBS Wed 8:00–9:00
REGULARS:
Tom Smothers
Dick Smothers

Pat Paulsen
Jim Stafford (1988)
Geoffrey Lewis (1989)
The Larry Cansler Orchestra (1988)
The Jack Elliott Orchestra (1989)

Yesterday once more. On February 3, 1988, CBS aired "The Smothers Brothers Comedy Hour 20th Reunion Show," a nostalgic look back at the contentious variety series of the '60s. (So what if it was actually twenty-*one* years since the original series premiered?) The special, which brought together many regulars and writers from the original show, drew a sizeable audience and good reviews, and CBS decided to try it as a series—again. The new effort was sharply written and topical, but there was certainly a sense of *déjà vu*—Tom and Dick's sibling rivalry was as strong as ever, Pat Paulsen was running for president again, and former regulars Jennifer Warnes and Leigh French turned up as guest stars. Even the set looked the same. Regularly featured was a segment in which Tom showed off his considerable skills with the yo-yo, as "The Yo-Yo Man."

SMOTHERS BROTHERS SHOW, THE (*Situation Comedy*)

FIRST TELECAST: *September 17, 1965*
LAST TELECAST: *September 9, 1966*
BROADCAST HISTORY:
Sep 1965–Sep 1966, CBS Fri 9:30–10:00
CAST:
Tom Smothers .... Himself
Dick Smothers .... Himself
Leonard J. Costello .... Roland Winters
Mrs. Costello .... Harriet MacGibbon
Janet .... Ann Elder

As a rising young executive at Pandora Publications, working for publisher Leonard J. Costello, Dick Smothers should have been enjoying the life of a prosperous bachelor. But one little thing kept getting in the way—his brother Tom. Not in ordinary ways, either. Tom had been lost at sea and two years later showed up as an apprentice angel, assigned to do good works on Earth to become a full-fledged regular angel. His efforts to help people did not always seem to work out the way he had planned, and he was forever seeking the aid of his earthly brother to help bail him out of some blunder he had created.

SMUSH (*Quiz/Audience Participation*)

BROADCAST HISTORY:
USA Network
30 minutes
Original episodes: *2001–2002*
Premiered: *December 3, 2001*
REGULARS:
Ken Ober
Lisa Dergan

A word game played by four contestants sitting around a table in a party setting (losers were sent away to the bar). The object was to put together names and words to create joke phrases—for example:

Q: "The actor who starred as McGarrett on *Hawaii 5-0*, and the Golding novel about English schoolkids stranded on an island."

A: "Jack Lord of the Flies."

Q: "Sixteenth-century dude who figured that Earth orbits the sun, and George's surname on *Seinfeld*."

A: "Copernicostanza."

In addition to regular questions there were picture questions, props, triple smushes, quadruple smushes, and smush chains (where contestants had to keep adding to an ongoing chain). In the final round the surviving contestant was given a root word and had to quickly add words to the beginning or end to claim the grand prize of $8,000.

Ken Ober was the sardonic host and Lisa Dergan, his shapely scorekeeper.

SNEAK PREVIEW (*Anthology*)

FIRST TELECAST: *July 3, 1956*
LAST TELECAST: *August 7, 1956*
BROADCAST HISTORY:
Jul 1956–Aug 1956, NBC Tue 9:00–9:30
HOST:
Nelson Case

The implication of this series was that the viewer would be seeing pilot films for series which might turn up on the fall schedule. None of them made it, however. Included were half-hour comedies starring Zsa Zsa Gabor, Ann Sheridan, and Celeste Holm. *Sneak Preview* was the 1956 summer replacement for *Jane Wyman's Fireside Theatre.*

SNOOP SISTERS, THE (*Detective Drama*)

FIRST TELECAST: *December 19, 1973*
LAST TELECAST: *August 20, 1974*
BROADCAST HISTORY:
Dec 1973, NBC Wed 8:30–10:00
Jan 1974–Aug 1974, NBC Tue 8:30–10:00
CAST:
Ernesta Snoop .... Helen Hayes
Gwen Snoop .... Mildred Natwick
Barney .... Lou Antonio
Lt. Steve Ostrowski .... Bert Convy

Ernesta and Gwen Snoop were two elderly sisters who were well named. Despite the fact that they were very successful mystery writers, or possibly because of it, they could not resist getting involved in real mysteries. Their experience working with clues in the fictitious stories they wrote for a living stood them in good stead when they were confronted with the urge to try to solve real crimes. All the physical work was handled for them by Barney, their combination chauffeur and bodyguard, and their nephew, police lieutenant Ostrowski. *The Snoop Sisters* was one of the four rotating elements in the 1973–1974 version of *The NBC Wednesday/Tuesday Mystery Movie.* The others were *Banacek, Faraday and Company,* and *Tenafly.*

SNOOPS (*Detective Drama*)

FIRST TELECAST: *September 22, 1989*
LAST TELECAST: *July 6, 1990*
BROADCAST HISTORY:
Sep 1989–Dec 1989, CBS Fri 8:00–9:00
Jul 1990, CBS Fri 8:00–9:00
CAST:
Chance Dennis .... Tim Reid
Micki Dennis .... Daphne Maxwell Reid
Hugo .... Troy Curvey, Jr.
Lt. Carl Akers .... John Karlen
Doug .... Adam Silbar

Jason .... Tim Reid II
Yolanda .... Tracy Camilla Johns

THEME:

"Curiosity," written by Steve Tyrell, Stephanie Tyrell, and Guy Moon; sung by Ray Charles

In the tradition of *The Thin Man*, this urbane drama series featured a sophisticated husband and wife team who, though not professional detectives, had a remarkable knack for getting involved in and solving crimes—crimes that always seemed to involve murder. Chance Dennis was a criminology professor at Georgetown University in Washington and his wife, Micki, was assistant to the Deputy Chief of Protocol for the State Department. With the help of their friend in the D.C. police department, Lt. Akers, and Hugo, Micki's State Department driver, the Dennises made life safer for the citizenry of the nation's capitol. Doug, Yolanda, and Jason were students in one of Chance's criminology courses at Georgetown.

Actress Tasha Scott was originally hired to play Chance's daughter but, by the time the series premiered, had been recast as his niece Katja. Although she appeared in only two of the episodes aired, she was featured in the opening credits every week.

SNOOPS (*Detective Drama*)

FIRST TELECAST: *September 26, 1999*
LAST TELECAST: *December 26, 1999*
BROADCAST HISTORY:

Sep 1999–Dec 1999, ABC Sun 9:00–10:00

CAST:

Glenn Hall .... Gina Gershon
Dana Plant .... Paula Marshall
Manny Lott .... Danny Nucci
Roberta Young .... Paula Jai Parker
Det. Greg McCormack .... Edward Kerr

Three delicious babes and one happy-go-lucky young guy made up Glenn Hall, Inc., a high-tech Santa Monica detective agency, in this flashy, lightweight series. Glenn, the savvy boss, had made her money rescuing the son of a billionaire (he was very grateful) and decided to use it to go into business with the best technology available. Besides computers, tracking devices, bugging equipment, tranquilizer guns and the like, her other secret weapon was simple: ignore the "rules" and get the bad guys any way you can (including sleeping with them, if necessary). Her latest recruit was Dana, a former police detective who had quit the Santa Monica PD because of all its rules, as well as a failed love affair with her boss, Det. McCormack. Dana had a little trouble adjusting ("You can't just tap phones!"), but she enjoyed her new freedom. Manny was their tech guy, a happy sort who loved practical jokes, high-tech toys and loud rock music, which seemed to follow him everywhere; Roberta was the sexy black assistant and wannabe detective. Greg hated Glenn and her rule breaking, but still had the hots for Dana and so gave the team leeway in their investigations, which usually involved multiple counts of trespassing, wiretapping, computer hacking, entrapment and high-speed chases in their BMW.

Only ten episodes of the series were aired. In three additional episodes that were filmed but not telecast, Dana was killed and former FBI agent Jessalyn Gilsig (Suzanne Shivers) took her place, but the gang then broke up.

SNOWY RIVER: THE MCGREGOR SAGA

(*Adventure*)

BROADCAST HISTORY:

The Family Channel
60 minutes
Produced: *1993–1996* (32 episodes)
Premiered: *August 28, 1993*

CAST:

Matt McGregor .... Andrew Clarke
Luke McGregor (1993–1994) .... Joshua Lucas
Colin McGregor .... Brett Climo
Rob McGregor .... Guy Pearce
Danni McGregor .... Joelene Crnogorac
Emily McGregor .... Sheryl Munks
Kathleen O'Neil .... Wendy Hughes
Frank Blackwood .... Rodney Bell
Victoria Blackwood .... Amanda Douge
Oliver Blackwood .... John Stanton

A hardy family carved out a life on the Australian frontier in the late 1800s in this cartoonish adventure cum soap opera. Noble rancher Matt headed the McGregor clan, consisting of sons Colin and Rob and daughters Danni and Emily. Matt not only ran the family's sprawling Langara ranch but was also a leading citizen of the nearby town of Patterson's Ridge and the local member of parliament. Representing the forces of evil in the area were the Blackwoods, who had bribed and cheated their way to great wealth. After the disappearance of Oliver Blackwood, that family was headed by his son, Frank, a vain, oily young man who habitually dressed in black and who bickered with his sister, Victoria, at the family's palatial estate, Balmoral.

Matt's chief ally in his battles with the scheming Blackwoods was Kathleen, an independent woman who ran a ranch, operated the local newspaper, and taught school. Widower Matt could use a woman with that many talents around the house, but feisty Kathleen was not ready to marry—not quite yet. Continuing stories included the death of Matt's vengeful nephew, Luke; the disappearance of Frank and Victoria's father, Oliver; assorted romances; and Emily's pregnancy.

Based on A. B. "Banjo" Paterson's ballad "The Man from Snowy River." Previous versions of the saga included two movies, *The Man from Snowy River* starring Kirk Douglas (1982) and its sequel, *Return to Snowy River* (1988). Filmed in the Snowy River mountain country of Australia, with its sweeping panoramas.

SO THIS IS HOLLYWOOD (*Situation Comedy*)

FIRST TELECAST: *January 1, 1955*
LAST TELECAST: *August 19, 1955*
BROADCAST HISTORY:

Jan 1955–Jun 1955, NBC Sat 8:30–9:00
Jul 1955–Aug 1955, NBC Fri 10:30–11:00

CAST:

Queenie Dugan .... Mitzi Green
Kim Tracy .... Virginia Gibson
Andy Boone .... Jimmy Lydon
Hubie Dodd .... Gordon Jones
April Adams .... Peggy Knudsen

So This Is Hollywood was the story of two young women trying to make it in show business. Queenie Dugan was a stunt woman who had been around

Hollywood long enough to know how to avoid being hustled and to realize that she wasn't ever going to be a star herself. Her roommate, Kim Tracy, was a young starlet and movie extra who, despite the efforts of her agent, Andy, seemed unable to get the one big break that would make her a star. Queenie was always trying to find ways to promote Kim's career, as were both Andy and Queenie's stunt-man boyfriend Hubie.

SO WEIRD (*Fantasy Drama*)

BROADCAST HISTORY:

Disney Channel
30 minutes
Original episodes: *1999–2001* (65 episodes)
Premiered: *January 18, 1999*

CAST:

Fiona "Fi" Phillips (age 13) (1999–2000) .... Cara DeLizia
Jack Phillips (15) .... Patrick Levis
Molly Phillips .... Mackenzie Phillips
Clu Bell (1999–2000) .... Erik von Detten
Irene Bell .... Belinda Metz
Ned Bell .... Dave "Squatch" Ward
Carey Bell .... Eric Lively
Annie Thelan (13) (2000–2001) .... Alexz Johnson

THEME:

"In the Darkness," sung by Mackenzie Phillips

So Weird was a sort of updated *Nancy Drew Mysteries* crossed with *The X-Files,* in which a computer-literate 13-year-old named Fi Phillips used her ever-present laptop computer to investigate paranormal occurrences while touring the country in a bus with her widowed, rock-star mom, Molly (who was on the road trying to make a comeback). Jack was Fi's skeptical brother and Clu, her somewhat dense teen friend. Clu's dad, Ned, was their chief technician, roadie, and wise adviser; Irene, his sensible wife. Coming aboard after the first few episodes was Clu's older brother, Carey. Also seen from time to time was Fi's dead father, Rick (Chris Gibson), with whom she tried to communicate in the afterlife.

Aliens, haunted buildings, and portals into other worlds seemed to confront the little troupe at every stop, and after two years of fighting off the spirits Fi decided to leave the road and settle down in Seattle. She turned over her magical ring to newcomer Annie, a talented young musician who joined the troupe. Around the same time, Clu left for college, although he occasionally returned to visit. Musical performances by Mackenzie Phillips and later by Alexz Johnson were featured in the show.

SO YOU WANT TO LEAD A BAND, see *Sammy Kaye Show, The*

SOAP (*Situation Comedy*)

FIRST TELECAST: *September 13, 1977*

LAST TELECAST: *April 20, 1981*

BROADCAST HISTORY:

Sep 1977–Mar 1978, ABC Tue 9:30–10:00
Sep 1978–Mar 1979, ABC Thu 9:30–10:00
Sep 1979–Mar 1980, ABC Thu 9:30–10:00
Oct 1980–Jan 1981, ABC Wed 9:30–10:00
Mar 1981–Apr 1981, ABC Mon 10:00–11:00

CAST:

Chester Tate .... Robert Mandan
Jessica Tate .... Katherine Helmond
Corrine Tate (1977–1980) .... Diana Canova
Eunice Tate .... Jennifer Salt
Billy Tate .... Jimmy Baio
Benson (1977–1979) .... Robert Guillaume
The Major .... Arthur Peterson
Mary Dallas Campbell .... Cathryn Damon
Burt Campbell .... Richard Mulligan
Jodie Dallas .... Billy Crystal
Danny Dallas .... Ted Wass
The Godfather (1977–1978) .... Richard Libertini
Claire (1977–1978) .... Kathryn Reynolds
Peter Campbell .... Robert Urich
Chuck/Bob Campbell .... Jay Johnson
Dennis Phillips (1978) .... Bob Seagren
Father Timothy Flotsky (1978–1979) ... Sal Viscuso
Carol David (1978–1981) .... Rebecca Balding
Elaine Lefkowitz (1978–1979) .... Dinah Manoff
Dutch (1978–1981) .... Donnelly Rhodes
Sally (1978–1979) .... Caroline McWilliams
Detective Donahue (1978–1980) .... John Byner
Alice (1979) .... Randee Heller
Mrs. David (1979–1981) .... Peggy Pope
Millie (1979) .... Candace Azzara
Leslie Walker (1979–1981) .... Marla Pennington
Polly Dawson (1979–1981) .... Lynne Moody
Saunders (1980–1981) .... Roscoe Lee Browne
Dr. Alan Posner (1980–1981) .... Allan Miller
Attorney E. Ronald Mallu (1978–1981) .... Eugene Roche
Carlos "El Puerco" Valdez (1980–1981) .... Gregory Sierra
Maggie Chandler (1980–1981) .... Barbara Rhoades
Gwen (1980–1981) .... Jesse Welles

Soap was undoubtedly the most controversial new series of the 1977–1978 "season of sex." Even before it went on the air ABC had received 32,000 letters about the show—all but nine of them against it—ABC affiliates had been picketed for planning to air it, and sponsors had been urged to boycott the show (which a few did). Some ABC affiliates refused to carry it, and many who did ran it late at night.

The object of all this ire was a half-hour comedy which was billed as a satire on soap operas. It had a continuing story line of sorts, but was populated by a cast such as was seldom seen on any serious dramatic show. Stories centered on the wealthy Tates and the blue-collar Campbells. Chester Tate was a pompous businessman with an affinity for extramarital affairs; no wonder, since his wife, Jessica, was a spaced-out, fluttery idiot. Of their three children, sexy Corrine was always putting her best attributes forward; Eunice was quieter and more conservative; and Billy, 14, was a wisecracking brat. Living with the Tates were Jessica's father, "the Major," who crawled around the floor in his old army uniform, still fighting World War II; and Benson, the insolent and obnoxious black servant and cook, who commented on the proceedings.

Across town lived Jessica's sister, Mary Campbell. Her husband, Burt, was a "working stiff" whose main problem lay in dealing with stepsons Jodie (who was gay) and Danny (who was involved with organized crime). Surreptitious sex was on practically everyone's mind, and formed the basis of many of the stories.

The major development during the first season was the murder of Peter, the handsome tennis pro (and Burt's son), who had been luring most of his female students into bed with him. First Corrine was accused, but then Jessica was arrested and subsequently convicted of the crime. In the last episode of the 1977–1978 season, an off-screen narrator informed viewers that she didn't really do it, and as the following season opened, Chester confessed to the crime.

Chester was sent to prison but soon escaped with Dutch, a convicted murderer. Soon thereafter Chester lost his memory and wandered out west, where he became a fry cook. Dutch, on the other hand, eloped with Eunice. Jessica fell in love with Detective Donahue, whom she had hired to find Chester, and when Chester finally returned she had to choose between them. She chose Chester, but only for a while; after a fling with South American revolutionary "El Puerco," she and Chester were divorced.

Life was not dull for the rest of the family, either. Benson the butler departed for greener pastures (his own series) in 1979, after rescuing Billy from a religious cult, the Sunnies. The new butler was named Saunders. Daughter Corrine Tate married ex-priest Timothy Flotsky, but their union produced—after six weeks—a baby possessed by the devil, and the Tates had to band together to exorcise the spirit. Across town, Burt found himself kidnapped and cloned by aliens; at least Mary got a few nights of uninhibited sex from the clone. But who, then, was the father of the baby that resulted? Jodie, Burt's gay son, decided that women are fun too and sired his own baby by Carol, but wound up in an ugly custody fight. Then Burt got himself elected sheriff, resulting in a run-in with the racketeer Tibbs and his hooker, Gwen. Danny, who had previously been in love with Elaine, Millie, and Polly, sort of liked her.

Soap attracted a large and loyal audience, and the controversy over it was confined largely to the first season. ABC intimated that the program represented a major breakthrough in TV comedy, and claimed that "through the Campbells and the Tates many of today's social concerns will be dealt with in a comedic manner." Others considered *Soap* nothing more than an extended dirty joke being piped into America's living rooms. Much of the opposition to the program was led by religious groups, including the National Council of Churches. Rev. Everett Parker, a longtime critic of TV, called *Soap* "a deliberate effort to break down any resistance to whatever the industry wants to put into prime time. . . . Who else besides the churches is going to stand against the effort of television to tear down our moral values and make all of us into mere consumers?"

See *ABC Late Night* for summer rerun dates for this series.

SOAP BOX THEATRE (*Dramatic Anthology*)
FIRST TELECAST: *June 24, 1950*
LAST TELECAST: *December 3, 1950*
BROADCAST HISTORY:
Jun 1950–Oct 1950, ABC Sun 9:30–10:00
Oct 1950–Dec 1950, ABC Sun 9:00–9:30

This was a series of filmed dramas.

SOAPNET (Network) (*General Entertainment Cable Network*)
LAUNCHED:
January 24, 2000
SUBSCRIBERS (MAY 2003):
30.7 million (29% U.S.)

A network for busy fans of daytime soap operas, who preferred to watch them at other times of the day. During the early 2000s the evening schedule consisted of same-day repeats of ABC afternoon soaps *All My Children, One Life to Live, General Hospital* and *Port Charles.* There were also marathons, classic soaps of the past *(Dynasty, Knots Landing, Hotel, Sisters)* and the original series *Soap Talk* (talk) with Lisa Rinna and Ty Treadway and *SoapCenter* (soap news) with Tanika Ray.

SOCIAL STUDIES (*Situation Comedy*)
FIRST TELECAST: *March 18, 1997*
LAST TELECAST: *August 5, 1997*
BROADCAST HISTORY:
Mar 1997–Apr 1997, UPN Tue 8:30–9:00
Jul 1997–Aug 1997, UPN Tue 8:30–9:00
CAST:
Frances Harmon .... Julia Duffy
Katherine "Kit" Weaver .... Bonnie McFarlane
Dan Rossini .... Adam Ferrara
Madison Lewis .... Lisa Wilhoit
Sara Valentine .... Vanessa Evigan
Jared Moore .... Rashaan Nall
Carla Stone .... Monica McSwain
Chip Wigley .... Corbin Allred
Matt .... Jordan Brower

Frances was the stuffy headmistress of the Woodbridge Academy, a coed boarding school on Manhattan's Upper West Side. Featured members of the staff were two twenty-somethings and fellow dorm supervisors: Kit, the cynical history teacher, and Dan, the gym teacher for whom Frances had the hots. Among the uniformed students were Chip, the spoiled son of an obnoxious wealthy businessman with a knack for getting anything for anybody; Madison, the free-spirited sexpot; Sara, bright, rich, and introverted; Carla, the studious African-American; Chip's buddy Jared, the emotionally retarded guy from the inner city; and Matt, the school hunk. Frances gave daily addresses to the students via a closed circuit TV system with monitors in the classrooms.

SOLDIER OF FORTUNE, INC. (*Adventure*)
BROADCAST HISTORY:
Syndicated only
60 minutes
Produced: *1997–1999* (37 episodes)
Released: *September 1997*
CAST:
Matt Shepherd .... Brad Johnson
Benny Ray Riddle .... Tim Abell
Margo Vincent .... Melinda Clarke
Jason "Chance" Walker (1997–1998) ... Real Andrews
Christopher "C.J." Yates (1997–1998) .... Mark A. Sheppard
Xavier Trout .... David Selby
Deacon "Deke" Reynolds (1998–1999) .... Dennis Rodman
Nick Delvecchio (1998–1999) ..... David Eigenberg
Debbie the Waitress (1998–1999) .. Julie Nathanson

Major Matthew Shepherd, formerly in the army's Special Forces, led a team of crack mercenaries, all former military personnel, who undertook high risk missions for the government where "plausible deniability was imperative." Their covert missions were under the auspices of Xavier Trout, a special consultant to the National Security Agency. Members of the team, which worked out of a warehouse in Venice Beach, California, were Yates, previously a pilot for the British Special Air Service, who specialized in demolition and electronic surveillance; Riddle, a former Marine staff sergeant who was a crack shot and weapons expert; Vincent, a sexy former C.I.A. case officer whose specialties were cryptography and languages; and Walker, a former pilot who excelled at close quarters combat. Their first mission was to rescue four Brits being held hostage in Iraq after their helicopter had crashed behind the lines. Later they captured a general wanted by the U.N. War Crimes Tribunal in Bosnia, prevented an AWOL marine in Cuba from killing Fidel Castro, rescued hostages (including Trout's daughter) from terrorists in Chile, and freed a hated former KGB agent from a high security prison to protect U.S. agents in Moscow.

When the series returned for its second season, the title had been changed to *SOF: Special Ops Force*. Walker and Yates were gone, and new to the team was Deke, a former Army helicopter pilot and demolitions expert, and super-cool dude who had been almost court-martialed for insubordination (played, appropriately, by professional basketball's resident bad boy, Dennis Rodman); and Nick, a former D.E.A. agent who loved going undercover. They had converted the warehouse to the Silver Star Bar, and were using it as a cover for their real activities. At the end of the May 1999 series finale viewers learned that Debbie, the perky waitress at the bar was an enemy agent monitoring their activities.

Filmed in Montreal, Canada

SOLDIER PARADE, see *Talent Patrol*

SOLDIERS, THE (*Situation Comedy*)

FIRST TELECAST: *June 25, 1955*
LAST TELECAST: *September 3, 1955*
BROADCAST HISTORY:
Jun 1955–Sep 1955, NBC Sat 8:00–8:30
CAST:
Hal .... Hal March
Tom .... Tom D'Andrea

This live summer comedy series, originating from Hollywood, starred Hal March and Tom D'Andrea in the roles they had played over the years on numerous variety shows. As two typical GIs who found nothing but trouble in the army, Tom and Hal complained about almost everything—the regimentation, the food, their superior officers, etc. Each episode contained one or more vignettes about a specific aspect of life in the army; getting letters from home, trying to get passes, being sent to an isolated location for a special assignment, and the problems of adjusting to civilian life after getting discharged.

SOLDIERS OF FORTUNE (*Adventure*)

BROADCAST HISTORY:
Syndicated only
30 minutes
Produced: *1955–1956* (52 episodes)
Released: *Early 1955*
CAST:
Tim Kelly .... John Russell
Toubo Smith .... Chick Chandler

Tim Kelly and Toubo Smith were two rugged adventurers-for-hire in this action series. They went anywhere for a price, and a typical episode might find them tramping through the African jungle, fighting their way out of a barroom brawl in Singapore, or pearl diving in the South Seas. Kelly was the serious one, a big, handsome hunk; and Toubo was the older, humorous sidekick.

SOLID GOLD (*Music*)

BROADCAST HISTORY:
Syndicated only
60 minutes
Produced: *1980–1988*
Released: *September 1980*
HOSTS:
Dionne Warwick (1980–1981, 1985–1986)
Marilyn McCoo (1981–1984, 1986–1988)
Andy Gibb (1981–1982)
Rex Smith (1982–1983)
Rick Dees (1984–1985)
REGULARS:
The Solid Gold Dancers
Wayland Flowers and Madame (1980–1984)
Marty Cohen (1980–1981)
Mack & Jamie (1982)
Jeff Altman (1982–1983)
Nina Blackwood (1986–1988)

Solid Gold was a countdown of the top ten records of the week, most of them accompanied by the high-energy dancing of the athletic and sexy Solid Gold Dancers. Also featured were other new releases, pick hits, and an occasional oldie. Some numbers were seen performed by the artists themselves, either in a video or in the studio, and there was even an occasional "joke" video of ordinary people lip-syncing to some famous hit. Even the star performances were lip-synced, in fact; unlike the situation in the prerock days of *Your Hit Parade*, the record (often an elaborate production), not the song, was now the hit.

There were a number of hosts on the program, most of them singers in their own right. During the first season Dionne Warwick hosted with the help of a different guest star each week. She was replaced by the team of Andy Gibb and Marilyn McCoo. Teenage heartthrob Gibb became increasingly unreliable by the end of the second season, missing several shows, and was replaced by Rex Smith for 1982–1983. Finally Miss McCoo—a beautiful woman who had once been a member of the group the Fifth Dimension—took over as sole host in 1983. Regulars included comedians Marty Cohen, Mack & Jamie, Jeff Altman, and Wayland Flowers and his foulmouthed puppet, Madame.

In the fall of 1984 disc jockey Rick Dees succeeded Miss McCoo as *Solid Gold*'s host, the first non-singer in that role. His tenure lasted one year, followed by the return of Dionne Warwick for the 1985–1986 season, and the return of Miss McCoo in the fall of 1986. That fall there were two new features added to *Solid Gold*—an interview segment in which disc jockey Nina Blackwood chatted with current rock stars and "Flashback," an opportunity for rock stars from the '50s, '60s, and '70s to re-create their big hits. The series was retitled *Solid Gold in Concert* at the start of the 1987–1988 season to reflect an increase in the number of live performances by the artists whose songs were performed on the show.

For a short time, during the summer of 1984, actor Grand Goodeve hosted a weekday half-hour spin-off series titled *Solid Gold Hits*.

SOME OF MY BEST FRIENDS (*Situation Comedy*)

FIRST TELECAST: *February 28, 2001*
LAST TELECAST: *April 11, 2001*
BROADCAST HISTORY:
Feb 2001–Mar 2001, CBS Wed 8:00–8:30
Mar 2001–Apr 2001, CBS Wed 8:30–9:00

CAST:
Frankie Zito .... Danny Nucci
Warren Fairbanks .... Jason Bateman
Meryl Doogan .... Jessica Lundy
Pino Palumbo .... Michael DeLuise
Vern Limoso .... Alec Mapa
Connie Zito .... Camille Saviola
Joe Zito .... Joe Grifasi

Macho young Frankie, an aspiring actor, was determined to get out of his parents' home in the Bronx. Sensitive, intellectual Warren's boyfriend had just moved out of his Greenwich Village apartment after a fight. Frankie responded to the ad Warren put in the paper seeking a roommate because he thought *GWM* meant "Guy With Money," not "Gay White Male." It wasn't until after Frankie moved in that they both realized what a mistake they had made but, by that time, they were actually starting to like each other, and decided to give it a try. Warren's twice-divorced sister, Meryl, managed the building, Pino was Frankie's beefy intellectually challenged buddy, and outlandish Vern was Warren's overtly gay Japanese best friend.

There were loads of gay jokes ("This whole fridge is filled with fairy food!"), but not much of an audience. Low ratings prompted CBS to pull the plug after five of the seven episodes produced had aired. Adapted from the 1997 film *Kiss Me Guido*.

SOMEONE LIKE ME (*Situation Comedy*)

FIRST TELECAST: *March 14, 1994*
LAST TELECAST: *April 25, 1994*
BROADCAST HISTORY:
Mar 1994–Apr 1994, NBC Mon 8:30–9:00

CAST:
Jean Stepjak .... Patricia Heaton
Steven Stepjak .... Anthony Tyler Quinn
Gabrielle (Gaby) Stepjak (age 11) .... Gaby Hoffman
Samantha (Sam) Stepjak .... Nikki Cox
Evan Stepjak (4) .... Joseph Tello
Dorie Schmidt .... Jane Morris
Jane Schmidt (12) .... Raegan Kotz
Neal Schmidt .... Matthew Thomas Carey
Marla .... Krystin Moore

Bright little sitcom about a glib 11-year-old chatterbox named Gaby and her world. Jean was her doting, all-American mom, given to natural foods and a squeaky-clean house. Her best friend, Jane, on the other hand, had a mom (Dorie) who let her do almost anything and whose house was a glorious mess. Steven was Gaby's earnest stepdad, an optician; Sam her scheming teenage sister, who was sometimes an ally, sometimes not; and Evan her little half brother. Neal was Jane's brother. Much of the action took place around the recreation-center pool, where Gaby was an ardent swimmer. Set in St. Louis.

SOMERSET MAUGHAM TV THEATRE (*Dramatic Anthology*)

FIRST TELECAST: *October 18, 1950*
LAST TELECAST: *December 10, 1951*
BROADCAST HISTORY:
Oct 1950–Mar 1951, CBS Wed 9:00–9:30
Apr 1951–Jun 1951, NBC Mon 9:30–10:30
Jul 1951–Aug 1951, NBC Mon 9:30–10:00
Sep 1951–Dec 1951, NBC Mon 9:30–10:30

HOST:
W. Somerset Maugham

This anthology series had the distinction of having as host the author of the novels and short stories that had been adapted for television presentation. The plays themselves were live, originating from New York, but the opening and closing remarks by the author had all been filmed prior to the start of the season at his home on the French Riviera. He would introduce each play and return at the end to thank the audience for watching and to announce the title of the next week's production. When it premiered on CBS as a half-hour series, its title was *Teller of Tales*. After three telecasts the title was changed to *Somerset Maugham TV Theatre*. On NBC during the spring and fall of 1951, a full-hour version of the show aired on alternate weeks with *Robert Montgomery Presents*. It ran during the summer of 1951 as a half-hour show every week.

SOMETHING IS OUT THERE (*Science Fiction*)

FIRST TELECAST: *October 21, 1988*
LAST TELECAST: *December 9, 1988*
BROADCAST HISTORY:
Oct 1988, NBC Fri 8:00–9:00
Oct 1988–Nov 1988, NBC Fri 9:00–10:00
Nov 1988–Dec 1988, NBC Fri 8:00–9:00

CAST:
Jack Breslin .... Joe Cortese
Ta'ra .... Maryam d'Abo
Lt. Victor Maldonado .... Gregory Sierra

A sci-fi yarn about a beautiful alien who teamed up with a skeptical cop to battle assorted terrors in a large American city. The series was based on a May 1988 NBC mini-series of the same name. Ta'ra was the medical officer of a spaceship that had been taken over by a ferocious monster. She escaped to Earth, only to discover that the monster—which hid in the bodies of its intended victims, ultimately destroying them—was here, too. But hiding within whom? Together, Ta'ra and Jack, the cop, tracked down the beast and saved the world. No one they met believed any of this, of course, so the following fall they were free to continue fighting Earth-bound criminals, as well as an occasional marauding alien. Ta'ra, who dressed in a sexy black jumpsuit, was a bit spacy (so to speak), but she had an impressive arsenal of laser weaponry as well as the useful ability to read minds. As for Jack, well, he knew the streets.

A recurring bit of humor revolved around the amazement of Ta'ra, an advanced alien, at Earth's primitive customs, not to mention at Jack's thoughts when he gazed at her slinky jumpsuit. Sex on Ta'ra's planet was consummated by merely touching hands.

Reading Jack's mind, she exclaimed "You want to do *what* with my body?"

SOMETHING SO RIGHT (*Situation Comedy*)

FIRST TELECAST: *September 17, 1996*

LAST TELECAST: *July 7, 1998*

BROADCAST HISTORY:

Sep 1996–Jun 1997, NBC Tue 8:30–9:00
Mar 1998–Apr 1998, ABC Tue 8:30–9:00
Apr 1998–May 1998, ABC Tue 9:30–10:00
May 1998–Jul 1998, ABC Tue 8:30–9:00

CAST:

Jack Farrell .... Jere Burns
Carly Davis .... Mel Harris
Nicole Farrell (age 16) .... Marne Patterson
Will Pacino (14) .... Billy L. Sullivan
Sarah Kramer (11) .... Emily Ann Lloyd
Grace (1996–1997) .... Carol Ann Susi
Paul Lardazzio (1998) .... Nick Gaza
**Stephanie Farrell* .... Christine Dunford
**Dante* .... Michael Milhoan
**Sheldon Kramer* .... Barry Jenner

*Occasional

"So we're not the Waltons," deadpanned Mom in this very '90s sitcom about a newlywed couple with three divorces and three kids between them. Jack was an amiable, divorced English teacher who had married twice-divorced Carly, a hyperactive corporate party planner. Passing through their busy Manhattan kitchen was a motley assortment of stepkids and ex's. Jack's daughter was scheming 16-year-old Nicole ("Dad-dy!"), while Carly's offspring were awkward Will, who had a major crush on Nicole, and brainy Sarah, who wanted to go live with her dad so she could have her own room again. Popping in from time to time were their friendly ex's, actress Stephanie, burly Dante, and rich, snotty Sheldon. Grace was Carly's technicolor coworker.

When *Something So Right* moved to ABC in 1998, Grace was gone, replaced by chubby, goofy delivery guy Paul, who had the hots for oblivious Nicole.

SOMETHING WILDER (*Situation Comedy*)

FIRST TELECAST: *October 1, 1994*

LAST TELECAST: *June 13, 1995*

BROADCAST HISTORY:

Oct 1994, NBC Sat 8:00–8:30
Dec 1994–Mar 1995, NBC Tue 8:30–9:00
Jun 1995, NBC Tues 8:30–9:00

CAST:

Gene Bergman .... Gene Wilder
Annie Bergman .... Hillary B. Smith
Gabe Bergman (age 4) .... Ian Bottiglieri
Sam Bergman (4) .... Carl Michael Lindner
Jack Travis .... Gregory Itzin
Richie Wainwright .... Jake Weber
Katy Mooney .... Raegan Kotz
Caleb .... Cleavant Derricks

THEME:

"You Brought a New Kind of Love to Me," by Sammy Fain, Irving Kahal, and Pierre Norman Connor (1930 pop song), sung by Gene Wilder

This gentle comedy starred Gene Wilder as a sensitive, emotional adman who rather late in life became the father of two supercute fraternal twins. And a doting dad he was. Restrained only slightly by sensible wife, Annie, and crabby partner, Jack (whose kids were grown), Gene hugged, mugged, and stopped work constantly to play with the little devils, who were seemingly always underfoot. Adding to the congestion was the fact that Gene and Jack's small agency, Berkshire Hills Advertising, was adjacent to their homes in rural Stockbridge, Massachusetts. Richie was Annie's irresponsible young brother (who worked for Gene), Katy her boy-crazy niece, and Caleb the handyman.

SON OF THE BEACH (*Situation Comedy*)

BROADCAST HISTORY:

FX
30 minutes
Original episodes: *2000–2002* (43 episodes)
Premiered: *March 14, 2000*

CAST:

Notch Johnson .... Timothy Stack
Jamaica St. Croix .... Leila Arcieri
B. J. Cummings .... Jaime Bergman
Kimberlee Clark .... Kim Oja
Chip Rommel .... Roland Kickinger
Mayor Anita Massengil .... Lisa Banes
Porcelain Bidet (2002) .... Amy Weber
**Kody Massengil* .... Jason Hopkins
**Professor Milosevic* .... Robert Stephen Ryan

*Occasional

Exceptionally raunchy sitcom about the intrepid lifeguards of Malibu Adjacent, California, led by flabby, out-of-shape—but resourceful—Notch Johnson. His buff team consisted of B. J., a part-time model who held the beach record for number of saves (52 mouth-to-mouth rescues); Jamaica, an inner-city sexpot with a "happening attitude" who became a lifeguard after her brother was killed in a swim-by shooting; Chip, a beefy German bodybuilder; and Kimberlee, whose intelligence made her severely overqualified for the "SPF 30" team. Kimberlee, it turned out, was a spy sent by scheming Mayor Massengil, who was plotting to get rid of Notch, but her loyalties quickly switched to the honest Notch. Kody was the mayor's fey, gay teenage son, who, like his uptight mother, lusted after Chip. Joining the team in 2002 was another beauty named Porcelain.

Among the unlikely threats that befell Notch and his "unit" were the toxic Unadumper, evil Professor Milosevic's female robot lifeguards, a mythical beast called the cocktopuss (part rooster, part octopus), and villains Stinkfinger and Heinous Anus (RuPaul). Nor were the adventures limited to Malibu Adjacent: Jamaica became the first black lifeguard in space, and the team traveled to Japan, South America, and the Middle East (where Notch became best friends with Israeli Noccus Johnstein, played by Gilbert Gottfried). A highlight of each episode was a fantasy sequence loosely tied to the plot, depicting such activities as amorously feeding grapes to members of the opposite sex, beautiful models slowly rubbing on sunscreen, etc.

This wild parody on *Baywatch* (or cesspool of double entendres, depending on your point of view) was created by none other than Howard Stern, the radio "shock jock."

SONG AND DANCE (*Music*)

FIRST TELECAST: *December 17, 1948*

LAST TELECAST: *June 21, 1949*

BROADCAST HISTORY:

Dec 1948–Jan 1949, NBC Fri 8:00–8:30
Jan 1949–Mar 1949, NBC Mon 8:00–8:30
Mar 1949–Apr 1949, NBC Mon 8:15–8:30
May 1949–Jun 1949, NBC Various nights and times

HOSTESS:

Roberta Quinlan (1948–1949)
Barbara Marshall (1949)

DANCERS:

Ellsworth & Fairchild

Live musical interlude featuring songs and dancing. Quite a number of "regular" singers and dancers came and went during the program's short run. Roberta Quinlan was the original hostess, replaced by Barbara Marshall in April 1949.

SONG SNAPSHOTS ON A SUMMER HOLIDAY,

see *Summer Holiday*

SONGS AT TWILIGHT (*Music*)

FIRST TELECAST: *July 3, 1951*
LAST TELECAST: *August 31, 1951*
BROADCAST HISTORY:

Jul 1951–Aug 1951, NBC Mon–Fri 7:30–7:45

REGULARS:

Bob Carroll
Buddy Greco
Johnny Andrews

Songs at Twilight was a live informal 15 minutes of song and talk by its host and his guest star of the evening. It spent the summer of 1951 filling the remainder of the half hour in which NBC aired its network news program. Holding on to a host was a problem for this series. When it premiered, singer Bob Carroll had the job. On July 16 he was replaced by singer-pianist Buddy Greco, who was replaced on July 30 by singer Johnny Andrews. Andrews somehow managed to last until the program went off the air.

SONGS FOR SALE (*Music*)

FIRST TELECAST: *July 7, 1950*
LAST TELECAST: *June 28, 1952*
BROADCAST HISTORY:

Jul 1950–Sep 1950, CBS Fri 9:00–10:00
Feb 1951, CBS Sat 7:30–8:00
Jun 1951–Feb 1952, CBS Sat 10:00–11:00
Mar 1952–Jun 1952, CBS Sat 9:30–11:00
Jun 1952, CBS Sat 8:00–9:00

EMCEE:

Jan Murray (1950–1951)
Steve Allen (1951–1952)

REGULARS:

Rosemary Clooney (1950–1951)
Tony Bennett (1950)
Richard Hayes (1950–1951)
Ray Bloch and His Orchestra
Mitch Miller (1951)
Peggy Lee (1951–1952)
Barry Gray (1952)

Songs for Sale was a showcase for the efforts of aspiring amateur songwriters. Each week a number of them (usually three) had their songs performed by professional singers and rated by a panel of judges. The winning song was guaranteed to be published, and the runners-up might be if a publisher who was listening liked them. The show, needless to say, was swamped with submissions. Originally there were two permanent singers on the show, and a rotating panel of judges. Rosemary Clooney and Tony Bennett were relatively unknown when the series began, but both immediately attracted considerable attention and went on to become major stars—they were probably more important "discoveries" of this show than any of the songs. (Both had previously been winners on *Arthur Godfrey's Talent Scouts.*) Bennett left the show after a month, but Rosemary Clooney continued, joined by Richard Hayes. Both of them remained until the show was temporarily shelved in the fall of 1950.

When it returned in 1951 singers were generally rotated, though Peggy Lee became a regular in December 1951 and remained for several months. Panelists changed too. For a period in the spring of 1951 Mitch Miller was a regular panelist, and Barry Gray served in a similar capacity in the spring of 1952. From its inception until September 1951, *Songs for Sale* was simulcast on radio and TV.

During its last season there were cash awards, up to $1,000, available to weekly winners whose songs also won a special run-off held once every five or six weeks, before an enlarged panel of judges.

SONGTIME (*Religion*)

FIRST TELECAST: *October 6, 1951*
LAST TELECAST: *May 17, 1952*
BROADCAST HISTORY:

Oct 1951–May 1952, ABC Sat 11:00–11:30

HOST:

Jack Wyrtzen

Hymns, gospel songs, and inspirational talks by youth leader Jack Wyrtzen. The program began locally in New York in November 1950, and was seen live over the network during the 1951–1952 season. Also known as *The Word of Life Songtime.*

SONNY AND CHER COMEDY HOUR, THE

(*Musical Variety*)

FIRST TELECAST: *August 1, 1971*
LAST TELECAST: *August 29, 1977*
BROADCAST HISTORY:

Aug 1971–Sep 1971, CBS Sun 8:30–9:30
Dec 1971–Jun 1972, CBS Mon 10:00–11:00
Sep 1972–Dec 1972, CBS Fri 8:00–9:00
Dec 1972–May 1974, CBS Wed 8:00–9:00
Feb 1976–Jan 1977, CBS Sun 8:00–9:00
Jan 1977–Mar 1977, CBS Fri 9:00–10:00
May 1977–Aug 1977, CBS Mon 10:00–11:00

REGULARS:

Sonny Bono
Cher Bono
Ted Zeigler
Chastity Bono (1973–1977)
Tom Solari (1971–1972)
Clark Carr (1971–1972)
Murray Langston (1971–1974)
Freeman King (1971–1974)
Peter Cullen (1971–1974)
The Jimmy Dale Orchestra (1971–1973)
The Marty Paich Orchestra (1973–1974)
Steve Martin (1972–1973)
Teri Garr (1973–1974)
Billy Van (1973–1976)
Bob Einstein (1973–1974)
Gailard Sartain (1976)
Jack Harrell (1976)

Robert Shields and Lorene Yarnell (1976–1977)
The Tony Mordente Dancers (1971–1974)
The Earl Brown Singers (1971–1974)
The Harold Battiste Orchestra (1976–1977)

THEME:

"The Beat Goes On," by Sonny Bono

After almost a decade performing in clubs and auditoriums, Sonny and Cher were given their own summer variety series on CBS. The interplay between the two stars—Sonny's ebullient enthusiasm and Cher's sardonic wit and continual put-downs of her husband—was one of the strong points of the program. The summer show did well and returned that December to become a hit regular series. During its initial run, *The Sonny and Cher Comedy Hour* utilized several recurring comedy sketches. There was a "Vamp" segment in which Cher would portray several of the more notorious women throughout history; a "Sonny's Pizza" segment featuring Sonny as the dumb owner of a pizzeria and Cher as his sexy, beautiful waitress Rosa; the "Dirty Linen" segment with housewife Laverne (Cher) giving her views on men to her friend Olivia (Teri Garr) at the laundromat; and a segment in which news headlines, both current and past, were treated in blackouts. Frequently seen were full-scale operettas based on legitimate operas, television commercials, types of TV programs, and almost anything else that could be spoofed.

All was going well, the ratings were good, the couple seemed to be the picture of happiness (they had even made their daughter a semiregular at the show's close when they would sing their record hit "I've Got You Babe"). Unfortunately, reality and appearances were two different things. The Bonos were having marital problems, and it was announced in the spring of 1974 that they were getting divorced and would give up the series. They went their separate ways. Sonny failed with *The Sonny Comedy Revue*, his own show on ABC that fall, and Cher had only middling success with *Cher*, her solo effort that began on CBS the following January. With her solo venture limping along after less than a year on the air, a professional reconciliation was arranged with Sonny so that they might work together again. Cher had since married rock singer Greg Allman and given birth to a son. The new venture was titled *The Sonny and Cher Show*, but it could never regain the magic of the original. Cher's put-downs of Sonny, which seemed funny when they were married, just didn't work as well after they were divorced. The new series limped along for two seasons and was canceled in the summer of 1977.

SONNY COMEDY REVUE, THE (*Comedy/Variety*)

FIRST TELECAST: *September 22, 1974*
LAST TELECAST: *December 29, 1974*
BROADCAST HISTORY:

Sep 1974–Dec 1974, ABC Sun 8:00–9:00

REGULARS:

Sonny Bono
Ted Zeigler
Billy Van
Peter Cullen
Freeman King
Murray Langston
Teri Garr
Lex De Azevedo Orchestra

After Sonny and Cher broke up their successful act, and marriage, in 1974, each of them tried continuing on their own. Sonny's effort was this short-lived comedy variety show in which he was supposed to play the Chaplinesque "little man," always beset by troubles, and always the underdog. A repertory company of young comedians appeared with him in sketches, as did assorted guests.

SONNY KENDIS SHOW, THE (*Music*)

FIRST TELECAST: *April 18, 1949*
LAST TELECAST: *January 6, 1950*
BROADCAST HISTORY:

Apr 1949–May 1949, CBS Mon/Wed 7:15–7:30
May 1949–Sep 1949, CBS Tue/Thu 7:45–7:55
Sep 1949–Jan 1950, CBS Mon/Tue/Thu/Fri 7:45–7:55

REGULARS:

Sonny Kendis
Gigi Durston

Pianist Sonny Kendis starred in this twice-to-four-times-per-week live musical series. His featured vocalist was Gigi Durston. Sonny was reputed to have such fast hands that they appeared to be a blur on the television screen when he played the piano rapidly.

SONNY SPOON (*Detective Drama*)

FIRST TELECAST: *February 12, 1988*
LAST TELECAST: *December 16, 1988*
BROADCAST HISTORY:

Feb 1988–Mar 1988, NBC Fri 10:00–11:00
May 1988–Jul 1988, NBC Fri 9:00–10:00
Oct 1988, NBC Fri 10:00–11:00
Oct 1988–Nov 1988, NBC Fri 8:00–9:00
Nov 1988–Dec 1988, NBC Fri 9:00–10:00

CAST:

Sonny Spoon .... Mario Van Peebles
Asst. D.A. Carolyn Gilder .... Terry Donahoe
Lucius DeLuce .... Joe Shea
Monique .... Jordana Capra
Johnny Skates .... Bob Wieland
Mel .... Melvin Van Peebles

"He's a scam, he's a sham, he's a flim-flam man," said the ad, which was bad, for this hip black lad. Sonny Spoon was certainly street-hip (though he didn't always rhyme), a smooth operator who had put his talents to work as a private eye. His office was a phone booth, and his friends and information sources mostly street people—Lucius the rotund newsstand operator, Monique the helpful hooker, and Skates, a legless man who zipped through crowds on a skateboard. When he needed a little heavy artillery Sonny turned to Carolyn, a rising star in the D.A.'s office who was skeptical about his scams, but liked the results he got. Mel was his dad, a bar owner. Sonny was particularly good at disguises, and might turn up, in the course of an episode, as anything from a bewildered Arab tourist, to a clergyman, to an old, fat woman. They all fit in with his bizarre cases, which were peopled with characters like Lame Larry, Insane Wayne, Tonsillitis (a blues singer), and an adorable little waif called Marilyn Monroe. Audiences could hardly keep up.

Hey, Sonny, keep shuckin' and jivin' . . . or else your ratings may start divin'.

SONS AND DAUGHTERS (*Drama*)

FIRST TELECAST: *September 11, 1974*
LAST TELECAST: *November 6, 1974*

BROADCAST HISTORY:

Sep 1974–Nov 1974, CBS Wed 8:00–9:00

CAST:

Jeff Reed .... Gary Frank
Anita Cramer.................... Glynnis O'Connor
Lucille Reed .... Jay W. Macintosh
Walter Cramer..................... John S. Ragin
Ruth Cramer.......................... Jan Shutan
Danny Reed...................... Michael Morgan
Stash Melnyck .... Scott Colomby
Murray "Moose" Kerner .... Barry Livingston
Mary Anne............................ Laura Siegel
Charlie Riddel .... Lionel Johnston
Evie Martinson..................... Debralee Scott
Cody........................... Christopher Nelson

In almost soap-opera fashion, *Sons and Daughters* attempted to portray what it was like to be teenagers in love in the mid-1950s. The two in love were Jeff and Anita, 16-year-old sweethearts and students at Southwest High School in Stockton, California. Jeff's dad had recently passed away and Anita's mother had just left her husband and moved in with another man. Their adjustments to the sudden changes in their home lives and the good and bad times they had with each other, with their friends, and with their families were told in the series. The peripheral relationships and involvements of the other cast members, despite the central focus on Jeff and Anita, gave *Sons and Daughters* an almost *Peyton Place* quality.

SONS & DAUGHTERS (*Drama*)

FIRST TELECAST: *January 4, 1991*
LAST TELECAST: *March 1, 1991*
BROADCAST HISTORY:

Jan 1991–Mar 1991, CBS Fri 10:00–11:00

CAST:

Tess Hammersmith .... Lucie Arnaz
Astrid Hammersmith (age 10) ...... Michelle Wong
Patty Hammersmith Lincoln...... Peggy Smithhart
Spud Lincoln........................ Rick Rossovich
Rocky Lincoln (16).................. Paul Scherrer
Paulette Lincoln (14) .... Kamie Harper
Ike Lincoln (7) .... Billy O'Sullivan
Gary Hammersmith .... Scott Plank
Lindy Hammersmith .... Stacy Edwards
Bing Hammersmith................... Don Murray
Mary Ruth Hammersmith.............. Lisa Blount
Bing Hammersmith, Jr. (4) ...... Aaron Brownstein
Grandpa Hank Hammersmith ... George D. Wallace

Set in Portland, Oregon, *Sons & Daughters* chronicled the intertwined lives of the large Hammersmith family. As the series opened, Bing Hammersmith had returned home to Portland with his much-younger second wife, Mary Ruth, and their young son, Bing, Jr. His return created a major problem for his neurotic daughter, Tess, a single parent who now had to share the family home in which she had been living with her adopted Korean daughter, Astrid. The problem was not her father, but his "hillbilly" bride with whom she could not get along. Bing's other daughter, Patty, the family peacemaker, was married to football coach Spud Lincoln. They had three children—Rocky, who dropped out of high school to become a male model; Paulette, who was trying to find herself; and precocious young Ike. Gary, the youngest of Bing's children, was a self-indulgent yuppie who, along with his wife, Lindy, was having problems adjusting to the changes in his lifestyle forced upon him by the birth of his daughter, Dakota.

SONS OF THUNDER (*Detective*)

FIRST TELECAST: *March 6, 1999*
LAST TELECAST: *April 17, 1999*
BROADCAST HISTORY:

Mar 1999–Apr 1999, CBS Sat 10:00–11:00

CAST:

Trent Malloy .... Jimmy Wlcek
Carlos Sandoval.................... Marco Sanchez
Marion "Butch" McMann................ Alan Autry
Kim Sutter............................ Dawn Maxey
Det. Art Ryan .... Neil Giuntoli

Sons of Thunder was a spin-off from *Walker, Texas Ranger.* Trent and Carlos, who had been featured on the latter series for the previous year, formed Thunder Investigations, a fledgling private detective agency. Trent was a former Army Ranger and third degree black belt in karate (who had been a protégé of Cordell Walker) and Carlos had just resigned from the Dallas Police Department. Their office was above Uppercuts, a popular sports bar in Dallas. Butch, the former boxer who ran Uppercuts, had been a P.I. himself before buying the bar and renting his former office to Trent and Carlos. He became their mentor, providing practical advice to the inexperienced detectives. In the second episode they hired Kim, a former night manager for a hotel, as their office manager to straighten out their finances. She also proved adept at using her computer skills to track down information. The guys often went undercover, and most episodes included several karate-filled fight scenes. In many respects *Thunder* looked like a more youthful version of *Walker.*

SOPRANOS, THE (*Crime Drama*)

BROADCAST HISTORY:

Home Box Office
60 minutes
Original episodes: *1999–*
Premiered: *January 10, 1999*

CAST:

Tony Soprano .... James Gandolfini
Carmela Soprano......................... Edie Falco
Meadow Soprano................. Jamie-Lynn Sigler
Anthony "A. J." Soprano, Jr. .... Robert Iler
Livia Soprano (1999–2000) ...... Nancy Marchand
Janice Soprano (2000–)............. Aida Turturro
Dr. Jennifer Melfi.................... Lorraine Bracco
Christopher Moltisanti .... Michael Imperioli
Paulie "Walnuts" Gualtieri .... Tony Sirico
Silvio Dante .... Steven Van Zandt
Salvatore "Big Pussy" Bonpensiero (1999–2000)
.... Vincent Pastore
Corrado "Uncle Junior" Soprano
.... Dominic Chianese
Adriana La Cerva .... Drea de Matteo
Rosalie Aprile........................ Sharon Angela
Artie Bucco .... John Ventimiglia
Charmaine Bucco .... Katherine Narducci
Jimmy Altieri (1999) .... Joe Badalucco, Jr.
Richie Aprile (2000)..................... David Proval
Furio Giunta (2000–2002) ... Federico Castelluccio
Gigi Cestone (2000–2001).................. John Fiore
Hugh DeAngelis (2000–) .... Tom Aldredge
Mary DeAngelis (2000–)..... Suzanne Shepherd
Ralph Cifaretto (2001–2002) .... Joe Pantoliano

Patsy Parisi (2001–).............. Dan Grimaldi
Vito Spatafore (2001–) .... Joseph R. Gannascoli
Eugene Pontecorvo (2001–) ...... Robert Funaro

One of the most popular and influential dramas of the late 1990s and early 2000s appeared on a premium cable channel, seen in only about one-third of U.S. television homes. Despite its limited distribution, *The Sopranos* sometimes drew larger audiences than programs running opposite it on the broadcast networks, and it won far more awards (including several Emmys). Tony Soprano was the cunning but conflicted boss of the northern New Jersey Mafia. A big, grinning bear of a man, he was by turns genial, a worried father—and a murderous thug. The drama came from the conflict between Tony's two dysfunctional "families," one personal and the other professional, and the show's unusual mixture of introspection and psychological tension, interspersed by occasional flashes of intense violence.

At Tony's opulent suburban home was his loyal but ambivalent wife, Carmela; his resentful teenage daughter, Meadow, a straight-A student embarrassed by the family "business"; and his adoring but uncommunicative son, A. J. His crime empire was run out of the Bada Bing Club, a local strip joint that he owned. Among his most loyal soldiers were old-school enforcer Paulie; somewhat dense Silvio; hefty, friendly Pussy; and green young nephew Christopher. When the series began, Tony was still a *capo*, but the old boss, Jackie Aprile, was on his deathbed. Tony and the other *capos* decided that Tony (whose father, Johnny Boy Soprano, had once been boss) should take over. This did not sit well with his father's older brother, Uncle Junior, however, and a power struggle ensued. In the course of the 1999 season, Uncle Junior plotted with Tony's bitter, ill mother Livia to order a hit on Tony; and henchman Jimmy Altieri was discovered wearing an F.B.I. wire and was "whacked" (killed). Tony's problems with his scheming family, as well as home problems with a resentful wife and rebellious kids, drove him to see a shrink, the beautiful and understanding Dr. Melfi. Melfi soon learned Tony's real occupation, but due to her fascination with him could not let go.

During 2000 Uncle Junior was jailed on a R.I.C.O. charge; unstable long-lost sister Janice flew in from Seattle to cause trouble, plotting with Jackie Aprile's brother Richie to overthrow Tony (Janice later killed Richie); trusted soldier Pussy ratted to the F.B.I. and was whacked; and there was a failed hit on Christopher.

In 2001 the F.B.I. made a major effort to get Tony, bugging his home, but failed. There were more problems at home with Meadow and A. J., and Tony's psychiatrist, Melfi, was brutally raped. (She tried to hide it from Tony, knowing what he would do.) Drunken, out-of-control Ralph took over Richie's businesses, causing more grief and a confrontation with Tony. Livia finally died, full of hatred and bile for her family. The following year saw Uncle Junior tried and acquitted (they fixed the jury), and Tony finally took care of the "Ralph" problem by brutally killing him. Carmela was increasingly despondent over her empty marriage to Tony. First she lusted for his handsome driver, Furio (who was promptly shipped back to Sicily); then, having had enough of his mistresses (including Adriana), she threw him out of the house and demanded a divorce. Bada bing.

SORORITY LIFE (*Documentary*)

BROADCAST HISTORY:

MTV
30 minutes
Original episodes: *2002–*
Premiered: *June 24, 2002*

Another of MTV's "slice of (teenage) life" documentaries, this one about sorority life. The first season followed six pledges as they tried to earn initiation into Sigma Alpha Epsilon Pi, a Jewish sorority at the University of California—Davis. Despite the house rules there was a lot of partying and drinking, as well as guys in their cutoffs hanging out, but in the end all the girls were inducted as full-fledged sisters. Season two was set at Delta Xi Omega sorority at the State University of New York at Buffalo. A spin-off series was called—what else?—*Fraternity Life*.

SOUL MAN (*Situation Comedy*)

FIRST TELECAST: *April 15, 1997*
LAST TELECAST: *September 15, 1998*
BROADCAST HISTORY:

Apr 1997, ABC Tue 8:30–9:00
Sep 1997–Oct 1997, ABC Tue 8:30–9:00
Oct 1997–Nov 1997, ABC Tue 8:00–8:30
Nov 1997–Feb 1998, ABC Tue 8:30–9:00
Apr 1998–May 1998, ABC Tue 8:30–9:00
May 1998–Jul 1998, ABC Tue 8:00–8:30
Jul 1998–Sep 1998, ABC Tue 8:30–9:00

CAST:

Rev. Mike Weber .... Dan Aykroyd
Kenny Weber (age 14) .... Kevin Sheridan
Andy Weber (11) .... Brendon Ryan Barrett
Meredith Weber (8) .... Courtney Chase
Fred Weber (1997) .... Spencer Breslin
Fred Weber (1997–1998) .... Michael Finiguerra
Bishop Jerome .... Dakin Matthews
Melinda McGraw .... Bridgette Collins
Nancy Boyd .... Helen Cates
Father Todd Tucker .... Anthony Clark

A gentle comedy about the homelife and churchlife of a widowed Episcopal minister raising four kids in Detroit. Reverend Mike had been something of a "wild child" in his younger days, motorcycle-riding, leather-jacketed, hanging out with the wrong crowd. Now he had to try to be a role model to his rambunctious brood: Kenny, the selfish teen, who thought church was dumb; Andy, the angelic little devil who was always trying weird experiments; and Meredith, the 8-year-old who lived to torture Fred, the youngest. His supervisor was straitlaced Bishop Jerome, who didn't approve of Mike's earthy sermons and little jokes, such as the devil hand puppet or taking phone calls while in the pulpit. Melinda, a snooping reporter who seemed to want to make Mike look bad in the local paper, was an inexplicable romantic interest.

When *Soul Man* returned in the fall, there was renewed focus on Mike and Kenny's dating activities, and two new cast members—Father Todd, an inept, neophyte assistant minister, and Nancy, a worldly divorcée who was the parish's new secretary and Mike's new potential love interest.

SOUND OFF TIME, see *Chesterfield Sound Off Time*

SOUPY SALES (*Children's*)

FIRST TELECAST: *July 4, 1955*

LAST TELECAST: *April 13, 1962*
BROADCAST HISTORY:
Jul 1955–Aug 1955, ABC Mon–Fri 7:00–7:15
Jan 1962–Apr 1962, ABC Fri 7:30–8:00
HOST:
Soupy Sales
ASSISTANT:
Clyde Adler

Soupy Sales, the world's leading authority on pie-throwing, was seen in a number of local and network series over the years, including two which ran in nighttime hours. His comedy featured outrageous puns, slapstick sketches, and a regular cast of puppet characters including White Fang, the giant dog (only his paw was seen); Black Tooth, the kindest dog in the U.S.; Marilyn Monwolf, a curvaceous friend of White Fang and Black Tooth; Herman the Flea; Willie the Worm; Pookie the Lion; and Hippy the Hippo.

Beginning with a local show, *Soupy's On,* in Detroit in 1953, he then had a 1955 summer series on the ABC network that originated live from that city. From 1959 to 1961 he was seen on the ABC network on Saturday afternoons in *Lunch with Soupy Sales,* and then in early 1962, Friday at 7:30 P.M., live from Hollywood. Soupy then moved to New York and held forth with a local show that premiered in 1964 and went into syndication the following year. By the late 1970s he was back on the West Coast, where a new syndicated series was produced in 1978–1979.

Remarkably, despite the more than 25-year span of his TV career, the late 1970s versions of *The Soupy Sales Show*—and Soupy himself—looked only slightly different from the original local version in Detroit in 1953.

SOURCE: ALL ACCESS, THE (*Music Magazine*)
BROADCAST HISTORY:
Syndicated only
60 minutes
Produced: *2000–2002*
Released: *September 2000*
REGULARS:
LisaRaye
Treach
Jeff Two Times

Following a dispute between Russell Simmons and the African Heritage Network syndication company, control of his series, *Russell Simmons' Oneworld Music Beat,* was given to *The Source* magazine. The show was restructured and the title was changed to *The Source: All Access.* LisaRaye and Treach, from the rap group Naughty By Nature, served as hosts, and Jeff Two Times was the resident DJ.

Among the regular features on *All Access* were Set Trippin'—videos in progress; Style File—fashions in clothing, hairstyles, etc.; One on One—interviews with African American celebrities ranging from athletes like basketball star Kobe Bryant to rap moguls like Suge Knight; All Access Live—rap performances; Ear to the Street—gossip hosted by various contributors to *The Source* magazine, and The Hot 5—the top songs in various categories, one category per show.

SOUTH BEACH (*Detective Drama*)
FIRST TELECAST: *June 6, 1993*
LAST TELECAST: *July 6, 1993*
BROADCAST HISTORY:
Jun 1993, NBC Sun 9:00–11:00
Jun 1993–Jul 1993, NBC Tue 9:00–10:00
CAST:
Kate Patrick .... Yancy Butler
Agent Roberts .... John Glover
Vernon Charday .... Eagle-Eye Cherry

The government has some surprising crime-fighting programs, at least on television, as con artist Kate Patrick found out in this hard-edged, sexy action show. Plying her trade on Miami's trendy South Beach, Kate was savvy and slick, but not quite slick enough to escape the clutches of a creepy federal agent named Roberts. He made her an offer: Work your cons for me, and stay out of the slammer. Each week Kate got a new partner (often con artists themselves), as she tracked down bigger fish for her mysterious boss, who somehow knew about all her clues before she found them. Vernon, a hip Jamaican, was a useful source of information in Miami's polyglot culture.

SOUTH CENTRAL (*Comedy Drama*)
FIRST TELECAST: *April 5, 1994*
LAST TELECAST: *August 30, 1994*
BROADCAST HISTORY:
Apr 1994–Aug 1994, FOX Tue 8:00–8:30
CAST:
Joan Mosley .... Tina Lifford
Deion (age 6) .... Keith Mbulo
Tasha Mosley (14) .... Tasha Scott
André Mosley (17) .... Larenz Tate
Rashad .... Lamont Bentley
Sweets .... Paula Kelly
Dr. Raymond McHenry .... Ken Page
Bobby Deavers .... Clifton Powell
Mayo Bonner .... Earl Billings
Lucille .... Jennifer Lopez
Nicole .... Maia Campbell

South Central Los Angeles was the setting for this remarkably hard-edged comedy/drama about a divorced, black single mother trying to raise her family in a tough inner-city neighborhood. Joan was adjusting to working for the neighborhood grocery coop after having been laid off from her higher-paying administrative job. Not only did she have to struggle financially, but she was trying to raise her family and protect them from the violence around them. Her older son, Marcus, had been killed by neighborhood gang members. Joan had two surviving children, André, a lazy but well-meaning high school senior whose grades left much to be desired, and Tasha, a diligent student who tended to tattle on her older brother. Living with them in her small house was little Deion, a foster child who never spoke. André had become infatuated with Nicole, a sexy girl who worked part-time for Dr. McHenry, a physician friend of his mother's. Although Nicole liked him, they had difficulty getting together since her successful parents didn't want their daughter to date someone from the 'hood. Others in the cast were Rashad, André's buddy from school; Sweets, Joan's neighbor and friend; Bobby, who ran the coop where Joan worked; and Mayo and Lucille, who also worked at the coop.

Critics loved *South Central* for its realistic portrayal of life in the inner city, even if the language was stronger than they would have liked. Avoiding most of the stereotypes of TV sitcoms, these were real people with real problems. Unfortunately, the series may have been too depressing to appeal to a mass audience. Despite a campaign to keep it on the air, it was canceled after its initial 13-episode run.

SOUTH OF SUNSET (*Detective Drama*)

FIRST TELECAST: *October 27, 1993*
LAST TELECAST: *October 27, 1993*
BROADCAST HISTORY:
Oct 1993, CBS Wed 9:00–10:00
CAST:
Cody McMahon........................ Glenn Frey
Ziggy Duane........................ Aries Spears
Gina Weston........................ Maria Pitillo

Cody, once head of security for a major motion picture studio (he had busted a powerful producer and gotten himself fired), was now a struggling private detective in Los Angeles, taking any jobs that would pay the bills, even spying on wayward spouses to provide evidence in divorce proceedings. Working with Cody were young Ziggy, a semireformed thief who helped with the legwork, and Gina, an aspiring actress who did his secretarial work between auditions.

South of Sunset was the disaster of the 1993–1994 season. Heavily promoted at the start of the season during CBS' coverage of the major-league baseball play-offs and World Series, the premiere attracted such a small audience that the network pulled the plug immediately and never aired a second episode.

Glenn Frey had been one of the founders of the rock music group The Eagles and was better known for his music than his acting. In 1994 MTV aired the episodes that had been produced but not aired on CBS in conjunction with other programming celebrating the reunion of The Eagles.

SOUTH PARK (*Cartoon*)

BROADCAST HISTORY:
Comedy Central
30 Minutes
Produced: *1997–*
Premiered: *August 13, 1997*
VOICES:
Stan Marsh, Eric Cartman, Mr. Herbert Garrison, Officer Barbrady, Terrance, Timmy, Ned Gerblanski, Randy Marsh, Stuart McCormick, Mr. Mackey, Mr. Hankey............ Trey Parker
Kyle Broflovski, Kenny McCormick, Gerald Broflovski, Pip Pirrup, Jesus, Jimbo, Phillip, Big Gay Al........................ Matthew Stone
Jerome "Chef" McElroy................ Isaac Hayes
Wendy Testaburger, Liane Cartman, Sheila Broflovski, Sharon Marsh, Shelly Marsh, Mrs. McCormick, Mayor McDaniels, Ms. Crabtree, Nurse Gollum (1997–1999)
...... Shannen Cassidy (aka Mary Kay Bergman)
Wendy Testaburger, Liane Cartman, Sharon Marsh, Shelly Marsh, Mrs. McCormick, Mayor McDaniels (1999–)....... Eliza Schneider (aka Blue Girl)
Sheila Broflovski, Linda Stotch (2000–)
.... Mona Marshall
Mrs. Mayor........................ Karri Turner

The most talked-about new series of the 1997 season was not on the broadcast networks, or even on one of the major cable networks (much to the dismay of them all). *South Park*, the outrageous cartoon about four foul-mouthed third-graders and their twisted little Rocky Mountain town, premiered on Comedy Central, which at the time was seen in less than half of America's TV homes. Word about it spread so quickly that by Christmas it was a smash hit, and *South Park* T-shirts, posters, and mugs were everywhere.

The setting was the permanently snowbound little town of South Park, Colorado. The kids were Stan, the sensible one who threw up whenever he got too close to the object of his affection, oblivious Wendy; Cartman, the fat, cursing bully who was thoroughly spoiled by his single mom (his favorite food: Cheesy Poofs); Kyle, the Jewish kid who was never quite sure what that meant; and Kenny, the shy little one who trailed along behind the others. Kenny's face was always hidden inside his heavy parka, and his voice was merely a mumble. Poor Kenny was killed in almost every episode in some gory accident, leading to the show's most popular catch phrase, "Oh my God, they killed Kenny!"

Everyday life for the kids was filled with encounters with aliens, maniacs, mad scientists, and screaming and/or clueless adults, all of whom they met with a mixture of foul language and wide-eyed, childish wonder. Among the town eccentrics were Mr. Garrison, the delusional teacher who spoke through a hand puppet he always carried with him; Pip, the British student; Shelly, Stan's bullying sister; Jimbo, a gun toting yokel; Mrs. Crabtree, the cranky school bus driver; Officer Barbrady, the dense constable; green-haired Mrs. Mayor; Canadian TV personalities Terrance and Phillip, who farted a lot; and Mr. Hankey, a friendly little piece of poo (i.e., feces). A frequently-seen feature on local cable TV was the show "Jesus & Pals," starring you-know-who. Keeping a watchful eye on the boys was Chef, a black former soul singer who ran the school lunch counter and who occasionally burst into a wholly inappropriate, sexually charged song as the little kids watched uncomprehendingly.

Guest stars sometimes appeared, and celebrities were often lampooned. George Clooney was rewarded for his early support of the show with the role of Stan's gay dog, Sparky (he only barked). Among the notorious early episodes were "Mecha-Streisand," a parody of old monster movies in which Barbra Streisand exploded into a towering, egomaniacal monster and stomped on the town, until she was stopped by Leonard Maltin, Sidney Poitier, and Robert Smith of The Cure; "Starvin' Marvin," in which the boys adopted a starving Ethiopian boy and met a corpulent Sally Struthers; and "Cartman's Mom is Still a Dirty Slut," in which Cartman discovered that his missing dad was actually his mom since she was a hermaphrodite.

Being slow learners, the boys entered the fourth grade in the fall of 2000. On a tragic note, Shannen Cassidy, the original voice of Wendy Testaburger, died in 1999, a suicide.

The idea for *South Park* originated with a video Christmas card called "The Spirit of Christmas," created in 1995 for Fox television executive Brian Graden by two young Hollywood animators, Trey Parker and Matt Stone. In it, Stan, Cartman, Kyle, and Kenny witnessed a knock-down, drag out fight between Jesus and Santa Claus over the meaning of Christmas. The animation was crude, but the twisted sensibility made the tape a cult item, copied and passed around by the Hollywood in-crowd, one early booster being actor George Clooney. The networks predictably passed on the show, but struggling Comedy Central had little to lose and ordered a limited number of episodes. It not only became a major hit but forced cable systems around the country to begin carrying Comedy Central, as subscribers demanded to see "that show" they had been hearing so much about.

SOUTHERNAIRES QUARTET (*Music*)
FIRST TELECAST: *September 19, 1948*
LAST TELECAST: *November 21, 1948*
BROADCAST HISTORY:
Sep 1948–Oct 1948, ABC Sun 9:00–9:30
Oct 1948–Nov 1948, ABC Sun 7:30–8:00
REGULARS:
The Southernaires

The Southernaires were a black gospel quartet who had been heard on radio throughout the 1940s. Members of the quartet were Roy Yeates, Lowell Peters, Jay Stone Toney, and William Edmunson, with accompaniment by pianist-arranger Clarence Jones. Their prime-time musical program in the fall of 1948 was one of the earliest network series starring black performers.

SPACE (*Drama*)
FIRST TELECAST: *July 4, 1987*
LAST TELECAST: *July 25, 1987*
BROADCAST HISTORY:
Jul 1987, CBS Sat 8:00–10:00
CAST:
Norman Grant .... James Garner
Elinor Grant .... Susan Anspach
Penny Hardesty Pope .... Blair Brown
Stanley Mott .... Bruce Dern
Rachel Mott .... Melinda Dillon
Leopold Strabismus (née Martin Scorcella) .... David Dukes
Dieter Kolff .... Michael York
Liesl Kolff .... Barbara Sukowa
Randy Claggett .... Beau Bridges
Debbie Dee Claggett .... Stephanie Faracy
John Pope .... Harry Hamlin
Senator Glancey .... Martin Balsam
Finnerty .... James Sutorius
Tucker Thomas .... G.D.Spradlin
Cindy Rhee .... Maggie Han
Funkhauser .... Wolf Kahler
Marcia Grant .... Jennifer Runyon
Skip Morgan .... David Spielberg

Originally aired as a five-part, 13-hour mini-series in April 1985, a re-edited 9-hour version of James A. Michener's *Space* was rerun on CBS during the summer of 1987.

This novelization of the evolution of the American space program began at the end of World War II, when the U.S. and Russians both sought to obtain the best German rocket scientists, and continued through the exploration of the moon in the early 1970s.

The central focus of *Space* was World War II naval hero Norman Grant who, after becoming a senator, used the space program as a platform to build a long-term power base. Norman's wife, Elinor, who never liked politics, became an alcoholic and got herself involved with con man Leopold Strabismus, who took advantage of the public's fascination with outer space, U.F.O.s, and extraterrestrials. Penny Pope was an ambitious lawyer working for the Senate Space Committee, chaired by Grant, with whom she had an affair. Her husband, John, and his buddy Randy Claggett, were fighter pilots in Korea, test pilots, and later astronauts. Most important to the success of the space program were the German rocket scientists, led by Dieter Kolff, who had been brought to the U.S. after the war. The man responsible for liberating the Germans, Georgia Tech astrophysicist Stanley Mott, continued to work with them over the years, despite the inherent problems dealing with both the federal bureaucracy and the rivalries among the different military services. It was their perseverance, along with the changing political climate, that eventually led to the creation of NASA under the Eisenhower administration and the highly successful space program of the 1960s. In the climactic episode of *Space*, astronauts Pope and Claggett were teamed on the successful voyage to the dark side of the moon.

SPACE: ABOVE AND BEYOND (*Science Fiction*)
FIRST TELECAST: *September 24, 1995*
LAST TELECAST: *June 30, 1996*
BROADCAST HISTORY:
Sep 1995–Mar 1996, FOX Sun 7:00–8:00
Apr 1996, FOX Fri 8:00–9:00
May 1996–Jun 1996, FOX Sun 7:00–8:00
CAST:
Lt. Nathan West .... Morgan Weisser
Capt. Shane Vansen .... Kristen Cloke
Lt. Cooper Hawkes .... Rodney Rowland
Lt. Vanessa Demphousse .... Lanei Chapman
Lt. Paul Wang .... Joel de la Fuente
Lt. Col. Tyrus Cassius "T.C." McQueen .... James Morrison
Commodore Glen Ross .... Tucker Smallwood
**Howard Sewell* .... Michael Mantell
**Feliciti OH* .... Kimberly Patton
**Lt. Kelly Anne Winslow* .... Tasia Valenza
**Kylen Celina* .... Amanda Douge
*Occasional

In the year 2063 settlers from Earth were establishing colonies on planets when two of their settlements were destroyed by hostile aliens, called Chigs, precipitating an interstellar war. The focus of this series was a group of hotshot young recruits in the war against the aliens. Their unit was the 58th Squadron (nicknamed the Wild Cards) of the U.S. Marine Corps Space Aviator Cavalry. The recruits were West, whose fiancée had been in one of the destroyed settlements; Vansen, a natural leader who had been orphaned when her parents were killed by rebellious human-looking robots (IA's or Silicates); Hawkes, a belligerent InVitro (the product of in vitro fertilization) with no real family; Demphousse, their Chief Engineer; and Wang, friendly, funny, and very insecure. Their leader aboard the intergalactic aircraft carrier *Saratoga* was McQueen, a tough battle-scarred veteran who was himself an InVitro. Commodore Ross was the commanding officer on the *Saratoga*.

Operation Round Hammer, the first counter-offensive by the Earth forces, began in an April 1996 episode. In a two-part story the 58th found an alien on a planet threatened by Chigs. They later found out it was, in fact, a Chig, when an envoy from the same race arrived on the *Saratoga* with a proposal for a cease-fire, eighteen months after the war had begun. Negotiations broke down, and during the subsequent action West found his missing fiancée, Kylen, with other P.O.W. colonists on an alien ship, Vansen and Demphousse were hit and forced to land their fighter on an alien planet, and Wang sacrificed himself so they could save the colonists.

SPACE CADET, see *Tom Corbett—Space Cadet*

SPACE CASES (*Science Fiction*)

BROADCAST HISTORY:

Nickelodeon
30 minutes
Produced: *1996*
Premiered: *March 2, 1996*

CAST:

Harlan Band .... Walter Emanuel Jones
Radu .... Kristian Ayre
Bova .... Rahi Azizi
Rosie Ianni .... Paige Christina
Catalina .... Jewel Staite
Suzee (pilot only) .... Rebecca Herbst
Comdr. Seth Goddard .... Paul Boretski
Miss T.J. Davenport .... Cary Lawrence
Thelma .... Anik Matern

Five Starcademy cadets from various parts of the galaxy found themselves trapped on a wandering spacecraft, struggling to get back to Earth, in this Saturday night kid's show. Harlan, a black kid, was the human leader; Radu, the long-haired Andromedan with oversized, supersensitive ears; Bova, the adventuresome kid with antlers; Rosie, the red-faced little Mercurian; and Catalina another girl (who replaced Suzee after the first episode.) There were adults on board, but they were not much help. Comdr. Goddard was a well-meaning klutz who had to be constantly rescued; Miss Davenport the fussy British teacher; and Thelma a jerky android. Their ship, which resembled a great Aztec bird, was called *The Christa*. The series was created by Bill Mumy (*Lost in Space*) and Peter David, with an opening narration by science fiction guru Harlan Ellison.

SPACE GHOST: COAST TO COAST (*Talk*)

BROADCAST HISTORY:

Cartoon Network
30 minutes
Produced: *1994–*
Premiered: *April 15, 1994*

VOICES:

Space Ghost (a.k.a. Tad Ghostal) ..... George Lowe
Zorak, Moltar .... C. Martin Croker
**Brak, Lokar* .... Andy Merrill
**Tanzit* .... Don Kennedy
**Black Widow* .... Judy Tenuta

*Occasional

What happens to a cartoon superhero when his time is past? Caped, jut-jawed Space Ghost, who had a successful run on Saturday mornings from 1966 to 1968 (and again, briefly, in the mid-1970s), returned as, of all things, a cable talk show host in 1994. The masked crusader was still a cartoon, but now he interacted with live guests who appeared on a TV screen on his "set," located on an asteroid circling Earth. Among his visitors were Dr. Joyce Brothers, Danny Bonaduce, Jim Carrey, Pat Boone, and the Bee Gees (whom he blew up in disgust). Leading the house band and constantly plotting against Space Ghost was the mantis Zorak, and in the control room was his old nemesis Moltar. Brak, Lokar, Tanzit, and Black Widow were occasionally seen members of the Council of Doom.

SPACE: 1999 (*Science Fiction*)

BROADCAST HISTORY:

Syndicated only
60 minutes
Produced: *1974–1976* (48 episodes)
Released: *September 1975*

CAST:

Commander John Koenig .... Martin Landau
Dr. Helena Russell .... Barbara Bain
Prof. Victor Bergman (1975–1976) ..... Barry Morse
Maya (1976–1977) .... Catherine Schell
First Officer Tony Verdeschi (1976–1977)
.... Tony Anholt
Capt. Alan Carter .... Nick Tate
Paul Morrow .... Prentis Hancock
David .... Clifton Jones
Sandra .... Zienia Merton

Moonbase Alpha was a research colony on the surface of the moon. When John Koenig was appointed base commander in September 1999, his orders were to oversee the launch of a deep-space probe. Unfortunately, due to the accidental detonation of nuclear wastes stored on the moon, there was a gigantic explosion and Koenig found himself launched into space, along with his 310 base colleagues. Their spaceship was the moon itself, blasted free from the Earth's gravitational force and hurtling toward distant galaxies.

En route they encountered all the alien life forms and intergalactic dangers familiar to sci-fi fans. Among them: a gigantic, people-swallowing squid; a blob of living foam; a man-turned-machine named Gwent; the sexy robots of the planet Piri; and the fearsome and mysterious Arra (played by Margaret Leighton), queen of the huge planet Astheria. There was plenty of futuristic hardware, including laser beams, giant spaceships, "Queller Drive" engines, "Camelot Locator" beams, and an omnipotent talking computer—which, in moments of crisis, was prone to bark lines like "Not enough data to formulate parameters. Human decision required."

Besides the stolid Koenig, the cast included stylish Dr. Helena Russell, chief medical officer of the base; Prof. Bergman, who had established the base and was Koenig's mentor; and Capt. Carter, the chief astronaut, responsible for reconnaissance missions. Bergman was written out of the show after the first season, as having died. Joining the cast for the second season were First Officer Tony Verdeschi, irreverent and sharp-tongued second in command, and his love interest Maya, a sensual alien from the planet Psychon. She had the unusual ability to transform herself into other forms for short periods, such as a gorilla, a lioness, or even an orange tree, by "rearranging molecules."

All this hokum arrived on TV screens in 1975 amid a huge splash of publicity, brought on by the fact that this was the most expensively produced show of its kind in the history of television (around $300,000 per episode). There were spectacular special effects by

England's Brian Johnson. The large cast was headed by husband-and-wife stars Landau and Bain, making a triumphal return to television after their success in *Mission: Impossible*. Even the futuristic, unisex jumpsuits they all wore were by the famous designer Rudi Gernreich. The program was set to run in more than 100 countries around the world. Nevertheless, all three U.S. networks had turned it down. So the English producers took it directly to individual stations, via syndication, and got it scheduled in practically every city in the country. Many stations preempted network programs to put it on, and there was much gloating in the press about how the all-powerful networks were about to get their comeuppance.

It didn't work out that way, however. After heavy curiosity viewing, audiences realized that *Space: 1999* had the same problem as most space epics: all hardware and no character development. The lovely Miss Bain, for one, walked through her role like a zombie. There were efforts made to remedy this in the second season, as Koenig and Russell developed a more explicit love life, as did Verdeschi and his elusive love Maya, but by then it was too late. *Space: 1999* never became the hit its makers anticipated, and production was stopped after 48 expensive episodes.

SPACE PATROL (*Children's*)
FIRST TELECAST: *June 9, 1951*
LAST TELECAST: *June 1, 1952*
BROADCAST HISTORY:
Jun 1951–Sep 1951, ABC Sat 6:00–6:30
Dec 1951–Jun 1952, ABC Sun 6:00–6:30
CAST:
Commander Buzz Corey .... Ed Kemmer
Cadet Happy .... Lyn Osborn
Carol Karlyle .... Virginia Hewitt
Tonga .... Nina Bara
Major Robbie Robertson .... Ken Mayer
Secretary General of the United Planets .... Norman Jolley
Mr. Proteus .... Marvin Miller
Prince Baccarratti, alias the Black Falcon .... Bella Kovacs
CREATED BY:
Mike Moser

Space Patrol began in early 1950 as a local program on the West Coast, and was seen until 1955. During most of its run it was an ABC network Saturday or Sunday daytime series. However, during the two periods shown above it was run at 6:00 P.M., and thus qualifies as a "nighttime" series.

Set in the 30th century A.D., *Space Patrol* made much use of time travel, depositing its heroes in various historical periods. Commander of the Space Patrol was Buzz Corey (played by real-life World War II flying hero Ed Kemmer), who battled assorted villains in the name of the United Planets of the Universe. His youthful sidekick, Cadet Happy, was always ready with a colorful rejoinder ("Smokin' rockets, Commander!") or a simplistic question to allow Buzz to explain some obvious truth to home viewers. Other leading characters were Carol, pretty daughter of the Secretary General of the United Planets, who had romantic designs on Buzz; Tonga, a beautiful villainess-turned-heroine; and frequent villains Mr. Proteus (played by Marvin Miller, later of *The Millionaire* fame), and Prince Baccarratti.

No one ever got killed on *Space Patrol*. The worst fate was to be rendered inanimate by Buzz's Paralyzer Ray Gun, and then shown the path of truth and justice by the Brainograph. Replicas of these and other devices were available to viewers as premiums. In what was perhaps the most spectacular of all the space-opera promotions, in 1954 a 30-foot model of Buzz's spaceship, the *Terra*, toured the U.S. (on the ground) and then was given away to a lucky viewer.

SPACE PRECINCT (*Science Fiction*)
BROADCAST HISTORY:
Syndicated only
60 minutes
Produced: *1994–1995* (22 episodes)
Released: *October 1994*
CAST:
Lt. Patrick Brogan .... Ted Shackelford
Off. Jack Haldane .... Rob Youngblood
Off. Jane Castle .... Simone Bendix
Off. Took .... Mary Woodvine
Sally Brogan .... Nancy Paul
Matt Brogan (age 14) .... Nic Klein
Liz Brogan (10) .... Megan Olive
Off. Hubble Orrin .... Richard James
Off. Fredo .... David Quilter
Capt. Rexton Podly .... Jerome Willis
Slomo (voice) .... Gary Martin
Off. Silas Romek .... Lou Hirsch

In the year 2040 Lt. Patrick Brogan and his partner, Jack Haldane, were policemen fighting crime in Demeter City on the planet Alitorp. Brogan, who had transferred from Earth's N.Y.P.D., lived with his wife, Sally, and their two children, Matt and Liz, on a space station in orbit over Demeter City. Among the grotesque (at least to human eyes) beings living and working on Alitorp were Tarns, who had a third eye in their foreheads, Creons, and Zyronites. Officer Castle's partner, Took, and all of the other police officers listed above were nonhumans, even though most of them wore police uniforms from the 1990s. Took, a Tarn female, was telepathic and had telekinetic abilities. Slomo was a knee-high police robot that wandered around the precinct assisting officers and staff.

Produced in England by veteran science fiction producer Gerry Anderson.

SPACE RANGERS (*Science Fiction*)
FIRST TELECAST: *January 6, 1993*
LAST TELECAST: *January 27, 1993*
BROADCAST HISTORY:
Jan 1993, CBS Wed 8:00–9:00
CAST:
Cmdr. Chennault .... Linda Hunt
Capt. John Boon .... Jeff Kaake
Doc .... Jack McGee
JoJo .... Marjorie Monaghan
Zylyn .... Cary-Hiroyuki Tagawa
Daniel Kincaid .... Danny Quinn
Mimmer .... Clint Howard
Erich Weiss .... Gottfried John

Short-lived tongue-in-cheek *Star Trek/Star Wars* wannabe. The Space Rangers were cranky, misfit lawmen at the edge of the intergalactic frontier in the year 2104. Based at Fort Hope on the planet Avalon, they tried to keep the peace on the fringe of the settled portion of the Milky Way galaxy, coping as best as they could with broken-down equipment, cutbacks in their operating budget, bureaucratic interference from Central Command, and their own idiosyncratic and cultural differences. Capt. John Boon was the veteran leader of the group. His crew consisted of Doc, the con-man engineer who could jury-rig almost anything (and was full of replacement parts himself); JoJo, the determined and gorgeous pilot; Zylyn, a huge and powerful beastlike native of the planet Grakka; and Kincaid, the ambitious young cadet. Others based at Fort Hope were Cmdr. Chennault, their diminutive but strong-willed commanding officer; Mimmer, the base's scientific genius; and Weiss, the humorless official who couldn't cope with their lack of discipline and refusal to do anything "by the book."

SPARKS (*Situation Comedy*)

FIRST TELECAST: *August 26, 1996*
LAST TELECAST: *August 31, 1998*
BROADCAST HISTORY:

Aug 1996–Dec 1996, UPN Mon 9:30–10:00
Dec 1996–Aug 1997, UPN Mon 9:00–9:30
Aug 1997–Mar 1998, UPN Mon 9:30–10:00
Jul 1998–Aug 1998, UPN Mon 9:30–10:00

CAST:

Alonzo Sparks .... James Avery
Wilma Cuthbert .... Robin Givens
Maxey Sparks .... Miguel A. Nunez, Jr.
Greg Sparks .... Terrence Howard
Darice Mayberry .... Kym A. Whitley
La Mar Hicks .... Arif S.Kinchen

Sparks, Sparks, & Sparks was a family-owned black inner city law firm in Compton, California, near Los Angeles. Alonzo, the patriarch who had founded the firm, was preparing to retire and leave it in the hands of his two sons, Maxey and Greg, who had very little in common. Maxey, the elder, was a flashy womanizer who wanted to market their law firm like a fast food restaurant, while Greg was conservative, serious, and cautious. About the only thing they agreed on was Wilma, the sexy Stanford Law School graduate that Greg had just hired as an associate. Maxey wanted to date her, while Greg, who was against dating people from work, wished his convictions were not so strong. Darice was their surly but efficient office manager and La Mar their hip young assistant who idolized Maxey. Wilma's fiancé in the pilot was Dallas Mavericks basketball player Jason Kidd, but in later episodes she was dating other guys.

In Fall 1997, Wilma and Maxey started dating but thought they were keeping it a secret from the rest of the office. They admitted it publicly in an October episode at Darice's aborted engagement party—after which Darice ended up sleeping with Greg. They were both a little drunk and regretted it in the morning. In the first November 1997 episode, Alonzo came back from a meeting in Las Vegas married to Carmen (Evelina Fernandez), a former client he hadn't seen in years. Planning to divorce her because of his impulsive mistake, Alonzo was won over by her ardor. In the spring Wilma broke up with Maxey and left for a more prestigious law firm. At episode's end, during a trial on which they were opposing counsel two months later, they had a passionate reconciliation.

SPARRING PARTNERS WITH WALTER KIERNAN (*Quiz*)

FIRST TELECAST: *April 8, 1949*
LAST TELECAST: *May 6, 1949*
BROADCAST HISTORY:

Apr 1949–May 1949, ABC Fri 9:30–10:00

EMCEE:

Walter Kiernan

This short-lived quiz show pitted a team of men against a team of women in a game using puppets in a miniature boxing ring.

SPEAK UP, AMERICA (*Human Interest/Audience Participation*)

FIRST TELECAST: *August 1, 1980*
LAST TELECAST: *October 10, 1980*
BROADCAST HISTORY:

Aug 1980–Oct 1980, NBC Fri 10:00–11:00

REGULARS:

Marjoe Gortner
Jayne Kennedy
Rhonda Bates
Sergio Aragones

This was one series in which the audience really got involved—in fact, the audience was the whole show. Each week audience reaction to a number of subjects and issues was solicited by the show's hosts, Marjoe Gortner (a hyperkinetic former evangelist), Jayne Kennedy, and Rhonda Bates (the tall, skinny one). Some of those asked for opinions were in the live studio audience and others appeared in segments filmed on location. Satirical cartoonist Sergio Aragones sketched appropriate scenes, depending on subject matter, after the segments. Although people with vested interests in specific issues were sometimes asked their opinions, for the most part *Speak Up, America* sought the attitudes of "ordinary, average Americans." Topics discussed included the 1980 Democratic and Republican conventions, the Equal Rights Amendment, whales facing extinction, the J.F.K. assassination, sex among the elderly in nursing homes, the actors' boycott of the Emmy Awards show, an all-nudist apartment house, the problems of the American automobile industry, and TV reruns.

On April 22 and 29, 1980, several months before this series premiered, NBC aired two *Speak Up, America* specials. Only Marjoe Gortner appeared on both the specials and the series. The other hosts on the specials were KNBC newswoman Felicia Jeter and U.S. Olympic hockey coach Herb Brooks.

SPEAKING OF EVERYTHING (*Interview/Discussion*)

BROADCAST HISTORY:

Syndicated only
60 minutes
Produced: *1988* (13 episodes)
Released: *January 1988*

HOST:

Howard Cosell

After a television career that had been centered almost completely on sports—as a reporter, football analyst, boxing commentator, and interviewer—Howard Cosell came out of broadcast retirement to host this series in which he chatted with personalities from, as its title would suggest, all walks of life. The literate, controversial, and outspoken Cosell, referred to by his detractors as "the mouth that roared," could be friendly or contentious, depending on his mood and his guests. Among them were columnist Liz Smith, his former boss at ABC Roone Arledge, General William Westmoreland, ABC White House correspondent Sam Donaldson, and comedian Billy Crystal.

SPECIAL UNIT 2 (*Science Fiction/Police Drama*)
FIRST TELECAST: *April 11, 2001*
LAST TELECAST: *February 13, 2002*
BROADCAST HISTORY:
Apr 2001–May 2001, UPN Wed 8:00–9:00
May 2001–Jun 2001, UPN Tue 9:00–10:00
Aug 2001–Feb 2002, UPN Wed 9:00–10:00
CAST:
Det. Nick O'Malley .... Michael Landes
Det. Kate Benson .... Alexandra Lee
Carl .... Danny Woodburn
Capt. Richard Page .... Richard Gant
Sean Redman (2001)................ Sean Whalen
Jonathan........................... Jonathan Togo

In the premiere of *Special Unit 2*, Kate Benson was suspended from the Chicago Police Department for filing a report about her confrontation with a Gargoyle, a stone creature that Det. Nick blew up with a special weapon. Nick then recruited her into Special Unit 2, a top-secret precinct with offices in an abandoned subway tunnel under a seedy Chinese laundry, the Golden Eagle Dry Cleaners. Capt. Page, who had retired from the regular force with a mechanical hand, ran the covert operation responsible for protecting the city from Links, the malicious species that were the missing link between man and beast. He told Kate that most of the creatures of childhood—monsters, dragons, trolls—were real. All except vampires. She was partnered with Nick, a fast talker with a short temper, who tended to shoot first and ask questions later, and Carl, a gnome and small-time thief who had been recruited as an informant in exchange for overlooking his crimes. Sean was the resident Link biologist, providing the officers with information on how to deal with the assorted monsters they confronted, including demons, werewolves, mummies, spider-women, chameleons, and witches.

When the show returned in the fall of 2001, Sean had been replaced by Jonathan, a young forensic specialist. In some respects this tongue-in-cheek series was an adaptation of the hit 1997 theatrical film *Men in Black*.

SPEED CHANNEL (Network) (*Informational/Instructional Cable Network*)
LAUNCHED:
January 1, 1996
SUBSCRIBERS (MAY 2003):
57.5 million (54% U.S.)

All about cars, boats, motorcycles, airplanes, and anything else with a motor. Mostly for guys who like *power!* The network featured coverage of auto races, boat shows, and other events in the field, along with documentaries on vehicles and drivers, and instructional programs. There was even *Lost Drive-in*, a weekly hot rod or biker flick hosted by Bruce Dern.

The network was launched in 1996 as SpeedVision, changing its name to Speed Channel in February 2002.

SPEIDEL SHOW, THE, see *Paul Winchell—Jerry Mahoney Show*

SPENCER (*Situation Comedy*)
FIRST TELECAST: *December 1, 1984*
LAST TELECAST: *July 5, 1985*
BROADCAST HISTORY:
Dec 1984–Jan 1985, NBC Sat 9:30–10:00
Mar 1985–May 1985, NBC Sat 9:30–10:00
Jun 1985–Jul 1985, NBC Fri 8:30–9:00
CAST:
Spencer Winger .... Chad Lowe
Spencer Winger (1985)................. Ross Harris
Doris Winger......................... Mimi Kennedy
George Winger........................ Ronny Cox
Andrea Winger....................... Amy Locane
Ben Sprague (1985) .... Harold Gould
Millie Sprague (1985).......... Frances Sternhagen
Benjamin Beanley............... Richard Sanders
Miss Spier .... Beverly Archer
Wayne............................... Grant Heslov
Herbie Bailey .... Dean Cameron

Spencer was a teenager coping with the pains of adolescence. At 16, he was a bit eccentric, tended to become involved with causes, and incidentally was having trouble finding the right girl. His chief nemesis was Mr. Beanley, the high school guidance counselor, who just didn't understand that Spencer was making a moral statement when he set free the laboratory mice to prevent them from being dissected. Spencer's parents, George and Doris, were understanding, but bewildered. Andrea was his rather mature younger sister, and Wayne and Herbie were two buddies.

When star Chad Lowe abruptly quit the show in a salary dispute after only a few episodes NBC decided to recast the role, alter the format, and change the title to *Under One Roof.* In this new version George had run off with a 23-year-old girl, leaving Doris to raise the kids alone. Doris' parents, Ben and Millie, moved in to help, taking Spencer's bedroom and forcing him to sleep in a room in the attic (more problems!). Mr. Beanley had become the school principal, and Miss Spier, who had been an English teacher in *Spencer*, now taught Spanish.

The reworked series was short-lived. To further confuse matters, reruns of the original *Spencer* aired in June and July.

SPENCER'S PILOTS (*Adventure*)
FIRST TELECAST: *September 17, 1976*
LAST TELECAST: *November 19, 1976*
BROADCAST HISTORY:
Sep 1976–Nov 1976, CBS Fri 8:00–9:00
CAST:
Cass Garrett .... Christopher Stone
Stan Lewis .... Todd Susman
Spencer Parish....................... Gene Evans
Linda Dann .... Margaret Impert
Mickey Wiggins .... Britt Leach

Spencer Aviation was a small charter airline service located in Southern California that would do everything from crop-dusting to transporting convicted criminals from one location to another for the police. Spencer Parish was the owner, Cass and Stan his two pilots, Linda the office manager, and Mickey the company's mechanic. This series never got off the ground, and was canceled after only two months on the air.

SPENSER: FOR HIRE (*Detective Drama*)
FIRST TELECAST: *September 20, 1985*
LAST TELECAST: *September 3, 1988*
BROADCAST HISTORY:
Sep 1985–Oct 1985, ABC Fri 10:00–11:00
Oct 1985–Sep 1986, ABC Tue 10:00–11:00
Sep 1986–May 1987, ABC Sat 10:00–11:00
Jun 1987–Sep 1987, ABC Tue 10:00–11:00
Sep 1987–Jan 1988, ABC Sun 8:00–9:00
Jan 1988–Jun 1988, ABC Sat 10:00–11:00
Jun 1988–Aug 1988, ABC Wed 10:00–11:00
Aug 1988–Sep 1988, ABC Sat 10:00–11:00
CAST:
Spenser .... Robert Urich
Hawk .... Avery Brooks
Susan Silverman (1985–1986, 1987–1988)
.... Barbara Stock
Lt. Martin Quirk (1985–1987) ...... Richard Jaeckel
Sgt. Frank Belson .... Ron McLarty
Asst. D.A. Rita Fiori (1986–1987)
.... Carolyn McCormick

Robert B. Parker's literate Boston detective was brought to television in this carefully crafted series. Spenser was not only well-read, he was a gourmet cook, an ex-boxer, and a former Boston policeman. Operating out of a converted firehouse (which the City of Boston took back at the start of the second season), he drove around town in a vintage Mustang solving crimes and protecting those who wanted a little class with their private detecting. His chief street contact and sometime backup was even more eccentric—a tall, menacing, yet intelligent black man who operated on both sides of the law. Hawk was a free-lance enforcer who would slowly call from the shadows, "Spen-sah!," in a way that made you wonder whose side he was on, just before he blew somebody away with his oversized Magnum pistol.

Lt. Quirk was Spenser's hard-nosed buddy on the Boston Police Dept., and Belson his slovenly, wisecracking subordinate. When Quirk was forced to retire after suffering a heart attack, Belson became Spenser's chief contact on the force. Spenser's girlfriend, Susan (he had asked her to marry him but she was afraid to marry a man who was always getting shot at), was a school guidance counselor; she left for San Francisco in the second season, to "think things over," but returned in the third. While she was gone Spenser's chief female foil was Asst. D.A. Rita, with whom he was often at odds. To give the series a more "literary" feel, Spenser himself functioned as narrator, as well as dispensing pretentious quotes from the classics in each episode.

Novelist Robert B. Parker served as a consultant and occasional writer for the series, but harbored no illusions about its fidelity to his original. In an interesting June 1987 *TV Guide* article he reflected on the differences between the Spenser of his books and that of the TV show, concluding that comparisons between the two media were pointless. "The business of television is to put on good television, not to replicate my books," he observed. "A thing is, after all, what it is, and not something else."

Filmed on location in Boston.

SPIDERMAN, see *The Amazing Spider-Man*

SPIES (*Espionage/Foreign Intrigue*)
FIRST TELECAST: *March 3, 1987*
LAST TELECAST: *April 14, 1987*
BROADCAST HISTORY:
Mar 1987–Apr 1987, CBS Tue 8:00–9:00
CAST:
Ian Stone .... George Hamilton
Ben Smythe .... Gary Kroeger
Thomas Brady .... Barry Corbin

Ian Stone had once been the most renowned spy in the world, and he was still irresistibly suave, debonair, and handsome. But the years had taken their toll. Ian had degenerated to being little more than a lazy, cynical womanizer. Thomas Brady, Ian's boss at the agency—referred to by his men as "C. of B." (Chairman of the Board)—would have fired him were it not for the intervention of Ben Smythe, an idealistic young agent to whom Ian's past exploits were legendary. Smythe became Ian's partner, more to keep him out of trouble than to help him on their assignments. Ian tried to get the uptight younger man to loosen up a little, and took great pleasure in managing to get away from Smythe for liaisons with assorted beautiful women. George Hamilton was perfectly cast for his role in this tongue-in-cheek espionage series, deftly caricaturing his real-life public image.

SPIKE JONES SHOW, THE (*Comedy/Variety*)
FIRST TELECAST: *January 2, 1954*
LAST TELECAST: *September 25, 1961*
BROADCAST HISTORY:
Jan 1954–May 1954, NBC Sat 8:00–8:30
Apr 1957–Aug 1957, CBS Tue 10:30–11:00
Aug 1960–Sep 1960, CBS Mon 9:30–10:00
Jul 1961–Sep 1961, CBS Mon 9:00–9:30
REGULARS:
Spike Jones
Helen Grayco
Billy Barty (1954, 1957)
Bill Dana (1960)
Joyce Jameson (1960)
Len Weinrib (1960)

Spike Jones and his singer wife, Helen Grayco, along with Spike's City Slicker Band, starred in this weekly fill-in series that appeared in four different seasons. Cowbells, foghorns, slide whistles, and other paraphernalia were the featured instruments in Spike's band, as virtually every type of music was reduced to mayhem. Spike, in his striped suit, presided over the merry band of musical lunatics. The nature of their work could probably best be described by one of their album titles—*Dinner Music for People Who Aren't Very Hungry*. The series included, along with the outrageous musical numbers, straight singing by Helen Grayco, appearances by guest stars, and comedy sketches. During the summer of 1960 there was a regular group of supporting comedians, the most famous being Bill Dana in his role as Jose Jimenez. Dana also produced the show. The members of the band all participated in the comedy skits and in general contributed to the frenetic nuttiness of the show.

SPIKE TV (Network), see TNN

SPIN CITY (*Situation Comedy*)
FIRST TELECAST: *September 17, 1996*
LAST TELECAST: *July 2, 2002*

BROADCAST HISTORY:

Sep 1996–Sep 1997, ABC Tue 9:30–10:00
Aug 1997–Sep 1997, ABC Wed 8:30–9:00
Sep 1997–Jul 1998, ABC Wed 8:00–8:30
Jul 1998–Jul 1999, ABC Tue 9:00–9:30
Mar 1999–Apr 1999, ABC Thu 9:30–10:00
Jul 1999–Dec 1999, ABC Tue 8:00–8:30
Nov 1999, ABC Tue 9:30–10:00
Jan 2000–Aug 2001, ABC Wed 9:30–10:00
Jul 2001–Oct 2001, ABC Tue 9:30–10:00
Nov 2001–Jan 2002, ABC Tue 8:30–9:00
Mar 2002–Apr 2002, ABC Tue 8:30–9:00
Jun 2002–Jul 2002, ABC Tue 8:00–9:00

CAST:

Dep. Mayor Michael Flaherty (1996–2000) .... Michael J. Fox
Mayor Randall Winston .... Barry Bostwick
Stuart Bondek .... Alan Ruck
Paul Lassiter .... Richard Kind
James Hobert (1996–2000) ... Alexander Chaplin**
Nikki Faber (1996–2000) .... Connie Britton
Carter Heywood .... Michael Boatman
Ashley Schaeffer (1996) .... Carla Gugino
**Helen Winston(1996–1997)* .... Deborah Rush
Janelle Cooper (1996–2000) .... Victoria Dillard
Karen (1996–1997) .... Taylor Stanley
Claudia Sacks (1997–1999) .... Faith Prince
Stacy Paterno (1997–1999) .... Jennifer Esposito
Caitlin Moore (1999–2002) .... Heather Locklear
Dep. Mayor Charlie Crawford (2000–2002) .... Charlie Sheen

*Occasional
**Originally Gaberman; named changed to Chaplin in '97

This topical comedy lampooned the politically cynical '90s, much as Michael J. Fox's earlier hit *Family Ties* had so accurately reflected the materialistic '80s. Deputy Mayor Mike was a *spinmeister* for bumbling New York City Mayor Winston, a distinguished-looking politician who was well-meaning but prone to political gaffes. Meeting a priest and a rabbi at an official function, hizzoner tried to make a joke ("So, both of you guys are in a rowboat . . ."); asked by a reporter if he'd be marching in a gay pride parade, he blurted out, "What, are you *drunk*?" Mike was always there to cover for him, explaining what he *really* meant, trying to patch things up, even if it meant getting the good Mayor to jump into the Hudson River to prove he really *did* think it was clean. With his boyish good looks and impish grin, the young Deputy Mayor was hard not to like. Much of the comedy took place in the Mayor's office, where Mike presided over a motley staff. Stuart was the sycophantic, ambitious number two man; Paul the loud, chunky, clueless press secretary; James the curly-haired, idealistic young speechwriter from the Midwest who was shocked by his sold-out colleagues; Nikki the accountant with a chaotic personal life; and Carter the gay, black activitist-attorney who was brought in to patch things up with the minority community after hizzoner made one too many "misunderstood" remarks.

Many stories revolved around their personal lives. Mike went through numerous girlfriends, beginning with aggressive reporter Ashley, and later including Nikki, a *Sports Illustrated* swimsuit model, and the manager of the election campaign of the Mayor's chief political opponent. Mayor Winston divorced his shrewish wife Helen at the end of the first season, and also entered the dating scene. Paul and Claudia had a long and tempestuous relationship, finally marrying in 1998. Carter had a number of boyfriends, which didn't stop him from sharing an apartment and several business schemes with the loudly heterosexual Stuart (one of their schemes was a bar in a gay neighborhood, which Carter pushed with the line "I'm here, I'm queer, let's sell a little beer!"). Janelle was Mike's original secretary, later promoted to mayoral assistant and replaced by Brooklyn spitfire Stacy. Rags was Carter's decrepit dog.

In the fall of 1999 Mike hired sexy, aggressive Caitlin to be campaign manager for the Mayor's ill-fated senatorial bid, only to find her jockeying with him for power. Later they dated. At the end of the season a mob-related scandal threatened to bring down the Mayor, and Mike took the fall, leaving city hall to become an environmental lobbyist in Washington, D.C. (actor Michael J. Fox, diagnosed with Parkinson's disease, had announced he was leaving the series). His chief nemesis in Congress: conservative Senator Alex P. Keaton! At the same time James, Nikki and Janelle all disappeared from the cast with no explanation, as had Stacy a few months earlier.

The following fall viewers were introduced to Mike's replacement, Charlie, who proved to be a trouble-prone womanizer with a lot of former girlfriends. He sparred with Caitlin, who broke off her long-distance relationship with the now absent Mike and for a time dated Tim (Scott Wolf). In November Claudia left Paul to become a nun. During the 2001–2002 season Mike visited, the mayor ran successfully for reelection while he dated Judge Claire (Farrah Fawcett) and Charlie dated the Mayor's opponent's campaign manager, Jennifer (Denise Richards). Charlie and his office rival Caitlin had a secret affair, but as the series came to a close their future was unresolved.

SPIN THE PICTURE (*Quiz/Audience Participation*)

FIRST TELECAST: *June 18, 1949*
LAST TELECAST: *February 4, 1950*
BROADCAST HISTORY:

Jun 1949–Jan 1950, DUM Sat 8:00–9:00
Jan 1950–Feb 1950, DUM Sat 8:00–8:30

EMCEE:

Carl Caruso (1949)
Eddie Dunn (1949)
Kathi Norris

REGULARS:

Gordon Dilworth
Shaye Cogan
Bob Dunn
Jerry Shad's Quartet
Alan Scott Trio

This was one early quiz show that gave away fairly large prizes. The first jackpot winner, who identified a "spinning picture" of composer Richard Rodgers, took home a cool $7,635. The bulk of the hour-long show consisted of dramatic sketches, songs, and other entertainment, with each act providing a clue to the name of a famous person, event, movie, etc. After each segment the host would call a viewer and ask if he could identify the name (viewers were asked to send in their phone numbers on postcards, and more than 25,000 did during the first weeks alone). The jackpot round presented a quickly flashed picture of a mystery celebrity, along with verbal clues to his identity.

SPONGEBOB SQUAREPANTS (*Cartoon*)

BROADCAST HISTORY:

Nickelodeon
30 minutes
Original episodes: *1999–*
Premiered: *July 17, 1999*

VOICES:

SpongeBob SquarePants, Gary, Mr. SquarePants, Patchy The Pirate, Narrator .... Tom Kenny
Patrick Star .... Bill Fagerbakke
Squidward Tentacles .... Rodger Bumpass
Sandy Cheeks .... Carolyn Lawrence
Mr. Eugene H. Krabs .... Clancy Brown
Pearl Krabs .... Lori Alan
Mermaid Man .... Ernest Borgnine
Mrs. Puff, Mrs. SquarePants .... Mary Jo Catlett
Barnacle Boy .... Tim Conway
Plankton, Larry the Lobster... Mr. (Doug) Lawrence
Various voices (including Scooter) .... Dee Bradley Baker

Square was beautiful in this charming cartoon that became a sensation among kids—and many adults—in the early 2000s. SpongeBob was a cheerful, hopelessly optimistic, square (literally) little sea sponge who lived in a pineapple in the bright underwater village of Bikini Bottom. He spent his days with his pet snail Gary (who meowed like a cat) and best friend, Patrick, a chubby and rather dense pink starfish. Squidward was his irritable neighbor, a squid who found solace playing his clarinet, while Sandy was an adventurous land squirrel who wore an air helmet and lived in a bubble. Other recurring characters included Mr. Krabs, the money-grubbing owner of the Krusty Krab, where SpongeBob and Squidward worked (SpongeBob loved his job while Squidward hated his, of course); Krabs' archrival Plankton, owner of the Chum Bucket, who was always trying to steal Krabs' business, and Krabs' whiny teenage daughter Pearl, who happened to be a whale. None of this made sense, of course, but amid the whimsy were lots of little lessons in being a good friend and getting along.

SPORTS CAMERA (*Sports Anthology*)

FIRST TELECAST: *September 12, 1950*
LAST TELECAST: *May 24, 1952*
BROADCAST HISTORY:

Sep 1950, ABC Tue 9:30–10:00
Sep 1951,, ABC Thu 10:45–11:00
Dec 1951–May 1952, ABC Sat 8:30–9:00
May 1952, ABC Sat 10:30–11:00

A collection of filmed short subjects on various sports and sports personalities. Known from December 1951 to March 1952 as *Sports on Parade*.

SPORTS FOCUS (*Sports News/Commentary*)

FIRST TELECAST: *June 3, 1957*
LAST TELECAST: *September 12, 1958*
BROADCAST HISTORY:

Jun 1957–Jul 1957, ABC Mon–Fri 7:00–7:15
Sep 1957–Sep 1958, ABC Mon–Fri 7:00–7:15

REPORTER:

Howard Cosell

Broadcast live from New York, this was Howard Cosell's first foray into the world of network television sports. Each night he summed up the day's news in the sports world, provided personal commentary on any currently controversial issues, and conducted interviews with sports personalities.

SPORTS FOR ALL, see *Fishing and Hunting Club*

SPORTS NEWSREEL, see *Gillette Summer Sports Reel*

SPORTS NIGHT (*Situation Comedy*)

FIRST TELECAST: *September 22, 1998*
LAST TELECAST: *May 16, 2000*
BROADCAST HISTORY:

Sep 1998–May 2000, ABC Tue 9:30–10:00

CAST:

Casey McCall .... Peter Krause
Dan Rydell .... Josh Charles
Dana Whitaker .... Felicity Huffman
Isaac Jaffee .... Robert Guillaume
Jeremy Goodwin .... Joshua Malina
Natalie Hurley .... Sabrina Lloyd
Elliott .... Greg Baker
Kim .... Kayla Blake
Chris .... Timothy Davis Reed
Dave .... Jeff Mooring
Will .... Ron Ostrow

A snappy workplace sitcom set behind the scenes at the late-night *Sports Night* program, flagship sportscast of the Continental Sports Channel (CSC), a fictional New York cable network. The two young egomaniacal anchors were Casey, a single dad just coming off a messy divorce, and his buddy Dan, a good-time kind of guy and loyal friend. Behind the cameras were Dana, their dedicated but overworked producer, who was always pushing them to do their best; Isaac, the demanding boss who alternated between laying down the law to his staff and fighting off interfering network brass; Jeremy, the nervous, bespectacled researcher with an encyclopedic knowledge of sports; and Natalie, the eager young associate producer who was constantly in motion (boss to Natalie: "Sit!"). Elliott, Kim, and Chris were among the more frequently seen technicians on the set. Episodes revolved around the pursuit of stories in the highly competitive world of sports journalism, often testing their journalistic ethics, and the personal lives of the harried but enthusiastic staff.

In the spring of 1999 Isaac suffered a stroke (actor Robert Guillaume had suffered a "slight stroke" in real life), left the office for a while, but then returned. During much of the following season he dealt with its aftermath. Also in the 1999–2000 season Dana broke up with her fiancé and began dating Casey. As the series came to a close CSC was in financial trouble, and it looked as if the show might move to the West Coast—or close down entirely.

SPORTS ON PARADE, see *Sports Camera*

SPORTS SPOT (*Sports Commentary*)

FIRST TELECAST: *June 13, 1951*
LAST TELECAST: *November 24, 1954*
BROADCAST HISTORY:

Jun 1951–Nov 1954, CBS Wed 10:45–11:00

HOST:

Jim McKay (1951)
Mel Allen (1951–1954)

This short live-sports program filled the time between the end of *Pabst Blue Ribbon Bouts* and the start of the local 11:00 P.M. news. It was primarily an interview show in which a sports celebrity chatted with the host about his career or sports in general. Jim McKay was the original host, and was succeeded by Mel Allen in October 1951.

SPORTS WITH JOE HASEL (*Sports News*)
FIRST TELECAST: *August 21, 1948*
LAST TELECAST: *April 26, 1949*
BROADCAST HISTORY:
Aug 1948–Jan 1949, ABC Sat 7:30–7:45
Jan 1949–Mar 1949, ABC Fri 9:30–9:45
Mar 1949–Apr 1949, ABC Tue 7:15–7:30
COMMENTATOR:
Joe Hasel
Weekly summary of the news from the world of sports—scores, commentary, and interviews with celebrities from various games.

SPORTSMAN'S QUIZ (*Sports Information*)
FIRST TELECAST: *April 26, 1948*
LAST TELECAST: *April 25, 1949*
BROADCAST HISTORY:
Apr 1948–Aug 1948, CBS Mon 8:00–8:05
Aug 1948–Dec 1948, CBS Fri 8:00–8:05
Dec 1948–Jan 1949, CBS Fri 8:30–8:35
Jan 1949–Apr 1949, CBS Mon 7:10–7:15
REGULARS:
Don Baker
Bernard Dudley
With the cooperation and assistance of the staff of *Sports Afield* magazine, the program's sponsor, this short weekly series posed questions about hunting, fishing, conservation, and wildlife, and then answered them with drawings, pictures, diagrams, or other visual aids. Bernard Dudley asked the questions and Don Baker provided the answers. Viewers were invited to send in questions of their own.

SPORTSREEL, see *Gillette Summer Sports Reel*

SPORTSWOMAN OF THE WEEK (*Interview*)
FIRST TELECAST: *September 9, 1948*
LAST TELECAST: *December 2, 1948*
BROADCAST HISTORY:
Sep 1948–Dec 1948, NBC Thu 7:45–7:50
HOSTESS:
Sarah Palfrey Cooke
This brief program was originally a documentary about a different notable woman each week, but soon changed to a straight interview show with tennis champion Sarah Cooke playing host to an outstanding woman guest from the world of sports. It was at first called *Girl of the Week.*

SPOTLIGHT (*Comedy/Variety*)
FIRST TELECAST: *July 4, 1967*
LAST TELECAST: *August 29, 1967*
BROADCAST HISTORY:
Jul 1967–Aug 1967, CBS Tue 8:30–9:30
REGULARS:
The Mike Sammes Singers
The Lionel Blair Dancers
Jack Parnell and His Orchestra
Produced in London, this 1967 summer replacement for *The Red Skelton Show* each week featured a different cast of stars in a variety format. At least one of the stars was a singer and at least one of them was a comic. The emphasis shifted depending on the talents of the performers, from music to comedy, with the majority of the shows highlighting the latter. Although the supporting acts were from all over the world, most of the stars were from America, especially the comics. Phil Silvers, Shelley Berman, Jack Carter, Frank Gorshin, and Bill Dana were among them. The singers included Barbara McNair, Paul Anka, Trini Lopez, Vikki Carr, Robert Goulet, Lainie Kazan, and then husband and wife Eddie Fisher and Connie Stevens. Welsh singer Tom Jones appeared as one of the stars, sharing that function with American Fran Jeffries, and eventually got a series of his own, *This Is Tom Jones,* on ABC.

SPOTLIGHT ON SPORTS (*Sports*)
FIRST TELECAST: *July 8, 1950*
LAST TELECAST: *September 3, 1950*
BROADCAST HISTORY:
Jul 1950, NBC Sat 7:30–8:00
Aug 1950–Sep 1950, NBC Sun 8:30–9:00
HOST:
Bill Stern
An interview and discussion program with various celebrities from the sports world. Bill Stern, NBC Sports Director, appeared on many telecasts on the network, including pre- and postgame shows and regular nightly reports, from 1949 through the 1950s. See the performer index for his other series.

SPOTLIGHT PLAYHOUSE (*Dramatic Anthology*)
FIRST TELECAST: *June 21, 1955*
LAST TELECAST: *September 22, 1959*
BROADCAST HISTORY:
Jun 1955–Sep 1959, CBS Tue 9:30–10:00 (Summer Only)
HOST:
Anita Louise (1958)
Julia Meade (1959)
Zachary Scott (1959)
For five summers *Spotlight Playhouse* filled in for the vacationing Red Skelton. All of the episodes telecast in the series were filmed reruns from other anthology series. During the first two seasons most of the plays came from *Schlitz Playhouse of Stars.* When reruns from *The Loretta Young Show* were used in 1958, Anita Louise was on hand to host the series. The following summer, with episodes coming from *G.E. Theater, Schlitz Playhouse,* and *The Jane Wyman Show,* Julia Meade and Zachary Scott served as hosts on alternate weeks.

SPY GAME (*Foreign Intrigue/Comedy*)
FIRST TELECAST: *March 3, 1997*
LAST TELECAST: *July 12, 1997*
BROADCAST HISTORY:
March 1997, ABC Mon 8:00–9:00
Jun 1997–Jul 1997, ABC Sat 10:00–11:00
CAST:
Lorne Cash .... Linden Ashby
Max London .... Allison Smith
Micah Simms .... Bruce McCarty
The Cold War was over but the spies lived on in this short-lived send-up of spy caper shows. Lorne

and Max were agents working for E.C.H.O., the Emergency Counter-Hostilities Organization, secretly established by the President to thwart former agents who, angry and out-of-work, were using their unique skills to cause no end of problems. Lorne was an old-fashioned fists and bravado type, surly, sarcastic, and almost uncontrollable; Max was sexy, athletic, techno-smart, and had a photographic memory. They battled the enemy and each other with ingenuity and style, pretty much ignoring their frustrated boss, young *wunderkind* Micah, despite the fact that he reported directly to the President (who was heard on speakerphones as a drawling, Southern buffoon). There was lots of high-tech gadgetry and in-jokes (like Robert Culp trying to blow up the Statue of Liberty), but the cartoonish series soon went the way of the out-of-work spies it lampooned.

SPY GROOVE (*Cartoon*)
BROADCAST HISTORY:
MTV
30 minutes
Original episodes: *2000* (6 episodes)
Premiered: *June 26, 2000*
VOICES:
Agent #1 .... Michael Gans
Agent #2 .... Richard Register
Mac .... Jessica Shaw
Helena Troy .... Fuschia
Narrator Carlo Fabrini .... Dean Elliott

Stylish, fast-paced parody on James Bond–style spy thrillers, following two hip young globe-trotting agents as they infiltrated the lairs of improbable villains such as Mr. Fish (who was bent on destroying trendy Miami Beach) and the slinky Contessa (out to destroy competing fashion houses and establish a haute couture dictatorship). Agent #1 was a brooding heartthrob always analyzing the situation; Agent #2, his impulsive, thrill-seeking companion; Mac, the scantily clad cocktail waitress and friend at their favorite hangout, the Maxi Bar; and Helena, the tough and sexy boss agent who gave them their orders over a picture-phone. "Without her," the narrator droned, "the agents would be nothing more than two extremely hip gas station attendants." The stories were filled with lot of high-tech jokes (the cherry-cam in their drinks, their anti-hypno contact lenses so they couldn't be hypnotized, a car that turned into an airplane and then a submarine), but it all lasted less than two months.

SPY TV (*Comedy*)
FIRST TELECAST: *June 21, 2001*
LAST TELECAST: *August 6, 2002*
BROADCAST HISTORY:
Jun 2001–Aug 2001, NBC Thu 8:30–9:00
Jun 2001–Sep 2001, NBC Tue 8:00–8:30
Oct 2001, NBC Sat 8:00–9:00
Jun 2002–Jul 2002, NBC Tue 8:00–9:00
Aug 2002, NBC Tue 8:00–8:30
HOST:
Michael Ian Black (2001)
Ali Landry (2002)

This rather mean-spirited *Candid Camera*–style prank show put ordinary people in uncomfortable situations in order to secretly record their uncensored reactions. Presumably NBC's lawyers were standing by as a car seller took an unsuspecting potential buyer for a hair-raising "test spin"; a guy in a wheelchair asked passersby for help as his chair took on a life of its own; the millionth-customer prize in a store went to a guy who cut in line; a delivery guy was drawn into bloody surgery being performed in a house where he made a delivery, and acrobats faked accidents on the street. The original host was Michael Ian Black, a young guy in a high-tech van filled with surveillance equipment and "operatives" in black miniskirts. He was replaced in season two by sexy Ali Landry, who had gained instant fame in a commercial for Doritos chips.

SQUARE PEGS (*Situation Comedy*)
FIRST TELECAST: *September 27, 1982*
LAST TELECAST: *September 12, 1983*
BROADCAST HISTORY:
Sep 1982–Mar 1983, CBS Mon 8:00–8:30
Apr 1983–May 1983, CBS Wed 8:30–9:00
May 1983–Sep 1983, CBS Mon 8:00–8:30
CAST:
Patty Greene .... Sarah Jessica Parker
Lauren Hutchinson .... Amy Linker
Jonny Slash .... Merritt Butrick
Marshall Blechtman .... John Femia
Jennifer DeNuccio .... Tracy Nelson
Muffy Tepperman .... Jami Gertz
LaDonna Fredericks .... Claudette Wells
Vinnie Pasetta .... Jon Caliri
Principal Dingleman .... Basil Hoffman
Mr. Donovan .... Steven Peterman
Ms. Loomis .... Catlin Adams
THEME:
"Square Pegs" written and performed by the Waitresses

The trials of high school life were the focus of this youthful comedy. Patty and Lauren were best friends who were new freshmen at Weemawee High School. They desperately wanted to be popular and to get into the right social clique, but were not quite cool enough to do it. Patty was skinny and wore glasses, and Lauren, horror of horrors, still had braces on her teeth. Marshall, the resident class clown, was one of their best friends, and even had a bit of a crush on Lauren. Johnny, the New Wave music freak, was Marshall's best friend and also spent much of his spare time with the girls. Then there were the people they could never get close to—wealthy Jennifer, whose life revolved around clothes and guys; Muffy, the preppie head cheerleader; LaDonna, the bigoted black sophisticate; and Vinnie, Weemawee's answer to John Travolta, a self-centered obnoxious hunk who knew he was God's gift to women.

STACCATO, see *Johnny Staccato*

STAGE A NUMBER (*Talent*)
FIRST TELECAST: *September 17, 1952*
LAST TELECAST: *May 20, 1953*
BROADCAST HISTORY:
Sep 1952–Apr 1953, DUM Wed 9:00–10:00
Apr 1953–May 1953, DUM Wed 8:30–9:00
EMCEE:
Bill Wendell

This was one of many low-budget talent shows on TV during the early years. The acts presented were young professionals, or aspiring professionals, who were introduced by a "sponsor" and then "staged their number" before a panel of show-business judges (producers, actors, etc.) Backdrops were simple, and accompaniment was usually just a piano or organ. The acts tended to be theatrical, such as dramatic acting or ballet, with several appearances by the Nina Youshkevitch Ballet Workshop, among others.

STAGE DOOR, THE (*Drama*)

FIRST TELECAST: *February 7, 1950*
LAST TELECAST: *March 28, 1950*
BROADCAST HISTORY:
Feb 1950–Mar 1950, CBS Tue 9:00–9:30
CAST:
Celia Knox .... Louise Allbritton
Hank Merlin .... Scott McKay
Rocco .... Tom Pedi

Life in and around the Broadway theater, as seen through the eyes of two young and aspiring performers, was the subject of this live dramatic series. It was based on the play *Stage Door* by Edna Ferber and George S. Kaufman. In addition to being struggling young performers, Celia and Hank, the two principals, were also madly in love with each other. The problems they had, both on- and offstage, were portrayed each week.

STAGE ENTRANCE (*Interview*)

FIRST TELECAST: *May 2, 1951*
LAST TELECAST: *March 9, 1952*
BROADCAST HISTORY:
May 1951–Aug 1951, DUM Wed 7:45–8:00
Sep 1951–Dec 1951, DUM Mon 8:00–8:30
Dec 1951–Mar 1952, DUM Sun 7:00–7:30
HOST:
Earl Wilson

Broadway columnist Earl Wilson ("The Midnight Earl") interviewed established stars and young hopefuls, and gave news of show business in this 1951–1952 TV version of his *New York Post* newspaper column.

STAGE 7 (*Dramatic Anthology*)

FIRST TELECAST: *December 12, 1954*
LAST TELECAST: *September 25, 1955*
BROADCAST HISTORY:
Dec 1954–Sep 1955, CBS Sun 9:30–10:00

This filmed anthology series featured Hollywood stars and a varied format that ranged from comedy, to Westerns, to melodrama. When it premiered in December 1954, its title was *Your Favorite Playhouse* and it was composed of reruns from other anthologies. Effective with the play that aired on January 30, 1955, the title changed to *Stage 7* and the plays were new ones created for this series. The best-known leading players who appeared were Frank Lovejoy, Vanessa Brown, Pat O'Brien, Dennis Morgan, Regis Toomey, George Brent, Alexis Smith, and Angela Lansbury.

STAGE SHOW (*Musical Variety*)

FIRST TELECAST: *July 3, 1954*
LAST TELECAST: *September 22, 1956*
BROADCAST HISTORY:
Jul 1954–Sep 1954, CBS Sat 8:00–9:00
Oct 1955–Feb 1956, CBS Sat 8:00–8:30
Feb 1956–Sep 1956, CBS Sat 8:30–9:00
REGULARS:
Tommy Dorsey
Jimmy Dorsey
The June Taylor Dancers
THEME:
"I'm Getting Sentimental over You," by Ned Washington and George Bassman

The opening of *Stage Show* was done with the camera used as the eyes of the home viewer. It entered the theater, moved down the aisle to its seat, and then awaited the start of the show. The theme song was "I'm Getting Sentimental over You," long identified with the Dorsey brothers. Tommy and Jimmy alternated as hosts and the show featured various guest stars. At the end of the program, the camera again became the eyes of the viewer, rising from its seat, leaving the theater, and moving out into the bustle of Manhattan on a Saturday night.

Stage Show was produced under the supervision of Jackie Gleason, and was the 1954 summer replacement for Gleason's Saturday night show. It aired intermittently in the Gleason time slot as a special during the 1954–1955 season, and when the half-hour *Honeymooners* became Gleason's regular series in the fall of 1955, *Stage Show* was used to fill the remainder of the hour every week. Gleason himself did the booking for the show.

Probably the most memorable night in the entire run was January 28, 1956, when the guest was a young country-rock singer from Memphis who was just beginning to attract national attention. This was the TV debut of Elvis Presley, the first time he had been seen or heard by most Americans, and he created pandemonium. He sang "Heartbreak Hotel" on that first telecast; released as a single record, it quickly became a multimillion seller. Elvis was booked for a total of six consecutive appearances on *Stage Show,* then went on to a career that dwarfed even that of the fabulous Dorseys. Ironically, the biggest superstar in the history of rock was introduced by two greats of the big-band swing era, in one of their last professional appearances.

Both Tommy and Jimmy Dorsey passed away shortly after this series ended its run, Tommy in November 1956 and brother Jimmy in June 1957.

STAGE 13 (*Dramatic Anthology*)

FIRST TELECAST: *April 19, 1950*
LAST TELECAST: *June 28, 1950*
BROADCAST HISTORY:
Apr 1950–Jun 1950, CBS Wed 9:30–10:00

Tales of mystery and suspense were told in this live anthology series that originated from New York. The title was supposed to convey the general feeling of the show, since 13 is an unlucky number and was avoided in numbering building floors, rooms, and the stages on movie lots. It was not particularly lucky for this series, either, which did not last even 13 weeks.

STAGE TWO REVUE (*Musical Variety*)

FIRST TELECAST: *July 30, 1950*
LAST TELECAST: *September 24, 1950*

BROADCAST HISTORY:

Jul 1950–Sep 1950, ABC Sun 8:00–8:30

REGULARS:

Georgia Lee
Buzz Adlam's Orchestra
Arlene Harris
Bob Carroll

Summer variety show, featuring Buzz Adlam's Orchestra, vocals by Georgia Lee, and guest acts.

STAGECOACH WEST (*Western*)

FIRST TELECAST: *October 4, 1960*
LAST TELECAST: *September 26, 1961*
BROADCAST HISTORY:

Oct 1960–Sep 1961, ABC Tue 9:00–10:00

CAST:

Luke Perry.......................... Wayne Rogers
Simon Kaye.......................... Robert Bray
David Kane.......................... Richard Eyer

There were very few Western series that paid any attention at all to the people who drove the stagecoaches back and forth from Missouri to California, in the days before the expanding railroad system made their jobs obsolete. This series focused on three. Luke Perry and Simon Kane were a team of drivers and Simon's son, David, went along to keep them company. The passengers they carried, the people they met, and the things that happened to them en route provided the stories told in this series.

STAINED GLASS WINDOWS (*Religion*)

FIRST TELECAST: *September 26, 1948*
LAST TELECAST: *October 16, 1949*
BROADCAST HISTORY:

Sep 1948–Nov 1948, ABC Sun 6:30–7:00
Jan 1949–Mar 1949, ABC Sun 7:15–7:45
Mar 1949–Oct 1949, ABC Sun 7:00–7:30

This early religious program included dramatizations, discussions dealing with viewers' moral problems, and films illustrating mission work around the world. The supervisor was Rev. Everett Parker of the Joint Radio-TV Commission

STAND BY FOR CRIME (*Police Drama*)

FIRST TELECAST: *January 11, 1949*
LAST TELECAST: *August 27, 1949*
BROADCAST HISTORY:

Jan 1949–Apr 1949, ABC Sat 9:30–10:00
May 1949–Aug 1949, ABC Sat 8:00–8:30

CAST:

Inspector Webb (Jan–Apr)............ Boris Aplon
Lt. Anthony Kidd (May–Aug)....... Myron Wallace
Sgt. Kramer (May–Aug) .... George Cisar

On January 11, 1949, New York and Chicago were first linked by television and this was the first program transmitted to Eastern audiences from Chicago. Though it was popular enough in the Midwest, Eastern reviewers found it rather crudely produced, and it did not last long.

It was a crime show with a novel twist. The drama was seen up to the point of the murder, with Inspector Webb (later Lt. Kidd of the homicide squad, whose assistant was Sgt. Kramer) sifting through the clues. Before the culprit was revealed, however, the action stopped and viewers were invited to phone in their guesses as to whodunit.

For a time guest "detectives" (celebrities) also appeared to offer their guesses as to who the guilty party might be.

The young actor who played Lt. Anthony Kidd would become one of television's most recognizable figures, but not until he gave up acting to return to his first love, journalism, and changed his first name from Myron to Mike. This was Mike Wallace's first network television exposure.

STAND BY YOUR MAN (*Situation Comedy*)

FIRST TELECAST: *April 5, 1992*
LAST TELECAST: *August 9, 1992*
BROADCAST HISTORY:

Apr 1992–Jun 1992, FOX Sun 10:00–10:30
Jun 1992–Aug 1992, FOX Sun 10:30–11:00

CAST:

Rochelle Dunphy........ Melissa Gilbert Brinkman
Lorraine Popowski............... Rosie O'Donnell
Artie Popowski .... Rick Hall
Roger Dunphy .... Sam McMurray
Adrienne Stone .... Miriam Flynn
Scab .... Don Gibb
Gloria.......................... Rusty Schwimmer
Sophie .... Ellen Ratners

Rochelle and Lorraine were two sisters living together for an unusual reason in this black comedy. Rochelle's husband, Roger, had been an apparently successful builder of sunrooms and patio enclosures, but he had actually been making most of his money robbing banks with the help of Lorraine's husband, Artie. After their men were sent to prison, cynical, earthy Lorraine sold her house trailer and moved into naive Rochelle's fancy mansion in Franklin Heights, New Jersey. Despite their money problems, Rochelle, who had been spoiled by Roger, was loath to get a job; Lorraine worked at a Bargain Circus discount store with Gloria and Sophie. They went to see their husbands in prison primarily because Rochelle was still madly in love with Roger. Lorraine just thought he was a crook who had gotten her gullible Artie involved in his criminal activities. Adrienne was Rochelle's next-door neighbor, a horny, status-conscious matron who made constant references to the jailbirds and the deterioration of the neighborhood—this despite her indiscriminate affairs with men, including Scab, Lorraine's illiterate biker friend.

Adapted from the British series *Birds of a Feather.*

STAND UP AND CHEER, see *Johnny Mann's Stand Up and Cheer*

STANLEY (*Situation Comedy*)

FIRST TELECAST: *September 24, 1956*
LAST TELECAST: *March 11, 1957*
BROADCAST HISTORY:

Sep 1956–Mar 1957, NBC Mon 8:30–9:00

CAST:

Stanley Peck...................... Buddy Hackett
Horace Fenton (voice only)........... Paul Lynde
Celia.............................. Carol Burnett
Marvin .... Reedy Talton
Mr. Phillips .... Frederic Tozere
Jane .... Jane Connell

Stanley Peck was the outgoing proprietor of a newsstand in a fancy New York hotel, the Sussex-Fenton. Because of his friendly nature he was also the hotel guests' source of all sorts of inside information on what to do and where to go in New York, and a confidant to his coworkers. Despite being short and fat, his personality made him very popular, and he was constantly involved in trying to help other people. The degree of this involvement often got him in trouble with his girlfriend, Celia, and with Mr. Phillips, the hotel's manager. Horace Fenton, the owner of the hotel chain, although never seen on camera, was heard regularly giving orders to members of the staff. *Stanley* was aired live from New York.

STAR DATES (*Documentary*)
BROADCAST HISTORY:
E! Entertainment
30 minutes
Original episodes: *2002–*
Premiered: *December 15, 2002*
HOST/CHAUFFEUR:
Jordan Black

Another trip to the land of the bizarre—er, Hollywood—on the E! cable network. On this one cameras followed as "ordinary people" (often show-business wannabes) went on blind dates with B-list and/or fading celebrities, to amusing results. On the premiere Butch Patrick of *The Munsters* went on two dates, spending a night on the town first with flirty Lisa Marie, then with sarcastic Eden. Later celebs included Dustin Diamond, Kim Fields and Phyllis Diller. Jordan was the hip black host, who doubled as each couple's chauffeur.

STAR GAMES, THE (*Sports*)
BROADCAST HISTORY:
Syndicated only
60 minutes
Produced: *1985* (26 episodes)
Released: *October 1985*
HOST:
Bruce Jenner
Pamela Sue Martin
REFEREE:
Dick Butkus

The Star Games was a variation on the concept that had been pioneered by ABC in its series of *Battle of the Network Stars* specials. Each week three teams of actors, each from a different television series, would compete in assorted sports events with the winners moving up in an elimination tournament. The sports included touch football, tennis, bicycle racing, swimming, and running events. Bruce Jenner and Pamela Sue Martin cohosted, with former football player Dick Butkus serving as a rather cantankerous referee.

STAR OF THE FAMILY (*Comedy/Variety*)
FIRST TELECAST: *September 22, 1950*
LAST TELECAST: *June 26, 1952*
BROADCAST HISTORY:
Sep 1950–Jun 1951, CBS Fri 10:00–10:30
Jul 1951–Jan 1952, CBS Sun 6:30–7:00
Jan 1952–Jun 1952, CBS Thu 8:00–8:30
HOST:
Morton Downey (1950–1951)
Peter Lind Hayes (1951–1952)
Mary Healy (1951–1952)
Carl Hoff Orchestra

The gimmick in this variety show was unique. The host of the show interviewed people who were related to famous celebrities without disclosing who the celebrities were. After the family members had chatted with the host, the "star of the family" was introduced, joined the conversation, and performed for the audience. Singer Morton Downey was the host during the first season, adding his songs to provide a change of pace from the interviews. He was replaced by Peter Lind Hayes and Mary Healy in the summer of 1951, and the emphasis shifted from music to comedy, depending of course on the talents of the celebrities whose relatives appeared on each week's telecast.

STAR OF THE FAMILY (*Situation Comedy*)
FIRST TELECAST: *September 30, 1982*
LAST TELECAST: *December 23, 1982*
BROADCAST HISTORY:
Sep 1982–Dec 1982, ABC Thu 8:30–9:00
CAST:
Buddy Krebs....................Brian Dennehy
Jennie Lee Krebs....................Kathy Maisnik
Douggie Krebs....................Michael Dudikoff
Feldman....................Todd Susman
Frank Rosetti....................George Deloy
Max....................Danny Mora
Moose....................Judy Pioli

The star of this family was 16-year-old Jennie Lee, whose singing talents (in the country/pop vein) were good enough to begin getting her show-business offers. Her dad, grumpy Fire Captain Buddy Krebs, was proud but worried, not wanting his little angel to grow up too soon—not for at least the next 20 or 30 years. That was only one of Buddy's troubles, though. His wife had run off with a bellhop, his 17-year-old son, Douggie, had muscles where he should have had brains, and his young charges down at the firehouse were a bunch of flakes: Feldman wrote to his mother telling her that he was a cardiologist, Rosetti had sex on the brain, and Max was a hotheaded Hispanic whose English was fractured. Then there was Moose, his daughter's amazon of a manager. You think you got troubles?

STAR PERFORMANCE, syndicated title for *Four Star Playhouse*

STAR SEARCH (*Talent*)
BROADCAST HISTORY:
Syndicated only
60 minutes
Produced: *1983–1995*
Released: *September 1983*
HOST:
Ed McMahon
Martha Quinn (1994–1995)

Ed McMahon hosted this big, glossy weekly talent show, which gave aspiring young performers a chance to compete in various categories: male and female vocalist, musical group, standup comedian, dance, dramatic, and "TV spokesmodel." The actors played a scene with a guest star like Joan Collins or Tony Geary, while the spokesmodel posed glamorously for a fashion photographer and read the rules of the competition. Each of the hopefuls was rated by a panel of producers and talent agents, with the winners coming back to face new challengers the following week. Some, like baby-faced vocalist Sam Harris, seemed to triumph week after week, while others (especially the comedians, who generally used up their best material quickly) were on and off in a week. Those who managed to survive to the end-of-season finals could win as much as $100,000.

Unlike some prior TV talent shows, *Star Search* produced many alumni who went on to careers in show business—according to some sources, 90% of those who appeared found employment in the field. Among the better-known alumni were the country/rock group Sawyer Brown, pop singers Tiffany, Britney Spears and Christina Aguilera, actors Brian Bloom *(As the World Turns)*, Sinbad *(A Different World)*, Amy Stock *(Dallas)*, Joseph Gian *(Hooperman)*, and Ami Dolenz *(General Hospital)*, and comics Rick Ducommun, Dennis Miller, Rosie O'Donnell, Drew Carey, Martin Lawrence, Chris Rock and Kim Coles.

Over the years there were changes in the categories, with the acting category being dropped to make room for more singing and dancing. In the 1991–1992 season, for example, the categories were Male Vocalist, Female Vocalist, Junior Vocalist, Teen Vocalist, Adult Dance, Junior Dance, Teen Dance, Comedy, and TV Spokesmodel.

In the fall of 1992 the series was retitled *Ed McMahon's Star Search* and restructured as a Monday–Friday half-hour show with the full-hour weekend edition featuring highlights from the weekday competition. The weekday version flopped and was dropped in November, and the weekend edition reverted to the original format. Origination of the series also moved from Los Angeles to Orlando, Florida, in 1992. In the fall of 1994 former MTV veejay Martha Quinn became Ed's cohost.

STAR SEARCH (*Talent*)
FIRST TELECAST: *January 8, 2003*
LAST TELECAST: *May 16, 2003*
BROADCAST HISTORY:
Jan 2003–May 2003, CBS Wed 8:00–9:00
Jan 2003–Feb 2003, CBS Thu 8:00–9:00
Feb 2003–May 2003, CBS Fri 8:00–9:00
HOST:
Arsenio Hall
REGULAR JUDGES:
Naomi Judd
Ben Stein
Carol Leifer
Ahmet Zappa

CBS revived *Star Search*, the venerable 1980s talent contest, with this updated version hosted by a remarkably restrained Arsenio Hall. The new *Star Search*, which aired twice a week live, featured aspiring performers in four categories—adult singer, junior singer, comic and supermodel—with two competitors in each category in the preliminary rounds. Each "season" ran for nine episodes. The winners on the first three episodes competed in a semifinal on episode four, then the winners on episodes five through seven faced each other in the second semifinal on episode eight. The ninth episode showcased the winners of the semi-finals, with $100,000 going to the grand finale winners in each category.

Voting was by a panel of celebrity judges and home viewers via the Internet, with each accounting for half of the total score. In addition to the regular judges, who were not always complimentary to the performers, there were a number of celebrity guest judges including Jessica Simpson, LeAnn Rimes, Lance Bass, Countess Vaughn and Earvin "Magic" Johnson. When the second "season" started in February the supermodel category was eliminated—a young dancer category took its place—and judge Carol Leifer was replaced by Ahmet Zappa.

STAR STAGE (*Dramatic Anthology*)
FIRST TELECAST: *September 9, 1955*
LAST TELECAST: *September 7, 1956*
BROADCAST HISTORY:
Sep 1955–Aug 1956, NBC Fri 9:30–10:00
Sep 1956, NBC Fri 9:00–9:30
HOST:
Jeffrey Lynn

Approximately two-thirds of the two-act plays aired on *Star Stage* were live and the remainder were filmed. The live dramas originated from both Hollywood and New York. Initially, there was no host, until Jeffrey Lynn assumed that post on November 18, 1955. One of the early telecasts was "On Trial" starring Joseph Cotten. He later hosted and starred in a courtroom series of the same name. A February 1956 telecast titled "Killer on Horseback," starring Rod Cameron, was the pilot for Cameron's syndicated series *State Trooper*. Others who were seen on *Star Stage* included Sylvia Sidney, Alan Young, Lorne Greene, Jeanne Crain, Dan Duryea, Ward Bond, Wendell Corey, and Polly Bergen.

STAR TIME (*Musical Variety*)
FIRST TELECAST: *September 5, 1950*
LAST TELECAST: *February 27, 1951*
BROADCAST HISTORY:
Sep 1950–Feb 1951, DUM Tue 10:00–11:00
REGULARS:
Frances Langford
Benny Goodman Sextet
Lew Parker
Kathryn Lee

In the fall of 1950 DuMont made another of its feeble efforts to launch a full-fledged prime-time variety hour with this series. Like most of the other attempts, it lacked the lure of a big-name (or rising) star who could attract viewers, and soon folded.

Star Time did have some good talent, however, including singer Frances Langford and the Benny Goodman Sextet as regulars. Comic Lew Parker and dancer Kathryn Lee also contributed, along with assorted, but not usually top-name, guests.

STAR TIME PLAYHOUSE (*Dramatic Anthology*)
FIRST TELECAST: *July 12, 1955*
LAST TELECAST: *September 13, 1955*
BROADCAST HISTORY:
Jul 1955–Sep 1955, CBS Tue 8:00–8:30

The filmed dramas in this series had never before been aired on television, tended to be on the serious side, and were headlined by well-known performers. Victor Jory starred in "The Man Who Escaped Devil's Island," and Ronald Reagan and Neville Brand in "Edge of Battle." Others appearing were Peter Lorre, Basil Rathbone, Broderick Crawford, and Angela Lansbury—she being the only woman to have star billing throughout *Star Time Playhouse*'s summer run.

STAR TONIGHT (*Dramatic Anthology*)
FIRST TELECAST: *February 3, 1955*
LAST TELECAST: *August 9, 1956*
BROADCAST HISTORY:
Feb 1955–Aug 1956, ABC Thu 9:00–9:30

Star Tonight was designed as a showcase for young actors and actresses working in New York. Each week a live play was telecast with a relative unknown in the lead, hopefully as a springboard to future stardom. The plays were chosen specifically for the individual young "stars" or written to suit their talents. Some of those who went on to greater things were Bruce Gordon, Joanne Woodward, Theodore Bikel, Neva Patterson, Kay Medford, and Robert Culp.

STAR TREK (*Science Fiction*)
FIRST TELECAST: *September 8, 1966*
LAST TELECAST: *September 2, 1969*
BROADCAST HISTORY:
Sep 1966–Aug 1967, NBC Thu 8:30–9:30
Sep 1967–Aug 1968, NBC Fri 8:30–9:30
Sep 1968–Apr 1969, NBC Fri 10:00–11:00
Jun 1969–Sep 1969, NBC Tue 7:30–8:30
CAST:
Capt. James T. Kirk .... William Shatner
Mr. Spock......................... Leonard Nimoy
Dr. Leonard McCoy................ DeForest Kelley
Yeoman Janice Rand (1966–1967)
.... Grace Lee Whitney
Sulu................................ George Takei
Uhura .... Nichelle Nichols
Engineer Montgomery Scott........ James Doohan
Nurse Christine Chapel .... Majel Barrett
Ensign Pavel Chekov (1967–1969) ... Walter Koenig

Set in the 23rd century, *Star Trek* followed the adventures of the starship U.S.S. *Enterprise*, a cruiser-sized spacecraft whose mission included reconnaissance of previously unexplored worlds and transporting supplies to Earth colonies in space. Confrontations with two alien races, Klingons and Romulans, provided recurring conflicts and there were numerous encounters with other "strange" forms of alien life as well. *Star Trek* differed from previous series such as *Captain Video* in that stories were often well written, serious science-fiction short stories, dealing with current social issues thinly disguised in extraterrestrial settings.

Captain James Kirk was cast in the classic hero mold but, if the truth were known, his alien first officer, Mr. Spock, had a following almost as large. Spock, a half-breed Vulcan whose father was an ambassador and mother was an Earth woman, had pointed ears and a decidedly green complexion. Although he tried, and usually succeeded, in maintaining a totally logical public self, there was turmoil within as he struggled to control his emotions. Even for a pure Vulcan this was an ongoing lifetime struggle, but in Spock's case, his human half made it even more difficult. Despite his Satanic appearance, Spock quickly became a favorite of viewers. The third principal cast member was Dr. Leonard "Bones" McCoy, a fine surgeon and diagnostician (no doubt helped by the advanced technology at his disposal) with a sarcastic sense of humor. Although Spock and McCoy did not always see eye to eye, they had great underlying respect for each other and were fiercely loyal to Captain Kirk. Supporting regulars were Sulu, the chief navigator; Lt. Uhura, the communications officer; Lt. Commander Montgomery "Scotty" Scott, the chief engineer; Dr. McCoy's assistant, Christine Chapel; and young Ensign Pavel Chekov, assistant navigator and aspiring executive office. During the first season Yeoman Janice Rand was a regular, but her character never seemed to develop and was dropped.

Although many of today's fans believe that *Star Trek* must have been a big hit, because of all the publicity about it, it was actually not very successful in its original run. It was regularly beaten in its time period by all sorts of competition, and it placed number 52 among all series in 1966–1967, its peak season, behind such programs as *Iron Horse* and *Mr. Terrific. Star Trek* was finally canceled by NBC in 1969 due to gradually declining audiences and the heavy proportion of teenagers and children in its viewership, which made it unattractive to network advertisers.

Since then, however, the program has been very successful in reruns, and developed a fanatical cult following in the 1970s. Its new fans, dubbed "trekkies" (they preferred to be called "trekkers"), organized themselves, lobbied to get the series brought back to network television, and even sponsored annual conventions in the U.S. and England. Probably no prime-time series had such a well-publicized "life after death" as *Star Trek*; it was practically the embodiment of TV nostalgia for the 1960s.

Star Trek did in fact return to the NBC-TV network, in modified form, as an animated cartoon series on Saturday morning, from 1973 to 1975. Original cast members supplied the voices. Then, in 1979, the years of lobbying, coupled with the box-office success of *Star Wars* and *Close Encounters of the Third Kind*, culminated in a theatrical motion-picture version of *Star Trek*. It reunited most of the original cast, cost some $40,000,000 to produce, and was a major disappointment to all concerned—especially its producer, Paramount Pictures. Despite the marginal success of the first film, a second, *Star Trek II: The Wrath of Khan,* reached theaters in 1982. Essentially a sequel to the "Space Seed" episode from the TV series, with "Space Seed" guest star Ricardo Montalban reprising his role, it was far more successful than the first film and was the basis for a continuing series of *Star Trek* motion pictures.

STAR TREK: DEEP SPACE NINE (*Science Fiction*)
BROADCAST HISTORY:
Syndicated only
60 minutes
Produced: *1992–1999* (176 episodes)
Released: *January 1993*
CAST:
Commander Benjamin Sisko .... Avery Brooks
Chief Operations Officer Miles O'Brien
.... Colm Meaney
Major Kira Nerys .... Nana Visitor
Constable Odo .... René Auberjonois
Dr. Julian Bashir.............. Alexander Siddig
Chief Science Officer Jadzia Dax (1993–1998)
.... Terry Farrell
Jake Sisko (age 14) .... Cirroc Lofton
Quark .... Armin Shimerman
**Keiko O'Brien (1992–1997)* .... Rosalind Chao
**Nog (1993, 1995–1999)* .... Aron Eisenberg

**Elim Garak* .... Andrew J. Robinson
**Gul Dukat* .... Marc Alaimo
**Rom*.............................. Max Grodenchik
**Kai Winn Adami* .... Louise Fletcher
**Founder (1994, 1996–1999)* .... Salome Jens
Lt. Commander Worf (1995–1999) ... Michael Dorn
**Leeta (1995–1999)* .... Chase Masterson
**Gen. Martok (1995–1999)*............. J. G. Hertzler
**Kasidy Yates (1995–1999)*.......... Penny Johnson
**Weyoun (1996–1999)* .... Jeffrey Combs
**Legate Damar (1996–1999)*............ Casey Biggs
Ziyal (1997)......................... Melanie Smith
**Vic Fontaine (1998–1999)* .... James Darren
Lt. Ezri-Dax (1998–1999)............ Nicole deBoer
**Admiral William Ross (1998–1999)* ... Barry Jenner

*Occasional

In this spin-off from *Star Trek: The Next Generation*, Deep Space Nine was a space station orbiting the planet Bajor after the Cardassians, who had been occupying it, withdrew after taking everything of value. The new commander on the station was Benjamin Sisko, a widower whose teenage son, Jake, was living with him on the station. Miles O'Brien, the station's chief operations officer, had been the transporter officer on *Next Generation*. Major Kira was the Bajoran liaison officer on Deep Space Nine who had been fighting for Bajoran independence and harbored some resentment about the Federation replacing the Cardassians as administrators. Sisko appointed her his first officer, and she eventually became more sympathetic to the Federation while retaining her hatred for the cruel Cardassians, who had virtually enslaved her people prior to the Federation's arrival. Others on the station were Quark, a conniving Ferengi who ran the gambling facility on the station; Odo, the chief of security, an alien shapeshifter with a love-hate relationship with Quark; Dr. Bashir, on his first assignment since graduating from Starfleet Medical; and Dax, from a joined species known as the Trill. The life form in Dax's symbiont humanoid body had lived in six previous host bodies, both male and female, was several hundred years old, and had been a friend of Sisko's when residing in its previous male body.

Deep Space Nine was situated near a wormhole that allowed instant transport to the far reaches of the galaxy. Its strategic location was coveted by many, including the Bajorans, who wanted to run it without interference, and the Cardassians, who wanted to regain control. There was plenty of conflict among the station's permanent residents as well as with those who visited it.

In the fall of 1994 the crew on Deep Space Nine faced a new threat, an organization called The Dominion. Sisko had obtained the *Defiant*, a stripped-down battleship originally designed to fight the Borg, to provide Deep Space Nine with some offensive weaponry to meet this and other threats. On its maiden voyage the crew discovered that The Dominion was run by The Founders, a race of changelings who had created it to take over control of other races and create order in the Universe. Odo, who found out that he was, himself, a Founder, decided to stay with the humanoids rather than be assimilated by his "people."

As the 1995–1996 season began, the crew was preparing for a possible invasion by The Dominion. Worf (previously a regular on *Star Trek: The Next Generation*) took over as the Strategic Operations officer following a confrontation with the Klingons, who had broken their twenty-year peace treaty with the Federation and invaded Cardassia. In the season finale most of the operating staff took an ailing Odo to the home world of The Founders in search of medical help. Once there, he faced judgment for having killed a Founder to save his friends earlier in the season, and as punishment was transformed into a solid humanoid. The Klingons declared war on the Federation, and Odo sensed that their leader was a Founder who had assumed Klingon form.

Late in the season Kira had become pregnant as a surrogate carrying a baby for Miles and Keiko, and in the episode airing the first week of February 1997, she gave birth to a baby boy. In the same episode Odo regained his ability as a shape-shifter when a dying Founder infant integrated itself with him. Threats posed to other races by The Dominion resulted in a new treaty between the Klingons and the Federation, with Gen. Martok added to Deep Space Nine's staff as the Klingon representative. Dr. Bashir was revealed to have been the product of genetic re-engineering as a 6-year-old child, and Nog, now a Star Fleet cadet, was learning skills on the station. At end of 1996–1997 season Rom and Leeta (who worked for Quark) got married, and the Cardassians, led by Gul Dukat, with the help of The Dominion, regained control of Deep Space Nine, which had been abandoned by Sisko. He was on the *Defiant*, waging war with the Federation fleet against the Cardassians and The Dominion.

In November 1997, Sisko, commanding the *Defiant*, led a confrontation between Federation forces (minus the Klingons, who were not willing to fight with them) and Dominion forces over control of the wormhole and Deep Space Nine. With the help of Quark, Dukat's daughter Ziyal, Rom, Kira, and Odo on the station, and the intervention of the inter-dimensional beings that lived in the wormhole, the Federation regained control of Deep Space Nine. At the end of the episode Dukat's assistant Dumar killed Ziyal during the Cardassian evacuation, leaving her father an unfocused mental case (he eventually recovered). The following week Dax and Worf, who had been dating for months, got married, and General Martak was named Supreme Commander of the Ninth Fleet. Sisko began an intermittent dating relationship with attractive freighter captain Kasidy Yates. In the season finale Sisko was planning an attack on Cardassia, and a pregnant Dax was killed by Dukat, who materialized while possessed by the spirit of a Bajoran demon he was carrying, determined to defeat both the Federation and the Bajoran "prophets." The demon destroyed the wormhole where the "prophets" resided, but Federation forces were successful in their attack on the Cardassian home world. Dr. Bashir was able to save the Trill symbiont, but Jadzia's body and personality died. As the episode ended, Sisko and his son Jake returned to Earth so he could sort things out—he believed he had failed Jadzia, the "prophets," and the Bajorans. Kira, now in command of the station, was promoted to colonel. During that season most of the crew found relaxation in the holosuite in a simulated Las Vegas, circa 1962, where lounge singer Vic Fontaine provided entertainment and good advice.

That fall Dax was in a new symbiont, Ezri-Dax, an ensign who joined the crew as a counselor. In an early season episode (à la *St. Elsewhere*'s finale) there were flashes of Sisko as Benny Russell, a patient in a contemporary mental hospital writing *Deep Space Nine* stories on the walls of his room, much to the chagrin of his doctors. Sisko went to the planet of Tyree, where he found an "orb of the prophets" that reopened the wormhole, and in November, Odo discovered that a plague was killing his people, the Founders. The war with The Dominion and the Romulans wore on.

In April 1999 Sisko married Kasidy Yates, who soon after discovered she was pregnant. Bashir figured out that a CIA-like Federation agency had actually created the virus causing the Founders' plague. He developed a cure, and used it to save the life of Odo, who had been infected. The Founders forged an alliance with the Breen to generate enough firepower to defeat the Federation, but in the midst of the climactic battle in the series finale, the Cardassians changed sides and joined forces with the Federation, turning the tide of the war. Odo beamed down to Bajor and linked with the Founder military leader, curing her of the disease and convincing her to stop the war. In return he promised to return to the Gamma Quadrant, cure his people, and show them that they could coexist with the solids. Dukat, who had insinuated himself into the confidence of power-hungry Bajoran leader Kai-Winn, had a confrontation with Sisko, who defeated him and was then taken by the prophets to their "Celestial Temple" to learn. Kasidy promised to wait until his return. In the aftermath Worf was named Federation Ambassador to the Klingon home world, Kira took over command of Deep Space Nine, and Miles returned to Earth.

STAR TREK: THE NEXT GENERATION (*Science Fiction*)

BROADCAST HISTORY:

Syndicated only
60 minutes
Produced: *1987–1994* (178 episodes)
Released: *October 1987*

CAST:

Capt. Jean-Luc Picard .... Patrick Stewart
Cdr. William Riker .... Jonathan Frakes
Lt. Geordi La Forge .... LeVar Burton
Lt. Tasha Yar (1987–1988) .... Denise Crosby
Lt. Worf .... Michael Dorn
Dr. Beverly Crusher (1987–1988, 1989–1994) .... Gates McFadden
Counselor Deanna Troi .... Marina Sirtis
Lt. Cmdr. Data .... Brent Spiner
Wesley Crusher (1987–1990) .... Wil Wheaton
Transporter Chief Miles O'Brien (1987–1993) .... Colm Meaney
Dr. Katherine "Kate" Pulaski (1988–1989) .... Diana Muldaur
**Guinan (1988–1993)* .... Whoopi Goldberg
**Keiko O'Brien (1991–1993)* .... Rosalind Chao
**Alexander Roshenko (1992–1994)* ... Brian Bonsall
Ensign Ro Laren (1992–1992) ...... Michele Forbes
Dr. Elissa Ogawa (1993–1994) .... Patti Yasutake

*Occasional

Over the years there had been numerous rumors that Paramount Pictures would bring *Star Trek* back to TV—the *Star Trek* motion pictures had become money-makers for the studio and the ancillary marketing of anything that could be associated with the series and films had become quite lucrative. Finally *Star Trek: The Next Generation* reached the air in 1987, 18 years after the original had ended.

There was a new *Enterprise*, a new crew, and better special effects. Most importantly, the man whose vision had been responsible for *Star Trek* in the first place, creator Gene Roddenberry, was back as executive producer of the new series. He used his influence to see that, as with the original series, the new *Star Trek* had a social conscience and relied heavily on stories which made moral points.

Star Trek: The Next Generation was set in the 24th century, 78 years after the original series. The new *Enterprise* was much larger than its twenty-third century predecessor—more than twice as long and with eight times as much interior space. Accordingly, the ship's crew, which now included children, numbered more than 2,000 people. Commanding the *Enterprise* was Captain Jean-Luc Picard, a more formal, fatherly, and much less emotional leader than Captain Kirk had been on the original series. Unlike Kirk, he generally preferred to remain on board and let his senior officers deal first-hand with crises that required a team to leave the ship. Second in command was Cdr. William Riker, the impetuous Kirk clone on this series. Riker and half-Betazoid Counselor Deanna Troi, who could sense the emotions of any living creature, were former lovers with the potential for rekindling their romance. Other officers on Picard's staff were Lt. Geordi La Forge, the blind helmsman who could "see" with the aid of a high-tech "visor" that sent video signals directly to his brain; Lt. Worf, the ship's Klingon officer (the Federation had made peace with the Klingons in the decades since Kirk's *Enterprise* had fought them); Lt. Tasha Yar, head of security; Lt. Cdr. Data, an android with total recall and the desire to become more "human"; and Dr. Beverly Crusher, the ship's medical officer with a soft spot for the captain. Dr. Crusher's son, Wesley, a brilliant and inventive youth who wanted eventually to become a Starfleet officer himself, helped get the crew out of jams on more than one occasion. When Tasha was killed by an alien in the spring of 1988 Lt. Worf assumed the duties of head of security.

In the fall of 1988 Dr. Crusher, who spent one season as head of Star Fleet Medical, was replaced by Dr. Pulaski. Geordi became chief engineer that season, with Wesley becoming an apprentice helmsman. Also showing up in 1988 was Guinan, the mysterious and incredibly intuitive humanoid bartender in the *Enterprise*'s Ten Forward Bar. Late in 1990 Wesley left the ship to enroll at Starfleet Academy. Early in 1993 transporter Chief Miles O'Brien left the *Enterprise* to become chief operations officer on Deep Space Nine, the space station that was the setting for *Star Trek: Deep Space Nine*, the third *Star Trek* series.

The last original episode of *Generation* had a very surrealistic quality about it. The mysterious Q (guest star John de Lancie), a superbeing who had been in the first episode of the series and had shown up on a number of occasions to "test" Picard and the crew, was back. His goal was to put Picard through another "test to expand his intelligence." He caused Picard to shift between the present, the time of his first arrival on the *Enterprise*, and the future, when he was retired and divorced from Dr. Crusher, whom he had apparently married after the series run had ended.

Late in 1994 *Star Trek: Generations*, the film that bridged the new series with the original *Star Trek*, arrived in theaters.

STAR TREK: VOYAGER (*Science Fiction*)
FIRST TELECAST: *January 16, 1995*
LAST TELECAST: *September 19, 2001*
BROADCAST HISTORY:

Jan 1995–Aug 1996, UPN Mon 8:00–9:00
Aug 1996–Oct 1997, UPN Wed 9:00–10:00
Nov 1997–Apr 1998, UPN Wed 8:00–9:00
Apr 1998–May 2001, UPN Wed 9:00–10:00
Sep 1999–Oct 1999, UPN Tue 9:00–10:00
May 2001–Aug 2001, UPN Wed 8:00–10:00
Aug 2001–Sep 2001, UPN Wed 8:00–9:00

CAST:

Capt. Kathryn Janeway .... Kate Mulgrew
First Officer Chakotay .... Robert Beltran
Security Chief Tuvok .... Tim Russ
Neelix .... Ethan Phillips
Doc .... Robert Picardo
Chief Engineer B'Elanna Torres
.... Roxann Biggs-Dawson
Kes (1995–1997) .... Jennifer Lien
Lt. Tom Paris .... Robert Duncan McNeill
Ensign Harry Kim .... Garrett Wang
**Seska (1995–1996)* .... Martha Hackett
Michael Jonas (1996) .... Raphael Sbarge
**Ensign Vorick (1996–1998)* ...... Alexander Enberg
Seven of Nine (1997–2001) .... Jeri Ryan
**Naomi Wildman (1999–2001)* ...... Scarlett Pomers
*Occasional

The fourth series in the *Star Trek* saga, *Voyager* was set in the same time period as *Deep Space Nine*. Unlike other *Trek* series, the ship in this one was relatively small, with a full crew complement of around 150. Originally in the vicinity of Deep Space Nine chasing a Maquis terrorist ship, *Voyager* was caught in a freak plasma storm and hurtled so far away (75,000 light-years) that it would take 75 years to get home. The Maquis ship, caught in the storm with them, was destroyed soon after, and its crew joined the *Voyager* crew in an uneasy alliance.

The biggest challenge for Kathryn Janeway, *Voyager*'s captain, was keeping her commingled crew working together while trying to get them back to a familiar part of the galaxy. Chakotay, captain of the Maquis ship, was a stolid Native American whom Janeway appointed First Officer of the combined crew. Others in the crew were Paris, an outgoing former fighter pilot with a zest for life and a tendency to get into trouble; Kim, a rookie out of Starfleet Academy not sure of his ability to live up to his own expectations; Torres, a moody, half-Klingon half-human from the Maquis ship who preferred her human side; and Tuvok, a Vulcan who had been on the Maquis ship as a Federation spy and was now, along with Janeway, keeper of the peace.

Since the ship's medical officer had died in the pilot episode, *Voyager*'s medical needs were met by Doc, an emergency medical program in the ship's computer that was, through holographic projection, able to assume a solid physical form to treat the injured and sick. Despite being a computer program, Doc did have a personality, albeit one of cynicism and impatience with the shortcomings of the crew's biological members. Neelix, one of the first aliens encountered by *Voyager* in this uncharted part of the galaxy, was a charming character looking for adventure who joined the crew as chef, handyman, and resident philosopher. With Neelix came Kes, his beautiful Ocampan lover, who worked with Doc to learn medical techniques. Since *Voyager* was so far from home, almost every race and entity its crew encountered was new, avoiding the familiar faces from the earlier *Trek* series.

Seska was a member of the crew who, a couple of months into the series run, turned out to be a surgically altered Kazon, a warrior race. She returned to her people, and early in 1996 another member of the crew, Jonas, began sending information to the Kazons via subspace communications, preparatory to an attack on *Voyager*, but he died in a fight with Neelix while trying to disable the ship's weapons systems. In the season finale the crew went into Kazon space, suckered into a trap set by Seska. While under attack, they lost contact with Tom, who was away in a shuttle craft. The Kazons took control of *Voyager* and dumped the crew on a hostile planet, similar to prehistoric Earth, without equipment or supplies. With the help of Doc and a lone crewman still on the ship, and the Talaxians Tom had recruited, the Kazons were defeated (Seska dying during the fight) and the crew beamed back aboard *Voyager* in the first episode that fall.

The 1997–1998 season premiere saw Seven of Nine, a Borg, added to *Voyager*'s crew when they managed to disengage her from the Borg Collective. Originally a human child named Anneka Hansen, who had been taken by the Borg almost two decades before, her human cells started to reassert themselves. She found it difficult adjusting to life as an individual and, despite a very sexy body, often acted more like a machine than a person. A week later Kes metamorphosed into a powerful energy being and, as a parting gift to the *Voyager* crew, gave the ship a huge shove, moving it 9,500 light-years closer to the Alpha Quadrant. In the spring, while they were stranded outside the ship, B'Elanna told Tom she loved him, and they began a serious relationship.

Tom was demoted to ensign in December 1998 after disobeying an order during what he considered a humanitarian mission to help an alien race. The following February, in a special two-hour episode, Seven of Nine was almost reassimilated by the Borg Collective but, with Janeway's help, was rescued. B'Elanna and Tom got married in March 1999. In April 2000, with the help of Reg Barkley (Dwight Shultz), an intergalactic communications link was established that enabled the crew to communicate with Starfleet Command in the Alpha Quadrant—but only for 11 minutes a day. In May 2001 Neelix was reunited with fellow Talaxians who were living on an asteroid. He helped them save their homes from miners and decided to stay with them as Starfleet ambassador to the Delta Quadrant.

The series finale opened on the 10th anniversary of Voyager's return after 23 years in transit back from the Delta Quadrant. Harry was now a captain; Tom was a writer of holo-novels; the daughter Tom had with B'Elanna was a Starfleet officer; Janeway was an admiral; and Tuvok was ailing. The doctor, who had taken the name Joe, had married a younger woman.

Janeway stole a Klingon device that enabled her to travel back in time through a wormhole in a quest to help her earlier self get *Voyager* back to Earth quicker and alter the future suffering that had originally beset the crew—Seven of Nine, who would marry Chakotay, would die from injuries suffered on an away mission, 23 other crew members would die, and Tuvok would suffer from a degenerative neurological condition that would not be curable when *Voyager* originally got back to the Alpha Quadrant. The admiral sacrificed herself to the Borg queen (Alice Krige) in a complicated plot that enabled *Voyager* to get back to Earth while simultaneously disrupting the ability of the Borg to assimilate other species.

STARGATE SG-1 (*Science Fiction*)

BROADCAST HISTORY:

Showtime, Sci-Fi Channel
60 minutes
Produced: *1997–2002* (Showtime, 110 episodes)
2002– (Sci-Fi Channel)
Premiered: *July 1997* (Showtime);
June 2002 (Sci-Fi Channel)

CAST:

Col. Jack O'Neill .... Richard Dean Anderson
Capt. Samantha "Sam" Carter ... Amanda Tapping
Dr. Daniel Jackson .... Michael Shanks
Teal'c .... Christopher Judge
Gen. George Hammond............... Don S. Davis
Dr. Janet Frasier...................... Teryl Rothery
**Sgt. Walter Davis*....................... Gary Jones
**Bra'tac* .... Tony Amendola
**Apophis (1997–2001)* .... Peter Williams
**Jacob Carter/Selmak (1998–)*
.... Carmen Argenziano
Jonas Quinn (2002–).............. Corin Nemec

*Occasional

In this sequel to the theatrical film *Stargate*, stuffy Gen. Hammond summoned heroic Col. Jack O'Neill to go on one last mission through the top secret Stargate—a huge, shimmering ring of glowing matter that allowed instant transport between different worlds. Since aliens could use it to get to Earth, as well as vice versa, it was supposed to be destroyed. But there was evidence that Egyptologist Daniel Jackson, presumed killed on the planet Abydos during the movie mission, might still be alive. O'Neill and his team found Jackson, who had discovered a hieroglyphic map of Stargates throughout the galaxy, making it possible to travel all over the universe. Following a confrontation with the vicious alien Goa'ulds, led by the evil Apophis, who had abducted Jackson's Abydon wife Sha're, they returned to Earth.

Once back, O'Neill formed a team based in the Air Force's Cheyenne Mountain complex, where Earth's Stargate was located, that was sent on missions to other planets. SG-1 (Stargate-1), was one of nine teams exploring the universe. The other members were shaggy-haired scientist Jackson, who hoped to one day rescue Sha're; Carter, a theoretical astrophysicist with high moral standards; and the muscular alien Teal'c, formerly a high-ranking guard/enforcer for Apophis, who had defected to the humans because he wanted to free his people, the Jaffa, from their subjugation by the Goa'uld. Other regulars were Sgt. Davis, the head Gate technician, and General Hammond's aide-de-camp, and Dr. Frasier, chief physician at Stargate Command. Using the Stargate portal to travel from planet to planet, O'Neill's team encountered civilizations ranging from primitive to technologically advanced, met friendly and hostile aliens, and had periodic confrontations with the Goa'uld.

Working with them, on occasion, were Teal'c's mentor, Bra'tac, and Sam's father, Jacob. Bra'tac, once a high-ranking aide to Apophis, was determined to free his people from their oppression by the Goa'uld. Jacob, a former general, was dying from cancer when, to save his life, he allowed his body to become the host for Selmak, a Tok'ra. The Tok'ra were a race committed to helping the humans fight the Goa'uld. Thor, commander of the Asgard military fleet, was another ally. The humans helped him in his ongoing conflict with the Replicators, a race of mechanical robotic creatures who ate technology, and he helped the humans fight the Goa'uld.

In 1999 Jackson found his wife, Sha're (Vaitiare Bandera), but she was carrying a Goa'uld symbiont of the evil Apophis and was pregnant with a human child. After the baby, a boy, was born, the symbiont took back control of her body. Daniel gave the infant to Sha're's father for safekeeping and she returned to Apophis. When she was killed later in the year Jackson almost resigned from the SG-1 team.

In June 2001 the SG-1 team captured the Goa'uld mother ship and with Jacob at its helm had a final confrontation with Apophis, who crashed into his home planet and was killed. A year later the team was trying to help the people of Kelowna prevent the destruction of their planet. To save thousands from dying Jackson exposed himself to a lethal dose of radiation, but before he died he ascended to another plane of existence. Quinn, a Kelownan diplomat who was partially responsible for Jackson's exposure, joined the SG-1 team as Jackson's replacement out of guilt and the desire to protect his home planet. With Apophis gone, the primary threat to humanity was Anubis, an aggressive Goa'uld leader who had partially ascended and existed between our universe and another plane.

Based on the 1995 theatrical film *Stargate*, starring Kurt Russell as O'Neill and James Spader as Jackson.

STARHUNTER (*Science Fiction*)

BROADCAST HISTORY:

Syndicated only
60 minutes
Produced: *2000–2001* (22 episodes)
Released: *September 2002*

CAST:

Dante Montana .... Michael Pare
Lucretia "Luc" Scott .... Claudette Roche
Percy Montana........................ Tanya Allen
Caravaggio .... Murray Melvin
Rudolpho .... Stephen Marcus

By the year 2275 Earth had colonized most of the solar system, but as its territory had expanded, its ability to maintain law and order—particularly in the outermost colonies—had diminished. The official police agencies were unable to cover the vast distances and, as a matter of convenience, had contracted with private bounty hunters, known as "starhunters," to bring the criminals running rampant in the colonies to justice—for a price. Dante Montana was one of them. Ten years earlier raiders had killed his wife, Penny, and taken his son, Travis. As a starhunter Dante could make a living while searching for his lost son. He was the captain of *The Tulip*, an aging luxury liner that had been modified to serve as a bounty-hunting vessel. Dante's niece Percy, whom he had adopted after her parents were killed by the same raiders who took his son, was the ship's saucy but brilliant young engineer. The other human crew member was Luc, a former marine and munitions expert who had been assigned to the ship by Rudolpho, Dante's boss and the owner of *The Tulip*. Rudolpho wanted her there to make sure that Dante spent more time hunting down criminals than searching for his son. Caravaggio, *The Tulip*'s sarcastic holographic maître d', had been reprogrammed to serve as its first mate.

Dante had no idea that Luc was actually an undercover agent for The Orchard, a secret organization run by her father that was trying to unravel the mystery of the Divinity Cluster, a sequence of four genes that, at some distant time in the development of the human race, had been hidden by aliens within the human genome. Luc knew that two of the genes were positive for human evolution while the other two were negative. She hoped to gain information from the criminals, who were trying to harness their power for their own ends, and prevent them from causing an evolutionary catastrophe.

Starhunter originally aired in Canada during the 2000–2001 season.

STARK RAVING MAD (*Situation Comedy*)
FIRST TELECAST: *September 23, 1999*
LAST TELECAST: *July 20, 2000*
BROADCAST HISTORY:
Sep 1999–Mar 2000, NBC Thu 9:30–10:00
Jul 2000, NBC Thu 9:30–10:00
CAST:
Henry McNeely................ Neil Patrick Harris
Ian Stark........................ Tony Shalhoub
Jake Donovan.................. Eddie McClintock
Maddie Keller................. Heather Paige Kent
Tess Faraday........................ Dorie Barton

Type-A obsessive met nut case in this oil-and-water sitcom. Henry was a fastidious, germophobic book editor who was constantly rubbing his hands with an antiseptic; he had been assigned by his publisher to look after eccentric horror writer Ian, whose first book, *Below Ground*, had been a best-seller but who was facing writer's block in producing a second. Ian was the kind who cleaned his teeth with a sword and loved staging dark and scary practical jokes, particularly on jittery Henry. Jake was Ian's dazed assistant, and Maddie the sensible barkeep in the restaurant below Ian's big New York loft, where he sometimes sang in a rock band. Tess was Henry's girlfriend. Edgar the hyperactive dog was played by "Marty."

STARLAND VOCAL BAND SHOW, THE (*Variety*)
FIRST TELECAST: *July 31, 1977*
LAST TELECAST: *September 2, 1977*
BROADCAST HISTORY:
Jul 1977–Aug 1977, CBS Sun 8:30–9:00
Aug 1977–Sep 1977, CBS Fri 8:30–9:00
REGULARS:
Bill Danoff
Taffy Danoff
Margot Chapman
Jon Caroll
Mark Russell
Dave Letterman
Jeff Altman
Phil Proctor
Peter Bergman
Milt Okun and His Orchestra

Four members of the popular music group The Starland Vocal Band (Bill, Taffy, Margot, and Jon) starred in this whimsical variety show which featured music and satirical comedy sketches. Political satirist Mark Russell was also a cast regular in this series, which was taped on location in such diverse places as a concert at Georgetown University in Washington, D.C., and at an outdoor picnic in Great Falls, Virginia. The group's main claim to fame, and the reason they got this summer series, was a 1976 hit record called "Afternoon Delight." Featured regularly in comedy sketches were three of the show's writers—Dave Letterman, Phil Proctor, and Peter Bergman.

STARLIGHT THEATRE (*Dramatic Anthology*)
FIRST TELECAST: *April 2, 1950*
LAST TELECAST: *October 4, 1951*
BROADCAST HISTORY:
Apr 1950–Jun 1950, CBS Sun 7:00–7:30
Jul 1950, CBS Mon 8:00–8:30
Jul 1950–Sep 1950, CBS Thu 9:00–9:30
Sep 1950, CBS Thu 9:30–10:00
Oct 1950, CBS Wed 9:00–9:30
Nov 1950–Oct 1951, CBS Thu 8:00–8:30

Stories of romance were presented on this live anthology series that bounced all over the CBS schedule during the 18 months it was on. The players came from both the legitimate theater and the motion-picture world. During its longest run in a single time slot, from November 1950 through October 1951, *Starlight Theatre* was reduced from a weekly to a biweekly series, alternating with *The George Burns and Gracie Allen Show*. Among the more familiar faces that showed up during the run were Barry Nelson, Mary Sinclair, Ernest Truex, Melvyn Douglas, Eve Arden, Julie Harris, Wally Cox, and John Forsythe.

STARLIT TIME (*Musical Variety*)
FIRST TELECAST: *April 9, 1950*
LAST TELECAST: *November 26, 1950*
BROADCAST HISTORY:
Apr 1950, DUM Sun 6:00–8:00
Apr 1950–Nov 1950, DUM Sun 7:00–8:00
REGULARS:
Bill Williams
Phil Hanna
Minnie Jo Curtis
Gordon Dilworth
Bibi Osterwald
Holly Harris
Allen Prescott
Ralph Stantley
Sondra Lee & Sam Steen
Roberto & Alicia
Eddie Holmes
Reggie Beane Trio
Cy Coleman Trio

Starlit Time was an early attempt by DuMont to compete in the Sunday night variety-show sweepstakes. Unfortunately a severe lack of budget, and therefore of big-name stars, hampered the show considerably. It premiered as an ambitious, two-hour affair consisting of two one-hour segments, "Welcome Mat," emceed by disc jockey Bill Williams, and "Phil Hanna Sings," emceed by vocalist Hanna. The two parts were linked together by Minnie Jo Curtis, who did a running bit as a celestial switchboard operator and who introduced some of the acts. Two hours proved unwieldy for such lightweight talent, and *Starlit Time* was soon reduced to a one-hour variety show co-hosted by Williams and Hanna. Among the regulars were folk singer Gordon Dilworth, dance teams Sondra Lee & Sam Steen and Roberto & Alicia, and assorted comics and vocalists.

During the summer months *Starlit Time* was known as *S.S. Holiday*.

STARMAN (*Science Fiction*)
FIRST TELECAST: *September 19, 1986*
LAST TELECAST: *September 4, 1987*
BROADCAST HISTORY:
Sep 1986–Mar 1987, ABC Fri 10:00–11:00
Mar 1987–May 1987, ABC Sat 8:00–9:00
Jun 1987, ABC Sat 10:00–11:00
Jul 1987, ABC Sat 8:00–9:00
Aug 1987–Sep 1987, ABC Fri 10:00–11:00
CAST:
Paul Forrester ("Starman") .... Robert Hays
Scott Hayden .... C. B. Barnes
George Fox .... Michael Cavanaugh

In this TV sequel to the 1984 theatrical movie of the same name, an alien who had fathered a child by an Earth woman returned—14 years later—to find his love, and help raise his son. Upon his arrival, the Starman (who apparently had no corporeal form of his own) assumed the body of Paul Forrester, a free-lance photographer who had been killed in a wilderness plane crash. He then located his son, Scott, in an orphanage, and together man and boy set out in search of Jenny, who had disappeared many years before.

Scott was naturally a bit skeptical about his alien origins, but was convinced when he saw Paul's unusual powers—and his own emerging paranormal abilities—which were triggered by the small, glowing spheres that Paul carried. It *was* handy at times to be able to levitate objects, or unlock doors without a key. In return, young Scott helped the innocent Paul understand Earth ways, sometimes in comical fashion. As they followed clues to Jenny's whereabouts they met and helped many people along the way, and the series took on an anthology quality. They could not stay anywhere for long: hot on their heels was the inevitable government agent, Fox, who had learned Starman's secret and was determined to capture him and take him to the lab "for testing." Some people have no sense of humor.

Everything turned out for the best in the end, however. In the final episode Starman and Scott finally found Jenny (played by Erin Gray), and they all went into cancellation together.

STARRING BORIS KARLOFF (*Suspense Anthology*)
FIRST TELECAST: *September 22, 1949*
LAST TELECAST: *December 15, 1949*
BROADCAST HISTORY:
Sep 1949–Oct 1949, ABC Thu 9:30–10:00
Nov 1949–Dec 1949, ABC Thu 9:00–9:30
STAR:
Boris Karloff
ORGANIST:
George Henniger

Tales of horror, starring Hollywood's best-known practitioner of that genre. The first telecast, titled "Five Golden Guineas," is illustrative. An English hangman unduly enjoys his work, which brings him payment of five guineas per hanging. He revels in the snap of the victim's neck, and the dangling arms. When his pregnant wife discovers his true occupation she leaves him. Twenty years later the hangman is called upon to execute a young man, which he does with pleasure, despite the fact that he has secret evidence that the youth is in fact innocent. Only then is he confronted by his ex-wife, who tells him that he has just hanged his own son. Enraged, he strangles his wife—and is subsequently sent to the gallows himself. Another hangman collects five golden guineas.

The title of this anthology series was changed to *Mystery Playhouse Starring Boris Karloff* effective with the October 27 telecast.

STARS IN ACTION (*Dramatic Anthology*)
FIRST TELECAST: *September 30, 1958*
LAST TELECAST: *September 29, 1959*
BROADCAST HISTORY:
Sep 1958–Sep 1959, CBS Tue 7:30–8:00

The filmed plays that were aired in this anthology series were reruns of episodes originally telecast on *Schlitz Playhouse*, an unusual practice for the start of a season. Reruns were frequently repackaged and retitled for use in the summer but rarely to fill a time slot for an entire season.

STARS OF JAZZ (*Music*)
FIRST TELECAST: *April 18, 1958*
LAST TELECAST: *November 30, 1958*
BROADCAST HISTORY:
Apr 1958–Jun 1958, ABC Fri 8:30–9:00
Jun 1958–Sep 1958, ABC Mon 9:00–9:30
Sep 1958–Oct 1958, ABC Thu 10:00–10:30
Nov 1958, ABC Sun 9:30–10:00
HOST:
Bobby Troup

Each week a different jazz musician or group was featured on this music series. Host Bobby Troup, himself a jazz musician, would introduce the week's guests, chat with them about their work, and sit back while they played for the audience.

STARS ON PARADE (*Musical Variety*)
FIRST TELECAST: *November 4, 1953*
LAST TELECAST: *June 30, 1954*
BROADCAST HISTORY:
Nov 1953–Jan 1954, DUM Wed 10:00–10:30
Jan 1954–May 1954, DUM Wed 9:30–10:00
May 1954–Jun 1954, DUM Wed 9:00–9:30
EMCEE:
Don Russell (1953)
Bobby Sherwood (1953–1954)
REGULAR:
Elliot Lawrence

Another of the military variety shows on television in the early 1950s. In addition to military bands, which were rehearsed for the occasion by civilian bandleader Elliot Lawrence, the talent included such stars as Perry Como, June Valli, Sarah Vaughan, and Errol Garner. The Glenn Miller Army Air Force Band also made an appearance. Don Russell was host for the first two telecasts only, being replaced on November 18 by Bobby Sherwood.

STARS OVER HOLLYWOOD (*Anthology*)

FIRST TELECAST: *September 6, 1950*
LAST TELECAST: *August 29, 1951*
BROADCAST HISTORY:
Sep 1950–Aug 1951, NBC Wed 10:30–11:00

Early filmed dramatic series, produced in Hollywood and generally featuring lesser-known actors and actresses. The star of the first presentation ("Beauty Is a Joy") was Mary Stuart, later to become the central character in CBS' long-running daytime serial *Search for Tomorrow*. Future star Raymond Burr was seen in two 1951 productions.

STARSKY AND HUTCH (*Police Drama*)

FIRST TELECAST: *September 3, 1975*
LAST TELECAST: *August 21, 1979*
BROADCAST HISTORY:
Sep 1975–Sep 1976, ABC Wed 10:00–11:00
Sep 1976–Jan 1978, ABC Sat 9:00–10:00
Jan 1978–Aug 1978, ABC Wed 10:00–11:00
Sep 1978–May 1979, ABC Tue 10:00–11:00
Aug 1979, ABC Tue 10:00–11:00

CAST:
Det. Dave Starsky .... Paul Michael Glaser
Det. Ken Hutchinson ("Hutch") .... David Soul
Capt. Harold Dobey .... Bernie Hamilton
Huggy Bear .... Antonio Fargas

MUSIC:
Lalo Schifrin, Tom Scott, Mark Snow

Starsky and Hutch was one of the light, youth-oriented police-action shows that populated TV in the 1970s. The two young plainclothes cops were both swinging bachelors, and their personalities meshed perfectly—they almost seemed to operate as one. Starsky was the streetwise member of the team, and Hutch the better-educated, soft-spoken one. Together they tackled cases in the roughest neighborhood in town (presumably Los Angeles), full of pimps, muggers, dope pushers, and big-time hoodlums. Sometimes they went undercover, but often they were highly visible, racing around the city, tires squealing, in Starsky's bright red hot-rod (a 1974 Ford Torino). Capt. Dobey was their quick-tempered but understanding boss, and Huggy Bear their flamboyant informant.

START OF SOMETHING BIG, THE (*Information/Interview*)

BROADCAST HISTORY:
Syndicated only
60 minutes
Produced: *1985–1986*
Released: *April 1985*

HOST:
Steve Allen

The primary focus of this series was on the roots of celebrity—how successful performers got started in show business. In addition to chatting with performers about the struggles, or lack thereof, early in their careers, host Steve Allen narrated feature pieces on the development of individual series like *Laugh-In*, *The Tonight Show*, *M*A*S*H*, and *Star Trek*. To provide a little variety, the inquisitive Mr. Allen also offered viewers segments on the origins of such things as the Boy Scouts, the bicycle, ice cream, the Barbie doll, credit cards, the Olympics, chocolate, and the toothbrush.

STARTIME (*Variety*)

FIRST TELECAST: *October 6, 1959*
LAST TELECAST: *May 31, 1960*
BROADCAST HISTORY:
Oct 1959–Jan 1960, NBC Tue 9:30–10:30
Jan 1960–May 1960, NBC Tue 8:30–9:30

PRODUCER:
Hubbell Robinson

The Ford Motor Company was the sponsor of this potpourri of hour-long specials that ran as a series during the 1959–1960 season. When it was sponsored by the Ford Division its full title was *Ford Startime—TV's Finest Hour*. When it was sponsored by the Lincoln-Mercury Division the title became *Lincoln-Mercury Startime*.

Serious dramatic presentations, musical comedies, and musical variety shows were all presented under the generic title *Startime*. One of the specials in this series that eventually became a series on its own was "Sing Along with Mitch," telecast on May 24, 1960, and back as a series the following January. Dean Martin, who would also eventually have a variety series on NBC, starred twice with variety specials. His former partner, Jerry Lewis, was also on *Startime*, but in the dramatic role of "The Jazz Singer," a version of Al Jolson's classic film. Ingrid Bergman made her American TV dramatic debut in "The Turn of the Screw" and so did Alec Guinness in "The Wicked Scheme of Jebal Deeks." The list of top-rank stars on this series was almost endless. Jimmy Stewart starred in "Cindy's Fella," a Western musical based loosely on "Cinderella," and Ed Wynn and Bert Lahr were featured in a straight comedy, "The Greatest Man Alive." Three of the most popular comedians of the century—Jack Benny, George Burns, and Eddie Cantor—starred together in a musical comedy revue.

STARTING FROM SCRATCH (*Situation Comedy*)

BROADCAST HISTORY:
Syndicated only
30 minutes
Produced: *1988–1989* (24 episodes)
Released: *October 1988*

CAST:
Dr. James Shepherd .... Bill Daily
Helen Shepherd DeAngelo .... Connie Stevens
Kate Shepherd (age 19) .... Heidi Helmer
Robbie Shepherd (14) .... Jason Marin
Rose .... Nita Talbot
**Frank DeAngelo* .... Carmine Caridi
*Occasional

This gentle family comedy centered on the life of veterinarian James Shepherd. James's ex-wife Helen, who had remarried but then quickly divorced again, spent more time around the house now than she had when she and James were married. Theirs was one of the friendliest divorces ever seen on TV. Helen would show up early in the morning to make breakfast for her kids, who were living with their father, before they went off to school. She was around to take Kate, who was in college, shopping. She was even there in the evenings. Good-natured, easy-going James was virtually unflappable, which probably explains how he had managed to live with his hyperkinetic ex-wife as long as he had, although he did occasionally muse over the amount of time she was spending at his home. His veterinary office was attached to his house and through its doors came a weekly menagerie of adorable dogs and cats, along with their sometimes eccentric owners. Rose was his cynical, worldly wise assistant who, at least according to herself, had been a beautiful showgirl in her youth.

STAT (*Situation Comedy*)
FIRST TELECAST: *April 16, 1991*
LAST TELECAST: *May 21, 1991*
BROADCAST HISTORY:
Apr 1991–May 1991, ABC Tue 9:30–10:00
CAST:
Dr. Tony Menzies .... Dennis Boutsikaris
Dr. Elizabeth Newberry............. Alison LaPlaca
Dr. Lewis "Cowboy" Doniger........... Casey Biggs
Jeanette Lemp .... Alix Elias
Anderson "Mary" Roche .... Ron Canada

This was a comedy set in New York City's Hudson Memorial Hospital, where paranoid doctors and harried nurses rushed about tending to equally nutty patients. Tony, the senior resident, was the relatively stable center of things; Elizabeth was an uncertain first-year resident; Lewis, a womanizing colleague; and Jeanette, the obsessive insurance adjuster. In the premiere a man went into labor along with his pregnant wife, and a cranky lawyer refused to sign the consent papers for his own emergency operation.

STATE, THE (*Comedy*)
BROADCAST HISTORY:
MTV
30 minutes
Produced: *1993–1995*
Premiered: *December 17, 1993*
REGULARS:
Kevin Allison
Michael Ian Black
Ben Garant
Todd Holoubek
Michael Patrick Jann
Kerri Kenney
Thomas Lennon
Joe Lo Truglio
Ken Marino
Michael Showalter
David Wain

Elaborately produced sketch comedy show satirizing movies, TV shows, baby-sitters, forgetful parents, even MTV itself. The comedy was primarily from a youthful point of view and often had a sexual edge. The original troupe was made up of New York University students.

STATE OF GRACE (*Drama*)
BROADCAST HISTORY:
Fox Family Channel
30 minutes
Original episodes: *2001–2002* (38 episodes)
Premiered: *June 25, 2001*
CAST:
Emma Grace McKee (age 12) .... Mae Whitman
Hannah Rayburn (12)................ Alia Shawkat
Narrator/Hannah (as adult; voice)
.... Frances McDormand
Tattie McKee........................... Faye Grant
Evelyn Rayburn.................... Dinah Manoff
David Rayburn .... Michael Mantell
Grandma Ida .... Erica Yohn
Uncle Heschie .... Jason Blicker
Cookie .... Patricia Forte
Greer .... Kingston DuCoeur
Shirley....................... Bonnie Bailey-Reed
THEME:
"Do You Believe in Magic?"

A gentle coming-of-age drama about two young girls from very different backgrounds in North Carolina in 1965. They met at St. Christina's in the Pines, an elite Catholic school. Hannah was the new girl in town, the daughter of a close-knit Jewish family who had just arrived to set up a furniture factory, and Grace was the fun-loving blond daughter of wealthy gentiles. Grace immediately "adopted" Hannah, and the reasons soon became clear: for all her money and status, Grace's home life was pretty barren. Tattie, her glamorous, globe-trotting mother, was a self-absorbed divorcée who was often away, leaving her in the care of housekeeper Cookie and chauffeur Greer. Hannah's family, on the other hand, was close to the point of smothering. Excitable mom Evelyn was a strong, controlling woman involved in running the family business as well as the household; dad David was intense, nervous, and a bit distracted; Grandma Ida fussed about the house; and Uncle Heschie was a nerdy bachelor in his late 20s, usually seen wearing a floppy fishing hat and hovering about like a bemused observer. The Rayburn household always seemed to be in an uproar, but there was plenty of love left over for Hannah's newfound friend Grace, who learned about Jewish customs as the Rayburns absorbed some of Grace's zest for life.

Stories were filled with sleepovers, school adventures, and *lots* of lessons about cultural differences, punctuated by music of the period ("The Times, They Are a-Changin'," "Wishin' and Hopin'," etc.). Midway through the run Tattie decided to marry millionaire Tommy Austin (Tom Verica), causing Grace great distress. The series was narrated, *Wonder Years* style, by journalist Hannah at age 47.

STATE POLICE (*Documentary*)
BROADCAST HISTORY:
Syndicated only
30 minutes
Produced: *2000–*
Released: *September 2000*
HOST:
Alex Paen

This series chronicled the activities of various state police departments around the country. Individual segments included reenactments of cases, and interviews with the actual officers and civilians who had been involved. Regular features included Police Blotter, footage of police in action; Evidence Locker, coverage of forensic techniques; and Safe & Sound, police rescues.

STATE TROOPER (*Police Drama*)
BROADCAST HISTORY:
Syndicated only
30 minutes
Produced: *1956–1959* (104 episodes)
Released: *January 1957*
CAST:
Trooper Rod Blake .... Rod Cameron

Lanky Rod Cameron brawled his way through murder cases, kidnappings, and other criminal investigations in this popular action series. Trooper Blake was chief investigator for the Nevada State Police, and as such got to track criminals in Las Vegas, Reno, Lake Tahoe, and across the Mojave Desert. Often he went undercover, assuming a variety of disguises to trap culprits.

State Trooper was supposedly based on actual Nevada police files. The pilot ran as an episode of NBC's *Star Stage* anthology in February 1956, but the series did not make the network schedule and was sold through syndication to local stations.

STATE V. (*Legal Documentary*)
FIRST TELECAST: *June 19, 2002*
LAST TELECAST: *July 17, 2002*
BROADCAST HISTORY:
Jun 2002–Jul 2002, ABC Wed 10:00–11:00
NARRATOR:
Cynthia McFadden

This unusual five-part documentary series was made possible by a special order from the Arizona Supreme Court that granted ABC behind-the-scenes access to several homicide cases in Maricopa County, which includes the city of Phoenix. Cameras were allowed to watch as prosecutors built their cases, lawyers conferred privately with clients, and trials took place; they were even allowed into jury rooms to watch the deliberations. Cases ranged from vehicular homicide to second-degree murder (a young man who shot his roommate in the head at point-blank range, and claimed self-defense). One case was covered per hour, in gripping and obviously real detail, but one thing was apparent—in cases such as these, nobody won.

STATLER BROTHERS SHOW, THE (*Variety*)
BROADCAST HISTORY:
The Nashville Network
60 minutes
Produced: *1991–1999*
Premiered: *October 12, 1991*
REGULARS:
The Statler Brothers (Jimmy Fortune, tenor; Phil Balsley, baritone; Don Reid, lead; Harold Reid, bass)
Rex Allen, Jr.
Janie Fricke
Bill Walker Orchestra

It has been said that "vaudeville never died, it just moved to Nashville," and this extremely popular series seemed to prove it. *The Statler Brothers Show,* a Saturday-night variety hour immediately following *Grand Ole Opry,* was a sensation on cable's TNN in the 1990s, quickly becoming the top-rated show on the network. Except for the substitution of country for pop music, the format was straight out of the Ed Sullivan era of the 1950s—musical acts alternating with comedians, ventriloquists, magicians, and even a juggler who performed with electric carving knives!

Known to popular audiences mostly for their 1965 novelty hit "Flowers on the Wall," the lively Statlers had been best-sellers in the country field for more than 25 years when this show premiered. Some of their biggest hits were country adaptations of pop songs ("That'll Be the Day," "Hello, Mary Lou"), but they also certainly had a sense of humor, with numbers such as "You Can't Have Your Kate and Edith, Too" and "Whatever Happened to Randolph Scott?" At times they masqueraded as "Lester 'Roadhog' Moran & His Cadillac Cowboys." As hosts of this show they oozed sincerity, although none of them was named Statler and only two were actually brothers. That's entertainment!

STEP BY STEP (*Situation Comedy*)
FIRST TELECAST: *September 20, 1991*
LAST TELECAST: *July 17, 1998*
BROADCAST HISTORY:
Sep 1991–Aug 1993, ABC Fri 8:30–9:00
Aug 1992–Sep 1992, ABC Tue 8:30–9:00
Aug 1993–Mar 1996, ABC Fri 9:00–9:30
Mar 1996, ABC Fri 9:30–10:00
Apr 1996–Sep 1996, ABC Fri 9:00–9:30
Mar 1997–May 1997, ABC Fri 9:30–10:00
Jun 1997–Aug 1997, ABC Fri 8:00–8:30
Sep 1997–Mar 1998, CBS Fri 9:30–10:00
Jun 1998–Jul 1998, CBS Fri 9:30–10:00
CAST:
Frank Lambert....................... Patrick Duffy
Carol Foster...................... Suzanne Somers
John Thomas ("J.T.") Lambert (age 15)
.... Brandon Call
Alicia ("Al") Lambert .... Christine Lakin
Brendan Lambert (7) (1991–1997)........ Josh Byrne
Dana Foster.......................... Staci Keanan
Karen Foster...................... Angela Watson
Mark Foster .... Christopher Castile
Lilly Lambert (1995–1996)
.... Lauren and Kristina Meyering
Lilly Lambert (1997–1998) .... Emily Mae Young
Ivy Baker (1991–1992) .... Peggy Rea
Penny Baker (1991–1992)........... Patrika Darbo
Cody (1991–1996)................. Sasha Mitchell
Jean-Luc Rieupeyroux (1997) ..... Bronson Pinchot
Rich Halke (1997–1998) .... Jason Marsden

Two appealing stars, winsome kids, and a can't-miss time slot in the middle of ABC's hit Friday lineup were more important than plot in the early success of this standard-issue family sitcom. Frank (Patrick Duffy of *Dallas*) was a freewheeling, divorced contractor who had impetuously married widowed beautician Carol (Suzanne Somers of *Three's Company*) when they met during separate vacations in Jamaica. They flew home to Port Washington, Wisconsin, where they both lived, told their kids—his three and her three—and all the problems of a merged family began. She was orderly, he was chaotic. The kids eyed each other suspiciously. Hers were teenager Dana, as compulsively neat as her mom, middle sis Karen, a budding fashion plate, and young worrier Mark. Frank's were teenage J.T., a cool customer, preteen Al, into insects and animals, and carefree Brendan. Working with Carol in her beauty salon next door were her mother Ivy and sister Penny. Cody was Frank's spaced-out 19-year-old nephew, whose nutty schemes and obsessions kept everyone in an uproar but who was really smarter than he seemed.

By the fourth season the oldest kids were approaching adulthood; Dana entered college, and J.T. was working as a car salesman. In May 1995, Carol gave birth to the couple's first child together, Lilly. Lilly grew rapidly, turning five and entering preschool in 1997. Other stories concerned the kids' growing pains, their exploits, and numerous girl- and boyfriends. At the center of many of them was Rich, J.T.'s best buddy and Dana's sometime boyfriend. A major excursion for the family—and a big advertisement for ABC owner the Walt Disney Co.—was a two-part trip to Disney World in May 1996, paid for by Frank's mother (June Lockhart). Showing up in early 1997 was Jean-Luc, a quirky hairdresser who opened a salon with Carol.

In the fall the series moved to CBS, and Carol decided to go to college, finding herself in the same classes as her freshman daughter Karen.

Perhaps after all that grief on *Dallas*, Bobby Ewing (Duffy) deserved some mindless laughs.

STEPHANIE MILLER SHOW, THE (*Talk*)

BROADCAST HISTORY:

Syndicated only
60 minutes
Produced: *1995–1996* (65 episodes)
Released: *September 15, 1995*

REGULARS:

Stephanie Miller
James
Hami

IRREGULAR REGULARS:

Carlos Alazraqui
Karen Maruyama
James Stephens III

Comedienne and former L.A. radio personality Stephanie Miller fronted this Monday through Friday late-night talk show that included comedy sketches (featuring her "irregular regulars") and patter with celebrities. She took "calls" from her "phone-in" studio audience at the beginning of most telecasts, and the entire show had a slightly raunchy quality—Ms. Miller's forte was what the producers described as her "brash humor and irreverent point of view." James was the show's black announcer and Hami its black one-man band. The show may have been too edgy and unpredictable for most viewers, and not attracting much of an audience, was canceled four months after its premiere.

STEPHEN KING'S GOLDEN YEARS (*Drama*)

FIRST TELECAST: *July 16, 1991*
LAST TELECAST: *August 22, 1991*
BROADCAST HISTORY:

Jul 1991, CBS Tue 9:00–11:00
Jul 1991–Aug 1991, CBS Thu 10:00–11:00

CAST:

Harlan Williams .... Keith Szarabajka
Gina Williams.................. Frances Sternhagen
Terry Spann .... Felicity Huffman
Jude Andrews .... R. D. Call
Gen. Louis Crewes.................. Ed Lauter
Dr. Richard Todhunter .... Bill Raymond
Fredericks .... Tim Guinee
Billy DeLois.................. Phil Lenkowsky

Harlan Williams was a 70-year-old custodian working at Falco Plains, a secret government research facility in upstate New York, whose life was changed forever when he was splashed with an exotic combination of chemicals after an explosion in the lab of Dr. Richard Todhunter, a mad scientist working on a process to regenerate destroyed animal tissue. Harlan made a miraculously quick recovery from his injuries and then, slowly, started to get younger—his hair, his skin, his eyesight, his general health, and his energy level all showing marked signs of improvement. There were side effects, of course—every once in a while his eyes would glow green in his sleep or his presence would cause objects to move and scare people half to death. His beloved wife Gina noticed it first and, before he could be made into a human guinea pig by Dr. Todhunter, they escaped with the help of Terry Spann, the head of security at Falco Plains. Terry had discovered that her one-time partner, ruthless Jude Andrews, an operative for a CIA-like agency called The Shop, was killing everyone who found out about Harlan and was about to grab Harlan. No one in authority would help them. Cold-blooded Jude was, in perceptive Harlan's words, "the devil himself." After several weeks on the run, in the final episode, elderly Gina's heart gave out and she died, Jude captured Harlan, and Terry and her boss, Gen. Crewes (now outlaws), escaped, hopefully to find a way to rescue Harlan. Although the last episode ended with "To Be Continued," there were no more episodes to resolve the story.

The series' creator, horror novel writer Stephen King, directed the first five episodes and had a cameo part as a bus driver in one of them.

When *Stephen King's Golden Years* subsequently aired on the Sci-Fi Channel, the ending was different. Harlan and Gina escaped, along with Terry and Gen. Crewes. Harlan's powers resurfaced, and he and Gina disappeared in the misty green glow. Terry killed Jude, and she and Gen. Crewes were discussing what they should do next as the final curtain fell.

STEVE ALLEN COMEDY HOUR, THE (*Comedy/Variety*)

FIRST TELECAST: *June 14, 1967*
LAST TELECAST: *August 16, 1967*
BROADCAST HISTORY:

Jun 1967–Aug 1967, CBS Wed 10:00–11:00

REGULARS:

Steve Allen
Jayne Meadows
Louis Nye
Ruth Buzzi
David Winters Dancers
John Byner
The Terry Gibbs Band

After an absence of several seasons, Steve Allen returned to prime-time television with this summer comedy variety series. With him were his wife, Jayne Meadows, comedian Louis Nye, comedienne Ruth Buzzi, and the David Winters Dancers. Although there was music in the series, the emphasis, regardless of who the week's guest stars were, was on comedy. Among the featured routines used regularly was the "Man on the Street Interview" in which Louis Nye played the suave, smug Gordon Hathaway. Although not listed by CBS as a regular, John Byner appeared in most of the episodes.

STEVE ALLEN COMEDY HOUR, THE (*Comedy/Variety*)

FIRST TELECAST: *October 18, 1980*
LAST TELECAST: *January 10, 1981*
BROADCAST HISTORY:

Oct 1980, NBC Sat 10:00–11:00
Dec 1980, NBC Tue 10:00–11:00
Jan 1981, NBC Sat 10:00–11:00

REGULARS:

Steve Allen
Joe Baker
Joey Forman
Tom Leopold
Bill Saluga
Bob Shaw
Helen Brooks
Carol Donelly
Fred Smoot
Nancy Steen
Catherine O'Hara
Kaye Ballard
Doris Hess
Tim Lund
Tim Gibbon
Terry Gibbs and His Band

Funnyman Steve Allen had been a fixture on network television throughout the 1950s, both in prime time and as host of the original *Tonight Show.* Following the cancellation of his primetime variety hour on ABC in 1961, Steve's projects had been mostly of the syndicated variety. On two occasions (1962–1964 and 1967–1969) he had hosted syndicated 90-minute variety series along the lines of *The Tonight Show* and in 1976 a variation on that type called *Steve Allen's Laugh Back,* in which his guests were all performers who had appeared with him in the 1950s. Steve had also produced and hosted the award-winning *Meeting of Minds* series for PBS starting in 1977, where he interviewed actors made up as historical figures. But, with the exception of a summer run on CBS in 1967 (see above), this was Steve's first commercial network prime-time series in almost two decades.

This *Steve Allen Comedy Hour* featured a large group of resident comics, collectively known as the Krelman Players. There were three recurring sketches on the show—a satirical spoof of local "Eyewitness News" shows, a revival of Steve's classic "Man on the Street" interviews, and "Camera on the Street," in which Steve ad-libbed observations about people and situations captured on tape by a hidden camera outside the studio at Hollywood and Vine in Los Angeles. There were guest stars, including Allen alumni Steve Lawrence and Tom Poston, but the thrust of the show was comedy, not personality. This series had a rather strange broadcast history, premiering in October with a single telecast, returning for the month of December, and closing with a single encore in mid-January.

STEVE ALLEN SHOW, THE (*Comedy/Variety*)

FIRST TELECAST: *December 25, 1950*
LAST TELECAST: *September 11, 1952*
BROADCAST HISTORY:

Dec 1950–Mar 1951, CBS Mon–Fri 7:00–7:30
Jul 1952–Sep 1952, CBS Thu 8:30–9:00

REGULAR:

Steve Allen

Steve Allen got his first network exposure on CBS with a live series that aired Monday–Friday at 7:00 P.M. and premiered on Christmas Day 1950. He played the piano, chatted with one or two guest stars, and had funny ad-lib interviews with both the guests and random members of the studio audience. When it left the early evening at the start of March 1951, the series was expanded to a full hour from 11:30 A.M. to 12:30 P.M. weekdays. He returned to CBS' nighttime lineup during the summer of 1952 on Thursday nights, running on alternate weeks with *Amos 'n' Andy.*

STEVE ALLEN SHOW, THE (*Comedy/Variety*)

FIRST TELECAST: *June 24, 1956*
LAST TELECAST: *December 27, 1961*
BROADCAST HISTORY:

Jun 1956–Jun 1958, NBC Sun 8:00–9:00
Sep 1958–Mar 1959, NBC Sun 8:00–9:00
Mar 1959, NBC Sun 7:30–9:00
Apr 1959–Jun 1959, NBC Sun 7:30–8:30
Sep 1959–Jun 1960, NBC Mon 10:00–11:00
Sep 1961–Dec 1961, ABC Wed 7:30–8:30

REGULARS:

Steve Allen
Louis Nye
Gene Rayburn (1956–1959)
Skitch Henderson (1956–1959)
Marilyn Jacobs (1956–1957)
Tom Poston (1956–1959, 1961)
Gabe Dell (1956–1957, 1958–1961)
Don Knotts (1956–1960)
Dayton Allen (1958–1961)
Pat Harrington, Jr. (1958–1961)
Cal Howard (1959–1960)
Bill Dana (1959–1960)
Joey Forman (1961)
Buck Henry (1961)
Jayne Meadows (1961)
John Cameron Swayze (1957–1958)
The Smothers Brothers (1961)
Tim Conway (1961)
Don Penny (1961)
Les Brown and His Band (1959–1961)

The multitalented Steve Allen—musician, composer, singer, comedian, author—was the star of this live weekly variety series that bore a strong resemblance to his informal, late-night *Tonight Show.* Although the program had elements of music and serious aspects, comedy was far and away its major component. Steve had with him one of the most versatile and talented collections of improvisational comics ever assembled. Among the features that were used at one time or another on a semi-regular basis were : "Letters to the Editor," "The Allen Report to the Nation," "Mad-Libs," "Crazy Shots," "Where Are They Now," "The Question Man," "The Allen Bureau of Standards," and "The Allen All Stars."

The most frequently used feature, and by far the most memorable, was the "Man on the Street Interview." It was here that the comics on the show developed their best-remembered characters: Louis Nye as suave, smug Gordon Hathaway, Tom Poston as the man who can't remember his own name, Skitch Henderson as Sidney Ferguson, Don Knotts as the extremely nervous and fidgety Mr. Morrison, Pat Harrington as Italian golf pro Guido Panzini, and Bill Dana as shy Jose Jimenez.

The Steve Allen Show spent three years on Sunday

evenings in head-to-head competition with *The Ed Sullivan Show.* On its second telecast, as a matter of fact, one of the guest stars was young rock 'n' roll singer Elvis Presley, a performer whose three appearances later that fall on Sullivan's show are better remembered than his stint with Steve Allen. In the fall of 1959, when the show moved to Monday evenings, it was retitled *The Steve Allen Plymouth Show*, a sop to its new full sponsor. When ABC picked up the show for a short run on Wednesdays in the fall of 1961, the title reverted to *The Steve Allen Show.* The series had originated from New York throughout its Sunday evening run but moved to Hollywood when it shifted to Mondays in the fall of 1959.

STEVE CANYON (*Adventure*)

FIRST TELECAST: *September 13, 1958*
LAST TELECAST: *September 8, 1960*
BROADCAST HISTORY:

Sep 1958–Jan 1959, NBC Sat 9:00–9:30
Jan 1959–Mar 1959, NBC Thu 8:00–8:30
Mar 1959–Sep 1959, NBC Tue 8:00–8:30
Apr 1960–Sep 1960, ABC Thu 7:30–8:00

CAST:

Lt. Col. Stevenson B. Canyon ...... Dean Fredericks
Police Chief Hagedorn (1959–1960) .... Ted DeCorsia
Major "Willie" Williston (1959–1960) .... Jerry Paris
Airman Abel Featherstone (1959–1960)
.... Abel Fernandez
Sgt. Charley Berger (1959–1960)........ Robert Hoy
Ingrid (1959–1960) .... Ingrid Goude

Milton Caniff's popular comic strip *Steve Canyon* was already 11 years old when this filmed series went on the air in the fall of 1958. Steve Canyon was a command pilot and troubleshooter for the air force and traveled from base to base around the country in the course of his work. Actual on-location footage of air force bases was used in the series, which had government approval and was considered a possible aid in recruiting drives. On January 3, 1959, Steve settled down as commanding officer of Big Thunder Air Force Base and acquired a regular supporting cast. Although based at Big Thunder in California, he still flew all over the world on special assignments. ABC aired reruns of the NBC series during the summer of 1960.

STEVE HARVEY SHOW, THE (*Situation Comedy*)

FIRST TELECAST: *August 25, 1996*
LAST TELECAST: *February 24, 2002*
BROADCAST HISTORY:

Aug 1996–Jun 1997, WB Sun 8:30–9:00
Jun 1997–Jul 1997, WB Sun 8:00–9:00
Jul 1997–Aug 1997, WB Wed 8:30–9:00
Aug 1997–Sep 1998, WB Wed 9:30–10:00
Jul 1998–Aug 1998, WB Sun 9:30–10:00
Sep 1998–Sep 1999, WB Thu 9:00–9:30
Aug 1999–Sep 1999, WB Sun 9:00–9:30
Sep 1999–Jul 2000, WB Fri 9:00–9:30
Apr 2000–Jun 2000, WB Fri 8:30–9:00
Jun 2000–Dec 2001, WB Sun 8:00–8:30
Feb 2001–Mar 2001, WB Sun 8:30–9:00
May 2001–Jun 2001, WB Sun 8:30–9:00
Jan 2002–Feb 2002, WB Sun 7:00–8:00

CAST:

Steve Hightower..................... Steve Harvey
Cedric Robinson .... Cedric "The Entertainer"
Romeo Santana .... Merlin Santana
Sophia Ortiz (1996–1997)............. Tracy Vilar
Stanley "Bullethead" Kuznocki.... William Lee Scott
Sara (1996–1997)...................... Netfa Perry
Principal Regina Grier.... Wendy Raquel Robinson
Lovita Jenkins (1997–2002)......... Terri J. Vaughn
Aesha (1997–1998)................ Ariyan Johnson
**Coretta (1998–2001)*............ Robin Yvette Allen
Lydia Guttman (1998–2002) .... Lori Beth Denberg

*Occasional

Steve had been lead singer in the soul group Steve Hightower and the Hightops, but with serious money problems ("I'm so broke they cut off my refrigerator light") he was forced to take a job teaching music at Booker T. Washington High School in inner city Chicago. Because of budget cutbacks he was also saddled with teaching drama and art, about which he knew nothing. Cedric, the lazy, fat sports coach with the insatiable appetite, was Steve's buddy. Principal Grier, a formerly fat (but now very svelte) classmate of his in high school, no longer had to take any nonsense from him. Steve caught the students' attention with his outlandish, bright 1970s-style suits and steady stream of one-liners. Among his students were Bullethead, a gofer for the administration who was dumb but conniving; Romeo, the black stud with the boom box who was always late to class because he had to make an entrance; Sophia, Romeo's sexpot girlfriend; and Sara, the sexy girl who became Romeo's girlfriend after he and Sophia broke up. Cedric moved in with Steve but they had their problems adjusting to each other's idiosyncracies. Despite their protestations, there was a sexual chemistry between Steve and Regina.

At the start of the 1997–1998 season Regina hired outspoken Lovita as her new secretary. Lovita and Cedric hit it off right away and began a serious romance, often spending time at the guys' apartment, much to Steve's chagrin. Steve and Regina did start dating, but he had trouble coping with her competitiveness. Then they broke up and she got back together with Warrington Steele (Dorien Wilson), an obnoxious rich ex-boyfriend. The following fall two female students became more prominent—Lydia, a bright white student, and Coretta, a beefy black with designs on Romeo.

A year later Steve was promoted to vice principal—although he still taught—and Cedric proposed to Lovita. Romeo and Bullethead had become an incompetent audiovisual team, and pushy Lydia had been assigned as a teaching assistant in Steve's class. For a time she also made the morning announcements over the public address system. In February, on the Friday after Valentine's Day, Cedric and Lovita got married.

In the fall of 2000 Steve's students were starting their senior year and he was going through a midlife crisis. Cedric and Lovita, who had been living with him, finally moved out of his apartment and into the one across the hall. Regina married her rich new boyfriend but returned from her honeymoon a widow; Jordan (Dwayne Adway) had suffered a fatal heart attack while they were making love. Depressed, she moved into Steve's apartment until she got herself back together—this despite having rejected Steve when he had admitted he loved her prior to the wedding. While Regina was recuperating, Steve took over as acting principal, but when she returned to work in December there was some friction. In January

Romeo's parents moved to New York and he moved in with Steve so he could finish his "last" senior year with the rest of the class. The following month, while on a school business trip, Steve and Regina finally made love. As graduation neared, Lydia, the class valedictorian, was accepted to Princeton, Lovita told Cedric she was pregnant, and Steve and Regina were having an affair. In the final original episode in February, the week after the graduation episode, Lovita and Cedric hit the Lotto jackpot—and she went into labor; Regina took a job as dean of a private school in California; and Steve, despite initial resistance, followed her there and effectively proposed to her.

STEVE LAWRENCE-EYDIE GORME SHOW, THE (*Musical Variety*)

FIRST TELECAST: *July 13, 1958*
LAST TELECAST: *August 31, 1958*
BROADCAST HISTORY:
Jul 1958–Aug 1958, NBC Sun 8:00–9:00
REGULARS:
Steve Lawrence
Eydie Gorme
Gene Rayburn
The Artie Malvin Singers
The Jack Kane Orchestra

The husband-and-wife singing team of Steve Lawrence and Eydie Gorme starred in this 1958 summer replacement for *The Steve Allen Show.* They sang separately and together, introduced and participated with their various guest stars in song, and occasionally acted in comedy skits. Gene Rayburn was the show's announcer.

The full title was *Steve Allen Presents the Steve Lawrence-Eydie Gorme Show.*

STEVE LAWRENCE SHOW, THE (*Musical Variety*)

FIRST TELECAST: *September 13, 1965*
LAST TELECAST: *December 13, 1965*
BROADCAST HISTORY:
Sep 1965–Dec 1965, CBS Mon 10:00–11:00
REGULARS:
Steve Lawrence
Charles Nelson Reilly
Betty Walker
The Ernie Flatt Dancers
The Dick Williams Singers
The Joe Guercio Orchestra

Singer Steve Lawrence was the host and star of this musical variety series. It featured appearances by guest stars, songs, comedy sketches, and production numbers. Comics Charles Nelson Reilly and Betty Walker were originally supposed to be featured regulars in the show, but were both gone by the end of September, leaving Steve and his guest stars to fend for themselves.

STEVE RANDALL (*Detective Drama*)

FIRST TELECAST: *November 7, 1952*
LAST TELECAST: *January 30, 1953*
BROADCAST HISTORY:
Nov 1952–Jan 1953, DUM Fri 8:00–8:30
CAST:
Steve Randall .... Melvyn Douglas

In this filmed series screen star Melvyn Douglas appeared as a disbarred lawyer who had turned sleuth in an attempt to regain his right to practice law. A suave, mustachioed detective, he greased his way through assorted cases of blackmail and murder before finally reaching his goal—reinstatement as a lawyer—in the final episode. There this short series ended.

Prior to the network run, some episodes of *Steve Randall* were seen locally under the title *Hollywood Off Beat.*

STILL STANDING (*Situation Comedy*)

FIRST TELECAST: *September 30, 2002*
LAST TELECAST:
BROADCAST HISTORY:
Sep 2002–Jun 2003, CBS Mon 9:30–10:00
Jun 2003– , CBS Mon 8:30–9:00
CAST:
Bill Miller............................ Mark Addy
Judy Miller .... Jami Gertz
Lauren Miller (age 13).............. Renee Olstead
Brian Miller (14)......................... Taylor Ball
Tina Miller (6) .... Soleil Borda
Linda.............................. Jennifer Irwin

In this traditional family sitcom Bill and Judy were a happily married middle-class couple raising their three children in Chicago. They had been high school sweethearts and were still madly in love after 15 years of marriage. Chunky, good-natured Bill was a salesman while Judy, his pretty wife, worked as a dental assistant. Their three children were Brian, a preppy-like intellectual who, despite being closer to his computer than to any of his classmates, longed to develop a social life; Lauren, a rebellious free spirit who chafed when compared unfavorably to her more studious older brother; and Tina, an uninhibited wide-eyed tyke who adored her parents. Judy's neurotic sister, Linda, showed up frequently to complain about her dating problems—she had no luck with men—and trade zingers with Bill.

STILL THE BEAVER, see *New Leave It to Beaver, The*

STINGRAY (*Drama*)

FIRST TELECAST: *March 4, 1986*
LAST TELECAST: *July 31, 1987*
BROADCAST HISTORY:
Mar 1986–May 1986, NBC Tue 10:00–11:00
Jun 1986–Aug 1986, NBC Fri 10:00–11:00
Jan 1987–Mar 1987, NBC Fri 8:00–9:00
Mar 1987–May 1987, NBC Fri 10:00–11:00
Jun 1987–Jul 1987, NBC Fri 8:00–9:00
CAST:
Stingray .... Nick Mancuso

"He's a Lone Ranger in a black sportscar!" trumpeted the ads. Stingray was an enigmatic adventurer with no traceable past who traveled from place to place fighting crime and helping people in trouble. He never charged for his services, but informed those he helped that someday he would need a favor from them, no questions asked; the favor would be used to help someone else. His real name was never revealed and he was known only by the vintage 1965 Corvette Stingray he drove; the curious were able to trace the registration only as far as the "White House West Coast motor pool."

STIR CRAZY (*Comedy/Adventure*)
FIRST TELECAST: *September 18, 1985*
LAST TELECAST: *January 7, 1986*
BROADCAST HISTORY:
Sep 1985–Oct 1985, CBS Wed 8:00–9:00
Dec 1985–Jan 1986, CBS Tue 8:00–9:00
CAST:
Harry Fletcher .... Larry Riley
Skip Harrington .... Joseph Guzaldo
Captain Betty (pilot only) .... Polly Holliday
Captain Betty (1985) .... Jeannie Wilson
Crawford (pilot only) .... Royce Applegate
Crawford (1985) .... Marc Silver

Harry and Skip were best friends who left their home in New York to pursue the American dream by starting a chain of ice cream stores in Glendale, Texas. Unfortunately, while trying to raise money, they got involved in a murder for which they were falsely accused, convicted, and sentenced to 132 years in prison. Undeterred, they escaped from a chain gang and set out, in bumbling fashion, after Crawford, the tattooed cowboy who had actually committed the murder. Hot on their trail, and determined to take them back into custody, was the humorless Captain Betty.

Although this series was loosely based on the 1980 theatrical film of the same name, which had starred Richard Pryor and Gene Wilder, *Stir Crazy* looked more like a silly version of *The Fugitive*.

STOCK CAR RACES (*Sports*)
FIRST TELECAST: *June 24, 1952*
LAST TELECAST: *August 26, 1952*
BROADCAST HISTORY:
Jun 1952–Aug 1952, ABC Tue 9:00–10:30
ANNOUNCER:
Chick Hearn

Live coverage of weekly late-model automobile racing from the 87th Street Speedway in Chicago.

STOCKARD CHANNING IN JUST FRIENDS (*Situation Comedy*)
FIRST TELECAST: *March 4, 1979*
LAST TELECAST: *August 11, 1979*
BROADCAST HISTORY:
Mar 1979–Jun 1979, CBS Sun 9:30–10:00
Jun 1979–Aug 1979, CBS Sat 8:30–9:00
CAST:
Susan Hughes .... Stockard Channing
Milt D'Angelo .... Lou Criscuolo
Leonard Scribner .... Gerrit Graham
Victoria .... Mimi Kennedy
Coral .... Sydney Goldsmith
Mrs. Fischer .... Joan Tolentino
Miss Yarnell .... Linda Rose
Mrs. Blanchard .... Rhonda Foxx

After separating from her husband, Susan Hughes decided to leave Boston and make a fresh start in sunny Los Angeles. There she found herself an apartment, a kooky neighbor named Leonard, and a job at a Beverly Hills health spa called the Fountain of Youth. Her boss at the spa was Milt D'Angelo, an oddball physical-fitness freak who resembled a mid-forties parody of Jack LaLanne. His fervor when discussing the merits of conditioning and exercise was pretty hard for anyone to take, including Susan, but he nevertheless liked his spunky new employee and quickly promoted her from exercise instructor to assistant manager. Susan's wealthy sister, Victoria, was always on the lookout for a nice, successful professional man for Susan, someone who would get her out of that horrid job and into a classy neighborhood. Coral was one of the instructors at the spa, and Mrs. Fischer, Mrs. Blanchard, and Miss Yarnell some of the patrons.

STOCKARD CHANNING SHOW, THE (*Situation Comedy*)
FIRST TELECAST: *March 24, 1980*
LAST TELECAST: *June 28, 1980*
BROADCAST HISTORY:
Mar 1980–Apr 1980, CBS Mon 8:30–9:00
Jun 1980, CBS Sat 8:30–9:00
CAST:
Susan Goodenow .... Stockard Channing
Brad Gabriel .... Ron Silver
Earline Cunningham .... Sydney Goldsmith
Gus Clyde .... Max Showalter
Mr. Kramer .... Jack Somack

This series was CBS' second attempt in less than a year to make a star out of Stockard Channing. The first venture, *Stockard Channing in Just Friends,* had cast the actress as a recently divorced woman working at a Beverly Hills health spa. This series cast her as a recently divorced woman working for a consumer advocate at a Los Angeles television station. Susan Goodenow had landed her job working for egotistical crusader Brad Gabriel because her friend Earline was a secretary at the station that aired Brad's program, "The Big Rip-Off." Mr. Clyde was the general manager of the station, which was owned by his wife. Mr. Kramer was the owner of the old apartment building in West Hollywood where Susan and Earline lived. His fatherly interest in Susan compensated for a notable lack of skill as a handyman.

There were many similarities between this series and Stockard Channing's previous effort. In both shows she was named Susan, she had recently ended a marriage, she was starting a new job in Los Angeles, and her friend and coworker was played by Sydney Goldsmith. The most telling similarity, however, was that neither show lasted more than a few months. CBS did not try again.

STONE (*Police Drama*)
FIRST TELECAST: *January 14, 1980*
LAST TELECAST: *March 17, 1980*
BROADCAST HISTORY:
Jan 1980–Feb 1980, ABC Mon 9:00–10:00
Mar 1980, ABC Mon 10:00–11:00
CAST:
Det. Sgt. Daniel Stone .... Dennis Weaver
Chief Paulton .... Pat Hingle
Det. Buck Rogers .... Robby Weaver
Jill Stone .... Nancy McKeon

Stone was a celebrity cop. His best-selling novels about police work, based on his own experiences, had made a lot of money and won him a host of female admirers who turned up wherever he went. Chief Paulton, his one-time mentor, was not too happy about that, but there was not much he could do about it; as long as Stone's writing was done on his own time, it was his private affair. In any event, Stone still managed to solve one tough case after another. Jill was his occasionally seen daughter.

Rookie detective Buck Rogers was played by Dennis Weaver's son Robby.

STONEY BURKE (*Western*)

FIRST TELECAST: *October 1, 1962*
LAST TELECAST: *September 2, 1963*
BROADCAST HISTORY:
Oct 1962–Sep 1963, ABC Mon 9:00–10:00
CAST:
Stoney Burke.......................... Jack Lord
Cody Bristol..................... Robert Dowdell
E. J. Stocker .... Bruce Dern
Ves Painter..................... Warren Oates
Red .... Bill Hart

Professional rodeo rider Stoney Burke was after one thing—the Golden Buckle, the award given to the world's champion saddle bronco rider. Unfortunately he didn't make it during the first season, which is as long as this contemporary Western series lasted, although he did survive a considerable array of violence and villainy along the way. Filmed in the Southwest.

STOP, LOOK AND LISTEN, see *Celebrity Time*

STOP ME IF YOU'VE HEARD THIS ONE (*Quiz/Panel*)

FIRST TELECAST: *March 4, 1948*
LAST TELECAST: *April 22, 1949*
BROADCAST HISTORY:
Mar 1948–Dec 1948, NBC Fri 8:30–9:00
Jan 1949–Apr 1949, NBC Fri 9:00–9:30
EMCEE:
Roger Bower (1948)
Leon Janney (1948–1949)
REGULAR PANELISTS:
Cal Tinney
Lew Lehr (1948)
Morey Amsterdam (1948)
Benny Rubin
George Givot (1949)

Live comedy game show in which the emcee read jokes sent in by viewers to a panel of three comedians. If one of the comics recognized the joke he would immediately shout "Stop!" and continue the story himself up to the punch line. For every wrong ending supplied by the comedians the viewer won a prize. Guest comedians were also sometimes seen on the panel of "gag-busters."

Based on the radio program of the same name, which was first heard in 1939 with Milton Berle as its star gagster.

STOP SUSAN WILLIAMS (*Serial*)

FIRST TELECAST: *February 27, 1979*
LAST TELECAST: *May 1, 1979*
BROADCAST HISTORY:
Feb 1979–Mar 1979, NBC Tue 8:00–8:20
Mar 1979–May 1979, NBC Tue 8:40–9:00
CAST:
Susan Williams .... Susan Anton
Bob Richards........................ Ray Walston
Jack Schoengarth.................. Michael Swan
Jennifer Selden...................... Marj Dusay
Anthony Korf .... Albert Paulsen
Gold Tooth .... John Hancock
Ti .... Ti Miratti

Beautiful young newspaper photographer Susan Williams was after the men who killed her brother in this "cliff-hanging" serial. Alan Williams, a reporter for the same Washington, D.C., newspaper that Susan worked for, had been on the verge of exposing a fiendish international conspiracy to set off a nuclear bomb near Camp David while the world's leaders were attending a peace conference there. Masterminding the plot was importer Anthony Korf, whose evil henchmen, Gold Tooth and Ti, tried to kill Susan in virtually every episode. Susan chased them all over the world, from Marrakesh to Nairobi to Switzerland. She barely escaped death by cobra bite, in a lion pit, going over a cliff in a sidecar, and in the final chapter telecast, she was trapped in the mine shaft where the nuclear bomb was about to explode. The episode of May 1, 1979, was supposed "to be continued," but it never was.

Bob Richards was Susan's editor (who turned out to be in cahoots with the bad guys) and Jennifer Selden was the owner of the paper. Jack Schoengarth, an old friend of her brother, helped Susan with her search. *Stop Susan Williams* was one of three serials telecast under the umbrella title *Cliff Hangers*.

Although network viewers of this series never found out what happened to Susan Williams, those who saw the re-edited movie version, *The Girl Who Saved the World,* did. In the movie version, which included footage shot for, but never aired on, NBC, Susan disarmed the nuclear bomb and escaped from the mine shaft. As the movie ended, Korf was hatching another evil plan, while Susan and Jack had fallen in love.

STOP THE MUSIC (*Quiz/Audience Participation*)

FIRST TELECAST: *May 5, 1949*
LAST TELECAST: *June 14, 1956*
BROADCAST HISTORY:
May 1949–Apr 1952, ABC Thu 8:00–9:00
Sep 1954–May 1955, ABC Tue 10:30–11:00
Sep 1955–Jun 1956, ABC Thu 8:30–9:00
EMCEE:
Bert Parks
VOCALISTS:
Estelle Loring (1949–1950)
Jimmy Blaine (1949–1952)
Betty Ann Grove (1949–1955)
Marion Morgan (1950–1951)
June Valli (1952)
Jaye P. Morgan (1954–1955)
ORCHESTRA:
Harry Salter

Stop the Music was introduced on radio in 1948, where it was an overnight sensation. The following year ABC brought it to TV, complete with Bert Parks and Harry Salter's orchestra, and it was a major hit there. It continued on radio as well.

The format was a mixture of musical entertainment and quiz. Bert, a cast of regular singers, and the orchestra would perform parts of songs, which contestants from the audience would be asked to identify for cash prizes. Viewers at home could get into the act by sending in official entry blanks with their names and phone numbers. Three lovely operators on stage would begin placing calls as Bert crooned a tune, and as soon as a connection was made, someone would yell, "Stop the music!" The home viewer would then be given a chance to identify the tune. It could be worth knowing, too, as a correct answer might be worth a jackpot of $20,000 or more. Mink coats and trips to Paris were also frequent prizes.

Various modifications in the basic format took place from time to time, such as a "mystery medley" and a competition between a contestant in the studio and a viewer at home on the telephone. There was also a good deal of turnover among vocalists on the show, with Betty Ann Grove having the longest run. Guest singers also appeared, and there were segments with straight musical entertainment and comedy sketches and interviews.

STOREFRONT LAWYERS (*Legal Drama*)
FIRST TELECAST: *September 16, 1970*
LAST TELECAST: *September 1, 1971*
BROADCAST HISTORY:
Sep 1970–Sep 1971, CBS Wed 7:30–8:30
CAST:
David Hansen .... Robert Foxworth
Deborah Sullivan .... Sheila Larkin
Gabriel Kaye .... David Arkin
Roberto Alvarez .... A Martinez
Gloria Byrd .... Pauline Myers
Devlin McNeil .... Gerald S. O'Loughlin

1970 was the year of relevance, and no series tried to be more relevant than *Storefront Lawyers.* In its premiere episode, young lawyer David Hansen gave up his position with the prestigious law firm of Horton, Troy, McNeil, Carroll and Clark, in plush Century City, California, to join two other young attorneys in a nonprofit practice. He, Deborah Sullivan, and Gabriel Kaye set up an office in a small store in a poor section of Los Angeles and offered their services to poor people who needed legal help but could not afford an expensive attorney. Following an unsuccessful fall, and a three-week hiatus in January, the series returned on February 3, 1971, with a new title, *Men at Law,* and a new format. The three young attorneys were now working for the fancy law firm that Hansen had left in the fall, under the guidance of senior partner Devlin McNeil, and the cases were more conventional. They still worked on cases involving the underprivileged, but also took on those of more affluent members of the community. At this point, the amount of each episode that actually took place in the courtroom also increased substantially.

STORK CLUB, THE (*Talk*)
FIRST TELECAST: *July 7, 1950*
LAST TELECAST: *July 24, 1955*
BROADCAST HISTORY:
Jul 1950, CBS Wed/Fri 7:45–8:00
Jul 1950–Sep 1950, CBS Mon/Wed/Fri 7:45–8:00
Sep 1950–Dec 1950, CBS Mon–Fri 7:00–7:30
Dec 1950–Jan 1951, CBS Tue/Thu/Sat 7:45–8:00
Jan 1951–Jun 1952, CBS Tue/Thu 7:45–8:00
Jul 1952–Oct 1953, CBS Sat 7:00–7:30
Sep 1954–Mar 1955, ABC Sat 10:00–10:30
Mar 1955–Jun 1955, ABC Sun 9:15–10:00
Jul 1955, ABC Sun 9:30–10:00
REGULARS:
Sherman Billingsley
Peter Lind Hayes (1950)
Mary Healy (1950)
Johnny Johnston (1950–1951)
Virginia Peine (1950–1951)

Stork Club owner Sherman Billingsley became a television celebrity through this series. It was unique in that it was broadcast live from a specially designed permanent set at the club itself. Guest celebrities were informally interviewed at the special "Table 50" and were often given Welsh terriers and boxers as gifts for appearing. Home viewers could also receive one of the pets by sending in particularly interesting questions to be asked of a specific guest. When the series began, Peter Lind Hayes and Mary Healy were regulars. They left in the fall of 1950, around the time Johnny Johnston and Virginia Peine (wife of writer Quentin Reynolds) were added. Johnny lasted only a couple of months and Miss Peine was on until the following June. At that point Sherman Billingsley decided to become the sole host of the show.

STORY OF THE WEEK (*Interview*)
FIRST TELECAST: *January 7, 1948*
LAST TELECAST: *January 5, 1949*
BROADCAST HISTORY:
Jan 1948–Nov 1948, NBC Wed 8:45–9:00
Nov 1948–Jan 1949, NBC Wed 7:15–7:30
HOST:
Richard Harkness

Public-affairs program from Washington, D.C. NBC political analyst Richard Harkness interviewed prominent public figures and commented on the latest events in the capital. Among the many notable guests was freshman Congressman Richard M. Nixon (Rep-Calif.), who commented on his solution to the problem of Communism.

STORYTELLERS (*Music*)
BROADCAST HISTORY:
VH1
60 minutes
Original episodes: *1997–* (66 episodes)
Premiered: *December 29, 1997*

An intimate performance series in which rock singer-songwriters played some of their best material and talked about the stories behind the songs. One artist was featured per show, among them Ray Davies, Elvis Costello, Melissa Etheridge, Garth Brooks, James Taylor, David Bowie, The Eurythmics, The Pretenders, Stone Temple Pilots and Bon Jovi. A few artists (Billy Joel, James Taylor) were so interesting they got two episodes.

STRAIGHTAWAY (*Adventure*)
FIRST TELECAST: *October 6, 1961*
LAST TELECAST: *July 4, 1962*
BROADCAST HISTORY:
Oct 1961–Dec 1961, ABC Fri 7:30–8:00
Jan 1962–Jul 1962, ABC Wed 8:00–8:30
CAST:
Scott Ross .... Brian Kelly
Clipper Hamilton .... John Ashley

Scott and Clipper were partners in the Straightaway Garage, where they designed, built, and serviced racing cars. Scott was primarily a designer, and Clipper was the better mechanic. Their involvement with lovers of speed and racing led to the adventures depicted in this series. Originally, the title was to be *The Racers*, but it had to be changed because of sponsor problems. Autolite, the maker of spark plugs, loved racing. But the Ford Motor Company bought Autolite between the commitment for the series and its actual premiere date. Ford makes cars and loves safety. The title had to be changed and many racing clips in the ten already finished episodes were deleted before broadcast, due to Ford's objections.

STRANGE FREQUENCY (*Horror Anthology*)

BROADCAST HISTORY:

VH1
60 minutes
Original episodes: *2001*
Premiered: *August 18, 2001*

HOST:

Roger Daltrey

A spooky anthology series in which the cursed were usually musicians or music industry types. In one story a musician kicked his drug habit only to become addicted to a beautiful woman who threatened to take his soul; in another, the lead singer of a goth band saw death take the life of a girl at one of her concerts and feared that she was next. Guest stars included Ally Sheedy, Jason Gedrick, Judd Nelson, Peter Strauss, Sebastian Bach, Wendie Malick, and Charisma Carpenter.

First seen as a TV movie telecast on January 24, 2001.

STRANGE LUCK (*Adventure*)

FIRST TELECAST: *September 15, 1995*
LAST TELECAST: *February 23, 1996*
BROADCAST HISTORY:

Sep 1995–Feb 1996, FOX Fri 8:00–9:00

CAST:

Chance Harper.................... D.B. Sweeney
Audrey Westin .... Pamela Gidley
Angie.................... Frances Fisher
Dr. Anne Richter .... Cynthia Martells

In this off-beat fantasy, Chance Harper was a free-lance photographer who took pictures for a local newspaper, *The Examiner*, and also provided photos for the tabloid *Eerie Enquirer*. His real name was Alex Sanders but he had been named Chance by the people who adopted him when, at the age of eleven months, he survived a plane crash in which his family and everyone else on board died. Chance had an odd knack for being in the wrong place at the right time to help people in need. In one not atypical day he prevented a suicide, witnessed a shooting, rescued a woman from a burning building, tracked down a killer, and stumbled across a suitcase full of money. Audrey, a former lover, was his editor at the paper, and Angie was the understanding waitress at the Blue Plate Diner where he hung out during his spare time. Dr. Richter was the therapist to whom he related his "strange luck" and his mixed feelings about helping people.

In the series finale Chance was reunited with his brother, Eric (Scott Plank), and his presumed dead father, Robert (Walter M. Dalton). He found out that "strange luck" ran in his family and that the plane crash had been an act of revenge by an enemy of his father who was still trying to kill them all.

STRANGE REPORT (*Detective Drama*)

FIRST TELECAST: *January 8, 1971*
LAST TELECAST: *September 10, 1971*
BROADCAST HISTORY:

Jan 1971–Sep 1971, NBC Fri 10:00–11:00

CAST:

Adam Strange.................... Anthony Quayle
Hamlyn Gynt .... Kaz Garas
Evelyn McLean .... Anneke Wills

Strange Report showcased the use of advanced scientific analytic methods as aids in the solution of complex crimes. Adam Strange was renowned as being the foremost authority on the workings of the criminal mind in the entire Western world. Operating out of his flat in the Paddington section of London, he handled special "problem" cases that the British government could not afford to be officially involved in. Adam and Hamlyn "Ham" Gynt, his American companion and assistant, traveled around town in Adam's unlicensed English taxicab working on cases. Gynt was a former Rhodes scholar whose formal job was in the research department of a London museum. Evelyn McLean, one of Adam's neighbors, was a model and aspiring artist whose friendship with him got her involved in many of his bizarre cases.

STRANGE UNIVERSE (*Paranormal Magazine*)

BROADCAST HISTORY:

Syndicated only
30 minutes
Produced: *1996–1998* (390 episodes)
Released: *September 1996*

HOSTS:

Dana Adams (1996–1997)
Emmett Miller

Unusual and unexplained events from around the world were covered in this quasi-newsmagazine series that described itself as "the Phenomenal Daily Newsmagazine." There were UFO reports, segments on possession, celebrities relating their paranormal experiences, and anything else that the producers found weird enough to meet their criteria for inclusion, including short takes on the nightly strange news roundup. In many respects this series was a nighty TV version of the preposterous tabloid *The Weekly World News*. Anchors Adams and Miller tried hard to play it straight, despite the ridiculous content of many of the stories.

In February of 1997 cohost Dana Adams was abruptly dropped and Emmett Miller was left to carry on alone.

STRANGE WORLD (*Detective Drama*)

FIRST TELECAST: *March 8, 1999*
LAST TELECAST: *March 16, 1999*
BROADCAST HISTORY:

Mar 1999, ABC Mon 10:00–11:00
Mar 1999, ABC Tue 10:00–11:00

CAST:

Paul Turner.................... Tim Guinee
Dr. Sydney MacMillan.................... Kristin Lehman
Major Lynne Reese.................... Saundra Quarterman
Japanese Woman.................... Vivian Wu

Paul Turner was a scientist with a malady and a mission. Exposed to an extremely deadly chemical while serving as a captain in the Gulf War, he somehow survived, fighting for his life for five years in army hospitals while being treated by Dr. Sydney MacMillan. Then something very strange happened: just as his degenerative disease was about to overtake him, a mysterious Japanese woman slipped him an unnamed drug that miraculously cured him. Released from the hospital, he found he could resume his life only in bits and pieces, because the "cure" was only temporary. When his next attack of sores and sweats began, the woman would unfailingly emerge from the shadows with another small dosage which, when injected heroin-style, revived him. Who she worked for, why they wanted him alive, and why they were keeping him under control this way, remained unknown.

The government wanted him too. Because of his knowledge, he was approached by his former commander Major Reese to work for USAMRIID, the United States Army Medical Research Institute for Infectious Diseases, which had broad powers to covertly combat those who would "abuse science." He reluctantly agreed, and was plunged into a world of cloning, rogue scientists, and dark conspiracies at the highest levels, all the while waiting for the next "fix" from the Japanese woman that would keep him alive. He could not tell Sydney, now his girlfriend, or his superiors, about the mysterious woman and her drug, or else it would stop. Perhaps the answer to who was controlling him was somewhere among the cases with which he now dealt. Paul got nowhere near that answer, unfortunately, as the series was canceled after just three episodes.

STRANGER, THE (*Crime Drama*)
FIRST TELECAST: *June 25, 1954*
LAST TELECAST: *February 11, 1955*
BROADCAST HISTORY:
Jun 1954–Feb 1955, DUM Fri 9:00–9:30
CAST:
The Stranger .... Robert Carroll

Mystery series dramatizing the adventures of a benevolent stranger who entered into the lives of people threatened by evildoers. The first episode told of a member of a ship's crew pursued by thieves who wanted his collection of beer steins from various ports. The sailor didn't know why they were after him, but "the stranger" did. Later episodes dealt with murder, kidnapping, etc., and at one point "the stranger" even went behind the Iron Curtain. He never accepted payment for his services, and disappeared as mysteriously as he had come after each case was solved.

STRANGERS WITH CANDY (*Situation Comedy*)
BROADCAST HISTORY:
Comedy Central
30 minutes
Produced: *1999–2000* (30 episodes)
Premiered: *April 7, 1999*
CAST:
Jerri Blank .... Amy Sedaris
Chuck Noblet .... Stephen Colbert
Geoffrey Jellineck .... Paul Dinello
Principal Onyx Blackman .... Greg Hollimon

In this "sick-com," a 46-year-old, sex- and drug-obsessed ex-con returned to high school as a freshman, bringing all her dreadful habits to high school life. Sweet, innocent, buck-toothed Jerri had been a teenage runaway; she then spent the next 32 years as a "boozer, a user, and a loser," and didn't understand why the popular kids now didn't want to be her friends. Mr. Noblet was the clueless geography teacher, Mr. Jellineck the somewhat hipper art teacher, and Blackman the deep-voiced, narcissistic principal of Flatpoint High. When not disrupting school life, Jerri lived at home with her catatonic father, stepmom, and disdainful teenage stepbrother Derek (Roberto Gari).

Created by Sedaris, Colbert, Dinello, and writer Mitch Rouse, all former members of the Second City Comedy troupe, and promoted as a parody of the preachy *Afterschool Specials*.

STRAUSS FAMILY, THE (*Romantic Drama*)
FIRST TELECAST: *May 5, 1973*
LAST TELECAST: *June 16, 1973*
BROADCAST HISTORY:
May 1973–Jun 1973, ABC Sat 9:00–10:00
CAST:
Johann Strauss, Sr. .... Eric Woolfe
Johann Strauss, Jr. .... Stuart Wilson
Anna Strauss .... Anne Stallybrass
Emilie Trampusch .... Barbara Ferris
Lanner .... Derek Jacobi
Josef .... Nicholas Simmonds
Hetti .... Margaret Whiting
Edi .... Tony Anholt
Annele .... Hilary Hardiman
Theresa .... Amanda Walker

True saga of the fabulous "waltz kings" of 19th-century Vienna, produced in England and aired in the U.S. as a seven-part mini-series. The family's history was certainly the stuff of good soap opera. Johann, Sr., was a famous composer and the toast of Vienna, but he was gradually being overshadowed by his ambitious son, who wrote such immortal melodies as "The Blue Danube Waltz" and "Tales from the Vienna Woods." Father and son clashed not only over musical prestige but over politics, women, and just about everything else, and Johann, Sr.'s wife, Anna, was torn between the two. Eventually she left Sr. to his mistress, Emilie, and devoted her full attention to aiding Jr.'s growing career. Romance, deaths, unfaithful lovers, and great political struggles swept through this epic, along with dozens of cast members, the most prominent of whom are listed above. Music was provided by members of the London Symphony Orchestra.

STRAW HAT THEATRE, see *ABC Dramatic Shorts—1952–1953*

STRAWHATTERS, THE (*Variety*)
FIRST TELECAST: *May 27, 1953*
LAST TELECAST: *September 8, 1954*
BROADCAST HISTORY:
May 1953–Sep 1953, DUM Wed 8:30–9:30
Jun 1954–Sep 1954, DUM Wed 9:00–10:00
EMCEE:
Johnny Olsen (1953)
Virginia Graham (1954)

This was essentially an hour-long advertisement for Palisades Amusement Park, located in New Jersey, across the Hudson River from New York City. It was (and looked like) a super-cheap production, consisting of a talent show, diving exhibitions in the park's big pool, musical entertainment in the ballroom, and pickups from other locations around the park. Much of the show was done outdoors.

The program was seen locally in New York in 1952 and went out over the full DuMont network (such as it was) from 1953–1954. The 1954 version was called *Summer in the Park*.

STREET, THE (*Police Drama*)

BROADCAST HISTORY:

Syndicated only
30 minutes
Produced: *1988* (65 episodes)
Released: *April 1988*

CAST:

Officer Bud Peluso .... Bruce MacVittie
Officer Arthur Scolari .... Stanley Tucci
Officer Jack Runyon .... Ron J. Ryan
Officer Shepard Scott .... Michael Beach

Shot on location in Newark and other cities of northern New Jersey, *The Street* was a five-nights-a-week cop show that focussed on several patrol car officers, both on and off duty. It was filmed mostly at night with hand-held cameras to give it a documentary/news look, and it exuded a gritty reality that made some viewers wince. Linking the segments together was patrol car 260, used by Peluso and Scolari on the 3:00–11:00 P.M. shift and Runyon and Cooper from 11:00 P.M.–7:00 A.M. The series began with Cooper being shot in the genitals with his own gun, by a female traffic offender with whom he tried to trade the ticket for sex. Runyon, with his somewhat racist attitudes, was none too comfortable to then be paired with black officer Scott, while waiting for Cooper to recover. Peluso and Scolari were squabbling friends, who had been best buddies since parochial school.

In addition to its cinema verité look, *The Street* used very frank language (there was an on-screen warning to this effect), and showed its officers to have real prejudices and shortcomings. Because of the subject matter and language, most stations aired it after 11:00 P.M.

$TREET, THE (*Drama*)

FIRST TELECAST: *November 1, 2000*
LAST TELECAST: *December 13, 2000*
BROADCAST HISTORY:

Nov 2000–Dec 2000, FOX Wed 9:00–10:00

CAST:

Jack Kenderson .... Tom Everett Scott
Alexandra "Alex" Brill .... Nina Garbiras
Tim Sherman .... Christian Campbell
Donna Pasqua .... Melissa De Sousa
Freddie Sacker .... Rick Hoffman
Chris McConnell .... Sean Maher
Catherine Miller .... Jennifer Connelly
Evan Mitchell .... Adam Goldberg
Bridget Deshiell .... Bridgette Wilson-Sampras
Tom Divack .... Giancarlo Esposito
Gillian Sherman .... Jennie Garth

The Wall Street firm Balmont Stevens was the setting for this fast-paced serial drama about aggressive young stockbrokers chasing sex and money. The principal characters were Catherine, the tough ("don't mess with me") new sales V.P. working on IPOs; Jack, a handsome trader working with her; Freddie, a ruthless, sexist, and rather homely equity trader who made women squirm; and Tim, a boyish young broker trainee. Intellectual Evan was the firm's chief investment strategist, and Tom was the manager to whom most of them reported.

Everyone rushed about wearing great suits that they frequently shed in bars, corridors, and even elevators. Jack found out that his fiancée, Alex, who made more at the firm than he did, had been chasing after her ex-boyfriend after she had accepted his proposal. He dumped her; in early December they reconciled, but when he found out she had lied to pressure him into committing, they broke up again. Jack was then romantically scammed by Bridget, who pretended to be a teacher while pumping him for info that enabled her to get a job at Balmont Stevens. Sleazy Freddie had incredible hots for her. Chris, another equity trader, was insecure because he had not gone to college and had a decidedly working-class background. He was trying to help Donna, the ambitious, sexy receptionist, "learn the business" (which she did mostly by sleeping around). Tim was the son of one of the owners of Dunkirk Sherman, a large paper company, although he did not tell the people at work that he and his sister Gillian, who showed up in late November, had money. Gillian worked at an arts foundation in New York; when Chris first met her at Tim's birthday party, he was seriously smitten.

The real stock market bubble had burst in the spring of 2000 and *The $treet*'s bubble burst after only seven of the 12 episodes produced had aired.

STREET HAWK (*Police Drama*)

FIRST TELECAST: *January 4, 1985*
LAST TELECAST: *May 16, 1985*
BROADCAST HISTORY:

Jan 1985–Mar 1985, ABC Fri 9:00–10:00
May 1985, ABC Thu 8:00–9:00

CAST:

Off. Jesse Mach .... Rex Smith
Norman Tuttle .... Joe Regalbuto
Capt. Leo Altobelli .... Richard Venture
Rachel Adams .... Jeannie Wilson

There's an old saying that there are two types of motorcyclists—those who have had an accident, and those who will have one. Jesse Mach evidently wanted to be in both groups. Jesse had been a top motorcycle cop until he was seriously injured, and assigned to desk duty. He was then approached by Norman, inventor of the super-secret Street Hawk police bike, with an offer he couldn't refuse: Norman would arrange for "experimental surgery" to repair Jesse's shattered leg if Jesse would agree to become the secret "test pilot" for Norman's incredible new baby. And so by night Jesse donned a futuristic black helmet and fought crime on city streets on the Street Hawk, with its 300 m.p.h. speed, computerized targeting system, high-energy particle beam (to blow things up), and ability to leap through the air. By day he maintained his cover at a desk in the police public information office. Drive carefully, Jesse.

STREET JUSTICE (*Adventure*)

BROADCAST HISTORY:

Syndicated only
60 minutes
Produced: *1991–1993* (44 episodes)
Released: *September 1991*

CAST:
Sgt. Adam Beaudreaux .... Carl Weathers
Grady Jamieson .... Bryan Genesse
Malloy .... Charlene Fernetz
Lt. Charles Pine .... Leam Blackwood
Off. Tricia Kelsey (1991–1992) .... Janne Mortil
Off. Paul Shuhan (1991–1992) .... Ken Tremblett
**Teddy Willis* .... Blu Mankuma
Miguel Mendez (1992–1993) .... Marcus Chong
Off. Eric Rothman (1992–1993) ... Eric McCormack
*Occasional

Adam Beaudreaux was a moody but dedicated police officer serving the people of an unnamed city in the Pacific Northwest, with a substantial Vietnamese community. When not on duty, he spent much of his time at Malloy's, a bar he owned jointly with his ex-partner's daughter. Living with Adam, and working at Malloy's, was 28-year-old Grady, the son of Canadian missionaries in Vietnam, who had been orphaned 20 years earlier when his parents had been killed by the Viet Cong. He had saved Adam's life and the two of them had lived together in Vietnam for six months before Adam was sent home. A martial arts expert, Grady spent so much time fighting crime that he might as well have been on the force himself. Lt. Pine was Adam's boss, Kelsey and Shuhan two of the officers who worked with him, and Miguel a former gang member befriended by Adam and Grady who sometimes helped them out. Shuhan and Kelsey, who were partners, got romantically involved in an October 1992 episode, and the following week Shuhan was killed in a shootout. Seen on occasion was Adam's Vietnam War buddy, Teddy Willis.

Filmed in Vancouver, British Columbia.

STREET MATCH (*Audience Participation*)

FIRST TELECAST: *July 28, 1993*
LAST TELECAST: *August 25, 1993*
BROADCAST HISTORY:
Jul 1993–Aug 1993, ABC Wed 8:30–9:00
HOST:
Ricky Paull Goldin

In this slice-of-life series, hip young daytime star Ricky Paull Goldin *(Another World)* played matchmaker on the streets of various cities, persuading complete strangers to go out on dates with each other. Cameras then followed them into their bathrooms and bedrooms as they prepared for the big date, went to a restaurant or club, and afterward until they put the lens cap on the camera.

STREET SMARTS (*Quiz*)

BROADCAST HISTORY:
Syndicated only
30 minutes
Produced: *2000–*
Released: *October 2000*
EMCEE:
Frank Nicotero

Contestants on *Street Smarts* were shown video clips of the host asking questions of people "on the street" at various locations around the country and won money by guessing whether or not the interviewees had answered correctly. There were three preliminary rounds. In the first, "Who Knew It," two contestants guessed which of three interviewees knew the correct answer to questions like, "Who is known as the Prince of Wales?" and got $100 for each correct guess. In the second round, "Who Blew It," the contestants guessed which two of the three interviewees missed a question, with each correct guess worth $200. In round three, "Pick Your Pony," each contestant chose one of the three interviewees and guessed what his or her answers were, with a correct guess worth $300. In rounds two and three a contestant could also put a dunce cap on his or her opponent and challenge that player's ability to guess correctly. A correct answer gave the challenged extra money, while an incorrect guess gave the money to the challenger.

The final round was "The Wager of Death," in which contestants were told the final question, picked an interviewee and guessed whether he or she had answered that question correctly, wagering whatever they wanted from their accumulated winnings. Contestants could win several thousand dollars on this show, which looked like it cost $1.98 to produce. Some of the interviewees were incredibly stupid and others seemed pretty intelligent, but it was obvious that the producers preferred to see people embarrass themselves.

STREET STORIES (*Magazine*)

FIRST TELECAST: *January 9, 1992*
LAST TELECAST: *August 6, 1993*
BROADCAST HISTORY:
Jan 1992–Apr 1993, CBS Thu 9:00–10:00
Jun 1993–Aug 1993, CBS Thu 9:00–10:00
HOST:
Ed Bradley
CORRESPONDENTS:
Bernard Goldberg (1992)
Victoria Corderi (1992)
Harold Dow
Bob McKeown
Peter Van Sant
Jerry Bowen
Richard Roth
Roberta Baskin
Deborah Norville (1993)

Unlike most other newsmagazine series, *Street Stories* focused on social issues almost exclusively through the personal stories of villains, victims, and heroes. There were segments on drunk drivers, a judge who made up his own rules based on his interpretation of what society needed, the problems of a small southern town coping with racial disharmony precipitated by the election of a black sheriff, students who took guns to school, a beautiful Mexican attorney getting rich dealing heroin in South Texas, children orphaned when their mothers were murdered, and New York newspaper columnist Ellis Henican, whose beat was the 730 miles of the New York City subway system. Almost all of CBS' reporters covered stories for this series, but only those listed above were considered correspondents.

STREETS OF SAN FRANCISCO, THE (*Police Drama*)

FIRST TELECAST: *September 16, 1972*
LAST TELECAST: *June 23, 1977*
BROADCAST HISTORY:
Sep 1972–Jan 1973, ABC Sat 9:00–10:00
Jan 1973–Aug 1974, ABC Thu 10:00–11:00
Sep 1974–Sep 1976, ABC Thu 9:00–10:00
Sep 1976–Jun 1977, ABC Thu 10:00–11:00

CAST:

Det. Lt. Mike Stone .... Karl Malden
Inspector Steve Keller (1972–1976) .... Michael Douglas
Inspector Dan Robbins (1976–1977) .... Richard Hatch
Lt. Lessing .... Lee Harris

EXECUTIVE PRODUCER:

Quinn Martin

There always seems to be room on TV for a police show set in San Francisco (remember *The Lineup*?). *The Streets of San Francisco* was such a show for the 1970s, following the cases of Lt. Mike Stone and his young partner as they used modern police methods to track down criminals, against the backdrop of the Bay Area. Mike was a 23-year veteran of the force, a widower, assigned to the Bureau of Inspectors Division of the San Francisco Police Department. His original partner was 28-year-old Steve Keller, a smart, college-educated man who rose from assistant inspector to inspector during his tenure on the show. In 1976 he left ("to enter teaching") and was replaced by the athletic Dan Robbins.

Mike's coed daughter was seen occasionally during the early years (played by Darleen Carr), but later the emphasis was shifted to the cases, rather than the home lives, of the principals. Some scenes in the series were filmed in actual San Francisco police buildings, such as the communications center, the morgue, etc.

Based on characters from the novel *Poor, Poor Ophelia*, by Carolyn Weston.

STRENGTH FOR A FREE WORLD, see *Marshall Plan in Action, The*

STRESSED ERIC (*Cartoon*)

FIRST TELECAST: *August 12, 1998*
LAST TELECAST: *August 26, 1998*
BROADCAST HISTORY:

Aug 1998, NBC Wed 9:30–10:00

VOICES:

Eric Feeble .... Hank Azaria
Claire Feeble, Heather Perfect .... Morwenna Banks
Maria, Alison .... Doon McKichan
Liz .... Rebecca Front
Ray Perfect .... Xander Armstrong
Mrs. Perfect .... Alison Steadman
Paul Power ("P.P.") .... Geoff McGivern
Doc .... Paul Shearer

Seldom has a cartoon character led such a relentlessly harried life as the appropriately named Stressed Eric. A divorced American dad living in London, Eric worked in the "data department" of a large company, where his runt of a boss, P.P., yelled at him, his secretary Alison chattered incessantly, and the cleaning lady threw out his hard work when he wasn't looking. At home his two kids, 10-year-old Brian and 7-year-old Claire, were always in trouble. Chubby Brian (who didn't speak) ate everything in sight, including the Baby Jesus doll in the school nativity play; Claire had a fondness for sweets, which made her tongue swell to horrendous proportions. Their punk nanny, Maria, did little to help, crawling home drunk after long nights on the town and throwing up a lot. Adding to Eric's misery was his selfish ex-wife Liz, who had dumped the kids on him, and the achingly perfect neighbors Mr. and Mrs. Perfect, with their perfect daughter Heather. Doc offered sensible advice, but when things got to be too much for Eric, his temples began to throb, as if his head was about to explode.

This cheery little domestic saga was canceled after just three weeks. Produced in England.

STRICTLY FOR LAUGHS (*Music*)

FIRST TELECAST: *November 22, 1949*
LAST TELECAST: *June 23, 1950*
BROADCAST HISTORY:

Nov 1949–Dec 1949, CBS Tue/Wed/Fri 7:00–7:15
Dec 1949, CBS Mon/Tue/Wed/Fri 7:00–7:15
Jan 1950, CBS Mon/Wed/Thu/Fri 7:00–7:15
Jan 1950–Jun 1950, CBS Mon–Fri 7:00–7:15

REGULARS:

The Kirby Stone Quintet

The light-hearted harmonizing of the Kirby Stone Quintet was featured in this live 15-minute musical program. Their songs were often pleasantly amusing, though not up to the level of silliness attained by the likes of Spike Jones. Rather, the lyrics tended to have subtle twists. Occasionally they were joined by guest performers. Effective with the telecast of April 3, 1950, the title of the series was changed to *The Kirby Stone Quintet*.

STRIKE FORCE (*Police*)

FIRST TELECAST: *November 13, 1981*
LAST TELECAST: *September 24, 1982*
BROADCAST HISTORY:

Nov 1981–May 1982, ABC Fri 10:00–11:00
Sep 1982, ABC Fri 10:00–11:00

CAST:

Capt. Frank Murphy .... Robert Stack
Det. Paul Strobber .... Dorian Harewood
Lt. Charlie Gunzer .... Richard Romanus
Det. Mark Osborn .... Michael Goodwin
Det. Rosie Johnson .... Trisha Noble
Deputy Commissioner Herbert Klein Herb Edelman

Capt. Frank Murphy headed this special unit within the Los Angeles Police Department dedicated to solving the toughest cases. Tackling only one case at a time, these men spent much of their time undercover, tracking mad bombers, rapists, assassins, fanatical cult leaders, and other undesirables who had proven too elusive for ordinary cops.

STRIKE IT RICH (*Quiz/Audience Participation*)

FIRST TELECAST: *July 4, 1951*
LAST TELECAST: *January 12, 1955*
BROADCAST HISTORY:

Jul 1951–Jan 1955, CBS Wed 9:00–9:30

EMCEE:

Warren Hull

Strike It Rich was one of the most hotly debated programs on television during the 1950s. To some it was TV's noblest hour, helping those less fortunate than most through the charity and goodwill of viewers. To others it was one of the most sickening spectacles ever seen on a TV screen, exploiting those same unfortunates for the vicarious thrill of viewers and the selfish gain of advertisers, a kind of video "kick the cripple." It was investigated by governmental bodies, limned by charitable organizations, and defended by others. Whichever way you looked at it, though, it was certainly popular, and perhaps the ultimate example of viewer-participation television.

Strike It Rich was created by producer Walt Framer

and was first heard on CBS radio in 1947. It consisted of a quiz show whose contestants were exclusively people in need of money—for medical treatment, for a destitute family, for a crippled children's hospital, for a little girl who had lost her dog. About a quarter of the contestants were actually representing someone else who was in need. The questions were easy and most contestants were winners—if you could classify anyone on a show like this a "winner"—but even if they lost, there was always the "Heart Line." After they told their tale of woe, emcee Hull would open up the telephone lines and ask viewers to pitch in what they could. And they did, thousands of dollars every broadcast, expensive therapeutic equipment, clothes, and furniture for those who had none, an endless stream of gifts from all over America to help ease the contestant's suffering.

The problem, besides the obvious ethical one, was that the program seemed to promise more than it could deliver. For every charity case that got on the air, hundreds were turned away (only "appealing" or "interesting" cases were wanted). From 3,000 to 5,000 letters a week poured in from desperate people, and despite the program's repeated advice to the contrary, dozens of them journeyed to New York in hopes of being picked out of the studio audience. Most of these wound up stranded in the city, and were forced to go to welfare agencies or the Salvation Army—which complained bitterly about the effect the show was having. The New York City Commissioner of Welfare called *Strike It Rich* "a disgusting spectacle and a national disgrace," and demanded that it be investigated. The supervisor of the Travelers Aid Society said, "We don't know if the successes on the show balance off against the human misery caused by it. But from what we see, I'd say they didn't. . . . Putting human misery on display can hardly be called right." The General Director of the Family Service Association of America said flatly, "Victims of poverty, illness, and everyday misfortune should not be made a public spectacle or seemingly be put in the position of begging for charity." A New York State legislative committee did look into the controversy, but then washed its hands of the affair, claiming that it did not have jurisdiction. As for CBS and NBC, the networks that carried the show on television and radio respectively, they were unconcerned. "We don't want to do anything that would antagonize the sponsor," said NBC.

And so the program that *TV Guide* called "a despicable travesty on the very nature of charity" continued untouched until it ended its normal run.

Strike It Rich remained on CBS' daytime TV schedule until January 1958. There were two attempts to revive it as a syndicated program in the 1970s, with Bert Parks as host in 1973 and Tom Kelly as host in 1978. Neither revival was successful.

Joe Garagiola hosted a syndicated quiz show that used the title *Strike It Rich* during the 1986–1987 season.

STRIP, THE (*Drama*)

FIRST TELECAST: *October 12, 1999*
LAST TELECAST: *September 22, 2000*
BROADCAST HISTORY:
Oct 1999–Jan 2000, UPN Tue 9:00–10:00
Jun 2000–Sep 2000, UPN Fri 8:00–9:00
CAST:
Elvis Ford .... Sean Patrick Flanery
Jesse Weir .... Guy Torry
Cameron Greene .... Joe Viterelli
Vanessa Weir .... Stacey Dash
Chad .... Brett Rickaby
Tad .... Keith Odett

Elvis and Jesse were undercover investigators in this violent buddy show set in Las Vegas. Elvis, the white one, was a slob who subsisted on junk food and lived on a landlocked, run-down sailboat he had named *Gonzo*. Jesse, the dapper black one, was married to beautiful Vanessa, who sold real estate. They had been undercover cops for the Vegas police department but now were working security for Cameron Greene, the jowly, gravel-voiced owner of Caesar's Palace casino (where this show was filmed). Among their cases was a ring of Japanese thugs who kidnapped showgirls and sold them into white slavery in Japan, the murder of a dancer who once worked for Greene, and the mysterious death of a magician who was killed while performing an illusion.

Despite Greene's frequent admonitions to the boys to "be discreet," *The Strip* was filled with squealing tires, flying bullets, and huge explosions. Produced, not surprisingly, by the people responsible for the *Lethal Weapon* feature films.

STRIP MALL (*Situation Comedy*)

BROADCAST HISTORY:
Comedy Central
30 minutes
Original episodes: *2000–2001* (20 episodes)
Premiered: *June 18, 2000*
CAST:
Tammi Tyler .... Julie Brown
Patty .... Victoria Jackson
Blunt/Blair/Blank .... Bob Koherr
Harvey Krudup .... Jim O'Heir
Sergei Zokolov .... Gregory Itzin
Josh MacIntosh .... Jonathan Mangum
Barry .... Chris Wylde
Tasha .... Tasha Taylor
Hedda Hummer .... Allison Dunbar
Fanny Sue Chang .... Amy Hill
Althea .... Loretta Fox
Rafe Barrett .... Maxwell Caulfield
Bettina Barrett .... Eliza Coyle
Dwight .... Tim Bagley

The sleazy denizens of the Plaza del Toro strip mall in Van Nuys, California, were the subjects of this twisted, soap opera–ish sitcom. The Funky Fox, a neighborhood bar, was home to Tammi, a waitress and former child star whose career had been derailed when she stabbed her adult costar, and Patty, a bartender with a metal plate in her head (something about an incident in Baghdad). Nearby was the Star Brite Laundry and Dry Cleaners, run by big, gross Harvey ("The King of Stains"); Wok Don't Run, a Chinese restaurant owned by a fat, gruff Asian American lesbian named Fanny and her sexy partner, Althea; the Good Things craft store, run by newly impoverished yuppies Rafe and Bettina; and We Shoot You Video, a photography studio run by a Ukrainian named Sergei, who serviced weddings and bar mitzvahs in the front and made pornographic films in the back. Assisting Sergei in his backroom studios were idealistic young director Josh, sold-out assistant Barry, secretary Tasha, and voluptuous "leading lady" Hedda, who could "do it" for the cameras with anyone or anything. Dwight was a local insurance agent.

Stories included gold digger Tammi's marriage to Harvey, whom she thought was worth millions, and her subsequent attempts to have him murdered by her biker boyfriend Blunt (or his identical brothers Blair and Blank); Sergei's riotous attempts to make a hit pornographic film; well-endowed Rafe secretly doing videos for Sergei to make money to keep his customerless shop afloat; and Fanny Sue and Althea's enthusiastic pursuit of the lesbian lifestyle, including a stint hosting "Lesbian Country Karaoke Night" at The Funky Fox.

Strip Mall was executive produced by star Julie Brown, and directed by comedian Bobcat Goldthwait.

STRIP POKER (*Quiz/Audience Participation*)

BROADCAST HISTORY:

USA Network
30 minutes
Original episodes: *2000–2001*
Premiered: *May 9, 2000*

REGULARS:

Graham Elwood
Jennifer Victoria Cole

This sex-drenched late-night game show was based on five-card stud poker, but the real object seemed to be to watch buff young hunks and hunkettes strip down to their undies. There were two teams, one consisting of two guys and the other of two girls, all young and good-looking. In the first two rounds the guys got "girl" questions while the girls had to answer "guy" questions, often of the titillating variety (for example, for the girls: "You were just charged two minutes for hooking; what sport were you playing?" Ans: Hockey). A correct answer won $50 to $100 and a card for the team's hand; wrong answers could lead to losing an item of clothing. In the Lightning Round the cards were dispensed with and the teams got a succession of pop-culture and trivia questions, with right answers winning money and wrong answers meaning that team members had to take off more items of clothing. All of this was accompanied by loud music, dancing, and whoops and hoots from the audience. Needless to say, everyone came dressed with plenty of layers, but at the end both teams often stripped off whatever they still had on (down to the undies, this being basic cable, after all) and boogied frantically.

Graham was the smarmy host and Jennifer, his sexpot assistant.

STRONG MEDICINE (*Medical Drama*)

BROADCAST HISTORY:

Lifetime
60 minutes
Original episodes: *2000–*
Premiered: *July 23, 2000*

CAST:

Dr. Luisa "Lu" Magdalena Delgado ..... Rosa Blasi
Dr. Dana Stowe (2000–2002) .... Janine Turner
Dr. Andy Campbell (2002–) .. Patricia Richardson
Lana Hawkins .... Jenifer Lewis
Nurse Peter Riggs .... Josh Coxx
Dr. Nick Biancavilla .... Brennan Elliott
Dr. Robert Jackson .... Philip Casnoff
Marc Delgado (2000–2001) ... Paul Robert Santiago
Marc Delgado (2001–) .... Chris Marquette

Rittenhouse Women's Health Clinic in Philadelphia was the setting for this earnest medical drama that tackled many women's health issues in its dramatic, *ER*-like stories. The clinic's original codirectors were Lu, a feisty product of the inner city whose storefront clinic had been absorbed into Rittenhouse, and Dana, a rather icy, Harvard-educated research physician whose emphasis was more on the disease than on the person. Of course they clashed, learned from each other, and ultimately worked together to help the women, rich and poor, who came through their doors. Lana was the saucy, worldly-wise receptionist, Peter the hunky male nurse-midwife with a sensitive side, Nick the brash young resident, and Jackson the uptight but supportive chief of staff. Marc was Lu's teenage son by a past relationship.

There were several continuing stories during the early seasons. Lu dealt with Marc's long-absent father, Bill, and later was date-raped by a prominent surgeon. Dana and Nick were romantic for a time; after trying unsuccessfully to become pregnant, she eventually adopted two young girls (one of them HIV-positive) and moved to Virginia to be with her family. She was replaced by Andy Campbell, a very different kind of doctor and former army colonel who brought discipline and field-hospital smarts to Rittenhouse. Andy had to deal with a tense family life involving two daughters and a bitter, unemployed husband.

Strong Medicine was created by Whoopi Goldberg, who appeared in the pilot episode as Dr. Lydia Emerson, the eminent physician who first brought Lu and Dana together.

STRUCK BY LIGHTNING (*Situation Comedy*)

FIRST TELECAST: *September 19, 1979*
LAST TELECAST: *October 3, 1979*

BROADCAST HISTORY:

Sep 1979–Oct 1979, CBS Wed 8:30–9:00

CAST:

Ted Stein .... Jeffrey Kramer
Frank .... Jack Elam
Nora .... Millie Slavin
Glenn Diamond .... Bill Erwin
Brian .... Jeff Cotler
Walt Calvin .... Richard Stahl

Jack Elam played Frankenstein for laughs in this extremely short-lived comedy. "Frank" was the caretaker of the ramshackle Brightwater Inn, on the Old Boston Post Road in modern-day rural Massachusetts. Ted Stein, a young science teacher who had recently inherited the inn, planned to sell it until he found out that Frank was in fact the 231-year-old Frankenstein monster, and that he, Ted, was the great-great-grandson of the original Dr. Frankenstein. Frank convinced Ted to keep the inn open and try to re-create his ancestor's life-sustaining formula. Unlike the monster of legend, Frank was kind and gentle, if a bit clumsy. Hanging out around the inn was Nora, who had been running the place before Ted arrived, her young son, Brian, a long-time boarder named Glenn, and real-estate agent Walt Calvin, who wanted Ted to sell the place through him.

Struck by Lightning wasn't, and the program was canceled after only three telecasts.

STU ERWIN SHOW, THE (*Situation Comedy*)

FIRST TELECAST: *October 21, 1950*
LAST TELECAST: *April 13, 1955*

BROADCAST HISTORY:

Oct 1950–Sep 1951, ABC Sat 7:30–8:00
Oct 1951–Apr 1952, ABC Fri 8:30–9:00
May 1952–Oct 1954, ABC Fri 7:30–8:00
Oct 1954–Apr 1955, ABC Wed 8:30–9:00

CAST:

Stu Erwin .... Himself
June Erwin .... June Collyer
Jackie Erwin .... Sheila James
Joyce Erwin (1950–1954) .... Ann Todd
Joyce Erwin (1954–1955) .... Merry Anders
Willie .... Willie Best
Harry (1954–1955) .... Harry Hayden
Jimmy Clark (1954–1955) .... Martin Milner

This was perhaps TV's leading bumbling-father series in the 1950s. Stu Erwin had made a long career of similar roles in movies and on radio before he came to TV in 1950. He was perfect for the role: he looked and acted like a well-meaning, folksy, but completely incompetent middle-aged suburban parent.

Stu was principal of Hamilton High School, which often served to get him involved in various civic activities. But most of the action was around the Erwins' own home, where Stu's every attempt to fix or improve things, surprise someone, or bring up the kids turned to disaster. Wife June (played by Erwin's real-life wife, June Collyer) generally came to the rescue. Teenage Joyce and tomboy Jackie rounded out the family, while Willie was the handyman and various neighbors came and went.

In 1954 Joyce began going steady with Jimmy Clark, and in a December telecast they were married. Also in the 1954–1955 season the producers made an effort to portray Stu as a little less blundering than he had been—something devoutly wished for by actor Erwin—but the series had run its course by early 1955.

The series was first known as *Life with the Erwins*, and later *The Trouble with Father* (which continued as its subtitle). During the final season, to emphasize the changes, it became *The New Stu Erwin Show*.

STUDIO 5-B (*Drama*)

FIRST TELECAST: *January 24, 1989*
LAST TELECAST: *February 5, 1989*
BROADCAST HISTORY:

Jan 1989, ABC Tue 9:00–10:00
Jan 1989–Feb 1989, ABC Sun 8:00–9:00

CAST:

Carla Montgomery .... Kerrie Keane
Gail Browning .... Wendy Crewson
Samantha ("Sam") Hurley .... Kim Myers
Jake Gallagher .... Justin Deas
David Chase .... Kenneth David Gilman
Douglas Hayward .... George Grizzard
Rosemary .... Kate Zentall
Woody .... William Thomas, Jr.
Lionel Goodman .... Jeffrey Tambor
J. J. McMillan .... David Ackroyd

The high-powered world of a TV network morning show was a soap opera behind the scenes in this short-lived series. All the stock characters were there: Carla, the ruthless anchor; Gail, the honest producer; Sam, the innocent newcomer; Jake, her former lover who showed up on the eve of her marriage; David, who was locked in an ugly divorce and custody battle; Douglas, the over-the-hill commentator; Lionel, the manipulative executive producer. It wasn't so safe for the show's guests, either—one was exposed as a hoax, another murdered on camera. Perhaps the show should have been called *Good Grief, America*?

STUDIO 57 (*Dramatic Anthology*)

FIRST TELECAST: *September 21, 1954*
LAST TELECAST: *September 6, 1955*
BROADCAST HISTORY:

Sep 1954–Oct 1954, DUM Tue 9:00–9:30
Oct 1954–Sep 1955, DUM Tue 8:30–9:00

This filmed dramatic series had few distinctions—the scripts were weak, the actors generally lesser known (at the time)—except that it was one of the last regularly scheduled series ever carried on the crumbling DuMont network. Only *What's the Story*, among non-sports series, lasted a few weeks longer. The title derived from the sponsor, "Heinz 57 Varieties."

Stories on *Studio 57* were generally mysteries or melodramas, set in various historical periods. Among the actors and actresses appearing were Craig Stevens, Natalie Wood, Hugh O'Brian, Pat Carroll, Peter Graves, Charles Coburn, and Brian Keith.

STUDIO 59, see *Into the Night*

STUDIO ONE (*Dramatic Anthology*)

FIRST TELECAST: *November 7, 1948*
LAST TELECAST: *September 29, 1958*
BROADCAST HISTORY:

Nov 1948–Mar 1949, CBS Sun 7:30–8:30
Mar 1949–May 1949, CBS Sun 7:00–8:00
May 1949–Sep 1949, CBS Wed 10:00–11:00
Sep 1949–Sep 1958, CBS Mon 10:00–11:00

COMMERCIAL SPOKESPERSON:

Betty Furness (1949–1958)

When *Studio One* premiered on CBS radio in the spring of 1947, there was little immediate concern at the network over the possible incursion of television as a competing medium. Little priority was given to TV, as CBS did not yet have a TV network. All that changed after the success of NBC's video coverage of the 1947 World Series. There was a crash development program at CBS and one of the principal components in that development was to be a live dramatic-anthology series. The radio version of *Studio One* lasted less than a year, but under the dynamic early leadership of producer Worthington Miner the new TV version became a major success, lasting for almost a full decade.

Miner's approach to television was somewhat different from that of many of the other producers of early dramatic shows. His concern was with the visual impact of the stories, for television was a visual medium, and he placed a greater emphasis on that than on the literary merit of the story. It was not that he produced second-rate plays—to the contrary, many of them were adaptations of classics and from the best young writers available (Miner personally did many of the adaptations during his tenure with *Studio One*)—but Miner's major contribution to television drama was more in his experimentation with camera techniques and other innovations in what the viewer saw, rather than in what was heard.

The premiere telecast of *Studio One*, on November 7, 1948, was an adaptation of the mystery play *The Storm*, starring stage and screen actress Margaret

Sullavan, one of the few established stars who was willing to perform on the new medium, especially considering the lowly pay (a maximum of $500 was budgeted for talent on early telecasts). The budgetary problems resulted in other interesting innovations. *Julius Caesar* was done twice in the spring of 1949, with Robert Keith in the lead and young Charlton Heston in a minor role, but lack of money forced the producers to stage it in modern dress. In 1955, with more cash available, *Julius Caesar* was done for a third time, in traditional period costumes, with Theodore Bikel starring.

Studio One had gone on the air without a sponsor, but it gained one in Westinghouse Electric in early 1949. On Westinghouse's third telecast the commercials were done by an actress named Betty Furness. She went on to become the most recognized and famous commercial spokesperson in the history of television. She would remain with the series until its cancellation in 1958 and continued with its successor, *Westinghouse Desilu Playhouse.* The picture of her demonstrating a range or opening a refrigerator and the slogan "You Can Be Sure if It's Westinghouse" were ingrained with a generation of Americans.

In the early years of *Studio One*, three performers were seen far more often than any others—Charlton Heston, Mary Sinclair, and Maria Riva—each with the lead roles in at least a dozen plays. Heston starred in adaptations of *Of Human Bondage*, *Jane Eyre* with Miss Sinclair, *The Taming of the Shrew*, with Phyllis Kirk, and *Wuthering Heights*, again with Miss Sinclair, and many lesser-known plays. Many of the better plays were repeated. The premiere presentation, *The Storm,* was redone in 1949 with Marsha Hunt in the lead role; *Jane Eyre* was done again in 1952; "Flowers from a Stranger" starred Yul Brynner in both 1949 and 1950; and *Julius Caesar*, as mentioned above, was done three times.

Doing live shows often presented problems. In a 1953 story, "Dry Run," whole sections of a submarine were built in the studio and the entire cast was almost electrocuted when the water that was used for special effects got very close to the power cables. Many young directors, such as Frank Schaffner, George Roy Hill, Sidney Lumet, and Paul Nickell, got their baptism under fire with this hectic live series. Authors like Rod Serling, Gore Vidal, Paul Monash, and Reginald Rose contributed teleplays for *Studio One* and it was Rose's "The Twelve Angry Men" in 1954 that won Emmys for writing (Rose), direction (Frank Schaffner), and performance by an actor in a drama (Bob Cummings).

Two months after "The Twelve Angry Men," another episode of *Studio One* aired that is remembered not for its dramatic merit, but for a song. The producers were planning to do a drama about skulduggery in the record industry and they needed a song, so they turned to Mitch Miller, head of recording for CBS' subsidiary, Columbia Records. Miller gave them an obscure ballad called "Let Me Go, Devil," and urged that it be sung on the soundtrack by an unknown songstress rather than by an established star, to heighten the dramatic impact. With remarkable foresight he then saw to it that, prior to the telecast, record stores were well stocked with her Columbia recording of the song.

There was little demand for the record until the night of the telecast (November 15, 1954). Now called "Let Me Go, Lover," and emotionally sung by Joan Weber, it was woven skillfully throughout the drama. The next morning record stores were deluged with customers wanting "that song that was on TV last night"—and "Let Me Go, Lover" became a phenomenal hit, selling more than 500,000 copies in the next five days (it eventually sold over one million). It was one of the few times in the history of television that a single telecast was directly responsible for a major song hit.

People appeared on *Studio One* who may now seem to have been somewhat out of place. Newsman Mike Wallace appeared in two dramas. Jackie Gleason and Art Carney, while still doing their live variety show, took time to star in a serious drama called "The Laugh Maker" in the spring of 1953, and later made other occasional appearances on the show separately. Ironically, Elizabeth Montgomery showed up on *Studio One* a few times in the mid-1950s. Her father was the host of *Robert Montgomery Presents*, the NBC Monday night dramatic showcase that was in direct competition with *Studio One* for most of its run. Even Edward R. Murrow was featured on the series, though not as an actor. He was the narrator of a 1957 documentary-drama, "The Night America Trembled," about Orson Welles's 1938 broadcast of "War of the Worlds."

With the first telecast in January 1958, *Studio One* moved to Hollywood, with the title appropriately changed to *Studio One in Hollywood*. It had moved because that was where the talent was, and the facilities for production were better than in New York. It was still done live, but only remained on the air for another nine months. Live drama was dying, as was New York origination of TV series.

In its decade on the air, *Studio One* presented nearly 500 plays. Literally thousands of actors and actresses appeared, but only a few of them were featured in at least half a dozen plays. Other than those already mentioned above, they were Katherine Bard, Richard Kiley, Priscilla Gillette, Judson Laire, Harry Townes, John Forsythe, Nina Foch, Hildy Parks, Sheppard Strudwick, Leslie Nielsen, James Daly, Everett Sloane, Betsy Palmer, Skip Homeier, James Gregory, Cathleen Nesbitt, Edward Andrews, Barbara O'Neill, Burt Brinckerhoff, Cliff Norton, Stanley Ridges, and Felicia Montealegre.

During the summers, when the regular *Studio One* production team was vacationing, the series was variously titled *Summer Theatre, Westinghouse Summer Theatre*, and *Studio One Summer Theatre*.

STUDIO 22 (*Magazine*)

BROADCAST HISTORY:

Syndicated only
30 minutes
Produced: *1991–1992*
Released: *September 1991*

ANCHOR:

Steve Kmetko
Dorothy Lucey

REGULARS:

Dennis Cunningham
Carol Martin

This weekly *Entertainment Tonight* clone was a collection of show business news, gossip, interviews, and features. Dennis Cunningham contributed reviews of films and videos, and Carol Martin offered celebrity interviews. Produced by the CBS television station division. *Studio 22* had aired for a year on the CBS-owned stations before going national in the fall of 1991. Anchors Kmetko and Lucey worked for KCBS-TV in Los Angeles, and Cunningham and Martin (who had replaced Jill Rappaport when the show went national) were seen on WCBS-TV in New York.

STUDS (*Comedy/Audience Participation*)

BROADCAST HISTORY:

Syndicated only
30 minutes
Produced: *1991–1993*
Released: *Summer 1991*

HOST:

Mark DeCarlo

Studs was a "dirty talk" cross between *The Dating Game* and *Love Connection*. Each night two guys and three gals discussed their dating experiences with each other, with much talk of the guys' great butts and hands up the gals' skirts. Each of the guys had gone out on a blind date with each of the three gals and, on the show, the guy who proved he knew the most about the gals was crowned "King Stud" and could win a fancy date paid for by the show. The gals had been asked various questions about the guys prior to the show—about phone impressions, first impressions after they had met, what they remembered most about the date, how romantic the guys were, which of the guys would be most likely to do various things, etc.—and the guys got points for figuring out which opinions of them had come from which gal. At the end of the show the guy with the most points was asked which of the gals he wanted to go out with again and, if she had also picked him, *Studs* sent them off on a fancy date. In case of ties, both guys got to pick.

STUDS LONIGAN (*Drama*)

FIRST TELECAST: *March 7, 1979*
LAST TELECAST: *March 21, 1979*

BROADCAST HISTORY:

Mar 1979, NBC Wed 9:00–11:00

CAST:

Studs Lonigan .... Harry Hamlin
Mrs. Lonigan .... Colleen Dewhurst
Mr. Lonigan .... Charles Durning
Martin .... John Friedrich
Lucy Scanlon .... Lisa Pelikan
Danny O'Neill .... Brad Dourif
Weary .... David Wilson
Loretta .... Jessica Harper
Fran .... Devon Ericson
Eileen .... Laurie Heineman
Paulie .... Michael Mullins
Catherine Banahan .... Diana Scarwid
Davey Cohen .... Sam Weisman
Phil Rolfe .... Jed Cooper

Set in Chicago, *Studs Lonigan* was the saga of an Irish-American family from the latter stages of World War I until the onset of the Great Depression, in 1930. It was an earthy story centering on young Studs, who was struggling into adulthood in a brawling city full of temptations. He watched as his buddies drifted away into various careers and greater success than he himself found. His social life was split between two extremes—quiet, sensitive Catherine and lusty, sensual Lucy. Underlying it all, as the prologue stated, was "a passionate and realistic echo of urban America as it used to be."

Studs Lonigan was based on the trilogy written by James T. Farrell. It aired as one of the *NBC Novels for Television*.

STUDS' PLACE (*Variety*)

FIRST TELECAST: *November 26, 1949*
LAST TELECAST: *January 28, 1952*

BROADCAST HISTORY:

Nov 1949–Dec 1949, NBC Sat 8:45–9:00
Apr 1950–May 1950, NBC Thu 8:00–8:30
May 1950–Aug 1950, NBC Thu 8:30–9:00
Oct 1950–Aug 1951, ABC Fri 10:30–11:00
Aug 1951–Jan 1952, ABC Mon 10:30–11:00

CAST:

Studs Terkel .... Himself
Grace, the Waitress (1950) .... Beverly Younger
Wynn (1950–1952) .... Win Stracke
Mr. Lord (1950) .... Phil Lord
Mr. Denby (1950) .... Jonathan Hole
Pianist (1950–1952) .... Chet Roble

Studs Terkel presided over this affable program of songs and stories, which was at first set in Studs' bar in New York, with Studs as the bartender. This version ran only about a month, and was then incorporated as a regular segment in the Saturday night series *Saturday Square*. When *Saturday Square* was canceled Studs returned again with his own series, this time cast as the proprietor of a Chicago barbecue restaurant frequented by a number of regulars. Among them were Wynn the folk-singing handyman, and Chet the jazz pianist. Both series were loosely plotted, with Studs' garrulous, philosophical ramblings the center of attention.

Telecast from Chicago.

STUMP THE AUTHORS (*Stories*)

FIRST TELECAST: *January 15, 1949*
LAST TELECAST: *April 2, 1949*

BROADCAST HISTORY:

Jan 1949–Apr 1949, ABC Sat 9:00–9:30

EDITOR:

Syd Breeze

AUTHORS:

Lou Zara
Dorothy Day
Jack Payne
Angel Casey

Ad-lib storytelling session in which three or four authors tried to spin yarns based on props given to them, which they had never seen before. From Chicago.

STUMP THE STARS, see *Pantomime Quiz*

STUNTMASTERS (*Documentary*)

BROADCAST HISTORY:

Syndicated only
60 minutes
Produced: *1991–1992* (26 episodes)
Released: *September 1991*

HOST:

Jack Scalia
Kendra King

The activities of thrill-seeking daredevils were chronicled in this weekly series. Among the recurring features were professional movie stunts, including detailed coverage of the preparations and setup, as well as the actual stunts; profiles of and interviews with professional stuntmen; historic film footage of famous stunts of the past; and new stunts created especially for the show. Viewers were encouraged to send in their ideas for "Stuntmasters Challenge" stunts. If the producers decided to use them, the viewers submitting the ideas were given free trips to Hollywood to see their stunts done.

Reminiscent of the 1972 Chuck Connors series *Thrill Seekers.*

STYLE & SUBSTANCE (*Situation Comedy*)
FIRST TELECAST: *January 5, 1998*
LAST TELECAST: *September 2, 1998*
BROADCAST HISTORY:
Jan 1998–Feb 1998, CBS Mon 9:30–10:00
Jul 1998–Sep 1998, CBS Wed 8:30–9:00
CAST:
Chelsea Stevens .... Jean Smart
Jane Sokol .... Nancy McKeon
Mr. John .... Joseph Maher
Trudy .... Linda Kash
Terry .... Heath Hyche
Earl .... Alan Autry

Chelsea Stevens was a dynamo whose knowledge of cooking, decorating, and entertaining had made her rich and famous. She had an estate in Connecticut and ran a media conglomerate that produced videos, books, a magazine, and a TV show. Unfortunately, she had virtually no people skills and alienated almost everyone with her lack of tact, need to be in control, and constant meddling in their personal lives. Chelsea's newly hired producer, Jane, was determined to make Chelsea more human, while minimizing the extent to which her boss interfered with her own personal life. She was not completely successful. With Jane's help Chelsea did try to change her self-absorbed image, but things didn't always go as planned. When Jane tutored a current-affairs ignorant Chelsea for an appearance on a *Politically Incorrect* type show, the topic was changed at the last minute. When Chelsea hosted a fund-raiser for a drug rehabilitation center, she accidentally served "magic mushrooms," leaving her social register guests stoned and confused. Others who worked for Chelsea were Mr. John, her gay interior designer; Trudy, the cynical food stylist; Terry, her gentle but incompetent secretary; and Earl, her muscular handyman.

This was the first of two CBS series parodying Martha Stewart that aired during the 1997–1998 season. When the second, *The Simple Life,* was canceled, *Style & Substance* took over the vacated time period.

SUDDENLY SUSAN (*Situation Comedy*)
FIRST TELECAST: *September 19, 1996*
LAST TELECAST: *June 27, 2000*
BROADCAST HISTORY:
Sep 1996–Jan 1997, NBC Thu 9:30–10:00
Feb 1997–May 1997, NBC Thu 8:30–9:00
Jun 1997–Aug 1997, NBC Thu 9:30–10:00
Jun 1997–Jul 1997, NBC Mon 9:30–10:00
Jul 1997–Jul 1998, NBC Mon 8:00–8:30
Jul 1998–Aug 1998, NBC Thu 8:30–9:00
Sep 1998–May 1999, NBC Mon 8:00–8:30
Jun 1999–Jul 1999, NBC Mon 8:00–9:00
Jul 1999–Jan 2000, NBC Mon 8:00–8:30
Jun 2000, NBC Tue 8:00–8:30
CAST:
Susan Keane .... Brooke Shields
Jack Richmond (1996–1999) .... Judd Nelson
Vicki Groener .... Kathy Griffin
Luis Rivera .... Nestor Carbonell
Todd Stites (1996–1999) .... David Strickland
Helen Keane (Nana) .... Barbara Barrie
**Pete (1996–1999)* .... Bill Stevenson
Maddy Piper (1997–1999) ...... Andrea Bendewald
Ian Maxtone-Graham (1999–2000) .... Eric Idle
Nate Knaborski (1999–2000) .... Currie Graham
Oliver Brown (1999–2000) .... Rob Estes
Miranda Charles (1999–2000) .... Sherri Shepherd
*Occasional

Young San Francisco copy editor Susan led a too-perfect life until she dumped her rich but boring fiancé at the altar and decided to try making it on her own in this bright workplace comedy. "Suddenly, Susan, you're interesting," growled her demanding boss Jack, promoting her to columnist at the hip local magazine, *The Gate.* Jack, interestingly, was the brother of her ex-fiancé. In her column, "Suddenly Susan," eager, innocent Susan wrote about her exploits in the singles world, including disastrous dates and the strange people she met. Vicki was her spunky, neurotic coworker, with whom she shared many adventures; Luis the darkly handsome photographer, who was very protective of Susan; and Todd the horny but harmless young music critic whose fixation with MTV had given him an extremely limited attention span. Susan's conservative parents Liz and Bill were aghast that she had walked away from all that money, but her wise, salty grandmother, Nana, said "Go for it!" egging her on. There was continuing sexual tension with Jack, an eccentric boss who had a rock climbing wall in his office, and after he divorced his shrewish wife Margo, he and Susan began an off-and-on relationship. Joining the gang in the third season was investigative reporter Maddy (previously a recurring character), who was Susan's high school rival and continued to irk her. Maddy later became Luis' love interest. Pete was the gay mailboy, and Susan's rarely seen parents were played in most appearances by Swoosie Kurtz and Ray Baker.

The third-season finale was a tribute to actor David Strickland, who had committed suicide; in it his character Todd was missing, and in searching for him the gang discovered many heartwarming facts about him they did not know. At the end of the episode they got a call from the police, but it was not clear what had happened to him. The fourth season brought major changes. *The Gate* was sold to eccentric former publishing whiz kid Ian, who was determined to turn it into a sleazy men's style magazine. He belittled everybody, especially Susan ("the modesty of your talent"), causing her to quit, and brought in star sportswriter Nate, bad-boy celebrity photographer Oliver and young black assistant Miranda. Susan came crawling back and was rehired, thanks to the intervention of Oliver, whom she later began dating. Their off-and-on romance lasted throughout the season, and in the series finale Oliver proposed but Susan was torn between marrying him and taking a glamorous New York job offer. The finale was not initially seen due to NBC's abrupt cancelation of the show. It finally aired, unbilled, on Christmas night, 2000, at 2 A.M. with three other previously unseen episodes.

This was a first series for famous actress Brooke Shields, who mined comedy by mocking her own glamorous image (and tall stature) in a manner reminiscent of Cybill Shepherd *(Moonlighting)* and Candice Bergen *(Murphy Brown)*.

SUE THOMAS, F.B.EYE. (*Crime Drama*)

FIRST TELECAST: *October 13, 2002*

LAST TELECAST:

BROADCAST HISTORY:

Oct 2002– , PAX Sun 9:00–10:00

Oct 2002–Dec 2002, PAX Mon 8:00–9:00

Jan 2003– , PAX Mon 9:00–10:00

CAST:

Sue Thomas .... Deanne Bray

Jack Hudson.......................... Yannick Bisson

Lucy Dotson.......................... Enuka Okuma

Dimitrius Gans.......................... Marc Gomes

Bobby Manning.......................... Rick Peters

Tara Williams .... Tara Samuel

Myles Leland III.......................... Ted Atherton

Ted Garrett.......................... Eugene Clark

THEME:

"Who Am I," performed by Jessica Andrews

After graduating from college Sue Thomas, a spunky deaf girl from the Midwest, moved to Washington where she started work with the F.B.I.—in a boring desk job analyzing fingerprints. Everything changed when she met handsome agent Jack Hudson who, after discovering how well she could read lips, convinced his boss to have her transferred to his surveillance team. Jack, to whom she was attracted, served as her trainer, and though she was supposed to work in support she sometimes got involved in the field taking down criminals. Other members of the team were Lucy and Tara, who worked primarily in the office, and Dimitrius, Bobby and Myles, who did most of the fieldwork. Almost everyone was friendly and supportive except for obnoxious, self-centered Myles, who resented her presence and took a while to come around. Sue and Lucy became close friends and, despite Sue's misgivings, they found an apartment to share. In November their original boss departed and was replaced by Ted Garrett. Levi was Sue's hearing-ear dog.

Based on the life of the real Sue Thomas who, despite being deaf since childhood, learned to read lips and eventually had a career working surveillance for the F.B.I. Actress Deanne Bray was herself deaf.

SUGAR AND SPICE (*Situation Comedy*)

FIRST TELECAST: *March 30, 1990*

LAST TELECAST: *May 25, 1990*

BROADCAST HISTORY:

Mar 1990–May 1990, CBS Fri 9:30–10:00

May 1990, CBS Fri 8:30–9:00

CAST:

Loretta Fontaine .... Loretta Devine

Vickilyn Fontaine Clayton ...... Vickilyn Reynolds

Toby Reed.......................... LaVerne Anderson

Ginger .... Dana Hill

Bonnie Buttram .... Stephanie Hodge

Cliff Buttram .... Gerrit Graham

Monsieur Jacques.......................... Leslie Jordan

The small town of Ponca City, Oklahoma, was the setting for this blue collar series about two middle-aged black sisters. Loretta and Vickilyn had very different personalities and outlooks on life. Vickilyn was conservative and quiet, a divorcee making her living with Small World Miniatures, a mail-order business run out of her converted garage. Her gregarious sister Loretta, an aspiring singer with a roving eye for good-looking men, was biding time working as a hostess at Cafe Jacques. Living with them was their teenage niece Toby, the only child of their late sister, whose good intentions were sometimes derailed when she took bad advice from her best friend Ginger. Bonnie, who had a tempestuous relationship with her trucker husband Cliff, was Vickilyn's assistant at Small World Miniatures.

SUGAR HILL TIMES (*Musical Variety*)

FIRST TELECAST: *September 13, 1949*

LAST TELECAST: *October 20, 1949*

BROADCAST HISTORY:

Sep 1949, CBS Tue 8:00–9:00

Oct 1949, CBS Thu 8:30–9:00

REGULARS:

Willie Bryant

Harry Bellafonte

Timmie Rogers

The Jubileers

Don Redman and His Orchestra

Sugar Hill Times was one of network television's first, short-lived attempts at showcasing black talent. All of the performers in the live weekly musical variety show were black. It aired three times as a full-hour show, and each time had a different title, premiering as *Uptown Jubilee*, changing to *Harlem Jubilee*, and finally settling on *Sugar Hill Times*, the title it also used during its two half-hour telecasts on October 6 and 20. It may have been an unintentional oversight on the part of the CBS press department at the time, but every press release for the show spelled singer Harry Belafonte's name as it's listed above, with two *l's*.

SUGAR TIME! (*Situation Comedy*)

FIRST TELECAST: *August 13, 1977*

LAST TELECAST: *May 29, 1978*

BROADCAST HISTORY:

Aug 1977–Sep 1977, ABC Sat 8:30–9:00

Apr 1978–May 1978, ABC Mon 8:00–8:30

CAST:

Maxx.......................... Barbi Benton

Maggie .... Marianne Black

Diane .... Didi Carr

Al Marks .... Wynn Irwin

Paul Landson.......................... Mark Winkworth

Popular singer/composer Paul Williams, wrote original songs and was musical supervisor for this comedy series about three beautiful young girls who were aspiring rock singers. The talented trio called themselves Sugar, and shared an apartment in California where they were attempting to launch their act, without pay, at Al Marks' Tryout Room. Maxx, beautiful and naive, worked as a hat-check girl: Diane, a wisecracking native of the Bronx, was a dental hygienist; and Maggie, the practical one, taught dancing to children. A constant threat to the group's success was Diane's indecision over whether she should marry her favorite dentist.

SUGARFOOT (*Western*)

FIRST TELECAST: *September 17, 1957*

LAST TELECAST: *July 3, 1961*

BROADCAST HISTORY:

Sep 1957–Sep 1960, ABC Tue 7:30–8:30

Oct 1960–Jul 1961, ABC Mon 7:30–8:30

CAST:

Tom "Sugarfoot" Brewster .... Will Hutchins

Western about the exploits of a young correspondence-school law student who rode west in search of adventure. Unfortunately, Tom Brewster was somewhat inept as a cowboy, and he promptly earned the nickname "Sugarfoot"—one grade lower than a tenderfoot—in the first episode. Undeterred, and with a redeeming sense of humor, he set out to lasso some outlaws and round up a few pretty girls, if possible.

Although it was a Western in the traditional sense, with plenty of action, *Sugarfoot* always had a light touch which set it apart from most examples of the genre. It ran on an alternate-week basis with *Cheyenne* from 1957–1959, with *Bronco* from 1959–1960, and then became one of three rotating elements of the *Cheyenne* anthology for its final season.

SUMMER BROTHERS SMOTHERS SHOW, THE (*Comedy/Variety*)

FIRST TELECAST: *June 23, 1968*

LAST TELECAST: *September 8, 1968*

BROADCAST HISTORY:

Jun 1968–Sep 1968, CBS Sun 9:00–10:00

REGULARS:

Glen Campbell

Pat Paulsen

Leigh French

John Hartford

The Jimmy Joyce Singers

Nelson Riddle & His Orchestra

This 1968 summer replacement for *The Smothers Brothers Comedy Hour* starred country singer Glen Campbell, who was later to get a regular series of his own, and two of the regulars from the Smothers Brothers group, comics Pat Paulsen and Leigh French. Regular features of the show were comedy sketches featuring Leigh French as a hippie, and Pat Paulsen doing improbable editorials and campaigning for President.

SUMMER CINEMA, see *Movies—Prior to 1961*

SUMMER FAIR, see *ABC Dramatic Shorts—1952–1953*

SUMMER FOCUS (*Documentary*)

FIRST TELECAST: *May 18, 1967*

LAST TELECAST: *August 31, 1967*

BROADCAST HISTORY:

May 1967–Aug 1967, ABC Thu 10:00–11:00

This series of documentaries included an examination of political protest in America, a debate on the limits of free speech in a democracy, a pictorial study of the paintings of Leonardo Da Vinci, an examination of health-care problems in America, and a look at the pollution problems facing both small and large cities.

SUMMER FUN (*Comedy Anthology*)

FIRST TELECAST: *July 22, 1966*

LAST TELECAST: *September 2, 1966*

BROADCAST HISTORY:

Jul 1966–Sep 1966, ABC Fri 8:00–8:30

ABC aired a collection of unsold pilots for projected situation comedy series for seven consecutive Fridays during the summer of 1966. Among them were shows starring Cliff Arquette, Bert Lahr, and Shelley Fabares.

SUMMER HOLIDAY (*Music*)

FIRST TELECAST: *June 24, 1954*

LAST TELECAST: *September 9, 1954*

BROADCAST HISTORY:

Jun 1954–Sep 1954, CBS Thu 7:45–8:00

Jul 1954–Aug 1954, CBS Tue 7:45–8:00

REGULARS:

Merv Griffin

Betty Ann Grove

This twice-weekly summer replacement for both *The Jo Stafford Show* and *The Jane Froman Show* was a live musical interlude that filled the remainder of the half hour in which CBS aired its network news program. The Tuesday edition was titled *Summer Holiday* and the Thursday edition *Song Snapshots on a Summer Holiday*. The format had the two singing stars portray camera bugs on an around-the-world tour, with sets and costumes of an appropriate nature, all to serve as a backdrop for their solos and duets.

SUMMER IN THE PARK, see *Strawhatters, The*

SUMMER NIGHT THEATER (*Anthology*)

FIRST TELECAST: *July 7, 1953*

LAST TELECAST: *July 28, 1953*

BROADCAST HISTORY:

Jul 1953, DUM Tue 10:00–10:30

A four-week series of filmed dramas, starring Gale Storm, Lloyd Bridges, and others. The series continued to be seen locally in New York for the remainder of the summer.

SUMMER PLAYHOUSE (*Anthology*)

FIRST TELECAST: *July 6, 1954*

LAST TELECAST: *September 6, 1965*

BROADCAST HISTORY:

Jul 1954–Aug 1954, NBC Tue 9:00–9:30

Jul 1957–Sep 1957, NBC Tue 9:30–10:00

Jul 1964–Sep 1964, CBS Sat 9:30–10:00

Jun 1965–Sep 1965, CBS Mon 8:30–9:00

HOST:

Nelson Case (1954)

Jane Wyman (1957)

These were all summer anthology series used to fill time until the fall season started. On the two occasions a program with the title *Summer Playhouse* aired on NBC, the episodes were reruns from other anthology series. The two CBS versions in the 1960s were made up of unsold pilots for projected regular series.

SUMMER SHOWCASE (*Documentary*)

FIRST TELECAST: *June 28, 1988*

LAST TELECAST: *August 30, 1988*

BROADCAST HISTORY:

Jun 1988–Aug 1988, NBC Tue 10:00–11:00

A series of mini-documentaries from NBC News. In most episodes two or three different reporters treated different aspects of the same story. For the debut, entitled "Of Macho and Men," Lucky Severson and Deborah Norville covered such subjects as male stereotypes in media, husband-beating, role shifts due to the increasing number of working wives, and how the law sometimes treats men more harshly than women. Subsequent telecasts dealt with handguns, aging, pension abuses, and "Women Behind Bars."

SUMMER SPORTS SPECTACULAR, THE (*Sports Anthology*)

FIRST TELECAST: *April 27, 1961*
LAST TELECAST: *September 28, 1961*
BROADCAST HISTORY:
Apr 1961–Sep 1961, CBS Thu 7:30–8:30
HOST:
Bud Palmer

CBS had premiered a weekly sports anthology on Sunday afternoons in January 1960 titled *The Sunday Sports Spectacular*. During the summer of 1961 it moved to Thursday evenings as *The Summer Sports Spectacular*. Host Bud Palmer covered a different type of sporting event each week. The premiere telecast was a figure-skating memorial tribute to the members of the 1960 U.S. Olympic figure skating team who had died tragically in an airplane crash. Subsequent episodes covered spring training with one of the two brand-new American League Baseball teams—Gene Autry's Los Angeles Angels—coverage of the European soccer championships, the Army-Navy lacrosse game, a gymnastics meet between the U.S. and Japan, and a motorcycle rally. In addition to actual event coverage, each telecast included background on the sport and interviews with participants.

The Sunday Sports Spectacular changed its name to *The CBS Sports Spectacular* in January 1963 and continued to run on a seasonal basis until the fall of 1967. It returned in January 1973 and has been on ever since, changing its name to *CBS Sports Saturday* and *CBS Sports Sunday* when it started airing episodes on both Saturdays and Sundays in the spring of 1981. The name was changed to *Eye on Sports* in 1994, *The CBS Sports Show* in 1995, and back to *The CBS Sports Spectacular* in 1998.

SUMMER SUNDAY U.S.A. (*Newsmagazine*)

FIRST TELECAST: *July 1, 1984*
LAST TELECAST: *September 7, 1984*
BROADCAST HISTORY:
Jul 1984–Sep 1984, NBC Sun 7:00–8:00
ANCHOR:
Andrea Mitchell
Linda Ellerbee

Summer Sunday was one of a long series of attempts by NBC to establish a prime-time newsmagazine program, but its scheduling directly opposite CBS' enormously popular *60 Minutes* was fatal. It was certainly different from NBC's previous efforts, however. The program originated live each week from outdoor locations around the country, and included such features as short quiz segments between the stories and "Trading Places," in which politicians were given a chance to question the reporters.

SUMMER THEATRE, see *Studio One*

SUMMER THEATRE (*Dramatic Anthology*)

FIRST TELECAST: *July 10, 1953*
LAST TELECAST: *September 11, 1953*
BROADCAST HISTORY:
Jul 1953–Sep 1953, ABC Fri 8:00–8:30

This filmed anthology series aired on ABC during the summer of 1953 as the replacement for *The Adventures of Ozzie & Harriet*. The title alternated from week to week because of sponsorship. One week it was *Summer Theatre* and on the alternate week it was *Interlude*. Among the presentations were "Myrt and Marge" with Franklin Pangborn and Lyle Talbot and "Foo Young" with Richard Loo.

SUMMERTIME U.S.A (*Music*)

FIRST TELECAST: *July 7, 1953*
LAST TELECAST: *August 27, 1953*
BROADCAST HISTORY:
Jul 1953–Aug 1953, CBS Tue/Thu 7:45–8:00
REGULARS:
Teresa Brewer
Mel Torme
The Honeydreamers
Ray Bloch & His Orchestra

This series was the 1953 summer replacement for another music series, *Jane Froman's U.S.A. Canteen*. The two stars, Teresa Brewer and Mel Torme, were seen in a different resort setting for each of the live telecasts. The scenic backgrounds ranged from Atlantic City and Niagara Falls on the domestic side, to Rio, Havana, and the Casbah on the international side.

SUNDAY AT HOME (*Music*)

FIRST TELECAST: *July 3, 1949*
LAST TELECAST: *July 31, 1949*
BROADCAST HISTORY:
Jul 1949, NBC Sun 7:15–7:30
REGULARS:
Obey ("Dad") Pickard, banjo, guitar, fiddle
Mom Pickard, autoharp
Obey Pickard, Jr. (Bud)
Charlie Pickard
Ruth Pickard Colwell
Ann Pickard Rhea

A short-lived summer show featuring the singing Pickard family, well-known country radio and recording artists. From a living room set, they sang and played folk songs and old favorites such as "Sourwood Mountain" and "I'm Forever Blowing Bubbles," always ending with a hymn. Filmed in Hollywood and originally seen on local station KNBH.

SUNDAY BEST (*Magazine*)

FIRST TELECAST: *February 3, 1991*
LAST TELECAST: *February 17, 1991*
BROADCAST HISTORY:
Feb 1991, NBC Sun 7:00–8:00
HOST:
Carl Reiner
CONTRIBUTORS:
Jeff Cesario
Linda Ellerbee
Harry Shearer
Merrill Markoe

This three-week wonder, one of the ratings disasters of the 1990–1991 season, seemed to have been devised by the NBC promotion people and accountants. The idea was to show clips from the same week's television shows (great promotion!), excerpts from the previous night's *Saturday Night Live* (more promotion!), plus nostalgic clips from great shows of the past (cheap!). Linda Ellerbee contributed one of her patented irreverent essays, Merrill Markoe filed a field report from an event such as a programming or electronics convention, and Shearer and Cesario did simple comic bits. To further cut costs, "Viewer Video Mail" offered viewers the chance to "write in" by sending NBC homemade video tapes. The first episode concluded with an entire chorus line of beaming, sweater-clad Jane Pauley clones dancing their way through a big plug for the next show on the NBC schedule, Pauley's *Real Life*.

SUNDAY COMICS, THE (*Comedy*)
FIRST TELECAST: *April 28, 1991*
LAST TELECAST: *March 22, 1992*
BROADCAST HISTORY:
Apr 1991–Dec 1991, FOX Sun 10:00–11:00
Feb 1992–Mar 1992, FOX Sun 10:30–11:00
HOST:
Jeff Altman
Lenny Clarke

Unlike *Comic Strip Primetime*, a showcase for standup comics which had preceded it in this time slot, *The Sunday Comics* was a mix of standup comedy, variety acts, and funny film shorts produced by a group of comics that included Bruce Baum, Gilbert Gottfried, Rich Hall, and Rick Overton. Originating primarily from the Palace Theatre in Hollywood, with occasional visits to other locations, this series brought viewers such familiar faces as Franklyn Ajaye, Dennis Wolfberg, Carol Leifer, John Mendoza, Jeff Joseph, Paul Provenza, George Wallace, Judy Tenuta, and Wayne Cotter. Jeff Altman, the original host, left at the end of June to star in *Nurses* on NBC and was replaced by Lenny Clarke, whose own sitcom *(Lenny)* had failed a few months earlier on CBS. When Clarke departed in October, *The Sunday Comics* instituted a policy of using guest hosts. Fox aired edited reruns of *The Sunday Comics* in the spring of 1992.

SUNDAY DATE (*Music*)
FIRST TELECAST: *August 21, 1949*
LAST TELECAST: *October 9, 1949*
BROADCAST HISTORY:
Aug 1949–Oct 1949, NBC Sun 7:15–7:30

Live musical interlude featuring an assortment of young, lesser-known singers and instrumentalists, and set in an imaginary sidewalk cafe just off New York's Central Park.

SUNDAY DINNER (*Situation Comedy*)
FIRST TELECAST: *June 2, 1991*
LAST TELECAST: *July 7, 1991*
BROADCAST HISTORY:
Jun 1991, CBS Sun 8:00–8:30
Jun 1991–Jul 1991, CBS Sun 8:30–9:00
CAST:
Ben Benedict .... Robert Loggia
TT Fagori .... Teri Hatcher
Vicky Benedict .... Martha Gehman
Kenneth Benedict .... Patrick Breen
Diana .... Kari Lizer
Rachel .... Shiri Appleby
Martha Benedict .... Marian Mercer

Set in New York's Long Island, *Sunday Dinner* chronicled the family conflicts caused by the engagement of the 56-year-old widowed owner of a printing business (Ben Benedict) to an environmental activist attorney (TT Fagori), 26 years his junior. His family thought he was crazy and kept referring to TT—behind her back—as "the bimbo." The squabbling Benedict clan consisted of Vicky (age 32), a twice-divorced atheist who had returned to college to get a Ph.D. in microbiology; Diana (30), an often incomprehensible airhead who had tried every fad religion and was still trying to find herself; Kenneth (25), a real estate salesman and aspiring yuppie forever on the lookout for ways to make a quick killing; Martha, Ben's conservative sister who ran his household; and Rachel, Vicky's younger daughter. TT, who deeply loved Ben, was a spiritual woman who talked regularly to God—addressing the deity as "chief"—when trying to sort out her emotions or find ways to deal with problems she was having with Ben's family.

This series was semi-autobiographical for producer Norman Lear, whose third wife was considerably younger than he; it also marked Lear's return to series television after an absence of many years. In an effort to attract an audience, CBS paired *Sunday Dinner* with selected reruns of his classic *All in the Family* on Sunday evenings. Unfortunately, the reruns did better than the new series.

SUNDAY LUCY SHOW, THE, see *I Love Lucy*

SUNDAY MYSTERY HOUR, THE, see *Chevy Mystery Show, The*

SUNDAY NIGHT (*Musical Variety*)
BROADCAST HISTORY:
Syndicated only
60 minutes
Produced: *1987–1990*
Released: *October 1987*
REGULARS:
David Sanborn
Jools Holland (1988–1989)
The Night Music Band (1989–1990)

A hip, unconventional hour of music from *Saturday Night Live* creator Lorne Michaels. The host, jazz musician David Sanborn, was a low-key performer who was more at home playing his saxophone than hosting. The music included everything from jazz and blues to gospel, country, rock, and even classical—sometimes all on the same show. *Sunday Night* was an offbeat hit with critics, who applauded its spare, uncluttered look, live performances, and selection of guests without regard to mainstream popularity. Airing on most stations in the wee hours after midnight on weekends, it never attracted a particularly large audience but was a must-view for its nucleus of devoted fans.

During the second season, Jools Holland, of the British pop group Squeeze, was added as cohost. Holland, a much more outgoing personality than Sanborn, spent much of his time chatting with the week's guest performers! When the show returned for a third season in the fall of 1989, it had a new title, *Michelob Presents Night Music* (Michelob beer was its sole sponsor and this way stations could air it on any night), and with Holland departed, emphasis was returned to the music rather than talk.

SUNDAY SHOWCASE (*Variety*)
FIRST TELECAST: *September 20, 1959*
LAST TELECAST: *May 1, 1960*

BROADCAST HISTORY:

Sep 1959–May 1960, NBC Sun 8:00–9:00

Sunday Showcase was actually a varied series of specials that aired in the 8:00–9:00 P.M. hour on Sunday evenings during the 1959–1960 season. Some of them were dramatic plays, some were comedy variety shows (such as "The Milton Berle Show"), some were musical comedies, and some were historical dramas (such as "Our American Heritage"). Among the other notable telecasts were a two-part version of Budd Schulberg's novel *What Makes Sammy Run* and the premiere offering, a "poetic drama" by S. Lee Pogostin called "People Kill People Sometimes," starring George C. Scott, Geraldine Page, and Jason Robards, Jr.

SUNSET BEAT (*Police Drama*)

FIRST TELECAST: *April 21, 1990*

LAST TELECAST: *April 28, 1990*

BROADCAST HISTORY:

Apr 1990, ABC Sat 8:00–9:00

CAST:

Chic Chesbro .... George Clooney
Tim Kelly .... Michael DeLuise
Bradley Coolidge .... Markus Flanagan
Tucson Smith .... Erik King
Ray Parker .... James Tolkan
Bickford .... Jack McGee

A team of young Los Angeles undercover cops posing as bikers got only two weeks to zoom around town in this quickly canceled series. They did manage to collar a crazed killer who dropped a dead cop from a helicopter onto the stage of a rock concert, and investigate a double murder in the X-rated movie business. Presumably their leather jackets and Harleys were donated to charity.

SUNSHINE (*Situation Comedy*)

FIRST TELECAST: *March 6, 1975*

LAST TELECAST: *June 19, 1975*

BROADCAST HISTORY:

Mar 1975–Jun 1975, NBC Thu 8:00–8:30

CAST:

Sam Hayden .... Cliff DeYoung
Jill .... Elizabeth Cheshire
Weaver .... Bill Mumy
Givits .... Corey Fischer
Nora .... Meg Foster

THEME:

"Sunshine on My Shoulders," by John Denver, Dick Kniss, and Mike Taylor

Set in Vancouver, British Columbia, *Sunshine* was the story of a young widower and his daughter trying to make ends meet. Sam Hayden's wife had died of cancer, leaving him to care for Jill, her five-year-old daughter by a previous marriage. Sam was a composer and, along with his two friends, Weaver and Givits, a member of a singing trio. With his musical career not generating much money, Sam sought all sorts of odd jobs to help support Jill and himself. He also tried to be both mother and father to Jill, who was always on the lookout for a likely candidate to marry her father. Helping Sam out, in addition to his two long-haired partners, was his neighbor and friend Nora. The easy and contemporary lifestyle led by Sam and Jill was cheered by some and condemned by others, and caused concern among those who felt it was not good for Jill's welfare. The title of the series referred to Jill's mother's favorite song.

Based on a CBS TV movie of the same name, which aired on November 9, 1973, with most of the same cast.

SUPER, THE (*Situation Comedy*)

FIRST TELECAST: *June 21, 1972*

LAST TELECAST: *August 23, 1972*

BROADCAST HISTORY:

Jun 1972–Aug 1972, ABC Wed 8:00–8:30

CAST:

Joe Girelli .... Richard Castellano
Francesca Girelli .... Ardell Sheridan
Joanne Girelli .... Margaret Castellano
Anthony Girelli .... Bruce Kirby, Jr.
Frankie Girelli .... Phil Mishkin
Officer Clark .... Ed Peck
Dottie Clark .... Virginia Vincent
Mrs. Stein .... Janet Brandt
Louie .... Louis Basile

All Joe wanted was a cold can of beer, a pizza, and a TV set. But big Joe (260 pounds) was superintendent of an old, walk-up apartment building in a lower-middle-class section of New York City, so what he got was tenants banging on the pipes, tenants complaining about him and about each other, a family that wouldn't leave him alone, and a city that wanted to condemn his building. Richard Castellano starred with his real-life daughter Margaret in this ethnic comedy (among the tenants were Italians, Irish, Poles, Jews, blacks, Puerto Ricans, homosexuals, social workers, cops, and revolutionaries). Francesca was his wife, Joanne and Anthony his disrespectful kids, and Frankie his big-shot lawyer brother.

SUPER ADVENTURE TEAM, THE (*Puppets*)

BROADCAST HISTORY:

MTV
30 minutes
Produced: *1998*
Premiered: *July 23, 1998*

VOICES:

Col. Buck Murdock .... Grant W. Wyllie
Dr. Benton Criswell .... Francis Mt. Pleasant
Talia Criswell .... Barbara St. Bill
Maj. Landon West .... James Penrod
Chief Engineer Head .... Benjamin Venom
Manfred Mordant .... Tim Marx

A rather racy satire on cartoon superheroes, using puppets. The members of the Super Adventure Team carried out the usual superhero assignments, saving the world from nefarious villains, but they had a harder time sorting out their own hang-ups. Col. Murdock was the jut-jawed, incompetent leader who was always grabbing the glory for what others did; he was also sleeping with Talia, the athletic wife of the clueless Dr. Criswell. Major West was the dense, hunky hero who always seemed to be having his clothes torn off, to the secret delight of young engineer Head, a closet homosexual. Mordant was their grouchy boss, seen on a TV screen. The puppets were animated by the "supermarionation" process pioneered by Gerry Anderson in the '60s in such classic kids' series as *Thunderbirds* and *Fireball XL5*.

SUPER BLOOPERS & NEW PRACTICAL JOKES,

see *TV's Bloopers & Practical Jokes*

SUPER DAVE'S VEGAS SPECTACULAR (*Situation Comedy*)

BROADCAST HISTORY:

USA Network
30 minutes
Produced: *1994* (6 episodes)
Premiered: *January 7, 1995*

CAST:

Super Dave Osborne.................Bob Einstein
Sandi Cosgrove....................Jennifer Grant
Donald Glanz..........................Don Lake
Fuji Hakayito........................Art Irizawa
Mike Walden..............................Himself
Super's twin bodyguards
........................Larry and David Powers
Morty Roth....................Keith MacKechnie
Guenter..............................Hans Tester
Hans...............................John Forristal
Tommy Keenan................Mike MacDonald

Slapstick sitcom about a disaster-prone stunt man. Super Dave was the owner of the big, glitzy Rio Hotel in Las Vegas, where each week he made plans to stage a spectacular stunt. Mishaps abounded as preparations took place, as Super and those around him were blown up, flattened, electrocuted, and otherwise mangled (never with any lasting effects). Sandi was Super's eager young public relations manager, Donald the goofball hotel manager, Fuji the incompetent stunt coordinator, Mike the old-fashioned announcer, Morty an agent who kept pitching Super ridiculous acts, Guenter and Hans a screwball animal act, and Tommy a gambling-obsessed USA Network executive. All seemed totally oblivious to the chaos, while tall, grinning Super Dave remained resplendent, and totally self-absorbed, in his gleaming white jumpsuit.

The Super Dave character had a long history. Writer/performer Bob Einstein created him in 1976 for the short-lived *Van Dyke and Company*, then continued the character on the Showtime sketch comedy series *Bizarre* (1979–1985) and in his own *Super Dave* series on Showtime from 1987 to 1992 (Fuji and Mike Walden also appeared in this series). He also appeared as Super Dave on *Late Night with David Letterman*, in commercials, and elsewhere. Just don't get too close to him when he's setting up a stunt.

SUPER FORCE (*Science Fiction/Police*)

BROADCAST HISTORY:

Syndicated only
30 minutes
Produced: *1990–1992* (52 episodes)
Released: *September 1990*

CAST:

Det. Zachary Stone....................Ken Olandt
F. X. Spinner........................Larry B. Scott
E. B. Hungerford (voice)...........Patrick Macnee
Capt. Carla Frost (1990)...............Lisa Niemi
**Zander Tyler (1991–1992)*.........Musetta Vander
**Sgt. Avery Merkel (1991–1992)*.......Tom Schuster

*Occasional

Set in the year 2020, *Super Force* was sort of a futuristic version of *Street Hawk*, an unsuccessful series that had aired on ABC in 1985. Zach Stone was a former astronaut who had become a policeman in Metroplex, a large city rife with corruption and crime. As the narrator intoned at the beginning of each episode, "in 2020 things are tough." To combat crime, Zach moonlighted as Super Force, a vigilante protected by a black, armored, Robocop-type suit that could activate a virtually impenetrable force field. He had state-of-the-art, computer-assisted weapons and rode a souped-up motorcycle with mounted machine guns. All of this special hardware had come from the late industrialist E. B. Hungerford, whose brain pattern and personality had been incorporated into a sentient computer that actually talked in E. B.'s voice. Maintaining the hardware, both for Zach and the computer system, was electronics expert F. X., the only person who knew of Zach's double life.

At the end of the first season Zach almost died but, in the second season premiere, with E. B.'s help and a mind link with psychic Zander Tyler, a friend of E. B.'s, Zack was revived. Zander was a member of the ESPER division of the police; her psychic powers proved very useful as she helped Zach and F. X. fight crime in Metroplex. In addition Zach, who had been neurally linked to E. B. to keep his body alive during his end-of-season ordeal, had acquired a number of computer-aided faculties—the strength of four men, accelerated motor functions, and enhanced vision and mental powers.

SUPER GHOST (*Quiz/Audience Participation*)

FIRST TELECAST: *July 27, 1952*
LAST TELECAST: *September 6, 1953*

BROADCAST HISTORY:

Jul 1952–Sep 1952, NBC Sun 7:00–7:30
Jul 1953–Sep 1953, NBC Sun 7:30–8:00

EMCEE:

Bergen Evans

PANELISTS:

Sherl Stern
Robert Pollack

Super Ghost was a live game show from Chicago, based on the old word game "ghost." Each of the contestants stood before a blackboard and was given three letters of the word being used. They would add letters, one at a time, the object of the game being to avoid completing the designated word. Each time they completed a word they would become one-third a ghost and when they had completed three words they became full ghosts and "disappeared" from the game. Home viewers submitted words for the show and won money if the panel members ended up completing their word. The only two panelists who were regulars throughout the two-summer run of *Super Ghost* were a local Chicago housewife, Sherl Stern, and former drama critic Robert Pollack. A variety of guests filled the other two seats on the panel.

SUPER JEOPARDY!, see *Jeopardy!*

SUPERBOY (*Adventure*)

BROADCAST HISTORY:

Syndicated only
30 minutes
Produced: *1988–1991* (78 episodes)
Released: *October 1988*

CAST:

Clark Kent/Superboy (1988–1989)
..........................John Haymes Newton
Clark Kent/Superboy (1989–1992)
...........................Gerard Christopher
Lana Lang...............................Stacy Haiduk

Trevor Jenkins White III (T. J.) (1988–1989)
.... Jim Calvert
**Lex Luthor (1988–1989)* .... Scott Wells
**Lex Luthor (1989–1992)* .... Sherman Howard
**Leo (1988–1989)* .... Michael Manno
**Lt. Zeke Harris (1988–1989)* .... Robert Pretto
Andy McAllister (1989–1990) .... Ilan Mitchell-Smith
**Darla (1990–1992)* .... Tracy Roberts
Matt Ritter (1990–1992) .... Peter Jay Fernandez
C. Dennis Jackson (1990–1992) ...... Robert Levine
*Occasional

Produced by the people responsible for the *Superman* movies starring Christopher Reeve, this series chronicled the adventures of "the boy of steel" during his college years. Clark Kent was a journalism major at Shuster University, who served as a reporter on the college newspaper. His roommate and best friend was T. J. White (nephew of Perry White of Clark's future), an aspiring photojournalist. Also attending Shuster were Lana Lang, Clark's high school girlfriend from Smallville, and Lex Luthor, well on his way to becoming the criminal genius who would be a continuing thorn in Superman's side years later. Seen infrequently were Clark's adoptive parents Jonathan (Stuart Whitman) and Mary (Salome Jens), with their first names taken from the *Superman* movies, not from the 1950's TV series.

The name Shuster University was a sly acknowledgment to one of *Superman*'s original creators, Joe Shuster and Jerry Siegel. The student union at Shuster was The Siegel Center.

When *Superboy* returned for its second season, there were a number of changes. There was a new actor playing Superboy (Newton had left in a contract dispute), Lex Luthor had undergone plastic surgery to age him and hide his identity from Superboy, T. J. had left school to go to work for the *Daily Planet*, and Clark got a new roommate, fast-talking Andy McAllister. Superboy's foes became more exotic than the ordinary crooks he had dealt with during the first season. There were aliens, vampires, witches, and, from the old comic strip, Mr. Mxyzptlk, the imp from the fifth dimension.

The 1990–1991 season brought a new title—*The Adventures of Superboy*—and a change in the setting. Clark and Lana had graduated from Shuster and were working at the Bureau of Extranormal Matters in Capital City. What better job in which to encounter even more strange and powerful earthly and extraterrestrial creatures? Matt Ritter was one of their coworkers and C. Dennis Jackson was their boss.

SUPERCARRIER (*Military Drama*)
FIRST TELECAST: *March 6, 1988*
LAST TELECAST: *August 27, 1988*
BROADCAST HISTORY:
Mar 1988–Apr 1988, ABC Sun 8:00–9:00
Jul 1988–Aug 1988, ABC Sat 8:00–9:00
CAST:
Capt. Jim Coleman .... Robert Hooks
Capt. Henry K. "Hank" Madigan .... Dale Dye
Lt. Jack "Sierra" DiPalma .... Ken Olandt
Lt. Doyle "Anzac" Sampson ...... John David Bland
Lt. Cdr. Ruth "Beebee" Rutkowski .... Cec Verrell
Master Chief Sam Rivers .... Richard Jaeckel
Master-at-Arms 1st Class Luis Cruz ... Gerardo Mejia
Ocean Specialist 1st Class Donald Willoughby
.... Michael Stuart Sharrett
Seaman Apprentice Raymond Lafitte
.... Matthew Walker
Yeoman 1st Class Rosie Henriques ..... Tasia Valenza
Billie Costello .... Marie Windsor

The above-and-below-deck world of the modern, peacetime navy was glorified in this Sunday action show. The handsome young fighter pilots were straight out of the hit movie *Top Gun*—"Sierra," "Anzac" and "Beebee" (the latter a woman who was better than any of them, but couldn't get sea duty because of her sex). In command of the pilots was Capt. Coleman, a black officer on his first big assignment, and worried about it. The ship's commander was Capt. Madigan; its equivalent of a town cop was Cruz, an earnest young military policeman who wanted to become a boxer; Rosie was a giggly medical assistant; and Willoughby was the expert young radarman.

The real star of the series, however, was the gigantic aircraft carrier itself, the U.S.S. *Georgetown*. How big? As the navy likes to say, "a floating city," 17 stories tall, population 5,630. There were plenty of shots of screaming jets being catapulted from its vast flight deck, or its towering bow looming over smaller craft nearby. It was the pride of San Miguel Naval Base, where off-duty personnel were welcomed by warm beds (and spouses) and by Billie's Bar, run by salty old Billie Costello.

The series was based on the book *Supercarrier* by George C. Wilson. At first the U.S. Navy cooperated fully with the producers, providing technical assistance, loaning aircraft, and allowing filming on the real-life U.S.S. *Kennedy*. However, upset by such nonregulation stories as an onboard love scene (which was deleted), hot-shot pilots crashing $20 million jets into the sea, and the discovery of cocaine on board, the navy later withdrew its support.

SUPERMAN, see *Adventures of Superman, The*

SUPERMARKET SWEEP (*Quiz/Audience Participation*)
CABLE HISTORY:
Lifetime Network
30 minutes
Produced: *1990–1998* (520 episodes)
Premiered: *February 5, 1990*
NETWORK HISTORY:
FIRST TELECAST: *April 5, 1999*
LAST TELECAST:
Apr 1999– , PAX Mon–Fri 6:00–6:30
Apr 2000–Jul 2000, PAX Mon–Fri 7:00–7:30
Oct 2000–Nov 2000, PAX Sat 7:00–7:30
Jul 2000–Sep 2002, PAX Mon–Fri 7:30–8:00
Feb 2003– , PAX Mon–Fri 7:00–7:30
EMCEE:
David Ruprecht

This fast-paced, physical game show was first seen in ABC daytime from 1965 to 1967, with Bill Malone as host, and was revived by cable's Lifetime as a daytime and early-evening entry in 1990. Whereas the 1960s show was staged at actual supermarkets around the country, the 1990s version was set in a big, brightly lit onstage supermarket. Three teams of two persons each competed to answer product-related questions; then, in the final round, they raced down the long, wide aisles, followed by hand-held cameras, filling up their carts with designated products and the most expensive items they could find. The grand prize winner could win as much as $10,000 or a car. David Ruprecht presided informally, with rolled-up sleeves, looking for all the world like the store manager.

Supermarket Sweep moved to Pax the year after it left Lifetime. In the preliminary rounds contestants answered product-related questions that gave them shopping merchandise value an added to the amount of time they had to "shop" in the final round—"The Big Sweep." Each team got their accumulated time to race through the supermarket, filling as many grocery carts as possible. There were special high-value prizes as well. The team that swept up the most money, merchandise and bonus prizes won the chance to win $5,000 in cash. They had one minute to find three products in the supermarket. Ruprecht gave them a clue to the first product; on the product was a clue to find the second product, and it contained a clue to the third product. If they found all three they won the $5,000 grand prize, added to their winnings from the preliminary rounds.

SUPERTRAIN (*Dramatic Anthology*)

FIRST TELECAST: *February 7, 1979*
LAST TELECAST: *July 28, 1979*
BROADCAST HISTORY:

Feb 1979–Mar 1979, NBC Wed 8:00–9:00
Apr 1979–Jul 1979, NBC Sat 10:00–11:00

CAST:

Conductor Harry Flood .... Edward Andrews
Dave Noonan .... Patrick Collins
Dr. Dan Lewis .... Robert Alda
Rose Casey .... Nita Talbot
Porter George Boone .... Harrison Page
Bartender Lou Atkins .... Michael Delano
Robert, the hairdresser .... Charlie Brill
Gilda, ... Aarika Wells
Wally .... William Nuckols
Engineer T.C. .... Anthony Palmer
Social Director Penny Whitaker .... Ilene Graff
Wayne Randall .... Joey Aresco

Supertrain was one of the most expensive failures in the history of network television. It was an anthology series set on a gigantic high-speed train that was appointed like a luxury liner. The massive locomotive pulled nine huge coaches from coast to coast at speeds in excess of 200 miles per hour. The train's passengers could use a 22-by-14-foot swimming pool, a gymnasium equipped with a steam room, a completely staffed and equipped medical center, and a swinging discotheque. The sets utilized in the production of *Supertrain*, both interiors and miniatures, were elaborate and expensive, costing millions of dollars. The train, apparently, was supposed to be the star of the show. Stories were an uneven mix of comedy, mystery, and adventure, and featured assorted guest stars, all interwoven with the activities of the regular train crew (as on ABC's *Love Boat*). Despite extensive advance publicity, which attracted a large audience of curious viewers to its premiere, *Supertrain*'s rating dropped like a rock in subsequent weeks and it was pulled from the NBC schedule barely one month after it had begun. Efforts were made to rework the concept, including cutting down on the number of regular crew members. When it returned after a month's hiatus, only conductor Harry Flood, Dr. Lewis, and chief porter Boone were left from the original crew. Two new members—chief operations officer Wayne Randall and social director Penny Whitaker—were added, and the behind-the-scenes production team had been changed, but it didn't help. Less than six months after its premiere, *Supertrain* was derailed for good.

SURE AS FATE (*Dramatic Anthology*)

FIRST TELECAST: *July 4, 1950*
LAST TELECAST: *April 3, 1951*
BROADCAST HISTORY:

Jul 1950, CBS Tue 8:00–9:00
Sep 1950–Apr 1951, CBS Tue 8:00–9:00

The themes that predominated in this live anthology series were of a melodramatic nature—stories of people confronted with situations not of their own making. *Sure as Fate* was tried for two weeks in July, received encouraging responses from the critics, and returned in September as a regular series. After a month as a weekly program it was cut back to alternate-week status with *Prudential Family Playhouse*. Among the performers featured were Rod Steiger, Leslie Nielsen, John Carradine, Kim Stanley, and Marsha Hunt.

SURFSIDE SIX (*Detective Drama*)

FIRST TELECAST: *October 3, 1960*
LAST TELECAST: *September 24, 1962*
BROADCAST HISTORY:

Oct 1960–Sep 1961, ABC Mon 8:30–9:30
Oct 1961–Sep 1962, ABC Mon 9:00–10:00

CAST:

Ken Madison .... Van Williams
Dave Thorne .... Lee Patterson
Sandy Winfield II .... Troy Donahue
Daphne Dutton .... Diane McBain
Cha Cha O'Brien .... Margarita Sierra
Lt. Snedigar (1960–1961) .... Donald Barry
Lt. Gene Plehan (1961–1962) .... Richard Crane
Mousie .... Mousie Garner

The success of *77 Sunset Strip* had prompted both its producers, Warner Bros, and its network, ABC, to try a series of cookie-cutter copies. *Surfside Six* fit the pattern. Just as in *Sunset Strip*, a trio of sexy, young private detectives (Ken, Dave, and Sandy) lived in an exciting city (Miami) and spent much time with beautiful women (Daphne and Cha Cha). All that was missing was a jive-talking parking-lot attendant. Surfside Six was the Miami telephone exchange that included the number of the houseboat that served as both home and office to the detectives. Anchored next to it was the yacht of kooky socialite Daphne Dutton, and across from it was the fabulous Fountainebleau Hotel, where Cha Cha worked as an entertainer in the Boom Boom Room.

Detective Ken Madison was a survivor of another private-eye show that had been seen in the same time slot during the previous season—*Bourbon Street Beat.* His Bourbon Street partner, Rex Randolph, latched on to another job too, joining the team on *77 Sunset Strip.* Warner Bros. certainly made the most of its characters.

SURREAL LIFE, THE (*Reality*)

FIRST TELECAST: *January 9, 2003*
LAST TELECAST: *February 20, 2003*

BROADCAST HISTORY:

Jan 2003–Feb 2003, WB Thu 9:00–9:30

The Surreal Life followed the activities of seven onetime celebrities—whose "stars" had dimmed considerably—as they lived together for two weeks in a luxurious home in the Hollywood Hills. The seven were super-cool MC Hammer, a major rap star of the '80s and now a minister; jokester Emmanuel Lewis, the former child star of *Webster*; beauty queen Brande Roderick, a former *Playboy* Playmate and actress on *Baywatch: Hawaii*; party guy Corey Feldman, a former child star; supermom Gabrielle Carteris, a one-time regular on *Beverly Hills 90210*; shaggy and surprisingly quiet Vince Neil, lead singer of the heavy-metal band Mötley Crüe; and touchy Jerri Manthey, who had gained notoriety as a bitchy contestant on *Survivor: The Australian Outback* ("I'll be nice as long as no one pisses me off").

The housemates had to work together to make the best of their living situation. They had no cars, computers, cell phones or personal staffs. Their only means of communication was a "pay" phone booth. Everything they did was filmed—cooking, shopping, cleaning, taking trips and establishing personal relationships. Among the activities were a camping trip, a talent show with Monty Hall showing up as the surprise host (Vince was the winner and won temporary use of the master bedroom), a trip to Las Vegas followed by a church service with Hammer serving as minister, a softball game, and the efforts of the other housemates to find the perfect date for Brande (she went out with Gabrielle's guy but there was no love connection).

The highlight of the last episode was Corey's wedding to his fiancée Susie Sprague. Throughout the two weeks he had gotten on everyone's nerves making plans and agonizing over whether he was making the right decision, and there was considerable relief when it was finally over. Hammer assisted the rabbi who conducted the service, and *Playboy* publisher Hugh Hefner was one of the guests.

The house that the housemates stayed in was the old Glen Campbell estate on Mullholland Drive.

SURVIVAL—ANGLIA, LTD. SERIES (*Wildlife/Nature*)

FIRST TELECAST: *June 24, 1976*
LAST TELECAST: *September 16, 1976*
BROADCAST HISTORY:

Jun 1976–Sep 1976, NBC Thu 8:00–9:00

This summer series was composed of a collection of documentaries on various animals. Some of them were originals and others were repeats of specials that had already aired on network television. Included were "Gorilla," narrated by David Niven, "Magnificent Monsters of the Deep," narrated by Orson Welles, and "Come into My Parlor" (about spiders), narrated by Peter Ustinov.

SURVIVOR (*Adventure/Competition*)

FIRST TELECAST: *May 31, 2000*
LAST TELECAST:
BROADCAST HISTORY:

May 2000–Aug 2000, CBS Wed 8:00–9:00
Feb 2001–May 2001, CBS Thu 8:00–9:00
Oct 2001–Jan 2002, CBS Thu 8:00–9:00
Feb 2002–May 2002, CBS Thu 8:00–9:00
Sep 2002–Dec 2002, CBS Thu 8:00–9:00
Feb 2003–May 2003, CBS Thu 8:00–9:00

HOST:

Jeff Probst

Survivor was a combination game show, soap opera and real-life adventure—a mix of elements that had never before been tried on American TV. Sixteen people were deposited on a remote island, where they had to fend for themselves, fighting the elements and their fellow contestants for the chance to win $1 million. They were separated into two "tribes" that competed in various challenges, mostly strenuous physical games. Every three days the losing tribe had to vote one of its members off the island at a tribal council where tribe members assembled carrying torches and the ousted contestant's torch was symbolically extinguished. After six people had been eliminated the survivors were merged into a single tribe, and it was every contestant for him- or herself. The contests fell into two basic categories: reward challenges for some luxury item (flashlight, waterproof matches, mosquito netting, candy bars, canned tuna, etc.), and immunity challenges, which temporarily protected the winner from being voted off the island. When there were just two contestants left, the previous seven who had been voted out returned as members of a jury, at the last tribal council, to choose the winner of the $1 million. You can imagine the infighting, politics and alliances that led up to the final vote!

CBS began promoting *Survivor* in October 1999, eight months before its premiere. By March 16 contestants had been chosen from among more than 6,000 applicants. The original eight male and eight female survivors represented a diverse group, ranging in age from 22 to 72. They were B. B. Andersen, Colleen Haskell, Gervase Peterson, Gretchen Cordy, Jenna Lewis, Joel Klug, Ramona Gray, Greg Buis, Dirk Been, Stacey Stillman, Rudy Boesch, Sonja Christopher, Richard Hatch, Kelly Wiglesworth, Sean Kenniff and Susan Hawk.

The 16 were flown to the remote island of Pulau Tiga, in the South China Sea, and marooned in an environment that was—to be charitable—pretty hostile. A nature preserve off Borneo in Malaysia, the island abounded with rats, poisonous snakes, scorpions, sand fleas, lizards and mosquitoes. The contestants had no tents, blankets, sleeping bags or any other creature comforts, and rice was the only food provided by the producers—they had to forage for anything else to eat. They were divided into the Tagi Tribe and the Pagong Tribe and cameras recorded everything that happened, including the struggles, romances, bickering, alliance building, mind games and double crossing as the contestants fought to keep from being voted off the island. Sonja, a sweet older lady with a ukulele, was the first to be voted off; bossy B. B. was next. Among the highlights were the surprising alliance between Richard, a hard-driving corporate trainer who was gay, and grizzled Rudy, a 72-year-old very masculine ex–Navy SEAL; and Richard walking around naked to celebrate his thirty-ninth birthday. It all culminated in the final tribal council, at which the previous seven who had been voted off each got to comment on the final two—Richard and Kelly—before voting for the winner. Tough-as-nails Sue summed it up in an unforgettable speech in which she called Richard an arrogant, pompous (but hardworking) snake, and Kelly a two-faced, manipulative rat, then said, "I feel we owe it to the island spirits that we have come to know to let it be, in the end, the way Mother Nature intended it to be—for the snake to eat the rat." Richard walked away with the $1 million.

Survivor was the TV phenomenon of the summer of 2000. By its fourth week on the air it was attracting more viewers than the other five networks combined and was the most talked-about show on TV. Viewers were obsessed with the relationships and conflicts among the contestants on the island. *Newsweek* called it the most addictive TV show of the year, and the morning after the final episode aired winner Hatch was on the front page of many of the nation's newspapers. CBS milked *Survivor*'s success for all it was worth, with contestants who had been voted off the island appearing on the next morning's CBS *Early Show*, as guests on *Late Show with David Letterman*, in promotional ads for the forthcoming CBS fall schedule and, in a few cases, in cameo roles on other CBS series.

Subsequent editions of *Survivor* were also highly successful. February 2001 brought *Survivor: The Australian Outback*. The two tribes for this incarnation were Ogakor and Kucha, and notorious episodes included tribesman Michael Skupin gleefully slaughtering a pig and later passing out and falling face-first into the campfire. Despite his agony a nearby cameraman did not come to his aid, but rather recorded the event for viewers—a decision that was widely criticized, but staunchly defended by the show's producer, Mark Burnett. He was helicoptered to a hospital for treatment of second- and third-degree burns; that was the only episode without a tribal council. The eventual winner was Tina Wesson, a nurse from Knoxville, Tennessee.

The third edition, *Survivor: Africa*, premiered in October 2001 with its contestants marooned in the Shaba National Reserve in Kenya. The two tribes were the Samburu and the Boran. On the fifth episode the producers introduced a twist. Each tribe had to select three of its "best" members and send them to host Probst for what they believed to be a reward challenge. Instead he told them that they were switching tribes, thereby forcing new alliances and disrupting whatever balance had previously existed. The $1 million went to Ethan Zohn, a curly-haired professional soccer player living in New York City.

Survivor: Marquesas, telecast the following February, took the show back to the South Pacific and a tiny abandoned island off Nuku Hiva, a distant neighbor of Tahiti. The two tribes were Maraamu (Wind) and Rotu (Rain). This time the switch took place on the fourth episode. The contestants were standing on small wooden disks and, when they stepped off and looked underneath the disks, they found bandannas indicating their new tribes. As with *Survivor: Africa*, three people from each tribe had to change. Vecepia Towery, an office manager from Portland, Oregon, won the $1 million.

September 2002 brought *Survivor: Thailand* set on Koh Tarutao, a remote island off the southeast coast of Thailand. This time the members of each tribe—Chuay Gahn and Sook Jai—were not preselected by the producers. Instead, the two oldest contestants, 53-year-old Jan and 61-year-old Jake, were designated to pick the members of their tribes. An additional twist was that the two tribes remained separate for an additional two weeks. In the final episode the $1 million went to Brian Heidik, a used-car salesman from Quartz Hill, California.

The rain forest of South America was the setting for *Survivor: The Amazon*, which premiered in February 2003. For the first time the contestants were segregated by sex—the Jabaru Tribe was all female and the Tambaqui Tribe, all male. Unlike the previous three *Survivors*, there were no unexpected twists and the tribes merged into one after the sixth contestant had been voted out. Jenna Morasca, a swimsuit model from Pittsburgh, Pennsylvania, won the $1 million.

SURVIVORS, THE (*Drama*)

FIRST TELECAST: *September 29, 1969*
LAST TELECAST: *September 17, 1970*
BROADCAST HISTORY:
Sep 1969–Jan 1970, ABC Mon 9:00–10:00
Jun 1970–Sep 1970, ABC Thu 10:00–11:00
CAST:
Tracy Carlyle Hastings .... Lana Turner
Philip Hastings .... Kevin McCarthy
Jeffrey Hastings .... Jan-Michael Vincent
Baylor Carlyle .... Ralph Bellamy
Duncan Carlyle .... George Hamilton
Belle .... Diana Muldaur
Jonathan .... Louis Hayward
Jean Vale .... Louise Sorel
Antaeus Riakos .... Rossano Brazzi
Miguel Santerra .... Robert Viharo
Marguerita .... Donna Baccala
Sheila .... Kathy Cannon
Tom .... Robert Lipton
Sen. Mark Jennings .... Clu Gulager
Eleanor Carlyle .... Natalie Schafer

Movie queen Lana Turner made her TV series debut—and swan song—in this adaptation of Harold Robbins's novel of love and lust among the jet set. Lana, as Tracy Hastings, was the center of the action as she struggled to protect her teenage son Jeffrey from (as the press release put it) "the forces that could destroy him." Among the other major protagonists were Tracy's philandering husband, Philip; her father, banking czar Baylor; and her playboy half brother, Duncan. Continuing story lines unfolded in a new "chapter" each week, and involved the Carlyles' entanglement with South American revolutionary Miguel Santerra, Tracy's old flame Riakos (eventually revealed to be Jeffrey's real father), Baylor's lingering death, and everybody's attempts to get their hands on his millions. Pure soap opera.

The Survivors was a big-name bust, lasting only three and a half months. ABC recouped some of its cost by running repeats during the summer of 1970.

The official title of the series was *Harold Robbins' "The Survivors."*

SUSAN RAYE (*Music*)

FIRST TELECAST: *October 2, 1950*
LAST TELECAST: *November 20, 1950*
BROADCAST HISTORY:
Oct 1950, DUM Mon/Fri 7:45–8:00
Oct 1950–Nov 1950, DUM Mon 7:30–7:45

HOSTESS:
Susan Raye

Musical interlude featuring the singing and piano stylings of Miss Raye.

SUSIE, syndicated title for *Private Secretary*

SUSPENSE (*Dramatic Anthology*)

FIRST TELECAST: *March 1, 1949*
LAST TELECAST: *September 9, 1964*
BROADCAST HISTORY:
Mar 1949–Jun 1950, CBS Tue 9:30–10:00 (OS)
Aug 1950–Aug 1954, CBS Tue 9:30–10:00
Mar 1964–Sep 1964, CBS Wed 8:30–9:00
HOST:
Sebastian Cabot (1964)

Suspense had been a fixture on the CBS Radio Network since 1942 (where it remained for 20 years). The radio version had won a Peabody Award and a special citation from the Mystery Writers of America. In the spring of 1949 it came to television. The television plays were broadcast live from New York and featured many well-known Hollywood and Broadway actors. All of the stories dealt with people in dangerous and threatening situations of one kind or another. Some were adaptations of classic horror tales like *Dr. Jekyll and Mr. Hyde,* done in 1950 with Ralph Bell in the lead role and again a year later with Basil Rathbone. A version of *Suspicion* starred Ernest Truex and his wife, Sylvia Field, William Prince had the lead in "The Waxworks," John Forsythe in Robert Louis Stevenson's "The Beach of Falsea," and Peter Lorre in "The Tortured Hand." Frequent performers during the live run of the series were Nina Foch, Mildred Natwick, Tom Drake, Barry Sullivan, and horror veterans Boris Karloff, John Carradine, and Henry Hull.

Not all of the stories were of the horror genre. Though the works of Poe and Stevenson were adapted frequently, there were straight mysteries by Charlotte Armstrong and Quentin Reynolds, among others. Rudyard Kipling's "The Man Who Would Be King" and numerous stories by Charles Dickens were also presented. On the more contemporary side, Grace Kelly starred in "50 Beautiful Girls," Arlene Francis and Lloyd Bridges in "Her Last Adventure," and Eva Gabor and Sidney Blackmer in a two-parter titled "This Is Your Confession." Jackie Cooper starred on occasion, and Cloris Leachman, Jacqueline Susann, and Mike Wallace showed up on *Suspense* as well.

In the spring of 1964, almost a full decade after the live version of *Suspense* left the air, a new series of filmed *Suspense* dramas arrived on CBS with Sebastian Cabot as host (there had never been a regular host for the live show). Some of the stars of these new stories—E. G. Marshall, James Daly, Basil Rathbone, and Skip Homeier—were returning home, as they had also starred in episodes of the live series in the 1950s. By the end of June, however, there were no new episodes being produced. Although it was still called *Suspense,* and Sebastian Cabot remained as host, all of the telecasts aired from July to September were actually reruns from *Schlitz Playhouse of Stars.*

SUSPENSE PLAYHOUSE (*Dramatic Anthology*)

FIRST TELECAST: *May 24, 1971*
LAST TELECAST: *July 31, 1972*
BROADCAST HISTORY:
May 1971–Jul 1971, CBS Mon 10:00–11:00
Jul 1972, CBS Mon 10:00–11:00

The filmed plays presented in this summer anthology series were all reruns of episodes originally telecast on *Premiere* during the summer of 1968. They were all unsold pilots for proposed regular series. The three episodes that aired in the summer of 1972 had also been seen within the 1971 run.

SUSPICION (*Suspense Anthology*)

FIRST TELECAST: *September 30, 1957*
LAST TELECAST: *September 6, 1959*
BROADCAST HISTORY:
Sep 1957–Sep 1958, NBC Mon 10:00–11:00
Jun 1959–Sep 1959, NBC Sun 7:30–8:30
HOST:
Dennis O'Keefe (1957)
Walter Abel (1959)

Suspicion was comprised of 20 filmed dramas and 20 live dramas that aired on NBC during the 1957–1958 season. The stories were meant to fascinate, mystify, and confound the audience, and generally dealt with people's fears and suspicions, often concerning murder. Alfred Hitchcock, who had his own series on CBS at this time, produced half of the filmed episodes. When it premiered, Dennis O'Keefe was to be the permanent host of the show. After two weeks, however, he left the series and was not replaced. In the summer of 1959 a number of the original episodes were rerun, with Walter Abel hosting them.

SUZANNE PLESHETTE IS MAGGIE BRIGGS
(*Situation Comedy*)

FIRST TELECAST: *March 4, 1984*
LAST TELECAST: *April 15, 1984*
BROADCAST HISTORY:
Mar 1984–Apr 1984, CBS Sun 8:00–8:30
CAST:
Maggie Briggs.................. Suzanne Pleshette
Walter Holden................. Kenneth McMillan
Connie Piscipoli.................... Shera Danese
Sherman Milslagle.................. Stephen Lee
Geoff Bennett.......................... John Getz
Melanie Bitterman................ Alison LaPlaca
Donny Bauer....................... Roger Bowen
Diana Barstow................. Michelle Nicastro

After 15 years as a hard-news reporter, Maggie Briggs was making the difficult adjustment to being a feature writer for the Modern Living Section of the *New York Examiner.* She really hadn't wanted to make the move but, out of loyalty to her friend and mentor, Walter Holden, who had also been transferred, she felt obligated to give it a chance. Working on human-interest stories was quite a change from her former criminal and political bylines. With her in her new area were Sherman, the neurotic food critic; Donny the religion editor; and fellow feature writers Melanie and Diana. Her new boss, editor of the Modern Living Section, was young, straight-arrow company man Geoff Bennett. Maggie's best friend was sexy but flaky clothing model Connie Piscipoli.

SWAMP THING (*Science Fiction/Adventure*)
BROADCAST HISTORY:
USA Network
30 minutes
Produced: *1990–1993* (72 episodes)
Premiered: *July 27, 1990*
CAST:
Swamp Thing/Dr. Alec Holland (voice) .... Dick Durock
**Dr. Alec Holland (flashbacks) (1991–1993)* .... Patrick Neil Quinn
Dr. Anton Arcane .... Mark Lindsay Chapman
Jim Kipp (1990) .... Jesse Ziegler
Will Kipp (1991–1993) .... Scott Garrison
Tressa Kipp .... Carrell Myers
Obo (1990) .... Anthony Galde
**Sheriff Ed Anderson* .... Marc Macaulay
**Dr. Hollister (1990)* .... William Whitehead
Abigail (1991–1993) .... Kari Wuhrer
Graham (1991–1993) .... Kevin Quigley
**Dr. Ann Fisk (1991–1993)* .... Janet Julian
*Occasional

"The swamp is my world," intoned the towering, leafy hero of this high-camp series at the beginning of each episode. "It is who I am. It is what I am. I was once a man. I know the evil men do. Do not bring your evil here. I warn you: beware the wrath of SWAMP THING!"

Swamp Thing had indeed once been a man, kind-hearted Dr. Alec Holland, until an environmental disaster caused by greedy Dr. Arcane had turned him into something resembling a large stick of broccoli. Now he lived in the pristine swamp near Houma, Louisiana, determined to protect it from all despoilers, especially the constantly scheming Arcane. Jim was a young boy who lived nearby with his divorced stepmother, Tressa. Neither had a clue that there was evil all around them, and they regularly had to be rescued by Swampy. Others came and went from the cartoonish series. Young Jim met a sad end (Arcane stuffed him in a box and shipped him to South America) and was replaced by handsome teenager Will, who had a sometime love interest in the mysterious Abigail. Graham was Arcane's craven assistant.

Swamp Thing was based on the popular environmental comic-book hero of the 1970s. The big guy was portrayed by Dick Durock in two movies, *Swamp Thing* (1982) and *The Return of Swamp Thing* (1989).

SWEATING BULLETS (*Detective*)
FIRST TELECAST: *April 8, 1991*
LAST TELECAST: *January 2, 1995*
BROADCAST HISTORY:
Apr 1991–Aug 1993, CBS Mon 11:30–12:30 A.M.
Jul 1991, CBS Fri 10:00–11:00
Sep 1993–Apr 1994, CBS Mon 12:35–1:35 A.M.
Apr 1994–Dec 1994, CBS Mon/Thu 12:35–1:35 A.M.
Dec 1994–Jan 1995, CBS Mon 1:05–2:05 A.M.
CAST:
Nick Slaughter .... Rob Stewart
Sylvie Girard .... Carolyn Dunn
Ian Stewart (1991–1992) .... John David Bland
Lt. Carillo (1991–1992) .... Pedro Armendariz
Ollie Porter (1991) .... Eugene Clark
Spider Garvin (1992–1993) .... Ian Tracey
Sgt. Gregory (1992–1993) .... Ari Sorko-Ram
Rollie (1992–1993) .... Alon Nashman

Nick Slaughter was a former Miami-based DEA agent with a ponytail and an attitude who opted for what he thought would be a safer, more laid-back, lifestyle: as a private eye on the sunny Caribbean island of Key Mariah. Life on the beach meant nubile gals in bikinis and guys with open shirts, which suited irresponsible Nick just fine. When he should have been looking for clients, he spent his time hanging out with his friend Ian, a former Australian rock star who had given it all up to run a beachfront bar and dive shop. Trying to keep Nick's mind on business was Sylvie, his sexy, superefficient partner (would they ever get involved romantically?), a computer whiz who had given up one marginal career as a travel agent for another one working for Nick. Also cruising the white silver sands were Lt. Carillo, head of the local police, and Ollie, a Philadelphia cop temporarily working as Carillo's assistant.

Filmed on location in Puerto Vallarta, Mexico, where bikinis and bare chests do indeed abound. Production was moved to Tel Aviv and Ellat in Israel in the fall of 1991 and to Mauritius (for beach scenes) and Pretoria, South Africa a year later. When Ian went back to rock and roll, Nick's friend Spider Garvin, a former tennis pro, took over the beach bar. Rollie was the nerdy medical examiner.

Although production of *Sweating Bullets* ended after the 1992–1993 season, CBS continued to air reruns until January 1995.

$WEEPSTAKE$ (*Dramatic Anthology*)
FIRST TELECAST: *January 26, 1979*
LAST TELECAST: *March 30, 1979*
BROADCAST HISTORY:
Jan 1979–Mar 1979, NBC Fri 10:00–11:00
CAST:
The Emcee .... Edd Byrnes

CBS had been quite successful in the 1950s with a series called *The Millionaire*, which each week showed a different recipient of a million dollars adjusting to sudden wealth. *$weepstake$* was an attempt to update the concept. Each week a different group of twelve finalists was in the running for $1 million tax-free, top prize in a state lottery. Every episode of *$weepstake$* concentrated on the lives of three of the finalists as the drawing approached and showed how the amount they won, whether it was the jackpot or the $1,000 given runners-up, affected their lives. Some of the stories were funny and some serious, and the most deserving people did not always win. Edd Byrnes, as the lottery drawing's emcee, was the only series regular. Among the performers appearing were Elaine Joyce, Frankie Avalon, Patrick Macnee, Adrienne Barbeau, Gary Burghoff, Elinor Donahue, Nipsey Russell, and Jack Jones.

SWEET JUSTICE (*Legal Drama*)
FIRST TELECAST: *September 15, 1994*
LAST TELECAST: *April 22, 1995*
BROADCAST HISTORY:
Sep 1994, NBC Thu 10:00–11:00
Sep 1994, NBC Sat 8:00–9:00
Sep 1994–Apr 1995, NBC Sat 9:00–10:00
CAST:
Carrie Grace Battle .... Cicely Tyson
Kate Delacroy .... Melissa Gilbert
James-Lee Delacroy .... Ronny Cox

Reese Daulkins.....................Cree Summer
Andy Del Sarto....................Greg Germann
Ross A. Ross.........................Jim Antonio
Bailey Connors....................Jason Gedrick
Anne Foley......................Megan Gallivan
**Harry Foley*.........................Scott Paetty
**Althea "Bunny" McClure*........Marcia Strassman
**Logan Wright*.................John Allen Nelson
Michael "T-Dog" Turner (1995)....Michael Warren

*Occasional

Magnolia blossoms wafted through the courtroom in this legal drama about a do-gooder daughter of the South who returned home to fight the Establishment. Young attorney Kate had been on the Wall Street fast track but came home for her stuck-up sister Anne's engagement party (to lawyer Harry) and decided to stay. But instead of joining the prestigious law firm headed by her arch conservative father, James-Lee, as expected, she joined forces with old civil rights warrior Carrie Grace Battle in Battle-Ross & Associates, the better to take on cases of women's rights, minority rights, and everyone else's rights. Dad was not pleased, grousing that Battle "dragged us kicking and screaming into the new South; some of us didn't think there was anything wrong with the old."

Battle's committed, low-rent staff included energetic single mom Reese, young upstart Andy, and methodical Ross. Bailey was a newspaperman and former flame of Kate's who helped her out while hoping that their flame might burn again one day. Bunny was a Southern belle out to wed James-Lee (and looked on with suspicion by his daughters), while T-Dog was a strong-willed black community leader who provided some love interest for Carrie.

SWEET SPOT, THE (*Situation Comedy*)

BROADCAST HISTORY:

Comedy Central
30 minutes
Original episodes: *2002* (5 episodes)
Premiered: *April 2, 2002*

CAST:

Bill Murray...............................Himself
Brian Doyle-Murray......................Himself
Joel Murray...............................Himself
John Murray...............................Himself

This brief series was essentially a vanity project for actor/golfer Bill Murray, and a chance to give three of his real-life brothers some work. It followed the fractious foursome as they teed off at five world-class golf courses, from Lake Geneva, Wisconsin, to Montego Bay, Jamaica, amid insults, sight gags, and silly sound effects. In each episode they competed for a cheap trophy called The Braggart's Cup. The idea for the series came, it was said, from Bill's 1980 film *Caddyshack*.

SWEET SURRENDER (*Situation Comedy*)

FIRST TELECAST: *April 18, 1987*
LAST TELECAST: *July 8, 1987*
BROADCAST HISTORY:

Apr 1987–May 1987, NBC Sat 8:30–9:00
Jul 1987, NBC Wed 9:30–10:00

CAST:

Georgia Holden......................Dana Delany
Ken Holden.............................Mark Blum
Bart Holden...........................Edan Gross
Lynnie Holden..........Rebecca and Sarah Simms
Vaughn Parker....................Christopher Rich
Frank Macklin.........................David Doyle
Joyce Holden........................Marjorie Lord
Marty Gafney.........................Thom Sharp
Lyla Gafney.......................Louise Williams
Taylor Gafney.....................Victor DiMattia
Cak....................................Viveka Davis

Domesticity was rampant in this routine little comedy about a wife (Georgia) who decided to put her business career on hold and become a full-time mom to her newborn baby Lynnie and young son, Bart. Hubby Ken was understanding, although his swaggering single friend (and coworker) Vaughn was constantly on hand to remind him that bachelorhood was more fun. Frank was Georgia's dad, Joyce was Ken's mother, the Gafneys were friends, and Cak the flaky teenage babysitter. Everybody offered advice, but nobody really understood just how *hard* a full-time mom's life could be!

SWIFT JUSTICE (*Detective Drama*)

FIRST TELECAST: *March 13, 1996*
LAST TELECAST: *July 31, 1996*
BROADCAST HISTORY:

Mar 1996–Jul 1996, UPN Wed 9:00–10:00

CAST:

Mac Swift.........................James McCaffrey
Det. Randall Paterson..............Gary Dourdan
Sgt. Al Swift............................Len Cariou

Mac was a tough New York undercover cop and former Navy SEAL, something of a loose cannon who broke the rules once too often and got busted from the force. He then became a private eye, helping those to whom justice had been denied because of the rules of conventional law enforcement. Paterson, his black former partner with dreadlocked hair, continued to be his friend and provided him with information on cases. Mac's father Al was a career beat officer now working as desk officer, who brought in the cavalry when necessary. Mac, a computer whiz, had an e-mail address through which clients could contact him. Cases included a wife whose ex-husband had kidnapped their son, and a rock star whose abusive husband refused to let her divorce him.

SWIFT SHOW, THE (*Musical Variety*)

FIRST TELECAST: *April 1, 1948*
LAST TELECAST: *August 4, 1949*
BROADCAST HISTORY:

Apr 1948–Aug 1949, NBC Thu 8:30–9:00

REGULARS:

Lanny Ross
Martha Logan
Sandra Gable (1948)
Eileen Barton (1948)
Susan Shaw (1948)
Martha Wright (1949)
Dulcy Jordan (1949)
Max Showalter (1949)
Ricki Hamilton (1949)
Frank Fontaine (1949)
Harry Simeone Orchestra & Chorus

Swift and Company, which had pioneered daytime commercial network television with the *Swift Home Service Club* in 1947, moved to prime time in early 1948 with a Thursday night half hour starring crooner

Lanny Ross. Although music and light comedy remained the central theme of the show throughout its run, the specific format changed several times during the next year.

At first the program was a combination of music and a quiz segment called the "Eye-Cue Game," which had been brought over from the *Swift Home Service Club.* Contestants were asked to identify various names, places, or events from a series of visual clues. By September the quiz segment had been dropped and the setting became Lanny's elegant penthouse apartment, with regular friends and special guests dropping by to entertain. Eileen Barton played the small-town girlfriend with a crush on Lanny. Soon Lanny began to get out of his apartment, in fanciful dreams set to music, and on dates with various girlfriends.

In March 1949 the penthouse and the dating story lines were dropped and the program became a straight musical revue, with Lanny singing songs and entertaining guests.

Two carryovers from the *Swift Home Service Club* were Martha Logan, who gave demonstrations and commercials in the Swift Kitchen (during the "apartment" phase she was the girl upstairs), and Sandra Gable, who modeled fashions and gave home-decorating ideas.

SWIFT SHOW WAGON, THE (*Variety*)

FIRST TELECAST: *January 8, 1955*
LAST TELECAST: *October 1, 1955*
BROADCAST HISTORY:

Jan 1955–Oct 1955, NBC Sat 7:30–8:00

HOST:

Horace Heidt

Each week this talent and variety show starring veteran bandleader Horace Heidt originated from a different state. It highlighted performers from that state, included interviews with local civic leaders, and presented one or two native sons who had gone on to become nationally known celebrities. Each show also included a salute to the "personality of the week," someone in the state who had performed a heroic deed. The show's title derived from the fact that it moved, not unlike a wagon, from place to place across the country. The full title was *The Swift Show Wagon with Horace Heidt and the American Way.*

SWISS FAMILY ROBINSON (*Adventure*)

FIRST TELECAST: *September 14, 1975*
LAST TELECAST: *April 11, 1976*
BROADCAST HISTORY:

Sep 1975–Apr 1976, ABC Sun 7:00–8:00

CAST:

Karl Robinson .... Martin Milner
Lotte Robinson .... Pat Delany
Fred Robinson .... Willie Aames
Ernie Robinson .... Eric Olson
Jeremiah Worth .... Cameron Mitchell
Helga Wagner .... Helen Hunt

PRODUCER:

Irwin Allen

Johann Wyss's classic children's story of a family shipwrecked in the early 1800s was brought to TV in this 1975 series. It didn't look much like the book, however. The TV *Swiss Family Robinson* was produced by Irwin Allen, famed for his "disaster" movies. Although he claimed that this was not going to be a "disaster of the week" series, there did seem to be a tidal wave, typhoon, earthquake, volcanic eruption, wild animal, or other natural calamity besetting the poor Robinsons in every episode—usually staged in a rather tacky fashion (you just don't have those movie budgets in TV). In their remarkably well-equipped tree house, Karl and Lotte Robinson were stoic through it all, while their children Fred and Ernie hung on for dear life in the teeth of every gale. Jeremiah was a rascally old sailor who had previously been marooned on the island, and Helga was the only other survivor of the Robinsons' shipwreck (she was the daughter of the captain).

Quite a few visitors passed through the Robinsons' "lost" island, including pirate Jean Lafitte, who stopped off to pick up some buried treasure on his way to help General Andrew Jackson at the Battle of New Orleans.

SWITCH (*Detective Drama*)

FIRST TELECAST: *September 9, 1975*
LAST TELECAST: *September 3, 1978*
BROADCAST HISTORY:

Sep 1975–Nov 1975, CBS Tue 9:00–10:00
Dec 1975–Jan 1977, CBS Tue 10:00–11:00
Jan 1977–Sep 1977, CBS Sun 9:00–10:00
Sep 1977, CBS Fri 10:00–11:00
Dec 1977–Jan 1978, CBS Mon 10:00–11:00
Jun 1978–Sep 1978, CBS Sun 10:00–11:00

CAST:

Pete Ryan .... Robert Wagner
Frank McBride .... Eddie Albert
Malcolm Argos .... Charlie Callas
Maggie .... Sharon Gless
Revel .... Mindi Miller
Lt. Griffin (1975–1976) .... Ken Swofford
Lt. Modeer (1976–1977) .... Richard X. Slattery
Lt. Shilton (1976–1978) .... William Bryant
Wang (1977–1978) .... James Hong

It was an unusual partnership. Pete was a former con man and Frank was a retired bunco cop. Together they had formed a private detective agency that specialized in pulling "switches" on the other con men still operating on the wrong side of the law. They would concoct elaborate schemes that would, hopefully, result in the swindlers swindling themselves. Based in Los Angeles, the two of them traveled far and wide on assorted cases. Malcolm, a small-time thief and con man who had gone straight and opened a restaurant was recruited by Pete and Frank to help them on cases, and Maggie was the firm's combination secretary-receptionist and all-around girl Friday.

By the middle of its second season, *Switch* had become a somewhat more traditional detective series, with fewer of the elaborate con games, and in the fall of 1977 Pete moved into a new apartment above Malcolm's bouzouki bar, where Revel was the hostess and Wang the new cook.

SWORD OF JUSTICE (*Adventure*)

FIRST TELECAST: *September 10, 1978*
LAST TELECAST: *August 11, 1979*
BROADCAST HISTORY:

Sep 1978, NBC Sun 8:00–10:00
Oct 1978, NBC Sat 10:00–11:00

Dec 1978, NBC Sun 10:00–11:00
Jul 1979, NBC Sat 9:00–10:00
Aug 1979, NBC Sat 10:00–11:00

CAST:

Jack Cole .... Dack Rambo
Hector Ramirez .... Bert Rosario
Arthur Woods .... Alex Courtney
Buckner .... Colby Chester

This series was billed as *Zorro* in contemporary garb. Jack Cole was not masked, but he certainly was an avenger, out to fight crime in high places, both public and private. Cole's motivation for this noble crusade was clear enough. A Park Avenue playboy, and heir to a great industrial fortune, he had suddenly been thrust from his pampered, jet-set existence into prison on a trumped-up charge of embezzlement after his father's death. While behind bars he learned the skills of the criminal's trade, lock picking, telephone bugging, and all the rest, and when he emerged he was determined to use these skills against the kind of white-collar criminals who had framed him. He resumed his playboy image, but only as a front for his (mostly) nocturnal crime-busting. His sign: a playing card. Helping was Hector, Jack's wise-cracking Puerto Rican excellmate, and always one step behind was Arthur Woods, formerly the Cole family attorney and now part of a government task force fighting high-level crime. Working with Woods was Federal Agent Buckner.

SYDNEY (*Situation Comedy*)

FIRST TELECAST: *March 21, 1990*
LAST TELECAST: *August 6, 1990*
BROADCAST HISTORY:

Mar 1990–Apr 1990, CBS Wed 8:30–9:00
Apr 1990–May 1990, CBS Wed 8:00–8:30
May 1990–Aug 1990, CBS Mon 8:30–9:00

CAST:

Sydney Kells .... Valerie Bertinelli
Billy Kells .... Matthew Perry
Matt Keating .... Craig Bierko
Ray .... Barney Martin
Jill .... Rebeccah Bush
Perry .... Perry Anzilotti
Cheezy .... Daniel Baldwin

THEME:

"Finish What Ya Started," written by Eddie Van Halen and performed by Van Halen

Sydney Kells was a bright, self-confident, single woman trying to make a living as a private detective in her native Los Angeles. Her first problem was getting anyone to take her seriously. Most of Sydney's assignments came from Matt Keating, an uptight young attorney who marveled at her professional skills but was embarrassed to admit to his superiors that he was using a good-looking young woman as an investigator. They thought Sydney was a man. Although Matt was engaged and very square, Sydney did find him attractive. Others in her life were Billy, her naive kid brother who had followed in their father's footsteps and become a cop; and Jill, her attractive neighbor who was forever fending off Billy's clumsy romantic overtures. Sydney spent much of her spare time at The Blue Collar, a neighborhood tavern whose owner/bartender Ray was a longtime family friend and surrogate father. Other regulars at the tavern were Perry, Sydney's most reliable snitch, and Cheezy, the crude, grubby guy who was constantly propositioning her.

The theme song for this mild-mannered comedy was written and performed by Ms. Bertinelli's husband, Eddie Van Halen.

SYMPHONY, THE, see *Chicago Symphony Chamber Orchestra*

SZYSZNYK (*Situation Comedy*)

FIRST TELECAST: *August 1, 1977*
LAST TELECAST: *January 25, 1978*
BROADCAST HISTORY:

Aug 1977, CBS Mon 8:30–9:00
Dec 1977–Jan 1978, CBS Wed 8:30–9:00

CAST:

Nick Szysznyk .... Ned Beatty
Ms. Harrison .... Olivia Cole
Sandi Chandler (1977) .... Susan Lanier
Leonard Kriegler .... Leonard Barr
Ralph .... Jarrod Johnson
Fortwengler .... Barry Miller
Tony La Placa .... Scott Colomby
Ray Gun .... Thomas Carter

Nick Szysznyk was a retired marine, used to the discipline and order of military life, who had taken on a new job as playground supervisor at the Northeast Community Center in a poor neighborhood in Washington, D.C. Coping with the bureaucracy in the city government that funded the center, his coworkers, and the street kids who used the center, all proved challenging to him—and to them as well. Highly successful in its initial run against repeat programming during the summer, *Szysznyk* returned in December 1977 against stronger competition and lasted only two months.

T

T. AND T. (*Detective Drama*)

BROADCAST HISTORY:

Syndicated and The Family Channel
30 minutes
Produced: *1987–1990*
Released: *January 1988*

CAST:

T. S. Turner.................................... Mr. T
Amanda "Amy" Taler (1988–1989)..... Alex Amini
Terri Taler (1990).................. Kristina Nicoll
Danforth (Dick) Decker............ David Nerman
Det. Jones (1988).......................... Ken James
Aunt Martha Robinson (1989)... Jackie Richardson
**Renee (1988)*..................... Rachael Crawford
**Sophie (1988)*.................... Catherine Disher
**Joe Casper (Fall 1988–1989)*........ Sean Roberge
**Det. Dick Hargrove (1990)*......... David Hemblen

*Occasional

The A-Team muscleman Mr. T in pinstripes. T. S. Turner was a tough former boxer who worked as a detective/investigator for attorney Amanda Taler. Though he still sported that distinctive Mohawk haircut, this time T was nattily attired in suits that were hard-pressed to contain his bulging muscles. However, when the need arose—and it did at least once in every episode—T.S. would charge off to his locker, change into a studded leather, street-chic outfit, and hunt down the bad guys. Not surprisingly, he found that the criminals were more intimidated by leather than pinstripes. Decker was a good friend who ran the gym where T.S. went to work out, Det. Jones, the cop who had developed a grudging respect for T.S., and Sophie, the secretary who worked for Amy. A bachelor, T.S. lived with his Aunt Martha and her attractive teenage daughter, Renee.

In the fall of 1988, when *T. and T.* returned for its second season, there were a number of changes. Gone, for the most part, were Turner's suits, gone was the stylized routine in the locker room, and gone were many of the supporting players. T.S. now worked out of an office in Decker's gym, dressed more informally, and got into fewer fights. The stories dealt more with social issues than violent crimes, and young Joe Casper, who lived with Decker and worked part time at the gym, was added to the cast.

In January 1990 *T. and T.* returned for a third season on cable's The Family Channel. T.S. had a new partner, Amanda Taler's younger sister Terri (with no explanation of what had happened to Amanda); a new contact on the police force, Detective Hargrove; and a return to somewhat more violent criminal cases.

TBS SUPERSTATION (Network) (*General Entertainment Cable Network*)

LAUNCHED:

December 17, 1976

SUBSCRIBERS (MAY 2003):

87.6 million (82% U.S.)

One of the most viewed cable channels, TBS built its schedule around action-oriented theatrical movies, reruns of network series, and high-profile sports coverage. Movies included the James Bond films and a seemingly endless number of Westerns starring Clint Eastwood and John Wayne. Among the network's sports highlights are Atlanta Braves baseball, NBA basketball, and the TBS-created Goodwill Games, which began in 1986. As for series, the network's "signature show" during the 1980s and early 1990s was the homey *Andy Griffith Show*, which found a whole new audience through its constant exposure on TBS.

TBS produces few original series of its own. Early examples were *Captain Planet & the Planeteers*, an environmentally conscious cartoon seen in the daytime, and *National Geographic Explorer*, a documentary series on Sunday nights. Later efforts included *Ripley's Believe It or Not* with Dean Cain, *Worst Case Scenario* and the unbelievable *Chimp Channel* (q.v.).

TBS Superstation is an outgrowth of a local TV station, WTBS, Channel 17, in Atlanta, which first fed its signal via satellite to cable systems around the country in 1976. It was founded by media mogul R. E. "Ted" Turner, one of the great pioneers of cable, who also launched CNN, TNT, and the Cartoon Network. It first reached 50 percent of U.S. television homes in February 1988. Turner's company also owns the MGM and RKO film libraries and the Hanna-Barbera animation studio, which provide much of the programming for his networks. TBS stands for "Turner Broadcasting System."

T.H.E. CAT (*Adventure*)

FIRST TELECAST: *September 16, 1966*
LAST TELECAST: *September 1, 1967*

BROADCAST HISTORY:

Sep 1966–Sep 1967, NBC Fri 9:30–10:00

CAST:

Thomas Hewitt Edward Cat......... Robert Loggia
Capt. MacAllister................. R. G. Armstrong
Pepe............................ Robert Carricart

T.H.E. Cat was a former circus aerialist and ex–cat burglar whose name fit him very well. His current profession was that of professional bodyguard. He fought crime by guarding those clients who had been marked for death. Only T.H.E. Cat stood between them and their would-be assassins. Declining to use weapons himself, Cat relied on his quickness and agility to protect his clients and himself. Living in San Francisco, he maintained an "office" at the Casa del Gato, a nightclub owned by his friend Pepe. Pepe was a Spanish gypsy whose life had once been saved by T.H.E. Cat, and he would remain loyal to Cat until the day he died. Capt. MacAllister was the police officer with whom Cat worked most closely.

T.J. HOOKER (*Police Drama*)

FIRST TELECAST: *March 13, 1982*
LAST TELECAST: *September 17, 1987*

BROADCAST HISTORY:

Mar 1982–Apr 1982, ABC Sat 8:00–9:00
Sep 1982–Sep 1985, ABC Sat 8:00–9:00
Sep 1985–Sep 1986, CBS Wed 11:30–12:40 A.M.
Sep 1986–Dec 1986, CBS Fri 11:30–12:40 A.M.
Dec 1986–Sep 1987, CBS Tue 11:30–12:40 A.M.
Sep 1987, CBS Tue–Thu 1:00–2:00 A.M.

CAST:

Sgt. T. J. Hooker.................. William Shatner
Officer Vince Romano (1982–1985)... Adrian Zmed
Officer Stacy Sheridan........... Heather Locklear

**Capt. Dennis Sheridan (1982–1985)*... Richard Herd
Fran Hooker (1982–1983) .... Lee Bryant
Vicki Taylor (1982).................... April Clough
Officer Jim Corrigan (1983–1986) .... James Darren

*Occasional

Star Trek's Captain Kirk (William Shatner) was back in uniform in this 1982 police show—but this time as a sergeant. Actually, Sgt. T. J. Hooker had been a detective, but gave up his gold shield and civvies for a uniformed street patrol because that's where he was needed. He was assigned to the Academy Precinct of the "L.C.P.D.," where he could lend advice to police trainees like Stacy and rookies like his eager new partner, Officer Vince Romano.

Hooker taught them more than street smarts, however. There was a good deal of anguish over the rights and wrongs of police work in this series. Hooker stood for traditional values, despite his own disappointments—a former partner killed in the line of duty, and a marriage that had ended in divorce (though he was still on good terms with his ex-wife, Fran). His two daughters, Cathy (played by Susan McClung) and Chrissie (Nicole Eggert, later Jennifer Beck), and young son Tommy (Andre Gower), were seen occasionally. Captain Sheridan was the by-the-book superior, and Stacy's father. In a February 1983 episode Hooker also encountered a familiar face from other times and other places—Leonard Nimoy, as a cop going off the deep end because his daughter had been raped. Celebrities such as Jerry Lee Lewis and the Beach Boys also had cameos from time to time.

In the fall of 1983 Stacy graduated to street patrol, with veteran patrolman Jim Corrigan as her partner. When ABC canceled *T.J. Hooker* in the spring of 1985, CBS picked it up, with new episodes, as an addition to its late-night schedule. The series went out of production at the end of the 1985–1986 season, but reruns continued to air on *CBS Late Night* for another year.

TLC (Network), see *Learning Channel, The*

TNN (NETWORK) (*General Entertainment Cable Network*)

LAUNCHED:

March 7, 1983

SUBSCRIBERS (MAY 2003):

85.5 million (80% U.S.)

For more than fifteen years the Nashville Network was TV's home for country music and middle-American values, providing programming ignored by the big, urban broadcast networks. Adult music and variety shows dominated the schedule, and daytime and weekends brought a range of how-to shows and hunting, fishing and racing.

The Mother Church of country music is of course the *Grand Ole Opry* in Nashville, and its long-running Saturday-night musical extravaganza had a spot on the TNN schedule from the beginning. Other standbys included talk-show host Ralph Emery *(Nashville Now)*; Lorianne Crook and Charlie Chase, country's answer to Regis and Kathie Lee *(Music City Tonight)*, and the Statler Brothers, whose Saturday-night variety hour following the *Opry* echoed the glory days of Ed Sullivan. Dance shows *(Club Dance, Dancin' at the Hot Spots)*, which looked a little like a cross-generational versions of *American Bandstand*, were also popular.

In 1988 the network introduced the annual *TNN Viewers' Choice Awards.* Although most of the network's schedule was original, it also offered occasional reruns, most notably the popular syndicated series *Hee-Haw*. TNN was basically adult-oriented in its programming, so in 1991 it acquired a small country music videos channel called CMT (Country Music Television, launched in 1983), which it operated for younger fans.

And then one day the city slickers came to town, in a long stream of black limousines.

In 1997 TNN and CMT were sold by their Nashville-based owners to Westinghouse Broadcasting Company, which then merged with CBS. In 1999 CBS began canceling the country music shows and shifting TNN to a "country lifestyle" network featuring movies and rerun series, some rather elderly *(Matt Houston, Cagney and Lacey)*. The network's guitar logo was dropped, and in January 2000 the first of a planned wave of original dramatic series, *18 Wheels of Justice*, premiered. Four months later Viacom, owner of MTV, bought CBS and announced that it would transform TNN into a general entertainment network to compete with USA and TNT. The official name of the network was changed to The National Network effective September 2000. A raft of original reality shows were introduced *(Small Shots, Lifegame, Pop Across America, The Conspiracy Zone, Oblivious)*—all of which failed. Keeping the network alive during this period were WWF/WWE wrestling and rerun series such as *Star Trek: The Next Generation, Baywatch, CSI* and *MadTV.* Finally, in early 2003, the new owners announced they were dropping the initials *TNN* altogether, renaming the network Spike TV, and turning it into a men's channel with testosterone-driven movies such as *Bladerunner* and *The Terminator* and male-oriented series offering raunchy humor, sexual innuendo, automotive news, and men's health tips. Stock market updates were also planned, on the premise that "guys like money, and girls like guys that have money."

TNN first reached more than half of all U.S. television homes in May 1989, and its principal original evening series after that date, and those of its successors, are listed in this book under their individual titles.

TNT (Network) (*General Entertainment Cable Network*)

LAUNCHED:

October 3, 1988

SUBSCRIBERS (MAY 2003):

86.2 million (81% U.S.)

TNT is owned by the company that operates TBS Superstation, and it features similar programming. Much of its schedule consists of movies, supplemented by rerun series *(Starsky and Hutch, In the Heat of the Night, Gilligan's Island, Law & Order)*, cartoons *(The Bugs Bunny Show)*, and sports coverage. The latter has included NFL football, NBA basketball, and the Winter Olympics in 1992 and 1994. The network debuted in 1988 with a telecast of *Gone With the Wind.*

TNT produces several original movies each year, many historical epics such as *A Man for All Seasons* starring Charlton Heston (1988), *Margaret Bourke-White* starring Farrah Fawcett (1989), *Geronimo* (1993), *Gettysburg* (1994) and *Andersonville* (1996).

For many years TNT produced no original series of its own, relying instead on its owners' vast library of network reruns. In the late '90s it began to tiptoe into the field, mostly airing new series that also aired at some point in syndication on broadcast stations. Among these were *The Lazarus Man* (1996), *The New Adventures of Robin Hood* (1997), *Babylon 5* (1998), and *Mortal Kombat: Conquest* (1998). Coming later were *Crusade* (1999) and *Witchblade* (2001).

TNT was founded by R. E. "Ted" Turner; the initials stand for Turner Network Television. It first reached more than half of all U.S. television homes in May 1990.

TV FUNHOUSE (*Comedy*)

BROADCAST HISTORY:

Comedy Central
30 minutes
Original episodes: *2000–2001* (8 episodes)
Premiered: *December 6, 2000*

CAST:

Doug .... Doug Dale
Jeffy (voice) .... Doug Dale
Fogey, Xabu, Triumph, Rocky (voices)
.... Robert Smigel
Hojo (voice) .... Jon Glaser
Chickie (voice) .... Dino Stamatopoulos
Whiskers (voice) .... Tommy Blacha
Larry (voice) .... David Juskow

"TV Funhouse, comin' through, with animals that pee and poo," began this twisted parody of a children's show, which was spun off from a sketch on *Saturday Night Live*. "Your pal Doug," the goofy host, was seen interacting with his "anipals" Xabu the dog, Whiskers the cat, Hojo the turtle, Chickie the chicken, and others—all portrayed by puppets. Rocky the fish flopped around on a counter and needed to be periodically doused with water. Doug would open the show by planning the day's activities, but then the animals would go off on their own, being seen in all sorts of unlikely human settings. The jokes were mostly of the sex and toilet-humor variety.

The series was created and produced by *SNL* writer Robert Smigel.

TV LAND (Network) (*General Entertainment Cable Network*)

LAUNCHED:

April 29, 1996

SUBSCRIBERS (MAY 2003)

78.6 million (74% U.S.)

A 24-hour sibling of Nick at Nite, featuring a wide range of elderly TV series dating from the 1950s to the 1980s. Whereas Nick at Night concentrated on sitcoms, TV Land aired numerous drama and action shows, including *Dragnet*, *Mannix*, *Gunsmoke*, and *Alfred Hitchcock Presents*. A few true antiques were seen on *The Museum of Television and Radio Showcase*, but most shows were baby boomer favorites. In fact, the whole channel projected a campy attitude, with bell bottoms and jokes about Gerald Ford abounding on variety shows such as *Sonny and Cher* and *The Flip Wilson Show*. Even the commercials, called "retromercials," were old.

For a complete guide to the channel, just read the rest of this book.

TV MOMENTS (*Documentary*)

BROADCAST HISTORY:

VH1
60 minutes
Original episodes: *2002–*
Premiered: *January 26, 2002*

Documentary that each week traced a different rock star's career on TV, with clips and interviews. The tone was generally reverential, even when dealing with such eccentrics as Michael Jackson, who was shown from his 1970s days of Day-Glo suits and bell-bottoms to his infamous crotch-grabbing video of later years.

TV NATION (*Comedy Newsmagazine*)

FIRST TELECAST: *July 19, 1994*
LAST TELECAST: *September 8, 1995*
BROADCAST HISTORY:

Jul 1994–Aug 1994, NBC Tue 8:00–9:00
Jul 1995–Sep 1995, FOX Fri 8:00–9:00

HOST:

Michael Moore

CORRESPONDENTS:

Merrill Markoe (1994)
Karen Duffy
Ben Hamper (1994)
Roy Sekoff (1994)
Louis Theroux
Jonathan Katz (1994)
Rusty Cundieff
Jane Morris (1994)
Janeane Garofalo (1995)
Jeff Stilson (1995)

Paunchy, rumpled, contrarian filmmaker Michael Moore produced and hosted this hilarious take on TV newsmagazines—*TV Guide* called it "the *Mad* magazine of [news] shows." The tone was much like his famous documentary *Roger and Me*, in which Moore pursued General Motors chairman Roger Smith seeking answers about a plant closing (which he never got), humorous, one-sided, and always from the little guy's point of view. Stories included happy dogs on Prozac, how workers get back at the boss with creative sabotage, going door to door with Avon ladies in the Amazon, Moore's challenge to corporate CEOs to service personally the products they sell (the head of IBM declined to format a disk, but the president of the Ford Motor Company did change his oil), and Moore's running campaign to get a game New York mayor Rudolph Giuliani to provide him with parking spaces and stronger water pressure in his shower.

A year after its cancellation by NBC, *TV Nation* turned up on Fox. New features included ridiculous poll results from the fictitious polling organization, Widgery and Associates; a weekly appearance by Crackers, the corporate crime-fighting chicken; and man-on-the-street interviews with ordinary people on Manhattan's Broadway.

TV 101 (*Drama*)

FIRST TELECAST: *November 29, 1988*
LAST TELECAST: *March 25, 1989*
BROADCAST HISTORY:

Nov 1988–Dec 1988, CBS Tue 8:00–9:00
Jan 1989–Feb 1989, CBS Wed 8:00–9:00
Feb 1989–Mar 1989, CBS Sat 9:00–10:00

CAST:

Kevin Keegan .... Sam Robards
Principal Edward Steadman .... Leon Russom
Emilie Walker .... Brynn Thayer
Sherman Fischer .... Andrew Cassese
Monique .... Stacey Dash
Holden Hines .... Alex Desert
Marty Voight .... Stewart Goddard
Chuck Bender .... Matt LeBlanc
Amanda Hampton .... Teri Polo
Penny Lipton .... Mary B. Ward
Vance Checker .... Andrew White
Angela Hernandez .... Monique Salcido
Mary Alice Peavy .... Cristine Rose
Skip the Janitor .... Matt Dearborn

In his years at Roosevelt High a decade earlier, Kevin Keegan had been a talented but disruptive student who found the regimentation and discipline stifling. Now he was back, at the behest of his former journalism teacher, Emilie Walker, attempting to instill some of his passion for journalism in a new generation of high school students. Recently divorced, and looking for a new direction in his life, Kevin had traded in his job as a TV news photographer to teach. But not the way he had been taught. Instead of a high school newspaper, his students produced a weekly cable TV news show, using video equipment donated to the school. Emilie gave him full support, which is more than could be said for principal Steadman, a rigid disciplinarian who remembered Kevin's student days all too well. After overcoming their initial skepticism, Kevin's students became enthusiastic and creative reporters, producing both light and serious pieces about their world.

TV READER'S DIGEST (*Dramatic Anthology*)

FIRST TELECAST: *January 17, 1955*
LAST TELECAST: *July 9, 1956*
BROADCAST HISTORY:

Jan 1955–Jul 1956, ABC Mon 8:00–8:30

HOST:

Hugh Reilly (1955)
Gene Raymond (1956)

Wholesome, frequently patriotic true stories from the pages of the *Reader's Digest* were dramatized in this filmed series. As in the *Digest*, little incidents from history and cameos from contemporary life were favorite subjects, and almost everything had a moral. Included were dramatizations of Stephen Foster's last days, the life of Pocahontas, the Scopes "Monkey" Trial of the 1920s, brainwashing attempts by the Communists in Korea, the story of a retired, old-time six-gun sheriff who was recalled by his town to stop a crime wave, etc. Performers were generally lesser known, but included some future stars such as Peter Graves, Chuck Connors, and Lee Marvin.

TV RECITAL HALL (*Music*)

FIRST TELECAST: *July 1, 1951*
LAST TELECAST: *September 6, 1954*
BROADCAST HISTORY:

Jul 1951–Aug 1951, NBC Sun 8:30–9:00
Aug 1954–Sep 1954, NBC Mon 9:00–9:30

Live performances of classical music, featuring performers in a recital-hall–type setting, were presented on a weekly basis. They originated from New York with a live audience and the selections and performers were introduced by an offstage announcer. Between August 1951 and August 1954 this show was seen on an intermittent basis, occasionally for periods on Sunday afternoons and sometimes as a one-time-only special. It returned in August 1954 with the title shortened to *Recital Hall*. Following its last primetime telecast, it returned to Sunday afternoons, where it remained until July 1955.

TV SOUNDSTAGE, see *Campbell Soundstage*

TV'S BLOOPERS & PRACTICAL JOKES

(*Comedy*)

FIRST TELECAST: *January 9, 1984*
LAST TELECAST: *August 8, 1998*
BROADCAST HISTORY:

Jan 1984–Feb 1986, NBC Mon 8:00–9:00
Feb 1986, NBC Mon 10:00–11:00
May 1988–Sep 1988, NBC Fri 8:00–9:00
Jan 1991, NBC Sun 7:00–8:00
Feb 1991, NBC Fri 8:00–9:00
Feb 1991–May 1991, NBC Sun 7:00–8:00
Jul 1993–Sep 1993, NBC Sat 8:00–9:00
Jan 1998–May 1998, NBC Sat 8:00–9:00
Jun 1998–Aug 1998, NBC Sun 7:00–8:00
Aug 1998, NBC Sat 8:00–9:00

HOST:

Ed McMahon (1984–1993)
Dick Clark
Suzanne Whang (1998)

REGULARS:

Julie Dees (1984)
Robert Klein (1984–1985)
Thom Sharp (1984–1988)
Len Cella (1984–1988)
Wil Shriner (1985–1986)

Bloopers, unintended pratfalls, and fluffed lines captured on film have been favorite showbiz entertainment for years, both behind the scenes and (at least for the cleaner clips) as features on various shows. In May 1981 NBC began a series of specials called "TV's Censored Bloopers" which proved so popular that the idea was spun off into a weekly series—which was promptly copied by ABC for a nearly identical show (see *Foul-Ups, Bleeps & Blunders*).

In addition to outtakes from movies, TV shows, and newscasts, the series featured classic commercials, humorous comments by children (interviewed by Julie Dees), and people on the street (interviewed by Robert Klein and David Letterman in New York and, beginning in the fall of 1984, by Thom Sharp in Hollywood). There were popular songs set to ironic visual clips, and Len Cella hosted a regular segment of short films that took an offbeat look at everyday life. A popular segment was practical jokes played on famous stars, while hidden cameras looked on; for example, Connie Sellecca of *Hotel* asked to take delivery of a truckload of pigs, Christopher Atkins of *Dallas* stopped by a cop for driving a "stolen" car, or James Coburn entering an apartment which then appeared to have no exit.

Johnny Carson, whose company coproduced this show (with Dick Clark Productions), occasionally narrated clips from *The Tonight Show*.

Whatever else could be said about this mélange, it

knew its roots. Each episode ended with a tribute to Kermit Schafer, the producer-writer who first popularized bloopers from radio in the 1940s and 1950s.

NBC aired selected reruns of this series during the summer of 1988 and continued to air periodic *Bloopers* specials into the 1990s. In early 1991 and 1993 the network brought the concept back as a short-run series (filling in time periods where other shows had failed), this time under the title *Super Bloopers & New Practical Jokes*. Dick Clark and Ed McMahon were the hosts of all these editions. In 1998 NBC aired yet another version, called *TV Censored Bloopers '98*, hosted by Clark and Suzanne Whang.

TV'S TOP TUNES (*Music*)
FIRST TELECAST: *July 2, 1951*
LAST TELECAST: *September 3, 1955*
BROADCAST HISTORY:
Jul 1951–Aug 1951, CBS Mon/Wed/Fri 7:45–8:00
Jun 1953–Aug 1953, CBS Mon/Wed/Fri 7:45–8:00
Jun 1954–Aug 1954, CBS Mon/Wed/Fri 7:45–8:00
Jul 1955–Sep 1955, CBS Sat 10:00–10:30
REGULARS:
Peggy Lee (1951)
Mel Torme (1951)
The Fontane Sisters (1951)
Mitchell Ayres Orchestra (1951, 1955)
The Skyliners (1954)
The Anthony Choir (1954)
Helen O'Connell (1953)
Bob Eberly (1953)
Ray Anthony & His Orchestra (1953, 1954)
Tommy Mercer (1954)
Marcie Mills (1954)
Julius LaRosa (1955)

In 1951, 1953, and 1954 various artists filled in for the vacationing Perry Como on *TV's Top Tunes*, a live thrice-weekly music show that filled the remainder of the half hour in which CBS aired its network news program. During the summer of 1955, when this series was expanded to a full half hour on Saturday nights, its star, Julius LaRosa, had another series, *The Julius LaRosa Show*, airing three times a week in the time period that *TV's Top Tunes* had occupied during previous summers.

TAB HUNTER SHOW, THE (*Situation Comedy*)
FIRST TELECAST: *September 18, 1960*
LAST TELECAST: *September 10, 1961*
BROADCAST HISTORY:
Sep 1960–Sep 1961, NBC Sun 8:30–9:00
CAST:
Paul Morgan .... Tab Hunter
Peter Fairfield III .... Richard Erdman
John Larsen .... Jerome Cowan
Thelma .... Reta Shaw

Paul Morgan was a swinging young bachelor who had made a living out of his lifestyle. As a cartoonist for Comics, Inc., he was the creator of the strip "Bachelor-at-Large," which detailed the adventures of an amorous young man living the good life in Southern California. The strip read almost like a diary, which it was, of the romantic exploits of its author. Paul's boss, John Larsen, never ceased to be amazed by the situations into which his prize cartoonist got himself. Paul's best friend was the wealthy, eligible, and stingy Peter Fairfield III, a fashion plate and car enthusiast who was regularly mixed up in Paul's romantic adventures. Keeping Paul's Malibu Beach apartment in order was his housekeeper, Thelma, who did not approve of his never-ending stream of beautiful women.

TABITHA (*Situation Comedy*)
FIRST TELECAST: *November 12, 1977*
LAST TELECAST: *August 25, 1978*
BROADCAST HISTORY:
Nov 1977–Jan 1978, ABC Sat 8:00–8:30
Jun 1978–Aug 1978, ABC Fri 8:00–8:30
CAST:
Tabitha Stephens .... Lisa Hartman
Paul Thurston .... Robert Urich
Marvin Decker .... Mel Stewart
Adam Stephens .... David Ankrum
Aunt Minerva .... Karen Morrow

This briefly seen comedy was a spin-off from ABC's long-running hit *Bewitched*. Tabitha was the daughter of Samantha, the leading character on *Bewitched*. She was seen as a child on that series, but by the time this one began she had grown into a bright young woman, just beginning her career as a television production assistant at station KLXA, in California. Tabitha worked for producer Marvin Decker, and her chief assignment was *The Paul Thurston Show*. Thurston was the station's handsome, but not-too-bright, star newscaster. Adam was Tabitha's brother and a fellow employee at KLXA, and Minerva was her meddlesome aunt.

Despite the similarity to *The Mary Tyler Moore Show*, Tabitha had something extra: as a witch, she could perform feats of magic, and get her own way, with a twitch of the nose. It didn't help. The series soon disappeared in a puff of Nielsen ratings.

TABOO (*Quiz*)
BROADCAST HISTORY:
TNN
30 minutes
Original episodes: *2003*
Premiered: *January 5, 2003*
EMCEE:
Chris Wylde

This noisy game show was played in a party atmosphere, with two teams of three people each. In the first and second rounds one member of each team was given a simple word or phrase such as *slumber party*, *wife* or *dam*, and told to describe it to the other two without using letters, rhymes or five "taboo" words (the most obvious clues). If the other two team members guessed the word they earned points for the team. The third and fourth rounds were similar except that the points and number of taboo words increased, and manic host Chris began distracting the contestants with noises, nerf balls and the like. The winning team was the one with the greatest number of points or, if there was a tie, the one that had accumulated the fewest taboos. The winning team then went on to a bonus "speed" round, in which they tried to guess six words in 60 seconds (without tripping over taboos), for a grand prize of $1,000 each and a vacation.

Based on the board game of the same name.

TAG THE GAG (*Quiz/Panel*)
FIRST TELECAST: *August 13, 1951*

LAST TELECAST: *August 20, 1951*
BROADCAST HISTORY:
Aug 1951, NBC Mon 8:00–8:30
MODERATOR:
Hal Block

In this comedy-quiz show a panel of comedians tried to guess the punch lines to jokes that were acted out by a group of performers. The performers would set up the punch line and it was up to the panelists to "tag the gag." Hal Block, who served as moderator, had created the idea for the show but, apparently, the joke was on him—it only lasted two weeks. The only panelist to appear on both telecasts was funnyman Morey Amsterdam.

TAINA (*Situation Comedy*)
BROADCAST HISTORY:
Nickelodeon
30 minutes
Original episodes: *2001–2002* (26 episodes)
Premiered: *January 14, 2001*
CAST:
Taina Maria Morales (age 14) .... Christina Vidal
Gloria Elena Morales .... Lisa Velez
Eduardo Morales .... Josh Cruze
Santito Morales .... Brandon Iglesias
Renee Aretha Jones .... Khaliah Adams
Daniel Nathaniel McDaniel .... David Oliver Cohen
LaMar Carlos Johnson ...... Christopher Knowings
Maritza Hogg .... LaTangela
Gregorio "Abuelo" Sanchez ..... Manolo Villaverde
Titi Rosa .... Selenis Leyva

Taina (pronounced Ty-ee-na) was a bright, enthusiastic, and ambitious Latina student at Manhattan's School of the Arts in this multicultural teen sitcom reminiscent of the 1980s series *Fame*. Together with her saucy black friend Renee, white guitarist Daniel (with whom she shared a locker), and goofball LaMar, she auditioned, staged musical numbers, and plotted her way to a show-biz career. (Periodically the students in this series would break out their instruments and stage big production numbers in the hallways, just as in *Fame*.) Maritza was her main foil, always tossing off put-downs and trying to upstage her (Renee to Maritza: "Maritza, shouldn't you slither away somewhere and eat your young?"). The gang sometimes performed at Papito's. At home her family consisted of doting parents Gloria and Eduardo, little brother Santito, and relative Rosa.

Taina's mom was played by 1980s pop icon Lisa Lisa, under her real name Lisa Velez.

TAKE A CHANCE (*Quiz/Audience Participation*)
FIRST TELECAST: *October 1, 1950*
LAST TELECAST: *December 24, 1950*
BROADCAST HISTORY:
Oct 1950–Dec 1950, NBC Sun 10:30–11:00
EMCEE:
Don Ameche

Each contestant on this live quiz program was drawn from the studio audience and given an initial $5. He was then asked a series of four questions. A correct answer to the first one enabled the contestant to keep the $5 and receive a small prize. Answers to the subsequent questions were worth unspecified other winnings, some big and some small. The contestant could quit whenever he or she no longer wanted to "take a chance," but there was an incentive to go on. Correctly answering all four questions gave the contestant a shot at the jackpot question—worth $1,000 in cash and 1,000 cakes of Sweetheart soap. If a question was not answered correctly, however, the contestant had to forfeit his last prize.

TAKE A GOOD LOOK (*Quiz/Panel*)
FIRST TELECAST: *October 22, 1959*
LAST TELECAST: *March 16, 1961*
BROADCAST HISTORY:
Oct 1959–Mar 1961, ABC Thu 10:30–11:00
HOST:
Ernie Kovacs
PANELISTS:
Hans Conried
Cesar Romero
Edie Adams (1960–1961)
Ben Alexander (1960)
Carl Reiner (1960–1961)
ACTORS:
Peggy Connelly
Bobby Lauher
Jolene Brand

Panelists were advised to "take a good look" at the contestants on this quiz show. Although they were relatively unknown, each of the contestants had once been a central figure in a headline-making news event, and the panel had to guess just who they were. To help, clues such as film clips or recordings were played, or Ernie Kovacs and a team of regulars acted out the clues. In addition to the regular panelists guest celebrities frequently appeared.

TAKE A GUESS (*Quiz/Audience Participation*)
FIRST TELECAST: *June 11, 1953*
LAST TELECAST: *September 10, 1953*
BROADCAST HISTORY:
Jun 1953–Sep 1953, CBS Thu 8:00–8:30
MODERATOR:
John K. M. McCaffery
PANELISTS:
Margaret Lindsay
Ernie Kovacs
Dorothy Hart
John Crawford
Robin Chandler
Hans Conried

Contestants on this summer quiz show were aided by members of a celebrity panel in trying to identify something that was known only to the moderator and the audience. Each contestant started with $150. As he looked on, the panel asked questions of the moderator to determine the identity of the mystery object. However, $5 was deducted from the $150 each time one of their questions received a "yes" answer, so the contestant had an incentive to guess as quickly as possible (he could take a maximum of four guesses). The contestant won whatever was left of the original $150 after the money for the "yes" answers was subtracted. If the entire $150 was used up (due to 30 "yes" answers), or the contestant had made four incorrect answers, there were no winnings at all.

TAKE FIVE (*Situation Comedy*)
FIRST TELECAST: *April 1, 1987*
LAST TELECAST: *April 8, 1987*

BROADCAST HISTORY:

Apr 1987, CBS Wed 8:30–9:00

CAST:

Andy Kooper .... George Segal
Dr. Noah Wolf .... Severn Darden
Al .... Derek McGrath
Monty .... Bruce Jarchow
Lenny Goodman .... Jim Haynie
Laraine McDermott .... Melanie Chartoff
Kevin Davis .... Todd Field
Max Davis .... Eugene Roche

Life was not going well for lanky Andy Kooper. His wife had divorced him and her father had fired him from his public relations job. Andy tried to get a handle on things by picking and singing with his buddies in the Lenny Goodman Quartet, a semi-pro Dixieland jazz band in which he sang and played banjo. The others in the quartet were Lenny, piano; Al, saxophone; and Monty, drums. The fact that Monty was dating Andy's ex-wife was a sour note but, hey, Andy could handle it. Andy did find a new job with Davis & Son public relations—where old Max Davis was retired and the new boss, his son Kevin, was incompetent. Unfortunately, the brightest person there, Laraine, hated Andy because she had pitched for the job he had gotten. Dr. Wolf was the psychiatrist to whom Andy told all.

Star George Segal, who played regularly with a Dixieland band much like the one in this series when he was not acting, managed to combine both his vocation and his avocation here—but not for long. *Take Five* never even got to five. It was canceled after only two episodes had aired.

TAKE IT FROM ME (*Situation Comedy*)

FIRST TELECAST: *November 4, 1953*
LAST TELECAST: *January 20, 1954*
BROADCAST HISTORY:

Nov 1953–Jan 1954, ABC Wed 9:00–9:30

CAST:

Wife .... Jean Carroll
Husband (Herbie) .... Alan Carney
Daughter .... Lynn Loring

Standup comedienne Jean Carroll starred as an "average" New York City housewife, complete with bumbling husband and moppet daughter, in this comedy. She opened each show with a monologue, then spiced the night's sketch with comic asides to the audience. Many of the stories involved her sly schemes to trick husband Herbie into doing whatever she wanted. The action took place in the couple's apartment and the surrounding neighborhood, which, though never identified, was presumably in Brooklyn or the Bronx. This New York orientation may have limited the show's appeal west of the Hudson River, and it lasted less than three months.

Also known as *The Jean Carroll Show.*

TALENT JACKPOT (*Talent*)

FIRST TELECAST: *July 19, 1949*
LAST TELECAST: *August 23, 1949*
BROADCAST HISTORY:

Jul 1949–Aug 1949, DUM Tue 9:00–9:30

EMCEE:

Vinton Freedley

ASSISTANT:

Bud Collyer

Summer talent show for aspiring professionals, emceed by Broadway producer Vinton Freedley and offering a maximum prize of $250 for each of the night's five acts. The amount each act won depended on the level reached by an audience applause meter. The top winner of the night got his own winnings as well as whatever was left over from the other acts' $250 maximums.

TALENT PATROL (*Talent/Variety*)

FIRST TELECAST: *January 19, 1953*
LAST TELECAST: *September 8, 1955*
BROADCAST HISTORY:

Jan 1953–Jul 1953, ABC Mon 9:30–10:00
Jul 1953–Aug 1953, ABC Mon 8:00–8:30
Sep 1953–Oct 1953, ABC Wed 8:00–8:30
Oct 1953–Jan 1954, ABC Sat 8:00–8:30
Jan 1954–Mar 1954, ABC Thu 9:00–9:30
Apr 1954–Jul 1954, ABC Thu 8:00–8:30
Jul 1954–Oct 1954, ABC Wed 7:30–8:00
Oct 1954–Nov 1954, ABC Sun 9:30–10:00
Dec 1954–Jan 1955, ABC Mon 8:00–8:30
Jan 1955–Jun 1955, ABC Thu 8:00–8:30
Jun 1955–Sep 1955, ABC Thu 8:00–9:00

EMCEE:

Steve Allen (1953)
Bud Collyer (1953)
Arlene Francis (1953–1955)
Richard Hayes (1955)

Talent Patrol began as a military talent show, sponsored by the army over the 88 stations of the ABC network as an aid to recruiting. All the contestants were GIs, performing a wide variety of nonmilitary skills—impersonations, folk singing, playing musical instruments, trampoline acts, and even hula dancing! Winners got a night on the town with a pretty actress. Even the runners-up came out ahead, however, with national TV exposure, not to mention a five-day pass to go to New York and rehearse for the show. Army bands provided the musical accompaniment.

In mid-1954 the program became more of a straight variety show, featuring army professional talent as well as celebrity guests, and the title was changed to *Soldier Parade.*

Steve Allen was the original host of the series, replaced "temporarily" by Bud Collyer after only three months and permanently by Arlene Francis in June 1953. When the program expanded to a full hour in June 1955 singer Richard Hayes, in the army himself at the time, joined Miss Francis in the capacity of cohost.

TALENT SCOUTS (*Talent/Variety*)

FIRST TELECAST: *July 3, 1962*
LAST TELECAST: *September 17, 1963*
BROADCAST HISTORY:

Jul 1962–Sep 1962, CBS Tue 10:00–11:00
Jul 1963–Sep 1963, CBS Tue 8:30–9:30

HOST:

Jim Backus (1962)
Merv Griffin (1963)

Each week a number of guest celebrities appeared on this show to introduce young professional performers who were being given their first network exposure on the series. In 1962 this was the summer replacement for *The Garry Moore Show* and in 1963 for *The Red Skelton Hour.* The most immediate success story from this series was impressionist Vaughn Meader. He did his imitation of President Kennedy on the first telecast of the 1962 series and had a subsequent smash recording—*The First Family.* Among the other young performers who appeared as newcomers were George Carlin, Charles Nelson Reilly, Louise Lasser, and Vic Dana.

This summer series was a revival of *Arthur Godfrey's Talent Scouts*, which had had a ten-year run on CBS ending in 1958.

TALENT VARIETIES (*Variety*)
FIRST TELECAST: *June 28, 1955*
LAST TELECAST: *November 1, 1955*
BROADCAST HISTORY:
Jun 1955–Sep 1955, ABC Tue 7:30–8:30
Sep 1955–Nov 1955, ABC Tue 10:00–10:30
REGULARS:
Slim Wilson
The Tall Timber Trio

Originating from Springfield, Missouri, this variety show had a country-and-western flavor. Each week emcee and singer Slim Wilson introduced assorted amateur talent and occasionally performed himself.

TALES FROM THE CRYPT (*Horror Anthology*)
FIRST TELECAST: *January 22, 1994*
LAST TELECAST: *July 14, 1995*
BROADCAST HISTORY:
Jan 1994–Aug 1995, FOX Sat 11:00–12:00 mid
May 1994–Aug 1994, FOX Tue 9:00–10:00
Jun 1995–Jul 1995, FOX Fri 8:00–9:00
(Also HBO cable)
VOICE:
The Cryptkeeper .... John Kassir

Tales from the Crypt was a ghoulish anthology series featuring a wide range of stories that often had gruesome surprise endings. Hosting the show was The Cryptkeeper, a talking skeleton with an evil sense of humor. Although most of the actors appearing were not well known at the time, some episodes did showcase more familiar faces. Among them were Demi Moore, Christopher Reeve, Teri Garr, Beau Bridges, Harry Anderson, Priscilla Presley, Donald O'Connor, Don Rickles, Martin Sheen, Margot Kidder, Joe Pesci, and Bruce Boxleitner.

The first three *Tales from the Crypt* episodes, adapted from the EC horror comic books of the 1950s, had aired as a trilogy on HBO on June 10, 1989, and new episodes continued to be produced for that cable network while reruns of older episodes aired on Fox. A total of 93 half hours were produced for HBO, with the last original episode premiering on July 19, 1996. In addition, there was an animated *Tales from the Cryptkeeper* that aired Saturday mornings on ABC from September 1993 to July 1995.

TALES FROM THE DARKSIDE
(*Horror/Supernatural*)
BROADCAST HISTORY:
Syndicated only
30 minutes
Produced: *1984–1988* (90 episodes)
Released: *September 1984*
NARRATOR:
Paul Sparer

Stylish if rather low-budget anthology of horror stories, many with O. Henry-ish surprise endings. *Tales from the Darkside* resembled the more macabre episodes of *The Twilight Zone* but, unlike the latter series, it never aired stories of a whimsical/fantasy nature. Watching it regularly could become a depressing experience. Performers were generally lesser-knowns or veteran character actors, among them Arnold Stang, Connie Stevens, Keenan Wynn, Fritz Weaver, Justine Bateman, Eddie Bracken, Peggy Cass, Harry Anderson, Jean Marsh, Bill Macy, Darren McGavin, and Phyllis Diller.

TALES OF E.S.P., see *E.S.P.*

TALES OF THE CITY, see *Willys Theater Presenting Ben Hecht's Tales of the City*

TALES OF THE GOLD MONKEY (*Adventure*)
FIRST TELECAST: *September 22, 1982*
LAST TELECAST: *July 6, 1983*
BROADCAST HISTORY:
Sep 1982–Feb 1983, ABC Wed 8:00–9:00
Mar 1983–Apr 1983, ABC Fri 10:00–11:00
Jun 1983–Jul 1983, ABC Wed 9:00–10:00
CAST:
Jake Cutter .... Stephen Collins
Corky .... Jeff MacKay
Sarah Stickney White .... Caitlin O'Heaney
Bon Chance Louis .... Roddy McDowall
Rev. Willie Tenboom .... John Calvin
Princess Koji .... Marta DuBois
Todo .... John Fujioka

The year was 1938, and the setting the tropical Marivella Islands in the South Pacific. Spies and schemers of many nationalities were found throughout the islands, especially in the languid port of Boragora. Their chief gathering spot was the elegant Monkey Bar, filled with wood carvings, tinkling piano music, and whispered information. Everyone in the place seemed to have a mysterious past, including Jake Cutter, whose worn leather flight jacket bore a Flying Tigers patch—legacy of past adventures. Jake was an American soldier of fortune and pilot with a wry sense of humor, whose battered seaplane, a Grumman Goose, provided the only inter-island air transportation. From this romantic setting Jake set out on a new adventure each week, rescuing kidnapped travelers, recovering stolen booty, and foiling the German and Japanese spies who infested the area.

Jake had two sidekicks, his loyal but frequently inebriated mechanic, Corky, and a one-eyed terrier named Jack (who never would forgive Jake for gambling away his jeweled glass eye). A shifty ally was the dapper but roguish Bon Chance Louis, the French magistrate in Boragora and proprietor of the Monkey Bar. Sarah was the willowy, contrary American singer at the bar, whose attraction to Jake kept getting in the way of her real purpose—she was an American agent keeping an eye on things in the islands. Others in the colorful cast were Rev. Willie Tenboom, a pompous Dutch minister who was really a German spy; Princess Koji, a beautiful Dragon Lady who maintained a large fleet of trading ships at Matuka in the Japanese sector of the island chain; and Todo, the fierce Samurai commander of the princess's private army.

TALES OF THE RED CABOOSE (*Adventure*)

FIRST TELECAST: *October 29, 1948*
LAST TELECAST: *January 14, 1949*
BROADCAST HISTORY:
Oct 1948–Jan 1949, ABC Fri 7:30–7:45

Early TV advertisers did not know what kind of use could be made of the new medium, and so can be forgiven shows like this one. *Tales of the Red Caboose* was sponsored by Lionel Trains, and consisted simply of model trains racing around on their tracks. Various races and miniaturized "adventures" were depicted, and a narrator, "Don Magee," spun yarns based on the lore of railroads.

For a similar program sponsored by rival A. C. Gilbert Co. (American Flyer) see *Roar of the Rails.*

TALES OF THE 77TH BENGAL LANCERS (*Adventure*)

FIRST TELECAST: *October 21, 1956*
LAST TELECAST: *June 2, 1957*
BROADCAST HISTORY:
Oct 1956–Jun 1957, NBC Sun 7:00–7:30

CAST:
Lt. Michael Rhodes .... Phil Carey
Lt. William Storm .... Warren Stevens
Col. Standish .... Patrick Whyte

Set in India in the late 19th century, the stories of this fictional outfit were based on the exploits of the real Bengal Lancers, the famed British Cavalry unit. Col. Standish was the commander of the "77th" and working under him were two lieutenants who were also close friends, Michael Rhodes and William Storm. Rhodes was portrayed as a Canadian because New Jersey–born Phil Carey had trouble mastering an English accent.

TALES OF THE TEXAS RANGERS (*Western*)

FIRST TELECAST: *December 22, 1958*
LAST TELECAST: *May 25, 1959*
BROADCAST HISTORY:
Dec 1958–May 1959, ABC Mon 7:30–8:00

CAST:
Ranger Jace Pearson.................. Willard Parker
Ranger Clay Morgan.................. Harry Lauter

As the title suggests, these were straightforward adventure stories concerning the exploits of one of America's most famous law-enforcement agencies. Although Rangers Pearson and Morgan were regulars, they appeared in a different setting each week, ranging from the Old West of the 1830s to modern-day Texas, using crime-detection methods appropriate to each era. The program was, in effect, a survey of the Rangers' activities over its 120-year history.

Tales of the Texas Rangers was seen on Saturday afternoons on CBS from September 1955 to May 1957. It then moved to ABC, where it ran at 5:00 P.M. on Sundays (September 1957 to June 1958) and later Thursdays (October 1958 to December 1958), just prior to its primetime run. *Tales of the Texas Rangers* was also heard as a radio series in the early 1950s, with Joel McCrea in the lead role of Ranger Pearson.

TALES OF THE UNEXPECTED (*Suspense Anthology*)

FIRST TELECAST: *February 2, 1977*
LAST TELECAST: *August 24, 1977*
BROADCAST HISTORY:
Feb 1977–Mar 1977, NBC Wed 10:00–11:00
Mar 1977, NBC Sun 9:00–11:00
Aug 1977, NBC Wed 10:00–11:00

NARRATOR:
William Conrad

EXECUTIVE PRODUCER:
Quinn Martin

This anthology show dealt in both psychological and occult suspense stories, all of which had unusual O. Henry–like twists to prolong the suspense until the very end of the episode. After five weeks on Wednesdays, the final two-hour episode of this series aired on a Sunday. Five months later, *Tales of the Unexpected* returned to its original time slot for two weeks with new episodes.

TALES OF THE UNKNOWN, see *Journey to the Unknown*

TALES OF TOMORROW (*Science Fiction Anthology*)

FIRST TELECAST: *August 3, 1951*
LAST TELECAST: *June 12, 1953*
BROADCAST HISTORY:
Aug 1951–Jun 1953, ABC Fri 9:30–10:00

Tales of Tomorrow was one of TV's earliest adult science-fiction series, using both classic and modern stories of strange and supernatural happenings. Among the stories were "The Monsters" (from Mars), "The Dark Angel" (about a woman who never aged), H. G. Wells' "The Crystal Egg," "The Flying Saucer," "Frankenstein," and a two-part version of Jules Verne's *20,000 Leagues Under the Sea.* The program was produced by George F. Foley, Jr., and used such talent as Franchot Tone, Lon Chaney, Jr., Veronica Lake, Boris Karloff, Eva Gabor, Leslie Nielsen, and Lee J. Cobb.

During 1951 and 1953 it alternated with other series. For a time during early 1953 the program was also heard on radio.

TALES OF WELLS FARGO (*Western*)

FIRST TELECAST: *March 18, 1957*
LAST TELECAST: *September 8, 1962*
BROADCAST HISTORY:
Mar 1957–Jul 1957, NBC Mon 8:30–9:00
Sep 1957–Sep 1961, NBC Mon 8:30–9:00
Sep 1961–Sep 1962, NBC Sat 7:30–8:30

CAST:
Jim Hardie .... Dale Robertson
Beau McCloud (1961–1962)............. Jack Ging
Jeb Gaine (1961–1962) .... William Demarest
Ovie (1961–1962) .... Virginia Christine
Mary Gee (1961–1962) .... Mary Jane Saunders
Tina (1961–1962)..................... Lory Patrick

During the five seasons in which *Tales of Wells Fargo* ran on Monday nights it had a single regular cast member, Wells Fargo agent Jim Hardie. Jim was a troubleshooter for the company, whose assignments ranged from helping employees out of personal jams to functioning as an unofficial lawman by fighting criminals who preyed on Wells Fargo shipments and passengers.

In the fall of 1961, *Tales of Wells Fargo* moved to Saturday nights and was expanded to a full hour. Also expanded was the regular cast. Although still a Wells Fargo agent, Jim Hardie was now also the owner of a ranch just outside of San Francisco. He had acquired a young assistant in Beau McCloud and a ranch foreman named Jeb Gaine. The ranch next door to his was owned by Widow Ovie, who lived with her two attractive daughters, Mary Gee and Tina. Ovie had her eye on Jeb as a possible second husband, despite his lack of interest. Most of the shows during this last season took place on the Hardie ranch and in San Francisco, although Jim still went on an occasional assignment in other parts of the West.

TALK SOUP (*Comedy*)

BROADCAST HISTORY:

E! Entertainment
30/60 minutes
Produced: *1991–2002*
Premiered: *December 26, 1991*

HOST:

Greg Kinnear (1991–1995)
John Henson (1995–1999)
Hal Sparks (1999–2000)
Aisha Tyler (2001–2002)

Just in case you thought the E! Entertainment cable network was merely a video flack for the entertainment industry, promoting every new film and TV show indiscriminately, consider this feisty little series. Airing daily, it "reviewed" the day's TV talk shows, from *Good Morning, America* to *Ricki Lake*, mocking their absurdities. As the talk shows became more and more outrageous, *Talk Soup* got funnier and funnier, attracting a cult following for the struggling cable network. Some of the major talk shows (including *Geraldo*, *Oprah Winfrey*, and *Sally Jesse Raphael*) were unamused, expecting more reverential treatment, and refused to allow clips to be used. However, plenty of others appreciated the publicity, and *Talk Soup* sailed merrily on despite the holdouts.

TALK TO ME (*Situation Comedy*)

FIRST TELECAST: *April 11, 2000*
LAST TELECAST: *May 2, 2000*
BROADCAST HISTORY:

Apr 2000–May 2000, ABC Tue 9:30–10:00

CAST:

Janey Munro .... Kyra Sedgwick
Rob .... David Newsom
Marshall .... Max Baker
Cam .... Mike Estime
Dr. Debra .... Beverly D'Angelo
Sandy .... Peter Jacobson
Kat .... Nicole Sullivan

Janey was a bubbly New York radio talk-show host given to manic activity and tight sweaters in this short-lived comedy. Her gang at WSJB included young co-host Rob, a handsome chap who provided the "male perspective"; Marshall, the sound-effects guy and general kibitizer with a British accent; and Cam, the witty black producer. There was rowdy interplay between the four during the show, plus input from guests such as Vampira and Gene Simmons (of KISS). Psychologist Dr. Debra was the stuck-up host of the conservative talk show scheduled after hers, and Sandy was the wimpy station manager, who owed his job to the fact that he was the son of the owner.

After the show the gang generally hung out at Janey's apartment, where she lived with her cheerful but somewhat clueless sister Kat.

TALL HOPES (*Situation Comedy*)

FIRST TELECAST: *August 25, 1993*
LAST TELECAST: *September 8, 1993*
BROADCAST HISTORY:

Aug 1993–Sep 1993, CBS Wed 8:30–9:00

CAST:

George Harris .... George Wallace
Lainie Harris .... Anna Maria Horsford
Chester Harris (age 16) ... Terrence Dashon Howard
Ernest Harris (14) .... Kenny Blank
DeeDee Harris (6) .... Karla Green

Gentle comedy about a 14-year-old black kid in the shadow of his big bro'. Ernest was a smart kid and an exceptional student. Unfortunately his father, George, a none-too-bright transit cop in Philadelphia, paid attention only to big brother Chester. "Chet the Jet" was even dumber than Dad, but he was Dad's pride and joy, a high school basketball star who George hoped would get an athletic scholarship to college. DeeDee was little sis, in her own world, and Lainie the screechy mom, who mediated when necessary. All of them dumped on poor short Ernest, so he talked about his dreams to his camcorder, and those little conversations became a centerpiece of the show.

Originally scheduled for a four-week summer run, *Tall Hopes* disappeared after only three episodes had been telecast.

TALL MAN, THE (*Western*)

FIRST TELECAST: *September 10, 1960*
LAST TELECAST: *September 1, 1962*
BROADCAST HISTORY:

Sep 1960–Sep 1962, NBC Sat 8:30–9:00

CAST:

Billy the Kid .... Clu Gulager
Dep. Sheriff Pat Garrett .... Barry Sullivan

Set in New Mexico during the 1870s, *The Tall Man* told fictionalized stories of the adventures of two real-life characters, Sheriff Pat Garrett and William H. Bonney. The latter was more popularly known as Billy the Kid, a youthful gunfighter with a penchant for getting himself into trouble. Billy and Pat, whose honesty and forthrightness had earned him the nickname "The Tall Man," were close friends despite the fact that they were often on opposite sides of the law. Pat looked upon Billy as a younger brother or son, but knew in the back of his mind that they would eventually be forced into a showdown. Although he too was pretty handy with a gun, Pat regarded it as a tool only to be used in an emergency where there was no alternative. Billy, on the other hand, looked at his gun as the great equalizer, compensating for his inferiority in size, strength, or intelligence. His criminal activities kept bringing him and Pat closer to the day of reckoning which, although never shown on the series, culminated in Pat's killing Billy.

TAMMY (*Situation Comedy*)

FIRST TELECAST: *September 17, 1965*
LAST TELECAST: *July 15, 1966*
BROADCAST HISTORY:

Sep 1965–Jul 1966, ABC Fri 8:00–8:30

CAST:

Tammy Tarleton .... Debbie Watson
Grandpa Tarleton .... Denver Pyle
Uncle Lucius .... Frank McGrath
John Brent .... Donald Woods

Steven Brent .... Jay Sheffield
Lavinia Tate .... Dorothy Green
Gloria Tate .... Linda Marshall
Peter Tate............................ David Macklin
Dwayne Whitt .... George Furth
Cousin Cletus Tarleton .... Dennis Robertson
Mrs. Brent............................ Doris Packer

Tammy was the story of a winsome, 18-year-old backwoods girl who moved back and forth between two worlds. One was the bayou houseboat where she and her kin lived. The other was "The Bowers," the plantation owned by wealthy John Brent, where she worked as Brent's secretary. Tammy's wistful, beguiling ways endeared her to almost everyone—except Lavinia Tate, the blue-blooded neighbor of the Brents who was always scheming to snatch some juicy plum away from Tammy for her own daughter, Gloria. Steven was John Brent's son, and Peter was Lavinia's son. Tammy's own kin included old codger Grandpa and scalawag Uncle Lucius, who had raised her after the death of her parents.

Based on the 1957 movie *Tammy and the Bachelor*, which starred Debbie Reynolds, and the movie's sequels starring Sandra Dee. In 1967 there was a feature-length theatrical motion picture called *Tammy and the Millionaire*, consisting of edited episodes of the TV series, in which Miss Watson and most of the principals from the series appeared.

TAMMY GRIMES SHOW, THE (*Situation Comedy*)
FIRST TELECAST: *September 8, 1966*
LAST TELECAST: *September 29, 1966*
BROADCAST HISTORY:
Sep 1966, ABC Thu 8:30–9:00
CAST:
Tammy Ward........................... Tammy Grimes
Uncle Simon.......................... Hiram Sherman
Terrence Ward .... Dick Sargent
Mrs. Ratchett .... Maudie Prickett

Tammy Ward was what the ABC press releases referred to as "a madcap heiress." Given her own way, she would have spent oodles of money on just anything that hit her fancy, regardless of how useful it might be. Trying to keep the purse strings from being opened too far was her banker, Uncle Simon, a much more pecunious soul than Tammy. In addition to not being able to get her hands on her money, she had to cope with an incredibly square twin brother named Terrence and a nosy housekeeper named Mrs. Ratchett. Both Tammy and Terrence worked for Uncle Simon at the Perpetual Bank of America. This series lasted just four weeks.

TARGET (*Dramatic Anthology*)
BROADCAST HISTORY:
Syndicated only
30 minutes
Produced: *1957–1958* (38 episodes)
Released: *March 1958*
HOST/OCCASIONAL STAR:
Adolphe Menjou

This anthology series featured stories of terror and suspense in which some ruthless force pursued its target—a man, a family, a place. In one, a helpless invalid became the target of a "mercy killer"; in another, a respected man was the target of a mining swindle. Adolphe Menjou, who had earlier presided over the somewhat gentler *Favorite Story* anthology series, was host and frequent star. Others appearing included Howard Duff, Kent Taylor, Hans Conried, Marie Windsor, and Lon Chaney, Jr.

TARGET: THE CORRUPTORS (*Newspaper Drama*)
FIRST TELECAST: *September 29, 1961*
LAST TELECAST: *September 21, 1962*
BROADCAST HISTORY:
Sep 1961–Sep 1962, ABC Fri 10:00–11:00
CAST:
Paul Marino .... Stephen McNally
Jack Flood......................... Robert Harland

Paul Marino was an investigative rackets reporter and Jack Flood was his undercover agent, sent to infiltrate suspected criminal-controlled or -threatened businesses to provide Marino with material for his newspaper exposés and for the police. A different form of underworld corruption was detailed each week in this dramatic series—everything from bookmaking and prostitution to phony charities and protection rackets.

TARZAN (*Adventure*)
FIRST TELECAST: *September 8, 1966*
LAST TELECAST: *September 10, 1969*
BROADCAST HISTORY:
Sep 1966, NBC Thu 7:30–8:30
Sep 1966–Sep 1968, NBC Fri 7:30–8:30
Jun 1969–Sep 1969, CBS Wed 7:30–8:30
CAST:
Tarzan.................................... Ron Ely
Jai .... Manuel Padilla, Jr.

Edgar Rice Burroughs's famous "Tarzan" character came to television in the person of Ron Ely, the 14th actor to play the role since *Tarzan of the Apes* had first been made as a silent movie almost half a century before. In the TV series Tarzan, who was actually the Earl of Greystoke, returned to his native jungle forest after years of formal schooling. Living among the wild creatures, with whom he could communicate, and possessed of incredibly acute senses, Tarzan waged war on renegades, poachers, and other interlopers in the jungle. Familiar with the civilized world, Tarzan preferred the honesty and openness of life in the jungle. His closest friend was the chimp Cheetah, but he was fond of all the creatures of the wilds. He was also very close to a small orphan boy named Jai. Ron Ely did many of his own stunts for this series. The famous Tarzan yell was actually a recording by another Tarzan, Johnny Weissmuller. CBS aired reruns of the NBC series during the summer of 1969, and some episodes were strung together and actually shown in theaters as feature-length films.

The character of Jane and the crude English Tarzan had used in the movie versions ("Me Tarzan—you Jane") were dropped for the purposes of this TV series.

TARZAN (*Adventure*)
BROADCAST HISTORY:
Syndicated only
30 minutes
Produced: *1991–1994* (75 episodes)
Released: *September 1991*
CAST:
Tarzan .... Wolf Larsen
Jane Porter........................... Lydie Denier

Roger Taft, Jr. .... Sean Roberge
Simon (1991–1992) .... Malick Bowens
Jack (1992–1993) .... Errol Slue
Dan Miller (1993–1994) .... William Taylor

There were a number of differences between this environmentally correct series and the first TV version of the Edgar Rice Burroughs classic. Unlike his glib predecessor, this Tarzan had had no formal schooling and spoke halting English. Jane, missing from the 1960s *Tarzan*, was here, but much changed from the Burroughs original. She was a French (not English) environmental scientist running an African wildlife institute, seeking ways to save endangered species. Working with Jane were 18-year-old Roger Taft, son of the New York millionaire businessman who was funding her research, and Simon, an English-educated African native. Tarzan was their friend, protector, and helper. Episodes dealt with polluters, poachers, smugglers, and other criminals; natural disasters; injured and sick travelers; and the wild animals, including Tarzan's pet chimp Cheetah, with which he had a unique way of communicating.

Although *Tarzan* was in production for three seasons, viewers in the U.S. saw only the first season's episodes during the series' original production run. The remaining episodes had aired around the world before they were released to the U.S. syndication market in Fall 1997. Simon had been replaced by Jack for the second season, and Dan Miller, who ran a small local air charter service, was added to the cast for the third.

Filmed in Mexico.

TARZAN: THE EPIC ADVENTURES (*Adventure*)

BROADCAST HISTORY:

Syndicated only
60 minutes
Produced: *1996–1997* (22 episodes)
Released: *September 1996*

CAST:

Tarzan .... Joe Lara
Themba .... Aaron Seville
Bolgani .... Don McLeod
Tasi .... Nkhensani Mangahyi
La .... Angela Harry

This version of the Tarzan saga was set in 1912. In the premiere episode Tarzan, first seen as the dandified Lord of Greystoke in London, returned to the jungle because he wasn't comfortable in the civilized world. Literate and well-spoken, Tarzan had a sixth sense and highly developed animal instincts. Themba was his bespectacled young friend, a prince of the Wogambi, who had also returned to the dark continent after obtaining a university education in Italy and England. Inept in jungle ways, he traveled with Tarzan after his native village was destroyed by the Leopard Men. They fought poachers, renegade tribesmen, an expatriate Roman emperor in a lost city, and assorted demons, zombies, witches, and other creatures who were constantly leaping from shadows or creeping up on them while they slept. Also seen were Tasi, a good friend; Bolgani, a wise witch doctor; and La, High priestess of the Forbidden City of Opar.

Tarzan's producers maintained that the stories told were all adapted from the 24 original Edgar Rice Burroughs Tarzan novels. Lara, the eighteenth actor to play Tarzan, had previously played the role in the 1989 CBS made-for-TV movie, *Tarzan in Manhattan*.

Filmed in Sun City, South Africa.

TATE (*Western*)

FIRST TELECAST: *June 8, 1960*
LAST TELECAST: *September 28, 1960*
BROADCAST HISTORY:

Jun 1960–Sep 1960, NBC Wed 9:30–10:00

CAST:

Tate .... David McLean

Tate was the 1960 summer replacement for the second half hour of *The Perry Como Show*, the first half hour being occupied by a situation comedy called *Happy*. Tate was a casualty of the Civil War. His left arm had been blasted into uselessness by an explosion during his wartime service. With only one good arm, he had found it almost impossible to get a job after the war ended. With little choice, he had become a wandering gunfighter, traveling from town to town looking for work as a fast gun. He was an imposing figure, with his shattered left arm wrapped in a rawhide-stitched black leather casing that ran from his fingertips to above the elbow.

TATTINGERS (*Drama/Situation Comedy*)

FIRST TELECAST: *October 26, 1988*
LAST TELECAST: *April 26, 1989*
BROADCAST HISTORY:

Oct 1988–Jan 1989, NBC Wed 10:00–11:00
Apr 1989, NBC Thu 9:30–10:00
Apr 1989, NBC Wed 9:30–10:00

CAST:

Nick Tattinger .... Stephen Collins
Hillary Tattinger .... Blythe Danner
Nina Tattinger .... Patrice Colihan
Winnifred Tattinger (1988) .... Chay Lentin
Winnifred Tattinger (1989) .... Jessica Prunell
Sid Wilbur .... Jerry Stiller
Sheila Bradey .... Mary Beth Hurt
Louis Chatham .... Roderick Cook
Sonny Franks (1988) .... Zach Grenier
Marco Bellini .... Rob Morrow
Billie Low .... Sue Francis Pai
Alphonse .... Yusef Bulos
Fr. Thomas Smaraldo .... Robert Clohessy
Norman Asher .... Simon Jones
Spin (1989) .... Chris Elliott
Marti (1989) .... Anna Levine

The restaurant business gave Nick Tattinger heartburn in this comedy-drama with a distinctively New York atmosphere. Nick had sold his swank Manhattan eatery and moved to Paris after being shot on the street by crazed drug dealer Sonny, but he couldn't stay away. Reclaiming the place from his inept successors, he installed a new chef (Sheila), and with the help of loyal maitre d' Sid, headwaiter Lou, bartender Marco, and pianist Billy, set about restoring it to its former glory. There was constant banter with his elegant ex-wife Hillary, now having an affair with boring Norman, as well as fatherly doting over his two spoiled teenage daughters, Nina and Winnifred. *Tattingers* was an odd mix of somber story lines (Sonny lurked in the shadows determined, for some reason, to kill Nick) juxtaposed with comic ones (an elderly gent died at his table in an episode entitled "Rest in Peas"). New York celebrities frequently came by, among them actress

Arlene Francis, basketball's Patrick Ewing, Broadway producer George Abbott, and pianist Bobby Short.

In an unusual move, NBC canceled the show in January but then brought it back in April, completely retooled, as a half-hour situation comedy called *Nick & Hillary*, with most of the cast intact. Flighty Hillary had taken over the restaurant while Nick was in Brazil and again, almost destroyed it. Careening on the edge of bankruptcy, they were now partners. After only two episodes in the new format, they beamed off into permanent TV hiatus together.

Tattingers was NBC's first drama to be filmed in New York since the 1950s.

TATTOOED TEENAGE ALIEN FIGHTERS FROM BEVERLY HILLS (*Science Fiction/Fantasy*)

BROADCAST HISTORY:

USA Network
30 minutes
Produced: *1994–1995* (40 episodes)
Premiered: *October 3, 1994*

CAST:

Gordon Henley (Taurus) .... Richard Nason
Laurie Foster (Scorpio) .... Leslie Danon
Drew Vincent (Centaur) .... K. Jill Sorgen
Swinton Sawyer (Apollo) .... Rugg Williams
Nimbar (voice) .... Glenn Shadix
Emperor Gorganus (voice) .... Ed Gilbert
Lechner (voice) .... David L. Lander

Nineteen ninety-four brought several rip-offs of the hit daytime kid's show *Mighty Morphin Power Rangers*, including this low-budget entry that ran in the late afternoon on the USA cable network. The alien fighters were handsome preppy Gordon, stuck-up cheerleader Laurie, middle-class Drew, and Swinton, a nerdy black kid who was also a computer genius. The four had been recruited by Nimbar, a bloblike entity, to become Galactic Sentinels and fight to save the universe from the evil Emperor Gorganus. Normally they hung out at school or at the Cafe Maison coffeehouse, but when their secret tattoos began to glow they would leap through a "power portal" into Nimbar's cavelike headquarters, get their orders, and then transform themselves into Sentinels by shouting their code names ("Scorpio! Taurus! Centaur! Apollo!").

Then, clad in tight-fitting Lycra, they would do battle with Gorganus's monsters in a fantasyland of bright colors and flashing lights. Although they had various types of laser guns, the emphasis was on kicks, flips, and karate. When the going got really tough they could lock arms and transform themselves into Nitron, a mighty combination fighter. Lechner was Gorganus's sarcastic pet bird.

TAXI (*Situation Comedy*)

FIRST TELECAST: *September 12, 1978*
LAST TELECAST: *July 27, 1983*
BROADCAST HISTORY:

Sep 1978–Oct 1980, ABC Tue 9:30–10:00
Nov 1980–Jan 1981, ABC Wed 9:00–9:30
Feb 1981–Jun 1982, ABC Thu 9:30–10:00
Sep 1982–Dec 1982, NBC Thu 9:30–10:00
Jan 1983–Feb 1983, NBC Sat 9:30–10:00
Mar 1983–May 1983, NBC Wed 9:30–10:00
Jun 1983–Jul 1983, NBC Wed 10:30–11:00

CAST:

Alex Rieger .... Judd Hirsch
Bobby Wheeler (1978–1981) .... Jeff Conaway
Louie De Palma .... Danny DeVito
Elaine Nardo .... Marilu Henner
Tony Banta .... Tony Danza
John Burns (1978–1979) .... Randall Carver
Latka Gravas .... Andy Kaufman
"Reverend Jim" Ignatowski (1979–1983) .... Christopher Lloyd
Simka Gravas (1981–1983) .... Carol Kane

The happy cabbies of New York's Sunshine Cab Company were the focal point of this comedy. Cab driving may be fun, but it was just a job for this crew, most of whom were working part-time as they tried to make it in other fields. Alex, the most experienced and most conservative of the group, was the only full-time driver. Bobby was a frustrated actor, waiting for his big break; Elaine was an art gallery receptionist, trying to pick up a few extra bucks; Tony, the boxer who never won a fight; and John, the student and all-around lost soul. Latka was the company's mechanic, of indeterminate nationality and fractured English, and Louie was the dispatcher, a pint-sized petty tyrant who ran things from a wire cage in the center of the garage. Joining the cast as a regular driver in the second season was Reverend Jim, a spaced-out ex-hippie.

During the 1980–1981 season Latka started to date a rather scatterbrained lady from his homeland named Simka, and at the end of that season they were married. Falling ratings led ABC to cancel *Taxi* in the spring of 1982 and, for a time, it seemed that the pay-cable network Home Box Office would pick up the series. That was not to be, however, as NBC decided to give *Taxi* a new life. Promotional announcements on NBC during the summer of 1982 showed series star Danny DeVito looking up at the camera and gloating, "Same time, better network!" Despite critical acclaim for the ensemble acting, the wit and charm of the writing, and the faith of a new network, *Taxi* obtained the same low ratings on NBC as it had in its last season ABC, and faded from sight the following summer.

TEACHERS ONLY (*Situation Comedy*)

FIRST TELECAST: *April 14, 1982*
LAST TELECAST: *May 21, 1983*
BROADCAST HISTORY:

Apr 1982–Jun 1982, NBC Wed 9:30–10:00
Sep 1982, NBC Thu 9:30–10:00
Feb 1983–May 1983, NBC Sat 9:30–10:00

CAST:

Diana Swanson .... Lynn Redgrave
Ben Cooper .... Norman Fell
Michael Dreyfuss (1982) .... Adam Arkin
Mr. Pafko (1982) .... Richard Karron
Mr. Brody (1982) .... Norman Bartold
Gwen Edwards (1982) .... Van Nessa Clarke
Lois McCardle (1982) .... Kit McDonough
Samantha "Sam" Keating (1983) .... Teresa Ganzel
Michael Horne (1983) .... Tim Reid
Spud Le Boone (1983) .... Joel Brooks
Shari (1983) .... Jean Smart

Most of the action in this short-lived school comedy took place in the faculty lunchroom and lounge, which was off limits to the students—hence the series title, *Teachers Only*. It was there that the faculty and staff of Millard Filmore High School talked about their successes and failures, both professional and personal. Diana Swanson was a high-principled, dedicated English teacher, popular with her students despite the rigors of her curriculum. Ben Cooper was the gruff, stubborn, but warm-hearted school principal who had developed an ulcer after many years of trying to balance the needs and wants of students, parents, faculty, and staff. Michael and Gwen were fellow teachers, Mr. Brody the assistant principal, and Mr. Pafko the janitor.

When *Teachers Only* returned in the spring of 1983 there were a number of changes. It was still set in Los Angeles, but the school (with no on-air explanation) was now Woodrow Wilson High. Only Diana, now a guidance counselor, and Ben, still the principal, returned. The remainder of the cast, teachers Sam Keating, Michael Horne, and Barney Betelman; gym teacher and coach Spud Le Boone; and Ben's secretary Shari, were all new. Apparently, the problem with the series was its premise, not its cast. Despite the infusion of new cast members, ratings as low as those it had obtained a year earlier prompted *Teachers Only* to be canceled again.

TEAM KNIGHT RIDER (*Adventure*)

BROADCAST HISTORY:

Syndicated only
60 minutes
Produced: *1997–1998* (22 episodes)
Released: *October 1997*

CAST:

Kyle Stewart .... Brixton Karnes
Erica West .... Kathy Trageser
Kevin "Trek" Sanders .... Nick Wechsler
Jenny Andrews .... Christine Steel
Duke DePalma .... Duane Davis
Kat (voice only) .... Andrea Beutner
Dante (voice only) .... Tom Kane
Plato (voice only) .... John Kassir
Beast (voice only) .... Kerrigan Mahan
Domino (voice only) .... Nia Vardalos
**Mobius* .... David McCallum
**Star* .... Marta Martin
**Shadow* .... Steve Forrest

*Occasional

This updated version of the popular 1980s series *Knight Rider* worked on the premise that more is better. As the voice-over announcer intoned at the beginning of each episode:

> "Ten years ago all it took was one man and one car. Now, the Foundation for Law and Government has assembled five highly skilled operatives and paired them with the most advanced state-of-the-art vehicles to take on a new breed of outlaw. They are Team Knight Rider."

Leader of the team was Kyle, a former CIA spy who drove Dante, a modified Ford Expedition S.U.V. with all its window glass—except the windshield—blacked out. The other members of the team were Erica, a con woman who tooled around in Kat, a special motorcycle with a sidecar; Trek, the teenage electronics genius who drove Plato, another customized motorcycle; onetime cop and ex-boxer Duke, handling Beast, a black Ford F-150 A.T.V. equipped with winches, cranes, and a laser cannon; and martial arts master Jenny, who drove Domino, a red Ford Mustang convertible with white racing stripes down its center. Their traveling maintenance facility and headquarters was a large transport plane which hovered, or landed in open spaces, and into which they drove their vehicles. All of the vehicles were equipped with intelligent, highly competitive talking computers with attitudes, as was the case with the original *Knight Rider* Pontiac Trans-Am.

Missions undertaken by the team included rescuing a Marine officer who had been kidnapped by terrorists, recovering a stolen top-secret experimental helicopter from an F.B.I. turncoat, and several confrontations with the diabolical wheelchair-bound genius Mobius. During the season the TKR team got occasional help from a mysterious figure they referred to as "Shadow."

Jenny, who had been adopted, initially joined F.L.A.G. because she was searching for information about her real father, Michael Long (the cop who had been physically reconstructed as Michael Knight, the original Knight Rider).

In the finale Mobius's henchmen used his special equipment to disable the TKR vehicles and capture all of the team, while taking control of a satellite to facilitate his development of a mind control device. At the end of the episode Mobius had stolen the "brain" of K.I.T.T. from TKR headquarters. The team went to a place where there was a tombstone for Michael Knight, but as the episode ended, they were met by a man who said he had been Michael Knight. Since the show was not renewed for a second season, viewers never learned what happened next.

TECHTV (Network) (*Informational Cable Network*)

LAUNCHED:

May 1998

SUBSCRIBERS (MAY 2003):

39.9 million (37% U.S.)

Remember the "Internet bubble" of the late 1990s, when the stock market, the economy and just about everything else was about to be taken over by the Internet? (We would buy on-line, work on-line, even vote on-line.) The folks at TechTV do, because that's when this network was bravely launched by Ziff-Davis Publications, publisher of leading computer and Internet magazines, to serve as the TV component of the computer revolution. Among its early programs were *The Money Machine* (how to use computers to make, save and manage money, with Carmine Gallo), *ZDTV News* (computer and Internet news, with Victoria Recano), *Internet Tonight* (information and commentary by Scott Herriot and Michaela Pereira), *Silicon Spin* (a roundtable discussion led by *PC Magazine*'s cranky columnist John C. Dvorak), *Fresh Gear* (hardware reviews with Jim Louderback) and *Call for Help* (a call-in show for those who couldn't make the *#@%*! thing work, with Leo Laporte).

The channel was originally called ZDTV, after Ziff-Davis, but was sold and renamed TechTV in 2000.

TED KNIGHT SHOW, THE (*Situation Comedy*)

FIRST TELECAST: *April 8, 1978*
LAST TELECAST: *May 13, 1978*
BROADCAST HISTORY:

Apr 1978–May 1978, CBS Sat 8:30–9:00

CAST:

Roger Dennis .... Ted Knight
Burt Dennis .... Normann Burton
Winston Dennis .... Thomas Leopold

Dottie .... Iris Adrian
Graziella .... Cissy Colpitts
Honey .... Fawne Harriman
Irma .... Ellen Regan
Philadelphia Phil Brown .... Tanya Boyd
Cheryl .... Janice Kent
Joy .... Deborah Harmon
Hobart Nalven .... Claude Stroud

Ted Knight, the handsome, empty-headed newscaster on *The Mary Tyler Moore Show*, landed his own series with this frothy comedy about an escort service in New York City. Dennis Escorts was a strictly high-class outfit, located in a posh Manhattan apartment building. It was staffed by some lovely young ladies, and headed by the suave, middle-aged Roger Dennis, who clucked over his brood like a mother hen. Complicating matters was Roger's no-nonsense businessman/brother, Burt, who had financed the enterprise and had incidentally saddled it with his wisecracking sister-in-law Dottie (who served as receptionist). Other cast members were Roger's college-age son, Winston, who was trying to break into the business and make time with the girls, and the mailman, Hobart, who had his eyes on Dottie.

TED KNIGHT SHOW, THE, see *Too Close For Comfort*

TED MACK FAMILY HOUR, THE (*Musical Variety*)
FIRST TELECAST: *January 7, 1951*
LAST TELECAST: *November 25, 1951*
BROADCAST HISTORY:
Jan 1951–Nov 1951, ABC Sun 6:00–7:00
REGULARS:
Ted Mack
The Mack Triplets
Jean Steel
Dick Byrd
Andy Roberts

Ted Mack, who was most famous for his *Original Amateur Hour,* also hosted this live Sunday night variety show during 1951. The emphasis was on family entertainment, and guest stars were generally cabaret and stage talent such as pianist Vincent Lopez, songstress Betty Ann Grove, and actor Bert Lytell. An occasional *Amateur Hour* champion also made his professional debut here.

TED STEELE SHOW, THE (*Music*)
FIRST TELECAST: *September 29, 1948*
LAST TELECAST: *August 3, 1949*
BROADCAST HISTORY:
Sep 1948–Oct 1948, NBC Wed/Fri Various 15 minute
Feb 1949–Apr 1949, DUM Sun 6:30–7:00
Apr 1949–Jul 1949, DUM Tue 9:00–9:30
Jul 1949–Aug 1949, CBS Tue/Wed/Thu 7:15–7:30
REGULARS:
Ted Steele
Mardi Bryant
Helen Wood
Michael Rich

Ted Steele was a versatile young (31) musician who had a blossoming career on radio in the 1940s. He was orchestra leader for several years on Perry Como's *Chesterfield Supper Club,* was a composer of some note ("Smoke Rings"), and also a singer, pianist, organist, and novachordist. His first break on TV came with a series of musical interludes on NBC, which originated in the WPTZ studios in Philadelphia. Ted later switched to DuMont, then to CBS, then became a local personality in New York.

TEECH (*Situation Comedy*)
FIRST TELECAST: *September 18, 1991*
LAST TELECAST: *October 16, 1991*
BROADCAST HISTORY:
Sep 1991–Oct 1991, CBS Wed 8:30–9:00
CAST:
Teech Gibson .... Phill Lewis
George Dubcek, Jr. .... Curnal Achilles Aulisio
Kenny Freedman .... Joshua Hoffman
Boyd Askew .... Ken Lawrence Johnston
Alby Nichols .... Jason Kristofer
Alfred W. Litton .... Steven Gilborn
Cassie Lee .... Maggie Han
Adrian Peterman .... Jack Noseworthy
THEME:
"Teach Me," written by Tom Snow, Norman Steinberg, and David Frankel; performed by B. B. King.

Music teacher Teech Gibson was the hip, token black instructor at Winthrop Academy, an exclusive private boarding school for boys in suburban Philadelphia. Among his students were Winthrop's notorious "gang of four"—George, the burly but dumb son of a former pro football player; Kenny, the intelligent ring leader and resident ladykiller: Boyd, the spoiled son of a socially prominent family; and Alby, the "Philly Cheese Steak Prince," heir to his family's lucrative fast food stand—the biggest troublemakers at the school. Others seen regularly were Alfred Litton, the school's autocratic headmaster, who tolerated Teech because he needed a token black on staff; Cassie, the sexy assistant headmaster who had hired him; and Adrian, the brown-nosing yuppie student forever trying to get the "gang of four" expelled.

TEEN ANGEL (*Situation Comedy*)
FIRST TELECAST: *September 26, 1997*
LAST TELECAST: *September 11, 1998*
BROADCAST HISTORY:
Sep 1997–Feb 1998, ABC Fri 9:30–10:00
May 1998–Sep 1998, ABC Fri 9:30–10:00
CAST:
Marty DePolo .... Mike Damus
Steve Beauchamp .... Corbin Allred
Judy Beauchamp .... Maureen McCormick
Katie Beauchamp .... Katie Volding
Jordan Lubell .... Jordan Brower
Aunt Pam .... Conchata Ferrell
The Head .... Ron Glass

This odd little comedy milked laughs from a dead teenager. No kidding. The teen of the title was Marty, a happy-go-lucky adolescent who met a sudden demise after eating a six-month-old hamburger he found under his pal Steve's bed. Transported to a place with white fluffy clouds and bright sunlight, he was given feathery wings and sent right back to Earth to be Steve's guardian angel, and hopefully help make the dorkiest kid in school a little cooler. Marty's new powers were awesome—he could make the school bully bang his own head against a locker, or summon up President James Monroe to help in a history exam—

but if he got too smart-alecky he would be called on the carpet by his boss, the Head, a disembodied cranium who popped up in unlikely places (and who explained that he was not God, but "God's cousin Rod"). Judy was Steve's single mom, Katie his bubbly little sis, Aunt Pam a disgruntled postal worker, and Jordan the coolest kid in school—who, with a little help from Marty, became Steve's friend.

TEEN TIME TUNES (*Music*)
FIRST TELECAST: *March 14, 1949*
LAST TELECAST: *July 15, 1949*
BROADCAST HISTORY:
Mar 1949–Jul 1949, DUM Mon–Fri 6:30–6:45
REGULARS:
Sue Benjamin (Bennett)
Alan Logan Trio

A pretty young vocalist named Sue Benjamin, just out of college, was the featured singer on this early program. It was typical of the extremely low-budget musical interludes favored by the networks—especially cash-poor ABC and Dumont—in the early days of TV. Miss Benjamin recalled that it was produced in a corner of the same studio used for Vincent Lopez, *The Small Fry Club*, Wendy Barrie, and others, and the set really consisted of no more than a drape with the musical trio (pianist Alan Logan, guitar, and bass) and herself in front. The program was just a supper-club combo on TV. Despite the "Teen" in the title, they played mostly standards and opened with an inane little ditty that went something like, "It's time, time, time/Time for 'Teen Time Tunes'!" Hardly a precursor of *American Bandstand*!

Miss Benjamin later changed her professional name to Sue Bennett and had a successful career on *Kay Kyser's Kollege of Musical Knowledge* and *Your Hit Parade*.

TEENAGE BOOK CLUB (*Discussion*)
FIRST TELECAST: *August 27, 1948*
LAST TELECAST: *October 29, 1948*
BROADCAST HISTORY:
Aug 1948–Oct 1948, ABC Fri 7:30–8:00
Oct 1948, ABC Fri 8:00–8:30

One of ABC's earlier series was this discussion program on books of interest to teenagers. Among the titles considered were Betty Betz's *Your Manners Are Showing*, Harry Haenigsen's comic strips, and a few classics such as *David Copperfield* and *Hamlet*.

TEKWAR (*Science Fiction*)
BROADCAST HISTORY:
USA Network
60 Minutes
Produced: *1994–1995* (18 episodes)
Premiered: *January 7, 1995*
CAST:
Jake Cardigan .... Greg Evigan
**Walter Bascom* .... William Shatner
Sid Gomez .... Eugene Clark
Sam Houston .... Maria Del Mar
Lt. Winger .... Maurice Dean Wint
Nika .... Natalie Radford
Shelley Grout .... Dana Brooks
Cowgirl .... Lexa Doig
Spaz .... Ernie Gruenwald
*Occasional

This action-packed sci-fi series was unusual in that it was set in the near rather than distant future. The year was 2045. There was no routine space travel or intergalactic battles but instead a much more relatable menace: tek, a highly addictive computer-based virtual reality "drug" that took its users into a fantasy world from which they might never escape. Tek was controlled by evil forces known as the teklords, and governments were losing (or corrupted by) the worldwide battle with them.

Enter Jake Cardigan, a former cop who had been cryogenically imprisoned on trumped-up charges because he got too close to the truth. Once out, disgraced, he was recruited by the mysterious Bascom, powerful head of the huge Cosmos security agency, to fight tek undercover. All the high-tech resources of Cosmos were at his disposal, including worldwide communications, holographic simulations of reality, the means to infiltrate enemy computers, space-age weapons, and Bascom's connections. In the end, though, Bascom's real agenda was never entirely clear, and Jake relied on his wits more than technology to save the day. Sid was Jake's first partner, succeeded by sexy Sam; Nika, a helpful computer jock at Cosmos; Cowgirl and Spaz, two cyberpunks who could literally "fly" into enemy computer networks using a kind of virtual reality; Winger, an android cop who was constantly on Jake's case; and Grout, a government agent who tried to foil him.

TekWar was based on a series of novels by actor William Shatner that were made into four syndicated TV movies seen during early 1994. Shatner was also executive producer of the series.

TELEPHONE TIME (*Dramatic Anthology*)
FIRST TELECAST: *April 8, 1956*
LAST TELECAST: *April 1, 1958*
BROADCAST HISTORY:
Apr 1956–Mar 1957, CBS Sun 6:00–6:30
Apr 1957–Jun 1957, ABC Thu 10:00–10:30
Jun 1957–Apr 1958, ABC Tue 9:30–10:00
HOST:
John Nesbitt (1956–1957)
Dr. Frank Baxter (1957–1958)

The plays presented in this film series had all been adapted from short stories by author John Nesbitt, who also served as the host of the show, introducing each episode. The subject matter ranged from contemporary to historical, with emphasis on the varied natures and qualities of people, both good and bad. He remained as the host of the series when it moved from CBS to ABC in the spring of 1957, although by this time the works of other authors had been included among the presentations. He was replaced as host in September 1957 by Dr. Frank Baxter. There were occasional appearances by such name talents as Judith Anderson, Thomas Mitchell, and Claudette Colbert, but most of the players in this series were not, at the time, major stars. A number of them—including Cloris Leachman, Michael Landon, Martin Milner, and Robert Vaughn—did become stars of their own television series in the 1960s and 1970s. On an unusual note, famed clown Emmett Kelly made his dramatic debut here in a story titled "Captain from Kopenick."

TELE-VARIETIES, see *Bristol-Myers Tele-Varieties*

TELEVISION: INSIDE AND OUT (*Magazine*)
FIRST TELECAST: *December 5, 1981*
LAST TELECAST: *January 2, 1982*
BROADCAST HISTORY:
Dec 1981–Jan 1982, NBC Sat 10:00–11:00
REGULARS:
Rona Barrett
Wil Shriner
Sylvester L. "Pat" Weaver
Gary Deeb

Hollywood gossip columnist Rona Barrett hosted this mix of information, opinion, reportage, and gossip about television. Pat Weaver, former chairman of the board of NBC, was on hand to do features about the past and present of TV, sometimes making editorial commentary and other times doing straight information pieces—as when he narrated a report on A. C. Nielsen, Jr., and his rating system. Humorist Wil Shriner looked at the funny side of the medium, and syndicated TV columnist Gary Deeb did a weekly report about current programs and personalities on TV. Rona did interviews à la Barbara Walters, with celebrities ranging from singers Mick Jagger and Lena Horne to actors Rock Hudson and Edward Asner.

TELEVISION PLAYHOUSE, see *Philco TV Playhouse*

TELEVISION PLAYHOUSE (*Dramatic Anthology*)
FIRST TELECAST: *December 4, 1947*
LAST TELECAST: *April 11, 1948*
BROADCAST HISTORY:
Dec 1947–Apr 1948, NBC Sun 8:40–9:10

This was an early series of live television dramas presented by NBC in cooperation with the American National Theater and Academy (ANTA), a federally sponsored theater group. Both light and serious fare were presented, many by famous authors but few starring actors of any note (they would not go near television in 1947). The first presentation was "The Last of My Solid Gold Watches" by Tennessee Williams. *Television Playhouse* was a semiregular program, generally appearing every third Sunday night during the period indicated.

TELEVISION SCREEN MAGAZINE (*Various*)
FIRST TELECAST: *November 17, 1946*
LAST TELECAST: *July 23, 1949*
BROADCAST HISTORY:
Nov 1946–Dec 1946, NBC Sun 8:00–8:30
Dec 1947–Mar 1948, NBC Thu Various (30 minutes)
Mar 1948–Sep 1948, NBC Tue Various (30 minutes)
Oct 1948–Jul 1949, NBC Sat Various (30 minutes)
EMCEE/"EDITOR":
George Putnam (1948)
Alan Scott (1948, 1949)
John K. M. McCaffery (1948)
Millicent Fenwick (1948)
Bob Stanton (1948)
Ray Forrest (1948–1949)
REGULAR:
Bill Berns

This grab bag of features, presented magazine-style once a week, was one of NBC's earliest network series and was seen initially in three cities (New York, Philadelphia, Schenectady). At first the format was highly informal and the guests were often ordinary people—seemingly anyone who could be lured into the studio. NBC employee Walter Law and his stamp collection was an early favorite, and the very first telecast (November 17, 1946) featured the Police Athletic League Chorus. Later the program became more tightly structured, with a regular host or "editor," occasional film features, and regular segments such as Bill Berns' "While Berns Roams."

The magazine format was emphasized by a shot of pages being flipped before each feature, and regular departments such as the fashion page, personality interviews, etc.

TELL IT TO GROUCHO (*Comedy/Interview*)
FIRST TELECAST: *January 11, 1962*
LAST TELECAST: *May 31, 1962*
BROADCAST HISTORY:
Jan 1962–May 1962, CBS Thu 9:00–9:30
REGULARS:
Groucho Marx
Jack Wheeler
Patty Harmon

This filmed series was the short-lived successor to Groucho's long-running *You Bet Your Life.* It was a vehicle designed to let Groucho demonstrate his wit by zinging the guests who appeared on the show to "tell it to Groucho." Guests were interviewed by Groucho about their hobbies, problems, and/or jobs. Assisting Groucho, and participating in the discussions with the guests, were two teenagers who had been "discovered" by Groucho when they had appeared as contestants on *You Bet Your Life.*

TELL IT TO THE CAMERA (*Interview*)
FIRST TELECAST: *December 25, 1963*
LAST TELECAST: *March 18, 1964*
BROADCAST HISTORY:
Dec 1963–Mar 1964, CBS Wed 8:30–9:00
HOST:
Red Rowe

Tell It to the Camera enabled everyday people from around the country to voice their opinions on network television. The filmed series sent a mobile unit to random locations at plants, shopping centers, schools, etc., and invited passersby to let their opinions be known, register complaints about almost anything that was bothering them, or tell what they felt were amusing or interesting stories. There was more than a coincidental resemblance between *Tell It to the Camera* and another series on the CBS schedule, *Candid Camera.* They were both produced by Allen Funt, whose entire career was wrapped up in showing normal people reacting to normal and abnormal situations.

TELLER OF TALES, see *Somerset Maugham TV Theater*

TELLTALE CLUE, THE (*Police Drama*)
FIRST TELECAST: *July 8, 1954*
LAST TELECAST: *September 23, 1954*
BROADCAST HISTORY:
Jul 1954–Sep 1954, CBS Thu 10:00–10:30
CAST:
Det. Lt. Richard Hale .... Anthony Ross

Detective Lieutenant Richard Hale was the head of the criminology department of the police department of a large, unnamed city. He used all of the scientific equipment and analytical skills at his disposal to find the flaws in what would have otherwise been "perfect" crimes. The step-by-step process by which he isolated the evidence that eventually led to an arrest enabled the home viewers to become familiar with modern police technology and, in certain respects, made this series a variation on the Ellery Queen–style whodunit.

TEMPERATURES RISING (*Situation Comedy*)

FIRST TELECAST: *September 12, 1972*
LAST TELECAST: *August 29, 1974*
BROADCAST HISTORY:

Sep 1972–Jan 1974, ABC Tue 8:00–8:30
Jul 1974–Aug 1974, ABC Thu 8:00–8:30

CAST (1972–1973):

Dr. Vincent Campanelli.......... James Whitmore
Dr. Jerry Noland.................... Cleavon Little
Nurse Annie Carlisle .... Joan Van Ark
Nurse Mildred MacInerny.............. Reva Rose
Student Nurse Ellen Turner............ Nancy Fox
Dr. David Amherst .... David Bailey

CAST (1973–1974):

Dr. Paul Mercy......................... Paul Lynde
Dr. Jerry Noland.................... Cleavon Little
Martha Mercy......................... Sudie Bond
Miss Tillis.......................... Barbara Cason
Nurse "Windy" Winchester .... Jennifer Darling
Dr. Lloyd Axton...................... Jeff Morrow
Dr. Charles Cleveland Claver......... John Dehner

CAST (SUMMER 1974):

Dr. Paul Mercy......................... Paul Lynde
Dr. Jerry Noland.................... Cleavon Little
Edwina Moffitt..................... Alice Ghostley
Nurse Ellen Turner...................... Nancy Fox
Nurse Amanda Kelly .... Barbara Rucker

ABC evidently had a good deal of faith in this medical comedy, trying three different casts and formats in two years before finally giving up. For the first season the show was set at Capital General Hospital in Washington, D.C., presided over by no-nonsense chief of surgery Dr. Vincent Campanelli and his all-nonsense staff. The latter consisted of prankster Jerry Noland, a free-swinging product of the ghetto and the hospital's chief bookie; sexy young nurse Annie Carlisle; her mischievous companion Mildred MacInerny; and Dr. David Amherst, the handsome love interest of practically every female in the place. There were also the patients: the old codger who liked to drag-race in his wheelchair, the paranoid young man who wanted his medication pretasted and then slipped under the door, etc.

The program returned for its second season retitled *The New Temperatures Rising Show*, with new producers, and almost completely recast. Capital General was now a private hospital, run by penny-pinching Dr. Paul Mercy (played by Paul Lynde) and owned by his meddlesome mother, Martha, who was permanently in residence and who kept calling her son via a beeper on his belt. Miss Tillis was the efficient accountant, "Windy" Winchester, the romantically inclined nurse, and Dr. Axton, the cheerfully fraudulent surgeon who had recently published two books, *Profit in Healing* and *Malpractice and Its Defense*. Only intern Jerry Noland remained from the first season.

The second version of *Termperatures Rising* was no more successful than the first, however, and lasted only through mid-season. Apparently viewers did not appreciate seeing doctors as the butt of comedy. The show did come back for another short run in the summer of 1974, with more new episodes, and still more changes in cast and plot. This time the meddling mother was gone, and Dr. Mercy ran the place with the help of his sister, Edwina. Intern Jerry Noland was back, along with a couple of nurses.

TEMPLE HOUSTON (*Western*)

FIRST TELECAST: *September 19, 1963*
LAST TELECAST: *September 10, 1964*
BROADCAST HISTORY:

Sep 1963–Sep 1964, NBC Thu 7:30–8:30

CAST:

Temple Houston .... Jeffrey Hunter
George Taggart......................... Jack Elam

Traveling the circuit courts in the Southwest during the 1880s was Temple Houston, the handsome attorney son of Texas immortal Sam Houston. Temple found his clients, both civil and criminal, wherever the circuit court happened to be in session. In spite of his vocation as a lawyer, Temple was also quite adept as a fast-shooting gunman. His appearance was one of elegance and his oratorical skills were renowned throughout the Southwest. Also traveling with the circuit court was George Taggart, an itinerant U.S. marshal and over-the-hill gunfighter. Taggart hired himself to the local towns and was either friend or foe of Houston, depending on the interests of Temple's clients. The real-life Temple Houston was a contemporary of both Bat Masterson and Billy the Kid, and was known to have engaged in shooting matches with them.

TEMPORARILY YOURS (*Situation Comedy*)

FIRST TELECAST: *March 5, 1997*
LAST TELECAST: *April 9, 1997*
BROADCAST HISTORY:

Mar 1997–Apr 1997, CBS Wed 8:30–9:00

CAST:

Deb DeAngelo......................... Debi Mazar
Joan Silver .... Joanna Gleason
David Silver .... Seth Green
Caesar Santos .... Saverio Guerra
Anne Marie........................ Nancy Cassaro

THEME:

by Branford Marsalis

This short-lived comedy certainly was compatible with its lead-in on the CBS schedule. What could be more appropriate than following a series about an aggressive, brassy Jewish girl from Queens (*The Nanny*) with a series about an aggressive, brassy Italian girl from Brooklyn?

Deb just couldn't find a job she really liked. She had just moved into a killer apartment in Manhattan after quitting her 27th job in the last two years. Her new job gave her hope for a better future. She went to work for Everything's Temporary, a fancy Upper East Side temp agency owned by the classy but neurotic Joan Silver. Joan wasn't sure how valuable an asset Deb's street smarts were, but there was something about her that appealed to her new boss. Since most of Deb's assignments lasted less than a week, she had little time to get bored and more opportunities to find the perfect job she was convinced was waiting for her. David was Joan's browbeaten son and assistant, Caesar the pushy superintendent of the building in which she lived, and Anne Marie her fast-talking married friend.

TEMPTATION ISLAND (*Dating/Reality*)

FIRST TELECAST: *January 10, 2001*

LAST TELECAST: *February 14, 2002*

BROADCAST HISTORY:

Jan 2001–Feb 2001, FOX Wed 9:00–10:00

Nov 2001–Feb 2002, FOX Thu 9:00–10:00

HOST:

Mark L. Walberg

Four young unmarried couples in supposedly committed relationships were sent to the tropical island of Ambergris Caye, Belize, to test their bonds. The men bunked in an area with sexy women to tempt them, and the women in an area with attractive guys. For two weeks they mixed, mingled, and dated the singles to test the strength of their relationships. With lots of hard bodies and tight buns in close proximity, there was plenty of temptation on *Temptation Island.*

The four couples on the initial season were Shannon and Andy (who had been together for 5 years), Mandy and Billy (1½ years), Valerie and Kaya (1½ years) and black couple Ytossie and Taheed (5½ years). On the first morning the couples were introduced to 26 singles, 13 guys and 13 girls, and the four females (as a group) and the four males were each given the opportunity to send home one single contestant of the opposite sex—whom they agreed looked like the most threatening. Each member of the couples could also designate which of the remaining singles their own partner could not date (by giving them a "no date" bracelet). On subsequent episodes couples members went on romantic dates with singles of the opposite sex chosen by the producers, and watched tapes of their partners doing the same. Some of what they did on their dates was shown, and everyone commented on what they thought of their latest date. Couples members could also periodically send video messages to their partners and vote incompatible singles off the island, at a bonfire ritual.

Early in the fourth episode, there was a crisis when Ytossie told one of the guys that she and Taheed had a baby. Afraid of endangering a child's welfare, the producers abruptly pulled the couple from the program. They were sent to a different location to work on their relationship, free from "temptation." The dating continued for the remaining couples, and as their time on the island drew to a close each picked a final dream date. Before seeing excerpts from the last dates, viewers saw Ytossie and Taheed saying they loved each other and would go to counseling to work out their problems.

After the dream dates, all three couples decided to spend the rest of their lives with the partners with whom they had come to the island. Andy proposed to Shannon, and she accepted. Billy and Mandy were still involved, although he had moved away to L.A. to try his luck as an actor, and Kaya, despite connecting with two of the women he had dated on the island, nevertheless decided to stay with a much-relieved Valerie. In November, prior to the start of *Temptation Island 2,* Fox aired a special that culminated in the wedding of Shannon and Andy.

Temptation Island 2, which took place at Playa Tambor, Costa Rica, was more "successful" at breaking up relationships. The four couples were Catherine and Edmundo (together 3 years), John and Shannon (10 months), Tommy and Nikkole (3½ years) and Tony and Genevieve (4½ years). At the end of the fifth episode Tony proposed to Genevieve and she accepted, leaving three couples. The following week a new couple arrived on the island, Mark and Kelley, who had been dating for 16 months. The other couples greeted them with mixed emotions, since the new arrivals got a lot of attention and had the potential to alter the game and relationships. At the end of the seventh episode a new wrinkle was added when host Walberg informed them that a new group of singles, chosen specifically to appeal to their individual desires, was arriving. The dating and relationship evaluating continued on to each person's dream date.

When the final decisions were made, Mark wanted to stay with Kelley but she broke up with him, and Nikkole and Tommy also broke up (they later got back together). John and insecure Shannon, who had tried to sneak notes to him that were intercepted by the producers, decided to stay together, as did Catherine and Edmundo. Hours after the show ended, however, Catherine and Edmundo also broke up.

TENAFLY (*Detective Drama*)

FIRST TELECAST: *October 10, 1973*

LAST TELECAST: *August 6, 1974*

BROADCAST HISTORY:

Oct 1973–Jan 1974, NBC Wed 8:30–10:00

Apr 1974–Aug 1974, NBC Tue 8:30–10:00

CAST:

Harry Tenafly .... James McEachin
Ruth Tenafly .... Lillian Lehman
Herb Tenafly .... Paul Jackson
Lorrie .... Rosanna Huffman
Lt. Sam Church .... David Huddleston

Harry Tenafly was a rarity among television's private detectives: he was black, and a dedicated and happy family man. He lived in Los Angeles with his wife, Ruth, and their son, Herb. The action in the series was divided between his home and his office life. His friend and confidant at the police department was Lt. Sam Church, who often got Harry out of jams. Unlike most private detectives, Harry was neither chasing nor being chased by beautiful women. He was happy with his family and saw his job as only a job. *Tenafly* was one of the four rotating elements in the 1973–1974 edition of *NBC Wednesday/Tuesday Mystery Movie.*

TENCHI MUYO! (*Cartoon*)

BROADCAST HISTORY:

Cartoon Network
30 minutes
Original episodes: *2000–*
Premiered: *July 3, 2000*

VOICES (U.S.):

Tenchi Masaki .... Matt K. Miller
Ryoko Hakubi .... Petrea Burchard
Ayeka Jurai .... Jennifer Darling
Sasami Jurai, Kiyone Makabi .... Sherry Lynn
Mihoshi Kurumitzu .... Rebecca Forstadt
Mihoshi Kurumitzu .... Ellen Gerstel

Washu Hakubi .... K. T. Vogt
Ryo-Ohki .... Debi Derryberry

An imaginative Japanese anime cartoon about a boy's wondrous world of adventure. The story line was complex and somewhat different in various versions of the show, but the principal character was Tenchi Masaki, a fun-loving teenager living in rural Japan with his father and grandfather, a Shinto priest. One day Tenchi accidently opened a nearby cave where the beautiful demon Ryoko had been sealed up for thousands of years due to past crimes. That began a sequence of events that brought Tenchi into contact with more beautiful women—two princesses of the planet Jurai, Ayeka and Sasami, galaxy police officer Mihoshi, and Ryoko's creator, the mad scientist Washu. They fought over shy Tenchi, who wanted nothing to do with them but eventually discovered that he was a member of the Jurai royal family and related to Ayeka and Sasami. He also had the power to wield a powerful but somewhat unreliable sword called "Tenchi," which proved handy in the outer-space battles and confrontations with monsters that followed. Among the other fantastic creature inhabiting Tenchi's world was Ryo-Ohki, a cat/rabbit creature that could transform into a spaceship or a young girl.

Tenchi Muyo! originated as a comic book and was first released on video in Japan in 1992 as *No Need for Tenchi*. It spawned several TV series and films, and came to American television in 2000, with voices dubbed by the actors listed above.

TENNESSEE ERNIE FORD SHOW, THE, see *Ford Show Starring Tennessee Ernie Ford, The*

TENSPEED AND BROWN SHOE (*Detective Drama*)
FIRST TELECAST: *January 27, 1980*
LAST TELECAST: *June 27, 1980*
BROADCAST HISTORY:
Jan 1980–Mar 1980, ABC Sun 8:00–9:00
May 1980–Jun 1980, ABC Fri 10:00–11:00
CAST:
E. L. Turner ("Tenspeed") .... Ben Vereen
Lionel Whitney ("Brown Shoe") ...... Jeff Goldblum

This was the odd couple of detective work. "Tenspeed" was a charming hustler and master of disguises, for whom legitimate employment (as a detective) was necessary to meet his parole requirements. "Brown Shoe"—an old term for bankers, stockbrokers, and other "straight" types—was his well-to-do and somewhat naive foil, a romantic whose idea of sleuthing was rooted in 1940s novels and old Bogart movies. This unlikely pair joined forces in their own agency, located two blocks off Sunset Boulevard in Los Angeles, and with lots of undercover work and high-speed chases they managed to crack all sorts of cases.

Tenspeed and Brown Shoe was launched with a tremendous promotional blitz in early 1980, and attracted a large audience for its first couple of episodes. It then declined rapidly and was soon canceled. The producer of this series was Stephen J. Cannell, whose name was used as "the author" of all the blood-and-guts detective novels Lionel was forever reading to help him hone his detective skills.

TEQUILA & BONETTI (*Police Comedy/Drama*)
FIRST TELECAST: *January 17, 1992*
LAST TELECAST: *April 18, 1992*
BROADCAST HISTORY:
Jan 1992–Apr 1992, CBS Fri 9:00–10:00
Apr 1992, CBS Fri 8:00–9:00
Apr 1992, CBS Sat 9:00–10:00
CAST:
Det. Nico Bonetti .... Jack Scalia
Off. Angela Garcia .... Mariska Hargitay
Tequila (voice) .... Brad Sanders
Capt Midian Knight .... Charles Rocket
Det. Lee .... W.K. Stratton
Sgt. Nuzo .... Terry Funk
Off. Vita .... Joe Vita

After being involved in a shootout that had generated a lot of negative public reaction, New York City police detective Nico Bonetti took a temporary assignment as a visiting detective on the South Coast police department in Southern California. Bonetti, a lover of fine jazz and a gourmet Italian cook, found it difficult to adjust to the laid-back California lifestyle and being given a dog as a partner. Tequila, a large French mastiff, was a junk-food addict, had a hip attitude, loved women and, like the basset hound Cleo in *The People's Choice*, provided the viewing audience with a running commentary on the action. Officer Angela Garcia was a pretty, widowed young policewoman who didn't succumb to Bonetti's charms and had problems dealing with his "shoot first and ask questions later" approach to police work. Midian Knight ("Captain Midnight"), their pretentious, image-conscious commanding officer, was more interested in making it as a movie scriptwriter than in his police work.

One of the problems this series had was in not deciding whether it was a police drama or a comedy. There was an uncomfortable mix of broad comedy and violent action in most episodes, and the show never attracted a large enough audience to stay on the air. Obviously inspired by the 1989 hit motion picture *Turner & Hooch*.

TEST, THE (*Talk*)
BROADCAST HISTORY:
FX
30 minutes
Original episodes: *2001*
Premiered: *April 23, 2001*
HOST:
Jillian Barberie

A late-night trifle in which four B-list celebrities compared their answers to provocative questions to those of ordinary people polled on the Internet. Questions were of the "What would you do if a sexy women gave you her key?" or "Do you consider cybersex cheating?" variety. Jillian Barberie was the loud, sexy host.

TEX AND JINX (*Talk*)
FIRST TELECAST: *April 20, 1947*
LAST TELECAST: *September 5, 1949*
BROADCAST HISTORY:
Apr 1947–Jun 1947, NBC Sun 8:00–8:15
Jun 1947–Aug 1947, NBC Sun 8:00–8:30
Mar 1949–Jul 1949, CBS Mon 8:00–8:30
Jul 1949–Sep 1949, CBS Mon 9:00–9:30
REGULARS:
Tex McCrary
Jinx Falkenburg

Newspaper columnist Tex McCrary and his actress-wife Jinx Falkenburg were frequently seen during the early days of television, both in guest appearances and as hosts of their own celebrity-interview series. First seen on NBC, they later moved to CBS, where their program was billed as *Preview*, "the living television magazine." In addition to these primetime appearances they hosted *The Swift Home Service Club* (1947–1948), which NBC says was the first sponsored network daytime program, an NBC radio series and various local programs in New York. Later, in the 1950s, they returned to daytime television.

Their primetime programs were variously known as *At Home with Tex and Jinx*, *The Tex and Jinx Film*, and *Preview with Tex and Jinx* in addition to *Tex and Jinx*.

TEXACO STAR THEATER, see *Milton Berle Show, The*

TEXACO STAR THEATER STARRING DONALD O'CONNOR, THE, see *Donald O'Connor Texaco Show, The*

TEXACO STAR THEATER STARRING JIMMY DURANTE, THE, see *Jimmy Durante Show, The*

TEXAN, THE (*Western*)

FIRST TELECAST: *September 29, 1958*
LAST TELECAST: *September 12, 1960*
BROADCAST HISTORY:
Sep 1958–Sep 1960, CBS Mon 8:00–8:30
CAST:
Bill Longley .... Rory Calhoun

He was not a law officer, but Big Bill Longley was often confronted with situations in which he might as well have been. In the years following the Civil War he made a name for himself throughout the state of Texas. He was a fast gun, a loyal and devoted friend, and a mortal enemy to those who broke the law or harassed the people whom he felt close to. As he traveled from town to town he helped those in need and found adventure, danger, and even an occasional romance.

ABC aired reruns of *The Texan* in its weekday daytime lineup from October 1960 to March 1962 and its Saturday morning lineup from February to May 1962.

TEXAS CONNECTION, THE (*Music*)

BROADCAST HISTORY:
The Nashville Network
30 minutes
Produced: *1990–1992*
Premiered: *March 31, 1990*

Concert series originating in San Antonio, featuring country music Texas-style. Among the early guests were Lyle Lovett, Jerry Jeff Walker, and Asleep at the Wheel.

TEXAS RODEO (*Sports Event*)

FIRST TELECAST: *April 30, 1959*
LAST TELECAST: *July 2, 1959*
BROADCAST HISTORY:
Apr 1959–Jul 1959, NBC Thu 7:30–8:00
COMMENTATOR:
Paul Crutchfield

All of the standard rodeo events were shown in this weekly series filmed on location before arena audiences at rodeos in Texas and elsewhere in the Southwest. Calf roping, bronc riding, bull riding, and steer wrestling were all standard features. Such special events as wild-cow milking and barrel racing were also included in some telecasts. Veteran rodeo announcer Paul Crutchfield did the commentary for this series.

TEXAS WHEELERS, THE (*Situation Comedy*)

FIRST TELECAST: *September 13, 1974*
LAST TELECAST: *July 24, 1975*
BROADCAST HISTORY:
Sep 1974–Oct 1974, ABC Fri 9:30 10:00
Jun 1975–Jul 1975, ABC Thu 8:30–9:00
CAST:
Zack Wheeler .... Jack Elam
Truckie Wheeler .... Gary Busey
Doobie Wheeler .... Mark Hamill
Boo Wheeler .... Karen Oberdiear
T. J. Wheeler .... Tony Becker
Sally .... Lisa Eilbacher
Bud .... Dennis Burkley
Lyle .... Bruce Kimball
THEME:
"Illegal Smile," composed and sung by John Prine (1974)

Earthy comedy about the four motherless Wheeler children and their no-account, cantankerous, "but lovable" father Zack. With Zack spending most of his time thinking of ways to avoid work, eldest son Truckie, 24, led the clan, which consisted of Doobie (16), Boo (12), and T.J. (10). Their adventures living in rural Texas, without much money but with a lot of spirit, provided the stories for this short-lived series.

THANKS (*Situation Comedy*)

FIRST TELECAST: *August 2, 1999*
LAST TELECAST: *September 6, 1999*
BROADCAST HISTORY:
Aug 1999–Sep 1999, CBS Mon 8:30–9:00
CAST:
James Winthrop .... Tim Dutton
Polly Winthrop .... Kirsten Nelson
Grammy Winthrop .... Cloris Leachman
Abigail Winthrop (age 14) .... Erika Christenson
Elizabeth Winthrop (10) .... Amy Centner
William Winthrop (8) .... Andrew Ducote
Cotton .... Jim Rash
Rev. Goodacre .... Keith Szarabajka
Magistrate .... Robert Machray

James was a young Pilgrim who had just survived his first Massachusetts winter in the New World with his family in this silly period comedy. He was an eternal optimist who ran the Plymouth general store with his outspoken wife, Polly. They had three children—Abigail, who suffered from raging hormones; Elizabeth, who may have been too intelligent for her own good (some people, including her sister, frequently accused her of being a witch); and William, the family dullard. Also living with them was sarcastic elderly Grammy, whose age didn't keep her from showing carnal interest in the young men of the community. James' best friend, Cotton, was the village idiot; Dr. Addington, the local dentist. There were lame jokes about the hardships of life in the New World, the religious fervor of the Pilgrims ("no fun allowed!"), stoning sinners, and the times in general.

THAT '80S SHOW (*Situation Comedy*)
FIRST TELECAST: *January 23, 2002*
LAST TELECAST: *May 29, 2002*
BROADCAST HISTORY:
Jan 2002–May 2002, FOX Wed 8:00–8:30
CAST:
Corey Howard.................... Glenn Howerton
Katie Howard..................... Tinsley Grimes
Roger Park............................ Eddie Chin
R. T. Howard...................... Geoff Pierson
Sophia.......................... Brittany Daniel
Tuesday (née June).................. Chyler Leigh
Margaret........................ Margaret Smith
Owen.............................. Josh Braaten

San Diego in 1984 was the setting for this comedy, a nostalgia-fest filled with music, styles, and language of the 1980s and obviously inspired by *That '70s Show.* Twenty-two-year-old Corey lived at home with his bubbly younger sister, Katie, and their father, R. T., an incredibly square marketing executive who had divorced their mother two years earlier. Uncertain about his future, Corey was biding his time working for Margaret, a burned-out 1960s hippie, at Permanent Record, a local record store. His coworker was Tuesday, a rude, leather-jacketed, spiked-hair punk rocker. Of course they were attracted to each other. They dated, and although she got skittish when he started talking about a "relationship," their affair got pretty serious. Sophia was Corey's beautiful former girlfriend, who had broken up with him after deciding she was bisexual, and who kept trying, unsuccessfully, to tempt naive Katie into a lesbian fling. Her biggest impediment was Owen, Katie's incredibly straight navy boyfriend. Corey's friend Roger, a Reagan conservative with the hots for Sophia, also lived with the Howards. In February he was fired because of a marketing idea he had gotten from R. T., who owned a mail-order fitness company that sold the Gut Whacker. After R. T. gave Sophia a job with his company, she started maneuvering to gain more control.

THAT GIRL (*Situation Comedy*)
FIRST TELECAST: *September 8, 1966*
LAST TELECAST: *September 10, 1971*
BROADCAST HISTORY:
Sep 1966–Apr 1967, ABC Thu 9:30–10:00
Apr 1967–Jan 1969, ABC Thu 9:00–9:30
Feb 1969–Sep 1970, ABC Thu 8:00–8:30
Sep 1970–Sep 1971, ABC Fri 9:00–9:30
CAST:
Ann Marie........................ Marlo Thomas
Don Hollinger........................ Ted Bessell
Lou Marie............................ Lew Parker
Helen Marie (1966–1970)...... Rosemary DeCamp
Judy Bessemer (1966–1967).......... Bonnie Scott
Dr. Leon Bessemer (1966–1967)... Dabney Coleman
Jerry Bauman...................... Bernie Kopell
Ruth Bauman (1967–1969)....... Carolyn Daniels
Ruth Bauman (1969–1971).......... Alice Borden
Harvey Peck (1966–1967).......... Ronnie Schell
George Lester (1966–1967)......... George Carlin
Seymour Schwimmer (1967–1968)..... Don Penny
Margie "Pete" Peterson (1967–1968).... Ruth Buzzi

Danny Thomas' daughter Marlo started a trend in TV comedies with this hit series. *That Girl* was the prototype for a wave of "independent woman" series, including *The Doris Day Show, Mary Tyler Moore,* and *Rhoda.* Marlo played Ann Marie, a high-spirited young actress who had left the comfort of her parents' home in rural Brewster, New York, to build a career in the big city. Her "big breaks" usually consisted of roles in TV commercials and bit parts in plays, so she supported herself with odd jobs in offices and department stores. New York City did bring one big break for Ann, however, as on the first telecast she met Don Hollinger, a junior executive for *Newsview* magazine, who became her first romance. They finally became engaged on a September 1970 telecast, but Don never did get to marry "that girl"—although he got as far as a stag party before the 1970–1971 season ended.

Others in Ann's world at various times were her parents, Lou (a restaurant owner) and Helen; her neighbors, the Bessemers; her friends the Baumans; and her agents, Harvey and George. Marcy (played by Reva Rose) was seen briefly as Ann Marie's married friend, during the 1970–1971 season. Danny Thomas made a few cameo appearances in the series in various roles.

Reruns of *That Girl* were shown as part of ABC's daytime lineup from June 1969 to March 1972.

THAT GOOD OLE NASHVILLE MUSIC (*Music*)
BROADCAST HISTORY:
Syndicated only
30 minutes
Produced: *1970–1985*
Released: *1970*

Widely carried country music series, featuring a different guest star each week. Produced in association with WSM-TV and Orpyland U.S.A., in Nashville. Also known as *That Nashville Music.*

THAT REMINDS ME (*Stories*)
FIRST TELECAST: *August 13, 1948*
LAST TELECAST: *October 1, 1948*
BROADCAST HISTORY:
Aug 1948–Oct 1948, ABC Fri 8:30–9:00
EMCEE:
Walter Kiernan
REGULARS:
Governor Harold Hoffman
"Uncle Jim" Harkins

This was simply a storytelling session with newsman Walter Kiernan joined by ex-New Jersey Governor Harold Hoffman and "Uncle Jim" Harkins. The stories were generally about humorous incidents in the lives of famous people, and members of the celebrity's family were often on hand to embellish the tales. It seemed like a good idea for TV in 1948.

THAT '70S SHOW (*Situation Comedy*)
FIRST TELECAST: *August 23, 1998*
LAST TELECAST:
BROADCAST HISTORY:
Aug 1998–Mar 1999, FOX Sun 8:30–9:00
Jun 1999–Oct 1999, FOX Mon 8:00–9:00
Sep 1999–Nov 1999, FOX Tue 8:30–9:00
Nov 1999–Jan 2003, FOX Tue 8:00–8:30
Feb 2000–Jul 2000, FOX Mon 8:00–8:30
Sep 2000–Oct 2000, FOX Sun 9:00–10:00
Jan 2001–May 2001, FOX Wed 8:00–8:30
Dec 2001–Jan 2002, FOX Wed 8:00–8:30
Mar 2002–Apr 2002, FOX Fri 8:00–8:30

Apr 2002–Jul 2002, FOX Tue 8:30–9:00
Oct 2002–Nov 2002, FOX Tue 8:30–9:00
Jan 2003– , FOX Wed 8:00–8:30
May 2003–Jun 2003, FOX Wed 8:30–9:00

CAST:

Eric Foreman .... Topher Grace
Jackie Burkhardt .... Mila Kunis
Michael Kelso .... Ashton Kutcher
Steve Hyde .... Danny Masterson
Donna Pinciotti .... Laura Prepon
Fez .... Wilmer Valderrama
Kitty Foreman .... Debra Jo Rupp
Red Foreman .... Kurtwood Smith
Midge Pinciotti (1998–2001) .... Tanya Roberts
Bob Pinciotti .... Don Stark
Laurie Foreman (1998–2000, 2003–)
.... Lisa Robin Kelly
Leo, the hippie (2000–2002) .... Tommy Chong
**Caroline (2001)* .... Allison Munn
**Big Rhonda (2001–2002)* ..... Cynthia LaMontagne
**Joanne (2001–)* .... Mo Gaffney
**Nina (2002–2003)* .... Joanna Canton

*Occasional

THEME:

"That '70s Song," written by Alex Chilton and Chris Bell, sung by Todd Griffin

Set in rural Point Place, Wisconsin, in 1976, this bright sitcom lampooned the activities of high school junior Eric Foreman and his friends during the height of the disco era. The other featured teens were Donna, the sexy redhead who lived next door and was sweet on Eric; hunky Kelso, who was incredibly naive and gullible; Jackie, Kelso's spoiled girlfriend; Hyde, a counter-culture conspiracy theorist; and Fez, a wide-eyed foreign exchange student. Signs of the times were everywhere: leisure suits, platform shoes, acid rock, long hair, and streaking. Eric's mother, Kitty, was a slightly flighty nurse, and his dad, Red, had recently been reduced to part-time work at the plant. His sister, Laurie, was a college freshman who, in February, was flunking out of the University of Wisconsin. Donna's pudgy, gross father, Bob, owned an appliance store and hired Red to work for him over the Christmas holidays. Much of the action took place in the Foreman basement, where the kids hung out.

In the fall of 1999 Hyde moved in with the Foremans because his parents had gone on a long trip (they had abandoned him), and Laurie, living at home since flunking out of college, was having recreational sex with dumb Kelso. When the plant closed down, Red got a job as a supervisor at the new Price Mart discount store. After the first of the year Eric and Donna finally made love and, soon after, their disapproving parents found out. Bob and Midge were so upset about it that they broke off their friendship with Red and Kitty. Jackie and Kelso broke up again after she found out he had been cheating on her with Laurie and they continued to fight.

That September Jackie decided she was in love with Hyde, who could barely stand her. In December Bob's appliance store went bankrupt because he couldn't compete with Price Mart. After the first of the year Kelso tried to get Jackie back but, to the relief of Fez who had the hots for her, he failed. Laurie decided to go to beauty school and was dropped from the credits early in 2001. Then Jackie made up with Kelso and they started dating again, while Fez was involved with psychotic, possessive Caroline, and Eric broke up with Donna because she had doubts about their long-term future.

Early in the 2001–2002 season Donna and Eric decided to be friends. In November Midge, who had not been seen since the start of the season, deserted her family and moved to California; Bob, when his initial depression lifted, started dating beefy Joanne. When her father found out that Jackie and Kelso were back together, he cut her off financially and she took a job at a cheese store to make money. In May Bob's divorce became final, Big Rhonda dumped Fez and Jackie tricked Kelso into asking her to marry him. At the end of the season Donna ran away to California to be with her mother, and Kelso, who didn't want to get married, went with her.

That fall Donna and Kelso came back home and Jackie was dating Hyde, who apparently had had a change of heart about her. Kitty announced she was pregnant (she later found out she was actually starting menopause) and started to have wild mood swings, none of which made Red very happy. When Kelso found out that Jackie was dating Hyde he got jealous and tried to break them up. Fez had a short-lived affair with Nina, his boss at the DMV, but she dumped him because he was too "needy." When Eric told his parents that he and Donna were engaged, Red was upset but he eventually gave them his blessing. After graduation, which the gang had missed because they overslept on a camping trip the night before, Donna and Eric were moving to Madison where they would be starting college in the fall, Jackie was undecided about whether to commit to Hyde or Kelso, and Laurie, who had moved back home a few weeks earlier, married Fez so that he could avoid being deported to his homeland—wherever that was.

THAT WAS THE WEEK THAT WAS (*News Satire*)

FIRST TELECAST: *January 10, 1964*
LAST TELECAST: *May 4, 1965*
BROADCAST HISTORY:

Jan 1964–Jul 1964, NBC Fri 9:30–10:00
Sep 1964–May 1965, NBC Tue 9:30–10:00

REGULARS:

Elliot Reid (1964)
Nancy Ames
David Frost
Henry Morgan (1964)
Phyllis Newman
Pat Englund
Buck Henry
Bob Dishy
Doro Merande (1964)
Alan Alda (1964)
Sandy Baron (1964)
Tom Bosley (1964)
Jerry Damon
Stanley Grover (1964)
Burr Tillstrom's Puppets
The Norman Paris Orchestra

Political satire came to American TV for the first time in this pioneering NBC series, known affectionately as "TW3." Based on a 1963 British TV series of the same name, it was first seen here as a special in November 1963, and premiered as a weekly series the following January. The setting and atmosphere resembled that of a cabaret, and the live origination (from New York) allowed the program to be highly topical.

Singer Nancy Ames was the "TW3" girl and sang the opening and closing numbers in addition to participating in the body of the show. The emphasis of the show was on poking fun at people in high places. Included in the format were comedy sketches, blackouts, musical production numbers, and news reports. Elliot Reid was the host during its first season. David Frost, who had hosted the British version of TW3 and been a contributor to the American series from the start, took over as host in the fall of 1964.

The satire could be very brutal. In one scene two good friends, a Catholic and a Jew, were discussing the fact that the Vatican had just exonerated the Jews from responsibility for Jesus' death. Well, they were off the hook for that one, after 2,000 years, but no, the Jew still couldn't join the Catholic's country club—that one hadn't been worked out yet. Then there was the news report from Jackson, Mississippi, where UN paratroopers had just been dropped by Guatemalan Air Force planes, to rescue Negro ministers, missionaries, and civil rights workers. The musical numbers were no less offensive. One telecast had "The Dance of the Liberal Republicans," and other such songs by writer-composer Tom Lehrer (who later recorded them on an album) as "National Brotherhood Week," "The Folk Song Army," "Smut," "Pollution," "Whatever Became of Hubert?" (Vice President Humphrey), and "The Vatican Rag."

TW3 attracted considerable attention and large audiences during its first few months on the air, and was easily renewed for the 1964–1965 season. But 1964 was an election year, and politicians—including Republican Presidential candidate Barry Goldwater—were among the show's favorite targets. Perhaps by chance, perhaps by design, TW3 was repeatedly preempted during the fall and replaced with low-rated political speeches and documentaries paid for by the Republicans. By the time the show reappeared after the election, its momentum was gone, and audiences had switched to the competition (*Peyton Place* on ABC and *Petticoat Junction* on CBS). TW3—and with it topical TV—was gone by the end of the season, but the example had been set. Political satire would appear in later years in *The Smothers Brothers Comedy Hour*, NBC's *Saturday Night Live*, and many other programs.

THAT WAS THEN (*Comedy/Drama*)

FIRST TELECAST: *September 27, 2002*
LAST TELECAST: *October 4, 2002*
BROADCAST HISTORY:

Sep 2002–Oct 2002, ABC Fri 9:00–10:00

CAST:

Travis Glass .... James Bulliard
Mickey Glass .... Bess Armstrong
Gary "Double G" Glass .... Jeffrey Tambor
Gregg Glass .... Brad Raider
Zooey Glass .... Andrea Bowen
Donnie Pinkus .... Tyler Labine
Claudia Wills-Glass .... Kiele Sanchez
Sophie Frisch .... Tricia O'Kelley

In this time-travel show a self-described 29-year-old loser got to go back in time and "make things right," but wound up learning that he should be careful what he wished for. Travis was a frustrated, unmarried salesman who lived with his widowed mom Mickey, adored his brother Gregg's ten-year-old son Ethan, and secretly pined for the girl he had lost years ago—Gregg's wife, Claudia. In his mind it all went wrong during one humiliating week in high school, when he botched a speech he was supposed to give and lost the girl.

Then one night while Travis was jamming to the Kinks' "Do It Again," a bolt of lightning hit the house and pow!—it was 1988, he was 16 again, and he knew everything that was about to happen. Of course he set about changing things, saving a friend he knew would be killed by an oncoming train, giving a great speech, and preventing the somewhat dense Gregg from getting together with Claudia. His best friend, and the only one who knew what Travis was doing, was gross, chubby Donnie (who showed his friendship by constantly jumping on Travis). Travis also reached out to his selfish, emotionally distant bookie dad, who had died some years later, trying to get him to take care of his health and pay more attention to his family. Then he zapped back to the present, and got a rude surprise. Things were even worse. He was married not to Claudia but to the smothering class chatterbox, former best friend Donnie hated him for inadvertently screwing up *his* life, and since Gregg and Claudia had never married, there was no Ethan. "I've got to get back!"

Go back he did, by putting on the Kinks again. The premise of the series, in fact, was that he would go back each week and change things again, but find that they worked out differently, and not so well, every time. Since the series only lasted for two weeks he never did get things back the way they started. Zooey was Travis' sarcastic kid sister.

THAT WONDERFUL GUY (*Situation Comedy*)

FIRST TELECAST: *December 28, 1949*
LAST TELECAST: *April 28, 1950*
BROADCAST HISTORY:

Dec 1949–Mar 1950, ABC Wed 9:00–9:30
Mar 1950–Apr 1950, ABC Fri 8:30–9:00

CAST:

Harold .... Jack Lemmon
Franklin Westbrook .... Neil Hamilton
Harold's girlfriend .... Cynthia Stone

A young Jack Lemmon starred in this early situation comedy about a pompous theatrical critic and his eager but bumbling valet. Lemmon, as the valet, was a lad fresh out of a Midwestern dramatic school and fresh into New York, looking for a chance to break into the Broadway big time as an actor. While waiting for opportunity to knock, he worked for suave, cynical drama critic Franklin Westbrook. Despite slick production and smooth performances by newcomer Lemmon and old pro Neil Hamilton, this series did not attract a sponsor and lasted only four months.

Lemmon himself did somewhat better than the valet he played here. After several more television roles (see Index) he landed a part in a Broadway play in 1953, then went to Hollywood in 1954 to begin a stellar motion-picture career.

Cynthia Stone, who played Harold's girlfriend, was Jack Lemmon's girlfriend in real life. Later in 1950 they were married.

THAT'S HOLLYWOOD (*Documentary*)

BROADCAST HISTORY:

Syndicated only
30 minutes

Produced: *1976–1982* (74 episodes)
Released: *Fall 1977*

NARRATOR:

Tom Bosley

This was a spin-off from the hit movie *That's Entertainment*, and was produced by Jack Haley, Jr., the same man responsible for the movie. Essentially, it was the same thing in small-screen format; scenes from great 20th Century–Fox movies of the past, strung together at a fast clip. Each show was built around a single theme, such as disaster scenes, popular detectives, musicals, amusing outtakes, etc. Two pilot episodes were aired on some stations during the 1976–1977 season (with Tony Franciosa as host of one), with the series proper debuting in the fall of 1977, with Tom Bosley as host.

THAT'S INCREDIBLE! (*Documentary*)

FIRST TELECAST: *March 3, 1980*
LAST TELECAST: *September 3, 1989*
BROADCAST HISTORY:

Mar 1980–Feb 1984, ABC Mon 8:00–9:00 (OS)
Apr 1984, ABC Thu 8:00–9:00
Apr 1984, ABC Mon 8:00–9:00
Oct 1988–Feb 1989, ABC Sun 7:00–8:00
Apr 1989–Sep 1989, ABC Sun 7:00–8:00

HOST:

John Davidson
Cathy Lee Crosby (1980–1984)
Fran Tarkenton (1980–1984)
Christina Ferrare (1988–1989)
Tracey Gold (1989)

A dentist who cures pain with clothespins! A man who catches arrows with his bare hands! An acrobat who leaps over cars speeding at him at 60 m.p.h.! A dog that catches sharks! A skydiver who jumps out of an airplane handcuffed and straitjacketed! A daredevil who catches a bullet in his teeth! (Six others lost their lives trying that last one.) ABC's *That's Incredible!*, conceived as an imitation of NBC's hit program *Real People*, seemed to be the freak-show annex of the earlier series. From a yogi sandwiched between two slabs of nails (sealed with a sledgehammer) to the band of karate experts leveling a barn, this show had less to do with "real people" than with those craving attention at any cost. When *Time* magazine announced its 1980 dubious achievement awards, "Most Sadistic Show" went to "ABC's *That's Incredible!*, which, in the search for thrills and ratings, had caused one man nearly to lose a foot, another to burn his fingers to stumps, and a third to suffer several fractures and a ruptured aorta." Even an exposé in a May 1982 issue of *TV Guide*, which revealed several of the program's stunts to be rigged or outright frauds, did not faze the series' producers.

To be fair, there were informative segments on breakthroughs in medicine and people overcoming their handicaps. But the show was perhaps best represented by the picture of a man juggling whirring chain saws, while a caption on the screen read, "Do not try this yourself!"

Four years after the program left the ABC schedule, it returned for an additional season, under the new title *Incredible Sunday*. Otherwise, little had changed. Smiling John Davidson was once again host, joined by Christina Ferrare (and in early 1989, by teen actress Tracey Gold). The feature story on the first episode in October 1988 was about a South African woman who became the surrogate mother for her own daughter; implanted with her daughter's fertilized eggs, she gave birth to her own grandchildren. *That*'s incredible!

THAT'S LIFE (*Music/Comedy*)

FIRST TELECAST: *September 24, 1968*
LAST TELECAST: *May 20, 1969*
BROADCAST HISTORY:

Sep 1968–May 1969, ABC Tue 10:00–11:00

CAST:

Robert Dickson .... Robert Morse
Gloria Quigley Dickson .... E. J. Peaker

MUSICAL DIRECTOR:

Elliot Lawrence

CHOREOGRAPHER:

Tony Mordente

This unusual comedy followed the romance and married life of a young couple through sketches, monologues, music, and dance. Though set in the mythical town of Ridgeville, it was otherwise relatively unstructured—in a sense, a predecessor of *Love, American Style*, which premiered the following fall. Both shows made heavy use of guest celebrities in cameo roles. For example, the first episode of *That's Life* opened with a monologue by George Burns, punctuated by short songs, dances, and skits. There followed a dream sequence in which Gloria imagined herself married to Rodney Wonderful (Tony Randall). Later, back in reality, Rodney arranged a blind date for Gloria and she met Bobby at a discotheque, where the music was provided by the rock group the Turtles. Their romance began, and was followed through subsequent shows as they married, set up housekeeping, had their first child, etc.

Other stars making appearances on *That's Life* included Sid Caesar, Paul Lynde, Ethel Merman, Alan King, Mahalia Jackson, Robert Goulet, Phil Silvers, the Muppets, Flip Wilson, Goldie Hawn, Louis Armstrong. Wally Cox, and many others. Creator and executive producer of the show was Marvin Marx, who was for many years Jackie Gleason's head writer.

THAT'S LIFE (*Situation Comedy*)

FIRST TELECAST: *March 10, 1998*
LAST TELECAST: *April 7, 1998*
BROADCAST HISTORY:

Mar 1998–Apr 1998, ABC Tue 9:30–10:00

CAST:

Mike .... Gerry Red Wilson
Patty .... Kellie Overbey
Catherine .... Nadia Dajani
Kieran (age 10) .... Michael Charles Roman
Lisa .... Pauley Perrette
Mitch .... Ron Livingston

It shoulda been one of the best days of his life. Big, blustery, blue collar Mike had just been promoted to "head of the meat department" at the Queens, New York, grocery store where he worked, and now he and his wife Patty wouldn't have to rent out the third floor of their row house. Instead he could turn it into "Guy Town," where he could hang out with his buddies, swill beer, fart, tell gross jokes, and grunt "How 'bout dem Jets?" Into this Elysian dream came Catherine, Patty's rich, snobbish sister from Manhattan, who had just broken up with her husband and needed a place to stay. In tow was her creepy son Kieran, who looked like a Stepford Child and didn't speak. Guy Town was put on hold.

Mike and Catherine spat at each other constantly, while long-suffering Patty interjected a zinger of her own once in a while. Lisa was Patty's 21-year-old sister, and Mitch was Mike's equally loutish friend. Nice folks. Gimme a beer.

THAT'S LIFE (*Comedy/Drama*)
FIRST TELECAST: *October 1, 2000*
LAST TELECAST: *January 26, 2002*
BROADCAST HISTORY:
Oct 2000, CBS Sun 8:15–9:15
Oct 2000–Apr 2001, CBS Sat 8:00–9:00
Jul 2001–Jan 2002, CBS Fri 9:00–10:00
Jan 2002, CBS Sat 9:00–10:00
CAST:
Lydia DeLucca .... Heather Paige Kent
Dolly DeLucca .... Ellen Burstyn
Frank DeLucca .... Paul Sorvino
Paulie DeLucca .... Kevin Dillon
Jackie O'Grady .... Debi Mazar
Dr. Victor Leski (2000–2001) .... Peter Firth
Candy Cooper (2000–2001) .... Kristin Bauer
Lou Buttafucco (2000–2001) ...... Sonny Marinelli
Plum Wilkinson .... Danielle Harris
Joe (2000–2001) .... Joseph Campanella
Carol (2000) .... Millicent Martin
Mrs. Paganini (2000–2001) .... Linda Lawson
Bob (2000–2001) .... Arell Blanton
Mrs. Messina .... Patience Cleveland
Dr. Eric Hackett (2001–2002) .... Titus Welliver
Ray Orozco (2001–2002) .... Jose Zuniga
Adele (2001–2002) .... Tammi Cubilette
THEME:
"That's Life," by Dean Kay and Kelly Gordon (2000–2001); "Learnin' As I Go," by Spencer Proffer and Steve Plunkett, performed by Heather Paige Kent (2001–2002)

Lydia was an earthy, sarcastic 32-year-old who, in the series premiere, made a decision that would change her life, enrolling as a freshman at nearby Montville State University. Nobody understood. Her toll collector father, Frank, and nagging mom Dolly just wanted her to get married and make babies. Her fiancé, Lou, complained about Lydia going to college so she broke their engagement, causing Dolly to fret that she was destined to become a lonely old maid. Lydia's kid brother Paulie, a somewhat goofy local cop who liked to needle her, thought she was screwing up her life. Her two best friends, Jackie, who ran a hair salon, and Candy, a former Miss New Jersey, tried to be supportive but also didn't understand why she wanted to get a degree and were upset because she spent so much time studying.

College was a struggle for Lydia, particularly the course taught by Dr. Leski, a psychology professor with a drinking problem who frequented the Afterlife, the local pub where she worked as a bartender. In January Leski and Jackie started to date. After losing her job at the Afterlife because she refused to serve Leski when he was drunk, Lydia moved back home to save money. Her dad quit the New Jersey Turnpike Authority and bought a local restaurant, with Paulie providing most of the money, and reopened it as Cucina DeLucca. Plum, who was dating Paulie, had a confrontation with her rich father, who cut her off financially. In the season finale she was tossed out of her dorm after she and Paulie were caught in her bed, and she temporarily moved in with the DeLuccas as well. While everyone was celebrating the senior DeLuccas' 35th wedding anniversary Paulie proposed to Plum.

That fall Lydia was having difficulty deciding on her major at college. Jackie found out she was pregnant with Leski's child but, in the season premiere, he died in a freak accident (falling off a horse) right after he proposed to her. Dr. Hackett, whom Lydia had met at the school's Sports Medicine Clinic, offered her a job as a physical therapy aide. They were attracted to each other but, even after he separated from his wife, were unable to establish a dating relationship. Paulie and Plum eloped but hid it from their families, who were planning a traditional wedding—which finally took place in December, just before Dolly was elected to city council. Ray, who worked for Frank at the restaurant and had been dating Jackie, proposed to her. She accepted but, when confronted with having to move with him to his native Mexico, changed her mind. That's life.

THAT'S MY BOY (*Situation Comedy*)
FIRST TELECAST: *April 10, 1954*
LAST TELECAST: *September 13, 1959*
BROADCAST HISTORY:
Apr 1954–Jan 1955, CBS Sat 10:00–10:30
Jun 1959–Sep 1959, CBS Sun 7:30–8:00
CAST:
"Jarring" Jack Jackson .... Eddie Mayehoff
Alice Jackson .... Rochelle Hudson
Junior Jackson .... Gil Stratton, Jr.
Henrietta Patterson .... Mabel Albertson
Bill Baker .... John Smith

"Jarring" Jack Jackson was a junior partner in the firm of Patterson and Jackson, made a comfortable living, and had a pleasant home in the suburbs. An ex-football star, and married to a former tennis star, Jack had delusions of grandeur about the future potential of his son, Junior, as an athlete. Unfortunately, Junior had neither the interest nor the ability to excel at sports. A quiet, intellectual sort, he was constantly hounded and prodded by his father into doing things he was not capable of succeeding at. Jack not only made life miserable for his son, but treating the world and everyone in it as though he was still calling signals in a football game, he also managed to make himself pretty hard for everyone else to take. During the summer of 1959, reruns of the original series were aired on Sunday evenings.

Based on the 1951 movie of the same name, which also starred Mayehoff (with Jerry Lewis as his son).

THAT'S MY BUSH (*Situation Comedy*)
BROADCAST HISTORY:
Comedy Central
30 minutes
Original episodes: *2001* (8 episodes)
Premiered: *April 4, 2001*
CAST:
President George W. Bush .... Timothy Bottoms
Laura Bush .... Carrie Quinn Dolin

Karl Rove .... Kurt Fuller
Princess Stevenson .... Kristen Miller
Maggie Hawley .... Marcia Wallace
Larry O'Shea .... John D'Aquino

Politics sometimes looks like a sitcom, and this unusual series took that idea to its extreme by portraying real-life incumbent George W. Bush and those around him as amiable bumblers in a sunny White House. George, a neat, mild-mannered man who looked a lot like the real thing, tried earnestly to deal with such hot-button issues as abortion, gun control, drugs, and the environment, but always managed to make things worse though his own ineptitude (pro- and anti-abortion advocates turned a White House dinner into a cake-throwing melee, Charlton Heston showed up to pick a fight over a ban on guns, George accidently got high at an anti-drug event, etc.). First Lady Laura was a little more sensible but mostly wanted him to pay more attention to *her*; sneaky political strategist Karl kept pushing him into issues he couldn't handle; sexy but dumb personal secretary Princess offered ill-advised advice; and saucy, seen-it-all White House maid Maggie weighed in with regular put-downs. Adding to the nonsense, "next-door neighbor" Larry dropped in to chat and help George put in an illegal cable hook-up.

In the last episode George was forced to resign, moved to a small, trashy apartment and tried becoming a pro wrestler, bartender and teacher.

That's My Bush marked the first time a fictional TV series was based on a real, incumbent president—and one of the few ever to portray a contemporary public figure. It lasted only two months, being canceled due to low ratings. The series was put together by *South Park* creators Trey Parker and Matt Stone, and was in development prior to the 2000 election, the plan being to portray either Bush or Al Gore, whoever won the election. One can only imagine a sitcom based on a Gore White House—or what this one would have looked like if it had lasted until the terrorist attacks of September 11, 2001.

THAT'S MY DOG (*Quiz/Audience Participation*)

BROADCAST HISTORY:
The Family Channel
30 minutes
Produced: *1991–1995* (100 episodes)
Premiered: *September 1, 1991*

HOST:
Steve Skrovan (1991–1993)
Susan Pari, assistant (1991–1993)
Wil Shriner (1993–1995)

An offbeat game show involving competition between two families and their dogs. The families answered questions, while the dogs were required to perform various tricks, retrieve objects, and find their way through a maze. Based on an English program.

THAT'S MY LINE (*Comedy/Variety*)

FIRST TELECAST: *August 9, 1980*
LAST TELECAST: *April 11, 1981*
BROADCAST HISTORY:
Aug 1980, CBS Sat 8:00–9:00
Feb 1981–Mar 1981, CBS Tue 8:00–9:00
Apr 1981, CBS Sat 9:00–10:00

REGULARS:
Bob Barker
Tiiu Leek
Suzanne Childs
Kerry Millerick (1981)

In the wake of NBC's hit series about *Real People* with unusual occupations, the producers of the 1950s and 1960s panel show *What's My Line* decided to bring back their old program—with a twist. Instead of making it a guessing game, they did filmed reports—à la *Real People*—on actual people with unusual ways of making a living. Among those seen were the world's fastest typist, a rodeo clown, professional flag raisers in Washington, D.C., a blind cabinetmaker, a man who designed skirts for men, the world's greatest hoaxer, and a 76-year-old man who delivered newspapers from an airplane.

Bob Barker was the host of *That's My Line*, and Tiiu Leek and Suzanne Childs were field reporters. When the series returned in 1981, following an initial three-week run the previous summer, a third reporter, Kerry Millerick, had been added. The thrust of the show also seemed to have changed: its initial effort to cover unusual occupations of all types had given way to an emphasis on the funny, bizarre, or ridiculous.

THAT'S MY MAMA (*Situation Comedy*)

FIRST TELECAST: *September 4, 1974*
LAST TELECAST: *December 24, 1975*
BROADCAST HISTORY:
Sep 1974–Sep 1975, ABC Wed 8:00–8:30
Sep 1975–Dec 1975, ABC Wed 8:30–9:00

CAST:
Clifton Curtis .... Clifton Davis
"Mama" Eloise Curtis .... Theresa Merritt
Earl Chambers .... Theodore Wilson
Tracy Curtis Taylor (1974–1975) ..... Lynne Moody
Tracy Curtis Taylor (1975) .... Joan Pringle
Leonard Taylor .... Lisle Wilson
Wildcat .... Jester Hairston
Josh .... DeForest Covan
Junior .... Ted Lange

This ethnic comedy centered on the world of Clifton Curtis, a young, hip barber in a black middle-class neighborhood of Washington, D.C. Clifton inherited the family barbershop, "Oscar's," after the death of his father. He liked his trade and his life as a bachelor, but Mama had different ideas for him, wanting him to find a nice, conservative mate, as his sister Tracy had done. Tracy's husband Leonard was successful, all right (he was an engineer), but far too square for Clifton. Others around the shop were Clifton's buddy Earl, the postman; old-timers Wildcat and Josh, who stopped in for jokes, checkers, and faulty advice; and Junior, the irrepressible street philosopher.

There were several cast changes in the fall of 1975, and Earl, the big talker with unworkable schemes, became Clifton's partner in the barbershop. (Note: Ed Bernard played Earl in the first two telecasts in 1974, while Theodore Wilson had another role in those episodes only.)

THAT'S SO RAVEN (*Situation Comedy*)

BROADCAST HISTORY:
Disney Channel
30 minutes
Original episodes: *2003–*
Premiered: *January 17, 2003*

CAST:
Raven Baxter (age 15) .. Raven (aka Raven-Symone)

Cory Baxter (10) .... Kyle Orlando Massey
Tonya Baxter .... T'Keyah Crystal Keymah
Victor Baxter.................... Rondell Sheridan
Eddie Thomas .... Orlando Brown
Chelsea Daniels .... Anneliese van der Pol

THEME:

performed by Def Jef

Raven was a bright, hyperactive teenager who had visions—flashes of the future, as it were—in this slapstick sitcom set in San Francisco. Trouble was, she would sometimes see only part of some future family event, misinterpret it, and send her family and friends off on a wild goose chase trying to fix things before they happened. Tonya was Raven's sensible mother; Victor, her goofy dad, a chef, and Cory, her annoying little brother, a chubby operator. Among her friends were Eddie, a lazy goofball who was a starting guard on the Bayside school basketball team, and Chelsea, a dense friend. Together they had silly little adventures, patching up misunderstandings, getting along with other kids and such. The show relied heavily on bright colors (even the walls of her house were red and purple), pratfalls and sight gags, and in some ways resembled a cross between a cartoon and a modern teen version of *I Love Lucy*.

THEA (*Situation Comedy*)

FIRST TELECAST: *September 8, 1993*
LAST TELECAST: *February 23, 1994*
BROADCAST HISTORY:

Sep 1993, ABC Wed 9:30–10:00
Sep 1993, ABC Wed 8:30–9:00
Sep 1993–Feb 1994, ABC Wed 8:00–8:30

CAST:

Thea Turrell .... Thea Vidale
Jarvis Turrell, Jr. (age 16)............. Adam Jeffries
Jerome Turrell (14)..................... Jason Weaver
Danesha Turrell (12)............... Brandy Norwood
James Turrell (7) .... Brenden Jefferson
Lynette .... Yvette Wilson
Charles .... Cleavant Derricks

THEME:

by Freddie Washington and Ben Wright

Thea was one TV mom whose kids did not get away with murder. Large, loud, and loving, she ruled her brood with a kind of "tough love" that left no doubt who was in charge. As a recent widow, she had many roles to juggle: a supermarket job during the day, courses in store management at night, part-time hairdresser, and full-time single parent.

Her four kids were serious Jarvis, schemer Jerome, shy Danesha, and cute little James. Basically good kids, they were sometimes rambunctious, but little escaped Mom's knowing gaze: "Thea knows all, Thea sees all." Lynette was Thea's sister and Charles her brother-in-law.

THEATER OF THE MIND (*Discussion*)

FIRST TELECAST: *July 14, 1949*
LAST TELECAST: *September 15, 1949*
BROADCAST HISTORY:

Jul 1949–Aug 1949, NBC Thu 9:30–10:00
Aug 1949–Sep 1949, NBC Thu 9:00–9:30

MODERATOR:

Dr. Houston Peterson

An early attempt to use television to help viewers meet emotional problems of home life. The first half of each telecast consisted of a playlet revolving around a problem such as a child's adjustment to a new baby in the home, inferiority complexes, domineering parents, old age, alcoholism, etc. After the dramatization a panel of psychiatrists and other experts discussed how the problem could be faced.

THEATER TIME (*Dramatic Anthology*)

FIRST TELECAST: *July 25, 1957*
LAST TELECAST: *September 26, 1957*
BROADCAST HISTORY:

Jul 1957–Sep 1957, ABC Thu 9:00–9:30

HOSTESS:

Anita Louise

The plays shown in this filmed series were all reruns of episodes originally aired as part of other anthology programs.

THEN CAME BRONSON (*Adventure*)

FIRST TELECAST: *September 17, 1969*
LAST TELECAST: *September 9, 1970*
BROADCAST HISTORY:

Sep 1969–Sep 1970, NBC Wed 10:00–11:00

CAST:

Jim Bronson .... Michael Parks

Following the suicide of his best friend, big-city reporter Jim Bronson pondered the meaning of his life and wondered about the satisfaction he was getting out of it. The conclusion he reached was that he really yearned to be free of the traditional commitments of urban living. So, he gave up his job, divested himself of most of his material possessions, and left town on his deceased friend's motorcycle in search of a more meaningful existence. The places he traveled to, the people he met, and the odd jobs he took to support himself in his wanderings across the country, provided the stories in this adventure series.

THEN CAME YOU (*Situation Comedy*)

FIRST TELECAST: *March 22, 2000*
LAST TELECAST: *April 26, 2000*
BROADCAST HISTORY:

Mar 2000–Apr 2000, ABC Wed 8:30–9:00

CAST:

Billie Thornton .... Susan Floyd
Aidan Wheeler .... Thomas Newton
Cheryl Sominsky..................... Miriam Shor
Ed .... Desmond Askew
Lewis Peters .... Colin Ferguson
Manuel.......................... Winston J. Rochas

Billie Thornton was a 33-year-old book editor and divorcé who moved into a fancy Chicago hotel and fell in love with a handsome young waiter in this May–December romantic comedy. Actually it was more like May–July, as Aidan was 22, only 11 years younger than she, but what a gulf, culturally and status-wise, it seemed to be to everyone. He had never even bought his music on vinyl! Billie's excitable friend Cheryl was dubious, and her ex, stuffy lawyer Lewis, downright disdainful ("Is this what you meant when you said you wanted children?"). More supportive were Aidan's goofball buddy Ed, who laughed a lot and traded barbs with Cheryl, and worldly dishwasher Manuel. But fluttery Billie and impulsive Aidan followed their dream, despite the wisecracks (Ed: "She's an older woman." Aidan: "Stop saying that, I keep thinking *Janet Reno*").

Based on the real-life experience of writer Betsy Thomas, a divorcée who fell in love with a waiter at L.A.'s Chateau Marmont Hotel.

THESE FRIENDS OF MINE, see *Ellen*

THEY STAND ACCUSED (*Courtroom Drama*)

FIRST TELECAST: *January 18, 1949*
LAST TELECAST: *December 30, 1954*
BROADCAST HISTORY:

Jan 1949–May 1949, CBS Tue 8:00–9:00
Sep 1949–Mar 1950, DUM Sun 9:00–10:00
Jun 1950–Oct 1950, DUM Sun 9:00–10:00
Oct 1950–Apr 1951, DUM Sun 10:00–11:00
Apr 1951–May 1951, DUM Sat 9:00–10:00
May 1951–Sep 1951, DUM Tue 10:00–11:00
Sep 1951–Oct 1952, DUM Sun 10:00–11:00
Sep 1954–Dec 1954, DUM Thu 8:00–9:00

They Stand Accused was one of the earliest and more popular network series to originate from Chicago. It was an unscripted, spontaneous courtroom trial with real lawyers and judges, and actors playing the parts of defendants and witnesses. Everyone ad-libbed his lines as he went along, according to the developing action. The studio audience served as the "jury," and determined the outcome of each case. Even the cases, though fictitious, had a ring of authenticity. They were plotted out by William Wines, Assistant Attorney General of the State of Illinois, who briefed the participants before each show as if they were principals in a real case about to go to trial, and then let the trial run its course.

Wines's cases sometimes involved murder, but just as often were property claims, divorces, or other civil matters. One week the jury might be deciding custody of a child; on another, whether a wealthy eccentric was capable of managing his own affairs. When it was murder there never was a question of who did it, but rather if self-defense, accident, or temporary insanity was a valid defense. So realistic was the presentation that many viewers were convinced that they were watching a real trial in progress.

They Stand Accused was first seen locally over WGN-TV in Chicago, in April 1948. One week after Chicago and New York were linked by coaxial cable in January 1949 the program was fed out to the CBS network, under the title *Cross Question.* It later moved to DuMont and changed its name to *They Stand Accused* in January 1950.

THEY'RE OFF (*Quiz*)

FIRST TELECAST: *June 30, 1949*
LAST TELECAST: *August 18, 1949*
BROADCAST HISTORY:

Jun 1949–Aug 1949, DUM Thu 8:30–9:00

EMCEE:

Tom Shirley

RACE CALLER:

Byron Field

Contestants were tested on films of historic horse races on this obscure early quiz show.

THICKE OF THE NIGHT (*Talk/Variety*)

BROADCAST HISTORY:

Syndicated only
90 minutes
Produced: *1983–1984*
Released: *September 5, 1983*

REGULARS:

Alan Thicke
Richard Belzer
Isabel Grandin
Mike McManus
Charles Fleischer
Chloe Webb (1983)
Gilbert Gottfried (1983)
Arsenio Hall (1984)
The Tom Canning Band
The John Toben Band (1984)

RECURRING PLAYERS:

Kent Skov
Bill Hudnut
Fred Willard
Rick Ducommun
Carl Wolfson
Cecille Frenette

Thicke of the Night arrived in the fall of 1983 amid a barrage of publicity: move over, Johnny Carson, a new, youth-oriented King of Late Night was here, produced by television's most famous programmer, Fred Silverman! More than one hundred stations agreed to carry the new Monday–Friday show, a few of them preempting Carson in the process and most of the rest running it in direct competition with *The Tonight Show.*

Johnny needn't have worried. Thicke, an amiable, good-looking Canadian who had been hovering around the U.S. television business for years (as an actor, producer, and songwriter), proved to be no competition. His show aimed for a more contemporary, improvisational feel than the *Tonight Show,* with rock songs, skits, and chatter among the regulars, as well as segments with guest stars like John Ritter, Rick Nelson, James Brown, Teri Copley, and Mr. T. Some guests turned up repeatedly, among them TV columnists Richard Hack and R. Couri Hay, talk-show host Wally George, rock-show emcee Kasey Kasem, and Thicke's wife at the time, actress-singer Gloria Loring. A large, open set, reminiscent of scaffolding (as if it were still under construction), added to the wide-open atmosphere. Despite energetic rock songs by Thicke and off-the-wall skits by a host of young comics, the show drew poor reviews and a small audience.

THICKER THAN WATER (*Situation Comedy*)

FIRST TELECAST: *June 13, 1973*
LAST TELECAST: *August 8, 1973*
BROADCAST HISTORY:

Jun 1973–Aug 1973, ABC Wed 8:00–8:30

CAST:

Nellie Paine .... Julie Harris
Ernie Paine .... Richard Long
Jonas Paine.................... Malcolm Atterbury
Lily............................... Jessica Myerson
Walter .... Lou Fant

This family comedy pitted a swinging brother (Ernie) and a staid, spinster sister (Nellie) in a battle of wits. The two were brought together by their ailing, octogenarian father, Jonas, who promised them each a $75,000 inheritance if they could both live at his home and together run the family pickle factory ("Paine's

Pure Pickles") for five years. As it turned out, old Jonas not only hung on to watch them bicker, but was probably going to outlive them both.

Lily was a cousin and Walter her husband. Based on the English TV series *Nearest and Dearest*.

THIEVES (*Adventure*)
FIRST TELECAST: *September 28, 2001*
LAST TELECAST: *November 23, 2001*
BROADCAST HISTORY:
Sep 2001–Nov 2001, ABC Fri 9:00–10:00
CAST:
Johnny.............................. John Stamos
Rita.............................. Melissa George
Agent Oliver Shue.................. Robert Knepper
Agent Al Trundel...................... Tone Loc

Echoes of *Moonlighting*! Johnny was a suave and handsome master thief who specialized in intricate plots, precision timing and the abundant use of charm instead of violence to get himself out of tight situations. Rita was a sexy, brassy no-holds-barred thief who preferred high-tech gadgets, explosives and a shoot-from-the-hip approach. They met while trying to pull off the same jewel heist, and were both captured by the unamused feds. That's when things got interesting. Shue, the prissy lead agent, offered them a deal: become thieves for the government, recovering national art treasures, underworld secrets, nuclear launch codes and the like, or spend the rest of their lives in jail. Johnny and Rita could barely stand each other, but under the circumstances they became a team. He smooth-talked people, she kicked 'em. He quietly picked locks (including her door while she was taking a bath; "I thought it was a test"), she blew them open ("Now do it *my* way!"). All the time, even while scaling buildings, dodging gunfire and defusing explosives, they bantered back and forth, insulting, teasing, and outsmarting the bad guys without half trying. There was lots of skin, and the sexual tension between these two smart, sexy thieves was palpable, but the series ended before viewers got to see where it might all lead.

THIN MAN, THE (*Detective/Comedy*)
FIRST TELECAST: *September 20, 1957*
LAST TELECAST: *June 26, 1959*
BROADCAST HISTORY:
Sep 1957–Jun 1959, NBC Fri 9:30–10:00
CAST:
Nick Charles......................... Peter Lawford
Nora Charles.......................... Phyllis Kirk
Lt. Ralph Raines (1957–1958)........ Stafford Repp
Lt. Steve King (1957–1958).............. Tol Avery
Lt. Harry Evans (1958–1959)........ Jack Albertson
Beatrice Dane (1958–1959)............ Nita Talbot
Hazel (1958–1959)................... Pat Donahue

Nick and Nora Charles were wealthy New York socialites living with their wire-haired fox terrier, Asta, in a luxurious Park Avenue apartment. When he married Nora, Nick retired from his occupation as a private detective, but his underworld friends were still around to haunt him. Out of her love for Nick, Nora tried to be hospitable to his friends from the seamier side of life. The friend she had the most trouble being courteous to was Beatrice Dane, a beautiful con-artist friend of Nick's who used the alias "Blondie Collins." Asta, with the mistaken notion that he was a bloodhound, spent much of his time sniffing out clues and suspects. Nick, Nora, and Asta were a team of super-sleuths, solving crimes together for the pure enjoyment of it.

Based on the characters created by novelist Dashiell Hammett, and portrayed in films for many years by William Powell and Myrna Loy. The name "thin man" did not refer to Nick Charles, incidentally, but to another character in the first (1934) *Thin Man* movie.

NBC aired reruns of *The Thin Man* as part of its daytime lineup from September 1959 to February 1960.

THINK FAST (*Quiz/Panel*)
FIRST TELECAST: *March 26, 1949*
LAST TELECAST: *October 8, 1950*
BROADCAST HISTORY:
Mar 1949–Apr 1949, ABC Sat 8:30–9:00
May 1949–Sep 1949, ABC Fri 8:00–8:30
Sep 1949–Jul 1950, ABC Sun 8:00–8:30
Jul 1950–Oct 1950, ABC Sun 7:00–7:30
MODERATOR:
Dr. Mason Gross (1949–1950)
Gypsy Rose Lee (1950)
PANELISTS:
Leon Janney
David Broekman
Eloise McElhone

The five panelists (three regulars and two guests) on this wordy quiz circled a large table, each getting a chance at the "King's" throne by outtalking the others on subjects thrown out by the host.

THINK FAST (*Quiz/Audience Participation*)
BROADCAST HISTORY:
Nickelodeon
30 minutes
Produced: *1989–1990* (106 episodes)
Premiered: *May 1, 1989*
HOST:
Skip Lackey

Fast-paced kids' quiz show combining memory skills, visual games, and physical stunts. The team with the most points went on to the "Locker Room," where they raced the clock in an effort to match pairs of characters or objects hidden behind the doors.

THIRD MAN, THE (*Intrigue*)
BROADCAST HISTORY:
Syndicated only
30 minutes
Produced: *1959–1962* (77 episodes)
Released (U.S.): *Fall 1960*
CAST:
Harry Lime......................... Michael Rennie
Bradford Webster.................. Jonathan Harris

Harry Lime was one of those sinister characters of literature who was cleaned up considerably for television (for two other notable examples, see *Boston Blackie* and *Hopalong Cassidy*). As introduced in Graham Greene's novel *The Third Man*, and portrayed by Orson Welles in the famous 1950 movie of the same name, Lime was a dark and treacherous man, a double-dealer whose only saving grace was that he usually swindled con men who were even more distasteful than himself. Harry could be very charming, but he always had an angle somewhere.

Television turned this blackguard into a suave and debonair ladies' man, the head of an import-export company in Vienna who traveled around the world acquiring works of art and solving mysteries. His criminal past was acknowledged, and he could still be a bit on the shady side. But, as actor Michael Rennie put it, "Justice is Harry Lime's major concern, his primary motive." Graham Greene must have howled at that! Bradford Webster, played by Jonathan Harris (later of *Lost in Space*), was Harry's sometime assistant.

The Third Man was an unusual joint British-American production, with approximately half the episodes filmed in England under the auspices of the BBC, and the other half in Hollywood by National Telefilm Associates. A radio version of *The Third Man*, starring Orson Welles, was syndicated in the early 1950s.

3RD ROCK FROM THE SUN (*Situation Comedy*)

FIRST TELECAST: *January 9, 1996*
LAST TELECAST: *May 22, 2001*
BROADCAST HISTORY:

Jan 1996–Apr 1996, NBC Tue 8:30–9:00
Apr 1996–Jul 1996, NBC Tue 8:00–8:30
Jul 1996–Aug 1996, NBC Thu 9:30–10:00
Aug 1996–Sep 1997, NBC Sun 8:00–8:30
Aug 1997–Sep 1997, NBC Thu 9:30–10:00
Sep 1997–May 1998, NBC Wed 9:00–9:30
Dec 1997–Feb 1998, NBC Wed 8:00–8:30
May 1998–Jun 1998, NBC Wed 8:00–8:30
Jun 1998–Dec 1998, NBC Wed 9:00–9:30
Jun 1998–Aug 1998, NBC Tue 9:30–10:00
Dec 1998–Jul 1999, NBC Tue 8:00–8:30
May 1999–Jun 1999, NBC Tue 9:30–10:00
Jul 1999–Feb 2000, NBC Tue 8:30–9:00
Feb 2000–Mar 2000, NBC Tue 8:00–9:00
Mar 2000–May 2000, NBC Tue 8:00–8:30
Jun 2000, NBC Thu 8:30–9:00
Jul 2000–Sep 2000, NBC Tue 8:00–8:30
Oct 2000–Jan 2001, NBC Tue 8:30–9:00
Jan 2001–Feb 2001, NBC Tue 8:00–8:30
Apr 2001–May 2001, NBC Tue 8:30–9:00

CAST:

Dr. Dick Solomon.................... John Lithgow
Sally Solomon .... Kristen Johnston
Harry Solomon .... French Stewart
Tommy Solomon .... Joseph Gordon-Levitt
Dr. Mary Albright..................... Jane Curtin
Nina Campbell....................... Simbi Khali
Alissa Strudwick (1998–2000) ...... Larisa Oleynik
Mrs. Mamie Dubcek.............. Elmarie Wendel
**Vicki Dubcek (1996–2000)* .... Jan Hooks
Officer Don Orville (1997–2001)..... Wayne Knight
**Judith Draper*.......................... Ileen Getz
**Pitman* .... Chris Hogan
**Caryn*........................... Danielle Nicolet
**Bug*.............................. David DeLuise
**Leon* .... Ian Lithgow

*Occasional

Four aliens landed on Earth to study the ways of the most unimportant of planets (the "3rd rock") in this loony comedy. The High Commander assumed the form of Dick, patriarch of the Solomon family and a professor of physics at Pendelton University in Rutherford, Ohio. His second-in-command, a male lieutenant, became sexy female Sally, while the other two occupied the bodies of doofus Harry and horny, shaggy-haired teenager Tommy (actually older than Dick). In addition to the confusion caused by the difference between their alien selves and the bodies they inhabited (Dick, learning that he can't swivel his head: "How are you supposed to lick your back?"), there were the inevitable misunderstandings as they bumbled their way through unfamiliar human customs and conventions (host: "May I take your coat?" Dick, looking perplexed: "If I can keep my pants."). Most people just thought they were eccentric.

Especially befuddled was Dick's office mate at the university, straitlaced Dr. Albright, whose sarcasm and own repressed lunacy added to the fun. Dick had a crush on her and wanted to get married, but was thwarted by the aliens' Supreme Leader, the Big Giant Head. Later Mary was promoted to Dean, making her Dick's supervisor, to his dismay. Nina was their sassy secretary, Alissa the daughter of a faculty member and Tommy's girlfriend, Mrs. Dubcek their landlady, and Officer Don, Sally's rotund boyfriend. Others frequently seen were Mrs. Dubcek's daughter (and Harry's girlfriend) Vicki, Mary's friend Judith, and students Pitman, Caryn, Bug and Leon. Liam Neesam (John Cleese) was Dick's occasionally seen malevolent alien nemesis.

In the May 1999 season finale the Solomons were visited by the Big Giant Head (William Shatner), a drunken reprobate who took the earth name "Stone Phillips," promoted Sally to High Commander because she looked sexy, and impregnated Vicki. Vicki's pregnancy came to term in a matter of moments and the gang rushed her to the hospital, where the nurse proclaimed, "I can see the head . . . boy, is that a big head!" Big Giant Head fled, leaving Dick back in charge. The May 2001 series finale brought closure. Don quit the police force, and Mary learned the aliens' secret when she saw Dick turn another alien into a monkey (after the alien tried to turn the Solomons into chimps). Because Dick had used a weapon against another alien the Big Giant Head canceled their mission and ordered them home. First, though, they threw a party (at which Elvis Costello sang "Fly Me to the Moon") using credit cards they knew they wouldn't have to pay off, and Dick invited Mary to come with them. She almost did, but chickened out at the last minute. The Solomons then got into their red Rambler, drove to a ridge above the city and began singing (badly) their group song, whereupon they were zapped into space.

THIRD WATCH (*Drama*)

FIRST TELECAST: *September 23, 1999*
LAST TELECAST:
BROADCAST HISTORY:

Sep 1999, NBC Thu 10:00–11:00
Sep 1999–Jan 2000, NBC Sun 8:00–9:00
Jan 2000–Jul 2001, NBC Mon 10:00–11:00
Aug 2001– , NBC Mon 9:00–10:00 (OS)

CAST:

Kim Zambrano......................... Kim Raver
Bobby Caffey (1999–2001) .... Bobby Cannavale
Monte "Doc" Parker .... Michael Beach
Carlos Nieto .... Anthony Ruivivar
Jimmy Doherty..................... Eddie Cibrian
Off. Maurice "Bosco" Boscorelli .... Jason Wiles
Off. Faith Yokas .... Molly Price

Off. John "Sully" Sullivan .... Skipp Sudduth
Off. Ty Davis, Jr. .... Coby Bell
Dr. Sarah Morales (1999–2001) .... Lisa Vidal
Alex Taylor (2000–) .... Amy Carlson
Fred Yokas .... Chris Bauer
**Lt. Swersky* .... Joe Lisi
**Lt. Johnson (2000–)* .... John Michael Bolger

*Occasional

The action-packed world of New York City street cops, paramedics and firefighters was the subject of this high-energy drama filled with burning buildings, shoot-outs, crack addicts, and screaming women going into labor in the subways. Ah, a typical day in Manhattan. Dealing with the chaos were two teams of paramedics, cool Kim and hotheaded Bobby, and battle-weary Doc and green young Carlos. Jimmy was Kim's ex, a buff firefighter who was tenacious at work and reckless in his personal life. Across the street from the paramedics, at the Fifty-fifth Precinct house, was glory-hungry Bosco, whose "supercop" mentality irritated his long-suffering partner Faith, a married mother of two. Sully was a paunchy and streetwise veteran (the only one here who didn't look like a model) saddled with bumbling and sometimes insubordinate young partner Ty. Seen in later seasons were courageous firefighter Alex and Faith's husband, Fred.

They all rushed around the city from one crisis to another, and when that became a little boring the show would devote an episode to some major disaster, such as a citywide blackout that led to widespread rioting, or the aftermath of the September 11, 2001, terrorist attacks. There were also continuing personal stories, including Faith and Fred's marital difficulties and her abortion, Jimmy's gambling problems and his fight with Kim for custody of their child Joey, Bosco's breakdown, Sully's drinking, Carlos' entanglement in a sexual molestation lawsuit, and liaisons between Bobby and Kim and Ty and Alex, among others. Bobby was killed in a 2001 episode.

13 EAST (*Situation Comedy*)
FIRST TELECAST: *July 29, 1989*
LAST TELECAST: *August 25, 1990*
BROADCAST HISTORY:

Jul 1989, NBC Sat 9:30–10:00
Jul 1989–Sep 1989, NBC Sat 8:30–9:00
Apr 1990–May 1990, NBC Sat 8:30–9:00
May 1990, NBC Sat 8:00–8:30
Aug 1990, NBC Sat 8:30–9:00

CAST:

Head Nurse Maggie Poole .... Diana Bellamy
Nurse Monique Roberts .... Jan Cobler
Nurse Kelly Morrison (1989) ...... Barbara Isenberg
Nurse Janet Tom (1989) .... Ellen Regan
Dr. Warren Newman (1989) .... Timothy Wade
Gertrude Boynton (1989) .... Marie Denn
Wayne Frazier .... Wayne Powers
Nurse A. J. Gilroy (1990) .... Rosemarie Jackson
Sidney Cooper (1990) .... Eric Glenn
Father Frankie (1990) .... Philip Proctor

Comedy set at the nursing station of Ward 13 East, at a large hospital. Maggie was the heavyset, heavy-handed boss nurse who thoroughly enjoyed being in charge. Her young subordinates were naive Kelly, socially conscious Janet, and sexy Monique, who was regularly being propositioned by horny Dr. Newman. Wandering about the floor were Gertrude, the absent-minded volunteer, and Frazier, the overbearing administrator. Several of these heavily stereotyped characters were jettisoned for the series' second brief run, only to be replaced by others: Sidney, the wisecracking orderly who aspired to be a standup comic, and A.J., the pretty nurse with no common sense, whose dates turned into disasters.

The series was produced by one-time actor Scoey Mitchlll.

13 QUEENS BOULEVARD (*Situation Comedy*)
FIRST TELECAST: *March 20, 1979*
LAST TELECAST: *July 24, 1979*
BROADCAST HISTORY:

Mar 1979–Apr 1979, ABC Tue 10:30–11:00
Jul 1979, ABC Tue 10:00–10:30

CAST:

Felicia Winters .... Eileen Brennan
Steven Winters .... Jerry Van Dyke
Elaine Dowling .... Marcia Rodd
Mildred Capestro .... Helen Page Camp
Annie Capestro .... Susan Elliot
Jill .... Louise Williams
Camille .... Karen Rushmore
Lois .... Frances Lee McCain

Adult comedy set in a garden apartment complex in Queens, a middle-class, residential borough of New York City. Felicia and Steven had been happily married for 15 years. Their neighbors included Felicia's best friend Elaine, a divorcée; Mildred Capestro; and Mildred's daughter, Jill.

After a four-week run in March–April, the series returned in July with three additional episodes.

30 SECONDS TO FAME (*Talent*)
FIRST TELECAST: *July 17, 2002*
LAST TELECAST:
BROADCAST HISTORY:

Jul 2002, FOX Wed 8:00–8:30
Aug 2002, FOX Wed 8:00–9:00
Oct 2002–Nov 2002, FOX Thu 8:00–9:00
May 2003– , FOX Thu 8:30–9:00

HOST:

Craig J. Jackson

This frenetic talent show was, in some respects, an updated version of *The Gong Show* of the 1970s. The acts ranged from the serious to the absurd. Mixed in with the legitimate singers and dancers were an assortment of nose flute players, rappers, jugglers, male strippers and contortionists. Many of the performers were talented, but others were embarrassingly bad. Each contestant was given 30 seconds to perform but could be voted out if the booing by the studio audience reached a predetermined level on the eliminator meter. After the first two preliminary rounds the studio audience voted for the three finalists, each of whom got another 30 seconds to perform before the final vote. The winner got $25,000; in the first episode a hefty black woman belted out "R-E-S-P-E-C-T" and took home the prize.

THIRTYSOMETHING (*Comedy/Drama*)
FIRST TELECAST: *September 29, 1987*
LAST TELECAST: *September 3, 1991*
BROADCAST HISTORY:

Sep 1987–Sep 1988, ABC Tue 10:00–11:00
Dec 1988–May 1991, ABC Tue 10:00–11:00
Jul 1991–Sep 1991, ABC Tue 10:00–11:00

CAST:

Michael Steadman .... Ken Olin
Hope Murdoch Steadman .... Mel Harris
Janey Steadman .... Brittany & Lacey Craven
Elliot Weston .... Timothy Busfield
Nancy Weston .... Patricia Wettig
Ethan Weston .... Luke Rossi
Brittany Weston .... Jordana "Bink" Shapiro
Melissa Steadman .... Melanie Mayron
Ellyn .... Polly Draper
Prof. Gary Shepherd .... Peter Horton
Miles Drentell (1989–1991) .... David Clennon
Susannah Hart (1989–1991) ..... Patricia Kalember
Billy Sidel (1990–1991) .... Erich Anderson

Ever since the term "yuppie" became popular the networks have been trying to fashion series about this elusive—and presumably heavy-consuming—audience segment. *thirtysomething* [sic] was the very picture of the viewers ABC wanted in its audience: 30-ish, upwardly mobile, preferably with children, and spending lots of money on consumer goods. Stories traced the relationships between two couples and three singles in Philadelphia, all friends. Michael and Elliot had worked together at a large advertising agency, then left to open their own. Michael's wife, Hope, a glamorous, driven, overachiever from Princeton, wanted to be a superstar in publishing but—for now—was raising their newborn baby, Janey. Elliot's wife, Nancy, a flower child of the '60s, had dreams of being an artist, but wound up raising their now school-age children, Ethan and Brittany; by early 1988 Elliot and Nancy were going through a painful separation. Melissa was Michael's sex-starved, want-it-all single cousin (an aging "JAP"), a photographer; Ellyn was Hope's girlhood friend, a worried career woman; and Gary, a long-haired, fun-loving Assistant Professor of Classics at a nearby college, who was Michael's best buddy.

All these pampered people worried constantly about the true meaning of their lives and marriages, pined for the youth they had left behind, and ran to see why the babies were crying. No one seemed to have a stable relationship. Elliot and Nancy's breakup took an entire season, at the end of which they suddenly decided to reconcile. Little Ethan was terrified that his parents might separate again, but a greater crisis awaited the family. Just as Nancy's self-esteem was boosted by the long-awaited publication of her children's book, *Whose Forest Is This?* (written "with Ethan"), she was diagnosed as having cancer. The treatment took another year.

Melissa and Ellyn each went through revolving door romances with a long series of men—Melissa had so many that at one point a gallery staged an exhibition of her work, which amounted to a pictorial chronicle of her failed relationships. Ellyn, after extended affairs with Woodman (Terry Kinney) and Jeffrey (Richard Gilliland) and some shorter flings with others, finally married a man she had discarded years before, Billy Sidel.

Professor Gary moved in with Susannah, who eventually bore him a child, Emma. Unfortunately he was fired from his teaching position (the college didn't like non-comformists), making it difficult to support his new family. Then, in early 1991, Gary suddenly died, devastating his circle of friends.

Even the Steadman marriage became increasingly rocky as Hope chafed in her mother-and-housewife role. She had a second child, Leo, in 1990, and spent a lot of time on an environmental campaign. Her husband's advertising career was a roller-coaster as Michael and Elliot's small agency went bankrupt, and they were forced to find work at a large shop, this one run by cold, cunning Miles Drentell, whose machinations kept everyone on edge. Was he Michael's sponsor or his exploiter, a scorpion ready to strike?

Who said that yuppies have it easy?

THIS COULD BE YOU, see *Bill Gwinn Show, The*

THIS IS AMERICA, CHARLIE BROWN (*Cartoon*)

FIRST TELECAST: *October 21, 1988*
LAST TELECAST: *July 25, 1990*
BROADCAST HISTORY:

Oct 1988–Nov 1988, CBS Fri 8:00–8:30
May 1990–Jul 1990, CBS Wed 8:00–8:30

Charles M. Schulz's "Peanuts" characters were transported through time to participate in significant events in American history in this educational, eight-part, animated mini-series. The first four episodes—"The Voyage of the Mayflower," "The Birth of the Constitution," "The Wright Brothers' Flight," and "The NASA Space Station"—aired weekly in the fall of 1988. The remaining episodes—"The Building of the Transcontinental Railroad," "The Great Inventors," "The Smithsonian and the Presidency," and "The Music and Heroes of America"—aired as monthly specials the following spring. Among the "Peanuts" characters participating were Charlie Brown, Snoopy and Woodstock, Lucy and Linus Van Pelt, Schroeder, Peppermint Patty, and Pig Pen.

CBS reran the entire mini-series during the summer of 1990.

THIS IS BROADWAY, see *This Is Show Business*

THIS IS GALEN DRAKE, see *Galen Drake Show, The*

THIS IS MUSIC (*Music*)

FIRST TELECAST: *November 29, 1951*
LAST TELECAST: *October 9, 1952*
BROADCAST HISTORY:

Nov 1951–Jun 1952, DUM Thu 8:00–8:30
Jun 1952–Oct 1952, DUM Thu 10:00–10:30

HOST:

Alexander Gray

REGULARS:

Nancy Carr
Bruce Foote
Lucille Reed
Jackie Van (1952)
Jacqueline James (1952)
Bill Snary
Robert Trendler Orchestra

DuMont favored pleasant, unassuming musical programs such as this one because they cost very little to telecast and could be relied upon to attract a respectable, if not really large, audience. The format consisted primarily of popular songs sung by a young cast of regulars.

THIS IS MUSIC (*Music*)

FIRST TELECAST: *June 13, 1958*
LAST TELECAST: *May 21, 1959*
BROADCAST HISTORY:

Jun 1958–Sep 1958, ABC Fri 8:30–9:00
Sep 1958, ABC Mon 7:30–8:00
Oct 1958, ABC Mon 10:00–10:30
Nov 1958–Feb 1959, ABC Thu 10:00–10:30
Mar 1959, ABC Mon 9:30–10:00
Apr 1959–May 1959, ABC Thu 10:00–10:30

EMCEE:

Colin Male

REGULARS:

Ramona Burnett
Lee Fogel
Paula Jane
Wanda Lewis
The O'Neill Dancers
Bud Chase
Bob Smith
Gail Johnson
Bob Shreeve

When the original artists mouthed the words to their hit records, as they did on *American Bandstand*, to make sure that it sounded right, it was called lip-syncing. On this live series, which originated from Cincinnati, Ohio, a group of regular performers did the same thing, but to records made famous by other artists. They mouthed the words while the records were played. *This Is Music* hopped all over the ABC schedule during the 1958–1959 season, filling otherwise empty time slots. Many of the larger stations, which scheduled syndicated programs to fill time slots that the network did not program on a regular basis, did not air this series.

THIS IS MY SONG, see *Bill Gwinn Show, The*

THIS IS NBC NEWS (*News*)

FIRST TELECAST: *June 3, 1962*
LAST TELECAST: *September 16, 1962*
BROADCAST HISTORY:

Jun 1962–Sep 1962, NBC Sun 6:30–7:00

HOST:

Ray Scherer

Anchorman Ray Scherer opened each edition of the 1962 summer season of *This Is NBC News* with a five-minute wrap-up of the day's news. The body of the show was then devoted to a series of reports by various NBC News correspondents, on tape or filmed, covering offbeat or entertaining news events from all over the world. At the end of each show, a short summary of the major news events that had occurred during the previous week was given by Mr. Scherer. A slightly different version of this show had aired earlier on Sunday evenings during the previous summer and this version continued on Sunday afternoons until March 24, 1963.

THIS IS SHOW BUSINESS (*Variety*)

FIRST TELECAST: *July 15, 1949*
LAST TELECAST: *September 11, 1956*
BROADCAST HISTORY:

Jul 1949–Sep 1949, CBS Fri 9:00–10:00
Oct 1949–Jan 1953, CBS Sun 7:30–8:00 (OS)
Jan 1953–Jun 1953, CBS Sat 9:00–9:30
Sep 1953–Mar 1954, CBS Tue 9:00–9:30
Jun 1956–Sep 1956, NBC Tue 8:30–9:00

EMCEE:

Clifton Fadiman

PANELISTS:

George S. Kaufman
Abe Burrows (1949–1951, 1956)
Sam Levenson (1951–1954)
Walter Slezak (1956)

The various entertainers who performed on this series were introduced by host/emcee Clifton Fadiman, who chatted with them briefly before they did their acts. Following each act—there were usually three on each show—the entertainers received the opportunity to ask the panel, composed of three show-business veterans, a few questions about the contestants' own acts or on general subjects related to the entertainment world. The title of this series was *This Is Broadway* during its Friday night run in the summer of 1949. When it moved to Sunday evenings that October the title was changed to *This Is Show Business.* During the period in which it was called *This Is Broadway*, the show was simulcast on radio and television. The NBC revival, for the summer of 1956, aired on alternate Tuesdays with *The Chevy Show.*

Probably the most famous moment in the entire run of the series came on the 1952 Christmas show, when acerbic author and panelist George S. Kaufman remarked on the commercialization of Christmas and then said, "Let's make this one program on which no one sings 'Silent Night.' " CBS received several hundred letters expressing viewer outrage at the comment, and Kaufman was briefly dropped from the show amid considerable publicity. Cooler heads prevailed, however, and he was soon reinstated.

THIS IS THE LIFE (*Religious Drama*)

FIRST TELECAST: *September 9, 1952*
LAST TELECAST: *October 26, 1953*
BROADCAST HISTORY:

Sep 1952–Oct 1952, DUM Fri 8:00–8:30
Oct 1952–Sep 1953, ABC Sun 9:30–10:00
Apr 1953–Aug 1953, DUM Mon 8:30–9:00
Sep 1953–Oct 1953, ABC Mon 10:00–10:30

CAST:

Mr. Fisher .... Onslow Stevens
Mrs. Fisher .... Nan Boardman
Emily Fisher (age 18) .... Randy Stuart
Pete Fisher (16) .... Michael Hall
Freddie Fisher (10) .... David Kasday
Grandpa Fisher .... Forrest Taylor
Pastor Martin .... Nelson Leigh

This religious series was produced by the Lutheran Church's Missouri Synod and depicted a Christian family's attempts to deal with the moral problems of everyday life. The "typical family" was the Fishers, who lived in the town of Middleburg, somewhere in the Midwest. Into their lives came a basketball player who had betrayed the trust of his team, a person victimized by rumors, a couple contemplating divorce, and others. The problem was unfolded in a dramatic presentation, then one member of the family, usually Grandpa or eldest child Emily, would deliver the "pitch"—the Christian solution.

The shows were provided free to any station that

would air them, and were seen locally in many cities as well as in the ABC and DuMont runs indicated above. The series was described by *TV Guide* in 1954 as "the most widely circulated TV show in the world."

This Is the Life continued in production until the 1980s, making it one of the longest-running series in television history. It won more than 70 awards, including four Emmies. The Fisher family was phased out in January 1956, and the title shortened from the original *This Is the Life Presents "The Fisher Family"* to simply *This Is the Life.* The program then followed an anthology format, with a different cast and setting each week. However, the objective remained the same: to illustrate through an interesting weekly drama the Christian solution to the problems of life.

THIS IS TOM JONES (*Musical Variety*)
FIRST TELECAST: *February 7, 1969*
LAST TELECAST: *January 15, 1971*
BROADCAST HISTORY:
Feb 1969–May 1969, ABC Fri 7:30–8:30
May 1969–Sep 1970, ABC Thu 9:00–10:00
Sep 1970–Jan 1971, ABC Fri 10:00–11:00
REGULARS:
Tom Jones
The Ace Trucking Company (1970–1971)
Big Jim Sullivan (1970–1971)
The Norman Maen Dancers
The Jack Parnell Orchestra (1969–1970)
The Johnnie Spence Orchestra (1970–1971)

Pop singer Tom Jones, he of the booming baritone, raw, driving energy, and ability to turn grown women into putty (read "sex appeal"), starred in his own musical variety series from 1969–1971. Jones is a Welshman and the first few telecasts originated in London and featured many English stars. Later the origination alternated between London and Hollywood, and top American stars, especially popular musicians, appeared as well. The show had a very contemporary quality, especially during the second season when the Ace Trucking Company, an improvisational comedy troupe consisting of four boys and one girl, joined as regulars.

After the last big, brassy musical number, dynamic Tom would wish his viewers good night in traditional Welsh, saying, "Gwyn eich byd a dymunaf i chwi lawenydd bob amser." Although there was some speculation about what he was really saying (how many Americans understand Welsh?), it meant, simply, "May you always be well and be happy."

THIS IS YOUR LIFE (*Testimonial*)
FIRST TELECAST: *October 1, 1952*
LAST TELECAST: *September 3, 1961*
BROADCAST HISTORY:
Oct 1952–Jun 1953, NBC Wed 10:00–10:30
Jun 1953–Aug 1953, NBC Tue 9:30–10:00
Jul 1953–Jun 1958, NBC Wed 9:30–10:00
Sep 1958–Sep 1960, NBC Wed 10:00–10:30
Sep 1960–Sep 1961, NBC Sun 10:30–11:00
HOST:
Ralph Edwards
ANNOUNCER:
Bob Warren

This Is Your Life was created by Ralph Edwards in the late 1940s and aired for one year each on NBC and CBS radio. It came to television in 1952 and remained on the air for nine seasons. Ralph Edwards was the host throughout the long network run and returned a decade later with a syndicated version.

The format of *This Is Your Life* was quite simple. Each show opened with Edwards surprising an unsuspecting individual, either in the studio or at some location not too far from it, and informing him or her that "this is your life." The guest of honor was then transported to the program's studio, where his life story was presented. Edwards would read from the honored guest's *This Is Your Life* book, chronologically covering the high points in his life, and would pause periodically in the narrative for the voice of an offstage guest. The guest of honor would try to guess whose voice it was—a relative, friend, teacher, minister, business associate, etc.—and then the offstage guest would come out to reminisce about their shared experiences. This would go on until the entire life story was unfolded.

At the end of the show, Ralph Edwards gathered all the guests together on the stage and personally presented the guest of honor with mementoes—a film of the show, a camera and projector to show it on, a charm bracelet with each charm depicting a significant event in the guest of honor's life, and various other prizes. After the show, the friends and family were taken to a party at the hotel where all out-of-town guests had been staying prior to the telecast. The subjects varied from ordinary people, to show-business celebrities, to well-known businessmen. *This Is Your Life* was presented live until the start of the 1959–1960 season, at which point many of the episodes were prerecorded.

Edwards's narration of the biographies of the subjects on *This Is Your Life* tended to wring the maximum amount of emotion from both subject and audience and there was plenty of nostalgic crying done by subjects and guests. To most of the guests of honor, the confrontation with Edwards came as a complete surprise, but there were a few exceptions. Eddie Cantor was told in advance because he had a heart condition and Edwards did not want to shock him into an attack. The most celebrated subject in the long history of *This Is Your Life*, singer Lillian Roth, was also told ahead of time, but for a very different reason. She had waged a long, successful battle with alcoholism and her story was just too personal to spring on her as a surprise. That telecast was extremely inspirational, had the full sanction of Alcoholics Anonymous, and was the only episode to be aired three times, twice on kinescopes after its original live presentation in 1953.

There was always a backup kinescope ready to roll in case something went wrong when Edwards sprang his little surprise on an unsuspecting guest, but it was never needed. There were occasions, though, when the plans had to be scrapped because the subject found out in advance what was being planned. According to the *This Is Your Life* staff, Ann Sheridan was one whose biography was canceled for this reason. There was one person who was definitely off limits—Ralph Edwards himself. He had told his staff, and he meant it, that he would fire every one of them if they ever tried to pull the switch and surprise him with his "life."

The first syndicated edition of *This Is Your Life*

lasted only the 1971–1972 season. For the 1983–1984 season a new syndicated version of *This Is Your Life* appeared, produced by Ralph Edwards but hosted by actor Joseph Campanella.

THIS WEEK IN COUNTRY MUSIC (*Magazine*)
BROADCAST HISTORY:
Syndicated only
30 minutes
Produced: *1983–1987*
Released: *September 1983*
HOST:
Lorianne Crook
Charlie Chase

This series aimed to do for country music what *Entertainment Tonight* did for the larger world of show business: provide news, gossip, and features on the stars and happenings in the field, on an up-to-the-minute basis. It was fed once a week via satellite to stations around the country.

THIS WEEK IN SPORTS (*Sports News*)
FIRST TELECAST: *September 20, 1949*
LAST TELECAST: *December 13, 1949*
BROADCAST HISTORY:
Sep 1949–Dec 1949, CBS Tue 10:00–10:15

Newsreel highlights of the week's activities in the world of sports were telecast in this series. Included were highlights from various events, films of outstanding individual plays, and short profiles of well-known sports personalities.

THIS WORLD—1954 (*Documentary*)
FIRST TELECAST: *August 4, 1954*
LAST TELECAST: *September 22, 1954*
BROADCAST HISTORY:
Aug 1954–Sep 1954, ABC Wed 9:00–9:30

Documentary films produced by the federal government on such subjects as Communism, good government, democracy, etc.

THORNS, THE (*Situation Comedy*)
FIRST TELECAST: *January 15, 1988*
LAST TELECAST: *March 11, 1988*
BROADCAST HISTORY:
Jan 1988–Feb 1988, ABC Fri 9:00–9:30
Mar 1988, ABC Fri 9:30–10:00
CAST:
Sloan Thorn .... Tony Roberts
Ginger Thorn .... Kelly Bishop
Rose Thorn .... Marilyn Cooper
Cricket .... Lori Petty
Toinette .... Mary Louise Wilson
Chad Thorn (age 16) .... Adam Biesk
Joey Thorn (14) .... Lisa Rieffel
Edmund Thorn (7) .... Jesse Tendler
Peggy/Mrs. Hamilton .... Maureen Stapleton
Katina Pappas .... Kathryn Macopulos
THEME:
"We're All Right," by John Kander and Fred Ebb, sung by Dorothy Loudon in an opening nightclub scene

Mike Nichols produced this caviar comedy about a family of rich, social-climbing snobs. Sharing an elegant New York City townhouse were Sloan, an insensitive, self-absorbed public relations executive; Ginger, his status-seeking wife; and their three insufferable children, Chad (a junior snob at 16), Joey, and Edmund. The most frequent form of parental discipline was to buy the kids off; the most frequent social activity, buying and lying one's way into all the right affairs. Cricket was the shapely mother's helper, and Toinette the contemptuous French maid.

Introducing a modicum of common sense were Sloan's no-nonsense mother, Rose, who moved in (horrors!) when her Brooklyn apartment burned down; and Peggy, the sensible maid to a fabulously rich, reclusive widow who lived nearby. (It turned out that Peggy was the widow herself, in disguise.)

Mike Nichols's previous contribution to television was the acclaimed dramatic series *Family*. With luck, this one will mercifully be forgotten.

THOSE AMAZING ANIMALS (*Animals*)
FIRST TELECAST: *August 24, 1980*
LAST TELECAST: *August 23, 1981*
BROADCAST HISTORY:
Aug 1980, ABC Sun 8:00–9:00
Sep 1980–May 1981, ABC Sun 7:00–8:00
Jul 1981–Aug 1981, ABC Sun 7:00–8:00
HOSTS:
Burgess Meredith
Priscilla Presley
Jim Stafford
REGULARS:
Jacques-Yves Cousteau
Joan Embrey
Ron and Valerie Taylor

Those Amazing Animals was a spin-off from the animal segments of *That's Incredible!* Like the parent program, and unlike most previous nature series (*Wild Kingdom,* etc.), it followed a newsmagazine format, with separate live or taped reports linked by studio discussion. There was also a studio audience.

Those Amazing Animals tried to play up the sensational aspects of wildlife wherever possible (A horse that can count! An elephant walks on Jim Stafford! "Reptile Man" hypnotizes hungry crocodiles! A 121-pound dog that chomps rearview mirrors off of passing cars!). Still, most of the reports were instructive, especially those contributed by world-famous explorer Jacques-Yves Cousteau, leading undersea photographers Ron and Valerie Taylor, and Joan Embrey of the San Diego Zoo. The program's hosts seemed to have been chosen mostly for their diversity: Burgess Meredith, the venerable actor, Priscilla Presley, ex-wife of Elvis, and Jim Stafford, a popular singer whose biggest hit was something called "Spiders and Snakes."

THOSE ENDEARING YOUNG CHARMS (*Situation Comedy*)
FIRST TELECAST: *March 30, 1952*
LAST TELECAST: *June 17, 1952*
BROADCAST HISTORY:
Mar 1952–Apr 1952, NBC Sun 6:30–7:00
May 1952–Jun 1952, NBC Tue/Thu 7:15–7:30
CAST:
Ralph Charm .... Maurice Copeland
Abbe Charm .... Fern Persons
Connie Charm .... Charon Follett
Clem Charm .... Gerald Garvey
Uncle Duff .... Clarence Hartzell

This live series, originating from Chicago, told of the adventures of the Charm family, who ran a mail-order business catering to collectors of household gadgets. The family business was run by Ralph Charm and his wife, Abbe, but all of the members of the household participated in it, including daughter Connie and son Clem. The strangest member of the household was Uncle Duff, whose hobby was memorizing mail-order catalogues. *Those Endearing Young Charms* had premiered on Sunday afternoons at the end of December 1951. It spent only two weeks in the 6:30–7:00 P.M. Sunday time slot and then returned early in May.

THOSE TWO (*Situation Comedy*)
FIRST TELECAST: *November 26, 1951*
LAST TELECAST: *April 24, 1953*
BROADCAST HISTORY:
Nov 1951–Apr 1953, NBC Mon/Wed/Fri 7:30–7:45
REGULARS:
Pinky Lee
Vivian Blaine (1951–1952)
Martha Stewart (1952–1953)

This live, loosely structured musical situation-comedy series was used to fill the remainder of the half hour in which NBC aired its network news program. Vivian was a nightclub singer whose accompanist, Pinky, was madly in love with her. Unfortunately for Pinky, she was in love with another man. The vestigial plot was primarily a backdrop allowing the stars to sing solos and duets. Miss Blaine left the series in May 1952 and was replaced by Martha Stewart.

THOSE WHITING GIRLS (*Situation Comedy*)
FIRST TELECAST: *July 4, 1955*
LAST TELECAST: *September 30, 1957*
BROADCAST HISTORY:
Jul 1955–Sep 1955, CBS Mon 9:00–9:30
Jul 1957–Sep 1957, CBS Mon 9:00–9:30
CAST:
Margaret Whiting .... Herself
Barbara Whiting .... Herself
Mrs. Whiting .... Mabel Albertson
Artie (1957) .... Jerry Paris

There were many similarities between the real lives of the Whiting sisters, Margaret and Barbara, and the roles they portrayed in this summer replacement for *I Love Lucy*. Margaret was, and played, a popular singer and Barbara was, and played, her younger sister. They lived in Los Angeles with their mother, and Barbara was a coed at UCLA. The adventures of the two girls and their relationship with their "mother" formed the bases for the stories told in the series. When it returned in 1957, Margaret had acquired an accompanist named Artie who was the one new regular in the cast.

THREE (*Foreign Intrigue*)
FIRST TELECAST: *February 2, 1998*
LAST TELECAST: *March 23, 1998*
BROADCAST HISTORY:
Feb 1998–Mar 1998, WB Mon 9:00–10:00
CAST:
Jonathan Vance .... Edward Atterton
Amanda Webb .... Julie Bowen
Marcus Miller .... Bumper Robinson
The Man (Spencer) .... David Warner

This squabbling team of crime-fighters was together only because they had been blackmailed by "The Man" into working for a top-secret crime solving agency that served "a combination of government and business interests" ("at higher levels, there is no difference"). Jonathan was a master jewel thief and ladies' man, Amanda a sexy, angry con artist ("Go to hell!"), and Marcus a computer hacker with a Robin Hood complex. Each had always worked alone until The Man recruited them to work together—if they refused, they would go to prison. Their assignments were given to them in a Manhattan brownstone where they lived quite well when not on duty. They prevented a master thief from stealing the Hope Diamond, recovered stolen $100-bill currency plates, and stopped an insane computer genius from launching a nuclear attack. In an episode in which Marcus got access to the organization's computer files, he found out that The Man's real name was Spencer, but was it his first or last name? There were lots of high-tech special effects, tense, *Mission Impossible*–type operations, and a pulsating rock soundtrack, but, alas, few viewers. The series lasted less than two months.

For a similar series the same season, see NBC's *Players*.

THREE ABOUT TOWN (*Music*)
FIRST TELECAST: *August 11, 1948*
LAST TELECAST: *October 27, 1948*
BROADCAST HISTORY:
Aug 1948–Sep 1948, ABC Wed 7:15–7:30
Sep 1948–Oct 1948, ABC Wed 8:45–9:00
HOSTESS:
Betsi Allison

Musical interlude featuring vocalist Betsi Allison and twin pianos, with songs and chatter about the theatrical world. Also seen as a local program in New York at various times during 1948.

THREE BLIND DATES (*Comedy*)
BROADCAST HISTORY:
Lifetime
30 minutes
Produced: *1997*
Premiered: *January 24, 1997*
REGULAR:
Cupid .... Johnny Biehle, Jr.

In this Friday night series, cameras followed three couples as they went out on blind dates. Viewers saw opposite versions of the same date (the girl's view and the guy's view), as well as humorous segments such as "Her Terrible Dates." Cupid, a nebbishy guy in an undershirt, introduced the segments.

THREE FLAMES SHOW, THE (*Music*)
FIRST TELECAST: *June 13, 1949*
LAST TELECAST: *August 20, 1949*
BROADCAST HISTORY:
Jun 1949, NBC Mon 10:00–10:30
Jul 1949–Aug 1949, NBC Mon 9:45–10:00
Jul 1949–Aug 1949, NBC Sat 10:00–10:30
REGULARS:
The Three Flames (Tiger Haynes, guitar; Roy Testamark, piano; Bill Pollard, bass)

Live program of music and patter by the Three Flames, a popular black vocal and instrumental trio whose biggest hit was the 1947 novelty "Open the Door, Richard." They performed, appropriately enough, before a backdrop of flames. Many, though not all, of their guests were black, including trumpet players Hot Lips Page and Dizzy Gillespie, singer Dinah Washington, and pianist Errol Garner.

The Three Flames were previously seen locally in New York as well as in a daytime program. They were among the first black performers to have a regular network series. (See *The Southernaires Quartet* for an earlier series featuring a black group, in 1948.)

THREE FOR THE ROAD (*Adventure*)
FIRST TELECAST: *September 14, 1975*
LAST TELECAST: *November 30, 1975*
BROADCAST HISTORY:
Sep 1975–Nov 1975, CBS Sun 7:00–8:00
CAST:
Pete Karras .... Alex Rocco
John Karras .... Vincent Van Patten
Endy Karras .... Leif Garrett

Free-lance photographer Pete Karras, a widower with two teenage sons, traveled around the country on various assignments. His mode of travel, and the means by which he kept his family together, was a mobile home. The nature of Pete's job and the people that he and his sons encountered in their travels provided the material for the stories in this series, which often tended to the moralistic (after beating a bad guy to a pulp, Pete told the boys that violence is not the answer, etc.). The series had a short run.

3 GIRLS 3 (*Variety*)
FIRST TELECAST: *March 30, 1977*
LAST TELECAST: *June 29, 1977*
BROADCAST HISTORY:
Mar 1977, NBC Wed 9:00–10:00
Jun 1977, NBC Wed 9:00–10:00
REGULARS:
Debbie Allen
Ellen Foley
Mimi Kennedy
Oliver Clark
Richard Byrd
Alan Johnson Dancers
Marvin Laird Orchestra

A novel programming idea, *3 Girls 3* was part musical variety show and part situation comedy. The three young stars, none of whom had any previous television experience, played three unknowns who auditioned for, and won, the starring roles in a network variety series. Part of each telecast consisted of their "show," where they were seen singing, dancing, and doing comedy sketches, and part depicted scenes at rehearsals and in their personal lives. Originally scheduled as a four-week mini-series in the spring of 1977, only the first telecast aired, with the three remaining episodes shown in June. A critical success, praised as a programming innovation, *3 Girls 3* never found much of an audience against *Baretta* and CBS movies.

THREE SISTERS (*Situation Comedy*)
FIRST TELECAST: *January 9, 2001*
LAST TELECAST: *February 5, 2002*
BROADCAST HISTORY:
Jan 2001–May 2001, NBC Tue 9:30–10:00
May 2001–Jun 2001, NBC Thu 8:30–9:00
Jul 2001–Aug 2001, NBC Tue 9:30–10:00
Sep 2001–Feb 2002, NBC Tue 8:30–9:00
CAST:
Bess Bernstein-Flynn Keats .... Katherine LaNasa
Steven Keats .... David Alan Basche
Nora Bernstein-Flynn .... Vicki Lewis
Annie Bernstein-Flynn .... A. J. Langer
Honey Bernstein-Flynn .... Dyan Cannon
George Bernstein-Flynn .... Peter Bonerz
Jake Riley .... Edward Kerr
Gordon .... Brian Scolaro
Elliot Quinn .... Paul Hipp

"I'm married to three women!" was the lament of the handsome Los Angeles architect Steven when he realized how close his new wife, Bess, and her two sisters were. He had gotten a true package deal. Bess was his fussy, overachieving wife, a Type A who tried to get dates for her pessimistic, divorced middle sister Nora, a documentary filmmaker. Annie (age 25) was the free-spirited youngest, who lived on Venice Beach, searched for the perfect wave and came up with harebrained schemes such as selling her eggs on eBay. Offering a little advice about the girls—mainly, to not even try to understand them—was their sarcastic dad, George. Honey was their vivacious mom, a meditation devotee who ran something called Beyond Yoga. Jake was Steven's horny business partner, Gordon was a bartender and Annie's romantic interest, and Elliot was Nora's "non-ex" (it turned out he didn't sign the divorce papers), a musician who as the series ended was getting ready to marry her again. Charlie was Bess and Steven's baby, whom everyone baby-sat from time to time.

3-SOUTH (*Cartoon*)
BROADCAST HISTORY:
MTV
30 minutes
Original episodes: *2002* (13 episodes)
Premiered: *November 7, 2002*
VOICES:
Sanford Riley .... Brian Dunkleman
Del Swanson, Todd .... Brian Posehn
Joe .... Mark Hentemann
Cindy, various .... Kathleen Wilhoite
Dean Earhart .... Jeffrey Tambor
ALSO:
Lori Alan
Rodger Bumpass
Tom Kenny
Phil LaMarr
Joel Murray
Eliza Schneider

College was a big goof for Sanford and Del, the two dumb slackers featured in this sitcom. They had somehow managed to get into Barder College (motto: "A Tradition of Adequacy"), where they roomed with studious pre-med student Joe, who was constantly frustrated with their clowning around. Cindy was Sanford's older sister, a junior, who had a penchant for booze and getting hit by cars; Todd, the blond, out-of-it resident advisor; and Earhart, the pompous dean.

THREE'S A CROWD (*Situation Comedy*)
FIRST TELECAST: *September 25, 1984*
LAST TELECAST: *September 10, 1985*

BROADCAST HISTORY:

Sep 1984–Oct 1984, ABC Tue 8:30–9:00
Oct 1984–Jul 1985, ABC Tue 8:00–8:30
Aug 1985–Sep 1985, ABC Tue 8:30–9:00

CAST:

Jack Tripper .... John Ritter
Vicky Bradford .... Mary Cadorette
James Bradford .... Robert Mandan
E. Z. Taylor .... Alan Campbell

After years of living platonically with two female roommates and chasing after a succession of beautiful girls, Jack Tripper finally found true love. He was smitten with pert flight attendant Vicky Bradford, much to the chagrin of her wealthy and straitlaced father, James. When Jack's roommates moved out, Jack decided it was finally time to get married. Unfortunately Vicky didn't agree—her parents' marriage had been turbulent and ended in divorce—and she preferred that she and Jack live together. Jack had misgivings, but they moved into an apartment over Jack's Bistro, the restaurant he now owned. Vicky's dad was apoplectic. In an effort to break them up, he bought the building, thus becoming their landlord, 10 percent owner of the restaurant, and constant surprise visitor. Beach bum E.Z. was Jack's eccentric assistant chef. Jessica Walter was seen occasionally as Vicky's mother, Claudia.

Three's a Crowd, a spin-off from the long-running hit series *Three's Company,* was adapted from the British series *Robin's Nest.*

ABC aired reruns of *Three's a Crowd* on weekday mornings from September 1985–January 1986.

THREE'S COMPANY (*Music*)

FIRST TELECAST: *May 18, 1950*
LAST TELECAST: *September 29, 1950*
BROADCAST HISTORY:

May 1950–Jun 1950, CBS Thu 7:45–8:00
Jun 1950, CBS Wed/Thu 7:45–8:00
Jul 1950–Sep 1950, CBS Tue/Thu 7:45–8:00
Sep 1950, CBS Mon/Wed/Fri 7:45–8:00
Sep 1950, CBS Sun 9:15–9:30.

REGULARS:

Martha Wright
Cy Walter
Stan Freeman
Judy Lynn

This live 15-minute music show, which filled the remainder of the half hour in which CBS aired its network news program during the summer of 1950, featured pianists Cy Walter and Stan Freeman and the vocals of Martha Wright. When Miss Wright left the show she was replaced, effective June 28, by Judy Lynn.

THREE'S COMPANY (*Situation Comedy*)

FIRST TELECAST: *March 15, 1977*
LAST TELECAST: *September 18, 1984*
BROADCAST HISTORY:

Mar 1977–Apr 1977, ABC Thu 9:30–10:00
Aug 1977–Sep 1977, ABC Thu 9:30–10:00
Sep 1977–May 1984, ABC Tue 9:00–9:30
May 1984–Sep 1984, ABC Tue 8:30–9:00

CAST:

Jack Tripper .... John Ritter
Janet Wood .... Joyce DeWitt
Chrissy Snow (1977–1981) .... Suzanne Somers
Helen Roper (1977–1979) .... Audra Lindley
Stanley Roper (1977–1979) .... Norman Fell
Larry Dallas (1978–1984) .... Richard Kline
Ralph Furley (1979–1984) .... Don Knotts
Lana Shields (1979–1980) .... Ann Wedgeworth
Cindy Snow (1980–1982) .... Jenilee Harrison
Terri Alden (1981–1984) .... Priscilla Barnes
Mike the bartender (occasional, 1981–1984)
.... Brad Blaisdell

THEME:

"Three's Company," by Don Nicholl and Joe Raposo, sung by Ray Charles and Julia Rinker

In this comedy, two contemporary young single girls found themselves in need of a roommate for their Santa Monica apartment so they decided to settle for the man they found sleeping in their bathtub—after a going-away party for their last roommate. Jack was harmless enough, but the problem was in convincing everyone else of that.

Parents objected and humorous misunderstandings abounded, but Jack stayed. In addition to his other virtues, he was the only one of the three roommates who could cook. His favorite ploy was to intimate that he was a homosexual, and therefore uninterested in the two sexy girls (in fact, nothing did go on between them). The landlady, Mrs. Roper, who lived downstairs, worried less about what was going on upstairs than about the fact that nothing was going on in *her* love life with her husband, Stanley. Away from their confused home life, Jack was studying for (and eventually got) his chef's diploma; Janet, the brunette, worked in a florist shop; and Chrissy, the frivolous blonde, was a typist.

After a short run in the spring of 1977 *Three's Company* was picked up as a regular series on ABC's fall 1977 schedule. The comedy was based almost entirely on sexual double-entendres, and religious leaders and critics found the program almost as objectionable as *Soap,* which followed it on the Tuesday night schedule. Nevertheless viewers made it one of the major hits of the 1977–1978 season, especially after it was featured on the cover of *Newsweek* magazine in February 1978. The cover photo was a staged shot of Chrissy with her undergarment seemingly falling off, and Jack leering over her shoulder—something that never happened on the show.

Norman Fell and Audra Lindley left the series in 1979 for their own show (see *The Ropers*), and were replaced by Don Knotts as the new landlord. Then, in 1980, Suzanne Somers, who had become a media celebrity as a result of this series, demanded a huge increase in salary plus a piece of the profits in recognition of her new importance. The producers adamantly refused, and her role was reduced to an occasional brief scene in which she was seen phoning her roommates long distance (she was supposed to be in Fresno caring for her sick mother). Eventually Somers was written out of the show altogether, and her career went into decline.

Jack and Janet promptly found a new roommate in Cindy, who was introduced as Chrissy's cute but clumsy cousin. She moved out in 1981 in order to study veterinary medicine at UCLA, though she continued to visit for another season. Her replacement was a smart, vivacious nurse named Terri.

Meanwhile Jack pursued his career as a chef, first at Angelino's Restaurant (whose owner, Frank Angelino, played by Jordan Charney, was seen occasionally). In 1982 Mr. Angelino and landlord Ralph Furley put up the money to open Jack's own place, called Jack's Bistro, specializing in French cuisine. When not at the restaurant or the apartment, the gang hung out at the Regal Beagle, a neighborhood pub.

When he lost his roommates (Janet got married and Terri moved to Hawaii) Jack moved in with his new girlfriend and a new series began in the fall of 1984. See *Three's A Crowd* for details.

Three's Company was based on the British series *Man About the House.*

ABC aired reruns on weekday mornings from June to September 1981.

THRILL SEEKERS (*Documentary*)

BROADCAST HISTORY:

Syndicated only
30 minutes
Produced: *1972–1974* (52 episodes)
Released: *January 1973*

HOST/NARRATOR:

Chuck Connors

This documentary focused on stunts, with films of motorcycle daredevils, cliff divers in Acapulco, practitioners of the Oriental martial arts, and others who sought danger for their kicks. Chuck Connors' excited narration tried to make everything seem equally death-defying, even a little girl with her pet lion.

THRILLER (*Suspense Anthology*)

FIRST TELECAST: *September 13, 1960*
LAST TELECAST: *July 9, 1962*
BROADCAST HISTORY:

Sep 1960–Sep 1961, NBC Tue 9:00–10:00
Sep 1961–Jul 1962, NBC Mon 10:00–11:00

HOST:

Boris Karloff

Stories of normal, everyday people caught in unexpected, often terrifying, situations were broadcast weekly on *Thriller.* Famous horror-movie star Boris Karloff was the host of the series, introducing all of the stories and occasionally starring in them. Generally lesser-known actors and actresses appeared in most of the productions, which bore such evocative titles as "Parasite Mansions," "The Terror in Teakwood," "Pigeons from Hell," and "The Premature Burial."

THROB (*Situation Comedy*)

BROADCAST HISTORY:

Syndicated only
30 minutes
Produced: *1986–1988* (48 episodes)
Released: *September 1986*

CAST:

Sandy Beatty .... Diana Canova
Jeremy Beatty (1986–1987) .... Paul W. Walker
Jeremy Beatty (1987–1988) .... Sean de Veritch
Zachary Armstrong .... Jonathan Prince
Meredith .... Maryedith Burrell
Blue (Prudence Anne Bartlett) .... Jane Leeves
Phil Gaines .... Richard Cummings, Jr.

THEME:

"Throb," written by Paul Cooper and performed by The Nylons and Diana Canova

A comedy that satirized the youth-oriented record business. Sandy was only 33, a divorcée with a teenage son, Jeremy, but she felt old when she went to work at New York's Throb Records. Throb was a small outfit with offices in a Manhattan loft, and it specialized in the more bizarre punk rock acts (you could tell them by their pink hair). The label was run by a very short and very energetic young man named Zachary. An eternal optimist, Zach had more than a platonic affection for Sandy, despite the fact that she was both older and taller than he. The other principal staffers at Throb were Phil, a hip but businesslike black, and Blue, a flightly young English girl who was more punk than most of the groups that paraded through the office. Meredeth was Sandy's best friend, a single teacher who lived in Sandy's building.

In the fall of 1987 Sandy fell in love with the newly vacated penthouse apartment in her building and took Blue in as a roommate to help with the rent. The conflicts between conservative Sandy and free-spirited Blue became even more pronounced when they were both living and working together.

THROUGH THE CRYSTAL BALL (*Dance*)

FIRST TELECAST: *April 18, 1949*
LAST TELECAST: *July 4, 1949*
BROADCAST HISTORY:

Apr 1949–Jul 1949, CBS Mon 9:00–9:30

REGULAR:

Jimmy Savo

Darmatization in dance form of popular fables were presented live on *Through the Crystal Ball.* Pantomimist Jimmy Savo was the original star, host, and narrator of the series. After he left in May there were no regular cast members. Various choreographers worked on the dance interpretation of such fables as *Alice in Wonderland*, "Cinderella," "Ali Baba," and "Casey at the Bat."

THROUGH THE CURTAIN (*Discussion*)

FIRST TELECAST: *October 21, 1953*
LAST TELECAST: *February 24, 1954*
BROADCAST HISTORY:

Oct 1953–Feb 1954, ABC Wed 8:15–8:30

HOST:

George Hamilton Combs

REGULAR:

Leo Gruliow

The curtain referred to here was the Iron Curtain. The program's object was to bring to the American viewer a concise summary of what the Soviet citizen got in his newspapers and magazines each week, with an analysis of what these publications revealed about Soviet society. Gruliow was editor of the *Current Digest of the Soviet Press.*

THROUGH WENDY'S WINDOW, see *Wendy Barrie Show, The*

THUNDER ALLEY (*Situation Comedy*)

FIRST TELECAST: *March 9, 1994*
LAST TELECAST: *July 25, 1995*
BROADCAST HISTORY:

Mar 1994–May 1994, ABC Wed 8:30–9:00
Aug 1994–Nov 1994, ABC Wed 8:00–8:30
Mar 1995–Jul 1995, ABC Tue 8:30–9:00

CAST:

Gil Jones .... Edward Asner
Bobbi Turner (1994) .... Diane Venora
Bobbi Turner (1994–1995) .... Robin Riker

Claudine Turner (age 11) .... Kelly Vint
Jenny Turner (8).................... Lindsay Felton
Harry Turner (5)................ Haley Joel Osment
Leland DuParte .... Jim Beaver
Walter (1994)...................... Ritch Brinkley

Gil Jones was an older, retired stock car driver with a nearly perfect life: his own successful Detroit garage, time to hang out with the boys, and a waiting room in which to charm the ladies who came in with their bent fenders. Into this masculine idea of paradise came divorced daughter Bobbi, with Gil's three grandchildren and some ideas of her own. The kids needed a father figure, and Gil would have to do. Moving in with her widower dad in his apartment over the garage, she tried to domesticate him. He barked, she retaliated. He was stubborn, she taught him little lessons. Of course nobody could resist those adorable kids, and they loved their grandpa, despite—or because of—the less-than-perfect role model he provided. Leland was Gil's mangy, droll chief mechanic.

THUNDER IN PARADISE (*Adventure*)

BROADCAST HISTORY:

Syndicated only
60 minutes
Produced: *1993–1994* (22 episodes)
Released: *March 1994*

CAST:

Randolph J. "Hurricane" Spencer
.... Terry "Hulk" Hogan
Martin "Bru" Brubaker .... Chris Lemmon
Kelly LaRue .... Carol Alt
Edward Whitaker................. Patrick Macnee
Megan Irene Whitaker Spencer (pilot)
.... Felicity Waterman
Jessica Whitaker Spencer (pilot only)
.... Robin Weisman
Jessica Whitaker Spencer (age 9) .... Ashley Gorrell
Thunder Voice .... Russ Wheeler
Trelawni (D. J. Moran)............... Kiki Shepard
Jimmy .... Jimmy Hart
**Allison Wilson* .... Heidi Mark
**Brutus* .... Ed "Brutus Beefcake" Leslie
**Kowalski* .... Jim "The Anvil" Neidhart
**Adam "Hammerhead" McCall*
.... Steve Borden "Sting"
**Kristen/T.C.*............................ Tai Collins

*Occasional

Baywatch with gunfire. In the pilot episode of *Thunder in Paradise* Megan Whitaker married hulking Hurricane Spencer to keep the Paradise Beach Hotel out of the hands of her grasping Uncle Edward. She had been running it but had to get married fast to honor a clause in her father's will. As for Spence, he needed money to bail out the debt-ridden *Thunder*, a super-high-tech boat he had built as a prototype to sell to the military, and he saw the marriage as a business deal. Between the pilot and the first regular episode Megan died in a car accident, leaving Spence to raise her young daughter, Jessica, who adored him. Uncle Edward fought with Spence over control of the hotel and custody of Jessica but finally agreed to let Spence adopt her in exchange for control of the hotel until she would inherit it when she turned 21.

With all this out of the way, the heavy action began. Spence loved action and adventure and, with the help of his buddy Bru, with whom he had been a navy SEAL in Vietnam, he took on assorted jobs for the navy and others. For $5,000 per day plus expenses clients got the two adventurers and *Thunder*, with its amazing high speed and loads of computer equipment, missile launcher, computer-controlled antitheft system that gave intruders severe electrical shocks, fully functional remote-control system, and stealth system that made it virtually undetectable on radar/sonar. Also seen regularly were Kelly, who wanted to be a sculptor but worked as a bartender at the Scuttlebutt Bar & Grill on the beach; Trelawni, a native girl who helped out at the bar, but, as it turned out, was in the witness-relocation program after testifying in a murder trial in Detroit; and lots of nubile bodies on the beach. A number of Hulk Hogan's friends from the wrestling world had minor supporting roles, including Sting, who showed up in several episodes as a former SEAL gone bad.

Filmed on location in Florida at Epcot Center. The Paradise Beach resort location was provided by Disney's Grand Floridian Beach Resort.

TIC TAC DOUGH (*Quiz/Audience Participation*)

FIRST TELECAST: *September 12, 1957*
LAST TELECAST: *December 29, 1958*
BROADCAST HISTORY:

Sep 1957–Oct 1958, NBC Thu 7:30–8:00
Oct 1958–Dec 1958, NBC Mon 7:30–8:00

EMCEE:

Jay Jackson (1957)
Win Elliot

The format of this nighttime quiz show was essentially the same as that of its daytime counterpart. Jay Jackson hosted the nighttime show, but only for its premiere episode. He was replaced the following week by Win Elliot, who remained with it until it was canceled. The game itself was a variation of tic-tac-toe in which each contestant put his *X* or *O* in a given box by answering a question in the category covering that box. After each round (one question for each contestant) the categories were rotated to different boxes. The value of the outside-box questions was $300 and the tougher center-box question was worth $500. The winner kept the cash value of the correct questions he had answered. In a tie game, the winnings were added to the value of the next game.

NBC aired a weekday daytime edition of *Tic Tac Dough* from July 1956 to October 1959. Emcees of the daytime version were Jack Barry, Gene Rayburn, and Bill Wendell. Nearly 20 years later, in 1978, *Tic Tac Dough* was revived as a daytime series on CBS and, simultaneously, a five-episodes-per-week syndicated series. Wink Martindale emceed both, with his work load cut in half when the CBS version was canceled in September after less than two months on the air. The syndicated version, however, remained in production through the 1985–1986 season. Jim Caldwell replaced Wink Martindale as emcee in the fall of 1985. The syndicated version of *Tic Tac Dough* was revived for the 1990–1991 season, with Patrick Wayne as host.

TICK, THE (*Fantasy*)

FIRST TELECAST: *November 8, 2001*
LAST TELECAST: *January 24, 2002*
BROADCAST HISTORY:

Nov 2001–Jan 2002, FOX Thu 8:30–9:00

CAST:

The Tick .... Patrick Warburton
Arthur .... David Burke
Captain Liberty (*née Janet*)............. Liz Vassey
Batmanuel .... Nestor Carbonell

Played primarily for laughs, *The Tick* was about a simple-minded klutzy super-hero in a cobalt-blue muscle-laden suit complete with quivering antennae, whose commentary consisted mostly of pompous absurdities. He was incredibly noble and naive and took everything anyone said literally. Arthur, his sidekick, a wimpy accountant and wannabe super-hero, wore a white moth jumpsuit complete with goggles and wings. They were friendly with two other "super-heroes"—Captain Liberty, a lonely super-woman whose personal life kept getting in the way of fighting crime, and Batmanuel, an ineffectual would-be ladies' man and self-promoter who always seemed to find reasons to avoid crime fighting. At night they fought crime in The City and hung out with other super-heroes at a local Chinese restaurant.

The Tick was originally a comic book created by Ben Edlund, who was an executive producer of this series. An animated version had previously aired on Fox's Saturday morning lineup from 1994 through 1997.

TIGHTROPE (*Police Drama*)

FIRST TELECAST: *September 8, 1959*
LAST TELECAST: *September 13, 1960*
BROADCAST HISTORY:

Sep 1959–Sep 1960, CBS Tue 9:00–9:30

CAST:

Undercover Agent .... Mike Connors

The task of infiltrating organized crime to expose its leaders and prevent the spread of corruption was the job of the unnamed police undercover agent who was the focus of this series. The "tightrope" he walked was treacherous, for many of the police he aided had no idea who he was and would have shot him in various situations without realizing he was working on their side.

The name used by the agent was part of his cover, and changed with each episode. Originally he was supposed to be named Nick Stone, but this idea was dropped before the first telecast and thereafter only occasionally was his real name mentioned—as "Nick."

TIM CONWAY COMEDY HOUR, THE (*Comedy/Variety*)

FIRST TELECAST: *September 20, 1970*
LAST TELECAST: *December 13, 1970*
BROADCAST HISTORY:

Sep 1970–Dec 1970, CBS Sun 10:00–11:00

REGULARS:

Tim Conway
McLean Stevenson
Art Metrano
The Tom Hansen Dancers
Sally Struthers
Bonnie Boland
Bruce Belland and Dave Somerville
The Jimmy Joyce Singers
The Nelson Riddle Orchestra

Comedian Tim Conway was the host and star of this variety show, which stressed sketch comedy. Tim's offbeat comedy did not attract much of an audience—many people were probably bewildered by musical production numbers in which Sally Struthers was the entire dancing chorus—and the show was canceled after only thirteen weeks.

TIM CONWAY SHOW, THE (*Situation Comedy*)

FIRST TELECAST: *January 30, 1970*
LAST TELECAST: *June 19, 1970*
BROADCAST HISTORY:

Jan 1970–Jun 1970, CBS Fri 8:00–8:30

CAST:

Spud Barrett .... Tim Conway
Herbert T. Kenworth .... Joe Flynn
Mrs. K. J. Crawford .... Anne Seymour
Ronnie Crawford .... Johnnie Collins III
Becky Parks .... Emily Banks
Harry Wetzel .... Fabian Dean
Sherman Bell .... Dennis Robertson

Spud Barrett was the clumsy, oafish, but well-meaning chief pilot for Triple-A, that is, Anywhere, Anytime Airline. He was the chief pilot primarily because he was also the only pilot. Owner of the airline, and Spud's boss, was cranky Herb Kenworth, who, despite being in the air-charter business, was terrified of flying. The airport out of which they flew was owned by Mrs. Crawford, who also ran her own more prosperous charter service.

TIM CONWAY SHOW, THE (*Comedy/Variety*)

FIRST TELECAST: *March 22, 1980*
LAST TELECAST: *August 31, 1981*
BROADCAST HISTORY:

Mar 1980–May 1980, CBS Sat 8:00–9:00
Aug 1980–Sep 1980, CBS Sat 8:30–9:00
Sep 1980–Oct 1980, CBS Sat 8:00–8:30
Nov 1980–Mar 1981, CBS Mon 8:30–9:00
Jun 1981–Aug 1981, CBS Mon 8:30–9:00

REGULARS:

Tim Conway
Eric Boardman (1980)
Jack Riley (1980)
Maggie Roswell
Miriam Flynn
Dick Orkin
Bert Berdis
Harvey Korman
The Peter Matz Orchestra
The Don Crichton Dancers
The Artie Malvin Singers

Tim Conway's second attempt at his own prime-time variety hour was essentially an offshoot of *The Carol Burnett Show*, on which he had been a supporting regular for several years. As with Carol's show, this *Tim Conway Show* relied on a small group of regulars in comedy sketches, supplemented by musical numbers and occasional guest stars. Since the series was produced by Miss Burnett's husband, Joe Hamilton, the similarity of formats was not surprising. An unusual feature was the dance group, the Don Crichton Dancers, all youngsters between the ages of 8 and 13.

The Tim Conway Show premiered as a full hour in the spring of 1980, but was trimmed to half an hour that summer. Carol Burnett, Vicki Lawrence, and Harvey Korman made guest appearances, with Harvey becoming a regular costar late in 1980. These alumni of the *Burnett* show even resurrected old running sketches from the former program when they guested here.

TIM CONWAY'S FUNNY AMERICA (*Comedy*)
FIRST TELECAST: *July 29, 1990*
LAST TELECAST: *September 2, 1990*
BROADCAST HISTORY:
Jul 1990–Sep 1990, ABC Sun 8:30–9:00
STAR:
Tim Conway
This was ABC's first, unsuccessful attempt to create a compatible "videos" program to follow its Sunday night hit *America's Funniest Home Videos.* Comedian Tim Conway traveled around the country adopting various disguises to perpetrate jokes on unsuspecting citizens while hidden cameras recorded their reactions. Among the gags were Conway as an old man tottering across the street, as a nutty denizen of a pet grooming salon, confronting passersby as a representative of the "fashion police," and in his Dorf character (a sort of half-height man) leading an aerobics class.

TIME EXPRESS (*Drama/Supernatural*)
FIRST TELECAST: *April 26, 1979*
LAST TELECAST: *May 17, 1979*
BROADCAST HISTORY:
Apr 1979–May 1979, CBS Thu 8:00–9:00
CAST:
Jason................................ Vincent Price
Margaret............................ Coral Browne
Conductor R. J. Walker .... James Reynolds
Engineer Callahan................. William Phipps
Ticket Clerk...................... Woodrow Parfey
This peculiar program was a sort of supernatural variation on *Fantasy Island.* Passengers who boarded the gleaming Time Express found themselves on an eerie train ride through a mist-filled sky, going back through time to destinations that were turning points in their lives. There they could disembark and attempt to alter decisions they had made long ago, in hopes of changing all that had subsequently happened to them as a result. The charming but mysterious couple who escorted the passengers to their destinations were Jason and Margaret, played by real-life married couple Vincent Price and Coral Browne. Among the voyagers who traveled back through time in this limited-run series were an advertising copywriter who wanted to recapture a romance he had forsaken, a rodeo cowboy seeking to find the daughter he had lost after a serious accident, and a former boxer who had thrown a championship fight and wanted to go back and win it after all.

TIME FOR REFLECTION (*Poetry*)
FIRST TELECAST: *May 7, 1950*
LAST TELECAST: *October 22, 1950*
BROADCAST HISTORY:
May 1950–Oct 1950, DUM Sun 6:45–7:00
HOST:
David Ross
Poetry readings by David Ross.

TIME OF YOUR LIFE (*Drama*)
FIRST TELECAST: *October 25, 1999*
LAST TELECAST: *June 21, 2000*
BROADCAST HISTORY:
Oct 1999–Jan 2000, FOX Mon 8:00–9:00
Jun 2000, FOX Wed 9:00–10:00
CAST:
Sarah Merrin................. Jennifer Love Hewitt
Romy Sullivan .... Jennifer Garner
Jesse "J. B." Byron.................... Diego Serrano
Cecelia Wiznarski.................. Pauley Perrette
John Maguire.................. Johnathon Schaech
Jocelyn "Joss" House .... Gina Ravera
In this spin-off from *Party of Five,* Bailey Salinger's longtime love Sarah moved from San Francisco to New York in search of her biological father. She moved into the East Greenwich Village apartment building in which her late birth mother had lived. Among her new friends were Romy, a struggling aspiring actress with no social life living in the apartment Sarah's mom had lived in 20 years earlier; J. B., the hunky hairstylist who lived in the building across the courtyard and showed romantic interest in Romy; Cecelia, the building's avaricious manager; Maguire, an eccentric guitarist who worked in a nearby record store; and Joss, the waitress who had had a casual sex relationship with Maguire and was living with him.

Despite an initial desire to go back to San Francisco when she found out that the man she thought was her father wasn't, Sarah decided to stay in New York and start a new life waiting tables at the bar where Joss worked. The following week Sarah got a Dear John letter from a frustrated Bailey. After Thanksgiving she started dating Maguire and Romy broke up with J. B. because he had a history of dating older women and accepting presents from them. Just before Christmas, in a despondent mood, Romy tossed Sarah out of her apartment—temporarily. Sarah, needing a place to crash, moved in with Maguire, whose apartment had just been burglarized. In addition to waiting tables, Sarah also had a part-time job as an au pair for an obnoxious young girl. In the last episode aired, Romy's recently arrived friend Molly died from stab wounds she received during a mugging. Everyone was traumatized, and Romy returned to Portland to sort things out.

Although 19 episodes were produced, dismally low ratings prompted Fox to pull *Time of Your Life* from the schedule after only 12 had aired.

TIME SQUAD (*Cartoon*)
BROADCAST HISTORY:
Cartoon Network
30 minutes
Original episodes: *2001–*
Premiered: *June 8, 2001*
VOICES:
Beauregard "Officer Buck" Tuddrussel
.... Rob Paulsen
The Larry 3000...................... Mark Hamill
Otto Osworth (age 8).......... Pamela Segall Adlon
The protection of history was in the hands of two incompetent time travelers and one smart kid in this fanciful cartoon. Officer Buck was a big, dumb time cop, with gleaming teeth and a propensity to beat people up (after which he said "sorry"); Larry 3000 was his skinny, cowardly robot, with an English accent. Neither of them knew anything about the historical events they were supposed to "put right," but fortunately they had bright little orphan Otto to help them out as they tried to convince Eli Whitney to invent the cotton gin instead of flesh-eating robots, and Albert Einstein that his true calling was mathematics, not be-

ing a car salesman. They operated out of a satellite in the year 100 million, traveling back in history when the History Instability Alarm went off and warned them that some historical event was about to go awry.

TIME TO SMILE, see *Alan Young Show, The* and *Ken Murray Show, The*

TIME TRAX (*Science Fiction*)

BROADCAST HISTORY:

Syndicated only
60 minutes
Produced: *1992–1994* (44 episodes)
Released: *January 1993*

CAST:

Capt. Darien Lambert .... Dale Midkiff
Selma .... Elizabeth Alexander
**Dr. Mordecai (Mo) Sahmbi* .... Peter Donat

*Occasional

In Washington, D.C., in the year 2193 Darien Lambert was a cop whose life was forever changed after he encountered evil scientist Mordecai Sahmbi, the driving force behind TRAX, a secret project that he had subverted to his own end. The TRAX machine enabled people to travel back in time, and Sahmbi was using it to transport criminals to 1993 to avoid capture. When Sahmbi was about to be captured he went back too, followed by Darien, whose mission was to track down all the future criminals now in the 20th century and use a device that looked like a garage-door remote control to send them back to the future. Darien communicated with the 2193 police by placing ads in 1993 newspapers that they read in archives and then acted upon. Helping him was Selma, a miniaturized sentient computer hidden in what looked like an AT&T MasterCard. Selma, who sometimes had trouble understanding the illogical functioning of humans, normally communicated by talking to him but could go visual, appearing as an attractively prim woman in early-20th-century clothing. Sahmbi, determined to kill Darien, showed up periodically with various plans—all unsuccessful—to dispose of his nemesis.

Filmed in Australia.

TIME TUNNEL, THE (*Science Fiction*)

FIRST TELECAST: *September 9, 1966*
LAST TELECAST: *September 1, 1967*
BROADCAST HISTORY:

Sep 1966–Jul 1967, ABC Fri 8:00–9:00
Jul 1967–Sep 1967, ABC Fri 7:30–8:30

CAST:

Dr. Tony Newman .... James Darren
Dr. Doug Phillips .... Robert Colbert
Dr. Ann MacGregor .... Lee Meriwether
Gen. Heywood Kirk .... Whit Bissel
Dr. Raymond Swain .... John Zaremba

CREATOR/PRODUCER:

Irwin Allen

Tony Newman and Doug Phillips were two young scientists working on a top-secret government project, deep below the Arizona desert. Their goal: to build a laser-actuated "time tunnel," leading to ages past and future. Unfortunately they were forced to plunge into the tunnel before it was fully tested, and found themselves lost in history, able to move from one point in time to another, but unable to get back to their starting point in the present.

While their associates, Drs. MacGregor and Swain, worked feverishly to free them from their bondage, Tony and Doug found themselves plunged into one famous historical event after another, always knowing the outcome in advance, but unable to change it. First they were deposited on the deck of the *Titanic*, just before you-know-what. Then it was in and out of the shadows of great events from the siege of Troy (500 B.C.) to a futuristic space flight to Mars. They tried to save Marie Antoinette and President Lincoln, opposed Cortez, and watched the Battle of Jericho as the walls came a-tumbling down. They chased one villain clear from one million B.C. to one million A.D. Who wanted to go back to Arizona?

TIME WILL TELL (*Quiz/Audience Participation*)

FIRST TELECAST: *August 20, 1954*
LAST TELECAST: *October 15, 1954*
BROADCAST HISTORY:

Aug 1954–Oct 1954, DUM Fri 10:30–11:00

EMCEE:

Ernie Kovacs

ANNOUNCER:

Bob Russell

This short-lived quiz show was intended to give comic Ernie Kovacs a chance to clown around with the contestants. And, indeed, Kovacs's interviews and asides were the principal attraction. The quiz portion consisted simply of a series of questions, most requiring one-word answers, delivered rapid-fire to a panel of three contestants for 90 seconds. The contestant with the most correct answers won.

TIMECOP (*Science Fiction*)

FIRST TELECAST: *September 22, 1997*
LAST TELECAST: *July 18, 1998*
BROADCAST HISTORY:

Sep 1997–Oct 1997, ABC Mon 8:00–9:00
Jun 1998–Jul 1998, ABC Sat 8:00–9:00

CAST:

Off. Jack Logan .... T. W. King
Off. Claire Hemmings .... Cristi Conaway
Eugene Matuzek .... Don Stark
Dr. Dale Easter .... Kurt Fuller

The year was 2007, and time travel—or to put it more precisely, "temporal displacement"—had been invented. Using this still-not-perfected technology for the common good was the T.E.C. (Time Enforcement Commission), the "time cops," whose mission was to "Protect the Past, Preserve the Future." Jack was a cocky, stubborn, but effective Timecop, who was sent out on missions whenever the T.E.C. team detected "ripples in history" that indicated bad guys were doing their own time traveling, changing things for their own maniacal ends. Scanning the pages of musty old newspapers to locate those ripples (i.e., some known historical fact had just changed) was nerdy but brilliant Dr. Dale; also on the team was wisecracking technician Claire and boss Eugene, whom Jack routinely ignored. When a ripple was found, Jack jumped into the time travel device, a kind of elaborate car on rails, buckled up, and roared off into the past, where he might encounter Jack the Ripper, Christopher Columbus, or the Nazis trying to "fix" World War II.

Based on the comic book and the 1994 Jean-Claude Van Damme movie.

TIMMY AND LASSIE, syndicated title for *Lassie*

TIN PAN ALLEY TV (*Musical Variety*)

FIRST TELECAST: *April 28, 1950*
LAST TELECAST: *September 29, 1950*
BROADCAST HISTORY:
Apr 1950–Sep 1950, ABC Fri 9:30–10:00
REGULARS:
Johnny Desmond
Gloria Van
Chet Roble, piano
Rex Maupin's Orchestra

This live musical program from Chicago showcased the songs of a different composer or lyricist each week. The one so honored was usually on hand; for example, lyricist Mitchell Parish watched the cast perform his "Deep Purple," "Star Dust," "Organ Grinder's Swing," and other standards on the premiere telecast. By early TV standards the production was quite elaborate, which at first gave the inexperienced studio crew some problems. *Variety* reported that on the premiere the singers were continually interrupted by loud thuds and clunks from offstage, that a dance team performing behind a vocalist worked nicely "when the camera could find them," and that a group of kids dancing around the man playing the organ grinder in "Organ Grinder's Swing" kept dancing right off the screen. Such were the problems of live TV in 1950. Presumably the problems were overcome as the series continued through the summer.

TITANS (*Drama*)

FIRST TELECAST: *October 4, 2000*
LAST TELECAST: *December 11, 2000*
BROADCAST HISTORY:
Oct 2000–Nov 2000, NBC Wed 8:00–9:00
Dec 2000, NBC Mon 8:00–9:00
CAST:
Richard Williams .... Perry King
Gwen Williams .... Victoria Principal
Chandler Williams .... Casper Van Dien
Peter Williams .... John Barrowman
Jack Williams .... Jack Wagner
Jenny Williams .... Elizabeth Bogush
Laurie Williams .... Josie Davis
Heather Lane Williams .... Yasmine Bleeth
David O'Connor .... Ingo Rademacher
Samantha Sanchez .... Lourdes Benedicto
Scott Littleton .... Jason Winston George
Ethan Benchley .... Kevin Zegers
Edward .... Clement von Franckenstein
Eve .... Michelle Holgate

This glossy, over-the-top soap opera about backstabbing among the rich and debauched harked back to the glory days of *Dallas* and *Dynasty*, but was not nearly as successful. Perhaps it was 20 years too late. Richard was the tyrannical president and CEO of Williams Global Enterprises, and Gwen his beautiful and savvy ex-wife, who lived in a mansion across from his in Beverly Hills. Richard's children were adopted Chandler, a jut-jawed navy pilot who had returned to claim his place in the family empire; wheeler-dealer Peter, who saw Chandler as a threat to his position as his father's right-hand man (although Richard treated Peter like dirt); younger brother Jack, who ran the European division and returned with romantic designs on his ex-stepmom, Gwen; alcoholic screw-up Jenny; and bossy Laurie, the "good sister" who worked diligently at Gwen's nightclub and hissed at slacker Jenny. The chief vixen (every soap needs one) was Heather, Richard's young, scheming new bride, who revealed early on that she was carrying Chandler's baby. Others in the large cast included handsome David, who ran Gwen's nightclub, Pulse; Samantha, the sexy daughter of the Williamses' former cleaning lady who wanted "her due"; Scott, Chander's black friend and coworker; Ethan, Gwen's lusty teen nephew, whom she took in; Edward the butler, and Eve the receptionist.

Major developments during the series' short run included Heather's marriage to Richard; his gift to her of Dress2K, a multimillion-dollar Internet company, which the rest of the family fought; Richard's heart attack while having sex with Heather, and his subsequent death; Peter's blackmail of Heather over the baby; Ethan's pursuit of the trouble-prone teen in the mansion next door; Heather's miscarriage; and Jenny's drug problems. All that in two months.

TITUS (*Situation Comedy*)

FIRST TELECAST: *March 20, 2000*
LAST TELECAST: *August 12, 2002*
BROADCAST HISTORY:
Mar 2000–Jul 2000, FOX Mon 8:30–9:00
Jul 2000–Aug 2001, FOX Tue 8:30–9:00
Jul 2001–Sep 2001, FOX Wed 9:00–9:30
Nov 2001–Mar 2002, FOX Wed 9:30–10:00
Jul 2002–Aug 2002, FOX Sun 9:00–10:00
CAST:
Christopher Titus .... Himself
Ken Titus .... Stacy Keach
Erin Fitzpatrick .... Cynthia Watros
Dave Titus .... Zach Ward
Tommy Shafter .... David Shatraw
Chris (age 10) (2000–2001) .... Phoenix Forsyth
Chris (10) (2001–2002) .... Evan Ellington
Chris (5) .... Dylan Capannelli
**Dave (5)* .... Adam Hicks
Nurse Kathy (2000–2001) .... Mary Lou Rosato
**Amy Fitzpatrick (15) (2001–2002)*
.... Rachel Roth

*Occasional

This very dark comedy was loosely based on the dysfunctional family life of its star. Slightly warped but well-meaning Chris owned Titus High Performance, a Southern California garage specializing in sports and racing cars. Working with him were his incompetent younger brother, Dave, and his neurotic best friend, Tommy, the organized detail man he desperately needed. Chris' girlfriend Erin was the only one who could keep Chris and his father, Ken, from total alienation—despite the fact that Ken called her a witch. Ken, the alcoholic patriarch of the Titus clan, was an obnoxious, sleazy slob who had been divorced five times and had driven Chris' manic-depressive mother, Juanita, into a mental institution that he had sensitively described to the child as "the wacko basket." As Chris said, "Normal people say what they mean. My dad's a pain in the ass, my girlfriend's constantly pissed at me, my brother's an idiot, and Tommy annoys the crap out of me. Life is beautiful."

Chris would frequently break the third wall by making observations to the audience about the people in his life, in black and white from a spartan room that housed what appeared to be an electric chair and was lit by a single bare, hanging lightbulb. There were also flashbacks featuring younger versions of himself.

Juanita escaped from the mental institution, showed up to make dinner (she drugged most of the family), and tried to kill Ken, but failed. Ken later faked a heart attack to save his driver's license after an auto accident, and then had a real one. In the fall Ken came home from the hospital and had sex with Kathy, the visiting nurse who was supposed to be helping him regain his health. They professed to be in love, and he proposed to her. When she moved in, she manipulated Chris into moving Dave's stuff out of the house, leaving him with no place to live. Ken and Kathy almost got married, but when Chris screwed things up at the pre-wedding dinner, Ken started working on the lady bartender. In early February Chris badmouthed guys from a hot-rod magazine and turned up on the cover of their magazine with a very negative article, which cost him his business. Tommy and Dave left to find other jobs, and Chris was forced to get a job at an auto parts store. The events drove him to drink. Erin, who had grown up in a home full of alcoholics, left him, too, but he eventually won her back. In May he was hurt when his car exploded during a drag race. He was brain dead in the hospital, but when they removed life support he miraculously recovered. In the season finale Chris and Erin were about to get married when his mother, Juanita, killed her current husband. The shock caused them to cancel the wedding and vow never to get married.

At the start of the 2001–2002 season, Chris' left arm was barely functioning after his accident. Much to his dismay, Erin's troubled niece, Amy, moved in with them, while Erin trained to become a social worker and started to do casework. In July Juanita, who had escaped from the mental hospital to reconcile with Chris, committed suicide. On the plane ride back from the funeral Chris, thinking he was schizophrenic, went berserk; the whole gang was arrested. At the end of the episode he entered a mental hospital for a three-month stay.

Chris' mother Juanita, who showed up a few times during the two-year run of the series, was played by three different actresses—once by Christine Estabrook, three times by Frances Fisher and twice by Connie Stevens.

TO HAVE & TO HOLD (*Drama*)
FIRST TELECAST: *September 30, 1998*
LAST TELECAST: *December 9, 1998*
BROADCAST HISTORY:
Sep 1998–Dec 1998, CBS Wed 9:00–10:00
CAST:
Det. Sean McGrail .... Jason Beghe
Annie Cornell .... Moira Kelly
Off. Michael McGrail .... Jason Wiles
Patrick McGrail .... Stephen Lee
Off. Tommy McGrail .... Stephen Largay
Fiona McGrail .... Fionnula Flanagan
Carolyn McGrail .... Colleen Flynn
Robert McGrail .... John Cullum

Sean was a calm, conservative detective with the Boston P.D., and Annie was a loud, feminist public defender, a situation that often caused these newlyweds to be at odds professionally. At home they sparred verbally but never went to bed angry—they made up the old-fashioned way, with great sex. Most of the rest of the cast was made up of Sean's large Irish-American family. Annie's closest confidante, her pregnant sister, Carolyn, was married to Sean's fireman brother, Patrick, whose drinking was creating problems. His other brothers, Michael and Tommy, both street patrolmen, and his parents, retired Robert and outspoken Fiona, all loved loud Annie. As Sean's dad put it, "There's nothing so wonderful as being with a woman you want to ravish one moment and strangle the next."

TO ROME WITH LOVE (*Situation Comedy*)
FIRST TELECAST: *September 28, 1969*
LAST TELECAST: *September 21, 1971*
BROADCAST HISTORY:
Sep 1969–Sep 1970, CBS Sun 7:30–8:00
Sep 1970–Jan 1971, CBS Tue 9:30–10:00
Jan 1971–Sep 1971, CBS Wed 8:30–9:00
CAST:
Michael Endicott .... John Forsythe
Aunt Harriet Endicott (1969–1970) ... Kay Medford
Alison Endicott .... Joyce Menges
Penny Endicott .... Susan Neher
Mary Jane (Pokey) Endicott ...... Melanie Fullerton
Mama Vitale .... Peggy Mondo
Gino Mancini .... Vito Scotti
Nico .... Gerald Michenaud
Grandpa Andy Pruitt (1970–1971) ... Walter Brennan

Following the death of his wife, college professor Michael Endicott decided to leave his native Iowa to accept a teaching position at the American Overseas School in Rome. The adjustments made by Michael and his three daughters to a wholly alien but fascinating environment provided much of the gentle humor of this series. Michael's sister Harriet, who tried constantly to get the family to return to Iowa, was living with them in their Rome apartment through the first half of the 1969–1970 season but gave up and returned home alone. At the start of the second season Andy Pruitt, the father of Michael's late wife, joined the cast. A crotchety Iowa farmer who had sold his farm in anticipation of moving to a retirement community, he arrived for a visit in Rome and somehow never left.

TO TELL THE TRUTH (*Quiz/Panel*)
FIRST TELECAST: *December 18, 1956*
LAST TELECAST: *May 22, 1967*
BROADCAST HISTORY:
Dec 1956–Sep 1958, CBS Tue 9:00–9:30
Sep 1958–Sep 1959, CBS Tue 8:30–9:00
Oct 1959–Jun 1960, CBS Thu 7:30–8:00
Jul 1960–Sep 1960, CBS Thu 10:30–11:00
Sep 1960–Sep 1966, CBS Mon 7:30–8:00
Dec 1966–May 1967, CBS Mon 10:00–10:30
EMCEE:
Bud Collyer
PANELISTS:
Polly Bergen (1956–1961)
Hy Gardner (1956–1959)
Hildy Parks (1956–1957)
Kitty Carlisle
Ralph Bellamy (1957–1959)
Tom Poston (1958–1967)
Orson Bean (1964–1967)
Peggy Cass (1964–1967)
PRODUCERS:
Mark Goodson and Bill Todman

Contestants on *To Tell the Truth* were introduced in threes. All of them purported to be the same individual. Following the introduction, emcee Bud Collyer would read an affidavit describing the life, activities, and/or unique experiences of the person whom all the contestants claimed to be. The panel then spent an amount of time asking questions of the three contestants, trying to determine which one was telling the truth and which two were lying. Following the question session, each panelist had to vote for whom he thought was really the person described in the affidavit. Wrong guesses were worth money to all three contestants, who split the winnings equally. The original title, which lasted only one episode, was *Nothing but the Truth*. The person whose description was read in the affidavit had to tell the truth, but the impostors, who had been given a briefing by the person they were pretending to be, could say anything. The famous closing line for each round: "Will the real —— please stand up!"

To Tell the Truth was also seen in daytime on CBS from June 1962 to September 1968. The emcee of the daytime version was also Bud Collyer and the regular panelists were the same ones as on the primetime edition.

Two of the regular panelists who were with the show when it left CBS in 1968—Kitty Carlisle and Peggy Cass—practically made careers out of *To Tell the Truth*. In the fall of 1969 it turned up in syndication with the two of them and Bill Cullen as regular panelists. They remained with the syndicated version until it left the air in 1977. Garry Moore was the emcee until the last year, with Joe Garagiola taking over at the end. Yet another syndicated version was produced during the 1980–1981 season with young Robin Ward as emcee, but without Carlisle and Cass.

NBC brought *To Tell the Truth* back as a daytime entry in the fall of 1990, with Gordon Elliott as emcee. Because of other contractual obligations, Elliott had to leave the series soon after its premiere, with former pro-football player Lynn Swann taking over. Swann was still emceeing when it left the air the following May. Actor John O'Hurley emceed a syndicated revival that premiered in the fall of 2000 and ran for two seasons.

TO THE QUEEN'S TASTE (*Cooking*)

FIRST TELECAST: *May 3, 1948*
LAST TELECAST: *December 29, 1949*
BROADCAST HISTORY:

May 1948–Aug 1948, CBS Mon 8:05–8:30
Aug 1948–Apr 1949, CBS Thu 8:00–8:30
May 1949–Jul 1949, CBS Thu 9:30–10:00
Jul 1949–Sep 1949, CBS Mon 8:00–8:30
Oct 1949–Dec 1949, CBS Thu 7:00–7:30

CHEF:

Dione Lucas

This early cooking show began as a local program in New York on October 9, 1947, originating from the Cordon Bleu (a Manhattan restaurant owned by Dione Lucas). Seven months later the show became a CBS network series. Cooking expert Lucas, the Julia Child of her day, showed viewers how to prepare exotic and tasty culinary treats from varied cuisines. This series was also known as *The Dione Lucas Show*, a title that was used for later local versions after it left the CBS network.

TOAST OF THE TOWN, THE, see *Ed Sullivan Show, The*

TODAY'S F.B.I. (*Police Drama*)

FIRST TELECAST: *October 25, 1981*
LAST TELECAST: *August 14, 1982*
BROADCAST HISTORY:

Oct 1981–Apr 1982, ABC Sun 8:00–9:00
Apr 1982, ABC Mon 8:00–9:00
Jun 1982–Aug 1982, ABC Sat 8:00–9:00

CAST:

Ben Slater .... Mike Connors
Nick Frazier .... Joseph Cali
Al Gordean .... Richard Hill
Dwayne Thompson (pilot only) ..... Charles Brown
Dwayne Thompson .... Harold Sylvester
Maggie Clinton .... Carol Potter

Today's F.B.I. was ABC's attempt to update its popular 1960s series, *The F.B.I.* Ben Slater, a 20-year veteran of the bureau, was the father figure and leader of a team of four bright young agents: Nick, a sometimes overeager young stud with a talent for undercover work; Al, an athletic type; Dwayne, a former marine intelligence officer; and Maggie, a trained psychologist who—in case that didn't work—was also a crack shot. They were all terribly efficient and, as *TV Guide* commented, "such a clean-cut bunch they could sell milk in the commercials." Their cases were often pursued with a moralistic zeal as well, accompanied by little lectures about how nuisances like First Amendment guarantees and restrictions on wire-taps got in the way of capturing slimy criminals. Organized crime, pornographers, kidnappers, and religious fanatics were typical villains, often caught through elaborate undercover operations.

This highly favorable portrait of the bureau was monitored and "approved" by the real-life FBI, which allowed use of its files for ideas for episodes.

TOGETHER WE STAND (*Situation Comedy*)

FIRST TELECAST: *September 22, 1986*
LAST TELECAST: *April 24, 1987*
BROADCAST HISTORY:

Sep 1986, CBS Mon 8:30–9:00
Oct 1986, CBS Wed 8:00–8:30
Oct 1986, CBS Wed 8:30–9:00
Feb 1987, CBS Sun 9:30–10:00
Mar 1987–Apr 1987, CBS Fri 8:00–8:30

CAST:

David Randall (1986) .... Elliott Gould
Lori Randall .... Dee Wallace Stone
Jack Randall (age 14) .... Scott Grimes
Amy Randall (16) .... Katie O'Neill
Sam (14) .... Ke Huy Quan
Sally (6) .... Natasha Bobo
Marion (1987) .... Julia Migenes

One of TV's many amalgam-family comedies, *Together We Stand* had a short, disrupted run during the 1986–1987 season. Originally it starred Elliott Gould as a former pro basketball coach for the Portland Trail Blazers, who stayed in the area after retiring to open a sporting goods store. Most of the action took place at home, where he and his wife, Lori, had a houseful of kids acquired from various sources. Amy, the oldest, had been adopted before Jack, the natural son they thought they could not have ("it was a miracle") was born. Seeing how well they did mixing a natural and adopted child, a pushy social worker then foisted on them two more adoptees, Asian-American Sam and a cute little black girl, Sally. Stories revolved around the cultural differences among the members of this suddenly multi-ethnic family and the adjustments that had to be made by all—Sam and Sally having parents for the first time, and Jack and Amy having to compete with the new arrivals for their folks' time and affection.

After a low-rated and often preempted fall season, *Together We Stand* was pulled from the schedule. It returned in February with a new title, *Nothing Is Easy*, and without star Elliott Gould. Lori was now a widow (David had been killed in an auto accident), coping with this United Nations of kids alone. She had gone back to work, was taking courses at night school to become a legal stenographer, and had to fend off the adoption agency, which had begun to think this was all a bit much for one woman. At least she gained a next-door neighbor, cynical Marion, who was a divorcée and also a single parent.

TOM (*Situation Comedy*)

FIRST TELECAST: *March 2, 1994*
LAST TELECAST: *June 13, 1994*
BROADCAST HISTORY:
Mar 1994–Apr 1994, CBS Wed 8:30–9:00
Jun 1994, CBS Mon 8:30–9:00
CAST:
Tom Graham .... Tom Arnold
Dorothy Graham .... Alison LaPlaca
Mike Graham .... Jason Marsden
Trevor Graham .... Josh Stoppelwerth
Emily Graham .... Tiffany Lubran
Charlotte Graham .... Kathryn Lubran
Donnie Graham .... Andrew Lawrence
Rodney Wilhoit .... Danton Stone
Kara Wilhoit .... Colleen Camp

Tom Graham was a big, grinning welder with a dream—to take over the family farm and build a dream house on the land. After he acquired the barely functioning, run-down farm, located next to the city dump, several miles from a small town in Kansas, Tom borrowed a construction trailer for temporary living quarters and moved his family in. His sensible wife, Dorothy, who had just started law school, tried to be supportive, but the kids gave the move mixed reviews. They all felt isolated out at the dump and hated being cramped into the trailer while their dad, who welded amusement-park rides with his brother-in-law Rodney during the day, made painfully slow progress with the house. Mike, the oldest, was good-looking, girl-crazy, and a manipulator; Trevor, fat and self-conscious, teased and bullied his siblings; Emily and Charlotte were relatively happy twins; and Donnie, the youngest, believed anything his brothers and sisters told him. Kara, Rodney's wife and Dorothy's sister, was a constant thorn in Tom's side, always putting him down and making fun of his slow progress on the house, which closely resembled a large hole in the ground.

TOM CORBETT, SPACE CADET (*Children's Science Fiction*)

FIRST TELECAST: *October 2, 1950*
LAST TELECAST: *September 26, 1952*
BROADCAST HISTORY:
Oct 1950–Dec 1950, CBS Mon/Wed/Fri 6:45–7:00
Jan 1951–Sep 1952, ABC Mon/Wed/Fri 6:30–6:45
Jul 1951–Sep 1951, NBC Sat 7:00–7:30
CAST:
Tom Corbett .... Frankie Thomas
Capt. Steve Strong (1950) .... Michael Harvey
Capt. Steve Strong (1951–1952) ..... Edward Bryce
Astro the Venusian .... Al Markim
Roger Manning .... Jan Merlin
Dr. Joan Dale .... Margaret Garland
TECHNICAL ADVISOR:
Willie Ley
WRITERS:
Frankie Thomas, Stu Brynes, Ray Morse

Tom Corbett was conceived by CBS in late 1950 to cash in on the enormous popularity of DuMont's *Captain Video.* The two programs were not directly competitive—in fact *Tom Corbett* (6:45–7:00 P.M.) led into *Captain Video* (7:00–7:30 P.M.) three nights a week—and they differed in substantial ways. *Tom Corbett* had a much larger budget and thus more realistic special effects, such as blastoffs, weightlessness, etc., all done live through various techniques of video hocus-pocus. And the emphasis was less on futuristic hardware (though there was plenty) and more on the adventures of the young cast.

Tom Corbett, curly-headed teenage cadet at the Space Academy, four centuries hence, was a figure with whom youngsters could identify. With him in training to become Solar Guards were wisecracking Cadet Roger Manning ("So what happens now, space heroes?" "Aw, go blow your jets!") and the quieter Astro, a Venusian (planetary boundaries were rather less important in the 24th century). Every week they blasted off in the spaceship *Polaris* to new adventures somewhere in space, usually against natural forces rather than the space villains who populated *Captain Video.* Their exploits were instructive as well as exciting. Program advisor Willie Ley, a noted scientist and author, worked in legitimate concepts such as variable gravity forces, asteroid belts, and anti-matter.

After three months on CBS *Tom Corbett* moved to ABC for a run of nearly two years. In addition kinescopes of the weekday serial were run on Saturdays on NBC during the summer of 1951—as summer replacement for Victor Borge! The series was also heard on ABC radio during 1952, with the same cast as the TV version. The *Tom Corbett* cast also made personal appearances to promote merchandise connected with the show (wonder if they offered the most popular of the Cadets' 24th-century aids—the Study Machine?). Late in 1952 the series moved to Saturday daytime, where it continued, off and on, until the summer of 1955.

Based on the novel *Space Cadet* by Robert A. Heinlein.

TOM, DICK AND MARY (*Situation Comedy*)

FIRST TELECAST: *October 5, 1964*
LAST TELECAST: *January 4, 1965*
BROADCAST HISTORY:
Oct 1964–Jan 1965, NBC Mon 8:30–9:00
CAST:
Dr. Tom Gentry .... Don Galloway
Mary Gentry .... Joyce Bulifant
Dr. Dick Moran .... Steve Franken
Dr. Krevoy .... John Hoyt
Horace Moran .... J. Edward McKinley

There is one thing you can always say for group living: it helps spread the costs of housing. It was for that reason that young Dr. Tom Gentry and his recent bride, Mary, were sharing an apartment with Tom's best friend, Dick. With Tom working as an intern and Mary as a medical secretary, the family income did not quite stretch far enough to afford their apartment at 90 Bristol Court. Dick was also an intern who had moved in with the Gentrys to share the costs of the apartment. The newlyweds were not thrilled having an extra person around, except when the rent was due. *Tom, Dick and Mary* was one of the three situation comedies that collectively made up the series *90 Bristol Court.* The other two were *Karen* and *Harris Against the World.*

TOM EWELL SHOW, THE (*Situation Comedy*)
FIRST TELECAST: *September 27, 1960*
LAST TELECAST: *July 18, 1961*
BROADCAST HISTORY:
Sep 1960–Jul 1961, CBS Tue 9:00–9:30
CAST:
Tom Potter .... Tom Ewell
Fran Potter .... Marilyn Erskine
Irene Brady .... Mabel Albertson
Carol Potter .... Cindy Robbins
Debbie Potter .... Sherry Alberoni
Sissie Potter .... Eileen Chesis

Tom Potter was a real estate agent whose entire life, away from the office, was dominated by women. His household resembled a multi-generational girl's dormitory. In addition to his wife Fran, and his three daughters (Carol, 15; Debbie, 11; and Sissie, 7), he had to cope with a live-in mother-in-law, Grandma Brady. The problems he had living in a woman's world provided the focus of this series.

TOM GREEN SHOW, THE (*Humor*)
BROADCAST HISTORY:
MTV
30 minutes
Produced: *1999–2000*
Premiered: *January 25, 1999*
REGULARS:
Tom Green
Glenn Humplik
Phil Giroux

Deadpan Canadian comic Tom Green built this show around his repertoire of man-in-the-street gags, in which he surprised passersby with stunts such as falling down (Green, bandaged and on crutches, would fall repeatedly in front of pedestrians while cameras captured their reactions), loudly buying a package of condoms, or serenading little old ladies on crosswalks. Some of the stunts were perpetrated on his own, unamused parents (e.g., painting "Slutmobile" on the family car), while others were simply intended to gross out the audience (sucking on a cow's teat). Green introduced the segments from a tacky little studio, assisted awkwardly by "real life friend" Glenn and by Phil, the constantly chortling guy-in-the-window.

TOM SHOW, THE (*Situation Comedy*)
FIRST TELECAST: *September 7, 1997*
LAST TELECAST: *March 15, 1998*
BROADCAST HISTORY:
Sep 1997–Oct 1997, WB Sun 9:00–9:30
Oct 1997–Dec 1997, WB Sun 8:30–9:00
Jan 1998–Mar 1998, WB Sun 7:30–8:00
CAST:
Tom Amross .... Tom Arnold
Charlie .... Ed McMahon
Florence Madison .... Shawnee Smith
Jonathan .... Michael Rosenbaum
Kenlon Amross (age 13) .... Lisa Wilhoit
Elissa Amross (9) .... Mika Boorem
Tonya Cole .... Tasha Smith
Brownie .... Danton Stone
**Maggie Amross* .... Shannon Tweed
Mrs. Martha Thompson .... Angela Paton
**Billy Swenson* .... John Caponera
*Occasional

Tom was a gregarious TV producer who moved back to his home town of St. Paul, Minnesota, with his two daughters after a messy divorce in which his ex-wife, talk show star Maggie, got the Hollywood mansion and most of the money. He got a job working with his old buddy Charlie, trying to boost the ratings of the latter's long-running local morning talk show, *Breakfast with Charlie,* on station KOGD. Tom's plan was to pair traditionalist Charlie with radical Madison, a young woman with a strong social conscience. The two of them got along like oil and water—he wanted to talk sports and food while she tried to discuss politics, the environment, cybersex, and body piercing. Tonya was the resentful former producer of Charlie's show who had recently been promoted to station manager. Other women in Tom's life included his agreeable younger daughter, Elissa, and teenage Kenlon, who found him over-protective and unwilling to accept her becoming a young woman. Others seen were Mrs. Thompson, the girls' babysitter; Brownie, Tom's buddy who owned a local bar where he hung out; and Billy, a cop who also spent time at the bar. Madison disappeared from the cast—without explanation—early in 1998 but was back in an episode that aired on March 1.

TOM SMOTHERS' ORGANIC PRIME TIME SPACE RIDE, see *Smothers Brothers Comedy Hour, The*

TOMA (*Police Drama*)
FIRST TELECAST: *October 4, 1973*
LAST TELECAST: *September 6, 1974*
BROADCAST HISTORY:
Oct 1973–Jan 1974, ABC Thu 8:00–9:00
Jan 1974–Sep 1974, ABC Fri 10:00–11:00
CAST:
Det. David Toma .... Tony Musante
Inspector Spooner .... Simon Oakland
Patty Toma .... Susan Strasberg
Jimmy Toma .... Sean Manning
Donna Toma .... Michelle Livingston

Like *Serpico* a few years later, *Toma* was based on the exploits of a real-life big-city cop, Det. David Toma of the Newark, New Jersey, police department. Toma was a loner, continually bucking the system, and in many ways a headache to his boss, Inspector Spooner. But he was also a master of disguise, and his quick-wittedness and unorthodox methods won him national fame as a highly effective undercover agent. His targets were usually crime syndicates, racketeers, and the like. Patty Toma was his worried wife, and Jimmy and Donna his young children.

The real-life Dave Toma played bit parts in this series.

In a rather unusual move, actor Tony Musante left the program after only one season because he just didn't like the weekly grind of production. ABC was not unhappy with the show's performance and planned to bring *Toma* back with a new actor in the lead role. It was originally to be called *Toma Starring Robert Blake*, but despite the strong similarities in the lead role, a number of minor changes in the format resulted in a new series titled *Baretta*.

TOMBSTONE TERRITORY (*Western*)

FIRST TELECAST: *October 16, 1957*
LAST TELECAST: *October 9, 1959*
BROADCAST HISTORY:
Oct 1957–Sep 1958, ABC Wed 8:30–9:00
Mar 1959–Oct 1959, ABC Fri 9:00–9:30
CAST:
Sheriff Clay Hollister .... Pat Conway
Harris Claibourne................ Richard Eastham
Deputy Riggs (1957) .... Gil Rankin

Western adventure set in Tombstone, Arizona, "the town too tough to die." Sheriff Hollister was the strong arm of the law, and Harris Claibourne, editor of *The Epitaph*, was the voice of the press. In addition to playing Claibourne, Eastham was also host/narrator of the series.

In an unusual move, new episodes of this series continued to be produced for a year after the program left the network, for sale in syndication.

TOMORROW PEOPLE, THE (*Science Fiction*)

BROADCAST HISTORY:
Nickelodeon
30 minutes
Produced: *1992–1995* (25 episodes)
Premiered: *January 29, 1994*
CAST:
Adam .... Kristian Schmid
Megabyte .... Christian Tessier
Kevin Wilson (episodes 1–10) .... Adam Pearce
Lisa (episodes 1–5) .... Kristen Ariza
Ami (episodes 6–20) .... Naomi Harris
Jade (episodes 21–25) .... Alexandra Milman

A serialized science fiction/adventure series about three teens with extraordinary powers who banded together to battle diabolical foes and save the world. Adam, Megabyte, and Lisa were the original team, teens who had "reached the next stage of human evolution" and were able to teleport, employ mental telepathy, and sense when one of the others was in danger. Their adventures unfolded in story arcs that spanned five episodes each. In one a mad scientist named Dr. Culex (Jean Marsh) developed a strain of robotic killer mosquitoes in order to take over the world. In another, a U.S. mobster and an urbane scientist created a rain-making machine with the same purpose. The team's young friend Kevin disappeared after the first two stories, and the female members changed as well (Ami in stories two, three, and four and Jade in number five).

The Tomorrow People was first seen on four consecutive nights from February 21–24, 1993, and was billed as "Nickelodeon's first mini-series." It became a weekly series the following January. Produced in England.

TOMORROW SHOW, THE (*Talk*)

FIRST TELECAST: *October 15, 1973*
LAST TELECAST: *January 28, 1982*
BROADCAST HISTORY:
Oct 1973–Sep 1980, NBC Mon–Thu 1:00–2:00 A.M.
Sep 1980–Jan 1982, NBC Mon–Thu 12:30–2:00 A.M.
HOST:
Tom Snyder
Rona Barrett (1980–1981)
REGULAR:
Nancy Friday (1980–1981)

For those insomniacs who were still looking for something other than old movies to watch in the wee hours, NBC offered *The Tomorrow Show* four nights each week. Hosted by brash newsman Tom Snyder, the topics covered ranged from nudism (including a remote pickup at a California nudist colony), to discussions with draft dodgers living in Canada, to all aspects of changing American lifestyles with a panel of psychologists. Tom Snyder's choreography often seemed to borrow a little from Edward R. Murrow's incisiveness and vintage Alan Burke guest-baiting. Tom could be sweet and ingenuous one moment, relentlessly probing the next.

Tomorrow was originally produced in Los Angeles, where host Snyder worked as an anchorman on the local KNBC-TV news. When it first went on the air there was no studio audience present at the taping, a situation that changed in less than four months. After an audience had been added, Snyder would often invite its members to ask questions of his guests. When his local news anchor duties shifted to New York, in December 1974, *The Tomorrow Show* went with him. In June 1977, Tom and the show returned to California, only to come back again to New York when Snyder became host of the newsmagazine *Prime Time Sunday* in 1979.

In the fall of 1980 *The Tomorrow Show* expanded from an hour to 90 minutes, as part of a general restructuring of NBC's late-night lineup. With an extra half-hour to fill, the *Tomorrow* staff was expanded and two new on-air personalities were added, Nancy Friday and Rona Barrett, and contemporary musical guests performed on most telecasts. Miss Friday, a psychologist who had been an occasional guest of Tom's in the past, became a semiregular as the resident "human relations commentator." Miss Barrett, the noted Hollywood gossip columnist, joined *Tomorrow* at the end of October (she had just left ABC's *Good Morning, America* to sign a long-term contract with NBC) as the West Coast–based cohost with Tom. She and Tom didn't get along well, with their strong egos conflicting almost immediately. Their feud boiled over on November 10, 1980, only two weeks after her first appearance on *Tomorrow*, when she refused to appear on the air. It took two months to resolve the dispute, and when Rona returned to the show on January 12, 1981, it had been retitled *Tomorrow Coast to Coast*. She left again later that year.

To those who were skeptical at the time of the practicality of televising anything this late at night, *Tomorrow*'s success was surprising. During its first two seasons it attracted an average of approximately three million viewers per night.

TOMORROW'S BOXING CHAMPIONS, see *Boxing*

TOMORROW'S CAREERS (*Informational*)
FIRST TELECAST: *March 26, 1955*
LAST TELECAST: *May 29, 1956*
BROADCAST HISTORY:
Mar 1955–Jun 1955, ABC Sat 7:00–7:30
Sep 1955–Jan 1956, ABC Sat 10:00–10:30
Jan 1956–May 1956, ABC Tue 10:00–10:30
HOST:
Lynn Poole
Each week Mr. Poole discussed opportunities in a particular career area with experts in that field. One week, it might be jobs in the antique field; another week, jobs with airlines; a third week, opportunities in movie direction. Emphasis was placed on openings for students graduating from school and for those in their middle years seeking to change career paths. During its March through June 1955 run, the title of this program was simply *Tomorrow.*

TONI TWIN TIME (*Variety*)
FIRST TELECAST: *April 5, 1950*
LAST TELECAST: *September 20, 1950*
BROADCAST HISTORY:
Apr 1950–Sep 1950, CBS Wed 9:00–9:30
REGULARS:
Jack Lemmon
Arlene Terry
Ardelle Terry
Ray Bloch Orchestra
This live variety show, hosted by young actor Jack Lemmon, alternated with *What's My Line* on Wednesday evenings during the summer of 1950. It was designed as a showcase for young talent, with Mr. Lemmon providing continuity and introductions. The "Toni Twins," Arlene and Ardelle Terry, acted as hostesses and did the commercials for the sponsor, whose slogan "Which Twin Has the Toni?" made home-permanent history in the late 1940s.

TONIGHT ON BROADWAY (*Interview/Play Excerpts*)
FIRST TELECAST: *April 20, 1948*
LAST TELECAST: *December 25, 1949*
BROADCAST HISTORY:
Apr 1948–May 1948, CBS Tue 7:00–7:30
Oct 1949–Dec 1949, CBS Sun 7:00–7:30
HOST:
John Mason Brown
Excerpts from current Broadway shows and interviews with the stars of those shows, broadcast directly from the stages of the theaters where the shows were being performed, were presented weekly on this series. It had originally begun as an experimental concept which premiered locally in New York on April 6, 1948, from the theater where *Mr. Roberts* was playing, moved to the CBS network two weeks later with *High Button Shoes,* and returned in the fall of 1949 for a three-month run. John Mason Brown, the host/interviewer/commentator of the series, was the president of the New York Drama Critics Circle.

TONIGHT SHOW, THE (*Talk/Variety*)
FIRST TELECAST: *September 27, 1954*
LAST TELECAST:
BROADCAST HISTORY:
Sep 1954–Oct 1956, NBC Mon–Fri 11:30–1:00 A.M.
Oct 1956–Jan 1957, NBC Mon–Fri 11:30–12:30 A.M.
Jan 1957–Dec 1966, NBC Mon–Fri 11:15–1:00 A.M.
Jan 1965–Sep 1966, NBC Sat or Sun 11:15–1:00 A.M.
Sep 1966–Sep 1975, NBC Sat or Sun 11:30–1:00 A.M.
Jan 1967–Sep 1980, NBC Mon–Fri 11:30–1:00 A.M.
Sep 1980–Aug 1991, NBC Mon–Fri 11:30–12:30 A.M.
Sep 1991– , NBC Mon–Fri 11:35–12:35 A.M.
Because of the unusual nature of *The Tonight Show*—the several complete overhauls of its cast and format—each of the individual versions is treated separately below:

TONIGHT
(September 27, 1954–January 25, 1957)
HOST:
Steve Allen
Ernie Kovacs (1956–1957)
REGULARS:
Gene Rayburn
Steve Lawrence
Eydie Gorme
Andy Williams
Pat Marshall (1954–1955)
Pat Kirby (1955–1957)
Hy Averback (1955)
Skitch Henderson and His Orchestra
Peter Hanley (1956–1957)
Maureen Arthur (1956–1957)
Bill Wendell (1956–1957)
Barbara Loden (1956–1957)
LeRoy Holmes & Orchestra (1956–1957)
Tonight began in June 1953 as a local show on WNBT-TV, the NBC flagship station in New York. Steve Allen was the original host, and he remained with the show when it moved to the network 15 months later. Under Allen, *Tonight* was very informal. He would open each evening seated at the piano, chatting and playing some of his own compositions (his most famous song, "This Could Be the Start of Something," was often heard). He then went to his desk, where he talked about anything that seemed to interest him. There were guest stars, in addition to his semiregulars—only announcer Gene Rayburn and orchestra leader Skitch Henderson were on every night—but the emphasis was on Steve and his comedic ad-libbing. He would go into the audience, work up impromptu sketches with other members of the cast, and do remotes outside the studio. Many of the remotes were comic man-in-the-street routines, but perhaps the most famous incident occurred when *Tonight* was doing some telecasts from Miami. Allen somehow talked the U.S. Marines into staging a nighttime landing on Miami Beach, for the benefit of his cameras—panicking tourists in nearby hotels, who thought an invasion was underway. In addition to the special features, there was a regular news summary given at about 12:30 A.M. by Gene Rayburn. The entire show was done live.

When Allen's primetime series premiered in the summer of 1956, he cut back his *Tonight* appearances to Wednesday through Friday. A series of guest hosts filled in on Mondays and Tuesdays until October 1st, when Ernie Kovacs took over as permanent Monday–Tuesday host. Kovacs had his own complete cast: Bill Wendell as announcer, and Peter Hanley, Maureen Arthur, and Barbara Loden as regulars. Ernie's format was very similar to that of his various primetime shows, with most of the same characters, as well as blackouts, satires, and slapstick humor.

TONIGHT! AMERICA AFTER DARK

(January 28, 1957–July 26, 1957)

HOST:

Jack Lescoulie (Jan–Jun)
Al "Jazzbo" Collins (Jun–Jul)

REGULARS:

Judy Johnson (Mar–Jul)
Lou Stein Trio (Jan–Mar)
Mort Lindsey Quartet (Mar–Jun)
Johnny Guarnieri Quarter (Jun–Jul)
Hy Gardner
Bob Considine
Earl Wilson (Jan–Jun)
Irv Kupcinet
Vernon Scott (Jan–Feb)
Paul Coates
Lee Giroux (Mar–Jun)

When Steve Allen left in January 1957, *Tonight* was replaced by a totally different type of program. It became much more like the early-morning *Today Show*, with an emphasis on news items. Its original host was *Today* veteran Jack Lescoulie. There were reports by contributing columnists in New York, Chicago, and Los Angeles, with live coverage from all three cities and elsewhere via remotes. Interviews with personalities in the news, in politics, or in show business were interspersed with live visits to nightclubs, Broadway openings, or such places as research hospitals and planetariums. Regular features were Bob Considine's summary of the news of the day. "The World Tonight"; a Hy Gardner interview segment, "Face to Face"; news of the entertainment world on "Hy Gardner Time"; and news commentary, human interest stories, and interviews on "Considine's Corner."

JACK PAAR SHOW, THE

(July 29, 1957–March 30, 1962)

HOST:

Jack Paar

REGULARS:

Hugh Downs
Jose Melis & Orchestra
Tedi Thurman (1957)
Dody Goodman (1957–1958)

SEMI-REGULARS:

Elsa Maxwell (1957–1958)
Bil Baird Puppets (1957–1958)
Betty Johnson (1957–1958)
Genevieve (1958–1962)
Cliff Arquette as *Charley Weaver* (1958–1962)
Pat Harrington, Jr., as *Guido Panzini* (1959–1962)
Hans Conried (1959–1962)
Peggy Cass (1958–1962)
Alexander King (1958–1962)
Joey Bishop (1958–1962)
Hermione Gingold (1958–1962)
Florence Henderson (1958–1962)
Buddy Hackett (1958–1962)
Renee Taylor (1959–1962)
Betty White (1959–1962)

Tonight! America After Dark was not successful with viewers or critics, so it was decided to return to a format closer to the original. The new host, a young comic named Jack Paar, was raided from CBS, where he had hosted several game and talk shows. Paar took over *The Tonight Show* six months after Steve Allen had left. Whereas Allen had depended on a frenetic pace and sketch comedy, Paar was at his best interviewing. He was incisive, witty, and highly emotional. He could easily get emotionally involved with his guests and their stories, and was not above crying on the air when he was moved. There were still sketches, and Paar would sometimes go into the audience for interviews. "It's All Relative" was a periodic spot in which a relative of a famous person would appear and the other guests would try to figure out who he was related to; "What Is It?" was a feature in which Paar would produce some strange-looking object and then explain what it was used for; there was a routine where baby pictures were shown to the audience and Paar would come up with funny captions for them; and Jose Melis had a "telephone game" in which he improvised melodies based on the last four digits of an audience member's telephone number.

Besides the fun and games, the show had a serious side. At one point Paar went on an extended crusade against the Batista dictatorship in Cuba, lauding Castro's revolution; later he tried to arrange a swap of tractors for prisoners from the Bay of Pigs invasion; several telecasts originated from the Berlin Wall; and presidential candidates Kennedy and Nixon were both guests, on separate occasions.

Paar's emotional outbursts were a major attraction of the show, and the cause of many of the controversies surrounding him. When he had first taken over as host, *The Tonight Show* was still being done live. Not too long after, it began taping early in the evening that it would be aired. It was NBC's ability to edit the tapes before air time that precipitated Paar's famous tearful walkout on the February 11, 1960, program. A "water closet" joke he had told the night before was considered in bad taste by the NBC censors and had been removed. Paar didn't think the joke was offensive and he left the show for a month. He later had a feud with Ed Sullivan over the fees paid guest stars—Paar's $320 versus Sullivan's several thousand—and eventually feuded with several newspaper columnists, notably Dorothy Kilgallen. Videotape did have its advantages, however, as it enabled Paar to cut down to a four-day week. Starting July 10, 1959, the Friday show was retitled *The Best of Paar* and was composed of reruns of previous shows.

TONIGHT SHOW, THE

(April 2, 1962–September 28, 1962)

ANNOUNCER:

Hugh Downs
Jack Haskell
Ed Herlihy

ORCHESTRA:

Skitch Henderson

After Jack Paar's departure from the series in March 1962, *The Tonight Show* aired with a succession of substitute hosts, while awaiting the arrival of Johnny Carson (who had to wait out an ABC contract). Hosts during this period were Art Linkletter, Joey Bishop, Bob Cummings, Merv Griffin, Jack Carter, Jan Murray, Peter Lind Hayes and Mary Healy, Soupy Sales, Mort Sahl, Steve Lawrence, Jerry Lewis, Jimmy Dean, Arlene Francis, Jack E. Leonard, Hugh Downs, Groucho Marx, Hal March, and Donald O'Connor. The format was unchanged.

TONIGHT SHOW STARRING JOHNNY CARSON, THE

(October 1, 1962–May 22, 1992)

HOST:

Johnny Carson

REGULARS:

Ed McMahon

Skitch Henderson (1962–1966)

Milton Delugg (1966–1967)

Doc Severinsen (1967–1992)

Tommy Newsom (1968–1992)

REGULAR GUEST HOST:

Joan Rivers (1983–1986)

Jay Leno (1987–1992)

THEME:

"Johnny's Theme," by Paul Anka and Johnny Carson

The contrast between Jack Paar and Johnny Carson was marked. As emotional and likely to blow up as Paar was, that is how calm and unflappable Carson was. Like Paar, Carson had been spirited away from another network; in fact he had previously had shows on both CBS and ABC. His biggest asset, other than his durability, was probably his knack for salvaging disasters with a perfect reaction take (a comic expression of resignation whenever something did not work). Carson opened each show with a monologue and then spent most of the remainder of the evening chatting with guests. Unlike Paar, Carson tended to avoid anything controversial and was usually content to keep his audience amused. Features that were used on his show with varying frequency included "Stump the Band," in which members of the studio audience would ask the band to try to play obscure songs by giving them only the titles; "Carnac the Magnificent" (first seen in 1964), with Carson as an inept magician; "Aunt Blabby" (1964); "The Mighty Carson Art Players" (1966), spoofing movies, TV shows, or events in the news; "Carswell" (1967), with Carson as a fortune-teller predicting the future; "The Great Carsoni" (1967); "Faharishi" (1968), with Carson as a yogi; "The Art Fern Tea Time Movie" (1971), with Carol Wayne as the original "Matinee Lady"; super-patriot "Floyd R. Turbo" (1977); "Father Time" (1977); and the one holdover from Paar, periodic displays of strange-looking contraptions with even stranger functions.

Perhaps the most celebrated telecast, and certainly the one with the most enormous audience, was that of December 17, 1969, on which Tiny Tim married Miss Vicki. Other highlights were seen on annual anniversary shows, in which Carson reprised often embarrassing moments from past years.

When Carson started, the show was originating from New York and was taped on the same evening that it aired. Johnny was on all five nights and began his monologue when the show began, at 11:15 P.M. (On his first show, Carson was introduced by Groucho Marx; Johnny's first words, reacting to the applause as he walked onstage for the first time: "Boy, you would think it was Vice President Nixon.") In February 1965 he refused to do the 11:15–11:30 P.M. segment any longer, leaving that to Ed McMahon and Skitch Henderson. Many local stations carried local news until 11:30 P.M., preempting the first fifteen minutes of *The Tonight Show*, and Carson wanted to save his monologue until the full network was in place. Two years later, on January 2, 1967, this first 15 minutes was dropped altogether. A few months later, in March 1967, Carson fought another skirmish with NBC, this time over money. This led to his walkout, which lasted for several weeks until he was finally lured back with a contract reported to provide more than $1 million per year.

In May 1972 *The Tonight Show* moved permanently from New York to Burbank (previously periodic telecasts were done from the West Coast), and for a time after that taping was done a day before the show aired. Because so much immediacy was lost, *Tonight* returned to same-night taping in May 1974. Carson also started cutting back on his appearances at about this time. After July 1971 he was no longer seen on Mondays. Then in March 1978 he obtained a highly publicized new $3-million-per-year contract that required him to work only three nights per week. (Steve Allen had worked only three hours per week for a time in 1956, although he also had a primetime show to do.) In 1980, after threats of a walkout, the program was cut back to an hour per night, with Carson on Tuesday through Friday. Carson's irregular appearances opened the way for a large number of substitute hosts, some of whom became almost as familiar to viewers as Johnny himself. Seen most often during the first 21 years were Joey Bishop (177 appearances as guest host), followed by Joan Rivers (93), Bob Newhart (87), John Davidson (87), David Brenner (70), McLean Stevenson (58), Jerry Lewis (52), and David Letterman (51). Joan Rivers was the "permanent" (and only) guest host from September 1983 until 1986, when she quit to launch her own ill-fated late-night show opposite Carson. *The Tonight Show* reverted to various guest hosts after Joan left, with Jay Leno the most frequent. Leno became the exclusive guest host in the fall of 1987.

Johnny's final telecast, on May 22, 1992, was a national event: A quiet reminicence (without big-name guests) about the show's golden moments over the past 30 years, it was, predictably, one of the top-rated programs of the year. Many, however, felt that the next-to-last show was the best; in it, Bette Midler sang a wistfully comic love song to Johnny that expressed what most viewers felt—there would never be another quite like him.

For more than a decade, from January 1965 until September 1975, taped repeats of *The Tonight Show* were offered to NBC stations for airing after the 11:00 P.M. news on Saturday or Sunday.

In the fall of 1985 a collection of edited comedy sketches from *The Tonight Show* was syndicated to local stations under the title *Carson Comedy Classics*.

TONIGHT SHOW WITH JAY LENO, THE

(May 25, 1992–)

HOST:

Jay Leno

REGULARS:

Branford Marsalis (1992–1995)

Kevin Eubanks (1995–)

Edd Hall (off-camera announcer)

"This is not your father's *Tonight Show*," quipped Jay Leno after one particularly hip musical act. The hefty, jut-jawed comic took over the show from the legendary Johnny Carson in the blinding glare of high expectations and from the start tried to give it his own spin—while not alienating the huge Middle American audience Carson had left him. It was a tough balancing act. Doc Severinsen was replaced by hip, black, jazz musician Branford Marsalis, and there was no Ed McMahon-style sidekick. The guests were still standard Hollywood A-list (Billy Crystal appeared on the first show), but musical acts tended toward the off-the-wall (Hootie and the Blowfish, Blue Man Group).

Among Jay's recurring bits were comic newspaper headlines, "Ask Jay Anything," "Police Blotter," fitness expert "Iron Jay," "Mr. Brain" (the smartest man in the universe), a "Jaywalking" man-in-the-street segment and "Evil Jay," his nefarious alter ego.

Ratings were fine for the first year, but when David Letterman—who had been passed over for the *Tonight* seat—launched *Late Show* opposite him on CBS in August 1993, *Tonight* dropped out of first place for the first time. Ratings later recovered as Jay introduced such newsmaking stunts as the "Dancing Itos" (a chorus of dancing, black-robed, Asian-American "jurists," mocking Judge Ito of O.J. Simpson trial fame). Kevin Eubanks took over as Jay's bandleader in January 1995.

TONY BENNETT SHOW, THE (*Musical Variety*)
FIRST TELECAST: *August 11, 1956*
LAST TELECAST: *September 8, 1956*
BROADCAST HISTORY:
Aug 1956–Sep 1956, NBC Sat 8:00–9:00
REGULARS:
Tony Bennett
The Frank Lewis Dancers
The Spellbinders
The Carl Hoff Orchestra

The Tony Bennett Show was one of three musical variety shows that served as 1956 summer replacements for *The Perry Como Show*. All three of them featured the Frank Lewis Dancers and the singing of the Spellbinders. The only difference between them was their star and host. Patti Page starred for the first month of the summer, and was followed by Julius LaRosa, who in turn was followed by Tony Bennett.

TONY DANZA SHOW, THE (*Situation Comedy*)
FIRST TELECAST: *September 24, 1997*
LAST TELECAST: *December 17, 1997*
BROADCAST HISTORY:
Sep 1997–Oct 1997, NBC Wed 8:00–8:30
Dec 1997, NBC Wed 8:30–9:00
CAST:
Tony DiMeo .... Tony Danza
Tina DiMeo (age 16) .... Majandra Delfino
Mickey DiMeo (11) .... Ashley Malinger
Frank DiMeo .... Dean Stockwell
Carmen Cruz .... Maria Canals
Stuey Mandelker .... Shaun Weiss

There were hugs and clichés galore in this rather pedestrian single-father sitcom. Tony was a freelance Manhattan sportswriter who was recently separated from his wife Susan, and got to raise their two daughters—awkwardly. Tina was the usual self-centered teen, prone to truancy, and Mickey the brainy young one with a thousand neuroses and phobias ("Dad, I'm writing a poem. What rhymes with 'cholera'?"). Tony had a phobia of his own, namely the computer on which he was supposed to write, so sexy computer whiz Carmen was frequently around, helping out, and periodically ranting in Spanish. Tony's old-world dad Frank owned a bakery in Little Italy where he offered incomprehensible advice. Stuey was the pudgy, mooching doorman, who also wandered in and out of the apartment. The theme song was something about "We got love . . . every day . . . ."

TONY MARTIN SHOW, THE (*Music*)
FIRST TELECAST: *April 26, 1954*
LAST TELECAST: *February 27, 1956*
BROADCAST HISTORY:
Apr 1954–Jun 1955, NBC Mon 7:30–7:45
Sep 1955–Feb 1956, NBC Mon 7:30–7:45
REGULARS:
Tony Martin
The Interludes
The Hal Bourne Orchestra (1954–1955)
David Rose and His Orchestra (1955–1956)

Singer Tony Martin starred in this live music series that filled the remainder of the half hour in which NBC aired its network news program. Backing up Mr. Martin was a mixed vocal group, the Interludes. The show originated from Hollywood and Mr. Martin had occasional guest stars who either performed or chatted with him or both.

TONY ORLANDO AND DAWN (*Musical Variety*)
FIRST TELECAST: *July 3, 1974*
LAST TELECAST: *December 28, 1976*
BROADCAST HISTORY:
Jul 1974, CBS Wed 8:00–9:00
Dec 1974–Jun 1976, CBS Wed 8:00–9:00
Sep 1976–Dec 1976, CBS Tue 8:00–9:00
REGULARS:
Tony Orlando
Telma Hopkins
Joyce Vincent Wilson
Alice Nunn
Lonnie Schorr
Adam Wade (1976)
George Carlin (1976)
Nancy Steen (1976)
Bob Holt (1976)
Susan Lanier (1976)
Jimmy Martinez (1976)
Edie McClurg (1976)
Jerry Jackson Singers
Bob Rozario Orchestra

After a number of hit records, most notably "Tie a Yellow Ribbon 'Round the Old Oak Tree," the singing group Tony Orlando and Dawn (Telma Hopkins and Joyce Vincent Wilson) was given a summer variety hour on CBS in the time slot that had been vacated by Sonny and Cher. The emphasis was on music, with guest stars joining the trio in song and comedy skits. A summer hit, it returned in December and had a very successful first year, but started to slip in the second. When it moved to Tuesday nights in the fall of 1976, there were a number of changes, including the title, which became *The Tony Orlando and Dawn Rainbow Hour*. Comedian George Carlin was added as a regular with a weekly comedy monologue, and a group of comics was also added to participate in sketches. Emphasis was shifted from music to comedy, but the series failed to last past the end of the year.

TONY RANDALL SHOW, THE (*Situation Comedy*)

FIRST TELECAST: *September 23, 1976*
LAST TELECAST: *March 25, 1978*
BROADCAST HISTORY:

Sep 1976–Dec 1976, ABC Thu 9:00–9:30
Dec 1976–Mar 1977, ABC Thu 9:30–10:00
Sep 1977–Jan 1978, CBS Sat 9:30–10:00
Jan 1978–Mar 1978, CBS Sat 8:30–9:00

CAST:

Judge Walter Franklin .... Tony Randall
Jack Terwilliger .... Barney Martin
Miss Janet Reubner .... Allyn Ann McLerie
Roberta "Bobby" Franklin (1976–1977)
.... Devon Scott
Roberta "Bobby" Franklin (1977–1978)
.... Penny Peyser
Oliver Wendell Franklin .... Brad Savage
Mrs. Bonnie McClellan .... Rachel Roberts
Mario Lanza .... Zane Lasky
Judge Eleanor Hooper .... Diana Muldaur
Wyatt Franklin (1977–1978) .... Hans Conried

This comedy concerned the courtroom and home life of a middle-aged Philadelphia judge. Court of Common Pleas Judge Walter Franklin was serious about his work, sometimes a bit stuffy, but kind at heart and always had a twinkle in his eye. After two years as a widower Walter was ready for a little romance, and his attempts to both keep his dignity and charm his dates provided much of the humor. Walter played the field, although Judge Eleanor Hooper was a recurring love interest.

Jack Terwilliger was Walter's longtime, ultra-accurate court reporter; Miss Reubner, the sharp-tongued, motherly secretary; Mario Lanza, the obnoxiously ingratiating assistant to the assistant District Attorney; and Mrs. McClellan, the nutty housekeeper. Walter's family consisted of 18-year-old daughter Bobby, who was very much involved with current issues, and precocious 11-year-old son Oliver. Wyatt Franklin was Walter's liberal-minded father, who considered his son something of a stuffed shirt.

TOO CLOSE FOR COMFORT (*Situation Comedy*)

FIRST TELECAST: *November 11, 1980*
LAST TELECAST: *September 15, 1983*
BROADCAST HISTORY:

Nov 1980–Sep 1982, ABC Tue 9:30–10:00
Sep 1982–Jun 1983, ABC Thu 9:00–9:30
Aug 1983–Sep 1983, ABC Thu 8:30–9:00
Sep 1983, ABC Thu 8:00–8:30
(In first-run syndication as *Too Close for Comfort* from January 1984–September 1985; and as *The Ted Knight Show* from April 1986–September 1986)

CAST:

Henry Rush .... Ted Knight
Muriel Rush .... Nancy Dussault
Jackie Rush (1980–1985)
.... Deborah Van Valkenburgh
Sara Rush (1980–1985) .... Lydia Cornell
Arthur Wainwright (1981) .... Hamilton Camp
Monroe Ficus .... J.M.J. Bullock
April Rush (1981–1982) .... Deena Freeman
Iris Martin (1982–1983) .... Audrey Meadows
Andrew Rush (1983–1984)
.... William Thomas Cannon
Andrew Rush (1983–1984)
.... Michael Philip Cannon
Andrew Rush (1984–1986) .... Joshua Goodwin
Lisa Flores (1986) .... Lisa Antille
Hope Stinson (1986) .... Pat Carroll

Henry Rush was a middle-aged, conservative, and very orderly professional illustrator. His greatest regret was that years ago he had gotten caught up in doing a kiddie cartoon called "Cosmic Cow," and now it seemed to rule his life. His second greatest regret was that his two college-aged daughters, wanting a little independence, had talked him into letting them live in the downstairs apartment of his two-apartment San Francisco town house. As boyfriends came and went, Henry agonized over his two little lambs.

Jackie, the brunette, worked at a bank; Sara, the blonde sex kitten, was a freshman at San Francisco State College. Among the others who drifted around this sex farce were Muriel, the understanding mom (an independent type who had once been a band singer and now was a successful free-lance photographer); Mr. Wainwright, Henry's diminutive publisher; Monroe, Sara's flaky student friend; and Henry's hand puppet, from which he derived inspiration for his comic strip and commiseration for his worries about his pretty daughters. Appearing occasionally was Mildred Rafkin (Selma Diamond), sister of the former downstairs tenant.

Among the developments in the second and third seasons were the arrival of April, Henry's hippie niece from Delaware, who stayed with the family for a year; and Muriel's pregnancy at age 42, culminating in the birth of a son, Andrew. Also arriving in 1982 were Muriel's nagging mother, Iris, who added further grief to Henry's life, and Jackie's fiancé, policeman Brad Turner (Jordan Suffin), who was seen occasionally.

Too Close for Comfort continued in production after being canceled by ABC in 1983, with the new episodes offered to local stations on a syndicated basis. With the title change to *The Ted Knight Show* came a change in format. Henry had purchased 49% of a weekly newspaper, *The Marin Bugler*, and he, Muriel, and Andrew had moved to a house in Mill Valley, north of San Francisco, to be close to his new place of business. Monroe, who had worked as a security guard after college, was still around, attempting to help out at the *Bugler*, where Muriel was also working as staff photographer, but Sara and Jackie (who had been dropped from the cast) were off on their own. New to the cast were the Rushes' Hispanic housekeeper, Lisa, and the publisher of the *Bugler*, Mrs. Stinson. She still owned 51% and loved her regular editorial disputes with Henry, her new partner and editor. *The Ted Knight Show* was scheduled to go into its second season of production when its star, who had been ill for several months, passed away during the summer of 1986.

ABC aired reruns of *Too Close for Comfort* on weekday mornings from June to September 1983.

Based on the British series *Keep It in the Family*.

TOO SOMETHING (*Situation Comedy*)

FIRST TELECAST: *October 1, 1995*
LAST TELECAST: *June 23, 1996*
BROADCAST HISTORY:

Oct 1995, FOX Sun 8:30–9:00
May 1996–Jun 1996, FOX Sun 8:30–9:00

CAST:

Eric McDougal .... Eric Schaeffer

Donny Reeves .... Donal Lardner Ward
Evelyn Lewis .... Lisa Gerstein
Maria Hunter .... Portia de Rossi
Daisy .... Mindy Seeger

Eric and Donny were roommates living in Manhattan who worked very hard at not becoming successful in this buddy comedy. Eric, a would-be author who never seemed to write anything, took menial jobs with companies. Donny, a long haired free-spirited photographer, took wonderful pictures but was afraid to show them to anyone who might actually find him paying work. They worked in the mailroom at Crown, Fink and Wagner, where they spent much of their time trying *not* to get noticed and promoted. Evelyn was their opinionated friend who had trouble sustaining relationships, while Daisy, a sarcastic dog walker, rented a room from Eric. Maria, who also lived in their building, was a pretty junior associate at the company where Eric and Donny worked. Eric had the hots for her.

The producers ran a viewer contest in 1995 to rename the series, but it was pulled from the schedule before the change took place. When it returned, in May 1996, it had a new title, *New York Daze*, and was introduced by Geri Dobson, the woman from Greensboro, North Carolina, who had won the contest. Nothing else had changed, and after another month on the air, the series was gone for good.

Stars Schaeffer and Ward, who had written and starred in the critically acclaimed independent film *My Life's in Turnaround*, were the creative forces behind this ill-fated comedy.

TOO YOUNG TO GO STEADY (*Situation Comedy*)
FIRST TELECAST: *May 14, 1959*
LAST TELECAST: *June 25, 1959*
BROADCAST HISTORY:
May 1959–Jun 1959, NBC Thu 8:30–9:00
CAST:
Mary Blake .... Joan Bennett
Tom Blake .... Donald Cook
Pam Blake .... Brigid Bazlen
Johnny Blake .... Martin Huston
Timmy .... Lorna Gillam

The problems of teenagers Pam and Johnny Blake were the focal points of this live series that aired in the spring of 1959. Pam was a 14-year-old trying to make the transition from tomboy to young lady. Her older brother, Johnny, got into almost as much trouble trying to help her as he did with his own life. Pam and her girlfriend Timmy were at that stage when love—or was it infatuation?—was the most important thing in their lives. Pam and Johnny's father, attorney Tom Blake, and their mother, Mary, kept a watchful eye on the activities of the kids and were generally understanding and interested in their happiness.

TOON DISNEY (Network) (*All Cartoon Cable Network*)
LAUNCHED:
April 1998
SUBSCRIBERS (MAY 2003):
39.0 million (37% U.S.)

If ever there was a "natural," it was a cartoon network from Disney. From the time it launched in 1998 Toon Disney has provided a wide array of relatively recent cartoons from the vast Disney vaults (there is surprisingly little original programming). Among them have been *Hercules the Series, The Lion King's Timon and Pumbaa, Disney's Doug, Teamo Supremo, Aladdin* and *Sabrina*. There were also some Disney animated feature films and occasional older classics such as Mickey Mouse and Donald Duck.

TOON NITE (*Cartoon Anthology*)
FIRST TELECAST: *April 17, 1991*
LAST TELECAST: *July 3, 1991*
BROADCAST HISTORY:
Apr 1991–Jul 1991, CBS Wed 8:00–8:30

Toon Nite was the umbrella title for a collection of animated reruns aired by CBS during the spring of 1991. Among them were an episode of *Teenage Mutant Ninja Turtles*, the Peanuts gang's "Snoopy's Reunion," two Bugs Bunny specials, and three episodes from the 1960s classic *Rocky and His Friends*.

TOP CARD (*Quiz/Audience Participation*)
BROADCAST HISTORY:
The Nashville Network
30 minutes
Produced: *1989–1990* (65 episodes)
Premiered: *April 3, 1989*
REGULARS:
Jim Caldwell (1989)
Blake Pickett (1989)
Dan Miller
Paige Brown

A short-lived quiz show, based on the card game 21, which ran in daytime and in the early evening on TNN. Contestants combined their knowledge of entertainment trivia with luck-of-the-draw to compete for prizes. Jim Caldwell and Blake Pickett were the original hosts; Dan Miller and Paige Brown replaced them.

TOP CAT (*Cartoon*)
FIRST TELECAST: *September 27, 1961*
LAST TELECAST: *September 26, 1962*
BROADCAST HISTORY:
Sep 1961–Sep 1962, ABC Wed 8:30–9:00
VOICES:
Top Cat .... Arnold Stang
Benny the Ball .... Maurice Gosfield
Choo Choo .... Marvin Kaplan
Spook/The Brain .... Leo DeLyon
Fancy-Fancy .... John Stephenson
Officer Dibble .... Allen Jenkins

Top Cat was the sophisticated, opportunistic leader of a pack of Broadway alley cats. Their homes were well-equipped ash cans, they made all their phone calls from the police phone on a nearby pole, got their milk and newspapers from nearby doorsteps, and ate scraps from the neighborhood delicatessen. Their only problem was Officer Dibble, the cop on the local beat. He did his best to control them but seldom succeeded.

Reruns of *Top Cat* aired for several year on Saturday mornings—on ABC from October 1962 to March 1963 and on NBC from April 1965 to May 1969.

TOP COPS (*Documentary*)
FIRST TELECAST: *July 18, 1990*
LAST TELECAST: *August 27, 1993*
BROADCAST HISTORY:
Jul 1990–Oct 1990, CBS Wed 10:00–11:00
Oct 1990–Feb 1991, CBS Thu 8:00–8:30

Feb 1991–Aug 1993, CBS Thu 8:00–9:00
Aug 1993, CBS Fri 10:00–11:00

Top Cops related the exploits of real police officers at work. Officers from police departments and government agencies around the country described incidents in which they had been involved, while actors performed dramatizations. Segments included a hostage crisis, shopping mall shooting, drug bust, prison escape, SWAT rescue team in action, suicide negotiation, kidnapping, gang violence, prostitution, car chase, and robbery. Each episode of *Top Cops* usually featured two or three separate segments.

TOP DOLLAR (*Quiz/Audience Participation*)

FIRST TELECAST: *March 29, 1958*
LAST TELECAST: *August 30, 1958*
BROADCAST HISTORY:
Mar 1958–Aug 1958, CBS Sat 8:30–9:00
EMCEE:
Toby Reed
WORD AUTHORITY:
Dr. Bergen Evans

Three contestants participated in each round of this word-spelling game that was a variation on the old party game "ghost." The object of the game was to keep adding letters to a potential word without completing it. Each letter, after the first three, was worth $100 to the winner, and after the first person was eliminated by making a word the two remaining contestants competed to determine the winner. As long as a contestant remained undefeated, he could continue to play. Dr. Bergen Evans was the final authority on whether or not a word had been made. An added attraction for home viewers was the announcement at the end of each telecast of the serial number of a dollar bill that, if presented to the show's producers, was worth $5,000 to the bearer. The serial number was determined by the regular game. The first eight letters of the "top dollar" word of the night (the longest one created by the contestants on the show) were matched to a telephone dial and converted to the digits of the jackpot serial number for the week.

CBS started a daytime version of *Top Dollar* two weeks before the primetime version left the air. The daytime version lasted until October 1959. Toby Reed also emceed the daytime version, but was succeeded by Jack Narz during its run.

TOP OF THE HEAP (*Situation Comedy*)

FIRST TELECAST: *April 14, 1991*
LAST TELECAST: *July 14, 1991*
BROADCAST HISTORY:
Apr 1991–Jul 1991, FOX Sun 9:30–10:00
CAST:
Charlie Verducci .... Joseph Bologna
Vinnie Verducci .... Matt LeBlanc
Alixandra Stone .... Rita Moreno
Emmet Lefebvre .... Leslie Jordan
Mona Mullins .... Joey Adams
THEME:
"Puttin' on the Ritz," sung by Kenny Yarbrough

This short-lived series, a spin-off from Fox's highly successful *Married . . . with Children,* centered on Al Bundy's best friend, Charlie Verducci, the divorced, sleazy, live-in superintendent of a run-down apartment building in Chicago. Charlie's main goal in life was to help his son Vinnie, a likable but incredibly dumb hunk, marry rich. The Verducci Master Plan was to put Vinnie in an environment full of rich women so that one of them would fall for the young stud. To that end, Vinnie got a job working at the exclusive Rolling Hills Country Club outside Chicago. The classy manager of the club, Alixandra Stone, had hired Vinnie because she thought the women members could use a little beefcake, and they certainly seemed to like it. Charlie, who found her very sexy, kept trying to get her to go out with him, but to no avail. Emmet, whose hormones always seemed to be raging, was the diminutive security guard at the club; and Mona was the Verducci's sexy 16-year-old neighbor who had the hots for Vinnie. As with *Married,* there was a lot of sexual innuendo and cheescake in this series.

TOP OF THE HILL (*Political Drama*)

FIRST TELECAST: *September 21, 1989*
LAST TELECAST: *December 7, 1989*
BROADCAST HISTORY:
Sep 1989–Dec 1989, CBS Thu 9:00–10:00
CAST:
Thomas Bell, Jr. .... William Katt
Thomas "Pat" Bell, Sr. .... Dick O'Neill
Susan Pengilly .... Jordan Baker
Mickey Stewart .... Robby Weaver
Link Winslow .... Tony Edwards

Curly-haired Representative Thomas Bell was the youngest (36), newest, and one of the most idealistic members of the U.S. Congress. When his dad Pat had been forced to step down because of a bad heart, Tom was elected to fill out his father's term. Unlike Pat, a grizzled veteran who had spent his life in the political trenches, ex-surfer Tom's only concerns were his conscience and the residents of the Northern California congressional district who had voted him into office. With the help of his three dedicated young aides—Susan, Mickey, and Link—Tom set out to fix the system. Although he sought his father's help in dealing with his fellow congressmen, he found it impossible to toe the party line when his heart told him it was wrong. Among the issues in which he got involved were adoptees' rights, union corruption, pollution of the environment, shelters for homeless teens, and military procurement.

TOP OF THE POPS (*Music*)

FIRST TELECAST: *September 25, 1987*
LAST TELECAST: *March 25, 1988*
BROADCAST HISTORY:
Sep 1987–Mar 1988, CBS Fri 11:30–12:30 A.M.
HOST:
Gary Davies
Nia Peeples

Top of the Pops was the third pop-music series CBS had aired in this Friday late-night time period in less than a year. Unlike the first two—*Keep on Cruisin'* and *In Person from the Palace*—which had been produced by American Dick Clark, this one was from the people responsible for the British series *Top of the Pops.* That venerable pop-music showcase had been running for 23 years at the time its American counterpart premiered. The American version was twice as long as the British version and actually consisted of two half-hour shows, one from London hosted by Gary Davies, and one from Los Angeles hosted by Nia Peeples. Among the performers appearing were Mick Jagger, Bananarama, David Bowie, Los Lobos, REO Speedwagon, Steve Winwood,

Cliff Richard, Def Leppard, Bon Jovi, Kiss, Sting, Santana, Squeeze, Pet Shop Boys, and the Bee Gees.

TOP PLAYS OF 1954 (*Dramatic Anthology*)
FIRST TELECAST: *June 1, 1954*
LAST TELECAST: *August 24, 1954*
BROADCAST HISTORY:
Jun 1954–Aug 1954, NBC Tue 9:30–10:00

This filmed anthology series was the 1954 summer replacement for *Armstrong Circle Theatre*. The plays which aired under this title were all reruns of episodes of *Ford Theatre* that had been telecast during the first half of 1954.

TOP PRO GOLF (*Sports*)
FIRST TELECAST: *April 6, 1959*
LAST TELECAST: *September 28, 1959*
BROADCAST HISTORY:
Apr 1959–Sep 1959, ABC Mon 9:30–10:30
COMMENTATOR:
Dick Danehe

Each week two professional golfers competed in an 18-hole match. The winner won $1,500 and the right to return the following week to defend his championship, while the loser took home $500. Filmed on location at various golf courses in Florida and Georgia, *Top Pro Golf* showed only the highlights of the round, avoiding coverage of holes that did not bear significantly on the outcome of the match. The big winner on this series was veteran Sam Snead. He had appeared early in the show's run and lost, but when he got another shot early in August he really took advantage of it. He won the last eight matches on this series.

The episodes that aired on Monday evenings as *Top Pro Golf* were actually reruns of a Saturday afternoon series on ABC titled *All Star Golf*. These episodes had first been seen during the 1959–1959 winter season on that series.

TOP TEN LUCY SHOWS, THE, see *I Love Lucy*

TOPPER (*Situation Comedy*)
FIRST TELECAST: *October 9, 1953*
LAST TELECAST: *October 14, 1956*
BROADCAST HISTORY:
Oct 1953–Sep 1955, CBS Fri 8:30–9:00
Oct 1955–Mar 1956, ABC Mon 7:30–8:00
Jun 1956–Oct 1956, NBC Sun 7:00–7:30
CAST:
Marion Kerby .... Anne Jeffreys
George Kerby .... Robert Sterling
Cosmo Topper .... Leo G. Carroll
Henrietta Topper .... Lee Patrick
Katie, the maid (1953–1954) .... Kathleen Freeman
Mr. Schuyler .... Thurston Hall
Maggie, the cook (1954–1955) .... Edna Skinner

On a skiing vacation in Europe, George and Marion Kerby were trapped in an avalance along with their would-be rescuer, a St. Bernard named Neil. All three of them died—only to return to the United States to haunt their former home, now occupied by banker Cosmo Topper. George and Marion developed quite an affection for the very proper Mr. Topper, but felt that he needed to be a little less stuffy. They did everything in their powers, and those powers were considerable, to help Cosmo loosen up. Between their antics and the wanderings of the ghostly Neil, who had a penchant for oversized, brim-full brandy snifters, life in the Topper household was kept very chaotic.

After two seasons on CBS, this series was canceled, only to show up in reruns for a full season on ABC and a summer on NBC. *Topper* was based on characters created by novelist Thorne Smith. These characters were also seen later in a series of movies. The one member of the TV cast that had not appeared in Mr. Smith's novels or the movies was Neil. In the original Smith story the Kerbys died in an automobile accident, not while skiing. Since no dog died with them, there was no dog to haunt with them.

TORKELSONS, THE (*Situation Comedy*)
FIRST TELECAST: *September 21, 1991*
LAST TELECAST: *July 3, 1993*
BROADCAST HISTORY:
Sep 1991–Nov 1991, NBC Sat 8:30–9:00
Nov 1991–Mar 1992, NBC Sun 7:30–8:00
May 1992–Jun 1992, NBC Sat 8:30–9:00
Feb 1993–Jul 1993, NBC Sat 8:00–8:30
CAST:
Millicent Torkelson .... Connie Ray
Dorothy Jane Torkelson (age 14) .... Olivia Burnette
Steven Floyd Torkelson (12) (1991–1992) .... Aaron Metchik
Ruth Ann Torkelson (10) (1991–1992) ... Anna Slotky
Chuckie Lee Torkelson (8) .... Lee Norris
Mary Sue Torkelson (6) .... Rachel Duncan
Wesley Hodges (1991–1992) ...... William Schallert
Kirby Scroggins (1991–1992) .... Paige Gosney
Riley Roberts (1991–1992) .... Michael Landes
Brian Morgan (1993) .... Perry King
Molly Morgan (1993) .... Brittany Murphy
Gregory Morgan (1993) .... Jason Marsden
THEME:
sung by the Judds

A sensitive teenager was mortified by her family in this bittersweet comedy about a working class family on the ropes. Dorothy Jane just wanted to be thought of as normal, like any 14-year-old, but how could she be: her father Randall had walked out on the family, they were perilously short of money, and might even lose their big old rambling house in Pyramid Corners, Oklahoma. Yet her perky, optimistic mom, Millicent, saw sunshine everywhere, even as men came to repossess the appliances. Her brothers and sisters—athletic Steven, spunky Ruth Ann, studious Chuckie Lee (the bug collector), and huggable little Mary Sue—acted as if nothing was wrong. Helping out at least a little was Mr. Hodges, a kindly older man who had rented a room in their basement.

After a single unsuccessful season *The Torkelsons* left the schedule, only to return in February 1993 with a new name, *Almost Home*. Millicent had moved to Seattle to become a nanny working for single dad Brian Morgan, who ran a successful catalogue business. She now had three kids (Steven and Ruth Ann evidently got left by the roadside), who mixed like oil and water with Brian's obnoxious offspring, Molly and Gregory.

Where did the producers get a name like Torkelson? Nearly 30 years before, a real Steven Floyd Torkelson had shared his bug collection, and a first kiss, with a little girl named Lynn Montgomery, who grew up to create this series. The name stayed with her and was immortalized on NBC's fall 1991 schedule.

Moral: be careful to whom you show your bug collection, you just might wind up in a sitcom.

TORTELLIS, THE (*Situation Comedy*)

FIRST TELECAST: *January 22, 1987*
LAST TELECAST: *May 12, 1987*
BROADCAST HISTORY:

Jan 1987, NBC Thu 9:30–10:00
Jan 1987–Apr 1987, NBC Wed 9:30–10:00
Apr 1987–May 1987, NBC Tue 9:30–10:00

CAST:

Nick Tortelli .... Dan Hedaya
Loretta Tortelli .... Jean Kasem
Anthony Tortelli .... Timothy Williams
Annie Tortelli .... Mandy Ingber
Charlotte Cooper .... Carlene Watkins
Mark Cooper .... Aaron Moffatt

In this spin-off from *Cheers*, slimy Nick Tortelli (onetime husband of Carla) moved to Las Vegas to try to reconcile with his new wife, a spaced-out blonde named Loretta who was trying to launch a show-biz career there. He swore he'd turned over a new leaf, but Loretta's level-headed sister Charlotte, who lived with them, was skeptical. Anthony was Nick's dumb teenage son, who helped him in his TV repair business, and Annie was Anthony's young bride.

TOTAL RECALL 2070 (*Science Fiction*)

BROADCAST HISTORY:

Showtime and syndication
60 minutes
Produced: *1999* (22 episodes)
Released: *March 1999* (Showtime); *January 2000* (Syndication)

CAST:

Det. David Hume .... Michael Easton
Det. Ian Farve .... Karl Pruner
Olivia Hume .... Cynthia Preston
Olan Chang .... Judith Krant
Lt. Martin Ehrenthal .... Michael Anthony Rawlins
James Calley .... Matthew Bennett

Earth in 2070 was still recovering from the economic and environmental collapse that had occurred early in the century. The entire planet was effectively under the control of The Consortium, six huge corporations. The most menacing of them was The Rekall Corporation, which was the largest manufacturer of virtual-reality technology while working on its own sinister modifications of both humans and androids. *Total Recall 2070* was set in a large, unnamed city in which clothing styles were virtually unchanged from what people were wearing in the 1990s. In this world the crime rate was much lower than during the previous century and police officers couldn't carry lethal weapons. There wasn't much privacy, since there were hidden cameras and monitors almost everywhere.

Veteran police detective David Hume worked for the Citizen's Protective Bureau, the global law enforcement agency that hunted down renegade androids and tried to keep huge multiworld corporations from running roughshod over the populace (despite the fact that most of the Bureau's funding came from them). Farve, Hume's partner, was an android, a new design that could pass for human, who wanted to learn more about being human. Since Hume hated androids and barely tolerated Farve, he was not much help. Other regulars were Olivia, Hume's wife who worked at Uber Braun, one of the six members of The Consortium and the largest manufacturer of androids (unlike most married couples on TV, they had great—and frequent—sex); Chang, the forensic specialist who spent most of her time in the lab; Ehrenthal, Hume's supportive boss at CPB; and Calley, a mysterious man who apparently oversaw the activities of the CPB and used his influence to get whatever he wanted.

Based on the 1990 theatrical film *Total Recall,* which starred Arnold Schwarzenegger and Sharon Stone. The film was adapted from the short story "We Can Remember It for You Wholesale," by Phillip K. Dick.

TOTAL SECURITY (*Detective Drama*)

FIRST TELECAST: *September 27, 1997*
LAST TELECAST: *November 15, 1997*
BROADCAST HISTORY:

Sep 1997–Nov 1997, ABC Sat 9:00–10:00

CAST:

Frank Cisco .... James Remar
Steve Wegman .... James Belushi
Jody Kiplinger .... Debrah Farentino
Ellie Jones .... Tracey Needham
Neville Watson .... Flex Alexander
George LaSalle .... Bill Brochtrup
Luis Escobar .... Tony Plana
Geneva Renault .... Kristin Bauer

This odd hour didn't seem to know what it wanted to be: action, comedy, or drama. Total Security was a high-tech security firm, investigating threats, tracking down missing persons, protecting important people from all manner of danger. Tough, grim, totally humorless Frank was its boss. Lots of tense standoffs, lots of gunfights. So far, sounds like an action show. Then there was Steve, a pushy, fumbling, wisecracking womanizer whose every move seemed to signal "comic relief." And Jody, a former cop preoccupied by her loyalty to an abusive, alcoholic husband and an intensifying romantic attachment to the dour Frank. Frank himself had been abandoned as a child, and in one episode he tracked down his mother, who, reunited with her son after many years, callously brushed him off. Sounds like drama. Others on the team were Ellie, a sophisticate whose classy charm could open many doors; Neville, a black technical wizard with spiked hair; and George, the studly office manager with his eye on the books ("Frank, get some cash flow!"). Luis was the suave manager of the exclusive Seven Palms Hotel, for which the firm did frequent work.

TOTALLY HIDDEN VIDEO (*Humor*)

FIRST TELECAST: *July 9, 1989*
LAST TELECAST: *August 7, 1992*
BROADCAST HISTORY:

Jul 1989–Jan 1990, FOX Sun 8:30–9:00
Dec 1989–Jul 1990, FOX Sat 8:30–9:00
Aug 1990–Jul 1991, FOX Sat 8:00–8:30
Jun 1991–Aug 1991, FOX Sun 7:00–7:30
Jul 1991–Nov 1991, FOX Sat 9:00–9:30
Nov 1991, FOX Fri 9:30–10:00
Dec 1991–Mar 1992, FOX Fri 9:00–9:30
Mar 1992–Apr 1992, FOX Fri 9:00–10:00
Apr 1992–Aug 1992, FOX Fri 9:30–10:00

HOST:

Steve Skrovan (1989–1990)
Mark Pitta (1991–1992)

When *Totally Hidden Video* premiered in the summer of 1989 it was embroiled in controversy. Allen Funt, to whose venerable *Candid Camera* this series bore more than a little resemblance, was suing the producers for both ripping off his idea—using hidden cameras to film ordinary people being made fools of in embarrassing and/or absurd situations set up by the producers—and using actors who knew what the gag was to portray the "ordinary people." The producers admitted that they had used actors in the original pilot for *Totally Hidden Video*, but swore that anything actually aired was legitimate. As for the basic series concept, Funt was unable to convince the court that there was anything copyrightable about the use of hidden cameras.

The stunts were vintage *Candid Camera* fare: Canadian mounties stop surprised motorists at a "border" station in the California desert and inform them that Congress has moved the Canadian border south; an actress in the audience at a wedding ceremony suddenly pipes up that the bride has been having an affair, and fingers an unsuspecting guest; a dog in a pet store talks to small children when their parents aren't looking. Original host Steve Skrovan, who also participated in some of the setups, left the show in the summer of 1990. That fall a number of comics served as guest hosts, with Mark Pitta taking over as the regular host the following January. When new episodes started airing in July of 1991, the series had a modified title, *Totally New Totally Hidden Video*, and a new feature, "Video Vengeance," in which the program helped viewers set up other people they knew to get even with them, and filmed the results for the show.

TOUCH OF GRACE, A (*Situation Comedy*)

FIRST TELECAST: *January 20, 1973*
LAST TELECAST: *June 16, 1973*
BROADCAST HISTORY:
Jan 1973–Jun 1973, ABC Sat 8:30–9:00
CAST:
Grace Simpson .... Shirley Booth
Herbert Morrison .... J. Patrick O'Malley
Walter Bradley .... Warren Berlinger
Myra Bradley .... Marian Mercer

Oscar, Emmy, and Tony winner Shirley Booth starred in this comedy as a recently widowed, sixtyish woman who moved in with her daughter and son-in-law. There the battle of the generations began—between Grace, a perky youngster at heart, and the young couple, a pair of conservative "squares," older than their years. Grace did a lot of dating, but her steady boyfriend was Herbert, a gravedigger. In the final telecast, he proposed and Grace accepted.

Based on the British TV series *For the Love of Ada.*

TOUCHED BY AN ANGEL (*Fantasy*)

FIRST TELECAST: *September 21, 1994*
LAST TELECAST: *April 27, 2003*
BROADCAST HISTORY:
Sep 1994–Dec 1994, CBS Wed 9:00–10:00
Feb 1995–Mar 1995, CBS Sat 9:00–10:00
Jun 1995–Sep 1996, CBS Sat 9:00–10:00
Aug 1996–Sep 2001, CBS Sun 8:00–9:00
Sep 2001–Jul 2002, CBS Sat 8:00–9:00
Jun 2002–Jul 2002, CBS Sun 8:00–9:00
Sep 2002–Apr 2003, CBS Sat 8:00–9:00
Apr 2003, CBS Sun 8:00–9:00
CAST:
Monica .... Roma Downey
Tess .... Della Reese
Andrew .... John Dye
**Special Agent Angel Sam (1995–1999)*
.... Paul Winfield
Rafael (1997–1998) .... Alexis Cruz
Gloria (2001–2003) .... Valerie Bertinelli
*Occasional
THEME:
"Walk with You," sung by Della Reese

Monica was an apprentice angel who had just been promoted to caseworker, a step up from her former work in search-and-rescue missions. She had been looking forward to the promotion because, as a caseworker, she could be seen by mortals and help and inspire them to change their lives for the better. Overseeing her work, offering advice, and occasionally helping herself was Tess, Monica's heavenly superior. The two of them traveled around the country in a vintage Cadillac convertible, using their common sense, concern, and an occasional minor miracle to help people improve themselves. Monica's cases included helping a bitter high school baseball coach come to terms with his mortality, keeping a successful writer with a drinking problem from being permanently estranged from her family, preventing a woman being blackmailed from committing suicide, and helping two orphaned brothers get through a difficult Christmas season.

At the start of the second season Andrew, the gentle Angel of Death, became a regular member of the cast, helping Tess and Monica and serving as a liaison from heaven. He could tell them when it was—or was not—someone's "time." In the special episode that aired on September 15, 1996, the Greene family was introduced, and two days later, got their own series, *Promised Land.* Special Agent Angel Sam showed up periodically, and Rafael, a young street-smart angel, was a regular during the 1997–1998 season.

In April 2001 a new angel, Gloria, was added to the cast. She was adjusting to people on Earth and was sorely in need of the guidance Monica provided. That fall Andrew's role expanded as he functioned as a caseworker. The two-part series finale opened with Monica being evaluated for promotion to supervisor. She helped a mysterious drifter (who turned out to be Jesus) and passed. After Monica said sad farewells to the others with whom she had been working, Tess, who was moving on to other work for God, gave her the keys to the big red Cadillac convertible and left.

TOUGH COOKIES (*Situation Comedy*)

FIRST TELECAST: *March 5, 1986*
LAST TELECAST: *April 23, 1986*
BROADCAST HISTORY:
Mar 1986–April 1986, CBS Wed 8:30–9:00
CAST:
Det. Cliff Brady .... Robby Benson
Rita .... Lainie Kazan
Danny Polchek .... Adam Arkin
Richie Messina .... Matt Craven
Lt. Iverson .... Art Metrano
Off. Connie Rivera .... Elizabeth Pena
Father McCaskey .... Alan North

Juvenile film star Robby Benson, just turned 30 but still saddled with a kid's image (one unkind critic called him "Cute as Bambi and twice as smarmy"), tried to establish an "adult" image by playing a tough cop in this 1986 series. It didn't work. Plainclothes detective Cliff Brady was on home turf, assigned to the precinct in a tough Southside Chicago neighborhood where he had grown up. He lived nearby, kept in touch with old friends, and tried to keep the area from deteriorating still further. His favored hangout (all tough cops have hangouts) was The Windbreaker, a local saloon run by outspoken Rita, a sort of surrogate mother. Boyhood friend Richie worked there as a bartender and another buddy, smooth-talking bookmaker Danny, hung out. Lt. Iverson was Cliff's even-tougher superior, Father McCaskey the understanding police chaplin, and Connie a fellow officer who couldn't have been more concerned about the welfare of the cute—er, tough—detective if she had been his sister.

TOUGH CROWD WITH COLIN QUINN (*Talk*)

BROADCAST HISTORY:

Comedy Central
30 minutes
Produced: *2003–*
Premiered: *March 10, 2003*

EMCEE:

Colin Quinn

Contentious comic Colin Quinn emceed this late-night gab-fest in which Quinn and four guest comedians discussed, half seriously, great issues of the day. The setting was a funky loftlike living room, and there was a lot of good-natured yelling, bleeps and interrupting as the group tackled subjects ranging from the 2003 Iraq war to advertising in movies. For example: "Why do we send an army full of 19-year-olds to Iraq? Send old angry guys who have been through divorces and stuff."

TOUGH ENOUGH (*Sports Competition*)

BROADCAST HISTORY:

MTV
30 minutes
Original episodes: *2001–*
Premiered: *June 21, 2001*

Shortly after WWF Wrestling's Smackdown moved to MTV, the network launched this spin-off reality series in which young wrestling hopefuls competed for a place in the league. Each season began with 13 guys and gals "chasing a dream" as they went through rigorous training under the watchful eyes of real WWF trainers and stars—a tough lot, if ever there was one. "When you get in the WWF you'll never have a moment when you're complete healthy," said one pro. "We work five days a week beat up." Still, the glamour of big-time professional wrestling kept the kids going as they were smashed around the ring to the sounds of loud thuds and groans. As the season progressed, the field was progressively narrowed until two winners emerged—in the first season it was Nidia Guenard and Maven Huffman. First-season trainers were Al Snow, Tazz, Tori, and Jacqueline.

TOUGH TARGET (*Information*)

BROADCAST HISTORY:

Syndicated only
30 minutes
Produced: *1994–1995* (26 episodes)
Released: *September 1994*

HOST:

J. J. Bittenbinder

Each episode of *Tough Target* showed real people describing how they had been victimized. The crimes were re-created, and the victims explained what they had done right and what they had done wrong. Host J. J. Bittenbinder, a police detective, followed up by providing viewers with advice on how they could avoid being in the same situation and prepare themselves to deal with crimes after they had occurred. Interviews with law enforcement professionals about programs that the public should be aware of were also included.

TOUR OF DUTY (*Military Drama*)

FIRST TELECAST: *September 24, 1987*
LAST TELECAST: *August 25, 1990*

BROADCAST HISTORY:

Sep 1987–Mar 1988, CBS Thu 8:00–9:00
Mar 1988–Aug 1988, CBS Sat 9:00–10:00
Jan 1989–Jun 1989, CBS Tue 8:00–9:00
Jun 1989–Jun 1990, CBS Sat 9:00–10:00
Jun 1990–Aug 1990, CBS Sat 10:00–11:00

CAST:

Sgt. Zeke Anderson .... Terence Knox
Capt. Rusty Wallace (1987–1988) .... Kevin Conroy
Lt. Myron Goldman .... Stephen Caffrey
Pvt. Roger Horn (1987–1988) .... Joshua Maurer
Pvt. "Doc" Randy Matsuda (1987–1988)
.... Steve Akahoshi
Cpl. Danny Percell .... Tony Becker
Pvt. Scott Baker (1987–1988) .... Eric Bruskotter
Pvt. Marvin Johnson (1987–1989) ...... Stan Foster
Pvt. Alberto Ruiz .... Ramon Franco
Pvt. Marcus Taylor .... Miguel A. Nunez, Jr.
Alex Devlin (1989–1990) .... Kim Delaney
Lt. John McKay (1989–1990) .... Dan Gauthier
Dr. Jennifer Seymour (1989) .... Betsy Brantley
Major Darling (1989) .... Richard Brestoff
Col. Brewster (1989–1990) .... Carl Weathers
Pvt. Francis "Doc Hock" Hockenbury (1989–1990)
.... John Dye
Major Duncan (1989–1990) .... Michael Christy
Col. Stringer (1989–1990) .... Alan Scarfe
Gen. Elliot (1989–1990) .... Peter Vogt
Pvt. William Griner (1990) .... Kyle Chandler
Pfc. Thomas "Pop" Scarlet (1990) ...... Lee Majors

THEME:

"Paint It Black," by Mick Jagger & Keith Richards, performed by The Rolling Stones

Set in Vietnam in 1967, *Tour of Duty* was a remarkably honest portrayal of a group of American soldiers fighting the most unpopular war in American history. The environment was hostile, most of the members of Company B were new recruits unprepared for the harsh realities of war, and many of their friends and relatives didn't support what they were doing. The real leader of B Company was Sgt. Anderson, a veteran serving his third tour of duty in Vietnam, whose friendliness, professionalism, and concern for the safety of his men made him very popular. His informal approach created conflict with Lt. Goldman, the platoon's uptight leader who was fresh out of officer candidate school. New to the platoon were Horn, a drafted pacifist from Chicago; Percell, a gung-ho volunteer from Iowa; Ruiz, a tough Puerto Rican from the Bronx; and Baker, a free-spirited surfer from Southern California. Johnson and Taylor were the two black veterans in the unit, the former, an experienced jungle fighter and the latter, a moody malcontent. Doc was the unit's medic and Capt. Wallace, the company commander. There was a gritty, depressing look to *Tour of Duty* and, as part of its attempt to be as realistic as possible, both Capt. Wallace and Doc died in action during the first six months the series was on the air.

When *Tour of Duty* returned for its second season, in January of 1989, the platoon had been reassigned to Tan Son Nhut airbase, just outside Saigon. Added to the cast were Alex Devlin, a pretty wire service reporter covering the war; Dr. Jennifer Seymour, a psychologist helping the men deal with their emotional problems; and Lt. Johnny McKay, a helicopter pilot who transported members of the platoon on their missions. The women brought the series a little romance—Anderson having an affair with Dr. Seymour while Goldman got involved with Alex. New that fall were Col. Brewster and Doc Hock, the company's new medic—a pacifist who was in Vietnam trying to save lives rather than to take them. Morale and discipline continued to deteriorate, with the impact on the platoon seen in the growing drug addiction of Percell. Even getting out didn't seem to help—when Johnson returned to the states after his tour ended he found people as confused and angry as the soldiers in Vietnam. It was much the same for Percell, Ruiz, and McKay when they returned home in the series' last original episode.

TOWNIES (*Situation Comedy*)

FIRST TELECAST: *September 18, 1996*

LAST TELECAST: *December 4, 1996*

BROADCAST HISTORY:

Sep 1996–Dec 1996, ABC Wed 8:30–9:00

CAST:

Carrie Donovan.................. Molly Ringwald
Shannon.......................... Jenna Elfman
Denise Rivaldi.................. Lauren Graham
Ryan................................ Billy Burr
Kurt............................ Ron Livingston
Kathy Donovan.................. Lee Garlington
Mike Donovan.................... Dion Anderson
Marge.......................... Conchata Ferrell
Jesse.......................... Joseph Reitman

Men were pigs—or at least day-old fish—in this girl-buddy sitcom set in the quaint fishing town of Gloucester, Massachusetts. The girls were three high school friends who were now twentysomething waitresses at a local restaurant. Carrie was the peacemaker, Shannon the loose liver liable to have naked guys in her apartment, and Denise the nervous wreck about to become a bride (if she could pull Ryan, the father of her baby, away from watching the Boston Celtics long enough). They hung out, bantered with the guys, and dreamt of getting out of Gloucester (Shannon: "The economy sucks, there's nothing to do, and everything I own smells like fish"). Kurt was Cassie's platonic pal, Kathy and Mike her traditional parents, Marge the raspy owner of the diner, and Jesse, Marge's son.

TOWNSEND TELEVISION (*Comedy/Variety*)

FIRST TELECAST: *September 12, 1993*

LAST TELECAST: *December 26, 1993*

BROADCAST HISTORY:

Sep 1993–Dec 1993, FOX Sun 7:00–8:00

REGULARS:

Robert Townsend
John Witherspoon
Barry Diamond
Paula Jai Parker
Roxanne Beckford
Darrel Heath
Lester Barrie
Biz Markie
The Paul Jackson Orchestra
The Russell Clark Dancers

The multitalented Robert Townsend starred in this variety series, which was a showcase for black performers. Townsend did standup comedy, participated in sketches, danced, sang, directed videotaped segments, and was one of the show's writers. There were spoofs of movies, videos, and commercials as well as comedy sketches and musical numbers by the regulars and guests. Two regular features were "Nigel Spider" short detective films starring Townsend as a black British detective, with Biz Markie as his strong-armed assistant Mad Dog, and "Tinseltown Talkies," black-and-white spoofs of silent movies with black casts and set in the 'hood. Several episodes featured unusual contests in which series regulars competed with each other and with guest performers—a comedy Olympics one week, a Motown singing showdown another—with the studio audience voting for the winners. Among the musical guest performers were the O'Jays, Ashford and Simpson, Aaron Neville, Taylor Dayne, and Queen Latifah.

TRACEY ULLMAN SHOW, THE (*Comedy/Variety*)

FIRST TELECAST: *April 5, 1987*

LAST TELECAST: *September 1, 1990*

BROADCAST HISTORY:

Apr 1987–May 1987, FOX Sun 8:30–9:00
May 1987–Sep 1987, FOX Sun 9:30–10:00
Sep 1987–Feb 1988, FOX Sun 9:00–9:30
Mar 1988–Jul 1988, FOX Sun 10:00–10:30
Jul 1988–Aug 1989, FOX Sun 9:30–10:00
Aug 1989–Mar 1990, FOX Sun 10:00–10:30
Apr 1990–Sep 1990, FOX Sun 9:30–10:00

REGULARS:

Tracey Ullman
Julie Kavner
Dan Castellaneta
Joe Malone
Sam McMurray
Anna Levine (1988–1989)

ANIMATION:

Gabor Csupo
Matt Groening

The multitalented British import Tracey Ullman—singer, dancer, actress, comedienne—starred in this critically acclaimed variety series. Each episode contained two or three comedy "playlets" featuring Miss Ullman and her small repertory group. Her recurring characterizations included South African golf pro Kiki Howard-Smith; materialistic Yuppie Sara Downey; anthropologist Ceci Beckwith, who was living with monkeys in the wilds of Africa; divorcée Ginny Tillman; Francesca, a teenager living with her gay father and his lover; Kay, an insecure spinster living with her mother; and Tina the postal worker. Short, bizarre animated segments aired between the live-action sketches; after a few months these began to focus on a rather strange family, the Simpsons, who became so popular that they got their own series. At the close of each show Miss Ullman came on stage without makeup, in her housecoat, to talk briefly to the studio audience. There was never any doubt when she was through, since her parting words were always the same—"Go home!!"

The Tracey Ullman Show was the only Fox Broadcasting series to be nominated for Emmy Awards during the fledgling fourth network's first season. At the 1990 Emmy Awards show, which aired two weeks after her series had gone off the air, Tracey Ullman did win an Emmy for the show.

TRACKDOWN (*Western*)
FIRST TELECAST: *October 4, 1957*
LAST TELECAST: *September 23, 1959*
BROADCAST HISTORY:
Oct 1957–Jan 1959, CBS Fri 8:00–8:30
Feb 1959–Sep 1959, CBS Wed 8:30–9:00
CAST:
Hoby Gilman .... Robert Culp

Set in the Southwest during the 1870s, *Trackdown* detailed the adventures of a mythical Texas Ranger, Hoby Gilman. Many of the stories told in the series were adapted from cases in the files of the Texas Rangers and it was for that reason that the show had the official approval of the State of Texas and the Rangers. That was a distinction that could be claimed by no other Western on the air.

TRACKER (*Science Fiction*)
BROADCAST HISTORY:
Syndicated only
60 minutes
Produced: *2001–2002* (22 episodes)
Released: *October 2001*
CAST:
Cole .... Adrian Paul
Mel Porter .... Amy Price-Francis
Jess .... Leanne Wilson
Dr. Zin .... Geraint Wyn Davies
Det. Victor Bruno .... Dean McDermott
Nestov .... Richard Yearwood

Cole was a security officer from Cirron 17, a planet in the Migar Solar System 100 light-years from Earth, whose mission was to recapture 218 prisoners who had escaped from an interplanetary prison and surfaced in Chicago. Since his own name was not pronounceable by humans, he had taken the name Cole—he saw it on an underwear billboard soon after arriving on Earth and taking human form. Adapting to life on Earth was not easy. He knew nothing about the planet and needed help to understand the culture and the people. That help was provided by Mel, an independent young woman who ran The Watchfire, a downtown Chicago bar that she had inherited from her grandmother and that, conveniently, never seemed to have any customers. Mel had found Cole wandering around soon after his arrival and took pity on him, providing him with a room above the bar and becoming his confidante.

Cole had extrasensory perception, could temporarily stop time and was a genius at adapting primitive Earth technology to help him track the escapees, all of whom had taken over human bodies. He captured them by using a small handheld device to suck their life force out of the bodies they were inhabiting and onto a little disk. Others seen regularly were Jess, the sexy barmaid who worked for Mel and had been told that Cole was a government agent working undercover; Vic, Mel's former boyfriend, who was still interested in her; and Nestov, a young Enixian con man and womanizer in the body of a bedraggled loser. Cole worked out a deal with Nestov, allowing him to stay in human form in exchange for his help tracking down the other fugitives. Zin, the mastermind behind the escape, was a diabolical scientist who had previously killed Cole's wife and daughter.

In February Jess received a proposal from a boyfriend in London and left to accept—but they were having problems when Cole and Mel went to visit her in May. While there Cole discovered that Zin had set up his criminal organization on Earth long before the prison break. Additionally, Mel had found a metal key suggesting that her father and grandmother may have been from Cole's home world. Cole analyzed the key, which provided access to a room beneath The Watchfire that in turn housed a power source Zin was looking for. In the series finale Cole found a way—with Mel's help—to send all of the remaining prisoners back to Sartop Prison simultaneously. Though his mission was complete, he decided to stay on Earth with her rather than return home. In the last scene, while they were celebrating, his computer screen showed the fugitive prisoners reappearing all over the U.S.

TRADE WINDS (*Drama*)
FIRST TELECAST: *August 27, 1993*
LAST TELECAST: *September 17, 1993*
BROADCAST HISTORY:
Aug 1993–Sep 1993, NBC Fri 10:00–11:00
CAST:
Christof Philips .... Efrem Zimbalist, Jr.
Robert Philips .... John Beck
Maxine Philips .... Michael Michele
Anthony Philips .... Ned Vaughn
Will Philips .... Sam Hennings
Marigot Philips .... Claudette Roche
Kyle Philips .... Allan Dean Moore
Grace Sommers .... Barbara Stock
Rick Sommers .... Stephen Meadows
Ocean Sommers .... Michael McLafferty
Ellen Sommers .... Rebecca Staub
Contessa Laetitia Philips Gabetti ..... Anita Morris
Joseph Gabetti .... Dean Tarolly
Madame DeGaulle .... Kim Hamilton
August DeGaulle .... Randi Ingerman
Maj. Hugo Rotterdam .... Lindsey Ginter
Nurse Lisa Topping .... Paula Trickey
Duncan Laurant .... G. McKinney
Chris .... Kent Burden

Soapsuds washed up on the white silver sands of Caribbean paradise St. Martin's in this short but convoluted summer series. Billed as the first in a series of romantic mini-series presented under the umbrella title *Great Escapes*, it involved the romantic and business rivalries of two families, the hardworking Sommers, owners of the Trade Winds resort, and the scheming Philips, owners of the Paradise Rum Company, who were determined to steal the resort from them. Of course there were also two star-crossed lovers who defied their families—hunky, ponytailed

Ocean Sommers and island beauty Maxine Philips (betrothed to ruthless prosecutor Joseph). The series ended after only four weeks with Ocean in jail for murder and the story unresolved.

A second "romantic novel"—*The Secrets of Lake Success*—followed under the *Great Escapes* banner, but it lasted only three weeks and thus does not quality as a "series" under the rigorous (where we want them to be) rules of this book. *Trade Winds* was published in book form, for those who care.

TRADERS (*Drama*)

BROADCAST HISTORY:

Lifetime
60 minutes
Produced: *1996* (13 episodes)
Premiered: *September 3, 1996*

CAST:

Sally Ross .... Sonja Smits
Cedric Ross .... David Gardner
Jack Larkin .... David Cubitt
Marty Stephens .... Patrick McKenna
Adam Cunningham .... Bruce Gray
Grant Jansky .... David Hewlett

Overcooked drama about romance and backstabbing at Gardner/Ross, a powerful investment house located in Toronto, Canada. Sally was the stylish young economist who took over when her father, senior partner Cedric Ross, was arrested for fraud. Swirling through the convoluted plots were Jack, a slick young hotshot from Vancouver trying to break into the big time; Marty, the chubby trader with a headset who ran the bull pen; and Adam, Cedric's arrogant partner who mixed with the old-line rich and powerful. The camera swooped and dodged across the trading floor, as if looking for a plot, and there were frequent extreme close-ups into characters' eyes (maybe the plot's in there?). American viewers found the manic activity more confusing than involving, and the Canadian-produced series soon foundered.

TRADING SPACES (*Instructional*)

BROADCAST HISTORY:

The Learning Channel
60 minutes
Original episodes: *2000–*
Premiered: *October 13, 2000*

HOST:

Alex McLeod (2000–2001)
Paige Davis (2001–)

REGULARS:

Frank Bielec, designer
Genevieve Gorder, designer
Dez Ryan, designer (2000–2001)
Hilda Santo-Tomas, designer
Roderick Shade, designer
Laurie Hickson-Smith, designer
Kia Steave-Dickerson, designer (2002–)
Edward Walker, designer (2002–)
Douglas Wilson, designer
Vern Yip, designer
Amy Wynn Pastor, carpenter
Ty Pennington, carpenter

This simple home design show captured viewers' imaginations in the early 2000s. Two sets of neighbors swapped keys, and each made over one room in the other's home in 48 hours—with the help of two professional designers, a carpenter and $1,000. The two teams (neither knew what the other was doing) talked about what their friends might like and with the help of the professionals stripped, painted and decorated, amid jokes and banter. At the end of the show there was a "reveal" in which each team returned to their own home and saw what their neighbors had done; reactions ranged from "Oh my God, I like it!" to "I don't know—I have to get used to it" (in the infamous "Crying Pam" episode a subject ran from her redecorated room sobbing). Usually the reaction was one of delight. Alex was the original perky host, replaced in the second season by perky Paige. A rotating stable of designers and carpenters assisted.

Based on the British series *Changing Rooms*.

TRAFFIC COURT (*Courtroom Drama*)

FIRST TELECAST: *June 18, 1958*
LAST TELECAST: *March 30, 1959*

BROADCAST HISTORY:

Jun 1958–Jul 1958, ABC Wed 9:30–10:00
Jul 1958–Oct 1958, ABC Sun 9:00–9:30
Oct 1958–Nov 1958, ABC Thu 10:00–10:30
Nov 1958, ABC Mon 10:00–10:30
Mar 1959, ABC Mon 10:00–10:30

CAST:

The Judge .... Edgar Allan Jones, Jr.
Bailiff .... Frank Chandler McClure
Court Clerk .... Samuel Whitson

This filmed series had a regular run during the summer of 1958, and was then used to fill numerous holes in the ABC schedule during the 1958–1959 season. It presented reenactments of actual traffic-court trials and arraignments. The judge was Edgar Allan Jones, Jr., who in real life was assistant dean of the U.C.L.A. law school.

TRAILMASTER, see *Wagon Train*

TRAILS WEST, see *Death Valley Days*

TRANSFORMERS ARMADA (*Cartoon*)

BROADCAST HISTORY:

Cartoon Network
30 minutes
Original episodes: *2002–*
Premiered: *August 23, 2002*

VOICES:

Rad .... Kirby Morrow
Carlos .... Matt Hill
Alexis .... Tabitha St. Germain
Billy .... Andrew Francis
Fred .... Tony Sampson
Optimus Prime .... Gary Chalk
Hotshot .... Brent Miller
Red Alert .... Brian Dobson
Megatron .... David Kaye
Starscream .... Michael Dobson
Demolisher .... Alvin Sanders
Cyclonus .... Donald Brown
Thrust .... Scott McNeil
Smokescreen .... Dale Wilson
Narrator .... Jim Conrad

Three kids from Lincoln Middle School, somewhere in the Southwest, stumbled into the middle of a long-running battle between two races of outer-space Transformers (robots) in this action-packed cartoon set in the year 2010. Rad, Carlos and Alexis were out hiking when they discovered a Pandora's Box from the ancient planet Cybertron, which attracted the attention of the battling Autobots and Decepticons. Both were after MiniCon robots, small units that when connected to themselves greatly enhanced their strength and power; apparently these MiniCons had been scattered on Earth many centuries earlier. The three kids befriended the relatively friendly Autobots (Optimus, Hotshot, Red Alert and others) and helped them in their battles with the Decepticons, led by Megatron and including Starscream, Demolisher and Cyclonus. Billy and his chubby friend Fred tagged along, and eventually discovered the secret of the robots as well.

The series was a revival of the earlier cartoons *The Transformers* (1985) and *Transformers: Generation 2* (1992), and was also represented by a Hasbro toy line.

TRAP, THE (*Dramatic Anthology*)

FIRST TELECAST: *April 29, 1950*
LAST TELECAST: *June 24, 1950*
BROADCAST HISTORY:
Apr 1950–Jun 1950, CBS Sat 9:00–10:00
NARRATOR:
Joseph DeSantis

The melodramas that were presented in this live anthology series were all concerned with people who had gotten themselves into situations over which they no longer had control. Fate would be the determinant of their future, of whether or not they survived the perilous predicament into which they had gotten themselves "trapped."

TRAPPER JOHN, M.D. (*Medical Drama*)

FIRST TELECAST: *September 23, 1979*
LAST TELECAST: *September 4, 1986*
BROADCAST HISTORY:
Sep 1979–Jan 1986, CBS Sun 10:00–11:00
Feb 1986–Mar 1986, CBS Tue 8:00–9:00
Jun 1986, CBS Thu 9:00–10:00
Aug 1986–Sep 1986, CBS Thu 10:00–11:00
CAST:
Dr. John McIntyre ("Trapper John") ... Pernell Roberts
Dr. George Alonzo Gates ("Gonzo") ... Gregory Harrison
Nurse Clara Willoughly ("Starch") (1979–1980) ... Mary McCarty
Nurse Gloria Brancusi ("Ripples") (1979–1985) ... Christopher Norris
Dr. Stanley Riverside II ... Charles Siebert
Dr. Justin Jackson ("Jackpot") ... Brian Mitchell
Nurse Shapiro (1979–1980) ... Marion Yue
Arnold Slocum (1979–1985) ... Simon Scott
Nurse Ernestine Shoop (1980–1986) ... Madge Sinclair
Dr. Sandler (1980–1984) ... Richard Schaal
Dr. Charlie Nichols (1980–1984) ... Michael Tucci
Nurse (1981–1985) ... Chris Hutson
Nurse Clover (1981–1984) ... Bebe Kelly
Nurse Andrews (1981–1986) ... Sarah Cunningham
Andrea Brancusi (1983–1985) ... Robin Ignico
E. J. Riverside (1983–1986) ... Marcia Rodd
Dr. John ("J.T.") McIntyre (1984–1986) .. Tim Busfield
Catherine Hackett (1985–1986) ... Janis Paige
Nurse Libby Kegler (1985–1986) ... Lorna Luft
Dr. Andy Pagano (1985–1986) ... Beau Gravitte
Fran Brennan (1985–1986) ... Andrea Marcovicci

This medical drama was a spin-off, of sorts, from the popular comedy *M*A*S*H*. In the 28 years since he had been discharged from the 4077th M.A.S.H. unit in Korea, balding Dr. John McIntyre had mellowed considerably. He not only learned to stop fighting the system, but became part of it, as chief of surgery at sprawling San Francisco Memorial Hospital. His concern for his patients still sometimes tempted him to violate "established hospital procedures," but Trapper had learned to mollify the hospital administration, represented by bookish Arnold Slocum. Working with Trapper was an admiring young doctor named Gonzo Gates, whose brash, irreverent attitude and love of life reminded Trapper of his own youth. Gonzo, the hospital Lothario (who lived in an R.V. parked in the hospital parking lot), had even served in an army M.A.S.H. unit himself, during the Vietnam War, and was a talented surgeon. Also featured was Trapper's scrub nurse, Starch, who went all the way back to his M.A.S.H. days (she was replaced by Nurse Shoop when actress Mary McCarty died during the hiatus between *Trapper John*'s first and second seasons); sexy young nurse Gloria Brancusi; and Doctors Jackson and Riverside, the latter a likable but officious chief of emergency services who, it was rumored, owed his job more to his father's position on the hospital's board of directors than to his own skill.

Major changes occurred in the personal lives of two of San Francisco Memorial's staff members early in 1983. Stanley Riverside got married to a woman dentist who also worked at the hospital, and Gloria adopted a sickly, homeless waif named Andrea. Trapper also had to deal with the occasional intrusions into his life by his ex-wife, Melanie (played by Jessica Walter).

Their son, J.T., recently graduated from medical school, arrived in the fall of 1984 to do his internship at San Francisco Memorial. The following fall saw the arrival of Libby Kegler to replace Gloria, attractive, mature Catherine Hackett as the new administrator, and young surgeon and emergency service helicopter pilot Andy Pagano. Early in 1986 Gonzo suffered a stroke (Gregory Harrison was leaving the series) and, although he regained most of his faculties, was unable to return to surgery. Trying to put his life back together, and unsure that he wanted to stay in medicine if he could not be a surgeon, Gonzo left the hospital on an extended vacation with his new bride, Fran.

TRAPS (*Police Drama*)

FIRST TELECAST: *March 31, 1994*
LAST TELECAST: *April 27, 1994*
BROADCAST HISTORY:
Mar 1994–Apr 1994, CBS Thu 10:00–11:00
Apr 1994, CBS Wed 9:00–10:00
CAST:
Joe Trapchek ... George C. Scott
Det. Chris Trapchek ... Dan Cortese
Cmdr. Laura Parkhurst ... Lindsay Crouse
Cora Trapchek ... Piper Laurie
Det. Jack Cloud ... Bill Nunn

Joe Trapchek was a retired chief of homicide in Seattle who had come out of retirement at the behest of Cmdr. Parkhurst to consult on tough cases. His return gave Joe an opportunity to rebuild a frayed relationship with his grandson, Chris, a young detective on the force. Chris, a free spirit who didn't always follow traditional police procedure, had been estranged from Joe ever since he had become a police officer. After his father, Dan, also a cop, had been killed by a criminal, Chris's relationship with Joe had deteriorated even further. It was tough trying to be his own man when there were two generations of Trapcheks with stellar records preceding him on the force. Helping to establish communication between the two was Chris's partner, Jack, who had been Dan's partner. While grandfather and grandson tried to work out their professional and personal conflicts they also had to deal with the deteriorating health of Joe's wife, Cora, who was suffering from Alzheimer's disease.

Filmed in Vancouver, British Columbia.

TRASH OR TREASURE, see *What's It Worth?*

TRASHED (*Quiz/Audience Participation*)

BROADCAST HISTORY:

MTV
30 minutes
Produced: *1994* (50 episodes)
Premiered: *February 14, 1994*

HOST:

Chris Hardwick

In this early-evening game show two teams of roommates competed to save their worldly possessions from total destruction.

TRAUMA CENTER (*Medical Drama*)

FIRST TELECAST: *September 22, 1983*
LAST TELECAST: *December 8, 1983*
BROADCAST HISTORY:

Sep 1983–Oct 1983, ABC Thu 8:00–9:00
Nov 1993–Dec 1983, ABC Thu 9:00–10:00

CAST:

Dr. Michael "Cutter" Royce .... James Naughton
Dr. Nate "Skate" Baylor .... Dorian Harewood
Dr. Brigitte Blaine .... Wendie Malick
Dr. "Beaver" Bouvier .... Bill Randolph
Amy Decker .... Eileen Heckart
Dr. Charles Sternhauser .... Arlen Dean Snyder
John Six .... Lou Ferrigno
Sidney "Hatter" Pacelli .... Alfie Wise
Buck Williams .... Jack Bannon
Nurse Hooter .... Jayne Modean

Life was just one disaster after another for the medics of *Trauma Center.* There were generally three or four "traumas" per show, ranging from an injured construction worker stuck in a high rise to golfers struck by lightning, victims of an explosion at a singles bar, a skyscraper climber whose foot slipped, and students mangled when the roof caved in on their high school prom. Youthful doctor "Cutter" Royce dealt with all this at the McKee Hospital Trauma Center, which had been set up to make maximum use of the "golden hour"—the first 60 minutes following an accident, in which many victims can be saved by fast action. Helping at the center and on the scene were young doctors Baylor, Blaine, and Bouvier, nursing supervisor Amy Decker and her ingenuous assistant Hooter, helicopter pilot Buck (well, they did have to move fast), and ambulance drivers Hatter and John Six. Six was played by brawny Lou Ferrigno, whose real-life partial deafness (and halting speech) was used to advantage in a story about a young boy coming to terms with his own accident-induced deafness. Dr. Sternhauser was the hospital administrator with whom Cutter was constantly fighting for new equipment and additional funds.

TRAUMA CENTER (*Documentary*)

BROADCAST HISTORY:

Syndicated only
30 minutes
Produced: *1994–1995* (26 episodes)
Released: *September 1994*

Taped in cinema verité style at a number of hospitals around the country, *Trauma Center* showcased the life-saving activities of the staffs of trauma centers and emergency room personnel. Each episode followed two or three patients at different hospitals from admittance to treatment to epilogues on what had happened to the patients since their hospitalizations. Although most of them had survived and were back leading normal lives, there were some who had been permanently disabled. Among the hospitals visited most frequently were Allegheny General Hospital in Pittsburgh, the University Medical Center of Southern Nevada in Las Vegas, St. Paul Ramsey Medical Center, and Loyola University Medical Center in Chicago.

TRAVEL CHANNEL, THE (Network)
(*Documentary Cable Network*)

LAUNCHED:

February 1, 1987

SUBSCRIBERS (MAY 2003):

70.8 million (66% U.S.)

For those who want to globe-trot from the comfort of their couch, cable's Travel Channel offers travelogues, travel advice, and coverage of exotic events such as the Mardi Gras in New Orleans and the Chinese New Year parade in San Francisco. In addition to original series about travel with names such as *Undersea Adventures* and *New England Outdoors,* the channel has aired reruns of appropriate broadcast shows, including *Lifestyles of the Rich and Famous* and *On the Road with Charles Kuralt.*

TRAVEL CORNER (*Documentary*)

FIRST TELECAST: *December 28, 1953*
LAST TELECAST: *September 4, 1954*
BROADCAST HISTORY:

Dec 1953–May 1954, ABC Mon 9:30–10:00
Jun 1954–Sep 1954, ABC Sat 10:00–10:30

Travel films.

TRAVELS OF JAIMIE MCPHEETERS, THE
(*Western*)

FIRST TELECAST: *September 15, 1963*
LAST TELECAST: *March 15, 1964*
BROADCAST HISTORY:

Sep 1963–Mar 1964, ABC Sun 7:30–8:30

CAST:

"Doc" Sardius McPheeters .... Dan O'Herlihy
Jaimie McPheeters .... Kurt Russell
John Murrel .... James Westerfield
Shep Baggott .... Sandy Kenyon
Jenny .... Donna Anderson
Matt Kissel .... Mark Allen
Mrs. Kissel .... Meg Wyllie
Kissel Brothers .... Osmond Brothers

Henry T. Coe .... Hedley Mattingly
Othello .... Vernett Allen III
Buck Coulter (1963) .... Michael Witney
Linc Murdock .... Charles Bronson

This adventure series followed a young boy on a westward-bound wagon train in 1849. Twelve-year-old Jaimie was surrounded by a colorful cast of characters, not the least of whom was his stovepipe-hatted father, an irresponsible scalawag M.D. (they had sneaked out of Paducah, Kentucky, just ahead of their creditors to join the wagon train). Traveling with the McPheeterses in the train was 17-year-old Jenny, a rather sexy orphan; the God-fearin' Kissel family (whose children, Micah, Leviticus, Deuteronomy, and Lamentations, were portrayed by the Osmond Brothers); and blue-blooded Henry T. Coe and his valet, Othello. Continual danger was posed by the Bible-quoting but cunning thief Murrel, and his shady partner, Baggott.

Adventure followed as the wagons made their way north to St. Louis, west across the North Platte River to Ft. Bridger, down to Salt Lake City, across the Humboldt Sink and the Sierra Nevada to the Feather River and finally the gold fields of California! Wagonmaster Buck Coulter lasted only a few weeks, until he was trampled to death in the process of saving Jaimie's life. Linc Murdock, a powerful but troubled man, then became the wagonmaster for the remainder of the show's single-season journey.

Based on Robert Lewis Taylor's 1958 Pulitzer Prize-winning novel of the same name.

TREASURE HUNT, see *What's It Worth?*

TREASURE HUNT (*Quiz/Audience Participation*)
FIRST TELECAST: *September 7, 1956*
LAST TELECAST: *June 17, 1958*
BROADCAST HISTORY:
Sep 1956–May 1957, ABC Fri 9:00–9:30
Dec 1957–Jun 1958, NBC Tue 7:30–8:00
EMCEE:
Jan Murray
ASSISTANT:
Marian Stafford (1956–1957, 1958)
Greta Thyssen (1957–1958)

Contestants on *Treasure Hunt*, usually one man and one woman, were asked a series of questions on a designated topic and got $50 for each correct answer. When one of the contestants had defeated the other in the quiz portion of the program, he won the opportunity to go on a "treasure hunt." There were a number of treasure chests on the stage and the winning contestant got to pick one. Whatever was in the chest went to the contestant. The prizes in the chests were not all winners. Everything from a head of cabbage to a check for a large sum of money was contained in various chests. The jackpot check in the ABC version was a flat $25,000. When NBC picked up *Treasure Hunt* for a nighttime version (NBC had begun airing it as a daytime show in August 1957) the jackpot check was a basic $10,000 plus $1,000 for each week that it was not discovered.

Jan Murray's sexy assistant, clad in a scanty pirate costume, was referred to on the show as the Pirate Girl. Marian Stafford was the Pirate Girl when the series was on ABC. Greta Thyssen was the first NBC nighttime pirate girl. When she left the show in January 1958, Marian, who had replaced Pat White in the daytime version in December, returned to the nighttime version as well.

Fourteen years after *Treasure Hunt* departed NBC's daytime lineup in December 1959, Chuck Barris purchased the rights to the title and brought out a syndicated series titled *The New Treasure Hunt*, emceed by Geoff Edwards. There was no quiz, only the opportunity for two contestants to pick the treasure chest with the $25,000 check. It was played to take advantage of the emotions of the contestants, and Barris was proud of the fact that one winner actually passed out on the stage. *The New Treasure Hunt* ran from 1973 to 1976.

TREASURE QUEST (*Quiz*)
FIRST TELECAST: *April 24, 1949*
LAST TELECAST: *September 2, 1949*
BROADCAST HISTORY:
Apr 1949–Jun 1949, ABC Sun 9:30–10:00
Jun 1949–Sep 1949, ABC Fri 8:30–9:00
HOST:
John Weigel

Quiz show in which contestants were required to identify various locations, from visual and verbal clues, with an expense-paid trip as prize. From Chicago.

Known during its first two weeks as *Bon Voyage*.

TREASURES IN YOUR HOME: THE WORLD OF COLLECTING (*Appraisal*)
FIRST TELECAST: *August 9, 1999*
LAST TELECAST: *July 26, 2000*
BROADCAST HISTORY:
Aug 1999–Jan 2000, PAX Mon–Fri 7:00–8:00
Jan 2000–Mar 2000, PAX Mon–Fri 7:30–8:00
Apr 2000–Jul 2000, PAX Mon–Fri 11:30–midnight
HOST:
John Burke
WEB PRODUCER:
Joshua Duenke

Some of the people who appeared with their collectibles on *Treasures in Your Home* related the circumstances under which they had acquired them, while others provided information on how to collect. What was unusual about this series was that home viewers could bid on items that the owners were willing to sell—on the show's Internet Web site—and could buy both the originals and replicas. The current high bid was displayed on screen. Among the frequent visitors were certified appraisers John Bruno and Cathy. Host Burke also asked collectible trivia questions and people who called in (and/or participated on the show's Web site) with the correct answers could win small prizes.

The same people produced *Collecting Across America* for PBS.

TREASURY MEN IN ACTION (*Crime Drama*)
FIRST TELECAST: *September 11, 1950*
LAST TELECAST: *September 30, 1955*
BROADCAST HISTORY:
Sep 1950–Dec 1950, ABC Mon 8:00–8:30
Apr 1951–Apr 1954, NBC Thu 8:30–9:00 (OS)
Oct 1954–Jun 1955, ABC Thu 8:30–9:00
Jun 1955–Sep 1955, ABC Fri 8:30–9:00
CAST:
The Chief .... Walter Greaza

Action dramas based on actual cases from the files of the U.S. Treasury Department and telecast live. Walter Greaza portrayed the chief of whatever division was involved in each week's case, running to earth such assorted scoundrels as smugglers, counterfeiters, gunrunners, tax evaders (a favorite!), and moonshiners. The program invariably ended with the moral that the government always wins, and thereby received several awards and commendations from official agencies for its public service. Actual government officials sometimes appeared on the show.

The supporting cast varied from week to week, but over the years included such names as Lee Marvin, Grace Kelly, Jason Robards, Jr., James Dean, Cliff Robertson, Jack Klugman, and Charles Bronson.

TREMORS (*Science Fiction*)

BROADCAST HISTORY:

Sci-Fi Channel
60 minutes
Original episodes: *2003–*
Premiered: *March 27, 2003*

CAST:

Burt Gummer .... Michael Gross
Tyler Reed .... Victor Browne
Jodi Chang .... Lela Lee
Nancy Sterngood .... Marcia Strassman
Rosalita Sanchez .... Gladise Jimenez
W. D. Twitchell .... Dean Norris

Hunky young Tyler was on his way to a desolate town in the Nevada desert to take over a tour business he had just bought when his car was swallowed by a giant worm. That was his first clue that something was odd about the town of Perfection. Rescuing Tyler from the same fate as his old Chevy was lanky survivalist Burt, who roared up in his camouflaged pickup truck and blasted the beast with a concussion grenade. Couldn't kill it, he explained, because it was an "endangered species" protected by the U.S. government. Tyler soon met the other oddballs in the tiny town: Jodi, the fast-talking, all-business manager of the general store, Rosalita, a sexy, resourceful ex–Las Vegas showgirl who ran a struggling local ranch, Nancy, a sweet but aging flower child who made her living creating ceramic action figures and hood ornaments modeled on heavily armed Burt and the monsters that threatened the town, and Twitchell, the fat, bossy agent from the Department of the Interior who kept watch over Perfection and its "endangered monsters."

As for that big worm, it was a Graboid called El Blanco—a 30-foot-long, sightless eating machine that roared around just under the surface of the ground lunging up from time to time to swallow unsuspecting animals, people or sometimes cars. Everyone in Perfection was equipped with a watchlike device that detected when El Blanco was heading for them, so they could jump onto the roof of a building or some other safe height (which was often). They also had to watch out for bipedal Shriekers, who morphed from the wormlike Graboids, and winged AssBlasters, who morphed from Shriekers and who carried the eggs of new Graboids, thus completing the monsters' life cycle. The citizens of Perfection treated these monsters and the havoc they wreaked with nonchalance, which gave the series a loony quality and left Tyler a little perplexed ("Aren't you guys kinda pushin' it out here?").

Tremors was based on the 1990 cult movie starring Kevin Bacon and Michael Gross. Gross also appeared in several made-for-video sequels.

TRIAL AND ERROR (*Situation Comedy*)

FIRST TELECAST: *March 15, 1988*
LAST TELECAST: *March 29, 1988*
BROADCAST HISTORY:

Mar 1988, CBS Tue 8:00–8:30

CAST:

John Hernandez .... Eddie Velez
Tony Rivera .... Paul Rodriguez
Bob Adams .... John de Lancie
Rhonda .... Debbie Shapiro
Edmund Kittle .... Stephen Elliott
Lisa .... Susan Saldivar

These two Hispanics had grown up together in the barrio in East L.A., and now they were roommates, but John and Tony had totally different approaches to life. Tony was a free spirit with limited financial aspirations, making a living selling T-shirts from a stand on Olvera Street near downtown Los Angeles. John, on the other hand, was recently graduated from law school and had joined the prestigious law firm of Kittle, Barnes, Fletcher & Gray. Although he disliked being the token Hispanic in the firm, and had to deal with condescending fellow attorney Bob Adams, John had the sincere support of senior partner Edmund Kittle. John's secretary, Rhonda, who had been with the firm for several years, knew much more about the internal politics and pecking order than he did. John and Tony were friends and they were roommates, but many were the times when Tony's blue-collar presence conflicted with, and potentially embarrassed, John's pinstripe-suited legal world.

TRIALS OF O'BRIEN, THE (*Legal Drama*)

FIRST TELECAST: *September 18, 1965*
LAST TELECAST: *May 6, 1966*
BROADCAST HISTORY:

Sep 1965–Nov 1965, CBS Sat 8:30–9:30
Dec 1965–May 1966, CBS Fri 10:00–11:00

CAST:

Daniel J. O'Brien .... Peter Falk
Katie .... Joanna Barnes
The Great McGonigle .... David Burns
Miss G. .... Elaine Stritch
Margaret .... Ilka Chase
Lt. Garrison .... Dolph Sweet

The Trials of O'Brien were not confined to those that took place in the court of law. Daniel J. O'Brien was a very talented—and expensive—New York attorney whose personal life was almost more trying than his professional life. He was behind in the rent on his luxurious penthouse apartment, behind in alimony payments to his beautiful ex-wife, Katie, and was one of the most unsuccessful gamblers in the city. Somehow, no matter how fast the money came in, it went out just a little bit faster. His secretary, Miss G., tried to help him maintain a better financial equilibrium, but it never quite worked out. The cases in this series were treated seriously, but O'Brien's personal problems were not. In certain ways, Peter Falk's characterization of O'Brien had parallels with his much more successful portrayal of Columbo in the 1970s. Both were extremely good at their jobs but rather sloppy and disorganized when it came to their personal lives.

TRIALS OF ROSIE O'NEILL, THE (*Legal Drama*)
FIRST TELECAST: *September 17, 1990*
LAST TELECAST: *May 30, 1992*
BROADCAST HISTORY:
Sep 1990–Jan 1992, CBS Mon 10:00–11:00
Jun 1991–Jul 1991, CBS Sun 10:00–11:00
Jul 1991–Dec 1991, CBS Thu 9:00–10:00
Apr 1992–May 1992, CBS Sat 10:00–11:00
CAST:
Fiona Rose "Rosie" O'Neill .... Sharon Gless
Hank Mitchell .... Dorian Harewood
Ben Meyer .... Ron Rifkin
Charlotte O'Neill .... Georgann Johnson
Doreen Morrison .... Lisa Banes
Kim Ginty (age 16) .... Lisa Rieffel
Barbara Navis .... Bridget Gless
Carole Kravitz .... Elaine Kagan
Udell Correy, III .... Geoffrey Lower
Pete Ramos (1990) .... Tony Perez
George Shaughnessy (1990–1991) ...... Al Pugliese
**D.A. Linda Vargas* .... Marisa Redanty
**D.A. Deb Grant (1990–1991)* .... Meg Foster
Walter Kovatch (1991–1992) .... Edward Asner
Valerie Whittaker (1991) .... Dayna Winston
Mason Pappas (1991) .... Victor Bevine
**D.A. Suzanne Ramey (1991–1992)* .... Karen Austin
Peter Donovan (1992) .... Robert Wagner
* Occasional
THEME:
"I Wish I Knew," written by Carole King and performed by Melissa Manchester during first season, instrumental thereafter

Rosie O'Neill was a successful, recently divorced 43-year-old attorney who had left the lucrative Beverly Hills law practice she had shared with her ex-husband to become a public defender. Rosie's life was one of constant anguish. Her new career did not sit well with either her friends or family, who couldn't understand why she would take such a frustrating low-paying job, and the personnel in the Los Angeles County Public Defenders Office thought she was slumming. Rosie's family included Charlotte, her conservative, socially prominent mother; Doreen, her married sister; and Kim, her ex-stepdaughter. Kim had grown so close to Rosie that, when she had trouble at home with her father's young third wife early in the second season, she moved in with Rosie.

The office staff consisted of Ben, Rosie's boss; Hank, the black public defender with whom she shared an office; Carole, the department secretary; Barbara, the young clerk (played by Ms. Gless' niece) who worked part time while attending law school; Udell, Mason, and Valerie, fellow public defenders; and investigators Pete, George, and, beginning in the fall of 1991, Walter Kovatch. Kovatch, a retired 35-year-veteran of the police force, was a hard-nosed, conservative constantly at odds with liberal Rosie's attitudes about her clients.

Most episodes of the series opened with neurotic Rosie in her analyst's office, talking about personal and professional problems she was trying to work out. The part of the analyst, always seen from the rear, was played by series producer Barney Rosenzweig, who had also produced Ms. Gless' previous series *Cagney & Lacey*. The two were living together when *Rosie* premiered, and they were married in the spring of 1991. Robert Wagner joined the show in 1992 in an attempt to save it from cancellation. He played suave Peter Donovan, the new editor of the *Los Angeles Chronicle* who became Rosie's lover. It became a bittersweet relationship for her when she discovered he was not divorced from his wife.

TRIBECA (*Dramatic Anthology*)
FIRST TELECAST: *March 23, 1993*
LAST TELECAST: *September 5, 1993*
BROADCAST HISTORY:
Mar 1993–May 1993, FOX Tue 9:00–10:00
Jul 1993–Sep 1993, FOX Sun 10:00–11:00
CAST:
Harry Arsharsky .... Philip Bosco
Off. Carleton Thomas .... Joe Morton

Manhattan provided the backdrop for this anthology series that might be a drama one week and a comedy the next. There were two peripheral characters who gave the series a little continuity—Harry, the understanding, fatherly owner of Muffin's Coffee House, and his friend Carleton, a mounted policeman for the N.Y.P.D. whose beat was the trendy Tribeca neighborhood where Muffin's was located. Although they might have some involvement in the weekly story lines, for the most part they were observers rather than participants. Larry Fishburne, Peter Boyle, Kathleen Quinlan, Ernie Hudson, Richard Kiley, Betty Buckley, Melanie Mayron, and Eli Wallach were some of the actors featured in individual episodes. Despite positive reviews and the added publicity value of having Robert De Niro as one of the executive producers, *Tribeca* never attracted much of an audience and only seven episodes were produced.

TRIGGER HAPPY TV (*Comedy*)
BROADCAST HISTORY:
Comedy Central
30 minutes
Original episodes: *2002–*
Premiered: *August 22, 2002*
REGULARS:
Dom Joly
Sam Cadman

British street comedy series, full of brief sight gags and candid camera bits, set to a rock-music soundtrack. Guest performers included Tim Rice, Alice Cooper, Bill Wyman, Buzz Aldrin, and Lord Bath.

TRINITY (*Drama*)
FIRST TELECAST: *October 16, 1998*
LAST TELECAST: *November 6, 1998*
BROADCAST HISTORY:
Oct 1998–Nov 1998, NBC Fri 9:00–10:00
CASTS:
Det. Bobby McCallister .... Justin Louis
Clarissa McCallister .... Kim Raver
Liam McCallister .... Sam Trammell
Kevin McCallister .... Tate Donovan
Fiona McCallister .... Charlotte Ross
Amanda McCallister .... Bonnie Root
Eileen McCallister .... Jill Clayburgh
Simon McCallister .... John Spencer
Det. Patricia Damiana .... Alicia Coppola

There were McCallisters of every stripe in this drama about a big, squabbling, inner-city Irish family. Bobby was the straight-arrow cop, trying to keep the family together while working the mean streets of New York City's Hell's Kitchen. His siblings were Liam, a wiry young operator who was ostensibly a union organizer but apparently was in the pocket of organized crime; Kevin, a curly-haired young priest struggling with his conscience; "good" sister Fiona, a successful stockbroker attracted to all the wrong men; and "bad" sister Amanda, a pregnant, frightened drug addict. They gathered weekly for dinner at the home of their parents, Eileen and Simon, who sighed a lot. A sixth sibling, teenager Mikey, had been killed several years earlier under mysterious circumstances. The only non-McCallister regularly seen was Det. Damiana, Bobby's partner, who naturally aroused the jealousy of Bobby's unhappy wife Clarissa, who took to hanging out with shifty Liam.

TROPICAL PUNCH (*Police Comedy*)
FIRST TELECAST: *July 11, 1993*
LAST TELECAST: *August 15, 1993*
BROADCAST HISTORY:
Jul 1993–Aug 1993, FOX Sun 7:45–8:00
CAST:
Capt. Mike Morgan .... Adam West
Det. Tom McCormick .... Billy Morrissette
Det. Al Hamoki .... Peter Navy Tuiasosopo
Cash .... Will MacMillan

A silly spoof of *Hawaii Five-O,* including a similar theme and opening montage. Morgan headed the Tropical Punch unit of the Honolulu Police Department. He was prone to falling asleep on the job and liked to go undercover but always looked ridiculous and stood out like a sore thumb. The lines were pretty hard to take—when he saw a Ninja threatening a frightened man, he asked the victim. "Did you order from Benihana?" Teamed with Morgan were Hamoki, his burly muscleman, and Tommy, a pretentious shrimp. When they caught the perpetrator, Morgan's stock line was "Tom, cuff 'em, book 'em)" (shades of *Hawaii Five-O*'s "Book 'em, Danno").

Tropical Punch was one of the elements of Fox's *Danger Theatre.*

TROUBLE WITH FATHER, syndicated title for *Stu Erwin Show, The*

TROUBLE WITH LARRY, THE (*Situation Comedy*)
FIRST TELECAST: *August 25, 1993*
LAST TELECAST: *September 8, 1993*
BROADCAST HISTORY:
Aug 1993–Sep 1993, CBS Wed 8:00–8:30
CAST:
Larry Burton .... Bronson Pinchot
Sally Easden Burton Flatt .... Shanna Reed
Gabriella Easden .... Courteney Cox
Boyd Flatt .... Perry King
Lindsay Flatt (age 9) .... Alex McKenna

Sally was living a quiet life in Syracuse, New York, with her very sensible, very predictable, very reliable, and very boring second husband, Boyd, along with Lindsay, her nine-year-old daughter from her first marriage. Sally's world was seriously disrupted when her first husband, Larry, who had been carried off by baboons during their African honeymoon and presumed dead, showed up in Syracuse after returning to America on a tramp steamer. Larry was everything Boyd was not—childlike, spontaneous, entertaining, adventuresome, and fun. After helping Sally save the lease on an art gallery she ran with her sexy younger sister, Gabriella, Larry talked his way into living temporarily with his ex-wife and her family. Boyd was uncomfortable with the manic Larry, Lindsay loved him, Gabriella hated him, and Sally wasn't sure how she felt about him.

CBS gave this series a head start on the 1993–1994 season by premiering it in late August. Unfortunately, the head start didn't help much. After scathing reviews and three weeks of low ratings, *The Trouble with Larry* left the air before the season of which it was supposed to be a part had even begun.

TROUBLE WITH NORMAL, THE (*Situation Comedy*)
FIRST TELECAST: *October 6, 2000*
LAST TELECAST: *November 10, 2000*
BROADCAST HISTORY:
Oct 2000–Nov 2000, ABC Fri 8:00–8:30
CAST:
Bob Wexler .... David Krumholtz
Max Perch .... Brad Raider
Zack Mango .... Jon Cryer
Stansfield Schlick .... Larry Joe Campbell
Claire Garletti .... Paget Brewster
Gary .... Jim Beaver
Lila .... Patricia Belcher

Paranoia was played for laughs in this pratfall sitcom, which might have been called *The Four Stooges.* Bob was a youthful, shaggy-haired Manhattan apartment dweller who thought everyone was spying on him—including his creepy neighbor Zack. Bob's pal Max, who worked at a spy goods store, thought so, too, so together they set up a trap and caught both Zack and his pudgy mailman friend Stansfield, who themselves were world-class neurotics (Zack so much so that he kept changing his last name to throw people off). After a certain amount of good-natured bumbling, the four found themselves in the basement of a local church attending a "neurotics support group" led by cute, sensible therapist Claire, who tried to convince them that the world was not spying on them. But of course it was—there were cameras in the ATMs, credit card companies knew everything they bought, HMOs kept records of their most intimate ailments. The dysfunctional four became so dependent on "normal" Claire that they started hanging out at her apartment, creating a whole new kind of singles gang.

TROUBLESHOOTERS (*Adventure*)
FIRST TELECAST: *September 11, 1959*
LAST TELECAST: *June 17, 1960*
BROADCAST HISTORY:
Sep 1959–Jun 1960, NBC Fri 8:00–8:30
CAST:
Kodiak .... Keenan Wynn
Frank Dugan .... Bob Mathias
Scotty .... Bob Fortier
Skinner .... Carey Loftin
Jim .... Bob Harris
Slats .... Chet Allen

The number-one troubleshooter of the Stenrud Corporation, a large heavy-construction firm specializing in both domestic and foreign building projects, was a grizzled old veteran named Kodiak. He had held that post for five years, during which time he had coped with the problems involved in building highways, dams, airfields, skyscrapers, and atomic installations all over the world. The pace had started to become too much for him to take, and he was in the slow process of training his assistant, Frank Dugan, to take over. Frank was all the things that Kodiak was not—well educated, socially polished, soft-spoken, and innocent of the evil ways of the world. As the two of them traveled from assignment to assignment they learned from each other and acquired qualities that would stand them in good stead in the future. Kodiak became somewhat less gruff and uncivilized and Frank became stronger and more assertive. Scotty, Skinner, Jim, and Slats were crew members who made frequent appearances.

TRUCKIN' U.S.A. (*Instruction*)

BROADCAST HISTORY:

The Nashville Network
30 minutes
Produced: *1989–1994*
Premiered: *April 2, 1989*

HOST:

Ed Bruce

A weekend series for the truck enthusiast, featuring trucking jamborees, museums, technical tips, and restorations.

TRUE, syndicated title for *General Electric True*

TRUE BLUE (*Police Drama*)

FIRST TELECAST: *December 3, 1989*
LAST TELECAST: *April 22, 1990*
BROADCAST HISTORY:

Dec 1989, NBC Sun 9:00–11:00
Dec 1989–Feb 1990, NBC Fri 9:00–10:00
Apr 1990, NBC Sun 8:00–9:00

CAST:

Officer Bobby Traverso .... John Bolger
Officer Jessica Haley .... Ally Walker
Officer Geno Toffenelli .... Nestor Serrano
Officer David Odom .... Darnell Williams
Officer Frankie Avila .... Eddie Velez
Officer Casey Pierce................... Grant Show
Sgt. Andy Wojeski .... Timothy Van Patten
Sgt. Mike Duffy...................... Dick Latessa
Officer Red Tollin.................. Leo Bermester
Connie Tollin .... Annie Golden
Lt. Bill Triplett .... Beau William Starr
Yuri .... Elya Baskin
Capt. Motte............................. Joe Lisi
Dep. Chief Servino .... Victor Arnold

The Emergency Services Unit of the New York City Police Dept. was glorified in this action-packed, reality-based hour. Blue ESU trucks constantly cruised the city in order to be first on the scene when terrorists, hostage-takers, and other violent criminals struck, or when someone needed immediate help—whether it was a "jumper," a child stuck in an elevator shaft, or a retarded man who had decided to make friends with the lions inside their cage at the city zoo. Besides the usual wailing sirens, the series placed a great deal of emphasis on "humanizing" the members of the team: Bobby, the handsome cop separated from his wife but uncomfortable being partnered with attractive Jessy, who was divorced and had a six-year-old daughter; Geno, the creepy-looking guy who was a master of disguises (he talked one deranged Elvis fan out of his gun by masquerading as the King himself); Odom, the master lock picker; Frankie, the marksman and mechanical wizard, who handled the team's high-tech robot Sammy III (wonder what happened to Sammy I and Sammy II?); Andy, the earnest young husband trying to father a child; Mike, the older, experienced member afraid of being involuntarily "retired"; Red, the Southern good ol' boy who handled Bird, the team's German shepherd; Casey, the young hunk; and Lt. Triplett, the fatherly boss. Yuri was a civilian who seemed to turn up at the scene of every disaster with his camera, to the team's initial suspicion and later, amusement.

Filmed on location in New York, *True Blue* was co-produced by Sonny Grosso, a 20-year veteran of the NYPD and partner of "Popeye" Doyle on the famous French Connection case.

TRUE COLORS (*Situation Comedy*)

FIRST TELECAST: *September 2, 1990*
LAST TELECAST: *August 23, 1992*
BROADCAST HISTORY:

Sep 1990, FOX Sun 8:30–9:00
Sep 1990–Jun 1991, FOX Sun 7:00–7:30
Jun 1991–Sep 1991, FOX Thu 8:30–9:00
Sep 1991–Jun 1992, FOX Sun 7:00–7:30
Jun 1992–Aug 1992, FOX Sun 7:30–8:00

CAST:

Ron Freeman (1990–1991) .... Frankie Faison
Ron Freeman (1991–1992)........... Cleavon Little
Terry Freeman (age 17) .... Claude Brooks
Lester Freeman (14) .... Adam Jeffries
Ellen Davis Freeman............. Stephanie Faracy
Katie Davis (15).............. Brigid Conley Walsh
Sara Bower......................... Nancy Walker
Twist (Robert) (1992) .... Norman D. Golden II

In the on-air promotional announcements for this interracial series, Fox proclaimed "It Ain't *The Brady Bunch*" and they were certainly right. Ron was a widowed black dentist with two teenage sons, and Ellen was a divorced white kindergarten teacher with a teenage daughter. They were newly married and living together in Ron's home in Baltimore. The three kids were very different—Terry, an uptight, conservative yuppie; Lester, a jive-talking free spirit; and Katie, a socially conscious environmental activist. Everyone was trying to make this unusual family work and they probably would have had less trouble were it not for the one other member of the household. Ellen's mother, Sara, was opinionated, contentious, and less than thrilled with her new son-in-law. While Ron and Ellen tried to smooth things over, Sara kept stirring them up. Nothing Ron did was right with her. Fortunately, as time went on, wisecracking Sara did develop a fondness for her step-grandchildren, particularly Lester. When *True Colors* began its second season Terry, who had graduated from high school, was attending Marshall State University.

TRUE DETECTIVES (*Detective*)

FIRST TELECAST: *December 28, 1990*
LAST TELECAST: *July 12, 1991*
BROADCAST HISTORY:

Dec 1990, CBS Fri 8:00–9:00
Mar 1991–Apr 1991, CBS Fri 10:00–11:00
Jun 1991–Jul 1991, CBS Fri 8:30–9:00

HOST:

Gregory Harrison

In the summer of 1990 CBS had premiered *Top Cops*, a series documenting the activities of real-life police officers. Five months later this series, documenting the exploits of real-life detectives, premiered. Hosted by Gregory Harrison, *True Detectives* told stories of professional and amateur detectives, with dramatic reenactments of the mysteries they had solved. Among them were a pharmacist who went undercover to expose a group of drug-dealing physicians, a mother working with the D.A.'s office to find her kidnapped daughter, a man tracking down the hit-and-run driver who killed his sister, and a communicable disease expert tracing the source of a rare tropical virus.

TRUTH OR CONSEQUENCES (*Quiz/Audience Participation*)

FIRST TELECAST: *September 7, 1950*
LAST TELECAST: *June 6, 1958*
BROADCAST HISTORY:

Sep 1950–May 1951, CBS Thu 10:00–10:30
May 1954–Sep 1955, NBC Tue 10:00–10:30
Sep 1955–Sep 1956, NBC Fri 8:00–8:30
Dec 1957–Jun 1958, NBC Fri 7:30–8:00

EMCEE:

Ralph Edwards (1950–1951)
Jack Bailey (1954–1956)
Steve Dunne (1957–1958)

Truth or Consequences had originally aired in 1940 as an NBC radio program with its creator, Ralph Edwards, as the emcee. A decade later it moved to television, on CBS, with its format and emcee unchanged. Contestants on the show were asked silly trick questions which they almost invariably failed to answer correctly. If they answered incorrectly, or failed to come up with any answer in a short time, Beulah the Buzzer went off. The emcee then told them that since they had failed to tell the truth, they would have to pay the consequences. Consequences consisted of elaborate stunts, some done in the studio and others done outside, some completed on that week's episode and others taking a week or more and requiring the contestant to return when the stunt was completed. Some of the stunts were funny, but more often they were also embarrassing, and occasionally they were sentimental (as when long-separated relatives were reunited within the context of the stunt).

The original TV version of this series, with Edwards as host, lasted only a single season. When it returned three years later on NBC, Jack Bailey was the emcee, later replaced by Steve Dunne. NBC aired a daytime version of the show from 1956 until 1965, first with Jack Bailey as host, succeeded by Bob Barker at the end of 1956. Barker made a career of the show after that, remaining with it through the rest of the daytime run and on into the original syndicated run from 1966 to 1974. A short-lived syndicated revival in 1977–1978 was emceed by Bob Hilton.

A decade later, in the fall of 1987, comic Larry Anderson turned up as the emcee of yet another syndicated *Truth or Consequences*. This version, in which the emcee was assisted by Murray (the Unknown Comic) Langston, quickly faded from the airwaves.

TRY AND DO IT (*Variety/Audience Participation*)

FIRST TELECAST: *July 4, 1948*
LAST TELECAST: *September 5, 1948*
BROADCAST HISTORY:

Jul 1948–Sep 1948, NBC Sun 8:30–9:00

HOST:

Jack Bright

REGULARS:

Thomas Leander Jones' Brass Band

Audience-participation show in which people from the studio audience performed various stunts—whistling through a mouthful of crackers, lacing up a right shoe on the left foot, etc. The program was set in a picnic ground, with Thomas Leander Jones's band providing schmaltzy music from an old-fashioned bandstand.

TUCKER (*Situation Comedy*)

FIRST TELECAST: *October 2, 2000*
LAST TELECAST: *October 23, 2000*
BROADCAST HISTORY:

Oct 2000, NBC Mon 8:30–9:00

CAST:

Tucker Pierce (age 14).............. Eli Marienthal
Jeannie Pierce .... Noelle Beck
Claire Wennick........................ Katey Sagal
Jimmy Wennick .... Casey Sander
Leon Wennick (15)............... Nathan Lawrence
McKenna Reed (15) .... Alison Lohman
Kenickie .... Andrew Lawrence

Tucker was a teenager whose life was seriously disrupted when he and his newly divorced mom were forced to move in with her bossy fussbudget sister, in the latter's big suburban house. Jeannie was his worrywart mom and Claire his aunt, who never let them forget how generous she was even while making Jeannie sleep on the couch (so she wouldn't have to give up her sewing room) and obsessing about her figurines. Uncle Jimmy, a pilot for Trans Globe Airlines, was a little more mellow, but their son Leon was a holy terror, fixated on wrestling (which he practiced by continually jumping on Tucker) and his collection of human hair. Tucker, who narrated, was a bright and outgoing lad who made the most of things and concocted many schemes, none of which seemed to work out. One bright spot was McKenna, a sexy neighbor kid, who alternately teased and flirted with him. Kenickie was a classmate.

NBC pulled the low-rated sitcom after four episodes; however, nine additional episodes were aired in the middle of the night March 6–27, 2001.

TUCKER'S WITCH (*Detective Drama*)

FIRST TELECAST: *October 6, 1982*
LAST TELECAST: *August 8, 1983*
BROADCAST HISTORY:

Oct 1982–Nov 1982, CBS Wed 10:00–11:00
Mar 1983–Jun 1983, CBS Thu 10:00–11:00
Jul 1983–Aug 1983, CBS Mon 9:00–10:00

CAST:

Rick Tucker .... Tim Matheson
Amanda Tucker .... Catherine Hicks
Ellen Hobbes .... Barbara Barrie
Lt. Sean Fisk .... Bill Morey
Marcia Fulbright .... Alfre Woodard
Stucky, the mortician .... Duncan Ross

Mix a little bit of *Mr. & Mrs. North* with a dash of *Bewitched* and you know what *Tucker's Witch* was like. Rick and Amanda Tucker were husband-and-wife partners in a private-detective agency. He was the conventional detective, working with evidence and utilizing his analytical skills, while she relied on her "intuition." In Amanda's case, however, there was a pretty substantial basis for her hunches, since she resorted to witchcraft for clues. Unfortunately, her ability to use witchcraft properly to solve cases was not always successful, since some of her spells didn't work exactly as planned, even with the help of her Siamese cat, Dickens, and the occasional assistance of her mother, Ellen, who was also a witch. Marcia was the Tuckers' secretary and Lt. Fisk the homicide detective with whom they were often at odds.

TUGBOAT ANNIE, see *Adventures of Tugboat Annie, The*

TURKS (*Police Drama*)

FIRST TELECAST: *January 21, 1999*
LAST TELECAST: *April 23, 1999*
BROADCAST HISTORY:
Jan 1999–Apr 1999, CBS Thu 9:00–10:00
Apr 1999, CBS Fri 9:00–10:00
CAST:
Sgt. Joe Turk .... William Devane
Off. Mike Turk .... David Cubitt
Off. Joey Turk .... Matthew John Armstrong
Paul Turk .... Michael Muhney
Mary Turk .... Helen Carey
Erin Turk .... Sarah Trigger
Ginny Antonucci .... Ashley Crow
Mark Turk .... Adam Tanguay
Off. Cliff Fowler .... Paul Adelstein
Off. Walt Keefer .... Rich Komenich
Donny (1999) .... Hank Johnston
Teri Gordon .... Kate Walsh
Off. Leigh Dixon .... Jacqueline Williams
Carolyn Fenwick .... Lisa Brenner
Richard Fenwick .... Dan Conway
Father Tom .... Tim Grimm
Christa Pierce .... Jennifer Anglin

This rather violent serial drama was about a family of Irish cops in Chicago. Joe, the patriarch, was a veteran desk sergeant in the 29th Precinct who was trying to salvage his failing marriage to Mary. Two of Joe's sons were cops working in his precinct—ambitious Mike, married to Erin, with a young son, Mark, and single Joey, whose affair with Teri ran hot and cold. Youngest son Paul had a gambling problem, and had quit college and become a stock trader to try to pay off his gambling debts. Paul had an affair with Carolyn, the daughter of his boss Richard, as well as with Richard's shark attorney Christa. Meanwhile, guilt-ridden Joe dallied with Ginny, a waitress at Emmits, the bar where the cops hung out. The April 1999 season finale was a cliffhanger which was never resolved, since the series was canceled. Mary miscarried, and Joey was last seen entering an abortion clinic he was assigned to protect just as a pipe bomb was tossed inside and exploded.

TURN BEN STEIN ON (*Discussion*)

BROADCAST HISTORY:
Comedy Central
30 minutes
Original episodes: *1999–2001*
Premiered: *December 2, 1999*
HOST:
Ben Stein

Witty writer and savant Ben Stein chatted with "pleasant and interesting people" on this low-key discussion show. Among them were actors Carl Reiner, Bob Saget, and Katy Wagner, musician Grace Slick, journalist Carl Bernstein, and futurist/author Alvin Toffler. Subjects tended to be offbeat, such as scientist Bill Nye and model Jody Ann Paterson talking about "the science of sex and attraction." Keeping costs low, Ben's cohost was his dog Puppy Wuppy.

TURN IT UP (*Quiz/Audience Participation*)

BROADCAST HISTORY:
MTV
30 minutes
Produced: *1990*
Premiered: *June 30, 1990*
HOST:
Jordan Brady

A loud rock 'n' roll game show in which contestants answered music-trivia questions. Telecast weeknights in the early evening on MTV.

TURN OF FATE, A, see *Alcoa Theatre* and *Goodyear TV Playhouse*

TURNABOUT (*Situation Comedy*)

FIRST TELECAST: *January 26, 1979*
LAST TELECAST: *March 23, 1979*
BROADCAST HISTORY:
Jan 1979–Feb 1979, NBC Fri 9:00–9:30
Feb 1979–Mar 1979, NBC Fri 9:30–10:00
CAST:
Sam Alston .... John Schuck
Penny Alston .... Sharon Gless
Jack Overmeyer .... Richard Stahl
Judy Overmeyer .... Bobbi Jordan
Geoffrey St. James .... James Sikking
Al Brennan .... Bruce Kirby

Everyone has, at one time or another, wished that they could change places with somebody else, and lead that other person's life. That was the wish that got Sam and Penny Alston into so much trouble. Over Sam's objections, Penny had purchased a small Buddha-like statue from a gypsy who claimed it had magic powers. Later, in a moment of boredom, the couple chanced to wish they could change places with each other and—*voilá!* the statue granted them their wish. While they slept, Sam's spirit moved into Penny's body and vice versa. Finding out the next morning that they had exchanged bodies was quite a shock—and that was only the beginning. Trying to maintain the illusion of normalcy, until they could get the statue to switch them back to their own bodies, was not easy. Sam (in Penny's body) had to learn all about the cosmetics industry, since she was an executive working for Geoffrey St. James; and Penny (in Sam's body) had to act the part of a gruff sportswriter to deal with boss Al Brennan. They also had personal habits and gestures that seemed inappropriate in their new bodies. Sam liked to smoke cigars and Penny was very dainty, among other things. The people most likely to notice the sudden "turnabout" were their nosy neighbors, the Overmeyers.

Based on the novel by Thorne Smith, who was also the author of the books on which another whimsical series, *Topper*, was based. The novel was also made into a movie, in 1940.

TURNER CLASSIC MOVIES (Network) (*Cable Movie Network*)

LAUNCHED:
April 14, 1994

SUBSCRIBERS (JAN. 2003):
63.9 million (60% U.S.)

A 24-hour commercial-free movie channel featuring older films made between the 1930s and the 1960s. Some were B-movies (viewers may have been surprised to learn that Dennis Morgan made so many films), but others featured stars like Bing Crosby, Fred Astaire, and Gregory Peck. TCM was launched by cable mogul Ted Turner to compete with American Movie Classics, utilizing the vast film library owned by Turner's companies.

As AMC "modernized" its schedule, TCM (and, to some extent, Fox Movie Channel) became the TV home of older classics, many from the '30s and '40s and some even older (Harold Lloyd silent films, Fritz Lang's *Metropolis*).

TURNING POINT (*Dramatic Anthology*)

FIRST TELECAST: *April 12, 1958*
LAST TELECAST: *Oct 4, 1958*
BROADCAST HISTORY:
Apr 1958–Oct 1958, NBC Sat 9:30–10:00

This was a collection of filmed reruns from other anthology series, with the addition of two unsold pilots for projected (but never scheduled) dramatic series.

TURNING POINT (*Documentary Newsmagazine*)

FIRST TELECAST: *March 9, 1994*
LAST TELECAST: *September 4, 1997*
BROADCAST HISTORY:
Mar 1994–Dec 1994, ABC Wed 10:00–11:00
Sep 1996–Dec 1996, ABC Thu 10:00–11:00
Feb 1997–Jul 1997, ABC Thu 10:00–11:00
Jul 1997–Sep 1997, ABC Thu 9:00–10:00

ROTATING ANCHORS:
Diane Sawyer
Barbara Walters
Forrest Sawyer

REGULAR CORRESPONDENTS:
Meredith Vieira (Chief Correspondent)
Deborah Amos
John Donvan
Don Kladstrup

Turning Point was a single-subject weekly news documentary, similar to CBS' *48 Hours*, which ran opposite it on Wednesday night. Subjects tended toward the sensational and exploitative, including the first interview with two repentant female followers of mass murderer Charles Manson, heroin use among the young and middle class, "eight women fighting for a second chance after killing partners they say abused them," and of course a great deal about accused murderer O.J. Simpson.

ABC presented three *Turning Point* specials in 1993 and early 1994 prior to the show's run as a regular series; it reverted to the status of occasional specials during 1995 and 1996, and then returned for another run as a series in 1996–1997.

TURNING POINT, THE, see *ABC Dramatic Shorts—1952–1953*

TURN-ON (*Comedy/Variety*)

FIRST TELECAST: *February 5, 1969*
LAST TELECAST: *February 5, 1969*
BROADCAST HISTORY:
Feb 1969, ABC Wed 8:30–9:00

REPERTORY COMPANY:
Bonnie Boland
Teresa Graves
Maura McGiveney
Cecile Ozorio
Mel Stuart
Alma Murphy
Hamilton Camp
Maxine Greene
Carlos Manteca
Chuck McCann
Bob Staats
Ken Greenwald

Turn-On is remembered as one of the most famous one-telecast fiascos in the history of television. It was publicized as the second coming of *Laugh-In*, and even had the same executive producer, George Schlatter. According to the producer, Digby Wolfe, it was to be a "visual, comedic, sensory assault involving . . . animation, videotape, stop-action film, electronic distortion, computer graphics—even people." The "star" of the show was a mock-up computer. Despite the ballyhoo, what it turned out to be was an exercise in extremely bad taste. When the show's rampant sexual double-entendres and complete depersonalization led many ABC affiliates to refuse to carry it after the first telecast, and Bristol-Myers dropped sponsorship, it was canceled.

Guest star on the first, and only, telecast was Tim Conway.

TWELVE O'CLOCK HIGH (*War Drama*)

FIRST TELECAST: *September 18, 1964*
LAST TELECAST: *January 13, 1967*
BROADCAST HISTORY:
Sep 1964–Jan 1965, ABC Fri 9:30–10:30
Jan 1965–Sep 1965, ABC Fri 10:00–11:00
Sep 1965–Sep 1966, ABC Mon 7:30–8:30
Sep 1966–Jan 1967, ABC Fri 10:00–11:00

CAST:
Brigadier General Frank Savage (1964–1965) .... Robert Lansing
Major General Wiley Crowe (1964–1965) .... John Larkin
Major Harvey Stovall .... Frank Overton
Major Joe Cobb (1964–1965) .... Lew Gallo
Major ("Doc") Kaiser .... Barney Phillips
Captain/Major/Colonel Joe Gallagher ... Paul Burke
Tech. Sgt. Sandy Komansky (1965–1967) .... Chris Robinson
Brigadier General Ed Britt (1965–1967) .... Andrew Duggan

EXECUTIVE PRODUCER:
Quinn Martin

This was one wartime action-adventure series in which the top brass did not stay behind the lines. It was the story of the 918th Bombardment Group of the U.S. Eighth Air Force, stationed near London during World War II. During the first season the stories centered on Brigadier General Frank Savage, as he personally led his pilots through bombing raids and narrow escapes over enemy territory. Major General

Crowe was his boss, and Major Harvey Stovall his adjutant on the ground.

The action was hot and heavy, and at the start of the second season it got a little too hot for General Savage, who was killed during a mission. Colonel Joe Gallagher then assumed command, and the lead in the series for the rest of its run. (Gallagher zoomed in rank from captain to colonel during the series' run, despite getting off to a bad start in the premiere telecast. He guest-starred then as a brash young man who felt that he deserved special treatment from Savage because his father was a three-star general.) Brigadier General Britt became the new superior officer in the second season, while Tech. Sgt. Komansky was Gallagher's gunner and flight engineer.

Based on the novel by Beirne Lay, Jr., and Sy Bartlett, which was also made into a movie starring Gregory Peck (1949).

20TH CENTURY, THE (*Documentary*)

NETWORK HISTORY:

FIRST TELECAST: *October 20, 1957*

LAST TELECAST: *January 4, 1970*

Oct 1957–May 1958, CBS Sun 6:30–7:00
Sep 1958–Aug 1961, CBS Sun 6:30–7:00
Sep 1961–Aug 1966, CBS Sun 6:00–6:30
Jan 1967–Oct 1967, CBS Sun 6:00–6:30
Jan 1968–Oct 1968, CBS Sun 6:00–6:30
Jan 1969–Sep 1969, CBS Sun 6:00–6:30
Jan 1970, CBS Sun 6:00–6:30

CABLE HISTORY:

A&E
60 minutes
Original episodes: *1994*
Premiered: *September 14, 1994*

NARRATOR:

Walter Cronkite (1957–1970)
Mike Wallace (1994)

CBS News correspondent Walter Cronkite was the narrator and host of this series throughout its original run. The objective of *The 20th Century* was to present filmed reports of the major events, movements, and personalities that had shaped modern world history. The subject matter ranged from politics and war to medicine and the arts. When the series returned to the air to start its tenth season in January 1967, the title and format were altered. Under the new title, *The 21st Century*, the subjects covered looked to the future, rather than the past. Advances that were taking place or were anticipated in medicine, transportation, space exploration, communications, the arts, and living conditions in general were all explored in depth.

A new series, hosted by Mike Wallace, premiered on A&E on September 14, 1994, and later appeared on The History Channel. More than 100 episodes of this version were filmed.

20TH CENTURY FOX-HOUR, THE (*Dramatic Anthology*)

FIRST TELECAST: *October 5, 1955*

LAST TELECAST: *September 18, 1957*

BROADCAST HISTORY:

Oct 1955–Sep 1957, CBS Wed 10:00–11:00

HOST:

Joseph Cotten (1955–1956)
Robert Sterling (1956–1957)

The filmed dramas that were presented in this series were produced by 20th Century-Fox in Hollywood. Many of them were short adaptations of films that had been released by Fox over its long history, but generally featured newer, lesser-known actors and actresses (few big-name movie stars appeared in this series). Among the adaptations presented were "The Ox-Bow Incident," "Junior Miss," "The Late George Apley," and "Miracle on 34th Street." *The 20th Century–Fox Hour* aired on alternate weeks with *The U.S. Steel Hour.*

TWENTIETH CENTURY TALES, see *ABC Dramatic Shorts—1952–1953*

21ST CENTURY, THE, see *20th Century, The*

TWENTY-ONE (*Quiz*)

FIRST TELECAST: *September 12, 1956*

LAST TELECAST: *October 16, 1958*

BROADCAST HISTORY:

Sep 1956–Jan 1957, NBC Wed 10:30–11:00
Jan 1957–Sep 1958, NBC Mon 9:00–9:30
Sep 1958–Oct 1958, NBC Thu 8:30–9:00

EMCEE:

Jack Barry

Fifteen months after the premiere of *The $64,000 Question*, which was the first and most popular of the big-money quiz shows, *Twenty-One* made its debut. The format was loosely based on the card game of the same name, also known as blackjack. Two contestants competed with each other to reach a point total of 21 and win the game. They were asked the questions while in individual isolation booths. At the start of each round they were informed of the category from which the questions would come and could choose to attempt a question worth from 1 to 11 points, with the difficulty increasing with rising point value. The value of each point was $500, with the winner progressing to face a new opponent. In case of a tie, a new game was started with the value of each point raised by $500, a process which would continue through succeeding ties until there was a winner. The only threat to a champion was that if he lost a future game, the amount of his opponent's winnings would be deducted from his final total.

When the quiz-show scandals surfaced in 1958, initiated by a former contestant on the game show *Dotto, Twenty-One* was one of the biggest losers. Its producers admitted that the game had been rigged; that contestants were often given answers in advance if the producers felt that they were desirable as winners in the sense that they were people the public could identify with; and that a fraud had indeed been perpetrated on the trusting American public. Herb Stempel, a former winner on *Twenty-One*, told the detailed story of how the game had been rigged. The most popular *Twenty-One* winner, college professor Charles Van Doren, who had acquired a regular position on NBC's *Today Show* after being dethroned with winnings of $129,000, was also forced eventually to admit that he had participated in the rigging. He lost his job on *Today*, was relieved of his teaching post, and suffered inestimable embarrassment. When the dust cleared the game shows were gone, but their records of generosity to contestants remained. The biggest winner on *Twenty-One* was Elfrida Von Nardroff, who apparently had not been a participant in the fixing of the show. She came away with a final total of $220,500. In the annals of the big-money quiz shows this total was only exceeded by the $224,000 won by 11-year-old genius Robert Strom and the $252,000 won by Teddy Nadler, both on CBS game shows, *The $64,000 Question* and *The $64,000 Challenge* respectively.

TWENTY-ONE (*Quiz*)
FIRST TELECAST: *January 9, 2000*
LAST TELECAST: *September 23, 2000*
BROADCAST HISTORY:
Jan 2000, NBC Sun 8:00–9:00
Jan 2000, NBC Wed 8:00–9:00
Jan 2000, NBC Mon 9:00–10:00
Mar 2000–Apr 2000, NBC Mon 9:00–10:00
Apr 2000–May 2000, PAX Sat 9:00–10:00
Jun 2000–Sep 2000, PAX Sat 8:00–9:00
EMCEE:
Maury Povich
ALSO:
John Cramer, announcer
Melissa Busby, "chaperone"
Mercedes Cornett, "chaperone"

The original *Twenty-One* was known for two things: its isolation booths (in which contestants were cut off from the outside world as they pondered difficult questions) and the fact that, along with *Dotto*, it was at the center of the game-rigging scandal that brought down the entire 1950s big-money quiz-show craze. No scandal tainted this revival, but it was a close recreation of the original, with much bigger prizes. Back were the isolation booths and the tough questions, worth from one to 11 points. A wrong answer resulted in a "strike"; three strikes and the contestant was out. Two people competed. The first round consisted of multiple-choice questions and was won one of three ways—by being the first to reach 21 points, by stopping the game with more points than one's opponent (since they were in isolation, contestants did not know how their opponents were doing), or by having an opponent strike out. A contestant had one "second chance" in which he or she could enlist the aid of a friend or relative. The winner went on to the "Perfect 21" bonus round, with six true-or-false questions.

Questions were mostly of the pop-culture variety (movies, music, television, commercials); for example, "True or false—the most mentioned man on the Internet is Bill Gates" (ans: false). Winnings were essentially unlimited since winners kept coming back until they were defeated, but could easily top $100,000. Winning was rather graphically illustrated by having host Povich drop wads of cash in a tote bag.

There was some criticism of the speed with which a contestant could win large sums on this show (as much as $100,000 in a first game), so in later episodes the prize structure was changed to make the first game worth $25,000, although a contestant who lasted for seven games could still reach a cool $1 million. The episodes airing on Pax were reruns of NBC episodes.

21 BEACON STREET (*Detective Drama*)
FIRST TELECAST: *July 2, 1959*
LAST TELECAST: *March 20, 1960*
BROADCAST HISTORY:
Jul 1959–Sep 1959, NBC Thu 9:30–10:00
Dec 1959–Mar 1960, ABC Sun 10:30–11:00
CAST:
Dennis Chase .... Dennis Morgan
Lola .... Joanna Barnes
Brian .... Brian Kelly
Jim .... James Maloney

Private investigator Dennis Chase operated out of an office at 21 Beacon Street, where he and his staff worked out methods of trapping criminals. The locale was not specified; it could have been any large American metropolis. Chase's staff consisted of sexy Lola, whose beauty could be used to charm information out of people; young law school graduate Brian; and Jim, a handyman with a knack for dialects. Unlike most private-detective shows, *21 Beacon Street* developed its crime situation before the hero entered the story, and then never had him take part in the actual apprehension. Chase preferred to send the police on that errand, after determining who the culprit was. *21 Beacon Street* was the 1959 summer replacement for *The Ford Show*, and was rerun on ABC in the middle of the 1959–1960 season.

21 JUMP STREET (*Police Drama*)
FIRST TELECAST: *April 12, 1987*
LAST TELECAST: *September 17, 1990*
BROADCAST HISTORY:
Apr 1987–Sep 1989, FOX Sun 7:00–8:00
Sep 1989–Sep 1990, FOX Mon 8:00–9:00
(In first-run syndication during 1990–1991 season)
CAST:
Off. Tom Hanson (pilot only) .... Jeff Yagher
Off. Tom Hanson (1987–1990) .... Johnny Depp
Off. Doug Penhall (1987–1990) .... Peter DeLuise
Off. Judy Hoffs .... Holly Robinson
Off. Harry Truman Ioki (1987–1990)
.... Dustin Nguyen
Capt. Richard Jenko (1987) .... Frederic Forest
Capt. Adam Fuller .... Steven Williams
Dorothy (1988–1989) .... Gina Nemo
Jackie Garrett (1988–1989) .... Yvette Nipar
Off. Dennis Booker (1988–1989) .... Richard Grieco
Sal "Blowfish" Banducci (1988–1990) .... Sal Jenco
Clavo (1990) .... Tony Dakota
Off. Anthony "Mac" McCann (1990–1991)
.... Michael Bendetti
Off. Joey Penhall (1990–1991) .... Michael DeLuise

The most popular of fledgling Fox Broadcasting's first-season shows was this teen-oriented police series. The four youthful officers featured were members of a special unit of the Los Angeles Police Department that fought crime in the schools. Hanson, Penhall, Hoffs, and Ioki could all pass as students, and went undercover every week in local high schools to deal with drug trafficking, extortion, school gangs, teenage prostitution, murders, and other "typical" teenage problems. The building in which the special unit was based was an abandoned chapel at 21 Jump Street, hence the show's title. Captain Jenko, an eccentric nonconformist, was the original supervisor of the group. He was killed by a drunk hit-and-run driver and was replaced by Adam Fuller, who preferred to do things by the book.

Most episodes ended with one of the cast members doing a public service announcement suggesting agencies or counseling services that were available to teens facing the problems dramatized in that week's story.

Officers Penhall and Hanson had their romantic

problems during the 1988–1989 season. Penhall's live-in girlfriend Dorothy dumped him, while Hanson had a terminal fight with his steady, Jackie Garrett, who worked in the D.A.'s office. It was also during that season that streetwise Dennis Booker joined the Jump Street team (he left in 1989 for his own series, *Booker*), as did Blowfish, a well-meaning but nerdy klutz who did maintenance work at the Jump Street precinct.

When Fox dropped *21 Jump Street* from its schedule in 1990, the series continued in first-run syndication. Two new officers were added to replace the departed Hanson and Ioki, Mac McCann and Doug Penhall's younger brother, Joey. Doug, who had been caring for his orphaned nephew Clavo, was still around, as was Judy Hoffs, the only original member of the team to have passed the test for promotion from officer to detective. In December 1990, after surviving a near-fatal shooting, Doug quit the force to become part owner of a bowling alley, not because of fear for himself, but to raise Clavo in a more stable environment.

Filmed in Vancouver, British Columbia.

24 (*Espionage*)

FIRST TELECAST: *November 6, 2001*

LAST TELECAST:

BROADCAST HISTORY:

Nov 2001– , FOX Tue 9:00–10:00 (OS)

Nov 2001–Jan 2002, FOX Fri 9:00–10:00

CAST:

Agent Jack Bauer .... Kiefer Sutherland
Teri Bauer (2001–2002) .... Leslie Hope
Kimberly Bauer .... Elisha Cuthbert
Sen./Pres. David Palmer .... Dennis Haysbert
Sherry Palmer .... Penny Johnson Jerald
Keith Palmer (2001–2002) ...... Vicellous Shannon
Nicole Palmer (2001–2002)
.... Megalyn Echikunwoke
Agent Nina Myers (2001–) .... Sarah Clarke
Agent Tony Almeida .... Carlos Bernard
Agent Aaron Pierce .... Glenn Morshower
Agent Jamey Farrell (2001–2002) .. Karina Arroyave
Dir. George Mason (2001–2003) ... Xander Berkeley
Alan York/Kevin Carroll (2001–2002)
.... Richard Burgi
Ira Gaines (2001–2002) .... Michael Massee
Dan (2001) .... Matthew Carey
Rick (2001–2002) .... Daniel Bess
Janet York (2001) .... Jacqui Maxwell
Patty Brooks (2001–2002) .... Tanya Wright
Carl Webb (2001–2002) .... Zach Grenier
Chief of Staff Mike Novick .... Jude Ciccolella
Milo Pressman (2001–2002) .... Eric Balfour
Alberta Green (2002) .... Tamara Tunie
Victor Drazen (2002) .... Dennis Hopper
Andre Drazen (2002) .... Zeljko Ivanek
Alexis Drazen (2002) .... Misha Collins
Melanie (2002) .... Navi Rawat
Kate Warner (2002–) .... Sarah Wynter
Marie Warner (2002–) .... Laura Harris
Bob Warner (2002–) .... John Terry
Reza Naiyeer (2002–2003) .... Phillip Rhys
Michelle Dessler (2002–) ...... Reiko Aylesworth
Gary Matheson (2002–2003) .... Billy Burke
Carla Matheson (2002) .... Tracy Middendorf
Megan Matheson (2002–2003)
.... Skye McCole Bartusiak
Lynne Kresge (2002–) .... Michelle Forbes
Paula Schaeffer (2002) .... Sara Gilbert
Miguel (2002–2003) .... Innis Casey
Roger Stanton (2002–) .... Harris Yulin
Syed Ali (2003) .... Francesco Quinn
Agent Tom Baker (2003) .... Daniel Dae Kim
Carrie Turner (2003–) .... Lourdes Benedicto
Yusuf Auda (2003) .... Donnie Keshawarz
Capt. Jonathan Wallace (2003) .... Gregg Henry
Vice Pres. Jim Prescott (2003–) .... Alan Dale
Dir. Ryan Chappelle (2003–) .... Paul Schulze

The structure of *24* was a radical departure from traditional dramatic television. Everything took place in real time, and each season consisted of 24 one-hour episodes that comprised a single action-packed day. Split screens were used to show different events happening simultaneously, and a constantly ticking digital clock at the bottom of the screen monitored the passage of time and heightened the sense of urgency.

The first season of *24* started at midnight on the day of the California presidential primary in Los Angeles. CIA agent Jack Bauer's mission was to thwart a plot to assassinate African American candidate David Palmer while looking for his own troubled daughter, Kimberly, who had sneaked out of the house to party with a friend. Jack had recently moved back home after a separation and was hoping to save his marriage to Teri. Agents working with him on the Counter Terrorism Unit (CTU) included Nina, with whom he had had an affair while he and Teri were separated; Tony, Nina's current lover; and Jamey, a computer specialist. District Dir. George Mason was their boss.

It was an unbelievably violent day, full of shootings, treachery and political intrigue. Kimberly and her friend Janet were kidnapped by Rick and Dan, operatives working for Gaines, who was coordinating the assassination of Sen. Palmer; Jamey was discovered to be a traitor within the CTU and committed suicide; Palmer's scheming wife, Sherry, plotted against him and tried to cover up a dark secret in their past involving their children Nicole (who had been raped) and Keith (who had killed the rapist); and Gaines was tracked down and killed by Jack. That was just the first few hours. It then turned out that Gaines was working for Andre Drazen, the son of Serbian war criminal Victor Drazen, who wanted Palmer dead because the senator had authorized a covert mission to kill him. Andre and his brother Alexis continued after both Palmer and Jack (who had been with the CIA in Kosovo when Victor's wife and daughter had been killed by the Americans), stalking Teri, kidnapping Kimberly and attempting to kill Palmer with a phone bomb. By the end of the long day the Drazens had been killed, Palmer told Sherry he wanted a divorce, and Nina was exposed as another traitor within the CTU—but not before she shot and killed Jack's wife, Teri.

Season two was, if anything, even more violent, with an alarming body count and treachery at the highest levels of government. It started at 8:00 on a morning 18 months later when a now-inactive agent Jack was called back by newly elected Pres. Palmer to deal with the most serious threat the United States had faced in years—terrorists known as Second Wave were planning to detonate a nuclear bomb in Los Angeles within the next 24 hours. First the terrorists bombed the CTU offices, killing agent Paula; Kate suspected that her sister Marie's fiancé Reza was a terrorist, only to discover that Marie, their wealthy father, Bob (who was duped), and terrorist leader Ali were all involved in the plot; George was poisoned by radioactive dust, and Jack discovered that last year's villain Nina was connected to the plot. He was forced to work with her and foreign agent Yusuf to track down the bomb—which, numerous dead bodies later, they found at Norton Airfield east of Los Angeles. Since the government bomb specialists were unable to disarm it, Jack and the dying George flew it over the desert, where it detonated after Jack parachuted to safety. Meanwhile, Jack's trouble-prone daughter Kim was entangled in a subplot involving abusive father Gary and his wife Carla, trying with the help of boyfriend Miguel to get abused daughter Megan out of their clutches.

In the wake of the nuclear catastrophe an audiotape surfaced that appeared to implicate three Middle Eastern countries, and NSA head Stanton and others agitated for military retaliation. Palmer resisted, but Stanton, Chief of Staff Novick and Vice Pres. Prescott—with the help of the president's vengeful ex-wife Sherry—plotted against him and staged a coup, convincing the cabinet to remove him from office as "unfit" under provisions of the Twenty-fifth Amendment. Prescott then ordered the attacks to proceed. The planes had almost reached their targets when it was revealed that Stanton had used a rogue military team led by Wallace to bring the bomb into the country, the tape was phony and the entire plot had been staged by industrialist Peter Kingsley (Tobin Bell) to start a war and increase the value of his Middle Eastern oil holdings. Palmer was reinstated as president and fired Novick. CTU director Chappelle, who had tried to shut down Jack and Tony's investigation, reversed himself and helped them track Kingsley to the Los Angeles Coliseum, where the übervillain was killed in a wild shootout.

Unfortunately there were no happy endings on this series. In the final scene, as a relieved Pres. Palmer left a press conference, a woman connected to the previous year's assassin Gaines reached out and shook his hand, impregnating him with a poison.

TWENTY QUESTIONS (*Quiz/Panel*)

FIRST TELECAST: *November 26, 1949*

LAST TELECAST: *May 3, 1955*

BROADCAST HISTORY:

Nov 1949–Dec 1949, NBC Sat 8:00–8:30
Mar 1950–Jun 1951, ABC Fri 8:00–8:30 (OS)
Jul 1951–Jun 1952, DUM Fri 8:00–8:30
Jul 1952–Sep 1952, DUM Fri 8:30–9:00
Oct 1952–Sep 1953, DUM Fri 10:00–10:30
Sep 1953–Apr 1954, DUM Mon 8:00–8:30
Apr 1954–May 1954, DUM Sun 10:00–10:30
Jul 1954–May 1955, ABC Tue 8:30–9:00

HOST:

Bill Slater (1949–1952)
Jay Jackson (1953–1955)

PANELISTS:

Fred Van De Venter
Florence Rinard
Herb Polesie
Johnnie McPhee (1949–1953)
Dickie Harrison (1953–1954)
Bobby McGuire (1954–1955)

This popular quiz show was something of a family affair, having been created by Van De Venter on radio in 1946 and featuring father (Fred), mother (Florence Rinard), and son (Bobby McGuire) together on the panel at various times. The format was based on the old parlor game of "animal, vegetable, or mineral." The panel, which consisted of four regulars and one celebrity guest, could ask up to 20 questions to identify the subject at hand. Each question would be answered only by a "yes" or "no." Questions were sent in by viewers, who won a prize if they stumped the panel.

Twenty Questions originated on the Mutual Radio Network in 1946 and when first seen on TV in 1949 was simulcast on radio. There was little turnover among regular panelists during its run, except in the "teenage" chair, where Johnnie McPhee was replaced by Dickie Harrison, who in turn gave way to the Van De Venters' own son, Bobby McGuire, who had been with the show on radio during the 1940s.

$25,000 PYRAMID, THE (*Quiz*)

BROADCAST HISTORY:

Syndicated and network daytime
30 minutes
Produced: *1974–1979, 1981, 1985–1988, 1991–1992, 2002–*
Released: *Fall 1974, Fall 1981, Fall 1985, January 1991, Fall 2002*

HOST:

Bill Cullen (1974–1979)
Dick Clark (1981, 1985–1988)
John Davidson (1991–1992)
Donny Osmond (2002–)

Television's most inflationary game show worked its way up from *The $10,000 Pyramid*, to *The $20,000 Pyramid*, to *The $25,000 Pyramid*, to *The $50,000 Pyramid*, to *The New $100,000 Pyramid* from its premiere on network daytime in 1973. The contest was a simple word-association game, played by two teams, each composed of one celebrity and one non-celebrity. One member of each team was given a list of seven words from a category chosen from among six categories displayed on a pyramid; the other member then had 30 seconds to identify as many of the words as possible from clues given by his partner. After three rounds, the winning team (most words identified) went into a playoff round in which the game was reversed—the pyramid listed a total of six categories and the person who could see it gave clues consisting of words that would fall into each category, hoping that his partner could figure out what the category was. Each correctly identified category had a dollar value, and a team identifying all six in 60 seconds won the jackpot.

The daytime version ran on CBS from 1973 to 1974, on ABC from 1974 to 1980, and returned to CBS in the fall of 1982. The jackpot value on the network version was increased from $10,000 to $20,000 in January 1976 and from $20,000 to $25,000 when it returned to CBS in 1982. Dick Clark was the only host of the network series. The syndicated version was *The $25,000*

Pyramid from 1974 to 1979, *The $50,000 Pyramid* in 1981, *The New $100,000 Pyramid* in 1985, and *The $100,000 Pyramid* in 1991.

In the fall of 2002 the series resurfaced in syndication under the title *Pyramid*, with former teen heartthrob Donny Osmond serving as host. Contestants could win a daily jackpot of $25,000 and the opportunity to participate in an elimination tournament in which the big winner could win $100,000.

26 MEN (*Western*)

BROADCAST HISTORY:

Syndicated only
30 minutes
Produced: *1957–1959* (78 episodes)
Released: *October 1957*

CAST:

Capt. Tom Rynning .... Tris Coffin
Ranger Clint Travis .... Kelo Henderson

26 Men was the Arizona equivalent of *Tales of the Texas Rangers*. It was based on historical fact; in 1901, the Arizona Territorial Legislature had authorized an armed force consisting of "one captain, one lieutenant, four sergeants, and 20 privates" to maintain law and order. "The reason there was only 26 of us was because the Territory couldn't afford no more," reminisced one of the original members, many years later.

In this straightforward action Western Tris Coffin played the captain, and Kelo Henderson a new recruit. Others of the 26 were seen from time to time, but none were regulars. The series was shot on location in Arizona, and many residents of Phoenix and Tucson were used in supporting roles.

20/20 (*Newsmagazine*)

FIRST TELECAST: *June 6, 1978*
LAST TELECAST:
BROADCAST HISTORY:

Jun 1978–Aug 1978, ABC Tue 10:00–11:00
Sep 1978–Apr 1979, ABC Various times
May 1979–Sep 1987, ABC Thu 10:00–11:00
Sep 1987–Sep 2001, ABC Fri 10:00–11:00
Sep 1997–Dec 1997, ABC Thu 10:00–11:00
Jan 1998–Aug 1998, ABC Mon 9:00–10:00
Sep 1998–Aug 2000, ABC Wed 10:00–11:00
Sep 1998–Aug 1999, ABC Sun 9:00–10:00
Feb 1999–Jan 2000, ABC Mon 8:00–9:00
Oct 1999–Sep 2000, ABC Thu 10:00–11:00
Sep 2000–Dec 2000, ABC Mon 8:00–9:00
Jun 2001–Jul 2001, ABC Mon 8:00–9:00
Aug 2001, ABC Wed 10:00–11:00
Jan 2002–Apr 2002, ABC Wed 10:00–11:00
Jan 2002– , ABC Fri 10:00–11:00

HOSTS:

Harold Hayes and Robert Hughes (first telecast only)
Hugh Downs (1978–1999)
Barbara Walters (1984–)
Diane Sawyer (1998–2000)
Sam Donaldson (1998–2002)
Connie Chung (1998–2002)
Charles Gibson (1998–2000)
Jack Ford (1999–2002)
John Miller (2002)

REGULAR CORRESPONDENTS:

Dave Marash (1978–1981)
Sylvia Chase (1978–1986, 1998–)
Dr. Carl Sagan (1978–1980)
Thomas Hoving (1978–1984)
Geraldo Rivera (1978–1985)
Tom Jarriel (1979–)
Bob Brown (1980–)
Steve Fox (1980–1983)
Barbara Walters (1981–1984)
John Stossel (1981–)
Lynn Sherr (1986–)
Stone Phillips (1986–1991)
Catherine Crier (1993–1995)
Brian Ross (1994–)
Arnold Diaz (1995–)
Deborah Roberts (1995–)
Bill Ritter (1997–)
Cynthia McFadden (1998–)
John Quinones (1998–)
Jay Schadler (1998–)
Chris Wallace (1998–)
Elizabeth Vargas (1999–)
Juju Chang (2000–)

This ABC newsmagazine set out to emulate the success of CBS' *60 Minutes*, but got off to a disastrous start. The elements were similar to those in *60 Minutes*—personality profiles, mini-documentaries, hard-hitting investigative reports—but the coverage was so shallow, and the production so full of gimmicks, that the premiere telecast received devastating reviews. *Variety* likened it to *The National Enquirer*. In one of the fastest cast changes in history, producer Bob Shanks fired his two cohosts—former magazine editor Harold Hayes and Australian art critic Robert Hughes—after just one telecast, brought in old pro Hugh Downs, and began tinkering with the contents. Subsequent shows were better received, though *20/20* did not rival *60 Minutes* as an audience attraction. Correspondents included Geraldo Rivera with investigative reports and Thomas Hoving on popular culture. Later contributors included hard-news reporter Tom Jarriel and showbiz correspondent Bob Brown, along with in-your-face investigative reporter John Stossel. Sometimes Stossel got a little *too* pushy; in one of the show's more celebrated moments, he was physically assaulted on camera by an angry wrestler. Dr. Carl Sagan, originally announced as a regular contributor on science, was seen relatively infrequently. At the start of the 1984–1985 season Barbara Walters was formally promoted from correspondent to cohost. Here, as in her specials, she was known primarily for her unique interviews, as when she asked feared Libyan dictator Mu'ammar Qaddafi directly, "Are you mad?" (His response: "Absolutely not.")

Nearly every telecast of *20/20* seemed to headline something sensational or celebrity-oriented, such as a profile of the latest rock star or an investigation into the circumstances surrounding the death of Elvis Presley, or something—anything—concerning sex. (In later years, sex in the military seemed to be a favorite topic.) There were also more substantive features over the years, among them a widely acclaimed special telecast on the secret Iranian hostage negotiations (aired just after the hostages were released), an exposé on the hazards of aluminum wiring, and Geraldo Rivera's report from inside war-torn Laos.

Two of *20/20*'s most widely publicized reports were aired in early 1991: Barbara Walters's exclusive interview with Gulf War hero Gen. Norman Schwarzkopf on March 15th, shortly after the hostilities ended; and less than a month later a vivid film of a real exorcism being performed by a Roman Catholic priest. Critics called it sensationalistic, but audiences were huge. Not every scoop worked out as well. Undoubtedly the show's most embarrassing moment occurred just months before, in October 1990, following an interview with former child star Buckwheat of the *Little Rascals*. The man turned out to be an imposter—the real Buckwheat had died ten years earlier.

In 1997 a second night of *20/20* was launched, and from then until 2002 the series fluctuated between two and four nights per week, for a time incorporating the staff of the discontinued *Primetime Live*. The Thursday version, specializing in urban-themed stories, was titled *20/20 Downtown* in the fall of 1999, and featured rotating hosts Vargas, Quinones, Schadler and McFadden (the *Downtown* name was sometimes used for short-run news hours in subsequent years as well). In early 2002 *20/20* was finally cut back to just its original Friday-night time slot, with Barbara Walters as host. Meanwhile ABC's other prime time news hour, *Primetime Live*, was relaunched in 2000 as *Primetime Thursday*.

TWICE IN A LIFETIME (*Fantasy*)

FIRST TELECAST: *August 25, 1999*

LAST TELECAST: *October 27, 2002*

BROADCAST HISTORY:

Aug 1999–Jun 2001, PAX Wed 8:00–9:00
Aug 1999–Sep 1999, PAX Sun 9:00–10:00
Sep 1999–Jan 2000, PAX Sun 10:00–11:00
Oct 1999–Mar 2000, PAX Mon 11:00–Midnight
Sep 2000–Feb 2001, PAX Sat 9:00–10:00
Jan 2001–Mar 2001, PAX Sun 11:00–Midnight
May 2001–Aug 2002, PAX Sat 11:00–Midnight
Sep 2002–Oct 2002, PAX Sun 11:00–Midnight

CAST:

Mr. Jones (1999–2000) .... Gordie Brown
Mr. Smith (2000–2001).............. Paul Popowich
Othniel .... Al Waxman

In this uplifting series in the spirit of *Highway to Heaven* and *Touched By an Angel*, Mr. Jones, a guardian angel, helped people who had ruined their lives. Each week he took a person who had just died to a hearing in front of a heavenly judge. Judge Othneil, a cherubic angel who spoke in epigrams, usually gave the deceased three days to unmake their Big Mistake. (In the first season Polly Bergen appeared a couple of times as Judge Deborah and Waxman, with a beard, as Judge Jepthat.) Mr. Jones then accompanied the people back in time, where they observed their younger selves and were given the opportunity to change the decisions that had negatively impacted their lives. If things worked out—and they always seemed to—their own lives and their impact on those around them were changed for the better. Among the well-known performers appearing were Mariette Hartley, Corbin Bernsen, Patrick Duffy and Markie Post.

In the second-season premiere a young man died in a church fire and his spirit was picked up by Othniel, who rechristened him "Mr. Smith" and charged him with taking over Mr. Jones' guardian role. Othniel offered him the chance to live his life again if he could help the firefighter who had tried to save him. Othniel gave the firefighter, who had been shot to death by his troubled son, the standard three days, with Mr. Smith's help, to go back in time and change things. After they succeeded Mr. Smith did not return to his old life but continued as a guardian. He realized that, despite not being an angel, he could still help others to change their lives for the better. Othniel was now seen on Earth and presided in assorted makeshift courtrooms rather than the heavenly one in which he had been seen during the first season.

Twice in a Lifetime was in production for two seasons but Pax continued to air reruns through the fall of 2002.

TWILIGHT THEATER (*Dramatic Anthology*)

FIRST TELECAST: *April 2, 1956*

LAST TELECAST: *July 15, 1959*

BROADCAST HISTORY:

Apr 1956–Jul 1956, ABC Mon 7:30–8:00
Jul 1958–Jul 1959, CBS Wed 7:30–8:00

The title *Twilight Theater* has been used several times for filmed primetime anthology series. In 1953 it was one of the titles under which ABC aired its inventory of miscellaneous dramatic films (see *ABC Dramatic Shorts—1952–1953* for details). ABC revived the name in 1956 for a summer series consisting of 30-minute dramas and comedies featuring such Hollywood standbys as Ethel Waters, Vera Miles, Hans Conried, Charles Coburn, and Hugh O'Brian. From 1958–1959 CBS used the title *Twilight Theater* for a series of reruns of films previously seen on *Schlitz Playhouse of Stars*.

TWILIGHT ZONE, THE (*Science Fiction Anthology*)

FIRST TELECAST: *October 2, 1959*

LAST TELECAST:

BROADCAST HISTORY:

Oct 1959–Sep 1962, CBS Fri 10:00–10:30
Jan 1963–Sep 1963, CBS Thu 9:00–10:00
Sep 1963–Sep 1964, CBS Fri 9:30–10:00
May 1965–Sep 1965, CBS Sun 9:00–10:00
Sep 1985–Apr 1986, CBS Fri 8:00–9:00
Jun 1986–Apr 1986, CBS Fri 8:00–9:00
Sep 1986–Oct 1986, CBS Sat 10:00–11:00
Dec 1986, CBS Thu 8:00–8:30
Jul 1987, CBS Fri 10:00–11:00
Sep 2002– , UPN Wed 9:00–10:00
(In first-run syndication during the 1987–1988 season)

HOST:

Rod Serling (1959–1965)
Forest Whitaker (2002–)

NARRATOR:

Charles Aidman (1985–1987)
Robin Ward (1987–1988)

THEME (1985–1987):

by the Grateful Dead

Playwright Rod Serling, who in the mid-1950s had been a prolific contributor of fine dramas for almost all of the prestigious live anthology series (his most famous being "Requiem for a Heavyweight" for *Playhouse 90*), turned to the world of science fiction with this series. In addition to serving as series host, he wrote many of the teleplays that were presented on *The Twilight Zone*. The stories were unusual and offbeat, often with ironic twists. For example, there was "Escape Clause," starring David Wayne as a hypochondriac who, in an effort to escape his dependence on pills and fear of his environment, made a pact with the Devil. In exchange for his soul he won immortality. Filled with self-assurance, he killed his intolerable shrew of a wife (expecting to be sentenced to die and knowing that was now impossible). Instead of the death penalty he got life imprisonment—an awfully long time for someone who was immortal. Another episode, "Time Enough at Last," starred Burgess Meredith as a bank teller who could never find enough time to read. One day at lunchtime, while he was squirreled away in the bank's vault reading a good book, there was a nuclear attack that killed everybody outside. Now he had all the time in the world to read. A happy ending—until he tripped and broke his glasses! In "The Eye of the Beholder," a young woman who had been born with a horrible facial deformity had just undergone the last possible operation to try and make her less hideous. Her head was swathed in bandages, and all the doctors and nurses were dimly seen standing in the shadows around her bed. Then the bandages were finally removed and there she was, beautiful—at least to us. Only then were the faces of the doctors and nurses revealed to be grotesque, for she lived in a world where our "beauty" was considered a horrible deformity. At the end of the telecast she was led away to her society's equivalent of a leper colony.

Some well-known actors appeared on *Twilight Zone*, but it was the stories rather than the performers that made the show work. Serling's original opening narration to the show set the scene appropriately. The opening: "There is a fifth dimension beyond that which is known to man. It is a dimension as vast as space and as timeless as infinity. It is the middle ground between light and shadow, between science and superstition, and it lies between the pit of man's fears and the summit of his knowledge. This is the dimension of imagination. It is an area we call *The Twilight Zone*."

After three successful seasons in a half-hour format, *The Twilight Zone* expanded to a full hour in January 1963. The longer format was abandoned the following fall, but some of the longer episodes were rerun during the summer of 1965.

In the fall of 1985, following the release of a 1983 theatrical feature of the same title, *The Twilight Zone* returned to TV. It had been two decades since the original had left the air, and a decade since the passing of its driving creative force, Rod Serling. The new version ran in an hour-long format, with two or three stories of varying length in each episode. It still had the same mix of straight science fiction, whimsy, fantasy, and the occult, but it was definitely a different show. It was now in color, the special effects were more elaborate and, although some of the original episodes were redone, most of the stories were new. The new theme music was by none other than The Grateful Dead. There was a minor furor when, late in 1985, science fiction writer Harlan Ellison, who had been serving as creative consultant, left the series in a dispute with the network over the content of the Christmas episode.

When the new color version of *The Twilight Zone* went into syndication in the fall of 1987, as a half-hour series, thirty first-run episodes were added to the ones that had aired on CBS. Robin Ward replaced Charles Aidman as the off-camera narrator of the syndicated episodes.

UPN revived *The Twilight Zone* in the fall of 2002, with actor/director/producer Forest Whitaker serving as host. Each hour-long telecast featured two self-contained stories.

TWIN PEAKS (*Serial Drama*)

FIRST TELECAST: *April 8, 1990*
LAST TELECAST: *June 10, 1991*
BROADCAST HISTORY:

Apr 1990, ABC Sun 9:00–11:00
Apr 1990–May 1990, ABC Thu 9:00–10:00
Aug 1990–Feb 1991, ABC Sat 10:00–11:00
Mar 1991–Apr 1991, ABC Thu 9:00–10:00
Jun 1991, ABC Mon 9:00–11:00

CAST:

Agent Dale Cooper .... Kyle MacLachlan
Sheriff Harry S. Truman .... Michael Ontkean
Jocelyn (Josie) Packard .... Joan Chen
Catherine Martell .... Piper Laurie
Pete Martell .... Jack Nance
Leland Palmer .... Ray Wise
Sarah Palmer .... Grace Zabriskie
Laura Palmer/Madeleine Ferguson ...... Sheryl Lee
Major Garland Briggs .... Don Davis
Bobby Briggs .... Dana Ashbrook
Big Ed Hurley .... Everett McGill
Nadine Hurley .... Wendy Robie
James Hurley .... James Marshall
Benjamin Horne .... Richard Beymer
Audrey Horne .... Sherilyn Fenn
Jerry Horne .... David Patrick Kelly
Donna Hayward .... Lara Flynn Boyle
Dr. William Hayward .... Warren Frost
Eileen Hayward .... Mary Jo Deschanel
Shelly Johnson .... Mädchen Amick
Leo Johnson .... Eric Da Re
Hank Jennings .... Chris Mulkey
Norma Jennings .... Peggy Lipton
Lucy Moran .... Kimmy Robertson
Dr. Lawrence Jacoby .... Russ Tamblyn
Deputy Andy Brennan .... Harry Goaz
Deputy Tommy "The Hawk" Hill .... Michael Horse
Mike Nelson .... Gary Hershberger
**Albert Rosenfield* .... Miguel Ferrer
**Mayor Dwayne Milford* .... John Boylan
**Blackie O'Reilly (1990)* .... Victoria Catlin
**Gordon Cole* .... David Lynch
Richard Tremayne .... Ian Buchanan
Margaret, the "Log Lady" ..... Catherine E. Coulson
Annie Blackburne (1991) .... Heather Graham
Windom Earle (1991) .... Kenneth Welsh

* Occasional

CREATORS/EXECUTIVE PRODUCERS:

David Lynch
Mark Frost

MUSIC:

"Falling," composed and conducted by Angelo Badalamenti

One of the most talked-about, but least-watched, TV experiments of the early '90s was ABC's surrealistic soap opera *Twin Peaks*. Created by avant-garde filmmaker David Lynch (*Blue Velvet*) and Mark Frost, it emphasized style over story; its eerie, non-linear visual and narrative quality left many initially intrigued viewers wondering "what's going on here?"—just before they changed channels.

The characters were hardly relatable, unless you happen to reside in an asylum. FBI Agent Cooper, a mystical loner, had come to the picturesque Pacific Northwest town of Twin Peaks, near the Canadian border, to investigate the murder of 17-year-old homecoming queen Laura Palmer. With the help of taciturn Sheriff Harry Truman, he began to explore the town's intricate web of affairs, plots, and eccentrics. The seemingly wholesome Laura had relationships with biker-poet James and hot-tempered Bobby, among others, and had been treated by weirdo psychiatrist Dr. Jacoby. She had been seen at One-Eyed Jacks, a bordello/casino just across the Canadian border, where drugs and sex flowed freely. The finger of suspicion pointed at many before the killer was finally revealed to be her own father Leland, an apparently upstanding citizen secretly possessed by "Killer BOB." (Before he was caught, and died in Cooper's arms, Leland/BOB also polished off Laura's lookalike cousin Madeleine.) Other principal stories included the plot by Catherine and developer Ben Horne to wrest the town's largest industry, Packard Sawmill, away from her brother's Asian widow Josie—who, it turned out, had paid Hank to kill the late Mr. Packard; the triangle between Shelly, Bobby, and Shelly's abusive husband Leo, who was eventually shot and turned into a drooling idiot; and the blue-collar triangle between Norma (owner of the Double-R Diner), Big Ed (service station owner and James's uncle), and Norma's ex-con hubby, the murderous Hank. Ed's one-eyed, Amazonian wife Nadine, who was certifiably crazy even by *Twin Peaks* standards, complicated matters.

With Laura's murder solved in late 1990, Agent Cooper stayed to investigate further murders; apparently "Killer BOB" lived on, inhabiting others. Cooper's principal nemesis became Windom Earle, his former FBI partner who had gone insane after his wife had been killed while in his and Cooper's custody. Earle, a master of disguises, played an elaborate chess game with Cooper via the mail and newspaper columns, taking a life every time he took a piece; half-witted Leo became his henchman. The vortex of deception and death finally drew the mystical Agent Cooper—who got many of his leads through dreams populated by dancing dwarfs and towering giants muttering epigrams—into the "Black Lodge," a terrifying, dreamlike place outside of reality where he confronted Earle, dead victims, and his own soul.

Lots of quirky little details added to the mood of *Twin Peaks*: the somber, slowly played guitar music; Agent Cooper's partiality for the town's "damn fine coffee" and cherry pie; his tape-recorded reports to his unseen secretary Diane; the "Log Lady" who always appeared with, yes, a log in her arms; Major Briggs's fuzzy investigation into "deep space" matters for the Air Force (if the series had continued, would aliens have arrived?). Hard-of-hearing Bureau Chief Cole, who turned up once in a while to confer with Cooper, was played by none other than producer David Lynch (i.e., the creator stepping into his own series to talk with the chief character!).

Portions of *Twin Peaks* were filmed on location in the Pacific Northwest, where the little community of Snoqualmie Falls, Washington, was used as a model for the fictional town. The large, rustic Salish Lodge was used for exteriors of the imposing Great Northern Hotel, where Cooper stayed in the series.

TWO (*Drama*)

BROADCAST HISTORY:

Syndicated only
60 minutes
Produced: *1996–1997* (24 episodes)
Released: *September 1996*

CAST:

Booth Hubbard/Gus McClain ...... Michael Easton
Agent Terry Carter .... Barbara Tyson
Agent Andy Forbes .... Lochlyn Munro
**Sara McClain* .... Allison Hossack
**Dir. James Fairchild* .... Andrew Johnston

*Occasional

Justice truly was blind in this dark knockoff of the '60s series *The Fugitive*. Gus McClain was happily married, with a new job as an assistant English professor at a college in Seattle, when his world was suddenly turned into a living hell. Unknown to Gus, he had a vicious, murderous twin brother named Booth who was determined to destroy his life. Why? It seems the brothers had been separated as infants, and adopted by different stepparents after their own parents were killed in a car accident. Gus was the lucky one, raised by a loving, generous couple, while Booth drew the short straw and grew up a psychotic criminal. As if that wasn't enough, Booth now had an aneurysm. Knowing he was going to die, he went on a killing rampage and then tracked down his hated brother to pin the crimes on him, and make Gus experience the miserable life he had lived. He killed Gus's wife Sara and framed Gus for the crime.

Enter Carter, an obsessed F.B.I. agent who was convinced that Gus had committed all these crimes, including the murder of her partner. Smug, smirking, and absolutely deaf to his side of the story, she even tried to shoot him in the back when he cornered her, then showed his honesty by handing over his gun (fortunately he had taken out the bullets). Andy was Carter's inept partner. Gus was left on the run, chased by the relentless Carter, while searching for evidence that Booth existed and was responsible for the murders. As Gus traveled, Booth sometimes showed up to wreak havoc that was invariably blamed on Gus. Viewers could tell them apart because Booth was a smoker and Gus was not. Gus' late wife Sara was seen in flashbacks during his understandably troubled dreams.

TWO FOR THE MONEY (*Quiz*)

FIRST TELECAST: *September 30, 1952*
LAST TELECAST: *September 7, 1957*
BROADCAST HISTORY:

Sep 1952–Aug 1953, NBC Tue 10:00–10:30
Aug 1953–Sep 1956, CBS Sat 9:00–9:30
Mar 1957–Jun 1957, CBS Sat 10:30–11:00
Jun 1957–Sep 1957, CBS Sat 8:30–9:00

EMCEE:

Herb Shriner (1952–1956)
Walter O'Keefe (1954)
Sam Levenson (1955, 1956, 1957)

QUIZ MODERATOR:
Dr. Mason Gross

Much in the manner of *You Bet Your Life,* this quiz show was designed more as a vehicle for the comic talents of its emcee than as a straight contest. Herb Shriner, with his country humor and tales of life in Indiana, was the original emcee and remained with the show until the spring of 1956. He was spelled during the summers by Walter O'Keefe in 1954 and Sam Levenson in 1955 and 1956. Levenson returned as the full-time emcee when the show returned in the spring of 1957. Three pairs of contestants vied for cash prizes during the actual quiz portion of the show and Dr. Mason Gross, Provost and Professor of Philosophy at Rutgers University, was the authority on correctness of answers.

240-ROBERT (*Adventure*)

FIRST TELECAST: *August 28, 1979*
LAST TELECAST: *September 19, 1981*
BROADCAST HISTORY:

Aug 1979, ABC Tue 8:30–10:00
Sep 1979–Dec 1979, ABC Mon 8:00–9:00
May 1980–Aug 1980, ABC Sat 8:00–9:00
Mar 1981, ABC Sat 8:00–9:00
Sep 1981, ABC Sat 8:00–9:00

CAST:

Deputy Theodore Roosevelt Applegate III ("Trap") .... John Bennett Perry
Deputy Dwayne Thibideaux (1979–1980) .... Mark Harmon
Deputy Morgan Wainwright (1979–1980) .... Joanna Cassidy
Kestenbaum .... Steve Tannen
Deputy C.B. (1979–1980) .... Lew Saunders
Deputy Roverino (1979–1980) .... JoeAl Nicassio
Terry (1979–1980) .... Thomas Babson
Deputy Bottendott (1981) .... Brant Von Hoffman
Deputy Brett Cueva (1981) .... Stephan Burns
Deputy Sandy Harper (1981) .... Pamela Hensley

One of TV's periodic "rescue" shows, *240-Robert* followed the exploits of the Los Angeles County Sheriff's Department Emergency Service Detail (E.S.D.). The principal characters were three bright-faced young deputies: Trap, the leader; Morgan, the pretty helicopter pilot; and Thib, the husky helper (played by former UCLA star quarterback Mark Harmon). Using choppers, motorcycles, boats, and a customized four-wheel-drive wagon, they managed to extract hapless citizens from various uncomfortable situations.

After its original run in the fall of 1979, and repeats the following summer, *240-Robert* returned briefly in early 1981 with a new female pilot (Sandy) and helper (Brett).

TWO GUYS, A GIRL AND A PIZZA PLACE (*Situation Comedy*)

FIRST TELECAST: *March 11, 1998*
LAST TELECAST: *June 6, 2001*
BROADCAST HISTORY:

Mar 1998–May 1998, ABC Wed 9:30–10:00
May 1998–Jul 1998, ABC Tue 9:30–10:00
Jul 1998–Mar 1999, ABC Wed 8:30–9:00
Apr 1999, ABC Fri 9:00–9:30
May 1999–Jul 1999, ABC Wed 8:30–9:00
Jul 1999–Apr 2000, ABC Wed 8:00–8:30
Aug 1999–Sep 1999, ABC Wed 9:30–10:00
Jun 2000–Sep 2000, ABC Wed 8:00–8:30
Jun 2000–Aug 2000, ABC Tue 9:30–10:00
Sep 2000–Dec 2000, ABC Fri 8:00–8:30
Jan 2001, ABC Fri 9:00–9:30
Feb 2001–Apr 2001, ABC Fri 8:00–8:30
May 2001, ABC Wed 8:30–9:00
May 2001–Jun 2001, ABC Wed 8:00–8:30

CAST:

Michael "Berg" Bergen .... Ryan Reynolds
Pete Dunville .... Richard R. Ruccolo
Sharon Carter .... Traylor Howard
Melissa (1998) .... Jennifer Westfeldt
Bill (1998) .... Julius Carry
Mr. Bauer (1998) .... David Ogden Stiers
Ashley Walker .... Suzanne Cryer
Johnny Donnelly .... Nathan Fillion
Irene (1999–2001) .... Jillian Bach
Germ (1999–2001) .... Giuseppe Andrews
Marti (2000) .... Tiffani Thiessen

The title pretty well summed up the premise of this happy-go-lucky sitcom, set in Boston. Berg and Pete were the two guys, sharing an apartment and working their way through graduate school as delivery boys for Beacon Street Pizza. Pete was a neurotic worrier, an architecture student trying vainly to stick to a blueprint of life; Berg was the tall, super-smart, easygoing one, coasting through his first year of medical school. The girl was sexy and successful Sharon, who lived upstairs and made big bucks selling chemicals. She worried about the moral implications of her work ("one more client for me, one less species of bird"), but didn't want to give up her Beemer. A true woman of the '90s. In the early episodes Melissa was Pete's girlfriend, Bill was their gruff boss, and Mr. Bauer the eccentric customer who told stories about his life that sounded suspiciously like scenes from old movies. In the fall Berg began wooing Ashley, a smart fellow student, while Pete played the field.

Stories revolved mostly around the threesome's dating antics. Johnny became Sharon's boyfriend, his penny-pinching contrasting with her free-spending ways. Pete had a crush on her, too, but Johnny and Sharon were married in 2000. Meanwhile both Berg and Pete quit the pizza place, Berg to pursue his medical training and Pete to become a fireman. Pete had a long-running relationship with his close-to-insane ex-girlfriend Irene (who had a tattoo of a tiger that covered her entire back, and who sometimes placed remarkably effective curses on people). He also dated Marti, a fellow fireman. Johnny also became a fireman. Germ was a dense teen who worked at the pizza place.

In the series finale it appeared that Sharon, Ashley or Irene might be pregnant. Viewers were invited to vote on-line to determine which one it would be, and the winner was Ashley. Four different endings had been taped for the episode, one for each of the women and one in which no one was pregnant; just before the credits viewers saw the other three. The title of the series was changed to *Two Guys and a Girl* effective September 1999.

TWO IN LOVE (*Quiz/Audience Participation*)

FIRST TELECAST: *June 19, 1954*
LAST TELECAST: *September 11, 1954*
BROADCAST HISTORY:

Jun 1954–Sep 1954, CBS Sat 10:30–11:00

EMCEE:

Bert Parks

Each week a couple—engaged, newly married, or celebrating a wedding anniversary—were the guests of emcee Bert Parks. Many of their relatives and friends were also invited to be on the show. The relatives and friends participated in an on-the-air discussion of the couple's romance and were asked other questions which, if answered correctly, added to the "nest egg" of cash that would be presented to the couple at the end of the show. After the first couple of weeks it was decided by the producers to have only engaged couples as guests.

TWO MARRIAGES (*Drama*)

FIRST TELECAST: *August 23, 1983*
LAST TELECAST: *April 26, 1984*
BROADCAST HISTORY:

Aug 1983, ABC Tue 9:30–11:00
Aug 1983–Sep 1983, ABC Wed 9:00–10:00
Mar 1984, ABC Thu 8:00–9:00
Apr 1984, ABC Thu 9:00–10:00

CAST:

Jim Daley .... Tom Mason
Ann Daley .... Karen Carlson
Willie Daley .... Ian Fried
Kim Daley .... Tiffany Toyoshima
Scott Morgan .... C. Thomas Howell
Dr. Art Armstrong .... Michael Murphy
Nancy Armstrong .... Janet Eilber
Eric Armstrong .... Kirk Cameron
Shelby Armstrong .... Louanne
Woody Daley .... John McLiam

The relationships within and between two middle-class, suburban American families were the subjects of this gentle drama, set in a pleasant Iowa community. The Daleys were the more contemporary couple: Ann was pursuing a successful career as a construction engineer, even while pregnant with another child, and Jim worked at his father Woody's dairy farm. Besides their rambunctious six-year-old, Willie, the bustling Daley household included two children from previous marriages, Jim's 11-year-old Vietnamese-American daughter, Kim, and Ann's rebellious teenage son, Scott. Across the well-mown lawn were their best friends the Armstrongs—Art the busy surgeon and Nancy the vaguely dissatisfied homemaker, who kept herself occupied with volunteer work and was always a bit envious of Ann's independent lifestyle. Shelby was the Armstrongs' 15-year-old, sensitive and wise beyond her years, and Eric their happy-go-lucky young son.

The contrast between traditional and "modern" marriages, and the joys and pains of families and friendships provided the stories.

TWO OF A KIND (*Situation Comedy*)

FIRST TELECAST: *September 25, 1998*
LAST TELECAST: *July 16, 1999*
BROADCAST HISTORY:

Sep 1998–Jul 1999, ABC Fri 8:00–8:30

CAST:

Kevin Burke .... Christopher Sieber
Mary-Kate Burke (age 11) .... Mary-Kate Olsen
Ashley Burke (11) .... Ashley Olsen
Carrie Moore .... Sally Wheeler

The adorable Olsen twins of *Full House* fame were back in another Friday night kid-com with this saccharine offering. They were the daughters of goofy, loving Kevin, a widowed science professor who lived with them in an apartment across from Wrigley Field in Chicago. Mary-Kate was the tomboy, into baseball, and Ashley the straight A student, who was just beginning to get interested in boys. Into their life came Carrie, a feisty young nanny who just happened to be one of Dad's students. Dad wasn't so sure having a student for a nanny was a good idea, but the twins loved her, and—well, in sitcom land you know the rest. Stories revolved around little misadventures, boyfriends, and Dad's dates, eventually with Carrie.

TWO OF US, THE (*Situation Comedy*)

FIRST TELECAST: *April 6, 1981*
LAST TELECAST: *August 10, 1982*
BROADCAST HISTORY:

Apr 1981, CBS Mon 8:30–9:00
Sep 1981–Jan 1982, CBS Mon 8:30–9:00
Jan 1982–Feb 1982, CBS Wed 8:30–9:00
Jun 1982–Aug 1982, CBS Tue 8:30–9:00

CAST:

Robert Brentwood .... Peter Cook
Nan Gallagher .... Mimi Kennedy
Cubby Royce .... Oliver Clark
Gabrielle "Gabby" Gallagher .... Dana Hill
Reggie Cavanaugh (1981–1982) ... Tim Thomerson

Robert Brentwood was a very proper English manservant thrust into a free-wheeling American household in this comedy of lifestyles. Nan Gallagher was a highly successful, divorced career woman, cohost of the New York City TV talk show "Mid-morning Manhattan." (The other host was the unseen Reggie Philbis—a takeoff on real Los Angeles talk show host Regis Philbin.) Nan's blind spot was housekeeping. Basically, she was a slob around the house, and she desperately needed someone to put her daily life in order. Enter Brentwood, quite by accident. Though initially repelled by the thought of working for a woman (with a child, yet!), he took the challenge. On the one hand sarcastic, sometimes overbearing, and always proper, he also happened to be a gourmet cook, a meticulous organizer, and conversant in several languages—skills which proved invaluable when Nan had to entertain a diverse parade of guests. If only he were a little less pompous! Cubby Royce was Nan's agent.

When *The Two of Us* returned in the fall of 1981 after a limited run in the spring, the name of Nan's cohost had been changed from Philbis to Cavanaugh and he was seen regularly in the person of actor Tim Thomerson. Reggie's ego was as big as all outdoors and he was so obnoxious that he had practically no real friends. Needless to say, Reggie and Nan were not the best of friends off camera.

2GETHER (*Sitcom*)

BROADCAST HISTORY:

MTV
30 minutes
Original episodes: *2000–2001* (19 episodes)
Premiered: *August 15, 2000*

CAST:

Jerry O'Keefe .... Evan Farmer
Mickey Parke .... Alex Solowitz
Jason "Q. T." McKnight .... Michael Cuccione

Chad Linus .... Noah Bastian
Doug Linus .... Kevin Farley
Tom Lawless .... Dave McGowan
**Glenn Brummer* .... Roger R. Cross
Elizabeth "Liz" Porter .... Brenda James

*Occasional

This parody on "boy bands" was spun off from MTV's first original movie, *2GE+HER*, in which a no-talent boy band called Whoa fired their manager Bob Buss (Alan Blumenfeld), only to have him pick out five more guys seemingly at random and form a competing group. The five young members of 2Gether were Jerry, "the heart throb"; Mickey, "the bad boy"; Q.T., "the cute one"; Chad, "the shy one"; and Chad's pudgy, balding brother, Doug—dubbed "the older brother"—who insisted on coming along because without him "Chad is like a lost puppy." Tom was their manager (later revealed to be gay) and Glenn, the vice president with their record label, What-Ev Records, who was later replaced by horny Liz. The group's single "The Hardest Part of Breaking Up (Is Getting Back Your Stuff)" grazed the bottom of the real-life *Billboard* charts, reaching number 87 in September 2000.

The movie aired on February 21, 2000. In a somber note, actor Michael Cuccione, who played Q. T., passed away from complications stemming from Hodgkin's disease on January 13, 2001, shortly after his 16th birthday.

2000 MALIBU ROAD (*Serial Drama*)

FIRST TELECAST: *August 23, 1992*
LAST TELECAST: *September 9, 1992*
BROADCAST HISTORY:

Aug 1992, CBS Sun 9:00–11:00
Aug 1992–Sep 1992, CBS Wed 9:00–10:00

CAST:

Jade O'Keefe .... Lisa Hartman
Lindsay Rule .... Drew Barrymore
Perry Quinn .... Jennifer Beals
Joy Rule .... Tuesday Knight
Eric Adler .... Brian Bloom
Scott Sterling .... Scott Bryce
Roger Tabor .... Michael T. Weiss
Sgt. Joe Muñoz .... Ron Marquette
Hal Lanford .... Robert Foxworth
Camilla .... Constance Towers
Porter .... Mitchell Ryan

Short-lived summer serial drama about four women living together in a luxurious home at the beach in the Mailbu section of Los Angeles. Jade, who owned the house, was a retired call girl who needed the money from her three roommates to afford the upkeep on it. Living with her were Lindsay, an aspiring actress; Lindsay's ruthless overweight older sister, Joy, who was managing her sibling's career with Svengali-like control; and Perry, an attractive attorney trying to put her life back together after the death of her fiancé. In the premiere episode Jade was linked to the murder of a woman who floated up on the beach near her house, a case that was not solved during the four weeks *2000 Malibu Road* was on the air. Also seen were Eric, a young neighbor of Jade's who was in love with Lindsay and wanted to use her in a movie he was planning; Scott, a DBS television network executive and one of Jade's former clients; Roger, a high school boyfriend of Perry's who had just come back into her life; Sgt. Muñoz, the police officer who had arrested Jade; Hal, her attorney; Camilla, Jade's mother who wanted her to get married and have children; and Porter, Jade's sleazy stepfather, who was running for governor.

227 (*Situation Comedy*)

FIRST TELECAST: *September 14, 1985*
LAST TELECAST: *July 28, 1990*
BROADCAST HISTORY:

Sep 1985–Jun 1986, NBC Sat 9:30–10:00
Jun 1986–May 1987, NBC Sat 8:30–9:00
Jun 1987–Jul 1987, NBC Sat 8:00–8:30
Jul 1987–Sep 1988, NBC Sat 8:30–9:00
Oct 1988–Jul 1989, NBC Sat 8:00–8:30
Sep 1989–Feb 1990, NBC Sat 8:30–9:00
Apr 1990–May 1990, NBC Sun 8:30–9:00
Jun 1990–Jul 1990, NBC Sat 8:00–8:30

CAST:

Mary Jenkins .... Marla Gibbs
Lester Jenkins .... Hal Williams
Rose Lee Holloway .... Alaina Reed-Hall
Sandra Clark .... Jackee (Harry)
Brenda Jenkins (age 14) .... Regina King
Tiffany Holloway (12) (1985–1986) .... Kia Goodwin
Pearl Shay .... Helen Martin
Calvin Dobbs .... Curtis Baldwin
Alexandria DeWitt (1988–1989) .. Countess Vaughn
Eva Rawley (1989–1990) .... Toukie A. Smith
Julian C. Barlow (1989–1990) .... Paul Winfield
Dylan McMillan (1989–1990) .... Barry Sobel
Travis Filmore (1989–1990) .... Stoney Jackson
**Warren Merriwether (1989–1990)* ... Kevin Peter Hall

* Occasional

Marla Gibbs, who played the insolent, wisecracking housekeeper on *The Jeffersons* for ten years, brought a somewhat toned-down variation of the character to this popular comedy about family life in a black neighborhood of Washington, D.C. Mary and her best friend, Rose, the landlady, liked to sit on the stoop of their apartment building (No. 227) and gossip about many things—especially the building's resident vamp, Sandra, who had the figure and mannerisms of a modern Mae West. While Sandra wiggled around in her tight dresses, Mary's daughter, Brenda, was just beginning to struggle with the pains of adolescence, her number-one pain being gangly boyfriend Calvin. Lester was Mary's level-headed husband, a small-time contractor, and Pearl a crochety old busybody (and Calvin's grandmother) who often leaned out her window to join in the front-stoop conversations. Tiffany, Rose's daughter and Brenda's friend, was rarely seen after the first season.

In the final two seasons, several new characters appeared. Alexandria was an exceptionally bright 11-year-old, a college freshman; Dylan, an eccentric white teacher who moved into the building; Travis, a limo driver; and Barlow, a cranky gentleman who bought the building from Rose and moved into the top floor penthouse. Rose found romance in the final season in the person of Warren (played by Alaina Reed-Hall's real-life husband, actor Kevin Peter Hall), a very tall young man whom she married in early 1990.

Daytime reruns of *227* appeared on NBC from September 1989 through July 1990. The series was based on a play, *227*, in which several of the principals (including Gibbs) had appeared.

TYCOON, THE (*Situation Comedy*)

FIRST TELECAST: *September 15, 1964*
LAST TELECAST: *September 7, 1965*
BROADCAST HISTORY:
Sep 1964–Sep 1965, ABC Tue 9:00–9:30
CAST:
Walter Andrews .... Walter Brennan
Pat Burns .... Van Williams
Herbert Wilson .... Jerome Cowan
Betty Franklin .... Janet Lake
Martha Keane .... Pat McNulty
Una Fields .... Monty Margetts

The chairman of the board of the giant Thunder Corporation was Walter Andrews, a cantankerous and eccentric millionaire. Walter did things his way, and despite the complaints and misgivings of his coworkers and business associates, his approach to problems usually worked. Not one to let protocol affect his operation, Walter was a constant problem for everyone from his young assistant and private pilot Pat Burns, to company president Herbert Wilson. Walter made his home with his cute little granddaughter Martha and housekeeper Una Fields.

U

UC: UNDERCOVER (*Police Drama*)
FIRST TELECAST: *September 30, 2001*
LAST TELECAST: *January 13, 2002*
BROADCAST HISTORY:
Sep 2001–Jan 2002, NBC Sun 10:00–11:00
CAST:
Frank Donovan .... Oded Fehr
Jake Shaw .... Jon Seda
Alex Cross .... Vera Farmiga
Monica Davis .... Bruklin Harris
Cody .... Jarrad Paul
Jack "Sonny" Walker .... William Forsythe

Viewers might have believed World War III had broken out if they happened on this extremely violent crime show, whose constant explosions and wild shoot-outs were staged with big-screen panache. The quick-on-the-trigger UC team was an "elite Justice Department crimefighting unit" that tackled the most dangerous criminals in America, most of them armed to the teeth. The team had been founded by Agent John Keller (Grant Show), who was forced out in the premiere and replaced by the tough Donovan, and consisted of pretty-boy Agent Jake, who was cool under pressure but hot to plunge into the most dangerous situations; sexy, irritable Alex; psychological profiler Monica, who advised them of the perp's likely next move; and tech-whiz Cody, who ran the team's high-tech surveillance gear. They chased extremely vicious criminals and psychos, chief among whom was arrogant Sonny, who robbed banks with his tight, heavily armed commando team. Other recurring villains included Sonny's girlfriend Carly Jacobs (Angie Everhard), imprisoned Carlos Cortez (Steven Bauer) and Quito Real (Ving Rhames). The undercover work was grim, dark and moody, with the action scenes lovingly played in slow motion as the bad guys went down in a hail of bullets.

UFO (*Science Fiction*)
BROADCAST HISTORY:
Syndicated only
60 minutes
Produced: *1970* (26 episodes)
Released (U.S.): *Fall 1972*
CAST:
Cdr. Edward Straker .... Ed Bishop
Col. Alec Freeman .... George Sewell
Capt. Peter Karlin .... Peter Gordeno
Lt. Gay Ellis .... Gabrielle Drake
Col. Paul Foster .... Michael Billington
Gen. Henderson .... Grant Taylor

This science-fiction adventure was set 10 years in the future—in the year 1980—when it was discovered that unidentified flying objects posed an imminent threat to Earth. The general public was not yet aware of this unfortunate development, so a secret multinational defense command was set up under a movie studio (!) and called SHADO—Supreme Headquarters, Alien Defense Organization. Its commander was Edward Straker, whose "cover" was that of a movie producer. Others included Col. Freeman, his second-in-command; Capt. Karlin, pilot of the "remarkable" Seagull X-ray craft; and Lt. Ellis, in charge of SHADO's Moon Base Control.

The stories were filled with violence, green-faced aliens, a number of very sexy females, and the usual array of scientific hardware. Among the gimmicks were an underwater airplane launcher, the ultra-futuristic Moon Base, and a Space Intruder Detector called SID.

The series was produced in England.

U.N.C.L.E., syndicated title for *Man from U.N.C.L.E., The* and *Girl from U.N.C.L.E., The*

U.N. CASEBOOK (*Documentary*)
FIRST TELECAST: *September 26, 1948*
LAST TELECAST: *March 6, 1949*
BROADCAST HISTORY:
Sep 1948–Oct 1948, CBS Sun 6:45–7:15
Oct 1948–Mar 1949, CBS Sun 6:30–7:00
NARRATOR:
Dr. Lyman Bryson
Quincy Howe

The many and varied functions of the United Nations were looked at individually in this documentary series. Dr. Lyman Bryson, CBS Counsellor on Public Affairs, and Quincy Howe interviewed international political and intellectual figures about the roles that the U.N. played and should play in its multiple areas of activity.

USA NETWORK (Network) (*General Entertainment Cable Network*)
LAUNCHED:
September 27, 1977
SUBSCRIBERS (MAY 2003):
86.2 million (81% U.S.)

A top-rated cable network and the cable channel that is most similar to the broadcast networks in content. Its schedule is a mix of movies, sports, and series, and it has long emphasized original production.

USA's first major venture into original series was in the mid-1980s with *Cover Story* (1984), *Seeing Stars* (1984), *Hollywood Insider* (1985), *Check It Out* (1985), *Robert Klein Time* (1986), and *Sanchez of Bel Air* (1986). None of these were particularly successful, so USA then began producing new episodes of series that had been canceled by (or acquired from) other sources, including *Airwolf* (1987, from CBS), *Alfred Hitchcock Presents* (1987, from NBC), *Ray Bradbury Theater* (1987, from HBO), *The Hitchhiker* (1989, from HBO), and *American Bandstand* (1989, from syndication).

The network finally began to hit its stride in original series in the 1990s. Among its more successful efforts were *Counterstrike* (1990), *Swamp Thing* (1990), *Silk Stalkings* (1991, originally coproduced with, and concurrently aired on, CBS), *Weird Science* (1994), and the offbeat but critically acclaimed *Duckman* (1994). Later successes included *Pacific Blue, La Femme Nikita, Dead Zone, Monk* and the eye-popping *Strip Poker.* A surprise hit in the late '90s was the wildly popular *WWF Raw* wrestling show on Monday nights (see under *Wrestling*).

USA began producing original movies in 1989 and later aired more than a dozen each year. Many were in the thriller genre and quite popular; one of them, *The China Lake Murders* (1990), ranked for many years as the highest-rated original basic cable movie. Others have ranged from the animated *Jonny's Golden Quest* to the acclaimed *Moby Dick*. The balance of the schedule over the years has consisted of sports (boxing, golf, U.S. Open tennis), cartoons (*Cartoon Express*), game shows (including some originals), and rerun series such as *MacGyver, Wings, Murder, She Wrote* and *Walker, Texas Ranger*.

The network was originally called the Madison Square Garden Network and was devoted primarily to sports programming. Its name was changed to USA Network in April 1980 to reflect a shift to more broad-based programming. It first reached more than half of all U.S. television homes in May 1988, and its principal original prime time series after that date (including those mentioned above) are listed in this book under their individual titles. The network's founder and longtime chief executive was Kay Koplovitz.

U.S.A. TODAY—THE TELEVISION SERIES (*Newsmagazine*)

BROADCAST HISTORY:

Syndicated only
30 minutes
Produced: *1988–1990*
Released: *September 1988*

ANCHOR/CORRESPONDENTS:

Edie Magnus (1988–1989)
Bill Macatee
Kenneth Walker (1988)
Robin Young (1988–1989)
Boyd Matson (1988)
Beth Ruyak
Dale Harimoto (1989–1990)

The national newspaper *U.S.A. Today*, with its short, punchy stories, emphasis on celebrities, and full-color graphics, was heavily influenced by television. Even its street corner vending machines were designed to look like TV sets. Ironically, this newspaper imitating TV became a daily TV show in the fall of 1988, with each episode modeled after an issue of the paper. There were four distinct "sections," each with its own correspondent: "U.S.A." (general interest headline stories anchored by Edie Magnus); "Sports" (with Bill Macatee); "Money" (financial and business news from Kenneth Walker); and "Life" (show business and lifestyles with Robin Young). Lavishly produced by former NBC president Grant Tinker and the Gannett Company, owners of *U.S.A. Today*, the series had a high-tech set, glitzy graphics, and a rapid-fire pace. It premiered amid a great burst of publicity but lasted less than 1½ years.

There were problems almost from the beginning. Designed to air between 6:00–8:00 P.M., *U.S.A. Today—The Television Series* opened with such dismal ratings that most stations quickly moved it to post-11:00 P.M. time slots—in some cases as late as 2:00 A.M. or 3:00 A.M. The show's original executive producer, Steve Friedman, former producer of *The Today Show*, was replaced by former *Entertainment Tonight* executive Jim Bellows two months after its premiere, and a reported $10,000,000 was poured in to retool a program that had already cost $40,000,000. The number of stories, initially 20–25 in a single half hour, was reduced to 5–7, and a concerted effort was made to reduce the series' fast-paced MTV look. Financial reporter Kenneth Walker and regular political reporter Boyd Matson were both gone before the end of the year, and in January the title was shortened to *U.S.A. Today on TV*. That spring Edie Magnus departed, with Beth Ruyak, anchor of the hour-long weekend edition of *U.S.A. Today on TV*, taking her place. Dale Harimoto replaced Robin Young as the show's entertainment reporter, and Tom Kirby arrived as its third producer in six months. Unfortunately, nothing seemed to help and, on January 5, 1990, *U.S.A. Today* (the title had been shortened again) aired for the last time.

U.S. CUSTOMS: CLASSIFIED (*Documentary*)

BROADCAST HISTORY:

Syndicated only
60 minutes
Produced: *1995–1996* (22 episodes)
Released: *September 1995*

HOST:

Stephen J. Cannell

Appearing in his busy "control center," bearded TV producer Stephen J. Cannell hosted this series featuring reenactments of actual cases from the files of the U.S. Customs Service, including, in some cases, actual surveillance footage. Episodes showed the service dealing with such problems as drug smugglers, illegal aliens, illegal trading of endangered species, and cults.

U.S. HIGHWAY 1954 (*Travelogue*)

FIRST TELECAST: *August 2, 1954*
LAST TELECAST: *September 27, 1954*
BROADCAST HISTORY:

Aug 1954–Sep 1954, ABC Mon 7:30–8:00

Travel films on American vacation spots and scenic areas such as the Grand Canyon, Yosemite National Park, Cape Cod, etc.

U.S. MARINE BAND (*Music*)

FIRST TELECAST: *July 9, 1949*
LAST TELECAST: *August 20, 1949*
BROADCAST HISTORY:

Jul 1949–Aug 1949, NBC Sat 8:00–8:30

A series of summer concerts originating in Washington, D.C., and featuring the 70-piece Marine Band, under the direction of Major William Santelmann.

U.S. MARSHALL see *Sheriff of Cochise, The*

U.S. ROYAL SHOWCASE, THE (*Comedy Variety*)

FIRST TELECAST: *January 13, 1952*
LAST TELECAST: *June 29, 1952*
BROADCAST HISTORY:

Jan 1952–Jun 1952, NBC Sun 7:00–7:30

HOST:

George Abbott
Jack Carson

This live comedy variety series originated from New York City. Each show was composed of three separate acts: a performance by a well-known star comedian, a singing interlude by a popular recording artist, and a performance by a promising young comedian. Broadway producer George Abbott directed the show and acted as the host, introducing the evening's performers, but he relinquished the on-camera hosting chores to comedian Jack Carson on April 13. The new-talent segment had been dropped from the show by the time Carson had taken over as host.

U.S. STEEL HOUR, THE (*Dramatic Anthology*)
FIRST TELECAST: *October 27, 1953*
LAST TELECAST: *June 12, 1963*
BROADCAST HISTORY:
Oct 1953–Jun 1955, ABC Tue 9:30–10:30
Jul 1955–Jun 1963, CBS Wed 10:00–11:00

United States Steel's initial venture into broadcast drama had been on ABC radio in 1945. Under the title *The Theatre Guild on the Air,* it was a showcase for authors and directors as well as performers, and presented plays from New York with distinguished casts. In 1953 the Theatre Guild moved the series to television, in effect bringing the Broadway stage to the nation's television viewers. Throughout its 10-year run as a live show originating from New York, *The U.S. Steel Hour* aired on alternate weeks with other dramatic anthologies. Ironically, *Armstrong Circle Theatre,* the show with which it shared the Wednesday time slot during most of its eight years on CBS, had been its competition during part of the time it was on ABC.

The two years on ABC produced primarily dramatic presentations. The premiere telecast, "P.O.W." starring Gary Merrill, Richard Kiley, and Sally Forrest, set the tone. Rex Harrison and his then wife, Lilli Palmer, were featured in "The Man in Possession," Tallulah Bankhead in an adaptation of Ibsen's *Hedda Gabler,* Thomas Mitchell and Dorothy Gish in a version of *The Rise and Fall of Silas Lapham,* and Wendell Corey and Keenan Wynn in "The Rack," by frequent contributor Rod Serling. Not all was serious, however, as Andy Griffith starred in "No Time for Sergeants" in 1955, before re-creating the role on both Broadway and film.

With the move to CBS, there was more diversity in the subject matter. To be sure, there were still moving dramas—Paul Newman, Albert Salmi, and George Peppard in "Bang the Drum Slowly" in 1956, almost 20 years before the movie of the same title; Teresa Wright, Dick Van Dyke, and George C. Scott in "Trap for a Stranger"; and Mona Freeman and Cliff Robertson in "The Two Worlds of Charlie Gordon" (which became the 1968 movie *Charly* for which Mr. Robertson received a Best Actor Academy Award for his portrayal of the title role)—but there was much more. Dorothy Collins and Edward Mulhare starred in an adaptation of Oscar Wilde's *The Importance of Being Earnest,* and Jack Carson, Basil Rathbone, Jimmy Boyd, and Florence Henderson were featured in a musical titled "Huck Finn," based on the Mark Twain novel. There was even a musical revue, with Fred MacMurray, Wally Cox, Edie Adams, Carol Burnett, and Hans Conried in a bit of fluff titled "The American Cowboy." Johnny Carson, not known primarily as an actor, appeared twice in light dramas in 1960, the first time with Anne Francis in "Queen of the Orange Bowl."

In ten years on the air, *The U.S. Steel Hour* presented more than 200 live plays, and the list of noted personalities who appeared in them is substantial. Numerous people made multiple appearances and, though some of them have already been mentioned, the names that follow were featured in at least four shows: Eddie Albert, Edward Andrews, Marty Astor, Ed Begley, Ralph Bellamy, Larry Blyden, Geraldine Brooks, Jack Carson, Hans Conried, James Daly, Jeff Donnell, Patty Duke, Faye Emerson, Nine Foch, Mona Freeman, Farley Granger, Arthur Hill, Richard Kiley, June Lockhart, Diana Lynn, Bill McGuire, Barry Morse, Meg Mundy, Betsy Palmer, Gene Raymond, Cliff Robertson, Franchot Tone, and Teresa Wright.

U TO U (*Kids' Magazine*)
BROADCAST HISTORY:
Nickelodeon
30 minutes
Produced: *1994–1996* (20 episodes)
Premiered: *December 3, 1994*
HOSTS:
Ali Rivera
Sertrone Starks

An interactive video magazine for kids. Among the segments were video letters from kids around the world, contests played by kids at home over the U-Phone, and big-screen video games played by the studio audience. Viewers could call, write, or send computer messages on Prodigy, share jokes, and ask questions of celebrities. Creativity was encouraged; a kid who sent in a song she or he had written might get time in a recording studio to record it and a professionally produced music video to go with it.

UGLIEST GIRL IN TOWN, THE (*Situation Comedy*)
FIRST TELECAST: *September 26, 1968*
LAST TELECAST: *January 30, 1969*
BROADCAST HISTORY:
Sep 1968–Jan 1969, ABC Thu 7:30–8:00
CAST:
Timothy Blair ("Timmie") .... Peter Kastner
Julie Renfield .... Patricia Brake
Gene Blair......................... Garry Marshall
Sondra Wolston .... Jenny Till
David Courtney................ Nicholas Parsons

This frothy bit of comedy had a male star dressed in women's clothes as its running gag. The situation was all very logical, though somewhat far-fetched. It seemed that young Hollywood talent agent Timothy Blair had fallen madly in love with an English starlet named Julie, while Julie was in town making a film. Then she flew back to London, and Timothy did not have the money to follow. Enter Timothy's brother Gene, a professional photographer assigned to shoot pictures of San Francisco hippies for a London magazine. At the last moment Gene's pictures were accidentally destroyed, and in desperation he dressed Timothy in a wig and hippie outfit and took pictures of *him* to send to London. London liked the pictures so much that they wanted that "girl"—for a major "Twiggy"-style modeling assignment.

Timothy (now dubbed "Timmie") went along with the ruse because it meant free airplane fare to England and his Julie, but once there he was faced with the necessity of maintaining the put-on in all sorts of awkward situations. What to do in a nude scene?

In almost less time than it took to explain all this, *The Ugliest Girl in Town* was on and off the ABC schedule.

ULTIMATE CHALLENGE, THE (*Documentary*)
FIRST TELECAST: *September 13, 1991*

LAST TELECAST: *November 1, 1991*
BROADCAST HISTORY:
Sep 1991–Nov 1991, FOX Fri 9:00–10:00
HOSTS:
Mike Adamle
Heather Thomas
Larry Hoff
John Long

Daredevils, professional stuntmen, and other thrill seekers were featured on this series that showed not only the actual stunts, but the detailed preparations that were needed to maximize the chance for success and minimize the risk of injury. High dives, sky diving, movie stunts, and cave exploration were just a few of the exploits showcased. Regular features were "Greg Stump's World of Extremes," in which Mr. Stump covered such subjects as stunt skiing, BMX biking, bungee jumping, etc.; automobile stunt driver Spanky Spangler's daredevil challenge; and a grueling outdoor collegiate obstacle course competition in and around Salmon River, Idaho.

A very similar program, *Stuntmasters*, premiered in syndication the same month this Fox series began. Neither was first with the idea: earlier stunt documentaries included *High Risk* (1988) and *Thrill Seekers* (1972).

ULTIMATE REVENGE (*Audience Participation*)
BROADCAST HISTORY:
TNN
30 minutes
Original episodes: *2001*
Premiered: *August 21, 2001*
HOST:
Ryan Seacrest

A short-lived cable series in which one party was helped in getting comic "revenge" on another. In one segment, a wife had her dumpy house garishly redecorated while her stick-in-the-mud husband was out; returning to find a fountain, a statue of David, and a gay designer in his living room, he barked, "What the hell is this?" In another, a husband who habitually drove too fast was set up to be stopped by phony cops.

UNCLE BUCK (*Situation Comedy*)
FIRST TELECAST: *September 10, 1990*
LAST TELECAST: *March 9, 1991*
BROADCAST HISTORY:
Sep 1990–Nov 1990, CBS Mon 8:00–8:30
Nov 1990, CBS Fri 8:00–8:30
Jan 1991–Mar 1992, CBS Sat 8:00–8:30
CAST:
Buck Russell .... Kevin Meaney
Tia Russell (age 16) .... Dah-ve Chodan
Miles Russell (8)........................ Jacob Gelman
Maizy Russell (6) .... Sarah Martineck
Maggie Hogoboom .... Audrey Meadows
Skank .... Dennis Cockrum
Rafer Freeman .... Thomas Mikal Ford
THEME:
"Uncle Buck," written by Steve Dorff and John Bettis, performed by Ronnie Milsap

Television, which is always testing the limits of taste, went over the edge in this short-lived, 8:00 P.M. "family" sitcom, which was denounced by critics and rejected by viewers. Buck was one of TV's more unlikely father figures—a pudgy, gruff, immature, cigar-smoking, beer-drinking slob. Nevertheless, following the deaths of his brother and sister-in-law in an accident, he had become guardian to their three children. Tia, the oldest, was a bright, but lazy, boy-crazy teenager who was forever trying to get around the household rules by donning miniskirts and black hose to get hot dates; Miles and Maizy were typical of TV's unending stream of wisecracking tots. The program gained its unfortunate reputation during the first few seconds of the opening episode when adorable little Maizy came through the kitchen door and abruptly yelled at her brother, "Miles, you suck!" When Uncle Buck objected mildly, she shot back "He called me a frecklebutt, and I don't have freckles on my butt. They're beauty marks." The laugh track roared, but parents, watching at home with their kids, were disgusted.

Gross-out humor permeated the show. Although Buck had moved into the children's neat suburban home, he continued to invite over his poker-playing buddies Skank and Rafer, much to the disgust of the kids' fearsome grandmother, Mrs. Hogoboom. She found little in Buck to trust as a positive role model and threatened to have his guardianship revoked, until she came to realize that above that beer belly was a heart of gold. He did love the kids and tried to guide them along the right path—even if he could not exactly lead by example.

Adapted from the 1989 movie of the same name starring John Candy.

UNCOVERED, syndicated title for *Vise, The*

UNDECLARED (*School Drama*)
FIRST TELECAST: *September 25, 2001*
LAST TELECAST: *March 12, 2002*
BROADCAST HISTORY:
Sep 2001–Mar 2002, FOX Tue 8:30–9:00
CAST:
Steven Karp........................ Jay Baruchel
Lloyd Haythe.................... Charlie Hunnam
Lizzie Exley.............................. Carla Gallo
Rachel Lindquist .... Monica Keena
Ron Garner............................ Seth Rogen
Marshall Nesbitt...................... Timm Sharp
Hal Karp .... Loudon Wainwright
Tina Ellroy .... Christina Payano
Perry .... Jarrett Grode

Bookish, awkward, and insecure Steven Karp was starting his freshman year at the University of North Eastern California. Steven had grown up 10 minutes from the campus, and his father, Hal, who was in the early stages of a divorce and had lost his job as a Saab salesman, spent a lot of his time hanging around the dorm. At age 48, and much to the chagrin of his son, Hal was acting like a teenager. Steven was infatuated with Lizzie, a psychology major who spent a lot of time on the phone with her jealous boyfriend, Eric (Jason Segel), who was out of school and working at the Kopy-Mat. Steven shared a suite with three other guys—Lloyd, a drama major from London and the dorm's resident ladies' man; Marshall, a music major from Fargo, North Dakota, who worked in the school cafeteria and was much smarter than he looked; and Ron, a sarcastic business major from Vancouver. Marshall had the hots for neurotic Rachel, a sexy art major from Marin County, who lived across the hall. Lizzie and Rachel's other roommate, Tina—who, like Steven, had failed to choose a major—was madly in love with Lloyd. After Eric broke up with Lizzie, she and Steven got more serious.

UNDER COVER (*Espionage/Foreign Intrigue*)
FIRST TELECAST: *January 7, 1991*
LAST TELECAST: *February 16, 1991*
BROADCAST HISTORY:
Jan 1991, ABC Mon 9:00–11:00
Jan 1991–Feb 1991, ABC Sat 9:00–10:00
CAST:
Dylan Del'Amico .... Anthony John Denison
Kate Del'Amico .... Linda Purl
Flynn .... John Rhys-Davies
Graham Parker .... John Slattery
Stewart Merriman .... Josef Sommer
Alex Robbins .... Kasi Lemmons
Megan .... Arlene Taylor
Grimbach .... Raye Birk
Emily Del'Amico (pilot) .... Sumer Stamper
Emily Del'Amico .... Marne Patterson
Marlon Del'Amico (pilot) .... Joshua South
Marlon Del'Amico .... Adam Ryen
Director Waugh (pilot) .... Dakin Matthews
Director Waugh .... G. W. Bailey

This espionage series got into trouble by reflecting world events a little too realistically. In the post-Cold War era, the operatives of the National Intelligence Agency, especially husband-and-wife Dylan and Kate, were concerned as much with their personal lives as with enemy spooks. Would Kate's youthful affair with a Soviet scientist come back to haunt her? How would they tell their teenage daughter Emily what her parents did for a living?

Their assignments dealt with leftover Soviet spies and third-world troublemakers, and it was one of the latter that caused the program so much grief. In a two-part story, a team was sent to Kuwait just before an Iraqi invasion. Part one aired on January 12th, but part two—in which Iraq plotted to fire virus-carrying missiles into Israel—would have appeared right after the real war broke out, and it was abruptly pulled from the schedule. It eventually aired on July 13, 1991 (preceded by a repeat of part one) as an *ABC Saturday Night Movie.* Two additional unaired episodes were telecast the following Saturday, July 20th, disguised as the movie *Spy Games.*

UNDER ONE ROOF, see *Spencer*

UNDER ONE ROOF (*Drama*)
FIRST TELECAST: *March 14, 1995*
LAST TELECAST: *April 18, 1995*
BROADCAST HISTORY:
Mar 1995–Apr 1995, CBS Tue 8:00–9:00
CAST:
Neb Langston .... James Earl Jones
Ron Langston .... Joe Morton
Maggie Langston .... Vanessa Bell Calloway
Charlotte "Charlie" Langston (age 15)
.... Essence Atkins
Derrick Langston (10) .... Ronald Joshua Scott
Ayesha (née Beverly) Langston ..... Monique Ridge
Marcus (16) .... Merlin Santana
Matt "Siggy" Sigalos .... Terence Knox

Neb was a widowed Seattle police officer sharing his suburban home with his extended family in this realistic depiction of the problems of a multi-generational black family. Living upstairs were his responsible son, Ron, who had returned from Germany after retiring from the Marines and just opened L&S Lumber and Hardware with his white partner, Siggy; Ron's sensible wife, Maggie, who graduated from college in the series' third episode and was going back to work for the first time in two decades; and their two children, Charlie, an engaging but sometimes self-centered teenager, and Derrick, an active young diabetic. Also in the house were Neb's independent daughter, Ayesha, who had recently moved back home, and Marcus, Neb's moody, troubled foster son who had a penchant for getting in trouble with the law. With such a large group living under the same roof there were conflicts, but there was love and understanding as well and everyone ultimately did his or her best to be supportive of each other.

UNDER ONE ROOF (*Competition/Reality*)
FIRST TELECAST: *March 22, 2002*
LAST TELECAST: *July 16, 2002*
BROADCAST HISTORY:
Mar 2002, UPN Fri 8:00–9:00
Jul 2002, UPN Tue 9:00–10:00
HOST:
Rob Nelson

This was a family-based reality series that sent five families to Koro, a remote island in Fiji, where they competed to win a luxurious beachfront home. First, however, they had to live in it together for three weeks "under one roof." There were two primary competitions, the Family Face Off and the Property Quest, examples being a field goal kickoff, a Fijian boat race and a spider crawl in which the object was to put as many spiders as possible on one's own family members. Winners of the Family Face Off chose between an advantage item that could help them in the next series of challenges, or a special prize, which they could enjoy back home. Property Quest winners were given ribbons that would eventually determine who got the deed to the house. At the end of every other episode the family with the fewest ribbons had to leave the island and, in the final episode, the last two families competed in a final quest for the deed to the house. In order to succeed the often bickering families had to put aside their problems with each other and work together to defeat the other families.

The five families were the Skofields from Las Vegas, characterized as "free-thinking, liberal new-age hippies"; the McRaes from Orlando, Florida, a close-knit family that had never owned a home of their own; the Paganis from Henderson, Nevada, trying to get back on track after the family business had failed and the parents separated; the Hatmakers from outside Galveston, Texas, who were still recovering a year after the accidental death of their dad (longtime friend Mark Anderson filled in as a surrogate dad); and the Distels from Huntington Beach, California, who convinced their teenage children to participate in a last family adventure before they left home and started their own lives.

When they arrived on Koro, each family was taken to a different location; the initial competition was to be the first to find the house. The Distels arrived first and took the two master suites in the four-bedroom house, while the Skofields, arriving second, took the other two bedrooms. When the McRaes arrived they took over the stove, laundry room, community bathroom and living room. Last to arrive were the Hatmakers and the Paganis, who slept on the floor. Host Nelson outlined the rules and told them that when they ran out of the food provided they would have to barter with the Fijians, who stood by laughing and clapping as the rich Americans competed for all this wealth.

At the end of the second episode the Distels were eliminated. Dismal ratings then prompted UPN to shelve *Under One Roof*. It resurfaced in early July and restarted from the beginning with reruns of the first two episodes. At the end of the third episode the Hatmakers were faced with possible elimination but, since UPN pulled the plug again, viewers never found out who won the Polynesian dream house.

UNDER SUSPICION (*Police Drama*)

FIRST TELECAST: *September 16, 1994*
LAST TELECAST: *August 9, 1995*
BROADCAST HISTORY:

Sep 1994–Mar 1995, CBS Fri 9:00–10:00
Nov 1994–Dec 1994, CBS Mon–Thu 12:35–1:40 A.M.
Jun 1995, CBS Wed 9:00–11:00
Jul 1995–Aug 1995, CBS Wed 10:00–11:00

CAST:

Det. Rose "Phil" Phillips .... Karen Sillas
Sgt. James Vitelli .... Philip Casnoff
Capt. Mickey Schwartz .... Seymour Cassel
Det. Desmond Beck .... Michael Beach
Chief Jack DeSort (1994) .... Ray Baker
Det. Patrick Clarke (1994) .... Paul McCrane
Det. Lou Barbini (1994) .... Richard Foronjy
Det. Costa "Doc" Papadakis ..... Anthony DeSando
Patsi Moosekian .... Arabella Field
Coroner Leon Hart .... Doug Baldwin
Elena .... Jeanette Aguilar Harris

This dark and moody cop show focused on Rose "Phil" Phillips, the only female homicide detective in an otherwise all-male precinct in Portland, Oregon. Not only did Phil have to fight crime, she also had to deal with the sexist attitudes of many of her fellow detectives, most notably Missing Persons Det. Barbini. Her confidant on the force was Vitelli, an internal affairs investigator with whom she had an on-again off-again romantic involvement. Having lost her original partner and mentor, Frank Fusco (Peter Onorati), in the pilot episode, Phil initially worked alone, later teaming up with Beck and Papadakis.

UNDERCURRENT (*Dramatic Anthology*)

FIRST TELECAST: *July 1, 1955*
LAST TELECAST: *September 19, 1958*
BROADCAST HISTORY:

Jul 1955–Sep 1958, CBS Fri 10:00–10:30 (Summers only)

For four summers *Undercurrent* was the replacement for *The Lineup*. During the first two years, the plays presented were all new to television. Starring in these dramas, which tended to be on the heavy side, were many future stars of television series. Among them were Brian Keith, Craig Stevens, Lloyd Bridges, Dale Robertson, Raymond Burr, and Vince Edwards. None of them, however, were major stars when these films aired. In 1957 and 1958, *Undercurrent* telecast reruns of episodes originally aired on other anthology series, the 1958 edition coming from NBC's *The Web*, which had aired the previous summer.

UNDERGRADS (*Cartoon*)

BROADCAST HISTORY:

MTV
30 minutes
Original episodes: *2001* (13 episodes)
Premiered: *April 22, 2001*

VOICES:

Parker "Nitz" Walsh, Justin "Gimpy" Taylan, Cal Evans, Rocko Gambiani .... Pete Williams
Kimmy Burton .... Susan Dalton

Four guys who had been friends since childhood shared their freshman year at college—even though each went to a different college in the same town. Nitz was the smart one, a slightly nerdy guy who habitually wore a baseball cap; Rocko, a big, hairy lug with considerably less brainpower ("What?"); Cal, a hunky, horny, but somewhat inept babe magnet; and Gimpy, a bug-eyed little computer geek who hardly looked human, and was usually found in front of a glowing screen. They hung out at a comic-book shop or at each other's messy dorm rooms, and talked about sex (with and without partners), partying, and how to avoid studying. Kimmy was Nitz' childhood crush.

UNDERSEA WORLD OF JACQUES COUSTEAU, THE (*Documentary*)

FIRST TELECAST: *May 23, 1976*
LAST TELECAST: *June 13, 1976*
BROADCAST HISTORY:

May 1976–Jun 1976, ABC Sun 7:00–8:00

PRODUCER:

Capt. Jacques-Yves Cousteau

NARRATOR:

Joseph Campanella

French scientist and explorer Capt. Jacques Cousteau has been producing TV documentaries longer than most people realize. His first network telecast was a feature on undersea archeology, presented on *Omnibus* on January 17, 1954. Widespread fame came in the late 1960s, however, when he began a long series of prime-time specials for ABC depicting outdoor nature adventures from pole to pole. It was ABC's answer to the *National Geographic Specials*.

At first the program dealt with sea life, as seen from Cousteau's exploration ship *Calypso* (the first special, on January 8, 1968, was "Sharks"). Later, as he began to run out of sea-born subjects, programs were done on land life as well. Rod Serling was the narrator until 1974, when he was replaced by Joseph Campanella.

The dates shown above reflect the single instance in which Cousteau specials ran consecutively for four weeks in the same time slot, qualifying as a "series" for the purposes of this book.

UNDRESSED (*Drama*)

BROADCAST HISTORY:

MTV
30 minutes
Original episodes: *1999–*
Premiered: *July 26, 1999*

MTV's young viewers evidently had one thing on their minds around 11:00 P.M.—sex—and this unusual serialized anthology provided them with plenty of, er, stimulation. Each episode looked in on three couples or sets of friends, each of whose stories continued over several episodes. The result was a constantly changing cast of characters and actors, all young, all nubile, all horny. Ages ranged from high schoolers to college graduate students, and couples represented various races, sexual preferences (including numerous gay, or discovering-I'm-gay, story lines), and even handicaps (a blind guy, another in a wheelchair). For example, two girls were thrown together in a college dorm room, where one had no inhibitions about having sex with various boys on the top bunk, to the dismay of her roommate below; four girls formed "the bitch squad" and plotted against boys; and a shy high school boy befriended his best friend's rejected girlfriend, and found himself attracted to her. There was much pulling off of shirts, unzipping of pants, and talk of sex and relationships, but little real nudity.

Given the nature of the series, hundreds of young actors were seen at various times, none of them famous names. During the first season the most frequently seen characters were Tina (Bree Turner) and her big sister Liz (Sarah Lancaster), who helped herself to Tina's boyfriend; and in the second season Jamie (Eddie Ebell) and his girlfriend Vanessa (Lackey Bevis).

UNHAPPILY EVER AFTER (*Situation Comedy*)

FIRST TELECAST: *January 11, 1995*
LAST TELECAST: *September 19, 1999*
BROADCAST HISTORY:

Jan 1995, WB Wed 8:30–9:00
Jan 1995–Jun 1995, WB Wed 9:00–9:30
May 1995–Jul 1996, WB Wed 9:30–10:00
Jul 1996–Aug 1996, WB Sun 9:00–10:00
Aug 1996–Jan 1997, WB Sun 9:00–9:30
Feb 1997, WB Sun 9:00–10:00
Feb 1997–Aug 1997, WB Sun 9:00–9:30
Sep 1997–Oct 1997, WB Sun 8:30–9:00
Oct 1997–Aug 1998, WB Sun 9:00–9:30
Aug 1998–Sep 1998, WB Sun 9:00–10:00
Sep 1998–Dec 1998, WB Sun 9:00–9:30
Dec 1998–Jan 1999, WB Sun 9:00–10:00
Jan 1999–Sep 1999, WB Sun 9:30–10:00

CAST:

Jack Malloy .... Geoff Pierson
Jennie Malloy (1995–1998) .... Stephanie Hodge
Ryan Malloy (age 16) .... Kevin Connolly
Tiffany Malloy (15) .... Nikki Cox
Ross Malloy (8) .... Justin Berfield
Maureen Slattery (1995–1996) .... Joyce Van Patten
Voice of Mr. Floppy .... Bobcat Goldthwait
**Amber Moss (1995–1997)* .... Dana Daurey
**Barry (1995–1997)* .... Ant
Sable O'Brien (1996–1997) .... Kristanna Loken
Muffy (1997–1998) .... Deborah Kellner
**Mr. Monteleone (1997–1998)* ..... Oliver Muirhead
Barbara Caulfield (1998–1999) ..... Wendy Benson

*Occasional

THEME:

Original theme performed by Bobcat Goldthwait. After a couple of months changed to "Hit the Road, Jack"

Produced by the same people responsible for Fox's *Married . . . with Children*, this comedy was similarly mean-spirited. After sixteen years of marriage Jennie Malloy, looking for more excitement in her life, had kicked husband Jack out of their Los Angeles home. Jack, who made $40,000 a year as a used car salesman for his soon-to-be-ex-father-in-law, was offered a divorce settlement by Jennie that would leave him with only $8,000 to live on. While they fought over the terms of the divorce he moved into a ratty apartment with only a stuffed bunny called Mr. Floppy for company. Young son Ross had given Mr. Floppy to his dad because he didn't want him to be lonely. Jack initially wondered about his sanity when the cynical Mr. Floppy actually started talking to him, but, not surprisingly, the stuffed bunny became this loser's only real friend. The two Malloy high schoolers were Ryan, a slob unable to find a girlfriend, and Tiffany, a self-absorbed young sexpot. Although none of the kids were thrilled to spend the weekends with Dad, they were more than willing to play their separated parents off against each other to get whatever they wanted. Jennie's chain-smoking, alcoholic mother, Maureen, who hated Jack, had moved into the house to help her raise the kids. Despite the separation, and the fact that they disliked each other intensely, there was a surprisingly strong physical attraction between Jennie and Jack, leading to periodic sexual encounters in both her house and his apartment.

In Fall 1995, Jack moved back into the house but was living in the basement since he had to court Jennie to get back into their bedroom (he never made it). A year later the series focus shifted from the parents' relationship to the activities of the kids, particularly sexy Tiffany and her new rival at school, Sable. Sable used Ryan as a doormat, but he was too stupid to realize it. In May, Tiffany was accepted to Harvard but couldn't go because Jack couldn't afford the $28,000 a year it would have cost. That fall Tiffany and Ryan went to Northridge Junior College, where she worked on the school paper, the *Northridge Journal*. On the September 21 episode Jennie died in a tanning-bed accident, leaving Jack free to date—but she was still around in ghostly form (visible only to her family) to keep interfering with everyone's lives. The following week she was brought back to life, when a real-life WB programming executive, Jordan Levin, showed up late in the episode and told the rest of the family that the ghostly Jennie wasn't as funny as they had thought it was going to be.

A year later Jennie was really gone from the show, having dumped Jack and gone to Europe with another woman. Ryan's hair was bleached blond, and Tiffany had a new rival at school, Barbara, the sexy blond brown-noser. They both had aspirations of transferring to Harvard and were in constant competition, academically and socially. In the series' finale they were both accepted to Harvard and Jack, in order to pay the high cost of the Ivy League school, motivated himself to become an incredibly successful car salesman to the stars.

UNION SQUARE (*Situation Comedy*)

FIRST TELECAST: *September 25, 1997*
LAST TELECAST: *January 22, 1998*
BROADCAST HISTORY:

Sep 1997–Jan 1998, NBC Thu 8:30–9:00

CAST:

Gabriella (Gaby) Diaz .... Constance Marie
Michael Weiss .... Michael Landes

Suzanne Barkley .... Harriet Sansom Harris
Vince .... Jeffrey Anderson-Gunter
Carrie .... Christine Burke
Albie .... Jonathan Slavin
Jack Pappas .... Jim Pirri

Another of the many friends-hanging-out sitcoms of the '90s, *Union Square* was set in a brightly colored Manhattan diner of that name—located in the same trendy neighborhood geographically (if not in terms of popularity) as *Seinfeld* and *Friends*. Among the regulars were Gaby, a fast-talking, excitable Latin sexpot who was looking for her big break as an actress; Michael, a struggling playwright with notably little self-confidence; and Suzanne, an acerbic real estate agent who would do anything for a sale. Trading quips with them were the staff, which included sarcastic, dreadlocked owner Vince; waitress and wannabe rock star Carrie; airheaded waiter Albie; and short-order cook Jack, a big dumb hunk who thought he was God's gift to women.

UNITED OR NOT (*Interview*)
FIRST TELECAST: *July 2, 1951*
LAST TELECAST: *October 27, 1952*
BROADCAST HISTORY:
Jul 1951–Sep 1951, ABC Mon 9:00–9:30
Oct 1951–Jun 1952, ABC Tue 9:00–9:30
Jun 1952–Aug 1952, ABC Tue 8:30–9:00
Sep 1952–Oct 1952, ABC Mon 8:30–9:00
MODERATOR:
John MacVane

Interviews and discussions with guests from the United Nations, including ambassadors, specialists from various technical branches, foreign government officials, and the Secretary General, Trygve Lie.

UNITED STATES (*Situation Comedy*)
FIRST TELECAST: *March 11, 1980*
LAST TELECAST: *April 29, 1980*
BROADCAST HISTORY:
Mar 1980–Apr 1980, NBC Tue 10:30–11:00
CAST:
Richard Chapin .... Beau Bridges
Libby Chapin .... Helen Shaver
Dylan Chapin .... Rossie Harris
Nicky Chapin .... Justin Dana

Produced by Larry Gelbart, who had developed *M*A*S*H* for TV nearly a decade earlier, *United States* was supposed to be a breakthrough in its blending of drama and comedy to explore the joys and the problems of contemporary marriage. Richard and Libby Chapin were a young, middle-class couple with two young children, and most of the action took place in their home. The series was certainly not a typical situation comedy. The frank discussions of problems, the open hostilities, and the inability to often reach long-term solutions all made difficult the Chapin's search for "united states," those moments when they felt at one with each other, a single entity. The subjects they discussed included death and dying, Libby's reunion with an old family friend who had molested her when she was eight, the mixed feelings they had had about becoming parents, their differing attitudes about their sexual relationship, and the admission that each of them had been unfaithful. Far from being funny, *United States* was often tedious, boring, and didactic. Viewers tuned out in droves. It lasted less than two months.

UNIVERSAL STAR TIME, Syndicated title for *Bob Hope Presents the Chrysler Theatre*

UNIVERSE (*Science Magazine*)
FIRST TELECAST: *July 12, 1980*
LAST TELECAST: *September 14, 1982*
BROADCAST HISTORY:
Jul 1980–Aug 1980, CBS Sat 8:00–9:00
Jun 1981–Sep 1981, CBS Tue 8:30–9:00
Jun 1982–Sep 1982, CBS Tue 8:00–8:30
ANCHORMAN:
Walter Cronkite

This summer series attempted to do for the world of science what *60 Minutes* did for general news subjects. *Universe* offered viewers insights on such topics as how EPA mileage ratings for new cars are computed and tested, the use of wind power in a world of shrinking energy reserves, the special-effects technology of movies like *Star Wars*, and a study of what causes motion sickness. Walter Cronkite was anchorman and chief correspondent, with contributions by other CBS News correspondents including Charles Osgood, Diane Sawyer, and Charles Crawford. In 1981 it was retitled *Walter Cronkite's Universe*.

UNIVERSITY HOSPITAL (*Medical Drama*)
BROADCAST HISTORY:
Syndicated only
60 minutes
Produced: *1994–1995* (22 episodes)
Released: *January 1995*
CAST:
Samantha "Sam" McCormick ... Alexandra Wilson
Jamie Fuller .... Hillary Danner
Megan Peterson .... Rebecca Cross
Tracy Stone .... Hudson Leick
Nurse Mary Jenkins .... Tonya Pinkins
Dr. Rob Daniels .... Doug Wert

University Hospital in fictional Seaside, Washington, was the setting for this sexy drama about the working and personal lives of four attractive young student nurses. Sam was the most efficient and prepared; her mother, grandmother, and great-grandmother had all been nurses. Jamie was looking to get a new start, having escaped from a live-in relationship with a domineering mobster/gambler at whose murder trial she later testified. Megan was the sweet, altruistic, sometimes naive farm girl from Sheridan, Montana. Tracy was the sexy bitch, more interested in finding a successful doctor or wealthy good-looking patient to share her bed with than in the quality of her work. Also seen were Nurse Jenkins, their strict but understanding training supervisor and Dr. Daniels, the resident who was sweet on Megan.

Filmed in Vancouver, British Columbia.

UNSOLVED MYSTERIES (*Public Service*)
FIRST TELECAST: *September 14, 1988*
LAST TELECAST: *August 13, 1999*
BROADCAST HISTORY:
Sep 1988–Sep 1994, NBC Wed 8:00–9:00
Sep 1994, NBC Sun 7:00–9:00
Oct 1994–Sep 1997, NBC Fri 8:00–9:00
Apr 1998–May 1998, CBS Fri 9:00–10:00
Jul 1998–Aug 1998, CBS Fri 9:00–10:00
Apr 1999–Aug 1999, CBS Fri 9:00–10:00

HOST:

Robert Stack
Virginia Madsen (1999)

CORRESPONDENT:

Keely Shaye Smith (1996–1997)

This unassuming documentary series was one of the most popular reality programs of the late 1980s and the inspiration for dozens of network and syndicated imitators. It began with a single special on the night of January 20, 1987, in which host Raymond Burr looked at four real-life mysteries: a Wyoming man found dead under mysterious circumstances three years after he disappeared from home; a 72-year-old Detroit woman who claimed to be the Siamese twin of a member of the Dodge auto family, separated at birth and put up for adoption, and now heir to the family fortune; the professional murder of a Tulsa executive at his country club; and two especially dangerous bank robbers who were then at large.

The special was so successful that six more were produced during 1987 and early 1988, the first two hosted by Karl Malden and the rest by Robert Stack. Then in the fall of 1988, *Unsolved Mysteries* became a weekly series. In addition to investigating baffling crimes, the series reunited missing persons, sought the heirs to unclaimed fortunes, and looked into persistent legends and even UFO sightings. Reenactments were routinely used, and the stories were produced as mini-dramas, usually three or four in an hour. In one episode the producers staged an elaborate re-creation of the famous 1962 escape attempt from Alcatraz prison, to determine if the escapees, who were never found, might have survived the chilly waters of San Francisco Bay. (They probably didn't.)

An 800 number was provided for viewers to call in clues, and by the end of the eighth season the show claimed to have been responsible for 87 reunions, the capture of 140 fugitives, and the solving of 250 cases. About forty percent of all wanted fugitives who were profiled were captured. Viewers might have wondered if there were enough cases to keep *Unsolved Mysteries* and all its imitators going. "If you read the F.B.I. Uniform Crime Report," said producer John Cosgrove, "I think there are 6,000 unsolved murders every year. There's certainly not a lack of cases to choose from."

CBS aired an *Unsolved Mysteries* special two months after its NBC cancellation, and brought the series back for two short runs the following spring and summer. When it surfaced again in Spring 1999, Virginia Madsen had been added as Stack's cohost. In 2001 and 2002 Lifetime, which had been airing reruns of *Unsolved Mysteries* for many years, produced dozens of new stories, which were intermixed with the older stories to create "partially new" episodes; in addition, updates were added describing recent developments in some of the unsolved cases. Robert Stack, by then in his eighties, returned with his trench coat and sepulchral voice to do new introductions, which looked and sounded little different from those he had done more than a decade earlier.

UNSUB (*Police Drama*)

FIRST TELECAST: *February 3, 1989*
LAST TELECAST: *April 14, 1989*
BROADCAST HISTORY:

Feb 1989–Apr 1989, NBC Fri 10:00–11:00

CAST:

John Westley Grayson ("Westy") .... David Soul
Ned Platt .... M. Emmet Walsh
Alan McWhirter .... Kent McCord
Norma McWhirter .... Andrea Mann
Tony D'Agostino .... Joe Maruzzo
Ann Madison .... Jennifer Hetrick
Jimmy Bello .... Richard Kind

Serial killers are a favorite theme for TV crime shows, and this one was built entirely around them. The Behavioral Science Unit of the U.S. Justice Department, headed by Westy Grayson, investigated the most baffling of these cases, using experts in psychological profiling and the latest high-tech equipment. Their targets—unknown subjects, or "unsubs"—gave the series its name.

UNTAMED WORLD (*Documentary*)

BROADCAST HISTORY:

Syndicated and network daytime
30 minutes
Produced: *1968–1975* (156 episodes)
Released: *1971*

NARRATOR:

Phil Carey

Nature documentary films about such subjects as snakes, predators and scavengers, primitive South American tribes, etc. The series first ran on NBC on Saturday afternoons from January to August 1969, then went into syndication with both repeats and new episodes.

UNTOUCHABLES, THE (*Police Drama*)

FIRST TELECAST: *October 15, 1959*
LAST TELECAST: *September 10, 1963*
BROADCAST HISTORY:

Oct 1959–Oct 1961, ABC Thu 9:30–10:30
Oct 1961–Sep 1962, ABC Thu 10:00–11:00
Sep 1962–Sep 1963, ABC Tue 9:30–10:30

CAST:

Eliot Ness .... Robert Stack
Agent Martin Flaherty (1959–1960) .... Jerry Paris
Agent William Youngfellow .... Abel Fernandez
Agent Enrico Rossi .... Nick Georgiade
Agent Cam Allison (1960) .... Anthony George
Agent Lee Hobson (1960–1963) .... Paul Picerni
Agent Rossman (1960–1963) .... Steve London
Frank Nitti .... Bruce Gordon

NARRATOR:

Walter Winchell

PRODUCER:

Quinn Martin

With the chatter of machine-gun fire and the squeal of tires on Chicago streets, *The Untouchables* brought furious controversy—and big ratings—to ABC in the early 1960s. It was perhaps the most mindlessly violent program ever seen on TV up to that time. Critics railed and public officials were incensed, but apparently many viewers enjoyed the weekly bloodbath, which sometimes included two or three violent shootouts per episode. As *TV Guide* observed, the show was highly consistent. "In practically every episode a gang leader winds up stitched to a brick wall and full of bullets, or face down in a parking lot (and full of bullets), or face up in a gutter (and still full of bullets), or hung up in an ice box, or run down in the street by a mug at the wheel of a big black Hudson touring car."

How did they get away with it? The first defense was that the program was historically accurate, being based on the life of a real treasury department gang-buster in the bullet-riddled Prohibition days of the early 1930s. The agent was Eliot Ness, and he had in fact played an important role in breaking the power of the notorious Al Capone in Chicago in 1931. Ness later wrote an autobiography, which served as the basis for a two-part semidocumentary dramatization of the Capone affair, presented on *Desilu Playhouse* in April 1959.

The special was an enormous hit, and led immediately to an ABC series the next fall. It followed Ness and his small band of incorruptible agents (dubbed by a Chicago newspaper "the Untouchables") as they battled one major crime lord after another. Capone had been packed off to prison at the conclusion of the April special, so the series began with the battle between his two top lieutenants, Jake "Greasy Thumb" Guzik and Frank "The Enforcer" Nitti, for control of his empire. As the series continued, and writers were pressed to find criminals famous enough for Ness to tackle, stories wandered farther and farther from the historical record. (Ness had in real life disbanded his Untouchables after cracking the Capone case, and had nothing to do with most of the cases dramatized on TV.) *The Untouchables* went after Bugs Moran (in whose garage the St. Valentine's Day Massacre took place), Ma Barker, and such East Coast hoods as Mad Dog Coll, Dutch Schultz, and Philadelphia crime boss Walter Legenza. There was even a two-part dramatization of the events leading up to the attempted assassination of President-elect Franklin D. Roosevelt at Miami Beach in 1933.

Some of this dramatic license caused problems, as when the FBI protested the depiction of Ness cornering Ma Barker (it was actually FBI agents). The estate of Al Capone sued the show for $1 million—not for inaccuracy, but for using Capone's name and likeness for profit. Italian-American groups protested the fact that so many of the hoods were given Italian names. Prison officials protested an episode which seemed to show Capone getting soft treatment in the Atlanta Penitentiary. Eventually the producers appended a disclaimer to the end of each episode stating that certain portions of *The Untouchables* had been "fictionalized."

Historical accuracy (or inaccuracy) aside, *The Untouchables* had another kind of appeal—and an excuse for violence. It was almost a fantasy, played by such colorful characters (the hoods), in such a one-dimensional style, and with such period trappings, that even the killings did not seem to be real. Eliot Ness was the upright, virtuous, and humorless enforcer of the law, and his opponents were greedy, sniveling animals. Robert Stack frankly admitted that he didn't really act in his role as Ness, but simply "reacted" to the over-played villains around him, and the contrast made the show work. Many fine character actors guest-starred as the thugs, such as Bruce Gordon (seen numerous times as Frank Nitti), Neville Brand (a look-alike for Capone), Nehemiah Persoff (Guzik), William Bendix (Legenza), Lloyd Nolan (Bugs Moran), Clu Gulager (baby-faced Mad Dog Coll), and Peter Falk (Nate Selko).

The Untouchables' success was spectacular but relatively short-lived. The program zoomed from the number 43 program on TV during its first season to number 8 in its second, but then, faced with the decidedly less violent competition of *Sing Along with Mitch* from 1961–1962, dropped back to number 41. There was frantic tinkering with the format during the final season—Ness became "more human," and the killings "more motivated." Investigators from other government bureaus began to appear, such as Barbara Stanwyck as a lieutenant from the Bureau of Missing Persons, and Dane Clark as an official of the U.S. Public Health Service. But *The Untouchables* was gone by 1963.

The Untouchables' original Desilu pilot and the initial episodes of the series were supervised by a young staff producer named Quinn Martin, starting a long string of TV crime-show hits for that gentleman.

UNTOUCHABLES, THE (*Police Drama*)

BROADCAST HISTORY:

Syndicated only
60 minutes
Produced: *1992–1994* (44 episodes)
Released: *January 1993*

CAST:

Eliot Ness .... Tom Amandes
Al Capone .... William Forsythe
Frank Nitti .... Paul Regina
Agent Mike Malone .... John Rhys-Davies
Agent Paul Robbins .... David James Elliott
Agent George Steelman (1993) .... Michael Horse
Agent Tony Pagano .... John Haymes Newton
**May Capone* .... Hynden Walch
Catherine Ness .... Nancy Everhard
Dorrie Greene (1993) .... Jenna Lyn Ward
Frankie Rio .... Valentino Cimo
Agent Sean Quinlan (1994) .... Shea Farrell

* Occasional

The saga of Eliot Ness and Al Capone returned to television in this syndicated revival of *The Untouchables* that mixed elements of the original series from the 1950s and the successful 1987 theatrical film version starring Kevin Costner and Sean Connery. Set in the 1930s, it chronicled the ongoing struggle between Eliot Ness and his small group of dedicated, incorruptible treasury agents and the Chicago mob run by Al Capone and his second in command, Frank Nitti. During the run of the series two of Ness's agents were killed, Steelman by Nitti in a fall 1993 episode and Malone by one of Capone's underlings in a February 1994 episode after he had planned to quit the Untouchables following his marriage to an Italian widow. In that same episode, Ness's wife, Catherine, decided to move in with relatives in Milwaukee to get away from the constant tension in Chicago. In April 1994 she wrote Eliot that she wanted a divorce. Capone also had one of Ness's friends, newspaper reporter Dorrie Greene, killed in October 1993 after she had written a story on the drunken mayor he controlled. As Prohibition ended, Capone planned to run for the Senate. The mob wanted to kill him for going straight, but Nitti decided to leak information about his tax-evasion crimes in order to put him in jail, the one place where he would be safe. The charge almost failed to hold up, but in the last episode a frightened bookkeeper provided information leading to Capone's conviction.

UP CLOSE (*Interview*)
FIRST TELECAST: *July 8, 2002*
LAST TELECAST: *January 24, 2003*
BROADCAST HISTORY:
Jul 2002–Jan 2003, ABC Mon–Fri 12:05–12:35 A.M.
ANCHOR:
Ted Koppel
This low-budget interview series was produced by ABC News to fill the late-night time slot between the end of *Politically Incorrect* and the debut of *Jimmy Kimmel Live.* It was anchored from a bare stage by *Nightline*'s Ted Koppel, who introduced filmed interviews conducted by ABC correspondents. The first subject was David Letterman, followed by a variety of writers, politicians and celebrities.

UP TO PAAR (*Quiz/Audience Participation*)
FIRST TELECAST: *July 28, 1952*
LAST TELECAST: *September 26, 1952*
BROADCAST HISTORY:
Jul 1952–Sep 1952, NBC Mon/Wed/Fri 7:00–7:30
EMCEE:
Jack Paar
Contestants on this live quiz show were drawn from the studio audience. They were interviewed by Mr. Paar and then asked a series of five questions based on current news stories. The value of each question increased, from $5 to $50. Winnings were given in the form of silver dollars and the money for each wrong answer went into the jackpot. At the end of the show all the contestants were asked the same jackpot question taken from that day's newspaper. They wrote their answers on a ballot and if anyone had the correct answer, he won $100 plus all the money lost by all the contestants on that night's show. This was Jack Paar's first network television series.

UPBEAT (*Music*)
FIRST TELECAST: *July 5, 1955*
LAST TELECAST: *September 22, 1955*
BROADCAST HISTORY:
Jul 1955–Sep 1955, CBS Tue/Thu 7:45–8:00
REGULARS:
The Honeydreamers
Russ Case Orchestra
The Tommy Morton Dancers
This twice-weekly summer series, which originated live from New York, filled the remainder of the half hour in which CBS aired its network news program. Each week there was a different singer as host, performing songs he or she had made popular. Among the singers who hosted the show were Tony Bennett, Teresa Brewer, Georgia Gibbs, Polly Bergen, and the Four Lads.

UPRIGHT CITIZENS BRIGADE (*Comedy*)
BROADCAST HISTORY:
Comedy Central
30 minutes
Produced: *1998–2000* (30 episodes)
Premiered: *August 19, 1998*
CAST:
Adair .... Matt Besser
Colby .... Amy Poehler
Antoine .... Ian Roberts
Trotter .... Matt Walsh
Sketch comedy series in which the four-person Upright Citizens Brigade, a dedicated team with unlimited resources and no government ties, pursued its mission to proliferate chaos within the everyday lives of ordinary citizens. Its slogan: "From the dawn of civilization they have existed in order to undermine it." After observing depressing normality on a large TV screen in their headquarters, they would swing into action, insinuating themselves into their subjects' lives by donning various disguises, and ensuring that chaos prevailed.

UPTOWN COMEDY CLUB, THE (*Comedy/Variety*)
BROADCAST HISTORY:
Syndicated only
60 minutes
Produced: *1992–1994* (44 episodes)
Released: *September 1992*
REGULARS:
Flex Alexander
Jim Breuer
Arceneaux & Mitchell
Ronda Fowler
Debra Wilson (1992–1993)
Macio
Corwin Moore (1992–1993)
Rob Magnotti
Monteria Ivey
Tracy Morgan (1993–1994)
Little Rascal (1993–1994)
Originating from a club in the Harlem section of Manhattan, *The Uptown Comedy Club* provided viewers with a mix of standup and sketch comedy by a troupe of comics, most of whom were black. Jim Breuer and Rob Magnotti were the only whites among the regulars. Guests included other standup comics and musical performers. The show was taped before a live studio audience, which participated in some of the sketches. Monteria Ivey served as host during the first season, and all the regulars rotated as host during the second.

URBAN ANGEL (*Adventure*)
FIRST TELECAST: *October 29, 1991*
LAST TELECAST: *September 10, 1993*
BROADCAST HISTORY:
Oct 1991–Feb 1992, CBS Tue 11:30–12:30 A.M.
Jan 1993–Mar 1993, CBS Tue 12:30–1:30 A.M.
Aug 1993–Sep 1993, CBS Mon–Fri 1:05–2:05 A.M.
CAST:
Victor Torres .... Justin Louis
Dino Moroni .... Vittorio Rossi
Francine Primeau .... Dorothee Berryman
Bob Vanverdan .... Jack Langedijk
Bill Rack .... Arthur Grosser
Rachel Kane .... Ellen Cohen
Hubie Collison .... Michael Rudder
Martine Beaudoin .... Jocelyne Zucco
Sylvia Belanger .... Sophie Lorain
Nicole .... Francois Robertson
Lt. Drabeck .... Vlasta Vrana
Alex Noble .... Berke Lawrence
This gritty drama focused on Victor Torres, a young investigative reporter for the *Montreal Tribune,* who frequently got into trouble while working under cover to break cases. Victor, an ex-con who had been

convicted of armed robbery, had taken the fall for his buddy Moroni, a local fence. Francine Primeau, the *Tribune*'s aggressive managing editor who believed, correctly, that Victor's underworld connections would prove invaluable, had hired him after his parole. Others on the paper's staff were Bob, the city editor who liked Victor and resented Francine's pushing him into dangerous situations; Bill, the veteran reporter who was biding time till retirement; Rachel, the insecure young reporter who was attracted to Victor; Hubie, the copy editor; Sylvie, the police reporter; and Martine, the staff photographer. Also seen were Nicole, the ex-hooker working as a waitress at Babes, where the *Tribune* staff hung out; Lt. Drabeck, the cop who wanted Victor to help him make a case against Moroni; and Alex, the former *Tribune* reporter who had kicked a drug problem and become the top network TV reporter in town.

Filmed on location in Montreal. CBS aired reruns of *Urban Angel* in late nighttime periods during 1993.

V

V (*Science Fiction*)

FIRST TELECAST: *October 26, 1984*

LAST TELECAST: *July 5, 1985*

BROADCAST HISTORY:

Oct 1984–Jan 1985, NBC Fri 8:00–9:00
Feb 1985–Mar 1985, NBC Fri 9:00–10:00
May 1985, NBC Fri 8:00–9:00
May 1985–Jul 1985, NBC Fri 9:00–10:00

CAST:

Mike Donovan .... Marc Singer
Dr. Julie Parrish .... Faye Grant
Diana .... Jane Badler
Nathan Bates .... Lane Smith
Robin Maxwell .... Blair Tefkin
Elizabeth (as teenager) .... Jennifer Cooke
Ham Tyler .... Michael Ironside
Elias .... Michael Wright
Willie .... Robert Englund
Kyle Bates .... Jeff Yagher
Lydia .... June Chadwick
Howard K. Smith .... Himself
Sean Donovan .... Nicky Katt
Mr. Chiang .... Aki Aleong
Charles .... Duncan Regehr
Lt. James (1985) .... Judson Scott
Martin/Philip (1985) .... Frank Ashmore

"V" stood for the "Visitors" in this science-fiction allegory of the takeover of Germany by the Nazis in the 1930s. The Visitors were aliens from a distant planet who came as friends, offering to help the world solve its problems through their high technology. All they asked for in exchange were some needed minerals. With the willing cooperation of a gullible world population and clever manipulation of the media they slowly and insidiously gained total control of Earth and then began methodically eliminating their enemies. As the story unfolded in two widely viewed mini-series broadcast in May 1983 and May 1984, the Visitors were finally unmasked by a small band of resistance fighters who discovered their true plan: to conquer the Earth and eat its population. Underneath the aliens' humanlike faces, they were actually lizards! A climactic battle ensued, and the Visitors were finally driven away with the help of a red dust bacteria.

As the weekly series began, the Visitors' captured leader, Diana, faced a Nuremberg-style trial. But she soon escaped and regained control of the Earth with the help of greedy human collaborators—notably the corrupt industrialist Nathan Bates, whose Scientific Frontiers Corp. (i.e., Krupp?) manufactured the dreaded Red Dust.

Leading the resistance were TV newsman Mike Donovan, who had originally discovered the Visitors' deceit; Julie, a brilliant scientist, and Ham and Elias. Their hideout was the Club Creole, and their allies included Willie, an alien who had turned against his leaders' diabolical plans. Another ally was a young woman named Robin, who had given birth to a half-human, half-alien baby following an affair with a Visitor. The child, named Elizabeth, had gone through a rapid metamorphosis, emerging as a beautiful teenager with extraordinary powers—and the key to the Visitors' destruction. Kyle was Nathan Bates' rebellious son, who aided the resistance; and Lydia was a Visitor military leader who plotted against Diana. Charles, Lt. James, and Martin were Visitor officers, with the latter sympathetic to and working with the resistance until his death. His twin brother Philip, a Visitor leader, also sided with those fighting for the Earth's freedom. In the last original episode (aired March 22, 1985), despite Diana's best efforts to ruin things, peace was reached between the Visitors and Earth. Elizabeth and Kyle (who stowed away because he loved her) returned to the Visitors' home planet, and Willie, who had grown fond of Earth, remained here with his new friends.

Former newsman Howard K. Smith portrayed himself as the anchorman of the Freedom Network newscast that opened each episode from November to January, with an update on the activities of both Visitors and resistance fighters around the world.

VH-1 (Network) (*Contemporary Music Cable Network*)

LAUNCHED:

January 1, 1985

SUBCRIBERS (MAY 2003):

83.8 million (79% U.S.)

Sister channel to MTV, featuring videos by established rock artists and aimed at a slightly older audience. Its original veejays were Don Imus and Jon "Bowzer" Bauman. Like MTV, VH-1 supplemented its videos with informational and entertainment series, although it tended to avoid non-musical series like MTV's *The Real World.* Among its series in the late 1980s were *Celebrity Hour* (interviews by veejays Bobby Rivers and Roger Rose), *FLIX* (movie reviews), and *My Generation* (vintage videos and interviews, hosted by Peter Noone of Herman's Hermits). The early '90s brought *Stand Up Spotlight* (comedians, hosted for a time by Rosie O'Donnell), *FT: Fashion TV* (fashion magazine), *Jonathan Ross Presents* (celebrity talk show), and *VH-1 to 1* (artist profiles).

For a period in the mid-'90s the channel downplayed series in favor of a steady diet of videos. It attracted a good deal of attention in 1996 with so-called "Pop-Up Videos," in which various wry comments and facts were superimposed on videos as they played. Renewed series development brought two biography series, *Legends* (1996) and *Behind the Music* (1997); *The RuPaul Show* (1996, a talk show); *My Generation* (1998, this version being a game show); *Rock & Roll Jeopardy* (1998, a quiz show); and *Vinyl Justice* (1998, a scripted comedy, in which two "music cops" raided people's record collections). A controversy arose when VH-1 premiered a series in October 2002 titled *Music Behind Bars,* in which convicts (including murderers) performed. Victim's families were outraged, and the show was quickly pulled from the schedule. (A similar incident occurred with the CourtTV series *Confessions.*)

VH-1 first reached more than half of all U.S. television homes in 1992.

VH1 CONFIDENTIAL (*Music Documentary*)

BROADCAST HISTORY:

VH1
60 minutes

Original episodes: *2000*
Premiered: *August 22, 2000*

Fast-paced tabloid documentary series about rock deaths and scandals. One episode looked at the death of Kurt Cobain (suicide or murder?), the rumored "death" of Paul McCartney in the 1960s, mass murderer Charles Manson as a rock-star wannabe, and whether Bob Marley was killed by the U.S. government by the unlikely means of "injecting him with cancer." To its credit, the show presented both sides of these dubious stories.

V.I.P. (*Adventure*)

BROADCAST HISTORY:

Syndicated only
60 minutes
Produced: *1998–2002* (88 episodes)
Released: *September 1998*

CAST:

Vallery Irons .... Pamela Anderson Lee
Tasha Dexter .... Molly Culver
Nikki Franco .... Natalie Raitano
Quick Williams .... Shaun Baker
Kay Simmons............................ Leah Lail
Maxine de la Cruz .... Angelle Brooks
Johnny Loh (2000–2002) .... Dustin Nguyen

Colt Arrow Security Services was struggling. Recently sold to its employees by its sleazy owner, who had to skip the country to avoid being nailed for tax evasion, it needed something to help generate business. Enter Vallery, a very sexy girl who had just moved to L.A. from the Midwest. While on a date with a movie star, he was attacked and she saved him—purely by accident. To avoid looking like a fool, the star told reporters Vallery was the top bodyguard in L.A. The Colt people promptly hired her as a front (and a nice front it was), renaming the firm Vallery Irons Protection. Despite their promise that she would not be in danger—just slink around in tight dresses and make lots of money—it didn't quite work out that way. Vallery was constantly in danger and had to learn the bodyguard business on-the-job. Tasha was a former espionage agent who did most of the work that Vallery got credit for. The other partners were Nikki, an expert on weapons and bombs; Quick, a former professional boxer and marksman with expertise in all forms of armaments; and Kay, the firm's mousy computer expert. Vallery's best friend Maxine provided her with good advice and helped her maintain her balance. There was plenty of skin, mostly Vallery's, in this tongue-in-cheek action adventure series.

As a recurring gimmick most episodes opened with cameos by well-known personalities who were being "protected" by Vallery. Among them were wrestler "Stone Cold" Steve Austin, *Tonight Show* host Jay Leno, basketball star Charles Barkley, rapper Coolio, talk show host Jerry Springer, and actor Alfonso Ribeiro.

When *V.I.P.* returned for its second season, the celebrity cameos had been dropped. The following fall Johnny, a former martial-arts star, joined Vallery Irons Protection and Ms. Anderson, who had separated from her husband, rock musician Tommy Lee, dropped the *Lee* from her name in the credits.

VISN (Network), see *Faith & Values Channel, The*

VR.5 (*Science Fiction*)

FIRST TELECAST: *March 10, 1995*
LAST TELECAST: *May 12, 1995*
BROADCAST HISTORY:

Mar 1995–May 1995, FOX Fri 8:00–9:00

CAST:

Sydney Bloom .... Lori Singer
Duncan Magnum.................. Michael Easton
Oliver Sampson........... Anthony Stewart Head
Dr. Joseph Bloom................. David McCallum
Mrs. Nora Bloom .... Louise Fletcher
Sydney Bloom (child) .... Kaci Williams
Samantha Bloom (child)......... Kimberly Cullum

Ever since she had survived the terrible accident that had killed her father and twin sister, Sydney had been haunted by the experience. She was only a child when her father, a brilliant computer scientist deeply worried about someone or something that was after them, had accidentally plunged their speeding car into a river and drowned along with her sister. Now, years later, Sydney was a lineperson for the Tel-Cal telephone company in San Francisco. Although she was a beautiful young woman, she had no social life, instead spending her spare time in her apartment crammed with personal computer equipment and the latest virtual reality (VR) gear. By donning the special goggles and gloves attached to her PC she could escape into a vivid, computer-created fantasy world.

While doing this she stumbled into the fabled "fifth level" of virtual reality, a fantasy world that affected events in the real world. When she called someone and connected the phone into her computer's modem, they too were sucked into her VR world, with unexpected results. This fifth level of VR was brightly colored, surrealistic, and not always hospitable. She might see how a real-life murderer had committed his crime but almost become the victim herself, or a neighborhood bully might almost be killed before her eyes by giant blue rats. She also used VR.5 to probe her own dangerous demons, as when she tried to communicate with her mother, who had been institutionalized in a catatonic state since the drowning. The VR journeys could be frightening because she was not entirely in control of the outcome.

Frightening too were those in the real world who wanted to use her unique ability to enter VR.5. The first was Dr. Frank Morgan (Will Patton), a professor of computer science at a local university who was her original contact with The Committee, a shadowy organization with mixed motives that made use of her ability and sent her on missions into the world of VR. Another was the mysterious Oliver—the same man who had terrified her father the night he had died, 20 years before. When Morgan was killed by an assassin as a result of one of Sydney's VR.5 assignments for The Committee, she felt responsible for his death. Sydney's only true friend and anchor in the real world was her neighbor Duncan, a free-spirited, insightful young man she had known since childhood.

In the last original episode in May 1995, Sydney found out that her father Joseph and sister Samantha (Tracey Needham) were still alive, prisoners of an evil faction of The Committee that was trying to use Dr. Bloom's discoveries to take over the world. The "accident" which she so vividly remembered was a "false memory" they had implanted in her brain. In the cliffhanger ending, Sydney fought off evil Committee operatives with the help of Oliver and Samantha and used the truth to bring her mother out of her catatonic state, but then plunged into unconsciousness herself.

Appropriately, Fox established a site on the Internet (vr5@delphi.com) for fans of the show to discuss what—if anything—it all meant.

VACATION PLAYHOUSE (*Anthology*)
FIRST TELECAST: *July 22, 1963*
LAST TELECAST: *August 28, 1967*
BROADCAST HISTORY:
Jul 1963–Sep 1963, CBS Mon 8:30–9:00
Jun 1964–Sep 1964, CBS Mon 8:30–9:00
Jun 1965–Sep 1965, CBS Fri 9:30–10:00
Jul 1966–Sep 1966, CBS Mon 8:30–9:00
Jul 1967–Aug 1967, CBS Mon 8:30–9:00

Vacation Playhouse collected pilots for proposed series that had not been sold and aired them as a summer replacement series. In the four years that this show ran on Monday nights it was the replacement for *The Lucy Show* and all of the episodes were situation comedies. In 1965, when it aired as the replacement for *Gomer Pyle U.S.M.C.* on Friday nights, the episodes were adventure and mystery pilots.

VAL DOONICAN SHOW, THE (*Musical Variety*)
FIRST TELECAST: *June 5, 1971*
LAST TELECAST: *August 14, 1971*
BROADCAST HISTORY:
Jun 1971–Aug 1971, ABC Sat 8:30–9:30
REGULARS:
Val Doonican
Bernard Cribbins
Bob Todd
The Norman Maen Dancers
The Mike Sammes Singers
Kenny Woodman's Orchestra
THEME:
"I Believe My Love Loves Me," by Tom Paxton.

Irish singer Val Doonican was the star and host of this summer variety series that was taped in England. Comedians Bernard Cribbins and Bob Todd were featured regulars on the series, which also showcased both American and British guest stars.

VALENTINE'S DAY (*Situation Comedy*)
FIRST TELECAST: *September 18, 1964*
LAST TELECAST: *September 10, 1965*
BROADCAST HISTORY:
Sep 1964–Sep 1965, ABC Fri 9:00–9:30
CAST:
Valentine Farrow .... Tony Franciosa
Rockwell "Rocky" Sin .... Jack Soo
Libby Freeman .... Janet Waldo
Molly .... Mimi Dillard
O. D. Dunstall .... Jerry Hausner
Grover Cleveland Fipple .... Eddie Quillan

The life of Valentine Farrow, a debonair young New York publishing executive, was depicted in this comedy. Valentine was continually being chased by beautiful girls, both in and out of his Park Avenue office at the publishing firm of Brackett and Dunstall, where he was senior nonfiction editor. Libby was his pretty secretary, Molly his receptionist, and O. D. Dunstall his nervous boss. At home, Valentine was no hero to his valet, the scrounging, poker-playing, con man "Rocky" Sin. Rocky had been Valentine's buddy in the army, and had saved his neck. Now he was his chief confidant and bottle-washer. Living in the basement of Valentine's elegant East Side town house was Mr. Fipple, the handyman.

After a series of amorous adventures Valentine finally fell in love in the last episode, with a pretty research assistant at Brackett and Dunstall. The series didn't return for a second season, however, so it never got any further than that.

Seen in a guest role was opera singer Helen Traubel as Valentine's mother, Muriel Farrow.

VALENTINO (*Romantic Monologue*)
FIRST TELECAST: *December 18, 1952*
LAST TELECAST: *March 5, 1953*
BROADCAST HISTORY:
Dec 1952–Mar 1953, ABC Thu 9:30–10:00
HOST:
Barry Valentino

Poetry readings, songs, and romantic monologues by Barry Valentino, who even looked a bit like his namesake, Rudolph Valentino. An obvious copy of CBS' soft-lights-and-sweet-music show, *The Continental.*

Also seen for a time as a local program in New York.

VALERIE, see *The Hogan Family*

VALIANT YEARS, THE see *Winston Churchill—The Valiant Years*

VAN CAMP'S LITTLE SHOW (*Music*)
FIRST TELECAST: *June 27, 1950*
LAST TELECAST: *November 22, 1951*
BROADCAST HISTORY:
Jun 1950–Nov 1951, NBC Tue/Thu 7:30–7:45
REGULARS:
John Conte
Jesse Bradley Trio

Intimate musical variety program featuring musical-comedy star Conte with a different female vocalist, and sometimes with other guests, on each show. Also known as *John Conte's Little Show* and *The Little Show.*

VAN DYKE AND COMPANY (*Comedy/Variety*)
FIRST TELECAST: *September 20, 1976*
LAST TELECAST: *December 30, 1976*
BROADCAST HISTORY:
Sep 1976, NBC Mon 10:00–11:00
Oct 1976, NBC Thu 10:00–11:00
Nov 1976–Dec 1976, NBC Thu 8:00–9:00
REGULARS:
Dick Van Dyke
The L.A. Mime Company
Andy Kaufman
Marilyn Sokol
Pat Proft
Bob Einstein
Richard Kiel
Chuck McCann

This short-lived series starred comedian Dick Van Dyke, whose previous success had been in situation comedies rather than variety programs. A true devotee of the art of pantomime, and renowned for his impression of Stan Laurel, Van Dyke made nonverbal comedy a prime ingredient in this show. In addition to the mime segments, and recurring "bright family" sketch about the dumbest family in the world, there were appearances by guest stars from the music and comedy worlds.

VAN DYKE SHOW, THE (*Situation Comedy*)
FIRST TELECAST: *October 26, 1988*
LAST TELECAST: *December 7, 1988*
BROADCAST HISTORY:
Oct 1988–Dec 1988, CBS Wed 8:00–8:30
CAST:
Dick Burgess .... Dick Van Dyke
Matt Burgess .... Barry Van Dyke
Chris Burgess .... Kari Lizer
Noah Burgess (age 7) .... Billy O'Sullivan
Doc Sterling .... Whitman Mayo
Jillian Ryan .... Maura Tierney
Eric Olander .... Paul Scherrer

Trying to make a success of the small regional theater he was running in rural Pennsylvania was not easy for Matt Burgess. When his dad, Broadway musical star Dick Burgess, decided to give up the Great White Way to live and work with Matt and get to know his family, things didn't get much easier. Dick was a big audience draw, but both men were proud and stubborn and comically disagreed about everything, particularly when it related to the theater—choice of plays, staging, and casting. Fortunately for all concerned, Matt's wife Chris was usually around to keep things from getting completely out of hand. Featured members of the theater's staff were Doc, the ancient stage manager with an encylcopedic knowledge of theatrical trivia; Jillian, Matt's secretary; and Eric, Matt's enthusiastic young helper.

This short-lived series did give real-life father and son Dick and Barry their first opportunity to work together professionally.

VANISHED (*Documentary*)
FIRST TELECAST: *June 17, 1999*
LAST TELECAST: *July 22, 1999*
BROADCAST HISTORY:
Jun 1999–Jul 1999, ABC Thu 10:00–11:00

ABC News produced this investigative documentary series about missing persons, some of whom may have disappeared on their own, and some of whom were victims of foul play. Cases ranged from the abduction of Charles Lindbergh's baby in 1932 to the fishing boat lost in "The Perfect Storm" in 1991. After its original six-episode run in the summer of 1999, *Vanished* became a series of occasional specials, with two or three airing each year from 2000 to 2002. There was no regular host.

VANISHING SON (*Adventure*)
Syndicated only
60 minutes
Produced: *1994–1995* (13 episodes)
Released: *January 1995*
CAST:
Jian-Wa Chang .... Russell Wong
Agent Dan Sandler .... Jason Adams
Agent Judith Phillips .... Stephanie Niznik
**Wago Chang* .... Chi Muoi Lo

* Occasional

Jian-Wa was a muscular but thoughtful student and musician, skilled in the martial arts, who had come to America from Beijing with his hot-headed younger brother, Wago, in search of freedom. Wago fell in with a gang, and when Jian-Wa tried to get him out, Wago and two federal agents were murdered. The real culprit was "The General," a Vietnamese expatriate who was making millions in the U.S. while serving as an informant for the government. Sandler, the immediate superior of the murdered federal agents, was sure Jian-Wa was the culprit and was chasing him to bring him to justice. Phillips, the newest member of Sandler's team, had doubts about Jian-Wa's guilt and was more willing to look for possible proof of his innocence than her aggressive boss. In this *The Fugitive* meets *Kung Fu* series, Jian-Wa traveled from place to place helping people in trouble and trying to find the proof of his innocence while avoiding capture by the feds. The spirit of his dead brother, Wago, showed up when he needed his help. Each episode opened and closed with Jian-Wa as narrator providing philosophical observations about life and people as they related to the episode's story line.

Several *Vanishing Son* TV movies had aired in 1994; this weekly series premiered early the following year.

VARIETY (*Various*)
FIRST TELECAST: *April 11, 1948*
LAST TELECAST: *September 26, 1948*
BROADCAST HISTORY:
Apr 1948–Jun 1948, NBC Sun 8:30–9:00
Jul 1948–Sep 1948, NBC Sun 9:00–9:30

NBC presented what amounted to a series of specials under this umbrella title in 1948. The shows ranged from music and comedy acts to full-scale plays. Some plays were light entertainment, such as Gilbert & Sullivan; others were serious dramas. There was no host or continuing cast.

Variety was also known at times as *NBC Playhouse* or *The Players*.

VAUDEO VARIETIES (*Variety*)
FIRST TELECAST: *January 14, 1949*
LAST TELECAST: *April 15, 1949*
BROADCAST HISTORY:
Jan 1949–Apr 1949, ABC Fri 8:00–9:00
EMCEE:
Eddie Hubbard

Hour-long variety show from Chicago, featuring emcee Eddie Hubbard and five different acts each week.

VAUDEVILLE SHOW (*Musical Variety*)
FIRST TELECAST: *December 9, 1953*
LAST TELECAST: *December 30, 1953*
BROADCAST HISTORY:
Dec 1953, ABC Wed 9:30–10:00
ORCHESTRA:
Glenn Osser

A four-week series of re-creations of an old-time vaudeville show. Each telecast had five acts, including singers, dancers, tumblers, magicians, etc.

VAUGHN MONROE SHOW, THE (*Musical Variety*)
FIRST TELECAST: *October 10, 1950*
LAST TELECAST: *September 8, 1955*
BROADCAST HISTORY:
Oct 1950–Jul 1951, CBS Tue 9:00–9:30

Aug 1954–Sep 1954, NBC Tue/Thu 7:30–7:45
Jul 1955–Sep 1955, NBC Tue/Thu 7:30–7:45

REGULARS:

Vaughn Monroe
Shaye Cogan (1950–1951)
Ziggy Talent (1950–1951)
Olga Suarez (1950–1951)
Kenny Davis (1950–1951)
The Satisfiers (1954)
The Richard Hayman Orchestra (1954)
The Richard Maltby Orchestra (1955)

THEME:

"Racing with the Moon," by Vaughn Monroe, Johnny Watson, and Pauline Pope

Singer and orchestra leader Vaughn Monroe was one of the leading musical stars on radio during the late 1940s and early 1950s with his *Camel Caravan,* a Saturday night CBS variety show which ran from 1946 to 1954. He took his first plunge into the new medium of television on CBS in 1950, with a half-hour series that featured singer Shaye Cogan and comedian Ziggy Talent, plus guest stars. Most of the crooning was done by Vaughn himself, however, with his deep baritone voice and raft of melodious hits ("Racing with the Moon," "There I've Said It Again," "Ghost Riders in the Sky," etc.). After a single season as a TV series star, he returned to radio and occasional TV guest shots, but in 1954 and 1955 was back with an NBC program that served as summer replacement for *The Dinah Shore Show.* Like the CBS series it was telecast live, but the 15-minute length allowed time for little more than a few songs. By 1955 Vaughn's kind of music was becoming more nostalgic than contemporary, and thereafter he was seen with decreasing frequency in guest appearances on other shows. Perhaps his best-remembered role in TV was as commercial spokesman for RCA products. He died in 1973.

VEGA$ (*Detective Drama*)

FIRST TELECAST: *September 20, 1978*
LAST TELECAST: *September 16, 1981*
BROADCAST HISTORY:

Sep 1978–Jun 1981, ABC Wed 10:00–11:00
Aug 1981–Sep 1981, ABC Wed 9:00–10:00

CAST:

Dan Tanna.......................... Robert Urich
Beatrice Travis...................... Phyllis Davis
Binzer (Bobby Borso)............. Bart Braverman
Angie Turner (1978–1979)........... Judy Landers
Sgt. Bella Archer (1978–1979)...... Naomi Stevens
Lt. David Nelson (1979–1981)......... Greg Morris
Philip Roth.......................... Tony Curtis

TV audiences never seem to tire of handsome, wisecracking private eyes, and Dan Tanna was the very latest 1978 model. Blue jeans, a sports car (a vintage red Thunderbird), sexy assistants, glamorous Las Vegas settings, and a new homicide every Wednesday night helped make this one of the hits of the 1978–1979 season. Dan was on retainer to Philip Roth, the fast-talking, millionaire owner of several of Vegas' bigger casino-hotels—including the Desert Inn, on whose grounds Tanna's office/apartment was located. Binzer, a reformed hood, was his inept but enthusiastic legman; Angie, his sexy but not very bright receptionist; and Beatrice, his equally sexy and very efficient secretary/assistant. Both women were also showgirls, though the older Beatrice was more often seen teaching the chorus line routines than participating in them. Dan's original contact on the Vegas police department was Sgt. Archer, who gradually faded from the scene after Lt. Nelson was added to the cast midway through the first season. Seen occasionally were Dan's boss, Philip Roth, who Tanna affectionately nicknamed "Slick"; Chief Harlon Two Leaf (played by Will Sampson), a friend of Dan's; and a stylish but hefty gambler named Diamond Jim (Victor Buono).

VENGEANCE UNLIMITED (*Detective*)

FIRST TELECAST: *September 29, 1998*
LAST TELECAST: *February 25, 1999*
BROADCAST HISTORY:

Sep 1998, ABC Tue 10:00–11:00
Oct 1998, ABC Thu 8:00–9:00
Dec 1998–Feb 1999, ABC Thu 8:00–9:00

CAST:

Mr. Chapel...................... Michael Madsen
KC Griffin......................... Kathleen York

Revenge, pure and simple, was the premise of this rather creepy series, from the creator of *Profit.* The avenger was Mr. Chapel, a tough, rumpled character whose past was deliberately shadowy. He had been wronged in some way, and now had dedicated his life to seeking revenge for others who had been wronged. His fee? One million dollars in cash, or a favor, to be redeemed at some future time when he needed it to help someone else. His targets were usually the rich and powerful, who had stolen, destroyed people, or committed murder (in the pilot, a ruthless businessman killed his knew-too-much secretary by slamming her into a copier and photocopying her dying face) and, thanks to their high-priced lawyers, gotten away with it. In fact, they usually walked out of the courthouse laughing. They stopped laughing when Chapel caught up with them. Unfortunately, his methods were as ruthless and extra-legal as theirs, such as stalking, abduction, and torture. Feeding Chapel information, and trying to keep him from going completely over the edge, was KC Griffin, a paralegal in the D.A.'s office and a former victim he had "helped."

The series at least knew how unsettling this all could be. When Chapel had finished collecting a favor, he would tell the former victim,"I'm out of your life forever." They would usually answer, "Thank God."

VERDICT (*Documentary*)

FIRST TELECAST: *June 21, 1991*
LAST TELECAST: *September 5, 1991*
BROADCAST HISTORY:

Jun 1991–Aug 1991, CBS Fri 8:00–8:30
Sep 1991, CBS Thu 10:00–11:00

Verdict was a summer series designed to give viewers a real view of the legal system at work. Each week a single case was covered, with background provided by CBS correspondents, excerpted coverage of the actual trial, and the verdict reached by the jury. The background might include an explanation of the issues, the circumstances that led to the case going to court, and behind-the-scenes looks at the strategies of the opposing attorneys. The cases included those of a con man accused of murdering an older woman he had taken for a lot of money, a 13-year-old who had accidentally shot and killed his best friend, a Vietnam veteran charged with shooting a neighbor to death during an argument, an adopted son on trial for murdering his parents, and a man on trial for rape. A different CBS correspondent covered each case and served as the host for each episode.

VERDICT IS YOURS, THE (*Courtroom Drama*)
FIRST TELECAST: *July 3, 1958*
LAST TELECAST: *September 25, 1958*
BROADCAST HISTORY:
Jul 1958–Sep 1958, CBS Thu 8:30–9:30
COURT REPORTER:
Jim McKay

Reenactments of actual trials were presented on this nighttime version of *The Verdict Is Yours.* Real lawyers tried the cases and real judges were on the bench. The jury was made up of members of the studio audience. Jim McKay, in the role of court reporter, established the background for each case and filled in missing details during the "trial." He also performed the same task on the daytime version which had premiered in 1957 and ran until 1962.

VERITAS: THE QUEST (*Adventure*)
FIRST TELECAST: *January 27, 2003*
LAST TELECAST: *March 17, 2003*
BROADCAST HISTORY:
Jan 2003–Mar 2003, ABC Mon 8:00–9:00
CAST:
Nicholas "Nikko" Zond............ Ryan Merriman
Solomon Zond.......................... Alex Carter
Calvin Raines.......................... Eric Balfour
Vincent Siminou .... Arnold Vosloo
Maggie Hayes....................... Cynthia Martells
Juliet Droil.......................... Cobie Smulders

The spirit, if not the style, of *Indiana Jones* was brought to the screen once again in this rip-roaring series about a rebellious teenager and his archeologist/adventurer dad. Nikko had been shuttled from one boarding school to another since the death of his beloved archeologist mother on a mission some years earlier. A cocky and extremely smart young man, he teamed up with his workaholic father, Solomon, when he learned that the latter was not a university professor as he had thought, but rather the head of a shadowy organization called the Veritas Foundation, whose agenda was to uncover the mysteries of history and civilization. Father and son were uncertain about working together, and both had strong egos, but gradually they gained each other's respect. Solomon's team included Calvin, a tall, brilliant, high-strung young man with degrees in archeology, astronomy and paleontology; Vincent, a tough "protector" who added muscle, and Maggie, a tech whiz who communicated with the team in the field by computer, tracking their movements and warning them of approaching danger (which was frequent). Together the globe-trotting team raided hidden temples, ancient tombs and Nazi hideaways, retrieving mysterious and powerful artifacts and seeking to keep "the power to rule the world" out of the hands of those evil guys in dark suits and Mercedes who were constantly on their tail.

Juliet was Nikko's sexy tutor and confidante.

VERONICA CLARE (*Detective Drama*)
BROADCAST HISTORY:
Lifetime Network
60 minutes
Produced: *1991* (9 episodes)
Released: *July 23, 1991*
CAST:
Veronica Clare..................... Laura Robinson
Duke Rado.......................... Robert Beltran
Kelsey Horne..................... Christina Pickles
Nikki Swarcek............................ Tony Plana
Sgt. Tweed............................ Robert Ruth
Rocco .... Robert Sutton
Jimmy................................ Wayne Chou

Detective series with a 1940s, film noir feel about a sultry and enigmatic female private eye. Veronica was part owner (with Duke) of a posh 'forties-style jazz club in L.A.'s Chinatown and also a detective. She took on cases that interested her, such as missing persons, battered women, and sometimes a murder mystery, none of which involved much violence. Her long flowing hair and reserved demeanor gave her a Lauren Bacall look (or was it one of the Andrews Sisters?), but she revealed little of her mysterious past. Viewers were supposed to learn more as the series unfolded, but few stopped by the club and the program was quickly canceled. Veronica's secrets are safe.

VERONICA'S CLOSET (*Situation Comedy*)
FIRST TELECAST: *September 25, 1997*
LAST TELECAST: *June 27, 2000*
BROADCAST HISTORY:
Sep 1997–May 1998, NBC Thu 9:30–10:00
Jun 1998, NBC Thu 8:30–9:00
Jun 1998–Jul 1998, NBC Mon 9:30–10:00
Sep 1998–May 1999, NBC Thu 9:30–10:00
Jul 1999–Dec 1999, NBC Mon 8:30–9:00
Jan 2000–Feb 2000, NBC Tue 9:30–10:00
Jun 2000, NBC Tue 8:30–9:00
CAST:
Veronica "Ronnie" Chase .... Kirstie Alley
Olive Massery....................... Kathy Najimy
Josh Blair .... Wallace Langham
Perry Rollins.......................... Dan Cortese
Leo Michaels............... Daryl "Chill" Mitchell
Virginia (1997–1998) .... Cynthia Mann
**Pat Chase (1997–1998)* .... Robert Prosky
**Bryce Anderson (1997–1998)*
.... Christopher McDonald
**Pepper (1997–1998)*............... Ever Carradine
Alec Bilson (1998–1999) .... Ron Silver
June Bilson (1999–2000) .... Lorri Bagley
Chloe (1999–2000) .... Mary Lynn Rajskub
*Occasional

Ronnie Chase was a model for women everywhere—a successful businesswoman, head of trendy mail-order lingerie and book company Veronica's Closet, and author of *The Guide to a Fairy Tale Marriage.* Unfortunately her own husband, womanizing Bryce, had run off with a dippy sexpot named Pepper, and her famous figure (a feature of her catalogs) was beginning to sag, leaving Ronnie to vent her frustrations on her long-suffering staff in this workplace comedy. Olive was her chubby, wisecracking top executive, who gave her moral as well as professional support; Josh, her fussy, sexually confused assistant who was constantly denying he was gay ("Oh, please!"); Perry, her handsome publicist, a former underwear model; and Leo her insecure, harried marketing manager. Huggable Pat was her soused dad, who worked as her chauffeur. At the beginning of the second season wealthy Alec bought a controlling share of the company, leaving Ronnie in charge of creative matters while he managed the business side. Sharing an office, they sparred constantly, and a mutual sexual attraction soon followed. Ronnie published a new book, *When Love Goes,* this one about surviving divorce.

Yet another change took place in the third season, as Alec died in a bizarre accident (he fell into a volcano while on vacation) and left his interest in the company to his new blond-bimbo wife, June, who sparred with Ronnie for the next year. As the series run on NBC came to a close, Josh was about to marry Chloe, but at the last minute decided he really was gay and took up with boyfriend Brian (Alan F. Smith). NBC canceled *Veronica's Closet* before the series-ending episodes could be shown. They were later seen in syndication, and in them Olive made $20 million in a business deal, bought out June, and became Ronnie's new partner.

VERSATILE VARIETIES (*Variety/Children's*)
FIRST TELECAST: *August 26, 1949*
LAST TELECAST: *December 14, 1951*
BROADCAST HISTORY:
Aug 1949–Jan 1951, NBC Fri 9:00–9:30 (OS)
Sep 1951–Dec 1951, ABC Fri 9:30–10:00
EMCEE:
George Givot (1949)
Harold Barry (1949–1950)
Bob Russell (1950–1951)
Lady Iris Mountbatten (1951)
"BONNY MAID":
Anne Francis (1949–1950)
ORCHESTRA:
Jerry Jerome (1949–1950)
Bernie Sands (1950–1951)

This began as a live variety show set in a nightclub, with guest singers, comedians, performing dogs, etc. Nonperforming guest celebrities were sometimes seen seated at ringside tables. George Givot, "the Greek Ambassador of Good Will," was the original host, succeeded after two months by comedian Harold Barry. Singer Bob Russell took over in the fall of 1950, as the program tended more to a presentation of new talent. Anne Francis appeared in the commercials (for floor coverings) as "Bonny Maid," assisted by two other Bonny Maids and the team of "Wear and Tear."

Versatile Varieties returned in the fall of 1951 with a somewhat different format, featuring Lady Iris Mountbatten and a cast of kids who presented various children's stories and skits.

During its NBC run the program was also known as *Bonny Maid Versatile Varieties.*

VIBE (*Talk/Music*)
BROADCAST HISTORY:
Syndicated only
60 minutes
Produced: *1997–1998*
Released: *August 4, 1997*
HOST:
Chris Spencer (1997)
Sinbad
MUSICAL DIRECTOR:
Greg Phillinganes
EXECUTIVE PRODUCER:
Quincy Jones

This urban-oriented talk show premiered on the same night as the similar *Keenen Ivory Wayans Show* and, although it outlasted *Wayans,* never attracted enough viewers to be renewed for a second season. *Vibe* placed more emphasis on music than talk, not surprising considering that it was named after a music magazine and its executive producer was music mogul Quincy Jones. Host Chris Spencer, a standup comedian, conducted some of his chats in-studio and some with people in remote locations who were seen on a TV monitor. In late October the producers replaced Spencer, who never seemed entirely comfortable as host, with the better known and more relaxed Sinbad, but it didn't help. The last original episode aired in the spring with reruns continuing on most stations through the summer.

The show's band was referred to as Greg Phillinganes Mouse and the Mouse Trap.

VIC DAMONE SHOW, THE, see *Dean Martin Presents Vic Damone* and *Dean Martin Summer Show, The*

VIC DAMONE SHOW, THE (*Musical Variety*)
FIRST TELECAST: *July 2, 1956*
LAST TELECAST: *September 11, 1957*
BROADCAST HISTORY:
Jul 1956–Sep 1956, CBS Mon 9:30–10:00
Jul 1957–Sep 1957, CBS Wed 8:00–9:00
REGULARS:
Vic Damone
The Spellbinders (1957)
The Tutti Camarata Orchestra (1956)
The Bert Farber Orchestra (1957)

Singer Vic Damone spent the summer of 1956 filling in for *December Bride* with a musical variety show. In addition to songs by himself and his guests, it featured aspects of Vic's personal life and interaction with the guests, many of whom were off-screen friends. The following summer Vic returned on a different night with an expanded, full-hour variety show. The format of the 1957 series was more traditional than his first one had been, with musical and comedy numbers filling the entire hour and no side trips into Vic's personal life. A singing group, the Spellbinders, was featured regularly on the 1957 show.

VICEROY STAR THEATRE (*Dramatic Anthology*)
FIRST TELECAST: *July 2, 1954*
LAST TELECAST: *September 24, 1954*
BROADCAST HISTORY:
Jul 1954–Sep 1954, CBS Fri 10:00–10:30

The plays presented in this filmed summer anthology series were all on the melodramatic and suspenseful side and starred personalties from the motion-picture world. Appearing were Zachary Scott, Katy Jurado, Lynn Bari, and Dennis Morgan, among others.

VICTOR BORGE SHOW, THE (*Comedy/Variety*)
FIRST TELECAST: *February 3, 1951*
LAST TELECAST: *June 30, 1951*
BROADCAST HISTORY:
Feb 1951–Jun 1951, NBC Sat 7:00–7:30
REGULARS:
Victor Borge
The Phil Ingalls Orchestra

Internationally known pianist and comic interpreter of music Victor Borge starred in this live variety series. His satirical interpretations of classical music were only one part of the show, however, and he did play at least one piece in a straight concert rendition each week. Perhaps his most famous routine, and one that he featured periodically, was "Phonetic Punctuation," in which each punctuation mark was represented by a different noise—"Ffftt!," "Sscht!," etc. When he read quickly through an entire paragraph, substituting "Ffftt's" and "Sscht's" for every dash, comma, and period, the effect could be hilarious.

Guest stars were also a regular feature of the show, and would chat with Borge in addition to performing.

VIDEO CHALLENGE (*Talent Contest*)

BROADCAST HISTORY:

Syndicated only
30 minutes
Produced: *1990–1991* (39 episodes)
Released: *September 1990*

HOST:

Steve Kelley

In this ripoff of ABC's popular *America's Funniest Home Videos*, viewers sent in their homemade videos hoping to win prize money. There were four categories—music, children, comedy, and real-life events—with a $25,000 grand prize for the best video in each category. The producers claimed that they would award $1,000,00 in total prize money during the season.

Also known as *$1,000,000 Video Challenge*.

VIDEO VILLAGE (*Quiz/Audience Participation*)

FIRST TELECAST: *July 1, 1960*
LAST TELECAST: *September 16, 1960*
BROADCAST HISTORY:

Jul 1960–Sep 1960, CBS Fri 9:00–9:30

EMCEE:

Jack Narz

ASSISTANT:

Joanne Copeland

ANNOUNCER:

Ken Williams

In a novel approach to television game shows, *Video Village* was a living board game. The contestants were the pieces, moving from square to square as determined by the roll of a giant die in a chuck-a-luck cage. The roll was accomplished with the aid of a friend or relative of the contestant. Various cash and merchandise prizes were awarded for landing on specified squares, while landing on others might cause loss of a turn, having to answer questions, or moving to another part of the board. The first person to reach the end of the board was the winner and started over again with a new contestant. Emcee Jack Narz was the mayor, assistant Joanne Copeland the assistant mayor, and announcer Ken Williams the town crier. The daytime version of this series started one week after the nighttime version and remained on the air through June 1962.

Monty Hall took over for Jack Narz when he left the daytime version, and Eileen Barton similarly replaced Joanne Copeland. There was also a Saturday morning children's version, *Video Village Jr. Edition*, during the 1961–1962 season, with Hall and Barton and a collection of young contestants vying for prizes appropriate for children.

VILLAGE BARN (*Musical Variety*)

FIRST TELECAST: *May 17, 1948*
LAST TELECAST: *May 29, 1950*
BROADCAST HISTORY:

May 1948–Oct 1948, NBC Mon 9:10–10:00
Oct 1948–Jan 1949, NBC Wed 10:10–11:00
Jan 1949–May 1949, NBC Wed 8:30–9:00
May 1949–Jul 1949, NBC Mon 10:00–10:30
Jul 1949–Sep 1949, NBC Thu 10:00–10:30
Jan 1950–May 1950, NBC Mon 9:30–10:00

EMCEE:

Zebe Carver (1948)
Dick Thomas & Dick Dudley (1948–1949)
Dick Dudley (1949)
Bob Stanton (1949)
Ray Forrest (1949)

REGULARS:

Romolo De Spirito (as The Road Agent, also known as The Masked Singer) (1949)
Piute Pete (1948–1949)
Pappy Howard and His Tumbleweed Gang
Bill Long and His Ranch Girls

Country music and down-home humor originating from New York's Village Barn, a popular night spot located at 52 West 8th Street. This was perhaps the first regular series to originate live from an actual nightclub. In addition to the music of such groups as Pappy Howard and His Tumbleweed Gang, Harry Ranch and His Kernels of Korn, and Bill Long's Ranch Girls, there was square dancing (with calls by Piute Pete), audience participation in potato sack, hobby horse, and kiddie-car races, and other unsophisticated entertainment.

VINCENT LOPEZ (*Musical Variety*)

FIRST TELECAST: *March 7, 1949*
LAST TELECAST: *July 22, 1950*
BROADCAST HISTORY:

Mar 1949–May 1949, DUM Mon/Wed/Fri 6:45–7:00
May 1949–Jul 1949, DUM Mon–Fri 6:45–7:00
Jul 1949–Jun 1950, DUM Mon–Fri 7:30–7:45
Jan 1950–Jul 1950, DUM Sat 8:00–8:30

REGULARS:

Vincent Lopez
Ann Warren (1950)
Lee Russell (1950)
Ray Barr

ANNOUNCER:

Fred Scott

Veteran bandleader and pianist Vincent Lopez ("Lopez speaking!") was seen on two different programs on the DuMont network from 1949–1950. The first was an early-evening musical interlude, running three to five nights a week with Lopez and Barr on twin pianos. The other, seen during 1950, was a full-fledged Saturday night variety show called *Dinner Date with Vincent Lopez* and originating live from the Grill Room of the Hotel Taft in New York, where Lopez had been holding forth for many years. Featured were his full orchestra, guest performers such as Cab Calloway, Arthur Tracy, and Woody Herman, and his own regular vocalists, Ann Warren and Lee Russell. In addition to serving as emcee, Lopez did numerous interviews, made song predictions, and improvised original themes based on the letters or names of viewers writing in.

VINCENT LOPEZ SHOW, THE (*Music*)
FIRST TELECAST: *February 9, 1957*
LAST TELECAST: *March 9, 1957*
BROADCAST HISTORY:
Feb 1957–Mar 1957, CBS Sat 7:00–7:30
REGULARS:
Vincent Lopez
Danny Davis
Judy Lynn
Johnny Messner
Teddy Norman
Eddie O'Connor
Johnny Amorosa
Joe Ortalano

In October 1956, six years after his departure from DuMont, Vincent Lopez turned up with an early Saturday evening music series on CBS' local station in New York. After four highly successful months, *The Vincent Lopez Show* expanded in February from 45 minutes to an hour, with the second half hour carried on the full CBS network. Among the featured vocalists were several members of the Lopez band—saxophonist Teddy Norman, guitarist Eddie O'Connor, trumpet player Johnny Amorosa, and trombonist Joe Ortalano. Although it only lasted five weeks on the network, *The Vincent Lopez Show* remained on the air locally until the end of April.

VINNIE & BOBBY (*Situation Comedy*)
FIRST TELECAST: *May 30, 1992*
LAST TELECAST: *September 5, 1992*
BROADCAST HISTORY:
May 1992–Sep 1992, FOX Sat 9:30–10:00
CAST:
Vinnie Verducci .... Matt LeBlanc
Bobby Grazzo .... Robert Torti
William Melvin Belli ("Bill") .... John Pinette
Mona .... Joey Adams
Stanley .... Ron Taylor
Fred Slacker .... Fred Stoller
Winnie, the mail lady .... Sharyn Leavitt
Casey .... Colleen Morris
Carl Sweetwater .... Vidal Peterson

In this spin-off from *Top of the Heap*, hunky but dimwitted Vinnie Verducci was no longer living with his social-climbing dad. He was still in the same run-down apartment but was now living with his freeloading childhood friend Bobby. Vinnie, a construction worker, did want to make something of his life and, to that end, was taking night courses at Dick Butkus Community College in Chicago. Bobby, a lazy, obnoxious guy who was convinced he was God's gift to women, was forever taking advantage of his good-natured friend. Mona was the sexy teenage girl who lived in Vinnie's building and had the hots for him. Bill, Stanley, Fred, and Casey were his fellow construction workers, and Carl was Mona's nerdy would-be boyfriend.

VINYL JUSTICE (*Humor*)
BROADCAST HISTORY:
VH1
30 minutes
Produced: *1998–1999*
Premiered: *August 25, 1998*
REGULARS:
Off. Barry Sobel
Off. Wayne Brady

The musically un-hip—a substantial portion of the American public, we're told—were brought to justice in this goofy parody of *Cops*-type reality shows. Uniformed "Officers" Sobel and Brady drove the streets of Los Angeles in an authentic-looking squad car, listening for violations such as a nerdy white guy rapping in his Volvo, or "Achy-Breaky Heart" wafting from a suburban window. Celebrities were not above the law. With cameras in tow, the music cops raided the home of '70s icon Erik Estrada, discovering 8-tracks and a CD called "Macarena Mix"; questioned Ed McMahon on his musical tastes; and interrogated an indignant Estelle Getty about her workout video. Ofttimes, though, Sobel and Brady ended up dancing with the perps, especially if they were pretty girls.

Better check your record collection. You could be next.

VIPER (*Police Drama/Science Fiction*)
FIRST TELECAST: *January 2, 1994*
LAST TELECAST: *April 1, 1994*
BROADCAST HISTORY:
Jan 1994, NBC Sun 9:00–11:00
Jan 1994–Apr 1994, NBC Fri 8:00–9:00
(In first-run syndication from September 1996 to September 1999)
CAST:
Joe Astor/Michael Payton (1994, 1998–1999)
.... James McCaffrey
Julian Wilkes (1994) .... Dorian Harewood
Frankie Waters .... Joe Nipote
Cdr. Delia Thorne (1994) .... Lee Chamberlin
Thomas Cole (1996–1998) .... Jeff Kaake
Det. Cameron Westlake (1996–1999)
.... Heather Medway
Allie Farrell (1996–1997) .... Dawn Stern
Sherman Catlett (1996–1999) .... J. Downing

In the cold, violent world of the "near future," a big city fought the heavily armed forces of organized crime ("The Outfit") with its own ultimate weapon—an armor-plated, high-tech pursuit vehicle called The Viper. A modified Dodge Viper sports car, it had been built by brilliant black scientist Julian Wilkes, but since he was in a wheelchair he could not drive it very well. In fact, hardly anyone could, so the authorities took a hotshot mob driver named Payton who had almost been killed, erased his memory, and created "Joe Astor." Joe slipped easily behind the wheel of this new power machine, which was equipped with computers, grappling hooks, zappers, and a detachable flying "spy camera" that could follow the fleeing bad guys. At high speeds it even morphed into a different shape.

Unfortunately, egotistical Joe was almost as hard to control as the Viper. Politics and corruption soon drove him and his new rod underground, and he operated as a vigilante out of a sort of bat cave under a remote hydroelectric plant. Helping him were Julian and Frankie, an eager-beaver scam artist whose job at the police motor pool gave them inside information.

Two years after its network cancellation, *Viper* returned as a syndicated series. The Viper team now consisted of the quiet, hunky Cole, a C.I.A.-trained security specialist and top evasive driver for the diplomatic corps; Allie, an electronics genius and systems designer (who was dropped at the end of the first season); and mechanic Frankie, the only holdover from the original team. Cameron, a tough-talking Metro

City patrol cop, served as liaison officer for the top secret Viper project and became an active member of the team. Wilkes had taken a position in Washington, and the new car had been developed with federal funding, with Metro City chosen as the test city. Headquarters was the central station for an unbuilt subway system—giving them tunnel access to any part of town in less than ten minutes. The new car had side-mounted .50-caliber machine guns and missile delivery tubes, front and rear battering rams, and a self-propelled miniature flying surveillance probe with its own weapons. Catlett was an obnoxious, marginally competent F.B.I. agent with a penchant for messing things up. Seen occasionally during the first season, he became a regular the following fall when he was assigned as liaison between the F.B.I. and all local law enforcement agencies, including the Viper team.

In the second season finale the Viper was destroyed to keep a Cole look-alike from using it to kill Cole and Frankie. At the end of the episode the team was admiring a computer-generated hologram prototype of the car to replace the one that had been destroyed—a new Viper. That fall Cole had been reassigned, and Joe, the original Viper driver, reluctantly returned to drive the new Viper.

VIRGINIAN, THE (*Western*)
FIRST TELECAST: *September 19, 1962*
LAST TELECAST: *September 8, 1971*
BROADCAST HISTORY:
Sep 1962–Sep 1971, NBC Wed 7:30–9:00
CAST:
Judge Henry Garth (1962–1966) .... Lee J. Cobb
The Virginian .... James Drury
Trampas .... Doug McClure
Steve (1962–1964) .... Gary Clarke
Molly Wood (1962–1963) .... Pippa Scott
Betsy Garth (1962–1965) .... Roberta Shore
Randy Benton (1964–1966) .... Randy Boone
Emmett Ryker (1964–1966, 1967–1968)
.... Clu Gulager
Belden (1964–1967) .... L. Q. Jones
Jennifer Garth (1965–1966) .... Diane Roter
John Grainger (1966–1967) .... Charles Bickford
Stacy Grainger (1966–1968) .... Don Quine
Elizabeth Grainger (1966–1970) .... Sara Lane
Sheriff Mark Abbott (1966–1970) .... Ross Elliott
Clay Grainger (1967–1970) .... John McIntire
Holly Grainger (1967–1970) .... Jeanette Nolan
David Sutton (1968–1969) .... David Hartman
Jim Horn (1969–1970) .... Tim Matheson
Col. Alan MacKenzie (1970–1971)
.... Stewart Granger
Roy Tate (1970–1971) .... Lee Majors
Parker (1970–1971) .... John McLiam

This long-running drama was the first 90-minute Western series. It starred James Drury as the laconic, mysterious "Virginian," who never revealed his real name and who "forced his idea of law and order on a Wyoming Territory community in the 1890s"; and Doug McClure as the wild young cowhand Trampas. Setting for the saga was the Shiloh Ranch, owned successively by Judge Garth, the two Grainger brothers (John and Clay), and finally Col. Alan MacKenzie. Col. MacKenzie took over during the last season, at which time the program was retitled *The Men from Shiloh* and the historical period was moved up a few years.

The Virginian was one of the leading "adult Westerns," relying on strong characterizations by both regular cast and guest stars rather than on gimmicks. In many respects it resembled a weekly movie feature. Many actors and actresses appeared in regular supporting roles for varying lengths of time, among them David Hartman in 1968 and Lee Majors in 1970.

The Virginian was based on the classic 1902 novel of the same name by Owen Wister, which had been produced three times as a motion picture (the most famous being the 1929 version starring Gary Cooper and Walter Huston).

An interesting sidelight was that the original pilot for this series, produced in the late 1950s, cast Drury as a Western dandy replete with shiny hunting boots, skintight pants, lace cuffs, and a tiny pistol. It didn't sell, and so was remade several years later without the foppish accoutrements—to become one of TV's biggest hits.

VISE, THE (*Suspense Anthology*)
FIRST TELECAST: *October 1, 1954*
LAST TELECAST: *December 16, 1955*
BROADCAST HISTORY:
Oct 1954–Dec 1955, ABC Fri 9:30–10:00
HOST:
Ron Randell

Filmed drama series produced in London, depicting people caught in "the vise" of fate due to their own misdeeds. Schemers, blackmailers, and other unseemly types always got their due in this program, and viewers invariably got a look at some very pretty girls, who always seemed to play roles in each of these internationally flavored stories. The actors were generally lesser-known British performers, but some talented newcomers who would later become internationally famous were seen here, including Honor Blackman, Patrick McGoohan, and Petula Clark. Australian actor Ron Randell was the host.

The series ended in December 1955, after which the time slot and the title *The Vise* were taken over by a new series of *Mark Saber* episodes.

VISIT WITH THE ARMED FORCES (*Documentary*)
FIRST TELECAST: *July 3, 1950*
LAST TELECAST: *January 1, 1951*
BROADCAST HISTORY:
Jul 1950–Jan 1951, DUM Mon 8:00–8:30

Documentary films about the armed forces.

VISITOR, THE, syndicated title for *Doctor, The*

VISITOR, THE (*Science Fiction*)
FIRST TELECAST: *September 19, 1997*
LAST TELECAST: *January 16, 1998*
BROADCAST HISTORY:
Sep 1997–Jan 1998, FOX Fri 8:00–9:00
CAST:
Adam MacArthur .... John Corbett
Agent Douglas Wilcox .... Grand L. Bush
Agent Nicolas LaRue .... Leon Rippy
Agent Craig Van Patten .... John Storey
Col. James Vise .... Steve Railsback
Michael Ryan ("The Hunter") .... Adam Baldwin

Adam had vanished in the Bermuda Triangle in 1947, abducted by aliens, only to return in 1997 in an alien ship that was shot down by the Air Force. He had not aged appreciably in the half century since his abduction, and now had powers—given to him by his abductors—that made him a target of both the military and the F.B.I. He wandered from place to place helping people while trying to evade capture. Adam could communicate with animals, stop his wounds from bleeding, heal himself and others, read more than 100 pages a minute, levitate, and read other people's thoughts. The aliens, after having abducted many humans for experiments, had reached the conclusion humanity was on the road to its own destruction. Adam was determined to prevent that from happening.

Every time he used computers to access restricted Pentagon files, the C.I.A. tried to seal them off and trace his location, but he was always one step ahead of them. His mission was to prevent mankind from destroying itself with pollution and runaway bad technology. As he said, "All life is connected, you just have to open your eyes." For a time Adam was also chased by "The Hunter," another abductee who didn't want him to alter history or save mankind from extinction. The Hunter was killed by a crazed Colonel Vise, one of his own childhood friends who had been haunted by the abduction of a group of his friends in 1975.

At the beginning of the last episode Adam was cornered by the F.B.I., but before they could take him into custody, a UFO beamed him aboard, with the wounded Vise (who later died) left behind. On the ship he was put on trial by his fellow abductees for tampering with the future. Ryan (his body now occupied by another who had been saved by Adam) served as his defense counsel. Meanwhile, mysterious people in the U.S. government disbanded the group that had been chasing him because they now believed in UFOs. Adam was returned from the UFO to resume his mission—as decreed by the never-seen alien "Elders" as his sentence for having caused problems in the first place.

VITAL SIGNS (*Medical Documentary*)

FIRST TELECAST: *February 27, 1997*
LAST TELECAST: *July 3, 1997*
BROADCAST HISTORY:
Feb 1997–Jul 1997, ABC Thu 9:00–10:00
HOST:
Robert Urich

The image most viewers took away from this series was the startling sight of matinee idol Robert Urich, completely bald, talking about medical emergencies—including his own. Urich was at the time fighting a rare form of cancer (which later went into temporary remission), and the chemotherapy had caused the baldness. Other stories, handled documentary-style, included an expectant mother's aneurysm, the aftermath of a motorcycle accident, and the three-year-old victim of a dog attack. The series was bloody but informative.

VIVA VALDEZ (*Situation Comedy*)

FIRST TELECAST: *May 31, 1976*
LAST TELECAST: *September 6, 1976*
BROADCAST HISTORY:
May 1976–Sep 1976, ABC Mon 8:00–8:30
CAST:
Luis Valdez .... Rodolfo Hoyos
Sophia Valdez .... Carmen Zapata
Victor Valdez .... James Victor
Ernesto Valdez .... Nelson D. Cuevas
Connie Valdez .... Lisa Mordente
Pepe Valdez .... Claudio Martinez
Jerry Ramirez .... Jorge Cervera, Jr.

Noisy "gang" comedy about a close-knit Mexican-American family living in East Los Angeles. Louis ran a plumbing business with his eldest son, Victor. Sophia was the mama; Ernesto, an artistic lad in training with the telephone company; Connie, the irrepressible teenager; and Pepe, the 12-year-old baseball fanatic. Jerry was a cousin newly arrived from Mexico.

VIVA VARIETY (*Comedy Variety*)

BROADCAST HISTORY:
Comedy Central
30 minutes
Produced: *1997–1998*
Premiered: *April 1, 1997*
REGULARS:
Mr. Laupin .... Thomas Lennon
Mrs. Laupin .... Kerri Kenney
Johnny Bluejeans .... Michael Ian Black

This English lampoon on TV variety shows was hosted by a divorced couple, the slick but inept Mr. Laupin and his statuesque ex-wife. They were assisted (if that is the word) by a rather dumb, sexy young man named Johnny, who dressed in vinyl suits and greased his hair à la Elvis. Amid the put-downs and general confusion real guests appeared, including celebrities (Ben Stiller, Janeane Garofalo), avant-garde bands (They Might Be Giants, The Mighty Mighty Bosstones, Shudder to Think), and a variety of freak acts ("The World's Only Contortionist Fiddle Player," "Scotland's Premiere Regurgitator"). The dancers were called the Swimsuit Squad.

VIVIEN KELLEMS, see *Power of Women, The*

VOICE OF FIRESTONE, THE (*Music*)

FIRST TELECAST: *September 5, 1949*
LAST TELECAST: *June 16, 1963*
BROADCAST HISTORY:
Sep 1949–Jun 1954, NBC Mon 8:30–9:00
Jun 1954–Jun 1957, ABC Mon 8:30–9:00
Sep 1957–Jun 1959, ABC Mon 9:00–9:30 (OS)
Sep 1962–Jun 1963, ABC Sun 10:00–10:30
NARRATOR:
John Daly (1958–1959)
REGULARS:
Howard Barlow conducting the Firestone Concert Orchestra
THEME MUSIC:
"If I Could Tell You" and "In My Garden," both composed by Mrs. Harvey Firestone

Radio's venerable Monday night program of classical and semiclassical music, which had been on the air since 1928, became a TV series in 1949, when regular simulcasts began with the radio program. It survived on TV for a total of twelve seasons, but not without sparking a bitter controversy over the role that ratings and mass-audience appeal should play in TV programming. It was canceled three times, eventually leaving the air permanently in 1963, a victim of the basic rule that on American television "best" is not enough—only "biggest" counts.

The format of *Voice* changed little over the years. Stars of grand opera were the usual guests, although occasionally more "popular" talent would also appear singing Broadway show tunes and pop standards. The 25th anniversary telecast, in 1953, was an especially gala affair, with speeches and performances by many of the great stars who had appeared on *Voice* over the years, including Eleanor Steber, Rise Stevens, Thomas L. Thomas, Brian Sullivan, Robert Rounseville, and Jerome Hines. Worthy causes were frequently promoted on the show, such as highway safety, 4-H, and the UN, and in 1954 there was an essay contest on the theme "I Speak for Democracy." The winner, a 16-year-old Akron, Ohio, schoolgirl, appeared on the program to read her essay.

Though the program was certainly prestigious, to be truthful it was a bit stiff—pleasing to hear, but sometimes boring to watch. Tuxedos and starched shirts were the order of the evening, with staging to match. There were few concessions to popular taste. During the early 1950s only occasional popular talent appeared (notably Jane Froman), but from 1958–1959 a new format was announced which struck a much more equal balance between the classics and the "better" pops on each show. Jo Stafford, Fred Waring, Xavier Cugat, and Gordon MacRae were among those who appeared, along with Carlos Montoya, the Philadelphia Symphony, the Ballet Russe of Monte Carlo, and the Vienna Boys' Choir from the "serious" side. John Daly, urbane and witty as always, was added as narrator.

A further change took place from 1962–1963 when Howard Barlow was phased out as permanent conductor (he still appeared occasionally) and a rotating roster of maestros was introduced. Most frequently seen were Arthur Fiedler, Wilfred Pelletier, and Harry John Brown. James McCracken made his network TV debut during this season, and Rudolf Nureyev also appeared.

Although the audience for *Voice* was relatively small by TV standards (about two to three million viewers per week), the appreciation of those who did watch, and the considerable prestige, made Firestone quite content to continue funding the show. But in 1954, after carrying *Voice* on Monday nights at 8:30 P.M. for 26 years (first on radio and then TV), NBC insisted that a change had to be made. The program's low ratings were affecting the entire Monday night NBC lineup, and the network was finding it impossible to sell the succeeding half hour. Firestone refused to budge, arguing that many of the program's faithful viewers would not be able to watch in a less desirable time period. So the show, both radio and TV versions, moved to ABC the following fall. ABC was at the time happy to have the business, but by 1959 that network too was beginning to taste big ratings in other parts of its schedule. A new, sales-oriented ABC management determined that *Voice* must move to 10:00 P.M. so as not to hurt the shows that followed it. Again, Firestone objected, and this time the show went off the air.

Though the audiences had been small, the hue and cry when *Voice* was dropped was deafening. Sen. Mike Monroney bitterly attacked ABC for following in the footsteps of NBC in dropping the "best" of TV. There were threats of action through the FCC, and critics were unrelenting. ABC tried to appease them by putting on a similar program called *Music for a Summer Night* using the same producers, but with a smaller budget. It was not the same. All three networks offered various fringe time slots to *Voice*, which Firestone rejected. For an investment of more than $1 million per year, Firestone felt that it deserved the best. Finally in 1962, after a change of management, ABC took it back, this time at 10:00 P.M. Commendations were immediately forthcoming (Sen. Thomas E. Dodd: "You're bringing back *Voice of Firestone*, and I find that commendable"). But again "only" two and a half million viewers chose to watch, and by mid-1963 *Voice* was once again gone—this time for good.

VOICE OF FIRESTONE TELEVUES (*Documentary*)
FIRST TELECAST: *April 10, 1944*
LAST TELECAST: *January 20, 1947*
BROADCAST HISTORY:
Apr 1944–Jan 1947, NBC Mon Various (10–15 minutes)

The Firestone Tire and Rubber Co. was one of television's earliest advertisers, beginning this Monday night series of "Televues" on NBC's New York station on November 29, 1943, and sponsoring it continuously for more than three years. The presentations were a varied selection of short documentary films on different subjects, such as dairy farming, football, vocational guidance, etc. There was a live opening and closing for each show.

The program became one of the first network series when NBC began feeding its Monday night schedule to stations in Philadelphia and Schenectady in April 1944.

VOLUME ONE (*Dramatic Anthology*)
FIRST TELECAST: *June 16, 1949*
LAST TELECAST: *July 21, 1949*
BROADCAST HISTORY:
Jun 1949–Jul 1949, ABC Thu 9:30–10:00
PRODUCER/DIRECTOR/NARRATOR:
Wyllis Cooper

Famed radio writer Wyllis Cooper tried his hand at television in this six-telecast series of original dramas. Cooper was the Rod Serling of radio, producing eerie, surrealistic stories of horror and suspense, often based more on psychological terror than on actual violence. He had created, among other shows, *Lights Out* and *Quiet, Please*. His first telecast starred Jack Lescoulie, Nancy Sheridan, and Frank Thomas, Jr., in an intelligent psychological thriller which drew rave reviews. Nevertheless the series lasted for only the scheduled six weeks.

Each telecast was numbered: "Volume One, Number One," "Volume One, Number Two," etc. The radio title *Quiet, Please* was originally to be used for the series, but had to be dropped at the last minute.

VOYAGE TO THE BOTTOM OF THE SEA (*Science Fiction*)
FIRST TELECAST: *September 14, 1964*
LAST TELECAST: *September 15, 1968*
BROADCAST HISTORY:
Sep 1964–Sep 1965, ABC Mon 7:30–8:30
Sep 1965–Sep 1968, ABC Sun 7:00–8:00

CAST:

Adm. Harriman Nelson .... Richard Basehart
Cdr./Capt. Lee Crane .... David Hedison
Lt. Cdr. Chip Morton............... Robert Dowdell
Chief Petty Officer Curley Jones (1964–1965)
.... Henry Kulky
Chief Sharkey (1965–1968) .... Terry Becker
Stu Riley (1965–1967)................ Allan Hunt
Kowalsky .... Del Monroe
Crewman Patterson .... Paul Trinka
Crewman Sparks .... Arch Whiting
Doctor .... Richard Bull

CREATOR/PRODUCER:

Irwin Allen

One of TV's all-time favorite science-fiction adventure series, this followed the exploits of the officers and men of the *Seaview,* a glass-nosed atomic submarine that roamed the seven seas fighting villains both human and alien. The *Seaview* was the brainchild of retired Adm. Harriman Nelson, director of the super-secret Nelson Institute of Marine Research at Santa Barbara, California. The time was ten years into the future. Originally there were two subs, but the *Seaview*'s sister ship, the *Polidor,* was sunk in the third episode. Nelson's chief assistant and the commander of the *Seaview* then became Cdr. Lee Crane (he was promoted to captain in the second season). Their opponents included such dastardly villains as Dr. Gamma (Theodore Marcuse) and the sneaky Prof. Multiple (Vincent Price)—he came aboard under the pretext of presenting a puppet show, only to have the puppets come to life and run amok—plus assorted unreconstructed Nazis, lost worlds, giant orchids quivering with alien energy, globular masses of "pure intelligence" that threatened to devour the entire sub, and other fantastic creatures (remarkable, what's down there!). Some episodes were less obvious. On one, the *Seaview* picked up Old John (Carroll O'Connor), an enigmatic stranger found floating placidly in a rowboat in the middle of the Pacific.

During the second season the emphasis on gadgetry was increased, with the *Seaview* gaining the *Sea Crab,* a self-propelled two-man explorer, and the *Flying Fish,* a mini-sub which could fly through the air at fantastic speeds. Some cast changes were made, including the addition of fast-talking, handsome young surfer Stu Riley, as a kind of on-shore ally.

The series was based on Irwin Allen's 1961 movie of the same name, and used many of the sets from that film.

VOYAGERS (*Science Fiction*)

FIRST TELECAST: *October 3, 1982*

LAST TELECAST: *July 31, 1983*

BROADCAST HISTORY:

Oct 1982–Mar 1983, NBC Sun 7:00–8:00
Jun 1983–Jul 1983, NBC Sun 7:00–8:00

CAST:

Phineas Bogg .... Jon-Erik Hexum
Jeffrey Jones .... Meeno Peluce

Designed primarily to appeal to children, this educational science-fiction series chronicled the adventures of two time travelers taking part in great events of human history. The show began with the curious premise that a group of trained travelers, or "Voyagers," journeyed back and forth through the ages making sure that great events turned out as intended. Phineas Boggs was one such Voyager, but a somewhat klutzy one. When his Omni—his time-travel device—malfunctioned, Phineas crashed into the Manhattan bedroom of young Jeffrey Jones. Phineas' guidebook to history was then eaten by Jeffrey's dog, Ralph, leaving the traveler without his source of information on how great events were supposed to turn out. Fortunately young Jeffrey was a history buff, and knew more about the subject than his embarrassed guest, so he agreed to travel with him and help him on assignments.

Most episodes featured two or three notable moments in history, with the Voyagers on hand to keep things on the right track. They gave directions to Lewis and Clark, helped General MacArthur get away from Pearl Harbor just before the Japanese attack in 1941, made sure the baby Moses was discovered by the Pharaoh's daughter, got the Wright Brothers back to working on their airplane, prevented President Teddy Roosevelt from being killed by Billy the Kid, and helped Spartacus escape from jail to lead a revolt against Roman oppression. Because Phineas' Omni was damaged, they could not go any later than the year 1982, except when the Voyagers brought them back to Phineas' home time (never specified) to try him for violating the Voyager code by using Jeffrey as a guide (he was acquitted). At the conclusion of each show, series star Meeno Peluce would suggest to young viewers that they go to the library to get more information about the historical periods featured on that episode.

WE: WOMEN'S ENTERTAINMENT (Network)

(*General Entertainment Cable Network*)

LAUNCHED:

January 1, 1997

SUBSCRIBERS (MAY 2003):

52.0 million (49% U.S.)

This women's network was originally launched as a movie channel called Romance Classics, a subsidiary of American Movie Classics, specializing in romantic movies, dramas and specials. Many of the films were lesser-known theatrical titles of the '80s, made for television, or imported—but then, love knows no boundaries, does it?

In 2000 the network was relaunched as WE: Women's Entertainment, a full-service women's network with movies still constituting a major part of the schedule. Supplementing them were such original series as *Cool Women* (documentary about women of achievement, hosted by Debbie Allen), *Everyday Elegance* (advice on entertaining, with Colin Cowie), *Style World* (a worldwide shopping binge with Daisy Fuentes), *Journey Women Off the Map* (outdoor adventures) and *Great Romances of the 20th Century*. Later entries included *Winning Women* (sports bios) with Alexandra Paul.

W.E.B. (*Drama*)

FIRST TELECAST: *September 13, 1978*
LAST TELECAST: *October 5, 1978*
BROADCAST HISTORY:

Sep 1978, NBC Wed 10:00–11:00
Sep 1978–Oct 1978, NBC Thu 10:00–11:00

CAST:

Ellen Cunningham .... Pamela Bellwood
Jack Kiley .... Alex Cord
Gus Dunlap .... Richard Basehart
Dan Costello .... Andrew Prine
Walter Matthews .... Howard Witt
Harvey Pearlstein .... Lee Wilkof
Christine .... Tisch Raye
Kevin .... Peter Coffield

Television showed the ability to caricature even itself in this primetime soap opera set behind the scenes at a "major television network"—Trans Atlantic Broadcasting. Ellen Cunningham, an ambitious, talented female executive who had clawed her way up in a man's world, was head of Special Events Programming. Surrounding her was an executive suite full of unsavory characters: Jack Kiley, the ruthless head of programming; Gus Dunlap, news chief and a drunken has-been; Dan Costello, fast-talking, inebriated sales chief; Walter Matthews, hard-driving head of operations; and Harvey Pearlstein, the research head obsessed with ratings. There was plenty of backbiting, maneuvering, and high-level treachery behind the smiling screen at T.A.B. This series was no doubt inspired by the movie *Network*, and was produced by Lin Bolen, who in real life had been one of the industry's first female programming chiefs (at NBC).

WIOU (*Drama*)

FIRST TELECAST: *October 24, 1990*
LAST TELECAST: *March 20, 1991*
BROADCAST HISTORY:

Oct 1990–Jan 1991, CBS Wed 10:00–11:00
Mar 1991, CBS Wed 10:00–11:00

CAST:

Hank Zaret .... John Shea
Kelby Robinson .... Helen Shaver
Neal Frazier .... Harris Yulin
Floyd Graham .... Dick Van Patten
Liz McVay .... Mariette Hartley
Taylor Young .... Kate McNeil
Eddie Bock .... Phil Morris
Willis Teitlebaum .... Wallace Langham
Ann Hudson .... Jayne Brook
Tony Pro .... Joe Grifasi
Kevin Dougherty .... Robin Gammell
Marc Adamson .... Eric Pierpoint
Rick Singer .... Steven Eckholdt
Floor Director .... Scott Harlan
Director .... Robert Crow

Hank Zaret was the new news director at TV station WNDY, sent by executives at the network which owned the station to bolster its sagging news ratings. Hank, who had gotten his start there years before, returned to a station in such financial trouble its staff had nicknamed it WIOU. The principal WNDY on-camera news personnel were anchor Neal Frazier, an overbearing womanizer with an inflated ego and a wandering eye; newly appointed coanchor Kelby Robinson, a dedicated journalist who had once been Hank's lover; weatherman Floyd Graham, a lovable veteran who was going blind from glaucoma; reporter Eddie Bock, an ambitious black newsman with minimal scruples when it came to furthering his career; and reporter Taylor Young, a recent arrival from Tampa with a mind-set almost identical to Eddie's. Others on the news staff were longtime executive producer Liz McVay, who felt she had been passed over when Hank had been hired; committed young field producer Ann Hudson, who was dating wealthy yuppie Rick Singer; news intern Willis Teitlebaum, who had a crush on Ann; and unprincipled cameraman Marc Adamson, who worked with Taylor to further both their careers. Tony Pro was WNDY's fast-talking public relations director and Kevin Dougherty its anxiety ridden general manager, fearful that if the ratings didn't get better, he'd be out of a job. Although no city was ever mentioned, with the call letters WNDY, this series could have been set in Chicago.

Despite lavish praise from critics, and a cast that gave *WIOU* a very real look, the ratings for the series were even lower than the news ratings for fictional WNDY. The series never found an audience and was canceled, with five of the eighteen episodes produced never having aired.

WKRP IN CINCINNATI (*Situation Comedy*)

FIRST TELECAST: *September 18, 1978*
LAST TELECAST: *September 20, 1982*
BROADCAST HISTORY:

Sep 1978–Nov 1978, CBS Mon 8:00–8:30
Jan 1979–Dec 1979, CBS Mon 9:30–10:00
Dec 1979–Jul 1980, CBS Mon 8:00–8:30
Jul 1980–Aug 1980, CBS Mon 8:30–9:00
Aug 1980–Sep 1980, CBS Sat 8:00–8:30
Sep 1980–Oct 1980, CBS Mon 9:30–10:00
Nov 1980–May 1981, CBS Sat 8:00–8:30

Jun 1981–Sep 1981, CBS Mon 8:00–8:30
Oct 1981–Jan 1982, CBS Wed 8:30–9:00
Jan 1982–Feb 1982, CBS Wed 8:00–8:30
Mar 1982–Apr 1982, CBS Wed 9:00–9:30
Jun 1982–Sep 1982, CBS Mon 8:30–9:00
(In first-run syndication from September 1991 to September 1993)

CAST:

Andy Travis (1978–1982) .... Gary Sandy
Arthur Carlson ("Big Guy") .... Gordon Jump
Jennifer Marlowe (1978–1982) ...... Loni Anderson
Les Nessman .... Richard Sanders
Gordon Sims (Venus Flytrap) (1978–1982) .... Tim Reid
Herb Tarlek .... Frank Bonner
Bailey Quarters (1978–1982) .... Jan Smithers
Johnny Caravella (Dr. Johnny Fever) .... Howard Hesseman
Lillian "Mama" Carlson (pilot only) ... Sylvia Sidney
**Lillian "Mama" Carlson (1979–1992)* .... Carol Bruce
Donovan Aderhold (1991–1993) .... Mykel T. Williamson
Dana Burns (1991–1992) .... Kathleen Garrett
Jack Allen (1991–1992) .... Michael Des Barres
Mona Loveland (1991–1993) .... Tawny Kitaen
Claire Hartline (1991–1992) .... Hope Alexander-Willis
Arthur Carlson, Jr. (1991–1992) ... Lightfield Lewis
Ronnie Lee (1991) .... Wendy Davis
Buddy Dornster (1991–1993) .... John Chappell
Nancy Braithwaite (1992–1993) .... Marla Jeanette Rubinoff
Razor Dee (1992–1993) .... French Stewart

*Occasional

The arrival of a new program director, Andy Travis, brought sudden and dramatic changes to WKRP, a Cincinnati radio station that had been losing money for years by playing sedate music. Andy's decision to turn WKRP into a "top 40" rock 'n' roll station alienated its elderly audience, and also its few sponsors, such as the Shady Hill Rest Home and Barry's Fashions for the Short and Portly. It also created a trying situation for Arthur Carlson, the inept and bumbling general manager who held his job only because his mother owned the station. But Mother Carlson, who had dollar signs in her eyes, decided to give Andy's plan a try—as long as the station turned a profit.

The staff of WKRP was full of offbeat characters. Les Nessman was the naive, gullible, and pompous news director, more concerned with his farm reports than with national and international stories. Bailey Quarters was Andy's enthusiastic young assistant, who handled billing and traffic and was eventually given the added responsibilities of backup news reporter working with Les. The two WKRP disc jockeys seen regularly were morning man Dr. Johnny Fever, a jive-talking counterculture type who seemed constantly spaced out, and night man Venus Flytrap, a hip black who had worked with Andy at other stations.

Jennifer Marlowe, the sexy but efficient receptionist, actually had a lot to do with holding the station together—she knew far more about what was going on than did her boss, Mr. Carlson. Loni Anderson, who played Jennifer, quickly became the star of the show, and one of the major sex symbols of the late 1970s. The Farrah Fawcett-Majors posters of a few years earlier gave way to posters of the buxom Loni. She guested constantly on other programs, and soon landed the juicy role of Jayne Mansfield in a made-for-television movie about the life of that sex symbol of an earlier era. All the adulation went to her—or her agent's—head, and, like Farrah, she quickly demanded a huge increase in salary or she would leave the show. Unlike Farrah, she got it, and stayed.

The final regular was Herb Tarlek, WKRP's high-pressure advertising salesman who, though married, spent much of his time making passes at Jennifer. He proved to be more talk than action, however, as he was totally intimidated when she indicated she was willing to take him up on his offer in one touching episode. Station owner Mrs. Carlson was a constant threat to them all but, fortunately, only showed up occasionally, usually to complain about something they either were or weren't doing with the station.

Nine years after *WKRP in Cincinnati* left CBS, it returned to the air in first-run syndication with three returning characters from the network series—bumbling station manager Arthur Carlson, sleazy salesman Herb Tarlek, and nerdy news director Les Nessman. New to the station were Donovan Aderhold, the recently hired black program director; Burns and Allen, the quarrelsome married couple who were known on the air as "the morning maniacs"; Mona Loveland, the sexy late-night disc jockey; Claire, WKRP's cynical traffic manager; Ronnie, the young receptionist; Buddy, the station's portly rumpled engineer; and Mr. Carlson's son, Arthur, Jr., an ambitious and rather arrogant apprentice salesman working with Herb. Nancy, a sexy but dopey receptionist, replaced Ronnie early in 1992, and a number of cast changes were made that fall. Gone were "the morning maniacs," replaced by Razor Dee, a spaced-out younger version of Johnny Fever; Dee lived in a trailer he had conned Les into leaving in his backyard. Fever himself, who had shown up several times during the previous season, was back full-time on the graveyard shift, and Art Jr., who had been a pain for Herb, had given up selling to go to graduate school. Seen occasionally during the syndicated run, as well as during the original network run, was Herb's perky wife, Lucille, played by Edie McClurg.

WACKIEST SHIP IN THE ARMY, THE (*War/Adventure*)

FIRST TELECAST: *September 19, 1965*
LAST TELECAST: *September 4, 1966*
BROADCAST HISTORY:

Sep 1965–Sep 1966, NBC Sun 10:00–11:00

CAST:

Major Simon Butcher .... Jack Warden
Lt. (j.g.) Richard "Rip" Riddle .... Gary Collins
Chief Petty Officer Willie Miller .... Mike Kellin
Gunner's Mate Sherman Nagurski ..... Rudy Solari
Ship's Cook Charles Tyler .... Don Penny
Radioman Patrick Hollis .... Mark Slade
Machinist's Mate Seymour Trivers ..... Fred Smoot
Gen. Cross .... William Zuckert
Admiral Vincent Beckett .... Charles Irving

In the spring of 1942, only months after the Japanese bombing of Pearl Harbor, the government of New Zealand presented to the United States the *Kiwi*, a 70-year-old twin-masted schooner. Obsolete and badly in need of repairs, the ship was staffed with a token crew while the U.S. Navy tried to figure out what to do with it. The navy soon discovered that it possessed certain unique qualities that made it a useful espionage weapon. Its wooden hull did not show up on radar, its sailing power did not register on sonar, and its shallow draft allowed it to travel in waters not deep enough for larger ships. And so the *Kiwi* went to war. It was commanded by young Lt. Rip Riddle when at sea and by Maj. Simon Butcher of the army when in port, a situation which caused numerous problems because Rip and Simon had very different views on war strategy, women, protocol, and their respective roles on the ship. Complicating things even more was the fact that Maj. Butcher, although higher in rank than Lt. Riddle, had to report to the younger man whenever the *Kiwi* was at sea, while their roles were reversed whenever it made port. The adventures of the crew in the South Pacific during the early days of the war constituted the stories, which were based on the real-life exploits of the *Echo*, a leaky two-masted schooner which New Zealand's government gave to the U.S. in 1942. The story of the *Echo* had been made into a comedy-adventure movie in 1960.

WACKY WORLD OF JONATHAN WINTERS, THE

(*Comedy/Variety*)

BROADCAST HISTORY:

Syndicated only
30 minutes
Produced: *1972–1974* (52 episodes)
Released: *Fall 1972*

REGULARS:

Jonathan Winters
Marian Mercer
Mary Gregory
Soul Sisters (1972–1973)
The Golddiggers (1973–1974)
Van Alexander Orchestra

Comedian Jonathan Winters, who had a number of network series (see Index), returned to TV in 1972 with this syndicated comedy variety show. The emphasis was on improvisational sketches, with Maudie Frickert and the other fanciful Winters characters appearing frequently. There was a regular supporting cast in the first season, and multiple guest appearances by John Davidson, Tony Orlando and Dawn, Charo, the Staple Singers, John Stewart, the Ding-a-Lings, and Lynn Anderson.

WAGON TRAIN (*Western*)

FIRST TELECAST: *September 18, 1957*
LAST TELECAST: *September 5, 1965*

BROADCAST HISTORY:

Sep 1957–Sep 1962, NBC Wed 7:30–8:30
Sep 1962–Sep 1963, ABC Wed 7:30–8:30
Sep 1963–Sep 1964, ABC Mon 8:30–10:00
Sep 1964–Sep 1965, ABC Sun 7:30–8:30

CAST:

Major Seth Adams (1957–1961) .... Ward Bond
Flint McCullough (1957–1962) ...... Robert Horton
Bill Hawks .... Terry Wilson
Charlie Wooster .... Frank McGrath
Duke Shannon (1961–1964) .... Scott Miller
Christopher Hale (1961–1965) .... John McIntire
Barnaby West (1963–1965) .... Michael Burns
Cooper Smith (1963–1965) .... Robert Fuller

Wagon Train was one of the most popular "big" Western series during the heyday of TV Westerns, in the late 1950s and early 1960s. It was big in scope (the whole American West, it seemed), big in cast (many top-name guests), and big in format (60 minutes most seasons, 90 minutes in one). The setting was a California-bound wagon train in the post–Civil War days, starting out each season from "St. Joe" (St. Joseph, Missouri) and making its way west until reaching California in the spring. In between there were endless adventures on the vast, Indian-controlled Great Plains, the endless deserts, and the towering passes of the Rocky Mountains. But what made *Wagon Train* work were the characters who passed in and out of its episodes. The program was actually a series of character studies, each week revolving around a different member of the party or a different person encountered by the train along the way. Some were God-fearin' settlers, others young adventurers, others scoundrels. The regulars in the cast, who composed the "staff" of the wagon train, were seen in costarring or sometimes even secondary roles.

Wagon Train had only two wagonmasters in its eight years of crisscrossing the country. The first was fatherly Major Adams, replaced in the spring of 1961 by Chris Hale (actor Ward Bond had died the previous November in the middle of shooting the 1960–1961 season's episodes). Flint McCullough was the original frontier scout who rode out ahead to clear the way and make peace, if possible, with often unfriendly Indians. When Robert Horton left the series (supposedly he was "fed up" with Westerns), McCullough was replaced by Duke Shannon and young Cooper Smith. Bill Hawks went all the way as the assistant wagonmaster and lead wagon driver, as did grizzled old Charlie Wooster as the cook. Barnaby West joined the regular cast during the last couple of seasons as a 13-year-old orphan boy found trudging along the trail heading west on his own.

Those were the continuing cast members, but the regular infusion of guest stars and the focus on different personalities in each episode made *Wagon Train* seem more like a new Western film every week than an ordinary TV series. The series took a season to catch on, but in its second year it was in the top ten. After three years of placing a close second to *Gunsmoke*, it became the number-one program on television in the 1961–1962 season.

Reruns of the episodes featuring Ward Bond aired as part of the ABC weekday daytime lineup under the title *Major Adams—Trailmaster* from September 1963 to September 1965 and on Sunday afternoons from January 1963 to May 1964.

WAIT TILL YOUR FATHER GETS HOME (*Cartoon*)

BROADCAST HISTORY:

Syndicated only
30 minutes
Produced: *1972–1974* (48 episodes)
Released: *Fall 1972*

VOICES:

Harry Boyle .... Tom Bosley
Irma Boyle .... Joan Gerber
Alice Boyle .... Kristina Holland
Chet Boyle .... David Hayward
Jamie Boyle .... Jackie Haley
Ralph .... Jack Burns

This rather unsubtle animated comedy was an attempt to cash in on the enormous success of *All in the Family*. Harry Boyle was a conservative businessman-father who was continually exasperated by the excesses of his hippie son, Chet, and sexually liberated daughter, Alice. His allies were obedient youngest son, Jamie, and Neanderthal neighbor, Ralph, who gave his family close-order drill against the day of the Communist invasion. Wife Irma was neutral.

A good many celebrities appeared on the show, sometimes voicing cartoon representations of themselves. Among them were Don Knotts, Phyllis Diller, Don Adams, Rich Little, Jonathan Winters, and Monty Hall.

WAITING FOR THE BREAK (*Variety*)

FIRST TELECAST: *March 18, 1950*

LAST TELECAST: *April 8, 1950*

BROADCAST HISTORY:

Mar 1950–Apr 1950, NBC Sat 7:30–8:00

HOST:

Hank Ladd

Four-week variety series featuring the understudies and chorus people from current Broadway hits, performing scenes and songs from their shows.

WALKER, TEXAS RANGER (*Western*)

FIRST TELECAST: *April 21, 1993*

LAST TELECAST: *July 28, 2001*

BROADCAST HISTORY:

Apr 1993, CBS Wed 9:00–11:00
Apr 1993–May 1993, CBS Sat 10:00–11:00
Sep 1993–Jun 2000, CBS Sat 10:00–11:00
Jun 2000–Aug 2001, CBS Sat 9:00–10:00
Jul 2000–Sep 2000, CBS Sat 10:00–11:00
Oct 2000–Feb 2001, CBS Sat 9:00–10:00
Apr 2001–Jun 2001, CBS Sat 8:00–9:00
Apr 2001–Jul 2001, CBS Sat 9:00–10:00

CAST:

Cordell "Cord" Walker .... Chuck Norris
James "Jimmy" Trivette .... Clarence Gilyard
Asst. D.A. Alex Cahill .... Sheree J. Wilson
C. D. Parker (pilot only) .... Gailard Sartain
C. D. Parker (1993–1999)......... Noble Willingham
Uncle Ray Firewalker (1993–1994)
.... Floyd Red Crow Westerman
Det. Carlos Sandoval (1998–1999) ... Marco Sanchez
Trent Malloy (1998–1999)........... Jimmy Wlcek
Francis Gage (1999–2001) .... Judson Mills
Sydney Cooke (1999–2001) .... Nia Peeples

Cordell Walker was a contemporary Texas Ranger working out of the Dallas office who believed in dealing with criminals the old-fashioned way—by beating them up. Despite the rules that governed the way law-enforcement officers were supposed to act, Walker's approach closely resembled the "an eye for an eye" school of crime fighting. His partner was young Ranger Jimmy Trivette, who had grown up in the slums of Baltimore and used football as his ticket to a college education and a career with the Dallas Cowboys until he tore up a knee. Despite Jimmy's belief in computers and scientific criminology, working with Walker always seemed to leave him bruised and sore—when Walker was trying to get information or take people into custody it was more than likely there would be a fistfight or karate kicks. County Assistant D.A. Alex Cahill, his sometimes girlfriend, frowned on Walker's methods, even if they did get results. When not on duty Walker and the others hung out at C.D.'s, the saloon/restaurant owned by his buddy C. D. Parker, a former Ranger forced to retire after taking a bullet in the knee, who still provided help and advice on cases. Uncle Ray was the wise old Native American who had raised Walker.

In March 1998, Walker rescued his friend Carlos, a Dallas police detective, who was in trouble on an undercover drug assignment. Trent Malloy, a mutual friend and one of Walker's former students who now ran his own karate school, helped out. For the next year, until Carlos left the force and became Trent's partner in a detective agency (see *Sons of Thunder*), they showed up regularly on *Walker*. In the May 1998 season finale Walker was about to ask Alex to marry him when she was shot by an ex-con who blamed her for his incarceration. She almost died but eventually recovered, and they got engaged that fall.

In the fall of 1999 two new Rangers who often worked undercover, Gage and Cooke, were added to Walker's team, and that December C. D. made his last on-screen appearance. The following May Cordell and Alex finally got married. In the series finale it was revealed that a vindictive criminal on a vendetta to kill a dozen Rangers, culminating with Walker, had poisoned C. D. (who had died mysteriously from a heart attack the previous October). The criminal helped a number of his colleagues escape from a high-security prison, and they went on a rampage. They first shot and killed one Ranger from long range, then rigged Trivette's car to crash and burn—but he had been thrown from it as it rolled and survived. When Walker and Alex went to see Trivette in the hospital, she went into labor and gave birth to a daughter, Angela. In the final confrontation Walker killed the criminal by pulling the pin on a grenade he had tied to his belt.

Star Chuck Norris, a former karate champion and movie star, played Walker in the deadpan unemotional style he had used in most of his feature films. Nothing ever seemed to excite him, and the violence on the show had a cartoon quality about it. There was a surrealistic efficiency about Walker—he almost never broke a sweat, got hurt, or wasted a blow—using violence because it was necessary but never glorying in it.

WALKING TALL (*Police Drama*)

FIRST TELECAST: *January 17, 1981*

LAST TELECAST: *June 6, 1981*

BROADCAST HISTORY:

Jan 1981–Feb 1981, NBC Sat 9:00–10:00
Mar 1981–Apr 1981, NBC Tue 10:00–11:00
Apr 1981–Jun 1981, NBC Sat 10:00–11:00

CAST:

Sheriff Buford Pusser.................. Bo Svenson
Michael Pusser .... Rad Daly
Dwana Pusser.................. Heather McAdams
Carl Pusser .... Walter Barnes
Deputy Aaron Fairfax .... Harold Sylvester
Deputy Grady Spooner.................. Jeff Lester
Deputy Joan Litton .... Courtney Pledger

Buford Pusser was a man with a deeply moral sense of right and wrong, which he enforced none too subtly with a large club. The sheriff of rural McNeal County, Tennessee, he was a big, two-fisted brawler who often used force to convince wrongdoers of the error of their ways. The local purveyors of gambling and prostitution hated Buford, who, carrying a four-foot-long club to mete out justice (his "pacifier"), was certainly an imposing sight. He had been beaten, threatened, and shot at—one assassination attempt had killed his wife, Pauline, by mistake, leaving Buford to raise his two young children with the help of his father, Carl.

There had been a real Buford Pusser, and his actual exploits were brought to theaters in 1973 in the film version of *Walking Tall*. Joe Don Baker played the role in the original film, and Bo Svenson took it over in the two sequels. Pusser was to have played himself in the second movie sequel, but died in an automobile crash before the film went into production. Although it could not be proven, the nature of the crash led some to suspect that the criminals had finally gotten rid of him.

WALT DISNEY (*Anthology*)

FIRST TELECAST: *October 27, 1954*

LAST TELECAST: *September 9, 1990*

BROADCAST HISTORY:

Oct 1954–Sep 1958, ABC Wed 7:30–8:30
Sep 1958–Sep 1959, ABC Fri 8:00–9:00
Sep 1959–Sep 1960, ABC Fri 7:30–8:30
Sep 1960–Sep 1961, ABC Sun 6:30–7:30
Sep 1961–Aug 1975, NBC Sun 7:30–8:30
Sep 1975–Sep 1981, NBC Sun 7:00–8:00
Sep 1981–Jan 1983, CBS Sat 8:00–9:00
Jan 1983–Feb 1983, CBS Tue 8:00–9:00
Jul 1983–Sep 1983, CBS Sat 8:00–9:00
Feb 1986–Sep 1987, ABC Sun 7:00–9:00
Sep 1987–Sep 1988, ABC Sun 7:00–8:00
Oct 1988–Jul 1989, NBC Sun 7:00–8:00
Jul 1989, NBC Sun 8:00–9:00
Aug 1989–May 1990, NBC Sun 7:00–8:00
May 1990–Jul 1990, NBC Sun 7:00–9:00
Jul 1990–Aug 1990, NBC Sun 8:00–9:00
Aug 1990–Sep 1990, NBC Sun 7:00–8:00

EXECUTIVE PRODUCER/HOST:

Walt Disney (1954–1966)
Michael Eisner (1986–1990)

Walt Disney under its various names, holds the record as the longest-running prime-time series in network history—thirty-four seasons (and we wouldn't take bets that it won't be back one day for more). It is also historic for another reason. When it premiered in 1954 it marked the first big plunge by a major Hollywood movie studio into television production. Disney changed the face of television in many ways. Previously the big studios, afraid of competition from the new medium, were television's sworn enemies, not only refusing to produce programming but denying TV the use of any of the latest or best theatrical films. Until Disney led the way, the lavish movie-style series so familiar today were an impossibility.

Luring Disney into television was a major coup for struggling ABC. Both CBS and NBC had negotiated with the moviemaker, but neither could agree to his seemingly exorbitant terms. Among other things, Mr. Disney wanted the network to help finance his proposed amusement park in Anaheim, California. Only ABC was willing to take a chance, paying a then-fabulous $500,000 plus $50,000 per program. ABC won big. Both the TV series and the park, Disneyland, were fabulous successes. The program *Disneyland* was, in fact, ABC's first major hit series.

Disneyland consisted of a mixture of cartoons, live-action adventures, documentaries, and nature stories, some made especially for TV and some former theatrical releases. A liberal number of repeat telecasts was included with each season's originals. At first *Disneyland* was divided into four rotating segments, listed at the beginning of each week's show by the cartoon character Tinkerbell (from *Peter Pan*). They were Frontierland, Fantasyland, Tomorrowland, and Adventureland. The first telecast was a variety show, but what really got *Disneyland* off the ground was a three-part series of Frontierland adventures which began less than two months later—*Davy Crockett*. The exploits of the famed real-life frontiersman of the early 1800s took America by storm. The title role was played by Fess Parker (whom Disney had seen playing a bit part in the horror movie *Them*). Buddy Ebsen played his sidekick, George Russel. *Davy Crockett* lifted Fess Parker from obscurity to stardom overnight. Davy's trademark coonskin cap and other Crockett merchandise sold like wildfire to the nation's youth, and a recording of the theme song, "The Ballad of Davy Crockett," was one of the biggest hits of the mid-1950s. (Fess Parker recorded the song, but ironically a minor-league singer named Bill Hayes beat him to it and had the big hit recording.)

The three original Crockett episodes were "Davy Crockett, Indian Fighter" (first aired December 15, 1954), "Davy Crockett Goes to Congress" (January 26, 1955), and "Davy Crockett at the Alamo" (February 23, 1955). Crockett was killed in the last episode, which created an embarrassing situation when the public began clamoring for more. Eventually a few more episodes were made, depicting incidents earlier in his life, but Crockett, for some reason, never did become a series in its own right.

Flushed with the spectacular success of Davy Crockett, Disney tried several more times to base multi-part stories on actual Western heroes. In 1957–1958 there was "The Saga of Andy Burnett" (Jerome Courtland as the young frontiersman), followed by "The Nine Lives of Elfego Baca" (starring Robert Loggia as a peace-loving but determined lawman in Tombstone, Arizona), "Texas John Slaughter" (Tom Tryon in the lead role), and "Swamp Fox" (Leslie Nielsen as Francis Marion, the Revolutionary War hero). Even Fess Parker got another shot at superstardom playing John Grayson in the film *Westward Ho! The Wagons*, which later turned up on the TV series. That time Parker made sure he got his recording of the theme song out before Bill Hayes did, but it didn't matter because neither the show nor the song was a hit.

There were many other presentations on *Disney* beyond the boundaries of Frontierland. Some were adaptations of classics such as *Alice in Wonderland*, *The Legend of Sleepy Hollow* (narrated by Bing Crosby), *Robin Hood*, *Treasure Island*, and *Babes in Toyland* (with Annette Funicello, Tommy Sands, and Ray Bolger). The animated shows tended to feature well-known Disney characters such as Mickey Mouse (voice originally provided by Walt himself), Donald Duck, Pluto, and Goofy, sometimes in full-length stories, sometimes "narrating" documentaries on various subjects. When the series moved to NBC in 1961 a new character was added, Professor Ludwig Von Drake (voice by Paul Frees), who was supposed to be Donald's eccentric uncle and who cohosted many of the shows with Walt.

Documentaries within the series covered subjects

ranging from space travel to how cartoons are made, and were always entertainingly presented. And of course there were plenty of plugs for the Disneyland park and, later, its Florida counterpart, Disney World, including reports on construction in progress, big opening galas, and, later, on-location variety shows. One of the latter, "Disneyland After Dark" in April 1962, marked the network TV debut of the Osmond Brothers, who were then performing at the park.

Every season of *Disney* brought all types of presentations, but the mix changed with the times. In the late 1950s and early 1960s there were many Westerns and other early-American adventures. Then the emphasis shifted more to nature stories, often about animals and their young human companions. *Disney,* in fact, produced quite a menagerie of nonhuman "stars," to wit: "Sammy, the Way Out Seal," "Greta, the Misfit Greyhound," "Ida, the Offbeat Eagle," "Joker, the Amiable Ocelot," "Boomerang, Dog of Many Talents," "Inky the Crow," "The Horse in the Grey Flannel Suit," "Salty, the Hijacked Harbor Seal," "Ringo, the Refugee Raccoon," "Stub, Best Cow Dog in the West," "Deacon, the High Noon Dog," "Twister, Bull from the Sky," and "Lefty, the Ding-a-Ling Linx." Not to mention "The Horse with the Flying Tail" and "The Hound That Thought He Was a Raccoon." The most frequent narrator of these animal stories was cowboy star Rex Allen, although producer-writer Winston Hibler and others were also used.

For many years Walt Disney himself introduced the telecasts, and it was through television that the master showman became a national celebrity. He was such an institution that it was a distinct shock when Walt passed away suddenly on December 15, 1966. On the next Sunday's telecast the prefilmed introductions by Disney were deleted, and tributes by Chet Huntley and Dick Van Dyke were substituted. But the program itself went on as planned—appropriately, it was a tour led by Walt himself through his pride and joy, Disneyland.

In subsequent seasons there was no opening and closing host, simply voice-over narration by announcer Dick Wesson.

In later years, *Disney* suffered the same fate as many long-running series, gradually declining in audience because viewers apparently took it for granted, or considered it "old hat." The fact that such programs might continue to provide first-rate entertainment meant little in the quest for "novelty." Each year *Disney*'s renewal became more doubtful until NBC finally announced its cancellation in 1981. The Disney magic refused to die, however. The series was picked up by CBS for two seasons (1981–1983), and then after a two-year hiatus returned to its original network, ABC. This latter version consisted of films (theatrical and made-for-TV), and revived the custom of specially filmed introductions by the head of the Disney studio—now a young executive named Michael D. Eisner.

After more than two years on ABC, *Disney* moved back to NBC in 1988, amid great fanfare that the venerable program would now become a "wheel" with four rotating elements, three of them revivals of past Disney hits as continuing series. One of these would be seen each week, while every fourth week viewers would get the usual potpourri of specials. The plan did not come to pass, however, as only two episodes were produced of each of the three revivals. *Davy Crockett* starred Tim Dunigan as the young frontiersman, with Gary Grubbs as his sidekick, Georgie Russel (Johnny Cash appeared as an older Davy looking back on his youthful days); *The Absent-Minded Professor* had Harry Anderson as the wacky inventor of flubber; and *The Parent Trap* returned Hayley Mills to her famous role as mischievous identical twins, now grown, one of whom married a widower (Barry Bostwick), with teenage identical triplets of his own.

Disney attempted to launch another series-within-a-series the following year, *Brand New Life,* starring Barbara Eden and Don Murray as middle-aged newlyweds who combine their families from previous marriages with chaotic results (sort of an updated *Brady Bunch*). Only five episodes of that were produced, scheduled at irregular intervals under the *Disney* umbrella. The "wheel" having gone flat, *Disney* sputtered along with a mix of specials and movies until the end of the 1989–1990 season, after which the company concentrated on producing original series airing under their own names (see, for example, *Disney Presents the 100 Lives of Black Jack Savage*).

The Disney series was originally titled *Disneyland,* changed to *Walt Disney Presents* in 1958, to *Walt Disney's Wonderful World of Color* in 1961 (when many of the films previously seen in black-and-white on ABC were repeated in color on NBC), to *The Wonderful World of Disney* in 1969, and to *Disney's Wonderful World* in 1979. The 1981 CBS version was titled simply *Walt Disney,* the 1986 ABC revival, *The Disney Sunday Movie,* and the NBC 1988–1990 version, *The Magical World of Disney.*

In the fall of 1997, ABC (then owned by Disney) revived *The Wonderful World of Disney* as an umbrella title for the family-oriented theatrical films and made-for-TV movies it aired on Sunday nights from 7:00–9:00 P.M.

WALTER AND EMILY (*Situation Comedy*)

FIRST TELECAST: *November 16, 1991*

LAST TELECAST: *February 22, 1992*

BROADCAST HISTORY:

Nov 1991–Feb 1992, NBC Sat 8:30–9:00

CAST:

Walter Collins .... Brian Keith
Emily Collins .... Cloris Leachman
Matt Collins .... Christopher McDonald
Zach Collins (age 11)............ Matthew Lawrence
Hartley................................ Edan Gross
**Stan*................................. Sandy Baron
**Albert* .... Shelley Berman

*Occasional

Noisy multigenerational comedy in which gruff Walter and busybody Emily realized every grandparent's dream—to show the next generation how to raise *their* kids. Walter's divorced son, Matt, a sportswriter, was frequently on the road and had custody of towheaded Zach only on the condition that his grandparents would be around to help raise him. Walter and Emily squabbled incessantly but still managed to smother the kid with attention as long-suffering Matt looked on helplessly. Hartley was Zach's pal, with whom he sometimes got into trouble.

Sandy Baron and Shelley Berman appeared occasionally as Walter's buddies from his salesman days.

WALTER CRONKITE'S UNIVERSE, see *Universe*

WALTER WINCHELL FILE, THE (*Crime Anthology*)
FIRST TELECAST: *October 2, 1957*
LAST TELECAST: *March 28, 1958*
BROADCAST HISTORY:
Oct 1957–Dec 1957, ABC Wed 9:30–10:00
Jan 1958–Mar 1958, ABC Fri 10:00–10:30
HOST/NARRATOR:
Walter Winchell

The crime dramas presented in this anthology were adapted from stories that Walter Winchell had uncovered while working the police beat in New York City. In addition to hosting the show, he functioned as the narrator, tying together the various elements that led to the drama that was actually shown on the air.

WALTER WINCHELL SHOW, THE (*News/Commentary*)
FIRST TELECAST: *October 5, 1952*
LAST TELECAST: *November 6, 1960*
BROADCAST HISTORY:
Oct 1952–Apr 1953, ABC Sun 6:45–7:00
Apr 1953–Jul 1953, ABC Sun 6:30–6:45
Sep 1953–Jan 1954, ABC Mon 7:00–7:15
Sep 1953–Jun 1955, ABC Sun 9:00–9:15
Oct 1960–Nov 1960, ABC Sun 10:30–11:00
REPORTER:
Walter Winchell

Syndicated newspaper columnist Walter Winchell had a highly successful radio series in the 1930s and 1940s which gave him the opportunity to report the headlines he deemed important in his uniquely fast-paced and highly opinionated style. His crusades and grudges were legendary, but everything was delivered with a theatricality (Winchell had once been in vaudeville) that kept listeners entranced. After the war he went on an extended crusade against Communism, and eventually became a staunch supporter of Senator Joseph McCarthy.

In the fall of 1952 Winchell began simulcasting his famous Sunday night news show. The sight of the grizzled reporter was a surprise to many viewers. He always wore his hat while on the air, he was noticeably older (in his 50s) than many had imagined, and he personally ran the telegraph key that was used to punctuate the news and gossip of the world that he related (though the "code" he punched out was actually meaningless garble). Even his opening line, "Good evening, Mr. and Mrs. North and South America and all the ships at sea . . . let's go to press," seemed somewhat dated on TV. The television version of his news show, although not the success that his radio program had been, remained on the air until Winchell resigned in a huff in 1955 after a disagreement with ABC executives. Five years later, it was brought back in a longer version. The revival was an immediate failure and lasted for only six weeks.

Winchell died in 1972.

WALTER WINCHELL SHOW, THE (*Variety*)
FIRST TELECAST: *October 5, 1956*
LAST TELECAST: *December 28, 1956*
BROADCAST HISTORY:
Oct 1956–Dec 1956, NBC Fri 8:30–9:00
HOST:
Walter Winchell

In the fall of 1956, NBC gave Walter Winchell the opportunity to show that he could be as successful as his fellow columnist Ed Sullivan as the host of a weekly live variety show. The program originated from New York for its first nine weeks and then moved to Hollywood. Despite the ability of Winchell to attract as guests show-business celebrities who owed him favors, and a reasonably well-paced production, the series never caught on and was canceled after 13 weeks.

WALTONS, THE (*Drama*)
FIRST TELECAST: *September 14, 1972*
LAST TELECAST: *August 20, 1981*
BROADCAST HISTORY:
Sep 1972–Aug 1981, CBS Thu 8:00–9:00
CAST:
John Walton .... Ralph Waite
Olivia Walton (1972–1980) ...... Michael Learned
Zeb (Grandpa) Walton (1972–1978) ...... Will Geer
Esther (Grandma) Walton (1972–1979) .. Ellen Corby
John Boy Walton (1972–1977)..... Richard Thomas
John Boy Walton (1979–1981).... Robert Wightman
Mary Ellen Walton Willard ..... Judy Norton-Taylor
Jim-Bob Walton .... David W. Harper
Elizabeth Walton..................... Kami Cotler
Jason Walton....................... Jon Walmsley
Erin Walton .... Mary Elizabeth McDonough
Ben Walton............................ Eric Scott
Ike Godsey............................ Joe Conley
Corabeth Godsey (1974–1981)
.... Ronnie Claire Edwards
Sheriff Ep Bridges .... John Crawford
Mamie Baldwin....................... Helen Kleeb
Emily Baldwin .... Mary Jackson
Verdie Foster .... Lynn Hamilton
Rev. Matthew Fordwick (1972–1977).... John Ritter
Rosemary Hunter Fordwick (1973–1977)
.... Mariclare Costello
Yancy Tucker (1972–1979) .... Robert Donner
Flossie Brimmer (1972–1977) .... Nora Marlowe
Maude Gormsley (1973–1979) .... Merie Earle
Dr. Curtis Willard (1976–1978)......... Tom Bower
Rev. Hank Buchanan (1977–1978)........ Peter Fox
J. D. Pickett (1978–1981) .... Lewis Arquette
John Curtis Willard (alternating; 1978–1981)
.... Marshall Reed
John Curtis Willard (alternating; 1978–1981)
.... Michael Reed
Cindy Brunson Walton (1979–1981) .. Leslie Winston
Rose Burton (1979–1981)................ Peggy Rea
Serena Burton (1979–1980) .... Martha Nix
Jeffrey Burton (1979–1980).......... Keith Mitchell
Toni Hazleton (1981) .... Lisa Harrison
Arlington Wescott Jones (Jonesy) (1981)
.... Richard Gilliland
NARRATOR:
Earl Hamner, Jr.

Life in the South during the Depression was the subject of *The Waltons.* John and Olivia Walton and their seven children all lived together on Walton's Mountain, in the Blue Ridge Mountains of rural Jefferson County, Virginia. The family's modest income came from the lumber mill run by John and Grandpa Zeb. It was a close-knit family, with everyone helping out most of the time, and moralistic homilies abounded. There was no sex, no violence—just a warm family drama. Everything was seen through the eyes of John

Boy, the oldest son, who had wanted to be a novelist for as long as he could remember. After high school he had enrolled as an English major at the local college, and at the start of the 1976–1977 season he began publishing his own local paper, *The Blue Ridge Chronicle*. By the end of the season, when his novel had been accepted by a publisher, he decided to move to New York. That season had been full of changes, including the marriage of Mary Ellen, who was in nursing school, to young Dr. Curtis Willard in November, and leading to the birth of their baby in 1978.

At the start of the 1977–1978 season *The Waltons* moved out of the Depression and into World War II. Young Rev. Fordwick enlisted in the army (John Ritter, who played the role, had a starring role in ABC's *Three's Company* that season) and was replaced by young Rev. Buchanan. Grandma Walton was ill (actress Ellen Corby had suffered a stroke) and was not seen until the last episode of the season, when she finally came home to Walton's Mountain, even though she was still partially incapacitated. She was seen only occasionally thereafter. The reunion was tearful, but brief. In April 1978, shortly after the close of the regular season, actor Will Geer, who played Grandpa Walton, died at the age of 76.

The 1978–1979 season saw much suffering on Walton's Mountain. Mary Ellen's husband, Curt, was killed in the Japanese attack on Pearl Harbor, and Olivia found out she had tuberculosis and went to a sanitarium for treatment (Michael Learned's contract had expired and she asked to be written out of the show to pursue other roles). In the spring Ben eloped with a young girl named Cindy. Olivia returned from the sanitarium and went off to a domestic army hospital to serve as a nurse. With Olivia gone and Grandpa having passed away, Olivia's cousin Rose arrived to run the Walton household—adding her two grandchildren to the group. Jason, John Boy, Jim-Bob, and Ben were all in the military, and a shortage of both materials and help forced John Walton to close his lumber mill temporarily. As the war drew to a close Jason got engaged to WAC Toni Hazleton (played by Jon Walmsley's real-life wife, Lisa Harrison), and Mary Ellen, taking courses in premed, found a new love with Jonesy. Her romance was almost aborted when she found that Curt had not died at Pearl Harbor after all, but their marriage was over and she stayed with Jonesy. As the series ended, John sold Walton's Mill to son Ben and moved to Arizona to be with his wife while she recuperated from a relapse of her TB.

Although *The Waltons* stopped production as a series in the spring of 1981, three more episodes aired as made-for-TV movies on NBC in February, May, and November of 1982. Erin Walton married her brother Ben's partner in the lumber business in February, Mary Ellen married Jonesy in May, and the family got together for Thanksgiving in the November episode, which aired almost 11 years after the made-for-TV film "The Homecoming," the original pilot for *The Waltons*.

Author Earl Hamner, Jr., was the creator and narrator of *The Waltons*, which was based on reminiscences of his own childhood (previously portrayed in a somewhat different fashion in the 1963 Henry Fonda movie *Spencer's Mountain*). It was the most wholesome of TV programs and, surprisingly, did extremely well in the ratings. When it premiered in 1972 its competition was *The Flip Wilson Show* on NBC, then one of the most popular shows on television. To the surprise of both critics and TV executives *The Waltons* not only survived, but it forced Flip Wilson off the air and itself became one of the most viewed programs on TV. It was never a big hit in large cities, but it struck a chord in middle and rural America that guaranteed it a long and prosperous run.

WANDA AT LARGE (*Situation Comedy*)

FIRST TELECAST: *March 26, 2003*

LAST TELECAST:

BROADCAST HISTORY:

Mar 2003–Apr 2003, FOX Wed 9:30–10:00

CAST:

Wanda Hawkins.................... Wanda Sykes
Keith.............................. Dale Godboldo
Bradley Grimes........................ Phil Morris
Rita Dahlberg..................... Ann Magnuson
Roger............................. Jason Kravits
Jenny Hawkins.................... Tammy Lauren
Barris Hawkins (age 13).......... Robert Bailey, Jr.
Holly Hawkins (17)............... Jurnee Smollett

Wanda was an unemployed stand-up comic in Washington, D.C., whose life changed radically when she met her friend Keith's boss, Roger. Keith was a segment producer for *The Beltway Gang*, a local political talk show on WHDC-TV, and Roger, after meeting her, decided that her outspoken in-your-face attitude would make her the perfect on-air correspondent to liven up his boring show. Wanda, who was very opinionated and got down and dirty on the air, clashed with the show's two anchors—stuffy Rita, who sometimes found her amusing, and uptight Bradley, who couldn't stand her—and the sparks flew. It was good for ratings but certainly strained relationships, and manipulative Roger kept stirring the pot to maintain the friction. Wanda lived across the hall from her widowed sister-in-law, Jenny, who was raising two teenage children, Barris and Holly, with Wanda's "help." Each episode opened with Wanda doing an outrageous out-of-studio segment on a topic of the day, such as gun buyers or plastic surgery, followed by the bemused, befuddled or repulsed reactions of the other members of *The Beltway Gang* panel.

WANTED (*Documentary*)

FIRST TELECAST: *October 20, 1955*

LAST TELECAST: *January 5, 1956*

BROADCAST HISTORY:

Oct 1955–Jan 1956, CBS Thu 10:30–11:00

NARRATOR:

Walter McGraw

There were no actors in *Wanted*. All of the participants played themselves, be they policemen, informers, or witnesses, as this filmed documentary series reenacted the process by which wanted criminals were pursued by law-enforcement officers. Each week an actual case was followed from the criminal act and then through the process of detection. All of the cases, which were drawn from FBI files, were still active, and the criminals whose stories were shown were asked over the air to give themselves up. There were interviews with victims and members of the wanted party's family as well as the crime-and-detection aspects of the show. The narrator, Walter McGraw, also produced *Wanted.*

WANTED: DEAD OR ALIVE (*Western*)

FIRST TELECAST: *September 6, 1958*
LAST TELECAST: *March 29, 1961*
BROADCAST HISTORY:

Sep 1958–Sep 1960, CBS Sat 8:30–9:00
Sep 1960–Mar 1961, CBS Wed 8:30–9:00

CAST:

Josh Randall .... Steve McQueen
Jason Nichols (1960) .... Wright King

Bounty hunters were very common in the Old West during the last half of the 19th century. They made a living from the rewards offered for capturing wanted criminals. Since it didn't matter whether or not the criminals were brought back alive, bounty hunters were not bound by the constraints that hampered lawmen, and did pretty much as they pleased. Such a man was Josh Randall. He felt little apparent emotion and was a man of few words. He was also adept at using his gun, not a normal pistol but an unusual cross between a handgun and a rifle. His "Mare's Leg" was a .30–.40 sawed-off carbine that could be handled almost like a pistol but had much more explosive impact when its cartridges hit a target. In the spring of 1960 Josh acquired a sidekick in young Jason Nichols. Apparently things didn't work out, for by the fall of that year Josh was once again riding alone.

The pilot for this program was aired in March 1958 as an episode of the series *Trackdown.*

WAR NEXT DOOR, THE (*Situation Comedy*)

BROADCAST HISTORY:

USA Network
30 minutes
Original episodes: *2000* (13 episodes)
Premiered: *July 23, 2000*

CAST:

Kennedy Smith .... Linden Ashby
Lili Smith .... Susan Walters
Lucas Smith .... Mark Rendall
Ellis Smith .... Nicole Dicker
Alan Kriegman .... Damian Young
Barbara Bush .... Tara Rosling

Kennedy Smith was a mild-mannered dad who used to be a secret agent for the C.I.A. in this nutty sitcom. Despite the fact that he knew 29 ways to kill a man with a spoon, he had promised his loving wife, Lili, he would give up his violent occupation and settle down in the nice quiet suburbs. Unfortunately, his diabolical archenemy Kriegman, a dapper evil genius dressed all in black, refused to give up their "eternal dance of death" and moved in next door so that he could continue to torment him. Automatic gunfire and explosions rattled the neatly trimmed lawns, but Lili, a perfect Donna Reed–type mom, was oblivious, as were the Smith kids, Lucas and Ellis. Kriegman ruined a Smith family barbecue by blowing things up with his laser, and Kennedy retaliated by turning the laser back on Kriegman with a spoon, incinerating him. Despite the mayhem, everybody was back again next week to start over. Barbara was Kriegman's slinky, dominatrix partner, who had been trying to seduce Kennedy for years without success.

USA "spooned" the series after eight weeks, with five remaining episodes unaired.

WAR OF THE WORLDS (*Science Fiction*)

BROADCAST HISTORY:

Syndicated only
60 minutes
Produced: *1988–1990*
Released: *October 1988*

CAST:

Dr. Harrison Blackwood .... Jared Martin
Dr. Suzanne McCullough...... Lynda Mason Green
Norton Drake (1988–1989) .... Philip Akin
Lt. Col. Paul Ironhorse (1988–1989)
.... Richard Chaves
Debi McCullough (age 11)........ Rachel Blanchard
**Mrs. Pennyworth (1988–1989)* ..... Corinne Conley
John Kincaid (1989–1990) .... Adrian Paul
Advocate #1 (1988–1989)
.... Richard Comar & David Calderisi
Advocate #2 (1988–1989)........... Ilse von Glatz
Advocate #3 (1988–1989) .... Michael Rudder
Malzor (1989–1990) .... Denis Forest
Mana (1989–1990) .... Catherine Disher
Ardix (1989–1990)................ Julian Richings

*Occasional

In this expensive sequel to the 1953 movie of the same name (from which footage was used), a small team of specialists attempted to thwart the efforts of a group of aliens from the planet Mortax, 40 light years from Earth, to take over our planet. The team, which worked out of a hidden pastoral military facility known as "The Cottage," consisted of Harrison Blackwood, an astrophysicist; Norton Drake, a paraplegic black computer whiz with a voice-activated wheelchair named Gertrude; Suzanne McCullough, a divorced microbiologist with a young daughter; and Paul Ironhorse, a by-the-book military man of Indian descent.

In the story line there had been an alien reconnaissance mission in 1938 (the year of the Orson Welles radio broadcast) and a first war in 1953 (the year of the theatrical movie). It was now 35 years later, and the aliens from the first war, who were not dead but had been kept in special storage tanks, had gotten loose and were attempting to mass their fellows for a new war. The aliens, and their hooded leaders, known only as "advocates," were based in an abandoned underground nuclear test site in Nevada. The outside world was unaware of them because they could absorb human bodies and take on their appearance while they sought weapons and supplies. The giveaway was that their high radiation level caused the bodies to gradually deteriorate, giving them the appearance of leprosy. When killed, the bodies dissolved into a slimy mess.

When the series returned for its second season in the fall of 1989, there were a number of changes. It had been retitled *War of the Worlds—The Second Invasion,* opened with Earth suffering strange storms and political anarchy, and introduced new invaders—humanoid refugees from the recently destroyed world Morthrai. The aliens from the first season were "soldiers" for Morthrai who were executed in the season opener for their failure to take over Earth. Also killed off were Ironhorse and Norton and, for the rest of the season,

Harrison, Suzanne, and another former soldier, John Kincaid, fought the new aliens from an underground hideaway in the ruins of what had once been a great city that was now overrun by people who did as they pleased because there was no legal system left.

The aliens, led by Malzor and Mana, along with their chief scientist, Ardix, wanted to "purify" the Earth to make it more suitable to their people. Along with their other technical wonders, they could create clones of humans to take the place of real people and do their bidding. The beings from Morthrai had one thing in common with their predecessors from Mortax; when they were killed, they didn't just die—they turned an iridescent green and dissolved. In the last original episode Malzor was revealed to his own people as evil and killed, leaving the few remaining aliens to seek peaceful coexistence with the people of Earth.

WARNER BROS. PRESENTS (*Various*)
FIRST TELECAST: *September 13, 1955*
LAST TELECAST: *September 11, 1956*
BROADCAST HISTORY:
Sep 1955–Sep 1956, ABC Tue 7:30–8:30
HOST/NARRATOR:
Gig Young

When ABC first approached the giant Warner Bros. film company it was for the purpose of obtaining the rights to theatrical films for telecasting on the network. But Warner was interested in getting into TV production, and the result was *Warner Bros. Presents,* an umbrella title for three rotating series, each based on a successful movie: *Kings Row, Cheyenne,* and *Casablanca.* From this start Warner Bros. went on to produce dozens of hit programs, and it is today an important producer of TV series.

Warner's first effort was a mixed success, however. Viewers and critics alike objected to the 10–15 minute segment at the end of each week's presentation devoted to plugging current Warner Bros. movies, and this was eventually dropped. (Gig Young was host of this segment, as well as narrator for the entire series.) *Kings Row* proved unsuccessful and was canceled at mid-season, followed soon after by *Casablanca.* Only *Cheyenne* caught on, lasting for a total of eight years on the ABC schedule. The *Warner Bros. Presents* title was discontinued after the 1955–1956 season.

See separate element titles for details.

WARREN HULL SHOW, THE, see *Ben Grauer Show, The*

WASHDAY THEATRE, see *Movies—Prior to 1961*

WASHINGTON EXCLUSIVE (*Discussion*)
FIRST TELECAST: *June 21, 1953*
LAST TELECAST: *November 1, 1953*
BROADCAST HISTORY:
Jun 1953–Nov 1953, DUM Sun 7:30–8:00
MODERATOR:
Frank McNaughton

Public-affairs discussion program in which six former senators discussed the civil and military affairs of the nation. Produced by Martha Rountree and Lawrence Spivak.

WASHINGTON REPORT (*Discussion*)
FIRST TELECAST: *May 22, 1951*
LAST TELECAST: *August 31, 1951*
BROADCAST HISTORY:
May 1951–Aug 1951, DUM Tue/Fri 7:45–8:00
MODERATOR:
Tris Coffin

Newsman Tris Coffin and distinguished guests from government, business, and labor discussed current events in this series originating from Washington, D.C.

WASTELAND (*Drama*)
FIRST TELECAST: *October 7, 1999*
LAST TELECAST: *October 28, 1999*
BROADCAST HISTORY:
Oct 1999, ABC Thu 9:00–10:00
CAST:
Dawnie Parker.................. Marisa Coughlan
Tyler (Ty) Swindell.................. Brad Rowe
Samantha (Sam) Price.......... Rebecca Gayheart
Vandy.................................. Eddie Mills
Jesse Presser...................... Sasha Alexander
Russell Baskin.................. Dan Montgomery
Vince Lewis...................... Jeffrey D. Sams
Phillip, the coffee boy................. Adam Scott

Seven gorgeous twenty-something friends in Manhattan fretted over the really important things in life, like who to date and who to sleep with, in this shallow and short-lived drama. At the center was Dawnie, a 26-year-old graduate student in anthropology who was writing a thesis on how her generation used their twenties as a second coming of age. A perky little chatterbox, she was still a virgin. Ty was the cute boyfriend she had broken up with six years earlier; he still pursued her, which she reacted to by regularly slapping him. Sam was a legal assistant with a rich daddy who had broken up with her singer-guitarist boyfriend Vandy, whom she regularly berated (no slaps, though). Jesse was a black-clad, chain-smoking publicist with an active but indiscriminate sex life and a tendency to dominate men (date to Jesse: "You suck the air dry!"). Russell was the closet gay friend, a hunky soap opera actor who feared being outed, and Vince was Sam's handsome, ambitious young boss in the D.A.'s office.

Only three episodes were aired on ABC, but ten others turned up on Showtime's ShowNext cable network in 2001.

WATCH MR. WIZARD (*Educational*)
FIRST TELECAST: *May 26, 1951*
LAST TELECAST: *February 19, 1955*
BROADCAST HISTORY:
May 1951–Feb 1952, NBC Sat 6:30–7:00
Mar 1952–Feb 1955, NBC Sat 7:00–7:30
CAST:
Mr. Wizard.......................... Don Herbert

Watch Mr. Wizard was one of the longest-running educational children's programs in the history of commercial television. It originated from Chicago from its inception on March 3, 1951 (late on Saturday afternoons), through the conclusion of the 1954–1955 season. When it moved to New York at the start of the 1955–1956 season, it was part of the NBC Saturday morning lineup. It remained as part of that lineup until June 27, 1965, and was revived for another season from 1971–1972. New episodes, under the title *Mr. Wizard's World,* aired on the Nickleodeon cable channel from 1983 to 1992. Seventy-eight *Mr. Wizard's World* episodes were produced; the last originals premiered early in 1991.

Don Herbert was the star of the show for its entire run. As Mr. Wizard, he would show his young helper how to do interesting scientific experiments with simple things found around the house. In addition to the demonstrations, Mr. Wizard would explain the principles behind them. The original helper was Mr. Wizard's 11-year-old neighbor, a boy named Willy. By the start of the 1953–1954 season, a boy and a girl alternated as Mr. Wizard's assistant. There was considerable turnover in the children who acted as his assistants, but they were all ready with an excited "Gee, Mr. Wizard!" whenever he popped one of his scientific tricks.

WATCH THE WORLD (*Documentary*)
FIRST TELECAST: *July 2, 1950*
LAST TELECAST: *August 20, 1950*
BROADCAST HISTORY:
Jul 1950–Aug 1950, NBC Sun 7:30–8:00
COMMENTATOR:
Don Goddard

Current events and features especially designed for youngsters, produced by NBC News in cooperation with the National Education Association. *Watch the World* was seen on Sunday afternoons during most of its 14-month run (April 1950–June 1951), with John Cameron Swayze and his family hosting. During the program's summer prime-time run, newscaster Don Goddard took over, with the vacationing Swayzes (John, his wife, son, and daughter) continuing to appear in periodic filmed reports.

WATCHER, THE (*Dramatic Anthology*)
FIRST TELECAST: *January 17, 1995*
LAST TELECAST: *April 11, 1995*
BROADCAST HISTORY:
Jan 1995–Apr 1995, UPN Tue 9:00–10:00
CAST:
The Watcher ..... Sir Mix-A-Lot (neé Anthony Ray)
Lori Danforth .... Bobbie Phillips

Hefty rap artist Sir Mix-A-Lot was The Watcher, the mysterious commentator/host of this anthology series set in Las Vegas. From his suite atop the Desert Flower Casino overlooking the city, filled with scores of TV surveillance monitors he could switch among at will, The Watcher followed the activities of the myriad people who lived, worked, and visited the "city that never sleeps." Not only did he watch what was going on, he anticipated what they were going to do and how their decisions would affect them, providing his observations in sometimes cryptic verse. Each episode followed the activities of a number of people—good and bad, rich and poor, celebrities and common folk. Most of the actors appearing were relatively unknown; Max Wright, Jamie Rose, Gilbert Gottfried, and Terri Austin were among the more familiar faces. The only regular other than The Watcher was pretty young limousine driver Lori Danforth.

WATCHING ELLIE (*Situation Comedy*)
FIRST TELECAST: *February 26, 2002*
LAST TELECAST: *May 20, 2003*
BROADCAST HISTORY:
Feb 2002–Apr 2002, NBC Tue 8:30–9:00
Apr 2003–May 2003, NBC Tue 9:30–10:00
CAST:
Eleanor "Ellie" Riggs .... Julia Louis-Dreyfus
Susan Riggs-Reyer .... Lauren Bowles
Ingvar (2002) .... Peter Stormare
Edgar Price .... Steve Carell
Ben Raffield .... Darren Boyd
Dr. Zimmerman .... Don Lake

Seinfeld alumna Julia Louis-Dreyfus starred as a jazz nightclub singer in this quirky comedy, which in some ways resembled her earlier show. The setting was Los Angeles, but the tone was New York cosmopolitan and the stories day-in-the-life vignettes, just like *Seinfeld*. Inhabiting Ellie's single world were Ben, her married British boyfriend and the guitarist in her band; obnoxious former boyfriend Edgar, who chased her relentlessly; Susan, her much-too-pretty married younger sister; Ingvar, the oddball neighbor who was infatuated with her; and Dr. Zimmerman, a nutty, balding middle-age veterinarian who also lived nearby. There was a lot of jazzy music and a certain amount of playful sexuality, as well as physical comedy. A gimmick in early episodes was a clock in the lower left-hand corner of the screen, starting at 22 minutes and counting down to the end of the story, which was told in real time. Sometimes it even cut off the last scene. When the series returned in the spring of 2003, it used a more traditional sitcom format (not real time) and dispensed with the clock.

Watching Ellie was created by Louis-Dreyfus' husband, actor Brad Hall, and co-starred her real-life sister as her sister Susan.

WATERFRONT (*Adventure*)
BROADCAST HISTORY:
Syndicated only
30 minutes
Produced: *1953–1956* (78 episodes)
Released: *February 1954*
CAST:
Capt. John Herrick .... Preston Foster
May (Mom) Herrick .... Lois Moran
Jim Herrick .... Harry Lauter
Carl Herrick .... Douglas Dick
Tip Hubbard .... Pinky Tomlin
Terry Van Buren .... Kathleen Crowley
Sid .... Allen Jenkins
Willie Slocum .... Willie Best
Tom Bailey .... Raymond Haddon
Wally .... Sid Saylor
Capt. Winant .... Miles Halpin
Joe Johnson .... Louis Jean Heydt

One of TV's earlier seagoing adventures was this syndicated series, focusing on tugboat captain Carl Herrick, his crew, and his family. Cap'n John ran the *Cheryl Ann* around San Pedro–Los Angeles harbor, encountering all sorts of smugglers, saboteurs, escaped convicts, and other seaborne criminals. Some episodes revolved around the doings of his family. The large cast included his wife, May, son Jim (a police detective), and the crew of the *Cheryl Ann*—son Carl, Tip, and Willie. Terry was Carl's fiancée, the daughter of a wealthy stockbroker.

Filmed on location in Los Angeles Harbor.

WAVERLY WONDERS, THE (*Situation Comedy*)
FIRST TELECAST: *September 7, 1978*
LAST TELECAST: *October 6, 1978*

BROADCAST HISTORY:

Sep 1978–Oct 1978, NBC Fri 8:00–8:30

CAST:

Joe Casey .... Joe Namath
John Tate .... Charles Bloom
Tony Faguzzi .... Joshua Grenrock
Connie Rafkin .... Kim Lankford
Alan Kerner .... James Staley
Hasty Parks .... Tierre Turner
Linda Harris .... Gwynne Gilford
George Benton .... Ben Piazza

Former pro football quarterback Joe Namath took a flyer in TV comedy in this 1978 series. He starred as Joe Casey, a washed-up pro basketball player turned history teacher and coach at Waverly High, in Eastfield, Wisconsin. It was questionable who was more inept, Joe in the classroom (he knew nothing about history) or his team, the Waverly Wonders, on the court (they hadn't won a game in three years). Nice kids, though: Tate, so shy he wouldn't take a shot; Faguzzi, the fumbling "Italian Stallion"; Parks, the fast-talking con artist; and Connie, the cute tomboy who was the best player of the lot. Linda Harris was the attractive principal and George Benton the stodgy former coach, known affectionately as "old prune face."

WAY OUT (*Dramatic Anthology*)

FIRST TELECAST: *March 31, 1961*
LAST TELECAST: *July 14, 1961*
BROADCAST HISTORY:

Mar 1961–Jul 1961, CBS Fri 9:30–10:00

HOST:

Roald Dahl

The host for this dramatic anthology was well chosen. Roald Dahl was a writer of short, macabre stories about people in strange and unsettling situations. The dramas in this series all fell into that category. In many respects it was like another CBS anthology series that was being aired in the following half hour, *The Twilight Zone. Way Out* was noticeably less successful, however, and lasted for only three and a half months.

WAYANS BROS., THE (*Situation Comedy*)

FIRST TELECAST: *January 11, 1995*
LAST TELECAST: *September 9, 1999*
BROADCAST HISTORY:

Jan 1995–Jun 1995, WB Wed, 8:00–8:30
Jun 1995–Feb 1997, WB Wed 9:00–9:30
Jul 1996–Aug 1996, WB Wed 9:30–10:00
Mar 1997–Aug 1997, WB Wed 9:30–10:00
Jun 1997–Aug 1997, WB Sun 9:30–10:00
Aug 1997–Sep 1998, WB Wed 9:00–9:30
Jul 1998–Sep 1998, WB Wed 8:00–8:30
Sep 1998–Sep 1999, WB Thu 8:00–8:30

CAST:

Shawn Williams .... Shawn Wayans
Marlon Williams .... Marlon Wayans
John "Pops" Williams .... John Witherspoon
Lisa Saunders (1995) .... Lela Rochon
Benny (1995) .... Benny Quan
Lupe (1995) .... Joanna Sanchez
Monique Lattimore (1995–1996) ... Paula Jai Parker
Lou Malino (1995) .... Jill Tasker
Dee Baxter .... Anna Maria Horsford
**T.C. (Thelonius Capricornio) (1995–1998)*
.... Phill Lewis
**White Mike (1995–1996)* .... Mitch Mullany
**Grandma Ellington (1996–1997)* ..... Ja'net DuBois

*Occasional

Shawn and Marlon were two brothers living together in this physical comedy series. Shawn, a driver for the APS overnight delivery service, was the more serious brother, hoping to get promoted or find a new career that would give him enough money to marry his girlfriend, Lisa, a college student whose father was a successful physician. Marlon, his free-spirited kid brother, worked part-time in the kitchen of their father's small Manhattan diner, Pops' Place, located adjacent to the lobby of the Neidermeyer Building. Happy-go-lucky Marlon always seemed to be getting himself and his brother in some kind of trouble. Pops wanted to be proud of both of his sons, but Marlon's antics didn't make it easy. Benny was the short-order cook at Pops' Place and Lupe the waitress who also worked the register.

In Fall 1995, Shawn was laid off and bought the newsstand in the lobby of the Neidermeyer Building with money he borrowed from his dad. Marlon worked busing tables at the diner and helped out at the newsstand. Added to the cast was Monique, a sexy woman from a rich family whose financial reverses had forced her to take a job as a clerk in the hotel's card shop. She and Shawn sparred verbally while Marlon had the hots for her. Lou was the feisty but petite security guard at the Neidermeyer Building, replaced late in the year by hefty Dee. Two recurring characters were bumbling White Mike and T. C., a con man forever looking to make his big score.

During the 1997–1998 season Marlon tried to get work as an actor. In the season finale an electrical fire destroyed Shawn's newsstand, but that fall he rebuilt it. Marlon got a regular role on the NBC sitcom *Everybody Loves Everybody* and Shawn became his business manager—for fifty percent of what he earned.

Shawn and Marlon, two of the younger members of the talented Wayans clan—their older brother, Keenen, had been the creative force behind *In Living Color* on which they both had appeared—were the creators of this series.

WAYNE AND SHUSTER TAKE AN AFFECTIONATE LOOK AT . . . (*Documentary*)

FIRST TELECAST: *June 17, 1966*
LAST TELECAST: *July 29, 1966*
BROADCAST HISTORY:

Jun 1966–Jul 1966, CBS Fri 10:00–11:00

HOSTS:

Johnny Wayne
Frank Shuster

Each week Canadian comedians Wayne and Shuster hosted a documentary that profiled top comedians of the 20th century. Film clips were used to provide background and examples of the work of the comedians being profiled, with Wayne and Shuster providing running commentary. The people whose careers were chronicled were Bob Hope and Bing Crosby, Jack Benny, W. C. Fields, the Marx Brothers, and George Burns. In addition to the profiles of comedians, one episode presented an affectionate look at one movie form native to America, the Western.

WAYNE BRADY SHOW, THE (*Comedy/Variety*)
FIRST TELECAST: *August 8, 2001*
LAST TELECAST: *March 11, 2002*
BROADCAST HISTORY:
Aug 2001–Sep 2001, ABC Wed 8:30–9:00
Mar 2002, ABC Mon 8:30–9:00
REGULARS:
Wayne Brady
Brooke Dillman
Jonathan Mangum
J. P. Manoux
Missi Pyle
Peter Michael Escovedo, orchestra leader

Wayne Brady, the upbeat black guy from Drew Carey's *Whose Line Is It Anyway?*, here fronted his own mostly improvisational comedy show, which included a lot of music. Using suggestions from the audience as well as his own ideas as starting points, he served up wild impressions of stars such as Little Richard, Michael Jackson, Louis Armstrong and Sammy Davis, Jr.; turned a singing newscast into a full-scale musical; sang doo-wop in the toilet stalls; and showed energetic dancers invading an office scene. Guest stars included Justin Timberlake and Brian McKnight, appearing in sketches as well as in musical performances.

WAYNE KING (*Music*)
FIRST TELECAST: *September 29, 1949*
LAST TELECAST: *June 26, 1952*
BROADCAST HISTORY:
Sep 1949–Jun 1952, NBC Thu 10:30–11:00 (OS)
REGULARS:
Wayne King
Nancy Evans (1949–1951)
Harry Hall
Gloria Van (1951–1952)
Barbara Becker (1951–1952)
Bob Morton (1951–1952)
The Don Large Chorus

Live program from Chicago featuring the smooth, somewhat sedate music of Wayne King and His Orchestra. Typical, and best known, of his numbers was "The Waltz You Saved for Me." Seen only on NBC's Midwest network.

WE GOT IT MADE (*Situation Comedy*)
FIRST TELECAST: *September 8, 1983*
LAST TELECAST: *March 30, 1984*
BROADCAST HISTORY:
Sep 1983–Dec 1983, NBC Thu 9:00–9:30
Jan 1984–Mar 1984, NBC Sat 9:00–9:30
(In first-run syndication for the 1987–1988 season)
CAST:
Mickey McKenzie...................... Teri Copley
Jay Bostwick.......................... Tom Villard
David Tucker (1983–1984)........... Matt McCoy
David Tucker (1987–1988)........... John Hillner
Claudia (1983–1984)............ Stepfanie Kramer
Beth Sorenson (1983–1984)......... Bonnie Urseth
Max Papavasilios, Sr. (1987–1988)... Ron Karabatsos
Max Papavasilios, Jr. (1987–1988)
.... Lance Wilson-White

Frothy comedy in which two young New York City bachelors hired a sexy live-in maid to clean up their sloppy apartment. David was a button-down lawyer, disgusted by the mess created by goofy roommate Jay, a free-thinking importer and "idea man." Along came Mickey, a bubbly and apparently air-headed blonde who just happened to be a crackerjack housekeeper. David and Jay's girlfriends (neurotic Claudia and ingenuous Beth, respectively) were naturally suspicious, but it was all quite innocent—of course.

Three years after leaving NBC, *We Got It Made* surfaced again with new episodes in first-run syndication. The relationship between Mickey and her bosses had not changed but David and Jay's regular girlfriends were gone. New to the cast were Max, a cop living in the apartment across the hall, and his awkward teenage son. Max, Jr., who had the hots for Mickey, often sought her advice about dealing with women.

WE TAKE YOUR WORD (*Quiz Panel*)
FIRST TELECAST: *April 1, 1950*
LAST TELECAST: *June 1, 1951*
BROADCAST HISTORY:
Apr 1950, CBS Sat 9:00–9:30
Jun 1950–Jul 1950, CBS Fri 8:00–8:30
Aug 1950, CBS Sun 9:30–10:00
Aug 1950–Sep 1950, CBS Mon 9:30–10:00
Oct 1950–Jan 1951, CBS Tue 10:30–11:00
Mar 1951–Jun 1951, CBS Fri 10:30–11:00
WORDMASTER:
John K. M. McCaffery
John Daly
PANELISTS:
Abe Burrows
Lyman Bryson (1950)

The panelists on *We Take Your Word* sought to provide the definitions, derivations, and histories of words that were sent in by viewers. Any word used on the program won for its submitter a book prize and, if the panel bungled their attempt to define it, $50. The series began on radio in January 1950 and was tried on television that April. John K. M. McCaffery was the wordmaster (moderator) of the radio version and also of the experimental TV version in April. He was replaced by John Daly when the show returned to television in June. John Daly stayed with the show through January 1951, to be replaced by its original host for its last three months. Initially there were two regular panelists and one guest. When Lyman Bryson left the show at the end of August 1950, Abe Burrows became the sole regular, with two guest panelists each week.

WE, THE PEOPLE (*Interview*)
FIRST TELECAST: *June 1, 1948*
LAST TELECAST: *September 26, 1952*
BROADCAST HISTORY:
Jun 1948–Oct 1949, CBS Tue 9:00–9:30
Nov 1949–Jun 1951, NBC Fri 8:30–9:00
Sep 1951–Sep 1952, NBC Fri 8:30–9:00
HOST:
Dwight Weist (1948–1950)
Dan Seymour (1950–1952)

We, the People had been a feature on radio for 12 years when it moved to television in the summer of 1948. It was the first regularly scheduled series to be simulcast on both network radio and network television. Host Dwight Weist (replaced by Dan Seymour in April

1950) interviewed various guests about important events in their lives. Entertainers, politicians, and ordinary Americans appeared on the series to chat informally, often about experiences of deep personal suffering or triumph over adversity. Members of public-service organizations and individuals who had done some form of humanitarian work appeared frequently. The guests were introduced with the line, "We, the people . . . speak." The radio-TV simulcasts continued until July 1950, after which date the radio and television versions were aired at different times.

WEAKEST LINK, THE (*Quiz*)

FIRST TELECAST: *April 16, 2001*

LAST TELECAST:

BROADCAST HISTORY:

Apr 2001–May 2001, NBC Mon 8:00–9:00
May 2001–Aug 2001, NBC Mon 9:00–10:00
Jun 2001–Apr 2002, PAX Fri 8:00–9:00
Jun 2001–Aug 2001, NBC Sun 10:00–11:00
Aug 2001–Dec 2001, NBC Mon 8:00–9:00
Sep 2001–Jul 2002, NBC Sun 8:00–9:00
Apr 2002–May 2002, PAX Fri 10:00–11:00
May 2002–Aug 2002, PAX Fri 8:00–9:00
Sep 2002–Jun 2003, PAX Tue 8:00–9:00
Jul 2003–, PAX Mon-Fri 6:30–7:00

(New episodes in first-run syndication from January 2002)

EMCEE:

Anne Robinson

This imported British quiz show had a real edge but was played with such a wink and a nod that it became one of the hits of the early 2000s game-show craze. Eight contestants stood behind podiums in a semi-circle around the host on a dark, eerily lit stage, and tried to create a "chain" of correct answers to eight fast-paced questions. If they succeeded they could win $125,000 for the team; or if one of them said "bank" before a question all the money won thus far was put into the bank, and they started over on another chain. Where it got interesting was at the end of each round, when the team had to vote off one member as "the weakest link." The audience was shown who had been the weakest player numerically, but the team could vote off anyone, often someone who merely hesitated when giving answers.

The icy host, Britisher Anne Robinson, appeared in a long black leather jacket with her hands clasped behind her back. She dismissed the contestant voted off with an abrupt and imperious, "You *are* the weakest link—g'bye." She grilled the remaining contestants on the reasons for their votes (inviting backbiting), and the dismissed contestants got to give their side from backstage (more backbiting). The questions then resumed, a little faster, and with one fewer contestant each round, until at the end the last two played for the accumulated bank in a series of five alternating questions, with the winner taking home as much as $1 million—and the loser getting nothing.

Robinson also hosted the British version, where she was known for her snide demeanor, but apparently NBC felt American audiences might not get the joke and had her give a little wink at the end of each episode. Her trademark "You *are* the weakest link" became a catchphrase. Reruns of the NBC episodes appeared on both Pax and the Game Show Network, which also ran some previously unaired episodes. There was also a syndicated version in daytime, hosted by comedian George Gray, who also dressed in black but could not match Robinson's sangfroid. In January 2003 PAX replaced NBC episodes with reruns of the syndicated episodes.

WEATHER CHANNEL, THE (Network) (*Cable Weather Network*)

LAUNCHED:

May, 1982

SUBSCRIBERS (MAY 2003):

85.2 million (80% U.S.)

Nothing epitomizes the specialty services of cable quite like The Weather Channel. It does one thing, and one thing only, 24 hours a day, and does it so matter-of-factly that it has been the butt of sitcom jokes. More than one sitcom character has been seen transfixed, staring at the hypnotic, routinized presentation for hours on end. The nameless forecasters glide effortlessly back and forth before their national weather maps, never obscuring the East or West Coast for more than a moment, never attracting attention to themselves; local forecasts ("accurate and dependable . . .") scroll by on the screen to the soporific sound of elevator music. How did the precable age live without this!

The channel is as well oiled off screen as on. Computers gather weather information from all over the country (and the world) and feed it to local cable systems, where it automatically triggers "your local forecast" on screen via high-tech equipment called the Star system. There are virtually no series as such, but the channel does have occasional specials about disasters it loves (*The Year the Sky Fell, The Burning Season*) and even sells videotapes of tornadoes to people who can't get enough of the real thing.

The Weather Channel was founded in 1982 by John Coleman, a Chicago TV weatherman. It first reached more than half of all U.S. television homes in September 1990.

WEB, THE (*Dramatic Anthology*)

FIRST TELECAST: *July 11, 1950*

LAST TELECAST: *October 6, 1957*

BROADCAST HISTORY:

Jul 1950–Aug 1950, CBS Tue 9:30–10:00
Aug 1950–Jul 1952, CBS Wed 9:30–10:00
Sep 1952–Sep 1954, CBS Sun 10:00–10:30
Jul 1957–Oct 1957, NBC Sun 10:00–10:30

HOST/NARRATOR:

Jonathan Blake (1950–1954)
William Bryant (1957)

PRODUCERS:

Mark Goodson and Bill Todman (1950–1954)

Normal, everyday people who found themselves in situations beyond their control populated the dramas telecast in this live CBS anthology series. Its producers, ironically, were Mark Goodson and Bill Todman of game-show fame.

All of the plays were adaptations of stories written by members of the Mystery Writers of America. Walter C. Brown and Hugh Pentecost were frequent contributors and even an occasional Charlotte Armstrong story, like "All the Way Home," turned up on *The Web*. Most of the actors and actresses appearing on the show were performers based in New York, where the show was produced. Included were Richard Kiley, James Daly, Eli Wallach, James Gregory, Patricia Wheel, Mary Sinclair, John Newland, and Phyllis Kirk.

Some future stars who were seen on *The Web* early in their careers were Grace Kelly in "Mirror of Delusion" in 1950, Jack Palance and Eva Marie Saint in "Last Chance" in 1953, and Paul Newman twice that summer, the second time in "One for the Road" on September 20, at the same time he was appearing on Broadway in the play *Picnic*. Newman's future wife, Joanne Woodward (they would marry in 1958), starred in "Welcome Home," the final telecast of CBS' version of *The Web*, on September 26, 1954.

Hollywood veterans taking lead roles in episodes of *The Web* on CBS included John Carradine, Mildred Dunnock, Sidney Blackmer, Mildred Natwick, Henry Hull, and Chester Morris. On occasion the leads went to performers not noted for their dramatic acting ability, such as singer Jane Morgan in "Rehearsal for Death" and musical-comedy star John Raitt in "The Dark Shore." The real stars on *The Web* were the stories, however, not the performers. The overall quality of the productions was attested to when *The Web* became the first television series to win the Edgar Allan Poe Award for excellence in the presentation of suspense stories during the 1951–1952 season.

In the summer of 1957, NBC revived the title *The Web* for a series of filmed dramas with essentially the same format as the live CBS series of the early 1950s. Again, the emphasis was on story rather than star, with Alexander Scourby, Beverly Garland, James Darren, and Rex Reason the most familiar performers appearing. The NBC edition was the summer replacement for *The Loretta Young Show*.

WEBER SHOW, THE, see *Cursed*

WEBSTER (*Situation Comedy*)

FIRST TELECAST: *September 16, 1983*
LAST TELECAST: *September 11, 1987*
BROADCAST HISTORY:

Sep 1983–Mar 1985, ABC Fri 8:30–9:00
Mar 1985–Mar 1987, ABC Fri 8:00–8:30
Mar 1987–Apr 1987, ABC Fri 8:30–9:00
May 1987, ABC Fri 8:00–8:30
Jun 1987–Aug 1987, ABC Sat 8:00–8:30
Aug 1987–Sep 1987, ABC Fri 8:00–8:30
(In first-run syndication during the 1987–1988 season)

CAST:

Webster Long .... Emmanuel Lewis
George Papadapolis .... Alex Karras
Katherine Calder-Young Papadapolis .. Susan Clark
Jerry Silver .... Henry Polic II
Bill Parker (1984–1986) .... Eugene Roche
Cassie Parker (1984–1986) .... Cathryn Damon
Uncle Phillip Long (1984–1985) .... Ben Vereen
*"*Papa" Papadapolis (1985–1987)* ... Jack Kruschen
Rob Whitaker/Joiner (1985–1986) ...... Chad Allen
**Tommy (1987)* .... Gabe Witcher
**Roger (1986–1987)* .... Carl Steven
**Andy (1986–1987)* .... Danny McMurphy
**Benny (1987)* .... Nick DeMauro
Nicky Papadapolis (1987–1988)
.... Corin "Corky" Nemec

*Occasional

THEME:

"Then Came You," by Steve Nelson and Madeline Sunshine

Emmanuel Lewis was 40 inches tall, cute as a button, and the comic find of the 1983–84 season. He was 12 years old, but looked half that. A network executive spotted him in a Burger King commercial and signed him on the spot—then ordered his writers to think up a series for him fast, before the little fellow grew another inch.

The series they came up with may have been a bit farfetched, but it did showcase young Lewis' talents. George was a burly former pro-football player turned sportscaster on WBJX-TV, Katherine a fluttery socialite with a career as a consumer advocate (later she became a psychologist). They had met on a Greek cruise and—though total opposites—married on impulse. George was generally an impulsive guy. No sooner did they arrive back in Chicago than they discovered at their door the result of one of George's past impulses: a cute black seven-year-old named Webster. It seemed that George was Webster's godfather. He had promised the boy's parents, teammate and best friend Travis and his wife Gert, that if anything ever happened to them he would look after their child. Well, something did (they were killed in a car crash), there were no next of kin, and here was Webster.

Adjustments were made by all, particularly Katherine, who was totally inept as a housewife or mother. Webster was cute enough to melt even her Tiffany heart, however, when he told her why he always called her Ma'am—"cause it kinda sounds like 'mom.' " (*Awwwww,* sighs the audience.) As for George, beneath that hulk beat the heart of a pussycat. Most of the stories in this syrupy series were of the "Webster can't sleep without this teddy bear" variety, but a few dealt with more serious subjects such as retarded children, and the day they had to explain to Webster that his parents were not just "away."

Jerry was Katherine's sarcastic male secretary, Cassie and Bill owned the large Victorian house into which the Papadapolises moved in the fall of 1984 (they later bought it), and Phillip was Webster's uncle—who arrived planning to fight for custody of the little guy, much to everyone's discomfort. He later moved to Hollywood to start a movie career. A major change occured in the fall of 1987 when George's brother and sister-in-law decided to relocate to Nigeria to work on a UN agricultural project, and their 14-year-old son Nicky moved in with George and his family. Nicky and Webster got along famously, and the older boy provided Webster with the "brother" he had never had.

ABC aired reruns of *Webster* on weekday mornings from December 1986 to July 1987.

WEDNESDAY NIGHT FIGHTS, THE, see *Boxing*

WEDNESDAY 9:30 (8:30 CENTRAL) (*Situation Comedy*)

FIRST TELECAST: *March 27, 2002*
LAST TELECAST: *June 12, 2002*
BROADCAST HISTORY:

Mar 2002–Apr 2002, ABC Wed 9:30–10:00
May 2002–Jun 2002, ABC Wed 9:30–10:00

CAST:

David Weiss .... Ivan Sergei
Paul Weffler .... Ed Begley, Jr.
Mike McClarren .... James McCauley
Lindsay Urich .... Melinda McGraw
Joanne Walker .... Sherri Shepherd
Red Lansing .... John Cleese

The inner workings of the television industry were lampooned in this raucous comedy, which was as fleeting as the shows it mocked. David was a midwestern innocent, a young Minneapolis theatrical producer who had been lured to shameless, immoral Hollywood by the owner of the IBS network, Red Lansing, to help his network climb out of the ratings cellar by tapping into the "average American mind." As soon as David arrived he collided with an office full of stereotypes. There was Paul, the indecisive network president, who constantly fretted about keeping his job; Mike, the senior VP of programming, who had converted to Judaism to gain an edge and pretended to be gay whenever it was to his advantage; Lindsay, the neurotic vice president of comedy, who resented David's incursion on her turf; and chubby black Joanne, a "quota babe" (and proud of it) who had gone from fired crouton maker to vice president of programming in five months.

David might have appeared clueless, but he caught on fast to the machinations of colleagues and stars. He groveled to get John Ritter on the network, fought off Red's attempts to televise a live execution to boost ratings, and romanced Lori Loughlin, who promptly slapped him with a sexual harassment suit. Meanwhile the network scheduling board was inadvertently rearranged into a winning lineup by a temperamental chimpanzee.

Pulled after two weeks, *Wednesday 9:30 (8:30 Central)* returned at the beginning of the summer with a new title, *My Adventures in Television,* but was no more successful.

WEEK IN RELIGION, THE (*Religion*)

FIRST TELECAST: *March 16, 1952*
LAST TELECAST: *October 18, 1954*
BROADCAST HISTORY:
Mar 1952–Sep 1952, DUM Sun 6:00–7:00
Jul 1953–Sep 1953, DUM Sun 6:00–7:00
Sep 1953–Oct 1954, DUM Sun 6:00–6:30

This ecumenical religious program was originally one hour long and divided into three 20-minute segments: 20 minutes for the Protestants, 20 minutes for the Catholics, and 20 minutes for the Jews. A representative of each faith reported on the latest news and happenings in his denomination. There is no record of who, if anyone, got cut when the program was reduced to a half hour.

WEEKEND (*Newsmagazine*)

FIRST TELECAST: *October 20, 1974*
LAST TELECAST: *April 22, 1979*
BROADCAST HISTORY:
Oct 1974–Jun 1978, NBC Sat 11:30–1:00 A.M.
Dec 1978, NBC Sat 10:00–11:00
Jan 1979–Apr 1979, NBC Sun 10:00–11:00
REGULARS:
Lloyd Dobyns
Linda Ellerbee (1978–1979)

Weekend was one of the more unusual news programs attempted in the 1970s. Hosted by sardonic Lloyd Dobyns, it was an odd mixture of serious and frivolous features, packaged in a most irreverent fashion. There were serious investigative stories on killer bees invading Central America, American women in Colombian prisons, and the competition to enter medical school, juxtaposed with topics like "Frisbees Are a Way of Life," "Slots on the Rhine," "The Pigeon Wars," and "My Son-in-Law, the President" (in which people talked about their relatives running for president). Adding to the light flavor of the program was the extensive use of animation, in running cartoon features like "Feeble Fables" and "Mr. Hipp Goes to Town," and in short sequences that commented, often sarcastically, on the main stories.

It was all very hip, and certainly compatible with *Saturday Night Live*, with which it alternated during most of its late-night run. (*Weekend* aired approximately once every four weeks.) But in 1978, entranced with visions of an irreverent hit show for prime time, NBC moved it to 10 P.M. To the larger (and older) prime-time audience such flippancy seemed out of place on a news program, and *Weekend* did poorly, finally being replaced by the more traditional *Prime Time Sunday* in 1979. Linda Ellerbee appeared as cohost during *Weekend*'s prime-time run.

WEEKEND VIBE (*Magazine*)

BROADCAST HISTORY:
Syndicated only
60 minutes
Produced: *2002–*
Released: *September 2002*
REGULARS:
Bryce Wilson
Mimi Valdez

Bryce Wilson hosted this urban magazine show produced by *Vibe* magazine. Originating from New York, it was billed as "the voice and soul of urban culture." Among the regular features were V Style (fashion), The Rant (commentary and/or complaints by a celebrity), V Props (awards and presentations), Video Mix (excerpts from popular music videos), Do the Right Thing (how celebrities gave back to the community) and Next (spotlight on emerging artists). Mimi Valdez, *Vibe* editor at large, presented a weekly summary of urban show-business news.

WEEKLY WORLD NEWS (*Satire*)

BROADCAST HISTORY:
USA Network
30 minutes
Produced: *1995–1996* (13 episodes)
Premiered: *January 6, 1996*
REGULARS:
Edwin Newman
Randy Kagan

Few viewers who caught this short-lived Saturday night parody on TV newsmagazines will ever forget it. Based on the satirical newsstand tabloid, *The Weekly World News,* it featured stories unlikely to appear on *60 Minutes*—the bleeding teenager who delivered a pizza despite a gunshot wound; the South Seas island tribe that worshiped Don King; the doctor who performed hernia surgery on himself; the day-care center run by Hell's Angels; and a comic who told killer jokes. If you believe any of this, you *should* be reading the tabloids. Former NBC newsman Edwin Newman, evidently a man with a sense of humor, delivered the deadpan introductions.

WEIRD SCIENCE (*Situation Comedy*)

BROADCAST HISTORY:
USA Network
30 minutes

Produced: *1994–1998* (88 episodes)
Premiered: *March 5, 1994*

CAST:

Lisa .... Vanessa Angel
Gary Wallace .... John Mallory Asher
Wyatt Donnelly .... Michael Manasseri
Chett Donnelly .... Lee Tergesen
**Wayne Donnelly (1994)* .... Richard Fancy
**Wayne Donnelly (1994–1998)* ...... Andrew Prine
**Marcia Donnelly* .... Melendy Britt
**Al Wallace* .... Jeff Doucette
**Emily Wallace* .... Joyce Bulifant
**Principal Clive Scampi* .... Bruce Jarchow

*Occasional

Lightweight sitcom in which two nerdy, dateless students at Farber High, fun-loving Gary and studious Wyatt, created the living babe of their dreams on Wyatt's home computer. Lisa was not quite what the boys expected, however. She was curvaceous all right, but also smart, and while she could grant their wishes for short intervals (if she wished), she mostly used her powers to help them learn little lessons in growing up. Chett was Wyatt's bossy but dense older brother (often the target of the boys' pranks), Wayne his ad exec dad, and Marcia his mother. Gary's blue-collar parents were Al and Emily. *Weird Science* was canceled abruptly by USA Network in October 1997. Six unaired episodes turned up in July 1998, on Saturday morning, on sister network the Sci-Fi Channel.

Based on the 1985 movie of the same name.

WELCOME ABOARD (*Musical Variety*)

FIRST TELECAST: *October 3, 1948*
LAST TELECAST: *February 20, 1949*
BROADCAST HISTORY:

Oct 1948–Feb 1949, NBC Sun 7:30–8:00

REGULARS:

Russ Morgan and His Orchestra (Oct–Nov 1948)
Vincent Lopez and His Orchestra
(Nov 1948–Feb 1949)

THEME:

"Sailor's Hornpipe"

Live musical variety program with a nautical theme, including the members of the orchestra dressed in sailor suits. Top-name singers and comedians appeared as guests, with Phil Silvers and Martin and Lewis featured on the first telecast. Toward the end of the run one of the guests would serve as the emcee, with bandleader Lopez assuming a background role. The series was originally known as *Admiral Presents the Five Star Revue—Welcome Aboard*, but became *Welcome Aboard* when Admiral dropped sponsorship in December.

WELCOME BACK, KOTTER (*Situation Comedy*)

FIRST TELECAST: *September 9, 1975*
LAST TELECAST: *August 10, 1979*
BROADCAST HISTORY:

Sep 1975–Jan 1976, ABC Tue 8:30–9:00
Jan 1976–Aug 1978, ABC Thu 8:00–8:30
Sep 1978–Oct 1978, ABC Mon 8:00–8:30
Oct 1978–Jan 1979, ABC Sat 8:00–8:30
Feb 1979–Mar 1979, ABC Sat 8:30–9:00
May 1979–Aug 1979, ABC Fri 8:30–9:00

CAST:

Gabe Kotter .... Gabriel Kaplan
Julie Kotter .... Marcia Strassman
Vinnie Barbarino .... John Travolta
Juan Luis Pedro Phillipo de Huevos Epstein
.... Robert Hegyes
Freddie "Boom Boom" Washington
.... Lawrence-Hilton Jacobs
Arnold Horshack .... Ron Palillo
Mr. Michael Woodman .... John Sylvester White
Rosalie Totzie (1975–1976) .... Debralee Scott
Verna Jean (1975–1977) .... Vernee Watson
Judy Borden (1975–1977) .... Helaine Lembeck
Todd Ludlow (1975–1977) .... Dennis Bowen
Maria (1975–1976) .... Catarina Cellino
Angie Globagoski (1978) .... Melonie Haller
Beau De Labarre (1978–1979) ... Stephen Shortridge
Carvelli (1978–1979) .... Charles Fleischer
Murray (1978–1979) .... Bob Harcum
Mary Johnson (1978–1979) .... Irene Arranga

CREATED BY:

Gabriel Kaplan and Alan Sacks

THEME:

"Welcome Back," composed and performed by John Sebastian

Welcome Back, Kotter was one of the more realistic comedies of the 1970s. Gabriel Kaplan portrayed Kotter, a Brooklyn-born teacher who returned to the inner-city high school from which he had graduated 10 years earlier to teach the toughest cases—a remedial academics group. Gabe's "sweathogs" were the outcasts of the academic system, streetwise but unable or unwilling to make it in normal classes. They were the toughest, and also the funniest, kids in school. Gabe was just as hip as they were, and with fine disregard for rules and a sense of humor he set out to help them pick up a little bit of practical, if not academic, knowledge, during their years at James Buchanan High. The four original "sweathogs" were Epstein, the Jewish Puerto Rican; "Boom Boom," the hip black; Horshack, the class yo-yo; and Barbarino, the cool, tough leader. John Travolta, playing Barbarino, became a major star through this series. He branched into popular music, where he had several hit records beginning in the summer of 1976 (although the big song hit to come out of this show was the theme, as recorded by its composer John Sebastian). Travolta also began a successful movie career, with such films as *Carrie* and *Saturday Night Fever*, while he was still starring on *Kotter*. By 1978 he was seen only occasionally on the series.

Dozens of other students passed through the series, most seen only briefly. Those with the most appearances are listed above. Other regulars were Gabe's wife, Julie, and Mr. Woodman, the assistant principal. Julie became pregnant at the end of the 1976–1977 season, and gave birth to twins Rachel and Robin in the fall of 1977, adding to the confusion and crowding in the Kotters' small apartment, and putting new strains on Gabe's limited income. In other developments, Angie turned up in early 1978 with the announcement that she was becoming the first female "sweathog" (she didn't last long), and a slick southerner, Beau De Labarre, joined the class the following fall. Also in the fall of 1978 Kotter was promoted to vice principal and Mr. Woodman to principal. The sweathogs got part-time jobs, with Vinnie becoming an orderly at a nearby hospital.

Welcome Back, Kotter was based on a real high school and the real experiences of Gabriel Kaplan.

Kaplan had once attended the equivalent of James Buchanan High School, in Bensonhurst, Brooklyn, New York, and had been a student in a remedial class there. He credits a Miss Shepard as the teacher who inspired him, and who led, indirectly, to *Welcome Back, Kotter*. Like Kotter, she cared about her "unteachable" students.

WELCOME FRESHMEN (*Situation Comedy*)

BROADCAST HISTORY:

Nickelodeon
30 minutes
Produced: *1991–1993* (52 episodes)
Premiered: *February 16, 1991*

CAST:

Alex Moore .... Jocelyn Steiner
Walter Patterson .... Rick Galloway
Kevin St. James .... Chris Lobban
Merv (1991–1992).................. David Phoden
Tara (1991–1992) .... Jill Setter
Erin Kelly (1992–1993) .... Arian Ash
Grant Kelly (1992–1993) .... Brock Bradley
Manny Barrington (1992) .... Nicholas Caruso
Mr. Elliott Lippman .... Mike Speller
Miss Petruka .... Janis Benson

In the wake of the success of NBC's frothy high school sitcom *Saved by the Bell*, Nickelodeon launched this close copy set at Hawthorne High, Anytown, USA. The characters were equally generic: bumbling schemer Walter, spacey black student Kevin, dumb jock Grant, Grant's lovelorn girlfriend Alex, and earnest Erin (Grant's sister). Mr. Lippman was the bald, nasal vice principal, a total nutcase who was constantly bumbling into trouble, and Miss Petruka was his absentminded secretary. The series began as a sketch comedy and evolved into a situation comedy during the second 26 episodes, with stories revolving around pranks and puppy loves that invariably went astray.

WELCOME MAT, see *Starlit Time*

WELCOME TO NEW YORK (*Situation Comedy*)

FIRST TELECAST: *October 11, 2000*
LAST TELECAST: *January 17, 2001*
BROADCAST HISTORY:

Oct 2000–Jan 2001, CBS Wed 8:30–9:00

CAST:

Marsha Bickner .... Christine Baranski
Jim Gaffigan .... Himself
Adrian Spencer .... Rocky Carroll
Amy Manning .... Sara Gilbert
Vince Verbena .... Anthony DeSando
Connie .... Mary Birdsong
Stage Manager.......................... Wendy Way

Genial, easygoing Fort Wayne weatherman Jim Gaffigan had just gotten his big break. He had left Indiana to start a new job as the meteorologist on *AM New York*, a local morning TV news show on WNYD, Channel 6. It wasn't easy for trusting Jim to adjust to living and working in cutthroat New York. The pace, the prices, and the pressures at work were all new to him. Marsha, the show's manic producer and his new boss, was demanding, sarcastic and verbally abusive. Adrian, *AM New York*'s male coanchor, was arrogant and condescending, and seemed to believe that everybody else was as self-absorbed as he. Others at the station were Amy, Marsha's unflappable assistant and Jim's assistant, Vince, who would do almost anything to make his new boss happy. Unfortunately, Vince was prone to promise things he couldn't deliver. Connie, the counter girl at the neighborhood deli, was Jim's confidante.

WELCOME TO PARADOX (*Science Fiction Anthology*)

BROADCAST HISTORY:

Sci-Fi Channel
60 minutes
Produced: *1998*
Premiered: *August 17, 1998*

HOST:

Paradox .... Michael Philip

A rather creepy anthology series which looked to the future and warned, "Be careful what you wish for." The citizens of the future had built a domed city called Betaville, where technology served their every need. Society appeared to have realized its fondest dreams—no apparent crime, disease, hostility, or stress. But human frailties being what they are, the greedy, the criminal, and the emotionally distraught were constantly tempted to exploit the wondrous scientific advances for their own ends. Among the guest stars in these cautionary tales were Mayim Bialik, A Martinez, and Ice-T. The only regular was the host, called Paradox, who introduced each episode.

WE'LL GET BY (*Situation Comedy*)

FIRST TELECAST: *March 14, 1975*
LAST TELECAST: *May 30, 1975*
BROADCAST HISTORY:

Mar 1975–May 1975, CBS Fri 8:30–9:00

CAST:

George Platt .... Paul Sorvino
Liz Platt .... Mitzi Hoag
Muff Platt .... Jerry Houser
Kenny Platt............................ Willie Aames
Andrea Platt.......................... Devon Scott

The Platt family was a normal middle-class group living in a modest home in the New Jersey suburbs just outside of New York City, where George Platt worked as a lawyer. He and his wife, Liz, had three teenage children. Life in the Platt household, with all its conflicts, was one of love and understanding. The program was created by Alan Alda.

WELLS FARGO, see *Tales of Wells Fargo*

WENDY AND ME (*Situation Comedy*)

FIRST TELECAST: *September 14, 1964*
LAST TELECAST: *September 6, 1965*
BROADCAST HISTORY:

Sep 1964–Sep 1965, ABC Mon 9:00–9:30

CAST:

George Burns .... Himself
Wendy Conway.................... Connie Stevens
Jeff Conway .... Ron Harper
Danny Adams....................... James Callahan
Mr. Bundy .... J. Pat O'Malley
Willard Norton .... Bartlett Robinson

This comedy was roughly patterned after the old

Burns and Allen Show of the 1950s, and was another attempt to find a suitable format for George Burns after the retirement of his wife, Gracie Allen. The setting was an apartment house in Southern California whose principal tenants were Wendy Conway, a slightly daft young bride, and her airline-pilot husband Jeff. Jeff's copilot and best friend was Danny, a girl-chasing bachelor who was inordinately proud of his "little black book" and "little red book." Mr. Bundy was the building superintendent.

Into the picture came George Burns, as himself. He had bought the building so he would have a place to practice his vaudeville routine—just in case anyone should ask him to perform it again. George's singing was not exactly widely admired, so he had written into every lease a provision that no tenant could evict the landlord. George, with his familiar cigar in hand, spent most of his time serving as onscreen narrator of the series. He followed Wendy through her day, commenting on the action in asides to the audience. Then he would step into the action himself.

WENDY BARRIE SHOW, THE (*Interview*)
FIRST TELECAST: *March 14, 1949*
LAST TELECAST: *September 27, 1950*
BROADCAST HISTORY:
Mar 1949–Jun 1949, DUM Mon/Wed/Fri 7:00–7:30
Jun 1949–Jul 1949, DUM Wed 7:00–7:30
Sep 1949–Oct 1949, ABC Mon 8:30–9:00
Nov 1949–Dec 1949, ABC Wed 8:00–8:30
Dec 1949–Feb 1950, ABC Thu 9:00–9:30
Feb 1950–Jun 1950, NBC Tue/Thu 7:30–7:45
Jul 1950–Aug 1950, NBC Mon/Wed/Fri 7:30–7:45
Aug 1950–Sep 1950, NBC Wed 8:15–8:30
REGULARS:
Wendy Barrie
Dave Davis (1949)

Celebrity-interview and gossip show, hosted by one-time Hollywood starlet and early TV personality Wendy Barrie. Wendy's movie heyday was past by the time she went into the infant medium of television, but her vivacious charm was quite intact. Each night she welcomed viewers into a plush setting that was supposed to be her own Manhattan apartment, with outstretched arms, and such endearments as "sweet bunny," "sweetie," and "dearie" (her sign-off was always "be a good bunny"). All sorts of celebrities dropped in to chat with Wendy, and sometimes to perform, and there was show-business gossip as well as banter (Wendy had a marvelous sense of humor, even about herself). There was a definite air of glamour about it all.

Her first nighttime network series was produced in cooperation with *Photoplay* magazine and was called *Inside Photoplay*, then *Photoplay Time* (September 1949). Later it became *The Wendy Barrie Show* (December 1949) and finally *Through Wendy's Window* (August 1950). Miss Barrie was later seen on afternoon shows and on local television in New York.

WEREWOLF (*Supernatural*)
FIRST TELECAST: *July 11, 1987*
LAST TELECAST: *August 21, 1988*
BROADCAST HISTORY:
Jul 1987–Aug 1987, FOX Sat 9:00–9:30
Aug 1987–Oct 1987, FOX Sat 8:00–8:30
Oct 1987–Mar 1988, FOX Sun 8:00–8:30
Apr 1988, FOX Sat 9:00–10:00
May 1988–Aug 1988, FOX Sun 10:30–11:00
CAST:
Eric Cord .... John J. York
Alamo Joe Rogan .... Lance LeGault
**Janos Skorzeny (1987–1988)* .... Chuck Connors
Nicholas Remy (1988) .... Brian Thompson
*Occasional

Eric Cord was a graduate student in college whose life took a bizarre twist when his best friend Ted asked Eric to kill him with a pistol loaded with a silver bullet—because Ted was a werewolf! Eric thought his friend was off his rocker, but was forced to oblige when Ted turned into a werewolf and attacked him. Unfortunately Eric was bitten in the attack, and found that *he* was now afflicted with the deadly curse. The only way to rid himself of it was to find and kill "the source of the bloodline," the mysterious Captain Janos Skorzeny. Eric embarked on a cross-country hunt for the swaggering Skorzeny while he, in turn, was being tracked by bounty hunter Alamo Joe. Although Eric was now prone to turn into a werewolf under the full moon, fortunately for the honest citizenry he only seemed to attack criminals, evil folk, and other werewolves.

Eric finally found and killed Skorzeny, but another complication arose; it turned out the source of the bloodline was actually Nicholas Remy, a remarkably well-preserved, powerful, and diabolical 2,000-year-old werewolf. Eric's quest to rid himself of his curse continued. Viewers never found out if he succeeded, however, since the series was canceled soon after Remy's arrival.

Werewolf was a very atmospheric series with vivid, even terrifying, special effects. The Fox network promoted the show heavily during the fall of 1987, and straight-faced announcements were aired giving viewers a toll-free number to call if they had sighted a werewolf. More than 400,000 calls were received. Later announcements featured Dr. Stephen Kaplan, an instructor of parapsychology, providing information about werewolves.

WESLEY (*Situation Comedy*)
FIRST TELECAST: *May 8, 1949*
LAST TELECAST: *August 30, 1949*
BROADCAST HISTORY:
May 1949–Jul 1949, CBS Sun 7:30–8:00
Jul 1949–Aug 1949, CBS Tue 9:30–10:00
Aug 1949, CBS Tue 8:00–8:30
CAST:
Wesley Eggleston (May–Jul) .... Donald Devlin
Wesley Eggleston (Jul–Aug) .... Johnny Stewart
Mr. Eggleston .... Frank Thomas
Mrs. Eggleston .... Mona Thomas
Grandpa .... Joe Sweeney
Elizabeth Eggleston .... Joy Reese
Alvin .... Billie Nevard

Wesley was a 12-year-old boy who was making, but ever so slowly, the transition from childhood to adulthood. He liked to play with his good buddy, Alvin, with whom he had an almost brotherly relationship, fight with his teenage sister, Elizabeth, and find ways of getting around his parents. This live situation comedy told of his adventures in a small rural community. The relationship between Wesley and his parents was, despite the problems inherent in all parent-child relationships, a warm and loving one.

WEST 57TH (*Newsmagazine*)
FIRST TELECAST: *August 13, 1985*
LAST TELECAST: *September 9, 1989*
BROADCAST HISTORY:
Aug 1985–Sep 1985, CBS Tue 10:00–11:00
Apr 1986–Jun 1986, CBS Wed 8:00–9:00
Jun 1986–Jul 1986, CBS Wed 10:00–11:00
Apr 1987, CBS Mon 10:00–11:00
May 1987–Jun 1987, CBS Tue 8:00–9:00
Jun 1987–Sep 1989, CBS Sat 10:00–11:00
CORRESPONDENTS:
John Ferrugia
Bob Sirott (1985–1988)
Meredith Vieira
Jane Wallace (1985–1988)
Steve Kroft (1987–1989)
Selina Scott (1987–1989)
Karen Burnes (1988–1989)
Stephen Schiff (1988–1989)

West 57th premiered as a summer magazine series that was a fast-paced "yuppie" version of *60 Minutes*. The four original correspondents were all under 40, and the stories they covered were oriented to a younger audience. There were multiple pieces on the drug problem—steroids for athletes, the use and abuse of legal "designer" drugs, and the problems with "Angel Dust"; a story on the growing popularity of cosmetic surgery; a feature about the increasing incidence of arson among teens; and coverage of the competition between American and Japanese companies searching for a cure for cancer. On the lighter side were profiles of actors Chuck Norris and John and Angelica Huston, singers Billy Joel and John Cougar Mellencamp, and comic Martin Short, as well as a story on the never-ending labors of an exterminator trying to control the pest population in the Pentagon.

After two years as a summer show, *West 57th* returned to the CBS schedule, in April 1987, on a full-time basis. That fall Steve Kroft joined the correspondents, as did Britisher Selina Scott, whose forte was European-based pieces on the music industry. When Jane Wallace left the show at the end of the year she was replaced by Karen Burnes.

WEST POINT STORY, THE (*Military Anthology*)
FIRST TELECAST: *October 5, 1956*
LAST TELECAST: *July 1, 1958*
BROADCAST HISTORY:
Oct 1956–Sep 1957, CBS Fri 8:00–8:30
Oct 1957–Jul 1958, ABC Tue 10:00–10:30
HOST:
Donald May (as *Cadet Charles C. Thompson*) (1956)

Produced with the cooperation of the Department of Defense, the Department of the Army, and the United States Military Academy, this series dramatized actual events and persons from the files of West Point. The names and dates of the people and situations involved were changed, but the events were real. The dramas showed cadets as real people, with the problems, joys, and tragedies that are part of every person's life. Not all of the episodes were based on contemporary life at the military academy; some looked at the academy at different periods in its history and the men who were a part of that history. Donald May was the host, in character, when *The West Point Story* premiered, but was phased out before the end of 1956.

WEST WING, THE (*Political Drama*)
FIRST TELECAST: *September 22, 1999*
LAST TELECAST:
BROADCAST HISTORY:
Sep 1999–   , NBC Wed 9:00–10:00
CAST:
President Josiah Bartlet .... Martin Sheen
Abigail Bartlet .... Stockard Channing
**Zoey Bartlet* .... Elizabeth Moss
Chief of Staff Leo McGarry .... John Spencer
Dep. Chief of Staff Josh Lyman ... Bradley Whitford
Press Secretary C. J. Cregg .... Allison Janney
Communications Dir. Toby Ziegler .. Richard Schiff
Dep. Communications Dir. Sam Seaborn (1999–2003) .... Rob Lowe
Madeline "Mandy" Hampton (1999–2000) .... Moira Kelly
Danny Concannon (1999–2000) .. Timothy Busfield
Donna Moss .... Janel Moloney
Charlie Young (2000–   ) .... Dulé Hill
**Delores Landingham (1999–2001)* .... Kathryn Joosten
Margaret .... NiCole Robinson
Carol .... Melissa Fitzgerald
**Bonnie* .... Devika Parikh
**Vice President John Hoynes* .... Tim Matheson
*Occasional

The majesty and drama of the White House was the setting for this series, which mixed personal stories with political intrigue. Josiah Bartlet was a liberal New Hampshire Democrat who brought to the presidency a JFK-like intensity and single-mindness of purpose. His intense and loyal staff included Chief of Staff Leo, an experienced operator who was the president's closest ally and at the center of almost every crisis; Leo's opinionated deputy Josh, a skilled strategist who sometimes blurted out the truth at inopportune moments; Josh's sarcastic assistant Donna; Press Secretary C. J., a tall, wired woman who deftly handled the resulting uproars; rumpled Communications Director Toby, whose cynical sense of humor got him through many dicey political situations, and Toby's deputy Sam, a smooth political operator and ladies' man. Abigail was the first lady, a doctor who was dedicated to her husband but not afraid to put him in his place; Zoey was their daughter. Others seen frequently in the bustling White House corridors included political consultant Mandy (Josh's ex-girlfriend), reporter Danny, Bartlet's devoted secretary Delores, C. J.'s secretary Carol, communications aide Bonnie and unsupportive Vice President Hoynes.

Major stories included an assassination attempt in 2000, which proved to have been aimed not at Bartlet but at his young black personal aide, Charlie; the revelation in 2001 that Bartlet had multiple sclerosis, which he hid until after his renomination and which led to a congressional investigation and charges of a cover-up; and his reelection campaign in 2001–2002 against conservative Gov. Robert Ritchie (James Brolin), which Bartlet won by a landslide.

Though by nature a political animal, Bartlet was not afraid to show his beliefs, as in the premiere when he got into an argument with a contentious group representing the religious right and pointedly showed them the door. The producers denied that this was a slap at Rev. Jerry Falwell and the Moral Majority, but Bartlet's liberal leanings were so apparent that wags dubbed the show "The Left Wing."

WESTERN HOUR, THE, syndicated title for *Rifleman, The* and *Dick Powell's Zane Grey Theater* (packaged as an hour show)

WESTERN STAR THEATRE, see *Death Valley Days*

WESTERNER, THE (*Western*)
FIRST TELECAST: *September 30, 1960*
LAST TELECAST: *December 30, 1960*
BROADCAST HISTORY:
Sep 1960–Dec 1960, NBC Fri 8:30–9:00
CAST:
Dave Blassingame .... Brian Keith
Burgundy Smith...................... John Dehner

Dave Blassingame was one of many adventurers wandering the TV version of the Old West. He was accompanied by a large mongrel named Brown (played by the same dog that had been featured in the Walt Disney movie *Old Yeller*). Though not a particularly friendly or outgoing type, Dave found settlers to defend, villains to fight, and causes to champion throughout the portion of the Southwest along the Mexican border. His avowed aim was to settle down on a ranch of his own and breed quarter horses, but his concern for the exploited pioneers he met constantly kept him postponing that move. One person Dave kept running into as he traveled was Burgundy Smith, an enterprising con man, who was constantly trying to fleece the citizenry.

WESTERNERS, THE, syndicated title for *Black Saddle, Johnny Ringo, Law of the Plainsman, The,* and *Westerner, The* (packaged as a single series)

WESTINGHOUSE DESILU PLAYHOUSE (*Dramatic Anthology*)
FIRST TELECAST: *October 13, 1958*
LAST TELECAST: *June 10, 1960*
BROADCAST HISTORY:
Oct 1958–Sep 1959, CBS Mon 10:00–11:00
Oct 1959–Jun 1960, CBS Fri 9:00–10:00
HOST:
Desi Arnaz
COMMERCIAL SPOKESPERSON:
Betty Furness

When *Studio One*'s live weekly anthology series went off the air after almost a full decade, sponsor Westinghouse Electric kept the time period with this series of filmed dramas. Betty Furness, who had been the spokesperson for *Studio One*, continued to show off refrigerators and ranges throughout the two years that *Desilu Playhouse* was on. The premiere telecast featured young Pier Angeli in "Bernadette," but the material ranged from light to serious. During the first season, host Desi Arnaz, whose production company was making the series, made no appearances as a performer, but two of his *I Love Lucy* gang did. Lucille Ball starred with William Lundigan and Aldo Ray in "K.O. Kitty," and William Frawley worked with Dan Duryea in "Comeback." William Bendix and Martin Balsam were featured in "The Time Element," a science-fiction story written by Rod Serling (and possibly the genesis of his later series *The Twilight Zone*). The most memorable program was a two-part story aired on April 20 and 27, 1959. Walter Winchell was the narrator, Robert Stack the star, and Keenan Wynn, Neville Brand, and Barbara Nichols featured players in "The Untouchables," which was destined to become a very successful and highly controversial series on ABC that fall.

Desi himself starred in two plays aired during the second season, "So Tender So Profane" and "Thunder in the Night," and another "Untouchables"-type story, "Meeting at Apalachin" starring Luther Adler, Cameron Mitchell, and Jack Warden and narrated by Bob Considine, was tried. Airing roughly once every five weeks within the series were a number of *Westinghouse Lucille Ball-Desi Arnaz Shows* in which the two stars re-created their roles from *I Love Lucy* along with Vivian Vance, William Frawley, and Richard Keith.

WESTINGHOUSE PLAYHOUSE (*Situation Comedy*)
FIRST TELECAST: *January 6, 1961*
LAST TELECAST: *July 7, 1961*
BROADCAST HISTORY:
Jan 1961–Apr 1961, NBC Fri 8:30–9:00
May 1961–Jul 1961, NBC Fri 9:30–10:00
CAST:
Nan McGovern .... Nanette Fabray
Dan McGovern.................... Wendell Corey
Buddy .... Bobby Diamond
Nancy......................... Jacklyn O'Donnell
Mrs. Harper....................... Doris Kemper

The full title of this comedy was *Westinghouse Playhouse Starring Nanette Fabray and Wendell Corey.* It was created by Miss Fabray's husband, writer-director Ranald MacDougall, and was based somewhat on her own life. Nan McGovern was a successful Broadway star who fell madly in love with Dan McGovern (whose wife had died six years previously) and married him after a very short courtship. On their way back to his hometown of Hollywood, Dan admitted to Nan that he had not told his children about her. When they arrived at his home in Beverly Hills Nan found herself confronted with two rude and indifferent stepchildren and a less-than-enthusiastic housekeeper. Her efforts to cope with the situation and become close to her new family provided the material for the episodes in this series.

WESTINGHOUSE PREVIEW THEATRE (*Comedy Anthology*)
FIRST TELECAST: *July 14, 1961*
LAST TELECAST: *September 22, 1961*
BROADCAST HISTORY:
Jul 1961–Sep 1961, NBC Fri 9:30–10:00

This summer series consisted of ten unsold pilots for potential situation comedy series, starring assorted TV and film personalities, and one musical program, "The Benny Goodman Show," which aired on September 15.

WESTINGHOUSE SUMMER THEATRE, see *Studio One*

WESTSIDE MEDICAL (*Medical Drama*)
FIRST TELECAST: *March 15, 1977*
LAST TELECAST: *August 25, 1977*
BROADCAST HISTORY:
Mar 1977–Apr 1977, ABC Thu 10:00–11:00
Jun 1977–Aug 1977, ABC Thu 10:00–11:00
CAST:
Dr. Sam Lanagan .... James Sloyan
Dr. Janet Cottrell .... Linda Carlson
Dr. Philip Parker .... Ernest Thompson
Carrie .... Alice Nunn
TECHNICAL CONSULTANT:
Walter D. Dishell, M.D.

Set in Southern California, this short-lived medical drama centered around three dedicated young doctors who opened their own clinic to provide total, personalized care to their patients. Carrie was the receptionist. *Westside Medical* returned at the end of June to run for another two months with both original and repeat episodes.

WE'VE GOT EACH OTHER (*Situation Comedy*)
FIRST TELECAST: *October 1, 1977*
LAST TELECAST: *January 14, 1978*
BROADCAST HISTORY:
Oct 1977–Jan 1978, CBS Sat 8:30–9:00
CAST:
Stuart Hibbard .... Oliver Clark
Judy Hibbard .... Beverly Archer
Damon Jerome .... Tom Poston
Dee Dee Baldwin .... Joan Van Ark
Donna .... Ren Woods
Ken Redford .... Martin Kove

The trials of a married couple whose marital roles were somewhat reversed formed the crux of this comedy. Stuart worked at home, as a copywriter for the "Herman Gutman Mail Order Catalogue" (full of improbable and useless gadgets), and did most of the cleaning and cooking. Judy commuted every day to downtown Los Angeles, where she was the assistant to professional photographer Damon Jerome, a hypertense, absentminded man who was great with a camera but terrible at the practical aspects of his business. Both Stuart and Judy had primary sources of aggravation, his being next-door neighbor Ken Redford and hers being model Dee Dee Baldwin, who was sarcastic, demanding, and incredibly self-centered. Donna, the office secretary, tried to maintain an uneasy truce between Judy and Dee Dee, but it was almost impossible.

WHAMMY! THE ALL NEW PRESS YOUR LUCK (*Quiz*)
BROADCAST HISTORY:
Game Show Network
30 minutes
Original episodes: *2002–*
Premiered: *April 15, 2002*
EMCEE:
Todd Newton

This fast, noisy game show was a new version of the daytime classic *Press Your Luck*, named after the dreaded "whammy" position on its board. Three contestants began with $1,000 each. Lights started rotating on a big neon board and a contestant yelled "stop!" to win whatever was in the box that the light landed on (cash or prize); but if it landed on a "whammy," signified by a little grinning devil character, the contestant lost all winnings up to that point. Whammy boxes multiplied as the game progressed. In round two the contestants answered questions to win additional spins, and then in round three they used those spins to win further money. Now, however, there were "double whammies"—which, if hit, resulted in the contestant getting spritzed with water, doused in popcorn or suffering some other indignity. Four whammies (total) and a contestant was out of the game. In the final round contestants could give their remaining spins to opponents, hoping *they* would get caught by a whammy. Winnings were usually in the $5,000–10,000 range.

The original *Press Your Luck* ran in CBS daytime 1983–1986, emceed by Peter Tomarken. It is perhaps best remembered for one 1984 contestant, Paul Michael Larson, who figured out the board patterns at home, went on the show and won $110,000 in cash and prizes—the biggest total ever won by a game-show player in one sitting. CBS subsequently reprogrammed its computers to prevent anyone else from "beating" the game this way.

WHAT A COUNTRY (*Situation Comedy*)
BROADCAST HISTORY:
Syndicated only
30 minutes
Produced: *1986–1987* (26 episodes)
Released: *September 1986*
CAST:
Nikolai Rostapovich .... Yakov Smirnoff
Taylor Brown .... Garrett M. Brown
Principal Joan Courtney .... Gail Strickland
Ali Nadeem .... Vijay Amritraj
Laslo Gabov .... George Murdock
Robert Muboto .... Harry Waters, Jr.
Maria Conchita Lopez .... Ada Maris
Victor Ortega .... Julian Reyes
Yung Hi .... Leila Hee Olsen
Principal F. Jerry "Bud" McPherson (1987)
.... Don Knotts

Real-life Russian immigrant Yakov Smirnoff starred in this series about resident aliens hoping to become American citizens. The series was set in Los Angeles where young Taylor Brown taught a night school course to help immigrants pass the American citizenship test. The members of his class were Nikolai, an effervescent Russian cab driver; Laslo, a grumpy, retired Hungarian physician; Ali, a Pakistani who took everything quite literally; Robert, the pretentious son of a deposed African king; Maria, the sexy housekeeper for a wealthy Beverly Hills family; Victor, a young Hispanic lady-killer in love with Maria; and Yung Hi, an incredibly shy and sensitive Chinese girl. Joan Courtney was the rather pushy principal of the school (replaced by Bud McPherson early in 1987). Stories revolved around their problems with American language and customs, as well as the ways in which they related to each other.

What a Country was adapted from the British series *Mind Your Language*.

WHAT A DUMMY (*Situation Comedy*)
BROADCAST HISTORY:
Syndicated only
30 minutes

Produced: *1990–1991* (24 episodes)
Released: *September 1990*

CAST:

Tucker Brannigan (age 16)........... Stephen Dorff
Cory Brannigan (11)................ Joshua Rudoy
Ed Brannigan........................ David Doty
Polly Brannigan................. Annabel Armour
Maggie Brannigan (6)............. Janna Michaels
Buzz (voice only) .... Loren Freeman
Mrs. Treva Travalony................ Kaye Ballard

Ed Brannigan's life took a bizarre turn when his great uncle Jackie died and left him a trunk full of props from his days as a ventriloquist. Locked in the trunk for 50 years had been Jackie's dummy, Buzz, and boy, was he achin' to get out! Buzz, it seems, could think and talk. And talk. And talk.

Having a bright, cynical ventriloquist's dummy with a mind of his own around the house was a mixed blessing. Buzz was forever giving everyone advice. The Brannigans couldn't tell anyone they had a "live" dummy living with them, yet Buzz was constantly making sarcastic comments when other people were around. The other members of the household were Ed's wife Polly and their three children—Tucker the carefree, girl-crazy teenager, Cory, the wise-beyond-his-years intellectual, and cute-as-a-button Maggie. Their next door neighbor in beautiful Secaucus, New Jersey, was pushy Mrs. Travalony. Maybe they could put *her* in the trunk.

WHAT ABOUT JOAN? (*Situation Comedy*)

FIRST TELECAST: *March 27, 2001*
LAST TELECAST: *October 9, 2001*
BROADCAST HISTORY:

Mar 2001–May 2001, ABC Tue 9:30–10:00
Oct 2001, ABC Tue 8:30–9:00

CAST:

Joan Gallagher....................... Joan Cusack
Jake Evans .... Kyle Chandler
Betsy Morgan....................... Jessica Hecht
Mark Ludlow .... Wallace Langham
Dr. Ruby Stern.................... Donna Murphy
Alice Adams........... Kellie Shanygne Williams
Steinie .... Jeff Garlin

Joan was a high school English teacher whose personal life was a bit of a shambles until handsome young investment banker Jake—whom she had been dating for just six weeks—suddenly proposed. This sent her into a series of anxiety attacks, and off to seek advice from her motley group of friends: Betsy, the insecure music teacher who was having an off-again, on-again affair with fellow teacher Mark; Ruby, a psychiatrist with troubles of her own, and student teacher Alice, perhaps the most sensible of the lot. Joan and Jake decided to "go slow," but Betsy and Mark abruptly married in May. Joining the cast during the short fall run was Jake's pal Steinie, who managed a bar. Filmed in Chicago, where the show was presumably set.

WHAT DO YOU HAVE IN COMMON? (*Quiz/Audience Participation*)

FIRST TELECAST: *July 1, 1954*
LAST TELECAST: *September 23, 1954*
BROADCAST HISTORY:

Jul 1954–Sep 1954, CBS Thu 9:00–9:30

EMCEE:

Ralph Story

Contestants on *What Do You Have in Common?* were brought to the stage in groups of three and informed by emcee Ralph Story that they had something in common that they must try to figure out by cross-examining each other. The first to figure out their common bond (which had been flashed on the TV screen to the viewers at home) won $500. Three groups of three participated on each show and the group that had taken the least time to figure out what they had in common won the opportunity to try for an extra $1,000 by guessing the similarity in the lives of three pictured celebrities.

WHAT DO YOU THINK? (*Discussion*)

FIRST TELECAST: *January 17, 1949*
LAST TELECAST: *February 14, 1949*
BROADCAST HISTORY:

Jan 1949–Feb 1949, ABC Mon 8:30–9:00

Book-discussion program produced by the Great Books Foundation Forum. From Chicago.

WHAT HAPPENED (*Quiz/Panel*)

FIRST TELECAST: *August 7, 1952*
LAST TELECAST: *August 21, 1952*
BROADCAST HISTORY:

Aug 1952, NBC Thu 8:30–9:00

MODERATOR:

Ben Grauer

PANELISTS:

Lisa Ferraday
Roger Price
Maureen Stapleton
Frank Gallop

Six weeks after *I've Got a Secret* premiered on CBS this very similar show turned up on the NBC schedule. Contestants on *What Happened* were all people who had had something happen to them that had been reported in a newspaper. The panelists, by asking questions to which the contestant answered yes or no, attempted to guess "what happened" to the contestant that was newsworthy. *I've Got a Secret* lasted 15 years in its original prime-time run. This shabby imitation lasted only three weeks.

WHAT HAPPENED? (*Documentary*)

FIRST TELECAST: *September 25, 1992*
LAST TELECAST: *October 16, 1992*
BROADCAST HISTORY:

Sep 1992–Oct 1992, NBC Fri 8:30–9:00

HOST:

Ken Howard

This reality series used scientific techniques such as computer simulations and analysis of film footage to probe various man-made accidents and disasters and speculate in each case what really happened. The tone was sensational and the cases usually high-profile: why Ricky Nelson's plane crashed in flames, why a gun turret blew up on the U.S.S. *Iowa* killing 47, why James Dean's car crashed, why a hotel elevator plunged 22 floors to the ground, and much more. The show even reexamined such well-worn cases as the JFK assassination and the Three Mile Island nuclear disaster. A consulting firm called Failure Analysis Associates carried out the high-tech reconstructions.

WHAT I LIKE ABOUT YOU (*Situation Comedy*)

FIRST TELECAST: *September 20, 2002*

LAST TELECAST:

BROADCAST HISTORY:

Sep 2002–Jun 2003, WB Fri 8:00–8:30

Jun 2003– , WB Fri 8:30–9:00

CAST:

Holly Tyler.......................... Amanda Bynes

Valerie Tyler .... Jennie Garth

Gary Thorpe .... Wesley Jonathan

Jeff .... Simon Rex

THEME:

"What I Like About You," performed by Lillix

This slapstick sitcom centered on two sisters with very different personalities living together in an apartment on Manhattan's Upper West Side. Sixteen-year-old Holly had moved in with her 28-year-old sister Valerie when their father took a job in Japan. Impulsive Holly was full of energy and enthusiasm, and loved being in the Big Apple. Val, a public relations executive with the firm of Harper & Diggs, was uptight and regimented, and needed her kid sister's help to loosen up. Despite Holly's penchant for getting herself—and often Val—into awkward or embarrassing situations, things always seemed to work out. Jeff, Val's commitment-phobic boyfriend, managed a local restaurant owned by his father, and Holly's friend Gary, who had a barely concealed crush on Val, worked at a local copy shop. There was a lot of physical comedy; simply getting off an elevator with luggage escalated into a major comedy bit.

In February Val and Jeff broke up when he told her he never wanted to get married and she went into a funk. When his father decided to close the restaurant, Holly helped Jeff get a job managing the restaurant where she hung out.

WHAT IN THE WORLD (*Quiz*)

FIRST TELECAST: *February 7, 1953*

LAST TELECAST: *September 5, 1953*

BROADCAST HISTORY:

Feb 1953–Sep 1953, CBS Sat 6:30–7:00

MODERATOR:

Dr. Froelich Rainey

PANELISTS:

Dr. Carleton Coon

Dr. Schuyler Cammann

The moderator of this live museum quiz was Dr. Froelich Rainey, director of the University of Pennsylvania Museum. Each week the two regular panelists, both professors in the anthropology department of the University of Pennsylvania, along with a third guest panelist, were shown works of art from the museum and asked to identify them. The identifications included background on the origins and original uses of the pieces, as well as possible explanations of the circumstances surrounding their discovery. This Peabody Award–winning series, broadcast live from Philadelphia, had actually premiered in April 1951 and continued until March 1955. For most of its run, however, it aired as a Saturday or Sunday afternoon program.

WHAT REALLY HAPPENED TO THE CLASS OF '65? (*Dramatic Anthology*)

FIRST TELECAST: *December 8, 1977*

LAST TELECAST: *July 27, 1978*

BROADCAST HISTORY:

Dec 1977–Mar 1978, NBC Thu 10:00–11:00

May 1978–Jul 1978, NBC Thu 10:00–11:00

CAST:

Sam Ashley................................ Tony Bill

A different graduate of Bret Harte High School, class of '65, was the subject of this dramatic anthology each week. Their post–high school stories were told from the perspective of a decade later: the class hustler, who had become a Vietnam War amputee; the class dreamers, who had become involved in a get-rich-quick scheme; "everybody's girl," who could never escape from her reputation for promiscuity.

A different cast appeared each week, with the only continuing role being that of Sam Ashley, who was a graduate of the class himself and who had returned to teach at the school. He served solely as narrator. Others appearing in individual telecasts included Leslie Nielsen, Jane Curtin, Larry Hagman, Linda Purl, and Meredith Baxter-Birney.

The series was based on the book of the same name.

WHAT SHOULD YOU DO? (*Information*)

BROADCAST HISTORY:

Lifetime

60 minutes

Original episodes: *2003–*

Premiered: *April 14, 2003*

REGULARS:

Candice DeLong

Dr. Winnie King

Charles Ingram

This helpful program showed viewers what to do in dangerous, but realistic, situations, by means of action-packed re-creations and expert advice. Examples included a child in a classroom who was accidently impaled with a pencil through the heart (the teacher kept pressure on the wound and *did not remove the pencil*); a woman kidnapped at gunpoint and forced into the trunk of her car (using her wits, she got out); and a couple caught in an avalanche (using a swimming motion, they stayed on the surface and grabbed onto passing trees and rocks).

The regular experts were former FBI agent Candice DeLong, emergency room physician Dr. Winnie King and emergency medical technician/rescue expert Charles Ingram. Sometimes their advice was a little challenging (if a gunman threatening you is distracted, you can try running away using a zigzag pattern and you "probably" won't get hit), but mostly it was good common sense. Now, do *you* know how to get out of your trunk?

WHAT WOULD YOU DO? (*Humor/Audience Participation*)

BROADCAST HISTORY:

Nickelodeon

30 minutes

Produced: *1991–1993* (90 episodes)

Premiered: *August 31, 1991*

HOST:

Marc Summers

One of those messy Nickelodeon game shows in which volunteers from the studio audience were asked if they would attempt stunts like kissing a chimp, picking up a cockroach, or sliding headfirst down the "pie slide" into a huge vat of whipped cream. In other segments, audience members voted on whether they thought people outside the studio would do bizarre things if asked and then saw via hidden cameras what actually happened when they did them.

WHATEVER HAPPENED TO ROBOT JONES?

(*Cartoon*)

BROADCAST HISTORY:

Cartoon Network
30 minutes
Original episodes: *2002–*
Premiered: *July 19, 2002*

VOICES:

Robot Jones .... himself
Mom Unit, Shannon Westaberg .... Grey Delisle
Robot Dad .... Maurice LaMarche
Timothy "Socks" Martin .... Kyle Sullivan
Cubey .... Myles Jeffrey
Lenny Yogman .... Josh Peck
Denny Yogman .... Austin Stout
Principal Madman .... Jeff Bennett
Mr. Rucoat .... Dee Bradley Baker
Tim Baines, Little Kevin .... Jonathan Osser
Mr. McMcmc .... Rip Taylor

Robot Jones was a diminutive robot with a large clear dome on top of his head and a monotone, synthesized voice, who had to deal with both being "different" (a robot) and growing up. Mom and Dad had sent him to Polyneux Jr. High School to study that strange race known as humans. Robot could be rather definite in his opinions ("Humans are illogical and inefficient"), but he did want to get along as he interacted with his friends Socks and Cubey, the infuriating Yogman twins, the oppressive Principal Madman, and gym teacher Mr. Rucoat. Shannon, a geeky girl with an artificial leg and teeth in a huge brace, was the object of his affection. While his mechanical brain and body gave him physical advantages, social interaction was another matter, and he had to be careful; for example, when ordered into the showers he was afraid he would rust! At the end of each episode the lessons he had learned became an entry in his data log.

WHAT'S GOING ON? (*Quiz/Panel*)

FIRST TELECAST: *November 28, 1954*
LAST TELECAST: *December 26, 1954*

BROADCAST HISTORY:

Nov 1954–Dec 1954, ABC Sun 9:30–10:00

MODERATOR:

Lee Bowman

PANELISTS:

Kitty Carlisle
Hy Gardner
Audrey Meadows
Cliff Norton
Gene Raymond
Susan Oakland

This show featured a panel of six celebrities, divided into two groups, the "ins" and the "outs." The "ins" remained inside the studio and had to guess what the "outs," gathered outside at some remote location, were doing. The program lasted exactly five weeks.

WHAT'S HAPPENING!! (*Situation Comedy*)

FIRST TELECAST: *August 5, 1976*
LAST TELECAST: *April 28, 1979*

BROADCAST HISTORY:

Aug 1976, ABC Thu 8:30–9:00
Nov 1976–Dec 1976, ABC Sat 8:30–9:00
Dec 1976–Jan 1978, ABC Thu 8:30–9:00
Jan 1978–Apr 1978, ABC Sat 8:00–8:30
Apr 1978–Jan 1979, ABC Thu 8:30–9:00
Feb 1979–Mar 1979, ABC Fri 8:30–9:00
Mar 1979–Apr 1979, ABC Sat 8:00–8:30
(In first-run syndication from September 1985–September 1988)

CAST:

Roger Thomas ("Raj") .... Ernest Thomas
Freddie Stubbs ("Rerun")(1976–1986) ... Fred Berry
Dwayne Clemens .... Haywood Nelson
Mrs. Thomas (Mama) (1976–1979)..... Mabel King
Dee Thomas .... Danielle Spencer
Shirley Wilson.................. Shirley Hemphill
Bill Thomas (1976–1977)........ Thalmus Rasulala
Marvin (1976–1977) .... Bryan O'Dell
Big Earl Babcock (1978–1979)*......... John Welsh
Little Earl (1978–1979) .... David Hollander
"The Snake" (1978–1979)........... Leland Smith
Nadine Hudson Thomas (1985–1988) .... Anne-Marie Johnson
Carolyn (1985–1986).................. Reina King
Maurice Warfield (1987–1988) ... Martin Lawrence
Darryl (1987–1988)..................... Ken Sagoes

*Later called Barnett, then Barrett

MUSIC:

Henry Mancini

Urban comedy about three spirited black kids in a big city. Raj was the studious dreamer, who wanted to be a writer; Rerun, the jolly, overweight clown who often wound up with his foot in his mouth; and Dwayne, the shy tag-along, always striving to be "cool." When not involved in some sort of scrape, the three could be found hanging out at Rob's, a diner near their school, where Shirley was the waitress. Family problems arose when Raj clashed with his no-nonsense mother, who worked as a maid, and with his pesky little sister, Dee. Mama's no-good ex-husband Bill, the kids' father, was seen occasionally, as was Marvin, the gossipy reporter for the high school newspaper.

In 1978 Raj and Rerun graduated from high school and moved into a shared apartment nearby, while Raj entered college and Rerun went to work. Their new neighbors were Big Earl, a police detective, and his smart-mouthed son, Little Earl. "The Snake" was the college basketball star.

First seen as a summer replacement show, *What's Happening!!* was given a spot on the regular ABC schedule in the fall of 1976. Six years after leaving ABC in 1979 it returned to television with a new title, *What's Happening Now!!*, and most of the original cast. In the syndicated version Raj was newly married and trying to make it as a writer, and Rerun and Dwayne, now a used car salesman and a computer programmer, respectively, were sharing an apartment. Shirley and Raj were also partners running Rob's, and Dee (who only showed up occasionally) was in college. Raj and Nadine, who were living in the house he had grown up in, took in a foster child named Caroline for a time. Added to the cast in the fall of 1987 were a local high school student named Maurice, who worked part-time as a busboy at Rob's, and his buddy, Darryl. It was also during that season that Dwayne gave up corporate life to open a small magic supplies shop.

The series was loosely based on the movie *Cooley High*.

WHAT'S HAPPENING TO AMERICA (*Discussion*)
FIRST TELECAST: *July 12, 1968*
LAST TELECAST: *August 16, 1968*
BROADCAST HISTORY:
Jul 1968–Aug 1968, NBC Fri 10:00–11:00
HOST:
Edwin Newman
NBC News correspondent Edwin Newman was the host and moderator of this series of four discussions with prominent figures about the contradictions in American life: the gap between the rich and the poverty-stricken, the disparity between the good times experienced by some and the bad times by others, and the recently apparent tension and violence on the political scene. This series did not air on either August 2 or August 9.

WHAT'S IN A WORD (*Quiz/Panel*)
FIRST TELECAST: *July 22, 1954*
LAST TELECAST: *September 9, 1954*
BROADCAST HISTORY:
Jul 1954–Sep 1954, CBS Thu 8:00–8:30
MODERATOR:
Clifton Fadiman
PANELISTS:
Faye Emerson
Audrey Meadows
Jim Moran
Mike Wallace
Contestants on this word-association panel show made up simple two-word rhymes, like Fickle Pickle or Nice Rice, and won money depending on how successful the panel was at guessing what the rhyme was. The moderator provided clues to the noun portion of the rhyme and, to narrow down the possibilities, the panelists tried to make an association that was correct. The contestant won $5 for each clue used before the panel narrowed down and correctly identified the noun. At that point the moderator would give a definition of the adjective. The contestant then won an additional $5 for each wrong guess until the panel identified the adjective to complete the rhyme.

WHAT'S IT ALL ABOUT, WORLD? (*Comedy/Variety*)
FIRST TELECAST: *February 6, 1969*
LAST TELECAST: *May 1, 1969*
BROADCAST HISTORY:
Feb 1969–May 1969, ABC Thu 9:00–10:00
HOST:
Dean Jones
REGULARS:
Dick Clair
Jenna McMahon
Gerri Granger
Alex Dreier
Dennis Allen
Scoey Mitchlll
Ron Prince
Maureen Arthur
Bayn Johnson
Kevin Carlisle Dancers
Denny Vaughn Orchestra
Not exactly a *Laugh-In*, not as bitingly satirical as *That Was the Week That Was*, not as controversial as *The Smothers Brothers Show*, *What's It All About, World?* nevertheless had some elements of each of those programs. It was a satirical revue that made fun of contemporary mores and hallowed institutions in a light, relatively inoffensive way. Comedy routines, fake documentaries, and musical production numbers were included, such as "The Rumor Factory" and "Hollywood Behind the Nixons." Among the regulars were the comedy team of Clair and McMahon, singer Gerri Granger, commentator Alex Dreier, and nine-year-old Bayn Johnson.

The show was produced by Saul Ilson and Ernest Chambers, who were also responsible for *The Smothers Brothers Show* (the Smothers Brothers made a guest appearance here).

WHAT'S IT FOR (*Quiz/Panel*)
FIRST TELECAST: *October 12, 1957*
LAST TELECAST: *January 4, 1958*
BROADCAST HISTORY:
Oct 1957–Jan 1958, NBC Sat 10:00–10:30
EMCEE:
Hal March
PANELISTS:
Betsy Palmer
Hans Conried
Abe Burrows
Toni Gilman (1957)
Lisa Ferraday
Strange inventions with presumably practical uses (an automatic hammock swinger, an umbrella skirt, etc.) were demonstrated each week for the panelists and audience of this program. After the demonstration an offstage announcer would inform the audience what the purpose of the invention was. The panel then had four minutes, one for each panel member, to guess the use of the invention by asking questions of the inventor or the inventor's representative, who had performed the demonstration. If the panel was stumped, the inventor received $100, and if they guessed the function of the invention he received $50. The three original regular panel members were Betsy Palmer, Hans Conried, and Abe Burrows, with a rotating fourth member. Toni Gilman became a fourth regular member in November and Lisa Ferraday replaced Miss Gilman in December.

WHAT'S IT WORTH (*Art Appraisal*)
FIRST TELECAST: *May 21, 1948*
LAST TELECAST: *October 11, 1953*
BROADCAST HISTORY:
May 1948–Jun 1948, CBS Fri 9:00–9:30
Jul 1948–Dec 1948, CBS Fri 8:00–8:30
Dec 1948–Jan 1949, CBS Fri 8:30–9:00
Jan 1949–Mar 1949, CBS Tue 9:30–10:00
Oct 1952, DUM Wed 8:30–9:00
Nov 1952–Sep 1953, DUM Thu 9:00–9:30
Sep 1953–Oct 1953, DUM Sun 6:00–6:30
APPRAISER:
Sigmund Rothschild
EMCEE:
Gil Fates (1948–1949)
Nelson Case (1952–1953)
Bill Wendell (1953)
As the resident authority on *What's It Worth?*, art restorer and copyist Sigmund Rothschild invited viewers to submit objects for appraisal. The objects could be family heirlooms, things discovered buried in attics, pets, or anything else of questionable value.

Aided by visiting appraisers, Mr. Rothschild would establish the value of the object and discuss its discovery or history with its owners. The series left network TV in March 1949 but remained on as a local program in New York for another three months.

A little over a year later, on November 9, 1950, Mr. Rothschild made his first appearance as an occasional visitor to the late afternoon weekday daytime series *The Kate Smith Hour*. He did essentially the same thing he had done on CBS—pointing out the distinguishing characteristics that made objects either valuable or worthless. He left Miss Smith in January 1952 but turned up that fall on DuMont with his own show, *Trash or Treasure*, the same title his feature had used within *The Kate Smith Hour*. The DuMont show utilized Nelson Case as emcee until March 1953, and Bill Wendell thereafter. The title was changed to *Treasure Hunt* (not to be confused with the later quiz show of that name) in April 1953.

WHAT'S MY LINE (*Quiz/Panel*)
FIRST TELECAST: *February 16, 1950*
LAST TELECAST: *September 3, 1967*
BROADCAST HISTORY:
Feb 1950–Mar 1950, CBS Thu 8:00–8:30
Apr 1950–Sep 1950, CBS Wed 9:00–9:30
Oct 1950–Sep 1967, CBS Sun 10:30–11:00
MODERATOR:
John Daly
PANELISTS:
Arlene Francis
Dorothy Kilgallen (1950–1965)
Louis Untermeyer (1950–1951)
Hal Block (1950–1953)
Bennett Cerf (1951–1967)
Steve Allen (1953–1954)
Fred Allen (1954–1956)
PRODUCERS:
Mark Goodson and Bill Todman

What's My Line was the longest-running game show in the history of prime-time network television. It ran for 18 seasons, on alternate weeks from February to September 1950, then every Sunday at 10:30 P.M. for the next 17 years. The format was exceedingly simple. Contestants were asked simple yes-or-no questions by the panel members, who tried to determine what interesting or unusual occupation the contestant had. Each time the contestant could answer no to a question, he got $5, and a total of 10 no's ended the game. The panel was forced to don blindfolds for the "mystery guest," a celebrity who tried to avoid identification by disguising his voice.

That little game, by itself, hardly warranted an 18-year run, when other panel shows of the early 1950s came and went every month. But *What's My Line* was something special, both for the witty and engaging panel, and for a certain élan which few other shows have ever captured. There were no flashy celebrities-of-the-moment or empty-headed pretty faces on this panel; they were obviously very intelligent people all, out to have some genteel fun with an amusing parlor game. Like John Daly with his bow tie and perfect manners, it reeked of urbanity ("That's three down and seven to go. Mr. Cerf?").

The panelists who created this special atmosphere were an elite group. The panel on the initial telecast consisted of Park Avenue psychiatrist Dr. Richard Hoffman, poet and critic Louis Untermeyer, former New Jersey Governor Harold Hoffman, and columnist Dorothy Kilgallen. (Their first contestant: a lissome blond hat-check girl from the Stork Club.) Arlene Francis joined the panel on the second telecast, and Bennett Cerf in March 1951. Kilgallen, Cerf, and Francis were continuing regulars for the next 15 years.

Of the other early panelists, Untermeyer was perhaps the most tragic loss—forced off the show, and off television, by McCarthy Era political blacklisting. Gag writer Hal Block was a panelist for a time, as were acerbic Fred Allen and multi-talented Steve Allen (who, in trying to determine size as quickly as possible within the show's yes-or-no format, conjured up the program's classic question: "Is it bigger than a breadbox?"). After the death of Fred Allen in 1956, the fourth seat on the panel was left permanently open for a different guest panelist each week. Little changed until the mid 1960s. In 1965 Dorothy Kilgallen died suddenly, of an overdose of medication, following her appearance on the November 7 program. A much-publicized talent hunt ensued for a permanent replacement, but in the end her chair was also left open, filled by another guest panelist each week.

Finally in 1967, hoary with age, *What's My Line* left the network, only to surface less than a year later in a considerably less sophisticated and more slapstick syndicated version. Arlene Francis was the only holdover, joined by Soupy Sales as a regular panelist and Wally Bruner as a moderator (replaced by Larry Blyden in 1972). The syndicated version lasted until 1975.

WHAT'S MY NAME, see *Paul Winchell—Jerry Mahoney Show, The*

WHAT'S NEW, see *Gulf Road Show Starring Bob Smith, The*

WHAT'S ON YOUR MIND, see *How Did They Get That Way*

WHAT'S SO FUNNY? (*Comedy*)
FIRST TELECAST: *December 3, 1995*
LAST TELECAST: *December 31, 1995*
BROADCAST HISTORY:
Dec 1995, FOX Sun 9:30–10:00
HOSTS:
Nick Bakay
Julie Hayden
CORRESPONDENT:
Suli McCullough

Each week *What's So Funny?* took an off-center look at amusing things that had occurred during the previous week in movies, television, sports, news, and videos. Hayden did the roundup of funny clips from TV shows airing during the week. McCullough was the show's special correspondent covering the world of computers and video games.

WHAT'S THE STORY? (*Quiz/Panel*)
FIRST TELECAST: *July 25, 1951*
LAST TELECAST: *September 23, 1955*
BROADCAST HISTORY:
Jul 1951–Oct 1951, DUM Wed 9:00–9:30
Oct 1951–Feb 1952, DUM Tue 8:00–8:30

Feb 1952–May 1952, DUM Tue 10:30–11:00
Jun 1952–May 1953, DUM Thu 9:30–10:00
May 1953–Jun 1953, DUM Wed 7:30–8:00
Jun 1953–Sep 1953, DUM Sun 10:00–10:30
Sep 1953–Apr 1954, DUM Thu 9:00–9:30
Apr 1954–Sep 1954, DUM Thu 8:00–8:30
Sep 1954–Feb 1955, DUM Thu 9:00–9:30
Mar 1955–Jun 1955, DUM Wed 8:00–8:30
Jul 1955–Sep 1955, DUM Fri 7:30–8:00

MODERATOR:
Walt Raney (1951)
Walter Kiernan (1951–1953)
Al Capp (1953)
John K. M. McCaffery (1953–1955)

PANELISTS:
Harriet Van Horne (1952–1955)
Robert Sullivan (1952–1953)
Jimmy Cannon (1952–1955)

To this innocuous panel show belongs the unique distinction of being the last surviving entertainment show on the dying DuMont TV network—only a few scattered sports events were continued into 1956. After *What's the Story?* left the air in September 1955, and the remaining boxing matches petered out in 1956, the DuMont network was but a memory.

For four years, however, *What's the Story?* had a reasonably successful career. It consisted of a celebrity panel which attempted to identify important news events from clues provided by the moderator and his helpers. Panelists were generally well-known newspaper columnists, with Harriet Van Horne of the *New York World Telegram*, Robert Sullivan of the New York *Daily News* and Jimmy Cannon of the *Post* the longest-running regulars. Bosley Crowther of the *New York Times* made frequent guest appearances, and John McCaffery's English bulldog, Porthos, was the show's mascot for a time.

WHAT'S YOUR BID (*Auction*)

FIRST TELECAST: *February 14, 1953*
LAST TELECAST: *July 5, 1953*
BROADCAST HISTORY:
Feb 1953–Apr 1953, ABC Sat 7:30–8:00
May 1953–Jul 1953, DUM Sun 10:00–10:30

HOST:
Leonard Rosen (ABC)
Robert Alda (DUM)

ANNOUNCER:
John Reed King (ABC)
Dick Shepard (DUM)

MODEL:
Roslyn Woods (ABC)

What's Your Bid was a switch on the usual TV giveaway in that the studio audience was supposed to bring its own money to the show—and use it to bid on merchandise such as radios, cars, mink coats, home freezers, etc. Bidders at least got their money's worth (if they bid more than an item was worth, something extra was thrown in) and the proceeds all went to charity. A feature of each show was the auctioning of an item brought in by a famous celebrity, and having some special connection with that celebrity. Some straight giveaway segments were also worked in, but this early form of "pay TV" did not catch on and was soon canceled. Leonard Rosen, the first host and auctioneer, was known on the show as "Liberal Bill."

WHEEL OF FORTUNE (*Quiz/Audience Participation*)

FIRST TELECAST: *July 7, 1953*
LAST TELECAST: *September 15, 1953*
BROADCAST HISTORY:
Jul 1953–Sep 1953, CBS Tue 8:30–9:00

HOST:
Todd Russell

All of the contestants on this early series were people who had distinguished themselves as good samaritans or heroes. They were brought on the show and received rewards for their good deeds. After host Todd Russell related their individual stories for the audience, a giant carnival-type wheel was spun to determine the nature of the "reward" that they would receive. A special "lucky" section on the wheel could bring the contestant a $1,000 bonus if he could answer a special jackpot question correctly. This summer series was identical to the daytime version that had premiered the previous October, and ran until Christmas Day 1953.

WHEEL OF FORTUNE (*Quiz*)

BROADCAST HISTORY:
Syndicated and network daytime
30 minutes
Produced: *1983–*
Released: *September 1983*

HOST:
Pat Sajak

ASSISTANT:
Vanna White

This series was a rather straightforward game show in which contestants spun a large wheel to determine whether they could attempt to fill in one letter of a mystery phrase. Depending on where the wheel stopped, they might win a corresponding amount of money (if the letter they guessed was in the phrase); lose control to another contestant; or go "bankrupt," losing all their winnings to date. The first contestant to guess the phrase got to use his or her accumulated money to buy prizes.

Wheel of Fortune premiered in NBC daytime in January 1975, with Chuck Woolery as host, later replaced by Pat Sajak. A syndicated evening version began production in 1983 and it became the most popular syndicated series of the 1980s.

When Pat Sajak's late-night talk show premiered on CBS in January 1989, he left the network (but not the syndicated) version of *Wheel of Fortune.* Rolf Benirschke took over but was, in turn, replaced by Bob Goen when it moved from NBC to CBS that July. Goen stayed with the network daytime version when it moved back to NBC in January 1991 and remained with it until its cancellation that September. Vanna White continued to serve as hostess of both the network and the syndicated versions.

The program was created and produced by Merv Griffin.

WHEELS (*Drama*)

FIRST TELECAST: *April 4, 1979*
LAST TELECAST: *April 18, 1979*
BROADCAST HISTORY:
Apr 1979, NBC Wed 9:00–11:00

CAST:
Adam Trenton .... Rock Hudson

Erica Trenton .... Lee Remick
Greg Trenton .... Howard McGillin
Kirk Trenton .... James Carroll Jordan
Hub Hewitson .... Tim O'Connor
Rusty Horton .... Gerald S. O'Loughlin
Rollie Knight .... Harold Sylvester
Teresa Chapman .... Adele Mara
Lowell Baxter .... Ralph Bellamy
Jody Horton .... Lisa Eilbacher
Smokey Stephenson .... Tony Franciosa
Barbara Lipton .... Blair Brown
Leonard Wingate .... Fred Williamson
Ursula .... Jessica Walter
Newkirk .... Al White

Set in Detroit in the late 1960s, *Wheels* was the story of boardroom intrigue at National Motors, a giant automobile company struggling for its life in a highly competitive industry. The central character was Adam Trenton, Vice President of Product Development, who had put his career on the line by developing and pushing the Hawk, a radically new, sporty model designed to win back the youth market. Opposing him were scheming President Hub Hewitson and conservative Board Chairman Lowell Baxter, Adam's father-in-law. Adam's total commitment to his work put his marriage on the line, as well. His wife, Erica, began an affair with a race driver, his younger son, Greg, ran away from home, and his older son, Kirk, began an affair with Adam's own mistress, Barbara Lipton.

Wheels was based on the best-selling novel by Arthur Hailey. It first aired as a five-part mini-series from May 7–15, 1978, and was highly successful. When it was repeated a year later, however, as part of *NBC Novels for Television*, hardly anyone watched—leading to one of the fastest re-editing jobs ever seen on network television. The repeat was supposed to run for five consecutive weeks, but when the network saw the disastrously low ratings for parts one and two it quickly compressed parts three, four, and five into a single concluding episode. Next week, surprised viewers saw the entire remainder of the novel flash by—and disappear.

WHEN THE WHISTLE BLOWS (*Situation Comedy*)

FIRST TELECAST: *March 14, 1980*
LAST TELECAST: *July 27, 1980*
BROADCAST HISTORY:
Mar 1980–Apr 1980, ABC Fri 8:00–9:00
Jun 1980, ABC Sat 10:00–11:00
Jul 1980, ABC Sun 8:00–9:00
CAST:
Buzz Dillard .... Doug Barr
Randy Hartford .... Philip Brown
Lucy Davis .... Susan Buckner
Martin "Hunk" Kincaid .... Tim Rossovich
Norm Jenkins .... Dolph Sweet
Dottie Jenkins .... Alice Hirson
Ted Hanrahan .... Gary Allen
Bulldog .... Noble Willingham
Darlene Ridgeway .... Sue Ane Langdon

Comedy about a gang of young construction workers out to have a good time, on the job and off. Lucy was the only woman on the crew, and just "one of the guys" at that. Randy was the college graduate; Buzz, the complete extrovert; and Hunk, the resident hulk. Others around the ol' construction site were Norm Jenkins, the older guy whose wife, Dottie, wished he would slow down; Bulldog, another worker; Hanrahan, the foreman; and Darlene, the operator of the gang's favorite hangout.

WHEN THINGS WERE ROTTEN (*Situation Comedy*)

FIRST TELECAST: *September 10, 1975*
LAST TELECAST: *December 24, 1975*
BROADCAST HISTORY:
Sep 1975–Dec 1975, ABC Wed 8:00–8:30
CAST:
Robin Hood .... Dick Gautier
Friar Tuck .... Dick Van Patten
Alan-a-Dale .... Bernie Kopell
Bertram/Renaldo .... Richard Dimitri
The Sheriff of Nottingham .... Henry Polic II
Maid Marian .... Misty Rowe
Little John .... David Sabin
Prince John .... Ron Rifkin
Princess Isabelle .... Jane A. Johnston
CREATOR PRODUCER:
Mel Brooks

Mel Brooks created this wild satire on Robin Hood and His Merry Men of Sherwood Forest in 12th-century England. Instead of the boldly heroic Robin of legend, he was portrayed as a complete nitwit, and his men a band of incompetents who only succeeded because of the even greater incompetence of the evil Prince John and his henchman, the sheriff of Nottingham. Much of the humor in this fast-paced, movie-style comedy was based on non sequiturs and historical anachronisms, such as the episode in which Prince John hired the four fastest woodcutters in the kingdom to chop down the entire Sherwood Forest—to make way for a new housing development for wealthy burghers. In the premiere telecast, the prince lured Robin into a trap by staging an archery contest to determine who was the greatest bowman in the land. Robin, vain as ever, came in disguise to win the title but was seized and thrown into the dungeon. Whereupon his men disguised themselves as a traveling conga band and bongoed their way into the castle to rescue him.

Maid Marian was Robin's sexy but empty-headed love interest.

Critics applauded this series as one of the most inventive of the season, but viewers paid no attention to it and it was soon canceled.

WHERE I LIVE (*Situation Comedy*)

FIRST TELECAST: *March 5, 1993*
LAST TELECAST: *November 20, 1993*
BROADCAST HISTORY:
Mar 1993–May 1993, ABC Fri 9:30–10:00
Aug 1993, ABC Tue 8:30–9:00
Nov 1993, ABC Sat 8:30–9:00
CAST:
Douglas St. Martin (age 17) .... Doug E. Doug
James St. Martin .... Sullivan Walker
Marie St. Martin .... Lorraine Toussaint
Sharon St. Martin (14) .... Yunoka Doyle
Reggie Coltrane .... Flex Alexander
Malcolm .... Shaun Baker
Kwanzie .... Jason Bose Smith
Vonzella .... Alma Yvonne

Easygoing, low-key sitcom about three black teenage

buddies who hung out on a Harlem stoop ("the center of the universe"), jived about sports and girls, and generally tried to figure out what life was all about. Doug was the carefree center of things, a hip kid in dreadlocks who was not as sure of himself as he looked; Reggie the self-styled ladies' man; and Malcolm the impulsive, opportunistic one. Just when their plans got bigger than their hip, oversized threads, in would roll the clouds of reality in the form of stern father James and sensible mom Marie. Meanwhile bookish little sis Sharon kept busy fighting off the advances of pint-sized Lothario Kwanzie.

Where I Live drew praise for its realistic characters and absence of the usual sitcom stereotypes. Despite disappointing ratings during the spring of 1993, fans (including Bill Cosby) persuaded ABC to give it a second chance in the fall. By then good-student Reggie had been accepted to a college and Doug, though no whiz at school, succumbed to family pressures and enrolled in a junior college. Only Malcolm stayed behind, dropping out of school and working as a stock clerk. Buried in a little-viewed Saturday-night time period (after a turkey called *George*), the series expired after just three more episodes.

WHERE WAS I? (*Quiz/Panel*)
FIRST TELECAST: *September 2, 1952*
LAST TELECAST: *October 6, 1953*
BROADCAST HISTORY:
Sep 1952–May 1953, DUM Tue 9:00–9:30
May 1953–Jun 1953, DUM Tue 10:00–10:30
Jul 1953–Oct 1953, DUM Tue 9:30–10:00
EMCEE:
Dan Seymour (1952)
Ken Roberts (1952)
John Reed King (1952–1953)
PANELISTS:
Nancy Guild
Peter Donald
Samuel Grafton (1953)
Virginia Graham (1952)
Bill Cullen (1953)
Barbara Barondess MacLean (1953)
Skitch Henderson (1953)
Mort Greene (1953)

In this picture quiz the panel had to identify a given location from a set of photographs and some verbal clues. The original host, Dan Seymour, lasted less than a month, followed by Ken Roberts for about two months and then John Reed King for the remainder of the run of the show. There was quite a bit of turnover in panelists as well.

WHERE'S HUDDLES (*Cartoon*)
FIRST TELECAST: *July 1, 1970*
LAST TELECAST: *September 9, 1970*
BROADCAST HISTORY:
Jul 1970–Sep 1970, CBS Wed 7:30–8:00
VOICES:
Bubba McCoy .... Mel Blanc
Sports Announcer .... Dick Enberg
Freight Train .... Herb Jeffries
Claude Pertwee .... Paul Lynde
Fumbles .... Don Messick
Ed Huddles .... Cliff Norton
Mad Dog Maloney .... Alan Reed
Marge Huddles .... Jean VanderPyl
Penny McCoy .... Marie Wilson

This animated summer series was the story of two professional football players for the Rhinos, quarterback Ed Huddles and center Bubba McCoy. They were next-door neighbors and best friends, as well as teammates, and their adventures on and off the field were the subjects of the episodes of the show.

Reruns of *Where's Huddles* aired the following summer on CBS' late Sunday afternoon schedule.

WHERE'S RAYMOND?, see *Ray Bolger Show, The*

WHILE YOU WERE OUT (*Instructional*)
BROADCAST HISTORY:
The Learning Channel
60 minutes
Original episodes: *2002–*
Premiered: *July 6, 2002*
HOST:
Anna Bocci (2002)
Teresa Strasser
REGULARS:
Chayse Dacoda, designer
Stephen Saint-Onge, designer
Mayita Dinos, landscape designer
Peter BonSey, garden designer
Leslie Segrete, carpenter
Andrew Dan-Jumbo, carpenter

In this variation on TLC's popular *Trading Spaces* a person conspired to get his or her housemate (usually a wife or husband) out of the house for 48 hours while a designer and two carpenters swooped in and redecorated the housemate's favorite room, garden or backyard space. Meanwhile the housemate was trailed with hidden cameras. When the housemate returned, his or her surprised (and usually delighted) reaction was recorded.

WHIPLASH (*Western*)
BROADCAST HISTORY:
Syndicated only
30 minutes
Produced: *1960–1961* (34 episodes)
Released (U.S.): *1961*
CAST:
Christopher Cobb .... Peter Graves
Dan .... Anthony Wickert

This was an Australian Western. Set in the 1850s, it traced the exploits of American Chris Cobb as he fought gunslingers, robbers, and swindlers to establish Cobb & Co., the first stagecoach line on the continent. Although filmed in Australia, the series did all it could to look American—even the bad guys were émigrés. The locals were mostly reduced to lines like, "You're an American—you're the only one who can stop them." Cobb, at least, showed some sensitivity to local feelings by using bullwhips and boomerangs to corral the villains.

WHIRLYBIRDS, THE (*Adventure*)
BROADCAST HISTORY:
Syndicated only
30 minutes
Produced: *1956–1959* (111 episodes)
Released: *January 1957*
CAST:
Chuck Martin .... Ken Tobey

Pete ("P.T.") Moore .... Craig Hill
Janet Culver (1956–1957)........... Sandra Spence
Helen Carter (1957–1959)............. Nancy Hale

Helicopters were substituted for horses in this contemporary Western. Chuck and P.T. were pilot partners in an outfit called Whirlybirds, Inc., located in Southern California. They hired out for all sorts of jobs, such as locating lost prospectors, delivering vital supplies, and even chasing a bad guy or two. There were plenty of stunt scenes, where one of the heroes would dangle from the end of a rope to pluck a client out of danger, or even leap from the chopper onto the back of a villain galloping away on horseback. Janet Culver was their original pretty secretary, replaced after the first season by Helen Carter.

The series was originally made to run on the CBS network, but instead was put into syndication by CBS Films. It became a substantial hit with the younger set.

WHISPERING SMITH (*Western/Detective*)

FIRST TELECAST: *May 15, 1961*
LAST TELECAST: *September 18, 1961*
BROADCAST HISTORY:
May 1961–Sep 1961, NBC Mon 9:00–9:30
CAST:
Det. Tom "Whispering" Smith ...... Audie Murphy
Det. George Romack .... Guy Mitchell
Chief John Richards .... Sam Buffington

Set in Denver, Colorado, in the 1870s, *Whispering Smith* was based on the adventures of the first police detective to bring modern methods of analysis, tracing technique, and apprehension to the practice of law enforcement in the West. Denver police detective Tom Smith, better known by his nickname "Whispering," was this pioneer Western criminologist. His partner and sidekick, George Romack, was played by singer-turned-actor Guy Mitchell. Sam Buffington, who played the chief of the Denver Police Department, died during the filming of the series and was seen in only a portion of the episodes. Actual cases from the files of the Denver Police Department provided the cases depicted in *Whispering Smith*.

This series was originally scheduled for the 1959–1960 fall season but, after costar Guy Mitchell suffered a broken shoulder with only seven episodes completed, it was temporarily postponed. Based rather loosely on the 1948 Alan Ladd film of the same name.

WHITE CAMELLIA, THE, see *ABC Dramatic Shorts—1952–1953*

WHITE SHADOW, THE (*Drama*)

FIRST TELECAST: *November 27, 1978*
LAST TELECAST: *August 12, 1981*
BROADCAST HISTORY:
Nov 1978–Jan 1979, CBS Mon 8:00–9:00
Jan 1979–Feb 1979, CBS Sat 8:00–9:00
Mar 1979–Dec 1979, CBS Mon 8:00–9:00
Dec 1979–Sep 1980, CBS Tue 8:00–9:00
Dec 1980–Jan 1981, CBS Tue 8:00–9:00
Feb 1981–Mar 1981, CBS Mon 8:00–9:00
Jun 1981–Aug 1981, CBS Wed 8:00–9:00
CAST:
Ken Reeves........................... Ken Howard
Jim Willis (first episode)............. Jason Bernard
Jim Willis (1978–1980)................ Ed Bernard
Sybil Buchanan .... Joan Pringle
James Hayward (1978–1980) .... Thomas Carter
Morris Thorpe .... Kevin Hooks
Curtis Jackson (1978–1980)......... Eric Kilpatrick
Milton Reese (1978–1980)............ Nathan Cook
Mario Pettrino (Salami)........ Timothy Van Patten
Abner Goldstein (1978–1980) ..... Ken Michelman
Ricky Gomez (1978–1980) .... Ira Angustain
Warren Coolidge.................. Byron Stewart
Katie Donahue (1978–1979)............ Robin Rose
Bill Donahue (1978–1979).............. Jerry Fogel
Nick Vitaglia (1979–1981)........... John Mengatti
Manager Phil Jefferson (1979–1981)
.... Russell Phillip Robinson
Wardell Stone (1980–1981) .... Larry Flash Jenkins
Jesse B. Mitchell (1980–1981)....... Stoney Jackson
Teddy Rutherford (1980–1981) .... Wolfe Perry
Eddie Franklin (1980–1981) .... Art Holliday
Paddy Falahey (1980–1981)......... John Laughlin

After a succession of knee problems forced Ken Reeves to retire from his job as a forward on the Chicago Bulls professional basketball team, his college friend Jim Willis convinced him to take a shot at being the basketball coach of Carver High in Los Angeles. Carver was in a tough inner-city, lower-middle-class neighborhood, with a racially mixed student body and team. It was a hard job, especially for someone unfamiliar with street-wise kids and coaching them in a game he knew best as a player. Ken could have earned more doing something else, as his sister Katie kept reminding him, but he found greater satisfaction working with these teenagers. Ken's old friend Jim was Carver's principal, and Sybil Buchanan was the vice principal (who became principal in the fall of 1980).

The White Shadow was more than just a basketball show, it was also the story of young people and their adjustments to life in an often hostile world. Within the framework of a high school basketball team were stories of personal conflict, drug problems, teenage crime, and the dangers in a tough area. In fact, in the spring of 1980 one of Ken's players, Curtis Jackson, was shot to death while witnessing a liquor-store holdup. Students moved on, as in real life. In the spring of 1980, after the team had won the Los Angeles City Basketball Championship, several players graduated from Carver and were replaced by new players in the fall. The series treated its subjects realistically and sympathetically, and was lauded by numerous educational organizations, although its audience size remained marginal throughout its run.

WHIZ KIDS (*Detective/Adventure*)

FIRST TELECAST: *October 5, 1983*
LAST TELECAST: *June 2, 1984*
BROADCAST HISTORY:
Oct 1983–Dec 1983, CBS Wed 8:00–9:00
Jan 1984–Jun 1984, CBS Sat 8:00–9:00
CAST:
Richie Adler .... Matthew Laborteaux
Hamilton Parker .... Todd Porter
Jeremy Saldino .... Jeffrey Jacquet
Llewellen Farley, Jr. .... Max Gail
Alice Tyler .... Andrea Elson
Cheryl Adler......................... Melanie Gaffin
Lt. Neal Quinn .... A Martinez
Irene Adler .... Madelyn Cain

Ms. Vance .... Linda Scruggs
Carson Marsh (1984) .... Dan O'Herlihy

If you were going to do a show about kids and computers, what better place than California, home of Silicon Valley, high-tech, and trend setters? It was there, in the suburban Los Angeles community of Calabasas, that the *Whiz Kids* lived. Richie was the bright computer "hacker" who, with the aid of Ham, Jeremy, and Alice, his buddies and schoolmates at Canyon High School, worked as an amateur detective in his spare time. Farley was their friend and information source, a reporter with the *Los Angeles Gazette* who sometimes asked them for help on stories he was working on and at other times got involved with cases on which they were already working. Farley's brother-in-law Neal Quinn, who ran the police department's MDT's (Mobile Data Terminals), also provided Farley and the kids with some help, albeit grudgingly, when they needed access to police computer information.

The real star of the show, however, may have been Richie's talking computer, Ralf. With Richie's expert programming, Ralf provided clues, graphic images, answers to problems, and access to other computer information banks that were supposedly protected against unauthorized use. Everyone in Richie's home got involved with technological toys and services. His little sister, Cheryl, had a small robot (instead of a doll) named Herman, and his divorced mother, Irene, had been enrolled (by Richie) in a computer dating service. At midseason the mysterious Carson Marsh was added to the cast, an elderly gentleman who, as head of the Athena Society, had contacts and access to data that not even Richie or the police could get to. Occasionally, when the kids got in over their heads, Carson helped bail them out.

WHO IN THE WORLD (*Interview*)

FIRST TELECAST: *June 24, 1962*
LAST TELECAST: *September 16, 1962*
BROADCAST HISTORY:
Jun 1962–Sep 1962, CBS Sun 9:30–10:00
HOST:
Warren Hull

Each week host Warren Hull interviewed three to five people who had made headlines in the nation's newspapers during the previous seven days. At least that was the original idea behind the show. A shortage of available headline-makers forced the area from which guests were drawn to be broadened to include people who had human-interest stories to tell. The program's producer found the world's first airline stewardess and the 1,000th member of the Peace Corps, among others, for Warren Hull to chat with.

WHO PAYS (*Quiz/Panel*)

FIRST TELECAST: *July 2, 1959*
LAST TELECAST: *September 24, 1959*
BROADCAST HISTORY:
Jul 1959–Sep 1959, NBC Thu 8:00–8:30
EMCEE:
Mike Wallace
PANELISTS:
Gene Klavan
Cedric Hardwicke
Celeste Holm

The object of *Who Pays* was for the three regular panelists to determine which celebrity or public figure was the employer of each pair of contestants. The employees were questioned by the panelists in two rounds. The first round gave each panelist one minute to ask specific questions of the two employees (who were chauffeurs, doctors, gardeners, hair stylists, etc.). At the end of the round the panelists pooled their information and decided whether or not to guess the identity of the employer. If they guessed correctly, the employees split $100 and if they guessed incorrectly the employees split $200. If the panelists felt they had too little information to hazard a guess, a second round was played with the dollar value to the employees doubling.

WHO SAID THAT? (*Quiz/Panel*)

FIRST TELECAST: *December 9, 1948*
LAST TELECAST: *July 26, 1955*
BROADCAST HISTORY:
Dec 1948–Jan 1949, NBC Mon 10:00–10:30
Jan 1949–Mar 1949, NBC Sun 10:30–11:00
Apr 1949–Dec 1949, NBC Sat 9:00–9:30
Jan 1950–Jul 1954, NBC Mon 10:30–11:00
Feb 1955–Apr 1955, ABC Wed 9:00–9:30
May 1955–Jul 1955, ABC Tue 8:30–9:00
EMCEE:
Robert Trout (1948–1951)
Walter Kiernan (1951–1954)
John Daly (1955)
PANELISTS:
John Cameron Swayze (1948–1951)
Bill Henry (1952–1953)
June Lockhart (1952–1955)
Morey Amsterdam (1954)
H. V. Kaltenborn (1954)
Bob Considine (1955)
John Mason Brown (1955)

Live quiz show based on quotations from the news. A panel of newsmen and celebrities was read a quotation from the current headlines, and then asked to identify "who said that," and something about the circumstances. Failure to come up with the correct answer resulted in forfeiture of cash to the prize jackpot, which at one time was represented by a goldfish bowl into which panel members stuffed bills. The jackpot was awarded to a home viewer if the quote had been sent in by one, or to a charity. Variations such as a famous guest who, seen only in silhouette, personally delivered his own quote, famous quotes from the past, and partial quotes which had to be completed were also introduced from time to time. During most of the show's run there was only a single permanent panelist (or "anchorman"), plus guests, but toward the end several permanent panelists were used. Among the panelists appearing irregularly, but frequently, were Frank Coniff, Earl Wilson, Al Capp, Quentin Reynolds, Bennett Cerf, Oscar Levant, and Kitty Carlisle.

The program was originally edited by Fred Friendly, and was also heard on radio for a time.

WHO WANTS TO BE A MILLIONAIRE? (*Quiz*)

FIRST TELECAST: *January 8, 2000*
LAST TELECAST: *June 27, 2002*
BROADCAST HISTORY:
Jan 2000, ABC Sat 8:00–9:00
Jan 2000–Sep 2001, ABC Sun 9:00–10:00
Jan 2000–Dec 2000, ABC Tue 8:00–9:00

Jan 2000–Jun 2002, ABC Thu 9:00–10:00
May 2000–Jun 2000, ABC Wed 8:00–9:00
Sep 2000–Mar 2001, ABC Wed 8:00–9:00
Jan 2001, ABC Fri 8:00–8:30
Feb 2001–Sep 2001, ABC Fri 9:00–10:00
Mar 2001–Sep 2001, ABC Tue 8:00–9:00
May 2001, ABC Wed 10:00–11:00
Sep 2001–Feb 2002, ABC Mon 8:00–9:00
(New episodes in first-run syndication beginning September 2002)

EMCEE:
Regis Philbin

Who Wants to Be a Millionaire? was one of those shooting stars that occasionally flashes across the TV firmament, an enormous hit that had all of America talking, then disappeared almost as quickly as it had begun. But what a hit it was. The premise was basically a big-money quiz show with some ingenious and dramatic trappings. Anybody could try out for the show by calling a 900 number and taking a short quiz; those who did best competed in a second telephone quiz, and the winners of that were invited to New York to appear on the show.

The show was set in a cavernous studio-in-the-round, with strobes, ominous music, and gregarious host Regis Philbin on a raised platform in the center, usually dressed in black. He began with ten contestants who competed to be the first to punch in the answer to a question. The winner came up on stage and sat opposite Regis, each of them facing a television monitor, in a kind of high-tech inquisition, with music (and pulses) pounding. There were 15 multiple-choice questions of increasing difficulty, the first worth $100, then continuously doubling, more or less, to the fifteenth, which was worth $1 million. Contestants could stop at any time and leave with their winnings, which were locked in at levels five ($1,000) and ten ($32,000). If stumped they could use three "Lifelines" allowed during the course of the game. The first, "50/50," eliminated two of the four multiple-choice answers; the second polled the audience to see what *they* thought the correct answer was; and the third was a phone call to a person of the contestant's choosing, to get advice. Except for the first few, the questions were not particularly easy—for example, "What's a mackintosh?" or "Where did Ted Kaczynski teach?"

Regis presided with panache, allowing contestants to ponder as long as they wanted (the overly long ones were edited down for broadcast). His habitual response when the contestant finally spoke up—"Is that your final answer?"—became a catchphrase.

The show was first telecast as a special event on August 16, 1999, with episodes telecast most nights for the next two weeks. It was such an enormous hit that ABC rushed more episodes into production, which aired November 7–20, 1999. It then launched as a regular series in January, airing on as many as five nights a week. Many, in fact, thought that massive overexposure by ratings-starved ABC is what ultimately killed the show. There were periodic celebrity editions, and other variations, but the basic game remained the same. Most contestants bailed out, or flunked out, well short of the $1 million, but as early as November 1999 an IRS officer (!) won the top prize. Later a bonus pool was established, raising the potential grand prize to over $2 million.

A syndicated version of the show, hosted by Meredith Vieira, premiered in September 2002. Adapted from the British hit of the same name.

WHODUNNIT? (*Quiz/Audience Participation*)

FIRST TELECAST: *April 12, 1979*
LAST TELECAST: *May 17, 1979*
BROADCAST HISTORY:
Apr 1979, NBC Thu 8:00–8:30
May 1979, NBC Thu 8:30–9:00

EMCEE:
Ed McMahon

REGULAR PANELISTS:
F. Lee Bailey
Melvin Belli

This odd program was a hybrid of drama and quiz show. Each week three contestants and a panel of three experts watched a dramatization of a murder mystery. The action stopped just before the villain was revealed, and the object was for the contestants to match wits with the experts in determining "whodunnit." Clues were provided, some relevant and some not, and the "suspects" were interrogated by a law-enforcement officer. The panel also cross-examined the suspects, but if any contestant could guess the actual murderer before they did he won $10,000. The panel then offered their opinion of who the actual murderer was. With all this information, the contestants made their choices; if they were right, and the panel was wrong, they won $5,000. If they and the panel both nailed the right suspect, they got $2,500.

Ed McMahon hosted the show, and celebrity attorneys F. Lee Bailey and Melvin Belli were the most frequent panelists. An added feature was the appearance of famous guest stars such as Jack Klugman, Erik Estrada, and Loni Anderson as the murder victims.

Although NBC billed this as television's first mystery game show, the format, and variations on it, were in fact rather popular in the very early days of TV: see *Stand By for Crime* (1949), *Chicagoland Mystery Players* (1949), and *Crawford Mystery Theatre* (1951), among others.

WHOLE NEW BALLGAME, A (*Situation Comedy*)

FIRST TELECAST: *January 9, 1995*
LAST TELECAST: *March 13, 1995*
BROADCAST HISTORY:
Jan 1995–Mar 1995, ABC Mon 8:30–9:00

CAST:
Brett Sooner .... Corbin Bernsen
Meg O'Donnell .... Julia Campbell
Dwight Kling .... Richard Kind
Dr. Warner Brakefield .... Stephen Tobolowsky
Libby Desoto .... Kari Coleman
Tad Sherman .... John O'Hurley
Mickey .... Shashawnee Hall
Pat .... Pat Millicano

Stereotype-laden sitcom modeled on *WKRP in Cincinnati* and *The Mary Tyler Moore Show.* Brett Sooner was an egotistical baseball star sidelined by the Great Baseball Strike of 1994 who was hired by the owner of Milwaukee TV station WPLP as its celebrity sportscaster. A true male sexist pig, he immediately clashed with liberated station manager Meg; unfortunately for her, his sloppy, unconventional on-air style was a hit with viewers, so she was stuck with him. Though they squabbled, there was an undeniable attraction between them. Looking on was the usual cast of broadcasting loonies: crass sales manager Dwight, dopey weatherman Warner, pompous anchorman Ted (er, Tad—we must have been thinking of Ted Baxter), and zealous secretary Libby, who mooned over handsome Brett. Mickey ran the sports bar where Brett hung out when he wasn't sparring with Meg.

WHOOPI GOLDBERG SHOW, THE (*Talk*)

BROADCAST HISTORY:

Syndicated only
30 minutes
Produced: *1992–1993* (200 episodes)
Released: *September 1992*

HOSTESS:

Whoopi Goldberg

Each weeknight actress/comedienne Whoopi Goldberg and her guest sat across from each other in overstuffed chairs chatting informally. Most of the people who appeared were show business celebrities—Elizabeth Taylor, Ted Danson, Elton John, Robin Williams, Burt Reynolds, and Billy Crystal appeared in the first two weeks—but there were others. Among them were vice presidential candidate Al Gore, baseball player Bo Jackson, former California governor Edmund G. Brown, Jr., former San Francisco mayor Dianne Feinstein, political activist the Reverend Al Sharpton, and boxer Evander Holyfield. Whoopi's questions were decidedly nonthreatening, and the mood was rather low-key.

WHO'S THE BOSS? (*Quiz/Panel*)

FIRST TELECAST: *February 19, 1954*
LAST TELECAST: *August 20, 1954*

BROADCAST HISTORY:

Feb 1954–Jun 1954, ABC Fri 9:30–10:00
Jul 1954–Aug 1954, ABC Fri 8:30–9:00

EMCEE:

Walter Kiernan (Feb–Jul)
Mike Wallace (Jul–Aug)

PANELISTS:

Peggy McKay
Dick Kollmar
Sylvia Lyons
Horace Sutton

Secretaries to famous personalities from the worlds of show business, politics, and sports were the guests on this show. The panel attempted to identify the names of their bosses through indirect questioning, with prizes being awarded after each round that the secretary continued to stump the panel.

WHO'S THE BOSS? (*Situation Comedy*)

FIRST TELECAST: *September 20, 1984*
LAST TELECAST: *September 10, 1992*

BROADCAST HISTORY:

Sep 1984, ABC Thu 8:30–9:00
Oct 1984–Apr 1985, ABC Tue 8:30–9:30
Apr 1985–Jul 1985, ABC Tue 9:00–9:30
Aug 1985–Aug 1991, ABC Tue 8:00–8:30
Aug 1991–Sep 1991, ABC Tue 8:30–9:00
Sep 1991–Jan 1992, ABC Sat 8:00–8:30
Feb 1992–Mar 1992, ABC Sat 8:30–9:00
Mar 1992–Jun 1992, ABC Sat 8:00–8:30
Jun 1992–Jul 1992, ABC Wed 9:30–10:00
Jul 1992–Sep 1992, ABC Thu 8:00–8:30

CAST:

Angela Bower .... Judith Light
Tony Micelli .... Tony Danza
Samantha Micelli .... Alyssa Milano
Jonathan Bower .... Danny Pintauro
Mona Robinson .... Katherine Helmond
**Geoffrey Wells (1986–1987)* .... Robin Thomas
**Bonnie (1986–1991)* .... Shana Lane-Block
**Jesse Nash (1987–1988)* .... Scott Bloom
**Mrs. Rossini* .... Rhoda Gemignani
Billy (age 5)(1990–1991) .... Jonathan Halyalkar
**Kathleen Sawyer (1990)* .... Kate Vernon
**Andy (1990)* .... Doug Ballard
Hank Thomopolous (1992)
.... Curnal Achilles Aulisio

*Occasional

THEME:

"Brand New Life," by Larry Carlton, Robert Kraft, Martin Cohan, and Blake Hunter

1984 was the year of male role reversal on television. That fall, both *Who's the Boss?* and *Charles in Charge* featured macho guys working as domestics for women who didn't have time to raise the kids. Tony was a former second baseman for the St. Louis Cardinals and a widower with a kid of his own, young Samantha. Fed up with the congestion and bustle of New York City, he sought refuge working as a domestic for Angela Bower, the high-powered but somewhat disorganized President of the Wallace and McQuade Advertising Agency, who lived in suburban Connecticut. Angela, a divorcée with a rambunctious young son named Jonathan, had doubts about the arrangement, but her mother, Mona, quickly observed that "a man can do meaningless, unproductive work as well as a woman." Tony proved to be very good at his new job, bringing order to Angela's chaotic household and providing a needed father figure to Jonathan.

Angela, who worried constantly about her career, was abruptly fired in 1986, whereupon she opened her own ad agency, with Mona pitching in. At about the same time romance entered her life in the person of handsome Geoffrey Wells—which served to bring into focus her growing fondness for Tony. However, for the time being, at least, they would not become an "item." Also in 1986, Samantha entered high school where, a year later, she found a boyfriend in Jesse. Not to be left out Mona was courted, off and on, by mature, dashing Max Muldoon (Leslie Nielsen).

Inspired by Angela's upscale lifestyle, Tony began taking college courses, and when Sam graduated from high school she enrolled at the same college. Among her boyfriends were Andy and Eric (the latter seemingly played by a different actor each time he appeared); Jonathan, meanwhile, entered high school. Things weren't as uproarious without a little kid in the house—and in the plots—so the writers introduced Billy, a five-year-old from Tony's Brooklyn neighborhood who was taken in for a season. Tony maintained his ties with Brooklyn, where his pal Al (William Gallo) and "second mom" Mrs. Rossini were his chief contacts. The family dog was Grover.

The running theme of *Who's the Boss?* was Tony and Angela's evolving relationship, which must have been one of the longest courtships in sitcom history. For the first few seasons it was easy banter and no more. Whenever they started to get close, they would call a halt and start seeing others (among Tony's more frequent dates was Kathleen). By 1991, seven years after they met, the uptown lady and Brooklyn mug admitted they were in love. Sam and her boyfriend Hank got married during the last season, and Tony and Angela had several close calls. In the spring when Tony got a job as baseball coach for a small college in Iowa Angela tried living with him there (she missed her job) and then having a long distance relationship (it didn't work). At the end of the last episode, having given up hope and in the market for a new housekeeper, Angela answered the door to find Tony, who had decided their relationship was more important than his coaching career, applying for the job. They still weren't married but they were going to give it another try.

ABC aired reruns of *Who's the Boss?* on weekday mornings from June 1987 to July 1988.

WHO'S THERE (*Quiz/Audience Participation*)

FIRST TELECAST: *July 14, 1952*
LAST TELECAST: *September 15, 1952*
BROADCAST HISTORY:
Jul 1952–Sep 1952, CBS Mon 9:30–10:00
EMCEE:
Arlene Francis
PANELISTS:
Bill Cullen
Robert Coote
Roger Price

The panelists on *Who's There* tried to identify famous celebrities from various articles of clothing or props that had been characteristic of, or identified with, the celebrities. There were two regular panelists—originally Bill Cullen and Robert Coote—and one guest panelist. Cullen was replaced in midsummer by Roger Price.

WHO'S WATCHING THE KIDS (*Situation Comedy*)

FIRST TELECAST: *September 22, 1978*
LAST TELECAST: *December 15, 1978*
BROADCAST HISTORY:
Sep 1978–Dec 1978, NBC Fri 8:30–9:00
CAST:
Stacy Turner .... Caren Kaye
Angie Vitola .... Lynda Goodfriend
Frankie "the Fox" Vitola .... Scott Baio
Melissa Turner .... Tammy Lauren
Mitzi Logan .... Marcia Lewis
Larry Parnell .... Larry Breeding
Memphis O'Hara .... Lorrie Mahaffey
Bert Gunkel .... Jim Belushi
Venus .... Shirley Kirkes
Bridget .... Elaine Bolton

The kids in this comedy were 15-year-old Frankie and 9-year-old Melissa, two hyperactive and worldly-wise youngsters who lived with their showgirl older sisters in a Las Vegas apartment. Angie and Stacy spent much of their time performing at a third-rate local nightspot, the Club Sand Pile, so help was enlisted from neighbor Larry Parnell to "watch the kids." Macho, street-wise Frankie and bookish, know-it-all Melissa were more than a match for all three adults. Larry was a reporter whose ambition was to become a hard-hitting investigative journalist, but so far he had made it only to reading the weather and garden news on a local TV station. Mitzi was the rotund emcee at the Club Sand Pile, and also the girls' landlady; Memphis was a singer at the club.

The pilot for this comedy, which had a slightly different story line, aired on May 19, 1978, under the title *Legs*.

WHO'S WHO (*Newsmagazine*)

FIRST TELECAST: *January 4, 1977*
LAST TELECAST: *June 26, 1977*
BROADCAST HISTORY:
Jan 1977–May 1977, CBS Tue 8:00–9:00
Jun 1977, CBS Sun 10:00–11:00
REPORTERS:
Dan Rather
Barbara Howar
Charles Kuralt

If *60 Minutes* was the television equivalent of *Time* magazine, this series, produced by the same team, was patterned after *People* magazine. Although *60 Minutes* often did profiles on individuals, it also included in-depth studies of broader issues. *Who's Who* concentrated only on people. Dan Rather and Barbara Howar did pieces on the famous—Richard Burton, Leopold Stokowski, Lily Tomlin, Jodie Foster, Jack Nicklaus, UN Ambassador Andrew Young, and First Lady Rosalynn Carter. Charles Kuralt focused on more obscure subjects. His "On the Road" segment included chats with an 89-year-old kite flyer in Farmland, Indiana; a champion boomerang thrower living on an island in the Gulf of Mexico; a nightclub owner in Vicksburg, Mississippi, who had booked top black jazz performers into his place in the 1930s and 1940s; and the inventor of the supermarket shopping cart, in Oklahoma City.

WHO'S WHOSE (*Quiz/Audience Participation*)

FIRST TELECAST: *June 25, 1951*
LAST TELECAST: *June 25, 1951*
BROADCAST HISTORY:
Jun 1951, CBS Mon 9:30–10:00
EMCEE:
Phil Baker
PANELISTS:
Robin Chandler
Art Ford
Basil Davenport
Emily Kimbrough

The object of this summer show was for the celebrity panel (three regulars and one guest) to guess which of three people was the spouse of a fourth contestant. The panelists had an opportunity to question all four people, three of one sex and the fourth of the other, in the attempt to determine who was whose. Since the show only lasted one week, it obviously did not work too well.

WHOSE LINE IS IT ANYWAY? (*Comedy Quiz*)

FIRST TELECAST: *August 5, 1998*
LAST TELECAST:
BROADCAST HISTORY:
Aug 1998–Sep 1998, ABC Wed 9:30–10:00
Dec 1998–Mar 1999, ABC Wed 9:30–10:00
Jun 1999–Aug 1999, ABC Wed 9:30–10:00
Aug 1999–Jun 2002, ABC Thu 8:00–9:00
Apr 2001, ABC Wed 8:30–9:00
Oct 2001–Dec 2001, ABC Wed 9:30–10:00
Jul 2002–Aug 2002, ABC Fri 9:00–10:00
Sep 2002–Oct 2002, ABC Mon 8:30–9:00
Nov 2002–Dec 2002, ABC Fri 9:30–10:00

Dec 2002–Jan 2003, ABC Fri 9:00–9:30
Mar 2003–May 2003, ABC Thu 8:00–9:00
Jun 2003– , ABC Fri 9:00–10:00

MODERATOR:

Drew Carey

REGULARS:

Ryan Stiles
Colin Mochrie
Wayne Brady
*Greg Proops
*Brad Sherwood
*Chip Esten
*Kathy Greenwood
Laura Hall, musical accompaniment

*Occasional

This improvisational comedy show began as a summer time filler, but proved popular enough to be added to the regular ABC schedule the following winter. It consisted of four comics on a bare stage, improvising sketches and impressions based on lines given to them by the moderator, and sometimes suggested by the audience. It sounds easy, but how do you improvise a video dating service, a song about accountants, or a foal being born? The sketches were usually short, very physical, and sometimes risque. A rotating cast of comics was used, the most frequently seen being tall, gawky Stiles, goofy, balding Mochrie, ingenious black comic Brady, and stuffy Proops. Presiding over the mayhem was loosey-goosey host Drew Carey, who awarded points and declared winners "purely arbitrarily," which didn't matter much since there were no prizes.

The producers called this unscripted show "comedy without a net," although each half hour was actually distilled from taping sessions that ran as long as two hours. Nevertheless it was highly unusual for American television. The show was based on the British series of the same name, which began in 1988 and on which Stiles, Mochrie, Brady, Proops, and Sherwood sometimes appeared. The British series aired in the U.S. on Comedy Central and its predecessor Ha! from 1990 to 1997.

WHY? (*Quiz/Panel*)

FIRST TELECAST: *January 12, 1953*
LAST TELECAST: *April 20, 1953*
BROADCAST HISTORY:

Jan 1953–Apr 1953, ABC Mon 10:00–10:30

EMCEE:

John Reed King

ASSISTANT:

Bill Cullen

In this quiz show based on the old "five W's," Bill Cullen read the panel the who, what, where, and when of a situation. The panel then had to guess the "why." The three members of each night's panel were drawn from all walks of life.

WICHITA TOWN (*Western*)

FIRST TELECAST: *September 30, 1959*
LAST TELECAST: *September 23, 1960*
BROADCAST HISTORY:

Sep 1959–Apr 1960, NBC Wed 10:30–11:00
Jun 1960–Sep 1960, NBC Fri 8:30–9:00

CAST:

Marshal Mike Dunbar .... Joel McCrea
Ben Matheson .... Jody McCrea
Rico Rodriguez .... Carlos Romero
Dr. Nat Wyndham .... George Neise
Aeneas MacLinahan .... Bob Anderson
Joe Kingston .... Robert Foulk

In the decade following the Civil War the town of Wichita, on the fringes of the lawless Western frontier in the Kansas Territory, was a young city trying to grow and prosper. The town's leading citizen was Mike Dunbar, a man who had led a cattle drive to Wichita and decided to stay on as marshal to help establish law and order in the community. Dunbar was aided by his two deputies, Ben Matheson and Rico Rodriguez, the former a foreman at the nearby Circle J Ranch, and the latter a reformed Mexican gunfighter. Also seen regularly in the series were Dr. Nat Wyndham, Wichita's first doctor, Aeneas MacLinahan, the town blacksmith, and Joe Kingston, the bartender in the local saloon.

Joel and Jody McCrea, who played marshal and deputy in this Western, were in real life father and son.

Wichita Town was based on the 1955 film in which McCrea had played Wyatt Earp.

WIDE COUNTRY, THE (*Western*)

FIRST TELECAST: *September 20, 1962*
LAST TELECAST: *September 12, 1963*
BROADCAST HISTORY:

Sep 1962–Sep 1963, NBC Thu 7:30–8:30

CAST:

Mitch Guthrie .... Earl Holliman
Andy Guthrie .... Andrew Prine

Western drama revolving around champion bronco rider Mitch Guthrie, as he encountered the adventures of contemporary rodeo life, while trying to persuade his kid brother Andy not to become a "rodeo bum" like himself.

WIDOWS (*Drama*)

FIRST TELECAST: *August 6, 2002*
LAST TELECAST: *August 27, 2002*
BROADCAST HISTORY:

Aug 2002, ABC Tue 10:00–11:00

CAST:

Dolly Rawlins .... Mercedes Ruehl
Shirley Heller .... Brooke Shields
Linda Pirelli .... Rosie Perez
Bella .... N'Bushe Wright
Harry Rawlins .... Nigel Bennett
Jimmy Rawlins .... Michael Rhoades
Lt. Maynard .... Jay O. Sanders
Mike Resnick .... Aidan Devine
Sara Sellick .... Jenna Stern
Sgt. Hodges .... Jonathan Higgins
Det. Dexter .... Kedar Brown
Audrey .... Jayne Eastwood
Arnold Stein .... Colm Feore
Rudi Sellick .... Rod Wilson
Terry Heller .... Bobby Johnston
Joe Pirelli .... Roman Rodhora

Widows was a miniseries, telecast over four consecutive weeks and thus qualifying for this book. The convoluted plot involved three widows from very different backgrounds who shared a common bond: their husbands had been killed by unknown parties as they were attempting a major heist at Boston's Stein Art Gallery. Dolly was the upper-middle-class ringleader, determined to find out who was behind the killings, and finish the heist; Shirley a rather innocent aspiring actress; and Linda a wisecracking blue-collar type who worked at a used-car dealership. Joining them was Bella, an exotic dancer whose missing boyfriend may also have been involved in the caper. As they tracked down clues and planned their own heist, they encountered Lt. Maynard, who was suspicious of them, Det. Resnick, who seemed to have been involved in the crime, and rich, arrogant gallery owner Stein, who may have been behind it all, in a elaborate scheme to switch paintings. In the conclusion Resnick, the dirty cop who set their husbands up, was killed by Dolly's crooked husband Harry (who was not dead after all); Harry was then killed by his girlfriend Sara, whom he had planned to dump, and Dolly found the real painting they had all been after. She turned it in for a $20 million reward, which she split with the other widows.

Based on the 1983 British miniseries of the same name.

WIFE SAVER, THE (*Household Hints*)
FIRST TELECAST: *May 22, 1947*
LAST TELECAST: *June 26, 1947*
BROADCAST HISTORY:
May 1947–Jun 1947, NBC Thu 8:30–9:00
HOST:
Allen Prescott

Longtime radio favorite Allen Prescott tried his popular *Wife Saver* routine (first heard in 1932) on television in 1947. The format consisted of Prescott in the kitchen demonstrating household gadgets and explaining ways of solving problems around the house, such as keeping twine untangled or bureau drawers unstuck, all interspersed with a steady patter of gags. The humor plus the useful hints should have made this a popular show, but it lasted only six weeks.

WILD & CRAZY KIDS (*Sports/Audience Participation*)
BROADCAST HISTORY:
Nickelodeon
30 minutes
Produced: *1990–1992* (65 episodes)
Premiered: *July 4, 1990*
HOST:
Omar Gooding
Donnie Jeffcoat
Annette Chavez (1990–1991)
Jessica Gaynes (1991–1992)

Physical competition in unusual settings was the theme of this early-evening series on Nick. Teams of well-padded kids competed in fast-paced games using go-carts, bumper boats, tennis guns, and slime slides; sometimes the youthful hosts joined in as well.

WILD BILL HICKOK, see *Adventures of Wild Bill Hickok, The*

WILD KINGDOM (*Wildlife/Nature*)
FIRST TELECAST: *January 7, 1968*
LAST TELECAST: *April 11, 1971*
BROADCAST HISTORY:
Jan 1968–Jun 1968, NBC Sun 7:00–7:30
Jan 1969–Jun 1969, NBC Sun 7:00–7:30
Sep 1969–Jun 1970, NBC Sun 7:00–7:30
Sep 1970–Apr 1971, NBC Sun 7:00–7:30
(In first-run syndication from fall 1971–fall 1988)
REGULARS:
Marlin Perkins
Jim Fowler
Stan Brock

The full title of this long-running nature series was *Mutual of Omaha's Wild Kingdom.* It starred famed naturalist and zoo director Marlin Perkins, with the aid of fellow naturalist Jim Fowler and, later, Stan Brock. The series covered such diverse topics as animal survival in the wilds, treatment of animals in captivity, the environments of primitive peoples, and the interrelationships between both primitive peoples and their animal neighbors and different species of animals with each other. An outgrowth of an earlier NBC series, *Zoo Parade,* which had originated almost exclusively from Chicago's Lincoln Park Zoo and which also starred Mr. Perkins, *Wild Kingdom* spent much more time away from the zoo setting. When it premiered on January 6, 1963, *Wild Kingdom* was telecast on Sunday afternoons, as its predecessor had been. It moved into the evening hours in January 1968. Following its cancellation by NBC at the end of the 1970–1971 season, *Wild Kingdom* went into syndication. Although many of the episodes shown in the syndicated version were reruns of those seen previously on NBC, new episodes continued to be produced. Perkins and Fowler were featured in these new episodes until failing health forced Perkins to leave the series in 1985 (he died the following year). Fowler's new assistant was Peter Eros.

WILD OATS (*Situation Comedy*)
FIRST TELECAST: *September 4, 1994*
LAST TELECAST: *September 25, 1994*
BROADCAST HISTORY:
Sep 1994, FOX Sun 9:30–10:00
CAST:
Jack Slayton .... Tim Conlon
Brian Grant .... Paul S. Rudd
Shelly Thomas .... Paula Marshall
Liz Bradford .... Jana Marie Hupp
Tanya Kavasi .... Karri Turner
Natasha Kavasi .... Tamara Olson
Kathee .... Christine Cavanaugh
Gordon Walker .... Timothy Fall

This was a comedy about the social lives of twenty-somethings in Chicago. Jack was a self-centered professional photographer used to getting his way. His lifelong best friend and roommate, Brian, was a sensitive social worker who between jobs worked for a temp agency. Shy Brian was dating Jack's former girlfriend, Shelly, a fifth-grade teacher, rekindling Jack's ardor for her. Shelly's dizzy roommate, Liz, was an insecure hairdresser who couldn't sustain a romantic relationship. Most of the action took place in their apartments and at The Hanger, a neighborhood singles club where they talked about important things like feelings, dates, and sex, sex, sex. Habitués there included the Kavasi sisters, sex-crazed dumb blonde bimbos who had moved to Chicago from their European homeland; Kathee, a cynical waitress/musician waiting for her big break; and Gordon, an obnoxious nerdy regular with the hots for Liz.

WILD ON (*Documentary*)
BROADCAST HISTORY:
E! Entertainment
60 minutes

Original episodes: *1999–*
Premiered: *1999*

HOSTS:
Eleanor Mondale (1997)
Jules Asner (1997–1999)
Brooke Burke (1999–2002)
Cindy Taylor (2002–)

This sex-drenched travelogue, a spin-off from E!'s *Sex On* series, explored the party scene in exotic locales all over the world, from New Orleans' Mardi Gras to the crystal waters of Australia's Great Barrier Reef. The focus was generally on local food, customs and especially nightclubs, where revelry and occasional nudity prevailed. Appropriately, the host was a scantily clad beauty, originally Eleanor Mondale (daughter of onetime presidential candidate Walter Mondale), succeeded by glamour queens Jules Asner and Brooke Burke. When Burke quit the show in 2002 (too many drooling drunks and leering locals, evidently), the network held an eight-episode competition to find her replacement, culminating at the Skin Pool Lounge in Las Vegas. Surprise, the winner was the finalist with the skimpiest bikini of all, Cindy Taylor!

WILD THINGS (*Wildlife Documentary*)

BROADCAST HISTORY:
Syndicated only
60 minutes
Produced: *1997–2000* (72 episodes)
Released: *September 1997*

The producers of this series traveled around the world filming animals in their natural habitats. Wildlife experts were seen on location and provided commentary on the action. Segments included rescuing a ten-foot-long anaconda in Brazil, birthing a seal in Argentina, an orphan rhino in Kenya, saving an elephant from drowning in mud in Namibia, spying polar bears swimming in Alaska, and tracking alligator hunters in Florida.

WILD THORNBERRYS, THE (*Cartoon*)

BROADCAST HISTORY:
Nickelodeon
30 minutes
Produced: *1998–*
Premiered: *September 1, 1998*

VOICES:
Eliza Thornberry (age 12) .... Lacey Chabert
Debbie Thornberry (16) .... Danielle Harris
Donnie Thornberry (4) .... Flea
Nigel Thornberry .... Tim Curry
Marianne Thornberry .... Jodi Carlisle
Darwin, the chimp .... Tom Kane
Kip O'Donnell .... Keith Szarabajka
Neil Biedermann .... Jerry Sroka

Hey kids, how'd you like to live in a big, high-tech RV, roaming the world with your family and filming nature documentaries about exotic animals of all kinds? If you were an inquisitive 12-year-old like Eliza, you'd probably find it cool. If you were a whiny 16-year-old grunge princess like Debbie, it would be, like, the pits. And if you were 4-year-old Donnie, you'd just crawl around and explore. The Thornberrys certainly led an unusual life. Nigel, the father, with his big red mustache and booming British voice ("Smashing!"), hosted the documentaries, while Marianne, his somewhat more cautious wife, served as cameraman and producer. Darwin was a talking chimp, with an English accent, who traveled with them, and Kip a villainous poacher with whom they had run-in's. Settings ranged from the Amazon to Africa, and not all of the wildlife they encountered was particularly friendly, but bright Eliza had the ability to talk to the animals, which got the family out of many a scrape.

WILD WEST SHOWDOWN (*Competition*)

BROADCAST HISTORY:
Syndicated only
60 minutes
Produced: *1994* (26 episodes)
Released: *October 1994*

HOST:
Alex Cord ("West")
Lisa Coles ("K.C. Clark")

ANNOUNCER:
Joe Fowler

OUTLAWS:
Sandy Berumen ("Alibi")
Craig Branham ("Three Fingers")
Tremel James ("Badger")
Lynn "Jonnie" Jonckowski ("Chance")
Kerry Maureen Mellin ("Faro")
Cheryl Lawson ("Silk")
Juddson Linn ("George")
Jeff Manazanares ("Bull")
Randall Oliver ("Godbreath")
Jason Reins-Rodriguez ("Kid Kidd")
Con Schell ("Snakebite")

Yet another variation on *American Gladiators*, *Wild West Showdown* gave average people the opportunity to compete as "cowboys" in such events as The Grand Stampede, Rider in the Sky, Shootout, and Bull Run, with $100 going to the winner of each individual event. Normally there were three contestants, two males and one female. Events included riding and roping, and everything had a Western flavor. The weekly winner could win $5,000 by defeating a selected outlaw in the final showdown. Events took place in and around the town of Broken Neck, and everything was designed to have the good guys helping rid Broken Neck of its outlaws. There were also lots of stuntmen doing Western stunts between events. West was the narrator and K.C. was the editor of the *Broken Neck Gazette*, who talked with the contestants and awarded the prize money.

WILD WILD WEST, THE (*Western*)

FIRST TELECAST: *September 17, 1965*
LAST TELECAST: *September 7, 1970*
BROADCAST HISTORY:
Sep 1965–Sep 1969, CBS Fri 7:30–8:30
Jul 1970–Sep 1970, CBS Mon 10:00–11:00

CAST:
James T. West .... Robert Conrad
Artemus Gordon .... Ross Martin
**President Ulysses S. Grant* .... James Gregory
Jeremy Pike (1968–1969) .... Charles Aidman

*Occasional

James T. West was the James Bond of Westerns. West was an undercover agent for President Grant whose assignments usually involved exposing or undermining the attempts of various radical, revolutionary, or criminal groups to take over all or part of the U.S. Helping him was his fellow Secret Service agent, Artemus Gordon, a master of disguises and dialects. The two of them traveled in a special railroad car that supplied them with the materials to concoct all sorts of bizarre weapons and devices to foil their adversaries. Beautiful women, contrived situations, and fantastic devices populated this series throughout its four-year run. One villain who had a remarkable facility for evading capture, or escaping from prison if caught, was the evil genius Dr. Miguelito Loveless (played by dwarf Michael Dunn). Dr. Loveless was to James West what Prof. Moriarty was to Sherlock Holmes—a brilliant antagonist bent on taking over the world. For part of the 1968–1969 season West was assisted by Jeremy Pike while costar Ross Martin was recovering from a heart attack.

CBS aired reruns during the summer of 1970.

WILD, WILD WORLD OF ANIMALS, THE
(*Wildlife/Nature*)

BROADCAST HISTORY:
Syndicated only
30 minutes
Produced: *1973–1978* (129 episodes)
Released: *Fall 1973*

NARRATOR:
William Conrad

This popular wildlife documentary series was produced by Time-Life Films.

WILDSIDE (*Western*)

FIRST TELECAST: *March 21, 1985*
LAST TELECAST: *April 25, 1985*
BROADCAST HISTORY:
Mar 1985–Apr 1985, ABC Thu 8:00–9:00

CAST:
Brodie Hollister .... William Smith
Sutton Hollister .... J. Eddie Peck
Bannister Sparks .... Howard E. Rollins, Jr.
Varges De La Cosa .... John DiAquino
Prometheus Jones .... Terry Funk
Cally Oaks .... Meg Ryan
Governor J. Wendell Summerhayes ... Sandy McPeak
Keye Ahn .... Jon Fong
Elliot Thogmorton .... Kurt Fuller
Alice Freeze .... Robin Hoff
Skillet .... Timothy Scott
Zeke .... Jason Hervey

Five upstanding citizens of Wildside County, California, constituted the "Wildside Chamber of Commerce"—a secret law-enforcement group—in this action series set in the Old West. Brodie was a rancher and the "fastest gun in the West"; Sutton, his son; Bannister, the debonair black explosives expert; Varges, the knife-wielding gunsmith; and Prometheus a gentle giant who was also a veterinarian and expert with the lariat. Their assignments generally came from the Governor, and adversaries ranged from local gangs to wandering ex-Confederate platoons and renegade British cavalry units left over from the Crimean War.

WILL & GRACE (*Situation Comedy*)

FIRST TELECAST: *September 21, 1998*
LAST TELECAST:
BROADCAST HISTORY:
Sep 1998–Nov 1998, NBC Mon 9:30–10:00
Dec 1998–Mar 1999, NBC Tue 9:30–10:00
Apr 1999–May 1999, NBC Thu 8:30–9:00
May 1999–Jul 1999, NBC Thu 9:30–10:00
Jun 1999–Sep 1999, NBC Tue 9:30–10:00
Aug 1999–Jul 2000, NBC Thu 9:00–9:30
May 2000, NBC Tue 8:30–9:00
Jul 2000– , NBC Thu 9:00–9:30
Aug 2000–Sep 2000, NBC Thu 8:30–9:00
Jan 2002, NBC Thu 8:30–9:00
Aug 2002–Sep 2002, NBC Thu 9:30–10:00

CAST:
Will Truman .... Eric McCormack
Grace Adler .... Debra Messing
Jack McFarland .... Sean Hayes
Karen Walker .... Megan Mullally
Rosario Salazar McFarland (1999–)
.... Shelley Morrison
Elliot (2001–) .... Michael Angarano
**Dr. Leo Markus (2002–)* .... Harry Connick, Jr.

*Occasional

The yuppie roommates in this comedy were an unusual pair for television: he was a handsome, gay attorney, she a heterosexual interior designer who had just dumped her fiancé at the altar. Best friends for years, they decided to share a Manhattan apartment without the sexual sparks that usually arc all over shows like this, despite a mutual love for French films, poker nights with the guys, and the home version of *The $10,000 Pyramid.* Like brother and sister, they supported each other as each played the field. Will's sexual orientation was subdued, but not that of his flamboyant friend Jack, who was constantly taking abuse (and loving it) for his wildly exaggerated mannerisms. Karen was Grace's fluttery business assistant, a slumming socialite who liked to work because it kept her "down to earth" (when late for work she would write Grace a check). Jack's pet parrot was named Guapo.

During the following seasons Will, Grace and Jack each had numerous boyfriends. Hers, who tended to be a little more long term, included Josh (Corey Parker), Ben Doucette (Gregory Hines) and Nathan (Woody Harrelson). Despite his sexual orientation Jack married Karen's El Salvadoran housekeeper Rosario in 1999 to keep her from being deported, but they later divorced. Then in 2001 Jack learned that he was the biological father of teenager Elliot, via a sperm bank donation, and he had to deal with the boy's fiesty mother Bonnie (Rosie O'Donnell) while learning to be a father. In 2002 Will heard his "biological clock" ticking and convinced Grace to be impregnated with his sperm so that he could be a father, too, but on her way to the fertility clinic she was swept off her feet by dashing Dr. Leo Markus. They fell in love and in the fall of 2002 were married.

Numerous celebrities made guest appearences on the popular show, either as themselves or as eccentric characters. Among them were Cher (whom Jack mistook for a drag queen), Gene Wilder (as Will's boss Mr. Stein), Beau Bridges, Blythe Danner, Ellen DeGeneres, Elton John, Glenn Close, Katie Couric, Kevin Bacon, Matt Damon, Piper Laurie, Sandra Bernhard and Tom Poston.

WILLY (*Situation Comedy*)

FIRST TELECAST: *September 18, 1954*
LAST TELECAST: *July 7, 1955*
BROADCAST HISTORY:
Sep 1954–Mar 1955, CBS Sat 10:30–11:00
Apr 1955–Jul 1955, CBS Thu 10:30–11:00

CAST:

Willa Dodger .... June Havoc
Franklin Sanders .... Danny Richards, Jr.
Emily Dodger .... Mary Treen
Papa Dodger .... Lloyd Corrigan
Charlie Bush .... Whitfield Connor
Perry Bannister (1955) .... Hal Peary
Harvey Evelyn (1955) .... Sterling Holloway

Following her graduation from law school, Willa Dodger opened a legal practice in her hometown of Renfrew, New Hampshire. There were not many exciting cases in that little hamlet so, in mid-season, Willa got an offer to work as legal counsel to a vaudeville organization run by Perry Bannister. She left her family and her boyfriend, Charlie Bush, and relocated to the big city. Her adventures, whether in rural New England or cosmopolitan New York, were on the lighter side and rarely involved her in serious legal cases.

WILLYS THEATRE PRESENTING BEN HECHT'S TALES OF THE CITY (*Dramatic Anthology*)

FIRST TELECAST: *June 25, 1953*
LAST TELECAST: *September 17, 1953*
BROADCAST HISTORY:
Jun 1953–Sep 1953, CBS Thu 8:30–9:00
NARRATOR:
Ben Hecht

Author Ben Hecht, whose most famous and award-winning work was the play *The Front Page,* was the narrator of this anthology series composed of adaptations of his stories. He was never seen onscreen, only heard with his introductions and closing remarks. The live dramas aired on alternate weeks with *Four Star Playhouse.*

WILTON NORTH REPORT, THE (*Comedy/Newsmagazine*)

FIRST TELECAST: *December 11, 1987*
LAST TELECAST: *January 8, 1988*
BROADCAST HISTORY:
Dec 1987–Jan 1988, FOX Mon–Fri 11:00–12:00 midnight
REGULARS:
Phil Cowan
Paul Robins
Nancy Collins
Greg Jackson
Wayne Satz
Paul Krassner
Jack LaLanne

This example of guerilla television was an odd mixture of serious news features and thoroughly ridiculous stories and comic bits, all in the guise of a nightly newsmagazine. It was produced by the former producer of *Late Night with David Letterman,* and was apparently an attempt to see what would happen if someone like Letterman took over *60 Minutes.* Hosted by the young comedy team of Phil Cowan and Paul Robins, *Wilton North* covered in documentary fashion such burning subjects as a woman claiming to be an extraterrestrial who had lived on 37 planets, the funniest inmate in Chino prison, a man who collected things that glowed in the dark, a visit to an alligator farm, lady wrestlers, and a woman who was convinced the devil was living in her toaster. On the more serious side were interviews with a professional matchmaker in New York, the woman president of Motown productions, the daughter of presidential candidate Gary Hart, and FBI informant Jimmie "The Weazel" Fratiano. Although there were many contributors to *Wilton North,* the most frequently seen were tongue-in-cheek investigative reporter Wayne Satz, satirical commentator Paul Krassner, health and science editor Jack LaLanne, and serious interviewers Nancy Collins and Greg Jackson. The title of the series referred to the location of the Hollywood building from which it was aired.

The Wilton North Report was fraught with problems. Its premiere was delayed for several weeks while producer Barry Sand tried to get the kinks out of the format. When it reached the air television critics crucified it as stupid, disjointed, and amateurish. What Fox executives had hoped would be an appealingly distinctive late-night viewing alternative drew small audiences and was yanked from the schedule less than a month after its first telecast.

WIN BEN STEIN'S MONEY (*Quiz*)

BROADCAST HISTORY:
Comedy Central
30 minutes
Produced: *1997–*
Premiered: *July 28, 1997*
REGULARS:
Ben Stein
Jimmy Kimmel, cohost/announcer (1997–2001)
Nancy Pimental, cohost/announcer (2001–2002)
Sal Iacono, cohost/announcer (2002–)

In this unusual quiz show, former Nixon speech writer, author, and actor *(Ferris Bueller's Day Off)* Ben Stein bet his own paycheck that he could outsmart contestants in a series of difficult questions. The show began with a $5,000 "pot." If Stein could beat the contestants, he could keep it all; the more they won, the less he got. What did he think of the concept? "It was not my idea and I don't like it," he deadpanned. However, fortunately for him, Stein was a pretty brainy guy, and he usually managed to hang on to a portion, if not all, of the money. Adding to the levity was his rather dry, superior manner, and the contemptuous asides of his sidekick, Los Angeles radio announcer Jimmy Kimmel.

WIN, LOSE OR DRAW (*Quiz/Panel*)

BROADCAST HISTORY:
Syndicated and network daytime
30 minutes
Produced: *1987–1990*
Released: *September 1987*
HOST:
Bert Convy (1987–1989)
Robb Weller (1989–1990)

Movie star Burt Reynolds invented this celebrity game for his friends' amusement in his own living room. The set, with its plush couches and plants, was even supposed to *look* like Burt's living room ("The john's down that way," he volunteered on one show). The game was, essentially, charades with pictures. Two teams competed, three men vs. three women. One person from a team was given a name or phrase (like "Neil Diamond" or "A Heart-to-Heart Talk"), and then had to communicate it to his or her teammates by quickly drawing a series of pictures on a large board. If the team failed to guess the phrase, the other team got to guess it. A speed round consisted of guessing as many words as possible in 90 seconds.

Prizes were not large, but two out of the three members on each team were celebrities, so the appeal was largely in watching the stars in a fast-paced, party-like setting. (The prize money went to the one noncelebrity on the winning team.) Burt himself often appeared, as did his Hollywood friends, including Loni Anderson, Dom DeLuise, Betty White, and other famous faces. A daytime version of *Win, Lose or Draw*, hosted by Vicki Lawrence, aired on NBC from September 1987 to September 1989.

WIN WITH A WINNER (*Quiz/Audience Participation*)

FIRST TELECAST: *June 24, 1958*
LAST TELECAST: *September 9, 1958*
BROADCAST HISTORY:
Jun 1958–Sep 1958, NBC Tue 7:30–8:00
EMCEE:
Sandy Becker
Win Elliot
POSTCARD GIRL:
Marilyn Toomey
Rita Hayes

This rather complicated summer quiz show encouraged home viewers to root for their favorite contestant and possibly share in the prizes. At the end of each show the next week's contestants were introduced, and viewers were invited to write in with their prediction of who would be the top money winner, as well as (during the first month at least) the order of finish. Those with the right choice were candidates for cash prizes, and anyone predicting the entire order of finish got a bonus prize.

The game itself generally resembled a horse race. The five (later four) contestants were each given the same question. A correct answer added the value of that question, usually $100 or $200, to their total, while a wrong answer subtracted the same amount from their previous winnings. In addition one contestant in each round had the opportunity to double his winnings—or losses. A running tally was kept of each contestant's total in the race, but only the top winner got to keep his money. The others got consolation prizes.

A "postcard girl" picked home-viewer predictions out of a large drum during the course of the show, and all of those predicting the top contestant would "win with the winner," splitting the same amount of money that he had won.

Sandy Becker and Marilyn Toomey, the original host and postcard girl, were replaced by Win Elliot and Rita Hayes on July 22.

WIND ON WATER (*Adventure*)

FIRST TELECAST: *October 17, 1998*
LAST TELECAST: *October 24, 1998*
BROADCAST HISTORY:
Oct 1998, NBC Sat 8:00–9:00
CAST:
Ciel Connolly .... Bo Derek
Cole Connolly .... William Gregory Lee
Kelly Connolly .... Brian Gross
Gardner Poole .... Lee Horsley
Val Poole .... Shawn Christian
Kate Poole .... Jacinda Barrett
Charlie Flanagan .... Matt George
Kai .... Matthew Stephen Liu
Tracy Poole .... Heidi Hannsz

One of the fastest casualties of the 1998–1999 season (canceled after two episodes), *Wind on Water* was supposed to be the saga of the Connolly clan as they fought to save their cattle ranch on the big island of Hawaii. Both the casting and the plot were fairly preposterous. Bo Derek starred as the sexy, widowed "matriarch" of the clan, often clad in a swimsuit (and looking as good as in her famous 1979 movie *10*). Moody Cole and cocky, baby-faced Kelly were her two hunky sons, who aimed to raise money to save the ranch by competing in extreme sports competitions, leading to lots of striking footage amid crashing surf (surfboarding), towering mountains (snowboarding), and blue sky (skydiving). Gardner Poole was the evil developer (Is there any other kind?) who schemed to take over Ciel's land; he fairly oozed oily charm as he stopped by with his young trophy wife, Tracy, and ruthless son Val. His rebellious daughter Kate was another matter, hanging out with the handsome Connolly brothers, despite her father's disapproval. Charlie was a Connolly family friend, and Kai one of the boys' surfing buddies.

Although the show got a quick hook from NBC, eight episodes were filmed and ten scripts completed, so we know that the character of Tracy was eventually recast, and that Lee Horsley was written out of the show by having his white Mercedes go over a cliff, even if viewers didn't get to savor that delectable moment.

WINDOW ON MAIN STREET (*Situation Comedy*)

FIRST TELECAST: *October 2, 1961*
LAST TELECAST: *September 12, 1962*
BROADCAST HISTORY:
Oct 1961–Feb 1962, CBS Mon 8:30–9:00
Feb 1962–Sep 1962, CBS Wed 8:00–8:30
CAST:
Cameron Garrett Brooks .... Robert Young
Chris Logan .... Constance Moore
Lloyd Ramsey .... Ford Rainey
Arny Logan .... Brad Berwick
Wally Evans .... James Davidson
Peggy Evans .... Carol Byron
Miss Wycliffe .... Coleen Gray
Harry McGill .... Warner Jones
Roddy Miller .... Tim Matheson

Writer Cameron Brooks returned to his hometown of Millsburg in search of material for stories. He moved into the Majestic Hotel and resumed an old friendship with Lloyd Ramsey, editor of the local newspaper. The people he knew, as well as those he met at the hotel, served as subjects for his stories. In the spring, when the Majestic was temporarily closed for renovations, Cameron took a room in the home of Wally and Peggy Evans.

Robert Young, the star of this series, had just completed a six-year run in the highly popular *Father Knows Best* (reruns of which were still being telecast in prime time). He was looking for a different type of series to display his talents, but *Window on Main Street* was not successful and so Young subsequently went into retirement—until 1969, when *Marcus Welby* came along.

WINDOW ON THE WORLD (*Variety*)

FIRST TELECAST: *January 27, 1949*
LAST TELECAST: *April 14, 1949*

BROADCAST HISTORY:

Jan 1949–Apr 1949, DUM Thu 9:00–9:30

REGULAR:

Merle Kendrick Orchestra

Variety acts from different parts of the world were featured on this program, with film clips of their native lands setting the scene. Among the American performers appearing were Hollywood comedian Gil Lamb and actress-singer Irene Manning. There was no regular emcee.

WINDOWS (*Dramatic Anthology*)

FIRST TELECAST: *July 8, 1955*

LAST TELECAST: *August 26, 1955*

BROADCAST HISTORY:

Jul 1955–Aug 1955, CBS Fri 10:30–11:00

This live dramatic series, originating from New York, was the 1955 summer replacement for *Person to Person*. Each episode of the series opened on an ordinary window through which the camera moved to begin the unfolding of the story. All of the stories were designed to show real people confronting real problems, such as a woman alcoholic and her effect on her family, a boy's adulation for an ex-circus clown, and an illiterate woman's determined struggle to learn how to read.

WINDY CITY JAMBOREE (*Country Music*)

FIRST TELECAST: *March 19, 1950*

LAST TELECAST: *June 18, 1950*

BROADCAST HISTORY:

Mar 1950–Jun 1950, DUM Sun 9:00–10:00

REGULARS:

Danny O'Neil
Gloria Van
Julian Stockdale Orchestra

Barn dance with variety acts, originating from Chicago.

WINGO (*Quiz*)

FIRST TELECAST: *April 1, 1958*

LAST TELECAST: *May 6, 1958*

BROADCAST HISTORY:

Apr 1958–May 1958, CBS Tue 8:30–9:00

EMCEE:

Bob Kennedy

This short-lived entry in the big-money quiz-show sweepstakes pitted two contestants against each other in answering questions of general and varied knowledge. The winner of each round won $1,000, the opportunity to continue against a new challenger, and a shot at the "Wingo" portion of the show. This part of the game, which depended on pure luck, offered the ultimate jackpot of $250,000 to any contestant who succeeded in matching the letters spelling the show's title in an elaborate word game. Contestants who continued to compete risked a part of their winnings in the event that they were defeated by a subsequent challenger.

WINGS (*Situation Comedy*)

FIRST TELECAST: *April 19, 1990*

LAST TELECAST: *September 17, 1997*

BROADCAST HISTORY:

Apr 1990–May 1990, NBC Thu 9:30–10:00
Sep 1990, NBC Thu 9:30–10:00
Sep 1990–Dec 1990, NBC Fri 9:30–10:00
Jan 1991–Mar 1991, NBC Thu 9:30–10:00
Jun 1991–Jan 1993, NBC Thu 9:30–10:00
Aug 1992–Sep 1992, NBC Wed 9:30–10:00
Feb 1993–Aug 1994, NBC Thu 8:30–9:00
Jul 1994–Aug 1994, NBC Tue 9:30–10:00
Sep 1994– Apr 1996, NBC Tue 8:00–8:30
Apr 1996–Jun 1996, NBC Tue 8:30–9:00
Jun 1996–Jul 1996, NBC Tue 9:30–10:00
Aug 1996–Feb 1997, NBC Wed 8:00–8:30
Mar 1997–Jul 1997, NBC Wed 9:00–9:30
Jul 1997, NBC Wed 9:00–10:00
Jul 1997–Aug 1997, NBC Mon 9:30–10:00
Sep 1997, NBC Wed 8:00–9:00

CAST:

Joe Hackett .... Timothy Daly
Brian Hackett .... Steven Weber
Helen Chappel Hackett .... Crystal Bernard
Roy Biggins .... David Schramm
Faye Evelyn Cochran .... Rebecca Schull
Lowell Mather (1990–1995) .. Thomas Haden Church
Antonio Scarpacci (1991–1997) .... Tony Shalhoub
Alex Lambert (1992–1994) .... Farrah Forke
Casey Davenport (1994–1997) .... Amy Yasbeck

THEME:

Piano Sonata in A Major, Catalogue #D-959, from the Fourth Movement, "Rondo," by Franz Schubert. Arranged by Antony Cooke and entitled "Wings"

This easygoing character comedy might have been called *Cheers II*. It was produced by the same people, structured somewhat like *Cheers*, set near *Cheers*' hometown of Boston, and scheduled immediately following *Cheers* on the NBC Thursday night lineup.

Instead of a bar, the location was the waiting room and lunch counter of a small airfield on the resort island of Nantucket, off the Massachusetts coast. The regular "gang" included brothers Joe and Brian Hackett, both pilots, who ran a one-plane commuter service called Sandpiper Air from the airport. They had little else in common. Joe was buttoned-down, organized, and serious (like *Cheers*' Rebecca), and Brian a hang-loose free spirit (rather like Sam Malone). Their mutual best friend since childhood was Helen, a once-chubby but now beautiful aspiring concert cellist who ran the lunch counter. These three lifelong friends were "the three musketeers." By the end of the first season Helen and Joe were having a serious affair, while Brian played the field. Other denizens of Nantucket Airport were Roy, the heavyset, blustery owner of a rival air service; Faye, the perky, sixtyish ex-stewardess who ran the ticket counter; and Lowell, the eccentric maintenance man and cosmic philosopher. Not exactly Norm or Cliff (of *Cheers*), but close. They all sat around, traded friendly jibes, and generally got involved in each other's lives. Sound familiar?

Joining the cast in later seasons were Antonio, the hopelessly romantic Italian cabbie; Alex, a brassy lady helicopter pilot; and Casey, Helen's divorced older sister from San Francisco whose "perfect marriage" didn't work out. Helen and Joe continued their on-again, off-again affair (interrupted by her brief marriage of convenience to Antonio!), and in the spring of 1995 they were married. With Helen and Joe married, the dating action shifted to Brian and Casey, whose romance became so hot and heavy they accidently burned Joe's house down in 1996. The following season Brian's house burned down, and the brothers were so strapped for cash they lost control of Sandpiper Air for a time.

The last original episode, on May 21, 1997, brought

the series full circle. In the 1990 premiere the long-separated brothers had been brought together via a "treasure hunt" resulting from a trail of notes left by their deceased father. Now, eight years later, they found another of his notes, which after a long chase eventually led them to a $250,000 inheritance hidden in an airport locker. After some squabbling, they decided to use it to help Helen realize her dream to study the cello under the world's leading cellist, in Vienna.

WINNER TAKE ALL (*Quiz/Audience Participation*)
FIRST TELECAST: *July 8, 1948*
LAST TELECAST: *October 3, 1950*
BROADCAST HISTORY:
Jul 1948–Aug 1948, CBS Thu 9:30–10:00
Aug 1948–Jan 1949, CBS Wed 8:30–9:00
Apr 1950–Jul 1950, CBS Thu 9:45–10:30
Jul 1950–Oct 1950, CBS Tue 9:00–9:30
EMCEE:
Bud Collyer

The format of *Winner Take All* was very simple. Two contestants competed with each other answering questions given them by the emcee. One of them had a bell and the other had a buzzer. The first one to announce his/her readiness to answer (by ringing or buzzing) was given an opportunity to answer the question. Each correct answer was worth a point and three points won the game. The winner won merchandise prizes and the right to meet new challengers until defeated. *Winner Take All* had been on CBS radio since the mid-1940s and the radio version, with a different emcee, was still being aired when the show moved to television in 1948. During the 15 months that it was not on the network, from January 1949 to April 1950, it continued as a local program in New York, returning to the network for its final six months as a nighttime series. It then became a daytime show, running first on CBS (with Barry Gray as emcee) and then on NBC (with Bill Cullen), until its final telecast in April 1952. The daytime version was much different from the evening *Winner Take All*. Regular members of the daytime cast performed sketches to challenge contestants' knowledge, and did song and dance numbers as well.

WINNETKA ROAD (*Serial Drama*)
FIRST TELECAST: *March 12, 1994*
LAST TELECAST: *April 16, 1994*
BROADCAST HISTORY:
Mar 1994–Apr 1994, NBC Sat 10:00–11:00
CAST:
Terry Mears .... Paige Turco
Nicky (Nicholas) .... Kellen Hathaway
Stan Oldman .... Harley Venton
Jack Passion .... Josh Brolin
Nicole Manning .... Megan Ward
Glenn Barker .... Ed Begley, Jr.
Jeannie Barker .... Catherine Hicks
Patti .... Jayne Frazer
Jason .... Richard Gilliland
Kevin Page .... Kurt Deutsch
George Grace .... Meg Tilly
Sterling Grace .... Sandy McPeak
Father Burke .... Eddie Bracken
Mike .... Richard Herd
Maybeth .... Kristen Cloke

Short-lived soap opera set in the Chicago suburb of Oak Bluff, Illinois, where tight jeans, bare chests, and easy sex seemed as much in evidence as on the beaches of Southern California. Several entanglements filled its short run: failed B-movie actress Terry's fight with her rich ex, Stan, over custody of their son, Nicky; hunky policeman Jack's vacillation between old flame Terry and new flame Nicole; Glenn's midlife crisis, which had him leaving estranged wife Jeannie for sexy young aerobics instructor Patti; and the triangle between bohemian artist George (a she), her rich but possessive husband, Sterling, and unemployed but boyish Kevin. Kindly Father Burke was a blind priest who looked after little Nicky while the rest of the cast pursued their worldly pleasures.

WINNING LINES (*Quiz*)
FIRST TELECAST: *January 8, 2000*
LAST TELECAST: *February 18, 2000*
BROADCAST HISTORY:
Jan 2000–Feb 2000, CBS Sat 8:00–8:30
Feb 2000, CBS Fri 8:30–9:00
EMCEE:
Dick Clark

This quiz show started with 49 contestants on a big blue wall. Six simple questions were asked, each of which had a numerical answer (Q: "What is a baker's dozen plus one?" A: "Fourteen"). The first contestant to punch in the correct answer advanced to the next round. In round two the six survivors were each assigned a number, and then faced a sudden-death situation in which the numerical answers to the questions were the same as the numbers they had been assigned. The first person to answer each question either advanced (if it was their number), eliminated another contestant (if it was that contestant's number), or eliminated themselves (if it was the wrong answer).

The finalist went on to the Wonderwall where she was guaranteed a minimum of $2,500 and could win as much as $1,000,000. There were 49 numbered questions; the object was to shout out 20 question numbers and their corresponding numerical answers in three minutes. Three strikes (wrong answers) and the contestant was out, but he could use two 15-second pit stops, and could pass on two questions. The contestant could also bail out and keep his accumulated winnings to that point.

Viewers could also win. The second digit of each of the six first-round winners' assigned numbers were combined with the second digit from the last winning question from the Wonderwall to provide seven numbers. Home viewers whose phone numbers consisted of these seven numbers, in any order, could call an 800 number for a random chance to win $50,000. One of the coauthors of this book scored a match and called the number—but so, unfortunately, did far too many others.

This complicated quiz show was based on the successful British series of the same name and was CBS' response to ABC's hugely successful *Who Wants to Be a Millionaire?* Apparently it was too complicated to hold viewers, and was gone after six weeks. Nobody hit the jackpot, but one contestant walked away with $500,000.

WINSTON CHURCHILL—THE VALIANT YEARS (*Documentary*)
FIRST TELECAST: *November 27, 1960*

LAST TELECAST: *April 5, 1963*
BROADCAST HISTORY:
Nov 1960–Jun 1961, ABC Sun 10:30–11:00
Sep 1962–Dec 1962, ABC Sun 6:30–7:00
Dec 1962–Apr 1963, ABC Fri 7:30–8:00
NARRATOR:
Gary Merrill
Richard Burton

Churchill's role in the years leading into and during World War II was chronicled in this award-winning documentary series. The basis for each episode was the memoirs that Churchill the historian had kept to describe the activities of Churchill the statesman. Old film clips, letters, and contemporary backgrounds were woven together to paint a picture of Churchill's role at that critical period of world history. Gary Merrill was the narrator with Richard Burton reading from Churchill's memoirs. The series was rerun in its entirety during the 1962–1963 season.

WINTUITION (*Quiz*)
BROADCAST HISTORY:
Game Show Network
30 minutes
Original episodes: *2002–*
Premiered: *December 2, 2002*
EMCEE:
Marc Summers

Players competed for tuition money in this game, which was billed as "turning knowledge into college." Three contestants answered general academic questions graded by difficulty, first at the elementary school level, and then middle school. In the third round the two highest-scoring contestants moved on to high-school-level questions, and in the fourth the finalist was faced with questions of college-level difficulty. The grand prize was $50,000 in tuition money, with other appropriate prizes (such as free Domino's pizza for a year) along the way.

WIRE, THE (*Magazine*)
BROADCAST HISTORY:
Lifetime
30 minutes
Produced: *1997*
Premiered: *January 24, 1997*

A women's lifestyles magazine, with features on makeup, travel, shopping, and everyday living. Many of the subjects were intensely practical, such as how to pack a suitcase and how to do the laundry. For those mystified by the male species, there was a women's explanation of football. A rotating stable of hip young reporters, including such characters as "The Nutrition Lady" and "The Laundry Lieutenant," offered the helpful tips.

WIRE SERVICE (*Newspaper Drama*)
FIRST TELECAST: *October 4, 1956*
LAST TELECAST: *September 13, 1959*
BROADCAST HISTORY:
Oct 1956–Feb 1957, ABC Thu 9:00–10:00
Feb 1957–Sep 1957, ABC Mon 7:30–8:30
Feb 1959–Sep 1959, ABC Sun 9:30–10:30
CAST:
Dan Miller .... Dane Clark
Dean Evans .... George Brent
Katherine Wells .... Mercedes McCambridge

The three stars of this series each played a roving reporter for the Trans-Globe wire service. Each of them traveled all over the country and the world, tracking down stories involving crime and high adventure. The three reporters worked independently and appeared in separate stories, on a rotating basis.

In 1959 the *Wire Service* episodes starring Dane Clark were rerun under the title *Deadline for Action.*

WISDOM OF THE AGES (*Discussion*)
FIRST TELECAST: *December 16, 1952*
LAST TELECAST: *June 30, 1953*
BROADCAST HISTORY:
Dec 1952–Jun 1953, DUM Tue 9:30–10:00
MODERATOR:
Jack Barry
PANELISTS:
Ronnie Mulluzzo (age 8)
Marcia Van Dyke (28)
Leo Cherne (40)
Mrs. H. V. Kaltenborn (64)
Thomas Clark (82)

Quizmaster Jack Barry had been highly successful with a panel show featuring youngsters *(Juvenile Jury)* and another with oldsters *(Life Begins at Eighty),* so it was natural to try a show that spanned all age groups. As on the prototype programs, the format was simply for the panel to discuss, from the perspective of their various generations, the often humorous problems and questions submitted by viewers. The panel consisted of one member under 20, one 20–40, one 40–60, one 60–80, and one over 80. The panelists most frequently seen during the show's six-month run are listed above. Interestingly enough, though each age group had its own unique point of view, it was the two extremes—the 8- and the 82-year-old—who were most often in agreement.

WISEGUY (*Police Drama*)
FIRST TELECAST: *September 16, 1987*
LAST TELECAST: *December 8, 1990*
BROADCAST HISTORY:
Sep 1987, CBS Wed 9:00–11:00
Sep 1987–Nov 1987, CBS Thu 9:00–10:00
Jan 1988–Mar 1988, CBS Mon 10:00–11:00
Jun 1988–Apr 1990, CBS Wed 10:00–11:00
Jun 1990–Jul 1990, CBS Thu 9:00–10:00
Nov 1990–Dec 1990, CBS Sat 10:00–11:00
CAST:
Vinnie Terranova (1987–1990) .... Ken Wahl
Michael Santana (1990) .... Steven Bauer
Frank McPike .... Jonathan Banks
"Lifeguard" (Daniel Benjamin Burroughs)
.... Jim Byrnes
Fr. Peter Terranova (1987, 1989) ... Gerald Anthony
Sonny Steelgrave (1987) .... Ray Sharkey
Paul Patrice (1987) .... Joe Dallesandro
Sid Royce (1987) .... Dennis Lipscomb
Harry "The Hunchback" Schanstra (1987)
.... Eric Christmas
Roger LoCocco (1988) .... William Russ
Susan Profitt (1988) .... Joan Sevarance
Mel Profitt (1988) .... Kevin Spacey
Herb Ketcher (1988) .... David Spielberg
Carlotta Terranova Aiuppo (1987–1989)
.... Elsa Raven
Beckstead (1988–1990) .... Ken Jenkins

Eli Sternberg (1988–1989) .... Jerry Lewis
David Sternberg (1988–1989) .... Ron Silver
Carole Sternberg (1988–1989)
.... Patricia Charbonneau
Rick Pinzolo (1988–1989) .... Stanley Tucci
Phil Bernstein (1988–1989) .... Harry Goz
Bobby Travis (1989) .... Glenn Frey
Isaac Twine (1989) .... Paul Winfield
Amber Twine (1989) .... Patti D'Arbanville
Winston Newquay (1989) .... Tim Curry
Don Rudy Aiuppo (1988–1989) .... George O. Petrie
Poochy Pompio (1988–1989) .... Tony Romano
Grosset (1989) .... John Snyder
Mark Volchek (1990) .... Steve Ryan
Rogosheske (1990) .... James Stacy
Lacey (1990) .... Darlanne Fluegel
Amado Guzman (1990) .... Maximillian Schell
Rafael Santana (1990) .... Manolo Villaverde
Hillary Stein (1990) .... Cecil Hoffmann
Dahlia Mendez (1990) .... Martika

Vinnie Terranova was an undercover agent for the Organized Crime Bureau who went from assignment to assignment infiltrating the most dangerous criminal organizations in America. Because of his brash attitude and street smarts, Vinnie made a perfect mob lieutenant. His boss at O.C.B. was cynical Frank McPike; "Lifeguard," Vinnie's only link to McPike while he was on assignment, served as a sympathetic conduit, as well as providing Vinnie with the information necessary to maintain his cover. Maintaining that cover was literally a matter of life or death—Vinnie was always "on the edge"—and it meant that everybody Vinnie knew, with the single exception of his brother, Peter (a priest), really thought he had become a crook.

Once he had contributed to the downfall of a mobster Vinnie moved on and, as a result, there was periodic turnover in the supporting cast. His first assignment was to bring down Atlantic City mob boss Sonny Steelgrave (played by Ray Sharkey in a bravura performance). From there he went on to disrupt the international smuggling operation (contraband, munitions, drugs, etc.) of crazed Mel Profitt and his beautiful sister Susan. Mel was involved with a deposed Caribbean dictator who was planning a coup but, when the plan fell apart, he committed suicide. His emotionally unstable sister, Susan, wound up in a mental hospital and Vinnie found out that the coup had in fact been orchestrated as an unauthorized CIA operation by Herb Ketcher through undercover agent Roger LoCocco, who was also a "wiseguy"—posing as a hit man for the Profitts. When the whole tangled affair came out in Senate hearings LoCocco was assassinated (or was he?), Ketcher committed suicide, and Vinnie—disillusioned with the entire U.S. government—quit the O.C.B.

That fall Vinnie was working at a gas station in his old Brooklyn neighborhood while trying to forget the O.C.B. Unfortunately, exposure to the racists in the neighborhood, who were as bad as the criminals he had been fighting for the O.C.B., convinced him he could bring them down by going back to the Bureau. He then went undercover as a garment center security consultant to save Eli Sternberg's Elrose Fashions dress firm from the clutches of mobster Rick Pinzolo. Vinnie's next undercover job, as the owner of Dead Dog Records, gave him the chance to nail corrupt players in the big-money rock music business. It also resulted in a torrid love affair with Amber Twine, the wife of his music business partner, Isaac Twine.

Meanwhile, Vinnie's mother, Carlotta, had married Rudy Aiuppo, the most powerful organized crime boss in New York. An assassination attempt on Don Aiuppo, ironically, left Vinnie with his seat on The Commission, the governing body of New York's organized crime. While his stepfather recovered in the hospital, Vinnie worked to track down the people responsible for the hit as well as to provide information to the O.C.B. Pressure from politicians who believed Vinnie was a mobster forced him out of that position, but not before Don Aiuppo found out his stepson was a Fed. Vinnie's last major case for the O.C.B. took him to rural Lynchboro where, as Vince Kozak, he sought to bring down reclusive Mark Volchek, the demented man who ran the town. After witnessing the electrocution/suicide of Lynchboro's sheriff, Vinnie went into an emotional funk and disappeared, taking menial work and trying to get himself together. He was last seen in a wharfside church where a former foe, seeking revenge, tried to take him out, killing the priest and wounding McPike instead.

When *Wiseguy* returned to the air in late 1990 McPike was out of the hospital and Vinnie had disappeared again (series star Ken Wahl had left the show in a disagreement with the producers). Because McPike thought Vinnie might have been the target of a Salvadoran death squad, he forged an uneasy alliance with Michael Santana (the series' new star), a disbarred Cuban-American Federal prosecutor whom Vinnie had contacted shortly before his disappearance. Santana went undercover to expose the corruption of wealthy businessman Amado Guzman, the man for whom his father worked.

WISH YOU WERE HERE (*Comedy/Adventure*)
FIRST TELECAST: *July 20, 1990*
LAST TELECAST: *August 24, 1990*
BROADCAST HISTORY:
Jul 1990–Aug 1990, CBS Fri 9:30–10:00
CAST:
Donny Cogswell .... Lew Schneider

An unusual comedy built around the latest American middle-class craze, the camcorder.

Donny Cogswell was too free a spirit to be tied down with a job on Wall Street. After a particularly bad day, he decided to pack it all in and recharge his batteries with a trip around Europe. With him was his trusty camcorder, which he used to record his experiences as he traveled. Rather than send letters back home to lovers, friends, and family, Donny sent videotapes.

Filmed on location, with local television and film stars (familiar in their homelands but not to American viewers) providing the supporting cast, *Wish You Were Here* traveled to Paris, Budapest, Barcelona, Morocco, and the French Riviera.

WITCHBLADE (*Adventure*)
BROADCAST HISTORY:
TNT
60 minutes
Original episodes: *2001–2002* (23 episodes)
Premiered: *June 12, 2001*
CAST:
Det. Sara "Pez" Pezzini .... Yancy Butler

Det. Jake McCartey .... David Chokachi
Det. Danny Woo .... Will Yun Lee
Kenneth Irons .... Anthony Cistaro
Ian Nottingham .... Eric "Kaos" Etebari
Gabriel Bowman..................... John Hensley
Vicky Po .... Kathryn Winslow
**Conchobar*........................ Kim De Lury
**Captain Bruno Dante* .... Nestor Serrano

*Occasional

Tough, stubborn New York City detective Sara Pezzini was the unwilling recipient of a powerful and dangerous weapon in this action-packed series. During a shoot-out in a museum, an ancient gauntlet (a kind of armored medieval glove, worn in combat) flew through the air and affixed itself to her arm, making her virtually invincible. The Witchblade, it seemed, had a long history, empowering select female warriors through the ages, such as Joan of Arc. It could deflect bullets, serve as a powerful sword, allow her to fly through the air, and do other neat tricks, but it had a mind of its own and might fail her at critical moments. Control freak Sara didn't really want it, but she had no choice—she was this generation's "chosen one." Danny was Sara's late partner, killed in a shoot-out with a mobster, who thanks to the Witchblade appeared to her as a ghost and served as her guardian angel. Her current partner was Jake, a boyish ex-surfer who wasn't quite sure what Sara was up to. On the dark side were Kenneth Irons, a mysterious billionaire who wanted the Witchblade but couldn't wield it and so became obsessed with Sara, and Ian, his dark, and very lethal henchman. Others seen included Internet art dealer Gabriel, Irish rock musician (and sometime ally) Conchobar, and corrupt cop Captain Dante.

Witchblade was first seen as a TV movie telecast on August 27, 2000. The series was canceled abruptly after only two seasons, despite good ratings. Speculation as to why centered on star Yancy Butler's well-publicized battles with alcohol, but TNT gave no real explanation. Based on a Top Cow comic book of the same name.

WITH THIS RING (*Quiz/Audience Participation*)

FIRST TELECAST: *January 28, 1951*
LAST TELECAST: *March 18, 1951*
BROADCAST HISTORY:
Jan 1951–Mar 1951, DUM Sun 9:30–10:00
HOST:
Bill Slater
Martin Gabel

This gentle quiz show drew its contestants from lists of young couples who had recently applied for a marriage license. Two couples were chosen and presented with questions about marriage sent in by viewers. After they gave their ideas about how they would handle the situations posed, a pair of celebrity judges—both married and therefore experienced—evaluated the answers. The winning couple got a free honeymoon trip.

Martin Gabel succeeded Bill Slater as host on the last two telecasts. The program was originally known as *Happily Ever After.*

WITHOUT A TRACE (*Police Drama*)

FIRST TELECAST: *September 26, 2002*
LAST TELECAST:
BROADCAST HISTORY:
Sep 2002– , CBS Thu 10:00–11:00
CAST:
Jack Malone .... Anthony LaPaglia
Samantha Spade .... Poppy Montgomery
Vivian Johnson............ Marianne Jean-Baptiste
Danny Taylor................... Enrique Murciano
Martin Fitzgerald .... Eric Close

New York City was the setting for this methodical drama about the work of the FBI's Missing Persons Squad. Each episode opened with a scene at the end of which someone had disappeared, and the rest of the hour was devoted to the efforts of the Missing Persons Squad to find him or her. The squad kept track of the clues on a big timeline board at headquarters that tracked when and where the missing person had been in the hours leading up to the disappearance. They interviewed family, friends, coworkers and anyone else who might be able to help, and used psychological profiling techniques, surveillance equipment and computer records. There were periodic flashbacks that reflected the latest information the team had obtained and constant on-screen reminders of how long it had been since the disappearance. Cases involved people who had been kidnapped, murdered, committed suicide or just wanted to get away.

Senior agent Jack Malone was the team leader, a serious, fatherly veteran who was well aware that the longer it took to find someone, the less likely it was that he or she would ever be found. The other members of the team were good-looking Samantha, driven Vivian, intense Danny and rookie Martin, who had to prove himself because his previous experience had been fighting white-collar crime.

At the end of each episode viewers were shown the picture of a real missing person and asked to call their local FBI office if they had seen the person or had any relevant information about the case.

WITNESS, THE (*Courtroom Anthology*)

FIRST TELECAST: *September 29, 1960*
LAST TELECAST: *January 26, 1961*
BROADCAST HISTORY:
Sep 1960–Dec 1960, CBS Thu 7:30–8:30
Dec 1960–Jan 1961, CBS Thu 9:00–10:00
CAST:
Court Reporter........................ Verne Collett
Court Clerk .... William Griffis
COMMITTEE MEMBERS:
Charles Haydon
Paul McGrath
William Smithers
Frank Milan

In a format that was similar to a Congressional investigation, this series attempted to dramatize the exploits and lifestyles of gangsters and rogues from the past and present. Detailed research was done on all of the "witnesses" who were brought before the committee to explain and/or defend their activities. The first of these hearings starred Telly Savalas as Charles "Lucky" Luciano. Among the other figures whose lives were exposed on this show were Bugsy Siegel, Dutch Schultz, Al Capone, John Dillinger, James Walker (former New York City mayor), and Ma Barker. The committee members asking the questions were all real attorneys and members of the New York Bar Association.

WIZARD, THE (*Adventure/Foreign Intrigue*)
FIRST TELECAST: *September 9, 1986*
LAST TELECAST: *July 7, 1987*
BROADCAST HISTORY:
Sep 1986–Oct 1986, CBS Tue 8:00–9:00
Nov 1986, CBS Sat 8:00–9:00
Dec 1986–Feb 1987, CBS Tue 8:00–9:00
Feb 1987–Apr 1987, CBS Thu 8:00–9:00
Jun 1987–Jul 1987, CBS Tue 8:00–9:00
CAST:
Simon McKay.................... David Rappaport
Alex Jagger........................... Douglas Barr
Tillie Russell............................. Fran Ryan

Although he made his living as an inventor of exotic and ingenious toys, diminutive Simon McKay (just four feet tall) spent much of his time helping people. He was a good samaritan who would track down people in need, design special devices to help the handicapped, and had, in the past, made contraptions for government agencies. It was this latter skill that had prompted the government to assign agent Alex Jagger to work with Simon. They were afraid that criminals or foreign powers who were aware of Simon's talents would kidnap him and force him to work for them. The two of them made quite a pair—impish, fun-loving Simon and serious, almost-humorless Alex. Together they traveled all over the world, at times on Simon's charitable missions and at others fighting the forces of evil. Tillie was the housekeeper who kept Simon's home in perfect order.

WIZARDS AND WARRIORS (*Adventure*)
FIRST TELECAST: *February 26, 1983*
LAST TELECAST: *May 14, 1983*
BROADCAST HISTORY:
Feb 1983–May 1983, CBS Sat 8:00–9:00
CAST:
Prince Erik Greystone................ Jeff Conaway
Marko........................... Walter Olkewicz
Prince Dirk Blackpool............. Duncan Regehr
Princess Ariel.......................... Julia Duffy
Wizard Vector.......................... Clive Revill
King Baaldorf............................. Tom Hill
Wizard Tranquil........................... Ian Wolfe
Geoffrey Blackpool................... Tim Dunigan
Justin Greystone............................ Jay Kerr
Queen Lattinia.......................... Julie Payne
Bethel................................. Randi Brooks
Cassandra............................. Phyllis Katz
Oriental Guard........................ Lonnie Wun

This period adventure with a sense of humor was set in the time of King Arthur's Court, when brave knights battled the forces of evil, with magic, sorcery, and sheer courage. The prize was the legendary Kingdom of Camarand, ruled by good King Baaldorf and Queen Lattinia. Their daughter, Princess Ariel, was betrothed to handsome Prince Erik Greystone, who, aided by his burly vassal Marko, was the principal defender of the realm. Evil Prince Dirk Blackpool was the archvillain, seeking to conquer Camarand through the black arts of Wizard Vector and sexy, decadent Witch Bethel. Prince Erik sometimes had the help of aged Wizard Tranquil, but often had to cope with no magical assistance at all. Justin was Erik's ne'er-do-well playboy brother, while Geoffrey was Blackpool's incompetent brother. Elaborate special effects such as ghosts, demons, powerful amulets, and fiery swords added visual impact to this short-lived fantasy.

WOLF (*Detective Drama*)
FIRST TELECAST: *September 13, 1989*
LAST TELECAST: *January 25, 1991*
BROADCAST HISTORY:
Sep 1989, CBS Wed 9:00–11:00
Sep 1989–Nov 1989, CBS Tue 9:00–10:00
Jun 1990, CBS Thu 10:00–11:00
Jul 1990–Sep 1990, CBS Wed 11:30–12:40 A.M.
Sep 1990, CBS Tue 12:40–1:45 A.M.
Oct 1990–Dec 1991, CBS Tue 1:10–2:15 A.M.
Jan 1991, CBS Tue–Fri 1:10–2:15 A.M.
Jan 1991, CBS Mon–Fri 12:00 midnight–1:10 A.M.
CAST:
Tony Wolf.............................. Jack Scalia
Sal Wolf............................ Joseph Sirola
Dylan Elliott..................... Nicolas Surovy
Melissa Shaw Elliott................. Judith Hoag
Connie Bacarri........................ Mimi Kuzyk
Angeline Bacarri..................... J. C. Brandy

Tony Wolf was an ex-San Francisco cop who had been too good for his own good—at least that's what the crooks who had set him up two years ago in a drug bust had thought. Although he had been framed, his superiors never found out. Now he was back working as a private investigator for, among others, Dylan Elliott, the attorney who had been instrumental in getting him thrown off the force. Dylan had come to believe he might have been wrong and helped Tony clear his name. Tony lived on *The Sea Wolf*, a family boat constantly in need of repair; had a crusty old father, Sal, with whom he was trying to reconcile; and spent much of his free time with Connie, his divorced high school sweetheart who worked at a small restaurant on Fisherman's Wharf. He also tried to help her deal with her tomboyish daughter, Angie.

One of the early casualties of the 1989–1990 season, *Wolf* was put on hiatus in November, returned briefly in June, and was banished to CBS' late-night lineup the following month. A number of first-run episodes aired there, along with reruns of those that had previously been seen in prime time.

WOLF LAKE (*Supernatural Drama*)
FIRST TELECAST: *September 19, 2001*
LAST TELECAST: *June 26, 2002*
BROADCAST HISTORY:
Sep 2001–Oct 2001, CBS Wed 10:00–11:00
Apr 2002–June 2002, UPN Wed 9:00–10:00
CAST:
John Kanin................. Lou Diamond Phillips
Sheriff Matthew Donner............ Tim Matheson
Sherman Blackstone............. Graham Greene
Sophia Donner (age 16).. Mary Elizabeth Winstead
Luke Cates...................... Paul Wasilewski
Ruby Wilder Cates.................. Mia Kirshner
Vivian Cates.................... Sharon Lawrence
Tyler Creed........................ Scott Bairstow
Willard Cates (2001)................ Bruce McGill
Presley................................ Fiona Scott
Miranda Devereaux................ Kellie Waymire
Dep. Molly Bloom.................. Carmen Moore
Buddy Hooks.................... Christian Bocher

Dark shadows and creepy music marked this short-lived melodrama. John Kanin was a moody young Seattle police officer whose girlfriend, Ruby, had disappeared after apparently being assaulted in her car. Receiving a tip about her whereabouts, he roared out of Seattle on his motorcycle and rode to the remote town of Wolf Lake to find her. What Kanin didn't know was that Ruby, her family and most of the residents of Wolf Lake were werewolves. Sheriff Donner, who befriended Kanin and eventually offered him a position with the Wolf Lake Police Department, was a "reformed" werewolf who quietly fought the town's scourge ("the beast within us"). The only other person in town who was willing to help was Sherman, the enigmatic Native American biology teacher who seemed to know everything about everybody.

Sheriff Donner's daughter, Sophia, who worked part-time at the local diner, had attracted the attention of Ruby's brother, Luke, which upset her father. Ruby and Luke's father was Willard Cates, a wealthy businessman, town boss and "high priest" of the werewolf pack—who was, however, dying. Vivian, his wife, had been having an affair with evil developer Tyler, who wanted to take Willard's place and control the pack. Ruby had originally fled Wolf Lake because her father had arranged her marriage to Tyler, whom she hated. Now she was being held captive in a cabin outside of town where Tyler was trying, unsuccessfully, to convince her to marry him.

In October Willard suffered a stroke. Then, while he was taking a "wolfen" run, he was caught in a trap and shot to death by a mystery man. After his death Ruby reluctantly married Tyler, which she hoped would protect Kanin from Tyler. When the pack gathered to choose a new leader (nominally the election was for presidency of Wolf Lake Brewery), the surprise winner, after a bloody, violent evening, was Willard's widow, Vivian.

Wolf Lake failed to attract much of an audience during its initial run on CBS and was pulled from the lineup after only five episodes. When it resurfaced on UPN the following spring, the CBS episodes were repeated, followed by four that had not previously been seen.

WOMAN TO REMEMBER, A (*Romantic Drama*)

FIRST TELECAST: *May 2, 1949*
LAST TELECAST: *July 15, 1949*
BROADCAST HISTORY:
May 1949–Jul 1949, DUM Mon–Fri 7:30–7:45
CAST:
Christine Baker .... Patricia Wheel
Steve Hammond........................ John Raby
Charley Anderson .... Frankie Thomas
Bessie Thatcher .... Ruth McDevitt
Carol Winstead .... Joan Catlin

A Woman to Remember was an early attempt to bring soap opera—radio soap opera, at that—to early-evening television. The leading character, Christine Baker, was even depicted as a radio soap-opera queen, engaged to handsome Steve Hammond, but beset by scheming rivals, notably shrewish Carol Winstead. Charley Anderson, the young sound man on Christine's show, and Bessie, another actress, were allies.

A Woman to Remember was first seen as a daytime serial, beginning February 21, 1949.

WOMEN DOCS (*Documentary*)

BROADCAST HISTORY:
Lifetime
60 minutes
Original episodes: *2001–2002* (23 episodes)
Premiered: *August 11, 2001*
NARRATOR:
Carolyn McCormick

Fast-paced documentary series focusing on women doctors in a different big-city hospital each week.

WOMEN IN PRISON (*Situation Comedy*)

FIRST TELECAST: *October 11, 1987*
LAST TELECAST: *April 2, 1988*
BROADCAST HISTORY:
Oct 1987, FOX Sun 8:30–9:00
Oct 1987–Apr 1988, FOX Sat 8:30–9:00
CAST:
Vicki Springer .... Julia Campbell
Asst. Warden Clint Rafferty .... Blake Clark
Dawn Murphy.................... C. C. H. Pounder
Eve Shipley............................ Peggy Cass
Bonnie Harper................... Antoinette Byron
Pam .... Wendie Jo Sperber
Meg Bando .... Denny Dillon

Twelve years after ABC failed with a comedy set in a men's prison *(On the Rocks),* Fox Broadcasting gave women equal time. The setting for this bizarre comedy was Bass Women's Prison in Wisconsin, where the inmates in cellblock J never seemed to be locked in their cells. Among the incarcerated skirts were naive Vicki, a pampered suburban housewife who had been framed for shoplifting by her philandering husband; Dawn, a tough black who had murdered her husband; Bonnie, a sexy, gay English hooker; and Eve, an aging, forgetful bank robber who had lived there for decades. In the adjoining cell, with a computer terminal but no roommates, was Pam, a brilliant but sarcastic woman who was serving time for computer embezzlement. Meg was cellblock J's short, frumpy, sadistic guard, and Warden Rafferty the grumpy boss, for whom Vicki worked as a secretary.

None of this was meant to be taken the least bit seriously, it seems. The garish theme song thundered lines like "So misunderstood, now you're missing a life that was so good. . . . While other girls make dates, you make license plates. . . . you're in JAIL!!"

WOMEN OF THE HOUSE (*Situation Comedy*)

FIRST TELECAST: *January 4, 1995*
LAST TELECAST: *March 20, 1995*
BROADCAST HISTORY:
Jan 1995–Feb 1995, CBS Wed 8:00–8:30
Mar 1995, CBS Mon 8:30–9:00
CAST:
Suzanne Sugarbaker .... Delta Burke
Sissy Emerson .... Teri Garr
Jim Sugarbaker.................... Jonathan Banks
Natalie Hollingsworth .... Patricia Heaton
Jennifer Malone................. Valerie Mahaffey
Jennifer Malone......................... Julie Hagerty
Desiree Sugarbaker .... Brittany Parkyn
THEME:
"Something to Talk About," performed by Shirley Elkhard

Following the death of 76-year-old Ray, her fifth husband, Suzanne Sugarbaker moved to Washington to fill out his term in the House of Representatives. With her were her young adopted daughter, Desiree, and her mentally retarded brother, Jim. Since nobody in Washington expected her to be around long—she was considered a political lightweight who would be gone after the next election—few people were interested in being on her staff, so she hired the three who were at her office when she arrived. They were chief of staff Natalie, former lover and chief aide to a congressman who was now in prison; press secretary Sissy, former *Washington Post* reporter whose drinking had gotten her fired; and naive receptionist Jennifer, whose football coach husband had run off with a Washington Redskins cheerleader and left her with no money and two sons to raise. Natalie had hopes of shaping Suzanne into her own highly efficient and politically savvy image but found the self-centered, out-spoken, and flamboyant Miss Sugarbaker difficult to mold. She did what she wanted to do, said what ever came to mind, and was oblivious to Washington protocol.

For star Delta Burke, this was a strange homecoming. She had been fired from *Designing Women* after feuding with series producers Linda Bloodworth-Thomason and Harry Thomason. Now, four years later, she reprised the role and coproduced the series with her former employers. The Thomasons' original choice for the role of Jennifer was Julie Hagerty, who was in a play when production began. Valerie Mahaffey filled in for her until she was available and ended up back in the part when Hagerty quit after taping only two episodes.

Five months after its original run had ended, CBS aired a single episode of *Women of the House*. Three weeks later, on September 8, Lifetime Cable presented the four remaining originial episodes as a two-hour special.

WONDER WOMAN (*Adventure*)

FIRST TELECAST: *December 18, 1976*
LAST TELECAST: *September 11, 1979*
BROADCAST HISTORY:

Dec 1976–Jan 1977, ABC Sat 8:00–9:00
May 1977–Jul 1977, ABC Sat 8:00–9:00
Sep 1977–Feb 1979, CBS Fri 8:00–9:00
Aug 1979–Sep 1979, CBS Tue 8:00–9:00

CAST:

Yeoman Diana Prince/"Wonder Woman" .... Lynda Carter
Maj. Steve Trevor/Steve Trevor, Jr. .... Lyle Waggoner
Gen. Blankenship (1976–1977) ... Richard Eastham
Corp. Etta Candy (1976–1977) ...... Beatrice Colen
Joe Atkinson (1977) .... Normann Burton
Eve (1977–1979) .... Saundra Sharp
Voice of I.R.A. (1977–1979) .... Tom Kratochzil

Wonder Woman, based on Charles Moulton's comic-book superheroine of the 1940s, developed gradually into a regular TV series. It was first seen as a TV movie in March 1974 (with Cathy Lee Crosby in the title role), then in another try in November 1975 (with Lynda Carter), then in a series of specials called *The New Original Wonder Woman* beginning in March 1976. After popping up in various spots all over the ABC schedule, it had a short consecutive-weeks run in December 1976–January 1977. Finally, in the fall of 1977, it moved to CBS and became a regular weekly series.

The show was comic-strip, pure and simple, set in the 1940s. Wonder Woman came from a "lost" island where a band of Amazon women had fled *ca.* 200 B.C. to escape male domination by the ancient Greeks and Romans. On Paradise Island they found the magic substance Feminum, which when molded into a golden belt gave them superhuman strength and in golden bracelets could deflect bullets. It didn't help their love life much, though, so when Major Steve Trevor of the U.S. army crash-landed on the island during World War II, Wonder Woman fell in love and returned with him to the U.S. in the guise of his secretary. Major Trevor did not know of her powers, but when trouble threatened, Yeoman Prince could disappear for a while, and whirl herself into Wonder Woman! She then reappeared, clad in sexy tights and draped in a cape that looked something like the American flag.

Her opponents were mostly Nazi agents, plus a few aliens from outer space, all of whom were dispatched in slam-bang-biff-pow style. Once the Nazis even found and occupied Paradise Island in their quest for Feminum, and they had their own Wonder Woman in Fausta. Seen occasionally on Diana's side was her younger sister, Drusilla, the "Wonder Girl" (played by Debra Winger).

When the series moved to CBS in the fall of 1977 there were a number of changes made. The title was now *The New Adventures of Wonder Woman* and the period was contemporary, rather than World War II. The heroine returned to America to fight terrorists and subversive elements for the Inter-Agency Defense Command (IADC), where her boss was Joe Atkinson. Working closely with her was Steve Trevor, Jr., the son of the Major Trevor with whom she had been associated during World War II. Since she had not aged at all—residents of Paradise Island had life spans measured in centuries, not decades—and Steve, Jr., was a dead ringer for his father, the couple seemed virtually unchanged. Eve was Steve's secretary. By the end of 1977 Mr. Atkinson had been phased out of the show and Steve had been promoted to Diana Prince's boss, leaving her to go alone on missions. A primary source of information for all IADC agents was the Internal Retrieval Associative computer. This wonderful device, called IRA by the staff, could actually communicate by voice with the agents. Despite the fact that Diana was no longer wearing glasses to conceal her real identity, as she had done in the ABC version of *Wonder Woman*, only IRA knew who she really was.

Lynda Carter, who portrayed Wonder Woman, did fit the part. A former "Miss World—U.S.A.," she was very athletic, tall (5'10", not 6' as some publicity releases claimed), and extremely well-endowed.

WONDER YEARS, THE (*Situation Comedy*)

FIRST TELECAST: *March 15, 1988*
LAST TELECAST: *September 1, 1993*
BROADCAST HISTORY:

Mar 1988–Apr 1988, ABC Tues 8:30–9:00
Oct 1988–Feb 1989, ABC Wed 9:00–9:30
Feb 1989–Aug 1990, ABC Tue 8:30–9:00
Aug 1990–Aug 1991, ABC Wed 8:00–8:30
Aug 1991–Feb 1992, ABC Wed 8:30–9:00
Mar 1992–Sep 1993, ABC Wed 8:00–8:30

CAST:

Kevin Arnold (age 12) .... Fred Savage
Kevin (as adult; voice only) .... Daniel Stern
Wayne Arnold .... Jason Hervey

Karen Arnold (1988–1992) .... Olivia d'Abo
Norma Arnold .... Alley Mills
Jack Arnold .... Dan Lauria
Paul Pfeiffer .... Josh Saviano
Winnie (Gwendolyn) Cooper ...... Danica McKellar
**Coach Cutlip* .... Robert Picardo
**Becky Slater* .... Crystal McKellar
**Mrs. Ritvo (1988–1989)* .... Linda Hoy
**Kirk McCray (1988–1989)* .... Michael Landes
**Carla Healy (1988–1990)* .... Krista Murphy
**Mr. DiPerna (1988–1991)* .... Raye Birk
**Mr. Cantwell (1988–1991)* .... Ben Stein
**Doug Porter (1989–1991)* .... Brandon Crane
**Randy Mitchell (1989–1993)* ...... Michael Tricario
**Craig Hobson (1989–1990)* .... Sean Baca
Ricky Halsenback (1991–1993) .... Scott Nemes
Jeff Billings (1992–1993) .... Giovanni Ribisi
**Michael (1992)* .... David Schwimmer

*Occasional

THEME:

"With a Little Help from My Friends," sung by Joe Cocker

A whimsical view of growing up in suburban America of the '60s, as seen through the eyes of a 12-year-old. In 1968 Kevin was just entering Robert F. Kennedy Junior High School. Vietnam protests, Beatles music and America's space program were in the air, but Kevin's concerns were closer to home. His teenage brother, Wayne, existed only to torture and humiliate him, or so it seemed; his older sister Karen was in her own world of love beads and social protest. Mom (Norma) and Dad (Jack) were a little distant—especially Dad, an intimidating presence who came home tired from work each day, and always seemed to get in an argument with someone. The family dog was Buster. Fitting in at school was an awesome challenge, shared with best friend Paul and hoped-for girlfriend Winnie. But Kevin, a rambunctious kid with an angelic face, would try.

A wide variety of teachers, dates, friends, and tormentors were seen from time to time, as stories explored Kevin's relationships with adults and peers—and especially with Paul and Winnie. Perhaps the most memorable were fearsome Coach Cutlip (played to the hilt by Robert Picardo, who was appearing simultaneously in a very different role on ABC's *China Beach*) and "steady date" Becky, the best alternative to beloved Winnie.

By the end of the series' run the time had advanced to the early 1970s. Dad gave up his bureaucratic job at Norcom and started his own furniture-making business; Wayne graduated from McKinley High and got his first job—at the same company his father had left. He lived downstairs in the family rec room. At the end of the 1991–1992 season Karen married Michael, in an outdoor "hippie" celebration that upset her family, and moved to Alaska.

The final episode in 1993 looked ahead nostalgically, as if skimming the remaining pages in the family album. Kevin finally broke with his domineering father but made up before Jack died, two years after the series ended. Wayne took over the family's business upon his father's death. Karen had a son, and best friend Paul went to Harvard and became a lawyer. And Winnie, the love of Kevin's life? She went to Paris to study art, leaving Kevin to marry another, with whom he had a son. But he would always remember . . .

The series was narrated by an unseen, adult Kevin; news clips and music from the period also contributed to the nostalgic flavor. One critic called it "A *Leave It to Beaver* with bite." A special preview of the series was telecast on January 31, 1988, following the Super Bowl.

WONDERFUL JOHN ACTON, THE (*Drama*)

FIRST TELECAST: *July 5, 1953*
LAST TELECAST: *September 22, 1953*
BROADCAST HISTORY:

July 1953–Aug 1953, NBC Sun 10:00–10:30
Sep 1953, NBC Tue 8:30–9:00

CAST:

John Acton .... Harry Holcombe
Uncle Terrence .... Ian Martin
Julia Acton .... Virginia Dwyer
Kevin Acton .... Ronnie Walken
Aunt Bessie .... Jane Rose
Peter Bodkin, Sr. .... Pat Harrington
Birdie Bodkin .... Mary Michael
Narrator .... Luis Van Rooten

Set in the Ohio River Valley town of Ludlow, Kentucky, *The Wonderful John Acton* was the story of an Irish family in 1919. John Acton was the county clerk and owned a combination candy and notions store, with his living quarters in the back. The stories were narrated by John's grandson, Kevin Acton, who reminisced about his childhood growing up in small-town America. Kevin revered his grandfather and had always considered him someone "wonderful." As narrator, the adult Kevin was never seen in this live dramatic series.

WONDERFUL WORLD OF DISNEY, THE, see *Walt Disney*

WONDERLAND (*Medical Drama*)

FIRST TELECAST: *March 30, 2000*
LAST TELECAST: *April 6, 2000*
BROADCAST HISTORY:

Mar 2000–Apr 2000, ABC Thu 10:00–11:00

CAST:

Dr. Robert Banger .... Ted Levine
Dr. Neil Harrison .... Martin Donovan
Dr. Lyla Garrity .... Michelle Forbes
Dr. Abe Matthews .... Billy Burke
Dr. Derrick Hatcher .... Michael Jai White
Dr. Heather Miles .... Joelle Carter
Julie McCray .... Michelle Barker

THEME:

co-composed and performed by Madonna

This dark, violent series combined psychiatry, criminology and medical drama at New York's Rivervue Psychiatric Hospital. Dr. Banger was the bearded chief of forensic psychiatry, responsible for some of the city's worst criminal crazies; in addition to his high-stress job, he was dealing with a bitter divorce in which he had to fight tooth and nail for joint custody of his two young sons. Dr. Harrison was the rather self-righteous husband of pregnant Dr. Garrity, who in the opening had to deal with the aftermath of her decision to release a patient who subsequently went on a shooting rampage, killing five people in Times Square. Dr. Matthews was a commitment-phobic womanizer (every medical show has one), and Dr. Hatcher a stressed-out single parent, who was responsible for training the hospital's young med students. Some patients were violent, others just yelled a lot or had "visions," but the whole atmosphere was one of tremendous noise, distraction and depression. Critics were impressed, but viewers fled.

WOOPS! (*Situation Comedy*)
FIRST TELECAST: *September 27, 1992*
LAST TELECAST: *December 6, 1992*
BROADCAST HISTORY:
Sep 1992–Dec 1992, FOX Sun 10:30–11:00
CAST:
Jack Connors .... Fred Applegate
Curtis Thorpe.................... Lane Davies
Dr. Frederick Ross.............. Cleavant Derricks
Alice McConnell.................. Meagan Fay
Suzanne Stillman .... Marita Geraghty
Mark Braddock .... Evan Handler

In this bizarre postapocalyptic comedy, kids playing with an electronic toy at a small Midwestern parade accidentally set off a nuclear missile that triggered a nuclear holocaust that wiped out almost the entire world population in less than an hour. However, six people survived, just enough to stock this Fox comedy. Mark, the narrator, had survived because he was in his Volvo; he had driven through devastation until he ran out of gas and found a lone farmhouse where the other five had found each other. A former English teacher, he kept a journal of the group's progress and was chosen as the leader because he was the least opinionated.

The other survivors were Alice, an idealistic feminist and somewhat spacey intellectual who had been in her bookstore basement, which had been built as a bomb shelter in the 1960s; Curtis, an arrogant, yuppie stock analyst who had been in the vault in his brokerage office; Jack, a perpetually cheery and optimistic homeless person with a penchant for joking around who had been living under the interstate; Frederick, a pessimistic black pathologist who had been in an underground morgue; and Suzanne, a sexy but dumb manicurist with no discernible opinions about anything. Occasional mutant insects (such as a gigantic grasshopper) intruded, but most of the action took place in the farmhouse as the six tried various nutty schemes to organize their new, "better world."

WORD OF LIFE SONGTIME, THE, see *Songtime*

WORDS AND MUSIC (*Music*)
FIRST TELECAST: *August 2, 1949*
LAST TELECAST: *September 8, 1949*
BROADCAST HISTORY:
Aug 1949–Sep 1949, NBC Tue/Thu 7:30–7:45
REGULARS:
Barbara Marshall
Jerry Jerome Trio

Live musical interlude featuring singer-pianist Barbara Marshall.

WORK WITH ME (*Situation Comedy*)
FIRST TELECAST: *September 29, 1999*
LAST TELECAST: *October 20, 1999*
BROADCAST HISTORY:
Sep 1999–Oct 1999, CBS Wed 8:30–9:00
CAST:
Julie Better .... Nancy Travis
Jordan Better......................... Kevin Pollak
Sebastian .... Ethan Embry
Stacy .... Emily Rutherfurd
A.J................................... Bray Poor

Two married attorneys in their mid-30s living in Manhattan decided to work together in this short-lived sitcom. When Jordan failed to make partner after 10 years at a stuffy Wall Street law firm, he quit and went into partnership with his wife, Julie, who ran her own legal practice from a small office. He was convinced that it would be good for their relationship, since their heavy workloads had made it difficult to find time together, but their divergent styles created a big problem. Compulsive Jordan was a hyperactive planner, while impulsive Julie preferred to go with the flow (she to he: "How do you not give *yourself* a headache?"). Stacy and Sebastian, their young assistants who had been having a secret affair for months, were now forced to cope with the temptations of working in the same office. A. J., the rather hyper relaxation therapist with an office next door, showed up regularly to offer advice.

WORKING (*Situation Comedy*)
FIRST TELECAST: *October 8, 1997*
LAST TELECAST: *January 25, 1999*
BROADCAST HISTORY:
Oct 1997–May 1998, NBC Wed 9:30–10:00
May 1998–Jun 1998, NBC Wed 8:30–9:00
Jun 1998–Jul 1998, NBC Wed 9:30–10:00
Jun 1998–Jul 1998, NBC Sun 8:30–9:00
Sep 1998–Dec 1998, NBC Tue 9:30–10:00
Jan 1999, NBC Mon 9:30–10:00
CAST:
Matt Peyser........................... Fred Savage
Tim Deale .... Maurice Godin
Hal (1997–1998)...................... Sarah Knowlton
Val (1998–1999)...................... Rebecca McFarland
Abby Cosgrove......................... Arden Myrin
John Delaney .... Steve Hytner
Jimmy Clarke (1997–1998) .... Dana Gould
Evelyn Smalley........................ Yvette Freeman
Liz Tricolli (1998–1999)............. Debi Mazar
THEME:
"Working in the Coal Mine" (Lee Dorsey/Devo pop song), recorded by Mark Mothersbaugh

Matt was a young, eager office worker starting his first job in a huge, faceless corporation in this raucous, almost surrealistic burlesque on the modern corporate workplace. His new employer was Upton/Weber, a massive international conglomerate, although exactly what the company did remained a mystery. Its headquarters was a gleaming skyscraper, complete with circling vultures. Inside was a beehive of activity, although if you looked closely nobody was actually doing anything meaningful. Matt's boss was Tim Deale, a weasily corporate politician whose credo seemed to be make no commitments, don't work too hard, and never get caught. Others in his department were Hal, the sexy, Yale-educated, wildly overqualified secretary; Abby, the perky, eager-to-please social organizer; John, the sarcastic loner (who rebelled by wearing a loose tie); Jimmy, the young worker who ratted on everyone; and Evelyn, the brusque, demanding officer manager (her scowling visage was seen on computer screen-savers in the background). The second season saw the arrival of Liz, a saucy, ambitious worker, and Hal's replacement by the nearly identical Val. Stories revolved around office projects and politics, the nonsensical decisions of management, and excursions outside the office. Elaborately produced mock commercials for Upton/Webber were seen between the acts, but they did little to clarify what the company did ("Upton/Webber . . . Making the products that make you buy more of our products, since 1892").

WORKING GIRL (*Situation Comedy*)
FIRST TELECAST: *April 16, 1990*
LAST TELECAST: *July 30, 1990*
BROADCAST HISTORY:
Apr 1990–May 1990, NBC Mon 8:30–9:00
Jul 1990, NBC Mon 8:30–9:00
CAST:
Tess McGill .... Sandra Bullock
Bryn Newhouse .... Nana Visitor
Lana Peters .... Judy Prescott
Everett Rutledge .... George Newbern
Libby Wentworth .... Edye Byrde
A. J. Trask .... Tom O'Rourke
Sal Pascarella .... Anthony Tyler Quinn
Joe McGill .... David Schramm
Fran McGill .... B. J. Ward

Another hit movie that failed as a TV series was *Working Girl*. The 1988 film starred Melanie Griffith in the title role, with Sigourney Weaver as her insufferable boss, but the TV series had to settle for lesser-known talent. Tess, the spunky, independent secretary who suddenly becomes a junior executive after charming company owner A. J. Trask, was portrayed here by newcomer Sandra Bullock (Nancy McKeon of *Facts of Life* was originally supposed to play the role). Tess' first challenge was to survive working for her antagonistic, uptight immediate boss, Ms. Newhouse, also known as the "company witch." Lana, a secretary, was Tess' best pal, more interested in doing her nails and rooting for Tess than in getting ahead herself; Everett was a fellow junior executive who was charming but too eager to please; and Libby was Tess' worldly wise, "permanent temporary" secretary, a moonlighting musician. Back home each night on Staten Island, Tess had to contend with her doting parents Joe and Fran, and with Sal, the blue-collar neighborhood Romeo who constantly pursued her.

WORKING IT OUT (*Situation Comedy*)
FIRST TELECAST: *August 22, 1990*
LAST TELECAST: *December 26, 1990*
BROADCAST HISTORY:
Aug 1990, NBC Wed 9:00–9:30
Sep 1990–Nov 1990, NBC Sat 8:30–9:00
Nov 1990–Dec 1990, NBC Wed 9:30–10:00
CAST:
Sarah Marshall .... Jane Curtin
David Stuart .... Stephen Collins
Andy .... Mary Beth Hurt
Stan .... David Garrison
Molly Marshall (age 9) .... Kyndra Joy Casper
Sophie .... Chevi Colton

A romantic comedy about the mating dance between two divorced, single parents; conservative, uptight Sarah and easygoing professional photographer David. Each was quite content with the single life and not thinking of serious dating until they met one night at a Manhattan cooking class (the kind populated mostly by singles looking for mates). There, across the linguine, their eyes met, and a stop-and-go courtship began. Sarah's best friend Andy told her men were not interested in women with small children, and David's pal Stan advised him to avoid the same. But to no avail. Sarah's 9-year-old daughter Molly was regularly seen, but David's two older daughters were away at college and probably missed this short-lived series altogether.

WORKING STIFFS (*Situation Comedy*)
FIRST TELECAST: *September 15, 1979*
LAST TELECAST: *October 6, 1979*
BROADCAST HISTORY:
Sep 1979–Oct 1979, CBS Sat 8:00–8:30
CAST:
Ernie O'Rourke .... Jim Belushi
Mike O'Rourke .... Michael Keaton
Al Steckler .... Val Bisoglio
Frank Falzone .... Phil Rubinstein
Mitch Hannigan .... Alan Arbus
Nikki Evashevsky .... Lorna Patterson

One of the first casualties of the 1979–1980 season, *Working Stiffs* was the story of two young brothers trying to get started in the business world. Ernie and Mike O'Rourke were ambitious, but incredibly clumsy janitors planning to work their way up from the bottom in the building-management field. The Chicago office building where they worked was owned by their uncle, Al Steckler, and Frank Falzone was their immediate superior, the building manager. Ernie and Mike lived in a small apartment over the Playland Cafe, where they spent much of their spare time with owner Mitch Hannigan and waitress Nikki Evashevsky. Dismal ratings cut the life of this slapstick comedy to less than a month.

WORLD IN YOUR HOME, THE (*Documentary*)
FIRST TELECAST: *December 22, 1944*
LAST TELECAST: *January 9, 1948*
BROADCAST HISTORY:
Dec 1944–Jan 1948, NBC Fri 8:45–9:00 (approx.)

One of the very earliest regular network features on TV seems to have been this weekly educational film sponsored by RCA Victor. It ran for more than three years in the same time slot, from 1944 to 1948. Network records are sketchy that far back and it is not known exactly when *The World in Your Home* became a network show (it originated from New York), but New York, Philadelphia, and Schenectady were linked by NBC-TV in 1944 and it is quite possible that it was fed to all three stations from the beginning.

WORLD OF DISCOVERY (*Documentary*)
FIRST TELECAST: *June 23, 1997*
LAST TELECAST: *July 28, 1997*
BROADCAST HISTORY:
Jun 1997–Jul 1997, ABC Mon 8:00–9:00
HOST:
James Brolin

A weekly series of nature documentaries, most of them previously shown on the network as specials between 1993 and 1996. Among them were "Polar Bears, Arctic Terror," "Blue Whale: Largest Animal on Earth," and "Last Charge of the Rhinos." Also known as *ABC's World of Discovery*.

WORLD OF MR. SWEENEY, THE (*Situation Comedy*)

FIRST TELECAST: *June 30, 1954*
LAST TELECAST: *August 20, 1954*
BROADCAST HISTORY:
Jun 1954–Aug 1954, NBC Tue–Fri 7:30–7:45
CAST:
Cicero P. Sweeney .... Charlie Ruggles
Kippy Franklin .... Glenn Walken
Marge Franklin .... Helen Wagner

Following a season as one of the segments of *The Kate Smith Evening Hour, The World of Mr. Sweeney* struck out on its own during the summer of 1954. Cicero P. Sweeney was the owner of a small-town general store who, in addition to providing groceries to the townspeople, was a sounding board for their problems and provider of good advice. Each episode revolved around different members of the local community and Sweeney's solutions to their problems. The only regulars other than Sweeney himself were his grandson, Kippy, and Kippy's mother, Marge. *The World of Mr. Sweeney* was produced live from New York throughout its nighttime run. In October 1954 it moved to the NBC Monday–Friday daytime lineup, where it stayed until December 1955.

Despite its relatively short run, *The World of Mr. Sweeney* was once cited as holding the all-time record for the largest number of episodes of a comedy series ever presented on the NBC network—mostly because of its 14 months in daytime, where it ran five times a week. In all, 345 installments were presented.

WORLD OF TALENT, see *Dick Clark's World of Talent*

WORLD WAR I (*Documentary*)

FIRST TELECAST: *September 22, 1964*
LAST TELECAST: *September 5, 1965*
BROADCAST HISTORY:
Sep 1964–Dec 1964, CBS Tue 8:00–8:30
Dec 1964–Sep 1965, CBS Sun 6:30–7:00
NARRATOR:
Robert Ryan

This was a documentary series recalling the background causes, conduct, and aftermath of World War I. The emotional reactions of the leaders and peoples most directly involved, as well as the social, political, and economic fabric of the times, were analyzed in depth.

WORLD WIDE '60 (*Documentary*)

FIRST TELECAST: *January 23, 1960*
LAST TELECAST: *August 27, 1960*
BROADCAST HISTORY:
Jan 1960–Aug 1960, NBC Sat 9:30–10:30
HOST:
Frank McGee

NBC News correspondent Frank McGee served as host and narrator of this series of public-affairs documentaries. The subject matter ranged from alcoholism, to old age, to architecture, to missiles, to jazz, to the problems of refugees. The premiere telecast of this series covered the first year of Fidel Castro's regime in Cuba.

WORLD'S FUNNIEST!, THE (*Comedy*)

FIRST TELECAST: *September 21, 1997*
LAST TELECAST: *January 30, 2000*
BROADCAST HISTORY:
Sep 1997–Aug 1998, FOX Sun 7:00–8:00
Aug 1998–Oct 1998, FOX Sun 7:00–7:30
Nov 1998–Jun 1999, FOX Sun 7:00–8:00
Dec 1998–Jan 1999, FOX Tue 8:30–9:00
Jun 1999–Oct 1999, FOX Sun 7:00–7:30
Jun 1999–Aug 1999, FOX Fri 8:00–9:00
Dec 1999–Jan 2000, FOX Sun 7:00–7:30
HOST:
James Brown

During the 1996–1997 season Fox had aired a number of blooper and outtake specials, and the following fall decided to turn the specials into a weekly series. In addition to outtakes from films and TV series, material included commercials from around the world, filmed and taped pieces about ordinary people in funny situations, hidden camera pranks, and segments on animals and small children.

Viewers were encouraged to send in amusing and/or embarrassing videos. If the videos were used on the show, the sender received $200 (raised to $500 in 1998) and, if it was voted the most embarrassing on the show, they won $5,000.

WORLD'S FUNNIEST VIDEOS (*Comedy*)

FIRST TELECAST: *February 1, 1996*
LAST TELECAST: *June 20, 1996*
BROADCAST HISTORY:
Feb 1996–Jun 1996, ABC Thu 8:00–8:30
HOSTS:
Dave Coulier
Eva LaRue

Another home videos show, this one featuring candid tapes from around the world: e.g., a man crooning in his bathtub, complete with keyboard and dark glasses; a parrot having a martini. Some segments were taped at Disney World's Epcot Center in Florida. The show's theme song was called "The Whole World's Watching You."

WORLD'S MOST AMAZING VIDEOS (*Reality*)

FIRST TELECAST: *March 3, 1999*
LAST TELECAST: *January 14, 2001*
BROADCAST HISTORY:
Mar 1999–Sep 1999, NBC Wed 9:00–10:00
Jun 1999, NBC Sun 7:00–8:00
Nov 1999–Jan 2000, NBC Sat 10:00–11:00
Feb 2000, NBC Sun 7:00–8:00
Jun 2000–Jul 2000, NBC Sun 7:00–8:00
Dec 2000–Jan 2001, NBC Sun 7:00–7:30
NARRATOR:
Stacy Keach

Another of TV's many "shockumentary" series, featuring graphic real-life footage of police chases, natural disasters, and people in distress. Among them: an escape artist who was buried alive, a pilot sucked into a jet engine, a race car crashing into a TV cameraman, a pregnant woman leaping from a burning building, an exploding rocket-fuel factory, and canoers caught in raging rapids.

WORLD'S WILDEST POLICE VIDEOS (*Police Documentary*)

FIRST TELECAST: *April 2, 1998*
LAST TELECAST: *September 7, 2001*
BROADCAST HISTORY:
Apr 1998–Oct 1999, FOX Thu 8:00–9:00

Jan 2000–May 2000, FOX Fri 8:00–9:00
Oct 2000–Sep 2001, FOX Fri 8:00–9:00

HOST:
John Bunnell

Fox had aired a succession of extremely violent specials during the year before this series premiered. Among them were "Moment of Impact," "Prisoners Out of Control," "Cheating Death," "World's Scariest Police Stings," "World's Scariest Police Shootouts," and four different "World's Scariest Police Chases." Despite receiving a lambasting from critics for pandering to the blood lust of viewers, Fox turned the specials into a weekly series because of the high ratings they had received. Bunnell, a retired sheriff from Portland, Oregon, excitedly hosted this collection of car chases, surveillance footage of robberies in progress, SWAT team action, and shootouts, many captured by dash-mounted squad car video cameras.

The series' title was shortened to *Police Videos* in May 2000.

WORST CASE SCENARIO (*Documentary*)

BROADCAST HISTORY:
TBS
60 minutes
Original episodes: *2002–*
Premiered: *July 10, 2002*

REGULARS:
Mike Rowe
Danielle Burgio ("Gear Girl")

This ridiculous reality show opened at The Worst Case Institute, a large room filled with what appeared to be surplus scientific equipment, where host Mike Rowe solemnly informed viewers that they were about to learn how to get out of dangerous situations. What followed were reenactments containing a confusing jumble of practical tips (how to kick down a door in an emergency: aim for the area of the doorknob) and dubious advice (how to jump off a three-story building: look for a Dumpster with nothing sharp in it to land in), plus challenges between experts (two lost survivalists competed to see who could get out of the woods fastest). One frightened woman was challenged to overcome her fears and jump 40 feet off a cliff into the water below (tip: keep your feet together!). Well, maybe someday she'll be chased by a bear. Helping demonstrate were some remarkably sexy stuntwomen, and a "Gear Girl." Based on the *Worst Case Scenario* book series.

WRANGLER (*Western*)

FIRST TELECAST: *August 4, 1960*
LAST TELECAST: *September 15, 1960*
BROADCAST HISTORY:
Aug 1960–Sep 1960, NBC Thu 9:30–10:00

CAST:
Pitcairn, the Wrangler .... Jason Evers

Wrangler was the 1960 summer replacement for *The Ford Show Starring Tennessee Ernie Ford.* Pitcairn, the Wrangler, was an adventurer who traveled about the Old West working sometimes as a ranch hand, sometimes as a gunfighter, and sometimes as a good samaritan. This short-lived summer series was filled with rustlers, horse thieves, hostile Indians, and all the other low-brow characters so prevalent in superficial Western shoot-'em-ups.

WREN'S NEST (*Situation Comedy*)

FIRST TELECAST: *January 13, 1949*
LAST TELECAST: *April 30, 1949*
BROADCAST HISTORY:
Jan 1949–Apr 1949, ABC Thu/Fri/Sat 7:15–7:30

CAST:
Sam Wren
Virginia Sale

One of the many "Mr. and Mrs." comedies of early television was this thrice-weekly series about the home life of a suburban New York couple and their 12-year-old twins. The Wrens were also married in real life, and both had appeared in numerous Hollywood films. (Virginia's screen career lasted from the 1920s to the 1960s, and later at the age of 80, she completed a one-woman national tour doing her comedy-drama act in theaters, schools, and clubs.)

WRESTLING (*Sports*)

FIRST TELECAST: *July 30, 1948*
LAST TELECAST:
BROADCAST HISTORY:

Monday
Sep 1949–Jan 1950, DUM 9:30–11:00
Jan 1950–Feb 1952, DUM 9:00–11:00
Feb 1952–Mar 1952, DUM 9:30–11:00

Tuesday
Oct 1948–Jul 1949, NBC 10:00–Conclusion
Jan 1950–Aug 1950, CBS 10:00–Conclusion

Wednesday
Aug 1948–Sep 1950, ABC 9:30–Conclusion
Sep 1950–Apr 1951, ABC 10:00–Conclusion
Apr 1951–Sep 1951, ABC 9:30–11:00
Jun 1952–Sep 1952, ABC 10:00–11:15
Sep 1952–Oct 1953, ABC 9:30–11:15
Oct 1953–Sep 1954, ABC 10:00–midnight

Thursday
Oct 1948–Jan 1949, DUM 9:00–Conclusion
Aug 1999– , UPN Thu 8:00–10:00

Friday
Jul 1948–Dec 1948, DUM 9:00–Conclusion

Saturday
Sep 1949–May 1951, DUM 10:00–Conclusion
May 1951–Mar 1955, DUM 9:30–Conclusion

Professional wrestling, the world of the "grunt and groaners," was a regular and popular form of entertainment on early, live network television, particularly on ABC and DuMont. Names like Gorgeous George, Antonino "Argentina" Rocca, and The Mighty Atlas were household words among the owners of TV sets in the late 1940s and early 1950s, as well as among those who watched the matches at their local bars. The two longest-running wrestling shows originated from Chicago—Jack Brickhouse doing the play-by-play from Marigold Garden every Saturday night on DuMont for almost six years and Wayne Griffin announcing from Rainbow Arena for ABC for roughly the same length of time. DuMont's other long-running wrestling show originated from various arenas around the New York City area (Jerome Arena, Jamaica Arena, Sunnyside Gardens, and Columbia Park Arena) with Dennis James at the mike. Bill Johnston, Jr., did commentary for CBS' New York–based show (from the Bronx Winter Garden Arena and St. Nicholas Arena), and NBC's show was covered by Bob Stanton (from St. Nicholas Arena).

The most famous of these early wrestling announcers was probably DuMont's Dennis James, whose simplified explanations and infectious enthusiasm made the sport palatable even to little old ladies. His oft-repeated phrase "Okay, Mother" became so identified with him that it was later used for the title of one of his numerous daytime game shows. That a game show emcee like James could become wrestling's most famous commentator was perhaps symbolic of the fact that on TV, wrestling was more show business than sport.

In the 1980s, wrestling experienced tremendous growth in popularity, not on broadcast TV, but on cable. Coverage on the USA Network and Superstation WTBS took what had been regional wrestling federations for decades, the WWF and the NWA (later renamed WCW), and gave them national exposure. For wrestling aficionados, people like Ric Flair, Dusty Rhodes, Roddy Piper, Andre the Giant, Sergeant Slaughter, the Road Warriors, Larry Zbyszko, and Jesse "the Body" Ventura became household names. But the biggest wrestling star of the '80s and early '90s, and the one given the most credit for its resurgence during that period, was Hulk Hogan. He was so popular that he starred in movies—albeit forgettable films such as *No Holds Barred, Suburban Commando,* and *Mr. Nanny*—and had his own TV series *(Thunder in Paradise).*

As wrestling moved closer to the millennium, it reached new levels of popularity. The promoters, most notably the WWF's Vince McMahon, publicly acknowledged that the matches were scripted and began referring to professional wrestling as "sports entertainment" rather than a sport. The amount of extracurricular activity—interviews, posturing, threatening each other, fighting in the locker rooms, the parking lots and anyplace other than the ring—expanded by the week. Beefy wrestlers bellowed at each other ("I'm gonna whup yo' ass!") and high-volume ringside announcers shrieked ("Did you see *that*??"). Convoluted continuing story lines pitted faction against faction, wrestlers vs. their bosses, tough guys against the world, making pro wrestling look like an action-packed beefcake soap opera.

The WWF, trying to rebuild its audience after a rough period earlier in the '90s when it was hurt by a steroid scandal and then lost many of its stars to the better-funded WCW, became progressively raunchier. Foul language, rude hand gestures, overt sexuality, and out-of-the-ring fighting became staples as it evolved into a musclebound theater of the absurd. "Stone Cold" Steve Austin epitomized the new WWF—nasty, profane, and stopping at nothing to win. Other stars included the glowering, six-foot-ten-inch Undertaker, the masked Mankind, sexy Sable (yes, there were women in the new pro wrestling), and real-life owner Vince McMahon, who portrayed himself onscreen as, of all things, the incarnation of corporate greed! Meanwhile the WCW was not far behind, having renamed longtime good guy Hulk Hogan, a defector from the WWF, "Hollywood" Hulk Hogan and making him the head of the NWO (New World Order), a collection of wrestling bad boys who made life miserable for other factions in the WCW, including its new star, Bill Goldberg.

All this, coupled with major marketing and merchandising, made pro wrestling far and away the most popular programming on cable television in the late '90s, particularly among teens and young men, who loved the almost cartoon violence and flaunting of authority. Ratings for shows like the WWF's *Monday Night Raw* on USA and the WCW's *Monday Nitro* on TNT, which aired head-to-head, dwarfed the audiences for most other basic cable programs and routinely attracted more young male viewers than the broadcast networks—a first for cable television. Pay-Per-View pro wrestling events (each organization aired one every couple of months), highlighted by the WWF's Wrestlemania, which had been an annual event since 1985, were also top attractions.

Nor did the wrestling boom stop there. In a bit of irony that may have said something about the state of politics in America, former wrestler Jesse Ventura, who had retired from the "sport" in the 1980s, was elected governor of Minnesota in 1998.

In August 1999 *WWF Smackdown* premiered on UPN, the first regularly scheduled wrestling series on broadcast network television in more than four decades, and immediately became the most-watched series on UPN. Story lines were intertwined with those on the long-running USA Network WWF shows to motivate viwers to watch both the cable and broadcast series. That same month Extreme Championship Wrestling (ECW), previously seen in syndication, premiered on TNN. TNN toned down the level of violence—ECW matches had a reputation for being bloodier and more violent than those seen on the WWF or WCW—then dumped ECW in October 2000 when, after a protracted legal fight with the USA Network, it won the telecast rights to the WWF.

The following March TNT's declining WCW was sold to the WWF. On the last telecast of *Monday Nitro* Vince McMahon showed up to announce the purchase and then, within the ongoing WWF story line, his son Shane, who had been "feuding" with his dad, announced that he had purchased the WCW and would run it as a separate entity. Although all matches now aired on WWF shows, there were WWF wrestlers and WCW wrestlers, and the feud between the senior and junior McMahon continued to fester. That summer the ECW, which had gone bankrupt, was reconstituted when it "merged" with the WCW and Shane announced that his sister, Stephanie McMahon-Helmsley, was the new owner of ECW.

In May 2002, to settle a trademark dispute with the World Wildlife Fund, the WWF (World Wrestling Federation) changed its name to WWE (World Wrestling Entertainment), and the title of the UPN series was changed to *WWE Smackdown.*

WRIGHT VERDICTS, THE (*Legal Drama*)
FIRST TELECAST: *March 31, 1995*
LAST TELECAST: *June 11, 1995*
BROADCAST HISTORY:
Mar 1995–Apr 1995, CBS Fri 9:00–10:00
Jun 1995, CBS Sun 8:00–9:00

CAST:

Charles Wright .... Tom Conti
Sandy Hamor.......................... Margaret Colin
Lydia .... Aida Turturro

Onetime British barrister Charles Wright had spent the last 15 years building a reputation as one of the premiere criminal attorneys in the United States. Living in New York, he was unusual in that, unlike most lawyers, he worked both sides of the street, on occasion serving as special prosecutor although he was primarily a defense attorney. Sandy, a street-smart former N.Y.P.D. detective who liked to play the horses and shoot pool, was Wright's investigator, and Lydia was his highly efficient assistant. Although he sometimes seemed absentminded, Wright had a mind like a steel trap and a flamboyant courtroom style that featured histrionics designed to impress and sway the jury.

WUBBULOUS WORLD OF DR. SEUSS, THE

(*Children's*)

BROADCAST HISTORY:

Nickelodeon
30 minutes
Produced: *1996*
Premiered: *October 13, 1996*

Stories by the beloved children's author were dramatized with Muppets in this short-lived Sunday night series, which was "hosted" by the Cat in the Hat.

WYATT EARP, see *Life and Legend of Wyatt Earp, The*

XAVIER CUGAT SHOW, THE (*Music*)

FIRST TELECAST: *February 27, 1957*
LAST TELECAST: *May 24, 1957*
BROADCAST HISTORY:
Feb 1957–May 1957, NBC Wed/Fri 7:30–7:45
REGULARS:
Xavier Cugat
Abbe Lane

Latin bandleader Xavier Cugat and his then wife, Abbe Lane, starred in this live 15-minute musical variety show that filled the remainder of the half hour in which NBC aired its nightly network news program. Cugie led the band and played his violin, Abbe sang Latin numbers and danced, and occasional guest stars joined them for variety.

X-FILES, THE (*Fantasy Drama*)

FIRST TELECAST: *September 10, 1993*
LAST TELECAST: *August 9, 2002*
BROADCAST HISTORY:
Sep 1993–Oct 1996, FOX Fri 9:00–10:00
Nov 1994, FOX Sun 7:00–8:00
Oct 1996–May 2002, FOX Sun 9:00–10:00
May 2002–Aug 2002, FOX Fri 9:00–10:00
CAST:
Fox Mulder .... David Duchovny
Dana Scully .... Gillian Anderson
Deep Throat (1993–1994) .... Jerry Hardin
**Asst. Dir. Walter Skinner* .... Mitch Pileggi
**Cigarette Smoking Man* .... William B. Davis
**Mr. X (1994–1996)* .... Steven Williams
**John Byers (1994–2002)* .... Bruce Harwood
**Melvin Frohike (1994–2002)* .... Tom Braidwood
**Ringo Langly (1994–2002)* .... Dean Haglund
**Agent Alex Krycek (1994–2002)* .... Nicholas Lea
**Alien Bounty Hunter (1995–2000)* .... Brian Thompson
**Well-Manicured Man (1995–1999)* .... John Neville
**Agent Pendrell (1995–1997)* .... Brendan Beiser
**Marita Covarrubias (1996–2000)* .... Laurie Holden
**Agent Jeffrey Spender (1998–1999)* .... Chris Owens
**Cassandra Spender (1998–1999)* .... Veronica Cartwright
**Asst. Dir. Alvin Kersh (1998–2002)* .... James Pickens, Jr.
**Special Agent Diana Fowley (1998–1999)* .... Mimi Rogers
**Agent Gene Crane (2000–2001)* .... Kirk B. R. Woller
Special Agent John Doggett (2000–2002) .... Robert Patrick
Agent Monica Reyes (2001–2002) .... Annabeth Gish
**Knowle Rohrer (2001–2002)* .... Adam Baldwin
**Asst. Dir. Brad Follmer (2001–2002)* .... Cary Elwes
Baby William Scully (2001–2002) .... James & Travis Riker

*Occasional

Mulder and Scully were F.B.I. agents charged with investigating unsolved cases categorized as "X-Files" by the bureau—those that dealt with phenomena and situations that defied conventional explanations. They investigated UFO sightings, telepaths, genetically altered beings, aliens, a mutant that surfaced from a cocoon every 30 years to kill people, evil children resulting from cloning, people with telekinetic powers, and a man-sized parasite living in the Newark, New Jersey, sewer system. Unfortunately, at the end, the physical evidence always slipped through their hands. Mulder, whose sister had been the victim of an alien abduction, was the true believer, while Scully, trained in medicine and the physical sciences, was the skeptic. *The X-Files* suggested that there were secret government agencies engaged in research the general public never found out about and/or that they were hiding the truth about extraterrestrial discoveries. Somewhere in a top-secret government storage area was The Truth.

In the last episode of the 1993–1994 season Deep Throat, their mysterious source of information about the government conspiracy, was killed by agents intent on reclaiming the bottled remains of a tiny alien used to generate biological mutation in human guinea pigs. At the start of the second season the X-files investigative unit had been mothballed and Mulder and Scully reassigned, he on regular investigations monitoring wiretaps and she teaching forensics at the F.B.I. academy in Quantico, Virginia. Mulder balked at the reassignment and was still chasing U.F.O.s when Mr. X, a new mystery "friend at the F.B.I.," surfaced. He apparently had his own agenda, alienated his superiors, and was killed on Mulder's doorstep in 1996. In a two-part episode in October, Scully was abducted by aliens and, with indications that a covert government operation was involved, Mulder got his boss, Skinner, to reopen the X-Files unit and allow him to work on them alone. She was returned, after having suffered some physical harm, and went back to work with Mulder after she recovered. Scully, the original skeptic, had become an X-file case herself.

In Spring 1996, Mulder retrieved a weapon hidden in a lamp in his parents' vacation home that was used to pierce the necks of the evil aliens among us—it was the only means of killing them. The aliens could assume any human-looking identity and had the ability—if they wanted to use it—to heal the mortally wounded or the terminally ill. The mysterious Cigarette Smoking Man (CSM), who appeared to be at the center of the alien conspiracy, knew exactly what had been going on. That November it was shown that, earlier in his career, CSM was involved in the assassinations of John F. Kennedy and Martin Luther King—although Deep Throat had done the actual killing.

There were a number of other recurring characters in the episodes that dealt with the conspiracy. The Well-Manicured Man was the head of the Consortium that seemed to be in control, and everyone, from Skinner to CSM, deferred to him. Special Agent Krycek was the most difficult to assess. Initially he was partnered with Mulder investigating strange murders of Vietnam vets, but he was later revealed to be a minion of CSM. Then he murdered Mulder's father, attempted to murder Mulder himself, accidentally killed Scully's sister, became an informer for Mulder, and apparently turned out to be a Soviet double agent. Spender, an F.B.I. agent who surfaced in 1998 working on cases with Mulder and Scully, was also an agent for CSM and, as it turned out, was CSM's son.

Several people provided Mulder with useful information. Pendrell, an F.B.I. scientist with a crush on Scully, was a valuable source until he took a bullet meant for her and died. Covarrubias, who worked at the U.N., provided him with leads and documents despite, as viewers discovered, being on CSM's payroll. Mulder also received periodic help from three brilliant but nerdy eccentrics—Byers, Langly, and Frohike—who worked for *The Lone Gunman*, a publication that attempted to expose perceived government conspiracies. Not only did they provide him with information, but they also relished being active, if not always effective, participants.

At the start of the 1997–1998 season Scully almost died from a cancer she had been infected with during her abduction (but it went into remission), Mulder obtained proof that there was a conspiracy, and CSM was shot in his office by a sniper. In the spring, however, he turned up living in a wilderness cabin and was brought back, by Krycek, to work again for the people who had tried to assassinate him. At end of the season the government was again planning to shut down the X-files unit and Mulder's files were destroyed by agents in a fire, setting up the theatrical feature released five weeks later. The *X-Files* movie didn't resolve the mystery and only did moderately well at the box office. Fans of the show loved it but moviegoers unfamiliar with the series found it ponderous and confusing.

A two-part episode in February 1999 clarified most of the conspiracy. It had apparently begun with the famous U.F.O. incident in Roswell, New Mexico, in 1947. Aliens who had landed there recruited a number of powerful, highly placed government operatives to assist them in preparing Earth for colonization by their scientifically advanced race and to create a slave race of human-alien hybrids. What got in the way was the arrival of the Rebels, another group of aliens that wanted to expose the conspiracy and prevent the subjugation of Earth and its inhabitants. The Rebels had infiltrated the Consortium, among other organizations, and were a constant thorn in the side of the original invaders. At the end of the two-parter, the Rebels lured most members of the Consortium to a hangar and killed them, while CSM, who escaped, killed his own son Jeffrey, whom he thought had betrayed him.

That fall the CSM formally revealed that he was, in fact, Mulder's father. At the end of the season Mulder and Scully were under evaluation for their excessive expenses by a bean counter who didn't believe in aliens or the supernatural. CSM, who appeared to be dying and could only smoke through an airhole in his neck, bailed Krycek out of a foreign prison and told him an alien spacecraft had collided with a commercial airplane in Oregon; this, he added, gave them the opportunity to rebuild the project that had gone up in smoke the previous spring. The alien bounty hunter was on the ship and rounding up all of the subjects of their previous tests. At the end of the episode Mulder and the others were transported into the ship—which took off; Krycek forced CSM off his wheelchair down a stairway to his apparent death; Skinner was trying to deal with having seen Mulder taken away in the alien ship; and Scully found out she was pregnant.

The 2000–2001 season began with an F.B.I. task force investigating Mulder's disappearance. Heading the task force was John Doggett, appointed to the job by recently promoted Deputy Director Kersh. Doggett and Kersh, however, wanted nothing to do with "aliens or alien abductions"—which didn't endear them to Scully or Skinner. Despite his skepticism, Doggett was assigned as Scully's new partner, investigating X-files. In February clues about Mulder started to surface. It was revealed that he had contributed the sperm that was used to inseminate Scully, although it was possible she was carrying an alien fetus—because her gynecologist was mixed up in other pregnancies that had resulted in nonhuman births. At the end of February Mulder was returned by a U.F.O. and found wrapped in a blanket—dead. Three months later Doggett was offered a promotion out of the X-files unit but, since he had become believer, turned it down. Scully was about to go on maternity leave, and if she was gone Kersh would shut the unit down completely. When another abductee who had been taken at the same time as Mulder turned up in a state of semi-suspended animation, Mulder was disinterred. He was also in a form of suspended animation and, after being treated in the hospital for an alien virus, recovered.

Mulder wanted to go back to the X-files, but Kersh gave him a desk job and was determined to keep him away from his old beat. He persisted and was investigating an alien plot to abduct certain individuals and replace them with alien facsimiles. At the end of April Mulder resigned from the agency so Doggett could keep the X-files unit alive. Scully went on maternity leave; in the season finale it was revealed that the baby she was carrying was a genetically engineered human embryo. She had been abducted by the military, and the chip in the back of her neck had made her pregnant. Bad aliens feared the birth of the baby and wanted to kill it—and Scully, if necessary. They sent a number of almost indestructible human replicants to stop the birth, but Scully and Reyes drove to Georgia to find safety and deliver her baby. In Washington, Skinner killed Krycek, who was about to shoot Mulder in a parking garage. Reyes delivered the baby boy, William, with a number of replicants observing, just before Mulder arrived. Afterward Scully asked Mulder if he had any idea why the replicants had not taken the baby; he opined that the baby may not have been what they thought it was going to be. In the last scene he implied that he might have been the father and kissed her.

The final season opened with Mulder gone and Scully still wondering why the aliens hadn't taken her baby. Although warned not to investigate F.B.I. involvement in an alien conspiracy by Assistant Director Follmer, Doggett and Reyes, his new partner, searched for proof of Mulder's theories. Scully found out that the government was after William, a seventh-generation mutated embryonic super-soldier who, as an infant, was manifesting telekinetic abilities. In the spring she and Reyes gave William to the Lone Gunmen for safekeeping, but he was kidnapped by a woman who belonged to a U.F.O. cult that believed he would grow up to start an alien race of super-soldiers. Scully and Reyes recovered William after the cult leader entered the hatch of the U.F.O. his group had been worshiping, and the ship flew off. At the end of April Doggett caught a badly disfigured man in the

X-files office looking for documents about Mulder's sister. Scully's fears for William's safety were exacerbated when the disfigured man, who turned out to be Mulder's presumed-dead half brother Jeffrey Spender, injected William with an unknown substance. In an attempt to protect him, Scully decided to send William to a foster home.

The *X-Files* series finale began with Mulder on trial at a military tribunal for killing Knowle Rohrer, but since Rohrer was a super-soldier and couldn't really be killed, there was no body. Kersh was presiding and Skinner was Mulder's defense counsel. Scully testified that she believed life came to Earth millions of years ago in a meteor from Mars, along with a virus that infected life on Earth but died in the last ice age. The virus, dormant in underground oil reservoirs, resurfaced and signaled to other aliens, who crashed at Roswell in 1947. The government caught the aliens and learned of their plans to retake Earth. Skinner then called Jeffrey Spender, who said that his father had been in charge of the conspiracy to hide the existence of extraterrestrials. Covarrubias testified that the Corsortium, working on a vaccine for the alien virus, had been destroyed by renegade aliens, but the conspiracy was still active and the super-soldiers were alien replacements. Scully and Reyes went to Quantico where Scully examined the alleged body of Rohrer but, when she returned and testified that it wasn't him, Kersh had her removed because her examination was unauthorized. Mulder was convicted of first-degree murder and sentenced to die by lethal injection.

Doggett and Skinner broke Mulder out of prison just before Rohrer entered his cell, found him missing, and sounded the alarm. Kersh, who had finally seen the light, met the fugitives and helped them escape. Scully and Mulder drove to an ancient Anasazi pueblo in New Mexico where they met the wise man—CSM with long gray hair and a tracheotomy device in his throat. He told them that Indian wisemen hid here because the pueblo contained magnetite, which protected it from the aliens. Doggett and Reyes, who had arrived by helicopter to warn Mulder that the super-soldiers were after him, approached the pueblo. Then Rohrer arrived, was pulled into the rock wall by the magnetite, and exploded. Mulder and Scully left in Rohrer's vehicle just before helicopters arrived with rockets that destroyed the pueblo and killed CSM. In the last scene Scully and Mulder were in a motel room in Roswell musing over what they had learned. His last observation was that he believed "the dead are not lost to us, and if we listen to them they can give us the power to save ourselves. Maybe there's hope."

The X-Files was a cult hit with viewers who either believed there was indeed a government cover-up or just loved the scary, spooky, moody special effects of the well-produced series. Ironically, in a March 1995 *TV Guide* article on *The X-Files*, Duchovny (Mulder) admitted he didn't believe in U.F.O.s while Anderson (Scully) said she believed they were real.

X SHOW, THE (*Talk/Magazine*)

BROADCAST HISTORY:

FX
60 minutes
Original episodes: *1999–2001*
Premiered: *May 31, 1999*

REGULARS:

Mark DeCarlo (1999–2000)
Derick Alexander
Justin Walker
John Webber
Craig J. Jackson
Jon Ernst, Musical Director

Dubbed "the show for men and the women who put up with them," *The X Show* was a late-night comedy chat-fest for guys interested in the really important things in life—mainly sex and sports. Typical features included Girls in Guys (models in men's pajamas and underwear), Penis Mistakes (real medical advice delivered in comic fashion), Getting It (need we elaborate?), Know the Rules (how to play seven-card stud and smoke cigars), and Sports Picks. Filmed street gags included trying to get girls to give up their panties for puppies. Besides the hosts listed above, a rotating stable of guest experts appeared, including Internet expert Courtney Birch, movie correspondent Ashley Degenford, film critic Chris Gore ("The Gorey Details"), book critic Sandra Taylor, and cohost Jillian Barberie, along with the hosts' beloved dog Knuckles.

The X Show premiered at about the same time as the similar *Man Show* on Comedy Central.

XENA: WARRIOR PRINCESS (*Adventure*)

BROADCAST HISTORY:

Syndicated only
60 minutes
Produced: *1995–2000* (134 episodes)
Released: *September 1995*

CAST:

Xena .... Lucy Lawless
Gabrielle .... Renee O'Connor
Joxer (1996–2000) .... Ted Raimi
**Autolycus (1996–1999)* .... Bruce Campbell
**Ares (1996–2001)* .... Kevin Smith
**Salmoneus (1995–1997)* .... Robert Trebor
**Callisto (1996, 1998–2000)* .... Hudson Leick
**Aphrodite (1998–2001)* .... Alexandra Tydings
Amarice (1999) .... Jennifer Sky
**Eli (1999–2000)* .... Timothy Omundson
Livia (Eve) (2000–2001) .... Adrienne Wilkinson
**Virgil (2000)* .... William Gregory Lee
**Archangel Michael (2000–2001)* ... Charles Mesure

*Occasional

The great success of *Hercules: The Legendary Journeys* brought this spin-off series that ultimately proved more popular than the original. Xena—sexy, muscular, tall, and dressed in leather—was an evil warrior princess who battled Hercules, but in her last appearance on his series she vowed to change her ways. She traveled from place to place helping those in trouble, wielding a sword and a chakram, a razor-sharp, discus-like weapon which she hurled at enemies with astonishing speed. Also in her bag of tricks were acrobatic flips, karate-type blows, and the "Xena touch," a two-fingered pinch on the neck with which she extracted information from otherwise uncooperative antagonists. Traveling with her, and sometimes adding comic relief, was Gabrielle, who suspiciously resembled (and sometimes talked like) a modern "valley girl." Joxer was their well-meaning but klutzy friend, who showed up frequently to "help." Argo was Xena's horse; for some reason, Gabrielle was almost always on foot. One recurring villainess was Callisto, sent to Hades after being defeated by Xena, who returned in various forms to give her trouble. Seen occasionally, as they were on *Hercules*, were Autolycus, the conniving prince of thieves, and Ares, the god of war. In addition there were numerous monsters and renegade gods, rendered with spectacular and imaginative special effects.

During the 1997–1998 season Gabrielle's evil daughter Hope, born of her mother's unwitting union with the sinister deity Dahak, murdered Xena's son and was apparently poisoned. At the end of the season she returned, emerging from a cocoon and looking exactly like Gabrielle. Her mission: to serve Dahak and prepare for his New World Order, in which all goodness would be snuffed out! In the battle that ensued, Gabrielle sacrificed herself by leaping into a bottomless pit in order to save Xena, and Callisto, henchperson of Hope and Ares, was stabbed to death by Xena. That fall, Xena was searching for Gabrielle, whose spirit had been cast into a sort of mythological Purgatory. They were reunited after Xena managed to get Hope's dying monster child to kill Hope by mistake, freeing Gabrielle. In May 1999 Xena and Gabrielle saved the Amazons from Caesar, with Amarice, a young Amazon, joining them. Caesar sought revenge on Xena and allied himself with Callisto, who wanted to make sure Xena went to Hades. Xena and Gabrielle were captured by Caesar's men and were crucified on the same day Brutus assassinated him. At episode's end, their spirits transcended their crucifixion.

That fall Joxer arrived to take Xena and Gabrielle's bodies back to Greece but their spirits were caught in an afterlife battle between demons and angels. Gabrielle was taken by a demon, and Xena went after her. Callisto was one of the demons who, after she had been saved to Heaven by Xena's effort to sacrifice herself for Gabrielle, aided healer Eli in bringing Xena and Gabrielle back to life. In October Gabrielle tamed a wild horse so she could ride with Xena after four years of walking behind her; in the same episode, Xena found out she was pregnant (as was star Lucy Lawless in real life). In January a vengeful Ares, upset over Eli's preaching of peace to the masses, killed him. Callisto, now a resident of Heaven and Xena's new spirit guide and conscience, revealed that she was about to be reincarnated as Xena's child and had been responsible for the pregnancy in the first place. According to legend, when Xena's child, not begotten by man, was born, it would mean the end of the rule of the gods. Zeus wanted to kill the unborn child but Hercules, with the surprising help of Hera, fought to prevent it and killed his father to keep him from killing Xena's baby, Eve. With Zeus gone, most of the other gods were after Xena and the baby, because only by killing Eve could they prevent their own destruction. Xena faked her and Gabrielle's deaths so well that Ares placed the bodies in secret crypts of ice in which they spent the next 25 years in a form of suspended animation.

When they awoke they discovered that an adult Eve, using the name Livia, had become a ruthless commander of the Roman legions. She was having an affair with Ares and planned to kill all of the pacifist followers of Eli. Xena and Gabrielle joined with Joxer, who had aged badly, and his son, Virgil, to fight Livia. Joxer gave Xena Argo II, the daughter of the horse she had ridden before her long sleep. The Roman emperor, Octavius, planned to marry Livia and told Xena, when she confronted him, that if the gods found out that Livia was Eve, they would hunt her down and kill her. Livia didn't believe Xena was her mother and challenged her to a fight to the death in the Arena. Xena defeated Livia, but wouldn't kill her, and the resentful Livia, goaded on by Ares, stalked off to seek her revenge—with her and her men slaughtering hundreds of followers of Eli. Xena, Gabrielle, Joxer and Virgil were in pursuit but, in a confrontation, Joxer was stabbed to death by Livia while trying to keep her from killing Gabrielle. When Livia was about to kill Xena, who had been unable to kill her when she had the chance, the spirits of Eli and Callisto stopped her and forced her to see the light; she wandered off acknowledging that her name was Eve. In the season finale Ares told the other gods that Eve was alive, and Aphrodite made plans to kill her by using the Furies to confuse Gabrielle and make her kill Eve. One of the gods accidentally killed Neptune, and Xena killed Discord. She had been chosen as the mother of Eve, the messenger, and had the ability to kill gods as long as Eve lived. When Gabrielle stabbed Eve, Xena, trying to stop it, almost killed her. Sympathetic Aphrodite took Xena to Olympus to make a deal after she killed a couple more gods; all seemed lost when Ares, who really loved Xena, saved Eve and Gabrielle by giving them his immortality, allowing Xena to kill Athena.

In the fall of 2000 Xena was traveling with Gabrielle and Eve; for a while Virgil traveled with them. Ares, now a mortal, had lost his powers and unsuccessfully tried to convince Xena to help him get his godhood back. In November Xena was in the land of the Vikings and, while facing the monster Grindl, put on the Rheingold ring (usable only by those who had forsaken love) to give herself extra strength. As a result, she lost her memory and Gabrielle was put into a trance protected by the flames of Brunhilda. The following week (a year had passed), Beowulf sought Xena's help to rescue Gabrielle while Odin, the Norse god with whom she had had an affair during her youth, hoped to get his hands on the Rheingold ring. Xena freed Gabrielle and returned the Rheingold ring to its owners. In January Xena and Gabrielle tried to help the mortal Ares avoid being killed by bounty hunters; in February Xena saved Eve, who was spreading the gospel of Eli, in a confrontation with evil Caligula. In that episode the angels took away her power to kill gods. Later that month Xena defeated Odin and took a golden apple that restored godhood to Ares and Aphrodite. Gabrielle became queen of the Amazons during a war with the half-god son of Artemis, who was ultimately killed by Xena. In the series finale Xena realized that during her evil younger days she had been responsible for the deaths of 40,000 people whose souls were enslaved by Yodoshi, a Samurai spirit. Determined to defeat Yodoshi and free the enslaved souls, she allowed herself to be killed by Japanese soldiers, who beheaded her, because she could only defeat Yodoshi if she was a spirit. She succeeded but, despite Gabrielle's objections, refused to have her body and soul restored in the magical waters atop Mount Fuji. She had to remain dead to avenge and free the 40,000 souls for whose deaths she had been responsible so many years earlier. In the last scene Xena's spirit did, however, promise to always be at Gabrielle's side.

Filmed in New Zealand.

YANCY DERRINGER (*Action/Adventure*)
FIRST TELECAST: *October 2, 1958*
LAST TELECAST: *September 24, 1959*
BROADCAST HISTORY:
Oct 1958–Sep 1959, CBS Thu 8:30–9:00
CAST:
Yancy Derringer .... Jock Mahoney
Pahoo-Ka-Ta-Wah .... X. Brands
John Colton .... Kevin Hagen
Amanda Eaton .... Julie Adams
Madame Francine .... Frances Bergen

Set in New Orleans in the years after the Civil War, *Yancy Derringer* followed the exploits of an ex-Confederate soldier turned cardshark and adventurer in a wide-open city. Yancy did have a steady occupation, that of special agent working for John Colton, civil administrator of the city of New Orleans. His job was to prevent crimes when possible, and to capture the criminals when it was not. Yancy was a smooth operator, dapper and suave with the ladies, and he carried a tiny pistol in his fancy hat. His constant companion and aide was an Indian named Pahoo. Together they formed a team that was not police, not detective, and not secret agent, but a little bit of all three.

YEAR AT THE TOP, A (*Situation Comedy*)
FIRST TELECAST: *August 5, 1977*
LAST TELECAST: *September 4, 1977*
BROADCAST HISTORY:
Aug 1977, CBS Fri 8:00–8:30
Aug 1977–Sep 1977, CBS Sun 8:30–9:00
CAST:
Greg .... Greg Evigan
Paul .... Paul Shaffer
Frederick J. Hanover .... Gabriel Dell
Miss Worley .... Priscilla Morrill
Trish .... Julie Cobb
Grandma Belle Durbin .... Nedra Volz
EXECUTIVE PRODUCER:
Norman Lear
MUSIC SUPERVISOR:
Don Kirshner

This summer series, long delayed in getting on the air because of production and conceptual problems (it was originally supposed to premiere in January, with a completely different cast), was about two young rock musicians in search of fame and fortune. Greg and Paul moved to Hollywood from their home in Boise, Idaho, and were looking for an agent to help them get their big break. The promoter they found was Frederick J. Hanover, renowned for discovering and creating pop music stars. He offered them a chance at stardom, but there was one little catch. Hanover was the son of the Devil and, in exchange for this year as pop music superstars, Greg and Paul would have to sign away their souls. Hanover gave them tastes of what their "year at the top" could be like, and tried various ways of tempting them to sign the contract, but circumstances and misgivings on Greg and Paul's part prevented it from happening, at least in the five weeks that *A Year at the Top* ran.

YEAR IN THE LIFE, A (*Drama*)
FIRST TELECAST: *August 24, 1987*
LAST TELECAST: *April 20, 1988*
BROADCAST HISTORY:
Aug 1987–Sep 1987, NBC Mon 9:00–11:00
Sep 1987–Feb 1988, NBC Wed 9:00–10:00
Mar 1988, NBC Wed 10:00–11:00
Apr 1988, NBC Wed 9:00–10:00
CAST:
Joe Gardner .... Richard Kiley
Anne Gardner Maxwell .... Wendy Phillips
David Sisk .... Trey Ames
Sunny Sisk .... Amanda Peterson
Lindley Gardner Eisenberg .... Jayne Atkinson
Jim Eisenberg .... Adam Arkin
Jack Gardner .... Morgan Stevens
Sam Gardner .... David Oliver
Kay Ericson Gardner .... Sarah Jessica Parker
Dr. Alice Foley .... Diana Muldaur

This warm family drama, a spin-off from the acclaimed December 1986, mini-series of the same name, sensitively explored the lives of three generations of a large, prosperous Seattle family. Joe Gardner was the patriarch, a strong-willed but basically decent man who had grown up during the Depression (the kids were never allowed to forget it!) and built the family's successful plastics business. In the mini-series, the death of his wife had brought his four grown children back together, despite their various problems. Anne, 35, was an ex-hippie, who had been shattered by the failure of her second marriage and had moved back into the house with her two teenage children (David and Sunny) from her first marriage. Daughter Lindley, 31, was struggling to balance her career as a sales representative for Gardner Plastics with being a mother to her new baby, Ruthie, and wife to amiable patent attorney Jim. Jack, 30, was the black sheep of the family, a rebellious drifter still trying to "find himself"—to the disgust of his father. And Sam, 24, was a handsome, conservative preppie-type who had inexplicably married the flighty, free-spirited Kay; he also worked for the family firm and lived in the guest house while saving for a home of his own.

Stories revolved around the tears and joys of these marriages and family relationships. Alice was Joe's on-again, off-again romantic interest.

YEARBOOK (*Documentary*)
FIRST TELECAST: *March 7, 1991*
LAST TELECAST: *July 6, 1991*
BROADCAST HISTORY:
Mar 1991, FOX Thu 8:30–9:00
Mar 1991–Jul 1991, FOX Sat 8:30–9:00
NARRATOR:
Ken Dashow

The Fox network gave the real-life students of Glenbard West High school, in Glen Ellyn, Illinois, a most unusual senior yearbook in 1991. With the students' permission, this series' cameras used the *cinéma vérité* style to follow, up close, both the school and home lives of a group of Glenbard students during their senior year. The subjects covered were both public and private: homecoming, sports competition, dating, worries about the war in Iraq, personal tragedies (one student's mother was diagnosed with cancer), and the pressure to get good grades and get into college.

YELLOW ROSE, THE (*Drama*)
FIRST TELECAST: *October 2, 1983*
LAST TELECAST: *August 3, 1990*
BROADCAST HISTORY:

Oct 1983, NBC Sun 10:00–11:00
Oct 1983–Jan 1984, NBC Sat 10:00–11:00
Mar 1984–May 1984, NBC Sat 10:00–11:00
Jul 1990–Aug 1990, NBC Fri 9:00–10:00

CAST:

Chance McKenzie .... Sam Elliott
Colleen Champion .... Cybill Shepherd
Roy Champion .... David Soul
Quisto Champion .... Edward Albert
Jeb Hollister .... Chuck Connors
Juliette Hollister .... Deborah Shelton
Grace McKenzie (1983) .... Susan Anspach
Luther Dillard .... Noah Beery, Jr.
Hoyt Coryell .... Ken Curtis
Whit Champion .... Tom Schanley
L. C. Champion .... Michelle Bennett
Caryn Cabrera .... Kerrie Keane
John Stronghart .... Will Sampson

Soap opera set on a huge, modern-day west Texas ranch. All the usual ingredients were there—money, lust, power, mysterious pasts, and family entanglements—along with a few not usually found in modern soaps (cattle drives, campfires out in the wide open spaces). The Yellow Rose, a 200,000 acre spread, had been built by the late Wade Champion, and now his offspring were fighting among themselves and against the world to keep it going. Wade's sons Roy and Quisto (a lawyer), and his 29-year-old widow, Colleen, ran the place. Roy found himself fighting both family arch-enemy Jeb Hollister, who thought the ranch should belong to him, and his own passion for his beautiful young stepmother. Colleen, on the other hand, was drawn to Chance, a lanky, taciturn stranger who arrived in the first episode and was the man with a past; it turned out he (1) had served time for murder, and (2) was Wade's illegitimate son. Other stories involved the smuggling of drugs and illegal aliens across the nearby border.

L.C. ("Love Child") was Colleen's 12-year-old daughter, and Whit was Roy's sexually curious teenage son. Also near the center of things were Grace, the sensual housekeeper, ranch hands Dillard and Coryell, and Jeb's daughter Juliette. Midway through the season it was announced that Jane Russell would join the cast as Chance's long-lost mother, Rose Hollister, but she showed up for only a couple of episodes.

NBC aired reruns of *The Yellow Rose* during the summer of 1990.

YES, DEAR (*Situation Comedy*)
FIRST TELECAST: *October 2, 2000*
LAST TELECAST:
BROADCAST HISTORY:

Oct 2000–Jun 2003, CBS Mon 8:30–9:00
Apr 2002, CBS Mon 8:00–8:30
Jun 2003– , CBS Mon 8:00–8:30

CAST:

Greg Warner .... Anthony Clark
Kim Warner .... Jean Louisa Kelly
Jimmy Hughes .... Mike O'Malley
Christine Hughes .... Liza Snyder
Sam Warner (infant) .... Anthony and Michael Bain
Dominick Hughes (age 4) (first two episodes)
.... Connor and Keenan Merkovich
Dominick Hughes (2000–) .... Joel Homan
Logan Hughes (1) (pilot only)
.... Blake, Easton and Hunter Draut
Logan Hughes (2000–2002)
.... Christopher and Nicolas Berry
Logan Hughes (2002) ....
.... Alexander and Shawn Shapiro
Logan Hughes (2002–) .... Brendon Baerg
**Billy (2001–)* .... Billy Gardell
**Mr. Savitsky (2002–)* .... Brian Doyle-Murray

*Occasional

Greg and Kim Warner were raising their infant son, Sam, in the suburban sprawl of Los Angeles. They were both well-meaning and attentive parents, but since they were also neurotic and uncertain about what was right for their son, they tended to wear on each other. They wanted everything to be perfect for Sam. It didn't help that Kim's free-spirited sister, Christine, was living with her goofball husband, Jimmy, and their two young children in the Warner's guest house. Christine and unemployed Jimmy just coasted through life, assuming everything, including parenting, would work itself out. Jimmy's carefree attitude drove uptight Greg crazy.

In the fall of 2000 Jimmy got a job as a security guard at Radford Studios, where Greg was executive manager of business affairs. The following January Jimmy's unreliable best friend, Billy, showed up and got an acting job on *The District*, but later lost it. At the start of the 2001–2002 season Christine started taking college classes and Jimmy got Billy a job working with him as a security guard at the studio. Little Sam and dumb Logan started nursery school together in January. In April Greg's boss, Mr. Savitsky, promoted him to executive director of business affairs because Jimmy had hit a home run for his team in the studio softball game—not because Greg was the best choice—which grated on Greg. In the season finale Kim found out she was pregnant and, the following November, gave birth to a daughter, Emily.

Various parents showed up from time to time, including Tim Conway and Vicki Lawrence as Greg's mom and dad.

YES YES NANETTE, syndicated title for
Westinghouse Playhouse

YESTERDAY & TODAY (*Music Documentary*)
BROADCAST HISTORY:

The Nashville Network
60 minutes
Produced: *1997–1998*
Premiered: *March 25, 1997*

A reverential prime-time documentary series celebrating the history and stars of country music. Subjects included artists who came from the gospel field, performing families, country radio, the "Urban Cowboy Era," and stars with humble backgrounds (ain't that all of 'em?).

YESTERYEAR (*Documentary*)
BROADCAST HISTORY:

The Nashville Network
60 minutes
Produced: *1994–1996*
Premiered: *September 30, 1994*

HOSTS:
Rex Allen, Jr.
Lisa Stewart

A nostalgic look at a year in the past in country music, with clips of famous artists.

YOU AGAIN? (*Situation Comedy*)
FIRST TELECAST: *February 27, 1986*
LAST TELECAST: *March 30, 1987*
BROADCAST HISTORY:
Feb 1986, NBC Thu 8:30–9:00
Mar 1986–Jun 1986, NBC Mon 8:00–8:30
Jun 1986–Jan 1987, NBC Wed 9:30–10:00
Mar 1987, NBC Mon 10:30–11:00

CAST:
Henry Willows .... Jack Klugman
Matt Willows .... John Stamos
Enid Tompkins .... Elizabeth Bennett
Pam .... Valerie Landsburg
Maggie Davis .... Barbara Rhoades
Louis Robles .... Luis Avalos
Harry .... Guy Marks

Ever since his bitter divorce ten years before, supermarket manager Henry Willows had been leading a quiet, peaceful life—and getting very set in his ways. Until, that is, his 17-year-old son Matt, whom he had not seen since the divorce, turned up on his doorstep. Henry's life was thrown into turmoil. Matt was a girl-chasing, borderline juvenile delinquent, and more than his conservative father could deal with. There was much yelling, and a lot of difficult adjustments to make on both sides, but underneath it all—as in all sitcoms—genuine affection. Henry's sarcastic British housekeeper, Enid, tossed in a few wisecracks from the woman's point of view.

Adapted from the British series *Home to Roost*, which was still running in that country. *You Again?* boasted at least one TV first. Actress Elizabeth Bennett played the same role (Enid) in both series simultaneously, requiring her to regularly commute between Los Angeles and London.

YOU ARE AN ARTIST, see *Ben Grauer Show, The*

YOU ARE AN ARTIST (*Art Instruction*)
FIRST TELECAST: *November 1, 1946*
LAST TELECAST: *January 17, 1950*
BROADCAST HISTORY:
Nov 1946–Dec 1946, NBC Fri 8:15–8:30
Dec 1946–Aug 1948, NBC Thu 9:00–9:15
Sep 1948–Oct 1948, NBC Wed 7:30–7:50
Nov 1948–Mar 1949, NBC Tue 7:30–7:45
Mar 1949–Apr 1949, NBC Thu 7:30–7:45
Jul 1949–Sep 1949, NBC Sat 7:30–7:45
Jan 1950, NBC Tue 11:00–11:15

HOST:
Jon Gnagy

Jon Gnagy might seem an unlikely choice to be one of the very first personalities to have his own network television series. An obscure but articulate young artist, he first appeared on NBC's *Radio City Matinee*, a grab bag of features telecast locally over WNBT, New York, in the early and mid-1940s. In November 1946, he was given a 15-minute time slot of his own and his program, *You Are an Artist*, was fed to a small network of stations on the East Coast. A month later the Gulf Oil Company was persuaded to assume sponsorship of the show, thus insuring its survival (and making Gulf one of the first sponsors of a network series).

Sporting a goatee, a plaid shirt, and sometimes a beret, Gnagy would execute drawings before the camera while describing his technique in simple, understandable terms as he went along. Later he added a segment in which he analyzed a famous painting lent by the Museum of Modern Art (and brought into the studio by two armed guards). He varied little from this simple format from 1946 to 1949, but around him the medium of television changed dramatically. In 1949 the program, by then a gentle reminder of an earlier day (only three years back!), quietly moved into daytime, then became a local New York show. It had a final three-week run on the network in January 1950.

Though soon forgotten amid the rush of the superproductions and big names flooding into the new medium, Jon Gnagy and *You Are an Artist* were true video pioneers. Gnagy died in 1981.

YOU ARE THERE (*Documentary Drama*)
FIRST TELECAST: *February 1, 1953*
LAST TELECAST: *October 13, 1957*
BROADCAST HISTORY:
Feb 1953–Jun 1953, CBS Sun 6:00–6:30
Sep 1953–Oct 1957, CBS Sun 6:30–7:00 (OS)

REPORTER:
Walter Cronkite

Reenactments of major events in the history of the world, with the emphasis on those of the last century, were presented on this weekly series. CBS News correspondent Walter Cronkite served as the anchorman as the events "occurred" and reports and interviews came in from various reporters. The initial telecast was "The Landing of the Hindenburg" and the last one was "The Scuttling of the Graf Spee." In between there were programs on "The Salem Witchcraft Trials," "The Gettysburg Address," and "The Fall of Troy."

Perhaps best remembered are the program's closing lines: "What sort of a day was it? A day like all days, filled with those events that alter and illuminate our times . . . and you were there."

You Are There was first heard as a CBS radio show in 1947, with John Daly as host.

YOU ASKED FOR IT (*Audience Participation*)
FIRST TELECAST: *December 29, 1950*
LAST TELECAST: *September 5, 1999*
BROADCAST HISTORY:
Dec 1950–Dec 1951, DUM Fri 8:30–9:00
Dec 1951–Mar 1952, ABC Mon 9:00–9:30
Apr 1952–Jan 1958, ABC Sun 7:00–7:30
Jan 1958–Apr 1958, ABC Sun 9:30–10:00
Apr 1958–Sep 1959, ABC Sun 7:00–7:30
Aug 1999–Sep 1999, NBC Sun 8:00–9:00
(New episodes in syndication, 1971–1977, 1981–1983)

HOST:
Art Baker (1950–1958)
Jack Smith (1958–1959)
Phil Morris (1999)

When this series premiered on the DuMont television network in December 1950, it was named *The Art Baker Show*, after its creator and host. That title was changed on April 13, 1951, to the more descriptive *You Asked for It*.

The format of the show was very simple. Viewers were asked to send in a postcard describing something they wanted to see and the program's staff made every attempt to provide it. For almost a decade *You Asked for It* thrived, taking viewers into the vault at Fort Knox, bringing to them strange people with unusual talents, showing them $1,000,000 in one-dollar bills, and almost anything else that the viewers wanted to see.

Jack Smith replaced Art Baker as host when the program moved to 9:30 P.M. Sunday night on January 26, 1958.

Although *You Asked for It* is most associated with this particular format, it was actually anticipated by a nearly identical program on NBC from 1948–1949 called *I'd Like to See.*

Jack Smith also hosted the syndicated version of *You Asked for It* that appeared during the 1971–1972 season and which continued in production on an erratic basis until 1977. A new syndicated version surfaced from 1981 to 1983, with impressionist Rich Little as host. Jack Smith was on hand to narrate clips from the older versions, many of them in black-and-white, while Little and his assistant, Jayne Kennedy, narrated the new stories.

Yet another version appeared in 1999 during the network vogue for "shocking documentaries" (*When Animals Attack,* etc.), hosted by actor Phil Morris, the son of 1960s star Greg Morris. Somewhat tamer than its 1990s counterparts, it featured a combination of new clips and segments from earlier versions of the show, some in black-and-white. Like his predecessors, Morris read requests from viewers. The most requested clip was said to be the old film of a huge suspension bridge twisting in a high wind, and then collapsing.

YOU ASKED FOR IT, AGAIN (*Audience Participation*)

BROADCAST HISTORY:

The Family Channel
30 minutes
Produced: *1991–1992* (22 episodes)
Premiered: *September 1, 1991*

HOST:

Jimmy Brogan

A revival of the venerable series that used a combination of old clips and new material. Some requests came from the studio audience.

YOU BET YOUR LIFE (*Quiz*)

FIRST TELECAST: *October 5, 1950*
LAST TELECAST: *September 21, 1961*
BROADCAST HISTORY:

Oct 1950–Jun 1951, NBC Thu 8:00–8:30
Oct 1951–Sep 1958, NBC Thu 8:00–8:30
Sep 1958–Sep 1961, NBC Thu 10:00–10:30

EMCEE:

Groucho Marx

ANNOUNCER:

George Fenneman

THEME:

"Hooray for Captain Spaulding," by Bert Kalmar and Harry Ruby

Comedian Groucho Marx, of the rapierlike wit and sarcastic asides, was the emcee and star of this filmed quiz show, which had begun on radio in 1947. Although it was ostensibly a quiz, the series' most important asset was the humor injected by Groucho into the interviews he did with contestants before they had a chance to play the game. Contestants were picked primarily on the potential they had to be foils for Groucho's barbs, which they seemed to love.

At the start of each show the audience was informed of the night's secret word—"It's a common word, something you see every day." If any of the contestants happened to say it while they were on the air, they won an extra $100. When they said the word a dilapidated stuffed duck would drop from the ceiling with the $100 attached. The quiz consisted of question-and-answer rounds in which contestants bet all or part of an initial purse on their ability to answer the questions in a chosen category. The questions were not really difficult, and the two members of a team could collaborate ("Remember, only one answer between you"), but sometimes they lost the whole thing. Then there was always the consolation prize, which could be won by answering a nonsense question like "Who is buried in Grant's Tomb?" As Groucho liked to say, "Nobody leaves here broke."

During the period in which *You Bet Your Life* was aired on both TV and radio, an hour-long session was filmed and then edited down to provide both 30-minute versions of the show—as well as to edit out any risqué remarks by Groucho. The same contestants appeared on both radio and TV versions, though the two were not exactly alike. The reruns that aired on TV during the summer were titled *The Best of Groucho* and the entire program was retitled *The Groucho Show* during its last season.

Along with the title change came a slight change in format. The mangy duck announcing the secret word was still around, but sometimes it was replaced by other ways of revealing the "word"—a pretty girl on a swing, a ballerina dancing across the stage, tumblers dropping from the ceiling with it on a sign, etc.

A syndicated version of *You Bet Your Life,* hosted by comic Buddy Hackett, turned up briefly in the fall of 1980. In the fall of 1992, following the conclusion of his highly rated sitcom, *The Cosby Show,* Bill Cosby starred in another revival of *You Bet Your Life.* Pretty young Robbi Chong was on hand as his announcer/assistant, but because of possible legal issues, the mangy duck had been replaced by a black goose. Cosby fared little better than Hackett had more than a decade before. By the end of 1992 it was obvious that viewers were not in love with the show—many stations had moved it to a postmidnight time slot—and the producers announced it would cease production at the end of the season.

YOU CAN BE A STAR (*Talent*)

BROADCAST HISTORY:

The Nashville Network
30 minutes
Produced: *1983–1989, 1991–1992*
Premiered: *September 5, 1983*

REGULARS:

Jim Ed Brown (1983–1989)
Bobby Randall (1991–1992)
Lisa Foster (1991–1992)

One of TNN's earliest regular series was this daily country talent show for amateurs, originating from Nashville. After a six-year run as *You Can Be a Star*, it was revived in 1991 with a new name *(Be a Star)*, new hosts, and prizes that included $50,000 in cash, television appearances, and recording contracts.

YOU CAN'T TAKE IT WITH YOU (*Situation Comedy*)

BROADCAST HISTORY:

Syndicated only
30 minutes
Produced: *1987–1988* (26 episodes)
Released: *September 1987*

CAST:

Martin Vanderhof .... Harry Morgan
Penny Vanderhof Sycamore .... Lois Nettleton
Paul Sycamore .... Richard Sanders
Alice Sycamore .... Lisa Aliff
Essie Sycamore .... Heather Blodgett
Durwood M. Pinner .... Theodore Wilson

A turn-of-the-century Victorian home in New York City's suburban borough of Staten Island was the setting for this multigenerational comedy about a family of eccentrics. Martin Vanderhof was the patriarch of the clan, an independent curmudgeon who also served as the series' narrator. Martin, a widower, lived with his bubbly, somewhat scatter-brained daughter, Penny, and her family. That family consisted of Penny's husband, Paul, an inventor of toys, with no apparent regular source of income; their idealistic teenage daughter, Essie; and their older daughter, Alice, who worked for a Manhattan brokerage firm. Mr. Pinner was a neighbor and friend who constructed prototypes for the toys Paul invented.

Adapted from the Pulitzer Prize–winning 1936 play of the same name written by Moss Hart and George S. Kaufman, which will be remembered long after this routine comedy is not.

YOU DON'T KNOW JACK (*Quiz*)

FIRST TELECAST: *June 20, 2001*
LAST TELECAST: *July 18, 2001*
BROADCAST HISTORY:

Jun 2001–Jul 2001, ABC Wed 8:30–9:00

HOST:

Paul Reubens (as *Troy Stevens*)

This wild summer entry was half comedy, half quiz show. Three contestants attempted to answer offbeat questions as manic host Troy Stevens mugged and shouted. Each question started off worth $2 million, but money was subtracted so fast—even while Troy read the question—that by the time a contestant got to buzz in the answer it might be down to $191. A sample question: "Fidel Castro is to military fatigues as the Jolly Green Giant is to what? 1: Pesticide, 2: Corn, 3: Leaves, 4: Speedos." In addition there were constant distractions, such as a mariachi band marching across the stage as the contestants tried to think, a crying, peeing baby or a belly dancer performing.

YOU DON'T SAY (*Quiz/Audience Participation*)

FIRST TELECAST: *January 7, 1964*
LAST TELECAST: *May 5, 1964*
BROADCAST HISTORY:

Jan 1964–May 1964, NBC Tue 8:30–9:00

EMCEE:

Tom Kennedy

You Don't Say was a game in which two teams of two members each (one member being the contestant and the other member a celebrity) competed in trying to guess the name of a famous person. One member of each team would be told the identity of the person and would then give clues to his partner in the form of incomplete sentences, with the missing word at the end of the sentence being the clue. The winner of each game got $100 and the chance to go to the bonus board to win more money. The board contained word clues to a different famous person's name. The clues were revealed, one at a time, and the members of the winning team tried to guess who the famous person was. Correct identification after one clue was worth $300, after two clues worth $200, and after all three clues worth $100. The daytime version of *You Don't Say*, on which the nighttime version was based, ran from April 1963 to September 1969 and was revived for a six-month period in 1975. Tom Kennedy was the emcee of all network versions of the show.

When *You Don't Say* returned to the air on a first-run syndicated basis during the 1978–1979 season. Jim Peck was the new emcee.

YOU TAKE THE KIDS (*Situation Comedy*)

FIRST TELECAST: *December 15, 1990*
LAST TELECAST: *January 12, 1991*
BROADCAST HISTORY:

Dec 1990–Jan 1991, CBS Sat 8:00–8:30

CAST:

Nell Kirkland .... Nell Carter
Michael Kirkland .... Roger E. Mosley
Raymond Kirkland (age 16) .... Dante Beze
Lorette Kirkland (14) .... Caryn Ward
Peter Kirkland (12) .... Marlon Taylor
Nate Kirkland (10) .... Trent Cameron
Helen .... Leila Danette

THEME:

"Nobody's Got It Easy," written by Jeff Moss and performed by Nell Carter

Short-lived comedy about a blue-collar family living in Pittsburgh's inner city. Michael Kirkland made a modest living as a school-bus driver, a job he had held for years. Nell, his wife of 17 years, opinionated but loving, taught piano at home to provide a little extra money for the family. Together they were raising their four children—Raymond, whose only apparent goal in life was to stay cool; Lorette, who was desperate to get a boyfriend; Peter, the family intellectual who wanted to become a doctor; and Nate, the resident pint-sized con artist. Living in the basement was Nell's loudmouthed mother, Helen, who wished her daughter had married better and was not shy about saying it in front of poor Michael.

YOU WISH (*Situation Comedy*)

FIRST TELECAST: *September 26, 1997*
LAST TELECAST: *September 4, 1998*
BROADCAST HISTORY:

Sep 1997–Nov 1997, ABC Fri 9:00–9:30
May 1998–Sep 1998, ABC Fri 8:30–9:00

CAST:

Gillian Apple .... Harley Jane Kozak
Mickey Apple (age 14) .... Alex McKenna
Travis Apple (11) .... Nathan Lawrence

Genie .... John Ales
**Mustafa* .... John Rhys-Davies
**Grandpa Max*.................... Jerry Van Dyke

*Occasional

A bright Friday night kid-com about a genie who brought some fun into a family's life—despite mom. Single mom Gillian and her two kids had wandered into Mustafa's quaint little Los Angeles carpet store looking for a bathroom rug. When she unrolled an old-looking purple rug, out popped Genie, who had been imprisoned there for 2,000 years as punishment for a serious genie offense: he had fallen in love with his last, female "master." Having had no love for 2,000 years, ebullient, curly-haired Genie was desperate to get out, and begged the Apples to become his new masters. He would grant their every wish. Gillian, a practical, no-nonsense '90s mom, didn't want the "disruption," but the kids pleaded and she finally relented. Happy, optimistic Genie could make wonderful things happen by just snapping his fingers, and the kids thought he was great. Even mom had to admit he could be fun.

YOU WRITE THE SONGS (*Music/Competition*)

BROADCAST HISTORY:

Syndicated only
30 minutes
Produced: *1986–1987* (26 episodes)
Released: *September 1986*

REGULARS:

Ben Vereen
The New Song Dancers (choreographed by Jaime Rogers)
Sam Harris
Monica Page
Kenny James
Catte Adams

Aspiring songsmiths were given exposure on this weekly series which presented offerings from three different amateur songwriters each week. The songs were performed by the show's regular singers, all alumni from *Star Search*, and were judged by a rotating celebrity panel with the weekly winners advancing toward a $100,000 grand prize. Host Ben Vereen introduced the songs and chatted with the weekly celebrity guests. Among those appearing on the show were Stevie Wonder, Donna Summer, Carole Bayer Sager, Melissa Manchester, Smokey Robinson, and Neil Sedaka.

For a similar series 36 years earlier, see *Songs for Sale*.

YOU'll NEVER GET RICH, see *Phil Silvers Show, The*

YOUNG AMERICANS (*School Drama*)

FIRST TELECAST: *July 12, 2000*
LAST TELECAST: *August 30, 2000*
BROADCAST HISTORY:

Jul 2000–Aug 2000, WB Wed 9:00–10:00
Jul 2000–Aug 2000, WB Fri 9:00–10:00

CAST:

Will Krudski .... Rodney Scott
Scout Calhoun .... Mark Famiglietti
Hamilton Fleming............... Ian Somerhalder
Finn .... Ed Quinn
Bella Banks .... Kate Bosworth
Jacqueline "Jake" Pratt......... Katherine Moening
Charlie Banks .... Ed Fry
Susan Krudski.................... Deborah Hazlett
Ryder Forrest .... Charlie Hunnam
Sean McGrail .... Matt Czuchry

THEME:

"Six Pacs," written by Kristian Ottestad and Espen Norweger, performed by The Getaway People

Will, a local boy from the poor side of town, was starting the summer session on scholarship at fancy Rawley Academy, a boarding school in New Rawley. His mother, Susan, was thrilled but his father, with whom he was having problems, was less than enthusiastic. Early on Will admitted to his wealthy roommate, Scout, that he had cheated on the entrance exam to get away from his dad. One of the other entering students was Hamilton who, despite being the dean's son, was totally anti-establishment. Bella, a pretty local girl who worked at her family's gas station—and was the object of every horny Rawley student's desire—had grown up with Will and treated him like a brother. Jake, also an outsider, was a tomboy masquerading as a guy who was working her way through every prep school in the Northeast. Finn, the crew coach and eccentric but idealistic lit professor, figured out that Will had cheated to get in but was convinced that Will belonged at Rawley and had real writing talent. In the premiere episode Bella's father told Scout, who was dating her, that she was actually his half sister, and Bella subsequently started dating townie Sean. Jake finally admitted to Hamilton—who feared he was gay—that she was a girl, and they surreptitiously started to date. Bella had figured out that Jake was a girl and they shared her secret, too. In the finale, as the summer term was ending, Bella had unsuccessfully tried to keep her mother from putting the gas station/home where she and her divorced dad lived up for auction; Jake, whose masquerade as a boy was becoming common knowledge, was heading home to New York for the rest of the summer; and Will had decided to spend the last few weeks of the summer with Scout on the island of St. Martin.

Rodney Scott had appeared as Will Krudski in a few episodes of *Dawson's Creek* earlier in 2000.

YOUNG AND GAY, see *Girls, The*

YOUNG BROADWAY, (*Music*)

FIRST TELECAST: *December 22, 1948*
LAST TELECAST: *June 23, 1949*
BROADCAST HISTORY:

Dec 1948–Mar 1949, NBC Wed 7:30–7:50
Apr 1949–Jun 1949, NBC Thu 10:00–10:30

Live musical program featuring young performers who were just getting their start in show business. For a time each program was built around a current Broadway play, but with the understudies rather than the stars performing the lead roles. Performers as varied as Roberta Quinlan and Marguerite Piazza appeared.

YOUNG DAN'L BOONE (*Adventure*)

FIRST TELECAST: *September 12, 1977*
LAST TELECAST: *October 4, 1977*
BROADCAST HISTORY:

Sep 1977, CBS 8:00–9:00
Oct 1977, CBS Tue 8:00–9:00

CAST:

Daniel Boone .... Rick Moses
Rebecca Bryan .... Devon Ericson
Hawk .... Ji-Tu Cumbuka
Peter Dawes .... John Joseph Thomas
Tsiskwa .... Eloy Phil Casados

Fess Parker had spent six successful seasons in the latter half of the 1960s playing an older version of the legendary Daniel Boone and CBS brought a younger version of the Kentucky woodsman to television in the fall of 1977. In his mid-20s, and not yet married, Daniel did his exploring with Peter Dawes, a 12-year-old English boy; Hawk, a runaway slave; and a Cherokee Indian friend named Tsiskwa. Waiting for him to settle down was his sweetheart, Rebecca. One of the failures of the 1977–1978 season, *Young Dan'l Boone* lasted only four weeks, three in its original Monday time slot and a fourth on Tuesday, October 4.

YOUNG INDIANA JONES CHRONICLES, THE (*Adventure*)

FIRST TELECAST: *March 4, 1992*
LAST TELECAST: *July 24, 1993*
BROADCAST HISTORY:

Mar 1992–Apr 1992, ABC Wed 9:00–10:00
Aug 1992–Nov 1992, ABC Mon 8:00–9:00
Mar 1993–Apr 1993, ABC Sat 8:00–9:00
Jun 1993–Jul 1993, ABC, Sat 8:00–9:00

CAST:

Indiana Jones (age 16) .... Sean Patrick Flanery
Indiana Jones (10) .... Corey Carrier
Indiana Jones (93) .... George Hall
Remy .... Ronny Coutteure
**Professor Jones* .... Lloyd Owen
**Anna Jones* .... Ruth DeSosa

*Occasional

EXECUTIVE PRODUCER:

George Lucas

Movie mogul George Lucas brought his big-screen, slam-bang epic *Indiana Jones* to the small screen in this series—and found it didn't fit. Though lavishly produced (in eleven countries), the series lacked the sprawling, nonstop action of the films and, oddly, was didactic. Indy was seen at three stages in life (sometimes in the same episode), as a child, a teenager, and an old man recalling his great adventures. In those adventures the young archeologist/explorer seemed to bump into every historical figure imaginable, from Pancho Villa to Sigmund Freud, Thomas A. Edison, Lawrence of Arabia, Norman Rockwell, George Patton, and Teddy Roosevelt. And, of course, dear viewer, we learned a little bit about each one.

Remy was Indy's pal and confederate. Indy's parents were occasionally seen, and Harrison Ford (the movie Indy) made a guest appearance in March 1993 as the adventurer at age 50.

YOUNG LAWYERS, THE (*Legal Drama*)

FIRST TELECAST: *September 21, 1970*
LAST TELECAST: *May 5, 1971*
BROADCAST HISTORY:

Sep 1970–Jan 1971, ABC Mon 7:30–8:30
Jan 1971–May 1971, ABC Wed 10:00–11:00

CAST:

Attorney David Barrett .... Lee J. Cobb
Aaron Silverman .... Zalman King
Pat Walters .... Judy Pace
Chris Blake (1971) .... Philip Clark

Drama about law students operating a Boston "Neighborhood Law Office" that provided free legal assistance to indigent clients. Slumlords, drug busts, police brutality, and rip-offs of the poor constituted most of their cases. In TV fashion the crew was suitably mixed: Aaron was the scrappy, tousle-haired young idealist, Pat was the well-educated but street-wise black chick, and Chris the earnest young middle-class WASP who was added to the cast in January, for contrast. Their experienced supervisor was David Barrett.

YOUNG MAVERICK (*Western*)

FIRST TELECAST: *November 28, 1979*
LAST TELECAST: *January 16, 1980*
BROADCAST HISTORY:

Nov 1979–Jan 1980, CBS Wed 8:00–9:00

CAST:

Ben Maverick .... Charles Frank
Nell McGarrahan .... Susan Blanchard
Marshal Edge Troy .... John Dehner

Revivals have had a generally dismal record on network television, and this one was no exception. The original *Maverick* was one of the biggest hits of the late 1950s, and widely remembered for its laid-back, easygoing sense of humor. The secret of its success was James Garner, a magnetic personality with just the right sardonic touch, and when CBS tried to bring it all back without him 20 years later the effect was like sarsaparilla gone flat.

Garner did appear briefly in the opening scene of the first episode, meeting his successor on the trail, but it was Charles Frank who had the unenviable task of trying to fill his boots as the permanent lead. Ben Maverick was Bret's cousin (which brought the number of Maverick kin appearing on the two series up to five: Ben, Beau, Bart, Bret, and Brent). He was Harvard-educated and inheritor of the Maverick family traditions of gambling artistry, disarming good looks, a willingness to bend the law wherever profitable, and an abiding belief in cowardice as the best way to avoid getting killed on the rough frontier. He was a little more of a dandy than Bret, having learned much from his father Beau. Ben's nemesis, partner, and romantic interest was Nell McGarrahan, a pretty slick operator in her own right, who hoped to marry him someday. Marshal Edge Troy always seemed to arrive on the scene just in time to save Ben from bodily harm. He never quite understood Ben's sense of humor, or anybody else's for that matter. He was all business. Marshal Troy's territory was the area of Idaho where Ben and Nell did their gambling and ran an occasional con game.

Series stars Charles Frank and Susan Blanchard were already well acquainted before this series premiered. They had spent several years playing husband and wife on the ABC daytime soap opera *All My Children*, and were married in real life as well.

YOUNG MR. BOBBIN (*Situation Comedy*)

FIRST TELECAST: *August 26, 1951*
LAST TELECAST: *May 18, 1952*
BROADCAST HISTORY:

Aug 1951–May 1952, NBC Sun 7:30–8:00

CAST:

Alexander Hawthorne Bobbin .... Jackie Kelk
Aunt Clara .... Jane Seymour

Aunt Bertha .... Nydia Westman
Nancy .... Pat Hosley
Susie .... Laura Weber
Mr. Deacon .... Cameron Prud'homme
Mr. Willis .... Cort Benson

At age 18, Alexander Bobbin had just graduated from high school and begun seeking his fortune. At his age, however, his aspirations tended to exceed his abilities. This live situation comedy focused on the struggles of the young man to establish himself and attain maturity. Alexander lived in an old house with the two maiden aunts who had raised him: organized, resourceful Aunt Clara, and confused, flighty Aunt Bertha. He was in love with Nancy, the girl next door, who liked him but was determined not to let him think he was the only man in her life. His strongest ally in his effort to win Nancy was Susie, her tomboy sister who tried to help him despite her apparent teasing.

YOUNG PEOPLE'S CHURCH OF THE AIR, see *Youth on the March*

YOUNG REBELS, THE (*Adventure*)

FIRST TELECAST: *September 20, 1970*
LAST TELECAST: *January 3, 1971*
BROADCAST HISTORY:

Sep 1970–Jan 1971, NBC Sun 7:00–8:00

CAST:

Jeremy Larkin .... Rick Ely
Isak Poole .... Louis Gossett, Jr.
Henry Abington .... Alex Henteloff
Elizabeth Coates .... Hilary Thompson
General the Marquis de Lafayette . Philippe Forquet

This series was supposed to allow the youthful social rebels of the late 1960s and early 1970s (or those who fantasized along with them) to relate to the American Revolution. The four young leads were members of the fictional Yankee Doodle Society, based in Chester, Pennsylvania, in the year 1777. Their goal was to harass the British behind their lines and to serve as spies for the American forces. Everyone was under 30, and British rule was the "system" they sought to overturn. Jeremy, the son of the town's mayor, was the long-haired leader; Elizabeth, his teenage girlfriend and helper; Isak, an ex-slave; and Henry, the brains of the outfit. Henry greatly admired Benjamin Franklin, and even looked a lot like him, with a calm, intellectual detachment and tiny spectacles on his nose. General Lafayette, the 20-year-old French nobleman who had come to aid the rebels, was a frequent ally, and various other youthful patriots also passed through the stories (including that eternal teenager Brandon De Wilde as young Nathan Hale).

YOUNG RIDERS, THE (*Western*)

FIRST TELECAST: *September 20, 1989*
LAST TELECAST: *July 23, 1992*
BROADCAST HISTORY:

Sep 1989, ABC Wed 8:30–9:30
Sep 1989–Apr 1990, ABC Thu 9:00–10:00
May 1990, ABC Mon 8:00–9:00
May 1990–Sep 1990, ABC Thu 9:00–10:00
Sep 1990–Aug 1991, ABC Sat 8:00–9:00
Sep 1991–Jan 1992, ABC Sat 9:00–10:00
May 1992–Jul 1992, ABC Thu 8:00–9:00

CAST:

Teaspoon Hunter .... Anthony Zerbe
The Kid .... Ty Miller
William "Billy" Cody .... Stephen Baldwin
Jimmy Hickok .... Josh Brolin
Ike McSwain (1989–1991) .... Travis Fine
Little Buck Cross .... Gregg Rainwater
Lou McCloud .... Yvonne Suhor
Emma Shannon (1989–1990) .... Melissa Leo
Marshal Sam Cain (1989–1990) .... Brett Cullen
Noah Dixon (1990–1992) .... Don Franklin
Rachel Dunn (1990–1992) .... Clare Wren
Tompkins .... Don Collier
Jesse James (1991–1992) .... Christopher Pettiet

The Pony Express rode again in this revisionist view of the Old West, which strove mightily to make Westerns palatable to the socially sensitive 1990s. The year was 1860, the place a prairie station near Sweetwater on the Central Overland Express line, which stretched 2,000 miles from St. Joseph to Sacramento. Grizzled, understanding old Teaspoon Hunter was the stationmaster, while his young riders were an unlikely mix of races, sexes, and famous-names-to-be: crack shot Jimmy, "Wild Bill" Hickok; the future Buffalo Bill Cody; handsome Kid (no other name); bald, mute Ike, the handicapped member (killed in 1991); minority representative Buck, half Kiowa Indian; and cross-dresser "Lou," a girl who masqueraded as a boy so she could be a Rider, too. The second season added Noah, an educated, freeborn black, and the third eager, young Jesse James, age 14, who helped out around the station. Emma was the original cook and housemother, replaced by the more mysterious Rachel in the second season after Emma ran off with Marshal Cain.

The riders did deliver some mail from time to time in their "mochila" pouch, but spent most of their time rescuing escaped slaves, protecting the innocent, and being nice to the Indians. Rumblings of the imminent Civil War allowed some moralizing on that subject. In the third season the entire crew moved to the larger town of Rock Creek, on the Nebraska-Kansas-Missouri border, to allow for the introduction of more "urban" concerns. Perhaps AIDS, or a crack epidemic? Teaspoon became a U.S. Marshal.

In the final episode Noah was refused enlistment into the white man's army (they were sorry), then was killed along with some soldiers in an ambush by a gang. Lou and the Kid were married (he wouldn't even give the preacher his real name!), and young Jesse ran off with his evil brother Frank after betraying his friends.

The real Pony Express was established in April 1860 and did use boys and small men as riders, but operated for only 1½ years. Fourteen-year-old "Buffalo Bill" Cody was, in fact, a member, but he was probably galloping too fast to stop and right wrongs along the way. Indeed, given his later descriptions of his "expert scalping" of Indians, it is unlikely that he was terribly sensitive to Native American issues.

YOUR BIG BREAK (*Talent*)

BROADCAST HISTORY:

Syndicated only
60 minutes
Produced: *1999–2001*
Released: *September 1999*

HOSTS:
Christopher "Kid" Reid (1999–2000)
Alfonso Ribeiro (2000–2001)
EXECUTIVE PRODUCER:
Dick Clark

On each telecast of this series five amateur singers with dreams of professional success competed by performing the hits of their favorite singers. They didn't lip-sync but actually sang the songs themselves. Before they appeared on stage, the contestants' real lives were profiled individually. At the end of the show the studio audience voted for their favorite act based on sound, looks and presentation. Weekly winners advanced to the semi-finals, with the eventual top prize of $25,000, a contract with a major record label, and the opportunity to compete in the international version of *Your Big Break*.

YOUR BIG MOMENT, see *Blind Date*

YOUR CHEVROLET SHOWROOM (*Variety*)
FIRST TELECAST: *November 20, 1953*
LAST TELECAST: *February 12, 1954*
BROADCAST HISTORY:
Nov 1953–Feb 1954, ABC Fri 10:00–11:00
EMCEE:
Cesar Romero

This hour of music and comedy premiered locally in New York on October 25, 1953, and went on the full ABC network a month later. Unfortunately the biggest name guests appeared on the first few telecasts, which were seen only in New York, and by the time network telecasting had begun, Cesar Romero found himself playing host to good but non-superstar acts such as Earl Wrightson, Connee Boswell, and the Russ Morgan Orchestra, plus legions of unknown singers, dancers, and comedians. The program was known for its first weeks simply as *Chevrolet Showroom*.

YOUR ESSO REPORTER (*News*)
FIRST TELECAST: *July 12, 1951*
LAST TELECAST: *September 13, 1951*
BROADCAST HISTORY:
Jul 1951–Sep 1951, CBS Thu 9:00–9:30

Your Esso Reporter had been a regular feature of CBS radio since the late 1930s, and the company had also sponsored one of the very earliest regular network TV newscasts, which began almost as soon as NBC was able to organize its first three-station East Coast network in 1946. During the summer of 1951 Esso sponsored this weekly roundup of the major news events from around the world, with the CBS News correspondents based in various world capitals all participating. In a rather unusual situation, the 1951 series was seen only in the East and the Far West, where Esso was marketed. The midwest portion of the CBS-TV network got *Meet Corliss Archer* instead.

YOUR FAVORITE GIRL NEXT DOOR (*Talent*)
BROADCAST HISTORY:
FX
30 minutes
Original episodes: *2000*
Premiered: *March 15, 2000*
HOSTS:
Brian Palermo
Stephanie Lydecker

A beauty contest for "ordinary people," in which female viewers were invited to submit home videos of themselves modeling swimsuits and engaging in various physical activities (the more bounce, the better). Each week the audience voted on five taped submissions, and the two with the highest vote totals were invited to the studio to chat with the hosts and do a little act. After another vote, the grand prize winner got $10,000.

YOUR FUNNY, FUNNY FILMS (*Comedy*)
FIRST TELECAST: *July 8, 1963*
LAST TELECAST: *September 9, 1963*
BROADCAST HISTORY:
Jul 1963–Sep 1963, ABC Mon 8:30–9:00
HOST:
George Fenneman

Home movies taken by amateurs, with the emphasis on intentionally (and sometimes unintentionally) humorous sequences. A few celebrities also appeared with their home movies. The first telecast consisted of (1) a five-year-old's birthday party, as he demolished a cake, then learned to ride a bicycle and roller skate; (2) a World War II "epic" made by a 12-year-old and his friends; (3) some amateur films made in the 1920s. The "Short Shorts" feature consisted of a string of brief clips, such as a youngster experimenting with shoe polish, a woman ostensibly climbing a mountain, a little girl dancing, a wood-chopping scene, and a tiny Romeo trying to steal a kiss from his little girlfriend. A lot of kids were seen in this series, which in some ways resembled *Candid Camera*.

YOUR HIT PARADE (*Music*)
FIRST TELECAST: *July 10, 1950*
LAST TELECAST: *August 30, 1974*
BROADCAST HISTORY:
Jul 1950–Aug 1950, NBC Mon 9:00–9:30
Oct 1950–Jun 1958, NBC Sat 10:30–11:00 (OS)
Oct 1958–Apr 1959, CBS Fri 7:30–8:00
Aug 1974, CBS Fri 8:00–8:30
VOCALISTS:
Eileen Wilson (1950–1952)
Snooky Lanson (1950–1957)
Dorothy Collins (1950–1957, 1958–1959)
Sue Bennett (1951–1952)
June Valli (1952–1953)
Russell Arms (1952–1957)
Gisele MacKenzie (1953–1957)
Tommy Leonetti (1957–1958)
Jill Corey (1957–1958)
Alan Copeland (1957–1958)
Virginia Gibson (1957–1958)
Johnny Desmond (1958–1959)
Kelly Garrett (1974)
Chuck Woolery (1974)
Sheralee (1974)
DANCERS:
The Hit Paraders (chorus & dancers) (1950–1958)
Peter Gennaro Dancers (1958–1959)
Tom Hansen Dancers (1974)
ANNOUNCER:
Andre Brauch (1950–1957)
Del Sharbutt (1957–1958)
ORCHESTRA:
Raymond Scott (1950–1957)
Harry Sosnik (1958–1959)
Milton Delugg (1974)

THEME:

"Be Happy, Go Lucky" (open); "So Long for Awhile" (closing)

The legendary *Lucky Strike Hit Parade*, which had been a radio standby since 1935, was first seen on television during the summer of 1950, as a four-time-only replacement for *Robert Montgomery Presents*. It became a regular series the following October, simulcast with the radio version.

The format was essentially unchanged from radio, presenting the seven most popular songs in America as performed by a regular cast of singers and the Hit Parade Orchestra. Songs were not necessarily presented in rank order, although the rank of each was prominently featured and number one was always presented last, with great fanfare. Two or three "extras"—usually standards—were also included. Elaborate production numbers marked *Your Hit Parade*, and since many songs stayed on the charts for months, considerable ingenuity was required to vary the treatment of a song from week to week. Among the songs that remained in the number-one spot for long periods in the early 1950s were "Too Young" (12 weeks), "Because of You" (11 weeks), and "Hey There" (10 weeks).

The survey strove to sound official. Each week listeners were told that "*Your Hit Parade* survey checks the best sellers on sheet music and phonograph records, the songs most heard on the air and most played on the automatic coin machines . . . an accurate, authentic tabulation of America's taste in popular music." No explanation of exactly how the surveying was done was ever revealed, however, and the actual compiling took place in great secrecy at Batten, Barton, Durstine & Osborne, which was sponsor American Tobacco Company's advertising agency.

The ballads of the early 1950s were fine for TV presentation by a regular cast of singers, but trouble began to brew for *Your Hit Parade* in 1955 when a new kind of music invaded the charts—rock 'n' roll. Not only were the Hit Parade regulars ill-suited to perform this new, raucous music, but the youngsters who bought the records wanted to see only the original performers. There was something ludicrous about Snooky Lanson attempting "Hound Dog" in a different setting each week (usually as a childish novelty).

Although most of the *Hit Parade* singers were recording artists in their own right, only one of them ever had a hit big enough to appear on the program's top seven while a regular on the show. That was Gisele MacKenzie's "Hard to Get," which made the list briefly in 1955. Ironically, one-time *Hit Parade* regular June Valli had the biggest hit of her career, "Crying in the Chapel," only two months after leaving the show in June 1953.

In September 1957 the entire cast was replaced by a younger, more "contemporary" crew, none of whom were popular rock artists, however. The age-old format itself was extensively revamped the following February, with the hit parade reduced to five songs, plus five more melodious "extras" and a big $200,000 "Mystery Tune" contest. None of this tinkering solved the problems created by drastically changing musical styles, and after a final season on CBS (during which the top-tunes list was drawn from *Billboard* magazine) the program expired on April 24, 1959. An abortive attempt was made at reviving the show in the summer of 1974, with the emphasis on *Your Hit Parade* songs from selected broadcasts of specific weeks in the 1940s and 1950s, mixed with currently popular hits performed by the original artists.

YOUR KAISER DEALER PRESENTS KAISER-FRAZER "ADVENTURES IN MYSTERY" STARRING BETTY FURNESS IN "BYLINE", see *Byline*

YOUR LUCKY CLUE (*Quiz/Audience Participation*)

FIRST TELECAST: *July 13, 1952*

LAST TELECAST: *August 31, 1952*

BROADCAST HISTORY:

Jul 1952–Aug 1952, CBS Sun 7:30–8:00

EMCEE:

Basil Rathbone

Each week two teams competed with each other to solve dramatized mysteries. One team was composed of two professional detectives and the other of two amateur criminologists. The audience was made aware of where the clues were in each dramatization, but the contestants were not. Each team tried to solve the case before the other team did, and before the emcee disclosed the solution. Basil Rathbone, long known as the Sherlock Holmes of motion pictures (he played the role in most of the adaptations of A. Conan Doyle's stories), was a logical choice as emcee.

YOUR LUCKY STRIKE HIT PARADE, see *Your Hit Parade*

YOUR NEIGHBOR THE WORLD (*Documentary*)

FIRST TELECAST: *April 6, 1958*

LAST TELECAST: *October 8, 1959*

BROADCAST HISTORY:

Apr 1958–Jan 1959, ABC Sun Various (30 minutes)
May 1959–Oct 1959, ABC Thu 10:00–10:30

Documentary films about different peoples and cultures around the world, from high fashion in Paris to natives in the Belgian Congo.

YOUR PLAY TIME (*Dramatic Anthology*)

FIRST TELECAST: *June 14, 1953*

LAST TELECAST: *September 3, 1955*

BROADCAST HISTORY:

Jun 1953–Sep 1953, CBS Sun 7:30–8:00
Jun 1954–Sep 1954, CBS Sun 7:30–8:00
Jun 1955–Sep 1955, NBC Sat 10:30–11:00

For three consecutive summers series bearing the title *Your Play Time* aired as replacements for other shows. In 1953 and 1954, on CBS, the show was the summer replacement for two alternating CBS programs, *The Jack Benny Show* and *Private Secretary*. In 1953 some of the plays were done live and others on film. They tended to be on the melodramatic side with settings in foreign locales. 1954's offerings, both comedy and drama, were entirely on film and generally took place in domestic settings. Featured were such lesser-known stars as George Nader, Hillary Brooke, Jack Haley, Peter Graves, Ruth Warrick, and Tommy Rettig.

The *Your Play Time* that was telecast by NBC in the summer of 1955 was made up of reruns from other anthology series, primarily *Pepsi-Cola Playhouse* and *Studio 57*. It was the summer replacement for *Your Hit Parade*.

YOUR PRIZE STORY (*Dramatic Anthology*)
FIRST TELECAST: *April 2, 1952*
LAST TELECAST: *May 28, 1952*
BROADCAST HISTORY:
Apr 1952–May 1952, NBC Wed 10:00–10:30

This live weekly dramatic show was unique in that its sponsor, Hazel Bishop, requested viewers to submit story ideas. The person sending in a story that was accepted and adapted for television received a cash prize of $1,000. It had to be a true story and literary skill was not required. The viewer was to tell it in his own words and let the program's staff rewrite it for airing. The presentations were done with very little in the way of scenery or props, much in the manner of little-theater performances.

Evidently the public was not bubbling over with good ideas for TV shows, as the series lasted less than two months.

YOUR SHOW OF SHOWS (*Comedy/Variety*)
FIRST TELECAST: *February 25, 1950*
LAST TELECAST: *June 5, 1954*
BROADCAST HISTORY:
Feb 1950–Jun 1954, NBC Sat 9:00–10:30
REGULARS:
Sid Caesar
Imogene Coca
Carl Reiner
Howard Morris (1951–1954)
Robert Merrill (1950–1951)
Marguerite Piazza (1950–1953)
Bill Hayes (1950–1953)
Jerry Ross & Nellie Fisher (1950–1952)
Mata & Hari (1950–1953)
Tom Avera (1950)
Hamilton Dancers
Jack Russell
Billy Williams Quartet
Judy Johnson (1950–1953)
Earl Redding (1950–1951)
Aariana Knowles (1951–1952)
Dick DeFreitas (1950–1953)
Bambi Linn & Rod Alexander (1952–1954)
James Starbuck
Show of Shows Ballet Company
Charles Sanford Orchestra
PRODUCERS:
Max Liebman
WRITERS:
Mel Brooks, Neil Simon, Lucille Kallen, Larry Gelbart, Mel Tolkin, others

One of the classics of television's "Golden Age," *Your Show of Shows* was the successor to Caesar and Coca's 1949 *Admiral Broadway Revue*. At the outset, *Your Show of Shows* was actually half of a larger show, being the New York element of NBC's *Saturday Night Revue*. The other portion, from Chicago, was *The Jack Carter Show*, on between 8:00 and 9:00 P.M. At the end of the 1950–1951 season Carter and the *Saturday Night Review* umbrella title were dropped.

Your Show of Shows was surely one of the most ambitious undertakings on television, *ever*. It was 90 minutes of live, original comedy, every week. And it was good. In addition to Caesar and Coca's sketches there was a large corps of regular singers and dancers, plus top-name guest stars. As a matter of fact, the nominal host of each program was a different big-name guest star (Burgess Meredith hosted the first two shows). Ballet sequences and scenes from grand opera were also featured, to give the show an undeniably "classy" air.

But it was the comic genius of Caesar and Coca for which the program is remembered. They appeared in such regular routines as "History As She Ain't," Caesar's roving reporter, monologues and mime, as well as in large-scale satires on current films and other hit TV shows. Caesar and his writers were movie buffs, and many of Hollywood's most pretentious epics got the full treatment, ranging from antique silent films (the drunken father) to contemporary hits such as *Shane* (in which Caesar played the unbelievably fearless gunfighter Strange) and *From Here to Eternity* ("From Here to Obscurity").

Carl Reiner and Howard Morris, who joined the supporting cast in 1950 and 1951 respectively, were gradually given more prominent roles and by the final season Caesar, Coca, Reiner, and Morris constituted a four-person repertory group employed in many of the skits. Caesar could take on many roles. He was the double-talking foreigner (he was a master of dialects), the henpecked husband, or the greasy-haired cad. Coca was nearly as versatile, while Reiner would most often be the slick, presumptuous salesman type, and Howard Morris the little guy determined to prove that he was as good as *anybody*—even if he wasn't. Among the notable routines developed during the show's long run were Caesar and Coca's husband-and-wife skit, "The Hickenloopers"; the fable of the great clock in the little town of Baverhoff, Bavaria, whose mechanical figures always seemed to go haywire when the hour struck; Coca as the happy-go-lucky tramp; Caesar as an Italian opera star bubbling gibberish in *Galapacci*, or as the supercool jazz musician Progress Hornsby, or as the visiting authority on almost anything, usually being interviewed at the airport, with such dialogue as this:

ARCHEOLOGIST: "After many years, I haff found ze secret of Titten-Totten's Tomb!"

INTERVIEWER: (excitedly): "What is it, Professor?"

ARCHEOLOGIST: "I should tell *you*?"

Your Show of Shows finally left the air in June 1954, as Caesar and Coca parted to pursue separate careers. Most series end their runs forgotten or in reruns, but in what must have been one of the more unusual farewells in TV history, the last telecast of *Your Show of Shows* was a big, tearful, nostalgic recap of the best sketches of the past years, ending with the by-then famous finale number "Stars over Broadway." Even the president of NBC, Pat Weaver, showed up to thank everyone for four excellent years and to wish them well in their future separate series.

Caesar and Coca never again quite recaptured the magic of those four years, either separately or together. The combination of fresh talent, excellent supporting cast, gifted writers (including such future stars as Mel Brooks and Neil Simon), and perhaps the times themselves had been "right"—but only once. Excerpts from the shows were packaged by producer Max Liebman as a theatrical movie titled *Ten From Your Show of Shows*, in 1973, and as a series of 90-minute TV specials syndicated in 1976.

YOUR SHOW TIME (*Dramatic Anthology*)
FIRST TELECAST: *January 21, 1949*
LAST TELECAST: *July 15, 1949*
BROADCAST HISTORY:
Jan 1949–Jul 1949, NBC Fri 9:30–10:00
HOST:
Arthur Shields
Filmed dramatizations of classic short stories by many of the world's most famous authors, including Guy de Maupassant, Robert Louis Stevenson, Henry James, and Sir Arthur Conan Doyle. Each telecast opened in an old bookshop where host Arthur Shields was seen seated behind an old-fashioned desk, from which he introduced tonight's story.

This program was notable as the recipient of the very first Emmy award presented to a network show. The award was for the premiere telecast, "The Necklace," starring John Beal.

YOUR SPORTS SPECIAL (*Sports News*)
FIRST TELECAST: *October 8, 1948*
LAST TELECAST: *November 4, 1949*
BROADCAST HISTORY:
Oct 1948–Jan 1949, CBS Fri 7:00–7:15
Jan 1949–Nov 1949, CBS Various 7:00–7:15
REPORTER:
Carswell Adams
Dolly Stark
Sports reporter Carswell Adams and former major-league umpire Dolly Stark were the hosts of this sports news and interview show. Originally seen on Friday nights, it expanded in January 1949 to an irregular schedule that varied from two to five times per week for the next ten months.

YOUR STORY THEATRE (*Dramatic Anthology*)
FIRST TELECAST: *December 1, 1950*
LAST TELECAST: *February 2, 1951*
BROADCAST HISTORY:
Dec 1950–Feb 1951, DUM Fri 8:00–8:30
Series of half-hour filmed dramas, starring such Hollywood standbys as Robert Alda, Hurd Hatfield, Marjorie Lord, William Frawley, Sterling Holloway, etc. Stories included both original scripts and adaptations from Henry James, Robert Louis Stevenson, Frank R. Stockton ("The Lady or the Tiger"), and other noted authors.

YOUR —— TV THEATER, syndicated title for
Fireside Theatre

YOUR WITNESS (*Courtroom Drama*)
FIRST TELECAST: *September 19, 1949*
LAST TELECAST: *September 26, 1950*
BROADCAST HISTORY:
Sep 1949–Oct 1949, ABC Mon 8:00–8:30
Dec 1949–May 1950, ABC Sun 9:00–9:30
Aug 1950–Sep 1950, ABC Wed 9:00–9:30
WITH:
Edmund Lowe
Wednesday was courtroom night in 1950, with *Your Witness* following *On Trial* on the ABC schedule, and running opposite *Famous Jury Trials* on DuMont. This was a low-budget courtroom drama/mystery, and originated from Chicago.

YOU'RE IN THE PICTURE (*Quiz/Audience Participation*)
FIRST TELECAST: *January 20, 1961*
LAST TELECAST: *January 20, 1961*
BROADCAST HISTORY:
Jan 1961, CBS Fri 9:30–10:00
HOST:
Jackie Gleason
PANELISTS:
Pat Harrington, Jr.
Pat Carroll
Jan Sterling
Arthur Treacher
This was one of those rare series that was so bad it was canceled after exactly one telecast. It was certainly one of the major fiascos in Jackie Gleason's career. The four celebrity panelists on the show were seen situated behind an oversized comic cutout of the kind found in amusement-park photography booths. They had no idea what the picture through which they had stuck their heads, and sometimes their hands, represented. The object was for the panel to guess what the picture was by asking questions of host/emcee Gleason. When they had successfully identified the picture, a new one would be substituted and they would start over. Jackie's wit was supposed to add to the humor of the show, which was played primarily for laughs. Keenan Wynn was supposed to be one the panelists, and appeared in the promotional stills shot for the show, but was injured on the day of the premiere and was replaced by Pat Harrington, Jr.

The first telecast was so bad, however, that the program never aired again. On the following Friday night Jackie spent the entire half hour apologizing for the disastrous first episode. For the remainder of the season he filled the time slot with an interview show, hosting different celebrities each week, under the title *The Jackie Gleason Show* (not to be confused with his comedy variety series of the same name). *You're in the Picture* was never heard of again.

YOU'RE INVITED (*Comedy/Variety*)
FIRST TELECAST: *July 1, 1948*
LAST TELECAST: *September 20, 1948*
BROADCAST HISTORY:
Jul 1948–Aug 1948, ABC Wed 8:00–8:30
Aug 1948–Sep 1948, ABC Mon 9:00–9:30
EMCEE:
Romo Vincent
Jovial, rotund comic Romo Vincent hosted this early variety show, which took place in a houseparty setting. At the start of each show he greeted his audience at the front door and invited them in to see the singers, dancers, and ventriloquists who were that week's guests. There was also an audience-participation segment.

YOU'RE ON YOUR OWN (*Quiz/Audience Participation*)
FIRST TELECAST: *December 22, 1956*
LAST TELECAST: *March 16, 1957*

BROADCAST HISTORY:

Dec 1956–Mar 1957, CBS Sat 10:30–11:00

EMCEE:

Steve Dunne

Contestants on *You're on Your Own* had free access to anything on the stage that would help them find answers to the questions posed by emcee Steve Dunne. They need not know everything, only be able to use the correct source: directories, record albums, telephone books, etc. The faster they were at ferreting out the correct answers, the more money they could win—as much as $25,000 on a single night.

YOU'RE THE ONE (*Situation Comedy*)

FIRST TELECAST: *April 19, 1998*
LAST TELECAST: *April 26, 1998*
BROADCAST HISTORY:

Apr 1998, WB Sun 9:30–10:00

CAST:

Lindsay Metcalf .... Cynthia Geary
Mark Weitz .... Elon Gold
Chip Metcalf .... Jayce Bartok
Robin Weitz .... Julie Dretzin
Howie .... Troy Winbush
Bo Metcalf .... Leo Burmester
Mary Chase Metcalf .... Jessie Jones
Leanore Weitz .... Dori Brenner
Sy Weitz .... Lenny Wolpe

Opposites attracted, briefly, in this cartoonish comedy. Perky Lindsay was a WASPy Southern aristocrat, the great granddaughter of a Civil War general. Who should she fall for but Mark, a prototypical New Yawker and the great-grandson of a Rumanian horse trader? She was an elegant landscape architect, he ran a baseball website on the Internet, called The Score. Needless to say, their parents—especially hers—were aghast. Lindsay's blustery, gun-toting dad, Bo, constantly tested his new son-in-law ("understand you're a Jew"), buying The Score and saddling him with his timid teenage son, Chip. Mark's large, noisy clan (including mom and dad Leanore and Sy) descended on the newlyweds, nattering over everything. Stereotypes abounded as the two clans met (Grandpa Weitz: "Hello. Where's the toilet?"). It all ended, mercifully, after two episodes.

YOURS FOR A SONG (*Quiz*)

FIRST TELECAST: *November 14, 1961*
LAST TELECAST: *September 18, 1962*
BROADCAST HISTORY:

Nov 1961–Sep 1962, ABC Tue 9:30–10:00

EMCEE:

Bert Parks

Contestants on this live half-hour game show won money by filling in the missing words to song lyrics that were flashed on a screen. Whenever a contestant won a round, in addition to the prize money he won the right to face a new challenger. In addition to serving as quizmaster, Bert Parks got a chance to sing in this one. A few weeks after this prime-time version premiered, ABC added a daytime version that ran until March 1963.

YOUTH ON THE MARCH (*Religion*)

FIRST TELECAST: *October 9, 1949*
LAST TELECAST: *June 7, 1953*
BROADCAST HISTORY:

Oct 1949–May 1952, ABC Sun 10:30–11:00 (OS)
Oct 1952–Jun 1953, DUM Sun 10:30–11:00

HOST:

Rev. Percy Crawford

This program of inspirational songs, hymns, and sermons was a fixture on Sunday nights for nearly four years, first on ABC and then on DuMont. It was presented by the Young People's Church of the Air and was presided over by Rev. Percy Crawford, with mixed choir and men's glee club.

YOUTH TAKES A STAND (*Discussion*)

FIRST TELECAST: *August 18, 1953*
LAST TELECAST: *September 15, 1953*
BROADCAST HISTORY:

Aug 1953–Sep 1953, CBS Tue 10:30–11:00

MODERATOR:

Marc Cramer
Alan Jackson

In an effort to get intelligent audience feedback to its television news effort, CBS invited four young scholars from high schools and junior colleges to participate in a discussion of current events and world affairs with a different CBS-TV reporter each week. The first moderator for the sessions during the show's prime-time run was the series' coproducer, Marc Cramer. A different panel of students, selected by CBS stations around the country in cooperation with various public, parochial, and private school organizations, appeared on each telecast to chat with such reporters as Charles Collingwood and Douglas Edwards. Mr. Cramer was replaced by CBS News reporter Alan Jackson before the series moved into a late-afternoon time slot on Sundays. It remained on the air until March 1955 with Jim McKay replacing Jackson as moderator in March 1954.

YOUTH WANTS TO KNOW (*Forum*)

FIRST TELECAST: *September 8, 1951*
LAST TELECAST: *August 24, 1954*
BROADCAST HISTORY:

Sep 1951–Oct 1951, NBC Sat 7:00–7:30
Jun 1952–Sep 1952, NBC Wed 8:30–9:00
Jul 1954–Aug 1954, NBC Sat 7:30–8:00

MODERATOR

Theodore Granik

This series gave high school and college students the opportunity to ask questions of major figures in the world of politics, business, and international affairs. The subjects covered were generally related to major issues that affected large parts of the world and large numbers of its people. *Youth Wants to Know* originated live from Washington, D.C., and students from the Washington area participated. Mr. Granik and the guest were seated on a platform in front of the students and the entire operation was run like a press conference, with Mr. Granik picking the questioners. The students prepared their own questions. When this series premiered in 1951, its title was *The American Youth Forum.* It was changed to *Youth Wants to Know* in January 1952. At times, though not always, it was simulcast on radio, and it continued to run irregularly on Sunday afternoons until October 1958.

YU-GI-OH! (*Cartoon*)

BROADCAST HISTORY:

Cartoon Network
30 minutes

Original episodes: *2002–*
Premiered: *November 11, 2002*
(Seen in daytime on WB Kids' Network beginning Sep. 29, 2001)

VOICES (U.S.):

Yugi Moto, Yami Yugi .... Dan Green
Joey Wheeler, Shadi............... Wayne Grayson
Tea Gardner....................... Amy Birnbaum
Mai Valentine................ Megan Hollingshead
Maximillion Pegasus.............. Darren Dunstan
Seto Kaiba .... Eric Stuart
Mokuba Kaiba......................... Tara Jayne
Bakura Ryou, Yami Bakura, Bandit Keith
.... Ted Lewis
Serenity Wheeler....................... Lisa Ortiz
Weevil Underwood .... Jimmy Zoppi

Action-packed Japanese anime cartoon based on the popular kids' card game. Yugi Moto was the young, blond, spiky-haired hero who had unlocked the secret of the Millennium Puzzle, hidden away by the Egyptians 5,000 years before. Infused with its magical energies, Yugi played Duel Monsters in island tournaments, summoning up monsters and spells to counter those of his foes. Joey and Tea were pals who played also (sometimes against each other), but often needed rescuing; among the chief villains were Seto Kaiba and Pegasus, an evil millionaire who craved the power of the cards (such as that of the much-sought-after "Blue Eyes White Dragon"). It was Pegasus who had created Duel Monsters, based on the ancient Egyptians' Shadow Games, and who held the Millennium Eye, which allowed him to see into the minds of others. Points earned were shown on the screen, making this look much like a video game.

The U.S. series was a dubbed version of the popular series seen in Japan.

Z

ZANE GREY THEATER, see *Dick Powell's Zane Grey Theater*

ZOE, DUNCAN, JACK & JANE (*Situation Comedy*)
FIRST TELECAST: *January 17, 1999*
LAST TELECAST: *June 11, 2000*
BROADCAST HISTORY:
Jan 1999–Jul 1999, WB Sun 9:00–9:30
Jul 1999, WB Sun 8:30–9:00
Jan 2000–Feb 2000, WB Mon 9:30–10:00
Apr 2000–Jun 2000, WB Sun 9:30–10:00
CAST:
Zoe Bean .... Selma Blair
Duncan Milch .... David Moscow
Jack Cooper .... Michael Rosenbaum
Jane Cooper .... Azura Skye
Iris Bean (1999) .... Mary Page Keller
Breeny Kennedy (1999) .... Sara Rue
Doug McArthur Anderson (2000) ... Omar Gooding

This teenage variation on *Friends* focused on the social lives of four upper middle class kids who attended Fielding Mellish Prep, a private high school on Manhattan's Upper West Side. Zoe was earnest, sincere, and something of a dreamer; curly-haired Duncan had a temper, was uptight, and couldn't find girls to date; and cool Jack and "plain" Jane were twins—although he was self-assured, she sarcastic and insecure. Jane and Zoe confided in each other about everything—boys, food, clothes, school, etc. The four of them hung out in a local coffeehouse, Café N, in Greenwich Village, after school. Breeny, their cynical wheelchair-bound classmate, was incredibly nasty and abusive. Zoe's single mom, Iris, was in the opening credits but only appeared occasionally.

The four teens were frequently seen in subway stations on their way around Manhattan, and in between scenes viewers were shown a subway map indicating their movements from home to school to their hangout in the Village.

When the show returned for its second season in January 2000, the title had been shortened to *Zoe . . .* (with three dots); at the start of the premiere the words THREE YEARS LATER flashed on the screen. Zoe and her friends, except for Duncan, were now in college, and all were living on their own. Jane was Zoe's roommate and Jack was Duncan's. Gone were the traditional subway map scenes. Zoe worked part time as a hostess at The Shanghai Chinese restaurant where Jane waited tables and Doug, an aspiring playwright, was the bartender. Duncan worked for a company designing Internet home pages for businesses. At the end of February the guys got a fancy apartment at a low rent by working as the building supers—but it didn't work out. In the spring Zoe started dating Duncan's boss, Andy (Hamilton Von Watts), and the three dots were dropped from the title.

ZORRO (*Western*)
FIRST TELECAST: *October 10, 1957*
LAST TELECAST: *September 24, 1959*
BROADCAST HISTORY:
Oct 1957–Sep 1959, ABC Thu 8:00–8:30
CAST:
Don Diego de la Vega ("Zorro") .... Guy Williams
Don Alejandro .... George J. Lewis
Bernardo .... Gene Sheldon
Capt. Monastario (1957–1958) .... Britt Lomond
Sgt. Demetrio Lopez Garcia .... Henry Calvin
Don Ignacio (Nacho) Torres (1957) .... Jan Arvan
Magistrate Carlos Galindo (1958)
.... Vinton Hayworth
Padre Felipe (1957) .... Romney Brent
José Sebastian Varga (1958) .... Charles Korvin
Anna Maria Verdugo (1958–1959) .... Jolene Brand
Sénor Gregorio Verdugo (1958) ...... Eduard Franz
Cpl. Reyes (1958–1959) .... Don Diamond
PRODUCER:
Walt Disney
THEME:
"Theme from Zorro," by Norman Foster and George Bruns

Guy Williams starred as a swashbuckling masked hero in Spanish California in this popular series. The year was 1820, and young Don Diego, the only son of wealthy Don Alejandro, was returning home from Spain in response to his father's appeals. Monastario, a ruthless army officer, had become commandant of the Fortress de los Angeles, and was tyrannizing the local dons and their peons. Arriving in California, Don Diego presented himself as a lazy, foppish aristocrat, much to his father's dismay. Secretly, however, he donned mask and sword and set out to aid the oppressed and foil the schemes of the evil Monastario. His name on these forays was Zorro—for the sign of the "Z" he cut with his sword—and his loyal manservant was the mute Bernardo, who pretended to be deaf as well as mute to make it easier for him to eavesdrop for his master. Only Zorro knew that Bernardo could really hear.

The plots were pretty simple, and there was a lot of derring-do (especially in the sword fights), making *Zorro* a great favorite with children. Helping Zorro's crusade was the fact that his initial adversaries, Monastario and his second-in-command, the fat, dim-witted Sgt. Garcia, were both quite incompetent. Another element of interest was that the stories continued from episode to episode, in semi-serial fashion, even though they were so basic that they could be joined at any point.

In the first season Zorro defeated the oppressive Capt. Monastario and a series of crooked replacements, then foiled an elaborate plot by a mysterious villain known as "The Eagle" to overthrow Spanish rule in California. The second season saw a plot to assassinate the Governor, as well as a short-lived romantic interest for Zorro in the person of Anna Maria Verdugo. Among those seen in multi-episode story arcs were Nacho Torres, an escaped political prisoner, scheming Magistrate Galindo, José Sebastian Varga ("The Eagle"), and a young señorita named Anita Cabrillo, played by Annette Funicello, who even got a chance to sing a few songs on the show. Her role was a birthday present from series producer Walt Disney, who had originally brought Annette to stardom as a *Mickey Mouse Club* mouseketeer only a few years before. Zorro's black and white stallions were Tornado and Phantom.

The theme song from the show ("Zorro—the fox

so cunning and free / Zorro—make the sign of the Z!") was a hit-parade favorite in 1958. It was first recorded by Henry Calvin, of all people (fat Sgt. Garcia!), but the hit version was by a pop group, the Chordettes.

Zorro left the air due to a financial dispute between ABC and the Walt Disney studio, which produced the series. Four new one-hour episodes were aired on *Walt Disney Presents* during the 1960–1961 season.

The character of Zorro was created by author Johnston McCulley in the early 1900s and has been the subject of several movies, including features starring Douglas Fairbanks, Sr. (1920) and Tyrone Power (1940) and popular Republic serials in the 1930s.

ZORRO (*Western*)

BROADCAST HISTORY:

The Family Channel
30 minutes
Produced: *1989–1993* (88 episodes)
Premiered: *January 5, 1990*

CAST:

Don Diego de la Vega (Zorro)....... Duncan Regehr
Don Alejandro Sebastian de la Vega (1990)
.... Efrem Zimbalist, Jr.
Don Alejandro Sebastian de la Vega
.... Henry Darrow
Victoria Scalanti .... Patrice Cahmi Martinez
Sgt. Hymen Mendoza................ James Victor
The Alcalde (Luis Ramone) (1990–1991)
.... Michael Tylo
The Alcalde (Ignacio DeSoto) (1991–1994)
.... John Hertzler
Felipe........................... Juan Diego Botto

In 1990 Zorro galloped back onto the small screen once again in this new, rather straightforward version on The Family Channel. Filmed in Spain, it starred Duncan Regehr as the masked rider. At first Efrem Zimbalist, Jr., played his father, but he was replaced shortly after the premiere by Henry Darrow, who had himself worn the black mask in CBS' *Zorro and Son.*

Felipe was Zorro's mute aide, Victoria his love interest, and The Alcalde the villainous ruler of old Los Angeles. The first Alcalde, Ramone, killed because of his own greed in 1991, was replaced by DeSoto, a politically obsessed schemer who had been a student in Madrid with Don Diego.

ZORRO AND SON (*Situation Comedy*)

FIRST TELECAST: *April 6, 1983*
LAST TELECAST: *June 1, 1983*
BROADCAST HISTORY:

Apr 1983–Jun 1983, CBS Wed 8:00–8:30

CAST:

Don Diego de la Vega (Zorro Sr.)..... Henry Darrow
Don Carlos de la Vega (Zorro Jr.) .... Paul Regina
Commandante Paco Pico........... Gregory Sierra
Sgt. Sepulveda .... Richard Beauchamp
Bernardo................................ Bill Dana
Brothers Napa and Sonoma......... Barney Martin
Corporal Cassette.................. John Moschitta
Señorita Anita .... Catherine Parks
Peasant................................. Pete Leal

Played pretty much for laughs, this series updated the legend of Zorro, 20–25 years after the masked defender of the people had first made his name in old California. Age had taken its toll on Don Diego and, when he was injured while trying to live up to his reputation, his faithful manservant Bernardo decided something had to be done. Bernardo sent to Spain for young Don Carlos, Diego's son. Unlike his father, Don Carlos was a modern swinger who, though willing to help out his father, would not give up his gambling or his girl-chasing. Not only that, the elder Zorro, a traditionalist, had great difficulty adjusting to his son's use of guns, gas bombs, and other modern weapons, instead of a simple sword. The current oppressor of the people was Commandante Pico, assisted by Sgt. Sepulveda, and his human recording machine, Corp. Cassette. *Zorro and Son* was liberally laced with bad jokes—the Franciscan monk arrested for "selling wine before its time," young Don Carlos futilely trying to rally the people in a makeshift Zorro costume when his regular one was lost, etc.—and it rarely took itself seriously, despite being produced by Walt Disney Productions, the same company responsible for the original *Zorro* TV series more than 25 years earlier.

APPENDIX 1

PRIME TIME SCHEDULES: 1946–2002

On the following pages are complete prime time network schedules for each season from 1946–1947 through 2002–2003. Television programming changes constantly, and schedules such as these can only offer an approximation of what was on during any given week. However, the industry has long had a custom of introducing new series in September or October of each year, and it is these introductory "fall schedules" that are shown here.

During the 1950s and 1960s most of the series introduced in the fall of each year lasted for at least three months, and often for a full year, even when they were unsuccessful. Industry practice was to contract in advance for at least 13 original episodes of a series. In later years, however, intense network competition led to the dropping of unsuccessful series as soon as three or four weeks after their premieres, and occasionally a TV dud, like a Broadway flop, will even close on its opening night. The principal fall programs are shown here, no matter how short their actual runs.

Times given are those at which the programs were seen in most cities. Newscasts will be found in the main body of the book under *News*, feature film series under *Movies*, sports events under the name of the sport, etc. (Miscellaneous collections of film shorts, used to fill time, are included on the schedules but are not in the book.) A blank indicates that there was no network programming in the time slot. This does not necessarily mean there was nothing on TV—individual stations usually filled in with their own local or syndicated shows—although in the earliest days there sometimes was only a test pattern to watch.

Abbreviations

A = ABC

C = CBS

D = DuMont

F = Fox

N = NBC

U = UPN

W = WB

PRIME TIME SCHEDULE: FALL 1946

Day	Network	7:00 PM	7:30	8:00	8:30	9:00	9:30	10:00	10:30
SUNDAY	A								
	C								
	D			Western Movie	Western Movie				
	N			Face to Face / Geographically Speaking	Television Screen Magazine				
MONDAY	A								
	C								
	D								
	N		Esso Newsreel	†		Gillette Cavalcade of Sports	Gillette Cavalcade of Sports	Gillette Cavalcade of Sports	Gillette Cavalcade of Sports
TUESDAY	A								
	C								
	D			Play the Game		Serving Through Science			
	N								
WEDNESDAY	A								
	C								
	D					Faraway Hill			
	N								
THURSDAY	A								
	C								
	D					Cash and Carry			
	N		Esso Newsreel	Hour Glass	Hour Glass	Fight Film Filler			
FRIDAY	A								
	C								
	D								
	N			*	I Love to Eat / ‡		Gillette Cavalcade of Sports	Gillette Cavalcade of Sports	Gillette Cavalcade of Sports
SATURDAY	A								
	C								
	D								
	N								

*You Are an Artist / Let's Rhumba †Voice of Firestone Televues ‡The World in Your Home

PRIME TIME SCHEDULE: FALL 1947

Day	Network	7:00 PM	7:30	8:00	8:30	9:00	9:30	10:00	10:30
SUNDAY	A								
	C								
	D								
	N			Various Special Presentations					
MONDAY	A								
	C								
	D	Small Fry Club	Doorway to Fame						
	N			Americana		Esso Reporter	Gillette Cavalcade of Sports		
TUESDAY	A								
	C								
	D	Small Fry Club		Western Movie		Mary Kay and Johnny			
	N								
WEDNESDAY	A								
	C								
	D	Small Fry Club							
	N		Kraft Television Theatre		*				
THURSDAY	A								
	C								
	D	Small Fry Club	Birthday Party		Charade Quiz				
	N		†	Musical Merry-Go-Round	Eye Witness	You Are an Artist			
FRIDAY	A								
	C								
	D	Small Fry Club							
	N			Campus Hoopla	‡	Gillette Cavalcade of Sports			
SATURDAY	A								
	C								
	D								
	N								

*In the Kelvinator Kitchen †NBC TV Newsreel ‡The World in Your Home

PRIME TIME SCHEDULE: FALL 1948

Day	Net	7:00 PM	7:30	8:00	8:30	9:00	9:30	10:00	10:30
SUNDAY	A	Pauline Frederick	Southernaires Quartet	Hollywood Screen Test	Actors Studio	Movie			
SUNDAY	C	Newsweek in Review	Studio One / Various		Riddle Me This	Toast of the Town		America Speaks	News
SUNDAY	D	Original Amateur Hour							
SUNDAY	N	Mary Kay and Johnny; News	Welcome Aboard	Author Meets the Critics	Meet the Press	Philco TV Playhouse			
MONDAY	A	News	Kiernan's Corner	Quizzing the News	Film Shorts				
MONDAY	C	Places Please	News; Face the Music		Arthur Godfrey's Talent Scouts	Basketball			
MONDAY	D	Doorway to Fame	††; Champagne and Orchids	Court of Current Issues					
MONDAY	N		America Song; News	Chevrolet Tele-Theater	Americana	Newsreel; Boxing from St. Nicholas Arena			
TUESDAY	A	News	Movieland Quiz	Film Shorts	America's Town Meeting of the Air				
TUESDAY	C	Roar of the Rails	News; Face the Music			We, the People	People's Platform		
TUESDAY	D		††; INS Telenews			Boxing			
TUESDAY	N		Musical Miniatures; News	Texaco Star Theater		Mary Margaret McBride	News / Films	Wrestling from St. Nicholas Arena	
WEDNESDAY	A	News	Critic at Large	Gay Nineties Revue	Film Shorts; Three About Town	Wrestling from Washington, D.C.			
WEDNESDAY	C	Places Please	News; Face the Music	Kobbs Korner	Winner Take All		Boxing from Westchester		News
WEDNESDAY	D	Birthday Party	††; Film Shorts	Photographic Horizons	The Growing Paynes	Boxing from Jamaica Arena			
WEDNESDAY	N		You Are an Artist; News	Girl About Town; Picture This	Ted Steele; Story of the Week	Kraft Television Theatre		News Reel; Village Barn	
THURSDAY	A	News; Film Shorts		Fashion Story	Club Seven	Movie			
THURSDAY	C		News; Face the Music	To the Queen's Taste	Movies / Sports				
THURSDAY	D	Adventures of Okey Doky	††	Film Shorts	Charade Quiz	Wrestling / Football			
THURSDAY	N	‡	Musical Miniatures; *; News	NBC Presents; ‡‡	Swift Show	Gulf Road Show with Bob Smith	Bigelow Show		
FRIDAY	A	News	Tales of Red Caboose; Film Shorts	Teenage Book Club	Various	Break the Bank			
FRIDAY	C	Your Sports Special; Places Please	News; Face the Music	†; What's It Worth	Cap'n Billy's Mississippi Music Hall				
FRIDAY	D	Key to the Missing	††; Film Shorts	Fashions on Parade	Film Shorts	Wrestling from Jamaica Arena			
FRIDAY	N		Musical Merry-Go-Round; News	Musical Miniatures	Stop Me If You've Heard This One	I'd Like to See	News; Gillette Cavalcade of Sports		
SATURDAY	A	News; Film Shorts	Sports with Joe Hasel	Play the Game	Film Shorts	Basketball			
SATURDAY	C			Basketball					
SATURDAY	D								
SATURDAY	N		Televison Screen Magazine	Saturday Night Jamboree	Basketball				

*Sportswoman of the Week
†Sportsman's Quiz
††Camera Headlines (News)
‡Paris Cavalcade of Fashion
‡‡The Nature of Things

PRIME TIME SCHEDULE: FALL 1949

		7:00 PM	7:30	8:00	8:30	9:00	9:30	10:00	10:30
SUNDAY	A	Paul Whiteman's Goodyear Revue	ABC Penthouse Players	Think Fast	The Little Revue	Let There Be Stars		Celebrity Time	Youth on the March
	C	Tonight on Broadway	This is Show Business	Toast of the Town		Fred Waring Show		News	
	D	Front Row Center		Chicagoland Mystery Players	Cinema Varieties	Cross Question			
	N	Leave It to the Girls	Aldrich Family	Chesterfield Supper Club	Colgate Theatre	Philco TV Playhouse		Garroway at Large	
MONDAY	A	News							
	C	Roar of the Rails	News Sonny Kendis *	Silver Theater	Arthur Godfrey's Talent Scouts	Candid Camera	The Goldbergs	Studio One	
	D	Captain Video	‡ Vincent Lopez	Newsweek Views the News	Al Morgan	And Everything Nice	Wrestling		
	N	Kukla, Fran & Ollie	† News	Chevrolet Tele-Theater	Voice of Firestone	Lights Out	Cities Service Band of America	Quiz Kids	
TUESDAY	A	News						Tomorrow's Boxing Champions	
	C	Strictly for Laughs	News Sonny Kendis *	Movies / Specials		Actors Studio	Suspense	This Week in Sports	
	D	Captain Video	‡ Vincent Lopez	Court of Current Issues		The O'Neills	Feature Theatre		
	N	Kukla, Fran & Ollie	† News	Texaco Star Theater		Fireside Theater	Life of Riley	Original Amateur Hour	
WEDNESDAY	A	News		Photoplay Time	Look Photocrime	Author Meets the Critics	Wrestling from Chicago		
	C	Strictly for Laughs	News At Home	Arthur Godfrey & His Friends		Bigelow Show	Boxing from St. Nicholas Arena		
	D	Captain Video	‡ Vincent Lopez	Movies		††	Famous Jury Trials		
	N	Kukla, Fran & Ollie	† News	Crisis	The Clock	Kraft Television Show		Break the Bank	
THURSDAY	A	News	Lone Ranger	Stop the Music		Crusade in Europe	Starring Boris Karloff	Roller Derby	
	C	Dione Lucas	News Sonny Kendis *	Front Page	Inside U.S.A. / Romance		Boxing from Sunnyside Gardens		
	D	Captain Video	‡ Vincent Lopez	Mystery Theater		Morey Amsterdam Show			
	N	Kukla, Fran & Ollie	† News	Hollywood Premiere	Mary Kay and Johnny	Fireball Fun-For-All		Martin Kane Private Eye	
FRIDAY	A	News		Majority Rules	Blind Date	Auction-Aire	Fun for the Money	Roller Derby	
	C	Strictly for Laughs	News Sonny Kendis *	Mama	Man Against Crime	Ford Theatre / 54th Street Revue		People's Platform	Capitol Cloakroom
	D	Captain Video	‡ Vincent Lopez	Hands of Mystery	Headline Clues	Fishing and Hunting Club	Film	Amateur Boxing from Chicago	
	N	Kukla, Fran & Ollie	† News	One Man's Family	We, the People	Bonny Maid Versatile Varieties	Big Story / Various	Gillette Cavalcade of Sports	
SATURDAY	A		Hollywood Screen Test	Paul Whiteman's TV Teen Club		Roller Derby			
	C		Quincy Home-News Blues by Bargy *			Premiere Playhouse			
	D			Spin the Picture		Cavalcade of Stars		Wrestling from Chicago	
	N		‡‡ News	Twenty Questions	Sessions Stud's Place	Who Said That?	Meet the Press	Black Robe	

*Herb Shriner Show
†Mohawk Showroom
‡Manhattan Spotlight
††The Plainclothesman
‡‡The Nature of Things

PRIME TIME SCHEDULE: FALL 1950

<table>
<tr><th></th><th></th><th>7:00 PM</th><th colspan="2">7:30</th><th>8:00</th><th>8:30</th><th>9:00</th><th>9:30</th><th>10:00</th><th>10:30</th></tr>
<tr><td rowspan="4">SUNDAY</td><td>A</td><td>Paul Whiteman's Revue</td><td colspan="2">Showtime, U.S.A.</td><td>Hollywood Premiere Theatre</td><td>Sit or Miss</td><td>Soap Box Theatre</td><td>Marshall Plan in Action</td><td>Old Fashioned Meeting</td><td>Youth on the March</td></tr>
<tr><td>C</td><td>Gene Autry Show</td><td colspan="2">This is Show Business</td><td colspan="2">Toast of the Town</td><td colspan="2">Fred Waring Show</td><td>Celebrity Time</td><td>What's My Line</td></tr>
<tr><td>D</td><td colspan="3">Starlit Time</td><td>Rhythm Rodeo</td><td></td><td colspan="2">Arthur Murray Party</td><td colspan="2">They Stand Accused</td></tr>
<tr><td>N</td><td>Leave it to the Girls</td><td colspan="2">Aldrich Family</td><td colspan="2">Colgate Comedy Hour</td><td colspan="2">Philco TV Playhouse</td><td>Garroway at Large</td><td>Take a Chance</td></tr>
<tr><td rowspan="4">MONDAY</td><td>A</td><td>Club Seven</td><td colspan="2">Hollywood Screen Test</td><td>Treasury Men in Action</td><td>Dick Tracy</td><td>College Bowl</td><td>On Trial</td><td colspan="2">Feature Film</td></tr>
<tr><td>C</td><td>Stork Club</td><td>News</td><td>Perry Como</td><td>Lux Video Theatre</td><td>Arthur Godfrey's Talent Scouts</td><td>Horace Heidt Show</td><td>The Goldbergs</td><td colspan="2">Studio One</td></tr>
<tr><td>D</td><td>Captain Video</td><td>Susan Raye</td><td>*</td><td>Visit with the Armed Forces</td><td>Al Morgan</td><td colspan="4">Wrestling from Columbia Park</td></tr>
<tr><td>N</td><td>Kukla, Fran & Ollie</td><td>†</td><td>News</td><td>Special Show</td><td>Voice of Firestone</td><td>Lights Out</td><td colspan="2">Robert Montgomery Presents Lucky Strike Time/ Musical Comedy Time</td><td>Who Said That?</td></tr>
<tr><td rowspan="4">TUESDAY</td><td>A</td><td>Club Seven</td><td colspan="2">Beulah</td><td>Game of the Week</td><td>Buck Rogers</td><td>Billy Rose Show</td><td>Can You Top This?</td><td>Life Begins at Eighty</td><td>Roller Derby</td></tr>
<tr><td>C</td><td>Stork Club</td><td>News</td><td>Faye Emerson</td><td colspan="2">Prudential Family Playhouse / Sure as Fate</td><td>Vaughn Monroe Musical Variety</td><td>Suspense</td><td>Danger</td><td>We Take Your Word</td></tr>
<tr><td>D</td><td>Captain Video</td><td></td><td>Joan Edwards</td><td>Court of Current Issues</td><td>Johns Hopkins Science Review</td><td colspan="2">Cavalcade of Bands</td><td colspan="2">Star Time</td></tr>
<tr><td>N</td><td>Kukla, Fran & Ollie</td><td>Little Show</td><td>News</td><td colspan="2">Texaco Star Theater</td><td>Fireside Theatre</td><td>Circle Theatre</td><td colspan="2">Original Amateur Hour</td></tr>
<tr><td rowspan="4">WEDNESDAY</td><td>A</td><td>Club Seven</td><td colspan="2">Chance of a Lifetime</td><td colspan="2">First Nighter</td><td colspan="2">Don McNeill TV Club</td><td colspan="2">Chicago Wrestling</td></tr>
<tr><td>C</td><td>Stork Club</td><td>News</td><td>Perry Como</td><td colspan="2">Arthur Godfrey & His Friends</td><td colspan="2">Teller of Tales</td><td colspan="2">Blue Ribbon Bouts</td></tr>
<tr><td>D</td><td>Captain Video</td><td>Most Important People</td><td>*</td><td colspan="2"></td><td>Famous Jury Trials</td><td>The Plainclothesman</td><td>Broadway to Hollywood</td><td></td></tr>
<tr><td>N</td><td>Kukla, Fran & Ollie</td><td>†</td><td>News</td><td colspan="2">Four Star Revue</td><td colspan="2">Kraft Television Theatre</td><td>Break the Bank</td><td>Stars Over Hollywood</td></tr>
<tr><td rowspan="4">THURSDAY</td><td>A</td><td>Club Seven</td><td colspan="2">Lone Ranger</td><td colspan="2">Stop the Music</td><td>Holiday Hotel</td><td>Blind Date</td><td>I Cover Times Square</td><td>Roller Derby</td></tr>
<tr><td>C</td><td>Stork Club</td><td>News</td><td>Faye Emerson</td><td colspan="2">Show Goes On</td><td>Alan Young Show</td><td>Big Town</td><td>Truth or Consequences</td><td>Nash Airflyte Theater</td></tr>
<tr><td>D</td><td>Captain Video</td><td>*</td><td>Joan Edwards</td><td colspan="2"></td><td>Adventures of Ellery Queen</td><td colspan="3">Boxing from Dexter Arena</td></tr>
<tr><td>N</td><td>Kukla, Fran & Ollie</td><td>Little Show</td><td>News</td><td>You Bet Your Life</td><td>Hawkins Falls</td><td colspan="2">Kay Kyser's Kollege of Musical Knowledge</td><td>Martin Kane, Private Eye</td><td>Wayne King</td></tr>
<tr><td rowspan="4">FRIDAY</td><td>A</td><td>Club Seven</td><td colspan="2">Life with Linkletter</td><td>Twenty Questions</td><td>Pro Football Highlights</td><td colspan="2">Pulitzer Prize Playhouse</td><td>Penthouse Party</td><td>Stud's Place</td></tr>
<tr><td>C</td><td>Stork Club</td><td>News</td><td>Perry Como</td><td>Mama</td><td>Man Against Crime</td><td colspan="2">Ford Theatre / Magnavox Theater</td><td>Morton Downey Show</td><td>Beat the Clock</td></tr>
<tr><td>D</td><td>Captain Video</td><td>Most Important People</td><td>*</td><td>Film Filler</td><td>Hold That Camera</td><td>Hands of Mystery</td><td>Inside Detective</td><td colspan="2">Cavalcade of Stars</td></tr>
<tr><td>N</td><td>Kukla, Fran & Ollie</td><td>†</td><td>News</td><td>Quiz Kids</td><td>We, the People</td><td>Bonny Maid Versatile Varieties</td><td>Big Story / The Clock</td><td>Gillette Cavalcade of Sports</td><td>Greatest Fights</td></tr>
<tr><td rowspan="4">SATURDAY</td><td>A</td><td>Sandy Dreams</td><td colspan="2">Stu Erwin Show</td><td colspan="2">Paul Whiteman's TV Teen Club</td><td colspan="4">Roller Derby</td></tr>
<tr><td>C</td><td>Big Top</td><td>Week in Review</td><td>Faye Emerson</td><td colspan="2">Ken Murray Show</td><td colspan="2">Frank Sinatra Show</td><td colspan="2">Sing It Again</td></tr>
<tr><td>D</td><td>Captain Video</td><td colspan="2"></td><td colspan="2">Country Style</td><td colspan="4">Madison Square Garden</td></tr>
<tr><td>N</td><td>Hank McCune</td><td colspan="2">One Man's Family</td><td colspan="2">Jack Carter Show</td><td colspan="3">Your Show of Shows</td><td>Your Hit Parade</td></tr>
</table>

*Manhattan Spotlight †Mohawk Showroom

PRIME TIME SCHEDULE: FALL 1951

<table>
<tr><th></th><th></th><th colspan="2">7:00 PM</th><th colspan="2">7:30</th><th colspan="2">8:00</th><th colspan="2">8:30</th><th colspan="2">9:00</th><th colspan="2">9:30</th><th colspan="2">10:00</th><th colspan="2">10:30</th><th>11:00</th></tr>
<tr><td rowspan="4">SUNDAY</td><td>A</td><td colspan="2">Paul Whiteman's Goodyear Revue</td><td colspan="2">Music in Velvet</td><td colspan="4">Admission Free</td><td colspan="2">Film Filler</td><td colspan="2">Marshall Plan in Action</td><td colspan="2">Hour of Decision</td><td colspan="2">Youth on the March</td></tr>
<tr><td>C</td><td colspan="2">Gene Autry Show</td><td colspan="2">This is Show Business</td><td colspan="4">Toast of the Town</td><td colspan="4">Fred Waring Show</td><td colspan="2">Goodrich Celebrity Time</td><td colspan="2">What's My Line</td></tr>
<tr><td>D</td><td colspan="8"></td><td colspan="2">Rocky King, Detective</td><td colspan="2">The Plainclothesman</td><td colspan="4">They Stand Accused</td></tr>
<tr><td>N</td><td colspan="2">Chesterfield Sound Off Time</td><td colspan="2">Young Mr. Bobbin</td><td colspan="4">Colgate Comedy Hour</td><td colspan="4">Philco TV Playhouse / Goodyear TV Playhouse</td><td colspan="2">Red Skelton Show</td><td colspan="2">Leave It to the Girls</td></tr>
<tr><td rowspan="4">MONDAY</td><td>A</td><td>News</td><td></td><td colspan="2">Hollywood Screen Test</td><td colspan="2">*</td><td colspan="2">Life Begins at Eighty</td><td colspan="4">Curtain Up</td><td colspan="2">Bill Gwinn Show</td><td colspan="2">Stud's Place</td></tr>
<tr><td>C</td><td colspan="2"></td><td>News</td><td>Perry Como</td><td colspan="2">Lux Video Theatre</td><td colspan="2">Arthur Godfrey's Talent Scouts</td><td colspan="2">I Love Lucy</td><td colspan="2">It's News to Me</td><td colspan="4">Studio One</td></tr>
<tr><td>D</td><td colspan="2">Captain Video</td><td colspan="2"></td><td colspan="2">Stage Entrance</td><td colspan="2">Johns Hopkins Science Review</td><td colspan="8">Wrestling from Columbia Park</td></tr>
<tr><td>N</td><td colspan="2">Kukla, Fran & Ollie</td><td>†</td><td>News</td><td colspan="2">Speidel Show</td><td colspan="2">Voice of Firestone</td><td colspan="2">Lights Out</td><td colspan="4">Robert Montgomery Presents/ Somerset Maugham TV Theatre</td><td colspan="2"></td></tr>
<tr><td rowspan="4">TUESDAY</td><td>A</td><td colspan="2"></td><td colspan="2">Beulah</td><td colspan="2">Charlie Wild, Private Detective</td><td colspan="2">How Did They Get That Way</td><td colspan="2">United or Not</td><td colspan="2">On Trial</td><td colspan="2">Film Filler</td><td colspan="2">Chicago Symphony Chamber Orchestra</td></tr>
<tr><td>C</td><td colspan="2"></td><td>News</td><td>Stork Club</td><td colspan="4">Frank Sinatra Show</td><td colspan="2">Crime Syndicated</td><td colspan="2">Suspense</td><td colspan="2">Danger</td><td colspan="2"></td></tr>
<tr><td>D</td><td colspan="2">Captain Video</td><td colspan="2"></td><td colspan="2">What's the Story?</td><td colspan="2">Keep Posted</td><td colspan="4">Cosmopolitan Theatre</td><td colspan="2">Hands of Destiny</td><td colspan="2"></td></tr>
<tr><td>N</td><td colspan="2">Kukla, Fran & Ollie</td><td>Little Show</td><td>News</td><td colspan="4">Texaco Star Theater</td><td colspan="2">Fireside Theatre</td><td colspan="2">Armstrong Circle Theatre</td><td colspan="4">Original Amateur Hour</td></tr>
<tr><td rowspan="4">WEDNESDAY</td><td>A</td><td>News</td><td></td><td colspan="2">Chance of a Lifetime</td><td colspan="4">Paul Dixon Show</td><td colspan="2">Don McNeil's TV Club/Arthur Murray Party</td><td colspan="2">The Clock</td><td colspan="4">Celanese Theatre / King's Crossroads</td></tr>
<tr><td>C</td><td colspan="2"></td><td>News</td><td>Perry Como</td><td colspan="4">Arthur Godfrey & His Friends</td><td colspan="2">Strike It Rich</td><td colspan="2">The Web</td><td colspan="3">Pabst Blue Ribbon Bouts</td><td>Sports Spot</td></tr>
<tr><td>D</td><td colspan="2">Captain Video</td><td colspan="6"></td><td colspan="2">Gallery of Mme. Liu-Tsong</td><td colspan="2">Shadow of the Cloak</td><td colspan="4"></td></tr>
<tr><td>N</td><td colspan="2">Kukla, Fran & Ollie</td><td>†</td><td>News</td><td colspan="4">Kate Smith Evening Hour</td><td colspan="4">Kraft Television Theatre</td><td colspan="2">Break the Bank</td><td colspan="2">Freddy Martin Show</td></tr>
<tr><td rowspan="4">THURSDAY</td><td>A</td><td>News</td><td></td><td colspan="2">Lone Ranger</td><td colspan="4">Stop the Music</td><td colspan="2">Herb Shriner Show</td><td colspan="2">Gruen Guild Theater</td><td colspan="2">Paul Dixon Show</td><td>Masland at Home Show</td><td>Carmel Myers Show</td></tr>
<tr><td>C</td><td colspan="2"></td><td>News</td><td>Stork Club</td><td colspan="2">George Burns & Gracie Allen Show / Garry Moore Show</td><td colspan="2">Amos 'n' Andy</td><td colspan="2">Alan Young Show</td><td colspan="2">Big Town</td><td colspan="2">Racket Squad</td><td colspan="2">Crime Photographer</td></tr>
<tr><td>D</td><td colspan="2">Captain Video</td><td colspan="2"></td><td colspan="2">Georgetown University Forum</td><td colspan="2">Broadway to Hollywood</td><td colspan="2">Adventures of Ellery Queen</td><td colspan="2"></td><td colspan="2">Bigelow Theatre</td><td></td><td>Football This Week</td></tr>
<tr><td>N</td><td colspan="2">Kukla, Fran & Ollie</td><td>Little Show</td><td>News</td><td colspan="2">You Bet Your Life</td><td colspan="2">Treasury Men in Action</td><td colspan="4">Ford Festival</td><td colspan="2">Martin Kane, Private Eye</td><td colspan="2">Wayne King</td></tr>
<tr><td rowspan="4">FRIDAY</td><td>A</td><td>News</td><td></td><td colspan="2">Say it with Acting/Life with Linkletter</td><td colspan="2">Mystery Theatre</td><td colspan="2">Stu Erwin Show</td><td colspan="2">Crime with Father</td><td colspan="2">Tales of Tomorrow/ Versatile Varieties</td><td colspan="2">Dell O'Dell Show</td><td colspan="2">America in View</td></tr>
<tr><td>C</td><td colspan="2"></td><td>News</td><td>Perry Como</td><td colspan="2">Mama</td><td colspan="2">Man Against Crime</td><td colspan="4">Schlitz Playhouse of Stars</td><td colspan="2">Live Like a Millionaire</td><td colspan="2">Hollywood Opening Night</td></tr>
<tr><td>D</td><td colspan="2">Captain Video</td><td colspan="2"></td><td colspan="2">Twenty Questions</td><td colspan="2">You Asked for It</td><td colspan="2">Down You Go</td><td colspan="2">Front Page Detective</td><td colspan="4">Cavalcade of Stars</td></tr>
<tr><td>N</td><td colspan="2">Kukla, Fran & Ollie</td><td>†</td><td>News</td><td colspan="2">Quiz Kids</td><td colspan="2">We, the People</td><td colspan="2">Big Story</td><td colspan="2">Aldrich Family</td><td colspan="3">Gillette Cavalcade of Sports</td><td>Greatest Fights</td></tr>
<tr><td rowspan="4">SATURDAY</td><td>A</td><td colspan="2">Hollywood Theatre Time</td><td colspan="2">Jerry Colonna Show</td><td colspan="4">Paul Whiteman's TV Teen Club</td><td colspan="2">Lesson in Safety</td><td colspan="2">America's Health</td><td colspan="4"></td></tr>
<tr><td>C</td><td colspan="2">Sammy Kaye Variety Show</td><td colspan="2">Beat the Clock</td><td colspan="4">Ken Murray Show</td><td colspan="2">Faye Emerson's Wonderful Town</td><td colspan="2">Show Goes On</td><td colspan="4">Songs for Sale</td></tr>
<tr><td>D</td><td colspan="10"></td><td colspan="6">Pro Wrestling from Chicago</td></tr>
<tr><td>N</td><td colspan="2">American Youth Forum</td><td colspan="2">One Man's Family</td><td colspan="4">All Star Revue</td><td colspan="6">Your Show of Shows</td><td colspan="2">Your Hit Parade</td></tr>
</table>

*Mr. District Attorney/Amazing Mr. Malone

†Mohawk Showroom

PRIME TIME SCHEDULE: FALL 1952

Day	Network	7:00 PM	7:30	8:00	8:30	9:00	9:30	10:00	10:30
SUNDAY	A	You Asked for It	Hot Seat	All-Star News		Playhouse #7	This is the Life	Hour of Decision / Film Filler	Anywhere, U.S.A.
	C	Gene Autry Show	This is Show Business	Toast of the Town		Fred Waring Show	Break the Bank	The Web	What's My Line
	D	Georgetown University Forum				Rocky King, Detective	The Plainclothesman	Arthur Murray Show	Youth on the March
	N	Red Skelton Show	Doc Corkle	Colgate Comedy Hour		Philco TV Playhouse / Goodyear TV Playhouse		The Doctor	
MONDAY	A		Hollywood Screen Test	Inspector Mark Saber	United or Not	All-Star News			
	C		News / Perry Como	Lux Video Theatre	Arthur Godfrey's Talent Scouts	I Love Lucy	Life with Luigi	Studio One	
	D	Captain Video		Pentagon	Johns Hopkins Science Review	Guide Right	Football Sidelines / Famous Fights	Boxing from Eastern Parkway	
	N		Those Two / News	What's My Name	Voice of Firestone	Hollywood Opening Night	Robert Montgomery Presents		Who Said That?
TUESDAY	A		Beulah						
	C		News / Heaven for Betsy	Leave it to Larry	Red Buttons Show	Crime Syndicated/ City Hospital	Suspense	Danger	
	D	Captain Video		Power of Women	Keep Posted	Where Was I?	Quick on the Draw		
	N	Short Short Dramas	Dinah Shore / News	Texaco Star Theater		Fireside Theatre	Armstrong Circle Theatre	Two for the Money	Club Embassy / On the Line with Considine
WEDNESDAY	A		Name's the Same	All-Star News		Adventures of Ellery Queen	Chicago Wrestling		
	C		News / Perry Como	Arthur Godfrey & His Friends		Strike It Rich	Man Against Crime	Pabst Blue Ribbon Bouts	Sports Spot
	D	Captain Video	New York Giants Quarterback Huddle		Trash or Treasure	Stage a Number			
	N		Those Two / News	I Married Joan	Scott Music Hall/Cavalcade of America	Kraft Television Theatre		This Is Your Life	
THURSDAY	A		Lone Ranger	All-Star News	Chance of a Lifetime	Politics on Trial	On Guard		
	C		News / Heaven for Betsy	George Burns and Gracie Allen Show	Amos 'n' Andy/ Four Star Playhouse	Pick the Winner	Big Town	Racket Squad	I've Got a Secret
	D	Captain Video			Broadway to Hollywood	Pick the Winner	What's the Story?	Author Meets the Critics	
	N	Short Short Dramas	Dinah Shore / News	You Bet Your Life	Treasury Men in Action	Dragnet/ Gangbusters	Ford Theatre	Martin Kane, Private Eye	
FRIDAY	A		Stu Erwin Show	Adventures of Ozzie & Harriet	All-Star News		Tales of Tomorrow		
	C		News / Perry Como	Mama	My Friend Irma	Schlitz Playhouse of Stars	Our Miss Brooks	Mr. & Mrs. North	
	D	Captain Video		Steve Randall	Dark of Night	Life Begins at Eighty		Twenty Questions	Down You Go
	N	Herman Hickman Show	Those Two / News	RCA Victor Show	Gulf Playhouse	Big Story	Aldrich Family	Gillette Cavalcade of Sports	Greatest Fights
SATURDAY	A	Paul Whiteman's TV Teen Club	Live Like a Millionaire	Feature Playhouse					
	C	Stork Club	Beat the Clock	Jackie Gleason Show		Jane Froman's U.S.A. Canteen	Meet Millie	Balance Your Budget/Quiz Kids	Battle of the Ages
	D		Pet Shop				Pro Wrestling from Chicago		
	N	Mr. Wizard	My Little Margie	All Star Revue		Your Show of Shows			Your Hit Parade

PRIME TIME SCHEDULE: FALL 1953

Day	Net	7:00 PM	7:30	8:00	8:30	9:00	9:30	10:00	10:30
SUNDAY	A	You Asked for It	Frank Leahy Show; Notre Dame Football			Walter Winchell Show; Orchid Award	Peter Potter Show		Hour of Decision
SUNDAY	C	Quiz Kids	Jack Benny Show / Private Secretary	Toast of the Town		G.E. Theater / Fred Waring Show	Man Behind the Badge	The Web	What's My Line
SUNDAY	D	Georgetown University Forum	Washington Exclusive			Rocky King, Detective	The Plainclothesman	Dollar a Second	Man Against Crime
SUNDAY	N	Paul Winchell Show	Mr. Peepers	Colgate Comedy Hour		Philco TV Playhouse / Goodyear TV Playhouse		Letter to Loretta	Man Against Crime
MONDAY	A	Walter Winchell; News	Jamie	Sky King	Of Many Things	Junior Press Conference	Big Picture	This is the Life	
MONDAY	C		News; Perry Como	George Burns and Gracie Allen Show	Arthur Godfrey's Talent Scouts	I Love Lucy	Red Buttons Show	Studio One	
MONDAY	D	Captain Video		Twenty Questions	Big Issue	Boxing from Eastern Parkway			
MONDAY	N		Arthur Murray Party; News	Name That Tune	Voice of Firestone	RCA Victor Show Starring Dennis Day	Robert Montgomery Presents		Who Said That?
TUESDAY	A	News	Cavalcade of America			Make Room for Daddy	U.S. Steel Hour / Motorola TV Theatre		Name's the Same
TUESDAY	C		News; Jane Froman	Gene Autry Show	Red Skelton Show	This is Show Business	Suspense	Danger	See It Now
TUESDAY	D	Captain Video		Life is Worth Living	Pantomime Quiz				
TUESDAY	N		Dinah Shore; News	Buick Berle Show		Fireside Theatre	Armstrong Circle Theatre	Judge for Yourself	On the Line with Considine; *
WEDNESDAY	A	News	Inspector Mark Saber	At Issue; Through the Curtain	America in View	Wrestling from Rainbo			
WEDNESDAY	C		News; Perry Como	Arthur Godfrey & His Friends		Strike It Rich	I've Got a Secret	Pabst Blue Ribbon Bouts	Sports Spot
WEDNESDAY	D	Captain Video		Johns Hopkins Science Review	Joseph Schildkraut Presents	Colonel Humphrey Flack	On Your Way	Stars on Parade	Music Show
WEDNESDAY	N		Coke Time; News	I Married Joan	My Little Margie	Kraft Television Theatre		This Is Your Life	
THURSDAY	A	News	Lone Ranger	Quick as a Flash	Where's Raymond	Back That Fact	Kraft Television Theatre		
THURSDAY	C		News; Jane Froman	Meet Mr. McNutley	Four Star Playhouse	Lux Video Theatre	Big Town	Philip Morris Playhouse	Place the Face
THURSDAY	D	Captain Video		New York Giants Quarterback Huddle	Broadway to Hollywood	What's the Story?			
THURSDAY	N		Dinah Shore; News	You Bet Your Life	Treasury Men in Action	Dragnet	Ford Theatre	Martin Kane, Private Eye	
FRIDAY	A	News	Stu Erwin Show	Adventures of Ozzie & Harriet	Pepsi-Cola Playhouse	Pride of the Family	Comeback Story	Showcase Theater	
FRIDAY	C		News; Perry Como	Mama	Topper	Schlitz Playhouse of Stars	Our Miss Brooks	My Friend Irma	Person to Person
FRIDAY	D	Captain Video		Front Page Detective	Melody Street	Life Begins at Eighty	Nine Thirty Curtain	Chance of a Lifetime	Down You Go
FRIDAY	N		Coke Time; News	Dave Garroway Show	Life of Riley	Big Story	Campbell Soundstage	Gillette Cavalcade of Sports	Greatest Fights
SATURDAY	A	Paul Whiteman's TV Teen Club	Leave it to the Girls	Talent Patrol	Music at the Meadowbrook	Saturday Night Fights	Fight Talk	Madison Square Garden Highlights	
SATURDAY	C	Meet Millie	Beat the Clock	Jackie Gleason Show		Two for the Money	My Favorite Husband	Medallion Theater	Revlon Mirror Theatre
SATURDAY	D			Pro Football					
SATURDAY	N	Mr. Wizard	Ethel & Albert	Bonino	Original Amateur Hour	Your Show of Shows			Your Hit Parade

*It Happened in Sports

PRIME TIME SCHEDULE: FALL 1954

<table>
<tr><th></th><th></th><th colspan="2">7:00 PM</th><th colspan="2">7:30</th><th colspan="2">8:00</th><th colspan="2">8:30</th><th colspan="2">9:00</th><th colspan="2">9:30</th><th colspan="2">10:00</th><th colspan="2">10:30</th></tr>
<tr><td rowspan="4">SUNDAY</td><td>A</td><td colspan="2">You Asked for It</td><td colspan="2">Pepsi-Cola Playhouse</td><td colspan="2">Flight #7</td><td colspan="2">Big Picture</td><td>Walter Winchell Show</td><td>Martha Wright Show</td><td colspan="2">Dr. I.Q.</td><td colspan="2">Break the Bank</td><td colspan="2"></td></tr>
<tr><td>C</td><td colspan="2">Lassie</td><td colspan="2">Jack Benny Show/Private Secretary</td><td colspan="4">Toast of the Town</td><td colspan="2">G.E. Theater</td><td colspan="2">Honestly Celeste</td><td colspan="2">Father Knows Best</td><td colspan="2">What's My Line</td></tr>
<tr><td>D</td><td colspan="2">Author Meets the Critic</td><td colspan="2">Opera Cameos</td><td colspan="4"></td><td colspan="2">Rocky King Detective</td><td colspan="2">Life Begins at Eighty</td><td colspan="2">Music Show</td><td colspan="2"></td></tr>
<tr><td>N</td><td colspan="2">People Are Funny</td><td colspan="2">Mr. Peepers</td><td colspan="4">Colgate Comedy Hour</td><td colspan="4">Philco TV Playhouse/ Goodyear TV Playhouse</td><td colspan="2">Loretta Young Show</td><td colspan="2">The Hunter</td></tr>
<tr><td rowspan="4">MONDAY</td><td>A</td><td>Kukla, Fran & Ollie</td><td>News</td><td colspan="2">Name's the Same</td><td colspan="2">Come Closer</td><td colspan="2">Voice of Firestone</td><td colspan="2">Junior Press Conference</td><td colspan="6">Boxing from Eastern Parkway</td></tr>
<tr><td>C</td><td colspan="2"></td><td>News</td><td>Perry Como</td><td colspan="2">George Burns and Gracie Allen Show</td><td colspan="2">Arthur Godfrey's Talent Scouts</td><td colspan="2">I Love Lucy</td><td colspan="2">December Bride</td><td colspan="4">Studio One</td></tr>
<tr><td>D</td><td>Captain Video</td><td>News</td><td colspan="2"></td><td colspan="2">Ilona Massey Show</td><td colspan="2"></td><td colspan="8">Boxing from St. Nicholas Areana</td></tr>
<tr><td>N</td><td colspan="2"></td><td>Tony Martin</td><td>News</td><td colspan="4">Caesar's Hour</td><td colspan="2">Medic</td><td colspan="4">Robert Montgomery Presents</td><td colspan="2"></td></tr>
<tr><td rowspan="4">TUESDAY</td><td>A</td><td>Kukla, Fran & Ollie</td><td>News</td><td colspan="2">Cavalcade of America</td><td colspan="2"></td><td colspan="2">Twenty Questions</td><td colspan="2">Make Room for Daddy</td><td colspan="4">U.S. Steel Hour / Elgin TV Hour</td><td colspan="2">Stop the Music</td></tr>
<tr><td>C</td><td colspan="2"></td><td>News</td><td>Jo Stafford</td><td colspan="2">Red Skelton Show</td><td colspan="2">Halls of Ivy</td><td colspan="2">Meet Millie</td><td colspan="2">Danger</td><td colspan="2">Life with Father</td><td colspan="2">See it Now</td></tr>
<tr><td>D</td><td>Captain Video</td><td>News</td><td colspan="2"></td><td colspan="2">Life is Worth Living</td><td colspan="2">Studio 57</td><td colspan="2">One Minute Please</td><td colspan="6"></td></tr>
<tr><td>N</td><td colspan="2"></td><td>Dinah Shore</td><td>News</td><td colspan="4">Buick Berle Show</td><td colspan="2">Fireside Theatre</td><td colspan="2">Armstrong Circle Theatre</td><td colspan="2">Truth or Consequences</td><td colspan="2">It's a Great Life</td></tr>
<tr><td rowspan="4">WEDNESDAY</td><td>A</td><td>Kukla, Fran & Ollie</td><td>News</td><td colspan="4">Disneyland</td><td colspan="2">Stu Erwin Show</td><td colspan="2">Masquerade Party</td><td colspan="2">Enterprise</td><td colspan="4"></td></tr>
<tr><td>C</td><td colspan="2"></td><td>News</td><td>Perry Como</td><td colspan="4">Arthur Godfrey & His Friends</td><td colspan="2">Strike It Rich</td><td colspan="2">I've Got a Secret</td><td colspan="3">Pabst Blue Ribbon Bouts</td><td>Sports Spot</td></tr>
<tr><td>D</td><td>Captain Video</td><td>News</td><td colspan="6"></td><td colspan="4">Chicago Symphony</td><td colspan="2">Down You Go</td><td colspan="2"></td></tr>
<tr><td>N</td><td colspan="2"></td><td>Coke Time</td><td>News</td><td colspan="2">I Married Joan</td><td colspan="2">My Little Margie</td><td colspan="4">Kraft Television Theatre</td><td colspan="2">This Is Your Life</td><td colspan="2">Big Town</td></tr>
<tr><td rowspan="4">THURSDAY</td><td>A</td><td>Kukla, Fran & Ollie</td><td>News</td><td colspan="2">Lone Ranger</td><td colspan="2">Mail Story</td><td colspan="2">Treasury Men In Action</td><td colspan="2">So You Want to Lead a Band</td><td colspan="4">Kraft Television Theatre</td><td colspan="2"></td></tr>
<tr><td>C</td><td colspan="2"></td><td>News</td><td>Jane Froman</td><td colspan="2">Ray Milland Show</td><td colspan="4">Climax</td><td colspan="2">Four Star Playhouse</td><td colspan="2">Public Defender</td><td colspan="2">Name That Tune</td></tr>
<tr><td>D</td><td>Captain Video</td><td>News</td><td colspan="2"></td><td colspan="4">They Stand Accused</td><td colspan="2">What's the Story</td><td colspan="6"></td></tr>
<tr><td>N</td><td colspan="2"></td><td>Dinah Shore</td><td>News</td><td colspan="2">You Bet Your Life</td><td colspan="2">Justice</td><td colspan="2">Dragnet</td><td colspan="2">Ford Theatre</td><td colspan="4">Lux Video Theatre</td></tr>
<tr><td rowspan="4">FRIDAY</td><td>A</td><td>Kukla, Fran & Ollie</td><td>News</td><td colspan="2">Adventures of Rin Tin Tin</td><td colspan="2">Adventures of Ozzie & Harriet</td><td colspan="2">Ray Bolger Show</td><td colspan="2">Dollar a Second</td><td colspan="2">The Vise</td><td colspan="4"></td></tr>
<tr><td>C</td><td colspan="2"></td><td>News</td><td>Perry Como</td><td colspan="2">Mama</td><td colspan="2">Topper</td><td colspan="2">Schlitz Playhouse of Stars</td><td colspan="2">Our Miss Brooks</td><td colspan="2">The Lineup</td><td colspan="2">Person to Person</td></tr>
<tr><td>D</td><td>Captain Video</td><td>News</td><td colspan="6"></td><td colspan="2">The Stranger</td><td colspan="2"></td><td colspan="2">Chance of a Lifetime</td><td colspan="2">Time Will Tell</td></tr>
<tr><td>N</td><td colspan="2"></td><td>Coke Time</td><td>News</td><td colspan="2">Red Buttons Show</td><td colspan="2">Life of Riley</td><td colspan="2">Big Story</td><td colspan="2">Dear Phoebe</td><td colspan="3">Gillette Cavalcade of Sports</td><td>Great Moments In Sports</td></tr>
<tr><td rowspan="4">SATURDAY</td><td>A</td><td colspan="2"></td><td colspan="2">Compass</td><td colspan="4">Dotty Mack Show</td><td colspan="3">Saturday Night Fights</td><td>Fight Talk</td><td colspan="2">Stork Club</td><td colspan="2"></td></tr>
<tr><td>C</td><td colspan="2">Gene Autry Show</td><td colspan="2">Beat the Clock</td><td colspan="4">Jackie Gleason Show</td><td colspan="2">Two for the Money</td><td colspan="2">My Favorite Husband</td><td colspan="2">That's My Boy</td><td colspan="2">Willy</td></tr>
<tr><td>D</td><td colspan="4"></td><td colspan="12">Pro Football</td></tr>
<tr><td>N</td><td colspan="2">Mr. Wizard</td><td colspan="2">Ethel & Albert</td><td colspan="2">Mickey Rooney Show</td><td colspan="2">Place the Face</td><td colspan="2">Imogene Coca Show</td><td colspan="2">Texaco Star Theater</td><td colspan="2">George Gobel Show</td><td colspan="2">Your Hit Parade</td></tr>
</table>

PRIME TIME SCHEDULE: FALL 1955

		7:00 PM		7:30		8:00	8:30	9:00	9:30	10:00	10:30	11:00
SUNDAY	A	You Asked for It		Famous Film Festival				Chance of a Lifetime	Original Amateur Hour	Life Begins at Eighty		
	C	Lassie		Jack Benny Show/ Private Secretary		Ed Sullivan Show		G.E. Theater	Alfred Hitchcock Presents	Appointment with Adventure	What's My Line	
	N	It's a Great Life		Frontier		Colgate Variety Hour		Goodyear TV Playhouse / Alcoa Hour		Loretta Young Show	Justice	
MONDAY	A	Kukla, Fran & Ollie	News	Topper		TV Reader's Digest	Voice of Firestone	Dotty Mack Show	Medical Horizons	Big Picture		
	C		News	Adventures of Robin Hood		George Burns and Gracie Allen Show	Arthur Godfrey's Talent Scouts	I Love Lucy	December Bride	Studio One		
	N			Tony Martin Show	News	Caesar's Hour		Medic	Robert Montgomery Presents			
TUESDAY	A	Kukla, Fran & Ollie	News	Warner Brothers Presents			Life and Legend of Wyatt Earp	Make Room for Daddy	DuPont Cavalcade Theater	Talent Varieties		
	C		News	Name That Tune		Navy Log	You'll Never Get Rich	Meet Millie	Red Skelton Show	$64,000 Question	My Favorite Husband	
	N			Dinah Shore Show	News	Martha Raye Show / Milton Berle Show / Chevy Show		Fireside Theatre	Armstrong Circle Theatre / Pontiac Presents Playwrights '56		Big Town	
WEDNESDAY	A	Kukla, Fran & Ollie	News	Disneyland			MGM Parade	Masquerade Party	Break the Bank	Wednesday Night Fights		
	C		News	Brave Eagle		Arthur Godfrey & His Friends		The Millionaire	I've Got a Secret	20th Century-Fox Hour / U.S. Steel Hour		
	N			Coke Time	News	Screen Director's Playhouse	Father Knows Best	Kraft Television Theatre		This Is Your Life	Midwestern Hayride	
THURSDAY	A	Kukla, Fran & Ollie	News	Lone Ranger		Life Is Worth Living	Stop the Music	Star Tonight	Down You Go	Outside U.S.A.		
	C		News	Sgt. Preston of the Yukon		Bob Cummings Show	Climax		Four Star Playhouse	Johnny Carson Show	Wanted	
	N			Dinah Shore Show	News	You Bet Your Life	People's Choice	Dragnet	Ford Theatre	Lux Video Theatre		
FRIDAY	A	Kukla, Fran & Ollie	News	Adventures of Rin Tin Tin		Adventures of Ozzie & Harriet	Crossroads	Dollar a Second	The Vise	Ethel & Albert		
	C		News	Adventures of Champion		Mama	Our Miss Brooks	The Crusader	Schlitz Playhouse of Stars	The Lineup	Person to Person	
	N			Coke Time	News	Truth or Consequences	Life of Riley	Big Story	Star Stage	Gillette Cavalcade of Sports	Red Barber's Corner	
SATURDAY	A			Ozark Jubilee				Lawrence Welk Show		Tomorrow's Careers		
	C	Gene Autry Show		Beat the Clock		Stage Show	The Honeymooners	Two for the Money	It's Always Jan	Gunsmoke	Damon Runyon Theatre	
	N			Big Surprise		Perry Como Show		People Are Funny	Texaco Star Theater Starring Jimmy Durante	George Gobel Show	Your Hit Parade	

PRIME TIME SCHEDULE: FALL 1956

		7:00 PM	7:30	8:00	8:30	9:00	9:30	10:00	10:30
SUNDAY	A	You Asked for It	Original Amateur Hour		Press Conference	Omnibus			
	C	Lassie	Jack Benny Show / Private Secretary	Ed Sullivan Show		G.E. Theater	Alfred Hitchcock Presents	$64,000 Challenge	What's My Line
	N	Tales of the 77th Bengal Lancers	Circus Boy	Steven Allen Show		Goodyear TV Playhouse / Alcoa Hour		Loretta Young Show	National Bowling Champions
MONDAY	A	Kukla, Fran & Ollie / News	Bold Journey	Danny Thomas Show	Voice of Firestone	Life Is Worth Living	Lawrence Welk Talent Show		
	C	News	Adventures of Robin Hood	George Burns and Gracie Allen Show	Arthur Godfrey's Talent Scouts	I Love Lucy	December Bride	Studio One	
	N		Nat "King" Cole Show / News	Adventures of Sir Lancelot	Stanley	Medic	Robert Montgomery Presents		
TUESDAY	A	Kukla, Fran & Ollie / News	Conflict / Cheyenne		Life and Legend of Wyatt Earp	Broken Arrow	DuPont Theater	It's Polka Time	
	C	News	Name That Tune	Phil Silvers Show	The Brothers	Herb Shriner Show	Red Skelton Show	$64,000 Question	Do You Trust Your Wife?
	N		Jonathan Winters Show / News	Big Surprise	Noah's Ark	Jane Wyman Show	Armstrong Circle Theatre/ Kaiser Aluminum Hour		Break the $250,000 Bank
WEDNESDAY	A	Kukla, Fran & Ollie / News	Disneyland		Navy Log	Adventures of Ozzie & Harriet	Ford Theatre	Wednesday Night Fights	
	C	News	Giant Step	Arthur Godfrey Show		The Millionaire	I've Got a Secret	20th Century-Fox Hour / U.S. Steel Hour	
	N		Eddie Fisher Show / News	Adventures of Hiram Holliday	Father Knows Best	Kraft Television Theatre		This Is Your Life	Twenty-One
THURSDAY	A	Kukla, Fran & Ollie / News	Lone Ranger	Circus Time		Wire Service		Ozark Jubilee	
	C	News	Sgt. Preston of the Yukon	Bob Cummings Show	Climax		Playhouse 90		
	N		Dinah Shore Show / News	You Bet Your Life	Dragnet	People's Choice	Ford Show Starring Tennessee Ernie Ford	Lux Video Theatre	
FRIDAY	A	Kukla, Fran & Ollie / News	Adventures of Rin Tin Tin	Adventures of Jim Bowie	Crossroads	Treasure Hunt	The Vise	Ray Anthony Show	
	C	News	My Friend Flicka	West Point Story	Dick Powell's Zane Grey Theater	The Crusader	Schlitz Playhouse	The Lineup	Person to Person
	N		Eddie Fisher Show / News	Life of Riley	Walter Winchell Show	On Trial	Big Story	Gillette Cavalcade of Sports	Red Barber's Corner
SATURDAY	A		Famous Film Festival			Lawrence Welk Show		Masquerade Party	
	C	Beat the Clock	The Buccaneers	Jackie Gleason Show		Gale Storm Show	Hey Jeannie	Gunsmoke	High Finance
	N		People Are Funny	Perry Como Show		Caesar's Hour		George Gobel Show	Your Hit Parade

PRIME TIME SCHEDULE: FALL 1957

		7:00 PM	7:30	8:00	8:30	9:00	9:30	10:00	10:30
SUNDAY	A	You Asked for It	Maverick		Bowling Stars	Open Hearing	All-American Football Game of the Week		
	C	Lassie	Jack Benny Show / Bachelor Father	Ed Sullivan Show		G.E. Theater	Alfred Hitchcock Presents	$64,000 Challenge	What's My Line
	N	Original Amateur Hour	Sally	Steve Allen Show		Dinah Shore Chevy Show		Loretta Young Show	
MONDAY	A	News	American Bandstand	Guy Mitchell Show	Bold Journey	Voice of Firestone	Lawrence Welk's Top Tunes and New Talent Show		
	C	News	Adventures of Robin Hood	George Burns and Gracie Allen Show	Arthur Godfrey's Talent Scouts	Danny Thomas Show	December Bride	Studio One in Hollywood	
	N		Price Is Right	Restless Gun	Tales of Wells Fargo	Twenty-One	Turn of Fate	Suspicion	
TUESDAY	A	News	Cheyenne / Sugarfoot		Life and Legend of Wyatt Earp	Broken Arrow	Telephone Time	West Point Story	
	C	News	Name That Tune	Phil Silvers Show	Eve Arden Show	To Tell the Truth	Red Skelton Show	$64,000 Question	Assignment Foreign Legion
	N		Nat "King" Cole Show	Eddie Fisher Show / George Gobel Show		Meet McGraw	Bob Cummings Show	The Californians	
WEDNESDAY	A	News	Disneyland		Tombstone Territory	Adventures of Ozzie & Harriet	Walter Winchell File	Wednesday Night Fights	Famous Fights
	C	News	I Love Lucy	Big Record		The Millionaire	I've Got a Secret	Armstrong Circle Theatre/ U.S. Steel Hour	
	N		Wagon Train		Father Knows Best	Kraft Television Theatre		This Is Your Life	
THURSDAY	A	News	Circus Boy	Zorro	Real McCoys	Pat Boone—Chevy Showroom	O.S.S.	Navy Log	
	C	News	Sgt. Preston of the Yukon	Harbourmaster	Climax		Playhouse 90		
	N		Tic Tac Dough	You Bet Your Life	Dragnet	People's Choice	Ford Show Starring Tennessee Ernie Ford	Lux Show Starring Rosemary Clooney	Jane Wyman Show
FRIDAY	A	News	Adventures of Rin Tin Tin	Adventures of Jim Bowie	Patrice Munsel Show	Frank Sinatra Show	Date with the Angels	Colt .45	
	C	News	Leave It to Beaver	Trackdown	Dick Powell's Zane Grey Theatre	Mr. Adams & Eve	Schlitz Playhouse	The Lineup	Person to Person
	N		Saber of London	Court of Last Resort	Life of Riley	M Squad	Thin Man	Gillette Cavalcade of Sports	Red Barber's Corner
SATURDAY	A		Keep It in the Family	Country Music Jubilee		Lawrence Welk's Dancing Party		Mike Wallace Interviews	
	C		Perry Mason		Dick & the Duchess	Gale Storm Show	Have Gun, Will Travel	Gunsmoke	
	N		People Are Funny	Perry Como Show		Polly Bergen Show / Club Oasis	Gisele MacKenzie Show	What's It For	Your Hit Parade

PRIME TIME SCHEDULE: FALL 1958

Day	Network	7:00 PM	7:30	8:00	8:30	9:00	9:30	10:00	10:30	11:00
SUNDAY	A	You Asked for It	Maverick		The Lawman	Colt .45	Encounter			
SUNDAY	C	Lassie	Jack Benny Show / Bachelor Father	Ed Sullivan Show		G.E. Theater	Alfred Hitchcock Presents	$64,000 Question	What's My Line	
SUNDAY	N	Saber of London	Northwest Passage	Steve Allen Show		Dinah Shore Chevy Show		Loretta Young Show		
MONDAY	A	News	Jubilee U.S.A.		Bold Journey	Voice of Firestone	Anybody Can Play	This Is Music		
MONDAY	C	News	Name That Tune	The Texan	Father Knows Best	Danny Thomas Show	Ann Sothern Show	Desilu Playhouse		
MONDAY	N		Tic Tac Dough	Restless Gun	Tales of Wells Fargo	Peter Gunn	Alcoa / Goodyear TV Playhouse	Arthur Murray Party		
TUESDAY	A	News	Cheyenne / Sugarfoot		Life and Legend of Wyatt Earp	The Rifleman	Naked City	Confession		
TUESDAY	C	News	Stars in Action	Keep Talking	To Tell the Truth	Arthur Godfrey Show	Red Skelton Show	Garry Moore Show		
TUESDAY	N		Dragnet	George Gobel Show / Eddie Fisher Show		George Burns Show	Bob Cummings Show	The Californians		
WEDNESDAY	A	News	Lawrence Welk's Plymouth Show		Adventures of Ozzie & Harriet	Donna Reed Show	Patti Page Olds Show	Wednesday Night Fights		
WEDNESDAY	C	News	Twilight Theater	Pursuit		The Millionaire	I've Got a Secret	Armstrong Circle Theatre / U.S. Steel Hour		
WEDNESDAY	N		Wagon Train		Price Is Right	Milton Berle in the Kraft Music Hall	Bat Masterson	This Is Your Life		
THURSDAY	A	News	Leave It to Beaver	Zorro	Real McCoys	Pat Boone—Chevy Showroom	Rough Riders	Traffic Court		
THURSDAY	C	News	I Love Lucy	December Bride	Yancy Derringer	Dick Powell's Zane Grey Theatre	Playhouse 90			
THURSDAY	N		Jefferson Drum	Ed Wynn Show	Twenty-One	Behind Closed Doors	Ford Show Starring Tennessee Ernie Ford	You Bet Your Life	Masquerade Party	
FRIDAY	A	News	Adventures of Rin Tin Tin	Walt Disney Presents		Man with a Camera	77 Sunset Strip			
FRIDAY	C	News	Your Hit Parade	Trackdown	Jackie Gleason Show	Phil Silvers Show	Lux Playhouse/ Schlitz Playhouse	The Lineup	Person to Person	
FRIDAY	N		Buckskin	Adventures of Ellery Queen		M Squad	Thin Man	Gillette Cavalcade of Sports	Fight Beat	
SATURDAY	A		Dick Clark Show	Jubilee U.S.A.		Lawrence Welk's Dodge Dancing Party		Sammy Kaye's Music from Manhattan		
SATURDAY	C		Perry Mason		Wanted: Dead or Alive	Gale Storm Show	Have Gun, Will Travel	Gunsmoke		
SATURDAY	N		People Are Funny	Perry Como Show		Steve Canyon	Cimarron City		Brains & Brawn	

PRIME TIME SCHEDULE: FALL 1959

Day	Network	7:00 PM	7:30	8:00	8:30	9:00	9:30	10:00	10:30	11:00
SUNDAY	A	Colt .45	Maverick		The Lawman	The Rebel	The Alaskans		Dick Clark's World of Talent	
SUNDAY	C	Lassie	Dennis the Menace	Ed Sullivan Show		G.E. Theater	Alfred Hitchcock Presents	Jack Benny Show / George Gobel Show	What's My Line	
SUNDAY	N	Riverboat		Sunday Showcase		Dinah Shore Chevy Show		Loretta Young Show		
MONDAY	A		Cheyenne		Bourbon Street Beat		Adventures in Paradise		Man with a Camera	
MONDAY	C	News	Masquerade Party	The Texan	Father Knows Best	Danny Thomas Show	Ann Sothern Show	Hennessey	DuPont Show with June Allyson	
MONDAY	N		Richard Diamond, Private Detective	Love & Marriage	Tales of Wells Fargo	Peter Gunn	Alcoa / Goodyear TV Playhouse	Steve Allen Plymouth Show		
TUESDAY	A		Sugarfoot / Bronco		Life and Legend of Wyatt Earp	The Rifleman	Philip Marlowe	Alcoa Presents	Keep Talking	
TUESDAY	C	News		Dennis O'Keefe Show	Many Loves of Dobie Gillis	Tightrope	Red Skelton Show	Garry Moore Show		
TUESDAY	N		Laramie		Fibber McGee & Molly	Arthur Murray Party	Startime			
WEDNESDAY	A		Court of Last Resort	Hobby Lobby Show	Adventures of Ozzie & Harriet	Hawaiian Eye		Wednesday Night Fights		
WEDNESDAY	C	News	The Lineup		Men into Space	The Millionaire	I've Got a Secret	Armstrong Circle Theatre/ U.S. Steel Hour		
WEDNESDAY	N		Wagon Train		Price Is Right	Perry Como's Kraft Music Hall		This Is Your Life	Wichita Town	
THURSDAY	A		Gale Storm Show	Donna Reed Show	Real McCoys	Pat Boone—Chevy Showroom	The Untouchables		Take a Good Look	
THURSDAY	C	News	To Tell the Truth	Betty Hutton Show	Johnny Ringo	Dick Powell's Zane Grey Theatre	Playhouse 90 / Big Party			
THURSDAY	N		Law of the Plainsman	Bat Masterson	Staccato	Bachelor Father	Ford Show Starring Tennessee Ernie Ford	You Bet Your Life	The Lawless Years	
FRIDAY	A		Walt Disney Presents		Man from Blackhawk	77 Sunset Strip		Robert Taylor: The Detectives	Black Saddle	
FRIDAY	C	News	Rawhide		Hotel de Paree	Desilu Playhouse		Twilight Zone	Person to Person	
FRIDAY	N		People Are Funny	The Trouble-shooters	Bell Telephone Hour		M Squad	Gillette Cavalcade of Sports	Phillies Jackpot Bowling	
SATURDAY	A		Dick Clark Show	High Road	Leave It to Beaver	Lawrence Welk Show		Jubilee U.S.A.		
SATURDAY	C		Perry Mason		Wanted: Dead or Alive	Mr. Lucky	Have Gun, Will Travel	Gunsmoke	Markham	
SATURDAY	N		Bonanza		Man & the Challenge	The Deputy	Five Fingers		It Could Be You	

PRIME TIME SCHEDULE: FALL 1960

<table>
<tr><th></th><th></th><th>7:00 PM</th><th>7:30</th><th>8:00</th><th>8:30</th><th>9:00</th><th>9:30</th><th>10:00</th><th>10:30</th></tr>
<tr><td rowspan="3">SUNDAY</td><td>A</td><td>Walt Disney Presents</td><td colspan="2">Maverick</td><td>The Lawman</td><td>The Rebel</td><td colspan="2">The Islanders</td><td>Walter Winchell Show</td></tr>
<tr><td>C</td><td>Lassie</td><td>Dennis the Menace</td><td colspan="2">Ed Sullivan Show</td><td>G.E. Theater</td><td>Jack Benny Show</td><td>Candid Camera</td><td>What's My Line</td></tr>
<tr><td>N</td><td colspan="2">Shirley Temple's Storybook</td><td>National Velvet</td><td>Tab Hunter Show</td><td colspan="2">Dinah Shore Chevy Show</td><td>Loretta Young Show</td><td>This Is Your Life</td></tr>
<tr><td rowspan="3">MONDAY</td><td>A</td><td></td><td colspan="2">Cheyenne</td><td colspan="2">Surfside Six</td><td colspan="2">Adventures in Paradise</td><td>Peter Gunn</td></tr>
<tr><td>C</td><td>News</td><td>To Tell the Truth</td><td>Pete & Gladys</td><td>Bringing Up Buddy</td><td>Danny Thomas Show</td><td>Andy Griffith Show</td><td>Hennessey</td><td>Presidential Countdown</td></tr>
<tr><td>N</td><td></td><td colspan="2">Riverboat</td><td>Tales of Wells Fargo</td><td>Klondike</td><td>Dante</td><td>Barbara Stanwyck Show</td><td>Jackpot Bowling</td></tr>
<tr><td rowspan="3">TUESDAY</td><td>A</td><td>Expedition</td><td>Bugs Bunny Show</td><td>The Rifleman</td><td>Life and Legend of Wyatt Earp</td><td colspan="2">Stagecoach West</td><td>Alcoa Presents</td><td></td></tr>
<tr><td>C</td><td>News</td><td></td><td>Father Knows Best</td><td>Many Loves of Dobie Gillis</td><td>Tom Ewell Show</td><td>Red Skelton Show</td><td colspan="2">Garry Moore Show</td></tr>
<tr><td>N</td><td></td><td colspan="2">Laramie</td><td>Alfred Hitchcock Presents</td><td colspan="2">Thriller</td><td colspan="2"></td></tr>
<tr><td rowspan="3">WEDNESDAY</td><td>A</td><td></td><td colspan="2">Hong Kong</td><td>Adventures of Ozzie & Harriet</td><td colspan="2">Hawaiian Eye</td><td colspan="2">Naked City</td></tr>
<tr><td>C</td><td>News</td><td colspan="2">Aquanauts</td><td>Wanted: Dead or Alive</td><td>My Sister Eileen</td><td>I've Got a Secret</td><td colspan="2">Armstrong Circle Theatre/ U.S. Steel Hour</td></tr>
<tr><td>N</td><td></td><td colspan="2">Wagon Train</td><td>Price Is Right</td><td colspan="2">Perry Como's Kraft Music Hall</td><td>Peter Loves Mary</td><td></td></tr>
<tr><td rowspan="3">THURSDAY</td><td>A</td><td></td><td>Guestward Ho!</td><td>Donna Reed Show</td><td>Real McCoys</td><td>My Three Sons</td><td colspan="2">The Untouchables</td><td>Take a Good Look</td></tr>
<tr><td>C</td><td>News</td><td colspan="2">The Witness</td><td>Dick Powell's Zane Grey Theatre</td><td>Angel</td><td>Peck's Bad Girl</td><td>Person to Person</td><td>DuPont Show with June Allyson</td></tr>
<tr><td>N</td><td></td><td colspan="2">The Outlaws</td><td>Bat Masterson</td><td>Bachelor Father</td><td>Ford Show Starring Tennessee Ernie Ford</td><td>Groucho Show</td><td></td></tr>
<tr><td rowspan="3">FRIDAY</td><td>A</td><td></td><td>Matty's Funday Funnies</td><td>Harrigan & Son</td><td>The Flintstones</td><td colspan="2">77 Sunset Strip</td><td>Robert Taylor: The Detectives</td><td>Law & Mr. Jones</td></tr>
<tr><td>C</td><td>News</td><td colspan="2">Rawhide</td><td colspan="2">Route 66</td><td>Mr. Garlund</td><td>Twilight Zone</td><td>Eyewitness to History</td></tr>
<tr><td>N</td><td></td><td colspan="2">Dan Raven</td><td>The Westerner</td><td colspan="2">Bell Telephone Hour</td><td colspan="2">Michael Shayne</td></tr>
<tr><td rowspan="3">SATURDAY</td><td>A</td><td></td><td colspan="2">Roaring Twenties</td><td>Leave It to Beaver</td><td colspan="2">Lawrence Welk Show</td><td>Fight of the Week</td><td>Make That Spare</td></tr>
<tr><td>C</td><td></td><td colspan="2">Perry Mason</td><td colspan="2">Checkmate</td><td>Have Gun, Will Travel</td><td>Gunsmoke</td><td></td></tr>
<tr><td>N</td><td></td><td colspan="2">Bonanza</td><td>Tall Man</td><td>The Deputy</td><td colspan="2">Nation's Future</td><td></td></tr>
</table>

PRIME TIME SCHEDULE: FALL 1961

		7:00 PM	7:30	8:00	8:30	9:00	9:30	10:00	10:30
SUNDAY	A	Maverick	Follow the Sun		The Lawman	Bus Stop		Adventures in Paradise	
	C	Lassie	Dennis the Menace	Ed Sullivan Show		G.E. Theater	Jack Benny Show	Candid Camera	What's My Line
	N	Bullwinkle Show	Walt Disney's Wonderful World of Color		Car 54, Where Are You?	Bonanza		DuPont Show of the Week	
MONDAY	A	Expedition	Cheyenne		The Rifleman	Surfside Six		Ben Casey	
	C	News	To Tell the Truth	Pete & Gladys	Window on Main Street	Danny Thomas Show	Andy Griffith Show	Hennessey	I've Got a Secret
	N			National Velvet	Price Is Right	87th Precinct		Thriller	
TUESDAY	A		Bugs Bunny Show	Bachelor Father	Calvin & the Colonel	New Breed		Alcoa Premiere	
	C	News	Marshal Dillon	Dick Van Dyke Show	Many Loves of Dobie Gillis	Red Skelton Show	Ichabod & Me	Garry Moore Show	
	N		Laramie		Alfred Hitchcock Presents	Dick Powell Show		Cain's Hundred	
WEDNESDAY	A		Steve Allen Show		Top Cat	Hawaiian Eye		Naked City	
	C	News	Alvin Show	Father Knows Best	Checkmate		Mrs. G. Goes to College	U.S. Steel Hour/Armstrong Circle Theatre	
	N		Wagon Train		Joey Bishop Show	Perry Como's Kraft Music Hall		Bob Newhart Show	David Brinkley's Journal
THURSDAY	A		Adventures of Ozzie & Harriet	Donna Reed Show	Real McCoys	My Three Sons	Margie	The Untouchables	
	C	News	Frontier Circus		Bob Cummings Show	The Investigators		CBS Reports	
	N		The Outlaws		Dr. Kildare		Hazel	Sing Along with Mitch	
FRIDAY	A		Straightaway	The Hathaways	The Flintstones	77 Sunset Strip		Target: The Corruptors	
	C	News	Rawhide		Route 66		Father of the Bride	Twilight Zone	Eyewitness
	N		International Showtime		Robert Taylor's Detectives		Bell Telephone Hour / Dinah Shore Show		Here & Now
SATURDAY	A	Matty's Funday Funnies	Roaring Twenties		Leave It to Beaver	Lawrence Welk Show		Fight of the Week	Make That Spare
	C		Perry Mason		The Defenders		Have Gun, Will Travel	Gunsmoke	
	N		Tales of Wells Fargo		Tall Man	NBC Saturday Night Movie			

PRIME TIME SCHEDULE: FALL 1962

Day	Network	7:00 PM	7:30	8:00	8:30	9:00	9:30	10:00	10:30
SUNDAY	A	Father Knows Best	Jetsons	ABC Sunday Night Movie				Voice of Firestone	Howard K. Smith
SUNDAY	C	Lassie	Dennis the Menace	Ed Sullivan		Real McCoys	G.E. True Theater	Candid Camera	What's My Line
SUNDAY	N	Ensign O'Toole	Walt Disney's Wonderful World of Color		Car 54 Where Are You?	Bonanza		DuPont Show of the Week	
MONDAY	A		Cheyenne		Rifleman	Stoney Burke		Ben Casey	
MONDAY	C	News	To Tell the Truth	I've Got a Secret	Lucy Show	Danny Thomas Show	Andy Griffith Show	New Loretta Young Show	Stump the Stars
MONDAY	N		It's a Man's World		Saints & Sinners		Price Is Right	David Brinkley's Journal	
TUESDAY	A		Combat		Hawaiian Eye		The Untouchables		Bell & Howell Closeup
TUESDAY	C	News	Marshal Dillon	Lloyd Bridges Show	Red Skelton Hour		Jack Benny Show	Garry Moore Show	
TUESDAY	N		Laramie		Empire		Dick Powell Show		Chet Huntley Reporting
WEDNESDAY	A		Wagon Train		Going My Way		Our Man Higgins	Naked City	
WEDNESDAY	C	News	CBS Reports		Many Loves of Dobie Gillis	Beverly Hillbillies	Dick Van Dyke Show	Armstrong Circle Theatre/ U.S. Steel Hour	
WEDNESDAY	N		The Virginian			Perry Como's Kraft Music Hall		Eleventh Hour	
THURSDAY	A		Adventures of Ozzie & Harriet	Donna Reed Show	Leave It to Beaver	My Three Sons	McHale's Navy	Alcoa Premiere	
THURSDAY	C	News	Mr. Ed	Perry Mason		The Nurses		Alfred Hitchcock Hour	
THURSDAY	N		Wide Country		Dr. Kildare		Hazel	Andy Williams Show	
FRIDAY	A		Gallant Men		The Flintstones	I'm Dickens—He's Fenster	77 Sunset Strip		
FRIDAY	C	News	Rawhide		Route 66		Fair Exchange		Eyewitness
FRIDAY	N		International Showtime		Sing Along with Mitch		Don't Call Me Charlie	Jack Paar Show	
SATURDAY	A	Beany & Cecil	Roy Rogers & Dale Evans Show		Mr. Smith Goes to Washington	Lawrence Welk Show		Fight of the Week	Make That Spare
SATURDAY	C		Jackie Gleason Show		Defenders		Have Gun, Will Travel	Gunsmoke	
SATURDAY	N		Sam Benedict		Joey Bishop Show	NBC Saturday Night Movie			

PRIME TIME SCHEDULE: FALL 1963

		7:00 PM	7:30	8:00	8:30	9:00	9:30	10:00	10:30	11:00
SUNDAY	A		Travels of Jaimie McPheeters		Arrest and Trial			100 Grand	ABC News Reports	
	C	Lassie	My Favorite Martian	Ed Sullivan Show		Judy Garland Show		Candid Camera	What's My Line	
	N	Bill Dana Show	Walt Disney's Wonderful World of Color		Grindl	Bonanza		DuPont Show of the Week		
MONDAY	A		Outer Limits		Wagon Train			Breaking Point		
	C		To Tell the Truth	I've Got a Secret	Lucy Show	Danny Thomas Show	Andy Griffith Show	East Side / West Side		
	N		NBC Monday Night Movie				Hollywood & the Stars	Sing Along with Mitch		
TUESDAY	A		Combat		McHale's Navy	Greatest Show on Earth		The Fugitive		
	C		Marshal Dillon	Red Skelton Hour		Petticoat Junction	Jack Benny Show	Garry Moore Show		
	N		Mr. Novak		Redigo	Richard Boone Show		Bell Telephone Hour		
WEDNESDAY	A		Adventures of Ozzie & Harriet	Patty Duke Show	Price Is Right	Ben Casey		Channing		
	C		Chronicle / CBS Reports		Glynis	Beverly Hillbillies	Dick Van Dyke Show	Danny Kaye Show		
	N		The Virginian			Espionage		Eleventh Hour		
THURSDAY	A		The Flintstones	Donna Reed Show	My Three Sons	Jimmy Dean Show		Edie Adams Show / Sid Caesar Show		
	C		Password	Rawhide		Perry Mason		The Nurses		
	N		Temple Houston		Dr. Kildare		Hazel	Kraft Suspense Theater		
FRIDAY	A		77 Sunset Strip		Burke's Law		Farmer's Daughter	Fight of the Week	Make That Spare	
	C		Great Adventure		Route 66		Twilight Zone	Alfred Hitchcock Hour		
	N		International Showtime		Bob Hope Presents the Chrysler Theatre		Harry's Girls	Jack Paar Show		
SATURDAY	A		Hootenanny		Lawrence Welk Show		Jerry Lewis Show			
	C		Jackie Gleason Show		Phil Silvers Show	The Defenders		Gunsmoke		
	N		The Lieutenant		Joey Bishop Show	NBC Saturday Night Movie				

PRIME TIME SCHEDULE: FALL 1964

<table>
<tr><th></th><th></th><th>7:00 PM</th><th>7:30</th><th>8:00</th><th>8:30</th><th>9:00</th><th>9:30</th><th>10:00</th><th>10:30</th><th>11:00</th></tr>
<tr><td rowspan="3">SUNDAY</td><td>A</td><td></td><td colspan="2">Wagon Train</td><td>Broadside</td><td colspan="4">ABC Sunday Night Movie</td><td></td></tr>
<tr><td>C</td><td>Lassie</td><td>My Favorite Martian</td><td colspan="2">Ed Sullivan Show</td><td>My Living Doll</td><td>Joey Bishop Show</td><td>Candid Camera</td><td>What's My Line</td><td></td></tr>
<tr><td>N</td><td>Profiles in Courage</td><td colspan="2">Walt Disney's Wonderful World of Color</td><td>Bill Dana Show</td><td colspan="2">Bonanza</td><td colspan="2">The Rogues</td><td></td></tr>
<tr><td rowspan="3">MONDAY</td><td>A</td><td></td><td colspan="2">Voyage to the Bottom of the Sea</td><td>No Time for Sergeants</td><td>Wendy and Me</td><td>Bing Crosby Show</td><td colspan="2">Ben Casey</td><td></td></tr>
<tr><td>C</td><td></td><td>To Tell the Truth</td><td>I've Got a Secret</td><td>Andy Griffith Show</td><td>Lucy Show</td><td>Many Happy Returns</td><td colspan="2">Slattery's People</td><td></td></tr>
<tr><td>N</td><td></td><td colspan="3">90 Bristol Court: Karen/Harris Against the World/ Tom, Dick, and Mary</td><td colspan="2">Andy Williams Show</td><td colspan="2">Alfred Hitchcock Hour</td><td></td></tr>
<tr><td rowspan="3">TUESDAY</td><td>A</td><td></td><td colspan="2">Combat</td><td>McHale's Navy</td><td>The Tycoon</td><td>Peyton Place</td><td colspan="2">The Fugitive</td><td></td></tr>
<tr><td>C</td><td></td><td></td><td>World War I</td><td colspan="2">Red Skelton Hour</td><td>Petticoat Junction</td><td colspan="2">Doctors and the Nurses</td><td></td></tr>
<tr><td>N</td><td></td><td colspan="2">Mr. Novak</td><td colspan="2">Man from U.N.C.L.E.</td><td>That Was the Week That Was</td><td colspan="2">Bell Telephone Hour</td><td></td></tr>
<tr><td rowspan="3">WEDNESDAY</td><td>A</td><td></td><td>Adventures of Ozzie & Harriet</td><td>Patty Duke Show</td><td>Shindig</td><td>Mickey</td><td colspan="2">Burke's Law</td><td>ABC Scope</td><td></td></tr>
<tr><td>C</td><td></td><td colspan="2">CBS Reports</td><td>Beverly Hillbillies</td><td>Dick Van Dyke Show</td><td>Cara Williams Show</td><td colspan="2">Danny Kaye Show</td><td></td></tr>
<tr><td>N</td><td></td><td colspan="3">The Virginian</td><td colspan="4">NBC Wednesday Night Movie</td><td></td></tr>
<tr><td rowspan="3">THURSDAY</td><td>A</td><td></td><td>The Flintstones</td><td>Donna Reed Show</td><td>My Three Sons</td><td>Bewitched</td><td>Peyton Place</td><td colspan="2">Jimmy Dean Show</td><td></td></tr>
<tr><td>C</td><td></td><td>The Munsters</td><td colspan="2">Perry Mason</td><td>Password</td><td>Baileys of Balboa</td><td colspan="2">The Defenders</td><td></td></tr>
<tr><td>N</td><td></td><td colspan="2">Daniel Boone</td><td colspan="2">Dr. Kildare</td><td>Hazel</td><td colspan="2">Kraft Suspense Theater</td><td></td></tr>
<tr><td rowspan="3">FRIDAY</td><td>A</td><td></td><td>Jonny Quest</td><td>Farmer's Daughter</td><td>Addams Family</td><td>Valentine's Day</td><td colspan="2">Twelve O'Clock High</td><td></td><td></td></tr>
<tr><td>C</td><td></td><td colspan="2">Rawhide</td><td colspan="2">The Entertainers</td><td>Gomer Pyle, U.S.M.C.</td><td colspan="2">The Reporter</td><td></td></tr>
<tr><td>N</td><td></td><td colspan="2">International Showtime</td><td colspan="2">Bob Hope Presents the Chrysler Theatre</td><td>Jack Benny Program</td><td colspan="2">Jack Paar Show</td><td></td></tr>
<tr><td rowspan="3">SATURDAY</td><td>A</td><td></td><td colspan="2">Outer Limits</td><td colspan="2">Lawrence Welk Show</td><td colspan="2">Hollywood Palace</td><td></td><td></td></tr>
<tr><td>C</td><td></td><td colspan="2">Jackie Gleason Show</td><td>Gilligan's Island</td><td colspan="2">Mr. Broadway</td><td colspan="2">Gunsmoke</td><td></td></tr>
<tr><td>N</td><td></td><td>Flipper</td><td>Famous Adventures of Mr. Magoo</td><td>Kentucky Jones</td><td colspan="4">NBC Saturday Night Movie</td><td></td></tr>
</table>

PRIME TIME SCHEDULE: FALL 1965

<table>
<tr><th></th><th></th><th>7:00 PM</th><th>7:30</th><th>8:00</th><th>8:30</th><th>9:00</th><th>9:30</th><th>10:00</th><th>10:30</th><th>11:00</th></tr>
<tr><td rowspan="3">SUNDAY</td><td>A</td><td colspan="2">Voyage to the Bottom of the Sea</td><td colspan="2">The F.B.I.</td><td colspan="4">ABC Sunday Night Movie</td></tr>
<tr><td>C</td><td>Lassie</td><td>My Favorite Martian</td><td colspan="2">Ed Sullivan Show</td><td colspan="2">Perry Mason</td><td>Candid Camera</td><td>What's My Line</td></tr>
<tr><td>N</td><td>Bell Telephone Hour/Actuality Specials</td><td colspan="2">Walt Disney's Wonderful World of Color</td><td>Branded</td><td colspan="2">Bonanza</td><td colspan="2">Wackiest Ship in the Army</td></tr>
<tr><td rowspan="3">MONDAY</td><td>A</td><td></td><td colspan="2">Twelve O'Clock High</td><td>Legend of Jesse James</td><td>Man Called Shenandoah</td><td>Farmer's Daughter</td><td colspan="2">Ben Casey</td></tr>
<tr><td>C</td><td></td><td>To Tell the Truth</td><td>I've Got a Secret</td><td>Lucy Show</td><td>Andy Griffith Show</td><td>Hazel</td><td colspan="2">Steve Lawrence Show</td></tr>
<tr><td>N</td><td></td><td>Hullabaloo</td><td>John Forsythe Show</td><td>Dr. Kildare</td><td colspan="2">Andy Williams Show</td><td colspan="2">Run for Your Life</td></tr>
<tr><td rowspan="3">TUESDAY</td><td>A</td><td></td><td colspan="2">Combat</td><td>McHale's Navy</td><td>F Troop</td><td>Peyton Place</td><td colspan="2">The Fugitive</td></tr>
<tr><td>C</td><td></td><td colspan="2">Rawhide</td><td colspan="2">Red Skelton Hour</td><td>Petticoat Junction</td><td colspan="2">CBS Reports/News Hour</td></tr>
<tr><td>N</td><td></td><td>My Mother the Car</td><td>Please Don't Eat the Daisies</td><td>Dr. Kildare</td><td colspan="4">NBC Tuesday Night Movie</td></tr>
<tr><td rowspan="3">WEDNESDAY</td><td>A</td><td></td><td>Adventures of Ozzie & Harriet</td><td>Patty Duke Show</td><td>Gidget</td><td colspan="2">Big Valley</td><td colspan="2">Amos Burke—Secret Agent</td></tr>
<tr><td>C</td><td></td><td colspan="2">Lost in Space</td><td>Beverly Hillbillies</td><td>Green Acres</td><td>Dick Van Dyke Show</td><td colspan="2">Danny Kaye Show</td></tr>
<tr><td>N</td><td></td><td colspan="3">The Virginian</td><td colspan="2">Bob Hope Presents the Chrysler Theatre</td><td colspan="2">I Spy</td></tr>
<tr><td rowspan="3">THURSDAY</td><td>A</td><td></td><td>Shindig</td><td>Donna Reed Show</td><td>O.K. Crackerby</td><td>Bewitched</td><td>Peyton Place</td><td colspan="2">Long, Hot Summer</td></tr>
<tr><td>C</td><td></td><td>The Munsters</td><td>Gilligan's Island</td><td>My Three Sons</td><td colspan="4">CBS Thursday Night Movie</td></tr>
<tr><td>N</td><td></td><td colspan="2">Daniel Boone</td><td colspan="2">Laredo</td><td>Mona McCluskey</td><td colspan="2">Dean Martin Show</td></tr>
<tr><td rowspan="3">FRIDAY</td><td>A</td><td></td><td>The Flintstones</td><td>Tammy</td><td>Addams Family</td><td>Honey West</td><td>Peyton Place</td><td colspan="2">Jimmy Dean Show</td></tr>
<tr><td>C</td><td></td><td colspan="2">Wild Wild West</td><td>Hogan's Heroes</td><td>Gomer Pyle U.S.M.C.</td><td>Smothers Brothers Show</td><td colspan="2">Slattery's People</td></tr>
<tr><td>N</td><td></td><td>Camp Runamuck</td><td>Hank</td><td colspan="2">Convoy</td><td>Mr. Roberts</td><td colspan="2">Man from U.N.C.L.E.</td></tr>
<tr><td rowspan="3">SATURDAY</td><td>A</td><td></td><td>Shindig</td><td>King Family Show</td><td colspan="2">Lawrence Welk Show</td><td colspan="2">Hollywood Palace</td><td>ABC Scope</td></tr>
<tr><td>C</td><td></td><td colspan="2">Jackie Gleason Show</td><td colspan="2">Trials of O'Brien</td><td>The Loner</td><td colspan="2">Gunsmoke</td></tr>
<tr><td>N</td><td></td><td>Flipper</td><td>I Dream of Jeannie</td><td>Get Smart</td><td colspan="4">NBC Saturday Night Movie</td></tr>
</table>

PRIME TIME SCHEDULE: FALL 1966

<table>
<tr><th></th><th></th><th>7:00 PM</th><th>7:30</th><th>8:00</th><th>8:30</th><th>9:00</th><th>9:30</th><th>10:00</th><th>10:30</th><th>11:00</th></tr>
<tr><td rowspan="3">SUNDAY</td><td>A</td><td colspan="2">Voyage to the Bottom of the Sea</td><td colspan="2">The F.B.I.</td><td colspan="4">ABC Sunday Night Movie</td></tr>
<tr><td>C</td><td>Lassie</td><td>It's About Time</td><td colspan="2">Ed Sullivan Show</td><td colspan="2">Garry Moore Show</td><td>Candid Camera</td><td>What's My Line</td></tr>
<tr><td>N</td><td>Actuality Specials/Bell Telephone Hour</td><td colspan="2">Walt Disney's Wonderful World of Color</td><td>Hey Landlord</td><td colspan="2">Bonanza</td><td colspan="2">Andy Williams Show</td></tr>
<tr><td rowspan="3">MONDAY</td><td>A</td><td></td><td colspan="2">Iron Horse</td><td>Rat Patrol</td><td>Felony Squad</td><td>Peyton Place</td><td colspan="2">Big Valley</td></tr>
<tr><td>C</td><td></td><td>Gilligan's Island</td><td>Run Buddy Run</td><td>Lucy Show</td><td>Andy Griffith Show</td><td>Family Affair</td><td>Jean Arthur Show</td><td>I've Got a Secret</td></tr>
<tr><td>N</td><td></td><td>The Monkees</td><td>I Dream of Jeannie</td><td>Roger Miller Show</td><td colspan="2">Road West</td><td colspan="2">Run for Your Life</td></tr>
<tr><td rowspan="3">TUESDAY</td><td>A</td><td></td><td colspan="2">Combat</td><td>The Rounders</td><td>Pruitts of Southampton</td><td>Love on a Rooftop</td><td colspan="2">The Fugitive</td></tr>
<tr><td>C</td><td></td><td colspan="2">Daktari</td><td colspan="2">Red Skelton Hour</td><td>Petticoat Junction</td><td colspan="2">CBS News Hour</td></tr>
<tr><td>N</td><td></td><td colspan="2">Girl from U.N.C.L.E.</td><td>Occasional Wife</td><td colspan="4">NBC Tuesday Night Movie</td></tr>
<tr><td rowspan="3">WEDNESDAY</td><td>A</td><td></td><td>Batman</td><td colspan="2">The Monroes</td><td>Man Who Never Was</td><td>Peyton Place</td><td colspan="2">ABC Stage '67</td></tr>
<tr><td>C</td><td></td><td colspan="2">Lost in Space</td><td>Beverly Hillbillies</td><td>Green Acres</td><td>Gomer Pyle, U.S.M.C.</td><td colspan="2">Danny Kaye Show</td></tr>
<tr><td>N</td><td></td><td colspan="3">The Virginian</td><td colspan="2">Bob Hope Presents the Chrysler Theatre</td><td colspan="2">I Spy</td></tr>
<tr><td rowspan="3">THURSDAY</td><td>A</td><td></td><td>Batman</td><td>F Troop</td><td>Tammy Grimes Show</td><td>Bewitched</td><td>That Girl</td><td colspan="2">Hawk</td></tr>
<tr><td>C</td><td></td><td colspan="2">Jericho</td><td>My Three Sons</td><td colspan="4">CBS Thursday Night Movie</td></tr>
<tr><td>N</td><td></td><td colspan="2">Daniel Boone</td><td colspan="2">Star Trek</td><td>The Hero</td><td colspan="2">Dean Martin Show</td></tr>
<tr><td rowspan="3">FRIDAY</td><td>A</td><td></td><td>Green Hornet</td><td colspan="2">Time Tunnel</td><td colspan="2">Milton Berle Show</td><td colspan="2">Twelve O'Clock High</td></tr>
<tr><td>C</td><td></td><td colspan="2">Wild Wild West</td><td>Hogan's Heroes</td><td colspan="4">CBS Friday Night Movie</td></tr>
<tr><td>N</td><td></td><td colspan="2">Tarzan</td><td colspan="2">Man from U.N.C.L.E.</td><td>T.H.E. Cat</td><td colspan="2">Laredo</td></tr>
<tr><td rowspan="3">SATURDAY</td><td>A</td><td></td><td colspan="2">Shane</td><td colspan="2">Lawrence Welk Show</td><td colspan="2">Hollywood Palace</td><td>ABC Scope</td></tr>
<tr><td>C</td><td></td><td colspan="2">Jackie Gleason Show</td><td>Pistols 'n' Petticoats</td><td colspan="2">Mission: Impossible</td><td colspan="2">Gunsmoke</td></tr>
<tr><td>N</td><td></td><td>Flipper</td><td>Please Don't Eat the Daisies</td><td>Get Smart</td><td colspan="4">NBC Saturday Night Movie</td></tr>
</table>

PRIME TIME SCHEDULE: FALL 1967

		7:00 PM	7:30	8:00	8:30	9:00	9:30	10:00	10:30
SUNDAY	A	Voyage to the Bottom of the Sea		The F.B.I.		ABC Sunday Night Movie			
	C	Lassie	Gentle Ben	Ed Sullivan Show		Smothers Brothers Comedy Hour		Mission: Impossible	
	N		Walt Disney's Wonderful World of Color		Mothers-in-Law	Bonanza		High Chaparral	
MONDAY	A		Cowboy in Africa		Rat Patrol	Felony Squad	Peyton Place	Big Valley	
	C		Gunsmoke		Lucy Show	Andy Griffith Show	Family Affair	Carol Burnett Show	
	N		The Monkees	Man from U.N.C.L.E.		Danny Thomas Hour		I Spy	
TUESDAY	A		Garrison's Gorillas		The Invaders		N.Y.P.D.	Hollywood Palace	
	C		Daktari		Red Skelton Hour		Good Morning, World	CBS News Hour	
	N		I Dream of Jeannie	Jerry Lewis Show		NBC Tuesday Night Movie			
WEDNESDAY	A		Legend of Custer		Second 100 Years	ABC Wednesday Night Movie			
	C		Lost in Space		Beverly Hillbillies	Green Acres	He & She	Dundee and the Culhane	
	N		The Virginian			Kraft Music Hall		Run for Your Life	
THURSDAY	A		Batman	Flying Nun	Bewitched	That Girl	Peyton Place	Good Company	
	C		Cimarron Strip			CBS Thursday Night Movie			
	N		Daniel Boone		Ironside		Dragnet	Dean Martin Show	
FRIDAY	A		Off To See the Wizard		Hondo		Guns of Will Sonnett	Judd, for the Defense	
	C		Wild Wild West		Gomer Pyle, U.S.M.C.	CBS Friday Night Movie			
	N		Tarzan		Star Trek		Accidental Family	Actuality Specials/ Bell Telephone Hour	
SATURDAY	A		Dating Game	Newlywed Game	Lawrence Welk Show		Iron Horse		ABC Scope
	C		Jackie Gleason Show		My Three Sons	Hogan's Heroes	Petticoat Junction	Mannix	
	N		Maya		Get Smart	NBC Saturday Night Movie			

PRIME TIME SCHEDULE: FALL 1968

<table>
<tr><th></th><th></th><th>7:00 PM</th><th>7:30</th><th>8:00</th><th>8:30</th><th>9:00</th><th>9:30</th><th>10:00</th><th>10:30</th><th>11:00</th></tr>
<tr><td rowspan="3">SUNDAY</td><td>A</td><td colspan="2">Land of the Giants</td><td colspan="2">The F.B.I.</td><td colspan="4">ABC Sunday Night Movie</td><td></td></tr>
<tr><td>C</td><td>Lassie</td><td>Gentle Ben</td><td colspan="2">Ed Sullivan Show</td><td colspan="2">Smothers Brothers Comedy Hour</td><td colspan="2">Mission: Impossible</td><td></td></tr>
<tr><td>N</td><td>New Adventures of Huck Finn</td><td colspan="2">Walt Disney's Wonderful World of Color</td><td>Mothers-in-Law</td><td colspan="2">Bonanza</td><td colspan="2">Beautiful Phyllis Diller Show</td><td></td></tr>
<tr><td rowspan="3">MONDAY</td><td>A</td><td></td><td colspan="2">The Avengers</td><td>Peyton Place</td><td colspan="2">The Outcasts</td><td colspan="2">Big Valley</td><td></td></tr>
<tr><td>C</td><td></td><td colspan="2">Gunsmoke</td><td>Here's Lucy</td><td>Mayberry R.F.D.</td><td>Family Affair</td><td colspan="2">Carol Burnett Show</td><td></td></tr>
<tr><td>N</td><td></td><td>I Dream of Jeannie</td><td colspan="2">Rowan & Martin's Laugh-In</td><td colspan="4">NBC Monday Night Movie</td><td></td></tr>
<tr><td rowspan="3">TUESDAY</td><td>A</td><td></td><td colspan="2">Mod Squad</td><td colspan="2">It Takes a Thief</td><td>N.Y.P.D.</td><td colspan="2">That's Life</td><td></td></tr>
<tr><td>C</td><td></td><td colspan="2">Lancer</td><td colspan="2">Red Skelton Hour</td><td>Doris Day Show</td><td colspan="2">CBS News Hour / 60 Minutes</td><td></td></tr>
<tr><td>N</td><td></td><td colspan="2">Jerry Lewis Show</td><td>Julia</td><td colspan="4">NBC Tuesday Night Movie</td><td></td></tr>
<tr><td rowspan="3">WEDNESDAY</td><td>A</td><td></td><td colspan="2">Here Comes the Brides</td><td>Peyton Place</td><td colspan="4">ABC Wednesday Night Movie</td><td></td></tr>
<tr><td>C</td><td></td><td colspan="2">Daktari</td><td>Good Guys</td><td>Beverly Hillbillies</td><td>Green Acres</td><td colspan="2">Jonathan Winters Show</td><td></td></tr>
<tr><td>N</td><td></td><td colspan="3">The Virginian</td><td colspan="2">Kraft Music Hall</td><td colspan="2">The Outsider</td><td></td></tr>
<tr><td rowspan="3">THURSDAY</td><td>A</td><td></td><td>Ugliest Girl in Town</td><td>Flying Nun</td><td>Bewitched</td><td>That Girl</td><td colspan="2">Journey to the Unknown</td><td></td><td></td></tr>
<tr><td>C</td><td></td><td>Blondie</td><td colspan="2">Hawaii Five-O</td><td colspan="4">CBS Thursday Night Movie</td><td></td></tr>
<tr><td>N</td><td></td><td colspan="2">Daniel Boone</td><td colspan="2">Ironside</td><td>Dragnet</td><td colspan="2">Dean Martin Show</td><td></td></tr>
<tr><td rowspan="3">FRIDAY</td><td>A</td><td></td><td colspan="2">Operation: Entertainment</td><td>Felony Squad</td><td>Don Rickles Show</td><td>Guns of Will Sonnett</td><td colspan="2">Judd, for the Defense</td><td></td></tr>
<tr><td>C</td><td></td><td colspan="2">Wild Wild West</td><td>Gomer Pyle, U.S.M.C.</td><td colspan="4">CBS Friday Night Movie</td><td></td></tr>
<tr><td>N</td><td></td><td colspan="2">High Chaparral</td><td colspan="3">Name of the Game</td><td colspan="2">Star Trek</td><td></td></tr>
<tr><td rowspan="3">SATURDAY</td><td>A</td><td></td><td>Dating Game</td><td>Newlywed Game</td><td colspan="2">Lawrence Welk Show</td><td colspan="2">Hollywood Palace</td><td></td><td></td></tr>
<tr><td>C</td><td></td><td colspan="2">Jackie Gleason Show</td><td>My Three Sons</td><td>Hogan's Heroes</td><td>Petticoat Junction</td><td colspan="2">Mannix</td><td></td></tr>
<tr><td>N</td><td></td><td>Adam 12</td><td>Get Smart</td><td>Ghost & Mrs. Muir</td><td colspan="4">NBC Saturday Night Movie</td><td></td></tr>
</table>

PRIME TIME SCHEDULE: FALL 1969

		7:00 PM	7:30	8:00	8:30	9:00	9:30	10:00	10:30	11:00
SUNDAY	A	Land of the Giants		The F.B.I.		ABC Sunday Night Movie				
	C	Lassie	To Rome with Love	Ed Sullivan Show		Leslie Uggams Show		Mission: Impossible		
	N	Wild Kingdom	Walt Disney's Wonderful World of Color		Bill Cosby Show	Bonanza		Bold Ones: The New Doctors/The Lawyers/The Protectors		
MONDAY	A		Music Scene	New People		Harold Robbins' "The Survivors"		Love, American Style		
	C		Gunsmoke		Here's Lucy	Mayberry R.F.D.	Doris Day Show	Carol Burnett Show		
	N		My World and Welcome to It	Rowan & Martin's Laugh-In		NBC Monday Night Movie				
TUESDAY	A		Mod Squad		Movie of the Week			Marcus Welby, M.D.		
	C		Lancer		Red Skelton Hour		Governor & J.J.	CBS News Hour / 60 Minutes		
	N		I Dream of Jeannie	Debbie Reynolds Show	Julia	NBC Tuesday Night Movie				
WEDNESDAY	A		Flying Nun	Courtship of Eddie's Father	Room 222	ABC Wednesday Night Movie				
	C		Glen Campbell Goodtime Hour		Beverly Hillbillies	Medical Center		Hawaii Five-O		
	N		The Virginian			Kraft Music Hall		Then Came Bronson		
THURSDAY	A		Ghost & Mrs. Muir	That Girl	Bewitched	This Is Tom Jones		It Takes a Thief		
	C		Family Affair	Jim Nabors Hour		CBS Thursday Night Movie				
	N		Daniel Boone		Ironside		Dragnet	Dean Martin Show		
FRIDAY	A		Let's Make a Deal	Brady Bunch	Mr. Deeds Goes to Town	Here Comes the Brides		Jimmy Durante Presents Lennon Sisters		
	C		Get Smart	Good Guys	Hogan's Heroes	CBS Friday Night Movie				
	N		High Chaparral		Name of the Game			Bracken's World		
SATURDAY	A		Dating Game	Newlywed Game	Lawrence Welk Show		Hollywood Palace			
	C		Jackie Gleason Show		My Three Sons	Green Acres	Petticoat Junction	Mannix		
	N		Andy Williams Show		Adam 12	NBC Saturday Night Movie				

PRIME TIME SCHEDULE: FALL 1970

<table>
<tr><th></th><th></th><th>7:00 PM</th><th>7:30</th><th>8:00</th><th>8:30</th><th>9:00</th><th>9:30</th><th>10:00</th><th>10:30</th><th>11:00</th></tr>
<tr><td rowspan="3">SUNDAY</td><td>A</td><td colspan="2">Young Rebels</td><td colspan="2">The F.B.I.</td><td colspan="4">ABC Sunday Night Movie</td></tr>
<tr><td>C</td><td>Lassie</td><td>Hogan's Heroes</td><td colspan="2">Ed Sullivan Show</td><td colspan="2">Glen Campbell Goodtime Hour</td><td colspan="2">Tim Conway Comedy Hour</td></tr>
<tr><td>N</td><td>Wild Kingdom</td><td colspan="2">Wonderful World of Disney</td><td>Bill Cosby Show</td><td colspan="2">Bonanza</td><td colspan="2">Bold Ones: The New Doctors/The Lawyers/The Senator</td></tr>
<tr><td rowspan="3">MONDAY</td><td>A</td><td></td><td colspan="2">Young Lawyers</td><td>Silent Force</td><td colspan="4">ABC Monday Night Football</td></tr>
<tr><td>C</td><td></td><td colspan="2">Gunsmoke</td><td>Here's Lucy</td><td>Mayberry R.F.D.</td><td>Doris Day Show</td><td colspan="2">Carol Burnett Show</td></tr>
<tr><td>N</td><td></td><td>Red Skelton Show</td><td colspan="2">Rowan & Martin's Laugh-In</td><td colspan="4">NBC Monday Night Movie</td></tr>
<tr><td rowspan="3">TUESDAY</td><td>A</td><td></td><td colspan="2">Mod Squad</td><td colspan="3">Movie of the Week</td><td colspan="2">Marcus Welby, M.D.</td></tr>
<tr><td>C</td><td></td><td>Beverly Hillbillies</td><td>Green Acres</td><td colspan="2">Hee Haw</td><td>To Rome with Love</td><td colspan="2">CBS News Hour / 60 Minutes</td></tr>
<tr><td>N</td><td></td><td colspan="2">Don Knotts Show</td><td>Julia</td><td colspan="4">NBC Tuesday Night Movie</td></tr>
<tr><td rowspan="3">WEDNESDAY</td><td>A</td><td></td><td>Courtship of Eddie's Father</td><td>Make Room for Granddaddy</td><td>Room 222</td><td colspan="2">Johnny Cash Show</td><td colspan="2">Dan August</td></tr>
<tr><td>C</td><td></td><td colspan="2">Storefront Lawyers</td><td>Governor & J.J.</td><td colspan="2">Medical Center</td><td colspan="2">Hawaii Five-O</td></tr>
<tr><td>N</td><td></td><td colspan="3">Men from Shiloh</td><td colspan="2">Kraft Music Hall</td><td colspan="2">Four in One: McCloud/ San Francisco International Airport/Night Gallery/ The Psychiatrist</td></tr>
<tr><td rowspan="3">THURSDAY</td><td>A</td><td></td><td colspan="2">Matt Lincoln</td><td>Bewitched</td><td>Barefoot in the Park</td><td>Odd Couple</td><td colspan="2">The Immortal</td></tr>
<tr><td>C</td><td></td><td>Family Affair</td><td colspan="2">Jim Nabors Hour</td><td colspan="4">CBS Thursday Night Movie</td></tr>
<tr><td>N</td><td></td><td colspan="2">Flip Wilson Show</td><td colspan="2">Ironside</td><td>Nancy</td><td colspan="2">Dean Martin Show</td></tr>
<tr><td rowspan="3">FRIDAY</td><td>A</td><td></td><td>Brady Bunch</td><td>Nanny and the Professor</td><td>Partridge Family</td><td>That Girl</td><td>Love, American Style</td><td colspan="2">This Is Tom Jones</td></tr>
<tr><td>C</td><td></td><td colspan="2">The Interns</td><td>The Headmaster</td><td colspan="4">CBS Friday Night Movie</td></tr>
<tr><td>N</td><td></td><td colspan="2">High Chaparral</td><td colspan="3">Name of the Game</td><td colspan="2">Bracken's World</td></tr>
<tr><td rowspan="3">SATURDAY</td><td>A</td><td></td><td>Let's Make a Deal</td><td>Newlywed Game</td><td colspan="2">Lawrence Welk Show</td><td colspan="2">Most Deadly Game</td><td></td></tr>
<tr><td>C</td><td></td><td colspan="2">Mission: Impossible</td><td>My Three Sons</td><td>Arnie</td><td>Mary Tyler Moore Show</td><td colspan="2">Mannix</td></tr>
<tr><td>N</td><td></td><td colspan="2">Andy Williams Show</td><td>Adam 12</td><td colspan="4">NBC Saturday Night Movie</td></tr>
</table>

PRIME TIME SCHEDULE: FALL 1971

Day	Net	7:00 PM	7:30	8:00	8:30	9:00	9:30	10:00	10:30	11:00
SUNDAY	A			The F.B.I.		ABC Sunday Night Movie				
SUNDAY	C		CBS Sunday Night Movie				Cade's County			
SUNDAY	N		Wonderful World of Disney		Jimmy Stewart Show	Bonanza		Bold Ones: The New Doctors/The Lawyers		
MONDAY	A			Nanny & Professor		ABC Monday Night Football				
MONDAY	C			Gunsmoke		Here's Lucy	Doris Day Show	My Three Sons	Arnie	
MONDAY	N			Rowan & Martin's Laugh-In		NBC Monday Night Movie				
TUESDAY	A		Mod Squad		Movie of the Week			Marcus Welby, M.D.		
TUESDAY	C		Glen Campbell Goodtime Hour		Hawaii Five-O		Cannon			
TUESDAY	N		Ironside		Sarge		The Funny Side			
WEDNESDAY	A			Bewitched	Courtship of Eddie's Father	Smith Family	Shirley's World	Man and the City		
WEDNESDAY	C			Carol Burnett Show		Medical Center		Mannix		
WEDNESDAY	N			Adam 12	NBC Mystery Movie: Columbo/McCloud/McMillan and Wife			Night Gallery		
THURSDAY	A			Alias Smith & Jones		Longstreet		Owen Marshall		
THURSDAY	C			Bearcats		CBS Thursday Night Movie				
THURSDAY	N			Flip Wilson Show		Nichols		Dean Martin Show		
FRIDAY	A			Brady Bunch	Partridge Family	Room 222	Odd Couple	Love, American Style		
FRIDAY	C			Chicago Teddy Bears	O'Hara, U.S. Treasury		New CBS Friday Night Movie			
FRIDAY	N			The D.A.	NBC World Premiere Movie					
SATURDAY	A			Getting Together	ABC Movie of the Weekend			The Persuaders		
SATURDAY	C			All in the Family	Funny Face	New Dick Van Dyke Show	Mary Tyler Moore Show	Mission: Impossible		
SATURDAY	N			The Partners	The Good Life	NBC Saturday Night Movie				

PRIME TIME SCHEDULE: FALL 1972

<table>
<tr><th></th><th></th><th>7:00 PM</th><th>7:30</th><th>8:00</th><th>8:30</th><th>9:00</th><th>9:30</th><th>10:00</th><th>10:30</th><th>11:00</th></tr>
<tr><td rowspan="3">SUNDAY</td><td>A</td><td colspan="2"></td><td colspan="2">The F.B.I.</td><td colspan="4">ABC Sunday Night Movie</td></tr>
<tr><td>C</td><td></td><td>Anna and the King</td><td>M*A*S*H</td><td>Sandy Duncan Show</td><td>New Dick Van Dyke Show</td><td colspan="2">Mannix</td><td></td></tr>
<tr><td>N</td><td></td><td colspan="2">Wonderful World of Disney</td><td colspan="3">NBC Sunday Mystery Movie
Columbo/McCloud/McMillan and Wife/
Hec Ramsey</td><td>Night Gallery</td><td></td></tr>
<tr><td rowspan="3">MONDAY</td><td>A</td><td colspan="2"></td><td colspan="2">The Rookies</td><td colspan="4">ABC Monday Night Football</td></tr>
<tr><td>C</td><td colspan="2"></td><td colspan="2">Gunsmoke</td><td>Here's Lucy</td><td>Doris Day Show</td><td colspan="2">New Bill Cosby Show</td></tr>
<tr><td>N</td><td colspan="2"></td><td colspan="2">Rowan & Martin's Laugh-In</td><td colspan="4">NBC Monday Night Movie</td></tr>
<tr><td rowspan="3">TUESDAY</td><td>A</td><td colspan="2"></td><td>Temperatures Rising</td><td colspan="3">Tuesday Movie of the Week</td><td colspan="2">Marcus Welby, M.D.</td></tr>
<tr><td>C</td><td colspan="2"></td><td>Maude</td><td colspan="2">Hawaii Five-O</td><td colspan="3">New CBS Tuesday Night Movie</td></tr>
<tr><td>N</td><td colspan="2"></td><td colspan="2">Bonanza</td><td colspan="2">Bold Ones:
The New Doctors</td><td colspan="2">NBC Reports</td></tr>
<tr><td rowspan="3">WEDNESDAY</td><td>A</td><td colspan="2"></td><td>Paul Lynde Show</td><td colspan="3">Wednesday Movie of the Week</td><td colspan="2">Julie Andrews Hour</td></tr>
<tr><td>C</td><td colspan="2"></td><td colspan="2">Carol Burnett Show</td><td colspan="2">Medical Center</td><td colspan="2">Cannon</td></tr>
<tr><td>N</td><td colspan="2"></td><td>Adam 12</td><td colspan="3">NBC Wednesday Mystery Movie:
Madigan/Cool Million/Banacek</td><td colspan="2">Search</td></tr>
<tr><td rowspan="3">THURSDAY</td><td>A</td><td colspan="2"></td><td colspan="2">Mod Squad</td><td colspan="2">The Men:
Assignment Vienna/
Delphi Bureau/Jigsaw</td><td colspan="2">Owen Marshall</td></tr>
<tr><td>C</td><td colspan="2"></td><td colspan="2">The Waltons</td><td colspan="4">CBS Thursday Night Movie</td></tr>
<tr><td>N</td><td colspan="2"></td><td colspan="2">Flip Wilson Show</td><td colspan="2">Ironside</td><td colspan="2">Dean Martin Show</td></tr>
<tr><td rowspan="3">FRIDAY</td><td>A</td><td colspan="2"></td><td>Brady Bunch</td><td>Partridge Family</td><td>Room 222</td><td>Odd Couple</td><td colspan="2">Love, American Style</td></tr>
<tr><td>C</td><td colspan="2"></td><td colspan="2">Sonny & Cher Comedy Hour</td><td colspan="4">CBS Friday Night Movie</td></tr>
<tr><td>N</td><td colspan="2"></td><td>Sanford & Son</td><td>Little People</td><td colspan="2">Ghost Story</td><td colspan="2">Banyon</td></tr>
<tr><td rowspan="3">SATURDAY</td><td>A</td><td colspan="2"></td><td colspan="2">Alias Smith & Jones</td><td colspan="2">Streets of San Francisco</td><td colspan="2">The Sixth Sense</td></tr>
<tr><td>C</td><td colspan="2"></td><td>All in the Family</td><td>Bridget Loves Bernie</td><td>Mary Tyler Moore Show</td><td>Bob Newhart Show</td><td colspan="2">Mission: Impossible</td></tr>
<tr><td>N</td><td colspan="2"></td><td colspan="2">Emergency</td><td colspan="4">NBC Saturday Night Movie</td></tr>
</table>

PRIME TIME SCHEDULE: FALL 1973

<table>
<tr><th></th><th></th><th>7:00 PM</th><th>7:30</th><th>8:00</th><th>8:30</th><th>9:00</th><th>9:30</th><th>10:00</th><th>10:30</th><th>11:00</th></tr>
<tr><td rowspan="3">SUNDAY</td><td>A</td><td></td><td colspan="2">The F.B.I.</td><td colspan="4">ABC Sunday Night Movie</td><td></td></tr>
<tr><td>C</td><td></td><td colspan="2">New Adv. of Perry Mason</td><td colspan="2">Mannix</td><td colspan="2">Barnaby Jones</td><td></td></tr>
<tr><td>N</td><td></td><td colspan="2">Wonderful World of Disney</td><td colspan="4">NBC Sunday Mystery Movie: Columbo/McCloud/McMillan and Wife/Hec Ramsey</td><td></td></tr>
<tr><td rowspan="3">MONDAY</td><td>A</td><td colspan="2"></td><td colspan="2">The Rookies</td><td colspan="4">ABC Monday Night Football</td></tr>
<tr><td>C</td><td colspan="2"></td><td colspan="2">Gunsmoke</td><td>Here's Lucy</td><td>New Dick Van Dyke Show</td><td colspan="2">Medical Center</td></tr>
<tr><td>N</td><td colspan="2"></td><td>Lotsa Luck</td><td>Diana</td><td colspan="4">NBC Monday Night Movie</td></tr>
<tr><td rowspan="3">TUESDAY</td><td>A</td><td colspan="2"></td><td>Temperatures Rising</td><td colspan="3">Tuesday Movie of the Week</td><td colspan="2">Marcus Welby, M.D.</td></tr>
<tr><td>C</td><td colspan="2"></td><td>Maude</td><td colspan="2">Hawaii Five-O</td><td colspan="3">Tuesday Night CBS Movie: Hawkins/Shaft/The New CBS Tuesday Night Movie</td></tr>
<tr><td>N</td><td colspan="2"></td><td colspan="2">Chase</td><td colspan="2">The Magician</td><td colspan="2">Police Story</td></tr>
<tr><td rowspan="3">WEDNESDAY</td><td>A</td><td colspan="2"></td><td>Bob & Carol & Ted & Alice</td><td colspan="3">Wednesday Movie of the Week</td><td colspan="2">Owen Marshall</td></tr>
<tr><td>C</td><td colspan="2"></td><td colspan="2">Sonny & Cher Comedy Hour</td><td colspan="2">Cannon</td><td colspan="2">Kojak</td></tr>
<tr><td>N</td><td colspan="2"></td><td>Adam 12</td><td colspan="3">NBC Wednesday Mystery Movie: Madigan/Tenafly/Faraday & Company/The Snoop Sisters</td><td colspan="2">Love Story</td></tr>
<tr><td rowspan="3">THURSDAY</td><td>A</td><td colspan="2"></td><td colspan="2">Toma</td><td colspan="2">Kung Fu</td><td colspan="2">Streets of San Francisco</td></tr>
<tr><td>C</td><td colspan="2"></td><td colspan="2">The Waltons</td><td colspan="4">CBS Thursday Night Movie</td></tr>
<tr><td>N</td><td colspan="2"></td><td colspan="2">Flip Wilson Show</td><td colspan="2">Ironside</td><td colspan="2">NBC Follies</td></tr>
<tr><td rowspan="3">FRIDAY</td><td>A</td><td colspan="2"></td><td>Brady Bunch</td><td>Odd Couple</td><td>Room 222</td><td>Adam's Rib</td><td colspan="2">Love, American Style</td></tr>
<tr><td>C</td><td colspan="2"></td><td>Calucci's Dept.</td><td>Roll Out</td><td colspan="4">CBS Friday Night Movie</td></tr>
<tr><td>N</td><td colspan="2"></td><td>Sanford & Son</td><td>The Girl with Something Extra</td><td>Needles & Pins</td><td>Brian Keith Show</td><td colspan="2">Dean Martin Show</td></tr>
<tr><td rowspan="3">SATURDAY</td><td>A</td><td colspan="2"></td><td>Partridge Family</td><td colspan="3">ABC Suspense Movie</td><td colspan="2">Griff</td></tr>
<tr><td>C</td><td colspan="2"></td><td>All in the Family</td><td>M*A*S*H</td><td>Mary Tyler Moore Show</td><td>Bob Newhart Show</td><td colspan="2">Carol Burnett Show</td></tr>
<tr><td>N</td><td colspan="2"></td><td colspan="2">Emergency</td><td colspan="4">NBC Saturday Night Movie</td></tr>
</table>

PRIME TIME SCHEDULE: FALL 1974

Day	Network	7:00 PM	7:30	8:00	8:30	9:00	9:30	10:00	10:30
SUNDAY	A			Sonny Comedy Revue		ABC Sunday Night Movie			
SUNDAY	C		Apple's Way		Kojak		Mannix		
SUNDAY	N		Wonderful World of Disney		NBC Sunday Mystery Movie: Columbo/McCloud/McMillian and Wife/Amy Prentiss				
MONDAY	A			Rookies		ABC Monday Night Football			
MONDAY	C			Gunsmoke		Maude	Rhoda	Medical Center	
MONDAY	N			Born Free		NBC Monday Night Movie			
TUESDAY	A			Happy Days	Tuesday Movie of the Week			Marcus Welby, M.D.	
TUESDAY	C			Good Times	M*A*S*H	Hawaii Five-O		Barnaby Jones	
TUESDAY	N			Adam 12	NBC World Premiere Movie			Police Story	
WEDNESDAY	A			That's My Mama	Wednesday Movie of the Week			Get Christie Love	
WEDNESDAY	C			Sons & Daughters		Cannon		Manhunter	
WEDNESDAY	N			Little House on the Prairie		Lucas Tanner		Petrocelli	
THURSDAY	A			Odd Couple	Paper Moon	Streets of San Francisco		Harry-O	
THURSDAY	C			The Waltons		CBS Thursday Night Movie			
THURSDAY	N			Sierra		Ironside		Movin' On	
FRIDAY	A			Kodiak	Six Million Dollar Man		Texas Wheelers	Kolchak: The Night Stalker	
FRIDAY	C			Planet of the Apes		CBS Friday Night Movie			
FRIDAY	N			Sanford & Son	Chico and the Man	Rockford Files		Police Woman	
SATURDAY	A			The New Land		Kung Fu		Nakia	
SATURDAY	C			All in the Family	Paul Sand in Friends and Lovers	Mary Tyler Moore Show	Bob Newhart Show	Carol Burnett Show	
SATURDAY	N			Emergency		NBC Saturday Night Movie			

PRIME TIME SCHEDULE: FALL 1975

<table>
<tr><th></th><th></th><th>7:00 PM</th><th>7:30</th><th>8:00</th><th>8:30</th><th>9:00</th><th>9:30</th><th>10:00</th><th>10:30</th><th>11:00</th></tr>
<tr><td rowspan="3">SUNDAY</td><td>A</td><td colspan="2">Swiss Family Robinson</td><td colspan="2">Six Million Dollar Man</td><td colspan="4">ABC Sunday Night Movie</td></tr>
<tr><td>C</td><td colspan="2">Three for the Road</td><td colspan="2">Cher</td><td colspan="2">Kojak</td><td colspan="2">Bronk</td></tr>
<tr><td>N</td><td colspan="2">Wonderful World of Disney</td><td colspan="2">Family Holvak</td><td colspan="4">NBC Sunday Mystery Movie:
Columbo/McCloud/McMillan and Wife/McCoy</td></tr>
<tr><td rowspan="3">MONDAY</td><td>A</td><td colspan="2"></td><td colspan="2">Barbary Coast</td><td colspan="4">ABC Monday Night Football</td></tr>
<tr><td>C</td><td colspan="2"></td><td>Rhoda</td><td>Phyllis</td><td>All in the Family</td><td>Maude</td><td colspan="2">Medical Center</td></tr>
<tr><td>N</td><td colspan="2"></td><td colspan="2">Invisible Man</td><td colspan="4">NBC Monday Night Movie</td></tr>
<tr><td rowspan="3">TUESDAY</td><td>A</td><td colspan="2"></td><td>Happy Days</td><td>Welcome Back, Kotter</td><td colspan="2">The Rookies</td><td colspan="2">Marcus Welby, M.D.</td></tr>
<tr><td>C</td><td colspan="2"></td><td>Good Times</td><td>Joe and Sons</td><td colspan="2">Switch</td><td colspan="2">Beacon Hill</td></tr>
<tr><td>N</td><td colspan="2"></td><td colspan="2">Movin' On</td><td colspan="2">Police Story</td><td colspan="2">Joe Forrester</td></tr>
<tr><td rowspan="3">WEDNESDAY</td><td>A</td><td colspan="2"></td><td>When Things Were Rotten</td><td>That's My Mama</td><td colspan="2">Baretta</td><td colspan="2">Starsky & Hutch</td></tr>
<tr><td>C</td><td colspan="2"></td><td colspan="2">Tony Orlando & Dawn</td><td colspan="2">Cannon</td><td colspan="2">Kate McShane</td></tr>
<tr><td>N</td><td colspan="2"></td><td colspan="2">Little House on the Prairie</td><td colspan="2">Doctors' Hospital</td><td colspan="2">Petrocelli</td></tr>
<tr><td rowspan="3">THURSDAY</td><td>A</td><td colspan="2"></td><td>Barney Miller</td><td>On the Rocks</td><td colspan="2">Streets of San Francisco</td><td colspan="2">Harry-O</td></tr>
<tr><td>C</td><td colspan="2"></td><td colspan="2">The Waltons</td><td colspan="4">CBS Thursday Night Movie</td></tr>
<tr><td>N</td><td colspan="2"></td><td>The Montefuscos</td><td>Fay</td><td colspan="2">Ellery Queen</td><td colspan="2">Medical Story</td></tr>
<tr><td rowspan="3">FRIDAY</td><td>A</td><td colspan="2"></td><td colspan="2">Mobile One</td><td colspan="4">ABC Friday Night Movie</td></tr>
<tr><td>C</td><td colspan="2"></td><td>Big Eddie</td><td>M*A*S*H</td><td colspan="2">Hawaii Five-O</td><td colspan="2">Barnaby Jones</td></tr>
<tr><td>N</td><td colspan="2"></td><td>Sanford & Son</td><td>Chico and the Man</td><td colspan="2">Rockford Files</td><td colspan="2">Police Woman</td></tr>
<tr><td rowspan="3">SATURDAY</td><td>A</td><td colspan="2"></td><td colspan="2">Saturday Night Live with Howard Cosell</td><td colspan="2">S.W.A.T.</td><td colspan="2">Matt Helm</td></tr>
<tr><td>C</td><td colspan="2"></td><td>The Jeffersons</td><td>Doc</td><td>Mary Tyler Moore Show</td><td>Bob Newhart Show</td><td colspan="2">Carol Burnett Show</td></tr>
<tr><td>N</td><td colspan="2"></td><td colspan="2">Emergency</td><td colspan="4">NBC Saturday Night Movie</td></tr>
</table>

PRIME TIME SCHEDULE: FALL 1976

<table>
<tr><th></th><th></th><th>7:00 PM</th><th>7:30</th><th>8:00</th><th>8:30</th><th>9:00</th><th>9:30</th><th>10:00</th><th>10:30</th><th>11:00</th></tr>
<tr><td rowspan="3">SUNDAY</td><td>A</td><td colspan="2">Cos</td><td colspan="2">Six Million Dollar Man</td><td colspan="4">ABC Sunday Night Movie</td></tr>
<tr><td>C</td><td colspan="2">60 Minutes</td><td colspan="2">Sonny & Cher Show</td><td colspan="2">Kojak</td><td colspan="2">Delvecchio</td></tr>
<tr><td>N</td><td colspan="2">Wonderful World of Disney</td><td colspan="3">NBC Sunday Mystery Movie: Columbo/McCloud/McMillan/Quincy, M.E.</td><td colspan="3">Big Event</td></tr>
<tr><td rowspan="3">MONDAY</td><td>A</td><td colspan="2"></td><td colspan="2">Captain and Tennille</td><td colspan="4">ABC Monday Night Football</td></tr>
<tr><td>C</td><td colspan="2"></td><td>Rhoda</td><td>Phyllis</td><td>Maude</td><td>All's Fair</td><td colspan="2">Executive Suite</td></tr>
<tr><td>N</td><td colspan="2"></td><td colspan="2">Little House on the Prairie</td><td colspan="4">NBC Monday Night Movie</td></tr>
<tr><td rowspan="3">TUESDAY</td><td>A</td><td colspan="2"></td><td>Happy Days</td><td>Laverne & Shirley</td><td colspan="2">Rich Man, Poor Man—Book II</td><td colspan="2">Family</td></tr>
<tr><td>C</td><td colspan="2"></td><td colspan="2">Tony Orlando & Dawn Rainbow Hour</td><td>M*A*S*H</td><td>One Day at a Time</td><td colspan="2">Switch</td></tr>
<tr><td>N</td><td colspan="2"></td><td colspan="2">Baa Baa Black Sheep</td><td colspan="2">Police Woman</td><td colspan="2">Police Story</td></tr>
<tr><td rowspan="3">WEDNESDAY</td><td>A</td><td colspan="2"></td><td colspan="2">Bionic Woman</td><td colspan="2">Baretta</td><td colspan="2">Charlie's Angels</td></tr>
<tr><td>C</td><td colspan="2"></td><td>Good Times</td><td>Ball Four</td><td>All in the Family</td><td>Alice</td><td colspan="2">Blue Knight</td></tr>
<tr><td>N</td><td colspan="2"></td><td>The Practice</td><td colspan="3">NBC Movie of the Week</td><td colspan="2">The Quest</td></tr>
<tr><td rowspan="3">THURSDAY</td><td>A</td><td colspan="2"></td><td>Welcome Back, Kotter</td><td>Barney Miller</td><td>Tony Randall Show</td><td>Nancy Walker Show</td><td colspan="2">Streets of San Francisco</td></tr>
<tr><td>C</td><td colspan="2"></td><td colspan="2">The Waltons</td><td colspan="2">Hawaii Five-O</td><td colspan="2">Barnaby Jones</td></tr>
<tr><td>N</td><td colspan="2"></td><td colspan="2">Gemini Man</td><td colspan="2">NBC's Best Sellers</td><td colspan="2">Van Dyke & Company</td></tr>
<tr><td rowspan="3">FRIDAY</td><td>A</td><td colspan="2"></td><td colspan="2">Donny & Marie</td><td colspan="4">ABC Friday Night Movie</td></tr>
<tr><td>C</td><td></td><td>Campaign '76</td><td colspan="2">Spencer's Pilots</td><td colspan="4">CBS Friday Night Movie</td></tr>
<tr><td>N</td><td colspan="2"></td><td>Sanford & Son</td><td>Chico and the Man</td><td colspan="2">Rockford Files</td><td colspan="2">Serpico</td></tr>
<tr><td rowspan="3">SATURDAY</td><td>A</td><td colspan="2"></td><td>Holmes & Yo-Yo</td><td>Mr. T and Tina</td><td colspan="2">Starsky & Hutch</td><td colspan="2">Most Wanted</td></tr>
<tr><td>C</td><td colspan="2"></td><td>The Jeffersons</td><td>Doc</td><td>Mary Tyler Moore Show</td><td>Bob Newhart Show</td><td colspan="2">Carol Burnett Show</td></tr>
<tr><td>N</td><td colspan="2"></td><td colspan="2">Emergency</td><td colspan="4">NBC Saturday Night Movie</td></tr>
</table>

PRIME TIME SCHEDULE: FALL 1977

		7:00 PM	7:30	8:00	8:30	9:00	9:30	10:00	10:30	11:00
SUNDAY	A	Hardy Boys Mysteries/ Nancy Drew Mysteries		Six Million Dollar Man		ABC Sunday Movie				
	C	60 Minutes		Rhoda	On Our Own	All in the Family	Alice	Kojak		
	N	Wonderful World of Disney				Big Event				
MONDAY	A			San Pedro Beach Bums		Monday Night Football				
	C			Young Dan'l Boone		Betty White Show	Maude	Rafferty		
	N			Little House on the Prairie		NBC Monday Movie				
TUESDAY	A			Happy Days	Laverne & Shirley	Three's Company	Soap	Family		
	C			The Fitzpatricks		M*A*S*H	One Day at a Time	Lou Grant		
	N			Richard Pryor Show		Mulligan's Stew		Police Woman		
WEDNESDAY	A			Eight Is Enough		Charlie's Angels		Baretta		
	C			Good Times	Busting Loose	CBS Wednesday Movie				
	N			Life and Times of Grizzly Adams		Oregon Trail		Big Hawaii		
THURSDAY	A			Welcome Back, Kotter	What's Happening	Barney Miller	Carter Country	Redd Foxx Show		
	C			The Waltons		Hawaii Five-O		Barnaby Jones		
	N			CHiPS		Man from Atlantis		Rosetti and Ryan		
FRIDAY	A			Donny and Marie		ABC Friday Movie				
	C			New Adventures of Wonder Woman		Logan's Run		Switch		
	N			Sanford Arms	Chico and the Man	Rockford Files		Quincy, M.E.		
SATURDAY	A			Fish	Operation Petticoat	Starsky and Hutch		Love Boat		
	C			Bob Newhart Show	We've Got Each Other	The Jeffersons	Tony Randall Show	Carol Burnett Show		
	N			Bionic Woman		NBC Saturday Movie				

PRIME TIME SCHEDULE: FALL 1978

Day	Network	7:00 PM	7:30	8:00	8:30	9:00	9:30	10:00	10:30
SUNDAY	A	Hardy Boys Mysteries		Battlestar Galactica		ABC Sunday Movie			
SUNDAY	C	60 Minutes		Mary		All in the Family	Alice	Kaz	
SUNDAY	N	Wonderful World of Disney		Big Event				Lifeline	
MONDAY	A			Welcome Back, Kotter	Operation Petticoat	Monday Night Football			
MONDAY	C			WKRP in Cincinnati	People	M*A*S*H	One Day at a Time	Lou Grant	
MONDAY	N			Little House on the Prairie		NBC Monday Movie			
TUESDAY	A			Happy Days	Laverne & Shirley	Three's Company	Taxi	Starsky and Hutch	
TUESDAY	C			Paper Chase		CBS Tuesday Movie			
TUESDAY	N			Grandpa Goes to Washington		Big Event			
WEDNESDAY	A			Eight Is Enough		Charlie's Angels		Vega$	
WEDNESDAY	C			The Jeffersons	In the Beginning	CBS Wednesday Movie			
WEDNESDAY	N			Dick Clark's Live Wednesday		NBC Wednesday Movie			
THURSDAY	A			Mork & Mindy	What's Happening	Barney Miller	Soap	Family	
THURSDAY	C			The Waltons		Hawaii Five-O		Barnaby Jones	
THURSDAY	N			Project U.F.O.		Quincy, M.E.		W.E.B.	
FRIDAY	A			Donny and Marie		ABC Friday Movie			
FRIDAY	C			New Adventures of Wonder Woman		Incredible Hulk		Flying High	
FRIDAY	N			Waverly Wonders	Who's Watching the Kids	Rockford Files		Eddie Capra Mysteries	
SATURDAY	A			Carter Country	Apple Pie	Love Boat		Fantasy Island	
SATURDAY	C			Rhoda	Good Times	American Girls		Dallas	
SATURDAY	N			CHiPS		Specials		Sword of Justice	

PRIME TIME SCHEDULE: FALL 1979

<table>
<tr><th></th><th></th><th>7:00 PM</th><th>7:30</th><th>8:00</th><th>8:30</th><th>9:00</th><th>9:30</th><th>10:00</th><th>10:30</th><th>11:00</th></tr>
<tr><td rowspan="3">SUNDAY</td><td>A</td><td>Out of the Blue</td><td>A New Kind of Family</td><td>Mork & Mindy</td><td>The Associates</td><td colspan="4">ABC Sunday Movie</td><td></td></tr>
<tr><td>C</td><td colspan="2">60 Minutes</td><td>Archie Bunker's Place</td><td>One Day at a Time</td><td>Alice</td><td>The Jeffersons</td><td colspan="2">Trapper John, M.D.</td><td></td></tr>
<tr><td>N</td><td colspan="2">Disney's Wonderful World</td><td colspan="4">The Big Event</td><td colspan="2">Prime Time Sunday</td><td></td></tr>
<tr><td rowspan="3">MONDAY</td><td>A</td><td colspan="2"></td><td colspan="2">240-Robert</td><td colspan="4">Monday Night Football</td><td></td></tr>
<tr><td>C</td><td colspan="2"></td><td colspan="2">White Shadow</td><td>M*A*S*H</td><td>WKRP in Cincinnati</td><td colspan="2">Lou Grant</td><td></td></tr>
<tr><td>N</td><td colspan="2"></td><td colspan="2">Little House on the Prairie</td><td colspan="4">NBC Monday Movie</td><td></td></tr>
<tr><td rowspan="3">TUESDAY</td><td>A</td><td colspan="2"></td><td>Happy Days</td><td>Angie</td><td>Three's Company</td><td>Taxi</td><td colspan="2">Lazarus Syndrome</td><td></td></tr>
<tr><td>C</td><td colspan="2"></td><td colspan="2">California Fever</td><td colspan="4">CBS Tuesday Movie</td><td></td></tr>
<tr><td>N</td><td colspan="2"></td><td colspan="2">Misadventures of Sheriff Lobo</td><td colspan="4">NBC Tuesday Movie</td><td></td></tr>
<tr><td rowspan="3">WEDNESDAY</td><td>A</td><td colspan="2"></td><td colspan="2">Eight Is Enough</td><td colspan="2">Charlie's Angels</td><td colspan="2">Vega$</td><td></td></tr>
<tr><td>C</td><td colspan="2"></td><td>Last Resort</td><td>Struck by Lightning</td><td colspan="4">CBS Wednesday Movie</td><td></td></tr>
<tr><td>N</td><td colspan="2"></td><td colspan="2">Real People</td><td>Diff'rent Strokes</td><td>Hello Larry</td><td colspan="2">Best of Saturday Night Live</td><td></td></tr>
<tr><td rowspan="3">THURSDAY</td><td>A</td><td colspan="2"></td><td>Laverne & Shirley</td><td>Benson</td><td>Barney Miller</td><td>Soap</td><td colspan="2">20/20</td><td></td></tr>
<tr><td>C</td><td colspan="2"></td><td colspan="2">The Waltons</td><td colspan="2">Hawaii Five-O</td><td colspan="2">Barnaby Jones</td><td></td></tr>
<tr><td>N</td><td colspan="2"></td><td colspan="2">Buck Rogers in the 25th Century</td><td colspan="2">Quincy, M.E.</td><td colspan="2">Kate Loves a Mystery</td><td></td></tr>
<tr><td rowspan="3">FRIDAY</td><td>A</td><td colspan="2"></td><td colspan="2">Fantasy Island</td><td colspan="4">ABC Friday Movie</td><td></td></tr>
<tr><td>C</td><td colspan="2"></td><td colspan="2">Incredible Hulk</td><td colspan="2">Dukes of Hazzard</td><td colspan="2">Dallas</td><td></td></tr>
<tr><td>N</td><td colspan="2"></td><td colspan="2">Shirley</td><td colspan="2">Rockford Files</td><td colspan="2">Eischied</td><td></td></tr>
<tr><td rowspan="3">SATURDAY</td><td>A</td><td colspan="2"></td><td>The Ropers</td><td>Detective School</td><td colspan="2">Love Boat</td><td colspan="2">Hart to Hart</td><td></td></tr>
<tr><td>C</td><td colspan="2"></td><td>Working Stiffs</td><td>Bad News Bears</td><td colspan="2">Big Shamus, Little Shamus</td><td colspan="2">Paris</td><td></td></tr>
<tr><td>N</td><td colspan="2"></td><td colspan="2">CHiPS</td><td colspan="2">B.J. and the Bear</td><td colspan="2">A Man Called Sloane</td><td></td></tr>
</table>

PRIME TIME SCHEDULE: FALL 1980*

		7:00 PM	7:30	8:00	8:30	9:00	9:30	10:00	10:30	11:00
SUNDAY	A	Those Amazing Animals		Charlie's Angels		ABC Sunday Movie				
	C	60 Minutes		Archie Bunker's Place	One Day at a Time	Alice	The Jeffersons	Trapper John, M.D.		
	N	Disney's Wonderful World		CHiPS		The Big Event				
MONDAY	A			That's Incredible		Monday Night Football				
	C			Flo	Ladies' Man	M*A*S*H	House Calls	Lou Grant		
	N			Little House on the Prairie		NBC Monday Movie				
TUESDAY	A			Happy Days	Laverne & Shirley	Three's Company	Too Close For Comfort	Hart to Hart		
	C			White Shadow		CBS Tuesday Movie				
	N			Lobo		B.J. and the Bear		Steve Allen Comedy Hour		
WEDNESDAY	A			Eight Is Enough		Taxi	Soap	Vega$		
	C			Enos		CBS Wednesday Movie				
	N			Real People		Diff'rent Strokes	Facts of Life	Quincy, M.E.		
THURSDAY	A			Mork & Mindy	Bosom Buddies	Barney Miller	It's a Living	20/20		
	C			The Waltons		Magnum, P.I.		Knots Landing		
	N			Games People Play		NBC Thursday Movie				
FRIDAY	A			Benson	I'm a Big Girl Now	ABC Friday Movie				
	C			Incredible Hulk		Dukes of Hazzard		Dallas		
	N			Marie		Speak Up America		NBC Magazine with David Brinkley		
SATURDAY	A			Breaking Away		Love Boat		Fantasy Island		
	C			WKRP in Cincinnati	Tim Conway Show	Freebie and the Bean		Secrets of Midland Heights		
	N			Barbara Mandrell & the Mandrell Sisters		Walking Tall		Hill Street Blues		

*An actors' strike delayed the start of the 1980–1981 season for many programs. The shows indicated in this schedule represent the first series with new episodes to appear in each time period. Some of them premiered in September but others may not have started until January 1981.

PRIME TIME SCHEDULE: FALL 1981*

Day	Net	7:00 PM	7:30	8:00	8:30	9:00	9:30	10:00	10:30
SUNDAY	A	Code Red		Today's F.B.I.		ABC Sunday Movie			
	C	60 Minutes		Archie Bunker's Place	One Day at a Time	Alice	The Jeffersons	Trapper John, M.D.	
	N	Specials	Here's Boomer	CHiPS		NBC Sunday Movie			
MONDAY	A			That's Incredible		Monday Night Football			
	C			Pvt. Benjamin	Two of Us	M*A*S*H	House Calls	Lou Grant	
	N			Little House on the Prairie		NBC Monday Movie			
TUESDAY	A			Happy Days	Laverne & Shirley	Three's Company	Too Close for Comfort	Hart to Hart	
	C			Simon & Simon		CBS Tuesday Movie			
	N			Father Murphy		Bret Maverick		Flamingo Road	
WEDNESDAY	A			Greatest American Hero		Fall Guy		Dynasty	
	C			Mr. Merlin	WKRP in Cincinnati	Nurse		Shannon	
	N			Real People		Facts of Life	Love, Sidney	Quincy, M.E.	
THURSDAY	A			Mork & Mindy	Best of the West	Barney Miller	Taxi	20/20	
	C			Magnum, P.I.		Knots Landing		Jessica Novak	
	N			Harper Valley	Lewis & Clark	Diff'rent Strokes	Gimme a Break	Hill Street Blues	
FRIDAY	A			Benson	Bosom Buddies	Darkroom		Strike Force	
	C			Incredible Hulk		Dukes of Hazzard		Dallas	
	N			NBC Magazine		McClain's Law		Specials	
SATURDAY	A			Maggie	Making a Living	Love Boat		Fantasy Island	
	C			Walt Disney		CBS Saturday Movie			
	N			Barbara Mandrell and The Mandrell Sisters		Nashville Palace		Fitz and Bones	

*A writers' strike delayed the start of the 1981–1982 season for many programs. The shows indicated in this schedule represent the first series with new episodes to appear in each time period. Some of them premiered in September but others may not have started until several months later.

PRIME TIME SCHEDULE: FALL 1982

<table>
<tr><th></th><th></th><th>7:00 PM</th><th>7:30</th><th>8:00</th><th>8:30</th><th>9:00</th><th>9:30</th><th>10:00</th><th>10:30   11:00</th></tr>
<tr><td rowspan="3">SUNDAY</td><td>A</td><td colspan="2">Ripley's Believe It or Not</td><td colspan="2">Matt Houston</td><td colspan="4">ABC Sunday Movie</td></tr>
<tr><td>C</td><td colspan="2">60 Minutes</td><td>Archie Bunker's Place</td><td>Gloria</td><td>The Jeffersons</td><td>One Day at a Time</td><td colspan="2">Trapper John, M.D.</td></tr>
<tr><td>N</td><td colspan="2">Voyagers</td><td colspan="2">CHiPS</td><td colspan="4">NBC Sunday Movie</td></tr>
<tr><td rowspan="3">MONDAY</td><td>A</td><td colspan="2"></td><td colspan="2">That's Incredible</td><td colspan="4">Monday Night Football</td></tr>
<tr><td>C</td><td colspan="2"></td><td>Square Pegs</td><td>Pvt. Benjamin</td><td>M*A*S*H</td><td>Newhart</td><td colspan="2">Cagney & Lacey</td></tr>
<tr><td>N</td><td colspan="2"></td><td colspan="2">Little House: A New Beginning</td><td colspan="4">NBC Monday Movie</td></tr>
<tr><td rowspan="3">TUESDAY</td><td>A</td><td colspan="2"></td><td>Happy Days</td><td>Laverne & Shirley</td><td>Three's Company</td><td>9 to 5</td><td colspan="2">Hart to Hart</td></tr>
<tr><td>C</td><td colspan="2"></td><td colspan="2">Bring 'Em Back Alive</td><td colspan="4">CBS Tuesday Movie</td></tr>
<tr><td>N</td><td colspan="2"></td><td colspan="2">Father Murphy</td><td colspan="2">Gavilan</td><td colspan="2">St. Elsewhere</td></tr>
<tr><td rowspan="3">WEDNESDAY</td><td>A</td><td colspan="2"></td><td colspan="2">Tales of the Gold Monkey</td><td colspan="2">Fall Guy</td><td colspan="2">Dynasty</td></tr>
<tr><td>C</td><td colspan="2"></td><td colspan="2">Seven Brides for Seven Brothers</td><td>Alice</td><td>Filthy Rich</td><td colspan="2">Tucker's Witch</td></tr>
<tr><td>N</td><td colspan="2"></td><td colspan="2">Real People</td><td>Facts of Life</td><td>Family Ties</td><td colspan="2">Quincy, M.E.</td></tr>
<tr><td rowspan="3">THURSDAY</td><td>A</td><td colspan="2"></td><td>Joanie Loves Chachi</td><td>Star of the Family</td><td>Too Close for Comfort</td><td>It Takes Two</td><td colspan="2">20/20</td></tr>
<tr><td>C</td><td colspan="2"></td><td colspan="2">Magnum, P.I.</td><td colspan="2">Simon & Simon</td><td colspan="2">Knots Landing</td></tr>
<tr><td>N</td><td colspan="2"></td><td colspan="2">Fame</td><td>Cheers</td><td>Taxi</td><td colspan="2">Hill Street Blues</td></tr>
<tr><td rowspan="3">FRIDAY</td><td>A</td><td colspan="2"></td><td>Benson</td><td>New Odd Couple</td><td colspan="2">Greatest American Hero</td><td colspan="2">The Quest</td></tr>
<tr><td>C</td><td colspan="2"></td><td colspan="2">Dukes of Hazzard</td><td colspan="2">Dallas</td><td colspan="2">Falcon Crest</td></tr>
<tr><td>N</td><td colspan="2"></td><td colspan="2">Powers of Matthew Star</td><td colspan="2">Knight Rider</td><td colspan="2">Remington Steele</td></tr>
<tr><td rowspan="3">SATURDAY</td><td>A</td><td colspan="2"></td><td colspan="2">T. J. Hooker</td><td colspan="2">Love Boat</td><td colspan="2">Fantasy Island</td></tr>
<tr><td>C</td><td colspan="2"></td><td colspan="2">Walt Disney</td><td colspan="4">CBS Saturday Movie</td></tr>
<tr><td>N</td><td colspan="2"></td><td>Diff'rent Strokes</td><td>Silver Spoons</td><td>Gimme a Break</td><td>Love, Sidney</td><td colspan="2">Devlin Connection</td></tr>
</table>

PRIME TIME SCHEDULE: FALL 1983

		7:00 PM	7:30	8:00	8:30	9:00	9:30	10:00	10:30	11:00
SUNDAY	A	Ripley's Believe It or Not		Hardcastle & McCormick		ABC Sunday Movie				
	C	60 Minutes		Alice	One Day at a Time	The Jeffersons	Goodnight, Beantown	Trapper John, M.D.		
	N	First Camera		Knight Rider		NBC Sunday Movie				
MONDAY	A			That's Incredible		Monday Night Football				
	C			Scarecrow & Mrs. King		AfterMASH	Newhart	Emerald Point N.A.S.		
	N			Boone		NBC Monday Movie				
TUESDAY	A			Just Our Luck	Happy Days	Three's Company	Oh, Madeline	Hart to Hart		
	C			The Mississippi		CBS Tuesday Movie				
	N			The A-Team		Remington Steele		Bay City Blues		
WEDNESDAY	A			Fall Guy		Dynasty		Hotel		
	C			Whiz Kids		CBS Wednesday Movie				
	N			Real People		Facts of Life	Family Ties	St. Elsewhere		
THURSDAY	A			Trauma Center		9 to 5	It's Not Easy	20/20		
	C			Magnum, P.I.		Simon & Simon		Knots Landing		
	N			Gimme a Break	Mama's Family	We Got it Made	Cheers	Hill Street Blues		
FRIDAY	A			Benson	Webster	Lottery		Matt Houston		
	C			Dukes of Hazzard		Dallas		Falcon Crest		
	N			Mr. Smith	Jennifer Slept Here	Manimal		For Love and Honor		
SATURDAY	A			T.J. Hooker		Love Boat		Fantasy Island		
	C			Cutter to Houston		CBS Saturday Movie				
	N			Diff'rent Strokes	Silver Spoons	The Rousters		Yellow Rose		

PRIME TIME SCHEDULE: FALL 1984

Day	Network	7:00 PM	7:30	8:00	8:30	9:00	9:30	10:00	10:30	11:00
SUNDAY	A	Ripley's Believe It or Not		Hardcastle & McCormick		ABC Sunday Night Movie				
SUNDAY	C	60 Minutes		Murder, She Wrote		The Jeffersons	Alice	Trapper John, M.D.		
SUNDAY	N	Silver Spoons	Punky Brewster	Knight Rider		NBC Sunday Movie				
MONDAY	A			Call to Glory		Monday Night Football				
MONDAY	C			Scarecrow & Mrs. King		Kate & Allie	Newhart	Cagney & Lacey		
MONDAY	N			TV's Bloopers & Practical Jokes		NBC Monday Movie				
TUESDAY	A			Foul-Ups, Bleeps & Blunders	Three's a Crowd	Paper Dolls		Jessie		
TUESDAY	C			AfterMASH	E/R	CBS Tuesday Movie				
TUESDAY	N			The A-Team		Riptide		Remington Steele		
WEDNESDAY	A			Fall Guy		Dynasty		Hotel		
WEDNESDAY	C			Charles in Charge	Dreams	CBS Wednesday Movie				
WEDNESDAY	N			Highway to Heaven		Facts of Life	It's Your Move	St. Elsewhere		
THURSDAY	A			People Do the Craziest Things	Who's the Boss?	Glitter		20/20		
THURSDAY	C			Magnum P.I.		Simon & Simon		Knots Landing		
THURSDAY	N			Cosby Show	Family Ties	Cheers	Night Court	Hill Street Blues		
FRIDAY	A			Benson	Webster	Hawaiian Heat		Matt Houston		
FRIDAY	C			Dukes of Hazzard		Dallas		Falcon Crest		
FRIDAY	N			V		Hunter		Miami Vice		
SATURDAY	A			T.J. Hooker		Love Boat		Finder of Lost Loves		
SATURDAY	C			Airwolf		Mickey Spillane's Mike Hammer		Cover Up		
SATURDAY	N			Diff'rent Strokes	Gimme a Break	Partners in Crime		Hot Pursuit		

PRIME TIME SCHEDULE: FALL 1985

		7:00 PM	7:30	8:00	8:30	9:00	9:30	10:00	10:30	11:00
SUNDAY	A	Ripley's Believe It or Not		MacGyver		ABC Sunday Movie				
	C	60 Minutes		Murder, She Wrote		Crazy Like a Fox		Trapper John, M.D.		
	N	Punky Brewster	Silver Spoons	Amazing Stories	Alfred Hitchcock Presents	NBC Sunday Movie				
MONDAY	A			Hardcastle & McCormick		Monday Night Football				
	C			Scarecrow & Mrs. King		Kate & Allie	Newhart	Cagney & Lacey		
	N			TV's Bloopers & Practical Jokes		NBC Monday Movie				
TUESDAY	A			Who's the Boss?	Growing Pains	Moonlighting		Our Family Honor		
	C			Hometown		CBS Tuesday Movie				
	N			The A-Team		Riptide		Remington Steele		
WEDNESDAY	A			Insiders		Dynasty		Hotel		
	C			Stir Crazy		Charlie & Company	George Burns Comedy Week	The Equalizer		
	N			Highway to Heaven		Helltown		St. Elsewhere		
THURSDAY	A			Fall Guy		Lady Blue		20/20		
	C			Magnum, P.I.		Simon & Simon		Knots Landing		
	N			Cosby Show	Family Ties	Cheers	Night Court	Hill Street Blues		
FRIDAY	A			Webster	Mr. Belvedere	Diff'rent Strokes	Benson	Spenser: For Hire		
	C			Twilight Zone		Dallas		Falcon Crest		
	N			Knight Rider		Misfits of Science		Miami Vice		
SATURDAY	A			Hollywood Beat		Lime Street		Love Boat		
	C			Airwolf		CBS Saturday Movie				
	N			Gimme A Break	Facts of Life	Golden Girls	227	Hunter		

PRIME TIME SCHEDULE: FALL 1986

		7:00 PM	7:30	8:00	8:30	9:00	9:30	10:00	10:30	11:00
SUNDAY	A	Disney Sunday Movie				ABC Sunday Movie				
	C	60 Minutes		Murder, She Wrote		CBS Sunday Movie				
	N	Our House		Easy Street	Valerie	NBC Sunday Movie				
MONDAY	A			MacGyver		Monday Night Football				
	C			Kate & Allie	My Sister Sam	Newhart	Designing Women	Cagney & Lacey		
	N			Alf	Amazing Stories	NBC Monday Movie				
TUESDAY	A			Who's the Boss?	Growing Pains	Moonlighting		Jack and Mike		
	C			The Wizard		CBS Tuesday Movie				
	N			Matlock		Crime Story		1986		
WEDNESDAY	A			Perfect Strangers	Head of the Class	Dynasty		Hotel		
	C			Together We Stand	Better Days	Magnum, P.I.		The Equalizer		
	N			Highway to Heaven		Gimme a Break	You Again	St. Elsewhere		
THURSDAY	A			Our World		The Colbys		20/20		
	C			Simon & Simon		Knots Landing		Kay O'Brien		
	N			Cosby Show	Family Ties	Cheers	Night Court	Hill Street Blues		
FRIDAY	A			Webster	Mr. Belvedere	Sidekicks	Sledge Hammer	Starman		
	C			Scarecrow & Mrs. King		Dallas		Falcon Crest		
	N			The A-Team		Miami Vice		L. A. Law		
SATURDAY	A			Life with Lucy	Ellen Burstyn Show	Heart of the City		Spenser: For Hire		
	C			Downtown		New Mike Hammer		Twilight Zone		
	N			Facts of Life	227	Golden Girls	Amen	Hunter		

PRIME TIME SCHEDULE: FALL 1987

		7:00 PM	7:30	8:00	8:30	9:00	9:30	10:00	10:30	11:00
SUNDAY	A	Disney Sunday Movie		Spenser: For Hire		Dolly		Buck James		
	C	60 Minutes		Murder, She Wrote		CBS Sunday Movie				
	F	21 Jump Street		Werewolf	Married with Children	Tracey Ullman	Duet			
	N	Our House		Family Ties	My Two Dads	NBC Sunday Movie				
MONDAY	A			MacGyver		Monday Night Football				
	C			Frank's Place	Kate & Allie	Newhart	Designing Women	Cagney & Lacey		
	N			Alf	Valerie's Family	NBC Monday Movie				
TUESDAY	A			Who's the Boss?	Growing Pains	Moonlighting		Thirtysomething		
	C			Houston Knights		Jake and the Fatman		Law and Harry McGraw		
	N			Matlock		J. J. Starbuck		Crime Story		
WEDNESDAY	A			Perfect Strangers	Head of the Class	Hooperman	Slap Maxwell Story	Dynasty		
	C			Oldest Rookie		Magnum, P.I.		The Equalizer		
	N			Highway to Heaven		A Year in the Life		St. Elsewhere		
THURSDAY	A			Sledge Hammer	The Charmings	ABC Thursday Movie				
	C			Tour of Duty		Wiseguy		Knots Landing		
	N			Cosby Show	A Different World	Cheers	Night Court	L. A. Law		
FRIDAY	A			Full House	I Married Dora	Max Headroom		20/20		
	C			Beauty and the Beast		Dallas		Falcon Crest		
	N			Rags to Riches		Miami Vice		Private Eye		
SATURDAY	A			Once a Hero		Ohara		Hotel		
	C			My Sister Sam	Everything's Relative	Leg Work		West 57th		
	F			Mr. President	Women in Prison	New Adventures of Beans Baxter	Second Chance			
	N			Facts of Life	227	Golden Girls	Amen	Hunter		

PRIME TIME SCHEDULE: FALL 1988*

		7:00 PM	7:30	8:00	8:30	9:00	9:30	10:00	10:30
SUNDAY	A	Incredible Sunday		Mission: Impossible		ABC Sunday Movie			
	C	60 Minutes		Murder, She Wrote		CBS Sunday Movie			
	F	21 Jump Street		America's Most Wanted	Married with Children	It's Garry Shandling's Show	Tracey Ullman	Duet	
	N	Magical World of Disney		Family Ties	Day by Day	NBC Sunday Movie			
MONDAY	A			MacGyver		Monday Night Football			
	C			Newhart	Coming of Age	CBS Monday Movie			
	N			Alf	Hogan Family	NBC Monday Movie			
TUESDAY	A			Who's the Boss?	Roseanne	Moonlighting		Thirtysomething	
	C			High Risk		CBS Tuesday Movie			
	N			Matlock		In the Heat of the Night		Midnight Caller	
WEDNESDAY	A			Growing Pains	Head of the Class	Wonder Years	Hooperman	China Beach	
	C			Van Dyke Show	Annie McGuire	The Equalizer		Wiseguy	
	N			Unsolved Mysteries		Night Court	Baby Boom	Tattingers	
THURSDAY	A			Knightwatch		Dynasty		Specials	
	C			48 Hours		Paradise		Knots Landing	
	N			Cosby Show	A Different World	Cheers	Dear John	L. A. Law	
FRIDAY	A			Perfect Strangers	Full House	Mr. Belvedere	Just the Ten of Us	20/20	
	C			Beauty and the Beast		Dallas		Falcon Crest	
	N			Sonny Spoon		Something Is Out There		Miami Vice	
SATURDAY	A			Murphy's Law		Police Story			
	C			Dirty Dancing	Raising Miranda	Simon & Simon		West 57th	
	F			The Reporters		Beyond Tomorrow			
	N			227	Amen	Golden Girls	Empty Nest	Hunter	

*A writer's strike delayed the start of the 1988–1989 season for many programs. Most did not premiere until mid October or later, with some delayed until late November.

PRIME TIME SCHEDULE: FALL 1989

<table>
<tr><th></th><th></th><th>7:00 PM</th><th>7:30</th><th>8:00</th><th>8:30</th><th>9:00</th><th>9:30</th><th>10:00</th><th>10:30</th><th>11:00</th></tr>
<tr><td rowspan="4">SUNDAY</td><td>A</td><td colspan="2">Life Goes On</td><td>Free Spirit</td><td>Homeroom</td><td colspan="4">ABC Sunday Movie</td></tr>
<tr><td>C</td><td colspan="2">60 Minutes</td><td colspan="2">Murder, She Wrote</td><td colspan="4">CBS Sunday Movie</td></tr>
<tr><td>F</td><td colspan="2">Booker</td><td>America's Most Wanted</td><td>Totally Hidden Video</td><td>Married with Children</td><td>Open House</td><td>Tracey Ullman</td><td>It's Garry Shandling's Show</td></tr>
<tr><td>N</td><td colspan="2">Magical World of Disney</td><td>Sister Kate</td><td>My Two Dads</td><td colspan="4">NBC Sunday Movie</td></tr>
<tr><td rowspan="4">MONDAY</td><td>A</td><td colspan="2"></td><td colspan="2">MacGyver</td><td colspan="4">Monday Night Football</td></tr>
<tr><td>C</td><td colspan="2"></td><td>Major Dad</td><td>People Next Door</td><td>Murphy Brown</td><td>Famous Teddy Z</td><td>Designing Women</td><td>Newhart</td></tr>
<tr><td>F</td><td colspan="2"></td><td colspan="2">21 Jump Street</td><td colspan="2">Alien Nation</td><td colspan="2"></td></tr>
<tr><td>N</td><td colspan="2"></td><td>Alf</td><td>Hogan Family</td><td colspan="4">NBC Monday Movie</td></tr>
<tr><td rowspan="3">TUESDAY</td><td>A</td><td colspan="2"></td><td>Who's the Boss?</td><td>Wonder Years</td><td>Roseanne</td><td>Chicken Soup</td><td colspan="2">Thirtysomething</td></tr>
<tr><td>C</td><td colspan="2"></td><td colspan="2">Rescue 911</td><td colspan="2">Wolf</td><td colspan="2">Island Son</td></tr>
<tr><td>N</td><td colspan="2"></td><td colspan="2">Matlock</td><td colspan="2">In the Heat of the Night</td><td colspan="2">Midnight Caller</td></tr>
<tr><td rowspan="3">WEDNESDAY</td><td>A</td><td colspan="2"></td><td>Growing Pains</td><td>Head of the Class</td><td>Doogie Howser, M.D.</td><td>Anything but Love</td><td colspan="2">China Beach</td></tr>
<tr><td>C</td><td colspan="2"></td><td colspan="2">Peaceable Kingdom</td><td colspan="2">Jake and the Fatman</td><td colspan="2">Wiseguy</td></tr>
<tr><td>N</td><td colspan="2"></td><td colspan="2">Unsolved Mysteries</td><td>Night Court</td><td>Nutt House</td><td colspan="2">Quantum Leap</td></tr>
<tr><td rowspan="3">THURSDAY</td><td>A</td><td colspan="2"></td><td colspan="2">Mission: Impossible</td><td colspan="2">Young Riders</td><td colspan="2">Primetime Live</td></tr>
<tr><td>C</td><td colspan="2"></td><td colspan="2">48 Hours</td><td colspan="2">Top of the Hill</td><td colspan="2">Knots Landing</td></tr>
<tr><td>N</td><td colspan="2"></td><td>Cosby Show</td><td>A Different World</td><td>Cheers</td><td>Dear John</td><td colspan="2">L. A. Law</td></tr>
<tr><td rowspan="3">FRIDAY</td><td>A</td><td colspan="2"></td><td>Full House</td><td>Family Matters</td><td>Perfect Strangers</td><td>Just the Ten of Us</td><td colspan="2">20/20</td></tr>
<tr><td>C</td><td colspan="2"></td><td colspan="2">Snoops</td><td colspan="2">Dallas</td><td colspan="2">Falcon Crest</td></tr>
<tr><td>N</td><td colspan="2"></td><td colspan="2">Baywatch</td><td colspan="2">Hardball</td><td colspan="2">Mancuso, F.B.I.</td></tr>
<tr><td rowspan="4">SATURDAY</td><td>A</td><td colspan="2"></td><td>Mr. Belvedere</td><td>Living Dolls</td><td colspan="4">ABC Saturday Mystery*</td></tr>
<tr><td>C</td><td colspan="2"></td><td colspan="2">Paradise</td><td colspan="2">Tour of Duty</td><td colspan="2">Saturday Night With Connie Chung</td></tr>
<tr><td>F</td><td colspan="2"></td><td>Cops</td><td colspan="2">The Reporters</td><td>Beyond Tomorrow</td><td colspan="2"></td></tr>
<tr><td>N</td><td colspan="2"></td><td>227</td><td>Amen</td><td>Golden Girls</td><td>Empty Nest</td><td colspan="2">Hunter</td></tr>
</table>

*B.L. Stryker; Columbo; Kojak; Christine Cromwell

PRIME TIME SCHEDULE: FALL 1990

		7:00 PM	7:30	8:00	8:30	9:00	9:30	10:00	10:30	11:00
SUNDAY	A	Life Goes On		America's Funniest Home Videos	America's Funniest People	ABC Sunday Movie				
	C	60 Minutes		Murder, She Wrote		CBS Sunday Movie				
	F	True Colors	Parker Lewis Can't Lose	In Living Color	Get A Life	Married with Children	Good Grief	Against the Law		
	N	Hull High		Lifestories		NBC Sunday Movie				
MONDAY	A			MacGyver		Monday Night Football				
	C			Uncle Buck	Major Dad	Murphy Brown	Designing Women	Trials of Rosie O'Neill		
	F			Fox Night at the Movies						
	N			Fresh Prince of Bel Air	Ferris Bueller	NBC Monday Movie				
TUESDAY	A			Who's the Boss?	Head of the Class	Roseanne	Coach	Thirtysomething		
	C			Rescue 911		CBS Tuesday Movie				
	N			Matlock		In the Heat of the Night		Law & Order		
WEDNESDAY	A			Wonder Years	Growing Pains	Doogie Howser, M.D.	Married People	Cop Rock		
	C			Lenny	Doctor, Doctor	Jake and the Fatman		WIOU		
	N			Unsolved Mysteries		Fanelli Boys	Dear John	Hunter		
THURSDAY	A			Father Dowling Mysteries		Gabriel's Fire		Primetime Live		
	C			Top Cops	The Flash		Doctor, Doctor	Knots Landing		
	F			The Simpsons	Babes	Beverly Hills 90210				
	N			Cosby Show	A Different World	Cheers	Grand	L. A. Law		
FRIDAY	A			Full House	Family Matters	Perfect Strangers	Going Places	20/20		
	C			Evening Shade	Bagdad Cafe	Over My Dead Body		Dallas		
	F			America's Most Wanted		D.E.A.				
	N			Quantum Leap		Night Court	Wings	Midnight Caller		
SATURDAY	A			Young Riders		China Beach		Twin Peaks		
	C			Family Man	Hogan Family	E.A.R.T.H.Force		48 Hours		
	F			Totally Hidden Video	Haywire	Cops	American Chronicles			
	N			Parenthood	Working It Out	Golden Girls	Empty Nest	Carol & Company	American Dreamer	

PRIME TIME SCHEDULE: FALL 1991

Day	Network	7:00 PM	7:30	8:00	8:30	9:00	9:30	10:00	10:30	11:00
SUNDAY	A	Life Goes On		America's Funniest Home Videos	America's Funniest People	ABC Sunday Movie				
SUNDAY	C	60 Minutes		Murder, She Wrote		CBS Sunday Movie				
SUNDAY	F	True Colors	Parker Lewis Can't Lose	In Living Color	ROC	Married with Children	Herman's Head	Sunday Comics		
SUNDAY	N	Adventures of Mark and Brian	Eerie, Indiana	Man of the People	Pacific Station	NBC Sunday Movie				
MONDAY	A			MacGyver		Monday Night Football				
MONDAY	C			Evening Shade	Major Dad	Murphy Brown	Designing Women	Northern Exposure		
MONDAY	F			Fox Night at the Movies						
MONDAY	N			Fresh Prince of Bel Air	Blossom	NBC Monday Movie				
TUESDAY	A			Full House	Home Improvement	Roseanne	Coach	Homefront		
TUESDAY	C			Rescue 911		CBS Tuesday Movie				
TUESDAY	N			I'll Fly Away		In the Heat of the Night		Law & Order		
WEDNESDAY	A			Dinosaurs	Wonder Years	Doogie Howser, M.D.	Sibs	Anything but Love	Good & Evil	
WEDNESDAY	C			Royal Family	Teech	Jake and the Fatman		48 Hours		
WEDNESDAY	N			Unsolved Mysteries		Night Court	Seinfeld	Quantum Leap		
THURSDAY	A			Pros and Cons		FBI: The Untold Stories	American Detective	Primetime Live		
THURSDAY	C			Top Cops		Trials of Rosie O'Neill		Knots Landing		
THURSDAY	F			The Simpsons	Drexell's Class	Beverly Hills 90210				
THURSDAY	N			Cosby Show	A Different World	Cheers	Wings	L. A. Law		
FRIDAY	A			Family Matters	Step by Step	Perfect Strangers	Baby Talk	20/20		
FRIDAY	C			Princesses	Brooklyn Bridge	Carol Burnett Show		Palace Guard		
FRIDAY	F			America's Most Wanted		Ultimate Challenge				
FRIDAY	N			Real Life with Jane Pauley	Exposé	Dear John	Flesh 'N' Blood	Reasonable Doubts		
SATURDAY	A			Who's the Boss?	Growing Pains	Young Riders		The Commish		
SATURDAY	C			CBS Saturday Movie				P.S. I Luv U		
SATURDAY	F			Cops		Totally Hidden Video	Best of the Worst			
SATURDAY	N			Golden Girls	The Torkelsons	Empty Nest	Nurses	Sisters		

PRIME TIME SCHEDULE: FALL 1992

Day	Net	7:00 PM	7:30	8:00	8:30	9:00	9:30	10:00	10:30	11:00
SUNDAY	A	Life Goes On		America's Funniest Home Videos	America's Funniest People	ABC Sunday Movie				
	C	60 Minutes		Murder, She Wrote		CBS Sunday Movie				
	F	Great Scott!	Ben Stiller Show	In Living Color	ROC	Married with Children	Herman's Head	Flying Blind	Woops!	
	N	Secret Service		I Witness Video		NBC Sunday Movie				
MONDAY	A			Young Indiana Jones Chronicles		Monday Night Football				
	C			Evening Shade	Hearts Afire	Murphy Brown	Love & War	Northern Exposure		
	F			Fox Night at the Movies						
	N			Fresh Prince of Bel Air	Blossom	NBC Monday Movie				
TUESDAY	A			Full House	Hangin' with Mr. Cooper	Roseanne	Coach	Going to Extremes		
	C			Rescue 911		CBS Tuesday Movie				
	N			Quantum Leap		Reasonable Doubts		Dateline NBC		
WEDNESDAY	A			Wonder Years	Doogie Howser, M.D.	Home Improvement	Laurie Hill	Civil Wars		
	C			Hat Squad		In the Heat of the Night		48 Hours		
	F			Beverly Hills 90210		Melrose Place				
	N			Unsolved Mysteries		Seinfeld	Mad About You	Law & Order		
THURSDAY	A			Delta	Room for Two	Homefront		Primetime Live		
	C			Top Cops		Street Stories		Knots Landing		
	F			The Simpsons	Martin	The Heights				
	N			A Different World	Rhythm & Blues	Cheers	Wings	L. A. Law		
FRIDAY	A			Family Matters	Step by Step	Dinosaurs	Camp Wilder	20/20		
	C			Golden Palace	Major Dad	Designing Women	Bob	Picket Fences		
	F			America's Most Wanted		Sightings	Likely Suspects			
	N			Final Appeal	What Happened?	Round Table		I'll Fly Away		
SATURDAY	A			Covington Cross		Crossroads		The Commish		
	C			Frannie's Turn	Brooklyn Bridge	Raven		Angel Street		
	F			Cops		Code 3	The Edge			
	N			Here and Now	Out All Night	Empty Nest	Nurses	Sisters		

PRIME TIME SCHEDULE: FALL 1993

		7:00 PM	7:30	8:00	8:30	9:00	9:30	10:00	10:30	11:00
SUNDAY	A	America's Funniest Home Videos	America's Funniest People	Lois & Clark		ABC Sunday Movie				
	C	60 Minutes		Murder, She Wrote		CBS Sunday Movie				
	F	Townsend Television		Martin	Living Single	Married with Children	Daddy Dearest			
	N	I Witness Video		seaQuest DSV		NBC Sunday Movie				
MONDAY	A			Day One		Monday Night Football				
	C			Evening Shade	Dave's World	Murphy Brown	Love & War	Northern Exposure		
	F			Fox Night at the Movies						
	N			Fresh Prince of Bel Air	Blossom	NBC Monday Movie				
TUESDAY	A			Full House	Phenom	Roseanne	Coach	N. Y. P. D. Blue		
	C			Rescue 911		CBS Tuesday Movie				
	F			ROC	Bakersfield P. D.	America's Most Wanted				
	N			Saved by the Bell The College Years	Getting By	John Larroquette Show	Second Half	Dateline NBC		
WEDNESDAY	A			Thea	Joe's Life	Home Improvement	Grace Under Fire	Moon Over Miami		
	C			Hearts Afire	The Nanny	South of Sunset		48 Hours		
	F			Beverly Hills 90210		Melrose Place				
	N			Unsolved Mysteries		Now		Law & Order		
THURSDAY	A			Missing Persons		Matlock		Primetime Live		
	C			In the Heat of the Night		Eye to Eye With Connie Chung		Angel Falls		
	F			The Simpsons	The Sinbad Show	In Living Color	Herman's Head			
	N			Mad About You	Wings	Seinfeld	Frasier	L. A. Law		
FRIDAY	A			Family Matters	Boy Meets World	Step by Step	Hangin' with Mr. Cooper	20/20		
	C			It Had to Be You	Family Album	Bob	Specials	Picket Fences		
	F			Adventures of Brisco County, Jr.		The X-Files				
	N			Against the Grain		NBC Friday Movie				
SATURDAY	A			George	Where I Live	Paula Poundstone Show		The Commish		
	C			Dr. Quinn, Medicine Woman		Harts of the West		Walker, Texas Ranger		
	F			Cops		Front Page				
	N			The Mommies	Café Americain	Empty Nest	Nurses	Sisters		

PRIME TIME SCHEDULE: FALL 1994

<table>
<tr><th></th><th></th><th>7:00 PM</th><th>7:30</th><th>8:00</th><th>8:30</th><th>9:00</th><th>9:30</th><th>10:00</th><th>10:30</th><th>11:00</th></tr>
<tr><td rowspan="4">SUNDAY</td><td>A</td><td>America's Funniest Home Videos</td><td>On Our Own</td><td colspan="2">Lois & Clark</td><td colspan="4">ABC Sunday Movie</td><td></td></tr>
<tr><td>C</td><td colspan="2">60 Minutes</td><td colspan="2">Murder, She Wrote</td><td colspan="4">CBS Sunday Movie</td><td></td></tr>
<tr><td>F</td><td colspan="2">Fortune Hunter</td><td>The Simpsons</td><td>Hardball</td><td>Married with Children</td><td>Wild Oats</td><td colspan="2"></td><td></td></tr>
<tr><td>N</td><td colspan="2">Earth 2</td><td colspan="2">seaQuest DSV</td><td colspan="4">NBC Sunday Movie</td><td></td></tr>
<tr><td rowspan="4">MONDAY</td><td>A</td><td colspan="2"></td><td>Coach</td><td>Blue Skies</td><td colspan="4">Monday Night Football</td><td></td></tr>
<tr><td>C</td><td colspan="2"></td><td>The Nanny</td><td>Dave's World</td><td>Murphy Brown</td><td>Love & War</td><td colspan="2">Northern Exposure</td><td></td></tr>
<tr><td>F</td><td colspan="2"></td><td colspan="2">Melrose Place</td><td colspan="2">Party of Five</td><td colspan="2"></td><td></td></tr>
<tr><td>N</td><td colspan="2"></td><td>Fresh Prince of Bel Air</td><td>Blossom</td><td colspan="4">NBC Monday Movie</td><td></td></tr>
<tr><td rowspan="4">TUESDAY</td><td>A</td><td colspan="2"></td><td>Full House</td><td>Me and the Boys</td><td>Home Improvement</td><td>Grace Under Fire</td><td colspan="2">N. Y. P. D. Blue</td><td></td></tr>
<tr><td>C</td><td colspan="2"></td><td colspan="2">Rescue 911</td><td colspan="4">CBS Tuesday Movie</td><td></td></tr>
<tr><td>F</td><td colspan="2"></td><td colspan="4">Fox Night at the Movies</td><td colspan="2"></td><td></td></tr>
<tr><td>N</td><td colspan="2"></td><td>Wings</td><td>Martin Short Show</td><td>Frasier</td><td>John Larroquette Show</td><td colspan="2">Dateline NBC</td><td></td></tr>
<tr><td rowspan="4">WEDNESDAY</td><td>A</td><td colspan="2"></td><td>Thunder Alley</td><td>All-American Girl</td><td>Roseanne</td><td>Ellen</td><td colspan="2">Turning Point</td><td></td></tr>
<tr><td>C</td><td colspan="2"></td><td>Boys Are Back</td><td>Daddy's Girls</td><td colspan="2">Touched by an Angel</td><td colspan="2">48 Hours</td><td></td></tr>
<tr><td>F</td><td colspan="2"></td><td colspan="2">Beverly Hills 90210</td><td colspan="2">Models Inc.</td><td colspan="2"></td><td></td></tr>
<tr><td>N</td><td colspan="2"></td><td colspan="2">The Cosby Mysteries</td><td colspan="2">Dateline NBC</td><td colspan="2">Law & Order</td><td></td></tr>
<tr><td rowspan="4">THURSDAY</td><td>A</td><td colspan="2"></td><td colspan="2">My So-Called Life</td><td colspan="2">McKenna</td><td colspan="2">Primetime Live</td><td></td></tr>
<tr><td>C</td><td colspan="2"></td><td colspan="2">Due South</td><td colspan="2">Eye to Eye with Connie Chung</td><td colspan="2">Chicago Hope</td><td></td></tr>
<tr><td>F</td><td colspan="2"></td><td>Martin</td><td>Living Single</td><td colspan="2">New York Undercover</td><td colspan="2"></td><td></td></tr>
<tr><td>N</td><td colspan="2"></td><td>Mad About You</td><td>Friends</td><td>Seinfeld</td><td>Madman of the People</td><td colspan="2">ER</td><td></td></tr>
<tr><td rowspan="4">FRIDAY</td><td>A</td><td colspan="2"></td><td>Family Matters</td><td>Boy Meets World</td><td>Step by Step</td><td>Hangin' with Mr. Cooper</td><td colspan="2">20/20</td><td></td></tr>
<tr><td>C</td><td colspan="2"></td><td colspan="2">Diagnosis Murder</td><td colspan="2">Under Suspicion</td><td colspan="2">Picket Fences</td><td></td></tr>
<tr><td>F</td><td colspan="2"></td><td colspan="2">M. A. N. T. I. S.</td><td colspan="2">The X-Files</td><td colspan="2"></td><td></td></tr>
<tr><td>N</td><td colspan="2"></td><td colspan="2">Unsolved Mysteries</td><td colspan="2">Dateline NBC</td><td colspan="2">Homicide: Life on the Street</td><td></td></tr>
<tr><td rowspan="4">SATURDAY</td><td>A</td><td colspan="2"></td><td colspan="4">ABC Family Movie</td><td colspan="2">The Commish</td><td></td></tr>
<tr><td>C</td><td colspan="2"></td><td colspan="2">Dr. Quinn, Medicine Woman</td><td>Five Mrs. Buchanans</td><td>Hearts Afire</td><td colspan="2">Walker, Texas Ranger</td><td></td></tr>
<tr><td>F</td><td colspan="2"></td><td colspan="2">Cops</td><td colspan="2">America's Most Wanted</td><td colspan="2"></td><td></td></tr>
<tr><td>N</td><td colspan="2"></td><td>Something Wilder</td><td>Empty Nest</td><td colspan="2">Sweet Justice</td><td colspan="2">Sisters</td><td></td></tr>
</table>

PRIME TIME SCHEDULE: FALL 1995

Day	Net	7:00 PM	7:30	8:00	8:30	9:00	9:30	10:00	10:30	11:00
SUNDAY	A	America's Funniest Home Videos		Lois & Clark		ABC Sunday Movie				
	C	60 Minutes		Cybill	Almost Perfect	CBS Sunday Movie				
	F	Space: Above and Beyond		The Simpsons	Too Something	Married with Children	Misery Loves Company			
	N	Brotherly Love	Minor Adjustments	Mad About You	Hope & Gloria	NBC Sunday Movie				
	W	Pinky & the Brain	Sister, Sister	Kirk	Simon	Cleghorne!	First Time Out			
MONDAY	A			The Marshal		Monday Night Football				
	C			The Nanny	Can't Hurry Love	Murphy Brown	If Not For You	Chicago Hope		
	F			Melrose Place		Partners	Ned and Stacey			
	N			Fresh Prince of Bel Air	In the House	NBC Monday Movie				
	U			Star Trek: Voyager		Nowhere Man				
TUESDAY	A			Roseanne	Hudson Street	Home Improvement	Coach	N.Y.P.D. Blue		
	C			John Grisham's The Client		CBS Tuesday Movie				
	F			Fox Night at the Movies						
	N			Wings	NewsRadio	Frasier	Pursuit of Happiness	Dateline NBC		
	U			Deadly Games		Live Shot				
WEDNESDAY	A			Ellen	Drew Carey Show	Grace Under Fire	Naked Truth	Primetime Live		
	C			Bless This House	Dave's World	Central Park West		Courthouse		
	F			Beverly Hills 90210		Party of Five				
	N			seaQuest 2032		Dateline NBC		Law & Order		
	U			The Sentinel		Swift Justice				
	W			Sister, Sister	The Parent 'hood	Wayans Bros.	Unhappily Ever After			
THURSDAY	A			Charlie Grace		The Monroes		Murder One		
	C			Murder, She Wrote		New York News		48 Hours		
	F			Living Single	The Crew	New York Undercover				
	N			Friends	Single Guy	Seinfeld	Caroline in the City	ER		
FRIDAY	A			Family Matters	Boy Meets World	Step By Step	Hangin' with Mr. Cooper	20/20		
	C			Dweebs	Bonnie Hunt Show	Picket Fences		American Gothic		
	F			Strange Luck		The X-Files				
	N			Unsolved Mysteries		Dateline NBC		Homicide: Life on the Street		
SATURDAY	A			Jeff Foxworthy Show	Maybe This Time	ABC Saturday Movie				
	C			Dr. Quinn, Medicine Woman		Touched by an Angel		Walker, Texas Ranger		
	F			Martin	The Preston Episodes	Cops	America's Most Wanted			
	N			JAG		John Larroquette Show	Home Court	Sisters		

PRIME TIME SCHEDULE: FALL 1996

		7:00 PM	7:30	8:00	8:30	9:00	9:30	10:00	10:30	11:00
SUNDAY	A	America's Funniest Home Videos		Lois & Clark		ABC Sunday Movie				
	C	60 Minutes		Touched by an Angel		CBS Sunday Movie				
	F	Big Deal		The Simpsons	Ned and Stacey	The X-Files				
	N	Dateline NBC		3rd Rock from the Sun	Boston Common	NBC Sunday Movie				
	W	Kirk	Brotherly Love	The Parent 'hood	Steve Harvey Show	Unhappily Ever After	Life with Roger			
MONDAY	A			Dangerous Minds		Monday Night Football				
	C			Cosby	Pearl	Murphy Brown	Cybill	Chicago Hope		
	F			Melrose Place		Party Girl	Lush Life			
	N			Jeff Foxworthy Show	Mr. Rhodes	NBC Monday Movie				
	U			In the House	Malcolm & Eddie	Goode Behavior	Sparks			
	W			7th Heaven		Savannah				
TUESDAY	A			Roseanne	Life's Work	Home Improvement	Spin City	N.Y.P.D. Blue		
	C			Promised Land		CBS Tuesday Movie				
	F			Fox Night at the Movies						
	N			Mad About You	Something So Right	Frasier	Caroline in the City	Dateline NBC		
	U			Moesha	Homeboys in Outer Space	Burning Zone				
WEDNESDAY	A			Ellen	Townies	Grace Under Fire	Drew Carey Show	Primetime Live		
	C			The Nanny	Almost Perfect	CBS Wednesday Movie				
	F			Beverly Hills 90210		Party of Five				
	N			Wings	John Larroquette Show	NewsRadio	Men Behaving Badly	Law & Order		
	U			The Sentinel		Star Trek: Voyager				
	W			Sister, Sister	Nick Freno: Licensed Teacher	Wayans Bros.	Jamie Foxx Show			
THURSDAY	A			High Incident		Murder One		Turning Point		
	C			Diagnosis Murder		Moloney		48 Hours		
	F			Martin	Living Single	New York Undercover				
	N			Friends	Single Guy	Seinfeld	Suddenly Susan	ER		
FRIDAY	A			Family Matters	Sabrina, the Teenage Witch	Clueless	Boy Meets World	20/20		
	C			Dave's World	Everybody Loves Raymond	Mr. & Mrs. Smith		Nash Bridges		
	F			Sliders		Millennium				
	N			Unsolved Mysteries		Dateline NBC		Homicide: Life on the Street		
SATURDAY	A			Second Noah		Coach	Common Law	Relativity		
	C			Dr. Quinn, Medicine Woman		Early Edition		Walker, Texas Ranger		
	F			Cops		Married with Children	Love and Marriage			
	N			Dark Skies		The Pretender		Profiler		

PRIME TIME SCHEDULE: FALL 1997

Day	Net	7:00 PM	7:30	8:00	8:30	9:00	9:30	10:00	10:30	11:00
SUNDAY	A	Wonderful World of Disney				ABC Sunday Movie				
	C	60 Minutes		Touched by an Angel		CBS Sunday Movie				
	F	World's Funniest!		The Simpsons	King of the Hill	The X-Files				
	N	Dateline NBC		Men Behaving Badly	Jenny	NBC Sunday Movie				
	W	Nick Freno: Licensed Teacher	The Parent 'hood	Jamie Foxx Show	Unhappily Ever After	The Tom Show	Alright, Already			
MONDAY	A			Timecop		Monday Night Football				
	C			Cosby	Everybody Loves Raymond	Cybill	George & Leo	Brooklyn South		
	F			Melrose Place		Ally McBeal				
	N			Suddenly Susan	Fired Up	Caroline in the City	Naked Truth	Dateline NBC		
	U			In the House	Malcolm & Eddie	Good News	Sparks			
	W			7th Heaven		Buffy, the Vampire Slayer				
TUESDAY	A			Soul Man	Over the Top	Home Improvement	Hiller and Diller	N.Y.P.D. Blue		
	C			JAG		Michael Hayes		Dellaventura		
	F			Fox Night at the Movies						
	N			Mad About You	NewsRadio	Frasier	Just Shoot Me	Dateline NBC		
	U			Clueless	Moesha	Hitz	Head Over Heels			
WEDNESDAY	A			Spin City	Dharma & Greg	Drew Carey Show	Ellen	Primetime Live		
	C			The Nanny	Murphy Brown	Public Eye with Bryant Gumbel		Chicago Hope		
	F			Beverly Hills 90210		Party of Five				
	N			Tony Danza Show	Built to Last	3rd Rock from the Sun	Working	Law & Order		
	U			The Sentinel		Star Trek: Voyager				
	W			Sister, Sister	Smart Guy	Wayans Bros.	Steve Harvey Show			
THURSDAY	A			Nothing Sacred		Cracker		20/20		
	C			Promised Land		Diagnosis Murder		48 Hours		
	F			Living Single	Between Brothers	413 Hope Street				
	N			Friends	Union Square	Seinfeld	Veronica's Closet	ER		
FRIDAY	A			Sabrina, the Teenage Witch	Boy Meets World	You Wish	Teen Angel	20/20		
	C			Family Matters	Meego	Gregory Hines Show	Step by Step	Nash Bridges		
	F			The Visitor		Millennium				
	N			Players		Dateline NBC		Homicide: Life on the Street		
SATURDAY	A			C-16		Total Security		The Practice		
	C			Dr. Quinn, Medicine Woman		Early Edition		Walker, Texas Ranger		
	F			Cops		America's Most Wanted: America Fights Back				
	N			The Pretender		Sleepwalkers		Profiler		

PRIME TIME SCHEDULE: FALL 1998

		7:00 PM	7:30	8:00	8:30	9:00	9:30	10:00	10:30	11:00
SUNDAY	A	Wonderful World of Disney				20/20		The Practice		
	C	60 Minutes		Touched by an Angel		CBS Sunday Movie				
	F	World's Funniest	Holding the Baby	The Simpsons	That '70s Show	The X-Files				
	N	Dateline NBC		Dateline NBC		NBC Sunday Movie				
	W	7th Heaven Beginnings		Sister, Sister	Smart Guy	Unhappily Ever After	The Army Show			
MONDAY	A			Monday Night Football						
	C			Cosby	King of Queens	Everybody Loves Raymond	Brian Benben Show	L.A. Doctors		
	F			Melrose Place		Ally McBeal				
	N			Suddenly Susan	Conrad Bloom	Caroline in the City	Will & Grace	Dateline NBC		
	U			Guys Like Us	DiResta	Secret Diary of Desmond Pfeiffer	Malcolm & Eddie			
	W			7th Heaven		Hyperion Bay				
TUESDAY	A			Home Improvement	The Hughleys	Spin City	Sports Night	N.Y.P.D. Blue		
	C			JAG		CBS Tuesday Movie				
	F			King of the Hill	Costello	Guinness World Records: Primetime				
	N			Mad About You	Encore! Encore!	Just Shoot Me	Working	Dateline NBC		
	U			Moesha	Clueless	Mercy Point				
	W			Buffy, the Vampire Slayer		Felicity				
WEDNESDAY	A			Dharma & Greg	Two Guys, A Girl & a Pizza Place	Drew Carey Show	Secret Lives of Men	20/20		
	C			The Nanny	Maggie Winters	To Have & to Hold		Chicago Hope		
	F			Beverly Hills 90210		Party of Five				
	N			Dateline NBC		3rd Rock from the Sun	Newsradio	Law & Order		
	U			Seven Days		Star Trek: Voyager				
	W			Dawson's Creek		Charmed				
THURSDAY	A			Vengeance Unlimited		ABC Thursday Movie				
	C			Promised Land		Diagnosis Murder		48 Hours		
	F			World's Wildest Police Videos		Fox Files				
	N			Friends	Jesse	Frasier	Veronica's Closet	ER		
	U			UPN Thursday Movie						
	W			Wayans Bros.	Jamie Foxx Show	Steve Harvey Show	For Your Love			
FRIDAY	A			Two of a Kind	Boy Meets World	Sabrina, the Teenage Witch	Brother's Keeper	20/20		
	C			Kids Say the Darndest Things	Candid Camera	Buddy Faro		Nash Bridges		
	F			Living in Captivity	Getting Personal	Millennium				
	N			Dateline NBC		Trinity		Homicide: Life on the Street		
	U			Legacy		Love Boat: The Next Wave				
SATURDAY	A			America's Funniest Home Videos		Fantasy Island		Cupid		
	C			Early Edition		Martial Law		Walker, Texas Ranger		
	F			Cops		America's Most Wanted: America Fights Back				
	N			Wind on Water		The Pretender		Profiler		

PRIME TIME SCHEDULE: FALL 1999

		7:00 PM	7:30	8:00	8:30	9:00	9:30	10:00	10:30	11:00
SUNDAY	A	Wonderful World of Disney				Snoops		The Practice		
	C	60 Minutes		Touched by an Angel		CBS Sunday Movie				
	F	World's Funniest!	King of the Hill	The Simpsons	Futurama	The X-Files				
	N	Dateline NBC		Third Watch		NBC Sunday Movie				
	W	7th Heaven Beginnings		Felicity		Jack & Jill				
MONDAY	A			20/20		Monday Night Football				
	C			King of Queens	Ladies Man	Everybody Loves Raymond	Becker	Family Law		
	F			Time of Your Life		Ally McBeal				
	N			Suddenly Susan	Veronica's Closet	Law & Order: Criminal Intent		Dateline NBC		
	U			Moesha	The Parkers	Grown Ups	Malcolm & Eddie			
	W			7th Heaven		Safe Harbor				
TUESDAY	A			Spin City	It's Like You Know	Dharma & Greg	Sports Night	Once and Again		
	C			JAG		60 Minutes II		Judging Amy		
	F			Ally	That '70s Show	Party of Five				
	N			Just Shoot Me	3rd Rock from the Sun	Will & Grace	Mike O'Malley Show	Dateline NBC		
	U			Dilbert	Shasta McNasty	The Strip				
	W			Buffy, the Vampire Slayer		Angel				
WEDNESDAY	A			Two Guys and a Girl	The Norm Show	Drew Carey Show	Oh Grow Up	20/20		
	C			Cosby	Work with Me	CBS Wednesday Movie				
	F			Beverly Hills 90210		Get Real				
	N			Dateline NBC		West Wing		Law & Order		
	U			Seven Days		Star Trek: Voyager				
	W			Dawson's Creek		Roswell				
THURSDAY	A			Whose Line Is It Anyway?		Wasteland		20/20		
	C			Diagnosis Murder		Chicago Hope		48 Hours		
	F			World's Wildest Police Videos		Family Guy	Action			
	N			Friends	Jesse	Frasier	Stark Raving Mad	ER		
	U			WWF Smackdown						
	W			Popular		Charmed				
FRIDAY	A			The Hughleys	Boy Meets World	Sabrina, the Teenage Witch	Odd Man Out	20/20		
	C			Kids Say the Darndest Things	Love & Money	Now and Again		Nash Bridges		
	F			Ryan Caulfield: Year One		Harsh Realm				
	N			Providence		Dateline NBC		Cold Feet		
	U			UPN Friday Movie						
	W			Mission Hill	Jamie Foxx Show	Steve Harvey Show	For Your Love			
SATURDAY	A			ABC Saturday Movie						
	C			Early Edition		Martial Law		Walker, Texas Ranger		
	F			Cops		America's Most Wanted: America Fights Back				
	N			Freaks and Geeks		The Pretender		Profiler		

PRIME TIME SCHEDULE: FALL 2000

Day	Network	7:00 PM	7:30	8:00	8:30	9:00	9:30	10:00	10:30 – 11:00
SUNDAY	A	Wonderful World of Disney				Who Wants to Be a Millionaire?		The Practice	
SUNDAY	C	60 Minutes		Touched by an Angel		CBS Sunday Movie			
SUNDAY	F	Futurama	King of the Hill	The Simpsons	Malcolm in the Middle	The X-Files			
SUNDAY	N	Dateline NBC		Ed		NBC Sunday Movie			
SUNDAY	W	Jamie Foxx Show	For Your Love	Steve Harvey Show	The PJs	Hype	Nikki		
MONDAY	A			20/20 Downtown		Monday Night Football			
MONDAY	C			King of Queens	Yes, Dear	Everybody Loves Raymond	Becker	Family Law	
MONDAY	F			Boston Public		Ally McBeal			
MONDAY	N			Daddio	Tucker	Dateline NBC		Third Watch	
MONDAY	U			Moesha	The Parkers	The Hughleys	Girlfriends		
MONDAY	W			7th Heaven		Roswell			
TUESDAY	A			Who Wants to Be a Millionaire?		Dharma & Greg	Geena Davis Show	Once and Again	
TUESDAY	C			JAG		60 Minutes II		Judging Amy	
TUESDAY	F			That '70s Show	Titus	Dark Angel			
TUESDAY	N			Michael Richards Show	3rd Rock from the Sun	Frasier	Dag	Dateline NBC	
TUESDAY	U			UPN Tuesday Movie					
TUESDAY	W			Buffy, the Vampire Slayer		Angel			
WEDNESDAY	A			Who Wants to Be a Millionaire?		Drew Carey Show	Spin City	Gideon's Crossing	
WEDNESDAY	C			Bette	Welcome to New York	CBS Wednesday Movie			
WEDNESDAY	F			Malcolm in the Middle	Normal, Ohio	The $treet			
WEDNESDAY	N			Titans		West Wing		Law & Order	
WEDNESDAY	U			Seven Days		Star Trek: Voyager			
WEDNESDAY	W			Dawson's Creek		Felicity			
THURSDAY	A			Whose Line Is It Anyway?		Who Wants to Be a Millionaire?		Primetime Thursday	
THURSDAY	C			48 Hours		City of Angels		Diagnosis Murder	
THURSDAY	F			FOX Thursday Movie					
THURSDAY	N			Friends	Cursed	Will & Grace	Just Shoot Me	ER	
THURSDAY	U			WWF Smackdown					
THURSDAY	W			Gilmore Girls		Charmed			
FRIDAY	A			Two Guys and a Girl	Trouble with Normal	Norm	Madigan Men	20/20	
FRIDAY	C			The Fugitive		CSI: Crime Scene Investigation		Nash Bridges	
FRIDAY	F			Police Videos		FreakyLinks			
FRIDAY	N			Providence		Dateline NBC		Law & Order: Special Victims Unit	
FRIDAY	U			Freedom		Level 9			
FRIDAY	W			Sabrina, the Teenage Witch	Grosse Pointe	Popular			
SATURDAY	A			ABC Saturday Movie					
SATURDAY	C			That's Life		Walker, Texas Ranger		The District	
SATURDAY	F			Cops		America's Most Wanted: America Fights Back			
SATURDAY	N			NBC Saturday Movie					

PRIME TIME SCHEDULE: FALL 2001

Day	Net	7:00 PM	7:30	8:00	8:30	9:00	9:30	10:00	10:30
SUNDAY	A	Wonderful World of Disney				Alias		The Practice	
	C	60 Minutes		Education of Max Bickford		CBS Sunday Movie			
	F	Futurama	King of the Hill	The Simpsons	Malcolm in the Middle	The X-Files			
	N	Dateline NBC		Weakest Link		Law & Order: Criminal Intent		UC: Undercover	
	W	Ripley's Believe It or Not		Steve Harvey Show	Men, Women & Dogs	Nikki	Off Centre		
MONDAY	A			Who Wants to Be a Millionaire?		Monday Night Football			
	C			King of Queens	Yes, Dear	Everybody Loves Raymond	Becker	Family Law	
	F			Boston Public		Ally McBeal			
	N			Weakest Link		Third Watch		Crossing Jordan	
	U			The Hughleys	One on One	The Parkers	Girlfriends		
	W			7th Heaven		Angel			
TUESDAY	A			Dharma & Greg	What About Joan?	Bob Patterson	Spin City	Philly	
	C			JAG		The Guardian		Judging Amy	
	F			That '70s Show	Undeclared	Love Cruise: The Maiden Voyage			
	N			Emeril	Three Sisters	Frasier	Scrubs	Dateline NBC	
	U			Buffy, the Vampire Slayer		Roswell			
	W			Gilmore Girls		Smallville			
WEDNESDAY	A			My Wife and Kids	According to Jim	Drew Carey Show	Whose Line Is It Anyway?	20/20	
	C			60 Minutes II		Amazing Race		Wolf Lake	
	F			Various Sitcoms	Grounded for Life	Bernie Mac	Titus		
	N			Ed		West Wing		Law & Order	
	U			Enterprise		Special Unit 2			
	W			Dawson's Creek		Felicity			
THURSDAY	A			Whose Line Is It Anyway?		Who Wants to Be a Millionaire?		Primetime Thursday	
	C			Survivor: Africa		CSI: Crime Scene Investigation		The Agency	
	F			Family Guy	The Tick	Temptation Island 2			
	N			Friends	Inside Schwartz	Will & Grace	Just Shoot Me	ER	
	U			WWF Smackdown					
	W			Popstars 2	Elimidate Deluxe	Charmed			
FRIDAY	A			Mole II: The Next Betrayal		Thieves		Once and Again	
	C			The Ellen Show	Danny	That's Life		48 Hours	
	F			Dark Angel		Pasadena			
	N			Providence		Dateline NBC		Law & Order: Special Victims Unit	
	U			UPN Friday Movie					
	W			Sabrina, the Teenage Witch	Maybe It's Me	Reba	Raising Dad		
SATURDAY	A			ABC Saturday Movie					
	C			Touched by an Angel		Citizen Baines		The District	
	F			Cops		America's Most Wanted: America Fights Back			
	N			Various		NBC Saturday Movie			

PRIME TIME SCHEDULE: FALL 2002

Day	Network	7:00 PM	7:30	8:00	8:30	9:00	9:30	10:00	10:30	11:00
SUNDAY	A	Wonderful World of Disney				Alias		The Practice		
	C	60 Minutes		Becker	Bram and Alice	CBS Sunday Movie				
	F	Futurama	The Simpsons	The Simpsons	King of the Hill	Malcolm in the Middle	Malcolm in the Middle			
	N	Dateline NBC		American Dreams		Law & Order: Criminal Intent		Boomtown		
	W	Gilmore Girls Beginnings		Charmed		Angel				
MONDAY	A			Drew Carey Show	Whose Line Is It Anyway?	Monday Night Football				
	C			King of Queens	Yes, Dear	Everybody Loves Raymond	Still Standing	C.S.I.: Miami		
	F			Boston Public		Girls Club				
	N			Fear Factor		Third Watch		Crossing Jordan		
	U			The Parkers	One on One	Girlfriends	Half & Half			
	W			7th Heaven		Everwood				
TUESDAY	A			8 Simple Rules for Dating My Teenage Daughter	According to Jim	Life with Bonnie	Less than Perfect	N.Y.P.D. Blue		
	C			JAG		The Guardian		Judging Amy		
	F			That '70s Show	Grounded for Life	24				
	N			In-Laws	Just Shoot Me	Frasier	Hidden Hills	Dateline NBC		
	U			Buffy, the Vampire Slayer		Haunted				
	W			Gilmore Girls		Smallville				
WEDNESDAY	A			My Wife and Kids	George Lopez	The Bachelor		MDs		
	C			60 Minutes II		Amazing Race 3		Presidio Med		
	F			Bernie Mac	Cedric the Entertainer Presents	Fastlane				
	N			Ed		West Wing		Law & Order		
	U			Enterprise		Twilight Zone				
	W			Dawson's Creek		Birds of Prey				
THURSDAY	A			Monk		Push, Nevada		Primetime Thursday		
	C			Survivor: Thailand		CSI: Crime Scene Investigation		Without a Trace		
	F			FOX Thursday Movie						
	N			Friends	Scrubs	Will & Grace	Good Morning, Miami	ER		
	U			WWE Smackdown						
	W			Family Affair	Do Over	Jamie Kennedy Experiment	Off Centre			
FRIDAY	A			America's Funniest Home Videos		That Was Then		20/20		
	C			48 Hours Investigates		Hack		Robbery Homicide Division		
	F			Firefly		John Doe				
	N			Providence		Dateline NBC		Law & Order: Special Victims Unit		
	U			UPN Friday Movie						
	W			What I Like About You	Sabrina, the Teenage Witch	Reba	Greetings from Tucson			
SATURDAY	A			ABC Saturday Movie						
	C			Touched by an Angel		The District		The Agency		
	F			Cops		America's Most Wanted: America Fights Back				
	N			NBC Saturday Movie						

APPENDIX 2

EMMY AWARD WINNERS

The "Emmy" awards are given each year in recognition of excellence in television performance and production. The following are the principal awards presented over the years to nighttime network series and the people connected with them, including actors, writers, and directors. Also included, for the sake of completeness, are awards for nighttime "one-time-only" specials and Public Broadcasting Service programs, even though these are not otherwise within the scope of this book.

The National Academy of Television Arts and Sciences also presents many other "Emmy" awards not listed here, in such areas as local programming, daytime and sports programming, and in numerous technical areas such as film editing, sound mixing, and technical direction.

1948 (presented January 25, 1949)

BEST FILM MADE FOR TELEVISION: "The Necklace," *Your Show Time* (NBC)

1949 (presented January 27, 1950)

BEST LIVE SHOW: *The Ed Wynn Show* (CBS)
BEST KINESCOPE SHOW: *Texaco Star Theater* (NBC)
MOST OUTSTANDING LIVE PERSONALITY: Ed Wynn (CBS)
MOST OUTSTANDING KINESCOPE PERSONALITY: Milton Berle (NBC)
BEST FILM MADE FOR AND VIEWED ON TELEVISION: *The Life of Riley* (NBC)

1950 (presented January 23, 1951)

BEST ACTOR: Alan Young (CBS)
BEST ACTRESS: Gertrude Berg (CBS)
MOST OUTSTANDING PERSONALITY: Groucho Marx (NBC)
BEST VARIETY SHOW: *The Alan Young Show* (CBS)
BEST DRAMATIC SHOW: *Pulitzer Prize Playhouse* (ABC)
BEST GAME AND AUDIENCE PARTICIPATION SHOW: *Truth or Consequences* (CBS)

1951 (presented February 18, 1952)

BEST DRAMATIC SHOW: *Studio One* (CBS)
BEST COMEDY SHOW: *The Red Skelton Show* (CBS)
BEST VARIETY SHOW: *Your Show of Shows* (NBC)
BEST ACTOR: Sid Caesar (NBC)
BEST ACTRESS: Imogene Coca (NBC)
BEST COMEDIAN OR COMEDIENNE: Red Skelton (NBC)

1952 (presented February 5, 1953)

BEST DRAMATIC PROGRAM: *Robert Montgomery Presents* (NBC)
BEST VARIETY PROGRAM: *Your Show of Shows* (NBC)
BEST PUBLIC AFFAIRS PROGRAM: *See It Now* (CBS)
BEST MYSTERY, ACTION, OR ADVENTURE PROGRAM: *Dragnet* (NBC)
BEST SITUATION COMEDY: *I Love Lucy* (CBS)
BEST AUDIENCE PARTICIPATION, QUIZ, OR PANEL PROGRAM: *What's My Line* (CBS)
BEST ACTOR: Thomas Mitchell
BEST ACTRESS: Helen Hayes
BEST COMEDIAN: Jimmy Durante (NBC)
BEST COMEDIENNE: Lucille Ball (CBS)
MOST OUTSTANDING PERSONALITY: Bishop Fulton J. Sheen (DUM)

1953 (presented February 11, 1954)

BEST DRAMATIC PROGRAM: *The U.S. Steel Hour* (ABC)
BEST SITUATION COMEDY: *I Love Lucy* (CBS)
BEST VARIETY PROGRAM: *Omnibus* (CBS)
BEST PROGRAM OF NEWS OR SPORTS: *See It Now* (CBS)
BEST PUBLIC AFFAIRS PROGRAM: *Victory at Sea* (NBC)
BEST CHILDREN'S PROGRAM: *Kukla, Fran & Oillie* (NBC)
BEST NEW PROGRAMS: *Make Room for Daddy* (ABC) and *The U.S. Steel Hour* (ABC)
BEST MALE STAR OF REGULAR SERIES: Donald O'Connor, *Colgate Comedy Hour* (NBC)
BEST FEMALE STAR OF REGULAR SERIES: Eve Arden, *Our Miss Brooks* (CBS)
BEST SERIES SUPPORTING ACTOR: Art Carney, *The Jackie Gleason Show* (CBS)
BEST SERIES SUPPORTING ACTRESS: Vivian Vance, *I Love Lucy* (CBS)
BEST MYSTERY, ACTION, OR ADVENTURE PROGRAM: *Dragnet* (NBC)
BEST AUDIENCE PARTICIPATION, QUIZ, OR PANEL PROGRAM: *This Is Your Life* (NBC) and *What's My Line* (CBS)
MOST OUTSTANDING PERSONALITY: Edward R. Murrow (CBS)

1954 (presented March 7, 1955)

MOST OUTSTANDING NEW PERSONALITY: George Gobel (NBC)
BEST CULTURAL, RELIGIOUS, OR EDUCATIONAL PROGRAM: *Omnibus* (CBS)
BEST SPORTS PROGRAM: *The Gillette Cavalacade of Sports* (NBC)
BEST CHILDREN'S PROGRAM: *Lassie* (CBS)
BEST WESTERN OR ADVENTURE SERIES: *Stories of the Century* (syndicated)
BEST NEWS REPORTER OR COMMENTATOR: John Daly (ABC)
BEST AUDIENCE, GUEST PARTICIPATION, OR PANEL PROGRAM: *This Is Your Life* (NBC)
BEST ACTOR IN A SINGLE PERFORMANCE: Robert Cummings, "Twelve Angry Men," *Studio One* (CBS)
BEST ACTRESS IN A SINGLE PERFORMANCE: Judith Anderson, "Macbeth," *Hallmark Hall of Fame* (NBC)
BEST MALE SINGER: Perry Como (CBS)
BEST FEMALE SINGER: Dinah Shore (NBC)
BEST SUPPORTING ACTOR IN A REGULAR SERIES: Art Carney, *The Jackie Gleason Show* (CBS)
BEST SUPPORTING ACTRESS IN A REGULAR SERIES: Audrey Meadows, *The Jackie Gleason Show* (CBS)
BEST ACTOR STARRING IN A REGULAR SERIES: Danny Thomas, *Make Room for Daddy* (ABC)
BEST ACTRESS STARRING IN A REGULAR SERIES: Loretta Young, *The Loretta Young Show* (NBC)
BEST MYSTERY OR INTRIGUE SERIES: *Dragnet* (NBC)
BEST VARIETY SERIES INCLUDING MUSICAL VARIETIES: *Disneyland* (ABC)
BEST SITUATION COMEDY SERIES: *Make Room for Daddy* (ABC)
BEST DRAMATIC SERIES: *The U.S. Steel Hour* (ABC)
BEST INDIVIDUAL PROGRAM OF THE YEAR: "Operation Undersea," *Disneyland* (ABC)
BEST WRITTEN DRAMATIC MATERIAL: Reginald Rose, "Twelve Angry Men," *Studio One* (CBS)
BEST WRITTEN COMEDY MATERIAL: James Allardice, Jack Douglas, Hal Kanter, and Harry Winkler, *The George Gobel Show* (NBC)
BEST DIRECTION: Franklin Schaffner, "Twelve Angry Men," *Studio One* (CBS)

1955 (presented March 17, 1956)

BEST CHILDREN'S SERIES: *Lassie* (CBS)
BEST DOCUMENTARY PROGRAM (RELIGIOUS, INFORMATIONAL, EDUCATIONAL, OR INTERVIEW): *Omnibus* (CBS)
BEST AUDIENCE PARTICIPATION SERIES (QUIZ, PANEL, ETC.): *The $64,000 Question* (CBS)
BEST ACTION OR ADVENTURE SERIES: *Disneyland* (ABC)
BEST COMEDY SERIES: *The Phil Silvers Show* (CBS)
BEST VARIETY SERIES: *The Ed Sullivan Show* (CBS)
BEST MUSIC SERIES: *Your Hit Parade* (NBC)
BEST DRAMATIC SERIES: *Producers' Showcase* (NBC)
BEST SINGLE PROGRAM OF THE YEAR: "Peter Pan," *Producers' Showcase* (NBC)
BEST ACTOR (SINGLE PERFORMANCE): Lloyd Nolan, "The Caine Mutiny Court-Martial," *Ford Star Jubilee* (CBS)
BEST ACTRESS (SINGLE PERFORMANCE): Mary Martin, "Peter Pan," *Producers' Showcase* (NBC)
BEST ACTOR (CONTINUING PERFORMANCE): Phil Silvers, *The Phil Silvers Show* (CBS)
BEST ACTRESS (CONTINUING PERFORMANCE): Lucille Ball, *I Love Lucy* (CBS)
BEST ACTOR IN A SUPPORTING ROLE: Art Carney, *The Jackie Gleason Show* (CBS)
BEST ACTRESS IN A SUPPORTING ROLE: Nanette Fabray, *Caesar's Hour* (NBC)
BEST COMEDIAN: Phil Silvers (CBS)
BEST COMEDIENNE: Nanette Fabray (NBC)
BEST MALE SINGER: Perry Como (NBC)
BEST FEMALE SINGER: Dinah Shore (NBC)
BEST MC OR PROGRAM HOST (MALE OR FEMALE): Perry Como (NBC)
BEST NEWS COMMENTATOR OR REPORTER: Edward R. Murrow (CBS)
BEST ORIGINAL TELEPLAY WRITING: Rod Serling, "Patterns," *Kraft Television Theatre* (NBC)
BEST COMEDY WRITING: Nat Hiken, Barry Blitser, Arnold Auerbach, Harvey Orkin, Vincent Bogert, Arnold Rosen, Coleman Jacoby, Tony Webster, and Terry Ryan, *The Phil Silvers Show* (CBS)
BEST TELEVISION ADAPTATION: Paul Gregory and Franklin Schaffner, "The Caine Mutiny Court-Martial," *Ford Star Jubilee* (CBS)
BEST PRODUCER (LIVE SERIES): Fred Coe, *Producers' Showcase* (NBC)
BEST PRODUCER (FILM SERIES): Walt Disney, *Disneyland* (ABC)
BEST DIRECTOR (LIVE SERIES): Franklin Schaffner, "The Caine Mutiny Court-Martial," *Ford Star Jubilee* (CBS)
BEST DIRECTOR (FILM SERIES): Nat Hiken, *The Phil Silvers Show* (CBS)

1956 (presented March 16, 1957)

BEST SINGLE PROGRAM OF THE YEAR: "Requiem for a Heavyweight," *Playhouse 90* (CBS)
BEST NEW PROGRAM SERIES: *Playhouse 90* (CBS)
BEST SERIES (HALF HOUR OR LESS): *The Phil Silvers Show* (CBS)
BEST SERIES (ONE HOUR OR MORE): *Caesar's Hour* (NBC)
BEST PUBLIC SERVICE SERIES: *See It Now* (CBS)
BEST CONTINUING PERFORMANCE BY AN ACTOR IN A DRAMATIC SERIES: Robert Young, *Father Knows Best* (NBC)
BEST CONTINUING PERFORMANCE BY AN ACTRESS IN A DRAMATIC SERIES: Loretta Young, *The Loretta Young Show* (NBC)
BEST CONTINUING PERFORMANCE BY A COMEDIAN IN A SERIES: Sid Caesar, *Caesar's Hour* (NBC)

BEST CONTINUING PERFORMANCE BY A COMEDIENNE IN A SERIES: Nanette Fabray, *Caesar's Hour* (NBC)
BEST SINGLE PERFORMANCE BY AN ACTOR: Jack Palance, "Requiem for a Heavyweight," *Playhouse 90* (CBS)
BEST SINGLE PERFORMANCE BY AN ACTRESS: Claire Trevor, "Dodsworth," *Producers' Showcase* (NBC)
BEST SUPPORTING PERFORMANCE BY AN ACTOR: Carl Reiner, *Caesar's Hour* (NBC)
BEST SUPPORTING PERFORMANCE BY AN ACTRESS: Pat Carroll, *Caesar's Hour* (NBC)
BEST MALE PERSONALITY (CONTINUING PERFORMANCE): Perry Como (NBC)
BEST FEMALE PERSONALITY (CONTINUING PERFORMANCE): Dinah Shore (NBC)
BEST NEWS COMMENTATOR: Edward R. Murrow (CBS)
BEST TELEPLAY WRITING (HALF HOUR OR LESS): James P. Cavanagh, "Fog Closes In," *Alfred Hitchcock Presents* (CBS)
BEST TELEPLAY WRITING (ONE HOUR OR MORE): Rod Serling, "Requiem for a Heavyweight," *Playhouse 90* (CBS)
BEST COMEDY WRITING (VARIETY OR SITUATION COMEDY): Nat Hiken, Billy Friedberg, Tony Webster, Leonard Stern, Arnold Rosen, and Coleman Jacoby, *The Phil Silvers Show* (CBS)
BEST DIRECTION (HALF HOUR OR LESS): Sheldon Leonard, "Danny's Comeback," *The Danny Thomas Show* (ABC)
BEST DIRECTION (ONE HOUR OR MORE): Ralph Nelson, "Requiem for a Heavyweight," *Playhouse 90* (CBS)

1957 (presented April 15, 1958)

BEST SINGLE PROGRAM OF THE YEAR: "The Comedian," *Playhouse 90* (CBS)
BEST NEW PROGRAM SERIES OF THE YEAR: *The Seven Lively Arts* (CBS)
BEST DRAMATIC ANTHOLOGY SERIES: *Playhouse 90* (CBS)
BEST DRAMATIC SERIES WITH CONTINUING CHARACTERS: *Gunsmoke* (CBS)
BEST COMEDY SERIES: *The Phil Silvers Show* (CBS)
BEST MUSICAL, VARIETY, AUDIENCE PARTICIPATION, OR QUIZ SERIES: *The Dinah Shore Chevy Show* (NBC)
BEST PUBLIC SERVICE PROGRAM OR SERIES: *Omnibus* (ABC and NBC)
BEST CONTINUING PERFORMANCE BY AN ACTOR IN A LEADING ROLE IN A DRAMATIC OR COMEDY SERIES: Robert Young, *Father Knows Best* (NBC)
BEST CONTINUING PERFORMANCE BY AN ACTRESS IN A LEADING ROLE IN A DRAMATIC OR COMEDY SERIES: Jane Wyatt, *Father Knows Best* (NBC)
BEST CONTINUING PERFORMANCE (MALE) IN A SERIES BY A COMEDIAN, SINGER, HOST, DANCER, MC, ANNOUNCER, NARRATOR, PANELIST, OR ANY PERSON WHO ESSENTIALLY PLAYS HIMSELF: Jack Benny, *The Jack Benny Show* (CBS)
BEST CONTINUING PERFORMANCE (FEMALE) IN A SERIES BY A COMEDIENNE, SINGER, HOSTESS, DANCER, MC, ANNOUNCER, NARRATOR, PANELIST, OR ANY PERSON WHO ESSENTIALLY PLAYS HERSELF: Dinah Shore, *The Dinah Shore Chevy Show* (NBC)
ACTOR—BEST SINGLE PERFORMANCE (LEAD OR SUPPORT): Peter Ustinov, "The Life of Samuel Johnson," *Omnibus* (NBC)
ACTRESS—BEST SINGLE PERFORMANCE (LEAD OR SUPPORT): Polly Bergen, "The Helen Morgan Story," *Playhouse 90* (CBS)
BEST CONTINUING SUPPORTING PERFORMANCE BY AN ACTOR IN A DRAMATIC OR COMEDY SERIES: Carl Reiner, *Caesar's Hour* (NBC)
BEST CONTINUING SUPPORTING PERFORMANCE BY AN ACTRESS IN A DRAMATIC OR COMEDY SERIES: Ann B. Davis, *The Bob Cummings Show* (CBS and NBC)
BEST NEWS COMMENTARY: Edward R. Murrow, *See It Now* (CBS)
BEST TELEPLAY WRITING (HALF HOUR OR LESS): Paul Monash, "The Lonely Wizard," *Schlitz Playhouse of Stars* (CBS)
BEST TELEPLAY WRITING (ONE HOUR OR MORE): Rod Serling, "The Comedian," *Playhouse 90* (CBS)
BEST COMEDY WRITING: Nat Hiken, Billy Friedberg, Phil Sharp, Terry Ryan, Coleman Jacoby, Arnold Rosen, Sydney Zelinka, A. J. Russell, and Tony Webster, *The Phil Silvers Show* (CBS)
BEST DIRECTION (HALF HOUR OR LESS): Robert Stevens, "The Glass Eye," *Alfred Hitchcock Presents* (CBS)
BEST DIRECTION (ONE HOUR OR MORE): Bob Banner, *The Dinah Shore Chevy Show* (NBC)

1958–1959 (presented May 6, 1959)

MOST OUTSTANDING SINGLE PROGRAM OF THE YEAR: "An Evening with Fred Astaire" (NBC)
BEST DRAMATIC SERIES (ONE HOUR OR LONGER): *Playhouse 90* (CBS)
BEST DRAMATIC SERIES (LESS THAN ONE HOUR): *Alcoa-Goodyear Theatre* (NBC)
BEST COMEDY SERIES: *The Jack Benny Show* (CBS)
BEST MUSICAL OR VARIETY SERIES: *The Dinah Shore Chevy Show* (NBC)
BEST WESTERN SERIES: *Maverick* (ABC)
BEST PUBLIC SERVICE PROGRAM OR SERIES: *Omnibus* (NBC)
BEST NEWS REPORTING SERIES: *The Huntley-Brinkley Report* (NBC)
BEST PANEL, QUIZ, OR AUDIENCE PARTICIPATION SERIES: *What's My Line* (CBS)
BEST SPECIAL DRAMATIC PROGRAM (ONE HOUR OR LONGER): "Little Moon of Alban," *Hallmark Hall of Fame* (NBC)
BEST SPECIAL MUSICAL OR VARIETY PROGRAM (ONE HOUR OR LONGER): "An Evening with Fred Astaire" (NBC)
BEST ACTOR IN A LEADING ROLE (CONTINUING CHARACTER) IN A DRAMATIC SERIES: Raymond Burr, *Perry Mason* (CBS)
BEST ACTRESS IN A LEADING ROLE (CONTINUING CHARACTER) IN A DRAMATIC SERIES: Loretta Young, *The Loretta Young Show* (NBC)
BEST ACTOR IN A LEADING ROLE (CONTINUING CHARACTER) IN A COMEDY SERIES: Jack Benny, *The Jack Benny Show* (CBS)
BEST ACTRESS IN A LEADING ROLE (CONTINUING CHARACTER) IN A COMEDY SERIES: Jane Wyatt, *Father Knows Best* (CBS and NBC)
BEST SUPPORTING ACTOR (CONTINUING CHARACTER) IN A DRAMATIC SERIES: Dennis Weaver, *Gunsmoke* (CBS)

BEST SUPPORTING ACTRESS (CONTINUING CHARACTER) IN A DRAMATIC SERIES: Barbara Hale, *Perry Mason* (CBS)
BEST SUPPORTING ACTOR (CONTINUING CHARACTER) IN A COMEDY SERIES: Tom Poston, *The Steve Allen Show* (NBC)
BEST SUPPORTING ACTRESS (CONTINUING CHARACTER) IN A COMEDY SERIES: Ann B. Davis, *The Bob Cummings Show* (NBC)
BEST PERFORMANCE BY AN ACTOR (CONTINUING CHARACTER) IN A MUSICAL OR VARIETY SERIES: Perry Como, *The Perry Como Show* (NBC)
BEST PERFORMANCE BY AN ACTRESS (CONTINUING CHARACTER) IN A MUSICAL OR VARIETY SERIES: Dinah Shore, *The Dinah Shore Chevy Show* (NBC)
BEST SINGLE PERFORMANCE BY AN ACTOR: Fred Astaire, "An Evening with Fred Astaire" (NBC)
BEST SINGLE PERFORMANCE BY AN ACTRESS: Julie Harris, "Little Moon of Alban," *Hallmark Hall of Fame* (NBC)
BEST NEWS COMMENTATOR OR ANALYST: Edward R. Murrow (CBS)
BEST DIRECTION OF A SINGLE PROGRAM OF A DRAMATIC SERIES (LESS THAN ONE HOUR): Jack Smight, "Eddie," *Alcoa-Goodyear Theatre* (NBC)
BEST DIRECTION OF A SINGLE DRAMATIC PROGRAM (ONE HOUR OR LONGER): George Schaefer, "Little Moon of Alban," *Hallmark Hall of Fame* (NBC)
BEST DIRECTION OF A SINGLE PROGRAM OF A COMEDY SERIES: Peter Tewksbury, "Medal for Margaret," *Father Knows Best* (CBS)
BEST DIRECTION OF A SINGLE MUSICAL OR VARIETY PROGRAM: Bud Yorkin, "An Evening with Fred Astaire" (NBC)
BEST WRITING OF A SINGLE PROGRAM OF A DRAMATIC SERIES (LESS THAN ONE HOUR): Alfred Brenner and Ken Hughes, "Eddie," *Alcoa-Goodyear Theatre* (NBC)
BEST WRITING OF A SINGLE DRAMATIC PROGRAM (ONE HOUR OR LONGER): James Costigan, "Little Moon of Alban," *Hallmark Hall of Fame* (NBC)
BEST WRITING OF A SINGLE PROGRAM OF A COMEDY SERIES: Sam Perrin, George Balzer, Hal Goldman, and Al Gordon, "Jack Benny Show with Ernie Kovacs," *The Jack Benny Show* (CBS)
BEST WRITING OF A SINGLE MUSICAL OR VARIETY PROGRAM: Bud Yorkin and Herbert Baker, "An Evening with Fred Astaire" (NBC)

1959–1960 (presented June 20, 1960)

OUTSTANDING PROGRAM ACHIEVEMENT IN THE FIELD OF HUMOR: "The Art Carney Special" (NBC)
OUTSTANDING PROGRAM ACHIEVEMENT IN THE FIELD OF DRAMA: *Playhouse 90* (CBS)
OUTSTANDING PROGRAM ACHIEVEMENT IN THE FIELD OF VARIETY: " 'The Fabulous Fifties' " (CBS)
OUTSTANDING PROGRAM ACHIEVEMENT IN THE FIELD OF NEWS: *The Huntley-Brinkley Report* (NBC)
OUTSTANDING PROGRAM ACHIEVEMENT IN THE FIELD OF PUBLIC AFFAIRS AND EDUCATION: *The Twentieth Century* (CBS)
OUTSTANDING SINGLE PERFORMANCE BY AN ACTOR (LEAD OR SUPPORT): Laurence Olivier, "The Moon and Sixpence" (NBC)
OUTSTANDING SINGLE PERFORMANCE BY AN ACTRESS (LEAD OR SUPPORT): Ingrid Bergman, "The Turn of the Screw," *Ford Startime* (NBC)
OUTSTANDING PERFORMANCE BY AN ACTOR IN A SERIES (LEAD OR SUPPORT): Robert Stack, *The Untouchables* (ABC)
OUTSTANDING PERFORMANCE BY AN ACTRESS IN A SERIES (LEAD OR SUPPORT): Jane Wyatt, *Father Knows Best* (CBS)
OUTSTANDING PERFORMANCE IN A VARIETY OR MUSICAL PROGRAM OR SERIES: Harry Belafonte, "Tonight with Belafonte," *The Revlon Revue* (CBS)
OUTSTANDING WRITING ACHIEVEMENT IN DRAMA: Rod Serling, *The Twilight Zone* (CBS)
OUTSTANDING WRITING ACHIEVEMENT IN COMEDY: Sam Perrin, George Balzer, Al Gordon, and Hal Goldman, *The Jack Benny Show* (CBS)
OUTSTANDING WRITING ACHIEVEMENT IN THE DOCUMENTARY FIELD: Howard K. Smith and Av Westin, "The Population Explosion" (CBS)
OUTSTANDING DIRECTORIAL ACHIEVEMENT IN DRAMA: Robert Mulligan, "The Moon and Sixpence" (NBC)
OUTSTANDING DIRECTORIAL ACHIEVEMENT IN COMEDY: Ralph Levy and Bud Yorkin, *The Jack Benny Hour Specials* (CBS)

1960–1961 (presented May 16, 1961)

THE PROGRAM OF THE YEAR: "Macbeth," *Hallmark Hall of Fame* (NBC)
OUTSTANDING PROGRAM ACHIEVEMENT IN THE FIELD OF HUMOR: *The Jack Benny Show* (CBS)
OUTSTANDING PROGRAM ACHIEVEMENT IN THE FIELD OF DRAMA: "Macbeth," *Hallmark Hall of Fame* (NBC)
OUTSTANDING PROGRAM ACHIEVEMENT IN THE FIELD OF VARIETY: "Astaire Time" (NBC)
OUTSTANDING PROGRAM ACHIEVEMENT IN THE FIELD OF NEWS: *The Huntley-Brinkley Report* (NBC)
OUTSTANDING PROGRAM ACHIEVEMENT IN THE FIELD OF PUBLIC AFFAIRS AND EDUCATION: *The Twentieth Century* (CBS)
OUTSTANDING SINGLE PERFORMANCE BY AN ACTOR IN A LEADING ROLE: Maurice Evans, "Macbeth," *Hallmark Hall of Fame* (NBC)
OUTSTANDING SINGLE PERFORMANCE BY AN ACTRESS IN A LEADING ROLE: Judith Anderson, "Macbeth," *Hallmark Hall of Fame* (NBC)
OUTSTANDING PERFORMANCE BY AN ACTOR IN A SERIES (LEAD): Raymond Burr, *Perry Mason* (CBS)
OUTSTANDING PERFORMANCE BY AN ACTRESS IN A SERIES (LEAD): Barbara Stanwyck, *The Barbara Stanwyck Show* (NBC)
OUTSTANDING PERFORMANCE IN A SUPPORTING ROLE BY AN ACTOR OR ACTRESS IN A SINGLE PROGRAM: Roddy McDowall, "Not Without Honor," *Equitable's American Heritage* (NBC)
OUTSTANDING PERFORMANCE IN A SUPPORTING ROLE BY AN ACTOR OR ACTRESS IN A SERIES: Don Knotts, *The Andy Griffith Show* (CBS)

OUTSTANDING PERFORMANCE IN A VARIETY OR MUSICAL PROGRAM OR SERIES: Fred Astaire, "Astaire Time" (NBC)
OUTSTANDING WRITING ACHIEVEMENT IN DRAMA: Rod Serling, *The Twilight Zone* (CBS)
OUTSTANDING WRITING ACHIEVEMENT IN COMEDY: Sherwood Schwartz, Dave O'Brien, Al Schwartz, Martin Ragaway, and Red Skelton, *The Red Skelton Show* (CBS)
OUTSTANDING WRITING ACHIEVEMENT IN THE DOCUMENTARY FIELD: Victor Wolfson, *Winston Churchill—The Valiant Years* (ABC)
OUTSTANDING DIRECTORIAL ACHIEVEMENT IN DRAMA: George Schaefer, "Macbeth," *Hallmark Hall of Fame* (NBC)
OUTSTANDING DIRECTORIAL ACHIEVEMENT IN COMEDY: Sheldon Leonard, *The Danny Thomas Show* (CBS)

1961–1962 (presented May 22, 1962)

THE PROGRAM OF THE YEAR: "Victoria Regina," *Hallmark Hall of Fame* (NBC)
OUTSTANDING PROGRAM ACHIEVEMENT IN THE FIELD OF HUMOR: *The Bob Newhart Show* (NBC)
OUTSTANDING PROGRAM ACHIEVEMENT IN THE FIELD OF DRAMA: *The Defenders* (CBS)
OUTSTANDING PROGRAM ACHIEVEMENT IN THE FIELD OF VARIETY: *The Garry Moore Show* (CBS)
OUTSTANDING PROGRAM ACHIEVEMENT IN THE FIELD OF NEWS: *The Huntley-Brinkley Report* (NBC)
OUTSTANDING PROGRAM ACHIEVEMENT IN THE FIELD OF EDUCATIONAL AND PUBLIC AFFAIRS PROGRAMMING: *David Brinkley's Journal* (NBC)
OUTSTANDING SINGLE PERFORMANCE BY AN ACTOR IN A LEADING ROLE: Peter Falk, "The Price of Tomatoes," *The Dick Powell Show* (NBC)
OUTSTANDING SINGLE PERFORMANCE BY AN ACTRESS IN A LEADING ROLE: Julie Harris, "Victoria Regina," *Hallmark Hall of Fame* (NBC)
OUTSTANDING CONTINUED PERFORMANCE BY AN ACTOR IN A SERIES (LEAD): E. G. Marshall, *The Defenders* (CBS)
OUTSTANDING CONTINUED PERFORMANCE BY AN ACTRESS IN A SERIES (LEAD): Shirley Booth, *Hazel* (NBC)
OUTSTANDING PERFORMANCE IN A SUPPORTING ROLE BY AN ACTOR: Don Knotts, *The Andy Griffith Show* (CBS)
OUTSTANDING PERFORMANCE IN A SUPPORTING ROLE BY AN ACTRESS: Pamela Brown, "Victoria Regina," *Hallmark Hall of Fame* (NBC)
OUTSTANDING PERFORMANCE IN A VARIETY OR MUSICAL PROGRAM OR SERIES: Carol Burnett, *The Garry Moore Show* (CBS)
OUTSTANDING WRITING ACHIEVEMENT IN DRAMA: Reginald Rose, *The Defenders* (CBS)
OUTSTANDING WRITING ACHIEVEMENT IN COMEDY: Carl Reiner, *The Dick Van Dyke Show* (CBS)
OUTSTANDING WRITING ACHIEVEMENT IN THE DOCUMENTARY FIELD: Lou Hazam, "Vincent Van Gogh: A Self-Portrait" (NBC)
OUTSTANDING DIRECTORIAL ACHIEVEMENT IN DRAMA: Franklin Schaffner, *The Defenders* (CBS)
OUTSTANDING DIRECTORIAL ACHIEVEMENT IN COMEDY: Nat Hiken, *Car 54, Where Are You?* (NBC)

1962–1963 (presented May 26, 1963)

THE PROGRAM OF THE YEAR: "The Tunnel" (NBC)
OUTSTANDING PROGRAM ACHIEVEMENT IN THE FIELD OF HUMOR: *The Dick Van Dyke Show* (CBS)
OUTSTANDING PROGRAM ACHIEVEMENT IN THE FIELD OF DRAMA: *The Defenders* (CBS)
OUTSTANDING PROGRAM ACHIEVEMENT IN THE FIELD OF MUSIC: "Julie and Carol at Carnegie Hall" (CBS)
OUTSTANDING ACHIEVEMENT IN THE FIELD OF VARIETY: *The Andy Williams Show* (NBC)
OUTSTANDING PROGRAM ACHIEVEMENT IN THE FIELD OF PANEL, QUIZ, OR AUDIENCE PARTICIPATION: *The G. E. College Bowl* (CBS)
OUTSTANDING PROGRAM ACHIEVEMENT IN THE FIELD OF CHILDREN'S PROGRAMMING: *Walt Disney's Wonderful World of Color* (NBC)
OUTSTANDING ACHIEVEMENT IN THE FIELD OF DOCUMENTARY PROGRAMS: "The Tunnel," Reuven Frank (NBC)
OUTSTANDING ACHIEVEMENT IN THE FIELD OF NEWS: *The Huntley-Brinkley Report* (NBC)
OUTSTANDING PROGRAM ACHIEVEMENT IN THE FIELD OF NEWS COMMENTARY OR PUBLIC AFFAIRS: *David Brinkley's Journal* (NBC)
OUTSTANDING ACHIEVEMENT IN INTERNATIONAL REPORTING OR COMMENTARY: Piers Anderton, Berlin correspondent, "The Tunnel" (NBC)
OUTSTANDING SINGLE PERFORMANCE BY AN ACTOR IN A LEADING ROLE: Trevor Howard, "The Invincible Mr. Disraeli," *Hallmark Hall of Fame* (NBC)
OUTSTANDING SINGLE PERFORMANCE BY AN ACTRESS IN A LEADING ROLE: Kim Stanley, "A Cardinal Act of Mercy," *Ben Casey* (ABC)
OUTSTANDING CONTINUED PERFORMANCE BY AN ACTOR IN A SERIES (LEAD): E. G. Marshall, *The Defenders* (CBS)
OUTSTANDING CONTINUED PERFORMANCE BY AN ACTRESS IN A SERIES (LEAD): Shirley Booth, *Hazel* (NBC)
OUTSTANDING PERFORMANCE IN A SUPPORTING ROLE BY AN ACTOR: Don Knotts, *The Andy Griffith Show* (CBS)
OUTSTANDING PERFORMANCE IN A SUPPORTING ROLE BY AN ACTRESS: Glenda Farrell, "A Cardinal Act of Mercy," *Ben Casey* (ABC)
OUTSTANDING PERFORMANCE IN A VARIETY OR MUSICAL PROGRAM OR SERIES: Carol Burnett, "Julie and Carol at Carnegie Hall" (CBS) and "Carol and Company" (CBS)
OUTSTANDING WRITING ACHIEVEMENT IN DRAMA: Robert Thom and Reginald Rose, "The Madman," *The Defenders* (CBS)
OUTSTANDING WRITING ACHIEVEMENT IN COMEDY: Carl Reiner, *The Dick Van Dyke Show* (CBS)
OUTSTANDING DIRECTORIAL ACHIEVEMENT IN DRAMA: Stuart Rosenberg, "The Madman," *The Defenders* (CBS)
OUTSTANDING DIRECTORIAL ACHIEVEMENT IN COMEDY: John Rich, *The Dick Van Dyke Show* (CBS)

1963–1964 (presented May 25, 1964)

THE PROGRAM OF THE YEAR: "The Making of the President 1960" (ABC)

OUTSTANDING PROGRAM ACHIEVEMENT IN THE FIELD OF COMEDY: *The Dick Van Dyke Show* (CBS)

OUTSTANDING PROGRAM ACHIEVEMENT IN THE FIELD OF DRAMA: *The Defenders* (CBS)

OUTSTANDING PROGRAM ACHIEVEMENT IN THE FIELD OF MUSIC: *The Bell Telephone Hour* (NBC)

OUTSTANDING PROGRAM ACHIEVEMENT IN THE FIELD OF VARIETY: *The Danny Kaye Show* (CBS)

OUTSTANDING ACHIEVEMENT IN THE FIELD OF DOCUMENTARY PROGRAMS: "The Making of the President 1960" (ABC)

OUTSTANDING PROGRAM ACHIEVEMENT IN THE FIELD OF NEWS REPORTS: *The Huntley-Brinkley Report* (NBC)

OUTSTANDING PROGRAM ACHIEVEMENT IN THE FIELD OF NEWS COMMENTARY OR PUBLIC AFFAIRS: "Cuba: Parts I and II—The Bay of Pigs and the Missile Crisis," *NBC White Paper* (NBC)

OUTSTANDING SINGLE PERFORMANCE BY AN ACTOR IN A LEADING ROLE: Jack Klugman, "Blacklist," *The Defenders* (CBS)

OUTSTANDING SINGLE PERFORMANCE BY AN ACTRESS IN A LEADING ROLE: Shelley Winters, "Two Is the Number," *Bob Hope Presents the Chrysler Theatre* (NBC)

OUTSTANDING CONTINUED PERFORMANCE BY AN ACTOR IN A SERIES (LEAD): Dick Van Dyke, *The Dick Van Dyke Show* (CBS)

OUTSTANDING CONTINUED PERFORMANCE BY AN ACTRESS IN A SERIES (LEAD): Mary Tyler Moore, *The Dick Van Dyke Show* (CBS)

OUTSTANDING PERFORMANCE IN A SUPPORTING ROLE BY AN ACTOR: Albert Paulsen, "One Day in the Life of Ivan Denisovich," *Bob Hope Presents the Chrysler Theatre* (NBC)

OUTSTANDING PERFORMANCE IN A SUPPORTING ROLE BY AN ACTRESS: Ruth White, "Little Moon of Alban," *Hallmark Hall of Fame* (NBC)

OUTSTANDING PERFORMANCE IN A VARIETY OR MUSICAL PROGRAM OR SERIES: Danny Kaye, *The Danny Kaye Show* (CBS)

OUTSTANDING WRITING ACHIEVEMENT IN DRAMA (ORIGINAL): Ernest Kinoy, "Blacklist," *The Defenders* (CBS)

OUTSTANDING WRITING ACHIEVEMENT IN DRAMA (ADAPTATION): Rod Serling, "It's Mental Work" (from the story by John O'Hara), *Bob Hope Presents the Chrysler Theatre* (NBC)

OUTSTANDING WRITING ACHIEVEMENT IN COMEDY OR VARIETY: Carl Reiner, Sam Denoff, and Bill Persky, *The Dick Van Dyke Show* (CBS)

OUTSTANDING DIRECTORIAL ACHIEVEMENT IN DRAMA: Tom Gries, "Who Do You Kill," *East Side/West Side* (CBS)

OUTSTANDING DIRECTORIAL ACHIEVEMENT IN COMEDY: Jerry Paris, *The Dick Van Dyke Show* (CBS)

OUTSTANDING DIRECTORIAL ACHIEVEMENT IN VARIETY OR MUSIC: Robert Scheerer, *The Danny Kaye Show* (CBS)

1964–1965 (presented September 12, 1965)

OUTSTANDING PROGRAM ACHIEVEMENTS IN ENTERTAINMENT: *The Dick Van Dyke Show,* Carl Reiner, producer (CBS); "The Magnificent Yankee," *Hallmark Hall of Fame,* George Schaefer, producer (NBC); "My Name is Barbra," Richard Lewine, producer (CBS)

OUTSTANDING INDIVIDUAL ACHIEVEMENTS IN ENTERTAINMENT (ACTORS AND PERFORMERS): Lynn Fontanne, "The Magnificent Yankee," *Hallmark Hall of Fame* (NBC); Alfred Lunt, "The Magnificent Yankee," *Hallmark Hall of Fame* (NBC); Barbra Streisand, "My Name Is Barbra" (CBS); Dick Van Dyke, *The Dick Van Dyke Show* (CBS)

OUTSTANDING INDIVIDUAL ACHIEVEMENT IN ENTERTAINMENT (WRITER): David Karp, "The 700-Year-Old Gang," *The Defenders* (CBS)

OUTSTANDING INDIVIDUAL ACHIEVEMENT IN ENTERTAINMENT (DIRECTOR): Paul Bogart, "The 700-Year-Old Gang," *The Defenders* (CBS)

OUTSTANDING PROGRAM ACHIEVEMENTS IN NEWS, DOCUMENTARIES, INFORMATION, AND SPORTS: "I, Leonardo da Vinci," *The Saga of Western Man,* John H. Secondari and Helen Jean Rogers, producers (ABC); "The Louvre," Lucy Jarvis, producer, and John J. Sughrue, coproducer (NBC)

OUTSTANDING INDIVIDUAL ACHIEVEMENT IN NEWS, DOCUMENTARIES, INFORMATION, AND SPORTS (DIRECTOR): John J. Sughrue, "The Louvre" (NBC)

OUTSTANDING INDIVIDUAL ACHIEVEMENT IN NEWS, DOCUMENTARIES, INFORMATION, AND SPORTS (WRITER): Sidney Carroll, "The Louvre" (NBC)

1965–1966 (presented May 22, 1966)

OUTSTANDING COMEDY SERIES: *The Dick Van Dyke Show,* Carl Reiner, producer (CBS)

OUTSTANDING VARIETY SERIES: *The Andy Williams Show,* Bob Finkel, producer (NBC)

OUTSTANDING VARIETY SPECIAL: "Chrysler Presents the Bob Hope Christmas Special," Bob Hope, executive producer (NBC)

OUTSTANDING DRAMATIC SERIES: *The Fugitive,* Alan Armer, producer (ABC)

OUTSTANDING DRAMATIC PROGRAM: "The Ages of Man," David Susskind and Daniel Melnick, producers (CBS)

OUTSTANDING MUSICAL PROGRAM: "Frank Sinatra: A Man and His Music," Dwight Hemion, producer (NBC)

OUTSTANDING CHILDREN'S PROGRAM: "A Charlie Brown Christmas," Lee Mendelson and Bill Melendez, producers (CBS)

OUTSTANDING PERFORMANCE BY AN ACTOR IN A LEADING ROLE IN A DRAMA: Cliff Robertson, "The Game," *Bob Hope Presents the Chrysler Theatre* (NBC)

OUTSTANDING PERFORMANCE BY AN ACTRESS IN A LEADING ROLE IN A DRAMA: Simone Signoret, "A Small Rebellion," *Bob Hope Presents the Chrysler Theatre* (NBC)

OUTSTANDING CONTINUED PERFORMANCE BY AN ACTOR IN A LEADING ROLE IN A DRAMATIC SERIES: Bill Cosby, *I Spy* (NBC)

OUTSTANDING CONTINUED PERFORMANCE BY AN ACTRESS IN A LEADING ROLE IN A DRAMATIC SERIES: Barbara Stanwyck, *The Big Valley* (ABC)

OUTSTANDING CONTINUED PERFORMANCE BY AN ACTOR IN A LEADING ROLE IN A COMEDY SERIES: Dick Van Dyke, *The Dick Van Dyke Show* (CBS)

OUTSTANDING CONTINUED PERFORMANCE BY AN ACTRESS IN A LEADING ROLE IN A COMEDY SERIES: Mary Tyler Moore, *The Dick Van Dyke Show* (CBS)

OUTSTANDING PERFORMANCE BY AN ACTOR IN A SUPPORTING ROLE IN A DRAMA: James Daly, "Eagle in a Cage," *Hallmark Hall of Fame* (NBC)

OUTSTANDING PERFORMANCE BY AN ACTRESS IN A SUPPORTING ROLE IN A DRAMA: Lee Grant, *Peyton Place* (ABC)

OUTSTANDING PERFORMANCE BY AN ACTOR IN A SUPPORTING ROLE IN A COMEDY: Don Knotts, "The Return of Barney Fife," *The Andy Griffith Show* (CBS)

OUTSTANDING PERFORMANCE BY AN ACTRESS IN A SUPPORTING ROLE IN A COMEDY: Alice Pearce, *Bewitched* (ABC)

OUTSTANDING WRITING ACHIEVEMENT IN DRAMA: Millard Lampell, "Eagle in a Cage," *Hallmark Hall of Fame* (NBC)

OUTSTANDING WRITING ACHIEVEMENT IN COMEDY: Bill Persky and Sam Denoff, "Coast to Coast Big Mouth," *The Dick Van Dyke Show* (CBS)

OUTSTANDING WRITING ACHIEVEMENT IN VARIETY: Al Gordon, Hal Goldman, and Sheldon Keller, "An Evening with Carol Channing" (CBS)

OUTSTANDING DIRECTORIAL ACHIEVEMENT IN DRAMA: Sidney Pollack, "The Game," *Bob Hope Presents the Chrysler Theatre* (NBC)

OUTSTANDING DIRECTORIAL ACHIEVEMENT IN COMEDY: William Asher, *Bewitched* (ABC)

OUTSTANDING DIRECTORIAL ACHIEVEMENT IN VARIETY OR MUSIC: Alan Handley, "The Julie Andrews Show" (NBC)

ACHIEVEMENTS IN NEWS AND DOCUMENTARIES (PROGRAMS): "American White Paper: United States Foreign Policy," Fred Freed, producer (NBC); "KKK—The Invisible Empire," *CBS Reports*, David Lowe, producer (CBS); "Senate Hearings on Vietnam," Chet Hagen, producer (NBC)

SPECIAL CLASSIFICATIONS OF INDIVIDUAL ACHIEVEMENTS: Burr Tillstrom, "Berlin Wall" hand ballet, *That Was The Week That Was* (NBC)

1966–1967 (presented June 4, 1967)

OUTSTANDING COMEDY SERIES: *The Monkees*, Bert Schneider and Bob Rafelson, producers (NBC)

OUTSTANDING VARIETY SERIES: *The Andy Williams Show*, Edward Stephenson and Bob Finkel, producers (NBC)

OUTSTANDING VARIETY SPECIAL: "The Sid Caesar, Imogene Coca, Carl Reiner, Howard Morris Special," Jack Arnold, producer (CBS)

OUTSTANDING DRAMATIC SERIES: *Mission: Impossible*, Joseph Gantman and Bruce Geller, producers (CBS)

OUTSTANDING DRAMATIC PROGRAM: "Death of a Salesman," David Susskind and Daniel Melnick, producers (CBS)

OUTSTANDING MUSICAL PROGRAM: "Brigadoon," Fielder Cook, producer (ABC)

OUTSTANDING CHILDREN'S PROGRAM: "Jack and the Beanstalk," Gene Kelly, producer (NBC)

OUTSTANDING SINGLE PERFORMANCE BY AN ACTOR IN A LEADING ROLE IN A DRAMA: Peter Ustinov, "Barefoot in Athens," *Hallmark Hall of Fame* (NBC)

OUTSTANDING SINGLE PERFORMANCE BY AN ACTRESS IN A LEADING ROLE IN A DRAMA: Geraldine Page, "A Christmas Memory," *ABC Stage 67* (ABC)

OUTSTANDING CONTINUED PERFORMANCE BY AN ACTOR IN A LEADING ROLE IN A DRAMATIC SERIES: Bill Cosby, *I Spy* (NBC)

OUTSTANDING CONTINUED PERFORMANCE BY AN ACTRESS IN A LEADING ROLE IN A DRAMATIC SERIES: Barbara Bain, *Mission: Impossible* (CBS)

OUTSTANDING CONTINUED PERFORMANCE BY AN ACTOR IN A LEADING ROLE IN A COMEDY SERIES: Don Adams, *Get Smart* (NBC)

OUTSTANDING CONTINUED PERFORMANCE BY AN ACTRESS IN A LEADING ROLE IN A COMEDY SERIES: Lucille Ball, *The Lucy Show* (CBS)

OUTSTANDING PERFORMANCE BY AN ACTOR IN A SUPPORTING ROLE IN A DRAMA: Eli Wallach, "The Poppy Is Also a Flower," *Xerox Special* (ABC)

OUTSTANDING PERFORMANCE BY AN ACTRESS IN A SUPPORTING ROLE IN A DRAMA: Agnes Moorehead, "Night of the Vicious Valentine," *The Wild Wild West* (CBS)

OUTSTANDING PERFORMANCE BY AN ACTOR IN A SUPPORTING ROLE IN A COMEDY: Don Knotts, "Barney Comes to Mayberry," *The Andy Griffith Show* (CBS)

OUTSTANDING PERFORMANCE BY AN ACTRESS IN A SUPPORTING ROLE IN A COMEDY: Frances Bavier, *The Andy Griffith Show* (CBS)

OUTSTANDING WRITING ACHIEVEMENT IN DRAMA: Bruce Geller, *Mission: Impossible* (CBS)

OUTSTANDING WRITING ACHIEVEMENT IN COMEDY: Buck Henry and Leonard Stern, "Ship of Spies," *Get Smart* (NBC)

OUTSTANDING WRITING ACHIEVEMENT IN VARIETY: Mel Brooks, Sam Denoff, Bill Persky, Carl Reiner, and Mel Tolkin, "The Sid Caesar, Imogene Coca, Carl Reiner, Howard Morris Special" (CBS)

OUTSTANDING DIRECTORIAL ACHIEVEMENT IN DRAMA: Alex Segal, "Death of a Salesman" (CBS)

OUTSTANDING DIRECTORIAL ACHIEVEMENT IN COMEDY: James Frawley, "Royal Flush," *The Monkees* (NBC)

OUTSTANDING DIRECTORIAL ACHIEVEMENT IN VARIETY OR MUSIC: Fielder Cook, "Brigadoon" (ABC)

ACHIEVEMENTS IN NEWS AND DOCUMENTARIES (PROGRAMS): "China: The Roots of Madness," Mel Stuart, producer (syndicated); "Hall of Kings," Harry Rasky, producer (ABC); "The Italians," Bernard Birnbaum, producer (CBS)

ACHIEVEMENTS IN NEWS AND DOCUMENTARIES (INDIVIDUAL): Theodore H. White, writer, "China: The Roots of Madness" (syndicated)

SPECIAL CLASSIFICATIONS OF INDIVIDUAL ACHIEVEMENTS: Art Carney, *The Jackie Gleason Show* (CBS); Truman Capote and Eleanor Perry, adaptation of "A Christmas Memory," *ABC Stage 67* (ABC); Arthur Miller, adaptation of "Death of a Salesman" (CBS)

1967–1968 (presented May 19, 1968)

OUTSTANDING ACHIEVEMENT WITHIN REGULARLY SCHEDULED NEWS PROGRAMS: "1st Cavalry, Con Thien," and other segments, *The CBS Evening News with Walter Cronkite,* CBS news correspondent John Laurence and CBS news cameraman Keith Kay (CBS); "Crisis in the Cities," *Public Broadcast Laboratory,* Av Westin, executive producer (NET)

OUTSTANDING ACHIEVEMENT IN NEWS DOCUMENTARIES: "Africa," James Fleming, executive producer (ABC); "Summer '67: What We Learned," Fred Freed, producer (NBC); "CBS Reports: What about Ronald Reagan?" *CBS News Hour,* Harry Reasoner, writer (CBS); "Same Mud, Same Blood," Vo Huynh, cameraman (NBC)

OUTSTANDING ACHIEVEMENT IN CULTURAL DOCUMENTARIES: "Eric Hoffer, the Passionate State of Mind," *CBS News Hour,* Jack Beck, producer (CBS); "Gauguin in Tahiti: The Search for Paradise," *CBS News Hour,* Martin Carr, producer (CBS); "John Steinbeck's America and the Americans," Lee Mendelson, producer (NBC); "Dylan Thomas: The World I Breathe," *NET Festival,* Perry Miller Adato, producer (NET); Nathaniel Dorsky, art photographer, "Gauguin in Tahiti: The Search for Paradise," *CBS News Hour* (CBS); Harry Morgan, writer, "The Wyeth Phenomenon," *Who, What, When, Where, Why* (CBS); Thomas A. Priestley, director of photography, and Robert Loweree, film editor, "John Steinbeck's America and the Americans" (NBC)

OUTSTANDING NEWS AND DOCUMENTARY ACHIEVEMENTS: *The Twenty-first Century,* Isaac Kleinerman, producer (CBS); "Science and Religion: Who Will Play God?" *CBS News Special,* Ben Flynn, producer (CBS); *Our World,* George Delerue, composer (NET)

OUTSTANDING COMEDY SERIES: *Get Smart,* Burt Nodella, producer (NBC)

OUTSTANDING DRAMATIC SERIES: *Mission: Impossible,* Joseph E. Gantman, producer (CBS)

OUTSTANDING DRAMATIC PROGRAM: "Elizabeth the Queen," *Hallmark Hall of Fame,* George Schaefer, producer (NBC)

OUTSTANDING MUSICAL OR VARIETY SERIES: *Rowan & Martin's Laugh-In,* George Schlatter, producer (NBC)

OUTSTANDING MUSICAL OR VARIETY PROGRAM: "Rowan & Martin's Laugh-In Special," George Schlatter, producer (NBC)

OUTSTANDING SINGLE PERFORMANCE BY AN ACTOR IN A LEADING ROLE IN A DRAMA: Melvyn Douglas, "Do Not Go Gentle into That Good Night," *CBS Playhouse* (CBS)

OUTSTANDING SINGLE PERFORMANCE BY AN ACTRESS IN A LEADING ROLE IN A DRAMA: Maureen Stapleton, "Among the Paths to Eden," *Xerox Special Event* (ABC)

OUTSTANDING CONTINUED PERFORMANCE BY AN ACTOR IN A LEADING ROLE IN A DRAMATIC SERIES: Bill Cosby, *I Spy* (NBC)

OUTSTANDING CONTINUED PERFORMANCE BY AN ACTRESS IN A LEADING ROLE IN A DRAMATIC SERIES: Barbara Bain, *Mission: Impossible* (CBS)

OUTSTANDING CONTINUED PERFORMANCE BY AN ACTOR IN A LEADING ROLE IN A COMEDY SERIES: Don Adams, *Get Smart* (NBC)

OUTSTANDING CONTINUED PERFORMANCE BY AN ACTRESS IN A LEADING ROLE IN A COMEDY SERIES: Lucille Ball, *The Lucy Show* (CBS)

OUTSTANDING PERFORMANCE BY AN ACTOR IN A SUPPORTING ROLE IN A DRAMA: Milburn Stone, *Gunsmoke* (CBS)

OUTSTANDING PERFORMANCE BY AN ACTRESS IN A SUPPORTING ROLE IN A DRAMA: Barbara Anderson, *Ironside* (NBC)

OUTSTANDING PERFORMANCE BY AN ACTOR IN A SUPPORTING ROLE IN A COMEDY: Werner Klemperer, *Hogan's Heroes* (CBS)

OUTSTANDING PERFORMANCE BY AN ACTRESS IN A SUPPORTING ROLE IN A COMEDY: Marion Lorne, *Bewitched* (ABC)

OUTSTANDING WRITING ACHIEVEMENT IN DRAMA: Loring Mandel, "Do Not Go Gentle into That Good Night," *CBS Playhouse* (CBS)

OUTSTANDING WRITING ACHIEVEMENT IN COMEDY: Allan Burns and Chris Hayward, "The Coming-Out Party," *He & She* (CBS)

OUTSTANDING WRITING ACHIEVEMENT IN MUSIC OR VARIETY: Paul Keyes, Hugh Wedlock, Allan Manings, Chris Bearde, David Panich, Phil Hahn, Jack Hanrahan, Coslough Johnson, Marc London, and Digby Wolfe, *Rowan & Martin's Laugh-In* (NBC)

OUTSTANDING DIRECTORIAL ACHIEVEMENT IN DRAMA: Paul Bogart, "Dear Friends," *CBS Playhouse* (CBS)

OUTSTANDING DIRECTORIAL ACHIEVEMENT IN COMEDY: Bruce Bilson, "Maxwell Smart, Private Eye," *Get Smart* (NBC)

OUTSTANDING DIRECTORIAL ACHIEVEMENT IN MUSIC OR VARIETY: Jack Haley, Jr., "Movin' with Nancy" (NBC)

SPECIAL CLASSIFICATION OF OUTSTANDING INDIVIDUAL ACHIEVEMENT: Art Carney, *The Jackie Gleason Show* (CBS); Pat Paulsen, *The Smothers Brothers Comedy Hour* (CBS)

1968–1969 (presented June 8, 1969)

OUTSTANDING COMEDY SERIES: *Get Smart,* Arne Sultan, executive producer; Burt Nodella, producer (NBC)

OUTSTANDING DRAMATIC SERIES: *NET Playhouse,* Curtis Davis, executive producer (NET)

OUTSTANDING DRAMATIC PROGRAM: "Teacher, Teacher," Henry Jaffe, executive producer; George Lefferts, producer, *Hallmark Hall of Fame* (NBC)

OUTSTANDING MUSICAL OR VARIETY SERIES: *Rowan & Martin's Laugh-In,* George Schlatter, executive producer; Paul Keyes and Carolyn Raskin, producers (NBC)

OUTSTANDING VARIETY OR MUSICAL PROGRAM: "The Bill Cosby Special," Roy Silver, executive producer; Bill Hobin, Bill Persky, and Sam Denoff, producers (NBC)

OUTSTANDING SINGLE PERFORMANCE BY AN ACTOR IN A LEADING ROLE: Paul Scofield, "The Male of the Species," *Prudential's On Stage* (NBC)

OUTSTANDING SINGLE PERFORMANCE BY AN ACTRESS IN A LEADING ROLE: Geraldine Page, "The Thanksgiving Visitor" (ABC)

OUTSTANDING CONTINUED PERFORMANCE BY AN ACTOR IN A LEADING ROLE IN A DRAMATIC SERIES: Carl Betz, *Judd, for the Defense* (ABC)

OUTSTANDING CONTINUED PERFORMANCE BY AN ACTRESS IN A LEADING ROLE IN A DRAMATIC SERIES: Barbara Bain, *Mission: Impossible* (CBS)

OUTSTANDING CONTINUED PERFORMANCE BY AN ACTOR IN A LEADING ROLE IN A COMEDY SERIES: Don Adams, *Get Smart* (NBC)

OUTSTANDING CONTINUED PERFORMANCE BY AN ACTRESS IN A LEADING ROLE IN A COMEDY SERIES: Hope Lange, *The Ghost and Mrs. Muir* (NBC)

OUTSTANDING SINGLE PERFORMANCE BY AN ACTOR IN A SUPPORTING ROLE: no award given

OUTSTANDING SINGLE PERFORMANCE BY AN ACTRESS IN A SUPPORTING ROLE: Anna Calder-Marshall, "The Male of the Species," *Prudential's On Stage* (NBC)

OUTSTANDING CONTINUED PERFORMANCE BY AN ACTOR IN A SUPPORTING ROLE IN A SERIES: Werner Klemperer, *Hogan's Heroes* (CBS)

OUTSTANDING CONTINUED PERFORMANCE BY AN ACTRESS IN A SUPPORTING ROLE IN A SERIES: Susan Saint James, *The Name of the Game* (NBC)

OUTSTANDING WRITING ACHIEVEMENT IN DRAMA: J. P. Miller, "The People Next Door," *CBS Playhouse* (CBS)

OUTSTANDING WRITING ACHIEVEMENT IN COMEDY, VARIETY, OR MUSIC: Alan Blye, Bob Einstein, Murray Roman, Carl Gottlieb, Jerry Music, Steve Martin, Cecil Tuck, Paul Wayne, Cy Howard, and Mason Williams, *The Smothers Brothers Comedy Hour* (CBS)

OUTSTANDING DIRECTORIAL ACHIEVEMENT IN DRAMA: David Greene, "The People Next Door," *CBS Playhouse* (CBS)

OUTSTANDING PROGRAM ACHIEVEMENT (SPECIAL CLASSIFICATION): *Firing Line with William F. Buckley, Jr.*, Warren Steibel, producer (syndicated); *Wild Kingdom*, Don Meier, producer (NBC)

OUTSTANDING INDIVIDUAL ACHIEVEMENT (SPECIAL CLASSIFICATION): Arte Johnson, *Rowan & Martin's Laugh-In* (NBC); Harvey Korman, *The Carol Burnett Show* (CBS)

OUTSTANDING ACHIEVEMENT WITHIN REGULARLY SCHEDULED NEWS PROGRAMS: "Coverage of Hunger in the United States," *The Huntley-Brinkley Report*, Wallace Westfeldt, executive producer (NBC). "On the Road," *The CBS Evening News with Walter Cronkite*, Charles Kuralt, correspondent: James Wilson, cameraman; Robert Funk, soundman (CBS). "Police After Chicago," *The CBS Evening News with Walter Cronkite*, John Laurence, corespondent (CBS)

OUTSTANDING ACHIEVEMENT IN COVERAGE OF SPECIAL EVENTS: "Coverage of Martin Luther King Assassination and Aftermath," *CBS News Special Reports* and Broadcasts, Robert Wussler, Ernest Leiser, Don Hewitt, and Burton Benjamin, executive producers (CBS)

OUTSTANDING NEWS DOCUMENTARY PROGRAM ACHIEVEMENTS: "CBS Reports: Hunger in America," *CBS News Hour*, Martin Carr, producer (CBS); "Law and Order," *Public Broadcast Laboratory*, Frederick Wiseman, producer (NET)

OUTSTANDING NEWS DOCUMENTARY INDIVIDUAL ACHIEVEMENT: Perry Wolff and Andrew A. Rooney, writers, "Black History: Lost, Stolen or Strayed" *[Of Black America Series], CBS News Hour* (CBS)

OUTSTANDING CULTURAL DOCUMENTARY AND "MAGAZINE TYPE" PROGRAM OR SERIES ACHIEVEMENT (PROGRAMS): "Don't Count the Candles," *CBS News Hour*, William K. McClure, producer (CBS); "Justice Black and the Bill of Rights," *CBS News Special*, Burton Benjamin, producer (CBS); "Man Who Dances: Edward Villela," *The Bell Telephone Hour*, Robert Drew and Mike Jackson, producers (NBC); "The Great American Novel," *CBS News Hour*, Arthur Barron, producer (CBS)

OUTSTANDING CULTURAL DOCUMENTARY AND "MAGAZINE TYPE" PROGRAM OR SERIES ACHIEVEMENT (INDIVIDUAL): Walter Dombrow and Jerry Sims, cinematographers, "The Great American Novel," *CBS News Hour* (CBS); Tom Pettit, producer, "CBW: The Secrets of Secrecy," *First Tuesday* (NBC); Lord Snowden, cinematographer, "Don't Count the Candles," *CBS News Hour* (CBS)

1969–1970 (presented June 7, 1970)

OUTSTANDING COMEDY SERIES: *My World and Welcome to It*, Sheldon Leonard, executive producer; Danny Arnold, producer (NBC)

OUTSTANDING DRAMATIC SERIES: *Marcus Welby, M.D.*, David Victor, executive producer; David J. O'Connell, producer (ABC)

OUTSTANDING DRAMATIC PROGRAM: "A Storm in Summer," *Hallmark Hall of Fame*, M. J. Rifkin, executive producer; Alan Landsburg, producer (NBC)

OUTSTANDING VARIETY OR MUSICAL SERIES: *The David Frost Show*, Peter Baker, producer (syndicated)

OUTSTANDING VARIETY OR MUSICAL PROGRAM (VARIETY AND POPULAR MUSIC): "Annie, the Women in the Life of a Man," Joseph Cates, executive producer; Martin Charnin, producer (CBS)

OUTSTANDING VARIETY OR MUSICAL PROGRAM (CLASSICAL MUSIC): "Cinderella," John Barnes and Curtis Davis, executive producers; Norman Campbell, producer (NET)

OUTSTANDING NEW SERIES: *Room 222*, Gene Reynolds, producer (ABC)

OUTSTANDING SINGLE PERFORMANCE BY AN ACTOR IN A LEADING ROLE: Peter Ustinov, "A Storm in Summer," *Hallmark Hall of Fame* (NBC)

OUTSTANDING SINGLE PERFORMANCE BY AN ACTRESS IN A LEADING ROLE: Patty Duke, "My Sweet Charlie," *NBC World Premiere Movie* (NBC)

OUTSTANDING CONTINUED PERFORMANCE BY AN ACTOR IN A LEADING ROLE IN A DRAMATIC SERIES: Robert Young, *Marcus Welby, M.D.* (ABC)

OUTSTANDING CONTINUED PERFORMANCE BY AN ACTRESS IN A LEADING ROLE IN A DRAMATIC SERIES: Susan Hampshire, *The Forsythe Saga* (NET)

OUTSTANDING CONTINUED PERFORMANCE BY AN ACTOR IN A LEADING ROLE IN A COMEDY SERIES: William Windom, *My World and Welcome to It* (NBC)

OUTSTANDING CONTINUED PERFORMANCE BY AN ACTRESS IN A LEADING ROLE IN A COMEDY SERIES: Hope Lange, *The Ghost and Mrs. Muir* (ABC)

OUTSTANDING PERFORMANCE BY AN ACTOR IN A SUPPORTING ROLE IN DRAMA: James Brolin, *Marcus Welby, M.D.* (ABC)

OUTSTANDING PERFORMANCE BY AN ACTRESS IN A SUPPORTING ROLE IN DRAMA: Gail Fisher, *Mannix* (CBS)

OUTSTANDING PERFORMANCE BY AN ACTOR IN A SUPPORTING ROLE IN COMEDY: Michael Constantine, *Room 222* (ABC)

OUTSTANDING PERFORMANCE BY AN ACTRESS IN A SUPPORTING ROLE IN COMEDY: Karen Valentine, *Room 222* (ABC)

OUTSTANDING WRITING ACHIEVEMENT IN DRAMA: Richard Levinson and William Link, "My Sweet Charlie," *NBC World Premiere Movie* (NBC)

OUTSTANDING WRITING ACHIEVEMENT IN COMEDY, VARIETY, OR MUSIC: Gary Belkin, Peter Bellwood, Herb Sargent, Thomas Meehan, and Judith Viorst, "Annie, the Women in the Life of a Man" (CBS)

OUTSTANDING DIRECTORIAL ACHIEVEMENT IN DRAMA: Paul Bogart, "Shadow Game," *CBS Playhouse* (CBS)

OUTSTANDING DIRECTORIAL ACHIEVEMENT IN COMEDY, VARIETY, OR MUSIC: Dwight Hemion, "The Sound of Burt Bacharach," *Kraft Music Hall* (NBC)

SPECIAL CLASSIFICATION OF OUTSTANDING PROGRAM AND INDIVIDUAL ACHIEVEMENT: *Wild Kingdom*, Don Meier, producer (NBC)

OUTSTANDING ACHIEVEMENT WITHIN REGULARLY SCHEDULED NEWS PROGRAMS: "An Investigation of Teenage Drug Addiction—Odyssey House," *The Huntley-Brinkley Report*, Wallace Westfeldt, executive producer; Les Crystal, producer (NBC). "Can the World Be Saved?," *The CBS Evening News with Walter Cronkite*, Ronald Bonn, producer (CBS)

OUTSTANDING ACHIEVEMENT IN MAGAZINE-TYPE PROGRAMMING: *Black Journal*, William Greaves, executive producer (NET); Tom Pettit, reporter-writer, "Some Footnotes to 25 Nuclear Years," *First Tuesday* (NBC)

OUTSTANDING ACHIEVEMENT IN NEWS DOCUMENTARY PROGRAMMING: "Hospital," *NET Journal*, Frederick Wiseman, producer (NET). "The Making of the President 1968," M. J. Rifkin, executive producer; Mel Stuart, producer (CBS)

OUTSTANDING ACHIEVEMENT IN CULTURAL DOCUMENTARY PROGRAMMING: "Artur Rubinstein," George A. Vicas, producer (NBC). Artur Rubinstein, commentator, "Artur Rubinstein" (NBC). "Fathers and Sons," *CBS News Hour*, Ernest Leiser, executive producer; Harry Morgan, producer (CBS). "The Japanese," *CBS News Hour*, Perry Wolff, executive producer; Igor Oganesoff, producer (CBS). Edwin O. Reischauer, commentator, "The Japanese," *CBS News Hour* (CBS)

1970–1971 (presented May 9, 1971)

OUTSTANDING SERIES—COMEDY: *All in the Family*, Norman Lear, producer (CBS)

OUTSTANDING SERIES—DRAMA: *The Senator [The Bold Ones]*, David Levinson, producer (NBC)

OUTSTANDING SINGLE PROGRAM—DRAMA OR COMEDY: "The Andersonville Trial," *Hollywood Television Theatre*, Lewis Freedman, producer (PBS)

OUTSTANDING VARIETY SERIES—MUSICAL: *The Flip Wilson Show*, Monte Kay, executive producer; Bob Henry, producer (NBC)

OUTSTANDING VARIETY SERIES—TALK: *The David Frost Show*, Peter Baker, producer (syndicated)

OUTSTANDING SINGLE PROGRAM—VARIETY OR MUSICAL (VARIETY AND POPULAR MUSIC): "Singer Presents Burt Bacharach," Gary Smith and Dwight Hemion, producers (CBS)

OUTSTANDING SINGLE PROGRAM—VARIETY OR MUSICAL (CLASSICAL MUSIC): "Leopold Stokowski," *NET Festival*, Curtis W. Davis, executive producer, Thomas Stevin, producer (PBS)

OUTSTANDING NEW SERIES: *All in the Family*, Norman Lear, producer (CBS)

OUTSTANDING SINGLE PERFORMANCE BY AN ACTOR IN A LEADING ROLE: George C. Scott, "The Price," *Hallmark Hall of Fame* (NBC)

OUTSTANDING SINGLE PERFORMANCE BY AN ACTRESS IN A LEADING ROLE: Lee Grant, "The Neon Ceiling," *World Premiere NBC Monday Night at the Movies* (NBC)

OUTSTANDING CONTINUED PERFORMANCE BY AN ACTOR IN A LEADING ROLE IN A DRAMATIC SERIES: Hal Holbrook, *The Senator [The Bold Ones]* (NBC)

OUTSTANDING CONTINUED PERFORMANCE BY AN ACTRESS IN A LEADING ROLE IN A DRAMATIC SERIES: Susan Hampshire, *The First Churchills [Masterpiece Theatre]* (PBS)

OUTSTANDING CONTINUED PERFORMANCE BY AN ACTOR IN A LEADING ROLE IN A COMEDY SERIES: Jack Klugman, *The Odd Couple* (ABC)

OUTSTANDING CONTINUED PERFORMANCE BY AN ACTRESS IN A LEADING ROLE IN A COMEDY SERIES: Jean Stapleton, *All in the Family* (CBS)

OUTSTANDING PERFORMANCE BY AN ACTOR IN A SUPPORTING ROLE IN DRAMA: David Burns, "The Price," *Hallmark Hall of Fame* (NBC)

OUTSTANDING PERFORMANCE BY AN ACTRESS IN A SUPPORTING ROLE IN DRAMA: Margaret Leighton, "Hamlet," *Hallmark Hall of Fame* (NBC)

OUTSTANDING PERFORMANCE BY AN ACTOR IN A SUPPORTING ROLE IN COMEDY: Edward Asner, *The Mary Tyler Moore Show* (CBS)

OUTSTANDING PERFORMANCE BY AN ACTRESS IN A SUPPORTING ROLE IN COMEDY: Valerie Harper, *The Mary Tyler Moore Show* (CBS)

OUTSTANDING DIRECTORIAL ACHIEVEMENT IN DRAMA (SERIES): Daryl Duke, "The Day the Lion Died," *The Senator [The Bold Ones]* (NBC)

OUTSTANDING DIRECTORIAL ACHIEVEMENT IN DRAMA (SINGLE PROGRAM): Fielder Cook, "The Price," *Hallmark Hall of Fame (NBC)*

OUTSTANDING DIRECTORIAL ACHIEVEMENT IN COMEDY (SERIES): Jay Sandrich, "Toulouse-Lautrec Is One of My Favorite Artists," *The Mary Tyler Moore Show* (CBS)

OUTSTANDING DIRECTORIAL ACHIEVEMENT IN VARIETY OR MUSIC (SERIES): Mark Warren, *Rowan & Martin's Laugh-In,* 10/26/70 (NBC)

OUTSTANDING DIRECTORIAL ACHIEVEMENT IN VARIETY OR MUSIC (SPECIAL): Sterling Johnson, "Timex Presents Peggy Fleming at Sun Valley" (NBC)

OUTSTANDING WRITING ACHIEVEMENT IN DRAMA (SERIES): Joel Oliansky, "To Taste of Death but Once," *The Senator [The Bold Ones]* (NBC)

OUTSTANDING WRITING ACHIEVEMENT IN DRAMA, ORIGINAL TELEPLAY (SPECIAL): Tracy Keenan Wynn and Marvin Schwartz, "Tribes," *Movie of the Week* (ABC)

OUTSTANDING WRITING ACHIEVEMENT IN DRAMA, ADAPTATION (SPECIAL): Saul Levitt, "The Andersonville Trial" (PBS)

OUTSTANDING WRITING ACHIEVEMENT IN COMEDY (SERIES): James L. Brooks and Allan Burns, "Support Your Local Mother," *The Mary Tyler Moore Show* (CBS)

OUTSTANDING WRITING ACHIEVEMENT IN VARIETY OR MUSIC (SERIES): Herbert Baker, Hal Goodman, Larry Klein, Bob Weiskopf, Bob Schiller, Norman Steinberg, and Flip Wilson, *The Flip Wilson Show,* with Lena Horne and Tony Randall, 12/10/70 (NBC)

OUTSTANDING WRITING ACHIEVEMENT IN COMEDY, VARIETY, OR MUSIC (SPECIAL): Bob Ellison and Marty Farrell, "Singer Presents Burt Bacharach" (CBS)

OUTSTANDING ACHIEVEMENT WITHIN REGULARLY SCHEDULED NEWS PROGRAMS (PROGRAMS): "Five Part Investigation of Welfare," *The NBC Nightly News,* Wallace Westfeldt, executive producer; David Teitelbaum, producer (NBC)

OUTSTANDING ACHIEVEMENT WITHIN REGULARLY SCHEDULED NEWS PROGRAMS (INDIVIDUALS): Bruce Morton, correspondent, "Reports from the Lt. Calley Trial," *The CBS Evening News with Walter Cronkite* (CBS)

OUTSTANDING ACHIEVEMENT IN NEWS DOCUMENTARY PROGRAMMING (PROGRAMS): "The Selling of the Pentagon," Perry Wolff, executive producer; Peter Davis, producer (CBS). "The World of Charlie Company," Ernest Leiser, executive producer; Russ Bensley, producer (CBS). "NBC White Paper: Pollution Is a Matter of Choice," Fred Freed, producer (NBC)

OUTSTANDING ACHIEVEMENT IN NEWS DOCUMENTARY PROGRAMMING (INDIVIDUALS): John Laurence, correspondent, "The World of Charlie Company" (CBS); Fred Freed, writer, "NBC News White Paper: Pollution Is a Matter of Choice" (NBC)

OUTSTANDING ACHIEVEMENT IN MAGAZINE-TYPE PROGRAMMING (PROGRAMS): "Gulf of Tonkin Segment," *60 Minutes,* Joseph Wershba, producer; *The Great American Dream Machine,* A. H. Perlmutter and Jack Willis, executive producers (PBS)

OUTSTANDING ACHIEVEMENT IN MAGAZINE-TYPE PROGRAMMING (INDIVIDUALS): Mike Wallace, correspondent, *60 Minutes* (CBS)

OUTSTANDING ACHIEVEMENT IN CULTURAL DOCUMENTARY PROGRAMMING (PROGRAMS): "The Everglades," Craig Fisher, producer (NBC); "The Making of Butch Cassidy & the Sundance Kid," Ronald Preissman, producer (NBC); "Arthur Penn, 1922–   : Themes and Variants," Robert Hughes, producer (PBS)

OUTSTANDING ACHIEVEMENT IN CULTURAL DOCUMENTARY PROGRAMMING (INDIVIDUALS): Nana Mahomo, narrator, "A Black View of South Africa" (CBS); Robert Guenette and Theodore H. Strauss, writers, "They've Killed President Lincoln" (NBC); Robert Young, director, "The Eskimo Fight for Life" (CBS)

SPECIAL CLASSIFICATION OF OUTSTANDING INDIVIDUAL ACHIEVEMENT: Harvey Korman, *The Carol Burnett Show* (CBS)

1971–1972 (presented May 6, 1972)

OUTSTANDING SERIES—COMEDY: *All in the Family,* Norman Lear, producer (CBS)

OUTSTANDING SERIES—DRAMA: *Elizabeth R [Masterpiece Theatre],* Christopher Sarson, executive producer; Roderick Graham, producer (PBS)

OUTSTANDING SINGLE PROGRAM—DRAMA OR COMEDY: "Brian's Song," *Movie of the Week,* Paul Junger Witt, producer (ABC)

OUTSTANDING VARIETY SERIES—MUSICAL: *The Carol Burnett Show,* Joe Hamilton, executive producer; Arnie Rosen, producer (CBS)

OUTSTANDING VARIETY SERIES—TALK: *The Dick Cavett Show,* John Gilroy, producer (ABC)

OUTSTANDING SINGLE PROGRAM (VARIETY AND POPULAR MUSIC): "Jack Lemmon in 'S Wonderful, 'S Marvelous, 'S Gershwin," *Bell System Family Theatre,* Joseph Cates, executive producer; Martin Charnin, producer (NBC)

OUTSTANDING SINGLE PROGRAM (CLASSICAL MUSIC): "Beethoven's Birthday: A Celebration in Vienna with Leonard Bernstein," James Krayer, executive producer; Humphrey Burton, producer (CBS)

OUTSTANDING NEW SERIES: *Elizabeth R [Masterpiece Theatre],* Christopher Sarson, executive producer; Roderick Graham, producer (PBS)

OUTSTANDING SINGLE PERFORMANCE BY AN ACTOR IN A LEADING ROLE: Keith Michell, "Catherine Howard," *The Six Wives of Henry VIII* (CBS)

OUTSTANDING SINGLE PERFORMANCE BY AN ACTRESS IN A LEADING ROLE: Glenda Jackson, "Shadow in the Sun," *Elizabeth R [Masterpiece Theatre]* (PBS)

OUTSTANDING CONTINUED PERFORMANCE BY AN ACTOR IN A LEADING ROLE IN A DRAMATIC SERIES: Peter Falk, *Columbo [NBC Mystery Movie]* (NBC)

OUTSTANDING CONTINUED PERFORMANCE BY AN ACTRESS IN A LEADING ROLE IN A DRAMATIC SERIES: Glenda Jackson, *Elizabeth R [Masterpiece Theatre]* (PBS)

OUTSTANDING CONTINUED PERFORMANCE BY AN ACTOR IN A LEADING ROLE IN A COMEDY SERIES: Carroll O'Connor, *All in the Family* (CBS)

OUTSTANDING CONTINUED PERFORMANCE BY AN ACTRESS IN A LEADING ROLE IN A COMEDY SERIES: Jean Stapleton, *All in the Family* (CBS)

OUTSTANDING PERFORMANCE BY AN ACTOR IN A SUPPORTING ROLE IN DRAMA: Jack Warden, "Brian's Song," *Movie of the Week* (ABC)

OUTSTANDING PERFORMANCE BY AN ACTRESS IN A SUPPORTING ROLE IN DRAMA: Jenny Agutter, "The Snow Goose," *Hallmark Hall of Fame* (NBC)

OUTSTANDING PERFORMANCE BY AN ACTOR IN A SUPPORTING ROLE IN COMEDY: Edward Asner, *The Mary Tyler Moore Show* (CBS)

OUTSTANDING PERFORMANCE BY AN ACTRESS IN A SUPPORTING ROLE IN COMEDY: (TIE) Valerie Harper, *The Mary Tyler Moore Show* (CBS); Sally Struthers, *All in the Family* (CBS)

OUTSTANDING ACHIEVEMENT BY A PERFORMER IN MUSIC OR VARIETY: Harvey Korman, *The Carol Burnett Show* (CBS)

OUTSTANDING ACHIEVEMENT WITHIN REGULARLY SCHEDULED NEWS PROGRAMS (PROGRAMS): "Defeat of Dacca," *The NBC Nightly News,* Wallace Westfeldt, executive producer; Robert Mulholland and David Teitelbaum, producers (NBC)

OUTSTANDING ACHIEVEMENT WITHIN REGULARLY SCHEDULED NEWS PROGRAMS (INDIVIDUALS): Phil Brady, reporter, "Defeat of Dacca," *The NBC Nightly News* (NBC); Bob Schieffer, Phil Jones, Don Webster, and Bill Plante, correspondents, "The Air War," *The CBS Evening News with Walter Cronkite* (CBS)

OUTSTANDING ACHIEVEMENT FOR REGULARLY SCHEDULED MAGAZINE-TYPE PROGRAMS (PROGRAMS): *The Great American Dream Machine,* A. H. Perlmutter, executive producer (PBS); *Chronolog,* Eliot Frankel, executive producer (NBC)

OUTSTANDING ACHIEVEMENT FOR REGULARLY SCHEDULED MAGAZINE-TYPE PROGRAMS (INDIVIDUALS): Mike Wallace, correspondent, *60 Minutes* (CBS)

OUTSTANDING DOCUMENTARY PROGRAM ACHIEVEMENT (PROGRAMS OF CURRENT SIGNIFICANCE): "A Night in Jail, A Night in Court," *CBS Reports,* Burton Benjamin, executive producer; John Sharnik, producer (CBS). "This Child Is Rated X: An NBC News White Paper on Juvenile Justice," Martin Carr, producer (NBC)

OUTSTANDING DOCUMENTARY PROGRAM ACHIEVEMENT (CULTURAL PROGRAMS): "Hollywood: The Dream Factory," *The Monday Night Special,* Nicolas Noxon, executive producer; Irwin Rosten and Bud Friedman, producers (ABC). "A Sound of Dolphins," *The Undersea World of Jacques Cousteau,* Jacques Cousteau and Marshall Flaum, executive producers; Andy White, producer (ABC). "The Unsinkable Sea Otter," *The Undersea World of Jacques Cousteau,* Jacques Cousteau and Marshall Flaum, executive producers; Andy White, producer (ABC)

OUTSTANDING DOCUMENTARY PROGRAM ACHIEVEMENT (INDIVIDUALS): Louis J. Hazam, writer, "Venice Be Damned" (NBC); Robert Northshield, writer, "Suffer the Little Children—An NBC News White Paper on Northern Ireland" (NBC)

OUTSTANDING DIRECTORIAL ACHIEVEMENT IN DRAMA (SERIES): Alexander Singer, "The Invasion of Kevin Ireland," *The Lawyers [The Bold Ones]* (NBC)

OUTSTANDING DIRECTORIAL ACHIEVEMENT IN DRAMA (SINGLE PROGRAM): Tom Gries, "The Glass House," *The New CBS Friday Night Movies* (CBS)

OUTSTANDING DIRECTORIAL ACHIEVEMENT IN COMEDY (SERIES): John Rich, "Sammy's Visit," *All in the Family* (CBS)

OUTSTANDING DIRECTORIAL ACHIEVEMENT IN VARIETY OR MUSIC (SERIES): Art Fisher, *The Sonny and Cher Comedy Hour,* with Tony Randall, 1/31/72 (CBS)

OUTSTANDING DIRECTORIAL ACHIEVEMENT IN COMEDY, VARIETY, OR MUSIC (SPECIAL): Walter C. Miller and Martin Charnin, "Jack Lemmon in 'S Wonderful, 'S Marvelous, 'S Gershwin," *Bell System Family Theatre* (NBC)

OUTSTANDING WRITING ACHIEVEMENT IN DRAMA (SERIES): Richard L. Levinson and William Link, "Death Lends a Hand," *Columbo [NBC Mystery Movie]* (NBC)

OUTSTANDING WRITING ACHIEVEMENT IN DRAMA, ORIGINAL TELEPLAY: Allan Sloane, "To All My Friends on Shore" (CBS)

OUTSTANDING WRITING ACHIEVEMENT IN DRAMA, ADAPTATION: William Blinn, "Brian's Song," *Movie of the Week* (ABC)

OUTSTANDING WRITING ACHIEVEMENT IN COMEDY (SERIES): Burt Styler, "Edith's Problem," *All in the Family* (CBS)

OUTSTANDING WRITING ACHIEVEMENT IN VARIETY OR MUSIC (SERIES): Don Hinkley, Stan Hart, Larry Siegel, Woody Kling, Roger Beatty, Art Baer, Ben Joelson, Stan Burns, Mike Marmer, and Arnie Rosen, *The Carol Burnett Show,* with Tim Conway and Ray Charles, 1/26/72 (CBS)

OUTSTANDING WRITING ACHIEVEMENT IN COMEDY, VARIETY, OR MUSIC (SPECIAL): Anne Howard Bailey, "The Trial of Mary Lincoln," *NET Opera Theatre* (PBS)

SPECIAL CLASSIFICATION OF OUTSTANDING PROGRAM AND INDIVIDUAL ACHIEVEMENT (GENERAL PROGRAMMING): "The Pentagon Papers," *PBS Special,* David Prowitt, executive producer; Martin Clancy, producer (PBS)

SPECIAL CLASSIFICATION OF OUTSTANDING PROGRAM AND INDIVIDUAL ACHIEVEMENT (DOCU-DRAMA): "The Search for the Nile—Parts I–VI," Christopher Railing, producer (NBC)

SPECIAL CLASSIFICATION OF OUTSTANDING PROGRAM AND INDIVIDUAL ACHIEVEMENT (INDIVIDUALS): Michael Hastings and Derek Marlowe, writers, "The Search for the Nile—Parts I–IV" (NBC)

1972–1973 (presented May 22, 1973)

OUTSTANDING COMEDY SERIES: *All in the Family,* Norman Lear, executive producer; John Rich, producer (CBS)

OUTSTANDING DRAMA SERIES—CONTINUING: *The Waltons,* Lee Rich, executive producer; Robert L. Jacks, producer (CBS)

OUTSTANDING DRAMA/COMEDY—LIMITED EPISODES: *Tom Brown's Schooldays [Masterpiece Theatre],* John D. McRae, producer (PBS)

OUTSTANDING VARIETY MUSICAL SERIES: *The Julie Andrews Hour,* Nick Vanoff and William O. Harbach, producers (ABC)

OUTSTANDING SINGLE PROGRAM—DRAMA OR COMEDY: "A War of Children," *The New CBS Tuesday Night Movies,* Roger Gimbel, executive producer; George Schaefer, producer (CBS)

OUTSTANDING SINGLE PROGRAM—VARIETY AND POPULAR MUSIC: "Singer Presents Liza with a 'Z,' " Bob Fosse and Fred Ebb, producers (NBC)

OUTSTANDING SINGLE PROGRAM—CLASSICAL MUSIC: "The Sleeping Beauty," J. W. Barnes and Robert Kotlowitz, executive producers; Norman Campbell, producer (PBS)

OUTSTANDING NEW SERIES: *America*, Michael Gill, producer (NBC)

OUTSTANDING SINGLE PERFORMANCE BY AN ACTOR IN A LEADING ROLE: Laurence Olivier, "A Long Day's Journey into Night" (ABC)

OUTSTANDING SINGLE PERFORMANCE BY AN ACTRESS IN A LEADING ROLE: Cloris Leachman, "A Brand New Life," *Tuesday Movie of the Week* (ABC)

OUTSTANDING CONTINUED PERFORMANCE BY AN ACTOR IN A LEADING ROLE (DRAMA SERIES—CONTINUING): Richard Thomas, *The Waltons* (CBS)

OUTSTANDING CONTINUED PERFORMANCE BY AN ACTOR IN A LEADING ROLE (DRAMA/COMEDY—LIMITED EPISODES): Anthony Murphy, *Tom Brown's Schooldays [Masterpiece Theatre]* (PBS)

OUTSTANDING CONTINUED PERFORMANCE BY AN ACTRESS IN A LEADING ROLE (DRAMA SERIES—CONTINUING): Michael Learned, *The Waltons* (CBS)

OUTSTANDING CONTINUED PERFORMANCE BY AN ACTRESS IN A LEADING ROLE (DRAMA/COMEDY—LIMITED EPISODES): Susan Hampshire, *Vanity Fair [Masterpiece Theatre]* (PBS)

OUTSTANDING CONTINUED PERFORMANCE BY AN ACTOR IN A LEADING ROLE IN A COMEDY SERIES: Jack Klugman, *The Odd Couple* (ABC)

OUTSTANDING CONTINUED PERFORMANCE BY AN ACTRESS IN A LEADING ROLE IN A COMEDY SERIES: Mary Tyler Moore, *The Mary Tyler Moore Show* (CBS)

OUTSTANDING PERFORMANCE BY AN ACTOR IN A SUPPORTING ROLE IN DRAMA: Scott Jacoby, *That Certain Summer," Wednesday Movie of the Week* (ABC)

OUTSTANDING PERFORMANCE BY AN ACTRESS IN A SUPPORTING ROLE IN DRAMA: Ellen Corby, *The Waltons* (CBS)

OUTSTANDING PERFORMANCE BY AN ACTOR IN A SUPPORTING ROLE IN COMEDY: Ted Knight, *The Mary Tyler Moore Show* (CBS)

OUTSTANDING PERFORMANCE BY AN ACTRESS IN A SUPPORTING ROLE IN COMEDY: Valerie Harper, *The Mary Tyler Moore Show* (CBS)

OUTSTANDING ACHIEVEMENT BY A SUPPORTING PERFORMER IN MUSIC OR VARIETY: Tim Conway, *The Carol Burnett Show*, 2/17/73 (CBS)

OUTSTANDING DIRECTORIAL ACHIEVEMENT IN DRAMA (SERIES): Jerry Thorpe, "An Eye for an Eye," *Kung Fu* (ABC)

OUTSTANDING DIRECTORIAL ACHIEVEMENT IN DRAMA (SINGLE PROGRAM): Joseph Sargent, "The Marcus-Nelson Murders," *The CBS Thursday Night Movies* (CBS)

OUTSTANDING DIRECTORIAL ACHIEVEMENT IN COMEDY (SERIES): Jay Sandrich, "It's Whether You Win or Lose," *The Mary Tyler Moore Show* (CBS)

OUTSTANDING DIRECTORIAL ACHIEVEMENT IN VARIETY OR MUSIC (SERIES): Bill Davis, *The Julie Andrews Hour*, with "Liza Doolittle" and "Mary Poppins," 9/13/72 (ABC)

OUTSTANDING DIRECTORIAL ACHIEVEMENT IN VARIETY OR MUSIC (SPECIAL): Bob Fosse, "Singer Presents Liza with a 'Z' " (NBC)

OUTSTANDING WRITING ACHIEVEMENT IN DRAMA (SERIES): John McGreevey, "The Scholar," *The Waltons* (CBS)

OUTSTANDING WRITING ACHIEVEMENT IN DRAMA, ORIGINAL TELEPLAY (SINGLE PROGRAM): Abby Mann, "The Marcus-Nelson Murders," *The CBS Thursday Night Movies* (CBS)

OUTSTANDING WRITING ACHIEVEMENT IN DRAMA, ADAPTATION (SINGLE PROGRAM): Eleanor Perry, "The House without a Christmas Tree" (CBS)

OUTSTANDING WRITING ACHIEVEMENT IN COMEDY (SERIES): Michael Ross, Bernie West, and Lee Kalcheim, "The Bunkers and the Swingers," *All in the Family* (CBS)

OUTSTANDING WRITING ACHIEVEMENT IN VARIETY OR MUSIC (SERIES): Stan Hart, Larry Siegel, Gail Parent, Woody Kling, Roger Beatty, Tom Patchett, Jay Tarses, Robert Hilliard, Arnie Kogen, Bill Angelos, and Buz Kohan, *The Carol Burnett Show*, with Steve Lawrence and Lily Tomlin, 11/8/72 (CBS)

OUTSTANDING WRITING ACHIEVEMENT IN COMEDY, VARIETY, OR MUSIC (SPECIAL): Renee Taylor and Joseph Bologna, "Acts of Love—And Other Comedies" (ABC)

OUTSTANDING ACHIEVEMENT WITHIN REGULARLY SCHEDULED NEWS PROGRAMS (PROGRAM SEGMENTS): "The U.S./Soviet Wheat Deal: Is There a Scandal?" *The CBS Evening News with Walter Cronkite*, Paul Greenberg and Russ Bensley, executive producers; Stanhope Gould and Linda Mason, producers (CBS)

OUTSTANDING ACHIEVEMENT WITHIN REGULARLY SCHEDULED NEWS PROGRAMS (INDIVIDUALS): Walter Cronkite, Dan Rather, Daniel Schorr, and Joel Blocker, correspondents, "The Watergate Affair," *CBS Evening News with Walter Cronkite* (CBS); David Dick, Dan Rather, Roger Mudd, and Walter Cronkite, correspondents, "Coverage of the Shooting of Governor Wallace," *CBS Evening News with Walter Cronkite* (CBS); Eric Sevareid, correspondent, "LBJ—The Man and the President," *CBS Evening News with Walter Cronkite* (CBS)

OUTSTANDING ACHIEVEMENT FOR REGULARLY SCHEDULED MAGAZINE-TYPE PROGRAMS (PROGRAMS): "Poppy Fields of Turkey—The Heroin Labs of Marseilles—The New York Connection," *60 Minutes*, Don Hewitt, executive producer; William McClure, John Tiffin, and Philip Scheffler, producers (CBS). "The Selling of Colonel Herbert," *60 Minutes*, Don Hewitt, executive producer; Barry Lando, producer (CBS). *60 Minutes*, Don Hewitt, executive producer (CBS)

OUTSTANDING ACHIEVEMENT FOR REGULARLY SCHEDULED MAGAZINE-TYPE PROGRAMS (INDIVIDUALS): Mike Wallace, correspondent, "The Selling of Colonel Herbert," *60 Minutes* (CBS); Mike Wallace, correspondent, *60 Minutes* (CBS)

OUTSTANDING ACHIEVEMENT IN COVERAGE OF SPECIAL EVENTS (INDIVIDUALS): Jim McKay, commentator, "Coverage of the Munich Olympic Tragedy," *ABC Special* (ABC)

OUTSTANDING DOCUMENTARY PROGRAM ACHIEVEMENT (CURRENT EVENTS): "The Blue Collar Trap," *NBC News White Paper,* Fred Freed, producer (NBC). "The Mexican Connection," *CBS Reports,* Burton Benjamin, executive producer; Jay McMullen, producer (CBS). "One Billion Dollar Weapon and Now the War Is Over—The American Military in the 1970's," *NBC Reports,* Fred Freed, executive producer; Al Davis, producer (NBC)

OUTSTANDING DOCUMENTARY PROGRAM ACHIEVEMENT (CULTURAL): *America,* Michael Gill, executive producer (NBC). "Jane Goodall and the World of Animal Behavior—The Wild Dogs of Africa," Marshall Flaum, executive producer; Hugo Van Lawick, Bill Travers, and James Hill, producers (ABC)

OUTSTANDING DOCUMENTARY PROGRAM ACHIEVEMENT (INDIVIDUALS): Alistair Cooke, narrator, *America* (NBC); Alistair Cooke, writer, "A Fireball in the Night," *America* (NBC); Hugo Van Lawick, director, "Jane Goodall and the World of Animal Behavior—The Wild Dogs of Africa" (ABC)

SPECIAL CLASSIFICATION OF OUTSTANDING PROGRAM AND INDIVIDUAL ACHIEVEMENT: *The Advocates,* Greg Harney, executive producer; Tom Burrows, Russ Morash, and Peter McGhee, producers (PBS). "VD Blues," *The Special of the Week,* Don Fouser, producer (PBS)

1973–1974 (presented May 28, 1974)

OUTSTANDING COMEDY SERIES: *M*A*S*H,* Gene Reynolds and Larry Gelbart, producers (CBS)

OUTSTANDING DRAMA SERIES: *Upstairs, Downstairs [Masterpiece Theatre],* Rex Firkin, executive producer; John Hawkesworth, producer (PBS)

OUTSTANDING MUSIC-VARIETY SERIES: *The Carol Burnett Show,* Joe Hamilton, executive producer; Ed Simmons, producer (CBS)

OUTSTANDING LIMITED SERIES: *Columbo [NBC Sunday Mystery Movie],* Dean Hargrove and Roland Kibbee, executive producers; Douglas Benton, Robert F. O'Neill, and Edward K. Dodds, producers (NBC)

OUTSTANDING SPECIAL—COMEDY OR DRAMA (SINGLE SPECIAL PROGRAM): "The Autobiography of Miss Jane Pittman," Robert Christiansen and Rick Rosenberg, producers (CBS)

OUTSTANDING COMEDY-VARIETY, VARIETY, OR MUSIC SPECIAL (SINGLE SPECIAL PROGRAM): "Lily," Irene Pinn, executive producer; Herb Sargent and Jerry McPhie, producers (CBS)

OUTSTANDING CHILDREN'S SPECIAL (EVENING): "Marlo Thomas and Friends in Free to Be . . . You and Me," Marlo Thomas and Carole Hart, producers (ABC)

BEST LEAD ACTOR IN A COMEDY SERIES: Alan Alda, *M*A*S*H* (CBS)

BEST LEAD ACTOR IN A DRAMA SERIES: Telly Savalas, *Kojak* (CBS)

BEST LEAD ACTOR IN A LIMITED SERIES: William Holden, *The Blue Knight* (NBC)

BEST LEAD ACTOR IN A DRAMA (FOR A SPECIAL PROGRAM—COMEDY OR DRAMA; OR A SINGLE APPEARANCE IN A COMEDY OR DRAMA SERIES): Hal Holbrook, "Pueblo," *ABC Theatre* (ABC)

ACTOR OF THE YEAR—SERIES: Alan Alda, *M*A*S*H* (CBS)

ACTOR OF THE YEAR—SPECIAL: Hal Holbrook, "Pueblo," *ABC Theatre* (ABC)

BEST LEAD ACTRESS IN A COMEDY SERIES: Mary Tyler Moore, *The Mary Tyler Moore Show* (CBS)

BEST LEAD ACTRESS IN A DRAMA SERIES: Michael Learned, *The Waltons* (CBS)

BEST LEAD ACTRESS IN A LIMITED SERIES: Mildred Natwick, *The Snoop Sisters [NBC Tuesday Mystery Movie]* (NBC)

BEST LEAD ACTRESS IN A DRAMA (FOR A SPECIAL PROGRAM—COMEDY OR DRAMA; OR A SINGLE APPEARANCE IN A COMEDY OR DRAMA SERIES): Cicely Tyson, "The Autobiography of Miss Jane Pittman" (CBS)

ACTRESS OF THE YEAR—SERIES: Mary Tyler Moore, *The Mary Tyler Moore Show* (CBS)

ACTRESS OF THE YEAR—SPECIAL: Cicely Tyson, "The Autobiography of Miss Jane Pittman" (CBS)

BEST SUPPORTING ACTOR IN COMEDY (FOR SPECIAL PROGRAM; A ONE-TIME APPEARANCE IN A SERIES; OR A CONTINUING ROLE): Rob Reiner, *All in the Family* (CBS)

BEST SUPPORTING ACTOR IN DRAMA (FOR A SPECIAL PROGRAM; A ONE-TIME APPEARANCE IN A SERIES; OR CONTINUING ROLE): Michael Moriarty, "The Glass Menagerie" (ABC)

BEST SUPPORTING ACTOR IN COMEDY-VARIETY, VARIETY, OR MUSIC (FOR A SPECIAL PROGRAM; A ONE-TIME APPEARANCE IN A SERIES; OR A CONTINUING ROLE): Harvey Korman, *The Carol Burnett Show* (CBS)

SUPPORTING ACTOR OF THE YEAR: Michael Moriarty, "The Glass Menagerie" (ABC)

SUPPORTING ACTRESS IN COMEDY (FOR A SPECIAL PROGRAM; A ONE-TIME appearance in a series; OR A CONTINUING ROLE): Cloris Leachman, "The Lars Affair," *The Mary Tyler Moore Show,* 9/15/73 (CBS)

BEST SUPPORTING ACTRESS IN DRAMA (FOR A SPECIAL PROGRAM; A ONE-TIME APPEARANCE IN A SERIES; OR A CONTINUING ROLE): Joanna Miles, "The Glass Menagerie" (ABC)

BEST SUPPORTING ACTRESS IN COMEDY-VARIETY, VARIETY, OR MUSIC (FOR A SPECIAL PROGRAM; A ONE-TIME APPEARANCE IN A SERIES; OR A CONTINUING ROLE): Brenda Vaccaro, "The Shape of Things" (CBS)

SUPPORTING ACTRESS OF THE YEAR: Joanna Miles, "The Glass Menagerie" (ABC)

BEST DIRECTING IN DRAMA (A SINGLE PROGRAM OF A SERIES WITH CONTINUING CHARACTERS AND/OR THEME): Robert Butler, *The Blue Knight,* PART III, 11/15/73 (NBC)

BEST DIRECTING IN DRAMA (A SINGLE PROGRAM—COMEDY OR DRAMA): John Korty, "The Autobiography of Miss Jane Pittman" (CBS)

BEST DIRECTING IN COMEDY (A SINGLE PROGRAM OR A SERIES WITH CONTINUING CHARACTERS AND/OR THEME): Jackie Cooper, "Carry on Hawkeye," *M*A*S*H,* 11/24/73 (CBS)

BEST DIRECTING IN VARIETY OR MUSIC (A SINGLE PROGRAM OF A SERIES): Dave Powers, "The Australia Show," *The Carol Burnett Show,* 12/8/73 (CBS)

BEST DIRECTING IN COMEDY-VARIETY, VARIETY, OR MUSIC (A SPECIAL PROGRAM): Dwight Hemion, "Barbra Streisand . . . And Other Musical Instruments" (CBS)

DIRECTOR OF THE YEAR—SERIES: Robert Butler, *The Blue Knight,* Part III, 11/15/73 (NBC)

DIRECTOR OF THE YEAR—SPECIAL: Dwight Hemion, "Barbra Streisand . . . And Other Musical Instruments" (CBS)

BEST WRITING IN DRAMA (A SINGLE PROGRAM OF A SERIES WITH CONTINUING CHARACTERS AND/OR THEME): Joanna Lee, "The Thanksgiving Story," *The Waltons*, 11/15/73 (CBS)

BEST WRITING IN DRAMA, ORIGINAL TELEPLAY (A SINGLE PROGRAM—COMEDY OR DRAMA): Fay Kanin, "Tell Me Where It Hurts," *G. E. Theater* (CBS)

BEST WRITING IN DRAMA, ADAPTATION (A SINGLE PROGRAM—COMEDY OR DRAMA): Tracy Keenan Wynn, "The Autobiography of Miss Jane Pittman" (CBS)

BEST WRITING IN COMEDY (A SINGLE PROGRAM OF A SERIES WITH CONTINUING CHARACTERS AND/OR THEME): Treva Silverman, "The Lou and Edie Story," *The Mary Tyler Moore Show*, 10/6/73 (CBS)

BEST WRITING IN VARIETY OR MUSIC (A SINGLE PROGRAM OF A SERIES): Ed Simmons, Gary Belkin, Roger Beatty, Arnie Kogen, Bill Richmond, Gene Perret, Rudy De Luca, Barry Levinson, Dick Clair, Jenna McMahon, and Barry Harman, *The Carol Burnett Show*, with Tim Conway and Bernadette Peters, 2/16/74 (CBS)

BEST WRITING IN COMEDY-VARIETY, VARIETY, OR MUSIC (A SPECIAL PROGRAM): Herb Sargent, Rosalyn Drexler, Lorne Michaels, Richard Pryor, Jim Rusk, James R. Stein, Robert Illes, Lily Tomlin, George Yanok, Jane Wagner, Rod Warren, Ann Elder, and Karyl Geld, "Lily" (CBS)

WRITER OF THE YEAR—SERIES: Treva Silverman, "The Lou and Edie Story," *The Mary Tyler Moore Show*, 10/6/73 (CBS)

WRITER OF THE YEAR—SPECIAL: Fay Kanin, "Tell Me Where It Hurts," *G. E. Theater* (CBS)

SPECIAL CLASSIFICATION OF OUTSTANDING PROGRAM AND INDIVIDUAL ACHIEVEMENT: *The Dick Cavett Show*, John Gilroy, producer (ABC); Tom Snyder, host, *Tomorrow* (NBC)

OUTSTANDING INDIVIDUAL ACHIEVEMENT IN CHILDREN'S PROGRAMMING: Charles M. Shultz, writer, "A Charlie Brown Thanksgiving" (CBS)

OUTSTANDING ACHIEVEMENT WITHIN REGULARLY SCHEDULED NEWS PROGRAMS: "Coverage of the October War from Israel's Northern Front," *CBS Evening News with Walter Cronkite*, John Laurence, correspondent, October 1973 (CBS). "The Agnew Resignation," Spiro Agnew *CBS Evening News with Walter Cronkite*, Paul Greenberg, executive producer; Ron Bonn, Ed Fouhy, John Lane, Don Bowers, John Armstrong, and Robert Mean, producers; Walter Cronkite, Robert Schakne, Fred Graham, Robert Pierpoint, Roger Mudd, Dan Rather, John Hart, and Eric Sevareid, correspondents, 10/10/73 (CBS). "The Key Biscayne Bank Charter Struggle," *CBS Evening News with Walter Cronkite*, Ed Fouhy, producer; Robert Pierpoint, correspondent, 10/15–10/17/73 (CBS). "Reports on World Hunger," *NBC Nightly News*, Lester M. Crystal, executive producer; Richard Fischer and Joseph Angotti, producer; Tom Streithorst, Phil Brady, John Palmer, and Liz Trotta, correspondents, March–June 1974 (NBC)

OUTSTANDING ACHIEVEMENT FOR REGULARLY SCHEDULED MAGAZINE-TYPE PROGRAMS: "America's Nerve Gas Arsenal," *First Tuesday*, Eliot Frankel, executive producer; William B. Hill and Anthony Potter, producers; Tom Pettit, correspondent, 6/5/73 (NBC). "The Adversaries," *Behind the Lines*, Carey Winfrey, executive producer; Peter Forbath, producer/reporter, Brendan Gill, host/moderator, 3/28/74 (PBS); "A Question of Impeachment," *Bill Moyers' Journal*, Jerome Toobin, executive producer; Martin Clancy, producer; Bill Moyers, broadcaster, 1/22/74 (PBS)

OUTSTANDING DOCUMENTARY PROGRAM ACHIEVEMENTS (CURRENT EVENTS): "Fire!," *ABC News Close Up*, Pamela Hill, producer; Jules Bergman, correspondent/narrator (ABC). "CBS News Special Report: The Senate and the Watergate Affair," Lesley Midgley, executive producer; Hal Haley, Bernard Birnbaum, and David Browning, producers; Dan Rather, Roger Mudd, Daniel Schorr, and Fred Graham correspondents (CBS)

OUTSTANDING DOCUMENTARY PROGRAM ACHIEVEMENTS (CULTURAL): "Journey to the Outer Limits," *National Geographic Specials*, Nicholas Clapp and Dennis Kane, executive producers; Alex Grasshoff, producer (ABC). *The World at War*, Jeremy Isaacs, producer (syndicated). CBS "Reports: The Rockefellers," Burton Benjamin, executive producer; Howard Stringer, producer; Walter Cronkite, correspondent (CBS)

OUTSTANDING INTERVIEW PROGRAM (FOR A SINGLE PROGRAM OF A SERIES): "Solzhenitsyn," *CBS News Special*, Burton Benjamin, producer; Walter Cronkite, correspondent, 6/24/74 (CBS). "Henry Steele Commager," *Bill Moyers' Journal*, Jerome Toobin, executive producer; Martin Clancy, producer; Bill Moyers, broadcaster, 3/26/74 (PBS)

OUTSTANDING TELEVISION NEWS BROADCASTER: Harry Reasoner, *ABC News* (ABC); Bill Moyers, "Essay on Watergate," *Bill Moyers' Journal*, 10/31/73 (PBS)

1974–1975 (presented May 19, 1975)

OUTSTANDING COMEDY SERIES: *The Mary Tyler Moore Show*. James L. Brooks and Allan Burns, executive producers; Ed Weinberger and San Daniels, producers (CBS)

OUTSTANDING DRAMA SERIES: *Upstairs, Downstairs [Masterpiece Theatre]*, Rex Firkin, executive producer; John Hawkesworth, producer (PBS)

OUTSTANDING COMEDY-VARIETY OR MUSIC SERIES: *The Carol Burnett Show*, Joe Hamilton, executive producer; Ed Simmons, producer (CBS)

OUTSTANDING LIMITED SERIES: *Benjamin Franklin*, Lewis Freedman, executive producer; George Lefferts and Glenn Jordan, producers (CBS)

OUTSTANDING SPECIAL—DRAMA OR COMEDY: "The Law," *NBC World Premiere Movie*, William Sackheim, producer, 10/22/74 (NBC)

OUTSTANDING SPECIAL—COMEDY-VARIETY OR MUSIC: "An Evening with John Denver," Jerry Weintaub, executive producer; Al Rogers and Rich Eustis, producers (ABC)

OUTSTANDING CLASSICAL MUSIC PROGRAM (FOR A SPECIAL PROGRAM OR FOR A SERIES): "Profile in Music: Beverly Sills," *Festival '75*, Patricia Foy, producer, 3/10/75 (PBS)

OUTSTANDING LEAD ACTOR IN A COMEDY SERIES: Tony Randall, *The Odd Couple* (ABC)
OUTSTANDING LEAD ACTOR IN A DRAMA SERIES: Robert Blake, *Baretta* (ABC)
OUTSTANDING LEAD ACTOR IN A LIMITED SERIES: Peter Falk, *Columbo [NBC Sunday Mystery Movie]* (NBC)
OUTSTANDING LEAD ACTOR IN A SPECIAL PROGRAM—DRAMA OR COMEDY (FOR A SPECIAL PROGRAM; OR A SINGLE APPEARANCE IN A DRAMA OR COMEDY SERIES): Laurence Olivier, "Love Among the Ruins," *ABC Theatre* (ABC)
OUTSTANDING LEAD ACTRESS IN A COMEDY SERIES: Valerie Harper, *Rhoda* (CBS)
OUTSTANDING LEAD ACTRESS IN A DRAMA SERIES: Jean Marsh, *Upstairs, Downstairs [Masterpiece Theatre]* (PBS)
OUTSTANDING LEAD ACTRESS IN A LIMITED SERIES: Jessica Walter, *Amy Prentiss [NBC Sunday Mystery Movie]* (NBC)
OUTSTANDING LEAD ACTRESS IN A SPECIAL PROGRAM—DRAMA OR COMEDY (FOR A SPECIAL PROGRAM; OR A SINGLE APPEARANCE IN A DRAMA OR COMEDY SERIES): Katharine Hepburn, "Love Among the Ruins," *ABC Theatre* (ABC)
OUTSTANDING CONTINUING PERFORMANCE BY A SUPPORTING ACTOR IN A COMEDY SERIES: Ed Asner, *The Mary Tyler Moore Show* (CBS)
OUTSTANDING CONTINUING PERFORMANCE BY A SUPPORTING ACTOR IN A DRAMA SERIES: Will Geer, *The Waltons* (CBS)
OUTSTANDING CONTINUING OR SINGLE PERFORMANCE BY A SUPPORTING ACTOR IN VARIETY OR MUSIC (FOR A CONTINUING ROLE IN A REGULAR OR LIMITED SERIES; OR A ONE-TIME APPEARANCE IN A SERIES; OR A SPECIAL): Jack Albertson, *Cher,* 3/2/75 (CBS)
OUTSTANDING SINGLE PERFORMANCE BY A SUPPORTING ACTOR IN A COMEDY OR DRAMA SPECIAL: Anthony Quayle, "QB VII," Parts 1 & 2, *ABC Movie Special* (ABC)
OUTSTANDING SINGLE PERFORMANCE BY A SUPPORTING ACTOR IN A COMEDY OR DRAMA SERIES (FOR A ONE-TIME APPEARANCE IN A REGULAR OR LIMITED SERIES): Patrick McGoohan, "By Dawn's Early Light," *Columbo [NBC Sunday Mystery Movie],* 10/27/74 (NBC)
OUTSTANDING CONTINUING PERFORMANCE BY A SUPPORTING ACTRESS IN A COMEDY SERIES: Betty White, *The Mary Tyler Moore Show* (CBS)
OUTSTANDING CONTINUING PERFORMANCE BY A SUPPORTING ACTRESS IN A DRAMA SERIES: Ellen Corby, *The Waltons* (CBS)
OUTSTANDING CONTINUING OR SINGLE PERFORMANCE BY A SUPPORTING ACTRESS IN VARIETY OR MUSIC (FOR CONTINUING ROLE IN A REGULAR OR LIMITED SERIES; OR A ONE-TIME APPEARANCE IN A SERIES; OR A SPECIAL): Cloris Leachman, *Cher,* 3/2/75 (CBS)
OUTSTANDING SINGLE PERFORMANCE BY A SUPPORTING ACTRESS IN A COMEDY OR DRAMA SPECIAL: Juliet Mills, "QB VII," Parts 1 & 2, *ABC Movie Special* (ABC)
OUTSTANDING SINGLE PERFORMANCE BY A SUPPORTING ACTRESS IN A COMEDY OR DRAMA SERIES (FOR A ONE-TIME APPEARANCE IN A REGULAR OR LIMITED SERIES): (TIE) Cloris Leachman, "Phyllis Whips Inflation," *The Mary Tyler Moore Show,* 1/18/75 (CBS); Zohra Lampert, "Queen of the Gypsies," *Kojak,* 1/19/75 (CBS)
OUTSTANDING DIRECTING IN A DRAMA SERIES (A SINGLE EPISODE OF A REGULAR OR LIMITED SERIES WITH CONTINUING CHARACTERS AND/OR THEME): Bill Bain, "A Sudden Storm," *Upstairs, Downstairs [Masterpiece Theatre],* 12/22/74 (PBS)
OUTSTANDING DIRECTING IN A COMEDY SERIES (A SINGLE EPISODE OF A REGULAR OR LIMITED SERIES WITH CONTINUING CHARACTERS AND/OR THEME): Gene Reynolds, "O.R.," *M*A*S*H,* 10/8/74 (CBS)
OUTSTANDING DIRECTING IN A COMEDY-VARIETY OR MUSIC SERIES (A SINGLE EPISODE OF A REGULAR OR LIMITED SERIES): Dave Powers, *The Carol Burnett Show,* with Alan Alda, 12/21/74 (CBS)
OUTSTANDING DIRECTING IN A COMEDY-VARIETY OR MUSICAL SPECIAL: Bill Davis, "An Evening with John Denver" (ABC)
OUTSTANDING DIRECTING IN A SPECIAL PROGRAM—DRAMA OR COMEDY: George Cukor, "Love Among the Ruins," *ABC Theatre* (ABC)
OUTSTANDING WRITING IN A DRAMA SERIES (A SINGLE EPISODE OF A REGULAR OR LIMITED SERIES WITH CONTINUING CHARACTERS AND/OR THEME): Howard Fast, "The Ambassador," *Benjamin Franklin,* 11/21/74 (CBS)
OUTSTANDING WRITING IN A COMEDY SERIES (A SINGLE EPISODE OF A REGULAR OR LIMITED SERIES WITH CONTINUING CHARACTERS AND/OR THEME): Ed Weinberger and Stan Daniels, "Mary Richards Goes to Jail," *The Mary Tyler Moore Show,* 9/14/74 (CBS)
OUTSTANDING WRITING IN A COMEDY-VARIETY OR MUSIC SERIES (A SINGLE EPISODE OF A REGULAR OR LIMITED SERIES): Ed Simmons, Gary Belkin, Roger Beatty, Arnie Kogen, Bill Richmond, Gene Perret, Rudy De Luca, Barry Levinson, Dick Clair, and Jenna McMahon, *The Carol Burnett Show,* with Alan Alda, 12/21/74 (CBS)
OUTSTANDING WRITING IN A COMEDY-VARIETY OR MUSIC SPECIAL: Bob Wells, John Bradford, and Cy Coleman, "Shirley MacLaine: If They Could See Me Now" (CBS)
OUTSTANDING WRITING IN A SPECIAL PROGRAM—DRAMA OR COMEDY—ORIGINAL TELEPLAY: James Costigan, "Love Among the Ruins," *ABC Theatre* (ABC)
OUTSTANDING WRITING IN A SPECIAL PROGRAM—DRAMA OR COMEDY—ADAPTATION: David W. Rintels, "IBM Presents Clarence Darrow" (NBC)
OUTSTANDING CHILDREN'S SPECIAL (EVENING): "Yes Virginia, There Is a Santa Claus," Burt Rosen, executive producer; Bill Melendez and Mort Greene, producers (ABC)
SPECIAL CLASSIFICATION OF OUTSTANDING PROGRAM ACHIEVEMENT: "The American Film Institute Salute to James Cagney," George Stevens, Jr., executive producer; Paul W. Keyes, producer (CBS)
SPECIAL CLASSIFICATION OF OUTSTANDING INDIVIDUAL ACHIEVEMENT: Alistair Cooke, host, *Masterpiece Theatre* (PBS)

1975–1976 (presented May 17, 1976)

OUTSTANDING COMEDY SERIES: *The Mary Tyler Moore Show,* James L. Brooks and Allan Burns, executive producers; Ed Weinberger and Stan Daniels, producers (CBS)
OUTSTANDING DRAMA SERIES: *Police Story,* David Gerber and Stanley Kallis, executive producers; Liam O'Brien and Carl Pingitore, producers (NBC)

OUTSTANDING COMEDY-VARIETY OR MUSIC SERIES: *NBC's Saturday Night Live,* Lorne Michaels, producer (NBC)

OUTSTANDING LIMITED SERIES: *Upstairs, Downstairs [Masterpiece Theatre],* Rex Firkin, executive producer; John Hawkesworth, producer (PBS)

OUTSTANDING SPECIAL—DRAMA OR COMEDY: "Eleanor and Franklin," *ABC Theatre,* David Susskind, executive producer; Harry Sherman and Audrey Mass, producers (ABC)

OUTSTANDING SPECIAL—COMEDY-VARIETY OR MUSIC: "Gypsy in My Soul," William O. Harbach, executive producer; Cy Coleman and Fred Ebb, producers (CBS)

OUTSTANDING CLASSICAL MUSIC PROGRAM: "Bernstein and the New York Philharmonic," *Great Performances,* Klaus Hallig and Harry Kraut, executive producers; David Griffiths, producer, 11/26/75 (PBS)

OUTSTANDING LEAD ACTOR IN A COMEDY SERIES: Jack Albertson, *Chico and the Man* (NBC)

OUTSTANDING LEAD ACTOR IN A DRAMA SERIES: Peter Falk, *Columbo [NBC Sunday Mystery Movie]* (NBC)

OUTSTANDING LEAD ACTOR IN A LIMITED SERIES: Hal Holbrook, "Sandburg's Lincoln" (NBC)

OUTSTANDING LEAD ACTOR IN A DRAMA OR COMEDY SPECIAL: Anthony Hopkins, "The Lindbergh Kidnapping Case," *NBC World Premiere Movie* (NBC)

OUTSTANDING LEAD ACTOR FOR A SINGLE APPEARANCE IN A DRAMA OR COMEDY SERIES: Edward Asner, *Rich Man, Poor Man,* 2/1/76 (ABC)

OUTSTANDING LEAD ACTRESS IN A COMEDY SERIES: Mary Tyler Moore, *The Mary Tyler Moore Show* (CBS)

OUTSTANDING LEAD ACTRESS IN A DRAMA SERIES: Michael Learned, *The Waltons* (CBS)

OUTSTANDING LEAD ACTRESS IN A LIMITED SERIES: Rosemary Harris, *Notorious Woman [Masterpiece Theatre]* (PBS)

OUTSTANDING LEAD ACTRESS IN A DRAMA OR COMEDY SPECIAL: Susan Clark, "Babe" (CBS)

OUTSTANDING LEAD ACTRESS FOR A SINGLE APPEARANCE IN A DRAMA OR COMEDY SERIES: Kathryn Walker, "John Adams, Lawyer," *The Adams Chronicles,* 1/20/76 (PBS)

OUTSTANDING CONTINUING PERFORMANCE BY A SUPPORTING ACTOR IN A COMEDY SERIES: Ted Knight, *The Mary Tyler Moore Show* (CBS)

OUTSTANDING CONTINUING PERFORMANCE BY A SUPPORTING ACTOR IN A DRAMA SERIES: Anthony Zerbe, *Harry-O* (ABC)

OUTSTANDING CONTINUING OR SINGLE PERFORMANCE BY A SUPPORTING ACTOR IN VARIETY OR MUSIC: Chevy Chase, *NBC's Saturday Night Live,* 1/17/76 (NBC)

OUTSTANDING SINGLE PERFORMANCE BY A SUPPORTING ACTOR IN A COMEDY OR DRAMA SPECIAL: Ed Flanders, "A Moon for the Misbegotten," *ABC Theatre* (ABC)

OUTSTANDING SINGLE PERFORMANCE BY A SUPPORTING ACTOR IN A COMEDY OR DRAMA SERIES: Gordon Jackson, "The Beastly Hun," *Upstairs, Downstairs [Masterpiece Theatre],* 1/18/76 (PBS)

OUTSTANDING CONTINUING PERFORMANCE BY A SUPPORTING ACTRESS IN A COMEDY SERIES: Betty White, *The Mary Tyler Moore Show* (CBS)

OUTSTANDING CONTINUING PERFORMANCE BY A SUPPORTING ACTRESS IN A DRAMA SERIES: Ellen Corby, *The Waltons* (CBS)

OUTSTANDING CONTINUING OR SINGLE PERFORMANCE BY A SUPPORTING ACTRESS IN VARIETY OR MUSIC: Vicki Lawrence, *The Carol Burnett Show,* 2/7/76 (CBS)

OUTSTANDING SINGLE PERFORMANCE BY A SUPPORTING ACTRESS IN A COMEDY OR DRAMA SPECIAL: Rosemary Murphy, "Eleanor and Franklin," *ABC Theatre* (ABC)

OUTSTANDING SINGLE PERFORMANCE BY A SUPPORTING ACTRESS IN A COMEDY OR DRAMA SERIES: Fionnula Flanagan, *Rich Man, Poor Man,* 2/2/76 (ABC)

OUTSTANDING DIRECTING IN A DRAMA SERIES (A SINGLE EPISODE OF A REGULAR OR LIMITED SERIES WITH CONTINUING CHARACTERS AND/OR THEME): David Greene, "Episode 8," *Rich Man, Poor Man,* 3/15/76 (ABC)

OUTSTANDING DIRECTING IN A COMEDY SERIES (A SINGLE EPISODE OF A REGULAR OR LIMITED SERIES WITH CONTINUING CHARACTERS AND/OR THEME): Gene Reynolds, "Welcome to Korea," *M*A*S*H,* 9/12/75 (CBS)

OUTSTANDING DIRECTING IN A COMEDY-VARIETY OR MUSIC SERIES (A SINGLE EPISODE OF A REGULAR OR LIMITED SERIES): Dave Wilson, *NBC's Saturday Night Live,* with host Paul Simon, 10/18/75 (NBC)

OUTSTANDING DIRECTING IN A COMEDY-VARIETY OR MUSIC SPECIAL: Dwight Hemion, "Steve and Eydie: 'Our Love Is Here to Stay' " (CBS)

OUTSTANDING DIRECTING IN A SPECIAL PROGRAM—DRAMA OR COMEDY: Daniel Petrie, "Eleanor and Franklin," *ABC Theatre* (ABC)

OUTSTANDING WRITING IN A DRAMA SERIES (A SINGLE EPISODE OF A REGULAR OR LIMITED SERIES WITH CONTINUING CHARACTERS AND/OR THEME): Sherman Yellen, "John Adams, Lawyer," *The Adams Chronicles,* 1/20/76 (PBS)

OUTSTANDING WRITING IN A COMEDY SERIES (A SINGLE EPISODE OF A REGULAR OR LIMITED SERIES WITH CONTINUING CHARACTERS AND/OR THEME): David Lloyd, "Chuckles Bites the Dust," *The Mary Tyler Moore Show,* 10/25/75 (CBS)

OUTSTANDING WRITING IN A COMEDY-VARIETY OR MUSIC SERIES (A SINGLE EPISODE OF A REGULAR OR LIMITED SERIES): Anne Beatts, Chevy Chase, Al Franken, Tom Davis, Lorne Michaels, Marilyn Suzanne Miller, Michael O'Donoghue, Herb Sargent, Tom Schiller, Rosie Schuster, and Alan Zweibel, *NBC's Saturday Night Live,* with host Elliott Gould, 1/10/76 (NBC)

OUTSTANDING WRITING IN A COMEDY-VARIETY OR MUSIC SPECIAL: Jane Wagner, Lorne Michaels, Ann Elder, Christopher Guest, Earl Pomerantz, Jim Rusk, Lily Tomlin, Rod Warren, and George Yanok, "Lily Tomlin" (ABC)

OUTSTANDING WRITING IN A SPECIAL PROGRAM—DRAMA OR COMEDY—ORIGINAL TELEPLAY: James Costigan, "Eleanor and Franklin," *ABC Theatre* (ABC)

OUTSTANDING WRITING IN A SPECIAL PROGRAM—DRAMA OR COMEDY—ADAPTATION: David W. Rintels, "Fear on Trial" (CBS)

OUTSTANDING EVENING CHILDREN'S SPECIAL: "You're a Good Sport, Charlie Brown," Lee Mendelson, executive producer; Bill Melendez, producer (CBS). "Huckleberry Finn," Steven North, producer (ABC)

SPECIAL CLASSIFICATION OF OUTSTANDING PROGRAM AND INDIVIDUAL ACHIEVEMENT: *Bicentennial Minutes,* Bob Markell, executive producer; Gareth Davies and Paul Walgner, producers (CBS). *The Tonight Show Starring Johnny*

Carson, Fred De Cordova, producer (NBC). Ann Marcus, Jerry Adelman, and Daniel Gregory Browne, writers, *Mary Hartman, Mary Hartman* (syndicated)

1976–1977 (presented September 12, 1977)

OUTSTANDING COMEDY SERIES: *The Mary Tyler Moore Show,* Allan Burns and James L. Brooks, executive producers; Ed Weinberger and Stan Daniels, producers (CBS)

OUTSTANDING DRAMA SERIES: *Upstairs, Downstairs [Masterpiece Theatre],* John Hawkesworth and Joan Sullivan, producers (PBS)

OUTSTANDING COMEDY-VARIETY OR MUSIC SERIES: *Van Dyke and Company,* Bryon Paul, executive producer; Alan Blye and Bob Einstein, producers (NBC)

OUTSTANDING LIMITED SERIES: *Roots [ABC Novel for Television],* David L. Wolper, executive producer; Stan Margulies, producer (ABC)

OUTSTANDING SPECIAL—DRAMA OR COMEDY: "Eleanor and Franklin: The White House Years," *ABC Theatre,* David Susskind, executive producer; Harry R. Sherman, producer (ABC). "Sybil," *The Big Event/NBC World Premiere Movie,* Peter Dunne and Philip Capice, executive producers; Jacqueline Babbin, producer (NBC)

OUTSTANDING SPECIAL—COMEDY-VARIETY OR MUSIC: "The Barry Manilow Special," Miles Lourie, executive producer; Steve Binder, producer (ABC)

OUTSTANDING CLASSICAL PROGRAM IN THE PERFORMING ARTS: "American Ballet Theatre: Swan Lake Live from Lincoln Center," *Great Performances,* John Goberman, producer, 6/30/76 (PBS)

OUTSTANDING LEAD ACTOR IN A COMEDY SERIES: Carroll O'Connor, *All in the Family* (CBS)

OUTSTANDING LEAD ACTOR IN A DRAMA SERIES: James Garner, *The Rockford Files* (NBC)

OUTSTANDING LEAD ACTOR IN A LIMITED SERIES: Christopher Plummer, "The Moneychangers," *The Big Event/NBC World Premiere Movie* (NBC)

OUTSTANDING LEAD ACTOR IN A DRAMA OR COMEDY SPECIAL: Ed Flanders, "Harry S Truman: Plain Speaking" (PBS)

OUTSTANDING LEAD ACTOR FOR A SINGLE APPEARANCE IN A DRAMA OR COMEDY SERIES: Louis Gossett, Jr., *Roots*—Part Two, 1/24/77 (ABC)

OUTSTANDING LEAD ACTRESS IN A COMEDY SERIES: Beatrice Arthur, *Maude* (CBS)

OUTSTANDING LEAD ACTRESS IN A DRAMA SERIES: Lindsay Wagner, *The Bionic Woman* (ABC)

OUTSTANDING LEAD ACTRESS IN A LIMITED SERIES: Patty Duke Astin, *Captains and the Kings, NBC's Best Sellers* (NBC)

OUTSTANDING LEAD ACTRESS IN A DRAMA OR COMEDY SPECIAL: Sally Field, "Sybil," *The Big Event/NBC World Premiere Movie* (NBC)

OUTSTANDING LEAD ACTRESS FOR A SINGLE APPEARANCE IN A DRAMA OR COMEDY SERIES: Beulah Bondi, "The Pony Cart," *The Waltons,* 12/2/76 (CBS)

OUTSTANDING CONTINUING PERFORMANCE BY A SUPPORTING ACTOR IN A COMEDY SERIES: Gary Burghoff, *M*A*S*H* (CBS)

OUTSTANDING CONTINUING PERFORMANCE BY A SUPPORTING ACTOR IN A DRAMA SERIES: Gary Frank, *Family* (ABC)

OUTSTANDING CONTINUING OR SINGLE PERFORMANCE BY A SUPPORTING ACTOR IN A VARIETY OR MUSIC: Tim Conway, *The Carol Burnett Show* (CBS)

OUTSTANDING PERFORMANCE BY A SUPPORTING ACTOR IN A COMEDY OR DRAMA SPECIAL: Burgess Meredith, "Tailgunner Joe," *The Big Event,* 2/6/77 (NBC)

OUTSTANDING SINGLE PERFORMANCE BY A SUPPORTING ACTOR IN A COMEDY OR DRAMA SERIES: Edward Asner, *Roots*—Part One, 1/23/77 (ABC)

OUTSTANDING CONTINUING PERFORMANCE BY A SUPPORTING ACTRESS IN A COMEDY SERIES: Mary Kay Place, *Mary Hartman, Mary Hartman* (syndicated)

OUTSTANDING CONTINUING PERFORMANCE BY A SUPPORTING ACTRESS IN A DRAMA SERIES: Kristy McNichol, *Family* (ABC)

OUTSTANDING CONTINUING OR SINGLE PERFORMANCE BY A SUPPORTING ACTRESS IN VARIETY OR MUSIC: Rita Moreno, *The Muppet Show* (syndicated)

OUTSTANDING PERFORMANCE BY A SUPPORTING ACTRESS IN A COMEDY OR DRAMA SPECIAL: Diana Hyland, "The Boy in the Plastic Bubble," *The ABC Friday Night Movie,* 11/12/76 (ABC)

OUTSTANDING SINGLE PERFORMANCE BY A SUPPORTING ACTRESS IN A COMEDY OR DRAMA SERIES: Olivia Cole, *Roots*—Part Eight, 1/30/77 (ABC)

OUTSTANDING DIRECTING IN A DRAMA SERIES (A SINGLE EPISODE OF A REGULAR OR LIMITED SERIES WITH CONTINUING CHARACTERS AND/OR THEME): David Greene, *Roots*—Part One, 1/23/77 (ABC)

OUTSTANDING DIRECTING IN A COMEDY SERIES (A SINGLE EPISODE OF A REGULAR OR LIMITED SERIES WITH CONTINUING CHARACTERS AND/OR THEME): Alan Alda, "Dear Sigmund," *M*A*S*H,* 11/9/76 (CBS)

OUTSTANDING DIRECTING IN A COMEDY-VARIETY OR MUSIC SERIES (A SINGLE EPISODE OF A REGULAR OR LIMITED SERIES): Dave Powers, *The Carol Burnett Show,* with Eydie Gorme, 2/12/77 (CBS)

OUTSTANDING DIRECTING IN A COMEDY-VARIETY OR MUSIC SPECIAL: Dwight Hemion, "America Salutes Richard Rodgers: The Sound of His Music" (CBS)

OUTSTANDING DIRECTING IN A SPECIAL PROGRAM—DRAMA OR COMEDY: Daniel Petrie, "Eleanor and Franklin: The White House Years," *ABC Theatre* (ABC)

OUTSTANDING WRITING IN A DRAMA SERIES (A SINGLE EPISODE OF A REGULAR OR LIMITED SERIES WITH CONTINUING CHARACTERS AND/OR THEME): William Blinn, *Roots*—Part Two, 1/24/77 (ABC)

OUTSTANDING WRITING IN A COMEDY SERIES (A SINGLE EPISODE OF A REGULAR OR LIMITED SERIES WITH CONTINUING CHARACTERS AND/OR THEME): Allan Burns, James L. Brooks, Ed Weinberger, Stan Daniels, David Lloyd, and Bob Ellison, "The Final Show," *The Mary Tyler Moore Show,* 3/19/77 (CBS)

OUTSTANDING WRITING IN A COMEDY-VARIETY OR MUSIC SERIES (A SINGLE EPISODE OF A REGULAR OR LIMITED SERIES): Anne Beatts, Dan Aykroyd, Al Franken, Tom Davis, James Downey, Lorne Michaels, Marilyn Suzanne Miller, Michael O'Donoghue, Herb Sargent, Tom Schiller, Rosie Schuster, Alan Zweibel, John Belushi, and Bill Murray, *NBC's Saturday Night Live,* with host Sissy Spacek, 3/12/77 (NBC)

OUTSTANDING WRITING IN A COMEDY-VARIETY OR MUSIC SPECIAL: Alan Buz Kohan and Ted Strauss, "America Salutes Richard Rodgers: The Sound of His Music" (CBS)

OUTSTANDING WRITING IN A SPECIAL PROGRAM—DRAMA OR COMEDY—ORIGINAL TELEPLAY: Lane Slate, "Tailgunner Joe," *The Big Event,* 2/6/77 (NBC)

OUTSTANDING WRITING IN A SPECIAL PROGRAM—DRAMA OR COMEDY—ADAPTATION: Stewart Stern, "Sybil," *The Big Event/NBC World Premiere Movie* (NBC)

OUTSTANDING EVENING CHILDREN'S SPECIAL: "Ballet Shoes, Parts 1 & 2," *Piccadilly Circus,* 12/27 & 12/28/76 (PBS)

SPECIAL CLASSIFICATION OF OUTSTANDING PROGRAM ACHIEVEMENT: *The Tonight Show Starring Johnny Carson,* Fred De Cordova, producer (NBC)

1977–1978 (presented September 17, 1978)

OUTSTANDING COMEDY SERIES: *All in the Family,* Mort Lachman, executive producer; Milt Josefsberg, producer (CBS)

OUTSTANDING DRAMA SERIES: *The Rockford Files,* Meta Rosenberg, executive producer; Stephen J. Cannell, supervising producer; David Chase and Charles F. Johnson, producers (NBC)

OUTSTANDING COMEDY-VARIETY OR MUSIC SERIES: *The Muppet Show,* David Lazer, executive producer; Jim Henson, producer; The Muppets—Frank Oz, Jerry Nelson, Richard Hunt, Dave Goelz, and Jim Henson, stars (syndicated)

OUTSTANDING LIMITED SERIES: *Holocaust,* Herbert Brodkin, executive producer; Robert Berger, producer (NBC)

OUTSTANDING INFORMATION SERIES: *The Body Human,* Thomas W. Moore, executive producer; Alfred R. Kelman, producer (CBS)

OUTSTANDING SPECIAL—DRAMA OR COMEDY: "The Gathering," Joseph Barbera, executive producer; Harry R. Sherman, producer (ABC)

OUTSTANDING SPECIAL—COMEDY-VARIETY OR MUSIC: "Bette Midler—Old Red Hair Is Back," Aaron Russo, executive producer; Gary Smith and Dwight Hemion, producers; Bette Midler, star (NBC)

OUTSTANDING INFORMATION SPECIAL: "The Great Whales: National Geographic," Thomas Skinner and Dennis B. Kane, executive producers; Nicolas Noxon, producer (PBS)

OUTSTANDING CLASSICAL PROGRAM IN THE PERFORMING ARTS: "American Ballet Theatre; 'Giselle' Live from Lincoln Center," John Goberman, producer, 6/2/77 (PBS)

OUTSTANDING LEAD ACTOR IN A COMEDY SERIES: Carroll O'Connor, *All in the Family* (CBS)

OUTSTANDING LEAD ACTOR IN A DRAMA SERIES: Ed Asner, *Lou Grant* (CBS)

OUTSTANDING LEAD ACTOR IN A LIMITED SERIES: Michael Moriarty, *Holocaust* (NBC)

OUTSTANDING LEAD ACTOR IN A DRAMA OR COMEDY SPECIAL: Fred Astaire, "A Family Upside Down" (NBC)

OUTSTANDING LEAD ACTOR FOR A SINGLE APPEARANCE IN A DRAMA OR COMEDY SERIES: Barnard Hughes, "Judge," *Lou Grant,* 11/15/77 (CBS)

OUTSTANDING LEAD ACTRESS IN A COMEDY SERIES: Jean Stapleton, *All in the Family* (CBS)

OUTSTANDING LEAD ACTRESS IN A DRAMA SERIES: Sada Thompson, *Family* (ABC)

OUTSTANDING LEAD ACTRESS IN A LIMITED SERIES: Meryl Streep, *Holocaust* (NBC)

OUTSTANDING LEAD ACTRESS IN A DRAMA OR COMEDY SPECIAL: Joanne Woodward, "See How She Runs," *General Electric Theater* (CBS)

OUTSTANDING LEAD ACTRESS FOR A SINGLE APPEARANCE IN A DRAMA OR COMEDY SERIES: Rita Moreno, "The Paper Palace," *The Rockford Files,* 1/20/78 (NBC)

OUTSTANDING CONTINUING PERFORMANCE BY A SUPPORTING ACTOR IN A COMEDY SERIES: Rob Reiner, *All in the Family* (CBS)

OUTSTANDING CONTINUING PERFORMANCE BY A SUPPORTING ACTOR IN A DRAMA SERIES: Robert Vaughn, *Washington: Behind Closed Doors* (ABC)

OUTSTANDING CONTINUING OR SINGLE PERFORMANCE BY A SUPPORTING ACTOR IN VARIETY OR MUSIC: Tim Conway, *The Carol Burnett Show* (CBS)

OUTSTANDING PERFORMANCE BY A SUPPORTING ACTOR IN A COMEDY OR DRAMA SPECIAL: Howard Da Silva, "Verna: USO Girl," *Great Performances,* 1/25/78 (PBS)

OUTSTANDING SINGLE PERFORMANCE BY A SUPPORTING ACTOR IN A COMEDY OR DRAMA SERIES: Ricardo Montalban, *How the West Was Won*—Part II, 2/19/78 (ABC)

OUTSTANDING CONTINUING PERFORMANCE BY A SUPPORTING ACTRESS IN A COMEDY SERIES: Julie Kavner, *Rhoda* (CBS)

OUTSTANDING CONTINUING PERFORMANCE BY A SUPPORTING ACTRESS IN A DRAMA SERIES: Nancy Marchand, *Lou Grant* (CBS)

OUTSTANDING CONTINUING OR SINGLE PERFORMANCE BY A SUPPORTING ACTRESS IN VARIETY OR MUSIC: Gilda Radner, *NBC's Saturday Night Live* (NBC)

OUTSTANDING PERFORMANCE BY A SUPPORTING ACTRESS IN A COMEDY OR DRAMA SPECIAL: Eva La Gallienne, "The Royal Family," 11/9/77 (PBS)

OUTSTANDING SINGLE PERFORMANCE BY A SUPPORTING ACTRESS IN A COMEDY OR DRAMA SERIES: Blanche Baker, *Holocaust*—Part I, 4/16/78 (NBC)

OUTSTANDING DIRECTING IN A DRAMA SERIES (A SINGLE EPISODE OF A REGULAR OR LIMITED SERIES WITH CONTINUING CHARACTERS AND/OR THEME): Marvin J. Chomsky, *Holocaust,* entire series (NBC)

OUTSTANDING DIRECTING IN A COMEDY SERIES (A SINGLE EPISODE OF A REGULAR OR LIMITED SERIES WITH CONTINUING CHARACTERS AND/OR THEME): Paul Bogart, "Edith's 50th Birthday," *All in the Family,* 10/16/77 (CBS)

OUTSTANDING DIRECTING IN A COMEDY-VARIETY OR MUSIC SERIES (A SINGLE EPISODE OF A REGULAR OR LIMITED SERIES): Dave Powers, *The Carol Burnett Show,* with Steve Martin and Betty White, 3/5/78 (CBS)

OUTSTANDING DIRECTING IN A COMEDY-VARIETY OR MUSIC SPECIAL: Dwight Hemion, "The Sentry Collection Presents Ben Vereen—His Roots," 3/2/78 (ABC)

OUTSTANDING DIRECTING IN A SPECIAL PROGRAM—DRAMA OR COMEDY: David Lowell Rich, "The Defection of Simas Kudirka," 1/23/78 (CBS)

OUTSTANDING WRITING IN A DRAMA SERIES (A SINGLE EPISODE OF A REGULAR OR LIMITED SERIES WITH CONTINUING CHARACTERS AND/OR THEME): Gerald Green, *Holocaust,* entire series (NBC)

OUTSTANDING WRITING IN A COMEDY SERIES (A SINGLE EPISODE OF A REGULAR OR LIMITED SERIES WITH CONTINUING CHARACTERS AND/OR THEME): Bob Weiskopf, Bob Schiller, Barry Harman, and Harve Broston, "Cousin Liz," *All in the Family,* 10/9/77 (CBS)

OUTSTANDING WRITING IN A COMEDY-VARIETY OR MUSIC SERIES (A SINGLE EPISODE OF A REGULAR OR LIMITED SERIES): Ed Simmons, Roger Beatty, Rich Hawkins, Liz Sage, Robert Illes, James Stein, Franelle Silver, Larry Siegel, Tim Conway, Bill Richmond, Gene Perret, Dick Clair, and Jenna McMahon, *The Carol Burnett Show,* with Steve Martin and Betty White, 3/5/78 (CBS)

OUTSTANDING WRITING IN A COMEDY-VARIETY OR MUSIC SPECIAL: Chevy Chase, Tom Davis, Al Franken, Charles Grodin, Lorne Michaels, Paul Simon, Lily Tomlin, and Alan Zweibel, "The Paul Simon Special," 12/8/77 (NBC)

OUTSTANDING WRITING IN A SPECIAL PROGRAM—DRAMA OR COMEDY—ORIGINAL TELEPLAY: George Rubino, "The Last Tenant," 6/25/78 (ABC)

OUTSTANDING WRITING IN A SPECIAL PROGRAM—DRAMA OR COMEDY—ADAPTATION: Caryl Ledner, "Mary White," 11/18/77 (ABC)

OUTSTANDING EVENING CHILDREN'S SPECIAL: "Halloween Is Grinch Night," David H. DePatie and Friz Freleng, executive producers; Ted Geisel, producer, 10/29/77 (CBS)

SPECIAL CLASSIFICATION OF OUTSTANDING PROGRAM ACHIEVEMENT: *The Tonight Show Starring Johnny Carson,* Fred De Cordova, producer; Johnny Carson, star (NBC)

FIRST ANNUAL ATAS GOVERNOR'S AWARD: William S. Paley, Chairman of the Board, CBS

1978–1979 (presented September 9, 1979)

OUTSTANDING COMEDY SERIES: *Taxi,* James L. Brooks, Stan Daniels, David Davis, and Ed Weinberger, executive producers; Glen Charles and Les Charles, producers (ABC)

OUTSTANDING DRAMA SERIES: *Lou Grant,* Gene Reynolds, executive producer; Seth Freeman and Gary David Goldberg, producers (CBS)

OUTSTANDING LIMITED SERIES: *Roots: The Next Generations,* David L. Wolper, executive producer; Stan Margulies, producer (ABC)

OUTSTANDING SPECIAL—DRAMA OR COMEDY: "Friendly Fire," Martin Starger, executive producer; Philip Barry and Fay Kanin, producers (ABC)

OUTSTANDING COMEDY-VARIETY OR MUSIC PROGRAM (SPECIAL OR SERIES): "Steve and Eydie Celebrate Irving Berlin," Steve Lawrence and Gary Smith, executive producers; Gary Smith and Dwight Hemion, producers; Steve Lawrence and Eydie Gorme, stars, 8/22/78 (NBC)

OUTSTANDING INFORMATION PROGRAM (SPECIAL OR SERIES): "Scared Straight," Arnold Shapiro, producer (syndicated)

OUTSTANDING CLASSICAL PROGRAM IN THE PERFORMING ARTS: "Balanchine IV Dance in America," *Great Performances,* Jac Venza, executive producer; Merrill Brockway, series producer; Emile Ardolino, series coordinating producer; Judy Kunberg, producer, 3/7/79 (PBS)

OUTSTANDING ANIMATED PROGRAM (SPECIAL OR SERIES): "The Lion, the Witch, and the Wardrobe," David Connell, executive producer; Steve Melendez, producer (CBS)

OUTSTANDING CHILDREN'S PROGRAM (SPECIAL OR SERIES): "Christmas Eve on Sesame Street," Jon Stone, executive producer; Dulcy Singer, producer, 12/3/78 (PBS)

OUTSTANDING PROGRAM ACHIEVEMENT—SPECIAL EVENTS: "51st Annual Awards Presentation of the Academy of Motion Picture Arts and Sciences," Jack Haley, Jr., producer, 4/9/79 (ABC)

OUTSTANDING LEAD ACTOR IN A COMEDY SERIES (FOR A CONTINUING OR SINGLE PERFORMANCE IN A REGULAR SERIES): Carroll O'Connor, *All in the Family* (CBS)

OUTSTANDING LEAD ACTOR IN A DRAMA SERIES (FOR A CONTINUING OR SINGLE PERFORMANCE IN A REGULAR SERIES): Ron Leibman, *Kaz* (CBS)

OUTSTANDING LEAD ACTOR IN A LIMITED SERIES OR A SPECIAL: Peter Strauss, "The Jericho Mile," 3/18/79 (ABC)

OUTSTANDING LEAD ACTRESS IN A COMEDY SERIES (FOR A CONTINUING OR SINGLE PERFORMANCE IN A REGULAR SERIES): Ruth Gordon, "Sugar Mama," *Taxi,* 1/16/79 (ABC)

OUTSTANDING LEAD ACTRESS IN A DRAMA SERIES (FOR A CONTINUING OR SINGLE PERFORMANCE IN A REGULAR SERIES): Mariette Hartley, "Married," *The Incredible Hulk,* 9/23/78 (CBS)

OUTSTANDING LEAD ACTRESS IN A LIMITED SERIES OR A SPECIAL: Bette Davis, "Strangers: The Story of a Mother and Daughter," 5/13/79 (CBS)

OUTSTANDING SUPPORTING ACTOR IN A COMEDY OR COMEDY-VARIETY OR MUSIC SERIES (FOR A CONTINUING OR SINGLE PERFORMANCE IN A REGULAR SERIES): Robert Guillaume, *Soap* (ABC)

OUTSTANDING SUPPORTING ACTOR IN A DRAMA SERIES (FOR A CONTINUING OR SINGLE PERFORMANCE IN A REGULAR SERIES): Stuart Margolin, *The Rockford Files* (NBC)

OUTSTANDING SUPPORTING ACTOR IN A LIMITED SERIES OR A SPECIAL: Marlon Brando, *Roots: The Next Generations*—Episode Seven, 2/25/79 (ABC)

OUTSTANDING SUPPORTING ACTRESS IN A COMEDY OR COMEDY-VARIETY OR MUSIC SERIES (FOR A CONTINUING OR SINGLE PERFORMANCE IN A REGULAR SERIES): Sally Struthers, "California Here We Are," *All in the Family,* 12/17/78 (CBS)

OUTSTANDING SUPPORTING ACTRESS IN A DRAMA SERIES (FOR A CONTINUING OR SINGLE PERFORMANCE IN A REGULAR SERIES): Kristy McNichol, *Family* (ABC)

OUTSTANDING SUPPORTING ACTRESS IN A LIMITED SERIES OR A SPECIAL: Esther Rolle, "Summer of My German Soldier," 10/30/78 (NBC)

OUTSTANDING INDIVIDUAL ACHIEVEMENT—INFORMATIONAL PROGRAM: John Korty, director; "Who Are the Debolts—And Where Did They Get 19 Kids?," 12/17/78 (ABC)

OUTSTANDING INDIVIDUAL ACHIEVEMENT—SPECIAL EVENTS: Mikhail Baryshnikov, star; "Baryshnikov at the White House," 4/15/79 (PBS)

OUTSTANDING DIRECTING IN A COMEDY OR COMEDY-VARIETY OR MUSIC SERIES (A SINGLE EPISODE OF A REGULAR SERIES): Noam Pitlik, "The Harris Incident," *Barney Miller,* 11/30/78 (ABC)

OUTSTANDING DIRECTING IN A DRAMA SERIES (A SINGLE EPISODE OF A REGULAR SERIES): Jackie Cooper, "Pilot," *The White Shadow,* 11/27/78 (CBS)

OUTSTANDING DIRECTING IN A LIMITED SERIES OR A SPECIAL: David Greene, "Friendly Fire," 4/22/79 (ABC)

OUTSTANDING WRITING IN A COMEDY OR COMEDY-VARIETY OR MUSIC SERIES (A SINGLE EPISODE OF A REGULAR SERIES): Alan Alda, "Inga," *M*A*S*H,* 1/8/79 (CBS)

OUTSTANDING WRITING IN A DRAMA SERIES (A SINGLE EPISODE OF A REGULAR SERIES): Michele Gallery, "Dying," *Lou Grant,* 11/6/78 (CBS)

OUTSTANDING WRITING IN A LIMITED SERIES OR A SPECIAL: Patrick Nolan and Michael Mann, "The Jericho Mile," 3/18/79 (ABC)

SPECIAL CLASSIFICATION OF OUTSTANDING PROGRAM ACHIEVEMENT: *The Tonight Show Starring Johnny Carson,* Fred De Cordova, producer; Johnny Carson, star. *Lifeline,* Thomas W. Moore and Robert E. Fuisz, M.D., executive producers; Alfred Kelman and Geof Bartz, producers (NBC)

SECOND ANNUAL ATAS GOVERNOR'S AWARD: Walter Cronkite

1979–1980 (presented September 7, 1980)

OUTSTANDING COMEDY SERIES: *Taxi,* James L. Brooks, Stan Daniels, and Ed Weinberger, executive producers; Glen Charles and Les Charles, producers (ABC)

OUTSTANDING DRAMA SERIES: *Lou Grant,* Gene Reynolds, executive producer; Seth Freeman, producer (CBS)

OUTSTANDING LIMITED SERIES: *Edward & Mrs. Simpson,* Andrew Brown, producer (syndicated)

OUTSTANDING SPECIAL—DRAMA OR COMEDY: "The Miracle Worker," Raymond Katz and Sandy Gallin, executive producers; Fred Coe, producer, 10/14/79 (NBC)

OUTSTANDING VARIETY OR MUSIC PROGRAM (SPECIAL OR SERIES): "IBM Presents Baryshnikov on Broadway," Herman Krawitz, executive producer; Gary Smith and Dwight Hemion, producers; Mikhail Baryshnikov, star, 4/24/80 (ABC)

OUTSTANDING INFORMATION PROGRAM (SPECIAL OR SERIES): "The Body Human: The Magic Sense," Thomas W. Moore, executive producer; Alfred R. Kelman, Robert E. Fuisz, M.D., Charles A. Bangert, and Vivian R. Moss, producers, 9/6/79 (CBS)

OUTSTANDING CLASSICAL PROGRAM IN THE PERFORMING ARTS: "Live from Studio 8H: A Tribute to Toscanini," Alvin Cooperman and Judith De Paul, producers, 1/9/80 (NBC)

OUTSTANDING ANIMATED PROGRAM (SPECIAL OR SERIES): "Carlton, Your Doorman," Lorenzo Music and Barton Dean, producers, 5/21/80 (CBS)

OUTSTANDING PROGRAM ACHIEVEMENT—SPECIAL EVENTS: "The 34th Annual Tony Awards," Alexander H. Cohen, executive producer; Hildy Parks and Roy A. Somlyo, producers, 6/8/80 (CBS)

OUTSTANDING LEAD ACTOR IN A COMEDY SERIES (FOR A CONTINUING OR SINGLE PERFORMANCE IN A REGULAR SERIES): Richard Mulligan, *Soap* (ABC)

OUTSTANDING LEAD ACTOR IN A DRAMA SERIES (FOR A CONTINUING OR SINGLE PERFORMANCE IN A REGULAR SERIES): Ed Asner, *Lou Grant* (CBS)

OUTSTANDING LEAD ACTOR IN A LIMITED SERIES OR A SPECIAL: Powers Boothe, "Guyana Tragedy," 4/15–16/80 (CBS)

OUTSTANDING LEAD ACTRESS IN A COMEDY SERIES (FOR A CONTINUING OR SINGLE PERFORMANCE IN A REGULAR SERIES): Cathryn Damon, *Soap* (ABC)

OUTSTANDING LEAD ACTRESS IN A DRAMA SERIES (FOR A CONTINUING OR SINGLE PERFORMANCE IN A REGULAR SERIES): Barbara Bel Geddes, *Dallas* (CBS)

OUTSTANDING LEAD ACTRESS IN A LIMITED SERIES OR A SPECIAL: Patty Duke Astin, "The Miracle Worker," 10/14/79 (NBC)

OUTSTANDING SUPPORTING ACTOR IN A COMEDY OR COMEDY-VARIETY OR MUSIC SERIES (FOR A CONTINUING OR SINGLE PERFORMANCE IN A REGULAR SERIES): Harry Morgan, *M*A*S*H* (CBS)

OUTSTANDING SUPPORTING ACTOR IN A DRAMA SERIES (FOR A CONTINUING OR SINGLE PERFORMANCE IN A REGULAR SERIES): Stuart Margolin, *The Rockford Files* (NBC)

OUTSTANDING SUPPORTING ACTOR IN A LIMITED SERIES OR A SPECIAL: George Grizzard, "The Oldest Living Graduate," 4/7/80 (NBC)

OUTSTANDING SUPPORTING ACTRESS IN A COMEDY OR COMEDY-VARIETY OR MUSIC SERIES (FOR A CONTINUING OR SINGLE PERFORMANCE IN A REGULAR SERIES): Loretta Swit, *M*A*S*H* (CBS)

OUTSTANDING SUPPORTING ACTRESS IN A DRAMA SERIES (FOR A CONTINUING OR SINGLE PERFORMANCE IN A REGULAR SERIES): Nancy Marchand, *Lou Grant* (CBS)

OUTSTANDING SUPPORTING ACTRESS IN A LIMITED SERIES OR A SPECIAL: Mare Winningham, "Amber Waves," 3/9/80 (ABC)

OUTSTANDING INDIVIDUAL ACHIEVEMENT—SPECIAL CLASS: "Operation: Lifeline," Dr. James "Red" Duke, 8/13/79 (NBC)

OUTSTANDING DIRECTING IN A COMEDY SERIES (A SINGLE EPISODE OF A REGULAR SERIES): James Burrows, *Taxi,* 9/11/79 (ABC)

OUTSTANDING DIRECTING IN A DRAMA SERIES (A SINGLE EPISODE OF A REGULAR SERIES): Roger Young, "Cop," *Lou Grant,* 9/17/79 (CBS)

OUTSTANDING DIRECTING IN A LIMITED SERIES OR A SPECIAL: Marvin J. Chomsky, "Attica," 3/2/80 (ABC)

OUTSTANDING DIRECTING IN A VARIETY OR MUSIC PROGRAM (A SINGLE EPISODE OF A REGULAR OR LIMITED SERIES, OR FOR A SPECIAL): Dwight Hemion, "Baryshnikov on Broadway," 4/24/80 (ABC)

OUTSTANDING WRITING IN A COMEDY SERIES (A SINGLE EPISODE OF A REGULAR SERIES): Bob Colleary, "Photographer," *Barney Miller,* 9/20/79 (ABC)

OUTSTANDING WRITING IN A DRAMA SERIES (A SINGLE EPISODE OF A REGULAR SERIES): Seth Freeman, "Cop," *Lou Grant,* 9/17/79 (CBS)

OUTSTANDING WRITING IN A LIMITED SERIES OR A SPECIAL: David Chase, "Off the Minnesota Strip," 5/5/80 (ABC)

OUTSTANDING WRITING IN A VARIETY OR MUSIC PROGRAM (A SINGLE EPISODE OF A REGULAR OR LIMITED SERIES, OR FOR A SPECIAL): Buz Kohan and Shirley MacLaine, "Every Little Movement," 5/22/80 (CBS)

SPECIAL CLASSIFICATION OF OUTSTANDING PROGRAM ACHIEVEMENT: "Fred Astaire, Change Partners and Dance," David Heeley, producer, 3/14/80 (PBS)

THIRD ANNUAL ATAS GOVERNOR'S AWARD: Johnny Carson

1980–1981 (presented September 13, 1981)

OUTSTANDING COMEDY SERIES: *Taxi,* James L. Brooks, Stan Daniels, and Ed Weinberger, executive producers; Glen Charles and Les Charles, producers (ABC)

OUTSTANDING DRAMA SERIES: *Hill Street Blues,* Steven Bochco and Michael Kozoll, executive producers; Gregory Hoblit, producer (NBC)

OUTSTANDING LIMITED SERIES: *Shogun,* James Clavell, executive producer; Eric Bercovici, producer (NBC)

OUTSTANDING VARIETY, MUSIC, OR COMEDY PROGRAM: "Lily: Sold Out," Lily Tomlin and Jane Wagner, executive producers; Rocco Urbisci, producer (CBS)

OUTSTANDING DRAMA SPECIAL: "Playing for Time," Linda Yellen, executive producer; John E. Quill, coproducer (CBS)

OUTSTANDING INFORMATIONAL SERIES: *Steve Allen's Meeting of Minds,* Loring d'Usseau, producer (PBS)

OUTSTANDING INFORMATIONAL SPECIAL: "The Body Human: The Bionic Breakthrough," Thomas W. Moore, executive producer; Alfred R. Kelman and Robert E. Fuisz, M.D., producers; Charles A. Bangert and Nancy Smith, coproducers (CBS)

OUTSTANDING CLASSICAL PROGRAM IN THE PERFORMING ARTS: "Live from Studio 8H: An Evening of Jerome Robbins' Ballets with Members of the New York City Ballet," Alvin Cooperman and Judith De Paul, producers (NBC)

OUTSTANDING CHILDREN'S PROGRAM: "Donahue and Kids. Project Peacock," Walter Bartlett, executive producer; Don Mischer, producer; Jan Cornell, coproducer (NBC)

OUTSTANDING ANIMATED PROGRAM: "Life Is a Circus, Charlie Brown," Lee Mendelson, executive producer; Bill Melendez, producer (CBS)

OUTSTANDING LEAD ACTOR IN A DRAMA SERIES: Daniel J. Travanti, *Hill Street Blues* (NBC)

OUTSTANDING LEAD ACTOR IN A COMEDY SERIES: Judd Hirsch, *Taxi* (ABC)

OUTSTANDING LEAD ACTOR IN A LIMITED SERIES OR A SPECIAL: Anthony Hopkins, "The Bunker" (CBS)

OUTSTANDING LEAD ACTRESS IN A DRAMA SERIES: Barbara Babcock, *Hill Street Blues* (NBC)

OUTSTANDING LEAD ACTRESS IN A COMEDY SERIES: Isabel Sanford, *The Jeffersons* (CBS)

OUTSTANDING LEAD ACTRESS IN A LIMITED SERIES OR A SPECIAL: Vanessa Redgrave, "Playing for Time" (CBS)

OUTSTANDING SUPPORTING ACTOR IN A DRAMA SERIES: Michael Conrad, *Hill Street Blues* (NBC)

OUTSTANDING SUPPORTING ACTOR IN A COMEDY OR VARIETY OR MUSIC SERIES: Danny DeVito, *Taxi* (ABC)

OUTSTANDING SUPPORTING ACTOR IN A LIMITED SERIES OR A SPECIAL: David Warner, *Masada* (ABC)

OUTSTANDING SUPPORTING ACTRESS IN A DRAMA SERIES: Nancy Marchand, *Lou Grant* (CBS)

OUTSTANDING SUPPORTING ACTRESS IN A COMEDY OR VARIETY OR MUSIC SERIES: Eileen Brennan, *Private Benjamin* (CBS)

OUTSTANDING SUPPORTING ACTRESS IN A LIMITED SERIES OR A SPECIAL: Jane Alexander, "Playing for Time" (CBS)

OUTSTANDING INDIVIDUAL ACHIEVEMENT—SPECIAL CLASS: Sarah Vaughan, performer, "Rhapsody and Song—A Tribute to George Gershwin" (PBS)

OUTSTANDING DIRECTING IN A DRAMA SERIES (SINGLE EPISODE): Robert Butler, "Hill Street Station," *Hill Street Blues* (NBC)

OUTSTANDING DIRECTING IN A COMEDY SERIES (SINGLE EPISODE): James Burrows, "Elaine's Strange Triangle," *Taxi* (ABC)

OUTSTANDING DIRECTING IN A LIMITED SERIES OR A SPECIAL: James Goldstone, "Kent State" (NBC)

OUTSTANDING DIRECTING IN A VARIETY, MUSIC, OR COMEDY PROGRAM: Don Mischer, "The Kennedy Center Honors: A National Celebration of the Performing Arts" (CBS)

OUTSTANDING WRITING IN A DRAMA SERIES (SINGLE EPISODE): Michael Kozoll and Steven Bochco, "Hill Street Station," *Hill Street Blues* (NBC)

OUTSTANDING WRITING IN A COMEDY SERIES (SINGLE EPISODE): Michael Leeson, "Tony's Sister and Jim," *Taxi* (ABC)

OUTSTANDING WRITING IN A LIMITED SERIES OR A SPECIAL: Arthur Miller, "Playing for Time" (CBS)

OUTSTANDING WRITING IN A VARIETY, MUSIC, OR COMEDY PROGRAM: Jerry Juhl, David O'Dell, Chris Langham, Jim Henson, and Don Hinkley; "The Muppet Show with Carol Burnett" (syndicated)

FOURTH ANNUAL ATAS GOVERNOR'S AWARD: Elton H. Rule, President, American Broadcasting Company

1981–1982 (presented September 19, 1982)

OUTSTANDING COMEDY SERIES: *Barney Miller,* Danny Arnold and Roland Kibbee, executive producers; Frank Dungan and Jeff Stein, producers; Gary Shaw, coproducer (ABC)

OUTSTANDING DRAMA SERIES: *Hill Street Blues,* Steven Bochco, executive producer; Gregory Hoblit, supervising producer; David Anspaugh and Anthony Yerkovich, producers (NBC)

OUTSTANDING LIMITED SERIES: *Marco Polo,* Vincenzo Labella, producer (NBC)

OUTSTANDING VARIETY, MUSIC, OR COMEDY PROGRAM: "Night of 100 Stars," Alexander H. Cohen, executive producer; Hildy Parks, producer; Roy A. Somlyo, coproducer (ABC)

OUTSTANDING DRAMA SPECIAL: "A Woman Called Golda," Harve Bennett, executive producer; Gene Corman, producer (syndicated)

OUTSTANDING INFORMATIONAL SERIES: *Creativity with Bill Moyers,* Merton Koplin and Charles Grinker, executive producers; Betsy McCarthy, coordinating producer (PBS)

OUTSTANDING INFORMATIONAL SPECIAL: "Making of *Raiders of the Lost Ark,*" Sidney Ganis, executive producer; Howard Kazanjian, producer (PBS)

OUTSTANDING CLASSICAL PROGRAM IN THE PERFORMING ARTS: "*La Bohème,* Live from the Met," Michael Bronson, executive producer; Clement d'Alessio, producer (PBS)

OUTSTANDING CHILDREN'S PROGRAM: "The Wave," Virginia L. Carter, executive producer; Fern Field, producer (ABC)

OUTSTANDING ANIMATED PROGRAM: "Grinch Grinches the Cat in the Hat," David H. DePatie, executive producer; Ted Geisel and Friz Freleng, producers (ABC)

OUTSTANDING LEAD ACTOR IN A DRAMA SERIES: Daniel J. Travanti, *Hill Street Blues* (NBC)

OUTSTANDING LEAD ACTOR IN A COMEDY SERIES: Alan Alda, *M*A*S*H* (CBS)

OUTSTANDING LEAD ACTOR IN A LIMITED SERIES OR A SPECIAL: Mickey Rooney, "Bill" (CBS)

OUTSTANDING LEAD ACTRESS IN A DRAMA SERIES: Michael Learned, *Nurse* (CBS)

OUTSTANDING LEAD ACTRESS IN A COMEDY SERIES: Carol Kane, "Simka Returns," *Taxi* (ABC)

OUTSTANDING LEAD ACTRESS IN A LIMITED SERIES OR A SPECIAL: Ingrid Bergman, "A Woman Called Golda" (syndicated)

OUTSTANDING SUPPORTING ACTOR IN A DRAMA SERIES: Michael Conrad, *Hill Street Blues* (NBC)

OUTSTANDING SUPPORTING ACTOR IN A COMEDY OR VARIETY OR MUSIC SERIES: Christopher Lloyd, *Taxi* (ABC)

OUTSTANDING SUPPORTING ACTOR IN A LIMITED SERIES OR A SPECIAL: Laurence Olivier, *Brideshead Revisited* (PBS)

OUTSTANDING SUPPORTING ACTRESS IN A DRAMA SERIES: Nancy Marchand, *Lou Grant* (CBS)

OUTSTANDING SUPPORTING ACTRESS IN A COMEDY OR VARIETY OR MUSIC SERIES: Loretta Swit, *M*A*S*H* (CBS)

OUTSTANDING SUPPORTING ACTRESS IN A LIMITED SERIES OR A SPECIAL: Penny Fuller, "The Elephant Man" (ABC)

OUTSTANDING INDIVIDUAL ACHIEVEMENT—SPECIAL CLASS: Nell Carter, performer, "Ain't Misbehavin' " (NBC); Andre De Shields, performer, "Ain't Misbehavin' " (NBC)

OUTSTANDING DIRECTING IN A DRAMA SERIES (SINGLE EPISODE): Harry Harris, "To Soar and Never Falter," *Fame* (NBC)

OUTSTANDING DIRECTING IN A COMEDY SERIES (SINGLE EPISODE): Alan Rafkin, "Barbara's Crisis," *One Day at a Time* (CBS)

OUTSTANDING DIRECTING IN A LIMITED SERIES OR A SPECIAL: Marvin J. Chomsky, "Inside the Third Reich" (ABC)

OUTSTANDING WRITING IN A DRAMA SERIES (SINGLE EPISODE): Steve Bochco, Anthony Yerkovich, Jeffrey Lewis, and Michael Wagner, teleplay; Michael Kozoll and Steven Bochco, story; "Freedom's Last Stand," *Hill Street Blues* (NBC)

OUTSTANDING WRITING IN A COMEDY SERIES (SINGLE EPISODE): Ken Estin, "Elegant Iggy," *Taxi* (ABC)

OUTSTANDING WRITING IN A LIMITED SERIES OR A SPECIAL: Corey Blechman, teleplay; Barry Morrow, story; "Bill" (CBS)

FIFTH ANNUAL ATAS GOVERNOR'S AWARD: *The Hallmark Hall of Fame*

1982–1983 (presented September 25, 1983)

OUTSTANDING COMEDY SERIES: *Cheers,* James Burrows, Glen Charles, and Les Charles, producers; Ken Levine and David Isaacs, coproducers (NBC)

OUTSTANDING DRAMA SERIES: *Hill Street Blues,* Steven Bochco, executive producer; Gregory Hoblit, coexecutive producer; Anthony Yerkovich, supervising producer; David Anspaugh and Scott Brazil, producers (NBC)

OUTSTANDING LIMITED SERIES: *Nicholas Nickleby,* Colin Callender, producer (syndicated)

OUTSTANDING VARIETY, MUSIC, OR COMEDY PROGRAM: "Motown 25: Yesterday, Today, Forever," Suzanne de Passe, executive producer; Don Mischer and Buz Kohan, producers; Suzanne Coston, producer for Motown (NBC)

OUTSTANDING DRAMA SPECIAL: "Special Bulletin," Don Ohlmeyer, executive producer; Marshall Herskovitz and Edward Zwick, producers (NBC)

OUTSTANDING INFORMATIONAL SERIES: *The Barbara Walters Specials,* Beth Polson, producer; Barbara Walters, host (ABC)

OUTSTANDING INFORMATIONAL SPECIAL: "The Body Human: The Living Code," Thomas W. Moore, executive producer; Robert E. Fuisz, M.D., and Alfred R. Kelman, M.D., producers; Charles A. Bangert, Franklin Getchell, and Nancy Smith, coproducers (CBS)

OUTSTANDING CLASSICAL PROGRAM IN THE PERFORMING ARTS: "Pavarotti in Philadelphia: *La Bohème,*" Margaret Anne Everitt, executive producer; Clement D'Alessio, producer; Luciano Pavarotti, star (PBS)

OUTSTANDING CHILDREN'S PROGRAM: "Big Bird in China," Jon Stone, executive producer; David Liu, Kuo Bao-Xiang, and Xu Ja-Cha, producers (NBC)

OUTSTANDING ANIMATED PROGRAM: "Ziggy's Gift," Lena Tabori, executive producer; Richard Williams, Tom Wilson, and Lena Tabori, producers (ABC)

OUTSTANDING LEAD ACTOR IN A DRAMA SERIES: Ed Flanders, *St. Elsewhere* (NBC)

OUTSTANDING LEAD ACTOR IN A COMEDY SERIES: Judd Hirsch, *Taxi* (NBC)

OUTSTANDING LEAD ACTOR IN A LIMITED SERIES OR A SPECIAL: Tommy Lee Jones, "The Executioner's Song" (NBC)

OUTSTANDING LEAD ACTRESS IN A DRAMA SERIES: Tyne Daly, *Cagney & Lacey* (CBS)

OUTSTANDING LEAD ACTRESS IN A COMEDY SERIES: Shelley Long, *Cheers* (NBC)

OUTSTANDING LEAD ACTRESS IN A LIMITED SERIES OR A SPECIAL: Barbara Stanwyck, *The Thorn Birds*—Part 1 (ABC)
OUTSTANDING SUPPORTING ACTOR IN A DRAMA SERIES: James Coco, "Cora and Arnie," *St. Elsewhere* (NBC)
OUTSTANDING SUPPORTING ACTOR IN A COMEDY, VARIETY, OR MUSIC SERIES: Christopher Lloyd, *Taxi* (NBC)
OUTSTANDING SUPPORTING ACTOR IN A LIMITED SERIES OR A SPECIAL: Richard Kiley, *The Thorn Birds*—Part 1 (ABC)
OUTSTANDING SUPPORTING ACTRESS IN A DRAMA SERIES: Doris Roberts, "Cora and Arnie," *St. Elsewhere* (NBC)
OUTSTANDING SUPPORTING ACTRESS IN A COMEDY, VARIETY, OR MUSIC SERIES: Carol Kane, *Taxi* (NBC)
OUTSTANDING SUPPORTING ACTRESS IN A LIMITED SERIES OR A SPECIAL: Jean Simmons, *The Thorn Birds* (ABC)
OUTSTANDING INDIVIDUAL PERFORMANCE IN A VARIETY OR MUSIC PROGRAM: Leontyne Price, "Live from Lincoln Center: Leontyne Price, Zubin Mehta, and the New York Philharmonic" (PBS)
OUTSTANDING INDIVIDUAL ACHIEVEMENT—INFORMATIONAL PROGRAMMING: Alfred R. Kelman, M.D., and Charles Bangert, directors, "The Body Human: The Living Code"; Louis H. Gorfain and Robert E. Fuisz, M.D., writers, "The Body Human: The Living Code" (CBS)
OUTSTANDING DIRECTING IN A DRAMA SERIES (SINGLE EPISODE): Jeff Bleckner, "Life in the Minors," *Hill Street Blues* (NBC)
OUTSTANDING DIRECTING IN A COMEDY SERIES (SINGLE EPISODE): James Burrows, "Showdown, Part 2," *Cheers* (NBC)
OUTSTANDING DIRECTING IN A LIMITED SERIES OR A SPECIAL: John Erman, "Who Will Love My Children?" (ABC)
OUTSTANDING DIRECTING IN A VARIETY OR MUSICAL PROGRAM: Dwight Hemion, "Sheena Easton, Act I" (NBC)
OUTSTANDING WRITING IN A DRAMA SERIES (SINGLE EPISODE): David Milch, "Trial by Fury," *Hill Street Blues* (NBC)
OUTSTANDING WRITING IN A COMEDY SERIES (SINGLE EPISODE): Glen Charles and Les Charles, "Give Me a Ring Sometime," *Cheers* (NBC)
OUTSTANDING WRITING IN A LIMITED SERIES OR A SPECIAL: Marshall Herskovitz, teleplay; Edward Zwick and Marshall Herskovitz, story; "Special Bulletin" (NBC)
OUTSTANDING WRITING IN A VARIETY OR MUSICAL PROGRAM: John Candy, Joe Flaherty, Eugene Levy, Andrea Martin, Martin Short, Dick Blasucci, Paul Flaherty, John McAndrew, Doug Steckler, Bob Dolman, Michael Short, and Mary Charlotte Wilcox; "The Energy Ball/Sweeps Week," *SCTV Network* (NBC)
SIXTH ANNUAL ATAS GOVERNOR'S AWARD: Sylvester L. "Pat" Weaver, Jr., former President of the National Broadcasting Company

1983–1984 (presented September 23, 1984)

OUTSTANDING COMEDY SERIES: *Cheers,* James Burrows, Glen Charles, and Les Charles, producers (NBC)
OUTSTANDING DRAMA SERIES: *Hill Street Blues,* Steven Bochco, executive producer; Gregory Hoblit, coexecutive producer; Scott Brazil, supervising producer; Jeff Lewis and Sascha Schneider, producers; David Latt, coproducer (NBC)
OUTSTANDING LIMITED SERIES: "Concealed Enemies," *American Playhouse,* Lindsay Law and David Elstein, executive producers; Peter Cook, producer (PBS)
OUTSTANDING VARIETY, MUSIC, OR COMEDY PROGRAM: Nick Vanoff and George Stevens, Jr., producers; "The 6th Annual Kennedy Center Honors: A Celebration of the Performing Arts" (CBS)
OUTSTANDING DRAMA SPECIAL: "Something About Amelia," Leonard Goldberg, executive producer; Michele Rappaport, producer (ABC)
OUTSTANDING INFORMATIONAL SERIES: *A Walk Through the 20th Century,* Merton Y. Koplin, senior executive producer; Charles Grinker and Sanford H. Fisher, producers; Betsy McCarthy, coordinating producer; David Grubin and Ronald Blumer, producers; Bill Moyers, host (PBS)
OUTSTANDING INFORMATIONAL SPECIAL: "America Remembers John F. Kennedy," Thomas F. Horton, producer (syndicated)
OUTSTANDING CLASSICAL PROGRAM IN THE PERFORMING ARTS: "Placido Domingo Celebrates Seville," *Great Performances,* Horant H. Holfeld, executive producer; David Griffiths, producer; Placido Domingo, host (PBS)
OUTSTANDING CHILDREN'S PROGRAM: "He Makes Me Feel Like Dancin'," Edgar J. Scherick and Scott Rudin, executive producers; Emile Ardolino and Judy Kinberg, producers (NBC)
OUTSTANDING ANIMATED PROGRAM: "Garfield on the Town," Jay Poynor, executive producer; Lee Mendelson and Bill Melendez, producers (CBS)
OUTSTANDING LEAD ACTOR IN A DRAMA SERIES: Tom Selleck, *Magnum, P.I,* (CBS)
OUTSTANDING LEAD ACTOR IN A COMEDY SERIES: John Ritter, *Three's Company* (ABC)
OUTSTANDING LEAD ACTOR IN A LIMITED SERIES OR A SPECIAL: Sir Laurence Olivier, *King Lear* (syndicated)
OUTSTANDING LEAD ACTRESS IN A DRAMA SERIES: Tyne Daly, *Cagney & Lacey* (CBS)
OUTSTANDING LEAD ACTRESS IN A COMEDY SERIES: Jane Curtin, *Kate & Allie* (CBS)
OUTSTANDING LEAD ACTRESS IN A LIMITED SERIES OR A SPECIAL: Jane Fonda, *The Dollmaker* (ABC)
OUTSTANDING SUPPORTING ACTOR IN A DRAMA SERIES: Bruce Weitz, *Hill Street Blues* (CBS)
OUTSTANDING SUPPORTING ACTOR IN A COMEDY, VARIETY, OR MUSIC SERIES: Pat Harrington, Jr., *One Day at a Time* (CBS)
OUTSTANDING SUPPORTING ACTOR IN A LIMITED SERIES OR A SPECIAL: Art Carney, "Terrible Joe Moran" (CBS)
OUTSTANDING SUPPORTING ACTRESS IN A DRAMA SERIES: Alfre Woodard, "Doris in Wonderland," *Hill Street Blues* (NBC)
OUTSTANDING SUPPORTING ACTRESS IN A COMEDY, VARIETY, OR MUSIC SERIES: Rhea Perlman, *Cheers* (NBC)
OUTSTANDING SUPPORTING ACTRESS IN A LIMITED SERIES OR A SPECIAL: Roxana Zal, "Something About Amelia" (ABC)
OUTSTANDING INDIVIDUAL PERFORMANCE IN A VARIETY OR MUSIC PROGRAM: Cloris Leachman, "Screen Actors Guild 50th Anniversary Celebration" (CBS)
OUTSTANDING INDIVIDUAL ACHIEVEMENT—INFORMATIONAL PROGRAMMING: Emile Ardolino, director; "He Makes Me Feel Like Dancin' " (NBC) and Bill Moyers, writer; "Marshall, Texas—Marshall, Texas" (PBS)
OUTSTANDING DIRECTING IN A DRAMA SERIES (SINGLE EPISODE): Corey Allen, "Goodbye Mr. Scripps," *Hill Street Blues* (NBC)

OUTSTANDING DIRECTING IN A COMEDY SERIES (SINGLE EPISODE): Bill Persky, "Very Loud Family," *Kate & Allie* (CBS)

OUTSTANDING DIRECTING IN A LIMITED SERIES OR A SPECIAL: Jeff Bleckner, "Concealed Enemies," *American Playhouse* (PBS)

OUTSTANDING DIRECTING IN A VARIETY, MUSIC, OR COMEDY PROGRAM: Dwight Hemion, "Here's Television Entertainment" (PBS)

OUTSTANDING WRITING IN A DRAMA SERIES (SINGLE EPISODE): John Ford Noonan, teleplay; John Masius and Tom Fontana, story; "The Women," *St. Elsewhere* (NBC)

OUTSTANDING WRITING IN A COMEDY SERIES (SINGLE EPISODE): David Angell, "Old Flames," *Cheers* (NBC)

OUTSTANDING WRITING IN A LIMITED SERIES OR SPECIAL: William Hanley, "Something About Amelia" (ABC)

OUTSTANDING WRITING IN A VARIETY, MUSIC, OR COMEDY PROGRAM: Steve O'Donnell, Gerard Mulligan, Sandy Frank, Joe Toplyn, Chris Elliott, Matt Wickline, Jeff Martin, Todd Greenberg, David Yazbek, Merrill Markoe, and David Letterman; *Late Night with David Letterman,* with Dr. Ruth Westheimer and Teri Garr, 11/15/83 (NBC)

SEVENTH ANNUAL ATAS GOVERNOR'S AWARD: Bob Hope

1984–1985 (presented September 22, 1985)

OUTSTANDING COMEDY SERIES: *The Cosby Show,* Marcy Carsey and Tom Werner, executive producers; Earl Pomerantz and Elliot Schoenman, coexecutive producers; John Markus, supervising producer; Caryn Sneider, producer; Earle Hyman, Jerry Ross, and Michael Loman, coproducers (NBC)

OUTSTANDING DRAMA SERIES: *Cagney & Lacey,* Barney Rosenzweig, executive producer; Steven Brown, Terry Louise Fisher, and Peter Lefcourt, producers (CBS)

OUTSTANDING LIMITED SERIES: "The Jewel in the Crown," *Masterpiece Theatre,* Denis Forman, executive producer; Christopher Morahan, producer (PBS)

OUTSTANDING VARIETY, MUSIC, OR COMEDY PROGRAM: "Motown Returns to the Apollo," Suzanne de Passe, executive producer; Don Mischer, producer; Suzanne Coston and Michael Weisbarth, coproducers (NBC)

OUTSTANDING DRAMA/COMEDY SPECIAL: "Do You Remember Love?," Dave Bell, executive producer; Marilyn Hall, coexecutive producer; Wayne Threm and James E. Thompson, producers; Walter Halsey Davis, coproducer (CBS)

OUTSTANDING INFORMATIONAL SERIES: *The Living Planet: A Portrait of Earth,* Richard Brock, executive producer; Adrian Warren, Ned Kelly, Andrew Neal, and Richard Brock, producers (PBS)

OUTSTANDING INFORMATIONAL SPECIAL: "Cousteau: Mississippi," Jacques-Yves Cousteau and Jean-Michel Cousteau, executive producers; Andrew Solt, producer; Jacques-Yves Cousteau, host (SYN)

OUTSTANDING CLASSICAL PROGRAM IN THE PERFORMING ARTS: "*Tosca,* Live from the Met," Michael Bronson, executive producer; Samuel J. Paul, producer (PBS)

OUTSTANDING CHILDREN'S PROGRAM: "Displaced Person," *American Playhouse,* Allison Maher, Barry Solomon, Rick Traum, and Patrick Lynch, executive producers; Patrick Dromgoole, supervising executive producer; Barry Levinson, producer (PBS)

OUTSTANDING ANIMATED PROGRAM: "Garfield in the Rough," Jay Poynor, executive producer; Phil Roman, producer; Jim Davis, writer; Phil Roman, director (CBS)

OUTSTANDING LEAD ACTOR IN A DRAMA SERIES: William Daniels, *St. Elsewhere* (NBC)

OUTSTANDING LEAD ACTOR IN A COMEDY SERIES: Robert Guillaume, *Benson* (ABC)

OUTSTANDING LEAD ACTOR IN A LIMITED SERIES OR A SPECIAL: Richard Crenna, "The Rape of Richard Beck," *ABC Theatre* (ABC)

OUTSTANDING LEAD ACTRESS IN A DRAMA SERIES: Tyne Daly, *Cagney & Lacey* (CBS)

OUTSTANDING LEAD ACTRESS IN A COMEDY SERIES: Jane Curtin, *Kate & Allie* (CBS)

OUTSTANDING LEAD ACTRESS IN A LIMITED SERIES OR A SPECIAL: Joanne Woodward, "Do You Remember Love?" (CBS)

OUTSTANDING SUPPORTING ACTOR IN A DRAMA SERIES: Edward James Olmos, *Miami Vice* (NBC)

OUTSTANDING SUPPORTING ACTOR IN A COMEDY SERIES: John Larroquette, *Night Court* (NBC)

OUTSTANDING SUPPORTING ACTOR IN A LIMITED SERIES OR A SPECIAL: Karl Malden, "Fatal Vision" (NBC)

OUTSTANDING SUPPORTING ACTRESS IN A DRAMA SERIES: Betty Thomas, *Hill Street Blues* (NBC)

OUTSTANDING SUPPORTING ACTRESS IN A COMEDY SERIES: Rhea Perlman, *Cheers* (NBC)

OUTSTANDING SUPPORTING ACTRESS IN A LIMITED SERIES OR A SPECIAL: Kim Stanley, "Cat on a Hot Tin Roof," *American Playhouse* (PBS)

OUTSTANDING INDIVIDUAL PERFORMANCE IN A VARIETY OR MUSIC PROGRAM: George Hearn, "Sweeney Todd," *Great Performances* (PBS)

OUTSTANDING INDIVIDUAL ACHIEVEMENT—INFORMATIONAL PROGRAMMING—WRITING: Howard Enders, John G. Fox, Michael Joseloff, and Marc Siegel; "The Crucible of Europe," *Heritage: Civilization and the Jews* (PBS) and Brian Wilson, "Out of the Ashes," *Heritage: Civilization and the Jews* (PBS)

OUTSTANDING DIRECTING IN A DRAMA SERIES (SINGLE EPISODE): Arthur Karen, "Heat," *Cagney & Lacey* (CBS)

OUTSTANDING DIRECTING IN A COMEDY SERIES (SINGLE EPISODE): Jay Sandrich, "The Younger Woman," *The Cosby Show* (NBC)

OUTSTANDING DIRECTING IN A LIMITED SERIES OR A SPECIAL: Lamont Johnson, "Wallenberg: A Hero's Story" (NBC)

OUTSTANDING DIRECTING IN A VARIETY OR MUSIC PROGRAM: Terry Hughes, "Sweeney Todd," *Great Performances* (PBS)

OUTSTANDING WRITING IN A DRAMA SERIES (SINGLE EPISODE): Patricia M. Green, "Who Said It's Fair—Part II," *Cagney & Lacey* (CBS)

OUTSTANDING WRITING IN A COMEDY SERIES (SINGLE EPISODE): Ed Weinberger and Michael Leeson, premiere episode, *The Cosby Show* (NBC)

OUTSTANDING WRITING IN A LIMITED SERIES OR A SPECIAL: Vickie Patik, "Do You Remember Love?" (CBS)

OUTSTANDING WRITING IN A VARIETY OR MUSIC PROGRAM: Gerard Mulligan, Sandy Frank, Joe Toplyn, Chris Elliott, Matt Wickline, Jeff Martin, Eddie Gorodetsky, Randy Cohen, Larry Jacobson, Kevin Curran, Fred Graver, Merrill Markoe, and David Letterman; "Christmas with the Lettermans," show #491, *Late Night with David Letterman* (NBC)

EIGHTH ANNUAL ATAS GOVERNOR'S AWARD: Alistair Cooke

1985–1986 (presented September 20, 1986)

OUTSTANDING COMEDY SERIES: *The Golden Girls,* Paul Junger Witt and Tony Thomas executive producers; Paul Bogart, supervising producer; Paul Junger Witt, Tony Thomas, Kathy Speer, and Terry Grossman producers; Marsha Posner Williams coproducer (NBC)

OUTSTANDING DRAMA SERIES: *Cagney & Lacey,* Barney Rosenzweig, executive producer; Liz Coe, supervising producer; Ralph Singleton, Patricia Green, and Steve Brown, producers; P. K. Knelman, coproducer (CBS)

OUTSTANDING MINI-SERIES: "Peter the Great," Marvin J. Chomsky, producer; Konstantin Theoren, line producer (NBC)

OUTSTANDING VARIETY, MUSIC, OR COMEDY PROGRAM: "The Kennedy Center Honors: A Celebration of the Performing Arts," Nick Vanoff and George Stevens, Jr., producers (CBS)

OUTSTANDING DRAMA/COMEDY SPECIAL: "Love Is Never Silent," Marian Rees, executive producer; Juliana Field, coexecutive producer (NBC)

OUTSTANDING INFORMATIONAL SERIES: *Laurence Olivier—A Life,* Nick Evans and Nick Elliott, executive producers; Bob Bee, producer (PBS); *Planet Earth,* Thomas Skinner, executive producer; Gregory Andorfer, series producer; Georgann Kane, coordinating producer (PBS)

OUTSTANDING INFORMATIONAL SPECIAL: "W.C. Fields Straight Up," Robert B. Weide, executive producer; Ronald J. Fields, coproducer (PBS)

OUTSTANDING CLASSICAL PROGRAM IN THE PERFORMING ARTS: "Wolftrap Presents the Kirov: Swan Lake," Michael B. Styer, executive producer; Phillip Byrd, senior producer; John T. Potthast, producer (PBS)

OUTSTANDING CHILDREN'S PROGRAM: *Anne of Green Gables—Wonderworks,* Kevin Sullivan and Lee Polk executive producers; Kevin Sullivan and Ian McDougall producers (PBS)

OUTSTANDING ANIMATED PROGRAM: "Garfield's Halloween Adventure," Jay Poynor, executive producer (CBS)

OUTSTANDING LEAD ACTOR IN A DRAMA SERIES: William Daniels, *St. Elsewhere* (NBC)

OUTSTANDING LEAD ACTOR IN A COMEDY SERIES: Michael J. Fox, *Family Ties* (NBC)

OUTSTANDING LEAD ACTOR IN A MINI-SERIES OR A SPECIAL: Dustin Hoffman, "Death of a Salesman" (CBS)

OUTSTANDING LEAD ACTRESS IN A DRAMA SERIES: Sharon Gless, *Cagney & Lacey* (CBS)

OUTSTANDING LEAD ACTRESS IN A COMEDY SERIES: Betty White, *The Golden Girls* (NBC)

OUTSTANDING LEAD ACTRESS IN A MINI-SERIES OR A SPECIAL: Marlo Thomas, "Nobody's Child" (NBC)

OUTSTANDING SUPPORTING ACTOR IN A DRAMA SERIES: John Karlen, *Cagney & Lacey* (CBS)

OUTSTANDING SUPPORTING ACTOR IN A COMEDY SERIES: John Larroquette, *Night Court* (NBC)

OUTSTANDING SUPPORTING ACTOR IN A MINI-SERIES OR A SPECIAL: John Malkovich, "Death of a Salesman" (CBS)

OUTSTANDING SUPPORTING ACTRESS IN A DRAMA SERIES: Bonnie Bartlett, *St. Elsewhere* (NBC)

OUTSTANDING SUPPORTING ACTRESS IN A COMEDY SERIES: Rhea Perlman, *Cheers* (NBC)

OUTSTANDING SUPPORTING ACTRESS IN A MINI-SERIES OR A SPECIAL: Colleen Dewhurst, "Between Two Women" (ABC)

OUTSTANDING INDIVIDUAL PERFORMANCE IN A VARIETY OR MUSIC PROGRAM: Whitney Houston, "The 28th Annual Grammy Awards" (CBS)

OUTSTANDING GUEST PERFORMER IN A DRAMA SERIES: John Lithgow, *Amazing Stories* (NBC)

OUTSTANDING GUEST PERFORMER IN A COMEDY SERIES: Roscoe Lee Browne, *The Cosby Show* (NBC)

OUTSTANDING INDIVIDUAL ACHIEVEMENT IN CLASSICAL MUSIC/DANCE PROGRAMMING-PERFORMING: Placido Domingo, "Cavalleria Rusticana," *Great Performances* (PBS)

OUTSTANDING INDIVIDUAL ACHIEVEMENT—INFORMATIONAL PROGRAMMING—WRITING: John L. Miller, "The Spencer Tracy Legacy: A Tribute by Katharine Hepburn" (PBS)

OUTSTANDING DIRECTING IN A DRAMA SERIES (SINGLE EPISODE): Georg Stanford Brown, "Parting Shots," *Cagney & Lacey* (CBS)

OUTSTANDING DIRECTING IN A COMEDY SERIES (SINGLE EPISODE): Jay Sandrich, "Denise's Friend," *The Cosby Show* (NBC)

OUTSTANDING DIRECTING IN A MINI-SERIES OR A SPECIAL: Joseph Sargent, "Love Is Never Silent," *Hallmark Hall of Fame* (NBC)

OUTSTANDING DIRECTING IN A VARIETY OR MUSIC PROGRAM: Waris Hussein, "Copacabana," (CBS)

OUTSTANDING WRITING IN A DRAMA SERIES (SINGLE EPISODE): Tom Fontana, John Tinker, and John Masius, "Time Heals," *St. Elsewhere* (NBC)

OUTSTANDING WRITING IN A COMEDY SERIES (SINGLE EPISODE): Barry Fanaro and Mort Nathan, "A Little Romance," *The Golden Girls* (NBC)

OUTSTANDING WRITING IN A MINI-SERIES OR A SPECIAL: Ron Cowen and Daniel Lipman, teleplay; Sherman Yellen, story; "An Early Frost" (NBC)

OUTSTANDING WRITING IN A VARIETY OR MUSIC PROGRAM: David Letterman, Joe O'Donnell, Sandy Frank, Joe Toplyn, Chris Elliott, Matt Wickline, Jeff Martin, Gerard Mulligan, Randy Cohen, Larry Jacboson, Kevin Curran, Fred Graver, and Merrill Markoe; Fourth Anniversary Show, *Late Night with David Letterman* (NBC)

OUTSTANDING INDIVIDUAL ACHIEVEMENT IN CLASSICAL MUSIC/DANCE PROGRAMMING-WRITING: John Ardlon, "Gala of Stars 1986" (PBS)

NINTH ANNUAL ATAS GOVERNOR'S AWARD: Red Skelton

1986–1987 (presented September 20, 1987)

OUTSTANDING COMEDY SERIES: *The Golden Girls,* Paul Junger Witt, Tony Thomas, and Susan Harris, executive producers; Kathy Speer and Terry Grossman, producers; Mort Nathan, Barry Fanaro, Winifred Hervey, and Marsha Posner Williams, coproducers (NBC)

OUTSTANDING DRAMA SERIES: *L.A. Law,* Steven Bochco, executive producer; Gregory Hoblit, coexecutive producer; Terry Louise Fisher, supervising producer; Ellen S. Pressman and Scott Goldstein, producers; Phillip M. Goldfarb, coordinating producer (NBC)

OUTSTANDING MINI-SERIES: "A Year in the Life," Joshua Brand and John Falsey, executive producers; Stephen Cragg, producer (NBC)

OUTSTANDING VARIETY, MUSIC, OR COMEDY PROGRAM: "The 1987 Tony Awards," Don Mischer, executive producer; David J. Goldberg, producer (CBS)

OUTSTANDING DRAMA/COMEDY SPECIAL: "Promise," *Hallmark Hall of Fame,* Peter K. Duchow and James Garner, executive producers; Glenn Jordan, producer; Richard Friedenberg, coproducer (CBS)

OUTSTANDING INFORMATIONAL SERIES: *Smithsonian World,* Adrian Malone, executive producer; David Grubin, producer (PBS); "Unknown Chaplin," *American Masters,* Kevin Brownlow and David Gill, producers (PBS)

OUTSTANDING INFORMATIONAL SPECIAL: "Dance in America: Agnes, The Indomitable De Mille," *Great Performances,* Jac Venza, executive producer; Judy Kinberg, producer (PBS)

OUTSTANDING CLASSICAL PROGRAM IN THE PERFORMING ARTS: "Vladimir Horowitz: The Last Romantic," Peter Gelb, executive producer; Susan Froemke, producer; Vladimir Horowitz, star (PBS)

OUTSTANDING CHILDREN'S PROGRAM: *Jim Henson the Storyteller,* "Hans My Hedgehog," Jim Henson, executive producer; Mark Shivas, producer (NBC)

OUTSTANDING ANIMATED PROGRAM: "Cathy," Lee Mendelson, executive producer; Bill Melendez, producer; Cathy Guisewite, writer (CBS)

OUTSTANDING LEAD ACTOR IN A DRAMA SERIES: Bruce Willis, *Moonlighting* (ABC)

OUTSTANDING LEAD ACTOR IN A COMEDY SERIES: Michael J. Fox, *Family Ties* (NBC)

OUTSTANDING LEAD ACTOR IN A MINI-SERIES OR A SPECIAL: James Woods, "Promise," *Hallmark Hall of Fame* (CBS)

OUTSTANDING LEAD ACTRESS IN A DRAMA SERIES: Sharon Gless, *Cagney & Lacey* (CBS)

OUTSTANDING LEAD ACTRESS IN A COMEDY SERIES: Rue McClanahan, *The Golden Girls* (NBC)

OUTSTANDING LEAD ACTRESS IN A MINI-SERIES OR A SPECIAL: Gena Rowlands, "The Betty Ford Story" (ABC)

OUTSTANDING SUPPORTING ACTOR IN A DRAMA SERIES: John Hillerman, *Magnum, P.I.* (CBS)

OUTSTANDING SUPPORTING ACTOR IN A COMEDY SERIES: John Larroquette, *Night Court* (NBC)

OUTSTANDING SUPPORTING ACTOR IN A MINI-SERIES OR A SPECIAL: Dabney Coleman, "Sworn to Silence" (ABC)

OUTSTANDING SUPPORTING ACTRESS IN A DRAMA SERIES: Bonnie Bartlett, *St. Elsewhere* (NBC)

OUTSTANDING SUPPORTING ACTRESS IN A COMEDY SERIES: Jackee Harry, *227* (NBC)

OUTSTANDING SUPPORTING ACTRESS IN A MINI-SERIES OR A SPECIAL: Piper Laurie, "Promise," *Hallmark Hall of Fame* (CBS)

OUTSTANDING INDIVIDUAL PERFORMANCE IN A VARIETY OR MUSIC PROGRAM: Robin Williams, "A Carol Burnett Special: Carol, Carl, Whoopi & Robin" (ABC)

OUTSTANDING GUEST PERFORMER IN A DRAMA SERIES: Alfre Woodard, *L.A. Law* (NBC)

OUTSTANDING GUEST PERFORMER IN A COMEDY SERIES: John Cleese, *Cheers* (NBC)

OUTSTANDING INDIVIDUAL ACHIEVEMENT IN CLASSICAL MUSIC/DANCE PROGRAMMING: Albert Maysles and David Maysles, directors; "Vladimir Horowitz: The Last Romantic" (PBS)

OUTSTANDING INDIVIDUAL ACHIEVEMENT IN INFORMATIONAL PROGRAMMING: Robert McCrum and Robert MacNeil, writers; *The Story of English,* "A Muse of Fire" (PBS)

OUTSTANDING DIRECTING IN A DRAMA SERIES (SINGLE EPISODE): Gregory Hoblit, "Pilot," *L.A. Law* (NBC)

OUTSTANDING DIRECTING IN A COMEDY SERIES (SINGLE EPISODE): Terry Hughes, "Isn't It Romantic?," *The Golden Girls* (NBC)

OUTSTANDING DIRECTING IN A MINI-SERIES OR A SPECIAL: Glenn Jordan, "Promise," *Hallmark Hall of Fame* (CBS)

OUTSTANDING DIRECTING IN A VARIETY OR MUSIC PROGRAM: Don Mischer, "The Kennedy Center Honors: A Celebration of the Performing Arts" (CBS)

OUTSTANDING WRITING IN A DRAMA SERIES (SINGLE EPISODE): Terry Louise Fisher, "Venus Butterfly," *L.A. Law* (NBC)

OUTSTANDING WRITING IN A COMEDY SERIES (SINGLE EPISODE): Gary David Goldberg and Alan Uger, " 'A,' My Name Is Alex," *Family Ties* (NBC)

OUTSTANDING WRITING IN A MINI-SERIES OR A SPECIAL: Richard Friedenberg, teleplay; Kenneth Blackwell, Tennyson Flowers, and Richard Friedenberg, story; "Promise," *Hallmark Hall of Fame* (CBS)

OUTSTANDING WRITING IN A VARIETY OR MUSIC PROGRAM: Steve O'Donnell, Sandy Frank, Joe Toplyn, Chris Elliott, Matt Wickline, Jeff Martin, Gerard Mulligan, Randy Cohen, Larry Jacobson, Kevin Curran, Fred Graver, Adam Resnick, and David Letterman; Fifth Anniversary Special, *Late Night with David Letterman* (NBC)

TENTH ANNUAL ATAS GOVERNOR'S AWARD: Grant Tinker

1987–1988 (presented August 28, 1988)

OUTSTANDING COMEDY SERIES: *The Wonder Years,* Carol Black and Neil Marlens, executive producers; Jeff Silver, producer (ABC)

OUTSTANDING DRAMA SERIES: *thirtysomething,* Edward Zwick and Marshall Herskovitz, executive producers; Paul Haggis, supervising producer; Edward Zwick and Scott Winant, producers (ABC)

OUTSTANDING MINI-SERIES: "The Murder of Mary Phagan," George Stevens, Jr., producer (NBC)

OUTSTANDING VARIETY, MUSIC, OR COMEDY PROGRAM: "Irving Berlin's 100th Birthday Celebration," Don Mischer, executive producer; Jan Cornell and David J. Goldberg, producers; Sara Lukinson, coproducer (CBS)

OUTSTANDING DRAMA/COMEDY SPECIAL: "Inherit the Wind," Peter Douglas, executive producer; Robert A. Papazian, producer (NBC)

OUTSTANDING CLASSICAL PROGRAM IN THE PERFORMING ARTS: "Nixon in China," *Great Performances,* Jac Venza, executive producer; David Horn, series producer; Michael Bronson, producer; John Walker, coordinating producer (PBS)

OUTSTANDING INFORMATIONAL SERIES: *Buster Keaton: A Hard Act To Follow: American Masters,* Kevin Brownlow and David Gill, producers (PBS). *Nature,* David Heeley, executive producer; Fred Kaifman, series producer (PBS)

OUTSTANDING INFORMATIONAL SPECIAL: "Dear America: Letters Home from Vietnam," Bill Couturie and Thomas Bird, producers (HBO)

OUTSTANDING CHILDREN'S PROGRAM: "The Secret Garden," *Hallmark Hall of Fame,* Norman Rosemont, executive producer; Steven Lanning, producer (CBS)

OUTSTANDING ANIMATED PROGRAM: "A Claymation Christmas Celebration," Will Vinton, executive producer; David Altschul, producer; Will Vinton, director; Ralph Liddle, writer (CBS)

OUTSTANDING VARIETY/MUSIC EVENTS PROGRAMMING: "The 60th Annual Academy Awards," Samuel Goldwyn, Jr., producer (ABC)

OUTSTANDING LEAD ACTOR IN A DRAMA SERIES: Richard Kiley, *A Year in the Life* (NBC)

OUTSTANDING LEAD ACTOR IN A COMEDY SERIES: Michael J. Fox, *Family Ties* (NBC)

OUTSTANDING LEAD ACTOR IN A MINI-SERIES OR SPECIAL: Jason Robards, "Inherit the Wind" (NBC)

OUTSTANDING LEAD ACTRESS IN A DRAMA SERIES: Tyne Daly, *Cagney & Lacey* (CBS)

OUTSTANDING LEAD ACTRESS IN A COMEDY SERIES: Beatrice Arthur, *The Golden Girls* (NBC)

OUTSTANDING LEAD ACTRESS IN A MINI-SERIES OR SPECIAL: Jessica Tandy, "Foxfire," *Hallmark Hall of Fame* (CBS)

OUTSTANDING SUPPORTING ACTOR IN A DRAMA SERIES: Larry Drake, *L.A. Law* (NBC)

OUTSTANDING SUPPORTING ACTOR IN A COMEDY SERIES: John Larroquette, *Night Court* (NBC)

OUTSTANDING SUPPORTING ACTOR IN A MINI-SERIES OR SPECIAL: John Shea, "Baby M" (ABC)

OUTSTANDING SUPPORTING ACTRESS IN A DRAMA SERIES: Patricia Wettig, *thirtysomething* (ABC)

OUTSTANDING SUPPORTING ACTRESS IN A COMEDY SERIES: Estelle Getty, *The Golden Girls* (NBC)

OUTSTANDING SUPPORTING ACTRESS IN A MINI-SERIES OR SPECIAL: Jane Seymour, "Onassis: The Richest Man in the World" (ABC)

OUTSTANDING INDIVIDUAL PERFORMANCE IN A VARIETY OR MUSIC PROGRAM: Robin Williams, "ABC Presents a Royal Gala" (ABC)

OUTSTANDING GUEST PERFORMER IN A DRAMA SERIES: Shirley Knight, *thirtysomething* (ABC)

OUTSTANDING GUEST PERFORMER IN A COMEDY SERIES: Beah Richards, *Frank's Place* (CBS)

OUTSTANDING DIRECTING IN A DRAMA SERIES (SINGLE EPISODE): Mark Tinker, "Weigh In, Weigh Out," *St. Elsewhere* (NBC)

OUTSTANDING DIRECTING IN A COMEDY SERIES (SINGLE EPISODE): Gregory Hoblit, Pilot, *Hooperman* (ABC)

OUTSTANDING DIRECTING IN A MINI-SERIES OR A SPECIAL: Lamont Johnson, "Gore Vidal's Lincoln" (CBS)

OUTSTANDING DIRECTING IN A VARIETY OR MUSIC PROGRAM: Patricia Birch and Humphrey Burton, "Celebrating Gershwin," *Great Performances* (PBS)

OUTSTANDING WRITING IN A DRAMA SERIES (SINGLE EPISODE): Paul Haggis and Marshall Herskovitz, "Business As Usual, aka Michael's Father's Death," *thirtysomething* (ABC)

OUTSTANDING WRITING IN A COMEDY SERIES (SINGLE EPISODE): Hugh Wilson, "The Bridge," *Frank's Place* (CBS)

OUTSTANDING WRITING IN A MINI-SERIES OR A SPECIAL: William Hanley, "The Attic: The Hiding of Anne Frank," *General Foods Golden Showcase* (CBS)

OUTSTANDING WRITING IN A VARIETY OR MUSIC PROGRAM: Jackie Mason, "Jackie Mason on Broadway" (HBO)

OUTSTANDING INDIVIDUAL ACHIEVEMENT IN INFORMATIONAL PROGRAMMING—PERFORMING: Hal Holbrook, "New York City," *Portrait of America* (TBS)

OUTSTANDING INDIVIDUAL ACHIEVEMENT IN INFORMATIONAL PROGRAMMING—DIRECTING: Kevin Brownlow and David Gill, *Buster Keaton: A Hard Act to Follow,* Part 1, *American Masters* (PBS)

OUTSTANDING INDIVIDUAL ACHIEVEMENT IN INFORMATIONAL PROGRAMMING—WRITING: Kevin Brownlow and David Gill, *Buster Keaton: A Hard Act to Follow,* Part 1, *American Masters* (PBS); Bill Couturie and Richard Dewhurst, "Dear America: Letters Home from Vietnam" (HBO)

OUTSTANDING INDIVIDUAL ACHIEVEMENT IN CLASSICAL MUSIC/DANCE PROGRAMMING—DIRECTING: Kirk Browning, "The Metropolitan Opera Presents: Turandot" (PBS)

OUTSTANDING INDIVIDUAL ACHIEVEMENT IN CLASSICAL MUSIC/DANCE PROGRAMMING—WRITING: David Gordon, "Dance in America: David Gordon's Made in U.S.A.," *Great Performances* (PBS)

OUTSTANDING INDIVIDUAL ACHIEVEMENT IN SPECIAL EVENTS PROGRAMMING—PERFORMER: Billy Crystal, "The 30th Annual Grammy Awards" (CBS)

OUTSTANDING INDIVIDUAL ACHIEVEMENT IN SPECIAL EVENTS PROGRAMMING—DIRECTING: Marty Pasetta, "The 60th Annual Academy Awards" (ABC)

ELEVENTH ANNUAL ATAS GOVERNOR'S AWARD: William Hanna and Joseph Barbera

1988–1989 (presented September 17, 1989)

OUTSTANDING COMEDY SERIES: *Cheers,* James Burrows, Glen Charles, and Les Charles, executive producers; Cheri Eichen and Bill Steinkellner, producers; Tim Berry and Phoef Sutton, coproducers (NBC)

OUTSTANDING DRAMA SERIES: *L.A. Law,* Steven Bochco, executive producer; Rick Wallace, coexecutive producer; David E. Kelley, supervising producer; Scott Goldstein and Michele Gallery, producers; William M. Finkelstein and Judith Parker, coproducers; Phillip M. Goldfarb and Alice West, coordinating producers (NBC)

OUTSTANDING MINI-SERIES: "War and Remembrance," Dan Curtis, executive producer; Barbara Steele, producer (ABC)

OUTSTANDING VARIETY, MUSIC, OR COMEDY PROGRAM: *The Tracey Ullman Show*, James L. Brooks, Heide Perlman, Jerry Belson, Ken Estin, and Sam Simon, executive producers; Richard Sakai and Ted Bessell, producers; Marc Flanagan, coproducer; Tracey Ullman, host (FOX)

OUTSTANDING DRAMA/COMEDY SPECIAL: "Day One," *AT&T Presents,* Aaron Spelling and E. Duke Vincent, executive producers; David W. Rintels, producer (CBS); "Roe vs. Wade," Michael Manheim, executive producer; Gregory Hoblit, producer; Alison Cross, coproducer (NBC)

OUTSTANDING CLASSICAL PROGRAM IN THE PERFORMING ARTS: "Bernstein at 70!," *Great Performances,* Harry Kraut and Klaus Hallig, executive producers; Michael Bronson and Thomas Skinner, producers (PBS)

OUTSTANDING INFORMATIONAL SERIES: *Nature,* David Heeley, executive producer; Fred Kaifman, series producer (PBS)

OUTSTANDING INFORMATIONAL SPECIAL: "Lillian Gish: The Actor's Life for Me," *American Masters,* Freida Lee Mock and Susan Lacy, executive producers; Terry Sanders, producer; William T. Cartwright, coproducer (PBS)

OUTSTANDING CHILDREN'S PROGRAM: "Free to Be . . . a Family," Marlo Thomas and Christopher Cerf, executive producers, U.S.; Robert Dalrymple, producer, U.S.; Leonid Zolotarevsky, executive producer, USSR; Igor Menzelintsev, producer, USSR; Vern T. Calhoun, coproducer (ABC)

OUTSTANDING ANIMATED PROGRAM: "Garfield: Babes and Bullets," Phil Roman, producer; Jim Davis, writer; Phil Roman, director; John Sparey and Bob Nesler; codirectors (CBS)

OUTSTANDING SPECIAL EVENTS PROGRAMMING: "Cirque de Soleil" (The Magic Circus), Helene Dufresne, producer (HBO); "The 11th Annual Kennedy Center Honors: A Celebration of the Performing Arts," George Stevens, Jr., and Nick Vanoff, producers (CBS); "The 42nd Annual Tony Awards," Don Mischer, executive producer; David J. Goldberg, producer; Jeffrey Lane, coproducer (CBS); "The 17th Annual American Film Institute Life Achievement Award: A Salute to Gregory Peck," George Stevens, Jr., producer, Jeffrey Lane, coproducer (NBC)

OUTSTANDING LEAD ACTOR IN A DRAMA SERIES: Carroll O'Connor, *In the Heat of the Night* (NBC)

OUTSTANDING LEAD ACTOR IN A COMEDY SERIES: Richard Mulligan, *Empty Nest* (NBC)

OUTSTANDING LEAD ACTOR IN A MINI-SERIES OR SPECIAL: James Woods, "My Name is Bill W.," *Hallmark Hall of Fame* (ABC)

OUTSTANDING LEAD ACTRESS IN A DRAMA SERIES: Dana Delany, *China Beach* (ABC)

OUTSTANDING LEAD ACTRESS IN A COMEDY SERIES: Candice Bergen, *Murphy Brown* (CBS)

OUTSTANDING LEAD ACTRESS IN A MINI-SERIES OR SPECIAL: Holly Hunter, "Roe vs. Wade" (NBC)

OUTSTANDING SUPPORTING ACTOR IN A DRAMA SERIES: Larry Drake, *L.A. Law* (NBC)

OUTSTANDING SUPPORTING ACTOR IN A COMEDY SERIES: Woody Harrelson, *Cheers* (NBC)

OUTSTANDING SUPPORTING ACTOR IN A MINI-SERIES OR SPECIAL: Derek Jacobi, "The Tenth Man," *Hallmark Hall of Fame* (CBS)

OUTSTANDING SUPPORTING ACTRESS IN A DRAMA SERIES: Melanie Mayron, *thirtysomething* (ABC)

OUTSTANDING SUPPORTING ACTRESS IN A COMEDY: Rhea Perlman, *Cheers* (NBC)

OUTSTANDING SUPPORTING ACTRESS IN A MINI-SERIES OR SPECIAL: Colleen Dewhurst, "Those She Left Behind" (NBC)

OUTSTANDING INDIVIDUAL PERFORMANCE IN A VARIETY OR MUSIC PROGRAM: Linda Ronstadt, "Canciones de Mi Padre," *Great Performances* (PBS)

OUTSTANDING GUEST ACTOR IN A DRAMA SERIES: Joe Spano, "The Execution of John Saringo," *Midnight Caller* (NBC)

OUTSTANDING GUEST ACTOR IN A COMEDY SERIES: Cleavon Little, "Stand By Your Man," *Dear John* (NBC)

OUTSTANDING GUEST ACTRESS IN A DRAMA SERIES: Kay Lenz, "After It Happened . . . ," *Midnight Caller* (NBC)

OUTSTANDING GUEST ACTRESS IN A COMEDY SERIES: Colleen Dewhurst, "Mama Said," *Murphy Brown* (CBS)

OUTSTANDING DIRECTING IN A DRAMA SERIES (SINGLE EPISODE): Robert Altman, "The Boiler Room," *Tanner 88* (HBO)

OUTSTANDING DIRECTING IN A COMEDY SERIES (SINGLE EPISODE): Peter Baldwin, "Our Miss White," *The Wonder Years* (ABC)

OUTSTANDING DIRECTING IN A MINI-SERIES OR A SPECIAL: Simon Wincer, "Lonesome Dove" (CBS)

OUTSTANDING DIRECTING IN A VARIETY OR MUSIC PROGRAM: Jim Henson, "Dog City," *The Jim Henson Hour* (NBC)

OUTSTANDING WRITING IN A DRAMA SERIES (single episode): Joseph Dougherty, "First Day/Last Day," *thirtysomething* (ABC)

OUTSTANDING WRITING IN A COMEDY SERIES (SINGLE EPISODE): Diane English, "Respect," *Murphy Brown* (CBS)

OUTSTANDING WRITING IN A MINI-SERIES OR A SPECIAL: Abby Mann, Rubin Vote, and Ron Hutchinson, "Murderers Among Us: The Simon Wiesenthal Story" (HBO)

OUTSTANDING WRITING IN A VARIETY OR MUSIC PROGRAM: James Downey, head writer; John Bowman, A. Whitney Brown, Gregory Daniels, Tom Davis, Al Franken, Shannon Gaughan, Jack Handy, Phil Hartman, Lorne Michaels, Mike Myers, Conan O'Brien, Bob Odenkirk, Herb Sargent, Tom Schiller, Robert Smigel, Bonnie Turner, Terry Turner, and Christine Zander, writers; George Meyer, additional sketches, *Saturday Night Live* (NBC)

OUTSTANDING INDIVIDUAL ACHIEVEMENT IN INFORMATIONAL PROGRAMMING—PERFORMING: Hal Holbrook, "Alaska," *Portrait of America* (TBS)

OUTSTANDING INDIVIDUAL ACHIEVEMENT IN INFORMATIONAL PROGRAMMING—WRITING: John Heminway, "Search for Mind," *The Mind* (PBS)

OUTSTANDING INDIVIDUAL ACHIEVEMENT IN CLASSICAL MUSIC/DANCE PROGRAMMING—PERFORMING: Mikhail Baryshnikov, "Dance in America: Baryshnikov Dances Balanchine," *Great Performances* (PBS)

OUTSTANDING INDIVIDUAL ACHIEVEMENT IN SPECIAL EVENTS PROGRAMMING—PERFORMER: Billy Crystal, "The 31st Annual Grammy Awards" (CBS)

OUTSTANDING INDIVIDUAL ACHIEVEMENT IN SPECIAL EVENTS PROGRAMMING—DIRECTING: Dwight Hemion, "The 11th Annual Kennedy Center Honors: A Celebration of the Performing Arts" (CBS)

OUTSTANDING INDIVIDUAL ACHIEVEMENT IN SPECIAL EVENTS PROGRAMMING—WRITING: Jeffrey Lane, "The 42nd Annual Tony Awards" (CBS)

TWELFTH ANNUAL ATAS GOVERNOR'S AWARD: Lucille Ball

1989–1990 (presented September 16, 1990)

OUTSTANDING COMEDY SERIES: *Murphy Brown,* Diane English and Joel Shukovsky, executive producers; Korby Siamis, consulting producer; Tom Seeley, Norm Gunzenhauser, Russ Woody, Gary Dontzig, Steven Peterman, and Barnet Kellman, producers; Deborah Smith, coproducer (CBS)

OUTSTANDING DRAMA SERIES: *L.A. Law,* David E. Kelley, executive producer; Rick Wallace, coexecutive producer; William M. Finkelstein, supervising producer; Elodie Keene and Michael M. Robin, producers; Alice West, coordinating producer; Robert M. Breech, coproducer (NBC)

OUTSTANDING MINI-SERIES: "Drug Wars: The Camarena Story," Michael Mann, executive producer; Richard Abrams, coexecutive producer; Christopher Calahan, Rose Schacht, and Ann Powell, supervising producers; Branko Lustig, producer; Mark Allan, coproducer (NBC)

OUTSTANDING VARIETY, MUSIC, OR COMEDY PROGRAM: *In Living Color,* Keenen Ivory Wayans, executive producer; Kevin S. Bright, supervising producer; Tamara Rawitt, producer; Michael Petok, coproducer (FOX)

OUTSTANDING DRAMA/COMEDY SPECIAL: "Caroline?," *Hallmark Hall of Fame,* Dan Enright and Les Alexander, executive producers; Barbara Hiser and Joseph Broido, coexecutive producers; Dorothea G. Petrie, producer (CBS); "The Incident," *AT&T Presents,* Robert Halmi, executive producer; Bill Brademan and Ed Self, producers (CBS)

OUTSTANDING VARIETY, MUSIC, OR COMEDY SPECIAL: "Sammy Davis, Jr.'s 60th Anniversary Celebration," George Schlatter, producer; Buz Kohan, Jeff Margolis, and Gary Necessary, coproducers (ABC)

OUTSTANDING CLASSICAL PROGRAM IN THE PERFORMING ARTS: "Aida," *The Metropolitan Opera Presents,* Peter Gelb, executive producer (PBS)

OUTSTANDING INFORMATIONAL SERIES: *Smithsonian World,* Adrian Malone, executive producer; Sandra W. Bradley, producer (PBS)

OUTSTANDING INFORMATIONAL SPECIAL: "Dance in America: Bob Fosse Steam Heat," *Great Performances,* Jac Venza, executive producer; Judy Kinberg, producer (PBS); "Broadway's Dreamers: The Legacy of The Group Theater," *American Masters,* Jac Venza and Susan Lacy, executive producers; Joan Kramer and David Heeley, producers; Joanne Woodward, host/producer (PBS)

OUTSTANDING CHILDREN'S PROGRAM: "A Mother's Courage: The Mary Thomas Story," *The Magical World of Disney,* Ted Field and Robert W. Cort, executive producers; Patricia Clifford and Kate Wright, coexecutive producers; Richard L. O'Connor, producer; Chet Walker, coproducer (NBC)

OUTSTANDING ANIMATED PROGRAM: *The Simpsons* (series), James L. Brooks, Matt Groening, and Sam Simon, executive producers; Richard Sakai, producer; Al Jean, Mike Reiss, and Larina Jean Adamson, coproducers; Magot Pipkin, animation producer; Gabor Csupo, supervising animation director; David Silverman, director; John Swartzwelder, writer (FOX)

OUTSTANDING LEAD ACTOR IN A DRAMA SERIES: Peter Falk, *Columbo* (ABC)

OUTSTANDING LEAD ACTOR IN A COMEDY SERIES: Ted Danson, *Cheers* (NBC)

OUTSTANDING LEAD ACTOR IN A MINI-SERIES OR SPECIAL: Hume Cronyn, "Age-Old Friends" (HBO)

OUTSTANDING LEAD ACTRESS IN A DRAMA SERIES: Patricia Wettig, *thirtysomething* (ABC)

OUTSTANDING LEAD ACTRESS IN A COMEDY SERIES: Candice Bergen, *Murphy Brown* (CBS)

OUTSTANDING LEAD ACTRESS IN A MINI-SERIES OR SPECIAL: Barbara Hershey, "A Killing in a Small Town" (CBS)

OUTSTANDING SUPPORTING ACTOR IN A DRAMA SERIES: Jimmy Smits, *L.A. Law* (NBC)

OUTSTANDING SUPPORTING ACTOR IN A COMEDY SERIES: Alex Rocco, *The Famous Teddy Z* (CBS)

OUTSTANDING SUPPORTING ACTOR IN A MINI-SERIES OR SPECIAL: Vincent Gardenia, "Age-Old Friends" (HBO)

OUTSTANDING SUPPORTING ACTRESS IN A DRAMA SERIES: Marg Helgenberger, *China Beach* (ABC)

OUTSTANDING SUPPORTING ACTRESS IN A COMEDY SERIES: Bebe Neuwirth, *Cheers* (NBC)

OUTSTANDING SUPPORTING ACTRESS IN A MINI-SERIES OR SPECIAL: Eva Marie Saint, "People Like Us" (NBC)

OUTSTANDING INDIVIDUAL PERFORMANCE IN A VARIETY OR MUSIC PROGRAM: Tracey Ullman, "The Best of The Tracey Ullman Show" (FOX)

OUTSTANDING GUEST ACTOR IN A DRAMA SERIES: Patrick McGoohan, "Agenda for Murder," *Columbo* (ABC)

OUTSTANDING GUEST ACTOR IN A COMEDY SERIES: Darren McGavin, "Brown Like Me," *Murphy Brown* (CBS)

OUTSTANDING GUEST ACTRESS IN A DRAMA SERIES: Viveca Lindfors, "Save the Last Dance for Me," *Life Goes On* (ABC)

OUTSTANDING GUEST ACTRESS IN A COMEDY SERIES: Swoosie Kurtz, "Reunion," *Carol & Company* (NBC)

OUTSTANDING DIRECTING IN A DRAMA SERIES (SINGLE EPISODE): Thomas Carter, "Promises to Keep," *Equal Justice* (ABC)

OUTSTANDING DIRECTING IN A COMEDY SERIES (SINGLE EPISODE): Michael Dinner, "Good-Bye," *The Wonder Years* (ABC)

OUTSTANDING DIRECTING IN A MINI-SERIES OR A SPECIAL: Joseph Sargent, "Caroline?," *Hallmark Hall of Fame* (CBS)

OUTSTANDING DIRECTING IN A VARIETY OR MUSIC PROGRAM: Dwight Hemion, "The Kennedy Center Honors: A Celebration of the Performing Arts" (CBS)

OUTSTANDING WRITING IN A DRAMA SERIES (SINGLE EPISODE): David E. Kelley, "Blood, Sweat & Fears," *L.A. Law* (NBC)

OUTSTANDING WRITING IN A COMEDY SERIES (SINGLE EPISODE): Bob Brush, "Good-Bye," *The Wonder Years* (ABC)

OUTSTANDING WRITING IN A MINI-SERIES OR A SPECIAL: Terrence McNally, "Andre's Mother," *American Playhouse* (PBS)

OUTSTANDING WRITING IN A VARIETY OR MUSIC PROGRAM: Billy Crystal, "Billy Crystal: Midnight Train to Moscow" (HBO); James L. Brooks, Heide Perlman, Sam Simon, Jerry Belson, Marc Flanagan, Dinah Kirgo, Jay Kogen,

Wallace Wolodarsky, Ian Praiser, Marilyn Suzanne Miller, and Tracey Ullman, *The Tracey Ullman Show* (FOX)

OUTSTANDING INDIVIDUAL ACHIEVEMENT IN INFORMATIONAL PROGRAMMING—PERFORMING: George Burns, *A Conversation With . . .* (DIS)

OUTSTANDING INDIVIDUAL ACHIEVEMENT IN INFORMATIONAL PROGRAMMING—DIRECTING: Gene Lasko, "W. Eugene Smith—Photography Made Difficult," *American Masters* (PBS)

OUTSTANDING INDIVIDUAL ACHIEVEMENT IN CLASSICAL MUSIC/DANCE PROGRAMMING—PERFORMING: Katarina Witt, Brian Orser, and Brian Boitano, "Carmen on Ice" (HBO)

OUTSTANDING INDIVIDUAL ACHIEVEMENT IN CLASSICAL MUSIC/DANCE PROGRAMMING—DIRECTING: Peter Rosen, director; Alan Skog, director of concert performances, "The Eighth Van Cliburn International Piano Competition: How to Make Music" (PBS)

THIRTEENTH ANNUAL ATAS GOVERNOR'S AWARD: Leonard Goldenson

1990–1991 (presented August 25, 1991)

OUTSTANDING COMEDY SERIES: *Cheers,* James Burrows, Glen Charles, Les Charles, Cheri Eichen, Bill Steinkellner, and Phoef Sutton, executive producers; Tim Berry, producer; Andy Ackerman, Brian Pollack, Mert Rich, Dan O'Shannon, Tom Anderson, and Larry Balmagia, coproducers (NBC)

OUTSTANDING DRAMA SERIES: *L.A. Law,* David E. Kelley and Rick Wallace, executive producers; Patricia M. Green, supervising producer; Elodie Keene, James C. Hart, Alan Brennert, Robert M. Breech, and John Hill, producers; Alice West, coordinating producer (NBC)

OUTSTANDING VARIETY, MUSIC, OR COMEDY PROGRAM: "The 63rd Annual Academy Awards," Gilbert Cates, producer (ABC)

OUTSTANDING DRAMA/COMEDY SPECIAL OR MINI-SERIES: "Separate but Equal," George Stevens, Jr., and Stan Margulies, executive producers (ABC)

OUTSTANDING CLASSICAL PROGRAM IN THE PERFORMING ARTS: "The Tchaikovsky 150th Birthday Gala from Leningrad," Peter Gelb, executive producer; Helmut Rost, producer; Anne Cauvin and Laura Mitgang, coordination producers (PBS)

OUTSTANDING INFORMATIONAL SERIES: *The Civil War* (A General Motors Mark of Excellence Presentation), Ken Burns and Ric Burns, producers; Stephen Ives, Julie Dunfey, and Mike Hill, coproducers; Catherine Eisele, coordinating producer (PBS)

OUTSTANDING INFORMATIONAL SPECIAL: "Edward R. Murrow: This Reporter," *American Masters,* Susan Lacy, executive producer; Susan Steinberg, producer; Elizabeth Kreutz and Harlene Freezer, coproducers (PBS)

OUTSTANDING CHILDREN'S PROGRAM: "You Can't Go Home Again: a 3-2-1 Contact Extra," Anne MacLeod, executive producer; Tom Cammisa, producer (PBS)

OUTSTANDING ANIMATED PROGRAM: *The Simpsons* (series), James L. Brooks, Matt Groening, and Sam Simon, executive producers; Al Jean and Mike Reiss, supervising producers; Jay Kogen, Wallace Wolodarsky, Richard Sakai, and Larina Jean Adamson, producers; George Meyer, coproducer; Gabor Csupo, executive animation producer; Sherry Gunther, animation producer; Steve Pepoon, writer; Rich Moore, director (FOX)

OUTSTANDING LEAD ACTOR IN A DRAMA SERIES: James Earl Jones, *Gabriel's Fire* (ABC)

OUTSTANDING LEAD ACTOR IN A COMEDY SERIES: Burt Reynolds, *Evening Shade* (CBS)

OUTSTANDING LEAD ACTOR IN A MINI-SERIES OR SPECIAL: John Gielgud, "Summer's Lease," *Masterpiece Theatre* (PBS)

OUTSTANDING LEAD ACTRESS IN A DRAMA SERIES: Patricia Wettig, *thirtysomething* (ABC)

OUTSTANDING LEAD ACTRESS IN A COMEDY SERIES: Kirstie Alley, *Cheers* (NBC)

OUTSTANDING LEAD ACTRESS IN A MINI-SERIES OR SPECIAL: Lynn Whitfield, "The Josephine Baker Story" (HBO)

OUTSTANDING SUPPORTING ACTOR IN A DRAMA SERIES: Timothy Busfield, *thirtysomething* (ABC)

OUTSTANDING SUPPORTING ACTOR IN A COMEDY SERIES: Jonathan Winters, *Davis Rules* (ABC)

OUTSTANDING ACTOR IN A MINI-SERIES OR SPECIAL: James Earl Jones, "Heat Wave" (TNT)

OUTSTANDING SUPPORTING ACTRESS IN A DRAMA SERIES: Madge Sinclair, *Gabriel's Fire* (ABC)

OUTSTANDING SUPPORTING ACTRESS IN A COMEDY SERIES: Bebe Neuwirth, *Cheers* (NBC)

OUTSTANDING SUPPORTING ACTRESS IN A MINI-SERIES OR SPECIAL: Ruby Dee, "Decoration Day," *Hallmark Hall of Fame* (CBS)

OUTSTANDING INDIVIDUAL PERFORMANCE IN A VARIETY OR MUSIC PROGRAM: Billy Crystal "The 63rd Annual Academy Awards" (ABC)

OUTSTANDING GUEST ACTOR IN A DRAMA SERIES: David Opatoshu, "A Prayer for the Goldsteins," *Gabriel's Fire* (ABC)

OUTSTANDING GUEST ACTOR IN A COMEDY SERIES: Jay Thomas, "Gold Rush," *Murphy Brown* (CBS)

OUTSTANDING GUEST ACTRESS IN A DRAMA SERIES: Peggy McCay, "State of Mind," *The Trials of Rosie O'Neill* (CBS)

OUTSTANDING GUEST ACTRESS IN A COMEDY SERIES: Colleen Dewhurst, "Bob and Murphy and Ted and Avery," *Murphy Brown* (CBS)

OUTSTANDING DIRECTING IN A DRAMA SERIES (SINGLE EPISODE): Thomas Carter, "In Confidence," *Equal Justice* (ABC)

OUTSTANDING DIRECTING IN A COMEDY SERIES (SINGLE EPISODE): James Burrows, "Woody Interruptus," *Cheers* (NBC)

OUTSTANDING DIRECTING IN A MINI-SERIES OR A SPECIAL: Brian Gibson, "The Josephine Baker Story" (HBO)

OUTSTANDING DIRECTING IN A VARIETY OR MUSIC PROGRAM: Hal Gurnee, Show 1425, *Late Night with David Letterman* (NBC)

OUTSTANDING WRITING IN A DRAMA SERIES (SINGLE EPISODE): David E. Kelley, "On the Road Again," *L.A. Law* (NBC)

OUTSTANDING WRITING IN A COMEDY SERIES (SINGLE EPISODE): Gary Dontzig and Steven Peterman, "Jingle Hell, Jingle Hell, Jingle All the Way," *Murphy Brown* (CBS)

OUTSTANDING WRITING IN A MINI-SERIES OR A SPECIAL: Andrew Davies, "House of Cards," *Masterpiece Theatre* (PBS)

OUTSTANDING WRITING IN A VARIETY OR MUSIC PROGRAM: Hal Kanter, Buz Kohan, Billy Crystal, David Steinberg, Bruce Vilanch, and Robert Wuhl, "The 63rd Annual Academy Awards" (ABC)
OUTSTANDING INDIVIDUAL ACHIEVEMENT IN INFORMATIONAL PROGRAMMING—WRITING: Geoffrey C. Ward, Ric Burns, and Ken Burns, "The Better Angels of Our Nature," *The Civil War* (PBS); Todd McCarthy, "Preston Sturges: The Rise and Fall of an American Dreamer," *American Masters* (PBS)
OUTSTANDING INDIVIDUAL ACHIEVEMENT IN INFORMATIONAL PROGRAMMING—DIRECTING: Peter Gelb, Susan Froemke, Albert Maysles, and Bob Eisenhardt, "Soldiers of Music: Rostropovich Returns to Russia" (PBS)
OUTSTANDING INDIVIDUAL ACHIEVEMENT IN CLASSICAL MUSIC/DANCE PROGRAMMING—PERFORMING: Kurt Moll, "The Ring of the Nibelung," *The Metropolitan Opera Presents* (PBS); Yo-Yo-Ma, "Tchaikovsky 150th Birthday Gala from Leningrad" (PBS)
FOURTEENTH ANNUAL ATAS GOVERNOR'S AWARD: *Masterpiece Theatre* (PBS)

1991–1992 (presented August 30, 1992)

OUTSTANDING COMEDY SERIES: *Murphy Brown,* Diane English and Joel Shukovsky, executive producers; Steven Peterman and Gary Dontzig; supervising producers; Tom Palmer, cosupervising producer; Korby Siamis, consulting producer; Deborah Smith, producer; Peter Tolan, coproducer (CBS)
OUTSTANDING DRAMA SERIES: *Northern Exposure,* Joshua Brand and John Falsey, executive producers; Andrew Schneider, coexecutive producer; Diane Frolov, Jeff Melvoin, Cheryl Bloch, and Robin Green, supervising producers; Matthew Nodella and Rob Thompson, producers (CBS)
OUTSTANDING VARIETY, MUSIC, OR COMEDY PROGRAM: *The Tonight Show Starring Johnny Carson,* Fred De Cordova and Peter Lassally, executive producers; Jeff Sotzing, producer; Jim McCawley, coproducer; Johnny Carson, host (NBC)
OUTSTANDING MINI-SERIES: "A Woman Named Jackie," Lester Persky, executive producer; Lorin Bennett Salob, producer, Tomlinson Dean, coproducer (NBC)
OUTSTANDING MADE-FOR-TELEVISION MOVIE: "Miss Rose White," *Hallmark Hall of Fame,* Marian Rees, executive producer; Andrea Baynes and Francine LeFrak, coexecutive producers; Anne Hopkins, producer (NBC)
OUTSTANDING CLASSICAL PROGRAM IN THE PERFORMING ARTS: "Perlman in Russia," Robert Dalrymple, producer; Itzhak Perlman, performer (PBS)
OUTSTANDING INFORMATIONAL SERIES: *MGM: When the Lion Roars,* Joni Levin, producer (TNT)
OUTSTANDING INFORMATIONAL SPECIAL: "Abortion: Desperate Choices," Susan Froemke, executive producer (HBO)
OUTSTANDING CHILDREN'S PROGRAM: "Mark Twain and Me," Geoffrey Cowan and Julian Fowles, executive producers; Daniel Petrie, producer (The Disney Channel)
OUTSTANDING ANIMATED PROGRAM: "A Claymation Easter," Will Vinton, executive producer; Paul Diener, producer; Mark Gustafson, director-writer; Barry Bruce and Ryan Holznagel, writers (CBS)
OUTSTANDING LEAD ACTOR IN A DRAMA SERIES: Christopher Lloyd, *Avonlea* (The Disney Channel)
OUTSTANDING LEAD ACTOR IN A COMEDY SERIES: Craig T. Nelson, *Coach* (ABC)
OUTSTANDING LEAD ACTOR IN A MINI-SERIES OR SPECIAL: Beau Bridges, "Without Warning: The James Brady Story" (HBO)
OUTSTANDING LEAD ACTRESS IN A DRAMA SERIES: Dana Delany, *China Beach* (ABC)
OUTSTANDING LEAD ACTRESS IN A COMEDY SERIES: Candice Bergen, *Murphy Brown* (CBS)
OUTSTANDING LEAD ACTRESS IN A MINI-SERIES OR SPECIAL: Gena Rowlands, "Faces of a Stranger" (CBS)
OUTSTANDING SUPPORTING ACTOR IN A DRAMA SERIES: Richard Dysart, *L.A. Law* (NBC)
OUTSTANDING SUPPORTING ACTOR IN A COMEDY SERIES: Michael Jeeter, *Evening Shade* (CBS)
OUTSTANDING SUPPORTING ACTOR IN A MINI-SERIES OR SPECIAL: Hume Cronyn, "Broadway Bound" (ABC)
OUTSTANDING SUPPORTING ACTRESS IN A DRAMA SERIES: Valerie Mahaffey, *Northern Exposure* (CBS)
OUTSTANDING SUPPORTING ACTRESS IN A COMEDY SERIES: Laurie Metcalf, *Roseanne* (ABC)
OUTSTANDING SUPPORTING ACTRESS IN A MINI-SERIES OR SPECIAL: Amanda Plummer, "Miss Rose White," *Hallmark Hall of Fame* (NBC)
OUTSTANDING INDIVIDUAL PERFORMANCE IN A VARIETY OR MUSIC PROGRAM: Bette Midler, performer, *The Tonight Show Starring Johnny Carson* (NBC)
OUTSTANDING VOICEOVER PERFORMANCE: Nancy Cartwright, Jackie Mason, Julie Kavner, Yeardley Smith, Marcia Wallace, and Dan Castellaneta, *The Simpsons* (FOX)
OUTSTANDING DIRECTING IN A DRAMA SERIES (SINGLE EPISODE): Eric Laneuville, "All God's Children," *I'll Fly Away* (NBC)
OUTSTANDING DIRECTING IN A COMEDY SERIES (SINGLE EPISODE): Barnet Kellman, "Birth 101," *Murphy Brown* (CBS)
OUTSTANDING DIRECTING IN A MINI-SERIES OR A SPECIAL: Joseph Sargent, "Miss Rose White," *Hallmark Hall of Fame* (NBC)
OUTSTANDING DIRECTING IN A VARIETY OR MUSIC PROGRAM: Patricia Birch, "Unforgettable, with Love: Natalie Cole Sings the Songs of Nat King Cole," *Great Performances* (PBS)
OUTSTANDING WRITING IN A DRAMA SERIES (SINGLE EPISODE): Andrew Schneider and Diane Frolov, "Seoul Mates," *Northern Exposure* (CBS)
OUTSTANDING WRITING IN A COMEDY SERIES (SINGLE EPISODE): Elaine Pope and Larry Charles, "The Fix Up," *Seinfeld* (NBC)
OUTSTANDING WRITING IN A MINI-SERIES OR A SPECIAL: Joshua Brand and John Falsey, pilot, *I'll Fly Away* (NBC)
OUTSTANDING WRITING IN A VARIETY OR MUSIC PROGRAM: Hal Kanter, Buz Kohan, Billy Crystal, Mark Shaiman, David Steinberg, Bruce Vilanch, and Robert Wuhl, "The 64th Annual Academy Awards" (ABC)

OUTSTANDING INDIVIDUAL ACHIEVEMENT IN INFORMATIONAL PROGRAMMING—DIRECTING: George Hickenlooper, Fax Bahr, and Eleanor Coppola, "Hearts of Darkness: A Filmmaker's Apocalypse" (Showtime)

OUTSTANDING INDIVIDUAL ACHIEVEMENT IN CLASSICAL MUSIC/DANCE PROGRAMMING—PERFORMING: Placido Domingo and Kathleen Battle, "The Metropolitan Opera Silver Anniversary Gala" (PBS)

OUTSTANDING INDIVIDUAL ACHIEVEMENT IN CLASSICAL MUSIC/DANCE PROGRAMMING—DIRECTING: Brian Large, "The Metropolitan Opera Silver Anniversary Gala" (PBS)

FIFTEENTH ANNUAL ATAS GOVERNOR'S AWARD: R. E. "Ted" Turner

1992–1993 (presented September 19, 1993)

OUTSTANDING COMEDY SERIES: *Seinfeld,* Larry David, Andrew Sheinman, George Shapiro, and Howard West, executive producers; Larry Charles and Tom Cherones, supervising producers; Jerry Seinfeld, producer; Joan Van Horn, line producer; Tim Kaiser, coordinating producer (NBC)

OUTSTANDING DRAMA SERIES: *Picket Fences,* David E. Kelley, executive producer; Michael Pressman, coexecutive producer; Alice West, senior producer; Robert Breech and Mark B. Perry, producers; Jonathan Pontell, coproducer (CBS)

OUTSTANDING VARIETY, MUSIC, OR COMEDY SERIES: *Saturday Night Live,* Lorne Michaels, executive producer; James Downey and Al Franken, producers (NBC)

OUTSTANDING VARIETY, MUSIC, OR COMEDY SPECIAL: "Bob Hope: The First 90 Years," Linda Hope, executive producer; Nancy Malone, supervising producer; Don Mischer, producer (NBC)

OUTSTANDING MINI-SERIES: "Prime Suspect 2," *Mystery!,* Sally Head, executive producer; Paul Marcus, producer (PBS)

OUTSTANDING MADE-FOR-TELEVISION MOVIE: "Barbarians at the Gate," Thomas M. Hammel and Glenn Jordan, executive producers; Ray Stark, producer; Marykay Powell, coproducer (HBO); "Stalin," Mark Carliner, producer; Don West, line producer; Ilene Kahn, coproducer (HBO)

OUTSTANDING CLASSICAL PROGRAM IN THE PERFORMING ARTS: "Tosca in the Settings and at the Times of Tosca," Rada Rassimov, executive producer; Andrea Andermann, producer; Zubin Mehta, conductor (PBS)

OUTSTANDING INFORMATIONAL SERIES: *Healing and the Mind with Bill Moyers,* David Grubin, executive producer; Alice Markowitz, producer; Bill Moyers, editorial producer/host; Judith Davidson Moyers, editorial producer (PBS)

OUTSTANDING INFORMATIONAL SPECIAL: "Lucy and Desi: A Home Movie," Lucie Arnaz and Laurence Luckinbill, executive producers; Don Buford, producer (NBC)

OUTSTANDING CHILDREN'S PROGRAM: *Avonlea,* Kevin Sullivan and Trudy Grant, executive producers; Brian Leslie Parker, line producer (The Disney Channel); "Beethoven Lives Upstairs," Terence E. Robinson, executive producer; David Devine and Richard Moser, producers (HBO)

OUTSTANDING ANIMATED PROGRAM: *Batman: The Series,* Jean H. MacCurdy and Tom Ruegger, executive producers; Alan Burnett, Eric Radomski, and Bruce W. Timm, producers; Randy Rogel, writer; Dick Sebast, director (FOX)

OUTSTANDING LEAD ACTOR IN A DRAMA SERIES: Tom Skerritt, *Picket Fences* (CBS)

OUTSTANDING LEAD ACTOR IN A COMEDY SERIES: Ted Danson, *Cheers* (NBC)

OUTSTANDING LEAD ACTOR IN A MINI-SERIES OR SPECIAL: Robert Morse, "Tru," *American Playhouse* (PBS)

OUTSTANDING LEAD ACTRESS IN A DRAMA SERIES: Kathy Baker, *Picket Fences* (CBS)

OUTSTANDING LEAD ACTRESS IN A COMEDY SERIES: Roseanne Arnold, *Roseanne* (ABC)

OUTSTANDING LEAD ACTRESS IN A MINI-SERIES OR SPECIAL: Holly Hunter, "The Positively True Adventures of the Alleged Texas Cheerleader-Murdering Mom" (HBO)

OUTSTANDING SUPPORTING ACTOR IN A DRAMA SERIES: Chad Lowe, *Life Goes On* (ABC)

OUTSTANDING SUPPORTING ACTOR IN A COMEDY SERIES: Michael Richards, *Seinfeld* (NBC)

OUTSTANDING SUPPORTING ACTOR IN A MINI-SERIES OR SPECIAL: Beau Bridges, "The Positively True Adventures of the Alleged Texas Cheerleader-Murdering Mom" (HBO)

OUTSTANDING SUPPORTING ACTRESS IN A DRAMA SERIES: Mary Alice, *I'll Fly Away* (NBC)

OUTSTANDING SUPPORTING ACTRESS IN A COMEDY SERIES: Laurie Metcalf, *Roseanne* (ABC)

OUTSTANDING SUPPORTING ACTRESS IN A MINI-SERIES OR SPECIAL: Mary Tyler Moore, "Stolen Babies" (Lifetime)

OUTSTANDING INDIVIDUAL PERFORMANCE IN A VARIETY OR MUSIC PROGRAM: Dana Carvey, "Saturday Night Live's Presidential Bash," *Saturday Night Live* (NBC)

OUTSTANDING GUEST ACTOR IN A DRAMA SERIES: Laurence Fishburne, "The Box," *Tribeca* (FOX)

OUTSTANDING GUEST ACTOR IN A COMEDY SERIES: David Clennon, "For Peter's Sake," *Dream On* (HBO)

OUTSTANDING GUEST ACTRESS IN A DRAMA SERIES: Elaine Stritch, "Point of View" *Law & Order* (NBC)

OUTSTANDING GUEST ACTRESS IN A COMEDY SERIES: Tracey Ullman, "The Prima Dava," *Love & War* (CBS)

OUTSTANDING VOICEOVER PERFORMANCE: Dan Castellaneta, *The Simpsons* (FOX)

OUTSTANDING DIRECTING IN A DRAMA SERIES (SINGLE EPISODE): Barry Levinson, "Gone for Goode," *Homicide—Life on the Street* (NBC)

OUTSTANDING DIRECTING IN A COMEDY SERIES (SINGLE EPISODE): Betty Thomas, "For Peter's Sake," *Dream On* (HBO)

OUTSTANDING DIRECTING IN A MINI-SERIES OR A SPECIAL: James Sadwith, "Sinatra" (CBS)

OUTSTANDING DIRECTING IN A VARIETY OR MUSIC PROGRAM: Walter C. Miller, "The 1992 Tony Awards" (CBS)

OUTSTANDING WRITING IN A DRAMA SERIES (SINGLE EPISODE): Tom Fontana, "Three Men and Adena," *Homicide—Life on the Street* (NBC)

OUTSTANDING WRITING IN A COMEDY SERIES (SINGLE EPISODE): Larry David, "The Contest," *Seinfeld* (NBC)

OUTSTANDING WRITING IN A MINI-SERIES OR A SPECIAL: Jane Anderson, "The Positively True Adventures of the Alleged Texas Cheerleader-Murdering Mom" (HBO)

OUTSTANDING WRITING IN A VARIETY OR MUSIC PROGRAM: Judd Apatow, Robert Cohen, David Cross, Brent Forrester, Jeff Kahn, Bruce Kirschbaum, Bob Odenkirk, Sultan Pepper, Dino Stamatopoulos, and Ben Stiller, *The Ben Stiller Show* (FOX)

OUTSTANDING INDIVIDUAL ACHIEVEMENT IN INFORMATIONAL PROGRAMMING—HOST: Audrey Hepburn, "Flower Gardens," *Gardens of the World* (PBS)

OUTSTANDING INDIVIDUAL ACHIEVEMENT IN INFORMATIONAL PROGRAMMING—DIRECTING: Lee Stanley, "Gridiron Gang" (syndicated)

OUTSTANDING INDIVIDUAL ACHIEVEMENT IN CLASSICAL MUSIC/DANCE PROGRAMMING—PERFORMING: Catherine Malfitano "Tosca in the Settings and at the Times of Tosca" (PBS)

OUTSTANDING INDIVIDUAL ACHIEVEMENT IN CLASSICAL MUSIC/DANCE PROGRAMMING—DIRECTING: Giuseppe Patroni Griffi and Brian Large, "Tosca in the Settings and at the Times of Tosca" (PBS)

1993–1994 (presented September 11, 1994)

OUTSTANDING COMEDY SERIES: *Frasier,* Peter Casey, David Angell, and David Lee, executive producers; Christopher Lloyd, coexecutive producer; Denise Moss and Sy Dukane, supervising producers; Maggie Randell, producer; Linda Morris and Vic Rauseo, consulting producers (NBC)

OUTSTANDING DRAMA SERIES: *Picket Fences,* David E. Kelley, executive producer; Michael Pressman, coexecutive producer; Alice West, senior producer; Robert Breech and Ann Donahue, producers; Jonathan Pontell and Geoffrey Neigher, coproducers; Jack Philbrick, coordinating producer (CBS)

OUTSTANDING VARIETY, MUSIC, OR COMEDY SERIES: *Late Show with David Letterman,* Peter Lassally and Robert Morton, executive producers; Hal Gurnee, supervising producer; Jude Brennan, producer; David Letterman, host (CBS)

OUTSTANDING VARIETY, MUSIC, OR COMEDY SPECIAL: "The Kennedy Center Honors," George Stevens, Jr., and Don Mischer, producers (CBS)

OUTSTANDING MINI-SERIES: "Prime Suspect 3," *Mystery!,* Sally Head, executive producer; Paul Marcus, producer (PBS)

OUTSTANDING MADE-FOR-TELEVISION MOVIE: "And the Band Played On," Aaron Spelling and E. Duke Vincent, executive producers; Midge Sanford and Sarah Pillsbury, producers (HBO)

OUTSTANDING CULTURAL PROGRAM: "Vladimir Horowitz: A Reminiscence," Peter Gelb, executive producer; Pat Jaffe, producer (PBS)

OUTSTANDING INFORMATIONAL SERIES: *Later with Bob Costas,* Lou Del Prete and Matthew McArthy, executive producers; Fred Rothenberg and Bruce Cornblatt, senior producers; Michael L. Weinberg, producer; Bob Costas, host (NBC)

OUTSTANDING INFORMATIONAL SPECIAL: "I Am a Promise: The Children of Stanton Street Elementary School," Alan Raymond and Susan Raymond, producers (HBO)

OUTSTANDING CHILDREN'S PROGRAM: "Kids Killing Kids/Kids Saving Kids," Arnold Shapiro, executive producer; David J. Eagle and Kerry Neal, producers; Norman Marcus and Michael Killen, coproducers (CBS and FOX)

OUTSTANDING ANIMATED PROGRAM: "The Roman City," Bob Kurtz, producer-director-writer; Mark Olshaker, writer (PBS)

OUTSTANDING LEAD ACTOR IN A DRAMA SERIES: Dennis Franz, *N.Y.P.D. Blue* (ABC)

OUTSTANDING LEAD ACTOR IN A COMEDY SERIES: Kelsey Grammer, *Frasier* (NBC)

OUTSTANDING LEAD ACTOR IN A MINI-SERIES OR SPECIAL: Hume Cronyn, "To Dance with the White Dog," *Hallmark Hall of Fame* (CBS)

OUTSTANDING LEAD ACTRESS IN A DRAMA SERIES: Sela Ward, *Sisters* (NBC)

OUTSTANDING LEAD ACTRESS IN A COMEDY SERIES: Candice Bergen, *Murphy Brown* (CBS)

OUTSTANDING LEAD ACTRESS IN A MINI-SERIES OR SPECIAL: Kirstie Alley, "David's Mother" (CBS)

OUTSTANDING SUPPORTING ACTOR IN A DRAMA SERIES: Fyvush Finkel, *Picket Fences* (CBS)

OUTSTANDING SUPPORTING ACTOR IN A COMEDY SERIES: Michael Richards, *Seinfeld* (NBC)

OUTSTANDING SUPPORTING ACTOR IN A MINI-SERIES OR SPECIAL: Michael Goorjian, "David's Mother" (CBS)

OUTSTANDING SUPPORTING ACTRESS IN A DRAMA SERIES: Leigh Taylor-Young, *Picket Fences* (CBS)

OUTSTANDING SUPPORTING ACTRESS IN A COMEDY SERIES: Laurie Metcalf, *Roseanne* (ABC)

OUTSTANDING SUPPORTING ACTRESS IN A MINI-SERIES OR SPECIAL: Cicely Tyson, "Oldest Living Confederate Widow Tells All" (CBS)

OUTSTANDING INDIVIDUAL PERFORMANCE IN A VARIETY OR MUSIC PROGRAM: Tracey Ullman, "Tracey Ullman Takes on New York" (HBO)

OUTSTANDING GUEST ACTOR IN A DRAMA SERIES: Richard Kiley, "Buried Alive," *Picket Fences* (CBS)

OUTSTANDING GUEST ACTOR IN A COMEDY SERIES: Martin Sheen, "Angst for the Memories," *Murphy Brown* (CBS)

OUTSTANDING GUEST ACTRESS IN A DRAMA SERIES: Faye Dunaway, "It's All in the Game," *Columbo* (ABC)

OUTSTANDING GUEST ACTRESS IN A COMEDY SERIES: Eileen Heckart, "You Make Me Feel So Young," *Love & War* (CBS)

OUTSTANDING VOICEOVER PERFORMANCE: Christopher Plummer, narrator, *Madeline* (The Family Channel)

OUTSTANDING DIRECTING IN A DRAMA SERIES (SINGLE EPISODE): Daniel Sackheim, "Tempest in a C-Cup," *N.Y.P.D. Blue* (ABC)

OUTSTANDING DIRECTING IN A COMEDY SERIES (SINGLE EPISODE): James Burrows, "The Good Son," *Frasier* (NBC)

OUTSTANDING DIRECTING IN A MINI-SERIES OR SPECIAL: John Frankenheimer, "Against the Wall" (HBO)

OUTSTANDING DIRECTING IN A VARIETY OR MUSIC PROGRAM: Walter C. Miller, "The 1993 Tony Awards" (CBS)

OUTSTANDING WRITING IN A DRAMA SERIES (SINGLE EPISODE): Ann Biderman, "Steroid Roy," *N.Y.P.D. Blue* (ABC)

OUTSTANDING WRITING IN A COMEDY SERIES (SINGLE EPISODE): David Angell, Peter Casey, and David Lee, "The Good Son," *Frasier* (NBC)

OUTSTANDING WRITING IN A MINI-SERIES OR SPECIAL: Bob Randall, "David's Mother" (CBS)

OUTSTANDING WRITING IN A VARIETY OR MUSIC PROGRAM: Jeff Cesario, Mike Dugan, Eddie Feldmann, Gregory Greenberg, Dennis Miller, and Kevin Rooney, *Dennis Miller Live* (HBO)

OUTSTANDING INDIVIDUAL ACHIEVEMENT IN INFORMATIONAL PROGRAMMING—NARRATOR: George Stevens, Jr., "George Stevens: D-Day to Berlin" (The Disney Channel)

OUTSTANDING INDIVIDUAL ACHIEVEMENT IN INFORMATIONAL PROGRAMMING—DIRECTING: Robin Leahman, "Cats & Dogs, Dogs Segment" (TBS)

OUTSTANDING INDIVIDUAL ACHIEVEMENT IN INFORMATIONAL PROGRAMMING—WRITING: George Stevens, Jr., "George Stevens: D-Day to Berlin" (The Disney Channel); Todd Robinson, "The Legend of Billy the Kid" (The Disney Channel); Dereck Joubert, "Reflections on Elephants" (PBS); Dennis Watlington, "The Untold West" and "The Black West" (TBS)

OUTSTANDING INDIVIDUAL ACHIEVEMENT IN CULTURAL PROGRAMMING—PERFORMING: Itzhak Perlman, violinist, "The Dvořák Concert from Prague: A Celebration" (PBS); Seiji Ozawa, conductor, "The Dvořák Concert from Prague: A Celebration" (PBS)

OUTSTANDING INDIVIDUAL ACHIEVEMENT IN CULTURAL PROGRAMMING—WRITING: Nuala O'Conner, "Irish Music and America . . . A Musical Migration" (The Disney Channel)

1994–1995 (presented September 10, 1995)

OUTSTANDING COMEDY SERIES: *Frasier,* Peter Casey, David Angell, David Lee, and Christopher Lloyd, executive producers; Vic Rauseo and Linda Morris, coexecutive producers; Maggie Randell, Elias Davis, and David Pollock, producers; Chuck Ranberg, Anne Flett-Giordano, and Joe Keenan, coproducers (NBC)

OUTSTANDING DRAMA SERIES: *NYPD Blue,* Steven Bochco, David Milch, Gregory Hoblit, and Mark Tinker, executive producers; Michael E. Robin, Walon Green, Charles H. Eglee, and Channing Gibson, coexecutive producers; Ted Mann, producer; Burton Armus, Gardner Stern, and Steven DePaul, coproducers; Robert Doherty, coordinating producer; Bill Clark, consulting producer (ABC)

OUTSTANDING VARIETY, MUSIC, OR COMEDY SERIES: *The Tonight Show with Jay Leno,* Debbie Vickers, executive producer; Larry Goita, line producer; Bill Royce, coproducer; Jay Leno, host (NBC)

OUTSTANDING VARIETY, MUSIC, OR COMEDY SPECIAL: "Barbra Steisand: The Concert," Martin Erlichman and Gary Smith, executive producers; Barbra Streisand and Dwight Hemion, producers (HBO)

OUTSTANDING MINI-SERIES: "Joseph," Gerald Rafshoon, executive producer; Lorenzo Minoli, producer; Laura Fattori, line producer (TNT)

OUTSTANDING MADE-FOR-TELEVISION MOVIE: "Indictment: The McMartin Trial," Oliver Stone, Janet Yang, and Abby Mann, executive producers; Diana Pokorny, producer (HBO)

OUTSTANDING CULTURAL PROGRAM: "Verdi's *La Traviata* with the New York City Opera," *Live from Lincoln Center,* John Goberman, producer; Marc Bauman, coordinating producer (PBS)

OUTSTANDING INFORMATIONAL SERIES: *Baseball: A General Motors Mark of Excellence Production,* Ken Burns, producer-director; Lynn Novick, producer; Geoffrey C. Ward and Ken Burns, writers; John Chancellor, narrator (PBS); *TV Nation,* Michael Moore, executive producer-director-writer-host; Kathleen Glynn, producer; Jerry Kupfer, supervising producer; Eric Zicklin, Stephen Sherrill, Chris Kelly, and Randy Cohen, writers (NBC)

OUTSTANDING INFORMATIONAL SPECIAL: "Taxicab Confessions," Sheila Nevins, executive producer; Joe Gantz and Harry Gantz, producer-directors (HBO); "The United States Holocaust Memorial Museum Presents: One Survivor Remembers," Kary Antholis, producer; Sheila Nevins, senior producer; Michael Berenbaum and Raye Farr, coproducers (HBO)

OUTSTANDING CHILDREN'S PROGRAM: "The World Wildlife Fund Presents 'Going, Going, Almost Gone! Animals in Danger,' " Sheila Nevins, executive producer; Ellen Goosenberg Kent, producer; Carole Rosen, senior producer; Amy Schatz, coproducer (HBO)

OUTSTANDING ANIMATED PROGRAM: *The Simpsons,* David Mirkin, James L. Brooks, Matt Groening, and Sam Simon, executive producers; Jace Richdale, George Meyer, J. Michael Mendel, Greg Daniels, Bill Oakley, David Sacks, Josh Weinstein, Jonathan Collier, Richard Raynis, Richard Sakai, Mike Scully, and David Silverman, producers; Al Jean and Mike Reiss, consulting producers; Phil Roman, animation executive producer; Bill Schultz and Michael Wolf, animation producers; Greg Daniels, writer; Jim Reardon, director (FOX)

OUTSTANDING LEAD ACTOR IN A DRAMA SERIES: Mandy Patinkin, *Chicago Hope* (CBS)

OUTSTANDING LEAD ACTOR IN A COMEDY SERIES: Kelsey Grammer, *Frasier* (NBC)

OUTSTANDING LEAD ACTOR IN A MINI-SERIES OR SPECIAL: Raul Julia, "The Burning Season" (HBO)

OUTSTANDING LEAD ACTRESS IN A DRAMA SERIES: Kathy Baker, *Picket Fences* (CBS)

OUTSTANDING LEAD ACTRESS IN A COMEDY SERIES: Candice Bergen, *Murphy Brown* (CBS)

OUTSTANDING LEAD ACTRESS IN A MINI-SERIES OR SPECIAL: Glenn Close, "Serving in Silence: The Margarethe Cammermeyer Story" (NBC)

OUTSTANDING SUPPORTING ACTOR IN A DRAMA SERIES: Ray Walston, *Picket Fences* (CBS)

OUTSTANDING SUPPORTING ACTOR IN A COMEDY SERIES: David Hyde Pierce, *Frasier* (NBC)

OUTSTANDING SUPPORTING ACTOR IN A MINI-SERIES OR SPECIAL: Donald Sutherland, "Citizen X" (HBO)

OUTSTANDING SUPPORTING ACTRESS IN A DRAMA SERIES: Julianna Margulies, *ER* (NBC)

OUTSTANDING SUPPORTING ACTRESS IN A COMEDY SERIES: Christine Baranski, *Cybill* (CBS)

OUTSTANDING SUPPORTING ACTRESS IN A MINI-SERIES OR SPECIAL: Judy Davis, "Serving in Silence: The Margarethe Cammermeyer Story" (NBC); Shirley Knight, "Indictment: The McMartin Trial" (HBO)

OUTSTANDING INDIVIDUAL PERFORMANCE IN A VARIETY OR MUSIC PROGRAM: Barbra Streisand, "Barbra Steisand: The Concert" (HBO)

OUTSTANDING GUEST ACTOR IN A DRAMA SERIES: Paul Winfield, "Enemy Lines," *Picket Fences* (CBS)

OUTSTANDING GUEST ACTOR IN A COMEDY SERIES: Carl Reiner, "The Alan Brady Show," *Mad About You* (NBC)

OUTSTANDING GUEST ACTRESS IN A DRAMA SERIES: Shirley Knight, "Large Mouth Bass," *NYPD Blue* (ABC)

OUTSTANDING GUEST ACTRESS IN A COMEDY SERIES: Cyndi Lauper, "Money Changes Everything," *Mad About You* (NBC)

OUTSTANDING VOICE-OVER PERFORMANCE: Jonathan Katz, "Dr. Katz Professional Therapist," (Comedy Central)

OUTSTANDING DIRECTING IN A DRAMA SERIES (SINGLE EPISODE): Mimi Leder, "Love's Labor Lost," *ER* (NBC)

OUTSTANDING DIRECTING IN A COMEDY SERIES (SINGLE EPISODE): David Lee, "The Matchmaker," *Frasier* (NBC)

OUTSTANDING DIRECTING IN A MINI-SERIES OR A SPECIAL: John Frankenheimer, "The Burning Season" (HBO)

OUTSTANDING DIRECTING IN A VARIETY OR MUSIC PROGRAM: Jeff Margolis, "The 67th Annual Academy Awards" (ABC)

OUTSTANDING WRITING IN A DRAMA SERIES (SINGLE EPISODE): Lance A. Gentile, "Love's Labor Lost," *ER* (NBC)

OUTSTANDING WRITING IN A COMEDY SERIES (SINGLE EPISODE): Chuck Ranberg and Anne Flett-Giordano, "An Affair to Forget," *Frasier* (NBC)

OUTSTANDING WRITING IN A MINI-SERIES OR A SPECIAL: Alison Cross, "Serving in Silence: The Margarethe Cammermeyer Story" (NBC)

OUTSTANDING WRITING IN A VARIETY OR MUSIC PROGRAM: Eddie Feldmann, writing supervisor; Jeff Cesario, Ed Driscoll, David Feldman, Gregory Greenberg, Dennis Miller, and Kevin Rooney, writers, *Dennis Miller Live* (HBO)

OUTSTANDING INDIVIDUAL ACHIEVEMENT IN CULTURAL PROGRAMMING—DIRECTING: David Hinton, "Two By Dove," *Great Performances, Dance in America* (PBS)

ATAS GOVERNORS AWARD: PBS

1995–1996 (presented September 8, 1996)

OUTSTANDING COMEDY SERIES: *Frasier,* Peter Casey, David Angell, David Lee, Christopher Lloyd, Vic Rauseo, and Linda Morris, executive producers; Steven Levitan, coexecutive producer; Maggie Randell, Chuck Ranberg and Anne Flett-Giordano, producers; Joe Keenan, Jack Burditt, and Mary Fukuto, coproducers (NBC)

OUTSTANDING DRAMA SERIES: *ER,* John Wells and Michael Crichton, executive producers; Carol Flint, Mimi Leder, and Lydia Woodward, coexecutive producers; Chris Chulack, producer; Paul Manning, supervising producer; Wendy Spence, coproducer (NBC)

OUTSTANDING VARIETY, MUSIC, OR COMEDY SERIES: *Dennis Miller Live,* Dennis Miller, executive producer/host; Kevin C. Slattery, executive producer; Eddie Feldmann, producer (HBO)

OUTSTANDING VARIETY, MUSIC, OR COMEDY SPECIAL: "The Kennedy Center Honors," George Stevens, Jr., and Don Mischer, producers (CBS)

OUTSTANDING MINI-SERIES: "Gulliver's Travels," Robert Halmi, Sr., and Brian Henson, executive producers; Duncan Kenworthy, producer (NBC)

OUTSTANDING MADE-FOR-TELEVISION MOVIE: "Truman," Paula Weinstein and Anthea Sylbert, executive producers; Doro Bachrach, producer (HBO)

OUTSTANDING CULTURAL MUSIC-DANCE PROGRAM: "Itzhak Perlman: In the Fiddler's House," *Great Performances,* Jac Venza, executive producer; Glenn DuBose, executive producer/codirector; James Arntz, producer/writer; Bill Murphy, coordinating producer; Sara Lukinson, producer/writer; Don Lenzer, codirector; Itzhak Perlman, performer (PBS)

OUTSTANDING INFORMATIONAL SERIES: *Time Life's Lost Civilizations,* Joel Westbrook, executive producer; Jason Williams, producer; Robert Gardner; producer/director/writer; William Morgan, coordinating producer; Ed Fields, writer; Sam Waterston, host (NBC)

OUTSTANDING INFORMATIONAL SPECIAL: "Survivors of the Holocaust," Pat Mitchell, executive producer; Vivian Schiller, senior producer; June Beallor and James Moll, producers; Jacoba Atlas, supervising producer; Allan Holzman, director (TBS)

OUTSTANDING CHILDREN'S PROGRAM: "Peter and the Wolf," George Daugherty, executive producer; David Wong, coexecutive producer; Linda Jones Clough and Adrian Workman, producers; Christine Losecast, coproducer (ABC)

OUTSTANDING ANIMATED PROGRAM: "A Pinky & the Brain Christmas Special," Steven Spielberg, executive producer; Tom Ruegger, senior producer; Peter Hastings, producer/writer; Rusty Mills, producer/director (WB)

OUTSTANDING LEAD ACTOR IN A DRAMA SERIES: Dennis Franz, *NYPD Blue* (ABC)

OUTSTANDING LEAD ACTOR IN A COMEDY SERIES: John Lithgow, *3rd Rock from the Sun* (NBC)

OUTSTANDING LEAD ACTOR IN A MINI-SERIES OR SPECIAL: Alan Rickman, "Rasputin" (HBO)

OUTSTANDING LEAD ACTRESS IN A DRAMA SERIES: Kathy Baker, *Picket Fences* (CBS)

OUTSTANDING LEAD ACTRESS IN A COMEDY SERIES: Helen Hunt, *Mad About You* (NBC)

OUTSTANDING LEAD ACTRESS IN A MINI-SERIES OR SPECIAL: Helen Mirren, "Prime Suspect: Scent of Darkness" (PBS)

OUTSTANDING SUPPORTING ACTOR IN A DRAMA SERIES: Ray Walston, *Picket Fences* (CBS)

OUTSTANDING SUPPORTING ACTOR IN A COMEDY SERIES: Rip Torn, *The Larry Sanders Show* (NBC)

OUTSTANDING SUPPORTING ACTOR IN A MINI-SERIES OR SPECIAL: Tom Hulce, "The Heidi Chronicles" (TNT)

OUTSTANDING SUPPORTING ACTRESS IN A DRAMA SERIES: Tyne Daly, *Christy* (CBS)

OUTSTANDING SUPPORTING ACTRESS IN A COMEDY SERIES: Julia Louis-Dreyfus, *Seinfeld* (NBC)

OUTSTANDING SUPPORTING ACTRESS IN A MINI-SERIES OR SPECIAL: Greta Scacchi "Rasputin" (HBO)

OUTSTANDING INDIVIDUAL PERFORMANCE IN A VARIETY OR MUSIC PROGRAM: Tony Bennett, "Tony Bennett Live by Request: A Valentine Special" (A&E)

OUTSTANDING GUEST ACTOR IN A DRAMA SERIES: Peter Boyle, "Clyde Bruckman's Final Repose," *The X-Files* (FOX)

OUTSTANDING GUEST ACTOR IN A COMEDY SERIES: Tim Conway, "The Gardener," *Coach* (ABC)

OUTSTANDING GUEST ACTRESS IN A DRAMA SERIES: Amanda Plummer, "A Stitch in Time," *The Outer Limits* (Showtime)

OUTSTANDING GUEST ACTRESS IN A COMEDY SERIES: Betty White, "Here We Go Again," *The John Larroquette Show* (NBC)

OUTSTANDING DIRECTING IN A DRAMA SERIES (SINGLE EPISODE): Jeremy Kagan, "Leave of Absence," *Chicago Hope* (CBS)

OUTSTANDING DIRECTING IN A COMEDY SERIES (SINGLE EPISODE): Michael Lembeck, "The One After the Super Bowl," *Friends* (NBC)

OUTSTANDING DIRECTING IN A MINI-SERIES OR A SPECIAL: John Frankenheimer, *Andersonville* (TNT)

OUTSTANDING DIRECTING IN A VARIETY OR MUSIC PROGRAM: Louis J. Horvitz, "The Kennedy Center Honors" (CBS)

OUTSTANDING WRITING IN A DRAMA SERIES (SINGLE EPISODE): Darin Morgan, "Clyde Bruckman's Final Repose," *The X-Files* (FOX)

OUTSTANDING WRITING IN A COMEDY SERIES (SINGLE EPISODE): Joe Keenan, Christopher Lloyd, Rob Greenberg, Jack Burditt, Chuck Ranberg, Anne Flett-Giordano, Linda Morris, and Vic Rauseo, "Moon Dance," *Frasier* (NBC)

OUTSTANDING WRITING IN A MINI-SERIES OR A SPECIAL: Simon Moore, "Gulliver's Travels" (NBC)

OUTSTANDING WRITING IN A VARIETY OR MUSIC PROGRAM: Dennis Miller, Eddie Feldmann, David Feldman, Mike Gandolfi, Tom Hertz, Leah Krinsky, and Rick Overton, *Dennis Miller Live* (HBO)

ATAS GOVERNORS AWARD: "The Native American: Beyond the Legends, Beyond the Myths" (TBS); Erase the Hate Campaign (USA)

PRESIDENT'S AWARD: "Blacklist: Hollywood on Trial" (American Movie Classics)

1996–1997 (presented September 14, 1997)

OUTSTANDING COMEDY SERIES: *Frasier,* Peter Casey, David Angell, David Lee, and Christopher Lloyd, executive producers; Chuck Ranberg, Anne Flett-Giordano, Joe Keenan, and Michael B. Kaplan, supervising producers; Maggie Randell, William Lucas Walker, and Suzanne Martin, producers; Rob Greenberg and Mary Fukuto, coproducers (NBC)

OUTSTANDING DRAMA SERIES: *Law & Order,* Dick Wolf, Rene Balcer, and Ed Sherin, executive producers; Ed Zuckerman, coexecutive producer; Arthur Forney and Gardner Stern, supervising producers; Jeffrey Hayes, Lewis H. Gould, and Billy Fox, producers; Jeremy R. Littman, coproducer (NBC)

OUTSTANDING VARIETY, MUSIC, OR COMEDY SERIES: *Tracey Takes On . . . ,* Allan McKeown and Tracey Ullman, executive producers; Dick Clement and Ian La Frenais, supervising producers; Carey Dietrich, Thomas Schlamme, Robert Klane, Jenji Kohan, Molly Newman, and Gail Parent, producers; Allen J. Zipper, coordinating producer; Stephanie Cone, associate producer; Jerry Belson, consulting producer (HBO)

OUTSTANDING VARIETY, MUSIC, OR COMEDY SPECIAL: "Chris Rock: Bring the Pain," Chris Rock, Michael Rotenberg, and Sandy Chanley, executive producers; Tom Bull, producer (HBO)

OUTSTANDING MINI-SERIES: "Prime Suspect 5: Errors of Judgement," Gub Neal and Rebecca Eaton, executive producers; Lynn Horsford, producer (PBS)

OUTSTANDING MADE-FOR-TELEVISION MOVIE: "Miss Evers' Boys," Robert Benedetti and Laurence Fishburne, executive producers; Kip Konwiser and Derek Kavanagh, producers; Peter Stelzer and Kern Konwiser, coproducers (HBO)

OUTSTANDING CULTURAL MUSIC-DANCE PROGRAM: "*La Boheme* with the New York City Opera," *Live from Lincoln Center,* John Goberman, producer; Marc Bauman, coordinating producer (PBS)

OUTSTANDING INFORMATIONAL SERIES: *A&E Biography,* Michael Cascio, executive producer; CarolAnne Dolan, supervising producer; Diane Ferenczi, coordinating producer; Peter Graves and Jack Perkins, hosts (A&E); *The Great War and the Shaping of the 20th Century,* Blaine Baggett, executive producer-writer; Jay Winter, coproducer-writer; Carl Byker, producer-director-writer (PBS)

OUTSTANDING INFORMATIONAL SPECIAL: "Without Pity: A Film About Abilities," Sheila Nevins, executive producer; Michael Mierendorf, producer-director-writer; Jonathan Moss, coordinating producer; Christopher Reeve, narrator (HBO)

OUTSTANDING CHILDREN'S PROGRAM: "How Do You Spell God?" Sheila Nevins, executive producer; Carole Rosen, senior producer; Ellen Greenberg Kent and Amy Schatz, producers (HBO)

OUTSTANDING ANIMATED PROGRAM: "Homer's Phobia," *The Simpsons,* Bill Oakley, Josh Weinstein, Matt Groening, James L. Brooks, Sam Simon, Mike Scully, George Meyer, and Steve Tompkins, executive producers; Phil Roman, animation executive producer; Jonathan Collier, Ken Keeler, David S. Cohen, Richard Appel, J. Michael Mendel, Richard Raynis, David Silverman, Richard Sakai, Denise Sirkot, Colin A.B.V. Lewis, David Mirkin, Ian Maxtone-Graham, and Dan McGrath, producers; Bill Schultz and Michael Wolf, animation producers; Mike B. Anderson, director; Ron Hauge, writer (FOX)

OUTSTANDING LEAD ACTOR IN A DRAMA SERIES: Dennis Franz, *NYPD Blue* (ABC)

OUTSTANDING LEAD ACTOR IN A COMEDY SERIES: John Lithgow, *3rd Rock from the Sun* (NBC)

OUTSTANDING LEAD ACTOR IN A MINI-SERIES OR SPECIAL: Armand Assante, "Gotti" (HBO)

OUTSTANDING LEAD ACTRESS IN A DRAMA SERIES: Gillian Anderson, *The X-Files* (FOX)

OUTSTANDING LEAD ACTRESS IN A COMEDY SERIES: Helen Hunt, *Mad About You* (NBC)

OUTSTANDING LEAD ACTRESS IN A MINI-SERIES OR SPECIAL: Alfre Woodard, "Miss Evers' Boys" (HBO)
OUTSTANDING SUPPORTING ACTOR IN A DRAMA SERIES: Hector Elizondo, *Chicago Hope* (CBS)
OUTSTANDING SUPPORTING ACTOR IN A COMEDY SERIES: Michael Richards, *Seinfeld* (NBC)
OUTSTANDING SUPPORTING ACTOR IN A MINI-SERIES OR SPECIAL: Beau Bridges, "The Second Civil War" (HBO)
OUTSTANDING SUPPORTING ACTRESS IN A DRAMA SERIES: Kim Delaney, *NYPD Blue* (ABC)
OUTSTANDING SUPPORTING ACTRESS IN A COMEDY SERIES: Kristen Johnston, *3rd Rock from the Sun* (NBC)
OUTSTANDING SUPPORTING ACTRESS IN A MINI-SERIES OR SPECIAL: Diana Rigg, "Rebecca" (PBS)
OUTSTANDING INDIVIDUAL PERFORMANCE IN A VARIETY OR MUSIC PROGRAM: Bette Midler, "Bette Midler: Diva Las Vegas" (HBO)
OUTSTANDING GUEST ACTOR IN A DRAMA SERIES: Pruitt Taylor Vince, *Murder One* (ABC)
OUTSTANDING GUEST ACTOR IN A COMEDY SERIES: Mel Brooks, *Mad About You* (NBC)
OUTSTANDING GUEST ACTRESS IN A DRAMA SERIES: Dianne Wiest, *Avonlea* (Disney Channel)
OUTSTANDING GUEST ACTRESS IN A COMEDY SERIES: Carol Burnett, *Mad About You* (NBC)
OUTSTANDING VOICE-OVER PERFORMANCE: Jeremy Irons as the voice of Siegfried Sassoon, "The Great War and the Shaping of the 20th Century" (PBS); Rik Mayall as the voice of the Toad, "The Willows in Winter" (The Family Channel)
OUTSTANDING DIRECTING IN A DRAMA SERIES (SINGLE EPISODE): Mark Tinker, "Where's Swaldo," *NYPD Blue* (ABC)
OUTSTANDING DIRECTING IN A COMEDY SERIES (SINGLE EPISODE): David Lee, "To Kill a Talking Bird," *Frasier* (NBC)
OUTSTANDING DIRECTING IN A MINI-SERIES OR A SPECIAL: Andrei Konochalovsky, *The Odyssey* Part I and Part II (NBC)
OUTSTANDING DIRECTING IN A VARIETY OR MUSIC PROGRAM: Don Mischer, "Centennial Olympic Games: Opening Ceremonies" (NBC)
OUTSTANDING WRITING IN A DRAMA SERIES (SINGLE EPISODE): David Milch, Stephen Gaghan, and Michael R. Perry, "Where's Swaldo," *NYPD Blue* (ABC)
OUTSTANDING WRITING IN A COMEDY SERIES (SINGLE EPISODE): Ellen DeGeneres, story; Mark Driscoll, Dava Savel, Tracy Newman, and Jonathan Stark, teleplay, "The Puppy Episode," *Ellen* (ABC)
OUTSTANDING WRITING IN A MINI-SERIES OR A SPECIAL: Horton Foote, teleplay, "William Faulkner's Old Man," *Hallmark Hall of Fame* (CBS)
OUTSTANDING WRITING IN A VARIETY OR MUSIC PROGRAM: Chris Rock, writer, "Chris Rock: Bring the Pain" (HBO)
OUTSTANDING INDIVIDUAL ACHIEVEMENT IN CULTURAL PROGRAMMING—PERFORMANCE: Pilobolus Dance Theatre Performers, "John F. Kennedy Center 25th Anniversary Celebration" (PBS)
THE PRESIDENT'S AWARD: "Miss Evers' Boys" (HBO)

1997–1998 (presented September 13, 1998)

OUTSTANDING COMEDY SERIES: *Frasier,* Peter Casey, David Angell, David Lee, and Christopher Lloyd, executive producers; Joe Keenan, co–executive producer; Jay Kogen and Jeffrey Richman, supervising producers; Maggie Randell, Suzanne Martin, Rob Greenberg, and David Lloyd, producers; Mary Fukuto and Lori Kirkland, coproducers (NBC)
OUTSTANDING DRAMA SERIES: *The Practice,* David E. Kelley, executive producer; Jeffrey Kramer, coexecutive producer; Robert Breech, supervising producer; Ed Redlich, Gary Strangis, Jonathan Pontell, and Alice West, producers; Pam Wisne and Christina Musrey, coproducers (ABC)
OUTSTANDING VARIETY, MUSIC, OR COMEDY SERIES: *Late Show with David Letterman,* Rob Burnett, executive producer; Barbara Gaines and Maria Pope, producers; Jon Beckerman, supervising producer (CBS)
OUTSTANDING VARIETY, MUSIC, OR COMEDY SPECIAL: "The 1997 Tony Awards," Gary Smith, executive producer; Walter C. Miller, producer; Roy A. Somlyo, supervising producer (CBS)
OUTSTANDING MINI-SERIES: "From the Earth to the Moon," Tom Hanks, executive producer; Brian Grazer, Ron Howard, and Michael Bostick, producers; Tony To, coexecutive producer; John Melfi and Graham Yost, supervising producers; Janace Tashjian, Bruce Richmond, and Erik Bork, coproducers (HBO)
OUTSTANDING MADE-FOR-TELEVISION MOVIE: "Don King: Only in America," Thomas Carter, executive producer; David Blocker, producer (HBO)
OUTSTANDING CLASSICAL MUSIC-DANCE PROGRAM: "Yo-Yo Ma Inspired By Bach," Niv Fishman, producer; Patricia Rozema, director-writer (PBS)
OUTSTANDING NONFICTION SERIES: *(Truman) The American Experience,* Margaret Drain, executive producer; David Grubin, producer-writer; Mark Samuels, senior producer; Judy Crichton, consulting executive producer; Allyson Luchak, senior producer (PBS)
OUTSTANDING NONFICTION SPECIAL: "Vietnam POWs: Stories of Survival," *Discovery Sunday,* Bob Reid, executive producer; Jacinda A. Davis, coordinating producer; Brian Leonard, producer-director-writer (Discovery Channel)
OUTSTANDING CHILDREN'S PROGRAM: *Muppets Tonight,* Brian Henson and Dick Blasucci, executive producers; Paul Flaherty and Kirk R. Thatcher, supervising producers; Patric M. Verrone, Martin G. Baker, and Chris Plourde, producers (Disney Channel); "Nick News Special Edition: What Are You Staring At?" Linda Ellerbee and Rolfe Tessem, executive producers; Mark Lyons, senior producer; Anne-Marie Cunniffe, producer (Nickelodeon)
OUTSTANDING ANIMATED PROGRAM: "Trash of the Titans," *The Simpsons,* Mike Skully, Matt Groening, James L. Brooks, and Sam Simon, executive producers; George Meyer, David S. Cohen, and Richard Appel, coexecutive producers; Dan Greaney, Ron Hauge, Donick Carey, Colin A.B.V. Lewis, Bonita Pietila, J. Michael Mendel, Richard Raynis, Richard Sakai, and Denise Sirkot, producers; Ian Maxtone-Graham consulting producer-

writer; David Mirkin, Jace Richdale, Bill Oakley, and Josh Weinstein, consulting producers; Phil Roman, animation executive producer; Lolee Aries and Michael Wolf, animation producers; Brian Scully and Julie Thacker, coproducers; Jim Reardon, director (FOX)

OUTSTANDING LEAD ACTOR IN A DRAMA SERIES: Andre Braugher, *Homicide: Life on the Street* (NBC)

OUTSTANDING LEAD ACTOR IN A COMEDY SERIES: Kelsey Grammer, *Frasier* (NBC)

OUTSTANDING LEAD ACTOR IN A MINI-SERIES OR MOVIE: Gary Sinise, "George Wallace" (TNT)

OUTSTANDING LEAD ACTRESS IN A DRAMA SERIES: Christine Lahti, *Chicago Hope* (CBS)

OUTSTANDING LEAD ACTRESS IN A COMEDY SERIES: Helen Hunt, *Mad About You* (NBC)

OUTSTANDING LEAD ACTRESS IN A MINI-SERIES OR MOVIE: Ellen Barkin, "Before Women Had Wings" (ABC)

OUTSTANDING SUPPORTING ACTOR IN A DRAMA SERIES: Gordon Clapp, *NYPD Blue* (ABC)

OUTSTANDING SUPPORTING ACTOR IN A COMEDY SERIES: David Hyde Pierce, *Frasier* (NBC)

OUTSTANDING SUPPORTING ACTOR IN A MINI-SERIES OR MOVIE: George C. Scott, "12 Angry Men" (Showtime)

OUTSTANDING SUPPORTING ACTRESS IN A DRAMA SERIES: Camryn Manheim, *The Practice* (ABC)

OUTSTANDING SUPPORTING ACTRESS IN A COMEDY SERIES: Lisa Kudrow, *Friends* (NBC)

OUTSTANDING SUPPORTING ACTRESS IN A MINI-SERIES OR MOVIE: Mare Winningham, "George Wallace" (TNT)

OUTSTANDING INDIVIDUAL PERFORMANCE IN A VARIETY OR MUSIC PROGRAM: Billy Crystal, host, "The 70th Annual Academy Awards" (ABC)

OUTSTANDING GUEST ACTOR IN A DRAMA SERIES: John Larroquette, *The Practice* (ABC)

OUTSTANDING GUEST ACTOR IN A COMEDY SERIES: Mel Brooks, *Mad About You* (NBC)

OUTSTANDING GUEST ACTRESS IN A DRAMA SERIES: Cloris Leachman, *Promised Land* (CBS)

OUTSTANDING GUEST ACTRESS IN A COMEDY SERIES: Emma Thompson, *Ellen* (ABC)

OUTSTANDING VOICE-OVER PERFORMANCE: Hank Azaria, various voices, *The Simpsons* (FOX)

OUTSTANDING DIRECTING IN A DRAMA SERIES (SINGLE EPISODE): Mark Tinker, pilot, *Brooklyn South* (CBS)

OUTSTANDING DIRECTING IN A COMEDY SERIES (SINGLE EPISODE): Todd Holland, "Flip," *The Larry Sanders Show* (HBO)

OUTSTANDING DIRECTING IN A MINI-SERIES OR A MOVIE: John Frankenheimer, "George Wallace" (TNT)

OUTSTANDING DIRECTING IN A VARIETY OR MUSIC PROGRAM: Louis J. Horvitz, "The 70th Annual Academy Awards" (ABC)

OUTSTANDING WRITING IN A DRAMA SERIES (SINGLE EPISODE): David Milch, Nicholas Wootton, and Bill Clark, "Lost Israel, part II," *NYPD Blue* (ABC)

OUTSTANDING WRITING IN A COMEDY SERIES (SINGLE EPISODE): Peter Tolan and Garry Shandling, "Flip," *The Larry Sanders Show* (HBO)

OUTSTANDING WRITING IN A MINI-SERIES OR A SPECIAL: Kario Salem, "Don King: Only in America" (HBO)

OUTSTANDING WRITING IN A VARIETY OR MUSIC PROGRAM: Eddie Feldmann, head writer; Dennis Miller, David Feldman, Leah Krinsky, Jim Hanna, David Weiss, and Jose Arroyo, writers, *Dennis Miller Live* (HBO)

THE GOVERNORS AWARD: The Learning Channel

1998–1999 (presented September 12, 1999)

OUTSTANDING COMEDY SERIES: *Ally McBeal,* David E. Kelley, executive producer; Jeffrey Kramer and Jonathan Pontell, coexecutive producers; Mike Listo, Steve Robin, and Pamela Wisne, producers; Peter Burrell, coordinating producer (FOX)

OUTSTANDING DRAMA SERIES: *The Practice,* David E. Kelley, executive producer; Jeffrey Kramer and Robert Breech, coexecutive producers; Christina Musrey, Gary M. Strangis, and Pamela Wisne, producers (ABC)

OUTSTANDING VARIETY, MUSIC OR COMEDY SERIES: *Late Show with David Letterman,* Rob Burnett, executive producer; Barbara Gaines and Maria Pope, producers (CBS)

OUTSTANDING VARIETY, MUSIC OR COMEDY SPECIAL: "The 53rd Annual Tony Awards," Walter C. Miller, executive producer; Roy A. Somlyo, supervising producer; Rosie O'Donnell, producer (CBS)

OUTSTANDING MINISERIES: "Horatio Hornblower," Andrew Benson, producer, Delia Fine and Vernon Lawrence, executive producers (A&E)

OUTSTANDING MADE-FOR-TELEVISION MOVIE: "A Lesson Before Dying," Ellen Krass, Joel Stillerman, and Ted Demme, executive producers; Robert Benedetti, producer (HBO)

OUTSTANDING CLASSICAL MUSIC-DANCE PROGRAM: "Itzhak Perlman: Fiddling for the Future," Margaret Smilow, producer; Allan Miller, director; Itzhak Perlman, performer; Jac Venza, executive producer; Walter Scheuer, executive producer for the Four Oaks Foundation (PBS)

OUTSTANDING NONFICTION SERIES: *The American Experience,* Margaret Drain, executive producer; Mark Samuels, senior producer; Austin Hoyt, producer (PBS)

OUTSTANDING NONFICTION SPECIAL: "Thug Life in D.C.," Sheila Nevins, executive producer; Marc Levin, producer/director; Daphne Pinkerson, producer; Nancy Abraham, supervising producer (HBO)

OUTSTANDING CHILDREN'S PROGRAM: "The Truth About Drinking," *The Teen Files,* Arnold Shapiro, executive producer; Allison Grodner, supervising producer; Mike Rabb, producer (Syndicated)

OUTSTANDING ANIMATED PROGRAM (ONE HOUR OR LESS): "And They Call It Bobby Love," *King of the Hill,* Greg Daniels, Mike Judge, Howard Klein, Michael Rotenberg, and Richard Appel, executive producers; Jonathan Collier, coexecutive producer; Jonathan Aibel, Glenn Berger, Alan R. Cohen, and Alan Freedland, supervising producers; Joseph A. Boucher, Johnny Hardwick, Paul Lieberstein, producers; Norm Hiscock, producer/writer; Jim Dauterive and Mark McJimsey, coproducers; Jon Vitte, Cheryl Holliday, Richard Raynis, and David Zuckerman, consulting producers; Wesley Archer, supervising director; Cyndi Tang, director; Lolee Aries and David Pritchard, animation executive producers; Michael Wolf, animation producer (FOX)

OUTSTANDING ANIMATED PROGRAM (MORE THAN ONE HOUR): "Spawn," Todd McFarlane, executive producer; John Leekley, coexecutive producer/writer; Randall J. White, producer; Brad Rader, Jennifer Yuh, Thomas A. Nelson, Chuck Patton, and Mike Vosburg, directors; Rebekah Bradford, writer; Frank Paur, supervising director (HBO)
OUTSTANDING LEAD ACTOR IN A DRAMA SERIES: Dennis Franz, *N.Y.P.D. Blue* (ABC)
OUTSTANDING LEAD ACTOR IN A COMEDY SERIES: John Lithgow, *3rd Rock from the Sun* (NBC)
OUTSTANDING LEAD ACTOR IN A MINISERIES OR MOVIE: Stanley Tucci, "Winchell" (HBO)
OUTSTANDING LEAD ACTRESS IN A DRAMA SERIES: Edie Falco, *The Sopranos* (HBO)
OUTSTANDING LEAD ACTRESS IN A COMEDY SERIES: Helen Hunt, *Mad About You* (NBC)
OUTSTANDING LEAD ACTRESS IN A MINISERIES OR MOVIE: Helen Mirren, "The Passion of Ayn Rand" (Showtime)
OUTSTANDING SUPPORTING ACTOR IN A DRAMA SERIES: Michael Badalucco, *The Practice* (ABC)
OUTSTANDING SUPPORTING ACTOR IN A COMEDY SERIES: David Hyde Pierce, *Frasier* (NBC)
OUTSTANDING SUPPORTING ACTOR IN A MINISERIES OR MOVIE: Peter O'Toole, "Joan of Arc" (CBS)
OUTSTANDING SUPPORTING ACTRESS IN A DRAMA SERIES: Holland Taylor, *The Practice* (ABC)
OUTSTANDING SUPPORTING ACTRESS IN A COMEDY SERIES: Kristen Johnston, *3rd Rock from the Sun* (NBC)
OUTSTANDING SUPPORTING ACTRESS IN A MINISERIES OR MOVIE: Anne Bancroft, "Deep in My Heart" (CBS)
OUTSTANDING INDIVIDUAL PERFORMANCE IN A VARIETY OR MUSIC PROGRAM: John Leguizamo, star, "Freaks" (HBO)
OUTSTANDING GUEST ACTOR IN A DRAMA SERIES: Edward Herrmann, *The Practice* (ABC)
OUTSTANDING GUEST ACTOR IN A COMEDY SERIES: Mel Brooks, *Mad About You* (NBC)
OUTSTANDING GUEST ACTRESS IN A DRAMA SERIES: Debra Monk, *N.Y.P.D. Blue* (ABC)
OUTSTANDING GUEST ACTRESS IN A COMEDY SERIES: Tracey Ullman, *Ally McBeal* (FOX)
OUTSTANDING VOICEOVER PERFORMANCE: Ja'net DuBois, Mrs. Avery, *The PJs* (FOX)
OUTSTANDING DIRECTING FOR A DRAMA SERIES (SINGLE EPISODE): Paris Barclay, "Hearts and Souls," *N.Y.P.D. Blue* (ABC)
OUTSTANDING DIRECTING FOR A COMEDY SERIES (SINGLE EPISODE): Thomas Schlamme, pilot, *Sports Night* (ABC)
OUTSTANDING DIRECTING FOR A MINISERIES OR A MOVIE: Alan Arkush, "Temptations" (NBC)
OUTSTANDING DIRECTING FOR A VARIETY OR MUSIC PROGRAM: Paul Miller, "The 53rd Annual Tony Awards" (CBS)
OUTSTANDING WRITING FOR A DRAMA SERIES (SINGLE EPISODE): James Manos, Jr., and David Chase, "College," *The Sopranos* (HBO)
OUTSTANDING WRITING FOR A COMEDY SERIES (SINGLE EPISODE): Jay Kogen, "Merry Christmas, Mrs. Moskowitz," *Frasier* (NBC)
OUTSTANDING WRITING FOR A MINISERIES OR A MOVIE: Ann Peacock, "A Lesson Before Dying" (HBO)
OUTSTANDING WRITING FOR A VARIETY OR MUSIC PROGRAM: Tom Agna, Vernon Chatman, Louis C. K., Lance Crouther, Gregory Greenberg, Ali Leroi, Steve O'Donnell, Chris Rock, Frank Sebastiano, Chuck Sklar, Jeff Stilson, Wanda Sykes-Hall, and Mike Upchurch, "The Chris Rock Show" (HBO)
THE GOVERNORS AWARD: "Fight for Your Rights: Take a Stand Against Violence" (MTV); "Save Our History" (The History Channel)

1999–2000 (presented September 10, 2000)

OUTSTANDING COMEDY SERIES: *Will & Grace*, David Kohan, Max Mutchnick, and James Burrows, executive producers; Jeff Greenstein and Alex Herschlag, coexecutive producers; Adam Barr and Jhoni Marchinko, supervising producers; Tim Kaiser, producer (NBC)
OUTSTANDING DRAMA SERIES: *The West Wing*, Aaron Sorkin, Thomas Schlamme, and John Wells, executive producers; Kristin Harms and Llewellyn Wells, producers (NBC)
OUTSTANDING VARIETY, MUSIC OR COMEDY SERIES: *Late Show with David Letterman*, Rob Burnett, executive producer; Barbara Gaines and Maria Pope, producers (CBS)
OUTSTANDING VARIETY, MUSIC OR COMEDY SPECIAL: "Saturday Night Live: 25th Anniversary," Lorne Michaels, executive producer; Ken Aymong, supervising producer; Marci Klein and Michael Shoemaker, producers (NBC)
OUTSTANDING MINISERIES: "The Corner," Robert F. Colesberry, David Mills, and David Simon, executive producers; Nina Kostroff Noble, producer (HBO)
OUTSTANDING MADE-FOR-TELEVISION MOVIE: "Tuesdays with Morrie," Oprah Winfrey and Kate Forte, executive producers; Jennifer Ogden, supervising producer (ABC)
OUTSTANDING CLASSICAL MUSIC-DANCE PROGRAM: "American Ballet Theatre in Le Corsaire," *Dance in America*, Jac Venza, executive producer; Judy Kinberg, producer; Matthew Diamond, director (PBS)
OUTSTANDING NONFICTION SERIES: *American Masters: Hitchcock, Selznick and the End of Hollywood*, Susan Lacy, executive producer; Tamar Hacker, senior producer; Michael Epstein, producer/writer/director; Karen Bernstein, producer (PBS)
OUTSTANDING NONFICTION SPECIAL: "Children in War," Sheila Nevins, executive producer; John Hoffman, supervising producer; Alan Raymond and Susan Raymond, producer/writer/directors (HBO)
OUTSTANDING CHILDREN'S PROGRAM: "The Color of Friendship," Alan Sacks, executive producer; Christopher Morgan and Kevin Hooks, producers (The Disney Channel); "Goodnight Moon & Other Sleepytime Tales," Sheila Nevins, executive producer; Carole Rosen, supervising producer; Amy Schatz, producer (HBO)
OUTSTANDING ANIMATED PROGRAM (FOR PROGRAMMING ONE HOUR OR LESS): "Behind the Laughter," *The Simpsons*, Matt Groening, James L. Brooks, Al Jean, and Sam Simon, executive producers; George Meyer and Mike Scully, executive producer/writers; Dan Greaney, Frank Mula, Ian Maxtone-Graham, Rob LaZebnik, and Ron Hauge, coexecutive producers; Julie Thacker and Larina Jean Adamson, supervising producers; Bonita Pietila, Carolyn Omine, Denise Sirkot, Don Payne, Richard Raynis, Richard Sakai, Tom Martin, John Frink,

and Larry Doyle, producers; Matt Selman, producer/writer; David Pritchard and Lolee Aries, animation executive producers; Michael Wolf, animation producer; Tim Long, writer; Jim Reardon, supervising director; Mark Kirkland, director (FOX)

OUTSTANDING ANIMATED PROGRAM (FOR PROGRAMMING MORE THAN ONE HOUR): "Walking with Dinosaurs," John Lynch and Tomi Bednar Landis, executive producers; Jasper James and Tim Haines, producer/directors; Georgann Kane, writer; Mike Milne, computer animation director (The Discovery Channel)

OUTSTANDING LEAD ACTOR IN A DRAMA SERIES: James Gandolfini, *The Sopranos* (HBO)

OUTSTANDING LEAD ACTOR IN A COMEDY SERIES: Michael J. Fox, *Spin City* (ABC)

OUTSTANDING LEAD ACTOR IN A MINISERIES OR MOVIE: Jack Lemmon, "Tuesdays with Morrie" (ABC)

OUTSTANDING LEAD ACTRESS IN A DRAMA SERIES: Sela Ward, *Once and Again* (ABC)

OUTSTANDING LEAD ACTRESS IN A COMEDY SERIES: Patricia Heaton, *Everybody Loves Raymond* (CBS)

OUTSTANDING LEAD ACTRESS IN A MINISERIES OR MOVIE: Halle Berry, "Introducing Dorothy Dandridge" (HBO)

OUTSTANDING SUPPORTING ACTOR IN A DRAMA SERIES: Richard Schiff, *The West Wing* (NBC)

OUTSTANDING SUPPORTING ACTOR IN A COMEDY SERIES: Sean Hayes, *Will & Grace* (NBC)

OUTSTANDING SUPPORTING ACTOR IN A MINISERIES OR MOVIE: Hank Azaria, "Tuesdays with Morrie" (ABC)

OUTSTANDING SUPPORTING ACTRESS IN A DRAMA SERIES: Allison Janney, *The West Wing* (NBC)

OUTSTANDING SUPPORTING ACTRESS IN A COMEDY SERIES: Megan Mullally, *Will & Grace* (NBC)

OUTSTANDING SUPPORTING ACTRESS IN A MINISERIES OR MOVIE: Vanessa Redgrave, "If These Walls Could Talk 2" (HBO)

OUTSTANDING INDIVIDUAL PERFORMANCE IN A VARIETY OR MUSIC PROGRAM: Eddie Izzard, "Eddie Izzard: Dress to Kill" (HBO)

OUTSTANDING GUEST ACTOR IN A DRAMA SERIES: James Whitmore, *The Practice* (ABC)

OUTSTANDING GUEST ACTOR IN A COMEDY SERIES: Bruce Willis, *Friends* (NBC)

OUTSTANDING GUEST ACTRESS IN A DRAMA SERIES: Beah Richards, *The Practice* (ABC)

OUTSTANDING GUEST ACTRESS IN A COMEDY SERIES: Jean Smart, *Frasier* (NBC)

OUTSTANDING VOICEOVER PERFORMANCE: Seth MacFarlane, Stewie Griffin, *Family Guy* (FOX); Julie Harris, Susan B. Anthony, "Not for Ourselves Alone: The Story of Elizabeth Cady Stanton & Susan B. Anthony" (PBS)

OUTSTANDING DIRECTING FOR A DRAMA SERIES (SINGLE EPISODE): Thomas Schlamme, pilot, *The West Wing* (NBC)

OUTSTANDING DIRECTING FOR A COMEDY SERIES (SINGLE EPISODE): Todd Holland, pilot, *Malcolm in the Middle* (FOX)

OUTSTANDING DIRECTING FOR A MINISERIES, MOVIE OR A SPECIAL: Charles Dutton, "The Corner" (HBO)

OUTSTANDING DIRECTING FOR A VARIETY OR MUSIC PROGRAM: Louis J. Horvitz, "The 72nd Annual Academy Awards" (ABC)

OUTSTANDING WRITING FOR A DRAMA SERIES (SINGLE EPISODE): Aaron Sorkin and Rick Cleveland, "In Excelsis Deo," *The West Wing* (NBC)

OUTSTANDING WRITING FOR A COMEDY SERIES (SINGLE EPISODE): Linwood Boomer, pilot, *Malcolm in the Middle* (FOX)

OUTSTANDING WRITING FOR A MINISERIES OR A MOVIE: David Simon and David Mills, "The Corner" (HBO)

OUTSTANDING WRITING FOR A VARIETY MUSIC OR COMEDY PROGRAM: Eddie Izzard, "Eddie Izzard: Dress to Kill" (HBO)

THE GOVERNORS AWARD: Save the Music Foundation (VH1); *The Biography Project for Children* (A&E); "The Teen Files" (Arnold Shapiro Productions)

2000–2001 (presented November 4, 2001)

OUTSTANDING COMEDY SERIES: *Sex and the City,* Darren Star and Michael Patrick King, executive producers; Jenny Bicks, Cindy Chupack, and John Melfi, coexecutive producers; Sarah Jessica Parker, producer (HBO)

OUTSTANDING DRAMA SERIES: *The West Wing,* Aaron Sorkin, Thomas Schlamme, and John Wells, executive producers; Kevin Falls, coexecutive producer; Michael Hissrich, Lawrence O'Donnell, Jr., Kristin Harms, and Llewellyn Wells, producers (NBC)

OUTSTANDING VARIETY, MUSIC OR COMEDY SERIES: *Late Show with David Letterman,* Maria Pope, Barbara Gaines, and Rob Burnett, executive producers; Eric Strangel and Justin Strangel, producers (CBS)

OUTSTANDING VARIETY, MUSIC OR COMEDY SPECIAL: "Cirque du Soleil's Dralion," Peter Wagg, executive producer; Rocky Oldham, producer; Francis Berwick, producer for Bravo (Bravo)

OUTSTANDING MINISERIES: "Anne Frank," Hans Proppe, executive producer; David Kappes, producer (ABC)

OUTSTANDING MADE-FOR-TELEVISION MOVIE: "Wit," Mike Nichols and Cary Brokaw, executive producers; Simon Bosanquet, producer (HBO)

OUTSTANDING CLASSICAL MUSIC-DANCE PROGRAM: "La Traviata from Paris," *Great Performances,* Rada Rassimov, Paola Megas, and Jac Venza, executive producers; Andrea Andermann, John Walker, and David Horn, producers; Patroni Griffi, director; Zubin Mehta, conductor (PBS)

OUTSTANDING NONFICTION PROGRAM (REALITY): *American High,* R. J. Cutler, Erwin Moore, Brian Medavoy, and Cheryl Stanley, executive producers; Dan Partland, supervising producer; Rich Bye, Molly O'Brien, Jonathan Chinn, Nick Doob, and Jonathan Mednick, producers (FOX)

OUTSTANDING NONFICTION PROGRAM (SPECIAL CLASS): *Survivor,* Mark Burnett and Charlie Parsons, executive producers; Craig Piligian, coexecutive producer; Scott Messick and Tom Shelly, supervising producers; Maria Baltazzi, Jay Bienstock, John Russell Feist, and Teri Kennedy, producers; Jeff Probst, host (CBS)

OUTSTANDING NONFICTION SPECIAL (INFORMATIONAL): "Scottsboro: An American Tragedy," *American Experience,* Margaret Drain, executive producer; Barak Goodman, producer/director/writer; Daniel Anker, producer/codirector; Mark Samels, supervising producer (PBS)

OUTSTANDING NONFICTION SERIES (INFORMATIONAL): "Finding Lucy," *American Masters,* Susan Lacy, executive producer; Pamela Mason Wagner, producer/director; Thomas Wagner, producer/writer; Tamar Hacker, producer (PBS)

OUTSTANDING CHILDREN'S PROGRAM: "The Teen Files: Surviving High School," Arnold Shapiro, executive producer; Allison Grodner, supervising producer/writer/director; Karen Haystead Duzy, producer (UPN)

OUTSTANDING ANIMATED PROGRAM (LESS THAN ONE HOUR): "Homr," *The Simpsons,* Matt Groening, James L. Brooks, Al Jean, Mike Scully, George Meyer and Sam Simon, executive producers; Ian Maxtone-Graham, Ron Hauge, Dan Greaney, Frank Mula, and Rob LaZebnik, coexecutive producers; Julie Thacker and Larina Jean Adamson, supervising producers; Larry Doyle, Tom Martin, Carolyn Omine, John Frank, Don Payne, Matt Selman, Tim Long, Mike Reiss, Tom Gammill, Max Pross, David Mirkin, Richard Raynis, Bonita Pietila, Denise Sirkot, and Richard Sakai, producers; Jim Reardon, supervising director; Mike B. Anderson, director; John Hyde, Jon F. Vein, and John Bush, animation executive producers; Michael Wolf and Laurie Biernacki, animation producers (FOX)

OUTSTANDING ANIMATED PROGRAM (ONE HOUR OR MORE): "Allosaurus: A Walking with Dinosaurs Special," Mick Kaczorowski, executive producer; Sharon Reed and William Sargent, animation coexecutive producers; Tim Haines, animation producer; Kate Bartlett and Michael Olmert, writers; Mike Milne, animation director (The Discovery Channel)

OUTSTANDING LEAD ACTOR IN A DRAMA SERIES: James Gandolfini, *The Sopranos* (HBO)

OUTSTANDING LEAD ACTOR IN A COMEDY SERIES: Eric McCormack, *Will & Grace* (NBC)

OUTSTANDING LEAD ACTOR IN A MINISERIES OR MOVIE: Kenneth Branagh, "Conspiracy" (HBO)

OUTSTANDING LEAD ACTRESS IN A DRAMA SERIES: Edie Falco, *The Sopranos* (HBO)

OUTSTANDING LEAD ACTRESS IN A COMEDY SERIES: Patricia Heaton, *Everybody Loves Raymond* (CBS)

OUTSTANDING LEAD ACTRESS IN A MINISERIES OR MOVIE: Judy Davis, "Life with Judy Garland: Me and My Shadows" (ABC)

OUTSTANDING SUPPORTING ACTOR IN A DRAMA SERIES: Bradley Whitford, *The West Wing* (NBC)

OUTSTANDING SUPPORTING ACTOR IN A COMEDY SERIES: Peter MacNicol, *Ally McBeal* (FOX)

OUTSTANDING SUPPORTING ACTOR IN A MINISERIES OR MOVIE: Brian Cox, "Nuremberg" (TNT)

OUTSTANDING SUPPORTING ACTRESS IN A DRAMA SERIES: Allison Janney, *The West Wing* (NBC)

OUTSTANDING SUPPORTING ACTRESS IN A COMEDY SERIES: Doris Roberts, *Everybody Loves Raymond* (CBS)

OUTSTANDING SUPPORTING ACTRESS IN A MINISERIES OR MOVIE: Tammy Blanchard, "Life with Judy Garland: Me and My Shadows" (ABC)

OUTSTANDING INDIVIDUAL PERFORMANCE IN A VARIETY OR MUSIC PROGRAM: Barbra Streisand, "Barbra Streisand: Timeless" (FOX)

OUTSTANDING GUEST ACTOR IN A DRAMA SERIES: Michael Emerson, *The Practice* (ABC)

OUTSTANDING GUEST ACTOR IN A COMEDY SERIES: Sir Derek Jacobi, *Frasier* (NBC)

OUTSTANDING GUEST ACTRESS IN A DRAMA SERIES: Sally Field, *ER* (NBC)

OUTSTANDING GUEST ACTRESS IN A COMEDY SERIES: Jean Smart, *Frasier* (NBC)

OUTSTANDING VOICEOVER PERFORMANCE: Hank Azaria as various characters, "Worst Episode Ever," *The Simpsons* (FOX); Ja'net DuBois as Mrs. Avery, "Let's Get Ready to Rhumba," *The PJs* (WB)

OUTSTANDING DIRECTING FOR A DRAMA SERIES (SINGLE EPISODE): Thomas Schlamme, "In the Shadow of Two Gunmen," *The West Wing* (NBC)

OUTSTANDING DIRECTING FOR A COMEDY SERIES (SINGLE EPISODE): Todd Holland, "Bowling," *Malcolm in the Middle* (FOX)

OUTSTANDING DIRECTING FOR A MINISERIES, MOVIE OR A SPECIAL: Mike Nichols, "Wit" (HBO)

OUTSTANDING DIRECTING FOR A VARIETY OR MUSIC PROGRAM: David Mallet, "Cirque du Soleil's Dralion" (Bravo)

OUTSTANDING WRITING FOR A DRAMA SERIES (SINGLE EPISODE): Robin Green and Mitchell Burgess, "Employee of the Month," *The Sopranos* (HBO)

OUTSTANDING WRITING FOR A COMEDY SERIES (SINGLE EPISODE): Alex Reid, "Bowling," *Malcolm in the Middle* (FOX)

OUTSTANDING WRITING FOR A MINISERIES OR A MOVIE: Loring Mandel, "Conspiracy" (HBO)

OUTSTANDING WRITING FOR A VARIETY MUSIC OR COMEDY PROGRAM: Eric Drysdale, Jim Earl, Dan Goor, Charlie Grandy, JR Havlan, Tom Johnson, Kent Jones, Paul Mercurio, Chris Regan, Allison Silverman, and Jon Stewart, *The Daily Show with Jon Stewart* (Comedy Central)

THE GOVERNORS AWARD: CNN; Showtime

2001–2002 (presented September 22, 2002)

OUTSTANDING COMEDY SERIES: *Friends,* Kevin S. Bright, Marta Kauffman, David Crane, Scott Silvari, Shana Goldberg-Meehan, Andrew Reich, and Ted Cohen, executive producers; Todd Stevens, coexecutive producer; Sherry Bilsing-Graham, Ellen Plummer, Brian Buckner, and Sebastian Jones, supervising producers; Wendy Knoller, producer (NBC)

OUTSTANDING DRAMA SERIES: *The West Wing,* Aaron Sorkin, Thomas Schlamme, and John Wells, executive producers; Kevin Falls, coexecutive producer; Christopher Misiano and Alex Graves, supervising producers; Llewellyn Wells, Michael Hissrich, and Kristin Harms, producers (NBC)

OUTSTANDING VARIETY, MUSIC OR COMEDY SERIES: *Late Show with David Letterman,* Maria Pope, Barbara Gaines, and Rob Burnett, executive producers; Eric Strangel and Justin Strangel, producers (CBS)

OUTSTANDING VARIETY, MUSIC OR COMEDY SPECIAL: "America: A Tribute to Heroes," Joel Gallen, executive producer (ABC, CBS, FOX, and NBC)

OUTSTANDING MINISERIES: "Band of Brothers," Tom Hanks and Steven Spielberg, executive producers; Stephen E. Ambrose, Gary Goetzman, and Tony To, coexecutive producers; Erik Bork and Erik Jondresen, supervising producers; Mary Richards, producer (HBO)

OUTSTANDING MADE-FOR-TELEVISION MOVIE: "The Gathering Storm," Ridley Scott, Julie Payne, and Tony Scott, executive producers; Tracy Scoffield, executive producer for the BBC; Lisa Ellzey, coexecutive producer; Frank Doelger and David M. Thompson, producers (HBO)

OUTSTANDING CLASSICAL MUSIC-DANCE PROGRAM: "Sweeney Todd in Concert," Chase Mishkin, executive producer; Ellen M. Krass and Mort Swinsky, coexecutive producers; Iris Merlis and Jeff Thorsen, producers; Lonny Price, director (PBS)

OUTSTANDING NONFICTION PROGRAM (REALITY): *The Osbournes,* Lois Curren, R. Greg Johnston, and Jeff Stilson, executive producers; Jonathon Taylor, supervising producer; Sharon Osbourne and Rod Aissa, producers (MTV)

OUTSTANDING SPECIAL CLASS PROGRAM: "The West Wing: Documentary Special," Thomas Schlamme, John Wells, and Aaron Sorkin, executive producers; Kevin Falls, coexecutive producer; Michael Hissrich, Llewellyn Wells, and Anne Sandkuhler, producers; William Couturie, director/interview materials; Eli Attie and Felicia Willson, interview materials (NBC)

OUTSTANDING NONFICTION SPECIAL (INFORMATIONAL): "9/11," Jules Naudet, Gedeon Naudet, and James Hanlon, executive producer/directors; Susan Zirinsky, Graydon Carter, and David Friend, executive producers; Hal Gessner, supervising producer; Tom Forman, senior producer/writer; Richard Barber, Michael J. Maloy, Bruce Spiegel, Mead Stone, and Paul LaRossa, producers; Rob Klug, director; Greg Kandra, writer (CBS)

OUTSTANDING NONFICTION SERIES (INFORMATIONAL): *Biography,* CarolAnne Dolan and Kevin Burns, executive producers; Maryellen Cox and Kerry Jensen, supervising producers; Jeanne Begley, producer/director; Gidion Phillips, writer (A&E)

OUTSTANDING CHILDREN'S PROGRAM: "Nick News Special Edition: Nick Faces of Hope: The Kids of Afghanistan," Linda Ellerbee and Rolfe Tessem, executive producers; Wally Berger, supervising producer; Josh Veselke and Mark Lyons, producers (Nickelodeon)

OUTSTANDING ANIMATED PROGRAM (LESS THAN ONE HOUR): "Roswell That Ends Well," *Futurama,* Matt Groening and David X. Cohen, executive producers; Ken Keeler and Eric Horsted, coexecutive producers; Lewis Morton and Patric M. Verrone, supervising producers; J. Stewart Burns, supervising producer/writer; Bill Odenkirk, Eric Kaplan, Brian J. Cowan, and Claudia Katz, producers; Rich Moore, supervising producer/director; Gregg Vanzo, animation executive producer (FOX)

OUTSTANDING ANIMATED PROGRAM (ONE HOUR OR MORE): "Walking with Prehistoric Beasts," Tim Haines and Mick Kaczorowski, executive producers; Jasper James, producer/writer; Nigel Patterson, producer/director/writer; Sharon Reed and William Sargent, computer animation executive producers; Mike Milne, computer animation director; Kate Bartlett and Michael Olmert, writers (The Discovery Channel)

OUTSTANDING LEAD ACTOR IN A DRAMA SERIES: Michael Chiklis, *The Shield* (FX)

OUTSTANDING LEAD ACTOR IN A COMEDY SERIES: Ray Romano, *Everybody Loves Raymond* (CBS)

OUTSTANDING LEAD ACTOR IN A MINISERIES OR MOVIE: Albert Finney, "The Gathering Storm" (HBO)

OUTSTANDING LEAD ACTRESS IN A DRAMA SERIES: Allison Janney, *The West Wing* (NBC)

OUTSTANDING LEAD ACTRESS IN A COMEDY SERIES: Jennifer Aniston, *Friends* (NBC)

OUTSTANDING LEAD ACTRESS IN A MINISERIES OR MOVIE: Laura Linney, "Wild Iris" (Showtime)

OUTSTANDING SUPPORTING ACTOR IN A DRAMA SERIES: John Spencer, *The West Wing* (NBC)

OUTSTANDING SUPPORTING ACTOR IN A COMEDY SERIES: Brad Garrett, *Everybody Loves Raymond* (CBS)

OUTSTANDING SUPPORTING ACTOR IN A MINISERIES OR MOVIE: Michael Moriarty, "James Dean" (TNT)

OUTSTANDING SUPPORTING ACTRESS IN A DRAMA SERIES: Stockard Channing, *The West Wing* (NBC)

OUTSTANDING SUPPORTING ACTRESS IN A COMEDY SERIES: Doris Roberts, *Everybody Loves Raymond* (CBS)

OUTSTANDING SUPPORTING ACTRESS IN A MINISERIES OR MOVIE: Stockard Channing, "The Matthew Shepard Story" (NBC)

OUTSTANDING INDIVIDUAL PERFORMANCE IN A VARIETY OR MUSIC PROGRAM: Sting, "A&E in Concert: Sting in Tuscany . . . All This Time" (A&E)

OUTSTANDING GUEST ACTOR IN A DRAMA SERIES: Charles S. Dutton, *The Practice* (ABC)

OUTSTANDING GUEST ACTOR IN A COMEDY SERIES: Anthony LaPaglia, *Frasier* (NBC)

OUTSTANDING GUEST ACTRESS IN A DRAMA SERIES: Patricia Clarkson, *Six Feet Under* (HBO)

OUTSTANDING GUEST ACTRESS IN A COMEDY SERIES: Cloris Leachman, *Malcolm in the Middle* (FOX)

OUTSTANDING VOICEOVER PERFORMANCE: Pamela Segall Adlon as various characters, "Bobby Goes Nuts," *King of the Hill* (FOX); Peter Macon, "John Henry, The Steel Driving Man," *Animated Tales of the World* (HBO)

OUTSTANDING DIRECTING FOR A DRAMA SERIES (SINGLE EPISODE): Alan Ball, pilot, *Six Feet Under* (HBO)

OUTSTANDING DIRECTING FOR A COMEDY SERIES (SINGLE EPISODE): Michael Patrick King, "The Real Me," *Sex and the City* (HBO)

OUTSTANDING DIRECTING FOR A MINISERIES, MOVIE OR A DRAMATIC SPECIAL: David Frankel, Tom Hanks, David Leland, Richard Loncraine, David Nutter, Phil Alden Robinson, Mikael Salomon, and Tony To, "Band of Brothers" (HBO)

OUTSTANDING DIRECTING FOR A VARIETY OR MUSIC PROGRAM: Ron de Moraes, Kenny Ortega, and Bucky Gunts, "Opening Ceremony, Salt Lake City 2002 Olympic Winter Games" (NBC)

OUTSTANDING WRITING FOR A DRAMA SERIES (SINGLE EPISODE): Joel Surnow and Robert Cochran, "Midnight–1:00 A.M.," *24* (FOX)

OUTSTANDING WRITING FOR A COMEDY SERIES (SINGLE EPISODE): Larry Wilmore, pilot, *The Bernie Mac Show* (FOX)

OUTSTANDING WRITING FOR A MINISERIES MOVIE OR A DRAMATIC SPECIAL: Larry Ramin, story; Hugh Whitemore, teleplay/story, "The Gathering Storm" (HBO)

OUTSTANDING WRITING FOR A VARIETY MUSIC OR COMEDY PROGRAM: Tina Fey and Dennis McNicholas, head writers;

Doug Abeles, James Anderson, Max Brooks, James Downey, Hugh Fink, Charlie Grandy, Jack Handey, Steve Higgins, Erik Kenward, Lorne Michaels, Matt Murray, Paula Pell, Matt Piedmont, Ken Scarborough, Michael Schur, Frank Sebastiano, T. Sean Shannon, Robert Smigel, Emily Spivey, Andrew Steele, and Scott Wainio, *Saturday Night Live* (NBC)

THE GOVERNORS AWARD: "America: A Tribute to Heroes" (ABC, CBS, FOX, and NBC)

BOB HOPE HUMANITARIAN AWARD: Oprah Winfrey

APPENDIX 3

TOP-RATED PROGRAMS BY SEASON

The following are listings of the top-rated evening series during each season, ranked by audience size. The Nielsen rating is the percent of all TV-equipped homes tuned to the program on an average night, as measured by Nielsen Media Research. Thus a rating of 61.6 for the *Texaco Star Theater* from 1950–1951 means that on the average, 61.6 percent of all homes that had a TV were tuned to this show.

A. C. Nielsen changed its system of computing ratings in 1960, so ratings prior to and after that date are not precisely comparable. It should also be noted that since the Nielsen system is basically a service for advertisers, only sponsored programs are measured. However, it is unlikely that any unsponsored series (usually public affairs or news) has ever regularly achieved audience levels comparable to those of the commercial programs shown here.

October 1950–April 1951

Program	Network	Rating
1. Texaco Star Theater	NBC	61.6
2. Fireside Theatre	NBC	52.6
3. Philco TV Playhouse	NBC	45.3
4. Your Show of Shows	NBC	42.6
5. The Colgate Comedy Hour	NBC	42.0
6. Gillette Cavalcade of Sports	NBC	41.3
7. The Lone Ranger	ABC	41.2
8. Arthur Godfrey's Talent Scouts	CBS	40.6
9. Hopalong Cassidy	NBC	39.9
10. Mama	CBS	39.7
11. Robert Montgomery Presents	NBC	38.8
12. Martin Kane, Private Eye	NBC	37.8
13. Man Against Crime	CBS	37.4
14. Kraft Television Theatre	NBC	37.0
15. The Toast of the Town	CBS	36.5
16. The Aldrich Family	NBC	36.1
17. You Bet Your Life	NBC	36.0
18. Arthur Godfrey and His Friends	CBS	35.9
19. Armstrong Circle Theatre	NBC	35.6
Lights Out	NBC	35.6
Big Town	CBS	35.6
22. The Alan Young Show	CBS	34.4
23. Stop the Music	ABC	34.0
24. Studio One	CBS	33.8
25. The Big Story	NBC	33.7
26. Pabst Blue Ribbon Bouts	CBS	33.4
The Original Amateur Hour	NBC	33.4
28. The Ken Murray Show	CBS	32.1
29. Your Hit Parade	NBC	32.0
30. Lux Video Theatre	CBS	31.5
The Speidel Show	NBC	31.5

October 1951–April 1952

Program	Network	Rating
1. Arthur Godfrey's Talent Scouts	CBS	53.8
2. Texaco Star Theater	NBC	52.0
3. I Love Lucy	CBS	50.9
4. The Red Skelton Show	NBC	50.2
5. The Colgate Comedy Hour	NBC	45.3
6. Arthur Godfrey and His Friends	CBS	43.3
7. Fireside Theatre	NBC	43.1
8. Your Show of Shows	NBC	43.0
9. The Jack Benny Show	CBS	42.8
10. You Bet Your Life	NBC	42.1
11. Mama	CBS	41.3
12. Philco TV Playhouse	NBC	40.4
13. Amos 'n' Andy	CBS	38.9
14. Gangbusters	NBC	38.7
15. Big Town	CBS	38.5
16. Goodyear TV Playhouse	NBC	37.8
17. Pabst Blue Ribbon Bouts	CBS	37.5
18. The Lone Ranger	ABC	36.8
19. Gillette Cavalcade of Sports	NBC	36.5
20. All Star Revue	NBC	36.3
Dragnet	NBC	36.3
22. The Alan Young Show	CBS	35.8
23. Kraft Television Theatre	NBC	34.8
24. Armstrong Circle Theatre	NBC	34.7
25. Strike It Rich	CBS	34.5
26. Robert Montgomery Presents	NBC	34.4
27. The Roy Rogers Show	NBC	32.7
28. Hopalong Cassidy	NBC	32.2
29. Man Against Crime	CBS	32.0
Racket Squad	CBS	32.0

October 1952–April 1953

Program	Network	Rating
1. I Love Lucy	CBS	67.3
2. Arthur Godfrey's Talent Scouts	CBS	54.7
3. Arthur Godfrey and His Friends	CBS	47.1
4. Dragnet	NBC	46.8
5. Texaco Star Theater	NBC	46.7
6. The Buick Circus Hour	NBC	46.0
7. The Colgate Comedy Hour	NBC	44.3
8. Gangbusters	NBC	42.4
9. You Bet Your Life	NBC	41.6
10. Fireside Theatre	NBC	40.6
11. The Red Buttons Show	CBS	40.2
12. The Jack Benny Show	CBS	39.0
13. Life with Luigi	CBS	38.5
14. Pabst Blue Ribbon Bouts	CBS	37.9
15. Goodyear TV Playhouse	NBC	37.8
16. The Life of Riley	NBC	37.4
17. Philco TV Playhouse	NBC	37.3
18. Mama	CBS	37.0
19. Your Show of Shows	NBC	36.0
20. What's My Line	CBS	35.3
Strike It Rich	CBS	35.3
22. Our Miss Brooks	CBS	35.0
The Big Story	NBC	35.0
24. Gillette Cavalcade of Sports	NBC	34.7
25. Amos 'n' Andy	CBS	34.4
26. All Star Revue	NBC	34.3
27. Treasury Men in Action	NBC	34.2
28. The Red Skelton Show	NBC	33.7
The Lone Ranger	ABC	33.7
30. Ford Theatre	NBC	33.6

October 1953–April 1954

Program	Network	Rating
1. I Love Lucy	CBS	58.8
2. Dragnet	NBC	53.2
3. Arthur Godfrey's Talent Scouts	CBS	43.6
You Bet Your Life	NBC	43.6
5. The Milton Berle Show	NBC	40.2
6. Arthur Godfrey and His Friends	CBS	38.9
7. Ford Theatre	NBC	38.8
8. The Jackie Gleason Show	CBS	38.1
9. Fireside Theatre	NBC	36.4
10. The Colgate Comedy Hour	NBC	36.2
This Is Your Life	NBC	36.2
12. The Red Buttons Show	CBS	35.3
13. The Life of Riley	NBC	35.0
14. Our Miss Brooks	CBS	34.2
15. Treasury Men in Action	NBC	33.9
16. The Jack Benny Show	CBS	33.3
17. The Toast of the Town	CBS	33.0
18. Gillette Cavalcade of Sports	NBC	32.7
19. Philco TV Playhouse	NBC	32.5
20. The George Burns and Gracie Allen Show	CBS	32.4
21. Kraft Television Theatre	NBC	31.3
22. Goodyear TV Playhouse	NBC	31.0
23. Pabst Blue Ribbon Bouts	CBS	30.9
24. Private Secretary	CBS	30.3
25. I Married Joan	NBC	30.2
Mama	CBS	30.2
27. General Electric Theater	NBC	29.9
28. What's My Line	CBS	29.6
29. The Big Story	NBC	29.5
Martin Kane, Private Eye	NBC	29.5
Your Hit Parade	NBC	29.5

October 1954–April 1955

Program	Network	Rating
1. I Love Lucy	CBS	49.3
2. The Jackie Gleason Show	CBS	42.4
3. Dragnet	NBC	42.1
4. You Bet Your Life	NBC	41.0
5. The Toast of the Town	CBS	39.6
6. Disneyland	ABC	39.1
7. The Jack Benny Show	CBS	38.3
8. The George Gobel Show	NBC	35.2
9. Ford Theatre	NBC	34.9
10. December Bride	CBS	34.7
11. Buick-Berle Show	NBC	34.6
12. This Is Your Life	NBC	34.5
13. I've Got a Secret	CBS	34.0
14. Two for the Money	CBS	33.9
15. Your Hit Parade	NBC	33.6
16. The Millionaire	CBS	33.0
17. General Electric Theater	CBS	32.6
18. Arthur Godfrey's Talent Scouts	CBS	32.5
19. Private Secretary	CBS	32.2
20. Fireside Theatre	NBC	31.1
21. The Life of Riley	NBC	30.9
22. Arthur Godfrey and His Friends	CBS	29.8
23. The Adventures of Rin Tin Tin	ABC	29.5
24. Topper	CBS	29.4
25. Pabst Blue Ribbon Bouts	CBS	29.1
26. The George Burns and Gracie Allen Show	CBS	29.0
27. The Colgate Comedy Hour	NBC	28.0
28. The Loretta Young Show	NBC	27.7
29. My Little Margie	NBC	27.1
30. The Roy Rogers Show	NBC	26.9

October 1955–April 1956

Program	Network	Rating
1. The $64,000 Question	CBS	47.5
2. I Love Lucy	CBS	46.1
3. The Ed Sullivan Show	CBS	39.5
4. Disneyland	ABC	37.4
5. The Jack Benny Show	CBS	37.2
6. December Bride	CBS	37.0
7. You Bet Your Life	NBC	35.4
8. Dragnet	NBC	35.0
9. The Millionaire	CBS	33.8
10. I've Got a Secret	CBS	33.5
11. General Electric Theater	CBS	32.9
12. Private Secretary	CBS	32.4
Ford Theatre	NBC	32.4
14. The Red Skelton Show	CBS	32.3
15. The George Gobel Show	NBC	31.9
16. Arthur Godfrey's Talent Scouts	CBS	31.1
17. The Lineup	CBS	30.8
18. The Perry Como Show	NBC	30.3
19. The Honeymooners	CBS	30.2
20. The Adventures of Robin Hood	CBS	30.1
21. The Life of Riley	NBC	29.9
22. Climax	CBS	29.6
23. Your Hit Parade	NBC	29.1
24. Fireside Theatre	NBC	29.0
25. Lux Video Theatre	NBC	28.9
26. This is Your Life	NBC	28.8
27. People Are Funny	NBC	28.4
The George Burns and Gracie Allen Show	CBS	28.4
29. The Chevy Show	NBC	28.2
30. The Phil Silvers Show	CBS	28.1

October 1956–April 1957

Program	Network	Rating
1. I Love Lucy	CBS	43.7
2. The Ed Sullivan Show	CBS	38.4
3. General Electric Theater	CBS	36.9
4. The $64,000 Question	CBS	36.4
5. December Bride	CBS	35.2
6. Alfred Hitchcock Presents	CBS	33.9
7. I've Got a Secret	CBS	32.7
Gunsmoke	CBS	32.7
9. The Perry Como Show	NBC	32.6
10. The Jack Benny Show	CBS	32.3
11. Dragnet	NBC	32.1
12. Arthur Godfrey's Talent Scouts	CBS	31.9
13. The Millionaire	CBS	31.8
Disneyland	ABC	31.8
15. The Red Skelton Show	CBS	31.4
The Lineup	CBS	31.4
17. You Bet Your Life	NBC	31.1
18. The Life & Legend of Wyatt Earp	ABC	31.0
19. The Ford Show	NBC	30.7
20. The Adventures of Robin Hood	CBS	30.3
21. People Are Funny	NBC	30.2
22. The $64,000 Challenge	CBS	29.7
The Phil Silvers Show	CBS	29.7
24. Lassie	CBS	29.5
25. Private Secretary	CBS	29.0
26. Climax	CBS	28.9
What's My Line	CBS	28.9
28. The George Burns and Gracie Allen Show	CBS	27.8
29. The Jackie Gleason Show	CBS	27.6
30. Name That Tune	CBS	27.2

October 1957–April 1958

Program	Network	Rating
1. Gunsmoke	CBS	43.1
2. The Danny Thomas Show	CBS	35.3
3. Tales of Wells Fargo	NBC	35.2
4. Have Gun Will Travel	CBS	33.7
5. I've Got a Secret	CBS	33.4
6. The Life and Legend of Wyatt Earp	ABC	32.6
7. General Electric Theater	CBS	31.5
8. The Restless Gun	NBC	31.4
9. December Bride	CBS	30.7
10. You Bet Your Life	NBC	30.6
11. The Perry Como Show	NBC	30.5
12. Alfred Hitchcock Presents	CBS	30.3
Cheyenne	ABC	30.3
14. The Ford Show	NBC	29.7
15. The Red Skelton Show	CBS	28.9
16. The Gale Storm Show	CBS	28.8
17. The Millionaire	CBS	28.5
18. The Lineup	CBS	28.4
19. This Is Your Life	NBC	28.1
The $64,000 Question	CBS	28.1
21. Zane Grey Theater	CBS	27.9
22. Lassie	CBS	27.8
23. Wagon Train	NBC	27.7
Sugarfoot	ABC	27.7
Father Knows Best	NBC	27.7
26. Twenty-One	NBC	27.6
27. The Ed Sullivan Show	CBS	27.3
28. The Jack Benny Show	CBS	27.1
29. People Are Funny	NBC	27.0
30. The Loretta Young Show	NBC	26.6
Zorro	ABC	26.6
The Real McCoys	ABC	26.6

October 1958–April 1959

Program	Network	Rating	Program	Network	Rating
1. Gunsmoke	CBS	39.6	16. Wanted: Dead or Alive	CBS	28.0
2. Wagon Train	NBC	36.1	Peter Gunn	NBC	28.0
3. Have Gun Will Travel	CBS	34.3	18. Cheyenne	ABC	27.9
4. The Rifleman	ABC	33.1	19. Perry Mason	CBS	27.5
5. The Danny Thomas Show	CBS	32.8	20. The Ford Show	NBC	27.2
6. Maverick	ABC	30.4	21. Sugarfoot	ABC	27.0
7. Tales of Wells Fargo	NBC	30.2	The Ann Sothern Show	CBS	27.0
8. The Real McCoys	ABC	30.1	The Perry Como Show	NBC	27.0
9. I've Got a Secret	CBS	29.8	24. Alfred Hitchcock Presents	CBS	26.8
10. The Life and Legend of Wyatt Earp	ABC	29.1	25. Name That Tune	CBS	26.7
			General Electric Theatre	CBS	26.7
11. The Price Is Right	NBC	28.6	27. The Lawman	ABC	26.0
12. The Red Skelton Show	CBS	28.5	28. Rawhide	CBS	25.9
13. Zane Grey Theater	CBS	28.3	29. This Is Your Life	NBC	25.8
Father Knows Best	CBS	28.3	30. The Millionaire	CBS	25.6
15. The Texan	CBS	28.2			

October 1959–April 1960

Program	Network	Rating	Program	Network	Rating
1. Gunsmoke	CBS	40.3	16. Dennis the Menace	CBS	26.0
2. Wagon Train	NBC	38.4	17. Cheyenne	ABC	25.9
3. Have Gun Will Travel	CBS	34.7	18. Rawhide	CBS	25.8
4. The Danny Thomas Show	CBS	31.1	19. Maverick	ABC	25.2
5. The Red Skelton Show	CBS	30.8	20. The Life and Legend of Wyatt Earp	ABC	25.0
6. Father Knows Best	CBS	29.7	21. Mr. Lucky	CBS	24.4
77 Sunset Strip	ABC	29.7	Zane Grey Theater	CBS	24.4
8. The Price Is Right	NBC	29.2	General Electric Theater	CBS	24.4
9. Wanted: Dead or Alive	CBS	28.7	24. The Ann Sothern Show	CBS	24.2
10. Perry Mason	CBS	28.3	25. Alfred Hitchcock Presents	CBS	24.1
11. The Real McCoys	ABC	28.2	26. You Bet Your Life	NBC	24.0
12. The Ed Sullivan Show	CBS	28.0	27. What's My Line	CBS	23.9
13. The Rifleman	ABC	27.5	28. I've Got a Secret	CBS	23.5
14. The Ford Show	NBC	27.4	29. The Perry Como Show	NBC	23.1
15. The Lawman	ABC	26.2	Lassie	CBS	23.1

October 1960–April 1961

Program	Network	Rating	Program	Network	Rating
1. Gunsmoke	CBS	37.3	16. Perry Mason	CBS	24.9
2. Wagon Train	NBC	34.2	17. Bonanza	NBC	24.8
3. Have Gun Will Travel	CBS	30.9	18. The Flintstones	ABC	24.3
4. The Andy Griffith Show	CBS	27.8	19. The Red Skelton Show	CBS	24.0
5. The Real McCoys	ABC	27.7	20. General Electric Theater	CBS	23.4
6. Rawhide	CBS	27.5	21. Checkmate	CBS	23.2
7. Candid Camera	CBS	27.3	22. What's My Line	CBS	23.1
8. The Untouchables	ABC	27.0	23. The Many Loves of Dobie Gillis	CBS	23.0
The Price Is Right	NBC	27.0	24. The Ford Show	NBC	22.9
10. The Jack Benny Show	CBS	26.2	25. The Garry Moore Show	CBS	22.7
11. Dennis the Menace	CBS	26.1	26. The Lawman	ABC	22.3
12. The Danny Thomas Show	CBS	25.9	27. The Rifleman	ABC	22.1
13. My Three Sons	ABC	25.8	28. Cheyenne	ABC	22.0
77 Sunset Strip	ABC	25.8	29. Peter Gunn	NBC	21.9
15. The Ed Sullivan Show	CBS	25.0	30. Route 66	CBS	21.7

October 1961–April 1962

Program	Network	Rating
1. Wagon Train	NBC	32.1
2. Bonanza	NBC	30.0
3. Gunsmoke	CBS	28.3
4. Hazel	NBC	27.7
5. Perry Mason	CBS	27.3
6. The Red Skelton Show	CBS	27.1
7. The Andy Griffith Show	CBS	27.0
8. The Danny Thomas Show	CBS	26.1
9. Dr. Kildare	NBC	25.6
10. Candid Camera	CBS	25.5
11. My Three Sons	ABC	24.7
12. The Garry Moore Show	CBS	24.6
13. Rawhide	CBS	24.5
14. The Real McCoys	ABC	24.2
15. Lassie	CBS	24.0
Sing Along with Mitch	NBC	24.0
17. Dennis the Menace	CBS	23.8
18. Ben Casey	ABC	23.7
19. The Ed Sullivan Show	CBS	23.5
20. Car 54, Where Are You?	NBC	23.2
21. The Flintstones	ABC	22.9
The Many Loves of Dobie Gillis	CBS	22.9
23. Walt Disney's Wonderful World of Color	NBC	22.7
24. The Joey Bishop Show	NBC	22.6
25. The Perry Como Show	NBC	22.5
26. The Defenders	CBS	22.4
27. The Price Is Right	NBC	22.3
The Rifleman	ABC	22.3
29. Have Gun, Will Travel	CBS	22.2
30. The Donna Reed Show	ABC	21.9
77 Sunset Strip	ABC	21.9

October 1962–April 1963

Program	Network	Rating
1. The Beverly Hillbillies	CBS	36.0
2. Candid Camera	CBS	31.1
The Red Skelton Show	CBS	31.1
4. Bonanza	NBC	29.8
The Lucy Show	CBS	29.8
6. The Andy Griffith Show	CBS	29.7
7. Ben Casey	ABC	28.7
The Danny Thomas Show	CBS	28.7
9. The Dick Van Dyke Show	CBS	27.1
10. Gunsmoke	CBS	27.0
11. Dr. Kildare	NBC	26.2
The Jack Benny Show	CBS	26.2
13. What's My Line	CBS	25.5
14. The Ed Sullivan Show	CBS	25.3
15. Hazel	NBC	25.1
16. I've Got a Secret	CBS	24.9
17. The Jackie Gleason Show	CBS	24.1
18. The Defenders	CBS	23.9
19. The Garry Moore Show	CBS	23.3
To Tell the Truth	CBS	23.3
Lassie	CBS	23.3
22. Rawhide	CBS	22.8
23. Perry Mason	CBS	22.4
24. Walt Disney's Wonderful World of Color	NBC	22.3
25. Wagon Train	ABC	22.0
26. The Virginian	NBC	21.7
27. Route 66	CBS	21.3
28. My Three Sons	ABC	21.0
29. Have Gun, Will Travel	CBS	20.8
30. The Flintstones	ABC	20.5

October 1963–April 1964

Program	Network	Rating
1. The Beverly Hillbillies	CBS	39.1
2. Bonanza	NBC	36.9
3. The Dick Van Dyke Show	CBS	33.3
4. Petticoat Junction	CBS	30.3
5. The Andy Griffith Show	CBS	29.4
6. The Lucy Show	CBS	28.1
7. Candid Camera	CBS	27.7
8. The Ed Sullivan Show	CBS	27.5
9. The Danny Thomas Show	CBS	26.7
10. My Favorite Martian	CBS	26.3
11. The Red Skelton Show	CBS	25.7
12. I've Got a Secret	CBS	25.0
Lassie	CBS	25.0
The Jack Benny Show	CBS	25.0
15. The Jackie Gleason Show	CBS	24.6
16. The Donna Reed Show	ABC	24.5
17. The Virginian	NBC	24.0
18. The Patty Duke Show	ABC	23.9
19. Dr. Kildare	NBC	23.6
20. Gunsmoke	CBS	23.5
21. Walt Disney's Wonderful World of Color	NBC	23.0
22. Hazel	NBC	22.8
McHale's Navy	ABC	22.8
24. To Tell the Truth	CBS	22.6
What's My Line	CBS	22.6
26. Perry Mason	CBS	22.1
27. My Three Sons	ABC	21.9
28. The Fugitive	ABC	21.7
29. The Adventures of Ozzie and Harriet	ABC	21.6
30. The Danny Kaye Show	CBS	21.5
Bob Hope Presents the Chrysler Theatre	NBC	21.5

October 1964–April 1965

Program	Network	Rating
1. Bonanza	NBC	36.3
2. Bewitched	ABC	31.0
3. Gomer Pyle, U.S.M.C.	CBS	30.7
4. The Andy Griffith Show	CBS	28.3
5. The Fugitive	ABC	27.9
6. The Red Skelton Hour	CBS	27.4
7. The Dick Van Dyke Show	CBS	27.1
8. The Lucy Show	CBS	26.6
9. Peyton Place II	ABC	26.4
10. Combat	ABC	26.1
11. Walt Disney's Wonderful World of Color	NBC	25.7
12. The Beverly Hillbillies	CBS	25.6
13. My Three Sons	ABC	25.5
14. Branded	NBC	25.3
15. Petticoat Junction	CBS	25.2
The Ed Sullivan Show	CBS	25.2
17. Lassie	CBS	25.1
18. The Munsters	CBS	24.7
Gilligan's Island	CBS	24.7
20. Peyton Place I	ABC	24.6
21. The Jackie Gleason Show	CBS	24.4
22. The Virginian	NBC	24.0
23. The Addams Family	ABC	23.9
24. My Favorite Martian	CBS	23.7
25. Flipper	NBC	23.4
26. I've Got a Secret	CBS	23.0
27. Gunsmoke	CBS	22.6
28. The Patty Duke Show	ABC	22.4
29. McHale's Navy	ABC	22.3
30. The Lawrence Welk Show	ABC	22.0

October 1965–April 1966

Program	Network	Rating
1. Bonanza	NBC	31.8
2. Gomer Pyle, U.S.M.C.	CBS	27.8
3. The Lucy Show	CBS	27.7
4. The Red Skelton Hour	CBS	27.6
5. Batman (Thurs.)	ABC	27.0
6. The Andy Griffith Show	CBS	26.9
7. Bewitched	ABC	25.9
The Beverly Hillbillies	CBS	25.9
9. Hogan's Heroes	CBS	24.9
10. Batman (Wed.)	ABC	24.7
11. Green Acres	CBS	24.6
12. Get Smart	NBC	24.5
13. The Man from U.N.C.L.E.	NBC	24.0
14. Daktari	CBS	23.9
15. My Three Sons	CBS	23.8
16. The Dick Van Dyke Show	CBS	23.6
17. Walt Disney's Wonderful World of Color	NBC	23.2
The Ed Sullivan Show	CBS	23.2
19. The Lawrence Welk Show	ABC	22.4
I've Got a Secret	CBS	22.4
21. Petticoat Junction	CBS	22.3
22. Gilligan's Island	CBS	22.1
23. Wild, Wild West	CBS	22.0
The Jackie Gleason Show	CBS	22.0
The Virginian	NBC	22.0
26. Daniel Boone	NBC	21.9
27. Lassie	CBS	21.8
I Dream of Jeannie	NBC	21.8
29. Flipper	NBC	21.6
30. Gunsmoke	CBS	21.3

October 1966–April 1967

Program	Network	Rating
1. Bonanza	NBC	29.1
2. The Red Skelton Hour	CBS	28.2
3. The Andy Griffith Show	CBS	27.4
4. The Lucy Show	CBS	26.2
5. The Jackie Gleason Show	CBS	25.3
6. Green Acres	CBS	24.6
7. Daktari	CBS	23.4
Bewitched	ABC	23.4
The Beverly Hillbillies	CBS	23.4
10. Gomer Pyle, U.S.M.C.	CBS	22.8
The Virginian	NBC	22.8
The Lawrence Welk Show	ABC	22.8
The Ed Sullivan Show	CBS	22.8
14. The Dean Martin Show	NBC	22.6
Family Affair	CBS	22.6
16. The Smothers Brothers Comedy Hour	CBS	22.2
17. Friday Night Movies	CBS	21.8
Hogan's Heroes	CBS	21.8
19. Walt Disney's Wonderful World of Color	NBC	21.5
20. Saturday Night at the Movies	NBC	21.4
21. Dragnet	NBC	21.2
22. Get Smart	NBC	21.0
23. Petticoat Junction	CBS	20.9
Rat Patrol	ABC	20.9
25. Daniel Boone	NBC	20.8
26. Bob Hope Presents the Chrysler Theatre	NBC	20.7
27. Tarzan	NBC	20.5
28. ABC Sunday Night Movie	ABC	20.4
29. I Spy	NBC	20.2
CBS Thursday Movie	CBS	20.2
My Three Sons	CBS	20.2
The F.B.I.	ABC	20.2

October 1967–April 1968

Program	Network	Rating
1. The Andy Griffith Show	CBS	27.6
2. The Lucy Show	CBS	27.0
3. Gomer Pyle, U.S.M.C.	CBS	25.6
4. Gunsmoke	CBS	25.5
Family Affair	CBS	25.5
Bonanza	NBC	25.5
7. The Red Skelton Show	CBS	25.3
8. The Dean Martin Show	NBC	24.8
9. The Jackie Gleason Show	CBS	23.9
10. Saturday Night at the Movies	NBC	23.6
11. Bewitched	ABC	23.5
12. The Beverly Hillbillies	CBS	23.3
13. The Ed Sullivan Show	CBS	23.2
14. The Virginian	NBC	22.9
15. Friday Night Movie	CBS	22.8
Green Acres	CBS	22.8
17. The Lawrence Welk Show	ABC	21.9
18. The Smothers Brothers Comedy Hour	CBS	21.7
19. Gentle Ben	CBS	21.5
20. Tuesday Night at the Movies	NBC	21.4
21. Rowan & Martin's Laugh-In	NBC	21.3
22. The F.B.I.	ABC	21.2
23. Thursday Night Movie	CBS	21.1
24. My Three Sons	CBS	20.8
25. Walt Disney's Wonderful World of Color	NBC	20.7
26. Ironside	NBC	20.5
27. The Carol Burnett Show	CBS	20.1
Dragnet '67	NBC	20.1
29. Daniel Boone	NBC	20.0
30. Lassie	CBS	19.9
It Takes a Thief	ABC	19.9

October 1968–April 1969

Program	Network	Rating
1. Rowan & Martin's Laugh-In	NBC	31.8
2. Gomer Pyle, U.S.M.C.	CBS	27.2
3. Bonanza	NBC	26.6
4. Mayberry R.F.D.	CBS	25.4
5. Family Affair	CBS	25.2
6. Gunsmoke	CBS	24.9
7. Julia	NBC	24.6
8. The Dean Martin Show	NBC	24.1
9. Here's Lucy	CBS	23.8
10. The Beverly Hillbillies	CBS	23.5
11. Mission: Impossible	CBS	23.3
Bewitched	ABC	23.3
The Red Skelton Hour	CBS	23.3
14. My Three Sons	CBS	22.8
15. The Glen Campbell Goodtime Hour	CBS	22.5
16. Ironside	NBC	22.3
17. The Virginian	NBC	21.8
18. The F.B.I.	ABC	21.7
19. Green Acres	CBS	21.6
20. Dragnet	NBC	21.4
21. Daniel Boone	NBC	21.3
Walt Disney's Wonderful World of Color	NBC	21.3
23. The Ed Sullivan Show	CBS	21.2
24. The Carol Burnett Show	CBS	20.8
The Jackie Gleason Show	CBS	20.8
26. I Dream of Jeannie	NBC	20.7
27. The Smothers Brothers Comedy Hour	CBS	20.6
28. The Mod Squad	ABC	20.5
The Lawrence Welk Show	ABC	20.5
30. The Doris Day Show	CBS	20.4

October 1969–April 1970

Program	Network	Rating
1. Rowan & Martin's Laugh-In	NBC	26.3
2. Gunsmoke	CBS	25.9
3. Bonanza	NBC	24.8
4. Mayberry R.F.D.	CBS	24.4
5. Family Affair	CBS	24.2
6. Here's Lucy	CBS	23.9
7. The Red Skelton Hour	CBS	23.8
8. Marcus Welby, M.D.	ABC	23.7
9. Walt Disney's Wonderful World of Color	NBC	23.6
10. The Doris Day Show	CBS	22.8
11. The Bill Cosby Show	NBC	22.7
12. The Jim Nabors Hour	CBS	22.4
13. The Carol Burnett Show	CBS	22.1
14. The Dean Martin Show	NBC	21.9
15. My Three Sons	CBS	21.8
Ironside	NBC	21.8
The Johnny Cash Show	ABC	21.8
18. The Beverly Hillbillies	CBS	21.7
19. Hawaii Five-O	CBS	21.1
20. The Glen Campbell Goodtime Hour	CBS	21.0
Hee Haw	CBS	21.0
22. Movie of the Week	ABC	20.9
23. Mod Squad	ABC	20.8
24. Saturday Night Movie	NBC	20.6
Bewitched	ABC	20.6
The F.B.I.	ABC	20.6
27. The Ed Sullivan Show	CBS	20.3
28. Julia	NBC	20.1
29. CBS Thursday Movie	CBS	20.0
30. Mannix	CBS	19.9

October 1970–April 1971

Program	Network	Rating
1. Marcus Welby, M.D.	ABC	29.6
2. The Flip Wilson Show	NBC	27.9
3. Here's Lucy	CBS	26.1
4. Ironside	NBC	25.7
5. Gunsmoke	CBS	25.5
6. ABC Movie of the Week	ABC	25.1
7. Hawaii Five-O	CBS	25.0
8. Medical Center	CBS	24.5
9. Bonanza	NBC	23.9
10. The F.B.I.	ABC	23.0
11. Mod Squad	ABC	22.7
12. Adam-12	NBC	22.6
13. Rowan & Martin's Laugh-In	NBC	22.4
The Wonderful World of Disney	NBC	22.4
15. Mayberry R.F.D.	CBS	22.3
16. Hee Haw	CBS	21.4
17. Mannix	CBS	21.3
18. The Men from Shiloh	NBC	21.2
19. My Three Sons	CBS	20.8
20. The Doris Day Show	CBS	20.7
21. The Smith Family	ABC	20.6
22. The Mary Tyler Moore Show	CBS	20.3
23. NBC Saturday Movie	NBC	20.1
24. The Dean Martin Show	NBC	20.0
25. The Carol Burnett Show	CBS	19.8
The Partridge Family	ABC	19.8
NBC Monday Movie	NBC	19.8
28. ABC Sunday Movie	ABC	19.7
29. The Jim Nabors Hour	CBS	19.5
30. CBS Thursday Movie	CBS	19.3

October 1971–April 1972

Program	Network	Rating
1. All in the Family	CBS	34.0
2.The Flip Wilson Show	NBC	28.2
3. Marcus Welby, M.D.	ABC	27.8
4. Gunsmoke	CBS	26.0
5. ABC Movie of the Week	ABC	25.6
6. Sanford and Son	NBC	25.2
7. Mannix	CBS	24.8
8. Funny Face	CBS	23.9
Adam 12	NBC	23.9
10. The Mary Tyler Moore Show	CBS	23.7
Here's Lucy	CBS	23.7
12. Hawaii Five-O	CBS	23.6
13. Medical Center	CBS	23.5
14. The NBC Mystery Movie	NBC	23.2
15. Ironside	NBC	23.0
16. The Partridge Family	ABC	22.6
17. The F.B.I.	ABC	22.4
18. The New Dick Van Dyke Show	CBS	22.2
19. The Wonderful World of Disney	NBC	22.0
20. Bonanza	NBC	21.9
21. Mod Squad	ABC	21.5
22. Rowan & Martin's Laugh-In	NBC	21.4
23. The Carol Burnett Show	CBS	21.2
The Doris Day Show	CBS	21.2
25. Monday Night Football	ABC	20.9
26. ABC Sunday Movie	ABC	20.8
27. The Sonny and Cher Comedy Hour	CBS	20.2
28. Room 222	ABC	19.8
Cannon	CBS	19.8
30. CBS Friday Movie	CBS	19.5

October 1972–April 1973

Program	Network	Rating
1. All in the Family	CBS	33.3
2. Sanford and Son	NBC	27.6
3. Hawaii Five-O	CBS	25.2
4. Maude	CBS	24.7
5. Bridget Loves Bernie	CBS	24.2
The NBC Sunday Mystery Movie	NBC	24.2
7. The Mary Tyler Moore Show	CBS	23.6
Gunsmoke	CBS	23.6
9. The Wonderful World of Disney	NBC	23.5
10. Ironside	NBC	23.4
11. Adam 12	NBC	23.3
12. The Flip Wilson Show	NBC	23.1
13. Marcus Welby, M.D.	ABC	22.9
14. Cannon	CBS	22.4
15. Here's Lucy	CBS	21.9
16. The Bob Newhart Show	CBS	21.8
17. Tuesday Movie of the Week	ABC	21.5
18. Monday Night Football	ABC	21.0
19. The Partridge Family	ABC	20.6
The Waltons	CBS	20.6
Medical Center	CBS	20.6
22. The Carol Burnett Show	CBS	20.3
23. ABC Sunday Movie	ABC	20.0
The Rookies	ABC	20.0
25. Barnaby Jones	CBS	19.9
The Little People	NBC	19.9
ABC Wednesday Movie of the Week	ABC	19.9
28. NBC Monday Movie	NBC	19.3
29. ABC Monday Movie	ABC	19.2
The F.B.I.	ABC	19.2
Kung Fu	ABC	19.2

September 1973–April 1974

Program	Network	Rating
1. All in the Family	CBS	31.2
2. The Waltons	CBS	28.1
3. Sanford and Son	NBC	27.5
4. M*A*S*H	CBS	25.7
5. Hawaii Five-O	CBS	24.0
6. Maude	CBS	23.5
7. Kojak	CBS	23.3
The Sonny and Cher Comedy Hour	CBS	23.3
9. The Mary Tyler Moore Show	CBS	23.1
Cannon	CBS	23.1
11. The Six Million Dollar Man	ABC	22.7
12. The Bob Newhart Show	CBS	22.3
The Wonderful World of Disney	NBC	22.3
14. The NBC Sunday Mystery Movie	NBC	22.2
15. Gunsmoke	CBS	22.1
16. Happy Days	ABC	21.5
17. Good Times	CBS	21.4
Barnaby Jones	CBS	21.4
19. Monday Night Football	ABC	21.2
CBS Friday Night Movie	CBS	21.2
21. Tuesday Movie of the Week	ABC	21.0
22. The Streets of San Francisco	ABC	20.8
23. Adam 12	NBC	20.7
ABC Sunday Night Movie	ABC	20.7
25. The Rookies	ABC	20.3
26. ABC Monday Movie	ABC	20.2
27. The Carol Burnett Show	CBS	20.1
Kung Fu	ABC	20.1
29. Here's Lucy	CBS	20.0
30. CBS Thursday Movie	CBS	19.9

September 1974–April 1975

Program	Network	Rating
1. All in the Family	CBS	30.2
2. Sanford and Son	NBC	29.6
3. Chico and The Man	NBC	28.5
4. The Jeffersons	CBS	27.6
5. M*A*S*H	CBS	27.4
6. Rhoda	CBS	26.3
7. Good Times	CBS	25.8
8. The Waltons	CBS	25.5
9. Maude	CBS	24.9
10. Hawaii Five-O	CBS	24.8
11. The Mary Tyler Moore Show	CBS	24.0
12. The Rockford Files	NBC	23.7
13. Little House on the Prairie	NBC	23.5
14. Kojak	CBS	23.3
15. Police Woman	NBC	22.8
16. S.W.A.T.	ABC	22.6
17. The Bob Newhart Show	CBS	22.4
18. The Wonderful World of Disney	NBC	22.0
The Rookies	ABC	22.0
20. Mannix	CBS	21.6
Cannon	CBS	21.6
22. Cher	CBS	21.3
The Streets of San Francisco	ABC	21.3
The NBC Sunday Mystery Movie	NBC	21.3
25. Paul Sand in Friends and Lovers	CBS	20.7
Tony Orlando & Dawn	CBS	20.7
27. Medical Center	CBS	20.6
28. Gunsmoke	CBS	20.5
29. The Carol Burnett Show	CBS	20.4
30. Emergency	NBC	20.0

September 1975–April 1976

Program	Network	Rating
1. All in the Family	CBS	30.1
2. Rich Man, Poor Man	ABC	28.0
3. Laverne & Shirley	ABC	27.5
4. Maude	CBS	25.0
5. The Bionic Woman	ABC	24.9
6. Phyllis	CBS	24.5
7. Sanford and Son	NBC	24.4
Rhoda	CBS	24.4
9. The Six Million Dollar Man	ABC	24.3
10. ABC Monday Night Movie	ABC	24.2
11. Happy Days	ABC	23.9
12. One Day at a Time	CBS	23.1
13. ABC Sunday Night Movie	ABC	23.0
14. The Waltons	CBS	22.9
M*A*S*H	CBS	22.9
16. Starsky and Hutch	ABC	22.5
Good Heavens	ABC	22.5
18. Welcome Back, Kotter	ABC	22.1
19. The Mary Tyler Moore Show	CBS	21.9
20. Kojak	CBS	21.8
21. The Jeffersons	CBS	21.5
22. Baretta	ABC	21.3
23. The Sonny & Cher Show	CBS	21.2
24. Good Times	CBS	21.0
25. Chico and the Man	NBC	20.8
26. The Bob Newhart Show	CBS	20.7
Donny and Marie	ABC	20.7
The Streets of San Francisco	ABC	20.7
29. The Carol Burnett Show	CBS	20.5
30. Police Woman	NBC	20.2

September 1976–April 1977

Program	Network	Rating
1. Happy Days	ABC	31.5
2. Laverne & Shirley	ABC	30.9
3. ABC Monday Night Movie	ABC	26.0
4. M*A*S*H	CBS	25.9
5. Charlie's Angels	ABC	25.8
6. The Big Event	NBC	24.4
7. The Six Million Dollar Man	ABC	24.2
8. ABC Sunday Night Movie	ABC	23.4
Baretta	ABC	23.4
One Day at a Time	CBS	23.4
11. Three's Company	ABC	23.1
12. All in the Family	CBS	22.9
13. Welcome Back, Kotter	ABC	22.7
14. The Bionic Woman	ABC	22.4
15. The Waltons	CBS	22.3
Little House on the Prairie	NBC	22.3
17. Barney Miller	ABC	22.2
18. 60 Minutes	CBS	21.9
Hawaii Five-O	CBS	21.9
20. NBC Monday Night Movie	NBC	21.8
21. Rich Man, Poor Man, Book II	ABC	21.6
22. Monday Night Football	ABC	21.2
23. Eight Is Enough	ABC	21.1
24. The Jeffersons	CBS	21.0
25. What's Happening!!	ABC	20.9
26. Good Times	CBS	20.5
27. Sanford and Son	NBC	20.3
28. ABC Friday Night Movie	ABC	20.2
29. The Tony Randall Show	ABC	20.1
30. Alice	CBS	20.0

September 1977–April 1978

Program	Network	Rating
1. Laverne & Shirley	ABC	31.6
2. Happy Days	ABC	31.4
3. Three's Company	ABC	28.3
4. 60 Minutes	CBS	24.4
Charlie's Angels	ABC	24.4
All in the Family	CBS	24.4
7. Little House on the Prairie	NBC	24.1
8. Alice	CBS	23.2
M*A*S*H	CBS	23.2
10. One Day at a Time	CBS	23.0
11. How the West Was Won	ABC	22.5
12. Eight Is Enough	ABC	22.2
13. Soap	ABC	22.0
14. The Love Boat	ABC	21.9
15. NBC Monday Night Movie	NBC	21.7
16. Monday Might Football	ABC	21.5
17. Fantasy Island	ABC	21.4
Barney Miller	ABC	21.4
19. Project U.F.O.	NBC	21.2
20. ABC Sunday Night Movie	ABC	20.8
The Waltons	CBS	20.8
22. Barnaby Jones	CBS	20.6
23. Hawaii Five-O	CBS	20.4
24. ABC Monday Night Movie	ABC	20.3
25. Rhoda	CBS	20.1
26. The Incredible Hulk	CBS	19.9
Family	ABC	19.9
Welcome Back, Kotter	ABC	19.9
29. On Our Own	CBS	19.6
30. The Big Event-Sunday	NBC	19.4

September 1978–April 1979

Program	Network	Rating
1. Laverne & Shirley	ABC	30.5
2. Three's Company	ABC	30.3
3. Mork & Mindy	ABC	28.6
Happy Days	ABC	28.6
5. Angie	ABC	26.7
6. 60 Minutes	CBS	25.5
7. M*A*S*H	CBS	25.4
8. The Ropers	ABC	25.2
9. All in the Family	CBS	24.9
Taxi	ABC	24.9
11. Eight Is Enough	ABC	24.8
12. Charlie's Angels	ABC	24.4
13. Alice	CBS	23.2
14. Little House on the Prairie	NBC	23.1
15. ABC Sunday Night Movie	ABC	22.6
Barney Miller	ABC	22.6
17. The Love Boat	ABC	22.1
18. One Day at a Time	CBS	21.6
19. Soap	ABC	21.3
20. The Dukes of Hazzard	CBS	21.0
21. NBC Monday Night Movie	NBC	20.9
22. Fantasy Island	ABC	20.8
23. Vega$	ABC	20.6
24. Barnaby Jones	CBS	20.5
25. CHiPS	NBC	20.3
26. Stockard Channing in Just Friends	CBS	20.2
27. Diff'rent Strokes	NBC	19.9
28. Monday Night Football	ABC	19.8
What's Happening!!	ABC	19.8
30. Lou Grant	CBS	19.7

September 1979–April 1980

Program	Network	Rating
1. 60 Minutes	CBS	28.4
2. Three's Company	ABC	26.3
3. That's Incredible	ABC	25.8
4. Alice	CBS	25.3
M*A*S*H	CBS	25.3
6. Dallas	CBS	25.0
7. Flo	CBS	24.4
8. The Jeffersons	CBS	24.3
9. The Dukes of Hazzard	CBS	24.1
10. One Day at a Time	CBS	23.0
11. Archie Bunker's Place	CBS	22.9
12. Eight Is Enough	ABC	22.8
13. Taxi	ABC	22.4
14. House Calls	CBS	22.1
Real People	NBC	22.1
16. Little House on the Prairie	NBC	21.8
17. Happy Days	ABC	21.7
18. CHiPS	NBC	21.5
19. Trapper John, M.D.	CBS	21.2
20. Charlie's Angels	ABC	20.9
Barney Miller	ABC	20.9
22. WKRP in Cincinnati	CBS	20.7
23. Benson	ABC	20.6
The Love Boat	ABC	20.6
25. Soap	ABC	20.5
26. Diff'rent Strokes	NBC	20.3
27. Mork & Mindy	ABC	20.2
28. Fantasy Island	ABC	20.1
29. Tenspeed and Brown Shoe	ABC	20.0
ABC Sunday Night Movie	ABC	20.0
Vega$	ABC	20.0
Knots Landing	CBS	20.0

September 1980–April 1981

Program	Network	Rating
1. Dallas	CBS	34.5
2. The Dukes of Hazzard	CBS	27.3
3. 60 Minutes	CBS	27.0
4. M*A*S*H	CBS	25.7
5. The Love Boat	ABC	24.3
6. The Jeffersons	CBS	23.5
7. Alice	CBS	22.9
8. House Calls	CBS	22.4
Three's Company	ABC	22.4
10. Little House on the Prairie	NBC	22.1
11. One Day at a Time	CBS	22.0
12. Real People	NBC	21.5
13. Archie Bunker's Place	CBS	21.4
14. Magnum, P.I.	CBS	21.0
15. Happy Days	ABC	20.8
Too Close for Comfort	ABC	20.8
17. Fantasy Island	ABC	20.7
Trapper John, M.D.	CBS	20.7
Diff'rent Strokes	NBC	20.7
20. Monday Night Football	ABC	20.6
Laverne & Shirley	ABC	20.6
22. That's Incredible	ABC	20.5
23. Hart to Hart	ABC	19.9
24. ABC Sunday Night Movie	ABC	19.4
CHiPS	NBC	19.4
26. The Facts of Life	NBC	19.3
27. Lou Grant	CBS	19.1
28. Knots Landing	CBS	19.0
29. NBC Monday Night Movie	NBC	18.8
30. The Waltons	CBS	18.6

September 1981–April 1982

Program	Network	Rating
1. Dallas	CBS	28.4
2. 60 Minutes	CBS	27.7
3. The Jeffersons	CBS	23.4
4. Three's Company	ABC	23.3
5. Alice	CBS	22.7
6. The Dukes of Hazzard	CBS	22.6
Too Close for Comfort	ABC	22.6
8. ABC Monday Night Movie	ABC	22.5
9. M*A*S*H	CBS	22.3
10. One Day at a Time	CBS	22.0
11. Monday Night Football	ABC	21.8
12. Archie Bunker's Place	CBS	21.6
13. Falcon Crest	CBS	21.4
14. The Love Boat	ABC	21.2
15. Hart to Hart	ABC	21.1
Trapper John, M.D.	CBS	21.1
17. Magnum, P.I.	CBS	20.9
18. Happy Days	ABC	20.6
19. Dynasty	ABC	20.2
20. Laverne & Shirley	ABC	19.9
21. Real People	NBC	19.7
22. ABC Sunday Night Movie	ABC	19.5
23. House Calls	CBS	19.2
24. The Facts of Life	NBC	19.1
Little House on the Prairie	NBC	19.1
26. The Fall Guy	ABC	19.0
27. Hill Street Blues	NBC	18.6
28. That's Incredible	ABC	18.4
T.J. Hooker	ABC	18.4
30. Fantasy Island	ABC	18.3

September 1982–April 1983

Program	Network	Rating
1. 60 Minutes	CBS	25.5
2. Dallas	CBS	24.6
3. M*A*S*H	CBS	22.6
Magnum, P.I.	CBS	22.6
5. Dynasty	ABC	22.4
6. Three's Company	ABC	21.2
7. Simon & Simon	CBS	21.0
8. Falcon Crest	CBS	20.7
9. The Love Boat	ABC	20.3
10. The A-Team	NBC	20.1
Monday Night Football	ABC	20.1
12. The Jeffersons	CBS	20.0
Newhart	CBS	20.0
14. The Fall Guy	ABC	19.4
15. 9 to 5	ABC	19.3
16. One Day at a Time	CBS	19.1
17. Hart to Hart	ABC	18.9
18. Gloria	CBS	18.7
Trapper John, M.D.	CBS	18.7
20. Knots Landing	CBS	18.6
21. Hill Street Blues	NBC	18.4
22. That's Incredible	ABC	18.3
Archie Bunker's Place	CBS	18.3
24. ABC Monday Night Movie	ABC	18.0
25. Laverne & Shirley	ABC	17.8
26. ABC Sunday Night Movie	ABC	17.6
27. CBS Tuesday Night Movie	CBS	17.5
28. Happy Days	ABC	17.4
Little House: A New Beginning	NBC	17.4
29. Real People	NBC	17.2
The Dukes of Hazzard	CBS	17.2

September 1983–April 1984

Program	Network	Rating
1. Dallas	CBS	25.7
2. 60 Minutes	CBS	24.2
3. Dynasty	ABC	24.1
4. The A-Team	NBC	24.0
5. Simon & Simon	CBS	23.8
6. Magnum, P.I.	CBS	22.4
7. Falcon Crest	CBS	22.0
8. Kate & Allie	CBS	21.9
9. Hotel	ABC	21.1
10. Cagney & Lacey	CBS	20.9
11. Knots Landing	CBS	20.8
12. ABC Sunday Night Movie	ABC	20.4
ABC Monday Night Movie	ABC	20.4
14. TV's Bloopers & Practical Jokes	NBC	20.3
15. AfterMASH	CBS	20.1
16. The Fall Guy	ABC	19.9
17. The Love Boat	ABC	19.0
18. Riptide	NBC	18.8
19. The Jeffersons	CBS	18.6
20. Scarecrow & Mrs. King	CBS	18.3
21. Monday Night Football	ABC	18.1
NBC Monday Night Movie	NBC	18.1
23. Newhart	CBS	18.0
24. The Facts of Life	NBC	17.3
25. CBS Tuesday Night Movie	CBS	17.2
Webster	ABC	17.2
Alice	CBS	17.2
Knight Rider	NBC	17.2
Hardcastle & McCormick	ABC	17.2
30. Trapper John, M.D.	CBS	17.0

September 1984–April 1985

Program	Network	Rating
1. Dynasty	ABC	25.0
2. Dallas	CBS	24.7
3. The Cosby Show	NBC	24.2
4. 60 Minutes	CBS	22.2
5. Family Ties	NBC	22.1
6. The A-Team	NBC	21.9
7. Simon & Simon	CBS	21.8
8. Murder, She Wrote	CBS	20.1
9. Knots Landing	CBS	20.0
10. Falcon Crest	CBS	19.9
Crazy Like a Fox	CBS	19.9
12. Hotel	ABC	19.7
Cheers	NBC	19.7
14. Riptide	NBC	19.2
15. Magnum, P.I.	CBS	19.1
16. Newhart	CBS	18.4
17. Kate & Allie	CBS	18.3
18. NBC Monday Night Movie	NBC	18.2
19. Highway to Heaven	NBC	17.7
20. Night Court	NBC	17.6
21. ABC Sunday Night Movie	ABC	17.5
22. Scarecrow & Mrs. King	CBS	17.1
TV's Bloopers & Practical Jokes	NBC	17.1
The Fall Guy	ABC	17.1
25. Monday Night Football	ABC	17.0
Remington Steele	NBC	17.0
Webster	ABC	17.0
28. Cagney & Lacey	CBS	16.9
29. Trapper John, M.D.	CBS	16.8
30. Hill Street Blues	NBC	16.6

September 1985–April 1986

Program	Network	Rating
1. The Cosby Show	NBC	33.7
2. Family Ties	NBC	30.0
3. Murder, She Wrote	CBS	25.3
4. 60 Minutes	CBS	23.9
5. Cheers	NBC	23.7
6. Dallas	CBS	21.9
7. Dynasty	ABC	21.8
The Golden Girls	NBC	21.8
9. Miami Vice	NBC	21.3
10. Who's the Boss?	ABC	21.1
11. Night Court	NBC	20.9
12. CBS Sunday Night Movie	CBS	20.5
13. Highway to Heaven	NBC	20.1
14. Kate & Allie	CBS	20.0
15. Monday Night Football	ABC	19.8
16. Newhart	CBS	19.6
17. Knots Landing	CBS	19.5
Growing Pains	ABC	19.5
19. You Again	NBC	19.2
20. 227	NBC	18.8
21. NBC Sunday Night Movie	NBC	18.5
22. Hotel	ABC	18.3
NBC Monday Night Movie	NBC	18.3
24. Moonlighting	ABC	18.1
Falcon Crest	CBS	18.1
Valerie	NBC	18.1
27. The Facts of Life	NBC	17.7
28. Scarecrow and Mrs. King	CBS	17.4
29. Simon & Simon	CBS	17.2
30. The A-Team	NBC	16.9

September 1986–April 1987

Program	Network	Rating
1. The Cosby Show	NBC	34.9
2. Family Ties	NBC	32.7
3. Cheers	NBC	27.2
4. Murder, She Wrote	CBS	25.4
5. The Golden Girls	NBC	24.5
6. 60 Minutes	CBS	23.3
7. Night Court	NBC	23.2
8. Growing Pains	ABC	22.7
9. Moonlighting	ABC	22.4
10. Who's the Boss?	ABC	22.0
11. Dallas	CBS	21.3
12. Newhart	CBS	19.5
13. Amen	NBC	19.4
14. 227	NBC	18.9
15. Matlock	NBC	18.6
CBS Sunday Night Movie	CBS	18.6
NBC Monday Night Movie	NBC	18.6
18. Monday Night Football	ABC	18.4
19. Kate & Allie	CBS	18.3
20. NBC Sunday Night Movie	NBC	18.2
21. L.A. Law	NBC	17.4
My Sister Sam	CBS	17.4
23. Falcon Crest	CBS	17.3
24. Highway to Heaven	NBC	17.2
Dynasty	ABC	17.2
26. Knots Landing	CBS	16.8
Miami Vice	NBC	16.8
28. Alf	NBC	16.5
Hunter	NBC	16.5
30. Head of the Class	ABC	16.4

September 1987–April 1988

Program	Network	Rating
1. The Cosby Show	NBC	27.8
2. A Different World	NBC	25.0
3. Cheers	NBC	23.4
4. The Golden Girls	NBC	21.8
5. Growing Pains	ABC	21.3
6. Who's the Boss?	ABC	21.2
7. Night Court	NBC	20.8
8. 60 Minutes	CBS	20.6
9. Murder, She Wrote	CBS	20.2
10. Alf	NBC	18.8
The Wonder Years	ABC	18.8
12. Moonlighting	ABC	18.3
L.A. Law	NBC	18.3
14. Matlock	NBC	17.8
15. Amen	NBC	17.5
16. Monday Night Football	ABC	17.4
17. Family Ties	NBC	17.3
18. CBS Sunday Night Movie	CBS	17.2
19. In the Heat of the Night	NBC	17.0
20. My Two Dads	NBC	16.9
Valerie's Family	NBC	16.9
22. Dallas	CBS	16.8
23. NBC Sunday Night Movie	NBC	16.7
Head of the Class	ABC	16.7
25. Newhart	CBS	16.5
26. NBC Monday Night Movie	NBC	16.4
27. 227	NBC	16.3
28. Day by Day	NBC	16.2
29. Hunter	NBC	16.1
30. Aaron's Way	NBC	16.0

October 1988–April 1989

Program	Network	Rating
1. The Cosby Show	NBC	25.6
2. Roseanne	ABC	23.8
3. A Different World	NBC	23.0
4. Cheers	NBC	22.3
5. 60 Minutes	CBS	21.7
6. The Golden Girls	NBC	21.4
7. Who's the Boss?	ABC	20.8
8. Murder, She Wrote	CBS	19.9
9. Empty Nest	NBC	19.2
10. Anything But Love	ABC	19.0
11. Dear John	NBC	18.5
12. Matlock	NBC	17.7
13. L.A. Law	NBC	17.6
Growing Pains	ABC	17.6
15. Alf	NBC	17.5
Monday Night Football	ABC	17.5
17. Unsolved Mysteries	NBC	17.4
18. In the Heat of the Night	NBC	17.3
19. Hunter	NBC	17.2
20. Head of the Class	ABC	17.1
21. Night Court	NBC	16.9
22. The Hogan Family	NBC	16.3
NBC Sunday Night Movie	NBC	16.3
The Wonder Years	ABC	16.3
25. Amen	NBC	16.2
NBC Monday Night Movie	NBC	16.2
27. Knots Landing	CBS	16.1
CBS Sunday Movie	CBS	16.1
29. ABC Mystery Movie	ABC	15.4
Dallas	CBS	15.4

September 1989–April 1990

Program	Network	Rating
1. The Cosby Show	NBC	23.1
Roseanne	ABC	23.1
3. Cheers	NBC	22.7
4. A Different World	NBC	21.1
5. America's Funniest Home Videos	ABC	20.9
6. The Golden Girls	NBC	20.1
7. 60 Minutes	CBS	19.7
8. The Wonder Years	ABC	19.2
9. Empty Nest	NBC	18.9
10. Monday Night Football	ABC	18.1
11. Unsolved Mysteries	NBC	18.0
12. Who's the Boss?	ABC	17.9
13. Murder, She Wrote	CBS	17.7
Chicken Soup	ABC	17.7
15. Grand	NBC	17.6
16. L.A. Law	NBC	17.4
17. Dear John	NBC	17.1
18. Coach	ABC	17.0
19. In the Heat of the Night	NBC	16.9
20. Matlock	NBC	16.6
21. Growing Pains	ABC	15.4
22. Full House	ABC	15.3
Designing Women	CBS	15.3
24. CBS Sunday Movie	CBS	14.9
Hunter	NBC	14.9
26. Head of the Class	ABC	14.8
27. Murphy Brown	CBS	14.7
28. The Simpsons	FOX	14.5
Night Court	NBC	14.5
Doogie Howser, M.D.	ABC	14.5

September 1990–April 1991

Program	Network	Rating
1. Cheers	NBC	21.3
2. 60 Minutes	CBS	20.6
3. Roseanne	ABC	18.1
4. A Different World	NBC	17.5
5. The Cosby Show	NBC	17.1
6. Murphy Brown	CBS	16.9
7. Empty Nest	NBC	16.7
America's Funniest Home Videos	ABC	16.7
9. Monday Night Football	ABC	16.6
10. The Golden Girls	NBC	16.5
11. Designing Women	CBS	16.5
12. Murder, She Wrote	CBS	16.4
13. America's Funniest People	ABC	16.3
14. Full House	ABC	15.9
15. Family Matters	ABC	15.8
16. Unsolved Mysteries	NBC	15.7
17. Matlock	NBC	15.5
18. Coach	ABC	15.3
19. Who's the Boss?	ABC	15.0
CBS Sunday Movie	CBS	15.0
21. In the Heat of the Night	NBC	14.9
Major Dad	CBS	14.9
23. L.A. Law	NBC	14.8
24. Doogie Howser, M.D.	ABC	14.7
25. Grand	NBC	14.6
26. Head of the Class	ABC	14.5
27. Growing Pains	ABC	14.3
Baby Talk	ABC	14.3
Davis Rules	ABC	14.3
30. The Wonder Years	ABC	14.2

September 1991–April 1992

Program	Network	Rating
1. 60 Minutes	CBS	21.9
2. Roseanne	ABC	19.9
3. Murphy Brown	CBS	18.6
4. Cheers	NBC	17.5
Home Improvement	ABC	17.5
6. Designing Women	CBS	17.3
7. Full House	ABC	17.0
8. Murder, She Wrote	CBS	16.9
9. Major Dad	CBS	16.8
10. Coach	ABC	16.7
Room for Two	ABC	16.7
12. Monday Night Football	ABC	16.6
13. Unsolved Mysteries	NBC	16.5
14. CBS Sunday Night Movie	CBS	15.9
15. Evening Shade	CBS	15.6
16. Northern Exposure	CBS	15.5
17. A Different World	NBC	15.2
18. The Cosby Show	NBC	15.0
19. Wings	NBC	14.6
20. Americas Funniest Home Videos	ABC	14.5
21. 20/20	ABC	14.4
22. Fresh Prince of Bel Air	NBC	14.3
Empty Nest	NBC	14.3
24. NBC Monday Movie	NBC	13.9
25. America's Funniest People	ABC	13.8
ABC Monday Movie	ABC	13.8
27. Family Matters	ABC	13.5
28. L.A. Law	NBC	13.3
29. 48 Hours	CBS	13.2
30. In the Heat of the Night	NBC	13.1
The Golden Girls	NBC	13.1

September 1992–April 1993

Program	Network	Rating
1. 60 Minutes	CBS	21.9
2. Roseanne	ABC	20.7
3. Home Improvement	ABC	19.4
4. Murphy Brown	CBS	17.9
5. Murder, She Wrote	CBS	17.7
6. Coach	ABC	17.5
7. Monday Night Football	ABC	16.7
8. CBS Sunday Movie	CBS	16.1
Cheers	NBC	16.1
10. Full House	ABC	15.8
11. Northern Exposure	CBS	15.2
12. 20/20	ABC	15.1
Rescue: 911	CBS	15.1
14. CBS Tuesday Movie	CBS	14.8
15. Love & War	CBS	14.7
16. Fresh Prince of Bel Air	NBC	14.6
Hangin' with Mr. Cooper	ABC	14.6
The Jackie Thomas Show	ABC	14.6
19. Evening Shade	CBS	14.5
20. Hearts Afire	CBS	14.3
21. Unsolved Mysteries	NBC	14.2
22. Primetime Live	ABC	14.1
23. Dr. Quinn, Medicine Woman	CBS	14.0
24. NBC Monday Movie	NBC	13.9
25. Seinfeld	NBC	13.7
26. 48 Hours	CBS	13.5
Blossom	NBC	13.5
28. ABC Sunday Night Movie	ABC	13.3
Matlock	ABC	13.3
30. Wings	NBC	13.0
The Simpsons	FOX	13.0

September 1993–April 1994

Program	Network	Rating
1. 60 Minutes	CBS	20.9
2. Home Improvement	ABC	20.4
3. Seinfeld	NBC	19.4
4. Roseanne	ABC	19.1
5. Grace Under Fire	ABC	17.7
6. Coach	ABC	17.4
7. Frasier	NBC	16.8
8. Monday Night Football	ABC	16.5
9. Murphy Brown	CBS	16.3
10. CBS Sunday Movie	CBS	16.2
11. Murder, She Wrote	CBS	16.0
12. Thunder Alley	ABC	15.9
13. Love & War	CBS	14.5
14. Northern Exposure	CBS	14.4
15. 20/20	ABC	14.3
16. Full House	ABC	14.2
17. Primetime Live	ABC	14.0
18. N.Y.P.D. Blue	ABC	13.9
Wings	NBC	13.9
20. Turning Point	ABC	13.8
21. Dave's World	CBS	13.7
Fresh Prince of Bel Air	NBC	13.7
23. NBC Monday Movie	NBC	13.6
24. Homicide: Life on the Street	NBC	13.5
25. CBS Tuesday Movie	CBS	13.3
Dr. Quinn, Medicine Woman	CBS	13.3
27. Phenom	ABC	13.2
Evening Shade	CBS	13.2
Rescue: 911	CBS	13.2
30. ABC Sunday Night Movie	ABC	12.6
Family Matters	ABC	12.6

September 1994–April 1995

Program	Network	Rating
1. Seinfeld	NBC	20.6
2. ER	NBC	20.0
3. Home Improvement	ABC	19.5
4. Grace Under Fire	ABC	18.6
5. Monday Night Football	ABC	17.7
6. 60 Minutes	CBS	17.2
7. N.Y.P.D. Blue	ABC	16.5
8. Murder, She Wrote	CBS	15.6
Friends	NBC	15.6
10. Roseanne	ABC	15.5
11. Mad About You	NBC	15.2
12. Madman of the People	NBC	14.9
13. Ellen	ABC	14.8
14. Hope & Gloria	ABC	14.6
15. Frasier	ABC	14.5
16. Murphy Brown	CBS	14.1
17. 20/20	ABC	14.0
18. CBS Sunday Movie	CBS	13.7
19. NBC Monday Movie	NBC	13.6
20. Me and the Boys	ABC	13.1
21. Dave's World	CBS	12.9
22. Cybill	CBS	12.8
23. ABC Sunday Movie	ABC	12.7
24.The Nanny	CBS	12.5
25. Full House	CBS	12.4
26. Wings	NBC	12.3
27. Law & Order	NBC	12.2
28. NBC Sunday Night Movie	NBC	12.0
29. Chicago Hope	CBS	11.7
ABC Monday Night Movie	ABC	11.7
The Martin Short Show	NBC	11.7
Primetime Live	ABC	11.7

September 1995–May 1996

Program	Network	Rating
1. ER	NBC	22.0
2. Seinfeld	NBC	21.2
3. Friends	NBC	18.7
4. Caroline in the City	NBC	18.0
5. Monday Night Football	ABC	17.1
6. The Single Guy	NBC	16.7
7. Home Improvement	ABC	16.1
8. Boston Common	NBC	15.6
9. 60 Minutes	CBS	14.2
10. N.Y.P.D. Blue	ABC	14.1
11. 20/20	ABC	13.6
Frasier	NBC	13.6
13. Grace Under Fire	ABC	13.2
14. NBC Monday Movie	NBC	12.9
Coach	ABC	12.9
16. The Nanny	CBS	12.5
Roseanne	ABC	12.5
18. Walker, Texas Ranger	CBS	12.3
Primetime Live	ABC	12.3
Murphy Brown	CBS	12.3
21. NBC Sunday Movie	NBC	12.2
22. 3rd Rock from the Sun	NBC	12.1
23. Chicago Hope	CBS	11.9
24. Law & Order	NBC	11.4
CBS Sunday Movie	CBS	11.4
The Naked Truth	ABC	11.4
Can't Hurry Love	CBS	11.4
28. Dateline NBC—Tuesday	NBC	11.3
Dateline NBC—Wednesday	NBC	11.3
30. The Dana Carvey Show	ABC	11.2

September 1996–May 1997

Program	Network	Rating
1. ER	NBC	21.2
2. Seinfeld	NBC	20.5
3. Suddenly Susan	NBC	17.0
4. Friends	NBC	16.8
The Naked Truth	NBC	16.8
6. Fired Up	NBC	16.5
7. Monday Night Football	ABC	16.0
8. The Single Guy	NBC	14.1
9. Home Improvement	ABC	14.0
10. Touched by an Angel	CBS	13.6
11. 60 Minutes	CBS	13.3
12. 20/20	ABC	12.8
13. N.Y.P.D. Blue	ABC	12.5
14. CBS Sunday Movie	CBS	12.1
15. Primetime Live	ABC	11.9
16. Frasier	NBC	11.8
17. Spin City	ABC	11.7
18. NBC Sunday Movie	NBC	11.5
The Drew Carey Show	ABC	11.5
20. Dateline NBC—Tuesday	NBC	11.4
21. Cosby	CBS	11.2
The X-Files	FOX	11.2
23. Walker, Texas Ranger	CBS	11.0
Mad About You	NBC	11.0
Caroline in the City	NBC	11.0
NBC Monday Movie	NBC	11.0
27. Law & Order	NBC	10.8
3rd Rock from the Sun	NBC	10.8
29. Ellen	ABC	10.6
30. Chicago Hope	CBS	10.5
Dateline NBC—Friday	NBC	10.5
Cybill	CBS	10.5

September 1997–May 1998

Program	Network	Rating
1. Seinfeld	NBC	21.7
2. ER	NBC	20.4
3. Veronica's Closet	NBC	16.6
4. Friends	NBC	16.1
5. Monday Night Football	ABC	15.0
6. Touched by an Angel	CBS	14.2
7. 60 Minutes	CBS	13.8
8. Union Square	NBC	13.6
9. CBS Sunday Movie	CBS	13.1
10. Frasier	NBC	12.0
Home Improvement	ABC	12.0
12. Just Shoot Me	NBC	11.9
13. Dateline NBC—Tuesday	NBC	11.5
14. Dateline NBC—Monday	NBC	11.4
15. The Drew Carey Show	ABC	11.1
16. 20/20—Friday	ABC	10.9
17. N.Y.P.D. Blue	ABC	10.8
Primetime Live	ABC	10.8
19. The X-Files	FOX	10.6
20. Law & Order	NBC	10.2
21. 20/20—Monday	ABC	10.0
22. Diagnosis Murder	CBS	9.8
23. King of the Hill	FOX	9.7
Mad About You	NBC	9.7
25. Cosby	CBS	9.5
Dharma & Greg	ABC	9.5
27. NBC Sunday Night Movie	NBC	9.4
28. Hiller and Diller	ABC	9.3
Walker, Texas Ranger	CBS	9.3
30. Everybody Loves Raymond	CBS	9.2
The Simpsons	FOX	9.2

September 1998–May 1999

Program	Network	Rating
1. ER	NBC	17.8
2. Friends	NBC	15.7
3. Frasier	NBC	15.6
4. Monday Night Football	ABC	14.0
5. Veronica's Closet	NBC	13.7
Jesse	NBC	13.7
7. 60 Minutes	CBS	13.2
8. Touched by an Angel	CBS	13.1
9. CBS Sunday Movie	CBS	12.0
10. Home Improvement	ABC	11.0
11. Everybody Loves Raymond	CBS	10.6
12. N.Y.P.D. Blue	ABC	10.5
13. Law & Order	NBC	10.1
14. The Drew Carey Show	ABC	9.9
20/20—Friday	ABC	9.9
16. Providence	NBC	9.8
20/20—Wednesday	ABC	9.8
JAG	CBS	9.8
19. Dateline NBC—Tuesday	NBC	9.7
Dateline NBC—Monday	NBC	9.7
Becker	CBS	9.7
CBS Tuesday Movie	CBS	9.7
23. Ally McBeal	FOX	9.6
24. Dharma & Greg	ABC	9.3
25. Spin City	ABC	9.2
Walker, Texas Ranger	CBS	9.2
Dateline NBC—Friday	NBC	9.2
28. The X-Files	FOX	9.1
NBC Sunday Night Movie	NBC	9.1
30. 60 Minutes II	CBS	9.0
Diagnosis Murder	CBS	9.0

September 1999–May 2000

Program	Network	Rating
1. Who Wants to Be a Millionaire?—Tuesday	ABC	18.6
2. Who Wants to Be a Millionaire?—Thursday	ABC	17.5
3. Who Wants to Be a Millionaire?—Sunday	ABC	17.1
4. ER	NBC	16.9
5. Friends	NBC	14.0
6. Frasier	NBC	13.6
7. Monday Night Football	ABC	13.5
8. 60 Minutes	CBS	12.0
9. The Practice	ABC	11.8
10. Touched by an Angel	CBS	11.6
11. Law & Order	NBC	11.5
12. Everybody Loves Raymond	CBS	11.4
13. Jesse	NBC	11.3
14. CBS Sunday Movie	CBS	10.9
15. Stark Raving Mad	NBC	10.7
N.Y.P.D. Blue	ABC	10.7
17. Dharma & Greg	ABC	10.5
18. Becker	CBS	10.4
19. Judging Amy	CBS	10.2
20. JAG	CBS	9.7
21. The Drew Carey Show	ABC	9.5
22. Providence	NBC	9.4
23. 60 Minutes II	CBS	9.3
24. The West Wing	NBC	9.1
ABC Monday Movie	ABC	9.1
Spin City	ABC	9.1
27. Family Law	CBS	9.0
28. Dateline NBC—Friday	NBC	8.9
Malcolm in the Middle	FOX	8.9
30. Law & Order: Special Victims Unit	NBC	8.8
CBS Wednesday Movie	CBS	8.8

September 2000–May 2001

Program	Network	Rating
1. Survivor	CBS	17.4
2. ER	NBC	15.0
3. Who Wants to Be a Millionaire?—Wednesday	ABC	13.7
4. Who Wants to Be a Millionaire?—Tuesday	ABC	13.0
5. Friends	NBC	12.6
Monday Night Football	ABC	12.6
Everybody Loves Raymond	CBS	12.6
8. Who Wants to Be a Millionaire?—Sunday	ABC	12.4
9. Law & Order	NBC	12.3
10. The Practice	ABC	11.7
11. Who Wants to Be a Millionaire?—Thursday	ABC	11.6
CSI: Crime Scene Investigation	CBS	11.6
The West Wing	NBC	11.6
14. Will & Grace	NBC	11.3
15. 60 Minutes	CBS	11.1
16. Becker	CBS	10.9
17. Temptation Island	FOX	10.7
Frasier	NBC	10.7
19. Who Wants to Be a Millionaire?—Friday	ABC	10.5
20. Just Shoot Me	NBC	10.4
21. Judging Amy	CBS	9.9
22. Cursed/The Weber Show	NBC	9.7
N.Y.P.D. Blue	ABC	9.7
Touched by an Angel	CBS	9.7
25. Law & Order: Special Victims Unit	NBC	9.4
26. JAG	CBS	9.2
27. King of Queens	CBS	8.9
28. Yes, Dear	CBS	8.7
29. Family Law	CBS	8.6
The District	CBS	8.6
CBS Sunday Movie	CBS	8.6

September 2001–May 2002

Program	Network	Rating
1. Friends	NBC	15.0
2. CSI: Crime Scene Investigation	CBS	14.5
3. ER	NBC	14.2
4. Everybody Loves Raymond	CBS	12.8
5. Law & Order	NBC	12.6
6. Survivor	CBS	11.8
7. Monday Night Football	ABC	11.5
8. The West Wing	NBC	11.4
9. Will & Grace	NBC	11.0
Leap of Faith	NBC	11.0
11. Becker	CBS	10.7
12. Law & Order: Special Victims Unit	NBC	10.4
13. 60 Minutes	CBS	10.1
14. Frasier	NBC	9.9
JAG	CBS	9.9
16. Inside Schwartz	NBC	9.8
Judging Amy	CBS	9.8
18. Just Shoot Me	NBC	9.3
19. King of Queens	CBS	8.9
20. Yes, Dear	CBS	8.8
Crossing Jordan	NBC	8.8
22. The Guardian	CBS	8.4
23. The Practice	ABC	8.3
N.Y.P.D. Blue	ABC	8.3
25. Baby Bob	CBS	8.1
Dateline NBC—Friday	NBC	8.1
27. Fear Factor	NBC	7.9
Law & Order: Criminal Intent	NBC	7.9
Providence	NBC	7.9
30. 60 Minutes II	CBS	7.7
Family Law	CBS	7.7

September 2002–May 2003

Program	Network	Rating
1. CSI: Crime Scene Investigation	CBS	16.3
2. Friends	NBC	13.9
3. Joe Millionaire	FOX	13.3
4. ER	NBC	13.1
5. American Idol—Tuesday	FOX	12.6
6. American Idol—Wednesday	FOX	12.5
7. Survivor (Thailand & Amazon)	CBS	11.9
Everybody Loves Raymond	CBS	11.9
9. Law & Order	NBC	11.7
10. Monday Night Football	ABC	11.4
11. CSI: Miami	CBS	11.0
Will & Grace	NBC	11.0
13. Scrubs	NBC	10.3
14. Law & Order: Special Victims Unit	NBC	10.1
15. Without a Trace	CBS	10.0
16. The Bachelor/Bachelorette	ABC	9.9
17. 60 Minutes	CBS	9.6
18. Judging Amy	CBS	9.5
19. Law & Order: Criminal Intent	NBC	9.4
Still Standing	CBS	9.4
21. The West Wing	NBC	9.0
22. JAG	CBS	8.9
23. Good Morning, Miami	NBC	8.7
24. Yes, Dear	CBS	8.6
25. King of Queens	CBS	8.5
26. Frasier	NBC	8.4
27. The Guardian	CBS	8.3
28. My Big Fat Greek Life	CBS	8.0
29. N.Y.P.D. Blue	ABC	7.8
30. Fear Factor	NBC	7.7

APPENDIX 4

LONGEST-RUNNING SERIES

The following is a listing of the longest-running series on nighttime broadcast network television, excluding movies and newscasts. A series is counted as having aired in a season if it was on for at least two months during that season. Seasons in which a series aired at other times of the day (for example, in the daytime), or on local stations, are not counted. Also not counted are late-night reruns (on *ABC Late Night* and *The CBS Late Night Movies*) of series that originally aired in prime time (for example, *Baretta, Police Woman,* and *M*A*S*H*).

Meet the Press is the longest-running series in all of television, having been on the air continuously since 1947. Only the eighteen seasons that it spent on the nighttime schedule (post 6:00 P.M.) are counted here, however.

Alternate titles are given in parentheses. The 2002–2003 season is the last one counted.

49 Seasons

The Tonight Show

35 Seasons

60 Minutes

34 Seasons

Walt Disney

33 Seasons

Monday Night Football

28 Seasons

Saturday Night Live

26 Seasons

20/20

24 Seasons

The Ed Sullivan Show (The Toast of the Town)

22 Seasons

Late Show with David Letterman (Late Night with David Letterman)

20 Seasons

Gunsmoke
The Red Skelton Show (The Red Skelton Hour)

18 Seasons

Friday Night Videos
Meet the Press
Monday Night Baseball
What's My Line

17 Seasons

Candid Camera (Candid Microphone)
Lassie
The Lawrence Welk Show (Lawrence Welk's Dodge Dancing Party)

16 Seasons

America's Most Wanted
48 Hours
Kraft Television Theatre (Kraft Suspense Theater, Kraft Mystery Theater)

15 Seasons

Cops
I've Got a Secret
The Jack Benny Show
The Jackie Gleason Show (The Honeymooners)
The Perry Como Show (Chesterfield Supper Club)

14 Seasons

The Adventures of Ozzie & Harriet
Armstrong Circle Theatre (Circle Theatre)
Bonanza
Dallas
The Gillette Cavalcade of Sports (The Cavalcade of Sports)
Knots Landing
The Simpsons

13 Seasons

All in the Family (Archie Bunker's Place)
America's Funniest Home Videos
The Danny Thomas Show (Make Room for Daddy, Make Room for Granddaddy)
The Dinah Shore Show (The Dinah Shore Chevy Show)
Later
Law & Order

12 Seasons

Dateline NBC
Dragnet
Hawaii Five-O
The Lucy Show (Here's Lucy)
Murder, She Wrote
My Three Sons
The Original Amateur Hour
Pabst Blue Ribbon Bouts (International Boxing Club Bouts, The Wednesday Night Fights)
Primetime Live (Primetime Thursday)
The 20th Century (The 21st Century)

11 Seasons

Alfred Hitchcock Presents (The Alfred Hitchcock Hour)
Arthur Godfrey's Talent Scouts
The Arthur Murray Party
CBS Reports/News Hour/News Special
The Carol Burnett Show
Cheers
Fireside Theatre (Jane Wyman's Fireside Theater, The Jane Wyman Show)
General Electric Theater (General Electric True)
Happy Days
The Jeffersons
M*A*S*H
Married . . . with Children
The Milton Berle Show (The Texaco Star Theater, The Buick-Berle Show, Milton Berle Starring in the Kraft Music Hall)
Pantomime Quiz (Stump the Stars)
To Tell the Truth
Unsolved Mysteries
The Voice of Firestone
You Bet Your Life (The Groucho Show)

10 Seasons

Arthur Godfrey and His Friends (The Arthur Godfrey Show)
Beverly Hills 90210
Columbo
Frasier
Late Night with Conan O'Brien
Murphy Brown
N.Y.P.D. Blue
Perry Mason (The New Adventures of Perry Mason)
The Steve Allen Show (The Steve Allen Comedy Hour)
Studio One
The U.S. Steel Hour
Your Hit Parade

9 Seasons

ABC in Concert
Alice
The Andy Williams Show
Beat the Clock
The Beverly Hillbillies
Break the Bank
Coach
The Dean Martin Show
Dynasty
ER
The F.B.I.
The Facts of Life
Falcon Crest
Family Matters
Father Knows Best
Friends
Goodyear TV Playhouse (Goodyear Theater)
Little House on the Prairie (Little House: A New Beginning)
The Love Boat
Masquerade Party
Matlock
The Midnight Special
Mission: Impossible
Night Court
One Day at a Time
Roseanne
Seinfeld
This Is Your Life
Three's Company (Three's A Crowd)
The Tomorrow Show
Touched by an Angel
The Twilight Zone
The Virginian (The Men from Shiloh)
The Waltons
The X-Files
You Asked for It (The Art Baker Show)

8 Seasons

The Alcoa Hour (Alcoa Theatre, Alcoa Presents, Alcoa Premiere)
The Andy Griffith Show
Barnaby Jones
Barney Miller
The Bell Telephone Hour
Bewitched
The Big Story
Cheyenne
The Cosby Show
Diff'rent Strokes
The Donna Reed Show
The Drew Carey Show
Full House
The Garry Moore Show
The George Burns and Gracie Allen Show
The Golden Girls (The Golden Palace)
Home Improvement
I Love Lucy (The Sunday Lucy Show, The Top 10 Lucy Shows)
Ironside
JAG
L.A. Law
Laverne & Shirley
The Lone Ranger
The Loretta Young Show (A Letter to Loretta)
Lux Video Theatre (Lux Playhouse)
Mad TV
Magnum, P.I.
Mama
Mannix
Mark Saber (Mystery Theater, Inspector Mark Saber—Homicide Squad, The Vise, Saber of London)

Melrose Place
Midwestern Hayride
Newhart
People Are Funny
Perfect Strangers
Person to Person
Rawhide
Robert Montgomery Presents
Schlitz Playhouse of Stars (Schlitz Playhouse)
Simon & Simon
Wagon Train
Walker, Texas Ranger
Who's the Boss?
Wings

7 Seasons

Adam 12
Benson
Boy Meets World
Buffy the Vampire Slayer
Cagney & Lacey
Captain Video and His Video Rangers
Designing Women
Diagnosis Murder
The Dukes of Hazzard
The Eddie Fisher Show (Coke Time with Eddie Fisher)
Empty Nest
Everybody Loves Raymond
Family Ties
Fantasy Island
Ford Theatre
The Gene Autry Show
Growing Pains
Hill Street Blues
The Hollywood Palace
Homicide: Life on the Street
Hunter
In the Heat of the Night
Just Shoot Me
King of the Hill
Kukla, Fran & Ollie
Life Begins at Eighty
The Life of Riley
MacGyver
Mad About You
Marcus Welby, M.D.
The Mary Tyler Moore Show
McCloud
Medical Center
Name That Tune
Petticoat Junction
Philco TV Playhouse
The Practice
The Price Is Right
Quincy, M.E.
The Quiz Kids
Red Barber's Corner (Red Barber's Clubhouse, The Peak of the Sports News)
Rescue 911
Sabrina, the Teenage Witch
7th Heaven
Step By Step
Suspense
This Is Show Business
Trapper John, M.D.
Who Said That?

6 Seasons

The Author Meets the Critics
Big Town
The Bob Newhart Show
Boy Meets World
Broadway to Hollywood—Headline Clues
Chicago Hope
CHiPs
The Colgate Comedy Hour
Daniel Boone
Dawson's Creek
December Bride
Dick Powell's Zane Grey Theater
A Different World
Dr. Quinn, Medicine Woman
Down You Go
Emergency
The Flintstones
Focus
The Fred Waring Show
Fresh Prince of Bel Air
The George Gobel Show
The Gillette Summer Sports Reel
Gimme a Break
The Goldbergs
Gomer Pyle, U.S.M.C.
Good Times
Green Acres
Have Gun Will Travel
The Hogan Family (Valerie, Valerie's Family)
Hogan's Heroes
Hollywood Screen Test
Kate & Allie
Leave It to Beaver
The Life and Legend of Wyatt Earp
Life Is Worth Living
The Lineup
Man Against Crime
Maude
McMillan and Wife (McMillan)
The Millionaire
Mr. Belvedere
Moesha
NBC Mystery Movie (NBC Sunday/Tuesday/Wednesday Mystery Movie)
The Nanny
Nash Bridges
Northern Exposure
Ozark Jubilee (Country Music Jubilee, Jubilee U.S.A.)
Party of Five
Paul Whiteman's TV Teen Club
Politically Incorrect
The Real McCoys
Real People
The Rockford Files
Rocky King, Inside Detective (Inside Detective)
Rowan & Martin's Laugh-In
The Roy Rogers Show
St. Elsewhere
The Sammy Kaye Show (So You Want to Lead a Band, Music from Manhattan)
Sanford and Son

77 Sunset Strip
Sister, Sister
Sisters
The Sonny and Cher Comedy Hour (The Sonny and Cher Show)
Star Trek Voyager
The Steve Harvey Show
Stop the Music
Tales of Wells Fargo
That's Incredible (Incredible Sunday)
3rd Rock from the Sun
Twenty Questions
The Web
The Wonder Years

APPENDIX 5

THE TOP 100 SERIES OF ALL TIME

In 1985 we published a small paperback book called *TV's Greatest Hits*, which contained our first-ever ranking of the most popular TV series of all time. The following is an updated version of that ranking, including data through the 2002–2003 season. It reflects not our choices, but those of you, the viewer. It was compiled by assigning each prime-time series points based on the number of seasons it was telecast, and its audience size ranking each year. (Detailed information on these two measures will be found in the "Top-Rated Programs by Season" and "Longest-Running Series" appendixes.) Thus, series were given credit for both popularity and longevity.

Some series currently on the air are still moving up the list; *60 Minutes,* which ranked number nine on the 1985 all-time list, is by virtue of its continued popularity now number one.

Program	Network(s)	From	To
1. 60 Minutes	CBS	1968	——
2. Gunsmoke	CBS	1955	1975
3. The Red Skelton Show	NBC, CBS	1951	1971
4. Bonanza	NBC	1959	1973
5. All in the Family/Archie Bunker's Place	CBS	1971	1983
6. Walt Disney	ABC, NBC, CBS	1954	1990
7. The Ed Sullivan Show/Toast of the Town	CBS	1948	1971
8. The Lucy Show/Here's Lucy	CBS	1962	1974
9. ER	NBC	1994	——
10. Murder, She Wrote	CBS	1984	1996
11. Friends	NBC	1994	——
12. M*A*S*H	CBS	1972	1983
13. Cheers	NBC	1982	1993
14. Dallas	CBS	1978	1991
15. The Cosby Show	NBC	1984	1992
16. Frasier	NBC	1993	——
17. The Andy Griffith Show	CBS	1960	1968
18. Roseanne	ABC	1988	1997
19. Home Improvement	ABC	1991	1999
20. The Jack Benny Show	CBS, NBC	1950	1965
21. Three's Company/Three's a Crowd	ABC	1977	1985
22. I Love Lucy	CBS	1951	1961
23. The Danny Thomas Show	ABC, CBS	1953	1971
24. The Beverly Hillbillies	CBS	1962	1971
25. You Bet Your Life	NBC	1950	1961
26. Happy Days	ABC	1974	1984
27. 20/20	ABC	1978	——
28. I've Got a Secret	CBS	1952	1967
29. Dragnet/Dragnet '67	NBC	1952	1970
30. Arthur Godfrey's Talent Scouts	CBS	1948	1958
31. The Jeffersons	CBS	1975	1985
32. Seinfeld	NBC	1990	1998
33. Law & Order	NBC	1990	——
34. Hawaii Five-O	CBS	1968	1980
35. The Jackie Gleason Show	CBS	1952	1970
36. N.Y.P.D. Blue	ABC	1993	——
37. One Day at a Time	CBS	1975	1984
38. The Golden Girls/The Golden Palace	NBC, CBS	1985	1993
39. Laverne & Shirley	ABC	1976	1983
40. The Milton Berle Show	NBC, ABC	1948	1967
41. Sanford and Son	NBC	1972	1977
42. Murphy Brown	CBS	1988	1998
43. Gomer Pyle, U.S.M.C.	CBS	1964	1970
44. Alice	CBS	1976	1985
45. Dynasty	ABC	1981	1989
46. Wagon Train	NBC, ABC	1957	1965
47. A Different World	NBC	1987	1993
48. My Three Sons	ABC, CBS	1960	1972
49. Everybody Loves Raymond	CBS	1996	——
50. Candid Camera	CBS, NBC, ABC, PAX	1948	——

51. Bewitched	ABC	1964	1972
52. Who's the Boss?	ABC	1984	1992
53. The Love Boat	ABC	1977	1986
54. Fireside Theatre	NBC, ABC	1949	1963
55. Little House on the Prairie	NBC	1974	1983
56. Coach	ABC	1989	1997
57. The Waltons	CBS	1972	1981
58. Have Gun, Will Travel	CBS	1957	1963
59. Touched by an Angel	CBS	1994	2003
60. General Electric Theater	CBS	1953	1962
61. Falcon Crest	CBS	1981	1990
62. Arthur Godfrey and His Friends	CBS	1949	1959
63. The Mary Tyler Moore Show	CBS	1970	1977
64. Maude	CBS	1972	1978
65. Family Ties	NBC	1982	1989
66. Marcus Welby, M.D.	ABC	1969	1976
67. Magnum, P.I.	CBS	1980	1988
68. Ironside	NBC	1967	1975
69. The Colgate Comedy Hour	NBC	1950	1955
70. Rowan & Martin's Laugh-In	NBC	1968	1973
71. Full House	ABC	1987	1995
72. Knots Landing	CBS	1979	1993
73. December Bride	CBS	1954	1960
74. Family Affair	CBS	1966	1971
75. Night Court	NBC	1984	1992
76. The Dean Martin Show	NBC	1965	1974
77. Growing Pains	ABC	1985	1992
78. The Dukes of Hazzard	CBS	1979	1985
79. The Virginian	NBC	1962	1971
80. The Dick Van Dyke Show	CBS	1961	1966
81. Newhart	CBS	1982	1990
82. Lassie	CBS	1954	1971
83. The Real McCoys	ABC, CBS	1957	1963
84. Perry Mason	CBS	1957	1974
85. America's Funniest Home Videos	ABC	1990	—
86. Primetime Live/Primetime Thursday	ABC	1989	—
87. Simon & Simon	CBS	1981	1989
88. The Perry Como Show	NBC, CBS	1948	1963
89. Matlock	NBC, ABC	1986	1995
90. Empty Nest	NBC	1988	1995
91. Charlie's Angels	ABC	1976	1981
92. CSI: Crime Scene Investigation	CBS	2000	—
93. L.A. Law	NBC	1986	1994
94. The Flip Wilson Show	NBC	1970	1974
95. Columbo	NBC, ABC	1971	1993
96. Philco TV Playhouse	NBC	1948	1955
97. Adam 12	NBC	1968	1975
98. The A-Team	NBC	1983	1987
99. The Lawrence Welk Show	ABC	1955	1971
100. Green Acres	CBS	1965	1971

APPENDIX 6
PRIME TIME SERIES REUNION TELECASTS

A successful TV series is something to be treasured, remembered, and, often, revived. Although reunions took place as early as the 1960s, gathering together the casts of past series became increasingly popular in the 1980s, as producers sought to capitalize on a wave of TV nostalgia. Sometimes these reunions tested the waters for series revivals (*Make Room for Granddaddy* and *The New Leave It to Beaver* were launched this way), but more often they were one-time affairs. A unique case is *Perry Mason*; its 1985 reunion movie led to a continuing series of made-for-TV movies, with two or three new ones produced each year thereafter. The last of the twenty-six starring Raymond Burr aired on November 29, 1993, a couple of months after his death.

Following is a list of network TV series whose casts were reunited in a TV movie or special long after the series had left the air. Following the name of the original series is the title of the reunion episode and the date on which it aired. To qualify for this list the reunion must have occurred at least two years after the original series ended (eliminating quick follow-ups such as those for *Emergency*, *Little House on the Prairie, The Love Boat,* and *The Waltons*); it must have been produced for TV (not for the theater, as was the *Peter Gunn* film *Gunn* and the *Get Smart* film *The Nude Bomb*); and it must have featured a majority of the original series' cast (no *The New Gidget* or *Bonanza: The Next Generation* allowed) in character, in a new story. Not included are retrospective "clip shows," in which the original actors (or others) simply appeared to talk about the original series. Additionally, only series with a continuing story line and cast are included; revivals of variety or anthology programs such as *Alfred Hitchcock Presents, Candid Camera, The Smothers Brothers Comedy Hour, That's Incredible,* and *This Is Your Life* have been excluded.

The Addams Family—"Halloween with the Addams Family" (10/30/77)
The Adventures of Ozzie and Harriet—"Ozzie's Girls" (9/10/72)
Alf—"Project Alf" (2/17/96)
Alien Nation—"Alien Nation: Dark Horizon" (10/25/94)
Alien Nation—"Alien Nation: Body and Soul" (10/10/95)
Alien Nation—"Alien Nation: Millennium" (1/2/96)
Alien Nation—"The Enemy Within" (11/12/96)
The Andy Griffith Show—"Return to Mayberry" (4/13/86)
Babylon 5—"Babylon 5: The Legend of the Rangers" (1/19/02)
Baywatch—"Baywatch Hawaiian Wedding" (2/28/03)
Ben Casey—"The Return of Ben Casey" (2/13/88)
The Beverly Hillbillies—"The Return of the Beverly Hillbillies" (10/6/81)
The Beverly Hillbillies—"The Legend of the Beverly Hillbillies (5/24/93)
The Bionic Woman—"The Return of the Six Million Dollar Man and the Bionic Woman" (5/17/87)
The Bionic Woman—"Bionic Showdown" (4/30/89)
The Bionic Woman—"Bionic Ever After" (11/29/94)
The Bob Newhart Show—"The Bob Newhart Show 20th Anniversary Special" (11/23/91)
The Brady Bunch—"A Very Brady Christmas" (12/12/88)
The Brady Bunch—"The Brady Bunch in the White House" (11/29/02)
Cagney & Lacey—"Cagney & Lacey: The Reunion" (11/6/94)
Cagney & Lacey—"Cagney & Lacey: Together Again" (4/30/95)
Cagney & Lacey—"Cagney & Lacey: The View Through the Glass Ceiling" (10/25/95)
Cagney & Lacey—"Cagney & Lacey: True Convictions" (1/29/96)
Cannon—"The Return of Frank Cannon" (11/1/80)
CHiPS—"CHiPS 99" (10/27/98)
Christy—"Christy: The Movie" (11/19/00)
Christy—"Christy: Choices of the Heart" (5/13 & 14/01)
Columbo—"Columbo: Ashes to Ashes" (10/9/98)
Columbo—"Columbo: Murder with Too Many Notes" (3/12/01)
Columbo—"Columbo Likes the Nightlife" (1/30/03)
Dallas—"Dallas: J.R. Returns" (11/15/96)
Dallas—"Dallas: War of the Ewings" (4/24/98)
The Danny Thomas Show—"Make More Room For Daddy" (11/6/67)
The Danny Thomas Show—"Make Room For Granddaddy" (9/14/69)
Dr. Quinn, Medicine Woman—"Dr. Quinn, Medicine Woman: The Heart Within" (5/12/01)
The Dukes of Hazzard—"The Dukes of Hazzard Reunion" (4/25/97)
The Dukes of Hazzard—"Dukes of Hazzard: Hazzard in Hollywood" (5/19/00)
Dynasty—"Dynasty: The Reunion" (10/20 & 22/91)

Eight Is Enough—"Eight Is Enough: A Family Reunion"(10/18/87)
Eight Is Enough—"An Eight Is Enough Wedding" (10/15/89)
The Facts of Life—"The Facts of Life Reunion" (11/18/01)
Father Knows Best—"The Father Knows Best Reunion" (5/15/77)
Father Knows Best—"Father Knows Best: Home For Christmas" (12/18/77)
Get Smart—"Get Smart, Again" (2/26/89)
Gilligan's Island—"Rescue From Gilligan's Island" (10/14 & 21/78)
Gilligan's Island—"The Castaways on Gilligan's Island" (5/3/79)
Gilligan's Island—"The Harlem Globetrotters on Gilligan's Island" (5/15/81)
Gilligan's Island—"Surviving Gilligan's Island" (10/14/01)
Green Acres—"Return to Green Acres" (5/18/90)
Growing Pains—"The Growing Pains Movie" (11/5/00)
Gunsmoke—"Gunsmoke: Return to Dodge" (9/26/87)
Gunsmoke—"Gunsmoke: The Last Apache" (3/18/90)
Gunsmoke—"Gunsmoke III: To the Last Man" (1/10/92)
Gunsmoke—"Gunsmoke: The Long Ride" (5/8/93)
Gunsmoke—"Gunsmoke: One Man's Justice" (2/10/94)
Hart to Hart—"Hart to Hart Returns" (11/5/93) (Note: Subsequently, NBC aired several *Hart to Hart* movies as part of its *Friday Mystery Movie* series in 1994 and The Family Channel aired three more during the 1995–1996 season.)
Homicide: Life on the Street—"Homicide: The Movie" (2/13/00)
The Honeymooners—"The Honeymooners Second Honeymoon" (2/2/76)
The Honeymooners—"The Honeymooners Christmas" (11/28/77)
The Honeymooners—"The Honeymooners Valentine Special" (2/13/78)
The Honeymooners—"The Honeymooners Christmas Special" (12/10/78)
Hunter—"The Return of Hunter" (5/2/95)
Hunter—"Hunter: Return to Justice" (11/16/02)
I Dream of Jeannie—"I Dream of Jeannie: 15 Years Later" (10/20/85)
I Dream of Jeannie—"I Still Dream of Jeannie" (10/20/91)
I Spy—"I Spy Returns" (2/3/94)
The Incredible Hulk—"The Incredible Hulk Returns" (5/24/88)
The Incredible Hulk—"The Trial of the Incredible Hulk" (5/6/89)
The Incredible Hulk—"The Death of the Incredible Hulk" (2/18/90)
Ironside—"The Return of Ironside" (5/4/93)
Knight Rider—"Knight Rider 2000" (5/19/91)
Knots Landing—"Knots Landing: Back to the Cul-de-Sac" (5/7 & 9/97)
Kojak—"Kojak: The Belarus File" (2/16/85)
Kojak—"Kojak: The Price of Justice" (2/21/87)
Kung Fu—"Kung Fu the Movie" (2/1/86)
L.A. Law—"L.A. Law: The Movie" (5/12/02)
Leave It to Beaver—"Still the Beaver" (3/19/83)
The Life and Legend of Wyatt Earp—"Wyatt Earp: Return to Tombstone" (7/2/94)
The Life and Times of Grizzly Adams—"The Capture of Grizzly Adams" (2/1/82)
MacGyver—"MacGyver: Lost Treasure of Atlantis" (5/14/94)
MacGyver—"MacGyver: Doomsday" (11/24/94)
The Man From U.N.C.L.E.—"The Return of the Man From U.N.C.L.E.: The 15 Years Later Affair" (4/5/83)
The Many Loves of Dobie Gillis—"Whatever Happened to Dobie Gillis" (5/10/77)
The Many Loves of Dobie Gillis—"Bring Me the Head of Dobie Gillis" (2/21/88)
Marcus Welby, M.D.—"The Return of Marcus Welby"(5/16/84)
Marcus Welby, M.D.—"Marcus Welby, M.D.—A Holiday Affair" (12/19/88)
The Mary Tyler Moore Show—"Mary and Rhoda" (2/7/00)
Maverick—"The New Maverick" (9/3/78)
McCloud—"The Return of Sam McCloud" (11/12/89)
The Mod Squad—"The Return of the Mod Squad" (5/18/79)
The Munsters—"The Munsters' Revenge" (2/27/81)
Murder, She Wrote—"Murder, She Wrote: A Story to Die for" (5/18/00)
Murder, She Wrote—"Murder, She Wrote: The Last Free Man" (5/2/01)
Murder, She Wrote—"Murder, She Wrote: The Celtic Riddle" (5/9/03)
My Three Sons—"The Partridge Family—My Three Sons Reunion" (11/25/77)
The Odd Couple—"The Odd Couple" (9/24/93)
The Partridge Family—"The Partridge Family—My Three Sons Reunion" (11/25/77)
The Patty Duke Show—"The Patty Duke Show: Still Rockin' in Brooklyn Heights" (4/27/99)
Perry Mason—"Perry Mason Returns" (12/1/85)
Peyton Place—"Peyton Place: The Next Generation" (5/13/85)
The Rockford Files—"The Rockford Files: I Still Love L.A." (11/27/94)
The Rockford Files—"The Rockford Files: A Blessing in Disguise" (5/14/95)
The Rockford Files—"The Rockford Files: If the Frame Fits" (1/14/96)

The Rockford Files—"The Rockford Files: Godfather Knows Best" (2/18/96)
The Rockford Files—"The Rockford Files: Friends and Foul Play" (4/25/96)
The Rockford Files—"The Rockford Files: Punishment and Crime" (9/18/96)
The Rockford Files—"The Rockford Files: Murder and Misdemeanors" (11/21/97)
The Rockford Files—"The Rockford Files: If It Bleeds, It Leads" (4/20/99)
Simon & Simon—"Simon & Simon: In Trouble Again" (2/23/95)
The Six Million Dollar Man—"The Return of the Six Million Dollar Man and the Bionic Woman" (5/17/87)
The Six Million Dollar Man—"Bionic Showdown" (4/30/89)
The Six Million Dollar Man—"Bionic Ever After" (11/29/94)
Spenser For Hire—"Spenser: Ceremony" (3/14/94) and sequels on Lifetime
The Streets of San Francisco—"Back to the Streets of San Francisco" (1/27/92)
The Waltons—"A Walton Thanksgiving Reunion" (11/21/93)
The Waltons—"A Walton Wedding" (2/12/95)
The Waltons—"A Walton Easter" (3/30/97)
The Wild, Wild West—"The Wild, Wild West Revisited" (5/9/79)
The Wild, Wild West—"More Wild, Wild West" (10/7 & 8/80)
Wiseguy—"Wiseguy" (5/2/96)

APPENDIX 7
PRIME TIME SPIN-OFFS

Listed below are prime time series that are spin-offs from other prime-time series. A spin-off occurred when one or more characters from a series, usually supporting characters, subsequently appeared on another series. In most, but not all, cases the supporting characters from the original series became the stars of the spin-off series, and ceased to appear in the original series (assuming that the original series was still in production). In some cases, particularly when the spin-off was set in a period several years apart from the original series or was actually produced many years after the original series had ceased production, the common characters were portrayed by different actors in the spin-off than had portrayed them in the original.

A variation on the idea of a spin-off is sometimes used by the producers of a successful show when they want to launch another, essentially unrelated series. Characters who appeared only infrequently on the established show—not regulars—become the stars of the new show, which otherwise has nothing to do with the earlier series. Often, in fact, their appearance is nothing more than a promotion for the upcoming series; for example, Robin Williams appeared just once on *Happy Days* as the alien Mork before beginning his own series, *Mork & Mindy*. These "semi-spin-offs" based on occasional characters and one-time guests are indicated by an asterisk (*).

The all-time spin-off champion is *All in the Family*, which has spawned no fewer than five other series, three of them highly successful and two of them spin-offs from spin-offs (*Gloria*, *Maude*, *The Jeffersons*, *Good Times*, and *Checking In*). *Happy Days* is close behind with four spin-offs (*Joanie Loves Chachi*, *Laverne & Shirley*, *Mork & Mindy*, and *Out of the Blue*), although three of these were based on non-regular characters. Shows with three spin-offs include *The Danny Thomas Show* (it spun off *The Andy Griffith Show*, which, in turn, spun off *Gomer Pyle, U.S.M.C.* and *Mayberry, R.F.D.*), *The Mary Tyler Moore Show*, and *Sanford and Son*.

In the listing below, the spin-off series appears first, with the series from which it was spun off listed second.

The Adventures of Champion from **The Gene Autry Show**
AfterMASH from **M*A*S*H**
***The Andy Griffith Show** from **The Danny Thomas Show**
Baywatch Nights from **Baywatch**
Benson from **Soap**
Beverly Hills Buntz from **Hill Street Blues**
Billy from **Head of the Class**
The Bionic Woman from **The Six Million Dollar Man**
Booker from **21 Jump Street**
The Brady Brides from **The Brady Bunch**
Bret Maverick from **Maverick**
***Buddies** from **Home Improvement**
***CSI: Miami** from **CSI: Crime Scene Investigation**
Checking In from **The Jeffersons**
The Colbys from **Dynasty**
Crusade from **Babylon 5**
Daria from **The Beavis & Butt-head Show**
***Diagnosis Murder** from **Jake and the Fatman**
A Different World from **The Cosby Show**
***Dirty Sally** from **Gunsmoke**
***Empty Nest** from **The Golden Girls**
Enos from **The Dukes of Hazzard**
The Facts of Life from **Diff'rent Strokes**
Family Matters from **Perfect Strangers**
Fish from **Barney Miller**
Flo from **Alice**
Frasier from **Cheers**
***Getting Together** from **The Partridge Family**
The Girl from U.N.C.L.E. from **The Man from U.N.C.L.E.**
Gloria from **All in the Family**
The Golden Palace from **The Golden Girls**
Gomer Pyle, U.S.M.C. from **The Andy Griffith Show**

Good Times from **Maude**
Grady from **Sanford and Son**
Green Acres from **Petticoat Junction**
Highlander: The Raven from **Highlander**
***Honey West** from **Burke's Law**
Hotel Malibu from **Second Chances**
I Am Weasel from **Cow and Chicken**
The Jeffersons from **All in the Family**
Jesse Hawkes from **High Mountain Rangers**
Joanie Loves Chachi from **Happy Days**
***The Joey Bishop Show** from **The Danny Thomas Show**
***Just the Ten of Us** from **Growing Pains**
Knots Landing from **Dallas**
***Laverne & Shirley** from **Happy Days**
***The Law and Harry McGraw** from **Murder, She Wrote**
Law & Order: Criminal Intent from **Law & Order**
Law & Order: Special Victims Unit from **Law & Order**
***Law of the Plainsman** from **The Rifleman**
***Living Dolls** from **Who's the Boss?**
The Lone Gunmen from **The X-Files**
Lou Grant from **The Mary Tyler Moore Show**
A Man Called Hawk from **Spenser**
***Maude** from **All in the Family**
Mayberry R.F.D. from **The Andy Griffith Show**
***Melrose Place** from **Beverly Hills 90210**
The Misadventures of Sheriff Lobo from **B.J. & the Bear**
***Models, Inc.** from **Melrose Place**
***Mork & Mindy** from **Happy Days**
Open House from **Duet**
***Out of the Blue** from **Happy Days**
Pete and Gladys from **December Bride**
Phyllis from **The Mary Tyler Moore Show**
Ponderosa from **Bonanza**
The Prisoner from **Secret Agent**
***Promised Land** from **Touched by an Angel**
Redigo from **Empire**
Rhoda from **The Mary Tyler Moore Show**
***Richie Brockelman, Private Eye** from **The Rockford Files**
The Ropers from **Three's Company**
***Roxie** from **Kate & Allie**
The Sandy Duncan Show from **Funny Face**
Sanford from **Sanford and Son**
The Sanford Arms from **Sanford and Son**
***Sarge** from **Ironside**
The $64,000 Challenge from **The $64,000 Question**
Sons of Thunder from **Walker, Texas Ranger**
Star Trek: Deep Space Nine from **Star Trek: The Next Generation**
Surfside Six from **Bourbon Street Beat**
Tabitha from **Bewitched**
Three's a Crowd from **Three's Company**
***Top of the Heap** from **Married . . . with Children**
***The Tortellis** from **Cheers**
Trapper John, M.D. from **M*A*S*H**
Vinnie & Bobby from **Top of the Heap**
***Wanted: Dead or Alive** from **Trackdown**
Women of the House from **Designing Women**
***Young Americans** from **Dawson's Creek**
Young Maverick from **Maverick**
***Xena: Warrior Princess** from **Hercules: The Legendary Journeys**
Zorro and Son from **Zorro**

APPENDIX 8

PRIME TIME SERIES BASED ON MOVIES

One lesson that producers never seem to learn is that a show spun off from a hit theatrical movie has no better chance of becoming a hit on TV than does any other new series. The elements that make a movie money are quite different from those that make a series popular (broad audience appeal, likable characters, situations that can be taken in many different directions, etc.). And, of course, the stars and budget of the big screen are seldom available to TV. Nevertheless, every season brings new headlines about the latest theatrical blockbuster that's about to become a hit series. It seldom works. Of the top 100 series of all time, only *M*A*S*H* and *Alice* were adapted directly from movies—if you don't count such evergreen properties as *The Virginian* (first filmed in 1914) and *Lassie*.

In the interests of truth, justice, and setting the record straight, we present a list of series included in this book that were based on theatrical movies. The rules for inclusion are that the series must have been a direct adaptation of the movie, sharing characters and/or setting, and not a disguised version possibly "inspired by" a theatrical film (e.g., *Switch* by *The Sting*, *Hunter* by *Dirty Harry*, *Battlestar Galactica* by *Star Wars*, etc.). We have also not included stars who simply played themselves in both movies and TV (Gene Autry, Roy Rogers), or, for the most part, historical figures whose lives have been portrayed in many forms over the years (e.g., Henry VIII, Wild Bill Hickok, etc.). Some judgment was used about what to include. Notable films *are* listed even if they were, in turn, based on another source such as a book *(Lassie)*, play *(The Odd Couple)*, or radio show *(Amos 'n' Andy)*, however.

Dates prior to 1928 generally indicate silent films. Unless noted, dates reflect the *first* series and movie; if there were sequels or remakes, this is indicated by "& seq." An asterisk (*) indicates a syndicated series.

TV series (premiere)	Earliest Film Version (principal star, date)
1949	
The Front Page	The Front Page (Adolphe Menjou, Pat O'Brien, 1931 & seq.)
The Life of Riley	Life of Riley (William Bendix, 1949)
Mama	I Remember Mama (Irene Dunne, 1948)
1950	
Adventures of Ellery Queen (& seq.)	The Spanish Cape Mystery (Donald Cook, 1935 & seq.)
Big Town	Big Town (Philip Reed, 1947 & seq.)
Buck Rogers (& seq.)	Buck Rogers (aka Destination Saturn) (Buster Crabbe, 1939 & seq.)
*Cisco Kid	Began in silent films; first sound feature In Old Arizona (Warner Baxter, 1929 & seq.)
Dick Tracy	Dick Tracy (Ralph Byrd, 1937 & seq.)
The Girls	Our Hearts Were Young and Gay (Gail Russell, 1944 & seq.)
Stage Door	Stage Door (Katharine Hepburn, 1937)
1951	
Amos 'n' Andy	Check and Double Check (Freeman Gosden, Charles Correll, 1930)
*Boston Blackie	Boston Blackie's Little Pal (1919 & seq.); the 14 films starring Chester Morris made between 1941–1949 are best known
A Date with Judy	A Date with Judy (Jane Powell, Elizabeth Taylor, 1948)
1952	
Adventures of Superman	Theatrical cartoon (voice: Bud Collyer) in 1941; movie serial starring Kirk Alyn in 1948; feature starring George Reeves in 1951
Claudia, The Story of a Marriage	Claudia (Dorothy McGuire, Robert Young, 1943 & seq.)
Mr. & Mrs. North	Mr. and Mrs. North (Gracie Allen, William Post, Jr., 1941)
My Friend Irma	My Friend Irma (Marie Wilson, 1949 & seq.)

TV series (premiere)	Earliest Film Version (principal star, date)
1953	
*Flash Gordon	Flash Gordon (aka Spaceship to the Unknown) (Buster Crabbe, 1936 & seq.)
Life with Father	Life with Father (William Powell, 1947)
Topper	Topper (Cary Grant, Roland Young, 1937 & seq.)
1954	
The Adventures of Rin Tin Tin	The Man from Hell's River (Rin Tin Tin, Sr., 1922 & seq.)
Lassie (& seq.)	Lassie Come Home (Roddy McDowall, Elizabeth Taylor, 1943 & seq.)
That's My Boy	That's My Boy (Dean Martin, Jerry Lewis, 1951)
1955	
The Adventures of Robin Hood (& seq.)	First British version in 1909; first U.S. version in 1912; the most famous versions (of many) are those starring Douglas Fairbanks, Sr. (1922) and Errol Flynn (1938)
Casablanca (& seq.)	Casablanca (Humphrey Bogart, 1942)
Cheyenne	Cheyenne (Dennis Morgan, 1947)
*Dr. Hudson's Secret Journal	Magnificent Obsession (Robert Taylor, 1935 & seq.)
Kings Row	Kings Row (Ann Sheridan, 1942)
1956	
*The Adventures of Fu Manchu	First seen in the 1920s as a series of British two-reelers starring Harry Agar Lyons; then The Mysterious Dr. Fu Manchu (Warner Oland, 1929 & seq.); numerous others including a series with Christopher Lee in the 1960s
The Adventures of Sir Lancelot	First version in 1942; most famous, Knights of the Round Table, starring Robert Taylor in 1954
Broken Arrow	Broken Arrow (James Stewart, 1950)
My Friend Flicka	My Friend Flicka (Roddy McDowall, 1943 & seq.)
1957	
Blondie (& seq.)	Blondie (Penny Singleton, Arthur Lake, 1938 & 27 seq.)
Mickey Spillane's Mike Hammer (& seq.)	I, the Jury (Biff Elliot, 1953 & seq.)
*The New Adventures of Charlie Chan	Began as a minor character in House Without a Key (George Kuwa, 1926); became a major one in numerous films starring Warner Oland (beginning 1931) and others
The Thin Man	The Thin Man (William Powell, Myrna Loy, 1934 & seq.)
Zorro (& seq.)	The Mark of Zorro (Douglas Fairbanks, Sr., 1920 & seq.)
1958	
*The Adventures of Tugboat Annie	Tugboat Annie (Marie Dressler, 1933 & seq.)
*How to Marry a Millionaire	How to Marry a Millionaire (Marilyn Monroe, Betty Grable, Lauren Bacall, 1953)
Naked City	The Naked City (Barry Fitzgerald, 1948)
Northwest Passage	Northwest Passage (Spencer Tracy, 1940)
1959	
Five Fingers	Five Fingers (James Mason, 1952)
Mr. Lucky	Mr. Lucky (Cary Grant, 1943)
Peck's Bad Girl	Peck's Bad Boy (Jackie Coogan, 1921 & seq.)
Pete Kelly's Blues	Pete Kelly's Blues (Jack Webb, 1955)
Wichita Town	Wichita (Joel McCrea, 1955)
1960	
My Sister Eileen	My Sister Eileen (Rosalind Russell, 1942 & seq.)
*The Third Man	The Third Man (Orson Welles, 1950)
National Velvet	National Velvet (Mickey Rooney, Elizabeth Taylor, 1944 & seq.)
1961	
The Asphalt Jungle	The Asphalt Jungle (Sterling Hayden, 1950 & seq.)
Bus Stop	Bus Stop (Marilyn Monroe, 1956)

TV series (premiere)	Earliest Film Version (principal star, date)
Dr. Kildare	Interns Can't Take Money (Joel McCrea, 1937); the more famous series began with Young Dr. Kildare, starring Lew Ayres (1938 & 14 seq.)
87th Precinct	Cop Hater (Robert Loggia, 1958 & seq.)
Father of the Bride	Father of the Bride (Spencer Tracy, Elizabeth Taylor, 1950 & seq.)
Margie	Margie (Jeanne Crain, 1946)
Whispering Smith	Whispering Smith (Alan Ladd, 1948 & seq.)
1962	
Going My Way	Going My Way (Bing Crosby, 1944 & seq.)
Mr. Smith Goes to Washington	Mr. Smith Goes to Washington (James Stewart, 1939 & seq.)
Room for One More	Room for One More (Cary Grant, 1952)
The Virginian	First version in 1914 starred Dustin Farnum; the most famous remake was in 1929, starring Gary Cooper
1963	
The Farmer's Daughter	The Farmer's Daughter (Loretta Young, 1947)
1964	
Destry	Destry Rides Again (Tom Mix, 1932 & seq.); most famous version, in 1939, starred James Stewart, Marlene Dietrich
Flipper (& seq.)	Flipper (Chuck Connors, 1963)
No Time for Sergeants	No Time for Sergeants (Andy Griffith, 1958)
Peyton Place	Peyton Place (Lana Turner, 1957 & seq.)
Twelve O'Clock High	Twelve O'Clock High (Gregory Peck, 1949)
Voyage to the Bottom of the Sea	Voyage to the Bottom of the Sea (Walter Pidgeon, 1961)
1965	
Wackiest Ship in the Army	The Wackiest Ship in the Army (Jack Lemmon, 1960)
Gidget (& seq.)	Gidget (Sandra Dee, 1959 & seq.)
The Long Hot Summer	The Long Hot Summer (Paul Newman, 1958)
Mr. Roberts	Mister Roberts (Henry Fonda, 1955)
Please Don't Eat the Daisies	Please Don't Eat the Daisies (Doris Day, 1960)
Tammy	Tammy and the Bachelor (Debbie Reynolds, 1957 & seq.)
1966	
Daktari	Clarence, The Cross-Eyed Lion (Marshall Thompson, 1965)
The Rounders	The Rounders (Glenn Ford, Henry Fonda, 1965)
Shane	Shane (Alan Ladd, 1953)
Tarzan (& seq.)	Tarzan of the Apes (Elmo Lincoln, 1918); at least 37 later versions, the most famous in the '30s and '40s starring Johnny Weissmuller
1967	
Cowboy in Africa	Africa—Texas Style! (Hugh O'Brian, 1967)
Hondo	Hondo (John Wayne, 1953)
The Saint	The Saint in New York (Louis Hayward, 1938 & seq.)
1968	
The Ghost and Mrs. Muir	The Ghost and Mrs. Muir (Gene Tierney, 1947)
1969	
The Courtship of Eddie's Father	Courtship of Eddie's Father (Glenn Ford, Ronny Howard, 1963)
Mr. Deeds Goes to Town	Mr. Deeds Goes to Town (Gary Cooper, 1936)
1970	
Barefoot in the Park	Barefoot in the Park (Robert Redford, Jane Fonda, 1967)
The Interns	The Interns (Cliff Robertson, 1962)
McCloud	Coogan's Bluff (Clint Eastwood, 1968)
The Odd Couple (& seq.)	The Odd Couple (Jack Lemmon, Walter Matthau, 1968)

TV series (premiere)	Earliest Film Version (principal star, date)
1971	
*Doctor in the House	Doctor in the House (Dirk Bogarde, 1954 & seq.)
1972	
Anna and the King	Anna and the King of Siam (Irene Dunne, Rex Harrison, 1946); musical version in 1956, The King and I, starred Deborah Kerr, Yul Brynner
M*A*S*H	M*A*S*H (Donald Sutherland, 1970)
1973	
Adam's Rib	Adam's Rib (Spencer Tracy, Katharine Hepburn, 1949)
Bob & Carol & Ted & Alice	Bob & Carol & Ted & Alice (Natalie Wood, 1969)
Shaft	Shaft (Richard Roundtree, 1971 & seq.)
1974	
Born Free	Born Free (Virginia McKenna, 1966 & seq.)
The Cowboys	The Cowboys (John Wayne, 1972)
Paper Moon	Paper Moon (Ryan O'Neal, 1973)
Petrocelli	The Lawyer (Barry Newman, 1970)
Planet of the Apes	Planet of the Apes (Charlton Heston, 1968 & seq.)
1975	
Matt Helm	The Silencers (Dean Martin, 1966 & seq.)
Swiss Family Robinson	Swiss Family Robinson (Thomas Mitchell, 1940 & seq.)
1976	
Alice	Alice Doesn't Live Here Anymore (Ellen Burstyn, 1975)
Popi	Popi (Alan Arkin, Rita Moreno, 1969)
Serpico	Serpico (Al Pacino, 1973)
What's Happening!! (& seq.)	Cooley High (Glynn Turman, 1975)
1977	
Life and Times of Grizzly Adams	The Life and Times of Grizzly Adams (Dan Haggerty, 1976)
Logan's Run	Logan's Run (Michael York, 1976)
The Nancy Drew Mysteries (& seq.)	Nancy Drew, Detective (Bonita Granville, 1938 & seq.)
Operation Petticoat	Operation Petticoat (Cary Grant, 1959)
1978	
How the West Was Won	How The West Was Won (all-star cast, 1962)
The Paper Chase	The Paper Chase (John Houseman, 1973)
1979	
House Calls	House Calls (Walter Matthau, 1978)
Little Women	Little Women (Katharine Hepburn, 1933 & seq.)
The Bad News Bears	Bad News Bears (Walter Matthau, 1976 & seq.)
The Curse of Dracula (& seq.)	German film Nosferatu (Max Schreck, 1922) and many sequels, notably Dracula (Bela Lugosi, 1931)
Dear Detective	Dear Detective (Annie Giradot, 1977 & seq.)
Delta House	National Lampoon's Animal House (John Belushi, 1978)
From Here to Eternity	From Here to Eternity (Burt Lancaster, 1953)
Turnabout	Turnabout (John Hubbard, Carole Landis, 1940)
1980	
Beyond Westworld	Westworld (Richard Benjamin, 1973 & seq.)
Breaking Away	Breaking Away (Dennis Christopher, 1979)
Freebie and the Bean	Freebie and the Bean (James Caan, Alan Arkin, 1974)
Semi-Tough	Semi-Tough (Burt Reynolds, 1977)
1981	
Flamingo Road	Flamingo Road (Joan Crawford, 1949)
Foul Play	Foul Play (Goldie Hawn, Chevy Chase, 1978)
Harper Valley P.T.A.	Harper Valley P.T.A. (Barbara Eden, 1978)
Private Benjamin	Private Benjamin (Goldie Hawn, 1980)
Walking Tall	Walking Tall (Joe Don Baker, 1973)

TV series (premiere)	Earliest Film Version (principal star, date)
1982	
Fame	Fame (Irene Cara, 1980)
Herbie, The Love Bug	The Love Bug (Dean Jones, 1969 & seq.)
9 to 5	9 to 5 (Jane Fonda, 1980)
Seven Brides for Seven Brothers	Seven Brides for Seven Brothers (Howard Keel, 1954)
1983	
Gun Shy	The Apple Dumpling Gang (Bill Bixby, 1975)
Hotel	Hotel (Rod Taylor, 1967)
1984	
Blue Thunder	Blue Thunder (Roy Scheider, 1983)
The Four Seasons	The Four Seasons (Alan Alda, 1981)
1985	
Mr. Belvedere	Sitting Pretty (Clifton Webb, 1948 & seq.)
Stir Crazy	Stir Crazy (Gene Wilder, Richard Pryor, 1980)
1986	
Fast Times	Fast Times at Ridgemont High (Sean Penn, 1982)
Gung Ho	Gung Ho (Michael Keaton, 1986)
Starman	Starman (Jeff Bridges, 1984)
1987	
*Bustin' Loose	Bustin' Loose (Richard Pryor, 1981)
Nothing in Common	Nothing in Common (Tom Hanks, 1986)
Down and Out in Beverly Hills	Boudu Saved from Drowning (Michel Simon, 1932), remade as Down and Out in Beverly Hills (Nick Nolte, 1986)
*You Can't Take It with You	You Can't Take It with You (Jean Arthur, Lionel Barrymore, 1938)
1988	
*Freddy's Nightmares	Nightmare on Elm Street (Robert Englund, 1984 & seq.)
In the Heat of the Night	In the Heat of the Night (Sidney Poitier, Rod Steiger, 1967 & seq.)
Baby Boom	Baby Boom (Diane Keaton, 1987)
Dirty Dancing	Dirty Dancing (Jennifer Grey, Patrick Swayze, 1987)
Dirty Dozen: The Series	The Dirty Dozen (Lee Marvin, 1967)
*War of the Worlds	War of the Worlds (Gene Barry, 1953)
1989	
Alien Nation	Alien Nation (James Caan, 1988)
1990	
Adventures of the Black Stallion	The Black Stallion (Kelly Reno, Mickey Rooney, 1979)
Bagdad Cafe	Bagdad Cafe (Marianne Sagebrecht, 1988)
Ferris Bueller	Ferris Bueller's Day Off (Matthew Broderick, 1986)
The Outsiders	The Outsiders (C. Thomas Howell, 1983)
Parenthood	Parenthood (Steve Martin, 1989)
Swamp Thing	Swamp Thing (Louis Jourdan, Adrienne Barbeau, 1982)
Uncle Buck	Uncle Buck (John Candy, 1989)
Working Girl	Working Girl (Melanie Griffith, 1988)
1991	
Baby Talk	Look Who's Talking (Kirstie Alley, John Travolta, 1989 & seq.)
Eddie Dodd	True Believer (James Woods, 1989)
*Harry and the Hendersons	Harry and the Hendersons (John Lithgow, 1987)
1992	
Bill & Ted's Excellent Adventures	Bill and Ted's Excellent Adventure (Keanu Reeves, Alex Winter, 1989)
*Highlander (& seq.)	Highlander (Christopher Lambert, Sean Connery, 1986 & seq.)

TV series (premiere)	Earliest Film Version (principal star, date)
*The Untouchables	The Untouchables (Kevin Costner, Sean Connery, 1987)
The Young Indiana Jones Chronicles	Raiders of the Lost Ark (Harrison Ford, 1981)
1993	
A League of Their Own	A League of Their Own (Tom Hanks, Geena Davis, 1992)
Problem Child	Problem Child (John Ritter, 1990 & seq.)
Snowy River: The McGregor Saga	The Man from Snowy River (Kirk Douglas, 1982)
1994	
*RoboCop: The Series	RoboCop (Peter Weller, 1987 & seq.)
Weird Science	Weird Science (Anthony Michael Hall, Kelly LeBrock, 1985)
1995	
John Grisham's The Client	The Client (Susan Sarandon, Tommy Lee Jones, 1994)
1996	
The Big Easy	The Big Easy (Dennis Quaid, Ellen Barkin, 1987)
Clueless	Clueless (Alicia Silverstone, Stacey Dash, 1995)
Dangerous Minds	Dangerous Minds (Michelle Pfeiffer, 1995)
*FX: The Series	F/X (Bryan Brown, Brian Dennehy, 1986)
Party Girl	Party Girl (Parker Posey, 1995)
1997	
Buffy, The Vampire Slayer	Buffy, the Vampire Slayer (Kristy Swanson, Donald Sutherland, Luke Perry, 1992)
*Conan: The Television Series	Conan the Barbarian (Arnold Schwarzenegger, 1982)
*Disney's Honey, I Shrunk the Kids	Honey, I Shrunk the Kids (Rick Moranis, 1989)
La Femme Nikita	La Femme Nikita (Anne Parillaud, 1991), Point of No Return (Bridget Fonda, Gabriel Byrne, 1993)
*Police Academy: The Series	Police Academy (Steve Guttenberg, George Gaynes, Michael Winslow, 1984 & seq.)
*Stargate SG-1	Stargate (Kurt Russell, James Spader, 1995).
Timecop	Timecop (Jean-Claude Van Damme, 1994)
1998	
*The Crow: Stairway to Heaven	The Crow (Brandon Lee, Ernie Hudson, 1994)
The Magnificent Seven: The Series	The Magnificent Seven (Yul Brynner, Steve McQueen, Charles Bronson, James Coburn, Robert Vaughn, 1960)
*Mortal Kombat: Conquest	Mortal Kombat (Christopher Lambert, 1995 & seq.)
The Net	The Net (Sandra Bullock, 1995)
1999	
*Beastmaster	The Beastmaster (Marc Singer, Tanya Roberts, 1982)
*Total Recall 2070	Total Recall (Arnold Schwarzenegger, Sharon Stone, 1990)
2001	
Some of My Best Friends	Kiss Me Guido (Nick Scotti, Anthony Barrile, 1997)
2002	
The Dead Zone	The Dead Zone (Christopher Walken, Brooke Adams, 1983)
2003	
My Big Fat Greek Life	My Big Fat Greek Wedding (Nia Vardalos, John Corbett, 2002)
Tremors	Tremors (Kevin Bacon, 1990)

APPENDIX 9

PRIME TIME NETWORK TV SERIES THAT ALSO AIRED ON NETWORK RADIO

The ideas for network TV series come from many sources. Some are original creations and others are adapted from other media—novels, short stories, magazine articles, motion pictures, comic strips, etc. One of the most popular sources for series ideas, particularly in the early days of television, was network radio. Many of radio's most popular, and in some cases least popular, series found their way to television in the 1940s and 1950s. On rare occasions television returned the favor. *Have Gun, Will Travel* was first seen on CBS television in 1957—the following year an audio version turned up on CBS radio.

Following is a list of network TV series that also aired on network radio. In cases where the radio title differed from the title of the TV series, the radio title is in parentheses. Each listing includes the radio networks on which the series was aired (in alphabetical order, not sequential order) and the years in which the radio version was in production. In addition to the three networks familiar to TV viewers—ABC, CBS, and NBC—there is a fourth radio network, the Mutual Broadcasting System (MBS). It should be noted that ABC was formed in 1943 when NBC, which previously owned two separate radio networks, the "red" network and the "blue" network, sold the "blue" network to Edward J. Noble. The network indications in the listing below, for all programs aired prior to 1943, refer to the NBC red network as "NBC" and to the NBC blue network as "BLUE."

In addition to the network series that aired on network radio, this listing also includes radio entries for any syndicated TV series which have been included in the body of *The Complete Directory*. To distinguish the listings for syndicated TV series from their network TV counterparts, they are all preceded by an asterisk.

The sources for this radio information were three books—*Tune in Yesterday*, by John Dunning, Prentice-Hall, Inc., 1976; *The Big Broadcast*, by Frank Buxton and Bill Owen, Viking Press, 1972; and *A Thirty Year History of Programs Carried on National Radio Networks in the United States 1926–1956* by Harrison B. Summers, Arno Press and *The New York Times*, 1972.

***The Abbott and Costello Show**; ABC, NBC; 1940, 1942–1949
The Adventures of Ellery Queen (Ellery Queen); ABC, CBS, NBC; 1939–1948
***The Adventures of Fu Manchu (Fu Manchu)**; CBS, Syndicated; 1932–1933, 1939–1940
The Adventures of Ozzie and Harriet; ABC, CBS, NBC; 1944–1954
The Adventures of Rin Tin Tin (Rin-Tin-Tin); BLUE, CBS, MBS; 1930–1934, 1955–1956
***The Adventures of Superman**; ABC, MBS; 1940–1951
***The Adventures of Wild Bill Hickok (Wild Bill Hickok)**; MBS; 1951–1956
The Alan Young Show; ABC, NBC; 1944–1949
The Aldrich Family; BLUE, NBC; 1939–1953
The Amazing Dunninger (Dunninger the Mentalist); ABC; 1943–1944
The Amazing Mr. Malone (Murder and Mr. Malone); ABC; 1947–1950
American Forum of the Air; MBS, NBC; 1937–1956
America's Town Meeting (America's Town Meeting of the Air); ABC, NBC; 1935–1956
Amos 'n' Andy; BLUE, CBS, NBC; 1929–1960
Arthur Godfrey's Talent Scouts; CBS; 1946–1958
Author Meets the Critics; ABC, MBS, NBC; 1946–1950
Beat the Clock; CBS; 1948–1950
Believe It Or Not; ABC, BLUE, CBS, MBS, NBC; 1930–1938, 1942–1947
The Bell Telephone Hour; NBC; 1940–1958
Beulah; ABC, CBS, NBC; 1945–1954
The Big Story; NBC; 1947–1955
Big Town; CBS, NBC; 1937–1952
Blind Date; ABC, NBC; 1943–1946
Blondie; ABC, CBS, NBC; 1939–1950
Bob and Ray; ABC, CBS, MBS, NBC; 1951–1960
The Bob Hope Show; NBC; 1938–1958
***Bold Venture**; Syndicated; 1950–1951
***Boston Blackie**; NBC, Syndicated; 1944–1945
Break the Bank; ABC, MBS, NBC; 1945–1955
Buck Rogers (Buck Rogers in the Twenty-Fifth Century); CBS, MBS; 1932–1936, 1939–1947
Can You Top This; ABC, MBS, NBC; 1942–1954
Candid Camera (Candid Microphone); ABC, 1947–1948, 1950
Capitol Cloak Room (Capitol Cloakroom); CBS, MBS; 1948–1956
Cavalcade of America; CBS, NBC; 1935–1953
Chance of a Lifetime; ABC; 1949–1952

Charlie Wild, Private Detective; CBS; 1950–1951
*The Cisco Kid; MBS; 1942–1943, 1946–1947
Cities Service Band of America (Cities Service Concerts); NBC; 1926–1956
City Hospital; CBS; 1951–1956
The Clock; ABC; 1946–1948
Coke Time with Eddie Fisher (The Eddie Fisher Show); ABC, MBS; 1952–1957
Crime Photographer (Casey, Crime Photographer); CBS; 1943–1950, 1953–1955
*Dangerous Assignment; NBC; 1950–1953
The Danny Kaye Show; CBS; 1945–1946
A Date with Judy; ABC, NBC; 1941–1950
The Dave Garroway Show; NBC; 1949–1953
*Death Valley Days; BLUE, CBS; 1930–1945
Dick Powell's Zane Grey Theater (The Zane Grey Show); MBS; 1947–1948
Dick Tracy; ABC, MBS, NBC; 1935–1939, 1943–1948
The Dinah Shore Show; CBS, NBC; 1939–1947, 1953–1955
Dr. I.Q. (Dr. I.Q., The Mental Banker); ABC, NBC; 1939–1950
Dr. Kildare; MBS, Syndicated; 1949, 1951–1952
Don McNeill TV Club (The Breakfast Club); ABC, BLUE; 1933–1968
Double or Nothing; CBS, MBS, NBC; 1940–1952
Down You Go; MBS; 1952–1953
Dragnet; NBC; 1949–1956
Earn Your Vacation; CBS; 1949–1950
Easy Aces; BLUE, CBS; 1931–1945, 1948–1949
Escape; CBS; 1948–1954
Ethel and Albert; ABC; 1944–1950
Face the Nation; CBS; 1954–
Famous Jury Trials; ABC, BLUE, MBS, NBC; 1936–1949
Father Knows Best; NBC; 1949–1954
*Favorite Story; Syndicated; 1946–1949
Fibber McGee and Molly; BLUE, NBC; 1935–1957
*Flash Gordon; MBS; 1935–1936
Ford Show (The Tennessee Ernie Ford Show); ABC, CBS; 1952–1955
Ford Theatre; CBS, NBC; 1947–1949
The Frank Sinatra Show; ABC, CBS, NBC; 1944–1947, 1949, 1951, 1956–1958
The Fred Waring Show; CBS, NBC; 1932–1952
The Galen Drake Show; ABC, CBS; 1945–1955
Gangbusters (Gang Busters); ABC, BLUE, CBS, MBS, NBC; 1936–1957
The Garry Moore Show; CBS; 1949–1950
The Gay Nineties Review; CBS; 1940–1944
The George Burns and Gracie Allen Show (Burns and Allen); CBS, NBC; 1932–1950
The Goldbergs; CBS, MBS, NBC; 1929–1934, 1937–1945, 1949–1950
Grand Ole Opry; NBC; 1939–1957
The Green Hornet; ABC, BLUE, MBS, NBC; 1936–1952
Gunsmoke; CBS; 1952–1961
The Halls of Ivy; NBC; 1950–1952
Have Gun, Will Travel; CBS; 1958–1960
Hayloft Hoedown; ABC; 1945–1949
Herb Shriner Time; CBS; 1948–1949
Hobby Lobby; BLUE, CBS, MBS; 1937–1949
Hopalong Cassidy; CBS, MBS; 1950–1952
The Horace Heidt Show; ABC, CBS, NBC; 1932–1953
The Hour of Decision; ABC, MBS; 1950–1956
Information Please; BLUE, CBS, MBS, NBC; 1938–1948
It Pays to Be Ignorant; CBS, MBS; 1942–1949
It's Alec Templeton Time (Alec Templeton Time); BLUE, CBS, NBC; 1939–1943, 1947
The Jack Benny Show; BLUE, CBS, NBC; 1932–1958
The Jane Pickens Show; NBC; 1952–1956
The Jimmy Durante Show; CBS, NBC; 1943–1950
Juvenile Jury; MBS, NBC; 1946–1953
The Kate Smith Show; ABC, CBS, MBS, NBC; 1930–1951, 1957–1958
Kay Kyser's Kollege of Musical Knowledge; ABC, MBS, NBC; 1938–1949
The Kraft Music Hall; NBC; 1933–1949
Ladies Be Seated; ABC; 1943–1950
Lassie; ABC, NBC; 1947–1950
The Lawrence Welk Show; ABC; 1949–1956
Leave It to the Girls; MBS; 1945–1949
Life Begins at 80; ABC, MBS; 1948–1949

The Life of Riley; NBC; 1943–1951
Life with Linkletter (Art Linkletter's House Party); CBS; 1945–1967
Life with Luigi; CBS; 1948–1953
Lights Out; CBS, MBS, NBC; 1935–1947
The Lineup; CBS; 1950–1953
The Little Show; CBS; 1947
Live Like a Millionaire; ABC; 1950–1953
The Lone Ranger; ABC, BLUE, NBC, Syndicated; 1933–1955
Lux Video Theatre (The Lux Radio Theatre); CBS, NBC; 1934–1955
*The Man Called X; CBS, NBC; 1944–1948, 1950–1952
The Marriage; NBC; 1953–1954
Martin Kane, Private Eye (Martin Kane, Private Detective); MBS; 1949–1952
Mary Margaret McBride; ABC, CBS, NBC; 1937–1954
Meet Corliss Archer; ABC, CBS; 1943–1955
Meet Millie; CBS; 1951–1954
Meet the Press; NBC; 1945–
Michael Shayne; ABC, MBS; 1946–1952
The Milton Berle Show; NBC; 1941–1942, 1947–1948
Mr. and Mrs. North; CBS, NBC; 1941–1956
Mr. District Attorney; ABC, BLUE, NBC; 1939–1953
The Morey Amsterdam Show; CBS; 1948–1949
My Favorite Husband; CBS; 1948–1951
My Friend Irma; CBS; 1947–1954
My Little Margie; CBS, MBS; 1952–1955
My True Story; ABC, NBC; 1943–1961
Name That Tune; NBC; 1952–1953
The Nat "King" Cole Show ("King" Cole Trio Time); NBC; 1947–1948
The National Barn Dance; ABC, BLUE, NBC; 1933–1950
Nero Wolfe (The Adventures of Nero Wolfe); ABC, BLUE, NBC; 1943–1946, 1950–1951
*The New Adventures of Charlie Chan (Charlie Chan); ABC, BLUE, MBS; 1932–1933, 1937–1938, 1944–1948
Oboler Comedy Theatre (Arch Oboler Plays); MBS, NBC; 1939–1940, 1945
One Man's Family; NBC; 1932–1959
The O'Neills; CBS, MBS, NBC; 1934–1943
The Original Amateur Hour (Major Bowes' Original Amateur Hour); ABC, CBS, NBC; 1935–1946, 1948–1952
Our Miss Brooks; CBS; 1948–1957
Our Secret Weapon—The Truth; CBS; 1942–1943
The Paul Winchell and Jerry Mahoney Show; MBS; 1943–1944
The Pee Wee King Show; NBC; 1952–1955
People Are Funny; CBS, NBC; 1942–1959
The People's Platform; CBS; 1938–1952
The Perry Como Show (Chesterfield Supper Club); NBC; 1944–1950
Perry Mason; CBS; 1943–1955
Pete Kelly's Blues; NBC; 1951
The Peter Potter Show (Jukebox Jury); CBS; 1954–1956
Philip Marlowe (The Adventures of Philip Marlowe); CBS, NBC; 1947–1950
Presidential Timber; CBS; 1948
Public Prosecutor; MBS; 1954–1956
Pursuit; CBS; 1949–1952
Q.E.D. (Mystery File); ABC; 1950–1951
Quick as a Flash; ABC, MBS; 1944–1951
The Quiz Kids; ABC, BLUE, CBS, NBC; 1940–1953
The RCA Victor Show (A Day in the Life of Dennis Day); NBC; 1946–1951
RFD America; MBS, NBC; 1947–1949
The Ray Bolger Show; CBS; 1945
The Ray Milland Show (Meet Mr. McNutley); CBS; 1953–1954
The Red Skelton Show; CBS, NBC; 1941–1953
Richard Diamond, Private Detective; ABC, NBC; 1949–1952
The Robert Q. Lewis Show; CBS; 1951–1955
Romance; CBS; 1947–1960
The Roy Rogers Show; MBS, NBC; 1944–1955
The Saint; CBS, MBS, NBC; 1945–1952
The Screen Directors' Playhouse; NBC; 1949–1951
See It Now (Hear It Now); CBS; 1950–1951
Sergeant Preston of the Yukon; ABC, MBS; 1947–1955
Sheilah Graham in Hollywood (The Sheilah Graham Show); MBS; 1949–1950
The Show Goes On; CBS; 1949–1950
The Silver Theatre; CBS; 1937–1946

Sing It Again; CBS; 1948–1951
The Singing Lady (The Singing Story Lady); ABC, BLUE, MBS, NBC; 1932–1950
Sky King; ABC, MBS; 1946–1954
Smilin' Ed McConnell and His Buster Brown Gang; NBC; 1944–1952
Songs for Sale; CBS; 1950–1951
Space Patrol; ABC; 1950–1955
The Spike Jones Show; CBS; 1947–1949
Stars over Hollywood; CBS; 1941–1954
The Steve Allen Show; CBS; 1952–1953
Stop Me If You've Heard This One; MBS, NBC; 1939–1940, 1947–1948
Stop the Music; ABC, CBS; 1948–1955
Strike It Rich; CBS, NBC; 1947–1958
Studio One; CBS; 1947–1948
Suspense; CBS; 1942–1962
The TV Reader's Digest (The Radio Reader's Digest); CBS; 1942–1948
Tales of the Texas Rangers; NBC; 1950–1952
Tales of Tomorrow; ABC, CBS; 1953
Tarzan; CBS; 1952–1953
The Ted Steele Show; MBS; 1954–1955
Tex and Jinx (Meet Tex and Jinx); NBC; 1947–1948
The Thin Man (The Adventures of the Thin Man); ABC, CBS, NBC; 1941–1950
Think Fast; ABC; 1949–1950
***The Third Man**; Syndicated; 1950–1951
This Is Show Business; CBS; 1949–1954
This Is Your Life; NBC; 1948–1950
Tom Corbett, Space Cadet; ABC; 1952
Topper (The Adventures of Topper); NBC; 1945
Truth or Consequences; CBS, NBC; 1940–1957
Twenty Questions; MBS; 1946–1954
Two for the Money; CBS; 1952–1957
The U.S. Steel Hour; ABC, NBC; 1945–1953
Valentino; ABC; 1952–1956
The Victor Borge Show; NBC; 1945–1947
Vincent Lopez; ABC, MBS; 1949–1956
The Voice of Firestone; ABC, NBC; 1928–1956
The Walter Winchell Show (Walter Winchell's Journal); ABC, BLUE, MBS; 1932–1956
We Take Your Word; CBS; 1950–1951
We, the People; CBS, NBC; 1936–1951
What's My Line; CBS; 1952–1953
What's My Name; ABC, MBS, NBC; 1938–1942, 1949–1950
Who Said That?; NBC; 1948–1950
The Wife Saver; NBC; 1932–1942
Winner Take All; CBS; 1946–1952
You Are There; (CBS Is There); CBS; 1947–1950
You Bet Your Life; ABC, CBS, NBC; 1947–1959
Your Hit Parade; NBC; 1935–1959
Youth Wants to Know; NBC; 1951–1955

APPENDIX 10

HIT THEME SONGS FROM SERIES

Listed here are prime time series theme songs that reached the top 60 on *Billboard* magazine's top pop singles chart. The year and highest position reached is in parentheses. Not included are previously popular songs that were later adopted by a series—an increasingly prevalent practice in the 1980s and 1990s (e.g., "Love and Marriage" on *Married . . . with Children*, "Ob-La-Di, Ob-La-Da" on *Life Goes On*). For readers interested in detailed information on TV theme songs over the years and recorded versions of them, we recommend the *TV Theme Soundtrack Directory* by Craig W. Pattillo (Portland, OR: Braemar, Books, 1990) and *Television Theme Recordings* by Steve Gelfand (Popular Culture Ink, 1995).

Addams Family
("Addams Groove" incorporating "Addams Family Theme") Hammer (1991, #7)

All in the Family
("Those Were the Days") Carroll O'Connor & Jean Stapleton (1971, #43)

Ally McBeal
("Searchin' My Soul") Vonda Shepard (1998, airplay chart #16)

Angie
("Different Worlds") Maureen McGovern (1979, #18)

Baretta
("Keep Your Eye on the Sparrow"), Merry Clayton (1975, #45), Rhythm Heritage (1976, #20)

Batman, The Marketts (1966, #17) Neal Hefti & Orchestra (1966, #35)

Ben Casey, Valijean (1962, #28)

Beverly Hillbillies
("The Ballad of Jed Clampett") Lester Flatt & Earl Scruggs (1962, #44)

Bonanza, Al Caiola (1961, #19)

Charlie's Angels, Henry Mancini (1977, #45)

Cops
("Bad Boys"), Inner Circle (1993, #8)

Dr. Kildare
("Three Stars Will Shine Tonight") Richard Chamberlain (1962, #10)

Dragnet, Ray Anthony Orchestra (1953, #3)

The Dukes of Hazzard, Waylon Jennings (1980, #21)

Dynasty, Bill Conti (1982, #52)

Friends
("I'll Be There for You") The Rembrandts (1995, #17)

The Greatest American Hero
("Believe It or Not") Joey Scarbury (1981, #2)

Happy Days, Pratt & McClain (1976, #5)

Have Gun Will Travel
("Ballad of Paladin") Duane Eddy (1962, #33)

Hawaii Five-O, The Ventures (1969, #4)

The Heights
("How Do You Talk to an Angel"), The Heights (1992, #1)

Here Come the Brides
("Seattle") Perry Como (1969, #38)

Hill Street Blues, Mike Post, featuring Larry Carlton, guitar (1981, #10)

I Love Lucy
("Disco Lucy") Wilton Place Street Band (1977, #24)

Laverne and Shirley
("Making Our Dreams Come True") Cyndi Grecco (1976, #25)

Magnum, P.I., Mike Post (1982, #25)

Makin' It, David Naughton (1979, #5)

Medic
("Blue Star") Felicia Sanders (1955, #29)

The Men, Isaac Hayes (1972, #38)

Miami Vice, Jan Hammer (1985, #1)

Mission: Impossible, Lalo Schifrin (1968, #41), U2 (Adam Clayton & Larry Mullen) (1996, #7)

Mr. Lucky, Henry Mancini Orchestra (1960, #21)

Moonlighting, Al Jarreau (1987, #23)

My Three Sons, Lawrence Welk Orchestra (1961, #55)

Peter Gunn, Ray Anthony Orchestra (1959, #8), Duane Eddy (1960, #27), The Art of Noise (1986, #50)

The Rockford Files, Mike Post (1975, #10)

Route 66, Nelson Riddle Orchestra (1962, #30)

S.W.A.T., Rhythm Heritage (1975, #1)

Secret Agent
("Secret Agent Man") Johnny Rivers (1966, #3), The Ventures (1966, #54)

Then Came Bronson
("Long Lonesome Highway"), Michael Parks (1970, #20)

Welcome Back, Kotter
("Welcome Back") John Sebastian (1976, #1)

Zorro, The Chordettes (1958, #17)

Appendix 11
NETWORK WEB ADDRESSES

In the past few years the Internet has exploded into an enormous repository of information on television, among other things. TV fans were among the first to embrace the Web, and some have created extensive Web sites honoring their favorite shows, with episode guides, commentary and chat rooms. The Web is huge, unsupervised and unedited, so it can at times be frustrating to use. Aside from the advertising that constantly assaults you, the information you're looking for may be hard to find, incomplete or simply wrong. There is no *Complete Directory* on the Web, but there are a lot of good sites, so in the following section we offer some suggestions of sites you may want to check. Use them to look for more detail on your favorite shows, and to keep up to date between editions of *The Complete Directory.*

You can, of course, simply type the name of a show into one of the major search engines, such as google.com or msn.com, but get ready for a long night—you will probably get thousands of "hits" to weed through. Some search engines (like yahoo.com) have their own TV areas, but we've found the following more useful.

www.tvtome.com is a useful site with information on thousands of shows, many with episode guides. Each show's page is edited by a different volunteer fan, so the quality of information (and the spelling) can vary considerably. If a show has a dedicated fan willing to put in the time required to maintain its page, you'll find a lot; if it doesn't, you won't—and they'll ask if you want to become the editor for that show.

www.epguides.com. Similar to, and linked to, tvtome, this is an outgrowth of the site established by George Fergus and mentioned in our last edition. It is strongest on relatively recent shows, but some older ones are covered as well.

www.imdb.com is a giant database of information on TV, movies and other entertainment media. Larger but generally more superficial (and less accurate) than the previous two sites. Useful for tracing an actor's career.

www.zap2it.com contains pages on current shows and movies, and links to show-specific sites.

www.starseeker.com offers links to celebrity pages (actors, musicians, etc.).

Almost every broadcast and cable network has its own Web site now. These may be useful for shows that are currently airing, but few contain information on past series—in fact, canceled series (and departed actors) are usually deleted immediately. The goal is not so much to provide information as to entertain via clips and animation, and get you to watch.

Broadcast Networks:

ABC: www.abc.com
CBS: www.cbs.com
FOX: www.fox.com
NBC: www.nbc.com
PAX: www.paxtv.com
UPN: www.upn.com
WB: www.thewb.com

Cable Networks:

ABC Family Channel: www.abcfamily.com
American Movie Classics (AMC): www.amctv.com
Animal Planet: www.discovery.com
Arts & Entertainment Network (A&E): www.AandE.com
BBC America: www.bbcamerica.com
Black Entertainment Television (BET): www.bet.com
Bloomberg Television: www.bloomberg.com
Bravo: www.bravotv.com
C-SPAN: www.c-span.org
Cartoon Network: www.cartoonnetwork.com
CMT (Country Music Television): www.cmt.com
CNBC: http://moneycentral.msn.com/cnbc/tv/
CNN: www.cnn.com
Comedy Central: www.comedycentral.com
Court TV: www.courttv.com
Discovery Channel, The: www.discovery.com

Disney Channel, The: www.disneychannel.com
E! Entertainment Television: www.eonline.com
ESPN: www.espn.com
Food Network: www.foodtv.com
Fox Movie Channel: www.thefoxmoviechannel.com
Fox News Channel: www.foxnews.com
Fuse: www.fuse.tv
FX: www.fxnetworks.com
Galavision: www.galavision.com
Game Show Network: www.gameshownetwork.com
Golf Channel: www.thegolfchannel.com
Great American Country: www.countrystars.com
Hallmark Channel: www.hallmarkchannel.com
History Channel: www.historychannel.com
Home & Garden Television: www.hgtv.com
Home Box Office (HBO): www.hbo.com
Home Shopping Network: www.hsn.com
Independent Film Channel: www.ifctv.com
Learning Channel, The (TLC): www.discovery.com
Lifetime: www.lifetimetv.com
MSNBC: www.msnbc.com
MTV: Music Television: www.mtv.com
MuchMusic (U.S.)—see Fuse
National Geographic Channel: www.nationalgeographic.com/channel
Nickelodeon/Nick at Nite: www.nick.com
Noggin: www.noggin.com
Outdoor Life Network (OLN): www.olntv.com
Oxygen: www.oxygen.com
QVC: www.qvc.com
Sci-Fi Channel, The: www.scifi.com
ShopNBC: www.shopnbc.com
Showtime: www.sho.com
Soapnet: www.soapnet.com
Speed Channel: www.speedtv.com
Spike TV: www.spiketv.com
TBS Superstation: www.TBSsuperstation.com
TechTV: www.techtv.com
TNN: www.thenewtnn.com; see also Spike TV
TNT: www.tnt.tv
Toon Disney: www.toondisney.com
Travel Channel, The: www.discovery.com
Turner Classic Movies: www.turnerclassicmovies.com
TV Land: www.tvland.com
USA Network: www.usanetwork.com
VH-1: www.vh1.com
WE: Women's Entertainment: www.we.tv
Weather Channel, The: www.weather.com

Appendix 12

THE Ph.D. TRIVIA QUIZ

By Marc Berman

Long Running or Short-Lived?

1. What current regularly scheduled network series is the longest running in the history of television?
2. Name the actor who appeared in two different long-running Saturday-night series for a total of 16 years.
3. Which one of the following failed series aired for more than one episode?
   a) *Co-Ed Fever*
   b) *Push*
   c) *Turn-On*
   d) *South of Sunset*
   e) *You're in the Picture*
4. Historically, what actor had a regular featured role in the largest number of prime time series? How many shows in total were there? (For a bonus, how many of them can you name?)
5. How many years did Amanda Blake play Miss Kitty on *Gunsmoke*?
6. Name the TV show based on a movie that was on the air for the most number of years.
7. Name the longest-running prime time medical drama in the history of television.
8. Which "Angel" was on *Charlie's Angels* the shortest amount of time?
9. Name the first failed series McLean Stevenson appeared on following his stint on *M*A*S*H.*
10. What show did *60 Minutes* initially share its time period with?

Spin-Off Fever

11. True or false: *The Mary Tyler Moore Show* has spun off the largest number of prime time series in the history of television.
12. Name the two "grandchild series" of *All in the Family* (spin-offs from its spin-offs).
13. What show was short-lived comedy *Roxie* spun off from?
14. Name the series Oprah Winfrey headlined that was based on a 1989 miniseries.
15. How many actors from 1980 theatrical *Fame* reprised their roles on the same titled TV spin-off, and who are they?
16. Other than *Lou Grant* out of *The Mary Tyler Moore Show*, name another long-running drama that was spun off from a comedy.
17. What top-rated sitcom originated on *Love, American Style*?
18. Name the syndicated first-run comedy that featured Yakov Smirnoff.
19. The characters on *Mama's Family* were first seen on what variety hour?
20. On what show did *Beavis & Butt-head* originate?

TV Dads

21. What did Jim Anderson do for a living on *Father Knows Best*?
22. How many children did J. R. Ewing have?
23. Who worked as a newspaper columnist for the *Register* in Sacramento, California?
24. How did Ozzie Nelson make a living on *The Adventures of Ozzie & Harriet*?
25. Name the TV father whose character was a Tony-winning Broadway producer.
26. Who was the father of Molly Dodd's son?
27. Which TV father never had twin sons?
   a) Eric Camden
   b) Michael Hogan
   c) Jesse Katsopolis
   d) Jim Nash
   e) Jason Seaver
28. What newspaper does Ray Barone work for?
29. How many children did Charles Ingalls adopt?
30. What was Tim Taylor's nickname?

TV Moms

31. After the kids were all grown and out of the house, what did Carol Brady do for a living?
32. Where did Ida Morgenstern live?
33. What did Elyse Keaton do for a living?
34. How old was Murphy Brown when she gave birth to son Avery?
35. Who played Roseanne's mother?
36. Other than driving a taxi, what did Elaine Nardo do to make ends meet?

37. Who was the TV mom who wrote a children's book called *Whose Forest Is This?*
38. Name the TV mom who loved to gossip with her friend Mrs. Bloom.
39. What was the full name of Scarecrow's partner?

TV Kids

40. What was the name of Richie Cunningham's older brother?
41. How many people do you have if you add the siblings from *The Waltons, Eight Is Enough, Please Don't Eat the Daisies* and *Father Knows Best* together?
42. Name the original actress from *The Brady Bunch* who didn't appear in 1990 dramedy *The Bradys.*
43. Who was the voice of Mabel Buchman, Paul and Jamie's daughter, on *Mad About You*?
44. When *Knots Landing* first began, how many kids were living at TV's most famous cul-de-sac? How many kids were there when the show ended?
45. What was the name of the youngest child on sitcom *Just the Ten of Us*?
46. Who was Corey Baker's best friend?
47. How many grandchildren does Reba Hart have (as of 2003)?
48. How old was Theodore "Beaver" Cleaver when *Leave It to Beaver* ended?
49. How many years younger is Rory Gilmore than her mother Lorelei?
50. What was the name of the first singing group formed on the WB series *Popstars*?

Dead or Alive?

51. Name the featured regular character in a hit TV series who died by falling down an elevator shaft.
52. What was the cause of James Evans' death on *Good Times*?
53. If *The Wonder Years* ever had a reunion, which member of the family would not be there?
54. Who killed Ciji Dunne?
55. Which one of the students from *The White Shadow* was shot to death after witnessing a liquor store holdup?
56. How did Maggie Gioberti Channing meet her maker on *Falcon Crest*?
57. After Freddie Prinze passed away, what was the name of the character who replaced his character Chico on *Chico and the Man*?
58. How did Bobby Ewing come back to life after dying in a car crash on *Dallas*?
59. Who was living with Archie Bunker when his "dingbat" wife Edith passed away?
60. Who replaced Will Geer as Grandpa Walton after his death in 1978 at age 76?

Let's Eat!

61. On *Laverne & Shirley*, what was the name of the restaurant Frank and Edna De Fazio bought when they moved to California?
62. How many waitresses in total worked at Mel's Diner during *Alice*'s nine-year run?
63. What TV chef headed to prime time in a failed sitcom in the fall of 2001?
64. What was the name of the cooking show Sue Ann Nivens hosted on WJM-TV?
65. Name the TV character who owned a restaurant called Daniel's.
66. What was the name of the coffee shop the gang on *Seinfeld* often hung out at?
67. Name the show that featured outspoken waitress Cassie Cranston.
68. Where did Renate Malone's cooking show originate?
69. What did Angie Falco Benson do for a living after she sold her coffee shop?
70. Name the five TV characters who worked at Edna's Edibles.

TV Geography

71. Which one of the following shows was not set in San Francisco?
    a) *The Doris Day Show*
    b) *Full House*
    c) *Hooperman*
    d) *Ironsides*
    e) *One Day at a Time*
72. Name the city where radio station KLOW was located.
73. What city was the setting for *Hill Street Blues*?
74. What was the Bunkers' address on *All in the Family*?
75. What city did Russell and Claire Greene eventually settle in?
76. Which one of the following series didn't move to a new city toward the end of its run?
    a) *Baywatch*
    b) *Coach*
    c) *Gimme a Break*
    d) *I Love Lucy*
    e) *Lou Grant*
77. What city in Europe did Michael Endicott move to?
78. What was the name of the series that featured a judge named Luther Charbonnet?
79. Where did Mary Hartman live?
80. What was the name of the military base where Gomer Pyle was stationed?

TV Veterans

81. Name the TV series star who was 229 years old, attended high school for 122 years, was co-captain of the Bouillabaisseball team and ran his own phlegm dealership.
82. Who played Henry Rush's mother-in-law?
83. What was the name of the Yiddish comedian who began each day by singing, "Oh, What a Beautiful Morning"?
84. How old was Grandpa when *The Munsters* first began?
85. Who played Susie McNamera and Katy O'Connor?
86. How old was "Mother" Dexter on *Phyllis*?
87. Who was the original host of game show *The Price Is Right*?
88. What year did *Our Miss Brooks* premiere on TV?
89. Name the columnist who was forced off *What's My Line* because of McCarthy-era political blacklisting.
90. Who was the voice of Matt Dillon on the radio version of *Gunsmoke*?

Seeing Double (or More)

91. How many actresses played Billie Jo Bradley on *Petticoat Junction*?
92. How old were Brenda and Brandon Walsh when *Beverly Hills, 90210* began?
93. What were the names of Robbie and Katie's triplets on *My Three Sons*?
94. At its peak, how many times a week was ABC's *Who Wants to Be a Millionaire* regularly telecast?
95. How many shows did Tony Danza appear in regularly as a character named Tony?
96. Which one of the following actors did not appear on two regularly scheduled prime time series at the same time?
    a) Richard Anderson
    b) Frank Cady
    c) Stephen Collins
    d) Heather Locklear
    e) Robert Reed
97. Name the actor who has appeared on two different regularly scheduled prime time series on Pax TV.
98. Riddle me this. Frank Gorshin was not the only actor to portray giggling villain The Riddler on camp classic *Batman*. Who also played The Riddler?
99. Which one of the following series was not remade at a later time under the same name?
    a) *Burke's Law*
    b) *Fantasy Island*
    c) *Get Smart*
    d) *The Mod Squad*
    e) *The Smothers Brothers Comedy Hour*
100. How many versions of the Twilight Zone have aired to date?

The "A, B, C's" of TV Trivia

101. Name one of Theodore Cleaver's two featured schoolteachers.
102. What was John Boy Walton's major in college?
103. What was the name of the female "sweathog" on *Welcome Back, Kotter*?
104. What was the name of the high school on *Room 222*?
105. What was the name of the principal at Benjamin Harrison High?
106. What daytime talk-show host also starred as a high school science teacher in prime time?
107. Who was the teacher on *Little House: A New Beginning*?
108. What college did Sondra Huxtable attend?
109. If your TV teacher in college was Prof. Lasky, what subject would you be learning about?
110. What was the name of the boarding school teacher who taught the notorious "gang of four"?

New Beginnings/Sad Endings:

111. What happened in the last scene of the last episode of *Newhart*?
112. What lounge singer did Rhoda eventually date following her divorce from Joe Gerard?
113. What 1980s crime drama actually got a reprieve after it was canceled?
114. Name the crime fighter who joined the cast of *Batman* in its third, and final, season.
115. Who hosted the first telecast of *Saturday Night Live*?
116. Who was the original choice to play Lt. Columbo?
117. Who was Suzanne Somers' initial replacement on *Three's Company*?
118. Which cast member landed on a new series immediately following the demise of *Eight Is Enough*?
119. What was the original title of *The Hogan Family*?
120. What was revealed in the final scene of *St. Elsewhere*?

Cable Corner

121. After *The Paper Chase* was canceled by CBS, what cable network kept the series going with original episodes?
122. What cable network began as a local pay-television station in Wilkes-Barre, Pennsylvania?
123. Including HBO's *Sex and the City*, how many regularly scheduled prime time series has Sarah Jessica Parker appeared in?
124. What was the name of Ben Stein's sidekick on *Turn Ben Stein On*?

125. What now defunct cable network did E! Entertainment Television originate from?
126. After her stint on *Melrose Place*, what was the name of the cable drama that Brooke Langton starred in?
127. What did the initials *CNBC* initially stand for?
128. What cable network did the Oak Ridge Boys once have a show on?
129. Who was the original host of TLC's *Trading Spaces*?
130. What cable network was The History Channel spun off from?

Animation Antics

131. Prior to *The Simpsons*, what was the longest running prime time animated sitcom in the history of television?
132. On what series did *The Simpsons* originate?
133. Which one of the following live-action series never spun off an animated continuation?
    a) *The Brady Bunch*
    b) *The Odd Couple*
    c) *The Partridge Family*
    d) *Star Trek*
    e) *Starsky and Hutch*
134. John Ritter was the voice of Inspector Gil on what animated series?
135. How many animated series did ABC have on its fall prime time lineup in 1961–62?
136. What TV character was employed as a cartoonist drawing Cosmic Cow?

TV Pets

137. What was the name of the little boy who originally owned Lassie?
138. Name the sitcom that featured a sheep dog named Ladadog.
139. What tough-talking detective had a pet cockatoo named Fred?
140. Name the TV character who worked at the Los Angeles County Zoo.
141. What show was the "semi-wonder dog" on?
142. What was the name of the dog on *The Partridge Family*?
143. Name the two TV characters who died in an avalanche with a St. Bernard named Neil.
144. What TV character had a pet alligator named Elvis?
145. What was the name of the dog on *The Jetsons*?
146. How much did black bear Ben weigh?

Rated R

147. What was the "Venus Butterfly"?
148. Of the four principal girls on *The Facts of Life*, who lost her virginity first?
149. How many times was Suzanne Sugarbaker married?
150. What was Karen Charlene (K. C.) Koloski's occupation on the drama *China Beach*?
151. What organization did Bailey Salinger and Annie Mott both belong to?
152. Name the 1970s drama that changed its title to coincide with the lead character losing his virginity.

Look Who's Hosting

153. What was the name of the TV character who hosted fictional talk show *Open Mike*?
154. Who was Jay Leno's original bandleader on *The Tonight Show*?
155. Who was Danny Tanner's morning show cohost?
156. Funt-free: other than Allen Funt, who hosted a syndicated version of *Candid Camera*?
157. Which one of the following five celebrities never hosted a summer variety series?
    a) Ken Berry
    b) John Davidson
    c) John Denver
    d) Gladys Knight
    e) Tony Orlando

The Ratings Game

158. Which one of the following five long-running comedies never finished a season first overall in the ratings?
    a) *All in the Family*
    b) *The Beverly Hillbillies*
    c) *Cheers*
    d) *Laverne & Shirley*
    e) *M*A*S*H*
159. For how many seasons did *Bonanza* rank number one in the Nielsen ratings?
160. True or false: In its initial 1966–69 run, *Star Trek*'s best season ending rating was number 52 overall.
161. Which one of the following long-running dramas never finished a season in the top 20?
    a) *Cagney & Lacey*
    b) *Little House on the Prairie*
    c) *Mission: Impossible*
    d) *St. Elsewhere*
    e) *Walker, Texas Ranger*

162. Historically, what show once finished a season with a whopping 67.3 average rating?
163. Which one of the following shows was not the highest-rated comedy overall in its final season?
   a) *The Andy Griffith Show*
   b) *The Golden Girls*
   c) *I Love Lucy*
   d) *M*A*S*H*
164. What Alfred Hitchcock film ranks in the top 10 among the highest-rated movies in the history of television?

Emmy Time

165. What regularly scheduled series holds the record for the most number of Emmy wins?
166. Which two of the following comedies featured Emmy wins for all their principal stars?
   a) *All in the Family*
   b) *The Golden Girls*
   c) *I Love Lucy*
   d) *Roseanne*
   e) *Seinfeld*
167. True or false: Jackie Gleason never won an Emmy award.
168. Name the actor who won two additional supporting actor comedy Emmys even after exiting the series on a regular basis.
169. Who was the only actor or actress from the sitcom *227* to win an Emmy?
170. How many Emmy awards did Candice Bergen win for *Murphy Brown*?

This, That and Other Miscellaneous TV Questions

171. If you were a kid growing up in the 1970s, chances are you watched ABC on Friday night. Name the five shows that aired in the network's classic 1971–73 Friday lineup.
172. What was the first failed series Pat Morita starred in after leaving *Happy Days*?
173. Which one of the following series never changed networks during its original run?
   a) *Diff'rent Strokes*
   b) *Family Matters*
   c) *In the Heat of the Night*
   d) *My Three Sons*
   e) *Northern Exposure*
174. How much did CBS offer David Letterman to move from NBC in 1993?
175. What TV character was famous for saying, "Let's be careful out there"?
176. Which one of the following series titles was not used for two different series?
   a) *The Good Life*
   b) *Happy Days*
   c) *Harry*
   d) *Karen*
   e) *Sara*
177. Who starred in two different shows that had the same name?
178. What series was nicknamed Miami Nice?
179. Which one of the following original half-hour series did not eventually expand to an hour in length?
   a) *Alfred Hitchcock Presents*
   b) *The Price Is Right*
   c) *The Red Skelton Show*
   d) *The $64,000 Question*
   e) *The Twilight Zone*
180. What was Maxwell Smart's agent number on *Get Smart*?
181. Who played Felix and Oscar in the 1982–83 remake of *The Odd Couple*?
182. What now famous entertainer was once a "Fly Girl" on *In Living Color*?
183. Name the show that was based on the book called *The Fifteenth Pelican*.
184. What network shows did *The Waltons* compete with in its first season?
185. Which one of the following five choices was not the actual title of a prime time series?
   a) *Baa Baa Black Sheep*
   b) *Blue Skies*
   c) *Pink Cadillac*
   d) *The White Shadow*
   e) *The Yellow Rose*
186. Name the first five winners on *Survivor*.
187. Who provided the musical interludes on the final season of *The Love Boat*?
188. Name the syndicated action hour starring Terry "Hulk" Hogan.
189. What network did *Don Kirshner's Rock Concert* air on?
190. How many people to date have hosted *Family Feud*?
191. What is the title of the theme song on *Friends*?

192. What was the name of the sitcom Lauren Graham starred on immediately prior to *Gilmore Girls*?
193. Which one of the following former *Saturday Night Live* regulars has yet to appear regularly in a failed prime time sitcom?
  a) Dan Aykroyd
  b) Ellen Cleghorne
  c) Joan Cusack
  d) Anthony Michael Hall
  e) Martin Short
194. Although producer Dick Wolf is known for NBC's *Law & Order* trilogy, what was the name of his unsuccessful 2000–01 syndicated reality series?
195. What show did *Felicity* share its time period with in 2000–01?
196. Who was the runner-up on the original edition of *American Idol*?
197. How many cases did TV's Perry Mason lose?
198. Where did Dr. Neil Bernstein work?
199. What sitcom was animated comedy *Wait Till Your Father Gets Home* reminiscent of?
200. Which one of the following series debuted on Friday the Thirteenth?
  a) *Kolchak: The Night Stalker*
  b) *The Man from U.N.C.L.E.*
  c) *The Twilight Zone*
  d) *Twin Peaks*
  e) *Viper*

ANSWERS

1. NBC's *Meet the Press*, which debuted on Nov. 20, 1947.
2. Gavin MacLeod: *The Mary Tyler Moore Show* (CBS, 1970–77), *The Love Boat* (ABC, 1977–86).
3. b) *Push*, which aired on ABC for two episodes in April 1998.
4. Robert Urich appeared regularly (and prominently) in the following 14 series:
  Bob & Carol & Ted & Alice (ABC, 1973)
  S.W.A.T. (ABC, 1975–76)
  Tabitha (ABC, 1977–78)
  Soap (ABC, 1977–78)
  Vega$ (ABC, 1978–81)
  Gavilan (NBC, 1982–83)
  Spenser: For Hire (ABC, 1985–88)
  American Dreamer (NBC, 1990–91)
  Crossroads (ABC, 1992–93)
  It Had to Be You (CBS, 1993)
  The Lazarus Man (syn, 1995–96)
  Vital Signs (ABC, 1997)
  Love Boat: The Next Wave (UPN, 1998–99)
  Emeril (NBC, 2001)
5. 19 years (1955–74).
6. *M*A*S*H* (1972–83).
7. NBC's *ER*, which began in Sep. 1994 and is still running as of this writing.
8. Since *Charlie's Angels* was canceled in midseason, Julie Rogers, played by Tanya Roberts, appeared in only half a season.
9. *The McLean Stevenson Show* (NBC, 1976–77).
10. *CBS News Hour* (1968–71).
11. False. With five series (*Maude*, *The Jeffersons*, *Archie Bunker's Place*, *Gloria* and *704 Houser*), *All in the Family* has two more spin-offs than *The Mary Tyler Moore Show* (*Rhoda*, *Phyllis* and *Lou Grant*).
12. *Good Times* (from spin-off *Maude*) and *Checking In* (from spin-off *The Jeffersons*).
13. *Kate & Allie*.
14. *Brewster Place*.
15. Debbie Allen, Albert Hague, Gene Anthony Ray and Lee Curreri.
16. *Trapper John, M.D.* from *M*A*S*H*.
17. *Happy Days*.
18. *What a Country*.
19. *The Carol Burnett Show*.
20. *Liquid TV*.
21. An agent with The General Insurance Company.
22. Two—James and John Ross Ewing III on *Dallas*.
23. Tom Bradford on *Eight Is Enough*.
24. Although Ozzie did once refer to himself as a former orchestra leader, since he always seemed to be home he apparently wasn't very busy!
25. Maxwell Sheffield on *The Nanny*.
26. Nathaniel (Nat) Hawthorne on *The Days and Nights of Molly Dodd*.
27. e) Jason Seaver of *Growing Pains*.

28. *New York Newsday* on *Everybody Loves Raymond.*
29. Three—Albert, James and Cassandra on *Little House on the Prairie.*
30. Tool Man on *Home Improvement.*
31. She was a real estate agent on *The Brady Brides* and *The Bradys.*
32. The Bronx on *Rhoda.*
33. An architect on *Family Ties.*
34. 42
35. Estelle Parsons on *Roseanne.*
36. She worked as an art gallery receptionist on *Taxi.*
37. Nancy Weston on *thirtysomething.*
38. Molly Goldberg on *The Goldbergs.*
39. Amanda King on *Scarecrow and Mrs. King.*
40. Chuck Cunningham on *Happy Days.*
41. 22
42. Maureen McCormick.
43. Janeane Garofalo.
44. Three at the beginning and three at the end.
45. Melissa Lubbock.
46. Earl J. Waggedorn on *Julia.*
47. One on *Reba.*
48. 13.
49. 16 years on *Gilmore Girls.*
50. Eden's Crush.
51. Rosalind Shays on *L.A. Law.*
52. Car accident.
53. Jack Arnold (who died, according to the epilogue).
54. Chip Roberts on *Knots Landing.*
55. Curtis Jackson.
56. She drowned in a swimming pool.
57. Raul Garcia.
58. Bobby never really died—Pam had dreamt the entire season he wasn't on.
59. Niece Stephanie Mills on *Archie Bunker's Place.*
60. No one. Only Will Geer could be Grandpa Walton on *The Waltons.*
61. Cowboy Bill's.
62. Five—Alice, Flo, Vera, Belle and Jolene.
63. Emeril Lagasse on *Emeril.*
64. *The Happy Homemaker Show* on *The Mary Tyler Moore Show.*
65. Richard Avery on *Knots Landing.*
66. Monk's Diner.
67. *It's a Living*, which was also known as *Making a Living.*
68. Her walk-up apartment in Brooklyn on CBS sitcom *Mama Malone.*
69. She bought a beauty parlor on *Angie.*
70. Edna Garrett, Blair Warner, Jo Polniaczek, Natalie Green and Dorothy "Tootie" Ramsey on *The Facts of Life.*
71. e) *One Day at a Time*, which took place in Indianapolis.
72. Portland, Oregon, on *Hello, Larry.*
73. Although rumors pointed to Chicago, it was never officially determined.
74. 704 Houser Street, Queens, New York.
75. Denver on *The Promised Land.*
76. d) *Lou Grant*, which was always set in Los Angeles.
77. Rome on 1969–71 CBS sitcom *To Rome with Love.*
78. *Orleans*, which aired on CBS in 1997.
79. Fernwood, Ohio.
80. Camp Henderson, California.
81. ALF (aka Gordon Shumway) on *Alf.*
82. Audrey Meadows on *Too Close for Comfort.*
83. Menasha Skulnik on *Menasha the Magnificent.*
84. 350 years old.
85. Ann Sothern on *Private Secretary* and *The Ann Sothern Show.*
86. 87 years old.
87. Bill Cullen.
88. 1952
89. Louis Untermeyer.
90. William Conrad.
91. Three—Jeannine Rile, Gunilla Hutton, Meredith MacRae.
92. 16 years old.

93. Robbie II, Steve Douglas, Jr., and Charley Douglas.
94. Four.
95. Four: Tony Banta in *Taxi*, Tony Micelli in *Who's the Boss?*, Tony Canetti on *Hudson Street* and Tony Di Meo on *The Tony Danza Show*.
96. c) Stephen Collins.
97. Richard Thomas: reality hour *It's a Miracle* and drama *Just Cause*.
98. John Astin.
99. d) *The Mod Squad*.
100. Four, including the first-run syndicated version in 1987–88.
101. Miss Canfield or Miss Landers on *Leave It to Beaver*.
102. English.
103. Angie Globagoski.
104. Walt Whitman High.
105. Joe Danzig, played by Ed Asner, on *The Bronx Zoo*.
106. Montel Williams, who starred in1996 CBS drama *Matt Waters*.
107. Etta Plum (played by Leslie Landon).
108. Princeton University on *The Cosby Show*.
109. Anthropology *(Saved by the Bell: The College Years)*.
110. Teech Gibson on 1991 CBS comedy *Teech*.
111. Bob woke up next to his former TV wife Emily (Suzanne Pleshette) and realized it was all a dream!
112. Lounge singer Johnny Venture.
113. *Cagney & Lacey*.
114. Batgirl.
115. George Carlin.
116. Bing Crosby.
117. Jenilee Harrison.
118. Adam Rich—*Code Red* on ABC in 1981–82
119. *Valerie*, which later became *Valerie's Family* and, finally, *The Hogan Family*.
120. Dr. Westphall's autistic son Tommy was shown shaking a snow globe featuring St. Eligius hospital. Apparently, the entire series was a figment of his imagination.
121. Showtime.
122. HBO.
123. Four—*Square Pegs* (CBS, 1982–83), *A Year in the Life* (NBC, 1987–88), *Equal Justice* (ABC, 1990–91) and HBO's *Sex and the City*.
124. Puppy Wuppy.
125. Movietime.
126. *The Net*.
127. Consumer News and Business Channel.
128. The Nashville Network.
129. Alex McLeod.
130. A&E.
131. *The Flintstones* (ABC, 1960–66).
132. As a sketch on Fox's *The Tracey Ullman Show*.
133. e) *Starsky and Hutch*.
134. *Fish Police*.
135. Five—*The Bugs Bunny Show*, *Calvin & the Colonel*, *Top Cat*, *The Flintstones*, *Matty's Funday Funnies*.
136. Henry Rush on *Too Close for Comfort*.
137. Jeff Miller.
138. *Please Don't Eat the Daisies*.
139. Baretta, played by Robert Blake, in the show of the same name.
140. Rebecca Cafferty on *A Peaceable Kingdom*.
141. *Life Goes On*.
142. Simone.
143. George and Marion Kerby on *Topper*.
144. Sonny Crockett on *Miami Vice*.
145. Astro.
146. 650 lbs.
147. It was a sexual maneuver that Stuart Markowitz knew on *L.A. Law*.
148. Natalie.
149. Five times.
150. Hooker.
151. AA—Alcoholics Anonymous.
152. *James at 15*, which became *James at 16*.
153. Karen MacKenzie from *Knots Landing*.
154. Branford Marsalis.
155. Rebecca Donaldson on *Full House*.

156. Dom DeLuise.
157. c) John Denver.
158. e) *M*A*S*H.*
159. Three (1964–66).
160. True.
161. c) *St. Elsewhere.*
162. *I Love Lucy* in 1952–53.
163. b) *The Golden Girls.*
164. *The Birds*, tied at number seven overall with *True Grit* at a 38.9 rating.
165. *Frasier.*
166. a) *All in the Family* and b) *The Golden Girls.*
167. True.
168. Don Knotts, who won five Emmys from *The Andy Griffith Show.*
169. Jackee Harry.
170. Five.
171. *The Brady Bunch, The Partridge Family, Room 222, The Odd Couple, Love, American Style.*
172. *Mr. T and Tina.*
173. e) *In the Heat of the Night.*
174. $42 million.
175. Sgt. Phil Esterhaus on *Hill Street Blues.*
176. c) *Harry.*
177. George Clooney: sitcom *E/R* (CBS, 1984–85) and NBC drama *ER* 1994–99.
178. *The Golden Girls.*
179. d) *The $64,000 Question.*
180. 86.
181. Ron Glass and Demond Wilson.
182. Jennifer Lopez.
183. *The Flying Nun.*
184. ABC's *The Mod Squad* and NBC's *The Flip Wilson Show.*
185. c) Pink Cadillac.
186. Richard Hatch, Tina Wesson, Ethan Zohn, Vicepia Towery and Brian Heidik.
187. The Love Boat Mermaids, which featured Teri Hatcher pre *Lois & Clark—The New Adventures of Superman.*
188. *Thunder in Paradise.*
189. Because it was syndicated, it didn't air on any particular network.
190. Four: Richard Dawson, Ray Combs, Louie Anderson and Richard Karn.
191. "I'll Be There for You."
192. *M.Y.O.B.*
193. d) Anthony Michael Hall
194. *Arrest & Trial.*
195. *Jack & Jill.*
196. Justin Guarini.
197. None. Although he did officially lose one trial when a client refused to reveal evidence, Mason managed to clear the individual after finding the real culprit.
198. In a coroner's office in the 1997 ABC drama *Leaving L.A.*
199. *All in the Family.*
200. a) *Kolchak: The Night Stalker*, which was a fitting date to premiere considering that the series dealt with the supernatural.

INDEX

ABOUT THE AUTHORS

Courtesy of Howard Millard

Earle Marsh considers himself one of the Midwest's first television babies. In 1947, when he was barely speaking, his parents bought their first television set, a Sentinel with a 10-inch screen. He can still remember his folks setting up folding chairs on Tuesday nights for friends who came to watch Uncle Miltie. In his formative years he acquired such treasures as a Captain Video Space Helmet, a set of genuine Hopalong Cassidy cap pistols, a Davy Crockett coon skin cap (complete with snap-on tail that could be fixed when his friends pulled it off), and his own Mickey Mouse ears. While earning a degree in marketing at Northwestern University in the 1960s, he worked on the local campus radio station, WNUR-FM, and it was only natural that he would migrate to broadcasting. Following a stint with the A. C. Nielsen Company, during which he learned more about ratings than most people would care to know, he made two round trips between NBC and CBS, advancing through the ranks in network radio, network television, and local television research. His most recent corporate media position was as Vice President of Research for Showtime/The Movie Channel. Although Mr. Marsh is currently working in the computer services industry, he also serves as a media consultant, servicing, among others, some of the companies for which he previously worked. He also gives college lectures and makes numerous media appearances.

Tim Brooks is a television fan who is also an executive in the industry. He is currently Executive Vice President, Research, for Lifetime Television. Raised in Hampton, New Hampshire, and a graduate of Dartmouth College and Syracuse University, Tim got his start in TV as a promotion writer for an Albany, New York, station, followed by positions with CBS, Westinghouse Broadcasting Co., and NBC, for which he analyzed Nielsen ratings and conducted viewer surveys in the 1970s and '80s. He takes full credit for helping get your favorite show on the air, but had nothing to do with the ones you hated! In 1989 he joined the NW Ayer advertising agency as Senior Vice President/Media Research Director, and in 1991 moved to USA Networks, where he helped launch the Sci-Fi Channel as well as the company's international channels, interviewing TV viewers around the world. He joined Lifetime in 2000. He is active in industry organizations, and has served as Chairman of the Media Rating Council (which monitors Nielsen and other research services), the Advertising Research Foundation, and the Cable & Telecommunications Association for Marketing Research Committee. Tim has also taught television research and program history at Long Island University. His full professional bio is in *Who's Who in America*. He is the author of the biographical dictionary *The Complete Directory to Prime Time TV Stars* (Ballantine, 1987), as well as three books about his other love, the history of the recording industry: *Little Wonder Records* (1999), *The Columbia Master Book Discography* (a history and discography of Columbia Records, coauthor, 1999) and the soon-to-be-released *Lost Sounds: Blacks and the Birth of the Recording Industry.*